SHAKESPEARE

THE

Complete Works

EDITED BY G. B. HARRISON

HARCOURT, BRACE & WORLD, INC.

NEW YORK   CHICAGO   SAN FRANCISCO   ATLANTA

CONTENTS

GENERAL INTRODUCTION   I

    1. THE UNIVERSALITY OF SHAKESPEARE   2. RECORDS OF THE LIFE OF SHAKESPEARE
3. SHAKESPEARE'S ENGLAND   4. ELIZABETHAN DRAMA   5. THE ELIZABETHAN PLAY-
HOUSE   6. THE STUDY OF THE TEXT   7. THE DEVELOPMENT OF SHAKESPEARE'S ART
8. SHAKESPEARE AND THE CRITICS   9. SHAKESPEAREAN SCHOLARSHIP AND CRITICISM
1900–1950

THE PLATES   91

    NOTES ON THE PLATES

THE PLAYS

    THE FIRST PART OF KING HENRY THE SIXTH   103
    THE SECOND PART OF KING HENRY THE SIXTH   142
    THE THIRD PART OF KING HENRY THE SIXTH   182
    THE TRAGEDY OF KING RICHARD THE THIRD   221
    THE COMEDY OF ERRORS   270
    THE TRAGEDY OF TITUS ANDRONICUS   294
    THE TAMING OF THE SHREW   328
    THE TWO GENTLEMEN OF VERONA   365
    LOVE'S LABOR'S LOST   394
    THE TRAGEDY OF KING RICHARD THE SECOND   430
    THE TRAGEDY OF ROMEO AND JULIET   468
    A MIDSUMMER NIGHT'S DREAM   511
    THE LIFE AND DEATH OF KING JOHN   541
    THE MERCHANT OF VENICE   579
    THE FIRST PART OF KING HENRY THE FOURTH   613
    THE SECOND PART OF KING HENRY THE FOURTH   653
    MUCH ADO ABOUT NOTHING   697
    THE LIFE OF KING HENRY THE FIFTH   732
    AS YOU LIKE IT   773
    THE TRAGEDY OF JULIUS CAESAR   809
    TWELFTH NIGHT, OR WHAT YOU WILL   845

THE TRAGEDY OF HAMLET, PRINCE OF DENMARK 880

THE MERRY WIVES OF WINDSOR 935

THE TRAGEDY OF TROILUS AND CRESSIDA 973

ALL'S WELL THAT ENDS WELL 1018

THE TRAGEDY OF OTHELLO, THE MOOR OF VENICE 1056

MEASURE FOR MEASURE 1100

THE TRAGEDY OF KING LEAR 1136

THE TRAGEDY OF MACBETH 1184

THE TRAGEDY OF ANTONY AND CLEOPATRA 1219

THE TRAGEDY OF CORIOLANUS 1265

TIMON OF ATHENS 1315

PERICLES 1349

CYMBELINE 1382

THE WINTER'S TALE 1429

THE TEMPEST 1471

THE FAMOUS HISTORY OF THE LIFE OF KING HENRY THE EIGHTH 1502

THE POEMS

VENUS AND ADONIS 1545

THE RAPE OF LUCRECE 1561

THE PASSIONATE PILGRIM 1584

THE PHOENIX AND THE TURTLE 1590

SONNETS 1592

A LOVER'S COMPLAINT 1624

APPENDICES
1631

I. THE ELIZABETHAN IDEA OF THE UNIVERSE   2. THE ALMANAC   3. THE HUMORS
4. THE MELANCHOLIC HUMOR   5. BEARBAITING AND BULLBAITING   6. LETTERS AND
SEALS   7. HATS AND HEADS   8. BALLADS   9. HERALDS AND HERALDRY   10. TOR-
TURES AND PUNISHMENTS   II. CUCKOLDS AND HORNS   12. SIGNS   13. BOWLS
14. THE GREAT HOUSEHOLD   15. MARRIAGE CUSTOMS   16. FUNERAL CUSTOMS
17. THE POST   18. NATURE AND ART   19. BELLS   20. EQUIVOCATION   21. ALCHEMY
22. TIME PROBLEMS   23. WITCHES AND WITCHCRAFT   24. DANCES   25. THE FENC-
ING MATCH IN "HAMLET"   26. HAWKS AND HAWKING   27. MONEY VALUES
28. THE HISTORY BEHIND THE HISTORY PLAYS   29. THE ORDER OF THE GARTER
30. THE SHAKESPEAREAN ADDITION TO "THE BOOKE OF SIR THOMAS MORE"

READING LIST
1662

PREFACE

This edition of *Shakespeare's Complete Works* has been produced for college students in the hope that it will help them to understand, appreciate, and enjoy the works for themselves. It is not intended for the scholar, who is amply served elsewhere.

The choice of a text gave considerable difficulty. When the volume was first planned there was hot controversy whether to use the familiar Globe text or to print a text which would more closely follow the original quarto or folio. The problem was submitted to a plebiscite of some fifty experienced professors who voted decisively in favor of the Globe. As the work progressed I was the more convinced that this decision was right for this edition. However, the Globe text was no longer modern, and I did not hesitate to follow current American usage in spelling, punctuation, and capitalization. Again with the student in mind, I have preferred to use a diacritical mark to denote the accented *ed,* and to abandon the earlier (and never consistent) practice of omitting *e* when silent; thus we prefer *determined* to *determin'd;* when the final syllable is accented, we print it *determinèd*. There is no way to edit a classic; each reader prefers the text most suited to his needs. The text which gives most help will best suit the student who is studying Shakespeare as literature. When he becomes a scholar, nothing but the folio should satisfy him, but meanwhile to insist that he use a text prepared according to the current notions of bibliographers would be sheer pedantry.

The Notes are full, because I have tried consistently to explain words, phrases, customs, and objects which are not readily comprehensible to the normally alert student of today. I have also offered some guidance through the more obscure passages; and certain topics which needed larger annotation than was convenient for a footnote have been gathered into the Appendices. But I resisted (as far as was humanly possible) the temptation to theorize about Shakespeare or his plays; nor have I commented often on textual matters, or listed variant readings, which are a matter rather for the scholar than for the student.

As editor I echo the words of Dr. Johnson: " After the labours of all the editors, I found many passages which appeared to me likely to obstruct the greater number of readers, and thought it my duty to facilitate their passage. It is impossible for an expositor not to write too little for some, and too much for others. He can only judge what is necessary by his own experience; and how long soever he may deliberate, will at last explain many lines which the learned will think impossible to be mistaken, and omit many for which the ignorant will want his help. These are censures merely relative, and must be quietly endured. I have endeavoured to be neither superfluously copious, nor scrupulously reserved, and hope that I have made my authour's meaning accessible to many who before were frighted from perusing him, and contributed something to the publick, by diffusing innocent and rational pleasure." Yet Notes, no matter how full or how carefully compiled, are useless if they pass unnoticed. They are therefore placed at the bottom of each column of the text. Further, the symbol ° is used throughout to denote a word, phrase, or passage which is annotated. Text and notes are thus linked, and the student need neither despair at searching for help which does not exist nor accept his own guess when an explanation is below.

Students often miss much because they are unfamiliar with the appearance of many things which were part of everyday life in Shakespeare's England. The Plates have therefore been chosen to illustrate the text rather than to beautify the volume. They are an essential part of the commentary, and should be used accordingly. Whenever reference is made to a Plate, the Note on that Plate (see pp. 91–99) should also be consulted.

The reader should observe that each cross reference is not merely to a certain page, but to a specific column on that page, the left column being denoted *a,* the right, *b.* Thus the search is considerably narrowed. The line numbering of the plays follows the Globe edition.

The General Introduction is intended to give the student a knowledge of the background to Shakespeare which he will find useful in studying individual plays. In the chapter " Shakespeare and the Critics," it seemed better to offer pertinent passages from a dozen of the most significant critics than to present a list of a hundred names and dates. Similarly in the chapter " Shakespearean Scholarship and Criticism 1900–1950," I have confined myself to a few modern works which should be among the first to be presented to students. Scholars who feel that I have unfairly neglected or omitted works which they themselves regard more highly will doubtless supply the omissions in their teaching. In the Reading List I have included those works which are likely to stimulate or be useful to the college student; I have deliberately omitted more erudite studies which are better suited to the scholar.

In the last two decades there has been a vast explosion in Shakespeare studies. Between 1,500 and 2,000 items — books, articles, reviews — are now issued annually. To provide the student with some guide to the more important modern trends and interests, a new section (III) has been added to the Reading List, for which I am greatly indebted to Alvin B. Kernan.

My thanks are due to the many scholars who gave much valuable advice and help in the making of this edition, especially to R. C. Bald, Frank C. Baxter, Ben Black, W. E. Farnham, Anton A. Raven, G. C. Sedgewick, R. G. Shedd, Theodore Spencer, Harold C. Walley, and Virgil K. Whitaker. For help in gathering the illustrations I am particularly indebted to J. C. Adams, C. T. Currelly, Giles E. Dawson, Martin Holmes, Elizabeth Maw, James G. McManaway, Herman R. Mead, and Louis B. Wright. Acknowledgment for particular illustrations is made in the Notes to the Plates (pp. 91–99).

G. B. H.

GENERAL INTRODUCTION

and the Plates

GENERAL INTRODUCTION

1. THE UNIVERSALITY OF SHAKESPEARE, 3

2. RECORDS OF THE LIFE OF SHAKESPEARE, 8

3. SHAKESPEARE'S ENGLAND, 16

4. ELIZABETHAN DRAMA, 34

5. THE ELIZABETHAN PLAYHOUSE, 51

6. THE STUDY OF THE TEXT, 61

7. THE DEVELOPMENT OF SHAKESPEARE'S ART, 67

8. SHAKESPEARE AND THE CRITICS, 73

9. SHAKESPEAREAN SCHOLARSHIP AND CRITICISM 1900–1950, 84

THE PLATES

NOTES ON THE PLATES, 91

1. The Universality of Shakespeare

It is a common belief that there is some mystery about the life of William Shakespeare and that scholars, for all their bibliographies and footnotes, really know nothing about him. When the scholars protest that they do know more about the facts of Shakespeare's life than about that of any other Elizabethan dramatist, they are met with the incredulous retort that the facts are commonplace; somehow the author of *Hamlet* must have towered above his fellows. Can they produce nothing more interesting than the plump, staring bust on the Stratford monument, or the disreputable legend that Shakespeare stole deer from Charlecot Park, or the fact that he left the second-best bed to his widow? It is well to face this problem clearly and objectively.

Literary persons, even the greatest, are seldom spectacular. The man who leads a life of heroic action has neither the time nor usually the desire, even if he has the ability, to express himself in writing. Those who gallop down valleys of death do not sing about that experience; they leave it to gentle poets living comfortably in country retreats. Moreover, to be a great writer a man must spend much of his time at a table in the laborious but wholly prosaic act of writing. Few writers attract a Boswell, and unless the details of their lives, their sayings, and their oddities happen to be preserved in writing, they soon become little more than a name. Even with all the elaborate apparatus of modern publicity, few readers could without notice write more of the biography of any living writer than could be contained on a postcard. The work is always so much greater than the man.

Nevertheless all great works of literary art reflect and reveal their authors. We need no biography to tell us that the personality and environment of Jane Austen differed from that of Charles Dickens, or that Alfred Tennyson's habits, thoughts, and desires were not the same as the habits, thoughts, and desires of Robert Burns. And as soon as we are aware of these facts, we can go further and distill something of the experiences, the personality, and the attitude toward life of an author. We must not, of course, attempt too much. We cannot expect to discover from a comparison of " Tam o' Shanter " with " The Passing of Arthur " whether Burns had a more tranquil private life than Tennyson; but by studying their works as a whole we can legitimately and with some accuracy deduce their differing likes and prejudices, their beliefs and negations, their views on life and conduct, on God, on man, and on woman. No man can write a good book or play without revealing something of himself to the expert reader, and of all forms of writing drama is often the most revealing, because it is talk and thought. For even though the words of each character must naturally be appropriate, the author wrote the words; the sentiments have first occurred in his mind.

For the past three hundred and fifty years Shakespeare has been regarded as the greatest writer in the English tongue, and since it is unusual for one generation to worship the gods of its fathers, it follows that he has been admired for very different reasons, and that his plays possess an enduring vitality. This quality in art we call universality. When we try to analyze the universality of Shakespeare, we find that he is not particularly original as a thinker, nor is he the only great English writer. Others, in various ways, have written poetry as memorable. But he is the most universal of all, because he is the wisest; that is, he can understand and sympathize more than other men. He can see the whole picture of humanity and re-create it so that men of every kind, country, creed, and generation understand. Knowing humanity as no one else ever did, he is nevertheless neither a mocking nor a weeping philosopher. He views life with zest, and he is so great that he can refrain from moral judgments.

Accordingly when we read Shakespeare's plays we are always meeting our own experiences and are constantly surprised by some phrase which expresses what we thought to be our own secret or our own discovery. It is for this reason that so often, consciously or unconsciously, we can find no words more apt than his to express ourselves in exultation or depression, in holiday mood, in love, or in the very pit of sorrow:

> Why should a dog, a horse, a rat have life
> And thou no breath at all? Thou'lt come no
>   more,
> Never, never, never, never, never!

Anyone who has suffered bereavement knows that experience, and has felt it almost in those words.

Shakespeare is thus continually reminding us of our own experiences and expressing them for us. Moreover, as we grow older and the range of our experience widens, so his range grows too. He is always giving us back our own, so that we understand his plays more and ourselves better. The reward of the study of literature is that we are constantly deepening our own experience and understanding, and of all English literature the study of Shakespeare is the most valuable. It gives us the power of detaching ourselves from ourselves and seeing our own lives as part of universal life, as players playing out our own seven acts on the universal stage, and at the same time enjoying the experience of the play as players on the stage and as critics in the audience.

Now it follows that a man who can touch so many in so large a range of emotional experience must himself have lived a full life. Shakespeare was born in April 1564 at Stratford-on-Avon, an important little town in the west of England, for it stood at the crossing of the river Avon. His father was a man of influence in the town, and in time held most of its chief offices. His mother was of gentle birth; her home still stands, a substantial house of people of means. At eighteen he married; at nineteen he was a father, at twenty the father of twins; and then for seven years there is a gap in the records until, in 1592, he writes a play — *I Henry VI* — which is the success of the season. Thereafter we can trace the outline of his life firmly. In 1593 he writes *Venus and Adonis,* which puts him at once into the first rank of English poets. By 1598 he is recognized as the finest writer of drama yet produced by the English. We can watch him too, in sober records of fact, as a senior partner in the Lord Chamberlain's Company of players, helping to finance the building of the Globe playhouse and later the Blackfriars, and then in middle age returning to Stratford

as a man of means, to retire. On April 23, 1616, he died, leaving a very full will and a comfortable estate. It is the record of a prosperous career.

To some romantic readers it may seem disappointing that a great dramatist should have been nothing more than a prosperous actor. Nevertheless there is some hope, even for the romantic. Shakespeare was nearly twenty-eight when he first attracted notice as a writer, and we do not know what he had been doing in the previous seven years. A man achieves most of his vigorous experiences between the ages of eighteen and twenty-eight, and Shakespeare lived in a world as stirring for a young man as our own world of the 1940's. When Shakespeare was twenty-three, Drake sailed into the Cádiz Harbor and burned a Spanish fleet. When he was twenty-four, the Spanish Armada came and went. When he was twenty-five, the English admirals led a great expedition into Portugal. When he was twenty-seven, an expeditionary force was helping the French King to subdue his rebellious subjects. It may be that Shakespeare did not spend all his time between twenty and twenty-eight holding horses outside the theater, or stealing deer in Charlecot Park, or teaching school in the country.

When we come to look closely into Shakespeare's plays, it is clear that he had an extraordinary knowledge of soldiers. Critics have not appreciated this in the past because one needs to have been a soldier to realize it. It is not only that Shakespeare can express the heroics of battle, as in Henry V's great speech before Harfleur:

> Once more into the breach, dear friends, once
>   more. . . .

Any poet who has a proper flow of words can write heroics. It is rather that he knows how soldiers think and how they behave, as in the little scene in *Henry V* when the King wanders in disguise amongst his soldiers and hears some home truths from the company lawyer. This intimate knowledge is seen again and again in some casual image — " like a rich armor, worn in heat of day, that scalds with safety." Anyone who has served in a tank in a tropical climate knows the significance of that line. Or it may be a chance question, as in *Coriolanus,* to a messenger in battle: " How could'st thou in a mile confound an hour? " The first thing that a young recruit learns about messages is that he must always ascertain the time of origin. This is not the kind of fact that the heroic poet even dreams of, yet somehow Shakespeare came by such a knowledge of soldiering.

As notable is his use of the imagery of the sea, which recurs constantly throughout his plays. There are certain remarkable set pieces, such as Clarence's dream in *Richard III* or the shipwreck in *The Tempest*. These are not necessarily very significant. Any writer who wishes to create such effects can find his material. Far more important as reflections of Shakespeare's mind are the casual images of the sea used sometimes to illustrate something quite different:

Will all great Neptune's ocean wash this blood
Clean from my hand? No, this my hand will rather
The multitudinous seas incarnadine,
Making the green one red.

           Behold the threaden sails,
Borne with the invisible and creeping wind,
Draw the huge bottoms through the furrowed sea. . . .

For do but stand upon the foaming shore,
The chidden billow seems to pelt the clouds,
The wind-shaked surge, with high and monstrous mane,
Seems to cast water on the burning Bear,
And quench the guards of the ever-fixèd Pole. . . .

If after every tempest come such calms,
May the winds blow till they have wakened death!
And let the laboring bark climb hills of seas
Olympus-high, and duck again as low
As Hell's from Heaven!

Surely Shakespeare's vision of the sea was something greater than can be picked up from an afternoon's cruise on a summer vacation.

Or take a longer passage. King Henry IV, restless and troubled, addresses Sleep:

Wilt thou upon the high and giddy mast
Seel up the ship boy's eyes, and rock his brains
In cradle of the rude imperious surge
And in the visitation of the winds,
Who take the ruffian billows by the top,
Curling their monstrous heads and hanging them
With deafening clamor in the slippery clouds,
That with the hurly, death itself awakes?

Canst thou, O partial Sleep, give thy repose
To the wet sea boy in an hour so rude,
And in the calmest and most stillest night,
With all appliances and means to boot,
Deny it to a king?

How did Shakespeare come by the incident of the ship boy sleeping in the crow's-nest during the storm? It can only have been in one of three ways. He read of it, or he heard of it, or he saw it.

These images of the sea — and there are about two hundred of them — prove nothing; but they show that Shakespeare was sensitive and receptive to anything that had to do with the sea. A man does not use the sea to illustrate his thoughts unless such images are familiar and spontaneous to him, unless the sea has been an experience. Shakespeare is not the kind of author who is forever reshuffling in his own work phrases or ideas collected in reading. Pope was such a collector, as was Milton, and their work can be annotated accordingly.

So in our analysis of Shakespeare's poetry we can say that there are traces of a considerable knowledge of soldiers and of the sea. Until some lucky researcher finds Shakespeare's name in the records of a campaign or a voyage, we can go no further; but it follows that either he was — as George Bernard Shaw has drawn him in *The Dark Lady of the Sonnets* — a man with a notebook, jotting down everything he heard, or else he saw many more things with his own eyes than his biographers have hitherto recorded.

All this, however, is speculation. We are more firmly set when we try to recover Shakespeare's fundamental beliefs, his attitudes toward life. He had little use for those high-sounding proverbs of conduct or consolation which drip so readily from the lips of the professionally respectable, and he put into the mouth of Polonius a wonderful collection of such pearls of wisdom, which are often admiringly quoted by those ignorant of their context and of their irony.

Shakespeare himself had no rigid system of rules, of religion, of conduct, or of morality. He had no particular theories of any kind, but certain very marked instincts. While he never codified his thoughts into rules of right and wrong he has certainly left us his prejudices and fundamental instincts, as shown, for instance, in his views on love and marriage.

Here he is normally sane, conventional almost, in his instincts, differing thereby from the smart dramatists of his own day, or of the Restoration, or of modern Broadway. He regards marriage as the natural end and fulfillment of love between man and woman. Love outside marriage is disastrous. None of the lovers whom Shakespeare likes — and surely we can see who they are — falls in love without the most honorable intentions. Even in *Romeo and Juliet,* his one great story of youth overwhelmed by elemental, irresistible, passionate love, hero and heroine marry before they mate. Shakespeare goes to great trouble to make the story entirely respectable. The disaster which comes to them is not their fault or of their making. It comes because of the stupidity of their parents; and in Shakespeare's plays most parents, especially fathers of daughters, are incredibly stupid. His other favorite lovers, Rosalind and Orlando, Benedick and Beatrice, march naturally forward to love in wedlock. And in his later plays — *The Winter's Tale* and *The Tempest* — Florizel and Perdita, Ferdinand and Miranda, pairs of lovers whom Shakespeare abundantly blesses, have the nicest regard for the sanctity of marriage.

In this attitude Shakespeare differs noticeably from his contemporaries. Beaumont and Fletcher and others play with themes of love outside marriage, and regard infidelity as a natural topic for comedy. Shakespeare does not. He has plenty of jokes about cuckold's horns, as have all Elizabethan dramatists, but he sees nothing comic in unfaithfulness or unchastity, which always bring disaster. In *Measure for Measure* all the troubles which descend so freely on the chief persons are first caused by Claudio's unchastity. Angelo, having wronged Mariana, is made to offer her the only possible restitution in marriage. In *Troilus and Cressida,* the fickle Cressida is presented not as amusing or even particularly attractive, but as essentially rotten to all decent men.

Infidelity brings disaster. Even a suspicion of infidelity brings disaster on Hero, Desdemona, Imogen, and Hermione. Shakespeare apparently condones the behavior of the wronged lovers; yet he has at the same time a horror of suspicion. He thus instinctively accepts normal morality not because it accords with any rigid code or sanction, but because his instinct tells him that moral customs are founded on that system of conduct which has been found to work best.

As for his religion, all sects of Christianity have claimed him, Roman Catholics, Anglicans, even Puritans. There is a fairly early tradition that he died a Catholic, and there is some evidence that his parents were Catholics, even if secretly. Shakespeare's sympathies in his plays are usually with the older faith. He toned down the Protestant exuberance in the old play of *King John,* which he rewrote. The few friars in his plays are sympathetically treated. They are grave, wise, patient men, such as Friar Laurence in *Romeo and Juliet* or Friar Francis in *Much Ado about Nothing* or the priest in *Twelfth Night.* Shakespeare's parsons are few. Parson Evans in *The Merry Wives of Windsor* is amusing, and so is Sir Nathaniel, the curate in *Love's Labor's Lost;* but neither is a spiritual character. The parson in *As You Like It* is definitely a scamp. But all these are characters in plays. They speak their parts, and perhaps no more.

Shakespeare's own religion is neither Catholic, Anglican, nor Puritan. He belongs to no sect. His characters from time to time utter the phrases of conventional piety, but he has little conception of God as a loving Father, nor does he regard Him as a revenging Jehovah. At its most optimistic his faith is that:

> There's a divinity that shapes our ends,
> Roughhew them how we will.

At its most pessimistic:

> As flies to wanton boys are we to the gods,
> They kill us for their sport.

His general belief seems to have been halfway between the extremes:

> There's special providence in the fall of a sparrow. If it be now, 'tis not to come; if it be not to come, it will be now; if it be not now, yet it will come. The readiness is all. Since no man has aught of what he leaves, what is't to leave betimes?

Like Tennyson, he faintly trusts the larger hope.

His religion may be summed up as fulfillment. He seems not to have been greatly interested in the insoluble problems. He has none of Faustus's curiosity in the ultimate incomprehensibles, but he has an insatiable zest for all varieties of men and women. The universe is man's stage, but man holds the center, and it is a sign that Hamlet has lost his balance in the depths of despair when he finds that he can no longer appreciate humanity:

What a piece of work is a man! How noble in reason! How infinite in faculty! In form and moving how express and admirable! In action how like an angel! In apprehension how like a god! The beauty of the world! The paragon of animals! And yet, to me, what is this quintessence of dust? Man delights not me — no, nor woman neither.

Shakespeare had very little hope, or indeed interest, in any glorious or unending immortality. His one ghost who comes back to report on conditions hereafter gives a very gloomy picture of the next world. To Hamlet, death is a consummation devoutly to be wished so long as it means "to die, to sleep — no more." His fear is lest the sleep of death may be disturbed by those terrible dreams which make Claudio frantic when confronted by death. With Edgar in *Lear*, in dejection, the conclusion is that:

> Men must endure
> Their going hence, even as their coming hither.
> Ripeness is all.

Nevertheless, Shakespeare does not brood, as Donne or Marston or Webster brooded, on the horrors of physical death. He made his contributions to the literature of the charnel house in *Hamlet*, as might be expected, but even here in the gravedigging scene he is always sane. Hamlet in some of his moods is hypersensitive:

To what base uses we may return, Horatio. Why may not imagination trace the noble dust of Alexander, till he find it stopping a bunghole?

But Horatio's reply is:

'Twere to consider too curiously, to consider so,

and this seems also to have been Shakespeare's comment on all unprofitable speculations.

In *The Tempest* Shakespeare, if ever, speaks directly and deliberately out of part through Prospero. He sees the universe ultimately dissolving, to leave not a rack behind:

> We are such stuff
> As dreams are made on, and our little life
> Is rounded with a sleep.

Life is a flicker of consciousness between two eternities of oblivion. The thought is not original; the expression is superbly his own.

As for Shakespeare's social beliefs and political instincts, they are from time to time clearly revealed. Certain instincts lie deep in the Englishman's character; one is a horror of civil disorder. The long Wars of the Roses were brought to an end on Bosworth Field (1485) when Henry Tudor established himself as undisputed King. In the days of his grandchildren, King Edward VI and Queen Mary, it seemed for a while that anarchy would return, but thereafter for some forty years peace at home had been symbolized in the person of Queen Elizabeth. Most sane men hoped that this state would continue and most feared that it would not. It is not, therefore, surprising that Shakespeare believed in the divinity of kings. Nevertheless, he saw that kings, if officially divine, were also in fact human — and seldom admirable; but yet they had a terrible responsibility and loneliness. Shakespeare was one of the very few Englishmen who saw that behind the pomp lay the intolerable burden:

> Upon the King! Let us our lives, our souls,
> Our debts, our careful wives,
> Our children, and our sins lay on the King!
> We must bear all. Oh, hard condition,
> Twin-born with greatness, subject to the breath
> Of every fool, whose sense no more can feel
> But his own wringing!

To Shakespeare, as to many of his contemporaries, the universe was an ordered system, a chain or pyramid (see App. 1). At the apex was God; on earth the Sovereign was God's own immediate deputy; and below, ranged in degrees and orders down to the least, came lesser men. This fundamental belief he expressed in one of his finest philosophical utterances, Ulysses' great speech on degree or natural order in *Troilus and Cressida*. Everything, says Ulysses, from the planets and the sun and downward, observes degree. Once degree is broken, chaos follows. When Shakespeare wrote this speech, men's minds were troubled by threats at home of some vast revolution that was likely at any time to break down natural order. He wrote for the understanding of his contemporaries. Yet this speech is a fine instance of Shakespeare's universality; it means even more to our generation when degree and natural order and **decency** are still in the balance:

Take but degree away, untune that string,
And hark what discord follows! Each thing meets
In mere oppugnancy. The bounded waters
Should lift their bosoms higher than the shores,
And make a sop of all this solid globe.
Strength should be lord of imbecility,
And the rude son should strike his father dead.
Force should be right, or rather, right and wrong,
Between whose endless jar justice resides,
Should lose their names, and so should justice too.
Then everything includes itself in power,
Power into will, will into appetite,
And appetite, a universal wolf,
So doubly seconded with will and power,
Must make perforce a universal prey,
And last eat up himself.

When a man has so clearly indicated his political, religious, and social instincts, we can surely say we know something about him; and with a little patience in reading his plays we can discover for ourselves much more of the personality of the man Shakespeare. We may not always agree with what we find, as so often we disagree in our estimates of living acquaintances, but " the purpose of playing " — and of all creative literary art — " at the first and now was and is to hold as 'twere the mirror up to Nature," and it is the function of a mirror to give us back our own reflections. We look into Shakespeare's plays and find ourselves; it is for this reason that he is of all writers the most universal.

2. Records of the Life of Shakespeare

Apart from the legends, inferences, interpretations, and deductions of scholars and critics, the actual facts of Shakespeare's life, duly authenticated in indisputable records, are considerable. A student of Shakespeare should know where fact ends and guessing begins. In this chapter, facts only are given. The more important records, most of which mention Shakespeare by name, are as follows: [1]

1564. APRIL 26. The parish register of the Stratford-on-Avon church records the baptism of " Gulielmus filius Johannes Shakspere " — William son of John Shakspere.

There is no record of the date of birth, though Shakespeare's birthday is celebrated at Stratford-on-Avon and elsewhere on April 23, principally because this happens also to be the day of Saint George, the patron saint of England.

John Shakespeare had come to Stratford in the 1550's. He is variously described in records as yeoman (that is, a landowner), glover, and whitawer (one who cured glove skins). He had married Mary Arden, whose family were Roman

Catholic gentlefolk living at Wilmcote near Stratford. John Shakespeare became a leading citizen of Stratford. In 1564 he was chosen alderman, and in 1568 bailiff — the highest civic office in the town, the modern mayor. After 1577 the records show that he was disposing of his property and had ceased to attend meetings of the corporation. In 1587 another was chosen alderman in his place. In 1592 his name appeared in the list of those in Stratford who absented themselves from church, and it was noted that he and others " came not to church for fear of process for debt."

1582. NOVEMBER 28. A license was issued by the Bishop of Worcester to " William Shagspere " and " Anne Hathwey of Stratford " to solemnize matrimony upon once asking of the banns, provided that there was no legal objection.

The law required that the banns of marriage should be read out in church for three successive Sundays before the marriage. This was to enable anyone to show cause (such as precontract) why the marriage could not lawfully take place. When for any reason the parties wished to hasten the marriage, a special license from the bishop was required.

According to the inscription on the grave of Anne Shakespeare, she died on August 6, 1623, aged sixty-seven years. She was therefore born in 1556, and was thus eight years older than her husband.

1583. MAY 26. The parish register of the Strat-

---

[1] The spellings in records noted within quotes are original. There is no significance in the different spellings of Shakespeare's name; his contemporaries were very free in such matters. Indeed, I have encountered a case where a Lord Lieutenant of a county signed his own name in three different spellings on the same day in one set of documents. Marlowe's name appears in different documents as Marlo, Marle, Marley, Marlin, Merling, Marling, Morley. In Shakespeare's will, the scribe spelt the name "Shackspeare" on the first sheet and "Shackspere" on the third. Shakespeare himself signed the three sheets: on the first he wrote "William Shakspere," on the second "Willm Shakspere," on the third "By me William Shakspere."

ford-on-Avon church records the baptism of Susanna, daughter to William Shakespeare.

1585. FEBRUARY 2. The parish register of the Stratford-on-Avon church records the baptism of "Hamnet & Judeth, sonne and daughter to William Shakspere."

1588. MICHAELMAS. John and Mary Shakespeare claiming to some property formerly mortgaged to Edmund Barton, Mary Shakespeare's brother-in-law, joined their son William as a party in the suit.

1592. MARCH 3. Henslowe[2] records that he received £3 16s. 8d. at the first performance of *Harry the Sixth*. The play was repeated on March 7, 11, 16, 28, April 5, 13, 21, May 4, 9, 16, 22, 29, June 12 and 20. For the fifteen performances the gross takings were £32 8s. 6d. or an average of £2 3s. 3d. a performance. The average for all others plays over the period of three and three-quarter months was £1 14s. 10d.

It seems likely that this is Shakespeare's *I Henry VI.* Nashe in *Piers Penniless His Supplication to the Devil,* entered for publication (see p. 66a) on August 8, 1592, commented:

How would it have ioyed braue *Talbot* (the terror of the French) to thinke that after he had lyne two hundred yeares in his Tombe, hee should triumphe againe on the Stage, and haue his bones newe embalmed with the teares of ten thousand spectators at least (at seuerall times) who, in the Tragedian that represents his person, imagine they behold him fresh bleeding?

SEPTEMBER 3. Robert Greene, the pamphleteer, poet, and playwright, died in poverty (see p. 39a). Among his papers was a letter addressed "To those Gentlemen his quondam acquaintance, that spend their wits in making plaies," who are usually identified with Marlowe, Nashe, and Lodge. Greene's complaint was that the professional players had battened on the brains of university men like himself, and now they had forsaken him. He continued:

Base minded men all three of you, if by my miserie you be not warnd: for vnto none of you (like mee) sought those burres to cleaue: those Puppets (I meane) that spake from our mouths, those Anticks garnisht in our colours. Is it not strange, that I, to whom they all haue beene beholding: is it not like that you, to whome they all haue beene beholding, shall (were yee in that case as I am now) bee both at once of them forsaken? Yes trust them not:

²See p. 38b.

for there is an vpstart Crow, beautified with our feathers, that with his *Tygers hart wrapt in a Players hyde,* supposes he is as well able to bombast out a blanke verse as the best of you: and beeing an absolute *Iohannes fac totum,* is in his owne conceit the onely Shake-scene in a countrey. O that I might intreat your rare wits to be imploied in more profitable courses: & let those Apes imitate your past excellence, and neuer more acquaint them with your admired inuentions.

The phrase "Tygers hart wrapt in a Players hyde" is a parody of a line in *III Henry VI* — "O tiger's heart wrapped in a woman's hide!" — and Greene's passage is a bitter attack on Shakespeare. The letter was printed in Greene's *Groatsworth of Wit,* a short collection consisting of an unfinished novel and other scraps, and put together for the press by Henry Chettle. It was entered on September 20, 1592. Marlowe had been pointedly referred to in the letter as an atheist and warned to repent in time; he and Shakespeare apparently protested. On December 8, 1592, Chettle's *Kind Heart's Dream* was entered. To this book Chettle added a prefatory epistle in which he wrote:

With neither of them that take offence was I acquainted, and with one of them I care not if I neuer be: The other, whome at that time I did not so much spare, as since I wish I had, for that as I haue moderated the heate of liuing writers, and might have vsed my owne discretion (especially in such a case) the Author beeing dead, that I did not, I am as sorry as if the originall fault had beene my fault, because my selfe haue seene his demeanor no lesse ciuill than he exelent in the qualitie he professes: Besides, diuers of worship haue reported his uprightnes of dealing, which argues his honesty, and his facetious grace in writting that aprooues his Art.

From these records it seems likely that the Talbot scenes in *I Henry VI* were among the first that Shakespeare wrote. Further, if Shakespeare had been writing plays for some years, Greene could have hardly referred to him as an "upstart," nor could Chettle, in the very small world of the London theater, have pleaded that he had not previously known of him. Shakespeare therefore probably first began to write plays in 1591 or 1592; but some scholars dispute this and claim that he had been actor and playwright since 1587.

1593. APRIL 18. *Venus and Adonis* was entered

1.) *I HENRY VI*
2.) *VENUS + ADONIS*

for publication and was printed with the title page:

VENUS AND ADONIS

Vilia miretur vulgus: mihi flauus Apollo
Pocula Castalia plena ministret aqua.[3]

The poem was dedicated

To the Right Honourable Henrie Wriothesley,[4] Earle of Southampton, and Baron of Titchfield.

Right Honourable, I know not how I shall offend in dedicating my vnpolisht lines to your Lordship, nor how the worlde will censure mee for choosing so strong a proppe to support so weake a burthen, onelye if your Honour seeme but pleased, I account my selfe highly praised, and vowe to take aduantage of all idle houres, till I haue honoured you with some grauer labour. But if the first heire of my inuention proue deformed, I shall be sorie it had so noble a god-father: and neuer after eare so barren a land, for feare it yeeld me still so bad a haruest. I leaue it to your Honourable suruey, and your Honor to your hearts content, which I wish may alwaies answere your owne wish, and the worlds hopefull expectation.

Your Honors in all dutie,
WILLIAM SHAKESPEARE.

The Earl of Southampton was at this time nineteen years old. He was regarded as a young man of considerable promise and was conspicuous among the Queen's courtiers for his beauty and intelligence.

Venus and Adonis, though regarded by the sober-minded as an improper poem, established Shakespeare's reputation as a poet. It was reprinted at least nine times during his lifetime.

1594. MAY 9. *The Rape of Lucrece* was entered for printing. This poem too was dedicated

To the Right Honourable, Henry Wriothesley, Earle of Southampton, and Baron of Titchfield.

The loue I dedicate to your Lordship is without end: wherof this Pamphlet without beginning is but a superfluous Moity. The warrant I haue of your Honourable disposition, not the worth of my vntutord Lines makes it assured of acceptance. What I haue done is yours, what I haue to doe is yours, being part in all I haue, devoted yours. Were my worth greater, my duety would shew greater, meane time, as it is, it is bound to your

Lordship; To whom I wish long life still lengthened with all happinesse.

Your Lordships in all duety.
WILLIAM SHAKESPEARE

From the tone of the dedication it may be inferred that Southampton had shown considerable favor to Shakespeare during the previous twelve months.

1594. DECEMBER 26 AND 27. Payment for performances at Court was made to "William Kempe, William Shakespeare, & Richarde Burbage, seruantes to the Lord Chamberleyne." This is the first record which definitely names Shakespeare as a member of the company. Subsequent payments for Court performances were made to John Heminges, who seems to have acted as treasurer for the company.

1596. AUGUST 11. The parish register of the Stratford-on-Avon church records the burial of "Hamnet filius William Shakspere."

OCTOBER 20. William Dethick, Garter Principal King of Arms, granted to John Shakespeare the privilege of bearing a coat of arms, viz.:

Gould, on a Bend Sables, a Speare of the first steeled argent. And for his creast or cognizaunce a falcon his winges displayed Argent standing on a wrethe of his coullers: supporting a Speare Gould steeled as aforesaid sett vppon a helmett with mantelles & tasselles as hath ben accustomed and doth more playnely appeare depicted on this margent: Signefieing hereby & by the authorite of my office aforesaid ratefieing that it shalbe lawfull for the said John Shakespeare gentilman and for his children yssue & posterite (at all tymes & places convenient) to beare and make demonstracon of the same Blazon or Atchevment vppon theyre Shieldes, Targetes, escucheons, Cotes of Arms, pennons, Guydons, Seales, Ringes, edefices, Buyldinges, vtensiles, Lyveries, Tombes, or monumentes or otherwise for all lawfull warlyke factes or ciuile vse or exercises, according to the Lawes of Armes, and customes that to gentillmen belongethe without let or interruption of any other person or persons for vse or bearing the same.

Thus William Shakespeare in the right of his father was henceforward entitled to call himself "gentleman."

1596. NOVEMBER 29. In the Controlment Rolls of the Queen's Bench in the Public Record Office in London occurs an entry that William Wayte craved sureties of the peace against William Shakespeare, Francis Langley, Dorothy

---

[3] The crowd admires vile things; for me may yellow-haired Apollo prepare cups full of Castalian water (i.e., from the Muses' spring on Mount Parnassus). [4] Pronounced and occasionally spelled "Risley."

Soer, wife of John Soer, and Anne Lee for fear of death and so forth. A writ of attachment was issued to the Sheriff of Surrey, returnable on November 29.

This entry was discovered by Dr. Leslie Hotson and published in his *Shakespeare versus Shallow* (1931). Of the persons mentioned, Langley was owner of the Swan playhouse, which he had built about two years earlier. Wayte was the stepson of a rascally magistrate named William Gardener. Langley himself had claimed sureties of the peace against Gardener and Wayte less than a month earlier. Dr. Hotson discovered many details about Wayte and Gardener, but was unable to find how Shakespeare came into the business or how he had caused anyone to be in fear of his life.

1597. MAY 4. William Shakespeare purchased from William Underhill a house with two barns and two gardens in Stratford-on-Avon for £60 sterling.

This property, known as New Place, was a large house in the center of Stratford. It was then about a hundred years old, built of brick and timber, and of fair size, with a frontage of sixty feet and a depth of seventy feet. Only the foundations now remain.

AUGUST 29. Andrew Wise entered *Richard II* for publication. It appeared soon afterward with the title *The Tragedie of King Richard the second. As it hath beene publikely acted by the right Honourable the Lorde Chamberlaine his Seruants.* No author's name was given in the 1597 edition, but the play was twice reprinted in 1598 with the addition of *By William Shake-speare*.

OCTOBER 20. Andrew Wise entered for publication "The tragedie of kinge Richard the Third with the death of the Duke of Clarence," which appeared with the title *The Tragedy of King Richard the Third. Containing, His treacherous Plots against his brother Clarence: the pittiefull murther of his innocent nephewes: his tyrannicall vsurpation: with the whole course of his detested life, and most deserued death. As it hath been lately acted by the Right honourable the Lord Chamberlaine his seruants* (see Pl. 14a). No author's name was given in the 1597 edition, but in a second edition dated 1598 is added *By William Shake-speare*.

NOVEMBER 15. The commissioners appointed to collect the subsidy in the ward of Bishopsgate, London, sent in a list of those who had failed to pay their contribution to the subsidy. Included in the names was "William Shackspere," assessed to pay 5s. on £5. Shakespeare's name reappeared in several later lists, but the tax was apparently paid in 1600. These records show that before 1596 Shakespeare had lived in the parish of St. Helen's, near Bishopsgate, but afterward went to live on the south side of the Thames.

1598. FEBRUARY 4. Owing to a general shortage of corn due to bad summers, there was considerable hoarding of corn. A survey was made of the corn and malt held by individuals in Stratford-on-Avon. Among them it was found that "Wm. Shackespere" held ten quarters.[5]

FEBRUARY 25. Andrew Wise entered for publication "The historye of Henry the iiij^th with his battaile of Shrewsburye against Henry Hotspurre of the Northe with the conceipted mirthe of Sir John Ffalstoff," which was published under the title *The History of Henrie the Fourth; With the battell at Shrewsburie, betweene the King and Lord Henry Percy, surnamed Henrie Hotspur of the North. With the humorous conceits of Sir Iohn Falstaffe.* No author's name was given in the edition of 1598, but in the second edition printed in 1599 the words *Newly corrected by W. Shake-speare* were added.

JULY 22. James Roberts entered in the Stationers' Register "a booke of the Marchaunt of Venyce, or otherwise called the Jewe of Venyce, Prouided, that yt bee not prynted by the said James Robertes or anye other whatsoeuer without lycence first had from the Right honorable the lord Chamberlen." This is an example of a "blocking entry" (see p. 66a) whereby the players arranged with Roberts to enter a play to avoid its publication.

SEPTEMBER 7. *Palladis Tamia: Wit's Treasury* by Francis Meres was entered for publication. This book was a large collection of "similitudes" or parallel passages from a vast number of authors. Meres added "A comparatiue discourse of our English Poets with the *Greeke, Latine, and Italian Poets*." Shakespeare was mentioned more frequently than any of the other English writers, as one of eight by whom "the English tongue is mightily enriched, and gorgeouslie inuested in rare ornaments and resplendent abiliments," as one of six who had raised *monumentum aere perennius,* as one of

---

[5] 1 quarter = 8 bushels. "Corn" here means wheat, rye, and oats.

five who excelled in lyric poetry, as one of thirteen "best for Tragedie," as one of seventeen "best for Comedy." Shakespeare was also picked out for special mention not given to the others:

As the soule of *Euphorbus* was thought to liue in *Pythagoras:* so the sweete wittie soule of *Ouid* liues in mellifluous & hony-tongued *Shakespeare,* witnes his *Venus* and *Adonis;* his *Lucrece,* his sugred Sonnets among his priuate friends, &c.

As *Plautus* and *Seneca* are accounted the best for Comedy and Tragedy among the Latines: so *Shakespeare* among the English is the most excellent in both kinds for the stage; for Comedy, witnes his *Gentlemen of Verona,* his *Errors,* his *Loue Labors lost,* his *Loue labours wonne,* his *Midsummers night dreame,* & his *Merchant of Venice:* for Tragedy his *Richard the 2. Richard the 3. Henry the 4. King Iohn, Titus Andronicus* and his *Romeo and Iuliet.*

As *Epius Stolo* said, that the Muses would speake with *Plautus* tongue, if they would speak Latin: so I say that the Muses would speake with *Shakespeares* fine filed phrase, if they would speake English.

Meres's remarks are important; they show that by 1598 — even before the greatest tragedies were produced — Shakespeare had already firmly established his reputation; and they give a list of twelve plays already written — a valuable piece of evidence for establishing the dates of some of Shakespeare's plays. *Love's Labor's Won* has apparently been lost, unless it is an earlier title of one of the comedies.

SEPTEMBER 20. The Chamberlain's Men acted Ben Jonson's *Every Man in His Humor.* In the 1616 collection of his plays Jonson added the note:

This Comoedie was first Acted, in the yeere 1598. By the then L. Chamberlayne his Seruants. The principall Comoedians were.

Will. Shakespeare.	Ric. Burbadge.
Aug. Philips.	Ioh. Hemings.
Hen. Condel.	Tho. Pope.
Will. Slye.	Chr. Beeston.
Will. Kempe.	Ioh. Duke.

OCTOBER 25. Richard Quiney, a citizen of Stratford, being in London on business, partly private and partly on behalf of the corporation, wrote a letter from the Bell in Carter Lane asking for a loan of £30, addressed " To my Loveinge good ffrend & countreymann Mr. W^m. Shackespere." As the sum of £30 in cash was considerable at this time, the letter shows that Shakespeare was a man of some means.

During this year was printed, but without entry in the Stationers' Register, *A Pleasant Conceited Comedie Called, Loues labors lost. As it was presented before her Highnes this last Christmas. Newly corrected and augmented by W. Shakespere.*

1599. FEBRUARY 21. Documents in a lawsuit dated April 28, 1619, show that a lease of the ground on which the Globe playhouse was being built was agreed between Nicholas Brend on the one part, and on the other Cuthbert Burbadge, Richard Burbadge, William Shakespeare, Augustine Phillipps, Thomas Pope, John Heminges, and William Kempe. The details of the shares of the takings in the playhouse to be received by each are also recorded.

During this year appeared *The Passionate Pilgrime By W. Shakespeare.* The book was published by W. Jaggard and contains twenty poems, two of which are sonnets by Shakespeare and three poems from *Love's Labor's Lost.* The rest of the poems are by different writers. It was an indication of Shakespeare's reputation that a printer should pass off such a volume as entirely his.

1600. AUGUST 23. Andrew Wise and William Aspley entered for publication " Muche a Doo about nothinge " and " the second parte of the history of Kinge Henry the IIIJth with the humours of Sir John Falstaff: Wrytten by master Shakespere." This was the first time that Shakespeare's name was entered in the Stationers' Register. The plays appeared with the titles: *Much Adoe about Nothing. As it hath been sundrie times publikely acted by the right honourable, the Lord Chamberlaine his seruants. Written by William Shakespeare;* and *The Second part of Henrie the fourth, continuing to his death, and coronation of Henrie the fift. With the humours of sir John Falstaffe, and swaggering Pistoll. As it hath been sundrie times publikely acted by the right honourable, the Lord Chamberlaine, his seruants. Written by William Shakespeare.*

OCTOBER 8. Thomas Fisher entered for publication " A booke called A mydsommer nightes Dreame." The play appeared with the title: *A Midsommer nights dreame. As it hath beene sundry times publickely acted, by the Right honourable, the Lord Chamberlaine his seruants. Written by William Shakespeare.*

OCTOBER 28. Thomas Hays by consent of James

Roberts entered "a booke called the booke of the merchant of Venyce." The play appeared with the title: *The most excellent Historie of the Merchant of Venice. With the extreame crueltie of Shylocke the Iewe towards the sayd Merchant, in cutting a iust pound of his flesh: and the obtayning of Portia by the choyse of three chests. As it hath beene diuers times acted by the Lord Chamberlaine his Seruants. Written by William Shakespeare* (see Pl. 14b).

1601. SEPTEMBER 8. The parish register of the Stratford-on-Avon church records the burial of "Mr. Johannes Shakspeare." This was Shakespeare's father.

1602. JANUARY 18. John Busby entered, but immediately assigned to Arthur Johnson, "A booke called An excellent and pleasant conceited commedie of Sir John Faulstof and the merry wyves of Windesor." The quarto which followed is entitled: *A Most pleasaunt and excellent conceited Comedie, of Syr Iohn Falstaffe, and the merrie Wiues of Windsor, Entermixed with sundrie variable and pleasing humors, of Syr Hugh the Welch Knight, Iustice Shallow, and his wise Cousin M. Slender. With the swaggering vaine of Auncient Pistoll, and Corporall Nym. By William Shakespeare. As it hath bene diuers times Acted by the right Honorable my Lord Chamberlaines seruants. Both before her Maiestie, and else-where.*

The text of the play printed in this edition is a garbled and pirated version, very different from the play as known in the first folio.

MAY 1. William Combe and John Combe of Stratford-on-Avon sold to "William Shakespere" one hundred and seven acres of arable land in old Stratford for the sum of £320. The deed was delivered to Gilbert Shakespeare "to the use of the within named William Shakespere." Gilbert was Shakespeare's younger brother, and Shakespeare himself seems to have been in Stratford-on-Avon at the time.

JULY 26. James Roberts entered in the Stationers' Register "A booke called the Revenge of Hamlett Prince Denmarke as yt was latelie Acted by the Lord Chamberleyne his servantes." No edition of 1602 is known. This was apparently another "blocking entry" (see p. 66a).

SEPTEMBER 28. Walter Getley transferred a cottage in Walkers Street (alias Dead Lane) in Stratford-on-Avon to "William Shackespere."

1603. MAY 19. Queen Elizabeth died on March 24. The new King, James I, took over the Lord Chamberlain's players as the King's Men. A license was accordingly issued to "our Servauntes Lawrence Fletcher, William Shakespeare, Richard Burbage, Augustyne Phillippes, Iohn Heninges, Henrie Condell, William Sly, Robert Armyn, Richard Cowly, and the rest of theire Assosiates freely to vse and exercise the Arte and faculty of playing Comedies, Tragedies, histories, Enterludes, moralls, pastoralls, Stageplaies and Suche others like as theie haue alreadie studied or hereafter shall vse or studie aswell for the recreation of our lovinge Subjectes as for our Solace and pleasure when wee shall thincke good to see them duringe our pleasure."

During this year was acted Jonson's *Sejanus*. In the collected edition of 1616, Jonson stated that the principal tragedians were:

Ric. Burbadge.	Will. Shake-Speare.
Aug. Philips.	Ioh. Hemings.
Will. Sly.	Hen. Condel.
Ioh. Lowin.	Alex. Cooke.

During this year was printed a garbled and pirated version of *Hamlet* entitled: *The Tragicall Historie of Hamlet Prince of Denmarke By William Shake-speare. As it hath beene diuerse times acted by his Highnesse seruants in the Cittie of London: as also in the two Vniuersities of Cambridge and Oxford, and else-where.*

1604. MARCH. King James made a royal progress through the City of London, with his various servants in attendance. The players being Grooms of the Chamber, four yards of red cloth for liveries was given to "William Shakespeare, Augustine Phillips, Lawrence Fletcher, John Hemminges, Richard Burbidge, William Slye, Robert Armyn, Henry Cundell, and Richard Cowley."

During this year was printed a second version of *Hamlet* entitled: *The Tragicall Historie of Hamlet, Prince of Denmarke. By William Shakespeare. Newly imprinted and enlarged to almost as much againe as it was, according to the true and perfect Coppie* (see Pl. 14d). As copies of this version are dated 1604 and 1605, it was probably issued late in 1604.

1605. MAY 4. Augustine Phillips, one of the King's Men, made his will and died shortly afterward, leaving "to my Fellowe William Shakespeare a thirty shillings peece in gould."

To other members of the company he also left money, thirty shillings to Henry Condell and Christopher Beeston, and twenty shillings each to Lawrence Fletcher, Robert Armin, Richard Cowley, Alexander Cook, and Nicholas Tooley.

JULY 24. Ralph Huband, in consideration of the sum of £440, assigned to " William Shakespear " a half of all the tithes of Stratford, Old Stratford, Welcombe, and Bushopton, and half the tithes of the parish of " Stratford-upon-Avon." This investment yielded Shakespeare about £60 a year.

1607. JUNE 5. The parish register of the Stratford-on-Avon church records the marriage of " M. John Hall gentleman & Susanna Shaxspere." Susanna was Shakespeare's elder daughter, born in 1583. John Hall was a doctor of medicine well known in the neighborhood.

NOVEMBER 26. Nathaniel Butter and John Busby entered in the Stationers' Register a book called " Master William Shakespeare his historye of Kinge Lear, as yt was played before the Kinges maiestie at Whitehall, vppon Sainct Stephens night at Christmas Last [that is, December 26, 1606] by his maiesties servantes playinge vsually at the Globe on the Banksyde." A quarto was published in 1608.

1608. FEBRUARY 21. The parish register of the Stratford-on-Avon church records the christening of " Elizabeth dawghter to John Hall gentleman." This was Shakespeare's first grandchild.

AUGUST 9. William Ostler, gentleman, of London agreed to rent the Blackfriars playhouse to Richard Burbage, John Hemings, William Shakespeare, Cuthbert Burbage, Henry Condell, and Thomas Evans for a period of twenty-one years.

SEPTEMBER 9. The parish register of the Stratford-on-Avon church records the burial of " Mayry Shaxspere, wydowe." This was Shakespeare's mother.

DECEMBER 17. " William Shackspeare," gentleman, began to take proceedings in the Stratford court against John Addenbrooke, gentleman, to recover a debt of £6. The case went on for some months.

1609. JANUARY 28. Richard Bonion and Henry Walleys entered for publication " a booke called the history of Troylus and Cressida," which appeared under the title: *The Historie of Troylus*

and Cresseida. As it was acted by the Kings Maiesties seruants at the Globe. Written by William Shakespeare.

A second issue appeared in the same year with the title: *The Famous Historie of Troylus and Cresseid. Excellently expressing the beginning of their loues, with the conceited wooing of Pandarus Prince of Licia. Written by William Shakespeare.*

MAY 20. Thomas Thorpe entered for publication " a Booke called Shakespeares sonnettes," which appeared under the title " *Shakes-speares Sonnets. Neuer before Imprinted.*

During the year also appeared: *The Late, And much admired Play, Called Pericles, Prince of Tyre. With the true Relation of the whole Historie, aduentures, and fortunes of the said Prince: As also, The no lesse strange, and worthy accidents, in the Birth and Life, of his Daughter Mariana. As it hath been diuers and sundry times acted by his Maiesties Seruants, at the Globe on the Banck-side. By William Shakespeare.*

1611. JANUARY. " William Shackspeare " and others started a suit in the Court of Chancery arising out of the ownership of the tithes which Shakespeare had purchased in 1605.

SEPTEMBER 11. The name of " Mr. William Shackspere " occurs in a list of those contributing toward the prosecuting of a bill in Parliament for the better repair of the highways.

1612. MAY 11. " William Shakespeare " of Stratford-on-Avon in the County of Warwick, gentleman, of the age of forty-eight years or thereabouts, gave evidence in London in the case of Belott vs Mountjoy. The evidence in the case shows that in 1604 Shakespeare was lodging in the house of Christopher Mountjoy, a wigmaker of Huguenot origin, in Cripplegate Ward in the City of London. Shakespeare had helped to negotiate a marriage between Christopher Mountjoy's daughter Mary and Stephen Belott, Mountjoy's apprentice. At the time Mountjoy had promised a dowry, which was not paid. Belott therefore sued his father-in-law, and Shakespeare was summoned as witness to the promises made at the betrothal. Shakespeare however in his evidence could not remember the details. Shakespeare's signature was appended to his deposition; he signed his name as " Willm. Shakp."

1613. JANUARY 28. John Combe of Stratford

left £5 in his will to "Mr. William Shack-spere."

MARCH 10. Henry Walker, citizen and minstrel of London, in consideration of the sum of £140 conveyed a dwelling house erected over the great gate of the former Blackfriars Monastery to " William Shakespeare of Stratford Vpon Avon in the Countie of Warwick gentleman, William Johnson, citizein and Vintener of London [and host of the Mermaid Tavern], John Jackson, and John Hemmyng of London gentlemen." Shakespeare paid the money; the other three were apparently acting as his trustees. One copy of the agreement, now in the Guildhall, London, bears Shakespeare's signature, in which he spelled his name " William Shakspē."

MARCH 31. The steward of the Earl of Rutland recorded in his accounts the payment " to M^r. Shakspeare in gold about my Lorde's impreso, xliiijs; to Richard Burbage for paynting and making yt, in gold xliiijs."

This " impresa " was a symbolic device with appropriate motto borne on the shield of those taking part in a tilt or tournament. These tilts were usually held on the anniversary of the Sovereign's accession (Queen Elizabeth, November 17; King James, March 24). Burbage was well known as a painter as well as an actor.

OCTOBER 28. An agreement was made between " William Shackspeare, of Stretford in the county of Warwicke, gent," and William Replingham of Great Harborough in the County of Warwick that Replingham would recompense Shakespeare for any decrease in his yearly value of tithes which might occur by reason of any enclosure or decay of tillage meant and intended by the said William Replingham. Hereafter Shakespeare's name occurs several times in various Stratford records concerning tithes and enclosures.

1616. FEBRUARY 10. The parish register of the Stratford-on-Avon church recorded the marriage of " M. Tho Queeny tow Judith Shakspere," Shakespeare's younger daugher.

MARCH 25. William Shakespeare made his will. The will was written on three large sheets of parchment, and is now in Somerset House, London. The principal bequests were to his younger daughter Judith, £150, with a further £150 on trust; to his sister Joan Hart, £20, all wearing apparel, and the use for life of the house which she occupied; £5 to each of his nephews; to Elizabeth Hall, his granddaughter, all his plate except the broad silver-gilt bowl, which went to Judith; money to buy memorial rings to five Stratford friends; 26s. 8d. each to his fellows John Heminges, Richard Burbage, and Henry Condell to buy rings; to his wife his second-best bed, with its furniture; to his daughter Susanna Hall of New Place two houses in Henley Street, and all other lands; and the residue, including all plate and household goods, to Susanna Hall and her husband.

The will was much corrected and revised, and signed at the foot of each of the three pages. Shakespeare's bequest of the second-best bed, and nothing else, to his wife has been much discussed. As widow she was entitled to a third of the income of the estate and to remain in the house. There is therefore no reason to suppose the bequest of the second-best bed, made as an interlinear afterthought, was necessarily a sign either of contempt or of especial affection for the widow.

APRIL 23. The monument in the Stratford church records that Shakespeare died on April 23.

APRIL 25. The register in the Stratford church records the burial of " Will. Shakspere, gent."

Shakespeare was buried within the church in the chancel, and over the grave was laid a stone with the inscription:

GOOD FREND FOR IESVS SAKE FORBEARE,
TO DIGG THE DVST ENCLOASED HEARE!
BLESTE BE Y^E MAN Y^T SPARES THES STONES,
AND CVRST BE HE Y^T MOVES MY BONES.

A tablet was erected on the north wall of the chancel which contains a bust within an arch (see Pl. 1b). The inscription reads:

IVDICIO PYLIUM, GENIO SOCRATEM, ARTE MARONEM:
TERRA TEGIT, POPVLVS MÆRET, OLYMPVS HABET.

STAY PASSENGER, WHY GOEST THOV BY SO FAST?
READ IF THOV CANST, WHOM ENVIOVS DEATH HATH PLAST,
WITH IN THIS MONVMENT SHAKSPEARE: WITH WHOME,
QVICK NATVRE DIDE: WHOSE NAME DOTH DECK Y^S TOMBE,
FAR MORE THEN COST: SIEH ALL, Y^T HE HATH WRITT,
LEAVES LIVING ART, BVT PAGE, TO SERVE HIS WITT.
OBIIT AÑO DO^I 1616
ÆTATIS · 53 DIE 23 AP^R.

The records thus give a clear outline of Shakespeare's life. He was born in Stratford-on-Avon in 1564, married at the age of eighteen and a half, and was the father of three children at twenty. There is a gap until 1592, when he wrote a play which was successful, followed by two popular poems. From 1594 onward he wrote plays which were acted by the company first known as the Lord Chamberlain's Men and later as the King's Men. He was a principal shareholder in this company. He made money, and in his later years lived in his native town, where he died on April 23, 1616. The records are not in themselves exciting, and they tell little of the personality or intimate experience of the man. Much more may be inferred or deduced from other evidence, but these are sober records of fact.

3. Shakespeare's England

London

Shakespeare was born at Stratford-on-Avon in Warwickshire, but he made his name in London, which was then, as now, the heart of England. At the end of the sixteenth century London was a city of about 200,000 inhabitants; few other English cities exceeded 15,000. The old medieval city of London was at that time still surrounded by walls; indeed, the names of some of the gates survive today as stations on the Inner Circle of the Underground Railway system — Aldgate, Bishopsgate, Moorgate, Aldersgate. To the East, and downstream of the River Thames, stood (and still stands) the Tower of London, a great fort protecting the city from any invasion from the sea. The Tower was also a royal palace, though no longer used as such, a prison for offenders who had incurred the displeasure of the Sovereign, and the chief arsenal of the realm. At the West End, the city was entered by Ludgate, though the city boundary stretched farther west to Temple Bar, where Fleet Street joins the Strand.

Farther west and two miles upstream lay the Royal City of Westminster. Here was the Palace of Whitehall, the principal residence of the Queen, the Abbey Church of St. Peter (now called Westminster Abbey), where the Kings and Queens of England are crowned and where also many are buried, and the Parliament House and Westminster Hall, where the Queen's Courts of Justice sat to determine civil lawsuits. The City of Westminster and the City of London were legally and geographically quite distinct. Westminster (like Washington) was the seat of the national Government; London (like New York) was the center of **trade, commerce, and wealth.** The two cities were connected by the Strand, which ran parallel to the River Thames and was fringed by a double row of houses. To the north and beyond, there was park land or open country.

The city of London had many privileges, jealously guarded. The Sovereign did not enter the city without invitation, and although relations between Court and city were close and friendly during Shakespeare's lifetime, the city was quick to resent anything that might seem to infringe upon its privileges — an attitude which considerably affected the position of players and dramatists. The city itself was quite small; it was less than a square mile in area, and its boundaries were fixed.[1] The suburbs to the north were growing fast, but they were controlled by the magistrates of the County of Middlesex and not by the city authorities.

The River Thames was the main highway for traffic, and watermen with rowboats took the place of the modern taxi. South of the Thames was the suburb of Southwark in the County of Surrey. Southwark clustered around the south end of London Bridge, the only bridge over the Thames and therefore of great strategic importance. The bridge was one of the wonders of Elizabethan England. It had been built on brick piles as early as 1209. By Shakespeare's time the piles had been enlarged, and a double row of shops ran along the length of the bridge, which was broken by a drawbridge (see Pl. 3). The piers held back the waters of the river, which at high and low tide flowed through with great force. Under one of the piers was set the wheel which turned the city's corn mills.

[1] Nowadays the *City* of London is a small but highly privileged island in the vast area of Greater London. In Shakespeare's time the suburbs were not extensive.

St. Paul's

In the city itself, with its many churches, the great Cathedral of St. Paul's — known as Paul's — towered over all. The old building was a large Gothic church with a squat tower (see Pl. 2a). It was the social center for all classes. Here at eight o'clock every Sunday morning the Lord Mayor and the Aldermen came in state to hear the weekly Paul's Cross sermon, which was preached in the open air when the weather allowed. The sermon was an important event, for it brought the principal citizens together. Moreover the preacher was often inspired by the Government to deliver official news or views. Here, for instance, on February 15, 1601, was preached the official account of Essex's rebellion by Dr. John Hayward. A fortnight later Dr. William Barlow preached on Essex's trial and condemnation. On November 10, 1605, Dr. Barlow also gave from the same pulpit the first public account of the Gunpowder Plot.

The Gunpowder Plot was the most sensational event at home during Shakespeare's lifetime. When James I came to the English throne in 1603, both Catholics and Puritans expected that the restrictions on liberty of worship would be relaxed, but they soon realized that they had been misled. Some of the more desperate Catholics thereupon plotted to bring about a revolution. They rented a cellar under the Parliament House, where they accumulated a great store of gunpowder with the intention of exploding it when the King was addressing the Lords and Commons on the opening day. Had it succeeded, the plot would have destroyed in one blow the entire executive of government — the King, the Prince of Wales, all the nobility, the bishops, the Privy Council, and a large number of the principal gentlemen. The plot was timed for the state opening of Parliament of November 5, 1605; it was discovered less than twelve hours before the explosion was due. Few events in English history have caused more universal horror and consternation. On this occasion Dr. Barlow's Paul's Cross sermon was below his usual standard; he had not recovered from the shock of his own narrow escape, for he would himself " have been one of the hoisted number."

On weekdays Paul's was a regular meeting place. Unemployed servants stuck up bills there declaring their qualifications; lawyers met their clients; professional perjurers (known as " knights of the post ") offered their services to dishonest litigants who required evidence for a doubtful case; needy gentlemen waited hopefully by " Duke Humphrey's " tomb for a free meal; pickpockets hovered about the unwary countryman as he looked around at the tombs, confused by the noise and bustle. Dekker complained:

At one time, in one and the same rank, yea, foot by foot and elbow by elbow, shall you see walking, the knight, the gull [sucker], the gallant, the upstart, the gentleman, the clown, the captain, the apple squire [pimp], the lawyer, the usurer, the citizen, the bankerout [bankrupt], the scholar, the beggar, the doctor, the idiot, the ruffian, the cheater, the puritan, the cut-throat, the high-man, the low-man, the true-man, and the thief; of all trades and professions some, of all countries some.

The City

The city of London was governed by the Lord Mayor and the Council of Aldermen, by whom the Lord Mayor was elected annually from their own body. It was a most important office, for the smooth working of the administration of the state depended largely on the co-operation of the citizens of London through their representative, the Lord Mayor. To be Lord Mayor of London was the ambition of every wealthy merchant; but it was not an easy office, for Londoners were notoriously rowdy. There was, for instance, every year trouble over the slaying of meat in Lent. It was a regular practice of the Privy Council, renewed annually, to order that no cattle should be killed in Lent except for invalids; able-bodied Christians were expected to eat fish.

The Council's motive was not religious but economic, for it was hoped by this means to encourage the fishermen, who were so urgently needed to serve in the navy, and also to preserve the stock cattle. Accordingly, during Lent only six butchers were licensed for the whole City, and the rest, as well as innkeepers and victualers, were strictly forbidden to sell meat. The inspection and control of these regulations was entrusted to the wardens and members of the Fishmongers' Company as the most interested parties. But the butchers were always defiant, even when they were severely punished; in fact, the

Council was so wearied by the struggle that its printed orders, issued annually, began with this pessimistic sentence: "First her Majesty's pleasure is, upon her understanding of the great disorders heretofore, and *especially the last Lent. . . .*" Nevertheless the black market in meat flourished, and disobedient hostesses, such as Mrs. Quickly, continued to set legs of mutton before their guests.

Riots in the city and the suburbs were frequent, for there were always unruly apprentices, masterless men for whom no one was responsible, and unemployed ex-soldiers ready for trouble on the least provocation. There was no regular police force. The sheriffs were responsible for order in the city, which was divided into parishes. In each parish the constable represented the law; he was assisted by the watch, composed of responsible citizens who reluctantly took their turn at patrolling their parish by night. These amateur watchmen were much derided by unruly young gentlemen. Indeed they sometimes acted with incredible stupidity; but their behavior was unpredictable; on occasion they were just obstinately honest. In great emergency, the trained bands — a rudimentary form of militia — could be called out, for it was the duty of every fit man to be trained as a soldier. The training was not very burdensome; it consisted of one annual parade at Mile End on Midsummer Day.

Plague

Many of the troubles in the city were due to overcrowding. Statesmen realized that the continual drift of farm laborers away from the country would be disastrous, but they did not know how to stop it. Regulations were constantly made that no new houses should be built in the city of London, but rules were easily evaded. Men with large houses rented them room by room as apartments, and hovels were knocked together on any piece of unoccupied ground. As a result, the city was pestered by an ill-controlled, filthy, slum population. Bubonic plague broke out frequently. It is known nowadays that the plague was communicated by fleas carried by the rats which bred in the innumerable muck heaps; but in Shakespeare's time, though a few doctors, more intelligent than the rest, associated plague with dirt and stench, most people regarded it as the direct sign of God's anger toward a wicked people. Stray dogs were considered to be carriers, and during an epidemic they were destroyed in large numbers, with the result that the rats bred more freely than usual. There were two violent outbreaks during Shakespeare's lifetime. In 1592 and 1593 more than 22,000 died of plague, and in 1603 — the year that King James came to the throne — over 30,000; that is, in two epidemics within eleven years a quarter of the city's population died from plague. Plague was thus a constant fear to the civic authorities.

Sanitation

The city was incredibly dirty. Most of the houses, many of them very old, were built close together in dark, narrow, airless lanes. Moreover, there were no sewers or drains except for the gutter which ran down the middle of the street. Garbage pails were emptied into the gutter and the filth accumulated until the next heavy rain, when it drifted down into one of the ditches — such as the Fleet ditch or the Moor ditch — which became proverbial for their foul stench. Night soil was, however, collected into carts and carried out to sea in barges.

Nevertheless, in many ways Tudor London was singularly beautiful. There were no smoke fogs to reduce the buildings to a uniform grime. Many of the houses were half-timbered, and the Thames, which still ran clear and silver, was fringed with the great mansions and gardens of noblemen and men of wealth. Today little remains of Shakespeare's London, for the old city was almost completely wiped out in the Great Fire of 1666.

Country Life

In the country, life was simple. The parish was the unit of local administration. The chief persons in the village were the squire, who was sometimes also a magistrate, the parson, and a few farmers; often the rest of the villagers lived and died without ever going more than twenty miles from home. In the village the church, surrounded by its churchyard, was the center of community life. It was used as a place of worship on Sundays and holy days, and at other times for public meetings of all kinds. In the churchyard were buried most of the dead; men of wealth with their families were buried inside the church itself, often beneath large and elaborate monuments. The officers of the church were the parson, assisted by the clerk or sexton, and the churchwardens, who were responsible for the administration of the affairs of the parish, such as collection of dues, repairs to roads, relief of the poor, and maintenance of the church fabric.

The Church of England

The right to appoint a minister to a "living" or "cure of souls" was a private property which could be bought and sold. The owner or "patron" had the right to present the living to any duly ordained minister of the Church of England quite regardless of the wishes of the congregation, who were not even consulted. Livings were in the gift of all kinds of patrons — the Sovereign, the bishop of the diocese, colleges and universities, and private individuals. The living was usually endowed with an income drawn from the proceeds of some investment, almost invariably the rents from lands or houses. The parson had the free use of a house and land; he had also the right to exact a tithe, or one-tenth of the produce, of his parishioners. Tithe could, however, be alienated from the living and purchased from the owner. Shakespeare himself (see page 14a) bought tithes as an investment.[2] The parson had many privileges and few heavy responsibilities. Once appointed to a living he was entitled to enjoy its income for life and he could be turned out only if convicted in an ecclesiastical court of some gross offense against morals or doctrine. Usually he was a graduate of one of the two universities of Oxford and Cambridge, and sometimes he was a scholar; but on the whole the village parson was seldom a man of much distinction. Indeed, very

little was demanded of him. He had to conduct a certain minimum of services in the church and baptize, marry, or bury his parishioners. He was required to preach a sermon on four occasions during the year, and for those who were incapable of original composition a *Book of Homilies* was prescribed. The reason for this generally low level of ability was that the Church was a safe and comfortable profession and attracted the timid and unambitious. A curious illustration of this occurs in a sermon preached against simony in 1597. In attacking those patrons who appropriated for themselves part of the income of the livings in their gift, the preacher argued that such an action would ruin the universities. Men, he declared, underwent the expense of a university training because they expected at the end to be rewarded with a vicarage worth £40 to £50 a year. If the value of livings went down, then the university degree would no longer be a good investment.

Roads

Communication between villages and the nearest town was poor. Roads were bad; there was some attempt to keep them in order, but as each parish was responsible for its own section of road, the state of repair depended on the zeal of the parish officers. There was, however, little wheeled traffic except for farm carts and the few lumbering springless coaches used by men of wealth. Most traffic was by means of pack horses. Travelers rode on horseback or walked. Since communication was so difficult, the local markets, held weekly at the nearest town, or the fairs, held annually at the greater cities, became important places for the exchange of goods of all kinds.

Family Life

Under such conditions men and women seldom moved far from their homes. Family life was therefore strong, and the father of a large family an important person. Women had few legal rights of their own. A married woman owned no property; at marriage her possessions passed into the control of her husband. As a result an unmarried woman with money of her own had a wide choice of husbands, and none need remain alone for long.

---

[2] The terms used for the clergy of the Church of England sometimes cause confusion. A minister was first ordained to the probationary rank of deacon; after a year's service he was ordained priest and entitled to administer all the sacraments. A rector was a priest in full charge of a cure and enjoying all the privileges, including the collection of tithes. A vicar was a priest in charge of a cure, but with curtailed privileges. The word "parson" is applied to both vicars and rectors. A curate was any minister in charge of a cure, but the term was most commonly used for a minister substituting for the rector. It was a common abuse for one man to hold several cures and to pay a small stipend to a curate to carry out the duties in each.

Scandals and abuses were common. The law recognized that a legal contract of marriage had been made when the two parties agreed before witnesses to take each other as man and wife. Such betrothals were neither registered nor officially recorded, but either party could claim the fulfillment of the bargain and all that it implied. If either married some other party, that marriage was void. Should a dispute arise, it was taken to the courts; the parties produced their witnesses and the court decided. Marriage in church was the proper and conventional form of contract and gave additional safeguards in that it was a public ceremony before many witnesses and a record of the marriage was entered by the parson in the parish register. Betrothal, however, was regarded by many as equally binding, and many such marriages were consummated before or even without the blessing of the Church.

So easy a form of contract led to many abuses. It was not difficult to entrap one of the parties into some statement before unscrupulous witnesses which could be construed as a binding betrothal. A woman with property was thus an easy prey, and naturally she found a legal protector as soon as possible.

Elizabethan widows were notorious for the rapidity with which they remarried. There is a story told in the *Hundred Merry Tales* of a certain woman whose husband died leaving her with great wealth. A young gentleman thought that she would be a desirable match, but having nice feelings, he waited until the funeral of the late husband. Then he knelt beside the widow, who was at her prayers, and in a whisper asked if she would marry him. She replied that she was sorry but she was already bespoken. In this case, however, the lady had failed to observe the proper etiquette, for it was not considered seemly for a widow to accept a proposal so long as the corpse of her late husband was still in the house.

In theory, and usually in practice, the father was the supreme head of the family, and had the right to dispose of his daughters in marriage.[3] Indeed the elders usually negotiated marriages for their children, though it naturally gave the greatest satisfaction to all concerned if the young people's desires coincided with those of their parents. But since the purpose of marriage was

the procreation of children to prolong the family and increase its possessions, it was regarded as of first importance that the young wife should be able to bear healthy children and " to bring meat in her mouth."

Relations between fathers and their children were therefore without much sentiment, and though there were many happy marriages, in real life romantic love was discouraged. The good son addressed his parents as " sir " or " madam," and treated them with formal respect and reverence. Nor was there much sentiment between sons and mothers; no Elizabethan poet ever sang songs about his dear old mammy. The successful mother ruled her sons, and they obeyed her. There are indeed so many stories of shrews that it is clear that the mother was often the real ruler of the household. Women were by no means slaves. In the home they were in fact predominant, and formed their own freemasonry; the menfolk worked and found their own society outside.

The Queen

As the father was in theory the head of the family, so the Queen was the head of the state. Within the state, each person had his proper place in the whole pattern (see p. 7b). The child looked to the father, the servant to the master, the master to the lord, the lord to the Sovereign, who was directly under God. Queen Elizabeth was emphatic in the claim, which she often asserted, that she was responsible to God alone, and she quite genuinely believed that He was always personally concerned with her welfare. One of her proclamations begins with the words:

For as much as it is manifestly seen to all the world how it hath pleased Almighty God of His most singular favour to have taken this Our Realm into His special protection these many years, even from the beginning of Our reign, in the midst of the troubled estate of all other kingdoms next adjoining, with a special preservation of Our own person, as next under his Almightiness, supreme Governor of the same . . .

This conception of the Queen as God's vicegerent and a semidivine being was fostered by the elaborate ceremonial of the Court. A German who was present there in 1598 thus de-

[3] See App. 8, " The Ballad of Ulalia Page."

scribes Queen Elizabeth going to her private chapel on a Sunday morning:

We were admitted by an order from the Lord Chamberlain into the presence-chamber, hung with rich tapestry, and the floor after the English fashion strewed with hay, through which the Queen commonly passes on her way to chapel: at the door stood a gentleman dressed in velvet, with a gold chain, whose office was to introduce to the Queen any person of distinction, that came to wait on her: it was Sunday, when there is usually the greatest attendance of nobility. In the same hall were the Archbishop of Canterbury, the Bishop of London, a great number of Councillors of State, officers of the Crown, and gentlemen, who waited the Queen's coming out; which she did from her own apartment, when it was time to go to prayers, attended in the following manner. First went gentlemen, Barons, Earls, Knights of the Garter, all richly dressed and bareheaded; next came the Chancellor, bearing the seals in a red-silk purse, between two; one of which carried the royal sceptre, the other the sword of state, in a red scabbard, studded with golden *fleurs de lys,* the point upwards: next came the Queen, in the sixty-fifth year of her age, as we were told, very majestic; her face oblong, fair, but wrinked; her eyes small, yet black and pleasant; her nose a little hooked; her lips narrow; and her teeth black (a defect the English seem subject to, from their too great use of sugar); she had in her ears two pearls, with very rich drops; she wore false hair, and that red; upon her head she had a small crown, reported to be made of some of the gold of the celebrated Lunebourg table; her bosom was uncovered, as all the English ladies have it, till they marry; and she had on a necklace of exceeding fine jewels; her hands were small, her fingers long, and her stature neither tall nor low; her air was stately, her manner of speaking mild and obliging. That day she was dressed in white silk, bordered with pearls of the size of beans, and over it a mantle of black silk, shot with silver threads; her train was very long, the end of it borne by a Marchioness; instead of a chain, she had an oblong collar of gold and jewels. As she went along in all this state and magnificence, she spoke very graciously, first to one, then to another, whether foreign ministers, or those who attended for different reasons, in English, French, or Italian; for besides being well skilled in Greek, Latin, and the languages I have mentioned, she is mistress of Spanish, Scotch, and Dutch: whoever speaks to her, it is kneeling; now and then she raises some with her hand. While we were there, W. Slawata, a Bohemian Baron, had letters to present to her; and she, after pulling off her glove, gave him her right hand to kiss, sparkling with rings and jewels, a mark of particular favour: wherever she turned her face, as she was going along, everybody fell down on their knees. The ladies of the court followed next to her, very handsome and well shaped, and for the most part dressed in white; she was guarded on each side by the gentlemen pensioners, fifty in number, with gilt battle-axes. In the ante-chapel next the hall where we were, petitions were presented to her, and she received them most graciously, which occasioned the acclamation of, "Long live Queen Elizabeth!" She answered it with, "I thank you, my good people."[4]

Queen Elizabeth was no figurehead, and in so far as any one ruler or government is responsible for the fate of a nation, to her belongs the credit for the greatness of England at the end of the sixteenth century. The epoch is justly named the Elizabethan Age.

Just as the Queen was the head of her family of subjects, so she belonged to the family of rulers of other peoples; rulers were all brethren, especially chosen by God, and accordingly bound to each other by the special code of kingly behavior. Queen Elizabeth held, and said, that kings must behave as kings; and when other sovereigns did not come up to her standards, she did not hesitate to rebuke them. She was especially annoyed with Philip II of Spain because he so far forgot himself as to send assassins to murder her, and with King James VI of Scotland because he failed to keep his subjects in proper order.

Religion

In such a conception of society, there is a fundamental instinct for order. Among the more conservative this instinct was the stronger because Englishmen had not forgotten the generations of anarchy during the Wars of the Roses. At all costs order must be preserved, and since the Sovereign was the apex of human society and God's Deputy on earth, to rebel against the Sovereign was to rebel against God. This belief explains also why religious persecution was regarded as natural and right. In theory the structure of the state was founded on God's will and command, as expressed in the Scriptures and in the divine institution, the Church. But the Church of England, by law established under

---

[4] Quoted in *Shakespeare's England,* ed. by Sir Walter Raleigh. 2 vols., I, 91.

Queen Elizabeth, was itself a compromise. England had been a Roman Catholic country until the time of Henry VIII, who, in his quarrel with the Pope over his first divorce, had decreed that he was himself the Head of the Church of England. He had further widened the schism by dissolving the monasteries and religious houses and redistributing their enormous wealth among his own followers. He did not, however, encourage changes in doctrine, and the Church of England in its practice and dogma remained Catholic. At the death of Henry VIII in 1547, the guardians of his young son Edward VI began a thorough Protestant reform of the English Church, which involved the destruction of many of the finest specimens of English ecclesiastic art of the Middle Ages. When the boy King died in 1553, he was succeeded by his elder sister, Queen Mary. She was a zealous and conscientious Roman Catholic. She accepted the superiority of the Pope in ecclesiastical matters and married Philip II, King of Spain, the most powerful of the Catholic Sovereigns; but her zeal for the old faith was without much success, because too many of her wealthiest subjects had profited from the plunder of the abbeys and were not willing to disgorge their spoils. Queen Mary died in 1558, and was succeeded by her half-sister, Queen Elizabeth. After three upheavals in twenty-five years Englishmen were ready for a compromise.

Queen Elizabeth was no zealot in religious matters and was not much interested in the subtleties of theology. At her accession, the Anglican Church reverted to independence from the Pope, but in church practice and ritual much of the old ceremony remained. Foreign visitors noted that outwardly the ceremony in English churches (at least in London) was very much the same as in Catholic churches on the Continent, except that the language used was English and not Latin. The Queen's compromise was accepted by most Englishmen without disturbance, though many were secretly in sympathy with the old faith. Zealous Puritans, on the other hand, were eager for much wider reforms. Extremists of both parties rejected compromise. Catholics hoped that the old order would be restored so that England might remain inside the structure of Catholic Europe. If so, the Queen would have to accept the Pope's supremacy. Some zealots, including the Jesuit propagandist Father Parsons, were even willing to force the issue by bringing over foreign soldiers and by murdering the Queen.

Extreme Puritans, however, were held to be the greater danger at home, for they put forward the most advanced democratic views. They claimed that the Church of England, with its bishops and ecclesiastical organization, was anti-Christian, and they proposed to reorganize society on a Scriptural basis. Each congregation was to elect elders; the elders were to form local consistories; these would elect provincial synods; finally there would be a National Synod, which would be the supreme court for all affairs, political, religious, moral, and social. No important matter was to be decided without the consent of the National Synod, and the Queen was to be subject to its censure if she did not obey its wishes. The Puritans were indeed the champions of liberty of conscience, but it was for their own kind of liberty; they were as eager as any other sect to force everyone to conform with their views. The Queen and her Ministers felt that such views were alarming and revolutionary and that they should be suppressed accordingly.

Although the three main divisions of Christianity superficially disagreed on matters of interpretation of Scripture, their differences were as much political and social as doctrinaire. Those who wished to reform society justified their theories not by the teaching of economists or political scientists but by the Scriptures. Men were therefore perforce religious, for at any time a man might have to suffer for his religious opinions. Interest in theological controversy was strong. Sermons were eagerly heard and theological argument was keenly followed. This can be well seen from the *Diary* of John Manningham, a barrister, who went twice every Sunday to hear a sermon, which he summarized with comments. On the other six days of the week he was chiefly interested in gossip and jokes of the kind that editors indicate with a row of stars.

Organization of the State

There were as yet no political parties in England. The Queen was the head of the state and personally decided all matters of policy. Queen Elizabeth was a keen and energetic businesswoman, familiar with every detail of the machinery of state. Hundreds of her letters survive; they cover every kind of state business. The Queen chose her own Ministers to carry out her policies in their several departments. They were palace officials, and formed her Privy Council. The government could not therefore be rejected or overthrown except by rebellion or murder, or if the Sovereign was weak, by seizing his person and providing him with new Ministers. The Sovereign could, however, dismiss a Minister, though in fact Queen Elizabeth kept her chief Ministers until they died. The only Councilor to betray or desert her was the Earl of Essex, who was executed on February 25, 1601.

Robert Devereux, Earl of Essex

For a period of ten years before his death Robert Devereux, Earl of Essex, was the most conspicuous figure next to the Queen. He was born in 1566 or 1567, and first attracted notice at Court as the protégé of his stepfather, the great Earl of Leicester. After Leicester's death in 1588, he became conspicuous. As a young man he was intelligent, romantic, ambitious, and flamboyantly brave, and soon became the Queen's favorite. He took part in the expedition known as the Portugal Voyage, and in 1591 was in nominal command of the English forces taking part in the siege of Rouen (see p. 29a). At the early age of twenty-six he was made a member of the Privy Council, and was soon regarded as the natural champion of professional soldiers and Puritans with a grievance. His greatest triumph was at the expedition to Cádiz in 1596, where he shared the command with the old Lord Admiral, Lord Charles Howard, and where his bravery and chivalry were much noted. But chivalry soon degenerated into jealous vanity. He was, indeed, no great leader of men and was easily influenced, especially by anyone who flattered him. Moreover, to the Queen's annoyance, he courted the popularity of the citizens of London. After 1597 his fortunes declined rapidly. He lost much reputation over the expedition to the Azores of which he was commander. Indeed the failure of that expedition was due largely to his incompetent leadership. Thereafter he drifted into the dangerous position of being the natural leader of all malcontents.

Essex was the last of Queen Elizabeth's favorites. The Queen, who liked handsome and promising young men, promoted him before he was ready for responsibility, and granted him excessive favors which he came to regard as his own right. The relations between Essex and the Queen were always uneasy. Essex was very sensitive and resented criticism; the Queen was always more prone to blame than to praise. There were constant quarrels and emotional reconciliations.

The climax in their relationship occurred in the summer of 1598. There had recently been a great disaster in Ireland, and it was essential that a competent commander should be sent over to take charge. The problem of the Irish command was discussed by the Queen, Essex, Lord Charles Howard, and Sir Robert Cecil. Essex obstinately insisted that his own candidate should be chosen, and when the Queen refused he insolently turned his back on her. Thereupon she gave him a box on the ear and told him to go and be hanged. The horrified Lord Admiral shuffled Essex out of the chamber. This crude and embarrassing quarrel upset public business for two months, as neither would apologize. Ultimately a reconciliation was patched up, but Essex had been so critical of all candidates suggested for the Irish command that he found himself in the embarrassing position of being selected.

He went over to Ireland in March 1599 in command of a large army of over sixteen thousand men, and he failed completely. He frittered his army away in unnecessary forays and then continually wrote home demanding reinforcements and complaining bitterly that he was being betrayed. At last, instead of attacking Tyrone, the rebel leader, he came to terms with him and, in spite of direct orders to the contrary, suddenly left his command and appeared in London with a small party of his followers. The Court at the time was at Nonesuch in Surrey. Thither Essex and his party rode. Essex went straight into the palace and up to the Queen's private apartments unannounced. He broke into her bedchamber and found her newly out of bed and not yet made up. She was astonished to see him and at first greeted him kindly, but when she had recovered from the shock she ordered that he remain a prisoner under close arrest. For the next nine months he was banished from Court, and then in June 1600 he was brought before the Privy Council and publicly censured. After this humiliation he was released, but forbidden to come to Court.

Essex's fortunes were now perilous. He had long since mortgaged all his private estate, and his income depended on the grant of a tax on sweet wines which the Queen had given him some years before. This grant lapsed in October 1600, and everyone waited to see whether the Queen would renew it or reduce Essex to beggary. After some hesitation she declared that the grant would not be renewed. This was generally taken to be a sign that she had finally broken with him. For a while he was in great depression, but his followers, many of them men of desperate fortunes, urged him to take revenge. As Christmas came near it was clear that some seditious plan was being hatched in Essex House. Extreme Puritans were allowed to preach dangerous sermons, and men of broken fortune were his chief friends.

The suspicions of the Council increased, and on Saturday, February 7, 1601, it was noticed that the Chamberlain's Men put on the play of *Richard II* before a large and enthusiastic audience of Essex's followers (see p. 45a). That night an official messenger was sent to summon Essex to the Court to explain his conduct. He refused to go, declaring it was a plot to murder him. Essex now sent for his friends to gather at Essex House in the morning. About two hundred of them had assembled by ten o'clock on Sunday when a deputation of Privy Councilors from the Court presented itself at Essex House. They were admitted. Essex led the deputation into his library and ordered them to be held captive. Then he went down into the courtyard and with his particular friend, the Earl of Southampton, put himself at the head of his followers and began to march toward the city of London.

Essex fully expected that the citizens would rise and join him. No one stirred. Meanwhile loyal supporters of the Queen's party were gathering. By afternoon Essex realized that his position was hopeless and, after some fighting near Paul's, with a small party of his followers he went down to the river and was rowed back to Essex House. Late that night Essex, Southampton, and the rest of his party surrendered to a little army commanded by the Lord Admiral Howard. The rebellion caused the greatest excitement and alarm, although it was some days before the truth was known. It seemed incredible that such a movement could have occurred without wide preparations for a general revolution. On February 19 Essex and Southampton were brought to trial for high treason before a special commission in Westminster Hall. The trial lasted all day and Essex was allowed great freedom in his defense. Nevertheless, both Earls were condemned to death. Southampton was reprieved, but six days later Essex was beheaded in the Tower before a select audience of about one hundred persons.

Essex, as can now be seen, was not a great man, but his death caused a vast wave of feeling in England. His rise and fall was not merely the story of one man's folly and ruin. It affected the nation more deeply than any event since the Great Armada. Essex had long seemed to stand out as a symbol of nobility in a corrupted universe, for he had never lost that early charm of manner which distinguished him as a young courtier. Everywhere there was a growing sense of disappointment, failure, and frustration. The Puritans cried out against the Anglican clergy; the Catholics lamented the deaths of their martyrs and were quarreling among themselves; men of wealth found the burden of taxation intolerable. Intelligent young men who had grown up under the shadow of this interminable war against Spain were cynical and contemptuous of the older generation. With Essex's death vanished the last hope of a brave new world. It is more than coincidence that *Hamlet* as we now know it was written in the last months of Essex's decline and fall.

The Privy Council

After Essex's death the Privy Council was reduced to ten members. Four months later three new Councilors were appointed. The thirteen members were John Whitgift, Archbishop of Canterbury (and administrative head of the Established Church); Sir Thomas Egerton, Lord Keeper of the Great Seal (that is, administrative head of the legal profession); Lord Buckhurst, Lord Treasurer; Charles Howard, Earl of Nottingham, Lord High Admiral (responsible for all naval affairs); the Earl of Shrewsbury; the Earl of Worcester, Master of the Horse (or as he would now be called, Minister for War);

Lord Hunsdon, Lord Chamberlain (responsible for the organization of the palace and the royal household); Sir William Knollys, Controller of the Household; Sir John Stanhope, the Vice-Chamberlain; Sir Robert Cecil, the Queen's Principal Secretary (and as such the Minister most intimate with the Queen); Sir John Fortesque, Chancellor of the Exchequer; Sir John Popham, Lord Chief Justice; and Mr. John Herbert, one of the Queen's secretaries and assistant to Sir Robert Cecil.

The Privy Council was the supreme governing body in the state, and functioned in much the same way as the modern Cabinet. Privy Councilors were greatly privileged. Only Councilors had the right of direct access to the Queen herself; other men had to petition for an audience through a Councilor or one of the Queen's personal attendants. The Council was a hardworking body, and met in committee most days, sometimes under the chairmanship of the Queen herself. Many of its letter books survive and show how much business was transacted. Thus in a typical and quite uneventful week in March 1592, the agenda for the first concerned reinforcements to be levied from the city of London; precautions against desertion from the draft; instructions for Sir Roger Williams, commanding the troops in France; relief for a poor man unable to pay his taxes; action to be taken against a crafty attorney. On the second, the Council considered a change in the command of one of the companies. On the third, the Council was concerned with the Free School at Newark; circular letters to the Lords Lieutenant of thirteen counties concerning military munitions, with other similar letters to thirteen other counties; directions to the Warden of the Fishmongers Company concerning the supervision of butchers during Lent. On the fifth, the agenda dealt with a stay of proceedings in a case at Bedford; the repair of the church at Wymondham; a fraud in the City; a French merchant's complaint; the complaint of a widow of New Sarum; the case of a poor prisoner who had been unjustly kept in prison; relief from taxation of a poor man in Essex; protection of a debtor; a complaint in the Court of Chancery; the claims of an orphan in Ireland; a letter to the mustermaster in Normandy concerning pay rolls; evasions of public duties by citizens dwelling in the suburbs; a passport for a German citizen;

the private affairs of Sir Hugh Hopton; warrants for the arrest of two suspects; three questions from Ireland; the renewal of the commissions of the commissioners against Catholic recusants in three Lincolnshire towns; complaints against the Lord President and Council in the Welsh Marches; a charge of seditious speech. On the seventh, the only business concerned deserters hiding in London and a special warning to Sir Edmund York not to allow any of his reinforcements to desert.

Such a volume of business could only be transacted when the members of the Council were punctilious and exact in attending to its affairs, as is shown by the record of attendance. Lord Burleigh was present at some two hundred meetings each year. The Council also sat as a supreme court of law in the notorious Star Chamber — so called because the ceiling was decorated with stars — where it tried cases which did not come within the ordinary procedure of the civil or criminal courts. It decided such matters as cases of riot, seditious behavior, perjury, or offenses committed by noblemen. It could fine offenders, or send them to the pillory, or condemn them to lose their ears; but it did not punish by death. Cases of high treason, especially when committed by persons of rank, were usually tried by a special commission.

The Council issued orders through the Lords Lieutenant of the counties or the Lord Mayor of London or, for particular matters, through the local magistrate or mayor immediately concerned. The system worked well. Although to modern notions it may seem undemocratic, it could only function with the willing co-operation of all, for there was no regular police force or standing army to enforce commands. In practice it meant that no regulations were put into force which were against the general wish of the majority.

Noblemen

Next to the Queen in order of importance came the peers or noblemen of England. In Shakespeare's earlier days there were three degrees of nobility — Earl, Viscount, Baron. The highest degree, that of Duke, was at the moment not held by anyone, but that rank was restored when King James came to the throne in 1603. Noblemen were created as a peculiar mark of favor by a special patent bestowed by the Sovereign. The patent was an imposing document sealed with the Great Seal of England (see Pl. 11b). The patent bestowed a title of honor, which descended to the eldest son in perpetuity. Noblemen were beings apart and were treated with much respect and ceremony. They had great estates, many servants, and considerable responsibility. They enjoyed various privileges and special places at Court according to their degree; they were exempt from trial in the ordinary courts of law and could be tried only by their peers; but they were also expected to serve the state without reward whenever required. Privy Councilors were often promoted to the ranks of the nobility as a reward for their services and to give them greater dignity. Indeed the English nobility has always contained a number of noblemen who began life as commoners. When Parliament met, the peers sat apart in their own House, the House of Lords. With them sat the Lords Spiritual, the bishops.

The Bishops

Bishops in the sixteenth century had great power and ranked as noblemen, though their privileges did not pass to their children. The bishop was appointed by the Sovereign and was responsible for the spiritual welfare of his diocese. He had his own ecclesiastical court of law, before which offenders against accepted doctrine and morality were summoned and, if condemned, punished by fine or imprisonment. These courts were particularly hated by the Puritans because they gave the hated "anti-Christian" bishop supreme control over all matters of worship and belief. The bishops were richly rewarded: they had their palaces, and many servants and great estates; they controlled the clergy in their dioceses, and therefore wielded great influence and authority. Occasionally spiritually minded men were chosen, but the quality chiefly required of a bishop was the administrative ability to organize and keep in check a very miscellaneous flock of clergy.

Knights and Gentlemen

Next to the nobility in the chain of order came the knights and gentlemen. A man was made knight either by the Sovereign in person, or by her deputy, such as the general in the field. He then bore the title "Sir" before his name. The honor, which was personal and not hereditary, was given for many different reasons — for political services, for gallant service in the wars, or as a mark of esteem to rich men who had shown public spirit. Queen Elizabeth was particular in bestowing the honor, and it was one of her major causes of annoyance with the Earl of Essex that when in command of her armies he had made knighthood cheap by giving it away too easily. When King James came to the throne, he bestowed so many knighthoods in his first years that the title became a joke.

Next to knights were the gentlemen. Legally a gentleman was a person of good birth and independent means who was not employed in any trade or profession. A man became officially a "gentleman" when a coat of arms was granted to him by the College of Heralds (see p. 10b and App. 9). A gentleman was expected to set an example to his neighbors by giving much of his time freely to the public service, and by undertaking such duties as serving as a justice of the peace or representing his shire in Parliament as a member of the House of Commons.

Parliament

Parliament in Queen Elizabeth's time was of less importance than it became later. It met every three or four years to amend old laws, to make new ones, and to agree as to taxes to cover the extraordinary expenses of the wars. The normal expenses of the state were met out of the Queen's private income, which amounted only to about £300,000 in money of the time.[5] Parliament was not, as the Queen told its members, a standing council, and liberty of speech was not always allowed. In the Parliament of 1593, for instance, the Queen gave orders that members should not discuss the question of her successor. When one member named Peter Wentworth insisted on bringing up the matter, he was sent to the Tower, and remained there without trial until his death three years later. Parliament, however, was a very valuable means of discovering the state of public opinion, especially since members were not controlled by party bosses in their votes or speeches.

[5] Equivalent to about $12,000,000 in modern American money. See App. 27.

A notable instance of this ability of Parliament to reflect the temper of the people occurred in 1601, when the Queen and the Council were made aware of the bitter feelings caused by the excessive granting of monopolies to deal in certain commodities. It had long been a privilege of the Sovereign to grant, as a reward for faithful service, a monopoly or sole right to deal in certain commodities, but the privilege had been abused and extended to cover necessities. There were patents for currants, vinegar, coal, brushes, pots, oils of various kinds, and even salt. The indignation of the House of Commons was reported to the Queen. She sent for the Speaker and told him that measures should immediately be taken to remedy the abuse. When the Speaker reported to the House, they enthusiastically agreed that a deputation should go to the Queen to give her thanks. About a hundred and fifty members appeared before her in Whitehall Palace. When the Speaker finished his speech, the Queen answered him at length with great eloquence and feeling. Then she ended with these words:

To be a King and wear a crown is more glorious to them that see it than it is pleasure to them that bear it. For myself, I was never so much enticed with the glorious name of a King, or royal authority of a Queen, as delighted that God hath made me this instrument to maintain His truth and glory, and to defend this Kingdom from peril, dishonour, tyranny and oppression. There will never Queen sit in my seat with more zeal to my country, care to my subjects, and that will sooner with willingness yield and venture her life for your good and safety than myself. And though you have had and may have many Princes more mighty and wise sitting in this seat, yet you never had or shall have any that will be more careful and loving. Should I ascribe anything to myself and my sexly weakness, I were not worthy to live then, and of all most unworthy of the mercies I have had from God, Who hath ever yet given me a heart which never yet feared foreign or home enemies. I speak it to give God the praise as a testimony before you, and not to attribute anything to myself. For I, O Lord, what am I, whom practices and perils past should not fear! O what can I do — and these words she spake with great emphasis — that I should speak for any glory! God forbid.

This, Mr. Speaker, I pray you deliver unto the House, to whom heartily recommend me. And so I commit you all to your best fortunes and further counsels.

Thereafter the House returned with increased zeal to its business of lawmaking.

Crime and Punishment

Elizabethan laws, especially against crime, were harsh, and many crimes were punished with death. In theory, public punishments provided a warning to the young of the end which awaited the wicked; in fact, they were highly appreciated as spectacles. Many crimes were punished by hanging, usually on the three-cornered gallows at Tyburn, which stood near the present Marble Arch. Murderers and those who had committed notable acts of high treason were sometimes executed as near as possible to the scene of the crime. Women who poisoned their husbands were burned alive.

Those found guilty of high treason were condemned to be hung, drawn, and quartered. They were dragged through the city on hurdles to the place of execution, where after much speech-making and some prayers by the minister, and sometimes unseemly wrangling, the condemned was made to mount the ladder and then " turned off." Before he was unconscious he was cut down, his parts and entrails were cut out and burned in a fire, the body was then dismembered and dipped into boiling tar, and the pieces were displayed in various parts of the city. Traitors' heads were stuck up on top of London Bridge (see Pl. 3). The barbarity of this sentence was sometimes mitigated, for there was a recognized custom that when the condemned acted with notable courage, piety, and decorum, he was allowed to hang until he was dead, or at least insensible. Beheading with the ax was a privilege reserved for noblemen and gentlemen of high standing.

Another form of punishment was that known as peine forte et dure, or pressing to death. This was the penalty for "standing dumb at the bar," or refusing to plead guilty or not guilty. Without a plea the trial could not proceed, and thus the prisoner avoided legal condemnation, which carried with it forfeiture of all his goods to the Queen. By taking this course some hardy individuals saved their families from poverty, but it was an act of considerable heroism and self-sacrifice. The victim was stretched out upon spikes, then a board was laid on him and heavy weights piled on until he was pressed to death.

With such elementary police organization as existed, it is surprising that criminals were so often caught. But when a crime was discovered, everyone took a hand in aiding justice. A " hue and cry " was raised, and the whole parish turned out to chase the offender. If he ran into another parish, the pursuit was taken up from parish to parish until he was caught or escaped. Escape was not easy; in a small community the stranger is conspicuous and suspected.

Violent death was frequent, particularly as the result of the many fights with weapons which occurred. Marlowe was twice involved in a fatal quarrel. On the first occasion he and the poet Watson killed a man called Bradley; on the second he was himself the victim. Ben Jonson killed a fellow actor in 1598 (see p. 42b). Jonson was tried for manslaughter and found guilty, but he escaped by pleading " benefit of clergy," a survival of the times when " clerks " (that is, educated men who could read) were so valuable that they were given a second chance. The accused was required to read aloud a passage from the Psalms — known as the " neck verse " — in Court, and was then branded on the thumb with a T and released with the loss of his goods.

Lesser crimes and frauds were often the work of professional crooks, known as conycatchers (from " cony "; that is, a rabbit, or " sucker "). A most interesting account of these experts was written by Robert Greene in a series of pamphlets which were published in 1591–92. They worked in fraternities, and were regularly organized. Conycatching was a form of cardsharping, but the profession included " crossbiters," " courbers," " nips," and " foists." The crossbiter and his moll (known as a " traffic ") lured men into brothels and there stripped them under threats of violence or blackmail. Courbers went round the city at night and where they found an open window they thrust in a fishing rod with a hook at the end and drew out what they could catch. Nips and foists both worked on purses; the nip used a knife, cutting the purse from the girdle, but the foist used his hand and picked the pocket. Foists regarded themselves as belonging to a higher profession than the others, for to use a tool was the mark of a tradesman, and no gentleman practiced a trade.

These experts were members of the city fraternities. In the country there were other branches, such as wandering beggars who called at cottages or farms when the menfolk were away at work. Of these, the bedlam beggars were the fiercest and most terrifying; they were lunatics discharged from Bedlam (Bethlehem Hospital, the London madhouse). There were other unlawful travelers on the roads, of whom the Statute against Vagabonds gives a long catalogue; it includes fencers, bearwards (who trailed a tame performing bear), common players not licensed by a lord, minstrels, jugglers, peddlers, tinkers, scholars from the universities begging for money to finish their education, and shipwrecked sailors.

Sailors were not welcomed in the country, and sober citizens regarded them as likely to be thieves and pirates, as indeed many of them were. Modern romantic notions about the Elizabethan seamen were not shared by their countrymen; although the more farsighted realized that the sea was England's greatest asset, it is significant that while in Elizabethan plays there are many soldier characters, there is no seaman of any importance. The few that appear are either minor rogues or convenient captains who answer such questions as " What country, friend, is this? " Soldier characters are plentiful because the wars came close to every man. England was occupied with major wars for the last eighteen years of the Queen's reign.

The Wars

The most sensational event in the long war with Spain was the defeat of the Spanish Armada in 1588. Historians looking back are prone to take a complacent view of the Spanish danger, as if the destruction of the Armada ended the anxiety of Englishmen and the war thereafter died away. In fact, the defeat of the Armada in August 1588 may be compared with the defeat of the German Air Force in the Battle of Britain in August and September 1940. Both victories were decisive in the history of the world, but at the time each seemed to Englishmen to be but the prelude to greater dangers. Among Shakespeare's contemporaries the first feeling was one of incredible relief, quickly followed by the sobering thought that next time the Spaniards would not repeat their mistakes.

The war continued actively in 1589, when a naval and military force under the command of

Sir Francis Drake was sent to Portugal with the object of restoring Don Antonio, the former King, to the throne from which the Spaniards had driven him — the expedition known as the Portugal Voyage. It was not a success; the Portuguese were not prepared to support Antonio, and although Corunna and Lisbon were sacked, the losses by disease were heavy. In the same year the Queen sent aid to the Protestant French King Henry of Navarre who was fighting the Catholic League of Frenchmen who were allied with the Spaniards. In 1590 while English troops were helping the Dutch in the Low Countries in the struggle against the Spaniards, the Spaniards were slowly advancing in Brittany. In 1591 two small English expeditions were fighting in France — one in Brittany and the other in Normandy, where Essex was in command of a force aiding Henry at the unsuccessful siege of Rouen. In 1593 Henry came to terms with his Catholic subjects. He was converted to Catholicism and so brought an end to the civil war in France. For a time it appeared as if he might be about to abandon the war against the Spaniards, perhaps even to join with them, but he remained true to his alliance with Queen Elizabeth. In 1594 a second expedition to Brittany succeeded in capturing Brest; 1595 was a year of great danger and alarm. Intelligence reports showed that a new Spanish Armada was being made ready. At the same time the alliance with Henry was weakening, as he was quite unable to continue the war. But in the winter of that year orders went out that a large English fleet should be prepared for an expedition in the spring. The alliance continued for the next few months, and in April the Spaniards besieged Calais. Essex at the time was at Dover supervising the assembly of ships. He begged to be allowed to carry over such troops as he could raise to go to the rescue of Calais. On April 9, which was Good Friday, the Lord Mayor was suddenly called away from the Paul's Cross sermon and ordered to collect and dispatch one thousand soldiers at once, but the order was countermanded the same night. Two days later, on Easter Sunday, troops were again ordered. Officers were sent round to the city churches as the people were making their Easter communion and the parish constables shut the church doors until they had collected the necessary numbers. On April 14, the noise of the cannonading outside Calais was heard all day in London, but before the expedition could sail news came that Calais had fallen.

The preparations for the great expedition then went on, and fleet and army were assembled at Plymouth. The expedition, which consisted of more than one hundred and fifty ships and ten thousand soldiers, set sail at the beginning of June. On July 19 news reached London that a magnificent victory had been won. By luck and good generalship the English fleet had entered the Bay of Cádiz, where it destroyed three great Spanish galleons and captured two others. The army then landed, and after a brief fight occupied Cádiz, which was completely sacked and burned. The great fleet of Spanish merchantmen was destroyed by fire. The Queen, however, was very dissatisfied with the expedition. Although every man who took part had helped himself to rich plunder, her own share turned out to be meager.

In 1597 another expedition was prepared under the command of Essex to raid the coast of Spain, but the weather throughout the early part of the summer was stormy and tempestuous and the ships were scattered. It was not until August 19 that the fleet set out to raid the islands of the Azores and to wait for the Spanish treasure fleet from South America. The expedition was a failure. There had been constant bickering between the naval men under Ralegh and the military under Essex, and very little was accomplished. Meanwhile there was a great danger at home, for it was learned that a new Spanish Armada was at sea. It was, however, scattered by tempest before reaching the English coast.

It may be noted that Shakespeare wrote *1 Henry IV* while London was still swarming with returned soldiers and captains from the Islands Voyage.

In 1598 the war with Spain languished as the situation on the Continent was uncertain. Henry IV, though nominally an ally, was effecting very little, and in April, without consulting his allies, he made a separate peace with the Spaniards. Meanwhile the situation in Ireland, always uneasy, was worse than usual. For some years the Irish had been in a state of unrest and sporadic rebellion, and the control of the English, except in the district around Dublin called the English Pale, was uncertain. Irish rebels at this time were led by Hugh O'Neill, Earl of Tyrone. In the summer of 1598 the small English forces which garrisoned the Pale were sent out against Tyrone, and in a disastrous battle near Armagh were cut to pieces. Rebellion quickly spread through the rest of Ireland, and by the end of the year it appeared likely that all Ireland would be lost.

In 1599 Essex was sent to Ireland with a model army of sixteen thousand men and failed completely, but in 1600 a new force under Charles Blount, Lord Mountjoy, was sent over. Mountjoy, by establishing garrisons and continually harassing the rebels, gradually regained control.

In 1601 the war both on the Continent and in Ireland was fiercer than ever. There was renewed activity in the Low Countries, where the Spaniards were besieging Ostend. They also sent a small expedition of three thousand men which occupied Kinsale in Ireland. Nevertheless, at the end of the year there were great victories on both fronts. Mountjoy defeated the Irish rebels and forced the Spaniards in Kinsale to surrender, while the Anglo-Dutch force under Sir Francis Vere, consisting of only twelve hundred men, utterly defeated an assault by ten thousand Spaniards.

There were no decisive actions in 1602, but by the end of the year Tyrone, the leader of the Irish rebels, admitted defeat and asked for terms of surrender. The war between Spain and England ceased suddenly in 1603 when Queen Elizabeth died. Wars in those days were the private quarrels of kings, and her successor, James of Scotland, had no quarrel with the Spaniards. Peace was therefore soon negotiated, and was confirmed in 1604.

The burden of war during Shakespeare's manhood was thus heavy and continuous and, particularly after 1598, men were constantly being demanded from the counties. In July 1601 no less than eight thousand men were required. At a time when armies were small and "total war" still unknown this was a considerable reinforcement for a country of about four million people. The wars touched everyone, and many literary men of the time had some experience of war at first hand, among others, including Edmund Spenser, Thomas Lodge, Ben Jonson, Thomas Campion, John Donne, and Walter Ralegh.

The popular notion of the Elizabethan period

that after the defeat of the Armada peace reigned supreme is thus false to facts. Actually Englishmen passed through as great a period of anxiety as at any time in their history. It is not surprising, therefore, that the plays of the time should abound in military characters. Shakespeare drew many, of all kinds, types, and sizes, from Falstaff, who was a supreme example of the shady side of war, to Othello, Coriolanus, and Henry V.

Nevertheless, in spite of the wars, there was still no regular standing army, though there were always available a number of officers with considerable battle experience. When a campaign was to be fought, armies were levied either by calling for volunteers or by "impresting" men from the cities or the counties. The Council would send a demand for soldiers, who were equipped by the local authorities. Their quality depended on the honesty of the selecting magistrate, but since compulsory service was always unpopular and casualties were heavy, especially through sickness, a fine opportunity was provided to clear the jails or to rid a village of its most unruly bums.

The Army

The unit of the army was the company, commanded by a captain, with a lieutenant and an ensign. The captain was commissioned to collect his hundred men; he drew their pay and was allowed to keep 10 per cent, known as "dead pays." The system was easily and often abused. Dishonest captains, such as Falstaff, conscripted men of good class and then accepted bribes to let them go, or else claimed pay for men who were dead or sometimes men who had no existence except on a nominal roll; these were known as "shadows." In an attempt to keep a check, the mustermaster from time to time inspected the men and compared the nominal rolls with those on parade; but men could be borrowed from other companies for the occasion. In the Irish wars it was even a practice to borrow men from the enemy; they often ran away with their arms after the parade. The discipline of an army depended on the general in command, and such abuses were rare under the leadership of such keen soldiers as Charles Blount, Lord Mountjoy, or Sir Francis Vere. On the whole, the English soldiers fought well, though there were some regrettable incidents.

The best soldiers were the volunteers. Volunteers were not difficult to obtain when a campaign promised good loot. Distinguished noblemen recruited special companies from their own followers. Many gentlemen of good family accompanied Essex on his expeditions to Rouen, Cádiz, and the Azores, among them John Donne the poet. But it is not surprising that army service was unpopular. Although the pay was for the times good (see App. 27), and usually forthcoming, disabled soldiers received no regular pension, and at the end of the campaign were left to shift for themselves. The unemployed ex-soldier was always a problem; for it is a quite modern notion that the veteran deserves special rehabilitation grants or educational facilities.

Education

Elizabethan Englishmen were amply aware of the value of education, and in most places of any consequence schools were available. In London the headmasters of the three great schools — St. Paul's, Merchant Taylors, and Westminster — were men of distinction, whose indirect influence on English life and thought through their pupils was very considerable; and in the country grammar schools too the schoolmaster was often an eminent scholar. Hence not only were most men of any social standing in the provinces literate; many of them were highly cultured. Of the friends, for instance, of the Shakespeare family at Stratford-on-Avon, one was a Master of Arts of Oxford University and another read Latin for pleasure.

The universities, then as now, were the main avenues to preferment for the clever boy, but the prizes were far fewer than the applicants, and many young graduates who began with the highest ambitions had to content themselves in the end with insignificant and degrading occupations. In a play called *The Pilgrimage to Parnassus* performed at the University of Cambridge in 1597 two hopeful young freshmen who are about to enter Parnassus (Cambridge) are thus addressed by a disillusioned scholar:

What, I travel to Parnassus? Why, I have burnt my books, splitted my pen, rent my papers and cursed the cosening hearts that brought me up to no better fortune. I, after many years' study, having almost brought my brain into consumption, looking still when I should meet with some good Maecenas that liberally would reward my deserts. I fed so long upon hope till I had almost starved. Why, our empty-handed satin suits do make more account of some foggy falconer than of a witty scholar, had rather reward a man for setting a hair than a man of wit for making of a poem; each long-eared ass rides on his trappings and thinks it sufficient to give a scholar a majestic nod with his rude noddle. Go to Parnassus? Alas, Apollo is bankrupt, there is nothing but silver words and golden phrases for a man; his followers want the gold, while tapsters, ostlers, carters, and cobblers have a foaming pouch, a belching bag that serves for a chair of estate for *Regina Pecunia*. See'st thou not my host Johns of the Crown, who lately lived like a mole six years under the ground in a cellar, and cried, " anon, anon, sir," now is mounted upon a horse of 20 marks, and thinks the earth too base to bear the weight of his refined body. Why would it not grieve a man of good spirit to see Hobson [the famous Cambridge hostler] find more money in the tails of 12 jades than a scholar in 200 books?

These are the complaints of a man who has found out for himself the universal truth that

Learning and poverty will ever kiss.

While those who were disillusioned in their material hopes blamed the general prevalence of " barbarism " for their own misfortunes, others who had no need to earn a living were equally disappointed because the university failed to satisfy their intellectual longings and questionings. Lampatho, in Marston's play *What You Will* (1601) envies the ignorant fool who is undisturbed by such problems:

I was a scholar. Seven useful springs
Did I deflower in quotations
Of crossed opinions 'bout the soul of man.
The more I learned the more I learned to doubt.
Knowledge and wit, faith's foes, turn faith about.

The Inns of Court

After leaving the university, the richer student came to London to finish his education by the study of law at one of the Inns of Court, which were the center of the intellectual life of the country. The junior members were the pick of the universities, belonged to the best families, and were not too much occupied with their studies, so that writers and dramatists found in them their best patrons. The peculiar position of the Inns of Court is well seen in the " revels " which the gentlemen of Gray's Inn held in the winter of 1594–95, when they elected one of themselves as " Prince of Purpool " and for several weeks kept up an elaborate and at times impudent parody of the Court and ceremonies of the realm. Moreover, the members of the Privy Council, far from standing on their dignity, attended the revels with great satisfaction and amusement, the Lord Mayor of London asked the " Prince " to make a progress through the city and entertained him at a banquet, and the highmaster of St. Paul's School set his head boy to compose some Latin verses of welcome. The proceedings came to an end with a tournament at Court at which the " Prince," having greatly distinguished himself, was very kindly complimented by Queen Elizabeth herself.

Amongst the ceremonies was the establishment of a mock order of knighthood, and one of the articles imposed on new " knights " was that they should read all fashionable authors and also " frequent the Theatre, and such like places of experience; and resort to the better sort of ordinaries for conference, whereby they may not only become accomplished with civil conversations and able to govern a table with discourse, but also sufficient, if need be, to make epigrams, emblems and other devices appertaining to his Honour's learned revels." It is significant that during this time and for the next forty years many of the best poets and dramatists came from the Inns of Court. Here a man with new ideas could hope for an intelligent hearing, but he might also expect severe and sarcastic criticism. Here, too, the players and booksellers found their best customers.

Books

For the spread of new ideas the booksellers were not of less importance than intelligent readers, and the English mind is accurately reflected in the books which were published. Many of the booksellers' shops were situated by St. Paul's Churchyard. About two hundred publications of all kinds came out each year, of which about a quarter were concerned with current news, presented in various forms from the account of an eyewitness of some battle or state pageant to the doleful ballads which were

composed for the execution of criminals. So far the newspaper had not been invented, but a few new pamphlets contained one or more letters from foreign parts, and the art of headlines was well advanced. One of these news pamphlets bears this alluring title: *A true relation of the French King his good success in winning from the Duke of Parma his forts and trenches, and slaying 500 of his men, with the great famine that is now in the said Duke's camp. With other intelligences given by other letters since the second of May 1592. A most wonderful and rare example, the like whereof never happened since the beginning of the world, of a mountain in the Isle of Palme which burned continually for five or six weeks, with other both fearful and strange sights seen in the air over the same place.* The ballad in doggerel verse set to some well-known tune was, however, the most popular way of circulating news.[6]

Nevertheless Elizabethan Englishmen suffered greatly from lack of regular and reliable information. The issue of news pamphlets was quite erratic, and the most important news, especially when it was liable to embarrass the Council, was suppressed. From the first invention of printing, English printers were very carefully controlled by and through their trade organization, the Worshipful Company of Stationers. Printing was allowed only at London and the two university towns, Oxford and Cambridge, and the London printers and their printing presses were limited in number. In theory it was difficult for a seditious book to be issued, for the printer had first to get the book " allowed " by some responsible authority, then to enter its title in the Hall Book of the Company (better known as the Stationers' Register) and so secure his copyright. But, as with other Elizabethan regulations, these rules were often neglected, and many quite harmless books were published unentered; no one cared until some notorious book got abroad, and then there would be an inquiry, possibly a punishment, and for a few weeks the rules would be kept. It was not easy to publish a complete book in secret, but scurrilous ballads, printed on a single sheet, could be rapidly set up, printed off, and distributed; and a most effective means of annoying the Council was to sing rude songs about its members or praises of those whom it liked.

[6] See App. 8.

It is difficult in modern times to imagine a world without radio, telegraph, newspapers, or other means of rapidly dispersing news or opinion; but in Shakespeare's England most men had to rely on hearsay rumor and gossip. The chief members of the Council kept in touch with foreign affairs through regular reports from the ambassadors at the various European Courts. Some kept private correspondents abroad to maintain an information service; the most elaborate of these services was organized by Anthony Bacon for the Earl of Essex, whose influence in the Council was partly due to the fact that he was better informed on foreign affairs than anyone else in the kingdom. Returned travelers were expected to report to the Council on what they had heard and seen, and through them and their own agents the principal merchants in the city of London kept in touch with commercial affairs on the Continent. Such news was circulated daily by word of mouth at the Exchange. The gossipmonger with a friend at Court was much in demand. Londoners thus lived in a constant state of rumor, excitement, and panic.

Shakespeare has drawn a picture of such panic in *King John* (IV. ii. 185–202):

Old men and beldams in the streets
Do prophesy upon it dangerously.
Young Arthur's death is common in their
mouths,
And when they talk of him, they shake their
heads
And whisper one another in the ear;
And he that speaks doth gripe the hearer's wrist
Whilst he that hears makes fearful action,
With wrinkled brows, with nods, with rolling
eyes.
I saw a smith stand with his hammer thus
The whilst his iron did on that anvil cool,
With open mouth swallowing a tailor's news,
Who, with his shears and measure in his hand,
Standing on slippers which his nimble haste
Had falsely thrust upon contráry feet,
Told of a many thousand warlike French
That were embattailèd and ranked in Kent.
Another lean unwashed artificer
Cuts off his tale and talks of Arthur's death.

Next in popularity to news pamphlets came sermons, for which there was a good market. In Shakespeare's lifetime the most widely read author was the Reverend Henry Smith, rector of St. Clement's Dane in London. He began to publish his sermons only late in 1589, and he died in 1591, yet a hundred and twenty-seven editions of his works in various forms appeared before 1640; in the same period ninety-three of Shakespeare's and ninety-seven of Greene's works appeared.

A number of volumes of poetry were put out each year, but the poetry-reading public was select. Poetry for better-class readers was usually printed with considerable care in roman type, and some of the books are charming little editions for the pocket. On the other hand, romantic fiction and news pamphlets were hurriedly turned out and generally printed in the old black-letter type, which was still the normal type for popular reading. The fashion of publishing plays for the educated was rapidly spreading, and though at first these were roughly printed and intended rather for the ballad-reading public, by the end of the sixteenth century they were evidently attracting a more cultured type of reader.

Literary vogues were quite noticeable. The Elizabethan general reader, like the modern, had his whims and fancies. During the 1580's he was content with novels which followed the fashion set by Lyly in his *Euphues* and Sidney in the *Arcadia;* at the end of 1591 he turned to Greene's realistic *Conny-catching Pamphlets,* which were more successful than anything Greene had yet written. Six months later both Greene and Nashe produced allegorical prose satires — *The Quip for an Upstart Courtier* and *Piers Penniless* — which attracted much attention by their scurrilous attacks on recognizable persons, especially Dr. Gabriel Harvey, the Cambridge scholar with whom Nashe kept up a paper war between 1592 and 1599, when the Archbishop of Canterbury ordered that the books should be seized and no more printed. Another fashion which began in the 1590's was for commonplace books — collections of pithy sayings, either original or culled from old authors; of these the most famous is the first edition of Bacon's *Essays* in 1597.

Similarly in poetry, the publication of Sidney's sonnet sequence *Astrophel and Stella* in 1591 stirred all the other society poets to examine their own emotions under the stress of unsuccessful love. This phase lasted for about four years, and then long narrative poems came into fashion; of these the most famous are Shakespeare's *Venus and Adonis* and Marlowe's *Hero and Leander*. At the end of the decade, poets turned from introspection to invective satire aimed at their fellow creatures, either in lengthy imitations of Juvenal or in terse, scurrilous, and at times exceedingly witty epigrams.

Most of these poems were written by young gentlemen of good social position, for authorship was still scarcely a paying profession. There is very little record of the payments given to popular authors, though the fees paid to a dramatist varied from about £6 to £10 for a play, and a hard-working playwright might make about £60 a year (roughly $2400; see App. 27). But authors had a double means of profiting by their own work; they received something from the publisher, but they hoped also to make a little by a judicious dedication to some nobleman or rich patron who might be expected to reward the compliment. Most often, however, the author tried to attract notice by his efforts and so secure some post in a great man's household. Many of the well-known Elizabethan writers, such as Drayton, Daniel, Chapman, Nashe, Jonson, Marlowe, and probably Shakespeare, were supported at some time or other in this way. With the possible exception of Greene and one or two ballad-makers, such as Elderton or Deloney, few writers can have made a living solely from their publications.

The Traveler

Intelligent men, however, gained their views of life from other sources than books. Many of them had seen something of the world by travel. Greene had made the journey to Italy, Lodge served in Cavendish's unfortunate expedition to the South Seas, Donne was present at the capture of Cádiz, Jonson volunteered for the Lowlands, Marlowe had served as a government spy, Campion took his degree abroad. Elizabethan

literature is virile because its authors had lived varied and exciting lives.

Travel was encouraged by statesmen, for the information on foreign affairs given by returned travelers was valuable. But in popular opinion travel was bad for a man; at the worst it infected him with foreign vices and atheism, and even if he escaped these dangers he was likely to come back affecting a foreign accent, or else making ostentatious use of such effeminate toys as a toothpick or a fork to use instead of dipping his fingers in the common dish like a man. Says Rosalind to Jaques,

Farewell, Monsieur Traveler. Look you lisp, and wear strange suits. Disable all the benefits of your own country, be out of love with your nativity, and almost chide God for making you that countenance you are, or I will scarce think you have swam in a gondola.

Travel was supposed to have another ill effect —the returned traveler came back to criticize, and a man who criticized his country was suspected of being a malcontent, and therefore dangerous.

Nevertheless it is a mistake to imagine that Englishmen lived in a state of perpetual uneasy suppression, or even that they were crude or uncivilized. A generation which produced such men as Philip Sidney, Bacon, Ralegh, Drake, Spenser, Hooker, Marlowe, Chapman, Jonson, Donne, not to mention Shakespeare or Queen Elizabeth herself, can stand comparison with any. Nor should an age be judged solely by its sensational events. History is more often the record of the abnormal than of the usual. Normal decency and the uneventful daily round provide no copy for the newspaperman. In Shakespeare's England most men were humane, tolerant, decent, and honest, faithful to their wives, fond of their children, genuinely charitable, reasonably patriotic, and they died in their beds as peacefully as their physicians would allow them.

4. Elizabethan Drama

Mysteries and Moralities

Plays have been acted in England from the earliest times. By the fifteenth century the act-

ing of little religious dramas was frequent, popular, and elaborate; such dramas covered the whole story of the Christian faith from the creation of the world to the " Harrowing of Hell," when Jesus descended into Hell in the days between the Crucifixion and the Resurrection. A surprisingly large number of the texts of these playlets, known as mysteries, have survived. Apart from isolated episodes, there are four complete cycles, each of thirty to forty episodes, which were performed in the cities of Chester, York, Coventry, and Wakefield. As well as mystery plays dealing with the Christian story, there were also plays on the lives of the saints, which naturally portrayed their miracles and are accordingly called miracle plays.

Mystery plays were acted principally in one of two ways. In some places there was an arena or an auditorium where various houses or little stages were set up to represent such localities as Heaven, Hell, Solomon's Temple, and the like, and the action moved from house to house. In other cities carts were used, each being the stage for one episode. Each cart was drawn around to various locations in the city where the episode was repeated. It was often the custom for one of the trade guilds to take up an appropriate episode and present it. In the Chester cycle, for instance, the story of the Flood was appropriately acted by the water-drawers. There was thus healthy local rivalry between the various groups of actors. Moreover, since the population of a medieval city was seldom greater than five thousand, there was all the excitement of a college play where the chief players are well known to everyone in the audience.

Subjects were at first taken from the Bible, but though the Bible is full of good stories, there is usually little characterization or dialogue. So the script-writers began to expand and to improve on their sources. Certain characters were popular — Herod, for instance, was presented as a raging, roaring tyrant. One episode which particularly appealed — as it has to children of all ages — was the story of the Deluge, of Noah, his ark, and its miscellaneous freight. It was generally agreed that Noah's wife must have been a shrew, and Noah was presented as a patient, henpecked husband. Noah and the Flood were at least Scriptural, but though Noah's wife and children are mentioned in Genesis, no details of their home life are recorded.

Before long the Scriptures were not enough, and bolder writers freely invented entirely new episodes. One of the most famous and interesting is the story of Mack and the shepherds.

Mack was a rogue who stole a sheep from the shepherds of Bethlehem as they watched their flocks by night, and the whole story was dramatized as a farce occurring before the shepherds passed on to adore the Holy Babe. Englishmen in the fifteenth century took their religion joyously. Writers of mystery plays had some sense of the tragic, but far more of the comic.

Meanwhile toward the end of the fifteenth century another form of drama, known as the morality, was developed. A morality was an allegorical play wherein qualities, virtues, vices, and other abstract ideas were personified as characters; such plays appealed rather to the more intellectual audience. On the whole, except for an occasional work of genius, such as the play of *Everyman,* moralities are tedious.

Thus by the beginning of the sixteenth century the acting of plays was popular and universal — long before academic persons began to discuss theories of drama. In the earlier decades of the sixteenth century the interest in acting increased. New subjects and kinds of play were introduced, and by the middle of the century acting had become a profession. In the households of noblemen, plays were performed at Christmas time and, as the records show, the players would sometimes ask their lord for a license to repeat the show elsewhere. Sometimes the performances were given at Court before the Queen. So rivalries developed, and as the standard of acting improved, more time and care were needed for rehearsals, until playing became a full-time occupation.

At this time, and indeed until long after Shakespeare's death, professional actors were officially the servants of some great lord who was responsible for their good behavior. They wore his livery or badge, and when they traveled they carried his license. If they were in trouble, he would usually protect them as a matter of personal prestige, but the patron had no further responsibility for his players. Though he could call on them for a play on some special occasion, he did not pay them regular wages or allowances.

The First Theaters

By 1570 professional players had become so popular that the authorities of the city of London regarded them, for a number of good reasons, as a public nuisance. Plays, it was complained, contained unchaste speeches and seditious matter. They attracted great crowds, especially of young men, who wasted their time and money and neglected churchgoing. Where there were crowds there were also pickpockets, quarrels, improper assignations, and above all the risk of spreading the plague. The Lord Mayor and his brethren decided that if they could not forbid players to perform in the city, they would control them by severe regulations.

At this time the great Earl of Leicester's company of players was led by James Burbage, a violent, truculent, and not overhonest man. But Burbage had ideas; he realized that the best way to evade the Lord Mayor was to build his own playhouse in the suburbs of London, outside the legal limits of the city, where the Lord Mayor could not touch him. Accordingly, in 1576 Burbage borrowed money from his brother-in-law, rented a piece of ground in Shoreditch, north of the city, and there set up the first English playhouse, which he called the Theater. The speculation was a success, and soon another playhouse, called the Curtain, was erected near by.

The plays first acted in these playhouses were still crude, and gentlemen of culture did not patronize them; but in the same year, 1576, another kind of theater was opened. The choirboys of the Queen's Chapel Royal and of St. Paul's were often summoned to Court to give musical and dramatic entertainments, which required much rehearsal. The masters of the two choirs hit on the bright notion of giving these rehearsals to a select public who should pay for the privilege of a preview. A hall was rented in the old Blackfriars' Monastery in the city, and was converted into a small private playhouse.

For some years this playhouse prospered. The principal playwright for the boys was John Lyly, who had recently made a name for himself by his two novels, *Euphues* (1579) and *Euphues and His England* (1580). Lyly's plays are delicate trifles, founded on mythical stories and full of songs, witty dialogue, and long speeches in his own peculiar "euphuistic" style; they were never intended for the hearty public that thronged the Theater, and they had little influence on drama written for the public stage. This first Blackfriars Theater lasted until 1589, when the boys became involved in a controversy

which greatly excited Englishmen. The Puritans had succeeded in setting up a secret printing press and publishing a number of pamphlets against the bishops of the Church of England, alleged to be written by "Martin Marprelate," which were very witty and scurrilous, and highly entertaining to the ungodly. The press was harried from place to place, but it still continued to function in spite of the Archbishop of Canterbury and his zealous searchers. It was then decided that wit must be countered with wit. Professional writers, including Lyly, were brought in and a number of attacks appeared from the press with such fancy names as *Pap with a Hatchet, An Almond for a Parrot,* and *A Whip for an Ape.* The players were likewise encouraged, particularly the Paul's Boys. None of the anti-Martin plays have survived, but some of the incidents can be discovered from the pamphlets. Playwrights and players entered into the contest with such zest that they soon became a bigger nuisance even than Martin, and as a result the Boys and their playhouse were suppressed.

Edward Alleyn

Meanwhile the professional players were thriving. A third playhouse, called the Rose, had been erected outside the city limits, across the river on the Bankside in the disreputable suburb of Southwark (see p. 16b). Certain of the younger professional players were becoming famous; of these the greatest was Edward Alleyn, the first star actor in the English theater. Alleyn was a good businessman, and he realized that he needed better plays than had hitherto been available. He had the luck to acquire two which made a considerable sensation. They were Thomas Kyd's *Spanish Tragedy* and Christopher Marlowe's *Tamburlaine.*

Thomas Kyd

The *Spanish Tragedy* (c. 1586) is the first surviving specimen of the revenge play, and it remained a favorite for fifty years. The story tells how young Horatio, son of Hieronimo, the Chief Councilor of the King of Spain, is treacherously murdered in his father's orchard, how the old father ultimately finds out the murderers, and how he achieves a ghastly dramatic vengeance. The play was competently put together and full of incident: a ghost, a midnight murder by hanging, an assassination by pistol, a public execution, several mad scenes, a suicide, and in the final scene three murders and two suicides in quick succession. Apart from these exciting episodes, Kyd had considerable skill in blank verse, and Alleyn made the most of his opportunities in the part of the afflicted old father.

Not very much is known of Thomas Kyd. His father was a scrivener — that is, one who drew up legal documents — and the son was educated at the Merchant Taylors' School under the great headmaster Richard Mulcaster. Kyd apparently did not go up to either of the universities.

Christopher Marlowe

Far more is known of Christopher Marlowe. His father was a shoemaker in the city of Canterbury, a man of good standing and comfortable means. Christopher was baptized on February 26, 1564, and was thus two months older than Shakespeare. He went up to the University of Cambridge in 1581, took his Bachelor's degree in 1584, and then began to study for his M.A. He was ready to apply for his degree in the spring of 1587, but the university hesitated. Rumors were circulating that he, like many other discontented young graduates, was preparing to go abroad to one of the Catholic colleges. Actually he was at this time employed by the Privy Council on some secret mission, probably as a spy on the Catholics. The Council therefore intervened and Marlowe's degree was granted. Then Marlowe came to London and there attracted the notice of Sir Walter Ralegh. He became one of Ralegh's circle of intellectuals, who were greatly suspected of holding atheistic beliefs and committing other enormities.

Marlowe's *Tamburlaine* was as popular as the *Spanish Tragedy*. As a stage play it is far less successful, but Marlowe's verse was more sonorous, astounding, and magnificent than anything that had hitherto been heard on the stage. The character of the Scythian shepherd, who by the power of his personality and his utter ruthlessness conquered the world, gave Alleyn another sensational part, wholly suited to his noisy and robustious style of acting. The first part of *Tamburlaine* was soon followed by a second which carried the story to the death of Tamburlaine.

The third play which Marlowe wrote was *The Jew of Malta*. As a drama it was a great improvement, for Marlowe by this time had learned a good deal about the theater. The play opens with a prologue spoken by the ghost of Machiavelli, who claims the Jew as one of his own special pupils. Then the curtains at the back of the stage are drawn aside and Barabas the Jew is discovered in his countinghouse with his treasures about him. The opening soliloquy effectively creates an impression of enormous and princely wealth. Then comes the conflict. To pay their ransom to the Turk the Christian Maltese seize the Jew's wealth and convert his house into a nunnery. But Barabas has a daughter called Abigail, whom he persuades to pretend that she wishes to be converted to Christianity. She enters the nunnery and recovers a bag of jewels from a secret hiding place. So once more Barabas begins to prosper. His hate of Christians by this time has grown gigantic. Unfortunately, his daughter has two Christian lovers: Lodovic, her chosen, and Mathias, who is unwelcome. Barabas brings it about that the two men fight and kill each other. This so distresses Abigail that she turns nun indeed. Barabas is so angry that to punish his daughter and prevent her from revealing the murder of Lodovic he sends poisoned rice to the nuns and so wipes out the whole nunnery. Meanwhile, Barabas's fortunes are still rising, and when the Turks enter Malta they make him governor. Nevertheless he promises the Maltese that he will destroy the Turkish leader at a banquet by means of a trapdoor through which the Turk shall fall into a caldron of boiling water. The Maltese, however, betray him. Barabas is caught in his own trap and dies in agony. The end of the play is not as good as the beginning, but it is lusty, rousing melodrama. It gave Alleyn another fine part.

Robert Greene

Soon a third writer of repute was attracted to drama. This was Robert Greene, the best known of all popular writers at this time. Greene, born in 1558, took his Bachelor's degree at Cambridge in 1578, and for some months traveled abroad in Italy and Spain. He came back to Cambridge and took his Master's degree in 1583. Thence he went up to London and became the first successful professional novelist. He wrote a number of novels in the style of Lyly and was soon well known, but as much for his wild life and odd pranks as for his books. At first Greene refused to write for the stage; he considered it beneath the dignity of a scholar. But his needs were always greater than his means, and when he saw the success of Marlowe, he was persuaded to turn playwright.

Greene's first plays were written in imitation of Marlowe's style. They were *Alphonsus of Aragon, A Looking Glass for London* (in which he collaborated with Thomas Lodge), and *Orlando Furioso.* Of these, *A Looking Glass for London* is the most interesting. The play dramatizes the Book of Jonah. It opens with the wickedness of the Ninevites, shown in a series of episodes, some fantastic, others realistic and founded on the sordid experiences of the author. Then the prophet Jonas appears and so effectively denounces the Ninevites for their sins that all turn to repentance and fasting, except Adam the clown, who hides food and drink in his baggy breeches until the searchers find them and carry him off to be hanged, in spite of his protest that " *modicum non nocet ut medicus daret* " (" a little drop won't hurt so long as the doctor orders it "). Finally Jonas comes forward and addresses the audience, warning them that London is as wicked as Nineveh and may likewise expect destruction. *A Looking Glass* had no claims to be considered fine drama, but it was first-class entertainment.

Greene also wrote *James the Fourth, King of Scotland,* which, in spite of its title, has nothing to do with history but is a wild melodrama, and *Friar Bacon and Friar Bungay,* his most frequently read play. Friar Bacon, the famous Oxford scholar, and Edward, Prince of Wales, were historical persons, but the play is a mixture of legendary incidents, such as Friar Bacon's famous magical Head of Brass which spoke, and of romance, such as the love of Lacy, Earl of Lincoln, for the lowly-born daughter of the keeper of Fressingfield. Indeed, Greene's plays almost without alteration would serve as scenarios for Hollywood. Plays about magicians were popular; and not long afterward Marlowe wrote his most famous play, *The Tragedy of Dr. Faustus.*[1]

In February 1592 Alleyn came to act at the

[1] See the edition of the play by F. S. Boas.

Rose Theater, which was owned by Philip Henslowe. Henslowe was a good example of the shrewd boy who prospered by making the most of his opportunities. He had been apprenticed in the leather trade to a certain Master Woodward. On the death of his master, he married the widow and took over her considerable property, part of which he invested in the playhouse. A few months later Alleyn married Henslowe's stepdaughter, and thereafter the two worked together in partnership. As owner of the playhouse, Henslowe drew a share of the daily takings, and being a careful man of business, he entered each day in his account book the name of the play acted and the sum received. This book, known as Henslowe's *Diary* (see p. 65a), still survives, and is one of the most interesting and important documents in the history of the English stage, for it gives a complete record of the plays acted by one company for a period of five years. Later Henslowe acted as banker to the companies playing at his theaters, and he then recorded the sums paid out for new plays, costumes, properties, and other expenses. With the aid of the *Diary* it is possible to date with certainty the plays acted at Henslowe's house, for he noted the first performance of each new play. Unfortunately, there are only scattered and fragmentary records for the other playhouses and companies. Except probably for a few months in 1592, Shakespeare was not connected with Henslowe's ventures.

Shakespeare's First Plays

On March 3, 1592, Alleyn put on a new play called *Harry the Sixth,* which is almost certainly the first part of Shakespeare's *Henry VI.* The play was a great success. Indeed at its first performance the takings were the largest ever recorded in Henslowe's *Diary.* The scenes which showed the heroic English knight Sir John Talbot were especially popular.

Shakespeare at this time was almost twenty-eight years old. He was learning his business as a playwright working for Alleyn and his company, and his first models were Alleyn's great successes: *The Spanish Tragedy, Friar Bacon Tamburlaine,* and *The Jew of Malta.* It is not surprising that with Alleyn's voice and presence constantly before him, Shakespeare in his earliest plays should have imitated his masters. In

Titus Andronicus he outdid even the horrors of the *Spanish Tragedy,* and in *Richard III* he copied the technique of *The Jew of Malta.*

Alleyn's venture came to an abrupt end on June 11. There had been serious rioting in Southwark caused by apprentices trying to rescue a prisoner from the Marshalsea Prison. As the apprentices had gathered at the Rose on the pretext of watching a new play, the Council ordered all playing to cease until Michaelmas. Alleyn therefore took his company on tour. Soon afterward the plague broke out in London; at such times no playing was allowed.

The Deaths of Greene and Marlowe

Meanwhile, Robert Greene was dying in great poverty from the dropsy brought on by his excessive living. All his friends had left London because of the plague, and he grew very bitter as he contemplated the prosperity of the players who had grown rich on the products of university men like himself. Shakespeare's success especially seemed to upset him, and his annoyance may have been partly increased by the fact that *Henry VI* had been drawing far better houses than his own plays. It was in this mood that he penned the famous letter to his fellow playwrights warning them against " the upstart Crow, beautified with our feathers" (see p. 9b). Greene died on September 2, 1592.

Alleyn came back to London just before Christmas and playing began again at the Rose. The repertory then included *The Spanish Tragedy, The Jew of Malta, Titus Andronicus, Friar Bacon,* and, as new plays, Marlowe's *Massacre at Paris* — a dramatization of the massacre of St. Bartholomew's Day — and *The Jealous Comedy,* which some scholars believe to be the origin of the play afterward rewritten as *The Merry Wives of Windsor.* The plague, however, was still lurking, and in February 1593 the playhouses were again closed.

Marlowe survived Greene by only nine months. His end was sensational. It was a time of general uneasiness, and the Council suspected that some revolutionary movement was about to break out. Mysterious libels were being circulated warning the Flemish traders living in London to get out of the country. As a preliminary measure all writers who might be suspected were apprehended, and Thomas Kyd found himself in jail. When his papers were examined, some pages of a disputation denying the divinity of Jesus Christ were discovered. Kyd was asked to explain how he came to possess such a suspicious document. He declared that it was Marlowe's property and had been left behind when the two men had shared a study two years before. Marlowe was therefore summoned to appear before the Council and to explain himself. On May 30, 1593, while he was still awaiting further instructions, Marlowe, in company with three men named Frizer, Skeeres, and Poley, went to eat and drink in an eating-house in Deptford on the Thames. During the evening Marlowe and Frizer began to quarrel. Marlowe seized Frizer's dagger, but in the scuffle he himself was jabbed in the eye and killed.[2] As Marlowe had the reputation of being a violent and foul-mouthed atheist, the godly regarded his end as highly appropriate. Kyd also died before the end of 1594.

The plague continued all through the summer and autumn of 1593, and it was not until the late spring of 1594 that the players began to drift back to London. For a while the players of the Lord Admiral and the Lord Chamberlain united to play at a small theater in the suburb of Newington Butts. Their plays included *The Jew of Malta, Titus Andronicus, Hamlet,*[3] and *The Taming of the Shrew.* The arrangement, however, only lasted for a few days. Alleyn then went back to the Rose and there reorganized the Admiral's Men; the others combined to form a new Lord Chamberlain's Company. By autumn both companies were firmly established.

The Lord Chamberlain's Players

The Lord Chamberlain at this time was Henry Carey, first Lord Hunsdon. He died on July 22, 1596, and his players then took service with his son, George Carey, second Lord Hunsdon. They were thus for a time officially known as the Lord of Hunsdon's Servants and are so described on the title page of the first quarto of *Romeo and Juliet.* They resumed their former title when the second Lord Hunsdon was ap-

---

[2] The report of the inquest was discovered by Dr. Leslie Hotson in the Public Record Office in London and published in 1925. [3] In the early version. See *Haml* Intro. pp. 880b–881a.

pointed Lord Chamberlain on March 17, 1597.

In the new Lord Chamberlain's Company the leading members were Richard and Cuthbert Burbage, sons of James Burbage, the builder of the Theater, Will Kempe, and Shakespeare. Richard Burbage was beginning to make a reputation as a tragic actor almost as great as Alleyn's, Kempe had long been famous as a clown, and Shakespeare was now without a rival as a dramatist. It was a strong team.

By this time Shakespeare had written the three parts of *Henry VI, Richard III, Titus Andronicus, The Two Gentlemen of Verona, The Taming of the Shrew, The Comedy of Errors,* and *Love's Labor's Lost. Richard III* was one of the earliest successes of the Chamberlain's Men. Shakespeare followed it up with *Romeo and Juliet,* which was immediately popular and much quoted by connoisseurs of poetry. In the Christmas holidays of 1594 the Chamberlain's Men played at Court; they also acted *The Comedy of Errors* for the young gentlemen of Gray's Inn, as a contribution to the elaborate revels of that Christmas (see p. 32a).

Shakespeare next wrote *A Midsummer Night's Dream* — probably in 1595 — presumably for some society wedding, and *Richard II,* which was an attempt to rival Marlowe's *Edward the Second.* As Marlowe's play had been printed in 1593, Shakespeare had the pattern in print before him. The patriotic speeches of John of Gaunt were much noted and are quoted in collections of pearls from the poets. Apart from these two plays, this seems to have been a poor year for drama. No plays of note were produced at the Rose, and once more the playhouses suffered from interference from the authorities.

The summer of 1594 had been disastrously wet and the crops failed. The price of food rose; there were serious riots in the city; and on June 26 the playhouses were again shut for two months. In September the Lord Mayor made another attempt to persuade the Council to suppress plays altogether, on the ground that plays were responsible for instilling young persons with "lewd demeanors." There was, indeed, a general air of uneasiness and gloom, especially as it was widely (and accurately) believed that the Spanish were preparing a new and greater Armada to invade England.

The Lord Admiral's Men

Nevertheless in 1596 several notable plays were produced. On February 12, the Admiral's Men put on *The Blind Beggar of Alexandria,* written by George Chapman, in which Alleyn took the part of a shepherd's son who, by disguising himself successively as a duke, a beggar, a moneylender, and a swashbuckling count called Hermes, lives a quadruple life with a different wife fitted to each personality. It was a fantastic play, even for the Rose, but it has some importance in the history of drama because Count Hermes is the first notable specimen of a " humor " character, his particular humor [4] or whim being to wear a patch over one eye, to shroud himself in a large cloak in cold weather or hot, and to carry a pistol with which to emphasize his humor by shooting up his enemies.

To this year also is usually assigned Shakespeare's *King John,* which was a rewriting of an old anti-Catholic play that had belonged to the now defunct Queen's Players and had been published five years earlier. *King John* is a very uneven play, but it contains some good topical speeches which directly reflect the general alarms of this anxious year. It was followed by *The Merchant of Venice,* a play which owed a little to Marlowe's *The Jew of Malta.*

Meanwhile, the Chamberlain's Men had their troubles. The twenty-one years' lease of the ground on which the Theater had been built was due to lapse in 1597, and the landlord, whose name was Giles Alleyn (no relation to the player), was reluctant to renew it. Old James Burbage, whose business instincts were as keen as ever, realized that conditions in the playing profession were fast changing. In the last seven years the standard of plays had so vastly improved that gentlemen of means were now keen patrons of the playhouses. Burbage decided to revive the idea of a private playhouse where plays could be acted indoors, at a high price, to an exclusive audience. He therefore acquired the lease of the old dining hall of the Blackfriars' Monastery and, at great expense, converted it into a small theater. It was almost ready for opening when the aristocratic residents in the neighborhood objected to the presence of a playhouse and petitioned the Council to prohibit the scheme. Burbage was forbidden

[4] See App. 3.

to proceed with his plan and was thus left with a considerable loss. He died a few weeks later, leaving the Theater property to his son Cuthbert and the Blackfriars to Richard.

In March 1597 the Admiral's Men produced at the Rose another play by Chapman, *A Humorous Day's Mirth,* which was very well received. This was the first notable example of a "comedy of humors." In plays of this kind the author aimed at presenting on the stage contemporary types of folly. The particular types caricatured by Chapman were an elderly jealous husband, Count Labervele; his newly married young wife, Florilla, who was a Puritan; a foolish gentleman called Master Blanuel, who tries to show his good breeding by copying the mannerisms of gallants; and Dowsecer, a melancholic man. Dowsecer is the first conspicuous specimen of the melancholic character who scorns the world and stands conspicuously apart, wrapped in a large black cloak and his own bitter thoughts. The play is a good indication of the change of public taste; it was intended for an intellectual and sophisticated audience.

Ben Jonson

About the same time a new competitor appeared to rival both the Admiral's Men and the Chamberlain's Men. From each company some actors broke away to form a new company under the patronage of the Earl of Pembroke. They acted at the Swan playhouse on the Bankside, with some success. But they rashly chose to put on a new play, *The Isle of Dogs,* the work of Thomas Nashe, the most vitriolic of all the Elizabethan satirists, and one of the actors in the company, Benjamin Jonson, who for the first time became conspicuous. The play was a bitter satire and so full of "seditious and slanderous matter" that the Council took stern action. They caused all playhouses to be shut up forthwith, and then sent Jonson and two of his fellow players, Gabriel Spencer and Robert Shaw, to prison. Pembroke's Men thereupon dissolved, but the chief actors agreed that when they came out of prison they would join the Admiral's Men at the Rose.

The offenders were released in October, and both the Admiral's Men and the Chamberlain's Men began again to play. During the restraint,

Shakespeare's *Richard II* had been published, and was so popular that at least three editions were printed during the next year. Soon afterward, Shakespeare continued the story in *I Henry IV.* When the play first appeared the fat knight was named Sir John Oldcastle. The real Oldcastle had been burned as a Lollard heretic during the reign of Henry V, and was thus regarded as one of the first Protestant martyrs. Oldcastle, by right of marriage, had acquired the title of Lord Cobham. The contemporary Lord Cobham, an unpleasant young man who had newly succeeded to the title, objected to the appearance of his predecessor in so disreputable a guise. Shakespeare was therefore obliged to alter the name to Falstaff, who became the most popular of all his characters.

By this time, the rivalry between the Chamberlain's Company and the Admiral's Men was becoming keen, and in the scene where Falstaff acts the part of the King rebuking his prodigal son he assumes the tragic mannerisms of the great Alleyn in a heavy role. The first part of *Henry IV* was so successful that Shakespeare followed it with a second part, probably first produced in the early months of 1598. The parodies in the second part were more conspicuous; Ancient Pistol, a new character, ranted about the stage in a close imitation of Alleyn's mannerisms, uttering bombastic and unintelligible phrases which were culled from the more extravagant plays in the repertoire of the Rose playhouse. Falstaff, Pistol, Bardolph, and the rest of the gang were themselves "humor" characters, and in the list of persons printed in the first folio in 1623 (see p. 66b) are labeled "irregular humorists."

Shakespeare's next play was *Much Ado about Nothing,* the first of the three mature romantic comedies; it was probably produced during the summer of 1598. By this time, the Chamberlain's Men were acting at the Curtain playhouse, for the dispute between the Burbages and their landlord was still unsettled and they had to abandon the Theater.

Meanwhile, since his release from prison Ben Jonson had been writing plays for the Admiral's Men. Ben was the most colorful of the Elizabethan dramatists, and much is known of his life. According to his own account, given to the Scottish poet William Drummond of Hawthornden in 1619, his grandfather was a gentleman from the County of Cumberland; his father had been imprisoned in the time of Queen Mary, lost his estates, and then turned clergyman. Jonson himself was born in London in 1573, a month after his father's death. He was taught at Westminster School by the famous scholar William Camden; but his schooling was interrupted when his mother married a bricklayer, and Ben was put to the trade, which he disliked. Accordingly, he went as a soldier to the Low Countries and there — so he claimed — he killed one of the enemy in single combat. Then he came back to England and turned player. As a young man, he was self-opinionated, conceited, and quarrelsome.

The Comedy of Humors

Jonson's first connection with the Admiral's Men lasted only a few months, and in the late summer of 1598 he sold his first successful play to the Chamberlain's Men. It was called *Every Man in His Humor,* and was produced at the Curtain in September.

The version best known to students differs considerably from the play as first acted, for Jonson revised and rewrote it for the first collected volume of his plays, published in 1616. In the final version the play is set in London and the characters bear English names. In the first version the locality was nominally Florence, but the characters were nevertheless typical Londoners, each representing a different type very familiar to the audience at the Curtain.

Jonson was a student of the classics. He approved Aristotle's theories of drama as expressed in the *Poetics* — and misinterpreted by the Italian critics, who invented the "theory of the three unities" of time, place, and action. They held that drama should present an action which happened in one place and occupied the same time on the stage as the events took in real life. Jonson did not follow these rules too rigidly, but he took great care to plan his plays so that all the events occurred within a single day in the same city and all the characters might reasonably have met each other in the course of their natural occupations. Moreover he held, as did most serious critics of the time, that all literature had a moral purpose. The particular purpose of comedy was to chastise folly by making it ridiculous. Accordingly, in his plays he created char-

acters which were contemporary types, and so plotted the story that each "humor" (see App. 3) displays his own particular folly and is suitably punished for it.

In the early version of *Every Man in His Humor,* Lorenzo, Senior (afterward renamed Edward Knowell, Senior), was an overanxious father who suspected that his son, Lorenzo, Junior, was wasting his time in writing poetry and in the company of a young gentleman called Prospero (renamed Wellbred). Two foolish gentlemen join them: Stephano (Master Stephen), a wealthy fool from the country who wants to learn how to be a gentleman, and Matheo (Master Matthew), a young townsman who writes bad poetry and tries to pass himself off as an aesthete and an intellectual. Matheo is a great admirer of Signor Bodadilla (Bobadil), who poses as a professional soldier of great military experience and distinction. The plot is further elaborated by Thorello (afterward Master Kitely), a merchant inordinately jealous of his young wife. Most of the complications are effected by Brainworm, Lorenzo, Senior's, man-servant, who is full of mischief and ingenuity.

This conception of comedy was not new. It was indeed a direct adaptation of Latin comedy, but the characters and the situations were entirely English. Each character in turn reveals his foolishness in an intricate plot, which keeps to the unities of time and action. Finally, all are brought together in the house of a magistrate, Dr. Clement, and appropriately rewarded or punished.

Every Man in His Humor, especially in the revised version, is still an excellent stage play, though seldom acted, and it set Jonson in the first rank of Elizabethan dramatists. After the first production, there was an unhappy sequel Gabriel Spencer, now one of the Admiral's Players and only a few months before Jonson's companion in misfortune because of *The Isle of Dogs* (see p. 41a), waited for him when the play was over. The two fell to quarreling and went off to the fields to settle the matter with swords. Jonson was wounded, but he killed Spencer. He was arrested and tried for manslaughter, but he pleaded benefit of clergy (see p. 28a) and was released. Thus the Admiral's Men had first lost a promising poet and now an experienced player.

The Globe Playhouse

About this time the dispute between the Burbages and their landlord Giles Alleyn reached a climax. In the original lease of 1576 James Burbage had agreed that if the lease of the ground was not renewed at the end of the twenty-one years' occupancy, either the buildings were to be removed or they would become the property of the landlord. As Alleyn had promised to renew the lease, Cuthbert Burbage let the Theater stand. Finally, Alleyn produced a new lease, but the terms were impossible and Burbage refused to sign. This was Alleyn's intention. He proposed to seize the Theater, demolish it, and use its valuable timber. When the Burbages realized Alleyn's plan, they took counsel with the chief sharers in the Chamberlain's Company — Shakespeare, Heminges, Phillips, Pope, and Kempe — and all agreed to finance a new playhouse. They rented a piece of ground south of the Thames, not far from the Rose. Then, during the Christmas holidays, with a party of men armed with swords and other weapons they set about the old Theater, tore it down, and transported the materials to the new site. Here, seven months later, arose the new playhouse, the Globe, the finest theater that had yet been seen in England.

Meanwhile, in the spring of 1599 Shakespeare's *Henry V* was put on at the Curtain. A year had passed since *II Henry IV,* wherein Shakespeare promised to continue Falstaff; but now he allowed Falstaff to die off stage, though the rest of his gang continued — with the addition of a new character, Corporal Nym, who was forever prating of his humors.

The Globe was ready for occupancy about July, and thither the Chamberlain's Men moved. Three of their first plays were *As You Like It, Jonson's Every Man out of His Humor,* and *Julius Caesar. As You Like It* was another romantic comedy, but in Jaques Shakespeare created a specimen of the melancholic humor which was now becoming so fashionable.

Every Man out of His Humor was a failure. After the success of *Every Man in His Humor,* Jonson became very arrogant, and he prefaced the new play with an induction or introductory piece in which three characters, apparently spectators, come onto the stage to discuss his theory of the humors and the purpose and history of comedy. The play itself was not so good as its predecessor; the portraits of the humors were too exact and the plot too involved. Jonson also committed a gross error of taste by introducing Queen Elizabeth on the stage, probably idealized as Cynthia or Astraea, to bring the play to a close. This offending episode was dropped when the play was printed. After this failure, Jonson went back to the Admiral's Men and collaborated with Dekker in various pieces of hack writing which have not survived. Thomas Dekker had for some time been writing busily for the Admiral's Men, and in 1599 sold them one of his happiest plays, *The Shoemaker's Holiday.*

Now that the Chamberlain's Men were playing at the Globe and were therefore near neighbors of the Admiral's Men at the Rose, the rivalry between the two companies became more bitter. The parodies in the Falstaff plays especially irked the Admiral's Men. Accordingly, in October 1599 they planned to retaliate. They tried to revive the ill feeling caused two years before, when Shakespeare's fat knight had first appeared as Oldcastle,[5] by producing a play on the real Oldcastle. In the prologue they unctuously claim:

> It is no pampered glutton we present,
> Nor aged counselor to youthful sin.

The authors of the play were Munday, Drayton, Wilson, and Hathaway, and in writing it they borrowed a good deal from Shakespeare's Falstaff. This competition, however, between the two companies did not last much longer; both were threatened with dangerous rivals elsewhere.

The Paul's Boys and John Marston

In the autumn of 1599 after a break of ten years the Paul's Boys (see p. 36a) were re-established. They were financed by William Stanley, Earl of Derby, who was a keen amateur of the drama. The Boys were immediately popular. They played in a little private house in the precincts of St. Paul's, where a gentleman could be sure of the quality of the audience; he would not "be choked with the stench of garlic, nor pasted to the barmy jacket of a beer-brewer." Their dramatist was John Marston.

[5] See *I Hen IV* Intro. p. 615a-b.

John Marston, a young man of good family, was the son and heir of John Marston, a bencher of the Middle Temple; that is, a lawyer of high standing. The son was born in 1576, took his degree in the University of Oxford in 1594, and came to London to study law; but he was more attracted to poetry. In 1597 he published a little volume called *The Metamorphosis of Pygmalion's Image and Certain Satires.* He followed this in 1598 with another book of satires called *The Scourge of Villainy.* This was the most popular of all the satires which appeared in the 1590's, but it was an extravagant, ranting book. Marston experimented with words and phrases and created a new kind of poetic language, furious, bombastic, and abounding with strange words.

Marston was a gentleman of means. He would not have condescended to write plays for the professional players at the Globe or the Rose, but there was no disgrace in writing for the genteel audiences which patronized the little theater of the Paul's Boys.

Marston's plays in some ways were as extravagant as his satires. He was, nevertheless, a dramatist of considerable skill, particularly in creating scenes of horror. In the new playhouse, plays were acted by artificial light, and Marston was able to produce vivid effects by the use of a single flickering torch. Among his first plays were *Antonio and Mellida,* and its gory, dismal sequel, *Antonio's Revenge.* Both of these appeared in the autumn of 1599.

By Christmas the Admiral's Men realized that the old Rose could no longer compete with the new Globe. Accordingly, Edward Alleyn decided to move. On January 8, 1600, he and Henslowe signed a contract with Peter Street, who had built the Globe, to erect a new playhouse for them in the parish of St. Giles Cripplegate, north of the City. There were many vexatious delays, which can be traced in Henslowe's *Diary,* but the new house was at last finished in August 1600. It was called the Fortune.

Many difficulties came to the Chamberlain's Men in 1600. In the general uneasiness of the times (see p. 24b), players were obliged to be cautious, and for a while by order of the Council playing was even reduced to two performances a week. Moreover, it had long been the **regulation** that playing should **cease altogether**

during Lent, and although hitherto the rule had been as much neglected as obeyed, it seemed unsafe this year to incur the anger of the authorities. During this period of enforced idleness Will Kempe, the clown of the company, thought to make some money on the side by betting that he would dance from London to Norwich, a distance of about a hundred miles. He set out on February 10 and reached his destination in nine stages. On his arrival the Mayor and chief citizens gave him a civic reception. It was a triumphant progress and was talked of for years. Kempe was so greatly elated by his success that he planned a much more ambitious venture: to dance over the Alps to Rome. He therefore sold his share in the Globe Theater, left the Chamberlain's Men, and set out. The loss of their clown, always one of the most popular attractions of their playhouse, was serious.

The Children of Blackfriars

Soon after the Admiral's Men had moved into the Fortune, the Chamberlain's Men suffered from a new and far more dangerous rival company. The indoor playhouse in the Blackfriars which James Burbage had built at such expense in 1596 (see p. 40b) was still empty, and Richard Burbage had to find the rent. He was approached by a certain Henry Evans, a Welsh lawyer who had once been a sharer in Lyly's ventures. Burbage agreed to rent the playhouse to Evans, who was in league with Nathaniel Giles, choirmaster of the Queen's Chapel Royal, and the two planned to establish a second boys' company. They were joined by Ben Jonson, who had again parted from the Admiral's Men.

Ben had always longed to write exclusively for audiences of gentlemen and courtiers, and here was his chance. He produced for the Children of the Chapel a play called *Cynthia's Revels,* somewhat after the pattern of one of Lyly's plays, part satire, part masque, part allegory, which would — so he hoped — be produced at Court. The play has the usual crowd of humor characters — foolish courtiers with their fashionable ways, and another melancholic, Crites, the upright judge who neither fears nor favors fools. Crites, indeed, was intended as an idealized portrait of Jonson himself.

Essex's Rebellion

The two boys' companies soon became the fashion and drew off the best part of the usual audiences of the professional players. Moreover, the Chamberlain's Men were involved in trouble which might have been disastrous. By Christmas 1600 it was obvious to observers at Court that the Earl of Essex and his followers were hatching some plot which would soon break (see p. 24a). Shakespeare's *Richard II* had become linked in a curious way with Essex's fortunes. When first published in 1597, the play sold well because contemporaries saw a parallel, not so obvious nowadays, between Queen Elizabeth and King Richard II, with Essex as Bolingbroke. The parallels became more conspicuous when John Hayward brought out his book called *The First Part of the Life and Reign of King Henry the Fourth.* On February 6, 1601, some of Essex's friends went over the river to the Globe playhouse and there saw Phillips, one of the players. They asked that *Richard II* might be played on the next afternoon, which was a Saturday. The players were dubious. *Richard II,* they said, was an old play and would not draw an audience, but they foolishly consented when Essex's friends promised to add forty shillings to the takings. So the play was acted before a large party from Essex House. Next morning, Essex made his disastrous attempt to raise the city of London against the Queen.

The Council took a very serious view of the playing of *Richard II,* which was much stressed at the trials of the conspirators. The Chamberlain's Men were not, however, considered to be involved in the rebellion; indeed, they played at Court on February 24, the night before Essex's execution.

The War of the Theaters

The growing rivalry between the two boys' companies was soon increased by a personal quarrel between Marston and Jonson, their respective playwrights. Jonson disliked Marston and regarded his peculiar style as outrageous. Accordingly, in successive plays these two struck out at each other, and their hostility developed into a regular " war of the theaters." Jonson began the war by introducing into *Every Man out of His Humor* a pair of gulls who try to pass themselves off as wits by speaking in Marston's peculiar manner. In *Jack Drum's Entertainment* Marston retorted with

> . . . bombast wits,
> That are puffed up with arrogant conceit
> Of their own worth, as if Omnipotence
> Had hoisted them to such unequaled height
> That they surveyed our spirits with an eye
> Only create to censure from above.

Jonson followed, in *Cynthia's Revels,* by calling Marston " a strange arrogating puff." Marston in his next play, *What You Will,* which came out in the spring of 1601, replied more fiercely. He prefaced the play with an induction wherein, without mentioning names, he attacked Jonson for his pedantic insistence on rules and his insolent contempt for all who disagreed with him:

> Music and poetry were first approved
> By common sense, and that which pleasèd most,
> Held most allowèd pass. Know rules of art
> Were shaped to pleasure, not pleasure to your
> rules.

Jonson was furious. He determined to make Marston so ridiculous that he would be silent forever. Jonson was a slow writer, and hitherto he had produced a new play at intervals of about ten months. His next play was written in fifteen weeks. It was called *Poetaster, His Arraignment,* a clever, witty comedy, telling of the Court of the Roman Emperor Augustus, with its brilliant circle of artists, including the poets Virgil, Horace, and Ovid. In the play, Horace, as everyone knew, was Jonson himself. Horace is harassed by two inferior wits, Crispinus and Demetrius, whom he finally causes to be condemned after a public trial before the Emperor. As a punishment Crispinus (alias Marston) is given an emetic which makes him vomit up his turgid words; he is then dismissed with a warning to mend his manners. The play was acted by the Children of the Chapel at the Blackfriars in the early autumn of 1601.

Jonson had made many enemies, for apart from Crispinus other characters whom he satirized were recognizable individuals; he had also taken to sneering at the professional players. Before *Poetaster* appeared, the Chamberlain's Men heard of Jonson's forthcoming revenge and hired

STOP

Dekker to make an answer. Dekker was a very rapid writer, and soon he had the reply ready. It was called *Satiromastrix; or, The Untrussing of the Humorous Poet.*[6] As a play it was a fantastical hodgepodge. The main story told of the English King, William Rufus (1087–1100), and his lust for the bride of Sir Walter Tyrrel. The underplot was a comedy of contemporary middle-class intrigue. In the midst walked Roman Horace (alias Jonson), who was most viciously abused and finally crowned with nettles and made to swear that he would thereafter behave himself. Dekker knew Jonson well, and his Horace is a brutal but vivid and most amusing caricature. *Satiromastrix* was acted by the Chamberlain's Men and by the Paul's Boys. It brought an end to the stage war; Jonson was bitterly offended and withdrew from writing plays altogether for the time being.

Shakespeare himself took a hand in the stage war. At Christmas time the students at St. John's College, Cambridge, acted a play called *The Second Part of the Return from Parnassus,* in which two students played the parts of Richard Burbage and Will Kempe. Kempe was made to say:

Few of the university pen plays well, they smell too much of that writer Ovid and that writer Metamorphosis, and talk too much of Proserpina and Jupiter. Why, here's our fellow Shakespeare puts them all down — aye, and Ben Jonson too. Oh, that Ben Jonson is a pestilent fellow, he brought up Horace giving the poets a pill, but our fellow Shakespeare hath given him a purge that made him bewray his credit.

The incident has not been identified. It may be that a passage from one of Shakespeare's known plays — *Troilus and Cressida* or *Hamlet* are the most likely — has disappeared. It may be that in a play which has not survived there was an uproarious scene in which a close stool was the principal property.

Little is known of the other plays produced by the Chamberlain's Men in 1601. Parts of *Hamlet,* in the version now known, were certainly written during this year, and probably also *Twelfth Night,* but as a whole the year was the worst for the professional players since the plague years of 1592–94, and there was little call for new plays.

<hr/>

[6] Untruss, "to remove the pants."

Business improved considerably in 1602. On February 2 the Chamberlain's Men played *Twelfth Night* before the members of the Middle Temple. In this year Shakespeare probably wrote *Othello* and *All's Well That Ends Well.* Business with Henslowe and Alleyn also improved. By this time they had a strong team of writers. Dekker had returned to work for them and two newcomers appear in the *Diary,* John Day and John Webster. During the year twenty new plays were ordered for the Fortune.

In this year also another new company was formed under the patronage of the Earl of Worcester. Their most important actor was Will Kempe, who had returned to England in the previous September. Although he had fulfilled his bet to dance to Rome, the venture was not a success and now he was back in London; but he did not rejoin his old colleagues. Worcester's Men began to act at the Rose in August. Their most interesting play was Thomas Heywood's domestic tragedy *A Woman Killed with Kindness.*

The King's Players

The next year, 1603, was a turning point in the fortunes of the players. At first the prospects were gloomy. By the middle of March it was clear to the Council that Queen Elizabeth was dying, and in the general anxiety every precaution was taken to prevent disturbances. On the nineteenth, orders were sent out that all playing should cease. The Queen died on March 24. By midday King James of Scotland had been proclaimed in London as true and lawful King of England. Immediately there was a scramble for offices under the new King. Among the lucky ones were the Lord Chamberlain's Players, who on May 19 were granted a patent appointing them to be the King's Players and Grooms of the Chamber Extraordinary (see p. 13b). For Shakespeare's fellows this was a great change in fortune. Hitherto the profession of playing had been precarious. Players existed only by favor of the Queen, for the official reason given to the Lord Mayor of London and others when they petitioned that the theaters should be suppressed was that since the Queen enjoyed plays, the players must be allowed to keep in practice. Now all was changed; henceforward the players became royal servants and favorites who were constantly in demand at Court. In the last four years of Queen Elizabeth's reign the Chamberlain's Men played at Court fourteen times; in the first four years of the new reign they played forty-one times.

In the general excitement Ben Jonson forgot his grievances and emerged from retirement. He was reconciled with the King's Men, who produced his latest play, a tragedy called *Sejanus*. This was a most scholarly production, full of minute and accurate details of Roman customs, and based on wide reading in the Roman classics. The historical Sejanus was a favorite of the Emperor Tiberius, who allowed him to obtain such power in the state that Sejanus became a very real danger. The Emperor, thus forced to scheme against his favorite, persuaded the Senate to turn against him, and Sejanus was brutally executed. This play was another of Jonson's unlucky ventures. It was dull and overbookish, and the audience did not like it. Moreover, some members of the Council were disturbed by the theme. It was hardly more than two years since Essex had been beheaded, and a play on the rise and fall of a royal favorite seemed too close to recent events. Jonson was summoned before the Council to explain himself.

The bright hopes of the spring were soon disappointed. As summer came on the plague broke out in London and all the playhouses were closed. The King's Men abandoned the Globe and went on tour in the country. The plague lasted all through the summer and autumn, but by mid-November the weekly record of deaths had fallen to a hundred. The Court during these months had been on progress, and at the beginning of December King James came to Wilton, near Salisbury, the great house of the Earl of Pembroke. Hither the King's Players were summoned to perform before King James, and for their trouble and expense they were allowed £30.

By their appointment as players to the King, the Chamberlain's Men were marked out as the leading company. At the end of the year recognition came also to the Admiral's Men and to the Children of the Blackfriars; the young Prince Henry became the patron of Alleyn's company; the Children of the Chapel were appointed Children of the Queen's Revels, and Samuel Daniel, the poet, was made their overseer.

Unfortunately Henslowe had by this time ceased to record his theatrical transactions in his *Diary,* and henceforward dramatic records of all kinds are so scanty that no continuous history of the London companies is possible. Apart from scattered incidents and details, the account must necessarily be slight and haphazard.

There was much activity for the King's Men in the year 1604. On March 15 King James made a progress in state through the city of London, beginning at the Tower and ending at Ludgate. The King's Men walked in the procession, wearing their red liveries as Grooms of the Chamber. In August they were called on to attend the Spanish Commissioners, who had come to London to take part in the formal ceremonies of swearing the peace between England and Spain. Several new plays came out this year, including probably Shakespeare's *Measure for Measure*. In November the King's Men acted *Othello* for the King and the Court in Whitehall Palace, but in December they caused some offense by putting on a play called *The Tragedy of Gowry* — a dramatization of a sensational attempt to murder King James in 1600 — in which one of the players took the part of King James himself. In the Christmas holidays they played before the King *Measure for Measure, The Comedy of Errors, Love's Labor's Lost, Henry V,* and *Every Man out of His Humor*.

Of the plays acted by other companies in 1604 the best was John Marston's *Malcontent*. This was produced and owned by the Children of the Queen's Revels at the Blackfriars. It was also brought out by the King's Men — although the play was not theirs — in retaliation for the fact that the Children had acted one of their plays.

In the new reign Ben Jonson's fortunes likewise rose. Queen Anne, the Danish wife of King James, was especially fond of masques, and she and her ladies from time to time acted in them. The masque was an elaborate and costly form of entertainment presented by young courtiers of both sexes. Based on a mythological story in verse, the masque was usually intended as a compliment either to the royal family or to the special occasion, such as a marriage, for which it was written. The story was made the excuse for much singing, dancing, elaborate and extravagant costumes, and ingenious scenery. Ben Jonson was particularly successful in writing the kind of poetic dialogue and lyric required for masques. The costumes, scenery, and complicated devices necessary for the production were mostly designed by Inigo Jones, but the partnership between Jonson and Jones was uneasy, as each was very jealous of the other.

During the year 1605 the King's Men continued to display their repertory before their master, and on Sunday, February 12, they acted *The Merchant of Venice*. This so delighted King James that he ordered the performance to be repeated on the following Tuesday.

" *Eastward Ho* "

Now that the old restraints had been removed, the players grew bolder and held the mirror more closely up to nature. The Children especially were encouraged to comment on their betters. This led to troubles. In September the Children of the Queen's Revels acted a new play by Jonson, Chapman, and Marston called *Eastward Ho*. *Eastward Ho* is a very moral story of life in London. The chief characters are a goldsmith, his two prentices, and his two daughters. One of the apprentices is an extravagant spendthrift, the other is a very proper, hard-working, thrifty young man, who marries the younger daughter and prospers. The other daughter is a giddy creature and is encouraged by her mother to marry a shiftless knight called Sir Petronel Flash. Sir Petronel immediately spends his wife's money, and to avoid her indignation goes on board a ship that is about to sail to Virginia. He is joined by the extravagant apprentice, and when the ship is wrecked in the Thames they are both imprisoned for debt until, after edifying repentance, they are finally delivered by the kind-hearted goldsmith. The story in itself was harmless enough, but in speaking of the disreputable Sir Petronel, one of the characters, mimicking King James's Scots accent, remarked: " I ken the man weel. He is one of my thirty-pound knights." And of Virginia, Seagull, the dishonest captain, declared that it was as pleasant a country as ever the sun shined on:

And then you shall live freely there, without sergeants, or courtiers, or lawyers, or intelligencers, only a few industrious Scots, perhaps, who indeed are dispersed over the face of the whole earth. But as for them, there are no greater friends to Englishmen and England, when they are out on't in the world, than they are. And for my part, I would a hundred thousand of 'em were there, for we are all one countrymen now, ye know, and we should

find ten times more comfort of them there than we do here.

The King was very angry. Marston ran away, but Jonson and Chapman in spite of their indignant protests of innocence were for a while sent to prison.

This year, also, the King's Men probably acted a domestic comedy called *The London Prodigal,* which was published with Shakespeare's name as its author on the title page, though there is no other reason to believe that Shakespeare took any hand in it.

On November 5, the great Gunpowder Plot was discovered (see p. 17a). The horror and the general feeling of unrest and disillusion of the times are well reflected in the plays which came out during the months following. Early in 1606 the Children of the Blackfriars played a cynical and satirical comedy called *The Isle of Gulls,* the work of John Day. The play is interesting as a comment on the mood of the year and the increasing difficulties of dramatists with an audience that now had grown hypercritical. Nowadays, complained the prologue, spectators are of three kinds: either they insist on satire and invectives, or they call for bawdry, or else nothing will content them but furious and bombastic language. And if the play is not to their liking, they rise in the middle of the action and go out of the theater, leaving the poor Children to speak their lines to an empty house.

Although Ben Jonson was now mostly occupied with writing masques, he produced in 1606 a comedy for the King's Men which — just to show what he could do when he tried and to answer those who had mocked him for only writing one play a year — he completed in five weeks, without any assistance. It was called *Volpone; or, The Fox* and was Ben's bitterest satire on humanity.

During this year, Shakespeare wrote two of his greatest plays, *Macbeth* and *King Lear*. It is possible that *Macbeth* was written in a hurry as one of the three plays which the King's Men acted before the King of Denmark on a memorable state visit. *King Lear* was acted on December 26 as one of the plays presented during the Christmas holidays. There are many indications that Shakespeare had written it during the previous nine months.

About this time a new dramatist appeared, a

young man of about twenty-one named Francis Beaumont. His first play, called *The Woman-Hater* (1606), was one of the last to be acted by Paul's Boys, who had not received any special encouragement in the new reign and soon afterward disappeared entirely from the records. In the following year, Beaumont wrote *The Knight of the Burning Pestle* for the Children of the Queen's Revels. It is his best-known play and gives a most entertaining picture of drama in the private playhouses. Into the auditorium there stray a grocer, his wife, and their two apprentices. While the Children endeavor to perform their own play, the grocer insists that his apprentices shall also act a romantic drama in honor of grocers. The play, however, was a failure at its first production, probably because it satirizes the audience as well as the citizen; intellectual audiences do not always appreciate humor at their own expense.

During these months (1607–08) it is probable that the King's Men acted Shakespeare's *Antony and Cleopatra* and *Coriolanus*. Of plays by other dramatists, one of the most remarkable and powerful was *The Revenger's Tragedy* by Cyril Tourneur. In this play the idea of the humors is applied to tragedy, each of the principal characters in the play representing a type of vice.

The King's Men and the Blackfriars Playhouse

In March 1608 there occurred a scandal which had far-reaching and unfortunate effects on drama. From the very beginning the Children of the Queen's Revels had been very impudent. Many of their plays openly satirized prominent persons, and from time to time there had been trouble. In spite of the indignation which had been caused by *Eastward Ho,* Chapman and the Children offended again and more seriously with a play called *The Conspiracy and Tragedy of Biron.* The real Biron, who had occupied much the same position in France as Essex in England, visited Queen Elizabeth in 1601, and his execution in France in 1602 caused a great sensation. The play thus dealt with French history and scandal only six years old. In one scene Henri IV, the reigning French King, was brought onto the stage together with his wife and his mistress, Madame de Verneuil. The ladies quarreled and the Queen gave hard words and blows to her rival. The French ambassador protested to the Earl of Salisbury, and the Children were ordered not to repeat the play; but in spite of this, as soon as the Court was moved out of London, they acted it again.

Once more all theaters were closed, and some of the chief offenders were sent to prison. This was hardly fair to the other companies, who indeed, according to the French ambassador's dispatch to his King, offered 100,000 francs to be allowed to resume playing. As a result of this scandal, those in charge of the Children were obliged to give up the private Blackfriars Theater, which in August reverted to Burbage and the King's Men. Henceforward, the King's Men decided to use it as a winter playhouse and to retain the Globe for use only during the summer. The Globe, as they had learned from experience, had several disadvantages: in wintertime the spectators were obliged to cross the river by boat or to trudge over London Bridge; the location was inconvenient, and the approach muddy. As a result of the change, the King's Men found that their profits greatly increased. Henceforward, they naturally preferred to cater to the one-class, moneyed audience which frequented the Blackfriars.

In 1608 Shakespeare probably wrote *Timon of Athens,* the last of his misanthropic plays, and *Pericles,* the first of a batch of four which deal with two generations, wherein the wrongs committed by the elders are set right by the children.

Francis Beaumont and John Fletcher

From about this time dates the most famous of dramatic partnerships, when Francis Beaumont and John Fletcher began to write plays together. Fletcher was the son of a former Bishop of London. Very little is known of him, but the partnership was much noted because the friendship between the two seemed remarkably close. According to gossip, Beaumont and Fletcher lived together on the Bankside, not far from the playhouse; they were both bachelors and shared everything in common — clothes, cloaks, and even a mistress. Their partnership lasted for about five years, until 1613, when Beaumont married an heiress and thereafter ceased to be actively interested in drama. Although in published editions a large number of plays appear as the work of "Beaumont & Fletcher," they can, in fact, have collaborated on only about half a dozen; the rest were the work of Fletcher after Beaumont had left him.

In 1609 Jonson returned to the theater with a comedy called *Epicoene; or, The Silent Woman*, which was acted by the Children of the Queen's Revels; but *The Alchemist*, which he wrote in 1610, was acted by the King's Men. In publishing this play he added a list of those who had taken the chief parts. Shakespeare's name was not included, for by this time he was taking little part in the affairs of the theater.

Beaumont and Fletcher were now working for the King's Men, who produced *Philaster; or, Love Lies a-Bleeding*, one of the best specimens of that kind of play called tragicomedy, in which these two dramatists specialized, a play full of incident, sometimes tragic, yet ending happily for the chief persons concerned. It is a type of drama which has been popular ever since on the stage and in the films. The story of *Philaster* is a kind of mixture of *Hamlet* and *Twelfth Night*. The King is a usurper, but he dares not do away with Prince Philaster, who is the true heir to the throne. To oust Philaster, however, he brings in Pharamond, a Spaniard, to marry Arethusa, his daughter and heir. But Arethusa is in love with Philaster. So Philaster gives Arethusa his adoring page, a youth called Bellario, whom he had found in the country, to be the go-between in their secret love. Meanwhile, the Spanish Prince, having no success with his wooing of Arethusa, becames involved in scandal at Court. Arethusa's obvious liking for the page also causes scandal and misunderstanding, until, after a long series of excitements, it is revealed that the page was in fact the daughter of the King's Chief Councilor, who doted on Philaster and hoped to live near him. The play was quite fantastic, but excellent entertainment. Beaumont and Fletcher have none of the depth of Shakespeare, but they have great skill in writing dialogue, and an excellent stage sense. No one could sit in the theater and watch Shakespeare's greatest tragedies unmoved; Beaumont and Fletcher kept the audience interested and mildly excited from beginning to end, but they never seared the emotions. It is more than a coincidence that Shakespeare's next play, *Cymbeline*, with its enormous complexity, false emotion, and interminable explanation and reconciliation, should bear some resemblance to *Philaster*.

Shakespeare's Last Plays

In 1611 Shakespeare wrote *The Winter's Tale* and *The Tempest*, and Jonson tried his hand at another classical tragedy called *Catiline*. Beaumont and Fletcher's *King and No King*, another melodrama, was also put on by the King's Men. In the autumn of 1612, the great preparations being made for the marriage of the Princess Elizabeth with the Elector Palatine of Bohemia were for a while disturbed by the death of the young Prince of Wales in November. Nevertheless the King's Men acted as usual at Christmas, when their plays included the two parts of *Henry IV*, *Julius Caesar*, *Much Ado about Nothing*, *Othello*, *The Winter's Tale*, *The Tempest*, Jonson's *Alchemist*, and Beaumont and Fletcher's *Philaster*, *The Maid's Tragedy*, and *King and No King*. The wedding of the young Princess took place on February 14 — St. Valentine's Day — and during the days which followed the King's Men acted fourteen times.

On June 29, 1613, they suffered a great misfortune — the Globe playhouse was burned to the ground. There are several descriptions of this disaster. The most famous occurs in a letter written by Sir Henry Wotton:

Now, to let matters of state sleep, I will entertain you at the present with what has happened this week at the Bank's side. The King's players had a new play, called *All is True*, representing some principal pieces of the reign of Henry VIII, which was set forth with many extraordinary circumstances of pomp and majesty, even to the matting of the stage; the Knights of the Order with their Georges and garters, the Guards with their embroidered coats, and the like: sufficient in truth within a while to make greatness very familiar, if not ridiculous. Now, King Henry making a masque at the Cardinal Wolsey's house, and certain chambers [small cannon] being shot off at his entry, some of the paper, or other stuff, wherewith one of them was stopped, did light on the thatch, where being thought at first but an idle smoke, and their eyes more attentive to the show, it kindled inwardly, and ran round like a train [fuse], consuming within less than an hour the whole house, to the very grounds. This was the fatal period of that virtuous fabric, wherein yet nothing did perish but wood and straw, and a few forsaken cloaks; only one man had his breeches set on fire, that would perhaps have broiled him, if he had not by the benefit of a provident wit put it out with bottle ale.

The destruction of the Globe Theater was symbolical. During the fourteen years of its existence Shakespeare's greatest plays had first been produced on its stage; he had now ceased to write for the theater. A new Globe soon rose from the ashes, but it belonged to another generation, and catered to the taste of a new audience.

5. The Elizabethan Playhouse[1]

Of all forms of literary art, that called drama is most affected by external and material influences. An acted play needs a combination of all kinds of artists. At its most elaborate there is a company of professional players to present the characters and speak their words; a stage with scenery, lighting, and equipment; experts responsible for designing and manipulating the settings; designers and makers of costumes; musicians for the orchestra. Above all, a producer or director is needed to mold all these activities into unity. Even in the most elementary form of drama a number of players must combine to act a play in harmony.

The dramatist is thus confined by limitations which do not hamper other forms of art; his play needs living actors and a stage. He must therefore write a play which can be acted on that stage. If he is confined to a stage ten feet square, his characters must be few. Moreover, if his players are professionals and need wages, he must not write a play which will require more actors than the receipts will warrant. A place for the spectators is also needed; and as there are many or few spectators, so the whole structure of the play will be changed. A pageant to be acted in a stadium will require very different treatment from intimate comedy in a small college theater.

When Shakespeare was a boy, players were content with the simplest of equipment. They toured the country and acted wherever they could find a stand or attract an audience. Plays were performed in all kinds of places — churchyards, innyards, halls, and great houses. But London was their natural home, for only in London was there a population large enough to provide regular audiences.

Before playhouses were built, certain inns became associated with the playing companies.

The medieval inn was built on a standard pattern. Rooms were grouped around four sides of a courtyard, from which the street was reached by passing under an arch. The chambers of the guests opened onto a gallery which looked down into the courtyard (see Pl. 4a). At the farther end of the courtyard lay the stables. In the courtyard the players erected their stage on trestles or barrels, and there gave their show. They gathered money from the spectators in the yard; the innkeeper took his share by collecting from his guests in the gallery. Such a stage was bare and primitive, with no possibility for liberty of action or scenic devices. It was natural, therefore, for hearty and noisy speechmaking to take the place of subtle action. Very few inns of this kind survive in England, but in the city of Gloucester there is still the New Inn, built in the fourteenth century, which preserves the old form and is known to have been used by Elizabethan players.

Players also acted in great halls, the Court, and the Inns of Court. The medieval great hall, of which many specimens survive, was also built to a pattern (see Pl. 4b). It was intended chiefly as a community dining hall. Overhead there was a beamed roof. At one end was a dais, or raised platform, with a long table running across. There the chief persons sat. Below the platform in the main hall the tables ran lengthwise; there sat the servants and less important members of the household. Halls of this kind are still used daily in the colleges at Oxford and Cambridge. At the lower end of the hall ran a screen of paneled oak which occupied the whole width and was pierced by two wide doors through which the servers brought the food. Over the screen there was a gallery used by musicians and spectators on great occasions. With this screen as background, the players entertained the guests after the feast.

The pattern for the Elizabethan playhouse

[1] This chapter owes much to two modern studies of first rate importance, *The Globe Playhouse* by John C. Adams (1942) and *Shakespeare's Audience* by Alfred Harbage (1941).

was set by the first English playhouse, the Theater, built by James Burbage in 1576 (see p. 36a).
Burbage combined the seating arrangements of
the inn with the stage arrangements of the great
hall. This general pattern was modified and improved in the later playhouses, and by the time
the Globe was built in 1599 the playhouse had
become quite elaborate, with much stage machinery and many conveniences to enable the
play to be acted quickly and effectively.

Although scholars are generally agreed about
the arrangement and plan of the Elizabethan
playhouse, direct information from contemporary accounts is meager. The details have been
assembled by much patient and elaborate research from many sources, of which the chief
are:

1. PICTURES: There is only one contemporary
picture of an Elizabethan stage (see Pl. 5a).
This is a sketch of the Swan Theater made in
1596 from memory by a Dutch traveler called
De Witt; but his memory was as slight as the
drawing, and some of the details are demonstra-
bly wrong. There are also two or three small
engravings of plays in progress, dating from
about two generations later.

2. BUILDING CONTRACTS: Among the papers of
Philip Henslowe (see p. 65a) are two contracts,
the first for building the Fortune playhouse in
1600, the second for building the Hope in 1613.

3. STAGE DIRECTIONS IN PLAYS AND CASUAL REF-
ERENCES: Much can be deduced from a careful
observation of the original editions of Elizabethan plays. For instance, in *Antony and Cleopatra,* which was first printed in the folio of
1623, there appear the following:

*Flourish. Enter Pompey, at one doore with Drum
and Trumpet: at another Caesar, Lepidus, Anthony, Enobarbus, Mecenas, Agrippa, Menas with
Souldiers; Marching.*

*Enter Ventidius as it were in triumph, the dead
body of Pacorus borne before him.*

*Enter Agrippa at one doore, Enobarbus at an-
other.*

*Camidius Marcheth with his Land Army one
way over the stage, and Towrus the Lieutenant of
Caesar the other way: After their going in, is heard
the noise of a Sea fight. Alarum. Enter Enobarbus
and Scarus.*

Musicke of the Hoboyes is under the Stage.

*Enter Cleopatra, and her Maides aloft, with
Charmian & Iras.*

They heave Anthony aloft to Cleopatra.

From the stage directions in this one play
alone it is clear that the stage for which *Antony
and Cleopatra* was written had at least two doors
by which characters entered and which were
wide enough to admit bearers carrying a corpse;
that there was a place under the stage where
the musicians could play their oboes; that there
was a place aloft large enough for Cleopatra
and her maids, and solid enough to withstand
the heaving-up of Antony. By collecting all such
stage directions from the earliest texts [2] and the
many passages in dialogues which indicate action, a fairly accurate picture can be recon-
structed of the playhouse and its arrangements.

The Fortune contract gave a number of measurements in detail. The playhouse was a square
frame building with an outside measurement of
eighty feet on each side. [3] Inside, the yard was
fifty-five feet square, the space between outer
wall and yard being occupied by spectators' galleries. There were three tiers of galleries, the
lowest twelve feet high, the second eleven feet,
the third nine feet, each gallery jutting over the
one below. The stage was forty-three feet wide
and extended to the middle of the yard. Unfortunately, no plan survives, but the stage of the
Fortune was " contrived and fashioned like unto
the stage of the said playhouse called the Globe,"
and was built by the same builder.

The Globe, the most famous of all Elizabethan
playhouses, was, however, an octagonal building. On the outside each of the eight sides was
approximately thirty-six feet, and the diameter
of the whole was eighty-four feet. It was a frame
building, standing on low brick supports, and
the roof was thatched with straw. It was about
thirty-three feet high to the eaves. Inside ran
three galleries, one above the other, surrounding the yard, which was fifty-six feet in diameter. The galleries looked down upon the stage,
which was at one end and occupied about a
third of the yard. Three sections of the octagon

---

[2] The student must always consult the original quartos or
the first folio, because many of the stage directions in the modern
texts were first inserted by editors of the eighteenth century who
knew nothing of the methods of staging in Shakespeare's day.
[3] The reader will better appreciate the smallness of the playhouse if he takes the measurements of any familiar hall or large
room.

were used for backstage and the needs of the players; the remaining five sections were used for the spectators. The yard was open to the sky and the stage was lit by daylight.

A spectator entered from the street by a door facing the stage. If he wished to stand in the yard to watch the play, he placed one penny in a box held by the gatherer and went straight in. If he desired a seat in one of the upper galleries, he paid a second penny and went up by one of the staircases to the right or left. If he wished to go into the lowest and most expensive gallery, he paid a third penny. Spectators who stood in the yard were known as the "groundlings." They were the noisiest, cheapest, and least desirable patrons. In the galleries the spectators sat. In addition, on the lowest gallery on either side of the stage, there were "gentlemen's rooms" reserved for the more distinguished spectators, who had also the privilege of sitting on a cushion. And for a time it was fashionable for gallants to sit or sprawl on the stage itself.

There has been considerable argument among scholars about the capacity of the Elizabethan playhouse. Dr. Harbage points out that in the Fortune the space available for spectators was 1842.5 square feet in the yard and 5725.32 square feet in the galleries. Since a man standing requires on an average 2.5 square feet and a man sitting 3.75 square feet, the total capacity of the Fortune was: standing, 818, sitting, 1,526, a total of 2,344 persons. Other evidence suggests that a full house held between two thousand and three thousand spectators and that on an average day some 1,250 attended each of the playhouses. This means that in 1595, when the Chamberlain's Men and the Admiral's Men were playing in London, about fifteen thousand patrons attended their theaters weekly. Ten years later, when five companies were acting regularly, the weekly number rose perhaps to twenty-one thousand. Thus one in ten or even more of the population of London came to the theater weekly. The proportion of town dwellers nowadays who go weekly to the movies is far greater.

The audience at the playhouse was a fair cross section of the citizens of London; that is, much the same type of audience as now visits the theater in New York or Chicago. A play was the most democratic form of gathering of men and women of all classes. No one had any particular rights over the other; firstcomers got the best places, and there was no advanced booking of seats. Hence the audience was in its place and eager when the play began. There was none of that trampling over the toes of those in the front seats which disturbs a modern play for the first ten minutes. It was a keen audience and well trained. Some critics regret that Shakespeare had to demean himself to please the mob. This is a foolish criticism. Shakespeare's audience was his greatest asset, for it was composed neither wholly of half-wits nor wholly of highbrows, but was a well-proportioned mixture of all levels of taste. It had its intellectuals, young gentlemen from the Inns of Court, and the gallants, but it had also many citizens and their wives and prentices, and the latter, especially in the more skilled trades, had already received an education in rhetoric and the classics which would dumfound most modern high-school boys. After all, an audience which appreciated Shakespeare's plays and encouraged him to write for them is hardly to be despised.

On the other hand the theater had many enemies. Apart from the Puritans, who objected to the theater on moral grounds, the Council was always suspicious. Any form of entertainment that attracts crowds will also attract the parasites that prey on crowds — pickpockets, touts, and prostitutes — and the enemies of the stage were loud in their complaints. Drama, being an intelligent form of entertainment, attracts intelligent and critical spectators. It could therefore be used as propaganda, and in those times government did not approve of methods of propaganda which it could not wholly control. For this reason, the theaters were closely watched, and whenever there was any likelihood of disturbance, they were immediately closed. But, taking the records as a whole, it is surprising that there were so few cases of disturbance in the playhouses at a time when general disorder was common.

The stage differed considerably from the modern stage in its arrangements and in its conventions, and as a result the whole theory of Elizabethan drama differed. In the modern theater the stage resembles a picture frame covered with a curtain. When the play begins, the auditorium lights go out, leaving the stage bright in contrast with the surrounding darkness. There is thus a psychological barrier between spectators and actors. In theory, modern actors pretend to be living their parts oblivious of the audience, who are, as it were, spies through a fourth wall. When the act is finished, the curtain descends, the lights go up, and the audience is abruptly cut off from the world of illusion. Scenery is realistic, properties and costumes are as accurate as possible. Convention demands that the actors shall speak and behave naturally. In the modern theater, if we are to understand what is going on in a character's mind, some natural means must be taken to show it. We become self-conscious if the character thinks aloud, or reads letters audibly, or turns aside to comment in a stage whisper. Nevertheless, modern realism is itself a convention. Spectators willingly allow themselves to pretend that the actors are in reality the people whom they represent, and that the wall before them is made of bricks and not of canvas and plywood.

Elizabethan conventions were quite different. The stage jutted out into the yard and was surrounded on three sides by spectators. There was no curtain to conceal or reveal the main stage, no light but daylight. Hence contact between actors and spectators was close and intimate; both shared in one experience. As there was little attempt at scenery, so there was no realistic setting. All the illusion nowadays created by the electrician and the scene-painter had to be effected by the dramatist and the actors. Words and gestures alone kindled the imagination. When the modern director requires dawn or moonlight, he calls on the electrician. When Shakespeare needed dawn, he suggested it in the dialogue:

> But, look, the morn, in russet mantle clad,
> Walks o'er the dew of yon high eastward hill.

For night, the modern stage has its cyclorama with little electric lights that twinkle. Shakespeare, in *The Merchant of Venice,* evokes moonlight in words:

> How sweet the moonlight sleeps upon this bank!
> Here will we sit and let the sounds of music
> Creep in our ears. Soft stillness and the night
> Become the touches of sweet harmony.
> Sit, Jessica. Look how the floor of heaven
> Is thick inlaid with patines of bright gold.
> There's not the smallest orb which thou behold'st
> But in his motion like an angel sings,
> Still quiring to the young-eyed cherubins.

This is romantic moonlight and rather obvious. Far more subtle was his creation in *Macbeth* of the atmosphere of grim night, when there was neither moon nor stars:

> BAN. How goes the night, boy?
> FLE. The moon is down, I have not heard the clock.
> BAN. And she goes down at twelve.
> FLE. 　　　　　　　I tak't 'tis later, sir.
> BAN. Hold, take my sword. There's husbandry in heaven,
> Their candles are all out. Take thee that too.
> A heavy summons lies like lead upon me,
> And yet I would not sleep. Merciful powers,
> Restrain in me the cursèd thoughts that nature
> Gives way to in repose!

We owe the poetry of Shakespeare's plays to the barrenness of the Elizabethan stage and to the appreciation of the Elizabethan audience.

Although the playhouse was small, the main stage was large — a platform jutting out into the yard like an apron (see Pl. 5a). Here most of the action of the play was staged. On either side of the stage there were doors, the main entrances through which characters came on and went off. The doors themselves could be used symbolically. In a history play, one side of the stage might be France, the other England. One door at least had a knocker and a grille and was used as the door of a house, a tavern, a nunnery, a prison, or a tomb, or the gate of a city. As for scenery, since the spectators were accustomed to using their imaginations, all that was necessary was to indicate the locality. This was done not by sets or program notes but in the course of the dialogue. One reason why Shakespeare's plays are so vivid to read or to broadcast is that so much of the action is described and embedded in the words.

Thus in *Lear:*

> CORN. Bind fast his corky arms.
> GLO. What mean your Graces? Good my friends, consider
> You are my guests. Do me no foul play, friends.
> CORN. Bind him, I say.
> REG. Hard, hard. O filthy traitor!
> GLO. Unmerciful lady as you are, I'm none.
> CORN. To this chair bind him. Villain, thou shalt find ——
> GLO. By the kind gods, 'tis most ignobly done
> To pluck me by the beard.

Or in *Coriolanus* when Volumnia demonstrates the proper action to win back the people:

> I prithee now, my son,
> Go to them, with this bonnet in thy hand,
> And thus far having stretched it, here be with them,
> Thy knee bussing the stones — for in such business
> Action is eloquence, and the eyes of the ignorant
> More learnèd than the ears — waving thy head,
> Which often thus, correcting thy stout heart,
> Now humble as the ripest mulberry
> That will not hold the handling.

Or again when Hamlet takes a recorder from one of the players:

HAML. Oh, the recorders! Let me see one. To withdraw with you —— Why do you go about to recover the wind of me, as if you would drive me into a toil?

GUIL. O my lord, if my duty be too bold, my love is too unmannerly.

HAML. I do not well understand that. Will you play upon this pipe?

GUIL. My lord, I cannot.

HAML. I pray you.

GUIL. Believe me, I cannot.

HAML. I do beseech you.

GUIL. I know no touch of it, my lord.

HAML. 'This as easy as lying. Govern these ventages with your fingers and thumb, give it breath with your mouth, and it will discourse most eloquent music. Look you, these are the stops.

There is no need for stage directions to tell the actor or the reader what is happening.

Over the stage, supported on two lofty pillars and running parallel with the roof, was the "shadow," which protected the players from the rain. The pillars themselves were also a useful adjunct to the stage; they were often used as trees, masts, and the like. Beneath the stage were trapdoors, a large main one and four subsidiaries, through which ghosts and spirits appeared.

As early stage directions show, at the back of the main stage there was some kind of recess or inner stage called by such names as "the tiring house" (i.e., the players' dressing room) and "the place behind the stage" and which Dr. Adams labeled "the study." This inner stage was concealed by a curtain and was used for such scenes as Juliet's tomb, the discovery of Ferdinand and Miranda playing chess in *The Tempest,* the hovel in *Lear* (III.iv), and many others. Behind the curtain Falstaff slept in *I Henry IV* (II.iv) and Claudius and Polonius stood to overhear Hamlet's conversation with Ophelia (III.i). Dr. Adams believed that the inner stage was part of the permanent structure of the playhouse, and it is so shown in the model (see Pl. 5b).

More recently the existence of a permanent inner stage has been denied. There is none in the Swan drawing (Pl. 5a) and, though the Fortune contract (see p. 52b) mentions the tiring house, no details of locality or size are given. Nevertheless, some kind of inner stage is required for several of Shakespeare's plays, and perhaps for special occasions a temporary structure of curtains supported on poles was set up.

This inner stage was also needed for concealments, especially of corpses at the end of a tragedy. Sometimes the dead were carried away in a funeral procession as at the end of *Coriolanus* and *Hamlet,* as the stage directions and dialogue show. At other times corpses were hidden from sight. In the last act of *Romeo and Juliet,* Romeo and Juliet are lying dead on the bier with the body of Paris on the ground beside them. These bodies were concealed by closing the curtain over the inner stage, for which the Prince gives the cue (V.iii.216–17):

> Seal up the mouth of outrage for a while
> Till we can clear these ambiguities

There is a similar situation in *Othello*. Othello and Desdemona are dead on the bed; Emilia's corpse is on the floor. Again there is a cue for closing the curtains, in Lodovico's words (V.ii.364–65):

> The object poisons sight,
> Let it be hid.

It follows that the inner stage or recess, whether permanent or temporary, was wide and deep enough for a bed and several corpses.

On the second level, parallel with the second gallery and part of it, was the "chamber." When not required, this also was covered with a curtain. In front of it there jutted out a balcony which was used to represent the walls of a castle or a town. Here Richard II, as from the walls of Flint Castle, addresses Bolingbroke, who stands on the stage beneath. The chamber itself was the same size as the recess and could be used for a bedchamber or the living room in a house, or for any other purpose when the dramatist required characters on the upper level. On either side of the chamber there were windows. From one of these, in *The Merchant of Venice* Jessica speaks to Lorenzo before she elopes with him. The gallery was also useful as part of the main stage. As it jutted out, it provided a roof of sorts, which could become the eaves of a house, or a shed. Here, for instance, Conrade and Borachio, in *Much Ado about Nothing,* hold the conversation which is overheard by the Watch.

On the third level there was another chamber, normally used by the musicians, but available occasionally for scenes. The man who describes Othello's ship on the horizon presumably stands in this third chamber.

On the fourth level was the turret. It contained a bell frequently used to ring an alarum or to toll a knell. Here were created the sound effects. Cannon balls were rolled on boards to imitate thunder, and the noises of " alarums and excursions " were produced with drums and trumpets.

The most effective way of visualizing the production of plays on the Elizabethan stage is to follow one play through and endeavor, so far as is possible, to reconstruct its staging. *Romeo and Juliet* is a good example, because in the two early quartos the stage directions are very much fuller than usual.[5] In the following analysis of the action — which must necessarily be guess-work — are included stage directions from the first and second quartos. Those from Q1 are shown in italics and single quotes ('), those from Q2 in italics and double quotes (").

ACT I, SC. i:

" *Enter Sampson and Gregory with swords and bucklers of the House of Capulet,*" by the RIGHT door. At the LEFT door enter Abraham and Balthasar of the Montagues. Benvolio enters by the RIGHT door. Tybalt enters by the LEFT door. During the fight, " *enter three or four citizens with clubs or partisans,*" through the CURTAIN of the RECESS. " *Enter old Capulet, in his gown, and his wife,*" by the RIGHT door. " *Enter old Montague and his wife,*" by the LEFT door. " *Enter Prince Escalus with his train,*" through the CENTER. The Prince

goes out through the CENTER. Capulet and his party go out through the RIGHT door, leaving Montague, Lady Montague, and Benvolio. Romeo enters through the BACK curtain. Benvolio draws attention to his approach with the phrase: " See where he comes! So please you, step aside." (Some such phrase as " See where he comes " is the usual method of drawing attention to a character who is entering from the *rear* of the stage.) Montague and his wife go out by the LEFT door; after some talk Benvolio and Romeo follow them.

ACT I, SC. ii:

Capulet and Count Paris, followed by Peter, enter by the RIGHT door and go out again, leaving Peter. Benvolio and Romeo enter by the LEFT door and read the letter. At the end of the scene, Peter goes out RIGHT; Romeo and Benvolio go out LEFT.

ACT I, SC. iii:

The curtains in the CHAMBER above are opened, revealing Lady Capulet and Nurse. Juliet joins them. A servingman enters to say that the guests have arrived. The curtains over the CHAMBER are closed.

ACT I, SC. iv:

By the RIGHT door, " *enter Romeo and Mercutio, Benvolio and five or six other Maskers, torchbearers.*" After a while, " *they march about the stage and Servingmen come forth with napkins* " through the curtain of the RECESS. They remain on the stage, as

[ACT I, SC. v:][6]

the curtains on the RECESS are opened and at the back of the stage enter old Capulet with " *all the guests and gentlewomen to the Maskers. Music plays and they dance.*" Tybalt goes out RIGHT. At the end of the scene, Capulet's party goes out, on either side at the back of the RECESS. The others go out by the RIGHT and LEFT doors. The curtains of the RECESS are closed.

ACT II:

The Chorus comes through the curtains at the BACK, advances to the center of the stage, delivers his lines, and goes back.

ACT II, SC. i:

" *Enter Romeo alone,*" by the LEFT door. He advances to the front of the stage and says:

　" Can I go forward when my heart is here?

　Turn back, dull earth, and find thy center out.'

As he moves toward the back of the stage, Benvolio and Mercutio enter by the LEFT door. Romeo hides

---

[5] This demonstration should be followed with the aid of the illustration (Pl. 5b). "Right" means as the actor faces the audience; i.e., the reader's left. The reader will find it an interesting problem in Elizabethan staging to work over other plays in this manner, especially with the aid of the stage directions in a reprint of the original quarto or folio text.

[6] The scenes set off in brackets have been created by editors; in the original texts the action is not interrupted.

by the right pillar (i.e., he keeps the pillar between himself and the other two). Benvolio and Mercutio go out LEFT.

[ACT II, SC. ii:]
When they have gone, Romeo is about to continue his move to the back when Juliet opens the WINDOW and looks out. Romeo pauses and then goes toward her. They converse. A voice calls for Juliet; she goes from the WINDOW, but quickly returns. The lovers bid good night. Juliet closes the WINDOW, and Romeo goes out RIGHT.

ACT II, SC. iii:
" Enter Friar alone with a basket," through the curtains of the RECESS; he comes forward. Romeo enters by the RIGHT door. They go out together through the curtains of the RECESS.

ACT II, SC. iv:
Benvolio and Mercutio enter by the LEFT door. Romeo enters through the curtain of the RECESS. " Enter Nurse and her man " by the RIGHT door. Benvolio and Mercutio go out by the LEFT door. After his conversation with the Nurse, Romeo goes out LEFT, and she goes out RIGHT.

ACT II, SC. v:
The curtains in the CHAMBER above are opened, revealing Juliet. The Nurse enters. At the end of the scene the curtains of the CHAMBER are closed.

ACT II, SC. vi:
The curtains of the RECESS are opened revealing Friar Laurence and Romeo. The recess is now the Friar's cell. Through the door at the back of the RECESS ' enter Juliet, somewhat fast, and embraceth Romeo.' As the Friar prepares to marry the lovers the curtains of the RECESS are closed.

ACT III, SC. i:
" Enter Mercutio, Benvolio and men," by the LEFT door. By the RIGHT door, enter Tybalt and others. Romeo enters through the RECESS curtains. Tybalt draws attention to his entry with " Here comes my man." Tybalt and Mercutio fight; ' Tybalt under Romeo's arm thrusts Mercutio, in and flies ' through the RIGHT door. The page goes out by the LEFT door. Mercutio, supported by Benvolio, goes out through the LEFT door, whence Benvolio emerges to say that Mercutio is dead. Tybalt re-enters by the RIGHT door. Romeo and Tybalt fight and Tybalt is slain. Romeo runs out by the LEFT door. The citizens enter through the curtains of the RECESS, followed by the Prince. Capulet and his wife enter by the RIGHT door. Montague and his wife enter by the LEFT. At the end of the scene, all go out by the ways in which they have entered, the body of Tybalt being carried out through the RIGHT door.

ACT III, SC. ii:
The curtains of the CHAMBER above are opened, revealing Juliet alone. ' Enter Nurse, wringing her hands, with the ladder of cords in her lap.' At the end of the scene the curtains of the CHAMBER are closed.

ACT III, SC. iii:
The curtains of the RECESS are opened; the recess once more represents the Friar's cell. The Friar calls to Romeo, who comes in from the side. The Nurse knocks at the back of the door of the RECESS; she enters through the door at the back of the RECESS. At the end of the scene, the Nurse goes out by the door in the RECESS, and the curtains are closed.

ACT III, SC. iv:
Capulet, Lady Capulet, and Paris enter by the RIGHT door. Paris goes out by the RIGHT door as Capulet and Lady Capulet go out through the curtains of the RECESS.

ACT III, SC. v:
The curtains of the CHAMBER above are opened. ' Enter Romeo and Juliet at the window.' ' He goeth down ' by the ladder of cords and goes out LEFT. Juliet pulls up the ladder; ' she goeth down from the window.' She shuts the window and passes into the CHAMBER as Lady Capulet enters. Capulet and the Nurse come to them and go out again. The Nurse goes out, leaving Juliet alone. The curtains of the CHAMBER are closed.

ACT IV, SC. i:
The curtains of the RECESS are opened, disclosing Friar Laurence and Paris, as if in Friar Laurence's cell. Juliet enters by the door at the back of the RECESS. Paris goes out through the door at the back of the RECESS. The Friar closes the door at Juliet's words: " Oh, shut the door." At the end of the scene, the curtains are closed over the RECESS.

ACT IV, SC. ii:
" Enter Father Capulet, Mother, Nurse and Servingmen, two or three," by the RIGHT door. The Servingmen go out RIGHT. Juliet enters through the curtain at the back of the stage: " See where she comes from shrift with merry look." Juliet and the Nurse go out through the curtains of the RECESS. Capulet and his wife go out by the RIGHT door.

ACT IV, SC. iii:
The curtains of the CHAMBER above are opened, revealing Juliet and the Nurse laying clothes on

the bed. Lady Capulet enters. She goes out with the Nurse. Juliet takes the potion; ' *she falls upon her bed within the curtains.*' The curtains of the CHAMBER are closed.

ACT IV, SC. iv:

The curtains of the RECESS are opened; the inner stage has now become the hall of Capulet's house. Enter Lady Capulet and Nurse, ' *with herbs.*' Capulet enters. Lady Capulet and the Nurse go out at the side of the RECESS. " *Enter three or four with spits and logs and baskets,*" who pass across the RECESS and go out. Capulet calls for the Nurse, who comes back. He tells her to make haste to call the bride. She goes up the STAIRS at the back of the RECESS.

[ACT IV, SC. v:]

The Nurse from within opens the curtains of the CHAMBER. Juliet is revealed lying on her bed. The Nurse tries to awaken Juliet and at her cries Lady Capulet and then Capulet go up the STAIRS at the back of the RECESS and appear in the CHAMBER. The Friar and the Count enter the CHAMBER. After their lamentations, ' *they all but the Nurse go forth, casting rosemary on her and shutting the curtains.*' In the act of closing the curtains of the CHAMBER, the Nurse is left standing on the BALCONY in front of the closed curtains. Musicians enter on the stage below. She looks down from the balcony and speaks to them and then she passes into the CHAMBER through the closed curtains. Peter enters at the back of the RECESS, and talks to the musicians, who go out by the RIGHT door. The curtains of the RECESS are closed.

ACT V, SC. i:

Romeo enters by the LEFT door. ' *Enter Balthasar, his man, booted* ' — thereby indicating that he has come a long journey on horseback. Balthasar goes out by the LEFT door. Romeo goes over to the RIGHT door (which now becomes the entrance to the Apothecary's shop) and knocks. The Apothecary comes out; he delivers the poison to Romeo, goes back, and shuts the door. Romeo goes out by the LEFT door.

ACT V, SC. ii:

Friar John comes in by the RIGHT door as Friar Laurence enters through the curtains of the RECESS. Each goes out as he came in.

ACT V, SC. iii:

By the RIGHT door, ' *enter County Paris and his Page with flowers and sweet water.*' Paris goes up to the LEFT door (which now becomes the entrance to the burial vault of the Capulets). ' *Paris strews*

the tomb with flowers.' The Page whistles. Paris steps forward in front of the left pillar to watch. By the RIGHT door, ' *enter Romeo and Balthasar, with a torch, a mattock, and a crow of iron.*' Romeo goes up to the LEFT door. His man Balthasar crosses the stage as if to go out by the RIGHT door, but comes back and hides by the pillar. ' *Romeo opens the tomb* '; i.e., he puts his crowbar to the LEFT door and pries it open at the words " Thus I enforce thy rotten jaws to open." Paris steps forward. They fight. The Page runs out by the RIGHT door. As Paris dies, he says: " Open the tomb, lay me with Juliet." Romeo picks up the body, and at the words " I'll bury thee in a triumphant grave " passes through the open LEFT door. The curtains of the RECESS are opened, revealing Juliet lying on a bier, and the shrouded corpse of Tybalt. Romeo appears in the RECESS and lays Paris's body down. He takes the poison and falls dead. By the RIGHT door, " *enter Friar with lanthorn, crow and spade.*" He crosses the stage. ' *Friar stoops and looks on the blood and weapons.*' He goes in through the open LEFT door and reappears in the RECESS as Juliet begins to stir. Friar Laurence comes forward and runs away by the RIGHT door. Juliet speaks to her dead lover and as the boy and the Watch come in through the RIGHT door she stabs herself.

By the RIGHT door then enter, in succession, Balthasar, Friar Laurence and Watchmen, the Prince, Capulet and his wife, Montague. They pass to the back of the stage and stand round the bodies in the RECESS.

The Prince then leads them forward and commands: " Seal up the mouth of outrage for a while." At these words, the curtains across the RECESS are closed, concealing the four bodies, and the LEFT door is also closed. After Friar Laurence's tale and the closing words of the Prince, all go out in procession by the RIGHT door.

From this analysis of the action, it will be seen that an Elizabethan play proceeded rapidly, without pauses for change of scenery. It was thus possible for Shakespeare to have twenty or even more scenes in one play.

But although there was little attempt to indicate scenery, there were properties which took the place of scenery. Chairs or stools suggested a living room or a tavern. A bed denoted a bedchamber. A man wearing riding boots had come on a journey by horseback. A watchman with a torch or a lantern indicated nighttime. Properties in the Elizabethan theater were many and varied, and among Henslowe's papers there still exists a complete inventory of the properties belonging to the Admiral's Men in 1598. They include: a rock, a cage, three tombs, a Hell mouth, a bedstead, a beacon, a heifer, the City of Rome, a golden fleece, a lion's skin, a bear's skin, various heads and limbs, a tree of three golden apples, a number of foils, helmets, and shields, two coffins, a dragon, a lion, a great horse, a black dog, and a device for a realistic beheading. It is not known how " Hell mouth " or the " City of Rome " were represented.

Costumes were lavish and magnificent. Henslowe's companies carried a large stock of general costumes, but for most plays they added something special, and there are many entries in the *Diary* recording the purchases of materials of the finest quality.

Not much is known of the style of costuming, but if the picture of *Titus Andronicus* (see Pl. 13a) is in any way accurate, it suggests that plays were produced with a wild mixture of styles. Shakespeare certainly did not greatly care. His Romans in *Julius Caesar* and in *Coriolanus* wore Elizabethan doublets, cloaks, and large black hats. At the same time, it should not be assumed that Elizabethan players lacked all sense of period. Ben Jonson made painful and pedantic efforts to see that his details were accurate in the Roman tragedy *Sejanus;* he is not likely to have approved of doublets for Tiberius and the Senate. There are also occasional details in the records which show that, spasmodically, Elizabethan players had a feeling for accuracy. The well-known account of the burning of the Globe Theater (see p. 50b) reveals the particular care taken that *Henry VIII* should be staged realistically.

There are other instances of accurate costuming not so well known. In 1601, shortly after the execution of the Earl of Essex, Charles, Duke of Biron, paid a state visit to Queen Elizabeth, with a large train of followers. It was much noted at Court that the Frenchmen wore black without any kind of decoration. Sir Walter Ralegh spent all that night with his tailor and appeared at Court next morning with a black taffeta suit and a black saddle. A year later, Biron himself was executed, and within a few weeks the Admiral's Men put on a play about him (see p. 49a). Henslowe's *Diary* records the purchase of a black satin suit for this play.

Another example may be noted. In the reign of King Richard II, men's fashions were very extravagant. Gallants wore shoes with enormously long toes, attached to the knee with a chain. There exists a manuscript play called *Thomas of Woodstock* in which a courtier is brought on wearing a pair of these shoes. On the whole, however, the Elizabethan player costumed his plays without any regard for historical accuracy.

Elizabethan audiences liked noise. The early texts of plays abound with notes for different kinds of trumpet calls, such as sennets, tuckets, and flourishes. No king or royal person enters in state without a flourish on the trumpets. There is a whole series of noises for battles, such as alarums and retreats. In the prologue before Act III of *Henry V,* " chambers " (small cannon) were shot off to rouse the audience into the proper mood of excitement. These noises had considerable psychological effect. Some stage effects were elaborate. In the play *Arden of Faversham* there was a fog, caused presumably by smoke sent up through one of the traps. Lightning was produced by flashes of gunpowder. Wet blood is often indicated in scenes of killing.

The Elizabethan acting company was a " fellowship." It consisted of ten to fifteen sharers who formed the company, with perhaps another ten or dozen extras, three or four boys, who would ultimately become full sharers, money gatherers, who were sometimes women, stage hands, and the like. The members of the company remained constant, as in the modern repertory company. When, therefore, Shakespeare wrote a play, he had to think in terms of his company. He could not, like the modern playwright, expect the director to gather from the theatrical agencies a special cast for each new play. Being a practical working dramatist, Shakespeare made use of the physical features and talents of the individuals in his company. This is particularly noticeable in some of the women's parts. As yet there were no actresses; young women's parts were taken by boys, and Shakespeare wrote to suit the type and capacity of each boy actor. Thus in the three romantic comedies, *Much Ado about Nothing, As You Like It,* and *Twelfth Night,* all of which were written within a few months, one of the women is always small. Hero is " too low for a high praise, too brown for a fair praise, and too little for a great praise "; she is " Leonato's short daughter." Celia is " low and browner than her brother " — that is, Rosalind. Maria is the " little villain," "the youngest wren of nine." It is clear that the same boy took all three parts, and probably a second boy played Rosalind, Beatrice, and Viola. In contrast to the little "lady" is the tall, thin man with a hatchet face who often appears. He is Private Shadow in *II Henry IV* —"this same half-faced fellow, Shadow. Give me this man. He presents no mark to the enemy, the foeman may with as great aim level at the edge of a penknife." He reappears in *Twelfth Night* as Sir Andrew Aguecheek, "as tall a man as any's in Illyria," and also "a thin-faced knave." He is Master Slender in *The Merry Wives of Windsor* "a latten bilbo," a man with "a little wheyface." There was also a bright little boy who took the part of Falstaff's Page in *II Henry IV*. After Falstaff's death, he transferred his services to Pistol in *Henry V*.

Then there was the clown of the company. He was the low comedian and most plays gave him a chance to play a comic servant, or a watchman, or a gravedigger, or to indulge in some business of his own. In fact, the clown was so important a member of the cast that in stage directions in early texts he is usually designated as "clown" regardless of the part which he represents. When the Chamberlain's Men were formed in the autumn of 1594, their first clown was Will Kempe (see p. 39b). Kempe, who was older than the other chief members of the company, had already won a great reputation. His name survives in some of the stage directions in the early quartos. In *Much Ado about Nothing,* for instance, there is a stage direction "enter Kempe and Cowley," where the modern editions read "enter Dogberry and Verges." He also took the part of Peter in *Romeo and Juliet.* Kempe, however, fell foul of his fellows. He was an individualist, and a great favorite with the groundlings. He was particularly famous for his jigs, which he performed after the play was over. When the tone of plays improved and the players began to take themselves more seriously, Kempe became a nuisance. He left the company in 1600. Shakespeare's severe remarks on the clown in *Hamlet,* written after Kempe joined a rival company, were clearly directed against him. After Kempe's departure, a more intelligent and refined kind of clown is noticeable in Shakespeare's plays—Touchstone in *As You Like It,* Feste in *Twelfth Night,* and Lear's singing Fool. These parts were taken by Robert Armin.

The chief member of the Chamberlain's Men was Richard Burbage, the youngest son of the James Burbage who had built the Theater. Burbage first made his name in the part of Richard III, and his rendering of Richard's cry of despair

A horse! A horse! My kingdom for a horse!

was particularly famous. He also is known to have taken the parts of Hamlet, Lear, and Othello.

The Chamberlain's Men remained friends throughout their fellowship. Shakespeare first worked in partnership with Richard Burbage in 1594. Twenty-one years later, when he made his will, Shakespeare left to Burbage and two others of his surviving fellows twenty-two shillings and eightpence to buy rings as mementos. Of Burbage's style as an actor we know little, but we can guess much from Hamlet's advice to the players. Shakespeare could hardly have been so severe a critic of robustious playing had Burbage been a "ham" actor.

Plays were acted on the repertory system. Each afternoon a different play was presented, and the company kept in their program a series of plays to which they were constantly adding. If the lists of plays in Henslowe's *Diary* are any guide to general practice, they show that the average life of a play was about ten performances. Popular plays were acted more often; unsuccessful plays passed out of the repertory after the first or second performance. This meant that the company was constantly in rehearsal and was able to put on a new play very quickly. There is a tradition that Shakespeare wrote *The Merry Wives of Windsor* in a fortnight to please Queen Elizabeth; it may quite likely be true. It follows that the players can have had little time for elaborate production, but they did have the advantage of being a team, always playing together and, at a pinch, able to improvise. The Elizabethan play was thus a very live form of entertainment.

If by some miracle we could be transplanted to a holiday performance at the Globe, we should be surprised in many ways. The playhouse would strike us as very small, uncomfortably crowded, and far more intimate than any modern theater. The presentation would at first seem noisy and crude, but we should soon become used to the trumpet calls and the lack of scenery. The acting might appear embarrass-ingly emotional, but very slick and competent. Shakespeare is not the only dramatist to speak of the "two hours' traffic of the stage." Since the average play contains from eighteen thousand to twenty thousand words, there can have been little dawdling; the rate of speech must have been at least from a hundred and sixty to a hundred and eighty words a minute. Such pace is only possible when the audience is sensitive, keen, and alert. Indeed the greatest contrast to our modern theater would be in the spectators, who responded quickly and violently, unashamedly demonstrating their grief, pleasure, or amusement, and at times — if dissatisfied with the performance or the play — their anger. Shakespeare was lucky in his environment. He would doubtless have succeeded under any conditions, but as it happened, the kind of play which best suited his theater and his audiences needed also the highest kind of poetry.

6. The Study of the Text

Students are often bewildered by the amount of space and energy which an editor of Shakespeare devotes to textual problems. They can seldom find much satisfaction or interest in such a note as this on *Hamlet*, I.i.63:

> 63. the sledded Polacks (Malone): the sleaded pollax (Q1 Q2 Q3); the sleaded Pollax (Q4 Q5); the sledded Pollax (F1 F2); the sledded Polax (F3); the sledded Poll-Ax (Q 1683); the sledded Poleaxe (F4); the sledded Pollack (Pope).

Indeed, of all forms of study, textual notes are the dreariest until the reader has some firsthand knowledge of the facts and problems briefly summarized in these mysterious formulae.

Modern readers sometimes forget that the text in which they read a play of Shakespeare is very different in a variety of small ways from Shakespeare's own manuscript or from the first printed version of the play. The differences can best be realized by some examples.

1. HAMLET:
There are three early texts of *Hamlet*: The first quarto (Q1) of 1603, a pirated, garbled version; the second quarto (Q2) of 1604–05, probably set up by the printer from Shakespeare's own manuscript; and the text of the play as it appears in the first folio (F1) of 1623.

A typical example of the differences between the three versions occurs in III.iv; i.e., toward the end of the closet scene. Hamlet is here upbraiding his mother. The ghost of his father has appeared and speaks to him. The Queen sees nothing. In Q1 the text reads:

Ham. Why doe you nothing heare?
Queene. Not I.

Ham. Nor doe you nothing see?
Queene. No neither.
Ham. No, why see the king my father, my father, in the habite
As he liued, looke you how pale he lookes,
See how he steales away out of the Portall,
Looke, there he goes.   *exit ghost.*
Queene. Alas, it is the weakenesse of thy braine,
Which makes thy tongue to blazon thy hearts griefe:
But as I haue a soule, I sweare by heauen,
I neuer knew of this most horride murder:
But Hamlet, this is onely fantasie,
And for my loue forget these idle fits.
Ham. Idle, no mother, my pulse doth beate like yours,
It is not madness that possesseth Hamlet.
O mother, if euer you did my deare father loue,
Forbeare the adulterous bed to night,
And win your selfe by little as you may,
In time it may be you wil lothe him quite:
And mother, but assist mee in reuenge,
And in his death your infamy shall die.
Queene. Hamlet, I vow by that maiesty,
That knowes our thoughts, and lookes into our hearts,
I will conceale, consent, and doe my best,
What stratagem soe're thou shalt deuise.
Ham. It is enough, mother good night:
Come sir, I'le prouide for you a graue,
Who was in life a foolish prating knaue.
                Exit Hamlet with the dead body.

                Enter the King and Lordes.
King. Now Gertred, what sayes our sonne, how doe you finde him?

In Q2 the text reads:

Ham. Doe you see nothing there?
Ger. Nothing at all, yet all that is I see.

Ham Nor did you nothing heare?

Ger. No nothing but our selues.

Ham Why looke you there, looke how it steales
away,

My father in his habit as he liued,

Looke where he goes, euen now out at the portall.
                           Exit Ghost.

Ger. This is the very coynage of your braine,

This bodilesse creation extacie is very cunning in.

Ham. My pulse as yours doth temperatly keepe
time,

And makes as healthfull musicke, it is not madnesse

That I haue vttred, bring me to the test,

And the matter will reword, which madnesse

Would gambole from, mother for loue of grace,

Lay not that flattering vnction to your soule

That not your trespasse but my madnesse speakes,

It will but skin and filme the vlcerous place

Whiles ranck corruption mining all within

Infects vnseene, confesse your selfe to heauen,

Repent what's past, auoyd what is to come,

And doe not spread the compost on the weedes

To make them rancker, forgiue me this my vertue,

For in the fatnesse of these pursie times

Vertue it selfe of vice must pardon beg,

Yea curbe and wooe for leaue to doe him good.

Ger. O *Hamlet* thou hast cleft my hart in twaine.

Ham. O throwe away the worser part of it,

And leaue the purer with the other halfe,

Good night, but goe not to my Vncles bed,

Assume a vertue if you haue it not,

That monster custome, who all sence doth eate

Of habits deuill, is angell yet in this

That to the vse of actions faire and good,

He likewise giues a frock or Liuery

That aptly is put on to refraine night,

And that shall lend a kind of easines

To the next abstinence, the next more easie:

For vse almost can change the stamp of nature,

And either the deuill, or throwe him out

With wonderous potency: once more good night,

And when you are desirous to be blest,

Ile blessing beg of you, for this same Lord

I doe repent; but heauen hath pleasd it so

To punish me with this, and this with me,

That I must be their scourge and minister,

I will bestowe him and will answere well

The death I gaue him; so againe good night

I must be cruell only to be kinde,

This bad beginnes, and worse remaines behind.

One word more good Lady.

Ger. What shall I doe?

Ham. Not this by no meanes that I bid you doe,

Let the blowt King temp't you againe to bed,

Pinch wanton on your cheeke, call you his Mouse,

And let him for a paire of reechie kisses,

Or padling in your necke with his damn'd fingers.

Make you to rouell all this matter out

That I essentially am not in madnesse,

But mad in craft, t'were good you let him knowe,

For who that's but a Queen, faire, sober, wise,

Would from a paddack, from a bat, a gib,

Such deare concernings hide, who would doe so,

No, in dispight of sence and secrecy,

Vnpeg the basket on the houses top,

Let the birds fly, and like the famous Ape,

To try conclusions in the basket creepe,

And breake your owne necke downe.

Ger. Be thou assur'd, if words be made of breath

And breath of life, I haue no life to breath

What thou hast sayd to me.

Ham. I must to *England,* you knowe that.

Ger. Alack I had forgot.

Tis so concluded on.

Ham. Ther's letters seald, and my two Schoole-
fellowes,

Whom I will trust as I will Adders fang'd,

They beare the mandat, they must sweep my way

And marshall me to knauery: let it worke,

For tis the sport to haue the enginer

Hoist with his owne petar, an't shall goe hard

But I will delue one yard belowe their mines,

And blowe them at the Moone: ô tis most sweete

When in one line two crafts directly meete,

This man shall set me packing,

Ile lugge the guts into the neighbour roome;

Mother good night indeed, this Counsayler

Is now most still, most secret, and most graue,

Who was in life a most foolish prating knaue.

Come sir, to draw toward an end with you.

Good night mother.   *Exit.*

     *Enter King, and Queene, with Rosencraus
                 and Guyldensterne.*

King. There's matter in these sighes, these profound heaues,

You must translate, tis fit we vnderstand them,

Where is your sonne?

In F1 the text reads:

Ham. Do you see nothing there?

Qu. Nothing at all, yet all that is I see.

Ham. Nor did you nothing heare?

Qu. No, nothing but our selues.

Ham. Why look you there: looke how it steals
away:

My Father in his habite, as he liued,

Looke where he goes euen now out at the Portall.
                             Exit.

Qu. This is the very coynage of your Braine,

This bodilesse Creation extasie is very cunning in.

Ham. Extasie?

My Pulse as yours doth temperately keepe time,

And makes as healthfull Musicke. It is not madnesse

That I haue vttered; bring me to the Test
And I the matter will re-word: which madnesse
Would gamboll from. Mother, for loue of Grace,
Lay not a flattering Vnction to your soule,
That not your trespasse, but my madnesse speakes:
It will but skin and filme the Vlcerous place;
Whil'st ranke Corruption mining all within,
Infects vnseene. Confesse your selfe to Heauen,
Repent what's past, auoyd what is to come,
And do not spred the Compost or the Weedes
To make them ranke. Forgiue me this my Vertue,
For in the fatnesse of this pursie times,
Vertue it selfe, of Vice must pardon begge,
Yea courb, and woe, for leaue to do him good.
  Qu. Oh *Hamlet*,
Thou hast cleft my heart in twaine.
  Ham. O throw away the worser part of it,
And liue the purer with the other halfe.
Good night, but go not to mine Vnkles bed,
Assume a Vertue, if you haue it not, refraine to
    night;
And that shall lend a kinde of easinesse
To the next abstinence. Once more goodnight,
And when you are desirous to be blest,
Ile blessing begge of you. For this same Lord,
I do repent: but heauen hath pleas'd it so,
To punish me with this, and this with me,
That I must be their Scourge and Minister.
I will bestow him, and will answer well
The death I gaue him: so againe, good night.
I must be cruell, onely to be kinde;
Thus bad begins and worse remaines behinde.
  Qu. What shall I do?
  Ham. Not this by no meanes that I bid you do:
Let the blunt King tempt you againe to bed,
Pinch Wanton on your cheeke, call you his Mouse,
And let him for a paire of reechie kisses,
Or padling in your necke with his damn'd Fingers,
Make you to rauell all this matter out,
That I essentially am not in madnesse,
But made in craft. 'Twere good you let him know,
For who that's but a Queene, faire, sober, wise,
Would from a Paddocke, from a Bat, a Gibbe,
Such deere concernings hide, Who would do so,
No in despight of Sense and Secrecie,
Vnpegge the Basket on the houses top:
Let the Birds flye, and like the famous Ape
To try Conclusions in the Basket, creepe
And breake your owne necke downe.
  Qu. Be thou assur'd, if words be made of breath,
And breath of life: I haue no life to breath
What thou hast saide to me.
  Ham. I must to England you know that?
  Qu. Alacke I had forgot: 'Tis so concluded on.
  Ham. This man shall set me packing:
Ile lugge the Guts into the Neighbor roome,
Mother goodnight. Indeede this Counsellor

Is now most still, most secret, and most graue,
Who was in life, a foolish prating Knaue.
Come sir, to draw toward an end with you.
Good night Mother.
       Exit Hamlet tugging in Polonius.
       Enter King.
  King. There's matters in these sighes.
These profound heaues
You must translate; Tis fit we vnderstand them.
Where is your Sonne?

A comparison of these three versions shows that there are many differences. In Q1 the Queen swears that she had known nothing of the murder and further that she will help Hamlet in whatever he devises. There is nothing of this in the other versions. When F1 is compared with Q2, it will be seen that Hamlet's speeches have been considerably altered; F1 omits nineteen lines that occur in Q2. Further, the version in Q2 is so lightly punctuated that at times the sense is obscure. F1 is a more carefully prepared version, but probably not a direct printing from Shakespeare's manuscript. There is discrepancy also between the two versions at the end of the scene. In Q2, the scene ends at *Exit* and the next scene begins with: "*Enter King, and Queene, with Rosencraus and Guyldensterne,*" as if the Queen had gone out and come in again. In F1, Gertrude is left alone at the end of the scene for a few moments, and then the King enters alone. Rosencranz and Guildenstern do not enter until the King calls for them, at line 32.

Which version should an editor of a modern text prefer? Actually, editors ignore Q1 as a spurious text and produce a text which contains all passages omitted in Q2 or in F1; and where, as often happens, there is a difference in reading between the two versions, they choose that which seems to them to give the better sense.

2. KING LEAR:

Similar problems occur in *Lear*. Here there is a first quarto (1608) and the text as printed in F1. Q1 is more complete than F1, but the text is very corrupt, although apparently not a pirated version of the same kind as the *Hamlet* of Q1. There are indeed about five hundred differences between the two texts, but yet Q1, for all its shortcomings, will often give a better reading than F1. A typical passage illustrating the differences between the two occurs in III.vi.92-122.
  In Q1, the text reads:

Glost. Come hither friend, where is the King
   my maister.
   Kent. Here sir, but trouble him not his wits are
gon.
   Glost. Good friend — I prithy take him in thy
   armes,
I haue or'e heard a plot of death vpon him,
Ther is a Litter ready lay him in't, & driue to-
   wards Douer frend,
Where thou shalt meet both welcome & protection,
   take vp thy master,
If thou should'st dally halfe an houre, his life with
   thine
And all that offer to defend him stand in assured
   losse,
Take vp the King and followe me, that will to
   some prouision
Giue thee quicke conduct.
   Kent. Oppressed nature sleepes,
This rest might yet haue balmed thy broken sin-
   ewes,
Which if conuenience will not alow stand in hard
   cure,
Come helpe to beare thy maister, thou must not
   stay behind.
   Glost. Come, come away.   *Exit.*
   Edg. When we our betters see bearing our woes:
   we scarcely thinke, our miseries, our foes.
Who alone suffers suffers, most it'h mind,
Leauing free things and happy showes behind,
But then the mind much sufferance doth or'e scip,
When griefe hath mates, and bearing fellowship:
How light and portable my paine seemes now,
When that which makes me bend, makes the King
   bow.
He childed as I fathered, *Tom* away,
Marke the high noyses and thy selfe bewray,
When false opinion whose wrong thoughts defile
   thee,
In thy iust proofe repeals and reconciles thee,
What will hap more to night, safe scape the King,
Lurke, lurke.

In F1, the text reads:

Glou. Come hither Friend:
Where is the King my Master?
   Kent. Here Sir, but trouble him not, his wits are
gon.
   Glou. Good friend, I prythee take him in thy
   armes;
I haue ore-heard a plot of death vpon him:
There is a Litter ready, lay him in't,
And driue toward Douer friend, where thou shalt
   meete
Both welcome, and protection. Take vp thy Master,
If thou should'st dally halfe an houre, his life
With thine, and all that offer to defend him,

Stand in assured losse. Take vp, take vp,
And follow me, that will to some prouision
Giue thee quicke conduct. Come, come, away.
        Exeunt.

Here F1 is a far better text than Q1. The verse
lines are correctly divided and the punctuation
is good, yet F1 omits nineteen lines. Scholars
have not yet satisfactorily explained why these
great differences should exist or how Q1 was
put together. From a close comparison of the
two versions, it seems clear that F1 was set up
from a copy of Q1 which had been very carefully corrected.

In *Lear* also the editor will probably prefer
to base his text on the folio; when there is a
marked difference between F1 and Q1, he must
decide which to choose.

3. ROMEO AND JULIET:

An example of a different kind of problem
occurs in *Romeo and Juliet*, V.iii.101–21. There
are two quartos of this play. Q1 (1597) has long
puzzled editors, for though it differs in many
places from Q2, it is not corrupt in the same
way as the Q1 of *Hamlet*. Q2 was probably
printed from Shakespeare's manuscript. The
text in F1 was printed from a corrected copy
of Q2. In Q2 (and in F1) Romeo's last speech
appears thus:

        Ah deare *Iuliet*
Why art thou yet so faire? I will beleeue,
Shall I beleeue that vnsubstantiall death is amor-
   ous,
And that the leane abhorred monster keepes
Thee here in darke to be his parramour?   [5]
For feare of that I still will staie with thee,
And neuer from this pallat of dym night.
Depart againe, come lye thou in my arme,
Heer's to thy health, where ere thou tumblest in.
O true Appothecarie!   [10]
Thy drugs are quicke. Thus with a kisse I die.
Depart againe, here, here will I remaine,
With wormes that are thy Chamber-maides: O
   here
Will I set vp my euerlasting rest:
And shake the yoke of inauspicious starres,   [15]
From this world wearied flesh, eyes looke your
   last:
Armes take your last embrace: And lips, O you
The doores of breath, seale with a righteous kisse
A datelesse bargaine to ingrossing death:
Come bitter conduct, come vnsauoury guide,   [20]
Thou desperate Pilot, now at once run on

The dashing Rocks, thy seasick weary barke:
Heeres to my Loue. O true Appothecary:
Thy drugs are quicke. Thus with a kisse I die.

It will be noted that the final phrases, "O true Appothecary . . . die" are printed twice, at lines 10–11 and 23–24. This repetition is left out by modern editors. The natural inference is that Shakespeare rewrote the last speech. In the first version, the speech ended at line 11: "Thus with a kisse I die." Later Shakespeare revised the play and expanded the last lines, beginning at "pallat of dym night (line 7)," but the printer failed to notice that the last thirteen lines should have directly followed "dym night" and that the next four lines (8–11) should have been omitted.

These are but three examples of the kind of difficulty often encountered in editing any text of Shakespeare. They arise because in Shakespeare's time few dramatists were greatly concerned with the literary value of their plays. The manuscript of a play was sold outright to the players, and there the matter ended. The players were usually anxious to keep their plays from being printed, because there was no acting copyright and nothing to prevent the play from being acted by another company.

Toward the end of Shakespeare's career, it became a fashion for gentlemen to collect and read plays. Some authors, notably Ben Jonson, then grew jealous for their literary fame; Shakespeare seems not to have greatly cared. Certainly he never took any steps to have his plays carefully printed, and had it not been for the zeal of his surviving friends, many would have been lost.

Much information can be gathered from Henslowe's *Diary,* which records many payments to dramatists. Plays were offered or ordered. An author who had a good idea for a play explained the plot to the company; and if they approved, he was commissioned to write it. Many plays were written by syndicates of two, three, or four writers, sometimes in great haste. The price paid for plays was good for the times. It varied from £6 to £10 (about $240 to $400 in modern money).[1] This is a high price when it is remembered that the average life of a play was not much more than ten performances.

The history of a play manuscript was compli-

[1] See App. 27.

cated. It had first to be written by the author or authors. Sometimes, indeed, when they were short of money, they sold it act by act as it was finished. A play manuscript as delivered was not always in a fit condition for performance, so the prompter went over it and prepared it for production by adding the necessary notes of stage business. Next, the manuscript was handed to a copyist to prepare the parts for the individual actors. These were written out, as is still the custom, giving the actor's full part and the last few words of the previous speech as a cue. Among the Henslowe papers there still survives a part prepared for Edward Alleyn when he played Orlando in Greene's *Orlando Furioso.* It was originally in the form of a continuous roll which at rehearsals Alleyn held in his left hand while gesturing with his right.

The next stage was to have the play licensed. The Master of the Revels, the Court official responsible for entertainments, was the official censor. The play was sent to him for reading. If he disapproved, he noted on the manuscript the alterations which he required. If he was satisfied, he wrote a certificate to this effect in the manuscript itself, which was thus formally licensed for performance. The play then went into rehearsal and was acted, the original manuscript being used in the theater as prompt copy. When the play had ceased to be popular, the manuscript was put away, or possibly sold to a printer. In some instances, therefore, the text which reached the printer was the original manuscript copy.

It is generally believed nowadays by scholars that the texts of *Romeo and Juliet* (Q2), *Much Ado about Nothing,* and *Hamlet* (Q2), among others, were set directly from Shakespeare's own manuscript and therefore reproduce some of the peculiarities of his spelling.

Printers, as well as actors, were bound by government regulations. When printing was first invented at the end of the fifteenth century, it was soon clear to the Government of the day that an uncontrolled printing press could be a very dangerous instrument of propaganda. Printers were therefore organized into their own Guild, the Stationers' Company. No one was allowed to own a press or print a book who was not a member of that company. Before books were printed they had first to be licensed by an official appointed by the Archbishop of

Canterbury or by the Master of the Stationers' Company. When a printer had obtained his license, he took the book along to the Stationers' Hall and there entered it in the Stationers' Register, paying a fee of sixpence. This entry gave him the sole right to print the book; any other printer who stole his copyright was liable to be heavily punished by the Stationers' Company. The Stationers' Register still exists and is thus a most valuable record of all early printed books, but by no means all books were entered. Sometimes a printer, knowing that he had a salable book which might or might not be allowed, risked prosecution. At other times, he was casual (as were all Elizabethans) in obeying the law. From a third to a quarter of the books printed during Shakespeare's lifetime were never entered in the Stationers' Register.

It seems also to have been the custom for the Lord Chamberlain's Men occasionally to come to an arrangement with a printer called James Roberts, whereby he would enter the title of one of their plays in the Stationers' Register as his own property, but not print it. In this way the players were protected against unauthorized printing. Modern scholars call this method of control " blocking entry."

Most plays were printed in the form known as quarto; that is, the original sheet of paper was folded twice to form four leaves or eight pages. This was the normal form for printing small books. Plays were usually badly printed and full of mistakes. The printer set up the manuscript more or less as it lay before him. He did not expend much care on tidying it for press. As a result, early quartos preserve many of the peculiarities of the play manuscript. There is seldom any division into acts or scenes, and no indication of the place of the action. Punctuation is light, sometimes effective but often quite impossible. Spelling is quite arbitrary. English spelling as yet was not fixed, and printers either followed the odd spellings of their authors or spelled words to suit their own convenience. As a result, play quartos are usually very slovenly.

When Shakespeare died, fourteen of his plays had been regularly printed in properly authorized quartos. They were: *Richard III, Titus Andronicus, Love's Labor's Lost, Romeo and Juliet, A Midsummer Night's Dream, Richard II, Merchant of Venice, Henry IV* (both parts),

Much Ado about Nothing, Troilus and Cressida, Hamlet, Lear, Pericles. Othello was printed in 1622. Pirated quartos had also appeared of *Romeo and Juliet, Henry V, The Merry Wives of Windsor,* and *Hamlet.* These piracies are interesting, although of no great value as texts. As Shakespeare's fame grew, the demand for his plays in print became considerable. Since the players were unwilling to release the manuscript, dishonest printers sometimes " acquired " a stolen version. Pirated texts were vamped together from various sources. Sometimes a shorthand report was obtained. The pirated quarto of *Hamlet* is apparently based on the part of Marcellus, and it seems likely that one of the lesser players was bribed to produce as much of the original play as he could remember.

In 1623 appeared the first folio; it includes in one volume all Shakespeare's undisputed plays with the exception of *Pericles.* Heminges and Condell, who were mainly responsible for the collection, took considerable care, but they were not scholars, and as soon as the texts in the folio are carefully examined, it is clear that copy of different kinds was sent to the printer. Where a play had already appeared in quarto, this quarto was used, possibly with such changes as had been made in the theater since the play was first written. For some plays, it is likely that Shakespeare's own manuscript was used; but for others (such as *The Winter's Tale*) it is clear that the copy had been carefully prepared by a professional copyist. In some plays the proper division of acts and scenes is made; in others there is no division from beginning to end. A few even have a list of characters. Divisions of verse lines are more accurate than in the quartos, and the punctuation especially has been vastly improved.

Elizabethan punctuation is interesting. Authors and copyists punctuated not as in modern times to indicate the syntax of a sentence, but to " point " it for delivery. The result is that in reading a play in the folio, the punctuation at times enormously increases the pleasure of reading. It is very doubtful, however, whether Shakespeare himself was responsible for this punctuation. If the quartos are any guide, his own method was to punctuate very lightly.

These somewhat haphazard methods of publication sufficed for readers of Shakespeare's generation. After the Restoration, when Rowe brought out his edition of 1709, printers and readers had become far more particular. Rowe took great care to make his text orderly and smooth for the reader. He made the divisions into acts and scenes where these were wanting; he added place headings, and adopted a consistent punctuation. This practice has been followed ever since. For the general reader, many difficulties have been smoothed away by editors, though the scholar prefers to get back to the original quarto or folio.

Editing Shakespeare's texts is thus full of difficulty. The curious notes on textual problems which disturb the student in his early days are a record of the ceaseless care and ingenuity which has gone to the making of the modern text. The note quoted at the beginning of this chapter concerns the famous "crux" in *Hamlet* (see I.i.62–64, *n*):

> So frowned he once when, in an angry parle,
> He smote *the sledded Polacks* on the ice.

The formula shows that Malone (1790) was the first editor to read "sledded Polacks," which most editors have since followed. The phrase in Q1 (1603), Q2 (1604), and Q3 (1611) appears as "the sleaded pollax"; in Q4 (undated) and Q5 (1637) it became "the sleaded Pollax." In F1 (1623), followed by F2 (1632) the reading is "sledded Pollax," which in F3 (1664) became "sledded Polax"; a quarto of 1683 read "sledded Poll-Ax," while F4 (1685) printed "sledded Poleaxe." Pope in his edition (1725) was the first to emend the text to read "sledded Polack," which Malone altered to "Polacks."

7. The Development of Shakespeare's Art

The Early Period

Shakespeare learned his craft in the best of schools, the theater itself. When he began to write, Edward Alleyn was the leading star actor, and his favorite parts, Marlowe's Tamburlaine and the Jew of Malta and Kyd's Hieronimo, set a standard. At first Shakespeare copied his masters, but he soon learned to develop his own techniques, and to the end of his career he was constantly experimenting. The changes in his style are indeed so noticeable that his plays can be approximately dated by style alone.

Shakespeare's poetic style can conveniently be divided into four periods: Early, Balanced, Overflowing, and Final.

To the Early Period belong *I, II, III Henry VI, Richard III, Richard II, Titus Andronicus, Love's Labor's Lost, The Two Gentlemen of Verona, The Comedy of Errors, The Taming of the Shrew, Romeo and Juliet,* and *A Midsummer Night's Dream*. Plays of this period have certain common characteristics. The plots are, on the whole, well worked out; but except in *Romeo and Juliet* the characterization is usually superficial, the psychology seldom subtle, and the dialogue inclined to be stiff, artificial, and overlong. There is an abundance of such rhetorical devices as repetition of phrase, question, exclamation, alliteration, and excess of punning and word play. Thus at their first appearance in *Romeo and Juliet* (I.i.169), Benvolio and Romeo exchange the following conversation:

BEN. What sadness lengthens Romeo's hours?
ROM. Not having that, which, having, makes them short.
BEN. In love?
ROM. Out ——
BEN. Of love?
ROM. Out of her favor where I am in love.
BEN. Alas that love, so gentle in his view,
Should be so tyrannous and rough in proof!
ROM. Alas that love, whose view is muffled still,
Should without eyes see pathways to his will!
Where shall we dine? Oh me! What fray was here?
Yet tell me not, for I have heard it all.
Here's much to do with hate, but more with love.
Why then, O brawling love! O loving hate!
O anything, of nothing first create!
O heavy lightness! Serious vanity!
Misshapen chaos of well-seeming forms!
Feather of lead, bright smoke, cold fire, sick health!
Still-waking sleep, that is not what it is!
This love feel I, that feel no love in this.

There is an excess of poetic imagery, often self-conscious, elaborate, and clever rather than illuminating. Thus in *A Midsummer Night's*

Dream (III.ii.201–16) Helena tearfully protests against Hermia's unkindness, so cruel after their schoolgirl affection:

> Oh, is it all forgot?
> All school days' friendship, childhood innocence?
> We, Hermia, like two artificial gods,
> Have with our needles created both one flower,
> Both on one sampler, sitting on one cushion,
> Both warbling of one song, both in one key —
> As if our hands, our sides, voices, and minds
> Had been incorporate. So we grew together,
> Like to a double cherry, seeming parted
> But yet a union in partition —
> Two lovely berries molded on one stem.
> So, with two seeming bodies, but one heart,
> Two of the first, like coats in heraldry,
> Due but to one, and crownèd with one crest.
> And will you rent our ancient love asunder,
> To join with men in scorning your poor friend?

The imagery of the double cherries and the coat of arms is altogether too elaborate to illustrate the simple idea of long-established friendship, unless — as is very possible — Shakespeare is here deliberately parodying a failing common in his own early work.

Rhyme is very common, verse lines are monotonously regular, stresses even, and verse and sentence usually end together. At first Shakespeare composed his speeches line by line as if he were laying bricks one on top of the other; and he had an excessive taste for puns. These traits can be seen from a typical passage in *Richard II*, in the episode where the King visits the dying Gaunt (II.i.72–85). Richard asks: "What comfort, man? How is't with aged Gaunt?" To which Gaunt replies:

> Oh, how that name befits my composition!
> Old Gaunt indeed, and gaunt in being old.
> Within me grief hath kept a tedious fast,
> And who abstains from meat that is not gaunt?
> For sleeping England long time have I watched,
> Watching breeds leanness, leanness is all gaunt.
> The pleasure that some fathers feed upon
> Is my strict fast — I mean, my children's looks —
> And therein fasting, hast thou made me gaunt.
> Gaunt am I for the grave, gaunt as a grave,
> Whose hollow womb inherits naught but bones.

On all possible occasions characters are given long poetic speeches which may be admirable in themselves but are not always suitable in their context, and often retard the movement of the plot. Two good examples of this habit are the account of Clarence's dream in *Richard III* (I.iv.1–63) and Mercutio's outburst on Queen Mab in *Romeo and Juliet* (I.iv.53–103).

At this stage in his career, Shakespeare did not always have much to say, but he said it at great length, and all the time he was experimenting with the uses of words. He was more a conscious artist than an instinctive dramatist. Nevertheless the artificiality of Shakespeare's verse often has charm, and at times even considerable power. A good example of the early style at its best is to be found in *Richard III* in Gloucester's soliloquy after he has successfully wooed the Lady Anne (I.ii.228–64):

> Was ever woman in this humor wooed?
> Was ever woman in this humor won?
> I'll have her, but I will not keep her long.
> What! I, that killed her husband and his father,
> To take her in her heart's extremest hate,
> With curses in her mouth, tears in her eyes,
> The bleeding witness of her hatred by —
> Having God, her conscience, and these bars against me,
> And I nothing to back my suit at all
> But the plain Devil and dissembling looks,
> And yet to win her, all the world to nothing! . . .
>
> My dukedom to a beggarly denier,
> I do mistake my person all this while.
> Upon my life, she finds, although I cannot,
> Myself to be a marvelous proper man.
> I'll be at charges for a looking-glass,
> And entertain some score or two of tailors,
> To study fashions to adorn my body.
> Since I am crept in favor with myself,
> I will maintain it with some little cost.
> But first I'll turn yon fellow in his grave,
> And then return lamenting to my love.
> Shine out, fair sun, till I have bought a glass,
> That I may see my shadow as I pass.

Here Shakespeare was successfully writing for effect, and though meter and rhythm remain regular, he instills into Richard personality and grim humor.

Another good example is Richard II's speech of renunciation in the deposition scene. Bolingbroke asks, "Are you contented to resign the crown?" To which Richard replies (IV.i.201–22):

> Aye, no; no, aye; for I must nothing be;
> Therefore no no, for I resign to thee.
> Now mark me, how I will undo myself:
> I give this heavy weight from off my head

And this unwieldy scepter from my hand,
The pride of kingly sway from out my heart;
With mine own tears I wash away my balm,
With mine own hands I give away my crown,
With mine own tongue deny my sacred state,
With mine own breath release all duty's rites:
All pomp and majesty I do forswear;
My manors, rents, revenues I forego;
My acts, decrees, and statutes I deny:
God pardon all oaths that are broke to me!
God keep all vows unbroke that swear to thee!
Make me, that nothing have, with nothing
   grieved,
And thou with all pleased, that hast all achieved!
Long mayst thou live in Richard's seat to sit,
And soon lie Richard in an earthy pit!
God save King Harry, unkinged Richard says,
And send him many years of sunshine days!
What more remains?

From the first, however, Shakespeare's comic dialogue in prose was easy and mature. Bottom, Quince, and company in *A Midsummer Night's Dream* are as fully developed as any of the later clowns, such as Dogberry and Verges in *Much Ado about Nothing,* the gravedigger in *Hamlet,* or Stephano and Trinculo in *The Tempest.*

The Early Period passed gradually into the Balanced Period. At all times Shakespeare wrote magnificent passages of poetry, but in the early plays the set piece is noticeably finer than its surroundings; in the later plays the whole effect is more even, and the dialogue is less concerned with fine sayings than with what is immediately appropriate to the scene. The main difference between the Early and the Balanced styles is that as Shakespeare's experience deepened, his power of expression grew. Speeches are now written as a whole, in one sweep; run-on lines become more common, and though the formal pattern of the verse remains, the stresses no longer tick like an ill-balanced grandfather clock.

The Balanced Period

Early and Balanced merge in *The Merchant of Venice,* which is perhaps the first play where Shakespeare is completely master of his craft. There are few long speeches of poetry for its own sake. The casket scene where Bassanio wins Portia (III.ii.) is a little drawn-out, but the effect is deliberate and intentional, and leads up to the lyric moment when Portia gives herself to Bassanio. The verse has become easier, the rhythm more varied, the power and emotion deeper.

In *I Henry IV,* which was probably his next play, Shakespeare has achieved complete balance. The few poetic speeches are short and appropriate, and there is a new sense of humor and of power. Shakespeare was now so sure of himself that he could even venture to parody his own serious speeches, as Hotspur's excessive zeal for honor (I.iii.200) is parodied by Falstaff's cynical self-catechism (V.i.127), or the moving scene where the King rebukes his erring son (III.ii) is parodied in advance, and enhanced, not spoiled, by Falstaff in his extemporary play (II.iv.409-532).

The characterization also is elaborate and successful in *I Henry IV,* and well illustrates Shakespeare's methods of creating character. There are three principal methods by which character can be shown: by what is said of a man by his friends, and not less important by his enemies; by what he says of himself, and how he says it; and by his own actions. Description of a character is the most obvious method. Ben Jonson in his plays made a feature of elaborate descriptions, which mainly occur just before the person appears. Shakespeare, however, was much more subtle. He seldom wrote long or elaborate descriptions of his characters. Instead he built up a character stroke by stroke, revealing each trait as it was needed. The character of Hotspur is a good example of his technique.

Hotspur is first mentioned in the first scene by the King, who sighs enviously that Northumberland's son should be so much better than his " young Harry." The King then goes on to comment on Hotspur's pride in refusing to hand over his prisoners. The audience is thus given some notion of Hotspur's character, so that when he appears in I.iii, and is rebuked by the King, his angry outburst is not unexpected. His behavior throughout this scene reveals much: his impatience and hotheadedness, his waspish sense of humor, his complete lack of self-control when roused, his passion for honor, which so obsesses him that he becomes entirely self-absorbed. Three scenes later Shakespeare reveals quite a different side of Hotspur's nature. At home, sleeping or waking his first thoughts and dreams are always on war, but he is very fond of his wife, a gentle, gay, womanly creature, and once she appears these two tease each other like lovers.

Throughout the play there is a deliberate contrast between Hotspur and Prince Hal. Hotspur is revealed as the showier hero, Hal as the deeper, more intelligent nature. After the scene between Hotspur and his wife, the Prince casually remarks to Poins, " I am not yet of Percy's mind, the Hotspur of the North, he that kills me some six or seven dozen of Scots at a breakfast, washes his hands, and says to his wife, ' Fie upon this quiet life! I want work.' ' O my sweet Harry,' says she, ' how many hast thou killed today?' ' 'Give my roan horse a drench,' says he, and answers ' Some fourteen ' an hour after — ' a trifle, a trifle.'" The description is intentionally a caricature of what has gone before, but yet it adds to our understanding of Hotspur — and of Hal.

Hotspur's next appearance is at the council with Worcester, Mortimer, and Glendower (III.i). Here Shakespeare contrasts four men of very different character in such a way that each reveals his own nature and brings out the character of the others. Hotspur shows himself impatient, rude, and overbearing, contemptuous of anything that he does not understand, a shrewd bargainer until he gets his own way — but, as before, he is redeemed and made lovable at the end by the little conversation with his wife. Finally, in the battle scenes he is true to his name. For a moment he is abashed at the news that his father has deserted him, but he recovers quickly and is eager to try conclusions with Prince Hal. Here he shows himself the lesser nature, for the Prince's challenge is issued with modest sincerity; Hotspur receives it with jealousy and contempt. Even as the two join in fight Hotspur despises his rival as an unworthy opponent. Thus until the end of the play the character is still growing and developing.

The Balanced Period lasted from *Henry IV* to *Othello,* roughly from 1597 to 1603, and includes *Henry V, Much Ado about Nothing, The Merry Wives of Windsor, As You Like It, Julius Caesar, Hamlet, Twelfth Night, Troilus and Cressida, Measure for Measure,* and *All's Well That Ends Well.* During this time Shakespeare's own experience of life was deepening and his power of expression expanding. By the end he could write speeches which were not only full of the subtlest characterization but, by their choice of vocabulary and rhythm, could express the whole nature of the speaker. Thus the experience of the world now degenerating into a complacent senility in Polonius is perfectly expressed in his instructions to Reynaldo on the best way of finding out whether Laertes is making a fool of himself in Paris (II.i.37–68):

POL. Marry sir, here's my drift,
And I believe it is a fetch of warrant.
You laying these slight sullies on my son,
As 'twere a thing a little soiled i' the working,
Mark you,
Your party in converse, him you would sound,
Having ever seen in the prenominate crimes
The youth you breathe of guilty, be assured
He closes with you in this consequence ——
" Good sir," or so, or " friend," or " gentleman,"
According to the phrase or the addition
Of man and country.
REY. Very good, my lord.
POL. And then, sir, does he this — he does ——
What was I about to say? By the mass, I was about
to say something. Where did I leave?
REY. At " closes in the consequence," at " friend
or so," and " gentleman."
POL. At " closes in the consequence," aye, marry:
He closes thus: " I know the gentleman.
I saw him yesterday, or t'other day,
Or then, or then, with such, or such, and, as you say,
There was a' gaming, there o'ertook in's rouse,
There falling out at tennis." Or perchance,
" I saw him enter such a house of sale,"
Videlicet, a brothel, or so forth.
See you now,
Your bait of falsehood takes this carp of truth.
And thus do we of wisdom and of reach,
With windlasses and with assays of bias,
By indirections find directions out.
So by my former lecture and advice,
Shall you my son. You have me, have you not?

The breakdown into prose as Polonius loses the thread of his own verbosity is perfect.

There is, however, real poetry in abundance in *Hamlet,* and it is worth comparing Hamlet's soliloquy on suicide (III.i.56–88) with Richard II's soliloquy in prison (V.v.1–66) to see Shakespeare's increased power of writing this kind of philosophic reverie. In *Hamlet* the rhythm is easier and more natural, the imagery terser and sharper, the mind of the speaker more mature and subtle.

The growth of dramatic power can be seen also in Shakespeare's increasing knowledge of human character and a certain change in his interest and point of view. In his early plays, he tended rather to see the whole story objectively. Some characters naturally were more important, but each was treated alike. From about 1599, for the next six or seven years — that is, from *As You Like It* and *Julius Caesar* to *Lear* and *Macbeth* — Shakespeare often selected one or two characters in the play for special treatment, so that we see not only what happens to them, but also the working and development of their minds. Brutus, Hamlet, Iago, Edmund, and Macbeth are given soliloquies in which they lay bare not only their intentions but their very souls.

Soliloquy — where a character left to himself reveals his own mind in a direct speech to the audience — was not a new device. Shakespeare and indeed all Elizabethan dramatists used it frequently, but in his earlier plays soliloquy was used mainly for three purposes: to give necessary information of the speaker's intentions, as when, at the end of the first scene of *A Midsummer Night's Dream*, Helena explains that she will tell Demetrius of Hermia's flight; or to reveal that the speaker is playing a part and is not what he seems, as when Richard of Gloucester gloats over his treachery to his brother Clarence (*Rich III*, I.iii.324); or as an excuse for an outburst of sheer poetry, as when Juliet waiting for Romeo breaks into a lyric ecstasy on night and love (*R & J*, III.ii.1).

In the soliloquies of Shakespeare's more mature plays, as when Brutus ponders whether to join the conspiracy, or Iago broods over the best way to hurt Othello, or Macbeth recoils in horror from the murder of Duncan, we see a mind seething. The interest is not so much in what may ultimately happen as in the working and development of the personality of the speaker. It is as if Shakespeare for a while was more interested in men's motives than in their actions.

The Overflowing Period

When he came to write *Lear*, Shakespeare was again experimenting with language. By this time his thoughts and feelings were coming too thick and powerful for balanced expression. He entered into an Overflowing Period. The metrical line and the formal scheme of five stresses to the line were often neglected. The thought became too intense for clear, logical expression;

the idea in Shakespeare's mind did not always travel along the usual conductor of grammatical sentences, but leapt across in some mighty image which only laborious paraphrase can reduce to everyday speech. *Lear* and *Macbeth* are full of these passages, often packed with a complex imagery which suggests half a dozen different glints and meanings. Thus Lady Macbeth, in her terrible self-dedication to evil (I.v.41–55):

> Come, you spirits
> That tend on mortal thoughts, unsex me here,
> And fill me, from the crown to the toe, topfull
> Of direst cruelty! Make thick my blood,
> Stop up the access and passage to remorse,
> That no compunctious visitings of nature
> Shake my fell purpose, nor keep peace between
> The effect and it! Come to my woman's breasts,
> And take my milk for gall, you murdering ministers,
> Wherever in your sightless substances
> You wait on nature's mischief! Come, thick night,
> And pall thee in the dunnest smoke of Hell,
> That my keen knife see not the wound it makes,
> Nor Heaven peep through the blanket of the dark
> To cry " Hold, hold! "

The language in *Lear* is even more concentrated and overflowing with meaning. Not only with the old King himself at moments of high emotion; the other characters also speak in this concentrated way. Thus Cordelia, while she waits for her father to awake into a feeble sanity, comments (IV.vii.26–42):

> O my dear Father! Restoration hang
> Thy medicine on my lips; and let this kiss
> Repair those violent harms that my two sisters
> Have in thy reverence made! . . .
> Had you not been their father, these white flakes
> Had challenged pity of them. Was this a face
> To be opposed against the warring winds?
> To stand against the deep dread-bolted thunder?
> In the most terrible and nimble stroke
> Of quick, cross lightning? To watch — poor perdu! —
> With this thin helm? Mine enemy's dog,
> Though he had bit me, should have stood that night
> Against my fire, and wast thou fain, poor Father,
> To hovel thee with swine, and rogues forlorn
> In short and musty straw? Alack, alack!
> 'Tis wonder that thy life and wits at once
> Had not concluded all.

There was less of this excessive concentration in *Antony and Cleopatra,* which followed *Macbeth,* but in its place a new sense of poetry, a magnificence, a kind of haunting resonance which occurs nowhere else. The gorgeous account of Antony's first meeting with Cleopatra (II.ii.194–245) was a return to the earlier method of inserting long descriptive passages into the dialogue; but it was necessary to explain Cleopatra's mystery and fascination, which could so enslave the hard-bitten Antony. It was, as it were, the orchestral accompaniment to a play full of word music, which is most conspicuous at the high moments and becomes an echo as Cleopatra prepares to die:

> Show me, my women, like a Queen. Go fetch
> My best attires. I am again for Cydnus,
> To meet Mark Antony. Sirrah Iras, go.
> Now, noble Charmian, we'll dispatch indeed;
> And when thou hast done this chare I'll give thee leave
> To play till Doomsday. Bring our crown and all.

In his Overflowing Period, Shakespeare was not only unrestrained in his verse but also in his plots. In *Lear* and in *Antony and Cleopatra* there is an impatience in the construction, or rather an exuberance of incident. There are too many incidents and too much detail for either play to be easily followed. Both require an unusual concentration in reader and playgoer, and both are tributes to the attention and intelligence of Shakespeare's audience. The characterization, however, is as good as anywhere, and the incidents themselves as effective on the stage. And in the use of language, there is less concentration in *Antony and Cleopatra,* and a return to a more balanced manner of writing.

In *Antony and Cleopatra* and *Coriolanus,* both of which were based on North's *Plutarch,* Shakespeare also returned to his earlier manner of construction. He abandoned the elaborate analysis of character and the psychological soliloquy. Though the characterization remains perfect, Shakespeare's intention was now not so much the development of an individual as the presentation of a theme.

Coriolanus is a demonstration of the eternal futility of politicians who in fighting for their own cause destroy not only each other, but the general commonwealth. *Antony and Cleopatra* illustrates the truth expressed in Bacon's Essay of Love:

The stage is more beholding to love than the life of man. For as to the stage, love is ever matter of comedies, and now and then of tragedies; but in life it doth much mischief; sometimes like a siren, sometimes like a fury. You may observe that amongst all the great and worthy persons (whereof the memory remaineth, either ancient or recent), there is not one that hath been transported to the mad degree of love; which shows that great spirits and great business do keep out this weak passion. You must except, nevertheless, Marcus Antonius, the half partner of the empire of Rome, and Appius Claudius, the decemvir and lawgiver; whereof the former was indeed a voluptuous man, and inordinate; but the latter was an austere and wise man; and therefore it seems (though rarely) that love can find entrance not only into an open heart, but also into a heart well fortified, if watch be not well kept.

The Final Period

At the end of his career, Shakespeare reached a Final Period, shown particularly in his last play, *The Tempest,* where he achieved perfect mastery and balance between thought, phrase, and meaning. It is seen in such a speech as Prospero's farewell to his art:

> Ye elves of hills, brooks, standing lakes, and groves,
> And ye that on the sands with printless foot
> Do chase the ebbing Neptune and do fly him
> When he comes back; you demipuppets that
> By moonshine do the green sour ringlets make,
> Whereof the ewe not bites; and you whose pastime
> Is to make midnight mushrooms that rejoice
> To hear the solemn curfew, by whose aid —
> Weak masters though ye be — I have bedimmed
> The noontide sun, called forth the mutinous winds,
> And twixt the green sea and the azured vault
> Set roaring war. To the dread rattling thunder
> Have I given fire, and rifted Jove's stout oak
> With his own bolt. The strong-based promontory
> Have I made shake, and by the spurs plucked up
> The pine and cedar. Graves at my command
> Have waked their sleepers, oped, and let 'em forth
> By my so potent art. But this rough magic
> I here abjure, and when I have required
> Some heavenly music — which even now I do —
> To work mine end upon their senses, that
> This airy charm is for, I'll break my staff,
> Bury it certain fathoms in the earth,
> And deeper than did ever plummet sound
> I'll drown my book.

Beyond this the English language cannot reach.

The changes in Shakespeare's style can be felt, but they cannot be exactly or scientifically analyzed, though there was at one time a fashion for reducing Shakespeare's verse to statistics and tables.[1] These figures are of little value except as showing — what is obvious to any sensitive reader — that as Shakespeare developed, his verse was less restrained by metrical rules. But the judgment of style comes late, and only after much reading and experience — and there are no short cuts to the development of taste.

8. Shakespeare and the Critics

Beginnings

The greatness of Shakespeare's plays has been appreciated from the very beginning. The first recorded performance of *I Henry VI* was on March 3, 1592; by 1598, Shakespeare was recognized as the greatest writer yet produced by the English, at least by one young student named Francis Meres (see p. 11b), whose tribute is the more remarkable since it was made before any of Shakespeare's most mature plays were written.

Shakespeare's reputation grew steadily for the next ten years, and then for a while his plays seemed to go somewhat out of fashion. Drama was becoming more and more a genteel amusement for the wealthy, who found the plays of Beaumont and Fletcher and of Ben Jonson more to their taste. Indeed, if it had not been for a lucky chance, Shakespeare might almost have been forgotten, for when he died only fourteen of his plays were in print.

The First Folio, 1623

The beginnings of Shakespeare's literary fame date from the collection of thirty-six of his plays published in 1623 and known as the *First Folio*. It was a great undertaking for all concerned, and was put out as a genuine tribute of affection by those who knew him. The folio is prefaced by a note "To the great Variety of Readers," signed by John Heminges and Henry Condell, two of the surviving members of Shakespeare's company. In this preface they say:

It had been a thing, we confess, worthy to have been wished, that the Author himself had lived to have set forth and overseen his own writings; but since it hath been ordained otherwise, and he by death departed from that right, we pray you do not envy his friends, the office of their care, and pain, to have collected and published them; and so to have published them, as where before you were abused with divers stolen and surreptitious copies, maimed, and deformed by the frauds and stealths of injurious impostors, that exposed them; even those, are now offered to your view cured, and perfect of their limbs; and all the rest, absolute in their numbers, as he conceived them. Who, as he was a happy imitator of Nature, was a most gentle expresser of it. His mind and hand went together: and what he thought, he uttered with that easiness, that we have scarce received from him a blot in his papers.

But the most impressive tribute in the folio is a full-dress ode written by Ben Jonson:

> To the memory of my beloved,
> The AUTHOR
> Mr. WILLIAM SHAKESPEARE:
> And
> what he hath left us.

The ode itself is an overelaborate performance and poor poetry, except for a few famous lines:

> He was not of an age, but for all time!
>   And all the Muses still were in their prime,
> When like Apollo he came forth to warm
>   Our ears, or like a Mercury to charm!
> Nature herself was proud of his designs,
>   And joyed to wear the dressing of his lines!
> Which were so richly spun, and woven so fit,
>   As, since, she will vouchsafe no other Wit.
> The merry Greek, tart Aristophanes,
>   Neat Terence, witty Plautus, now not please;
> But antiquated, and deserted lie
>   As they were not of Nature's family.
> Yet must I not give Nature all: thy Art,
>   My gentle Shakespeare, must enjoy a part.
> For though the Poets matter, Nature be,
>   His Art doth give the fashion. And, that he,

[1] The curious reader will find a whole series of these tables in E. K. Chambers' *William Shakespeare*, II, 397.

Who casts to write a living line, must sweat,
　(Such as thine are) and strike the second heat
Upon the Muses' anvil: turn the same,
　(And himself with it) that he thinks to frame;
Or for the laurel, he may gain a scorn,
　For a good Poet's made, as well as born.
And such wert thou.

The folio was reprinted in 1632 and further tributes were added, including one by John Milton, then a young man.

Mr. Hales of Eton

Shakespeare's reputation was at its lowest in the 1630's and 1640's, as was but natural. He was not yet established as a classic and he was no longer a modern; to bright young playgoers he appeared just old-fashioned. Nevertheless he always had his champions, and the matter was debated on a famous occasion to which there are several allusions:

In a conversation between Sir John Suckling, Sir William D'Avenant, Endymion Porter, Mr. Hales of Eton, and Ben Jonson, Sir John Suckling, who was a professed admirer of Shakespeare, had undertaken his defence against Ben Jonson with some warmth. Mr. Hales, who had sat still for some time, hearing Ben frequently reproaching him with the want of learning, and ignorance of the Ancients, told him at last, "That if Mr. Shakespeare had not read the Ancients, he had likewise not stolen anything from 'em; (a fault the other made no conscience of) and that if he would produce any one topic finely treated by any of them, he would undertake to show something upon the same subject at least as well written by Shakespeare." [1]

As yet there was little serious attempt at "Shakespearean criticism," nor indeed had any English literary critic of merit appeared. During the period of the Commonwealth, 1642–60, plays were forbidden, but when in 1660 King Charles II was restored to his throne, the theaters were reopened, and naturally Shakespeare's plays were brought out with the others. Playgoers of the new generation were puzzled. They recognized Shakespeare's genius, but they were offended by his irregularities. The latest opinion among literary men was all for classic regularity in the construction of dramas, and there was

considerable argument whether ancient or modern plays were to be preferred, and of English writers of the older generation, whether Beaumont and Fletcher or Jonson or Shakespeare were best. The debate developed into an argument about the comparative advantages of "art" and "nature," and critics took sides, each championing his own man, as in Victorian times readers championed either Dickens or Thackeray. For the stage and the theatergoing public of the latter half of the seventeenth century, the plays of Beaumont and Fletcher and of Ben Jonson were indeed more suited.

John Dryden

The first sane and subtle criticism of Shakespeare was written by John Dryden in his *Essay of Dramatic Poesy* (1660), a discussion in dialogue form of the whole controversy. In the dialogue, Neander, one of the speakers, puts forward Jonson's *Silent Woman* as a perfect play, but before he begins his detailed examination he is asked to give his frank opinion whether or not Jonson is greater than all other writers, French or English.

" I fear," replied Neander, " that in obeying your commands I shall draw some envy on myself. Besides, in performing them, it will be first necessary to speak somewhat of Shakespeare and Fletcher, his rivals in poesy; and one of them, in my opinion, at least his equal, perhaps his superior.

" To begin, then, with Shakspeare. He was the man who of all modern, and perhaps ancient poets, had the largest and most comprehensive soul. All the images of Nature were still present to him, and he drew them, not laboriously, but luckily; when he describes anything, you more than see it, you feel it too. Those who accuse him to have wanted learning, give him the greater commendation: he was naturally learned; he needed not the spectacles of books to read Nature; he looked inwards, and found her there. I cannot say he is everywhere alike; were he so, I should do him injury to compare him with the greatest of mankind. He is many times flat, insipid; his comic wit degenerating into clenches, his serious swelling into bombast. But he is always great, when some great occasion is presented to him; no man can say he ever had a fit subject for his wit, and did not then raise himself as high above the rest of poets, *Quantum lenta solent inter viburna cupressi.* . . .[2]

" If I would compare him [Jonson] with Shak-

---

[1] *The Shakspere Allusion-Book: A Collection of Allusions to Shakspere from 1591 to 1700*, edited by John Munro (1909), I, 373.

[2] "As cypresses among lowly shrubs." Virgil, *Eclogues*, I, 26.

speare, I must acknowledge him the more correct poet, but Shakspeare the greater wit. Shakspeare was the Homer, or father of our dramatic poets; Jonson was the Virgil, the pattern of elaborate writing; I admire him, but I love Shakspeare."

Nicholas Rowe

A third reprint of the folio was produced in 1663–64 and a fourth in 1685. In 1709, Shakespeare definitely became a classic when Nicholas Rowe, a Restoration dramatist, brought out the first edited collection of his plays. Shakespeare was now sufficiently ancient for the public to need some information about him, and the taste of readers of plays had grown so much more particular that the earlier and cruder methods of printing were no longer suitable. Rowe added to his edition a short biographical introduction and some commendations of the passages which he most admired. He also considerably revised the text, adding place headings and stage directions. Rowe was largely responsible for the form in which Shakespeare's plays are still normally printed today.

Rowe's attitude toward Shakespeare was a genuine wonder that such greatness could have existed in so crude an age:

But certainly the greatness of this author's genius does nowhere so much appear as where he gives his imagination an entire loose and raises his fancy to a flight above mankind and the limits of the visible world. Such are his attempts in *The Tempest, Midsummer-Night's Dream, Macbeth* and *Hamlet.* Of these, *The Tempest,* however it comes to be placed the first by the former publishers of his works, can never have been the first written by him: it seems to me as perfect in its kind, as almost anything we have of his. One may observe, that the Unities are kept here with an exactness uncommon to the liberties of his writing: though that was what, I suppose, he valued himself least upon, since his excellencies were all of another kind. I am very sensible that he does, in this play, depart too much from that likeness to Truth which ought to be observed in these sort of writings; yet he does it so very finely, that one is easily drawn in to have more faith for his sake, than reason does well allow of. His magic has something in it very solemn and very poetical: and that extravagant character of Caliban is mighty well sustained, shows a wonderful invention in the author, who could strike out such a particular wild image, and is certainly one of the finest and most uncommon grotesques that

was ever seen. The observation, which I have been informed three very great men concurred in making upon this part, was extremely just. " That Shakespear had not only found out a new character in his Caliban, but had also devised and adapted a new manner of language for that character." Among the particular beauties of this piece, I think one may be allowed to point out the Tale of Prospero in the First Act; his speech to Ferdinand in the Fourth, upon the breaking up the Masque of Juno and Ceres; and that in the Fifth where he dissolves his charms, and resolves to break his magic rod.

Nevertheless, minor critics were often very condescending toward Shakespeare's lack of knowledge of the rules of construction and propriety, which revealed his ignorance of the essentials of a gentleman's education in the classics. Again and again the greatest critics of the age defended Shakespeare against this charge. Thus Addison, in *The Spectator,* No. 592, wrote:

Who would not rather read one of his plays, where there is not a single rule of the stage observed, than any production of a modern critic, where there is not one of them violated? Shakespear was indeed born with all the seeds of poetry, and may be compared to the stone in Pyrrhus's ring, which, as Pliny tells us, had the figure of Apollo and the Nine Muses in the veins of it, produced by the spontaneous hand of Nature, without any help from art.

In the eighteenth century, enthusiasm for Shakespeare grew rapidly, and he soon outstripped all his rivals. In 1616 Jonson had collected the best of his own plays then written in a folio volume; a second folio, with all Jonson's plays, came out in 1640; other editions appeared in 1692 and 1756. Beaumont and Fletcher's collected plays were printed in 1647, 1679, 1711, and 1778. Of Shakespeare's plays, no less than sixty complete editions, including reprints, appeared between 1709 and 1799.

Alexander Pope

After Rowe, Alexander Pope was the next editor; his edition came out during 1723–25. Pope was a highhanded editor. He believed that much rubbish had been foisted into Shakespeare's plays by the actors and he transferred what he regarded as the worst passages to the foot of the page. His preface, however, was full of enthusiasm and common sense:

> Of all English poets Shakespear must be confessed to be the fairest and fullest subject for criticism, and to afford the most numerous, as well as most conspicuous instances, both of beauties and faults of all sorts.

Pope had no respect for Shakespeare's audience, "generally composed of the meaner sort of people," who could have no knowledge or appreciation of " the model of the ancients," but he would not condemn Shakespeare for ignoring the practice of the ancients.

> To judge therefore of Shakespear by Aristotle's rules, is like trying a man by the laws of one country, who acted under those of another. He writ to the People; and writ at first without patronage from the better sort, and therefore without aims of pleasing them: without assistance or advice from the learned, as without the advantage of education or acquaintance among them: without that knowledge of the best models, the ancients, to inspire him with an emulation of them; in a word, without any views of reputation, and of what poets are pleased to call immortality: some or all of which have encouraged the vanity, or animated the ambition, of other writers.
>
> Yet it must be observed, that when his performances had merited the protection of his Prince, and when the encouragement of the Court had succeeded to that of the Town; the works of his riper years are manifestly raised above those of his former. The dates of his plays sufficiently evidence that his productions improved, in proportion to the respect he had for his auditors. And I make no doubt this observation would be found true in every instance, were but editions extant from which we might learn the exact time when every piece was composed, and whether writ for the Town, or the Court.
>
> Another cause (and no less strong than the former) may be deduced from our author's being a Player, and forming himself first upon the judgments of that body of men whereof he was a member. They have ever had a standard to themselves, upon other principles than those of Aristotle. As they live by the majority, they know no rule but that of pleasing the present humour, and complying with the wit in fashion; a consideration which brings all their judgment to a short point. Players are just such judges of what is right, as tailors are of what is graceful. And in this view it will be but fair to allow, that most of our author's faults are less to be ascribed to his wrong judgment as a Poet, than to his right judgment as a Player.

Yet Pope did not agree with those who despised Shakespeare's supposed want of learning:

> I am inclined to think this opinion proceeded originally from the zeal of the partisans of our author and Ben Jonson; as they endeavoured to exalt the one at the expense of the other. It is ever the nature of Parties to be in extremes; and nothing is so probable, as that because Ben Jonson had much the most learning, it was said on the one hand that Shakespear had none at all; and because Shakespear had much the most wit and fancy, it was retorted on the other, that Jonson wanted both. Because Shakespear borrowed nothing, it was said that Ben Jonson borrowed everything. Because Jonson did not write extempore, he was reproached with being a year about every piece, and because Shakespear wrote with ease and rapidity, they cried, he never once made a blot. Nay the spirit of opposition ran so high, that whatever those of the one side objected to the other, was taken at the rebound, and turned into praises; as injudiciously as their antagonists before had made them objections.

Samuel Johnson

Dr. Johnson's edition of Shakespeare's plays appeared in 1765. His Preface is one of the most valuable general estimates of Shakespeare in the eighteenth century. As a critic Johnson regarded himself as a judge of the Supreme Court. His pronouncements were delivered with weight and solemnity, after impartial consideration of the evidence on both sides, but they were always based on common sense and a strong feeling of morality. Johnson's admiration for Shakespeare was immense. In his view, Shakespeare's supreme merit was that he

> . . . above all writers, at least above all modern writers, is the poet of nature; the poet that holds up to his readers a faithful mirror of manners and of life. His characters are not modified by the customs of particular places, unpracticed by the rest of the world; by the peculiarities of studies or professions, which can operate but upon small numbers; or by the accidents of transient fashions or temporary opinions: they are the genuine progeny of common humanity, such as the world will always supply, and observation will always find. His persons act and speak by the influence of those general passions and principles by which all minds are agitated, and the whole system of life is continued in motion. In the writings of other poets a character is too often an individual; in those of Shakespeare it is commonly a species.

Nevertheless, Shakespeare was far from perfect and, having allowed himself to reveal unusual enthusiasm, Johnson felt that he was bound also to censure:

In his comic scenes, he is seldom very successful, when he engages his characters in reciprocations of smartness and contests of sarcasm; their jests are commonly gross, and their pleasantry licentious; neither his gentlemen nor his ladies have much delicacy, nor are sufficiently distinguished from his clowns by any appearance of refined manners. Whether he represented the real conversation of his time is not easy to determine; the reign of Elizabeth is commonly supposed to have been a time of stateliness, formality and reserve, yet perhaps the relaxations of that severity were not very elegant. There must, however, have been always some modes of gaiety preferable to others, and a writer ought to choose the best.

In tragedy his performance seems constantly to be worse, as his labour is more. The effusions of passion which exigence forces out are for the most part striking and energetic; but whenever he solicits his invention, or strains his faculties, the offspring of his throes is tumour, meanness, tediousness, and obscurity.

In narration he affects a disproportionate pomp of diction and a wearisome train of circumlocution, and tells the incident imperfectly in many words, which might have been more plainly delivered in few. Narration in dramatic poetry is naturally tedious, as it is unanimated and inactive, and obstructs the progress of the action; it should therefore always be rapid, and enlivened by frequent interruption. Shakespeare found it an encumbrance, and instead of lightening it by brevity, endeavoured to recommend it by dignity and splendour.

His declamations or set speeches are commonly cold and weak, for his power was the power of nature; when he endeavoured, like other tragic writers, to catch opportunities of amplification, and instead of inquiring what the occasion demanded, to show how much his stores of knowledge could supply, he seldom escapes without the pity or resentment of his reader.

It is always as well to turn to Johnson as a corrective to too much modern enthusiasm, even when, as so often happened, his views were warped by prejudice. Johnson judged Shakespeare by his own standards of universal morality; he would never have admitted, as explanation or excuse, that Shakespeare was bound by the conventions or restrictions of his stage or his generation.

Maurice Morgann

With Maurice Morgann, interest shifted from Shakespeare to his creations. Morgann's *Essay on the Dramatic Character of Sir John Falstaff* (1777) is the first important piece of romantic criticism. Morgann set out to prove that Falstaff was not a constitutional coward, and so was led to a full analysis of his character as a real man. Logically and morally Falstaff is reprehensible, if we take his actions one by one; but, Morgann argues, this is not the impression which Falstaff makes on us and

. . . in dramatic composition the impression is the fact; and the writer, who, meaning to impress one thing, has impressed another, is unworthy of observation.

It is a very unpleasant thing to have, in the first setting out, so many and so strong prejudices to contend with. All that one can do in such case, is, to pray the reader to have a little patience in the commencement; and to reserve his censure, if it must pass, for the conclusion. Under his gracious allowance, therefore, I presume to declare it, as my opinion, that cowardice *is not* the *impression,* which the *whole* character of Falstaff is calculated to make on the minds of an unprejudiced audience; though there be, I confess, a great deal of something in the *composition* likely enough to puzzle, and consequently to mislead the understanding. — The reader will perceive that I distinguish between *mental impressions* and the *understanding.* — I wish to avoid everything that looks like subtlety and refinement; but this is a distinction, which we all comprehend. — There are none of us unconscious of certain feelings or sensations of mind, which do not seem to have passed through the understanding; the effects, I suppose, of some secret influences from without, acting upon a certain mental sense, and producing feelings and passions in just correspondence to the force and variety of those influences on the one hand, and to the quickness of our sensibility on the other. Be the cause, however, what it may, the fact is undoubtedly so; which is all I am concerned in. And it is equally a fact, which every man's experience may avouch, that the understanding and those feelings are frequently at variance. The latter often arise from the most minute circumstances, and frequently from such as the understanding cannot estimate, or even recognize; whereas the understanding delights in abstraction, and in general propositions; which, however true considered as such, are very seldom, I had like to have said *never,* perfectly applicable to any particular case. And hence, among other causes, it is, that we often condemn or applaud characters and actions on the credit of some logical process, while our hearts revolt, and would fain lead us to a very different conclusion. . . .

We all like *Old Jack;* yet, by some strange perverse fate, we all abuse him, and deny him the possession of any one single good or respectable quality. There is something extraordinary in this: It must be a strange art in Shakespeare which can draw our liking and good will towards so offensive an object. He has wit, it will be said; cheerfulness and humour of the most characteristic and captivating sort. And is this enough? Is the humour and gaiety of vice so very captivating? Is the wit, characteristic of baseness and every ill quality capable of attaching the heart and winning the affections? Or does not the apparency of such humor, and the flashes of such wit, by more strongly disclosing the deformity of character, but the more effectually excite our hatred and contempt of the man? And yet this is not our *feeling* of Falstaff's character. When he has ceased to amuse us, we find no emotions of disgust; we can scarcely forgive the ingratitude of the Prince in the new-born virtue of the King, and we curse the severity of that poetic justice which consigns our old, good-natured, delightful companion to the custody of the *warden,* and the dishonours of the Fleet.

Charles Lamb

After Morgann, Shakespeare's characters came almost to have an independent life and to be discussed as human beings of whom the play presents some records from which other facts may be deduced. This was Charles Lamb's feeling. Indeed, some of Shakespeare's characters were to him so real that he resented the attempts of actors to impersonate them. He argued his objections in a famous essay *On the Tragedies of Shakspeare, Considered with Reference to Their Fitness for Stage Representation* (1811):

It may seem a paradox but I cannot help being of opinion that the plays of Shakspeare are less calculated for performance on a stage, than those of almost any other dramatist whatever. Their distinguishing excellence is a reason that they should be so. There is so much in them, which comes not under the province of acting, with which eye, and tone, and gesture, have nothing to do. . . .

So to see Lear acted — to see an old man tottering about the stage with a walking-stick, turned out of doors by his daughters in a rainy night, has nothing in it but what is painful and disgusting. We want to take him into shelter and relieve him. That is all the feeling which the acting of Lear ever produced in me. But the Lear of Shakspeare cannot be acted. The contemptible machinery by which they mimic the storm which he goes out in, is not more inadequate to represent the horrors of the real elements, than any actor can be to represent Lear: they might more easily propose to personate the Satan of Milton upon a stage, or one of Michael Angelo's terrible figures. The greatness of Lear is not in corporal dimension, but in intellectual: the explosions of his passion are terrible as a volcano: they are storms turning up and disclosing to the bottom that sea, his mind, with all its vast riches. It is his mind which is laid bare. This case of flesh and blood seems too insignificant to be thought on; even as he himself neglects it. On the stage we see nothing but corporal infirmities and weakness, the impotence of rage; while we read it, we see not Lear, but we are Lear — we are in his mind, we are sustained by a grandeur which baffles the malice of daughters and storms; in the aberrations of his reason, we discover a mighty irregular power of reasoning, immethodized from the ordinary purposes of life, but exerting its powers, as the wind blows where it listeth, at will upon the corruptions and abuses of mankind. What have looks, or tones, to do with that sublime identification of his age with that of the *heavens themselves,* when in his reproaches to them for conniving at the injustice of his children, he reminds them that " they themselves are old." What gesture shall be appropriate to this? What has the voice or the eye to do with such things? But the play is beyond all art, as the tamperings with it show: it is too hard and stony; it must have love-scenes, and a happy ending. It is not enough that Cordelia is a daughter, she must shine as a lover too. Tate has put his hook in the nostrils of this Leviathan,[3] for Garrick and his followers, the showmen of the scene, to draw the mighty beast about more easily. A happy ending! — as if the living martyrdom that Lear had gone through — the flaying of his feelings alive, did not make a fair dismissal from the stage of life the only decorous thing for him. If he is to live and be happy after, if he could sustain this world's burden after, why all this pudder and preparation — why torment us with all this unnecessary sympathy? As if the childish pleasure of getting his gilt robes and sceptre again could tempt him to act over again his misused station — as if at his years, and with his experience, anything was left but to die.

---

[3] Nahum Tate in 1681 rewrote Shakespeare's *Lear,* keeping about half of Shakespeare's lines and scenes. In this version Edgar falls in love with Cordelia, rescues her from robbers, and ultimately saves her life. The play ends happily with Lear, Gloucester, and Kent retiring to a peaceful old age while Edgar and Cordelia succeed to the throne. Tate's version was acted throughout the eighteenth century. Lamb, it may be noted, never had the opportunity of seeing Shakespeare's *Lear* on the stage.

Lear is essentially impossible to be represented on a stage.

Samuel Taylor Coleridge

To Samuel Taylor Coleridge, Shakespeare was not merely a great dramatist and poet but a divine genius, whose faults were not faults but inspired virtues. In a lecture delivered in 1818, he said:

Let me now proceed to destroy, as far as may be in my power, the popular notion that he was a great dramatist by mere instinct, that he grew immortal in his own despite, and sank below men of second or third-rate power, when he attempted aught beside the drama — even as bees construct their cells and manufacture their honey to admirable perfection; but would in vain attempt to build a nest. Now this mode of reconciling a compelled sense of inferiority with a feeling of pride, began in a few pedants, who having read that Sophocles was the great model of tragedy, and Aristotle the infallible dictator of its rules, and finding that the *Lear, Hamlet, Othello* and other master-pieces were neither in imitation of Sophocles, nor in obedience to Aristotle — and not having (with one or two exceptions) the courage to affirm, that the delight which their country received from generation to generation, in defiance of the alterations of circumstances and habits, was wholly groundless, — took upon them, as a happy medium and refuge, to talk of Shakespeare as a sort of beautiful *lusus naturæ,*[4] a delightful monster — wild, indeed, and without taste or judgment, but like the inspired idiots so much venerated in the East, uttering, amid the strangest follies, the sublimest truths. In nine places out of ten in which I find his awful name mentioned, it is with some epithet of " wild," " irregular," " pure child of nature," &c.

Coleridge indeed demanded almost blind worship from Shakespeare's readers:

Assuredly that criticism of Shakspeare will alone be genial which is reverential. The Englishman, who without reverence, a proud and affectionate reverence, can utter the name of William Shakspeare, stands disqualified for the office of critic. He wants one at least of the very senses, the language of which he is to employ, and will discourse at best. but as a blind man, while the whole harmonious creation of light and shade with all its subtle interchange of deepening and dissolving colours rises in silence to the silent *fiat* of the uprising Apollo. However inferior in ability I may be to

[4] freak.

some who have followed me, I own I am proud that I was the first in time who publicly demonstrated to the full extent of the position, that the supposed irregularity and extravagances of Shakspeare were the mere dreams of a pedantry that arraigned the eagle because it had not the dimensions of the swan. In all the successive courses of lectures delivered by me, since my first attempt at the Royal Institution, it has been, and it still remains, my object, to prove that in all points from the most important to the most minute, the judgment of Shakspeare is commensurate with his genius — nay. that his genius reveals itself in his judgment, as in its most exalted form.

Coleridge's pronouncements had a profound influence on Shakespearean critics for over a century, and none were more widely quoted than his remarks on *Hamlet:*

In Hamlet he seems to have wished to exemplify the moral necessity of a due balance between our attention to the objects of our senses, and our meditation on the workings of our minds — an *equilibrium* between the real and the imaginary worlds. In Hamlet this balance is disturbed: his thoughts, and the images of his fancy, are far more vivid than his actual perceptions, and his very perceptions, instantly passing through the *medium* of his contemplations, acquire, as they pass, a form and a colour not naturally their own. Hence we see a great, an almost enormous, intellectual activity, and a proportionate aversion to real action, consequent upon it, with all its symptoms and accompanying qualities. This character Shakspeare places in circumstances, under which it is obliged to act on the spur of the moment: — Hamlet is brave and careless of death; but he vacillates from sensibility and procrastinates from thought, and loses the power of action in the energy of resolve. Thus it is that this tragedy presents a direct contrast to that of Macbeth; the one proceeds with the utmost slowness, the other with a crowded and breathless rapidity.

The effect of this overbalance of the imaginative power is beautifully illustrated in the everlasting broodings and superfluous activities of Hamlet's mind, which, unseated from its healthy relation, is constantly occupied with the world within, and abstracted from the world without — giving substance to shadows, and throwing a mist over all commonplace actualities. It is the nature of thought to be indefinite — definiteness belongs to external imagery alone. Hence it is that the sense of sublimity arises, not from the sight of an outward object, but from the beholder's reflection upon it; — not from the sensuous impression, but from the imaginative reflex. Few have seen a celebrated waterfall without feeling something akin to disappointment: it is only subsequently that the image comes back full into the mind, and brings with it a train of grand or beautiful associations. Hamlet feels this; his senses are in a state of trance, and he looks upon external things as hieroglyphics. His soliloquy —

" O! that this too too solid flesh would melt, &c."

springs from that craving after the indefinite — for that which is not — which most easily besets men of genius; and the self-delusion common to this temper of mind is finely exemplified in the character which Hamlet gives of himself: —

> " — It cannot be
> But I am pigeon-livered, and lack gall
> To make oppression bitter."

He mistakes the seeing his chains for the breaking them, delays action till action is of no use, and dies the victim of mere circumstance and accident.

Some years later, in his *Table Talk*, Coleridge made an illuminating comment:

Hamlet's character is the prevalence of the abstracting and generalizing habit over the practical. He does not want courage, skill, will, or opportunity; but every incident sets him thinking; and it is curious, and, at the same time strictly natural, that Hamlet, who all the play seems reason itself, should be impelled, at last, by mere accident to effect his object. I have a smack of Hamlet myself, if I may say so.

William Hazlitt

There was much excellent Shakespearean criticism in the first quarter of the nineteenth century. Two writers are particularly important, William Hazlitt and Thomas De Quincey. Hazlitt's *Characters of Shakespear's Plays* (1817) was, in the words of the critic Jeffrey, "written less to tell the reader what Mr. H. *knows* about Shakespeare or his writings, than to explain to them what he *feels* about them — and *why* he feels so — and thinks that all who profess to love poetry should feel so likewise."

Hazlitt's book is full of gusto and is always worth reading. Of Othello he wrote:

It has been said that tragedy purifies the affections by terror and pity. That is, substitutes imaginary sympathy for mere selfishness. It gives us a high and permanent interest, beyond ourselves, in humanity as such. It raises the great, the remote, and the possible to an equality with the real, the little and the near. It makes man a partaker with his kind. It subdues and softens the stubbornness of his will. It teaches him that there are and have been others like himself, by showing him as in a glass what they have felt, thought, and done. It opens the chambers of the human heart. It leaves nothing indifferent to us that can affect our common nature. It excites our sensibility by exhibiting the passions wound up to the utmost pitch by the power of imagination or the temptation of circumstances; and corrects their fatal excesses in ourselves by pointing to the greater extent of sufferings and of crimes to which they have led others. Tragedy creates a balance of the affections. It makes us thoughtful spectators in the lists of life. It is the refiner of the species; a discipline of humanity. The habitual study of poetry and works of imagination is one chief part of a well-grounded education. A taste for liberal art is necessary to complete the character of a gentleman. Science alone is hard and mechanical. It exercises the understanding upon things out of ourselves, while it leaves the affections unemployed, or engrossed with our own immediate, narrow interest. — *Othello* furnishes an illustration of these remarks. It excites our sympathy in an extraordinary degree. The moral it conveys has a closer application to the concerns of human life than that of almost any other of Shakespear's plays. " It comes directly home to the bosoms and business of men." The pathos in *Lear* is indeed more dreadful and overpowering; but it is less natural, and less of every day's occurrence. We have not the same degree of sympathy with the passions described in *Macbeth*. The interest in *Hamlet* is more remote and reflex. That of *Othello* is at once equally profound and affecting. . . .

The character of Iago is one of the supererogations of Shakespear's genius. Some persons, more nice than wise, have thought this whole character unnatural because his villainy is *without a sufficient motive*. Shakespear, who was as good a philosopher as he was a poet, thought otherwise. He knew that the love of power, which is another name for the love of mischief, is natural to man. He would know this as well or better than if it had been demonstrated to him by a logical diagram, merely from seeing children paddle in the dirt or kill flies for sport. Iago in fact belongs to a class of character, common to Shakespear and at the same time peculiar to him; whose heads are as acute and active as their hearts are hard and callous. Iago is to be sure an extreme instance of the kind; that is to say, of diseased intellectual activity, with the most perfect indifference to moral good or evil, or rather with a decided preference of the latter, because it falls more readily in with his favourite propensity, gives greater zest to his thoughts and scope to his actions.

He is quite or nearly as indifferent to his own fate as to that of others; he runs all risks for a trifling and doubtful advantage; and is himself the dupe and victim of his ruling passion — an insatiable craving after action of the most difficult and dangerous kind. " Our ancient " is a philosopher, who fancies that a lie that kills has more point in it than an alliteration or an antithesis; who thinks a fatal experiment on the peace of a family a better thing than watching the palpitations in the heart of a flea in a microscope; who plots the ruin of his friends as an exercise for his ingenuity, and stabs men in the dark to prevent *ennui*. His gaiety, such as it is, arises from the success of his treachery; his ease from the torture he has inflicted on others. He is an amateur of tragedy in real life; and instead of employing his invention on imaginary characters, or long-forgotten incidents, he takes the bolder and more desperate course of getting up his plot at home, casts the principal parts among his nearest friends and connections, and rehearses it in downright earnest, with steady nerves and unabated resolution.

Thomas De Quincey

De Quincey's appreciation of Shakespeare was subtle and penetrating, and in his essay " On the Knocking at the Gate in Macbeth " (1823) he chose one moment in one play to illustrate Shakespeare's genius:

Or, if the reader has ever been present in a vast metropolis, on the day when some great national idol was carried in funeral pomp to his grave, and chancing to walk near the course through which it passed, has felt powerfully in the silence and desertion of the streets, and in the stagnation of ordinary business, the deep interest which at that moment was possessing the heart of man — if all at once he should hear the death-like stillness broken up by the sound of wheels rattling away from the scene, and making known that the transitory vision was dissolved, he will be aware that at no moment was his sense of the complete suspension and pause in ordinary human concerns so full and affecting, as at that moment when the suspension ceases, and the goings-on of human life are suddenly resumed. All action in any direction is best expounded, measured, and made apprehensible, by reaction. Now apply this to the case in *Macbeth*. Here, as I have said, the retiring of the human heart, and the entrance of the fiendish heart was to be expressed and made sensible. Another world has stept in; and the murderers are taken out of the region of human things, human purposes, human desires. They are transfigured: Lady Macbeth is " unsexed ": Macbeth has forgot that he was born of woman; both are conformed to the image of devils; and the world of devils is suddenly revealed. But how shall this be conveyed and made palpable? In order that a new world may step in, this world must for a time disappear. The murderers, and the murder must be insulated — cut off by an immeasurable gulf from the ordinary tide and succession of human affairs — locked up and sequestered in some deep recess; we must be made sensible that the world of ordinary life is suddenly arrested — laid asleep — tranced — racked into a dread armistice; time must be annihilated; relation to things without abolished; and all must pass self-withdrawn into a deep syncope and suspension of earthly passion. Hence it is, that when the deed is done, when the work of darkness is perfect, then the world of darkness passes away like a pageantry in the clouds: the knocking at the gate is heard; and it makes known audibly that the reaction has commenced; the human has made its reflux upon the fiendish; the pulses of life are beginning to beat again; and the re-establishment of the goings-on of the world in which we live, first makes us profoundly sensible of the awful parenthesis that had suspended them.

O mighty poet! Thy works are not as those of other men, simply and merely great works of art; but are also like the phenomena of nature, like the sun and the sea, the stars and the flowers; like frost and snow, rain and dew, hail-storm and thunder, which are to be studied with entire submission of our own faculties, and in the perfect faith that in them there can be no too much or too little, nothing useless or inert — but that, the farther we press in our discoveries, the more we shall see proofs of design and self-supporting arrangement where the careless eye had seen nothing but accident!

Thomas Carlyle

With De Quincey, as with Coleridge, Shakespeare was elevated into a god; he was still at least a demigod when Carlyle wrote the chapter on " The Hero as Poet " in *Heroes and Hero Worship* (1845):

Whoever looks intelligently at this Shakspeare may recognize that he too was a *prophet,* in his way; of an insight analogous to the Prophetic, though he took it up in another strain. Nature seemed to this man also divine; *un*speakable, deep as Tophet, high as Heaven: " We are such stuff as Dreams are made of! " That scroll in Westminster Abbey, which few read with understanding, is of the depth of any Seer. But the man sang; did not preach except musically. We called Dante the melodious Priest of Middle-Age Catholicism. May we not call Shakspeare the still more melodious Priest of a *true* Catholicism, the "Universal Church" of the Future and of all times? No narrow superstition, harsh asceticism, intolerance, fanatical fierceness or perversion: a Revelation, so far as it goes, that such a thousandfold hidden beauty and divineness dwells in all Nature; which let all men worship as they can.

In "The Hero as Poet" Carlyle drew a romantic picture of the Warwickshire peasant boy for which there was no real foundation in the facts known to scholars. Indeed in sane discussions of a writer long dead, critics and scholars must depend on each other. Until the scholar has established the facts of date and place, the critic is not equipped to discuss the life, the personality, or the development of an author. In Johnson's day, small attempt had been made to discover further facts about Shakespeare, and less to study his environment. Rowe had added a brief biography, but little had been discovered since Rowe's time. But by the end of the eighteenth century Shakespearean scholarship was beginning.

Beginnings of Scholarship

Of the early Shakespearean scholars the greatest was Edmund Malone, a zealous antiquarian who realized that to study Shakespeare a knowledge of his environment was needed. Malone gathered all the contemporary material that he could find and left a large collection of early plays, books, and pamphlets to the Bodleian Library at the University of Oxford. Malone also wrote the first good account of the Elizabethan stage.

In the early years of the nineteenth century, as part of the reaction against the tastes of the eighteenth, there was a considerable revival of interest in the literature of the pre-Restoration period and especially in its drama, but there was as yet no comprehensive collection for study. A studious reader could find, without much difficulty, old editions of the plays of Ben Jonson or of Beaumont and Fletcher or of Massinger, and some of the old plays were collected in Dodsley's *Old Plays* (1744). But there was no complete edition of Ford until 1811, of Marlowe until 1826, of Peele until 1828-39; Webster was first

collected in 1830, Greene in 1831, Middleton in 1840, Heywood in 1842-51, and Dekker so late as 1873.

In 1841 the first Shakespeare Society was founded. The chief interest of its members was to collect and edit records and contemporary books which illustrated Shakespeare's times. This group included John Payne Collier, one of the greatest of all Shakespearean scholars. Payne Collier was a tireless searcher in records, few of which had as yet been catalogued or calendared. Unfortunately his discoveries did not keep pace with his enthusiasm, and when he could not find documents to prove his theories he took to forging them. When his forgeries were exposed in 1853, Shakespearean scholarship received a great setback.

A second or New Shakespere Society was founded in 1873. Its leader was F. J. Furnivall, a medieval scholar, who set his followers to work on the collective project of establishing the order of the writing of Shakespeare's plays by observing all allusions to or within the plays, and by examining statistically the peculiarities of Shakespeare's style. The results, with some modifications, have been generally accepted by scholars. Thus in 1875, when Edward Dowden came to write *Shakspere: A Critical Study of His Mind and Art,* he began with a clear idea of the order in which Shakespeare's plays were written. This was something new in Shakespearean criticism.

Edward Dowden

Dowden was responsible for the conception that Shakespeare's "art life" could be divided into four periods: the years of experiment; the period when "he was gaining a sure grasp of the positive facts of life," shown at first in the *Henry IV* plays and later in *Much Ado about Nothing, As You Like It,* and *Twelfth Night;* the period of the great tragedies; and the last, or tranquil, period when Shakespeare, after some years of turmoil, reached serenity. Dowden thus projected Shakespeare's mental development into his plays, implying that they were a reflection of his own emotional development. The book is a good specimen of Victorian criticism at its best, though Dowden tends to see Shakespeare's artistic development almost as a deliberate and conscious process, uninfluenced by external or material causes. Thus, of *As You Like It* he wrote:

Shakspere, when he wrote this idyllic play was himself in his Forest of Arden. He had ended one great ambition — the historical plays — and not yet commenced his tragedies. It was a resting-place. He sends his imagination into the woods to find repose. Instead of the courts and camps of England, and the embattled plains of France, here was this woodland scene, where the palm-tree, the lioness, and the serpent are to be found; possessed of a flora and fauna that flourish in spite of physical geographers. There is an open-air feeling throughout the play. The dialogue, as has been observed, catches freedom and freshness from the atmosphere. Never is the scene within-doors, except when something discordant is introduced to heighten as it were the harmony. After the trumpet-tones of Henry V comes the sweet pastoral strain, so bright, so tender. Must it not be all in keeping? Shakspere was not trying to control his melancholy. When he needed to do that, Shakspere confronted his melancholy very passionately, and looked it full in the face. Here he needed refreshment, a sunlight tempered by forest-boughs, a breeze upon his forehead, a stream murmuring in his ears.

A. C. Bradley

The last and greatest example of Victorian criticism was A. C. Bradley's *Shakespearean Tragedy* (1904), in which he discusses *Hamlet, Othello, King Lear,* and *Macbeth.* No single volume of criticism has achieved a greater reputation. Bradley's intention was to examine the plays from a single point of view:

Our one object will be what, again in a restricted sense, may be called dramatic appreciation; to increase our understanding and enjoyment of these works as dramas; to learn to apprehend the action and some of the personages of each with a somewhat greater truth and intensity, so that they may assume in our imaginations a shape a little less unlike the shape they wore in the imagination of their creator.

He began with an essay on "The Substance of Shakespearean Tragedy," in which he endeavored to answer the question: "What is Shakespearean tragedy?" He concluded:

Thus we are left at last with an idea showing two sides or aspects which we can neither separate nor reconcile. The whole or order against which the individual part shows itself powerless seems to be animated by a passion for perfection: we cannot otherwise explain its behaviour towards evil. Yet it appears to engender this evil within itself, and in its effort to overcome and expel it it is agonised with pain, and driven to mutilate its own substance and to lose not only evil but priceless good. That this idea, though very different from the idea of a blank fate, is no solution of the riddle of life is obvious; but why should we expect it to be such a solution? Shakespeare was not attempting to justify the ways of God to men, or to show the universe as a Divine Comedy. He was writing tragedy, and tragedy would not be tragedy if it were not a painful mystery. Nor can he be said even to point distinctly, like some writers of tragedy, in any direction where a solution might lie. We find a few references to gods or God, to the influence of the stars, to another life: some of them certainly, all of them perhaps, merely dramatic — appropriate to the person from whose lips they fall. A ghost comes from Purgatory to impart a secret out of the reach of its hearer — who presently meditates on the question whether the sleep of death is dreamless. Accidents once or twice remind us strangely of the words, " There's a divinity that shapes our ends." More important are other impressions. Sometimes from the very furnace of affliction a conviction seems borne to us that somehow, if we could see it, this agony counts as nothing against the heroism and love which appear in it and thrill our hearts. Sometimes we are driven to cry out that these mighty or heavenly spirits who perish are too great for the little space in which they move, and that they vanish not into nothingness but into freedom. Sometimes from these sources and from others comes a presentiment, formless but haunting and even profound, that all the fury of conflict, with its waste and woe, is less than half the truth, even an illusion, " such stuff as dreams are made on." But these faint and scattered intimations that the tragic world, being but a fragment of a whole beyond our vision, must needs be a contradiction and no ultimate truth, avail nothing to interpret the mystery. We remain confronted with the inexplicable fact, or the no less inexplicable appearance, of a world travailing for perfection, but bringing to birth, together with glorious good, an evil which it is able to overcome only by self-torture and self-waste. And this fact or appearance is tragedy.

From this beginning Bradley proceeded to analyze the four tragedies as records of what passed in the minds of Shakespeare and of the characters. The analysis is long, penetrating, and suggestive. The objection, however, to this kind of criticism is that it ignores the practical facts of Elizabethan stage drama and attributes to

Shakespeare a minute care which he probably never took. Bradley, for instance, spent three and a half pages in a discussion of the question: "Where was Hamlet at the time of his father's death?"—a matter which Shakespeare ignored and which no one stops to consider when the play is being acted. However, *Shakespearean Tragedy* is still probably the most widely read of all single works of Shakespearean criticism.

9. Shakespearean Scholarship and Criticism 1900–1950

In the nineteenth century the most important contributions to Shakespearean study and criticism were made by English and German scholars and critics; but in the twentieth century the results of American scholarship have been most impressive. Before 1900 scholars were confined in their researches mainly to the great English collections of books and original documents in the British Museum and the Public Record Office in London and the Bodleian Library in Oxford. Today the Huntington Library in California and the Folger Shakespeare Library in Washington, D.C., rival the greatest English libraries. Moreover, generous benefactions and grants-in-aid of research have enabled American scholars to study wherever their interests lead, while the modern invention of microfilm enables a scholar to have inexpensive photographic reproductions of any book or manuscript available in his university library or even his own study.

In the last fifty years there has been an ever-increasing mass of Shakespearean studies of every kind; and a bibliography of any one year's work will record well over a hundred books, articles, and notes on a wide variety of topics. So vast indeed is the output that no single scholar can now hope to keep abreast of everything that is written about Shakespeare. Nevertheless, there are fashions in Shakespearean interest which follow the general changes in taste in other artistic matters. Four branches of study have been especially popular during the past fifty years. These are the exact study of the text; the Elizabethan theater; the background—historical and intellectual; and the minute analysis of Shakespeare's poetic and dramatic technique. Increased knowledge of all four has considerably deepened the understanding of Shakespeare's plays.

The Exact Study of the Text

When Bradley's *Shakespearean Tragedy* first appeared in 1904, it produced among students a feeling that the last word in Shakespearean criticism had been said, at least about the four great tragedies, and that the correct method of appreciating Shakespeare had been finally established. But an indirect reaction against this kind of approach had already begun. In the same year that *Shakespearean Tragedy* was published, there appeared also the first volumes of two monumental works of scholarship: W. W. Greg's edition of Henslowe's *Diary* and *Papers* (1904–08) and R. B. McKerrow's edition of the works of Thomas Nashe (1904–10). Henslowe's *Diary* (see p. 65a) is one of the most exciting books that a student can encounter; it takes him, as it were, into the manager's office of an Elizabethan playhouse and shows him a host of the human details that lie behind drama. McKerrow's *Nashe* was one of the first, and certainly one of the best, specimens of an elaborate study of an author which included a minute study of the text. Nashe, moreover, was the most popular writer of his generation, and his books abound in comments on current affairs and interests, all of which were illuminated by McKerrow's sane erudition. This edition is a model for scholars.

These two works, with others, turned scholars back to the study of Shakespeare's environment, and this led to the realization that it was foolish for the critic to theorize about *Hamlet* or *Macbeth* until he was first sure that he understood what the plays meant to Shakespeare and to the original audiences.

Hitherto most editions of Elizabethan plays had been "literary"; that is, the text was modernized in spelling, punctuation, act division, and stage direction. Such texts, though more readable for the common reader, were no longer adequate for scholarly purposes, and in 1907 the Malone Society (with Greg as General Editor) began to publish Elizabethan stage documents and exact reprints of Elizabethan plays.

The interest in the early texts of Shakespeare's plays spread. In 1909 A. W. Pollard published a study of *Shakespeare Folios and Quartos,* and in 1919, in *Shakespeare's Fight with the Pirates,* Pollard set out to demonstrate that some of the early quartos were probably set up by the printer direct from Shakespeare's own manuscripts and reproduced many of their peculiarities. As a result the early editions of the plays — quartos and first folio — became of supreme interest to scholars, and, thanks to the publication of photographic facsimiles of the first folio in 1904 and again in 1910, it was now possible to study the problems of the text at leisure and without a journey to one of the great libraries. Interest was further stimulated by the suggestion that a large fragment of Shakespeare's own handwriting still survived in a play manuscript. Edward Maunde Thompson, an expert paleographer, in writing his chapter on "Shakespeare's Handwriting" for *Shakespeare's England* (1916), re-examined in the British Museum the manuscript of an Elizabethan play called *The Booke of Sir Thomas More.* The manuscript is in six different handwritings, and it includes an addition of three and a half pages — a crowd scene in which More pacifies London rioters. Part of the scene reads as follows:

all	Shrieue moor moor more Shreue moore
moor	even by the rule yo^u haue among yor sealues
	comand still audience
all	Surrey Sury
Lincolne betts	peace peace scilens peace
moor	Yo^u that haue voyce and Credyt w^t the nvmber
	Comaund them to a stilnes
Lincolne	a plaigue on them they will not hold their peace the deule
	Cannot rule them
Moor	Then what a rough and ryotous charge haue yo^u
	to Leade those that the deule Cannot rule
	good masters heare me speake
Doll	I byth mas will we moor thart a good howskeeper and I
	thanck thy good worship for my Brother Arthur watchins
all	peace peace
moor	look what yo^u do offend yo^u Cry vppon
	that is the peace, not of yo^u heare present
	had there such fellowes, lyvd when yo^u wer babes
	that coold haue topt the peace as nowe yo^u woold
	the peace wherin yo^u haue till nowe growne vp
	had bin tane from yo^u, and the bloody tymes
	coold not haue brought yo^u to the state of men
	alas poor things what is yt yo^u haue gott
	although we graunt yo^u geat the thing yo^u seeke
Bett	marry the removing of the straingers wch cannot choose but
	much advauntage the poor handycraftes of the Cytty
moor	graunt them remoued and graunt that this yor noyce
	hath Chidd downe all the matie of Ingland
	ymagin that yo^u see the wretched straingers
	their babyes at their backs, and their poor lugage
	plodding tooth ports and costs for transportacion
	and that yo^u sitt as kings in your desyres
	aucthoryty quyte sylenct by yor braule
	and yo^u in ruff of yor opynions clothd

what had yoᵘ gott, I'le tell yoᵘ, yoᵘ had taught
how insolenc and strong hand shoold prevayle
how ordere shoold be quelld, and by this patterne
not on of yoᵘ shoold lyve an aged man
for other ruffians as their fancies wrought
with sealf same hand sealf reasons and sealf right
woold shark on yoᵘ and men lyke ravenous fishes
woold feed on on another

Doll before god thats as trewe as the gospell
Lincolne nay this a sound fellowe I tell yoᵘ lets mark him
moor Let me sett vp before yoʳ thoughts good freinds
on supposytion which if yoᵘ will marke
yoᵘ shall perceaue howe horrible a shape
yoʳ ynnovation beres, first tis a sinn
which oft thappostle did forwarne vs of vrging obedienc to aucthoryty
and twere no error yf I told yoᵘ all yoᵘ wer in armes gainst god
all marry god forbid that

Maunde Thompson concluded that the handwriting of these passages was Shakespeare's. In 1923 the case was presented in *Shakespeare's Hand in the Play of "Sir Thomas More"* by Greg, Pollard, Dover Wilson, Maunde Thompson, and R. W. Chambers. Each scholar approached the problem from a different angle, and though none of the separate studies was in itself conclusive, the whole argument was impressive. The case was hotly argued for years, and today the general conclusion is that, though not wholly proved, the claim for Shakespeare's handwriting is highly probable. It follows that if we have indeed a large fragment of Shakespeare's handwriting, we can often see how and why misprints in the quartos and folio arose. Certain letters in the manuscript are badly formed. In Elizabethan script *d* and *e* are similar and differ only in size; the writer of the three pages tended to make his *d*'s and *e*'s look alike. The letters *i* (used also for *j*), *n, u* (used also for *v*), *m,* and *w,* as written in the manuscript, can also easily be misread. Thus the word *find* can be misread as *fine* or *fiue* (*five*). Such misreadings are fairly common in the quartos and the folio. Also, some of the more unusual spellings in the three pages occur in the quartos. Editors of Shakespearean texts, when confronted with corrupt passages or obvious misprints, should therefore consider possible misreadings of the manuscript before proposing emendations.

One result of these textual studies was the publication of a new edition of Shakespeare's plays — the *New Shakespeare* — edited by Dover Wilson (and — for the comedies — A. T. Quiller-Couch), which was intended to give a text of the plays edited along new lines. The principles which the textual editor proposed to follow were laid down in the first volume — *The Tempest* — which appeared in 1920. Though always interesting and stimulating, the various theories that have been put forward by Dover Wilson to account for the peculiarities of the text of each of the plays are sometimes felt to be more romantic than convincing. Other scholars have published detailed but less ingenious studies of individual texts, such as Greg's edition of the bad quarto of *The Merry Wives of Windsor* (1910), Peter Alexander's *Shakespeare's Henry VI and Richard III* (1929), G. I. Duthie's *The 'Bad' Quarto of Hamlet* (1941) and his critical edition of *King Lear* (1949), and H. R. Hoppe's *The Bad Quarto of Romeo and Juliet* (1948).

The principles which should guide modern scholars in editing Elizabethan texts were discussed in McKerrow's *An Introduction to Bibliography for Literary Students* (1927) and *Prolegomena to the Oxford Shakespeare* (1939), and Greg's *The Editorial Problem in Shakespeare* (1942).

The Elizabethan Stage

In this branch of Shakespearean study, the publication of Henslowe's *Diary* and *Papers* (1904–08) was of the greatest importance, for it provided the student with a mass of original material. In 1910 C. W. Wallace, working in the Public Record Office in London, unearthed a number of records of the lawsuits connected with the Theater (see p. 36a) which James Burbage had built in 1576. By 1917 enough information was available for Joseph Quincy Adams to write a satisfactory account of *Shakespearean Playhouses*. Six years later E. K. Chambers in the four massive volumes of *The Elizabethan Stage* collected and analyzed most of what was known about every aspect of Elizabethan playing. Apart from the many studies of detailed problems, two works of particular importance have appeared since Chambers' book — Alfred Harbage's *Shakespeare's Audience* (1941) and John Cranford Adams' *The Globe Playhouse* (1942).

All this zeal for reconstructing the actual conditions under which Shakespeare wrote led to new critical approaches. Of these the most important were the *Prefaces* of Harley Granville-Barker.

Granville-Barker was unusually well equipped for the task of estimating the value of Shakespeare's plays in the theater. He first made his name in the 1900's as a young actor in Bernard Shaw's plays. In 1910–13 he directed productions on the London stage of *The Winter's Tale, A Midsummer Night's Dream,* and *Twelfth Night* which revolutionized Shakespearean acting and presentation. Up to that time the normal custom was to produce a Shakespearean play with elaborate scenery and a large cast of actors, while the style of speech was sonorous, rhetorical, and often quite meaningless. To allow time for elaborate sets to be erected, the texts of the plays were heavily cut and rearranged. Granville-Barker, realizing that an Elizabethan play needed Elizabethan treatment, substituted simple but lovely settings which could be changed in a moment so that the plays were acted rapidly, unedited and uncut. Above all, he insisted that each actor should know the full meaning of every word he spoke and should bring out the full poetic value of every speech.

Granville-Barker was not only a man of wide reading and an able Elizabethan scholar, but he had also (what is sometimes lacking in scholars) a wide knowledge of the world, and he possessed an enormous zest for Shakespeare which he was able to communicate. In 1923, a new and costly edition of Shakespeare's plays — *The Players' Shakespeare* — reproducing the folio text, was projected and Granville-Barker was invited to contribute a preface to each volume. This edition was soon abandoned, but the *Prefaces* were

separately published and from time to time additional prefaces were added; in all, studies of ten plays appeared. Granville-Barker approached the plays as a man of the theater, examining each to discover its meaning as a dramatic experience, to bring out the intention of the poetry, the nature of the characters, and the best way to produce each scene in the general harmony of the whole pattern.

A writer of very different background was E. E. Stoll. He combined wide literary and historical scholarship with vigorous criticism in such works as *Othello, An Historical and Comparative Study* (1915), *Hamlet* (1919), in which he stressed that *Hamlet* is an Elizabethan revenge play and must be judged as such, *Shakespeare Studies* (1927), and *Art and 'Artifice in Shakespeare* (1933), perhaps his most important work and one which should be read alongside some of the more recent critical and imagist studies. Stoll's claim and conclusion is that "the greatest of dramatists is careful, not so much for the single character, as for the drama; indeed, he observes not so much the probabilities of the action, or the psychology of the character, as the psychology of the audience, for whom both action and character are framed. Writing hastily, but impetuously, to be played, not read, he seizes upon almost every means of imitation and opportunity for excitement which this large liberty affords."

The Background

Meanwhile other scholars were at work on the reconstruction of the general background of Shakespeare's plays. To realize the actual meaning of Shakespeare's words some knowledge of the externals of life and of contemporary ideas is essential. As a glance at the illustrations in this book will show, even the simplest words, such as *hat, coat, hose, bed, gun, theater, ship, bottle,* conveyed a different picture to the minds of Shakespeare's audiences than to us, while the ideas and associations suggested by such words as *humor, degree, kingship, stars* were equally different. The study of the background thus includes not only the life of the age in its daily details but also its notions on such topics as the universe, religion, education, science, psychology, medicine, theories of criticism, and family life.

One of the most useful and interesting of

these works, which will be of value to the general student, is *Shakespeare's England* (1916), a generously illustrated account of life and manners of the age in the form of thirty studies, each by an expert in a particular field. In 1924, Edgar I. Fripp, who had edited the Minutes and Accounts of the Corporation of Stratford from 1553 to 1620 and possessed a minute knowledge of Elizabethan Stratford and its people, published an account of *Master Richard Quyny* — a friend of the Shakespeare family. Later he brought out *Shakespeare's Stratford* (1928), *Shakespeare's Haunts near Stratford* (1930), and *Shakespeare Studies: Biographical and Literary* (1930), all of which are full of information about Shakespeare's family, friends, and home environment.

Leslie Hotson in *I, William Shakespeare do appoint Thomas Russell, esquire* (1937) revealed many new facts about the man who was executor of Shakespeare's will, and about Shakespeare's acquaintances. Of greater intellectual and critical importance were Hardin Craig's *Enchanted Glass* (1936), a scholarly account of the intellectual background of the age, and Theodore Spencer's *Shakespeare and the Nature of Man* (1942), which discussed the turmoil of contemporary ideas on man's place in the universe. Lily B. Campbell in *Shakespeare's Tragic Heroes; Slaves of Passion* (1930) examined some of the tragedies in the light of contemporary ideas about morality and psychology, and in *Shakespeare's "Histories"* (1947) considered Elizabethan theories about history. W. W. Lawrence, in 1931, discussed *Shakespeare's Problem Comedies* in the light of medieval and Elizabethan ideas. In 1944, T. W. Baldwin in *William Shakspere's Small Latine and Lesse Greeke* provided a very full account of education at the English Grammar Schools. These, however, are but a small selection of the many scholarly works of the last half-century which have enriched our knowledge of the background of Shakespeare's plays.

The Study of Shakespeare's Imagery

In the 1930's a new movement in Shakespeare criticism became apparent. While the younger poets were evolving those new techniques and ways of expression which are sometimes called "modern poetry," the universal interest in psychology and the processes of the human mind so greatly stimulated by the work of Sigmund Freud led to a reconsideration of the nature of language itself, of poetry, and of the principles of criticism. It was natural that critics should reexamine Shakespeare's technique and especially his use of symbol and imagery. Awareness of Shakespeare's imagery was not indeed new; a generation earlier, Bradley in *Shakespearean Tragedy* had made acute observations on the imagery of *Macbeth*. But now two critics especially popularized this approach — Caroline Spurgeon and G. Wilson Knight.

Caroline Spurgeon, after two short publications — *Leading Motives in the Imagery of Shakespeare's Tragedies* (1930) and *Shakespeare's Iterative Imagery* (1931) — produced *Shakespeare's Imagery and What It Tells Us* in 1935. This book was an attempt to deal scientifically with Shakespeare's images.

Miss Spurgeon argued that the imagery used by a poet is a revelation, largely unconscious, "of the furniture of the mind, the channels of thought, the qualities of things, the objects and incidents he observes and remembers, and perhaps most significant of all those which he does not observe or remember." Accordingly, she and her assistants collected, tabulated, and categorized the images in Shakespeare's plays and, by way of comparison, the imagery of other Elizabethan dramatists. In the first part of the book the habits, likes, and dislikes of Shakespeare the man were deduced from his images: thus — "he was deft and nimble with his hands, and loved using them, particularly in the carpenter's craft, and contrary to our idea of most poets, he was probably a practical, neat and handy man about the house, as we know that he was a 'Johannes Factotum' about the stage."

Of far greater importance for critics were Miss Spurgeon's demonstrations of the "clusters" of significant images that occur in different plays. Thus *Romeo and Juliet* is full of images of light, *Hamlet* of images of ulcers and disease, *Troilus and Cressida* of images of food, *Macbeth* of images of ill-fitting clothes, and so forth.

The study of images is attractive to a "scientific" generation because, at first sight, it seems to be objective and capable of precise demonstration. Nevertheless, the perception of an image depends upon the experience of a reader. An ornithologist will see far more in one of Shakespeare's bird images than an unobservant town dweller, as was demonstrated in E. A. Armstrong's *Shakespeare's Imagination* (1946); a mariner (if he reads Shakespeare) will find special meanings in the scores of sea images, while a modern critic, steeped in the newer psychological notions, will find all kinds of subconscious significances, symbols, and patterns of which Shakespeare himself was unaware.

While Caroline Spurgeon based her conclusions on tables of images, Wilson Knight relied rather on intuition. In *The Wheel of Fire* (1930) he set out to " interpret " Shakespeare's somber tragedies. His approach, or process, was explained thus: When we watch or act Shakespeare for pure enjoyment we accept everything, but when we think critically we are on the lookout for faults. Knight argued, " we should interpret our original imaginative experience into the slower consciousness of logic and intellect, preserving something of that child-like faith which we possess, or should possess, in the theatre. It is exactly this translation from one order of consciousness to another that interpretation claims to perform. Uncritically, and passively, it receives the whole of the poet's vision; it then proceeds to re-express this experience in its own terms."

In the " right Shakespearean interpretation " there are four main principles: we must regard each play " as a visionary unit bound to obey none but its own self-imposed laws "; we must see each play as " an expanded metaphor by means of which the original vision was projected into forms roughly correspondent with its actuality "; we should analyze the poetic symbolism, especially when certain images recur in the same association; and we should consider the relation of the plays to each other in the " Shakespeare Progress." These principles were demonstrated in *The Wheel of Fire* and the volumes which followed — *The Imperial Theme* (1931) and *The Crown of Life* (1947).

In the last twenty years there have been many studies of Shakespeare's imagery, such as R. B. Heilman's *This Great Stage* (1948) — an elaborate study of image and structure in *King Lear* — and Donald Stauffer's *Shakespeare's World of Images* (1949), which traces the development of Shakespeare's moral ideas.

This intensive study of Shakespeare's poetic symbolism is, in a way, not so much a " new criticism " as a " neo-Victorian reaction." Victorian critics, in exalting Shakespeare the poet and genius, had forgotten that he was also a man of the theater. Critics in the 1920's put Shakespeare back in the Globe playhouse, and they reminded us that every professional dramatist has " to give the public what it wants." Fortunately, Shakespeare's public, being unusually intelligent, wanted what he gave them; yet, while it is salutary to remember that Shakespeare was a working Elizabethan playwright, it is equally wrong to regard him as nothing else.

The latest movement in literary criticism again fetches Shakespeare out of the theater and brings him back into the study; for the intricate relationships of images and ideas can be fully appreciated and understood only in close and leisurely reading. Thus Shakespeare the poet and philosopher is once more stressed and exalted, while Shakespeare the actor-dramatist is forgotten. Yet Shakespeare's lines, however subtle and symbolic, were written to be spoken rapidly on a stage and were accompanied by vivid, quick, and noisy action. If Shakespeare was consciously aware of his own " patterns of imagery " and deliberately used such symbolism as part of the dramatic structure of his plays, it follows that the more intelligent members of his audiences, who had received an elaborate training in formal rhetoric, must have been acutely sensitive to verbal subtleties. If this is so, it should increase our respect for their appreciation.

All these " studies " and " approaches " may well fill the student with despair. Must he, in order to read Shakespeare with pleasure or profit, first gnaw through a hundred thick volumes of scholarship or criticism? And what must be his attitude toward the conflicting claims of the scholars and the critics? The answer to the student's cry of distress is that with a minimum of preparation any intelligent reader can enjoy Shakespeare, but the wider his experience of the various branches of Shakespearean interest, the deeper will be his understanding, and his pleasure. No particular kind of criticism or scholarship contributes everything, but every kind will contribute something to the final comprehension so long as the student never commits the fatal error of regarding the commentary as more important than the text.

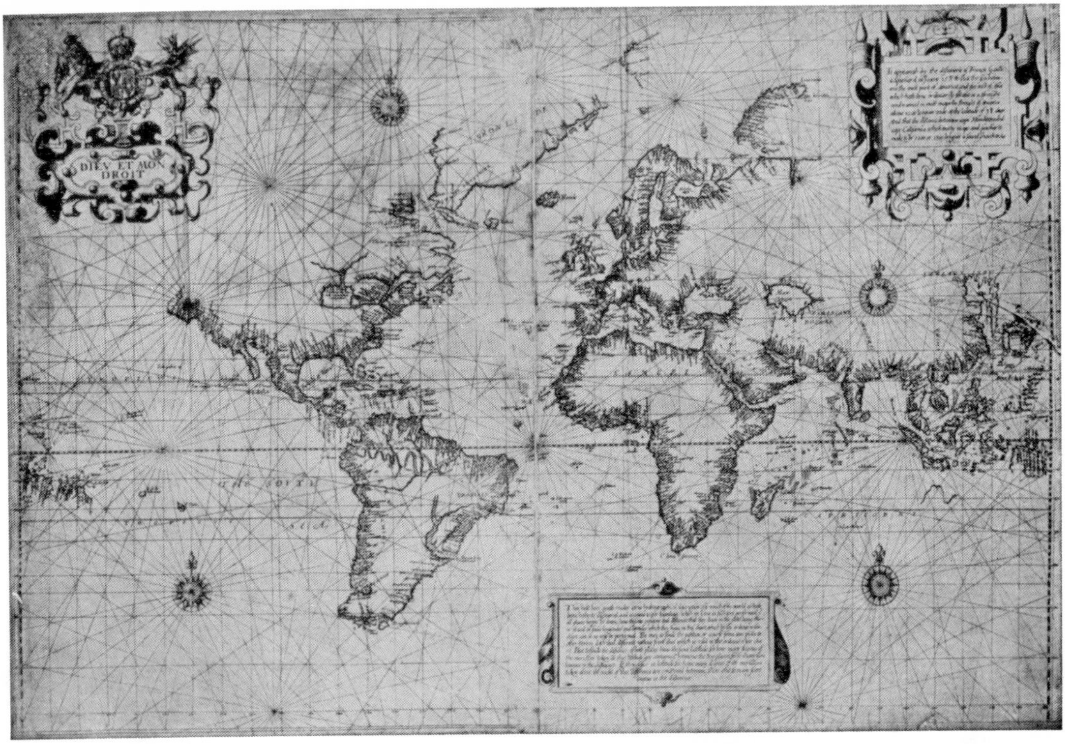

PLATE I

a. The World as known in 1600

b. William Shakespeare

PLATE 2

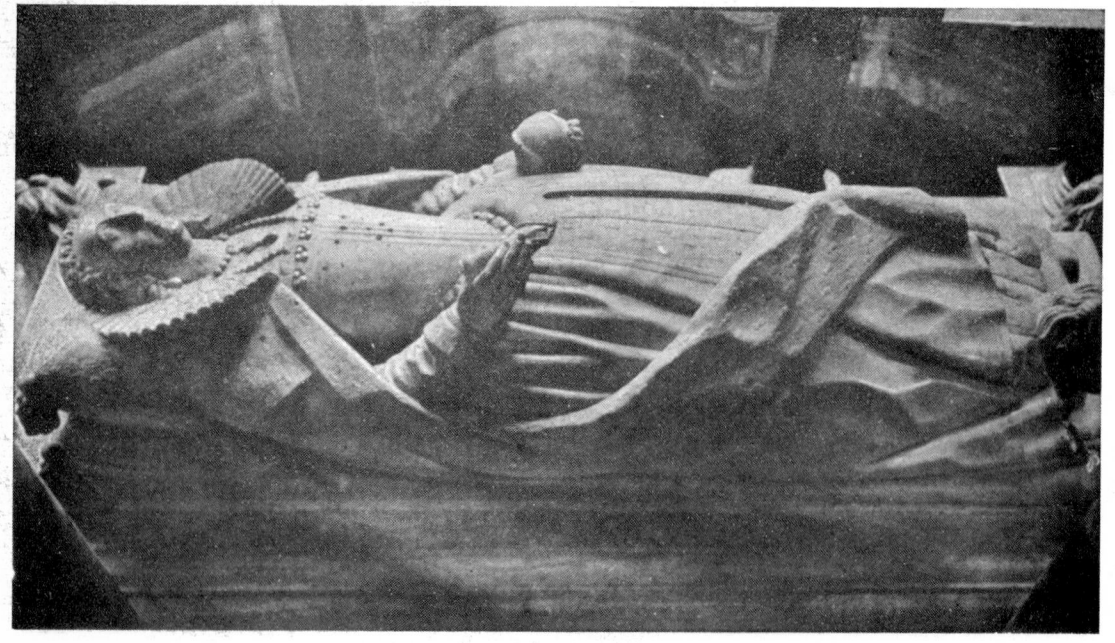

a. Shakespeare's London

b. Queen Elizabeth

PLATE 3

b. Queen Elizabeth attends a wedding, 1600

PLATE 4

THE EVOLUTION OF THE ELIZABETHAN STAGE

b. The Hall of the Middle Temple

a. The New Inn at Gloucester

PLATE 5

THE EVOLUTION OF THE ELIZABETHAN STAGE

b. The stage of the Globe (Irwin Smith's reconstruction)

a. The Swan playhouse

PLATE 6

a. Jonah and the whale

b. John Harvard's birthplace at Stratford-on-Avon   *c. Bare ruined choirs: Tintern Abbey*

PLATE 7

a. *Venus and Adonis*

b. *Princess Elizabeth leaves England, 1613*

PLATE 8   CONTEMPORARY COSTUME

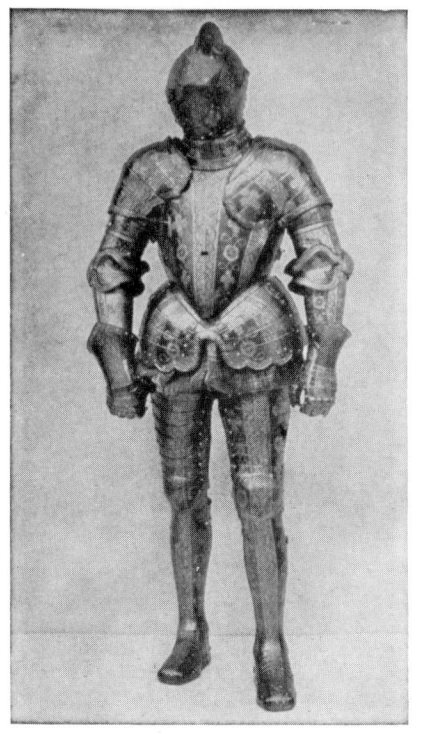

a. Armor   *b. A courtier's clothes*

c. German slops   *d. The Earl of Leicester*

a *b* *c* *d* *e*

a. A military funeral

f *g* *h* *l* *j*

k *l* *m* *n* *o*

b. Elizabethan types

PLATE 10

a. Elizabethan shilling, obverse and reverse   *b. Shilling of James I*

c. Gold angel   *d. Half groat*   *e. Gold half angel*

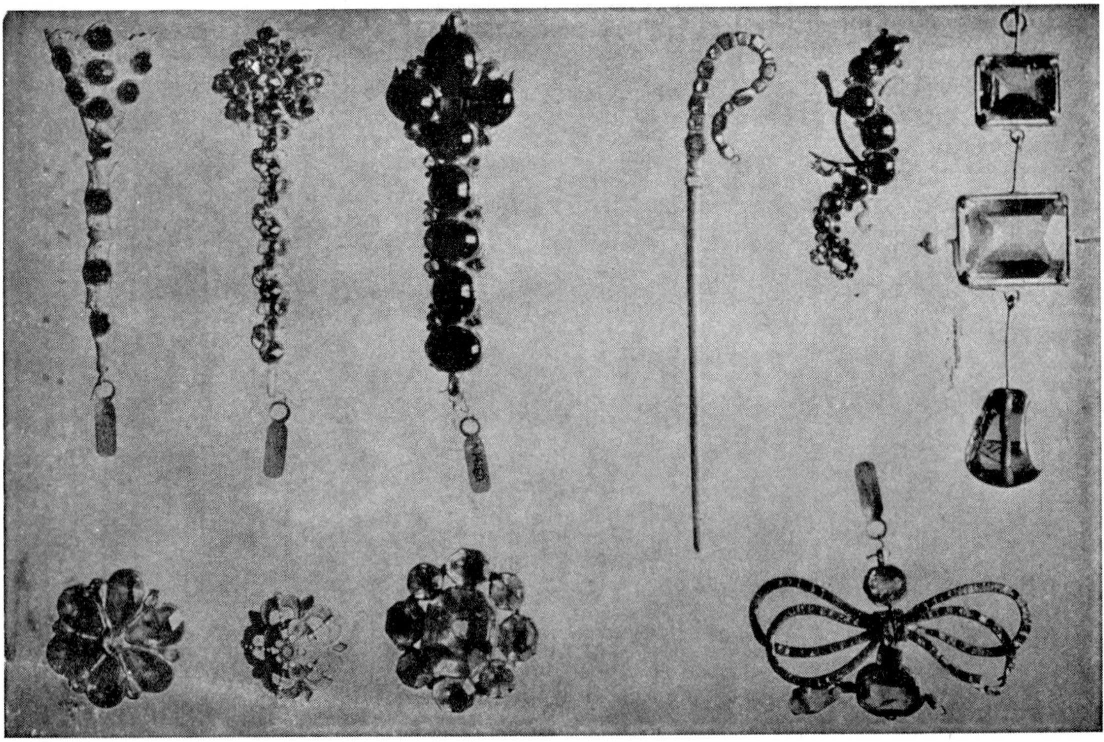

f. Elizabethan jewelry

PLATE II

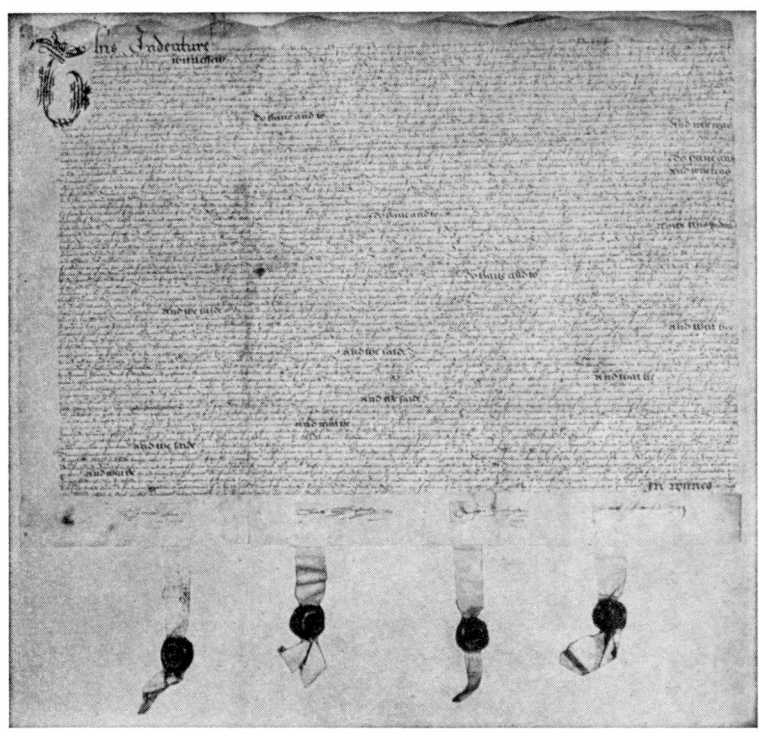

a. An indenture

b. A patent under the Great Seal

PLATE 12

a. The assault

d. A consort of music

b. A camp

e. The mandrake

c. Macbeth and the Three Weird Sisters

f. The Fool and Death

PLATE 13

a. Elizabethan stage costume: Titus Andronicus

b. The exchange of rapiers

c. A fool and a courtesan

d. Kempe dancing

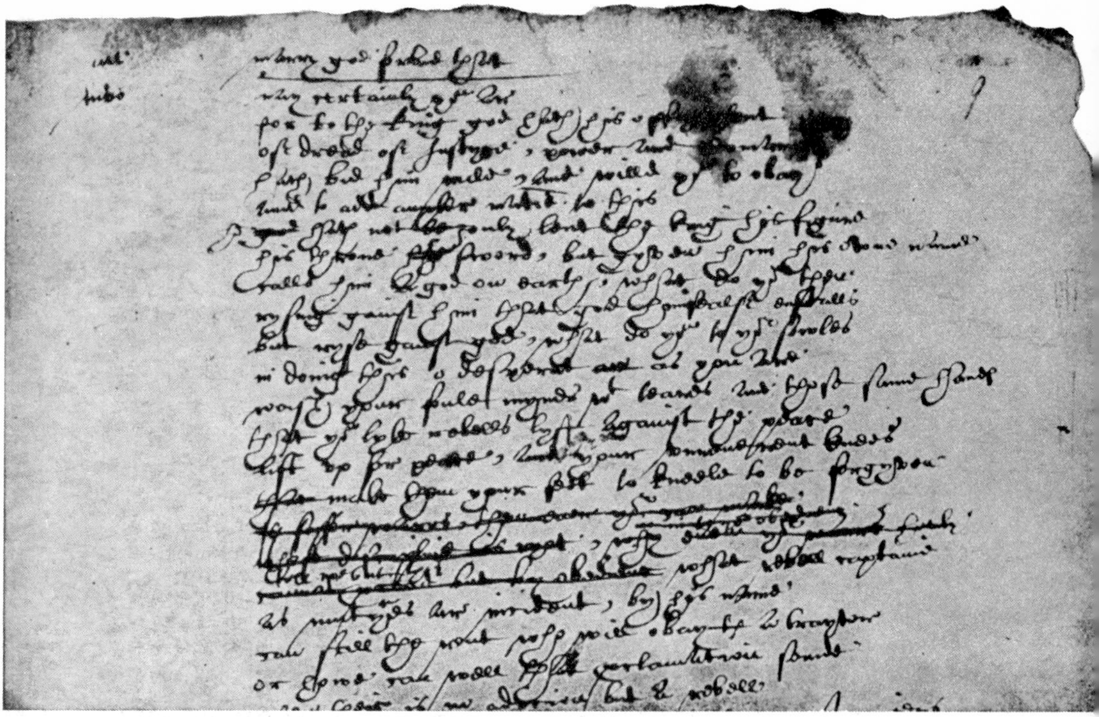

PLATE 14

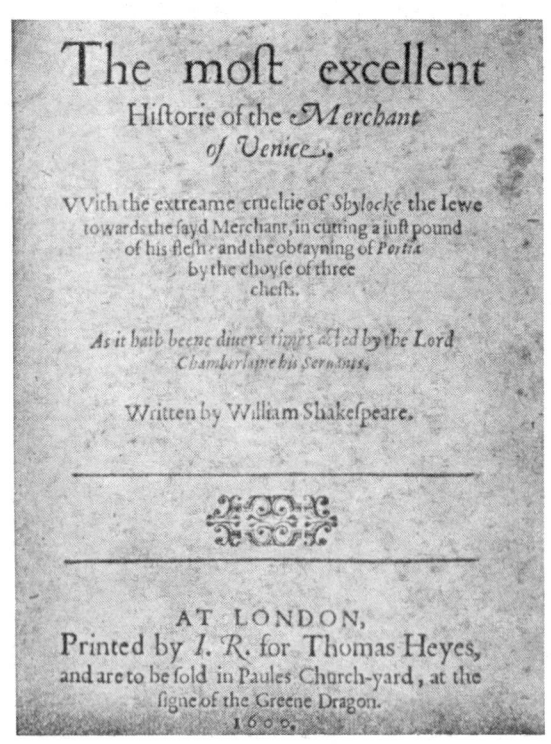

a. A portion in Hand D of the manuscript of The Booke of Sir Thomas More

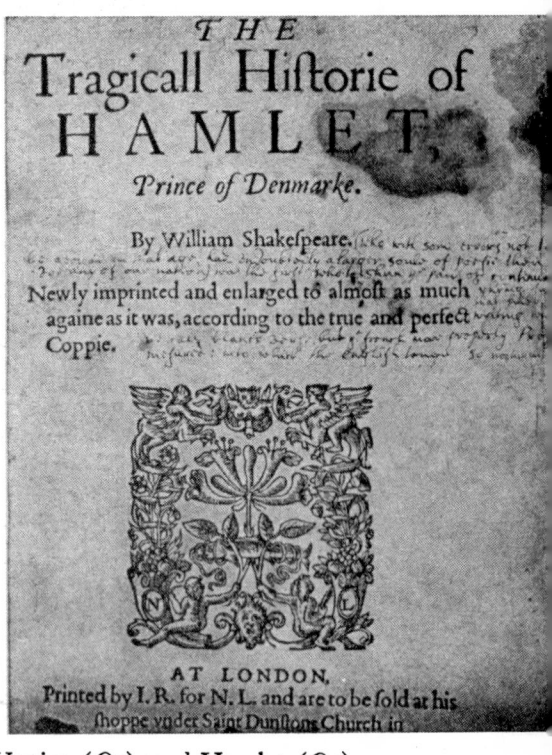

b. Title pages of two quartos: The Merchant of Venice (Q1) *and* Hamlet (Q2)

PLATE 15

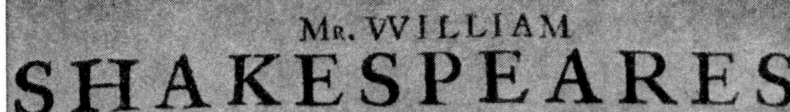

Title page of the first folio

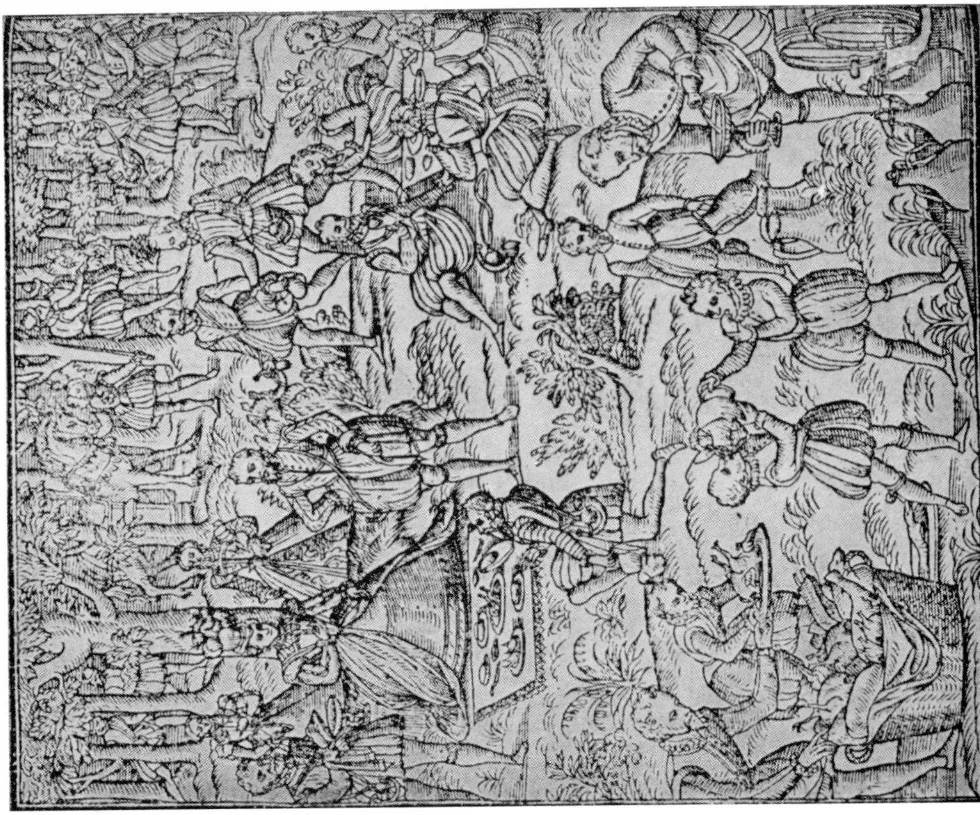

PLATE 16

b. The hunting party

a. A garden

a. *Joint stool*   b. *Great bed*   c. *Carved chest*

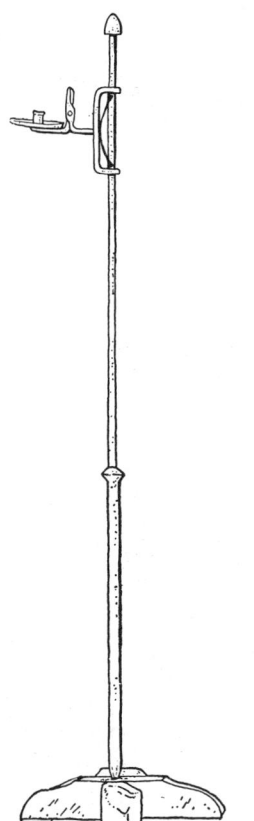

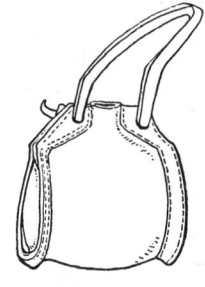

e. *Leather bottle* (8½″)

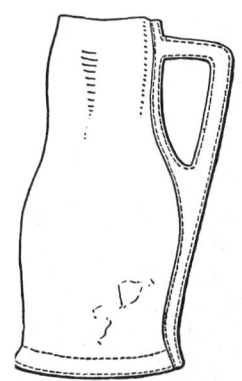

d. *Candleholder* (3′9″)   f. *Leather bombard* (12⅜″)

PLATE 18   MUSICAL INSTRUMENTS

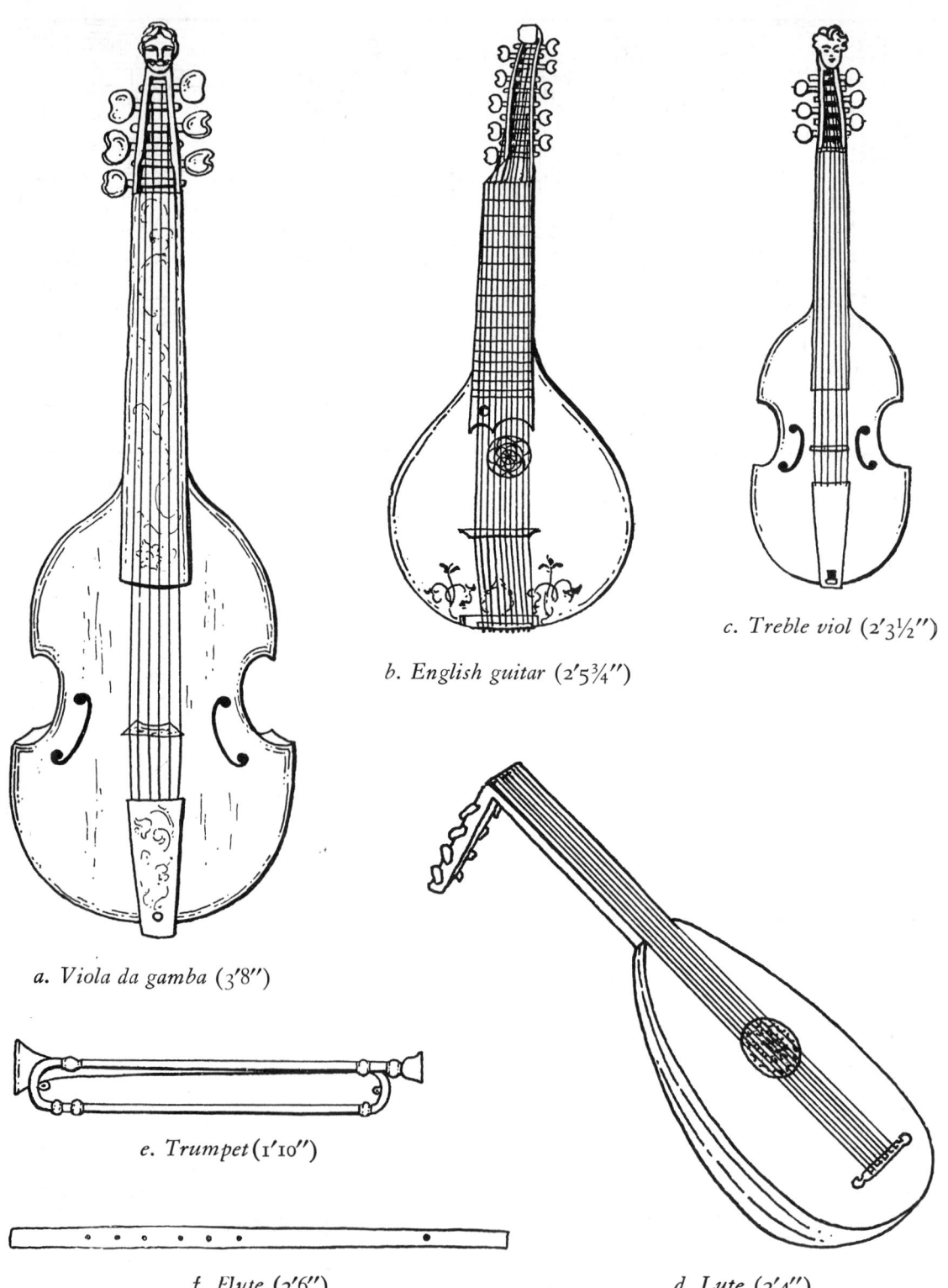

a. *Viola da gamba* (3'8")

b. *English guitar* (2'5¾")

c. *Treble viol* (2'3½")

e. *Trumpet* (1'10")

f. *Flute* (2'6")

d. *Lute* (2'4")

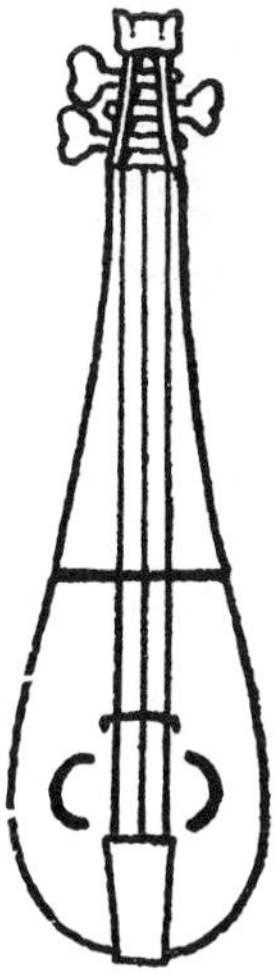

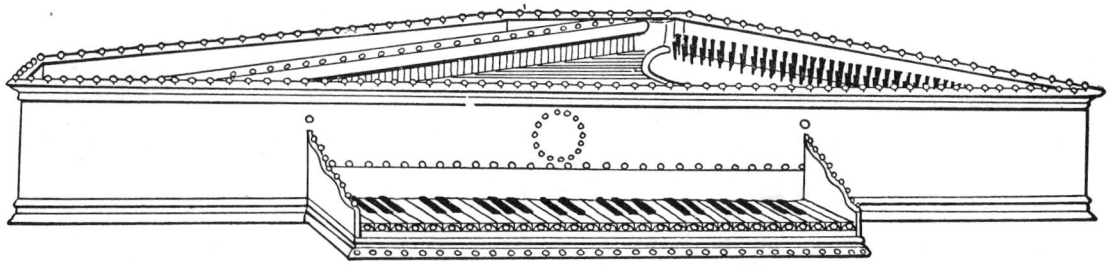

a. Rebec (1′10″)

b. Recorder (1′6″)

c. Cornet (2′2″)

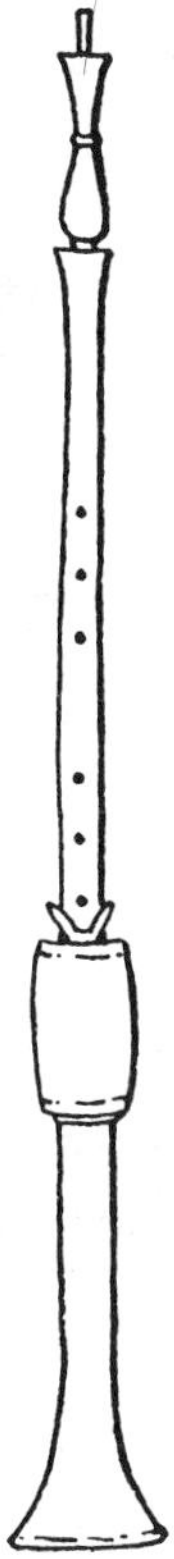

d. Shawm (3′2″)

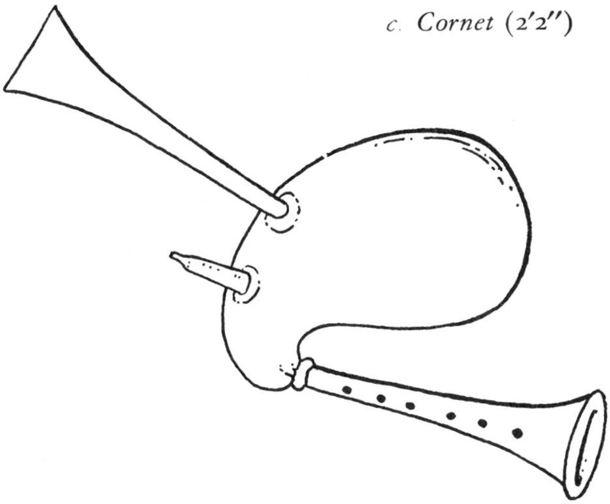

e. Bagpipe (3′6″)

f. Virginal (5′1⅜″)

PLATE 20   HOUSEHOLD FURNITURE AND UTENSILS: THE DINING ROOM

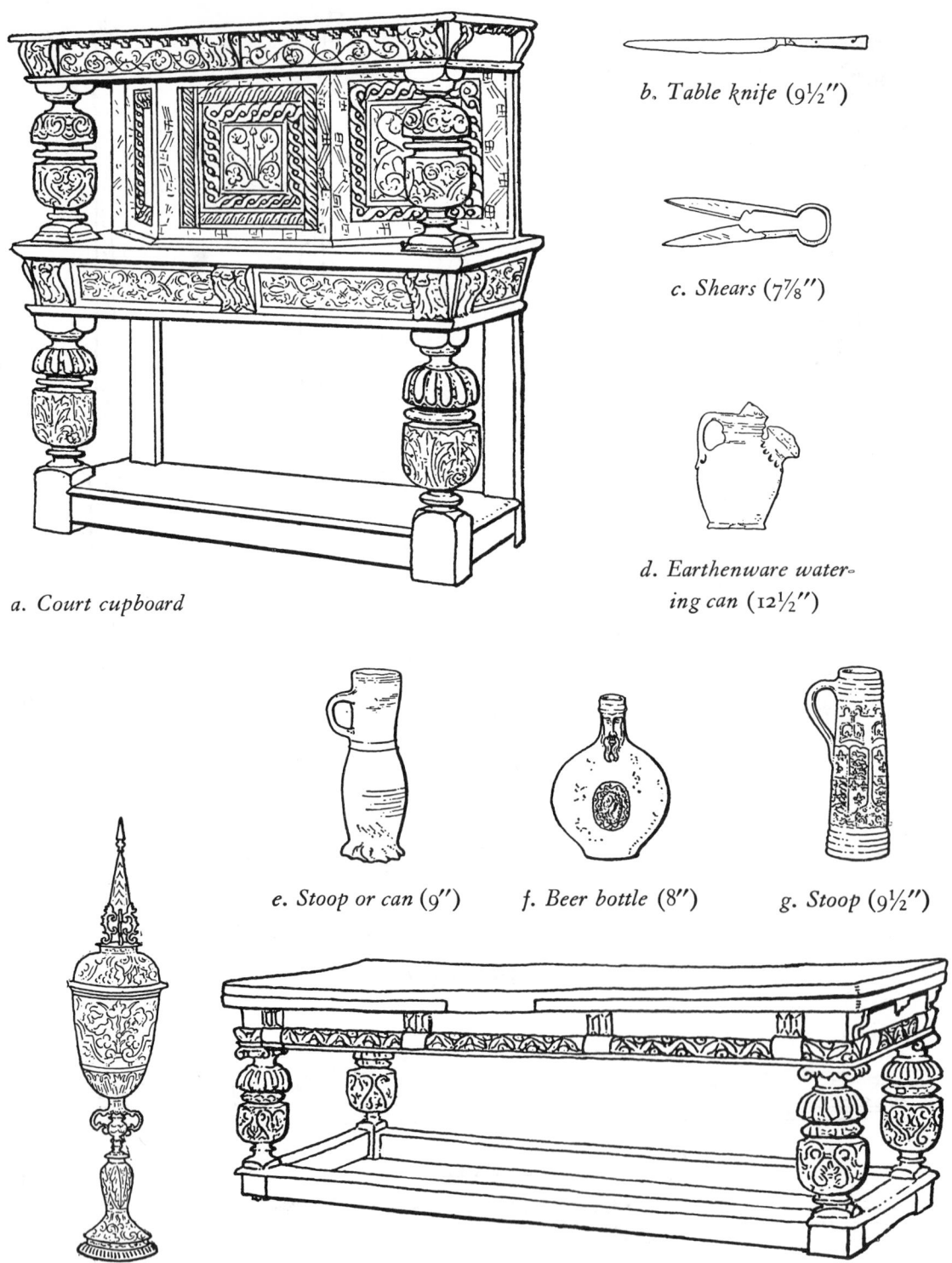

b. *Table knife* (9½″)

c. *Shears* (7⅞″)

a. *Court cupboard*

d. *Earthenware water-*
ing can (12½″)

e. *Stoop or can* (9″)   f. *Beer bottle* (8″)   g. *Stoop* (9½″)

h. *Standing cup* (1′8″)   i. *Table*

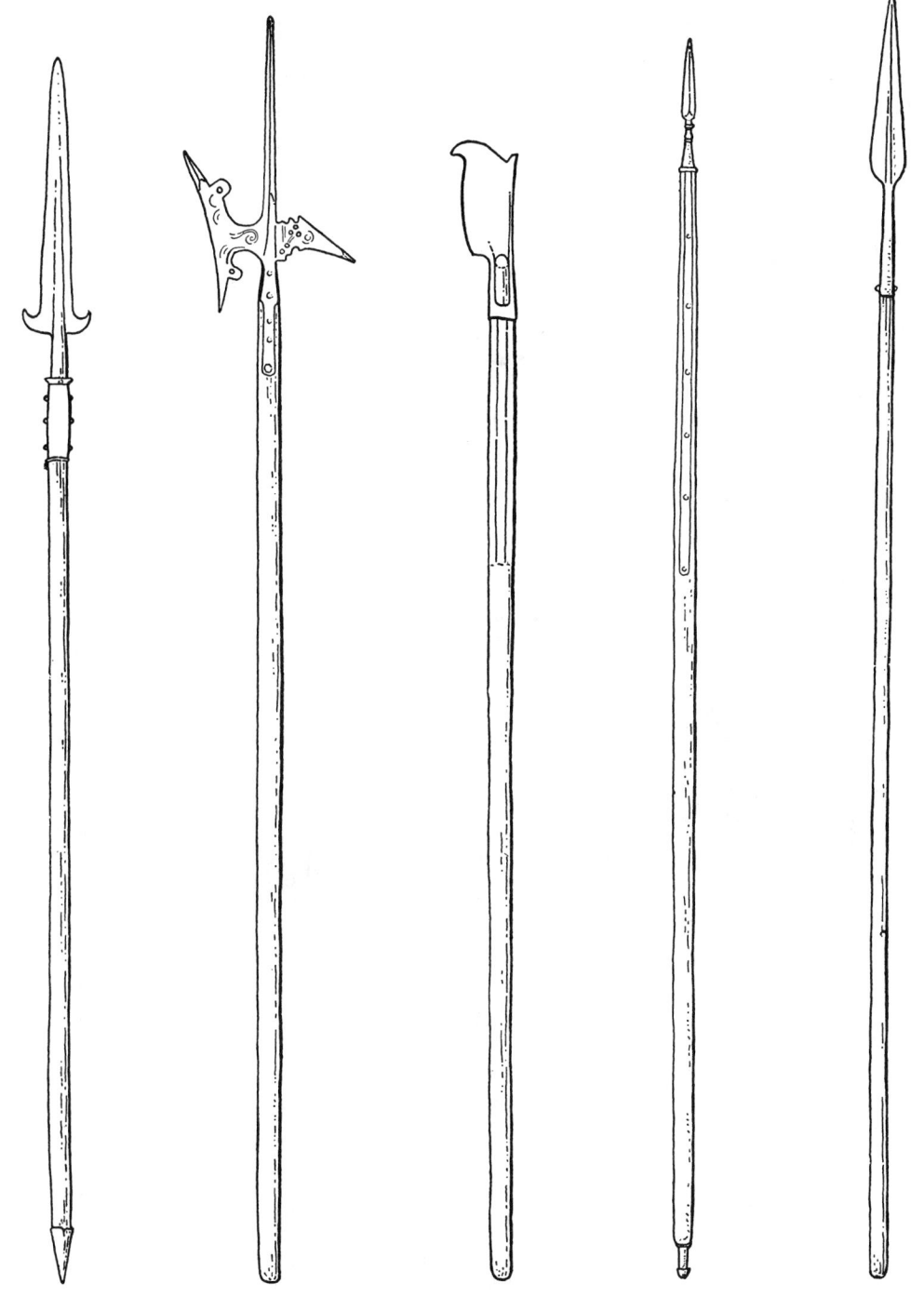

a. Partisan (9'2")   *b. Halberd* (7'2")   *c. Bill* (6'11")   *d. Pike* (9'3")   *e. Hunting spear*
(7'6")

PLATE 22

ARMS AND WEAPONS

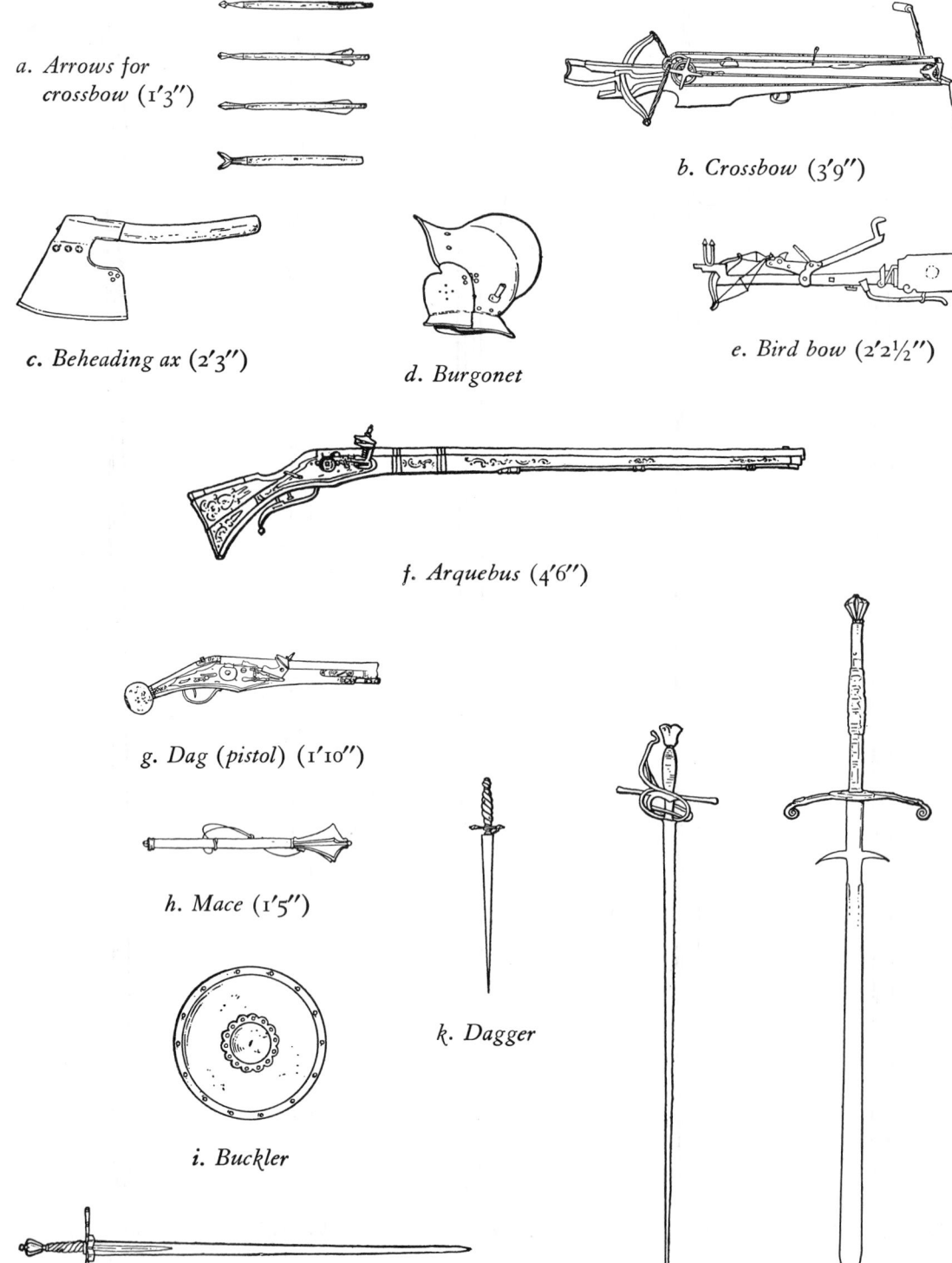

a. Arrows for crossbow (1′3″)

b. Crossbow (3′9″)

c. Beheading ax (2′3″)

d. Burgonet

e. Bird bow (2′2½″)

f. Arquebus (4′6″)

g. Dag (*pistol*) (1′10″)

h. Mace (1′5″)

k. Dagger

i. Buckler

j. Sword

l. Rapier

m. Two-handed sword

NOTES ON THE PLATES

Halftone Reproductions

1a. The World as known in 1600 (Huntington Library)

This map was drawn by Edward Wright, assisted by Richard Hakluyt, the compiler of Hakluyt's *Voyages,* and John Davis, an experienced sea captain. It depicts the world as known to Shakespeare's contemporaries and was the first map to be prepared on the principle known as Mercator's projection — showing the world as flat. Maria compares Malvolio's smiles to the many "rhumb lines" (lines radiating from a point to indicate comparative distances) so conspicuous on the map (*Twelfth Night* III.ii.84). The legend in the top right-hand corner reads:

It appeareth by the discoverie of Francis Gaulle a Spaniard in the yeare 1584 that the sea betweene the west part of America and the east of Asia (which hath bene ordinarily set out as a Straight and named in most maps the Straight of Aman) is above 1200 leagues wide at the latitude of 38 dgr. And that the distance betweene cape Mendocine and cape California which many maps and seacharts make to be 1200 or 1300 leagues is scarse so much as 600.

The legend at the bottom reads:

Thou hast here, gentle reader, a true hydrographical description of so much of the world as hath beene hetherto discovered, and is comme to our knowledge. Which we have in such sort performed, all places herein set downe, have the same positions and distances that they have in the globe, being therein placed in same longitudes and latitudes which they have in this chart; which by the ordinarie seachart can in no wise be performed. The way to finde the position, or course from any place to other herein described, differeth nothing from that which is used in the ordinary seachart. But to finde the distance; if both places have the same latitude, see how many degrees of the meridian taken at that latitude are contayned betweene the two places, for so many score leagues is the distance. If they differ in latitude, see how many degrees of the meridian taken about the midst of that difference are contayned betweene them and so many score leagues is the distance.

[1] The reader when referring to individual plates in the preceding pages should always consult also the relevant note. Notes on particular items of costume are grouped under Pl. 8.

1b. William Shakespeare (Ewing Galloway)

The memorial bust erected on the north wall of the Church of the Holy Trinity at Stratford-on-Avon sometime before 1623. It overlooks Shakespeare's grave in the chancel. The bust was the work of Gerard Johnson (or Janssen), one of a family of monument makers who came originally from Amsterdam. See Gen. Intro. p. 15b. This bust and the engraved portrait in the first folio (Pl. 15) are the only pictures of Shakespeare which are indisputably genuine; both probably derive from the same original sketch or painting, now lost.

2a–3a. Shakespeare's London (Folger Library)

This famous engraving of London was the work of John Visscher in 1616. The city is viewed from a point in Southwark on the south bank of the Thames, which here runs from west to east (i.e., from left to right). St. Paul's is the most conspicuous building. The Guildhall lies away to the north, over the large riverside warehouse known as Coleharbor. On the extreme east can be seen the Tower of London, with its central keep conspicuous with four domed turrets. All along the riverbank stand the warehouses and wharfs belonging to the chief merchants. London Bridge, with its houses and shops, connects north and south banks. The bridge is broken by a drawbridge, which can be seen between the first and second block of buildings. At the south end, the bridge is guarded by the Bridge Gate, above which are exposed the heads of traitors executed for high treason. On the south bank, to the west, the two conspicuous octagonal buildings are the Bear Garden and the Globe playhouse. The large church in the foreground is St. Mary Overeyes; it still stands, and is now known as Southwark Cathedral.

2b. Queen Elizabeth (Reproduced by permission of the Controller of His Britannic Majesty's Stationery Office from the Westminster Abbey volume of the Royal Commission on Historical Documents)

The recumbent marble effigy of the Queen on her tomb in Westminster Abbey, seen from above

3b. Queen Elizabeth attends a wedding, 1600 (Courtesy of Colonel F. J. B. Wingfield Digby, Sherborne Castle, Dorset)

From a painting by Marcus Gheerarts. The wedding took place in the Blackfriars on June 16, 1600, between Anne Russell (one of the Queen's maids of honor) and Lord Herbert, son of the Earl of Worcester. The Queen is seated in a canopied litter borne by courtiers. The other principal persons shown are: Charles Howard, Earl of Nottingham and Lord High Admiral, the white-headed figure looking to the left; George Carey, Lord Hunsdon, the Lord Chamberlain (and patron of Shakespeare's company), bearing his wand of office and with his left hand clasping his rapier, which is supported by a hanger; and Henry Brooke, Lord Cobham (the Queen's host for the occasion), carrying the sword of state. In the foreground, wearing white, is Edward Somerset, Earl of Worcester, the father of the bridegroom. The figure in white supporting the litter is the bridegroom himself. Behind the litter follow the Queen's maids of honor, preceded by the bride (in white) and the bridegroom's mother (shown between bridegroom and bride).

See also General Notes on Contemporary Costume, below.

4a. The New Inn at Gloucester (Raphael Tuck and Sons, Ltd.)

The New Inn was built in the fourteenth century to accommodate visitors to the tomb of Edward II. The illustration shows the typical yard and galleries. See Gen. Intro. p. 51b.

4b. The Hall of the Middle Temple

The Hall was a fine specimen of carved oak paneling of the Elizabethan period. Here on February 2, 1602, *Twelfth Night* was performed. The Hall was very badly damaged during a German air raid in 1940. See Gen. Intro. p. 51b.

5a. The Swan playhouse

A drawing made about 1596 by a Dutch traveler named Johannes de Witt.

5b. The stage of the Globe (Irwin Smith's reconstruction)

See Gen. Intro. pp. 52b–58b.

6a. Jonah and the whale (London Museum)

A Tudor wall painting (*c.* 1560) from an old house at Waltham Cross. It is typical of the kind of scene depicted on " painted cloth " — conventional illustrations of stories from the Bible or classical literature. Jonah is being thrown overboard from the waist of the ship; on the poop a sailor steers with a large oar; another on the forecastle is furling the topsail. The ship itself is of fantastic and semiclassical form, but the vessel in the background shows the usual Elizabethan type.

6b. John Harvard's birthplace at Stratford-on-Avon

This house and the neighboring house were built after a fire which largely destroyed Stratford-on-Avon in 1596. The two are typical town houses of the period, with exposed oak beams, leaded windows, and overhanging upper stories.

6c. Bare ruined choirs: Tintern Abbey

One of the many magnificent abbeys which had been looted and destroyed by the " reformers " in the days of Shakespeare's grandparents. Among folk in general, especially in the country, there was a common feeling that " 'twas never merry world since the friars were put down." See Sonnet 73, l. 4.

7a. Venus and Adonis (Victoria and Albert Museum, London)

The original is a hand-embroidered needlework panel, *c.* 1590. The story is shown in three episodes; the fight with the boar; Venus and her attendants lamenting over the dead youth; Venus returning to heaven in her chariot drawn by swans. Note the elaborate richness and detail of the decoration. Such scenes as these, rather than the nude figures of the Italian masters, were present in the imagination of Sidney, Shakespeare, Marlowe, and Spenser when they retold old tales.

7b. Princess Elizabeth leaves England, 1613

Painting by the Dutch artist Adam Willaerts, 1577–1664. (By permission of the Trustees of the National Maritime Museum, Greenwich, England.)

On February 14, 1613, Princess Elizabeth, daughter of King James I, married Prince Frederick, Elector Palatine and afterward King of

Bohemia. The wedding was the most elaborate of the many Court entertainments in the reign of King James. The picture shows the departure of the bride and bridegroom from Dover, and illustrates the different types of contemporary ships. In the *Tempest* Shakespeare has in mind a ship similar to that in the center of the picture.

8. CONTEMPORARY COSTUME:

General Notes

MEN'S COSTUME

The dress worn by men of rank and wealth was elaborate, richly embroidered, costly, and gay, and was made of various materials. The principal garments and accessories were:

a. DOUBLET. A short close-fitting coat, with fixed or detachable sleeves of various shapes and patterns, and buttoned up the front or sides with many buttons. **Pl. 8b** shows a fine specimen of actual doublet, elaborately embroidered. Leicester in **Pl. 8d** is wearing a BIG-BELLY or PEASECOD doublet, so called because it was cut to a point overhanging the stomach and so resembled the end of a pea pod; by contrast, a close-fitting doublet was sometimes called "THIN-BELLY."

b. JERKIN. A short sleeveless coat worn over the doublet. The foremost of the courtiers carrying the litter in **Pl. 3b** is wearing one. Jerkins of leather were worn by sergeants.

c. CLOAK. Cloaks of various lengths and shapes, often of velvet or other rich material, were worn over the doublet. The specimen shown in **Pl. 8b** is a short or Spanish cloak; for other specimens see the foremost lords in **Pl. 3b**, and **Pl. 9f** and **9n**.

d. GOWN. Worn usually by elderly and grave persons; see **Pl. 9j** and **9l**. Gowns worn by the wealthy were trimmed with fur (such as fox or sable) round the neck and down the front; see **Pl. 9l**.

e. HOSE. This word sometimes causes difficulty, as it was often used to describe any kind of breeches and also the whole set of garments from waist to knee. It was *not* used, as nowadays, for stockings. Of the various garments included under hose, the most common were:

i. ROUND HOSE, called also TRUNK HOSE, FRENCH HOSE, or FRENCH BREECHES. These were very short wide breeches, puffed out with padding, worn immediately below the doublet. See **Pl. 8b, 8d**, and the men in **3b**.

ii. Beneath the round hose and covering the thigh were worn close-fitting breeches called UPPERSTOCKS. See **Pl. 8d** and the men in **3b**.

iii. On the legs were worn stockings called NETHERSTOCKS, drawn up to or over the knee, and sometimes almost to the top of the thighs. See **Pl. 8d** and **3b**.

iv. VENETIANS, called also GASKINS or GALLIGASKINS, were wide breeches reaching down to the knees. In **Pl. 7a** Adonis is shown wearing VENETIANS.

v. SLOPS were excessively wide and baggy breeches, worn especially by Germans; see **Pl. 8c**. The word "slop," however, was sometimes used for any very wide breeches, including TRUNK HOSE. See *Romeo and Juliet*, II.iv.47.

vi. STROSSERS or TROUSERS were long underpants reaching to the ankle, rarely worn by Englishmen.

vii. CODPIECE. The white-bearded man in **Pl. 8c** wears a codpiece in front of his slops. The codpiece covered the opening in front of the breeches (hose). This accessory to male attire was often indelicately prominent. It was made in various forms, such as a bow of silk, a flap tied to the hose with laces, a small padded sausage-shaped cushion ornamented with pins, or a small bag used as a pocket.

f. STOCKINGS were cut from material and sewn; knitted stockings were however beginning to come into use by the end of the sixteenth century. Stockings were kept up by garters. CROSS GARTERS were passed round the leg beneath the knee, crossed at the back, and tied above the knee; they are being worn by the older man in **Pl. 8c**. and by the page (drinking) in **Pl. 16b**.

g. FOOTWEAR.

i. GREAT-BOOTS reaching to the knee were worn by riders or mounted soldiers. See **Pl. 9b, 9c**, and **12c**.

ii. SHOES were of various shapes and patterns. Sometimes they were adorned with rosettes, as in **Pl. 3b**, or with patterns made in the leather by cutting, slashing, or pinking, as in **Pl. 8c** and **13b.** The modern form of laced shoe was not used.

iii. BUSKINS were a kind of gaitered boot or sandal, and associated with gods, goddesses, and other ancient personages. They are worn by Titus Andronicus and the Moor in **Pl. 13a.**

h. SHIRTS were made usually of linen, often embroidered at neck and wrists. Longer shirts were worn as night attire.

i. A NIGHTGOWN was a long loosely fitting gown, like the modern dressing gown.

j. NECKWEAR:

i. The RUFF or BAND was a pleated collar, starched to keep it in shape, worn as a kind of frill round the neck, sometimes so wide that the head appeared to be sitting on a plate. See **Pl. 3b, 9f, 9j,** and **9n.**

ii. A FALLING BAND was a turned down collar, often ornamented with lace or embroidery; see **Pl. 8d, 9b–9e.**

iii. The WHISK was a plain or lace-edged band, semicircular in shape and stiffened with starch; see the portrait of Shakespeare himself on **Pl. 15.**

k. HEADGEAR. Hats were of various kinds and materials. Citizens often wore a FLAT CAP made of wool; see **Pl. 9l.** This kind of hat was known also as a STATUTE cap, because its use on Sunday was compulsory — a measure introduced to compensate hatmakers for the loss of trade caused by the introduction of felt hats. The flat cap was correct wear for apprentices at all times and for citizens when wearing a gown. Hats of this shape are still worn at academic ceremonies by doctors in English universities. Gallants wore hats of many shapes and kinds; see **Pl. 9b, 9f, 9j.** The specimen shown in **Pl. 8b** was called a COPINTANK or COPETAIN hat. THRUMMED hats are being worn by the right-hand figure in **Pl. 8c** and the nobleman in **Pl. 9n.** A BONNET was a cap of velvet or other soft material; see **Pl. 8d.**

l. Miscellaneous:

i. POINTS. Suspenders had not yet been invented. The hose was provided with a series of POINTS (resembling shoelaces), which were inserted from inside into eyelets or loops on the doublet, pulled through and then tied tight.

This process was called TRUSSING. A man taking his ease loosened (or *untrussed*) his points.

ii. GUARDS were ornamental stripes of braid or trimming sewn to doublet or cloak. The young nobleman in **Pl. 9f** wears a guarded cloak, and **9k** shows the guarded gown traditionally associated with citizens' wives.

iii. HANGER. A device for carrying the sword, consisting of a series of straps hanging from the sword belt. Hangers were often elaborately ornamented and costly. For a specimen see **Pl. 3b.**

WOMEN'S COSTUME

Women's costume was as complicated and elaborate as men's. The chief items of dress were:

a. BODY. Above the waist women wore a BODY (or bodice), often resembling a man's doublet. At one time it was fashionable for unmarried women to wear the front of the body very low. In front was worn a STOMACHER or PLACARD, a stiff embroidered front worn over the chest and stomach and sometimes ending in a point; see **Pl. 3b.**

b. KIRTLE. The outer skirt, called a KIRTLE, reached to the ground and was very full and voluminous; see **Pl. 9i, 7a.**

c. FARTHINGALE. The kirtle was made to stand out by means of a FARTHINGALE, which consisted either of a wire frame (made on the same principle as the hoops fashionable in the eighteenth century and the 1850's) or of a large roll of padding.

d. PETTICOAT. Over the farthingale and under the kirtle, one or more petticoats were worn. As it was customary to raise the skirt when walking, petticoats were embroidered; see **Pl. 9h, 9i, 9k** and **9m.**

e. GOWN. Women's gowns were of various kinds. A sleeveless gown for day wear was worn over body and kirtle, either left open in front as in **Pl. 9g** or gathered at the waist as in **Pl. 16b** or **Pl. 7a** (the kneeling figure with outstretched arms). Elderly ladies who had ceased to care for their figures wore a loose gown as the top garment; see **Pl. 9m.** A NIGHTGOWN was a long loose coat, much after the fashion of the modern house coat.

f. SMOCK. For night wear, a woman wore a SMOCK, a straight-cut nightshirt of linen embroidered at the neck and wrists. The smock was also used as an undergarment or chemise.

g. SLEEVES. Sleeves were separate from the main garment, to which they were attached by points or pins. Sleeves were usually embroidered and were of various shapes; a sleeve was an appropriate gift from a lover to his lady. A sleeve was Troilus' parting gift to Cressida. The CANNON or LEG-OF-MUTTON sleeve was very full at the shoulder and close-fitting at the wrist. SIDE SLEEVES were long sleeves covering the whole arm; see **Pl. 7a** and **Pl. 9g, 9i, 9k, 9m.** DOWN SLEEVES were open from the shoulder, and worn in addition to side sleeves; Queen Elizabeth is shown wearing them in **Pl. 3b.** The SLEEVEHAND was the ruffle of embroidery worn at the wrist.

h. NECKWEAR. The principal neckwear was the RUFF, either round of similar pattern to that worn by men (see **Pl. 9g, 9i, 9k, 9m,** and **Pl. 13c**) or else open at the throat and supported by a REBATO, a wire frame covered with linen which enabled the ruff to be bent up behind the neck to provide a kind of background to the face; see **Pl. 2b,** and **3b.**

i. Miscellaneous:

i. The PLACKET was the opening in front of the petticoat to enable the wearer to slip it over her head.

ii. CHOPINES were shoes mounted on a very high cork soles.

8a. Armor (Metropolitan Museum)

This suit of armor was made for George Clifford, Earl of Cumberland, about 1590, and used in the tilting contests before Queen Elizabeth. It is of russet steel, very richly decorated, and inlaid with goldsmith's work. Battle armor in the fifteenth and sixteenth centuries was made on the same general pattern, though fashion, details, and shape of different pieces were constantly changing. The technical names for the various protecting pieces are: (a) Head. CLOSE HELMET (CASQUE, ARMET), with the face protected by a visor which can be raised on a pivot. The BEAVER, often used loosely to describe the whole

helmet, was the lowest of the three sections remaining in place about the cheeks and chin when the remainder (the visor proper with its slits for sight, and the MEZAIL with its breathing holes) were raised. The foremost mounted man in **Pl. 12a** is shown with his visor in this position. (b) Throat. GORGET. (c) Shoulders. PAULDRONS. (d) Upper arm. REREBRACE. (e) Elbow. ELBOW COP or COUTER. (f) Forearm. VAMBRACE, or VAUNTBRACE (often used to denote the covering of the whole arm between pauldron and gorget). (g) Hand. GAUNTLET. (h) Chest and stomach. BACK AND BREAST, or "PAIR OF PLATES," from which hung the skirt of plate on the TASSETS, protecting the upper parts of the thighs. (i) Groin. A steel CODPIECE or a fringe of chain mail. (j) Thighs. CUISSES. (k) Knees. KNEECAPS. (l) Legs. GREAVES. (m) Feet. SABBATONS.

8b. A courtier's clothes (London Museum)

One of the very few original suits of Elizabethan clothes still surviving. It consists of embroidered velvet cloak, doublet, trunk hose, copetain hat, and embroidered gloves.

8c. German slops (Victoria and Albert Museum, London)

From Abraham de Bruyn, *Habitas variarum gentium,* 1581. The costumes are characteristically German. The figure on the reader's left is wearing slops, with a codpiece, crossed garters, and slashed or razed shoes.

8d. The Earl of Leicester (From a miniature by Nicholas Hilliard in the Victoria and Albert Museum, London)

Leicester is shown wearing a velvet bonnet, a falling band round his neck, a short velvet cloak with sleeves, a peasecod doublet, trunk hose, embroidered upperstocks, embroidered netherstocks, and shoes. On his left leg is the Order of the Garter, with the collar of the Order round his shoulders (from which hangs the " George " — the badge of Saint George slaying the dragon), and in his right hand the white staff of office. The walls are covered with plain hangings, probably of leather, and the table has a long tablecloth characteristic of the period.

9a. A military funeral

A section from Thomas Lant's engraving of the funeral of Sir Philip Sidney, 1587 (Victoria and Albert Museum, London). (a) The Captain's boy carries his master's target, a larger version of the buckler (see **Pl. 22i**). (b) The Captain (Thomas Smyth) wears a scarf across his right shoulder to denote his rank, and carries a partisan (see **Pl. 21a**) in his right hand, trailed point to the rear in sign of mourning. (c) The lieutenant trails a pike (see **Pl. 21d**). (d) Three " targeters " armed with swords and targets. (e) Three musketeers, with their muskets muzzle to the rear in sign of mourning. They carry in the other hand the forked rest, which was necessary because of the great weight of the musket, and they wear bandoliers from which are hung little bags, each containing one charge of gunpowder and bullets.

9b.   Elizabethan types

From Abraham de Bruyn, *Habitas variarum gentium,* 1581 (Victoria and Albert Museum, London). (f) A young nobleman (g) An elderly lady of rank. (h) A young unmarried woman. (i) A noblewoman. (j) A nobleman. (k) A city matron in her best. (l) A London citizen in full dress (i.e., wearing his civic gown). (m) An aged noblewoman. (n) A nobleman (o) A young man carrying sword and spiked buckler (see **Pl. 22 i** and **j**). Note the short Spanish cape of (f), the furred and " guarded " gowns of (j) and (l), the long riding cloak of (n), and the short cassocks (the citizens' alternative to the courtly doublet and hose) worn by (l) and (o). Citizens and servants frequently went about without cloaks, but the wearing or carrying of a cloak, even if it covered only one shoulder, was necessary to any man who claimed to be considered a gentleman.

10a–e.   Elizabethan coins (actual size) (Royal Ontario Museum)

(a) Elizabethan shilling, obverse and reverse. (b) Shilling of James I. (c) Gold angel. (d) Half groat. (e) Gold half angel. See App. 27.

10f.   Elizabethan jewelry (London Museum)

These are specimens from the Cheapside hoard, discovered in London in 1912. On the left, three examples of jeweled fan holders; below, three hat ornaments; an ornamented pin; on the right, a brooch and two pendants. The hoard contained small vessels of crystal, chains, buttons, ornaments of jewels and enamelwork, and a quantity of uncut and unset stones. It was probably the stock of a London jeweler about 1600.

11a.   An indenture (Folger Library)

See App. 6.

11b.   A patent under the Great Seal (Folger Library)

Grants from the sovereign of a title, lands, privileges, etc. were embodied in a document known as letters patent, and sealed with the Great Seal of England.

12a.   The assault

This woodcut from Holinshed's *Chronicles* illustrates the assault on a town after the walls have been breached in two places by cannon fire or mines. On the right, the attackers, armed with pikes and swords, are going in to the attack while others mount a scaling ladder. In the left foreground, a musketeer is loading his piece with the aid of a ramrod. In the center, the ordnance, protected by palisades, are being fired by the gunners' applying the lighted match at the end of the linstock. On the right cavalrymen in armor wait their turn. The foremost cavalryman is shown with his visor raised.

12b.   A camp

This woodcut from Holinshed's *Chronicles* shows life behind the lines. Note the length of the pikes propped against the tents, the drum, the caliver (center foreground), drinking vessels, etc.

12c.   Macbeth and the three Weird Sisters

In this woodcut from Holinshed's *Chronicles* Macbeth is shown wearing full hose and riding boots, with spurs. The costume of the Weird Sisters is quite imaginary.

12d.   A consort of music

From Holinshed's *Chronicles*. The consort (or " table ") of music consists of lute, bass viol, virginal, hautboy or recorder, and a singer. See also **Pl. 18 and 19.**

12e.   The mandrake (Folger Library)

From John Gerard's *Herbal,* 1597. The mandrake, because of its resemblance to the lower part of the human form, was believed to have magical properties: it flourished best under a gallows, it shrieked when pulled out of the ground, and its screams were so fatal that a dog was tied to the root and forced to draw it forth. In medicine it was used as an anodyne and a soporific.

12f. The Fool and Death

From an initial " A " in Anthony Munday's edition of *Stow's Survey* of London, 1618. The fool is wearing the cap with ass's ears. His bauble — a doll's head on a stick — lies in front under a skull which half conceals an hourglass.

13a. Elizabethan stage costume: *Titus Andronicus* (A drawing in the possession of the Marquis of Bath. Photo from the Cunliffe Collection, by permission of D. Appleton-Century Co.)

From a drawing made in 1595 by Henry Peacham, which in the original is followed by a transcript of *Titus Andronicus* I.i.104–21. The episode shows Tamora vainly appealing to Titus Andronicus to show mercy to her sons, who are about to be sacrificed. If, as is possible, Peacham's drawing was founded on his recollection of an actual performance, it gives some indication of the haphazard method of costuming in the Elizabethan playhouse. The two men on the left holding halberds are in Elizabethan costumes, the first figure being armed with a scimitar or falchion. Titus, Tamora's sons, and Aaron the Moor are in " Renaissance classical " costume, which is common in the better-class engravings of the period and was copied from ancient Roman statues. Tamora is in flowing draperies.

13b. The exchange of rapiers

This cut illustrates the episode in the fencing match in *Hamlet*. See App. 25.

13c. A fool and a courtesan

From the title page of Robert Greene's *Third Part of the Conny-catching*, 1592. The fool wears the cockscomb cap and bells, and the motley dress of his calling, which was particolored — right leg and left breast being of one color, left leg and right breast of another. This is the costume worn by Touchstone in *As You Like It,* Feste in *Twelfth Night,* and the Fool in *Lear.*

In the foreground the tools are a cutpurse's knife and a picklock.

13d. Kempe dancing

Woodcut from the title page of Kempe's *Nine Days' Wonder,* 1601, the pamphlet describing his famous dance to Norwich (see Gen. Intro. p. 44b) The famous clown is shown in morris-dancing costume, with bells tied round his knees. He is accompanied by his taborer, playing pipe and tabor, the typical instruments of shepherds and clowns.

14a. Portion of the *More* manuscript (Trustees of the British Museum) (see pp. 85–86 and App. 30 for the literal transcript)

14b. Title pages of two quartos: *The Merchant of Venice* (Q1) and *Hamlet* (Q2) (Folger Library)

The last two lines of *Hamlet* have been cut off in the binding. The remarks following *By William Shakespeare* were written in the Old English " secretary " hand about 1660; they read: "(who with some errors not to be avoided in that age, had undoubtedly a larger soule of poesie than for any of our nation) was the first who to shun ye pains of continuall rhyme Invented that kinde of writing which we call blanck verse but ye french more properly Prose mesured: into which the english tonge so nachurally falls."

15. Title page of the first folio (Folger Library)

16a. A garden (From *The Orchard and the Garden, 1594*)

The illustrations show typical contemporary gardens with formal flower beds and covered walks. In such a garden Malvolio was spied upon by the conspirators in *Twelfth Night,* and Benedick and Beatrice were betrayed by overheard conversations.

16b. The hunting party (From George Turberville, *Noble Arte of Venerie,* 1575, as reproduced in *Shakespeare's England,* Vol. II, p. 345)

Queen Elizabeth is shown being served at a picnic dinner in the woods — the kind of scene in Shakespeare's mind in *As You Like It.* Note the hunting horns carried by the gentlemen.

Line Cuts

17. Household furniture and utensils: the bed-room

a. Joint stool. This was the commonest piece of furniture, and used for most sitting purposes; chairs with backs and arms were few and reserved for persons of importance.

b. Great bed, with paneled back, canopy, carved posts, and curtains which were drawn close at night. The fringe round the side was called a valance. In a bed of this kind Desdemona was murdered.

c. Carved chest, used for clothes and linen, and often elaborately ornamented.

d. Candleholder. The candle (or taper) was held in the socket; the pincers were used for holding a rushlight (a taper made of a rush coated thinly with wax) which was used for carrying a light from place to place.

e. Leather bottle (called also a *costrel*), used for carrying liquor by such persons as shepherds, gravediggers, or drunken butlers.

f. Leather bombard, used for carrying liquor from cask to table.

18. Musical instruments

a. Viola de gamba, so called because it was held between the knees like the modern cello

b. English guitar

c. Treble viol

d. Lute, used commonly for the musical accompaniment of songs

e. Trumpet

f. Flute

19. Musical instruments

a. Rebec, a simple form of fiddle

b. Recorder, a popular form of woodwind instrument

c. Cornet, another woodwind instrument

d. Shawn, another woodwind instrument

e. Bagpipe

f. Virginal, played in the same way as the modern piano. In the virginal, however, the strings are plucked by quills held by jacks which are moved by the keys; in the spinet (and modern piano) the strings are struck by hammers.

20. Household furniture and utensils: the dining room

a. Court cupboard of carved oak, used for the display of silver plate

b. Table knife

c. Shears used by tailors for cutting out cloth

d. Earthenware watering can, used for sprinkling rushes and wooden floors to lay the dust

e. Stoop or can, a common stoneware type of drinking vessel, called also a *canater* or *cannikin*

f. Beer bottle of stoneware

g. Stoop or *canette* of stoneware, with the royal arms. These were made in large quantities at Siegburg in Germany for the English market.

h. Standing cup of silverware, 1612, called also a *covered goblet*

i. Table of carved oak, with leaves at either end which can be drawn out to give additional length

21. Weapons

a. Partisan. Carried chiefly by palace guards, a heavy weapon, used for close fighting in rooms and passages.

b. Halberd. The characteristic weapon of the Swiss infantry. It had a threefold purpose: the point was for thrusting, the axhead for a smashing blow, the spike for thrusting down scaling ladders or hooking horsemen from their horses.

c. Bill. Another infantry weapon for miscellaneous fighting. It was adapted from the tool used for cutting down branches of trees or trimming hedges. For use as a weapon it was fixed to a longer shaft and was deadly in the hands of an expert. It was also the normal weapon of a watchman.

d. Pike. The English infantryman's weapon. Pikes were usually mounted on a shaft 16 feet long. For resisting cavalry the butt was thrust into the ground and the point pushed forward. In attack it was used by men in close formation who pushed forward by sheer weight.

e. Hunting spear. In **Pl. 7a** Adonis is shown using a boar spear, which was a hunting spear especially adapted for hunting boar; it had a crossbar below the head to take the weight of a charging animal.

22. Arms and weapons

a. Arrows for crossbow, known also as *bolts,* of various types. The short, blunt kind is a bird bolt for killing small birds.

b. Crossbow. The crossbow has a steel spring too powerful to be bent by hand. It was set by winding up the handle until the string was caught on the projection of the trigger.

c. Beheading ax, used for executions. The specimen shown has a short handle; the handle was sometimes much longer. The blade is very broad and heavy.

d. Burgonet, a type of helmet with an open face used chiefly by horsemen as an alternative to the close helmet

e. Bird bow, a smaller type of crossbow

f. Arquebus. One of the four types of hand firearms, the others being the lighter caliver and the heavy musket (see **Pl. 9e**), and the dag or pistol (**g**). There was still great controversy among military men about the relative merits of the bow and the musket and other firearms. It was admitted that firearms exceeded in weight and effectiveness of the projectile, but they were heavy and cumbersome, and very slow to load; for it was necessary first to pour in the charge of loose gunpowder, then with the aid of a ramrod to tamp it down with a wad, to insert the bullets, and to tamp them down with a wad. To discharge the firearm some loose powder was placed in the little pan beside the butt end of the barrel and lit. There were various methods of discharging the arquebus. The simplest was to apply a lighted match to the touchhole at the base of the barrel and so set off the gunpowder by direct action. In other specimens (as in this plate) a flint, inserted into the hammer, was used; by the action of the trigger the flint struck a steel projection which caused a spark to fall into a little pan of loose gunpowder at the base of the barrel, whereby ignition was conveyed to the charge in the barrel. Gunpowder when discharged gave off a thick cloud of whitish smoke, so that after a volley the troops were completely enveloped in a heavy smoke screen.

g. Dag (pistol)

h. Mace. Carried by horsemen for use in close combat. The heavy end delivered a smashing blow which dented through the helmet and gave the wearer concussion of the brain. A miniature mace was carried by sergeants of the law as a badge of office.

i and **j.** Buckler and sword. The sword was the popular English weapon until superseded by the rapier toward the end of the sixteenth century. The sword was used mainly for a cutting stroke but could also be used for thrusting. The buckler was used with the sword. It was carried in the left hand for warding off the opponent's blows. The specimen illustrated has a flanged rim to catch the sword point and a round leather disk at the back to serve as a pad for the knuckles. Bucklers were sometimes provided with a spike, screwed into the center, for thrusting into the opponent's face; see also **Pl. 9o**.

k. Dagger. Carried in a sheath on the girdle, and used point upward in the left hand for parrying the strokes of the rapier.

l. Rapier. A long, light weapon with a thin blade of very finely tempered steel, introduced from Italy. In Shakespeare's time it was the fashionable weapon of young gallants. It was used mainly for thrusting, though as the blade was flat and as it had a very sharp cutting edge, it could also be used for hamstringing an opponent or slicing him over the eye so that he was blinded by his own blood. A rapier suitable only for thrusting was called an *estoc, stuck,* or *tuck*. Old gentlemen of the old school, such as Capulet (*Romeo and Juliet*) or Antonio (*Much Ado about Nothing*) despised the weapon; but in the hands of an expert it was more than a match for the sword.

m. Two-handed sword. A weapon more common on the Continent, used for a short heavy hammerlike blow.

ACKNOWLEDGEMENTS

The drawings for the line cuts were prepared by Miss Elizabeth Maw of the Royal Ontario Museum. Her sources were original objects and/or photographs from the following collections:

The Royal Ontario Museum, Toronto, Plates 17 a, b, c, d, f, 18; 19; 20 b, c, d; 21

The London Museum, Plates 17 e; 20 e, f, g, h.

The Metropolitan Museum, New York, Plates 20 a, i.

The collection of Mr. M. R. Holmes, FSA, Plates 22 d, i, j, h, k, l, m.

THE PLAYS
and the Poems

KING HENRY THE SIXTH

Introduction[1]

On March 3, 1592, Philip Henslowe noted in his famous *Diary* (see Gen. Intro. p. 38b) the performance of a new play called " harey the vi," for which his share of the takings was £3. 16s. 8d. This was the largest sum recorded for any of the 105 performances by the Lord Strange's players at the Rose playhouse between February 19 and June 22 when playing ceased in London for six months. *Harry the Sixth* was performed fifteen times during that period, and the takings were well above the average. The popularity of the play is further confirmed by the enthusiastic praise of Thomas Nashe in *Piers Penniless,* which was sent to the press in August (see Gen. Intro. p. 9a). Although Shakespeare's name does not appear in the *Diary,* it is likely that " harey the vi " is *I Henry VI* — unless some other writer at the same time wrote a rival play on the reign of Henry VI. Shakespeare's play thus seems to date from the end of 1591 or the beginning of 1592.

The Third Part (and presumably also the Second Part) was in existence by the summer of 1592. When Robert Greene in his last days made his bitter attack on the players in *The Groatsworth of Wit* (see Gen. Intro. p. 9a–b), he sneered at " an upstart Crow, beautified with our feathers," " with his Tiger's heart wrapped in a Player's hide," thereby parodying a line in *III Henry VI* — " O tiger's heart wrapped in a woman's hide " (I.iv.137). Greene died on September 3, 1592. Yet there is no trace of *II* or *III Henry VI* in Henslowe's *Diary,* and various conjectures have been made to explain the origin and ownership of the Second and Third Parts. It has indeed been suggested that the Second and Third Parts may have been written before the First, which was — as the *Diary* shows — the property of the company acting at the Rose Theater.

The First Part was not printed during Shakespeare's lifetime and did not appear in printed form until the first folio of 1623. The complete texts of the Second and Third Parts also first appeared in the first folio, but garbled versions of both had been printed in 1594 and 1595 respectively. These were entitled: *The First part of the Contention betwixt the two famous Houses of Yorke and Lancaster, with the death of the good Duke Humphrey: And the banishment and death of the Duke of Suffolke, and the Tragicall end of the proud Cardinall of Winchester, with the notable Rebellion of Iacke Cade: And the Duke of Yorkes first claime vnto the Crowne. London. Printed by Thomas Creed, for Thomas Millington, and are to be sold at his shop vnder Saint Peters Church in Cornwall. 1594.* And *The true Tragedie of Richard Duke of Yorke, and the death of good King Henrie the Sixt, with the whole contention betweene the two Houses Lancaster and Yorke, as it was sundrie times acted by the Right Honourable the Earle of Pembrooke his seruants. Printed at London by P. S. for Thomas Millington, and are to be sold at his shoppe vnder Saint Peters Church in Cornwal. 1595.*

Both quartos were reprinted in 1600, and again in 1619 when they were reissued as one play with the title — *The Whole Contention betweene the two Famous Houses, Lancaster and Yorke. With the Tragicall ends of the good Duke Humfrey, Richard Duke of Yorke, and King Henrie the sixt. Diuided into two Parts: And newly corrected and enlarged. Written by William Shakespeare, Gent. Printed at London, for T. P.* It will be noted that Shakespeare's name is added to the title page in this edition.

A comparison of these quartos with the folio texts of *II* and *III Henry VI* shows the same kind of similarity and of difference as is found in the bad quarto and the good F1 text of *Henry V.* The quartos are considerably shorter, and in the main they tell the story in similar episodes. Occasionally speeches or lines are identical in Q and F1; at other times the passage in Q is a paraphrase of F1; more usually there is only general resemblance. Thus, for example, King Henry's pathetic lamentation (*III Hen VI,* II.v.1–54) appears in *The True Tragedy* as follows:

[1] For the history behind these three plays, see also App.
28.

Oh gratious God of heauen looke downe on vs,
And set some endes to these incessant griefes,
How like a mastlesse ship vpon the Seas,
This wofull battaile doth coutinue still:
Now leaning this way, now to that side driue,
And none doth know to whome the day will fall.
O would my death might stay these cruell iarres;
Would I had neuer raignde, nor nere bin king.
Margret and *Clifford,* chide me from the field,
Swearing they had best successe when I was thence:
Would God that I were dead, so all were well,
Or would my crowne suffice, I were content,
To yeeld it them and liue a priuate life.

On the other hand, the last speech of King Henry (V.vi.35–56) is mostly the same, and Gloucester's speech (ll. 61–93) is almost identical in both versions.

Until modern scholars began to re-examine the original quartos (see Gen. Intro. p. 85a), it was generally assumed that the F1 versions of *II* and *III Henry VI* were revisions by Shakespeare of *The Contention* and *The True Tragedy,* which were the work of other dramatists. This theory, first proposed by Edmund Malone (see Gen. Intro. p. 82a), was based on Greene's words in *The Groatsworth of Wit* which were interpreted as Greene's accusation that his own work had been rewritten by Shakespeare. The argument was partially confirmed by some prefatory verses by "R.B." in a pamphlet called *Greene's Funerals,* which came out in 1594:

Greene gave the ground to all that wrote upon him.
Nay more the men that so eclipsed his flame
Purloined his plumes; can they deny the same?

Malone's theory thus involves two different proposals: (a) The F1 version of *II* and *III Henry VI* is a rewriting of *The Contention* and *The True Tragedy;* and (b) *Henry VI* is not Shakespeare's work, but his revision of the work of others.

It is now generally agreed by scholars that (a) is no longer tenable, and that both *The Contention* and *The True Tragedy* are in fact pirated versions of *II* and *III Henry VI,* put together for the press in much the same way as were the other pirated quartos (see Gen. Intro. p. 66b).

The second proposal (b) is not so easily confuted, for the answer depends solely on the judgment of style. There are manifest differences of style between various episodes and speeches in the *Henry VI* plays, and especially in the First Part. It is hard, for instance, to believe that all the speeches of the heroic Talbot are the work of one man. Thus, in I.v.9–39 his eloquence runs smooth and even, and in the same tone he laments over Salisbury (II.ii.4–21):

Bring forth the body of old Salisbury,
And here advance it in the market place,
The middle center of this cursèd town.
Now have I paid my vow unto his soul:
For every drop of blood was drawn from him
There hath at least five Frenchmen died tonight,
And that hereafter ages may behold
What ruin happened in revenge of him,
Within their chiefest temple I'll erect
A tomb, wherein his corpse shall be interred,
Upon the which, that everyone may read,
Shall be engraved the sack of Orleans,
The treacherous manner of his mournful death
And what a terror he had been to France.
But, lords, in all our bloody massacre,
I muse we met not with the Dauphin's Grace,
His new-come champion, virtuous Joan of Arc,
Nor any of his false confederates.

But the style of his speech to the King at the beginning of III.iv is a far less able piece of writing:

My gracious Prince, and honorable peers,
Hearing of your arrival in this realm,
I have awhile given truce unto my wars
To do my duty to my sovereign ——
In sign whereof, this arm, that hath reclaimed
To your obedience fifty fortresses,
Twelve cities, and seven wallèd towns of strength,
Beside five hundred prisoners of esteem,
Lets fall his sword before your Highness' feet.
And with submissive loyalty of heart
Ascribes the glory of his conquest got
First to my God and next unto your Grace.

Here the author laboriously builds up the speech line by line and stress by stress. Just before his death, Talbot for no very obvious reason drops into a ranting and strained rhyme as he addresses his gallant son (IV.vi.10–41):

When from the Dauphin's crest thy sword struck
      fire,
It warmed thy father's heart with proud desire
Of bold-faced victory. Then leaden age,
Quickened with youthful spleen and warlike rage,
Beat down Alençon, Orleans, Burgundy,

And from the pride of Gallia rescued thee.
The ireful bastard Orleans, that drew blood
From thee, my boy, and had the maidenhood
Of thy first fight, I soon encounterèd,
And interchanging blows I quickly shed
Some of his bastard blood, and in disgrace
Bespoke him thus: " Contaminated base
And misbegotten blood I spill of thine,
Mean and right poor, for that pure blood of mine
Which thou didst force from Talbot, my brave
  boy."
Here, purposing the Bastard to destroy,
Came in strong rescue. Speak, thy father's care,
Art thou not weary, John? How dost thou fare?
Wilt thou yet leave the battle, boy, and fly,
Now thou art sealed the son of chivalry?
Fly, to revenge my death when I am dead.
The help of one stands me in little stead.
Oh, too much folly is it, well I wot,
To hazard all our lives in one small boat!
If I today die not with Frenchmen's rage,
Tomorrow I shall die with mickle age.
By me they nothing gain an if I stay;

'Tis but the shortening of my life one day.
In thee thy mother dies, our household's name,
My death's revenge, thy youth, and England's
  fame.
All these and more we hazard by thy stay.
All these are saved if thou wilt fly away.

It may be that in these, his first plays, Shakespeare's touch was so unsure that he could vary in this manner, but it is more likely that *Henry VI* was the work of more than one author. Various names have been suggested — Greene, Marlowe, Peele, Nashe — but there is not sufficient evidence to identify the style of any one of them and the case cannot be proved either way. An inexperienced writer who has not yet developed his own style and technique is often powerfully influenced by the work of more established contemporaries, and Heminges and Condell would hardly have included the three parts of *Henry VI* in the folio unless they had believed that these plays were mainly Shakespeare's work.

The First Part of King Henry the Sixth

Shakespeare's plays dealing with English history, and other plays written by other dramatists, are often called " Chronicle plays " because they were based on the English Chronicles, particularly the volumes compiled by Raphael Holinshed in 1577, and reissued in 1587. Early chroniclers were not restricted by the laws of copyright or plagiarism, and they borrowed freely from their predecessors. Holinshed, for the period covered by the reign of Henry VI, copied or paraphrased Edward Halle's *Chronicle* so closely that one cannot now be certain whether Shakespeare was using Holinshed or Halle; probably he used both, for occasionally he adapted incidents which appear in Halle but not in Holinshed. In his later Chronicle plays — the two parts of *Henry IV* and *Henry V* — Shakespeare kept closely to history, but in *Henry VI* he was very free with historical facts. *The First Part of Henry VI,* for instance, opens with the funeral of Henry V, which occurred on November 7, 1422. As the procession pauses, Bedford and Gloucester pronounce their eulogies over the dead hero, but at once quarrels break out between Henry Beaufort, Bishop of Winchester, and Humphrey Duke of Gloucester. Gloucester taunts Winchester with his fondness for

an effeminate prince
Whom, like a schoolboy, you may overawe —

forgetting that the little King Henry VI was at this time less than a year old. Bedford stops the quarrel to utter a somewhat pagan invocation to Henry V's ghost, but he is himself interrupted by the arrival of three messengers. From the first messenger the English nobles learn of the loss of Guienne, Champagne, Rheims, Orleans, Paris, Guysors, Poictiers, and Rouen. Actually Rheims was surrendered in 1429, Paris in 1436, Guysors and Rouen in 1449. Moreover, Orleans and Poictiers were not in English hands at the death of Henry V. A second messenger enters to declare that Charles the Dauphin has been crowned in Rheims (an event that occurred in 1429); and a third messenger tells of the capture of Talbot, which happened on June 18, 1429 — some weeks after the siege of Orleans which is *later* shown in Act II.

I Henry VI is thus quite unreliable as sober history. In effect the play covers a period of twenty years, from the funeral of Henry V to the negotiations for the marriage of Henry VI to Margaret of Anjou (V.ii and v) in 1444; but the death of Sir John Talbot (IV.v and vi) — the most effective scene in the play — occurred in 1453, twenty-two years after the burning of Joan of Arc (V.iv).

Apart from this wild chronology, some of the episodes in the play are quite unhistorical. These include the famous incident of the plucking of the roses (II.iv) and the Countess of Auvergne's attempt to capture Talbot (II.ii).

Modern readers, however, are not greatly disturbed by such romantic inaccuracies; but they are acutely distressed by the unpleasant portrait of Joan of Arc, which is even further from actual history than George Bernard Shaw's *St. Joan*. In *I Henry VI* Joan is shown as mistress to Charles the Dauphin and a dabbler in the occult arts, who owes her abilities and successes to the infernal powers; and she is finally led to the stake as a witch and a strumpet. It is perhaps a slight excuse for her prosecutors in the play that the seasoned warriors whom she defeated could find no natural or divine explanation for the prowess and generalship of a girl of eighteen. Moreover, Shakespeare found most of the calumnies in Holinshed.

Some examples from Holinshed will show the use made of the *Chronicles* in the play.

1. THE COMING OF JOAN LA PUCELLE (cf. I.iv)

In the time of this siege at Orleans (French stories say) the first week of March 1429, unto Charles the Dolphin at Chinon, as he was in very great care and study how to wrestle against the English nation, by one Robert Badricourt, captain of Vacoleurs (made after Marshal of France by the Dolphin's creation), was carried a young wench of an eighteen years old, called Joan Arc, by name of her father (a sorry shepherd) James of Arc, and Isabel her mother; brought up poorly in their trade of keeping cattle; born at Domprin (therefore reported by Bale, Joan Domprin) upon Meuse in Loraine, within the diocese of Thoule. Of favor was she counted likesome, of person strongly made and manly, of courage great, hardy and stout withal; an understander of counsels though she were not at them; great semblance of chastity both of body and behavior; the name of Jesus in her mouth about all her businesses; humble, obdient; and fasting divers days in the week. A person (as their

books make her) raised up by power divine, only for succor to the French estate then deeply in distress; in whom, for planting a credit the rather, first the company that toward the Dolphin did conduct her, through places all dangerous, was holden by the English (where she never was afore) all the way and by nightertale [nighttime] safely did she lead: then at the Dolphin's sending by her assignment, from St. Katherine's church of Fierbois in Touraine (where she never had been and knew not) in a secret place there among old iron, appointed she her sword to be sought out and brought her (that with five flower-de-luces was graven on both sides), wherewith she fought and did many slaughters by her own hands. On warfare rode she in armor cap-a-pie [head to foot] and mustered [equipped] as a man; before her an ensign all white, wherein was Jesus Christ painted with a flower de luce in his hand.

Unto the Dolphin into his gallery when first she was brought, and he, shadowing himself behind, setting other gay Lords before him to try her cunning, from all the company with a salutation (that indeed mars all the matter) she picked him out alone; who thereupon had her to the end of the gallery, where she held him an hour in secret and private talk, that of his privy chamber was thought very long, and therefore would have broken it off; but he made them a sign to let her say on. In which (among other), as likely it was, she set out unto him the singular feats (for sooth) given her by revelation divine, that in virtue of that sword she should achieve; which were, how with honor and victory she would raise the siege at Orleans, set him in state of the crown of France, and drive the English out of the country, thereby he to enjoy the kingdom alone. Hereupon he heartened at full, appointed her a sufficient army with absolute power to lead them, and they obediently to do as she bade them. Then fell she to work, and first defeated, indeed, the siege at Orleans; by and by encouraged him to crown himself King of France at Reims, that a little before from the English she had won. Thus after pursued she many bold enterprises to our great displeasure a two year together; for the time she kept in state until she were taken and for heresy and witchery burned.

2. THE DEATH OF SALISBURY (cf. I.iv)

In the tower that was taken at the bridge end (as before you have heard) there was an high chamber, having a grate full of bars of iron, by the which a man might look all the length of the bridge into the city; at which grate many of the chief captains stood many times, viewing the city, and devising in what place it was best to give the assault. They within the city well perceived this tooting hole [spy hole], and laid a piece of ordnance directly against the window.

It so chanced that the nine and fiftieth day after the siege was laid, the Earl of Salisbury, Sir Thomas Gargrave and William Glasdale, with divers other went into the said tower, and so into the high chamber, and looked out at the grate; and, within a short space, the son of the master gunner, perceiving men looking out at the window, took his match (as his father had taught him; who was gone to dinner) and fired the gun; the shot whereof brake and shivered the iron bars of the grate, so that one of the same bars strake the Earl so violently on the head that it stroke away one of his eyes and the side of his cheek. Sir Thomas Gargrave was likewise stricken and died within two days.

3. THE CAPTURE OF ORLEANS (cf. II.i)

[Orleans was not captured in the manner shown in II.i of the play. This scene was based on the capture of Mans. The English withdrew from the town and reported to Talbot who sent out Matthew Gough to spy on the state of the French garrison.]

Matthew Gough so well sped his business that privily in the night he came into the castle, where he learned that the Frenchmen very negligently used themselves, without taking heed in their watch, as though they had been out of all danger; which well understood, he returned again, and within a mile of the city met the Lord Talbot and the Lord Scales, and opened unto them all things according to his credence. The Lords then to make haste in the matter (because the day approached) with all speed possible came to the postern gate, and alighting from their horses, about six of the clock in the morning, they issued out of the castle crying, " Saint George! Talbot! "

The Frenchmen, being thus suddenly taken, were sore amazed; in so much that some of them, being not out of their beds, got up in their shirts and leaped over the walls. Others ran naked out of the gates to save their lives, leaving all their apparel, horses, armor, and riches behind them: none was hurt but such as resisted.

4. THE END OF JOAN LA PUCELLE (cf. v.iv)

[Joan was tried before Peter Cauchon, Bishop of Beauvais, who] caused her life and belief, after order of law, to be inquired upon and examined. Wherein found though a virgin, yet first, shamefully rejecting her sex abominably in acts and apparel, to have counterfeit mankind, and then, all damnably faithless, to be a pernicious instrument to hostility and bloodshed in devilish witchcraft and sorcery, sentence accordingly was pronounced against her. Howbeit, upon humble confession of her iniquities with a counterfeit contrition pretending a careful sorrow for the same, execution spared and all mollified into this, that thenceforth she should cast off her unnatural wearing of man's habiliments and keep her to garments of her own kind, abjure her pernicious practices of sorcery and witchery, and have life and leisure in perpetual prison to bewail her misdeeds. Which to perform (according to the manner of abjuration) a solemn oath very gladly she took.

But herein (God help us!) she fully afore possessed of the fiend, not able to hold her own in any towardness of grace, falling straight into her former abominations (and yet seeking to eke out life as long as she might) stake not (though the shift were shameful) to confess herself a strumpet, and (unmarried as she was) to be with child.[1] For trial, the Lord Regent's lenity gave her nine month's stay, at the end whereof she (found herein as false as wicked in the rest, an eight days after, upon a further definitive sentence declared against her to be relapse and a renouncer of her oath and repentance) was thereupon delivered over to secular power, and so executed by consumption of fire in the old market place at Rouen, in the selfsame stead [place] where now St. Michael's Church stands: her ashes afterward without the town walls shaken into the wind.

The story of *I Henry VI* is thus mainly concerned with the wars in France, and it ends where the Second Part begins — with the marriage of the King, now grown up, with the French Princess Margaret.

[1] There was no truth in this calumny.

Henry VI Part I

DRAMATIS PERSONAE

KING HENRY *the Sixth*

DUKE OF GLOUCESTER, *uncle to the King, and Protector*

DUKE OF BEDFORD, *uncle to the King, and Regent of France*

THOMAS BEAUFORT, *Duke of Exeter, great-uncle to the King*

HENRY BEAUFORT, *great-uncle to the King, Bishop of Winchester, and afterward Cardinal*

JOHN BEAUFORT, *Earl, afterward Duke, of Somerset*

RICHARD PLANTAGENET, *son of Richard late Earl of Cambridge, afterward Duke of York*

EARL OF WARWICK

EARL OF SALISBURY

EARL OF SUFFOLK

LORD TALBOT, *afterward Earl of Shrewsbury*

JOHN TALBOT, *his son*

EDMUND MORTIMER, *Earl of March*

SIR JOHN FASTOLFE

SIR WILLIAM LUCY

SIR WILLIAM GLANSDALE

SIR THOMAS GARGRAVE

MAYOR OF LONDON

WOODVILE, *Lieutenant of the Tower*

VERNON, *of the White Rose or York faction*

BASSET, *of the Red Rose or Lancaster faction*

A LAWYER

MORTIMER'S KEEPERS

CHARLES, *Dauphin, and afterward King of France*

REIGNIER, *Duke of Anjou, and titular King of Naples*

DUKE OF BURGUNDY

DUKE OF ALENÇON

BASTARD *of Orleans*

GOVERNOR *of Paris*

MASTER GUNNER *of Orleans, and his son*

GENERAL *of the French forces in Bordeaux*

A FRENCH SERGEANT

A PORTER

AN OLD SHEPHERD, *father to Joan la Pucelle*

MARGARET, *daughter to Reignier, afterward married to King Henry*

COUNTESS OF AUVERGNE

JOAN LA PUCELLE, *commonly called Joan of Arc*

LORDS, WARDERS *of the Tower*, HERALDS, OFFICERS, SOLDIERS, MESSENGERS, *and* ATTENDANTS

FIENDS *appearing to La Pucelle*

SCENE — *Partly in England, and partly in France.*

Act I

SCENE I. *Westminster Abbey.*

[*Dead march. Enter the funeral of* KING HENRY *the Fifth, attended on by the* DUKE OF BEDFORD, *Regent of France, the* DUKE OF GLOUCESTER, *Protector, the* DUKE OF EXETER, *the* EARL OF WARWICK, *the* BISHOP OF WINCHESTER, HERALDS,° *&c.*]

BED. Hung be the heavens with black,° yield day to night!
Comets,° importing change of times and states,
Brandish° your crystal° tresses° in the sky,
And with them scourge the bad revolting stars
That have consented unto Henry's death!   5
King Henry the Fifth, too famous to live long!
England ne'er lost a king of so much worth.
   GLO. England ne'er had a king until his time.
Virtue he had, deserving to command.
His brandished sword did blind men with his beams.   10
His arms spread wider than a dragon's wings.
His sparkling eyes, replete with wrathful fire,
More dazzled and drove back his enemies
Than midday sun fierce bent against their faces.
What should I say? His deeds exceed all speech.   15
He ne'er lift° up his hand but conquerèd.
   EXE. We mourn in black. Why mourn we not in blood?
Henry is dead and never shall revive.
Upon a wooden° coffin we attend,
And death's dishonorable victory   20
We with our stately presence glorify,
Like captives bound to a triumphant car.°
What! Shall we curse the planets of mishap
That plotted thus our glory's overthrow?

Act I, Sc. i: s.d., **Heralds:** See App. 9.   **1. Hung . . . black:** Black curtains were used on the stage when a tragedy was being played. **2–5. Comets . . . death:** i.e., Henry's death is such a disaster that there should be signs and portents in the sky, as before the death of Julius Caesar. See *Caesar*, I.iii–II.ii, and II.ii.30–31. The notion of the evil influence of the stars is repeated in ll.23–24 and l.54. See App. 1. **3. Brandish:** flash. **crystal:** bright. **tresses:** The "tail" of a comet was likened to hair.

16. lift: lifted. **19. wooden:** i.e., useless. **22. car:** chariot.

Or shall we think the subtle-witted French   25
Conjurers and sorcerers that, afraid of him,
By magic verses° have contrived his end?
   WIN. He was a king blessed of the King of kings.
Unto the French the dreadful Judgment Day
So dreadful will not be as was his sight.   30
The battles of the Lord of Hosts he fought.
The Church's prayers made him so prosperous.
   GLO. The Church! Where is it? Had not church-
      men prayed,
His thread of life had not so soon decayed.
None do you like but an effeminate prince,   35
Whom, like a schoolboy, you may overawe.
   WIN. Gloucester, whate'er we like, thou art Pro-
      tector,°
And lookest to command the Prince and realm.
Thy wife is proud. She holdeth thee in awe°
More than God or religious churchmen may.   40
   GLO. Name not religion, for thou lovest the flesh,
And ne'er throughout the year to church thou go'st
Except it be to pray against thy foes.
   BED. Cease, cease these jars° and rest your minds
      in peace.
Let's to the altar. Heralds, wait on us.   45
Instead of gold, we'll offer up our arms,
Since arms avail not now that Henry's dead.
Posterity, await for wretched years
When at their mothers' moist eyes babe shall
      suck,
Our isle be made a nourish° of salt tears,   50
And none but women left to wail the dead.
Henry the Fifth, thy ghost I invocate:°
Prosper this realm, keep it from civil broils,
Combat with adverse planets° in the heavens!
A far more glorious star thy soul will make   55
Than Julius Caesar or bright ——
         [*Enter a* MESSENGER.]
   MESS. My honorable lords, health to you all!
Sad tidings bring I to you out of **France**
Of loss, of slaughter and discomfiture.
Guienne, Champagne, Rheims, Orleans   60
Paris, Guysors, Poictiers, are all quite lost.
   BED. What say'st thou, man, before dead Henry's
      corse?°
Speak softly, or the loss of those great towns
Will make him burst his lead° and rise from death.
   GLO. Is Paris lost? Is Rouen yielded up?   65
If Henry were recalled to life again,
These news would cause him once more yield the
      ghost.
   EXE. How were they lost? What treachery was
      used?

   MESS. No treachery, but want of men and money.
Amongst the soldiers this is mutterèd: 70
That here you maintain several factions,°
And whilst a field° should be dispatched and
      fought,
You are disputing of your generals.
One would have lingering wars with little cost.
Another would fly swift, but wanteth wings.   75
A third thinks, without expense at all,
By guileful fair words peace may be obtained.
Awake, awake, English nobility!
Let not sloth dim your honors new-begot.
Cropped are the flower-de-luces° in your arms;   80
Of England's coat one half is cut away.
   EXE. Were our tears wanting to this funeral,
These tidings would call forth their flowing tides.
   BED. Me they concern. Regent I am of France.
Give me my steelèd coat. I'll fight for France.   85
Away with these disgraceful wailing robes!°
Wounds will I lend the French instead of eyes
To weep their intermissive° miseries.
         [*Enter to them another* MESSENGER.]
   MESS. Lords, view these letters full of bad mis-
      chance.
France is revolted from the English quite,   90
Except some petty towns of no import.
The Dauphin° Charles is crownèd king in Rheims;
The Bastard of Orleans with him is joined;
Reignier, Duke of Anjou, doth take his part;
The Duke of Alençon flieth to his side.   95
   EXE. The Dauphin crownèd king! All fly to him!
Oh, whither shall we fly from this reproach?
   GLO. We will not fly, but to our enemies' throats.
Bedford, if thou be slack, I'll fight it out.
   BED. Gloucester, why doubt'st thou of my for-
      wardness?   100
An army have I mustered in my thoughts
Wherewith already France is overrun.
         [*Enter another* MESSENGER.]
   MESS. My gracious lords, to add to your laments
Wherewith you now bedew° King Henry's hearse,
I must inform you of a dismal fight   105
Betwixt the stout Lord Talbot and the French.
   WIN. What! Wherein Talbot overcame? Is 't so?
   MESS. Oh, no! Wherein Lord Talbot was o'er-
      thrown.
The circumstance I'll tell you more at large.
The tenth of August last this dreadful lord,   110
Retiring from the siege of Orleans,
Having full scarce six thousand in his troop,
By three and twenty thousand of the French

27. **verses:** incantations.   37. **Protector:** acting King during the infant King's minority.   39. **in awe:** i.e., afraid of her. 44. **jars:** wranglings.   50. **nourish:** nurse.   52. **invocate:** call upon, as if he were a saint in Heaven.   54. **adverse planets:** unlucky stars. See App. 1.   62. **corse:** corpse.   64. **lead:** The illustrious dead were inclosed in an inner coffin of lead.

71. **maintain . . . factions:** back up different parties.   72. **field:** combat force.   80. **flower-de-luces:** fleur-de-lis, the heraldic emblem for France, first set in the coat of arms of English kings by Edward I.   86. **wailing robes:** funeral cloaks. See App. 16. 88. **intermissive:** coming periodically.   92. **Dauphin:** the heir to the French throne, spelt "Dolphin" in the folio.   104. **bedew:** wet with tears.

Was round encompassèd and set upon.
No leisure had he to enrank his men.　　　115
He wanted pikes° to set before his archers,
Instead whereof sharp stakes plucked out of hedges
They pitchèd in the ground confusedly
To keep the horsemen off from breaking in.
More than three hours the fight continuèd,　　120
Where valiant Talbot above human thought
Enacted wonders with his sword and lance.
Hundreds he sent to Hell, and none durst stand
　　him.
Here, there, and everywhere, enraged he flew.
The French exclaimed the Devil was in arms.　125
All the whole army stood agazed on him.
His soldiers, spying his undaunted spirit,
" A Talbot! A Talbot! " cried out amain,
And rushed into the bowels of the battle.
Here had the conquest fully been sealed up,°　130
If Sir John Fastolfe had not played the coward.
He, being in the vaward, placed behind
With purpose to relieve and follow them,°
Cowardly fled, not having struck one stroke.
Hence grew the general wreck and massacre.　135
Enclosèd were they with their enemies.
A base Walloon,° to win the Dauphin's grace,
Thrust Talbot with a spear into the back,
Whom all France with their chief assembled
　　strength
Durst not presume to look once in the face.　140
　　BED. Is Talbot slain? Then I will slay myself
For living idly here in pomp and ease
Whilst such a worthy leader, wanting aid,
Unto his dastard foemen is betrayed.
　　MESS. Oh, no, he lives, but is took prisoner,　145
And Lord Scales with him, and Lord Hungerford.
Most of the rest slaughtered or took likewise.
　　BED. His ransom there is none but I shall pay.
I'll hale° the Dauphin headlong from his throne.
His crown shall be the ransom of my friend.　150
Four of their lords I'll change for one of ours.
Farewell, my masters; to my task will I.
Bonfires in France forthwith I am to make
To keep our great Saint George's feast° withal.
Ten thousand soldiers with me I will take,　155
Whose bloody deeds shall make all Europe quake.
　　MESS. So you had need, for Orleans is besieged.
The English army is grown weak and faint.
The Earl of Salisbury craveth supply
And hardly keeps his men from mutiny,　　160
Since they, so few, watch such a multitude.
　　EXE. Remember, lords, your oaths to Henry sworn
Either to quell the Dauphin utterly
Or bring him in obedience to your yoke.　　164

116. pikes: See Pl. 21d.　130. sealed up: completed. See App. 6.
132–33. being . . . them: i.e., being in the rear of the vanguard
(*vaward*) to act as reinforcement.　137. Walloon: inhabitant of
Walloon, now Belgium.　149. hale: pull, haul.　154. Saint . . .
feast: April 23rd.

　　BED. I do remember it, and here take my leave
To go about my preparation.°　　　[*Exit.*]
　　GLO. I'll to the Tower° with all the haste I can
To view the artillery and munition,
And then I will proclaim young Henry king.
　　　　　　　　　　　　　　　　　　　[*Exit.*]
　　EXE. To Eltham will I, where the young King is,
Being ordained his special governor,　　171
And for his safety there I'll best devise.　[*Exit.*]
　　WIN. Each hath his place and function to attend.
I am left out; for me nothing remains.
But long I will not be Jack out of office.　175
The King from Eltham I intend to steal
And sit at chiefest stern° of public weal.
　　　　　　　　　　　　　　　　　　[*Exeunt.*]

SCENE II. *France. Before Orleans.*

[*Sound a flourish.° Enter* CHARLES, ALENÇON, *and*
　REIGNIER, *marching with drum and* SOLDIERS.]
　　CHA. Mars his° true moving,° even as in the
　　　heavens
So in the earth, to this day is not known.
Late did he shine upon the English side.
Now we are victors. Upon us he smiles.
What towns of any moment but° we have?°　　5
At pleasure here we lie near Orleans.
Otherwhiles° the famished English, like pale
　　ghosts,
Faintly besiege us one hour in a month.
　　ALEN. They want° their porridge and their fat
　　　bull-beeves.°
Either they must be dieted like mules　　10
And have their provender tied to their mouths,
Or piteous they will look, like drownèd mice.
　　REI. Let's raise the siege. Why live we idly here?
Talbot is taken, whom we wont° to fear.
Remaineth none but mad-brained Salisbury,　15
And he may well in fretting spend his gall,°
Nor men nor money hath he to make war.
　　CHA. Sound, sound alarum!° We will rush on
　　　them.
Now for the honor of the forlorn French!
Him I forgive my death that killeth me　　20
When he sees me go back one foot or fly. [*Exeunt.*]

166. preparation: a five syllable word.　167. Tower: See Gen.
Intro. p. 16a and Pl. 2d.　177. at . . . stern: i.e., as chief steers-
man.
　　Sc. ii: s.d., flourish: trumpet call to announce the entrance of
an important personage.　1. Mars his: Mars's. Mars here is
both the planet and the god of war. See App. 1. true moving:
The course of the planet Mars had not as yet been accurately
traced.　5. What . . . have: i.e., all the chief towns are in our
hands. but: except.　7. Otherwhiles: at other times.　9. want:
lack. bull-beeves: bull-beef, regarded as the proper diet for
Englishmen. See *Hen V*, III.vii.160–64.　14. wont: were accustomed.　16. spend . . . gall: wear out his anger.　18. alarum:
trumpet call to arms.

[Here Alarum. They are beaten back by the Eng-
lish with great loss. Re-enter CHARLES, ALENÇON, *and*
    REIGNIER.*]*

CHA. Who ever saw the like? What men have I!
Dogs! Cowards! Dastards! I would ne'er have fled,
But that they left me 'midst my enemies.

    REI. Salisbury is a desperate homicide.   25
He fighteth as one weary of his life.
The other lords, like lions wanting food,
Do rush upon us as their hungry prey.

    ALEN. Froissart,° a countryman of ours, records
England all Olivers and Rowlands° bred   30
During the time Edward the Third did reign.
More truly now may this be verified,
For none but Samsons and Goliases°
It sendeth forth to skirmish. One to ten!   34
Lean raw-boned° rascals! Who would e'er suppose
They had such courage and audacity?

    CHA. Let's leave this town, for they are hare-
    brained slaves,
And hunger will enforce them to be more eager.
Of old I know them. Rather with their teeth   39
The walls they'll tear down than forsake the siege.

    REI. I think by some odd gimmors° or device
Their arms are set like clocks, still° to strike on,
Else ne'er could they hold out so as they do.
By my consent, we'll even let them alone.

    ALEN. Be it so.   45
    [Enter the BASTARD *of Orleans.]*

BAST. Where's the Prince Dauphin? I have news
    for him.

    CHA. Bastard of Orleans, thrice welcome to us.

    BAST. Methinks your looks are sad, your cheer
    appalled.°
Hath the late overthrow wrought this offense?
Be not dismayed, for succor is at hand.   50
A holy maid hither with me I bring,
Which by a vision sent to her from Heaven
Ordainèd is to raise this tedious siege
And drive the English forth° the bounds of France.
The spirit of deep prophecy she hath,   55
Exceeding the nine sibyls° of old Rome.
What's past and what's to come she can descry.
Speak, shall I call her in? Believe my words,
For they are certain and unfallible.°

    CHA. Go, call her in. *[Exit* BASTARD.*]* But first, to
    try her skill,   60

Reignier, stand thou as Dauphin in my place.
Question her proudly. Let thy looks be stern.
By this means shall we sound what skill she hath.
    [Re-enter the BASTARD *of Orleans, with* JOAN LA
    PUCELLE.°*]*

    REI. Fair maid, is 't thou wilt do these wondrous
    feats?

    PUC. Reignier, is 't thou that thinkest to beguile
    me?   65
Where is the Dauphin? Come, come from behind.
I know thee well, though never seen before.
Be not amazed, there's nothing hid from me.
In private will I talk with thee apart.
Stand back, you lords and give us leave awhile.   70
    [They stand back.]

    REI. She takes upon her° bravely at first dash.

    PUC. Dauphin, I am by birth a shepherd's daugh-
    ter,
My wit untrained in any kind of art.°
Heaven and our Lady gracious hath it pleased
To shine on my contemptible estate.   75
Lo, whilst I waited on my tender lambs,
And to sun's parching heat displayed my cheeks,
God's Mother° deignèd to appear to me,
And in a vision full of majesty
Willed me to leave my base vocation   80
And free my country from calamity.
Her aid she promised and assured success.
In cómplete glory she revealed herself;
And, whereas I was black and swart° before,
With those clear rays which she infused° on me   85
That beauty am I blessed with which you see.
Ask me what question thou canst possible,
And I will answer unpremeditated.
My courage try by combat if thou darest,
And thou shalt find that I exceed my sex.   90
Resolve on this,° thou shalt be fortunate
If thou receive me for thy warlike mate.

    CHA. Thou hast astonished me with thy high
    terms.°
Only this proof I'll of thy valor make.
In single combat thou shalt buckle° with me,   95
And if thou vanquishest, thy words are true;
Otherwise I renounce all confidence.

    PUC. I am prepared. Here is my keen-edged
    sword,
Decked with five flower-de-luces° on each side,
The which at Touraine, in Saint Katharine's
    churchyard,   100
Out of a great deal of old iron I chose forth.

---

29. Froissart: Jean Froissart (1338–1410), a famous French chronicler who recorded the wars of Edward III in France. **30. Olivers . . . Rowlands:** Rowland and Oliver, the most famous and doughty knights of Charlemagne, were much celebrated in legend. **33. Samsons . . . Goliases:** For the deeds of Samson and Goliath, see Judges 13–16 and I Samuel 17. **35. raw-boned:** fleshless skeletons. **41. gimmors:** "gimcrack trick," lit., a ring so made that it opens out into two rings. **42. still:** repeatedly. **48. cheer appalled:** cheerful looks made pale. **54. forth:** out of. **56. sibyls:** aged prophetesses. **59. unfallible:** infallible.

63. s.d., *La Pucelle:* the Maid. **71. takes . . . her:** plays her part. **73. art:** book learning. **78. God's Mother:** the Blessed Virgin. **84. swart:** dark. **85. infused:** shed. **91. Resolve on this:** if you decide to do this. **93. high terms:** lofty claims. **95. buckle:** join in close fight. **99. flower-de-luces:** See I.i.80,n and *I Hen VI* Intro. p. 106b.

CHA. Then come, o' God's name. I fear no
    woman.
PUC. And while I live, I'll ne'er fly from a man.
[*Here they fight, and* JOAN LA PUCELLE *overcomes.*]
CHA. Stay, stay thy hands! Thou art an Amazon,°
And fightest with the sword of Deborah.°   105
PUC. Christ's Mother helps me, else I were too
    weak.
CHA. Whoe'er helps thee, 'tis thou that must help
    me.
Impatiently I burn with thy desire.
My heart and hands thou hast at once subdued.
Excellent Pucelle, if thy name be so,   110
Let me thy servant° and not sovereign be.
'Tis the French Dauphin sueth to thee thus.
PUC. I must not yield to any rites of love,
For my profession's sacred from above.
When I have chasèd all thy foes from hence,   115
Then will I think upon a recompense.
CHA. Meantime look gracious on thy prostrate
    thrall.°
REI. My lord, methinks, is very long in talk.
ALEN. Doubtless he shrives this woman to her
    smock,°
Else ne'er could he so long protract his speech.   120
REI. Shall we disturb him, since he keeps no
    mean?°
ALEN. He may mean more than we poor men do
    know.
These women are shrewd tempters with their
    tongues.
REI. My lord, where are you? What devise you
    on?
Shall we give over Orleans, or no?   125
PUC. Why, no, I say, distrustful recreants!°
Fight till the last gasp. I will be your guard.
CHA. What she says I'll confirm. We'll fight it
    out.
PUC. Assigned am I to be the English scourge.
This night the siege assuredly I'll raise.   130
Expect Saint Martin's summer,° halcyon days,°
Since I have entered into these wars.
Glory is like a circle in the water
Which never ceaseth to enlarge itself
Till by broad spreading it disperse to nought.   135
With Henry's death the English circle ends.
Dispersèd are the glories it included.
Now am I like that proud insulting ship

Which Caesar and his fortune bare at once.°
    CHA. Was Mahomet inspirèd with a dove?°   140
Thou with an eagle art inspirèd then.
Helen,° the mother of great Constantine,
Nor yet Saint Philip's daughters,° were like thee.
Bright star of Venus, fall'n down on the earth,
How may I reverently worship thee enough?   145
    ALEN. Leave off delays, and let us raise the siege.
    REI. Woman, do what thou canst to save our
    honors.
Drive them from Orleans and be immortalized.
    CHA. Presently° we'll try. Come, let's away about
    it.   149
No prophet will I trust if she prove false. [*Exeunt.*]

SCENE III. *London. Before the Tower.*

[*Enter the* DUKE OF GLOUCESTER, *with his* SERVING-
MEN *in blue coats.*°]

GLO. I am come to survey the Tower this day.
Since Henry's death, I fear, there is conveyance.°
Where be these warders, that they wait not here?
Open the gates. 'Tis Gloucester that calls.
    1. WAR. [*Within*] Who's there that knocks so im-
    periously?   5
    1. SER. It is the noble Duke of Gloucester.
    2. WAR. [*Within*] Whoe'er he be, you may not be
    let in.
    1. SER. Villains, answer you so the Lord Protec-
    tor?
    1. WAR. [*Within*] The Lord protect him! So we
    answer him.
We do no otherwise than we are willed.°   10
    GLO. Who willed you? Or whose will stands but
    mine?
There's none protector of the realm but I.
Break up° the gates, I'll be your warrantize.°
Shall I be flouted thus by dunghill grooms?
[GLOUCESTER's *men rush at the Tower Gates, and*
WOODVILE, *the Lieutenant, speaks within.*]
    WOOD. What noise is this? What traitors have we
    here?   15
    GLO. Lieutenant, is it you whose voice I hear?
Open the gates. Here's Gloucester that would enter.

---

104. **Amazon:** See *MND*,I.i.l,n.   105. **Deborah:** a doughty
Hebrew prophetess who "judged" Israel. See Judges 4–5.
111. **servant:** lover. 117. **thrall:** slave. 119. **shrives . . .
smock:** is making love to her. 121. **mean:** moderation. 126. **recreants:** cowards. 131. **Saint . . . summer:** a patch of fine
weather in late autumn. St. Martin's Day is Nov. 11. **halcyon
days:** i.e., fine weather in winter. According to Pliny's *Natural
History*, for a week before and after midwinter's day, the sea is
calm so that the halcyon (kingfisher) may hatch her eggs.

138–139. **proud . . . once:** Plutarch, in his life of Julius Caesar,
wrote that when Caesar tried to cross over dangerous seas in a
small boat, he said to the reluctant master of the ship: "Good
fellow . . . fear not, for thou hast Caesar and his fortune with
thee." 140. **Mahomet . . . dove:** The prophet Mahomet was
said to have been divinely inspired by a dove or pigeon which
whispered in his ear. 142. **Helen:** St. Helena, the Christian
mother of the Emperor Constantine. 143. **Philip's daughters:**
See Acts 21: 8–9: "And we entered into the house of Philip the
Evangelist . . . and the same man had four daughters, virgins,
which did prophesy." 149. **Presently:** immediately.
    Sc. iii: s.d., **blue coats:** blue liveries. 2. **conveyance:** trick-
ery. 10. **willed:** ordered. 13. **Break up:** break down. **warrantize:** guarantee.

WOOD. Have patience, noble Duke. I may not
   open.
The Cardinal of Winchester forbids.
From him I have express commandment   20
That thou nor none of thine shall be let in.
   GLO. Faint-hearted Woodvile, prizest him 'fore
   me?
Arrogant Winchester, that haughty prelate
Whom Henry, our late sovereign, ne'er could
   brook?°
Thou art no friend to God or to the King.   25
Open the gates, or I'll shut thee out shortly.
   SERVINGMEN. Open the gates unto the Lord Pro-
   tector,
Or we'll burst them open if that you come not
   quickly.
   [*Enter to the Protector at the Tower Gates*
   WINCHESTER *and his men in tawny*° *coats.*]
   WIN. How now, ambitious Humphrey! What
   means this?
   GLO. Peeled° priest, dost thou command me to be
   shut out?   30
   WIN. I do, thou most usurping proditor,°
And not protector, of the King or realm.
   GLO. Stand back, thou manifest conspirator —
Thou that contrivedst to murder our dead lord,
Thou that givest whores indulgences to sin.   35
I'll canvass° thee in thy broad cardinal's hat
If thou proceed in this thy insolence.
   WIN. Nay, stand thou back; I will not budge a
   foot.
This be Damascus,° be thou cursèd Cain,
To slay thy brother Abel if thou wilt.   40
   GLO. I will not slay thee, but I'll drive thee back.
Thy scarlet robes as a child's bearing cloth°
I'll use to carry thee out of this place.
   WIN. Do what thou darest. I beard thee to thy
   face.
   GLO. What! Am I dared and bearded to my face?°
Draw, men, for all this privilegèd place.°   46
Blue coats to tawny coats! Priest, beware your
   beard!
I mean to tug° it and to cuff you soundly.
Under my feet I stamp thy cardinal's hat.
In spite of Pope or dignities of Church,   50
Here by the cheeks I'll drag thee up and down.

WIN. Gloucester, thou wilt answer this before the
   Pope.
   GLO. Winchester goose,° I cry, " A rope! A
   rope! "° —
Now beat them hence. Why do you let them
   stay? —
Thee I'll chase hence, thou wolf in sheep's array. 55
Out, tawny coats! Out, scarlet hypocrite!
[*Here* GLOUCESTER's *men beat out the* CARDINAL's
men, and enter in the hurly-burly° *the* MAYOR OF
LONDON *and his* OFFICERS.]
   MAY. Fie, lords, that you, being supreme magis-
   trates,
Thus contumeliously° should break the peace!
   GLO. Peace, Mayor! Thou know'st little of my
   wrongs.
Here's Beaufort, that regards nor God nor King,
Hath here distrained° the Tower to his use.   61
   WIN. Here's Gloucester, a foe to citizens,
One that still motions° war and never peace,
O'ercharging your free purses with° large fines,
That seeks to overthrow religion   65
Because he is Protector of the realm,
And would have armor here out of the Tower
To crown himself King and suppress the Prince.
   GLO. I will not answer thee with words, but
   blows.   [*Here they skirmish again.*]
   MAY. Naught rests for me in this tumultuous
   strife   70
But to make open proclamation.
Come, Officers. As loud as e'er thou canst,
Cry.
   OFF. All manner of men assembled here in arms
this day against God's peace and the King's, we 75
charge and command you, in His Highness' name,
to repair to your several° dwelling places, and not
to wear, handle, or use any sword, weapon, or dag-
ger henceforward, upon pain of death.
   GLO. Cardinal, I'll be no breaker of the law;   80
But we shall meet, and break° our minds at large.
   WIN. Gloucester, we will meet — to thy cost, be
   sure.
Thy heart blood I will have for this day's work.
   MAY. I'll call for clubs° if you will not away.
This Cardinal's more haughty than the Devil.   85
   GLO. Mayor, farewell. Thou dost but what thou
   mayst.
   WIN. Abominable Gloucester, guard thy head,
For I intend to have it ere long.

24. brook: endure. **28. s.d., tawny:** yellowish brown. **30. Peeled:**
i.e., with your head shaven. **31. proditor:** betrayer, traitor.
36. canvass: lit., toss (in a canvas sheet). **39. Damascus:** According to tradition the murder of Abel by Cain took place at
Damascus. **42. bearing cloth:** robe in which an infant was
carried to its christening. **45. bearded . . . face:** openly insulted. **46. privilegèd place:** The Tower, being a royal palace,
was invested with certain "privileges"; it was, e.g., a capital
offense to draw a sword in anger within the precincts of a palace.
48. tug: To pull a man by the beard was regarded as the deadliest
insult that could be offered. See *Haml,* II.ii.600 and *Lear,* III.
vii.35–36.

53. Winchester goose: See *Tr and Cr,* V.x.55,n. **A rope! A rope!:**
an abusive cry. **56. s.d., hurly-burly:** confusion. **58. con-
tumeliously:** contemptuously. **61. distrained:** seized. **63. motions:** proposes. **64. O'ercharging . . . with:** laying excessive
burdens on. **77. several:** separate. **81. break:** reveal.
84. call . . . clubs: the cry raised in the streets of London to call
on the apprentices to leave their shops and come out to assist
the city officers.

[*Exeunt, severally,* GLOUCESTER *and* WINCHESTER
with their SERVINGMEN.]

MAY. See the coast cleared, and then we will de-
part.   89
Good God, these nobles should such stomachs° bear!
I myself fight not once in forty year.   [*Exeunt.*]

SCENE IV. *Orleans.*°

[*Enter, on the walls, a* MASTER GUNNER *and his* BOY.]

M. GUN. Sirrah,° thou know'st how Orleans is be-
sieged,
And how the English have the suburbs won.
BOY. Father, I know, and oft have shot at them,
Howe'er unfortunate I missed my aim.
M. GUN. But now thou shalt not. Be thou ruled
by me.   5
Chief master gunner am I of this town.
Something I must do to procure me grace.°
The Prince's espials° have informèd me
How the English, in the suburbs close intrenched,
Wont° through a secret grate of iron bars   10
In yonder tower to overpeer° the city
And thence discover how with most advantage
They may vex us with shot or with assault.
To intercept this inconvenience,
A piece of ordnance 'gainst it I have placed;   15
And even these three days have I watched,
If I could see them.
Now do thou watch, for I can stay no longer.
If thou spy'st any, run and bring me word;   19
And thou shalt find me at the Governor's.   [*Exit.*]
BOY. Father, I warrant you, take you no care.
I'll never trouble you° if I may spy them.   [*Exit.*]
[*Enter, on the turrets, the* LORDS SALISBURY *and*
TALBOT, SIR WILLIAM GLANSDALE, SIR THOMAS
GARGRAVE, *and others.*]

SAL. Talbot, my life, my joy, again returned!
How wert thou handled, being prisoner?
Or by what means got'st thou to be released?   25
Discourse, I prithee, on this turret's top.
TAL. The Duke of Bedford had a prisoner
Called the brave Lord Ponton de Santrailles.
For him was I exchanged and ransomèd.
But with a baser man of arms° by far   30
Once in contempt they would have bartered° me;
Which I disdaining scorned, and cravèd death
Rather than I would be so vile-esteemed.
In fine,° redeemed I was as I desired.

But, oh, the treacherous Fastolfe wounds my
heart,   35
Whom with my bare fists I would execute
If I now had him brought into my power.
SAL. Yet tell'st thou not how thou wert enter-
tained.°
TAL. With scoffs and scorns and contumelious
taunts.
In open market place produced they me   40
To be a public spectacle to all.
Here, said they, is the terror of the French,
The scarecrow that affrights our children so.
Then broke I from the officers that led me,   44
And with my nails digged stones out of the ground
To hurl at the beholders of my shame.
My grisly countenance made others fly.
None durst come near for fear of sudden death.
In iron walls they deemed me not secure.
So great fear of my name 'mongst them was spread
That they supposed I could rend bars of steel,   51
And spurn in pieces posts of adamant;°
Wherefore a guard of chosen shot° I had
That walked about me every minute while,°
And if I did but stir out of my bed,   55
Ready they were to shoot me to the heart.
[*Enter the* BOY *with a linstock.*°]
SAL. I grieve to hear what torments you endured,
But we will be revenged sufficiently.
Now it is suppertime in Orleans.
Here, through this grate, I count each one,   60
And view the Frenchmen how they fortify.
Let us look in. The sight will much delight thee.
Sir Thomas Gargrave and Sir William Glansdale,
Let me have your express opinions
Where is best place to make our battery° next.   65
GAR. I think at the north gate, for there stand
lords.
GLAN. And I, here, at the bulwark of the bridge.
TAL. For aught I see, this city must be famished,
Or with light skirmishes enfeeblèd.   69
[*Here they shoot.* SALISBURY *and* GARGRAVE *fall.*]
SAL. O Lord, have mercy on us, wretched sinners!
GAR. O Lord, have mercy on me, woeful man!
TAL. What chance is this that suddenly hath
crossed us?
Speak, Salisbury, at least, if thou canst speak.
How farest thou, mirror of all martial men?°
One of thy eyes and thy cheek's side struck off!   75
Accursèd tower! Accursèd fatal hand
That hath contrived this woeful tragedy!
In thirteen battles Salisbury o'ercame.°
Henry the Fifth he first trained to the wars.   79

---

90. stomachs: proud tempers.
     Sc. iv: Orleans: See *I Hen VI* Intro. p. 107a. 1. Sirrah: a term
of address used to an inferior. 7. grace: favor. 8. espials: spies.
10. Wont: are accustomed. 11. overpeer: look down on. 22. I'll
. . . you: i.e., I'll shoot without waiting for you to come. 30. man
of arms: soldier. 31. bartered: exchanged. 34. fine: conclusion.

38. entertained: treated. 52. adamant: the hardest kind of
stone (or metal). 53. chosen shot: selected musketeers.
54. every . . . while: all the time. 56. s.d., linstock: match for
discharging a cannon. See Pl.12a and note on p.96b. 65. battery: bombardment, assault. 74. mirror . . . men: perfect example of what a soldier should be. 78. o'ercame: was victor.

Whilst any trump did sound, or drum struck
    up,
His sword did ne'er leave striking in the field.
Yet° livest thou, Salisbury? Though thy speech
    doth fail,
One eye thou hast, to look to Heaven for grace.
The sun with one eye vieweth all the world.
Heaven, be thou gracious to none alive   85
If Salisbury wants° mercy at thy hands!
Bear hence his body. I will help to bury it.
Sir Thomas Gargrave, hast thou any life?
Speak unto Talbot; nay, look up to him.
Salisbury, cheer thy spirit with this comfort: 90
Thou shalt not die whiles° ——
He beckons with his hand and smiles on me,
As who should say, " When I am dead and gone,
Remember to avenge me on the French."
Plantagenet, I will; and like thee, Nero,°   95
Play on the lute,° beholding the towns burn.
Wretched shall France be only in my name.
    [*Here an alarum, and it thunders and lightens.*]
What stir is this? What tumult's in the heavens?
Whence cometh this alarum and the noise?
    [*Enter a* MESSENGER.]
  MESS. My lord, my lord, the French have gathered
    head.   100
The Dauphin, with one Joan la Pucelle joined,
A holy prophetess new risen up,
Is come with a great power to raise the siege.
    [*Here* SALISBURY *lifteth himself up and groans.*]
  TAL. Hear, hear how dying Salisbury doth groan!
It irks his heart he cannot be revenged.   105
Frenchmen, I'll be a Salisbury to you.
Pucelle or puzzel,° dolphin or dogfish,
Your hearts I'll stamp out with my horse's heels,
And make a quagmire of your mingled brains.
Convey me° Salisbury into his tent,   110
And then we'll try what these dastard Frenchmen
    dare.   [*Alarum. Exeunt.*]

SCENE V. *The same.*

[*Here an alarum again, and* TALBOT *pursueth the*
DAUPHIN, *and driveth him. Then enter* JOAN LA
PUCELLE, *driving Englishmen before her, and exit
after them. Then re-enter* TALBOT.]
  TAL. Where is my strength, my valor, and my
    force?
Our English troops retire, I cannot stay them.
A woman clad in armor chaseth them.
    [*Re-enter* LA PUCELLE.]
Here, here she comes. I'll have a bout with thee.

Devil or Devil's dam,° I'll conjure thee!   5
Blood will I draw on thee, thou art a witch,
And straightway give thy soul to him thou servest.
  PUC. Come, come, 'tis only I that must disgrace
    thee.   [*Here they fight.*]
  TAL. Heavens, can you suffer Hell so to prevail?
My breast I'll burst with straining of my courage,
And from my shoulders crack my arms asunder,
But I will chastise this high-minded° strumpet.   12
    [*They fight again.*]
  PUC. Talbot, farewell. Thy hour is not yet come.
I must go victual Orleans forthwith.
    [*A short alarum. Then enter the town with
    soldiers.*]
O'ertake me, if thou canst. I scorn thy strength.   15
Go, go, cheer up thy hungry-starvèd men.
Help Salisbury to make his testament.°
This day is ours, as many more shall be.   [*Exit.*]
  TAL. My thoughts are whirlèd like a potter's
    wheel.
I know not where I am, nor what I do.   20
A witch by fear, not force, like Hannibal,°
Drives back our troops and conquers as she lists:
So bees with smoke and doves with noisome stench
Are from their hives and houses driven away.
They called us for our fierceness English dogs;   25
Now, like to whelps,° we crying run away.
    [*A short alarum.*]
Hark, countrymen! Either renew the fight,
Or tear the lions° out of England's coat.
Renounce your soil, give sheep in lions' stead.°
Sheep run not half so treacherous from the wolf,
Or horse or oxen from the leopard,   31
As you fly from your oft-subduèd° slaves.
    [*Alarum. Here another skirmish.*]
It will not be. Retire into your trenches.
You all consented unto Salisbury's death,
For none would strike a stroke in his revenge.   35
Pucelle is entered into Orleans
In spite of us or aught that we could do.
Oh, would I were to die with Salisbury!
The shame hereof will make me hide my head.
    [*Exit* TALBOT. *Alarum; retreat; flourish.*]

SCENE VI. *The same.*

[*Enter, on the walls,* LA PUCELLE, CHARLES, REIGNIER,
ALENÇON, *and* SOLDIERS.]
  PUC. Advance° our waving colors on the walls;
Rescued is Orleans from the English.

Sc. v.   **5. dam:** mother.   **12. high-minded:** arrogant.
17. testament: last will.   **21. Hannibal:** the Carthaginian leader
who so often defeated the Romans.   **26. whelps:** puppies.
28. lions: the three lions in the coat of arms of English kings.
29. sheep . . . stead: i.e., sheep are a more fitting emblem than
lions.   **32. your oft-subdued:** whom you have often beaten.
    Sc. vi: **1. Advance:** set up.

82. Yet: still.   **86. wants:** is without.   **91. whiles:** until.
95. Nero: the Roman Emperor who is said to have played on the
lute while Rome burned.   **96. lute:** See Pl. 18d.   **107. puzzel:**
slut.   **110. me:** for me.

Thus Joan la Pucelle hath performed her word.
  CHA. Divinest creature, Astraea's° daughter,
How shall I honor thee for this success?   5
Thy promises are like Adonis'° gardens
That one day bloomed and fruitful were the next.
France, triumph in thy glorious prophetess!
Recovered is the town of Orleans.
More blessed hap did ne'er befall our state.   10
  REI. Why ring not out the bells aloud throughout
    the town?
Dauphin, command the citizens make bonfires
And feast and banquet in the open streets
To celebrate the joy that God hath given us.
  ALEN. All France will be replete with mirth and
    joy   15
When they shall hear how we have played the
    men.°
  CHA. 'Tis Joan, not we, by whom the day is won;
For which I will divide my crown with her,
And all the priests and friars in my realm
Shall in procession sing her endless praise.   20
A statelier pyramis° to her I'll rear
Than Rhodope's or Memphis'° ever was.
In memory of her when she is dead,
Her ashes, in an urn more precious
Than the rich-jeweled coffer° of Darius,°   25
Transported shall be at high festivals
Before the kings and queens of France.
No longer on Saint Denis° will we cry,
But Joan la Pucelle shall be France's saint.°
Come in, and let us banquet royally   30
After this golden day of victory.

                          [Flourish. Exeunt.]

Act II

SCENE I. *Before Orleans.*

[Enter a SERGEANT *of a band, with two* SENTINELS.*]*
  SERG. Sirs, take your places and be vigilant.
If any noise or soldier you perceive

Near to the walls, by some apparent° sign
Let us have knowledge at the court of guard.°
  1. SENT. Sergeant, you shall.   *[Exit* SERGEANT.*]*
    Thus are poor servitors,°   5
When others sleep upon their quiet beds,
Constrained° to watch in darkness, rain and cold.
[Enter TALBOT, BEDFORD, BURGUNDY, *and forces, with
    scaling ladders,° their drums beating a dead
                    march.°]*

  TAL. Lord Regent, and redoubted Burgundy,
By whose approach the regions of Artois,
Wallon and Picardy are friends to us,   10
This happy night the Frenchmen are secure,°
Having all day caroused and banqueted.
Embrace we then this opportunity
As fitting best to quittance° their deceit
Contrived by art and baleful sorcery.   15
  BED. Coward of France! How much he wrongs
    his fame,
Despairing of his own arm's fortitude,
To join with witches and the help of Hell!
  BUR. Traitors have never other company.   19
But what's that Pucelle whom they term so pure?
  TAL. A maid, they say.
  BED.   A maid! And be so martial!
  BUR. Pray God she prove not masculine ere long
If underneath the standard of the French
She carry armor as she hath begun.
  TAL. Well, let them practice° and converse with
    spirits.   25
God is our fortress, in whose conquering name
Let us resolve to scale their flinty bulwarks.
  BED. Ascend, brave Talbot. We will follow thee.
  TAL. Not all together. Better far, I guess,
That we do make our entrance several ways,   30
That, if it chance the one of us do fail,
The other yet may rise against their force.
  BED. Agreed. I'll to yond corner.
  BUR.   And I to this.
  TAL. And here will Talbot mount, or make his
    grave.
Now, Salisbury, for thee, and for the right   35
Of English Henry, shall this night appear
How much in duty I am bound to both.
  SENT. Arm! Arm! The enemy doth make assault!
            [Cry, " Saint George!" "A Talbot!"]
*[The French leap over the walls in their shirts. En-
ter, several ways, the* BASTARD *of Orleans,* ALENÇON,
and REIGNIER, *half ready, and half unready.°]*
  ALEN. How now, my lords! What, all unready so?
  BAST. Unready! Aye, and glad we 'scaped so well.

---

4. **Astraea:** daughter of the god Jupiter, and a pattern of feminine beauty. The excessive use of classical names in this passage is typical of Shakespeare's early work.   6. **Adonis:** a beautiful youth, loved by Venus. See Shakespeare's *Venus and Adonis.* There is a long description of Adonis' Garden in Spenser's *Faerie Queene,* III.vi.29. See Pl. 7a.   16. **played . . . men:** proved ourselves heroes.   21. **pyramis:** pyramid.   22. **Rhodope's or Memphis':** According to the story Rhodope was a courtesan who married the King of Memphis (the Egyptian city near the great pyramids).   25. **coffer:** treasure chest. **Darius:** King of Persia, defeated by Alexander the Great.   28. **Saint Denis:** patron Saint of France.   29. **Joan . . . saint:** This prophecy was fulfilled when Joan of Arc was canonized on May 16, 1920.

Act II, Sc. i: 3. **apparent:** clear, unmistakable.   4. **court of guard:** guardroom.   5. **servitors:** private soldiers.   7. **Constrained:** forced.   s.d., **scaling ladders:** See Pl. 12a.   **dead march:** as for Salisbury's funeral.   11. **secure:** careless.   14. **quittance:** pay back.   25. **practice:** plot.   38. s.d., **unready:** undressed.

REI. 'Twas time, I trow, to wake and leave our
   beds,   41
Hearing alarums at our chamber doors.
ALEN. Of all exploits since first I followed arms,
Ne'er heard I of a warlike enterprise
More venturous or desperate than this.   45
  BAST. I think this Talbot be a fiend of Hell.
  REI. If not of Hell, the Heavens, sure, favor him.
  ALEN. Here cometh Charles. I marvel how he
   sped.°
  BAST. Tut, holy Joan was his defensive guard.
     [*Enter* CHARLES *and* LA PUCELLE.]
CHA. Is this thy cunning, thou deceitful dame?
Didst thou at first, to flatter us withal,   51
Make us partakers of a little gain,
That now our loss might be ten times so much?
  PUC. Wherefore is Charles impatient with his
   friend?°
At all times will you have my power alike?   55
Sleeping or waking must I still prevail,
Or will you blame and lay the fault on me?
Improvident soldiers! Had your watch been good,
This sudden mischief never could have fall'n.
  CHA. Duke of Alençon, this was your default   60
That, being captain of the watch tonight,
Did look no better to that weighty charge.°
  ALEN. Had all your quarters been as safely kept
As that whereof I had the government,
We had not been thus shamefully surprised.   65
  BAST. Mine was secure.
  REI.   And so was mine, my lord.
  CHA. And, for myself, most part of all this night,
Within her quarter and mine own precinct°
I was employed in passing to and fro
About relieving of the sentinels.   70
Then how or which way should they first break in?
  PUC. Question, my lords, no further of the case
How or which way. 'Tis sure they found some place
But weakly guarded, where the breach was made.
And now there rests no other shift° but this: 75
To gather our soldiers, scattered and dispersed,
And lay new platforms° to endamage them.
[*Alarum. Enter an* ENGLISH SOLDIER, *crying,* "A
Talbot! A Talbot!" *They fly, leaving their clothes
behind.*]
SOLD. I'll be so bold to take what they have left.
The cry of Talbot serves me for a sword,
For I have loaden° me with many spoils,   80
Using no other weapon but his name.   [*Exit.*]

48. sped: fared.   54. friend: lover.   62. charge: responsibility.
68. precinct: part of the camp.   75. shift: device.   77. plat-
forms: plans.   80. loaden: laden.

SCENE II. *Orleans. Within the town.*

[*Enter* TALBOT, BEDFORD, BURGUNDY, *a* CAPTAIN,
and others.]

BED. The day begins to break, and night is fled,
Whose pitchy mantle° overveiled the earth.
Here sound retreat, and cease our hot pursuit.
           [*Retreat sounded.*]
TAL. Bring forth the body of old Salisbury,
And here advance° it in the market place,   5
The middle center of this cursèd town.
Now have I paid my vow unto his soul:
For every drop of blood was drawn from him
There hath at least five Frenchmen died tonight.
And that hereafter ages may behold   10
What ruin happened in revenge of him,
Within their chiefest temple I'll erect
A tomb, wherein his corpse shall be interred,
Upon the which, that everyone may read,
Shall be engraved the sack of Orleans,   15
The treacherous manner of his mournful death
And what a terror he had been to France.
But, lords, in all our bloody massacre,
I muse we met not with the Dauphin's Grace,°
His new-come champion, virtuous Joan of Arc,   20
Nor any of his false confederates.
  BED. 'Tis thought, Lord Talbot, when the fight
   began,
Roused on the sudden from their drowsy beds,
They did amongst the troops of armèd men
Leap o'er the walls for refuge in the field.   25
  BUR. Myself, as far as I could well discern
For smoke and dusky vapors of the night,
Am sure I scared the Dauphin and his trull°
When arm in arm they both came swiftly running,
Like to a pair of loving turtle doves   30
That could not live asunder day or night.
After that things are set in order here,
We'll follow them with all the power we have.
         [*Enter a* MESSENGER.]
MESS. All hail, my lords! Which of this princely
   train
Call ye the warlike Talbot, for his acts   35
So much applauded through the realm of France?
  TAL. Here is the Talbot. Who would speak with
   him?
  MESS. The virtuous lady, Countess of Auvergne,
With modesty admiring thy renown,   39
By me entreats, great lord, thou wouldst vouchsafe
To visit her poor castle where she lies,
That she may boast she hath beheld the man
Whose glory fills the world with loud report.
  BUR. Is it even so? Nay, then, I see our wars
Will turn unto a peaceful comic sport,   45

Sc. ii: 2. pitchy mantle: black cloak. 5. advance: bring
forward. 19. Dauphin's Grace: i.e., His Grace the Dauphin
28. trull: whore.

When ladies crave to be encountered with.
You may not, my lord, despise her gentle suit.
    TAL. Ne'er trust me, then, for when a world of
        men
Could not prevail with all their oratory,
Yet hath a woman's kindness overruled;°   50
And therefore tell her I return great thanks
And in submission will attend on her.
Will not your Honors bear me company?
    BED. No, truly, it is more than manners will;°
And I have heard it said unbidden guests   55
Are often welcomest when they are gone.
    TAL. Well then, alone, since there's no remedy,
I mean to prove this lady's courtesy. —
Come hither, Captain. [*Whispers.*] You perceive
        my mind?
    CAP. I do, my lord, and mean accordingly.   60
                                        [*Exeunt.*]

SCENE III. *Auvergne. The* COUNTESS's *castle.*

        [*Enter the* COUNTESS *and her* PORTER.]
    COUNT. Porter, remember what I gave in charge,
And when you have done so, bring the keys to me.
    POR. Madam, I will.   [*Exit.*]
    COUNT. The plot is laid. If all things fall out right,
I shall as famous be by this exploit   5
As Scythian Tomyris° by Cyrus' death.
Great is the rumor of this dreadful knight,
And his achievements of no less account.
Fain would mine eyes be witness with mine ears
To give their censure° of these rare° reports.   10
        [*Enter* MESSENGER *and* TALBOT.]
    MESS. Madam,
According as your ladyship desired,
By message craved, so is Lord Talbot come.
    COUNT. And he is welcome. What! Is this the
        man?
    MESS. Madam, it is.
    COUNT.   Is this the scourge of France?   15
Is this the Talbot, so much feared abroad
That with his name the mothers still° their babes?
I see report is fabulous and false.
I thought I should have seen some Hercules,
A second Hector,° for his grim aspéct   20
And large proportion of his strong-knit limbs.
Alas, this is a child, a silly dwarf!

50. overruled: prevailed.   54. more . . . will: i.e., you won't
want us.
Sc. iii: 6. Scythian Tomyris: She was Queen of the Massage-
tae, a Scythian (South Russian) tribe against which Cyrus King
of Persia led an expedition. Cyrus was killed in battle, whereupon
Tomyris had his head cut off and enclosed in a bag of blood so
that he might have his fill.   10. censure: judgment. rare: wonderful.   17. still: quieten.   20. Hector: the doughty champion
of Troy.

It cannot be this weak and writhled° shrimp
Should strike such terror to his enemies.
    TAL. Madam, I have been bold to trouble you,   25
But since your ladyship is not at leisure,
I'll sort° some other time to visit you.
    COUNT. What means he now? Go ask him
        whither he goes.
    MESS. Stay, my Lord Talbot, for my lady craves
To know the cause of your abrupt departure.   30
    TAL. Marry,° for that she's in a wrong belief,
I go to certify her Talbot's here.
        [*Re-enter* PORTER *with keys.*]
    COUNT. If thou be he, then art thou prisoner.
    TAL. Prisoner! To whom?
    COUNT.   To me, blood-thirsty lord;
And for that cause I trained° thee to my house.   35
Long time thy shadow hath been thrall to me,
For in my gallery thy picture hangs.
But now the substance shall endure the like,
And I will chain these legs and arms of thine,
That hast by tyranny these many years   40
Wasted our country, slain our citizens,
And sent our sons and husbands captive.°
    TAL. Ha, ha, ha!
    COUNT. Laughest thou, wretch? Thy mirth shall
        turn to moan.
    TAL. I laugh to see your ladyship so fond°   45
To think that you have aught but Talbot's shadow
Whereon to practice your severity.
    COUNT. Why, art not thou the man?
    TAL.   I am indeed.
    COUNT. Then have I substance too.
    TAL. No, no, I am but shadow of myself.   50
You are deceived, my substance is not here;
For what you see is but the smallest part
And least proportion of humanity.
I tell you, madam, were the whole frame here,
It is of such a spacious lofty pitch°   55
Your roof were not sufficient to contain 't.
    COUNT. This is a riddling merchant for the
        nonce.°
He will be here, and yet he is not here.
How can these contrarieties agree?
    TAL. That will I show you presently.°   60
                [*Winds° his horn.*
            Drums strike up. A peal° of ordnance.]
                [*Enter* SOLDIERS.]
How say you, madam? Are you now persuaded
That Talbot is but shadow of himself?
These are his substance, sinews, arms, and strength
With which he yoketh your rebellious necks,

23. writhled: shriveled and wrinkled.   27. sort: choose.   31. Marry:
Mary, by the Virgin.   35. trained: lured, enticed.   42. captivate: captives.   45. fond: foolish.   55. pitch: height.   57. for
. . . nonce: lit., for the occasion — one of those rather meaningless expressions which are so useful in filling up a line of verse.
60. presently: immediately. s.d., Winds: sounds. peal: discharge.

Razeth your cities, and subverts° your towns,   65
And in a moment makes them desolate.
   COUNT. Victorious Talbot! Pardon my abuse.
I find thou art no less than fame hath bruited°
And more than may be gathered by thy shape.
Let my presumption not provoke thy wrath,   70
For I am sorry that with reverence
I did not entertain thee as thou art.
   TAL. Be not dismayed, fair lady, nor misconstrue
The mind of Talbot as you did mistake
The outward composition of his body.   75
What you have done hath not offended me;
Nor other satisfaction do I crave,
But only, with your patience, that we may
Taste of your wine and see what cates° you have,
For soldiers' stomachs always serve them well.   80
   COUNT. With all my heart, and think me honored
To feast so great a warrior in my house. [Exeunt.]

SCENE IV. *London. The Temple garden.*

[*Enter the* EARLS OF SOMERSET, SUFFOLK,
and WARWICK, RICHARD PLANTAGENET,
VERNON, *and another* LAWYER.]

   PLAN. Great lords and gentlemen, what means
     this silence?
Dare no man answer in a case of truth?
   SUF. Within the Temple Hall° we were too loud.
The garden here is more convenient.
   PLAN. Then say at once if I maintained the truth,
Or else was wrangling Somerset in the error?   6
   SUF. Faith, I have been a truant° in the law,
And never yet could frame my will to it;
And therefore frame the law unto my will.
   SOM. Judge you, my Lord of Warwick, then, be-
     tween us.   10
   WAR. Between two hawks, which flies the higher
     pitch;°
Between two dogs, which hath the deeper mouth;°
Between two blades, which bears the better temper;
Between two horses, which doth bear him best;   14
Between two girls, which hath the merriest eye?
I have perhaps some shallow spirit of judgment,
But in these nice sharp quillets° of the law,
Good faith, I am no wiser than a daw.°
   PLAN. Tut, tut, here is a mannerly forbearance.°
The truth appears so naked on my side   20
That any purblind° eye may find it out.
   SOM. And on my side it is so well appareled,

So clear, so shining, and so evident
That it will glimmer through a blind man's eye.
   PLAN. Since you are tongue-tied and so loath to
     speak,   25
In dumb significants° proclaim your thoughts.
Let him that is a true-born gentleman
And stands upon° the honor of his birth,
If he suppose that I have pleaded truth,
From off this brier pluck a white rose with me.   30
   SOM. Let him that is no coward nor no flatterer,
But dare maintain the party of the truth,
Pluck a red rose from off this thorn with me.
   WAR. I love no colors,° and without all color
Of base insinuating flattery   35
I pluck this white rose with Plantagenet.
   SUF. I pluck this red rose with young Somerset,
And say withal I think he held the right.
   VER. Stay, lords and gentlemen, and pluck no
     more
Till you conclude that he upon whose side   40
The fewest roses are cropped from the tree
Shall yield the other in the right opinion.
   SOM. Good Master Vernon, it is well objected.°
If I have fewest, I subscribe in silence.
   PLAN. And I.   45
   VER. Then for the truth and plainness of the case,
I pluck this pale and maiden blossom here,
Giving my verdict on the white rose side.
   SOM. Prick not your finger as you pluck it off,
Lest bleeding you do paint the white rose red   50
And fall on my side so, against your will.
   VER. If I, my lord, for my opinion bleed,
Opinion° shall be surgeon to my hurt
And keep me on the side where still I am.
   SOM. Well, well, come on. Who else?   55
   LAW. Unless my study and my books be false,
The argument you held was wrong in you,
                       [*To* SOMERSET]
In sign whereof I pluck a white rose too.
   PLAN. Now, Somerset, where is your argument?
   SOM. Here in my scabbard, meditating that   60
Shall dye your white rose in a bloody red.
   PLAN. Meantime your cheeks do counterfeit° our
     roses,
For pale they look with fear, as witnessing
The truth on our side.
   SOM.   No, Plantagenet,
'Tis not for fear but anger that thy cheeks   65
Blush for pure shame to counterfeit our roses,
And yet thy tongue will not confess thy error.
   PLAN. Hath not thy rose a canker,° Somerset?

65. subverts: overturns. 68. bruited: noised abroad. 79. cates:
delicacies.
   Sc. iv: 3. Temple Hall: the dining hall of the Temple, one of
the Inns of Court. See Gen. Intro. pp. 31b–32a. 7. truant: slack
student. 11. pitch: flight. See App. 26. 12. mouth: cry. See
MND, IV.i.127,n. 17. quillets: subtleties. 18. daw: jackdaw.
19. mannerly forbearance: polite refusal to take sides. 21. purblind: half blind.

26. significants: signs. 28. stands upon: insists on, is eager to
defend. 34. colors: pretenses. Puns on the various meanings
of color are common. See *T Night*, I.v.5–14. 43. objected:
argued. 52–53. opinion . . . Opinion: judgment . . . honor —
used with a double meaning, as so often in Shakespeare. 62. counterfeit: imitate. 68. canker: grub.

SOM. Hath not thy rose a thorn, Plantagenet?
PLAN. Aye, sharp and piercing, to maintain his
truth,　　　　70
Whiles thy consuming canker eats his falsehood.
SOM. Well, I'll find friends to wear my bleeding
roses
That shall maintain what I have said is true,
Where false Plantagenet dare not be seen.　　74
PLAN. Now, by this maiden blossom in my hand,
I scorn thee and thy fashion, peevish boy.°
SUF. Turn not thy scorns this way, Plantagenet.
PLAN. Proud Pole, I will, and scorn both him and
thee.
SUF. I'll turn my part thereof into thy throat.
SOM. Away, away, good William de la Pole!　80
We grace the yeoman° by conversing with him.
WAR. Now, by God's will, thou wrong'st him,
Somerset.
His grandfather was Lionel Duke of Clarence,
Third son to the third Edward, King of England.
Spring crestless° yeomen from so deep a root?　85
PLAN. He bears him on the place's privilege,°
Or durst not, for his craven heart, say thus.
SOM. By Him that made me, I'll maintain my
words
On any plot of ground in Christendom.　　89
Was not thy father, Richard Earl of Cambridge,
For treason executed in our late King's days?
And, by his treason, stand'st not thou attainted,°
Corrupted,° and exempt° from ancient gentry?
His trespass yet lives guilty in thy blood,
And, till thou be restored, thou art a yeoman.　95
PLAN. My father was attachèd,° not attainted,
Condemned to die for treason, but no traitor;
And that I'll prove on better men than Somerset,
Were growing time once ripened to my will.°
For your partaker° Pole and you yourself,　100
I'll note you in my book of memory
To scourge you for this apprehension.°
Look to it well, and say you are well warned.
SOM. Ah, thou shalt find us ready for thee still;
And know us by these colors for thy foes,　105
For these my friends in spite of thee shall wear.
PLAN. And, by my soul, this pale and angry rose,
As cognizance° of my blood-drinking hate,
Will I forever and my faction wear
Until it wither with me to my grave　　110

Or flourish to the height of my degree.
SUF. Go forward and be choked with thy ambi-
tion!
And so farewell until I meet thee next.　[*Exit.*]
SOM. Have with thee, Pole. Farewell, ambitious
Richard.　　　　　[*Exit.*]
PLAN. How I am braved° and must perforce en-
dure it!　　　　115
WAR. This blot that they object against your house
Shall be wiped out in the next Parliament,
Called for the truce of° Winchester and Gloucester;
And if thou be not then created York,
I will not live to be accounted Warwick.　120
Meantime, in signal of my love to thee,
Against proud Somerset and William Pole,
Will I upon thy party wear this rose.
And here I prophesy: this brawl today,
Grown to this faction° in the Temple garden,　125
Shall send between the red rose and the white
A thousand souls to death and deadly night.
PLAN. Good Master Vernon, I am bound to you
That you on my behalf would pluck a flower.
VER. In your behalf still will I wear the same.　130
LAW. And so will I.
PLAN. Thanks, gentle sir.
Come, let us four to dinner. I dare say
This quarrel will drink blood another day.
　　　　　　　　　　　　[*Exeunt.*]

SCENE V. *The Tower of London.*

[*Enter* MORTIMER, *brought in a chair, and* JAILERS.]
MOR. Kind keepers of my weak decaying age,
Let dying Mortimer here rest himself.
Even like a man new halèd° from the rack,°
So fare my limbs with long imprisonment,
And these grey locks, the pursuivants° of death, 5
Nestor-like° agéd in an age of care,
Argue° the end of Edmund Mortimer.
These eyes, like lamps whose wasting oil is spent,
Wax dim, as drawing to their exigent;°　　9
Weak shoulders, overborne with burdening grief,
And pithless° arms, like to a withered vine
That droops his sapless branches to the ground.
Yet are these feet, whose strengthless stay° is numb,
Unable to support this lump of clay,
Swift-wingèd with desire to get a grave,　　15
As witting° I no other comfort have.
But tell me, keeper, will my nephew come?

76. boy: youngster, a deadly insult. See *Cor*, V.vi.101.　81. grace
. . . yeoman: i.e., we honor this man, who is no gentleman, by
talking with him.　85. crestless: without a coat of arms. See
App. 9.　86. bears . . . privilege: i.e., he knows he is safe because fighting is not allowed in this place. See I.iii.46,n.　92. attainted: convicted.　93. Corrupted: regarded as of tainted blood.
exempt: excluded. The children of a nobleman condemned for
treason lost all the family privileges.　96. attached: arrested.
99. growing . . . will: i.e., if ever I get my opportunity.　100. partaker: supporter.　102. apprehension: notion.　108. cognizance: badge.

115. braved: insulted.　118. for . . . of: to make peace between.
125. faction: division, quarrel.
　Sc. v: 3. haled: hauled, fetched. rack: See App. 10.　5. pursuivants: officers attending on the heralds.　6. Nestor-like:
Nestor was the elder statesman among the Greeks at the siege
of Troy. See *Tr & Cr.*　7. Argue: indicate.　9. exigent: end.
11. pithless: lit., without marrow, feeble.　13. stay: support.
16. witting: knowing.

1. JAI. Richard Plantagenet, my lord, will come.
We sent unto the Temple, unto his chamber,
And answer was returned that he will come.   20
   MOR. Enough. My soul shall then be satisfied.
Poor gentleman! His wrong doth equal mine.
Since Henry Monmouth° first began to reign,
Before whose glory I was great in arms,
This loathsome sequestration° have I had;   25
And even since then hath Richard been obscured,
Deprived of honor and inheritance.
But now the arbitrator of despairs,
Just Death,° kind umpire of men's miseries,
With sweet enlargement° doth dismiss me hence.
I would his troubles likewise were expired,   31
That so he might recover what was lost.
             [*Enter* RICHARD PLANTAGENET.]
   1. JAI. My lord, your loving nephew now is come.
   MOR. Richard Plantagenet, my friend, is he come?
   PLAN. Aye, noble Uncle, thus ignobly used,   35
Your nephew, late despisèd Richard, comes.
   MOR. Direct mine arms I may embrace his neck,
And in his bosom spend my latter° gasp.
Oh, tell me when my lips do touch his cheeks,
That I may kindly give one fainting kiss.   40
And now declare, sweet stem from York's great
      stock,
Why didst thou say of late thou wert despised?
   PLAN. First, lean thine agèd back against mine
      arm,
And in that ease I'll tell thee my disease.
This day, in argument upon a case,   45
Some words there grew 'twixt Somerset and me,
Among which terms he used his lavish tongue
And did upbraid me with my father's death;
Which obloquy° set bars before my tongue,
Else with the like I had requited him.   50
Therefore, good Uncle, for my father's sake,
In honor of a true Plantagenet
And for alliance sake, declare the cause
My father, Earl of Cambridge, lost his head.
   MOR. That cause, fair Nephew, that imprisoned
      me   55
And hath detained me all my flowering youth
Within a loathsome dungeon, there to pine,
Was cursèd instrument of his decease.
   PLAN. Discover more at large what cause that
      was,
For I am ignorant and cannot guess.   60
   MOR. I will, if that my fading breath permit,
And death approach not ere my tale be done.
Henry° the Fourth, grandfather to this King,

Deposed his nephew Richard, Edward's son,
The first-begotten and the lawful heir   65
Of Edward, King, the third of that descent;
During whose reign the Percies of the North,
Finding his usurpation most unjust,
Endeavored my advancement to the throne.
The reason moved these warlike lords to this   70
Was for that — young King Richard thus removed,
Leaving no heir begotten of his body —
I was the next by birth and parentage;
For by my mother I derivèd am
From Lionel Duke of Clarence, the third son   75
To King Edward the Third, whereas he
From John of Gaunt doth bring his pedigree,
Being but fourth of that heroic line.
But mark: As in this haughty great attempt
They laborèd to plant the rightful heir,   80
I lost my liberty and they their lives.
Long after this, when Henry the Fifth,
Succeeding his father Bolingbroke, did reign,
Thy father, Earl of Cambridge, then derived°
From famous Edmund Langley, Duke of York,   85
Marrying my sister that thy mother was,
Again in pity of my hard distress
Levied an army, weening° to redeem
And have installed me in the diadem;°
But, as the rest, so fell that noble Earl   90
And was beheaded. Thus the Mortimers,
In whom the title rested, were suppressed.
   PLAN. Of which, my lord, your Honor is the last.
   MOR. True, and thou seest that I no issue° have,
And that my fainting words do warrant death.   95
Thou art my heir; the rest I wish thee gather.°
But yet be wary in thy studious care.
   PLAN. Thy grave admonishments prevail with
      me.
But yet, methinks, my father's execution
Was nothing less than bloody tyranny.   100
   MOR. With silence, Nephew, be thou politic.°
Strong-fixèd is the House of Lancaster,
And like a mountain not to be removed.
But now thy uncle is removing hence,   104
As princes do their courts when they are cloyed°
With long continuance in a settled place.
   PLAN. Oh, Uncle, would some part of my young
      years
Might but redeem the passage of your age!
   MOR. Thou dost then wrong me, as that slaugh-
      terer doth   109
Which giveth many wounds when one will kill.
Mourn not, except thou sorrow for my good.

---

23. Henry Monmouth: i.e., Henry V.   **25. sequestration:** separation, i.e., imprisonment.   **28–29. arbitrator . . . Death:** Death, who finally ends despair.   **30. enlargement:** release.   **38. latter:** last.   **49. obloquy:** disgrace.   **63–92: Henry . . . suppressed:** See *Rich II*, App. 28, and Genealogical Table A. The deposition of Richard II is the theme of Shakespeare's *Rich II*.   **84. derived:** descended from.   **88. weening:** thinking.   **89. installed . . . diadem:** crowned King.   **94. issue:** child.   **96. gather:** understand from hints.   **101. politic:** crafty.   **105. cloyed:** bored.

Only give order for my funeral.
And so farewell, and fair be all thy hopes,
And prosperous be thy life in peace and war!

           [*Dies.*]

PLAN. And peace, no war, befall thy parting soul!
In prison hast thou spent a pilgrimage,° 116
And like a hermit overpassed thy days.
Well, I will lock his counsel in my breast,
And what I do imagine, let that rest.
Keepers, convey him hence, and I myself 120
Will see his burial better than his life.

    [*Exeunt* JAILERS, *bearing out*
      the body of MORTIMER.]

Here dies the dusky° torch of Mortimer,
Choked with ambition of the meaner sort.
And for those wrongs, those bitter injuries,
Which Somerset hath offered to my house, 125
I doubt not but with honor to redress;
And therefore haste I to the Parliament,
Either to be restorèd to my blood°
Or make my ill the advantage of my good. [*Exit.*]

Act III

SCENE I. *London. The Parliament House.*

[*Flourish. Enter* KING, EXETER, GLOUCESTER,
WARWICK, SOMERSET, *and* SUFFOLK, *the* BISHOP OF
WINCHESTER, RICHARD PLANTAGENET, *and others.*
GLOUCESTER *offers to put up a bill.*° WINCHESTER
snatches it and tears it.]

WIN. Comest thou with deep premeditated
  lines,°
With written pamphlets studiously devised,
Humphrey of Gloucester? If thou canst accuse,
Or aught intend'st to lay unto my charge,
Do it without invention,° suddenly, 5
As I with sudden and extemporal speech
Purpose to answer what thou canst object.
 GLO. Presumptuous priest! This place° commands
  my patience,
Or thou shouldst find thou hast dishonored me.
Think not, although in writing I preferred° 10
The manner of thy vile outrageous crimes,
That therefore I have forged, or am not able
Verbatim to rehearse the method° of my pen.
No, prelate. Such is thy audacious wickedness,
Thy lewd, pestiferous and dissentious pranks, 15

As° very infants prattle of thy pride.
Thou art a most pernicious usurer,
Froward by nature, enemy to peace,
Lascivious, wanton, more than well beseems
A man of thy profession and degree. 20
And for thy treachery, what's more manifest?
In that thou laid'st a trap to take my life,
As well at London Bridge as at the Tower.
Beside, I fear me, if thy thoughts were sifted,
The King, thy sovereign, is not quite exempt 25
From envious malice of thy swelling heart.
 WIN. Gloucester, I do defy thee. Lords, vouch-
  safe
To give me hearing what I shall reply.
If I were covetous, ambitious, or perverse
As he will have me, how am I so poor? 30
Or how haps° it I seek not to advance
Or raise myself, but keep my wonted calling?
And for dissension, who preferreth peace
More than I do — except I be provoked?
No, my good lords, it is not that offends; 35
It is not that that hath incensed the Duke.
It is because no one should sway° but he,
No one but he should be about the King,
And that engenders thunder in his breast
And makes him roar these accusations forth. 40
But he shall know I am as good ——
 GLO.   As good!
Thou bastard° of my grandfather!
 WIN. Aye, lordly sir, for what are you, I pray,
But one imperious in another's throne?
 GLO. Am I not Protector, saucy priest? 45
 WIN. And am not I a prelate of the Church?
 GLO. Yes, as an outlaw in a castle keeps°
And useth it to patronage° his theft.
 WIN. Unreverent Gloucester!
 GLO.   Thou art reverent
Touching thy spiritual function, not thy life. 50
 WIN. Rome shall remedy this.
 WAR.   Roam thither, then.
 SOM. My lord, it were your duty to forbear.
 WAR. Aye, see the Bishop be not overborne.°
 SOM. Methinks my lord should be religious,
And know the office that belongs to such. 55
 WAR. Methinks his lordship should be humbler.
It fitteth not a prelate so to plead.
 SOM. Yes, when his holy state is touched so near.
 WAR. State holy or unhallowed, what of that?
Is not his Grace Protector to the King? 60
 PLAN. [*Aside*] Plantagenet, I see, must hold his
  tongue,
Lest it be said, "Speak, sirrah,° when you should;

---

116. **pilgrimage:** complete life. 122. **dusky:** smoking, extinguished. 128. **to . . . blood:** i.e., restored to my proper rank.
See II.iv.93,n.

 Act III, Sc. i: **s.d., put . . . bill:** set up a written statement.
1. **lines:** i.e., of writing. 5. **invention:** elaborate preparation.
8. **This place:** i.e., the presence of the King. 10. **preferred:** put forward. 13. **method:** argument.

---

16. **As:** that. 31. **haps:** happens. 37. **sway:** have power.
42. **bastard:** See App. 28, Genealogical Table C. Beaufort was born before his mother married Gaunt. 47. **keeps:** dwells.
48. **patronage:** protect. 53. **overborne:** overcome. 62. **sirrah:** See I.iv.1,n.

Must your bold verdict enter talk with lords? "°
Else would I have a fling at Winchester.

   KING. Uncles of Gloucester and of Winchester,
The special watchmen of our English weal,°   66
I would prevail, if prayers might prevail,
To join your hearts in love and amity.
Oh, what a scandal is it to our crown
That two such noble peers as ye should jar!   70
Believe me, lords, my tender years can tell
Civil dissension is a viperous worm°
That gnaws the bowels of the commonwealth.
   [*A noise within,* " Down with the tawny coats! "]
What tumult's this?

   WAR.   An uproar, I dare warrant,
Begun through malice of the Bishop's men.   75
   [*A noise again,* " Stones! Stones! "]
   [*Enter* MAYOR.]

   MAY. Oh, my good lords and virtuous Henry,
Pity the city of London, pity us!
The Bishop and the Duke of Gloucester's men,
Forbidden late to carry any weapon,
Have filled their pockets full of pebble stones,   80
And banding themselves in contrary parts,°
Do pelt so fast at one another's pate
That many have their giddy brains knocked out.
Our windows are broke down in every street,
And we for fear compelled to shut our shops.   85
   [*Enter* SERVINGMEN, *in skirmish, with bloody pates.*]

   KING. We charge° you, on allegiance° to ourself,
To hold your slaughtering hands and keep the
    peace.
Pray, Uncle Gloucester, mitigate° this strife.

   1. SERV. Nay, if we be forbidden stones, we'll fall
to it with our teeth.   90

   2. SERV. Do what ye dare, we are as resolute.
                        [*Skirmish again.*]

   GLO. You of my household, leave this peevish
    broil
And set this unaccustomed fight aside.

   3. SERV. My lord, we know your Grace to be a
    man
Just and upright, and, for your royal birth,   95
Inferior to none but to His Majesty;
And ere that we will suffer such a prince,
So kind a father of the commonweal,
To be disgracèd by an inkhorn mate,°
We and our wives and children all will fight   100
And have our bodies slaughtered by thy foes.

   1. SERV. Aye, and the very parings of our nails
Shall pitch a field° when we are dead.
                       [*Begin again.*]

   GLO.   Stay, stay, I say!
And if you love me, as you say you do,
Let me persuade you to forbear awhile.   105

   KING. Oh, how this discord doth afflict my soul!
Can you, my Lord of Winchester, behold
My sighs and tears and will not once relent?
Who should be pitiful if you be not?
Or who should study to prefer° a peace   110
If holy churchmen take delight in broils?

   WAR. Yield, my Lord Protector, yield, Winchester,
Except you mean with obstinate repulse
To slay your sovereign and destroy the realm.
You see what mischief and what murder too   115
Hath been enacted through your enmity.
Then be at peace, except ye thirst for blood.

   WIN. He shall submit, or I will never yield.

   GLO. Compassion on the King commands me
    stoop,
Or I would see his heart out, ere the priest   120
Should ever get that privilege of me.

   WAR. Behold, my Lord of Winchester, the Duke
Hath banished moody discontented fury,
As by his smoothèd brows it doth appear.
Why look you still so stern and tragical?   125

   GLO. Here, Winchester, I offer thee my hand.

   KING. Fie, Uncle Beaufort! I have heard you
    preach
That malice was a great and grievous sin;
And will not you maintain the thing you teach,
But prove a chief offender in the same?   130

   WAR. Sweet King! The Bishop hath a kindly
    gird.°
For shame, my Lord of Winchester, relent!
What, shall a child instruct you what to do?

   WIN. Well, Duke of Gloucester, I will yield to
    thee.
Love for thy love and hand for hand I give.   135

   GLO. [*Aside*] Aye, but, I fear me, with a hollow
    heart. —
See here, my friends and loving countrymen.
This token serveth for a flag of truce
Betwixt ourselves and all our followers.
So help me God, as I dissemble° not!   140

   WIN. [*Aside*] So help me God, as I intend it not!

   KING. O loving Uncle, kind Duke of Gloucester,
How joyful am I made by this contráct!
Away, my masters! Trouble us no more,   144
But join in friendship, as your lords have done.

   1. SERV. Content. I'll to the surgeon's.

   2. SERV.   And so will I.

   3. SERV. And I will see what physic the tavern
    affords.   [*Exeunt* SERVINGMEN, MAYOR, *&c.*]

   WAR. Accept this scroll, most gracious sovereign,
Which in the right of Richard Plantagenet   150

---

63. **bold . . . lords:** i.e., express your insolent opinion in the presence of your betters. **66. weal:** welfare. **72. viperous worm:** caterpillar. See *Rich II,* II.iii.166,n. **81. contrary parts:** opposing sides. **86. charge:** command. **on allegiance:** loyalty — the most solemn form of command that can be put on a subject; to disobey is high treason. **88. mitigate:** pacify. **99. inkhorn mate:** scribbling wretch. **103. pitch a field:** fight a battle.

110. prefer: propose. **131. kindly gird:** i.e., the King has given him a gentle rebuke. **140. dissemble:** cheat.

We do exhibit° to your Majesty.
    GLO. Well urged, my Lord of Warwick. For,
        sweet Prince,
An if° your Grace mark every circumstance,
You have great reason to do Richard right,
Especially for those occasions°   155
At Eltham Place I told your Majesty.
    KING. And those occasions, Uncle, were of force.°
Therefore, my loving lords, our pleasure is
That Richard be restorèd to his blood.
    WAR. Let Richard be restorèd to his blood;   160
So shall his father's wrongs be recompensed.
    WIN. As will the rest, so willeth Winchester.
    KING. If Richard will be true, not that alone
But all the whole inheritance I give
That doth belong unto the House of York,   165
From whence you spring by lineal descent.
    PLAN. Thy humble servant vows obedience
And humble service till the point of death.
    KING. Stoop then and set your knee against my
        foot;
And in reguerdon° of that duty done,   170
I gird thee with the valiant sword of York.
Rise, Richard, like a true Plantagenet,
And rise created princely Duke of York.
    PLAN. And so thrive Richard as thy foes may fall!
And as my duty springs, so perish they   175
That grudge one thought against your Majesty!
    ALL. Welcome, high Prince, the mighty Duke of
        York!
    SOM. [*Aside*] Perish, base Prince, ignoble Duke
        of York!
    GLO. Now will it best avail your Majesty
To cross the seas and to be crowned in France.   180
The presence of a king engenders love
Amongst his subjects and his loyal friends,
As it disanimates° his enemies.
    KING. When Gloucester says the word, King
        Henry goes;
For friendly counsel cuts off many foes.   185
    GLO. Your ships already are in readiness.
        [*Sennet.° Flourish. Exeunt all but* EXETER.]
    EXE. Aye, we may march in England or in
        France,
Not seeing what is likely to ensue.
This late dissension grown betwixt the peers
Burns under feignèd ashes of forged° love,   190
And will at last break out into a flame.
As festered members° rot but by degree
Till bones and flesh and sinews fall away,
So will this base and envious discord breed.
And now I fear that fatal prophecy   195
Which in the time of Henry named the Fifth

Was in the mouth of every sucking babe —
That Henry born at Monmouth should win all
And Henry born at Windsor lose all:
Which is so plain that Exeter doth wish   200
His days may finish ere that hapless time.   [*Exit.*]

SCENE II. *France. Before Rouen.*

[*Enter* LA PUCELLE *disguised, with four* SOLDIERS
with sacks upon their backs.]
    PUC. These are the city gates, the gates of Rouen,°
Through which our policy° must make a breach.
Take heed, be wary how you place your words.
Talk like the vulgar sort of market men
That come to gather money for their corn.   5
If we have entrance, as I hope we shall,
And that we find the slothful watch but weak,
I'll by a sign give notice to our friends,
That Charles the Dauphin may encounter them.
    1. SOLD. Our sacks shall be a mean° to sack the
        city,   10
And we be lords and rulers over Rouen.
Therefore we'll knock.   [*Knocks.*]
    WATCH. [*Within*] *Qui est là?*
    PUC. *Paysans, pauvres gens de France;*
Poor market folks that come to sell their corn.   15
    WATCH. Enter, go in. The market bell is rung.
    PUC. Now, Rouen, I'll shake thy bulwarks to the
        ground.   [*Exeunt.*]
[*Enter* CHARLES, *the* BASTARD *of Orleans,* ALENÇON,
        REIGNIER, *and* FORCES.]
    CHA. Saint Denis bless this happy stratagem!
And once again we'll sleep secure in Rouen.   19
    BAST. Here entered Pucelle and her practisants.°
Now she is there, how will she specify
Where is the best and safest passage in?
    REI. By thrusting out a torch from yonder tower,
Which, once discerned, shows that her meaning is
No way to that, for weakness,° which she entered.
[*Enter* LA PUCELLE *on the top, thrusting out a torch
        burning.*]
    PUC. Behold, this is the happy wedding torch   26
That joineth Rouen unto her countrymen,
But burning fatal to the Talbotites!   [*Exit.*]
    BAST. See, noble Charles, the beacon of our friend.
The burning torch in yonder turret stands.   30
    CHA. Now shine it like a comet of revenge,
A prophet to the fall of all our foes!
    REI. Defer no time, delays have dangerous ends.
Enter, and cry "The Dauphin!" presently,
And then do execution on the watch.   35
                              [*Alarum. Exeunt.*]

---

151. exhibit: present.   **153. An if:** if.   **155. occasions:** arguments.   **157. of force:** powerful.   **170. reguerdon:** ample reward.   **183. disanimates:** discourages.   **186. s.d., Sennet:**
trumpet notes to indicate the departure of a procession.
190. forged: false.   **192. festered members:** gangrened limbs.

Sc. ii: 1. Rouen: in Elizabethan times spelt and pronounced
"Roan" — a monosyllable.   **2. policy:** cunning.   **10. mean:**
means.   **20. practisants:** fellow conspirators.   **25. No . . .
weakness:** i.e., that is the best way to indicate a weak **pot.**

[*An alarum. Enter* TALBOT *in an excursion.*°]

TAL. France, thou shalt rue this treason with tiny
    tears
If Talbot but survive thy treachery.
Pucelle, that witch, that damnèd sorceress,
Hath wrought this hellish mischief unawares,   39
That hardly we escaped the pride° of France.
                      [*Exit.*]
[*An alarum. Excursions.* BEDFORD, *brought in sick
in a chair. Enter* TALBOT *and* BURGUNDY *without.
Within* LA PUCELLE, CHARLES, BASTARD, ALENÇON, *and*
REIGNIER, *on the walls.*]

PUC. Good morrow, gallants! Want ye corn° for
    bread?
I think the Duke of Burgundy will fast
Before he'll buy again at such a rate.
'Twas full of darnel.° Do you like the taste?   44

BUR. Scoff on, vile fiend and shameless courtesan!
I trust ere long to choke thee with thine own,
And make thee curse the harvest of that corn.

CHA. Your Grace may starve perhaps before that
    time.

BED. Oh, let no words, but deeds, revenge this
    treason!

PUC. What will you do, good grey-beard? Break
    a lance,   50
And run a tilt° at death within a chair?°

TAL. Foul fiend of France, and hag of all despite,°
Encompassed with thy lustful paramours!
Becomes it thee to taunt his valiant age
And twit with cowardice a man half dead?   55
Damsel, I'll have a bout with you again,
Or else let Talbot perish with this shame.

PUC. Are ye so hot, sir? Yet, Pucelle, hold thy
    peace.
If Talbot do but thunder, rain will follow.
    [*The English whisper together in council.*]
God speed the parliament! Who shall be the
    speaker?   60

TAL. Dare ye come forth and meet us in the field?

PUC. Belike your lordship takes us then for fools
To try if that our own be ours or no.

TAL. I speak not to that railing Hecaté,°
But unto thee, Alençon, and the rest.   65
Will ye, like soldiers, come and fight it out?

ALEN. Signior, no.

TAL. Signior, hang! Base muleters° of France!
Like peasant footboys° do they keep the walls,
And dare not take up arms like gentlemen.   70

PUC. Away, Captains! Let's get us from the walls,

For Talbot means no goodness by his looks.
God be wi' you, my lord! We came but to tell you
That we are here.   [*Exeunt from the walls.*]

TAL. And there will we be too, ere it be long,   75
Or else reproach be Talbot's greatest fame!
Vow, Burgundy, by honor of thy house,
Pricked on° by public wrongs sustained in France,
Either to get the town again or die;
And I, as sure as English Henry lives,   80
And as his father here was conqueror,
As sure as in this late-betrayèd town
Great Coeur-de-lion's° heart was buried,
So sure I swear to get the town or die.   84

BUR. My vows are equal partners with thy vows.

TAL. But ere we go, regard this dying Prince,
The valiant Duke of Bedford. Come, my lord,
We will bestow you in some better place,
Fitter for sickness and for crazy° age.

BED. Lord Talbot, do not so dishonor me.   90
Here will I sit before the walls of Rouen
And will be partner of your weal or woe.

BUR. Courageous Bedford, let us now persuade
    you.

BED. Not to be gone from hence; for once I read
That stout Pendragon° in his litter sick   95
Came to the field and vanquishèd his foes.
Methinks I should revive the soldiers' hearts,
Because I ever found them as myself.

TAL. Undaunted spirit in a dying breast!
Then be it so. Heavens keep old Bedford safe!   100
And now no more ado, brave Burgundy,
But gather we our forces out of hand°
And set upon our boasting enemy.
    [*Exeunt all but* BEDFORD *and* ATTENDANTS.]
[*An alarum. Excursions. Enter* SIR JOHN FASTOLFE
and a CAPTAIN.]

CAP. Whither away, Sir John Fastolfe, in such
    haste?

FAS. Whither away! To save myself by flight.
We are like to have the overthrow again.   106

CAP. What! Will you fly, and leave Lord Talbot?

FAS.   Aye,
All the Talbots in the world, to save my life.
                            [*Exit.*]

CAP. Cowardly knight! Ill fortune follow thee!
                            [*Exit.*]
[*Retreat. Excursions.* LA PUCELLE, ALENÇON, *and*
CHARLES *fly.*]

BED. Now, quiet soul, depart when Heaven
    please,   110
For I have seen our enemies' overthrow.
What is the trust or strength of foolish man?

---

35. s.d., excursion: *Excursions*, which usually in stage directions
are linked with "alarums," indicate that a party of soldiers runs
in and across the stage.   **40. pride:** proud strength.   **41. corn:**
grain, wheat.   **44. darnel:** a weed which grows among the wheat.
51. run a tilt: make a charge at. **within a chair:** from your
invalid's chair.   **52. hag . . . despite:** most malicious witch.
64. Hecate: goddess of witchcraft. See *Macb*, III.v. **68. muleters:** muleteers.   **69. footboys:** i.e., who walk beside their masters on foot. Gentlemen rode on horseback.

78. Pricked on: goaded.   **83. Coeur-de-lion:** Richard I, the
fiercest of the English warrior-kings. He died of a wound received
in France in 1199. His heart was separately buried in Rouen.
See App. 28: King John. **89. crazy:** decrepit. **95. Pendragon:**
Uther Pendragon, father of Arthur the legendary British hero.
102. out of hand: at once.

They that of late were daring with their scoffs
Are glad and fain° by flight to save themselves.
[BEDFORD *dies, and is carried in by two in his chair.*]
[*An alarum. Re-enter* TALBOT, BURGUNDY, *and the rest.*]

    TAL. Lost and recovered in a day again!   115
This is a double honor, Burgundy.
Yet Heavens have glory for this victory!
    BUR. Warlike and martial Talbot, Burgundy
Enshrines thee in his heart and there erects
Thy noble deeds as valor's monuments.   120
    TAL. Thanks, gentle Duke. But where is Pucelle now?
I think her old familiar° is asleep.
Now where's the Bastard's braves,° and Charles his gleeks?°
What, all amort?° Rouen hangs her head for grief
That such a valiant company are fled.   125
Now will we take some order in the town,
Placing therein some expert officers,
And then depart to Paris to the King,
For there young Henry with his nobles lie.   129
    BUR. What wills Lord Talbot pleaseth Burgundy.
    TAL. But yet, before we go, let's not forget
The noble Duke of Bedford late deceased,
But see his exequies° fulfilled in Rouen.
A braver soldier never couchèd° lance,
A gentler heart did never sway in Court;   135
But kings and mightiest potentates must die,
For that's the end of human misery.   [*Exeunt.*]

SCENE III. *The plains near Rouen.*

[*Enter* CHARLES, *the* BASTARD *of Orleans,* ALENÇON,
    LA PUCELLE, *and* FORCES.]

    PUC. Dismay not, Princes, at this accident,
Nor grieve that Rouen is so recoverèd.
Care° is no cure, but rather corrosive
For things that are not to be remedied.
Let frantic Talbot triumph for a while   5
And like a peacock sweep along his tail.
We'll pull his plumes and take away his train°
If Dauphin and the rest will be but ruled.°
    CHA. We have been guided by thee hitherto
And of thy cunning had no diffidence.°   10
One sudden foil° shall never breed distrust.
    BAST. Search out thy wit for secret policies,°
And we will make thee famous through the world.
    ALEN. We'll set thy statue in some holy place
And have thee reverenced like a blessèd saint.   15

Employ thee then, sweet virgin, for our good.
    PUC. Then thus it must be. This doth Joan devise:
By fair persuasions mixed with sugared° words
We will entice the Duke of Burgundy
To leave the Talbot and to follow us.   20
    CHA. Aye, marry, sweeting, if we could do that,
France were no place for Henry's warriors,
Nor should that nation boast it so with us,
But be extirpèd° from our provinces.
    ALEN. Forever should they be expulsed° from France,   25
And not have title of an earldom here.°
    PUC. Your Honors shall perceive how I will work
To bring this matter to the wishèd end.
    [*Drum sounds afar off.*]
Hark! By the sound of drum you may perceive
Their powers° are marching unto Parisward.   30
[*Here sound an English march.° Enter, and pass over at a distance,* TALBOT *and his* FORCES.]
There goes the Talbot with his colors spread,
And all the troops of English after him.
[*French march.° Enter the* DUKE OF BURGUNDY *and FORCES.*]
Now in the rearward comes the Duke and his.
Fortune in favor° makes him lag behind.
Summon a parley; we will talk with him.   35
    [*Trumpets sound a parley.°*]
    CHA. A parley with the Duke of Burgundy!
    BUR. Who craves a parley with the Burgundy?
    PUC. The princely Charles of France, thy countryman.
    BUR. What say'st thou, Charles? For I am marching hence.
    CHA. Speak, Pucelle, and enchant him with thy words.   40
    PUC. Brave Burgundy, undoubted hope of France!
Stay, let thy humble handmaid speak to thee.
    BUR. Speak on, but be not overtedious.
    PUC. Look on thy country, look on fertile France,
And see the cities and the towns defaced   45
By wasting ruin of the cruel foe.
As looks the mother on her lowly babe
When death doth close his tender dying eyes,
See, see the pining malady of France!
Behold the wounds, the most unnatural wounds,
Which thou thyself hast given her woeful breast.   51
Oh, turn thy edgèd sword another way;
Strike those that hurt, and hurt not those that help.

---

114. fain: eager.   122. familiar: familiar spirit.   123. braves: taunts. gleeks: scoffs.   124. amort: sick to death, dejected.   133. exequies: funeral ceremonies.   134. couched: laid in position for a charge on horseback.
    Sc. iii: 3. Care: sorrow.   7. train: long tail.   8. be . . . ruled: accept advice.   10. diffidence: distrust.   11. foil: repulse.   12. policies: tricks.

18. sugared: candycoated.   24. extirped: rooted out.   25. expulsed: expelled.   26. not . . . here: i.e., have no claim even to an earldom in France. The English Kings claimed the French Kingdom for reasons set out in *Hen V*, I.ii.33–95.   30. powers: army. s.d., march: marching tune.   32. s.d., French march: music for a slow march.   34. Fortune in favor: good luck.   35. s.d., parley: trumpet call summoning to negotiate.

One drop of blood drawn from thy country's
  bosom
Should grieve thee more than streams of foreign
  gore.   55
Return thee therefore with a flood of tears,
And wash away thy country's stainèd spots.
   BUR. Either she hath bewitched me with her
    words,
Or nature makes me suddenly relent.
   PUC. Besides, all French and France exclaims° on
    thee,   60
Doubting thy birth and lawful progeny.°
Who join'st thou with but with a lordly nation
That will not trust thee but for profit's sake?
When Talbot hath set footing once in France
And fashioned thee that instrument of ill,   65
Who then but English Henry will be lord,
And thou be thrust out like a fugitive?°
Call we to mind, and mark but this for proof,
Was not the Duke of Orleans thy foe?
And was he not in England prisoner?   70
But when they heard he was thine enemy,
They set him free without his ransom paid
In spite of Burgundy and all his friends.
See, then, thou fight'st against thy countrymen 74
And join'st with them will be thy slaughter-men.
Come, come, return, return, thou wandering lord.
Charles and the rest will take thee in their arms.
   BUR. I am vanquished. These haughty words of
    hers
Have battered me like roaring cannon-shot
And made me almost yield upon my knees.   80
Forgive me, country, and sweet countrymen,
And, lords, accept this hearty kind embrace.
My forces and my power of men are yours.
So farewell, Talbot. I'll no longer trust thee.
   PUC. [*Aside*] Done like a Frenchman. Turn, and
    turn again!°   85
   CHA. Welcome, brave Duke! Thy friendship
    makes us fresh.
   BAST. And doth beget new courage in our breasts.
   ALEN. Pucelle hath bravely played her part in this,
And doth deserve a coronet of gold.
   CHA. Now let us on, my lords, and join our
    powers,   90
And seek how we may prejudice° the foe.
          [*Exeunt.*]

60. exclaims: cries shame. 61. progeny: descent. 67. fugitive:
runaway from your own party. 85. Done . . . again: The English, when this play was written, were supporting Henry of
Navarre against his French subjects. Sneers at the Frenchmen's
changing of sides were common. See *John* Intro. p. 541b.
91. prejudice: injure.

SCENE IV. *Paris. The palace.*

[*Enter the* KING, GLOUCESTER, BISHOP OF WINCHESTER,
YORK, SUFFOLK, SOMERSET, WARWICK, EXETER,
VERNON, BASSET, *and others. To them with
his* SOLDIERS, TALBOT.]

   TAL. My gracious Prince, and honorable peers,
Hearing of your arrival in this realm,
I have awhile given truce unto my wars
To do my duty to my sovereign —
In sign whereof, this arm that hath reclaimed   5
To your obedience fifty fortresses,
Twelve cities, and seven wallèd towns of strength,
Beside five hundred prisoners of esteem,°
Lets fall his sword before your Highness' feet,
And with submissive loyalty of heart   10
Ascribes the glory of his conquest got
First to my God and next unto your Grace.
          [*Kneels.*]
   KING. Is this the Lord Talbot, Uncle Gloucester,
That hath so long been resident in France?
   GLO. Yes, if it please your Majesty, my liege.   15
   KING. Welcome, brave Captain and victorious
    lord!
When I was young, as yet I am not old,
I do remember how my father said°
A stouter champion never handled sword.
Long since we were resolvèd° of your truth,   20
Your faithful service, and your toil in war;
Yet never have you tasted our reward,
Or be reguerdoned with so much as thanks,
Because till now we never saw your face.   24
Therefore, stand up; and, for these good deserts,
We here create you Earl of Shrewsbury,
And in our coronation take your place.
   [*Sennet. Flourish. Exeunt all but* VERNON *and*
          BASSET.]
   VER. Now, sir, to you, that were so hot° at sea,
Disgracing of these colors that I wear
In honor of my noble Lord of York —   30
Darest thou maintain the former words thou
    spakest?
   BAS. Yes, sir, as well as you dare patronage°
The envious barking of your saucy tongue
Against my lord the Duke of Somerset.
   VER. Sirrah, thy lord I honor as he is.   35
   BAS. Why, what is he? As good a man as York.
   VER. Hark ye, not so — in witness, take ye that.
          [*Strikes him.*]
   BAS. Villain, thou know'st the law of arms is
    such
That whoso draws a sword,° 'tis present° death,

Sc. iv: 8. esteem: high rank. 18. I . . . said: See *I Hen VI*
Intro. p. 105b. 20. resolved: convinced. 28. hot: haughty.
32. patronage: uphold, maintain. 39. draws a sword: To
fight in the king's presence in the Court was a capital offense.
See I.iii.46,n. present: immediate.

Or else this blow should broach° thy dearest blood.
But I'll unto his Majesty, and crave   41
I may have liberty to venge this wrong.
When thou shalt see I'll meet thee to thy cost.
    VER. Well, miscreant,° I'll be there as soon as
        you,
And after, meet you sooner than you would.   45
                                        [*Exeunt.*]

Act IV

SCENE I. *Paris. A hall of state.*

[*Enter the* KING, GLOUCESTER, BISHOP OF WINCHESTER,
YORK, SUFFOLK, SOMERSET, WARWICK, TALBOT, EXETER,
    the GOVERNOR OF PARIS, *and others.*]

    GLO. Lord Bishop, set the crown upon his head.
    WIN. God save King Henry, of that name the
        sixth!
    GLO. Now, Governor of Paris, take your oath
That you elect no other King but him,
Esteem none friends but such as are his friends,   5
And none your foes but such as shall pretend°
Malicious practices against his state.
This shall ye do, so help you righteous God!
                        [*Enter* SIR JOHN FASTOLFE.]
    FAS. My gracious sovereign, as I rode from Calais
To haste unto your coronation,   10
A letter was delivered to my hands
Writ to your Grace from the Duke of Burgundy.
    TAL. Shame to the Duke of Burgundy and thee!
I vowed, base knight, when I did meet thee next,
To tear the Garter° from thy craven's° leg,   15
                        [*Plucking it off.*]
Which I have done, because unworthily
Thou wast installèd in that high degree.
Pardon me, princely Henry, and the rest.
This dastard,° at the battle of Patay,
When but in all I was six thousand strong   20
And that the French were almost ten to one,
Before we met or that a stroke was given
Like to a trusty squire° did run away;
In which assault we lost twelve hundred men,
Myself and divers° gentlemen beside   25
Were there surprised and taken prisoners.
Then judge, great lords, if I have done amiss,
Or whether that such cowards ought to wear

This ornament of knighthood, yea or no.
    GLO. To say the truth, this fact was infamous   30
And ill beseeming any common man,
Much more a knight, a captain and a leader.
    TAL. When first this Order° was ordained, my
        lords,
Knights of the Garter were of noble birth,
Valiant and virtuous, full of haughty courage,   35
Such as were grown to credit° by the wars,
Not fearing death, nor shrinking for distress,
But always resolute in most extremes.
He then that is not furnished in this sort°
Doth but usurp the sacred name of knight,   40
Profaning this most honorable Order,
And should, if I were worthy to be judge,
Be quite degraded, like a hedge-born° swain°
That doth presume to boast of gentle blood.
    KING. Stain to thy countrymen, thou hear'st thy
        doom!   45
Be packing, therefore, thou that wast a knight.
Henceforth we banish thee, on pain of death.
                        [*Exit* FASTOLFE.]
And now, my Lord Protector, view the letter
Sent from our uncle Duke of Burgundy.
    GLO. What means His Grace, that he hath
        changed his style?°   50
No more but, plain and bluntly,
"To the King!"
Hath he forgot he is his sovereign?
Or doth this churlish superscription°
Pretend° some alteration in good will?
What's here?
[*Reads.*] "I have, upon especial cause,   55
Moved with compassion of my country's wreck,
Together with the pitiful complaints
Of such as your oppression feeds upon,
Forsaken your pernicious faction,
And joined with Charles, the rightful King of
        France."   60
Oh, monstrous treachery! Can this be so,
That in alliance, amity, and oaths
There should be found such false dissembling
        guile?
    KING. What! Doth my Uncle Burgundy revolt?
    GLO. He doth, my lord, and is become your foe.
    KING. Is that the worst this letter doth contain?
    GLO. It is the worst, and all, my lord, he writes.
    KING. Why, then, Lord Talbot there shall talk
        with him,
And give him chastisement for this abuse.

---

40. broach: spill, lit., tap a wine cask.   44. miscreant: villain,
lit., unbeliever.
    Act IV, Sc. i: 6. pretend: purpose.   15. Garter: Order of the
Garter. See ll. 33–38. craven: coward.   19. dastard: coward.
23. trusty squire: *Squire* usually means "a gentleman below the
rank of knight," but is here used as a term of contempt, "fellow."
25. divers: various.

33. Order: See App. 29.   36. credit: fame.   39. furnished . . .
sort: i.e., of such a character.   43. hedge-born: born under a
hedge, hobo. swain: young man from the country.   50. style:
manner of address. In addressing a prince, it was customary to
inscribe a letter with all his titles. To neglect this courtesy was a
sign of deliberate contempt.   53. churlish superscription: ill-
mannered form of address (written on the outside of the letter)
54. Pretend: convey.

How say you, my lord? Are you not content?   70
TAL. Content, my liege!° Yes, but that I am pre-
    vented,°
I should have begged I might have been employed.
   KING. Then gather strength and march unto him
    straight.
Let him perceive how ill we brook° his treason,
And what offense it is to flout his friends.   75
   TAL. I go, my lord, in heart desiring still
You may behold confusion of your foes.   [*Exit.*]
      [*Enter* VERNON *and* BASSET.]
   VER. Grant me the combat,° gracious sovereign.
   BAS. And me, my lord, grant me the combat too.
   YORK. This is my servant. Hear him, noble
    Prince.   80
   SOM. And this is mine. Sweet Henry, favor him.
   KING. Be patient, lords, and give them leave to
    speak.
Say, gentlemen, what makes you thus exclaim?
And wherefore crave you combat? Or with whom?
   VER. With him, my lord, for he hath done me
    wrong.   85
   BAS. And I with him, for he hath done me wrong.
   KING. What is that wrong whereof you both
    complain?
First let me know, and then I'll answer you.
   BAS. Crossing the sea from England into France,
This fellow here, with envious carping tongue,   90
Upbraided me about the rose° I wear,
Saying the sanguine color of the leaves
Did represent my master's blushing cheeks
When stubbornly he did repugn° the truth
About a certain question in the law   95
Argued betwixt the Duke of York and him;
With other vile and ignominious terms.
In confutation of which rude reproach,
And in defense of my lord's worthiness,
I crave the benefit° of law of arms.   100
   VER. And that is my petition, noble lord.
For though he seem with forgèd quaint conceit°
To set a gloss° upon his bold intent,
Yet know, my lord, I was provoked by him,
And he first took exceptions at this badge,   105
Pronouncing that the paleness of this flower°
Bewrayed° the faintness of my master's heart.
   YORK. Will not this malice, Somerset, be left?°
   SOM. Your private grudge, my Lord of York, will
    out,
Though ne'er so cunningly you smother it.   110

   KING. Good Lord, what madness rules in brain-
    sick° men
When for so slight and frivolous a cause
Such factious emulations° shall arise!
Good Cousins both, of York and Somerset,
Quiet yourselves, I pray, and be at peace.   115
   YORK. Let this dissension first be tried by fight,
And then your Highness shall command a peace.
   SOM. The quarrel toucheth none but us alone.
Betwixt ourselves let us decide it then.
   YORK. There is my pledge.° Accept it, Somerset.
   VER. Nay, let it rest where it began at first.   121
   BAS. Confirm it so, mine honorable lord.
   GLO. Confirm it so! Confounded be your strife!
And perish ye, with your audacious prate!
Presumptuous vassals, are you not ashamed   125
With this immodest clamorous outrage
To trouble and disturb the King and us?
And you, my lords, methinks you do not well
To bear with their perverse objections,
Much less to take occasion° from their mouths   130
To raise a mutiny° betwixt yourselves.
Let me persuade you take a better course.
   EXE. It grieves His Highness. Good my lords, be
    friends.
   KING. Come hither, you that would be com-
    batants.
Henceforth I charge you, as you love our favor,
Quite to forget this quarrel and the cause.   136
And you, my lords, remember where we are —
In France, amongst a fickle wavering nation.
If they perceive dissension in our looks
And that within ourselves we disagree,   140
How will their grudging stomachs° be provoked
To wilful disobedience and rebel!
Beside, what infamy will there arise
When foreign princes shall be certified°
That for a toy,° a thing of no regard,   145
King Henry's peers and chief nobility
Destroyed themselves and lost the realm of France!
Oh, think upon the conquest of my father,
My tender years, and let us not forgo°
That for a trifle that was bought with blood!   150
Let me be umpire in this doubtful strife.
I see no reason, if I wear this rose,
      [*Putting on a red rose.*]
That anyone should therefore be suspicious
I more incline to Somerset than York.
Both are my kinsmen, and I love them both.   155
As well they may upbraid me with my crown,

---

71. liege: sovereign. prevented: forestalled.   74. brook: endure.   78. Grant . . . combat: give me leave to fight.   91. rose:
i.e., the Red Rose of the Lancastrian party. See II.iv.37–74.
94. repugn: oppose, reject.   100. benefit: right.   102. forged
. . . conceit: false, neat turn of phrase.   103. gloss: polish, fair
appearance.   106. paleness . . . flower: i.e., the White Rose.
107. Bewrayed: betrayed.   108. Will . . . left: i.e., will you
never cease being malicious?

111. brainsick: lunatic.   113. factious emulations: jealousy
which causes party strife.   120. There . . . pledge: Here he
throws down his glove as token that he will fight. See *Rich II*,
I.i.69–74 and IV.i.25–85, for similar challenges.   130. occasion:
opportunity, advantage.   131. mutiny: discord.   141. grudging
stomachs: discontented resentment.   144. certified: certainly
informed.   145. toy: trifle.   149. forgo: forfeit.

Because, forsooth, the King of Scots is crowned.
But your discretions better can persuade
Than I am able to instruct or teach;
And therefore, as we hither came in peace,   160
So let us still continue peace and love.
Cousin of York, we institute your Grace
To be our Regent in these parts of France;
And, good my Lord of Somerset, unite   164
Your troops of horsemen with his bands of foot,
And, like true subjects, sons of your progenitors,°
Go cheerfully together and digest°
Your angry choler° on your enemies.
Ourself, my Lord Protector and the rest
After some respite° will return to Calais;   170
From thence to England, where I hope ere long
To be presented, by your victories,
With Charles, Alençon and that traitorous rout.
              [*Flourish. Exeunt all but* YORK, WARWICK,
                            EXETER *and* VERNON.]
  WAR. My Lord of York, I promise you, the King
Prettily, methought, did play the orator.   175
  YORK. And so he did, but yet I like it not,
In that he wears the badge of Somerset.
  WAR. Tush, that was but his fancy, blame him
    not.
I dare presume, sweet Prince, he thought no harm.
  YORK. An if I wist he did°—but let it rest.   180
Other affairs must now be managèd.
                    [*Exeunt all but* EXETER.]
  EXE. Well didst thou, Richard, to suppress thy
    voice,
For, had the passions of thy heart burst out,
I fear we should have seen deciphered° there
More rancorous spite, more furious raging broils,
Than yet can be imagined or supposed.   186
But howsoe'er, no simple man that sees
This jarring discord of nobility,
This shouldering of each other in the Court,
This factious bandying° of their favorites,   190
But that it doth presage some ill event.
'Tis much° when scepters are in children's hands,
But more when envy breeds unkind° division;
There comes the ruin, there begins confusion.
                                    [*Exit.*]

SCENE II. *Before Bordeaux.*

              [*Enter* TALBOT, *with trump and drum.*]
  TAL. Go to the gates of Bordeaux, trumpeter.
Summon their General unto the wall.
[*Trumpet sounds. Enter* GENERAL *and others, aloft.*]
English John Talbot, Captains, calls you forth,

Servant in arms to Harry King of England
And thus he would: Open your city gates,   5
Be humble to us, call my sovereign yours
And do him homage as obedient subjects,
And I'll withdraw me and my bloody power;
But if you frown upon this proffered peace,
You tempt the fury of my three attendants —   10
Lean famine, quartering steel, and climbing fire° —
Who in a moment even with the earth
Shall lay your stately and air-braving° towers
If you forsake the offer of their love.   14
  GEN. Thou ominous and fearful owl° of death,
Our nation's terror and their bloody scourge!
The period° of thy tyranny approacheth.
On us thou canst not enter but by death,
For, I protest, we are well fortified
And strong enough to issue out and fight.   20
If thou retire, the Dauphin, well appointed,
Stands with the snares of war to tangle thee.
On either hand thee° there are squadrons pitched
To wall thee from the liberty of flight,
And no way canst thou turn thee for redress,   25
But death doth front° thee with apparent spoil,°
And pale destruction meets thee in the face.
Ten thousand French have ta'en the sacrament
To rive their dangerous artillery°
Upon no Christian soul but English Talbot.   30
Lo, there thou stand'st, a breathing valiant man
Of an invincible unconquered spirit!
This is the latest glory of thy praise
That I, thy enemy, due thee withal;°
For ere the glass that now begins to run   35
Finish the process of his sandy hour,°
These eyes, that see thee now well colorèd,
Shall see thee withered, bloody, pale, and dead.
                            [*Drum afar off.*]
Hark! Hark! The Dauphin's drum, a warning
    bell,°
Sings heavy music to thy timorous soul,   40
And mine shall ring thy dire departure° out.
                        [*Exeunt* GENERAL, *&c.*]
  TAL. He fables not. I hear the enemy.
Out, some light horsemen, and peruse° their wings.
Oh, negligent and heedless discipline!
How are we parked° and bounded in a pale,°   45
A little herd of England's timorous deer

166. progenitors: ancestors.   167. digest: get rid of.   168. choler: wrath.   170. respite: delay.   180. An . . . did: i.e., if I thought he did mean harm — but York does not finish the sentence.   184. deciphered: uncovered, revealed.   190. bandying: contending.   192. 'Tis much: it's a bad business.   193. unkind: unnatural.

Sc. ii: 11. Lean . . . fire: See *Hen V*, Act I.i. Chorus ll. 5–8.   13. air-braving: lofty.   15. owl: bird of evil omen.   17. period: end.   23. hand thee: side of thee.   26. front: face. apparent spoil: obvious destruction.   29. rive . . . artillery: discharge their firearms.   33–34. This . . . withal: this is the last time that I, your enemy, will bestow (*due thee*) praise upon your fame.   35–36. For . . . hour: before the sand in the hourglass has run through.   39. warning bell: i.e., passing bell. See App. 19.   41. departure: death.   43. peruse: reconnoiter.   45. parked: enclosed in a park. A park was originally so called because it was an enclosure for deer. The image of hunted deer is maintained to l. 53.   bounded . . . pale: lit., kept in by a fence.

Mazed° with a yelping kennel of French curs!
If we be English deer, be then in blood,°
Not rascal-like° to fall down with a pinch,°   49
But rather — moody-mad° and desperate stags —
Turn on the bloody hounds with heads of steel
And make the cowards stand aloof° at bay.
Sell every man his life as dear as mine,
And they shall find dear deer of us, my friends. 54
God and Saint George, Talbot and England's right,
Prosper our colors° in this dangerous fight!
                                        [*Exeunt.*]

SCENE III. *Plains in Gascony.*

[*Enter a* MESSENGER *that meets* YORK. *Enter* YORK
        with trumpet and many SOLDIERS.]
    YORK. Are not the speedy scouts returned again
That dogged the mighty army of the Dauphin?
    MESS. They are returned, my lord, and give it out
That he is marched to Bordeaux with his power
To fight with Talbot. As he marched along,   5
By your espials were discoverèd
Two mightier troops than that the Dauphin led,
Which joined with him and made their march for
        Bordeaux.
    YORK. A plague upon that villain Somerset,
That thus delays my promisèd supply°   10
Of horsemen that were levied for this siege!
Renownèd Talbot doth expect my aid,
And I am louted° by a traitor villain
And cannot help the noble chevalier.
God comfort him in this necessity!   15
If he miscarry,° farewell wars in France.
            [*Enter* SIR WILLIAM LUCY.]
    LUCY. Thou princely leader of our English
        strength,
Never so needful on the earth of France,
Spur to the rescue of the noble Talbot,
Who now is girdled with a waist of iron,   20
And hemmed about with grim destruction.
To Bordeaux, warlike Duke! To Bordeaux, York!
Else, farewell Talbot, France, and England's honor.
    YORK. Oh, God, that Somerset, who in proud
        heart
Doth stop my cornets,° were in Talbot's place!   25
So should we save a valiant gentleman
By forfeiting a traitor and a coward.
Mad ire and wrathful fury makes me weep,
That thus we die while remiss° traitors sleep.   29

    LUCY. Oh, send some succor to the distressed lord!
    YORK. He dies,° we lose; I break my warlike
        word;
We mourn, France smiles; we lose, they daily get;°
All 'long of° this vile traitor Somerset.
    LUCY. Then God take mercy on brave Talbot's
        soul,
And on his son young John, who two hours since
I met in travel toward his warlike father!   36
This seven years did not Talbot see his son,
And now they meet where both their lives are done.
    YORK. Alas, what joy shall noble Talbot have
To bid his young son welcome to his grave?   40
Away! Vexation almost stops my breath,
That sundered° friends greet in the hour of death.
Lucy, farewell. No more my fortune can
But curse the cause I cannot aid the man.
Maine, Blois, Poictiers, and Tours are won away,
'Long all° of Somerset and his delay.   46
                [*Exit, with his* SOLDIERS.]
    LUCY. Thus, while the vulture of sedition
Feeds in the bosom of such great commanders,
Sleeping neglection° doth betray to loss
The conquest of our scarce cold° conqueror,   50
That ever living man of memory,
Henry the Fifth. Whiles they each other cross,
Lives, honors, lands, and all hurry to loss. [*Exit.*]

SCENE IV. *Other plains in Gascony.*

[*Enter* SOMERSET *with his* ARMY, *a* CAPTAIN
        of TALBOT's *with him.*]
    SOM. It is too late. I cannot send them now.
This expedition was by York and Talbot
Too rashly plotted.° All our general force
Might with a sally of the very town
Be buckled with.° The overdaring Talbot
Hath sullied° all his gloss of former honor
By this unheedful, desperate, wild adventure.
York set him on to fight and die in shame,
That, Talbot dead, great York might bear the name.
    CAP. Here is Sir William Lucy, who with me   10
Set from our o'ermatched° forces forth for aid.
            [*Enter* SIR WILLIAM LUCY.]
    SOM. How now, Sir William! Whither were you
        sent?
    LUCY. Whither, my lord? From bought and sold
        Lord Talbot,
Who, ringed about with bold adversity.
Cries out for noble York and Somerset   15

47. **Mazed**: amazed.   48. **in blood**: in fine condition, and therefore courageous.   49. **rascal-like**: like deer in poor condition which give up without a struggle. **pinch**: a mere nip.   50. **moody-mad**: hot tempered.   52. **stand aloof**: keep their distance.   56. **colors**: standard.

Sc. iii: 10. **supply**: reinforcement.   13. **louted**: made a lout (fool) of.   16. **miscarry**: come to grief.   25. **cornets**: troops of cavalry.   29. **remiss**: careless.

31. **He dies**: i. e., if he dies.   32. **get**: gain.   33. **'long of**: along, because of.   42. **sundered**: parted.   46. **'Long all**: for "all 'long." See l. 33.   49. **neglection**: disregard.   50. **scarce cold**: Actually Henry V had been dead for thirty years!

Sc. iv: 3. **plotted**: planned.   5. **buckled with**: grappled with, overcome. See I.ii.95.   6. **sullied**: smeared.   11. **o'ermatched**: fighting against great odds.

To beat assailing death from his weak legions;
And whiles the honorable captain there
Drops bloody sweat from his war-wearied limbs,
And, in advantage lingering,° looks for rescue,
You, his false hopes, the trust of England's honor,
Keep off aloof with worthless emulation.°　　　21
Let not your private discord keep away
The levied succors that should lend him aid,
While he, renownèd noble gentleman,
Yields up his life unto a world of° odds.　　　25
Orleans the Bastard, Charles, Burgundy,
Alençon, Reignier, compass him about,
And Talbot perisheth by your default.°

SOM. York set him on. York should have sent him
　　aid.
LUCY. And York as fast upon your Grace ex-
　　claims,　　　30
Swearing that you withhold his levied host
Collected for this expedition.
SOM. York lies. He might have sent and had the
　　horse.
I owe him little duty and less love,
And take foul scorn° to fawn on him by sending.
LUCY. The fraud of England, not the force of
　　France,　　　36
Hath now entrapped the noble-minded Talbot.
Never to England shall he bear his life,
But dies, betrayed to fortune by your strife.
SOM. Come, go. I will dispatch the horsemen
　　straight.　　　40
Within six hours they will be at his aid.
LUCY. Too late comes rescue. He is ta'en or slain,
For fly he could not, if he would have fled,
And fly would Talbot never, though he might.
SOM. If he be dead, brave Talbot, then adieu!　　45
LUCY. His fame lives in the world, his shame in
　　you.　　　　　　　　　　　　　　[Exeunt.]

SCENE V. *The English camp near Bordeaux.*

[*Enter* TALBOT *and* JOHN *his son.*]
TAL. O young John Talbot! I did send for thee
To tutor° thee in stratagems of war,
That Talbot's name might be in thee revived
When sapless age and weak unable limbs
Should bring thy father to his drooping chair.　5
But, oh, malignant and ill-boding° stars!
Now thou art come unto a feast of death,
A terrible and unavoided° danger.
Therefore, dear boy, mount on my swiftest horse,

And I'll direct thee how thou shalt escape　　　10
By sudden flight. Come, dally not, be gone.
JOHN. Is my name Talbot? And am I your son?
And shall I fly? Oh, if you love my mother,
Dishonor not her honorable name
To make a bastard and a slave of me!　　　15
The world will say, " He is not Talbot's blood
That basely fled when noble Talbot stood."
TAL. Fly, to revenge my death if I be slain.
JOHN. He that flies so will ne'er return again.
TAL. If we both stay, we both are sure to die.　20
JOHN. Then let me stay, and, Father, do you fly.
Your loss is great, so your regard should be;°
My worth unknown, no loss is known in me.
Upon my death the French can little boast;
In yours they will, in you all hopes are lost.　　25
Flight cannot stain the honor you have won,
But mine it will, that no exploit have done.
You fled for vantage,° everyone will swear,
But if I bow,° they'll say it was for fear.
There is no hope that ever I will stay　　　30
If the first hour I shrink and run away.
Here on my knee I beg mortality,°
Rather than life preserved with infamy.
TAL. Shall all thy mother's hopes lie in one tomb?
JOHN. Aye, rather than I'll shame my mother's
　　womb.　　　35
TAL. Upon my blessing, I command thee go.
JOHN. To fight I will, but not to fly the foe.
TAL. Part of thy father may be saved in thee.
JOHN. No part of him but will be shame in me.
TAL. Thou never hadst renown, nor canst not lose
　　it.　　　40
JOHN. Yes, your renownèd name. Shall flight
　　abuse it?
TAL. Thy father's charge° shall clear thee from
　　that stain.
JOHN. You cannot witness for me, being slain.
If death be so apparent, then both fly.
TAL. And leave my followers here to fight and
　　die?　　　45
My age was never tainted with such shame.
JOHN. And shall my youth be guilty of such
　　blame?
No more can I be severed from your side
Than can yourself yourself in twain divide.
Stay, go, do what you will, the like do I;　　　50
For live I will not, if my father die.
TAL. Then here I take my leave of thee, fair son,
Born to eclipse° thy life this afternoon.
Come, side by side together live and die,
And soul with soul from France to Heaven fly.
　　　　　　　　　　　　　　　　[Exeunt.]

---

19. in . . . lingering: holding out because he has an advantageous position.　21. emulation: jealous rivalry.　25. world of: enormous.　28. default: failure.　35. take . . . scorn: regard it as a foul disgrace.
　Sc. v: 2. tutor: instruct.　6. ill-boding: foretelling evil. See App. I.　8. unavoided: unavoidable.

22. Your . . . be: i.e., you should consider how serious it will be for the English to lose you.　28. for vantage: i.e., for good strategic reasons.　29. bow: bend, yield.　32. mortality: death.　42. charge: direct order.　53. eclipse: i.e., extinguish.

SCENE VI. *A field of battle.*

[*Alarum. Excursions, wherein* TALBOT'S SON *is hemmed about, and* TALBOT *rescues him.*]

TAL. Saint George and victory! Fight, soldiers,
    fight!
The Regent hath with Talbot broke his word
And left us to the rage of France his sword.
Where is John Talbot? Pause, and take thy breath.
I gave thee life and rescued thee from death.   5
    JOHN. Oh, twice my father, twice am I thy son!
The life thou gavest me first was lost and done
Till with thy warlike sword, despite° of fate,
To my determined time° thou gavest new date.
    TAL. When from the Dauphin's crest thy sword
    struck fire,   10
It warmed thy father's heart with proud desire
Of bold-faced victory. Then leaden age,
Quickened with youthful spleen° and warlike rage,
Beat down Alençon, Orleans, Burgundy,
And from the pride of Gallia° rescued thee.   15
The ireful bastard Orleans, that drew blood
From thee, my boy, and had the maidenhood
Of thy first fight, I soon encounterèd,
And interchanging blows I quickly shed
Some of his bastard blood, and in disgrace   20
Bespoke him thus: "Contaminated base
And misbegotten blood I spill of thine,
Mean and right poor, for that pure blood of mine
Which thou didst force from Talbot, my brave
    boy."
Here, purposing the Bastard to destroy,   25
Came in strong rescue. Speak, thy father's care,
Art thou not weary, John? How dost thou fare?
Wilt thou yet leave the battle, boy, and fly,
Now thou art sealed° the son of chivalry?
Fly, to revenge my death when I am dead.   30
The help of one stands me in little stead.
Oh, too much folly is it, well I wot,°
To hazard all our lives in one small boat!
If I today die not with Frenchmen's rage,
Tomorrow I shall die with mickle° age.   35
By me they nothing gain an if I stay;
'Tis but the shortening of my life one day.
In thee thy mother dies, our household's name,
My death's revenge, thy youth, and England's fame.
All these and more we hazard by thy stay.   40
All these are saved if thou wilt fly away.
    JOHN. The sword of Orleans hath not made me
    smart.
These words of yours draw lifeblood from my heart.
On that advantage, bought with such a shame,
To save a paltry life and slay bright fame,   45

Before young Talbot from old Talbot fly
The coward horse that bears me fall and die!
And like° me to the peasant boys of France,
To be shame's scorn and subject of mischance!°
Surely, by all the glory you have won,   50
An if I fly, I am not Talbot's son.
Then talk no more of flight, it is no boot;°
If son to Talbot, die at Talbot's foot.
    TAL. Then follow thou thy desperate sire of
    Crete,
Thou Icarus.° Thy life to me is sweet.   55
If thou wilt fight, fight by thy father's side,
And, commendable proved, let's die in pride.
                  [*Exeunt.*]

SCENE VII. *Another part of the field.*

[*Alarum. Excursions. Enter old* TALBOT *led by a* SERVANT.]

    TAL. Where is my other life? Mine own is gone.
Oh, where's young Talbot? Where is valiant John?
Triumphant death, smeared with captivity,°
Young Talbot's valor makes me smile at thee.
When he perceived me shrink and on my knee,   5
His bloody sword he brandished over me
And, like a hungry lion, did commence
Rough deeds of rage and stern impatience.
But when my angry guardant° stood alone,
Tendering my ruin° and assailed of none,   10
Dizzy-eyed fury and great rage of heart
Suddenly made him from my side to start
Into the clustering battle of the French.
And in that sea of blood my boy did drench
His overmounting spirit, and there died,   15
My Icarus, my blossom, in his pride.
    SERV. O my dear lord, lo, where your son is borne!
[*Enter* SOLDIERS, *with the body of young* TALBOT.]
    TAL. Thou antic° Death, which laugh'st us here
    to scorn,
Anon, from thy insulting tyranny,
Coupled in bonds of perpetuity,   20
Two Talbots, wingèd through the lither° sky,
In thy despite shall 'scape mortality.°

48. **like:** liken.   49. **subject of mischance:** servant of (i.e., deserving) misfortune.   52. **boot:** advantage.   54–55. **sire . . . Icarus:** Daedalus of Crete and his son Icarus, hoping to escape from Minos, their King, attempted to fly by fastening wings on their shoulders. Daedalus successfully returned to earth, but Icarus crashed and was killed when the sun melted the wax by which his wings were fastened.   **Sc. vii: 3. Triumphant . . . captivity:** This line presumably means that Talbot welcomes death because neither he nor his son have disgraced themselves by surrender.   **9. guardant:** a heraldic term. A guardant lion is pictured as standing on his hind legs brandishing a sword.   **10. Tendering my ruin:** caring for me in my overthrow.   **18. antic:** grinning like a clown. See *Rich II,* III.ii.162,n. and Pl. 12f.   **21–22. Two . . . mortality:** i.e., we two Talbots will overcome Death and fly straight to Heaven. **lither:** supple.

Sc. vi: 8. **despite:** in spite.   9. **determined time:** fated end. 13. **spleen:** wrath; i.e., in my wrath I become like a young man.   15. **Gallia:** France.   29. **sealed:** i.e., guaranteed as true. 32. **wot:** know.   35. **mickle:** great.

O thou, whose wounds become hard-favored°
    death,
Speak to thy father ere thou yield thy breath!   24
Brave° Death by speaking, whether he will or no.
Imagine him a Frenchman and thy foe.
Poor boy! He smiles, methinks, as who should say,
"Had Death been French, then Death had died to-
    day."
Come, come and lay him in his father's arms.
My spirit can no longer bear these harms.   30
Soldiers, adieu! I have what I would have;
Now my old arms are young John Talbot's grave.

                       [Dies.]

[*Enter* CHARLES, ALENÇON, BURGUNDY, BASTARD, LA
    PUCELLE, *and* FORCES.]

CHA. Had York and Somerset brought rescue in,
We should have found a bloody day of this.
  BAST. How the young whelp of Talbot's, raging
    wood,°   35
Did flesh° his puny° sword in Frenchmen's blood!
  PUC. Once I encountered him, and thus I said:
"Thou maiden youth, be vanquished by a maid."
But, with a proud majestical high scorn,
He answered thus: "Young Talbot was not born
To be the pillage of a giglot° wench."   41
So, rushing in the bowels of the French,
He left me proudly, as unworthy fight.
  BUR. Doubtless he would have made a noble
    knight.
See where he lies inhearsèd° in the arms   45
Of the most bloody nurser of his harms!
  BAST. Hew them to pieces, hack their bones asun-
    der,
Whose life was England's glory, Gallia's wonder.
  CHA. Oh, no, forbear! For that which we have
    fled
During the life, let us not wrong it dead.   50

[*Enter* SIR WILLIAM LUCY, *attended*, HERALD *of the
    French preceding.*]

  LUCY. Herald, conduct me to the Dauphin's tent,
To know who hath obtained the glory of the day.
  CHA. On what submissive message art thou sent?
  LUCY. Submission, Dauphin! 'Tis a mere French
    word.
We English warriors wot not what it means.   55
I come to know what prisoners thou hast ta'en,
And to survey the bodies of the dead.
  CHA. For prisoners ask'st thou? Hell our prison
    is.°

But tell me whom thou seek'st.   59
  LUCY. But where's the great Alcides° of the field,
Valiant Lord Talbot, Earl of Shrewsbury,
Created, for his rare success in arms,
Great Earl of Washford, Waterford, and Valence;
Lord Talbot of Goodrig and Urchinfield,   64
Lord Strange of Blackmere, Lord Verdun of Alton,
Lord Cromwell of Wingfield, Lord Furnival of
    Sheffield,
The thrice-victorious Lord of Falconbridge;
Knight of the noble order of Saint George,
Worthy Saint Michael and the Golden Fleece;°
Great Marshal to Henry the Sixth   70
Of all his wars within the realm of France?
  PUC. Here is a silly stately style° indeed!
The Turk, that two and fifty kingdoms hath,
Writes not so tedious a style° as this.
Him that thou magnifiest with all these titles   75
Stinking and fly-blown lies here at our feet.
  LUCY. Is Talbot slain, the Frenchmen's only
    scourge,
Your kingdom's terror and black Nemesis?°
Oh, were mine eyeballs into bullets turned,
That I in rage might shoot them at your faces!   80
Oh, that I could but call these dead to life!
It were enough to fright the realm of France.
Were but his picture left amongst you here,
It would amaze the proudest of you all.   84
Give me their bodies, that I may bear them hence
And give them burial as beseems their worth.
  PUC. I think this upstart is old Talbot's ghost,
He speaks with such a proud commanding spirit.
For God's sake, let him have 'em. To keep them
    here,
They would but stink, and putrefy the air.   90
  CHA. Go, take their bodies hence.
  LUCY. I'll bear them hence; but from their ashes
    shall be reared
A phoenix° that shall make all France afeard.
  CHA. So we be rid of them, do with 'em what
    thou wilt.
And now to Paris in this conquering vein.   95
All will be ours, now bloody Talbot's slain.

                       [Exeunt.]

60. Alcides: Hercules. **69. Saint . . . Fleece:** two famous orders of Knighthood. St. Michael was a French order; the Golden Fleece was founded in 1429 by Philip Duke of Burgundy. **72. style:** the description of a man's titles. **73-74. The . . . style:** According to a pamphlet published in 1606, the Great Turk's style was "by the Grace of the High God Most Well-Beloved in Heaven, descended of the Line of the Great Prophet Mahomet, Champion of Babylon, God on Earth, Baron of Turkey, Lord of the Country of India, even unto the Earthly Paradise, Conqueror of Constantinople and of Greece, Governor of the High and Lower Seas, Commander of Hungary, and future Conqueror of Christendom." **78. Nemesis:** Avenging Justice. **93. phoenix:** See *Temp,* III.iii.23,n.

23. hard-favored: grim-faced. **25. Brave:** insult. **35. wood:** mad. **36. flesh:** draw blood for the first time. **puny:** inexperienced, lit., freshman. **41. giglot:** wanton. **45. inhearsèd:** encoffined. **58. Hell . . . is:** i.e., we have sent our prisoners to Hell — killed them.

Act V

SCENE I. *London. The palace.*

[*Sennet. Enter* KING, GLOUCESTER, *and* EXETER.]
KING. Have you perused the letters from the
    Pope,
The Emperor, and the Earl of Armagnac?
  GLO. I have, my lord, and their intent is this:
They humbly sue unto your Excellence
To have a godly peace concluded of   5
Between the realms of England and of France.
  KING. How doth your Grace affect their motion?°
  GLO. Well, my good lord, and as the only means
To stop effusion of our Christian blood
And stablish quietness on every side.   10
  KING. Aye, marry, Uncle, for I always thought
It was both impious and unnatural
That such immanity° and bloody strife
Should reign among professors° of one faith.
  GLO. Beside, my lord, the sooner to effect   15
And surer bind this knot of amity,
The Earl of Armagnac, near knit to Charles,
A man of great authority in France,
Proffers his only daughter to your Grace   19
In marriage, with a large and sumptuous dowry.
  KING. Marriage, Uncle! Alas, my years are young!
And fitter is my study and my books
Than wanton dalliance with a paramour.
Yet call the ambassadors, and, as you please,
So let them have their answers every one.   25
I shall be well content with any choice
Tends° to God's glory and my country's weal.
[*Enter* WINCHESTER *in cardinal's habit, a* LEGATE *and*
    two AMBASSADORS.]
  EXE. What! Is my Lord of Winchester installed
And called unto a cardinal's degree?
Then I perceive that will be verified   30
Henry the Fifth did sometime prophesy:
"If once he come to be a cardinal,
He'll make his cap coequal with the crown."
  KING. My Lords Ambassadors, your several suits
Have been considered and debated on.   35
Your purpose is both good and reasonable;
And therefore are we certainly resolved
To draw° conditions of a friendly peace,
Which by my Lord of Winchester we mean°
Shall be transported presently° to France.   40
  GLO. [*To* AMBASSADOR *from Armagnac.*] And for
    the proffer of my lord your master,
I have informed His Highness so at large,
As liking of the lady's virtuous gifts,

Her beauty, and the value of her dower,
He doth intend she shall be England's Queen.   45
  KING. In argument and proof of which contract,
Bear her this jewel, pledge of my affection.
And so, my Lord Protector, see them guarded
And safely brought to Dover, where, inshipped,
Commit them to the fortune of the sea.   50
    [*Exeunt all but* WINCHESTER *and* LEGATE.]
  WIN. Stay, my Lord Legate. You shall first re-
    ceive
The sum of money which I promisèd
Should be delivered to His Holiness
For clothing me in these grave ornaments.   54
  LEG. I will attend upon your lordship's leisure.
  WIN. [*Aside*] Now Winchester will not submit, I
    trow,
Or be inferior to the proudest peer.
Humphrey of Gloucester, thou shalt well perceive
That neither in birth or for authority
The Bishop will be overborne by thee.   60
I'll either make thee stoop and bend thy knee,
Or sack this country with a mutiny.   [*Exeunt.*]

SCENE II. *France. Plains in Anjou.*

[*Enter* CHARLES, BURGUNDY, ALENÇON, BASTARD,
    REIGNIER, LA PUCELLE, *and* FORCES.]
  CHA. These news, my lords, may cheer our droop-
    ing spirits:
'Tis said the stout Parisians do revolt
And turn again unto the warlike French.
  ALEN. Then march to Paris, royal Charles of
    France,
And keep not back your powers in dalliance.°   5
  PUC. Peace be amongst them, if they turn to us;
Else, ruin combat with their palaces!
    [*Enter* SCOUT.]
  SCOUT. Success unto our valiant General,
And happiness to his accomplices!°
  CHA. What tidings send our scouts? I prithee
    speak.   10
  SCOUT. The English army, that divided was
Into two parties, is now conjoined in one,
And means to give you battle presently.
  CHA. Somewhat too sudden, sirs, the warning is,
But we will presently provide for them.   15
  BUR. I trust the ghost of Talbot is not there.
Now he is gone, my lord, you need not fear.
  PUC. Of all base passions, fear is most accursed.
Command the conquest, Charles, it shall be thine.
Let Henry fret and all the world repine.   20
  CHA. Then on, my lords, and France be fortunate!
    [*Exeunt.*]

Act V, Sc. i: **7. affect . . . motion:** favor their proposal.
13. immanity: savagery.   **14. professors:** those who profess.
27. Tends: which tends.   **38. draw:** draw up.   **39. mean:**
intend.   **40. presently:** immediately.

Sc. ii: **5. dalliance:** trifling, lovemaking.   **9. accomplices:**
comrades.

SCENE III. *Before Angiers.*

[*Alarum. Excursions. Enter* LA PUCELLE.]
PUC. The Regent conquers, and the Frenchmen
    fly.
Now help, ye charming spells° and periapts,°
And ye choice spirits that admonish° me
And give me signs of future accidents.° [*Thunder.*]
You speedy helpers, that are substitutes   5
Under the lordly monarch of the North,°
Appear and aid me in this enterprise.
                    [*Enter* FIENDS.]
This speedy and quick appearance argues proof
Of your accustomed diligence to me.
Now, ye familiar spirits, that are culled°   10
Out of the powerful regions under earth,
Help me this once, that France may get the field.
                    [*They walk, and speak not.*]
Oh, hold me not with silence overlong!
Where I was wont to feed you with my blood,°
I'll lop a member° off and give it you   15
In earnest° of a further benefit,
So you do condescend to help me now.
                    [*They hang their heads.*]
No hope to have redress? My body shall
Pay recompense if you will grant my suit.
                    [*They shake their heads.*]
Cannot my body nor blood sacrifice   20
Entreat you to your wonted furtherance?°
Then take my soul, my body, soul and all,
Before that England give the French the foil.°
                    [*They depart.*]
See, they forsake me! Now the time is come
That France must vail° her lofty plumèd crest°   25
And let her head fall into England's lap.
My ancient incantations are too weak,
And Hell too strong for me to buckle with.
Now, France, thy glory droopeth to the dust.   29
                    [*Exit.*]
[*Excursions. Re-enter* LA PUCELLE *fighting hand to
    hand with* YORK. LA PUCELLE *is taken.
    The French fly.*]
YORK. Damsel of France, I think I have you fast.
Unchain your spirits now with spelling° charms,
And try if they can gain your liberty.
A goodly prize, fit for the Devil's Grace!°
See how the ugly witch doth bend her brows,

Sc. iii: **2. charming spells:** incantations which work enchantment. **periapts:** amulets, charms.   **3. admonish:** advise.
4. accidents: events.   **6. monarch . . . North:** The Devil and
evil spirits were regarded as dwelling in the darker northern
regions.   **10. culled:** collected.   **14. feed . . . blood:** Witches
were believed to feed their familiar spirits with their own blood.
Women accused of witchcraft were searched for marks indicating that their blood had been sucked.   **15. member:** limb.
16. earnest: money given on account of the full payment.
21. wonted furtherance: customary aid.   **23. foil:** repulse.
25. vail: lower. **lofty . . . crest:** plumed helmet. See Pl. 13a.
31. spelling: making magic spells.   **33. Devil's Grace:** i.e., His
Grace the Devil.

As if with Circe she would change my shape!°   35
    PUC. Changed to a worser shape thou canst not be.
    YORK. Oh, Charles the Dauphin is a proper° man.
No shape but his can please your dainty eye.
    PUC. A plaguing mischief light on Charles and
        thee!
And may ye both be suddenly surprised   40
By bloody hands in sleeping on your beds!
    YORK. Fell banning° hag, enchantress, hold thy
        tongue!
    PUC. I prithee give me leave to curse awhile.
    YORK. Curse, miscreant, when thou comest to the
        stake.   [*Exeunt.*]
[*Alarum. Enter* SUFFOLK, *with* MARGARET *in his
        hand.*]
    SUF. Be what thou wilt, thou art my prisoner.
                    [*Gazes on her.*]
O fairest beauty, do not fear nor fly!   46
For I will touch thee but with reverent hands.
I kiss these fingers for eternal peace,
And lay them gently on thy tender side.
Who art thou? Say, that I may honor thee.   50
    MAR. Margaret my name, and daughter to a
        King,
The King of Naples, whosoe'er thou art.
    SUF. An Earl I am, and Suffolk am I called.
Be not offended, nature's miracle,
Thou art allotted° to be ta'en by me.   55
So doth the swan her downy cygnets save,
Keeping them prisoner underneath her wings.
Yet, if this servile usage once offend,
Go and be free again as Suffolk's friend.°
                    [*She is going.*]
Oh, stay! I have no power to let her pass.   60
My hand would free her, but my heart says no.
As plays the sun upon the glassy streams,
Twinkling another counterfeited° beam,
So seems this gorgeous beauty to mine eyes.
Fain would I woo her, yet I dare not speak.   65
I'll call for pen and ink, and write my mind.
Fie, de la Pole! Disable not thyself.
Hast not a tongue? Is she not here?
Wilt thou be daunted at a woman's sight?
Aye, beauty's princely majesty is such,   70
Confounds the tongue and makes the senses rough.
    MAR. Say, Earl of Suffolk — if thy name be so —
What ransom must I pay before I pass?
For I perceive I am thy prisoner.
    SUF. How canst thou tell she will deny thy suit,
Before thou make a trial of her love?   76
    MAR. Why speak'st thou not? What ransom must
        I pay?

---

35. Circe . . . shape: Circe was an enchantress who lured men
into her palace and then by magic turned them into animals.
She was subdued by Odysseus (Ulysses). The story is told in
Homer's *Odyssey*, Bk. X.   **37. proper:** fine.   **42. Fell banning:**
fearful cursing.   **55. allotted:** fated.   **59. friend:** lover.
63. counterfeited: imitated, reflected.

SUF. She's beautiful and therefore to be wooed.
She is a woman, therefore to be won.°   79
   MAR. Wilt thou accept of ransom? Yea, or no.
   SUF. Fond man, remember that thou hast a wife.
Then how can Margaret be thy paramour?
   MAR. I were best to leave him, for he will not
     hear.
   SUF. There all is marred. There lies a cooling
     card.°
   MAR. He talks at random. Sure, the man is mad.
   SUF. And yet a dispensation° may be had.   86
   MAR. And yet I would that you would answer
     me.
   SUF. I'll win this Lady Margaret. For whom?
Why, for my King. Tush, that's a wooden° thing!
   MAR. He talks of wood. It is some carpenter.   90
   SUF. Yet so my fancy° may be satisfied,
And peace establishèd between these realms.
But there remains a scruple° in that too,
For though her father be the King of Naples,
Duke of Anjou and Maine, yet is he poor,   95
And our nobility will scorn the match.
   MAR. Hear ye, Captain, are you not at leisure?
   SUF. It shall be so, disdain they ne'er so much.
Henry is youthful and will quickly yield.
Madam, I have a secret to reveal.   100
   MAR. What though I be enthralled?° He seems a
     knight,
And will not any way dishonor me.
   SUF. Lady, vouchsafe to listen what I say.
   MAR. Perhaps I shall be rescued by the French,
And then I need not crave his courtesy.   105
   SUF. Sweet madam, give me hearing in a
     cause ——
   MAR. Tush, women have been captive ere now.
   SUF. Lady, wherefore talk you so?
   MAR. I cry you mercy, 'tis but quid for quo.
   SUF. Say, gentle Princess, would you not suppose
Your bondage happy to be made a queen?   111
   MAR. To be a queen in bondage is more vile
Than is a slave in base servility,
For princes should be free.
   SUF.   And so shall you
If happy England's royal King be free.   115
   MAR. Why, what concerns his freedom unto me?
   SUF. I'll undertake to make thee Henry's Queen,
To put a golden scepter in thy hand
And set a precious crown upon thy head
If thou wilt condescend to be my ——
   MAR.   What?   120
   SUF. His love.
   MAR. I am unworthy to be Henry's wife.

   SUF. No, gentle madam. I unworthy am
To woo so fair a dame to be his wife
And have no portion in the choice myself.   125
How say you, madam, are ye so content?
   MAR. An if my father please, I am content.
   SUF. Then call our captains and our colors forth.
And, madam, at your father's castle walls
We'll crave a parley to confer with him.   130
   [*A parley sounded. Enter* REIGNIER *on the walls.*]
See, Reignier, see, thy daughter prisoner!
   REI. To whom?
   SUF.   To me.
   REI.   Suffolk, what remedy?
I am a soldier, and unapt° to weep,
Or to exclaim on° Fortune's fickleness.
   SUF. Yes, there is remedy enough, my lord.   135
Consent, and for thy honor give consent,
Thy daughter shall be wedded to my King;
Whom I with pain° have wooed and won thereto.
And this her easy-held imprisonment
Hath gained thy daughter princely liberty.   140
   REI. Speaks Suffolk as he thinks?
   SUF.   Fair Margaret knows
That Suffolk doth not flatter, face,° or feign.
   REI. Upon thy princely warrant, I descend
To give thee answer of thy just demand.
                    [*Exit from the walls.*]
   SUF. And here I will expect thy coming.   145
   [*Trumpets sound. Enter* REIGNIER, *below.*]
   REI. Welcome, brave Earl, into our territories.
Command in Anjou what your Honor pleases.
   SUF. Thanks, Reignier, happy for so sweet a
     child,
Fit to be made companion with a king.   149
What answer makes your Grace unto my suit?
   REI. Since thou dost deign to woo her little worth
To be the princely bride of such a lord,
Upon condition I may quietly
Enjoy mine own, the country Maine and Anjou,
Free from oppression or the stroke of war,   155
My daughter shall be Henry's if he please.
   SUF. That is her ransom. I deliver her,
And those two counties° I will undertake
Your Grace shall well and quietly enjoy.
   REI. And I again, in Henry's royal name,   160
As deputy unto that gracious King,
Give thee her hand for sign of plighted faith.
   SUF. Reignier of France, I give thee kingly
     thanks,
Because this is in traffic of° a King.   164
   [*Aside*] And yet, methinks, I could be well content
To be mine own attorney° in this case.
I'll over then to England with this news,

78–79. She's . . . won: a frequent sentiment in Elizabethan authors; see *Rich III*, I.ii.228–29. 84. cooling card: a common proverbial phrase meaning "damper." 86. dispensation: permission from the Church. 89. wooden: useless; i.e., not interested in women 91. fancy: love. 93. scruple: objection. 101. enthralled: imprisoned.

133. unapt: not fitted, unaccustomed. 134. exclaim on: curse at. 138. pain: difficulty. 142. face: pretend. 158. counties: earldoms. A "county" was originally the territory governed by a count (or earl). 164. traffic of: i.e., acting as agent for. 166. attorney: pleader.

And make this marriage to be solemnized.
So farewell, Reignier. Set this diamond safe
In golden palaces, as it becomes.   170
   REI. I do embrace thee, as I would embrace
The Christian prince King Henry were he here.
   MAR. Farewell, my lord. Good wishes, praise, and
     prayers
Shall Suffolk ever have of Margaret.   [*Going.*]
   SUF. Farewell, sweet madam. But hark you,
     Margaret.   175
No princely commendations to my King?
   MAR. Such commendations as becomes a maid,
A virgin and his servant, say to him.
   SUF. Words sweetly placed and modestly directed.
But, madam, I must trouble you again.   180
No loving token to His Majesty?
   MAR. Yes, my good lord, a pure unspotted heart,
Never yet taint° with love, I send the King.
   SUF. And this withal.   [*Kisses her.*]
   MAR. That for thyself. I will not so presume   185
To send such peevish° tokens to a king.
      [*Exeunt* REIGNIER *and* MARGARET.]
   SUF. Oh, wert thou for myself! But, Suffolk, stay.
Thou mayst not wander in that labyrinth.°
There Minotaurs° and ugly treasons lurk.
Solicit Henry with her wondrous praise.   190
Bethink thee on her virtues that surmount,
And natural graces that extinguish art.°
Repeat their semblance° often on the seas,   193
That, when thou comest to kneel at Henry's feet,
Thou mayst bereave him of his wits with wonder.
          [*Exit.*]

SCENE IV. *Camp of the* DUKE OF YORK
in Anjou.

   [*Enter* YORK, WARWICK, *and others.*]
   YORK. Bring forth that sorceress condemned to
     burn.
   [*Enter* LA PUCELLE, *guarded, and a* SHEPHERD.]
   SHEP. Ah, Joan, this kills thy father's heart out-
     right!
Have I sought every country far and near,
And, now it is my chance to find thee out,
Must I behold thy timeless° cruel death?   5
Ah, Joan, sweet daughter Joan, I'll die with thee!
   PUC. Decrepit miser!° Base ignoble wretch!
I am descended of a gentler° blood.

---

183. taint: tainted.   **186. peevish:** silly.   **188. labyrinth:** maze.
189. Minotaurs: The Minotaur was a creature — half man,
half brute — who lived in Crete and to whom maidens were offered as a sacrifice. The Minotaur, who lived in the center of a
maze (*labyrinth*), was finally slain by the hero Theseus.   **192. art:**
i.e., made-up beauty.   **193. Repeat . . . semblance:** i.e., repeatedly imagine her beauty.
   Sc. iv: 5. timeless: untimely.   **7. miser:** wretch.   **8. gentler:**
nobler.

Thou art no father nor no friend of mine.
   SHEP. Out, out! My lords, an please you, 'tis not
     so.   10
I did beget her, all the parish knows.
Her mother liveth yet, can testify
She was the first fruit of my bachelorship.
   WAR. Graceless! Wilt thou deny thy parentage?
   YORK. This argues what her kind of life hath
     been —   15
Wicked and vile, and so her death concludes.
   SHEP. Fie, Joan, that thou wilt be so obstacle!°
God knows thou art a collop° of my flesh,
And for thy sake have I shed many a tear.
Deny me not, I prithee, gentle Joan.   20
   PUC. Peasant, avaunt! You have suborned° this
     man
Of purpose to obscure my noble birth.
   SHEP. 'Tis true, I gave a noble° to the priest
The morn that I was wedded to her mother.   24
Kneel down and take my blessing, good my girl.
Wilt thou not stoop? Now cursèd be the time
Of thy nativity!° I would the milk
Thy mother gave thee when thou suck'dst her
     breast
Had been a little ratsbane° for thy sake!
Or else, when thou didst keep my lambs a-field,   30
I wish some ravenous wolf had eaten thee!
Dost thou deny thy father, cursed drab?°
Oh, burn her, burn her! Hanging is too good.
          [*Exit.*]
   YORK. Take her away, for she hath lived too long
To fill the world with vicious qualities.   35
   PUC. First, let me tell you whom you have con-
     demned:
Not me begotten of a shepherd swain,
But issued from the progeny of kings,
Virtuous and holy, chosen from above
By inspiration of celestial grace   40
To work exceeding miracles on earth.
I never had to do with wicked spirits.
But you, that are polluted with your lusts,
Stained with the guiltless blood of innocents,
Corrupt and tainted with a thousand vices,   45
Because you want° the grace that others have,
You judge it straight a thing impossible
To compass wonders but by help of devils.
No, misconceived!° Joan of Arc hath been
A virgin from her tender infancy,   50
Chaste and immaculate in very thought;
Whose maiden blood, thus rigorously effused,°
Will cry for vengeance at the gates of Heaven.
   YORK. Aye, aye. Away with her to execution!
   WAR. And hark ye, sirs, because she is a maid,

---

17. obstacle: obstinate.   **18. collop:** slice. See *W Tale,* I.ii.137.
21. suborned: hired to commit perjury.   **23. noble:** 6s.8d.
See App. 27.   **27. nativity:** birth.   **29. ratsbane:** rat poison.
32. drab: harlot.   **46. want:** lack.   **49. misconceived:** misun-
derstood.   **52. rigorously effused:** cruelly shed.

Spare for no faggots, let there be enow.°   56
Place barrels of pitch upon the fatal stake,
That so her torture may be shortenèd.

PUC. Will nothing turn your unrelenting hearts?
Then, Joan, discover thine infirmity   60
That warranteth by law to be thy privilege.°
I am with child, ye bloody homicides.
Murder not then the fruit within my womb,
Although ye hale me to a violent death.

YORK. Now Heaven forfend!° The holy maid
  with child!   65

WAR. The greatest miracle that e'er ye wrought.
Is all your strict preciseness come to this?

YORK. She and the Dauphin have been juggling.
I did imagine what would be her refuge.°

WAR. Well, go to. We'll have no bastards live,
Especially since Charles must father it.   71

PUC. You are deceived. My child is none of his.
It was Alençon that enjoyed my love.

YORK. Alençon! That notorious Machiavel!°
It dies an if it had a thousand lives.   75

PUC. Oh, give me leave, I have deluded you.
'Twas neither Charles nor yet the Duke I named,
But Reignier, King of Naples, that prevailed.

WAR. A married man! That's most intolerable.

YORK. Why, here's a girl! I think she knows not
  well,   80
There were so many, whom she may accuse.

WAR. It's sign she hath been liberal and free.

YORK. And yet, forsooth, she is a virgin pure.
Strumpet, thy words condemn thy brat and thee.
Use no entreaty, for it is in vain.   85

PUC. Then lead me hence, with whom I leave my
  curse:
May never glorious sun reflex° his beams
Upon the country where you make abode,
But darkness and the gloomy shade of death
Environ you till mischief and despair   90
Drive you to break your necks or hang yourselves!
          [*Exit, guarded.*]

YORK. Break thou in pieces and consume to ashes,
Thou foul accursèd minister° of Hell!

[*Enter* CARDINAL BEAUFORT, BISHOP OF WINCHESTER,
  attended.]

CAR. Lord Regent, I do greet your Excellence
With letters of commission from the King.   95

For know, my lords, the states of Christendom,
Moved with remorse° of these outrageous broils,
Have earnestly implored a general peace
Betwixt our nation and the aspiring French;
And here at hand the Dauphin and his train°   100
Approacheth to confer about some matter.

YORK. Is all our travail turned to this effect?
After the slaughter of so many peers,
So many captains, gentlemen, and soldiers
That in this quarrel have been overthrown   105
And sold their bodies for their country's benefit,
Shall we at last conclude effeminate peace?
Have we not lost most part of all the towns,
By treason, falsehood and by treachery,
Our great progenitors had conquered?   110
Oh, Warwick, Warwick! I foresee with grief
The utter loss of all the realm of France.

WAR. Be patient, York. If we conclude a peace,
It shall be with such strict and severe covenants
As little shall the Frenchmen gain thereby.   115

[*Enter* CHARLES, ALENÇON, BASTARD, REIGNIER, *and
  Others.*]

CHA. Since, lords of England, it is thus agreed
That peaceful truce shall be proclaimed in France,
We come to be informèd by yourselves
What the conditions of that league must be.

YORK. Speak, Winchester, for boiling choler°
  chokes   120
The hollow passage of my poisoned voice
By sight of these our baleful° enemies.

CAR. Charles and the rest, it is enacted thus:
That, in regard King Henry gives consent
Of mere compassion and of lenity°   125
To ease your country of distressful war
And suffer you to breathe in fruitful peace,
You shall become true liegemen° to his Crown.
And, Charles, upon condition thou wilt swear
To pay him tribute and submit thyself,   130
Thou shalt be placed as Viceroy under him,
And still enjoy thy regal dignity.

ALEN. Must he be then as shadow of himself?
Adorn his temples with a coronet,°
And yet in substance and authority   135
Retain but privilege of a private man?
This proffer is absurd and reasonless.

CHA. 'Tis known already that I am possessed
With more than half the Gallian territories,
And therein reverenced for their lawful King.   140
Shall I, for lucre of the rest unvanquished,
Detract so much from that prerogative
As to be called but Viceroy of the whole?
No, Lord Ambassador, I'll rather keep
That which I have than, coveting for more,   145

---

56. enow: enough.   **61. warranteth . . . privilege**: A woman condemned to death could plead that she was pregnant. If the plea was accepted, her life was spared until the child had been born.
65. forfend: forbid.   **69. refuge**: defense.   **74. Machiavel**: Pietro Machiavelli, a Florentine, published his famous treatise *The Prince* (*Il Principe*) in 1513. Machiavelli's cynical and realistic advice on statecraft was regarded by contemporaries (especially by those who had never read it) as so immoral and devilish that the word "Machiavellian" was used to denote a man who utterly despised all religious, moral, and human laws. Richard Duke of Gloucester, afterward Richard III, was regarded as a typical specimen. See *III Hen VI*, III.ii.193.
87. reflex: reflect.   **93. minister**: servant.

97. remorse: pity.   **100. train**: followers.   **120. choler**: anger.
122. baleful: deadly.   **125. lenity**: mildness.   **128. liegemen**: subjects.   **134. coronet**: small crown, worn by one of less rank than a king.

Be cast° from possibility of all.
 YORK. Insulting Charles! Hast thou by secret means
Used intercession to obtain a league,
And, now the matter grows to compromise,°
Stand'st thou aloof upon comparison?° 150
Either accept the title thou usurp'st
Of benefit proceeding° from our King
And not of any challenge of desert,
Or we will plague thee with incessant wars.
 REI. My lord, you do not well in obstinacy 155
To cavil in the course of this contract.
If once it be neglected, ten to one
We shall not find like opportunity.
 ALEN. To say the truth, it is your policy°
To save your subjects from such massacre 160
And ruthless slaughters as are daily seen
By our proceeding in hostility,
And therefore take this compact° of a truce,
Although you break it when your pleasure serves.
 WAR. How say'st thou, Charles? Shall our condition stand? 165
 CHA. It shall;
Only reserved, you claim no interest
In any of our towns of garrison.°
 YORK. Then swear allegiance to His Majesty,
As thou art knight, never to disobey 170
Nor be rebellious to the Crown of England —
Thou, nor thy nobles, to the Crown of England.
So now dismiss your army when ye please.
Hang up your ensigns, let your drums be still, 174
For here we entertain a solemn peace. [*Exeunt.*]

SCENE V. *London. The royal palace.*

[*Enter* SUFFOLK *in conference with the* KING,
GLOUCESTER, *and* EXETER.]

 KING. Your wondrous rare description, noble Earl,
Of beauteous Margaret hath astonished me.
Her virtues gracèd with external gifts
Do breed love's settled passions in my heart;
And like as rigor of tempestuous gusts 5
Provokes the mightiest hulk against the tide,
So am I driven by breath of her renown
Either to suffer shipwreck or arrive
Where I may have fruition of her love.
 SUF. Tush, my good lord, this superficial tale 10
Is but a preface of her worthy praise.
The chief perfections of that lovely dame,
Had I sufficient skill to utter them,

Would make a volume of enticing lines
Able to ravish° any dull conceit.° 15
And, which is more, she is not so divine,
So full replete with choice of all delights,
But with as humble lowliness of mind
She is content to be at your command —
Command, I mean, of virtuous chaste intents, 20
To love and honor Henry as her lord.
 KING. And otherwise will Henry ne'er presume.
Therefore, my Lord Protector, give consent
That Margaret may be England's royal Queen.
 GLO. So should I give consent to flatter sin. 25
You know, my lord, your Highness is betrothed°
Unto another lady of esteem.
How shall we then dispense with that contract
And not deface° your honor with reproach?
 SUF. As doth a ruler with unlawful oaths, 30
Or one that, at a triumph having vowed
To try his strength, forsaketh yet the lists°
By reason of his adversary's odds,
A poor Earl's daughter° is unequal odds,
And therefore may be broke without offense. 35
 GLO. Why, what, I pray, is Margaret more than that?
Her father is no better than an earl,
Although in glorious titles he excel.
 SUF. Yes, my lord, her father is a King —
The King of Naples and Jerusalem, 40
And of such great authority in France
As his alliance will confirm our peace
And keep the Frenchmen in allegiance.
 GLO. And so the Earl of Armagnac may do
Because he is near kinsman unto Charles. 45
 EXE. Beside, his wealth doth warrant a liberal dower,
Where Reignier sooner will receive than give.
 SUF. A dower, my lords! Disgrace not so your King
That he should be so abject, base and poor,
To choose for wealth, and not for perfect love. 50
Henry is able to enrich his queen,
And not to seek a queen to make him rich:
So worthless peasants bargain for their wives,
As market men for oxen, sheep, or horse.
Marriage is a matter of more worth 55
Than to be dealt in by attorneyship.°
Not whom we will, but whom his Grace affects,°
Must be companion of his nuptial bed.
And therefore, lords, since he affects her most,
It most of all these reasons bindeth us 60
In our opinions she should be preferred.

146. cast: driven away. 149. compromise: agreement.
150. upon comparison: i.e., when the agreement comes to be signed; lit., when both copies of the agreement are compared before signature. 152. benefit proceeding: as an act of favor.
159. policy: best plan. 163. compact: agreement. 168. towns of garrison: fortified towns.

 Sc. v: 15. ravish: overcome. conceit: imagination.
26. betrothed: See V.i.1–27. 29. deface: disfigure. 32. lists: place of combat. 34. Earl's daughter: According to Hall's *Chronicle*, it had already been agreed that the King should marry the daughter of the "Earl of Arminack." 56. by attorneyship: i.e., as a business arrangement. 57. affects: likes.

For what is wedlock forcèd but a hell,
An age of discord and continual strife?
Whereas the contrary bringeth bliss,
And is a pattern° of celestial peace.   65
Whom should we match with Henry, being a King,
But Margaret, that is daughter to a King?
Her peerless feature, joinèd with her birth,
Approves her fit for none but for a king.
Her valiant courage and undaunted spirit,   70
More than in women commonly is seen,
Will answer our hope in issue of a king;
For Henry, son unto a conqueror,
Is likely to beget more conquerors
If with a lady of so high resolve   75
As is fair Margaret he be linked in love.
Then yield, my lords, and here conclude with me
That Margaret shall be Queen, and none but she.
    KING. Whether it be through force of your report,
My noble Lord of Suffolk, or for that   80
My tender youth was never yet attaint°
With any passion of inflaming love,
I cannot tell; but this I am assured:
I feel such sharp dissension in my breast,
Such fierce alarums both of hope and fear,   85
As I am sick with working of my thoughts.
Take, therefore, shipping. Post,° my lord, to France.

Agree to any covenants, and procure
That Lady Margaret do vouchsafe to come
To cross the seas to England, and be crowned   90
King Henry's faithful and anointed Queen.
For your expenses and sufficient charge,
Among the people gather up a tenth.
Be gone, I say! For till you do return,
I rest perplexèd with a thousand cares.   95
And you, good Uncle, banish all offense.
If you do censure° me by what you were,°
Not what you are, I know it will excuse
This sudden execution of my will.
And so, conduct me where, from company,   100
I may revolve and ruminate my grief.   [*Exit.*]
    GLO. Aye, grief, I fear me, both at first and last.
          [*Exeunt* GLOUCESTER *and* EXETER.]
    SUF. Thus Suffolk hath prevailed, and thus he goes,
As did the youthful Paris once to Greece,°
With hope to find the like event° in love;   105
But prosper better than the Trojan did.
Margaret shall now be Queen, and rule the King;
But I will rule both her, the King, and realm.
                                                  [*Exit.*]

65. pattern: type, model.   81. attaint: tainted.   87. Post: hasten.

97. censure: judge. you were: i.e., when you yourself were young. 104. Paris ... Greece: Paris, son of Priam King of Troy ran away with Helen, the beautiful wife of Menelaus King of Sparta. This was the cause of the ten years siege of Troy. See *Tr & Cr.* 105. event: result.

The Second Part of

KING HENRY THE SIXTH

Introduction

The Second Part of Henry VI continues the story from the marriage of the young King Henry VI and the Lady Margaret of Anjou to the victory of Richard Duke of York at the battle of St. Albans. Its theme is the beginning of the long civil wars in England between the Houses of Lancaster and York. As dramatic writing this Second Part shows more skill and unity of style than the First. The plot has more shape and is better developed, the characterization is more convincing, and the events are seen as the result of the clash of personalities and not just as a series of episodes. A general atmosphere of jealousy and hatred pervades the whole play. The young Queen Margaret is shown as a ruthless and domineering woman; she despises her meek husband and takes Suffolk as her lover; she resents and insults the Duchess of Gloucester and exults in her disgrace and in the downfall and death of Humphrey, the "good Duke of Gloucester." She hates York and his supporters and all his family — which is understandable — and she is the inspiration of the party of the Red Rose, the Lancastrians.

Opposed to the Queen and her followers are Richard Duke of York and his sons and supporters, especially the Earl of Warwick, known in English history as "the Kingmaker," the most powerful of all the English nobles. Richard of York is a good specimen of the ambitious villain — a type popular on the English stage in the early 1590's; but he is mild compared with his youngest son Richard, afterward Duke of Gloucester and King Richard III. York's motives, as he explains in the first soliloquy (I.i.214–59) are mixed — a desire to claim his rights as legal heir of Edward III, disgust at the "bookish" King's misrule, and a personal hatred of the House of Lancaster. At the beginning of the play he is overshadowed by Humphrey Duke of Gloucester, but he bides his time until Humphrey's fall. When he is sent off to deal with the rebellion in Ireland, he realizes that his opportu-

nity has come (III.i.309–83). He resolves that he will stir up troubles in England and then at the head of his army return to reap his harvest and win the crown.

The fourth act of the play is wholly concerned with the rebellion of Jack Cade. These scenes are interesting examples of the development of Shakespeare's art, for they are the first specimens of the "crowd scenes" which he later so successfully developed in *Julius Caesar* and *Coriolanus*. In spite of their grimness the episodes gave Shakespeare a chance of lowering the tone of the play to common people and their talk from the level of the high, heroic, and at times ranting speeches with which the scenes of the jarring nobility were so amply filled.

The play ends with York's return to claim the crown. The civil wars begin; at first the White Rose is victorious, and York and Warwick go forth in triumph to receive the submission of London.

In writing *II Henry VI* Shakespeare was still considerably under the influence of contemporary fashion in drama. The speeches are self-consciously poetical and high sounding, overfull of classical allusion, and usually too long. When a person has anything of importance to say, he needs from 25 to 50 lines to say it (e.g., I.i.75–103, 214–59, II.iv.27–57, III.i.4–42, 331–83, III.ii.73–121, IV.i.70–103). In his maturity Shakespeare could pack a world of meaning into a line or two. Nevertheless, he was rapidly absorbing the art of drama, of which one of the main secrets is to keep the audience continually alert by contrast and variety. Fine speech was amply appreciated, but he was learning that it needed to be varied by exciting episode and even at times by a good laugh. Apart from the set scenes when the great personages make speeches against one another, he introduced such varied episodes as the Duchess of Gloucester's séance with the spirits (I.iv), the false miracle (II.i), the comic combat of Horner and his man Peter (II.iii), the deathbed of Cardinal Beaufort (III.iii), and Jack Cade and his mob (IV.ii).

In *II Henry VI* Shakespeare was not quite so reckless with the facts of history and chronology as he had been in Part I, for here the episodes are fewer; but it may be noted that the quarrel between Queen Margaret and the Duchess of Gloucester could not have occurred, as the Duchess was disgraced three and a half years before Margaret came to England. Nor was Suffolk actually the Queen's lover. Moreover, certain episodes in the rebellion of Jack Cade were taken over from incidents in the Wat Tyler rebellion of seventy years earlier.

The sources for *II Henry VI*, as for *I Henry VI*, were for the most part the *Chronicles* of Halle and Holinshed. Some examples will show how Shakespeare used these sources.

1. THE CHARACTER OF HENRY VI

[Halle gives the following character sketch of Henry VI:]

King Henry was of stature goodly, of body slender, to which proportion all other members were correspondent; his face beautiful, in the which continually was resident the bounty of mind with which he was inwardly endowed. He did abhor of his own nature all the vices, as well of the body as of the soul; and from his very infancy he was of honest conversation and pure integrity; no knower of evil, and a keeper of all goodness; a despiser of all things which were wont to cause the minds of mortal men to slide or appair. Besides this, patience was so radicate in his heart that of all the injuries to him committed (which were no small number) he never asked vengeance nor punishment, but for that rendered to Almighty God, his Creator, hearty thanks, thinking that by this trouble and adversity his sins were to him forgotten and forgiven.

2. THE DEATH OF SUFFOLK (cf. IV.i)

But God's justice would not that so ungracious a person should so escape; for, when he shipped in Suffolk, intending to transport himself over into France, he was encountered with a ship of war, appertaining to the Duke of Exeter, Constable of the Tower of London, called *The Nicholas of the Tower*. The captain of that bark with small fight entered into the Duke's ship, and perceiving his person present, brought him to Dover Road [harbor] and there on the one side of a cockboat caused his head to be stricken off, and left his body with the head lying there on the sands.

3. THE DEATH OF CADE (cf. IV.x)

[Halle relates that when Cade saw his men suddenly disperse, he fled into Sussex in disguise.]

But all his metamorphosis or transfiguration little prevailed. For, after a proclamation made that whosoever could apprehend the said Jack Cade should have for his pain a thousand marks, many sought for him but few espied him, till one Alexander Iden, esquire of Kent, found him in a garden and there in his defense manfully slew the caitiff Cade and brought his dead body to London, whose head was set on London Bridge.

4. THE "MIRACLE" AT ST. ALBANS (cf. II.i.60–160)

[This episode was taken from Sir Thomas More's *Dialogue*, concerning the veneration and worship of images, etc.]

When the King was comen and the town full, suddenly this blind man at Saint Alban's Shrine had his sight again; and a miracle solemnly rongen and *Te Deum* songen [i.e., the bells were rung in token of a miracle], so that nothing was talked of in all the town but this miracle. So happened it that Duke Humphrey of Gloucester, a great wise man and very well learned, having great joy to see such a miracle, called the poor man unto him. And first showing himself joyous of God's glory, so showed in the getting of his sight; and exhorting him to meekness, and to none ascribing of any part the worship to himself, nor to be proud of the people's praise, which would call him a good and godly man thereby. At last he looked well into his eyen [eyes], and asked whether he could never see nothing at all in all his life before. And when as well his wife as himself affirmed fastly no, then he looked advisedly upon his eyen again and said, " I believe you very well, for me thinketh that ye cannot see so well yet." " Yes, sir," quoth he, " I thank God and his holy martyr, I can now see as well as any man." " Ye can? " quoth the Duke; " what color is my gown? " Then anon the beggar told him. " What color is this man's gown? " He told him also; and so forth, without any sticking, he told him the names of all the colors that could be showed him. And when my Lord saw that, he had him " walk, faitor [impostor]! " and made him be set openly in the stocks; for though he could have seen suddenly by miracle the difference between divers colors, yet he could not by the sight so suddenly tell the names of all these colors but if he had known them before, no more than the names of all the men that he should suddenly see.

II Henry VI as it stands is an incomplete play and needs its sequel to finish the story.

Henry VI, Part II

DRAMATIS PERSONAE

KING HENRY *the Sixth*
HUMPHREY, *Duke of Gloucester, his uncle*
CARDINAL BEAUFORT, *Bishop of Winchester, great-uncle to the King*
RICHARD PLANTAGENET, *Duke of York*
EDWARD *and* RICHARD, *his sons*
DUKE OF SOMERSET
DUKE OF SUFFOLK
DUKE OF BUCKINGHAM
LORD CLIFFORD
YOUNG CLIFFORD, *his son*
EARL OF SALISBURY
EARL OF WARWICK
LORD SCALES
LORD SAY
SIR HUMPHREY STAFFORD, *and* WILLIAM STAFFORD, *his brother*
SIR JOHN STANLEY
VAUX
MATTHEW GOFFE
A SEACAPTAIN, MASTER, *and* MASTER'S MATE, *and* WALTER WHITMORE
TWO GENTLEMEN, *prisoners with Suffolk*
JOHN HUME *and* JOHN SOUTHWELL, *priests*
BOLINGBROKE, *a conjurer*

THOMAS HORNER, *an armorer*
PETER, *his man*
CLERK *of Chatham*
MAYOR *of Saint Alban's*
SIMPCOX, *an impostor*
ALEXANDER IDEN, *a Kentish gentleman*
JACK CADE, *a rebel*
GEORGE BEVIS, JOHN HOLLAND, DICK *the butcher,* SMITH *the weaver,* MICHAEL, *&c., followers of Cade*
TWO MURDERERS

MARGARET, *Queen to King Henry*
ELEANOR, *Duchess of Gloucester*
MARGARET JOURDAIN, *a witch*
WIFE *to Simpcox*

LORDS, LADIES, *and* ATTENDANTS, PETITIONERS, ALDERMEN, *a* HERALD, *a* BEADLE, SHERIFF, *and* OFFICERS, CITIZENS, 'PRENTICES, FALCONERS, GUARDS, SOLDIERS, MESSENGERS, *&c*
A SPIRIT

SCENE — *England*

Act I

SCENE I. *London. The palace.*

[*Flourish of trumpets, then hautboys.°* Enter THE KING, HUMPHREY, DUKE OF GLOUCESTER, SALISBURY, WARWICK, *and* CARDINAL BEAUFORT, *on the one side,* THE QUEEN, SUFFOLK, YORK, SOMERSET, *and* BUCKINGHAM *on the other.*]

SUF. As° by your high imperial Majesty
I had in charge at my depart for France,
As procurator° to your Excellence,
To marry Princess Margaret for your Grace,
So, in the famous ancient city Tours,   5
In presence of the Kings of France and Sicil,
The Dukes of Orleans, Calaber,° Bretagne and Alençon,
Seven Earls, twelve Barons, and twenty reverend Bishops,
I have performed my task and was espoused,°

And humbly now upon my bended knee,   10
In sight of England and her lordly peers,
Deliver up my title° in the Queen
To your most gracious hands, that are the substance
Of that great shadow I did represent —
The happiest gift that ever marquess gave,   15
The fairest queen that ever king received.
KING. Suffolk, arise. Welcome, Queen Margaret.
I can express no kinder sign of love
Than this kind kiss. O Lord, that lends me life,
Lend me a heart replete with thankfulness!   20
For Thou hast given me in this beauteous face
A world of earthly blessings to my soul
If sympathy of love unite our thoughts.
QUEEN. Great King of England and my gracious lord,   24
The mutual conference that my mind hath had
By day, by night, waking and in my dreams,
In courtly company or at my beads,
With you, mine alder-liefest° sovereign,
Makes me the bolder to salute my King
With ruder terms such as my wit affords   30
And overjoy of heart doth minister.

Act I. Sc. i: s.d., hautboys: oboes.   1–16. As . . . received: The Second Part of the play resumes where the First Part concluded.   3. procurator: agent.   7. Caliber: Calabre. The list of notables is taken direct from Holinshed.   9. espoused: betrothed as your proxy.

12. title: claim.   28. alder-liefest: dearest of all.

KING. Her sight did ravish, but her grace in
  speech,
Her words y-clad° with wisdom's majesty,
Makes me from wondering fall to weeping joys;
Such is the fulness of my heart's content.   35
Lords, with one cheerful voice welcome my love.
    ALL. [*Kneeling*] Long live Queen Margaret, Eng-
  land's happiness!
    QUEEN. We thank you all.   [*Flourish.*]
    SUF. My Lord Protector, so° it please your Grace,
Here are the articles of contracted peace   40
Between our sovereign and the French king Charles,
For eighteen months concluded by consent.
    GLO. [*Reads.*] *" Imprimis,° it is agreed between*
the French king Charles and William de la Pole,
Marquess of Suffolk, Ambassador for Henry   45
King of England, that the said Henry shall espouse
the Lady Margaret, daughter unto Reignier, King
of Naples, Sicilia, and Jerusalem, and crown her
Queen of England ere the thirtieth of May next en-
suing. Item, that the Duchy of Anjou and the   50
County of Maine shall be released and delivered to
the King her father——"   [*Lets the paper fall.*]
    KING. Uncle, how now!
    GLO.   Pardon me, gracious lord.
Some sudden qualm° hath struck me at the heart
And dimmed mine eyes, that I can read no further.
    KING. Uncle of Winchester, I pray, read on.   56
    CAR. [*Reads.*] *" Item, It is further agreed between*
them that the duchies of Anjou and Maine shall be
released and delivered over to the King her father,
and she sent over of the King of England's own
proper cost and charges, without having any
dowry."   62
    KING. They please us well. Lord Marquess, kneel
  down.
We here create thee the first Duke of Suffolk
And gird thee with the sword. Cousin of York,   65
We here discharge your Grace from being Regent
I' the parts of France till term of eighteen months
Be full expired. Thanks, Uncle Winchester,
Gloucester, York, Buckingham, Somerset,
Salisbury, and Warwick.   70
We thank you all for this great favor done
In entertainment to my princely Queen.
Come, let us in, and with all speed provide
To see her coronation be performed.   74
    [*Exeunt* KING, QUEEN, *and* SUFFOLK.]
    GLO. Brave peers of England, pillars of the state,
To you Duke Humphrey must unload his grief,
Your grief, the common grief of all the land.
What! Did my brother Henry spend his youth,
His valor, coin, and people, in the wars?

Did he so often lodge in open field,   80
In winter's cold and summer's parching heat,
To conquer France, his true inheritance?
And did my brother Bedford toil his wits°
To keep by policy° what Henry got?
Have you yourselves, Somerset, Buckingham,   85
Brave York, Salisbury, and victorious Warwick,
Received deep scars in France and Normandy?
Or hath mine Uncle Beaufort and myself,
With all the learnèd Council of the realm,
Studied so long, sat in the council house   90
Early and late, debating to and fro
How France and Frenchmen might be kept in
  awe,°
And had His Highness in his infancy
Crownèd in Paris in despite° of foes?
And shall these labors and these honors die?   95
Shall Henry's conquest, Bedford's vigilance,
Your deeds of war and all our counsel die?
O peers of England, shameful is this league!
Fatal this marriage, canceling your fame,
Blotting your names from books of memory,   100
Razing° the characters° of your renown,
Defacing monuments of conquered France,
Undoing all as all had never been!
    CAR. Nephew, what means this passionate dis-
  course,
This peroration with such circumstance?°   105
For France, 'tis ours, and we will keep it still.
    GLO. Aye, Uncle, we will keep it if we can;
But now it is impossible we should.
Suffolk, the new-made Duke that rules the roast,°
Hath given the Duchy of Anjou and Maine   110
Unto the poor King Reignier, whose large style°
Agrees not with the leanness of his purse.
    SAL. Now, by the death of Him that died for all,
These counties were the keys of Normandy.   114
But wherefore weeps Warwick, my valiant son?
    WAR. For grief that they are past recovery.
For, were there hope to conquer them again,
My sword should shed hot blood, mine eyes no
  tears.
Anjou and Maine! Myself did win them both.   119
Those provinces these arms of mine did conquer.
And are the cities that I got with wounds
Delivered up again with peaceful words?
Mort Dieu!°
    YORK. For Suffolk's Duke, may he be suffocate
That dims the honor of this warlike Isle!   125
France should have torn and rent my very heart
Before I would have yielded to this league.

---

33. y-clad: clad.   **39. so:** if.   **43.** *Imprimis:* firstly — the
normal beginning in setting out the details of an agreement, the
clauses which follow being introduced by *Item* (likewise).
54. qualm: fainting attack.

83. toil . . . wits: scheme.   **84. policy:** statecraft.   **92. awe:**
obedience.   **94. despite:** spite.   **101. Razing:** erasing. characters: inscriptions which record.   **105. peroration . . . circumstance:** elaborately prepared oration.   **109. rules . . . roast:**
domineers at the feast.   **111. large style:** pompous title.
123. Mort Dieu: by God's death — an oath.

I never read but England's kings have had
Large sums of gold and dowries with their wives;
And our King Henry gives away his own   130
To match° with her that brings no vantages.
    GLO. A proper jest, and never heard before,
That Suffolk should demand a whole fifteenth°
For costs and charges in transporting her!
She should have stayed in France and starved in
    France   135
Before ——
    CAR. My Lord of Gloucester, now ye grow too hot.
It was the pleasure of my Lord the King.
    GLO. My Lord of Winchester, I know your mind.
'Tis not my speeches that you do mislike,   140
But 'tis my presence that doth trouble ye.
Rancor will out. Proud prelate, in thy face
I see thy fury. If I longer stay,
We shall begin our ancient bickerings.
Lordings,° farewell, and say, when I am gone,   145
I prophesied France will be lost ere long. [Exit.]
    CAR. So, there goes our Protector in a rage.
'Tis known to you he is mine enemy —
Nay, more, an enemy unto you all,
And no great friend, I fear me, to the King.   150
Consider, lords, he is the next of blood
And heir apparent to the English crown.
Had Henry got an empire by his marriage,
And all the wealthy kingdoms of the West,
There's reason he should be displeased at it.   155
Look to it, lords. Let not his smoothing words
Bewitch your hearts. Be wise and circumspect.
What though° the common people favor him,
Calling him "Humphrey, the good Duke of
    Gloucester,"   159
Clapping their hands, and crying with loud voice,
" Jesu maintain your royal Excellence! "
With " God preserve the good Duke Humphrey! "
I fear me, lords, for all this flattering gloss,°
He will be found a dangerous Protector.
    BUCK. Why should he, then, protect our sov-
    ereign,   165
He being of age to govern of himself?
Cousin of Somerset, join you with me,
And all together, with the Duke of Suffolk,
We'll quickly hoise° Duke Humphrey from his
    seat.
    CAR. This weighty business will not brook° de-
    lay.   170
I'll to the Duke of Suffolk presently.°   [Exit.]
    SOM. Cousin of Buckingham, though Hum-
    phrey's pride
And greatness of his place be grief to us,
Yet let us watch the haughty Cardinal.

His insolence is more intolerable   175
Than all the princes in the land beside.
If Gloucester be displaced, he'll be Protector.
    BUCK. Or thou or I, Somerset, will be Protector,
Despite Duke Humphrey or the Cardinal.   179
        [Exeunt BUCKINGHAM and SOMERSET.]
    SAL. Pride went before, ambition follows him.
While these do labor for their own preferment,
Behoves it us to labor for the realm.
I never saw but Humphrey Duke of Gloucester,
Did bear him like a noble gentleman.
Oft have I seen the haughty Cardinal,   185
More like a soldier than a man o' the Church,
As stout and proud as he were lord of all,
Swear like a ruffian and demean himself
Unlike the ruler of a commonweal.
Warwick, my Son, the comfort of my age,   190
Thy deeds, thy plainness,° and thy housekeeping°
Hath won the greatest favor of the commons,
Excepting none but good Duke Humphrey.
And, Brother York, thy acts in Ireland,
In bringing them to civil discipline,   195
Thy late exploits done in the heart of France
When thou wert regent for our sovereign,
Have made thee feared and honored of the people.
Join we together, for the public good,
In what we can to bridle and suppress   200
The pride of Suffolk and the Cardinal,
With Somerset's and Buckingham's ambition;
And, as we may, cherish Duke Humphrey's deeds
While they do tend the profit of the land.
    WAR. So God help Warwick, as he loves the land
And common profit of his country!   206
    YORK. [Aside] And so says York, for he hath
    greatest cause.
    SAL. Then let's make haste away, and look unto
    the main.°
    WAR. Unto the main! O Father, Maine is lost —
That Maine which by main force Warwick did
    win   210
And would have kept so long as breath did last!
Main chance, Father, you meant, but I meant
    Maine,
Which I will win from France, or else be slain.
        [Exeunt WARWICK and SALISBURY.]
    YORK. Anjou and Maine are given to the French.
Paris is lost. The state of Normandy   215
Stands on a tickle° point,° now they are gone.
Suffolk concluded on° the articles,
The peers agreed, and Henry was well pleased
To change two dukedoms for a duke's fair daugh-
    ter.

131. match: marry.   133. fifteenth: a tax of one-fifteenth levied
on the income from real estate.   145. Lordings: my lords.
158. What though: even if.   163. gloss: glittering outside.
169. hoise: hoist.   170. brook: endure.   171. presently: immediately.

191. plainness: honest dealing. housekeeping: hospitality.
208. main: a term in hazard, a dice game, with the inevitable
pun on "Maine." In hazard the caster called a main (i.e., 5, 6, 7,
8, or 9). If his opponent threw the main, he won the stake.
216. Stands . . . point: i.e., is in a delicate state. tickle: delicately balanced, easily upset.   217. concluded on: agreed to.

I cannot blame them all. What is 't to them?　220
'Tis thine they give away, and not their own.
Pirates may make cheap pennyworths° of their pil-
　lage,
And purchase friends and give to courtesans,
Still reveling like lords till all be gone,
While as the silly° owner of the goods　225
Weeps over them and wrings his hapless hands
And shakes his head and trembling stands aloof
While all is shared and all is borne away,
Ready to starve and dare not touch his own:
So York must sit and fret and bite his tongue　230
While his own lands are bargained for and sold.
Methinks the realms of England, France, and Ire-
　land
Bear that proportion to my flesh and blood
As did the fatal brand Althaea burned
Unto the Prince's heart° of Calydon.°　235
Anjou and Maine both given unto the French!
Cold news for me, for I had hope of France,
Even as I have of fertile England's soil.
A day will come when York shall claim his own,
And therefore I will take the Nevils'° parts　240
And make a show of love to proud Duke Hum-
　phrey;
And, when I spy advantage,° claim the crown,
For that's the golden mark I seek to hit.
Nor shall proud Lancaster° usurp my right,
Nor hold the scepter in his childish fist,　245
Nor wear the diadem upon his head,
Whose churchlike humors° fits not for a crown.
Then, York, be still awhile, till time do serve.
Watch thou and wake when others be asleep,
To pry into the secrets of the state,　250
Till Henry, surfeiting° in joys of love
With his new bride and England's dear-bought
　Queen,
And Humphrey with the peers be fall'n at jars.°
Then will I raise aloft the milk-white Rose,°　254
With whose sweet smell the air shall be perfumed,
And in my standard bear the arms of York
To grapple with the House of Lancaster;
And, force perforce, I'll make him yield the crown,
Whose bookish rule° hath pulled fair England
　down.　　　　　　　　　　　　　　　[*Exit.*]

222. **pennyworths:** "penn'oths" (bargains). 225. **silly:** helpless.
234–35. **Althaea . . . Calydon:** Althaea, at the birth of her son
Meleager, was told by the Fates that he would die when a firebrand then burning in the fire was consumed. She took the brand
from the fire and guarded it. Years later, Meleager having become Prince of Calydon, angered his mother by slaying her
brethren, whereupon in rage she cast the brand on the fire and
Meleager died. 235. **Unto . . . heart:** i.e., fatally. 240. **Nevils:**
See App. 28, *Henry VI*. 242. **spy advantage:** see my chance.
244. **Lancaster:** i.e., Henry VI, descended from John of Gaunt,
Duke of Lancaster. See App. 28, Table A. 247. **churchlike humors:** pious behavior. 251. **surfeiting:** enjoying to excess.
253. **be . . . jars:** has fallen out. 254. **milk-white Rose:** i.e., the
White Rose of York. See *I Hen VI*, II.iv.36. 259. **bookish
rule:** i.e., the King is a mere scholar, not a man of action.

SCENE II. *The* DUKE OF GLOUCESTER'S *house.*

[*Enter* DUKE HUMPHREY *and his wife* ELEANOR.]
DUCH. Why droops my lord, like overripened
　corn°
Hanging the head at Ceres'° plenteous load?
Why doth the great Duke Humphrey knit his
　brows,
As frowning at the favors of the world?
Why are thine eyes fixed to the sullen earth,　5
Gazing on that which seems to dim thy sight?
What seest thou there? King Henry's diadem,
Enchased° with all the honors of the world?
If so, gaze on, and grovel on thy face,
Until thy head be circled with the same.　10
Put forth thy hand, reach at the glorious gold.
What, is 't too short? I'll lengthen it with mine;
And, having both together heaved it up,
We'll both together lift our heads to Heaven
And never more abase our sight so low　15
As to vouchsafe one glance unto the ground.
GLO. O Nell, sweet Nell, if thou dost love thy
　lord,
Banish the canker° of ambitious thoughts.
And may that thought, when I imagine ill
Against my King and nephew, virtuous Henry,　20
Be my last breathing° in this mortal world!
My troublous dream this night doth make me sad.
DUCH. What dreamed my lord? Tell me, and I'll
　requite° it
With sweet rehearsal of my morning's dream.°
GLO. Methought this staff,° mine office badge in
　Court,　25
Was broke in twain — by whom I have forgot,
But, as I think, it was by the Cardinal —
And on the pieces of the broken wand
Were placed the heads of Edmund Duke of Som-
　erset,
And William de la Pole, first Duke of Suffolk.　30
This was my dream. What it doth bode,° God
　knows.
DUCH. Tut, this was nothing but an argument
That he that breaks a stick of Gloucester's grove
Shall lose his head for his presumption.
But list to me, my Humphrey, my sweet Duke.　35
Methought I sat in seat of majesty
In the cathedral church of Westminster
And in that chair where kings and queens are
　crowned,
Where Henry and Dame Margaret kneeled to me
And on my head did set the diadem.　40

Sc. ii: 1. **corn:** wheat. 2. **Ceres:** goddess of corn. 8. **En-
chased:** enriched with gems. 18. **canker:** grub causing rottenness. 21. **breathing:** breath. 23. **requite:** pay back, counterbalance. 24. **morning's dream:** It was believed that morning
dreams came true. 25. **staff:** the white staff of office borne by
the chief officers of state. See *Rich II*, II.ii.59,n. and Pl. 8d
31. **bode:** foretell.

GLO. Nay, Eleanor, then must I chide outright.
Presumptuous dame, ill-nurtured° Eleanor,
Art thou not second woman in the realm
And the Protector's wife, beloved of him?
Hast thou not worldly pleasure at command   45
Above the reach or compass of thy thought?
And wilt thou still be hammering° treachery
To tumble down thy husband and thyself
From top of honor to disgrace's feet?
Away from me, and let me hear no more!   50
   DUCH. What, what, my lord! Are you so choleric°
With Eleanor, for telling but her dream?
Next time I'll keep my dreams unto myself
And not be checked.°
   GLO. Nay, be not angry. I am pleased again.   55
           [*Enter* MESSENGER.]
   MESS. My Lord Protector, 'tis His Highness'
   pleasure
You do prepare to ride unto Saint Alban's,
Whereas° the King and Queen do mean to hawk.
   GLO. I go. Come, Nell, thou wilt ride with us?
   DUCH. Yes, my good lord, I'll follow presently.
       [*Exeunt* GLOUCESTER *and* MESSENGER.]
Follow I must; I cannot go before   61
While Gloucester bears this base and humble mind.
Were I a man, a duke, and next of blood,
I would remove these tedious stumbling blocks
And smooth my way upon their headless necks;   65
And, being a woman, I will not be slack
To play my part in Fortune's pageant.
Where are you there? Sir John!° Nay, fear not,
   man,
We are alone. Here's none but thee and I.
           [*Enter* HUME.]
   HUME. Jesus preserve your royal Majesty!   70
   DUCH. What say'st thou? Majesty! I am but
   Grace.°
   HUME. But by the grace of God, and Hume's ad-
   vice,
Your Grace's title shall be multiplied.
   DUCH. What say'st thou, man? Hast thou as yet
   conferred
With Margery Jourdain, the cunning witch.   75
With Roger Bolingbroke, the conjurer?
And will they undertake to do me good?
   HUME. This they have promised, to show your
   Highness
A spirit raised from depth of underground
That shall make answer to such questions   80
As by your Grace shall be propounded him.
   DUCH. It is enough. I'll think upon the questions.
When from Saint Alban's we do make return,
We'll see these things effected to the full.   84
Here, Hume, take this reward. Make merry, man,

With thy confederates in this weighty cause. [*Exit.*]
   HUME. Hume must make merry with the Duch-
   ess' gold.
Marry,° and shall. But, how now, Sir John Hume!
Seal up your lips and give no words but mum.
The business asketh silent secrecy.   90
Dame Eleanor gives gold to bring the witch.
Gold cannot come amiss, were she a devil.
Yet have I gold flies from another coast.°
I dare not say from the rich Cardinal
And from the great and new-made Duke of Suffolk,
Yet I do find it so; for, to be plain,   96
They, knowing Dame Eleanor's aspiring humor,°
Have hirèd me to undermine the Duchess
And buz these conjurations in her brain.
They say, "A crafty knave does need no broker";°
Yet am I Suffolk and the Cardinal's broker.   101
Hume, if you take not heed, you shall go near
To call them both a pair of crafty knaves.
Well, so it stands, and thus, I fear, at last
Hume's knavery will be the Duchess' wreck,   105
And her attainture° will be Humphrey's fall.
Sort how it will, I shall have gold for all.   [*Exit.*]

SCENE III. *The palace.*

[*Enter three or four* PETITIONERS, PETER, *the
armorer's man, being one.*]

   1. PETI. My masters, let's stand close. My Lord
Protector will come this way by and by, and then
we may deliver our supplications in the quill.°
   2. PETI. Marry, the Lord protect him, for he's a
good man! Jesu bless him!   6
         [*Enter* SUFFOLK *and* QUEEN.]
   PET. Here a'° comes, methinks, and the Queen
with him. I'll be the first, sure.
   2. PETI. Come back, fool. This is the Duke of Suffolk, and not my Lord Protector.   10
   SUF. How now, fellow! Wouldst anything with
me?
   1. PETI. I pray, my lord, pardon me. I took ye for
my Lord Protector.
   QUEEN. [*Reading*] "To my Lord Protector!"
Are your supplications to his lordship? Let me see
them. What is thine?   17
   1. PETI. Mine is, an 't° please your Grace, against
John Goodman, my Lord Cardinal's man, for keeping my house, and lands, and wife, and all, from
me.   21
   SUF. Thy wife too! That's some wrong, indeed.

---

88. Marry: Mary, by the Virgin.   **93. Yet . . . coast:** i.e., I am
being bribed by her enemies.   **97. humor:** mood, nature.
100. A . . . broker: a proverb meaning "A knave can do his own
dirty work." **broker:** agent.   **106. attainture:** condemnation,
disgrace.

Sc. iii: 4. in . . . quill: all together. The origin of the phrase
is unknown.   **7. a':** he.   **28. an't:** if it.

---

42. ill-nurtured: ill-bred, wicked.   **47. hammering:** thinking
out.   **51. choleric:** hot-tempered.   **54. checked:** rebuked.
58. Whereas: where.   **68. Sir John:** a priest. See *AYLI,*
III.iii.43,n.   **71. Grace:** the courtesy title of a duke or duchess.

What's yours? What's here! [*Reads.*] "Against the
Duke of Suffolk, for enclosing the commons° of
Melford." How now, sir knave!   25

2. PETI. Alas, sir, I am but a poor petitioner of our
whole township.

PET. [*Giving his petition*] Against my master,
Thomas Horner, for saying that the Duke of York
was rightful heir to the crown.   30

QUEEN. What say'st thou? Did the Duke of York
say he was rightful heir to the crown?

PET. That my master was? No, forsooth. My master said that he was, and that the King was an
usurper.   35

SUF. Who is there? [*Enter* SERVANT.] Take this
fellow in, and send for his master with a pursui-
vant° presently. We'll hear more of your matter
before the King.   [*Exit* SERVANT *with* PETER.]

QUEEN. And as for you that love to be protected
Under the wings of our Protector's grace,   41
Begin your suits anew, and sue to him.
                    [*Tears the supplications.*]
Away, base cullions!° Suffolk, let them go.

ALL. Come, let's be gone.   [*Exeunt.*]

QUEEN. My Lord of Suffolk, say, is this the
     guise,°   45
Is this the fashion in the Court of England?
Is this the government of Britain's isle,
And this the royalty of Albion's° King?
What, shall King Henry be a pupil° still
Under the surly Gloucester's governance?   50
Am I a Queen in title and in style,
And must be made a subject to a Duke?
I tell thee, Pole, when in the city Tours
Thou ran'st a tilt in honor of my love,
And stolest away the ladies' hearts of France,   55
I thought King Henry had resembled thee
In courage, courtship, and proportion.°
But all his mind is bent to holiness,
To number Ave Maries° on his beads.°
His champions are the prophets and apostles,   60
His weapons holy saws° of sacred writ,
His study is his tiltyard,° and his loves
Are brazen images of canonized saints.
I would the College of the Cardinals
Would choose him Pope and carry him to Rome,
And set the triple° crown upon his head.   66
That were a state fit for his holiness.

SUF. Madam, be patient. As I was cause
Your Highness came to England, so will I

In England work your Grace's full content.   70

QUEEN. Beside the haughty Protector, have we
     Beaufort
The imperious churchman, Somerset, Buckingham,
And grumbling York; and not the least of these
But can do more in England than the King.

SUF. And he of these that can do most of all   75
Cannot do more in England than the Nevils.
Salisbury and Warwick are no simple peers.

QUEEN. Not all these lords do vex me half so
     much
As that proud dame, the Lord Protector's wife.
She sweeps it° through the Court with troops of la-
     dies,   80
More like an empress than Duke Humphrey's wife.
Strangers in Court do take her for the Queen.
She bears a duke's revénues on her back,
And in her heart she scorns our poverty.
Shall I not live to be avenged on her?   85
Contemptuous base-born callet° as she is,
She vaunted 'mongst her minions° t' other day
The very train of her worst wearing gown
Was better worth than all my father's lands   89
Till Suffolk gave two dukedoms for his daughter.

SUF. Madam, myself have limed° a bush for her,
And placed a choir of such enticing° birds
That she will light to listen to the lays°
And never mount to trouble you again.
So, let her rest. And, madam, list to me,   95
For I am bold to counsel you in this.
Although we fancy not the Cardinal,
Yet must we join with him and with the lords
Till we have brought Duke Humphrey in disgrace.
As for the Duke of York, this late complaint   100
Will make but little for his benefit.
So, one by one, we'll weed them all at last,
And you yourself shall steer the happy helm.

[*Sound a Sennet.° Enter the* KING, DUKE HUMPHREY
OF GLOUCESTER, CARDINAL BEAUFORT, BUCKINGHAM,
    YORK, SOMERSET, SALISBURY, WARWICK, *and the*
           DUCHESS OF GLOUCESTER.]

KING. For my part, noble lords, I care not which.
Or Somerset or York, all's one to me.   105

YORK. If York have ill demeaned himself in
     France,
Then let him be denayed° the regentship.

SOM. If Somerset be unworthy of the place,
Let York be Regent. I will yield to him.

WAR. Whether your Grace be worthy, yea or no,
Dispute not that. York is the worthier.   111

CAR. Ambitious Warwick, let thy betters speak.

WAR. The Cardinal's not my better in the field.

BUCK. All in this presence are thy betters, War-
     wick.

24. **commons:** common lands. The *enclosing* of common lands by
the rich was one of the greatest scandals of the sixteenth century.
38. **pursuivant:** officer of the Court.   43. **cullions:** low fellows.
45. **guise:** fashion.   48. **Albion:** England.   49. **pupil:** i.e., not
his own master.   57. **proportion:** bodily grace.   59. **To . . .
beads:** i.e., to say his rosary. **Ave Maries:** the prayer beginning
"Hail Mary."   61. **saws:** sayings.   62. **tiltyard:** tilting ground,
where knights in full armor charged each other in friendly combat
— a form of contest which called for courage.   66. **triple:** i.e.,
papal.

80. **sweeps it:** stalks haughtily.   86. **callet:** low woman.
87. **minions:** hangers-on.   91. **limed:** prepared with birdlime.
92. **enticing:** decoy.   93. **lays:** songs.   103. **s.d., Sennet:**
trumpet call to announce a procession.   107. **denayed:** refused.

WAR. Warwick may live to be the best of all.   115

SAL. Peace, Son! And show some reason, Buckingham,

Why Somerset should be preferred in this.

QUEEN. Because the King, forsooth, will have it so.

GLO. Madam, the King is old enough himself   119
To give his censure.° These are no women's matters.

QUEEN. If he be old enough, what needs your Grace

To be Protector of His Excellence?

GLO. Madam, I am Protector of the realm,
And, at his pleasure, will resign my place.   124

SUF. Resign it then and leave thine insolence.
Since thou wert King — as who is King but thou? —
The commonwealth hath daily run to wreck.
The Dauphin hath prevailed beyond the seas,
And all the peers and nobles of the realm
Have been as bondmen to thy sovereignty.   130

CAR. The commons hast thou racked.° The clergy's bags°
Are lank and lean with thy extortions.

SOM. Thy sumptuous buildings and thy wife's attire
Have cost a mass of public treasury.

BUCK. Thy cruelty in execution°   135
Upon offenders hath exceeded law,
And left thee to the mercy of the law.

QUEEN. Thy sale of offices and towns in France,
If they were known, as the suspect is great,   139
Would make thee quickly hop without thy head.

[*Exit* GLOUCESTER. *The* QUEEN *drops her fan.*]

Give me my fan. What, minion! Can ye not?

[*She gives the* DUCHESS *a box on the ear.*]

I cry you mercy,° madam. Was it you?

DUCH. Was 't I! Yea, I it was, proud Frenchwoman.
Could I come near your beauty with my nails,
I'd set my ten commandments° in your face.   145

KING. Sweet Aunt, be quiet. 'Twas against her will.

DUCH. Against her will! Good King, look to 't in time.
She'll hamper thee and dandle thee like a baby.
Though in this place most master wear no breeches,°
She shall not strike Dame Eleanor unrevenged.   150
[*Exit.*]

BUCK. Lord Cardinal, I will follow Eleanor,
And listen after Humphrey, how he proceeds.

She's tickled° now. Her fume° needs no spurs;
She'll gallop far enough to her destruction. [*Exit.*]
[*Re-enter* GLOUCESTER.]

GLO. Now, lords, my choler° being overblown
With walking once about the quadrangle,   156
I come to talk of commonwealth affairs.
As for your spiteful false objections,
Prove them, and I lie open to the law.
But God in mercy so deal with my soul   160
As I in duty love my King and country!
But, to the matter that we have in hand.
I say, my sovereign, York is meetest man
To be your Regent in the realm of France.

SUF. Before we make election, give me leave
To show some reason of no little force   166
That York is most unmeet of any man.

YORK. I'll tell thee, Suffolk, why I am unmeet:
First, for I cannot flatter thee in pride;
Next, if I be appointed for the place,   170
My Lord of Somerset will keep me here
Without discharge, money, or furniture°
Till France be won into the Dauphin's hands.
Last time I danced attendance on his will
Till Paris was besieged, famished, and lost.   175

WAR. That can I witness, and a fouler fact
Did never traitor in the land commit.

SUF. Peace, headstrong Warwick!

WAR. Image of pride, why should I hold my peace?

[*Enter* HORNER, *the armorer, and his man* PETER, *guarded.*]

SUF. Because here is a man accused of treason.
Pray God the Duke of York excuse himself!   181

YORK. Doth anyone accuse York for a traitor?

KING. What mean'st thou, Suffolk? Tell me, what are these?

SUF. Please it your Majesty, this is the man
That doth accuse his master of high treason.   185
His words were these: that Richard Duke of York
Was rightful heir unto the English crown,
And that your Majesty was an usurper.

KING. Say, man, were these thy words?

HOR. An 't shall please your Majesty, I never   190
said nor thought any such matter. God is my witness, I am falsely accused by the villain.

PET. By these ten bones, my lords, he did speak
them to me in the garret one night as we were
scouring° my Lord of York's armor.   195

YORK. Base dunghill villain and mechanical,°
I'll have thy head for this thy traitor's speech.
I do beseech your royal Majesty,
Let him have all the rigor of the law.   199

HOR. Alas, my lord, hang me if ever I spake the
words. My accuser is my 'prentice, and when I did

120. censure: judgment.   **131. racked:** stretched; i.e., plundered. **bags:** purses.   **135. execution:** a five-syllable word. **142. cry . . . mercy:** a mock apology.   **145. ten commandments:** a slang phrase for fingers.   **149. most . . . breeches:** a proverb of which the modern form is "The wife wears the pants."

153. tickled: excited. **fume:** rage, lit., smoke.   **155. choler:** anger.   **172. furniture:** equipment.   **195. scouring:** cleaning. **196. mechanical:** laborer.

correct him for his fault the other day, he did vow
upon his knees he would be even with me. I have
good witness of this. Therefore I beseech your Majesty, do not cast away an honest man for a villain's
accusation.   206

KING. Uncle, what shall we say to this in law?

GLO. This doom, my lord, if I may judge:
Let Somerset be Regent o'er the French
Because in York this breeds suspicion.   210
And let these have a day appointed them
For single combat in convenient place,
For he hath witness of his servant's malice.
This is the law, and this Duke Humphrey's doom.

SOM. I humbly thank your royal Majesty.   215

HOR. And I accept the combat willingly.

PET. Alas, my lord, I cannot fight. For God's
sake, pity my case. The spite of man prevaileth
against me. O Lord, have mercy upon me! I
shall never be able to fight a blow. O Lord, my
heart!   221

GLO. Sirrah,° or° you must fight, or else be
hanged.

KING. Away with them to prison; and the day of
combat shall be the last of the next month.   225
Come, Somerset, we'll see thee sent away.

                        [Flourish. Exeunt.]

SCENE IV. GLOUCESTER'S *garden.*

[*Enter* MARGARET JOURDAIN, HUME, SOUTHWELL,
          and BOLINGBROKE.]

HUME. Come, my masters. The Duchess, I tell
you, expects performance of your promises.

BOL. Master Hume, we are therefore provided.
Will her ladyship behold and hear our exorcisms?°

HUME. Aye, what else? Fear you not her courage.   6

BOL. I have heard her reported to be a woman of
an invincible spirit; but it shall be convenient, Master Hume, that you be by her aloft while we   10
be busy below. And so, I pray you, go, in God's
name, and leave us. [*Exit* HUME.] Mother Jourdain,
be you prostrate and grovel on the earth. John
Southwell, read you, and let us to our work.   15

[*Enter* DUCHESS *aloft,* HUME *folowing.*]

DUCH. Well said, my masters, and welcome all.
To this gear° the sooner the better.

BOL. Patience, good lady. Wizards know their
times.
Deep night, dark night, the silent of the night,
The time of night when Troy was set on fire,   20
The time when screech owls cry, and ban-dogs°
    howl,

And spirits walk, and ghosts break up their graves,
That time best fits the work we have in hand.
Madam, sit you and fear not. Whom we raise,
We will make fast within a hallowed verge.°   25

[*Here they do the ceremonies belonging, and make
    the circle;* BOLINGBROKE *or* SOUTHWELL *reads,*
    "Conjuro te," &c. *It thunders and light-
    ens terribly. Then the* SPIRIT *riseth.*]

SPIR. *Adsum.*°

JOUR. Asmath,°
By the eternal God, whose name and power
Thou tremblest at, answer that I shall ask;   29
For till thou speak, thou shalt not pass from hence.

SPIR. Ask what thou wilt. That I had said and
    done!

BOL. [*Reading out of a paper.*] "First of the
    King. What shall of him become?"

SPIR. The Duke yet lives that Henry shall depose;
But him outlive, and die a violent death.   34

[*As the* SPIRIT *speaks,* SOUTHWELL
    writes the answer.]

BOL. "What fates await the Duke of Suffolk?"

SPIR. By water shall he die and take his end.

BOL. "What shall befall the Duke of Somerset?"

SPIR. Let him shun castles.
Safer shall he be upon the sandy plains
Than where castles mounted stand.   40
Have done, for more I hardly can endure.

BOL. Descend to darkness and the burning lake!
False fiend, avoid!°

            [*Thunder and lightning. Exit* SPIRIT.]

[*Enter the* DUKE OF YORK *and the* DUKE OF BUCKING-
    HAM *with their* GUARD *and break in.*]

YORK. Lay hands upon these traitors and their
    trash.
Beldam,° I think we watched you at an inch.°   45
What, madam, are you there? The King and com-
    monweal
Are deeply indebted for this piece of pains.
My Lord Protector will, I doubt it not,
See you well guerdoned° for these good deserts.

DUCH. Not half so bad as thine to England's
    King,   50
Injurious Duke, that threatest where's no cause.

BUCK. True, madam, none at all. What call you
    this?
Away with them! Let them be clapped up close°
And kept asunder.° You, madam, shall with us.
Stafford, take her to thee.   55

[*Exeunt above* DUCHESS *and* HUME, *guarded.*]
We'll see your trinkets here all forthcoming.
All, away!

---

222. **Sirrah:** form of address to an inferior. **or:** either.
   Sc. iv: 4. **exorcisms:** conjurations, lit., charms to expel spirits.
17. **gear:** business.   21. **ban-dogs:** watchdogs.

25. **fast . . . verge:** unable to escape from our magic circle.
26. *Adsum:* I am here.   27. **Asmath:** the name of the fiend.
43. **avoid:** begone.   45. **Beldam:** hag. **at an inch:** closely.
49. **guerdoned:** rewarded.   53. **clapped up close:** closely confined.   54. **asunder:** separate.

[*Exeunt* GUARD *with* JOURDAIN, SOUTHWELL, *&c.*]
YORK. Lord Buckingham, methinks, you watched
  her well.
A pretty plot, well chosen to build upon!
Now, pray, my lord, let's see the Devil's writ.   60
What have we here?   [*Reads.*]
" The Duke yet lives that Henry shall depose;
But him outlive, and die a violent death."
Why, this is just
" *Aio te, Aeacida, Romanos vincere posse.*"°   65
Well, to the rest:
" Tell me, what fate awaits the Duke of Suffolk?
By water shall he die, and take his end.
What shall betide the Duke of Somerset?
Let him shun castles.   70
Safer shall he be upon the sandy plains
That where castles mounted stand."
Come, come my lords.
These oracles are hardly attained
And hardly understood.°   75
The King is now in progress towards Saint Alban's,
With him the husband of this lovely lady.
Thither go these news as fast as horse can carry
  them —
A sorry breakfast for my Lord Protector.
  BUCK. Your Grace shall give me leave, my Lord
  of York,   80
To be the post, in hope of his reward.
  YORK. At your pleasure, my good lord. Who's
  within there, ho!
            [*Enter a* SERVINGMAN.]
Invite my Lords of Salisbury and Warwick
To sup with me tomorrow night. Away! [*Exeunt.*]

Act II

SCENE I. *Saint Alban's.*

[*Enter the* KING, QUEEN, GLOUCESTER, CARDINAL,
and SUFFOLK, *with* FALCONERS° *hallooing.*]
  QUEEN. Believe me, lords, for flying at the
  brook°
I saw not better sport these seven years' day.
Yet, by your leave, the wind was very high,

And, ten to one, old Joan had not gone out.°
  KING. But what a point,° my lord, your falcon
  made,   5
And what a pitch° she flew above the rest!
To see how God in all His creatures works!
Yea, man and birds are fain of climbing° high.
  SUF. No marvel, an it like° your Majesty,
My Lord Protector's hawks do tower° so well.   10
They know their master loves to be aloft,
And bears his thoughts above his falcon's pitch.
  GLO. My lord, 'tis but a base ignoble mind
That mounts no higher than a bird can soar.
  CAR. I thought as much. He would be above the
  clouds.   15
  GLO. Aye, my Lord Cardinal? How think you by
  that?
Were it not good your Grace could fly to Heaven?
  KING. The treasury of everlasting joy.
  CAR. Thy heaven is on earth. Thine eyes and
  thoughts
Beat on a crown, the treasure of thy heart.   20
Pernicious Protector, dangerous peer,
That smooth'st° it so with King and commonweal!
  GLO. What, Cardinal, is your priesthood grown
  peremptory?°
Tantaene animis coelestibus irae?°
Churchmen so hot? Good Uncle, hide such malice.
With such holiness can you do it?   26
  SUF. No malice, sir, no more than well becomes
So good a quarrel and so bad a peer.
  GLO. As who, my lord?
  SUF.   Why, as you, my lord,
An 't like your lordly Lord-Protectorship.   30
  GLO. Why, Suffolk, England knows thine inso-
  lence.
  QUEEN. And thy ambition, Gloucester.
  KING. I prithee, peace, good Queen,
And whet not° on these furious peers;
For blessed are the peacemakers on earth.   35
  CAR. Let me be blessèd for the peace I make
Against this proud Protector with my sword!
  GLO. [*Aside to* CARDINAL] Faith, holy Uncle,
  would 'twere come to that!
  CAR. [*Aside to* GLOUCESTER] Marry, when thou
  darest.
  GLO. [*Aside to* CARDINAL] Make up no factious
  numbers° for the matter.   40
In thine own person answer thy abuse.
  CAR. [*Aside to* GLOUCESTER] Aye, where thou dar-
  est not peep. An if thou darest,

62–65. The . . . *posse:* The prophecy has a double meaning,
as it is not clear whether the King or the Duke is to be deposed.
The answer, says York, is like the famous warning given by the
oracle to King Pyrrhus when about to war on the Romans: "I tell
you, son of Aeacus, you the Romans can conquer." Pyrrhus in
his pride erroneously assumed that victory was promised to himself.   74–75. hardly . . . understood: are obtained with difficulty
and are hard to understand.
    Act II, Sc. i: s.d., falconers: See App. 26.   1. flying . . .
brook: hawking for water birds such as duck or heron.

4. old . . . out: the old hawk [named Joan] would not have flown
away. Hawks are liable to fly off in a high wind.   5. point: place
of advantage from which to swoop.   6. pitch: height.   8. fain
of climbing: eager to climb.   9. an it like: if it please.
10. tower: fly high.   22. smooth'st: flatterest.   23. peremptory:
overbearing.   24. *Tantaene . . . irae:* is such anger fit for
heavenly minds?   34. whet not: do not encourage, lit., sharpen.
40. factious numbers: rebellious allies.

This evening, on the east side of the grove.
 KING. How now, my lords!
 CAR.   Believe me, Cousin Gloucester,
Had not your man put up the fowl so suddenly, 45
We had had more sport. [*Aside to* GLOUCESTER]
 Come with thy two-hand sword.
 GLO. True, Uncle.
 CAR. [*Aside to* GLOUCESTER] Are ye advised? The
 east side of the grove?
 GLO. [*Aside to* CARDINAL] Cardinal, I am with
 you.
 KING.   Why, how now, Uncle Gloucester!
 GLO. Talking of hawking, nothing else, my lord.
[*Aside to* CARDINAL] Now, by God's Mother,°
 priest, I'll shave your crown for this, 51
Or all my fence° shall fail.
 CAR. [*Aside to* GLOUCESTER] *Medice, teipsum* — °
Protector, see to 't well, protect yourself.
 KING. The winds grow high; so do your stom-
 achs,° lords. 55
How irksome is this music to my heart!
When such strings jar, what hope of harmony?
I pray, my lords, let me compound° this strife.
[*Enter a* TOWNSMAN *of Saint Alban's, crying,* "A
 miracle!"]
 GLO. What means this noise?
Fellow, what miracle dost thou proclaim? 60
 TOWN. A miracle! A miracle!
 SUF. Come to the King and tell him what mir-
 acle.
 TOWN. Forsooth, a blind man at Saint Alban's
 shrine
Within this half hour hath received his sight —
A man that ne'er saw in his life before. 65
 KING. Now, God be praised, that to believing
 souls
Gives light in darkness, comfort in despair!
[*Enter the* MAYOR *of Saint Alban's and his brethren,
bearing* SIMPCOX, *between two in a chair,* SIMPCOX's
WIFE *following.*]
 CAR. Here comes the townsmen on procession
To present your Highness with the man. 69
 KING. Great is his comfort in this earthly vale,
Although by his sight his sin be multiplied.°
 GLO. Stand by, my masters. Bring him near the
 King.
His Highness' pleasure is to talk with him.
 KING. Good fellow, tell us here the circumstance,
That we for thee may glorify the Lord. 75
What, hast thou been long blind and now restored?
 SIM. Born blind, an 't please your Grace.
 WIFE. Aye, indeed, was he.
 SUF. What woman is this?

WIFE. His wife, an 't like your Worship. 80
 GLO. Hadst thou been his mother, thou couldst
 have better told.
 KING. Where wert thou born?
 SIM. At Berwick in the North, an 't like your
 Grace.
 KING. Poor soul, God's goodness hath been great
 to thee.
Let never day nor night unhallowed° pass, 85
But still remember what the Lord hath done.
 QUEEN. Tell me, good fellow, camest thou here
 by chance,
Or of devotion, to this holy shrine?
 SIM. God knows, of pure devotion, being called
A hundred times and oftener, in my sleep, 90
By good Saint Alban, who said, " Simpcox, come,
Come, offer at my shrine, and I will help thee."
 WIFE. Most true, forsooth, and many time and oft
Myself have heard a voice to call him so.
 CAR. What, art thou lame?
 SIM.   Aye, God Almighty help me! 95
 SUF. How camest thou so?
 SIM.   A fall off of a tree.
 WIFE. A plum tree, master.
 GLO.   How long hast thou been blind?
 SIM. Oh, born so, master.
 GLO.   What, and wouldst climb a tree?
 SIM. But that in all° my life, when I was a youth.
 WIFE. Too true, and bought his climbing very
 dear. 100
 GLO. Mass,° thou lovedst plums well, that
 wouldst venture so.
 SIM. Alas, good master, my wife desired some
 damsons,
And made me climb, with danger of my life.
 GLO. A subtle knave! But yet it shall not serve.
Let me see thine eyes. Wink° now. Now open them.
In my opinion yet thou see'st not well. 106
 SIM. Yes, master, clear as day, I thank God and
 Saint Alban.
 GLO. Say'st thou me so? What color is this cloak
 of?
 SIM. Red, master, red as blood. 110
 GLO. Why, that's well said. What color is my
 gown of?
 SIM. Black, forsooth. Coal-black as jet.
 KING. Why, then, thou know'st what color jet is
 of?
 SUF. And yet, I think, jet did he never see.
 GLO. But cloaks and gowns, before this day, a
 many. 115
 WIFE. Never, before this day, in all his life.
 GLO. Tell me, sirrah, what's my name?
 SIM. Alas, master, I know not.
 GLO. What's his name?

---

51. **God's Mother:** the Virgin Mary. 52. **fence:** skill in fencing.
53. *Medice, teipsum:* physician [heal] thyself. 55. **stomachs:**
tempers. 58. **compound:** settle. 70–71. **Great . . . multiplied:**
he is greatly blessed on earth, but now that he can see he will
become a greater sinner; i.e., his temptations will increase.

85. **unhallowed:** unblessed. 99. **But . . . all:** only once.
101. **Mass:** by the Mass. 105. **Wink:** shut your eyes.

SIM. I know not.   120

GLO. Nor his?

SIM. No, indeed, master.

GLO. What's thine own name?

SIM. Saunder Simpcox, an if it please you, master.

GLO. Then, Saunder, sit there, the lyingest 125 knave in Christendom. If thou hadst been born blind, thou mightst as well have known all our names as thus to name the several colors we do wear. Sight may distinguish of colors, but suddenly to nominate° them all, it is impossible. My 130 lords, Saint Alban here hath done a miracle; and would ye not think his cunning to be great, that could restore this cripple to his legs again?

SIM. Oh, master, that you could!

GLO. My masters of Saint Alban's, have you not beadles° in your town, and things called whips?

MAY. Yes, my lord, if it please your Grace.

GLO. Then send for one presently.°   139

MAY. Sirrah, go fetch the beadle hither straight.
                 [*Exit an* ATTENDANT.]

GLO. Now fetch me a stool hither by and by. [*A stool brought.*] Now, sirrah, if you mean to save yourself from whipping, leap me over this stool and run away.

SIM. Alas, master, I am not able to stand alone. You go about to torture me in vain.   146

       [*Enter a* BEADLE *with whips.*]

GLO. Well, sir, we must have you find your legs. Sirrah Beadle, whip him till he leap over that same stool.

BEAD. I will, my lord. Come on, sirrah. Off with your doublet° quickly.   151

SIM. Alas, master, what shall I do? I am not able to stand. [*After the* BEADLE *hath hit him once, he leaps over the stool and runs away; and they follow and cry,* " A miracle! "]

KING. O God, seest Thou this, and bearest so long?

QUEEN. It made me laugh to see the villain run.

GLO. Follow the knave, and take this drab° away.

WIFE. Alas, sir, we did it for pure need.   157

GLO. Let them be whipped through every market town till they come to Berwick, from whence they came.   [*Exeunt* WIFE, BEADLE, MAYOR, *&c.*] 160

CAR. Duke Humphrey has done a miracle today.

SUF. True; made the lame to leap and fly away.

GLO. But you have done more miracles than I. You made in a day, my lord, whole towns to fly.

         [*Enter* BUCKINGHAM.]

KING. What tidings with our Cousin Buckingham?   165

BUCK. Such as my heart doth tremble to unfold. A sort of naughty° persons, lewdly bent,°

Under the countenance and confederacy° Of Lady Eleanor, the Protector's wife, The ringleader and head of all this rout,° 170 Have practiced° dangerously against your state, Dealing with witches and with conjurers; Whom we have apprehended in the fact,° Raising up wicked spirits from under ground, Demanding of King Henry's life and death, 175 And other of your Highness' Privy Council, As more at large your Grace shall understand.

CAR. [*Aside to* GLOUCESTER] And so, my Lord Protector, by this means Your lady is forthcoming yet at London. 179 This news, I think, hath turned your weapon's edge. 'Tis like, my lord, you will not keep your hour.°

GLO. Ambitious churchman, leave° to afflict my heart. Sorrow and grief have vanquished all my powers, And, vanquished as I am, I yield to thee, Or to the meanest groom.   185

KING. Oh, God, what mischiefs work the wicked ones, Heaping confusion on their own heads thereby!

QUEEN. Gloucester, see here the tainture° of thy nest, And look thyself be faultless, thou wert best. 189

GLO. Madam, for myself, to Heaven I do appeal How I have loved my King and commonweal. And, for my wife, I know not how it stands. Sorry I am to hear what I have heard. Noble she is, but if she have forgot Honor and virtue and conversed° with such 195 As, like to pitch, defile nobility, I banish her my bed and company, And give her as a prey to law and shame That hath dishonored Gloucester's honest name.

KING. Well, for this night we will repose us here. Tomorrow toward London back again   201 To look into this business thoroughly, And call these foul offenders to their answers, And poise° the cause in justice' equal scales, Whose beam stands sure, whose rightful cause prevails.   [*Flourish. Exeunt.*] 205

SCENE II. *London. The* DUKE OF YORK'S *garden.*

[*Enter* YORK, SALISBURY, *and* WARWICK.]

YORK. Now, my good Lords of Salisbury and Warwick, Our simple supper ended, give me leave

---

130. nominate: give names to.   136. beadles: parish officers, responsible for keeping order and inflicting minor punishments. 139. presently: immediately. 151. doublet: coat. 156. drab: slut. 167. naughty: wicked. bent: inclined.

168. confederacy: conspiracy. 170. rout: rabble. 171. practiced: plotted. 173. apprehended . . . fact: arrested in the act. 181. keep . . . hour: maintain your normal way of life. 182. leave: cease. 188. tainture: fouling. 195. conversed: had dealings. 204. poise: weigh.

In this close walk° to satisfy myself
In craving your opinion of my title,
Which is infallible,° to England's crown.   5
   SAL. My lord, I long to hear it at full.
   WAR. Sweet York, begin; and if thy claim be
     good,
The Nevils are thy subjects to command.
   YORK. Then thus:°
Edward the Third, my lords, had seven sons: 10
The first, Edward the Black Prince, Prince of
     Wales;
The second, William of Hatfield, and the third,
Lionel Duke of Clarence; next to whom
Was John of Gaunt, the Duke of Lancaster;
The fifth was Edmund Langley, Duke of York;   15
The sixth was Thomas of Woodstock, Duke of
     Gloucester;
William of Windsor was the seventh and last.
Edward the Black Prince died before his father,
And left behind him Richard, his only son,
Who, after Edward the Third's death, reigned as
     king   20
Till Henry Bolingbroke, Duke of Lancaster,
The eldest son and heir of John of Gaunt,
Crowned by the name of Henry the Fourth,
Seized on the realm, deposed the rightful King,
Sent his poor Queen to France, from whence she
     came,   25
And him to Pomfret, where, as all you know,
Harmless Richard was murdered traitorously.
   WAR. Father, the Duke hath told the truth.
Thus got the House of Lancaster the crown.
   YORK. Which now they hold by force and not by
     right;   30
For Richard, the first son's heir, being dead,
The issue of the next son should have reigned.
   SAL. But William of Hatfield died without an
     heir.
   YORK. The third son, Duke of Clarence, from
     whose line   34
I claim the crown, had issue, Philippe, a daughter,
Who married Edmund Mortimer, Earl of March.
Edmund had issue, Roger Earl of March;
Roger had issue, Edmund, Anne and Eleanor.
   SAL. This Edmund, in the reign of Bolingbroke,
As I have read, laid claim unto the crown,   40
And, but for Owen Glendower, had been king,
Who kept him in captivity till he died.
But to the rest.
   YORK.   His eldest sister, Anne,
My mother, being heir unto the crown,   44
Married Richard Earl of Cambridge, who was son
To Edmund Langley, Edward the Third's fifth son.
By her I claim the kingdom. She was heir

To Roger Earl of March, who was the son
Of Edmund Mortimer, who married Philippe,
Sole daughter unto Lionel Duke of Clarence.   50
So, if the issue of the elder son
Succeed before the younger, I am King.
   WAR. What plain proceeding is more plain than
     this?
Henry doth claim the crown from John of Gaunt,
The fourth son; York claims it from the third.   55
Till Lionel's issue fails, his° should not reign.
It fails not yet, but flourishes in thee
And in thy sons, fair slips° of such a stock.
Then, Father Salisbury, kneel we together,
And in this private plot° be we the first   60
That shall salute our rightful sovereign
With honor of his birthright to the crown.
   BOTH. Long live our sovereign Richard, Eng-
     land's King!
   YORK. We thank you, lords. But I am not your
     King
Till I be crowned and that my sword be stained   65
With heart-blood of the House of Lancaster;
And that's not suddenly to be performed,
But with advice° and silent secrecy.
Do you as I do in these dangerous days.
Wink at the Duke of Suffolk's insolence,   70
At Beaufort's pride, at Somerset's ambition,
At Buckingham and all the crew of them,
Till they have snared the shepherd of the flock,
That virtuous prince, the good Duke Humphrey.
'Tis that they seek, and they in seeking that   75
Shall find their deaths, if York can prophesy.
   SAL. My lord, break we off. We know your mind
     at full.
   WAR. My heart assures me that the Earl of War-
     wick
Shall one day make the Duke of York a King.
   YORK. And, Nevil, this I do assure myself: 80
Richard shall live to make the Earl of Warwick
The greatest man in England but the King.
                            [Exeunt.]

SCENE III. *A hall of justice.*

[*Sound trumpets. Enter the* KING, *the* QUEEN,
GLOUCESTER, YORK, SUFFOLK, *and* SALISBURY;
the DUCHESS OF GLOUCESTER, MARGARET JOUR-
DAIN, SOUTHWELL, HUME, *and* BOLINGBROKE,
under guard.]
   KING. Stand forth, Dame Eleanor Cobham,
     Gloucester's wife.
In sight of God and us, your guilt is great.
Receive the sentence of the law for sins

Sc. ii: **3. close walk:** enclosed garden path. See Pl. 16a.
5. infallible: indisputable. **9. Then thus:** See App. 28 and
Genealogical Tables. The history summarized in ll. 20–27 is the
theme of *Rich II.*

56. his: i.e., King Henry's. **58. slips:** cuttings from a tree used
for grafting or propagating new stock. **60. plot:** ground, place.
68. advice: careful thought.

Such as by God's book are adjudged to death.°
You four, from hence to prison back again;   5
From thence unto the place of execution.
The witch in Smithfield shall be burned to ashes,
And you three shall be strangled° on the gallows.
You, madam, for you are more nobly born,
Despoilèd of your honor in your life,   10
Shall, after three days' open penance done,
Live in your country here in banishment,
With Sir John Stanley, in the Isle of Man.

   DUCH. Welcome is banishment. Welcome were
    my death.

   GLO. Eleanor, the law, thou see'st, hath judged
    thee.   15
I cannot justify whom the law condemns.
    [*Exeunt* DUCHESS *and other prisoners, guarded.*]
Mine eyes are full of tears, my heart of grief.
Ah, Humphrey, this dishonor in thine age
Will bring thy head with sorrow to the ground!
I beseech your Majesty, give me leave to go.   20
Sorrow would° solace and mine age would ease.

   KING. Stay, Humphrey Duke of Gloucester. Ere
    thou go,
Give up thy staff.° Henry will to himself
Protector be; and God shall be my hope,
My stay, my guide and lantern to my feet.   25
And go in peace, Humphrey, no less beloved
Than when thou wert Protector to thy King.

   QUEEN. I see no reason why a King of years°
Should be to be protected like a child.
God and King Henry govern England's realm.   30
Give up your staff, sir, and the King his realm.

   GLO. My staff? Here, noble Henry, is my staff.
As willingly do I the same resign
As e'er thy father Henry made it mine;
And even as willingly at thy feet I leave it   35
As others would ambitiously receive it.
Farewell, good King. When I am dead and gone,
May honorable peace attend thy throne!   [*Exit.*]

   QUEEN. Why, now is Henry King, and Margaret
    Queen,   39
And Humphrey Duke of Gloucester scarce himself,
That bears so shrewd a maim:° two pulls at once —
His lady banished, and a limb lopped off.
This staff of honor raught,° there let it stand
Where it best fits to be, in Henry's hand.

   SUF. Thus droops this lofty pine and hangs his
    sprays;   45
Thus Eleanor's pride dies in her youngest days.

   YORK. Lords, let him go. Please it your Majesty,
This is the day appointed for the combat,
And ready are the appellant° and defendant,
The armorer and his man, to enter the lists,   50
So please your Highness to behold the fight.

   QUEEN. Aye, good my lord; for purposely there-
    fore
Left I the Court, to see this quarrel tried.

   KING. O' God's name, see the lists° and all things
    fit.
Here let them end it, and God defend the right!   55

   YORK. I never saw a fellow worse bested,°
Or more afraid to fight, than is the appellant,
The servant of this armorer, my lords.
[*Enter at one door,* HORNER, *the armorer, and his*
NEIGHBORS, *drinking to him so much that he is
drunk; and he enters with a drum before him and
his staff with a sandbag*° *fastened to it; and at the
other door* PETER, *his man, with a drum and sandbag, and* 'PRENTICES *drinking to him.*]

   1. NEIGH. Here, Neighbor Horner, I drink to you
in a cup of sack;° and fear not, Neighbor, you shall
do well enough.   61

   2. NEIGH. And here, Neighbor, here's a cup of
charneco.°

   3. NEIGH. And here's a pot of good double° beer,
Neighbor. Drink, and fear not your man.

   HOR. Let it come, i' faith, and I'll pledge you all;
and a fig for° Peter!   66

   1. 'PREN. Here, Peter, I drink to thee; and be not
afraid.

   2. 'PREN. Be merry, Peter, and fear not thy master.
Fight for credit of the 'prentices.   71

   PET. I thank you all. Drink and pray for me, I
pray you; for I think I have taken my last draught
in this world. Here, Robin, an if I die, I give thee
my apron; and, Will, thou shalt have my hammer;
and here, Tom, take all the money that I have. O
Lord, bless me! I pray God! For I am never able to
deal with my master, he hath learnt so much fence
already.   79

   SAL. Come, leave your drinking and fall to blows.
Sirrah, what's thy name?

   PET. Peter, forsooth.

   SAL. Peter! What more?

   PET. Thump.

   SAL. Thump! Then see thou thump thy master
    well.   86

   HOR. Masters, I am come hither, as it were upon
my man's instigation, to prove him a knave and myself an honest man; and touching the Duke of York,
I will take my death, I never meant him any ill, nor
the King, nor the Queen. And therefore, Peter, have
at thee with a downright blow!   93

Sc. iii: 4. God's . . . death: "Thou shalt not suffer a witch to live" (Exodus 22:18).   **8. strangled:** choked, hanged. **21. would:** wishes, i.e., needs.   **23. staff:** See I.ii.25,n.   **28. of years:** i.e., no longer a minor.   **41. shrewd a maim:** bitter mutilation.   **43. raught:** snatched.   **49. appellant:** challenger.

54. lists: barriers fencing off the place of combat.   **56. bested:** be-sted, in worse condition.   **58. s.d., sandbag:** This s.d. is from F1. A bag filled with sand is an effective weapon.   **60. sack:** wine from Spain. See *II Hen IV.*IV.iii.102–35.   **62: charneco:** a wine, probably from Portugal.   **63. double:** strong.   **66. fig for:** "to hell with." See *Hen V,* III.vi.59,n.

YORK. Dispatch. This knave's tongue begins to
    double.°
Sound, trumpets, alarum to the combatants!
[*Alarum. They fight, and* PETER *strikes him down.*]
    HOR. Hold, Peter, hold! I confess, I confess trea-
son.   [*Dies.*]
    YORK. Take away his weapon. Fellow, thank God,
and the good wine in thy master's way.   100
    PET. O God, have I overcome mine enemy in this
presence? O Peter, thou hast prevailed in right!
    KING. Go, take hence that traitor from our sight;
For by his death we do perceive his guilt.
And God in justice hath revealed to us   105
The truth and innocence of this poor fellow,
Which he had thought to have murdered wrong-
    fully.
Come, fellow, follow us for thy reward.
                [*Sound a flourish. Exeunt.*]

SCENE IV. *A street.*

[*Enter* GLOUCESTER *and his* SERVINGMEN, *in mourn-*
ing cloaks.°]

    GLO. Thus sometimes hath the brightest day a
    cloud;
And after summer, evermore succeeds
Barren winter with his wrathful nipping cold.
So cares and joys abound, as seasons fleet.°
Sirs, what's o'clock?
    SERV.   Ten, my lord.   5
    GLO. Ten is the hour that was appointed me
To watch the coming of my punished Duchess.
Uneath° may she endure the flinty streets,
To tread them with her tender-feeling feet.
Sweet Nell, ill can thy noble mind abrook°   10
The abject° people gazing on thy face,
With envious° looks laughing at thy shame,
That erst did follow thy proud chariot wheels
When thou didst ride in triumph through the
    streets.
But, soft! I think she comes; and I'll prepare   15
My tear-stained eyes to see her miseries.
[*Enter the* DUCHESS OF GLOUCESTER *in a white sheet,*
and a taper° *burning in her hand, with* SIR JOHN
STANLEY, *the* SHERIFF, *and* OFFICERS.]

    SERV. So please your Grace, we'll take her from
    the sheriff.
    GLO. No, stir not, for your lives. Let her pass by.
    DUCH. Come you, my lord, to see my open shame?
Now thou dost penance too. Look how they gaze!
See how the giddy multitude do point,   21
And nod their heads, and throw their eyes on thee!

Ah, Gloucester, hide thee from their hateful looks,
And, in thy closet° pent up, rue my shame,
And ban° thine enemies, both mine and thine!   25
    GLO. Be patient, gentle Nell. Forget this grief.
    DUCH. Ah, Gloucester, teach me to forget myself!
For whilst I think I am thy married wife,
And thou a prince, Protector of this land,
Methinks I should not thus be led along,   30
Mailed up° in shame, with papers on my back,°
And followed with a rabble that rejoice
To see my tears and hear my deep-fet° groans.
The ruthless flint doth cut my tender feet,
And when I start,° the envious people laugh   35
And bid me be advisèd how I tread.
Ah, Humphrey, can I bear this shameful yoke?
Trow'st° thou that e'er I'll look upon the world,
Or count them happy that enjoy the sun?
No. Dark shall be my light and night my day.   40
To think upon my pomp shall be my hell.
Sometime I'll say, I am Duke Humphrey's wife,
And he a prince and ruler of the land.
Yet so he ruled, and such a prince he was,
As he stood by whilst I, his forlorn Duchess,   45
Was made a wonder and a pointing stock°
To every idle rascal follower.
But be thou mild and blush not at my shame,
Not stir at nothing till the ax of death
Hang over thee, as, sure, it shortly will;   50
For Suffolk — he that can do all in all
With her that hateth thee and hates us all —
And York and impious Beaufort, that false priest,
Have all limed° bushes to betray thy wings,
And, fly thou how thou canst, they'll tangle thee.
But fear not thou until thy foot be snared,   56
Nor never seek prevention of thy foes.
    GLO. Ah, Nell, forbear! Thou aimest all awry;
I must offend before I be attainted,
And had I twenty times so many foes,   60
And each of them had twenty times their power,
All these could not procure me any scathe°
So long as I am loyal, true, and crimeless.
Wouldst have me rescue thee from this reproach?
Why, yet thy scandal were not wiped away,   65
But I in danger for the breach of law.
Thy greatest help is quiet, gentle Nell.
I pray thee, sort° thy heart to patience.
These few days' wonder will be quickly worn.°
                [*Enter a* HERALD.]
    HER. I summon your Grace to His Majesty's Par-
    liament,   70
Holden at Bury the first of this next month.
    GLO. And my consent ne'er asked herein before!

94. double: talk thick, i.e., drunkenly.
    Sc. iv: s.d., mourning cloaks: long black hooded cloaks,
covering everything but the face.   4. fleet: pass quickly.
8. Uneath: hardly.   10. abrook: endure.   11. abject: low.
12. envious: hateful.   16. s.d., taper: candle.

24. closet: a small private room.   25. ban: curse.   31. Mailed
up: enveloped. papers . . . back: a placard setting out the
offense.   33. deep-fet: deep-fetched.   35. start: flinch.
38. Trow'st: do you think.   46. pointing stock: thing pointed at.
54. limed: See I.iv.91,n.   62. scathe: harm.   68. sort: fit.
69. worn: forgotten.

This is close° dealing. Well, I will be there.
　　　　　　　　　　　　　　[*Exit* HERALD.]
My Nell, I take my leave. And, Master Sheriff,
Let not her penance exceed the King's commission.°
　　SHER. An 't please **your** Grace, here my commis-
　　sion stays,　　　　　　　　　　　　　76
And Sir John Stanley is appointed now
To take her with him to the Isle of Man.
　　GLO. Must you, Sir John, protect my lady here?
　　STAN. So am I given in charge, may 't please your
　　Grace.　　　　　　　　　　　　　80
　　GLO. Entreat° her not the worse in that I pray°
You use her well. The world may laugh again;
And I may live to do you kindness if
You do it her. And so, Sir John, farewell!
　　DUCH. What, gone, my lord, and bid me not fare-
　　well!　　　　　　　　　　　　　85
　　GLO. Witness my tears, I cannot stay to speak.
　　　　　　　[*Exeunt* GLOUCESTER *and* SERVINGMEN.]
　　DUCH. Art thou gone too? All comfort go with
　　thee!
For none abides with me. My joy is death —
Death, at whose name I oft have been afeared
Because I wished this world's eternity.　　90
Stanley, I prithee go, and take me hence;
I care not whither, for I beg no favor.
Only convey me where thou art commanded.
　　STAN. Why, madam, that is to the Isle of Man,
There to be used according to your state.　　95
　　DUCH. That's bad enough, for I am but reproach.
And shall I then be used reproachfully?
　　STAN. Like to a duchess, and Duke Humphrey's
　　lady.
According to that state you shall be used.　　99
　　DUCH. Sheriff, farewell, and better than I fare,
Although thou hast been conduct° of my shame.
　　SHER. It is my office; and, madam, pardon me.
　　DUCH. Aye, aye, farewell. Thy office is discharged.
Come, Stanley, shall we go?
　　STAN. Madam, your penance done, throw off this
　　sheet,　　　　　　　　　　　　105
And go we to attire you for our journey.
　　DUCH. My shame will not be shifted with **my**
　　sheet.
No, it will hang upon my richest robes
And show itself, attire me how I can.
Go, lead the way. I long to see my prison.　　110
　　　　　　　　　　　　　　[*Exeunt.*]

73. **close:** secret.　75. **commission:** formal command.　81. **En-**
treat: treat. **in . . . pray:** i.e., because I, who am out of favor,
ask it.　101. **conduct:** escort.

Act III

SCENE I. *The Abbey at Bury St. Edmund's.*

[*Sound a Sennet. Enter* KING, QUEEN, CARDINAL
BEAUFORT, SUFFOLK, YORK, BUCKINGHAM, SALISBURY
and WARWICK *to the Parliament.*]
　　KING. I muse° my Lord of Gloucester is not come.
'Tis not his wont to be the hindmost man,
Whate'er occasion keeps him from us now.
　　QUEEN. Can you not see? Or will ye not observe
The strangeness of his altered countenance?　　5
With what a majesty he bears himself,
How insolent of late he is become,
How proud, how peremptory,° and unlike himself?
We know the time since° he was mild and affable,
And if we did but glance a far-off look,　　10
Immediately he was upon his knee,
That all the Court admired° him for submission.°
But meet him now, and, be it in the morn,
When everyone will give the time of day,°
He knits his brow and shows an angry eye,　　15
And passeth by with stiff unbowèd knee,
Disdaining duty° that to us belongs.
Small curs are not regarded when they grin,°
But great men tremble when the lion roars,
And Humphrey is no little man in England.　　20
First note that he is near you in descent,
And should you fall, he is the next will mount.
Me seemeth,° then, it is no policy,
Respecting° what a rancorous mind he bears
And his advantage following your decease,　　25
That he should come about your royal person
Or be admitted to your Highness' Council.
By flattery hath he won the commons' hearts,
And when he please to make commotion,
'Tis to be feared they all will follow him.　　30
Now 'tis the spring, and weeds are shallow-rooted;
Suffer them now, and they'll o'ergrow the garden
And choke the herbs for want of husbandry.°
The reverent care I bear unto my lord
Made me collect° these dangers in the Duke.　　35
If it be fond,° call it a woman's fear,
Which fear, if better reasons can supplant,
I will subscribe° and say I wronged the Duke.
My Lord of Suffolk, Buckingham, and York,
Reprove° my allegation, if you can,　　40
Or else conclude my words effectual.
　　SUF. Well hath your Highness seen into this
　　Duke;

Act III, Sc. i: 1. **muse:** wonder.　8. **peremptory:** overbearing.
9. **We . . . since:** i.e., once he was.　12. **admired:** wondered at.
submission: loyal behavior.　14. **give . . . day:** say good morning.　17. **duty:** signs of respect.　18. **grin:** show the teeth.
23. **Me seemeth:** it seems to me.　24. **Respecting:** considering.
33. **husbandry:** cultivation.　35. **collect:** gather, perceive.
36. **fond:** foolish.　38. **subscribe:** acknowledge.　40. **Reprove:**
disprove.

And, had I first been put to speak my mind,
I think I should have told your Grace's tale.
The Duchess, by his subornation,°   45
Upon my life began her devilish practices.
Or, if he were not privy to° those faults,
Yet, by reputing of° his high descent,
As next the King he was successive° heir,
And such high vaunts of his nobility,   50
Did instigate the bedlam° brain-sick Duchess
By wicked means to frame° our sovereign's fall.
Smooth runs the water where the brook is deep;
And in his simple show he harbors treason.   54
The fox barks not when he would steal the lamb.
No, no, my sovereign. Gloucester is a man
Unsounded° yet and full of deep deceit.
   CAR. Did he not, contrary to form of law,
Devise strange deaths for small offenses done?
   YORK. And did he not, in his protectorship,   60
Levy great sums of money through the realm
For soldiers' pay in France, and never sent it?
By means whereof the towns each day revolted.
   BUCK. Tut, these are petty faults to faults un-
      known
Which time will bring to light in smooth Duke
      Humphrey.   65
   KING. My lords, at once.° The care you have of us
To mow down thorns that would annoy° our foot
Is worthy praise; but, shall I speak my conscience,
Our kinsman Gloucester is as innocent
From meaning treason to our royal person   70
As is the sucking lamb or harmless dove.
The Duke is virtuous, mild, and too well-given
To dream on evil or to work my downfall.
   QUEEN. Ah, what's more dangerous than this
      fond affiance!°
Seems he a dove? His feathers are but borrowed,
For he's disposèd as° the hateful raven.   76
Is he a lamb? His skin is surely lent him,
For he's inclined as is the ravenous wolf.
Who cannot steal a shape° that means deceit?
Take heed, my lord. The welfare of us all   80
Hangs on the cutting short that fraudful man.
         [Enter SOMERSET.]
   SOM. All health unto my gracious sovereign!
   KING. Welcome, Lord Somerset. What news from
      France?
   SOM. That all your interest in those territories
Is utterly bereft you. All is lost.   85
   KING. Cold news, Lord Somerset; but God's will
      be done!

   YORK. [Aside] Cold news for me, for I had hope
      of France
As firmly as I hope for fertile England.
Thus are my blossoms blasted in the bud,
And caterpillars eat my leaves away;   90
But I will remedy this gear° ere long,
Or sell my title for a glorious grave.
         [Enter GLOUCESTER.]
   GLO. All happiness unto my lord the King!
Pardon, my liege, that I have stayed so long.
   SUF. Nay, Gloucester, know that thou art come
      too soon   95
Unless thou wert more loyal than thou art.
I do arrest thee of high treason here.
   GLO. Well, Suffolk, thou shalt not see me blush
Nor change my countenance for this arrest.
A heart unspotted is not easily daunted.   100
The purest spring is not so free from mud
As I am clear from treason to my sovereign.
Who can accuse me? Wherein am I guilty?
   YORK. 'Tis thought, my lord, that you took bribes
      of France,
And, being Protector, stayed° the soldiers' pay,   105
By means whereof His Highness hath lost France.
   GLO. Is it but thought so? What are they that
      think it?
I never robbed the soldiers of their pay,
Nor ever had one penny bribe from France.   109
So help me God, as I have watched the night° —
Aye, night by night, in studying good for Eng-
      land! —
That doit° that e'er I wrested from the King,
Or any groat° I hoarded to my use,
Be brought against me at my trial day!   114
No! Many a pound of mine own proper° store,
Because I would not tax the needy commons,
Have I dispursèd to the garrisons,
And never asked for restitution.
   CAR. It serves you well, my lord, to say so much.
   GLO. I say no more than truth, so help me God!
   YORK. In your protectorship you did devise   121
Strange tortures for offenders never heard of,
That England was defamed° by tyranny.
   GLO. Why, 'tis well known that whiles° I was
      Protector,
Pity was all the fault that was in me;   125
For I should melt at an offender's tears,
And lowly words were ransom for their fault.
Unless it were a bloody murderer,
Or foul felonious thief that fleeced poor passengers,°
I never gave them condign° punishment.   130
Murder indeed, that bloody sin, I tortured

45. subornation: persuasion to commit a crime.   47. privy to:
secretly acquainted with.   48. reputing of: brooding on.
49. successive: next in succession.   51. bedlam: lunatic.
52. frame: design.   57. Unsounded: whose depth of treachery
has not been measured.   66. at once: i.e., you need say no more.
67. annoy: hurt.   74. affiance: confidence.   76. disposed as:
has the nature of.   79. steal a shape: assume a disguise.

91. gear: business.   105. stayed: kept back.   110. watched . . .
night: lain awake.   112. doit: small worthless coin, "cent."
113. groat: fourpence.   115. proper: private.   123. defamed:
made infamous for.   124. whiles: whilst.   129. passengers:
travelers on foot; i.e., poor men.   130. condign: well-deserved.

Above the felon° or what trespass else.

SUF. My lord, these faults are easy, quickly answered.

But mightier crimes are laid unto your charge,
Whereof you cannot easily purge yourself.   135
I do arrest you in His Highness' name,
And here commit you to my Lord Cardinal
To keep until your further time of trial.

KING. My Lord of Gloucester, 'tis my special hope
That you will clear yourself from all suspect.°   140
My conscience tells me you are innocent.

GLO. Ah, gracious lord, these days are dangerous.
Virtue is choked with foul ambition,
And charity chased hence by rancor's hand.
Foul subornation is predominant,   145
And equity° exiled your Highness' land.
I know their complot° is to have my life,
And if my death might make this island happy
And prove the period° of their tyranny,
I would expend it with all willingness.   150
But mine is made the prologue to their play;
For thousands more, that yet suspect no peril,
Will not conclude their plotted tragedy.
Beaufort's red sparkling eyes blab his heart's malice,
And Suffolk's cloudy brow his stormy hate.   155
Sharp Buckingham unburdens with his tongue
The envious load that lies upon his heart,
And doggèd York, that reaches at the moon,
Whose overweening arm I have plucked back,
By false accuse doth level° at my life.   160
And you, my sovereign lady, with the rest,
Causeless have laid disgraces on my head,
And with your best endeavor have stirred up
My liefest liege° to be mine enemy.
Aye, all of you have laid your heads together —   165
Myself had notice of your conventicles° —
And all to make away° my guiltless life.
I shall not want° false witness to condemn me,
Nor store of treasons to augment my guilt.
The ancient proverb will be well effected: 170
" A staff is quickly found to beat a dog."

CAR. My liege, his railing is intolerable.
If those that care to keep your royal person
From treason's secret knife and traitors' rage
Be thus upbraided, chid and rated at,   175
And the offender granted scope of speech,
'Twill make them cool in zeal unto your Grace.

SUF. Hath he not twit our sovereign lady here
With ignominious words, though clerkly couched,°
As if she had subornèd° some to swear   180
False allegations to o'erthrow his state?

QUEEN. But I can give the loser leave to chide.

GLO. Far truer spoke than meant. I lose, indeed.
Beshrew° the winners, for they played me false!
And well such losers may have leave to speak.   185

BUCK. He'll wrest the sense° and hold us here all day.
Lord Cardinal, he is your prisoner.

CAR. Sirs, take away the Duke, and guard him sure.

GLO. Ah! Thus King Henry throws away his crutch
Before his legs be firm to bear his body.   190
Thus is the shepherd beaten from thy side,
And wolves are gnarling who shall gnaw thee first.
Ah, that my fear were false! Ah, that it were!
For, good King Henry, thy decay I fear.
[Exit, guarded.]

KING. My lords, what to your wisdoms seemeth best,   195
Do or undo as if ourself were here.

QUEEN. What, will your Highness leave the Parliament?

KING. Aye, Margaret. My heart is drowned with grief
Whose flood begins to flow within mine eyes,
My body round engirt with misery,   200
For what's more miserable than discontent?
Ah, Uncle Humphrey! In thy face I see
The map° of honor, truth, and loyalty.
And yet, good Humphrey, is the hour to come
That e'er I proved thee false or feared thy faith.
What louring star now envies thy estate,   206
That these great lords and Margaret our Queen
Do seek subversion of thy harmless life?
Thou never didst them wrong nor no man wrong;
And as the butcher takes away the calf,   210
And binds the wretch, and beats it when it strays,
Bearing it to the bloody slaughterhouse,
Even so remorseless have they borne him hence;
And as the dam° runs lowing up and down,   214
Looking the way her harmless young one went,
And can do naught but wail her darling's loss,
Even so myself bewails good Gloucester's case
With sad unhelpful tears, and with dimmed eyes
Look after him and cannot do him good,
So mighty are his vowèd enemies.   220
His fortunes I will weep, and 'twixt each groan
Say, " Who's a traitor? Gloucester he is none."
[Exeunt all but QUEEN, CARDINAL BEAUFORT,
SUFFOLK, and YORK. SOMERSET remains apart.]

QUEEN. Free lords, cold snow melts with the sun's hot beams.
Henry my lord is cold in great affairs,
Too full of foolish pity, and Gloucester's show   225
Beguiles him, as the mournful crocodile°

131–32. Murder . . . felon: i.e., I punished murder severely, but other crimes lightly.   140. suspect: suspicion.   146. equity: justice.   147. complot: plot.   149. period: end.   160. level: aim.   164. liefest liege: dearest lord.   166. conventicles: meetings.   168. want: lack.   179. clerkly couched: politely phrased. 180 subornèd: procured to commit perjury.

184. Beshrew: ill luck to.   186. wrest . . . sense: distort the meaning.   203. map: i.e., picture, image.   214. dam: mother. 226. crocodile: It was believed that the crocodile first attracted the passer-by with its lamentations and then snapped him up.

With sorrow snares relenting passengers,
Or as the snake rolled in a flowering bank
With shining checkered° slough° doth sting a child
That for the beauty thinks it excellent.   230
Believe me, lords, were none more wise than I —
And yet herein I judge mine own wit good —
This Gloucester should be quickly rid the world
To rid us from the fear we have of him.
   CAR. That he should die is worthy policy;   235
But yet we want a color° for his death.
'Tis meet° he be condemned by course of law.
   SUF. But, in my mind, that were no policy.
The King will labor still° to save his life,
The commons haply rise to save his life;   240
And yet we have but trivial argument,
More than mistrust,° that shows him worthy death.
   YORK. So that, by this, you would not have him
     die.
   SUF. Ah, York, no man alive so fain° as I!
   YORK. 'Tis York that hath more reason for his
     death.   245
But, my Lord Cardinal, and you, my Lord of
     Suffolk,
Say as you think, and speak it from your souls.
Were 't not all one, an empty eagle were set
To guard the chicken from a hungry kite,°   249
As place Duke Humphrey for the King's Protector?
   QUEEN. So the poor chicken should be sure of
     death.
   SUF. Madam, 'tis true; and were 't not madness,
     then,
To make the fox surveyor of the fold?
Who being accused a crafty murderer,
His guilt should be but idly posted° over   255
Because his purpose is not executed.
No, let him die, in that he is a fox,
By nature proved an enemy to the flock,
Before his chaps° be stained with crimson blood,
As Humphrey, proved by reasons, to my liege. 260
And do not stand on quillets° how to slay him.
Be it by gins, by snares, by subtlety,
Sleeping or waking, 'tis no matter how,
So he be dead; for that is good deceit   264
Which mates° him first that first intends deceit.
   QUEEN. Thrice-noble Suffolk, 'tis resolutely spoke.
   SUF. Not resolute, except so much were done,
For things are often spoke and seldom meant.
But that my heart accordeth with my tongue,
Seeing the deed is meritorious,   270
And to preserve my sovereign from his foe,
Say but the word, and I will be his priest.°

CAR. But I would have him dead, my Lord of
     Suffolk,
Ere you can take due orders for a priest.
Say you consent and censure well the deed,   275
And I'll provide his executioner,
I tender so the safety of my liege.
   SUF. Here is my hand, the deed is worthy doing.
   QUEEN. And so say I.
   YORK. And I. And now we three have spoke it,
It skills° not greatly who impugns our doom.° 281
            [Enter a POST.]
   POST. Great lords, from Ireland am I come
     amain°
To signify that rebels there are up,
And put the Englishmen unto the sword.
Send succors, lords, and stop the rage betime,   285
Before the wound do grow uncurable;
For, being green,° there is great hope of help.
   CAR. A breach° that craves a quick expedient
     stop!
What counsel give you in this weighty cause?
   YORK. That Somerset be sent as Regent thither.
'Tis meet that lucky ruler be employed.   291
Witness the fortune he hath had in France.
   SOM. If York, with all his far-fet° policy,
Had been the Regent there instead of me,
He never would have stayed in France so long. 295
   YORK. No, not to lose it all, as thou hast done.
I rather would have lost my life betimes
Than bring a burden of dishonor home
By staying there so long till all were lost.
Show me one scar charactered° on thy skin.   300
Men's flesh preserved so whole do seldom win.
   QUEEN. Nay, then, this spark will prove a raging
     fire
If wind and fuel be brought to feed it with.
No more, good York. Sweet Somerset, be still. 304
Thy fortune, York, hadst thou been regent there,
Might happily have proved far worse than his.
   YORK. What, worse than naught? Nay, then, a
     shame take all!
   SOM. And, in the number, thee that wishest
     shame!
   CAR. My Lord of York, try what your fortune is.
The uncivil kernes° of Ireland are in arms   310
And temper° clay with blood of Englishmen.
To Ireland will you lead a band of men
Collected choicely, from each county some,
And try your hap against the Irishmen?
   YORK. I will, my lord, so please His Majesty.   315
   SUF. Why, our authority is his consent,
And what we do establish he confirms.
Then, noble York, take thou this task in hand.

---

229. checkered: patterned in square. slough: skin (pronounced
"sluff"). 236. color: excuse. 237. meet: fit. 239. still:
continually. 242. mistrust: suspicion. 244. fain: eager.
249. kite: the lowest of the birds of prey. 255. idly posted:
negligently passed over. 259. chaps: jaws. 261. quillets:
legal subtleties. 265. mates: confounds. 272. I . . . priest:
i.e., I will prepare him for death.

281. skills: matters. impugns . . . doom: calls our judgment in
question. 282. amain: speedily. 287. green: still fresh.
288. breach: gap. 293. far-fet: elaborate. 300. charactered:
inscribed, written. 310. kernes: Irish foot soldiers, greatly
dreaded by Shakespeare's contemporaries. 311. temper: mix.

YORK. I am content. Provide me soldiers, lords,
Whiles I take order for mine own affairs.   320
  SUF. A charge, Lord York, that I will see per-
    formed.
But now return we to the false Duke Humphrey.
  CAR. No more of him, for I will deal with him,
That henceforth he shall trouble us no more.
And so break off. The day is almost spent.   325
Lord Suffolk, you and I must talk of that event.
  YORK. My Lord of Suffolk, within fourteen days
At Bristol I expect my soldiers;
For there I'll ship them all for Ireland.
  SUF. I'll see it truly done, my Lord of York.   330
                [*Exeunt all but* YORK.]
  YORK. Now, York, or never, steel thy fearful°
    thoughts
And change misdoubt to resolution.
Be that thou hopest to be, or what thou art
Resign to death; it is not worth the enjoying.
Let pale-faced fear keep° with the mean-born
    man   335
And find no harbor in a royal heart.
Faster than spring-time showers comes thought on
    thought,
And not a thought but thinks on dignity.
My brain more busy than the laboring spider
Weaves tedious snares to trap mine enemies.   340
Well, nobles, well, 'tis politicly done,
To send me packing with an host of men.
I fear me you but warm the starvèd snake,
Who, cherished in your breasts, will sting your
    hearts.
'Twas men I lacked, and you will give them me.
I take it kindly. Yet be well assured   346
You put sharp weapons in a madman's hands.
Whiles I in Ireland nourish° a mighty band,
I will stir up in England some black storm   349
Shall blow ten thousand souls to Heaven or Hell;
And this fell tempest shall not cease to rage
Until the golden circuit° on my head,
Like to the glorious sun's transparent beams,
Do calm the fury of this mad-bred flaw.°
And, for a minister of my intent,   355
I have seduced a headstrong Kentishman,
John Cade of Ashford,
To make commotion, as full well he can,
Under the title of John Mortimer.
In Ireland have I seen this stubborn Cade   360
Oppose himself against a troop of kernes,
And fought so long till that his thighs with darts
Were almost like a sharp-quilled porpentine;
And, in the end being rescued, I have seen
Him caper° upright like a wild Morisco,°   365

Shaking the bloody darts as he his bells.
Full often, like a shag-haired° crafty kerne,
Hath he conversèd with the enemy,
And undiscovered come to me again
And given me notice of their villainies.   370
This devil here shall be my substitute,
For that John Mortimer, which now is dead,
In face, in gait, in speech, he doth resemble.
By this I shall perceive the commons' mind,
How they affect° the House and claim of York.
Say he be taken, racked,° and tortured,   376
I know no pain they can inflict upon him
Will make him say I moved him to those arms.
Say that he thrive, as 'tis great like he will,   379
Why, then from Ireland come I with my strength,
And reap the harvest which that rascal sowed.
For Humphrey being dead, as he shall be,
And Henry put apart, the next for me.   [*Exit.*]

SCENE II. *Bury St. Edmund's. A room of state.*

    [*Enter certain* MURDERERS, *hastily.*]
  1. MUR. Run to my Lord of Suffolk. Let him
    know
We have dispatched the Duke, as he commanded.
  2. MUR. Oh, that it were to do!° What have we
    done?
Didst ever hear a man so penitent?
           [*Enter* SUFFOLK.]
  1. MUR. Here comes my lord.   5
  SUF. Now, sirs, have you dispatched this thing?
  1. MUR. Aye, my good lord, he's dead.
  SUF. Why, that's well said. Go, get you to my
    house.
I will reward you for this venturous deed.
The King and all the peers are here at hand.   10
Have you laid fair the bed? Is all things well,
According as I gave directions?
  1. MUR. 'Tis, my good lord.
  SUF. Away! Be gone.   [*Exeunt* MURDERERS.]
[*Sound trumpets. Enter the* KING, *the* QUEEN,
CARDINAL BEAUFORT, SOMERSET, *with* ATTEND-
             ANTS.]
  KING. Go, call our uncle to our presence straight.
Say we intend to try His Grace today,   16
If he be guilty, as 'tis publishèd.
  SUF. I'll call him presently, my noble lord.
                     [*Exit.*]
  KING. Lords, take your places; and I pray you all
Proceed no straiter° 'gainst our Uncle Gloucester
Than from true evidence of good esteem   21

---

331. fearful: timid. **335. keep:** live. **348. nourish:** a one-syllable word. **352. golden circuit:** crown. **354. flaw:** gust of wind. **365. caper:** See App. 24: The Capriol, and Country Dances. **Morisco:** morris dancer. See Pl. 13d.

367. shag-haired: rough-haired. **375. affect:** incline to. **376. racked:** See App. 10.

Sc. ii: **3. Oh ... do:** i.e., that it had not been done. **20. straiter:** more strictly.

He be approved° in practice° culpable.
　QUEEN. God forbid any malice should prevail
That faultless may condemn a nobleman!
Pray God he may acquit him of suspicion!　　25
　KING. I thank thee, Nell.° These words content
　　me much.

[Re-enter SUFFOLK.]

How now! Why look'st thou pale? Why tremblest
　　thou?
Where is our uncle? What's the matter, Suffolk?
　SUF. Dead in his bed, my lord. Gloucester is
　　dead.
　QUEEN. Marry, God forfend!°　　　　　30
　CAR. God's secret judgment. I did dream tonight
The Duke was dumb and could not speak a word.

[The KING swoons.]

　QUEEN. How fares my lord? Help, lords! The
　　King is dead.
　SOM. Rear up his body. Wring him by the nose.°
　QUEEN. Run, go, help, help! O Henry, ope thine
　　eyes!　　　　　35
　SUF. He doth revive again. Madam, be patient.
　KING. O heavenly God!
　QUEEN.　　　　　How fares my gracious lord?
　SUF. Comfort, my sovereign! Gracious Henry,
　　comfort!
　KING. What, doth my Lord of Suffolk comfort
　　me?
Came he right now to sing a raven's note°　　40
Whose dismal tune bereft my vital powers,
And thinks he that the chirping of a wren,
By crying comfort from a hollow breast,
Can chase away the first-conceivèd sound?
Hide not thy poison with such sugared words.　　45
Lay not thy hands on me. Forbear, I say.
Their touch affrights me as a serpent's sting.
Thou baleful° messenger, out of my sight!
Upon thy eyeballs murderous tyranny
Sits in grim majesty, to fright the world.　　50
Look not upon me, for thine eyes are wounding.
Yet do not go away. Come, basilisk,°
And kill the innocent gazer with thy sight.
For in the shade of death I shall find joy,　　54
In life but double death, now Gloucester's dead.
　QUEEN. Why do you rate° my Lord of Suffolk
　　thus?
Although the Duke was enemy to him,
Yet he most Christian-like laments his death.
And for myself, foe as he was to me,
Might liquid tears, or heart-offending groans,　　60
Or blood-consuming sighs recall his life,

I would be blind with weeping, sick with groans,
Look pale as primrose with blood-drinking sighs,°
And all to have the noble Duke alive.
What know I how the world may deem of me?　　65
For it is known we were but hollow° friends.
It may be judged I made the Duke away;
So shall my name with slander's tongue be
　　wounded
And princes' courts be filled with my reproach.
This get I by his death. Aye me unhappy!　　70
To be a queen, and crowned with infamy!
　KING. Ah, woe is me for Gloucester, wretched
　　man!
　QUEEN. Be woe for me, more wretched than he is.
What, dost thou turn away and hide thy face?
I am no loathsome leper. Look on me.　　75
What! Art thou, like the adder, waxen deaf?°
Be poisonous too, and kill thy forlorn Queen.
Is all thy comfort shut in Gloucester's tomb?
Why, then, Dame Eleanor° was ne'er thy joy.
Erect his statuë° and worship it,　　80
And make my image but an alehouse sign.
Was I for this nigh wrecked upon the sea,
And twice by awkward° wind from England's
　　bank
Drove back again unto my native clime?
What boded this, but well forewarning wind　　85
Did seem to say, " Seek not a scorpion's nest,
Nor set no footing on this unkind shore "?
What did I then, but cursed the gentle gusts
And he that loosed them forth their brazen caves,
And bid them blow toward England's blessèd
　　shore,　　　　　90
Or turn our stern upon a dreadful rock?
Yet Aeolus° would not be a murderer,
But left that hateful office unto thee.
The pretty vaulting° sea refused to drown me,
Knowing that thou wouldst have me drowned on
　　shore　　　　　95
With tears as salt as sea, through thy unkindness.
The splitting rocks cowered in the sinking sands
And would not dash me with their ragged sides,
Because thy flinty heart, more hard than they,
Might in thy palace perish° Eleanor.　　100
As far as I could ken° thy chalky cliffs,
When from thy shore the tempest beat us back,
I stood upon the hatches in the storm,
And when the dusky sky began to rob

61–63. blood-consuming . . . sighs: It was believed that sighing consumed the heart's blood and so shortened life.　66. hollow: false, pretended.　76. waxen deaf: grown deaf.　It was a popular belief, founded on Psalm 58:4–5, that the adder resisted the music of the snake charmer by putting her tail in one ear and clapping the other to the ground.　79. Dame Eleanor: See l. 26,n.　80. statuë: a three-syllable word.　83. awkward: adverse.　89–92. he . . . Aeolus: god of the winds, who kept them imprisoned in a cave.　94. pretty vaulting: gently leaping.　100. perish: destroy.　101. ken: perceive.

22. approved: proved. practice: plotting.　26. Nell: Shakespeare has forgotten here and later (see ll. 79, 100, 120) that the Queen's name was not Eleanor, but Margaret.　30. forfend: forbid.　34. Wring . . . nose: i.e., rub his nose to bring him back to consciousness.　40. raven's note: The raven's croak was regarded as ill-omened.　48. baleful: deathly.　52. basilisk: See *Rich III*, I.ii.151,n.　56. rate: abuse.

My earnest-gaping sight of thy land's view,   105
I took a costly jewel from my neck —
A heart it was, bound in with diamonds —
And threw it toward thy land. The sea received it,
And so I wished thy body might my heart.
And even with this I lost fair England's view,   110
And bid mine eyes be packing° with my heart,
And called them blind and dusky spectacles
For losing ken of Albion's wishèd coast.
How often have I tempted Suffolk's tongue,
The agent of thy foul inconstancy,°   115
To sit and witch° me, as Ascanius° did,
When he to madding Dido would unfold
His father's acts commenced in burning Troy!
Am I not witched like her? Or thou not false like
   him?
Aye me, I can no more! Die, Eleanor!   120
For Henry weeps that thou dost live so long.

     [*Noise within. Enter* WARWICK, SALISBURY, *and
     many* COMMONS.]

   WAR. It is reported, mighty sovereign,
That good Duke Humphrey traitorously is mur-
   dered
By Suffolk and the Cardinal Beaufort's means.
The commons, like an angry hive of bees   125
That want° their leader, scatter up and down,
And care not who they sting in his revenge.
Myself have calmed their spleenful° mutiny,
Until they hear the order° of his death.
   KING. That he is dead, good Warwick, 'tis too
     true;   130
But how he died God knows, not Henry.
Enter his chamber, view his breathless corpse,
And comment then upon his sudden death.
   WAR. That shall I do, my liege. Stay, Salisbury,
With the rude multitude till I return.   [*Exit.*]
   KING. O Thou that judgest all things, stay my
     thoughts,   136
My thoughts, that labor to persuade my soul
Some violent hands were laid on Humphrey's life!
If my suspect° be false, forgive me, God,
For judgment only doth belong to Thee.   140
Fain would I go to chafe his paly° lips
With twenty thousand kisses, and to drain
Upon his face an ocean of salt tears,
To tell my love unto his dumb deaf trunk,
And with my fingers feel his hand unfeeling.   145
But all in vain are these mean obsequies,°
And to survey his dead and earthly image,
What were it but to make my sorrow greater?

   [*Re-enter* WARWICK *and others, bearing*
     GLOUCESTER's *body on a bed.*]

   WAR. Come hither, gracious sovereign, view this
     body.
   KING. That is to see how deep my grave is made.
For with his soul fled all my worldly solace;   151
For seeing him I see my life in death.
   WAR. As surely as my soul intends to live
With that dread King,° that took our state upon
     him
To free us from his Father's wrathful curse,   155
I do believe that violent hands were laid
Upon the life of this thrice-famèd Duke.
   SUF. A dreadful oath, sworn with a solemn
     tongue!
What instance° gives Lord Warwick for his vow?
   WAR. See how the blood is settled in his face.   160
Oft have I seen a timely parted° ghost,
Of ashy semblance, meager, pale, and bloodless,
Being all descended° to the laboring heart,
Who, in the conflict that it holds with death,   164
Attracts the same for aidance 'gainst the enemy;
Which with the heart there cools and ne'er re-
   turneth
To blush and beautify the cheek again.
But see, his face is black and full of blood,
His eyeballs further out than when he lived,
Staring full ghastly like a strangled man,   170
His hair upreared, his nostrils stretched with
     struggling,
His hands abroad displayed, as one that grasped
And tugged for life and was by strength subdued.
Look, on the sheets his hair, you see, is sticking,
His well-proportioned beard made rough and
     rugged,   175
Like to the summer's corn by tempest lodged.°
It cannot be but he was murdered here.
The least of all these signs were probable.
   SUF. Why, Warwick, who should do the Duke to
     death?
Myself and Beaufort had him in protection,   180
And we, I hope, sir, are no murderers.
   WAR. But both of you were vowed Duke Hum-
     phrey's foes,
And you, forsooth, had the good Duke to keep.
'Tis like you would not feast him like a friend,
And 'tis well seen he found an enemy.   185
   QUEEN. Then you, belike, suspect these noble-
     men
As guilty of Duke Humphrey's timeless° death.
   WAR. Who finds the heifer dead and bleeding
     fresh,
And sees fast by a butcher with an ax,   189

---

111. packing: be gone.   115. agent . . . inconstancy: i.e.,
Suffolk was the King's deputy at the wedding (see I.i.1–9) and so
to that extent responsible for Henry's loss of love.   116. witch:
bewitch. Ascanius: son of the Trojan Aeneas, whom Dido
Queen of Carthage loved madly. See *Temp*, II.i.76,n. The story
is told in Vergil's *Aeneid*.   126. want: are deprived of.
128. spleenful: angry-tempered.   129. order: manner, particulars.   139. suspect: suspicion.   141. paly: pale.   146. obsequies: rites paid to the dead.

154. King: i.e., Christ.   159. instance: proof.   161. timely
parted: who died naturally.   163. Being . . . descended: because all the blood has descended.   176. lodged: laid flat.
187. timeless: untimely.

But will suspect 'twas he that made the slaughter?
Who finds the partridge in the puttock's° nest,
But may imagine how the bird was dead,
Although the kite soar with unbloodied beak?
Even so suspicious is this tragedy.
    QUEEN. Are you the butcher, Suffolk? Where's
      your knife?   195
Is Beaufort termed a kite? Where are his talons?
    SUF. I wear no knife to slaughter sleeping men;
But here's a vengeful sword, rusted with ease,
That shall be scourèd in his rancorous heart   199
That slanders me with murder's crimson badge.°
Say, if thou darest, proud Lord of Warwickshire,
That I am faulty in Duke Humphrey's death.
    [Exeunt CARDINAL, SOMERSET, and others.]
    WAR. What dares not Warwick, if false Suffolk
    dare him?
    QUEEN. He dares not calm his contumelious°
    spirit,
Nor cease to be an arrogant controller,°   205
Though Suffolk dare him twenty thousand times.
    WAR. Madam, be still, with reverence may I say;
For every word you speak in his behalf
Is slander to your royal dignity.
    SUF. Blunt-witted lord, ignoble in demeanor!
If ever lady wronged her lord so much,   211
Thy mother took into her blameful bed
Some stern untutored churl, and noble stock
Was graft with crab-tree slip,° whose fruit thou
    art,
And never of the Nevils' noble race.   215
    WAR. But that the guilt of murder bucklers°
    thee,
And I should rob the deathsman° of his fee,
Quitting° thee thereby of ten thousand shames,
And that my sovereign's presence makes me mild,
I would, false murderous coward, on thy knee   220
Make thee beg pardon for thy passèd° speech
And say it was thy mother that thou meant'st,
That thou thyself wast born in bastardy,
And after all this fearful homage done,
Give thee thy hire° and send thy soul to Hell,   225
Pernicious bloodsucker of sleeping men!
    SUF. Thou shalt be waking while I shed thy
    blood,
If from this presence thou darest go with me.
    WAR. Away even now, or I will drag thee hence.
Unworthy though thou art, I'll cope° with thee   230
And do some service to Duke Humphrey's ghost.
    [Exeunt SUFFOLK and WARWICK.]

    KING. What stronger breastplate than a heart
    untainted!
Thrice is he armed that hath his quarrel just,
And he but naked, though locked up in steel,
Whose conscience with injustice is corrupted.   235
               [A noise within.]
    QUEEN. What noise is this?
    [Re-enter SUFFOLK and WARWICK, with their
          weapons drawn.]
    KING. Why, how now, lords! Your wrathful
    weapons drawn
Here in our presence! Dare you be so bold?
Why, what tumultuous clamor have we here?
    SUF. The traitorous Warwick with the men of
    Bury   240
Set all upon me, mighty sovereign.
    SAL. [To the COMMONS, entering] Sirs, stand
    apart. The King shall know your mind.
Dread lord, the commons send you word by me,
Unless Lord Suffolk straight be done to death,
Or banishèd fair England's territories,   245
They will by violence tear him from your palace
And torture him with grievous lingering death.
They say, by him the good Duke Humphrey died.
They say, in him they fear your Highness' death,
And mere instinct of love and loyalty,   250
Free from a stubborn opposite intent,°
As being thought to contradict your liking,°
Makes them thus forward in his banishment.
They say, in care of your most royal person,
That if your Highness should intend to sleep,   255
And charge that no man should disturb your rest
In pain of your dislike or pain of death,
Yet, notwithstanding such a strait° edict,
Were there a serpent seen, with forkèd tongue,
That slyly glided toward your Majesty,   260
It were but necessary you were waked,
Lest, being suffered in that harmful slumber,
The mortal worm° might make the sleep eternal;
And therefore do they cry, though you forbid,
That they will guard you, whether you will or no,
From such fell° serpents as false Suffolk is,   266
With whose envenomèd and fatal sting
Your loving uncle, twenty times his worth,
They say is shamefully bereft of life.
    COMMONS. [Within] An answer from the King,
    my Lord of Salisbury!   270
    SUF. 'Tis like° the commons, rude unpolished
    hinds,°
Could send such message to their sovereign.
But you, my lord, were glad to be employed
To show how quaint° an orator you are;
But all the honor Salisbury hath won   275

---

191. puttock: kite.   200. with . . . badge: i.e., by accusing me
of wearing the badge of murder.   204. contumelious: contemptuous.   205. controller: critic.   213–14. noble . . . slip:
a cutting from a base tree was engrafted into a noble stock; i.e.,
you are a bastard.   216. bucklers: shields.   217. deathsman:
executioner.   218. Quitting: ridding.   221. passèd: just
uttered.   225. hire: reward.   230. cope: encounter.

251. Free . . . intent: i.e., this demand is not merely stubborn opposition.   252. liking: desire.   258. strait: strict.   263. mortal
worm: deadly snake.   266. fell: fearful.   271. 'Tis like: it is
likely — said sarcastically.   hinds: boors.   274. quaint: clever.

Is that he was the Lord Ambassador
Sent from a sort° of tinkers to the King.
 COMMONS. [*Within*] An answer from the King,
  or we will all break in!
 KING. Go, Salisbury, and tell them all from me
I thank them for their tender loving care,   280
And had I not been cited° so by them,
Yet did I purpose as they do entreat;
For, sure, my thoughts do hourly prophesy
Mischance unto my state by Suffolk's means.
And therefore, by His majesty I swear,   285
Whose far unworthy deputy I am,
He shall not breathe infection° in this air
But three days longer, on the pain of death.
        [*Exit* SALISBURY.]
 QUEEN. O Henry, let me plead for gentle Suffolk!
 KING. Ungentle Queen, to call him gentle Suf-
  folk!   290
No more, I say. If thou dost plead for him,
Thou wilt but add increase unto my wrath.
Had I but said, I would have kept my word,
But when I swear, it is irrevocable.
If, after three days' space, thou here be'st found
On any ground that I am ruler of,   296
The world shall not be ransom for thy life.
Come, Warwick, come, good Warwick, go with me.
I have great matters to impart to thee.
    [*Exeunt all but* QUEEN *and* SUFFOLK.]
 QUEEN. Mischance and sorrow go along with you!
Heart's discontent and sour affliction   301
Be playfellows to keep you company!
There's two of you; the Devil make a third!
And threefold vengeance tend upon your steps!
 SUF. Cease, gentle Queen, these execrations, 305
And let thy Suffolk take his heavy leave.
 QUEEN. Fie, coward woman and soft-hearted
  wretch!°
Hast thou not spirit to curse thine enemy?
 SUF. A plague upon them! Wherefore should I
  curse them?
Would curses kill, as doth the mandrake's° groan,
I would invent as bitter-searching terms,   311
As curst,° as harsh and horrible to hear,
Delivered strongly through my fixèd teeth,
With full as many signs of deadly hate
As lean-faced Envy in her loathsome cave.   315
My tongue should stumble in mine earnest words.
Mine eyes should sparkle like the beaten flint,
Mine hair be fixed on end, as one distract.°
Aye, every joint should seem to curse and ban, 319
And even now my burdened heart would break
Should I not curse them. Poison be their drink!

Gall, worse than gall, the daintiest that they taste!
Their sweetest shade a grove of cypress° trees!
Their chiefest prospect murdering basilisks!
Their softest touch as smart° as lizards' stings!
Their music frightful as the serpent's hiss,   326
And boding° screech owls make the concert full!
All the foul terrors in dark-seated Hell——
 QUEEN. Enough, sweet Suffolk. Thou torment'st
  thyself,
And these dread curses, like the sun 'gainst glass,
Or like an overchargèd gun, recoil   331
And turn the force of them upon thyself.
 SUF. You bade me ban, and will you bid me
  leave?
Now, by the ground that I am banished from,
Well could I curse away a winter's night,   335
Though standing naked on a mountaintop
Where biting cold would never let grass grow,
And think it but a minute spent in sport.
 QUEEN. Oh, let me entreat thee cease. Give me
  thy hand,
That I may dew it with my mournful tears;   340
Nor let the rain of heaven wet this place
To wash away my woeful monuments.°
Oh, could this kiss be printed in thy hand,
That thou mightst think upon these by the seal°
Through whom a thousand sighs are breathed for
  thee!   345
So, get thee gone, that I may know my grief.
'Tis but surmised whiles thou art standing by,
As one that surfeits thinking on a want.°
I will repeal° thee, or, be well assured,
Adventure to be° banishèd myself;   350
And banishèd I am, if but from° thee.
Go. Speak not to me; even now be gone.
Oh, go not yet! Even thus two friends condemned
Embrace and kiss and take ten thousand leaves,
Loather a hundred times to part than die.   355
Yet now farewell, and farewell life with thee!
 SUF. Thus is poor Suffolk ten times banishèd:
Once by the King, and three times thrice by thee.
'Tis not the land I care for, wert thou thence.
A wilderness is populous enough,   360
So Suffolk had thy heavenly company.
For where thou art, there is the world itself
With every several° pleasure in the world,
And where thou art not, desolation.
I can no more. Live thou to joy thy life.   365
Myself no joy in naught but that thou livest.

---

277. **sort:** gang. 281. **cited:** incited. 287. **breathe infection:** breathe out poison. 307. **Fie . . . wretch:** These words are spoken to Suffolk because he does not immediately curse the King. From this point onwards Margaret becomes steadily more fiendlike. 310. **mandrake:** See Pl. 12e and Note on pp. 96b–97a. 312. **curst:** bitter. 318. **distract:** mad.

323. **cypress:** The dark evergreen cypress was regarded as a dismal tree, fit for graveyards. 325. **smart:** painful. 327. **boding:** ill-omened. 342. **woeful monuments:** i.e., the tears which remain imprinted on his hand — a far-fetched conceit. 344. **seal:** impression. 347–48. **'Tis . . . want:** I shall not realize the depth of my grief so long as you are with me, just as a well-fed man cannot imagine hunger. 349. **repeal:** recall from banishment. 350. **Adventure to be:** risk being. 351. **if . . . from:** if I am separated from. 363. **several:** separate, distinct.

[*Enter* VAUX.]

QUEEN. Whither goes Vaux so fast? What news,
　I prithee?
VAUX. To signify unto His Majesty
That Cardinal Beaufort is at point of death.
For suddenly a grievous sickness took him, 　370
That makes him gasp and stare and catch the air,
Blaspheming God and cursing men on earth.
Sometime he talks as if Duke Humphrey's ghost
Were by his side; sometime he calls the King,
And whispers to his pillow as to him 　375
The secrets of his overchargèd soul.
And I am sent to tell His Majesty
That even now he cries aloud for him.
　QUEEN. Go tell this heavy message to the King.
　　　　　　　　　　　　　　　[*Exit* VAUX.]
Aye me! What is this world! What news are these!
But wherefore grieve I at an hour's poor loss, 　381
Omitting Suffolk's exile, my soul's treasure?
Why only, Suffolk, mourn I not for thee,
And with the southern° clouds contend in tears,
Theirs for the earth's increase, mine for my sor-
　rows?
　　　　　　　　　　　　　　　　　　385
Now get thee hence. The King, thou know'st, is
　coming.
If thou be found by me,° thou art but dead.
　SUF. If I depart from thee, I cannot live,
And in thy sight to die, what were it else
But like a pleasant slumber in thy lap? 　390
Here could I breathe my soul into the air,
As mild and gentle as the cradle babe
Dying with mother's dug between its lips;
Where, from° thy sight, I should be raging mad,
And cry out for thee to close up mine eyes, 　395
To have thee with thy lips to stop my mouth;
So shouldst thou either turn my flying soul,
Or I should breathe it so into thy body,
And then it lived in sweet Elysium.
To die by thee were but to die in jest; 　400
From thee to die were torture more than death.
Oh, let me stay, befall what may befall!
　QUEEN. Away! Though parting be a fretful cor-
　rosive,°
It is applièd to a deathful wound.
To France, sweet Suffolk. Let me hear from thee;
For wheresoe'er thou art in this world's globe, 　406
I'll have an Iris° that shall find thee out.
　SUF. I go.

QUEEN. And take my heart with thee.
SUF. A jewel, locked into the woefull'st cask°
That ever did contain a thing of worth. 　410
Even as a splitted bark,° so sunder we.
This way fall I to death.
　QUEEN. 　　　This way for me. [*Exeunt severally.*]

SCENE III. *A bedchamber.*

[*Enter the* KING, SALISBURY, WARWICK, *to the*
CARDINAL *in bed.*]

　KING. How fares my lord? Speak, Beaufort, to
　thy sovereign.
　CAR. If thou be'st Death, I'll give thee England's
　treasure,
Enough to purchase such another island,
So thou wilt let me live and feel no pain.
　KING. Ah, what a sign it is it is of evil life, 　5
Where death's approach is seen so terrible!
　WAR. Beaufort, it is thy sovereign speaks to thee.
　CAR. Bring me unto my trial when you will.
Died he° not in his bed? Where should he die?
Can I make men live whether they will or no? 　10
Oh, torture me no more! I will confess.
Alive again? Then show me where he is.
I'll give a thousand pound to look upon him.
He hath no eyes, the dust hath blinded them. 　14
Comb down his hair. Look, look! It stands upright,
Like lime twigs set to catch my wingèd soul.
Give me some drink, and bid the apothecary
Bring the strong poison that I bought of him.
　KING. O Thou eternal Mover of the heavens,
Look with a gentle eye upon this wretch! 　20
Oh, beat away the busy meddling fiend
That lays strong siege unto this wretch's soul
And from his bosom purge this black despair!
　WAR. See how the pangs of death do make him
　grin! 　24
　SAL. Disturb him not. Let him pass peaceably.
　KING. Peace to his soul, if God's good pleasure
　be!
Lord Cardinal, if thou think'st on Heaven's bliss,
Hold up thy hand, make signal of thy hope.
He dies, and makes no sign. O God, forgive him!
　WAR. So bad a death argues a monstrous life. 　30
　KING. Forbear to judge, for we are sinners all.
Close up his eyes and draw the curtain close,
And let us all to meditation. 　　[*Exeunt.*]

384. southern: The south was the region from which wind, storm, and misfortune were believed to come. 387. by me: by my side. 394. from: away from. 403. fretful corrosive: Ointment containing corrosives was applied to tainted wounds. 407. Iris: the rainbow, one of the messengers of the gods.

409. cask: casket. 411. splitted bark: ship that breaks into two pieces.
Sc. iii: 9. he: i.e., Duke Humphrey, by whose murder the Cardinal is haunted in his delirium.

Act IV

SCENE I. *The coast of Kent.*

[*Alarum. Fight at sea. Ordnance goes off. Enter a*
CAPTAIN, *a* MASTER, *a* MASTER'S MATE, WALTER WHIT-
MORE, *and others; with them* SUFFOLK, *and others,*
PRISONERS.]

CAP. The gaudy, blabbing and remorseful° day
Is crept into the bosom of the sea;
And now loud-howling wolves arouse the jades°
That drag the tragic melancholy night, 4
Who, with their drowsy, slow, and flagging° wings,
Clip° dead men's graves, and from their misty jaws
Breathe foul contagious darkness in the air.
Therefore bring forth the soldiers of our prize;°
For whilst our pinnace anchors in the Downs,°
Here shall they make their ransom on the sand, 10
Or with their blood stain this discolored shore.
Master, this prisoner freely give I thee,
And thou that art his mate, make boot° of this.
The other, Walter Whitmore, is thy share.

1. GENT. What is my ransom, Master? Let me
　　know. 15

MAST. A thousand crowns, or else lay down your
　　head.

MATE. And so much shall you give, or off goes
　　yours.

CAP. What, think you much to pay two thousand
　　crowns,
And bear the name and port° of gentlemen?°
Cut both the villains' throats, for die you shall. 20
The lives of those which we have lost in fight
Be counterpoised° with such a petty sum!

1. GEN. I'll give it, sir, and therefore spare my life.

2. GEN. And so will I, and write home for it
　　straight. 24

WHIT. I lost mine eye in laying the prize aboard,°
And therefore to revenge it, shalt thou die;
[*To* SUFFOLK] And so should these, if I might have
my will.

CAP. Be not so rash. Take ransom, let him live.

SUF. Look on my George.° I am a gentleman.
Rate° me at what thou wilt, thou shalt be paid. 30

WHIT. And so am I. My name is Walter° Whitmore.
How now! Why start'st thou? What, doth death affright?

Act IV, Sc. i: 1. remorseful: full of pity. 3. jades: poor-
spirited nags. 5. flagging: drooping. 6. Clip: embrace.
8. soldiers . . . prize: i.e., those whom we have captured.
9. Downs: south coast of Kent. 13. boot: booty. 18–19. What
. . . gentlemen: do you two, who claim to be gentlemen, think
yourselves not worth 2000 crowns? port: bearing. 22. counterpoised: counterbalanced. 25. laying . . . aboard: boarding
the captured ship. 29. George: my badge as Knight of the
Garter. See App. 29 and Pl. 8d. 30. Rate: assess. 31. Walter:
pronounced "Water."

SUF. Thy name affrights me, in whose sound is
　　death.
A cunning man° did calculate my birth,°
And told me that by water I should die. 35
Yet let not this make thee be bloody-minded;
Thy name is Gualtier,° being rightly sounded.

WHIT. Gualtier or Walter, which it is, I care not.
Never yet did base dishonor blur our name,
But with our sword we wiped away the blot. 40
Therefore, when merchantlike I sell revenge,
Broke be my sword, my arms° torn and defaced,
And I proclaimed a coward through the world!

SUF. Stay, Whitmore, for thy prisoner is a prince,
The Duke of Suffolk, William de la Pole. 45

WHIT. The Duke of Suffolk, muffled up in rags!

SUF. Aye, but these rags are no part of the Duke.
Jove sometime went disguised, and why not I?

CAP. But Jove was never slain, as thou shalt be.

SUF. Obscure and lowly swain, King Henry's
　　blood, 50
The honorable blood of Lancaster,
Must not be shed by such a jaded° groom.
Hast thou not kissed thy hand and held my stirrup?
Bare-headed plodded by my footcloth mule,°
And thought thee happy when I shook° my head?
How often hast thou waited at my cup, 56
Fed from my trencher,° kneeled down at the board
When I have feasted with Queen Margaret?
Remember it, and let it make thee crestfallen,°
Aye, and allay° this thy abortive pride. 60
How in our voiding lobby° hast thou stood
And duly waited for my coming forth?
This hand of mine hath writ in thy behalf,
And therefore shall it charm thy riotous tongue.

WHIT. Speak, Captain, shall I stab the forlorn
　　swain? 65

CAP. First let my words stab him as he hath me.

SUF. Base slave, thy words are blunt, and so art
　　thou.

CAP. Convey him hence, and on our longboat's
　　side
Strike off his head.

SUF. Thou darest not, for thy own.

CAP. Yes, Pole.

SUF. Pole!

CAP. Pool! Sir Pool! Lord! 70
Aye, kennel,° puddle, sink, whose filth and dirt
Troubles the silver spring where England drinks.
Now will I dam up this thy yawning mouth
For swallowing the treasure of the realm.

---

34. cunning man: soothsayer. calculate my birth: cast my
horoscope. 37. Gualtier: French form of Walter. 42. arms:
coat of arms. 52. jaded: contemptible. 54. footcloth mule:
mule draped with an ornamental cloth which hung down to the
ground on either side, used on ceremonial occasions. 55. shook:
nodded. 57. trencher: platter. 59. crestfallen: humble —
like a defeated fighting cock. 60. allay: diminish, lit., water
down. 61. voiding lobby: waiting room. 71. kennel: gutter.

Thy lips that kissed the Queen shall sweep the
    ground,   75
And thou that smiledest at good Duke Humphrey's
    death
Against° the senseless winds shalt grin in vain,
Who in contempt shall hiss at thee again.
And wedded be thou to the hags of Hell
For daring to affy° a mighty lord   80
Unto the daughter of a worthless King,
Having neither subject, wealth, nor diadem.
By devilish policy art thou grown great,
And, like ambitious Sylla,° overgorged
With gobbets of thy mother's° bleeding heart.   85
By thee Anjou and Maine were sold to France.
The false revolting Normans thorough° thee
Disdain to call us lord, and Picardy
Hath slain their governors, surprised our forts,
And sent the ragged soldiers wounded home.   90
The princely Warwick and the Nevils all,
Whose dreadful swords were never drawn in vain,
As hating thee, are rising up in arms.
And now the House of York, thrust from the crown
By shameful murder of a guiltless King°   95
And lofty proud encroaching tyranny,
Burns with revenging fire; whose hopeful colors
Advance our half-faced sun,° striving to shine,
Under the which is writ, "*Invitis nubibus.*"°
The commons here in Kent are up in arms;   100
And, to conclude, reproach and beggary
Is crept into the palace of our King,
And all by thee. Away! Convey him hence.
  SUF. Oh, that I were a god, to shoot forth thun-
    der
Upon these paltry, servile, abject drudges!   105
Small things make base men proud. This villain
    here,
Being captain of a pinnace, threatens more
Than Bargulus the strong Illyrian pirate.
Drones suck not eagles' blood, but rob bee hives.
It is impossible that I should die   110
By such a lowly vassal as thyself.
Thy words move rage and not remorse in me.
I go of message from the Queen to France.
I charge thee waft° me safely cross the Channel.
  CAP. Walter——   115
  WHIT. Come, Suffolk, I must waft thee to thy
    death.
  SUF. *Gelidus timor occupat artus.*° It is thee I
    fear.

  WHIT. Thou shalt have cause to fear before I leave
    thee.
What, are ye daunted now? Now will ye stoop?
  I. GEN. My gracious lord, entreat him, speak him
    fair.   120
  SUF. Suffolk's imperial tongue is stern and rough,
Used to command, untaught to plead for favor.
Far be it we should honor such as these
With humble suit. No, rather let my head
Stoop to the block than these knees bow to any
Save to the God of Heaven and to my King,   126
And sooner dance upon a bloody pole
Than stand uncovered° to the vulgar groom.
True nobility is exempt from fear.
More can I bear than you dare execute.   130
  CAP. Hale him away, and let him talk no more.
  SUF. Come, soldiers, show what cruelty ye can,
That this my death may never be forgot!
Great men oft die by vile bezonians.°
A Roman sworder and banditto slave   135
Murdered sweet Tully;° Brutus' bastard hand
Stabbed Julius Caesar; savage islanders,
Pompey the Great; and Suffolk dies by pirates.
    [*Exeunt* WHITMORE *and others with* SUFFOLK.]
  CAP. And as for these whose ransom we have set,
It is our pleasure one of them depart.   140
Therefore come you with us and let him go.
    [*Exeunt all but the* FIRST GENTLEMAN.]
    [*Re-enter* WHITMORE *with* SUFFOLK's *body.*]
  WHIT. There let his head and lifeless body lie
Until the Queen his mistress bury it.   [*Exit.*]
  I. GEN. Oh, barbarous and bloody spectacle!
His body will I bear unto the King.   145
If he revenge it not, yet will his friends.
So will the Queen, that living held him dear.
    [*Exit with the body.*]

SCENE II. *Blackheath.*

    [*Enter* GEORGE BEVIS *and* JOHN HOLLAND.]
  BEV. Come, and get thee a sword, though made
of a lath.° They have been up these two days.
  HOL. They have the more need to sleep now, then.
  BEV. I tell thee, Jack Cade the clothier means   5
to dress the commonwealth, and turn it, and set a
new nap upon it.
  HOL. So he had need, for 'tis threadbare. Well, I
say it was never merry world in England since gentlemen came up.°   10
  BEV. Oh, miserable age! Virtue is not regarded in
handicraftsmen.
  HOL. The nobility think scorn to go in leather
aprons.

---

77. Against: in the face of.   **80. affy:** betroth.   **84. Sylla:** or
Sulla, dictator of Rome, notorious for his wholesale slaughter of
his political opponents.   **85. mother:** i.e., motherland.
87. thorough: through.   **95. guiltless King:** i.e., Richard II.
See App. 28.   **98. half-faced sun:** i.e., device of a sun shining
through the clouds.   **99. *Invitis nubibus:*** even if the clouds are
unwilling.   **114. waft:** transport.   **117. *Gelidus . . . artus:***
cold fear seizes my limbs.

128. uncovered: with my hat in my hand — as a sign of respect.
See App. 7.   **134. bezonians:** beggars.   **136. Tully:** Marcus
Tullius Cicero, murdered by order of Marcus Antonius.
  Sc. ii: 1. lath: strip of wood.   **10. came up:** rose in the world.

BEV. Nay, more, the King's Council are no good workmen.   16

HOL. True, and yet it is said, labor in thy vocation; which is as much to say as, let the magistrates be laboring men; and therefore should we be magistrates.   20

BEV. Thou hast hit it, for there's no better sign of a brave mind than a hard hand.

HOL. I see them! I see them! There's Best's son, the tanner of Wingham ——

BEV. He shall have the skins of our enemies to make dog's leather° of.   26

HOL. And Dick the butcher ——

BEV. Then is sin struck down like an ox, and iniquity's throat cut like a calf.

HOL. And Smith the weaver ——   30

BEV. Argo,° their thread of life is spun.

HOL. Come, come, let's fall in with them.

[*Drum. Enter* CADE, DICK *the butcher,* SMITH *the weaver, and a* SAWYER,° *with infinite numbers.*]

CADE. We John Cade, so termèd of our supposèd father° ——

DICK. [*Aside*] Or rather, of stealing a cade° of herrings.   36

CADE. For our enemies shall fall before us, inspired with the spirit of putting down kings and princes —— [*To* DICK] Command silence.

DICK. Silence!   40

CADE. My father was a Mortimer ——

DICK. [*Aside*] He was an honest man, and a good bricklayer.

CADE. —— My mother a Plantagenet ——   44

DICK. [*Aside*] I knew her well. She was a midwife.

CADE. —— My wife descended of the Lacies ——

DICK. [*Aside*] She was, indeed, a peddler's daughter, and sold many laces.   49

SMITH. [*Aside*] But now of late, not able to travel with her furred pack,° she washes bucks° here at home.

CADE. —— Therefore am I of an honorable house.

DICK. [*Aside*] Aye, by my faith, the field is honorable. And there was he born, under a hedge,° for his father had never a house but the cage.°   56

CADE. Valiant I am.

SMITH. [*Aside*] A' must needs, for beggary is valiant.

CADE. I am able to endure much.   60

DICK. [*Aside*] No question of that, for I have seen him whipped three market days together.

CADE. I fear neither sword nor fire.

SMITH. [*Aside*] He need not fear the sword, for his coat is of proof.°   65

DICK. [*Aside*] But methinks he should stand in fear of fire, being burnt i' the hand° for stealing of sheep.

CADE. Be brave, then, for your captain is brave and vows reformation. There shall be in England   70 seven half-penny loaves sold for a penny. The three-hooped pot° shall have ten hoops, and I will make it felony to drink small° beer. All the realm shall be in common, and in Cheapside shall my palfrey° go to grass. And when I am King, as King I will   75 be ——

ALL. God save your Majesty!

CADE. I thank you, good people. There shall be no money. All shall eat and drink on my score,° and I will apparel them all in one livery,° that   80 they may agree like brothers, and worship me their lord.

DICK. The first thing we do, let's kill all the lawyers.

CADE. Nay, that I mean to do. Is not this a   85 lamentable thing, that of the skin of an innocent lamb should be made parchment? That parchment, being scribbled o'er, should undo a man? Some say the bee stings; but I say, 'tis the bee's wax,° for I did but seal° once to a thing, and I was never mine own man since. How now! Who's there?   91

[*Enter some, bringing forward the* CLERK OF CHATHAM.]

SMITH. The clerk of Chatham. He can write and read and cast accompt.°

CADE. Oh, monstrous!

SMITH. We took him setting of boys' copies.°   95

CADE. Here's a villain!

SMITH. Has a book in his pocket with red letters in 't.

CADE. Nay, then, he is a conjuror.

DICK. Nay, he can make obligations,° and write court hand.°   101

CADE. I am sorry for 't. The man is a proper° man, of mine honor. Unless I find him guilty, he shall not die. Come hither, sirrah, I must examine thee. What is thy name?   105

CLERK. Emmanuel.

DICK. They use to write it on the top of letters.°

26. dog's leather: used for making gloves.   31. Argo: for *ergo*, therefore.   32. s.d., sawyer: one who saws lumber.   34. supposed father: Cade pretended that his real father was Mortimer. See III.ii.355–81.   35. cade: herring barrel.   51. furred pack: skin bag. bucks: dirty clothes.   55. under a hedge: i.e., as a homeless beggar.   56. cage: parish lockup.

65. coat . . . proof: lit., armor of fine tested quality, but Cade's coat has been tested by whipping.   67. burnt . . . hand: sheep stealers who escaped hanging were branded.   72. three-hooped pot: The quart drinking pot was made of wood with three hoops. A ten-hooped pot would contain more than three quarts.   73. small: weak.   74. palfrey: riding horse.   79. on my score: at my charge.   80. livery: uniform.   89. bee's wax: used for sealing wax.   90. seal: i.e., put my seal on an agreement.   93. cast accompt: keep accounts.   95. setting . . . copies: teaching boys to write.   100. obligations: contracts, bonds.   101. court hand: the type of handwriting used by lawyers.   102. proper: handsome.   106–07. Emmanuel . . . letters: It was a pious custom to head letters with the word *Emmanuel* (God with us).

'Twill go hard with you.

CADE. Let me alone. Dost thou use to write thy name? Or hast thou a mark to thyself,° like an honest plain-dealing man?   111

CLERK. Sir, I thank God, I have been so well brought up that I can write my name.

ALL. He hath confessed. Away with him! He's a villain and a traitor.   115

CADE. Away with him, I say! Hang him with his pen and inkhorn° about his neck.

[*Exit one with the* CLERK.]
[*Enter* MICHAEL.]

MICH. Where's our General?

CADE. Here I am, thou particular fellow.   119

MICH. Fly, fly, fly! Sir Humphrey Stafford and his brother are hard by,° with the King's forces.

CADE. Stand, villain, stand, or I'll fell thee down. He shall be encountered with a man as good as himself. He is but a knight, is a'?   125

MICH. No.

CADE. To equal him, I will make myself a knight presently. [*Kneels.*] Rise up, Sir John Mortimer.° [*Rises.*] Now have at him!

[*Enter* SIR HUMPHREY STAFFORD *and his* BROTHER, *with drum and* SOLDIERS.]

STAF. Rebellious hinds, the filth and scum of Kent,   130
Marked for the gallows, lay your weapons down. Home to your cottages, forsake this groom. The King is merciful if you revolt.

BRO. But angry, wrathful, and inclined to blood, If you go forward. Therefore yield, or die.   135

CADE. As for these silken-coated slaves, I pass° not.
It is to you, good people, that I speak, Over whom, in time to come, I hope to reign; For I am rightful heir unto the crown.

STAF. Villain, thy father was a plasterer,   140
And thou thyself a shearman,° art thou not?

CADE. And Adam was a gardener.

BRO. And what of that?

CADE. Marry, this: Edmund Mortimer, Earl of March,
Married the Duke of Clarence' daughter, did he not?   145

STAF. Aye, sir.

CADE. By her he had two children at one birth.

BRO. That's false.

CADE. Aye, there's the question, but I say 'tis true. The elder of them, being put to nurse,   150

Was by a beggar woman stolen away, And, ignorant of his birth and parentage, Became a bricklayer when he came to age. His son am I. Deny it if you can.

DICK. Nay, 'tis too true. Therefore he shall be king.   155

SMITH. Sir, he made a chimney in my father's house, and the bricks are alive at this day to testify it. Therefore deny it not.

STAF. And will you credit this base drudge's words,
That speaks he knows not what?   160

ALL. Aye, marry, will we. Therefore get ye gone.

BRO. Jack Cade, the Duke of York hath taught you this.

CADE. [*Aside*] He lies, for I invented it myself. Go to, sirrah, tell the King from me, that for his father's sake, Henry the Fifth, in whose time   165 boys went to span-counter° for French crowns, I am content he shall reign, but I'll be Protector over him.

DICK. And, furthermore, we'll have the Lord Say's head for selling the Dukedom of Maine.   170

CADE. And good reason, for thereby is England mained and fain to go with° a staff, but that my puissance° holds it up. Fellow Kings, I tell you that that Lord Say hath gelded the commonwealth   175 and made it a eunuch. And more than that, he can speak French, and therefore he is a traitor.

STAF. Oh, gross and miserable ignorance!

CADE. Nay, answer if you can. The Frenchmen are our enemies. Go to, then, I ask but this: 180 Can he that speaks with the tongue of an enemy be a good counselor, or no?

ALL. No, no, and therefore we'll have his head.

BRO. Well, seeing gentle words will not prevail, Assail them with the army of the King.   185

STAF. Herald, away, and throughout every town Proclaim them traitors that are up with Cade, That those which fly before the battle ends May, even in their wives' and children's sight, Be hanged up for example at their doors.   190
And you that be the King's friends, follow me.

[*Exeunt the two* STAFFORDS, *and* SOLDIERS.]

CADE. And you that love the commons, follow me. Now show yourselves men. 'Tis for liberty. We will not leave one lord, one gentleman. Spare none but such as go in clouted shoon,°   195 For they are thrifty honest men, and such As would, but that they dare not, take our parts.

DICK. They are all in order and march toward us.

CADE. But then are we in order when we are   199 most out of order. Come, march forward. [*Exeunt.*]

---

110. hast . . . thyself: do you use a mark instead of a signature. 117. inkhorn: portable ink pot. 121. hard by: nearby. 127–28. make . . . Mortimer: In the ceremony of knighthood, the recipient kneels before the king or his representative, who touches him on the shoulder with the blade of a sword, saying, "Rise, Sir John!" Cade knights himself. 136. pass: care. 141. shearman: one who shears woolen cloth.

166. span-counter: a game in which the first player tosses a counter or coin and the opponent throws another to hit it or come within a span (nine inches) of it. 172. fain . . . with: forced to go with the aid of. 173. puissance: might. 195. clouted shoon: patched shoes — the mark of a poor man.

SCENE III. *Another part of Blackheath.*

[*Alarums to the fight, wherein both the* STAFFORDS *are slain. Enter* CADE *and the rest.*]

CADE. Where's Dick, the butcher of Ashford?

DICK. Here, sir.

CADE. They fell before thee like sheep and oxen, and thou behavedst thyself as if thou hadst been in thine own slaughterhouse. Therefore thus will I   5
reward thee: The Lent° shall be as long again as it is, and thou shalt have a license to kill for a hundred lacking one.°

DICK. I desire no more.   10

CADE. And, to speak truth, thou deservest no less. This monument of the victory will I bear [*putting on* SIR HUMPHREY'S *brigandine*°], and the bodies shall be dragged at my horse heels till I do come to London, where we will have the Mayor's sword° borne before us.   16

DICK. If we mean to thrive and do good, break open the jails and let out the prisoners.

CADE. Fear not that, I warrant thee. Come, let's march towards London.   [*Exeunt.*]   20

SCENE IV. *London. The palace.*

(*Enter the* KING *with a supplication,° and the* QUEEN *with* SUFFOLK'S *head, the* DUKE OF BUCKINGHAM, *and the* LORD SAY.]

QUEEN. Oft have I heard that grief softens the mind
And makes it fearful and degenerate.
Think therefore on revenge, and cease to weep.
But who can cease to weep, and look on this?
Here may his head lie on my throbbing breast: 5
But where's the body that I should embrace?

BUCK. What answer makes your Grace to the rebels' supplication?

KING. I'll send some holy bishop to entreat,
For God forbid so many simple souls   10
Should perish by the sword! And I myself,
Rather than bloody war shall cut them short,
Will parley with Jack Cade their General.
But stay, I'll read it over once again.

QUEEN. Ah, barbarous villains! Hath this lovely face   15
Ruled, like a wandering planet,° over me,
And could it not enforce them to relent
That were unworthy to behold the same?

KING. Lord Say, Jack Cade hath sworn to have thy head.

SAY. Aye, but I hope your Highness shall have his.   20

KING. How now, madam!
Still lamenting and mourning for Suffolk's death?
I fear me, love, if that I had been dead,
Thou wouldest not have mourned so much for me.

QUEEN. No, my love, I should not mourn, but die for thee.   25

[*Enter a* MESSENGER.]

KING. How now! What news? Why comest thou in such haste?

MESS. The rebels are in Southwark.° Fly, my lord!
Jack Cade proclaims himself Lord Mortimer,
Descended from the Duke of Clarence' house,
And calls your Grace usurper openly,   30
And vows to crown himself in Westminster.
His army is a raggèd multitude
Of hinds and peasants, rude and merciless.
Sir Humphrey Stafford and his brother's death
Hath given them heart and courage to proceed.   35
All scholars, lawyers, courtiers, gentlemen,
They call false caterpillars° and intend their death.

KING. Oh, graceless men! They know not what they do.

BUCK. My gracious lord, retire to Killingworth
Until a power° be raised to put them down.   40

QUEEN. Ah, were the Duke of Suffolk now alive,
These Kentish rebels would be soon appeased!°

KING. Lord Say, the traitors hate thee.
Therefore away with us to Killingworth.

SAY. So might your Grace's person be in danger.
The sight of me is odious in their eyes,   46
And therefore in this city will I stay
And live alone as secret as I may.

[*Enter another* MESSENGER.]

MESS. Jack Cade hath gotten London Bridge.
The citizens fly and forsake their houses.   50
The rascal people, thirsting after prey,
Join with the traitor, and they jointly swear
To spoil° the city and your royal Court.

BUCK. Then linger not, my lord. Away, take horse!

KING. Come, Margaret. God, our hope, will succor us.   55

QUEEN. My hope is gone, now Suffolk is deceased.

KING. Farewell, my lord. Trust not the Kentish rebels.

BUCK. Trust nobody, for fear you be betrayed.

SAY. The trust I have is in mine innocence,
And therefore am I bold and resolute. [*Exeunt.*]   60

Sc. iii: 6. Lent: See Gen. Intro. pp. 17b–18a.   7. hundred . . . one: i.e., to supply meat for ninety-nine families.   13. s.d., brigandine: coat of mail. This stage direction was added by editors from the *Chronicle*.   15. Mayor's sword: A sword of state is still carried before the Lord Mayor of London on state occasions.
Sc. iv: s.d., supplication: petition.   16. wandering planet: See App. I.

27. Southwark: pronounced "Suth'ark." See Gen. Intro. p. 16b and Pl. 3a.   37. caterpillars: See *Rich II*, II.iii.166,n.   40. power: army.   42. appeased: pacified.   53. spoil: loot.

SCENE V. *London. The Tower.*

[*Enter* LORD SCALES *upon the Tower,°* walking.
Then enter two or three CITIZENS *below.*]

SCALES. How now! Is Jack Cade slain?

1. CIT. No, my lord, nor likely to be slain, for they have won the Bridge, killing all those that withstand them. The Lord Mayor craves aid of your 5 Honor from the Tower to defend the city from the rebels.

SCALES. Such aid as I can spare you shall command,

But I am troubled here with them myself.
The rebels have assayed to win the Tower.
But get you to Smithfield° and gather head,° 10
And thither I will send you Matthew Goffe.
Fight for your King, your country, and your lives.
And so, farewell, for I must hence again. [*Exeunt.*]

SCENE VI. *London. Cannon Street.*

[*Enter* JACK CADE *and the rest, and strikes his staff on London Stone.°*]

CADE. Now is Mortimer lord of this city. And here, sitting upon London Stone, I charge and command that, of the city's cost, the pissing conduit° run nothing but claret wine this first year of our reign. And now henceforward it shall be treason 5 for any that calls me other than Lord Mortimer.

[*Enter a* SOLDIER, *running.*]

SOLD. Jack Cade! Jack Cade!

CADE. Knock him down there. [*They kill him.*]

SMITH. If this fellow be wise, he'll never call 10 ye Jack Cade more. I think he hath a very fair warning.

DICK. My lord, there's an army gathered together in Smithfield.

CADE. Come, then, let's go fight with them; 15 but first go and set London Bridge on fire, and if you can, burn down the Tower too. Come, let's away. [*Exeunt.*]

SCENE VII. *London. Smithfield.*

[*Alarums.* MATTHEW GOFFE *is slain, and all the rest. Then enter* JACK CADE, *with his company.*]

CADE. So, sirs. Now go some and pull down the Savoy,° others to the Inns of Court.° Down with them all.

DICK. I have a suit° unto your lordship.

CADE. Be it a lordship, thou shalt have it for that word. 6

DICK. Only that the laws of England may come out of your mouth.

HOL. [*Aside*] Mass, 'twill be sore law, then, for he was thrust in the mouth with a spear, and 'tis not whole yet. 11

SMITH. [*Aside*] Nay, John, it will be stinking law, for his breath stinks with eating toasted cheese.

CADE. I have thought upon it, it shall be so. 15 Away, burn all the records of the realm. My mouth shall be the Parliament of England.

HOL. [*Aside*] Then we are like to have biting statutes,° unless his teeth be pulled out.

CADE. And henceforward all things shall be in common. 21

[*Enter a* MESSENGER.]

MESS. My lord, a prize, a prize! Here's the Lord Say, which sold the towns in France — he that made us pay one and twenty fifteens° and one shilling to the pound the last subsidy.° 25

[*Enter* GEORGE BEVIS, *with the* LORD SAY.]

CADE. Well, he shall be beheaded for it ten times. Ah, thou say, thou serge, nay, thou buckram° lord! Now art thou within point-blank° of our jurisdiction regal. What canst thou answer to my Majesty for giving up of Normandy unto Mounsieur 30 Basimecu,° the Dauphin° of France? Be it known unto thee by these presence, even the presence of Lord Mortimer, that I am the besom° that must sweep the Court clean of such filth as thou art. 35 Thou hast most traitorously corrupted the youth of the realm in erecting a grammar school. And whereas before, our forefathers had no other books but the score° and the tally,° thou hast caused 40 printing° to be used, and, contrary to the King, his crown, and dignity, thou hast built a papermill. It will be proved to thy face that thou hast men about thee that usually talk of a noun, and a verb, and such abominable words as no Christian ear can 45 endure to hear. Thou hast appointed justices of peace to call poor men before them about matters they were not able to answer. Moreover, thou hast

---

4. **suit:** petition.   19. **statutes:** acts of Parliament.   24. **fifteens:** tax of one-fifteenth on the rent of land.   25. **subsidy:** tax raised for a special purpose to supplement the king's regular income. 27. **say . . . serge . . . buckram:** puns on different kinds of material: *say* (silk cloth), *serge* (coarse woolen cloth), *buckram* (coarse linen, like denim).   28. **point-blank:** close range. 31. **Basimecu:** kiss-my-tail. **Dauphin:** the heir to the French throne.   33. **besom:** broom made out of twigs.   40. **score:** an account for drink written up in chalk on the inside of the tavern door. **tally:** a primitive method of keeping accounts. Creditor and debtor each kept a stick on which the account was recorded by cutting notches.   41. **printing:** an anachronism, as printing was first used in London in 1474. Cade's rebellion occurred in 1450.

Sc. v: s.d., **the Tower:** See Gen. Intro. p. 16a and Pl. 3a.
10. **Smithfield:** the butchers' quarter in London. **head:** forces.
Sc. vi: s.d., **London Stone:** a famous stone, of immemorial antiquity, used as a landmark.   3. **pissing conduit:** a well-known fountain in the City of London.
Sc. vii: 2. **Savoy:** a great house in London, near the Inns of Court, used as a guest house by those having business in the law courts.   **Inns of Court:** See Gen. Intro. pp. 31b–32a.

put them in prison, and because they could   49
not read,° thou hast hanged them, when, indeed,
only for that cause they have been most worthy to
live. Thou dost ride in a footcloth,° dost thou not?

SAY. What of that?

CADE. Marry, thou oughtest not to let thy horse
wear a cloak when honester men than thou go in
their hose and doublets.°   56

DICK. And work in their shirt too, as myself, for
example, that am a butcher.

SAY. You men of Kent——

DICK. What say you of Kent?   60

SAY. Nothing but this: 'Tis " *bona terra, mala
gens.*"°

CADE. Away with him, away with him! He speaks
Latin.

SAY. Hear me but speak, and bear me where you
will.
Kent, in the *Commentaries* Caesar writ,   65
Is termed the civil'st place of all this isle.
Sweet is the country, because full of riches,
The people liberal, valiant, active, wealthy,
Which makes me hope you are not void of pity.
I sold not Maine, I lost not Normandy,   70
Yet, to recover them, would lose my life.
Justice with favor° have I always done;
Prayers and tears have moved me, gifts could never.
When have I aught exacted at your hands
But to maintain the King, the realm, and you?   75
Large gifts have I bestowed on learnèd clerks
Because my book° preferred° me to the King,
And, seeing ignorance is the curse of God,
Knowledge the wing wherewith we fly to Heaven,
Unless you be possessed with devilish spirits,   80
You cannot but forbear to murder me.
This tongue hath parleyed unto foreign kings
For your behoof——

CADE. Tut, when struck'st thou one blow in the
field?   85

SAY. Great men have reaching° hands. Oft have
I struck
Those that I never saw, and struck them dead.

GEO. Oh, monstrous coward! What, to come behind folks?

SAY. These cheeks are pale for watching for your
good.   90

CADE. Give him a box o' the ear and that will
make 'em red again.

SAY. Long sitting to determine poor men's causes
Hath made me full of sickness and diseases.

CADE. Ye shall have a hempen caudle° then and
the help of hatchet.   96

DICK. Why dost thou quiver, man?

SAY. The palsy, and not fear, provokes me.

CADE. Nay, he nods at us, as who should say, " I'll
be even with you." I'll see if his head will   100
stand steadier on a pole, or no. Take him away, and
behead him.

SAY. Tell me wherein have I offended most?
Have I affected wealth or honor? Speak.
Are my chests filled up with extorted gold?   105
Is my apparel sumptuous to behold?
Whom have I injured, that ye seek my death?
These hands are free from guiltless blood-shedding,
This breast from harboring foul deceitful thoughts.
Oh, let me live!   111

CADE. [*Aside*] I feel remorse in myself with his
words; but I'll bridle it. He shall die, an it be but for
pleading so well for his life. Away with him! He
has a familiar° under his tongue. He speaks   115
not o' God's name. Go, take him away, I say, and
strike off his head presently; and then break into
his son-in-law's house, Sir James Cromer, and strike
off his head, and bring them both upon two poles
hither.

ALL. It shall be done.   120

SAY. Ah, countrymen! If when you make your
prayers,
God should be so obdurate° as yourselves,
How would it fare with your departed souls?
And therefore yet relent, and save my life.   124

CADE. Away with him and do as I command ye.

[*Exeunt some with* LORD SAY.]
The proudest peer in the realm shall not wear a
head on his shoulders unless he pay me tribute.
There shall not a maid be married, but she shall pay
to me her maidenhead ere they have it. Men   130
shall hold of me *in capite;*° and we charge and command that their wives be as free as heart can wish
or tongue can tell.

DICK. My lord, when shall we go to Cheapside
and take up commodities upon our bills?°   135

CADE. Marry, presently.

ALL. Oh, brave!

[*Re-enter one with the heads.*]

CADE. But is not this braver? Let them kiss one
another, for they loved well when they were alive.
Now part them again, lest they consult about   140
the giving up of some more towns in France. Soldiers, defer the spoil of the city until night; for with
these borne before us, instead of maces, will we ride
through the streets, and at every corner have them
kiss. Away!   [*Exeunt.*]   145

49-50. because . . . read: i.e., their "neck verse" to claim benefit
of clergy. See Gen. Intro. p. 28a.   52. footcloth: See IV.i.54,n.
56. hose . . . doublets: coat and breeches. Fashionable gentlemen
always wore a cloak in addition.   61. bona . . . gens: a good
country but an evil race.   72. favor: lenience.   77. book: i.e.,
book learning. preferred: promoted.   86. reaching: i.e., which
can influence many.

95. caudle: "nightcap," hot drink given to invalids.   115. familiar: familiar spirit.   122. obdurate: hard-hearted.   131. *in
capite:* by direct grant — a legal term.   135. take . . . bills:
lit., acquire goods on credit, with a pun on *bills* — weapons.

Let this my sword report what speech forbears.

CADE. By my valor, the most complete champion
that ever I heard! Steel, if thou turn the edge, or cut
not out the burly-boned° clown in chines° of   60
beef ere thou sleep in thy sheath, I beseech God on
my knees thou mayst be turned to hobnails. [*Here
they fight.* CADE *falls.*] Oh, I am slain! Famine and
no other hath slain me. Let ten thousand devils   65
come against me and give me but the ten meals I
have lost, and I'd defy them all. Wither, garden,
and be henceforth a burying place to all that do
dwell in this house, because the unconquered soul
of Cade is fled.   70

IDEN. Is 't Cade that I have slain, that monstrous
traitor?
Sword, I will hallow° thee for this thy deed,
And hang thee o'er my tomb when I am dead.
Ne'er shall this blood be wipèd from thy point,
But thou shalt wear it as a herald's coat°   75
To emblaze° the honor that thy master got.

CADE. Iden, farewell, and be proud of thy victory.
Tell Kent from me, she hath lost her best man,
and exhort all the world to be cowards; for I, that
never feared any, am vanquished by famine, not by
valor.   [*Dies.*]   81

IDEN. How much thou wrong'st me, Heaven be
my judge.
Die, damnèd wretch, the curse of her that bare thee;
And as I thrust thy body in with my sword,
So wish I, I might thrust thy soul to Hell.   85
Hence will I drag thee headlong by the heels
Unto a dunghill which shall be thy grave,
And there cut off thy most ungracious head,
Which I will bear in triumph to the King,   89
Leaving thy trunk for crows to feed upon.   [*Exit.*]

Act V

SCENE I. *Fields between Dartford
and Blackheath.*

[*Enter* YORK, *and his army of Irish, with drum and
colors.*°]

YORK. From Ireland thus comes York to claim his
right
And pluck the crown from feeble Henry's head.
Ring, bells, aloud! Burn, bonfires, clear and bright,
To entertain great England's lawful King.
Ah! *Sancta majestas,*° who would not buy thee
dear?   5

Let them obey that know not how to rule.
This hand was made to handle naught but gold.
I cannot give due action to my words
Except a sword or scepter balance it.
A scepter shall it have, have I° a soul,   10
On which I'll toss° the flower-de-luce° of France.
           [*Enter* BUCKINGHAM.]
Whom have we here? Buckingham, to disturb me?
The King hath sent him, sure. I must dissemble.°

BUCK. York, if thou meanest well, I greet thee
well.

YORK. Humphrey of Buckingham, I accept thy
greeting.   15
Art thou a messenger, or come of pleasure?

BUCK. A messenger from Henry, our dread liege,
To know the reason of these arms in peace;
Or why thou, being a subject as I am,
Against thy oath and true allegiance sworn,   20
Should raise so great a power without his leave,
Or dare to bring thy force so near the Court.

YORK. [*Aside*] Scarce can I speak, my choler° is
so great.
Oh, I could hew up rocks and fight with flint,
I am so angry at these abject terms;°   25
And now, like Ajax Telamonius,°
On sheep or oxen could I spend my fury.
I am far better born than is the King,
More like a king, more kingly in my thoughts.
But I must make fair weather° yet a while   30
Till Henry be more weak and I more strong. —
Buckingham, I prithee pardon me
That I have given no answer all this while.
My mind was troubled with deep melancholy.
The cause why I have brought this army hither   35
Is to remove proud Somerset from the King,
Seditious to his Grace and to the state.

BUCK. That is too much presumption on thy part.
But if thy arms be to no other end,
The King hath yielded unto thy demand.   40
The Duke of Somerset is in the Tower.

YORK. Upon thine honor, is he prisoner?

BUCK. Upon mine honor, he is prisoner.

YORK. Then, Buckingham, I do dismiss my pow-
ers. —
Soldiers, I thank you all. Disperse yourselves.   45
Meet me tomorrow in Saint George's Field,°
You shall have pay and everything you wish.
And let my sovereign, virtuous Henry,
Command my eldest son — nay, all my sons —
As pledges° of my fealty° and love.   50
I'll send them all as willing as I live.

---

10. have I: as sure as I have.   11. toss: carry aloft. flower-de-
luce: fleur-de-lys, the emblem of France.   13. dissemble: pretend, conceal my real feelings.   23. choler: anger.   25. abject
terms: insulting words.   26. Ajax Telamonius: See *T Andr*
I.i.379–81,n.   30. make . . . weather: fall in with the times.
46. Saint George's Field: an open space on the south bank of
the Thames.   50. pledges: pawns, hostages. fealty: loyalty.

---

60. burly-boned: hulking. chines: roasts.   72. hallow: treat
as a holy relic.   75. herald's coat: See App. 9.   76. emblaze:
paint, signify.

Act V. Sc. i: s.d., colors: flags.   5. *Sancta majestas:* sacred
majesty.

Lands, goods, horse, armor, anything I have
Is his to use, so Somerset may die.
　　BUCK. York, I commend this kind submission.
We twain will go into His Highness' tent.　　55
　　　　　[*Enter* KING *and* ATTENDANTS.]
　　KING. Buckingham, doth York intend no harm to
　　　us,
That thus he marcheth with thee arm in arm?
　　YORK. In all submission and humility
York doth present himself unto your Highness.
　　KING. Then what intends these forces thou dost
　　　bring?　　60
　　YORK. To heave the traitor Somerset from hence
And fight against that monstrous rebel Cade,
Who since I heard to be discomfited.
　　　　　[*Enter* IDEN, *with* CADE's *head.*]
　　IDEN. If one so rude and of so mean condition°
May pass into the presence of a king,　　65
Lo, I present your Grace a traitor's head,
The head of Cade, whom I in combat slew.
　　KING. The head of Cade! Great God, how just
　　　art Thou!
Oh, let me view his visage, being dead,
That living wrought me such exceeding trouble.　70
Tell me, my friend, art thou the man that slew
　　　him?
　　IDEN. I was, an 't like° your Majesty.
　　KING. How art thou called? And what is thy
　　　degree?
　　IDEN. Alexander Iden, that's my name;
A poor esquire of Kent, that loves his King.　75
　　BUCK. So please it you, my lord, 'twere not amiss
He were created knight for his good service.
　　KING. Iden, kneel down. [*He kneels.*] Rise up a
　　　knight.
We give thee for reward a thousand marks°
And will that thou henceforth attend on us.　　80
　　IDEN. May Iden live to merit such a bounty,
And never live but true unto his liege!°　[*Rises.*]
　　　　　[*Enter* QUEEN *and* SOMERSET.]
　　KING. See, Buckingham, Somerset comes with the
　　　Queen.
Go bid her hide him quickly from the Duke.
　　QUEEN. For thousand Yorks he shall not hide his
　　　head,　　85
But boldly stand and front him to his face.
　　YORK. How now! Is Somerset at liberty?
Then, York, unloose thy long-imprisoned thoughts
And let thy tongue be equal with thy heart.
Shall I endure the sight of Somerset?　　90
False King! Why hast thou broken faith with me,
Knowing how hardly I can brook abuse?°
King did I call thee? No, thou art not King,

Not fit to govern and rule multitudes,
Which darest not, no, nor canst not rule a traitor.
That head of thine doth not become a crown.　96
Thy hand is made to grasp a palmer's° staff,
And not to grace an awful princely scepter.
That gold° must round engirt° these brows of
　　mine,
Whose smile and frown, like to Achilles' spear,°
Is able with the change to kill and cure.　　101
Here is a hand to hold a scepter up,
And with the same to act controlling laws.
Give place. By Heaven, thou shalt rule no more
O'er him whom Heaven created for thy ruler.　105
　　SOM. Oh, monstrous traitor! I arrest thee, York,
Of capital° treason 'gainst the King and Crown.
Obey, audacious traitor. Kneel for grace.
　　YORK. Wouldst have me kneel? First let me ask
　　　of these
If they can brook I bow a knee to man.　　110
Sirrah, call in my sons to be my bail.
　　　　　　　　　[*Exit* ATTENDANT.]
I know, ere they will have me go to ward,°
They'll pawn their swords for my enfranchisement.°
　　QUEEN. Call hither Clifford. Bid him come
　　　amain°
To say if that the bastard boys of York　　115
Shall be the surety for their traitor father.
　　　　　　　　　[*Exit* BUCKINGHAM.]
　　YORK. O blood-bespotted Neapolitan,°
Outcast of Naples, England's bloody scourge!
The sons of York, thy betters in their birth,
Shall be their father's bail; and bane° to those　120
That for my surety will refuse the boys!
　　　　　[*Enter* EDWARD *and* RICHARD.]
See where they come. I'll warrant they'll make it
　　good.
　[*Enter* CLIFFORD *and his son,* YOUNG CLIFFORD.]
　　QUEEN. And here comes Clifford to deny their
　　　bail.
　　CLIF. Health and all happiness to my lord the
　　　King!　　　　　　　　[*Kneels.*]
　　YORK. I thank thee, Clifford. Say, what news with
　　　thee?　　125
Nay, do not fright us with an angry look.
We are thy sovereign, Clifford, kneel again.
For thy mistaking, so, we pardon thee.
　　CLIF. This is my King, York, I do not mistake,
But thou mistakest me much to think I do.　130
To Bedlam° with him! Is the man grown mad?

97. palmer: pilgrim.　**99. gold:** crown. **round engirt:** encircle.
100. Achilles' spear: made for him by Vulcan, the blacksmith
god. It was able to heal as well as kill by touch.　**107. capital:**
deserving death.　**112. ward:** prison.　**113. enfranchisement:**
liberty.　**114. amain:** speedily.　**117. Neapolitan:** because her
father was Reignier King of Naples. See I.i.47.　**120. bane:**
destruction.　**131. Bedlam:** i.e., Bethlehem, the London hospital
for lunatics.

64. condition: i.e., rank.　**72. an't like:** if it please.　**79. marks:**
13s 4d — two-thirds of a pound.　**82. liege:** lord.　**92. abuse:**
misuse, shameful treatment.

KING. Aye, Clifford, a bedlam and ambitious
    humor°
Makes him oppose himself against his King.
  CLIF. He is a traitor. Let him to the Tower
And chop away that factious pate° of his.   135
  QUEEN. He is arrested, but will not obey.
His sons, he says, shall give their words for him.
  YORK. Will you not, sons?
  EDW. Aye, noble Father, if our words will serve.
  RICH. And if words will not, then our weapons
    shall.   140
  CLIF. Why, what a brood of traitors have we
    here!
  YORK. Look in a glass, and call thy image so.
I am thy King, and thou a false-heart traitor.
Call hither to the stake° my two brave bears,
That with the very shaking of their chains   145
They may astonish these fell-lurking° curs.
Bid Salisbury and Warwick come to me.
  [*Enter the* EARLS OF WARWICK *and* SALISBURY.]
  CLIF. Are these thy bears? We'll bait thy bears to
    death
And manacle the bearward° in their chains
If thou darest bring them to the baiting place. 150
  RICH. Oft have I seen a hot o'erweening° cur
Run back and bite because he was withheld;
Who, being suffered with the bear's fell paw,
Hath clapped his tail between his legs and cried.
And such a piece of service will you do   155
If you oppose yourselves to match Lord Warwick.
  CLIF. Hence, heap of wrath, foul indigested
    lump,°
As crooked in thy manners as thy shape!
  YORK. Nay, we shall heat° you thoroughly anon.
  CLIF. Take heed, lest by your heat you burn
    yourselves.   160
  KING. Why, Warwick, hath thy knee forgot to
    bow?
Old Salisbury, shame to thy silver hair,
Thou mad misleader of thy brain-sick son!
What, wilt thou on thy deathbed play the ruffian,
And seek for sorrow with thy spectacles?   165
Oh, where is faith? Oh, where is loyalty?
If it be banished from the frosty° head,
Where shall it find a harbor in the earth?
Wilt thou go dig a grave to find out war,
And shame thine honorable age with blood?   170
Why art thou old, and want'st experience?
Or wherefore dost abuse it, if thou hast it?
For shame! In duty bend thy knee to me,

That bows unto the grave with mickle° age.
  SAL. My lord, I have considered with myself 175
The title of this most renownèd Duke,
And in my conscience do repute His Grace
The rightful heir to England's royal seat.
  KING. Hast thou not sworn allegiance unto me?
  SAL. I have.   180
  KING. Canst thou dispense° with Heaven for
    such an oath?
  SAL. It is great sin to swear unto a sin,
But greater sin to keep a sinful oath.
Who can be bound by any solemn vow
To do a murderous deed, to rob a man,   185
To force a spotless virgin's chastity,
To reave° the orphan of his patrimony,
To wring the widow from° her customed right,
And have no other reason for this wrong
But that he was bound by a solemn oath?   190
  QUEEN. A subtle traitor needs no sophister.°
  KING. Call Buckingham, and bid him arm him-
    self.
  YORK. Call Buckingham, and all the friends thou
    hast.
I am resolved for death or dignity.
  CLIF. The first I warrant thee, if dreams prove
    true.   195
  WAR. You were best to go to bed and dream again
To keep thee from the tempest of the field.
  CLIF. I am resolved to bear a greater storm
Than any thou canst conjure up today,
And that I'll write upon thy burgonet,°   200
Might I but know thee by thy household badge.°
  WAR. Now, by my father's badge, old Nevil's crest,
The rampant° bear chained to the ragged° staff,
This day I'll wear aloft my burgonet,
As on a mountain top the cedar shows   205
That keeps his leaves in spite of any storm,
Even to affright thee with the view thereof.
  CLIF. And from thy burgonet I'll rend° thy bear
And tread it under foot with all contempt,
Despite the bearward that protects the bear. 210
  Y. CLIF. And so to arms, victorious Father,
To quell the rebels and their complices.°
  RICH. Fie! Charity, for shame! Speak not in spite,
For you shall sup° with Jesu Christ tonight.
  Y. CLIF. Foul stigmatic,° that's more than thou
    canst tell.   215
  RICH. If not in Heaven, you'll surely sup in Hell.
    [*Exeunt severally.*]

---

132. humor: whim.   135. factious pate: rebellious head.
144–54. stake . . . cried: This elaborate image is taken from the
sport of bearbaiting. See App. 5.   146. fell-lurking: treacherous.
149. bearward: bearkeeper.   151. o'erweening: too proud.
157. foul . . . lump: For the physical deformities of Richard,
afterward Duke of Gloucester and King, see *III Hen VI*,
III.ii.152–62.   159. heat: anger.   167. frosty: white-haired.
174. mickle: great.   181. dispense: come to terms with.
187. reave: rob.   188. wring . . . from: remove by force.
191. sophister: clever debater.   200. burgonet: helmet. See
Pl. 22d.   201. household badge: family crest — described in
l. 203.   203. rampant: standing on its hind legs. ragged:
rough.   208. rend: tear.   212. complices: accomplices.
214. sup: i.e., in Heaven.   215. stigmatic: branded; i.e.,
marked as foul by your deformity.

SCENE II. *Saint Alban's.*

[Alarums to the battle. Enter WARWICK.*]*

WAR. Clifford of Cumberland, 'tis Warwick calls.
And if thou dost not hide thee from the bear,
Now, when the angry trumpet sounds alarum
And dead men's cries do fill the empty air,
Clifford, I say, come forth and fight with me.   5
Proud northern lord, Clifford of Cumberland,
Warwick is hoarse with calling thee to arms.

[Enter YORK.*]*

How now, my noble lord! What, all afoot?
   YORK. The deadly-handed Clifford slew my steed,
But match to match I have encountered him   10
And made a prey for carrion kites and crows
Even of the bonny beast he loved so well.

[Enter CLIFFORD.*]*

   WAR. Of one or both of us the time is come.
   YORK. Hold, Warwick, seek thee out some other
     chase,°
For I myself must hunt this deer to death.   15
   WAR. Then, nobly, York. 'Tis for a crown thou
     fight'st.
As I intend, Clifford, to thrive today,
It grieves my soul to leave thee unassailed.   *[Exit.]*
   CLIF. What seest thou in me, York? Why dost
     thou pause?
   YORK. With thy brave bearing° should I be in
     love,   20
But that thou art so fast mine enemy.
   CLIF. Nor should thy prowess want praise and
     esteem
But that 'tis shown ignobly and in treason.
   YORK. So let it help me now against thy sword,
As I in justice and true right express it.   25
   CLIF. My soul and body on the action both!
   YORK. A dreadful lay!° Address thee instantly.

[They fight, and CLIFFORD *falls.]*

   CLIF. *La fin couronne les oeuvres.*°   *[Dies.]*
   YORK. Thus war hath given thee peace, for thou
     art still.
Peace with his soul, Heaven, if it be Thy will!   30
         [Exit.]

[Enter YOUNG CLIFFORD.*]*

Y. CLIF. Shame and confusion! All is on the rout.
Fear frames° disorder, and disorder wounds
Where it should guard. O War, thou son of Hell,
Whom angry Heavens do make their minister,
Throw in the frozen° bosoms of our part°   35
Hot coals of vengeance! Let no soldier fly.
He that is truly dedicate to war
Hath no self-love, nor he that loves himself
Hath not essentially but by circumstance

The name of valor.° *[Seeing his dead father]* Oh,
   let the vile world end   40
And the premisèd° flames of the last day
Knit earth and Heaven together!
Now let the general trumpet blow his blast,
Particularities° and petty sounds
To cease! Wast thou ordained, dear Father,   45
To lose thy youth in peace, and to achieve
The silver livery of advisèd° age,
And, in thy reverence and thy chair days,° thus
To die in ruffian battle? Even at this sight
My heart is turned to stone; and while 'tis mine,   50
It shall be stony. York not our old men spares;
No more will I their babes. Tears virginal°
Shall be to me even as the dew to fire,
And beauty that the tyrant oft reclaims°
Shall to my flaming wrath be oil and flax.   55
Henceforth I will not have to do with pity.
Meet I an infant of the House of York,
Into as many gobbets° will I cut it
As wild Medea young Absyrtus° did.
In cruelty will I seek out my fame.   60
Come, thou new ruin of old Clifford's house.
As did Aeneas old Anchises° bear,
So bear I thee upon my manly shoulders;
But then Aeneas bare a living load,
Nothing so heavy as these woes of mine.   65
     [Exit, bearing off his father.]
[Enter RICHARD *and* SOMERSET *to fight.* SOMERSET *is
     killed.]*

   RICH. So, lie thou there.
For underneath an alehouse' paltry sign,
The Castle in Saint Alban's, Somerset
Hath made the wizard famous in his death.°   69
Sword, hold thy temper.° Heart, be wrathful still.
Priests pray for enemies, but princes kill.   *[Exit.]*
[Fight. Excursions.° Enter KING, QUEEN, *and
     others.]*

   QUEEN. Away, my lord! You are slow. For
     shame, away!
   KING. Can we outrun the Heavens? Good
     Margaret, stay.
   QUEEN. What are you made of? You'll nor fight
     nor fly.

38–40: nor . . . valor: the man that has any thought for himself
is not truly brave, but only by accident.   41. premised: foreordained.   44. Particularities: trifles.   47. advised: wise.
48. chair days: i.e., when you ought to be at ease in your chair.
52. virginal: of virgins.   54. reclaims: subdues.   58. gobbets:
small pieces of meat.   59. Medea . . . Absyrtus: Jason, the
Greek hero, won the Golden Fleece with the aid of the sorceress
Medea, with whom he fled away. To delay pursuit by her father,
Medea slew her brother Absyrtus and cut his body into pieces.
62. Aeneas . . . Anchises: See *Caesar*, I.ii.112,n.   67–69. For
. . . death: Margaret Jourdain's spirit had warned Somerset to
"shun castles" (I.iv. 37–40). Somerset was killed in the streets
of St. Albans, beneath the sign of the Castle Alehouse.
70. temper: quality, hardness.   71. s.d., Excursions: men running to and fro, indicating the fury of battle.

Sc. ii: 14. chase: game.   20. bearing: behavior.   27. lay:
bet, stake.   28. La . . . oeuvres: the end crowns the work.
32. frames: makes.   35. frozen: cold, cowardly. part: party.

Now is it manhood, wisdom, and defense   75
To give the enemy way, and to secure° us
By what we can, which can no more but fly.
                [*Alarum afar off.*]
If you be ta'en, we then should see the bottom
Of all our fortunes; but if we haply scape,
As well we may, if not through your neglect,   80
We shall to London get, where you are loved,
And where this breach° now in our fortunes made
May readily be stopped.
        [*Re-enter* YOUNG CLIFFORD.]
  Y. CLIF. But that my heart's on future mischief
    set,
I would speak blasphemy ere bid you fly.   85
But fly you must. Uncurable discomfit°
Reigns in the hearts of all our present parts.
Away, for your relief, and we will live
To see their day and them our fortune give.°
Away, my lord, away!   [*Exeunt.*]   90

SCENE III. *Fields near St. Alban's.*

[*Alarum. Retreat. Enter* YORK, RICHARD, WARWICK,
   and SOLDIERS, *with drum and colors.*]
  YORK. Of Salisbury, who can report of him,
That winter lion, who in rage forgets
Aged contusions° and all brush° of time,
And, like a gallant in the brow of youth,
Repairs him with occasion?° This happy day   5

Is not itself, nor have we won one foot,
If Salisbury be lost.
  RICH.   My noble Father,
Three times today I holp him to his horse,
Three times bestrid° him. Thrice I led him off,
Persuaded him from any further act.   10
But still, where danger was, still there I met him;
And like rich hangings° in a homely house,
So was his will in his old feeble body.
But, noble as he is, look where he comes.
        [*Enter* SALISBURY.]
  SAL. Now, by my sword, well hast thou fought   15
By the Mass, so did we all. I thank you, Richard.
God knows how long it is I have to live,
And it hath pleased Him that three times today
You have defended me from imminent death.
Well, lords, we have not got that which we have.°
'Tis not enough our foes are this time fled,   21
Being opposites of such repairing nature.°
  YORK. I know our safety is to follow them;
For, as I hear, the King is fled to London
To call a present Court of Parliament.   25
Let us pursue him ere the writs° go forth.
What says Lord Warwick? Shall we after them?
  WAR. After them! Nay, before them, if we can.
Now, by my faith, lords, 'twas a glorious day.
Saint Alban's battle won by famous York   30
Shall be eternized in all age to come.
Sound drums and trumpets, and to London all.
And more such days as these to us befall!
                [*Exeunt.*]

---

76. **secure:** make safe.   82. **breach:** gap.   86. **discomfit:** discouragement.   89. **To . . . give:** to see their unlucky day when they have our bad luck.
   Sc. iii: 3. **contusions . . . brush:** both words mean bruise.
5. **Repairs . . . occasion:** i.e., renews his youth.

9. **bestrid:** stood over when prostrate. See *I Hen IV*, V.i.122.
12. **hangings:** costly tapestry.   20. **got . . . have:** i.e., our victory is not yet complete.   22. **opposites . . . nature:** opponents who can recover their strength.   26. **writs:** official summons to attend.

The Third Part of
KING HENRY THE SIXTH

Introduction

In *III Henry VI*, the pattern of the drama somewhat changes. Hitherto the play has shown certain historical events and persons, as " scenes from history." Now a theme of moral order becomes discernible. Those who commit crimes against divine justice and mercy flourish for a while but end wretchedly.

Richard Duke of York is the first victim of overweening ambition. The Second Part of *Henry VI* had concluded with the triumph of York and Warwick at the battle of St. Albans. The Third Part begins with a scene in Parliament — more symbolic than realistic — in which Richard sets himself on the throne and treats King Henry VI with deliberate contempt. York, however, agrees to the compromise that Henry shall remain nominally King for life but that Richard shall succeed on his death. Queen Margaret and her friends, especially Clifford, will have none of this weakness and withdraw to renew the war. York, on the advice of his youngest son Richard (afterward Duke of Gloucester and King Richard III), breaks his oath to Henry. But at the battle of Wakefield Fortune turns against him; his young son Rutland is cruelly murdered and he himself is captured by the ruthless Margaret, who mocks and taunts him vilely before she herself aids Clifford to stab him.

The claims of York thus fall to his eldest son Edward Earl of March, who still has the all-powerful support of Warwick. For a while, however, the Red Rose of Lancaster is in the ascendant. The two parties defy each other and battle is joined; Edward and his party are defeated and flee for their lives. During the turmoil the poor King wanders in alone and sits down to lament his hard fate — called to be a King yet despised by Queen, friends, and foes. Then Fortune once more changes sides. Clifford, the most ferocious of Queen Margaret's party, is killed, and Edward marches off to London to be crowned King, his first act being to promote his two brothers — Richard to be Duke of Gloucester and George to be Duke of Clarence — while Warwick remains the acknowledged chief prop of the new reign.

In the third act Edward commits the fatal error which ultimately brings about the downfall of his house. While Warwick is in France negotiating a marriage with the French King's sister-in-law, Lady Bona, Edward — always a lustful man — makes love to Lady Grey, a widow who has come to beg for restitution of her husband's lands; but she resists his suggestions until he asks her to marry him and become his Queen.

Richard Duke of Gloucester now reveals himself in a tremendous soliloquy (III.ii.124–95); and from this point until his death in *Richard III* (V.v) he is the dominant figure, a colossal monster of unmitigated evil. Edward's ill-advised marriage alienates Warwick (and even turns him into the ally of the exiled Queen Margaret). It also annoys the King's brothers, Clarence and Gloucester, so that when Warwick returns he justifies his name of " the Kingmaker " by unkinging Edward and restoring Henry VI. However, Edward escapes from his captivity, with the aid of Richard, and rallies his friends. In the battle of Barnet, Warwick is killed (V.ii) and in the final battle at Tewkesbury (V.iii and iv) the last hopes of the Lancastrians are destroyed. Margaret and her son, the young Edward Prince of Wales, are captured, and the boy is mercilessly slain before the eyes of his mother by King Edward and his brothers; Richard rides off to London to murder the saintly King Henry in the Tower. The play thus ends with the triumph of the White Rose of York. Yet a fourth play was needed — *Richard III*, the best of the series — to show the destruction of the House of York and the final restitution of moral order and the triumph of divine retribution.

Although *III Henry VI* is far from being one of Shakespeare's greater plays, it contains some patches of writing that were better than any

Shakespeare had as yet achieved, particularly in the last speeches of York (I.iv.111–68), and the lament of the unhappy King Henry VI (II.v.1–54) which foreshadows the pathos of Richard II in the later play (see especially *Rich II*, III.iii.143–83 and V.v.1–66). There is considerable power, also, in the utterances of Richard of Gloucester, especially in his soliloquies (III.ii.124–95 and V.vi.61–93).

The three parts of *Henry VI* are not much read except by students, yet they have a considerable place in the development of Elizabethan drama, for they were at the time of their writing the best history plays that had yet appeared.

As with *I* and *II Henry VI* the source of the Third Part was mainly the *Chronicles* of Halle and Holinshed, of which the following passages are representative:

1. THE CRUELTY OF CLIFFORD (cf. I.iii and iv)

[Halle tells that during the battle of Wakefield:]

A priest called Sir Robert Aspall, chaplain and schoolmaster to the young Earl of Rutland (second son to the above named Duke of York, scarce of the age of twelve years, a fair gentleman and a maidenlike person), perceiving that flight was more safeguard than tarrying both for him and his master, secretly conveyed the Earl out of the field, by the Lord Clifford's band, toward the town; but, or [before] he could enter into a house, he was by the said Lord Clifford espied, followed, and taken, and by reason of his apparel demanded what he was. The young gentleman, dismayed, had not a word to speak, but kneeled on his knees, imploring mercy and desiring grace, both with holding up his hands and making dolorous countenance, for his speech was gone for fear. " Save him," said his chaplain, " for he is a Prince's son, and peradventure may do you good hereafter." With that word, the Lord Clifford marked him and said, " By God's blood! Thy father slew mine, and so will I do thee and all thy kin!" And with that word, stack the Earl to the heart with his dagger, and bade his chaplain bear the Earl's mother and brother word what he had done and said. In this act the Lord Clifford was accounted a tyrant and no gentleman, for the property of the lion (which is a furious and unreasonable beast) is to be cruel to them that withstand him, and gentle to such as prostrate or humiliate themselves before him.

2. THE WOOING OF THE LADY GREY (cf. III.ii)

[Both Halle and Holinshed record that the King first met the Lady Elizabeth Grey while he was **out hunting.**]

When the King beheld and heard her speak, as she was both fair and of a goodly favor, moderate of stature, well made and very wise, he not only pitied her but also waxed enamored of her. And, taking her afterward secretly aside, began to enter in talking more familiarly. Whose appetite when she perceived, she virtuously denied him.

But that she did so wisely, and with so good manner, and words so well set, that she rather kindled his desire than quenched it. And finally after many a meeting, much wooing, and many great promises, she well espied the King's affection toward her so greatly increased that she durst the more boldly say her mind as to him whose heart she perceived more fervently set than to fall off for a word. And in conclusion she showed him plain that, as she wist herself too simple to be his wife, so she thought herself too good to be his concubine. The King, much marveling at her constancy (as he that had not been wont elsewhere to be so stiffly said nay) so much esteemed her continency and chastity that he set her virtue in the stead of possession and riches; and thus taking counsel of his desire, determined in all possible haste to marry her.

3. THE ANGER OF WARWICK (cf. III.iii)

The French King was not well pleased to be thus dallied with; but he shortly (to appease the grief of his wife and her sister, the Lady Bona) married the said Lady Bona to the Duke of Milan.

Now when the Earl of Warwick had knowledge by letters sent to him out of England from his trusty friends that King Edward had gotten him a new wife, he was not a little troubled in his mind; for that he took it his credence [credit] thereby was greatly minished, and his honor much stained, namely, in the Court of France, for that it might be judged he came rather like an espial, to move a thing never minded, and to treat a marriage determined before not to take effect. Surely he thought himself evil used, that when he brought the matter to his purposed intent and wished conclusion, then to have it quail on his part; so as all men might think at the least wise that his Prince made small account of him to send him on such a sleeveless [futile] errand.

All men for the most part agree that this marriage was the only cause why the Earl of Warwick conceived an hatred against King Edward whom he so much before favored.

At the end of *III Henry VI*, the audience is prepared for *Richard III* which shows how the civil wars finally ended in the establishment of the Tudor dynasty and lasting peace.

Henry VI, Part III

DRAMATIS PERSONAE

KING HENRY *the Sixth*
EDWARD, PRINCE OF WALES, *his son*
LEWIS *the Eleventh, King of France*
DUKE OF SOMERSET
DUKE OF EXETER
EARL OF OXFORD
EARL OF NORTHUMBERLAND
EARL OF WESTMORELAND
LORD CLIFFORD
RICHARD PLANTAGENET, *Duke of York*
EDWARD, *Earl of March, afterward*
  King Edward IV
EDMUND, *Earl of Rutland* }
GEORGE, *afterward Duke of Clarence* } *his sons*
RICHARD, *afterward Duke of Gloucester* }
DUKE OF NORFOLK
MARQUESS OF MONTAGUE
EARL OF WARWICK
EARL OF PEMBROKE
LORD HASTINGS
LORD STAFFORD

SIR JOHN MORTIMER }
SIR HUGH MORTIMER } *uncles to the Duke of York*
HENRY, *Earl of Richmond, a youth*
LORD RIVERS, *brother to Lady Grey*
SIR WILLIAM STANLEY
SIR JOHN MONTGOMERY
SIR JOHN SOMERVILE
TUTOR *to Rutland*
MAYOR *of York*
LIEUTENANT *of the Tower*
A NOBLEMAN
TWO KEEPERS
A HUNTSMAN
A SON *that has killed his father*
A FATHER *that has killed his son*

QUEEN MARGARET
LADY GREY, *afterward Queen to Edward IV*
BONA, *sister to the French Queen*

SOLDIERS, ATTENDANTS, MESSENGERS, WATCHMEN, *&c.*

SCENE — *England and France.*

Act I

SCENE I. *London. The Parliament House.*

[*Alarum.*° *Enter the* DUKE OF YORK, EDWARD,
RICHARD, NORFOLK, MONTAGUE, WARWICK, *and*
SOLDIERS.]
WAR. I wonder how the King escaped our hands.
YORK. While we pursued the horsemen of the
  North,
He slyly stole away and left his men;
Whereat the great Lord of Northumberland,
Whose warlike ears could never brook° retreat, 5
Cheered up the drooping army, and himself,
Lord Clifford, and Lord Stafford, all abreast,
Charged our main battle's front and, breaking in,
Were by the swords of common soldiers slain.
  EDW. Lord Stafford's father, Duke of Bucking-
  ham,   10
Is either slain or wounded dangerously.
I cleft his beaver° with a downright blow.
That this is true, Father, behold his blood.
  MONT. And, Brother, here's the Earl of Wilt-
  shire's blood,

Whom I encountered as the battles joined.   15
  RICH. Speak thou for me, and tell them what I
  did.
    [*Throwing down the* DUKE OF SOMERSET'S *head.*]
  YORK. Richard hath best deserved of all my sons.
But is your Grace dead, my Lord of Somerset?
  NORF. Such hope have all the line of John of
  Gaunt!
  RICH. Thus do I hope to shake King Henry's
  head.   20
  WAR. And so do I. Victorious Prince of York,
Before I see thee seated in that throne
Which now the House of Lancaster usurps,
I vow by Heaven these eyes shall never close.
This is the palace of the fearful° King,   25
And this the regal seat. Possess it, York,
For this is thine, and not King Henry's heirs'.
  YORK. Assist me, then, sweet Warwick, and I
  will,
For hither we have broken in by force.   29
  NORF. We'll all assist you. He that flies shall die.
  YORK. Thanks, gentle Norfolk. Stay by me, my
  lords;
And, soldiers, stay and lodge by me this night.
    [*They go up.*]

Act I, Sc. i: s.d., Alarum: noises of battle.   5. brook: endure.
12. beaver: helmet, lit., the face piece. See Pl. 8a.

25. fearful: full of fear.

WAR. And when the King comes, offer him no
    violence
Unless he seek to thrust you out perforce.°
    YORK. The Queen this day here holds her Par-
      liament,   35
But little thinks we shall be of her council.
By words or blows here let us win our right.
    RICH. Armed as we are, let's stay within this
      house.
    WAR. The bloody Parliament shall this be called
Unless Plantagenet, Duke of York, be King   40
And bashful Henry deposed, whose cowardice
Hath made us bywords to our enemies.
    YORK. Then leave me not, my lords. Be resolute.
I mean to take possession of my right.
    WAR. Neither the King, nor he that loves him
      best,   45
The proudest he that holds up Lancaster,
Dares stir a wing if Warwick shake his bells.°
I'll plant Plantagenet, root him up who dares.
Resolve thee, Richard. Claim the English crown.
    [*Flourish. Enter* KING HENRY, CLIFFORD,
      NORTHUMBERLAND, WESTMORELAND,
        EXETER, *and the rest.*]
    K. HEN. My lords, look where the sturdy rebel
      sits,   50
Even in the chair of state. Belike° he means,
Backed by the power of Warwick, that false peer,
To aspire unto the crown and reign as King.
Earl of Northumberland, he slew thy father,
And thine, Lord Clifford; and you both have
    vowed revenge   55
On him, his sons, his favorites, and his friends.
    NORTH. If I be not, Heavens be revenged on me!
    CLIF. The hope thereof makes Clifford mourn
      in steel.°
    WEST. What, shall we suffer this? Let's pluck him
      down.
My heart for anger burns. I cannot brook it.   60
    K. HEN. Be patient, gentle Earl of Westmoreland.
    CLIF. Patience is for poltroons,° such as he.
He durst not sit there, had your father lived.
My gracious lord, here in the Parliament
Let us assail the family of York.   65
    NORTH. Well hast thou spoken, Cousin. Be it so.
    K. HEN. Ah, know you not the city° favors them,
And they have troops of soldiers at their beck?°
    EXE. But when the Duke is slain, they'll quickly
      fly.
    K. HEN. Far be the thought of this from Henry's
      heart   70

To make a shambles of the Parliament House!
Cousin of Exeter, frowns, words, and threats
Shall be the war that Henry means to use. —
Thou factious° Duke of York, descend my throne,
And kneel for grace and mercy at my feet.   75
I am thy sovereign.
    YORK.   I am thine.
    EXE. For shame, come down. He made thee
      Duke of York.
    YORK. 'Twas my inheritance, as the Earldom°
      was.
    EXE. Thy father was a traitor to the Crown.°
    WAR. Exeter, thou art a traitor to the Crown   80
In following this usurping Henry.
    CLIF. Whom should he follow but his natural
      King?
    WAR. True, Clifford, and that's Richard Duke of
      York.
    K. HEN. And shall I stand, and thou sit in my
      throne?   84
    YORK. It must and shall be so. Content thyself.
    WAR. Be Duke of Lancaster. Let him be King.
    WEST. He is both King and Duke of Lancaster,
And that the Lord of Westmoreland shall maintain.
    WAR. And Warwick shall disprove it. You forget
That we are those which chased you from the field,
And slew your fathers, and with colors° spread   91
Marched through the city to the palace gates.
    NORTH. Yes, Warwick, I remember it to my grief,
And, by his soul, thou and thy house shall rue it.
    WEST. Plantagenet, of thee and these thy sons,   95
Thy kinsmen, and thy friends, I'll have more lives
Than drops of blood were in my father's veins.
    CLIF. Urge it no more, lest that, instead of words,
I send thee, Warwick, such a messenger
As shall revenge his death before I stir.   100
    WAR. Poor Clifford! How I scorn his worthless
      threats!
    YORK. Will you we show our title to the crown?
If not, our swords shall plead it in the field.
    K. HEN. What title hast thou, traitor, to the
      crown?
Thy father was, as thou art, Duke of York;   105
Thy grandfather, Roger Mortimer, Earl of March.
I am the son of Henry the Fifth,
Who made the Dauphin and the French to stoop
And seized upon their towns and provinces.
    WAR. Talk not of France, sith° thou hast lost it
      all.   110
    K. HEN. The Lord Protector lost it, and not I.
When I was crowned I was but nine months old.

---

34. perforce: by force.   **47. shake . . . bells:** a metaphor from hawking. Bells were fastened to the hawk's leg. See App. 26. **51. Belike:** it is likely that.   **58. in steel:** i.e., wearing armor, and not the customary mourning cloak.   **62. poltroons:** lazy cowards.   **67. city:** i.e., London.   **68. beck:** bidding, lit., when they beckon

74. factious: rebellious.   **78. Earldom:** York inherited the Earldom of March from his mother, through whom he claimed the crown. See *II Hen VI*, II.ii.9–52.   **79. father . . . Crown:** He was Richard Earl of Cambridge, executed by Henry V. See *Hen V*, II.ii.   **91. colors:** flags.   **110. sith:** since.

RICH. You are old enough now, and yet, me-
thinks, you lose.
Father, tear the crown from the usurper's head.
   EDW. Sweet Father, do so. Set it on your head.
   MONT. Good Brother, as thou lovest and honorest
arms,   116
Let's fight it out, and not stand caviling thus.
   RICH. Sound drums and trumpets, and the King
will fly.
   YORK. Sons, peace!
   K. HEN. Peace, thou! And give King Henry leave
to speak.   120
   WAR. Plantagenet shall speak first. Hear him,
lords,
And be you silent and attentive too,
For he that interrupts him shall not live.
   K. HEN. Think'st thou that I will leave my kingly
throne,
Wherein my grandsire and my father sat?   125
No. First shall war unpeople this my realm.
Aye, and their colors, often borne in France,
And now in England to our heart's great sorrow,
Shall be my winding sheet.° Why faint you,°
lords?
My title's good, and better far than his.   130
   WAR. Prove it, Henry, and thou shalt be King.
   K. HEN. Henry the Fourth by conquest got the
crown.
   YORK. 'Twas by rebellion against his King.
   K. HEN. [*Aside*] I know not what to say. My
title's weak. —
Tell me, may not a king adopt an heir?   135
   YORK. What then?
   K. HEN. An if° he may, then am I lawful King;
For Richard, in the view of many lords,
Resigned the crown to Henry the Fourth,
Whose heir my father was, and I am his.   140
   YORK. He rose against him, being his sovereign,
And made him to resign his crown perforce.
   WAR. Suppose, my lords, he did it unconstrained,
Think you 'twere prejudicial to his crown?   144
   EXE. No, for he could not so resign his crown
But that the next heir should succeed and reign.
   K. HEN. Art thou against us, Duke of Exeter?
   EXE. His is the right, and therefore pardon me.
   YORK. Why whisper you, my lords, and answer
not?
   EXE. My conscience tells me he is lawful King.
   K. HEN. [*Aside*] All will revolt from me and
turn to him.   151
   NORTH. Plantagenet, for all the claim thou lay'st,
Think not that Henry shall be so deposed.
   WAR. Deposed he shall be, in despite° of all.
   NORTH. Thou art deceived. 'Tis not thy southern
power   155

Of Essex, Norfolk, Suffolk, nor of Kent,
Which makes thee thus presumptuous and proud,
Can set the Duke up in despite of me.
   CLIF. King Henry, be thy title right or wrong,
Lord Clifford vows to fight in thy defense.   160
May that ground gape and swallow me alive,
Where I shall kneel to him that slew my father!
   K. HEN. O Clifford, how thy words revive my
heart!
   YORK. Henry of Lancaster, resign thy crown.
What mutter you, or what conspire you, lords?   165
   WAR. Do right unto this princely Duke of York,
Or I will fill the house with armèd men,
And over the chair of state, where now he sits,
Write up his title with usurping blood.
         [*He stamps with his foot, and the
                 SOLDIERS show themselves.*]
   K. HEN. My Lord of Warwick, hear me but one
word.   170
Let me for this my lifetime reign as King.
   YORK. Confirm the crown to me and to mine
heirs,
And thou shalt reign in quiet while thou livest.
   K. HEN. I am content. Richard Plantagenet,
Enjoy the kingdom after my decease.   175
   CLIF. What wrong is this unto the Prince your
son!
   WAR. What good is this to England and himself!
   WEST. Base, fearful, and despairing Henry!
   CLIF. How hast thou injured both thyself and
us!
   WEST. I cannot stay to hear these articles.°   180
   NORTH. Nor I.
   CLIF. Come, Cousin, let us tell the Queen these
news.
   WEST. Farewell, faint-hearted and degenerate
King,
In whose cold blood no spark of honor bides.
   NORTH. Be thou a prey unto the House of York,
And die in bands° for this unmanly deed!   186
   CLIF. In dreadful war mayst thou be overcome,
Or live in peace, abandoned and despised!
         [*Exeunt* NORTHUMBERLAND, CLIFFORD,
                 and WESTMORELAND.]
   WAR. Turn this way, Henry, and regard them
not.
   EXE. They seek revenge and therefore will not
yield.   190
   K. HEN. Ah, Exeter!
   WAR.   Why should you sigh, my lord?
   K. HEN. Not for myself, Lord Warwick, but my
son,
Whom I unnaturally shall disinherit.
But be it as it may. I here entail°
The crown to thee and to thine heirs forever,   195

---

129. winding sheet: shroud in which a corpse is wrapped. **faint you:** are you dispirited? **137. An if:** if. **154. despite:** spite.

180. articles: clauses in a document. **186. bands:** bonds, captivity. **194. entail:** settle an estate on someone and his heirs.

Conditionally that here thou take an oath
To cease this civil war, and, whilst I live,
To honor me as thy King and sovereign,
And neither by treason nor hostility
To seek to put me down and reign thyself.   200
  YORK. This oath I willingly take and will per-
    form.
  WAR. Long live King Henry! Plantagenet, em-
    brace him.
  K. HEN. And long live thou and these thy for-
    ward sons!
  YORK. Now York and Lancaster are reconciled.
  EXE. Accursed be he that seeks to make them
    foes!   [*Sennet.° Here they come down.*]
  YORK. Farewell, my gracious lord. I'll to my
    castle.   206
  WAR. And I'll keep London with my soldiers.
  NORF. And I to Norfolk with my followers.
  MONT. And I unto the sea from whence I came.
    [*Exeunt* YORK *and his* SONS, WARWICK, NORFOLK,
      MONTAGUE, *their* SOLDIERS, *and* ATTENDANTS.]
  K. HEN. And I, with grief and sorrow, to the
    Court.   210
[*Enter* QUEEN MARGARET *and the* PRINCE OF WALES.]
  EXE. Here comes the Queen, whose looks be-
    wray° her anger.
I'll steal away.
  K. HEN.   Exeter, so will I.
  Q. MAR. Nay, go not from me. I will follow thee.
  K. HEN. Be patient, gentle Queen, and I will stay.
  Q. MAR. Who can be patient in such extremes?
Ah, wretched man! Would I had died a maid   216
And never seen thee, never borne thee son,
Seeing thou hast proved so unnatural a father!
Hath he deserved to lose his birthright thus?
Hadst thou but loved him half so well as I,   220
Or felt that pain which I did for him once,
Or nourished him as I did with my blood,
Thou wouldst have left thy dearest heartblood
    there,
Rather than have made that savage Duke thine heir
And disinherited thine only son.   225
  PRIN. Father, you cannot disinherit me.
If you be King, why should not I succeed?
  K. HEN. Pardon me, Margaret. Pardon me, sweet
    Son.
The Earl of Warwick and the Duke enforced me.
  Q. MAR. Enforced thee! Art thou King and wilt
    be forced?   230
I shame to hear thee speak. Ah, timorous wretch!
Thou hast undone thyself, thy son, and me,
And given unto the House of York such head°
As thou shalt reign but by their sufferance.
To entail him and his heirs unto the crown,   235
What is it, but to make thy sepulcher

And creep into it far before thy time?
Warwick is Chancellor and the Lord of Calais,
Stern Falconbridge commands the Narrow Seas,°
The Duke is made Protector of the realm,   240
And yet shalt thou be safe? Such safety finds
The trembling lamb environèd° with wolves.
Had I been there, which am a silly woman,
The soldiers should have tossed° me on their
    pikes.°
Before I would have granted to that act.   245
But thou preferr'st thy life before thine honor.
And seeing thou dost, I here divorce myself
Both from thy table, Henry, and thy bed
Until that Act of Parliament be repealed
Whereby my son is disinherited.   250
The Northern lords that have forsworn° thy colors
Will follow mine if once they see them spread;
And spread they shall be, to thy foul disgrace
And utter ruin of the House of York.
Thus do I leave thee. Come, Son, let's away.   255
Our army is ready. Come, we'll after them.
  K. HEN. Stay, gentle Margaret, and hear me
    speak.
  Q. MAR. Thou hast spoke too much already. Get
    thee gone.
  K. HEN. Gentle Son Edward, thou wilt stay with
    me?   259
  Q. MAR. Aye, to be murdered by his enemies.
  PRIN. When I return with victory from the field
I'll see your Grace. Till then I'll follow her.
  Q. MAR. Come, Son, away! We may not linger
    thus.
    [*Exeunt* QUEEN MARGARET *and the* PRINCE.]
  K. HEN. Poor Queen! How love to me and to her
    son
Hath made her break out into terms° of rage!   265
Revenged may she be on that hateful Duke
Whose haughty spirit, wingèd with desire,
Will cost my crown and, like an empty eagle,
Tire° on the flesh of me and of my son!
The loss of those three lords torments my heart.
I'll write unto them and entreat them fair.   271
Come, Cousin, you shall be the messenger.
  EXE. And I, I hope, shall reconcile them all.
                            [*Exeunt.*]

SCENE II. *Sandal Castle.*

[*Enter* RICHARD, EDWARD, *and* MONTAGUE.]
  RICH. Brother, though I be youngest, give me
    leave.
  EDW. No, I can better play the orator.

---

205. s.d., Sennet: trumpet notes to signify an important entry on
the stage.   **211. bewray:** betray.   **233. head:** superiority.
239. Narrow Seas: English Channel.   **242. environed:** surrounded.   **244. tossed:** speared. **pikes:** See Pl. 21d.   **251. for-**
sworn: deserted, sworn not to follow.   **265. terms:** expressions.
269. Tire: feed greedily.

MONT. But I have reasons strong and forcible.
    [*Enter the* DUKE OF YORK.]
YORK. Why, how now, Sons and Brother! At a
    strife?
What is your quarrel? How began it first?   5
EDW. No quarrel, but a slight contention.
YORK. About what?
RICH. About that which concerns your Grace and
    us —
The crown of England, Father, which is yours. 9
YORK. Mine, boy? Not till King Henry be dead.
RICH. Your right depends not on his life or death.
EDW. Now you are heir, therefore enjoy it now.
By giving the House of Lancaster leave to breathe,
It will outrun you, Father, in the end.
YORK. I took an oath that he should quietly
    reign.   15
EDW. But for a kingdom any oath may be broken.
I would break a thousand oaths to reign one year.
RICH. No, God forbid your Grace should be for-
    sworn.°
YORK. I shall be if I claim by open war.
RICH. I'll prove the contrary if you'll hear me
    speak.   20
YORK. Thou canst not, Son. It is impossible.
RICH. An oath is of no moment,° being not took
Before a true and lawful magistrate
That hath authority over him that swears.
Henry had none, but did usurp the place.   25
Then, seeing 'twas he that made you to depose,°
Your oath, my lord, is vain and frivolous.
Therefore, to arms! And, Father, do but think
How sweet a thing it is to wear a crown,
Within whose circuit is Elysium°   30
And all that poets feign of bliss and joy.
Why do we linger thus? I cannot rest
Until the White Rose that I wear be dyed
Even in the lukewarm blood of Henry's heart.
YORK. Richard, enough. I will be King or die. 35
Brother, thou shalt to London presently°
And whet on Warwick to this enterprise.
Thou, Richard, shalt to the Duke of Norfolk
And tell him privily° of our intent.
You, Edward, shall unto my Lord Cobham,   40
With whom the Kentishmen will willingly rise.
In them I trust, for they are soldiers,
Witty, courteous, liberal, full of spirit.
While you are thus employed, what resteth more
But that I seek occasion how to rise,   45
And yet the King not privy to° my drift,°
Nor any of the House of Lancaster?
    [*Enter a* MESSENGER.]
But stay. What news? Why comest thou in such
    post?°

MESS. The Queen with all the Northern Earls and
    lords
Intend here to besiege you in your castle.   50
She is hard by with twenty thousand men,
And therefore fortify your hold,° my lord.
YORK. Aye, with my sword. What! Think'st thou
    that we fear them?
Edward and Richard, you shall stay with me.
My brother Montague shall post to London.   55
Let noble Warwick, Cobham, and the rest
Whom we have left protectors of the King,
With powerful policy° strengthen themselves
And trust not simple Henry nor his oaths.   59
MONT. Brother, I go. I'll win them, fear it not.
And thus most humbly I do take my leave. [*Exit*]
    [*Enter* SIR JOHN MORTIMER *and* SIR HUGH
        MORTIMER.]
YORK. Sir John and Sir Hugh Mortimer, mine
    Uncles,
You are come to Sandal in a happy° hour.
The army of the Queen mean to besiege us
SIR JOHN. She shall not need. We'll meet her in
    the field.   65
YORK. What, with five thousand men?
RICH. Aye, with five hundred, Father, for a
    need.°
A woman's General. What should we fear?
    [*A march afar off.*]
EDW. I hear their drums. Let's set our men in
    order
And issue forth and bid them battle straight. 70
YORK. Five men to twenty! Though the odds be
    great,
I doubt not, Uncle, of our victory.
Many a battle have I won in France
When as° the enemy hath been ten to one.
Why should I not now have the like success? 75
    [*Alarum. Exeunt.*]

SCENE III. *Field of battle betwixt Sandal
    Castle and Wakefield.*

    [*Alarums. Enter* RUTLAND *and his* TUTOR.]
RUT. Ah, whither shall I fly to 'scape their hands?
Ah, tutor, look where bloody Clifford comes!
    [*Enter* CLIFFORD *and* SOLDIERS.]
CLIF. Chaplain, away! Thy priesthood saves thy
    life.
As for the brat of this accursèd Duke,
Whose father slew my father, he shall die.   5
TUT. And I, my lord, will bear him company.
CLIF. Soldiers, away with him!
TUT. Ah, Clifford, murder not this innocent
    child,

Sc. ii: **18. forsworn:** perjured.   **22. moment:** importance.
26. depose: swear an oath.   **30. Elysium:** Heaven.   **36. presently:** immediately.   **39. privily:** secretly.   **46. privy to:** acquainted with. **drift:** intention.   **48. post:** haste.

52. hold: castle.   **58. policy:** cunning.   **63. happy:** lucky.
67. for a need: if necessary.   **74. When as:** when.

Lest thou be hated both of God and man!
              [*Exit, dragged off by* SOLDIERS.]
  CLIF. How now! Is he dead already? Or is it
    fear   10
That makes him close his eyes? I'll open them.
  RUT. So looks the pent-up° lion o'er the wretch
That trembles under his devouring paws,
And so he walks, insulting° o'er his prey,
And so he comes, to rend his limbs asunder.   15
Ah, gentle Clifford, kill me with thy sword,
And not with such a cruel threatening look.
Sweet Clifford, hear me speak before I die.
I am too mean a subject for thy wrath.
Be thou revenged on men, and let me live.   20
  CLIF. In vain thou speak'st, poor boy. My father's
    blood
Hath stopped the passage where thy words should
    enter.
  RUT. Then let my father's blood open it again.
He is a man, and, Clifford, cope with° him.
  CLIF. Had I thy brethren here, their lives and
    thine   25
Were not revenge sufficient for me.
No, if I digged up thy forefathers' graves
And hung their rotten coffins up in chains,
It could not slake mine ire, nor ease my heart.
The sight of any of the House of York   30
Is as a fury to torment my soul,
And till I root out their accursed line
And leave not one alive, I live in Hell.
Therefore ——   [*Lifting his hand*.]
  RUT. Oh, let me pray before I take my death! 35
To thee I pray. Sweet Clifford, pity me!
  CLIF. Such pity as my rapier's point affords.
  RUT. I never did thee harm. Why wilt thou slay
    me?
  CLIF. Thy father hath.
  RUT.   But 'twas ere I was born.
Thou hast one son. For his sake pity me,   40
Lest in revenge thereof, sith God is just,
He be as miserably slain as I.
Ah, let me live in prison all my days,
And when I give occasion of offense,
Then let me die, for now thou hast no cause. 45
  CLIF. No cause!
Thy father slew my father. Therefore, die.
                      [*Stabs him*.]
  RUT. *Di faciant laudis summa sit ista tuae!*°
                        [*Dies*.]
  CLIF. Plantagenet! I come, Plantagenet!
And this thy son's blood cleaving to my blade 50
Shall rust upon my weapon till thy blood,
Congealed with this, do make me wipe off both.
                       [*Exit*.]

Sc. iii: **12. pent-up:** frustrated.   **14. insulting:** triumphing.
24. cope with: encounter.   **48. Di . . . tuae:** may the gods make
this your most famous act; i.e., the slaughter of an innocent.

SCENE IV. *Another part of the field.*

[*Alarum. Enter* RICHARD *Duke of York.*]
  YORK. The army of the Queen hath got the field.
My uncles both are slain in rescuing me,
And all my followers to the eager foe
Turn back and fly, like ships before the wind,
Or lambs pursued by hunger-starvèd wolves.   5
My sons, God knows what hath bechancèd them.
But this I know, they have demeaned° themselves
Like men born to renown by life or death.
Three times did Richard make a lane to me,
And thrice cried, "Courage, Father! Fight it
    out!"   10
And full as oft came Edward to my side,
With purple falchion,° painted to the hilt
In blood of those that had encountered him.
And when the hardiest warriors did retire,
Richard cried, "Charge, and give no foot of
    ground!"   15
And cried, "A crown, or else a glorious tomb!
A scepter, or an earthly sepulcher!"
With this, we charged again. But, out, alas!
We bodged° again, as I have seen a swan
With bootless° labor swim against the tide   20
And spend her strength with overmatching° waves.
                  [*A short alarum within*.]
Ah, hark! The fatal followers do pursue,
And I am faint, and cannot fly their fury.
And were I strong, I would not shun their fury.
The sands° are numbered that make up my life.
Here must I stay, and here my life must end.   26
      [*Enter* QUEEN MARGARET, CLIFFORD,
NORTHUMBERLAND, *the young* PRINCE, *and* SOLDIERS.]
Come, bloody Clifford, rough Northumberland,
I dare your quenchless fury to more rage.
I am your butt,° and I abide your shot.   29
  NORTH. Yield to our mercy, proud Plantagenet.
  CLIF. Aye, to such mercy as his ruthless arm,
With downright payment, showed unto my father.
Now Phaëthon° hath tumbled from his car°
And made an evening at the noontide prick.°
  YORK. My ashes, as the phoenix,° may bring forth
A bird that will revenge upon you all;   36
And in that hope I throw mine eyes to Heaven,
Scorning whate'er you can afflict me with.
Why come you not? What! Multitudes, and fear?
  CLIF. So cowards fight when they can fly no
    further;   40
So doves do peck the falcon's piercing talons;
So desperate thieves, all hopeless of their lives,

Sc. iv: **7. demeaned:** behaved.   **12. falchion:** curved sword.
19. bodged: bungled.   **20. bootless:** vain.   **21. overmatching:**
overcoming.   **25. sands:** i.e., in the hourglass.   **29. butt:**
target.   **33. Phaëthon:** the son of the sun god, who tried to drive
his father's horses but was thrown out of the chariot and killed.
car: chariot.   **34. prick:** mark on the dial showing noon.
35. phoenix: See *Temp*, III.iii.23,n.

Breathe out invectives 'gainst the officers.

YORK. O Clifford, but bethink thee once again,
And in thy thought o'errun my former time;   45
And, if thou canst for blushing, view this face,
And bite thy tongue that slanders him with cow-
ardice
Whose frown hath made thee faint and fly ere this!

CLIF. I will not bandy° with thee word for word,
But buckle° with thee blows, twice two for one.   50

Q. MAR. Hold, valiant Clifford! For a thousand
causes
I would prolong awhile the traitor's life.
Wrath makes him deaf. Speak thou, Northumberland.

NORTH. Hold, Clifford! Do not honor him so
much
To prick thy finger, though to wound his heart.
What valor were it, when a cur doth grin,°   56
For one to thrust his hand between his teeth
When he might spurn him with his foot away?
It is war's prize to take all vantages,
And ten to one is no impeach° of valor.   60

    [*They lay hands on* YORK, *who struggles.*]

CLIF. Aye, aye, so strives the woodcock with the
gin.°

NORTH. So doth the cony° struggle in the net.

YORK. So triumph thieves upon their conquered
booty;
So true men yield, with robbers so o'ermatched.

NORTH. What would your Grace have done unto
him now?   65

Q. MAR. Brave warriors, Clifford and Northumber-
land,
Come, make him stand upon this molehill here,
That raught° at mountains with outstretchèd arms,
Yet parted but° the shadow with his hand.
What! Was it you that would be England's king?
Was 't you that reveled° in our Parliament   71
And made a preachment° of your high descent?
Where are your mess° of sons to back you now?
The wanton Edward and the lusty George?
And where's that valiant crookback prodigy,°   75
Dicky your boy, that with his grumbling voice
Was wont to cheer his dad in mutinies?
Or, with the rest, where is your darling Rutland?
Look, York. I stained this napkin with the blood
That valiant Clifford, with his rapier's point,   80
Made issue from the bosom of the boy;
And if thine eyes can water for his death,
I give thee this to dry thy cheeks withal.
Alas, poor York! But that I hate thee deadly,

I should lament thy miserable state.   85
I prithee grieve to make me merry, York.
What, hath thy fiery heart so parched° thine en-
trails
That not a tear can fall for Rutland's death?
Why art thou patient, man? Thou should'st be mad;
And I, to make thee mad, do mock thee thus.   90
Stamp, rave, and fret, that I may sing and dance.
Thou wouldst be fee'd,° I see, to make me sport.
York cannot speak unless he wear a crown.
A crown for York! And, lords, bow low to him.
Hold you this hands whilst I do set it on.   95

    [*Putting a paper crown on his head.*]

Aye, marry,° sir, now looks he like a king!
Aye, this is he that took King Henry's chair,
And this is he was his adopted heir.
But how is it that great Plantagenet
Is crowned so soon and broke his solemn oath?   100
As I bethink me, you should not be King
Till our King Henry had shook hands with death.
And will you pale° your head in Henry's glory
And rob his temples of the diadem,
Now in his life, against your holy oath?   105
Oh, 'tis a fault too too unpardonable!
Off with the crown, and, with the crown, his head,
And, whilst we breathe,° take time to do him dead.

CLIF. That is my office, for my father's sake.

Q. MAR. Nay, stay. Let's hear the orisons° he
makes.   110

YORK. She-wolf of France, but worse than wolves
of France,
Whose tongue more poisons than the adder's
tooth!
How ill-beseeming is it in thy sex
To triumph, like an Amazonian° trull,°
Upon their woes whom fortune captivates!°   115
But that thy face is, vizardlike,° unchanging,
Made impudent with use of evil deeds,
I would assay,° proud Queen, to make thee blush.
To tell thee whence thou camest, of whom derived,
Were shame enough to shame thee, wert thou not
shameless.   120
Thy father bears the type° of King of Naples,
Of both the Sicils and Jerusalem,
Yet not so wealthy as an English yeoman.°
Hath that poor monarch taught thee to insult?
It needs not, nor it boots° thee not, proud Queen,
Unless the adage must be verified°   126
That beggars mounted run their horse to death.
'Tis beauty that doth oft make women proud,

---

49. **bandy:** exchange, lit., hit the ball to and fro in tennis.
50. **buckle:** grapple.   56. **grin:** show his teeth.   60. **impeach:**
calling in question.   61. **gin:** snare.   62. **cony:** rabbit.
68. **raught:** reached.   69. **parted but:** only pushed aside.
71. **reveled:** played the drunkard.   72. **preachment:** sermon.
73. **mess:** lit., a set of four eating at one table.   75. **prodigy:**
i.e., the deformed Richard; see III.ii.154–71.

87. **parched:** dried up.   92. **fee'd:** rewarded.   96. **marry:** Mary,
by the Virgin.   103. **pale:** fence in, enclose.   108. **breathe:**
rest.   110. **orisons:** prayers.   114. **Amazonian:** The Amazons
were a legendary race of female warriors who lived in South
Russia. **trull:** strumpet.   115. **captivates:** reduces to captivity.   116. **vizardlike:** masklike.   118. **assay:** attempt.   121. **type:**
badge, crown.   123. **yeoman:** farmer.   125. **boots:** advantages.
126. **adage . . . verified:** proverb must be proved true.

But, God He knows, thy share thereof is small.
'Tis virtue that doth make them most admired;
The contrary doth make thee wondered at.   131
'Tis government° that makes them seem divine;
The want thereof makes thee abominable.
Thou art as opposite to every good
As the Antipodes° are unto us,   135
Or as the South to the septentrion.°
O tiger's heart wrapped in a woman's hide!°
How couldst thou drain the lifeblood of the child
To bid the father wipe his eyes withal,
And yet be seen to bear a woman's face?   140
Women are soft, mild, pitiful, and flexible —
Thou, stern, obdúrate, flinty, rough, remorseless.
Bid'st thou me rage? Why, now thou hast thy wish.
Wouldst have me weep? Why, now thou hast thy
    will.
For raging wind blows up incessant showers,   145
And when the rage allays, the rain begins.
These tears are my sweet Rutland's obsequies,°
And every drop cries vengeance for his death
'Gainst thee, fell° Clifford, and thee, false French-
    woman.
    NORTH. Beshrew° me, but his passion° moves me
        so   150
That hardly can I check my eyes from tears.
    YORK. That face of his the hungry cannibals
Would not have touched, would not have stained
    with blood;
But you are more inhuman, more inexorable,°
Oh, ten time more, than tigers of Hyrcania.°   155
See, ruthless Queen, a hapless father's tears.
This cloth thou dip'dst in blood of my sweet boy,
And I with tears do wash the blood away.
Keep thou the napkin, and go boast of this.
And if thou tell'st the heavy story right,   160
Upon my soul, the hearers will shed tears.
Yea, even my foes will shed fast-falling tears
And say, " Alas, it was a piteous deed! "
There, take the crown, and, with the crown, my
    curse;
And in thy need such comfort come to thee   165
As now I reap at thy too cruel hand!
Hard-hearted Clifford, take me from the world.
My soul to Heaven, my blood upon your heads!
    NORTH. Had he been slaughterman to all my kin,
I should not for my life but weep with him   170
To see how inly° sorrow gripes his soul.
    Q. MAR. What, weeping-ripe,° my Lord North-
        umberland?
Think but upon the wrong he did us all,

And that will quickly dry thy melting tears.
    CLIF. Here's for my oath, here's for my father's
        death.   [*Stabbing him.*] 175
    Q. MAR. And here's to right our gentle-hearted
        King.   [*Stabbing him.*]
    YORK. Open Thy gate of mercy, gracious God!
My soul flies through these wounds to seek out
    Thee.   [*Dies.*]
    Q. MAR. Off with his head and set it on York
        gates;
So York may overlook the town of York.   180
                    [*Flourish. Exeunt.*]

Act II

SCENE I. *A plain near Mortimer's Cross
in Herefordshire.*

[*A march. Enter* EDWARD, RICHARD, *and their
power.*°]

    EDW. I wonder how our princely father 'scaped,
Or whether he be 'scaped away or no
From Clifford's and Northumberland's pursuit. 3
Had he been ta'en, we should have heard the news;
Had he been slain, we should have heard the news;
Or had he 'scaped, methinks we should have heard
The happy tidings of his good escape.
How fares my brother? Why is he so sad?
    RICH. I cannot joy until I be resolved
Where our right valiant father is become.°   10
I saw him in the battle range° about,
And watched him how he singled Clifford forth.
Methought he bore him in the thickest troop
As doth a lion in a herd of neat,°
Or as a bear, encompassed round with dogs,   15
Who having pinched a few and made them cry,
The rest stand all aloof and bark at him.°
So fared our father with his enemies;
So fled his enemies° my warlike father.
Methinks, 'tis prize enough to be his son.   20
See how the morning opes her golden gates
And takes her farewell of the glorious sun!
How well resembles it the prime of youth,
Trimmed like a younker° prancing to his love!
    EDW. Dazzle mine eyes,° or do I see three suns?
    RICH. Three glorious suns, each one a perfect
        sun,   26
Not separated with the racking° clouds,

132. government: self-control, nice manners.   135. Antipodes:
the opposite side of the world.   136. septentrion: north.
137. O . . . hide: See Gen. Intro. p. 9b.   147. obsequies: funeral
rites.   149. fell: cruel.   150. Beshrew: bad luck to. passion:
emotion.   154. inexorable: merciless.   155. Hyrcania: the
Caspian Sea, the traditional home of fierce tigers. See *Haml,*
II.ii.472.   171. inly: inwardly.   172. weeping-ripe: full of tears.

Act II, Sc. i: s.d., power: army.   10. Where . . . become:
what has happened to.   11. range: roam.   14. neat: cattle.
15–17. bear . . . him: See App. 5.   19. fled . . . enemies: i.e.,
his enemies fled from.   24. Trimmed . . . younker: dressed out
in his best like a young man.   25. Dazzle . . . eyes: are my eyes
dimmed?   27. racking: drifting.

But severed in a pale clear-shining sky.
See, see! They join, embrace, and seem to kiss,
As if they vowed some league inviolable.   30
Now are they but one lamp, one light, one sun.
In this the heaven figures° some event.
   EDW. 'Tis wondrous strange, the like yet never
     heard of.
I think it cites° us, Brother, to the field,
That we, the sons of brave Plantagenet,   35
Each one already blazing by our meeds,°
Should notwithstanding join our lights together
And overshine the earth as this the world.
Whate'er it bodes, henceforward will I bear
Upon my target° three fair-shining suns.   40
   RICH. Nay, bear three daughters. By your leave
     I speak it,
You love the breeder° better than the male.
            [*Enter a* MESSENGER.]
But what art thou, whose heavy looks foretell
Some dreadful story hanging on thy tongue?
   MESS. Ah, one that was a woeful looker-on   45
When as the noble Duke of York was slain,
Your princely father and my loving lord!
   EDW. Oh, speak no more, for I have heard too
     much.
   RICH. Say how he died, for I will hear it all.
   MESS. Environèd° he was with many foes,   50
And stood against them, as the hope of Troy°
Against the Greeks that would have entered Troy.
But Hercules himself must yield to odds,
And many strokes, though with a little ax,
Hew down and fell the hardest-timbered oak.   55
By many hands your father was subdued,
But only slaughtered by the ireful° arm
Of unrelenting Clifford and the Queen,
Who crowned the gracious Duke in high despite,
Laughed in his face; and when with grief he wept,
The ruthless Queen gave him to dry his cheeks   61
A napkin steepèd in the harmless blood
Of sweet young Rutland, by rough Clifford slain.
And after many scorns, many foul taunts,
They took his head, and on the gates of York   65
They set the same; and there it doth remain,
The saddest spectacle that e'er I viewed.
   EDW. Sweet Duke of York, our prop to lean
     upon,
Now thou art gone, we have no staff, no stay.
O Clifford, boisterous Clifford! Thou hast slain   70
The flower of Europe for his chivalry,
And treacherously hast thou vanquished him,
For hand to hand he would have vanquished thee.
Now my soul's palace is become a prison.°   74
Ah, would she break from hence, that this my body

Might in the ground be closèd up in rest!
For never henceforth shall I joy again,
Never, oh never, shall I see more joy!
   RICH. I cannot weep, for all my body's moisture
Scarce serves to quench my furnace-burning
     heart.   80
Nor can my tongue unload my heart's great bur-
     den;
For selfsame wind that I should speak withal
Is kindling coals that fires all my breast
And burns me up with flames that tears would
     quench.
To weep is to make less the depth of grief.   85
Tears then for babes; blows and revenge for me!
Richard, I bear thy name. I'll venge thy death,
Or die renownèd by attempting it.
   EDW. His name that valiant Duke hath left with
     thee.
His dukedom and his chair° with me is left.   90
   RICH. Nay, if thou be that princely eagle's bird,
Show thy descent by gazing 'gainst the sun.°
For chair and dukedom, throne and kingdom say;
Either that is thine, or else thou wert not his.
     [*March. Enter* WARWICK, MARQUESS OF MONTAGUE,
          and their army.]
   WAR. How now, fair lords! What fare? What
     news abroad?   95
   RICH. Great Lord of Warwick, if we should re-
     count
Our baleful° news and at each word's deliverance
Stab poniards° in our flesh till all were told,
The words would add more anguish than the
     wounds.
O valiant lord, the Duke of York is slain!   100
   EDW. O Warwick, Warwick! That Plantagenet,
Which held thee dearly as his soul's redemption,°
Is by the stern Lord Clifford done to death.
   WAR. Ten days ago I drowned these news in tears;
And now, to add more measure to your woes,   105
I come to tell you things sith then befall'n.
After the bloody fray at Wakefield fought,
Where your brave father breathed his latest° gasp,
Tidings, as swiftly as the posts° could run,
Were brought me of your loss and his depart.°   110
I, then in London, Keeper of the King,
Mustered my soldiers, gathered flocks of friends,
And very well appointed,° as I thought,
Marched toward Saint Alban's to intercept the
     Queen,
Bearing the King in my behalf along;   115
For by my scouts I was advertisèd°
That she was coming with a full intent

---

32. figures: foretells.   34. cites: summons.   36. meeds: deserts.
40. target: shield.   42. breeder: female — Edward's wantonness
being notorious.   50. Environed: surrounded. See I.i.242.
51. hope of Troy: Hector.   57. ireful: wrathful.   74. soul's . . .
prison: a fanciful way of saying "I do not care to live longer."

90. chair: i.e., the throne which York had claimed.   **92. gazing
. . . sun:** It was believed that the eagle's eyes were so strong that
it could look into the sun. See *LLL* IV.iii.334.   **97. baleful:**
deadly.   **98. poniards:** daggers.   **102. redemption:** salvation.
108. latest: last.   **109. posts:** See App. 17.   **110. depart: death.**
113. appointed: equipped.   **116. advertised:** informed.

To dash° our late decree in Parliament
Touching King Henry's oath and your succession.
Short tale to make, we at Saint Alban's met,   120
Our battles° joined, and both sides fiercely fought.
But whether 'twas the coldness of the King,
Who looked full gently on his warlike Queen,
That robbed my soldiers of their heated spleen,°
Or whether 'twas report of her success,   125
Or more than common fear of Clifford's rigor,°
Who thunders to his captives blood and death,
I cannot judge. But, to conclude with truth,
Their weapons like to lightning came and went.
Our soldiers', like the night owl's lazy flight,   130
Or like an idle thresher with a flail,°
Fell gently down, as if they struck their friends.
I cheered them up with justice of our cause,
With promise of high pay and great rewards.
But all in vain. They had no heart to fight,   135
And we in them no hope to win the day;
So that we fled — the King unto the Queen,
Lord George your brother, Norfolk and myself,
In haste, posthaste,° are come to join with you.
For in the Marches° here we heard you were,   140
Making another head° to fight again.
    EDW. Where is the Duke of Norfolk, gentle
      Warwick?
And when came George from Burgundy to Eng-
land?
    WAR. Some six miles off the Duke is with the
      soldiers;
And for your brother, he was lately sent   145
From your kind aunt, Duchess of Burgundy,
With aid of soldiers to this needful war.
    RICH. 'Twas odds, belike,° when valiant War-
      wick fled.
Oft have I heard his praises in pursuit,
But ne'er till now his scandal of retire.°   150
    WAR. Nor now my scandal, Richard, dost thou
      hear.
For thou shalt know this strong right hand of mine
Can pluck the diadem from faint Henry's head
And wring the awful° scepter from his fist,
Were he as famous and as bold in war   155
As he is famed for mildness, peace, and prayer.
    RICH. I know it well, Lord Warwick. Blame me
      not.
'Tis love I bear thy glories makes me speak.
But in this troublous time what's to be done?
Shall we go throw away our coats of steel   160
And wrap our bodies in black mourning gowns,

Numbering our Ave Maries° with our beads?
Or shall we on the helmets of our foes
Tell our devotion° with revengeful arms?
If for the last, say aye, and to it, lords.   165
    WAR. Why, therefore Warwick came to seek
      you out;
And therefore comes my brother Montague.
Attend° me, lords. The proud insulting Queen,
With Clifford and the haught° Northumberland,
And of their feather many moe° proud birds,   170
Have wrought° the easy-melting King like wax.
He swore consent to your succession,
His oath enrollèd in the Parliament;
And now to London all the crew are gone
To frustrate both his oath and what beside   175
May make against the House of Lancaster.
Their power, I think, is thirty thousand strong.
Now, if the help of Norfolk and myself,
With all the friends that thou, brave Earl of
    March,
Amongst the loving Welshmen canst procure,   180
Will but amount to five and twenty thousand,
Why, *Via!*° To London will we march amain,
And once again bestride our foaming steeds,
And once again cry, " Charge upon our foes! "
But never once again turn back and fly.   185
    RICH. Aye, now methinks I hear great Warwick
      speak.
Ne'er may he live to see a sunshine day
That cries, " Retire," if Warwick bid him stay.
    EDW. Lord Warwick, on thy shoulder will I lean.
And when thou fail'st — as God forbid the hour! —
Must Edward fall, which peril Heaven forfend!°
    WAR. No longer Earl of March, but Duke of
      York.   192
The next degree° is England's royal throne;
For King of England shalt thou be proclaimed
In every borough as we pass along,   195
And he that throws not up his cap for joy
Shall for the fault make forfeit of his head.
King Edward, valiant Richard, Montague,
Stay we no longer, dreaming of renown,
But sound the trumpets, and about our task.   200
    RICH. Then, Clifford, were thy heart as hard as
      steel,
As thou hast shown it flinty by thy deeds,
I come to pierce it, or to give thee mine.
    EDW. Then strike up drums. God and Saint
      George for us!
          [*Enter a* MESSENGER.]
    WAR. How now! What news?   205
    MESS. The Duke of Norfolk sends you word by me
The Queen is coming with a puissant° host,

---

118. **dash:** upset.   121. **battles:** armies.   124. **spleen:** wrath.
126. **rigor:** ferocity.   131. **flail:** implement for extracting wheat
from the ear, made of two heavy sticks joined by a leather thong
with which the straw was threshed (or beaten).   139. **posthaste:**
urgent speed. See App. 17.   140. **Marches:** borders (of Wales).
141. **head:** force.   148. **'Twas . . . belike:** the odds against him
must have been heavy.   150. **scandal of retire:** that he was disgraced by having to retreat.   154. **awful:** causing fear.

162. **Ave Maries:** the prayer beginning "Hail Mary."   164. **Tell
. . . devotion:** say our prayers.   168. **Attend:** listen to.
169. **haught:** haughty.   170. **moe:** more.   171. **wrought:**
worked on.   182. *Via:* away!   191. **forfend:** forbid.   193. **degree:** step.   207. **puissant:** powerful.

And craves your company for speedy counsel.
WAR. Why then it sorts.° Brave warriors, let's
　　away.　　　　　　　　　　　　　　[*Exeunt.*]

SCENE II. *Before York.*

[*Flourish. Enter* KING HENRY, QUEEN MARGARET, *the*
PRINCE OF WALES, CLIFFORD, *and* NORTHUMBERLAND,
　　　　with drum and trumpets.]
Q. MAR. Welcome, my lord, to this brave town of
　　York.
Yonder's the head of that archenemy
That sought to be encompassed with your crown.
Doth not the object cheer your heart, my lord?
　K. HEN. Aye, as the rocks cheer them that fear
　　their wreck.　　　　　　　　　　　　　5
To see this sight, it irks my very soul.
Withhold revenge, dear God! 'Tis not my fault,
Nor wittingly° have I infringed my vow.
　CLIF. My gracious liege,° this too much lenity°
And harmful pity must be laid aside.　　　10
To whom do lions cast their gentle looks?
Not to the beast that would usurp their den.
Whose hand is that the forest bear doth lick?
Not his that spoils° her young before her face.
Who 'scapes the lurking serpent's mortal sting?°
Not he that sets his foot upon her back.　　16
The smallest worm will turn being trodden on,
And doves will peck in safeguard of their brood.
Ambitious York did level° at thy crown,
Thou smiling while he knit his angry brows.　20
He, but a Duke, would have his son a king,
And raise his issue° like a loving sire;
Thou, being a King, blest with a goodly son,
Didst yield consent to disinherit him,
Which argued thee a most unloving father.　25
Unreasonable creatures° feed their young;
And though man's face be fearful to their eyes,
Yet, in protection of their tender ones,
Who hath not seen them, even with those wings
Which sometime they have used with fearful
　　flight,　　　　　　　　　　　　　30
Make war with him that climbed unto their nest,
Offering their own lives in their young's defense?
For shame, my liege, make them your precedent!
Were it not pity that this goodly boy
Should lose his birthright by his father's fault　35
And long hereafter say unto his child,
" What my great-grandfather and grandsire got
My careless father fondly° gave away "?
Ah, what a shame were this! Look on the boy,
And let his manly face, which promiseth　　40

Successful fortune, steel thy melting heart
To hold thine own and leave thine own with him.
　K. HEN. Full well hath Clifford played the orator,
Inferring° arguments of mighty force.
But, Clifford, tell me, didst thou ever hear　　45
That things ill-got had ever bad success?
And happy always was it for that son
Whose father for° his hoarding went to Hell?
I'll leave my son my virtuous deeds behind,
And would my father had left me no more!　　50
For all the rest is held at such a rate
As brings a thousandfold more care to keep
Than in possession any jot° of pleasure.
Ah, Cousin York! Would thy best friends did know
How it doth grieve me that thy head is here!　55
　Q. MAR. My lord, cheer up your spirits. Our foes
　　are nigh,
And this soft courage makes your followers faint.
You promised knighthood to our forward son.
Unsheathe your sword, and dub° him presently.
Edward, kneel down.　　　　　　　　　60
　K. HEN. Edward Plantagenet, arise a knight,
And learn this lesson: Draw thy sword in right.
　PRIN. My gracious Father, by your kingly leave,
I'll draw it as apparent° to the crown,
And in that quarrel use it to the death.　　65
　CLIF. Why, that is spoken like a toward° prince.
　　　　　　　[*Enter a* MESSENGER.]
　MESS. Royal commanders, be in readiness.
For with a band of thirty thousand men
Comes Warwick, backing of the Duke of York,°
And in the towns, as they march along,　　70
Proclaims him King, and many fly to him.
Darraign your battle,° for they are at hand.
　CLIF. I would your Highness would depart the
　　field.
The Queen hath best success when you are absent.
　Q. MAR. Aye, good my lord, and leave us to our
　　fortune.　　　　　　　　　　　　75
　K. HEN. Why, that's my fortune too. Therefore
　　I'll stay.
　NORTH. Be it with resolution, then, to fight.
　PRIN. My royal Father, cheer these noble lords
And hearten those that fight in your defense.
Unsheathe your sword, good Father. Cry, " Saint
　　George! "　　　　　　　　　　　80
[*March. Enter* EDWARD, GEORGE, RICHARD, WARWICK,
　　NORFOLK, MONTAGUE, *and* SOLDIERS.]
　EDW. Now, perjured Henry! Wilt thou kneel for
　　grace
And set thy diadem upon my head,
Or bide° the mortal° fortune of the field?

209. sorts: turns out well.
　　Sc. ii: 8. wittingly: intentionally.　9. liege: lord. lenity:
gentleness.　14. spoils: destroys.　15. sting: It was generally
believed that snakes stung with their tails.　19. level: aim.
22. raise . . . issue: promote his children.　26. Unreasonable
creatures: animals that have no power of reason.　38. fondly:
foolishly.

44. Inferring: producing.　48. for: because of.　53. jot: lit.,
little mark.　59. dub: bestow knighthood upon. See *II Hen
II*, IV.ii.127–28,n.　64. apparent: heir.　66. toward: bold.
69. Duke of York: i.e., Edward. See II.i.192.　72. Darraign . . .
battle: set in order your army.　83. bide: await. mortal:
deadly.

Q. MAR. Go, rate° thy minions,° proud insulting
    boy!
Becomes it thee to be thus bold in terms°   85
Before thy sovereign and thy lawful King?
    EDW. I am his King, and he should bow his knee.
I was adopted heir by his consent;
Since when, his oath is broke, for, as I hear,
You, that are King, though he do wear the crown,
Have caused him, by new Act of Parliament,   91
To blot out me and put his own son in.
    CLIF. And reason too.
Who should succeed the father but the son?   94
    RICH. Are you there, butcher? Oh, I cannot speak!
    CLIF. Aye, crookback, here I stand to answer thee,
Or any he the proudest of thy sort.°
    RICH. 'Twas you that killed young Rutland, was
    it not?
    CLIF. Aye, and old York, and yet not satisfied.
    RICH. For God's sake, lords, give signal to the
    fight.   100
    WAR. What say'st thou, Henry, wilt thou yield
    the crown?
    Q. MAR. Why, how now, long-tonguèd Warwick!
    Dare you speak?
When you and I met at Saint Alban's last,
Your legs did better service than your hands.
    WAR. Then 'twas my turn to fly, and now 'tis
    thine.   105
    CLIF. You said so much before, and yet you fled.
    WAR. 'Twas not your valor, Clifford, drove me
    thence.
    NORTH. No, nor your manhood that durst make
    you stay.
    RICH. Northumberland, I hold thee reverently.
Break off the parley, for scarce I can refrain   110
The execution of° my big-swoln° heart
Upon that Clifford, that cruel child-killer.
    CLIF. I slew thy father. Call'st thou him a child?
    RICH. Aye, like a dastard° and a treacherous
    coward,
As thou didst kill our tender brother Rutland;   115
But ere sunset I'll make thee curse the deed.
    K. HEN. Have done with words, my lords, and
    hear me speak.
    Q. MAR. Defy them then, or else hold close thy
    lips.
    K. HEN. I prithee, give no limits° to my tongue.
I am a King, and privileged to speak.   120
    CLIF. My liege, the wound that bred this meeting
    here
Cannot be cured by words. Therefore be still.
    RICH. Then, executioner, unsheathe thy sword.
By Him that made us all, I am resolved°   124

That Clifford's manhood lies upon his tongue.°
    EDW. Say, Henry, shall I have my right, or no?
A thousand men have broke their fasts today
That ne'er shall dine unless thou yield the crown.
    WAR. If thou deny, their blood upon thy head,
For York in justice puts his armor on.   130
    PRIN. If that be right which Warwick says is
    right,
There is no wrong, but everything is right.
    RICH. Whoever got thee, there thy mother
    stands;°
For, well I wot,° thou hast thy mother's tongue.
    Q. MAR. But thou art neither like thy sire nor
    dam,°   135
But like a foul misshapen stigmatic,°
Marked by the destinies to be avoided
As venom° toads, or lizards' dreadful stings.
    RICH. Iron° of Naples hid with English gilt,
Whose father bears the title of a King —   140
As if a channel° should be called the sea —
Shamest thou not, knowing whence thou art ex-
    traught,°
To let thy tongue detect° thy base-born heart?
    EDW. A wisp of straw° were worth a thousand
    crowns
To make this shameless callet° know herself.   145
Helen of Greece was fairer far than thou,
Although thy husband may be Menelaus,
And ne'er was Agamemnon's° brother wronged
By that false woman as this King by thee
His father reveled in the heart of France   150
And tamed the King, and made the Dauphin
    stoop;
And had he matched° according to his state,
He might have kept that glory to this day,
But when he took a beggar to his bed
And graced thy poor sire with his bridal day,   155
Even then that sunshine brewed a shower for him,
That washed his father's fortunes forth° of France
And heaped sedition on his crown at home.
For what hath broached° this tumult but thy pride?
Hadst thou been meek, our title° still had slept,
And we, in pity of the gentle King,   161
Had slipped our claim until another age.
    GEO. But when we saw our sunshine made thy
    spring

125. manhood . . . tongue: i.e., his courage is nothing but words.
133. Whoever . . . stands: whoever may have been your father,
you are certainly like your mother.   134. wot: know.
135. dam: mother.   136. stigmatic: See *II Hen VI*, V.i.215,n.
138. venom: poisonous.   139. Iron: i.e., worthless metal. See
I.iv.121–27.   141. channel: ditch.   142. extraught: extracted,
derived.   143. detect: reveal.   144. wisp of straw: Scolds were
punished by being made to wear a crown of straw.   145. callet:
lewd woman.   147–48. Menelaus . . . Agamemnon's: Menelaus,
King of Sparta, was husband of Helen, who ran away with Paris
of Troy. Agamemnon was King of Mycenae, leader of the Greek
army against Troy, and Menelaus's brother. See *Tr & Cr.*
152. matched: married.   157. forth: out.   159. broached:
made to flow.   160. title: claim to the throne.

84. rate: chide. minions: favorites.   85. terms: words.
97. sort: gang.   111. execution of: lit., action resulting from.
big-swoln: swollen to bursting.   114. dastard: sneaking coward.
119. limits: boundaries.   124. resolved: sure, convinced.

And that thy summer bred us no increase,
We set the ax to thy usurping° root;   165
And though the edge hath something hit our-
selves,
Yet, know thou, since we have begun to strike,
We'll never leave till we have hewn thee down
Or bathed thy growing with our heated bloods.
    EDW. And, in this resolution, I defy thee,   170
Not willing any longer conference,
Since thou deniest the gentle King to speak.
Sound trumpets! Let our bloody colors wave!
And either victory, or else a grave.
    Q. MAR. Stay, Edward.   175
    EDW. No, wrangling woman, we'll no longer
stay.
These words will cost ten thousand lives this day.
        [*Exeunt.*]

SCENE III. *A field of battle between Towton
    and Saxton, in Yorkshire.*

    [*Alarum. Excursions.*° *Enter* WARWICK.]
    WAR. Forspent° with toil, as runners with a race,
I lay me down a little while to breathe,
For strokes received, and many blows repaid,
Have robbed my strong-knit sinews of their
    strength,
And spite of spite° needs must I rest awhile.   5
        [*Enter* EDWARD, *running.*]
    EDW. Smile, gentle Heaven! Or strike, ungentle
    death!
For this world frowns, and Edward's sun is
    clouded.
    WAR. How now, my lord! What hap?° What
    hope of good?
        [*Enter* GEORGE.]
    GEO. Our hap is loss, our hope but sad despair.
Our ranks are broke, and ruin follows us.   10
What counsel give you? Whither shall we fly?
    EDW. Bootless is flight, they follow us with wings,
And weak we are and cannot shun pursuit.
        [*Enter* RICHARD.]
    RICH. Ah, Warwick, why hast thou withdrawn
    thyself?   14
Thy brother's blood the thirsty earth hath drunk,
Broached with the steely point of Clifford's lance,
And in the very pangs of death he cried,
Like to a dismal clangor° heard from far,
"Warwick, revenge! Brother, revenge my death!"
So, underneath the belly of their steeds,   20
That stained their fetlocks° in his smoking blood,
The noble gentleman gave up the ghost.

    WAR. Then let the earth be drunken with our
    blood.
I'll kill my horse, because I will not fly.
Why stand we like soft-hearted women here,   25
Wailing our losses, whiles° the foe doth rage,
And look upon, as if the tragedy
Were played in jest by counterfeiting actors?
Here on my knee I vow to God above,
I'll never pause again, never stand still,   30
Till either death hath closed these eyes of mine,
Or fortune given me measure of revenge.
    EDW. O Warwick, I do bend my knee with thine,
And in this vow do chain my soul to thine!
And ere my knee rise from the earth's cold face,   35
I throw my hands, mine eyes, my heart to Thee,
Thou setter up and plucker down of kings,
Beseeching Thee, if with Thy will it stands
That to my foes this body must be prey,
Yet that Thy brazen gates of Heaven may ope   40
And give sweet passage to my sinful soul!
Now, lords, take leave until we meet again,
Where'er it be, in Heaven or in earth.
    RICH. Brother, give me thy hand, and, gentle
    Warwick,
Let me embrace thee in my weary arms.   45
I, that did never weep, now melt with woe
That winter should cut off our springtime so.
    WAR. Away, away! Once more, sweet lords, fare-
    well.
    GEO. Yet let us all together to our troops,
And give them leave to fly that will not stay,   50
And call them pillars that will stand to us;
And, if we thrive, promise them such rewards
As victors wear at the Olympian games.
This may plant courage in their quailing° breasts,
For yet is hope of life and victory.   55
Forslow° no longer, make we hence amain.°
        [*Exeunt.*]

SCENE IV. *Another part of the field.*

    [*Excursions. Enter* RICHARD *and* CLIFFORD.]
    RICH. Now, Clifford, I have singled thee alone.
Suppose this arm is for the Duke of York,
And this for Rutland — both bound to revenge,
Wert thou environed° with a brazen wall.
    CLIF. Now, Richard, I am with thee here alone.
This is the hand that stabbed thy father York,   6
And this the hand that slew thy brother Rutland,
And here's the heart that triumphs in their death
And cheers these hands, that slew thy sire and
    brother,
To execute the like upon thyself;   10

---

165. usurping: because as Henry's Queen she is a usurper.
    Sc. iii: s.d. **Excursions:** rapid movements indicating a battle.
1. Forspent: exhausted.   **5. spite of spite:** whatever happens.
8. hap: fortune.   **18. clangor:** clanging sound.   **21. fetlocks:**
the tuft of hair above the hoof of a horse.

26. whiles: while.   **54. quailing:** shrinking.   **56 Forslow:** delay.
amain: with full force.
    Sc. iv: 4. environed: surrounded.

And so, have at thee!
    [*They fight.* WARWICK *comes.* CLIFFORD *flies.*]
  RICH. Nay, Warwick, single out some other
    chase,°
For I myself will hunt this wolf to death.
                        [*Exeunt.*]

SCENE V. *Another part of the field.*

    [*Alarum. Enter* KING HENRY *alone.*]
  K. HEN. This battle fares like to the morning's
    war,
When dying clouds contend with growing light,
What time the shepherd, blowing of° his nails,
Can neither call it perfect day nor night.
Now sways it this way, like a mighty sea   5
Forced by the tide to combat with the wind.
Now sways it that way, like the selfsame sea
Forced to retire by fury of the wind.
Sometime the flood prevails, and then the wind,
Now one the better, then another best,   10
Both tugging to be victors, breast to breast,
Yet neither conqueror nor conquerèd:
So is the equal poise° of this fell war.
Here on this molehill will I sit me down.
To whom God will, there be the victory!   15
For Margaret my Queen, and Clifford too,
Have chid° me from the battle, swearing both
They prosper best of all when I am thence.
Would I were dead, if God's good will were so,
For what is in this world but grief and woe?   20
Oh, God! Methinks it were a happy life
To be no better than a homely swain,°
To sit upon a hill, as I do now,
To carve out dials quaintly, point by point,°
Thereby to see the minutes how they run —   25
How many make the hour full complete,
How many hours bring about the day,
How many days will finish up the year,
How many years a mortal man may live.
When this is known, then to divide the times —   30
So many hours must I tend my flock,
So many hours must I take my rest,
So many hours must I contemplate,
So many hours must I sport myself;
So many days my ewes have been with young,   35
So many weeks ere the poor fools will ean,°
So many years ere I shall shear the fleece.
So minutes, hours, days, months, and years,
Passed over to the end they were created,
Would bring white hairs unto a quiet grave.   40
Ah, what a life were this! How sweet! How lovely!
Gives not the hawthorn bush a sweeter shade

To shepherds looking on their silly° sheep
Than doth a rich embroidered canopy
To kings that fear their subjects' treachery?   45
Oh, yes, it doth, a thousandfold it doth.
And to conclude, the shepherd's homely curds,°
His cold thin drink out of his leather bottle,°
His wonted sleep under a fresh tree's shade,
All which secure° and sweetly he enjoys,   50
Is far beyond a prince's delicates,°
His viands sparkling in a golden cup,
His body couchèd in a curious° bed,
When care, mistrust, and treason waits on him.
[*Alarum. Enter a* SON *that has killed his father,*
dragging in the body.]
  SON. Ill blows the wind that profits nobody.   55
This man, whom hand to hand I slew in fight,
May be possessèd with some store of crowns;
And I, that haply° take them from him now,
May yet ere night yield both my life and them
To some man else, as this dead man doth me.   60
Who's this? O God! It is my father's face,
Whom in this conflict I, unwares, have killed.
O heavy times, begetting such events!
From London by the King was I pressed° forth.
My father, being the Earl of Warwick's man,   65
Came on the part of York, pressed by his master.
And I, who at his hands received my life,
Have by my hands of life bereavèd him.
Pardon me, God, I knew not what I did!
And pardon, Father, for I knew not thee!   70
My tears shall wipe away these bloody marks,
And no more words till they have flowed their fill.
  K. HEN. Oh, piteous spectacle! Oh, bloody times!
Whiles lions war and battle for their dens,
Poor harmless lambs abide° their enmity.   75
Weep, wretched man, I'll aid thee tear for tear,
And let our hearts and eyes, like civil war,
Be blind with tears, and break o'ercharged° with
    grief.
[*Enter a* FATHER *that has killed his son, bringing in*
the body.]
  FATH. Thou that so stoutly hast resisted me,
Give me thy gold if thou hast any gold,   80
For I have bought it with an hundred blows.
But let me see. Is this our foeman's face?
Ah, no, no, no, it is mine only son!
Ah, boy, if any life be left in thee,
Throw up thine eye! See, see what showers arise,
Blown with the windy tempest of my heart   86
Upon thy wounds, that kill mine eye and heart!
Oh, pity, God, this miserable age!
What stratagems,° how fell, how butcherly,

12. chase: prey.
  Sc. v: 3. of: on — to keep them warm.   13. poise: balance.
17. chid: roughly ordered.   22. swain: rustic.   24. carve . . .
point: i.e., cut out a sundial on the turf.   36. ean: bring forth
young.

43. silly: simple.   47. homely curds: simple food made of milk
curd.   48. leather bottle: See Pl. 17e.   50. secure: without a
care.   51. delicates: delicacies.   53. curious: elaborate. See
Pl. 17b.   58. haply: luckily.   64. pressed: conscripted.
75. abide: endure.   78. o'ercharged: filled to overflowing
98. stratagems; violent deeds.

Erroneous, mutinous and unnatural, 90
This deadly quarrel daily doth beget!
O boy, thy father gave thee life too soon,
And hath bereft thee of thy life too late!
  K. HEN. Woe above woe! Grief more than common grief!
Oh, that my death would stay these ruthful°
  deeds! 95
Oh, pity, pity, gentle Heaven, pity!
The red rose and the white are on his face,
The fatal colors of our striving houses.
The one his purple blood right well resembles,
The other his pale cheeks, methinks, presenteth.
Wither one rose, and let the other flourish. 101
If you contend, a thousand lives must wither.
  SON. How will my mother for a father's death
Take on with me and ne'er be satisfied!
  FATH. How will my wife for slaughter of my son
Shed seas of tears and ne'er be satisfied! 106
  K. HEN. How will the country for these woeful
  chances
Misthink° the King and not be satisfied!
  SON. Was ever son so rued a father's death?
  FATH. Was ever father so bemoaned his son? 110
  K. HEN. Was ever king so grieved for subjects'
  woe?
Much is your sorrow, mine ten times so much.
  SON. I'll bear thee hence, where I may weep my
  fill.   [*Exit with the body.*]
  FATH. These arms of mine shall be thy winding
  sheet,
My heart, sweet boy, shall be thy sepulcher. 115
For from my heart thine image ne'er shall go.
My sighing breast shall be thy funeral bell,°
And so obsequious° will thy father be,
Even for the loss of thee, having no more,
As Priam° was for all his valiant sons. 120
I'll bear thee hence, and let them fight that will,
For I have murdered where I should not kill.
             [*Exit with the body.*]
  K. HEN. Sad-hearted men, much overgone° with
  care,
Here sits a King more woeful than you are.
[*Alarums. Excursions. Enter* QUEEN MARGARET, *the*
    PRINCE, *and* EXETER.]
  PRIN. Fly, Father, fly! For all your friends are
  fled, 125
And Warwick rages like a chafèd° bull.
Away! For death doth hold us in pursuit.
  Q. MAR. Mount you, my lord. Toward Berwick
  post amain.
Edward and Richard, like a brace of greyhounds
Having the fearful flying hare in sight, 130

With fiery eyes sparkling for very wrath
And bloody steel grasped in their ireful hands,
Are at our backs; and therefore hence amain.
  EXE. Away! For vengeance comes along with
  them.
Nay, stay not to expostulate,° make speed, 135
Or else come after. I'll away before.
  K. HEN. Nay, take me with thee, good sweet Exeter.
Not that I fear to stay, but love to go
Whither the Queen intends. Forward, away!
                [*Exeunt.*]

SCENE VI. *Another part of the field*

[*A loud alarum. Enter* CLIFFORD, *wounded.°*]
  CLIF. Here burns my candle out. Aye, here it dies,
Which, whiles it lasted, gave King Henry light.
O Lancaster, I fear thy overthrow
More than my body's parting with my soul!
My love and fear° glued many friends to thee, 5
And, now I fall, thy tough commixture° melts.
Impairing Henry, strengthening misproud° York,
The common people swarm like summer flies,
And whither fly the gnats but to the sun?
And who shines now but Henry's enemies? 10
O Phoebus,° hadst thou never given consent
That Phaëthon° should check thy fiery steeds,
Thy burning car never had scorched the earth!
And, Henry, hadst thou swayed° as kings should
  do,
Or as thy father and his father did, 15
Giving no ground unto the House of York,
They never then had sprung like summer flies,
I and ten thousand in this luckless realm
Had left no mourning widows for our death,
And thou this day hadst kept thy chair in peace. 20
For what doth cherish weeds but gentle air?
And makes robbers bold but too much lenity?
Bootless are plaints, and cureless are my wounds;
No way to fly, nor strength to hold out flight.
The foe is merciless and will not pity, 25
For at their hands I have deserved no pity.
The air hath got into my deadly wounds,
And much effuse° of blood doth make me faint.
Come, York and Richard, Warwick and the rest.
I stabbed your fathers' bosoms, split my breast. 30
                [*He faints.*]
[*Alarum and retreat.° Enter* EDWARD, GEORGE,
RICHARD, MONTAGUE, WARWICK, *and* SOLDIERS.]

135. expostulate: argue.
Sc. vi: s.d., wounded: The *Contention* adds the detail "with
an arrow in his neck." 5. fear: i.e., of me. 6. commixture:
union of love and fear. 7. misproud: wrongfully proud.
11. Phoebus: the sun god. 12. Phaëthon: See I.iv.33,n.
14. swayed: ruled. 28. effuse: effusion, loss. 30. s.d., retreat:
battle noises.

95. ruthful: piteous. 108. Misthink: misjudge. 117. funeral
bell: See App. 19. 118. obsequious: mourning. 120. Priam:
King of Troy who had fifty sons, all slain during the Trojan War.
123. overgone: overcome. 126. chafed: enraged.

EDW. Now breathe we, lords. Good fortune bids
  us pause
And smooth the frowns of war with peaceful looks.
Some troops pursue the bloody-minded Queen,
That led calm Henry, though he were a King,
As doth a sail, filled with a fretting gust,   35
Command an argosy° to stem° the waves.
But think you, lords, that Clifford fled with them?
  WAR. No, 'tis impossible he should escape,
For, though before his face I speak the words,
Your brother Richard marked him for the grave,
And wheresoe'er he is, he's surely dead.   41
          [CLIFFORD *groans, and dies.*]
  EDW. Whose soul is that which takes her heavy
    leave?
  RICH. A deadly groan, like life and death's de-
    parting.°
  EDW. See who it is. And, now the battle's ended,
If friend or foe, let him be gently used.   45
  RICH. Revoke that doom of mercy, for 'tis Clif-
    ford,
Who not contented that he lopped the branch
In hewing Rutland when his leaves put forth,°
But set his murdering knife unto the root
From whence that tender spray° did sweetly
    spring —   50
I mean our princely father, Duke of York.
  WAR. From off the gates of York fetch down the
    head,
Your father's head, which Clifford placèd there;
Instead whereof let this supply the room.°
Measure for measure must be answerèd.   55
  EDW. Bring forth that fatal screech owl° to our
    house
That nothing sung but death to us and ours.
Now death shall stop his dismal threatening sound,
And his ill-boding° tongue no more shall speak.
  WAR. I think his understanding is bereft.   60
Speak, Clifford, dost thou know who speaks to
    thee?
Dark cloudy death o'ershades his beams of life,
And he nor° sees, nor hears us what we say.
  RICH. Oh, would he did! And so perhaps he doth.
'Tis but his policy° to counterfeit   65
Because he would avoid such bitter taunts
Which in the time of death he gave our father.
  GEO. If so thou think'st, vex him with eager
    words.
  RICH. Clifford, ask mercy and obtain no grace.

  EDW. Clifford, repent in bootless penitence.   70
  WAR. Clifford, devise excuses for thy faults.
  GEO. While we devise fell tortures for thy faults.
  RICH. Thou didst love York, and I am son to
    York.
  EDW. Thou pitied'st Rutland. I will pity thee.
  GEO. Where's Captain Margaret, to fence° you
    now?   75
  WAR. They mock thee, Clifford. Swear as thou
    wast wont.
  RICH. What, not an oath? Nay, then the world
    goes hard
When Clifford cannot spare his friends an oath.
I know by that he's dead; and, by my soul,
If this right hand would buy two hours' life,   80
That I in all despite might rail at him,
This hand should chop it off, and with the issuing
    blood
Stifle the villain, whose unstanched° thirst
York and young Rutland could not satisfy.
  WAR. Aye, but he's dead. Off with the traitor's
    head   85
And rear° it in the place your father's stands.
And now to London with triumphant march,
There to be crownèd England's royal King;
From whence shall Warwick cut° the sea to
    France,
And ask the Lady Bona for thy queen.   90
So shalt thou sinew° both these lands together,
And, having France thy friend, thou shalt not
    dread
The scattered foe that hopes to rise again.
For though they cannot greatly sting to hurt,
Yet look to have them buzz to offend thine ears.
First will I see the coronation,   96
And then to Brittany I'll cross the sea
To effect this marriage, so it please my lord.
  EDW. Even as thou wilt, sweet Warwick, let it be;
For in° thy shoulder do I build my seat,   100
And never will I undertake the thing
Wherein thy counsel and consent is wanting.
Richard, I will create thee Duke of Gloucester,
And George, of Clarence. Warwick, as ourself,
Shall do and undo as him pleaseth best.   105
  RICH. Let me be Duke of Clarence, George of
    Gloucester,
For Gloucester's dukedom is too ominous.°
  WAR. Tut, that's a foolish observation.
Richard, be Duke of Gloucester. Now to London
To see these honors in possession. [*Exeunt.*] 110

---

36. argosy: great merchant vessel. stem: cut through with the
prow.   43. departing: parting company.   48. when . . . forth:
i.e., in his youth.   50. spray: young branch.   54. supply . . .
room: take the place.   56. screech owl: regarded as a bird of
evil omen.   59. ill-boding: prophesying evil.   63. nor: neither.
65. policy: cunning.

75. fence: protect.   83. unstanched: unquenchable.   86. rear:
set up.   89. cut: cut through, cross.   91. sinew: join.   100. in:
on.   107. ominous: The title Duke of Gloucester had been
borne by Humphrey (see *II Hen VI*, III.ii), Thomas of Woodstock (see *Rich II*, I.i.98–102), and Hugh Spenser, favorite of
Edward II, all of whom had died violently.

Act III

SCENE I. *A forest in the North of England.*

[*Enter two* KEEPERS, *with crossbows° in their hands.*]

1. KEEP. Under this thick-grown brake° we'll
    shroud° ourselves,
For through this laund° anon° the deer will come;
And in this covert will we make our stand,
Culling° the principal of all the deer.   4
  2. KEEP. I'll stay above the hill so both may shoot.
  1. KEEP. That cannot be. The noise of thy cross-
    bow
Will scare the herd, and so my shoot is lost.
Here stand we both, and aim we at the best;
And, for the time shall not seem tedious,
I'll tell thee what befell me on a day   10
In this self° place where now we mean to stand.
  2. KEEP. Here comes a man. Let's stay till he be
    past.
[*Enter* KING HENRY, *disguised, with a prayer book.*]
  K. HEN. From Scotland am I stol'n, even of pure
    love,
To greet mine own land with my wishful° sight.   15
No, Harry, Harry, 'tis no land of thine.
Thy place is filled, thy scepter wrung from thee,
Thy balm° washed off wherewith thou wast
    anointed.
No bending knee will call thee Caesar now,
No humble suitors press to speak for right,
No, not a man comes for redress of thee;°   20
For how can I help them, and not myself?
  1. KEEP. Aye, here's a deer whose skin's a keeper's
    fee.
This is the quondam° King. Let's seize upon him.
  K. HEN. Let me embrace thee, sour Adversity,
For wise men say it is the wisest course.   25
  2. KEEP. Why linger we? Let us lay hands upon
    him.
  1. KEEP. Forbear awhile. We'll hear a little more.
  K. HEN. My Queen and son are gone to France
    for aid,
And, as I hear, the great commanding Warwick
Is thither gone to crave the French King's sister   30
To wife for Edward. If this news be true,
Poor Queen and Son, your labor is but lost;
For Warwick is a subtle orator,
And Lewis a prince soon won with moving words.
By this account then Margaret may win him,   35
For she's a woman to be pitied much.
Her sighs will make a battery in his breast,

Her tears will pierce into a marble heart,
The tiger will be mild whiles she doth mourn,
And Nero° will be tainted with remorse°   40
To hear and see her plaints,° her brinish° tears.
Aye, but she's come to beg, Warwick, to give;
She, on his left side, craving aid for Henry,
He, on his right, asking a wife for Edward.
She weeps and says her Henry is deposed;   45
He smiles and says his Edward is installed;
That she, poor wretch, for grief can speak no more,
Whiles Warwick tells his title,° smooths the wrong,
Inferreth° arguments of mighty strength,
And in conclusion wins the King from her   50
With promise of his sister, and what else,
To strengthen and support King Edward's place.
O Margaret, thus 'twill be; and thou, poor soul,
Art then forsaken, as thou went'st forlorn!
  2. KEEP. Say, what art thou that talk'st of kings
    and queens?   55
  K. HEN. More than I seem, and less than I was
    born to.
A man at least, for less I should not be;
And men may talk of kings, and why not I?
  2. KEEP. Aye, but thou talk'st as if thou wert a
    King.
  K. HEN. Why, so I am, in mind, and that's
    enough.   60
  2. KEEP. But if thou be a King, where is thy
    crown?
  K. HEN. My crown is in my heart, not on my
    head,
Not decked with diamonds and Indian stones,°
Nor to be seen. My crown is called content.
A crown it is that seldom kings enjoy.   65
  2. KEEP. Well, if you be a King crowned with
    content,
Your crown content and you must be contented
To go along with us; for, as we think,
You are the King King Edward hath deposed,
And we his subjects sworn in all allegiance   70
Will apprehend you as his enemy.
  K. HEN. But did you never swear, and break an
    oath?
  2. KEEP. No, never such an oath, nor will not
    now.
  K. HEN. Where did you dwell when I was King
    of England?
  2. KEEP. Here in this country where we now re-
    main.   75
  K. HEN. I was anointed King at nine months old.
My father and my grandfather were Kings,
And you were sworn true subjects unto me.

Act III, Sc.i: s.d., **crossbows**: See Pl. 22b. 1. **brake**: thicket.
shroud: cover. 2. **laund**: lawn, open space in a forest. **anon**:
by and by. 4. **Culling**: selecting. 11. **self**: same. 14. **wish-
ful**: longing. 17. **balm**: sacred oil. 20. **for . . . thee**: to thee
for redress. 23. **quondam**: former.

40. **Nero**: the Roman Emperor who is the standard example of
cruelty. **tainted . . . remorse**: lose his proper nature through
pity. 41. **plaints**: lamentations. **brinish**: salt. 48. **tells . . .
title**: i.e., explains Edward's claim to the throne. 49. **Inferreth**:
produces. 63. **Indian stones**: pearls. See *Tr & Cr*, I.i.105.

And tell me, then, have you not broke your oaths?
1. KEEP. No,   80
For we were subjects but while° you were King.
K. HEN. Why, am I dead? Do I not breathe a
man?
Ah, simple men, you know not what you swear!
Look, as I blow this feather from my face,
And as the air blows it to me again,   85
Obeying with my wind when I do blow
And yielding to another when it blows,
Commanded always by the greater gust,
Such is the lightness of you common men.
But do not break your oaths, for of that sin   90
My mild entreaty shall not make you guilty.
Go where you will, the King shall be commanded;
And be you kings. Command, and I'll obey.
1. KEEP. We are true subjects to the King, King
Edward.
K. HEN. So would you be again to Henry   95
If he were seated as King Edward is.
1. KEEP. We charge you, in God's name and the
King's,
To go with us unto the officers.
K. HEN. In God's name, lead. Your King's name
be obeyed.   99
And what God will, that let your King perform;
And what he will, I humbly yield unto. [*Exeunt.*]

SCENE II. *London. The palace.*

[*Enter* KING EDWARD, GLOUCESTER, CLARENCE, *and*
LADY GREY.]

K. EDW. Brother of Gloucester, at Saint Alban's
field
This lady's husband, Sir Richard Grey, was slain,
His lands then seized on by the conqueror.
Her suit is now to repossess those lands,
Which we in justice cannot well deny,   5
Because in quarrel of the House of York
The worthy gentleman did lose his life.
GLO. Your Highness shall do well to grant her
suit.
It were dishonor to deny it her.
K. EDW. It were no less, but yet I'll make a pause.
GLO. [*Aside to* CLARENCE] Yea, is it so?   11
I see the lady hath a thing to grant
Before the King will grant her humble suit.
CLAR. [*Aside to* GLOUCESTER] He knows the
game. How true he keeps the wind!°
GLO. [*Aside to* CLARENCE] Silence!   15
K. EDW. Widow, we will consider of your suit;
And come some other time to know our mind.
GREY. Right gracious lord, I cannot brook delay.

May it please your Highness to resolve me now,
And what your pleasure is shall satisfy me.   20
GLO. [*Aside to* CLARENCE] Aye, widow? Then I'll
warrant° you all your lands
An if what pleases him shall pleasure you.
Fight closer, or, good faith, you'll catch a blow.
CLAR. [*Aside to* GLOUCESTER] I fear her not, un-
less she chance to fall.
GLO. [*Aside to* CLARENCE] God forbid that! For
he'll take vantages.   25
K. EDW. How many children hast thou, widow?
Tell me.
CLAR. [*Aside to* GLOUCESTER] I think he means to
beg a child of her.
GLO. [*Aside to* CLARENCE] Nay, whip me then.
He'll rather give her two.
GREY. Three, my most gracious lord.
GLO. [*Aside to* CLARENCE] You shall have four if
you'll be ruled by him.   30
K. EDW. 'Twere pity they should lose their father's
lands.
GREY. Be pitiful, dread lord, and grant it then.
K. EDW. Lords, give us leave. I'll try this widow's
wit.
GLO. [*Aside to* CLARENCE] Aye, good leave have
you, for you will have leave
Till youth take leave and leave you to the crutch.°
[GLOUCESTER *and* CLARENCE *retire.*]
K. EDW. Now tell me, madam, do you love your
children?   36
GREY. Aye, full as dearly as I love myself.
K. EDW. And would you not do much to do them
good?
GREY. To do them good I would sustain some
harm.
K. EDW. Then get your husband's lands to do
them good.   40
GREY. Therefore I came unto your Majesty.
K. EDW. I'll tell you how these lands are to be got.
GREY. So shall you bind me to your Highness'
service.
K. EDW. What service wilt thou do me if I give
them?   44
GREY. What you command that rests in me to do.
K. EDW. But you will take exceptions to my boon.°
GREY. No, gracious lord, except I cannot do it.
K. EDW. Aye, but thou canst do what I mean to
ask.
GREY. Why, then I will do what your Grace com-
mands.
GLOU. [*Aside to* CLARENCE] He plies° her hard,
and much rain wears the marble.   50
CLAR. [*Aside to* GLOUCESTER] As red as fire! Nay,
then her wax must melt.

---

81. **but while:** only so long as.

Sc. ii: 14. **keeps . . . wind:** hunts contrary to the wind — so
that the deer shall not perceive him.

21. **warrant:** guarantee.   35. **leave . . . crutch:** i.e., until you're
too old for lovemaking.   46. **boon:** favor asked.   50. **plies:**
urges.

GREY. Why stops my lord? Shall I not hear my
    task?

K. EDW. An easy task — 'tis but to love a king.

GREY. That's soon performed, because I am a sub-
    ject.

K. EDW. Why, then, thy husband's lands I freely
    give thee.   55

GREY. I take my leave with many thousand
    thanks.

GLO. [*Aside to* CLARENCE] The match is made.
    She seals it with a curt'sy.

K. EDW. But stay thee, 'tis the fruits of love I
    mean.

GREY. The fruits of love I mean, my loving liege.

K. EDW. Aye, but, I fear me, in another sense.   60
What love think'st thou I sue so much to get?

GREY. My love till death, my humble thanks, my
    prayers;
That love which virtue begs and virtue grants.

K. EDW. No, by my troth,° I did not mean such
    love.

GREY. Why, then you mean not as I thought you
    did.   65

K. EDW. But now you partly may perceive my
    mind.

GREY. My mind will never grant what I perceive
Your Highness aims at, if I aim aright.

K. EDW. To tell thee plain, I aim to lie with thee.

GREY. To tell you plain, I had rather lie in prison.

K. EDW. Why, then thou shalt not have thy hus-
    band's lands.   71

GREY. Why, then mine honesty shall be my
    dower,
For by that loss I will not purchase them.

K. EDW. Therein thou wrong'st thy children
    mightily.

GREY. Herein your Highness wrongs both them
    and me.   75
But, mighty lord, this merry inclination
Accords not with the sadness° of my suit.
Please you dismiss me, either with " aye " or " no."

K. EDW. Aye, if thou wilt say " aye " to my re-
    quest;
No, if thou dost say " no " to my demand.   80

GREY. Then, no, my lord. My suit is at an end.

GLO. [*Aside to* CLARENCE] The widow likes him
    not; she knits her brows.

CLAR. [*Aside to* GLOUCESTER] He is the bluntest
    wooer in Christendom.

K. EDW. [*Aside*] Her looks do argue her replete
    with° modesty.
Her words do show her wit incomparable.   85
All her perfections challenge sovereignty.
One way or other, she is for a king,
And she shall be my love, or else my Queen. —

Say that King Edward take thee for his Queen?

GREY. 'Tis better said than done, my gracious
    lord.   90
I am a subject fit to jest withal,
But far unfit to be a sovereign.

K. EDW. Sweet widow, by my state° I swear to
    thee
I speak no more than what my soul intends,
And that is to enjoy thee for my love.   95

GREY. And that is more than I will yield unto.
I know I am too mean to be your Queen,
And yet too good to be your concubine.

K. EDW. You cavil,° widow. I did mean my
    Queen.

GREY. 'Twill grieve your Grace my sons should
    call you father.   100

K. EDW. No more than when my daughters call
    thee mother.
Thou art a widow, and thou hast some children;
And, by God's Mother,° I, being but a bachelor,
Have other some.° Why, 'tis a happy thing
To be the father unto many sons.   105
Answer no more, for thou shalt be my Queen.

GLO. [*Aside to* CLARENCE] The ghostly father now
    hath done his shrift.°

CLAR. [*Aside to* GLOUCESTER] When he was made
    a shriver,° 'twas for shift.°

K. EDW. Brothers, you muse what chat we two
    have had.

GLO. The widow likes it not, for she looks very
    sad.   110

K. EDW. You'd think it strange if I should marry
    her.

CLAR. To whom, my lord?

K. EDW.   Why, Clarence, to myself.

GLO. That would be ten days'° wonder at the
    least.

CLAR. That's a day longer than a wonder lasts.

GLO. By so much is the wonder in extremes.   115

K. EDW. Well, jest on, Brothers. I can tell you
    both
Her suit is granted for her husband's lands.

[*Enter a* NOBLEMAN.]

NOB. My gracious lord, Henry your foe is taken
And brought your prisoner to your palace gate.

K. EDW. See that he be conveyed unto the Tower,
And go we, Brothers, to the man that took him,
To question of his apprehension.   122
Widow, go you along. Lords, use her honorably.

[*Exeunt all but* GLOUCESTER.]

93. state: kingship.   99. cavil: raise frivolous objections.
103. Mother: the Blessed Virgin.   104. other some: i.e., children
of my own.   107. The . . . shrift: During their conversation
Lady Grey has been kneeling before Edward, like a penitent
at confession (*shrift*). She now rises to her feet.   108. shriver:
lit., priest, one able to give absolution from sins. shift: trickery.
113. ten days': i.e., even greater than the usual Nine Days'
Wonder.

64. troth: truth.   77. sadness: seriousness.   84. replete with:
full of.

GLO. Aye, Edward will use women honorably.
Would he were wasted, marrow, bones and all,
That from his loins no hopeful branch may spring
To cross° me from the golden time° I look for!
And yet, between my soul's desire and me — 128
The lustful Edward's title buried —
Is Clarence, Henry, and his son young Edward,
And all the unlooked for° issue of their bodies,
To take their rooms, ere I can place myself. 132
A cold premeditation° for my purpose!
Why, then, I do but dream on sovereignty,
Like one that stands upon a promontory 135
And spies a far-off shore where he would tread,
Wishing his foot were equal with his eye,
And chides the sea that sunders° him from thence,
Saying he'll lade° it dry to have his way:
So do I wish the crown, being so far off, 140
And so I chide the means that keeps me from it,
And so I say I'll cut the causes off,
Flattering me with impossibilities.°
My eye's too quick, my heart o'erweens° too much,
Unless my hand and strength could equal them.
Well, say there is no kingdom then for Richard.
What other pleasure can the world afford? 147
I'll make my heaven in a lady's lap,
And deck my body in gay ornaments,
And witch° sweet ladies with my words and looks.
Oh, miserable thought, and more unlikely 151
Than to accomplish twenty golden crowns!
Why, love forswore me in my mother's womb
And, for I should not° deal in her soft laws,
She did corrupt frail nature with some bribe 155
To shrink mine arm up like a withered shrub,
To make an envious° mountain on my back,
Where sits deformity to mock my body,
To shape my legs of an unequal size,
To disproportion me in every part, 160
Like to a chaos,° or an unlicked bear whelp°
That carries no impression° like the dam.
And am I then a man to be beloved?
Oh, monstrous fault, to harbor such a thought!
Then, since this earth affords no joy to me 165
But to command, to check,° to o'erbear such
As are of better person than myself,
I'll make my heaven to dream upon the crown
And, whiles I live, to account this world but Hell
Until my misshaped trunk that bears this head 170

Be round impalèd° with a glorious crown.
And yet I know not how to get the crown,
For many lives stand between me and home.°
And I — like one lost in a thorny wood,
That rends the thorns and is rent with the thorns,
Seeking a way and straying from the way, 176
Not knowing how to find the open air,
But toiling desperately to find it out —
Torment myself to catch the English crown.
And from that torment I will free myself, 180
Or hew my way out with a bloody ax.
Why, I can smile, and murder whiles I smile,
And cry " Content "° to that which grieves my
    heart,
And wet my cheeks with artificial tears,
And frame my face° to all occasions. 185
I'll drown more sailors than the mermaid° shall;
I'll slay more gazers than the basilisk;°
I'll play the orator as well as Nestor,°
Deceive more slyly than Ulysses° could,
And, like a Sinon,° take another Troy. 190
I can add colors to the chameleon,
Change shapes with Proteus° for advantages,
And set the murderous Machiavel° to school.
Can I do this, and cannot get a crown? 194
Tut, were it farther off, I'll pluck it down. [*Exit.*]

SCENE III. *France. The* KING'S *palace.*

[*Flourish. Enter* LEWIS *the French King, his sister*
BONA, *his Admiral, called* BOURBON, PRINCE EDWARD,
QUEEN MARGARET, *and the* EARL OF OXFORD. LEWIS
sits, and riseth up again.]

K. LEW. Fair Queen of England, worthy Marga-
    ret,
Sit down with us. It ill befits thy state
And birth that thou shouldst stand while Lewis
    doth sit.
Q. MAR. No, mighty King of France. Now Mar-
    garet
Must strike° her sail and learn a while to serve 5
Where kings command. I was, I must confess,
Great Albion's° Queen in former golden days;
But now mischance hath trod my title down
And with dishonor laid me on the ground,

---

127. cross: thwart, prevent. golden time: i.e., enjoyment of the crown. 131. unlooked for: as yet unseen. 133. cold premeditation: hopeless reflection. 138. sunders: separates. 139. lade: bale. 142–43. And . . . impossibilities: i.e., I'll pretend that I can destroy those who stand in my way, deceiving myself with what is impossible. 144. o'erweens: is proud. 150. witch: bewitch. 154. for . . . not: lest. 157. envious: hateful. 161. chaos: shapeless mass. unlicked . . . whelp: It was believed that a bear cub was born shapeless but was licked into shape by its mother. 162. impression: shape. 166. check: rebuke.

171. impaled: surrounded. 173. home: i.e., my destination. 183. Content: agreed. 185. frame my face: suit my looks. 186. mermaid: See *Errors*, III.ii.45,n. 187. basilisk: See *Rich III*, I.ii.151,n. 188. Nestor: the old Greek veteran of the Trojan war. See *Tr & Cr*. 189. Ulysses: the cunning general by whose device the Wooden Horse Troy was ultimately taken. 190. Sinon: a Greek who pretended to desert to the Trojans. He persuaded them to take into the city the Wooden Horse filled with armed Greeks. When night came, Sinon released his friends from the Horse. 192. Proteus: the "Old Man of the Sea," who cared for the sea god's seals. If seized, he changed himself into some other shape. 193. Machiavel: See *I Hen VI*, V.iv.74,n.
    Sc. iii: 5. strike: lower in sign of submission. 7. Albion: England.

Where I must take like seat unto my fortune   10
And to my humble seat conform myself.
    K. LEW. Why, say, fair Queen, whence springs
    this deep despair?
    Q. MAR. From such a cause as fills mine eyes with
    tears
And stops my tongue, while heart is drowned in
  cares.
    K. LEW. Whate'er it be, be thou still like thyself,
And sit thee by our side. [*Seats her by him.*] Yield
  not thy neck   16
To fortune's yoke, but let thy dauntless mind
Still ride in triumph over all mischance.
Be plain, Queen Margaret, and tell thy grief.
It shall be eased if France can yield relief.   20
    Q. MAR. Those gracious words revive my droop-
    ing thoughts
And give my tongue-tied sorrows leave to speak.
Now, therefore, be it known to noble Lewis
That Henry, sole possessor of my love,
Is of° a King become a banished man,   25
And forced to live in Scotland a forlorn,°
While proud ambitious Edward Duke of York
Usurps the regal title and the seat
Of England's true-anointed lawful King.
This is the cause that I, poor Margaret,   30
With this my son, Prince Edward, Henry's heir,
Am come to crave thy just and lawful aid,
And if thou fail us, all our hope is done.
Scotland hath will to help, but cannot help.
Our people and our peers are both misled,   35
Our treasure seized, our soldiers put to flight,
And, as thou seest, ourselves in heavy plight.
    K. LEW. Renownèd Queen, with patience calm the
    storm
While we bethink a means to break it off.
    Q. MAR. The more we stay,° the stronger grows
    our foe.   40
    K. LEW. The more I stay, the more I'll succor thee.
    Q. MAR. Oh, but impatience waiteth on true sor-
    row.
And see where comes the breeder of my sorrow!
      [*Enter* WARWICK.]
    K. LEW. What's he approacheth boldly to our
    presence?
    Q. MAR. Our Earl of Warwick, Edward's greatest
    friend.   45
    K. LEW. Welcome, brave Warwick! What brings
    thee to France?   [*He descends. She ariseth.*]
    Q. MAR. Aye, now begins a second storm to rise,
For this is he that moves both wind and tide.
    WAR. From worthy Edward, King of Albion,
My lord and sovereign, and thy vowèd friend,   50
I come, in kindness and unfeignèd love,
First, to do greetings to thy royal person,

And then, to crave a league of amity,
And lastly, to confirm that amity
With nuptial knot if thou vouchsafe to grant   55
That virtuous Lady Bona, thy fair sister,
To England's King in lawful marriage.
    Q. MAR. [*Aside*] If that go forward, Henry's hope
    is done.
    WAR. [*To* BONA] And, gracious madam, in our
    King's behalf,
I am commanded, with your leave and favor,   60
Humbly to kiss your hand, and with my tongue
To tell the passion of my sovereign's heart,
Where fame, late entering at his heedful ears,
Hath placed thy beauty's image and thy virtue.
    Q. MAR. King Lewis and Lady Bona, hear me
    speak   65
Before you answer Warwick. His demand
Springs not from Edward's well-meant honest love,
But from deceit bred by necessity.
For how can tyrants safely govern home
Unless abroad they purchase great alliance?   70
To prove him tyrant this reason may suffice:
That Henry liveth still. But were he dead,
Yet here Prince Edward stands, King Henry's son.
Look, therefore, Lewis, that by this league and
  marriage
Thou draw not on thy danger and dishonor;   75
For though usurpers sway the rule a while,
Yet Heavens are just, and time suppresseth wrongs.
    WAR. Injurious° Margaret!
    PRIN.   And why not Queen?
    WAR. Because thy father Henry did usurp,
And thou no more art Prince than she is Queen.
    OXF. Then Warwick disannuls° great John of
    Gaunt,   81
Which did subdue the greatest part of Spain;
And, after John of Gaunt, Henry the Fourth,
Whose wisdom was a mirror to the wisest;
And, after that wise prince, Henry the Fifth,   85
Who by his prowess conquerèd all France.
From these our Henry lineally descends.
    WAR. Oxford, how haps it, in this smooth dis-
    course,
You told not how Henry the Sixth hath lost
All that which Henry the Fifth had gotten?   90
Methinks these peers of France should smile at that.
But for the rest, you tell a pedigree
Of threescore and two years — a silly time
To make prescription for a kingdom's worth.°
    OXF. Why, Warwick, canst thou speak against
    thy liege,   95
Whom thou obeyed'st thirty and six years,

---

25. of: from being.   **26. forlorn:** a man abandoned.   **40. stay:**
wait.

78. Injurious: insulting.   **81. disannuls:** cancels out.
92–94. But . . . worth: but in conclusion (*for the rest*), you are
making a claim (*tell a pedigree*) which is sixty-two years old —
a senseless (*silly*) period for making a claim (*presumption*) to the
riches of a kingdom. The episode shown in this scene occurred in
1461 — 62 years after Henry IV deposed Richard II.

And not bewray thy treason with a blush?

WAR. Can Oxford, that did ever fence the right,
Now buckler° falsehood with a pedigree?   99
For shame! Leave Henry, and call Edward, King.

OXF. Call him my King by whose injurious doom
My elder brother, the Lord Aubrey Vere,
Was done to death? And more than so, my father,
Even in the downfall of his mellowed years,   104
When nature brought him to the door of death?
No, Warwick, no. While life upholds this arm,
This arm upholds the House of Lancaster.

WAR. And I the House of York.

K. LEW. Queen Margaret, Prince Edward, and
Oxford,
Vouchsafe, at our request, to stand aside   110
While I use further conference with Warwick.
                         [*They stand aloof.*]

Q. MAR. Heavens grant that Warwick's words
bewitch him not!

K. LEW. Now, Warwick, tell me, even upon thy
conscience,
Is Edward your true King? For I were loath   114
To link with him that were not lawful chosen.

WAR. Thereon I pawn my credit and mine honor.

K. LEW. But is he gracious in the people's eye?

WAR. The more that Henry was unfortunate.

K. LEW. Then further, all dissembling° set aside,
Tell me for truth the measure of his love   120
Unto our sister Bona.

WAR.   Such it seems
As may beseem° a monarch like himself.
Myself have often heard him say and swear
That this his love was an eternal plant   124
Whereof the root was fixed in virtue's ground,
The leaves and fruit maintained with beauty's sun,
Exempt from envy, but not from disdain,
Unless the Lady Bona quit his pain.°   128

K. LEW. Now, Sister, let us hear your firm resolve.

BONA. Your grant, or your denial, shall be mine.
[*To WARWICK*] Yet I confess that often ere this day,
When I have heard your King's desert recounted,
Mine ear hath tempted judgment to desire.

K. LEW. Then, Warwick, thus: Our sister shall be
Edward's;
And now forthwith shall articles be drawn   135
Touching the jointure° that your King must make,
Which with her dowry shall be counterpoised.°
Draw near, Queen Margaret, and be a witness
That Bona shall be wife to the English King.   139

PRIN. To Edward, but not to the English King.

Q. MAR. Deceitful Warwick! It was thy device
By this alliance to make void my suit.

---

99. **buckler**: shield.   119. **dissembling**: pretense.   122. **be-**
seem: become.   127–28. **Exempt ... pain**: if the Lady Bona
does not repay (*quit*) his passion (*pain*) with love, he will bear no
malice (*envy*), but he will certainly suffer contempt (*disdain*).
136. **jointure**: marriage settlement given to the wife.   137. **coun-**
terpoised: equally weighed.

Before thy coming Lewis was Henry's friend.

K. LEW. And still is friend to him and Margaret.
But if your title to the crown be weak,   145
As may appear by Edward's good success,
Then 'tis but reason that I be released
From giving aid which late I promisèd.
Yet shall you have all kindness at my hand
That your estate requires and mine can yield.   150

WAR. Henry now lives in Scotland at his ease,
Where having nothing, nothing can he lose.
And as for you yourself, our quondam Queen,
You have a father able to maintain you,   154
And better 'twere you troubled him than France.

Q. MAR. Peace, impudent and shameless Warwick,
peace,
Proud setter up and puller down of kings!
I will not hence till, with my talk and tears,
Both full of truth, I make King Lewis behold
Thy sly conveyance° and thy lord's false love;   160
For both of you are birds of selfsame feather.
                  [POST *blows a horn° within.*]

K. LEW. Warwick, this is some post to us or thee.
                         [*Enter a* POST.]

POST. [*To* WARWICK] My Lord Ambassador, these
letters are for you,
Sent from your brother Marquess Montague,
[*To* LEWIS] These from our King unto your Majesty,   165
[*To* MARGARET] And, madam, these for you, from
whom I know not. [*They all read their letters.*]

OXF. I like it well that our fair Queen and mistress
Smiles at her news, while Warwick frowns at his.

PRIN. Nay, mark how Lewis stamps, as he were
nettled.
I hope all's for the best.   170

K. LEW. Warwick, what are thy news? And
yours, fair Queen?

Q. MAR. Mine, such as fill my heart with unhoped
joys.

WAR. Mine, full of sorrow and heart's discontent.

K. LEW. What! Has your King married the Lady
Grey?
And now, to soothe your forgery° and his,   175
Sends me a paper to persuade me patience?
Is this the alliance that he seeks with France?
Dare he presume to scorn us in this manner?

Q. MAR. I told your Majesty as much before.
This proveth Edward's love and Warwick's honesty!   180

WAR. King Lewis, I here protest, in sight of
Heaven
And by the hope I have of heavenly bliss,
That I am clear from this misdeed of Edward's —
No more my King, for he dishonors me,

---

160. **conveyance**: fraud.   161. s.d., **Post ... horn**: See App. 17
175. **forgery**: deceit.

But most himself,° if he could see his shame.   185
Did I forget that by the House of York
My father came untimely to his death?
Did I let pass the abuse done to my niece?°
Did I impale° him with the regal crown?
Did I put Henry from his native right?   190
And am I guerdoned° at the last with shame?
Shame on himself! For my desert is honor;
And to repair my honor lost for him,
I here renounce him and return to Henry.
My noble Queen, let former grudges pass,   195
And henceforth I am thy true servitor.
I will revenge his wrong to Lady Bona
And replant Henry in his former state.

    Q. MAR. Warwick, these words have turned my
    hate to love,
And I forgive and quite forget old faults,   200
And joy that thou becomest King Henry's friend.

    WAR. So much his friend, aye, his unfeignèd
    friend,
That if King Lewis vouchsafe to furnish us
With some few bands of chosen soldiers,
I'll undertake to land them on our coast   205
And force the tyrant from his seat by war.
'Tis not his new-made bride shall succor him.
And as for Clarence, as my letters tell me,
He's very likely now to fall from him   209
For matching° more for wanton lust than honor,
Or than for strength and safety of our country.

    BONA. Dear Brother, how shall Bona be revenged
But by thy help to this distressèd Queen?

    Q. MAR. Renownèd Prince, how shall poor Henry
    live
Unless thou rescue him from foul despair?   215

    BONA. My quarrel and this English Queen's are
    one.

    WAR. And mine, fair Lady Bona, joins with
    yours.

    K. LEW. And mine with hers, and thine, and
    Margaret's.
Therefore at last I firmly am resolved
You shall have aid.   220

    Q. MAR. Let me give humble thanks for all at
    once.

    K. LEW. Then, England's messenger, return in
    post
And tell false Edward, thy supposèd King,
That Lewis of France is sending over masquers°

To revel it with him and his new bride.   225
Thou seest what's past, go fear° thy King withal.°

    BONA. Tell him, in hope he'll prove a widower
    shortly,
I'll wear the willow garland° for his sake.

    Q. MAR. Tell him my mourning weeds° are laid
    aside,
And I am ready to put armor on.   230

    WAR. Tell him from me that he hath done me
    wrong,
And therefore I'll uncrown him ere 't be long.
There's thy reward. Be gone.   [*Exit* POST.]

    K. LEW.   But, Warwick,
Thou and Oxford, with five thousand men,   234
Shall cross the seas and bid false Edward battle;
And, as occasion serves, this noble Queen
And Prince shall follow with a fresh supply.
Yet, ere thou go, but answer me one doubt:
What pledge have we of thy firm loyalty?

    WAR. This shall assure my constant loyalty: 240
That if our Queen and this young Prince agree,
I'll join mine eldest daughter and my joy
To him forthwith in holy wedlock bands.

    Q. MAR. Yes, I agree, and thank you for your mo-
    tion.
Son Edward, she is fair and virtuous.   245
Therefore delay not, give thy hand to Warwick,
And, with thy hand, thy faith irrevocable
That only Warwick's daughter shall be thine.

    PRIN. Yes, I accept her, for she well deserves it;
And here, to pledge my vow, I give my hand.   250
            [*He gives his hand to* WARWICK.]

    K. LEW. Why stay we now? These soldiers shall
    be levied,
And thou, Lord Bourbon, our High Admiral,
Shalt waft° them over with our royal fleet.
I long° till Edward fall by war's mischance,
For mocking marriage with a dame of France.   255
            [*Exeunt all but* WARWICK.]

    WAR. I came from Edward as ambassador,
But I return his sworn and mortal foe.
Matter of marriage was the charge he gave me,
But dreadful war shall answer his demand.
Had he none else to make a stale° but me?   260
Then none but I shall turn his jest to sorrow.
I was the chief that raised him to the crown,
And I'll be chief to bring him down again;
Not that I pity Henry's misery,   264
But seek revenge on Edward's mockery.   [*Exit.*]

---

185. But . . . himself: i.e., he dishonors himself more than me.
188. abuse . . . niece: Edward had attempted to seduce the lady.
189. impale: See III.ii.171,n.   191. guerdoned: rewarded.
210. matching: marrying.   224. masquers: revelers — said
ironically, in contempt for Edward's wanton habits.

226. fear: frighten. withal: with this.   228. willow garland: the
badge of a deserted lover.   229. weeds: garments.   253. waft:
convoy.   254. long: am impatient.   260. stale: decoy.

Act IV

SCENE I. *London. The palace.*

[*Enter* GLOUCESTER, CLARENCE, SOMERSET, *and*
MONTAGUE.]

GLO. Now tell me, Brother Clarence, what think
you
Of this new marriage with the Lady Grey?
Hath not our brother made a worthy choice?
    CLAR. Alas, you know, 'tis far from hence to
France.
How could he stay till Warwick made return?   5
    SOM. My lords, forbear this talk. Here comes the
King.
    GLO. And his well-chosen bride.
    CLAR. I mind to tell him plainly what I think.

[*Flourish. Enter* KING EDWARD, *attended,* LADY GREY,
as Queen (ELIZABETH), PEMBROKE, STAFFORD,
HASTINGS, *and others.*]

    K. EDW. Now, Brother of Clarence, how like you
our choice
That you stand pensive, as half malcontent?°   10
    CLAR. As well as Lewis of France or the Earl of
Warwick,
Which° are so weak of courage and in judgment
That they'll take no offense at our abuse!°
    K. EDW. Suppose they take offense without a
cause,   14
They are but Lewis and Warwick. I am Edward,
Your King and Warwick's, and must have my
will.°
    GLO. And shall have your will, because our King.
Yet hasty marriage seldom proveth well.
    K. EDW. Yea, Brother Richard, are you offended
too?
    GLO. Not I.   20
No, God forbid that I should wish them severed
Whom God hath joined together. Aye, and 'twere
pity
To sunder them that yoke so well together.
    K. EDW. Setting your scorns and your mislike
aside,
Tell me some reason why the Lady Grey   25
Should not become my wife and England's Queen.
And you too, Somerset and Montague,
Speak freely what you think.
    CLAR. Then this is mine opinion: that King Lewis
Becomes your enemy for mocking him   30
About the marriage of the Lady Bona.
    GLO. And Warwick, doing what you gave in
charge,°

Is now dishonored by this new marriage.
    K. EDW. What if both Lewis and Warwick be ap-
peased
By such invention° as I can devise?   35
    MONT. Yet, to have joined with France in such
alliance
Would more have strengthened this our common-
wealth
'Gainst foreign storms than any home-bred mar-
riage.
    HAST. Why, knows not Montague that of itself
England is safe, if true within itself?   40
    MONT. But the safer when 'tis backed with
France.
    HAST. 'Tis better using France than trusting
France.
Let us be backed with God and with the seas,
Which He hath given for fence impregnable,
And with their helps only defend ourselves.   45
In them and in ourselves our safety lies.
    CLAR. For this one speech Lord Hastings well de-
serves
To have the heir of the Lord Hungerford.
    K. EDW. Aye, what of that? It was my will and
grant,
And for this once my will shall stand for law.   50
    GLO. And yet methinks your Grace hath not done
well
To give the heir and daughter of Lord Scales
Unto the brother of your loving bride.
She better would have fitted me or Clarence.
But in your bride you bury brotherhood.°   55
    CLAR. Or else you would not have bestowed the
heir
Of the Lord Bonville on your new wife's son,
And leave your brothers to go speed° elsewhere.
    K. EDW. Alas, poor Clarence! Is it for a wife
That thou art malcontent? I will provide thee.   60
    CLAR. In choosing for yourself, you showed your
judgment,
Which being shallow, you shall give me leave
To play the broker° in mine own behalf;
And to that end I shortly mind to leave you.
    K. EDW. Leave me, or tarry, Edward will be King,
And not be tied unto his brother's will.   66
    Q. ELIZ. My lords, before it pleased His Majesty
To raise my state to title of a Queen,
Do me but right, and you must all confess
That I was not ignoble of descent,   70
And meaner than myself have had like fortune.
But as this title honors me and mine,
So your dislike, to whom I would be pleasing,
Doth cloud my joys with danger and with sorrow.

Act IV, Sc. i: **10. malcontent:** one who disapproves of the
state of things. See App. 4.   **12. Which:** who.   **13. our abuse:**
the wrong we have committed.   **16. will:** The word has several
shades of meaning from "determination" to "lust." See Sonnet
135.   **32. gave in charge:** instructed him to do.

35. invention: plan.   **55. But . . . brotherhood:** in favoring your
wife you forget the claims of your own brothers.   **58. speed:**
try their luck, look after themselves.   **63. broker:** agent.

K. EDW. My love, forbear to fawn upon their
    frowns.   75
What danger or what sorrow can befall thee
So long as Edward is thy constant friend
And their true sovereign, whom they must obey?
Nay, whom they shall obey, and love thee too,
Unless they seek for hatred at my hands;   80
Which if they do, yet will I keep thee safe,
And they shall feel the vengeance of my wrath.
    GLO. [*Aside*] I hear, yet say not much, but think
    the more.

> [*Enter a* POST.]

    K. EDW. Now, messenger, what letters or what
    news
From France?   85
    POST. My sovereign liege, no letters, and few
    words,
But such as I, without your special pardon,
Dare not relate.
    K. EDW. Go to,° we pardon thee. Therefore, in
    brief,
Tell me their words as near as thou canst guess
    them.   90
What answer makes King Lewis unto our letters?
    POST. At my depart, these were his very words:°
"Go tell false Edward, thy supposèd King,
That Lewis of France is sending over masquers
To revel it with him and his new bride."   95
    K. EDW. Is Lewis so brave?° Belike he thinks me
    Henry.
But what said Lady Bona to my marriage?
    POST. These were her words, uttered with mild
    disdain:
"Tell him, in hope he'll prove a widower shortly,
I'll wear the willow garland for his sake."   100
    K. EDW. I blame not her, she could say little less.
She had the wrong. But what said Henry's Queen?
For I have heard that she was there in place.
    POST. "Tell him," quoth she, "my mourning
    weeds are done,
And I am ready to put armor on."   105
    K. EDW. Belike she minds to play the Amazon.°
But what said Warwick to these injuries?
    POST. He, more incensed against your Majesty
Than all the rest, discharged me with these words:
"Tell him from me that he hath done me wrong,
And therefore I'll uncrown him ere 't be long."   111
    K. EDW. Ha! Durst the traitor breathe out so
    proud words?
Well, I will arm me, being thus forewarned.
They shall have wars and pay for their presumption.
But say, is Warwick friends with Margaret?   115
    POST. Aye, gracious sovereign. They are so linked
    in friendship

That young Prince Edward marries Warwick's
    daughter.
    CLAR. Belike the elder; Clarence will have the
    younger.
Now, Brother King, farewell, and sit you fast,
For I will hence to Warwick's other daughter,   120
That, though I want° a kingdom, yet in marriage
I may not prove inferior to yourself.
You that love me and Warwick, follow me.

> [*Exit* CLARENCE, *and* SOMERSET *follows.*]

    GLO. [*Aside*] Not I.
My thoughts aim at a further matter. I   125
Stay not for the love of Edward, but the crown.
    K. EDW. Clarence and Somerset both gone to War-
    wick!
Yet am I armed against the worst can happen,
And haste is needful in this desperate case.
Pembroke and Stafford, you in our behalf   130
Go levy men and make prepare for war.
They are already, or quickly will be, landed.
Myself in person will straight follow you.

> [*Exeunt* PEMBROKE *and* STAFFORD.]

But, ere I go, Hastings and Montague,
Resolve my doubt. You twain, of all the rest,   135
Are near to Warwick by blood and by alliance.
Tell me if you love Warwick more than me.
If it be so, then both depart to him.
I rather wish you foes than hollow friends.
But if you mind to hold your true obedience,   140
Give me assurance with some friendly vow,
That I may never have you in suspect.
    MONT. So God help Montague as he proves true!
    HAST. And Hastings as he favors Edward's cause!
    K. EDW. Now, brother Richard, will you stand by
    us?   145
    GLO. Aye, in despite of all that shall withstand
    you.
    K. EDW. Why, so! Then am I sure of victory.
Now therefore let us hence, and lose no hour,
Till we meet Warwick with his foreign power.

> [*Exeunt.*]

SCENE II. *A plain in Warwickshire.*

> [*Enter* WARWICK *and* OXFORD, *with* FRENCH
> SOLDIERS.]

WAR. Trust me, my lord, all hitherto goes well.
The common people by numbers swarm to us.

> [*Enter* CLARENCE *and* SOMERSET.]

But see where Somerset and Clarence comes!
Speak suddenly,° my lords, are we all friends?
    CLAR. Fear not that, my lord.   5
    WAR. Then, gentle Clarence, welcome unto War-
    wick;

---

89. Go to: an exclamation — "all right!"   **92. words:** See
III.iii.223-32.   **96. brave:** full of spirit.   **106. Amazon:** See
I.iv.114,n.

121. want: am without, lack.
    Sc. ii: 4. suddenly: quickly.

And welcome, Somerset. I hold it cowardice
To rest mistrustful where a noble heart
Hath pawned° an open hand in sign of love.
Else might I think that Clarence, Edward's
    brother,   10
Were but a feignèd friend to our proceedings.
But welcome, sweet Clarence. My daughter shall be
    thine.
And now what rests but, in night's coverture,°
Thy brother being carelessly encamped,
His soldiers lurking in the towns about,   15
And but attended by a simple guard,
We may surprise and take him at our pleasure?
Our scouts have found the adventure very easy;
That as Ulysses and stout Diomede   19
With sleight and manhood stole to Rhesus' tents
And brought from thence the Thracian fatal
    steeds,°
So well covered with the night's black mantle,
At unawares may beat down Edward's guard
And seize himself. I say not, slaughter him,
For I intend but only to surprise him.   25
You that will follow me to this attempt,
Applaud the name of Henry with your leader.
                  [They all cry, " Henry! "]
Why, then, let's on our way in silent sort,°
For Warwick and his friends, God and Saint
    George!   *[Exeunt.]*

SCENE III. EDWARD'S *camp, near* WARWICK.

[Enter three WATCHMEN, *to guard the* KING'S *tent.]*
    1. WATCH. Come on, my masters, each man take
    his stand.
The King by this is set him down to sleep.
    2. WATCH. What, will he not to bed?
    1. WATCH. Why, no, for he hath made a solemn
    vow
Never to lie and take his natural rest   5
Till Warwick or himself be quite suppressed.
    2. WATCH. Tomorrow, then, belike shall be the
    day,
If Warwick be so near as men report.
    3. WATCH. But say, I pray, what nobleman is that
That with the King here resteth in his tent?   10
    1. WATCH. 'Tis the Lord Hastings, the King's
    chiefest friend.
    3. WATCH. Oh, is it so? But why commands the
    King
That his chief followers lodge in towns about him,

While he himself keeps in the cold field?
    2. WATCH. 'Tis the more honor, because more
    dangerous.   15
    3. WATCH. Aye, but give me worship° and quiet-
    ness.
I like it better than a dangerous honor.
If Warwick knew in what estate° he stands,
'Tis to be doubted he would waken him.
    1. WATCH. Unless our halberds° did shut up his
    passage.   20
    2. WATCH. Aye, wherefore else guard we his royal
    tent,
But to defend his person from night foes?
[Enter WARWICK, CLARENCE, OXFORD, SOMERSET, *and*
             FRENCH SOLDIERS, *silent all.]*
    WAR. This is his tent, and see where stand his
    guard.
Courage, my masters! Honor now or never!
But follow me, and Edward shall be ours.   25
    1. WATCH. Who goes there?
    2. WATCH. Stay, or thou diest!
        *[*WARWICK *and the rest cry all, "* Warwick!
Warwick! *" and set upon the* GUARD, *who fly, crying,*
" Arm! Arm! *"* WARWICK *and the rest following*
                  them.]
[The drum playing and trumpet sounding, re-enter
WARWICK, SOMERSET, *and the rest, bringing the* KING
out in his gown,° sitting in a chair. RICHARD *and*
      HASTINGS *fly over° the stage.]*
    SOM. What are they that fly there?
    WAR. Richard and Hastings. Let them go. Here is
The Duke.
    K. EDW. The Duke! Why, Warwick, when we
    parted,   30
Thou call'dst me King.
    WAR.   Aye, but the case is altered.
When you disgraced me in my embassade,°
Then I degraded you from being King
And come now to create you Duke of York.
Alas! How should you govern any kingdom,   35
That know not how to use ambassadors,
Nor how to be contented with one wife,
Nor how to use your brothers brotherly,
Nor how to study for the people's welfare,
Nor how to shroud yourself from enemies?   40
    K. EDW. Yea, Brother of Clarence, art thou here
    too.
Nay, then I see that Edward needs must down.
Yet, Warwick, in despite of all mischance,
Of thee thyself and all thy complices,°
Edward will always bear himself as King.   45
Though Fortune's malice overthrow my state,
My mind exceeds the compass of her wheel.°

9. **pawned:** pledged.   13. **coverture:** overshadowing.
19-21. **Ulysses . . . steeds:** The story is told in the *Iliad*, Bk. X.
It had been declared by the oracle that if the horses of Rhesus
(King of Thrace, who came to help the Trojans) grazed on the
plains of Troy, the city would never be taken. Ulysses and Diomedes were sent by the Greeks to intercept Rhesus. In a night
foray they killed the King and took his horses.   28. **sort:** manner.

Sc. iii: 16. **worship:** dignity, comfort.   18. **estate:** condition.
20. **halberds:** See Pl. 21b.   27. s.d., **gown:** dressing gown. **fly
over:** flee across.   32. **embassade:** embassy.   44. **complices:**
accomplices.   47. **wheel:** See *Hen V*, III.vi.31-40 for Fluellen's
discourse on Fortune's wheel.

WAR. Then, for his mind, be Edward England's
  King;   [*Takes off his crown.*]
But Henry now shall wear the English crown
And be true King indeed, thou but the shadow.   50
My Lord of Somerset, at my request,
See that forthwith Duke Edward be conveyed
Unto my brother, Archbishop of York.
When I have fought with Pembroke and his fellows,
I'll follow you and tell what answer   55
Lewis and the Lady Bona send to him.
Now, for a while farewell, good Duke of York.
           [*They lead him out forcibly.*]
    K. EDW. What fates impose, that men must needs
    abide.
It boots not° to resist both wind and tide.
           [*Exit, guarded.*]
    OXF. What now remains, my lords, for us to do
But march to London with our soldiers?   61
    WAR. Aye, that's the first thing that we have to do,
To free King Henry from imprisonment
And see him seated in the regal throne.   [*Exeunt.*]

SCENE IV. *London. The palace.*

[*Enter* QUEEN ELIZABETH *and* RIVERS.]
    RIV. Madam, what makes you in this sudden
    change?°
    Q. ELIZ. Why, Brother Rivers, are you yet to learn
What late misfortune is befall'n King Edward?
    RIV. What! Loss of some pitched battle against
    Warwick?
    Q. ELIZ. No, but the loss of his own royal person.
    RIV. Then is my sovereign slain?   6
    Q. ELIZ. Aye, almost slain, for he is taken prisoner,
Either betrayed by falsehood of his guard,
Or by his foe surprised at unawares,
And, as I further have to understand,   10
Is new committed to the Bishop of York,
Fell Warwick's brother and by that our foe.
    RIV. These news I must confess are full of grief.
Yet, gracious madam, bear it as you may.
Warwick may lose, that now hath won the day.   15
    Q. ELIZ. Till then fair hope must hinder life's
    decay.
And I the rather wean me from despair
For love of Edward's offspring in my womb.
This is it that makes me bridle° passion
And bear with mildness my misfortune's cross.°   20
Aye, aye, for this I draw in many a tear
And stop the rising of blood-sucking° sighs,
Lest with my sighs or tears I blast or drown
King Edward's fruit, true heir to the English crown.

    RIV. But, madam, where is Warwick then be-
    come?   25
    Q. ELIZ. I am informed that he comes toward
    London
To set the crown once more on Henry's head.
Guess thou the rest. King Edward's friends must
    down,
But, to prevent° the tyrant's violence —
For trust not him that hath once broken faith —   30
I'll hence forthwith unto the sanctuary
To save at least the heir of Edward's right.
There shall I rest secure from force and fraud.
Come, therefore, let us fly while we may fly.   34
If Warwick take us, we are sure to die.   [*Exeunt.*]

SCENE V. *A park near Middleham Castle in Yorkshire.*

[*Enter* GLOUCESTER, LORD HASTINGS, SIR WILLIAM
    STANLEY, *and others.*]
    GLO. Now, my Lord Hastings and Sir William
    Stanley,
Leave off to wonder why I drew you hither
Into this chiefest thicket° of the park.
Thus stands the case: You know our King, my
    brother,
Is prisoner to the Bishop here, at whose hands   5
He hath good usage and great liberty,
And, often but° attended with weak guard,
Comes hunting this way to disport himself.
I have advertised him° by secret means
That if about this hour he make this way   10
Under the color° of his usual game,
He shall here find his friends with horse and men
To set him free from his captivity.
[*Enter* KING EDWARD *and a* HUNTSMAN *with him.*]
    HUNT. This way, my lord, for this way lies the
    game.
    K. EDW. Nay, this way, man. See where the hunts-
    men stand.   15
Now, Brother of Gloucester, Lord Hastings, and
    the rest,
Stand you thus close to steal the Bishop's deer?
    GLO. Brother, the time and case requireth haste.
Your horse stands ready at the park corner.
    K. EDW. But whither shall we then?
    HAST.   To Lynn, my lord,   20
And ship from thence to Flanders.
    GLO. Well guessed, believe me, for that was my
    meaning.
    K. EDW. Stanley, I will requite thy forwardness.°
    GLO. But wherefore stay we? 'Tis no time to talk.

---

59. boots not: is no use.
    Sc. iv: 1. makes . . . change: causes you to be changed so
suddenly.   **19. bridle:** rein in, restrain.   **20. cross:** grief.
22. blood-sucking: It was believed that sighing wasted the
heart's blood.

29. prevent: forestall.
    Sc. v: 3. chiefest thicket: thickest part.   **7. but:** only.
9. advertised him: given him warning.   **11. color:** pretext.
23. forwardness: zeal.

K. EDW. Huntsman, what say'st thou? Wilt thou
    go along? 25
HUNT. Better do so than tarry and be hanged.
GLO. Come then, away. Let's ha' no more ado.
K. EDW. Bishop, farewell. Shield thee from War-
    wick's frown,
And pray that I may repossess the crown.
                         [*Exeunt.*]

SCENE VI. *London. The Tower.*

[*Flourish. Enter* KING HENRY, CLARENCE, WARWICK,
SOMERSET, *young* RICHMOND, OXFORD, MONTAGUE, *and*
LIEUTENANT° *of the Tower.*]

    K. HEN. Master Lieutenant, now that God and
    friends
Have shaken Edward from the regal seat
And turned my captive state to liberty,
My fear to hope, my sorrows unto joys,
At our enlargement° what are thy due fees?° 5
    LIEU. Subjects may challenge nothing of their
    sovereigns,
But if an humble prayer may prevail,
I then crave pardon of your Majesty.
    K. HEN. For what, Lieutenant? For well using
    me?
Nay, be thou sure I'll well requite thy kindness, 10
For that it made my imprisonment a pleasure —
Aye, such a pleasure as incagèd birds
Conceive when, after many moody thoughts,
At last, by notes of household harmony,
They quite forget their loss of liberty. 15
But, Warwick, after God, thou set'st me free,
And chiefly therefore I thank God and thee.
He was the author, thou the instrument.
Therefore, that I may conquer Fortune's spite
By living low, where Fortune cannot hurt me, 20
And that the people of this blessèd land
May not be punished with my thwarting stars,°
Warwick, although my head still wear the crown,
I here resign my government to thee,
For thou art fortunate in all thy deeds. 25
    WAR. Your Grace hath still° been famed for vir-
    tuous,
And now may seem as wise as virtuous
By spying and avoiding Fortune's malice,
For few men rightly temper with the stars.°
Yet in this one thing let me blame your Grace, 30
For choosing me when Clarence is in place.
    CLAR. No, Warwick, thou art worthy of the
    sway,
To whom the Heavens in thy nativity

Adjudged an olive branch and laurel crown
As likely to be blest in peace and war; 35
And therefore I yield thee my free consent.
    WAR. And I choose Clarence, only, for Protector.
    K. HEN. Warwick and Clarence, give me both
    your hands.
Now join your hands, and with your hands your
    hearts,
That no dissension hinder government. 40
I make you both Protectors of this land,
While I myself will lead a private life
And in devotion spend my latter days
To sin's rebuke and my Creator's praise.
    WAR. What answers Clarence to his sovereign's
    will? 45
    CLAR. That he consents if Warwick yield con-
    sent;
For on thy fortune I repose myself.
    WAR. Why, then, though loath, yet must I be
    content.
We'll yoke together, like a double shadow
To Henry's body, and supply° his place — 50
I mean, in bearing weight of government,
While he enjoys the honor and his ease.
And, Clarence, now then it is more than needful
Forthwith that Edward be pronounced a traitor
And all his lands and goods be confiscate. 55
    CLAR. What else? And that succession be deter-
    mined.
    WAR. Aye, therein Clarence shall not want his
    part.
    K. HEN. But, with the first of all your chief affairs,
Let me entreat, for I command no more,
That Margaret, your Queen, and my son Edward
Be sent for to return from France with speed; 61
For, till I see them here, by doubtful fear
My joy of liberty is half eclipsed.
    CLAR. It shall be done, my sovereign, with all
    speed.
    K. HEN. My Lord of Somerset, what youth is that
Of whom you seem to have so tender care? 66
    SOM. My liege, it is young Henry° Earl of Rich-
    mond.
    K. HEN. Come hither, England's hope. [*Lays his
    hand on his head.*] If secret powers
Suggest but truth to my divining thoughts,
This pretty lad will prove our country's bliss. 70
His looks are full of peaceful majesty,
His head by nature framed to wear a crown,
His hand to wield a scepter, and himself
Likely in time to bless a regal throne.
Make much of him, my lords, for this is he 75
Must help you more than you are hurt by me.
                [*Enter a* POST.]
    WAR. What news, my friend?

Sc. vi: s.d., Lieutenant: Deputy Warden. **5. enlargement:**
release. fees: Prisoners were charged for food and maintenance
by their keepers. **22. thwarting stars:** unlucky Fate. See
App. 1. **26. still:** always. **29. temper . . . stars:** accommodate
themselves to their fate.

50. supply: fill. **67. young Henry:** Ultimately Henry of Richmond became King as Henry VII. See *Rich III*, V.v.

POST. That Edward is escapèd from your brother
And fled, as he hears since, to Burgundy.   79
   WAR. Unsavory news! But how made he escape?
POST. He was conveyed by Richard Duke of
   Gloucester
And the Lord Hastings, who attended him
In secret ambush on the forest side
And from the Bishop's huntsmen rescued him;
For hunting was his daily exercise.   85
   WAR. My brother was too careless of his charge.
But let us hence, my sovereign, to provide
A salve° for any sore that may betide.°
[*Exeunt all but* SOMERSET, RICHMOND, *and* OXFORD.]
   SOM. My lord, I like not of this flight of Edward's,
For doubtless Burgundy will yield him help,   90
And we shall have more wars before 't be long.
As Henry's late presaging° prophecy
Did glad my heart with hope of this young Rich-
   mond,
So doth my heart misgive me, in these conflicts
What may befall him, to his harm and ours.   95
Therefore, Lord Oxford, to prevent the worst,
Forthwith we'll send him hence to Brittany
Till storms be past of civil enmity.
   OXF. Aye, for if Edward repossess the crown,
'Tis like that Richmond with the rest shall down.
   SOM. It shall be so. He shall to Brittany.   101
Come, therefore, let's about it speedily.   [*Exeunt.*]

SCENE VII. *Before York.*

[*Flourish. Enter* KING EDWARD, GLOUCESTER,
HASTINGS, *and* SOLDIERS.]
   K. EDW. Now, Brother Richard, Lord Hastings,
   and the rest,
Yet thus far Fortune maketh us amends
And says that once more I shall interchange
My wanèd° state for Henry's regal crown.
Well have we passed and now repassed the seas,   5
And brought desirèd help from Burgundy.
What then remains, we being thus arrived
From Ravenspurgh haven before the gates of York
But that we enter, as into our dukedom?
   GLO. The gates made fast! Brother, I like not this,
For many men that stumble at the threshold°   11
Are well foretold that danger lurks within.
   K. EDW. Tush, man, abodements° must not now
   affright us.
By fair or foul means we must enter in,
For hither will our friends repair to us.   15
   HAST. My liege, I'll knock once more to summon
   them.

[*Enter, on the walls, the* MAYOR OF YORK *and his
brethren.*]
   MAY. My lords, we were forewarnèd of your
   coming
And shut the gates for safety of ourselves,
For now we owe allegiance unto Henry.
   K. EDW. But, Master Mayor, if Henry be your
   King,   20
Yet Edward at the least is Duke of York.
   MAY. True, my good lord, I know you for no less.
   K. EDW. Why, and I challenge nothing but my
   dukedom,
As being well content with that alone.
   GLO. [*Aside*] But when the fox hath once got in
   his nose,   25
He'll soon find means to make the body follow.
   HAST. Why, Master Mayor, why stand you in a
   doubt?
Open the gates. We are King Henry's friends.
   MAY. Aye, say you so? The gates shall then be
   opened.   [*They descend.*]
   GLO. A wise stout captain, and soon persuaded!
   HAST. The good old man would fain° that all
   were well,   31
So 'twere not 'long of him.° But being entered,
I doubt not, I, but we shall soon persuade
Both him and all his brothers unto reason.
[*Enter the* MAYOR *and two* ALDERMEN, *below.*]
   K. EDW. So, Master Mayor. These gates must not
   be shut   35
But in the night or in the time of war.
What! Fear not, man, but yield me up the keys;
     [*Takes his keys.*]
For Edward will defend the town and thee,
And all those friends that deign° to follow me.
[*March. Enter* MONTGOMERY, *with drum and
SOLDIERS.*]
   GLO. Brother, this is Sir John Montgomery,   40
Our trusty friend, unless I be deceived.
   K. EDW. Welcome, Sir John! But why come you
   in arms?
   MONT. To help King Edward in his time of storm,
As every loyal subject ought to do.
   K. EDW. Thanks, good Montgomery. But we now
   forget   45
Our title to the crown and only claim
Our dukedom till God please to send the rest.
   MONT. Then fare you well, for I will hence again.
I came to serve a king, and not a duke.
Drummer, strike up, and let us march away.   50
     [*The drum begins to march.*]
   K. EDW. Nay, stay, Sir John, a while, and we'll
   debate
By what safe means the crown may be recovered.
   MONT. What talk you of debating? In few words,

---

88. **salve:** healing ointment. **betide:** befall.   92. **presaging:**
foretelling.
   Sc. vii: 4. **waned:** reduced.   11. **stumble . . . threshold:** regarded as a sign of ill luck to come. See *R & J*, V.iii.122.
13. **abodements:** forebodings.

31. **fain:** be glad.   32. **So . . . him:** so long as it was not his
responsibility.   39. **deign:** are willing.

If you'll not here proclaim yourself our King,
I'll leave you to your fortune and be gone   55
To keep them back that come to succor you.
Why shall we fight if you pretend° no title?
   GLO. Why, Brother, wherefore stand you on nice
     points?°
   K. EDW. When we grow stronger, then we'll make
     our claim.
Till then, 'tis wisdom to conceal our meaning.   60
   HAST. Away with scrupulous wit! Now arms
     must rule.
   GLO. And fearless minds climb soonest unto
     crowns.
Brother, we will proclaim you out of hand.°
The bruit° thereof will bring you many friends.
   K. EDW. Then be it as you will; for 'tis my right,
And Henry but usurps the diadem.   66
   MONT. Aye, now my sovereign speaketh like him-
     self,
And now will I be Edward's champion.
   HAST. Sound trumpet. Edward shall be here pro-
     claimed.   69
Come, fellow soldier, make thou proclamation.
                       [Flourish.]
   SOLD. Edward the Fourth, by the grace of God,
     King of
England and France, and Lord of Ireland, &c.
   MONT. And whosoe'er gainsays King Edward's
     right,
By this I challenge him to single fight.   75
             [Throws down his gauntlet.]
   ALL. Long live Edward the Fourth!
   K. EDW. Thanks, brave Montgomery, and thanks
     unto you all.
If Fortune serve me, I'll requite this kindness.
Now, for this night, let's harbor here in York,
And when the morning sun shall raise his car°   80
Above the border of this horizon,
We'll forward toward Warwick and his mates;
For well I wot° that Henry is no soldier.
Ah, froward Clarence! How evil it beseems thee
To flatter Henry and forsake thy brother!   85
Yet, as we may, we'll meet both thee and War-
   wick.
Come on, brave soldiers. Doubt not of the day,
And, that once gotten, doubt not of large pay.
                          [Exeunt.]

SCENE VIII. *London. The palace.*

[Flourish. Enter KING HENRY, WARWICK, MONTAGUE,
     CLARENCE, EXETER, *and* OXFORD.*]*
   WAR. What counsel, lords? Edward from Belgia,

With hasty Germans and blunt Hollanders,
Hath passed in safety through the Narrow Seas,
And with his troops doth march amain to London;
And many giddy people flock to him.   5
   K. HEN. Let's levy men and beat him back again.
   CLAR. A little fire is quickly trodden out,
Which, being suffered, rivers cannot quench.
   WAR. In Warwickshire I have true-hearted
     friends,
Not mutinous in peace, yet bold in war.   10
Those will I muster up. And thou, Son Clarence,
Shalt stir up in Suffolk, Norfolk, and in Kent
The knights and gentlemen to come with thee.
Thou, Brother Montague, in Buckingham,
Northampton, and in Leicestershire shalt find   15
Men well inclined to hear what thou command'st.
And thou, brave Oxford, wondrous well beloved,
In Oxfordshire shalt muster up thy friends.
My sovereign, with the loving citizens,
Like to his island girt in with the ocean,   20
Or modest Dian° circled with her nymphs,
Shall rest in London till we come to him.
Fair lords, take leave and stand not to reply.
Farewell, my sovereign.
   K. HEN. Farewell, my Hector,° and my Troy's
     true hope.   25
   CLAR. In sign of truth, I kiss your Highness'
     hand.
   K. HEN. Well-minded Clarence, be thou fortu-
     nate!
   MONT. Comfort, my lord, and so I take my leave.
   OXF. And thus I seal° my truth and bid adieu.
   K. HEN. Sweet Oxford, and my loving Montague,
And all at once, once more a happy farewell.   31
   WAR. Farewell, sweet lords. Let's meet at Coven-
     try. *[Exeunt all but* KING HENRY *and* EXETER.*]*
   K. HEN. Here at the palace will I rest a while.
Cousin of Exeter, what thinks your lordship?
Methinks the power that Edward hath in field   35
Should not be able to encounter mine.
   EXE. The doubt° is that he will seduce the rest.
   K. HEN. That's not my fear. My meed hath got
     me fame.°
I have not stopped mine ears to their demands,
Nor posted off° their suits with slow delays.   40
My pity hath been balm to heal their wounds,
My mildness hath allayed their swelling griefs,
My mercy dried their water-flowing tears.
I have not been desirous of their wealth,
Nor much oppressed them with great subsidies,   45
Nor forward of revenge, though they much erred.
Then why should they love Edward more than me?
No, Exeter, these graces challenge° grace;

   Sc. viii: **21. Dian:** Diana.   **25. Hector:** i.e., champion.
29. seal: confirm. Here he kisses the King's hand.   **37. doubt:**
fear.   **38. My . . . fame:** my merit in dealing justly has won
me support.   **40. posted off:** put off.   **48. challenge:** claim as
their due.

57. pretend: claim.   **58. stand . . . points:** are you so over-
particular.   **63. out of hand:** forthwith.   **64. bruit:** report.
80. car: chariot.   **83. wot:** know.

And when the lion fawns upon the lamb,
The lamb will never cease to follow him.   50
    [*Shout within,* "A Lancaster! A Lancaster!"]
EXE. Hark, hark, my lord! What shouts are
  these?
[*Enter* KING EDWARD, GLOUCESTER, *and* SOLDIERS.]
    K. EDW. Seize on the shame-faced Henry, bear
  him hence,
And once again proclaim us King of England.
You are the fount that makes small brooks to flow.
Now stops thy spring. My sea shall suck them dry
And swell so much the higher by their ebb.   56
Hence with him to the Tower. Let him not speak.
    [*Exeunt some with* KING HENRY.]
And, lords, toward Coventry bend we our course,
Where peremptory° Warwick now remains.
The sun shines hot, and if we use delay,   60
Cold biting winter mars our hoped-for hay.
    GLO. Away betimes, before his forces join
And take the great-grown traitor unawares.
Brave warriors, march amain toward Coventry.
                    [*Exeunt.*]

Act V

SCENE I. *Coventry.*

[*Enter* WARWICK, *the* MAYOR OF COVENTRY, *two*
  MESSENGERS, *and others upon the walls.*]
  WAR. Where is the post that came from valiant
  Oxford?
How far hence is thy lord, mine honest fellow?
    1. MESS. By this at Dunsmore, marching hither-
  ward.
  WAR. How far off is our brother Montague?
Where is the post that came from Montague?   5
    2. MESS. By this at Daintry,° with a puissant
  troop.
           [*Enter* SIR JOHN SOMERVILE.]
  WAR. Say, Somervile, what says my loving son?
And by thy guess how nigh is Clarence now?
    SOM. At Southam I did leave him with his forces,
And do expect him here some two hours hence. 10
                     [*Drum heard.*]
  WAR. Then Clarence is at hand. I hear his drum.
  SOM. It is not his, my lord. Here Southam lies.
The drum your Honor hears marcheth from War-
  wick.
  WAR. Who should that be? Belike, unlooked-for
  friends.
  SOM. They are at hand, and you shall quickly
  know.   15

---

59. peremptory: overbearing.
  Act V, Sc. i: 6. Daintry: now spelt Daventry.

[*March. Flourish. Enter* KING EDWARD, GLOUCESTER,
  and SOLDIERS.]
  K. EDW. Go, trumpet, to the walls, and sound a
  parle.
  GLO. See how the surly Warwick mans the wall!
  WAR. Oh, unbid spite! Is sportful Edward come?
Where slept our scouts, or how are they seduced,
That we could hear no news of his repair?°   20
  K. EDW. Now, Warwick, wilt thou ope the city
  gates,
Speak gentle words and humbly bend thy knee,
Call Edward king, and at his hands beg mercy?
And he shall pardon thee these outrages.
  WAR. Nay, rather, wilt thou draw thy forces
  hence,   25
Confess who set thee up and plucked thee down?
Call Warwick patron and be penitent,
And thou shalt still remain the Duke of York.
  GLO. I thought, at least, he would have said the
  King.
Or did he make the jest against his will?   30
  WAR. Is not a dukedom, sir, a goodly gift?
  GLO. Aye, by my faith, for a poor Earl to give.
I'll do thee service for so good a gift.
  WAR. 'Twas I that gave the kingdom to thy
  brother.
  K. EDW. Why then 'tis mine, if but by Warwick's
  gift.   35
  WAR. Thou art no Atlas° for so great a weight;
And, weakling, Warwick takes his gift again,
And Henry is my King, Warwick his subject.
  K. EDW. But Warwick's King is Edward's pris-
  oner.
And, gallant Warwick, do but answer this: 40
What is the body when the head is off?
  GLO. Alas, that Warwick had no more forecast,
But, whiles he thought to steal the single ten,°
The king was slyly fingered from the deck!
You left poor Henry at the Bishop's palace,   45
And, ten to one, you'll meet him in the Tower.
  K. EDW. 'Tis even so. Yet you are Warwick still.
  GLO. Come, Warwick, take the time. Kneel down,
  kneel down.
Nay, when? Strike now, or else the iron cools.
  WAR. I had rather chop this hand off at a blow
And with the other fling it at thy face   51
Than bear so low a sail, to strike° to thee.
  K. EDW. Sail how thou canst, have wind and tide
  thy friend,
This hand, fast wound about thy coal-black hair,
Shall, whiles thy head is warm and new cut off, 55
Write in the dust this sentence with thy blood,
"Wind-changing Warwick now can change no
  more."

---

20. repair: approach.   **36. Atlas:** In classical mythology Atlas
carries the world on his shoulders.   **43. single ten:** i.e., the
highest of the plain cards.   **52. strike:** lower my sail in token of
surrender — with a pun on *strike* in l. 49. See III.iii.5.

[*Enter* OXFORD, *with drum and colors.*]

WAR. O cheerful colors! See where Oxford comes!

OXF. Oxford, Oxford, for Lancaster!

        [*He and his forces enter the city.*]

GLO. The gates are open, let us enter too.   60

K. EDW. So other foes may set upon our backs.

Stand we in good array, for they no doubt

Will issue out again, and bid us battle.

If not, the city being but of small defense,

We'll quickly rouse° the traitors in the same. 65

  WAR. Oh, welcome, Oxford! For we want thy
    help.

[*Enter* MONTAGUE, *with drum and colors.*]

MONT. Montague, Montague, for Lancaster!

        [*He and his forces enter the city.*]

GLO. Thou and thy brother both shall buy this
  treason

Even with the dearest blood your bodies bear.

K. EDW. The harder matched, the greater victory.

My mind presageth happy gain and conquest. 71

  [*Enter* SOMERSET, *with drum and colors.*]

SOM. Somerset, Somerset, for Lancaster!

        [*He and his forces enter the city.*]

GLO. Two of thy name, both Dukes of Somerset,

Have sold their lives unto the house of York,

And thou shalt be the third, if this sword hold. 75

  [*Enter* CLARENCE, *with drum and colors.*]

WAR. And lo, where George of Clarence sweeps
  along,

Of force enough to bid his brother battle;

With whom an upright zeal to right prevails

More than the nature of a brother's love!

Come, Clarence, come. Thou wilt, if Warwick
  call.   80

  CLAR. Father of Warwick, know you what this
    means? [*Taking his red rose out of his hat.*°]

Look here, I throw my infamy at thee.

I will not ruinate my father's house,

Who gave his blood to lime° the stones together

And set up Lancaster. Why, trow'st° thou, Warwick,   85

That Clarence is so harsh, so blunt, unnatural,

To bend the fatal instruments of war

Against his brother and his lawful King?

Perhaps thou wilt object° my holy oath.

To keep that oath were more impiety 90

Than Jephthah's° when he sacrificed his daughter.

I am so sorry for my trespass made

That, to deserve well at my brother's hands,

I here proclaim myself thy mortal foe,

With resolution, wheresoe'er I meet thee — 95

As I will meet thee if thou stir abroad —

To plague thee for thy foul misleading me.

And so, proud-hearted Warwick, I defy thee,

And to my brother turn my blushing cheeks.

Pardon me, Edward, I will make amends; 100

And, Richard, do not frown upon my faults,

For I will henceforth be no more unconstant.°

  K. EDW. Now welcome more, and ten times more
    beloved,

Than if thou never hadst deserved our hate. 104

  GLO. Welcome, good Clarence. This is brotherlike.

  WAR. Oh, passing° traitor, perjured and unjust!

  K. EDW. What, Warwick, wilt thou leave the
    town and fight?

Or shall we beat the stones about thine ears?

  WAR. Alas, I am not cooped here for defense!

I will away toward Barnet presently,° 110

And bid thee battle, Edward, if thou darest.

  K. EDW. Yes, Warwick, Edward dares, and leads
    the way.

Lords, to the field. Saint George and victory!

    [*Exeunt* KING EDWARD *and his company. March.*
    WARWICK *and his company follow.*]

SCENE II. *A field of battle near Barnet.*

[*Alarum and excursions. Enter* KING EDWARD, *bringing forth* WARWICK *wounded.*]

  K. EDW. So, lie thou there. Die thou, and die our
    fear;

For Warwick was a bug° that feared° us all.

Now, Montague, sit fast. I seek for thee

That Warwick's bones may keep thine company.

                         [*Exit.*]

  WAR. Ah, who is nigh? Come to me, friend or
    foe, 5

And tell me, who is victor, York or Warwick?

Why ask I that? My mangled body shows,

My blood, my want of strength, my sick heart
  shows,

That I must yield my body to the earth

And, by my fall, the conquest to my foe. 10

Thus yields the cedar to the ax's edge

Whose arms gave shelter to the princely eagle

Under whose shade the ramping° lion slept,

Whose top branch overpeered° Jove's spreading
  tree°

And kept low shrubs from winter's powerful wind.

These eyes that now are dimmed with death's
  black veil 16

Have been as piercing as the midday sun

To search the secret treasons of the world.

The wrinkles in my brows, now filled with blood,

---

65. **rouse:** lit., to drive an animal from its den or hole. 81. s.d., **Taking . . . hat:** The s.d. in *The True Tragedy* reads: "*Sound a parley, and Richard and Clarence whisper together, and then Clarence takes his red rose out of his hat and throws it at Warwick.*" 84. **lime:** cement. 85. **trow'st:** thinkest. 89. **object:** reproach me with. 91. **Jephthah's:** See *Haml*, II.ii.422,n.

102. **unconstant:** shifty, changing sides. 106. **passing:** surpassing. 110. **presently:** immediately.

    Sc. ii: 2. **bug:** hobgoblin. **feared:** frightened. 13. **ramping:** rearing up, enraged. 14. **overpeered:** overlooked. **Jove's . . . tree:** the oak.

Were likened oft to kingly sepulchers.　　　　20
For who lived king, but I could dig his grave?
And who durst smile when Warwick bent his
　　brow?
Lo, now my glory smeared in dust and blood!
My parks, my walks, my manors that I had
Even now forsake me, and of all my lands　　25
Is nothing left me but my body's length.
Why, what is pomp, rule, reign, but earth and
　　dust?
And, live we how we can, yet die we must.
　　　　　　[*Enter* OXFORD *and* SOMERSET.]
　　SOM. Ah, Warwick, Warwick! Wert thou as we
　　are,
We might recover all our loss again.　　　　30
The Queen from France hath brought a puissant
　　power.
Even now we heard the news. Ah, couldst thou fly!
　　WAR. Why, then I would not fly. Ah, Montague,
If thou be there, sweet Brother, take my hand
And with thy lips keep in my soul a while!　35
Thou lovest me not, for, Brother, if thou didst,
Thy tears would wash this cold congealèd blood
That glues my lips and will not let me speak.
Come quickly, Montague, or I am dead.
　　SOM. Ah, Warwick! Montague hath breathed his
　　last,　　　　　　　　　　　　　　　　　40
And to the latest gasp cried out for Warwick,
And said, "Commend me to my valiant brother."
And more he would have said, and more he spoke
Which sounded like a clamor in a vault
That mought° not be distinguished; but at last　45
I well might hear, delivered with a groan,
"Oh, farewell, Warwick!"
　　WAR. Sweet rest his soul! Fly, lords, and save
　　yourselves,
For Warwick bids you all farewell, to meet in
　　Heaven.　　　　　　　　　　　　　　[*Dies.*]
　　OXF. Away, away, to meet the Queen's great
　　power!　　　　　　　　　　　　　　　50
　　　　　　[*Here they bear away his body. Exeunt.*]

SCENE III. *Another part of the field.*

[*Flourish. Enter* KING EDWARD *in triumph, with*
　　GLOUCESTER, CLARENCE, *and the rest.*]
　　K. EDW. Thus far our fortune keeps an upward
　　course,
And we are graced with wreaths of victory;
But in the midst of this bright-shining day,
I spy a black, suspicious, threatening cloud
That will encounter with our glorious sun　　5
Ere he attain his easeful western bed.
I mean, my lords, those powers that the Queen

45. **mought:** might.

Hath raised in Gallia° have arrived our coast,
And, as we hear, march on to fight with us.
　　CLAR. A little gale will soon disperse that cloud
And blow it to the source from whence it came.　11
Thy very beams will dry those vapors up,
For every cloud engenders° not a storm.
　　GLO. The Queen is valued thirty thousand strong,
And Somerset, with Oxford, fled to her.　　15
If she have time to breathe, be well assured
Her faction° will be full as strong as ours.
　　K. EDW. We are advértised by our loving friends
That they do hold their course toward Tewkes-
　　bury.
We, having now the best at Barnet field,　　20
Will thither straight, for willingness rids way,°
And as we march, our strength will be augmented
In every county as we go along.
Strike up the drum! Cry, "Courage!" and away.
　　　　　　　　　　　　　　　　[*Exeunt.*]

SCENE IV. *Plains near Tewkesbury.*

[*March. Enter* QUEEN MARGARET, PRINCE EDWARD,
　　SOMERSET, OXFORD, *and* SOLDIERS.]
　　Q. MAR. Great lords, wise men ne'er sit and wail
　　their loss,
But cheerly° seek how to redress their harms.
What though the mast be now blown overboard,
The cable broke, the holding anchor lost,
And half our sailors swallowed in the flood?　5
Yet lives our pilot still. Is 't meet that he
Should leave the helm and, like a fearful lad,
With tearful eyes add water to the sea
And give more strength to that which hath too
　　much,
Whiles, in his moan, the ship splits on the rock　10
Which industry and courage might have saved?
Ah, what a shame! Ah, what a fault were this!
Say Warwick was our anchor. What of that?
And Montague our topmast. What of him?
Our slaughtered friends the tackles.° What of
　　these?　　　　　　　　　　　　　　　15
Why, is not Oxford here another anchor?
And Somerset another goodly mast?
The friends of France our shrouds° and tacklings?
And, though unskillful, why not Ned and I
For once allowed the skillful pilot's charge?°　20
We will not from the helm to sit and weep,
But keep our course, though the rough wind say no,
From shelves° and rocks that threaten us with
　　wreck.
As good to chide the waves as speak them fair.

Sc. iii: 8. **Gallia:** France.　13. **engenders:** begets.　17. **faction:** party.　21. **rids way:** takes away the toil of the journey.
　　Sc. iv: 2. **cheerly:** cheerfully.　15. **tackles:** ropes.
18. **shrouds:** sails.　20. **allowed . . . charge:** be allowed to steer the ship.　23. **shelves:** shoals, sandbanks.

And what is Edward but a ruthless sea?   25
What Clarence but a quicksand of deceit?
And Richard but a ragged fatal rock?
All these the enemies to our poor bark.°
Say you can swim — alas, 'tis but a while!
Tread on the sand — why, there you quickly sink.
Bestride the rock — the tide will wash you off,   31
Or else you famish; that's a threefold death.
This speak I, lords, to let you understand,
If case° some one of you would fly from us,
That there's no hoped-for mercy with the brothers
More than with ruthless waves, with sands and
    rocks.   36
Why, courage then! What cannot be avoided
'Twere childish weakness to lament or fear.
   PRIN. Methinks a woman of this valiant spirit
Should, if a coward heard her speak these words,
Infuse his breast with magnanimity   41
And make him, naked, foil a man at arms.°
I speak not this as doubting any here,
For did I but suspect a fearful man,
He should have leave to go away betimes,   45
Lest in our need he might infect another
And make him of like spirit to himself.
If any such be here — as God forbid! —
Let him depart before we need his help.   49
   OXF. Women and children of so high a courage,
And warriors faint! Why, 'twere perpetual shame.
O brave young Prince! Thy famous grandfather
Doth live again in thee. Long mayst thou live
To bear his image and renew his glories!
   SOM. And he that will not fight for such a hope,
Go home to bed, and like the owl by day,   56
If he arise, be mocked and wondered at.
   Q. MAR. Thanks, gentle Somerset. Sweet Oxford,
    thanks.
   PRIN. And take his thanks that yet hath nothing
    else.
          [Enter a MESSENGER.]
   MESS. Prepare you, lords, for Edward is at hand,
Ready to fight. Therefore be resolute.   61
   OXF. I thought no less. It is his policy
To haste thus fast to find us unprovided.
   SOM. But he's deceived. We are in readiness.
   Q. MAR. This cheers my heart, to see your for-
    wardness.   65
   OXF. Here pitch our battle.° Hence we will not
    budge.
     [Flourish and March. Enter KING EDWARD,
      GLOUCESTER, CLARENCE, *and* SOLDIERS.]
   K. EDW. Brave followers, yonder stands the
    thorny wood
Which, by the Heavens' assistance and your
    strength,

Must by the roots be hewn up yet ere night.
I need not add more fuel to your fire,   70
For well I wot° ye blaze to burn them out.
Give signal to the fight, and to it, lords!
   Q. MAR. Lords, knights, and gentlemen, what I
    should say
My tears gainsay.° For every word I speak,
Ye see I drink the water of mine eyes.   75
Therefore, no more but this: Henry, your sover-
   eign,
Is prisoner to the foe, his state usurped,
His realm a slaughterhouse, his subjects slain,
His statutes canceled, and his treasure spent;
And yonder is the wolf that makes this spoil.   80
You fight in justice. Then, in God's name, lords,
Be valiant, and give signal to the fight.
     [Alarum. Retreat. Excursions. Exeunt.]

   SCENE V. *Another part of the field.*

   [Flourish. Enter KING EDWARD, GLOUCESTER,
CLARENCE, *and* SOLDIERS; *with* QUEEN MARGARET,
   OXFORD, *and* SOMERSET, *prisoners.*]
   K. EDW. Now here a period° of tumultuous
    broils.
Away with Oxford to Hames Castle straight.
For Somerset, off with his guilty head.
Go, bear them hence. I will not hear them speak.
   OXF. For my part, I'll not trouble thee with
    words.   5
   SOM. Nor I, but stoop with patience to my for-
    tune. *[Exeunt* OXFORD *and* SOMERSET, *guarded.*]
   Q. MAR. So part we sadly in this troublous world,
To meet with joy in sweet Jerusalem.°
   K. EDW. Is proclamation made that who finds
    Edward
Shall have a high reward, and he his life?   10
   GLO. It is; and lo, where youthful Edward
    comes!
     [Enter SOLDIERS, *with* PRINCE EDWARD.]
   K. EDW. Bring forth the gallant, let us hear him
    speak.
What! Can so young a thorn begin to prick?
Edward, what satisfaction° canst thou make
For bearing arms, for stirring up my subjects,   15
And all the trouble thou hast turned me to?
   PRIN. Speak like a subject, proud ambitious
    York!
Suppose that I am now my father's mouth.
Resign thy chair, and where I stand kneel thou,
Whilst I propose the selfsame words to thee   20
Which, traitor, thou wouldst have me answer to.
   Q. MAR. Ah, that thy father had been so resolved!

---

28. bark: vessel.   34. If case: in case.   42. foil . . . arms:
overthrow an armed soldier.   66. pitch . . . battle: draw up our
army.

71. wot: know.   74. gainsay: forbid.
   Sc. v: 1. period: end.   8. Jerusalem: Heaven.   14. satisfaction: recompense.

GLO. That you might still have worn the petticoat,
And ne'er have stol'n the breech° from Lancaster.
    PRIN. Let Aesop° fable in a winter's night.   25
His currish° riddles sort° not with this place.
    GLO. By Heaven, brat, I'll plague ye for that
word.
    Q. MAR. Aye, thou wast born to be a plague to
men.
    GLO. For God's sake, take away this captive
scold.
    PRIN. Nay, take away this scolding crookback
rather.   30
    K. EDW. Peace willful boy, or I will charm your
tongue.°
    CLAR. Untutored lad, thou art too malapert.°
    PRIN. I know my duty. You are all undutiful.
Lascivious Edward, and thou perjured George,
And thou misshapen Dick, I tell ye all   35
I am your better, traitors as ye are,
And thou usurp'st my father's right and mine.
    K. EDW. Take that, thou likeness of this railer
here.   [*Stabs him.*]
    GLO. Sprawl'st thou? Take that, to end thy
agony.   [*Stabs him.*]
    CLAR. And there's for twitting me with perjury.
        [*Stabs him.* PRINCE EDWARD *dies.*]
    Q. MAR. Oh, kill me too!   41
    GLO. Marry,° and shall.   [*Offers to kill her.*]
    K. EDW. Hold, Richard, hold, for we have done
too much.
    GLO. Why should she live to fill the world with
words?
    K. EDW. What, doth she swoon? Use means for
her recovery.   45
    GLO. Clarence, excuse me to the King my brother.
I'll hence to London on a serious matter.
Ere ye come there, be sure to hear some news.
    CLAR. What? What?
    GLO. The Tower, the Tower.   [*Exit.*]   50
    Q. MAR. O Ned, sweet Ned! Speak to thy mother,
boy!
Canst thou not speak? Oh, traitors! Murderers!
They that stabbed Caesar shed no blood at all,
Did not offend, nor were not worthy blame,
If this foul deed were by to equal it.   55
He was a man; this, in respect,° a child;
And men ne'er spend their fury on a child.
What's worse than murderer, that I may name it?
No, no, my heart will burst an if I speak;
And I will speak that so my heart may burst.   60
Butchers and villains! Bloody cannibals!

How sweet a plant have you untimely cropped!
You have no children, butchers! If you had,
The thought of them would have stirred up re-
morse.
But if you ever chance to have a child,   65
Look in his youth to have him so cut off
As, deathsmen, you have rid° this sweet young
Prince!
    K. EDW. Away with her. Go, bear her hence per-
force.
    Q. MAR. Nay, never bear me hence, dispatch me
here.   69
Here sheathe thy sword, I'll pardon thee my death.
What, wilt thou not? Then, Clarence, do it thou.
    CLAR. By Heaven, I will not do thee so much
ease.
    Q. MAR. Good Clarence, do. Sweet Clarence, do
thou do it.
    CLAR. Didst thou not hear me swear I would not
do it?
    Q. MAR. Aye, but thou usest to forswear thyself.°
'Twas sin before, but now 'tis charity.   76
What, wilt thou not? Where is that Devil's butcher,
Hard-favored° Richard? Richard, where art thou?
Thou art not here. Murder is thy almsdeed;°
Petitioners for blood thou ne'er put'st back.°   80
    K. EDW. Away, I say. I charge ye, bear her hence.
    Q. MAR. So come to you and yours as to this
Prince!   [*Exit, led out forcibly.*]
    K. EDW. Where's Richard gone?
    CLAR. To London, all in post,° and, as I guess,
To make a bloody supper in the Tower.   85
    K. EDW. He's sudden if a thing comes in his
head.
Now march we hence. Discharge the common sort
With pay and thanks, and let's away to London
And see our gentle Queen how well she fares.   89
By this, I hope, she hath a son for me.   [*Exeunt.*]

SCENE VI. *London. The Tower.*

[*Enter* KING HENRY *and* GLOUCESTER, *with the*
LIEUTENANT, *on the walls.*]
    GLO. Good day, my lord. What, at your book so
hard?
    K. HEN. Aye, my good lord — my lord, I should
say rather.
'Tis sin to flatter; " good " was little better.
" Good Gloucester " and " good Devil " were alike,
And both preposterous.° Therefore, not " good
lord."   5

---

24. **breech:** breeches.   25. **Aesop:** a Greek of the 6th century
B.C. who devised moral fables much read and quoted. He was
said to have been monstrously ugly and deformed. 26. **currish:**
doglike. **sort:** suit.   31. **charm . . . tongue:** make you quiet.
32. **malapert:** impudent. 42. **Marry:** Mary, by the Virgin.
56. **in respect:** by comparison.

67. **rid:** cut off.   75. **forswear thyself:** break your oath.
78. **Hard-favored:** grim-faced.   79. **almsdeed:** charitable action.
80. **Petitioners . . . back:** you never refuse anyone who asks
leave to commit murder.   84. **post:** haste.
Sc. vi: 5. **preposterous:** unnatural.

GLO. Sirrah,° leave us to ourselves. We must confer.   [*Exit* LIEUTENANT.]

K. HEN. So flies the reckless shepherd from the wolf;
So first the harmless sheep doth yield his fleece
And next his throat unto the butcher's knife.
What scene of death hath Roscius° now to act?   10

GLO. Suspicion always haunts the guilty mind.
The thief doth fear each bush an officer.

K. HEN. The bird that hath been limèd° in a bush,
With trembling wings misdoubteth° every bush;
And I, the hapless male to one sweet bird,   15
Have now the fatal object in my eye
Where my poor young was limed, was caught, and killed.

GLO. Why, what a peevish fool° was that of Crete
That taught his son the office° of a fowl!
And yet, for all his wings, the fool was drowned.

K. HEN. I, Daedalus; my poor boy, Icarus;   21
Thy father, Minos, that denied our course;
The sun that seared° the wings of my sweet boy,
Thy brother Edward, and thyself, the sea
Whose envious gulf° did swallow up his life.   25
Ah, kill me with thy weapon, not with words!
My breast can better brook thy dagger's point
Than can my ears that tragic history.
But wherefore dost thou come? Is 't for my life?

GLO. Think'st thou I am an executioner?   30

K. HEN. A persecutor, I am sure, thou art.
If murdering innocents be executing,
Why, then thou art an executioner.

GLO. Thy son I killed for his presumption.

K. HEN. Hadst thou been killed when first thou didst presume,   35
Thou hadst not lived to kill a son of mine.
And thus I prophesy: that many a thousand,
Which now mistrust no parcel of my fear,°
And many an old man's sigh and many a widow's,
And many an orphan's water-standing° eye —   40
Men for their sons, wives for their husbands,
And orphans for their parents' timeless death —
Shall rue the hour that ever thou wast born.
The owl shrieked at thy birth — an evil sign.
The night crow cried, aboding luckless time.°   45
Dogs howled, and hideous tempest shook down trees.
The raven rooked her° on the chimney's top,

And chattering pies° in dismal discords sung.
Thy mother felt more than a mother's pain,
And yet brought forth less than a mother's hope —
To wit, an indigested and deformèd lump,   51
Not like the fruit of such a goodly tree.
Teeth hadst thou in thy head when thou wast born,
To signify thou camest to bite the world.
And, if the rest be true which I have heard,   55
Thou camest ——

GLO. I'll hear no more. Die, prophet, in thy speech.   [*Stabs him.*]
For this, amongst the rest, was I ordained.

K. HEN. Aye, and for much more slaughter after this.
Oh, God forgive my sins and pardon thee!   [*Dies.*]

GLO. What, will the aspiring° blood of Lancaster
Sink in the ground? I thought it would have mounted.   62
See how my sword weeps for the poor King's death!
Oh, may such purple tears be always shed
From those that wish the downfall of our house!
If any spark of life be yet remaining,   66
Down, down to Hell, and say I sent thee thither,
                                    [*Stabs him again.*]
I, that have neither pity, love, nor fear.
Indeed, 'tis true that Henry told me of,
For I have often heard my mother say   70
I came into the world with my legs forward.
Had I not reason, think ye, to make haste
And seek their ruin that usurped our right?
The midwife wondered, and the women cried,
" Oh, Jesus bless us, he is born with teeth! "   75
And so I was, which plainly signified
That I should snarl and bite and play the dog.
Then, since the Heavens have shaped my body so,
Let Hell make crooked my mind to answer it.
I have no brother, I am like no brother;   80
And this word " love," which greybeards call divine,
Be resident in men like one another,
And not in me. I am myself alone.
Clarence, beware. Thou keep'st me from the light;
But I will sort a pitchy day° for thee,   85
For I will buzz abroad such prophecies
That Edward shall be fearful of his life,
And then, to purge his fear, I'll be thy death.
King Henry and the Prince his son are gone.
Clarence, thy turn is next, and then the rest,   90
Counting myself but bad till I be best.
I'll throw thy body in another room
And triumph, Henry, in thy day of doom.
                                    [*Exit, with the body.*]

---

6. **Sirrah:** term of address used to an inferior.   10. **Roscius:** i.e., this play actor. Roscius was a famous Roman actor. See *Haml,* II.ii.410.   13. **limed:** caught by birdlime.   14. **misdoubteth:** suspects.   18–25. **fool . . . life:** See *I Hen VI,* IV.vi.54–55,n.   19. **office:** business.   23. **seared:** scorched.   25. **envious gulf:** hateful whirlpool.   38. **mistrust . . . fear:** do not suspect (*mistrust*) any part (*parcel*) of what I fear.   40. **water-standing:** brimming with tears.   45. **aboding . . . time:** foretelling evil days.   47. **rooked her:** crouched.

48. **pies:** magpies, regarded as unlucky birds.   61. **aspiring:** soaring.   85. **sort . . . day:** find out a black day.

SCENE VII. *London. The palace.*

[*Flourish. Enter* KING EDWARD, QUEEN ELIZABETH,
CLARENCE, GLOUCESTER, HASTINGS, *a* NURSE *with the
young* PRINCE, *and* ATTENDANTS.]
  K. EDW. Once more we sit in England's royal
    throne,
Repurchased with the blood of enemies.
What valiant foemen, like to autumn's corn,°
Have we mowed down in tops of all their pride!
Three Dukes of Somerset, threefold renowned   5
For hardy and undoubted champions;
Two Cliffords, as the father and the son;
And two Northumberlands — two braver men
Ne'er spurred their coursers° at the trumpet's
    sound.
With them, the two brave bears,° Warwick and
    Montague,   10
That in their chains fettered the kingly lion
And made the forest tremble when they roared.
Thus have we swept suspicion from our seat
And made our footstool of security.°
Come hither, Bess, and let me kiss my boy.   15
Young Ned, for thee thine uncles and myself
Have in our armors watched the winter's night,
Went all afoot in summer's scalding heat,
That thou mightst repossess the crown in peace.
And of our labors thou shalt reap the gain.   20
  GLO. [*Aside*] I'll blast his harvest if your head
    were laid;°

Sc. vii: **3. corn:** wheat.   **9. coursers:** war horses.   **10. bears:**
The crest of the earls of Warwick was a bear tied to a ragged tree.
14. footstool of security: made safety our footstool.   **21. laid:**
laid flat.

For yet I am not looked on in the world.
This shoulder was ordained so thick to heave,
And heave it shall some weight, or break my back.
Work thou the way — and thou shalt execute.   25
  K. EDW. Clarence and Gloucester, love my lovely
    Queen,
And kiss your princely nephew, Brothers both.
  CLAR. The duty that I owe unto your Majesty
I seal upon the lips of this sweet babe.
  Q. ELIZ. Thanks, noble Clarence. Worthy Brother,
    thanks.   30
  GLO. And, that I love the tree from whence thou
    sprang'st,
Witness the loving kiss I give the fruit.
[*Aside*] To say the truth, so Judas kissed his Master,
And cried, " All hail! " when as he meant all
    harm.°
  K. EDW. Now am I seated as my soul delights,
Having my country's peace and brothers' loves.
  CLAR. What will your Grace have done with Mar-
    garet?   37
Reignier, her father, to the King of France
Hath pawned the Sicils and Jerusalem,
And hither have they sent it for her ransom.   40
  K. EDW. Away with her, and waft° her hence to
    France.
And now what rests but that we spend the time
With stately triumphs, mirthful comic shows,
Such as befits the pleasure of the Court?   44
Sound drums and trumpets! Farewell sour annoy!
For here, I hope, begins our lasting joy. [*Exeunt.*]

33–34. Judas . . . harm: See Matthew 26:47–49.   **41. waft:**
convoy.

The Tragedy of

KING RICHARD THE THIRD

Introduction

The Tragedy of King Richard the Third was the fourth and concluding play of the series which Shakespeare began with *I Henry VI*.[1] It was probably written in 1592 or 1593 at a time when Shakespeare was still a learner and an imitator; indeed some scholars have believed that some of the scenes were written by Marlowe.

The main source of the story, as with the other historical plays, was Raphael Holinshed's *Chronicles of England, Scotland, and Ireland,* published in 1577, and reissued in a second edition in 1587. For the events of the life and reign of Richard, Duke of Gloucester, afterward Richard III, Holinshed reprinted almost verbatim from Edward Halle's *Chronicle.* Halle had in turn used Sir Thomas More's life of Richard the Third and Polydore Vergil's *Historia Angliae.* More's life dealt only with the months from the death of Edward IV to the rebellion of Buckingham; Polydore Vergil covered the whole period to the Battle of Bosworth. Shakespeare may have used both chronicles, but he was mainly indebted to Holinshed.

Shakespeare borrowed from his sources freely, selecting a few incidents but inventing others to illustrate the theme that blood will have blood, and to show how the curse laid on the House of Lancaster when Henry IV usurped the throne was at last fulfilled, and how the many troubles caused by that crime were finally purged when Henry of Richmond became King; for by his marriage with Elizabeth of York he united the White Rose and the Red, and thereby became the grandfather of Shakespeare's Queen Elizabeth.

Shakespeare's debt to Holinshed may be illustrated by some extracts:

I. THE CHARACTER OF RICHARD, DUKE OF GLOUCESTER

Richard, the third son, of whom we now intreat, was in wit and courage equal with either of them [Edward IV and Clarence], in body and prowess

---
[1] For the history behind this play, see Appendix 28.

---

far under them both; little of stature, ill-featured of limbs, crookbacked, his left shoulder much higher than his right, hard-favored of visage, and such as is in states called "warly" [warlike], in other men otherwise; he was malicious, wrathful, envious, and from afore his birth ever froward. It is for truth reported that the Duchess his mother had so much ado in her travail that she could not be delivered of him uncut; and that he came into the world with the feet forward, as men be borne outward, and (as the fame runneth also) not untoothed . . .

None evil captain was he in the war, as to which his disposition was more meetly than for peace. Sundry victories had he, and sometimes overthrows, but never on default as for his own person, either of hardiness or politic order. Free was he called of dispense, and somewhat above his power liberal; with large gifts he gat him unsteadfast friendship, for which he was fain to pill [pillage] and spoil in other places, and got him steadfast hatred. He was close and secret, a deep dissembler, lowly of countenance, arrogant of heart, outwardly companionable where he inwardly hated, not letting [hindering; that is, allowing himself] to kiss whom he thought to kill; despitious [full of spite] and cruel, not for evil will alway, but ofter of ambition and either for the surety or increase of his estate.

Friend and foe was much what indifferent, where his advantage grew; he spared no man's death whose life withstood his purpose . . .

As he was small and little of stature, so was he of body greatly deformed, the one shoulder higher than the other. His face was small, but his countenance cruel, and such that at the first aspect a man would judge it to savor and smell of malice, fraud, and deceit. When he stood musing, he would bite and chaw busily his nether lip, as who said that his fierce nature in his cruel body always chafed, stirred, and was ever unquiet. Beside that, the dagger which he ware, he would, when he studied [meditated] with his hand pluck up and down in the sheath to the midst, never drawing it fully out. He was of a ready, pregnant, and quick wit, wily to feign, and apt to dissemble. He had a proud mind, and an arrogant stomach, the which accompanied him even to his death; rather choosing to suffer the same by dint of sword than, being forsaken and left helpless of his unfaithful companions, to preserve by cowardly flight such a frail and uncertain life, which by malice, sickness, or condign punishment was like shortly to come to confusion.

2. THE DEATH OF HASTINGS (cf. III.IV)

[On June 13, 1483] many lords assembled in the Tower, and there sat in council, devising the honorable solemnity of the King's [Edward V's] coronation, of which the time appointed then so near approached that the pageants and subtleties were in making day and night at Westminster, and much victuals killed therefor that afterward was cast away. These lords so sitting together communing of this matter, the Protector came in amongst them, first about nine of the clock, saluting them courteously, and excusing himself that he had been from them so long, saying merrily that he had been a sleeper that day.

After a little talking with them, he said unto the Bishop of Ely: "My lord, you have very good strawberries at your garden in Holborn. I require you let us have a mess of them." "Gladly, my lord," quoth he. "Would God I had some better thing as ready to your pleasure as that." And therewithal in all the haste he sent his servant for a mess of strawberries. The Protector set the lords fast in communing, and thereupon, praying them to spare him for a little while, departed thence. And soon after one hour, between ten and eleven, he returned into the chamber amongst them, all changed, with a wonderful sour angry countenance, knitting the brows, frowning, and fretting and gnawing on his lips, and so sat him down in his place.

All the lords were much dismayed, and sore marveled at this manner of sudden change, and what thing should ail him. Then, when he had sitten still awhile, he thus began: "What were they worthy to have that compass and imagine the destruction of me, being so near of blood unto the King, and Protector of his royal person and his realm?" At this question all the lords sat sore astonied, musing much by whom this question should be meant, of which every man wist himself clear. Then the Lord Chamberlain [Hastings], as he that for the love between them thought he might be boldest with him, answered and said that they were worthy to be punished as heinous traitors, whatsoever they were. And all the other affirmed the same. "That is," quoth he, "yonder sorceress my brother's wife, and other with her" (meaning the Queen).

At these words many of the lords were greatly abashed that favored her. But the Lord Hastings was in his mind better content that it was moved by her than by any other whom he loved better [that is, Jane Shore], albeit his heart somewhat grudged that he was not afore made of counsel in this matter

as he was of the taking of her kindred and of their putting to death, which were by his assent before devised to be beheaded at Pomfret this selfsame day; in which he was not ware that it was by other devised that he himself should be beheaded that same day at London. Then said the Protector: "You shall see in what wise that sorceress, and that other witch of her counsel, Shore's wife, with her affinity, have by their sorcery and witchcraft wasted my body." And therewith he plucked up his doublet sleeve to his elbow, upon his left arm, where he showed a weerish [sickly-looking] withered arm, and small as it was never other.

Hereupon every man's mind sore misgave him, well perceiving that this matter was but a quarrel. For they well wist that the Queen was too wise to go about any such folly. And also, if she would, yet would she of all folk least make Shore's wife of her counsel, whom of all women she most hated as that concubine whom the King her husband had most loved. And also no man was there present but well knew that his arm was ever such since his birth.

Naithless, the Lord Chamberlain (which from the death of King Edward kept Shore's wife, on whom he had somewhat doted in the King's life, saving, as it is said, he that while forbear her of reverence toward the King, or else of a certain kind of fidelity to his friend), answered and said: "Certainly, my lord, if they have so heinously done, they be worthy heinous punishment."

"What," quoth the Protector, "thou servest me, I ween, with 'ifs' and with 'ands.' I tell thee they have so done, and that I will make good on thy body, traitor." And therewith, as in a great anger, he clapped his fist upon the board a great rap. At which token one cried "Treason!" without the chamber. Therewith a door clapped, and in come there men in harness [armor], as many as the chamber might hold. And anon the Protector said to the Lord Hastings: "I arrest thee, traitor!" "What me, my lord?" quoth he. "Yea, thee, traitor!" quoth the Protector. . . .

Then were they all quickly bestowed in divers chambers, except the Lord Chamberlain, whom the Protector bade speed and shrive him [confess his sins and receive absolution] apace, "for by Paul," quoth he, "I will not to dinner till I see thy head off!" It booted him not to ask why, but heavily he took a priest at adventure and made a short shrift; for a longer would he not be suffered, the Protector made so much haste to dinner, which he might not go to until this were done for saving of his oath.

3. THE MURDER OF THE PRINCES (cf. IV.ii AND iii)

Sir James Tyrrel devised that they should be murdered in their beds. To the execution whereof he appointed one Miles Forrest, one of the four that kept them, a fellow fleshed in murder beforetime. To him he joined one John Deighton, his own horsekeeper, a big, broad, square, and strong knave.

Then all the other being removed from them, this Miles Forrest and John Deighton about midnight (the silly [simple, innocent] children lying in their beds) came into the chamber, and suddenly lapping them up among the clothes, so to-bewrapped them and entangled them, keeping down by force the feather bed and pillows hard unto their mouths, that within a while, smothered and stifled, their breath failing, they gave up to God their innocent souls into the joys of Heaven, leaving to the tormentors their bodies dead in the bed. Which after that the wretches perceived, first by the struggling with the pains of death, and after long lying still, to be thoroughly dead, they laid their bodies naked out upon the bed, and fetched Sir James to see them, which, upon the sight of them, caused those murderers to bury them at the stair foot, meetly deep in the ground under a great heap of stones.

Then rode Sir James in great haste to King Richard and showed him all the manner of the murder, who gave him great thanks, and (as some say) then made him knight. But he allowed not (as I have heard) the burying in so vile a corner, saying that he would have them buried in a better place, because they were a King's sons. . . . Whereupon, they say that a priest of Sir Robert Brakenbury's took up the bodies again and secretly interred them in such a place as by the occasion of his death, which only knew it, could never since come to light.

4. RICHARD DREAMS BEFORE BOSWORTH (cf. v.iii)

[The episode of the ghosts which appeared to Richard on the night before he was killed was based on the following paragraph.]

The fame went that he had the same night a dreadful and terrible dream; for it seemed to him being asleep that he did see divers images like terrible devils, which pulled and haled him, not suffering him to take any quiet or rest. The which strange vision not so suddenly strake his heart with a sudden fear, but it stuffed his head and troubled his mind with many busy and dreadful imaginations. For incontinent after, his heart being almost damped, he prognosticated before the doubtful chance of the battle to come, not using the alacrity and mirth of mind and countenance as he was accustomed to do before he came toward the battle. At least that it might be suspected that he was abashed for fear of his enemies, and for that cause looked so piteously, he recited and declared to his familiar friends in the morning his wonderful vision and fearful dream.

5. THE DEATH OF RICHARD AT THE BATTLE OF BOSWORTH (cf. v.iv AND v)

King Richard set on so sharply at the first brunt that he overthrew the Earl's [Richmond's] standard and slew Sir William Brandon his standard-bearer (which was father to Sir Charles Brandon, by King Henry the Eighth created Duke of Suffolk) and matched hand to hand with Sir John Cheney, a man of great force and strength, which would have resisted him; but the said John was by him manfully overthrown. And so, he making passage by dint of sword as he went forward, the Earl of Richmond withstood his violence, and kept him at the sword's point without advantage longer than his companions either thought or judged; which being almost in despair of victory were suddenly recomforted by Sir William Stanley, which came to his succors with three thousand tall men. At which very instant King Richard's men were driven back and fled, and he himself, manfully fighting in the middle of his enemies, was slain, and (as he worthily had deserved) came to a bloody death as he had led a bloody life . . .

When the loss of the battle was imminent and apparent, they brought him a swift and light horse to convey him away. He which was not ignorant of the grudge and ill will that the common people bare toward him, casting away all hope of fortunate success and happy chance to come, answered (as men say) that on that day he would make an end of all battles, or else there finish his life.

Richard III was entered for publication in the Stationers' Register to Andrew Wise on October 20, 1597, as " The tragedie of kinge Richard the Third with the death of the Duke of Clarence." A first quarto appeared in the same year with the title: *The Tragedy of King Richard the Third. Containing, His treacherous Plots against his brother Clarence: the pittiefull murther of his innocent nephewes; his tyrannicall usurpation: with the whole course of his detested life, and most deserved death. As it hath beene lately Acted by the Right Honourable the Lord Chamberlaine his servants.* Other quartos appeared in 1598, 1602, 1605, 1616, and 1622. These were printed one from the other, but when the play was reprinted in the first folio of 1623 the text was set up from a copy corrected from some different original. There are considerable variations between the quarto and folio versions. The folio adds certain passages: I.ii.156–67; II.ii.89–110; II.ii.123–40; III.vii.144–53; IV.iv.221–34; IV.iv. 288–42. As the play is considerably longer than the average, these passages may have been cut in the acting version. On the other hand, the folio omits IV.ii.101–19 and some shorter passages and there are many minor differences between the two versions. Either the folio text was based on the playhouse copy and the quarto on an inferior original, or the quarto version is the earlier and the folio a revision. The text of the play is thus difficult. The modern text is a compound of both versions, each editor giving the reading which appears to him best.

In writing *Richard III* Shakespeare imitated his predecessors in several ways. The obvious dramatic ironies, the prophecies and curses, the ghosts, and the symbolic figure of the aged Queen Margaret are in the manner of Kyd and of the Roman dramatist Seneca, whom earlier Elizabethan dramatists admiringly copied; but Shakespeare owed most to Marlowe. Like *Tamburlaine* and *The Jew of Malta, Richard III* is a play with one star part; it is the portrayal of a colossal villain. There is little opportunity for other members of the company to distinguish themselves except in individual scenes. The hero, like Barabas in *The Jew of Malta,* is a " Machiavellian," and the play opens in the same way, with the chief character coming forward alone to explain himself in a long soliloquy. Richard as Duke of Gloucester had already shown his ruthless nature in the *III Henry VI,* which ended with Richard murdering King Henry VI in the Tower as King Edward IV was restored to the throne.

Richard III begins with Richard announcing that since he is lame, ugly, and repulsive in body he is "determined to prove a villain." He is thus an unnatural monster who delights in wickedness for its own sake. His first step will be the destruction of his brother Clarence, which he effects by persuading King Edward IV to have Clarence murdered, while at the same time he pretends to Clarence to be his true friend. By the end of the first scene Richard has already shown that his ambitions are leading him to the crown.

His next step is to marry Anne, the daughter of the late Earl of Warwick, even though he had murdered her husband and her father-in-law. In the second scene Richard is shown carrying out this plan: As the funeral of King Henry VI passes by, with the Lady Anne as chief mourner, Richard intercepts the procession and proceeds first to overcome the loathing of Anne and then to persuade her to accept his monstrous offer of marriage. Richard did in fact marry Prince Edward's widow, but the wooing as shown in the play is wholly unhistorical and highly artificial in conception and dialogue, yet in an extravagant way theatrically effective. It abounds in those devices which mark Shakespeare's early style — puns, conceits, elaborate imagery, repetitions, word play in which one word is used in two or three different meanings, and a general delight in cleverness rather than in psychological insight. Thus Richard addresses Anne (I.ii.75–78):

> Vouchsafe, divine perfection of a woman,
> Of these supposèd evils to give me leave,
> By circumstance, but to acquit myself.

Anne retorts phrase for phrase:

> Vouchsafe, defused infection of a man,
> For these known evils but to give me leave,
> By circumstance, to curse thy cursèd self.

This kind of elaborate cleverness is not to be found in the plays of Shakespeare's maturity. Richard has made a good beginning, but he is in considerable danger. The King's relations, who occupy the highest offices in the state, loathe him. Further, Edward IV is ailing. While his relations are anxiously debating the King's health, Richard joins them, and during the wrangle that follows there enters the aged Queen Margaret, widow of King Henry VI, and once champion of the House of Lancaster. Her presence among her enemies is quite fantastic, but she is brought in as a prophetess of woe and doom to rain curses on her many enemies of the House of York and to foretell their downfall. Act I ends with the murder of Clarence — a scene which includes a fine piece of epic description in Clarence's account of his dream.

Act II begins with the dying King's vain efforts to bring about a reconciliation between his jarring relatives. Upon Edward's death the women of his family — his wife and his mother — lament for him, but Richard and his ally, Buckingham, at once take steps to seize the boy King, Edward V. At this point Shakespeare interposed a short scene (II.iii) in which two citizens in their conversation reveal the general fears that dangerous times are at hand.

In Act III, Richard and Buckingham, having captured the young King and his brother, the precocious little Duke of York, lead the two boys to the Tower. Richard is now feeling after the crown. The first step is to eliminate possible opponents. Of these the most dangerous is the Lord Chamberlain, Lord Hastings. Richard sends his man Catesby to sound him out; Catesby finds that Hastings, as Richard had suspected, is loyal to the boy King. At a meeting of the Council Richard suddenly denounces Hastings and commands his instant execution. Then he sends Buckingham to try to win over the Lord Mayor and the citizens of London to his support. The citizens are cold, but Buckingham persuades the Lord Mayor to lead a deputation to beg Richard to assume the crown. Richard now becomes King. He sends for Tyrrel, a conscienceless villain, and orders the murder of the two little Princes. Anne dies, evidently by Richard's orders. But new difficulties are showing themselves; Buckingham is no longer as subservient as before. Tyrrel returns with the news of the death of the boys. Then follows a scene where Queen Margaret once more appears to gloat over the downfall of her enemies and to indulge in a contest of lamentation with Elizabeth, widow of Edward IV, and the aged Duchess of York. Though Margaret hates them both, they are at least united in their common hatred of Richard, and they curse him as he passes by. But Richard with his old cynicism approaches Elizabeth and in a long dialogue between them (which parallels the earlier wooing of Anne) tries to win her over to agree to his marriage with her daughter Elizabeth. The tide has now turned; news comes to Richard that his enemies are everywhere rising to join with Henry Richmond, the last survivor of the House of Lancaster and Buckingham is among them. Buckingham, however, is taken.

The last act opens with a brief scene showing Buckingham on his way to execution. He pauses to lament his treacheries, which have now come back on his own head. The scene then shifts to the field of Bosworth on the night before the battle. On either side of the stage the tents of Richard and Richmond are set up. One by one the ghosts of Richard's victims rise — Prince Edward, Margaret's son, Henry VI, Clarence, Rivers, Vaughan, Grey, the two Princes, Anne, Buckingham. They curse Richard, bless Richmond, and disappear. The episode is symbolic and a fitting summary of Richard's career. A short battle scene follows. Richard is killed, Henry Richmond is saluted as King, and the play ends with a prayer that England may be spared another civil war.

To anyone unfamiliar with an intricate period of English history, *Richard III* is difficult to follow in the reading. On the stage it is effective in a melodramatic way; it demands extravagant acting and a certain lack of sophistication in the audience. In its own times it was a popular success, and Burbage's acting of the part of Richard was much admired. Indeed his rendering of Richard's last speech — "A horse! A horse! My kingdom for a horse!" — was almost as much quoted and parodied as some of the famous lines in Kyd's *Spanish Tragedy*. But Shakespeare and his fellows soon abandoned this ranting kind of drama as they came to realize that to make a good play something more was needed than verbal cleverness and a star actor.

Richard III

DRAMATIS PERSONAE

KING EDWARD *the Fourth*

EDWARD, *Prince of Wales, afterward King Edward V*

RICHARD, *Duke of York* } *sons to the King*

GEORGE, *Duke of Clarence*

RICHARD, *Duke of Gloucester, afterward King Richard III* } *brothers to the King*

A young son of Clarence

HENRY, *Earl of Richmond, afterward King Henry VII*

CARDINAL BOURCHIER, *Archbishop of Canterbury*

THOMAS ROTHERHAM, *Archbishop of York*

JOHN MORTON, *Bishop of Ely*

DUKE OF BUCKINGHAM

DUKE OF NORFOLK

EARL OF SURREY, *his son*

EARL RIVERS, *brother to Elizabeth*

MARQUIS OF DORSET *and* LORD GREY, *sons to Elizabeth*

EARL OF OXFORD

LORD HASTINGS

LORD STANLEY, *called also* EARL OF DERBY

LORD LOVEL

SIR THOMAS VAUGHAN

SIR RICHARD RATCLIFF

SIR WILLIAM CATESBY

SIR JAMES TYRREL

SIR JAMES BLOUNT

SIR WALTER HERBERT

SIR ROBERT BRAKENBURY, *Lieutenant of the Tower*

SIR WILLIAM BRANDON

CHRISTOPHER URSWICK, *a priest. Another Priest*

TRESSEL *and* BERKELEY, *gentlemen attending on the Lady Anne*

LORD MAYOR *of London*

SHERIFF *of Wiltshire*

ELIZABETH, *queen to King Edward IV*

MARGARET, *widow of King Henry VI*

DUCHESS OF YORK, *mother to King Edward IV*

LADY ANNE, *widow of Edward Prince of Wales, son to King Henry VI; afterward married to Richard*

A young daughter of Clarence (MARGARET PLANTAGENET)

GHOSTS *of those murdered by Richard III,* LORDS *and other* ATTENDANTS; *a* PURSUIVANT, SCRIVENER, CITIZENS, MURDERERS, MESSENGERS, SOLDIERS, ETC.

SCENE — *England*.

Act I

SCENE I. *London. A street.*

[*Enter* RICHARD, DUKE OF GLOUCESTER, *solus.*]
GLO. Now is the winter of our discontent
Made glorious summer by this sun of York,°
And all the clouds that lowered upon our house
In the deep bosom of the ocean buried.
Now are our brows bound with victorious wreaths,
Our bruisèd arms hung up for monuments,　　6
Our stern alarums changed to merry meetings,
Our dreadful marches to delightful measures.°
Grim-visaged war hath smoothed his wrinkled front,°
And now, instead of mounting barbèd° steeds　10
To fright the souls of fearful adversaries,
He capers nimbly in a lady's chamber
To the lascivious pleasing of a lute.°
But I, that am not shaped for sportive tricks,
Nor made to court an amorous looking-glass;　15
I, that am rudely stamped, and want love's majesty
To strut before a wanton ambling nymph;
I, that am curtailed° of this fair proportion,°
Cheated of feature by dissembling° nature,
Deformed, unfinished, sent before my time　20
Into this breathing world, scarce half made up,
And that so lamely and unfashionable
That dogs bark at me as I halt° by them —
Why, I, in this weak piping time° of peace,
Have no delight to pass away the time,　25
Unless to spy my shadow in the sun
And descant° on mine own deformity.
And therefore, since I cannot prove a lover,
To entertain° these fair well-spoken days,
I am determinèd to prove a villain　30
And hate the idle pleasures of these days.
Plots have I laid, inductions° dangerous,
By drunken prophecies, libels, and dreams,
To set my brother Clarence and the King

Act I, Sc. i: **2. sun . . . York:** a triple pun. Edward IV was son of the Duke of York, and bore a sun as his badge. He was also the bright sun of the Yorkist party now in power.　**8. measures:** dances. See App. 24.　**9. wrinkled front:** frowning forehead.　**10. barbed:** armed.　**13. lute:** See Pl. 18d.

18. curtailed: cut short. **proportion:** shape.　**19. dissembling:** cheating.　**23. halt:** limp.　**24. piping time:** i.e., when shepherds play their pipes.　**27. descant:** warble, "make a song about."　**29. entertain:** pass away.　**32. inductions:** introductions — the first steps in an undertaking.

In deadly hate the one against the other.   35
And if King Edward be as true and just
As I am subtle, false, and treacherous,
This day should Clarence closely be mewed up,°
About a prophecy, which says that G
Of Edward's heirs the murderer shall be.   40
Dive, thoughts, down to my soul — here Clarence
    comes.
    [*Enter* CLARENCE, *guarded, and* BRAKENBURY.]
Brother, good day. What means this armèd guard
That waits upon your Grace?
    CLAR.   His Majesty,
Tendering my person's safety, hath appointed
This conduct to convey me to the Tower.   45
    GLO. Upon what cause?
    CLAR.   Because my name is George.
    GLO. Alack, my lord, that fault is none of yours.
He should, for that, commit your godfathers.
Oh, belike His Majesty hath some intent
That you shall be new-christened in the Tower.   50
But what's the matter, Clarence? May I know?
    CLAR. Yea, Richard, when I know, for I protest
As yet I do not. But, as I can learn,
He hearkens after prophecies and dreams;
And from the crossrow° plucks the letter G,   55
And says a wizard told him that by G
His issue disinherited should be;
And, for my name of George begins with G,
It follows in his thought that I am he.
These, as I learn, and suchlike toys° as these   60
Have moved His Highness to commit me now.
    GLO. Why, this it is, when men are ruled by
    women.
'Tis not the King that sends you to the Tower;
My Lady Grey his wife, Clarence, 'tis she
That tempers° him to this extremity.   65
Was it not she and that good man of worship,
Anthony Woodville, her brother there,
That made him send Lord Hastings to the Tower,
From whence this present day he is delivered?
We are not safe, Clarence, we are not safe.   70
    CLAR. By Heaven, I think there's no man is secure
But the Queen's kindred and nightwalking heralds
That trudge betwixt the King and Mistress Shore.°
Heard ye not what a humble suppliant
Lord Hastings was to her for his delivery?   75
    GLO. Humbly complaining to her deity
Got my Lord Chamberlain his liberty.
I'll tell you what — I think it is our way,
If we will keep in favor with the King,
To be her men and wear her livery.   80
The jealous o'erworn widow and herself,

Since that our brother dubbed° them gentlewomen,
Are mighty gossips° in this monarchy.
    BRAK. I beseech your Graces both to pardon me —
His Majesty hath straitly° given in charge   85
That no man shall have private conference,
Of what degree° soever, with his brother.
    GLO. Even so, an 't° please your Worship, Brak-
    enbury,
You may partake of anything we say.
We speak no treason, man. We say the King   90
Is wise and virtuous, and his noble Queen
Well struck in years, fair, and not jealous.
We say that Shore's wife hath a pretty foot,
A cherry lip, a bonny eye, a passing° pleasing
    tongue.
And that the Queen's kindred are made gentlefolk.
How say you, sir? Can you deny all this?   96
    BRAK. With this, my lord, myself have naught to
    do.
    GLO. Naught to do with Mistress Shore! I tell
    thee, fellow,
He that doth naught with her, excepting one,
Were best he do it secretly alone.   100
    BRAK. What one, my lord?
    GLO. Her husband, knave. Wouldst thou betray
    me?
    BRAK. I beseech your Grace to pardon me, and
    withal
Forbear your conference with the noble Duke.
    CLAR. We know thy charge,° Brakenbury, and
    will obey.   105
    GLO. We are the Queen's abjects,° and must obey.
Brother, farewell. I will unto the King,
And whatsoever you will employ me in,
Were it to call King Edward's widow° sister,
I will perform it to enfranchise° you.   110
Meantime, this deep disgrace in brotherhood°
Touches me deeper than you can imagine.
    CLAR. I know it pleaseth neither of us well.
    GLO. Well, your imprisonment shall not be long.
I will deliver you, or else lie for you.°   115
Meantime, have patience.
    CLAR.   I must perforce. Farewell.
    [*Exeunt* CLARENCE, BRAKENBURY, *and* GUARD.]
    GLO. Go tread the path that thou shalt ne'er re-
    turn,
Simple, plain Clarence! I do love thee so
That I will shortly send thy soul to Heaven,

38. mewed up: confined.   **55. crossrow:** alphabet. Boys learned their alphabet from a printed sheet covered with horn, and known as the hornbook. As the first sign on the page was a cross (✠), the alphabet was sometimes called the christcross-row. **60. toys:** trifles. **65. tempers:** molds. **73. Mistress Shore:** wife of a London goldsmith and Edward IV's mistress.

82. dubbed: promoted. **83. gossips:** close friends who exchange gossip. **85. straitly:** strictly. **87. degree:** rank. **88. an 't:** if it. **94. passing:** exceedingly. **105. charge:** instructions. **106. abjects:** lowly servants, here used ironically for "subjects." **109. widow:** the widow whom Edward IV had married — Lady Elizabeth Woodville. **110. enfranchise:** set free. **111. disgrace in brotherhood:** The phrase, as is common in this play, has various meanings — "unnatural behavior in a brother (the King)," "disgrace to a brother (Clarence)," and "my own disgraceful conduct." **115. lie . . . you:** with double meaning — "take your place in prison" and "tell lies on your behalf."

If Heaven will take the present at our hands.   120
But who comes here? The new-delivered Hastings?

            [*Enter* LORD HASTINGS.]

    HAST. Good time of day unto my gracious lord!
    GLO. As much unto my good Lord Chamberlain!
Well are you welcome to the open air.   124
How hath your lordship brooked° imprisonment?
    HAST. With patience, noble lord, as prisoners
      must.
But I shall live, my lord, to give them thanks
That were the cause of my imprisonment.
    GLO. No doubt, no doubt, and so shall Clarence
      too;
For they that were your enemies are his,   130
And have prevailed as much on him as you.
    HAST. More pity that the eagle should be mewed°
While kites° and buzzards° prey at liberty.
    GLO. What news abroad?   134
    HAST. No news so bad abroad as this at home:
The King is sickly, weak, and melancholy,
And his physicians fear° him mightily.
    GLO. Now, by Saint Paul, this news is bad in-
      deed.
Oh, he hath kept an evil diet long,
And overmuch consumed his royal person.   140
'Tis very grievous to be thought upon.
What, is he in his bed?
    HAST.   He is.
    GLO. Go you before, and I will follow you.

                     [*Exit* HASTINGS.]

He cannot live, I hope, and must not die   145
Till George be packed with post horse° up to
    Heaven.
I'll in, to urge his hatred more to Clarence,
With lies well steeled° with weighty arguments;
And if I fail not in my deep intent,
Clarence hath not another day to live.   150
Which done, God take King Edward to His
    mercy,
And leave the world for me to bustle in!
For then I'll marry Warwick's youngest daughter.
What though I killed her husband and her father?
The readiest way to make the wench amends   155
Is to become her husband and her father —
The which will I, not all so much for love
As for another secret close intent
By marrying her which I must reach unto.
But yet I run before my horse to market.°   160
Clarence still breathes, Edward still lives and
    reigns.
When they are gone, then must I count my gains.

                       [*Exit.*]

SCENE II. *The same. Another street.*

[*Enter the corpse of* KING HENRY *the Sixth,* GENTLE-
MEN *with halberds*° *to guard it,* LADY ANNE *being
the mourner.*]

    ANNE. Set down, set down your honorable load —
If honor may be shrouded in a hearse —
Whilst I awhile obsequiously° lament
The untimely fall of virtuous Lancaster.
Poor key-cold figure of a holy King!   5
Pale ashes of the House of Lancaster,
Thou bloodless remnant of that royal blood!
Be it lawful that I invocate thy ghost
To hear the lamentations of poor Anne,
Wife to thy Edward, to thy slaughtered son,   10
Stabbed by the selfsame hand that made these
    wounds!
Lo, in these windows that let forth thy life
I pour the helpless balm of my poor eyes.
Cursed be the hand that made these fatal holes!
Cursed be the heart that had the heart to do it!   15
Cursèd the blood that let this blood from hence!
More direful hap betide° that hated wretch
That makes us wretched by the death of thee
Than I can wish to adders, spiders, toads,
Or any creeping venomed thing that lives!   20
If ever he have child, abortive° be it,
Prodigious,° and untimely brought to light,
Whose ugly and unnatural aspect°
May fright the hopeful mother at the view,
And that be heir to his unhappiness!°   25
If ever he have wife, let her be made
As miserable by the death of him
As I am made by my poor lord and thee!
Come, now toward Chertsey° with your holy load,
Taken from Paul's° to be interrèd there;   30
And still,° as° you are weary of the weight,
Rest you whiles I lament King Henry's corse.°

                     [*Enter* GLOUCESTER.]

    GLO. Stay, you that bear the corse, and set it
      down.
    ANNE. What black magician conjures up this
      fiend
To stop devoted charitable deeds?   35
    GLO. Villains, set down the corse, or, by Saint
      Paul,
I'll make a corse of him that disobeys.
    GENT. My lord, stand back, and let the coffin pass.
    GLO. Unmannered dog! Stand thou when I com-
      mand.
Advance thy halberd higher than my breast,   40
Or, by Saint Paul, I'll strike thee to my foot

---

125. **brooked:** endured.   132. **mewed:** caged.   133. **kites:** the lowest of the birds of prey. **buzzards:** an inferior species of hawk.   137. **fear:** fear for, are anxious about.   146. **post horse:** See App. 17.   148. **steeled:** with steel points.   160. **I ... market:** a proverb like "Count my chickens before they are hatched."

Sc. ii: s.d., **halberds:** See Pl. 21b.   3. **obsequiously:** as be-fits a mourner with obsequies.   17. **hap betide:** fortune befall. 21. **abortive:** unnatural.   22. **Prodigious:** monstrous.   23. **aspect:** look.   25. **unhappiness:** evil nature.   29. **Chertsey:** a town in Surrey.   30. **Paul's:** St. Paul's Church. See Gen. Intro. p. 17a, and Pl. 2a.   31. **still:** meanwhile. **as:** since.   32. **corse:** corpse.

And spurn upon thee, beggar, for thy boldness.
   ANNE. What, do you tremble? Are you all afraid?
Alas, I blame you not, for you are mortal,
And mortal eyes cannot endure the Devil.   45
Avaunt,° thou dreadful minister° of Hell!
Thou hadst but power over his mortal body,
His soul thou canst not have, therefore be gone.
   GLO. Sweet saint, for charity, be not so curst.°
   ANNE. Foul devil, for God's sake, hence, and
     trouble us not,   50
For thou hast made the happy earth thy Hell,
Filled it with cursing cries and deep exclaims.
If thou delight to view thy heinous deeds,
Behold this pattern° of thy butcheries.
O gentlemen, see, see! Dead Henry's wounds   55
Open their congealed mouths and bleed afresh.°
Blush, blush, thou lump of foul deformity,
For 'tis thy presence that exhales° this blood
From cold and empty veins where no blood dwells;
Thy deed, inhuman and unnatural,   60
Provokes this deluge most unnatural.
O God, which this blood mad'st, revenge his death!
O earth, which this blood drink'st, revenge his
    death!
Either Heaven with lightning strike the murderer
    dead,
Or earth, gape open wide and eat him quick,°   65
As thou dost swallow up this good King's blood,
Which his Hell-governed arm hath butchered!
   GLO. Lady, you know no rules of charity,
Which renders good for bad, blessings for curses.
   ANNE. Villain, thou know'st no law of God nor
    man.   70
No beast so fierce but knows some touch of pity.
   GLO. But I know none, and therefore am no beast.
   ANNE. Oh, wonderful when devils tell the truth!
   GLO. More wonderful when angels are so angry.
Vouchsafe, divine perfection of a woman,   75
Of these supposèd evils to give me leave,
By circumstance,° but to acquit myself.
   ANNE. Vouchsafe, defused° infection of a man,
For these known evils but to give me leave,
By circumstance, to curse thy cursèd self.   80
   GLO. Fairer than tongue can name thee, let me
    have
Some patient leisure to excuse myself.
   ANNE. Fouler than heart can think thee, thou
    canst make
No excuse current° but to hang thyself.
   GLO. By such despair I should accuse myself.   85
   ANNE. And, by despairing, shouldst thou stand
    excused

For doing worthy vengeance on thyself,
Which didst unworthy slaughter upon others.
   GLO. Say° that I slew them not?
   ANNE.   Why, then they are not dead.
But dead they are, and, devilish slave, by thee.   90
   GLO. I did not kill your husband.
   ANNE.   Why, then he is alive.
   GLO. Nay, he is dead, and slain by Edward's
    hand.
   ANNE. In thy foul throat thou liest. Queen Mar-
    garet saw
Thy murderous falchion° smoking in his blood,
The which thou once didst bend against her
    breast,   95
But that thy brothers beat aside the point.
   GLO. I was provokèd by her slanderous tongue,
Which laid their guilt upon my guiltless shoulders.
   ANNE. Thou wast provokèd by thy bloody mind,
Which never dreamed on aught but butcheries.   100
Didst thou not kill this King?
   GLO.   I grant ye.
   ANNE. Dost grant me, hedgehog?° Then, God
    grant me too
Thou mayst be damnèd for that wicked deed!
Oh he was gentle, mild, and virtuous!
   GLO. The fitter for the King of Heaven, that hath
    him.   105
   ANNE. He is in Heaven, where thou shalt never
    come.
   GLO. Let him thank me that holp° to send him
    thither,
For he was fitter for that place than earth.
   ANNE. And thou unfit for any place but Hell.
   GLO. Yes, one place else, if you will hear me
    name it.   110
   ANNE. Some dungeon.
   GLO.   Your bedchamber.
   ANNE. Ill rest betide the chamber where thou
    liest!
   GLO. So will it, madam, till I lie with you.
   ANNE. I hope so.
   GLO.   I know so. But, gentle Lady Anne,
To leave this keen encounter of our wits   115
And fall somewhat into a slower method,
Is not the causer of the timeless° deaths
Of these Plantagenets, Henry and Edward,
As blameful as the executioner?
   ANNE. Thou art the cause, and most accursed
    effect.°   120
   GLO. Your beauty was the cause of that effect—
Your beauty, which did haunt me in my sleep
To undertake the death of all the world
So I might live one hour in your sweet bosom.
   ANNE. If I thought that, I tell thee, homicide,

---

46. **Avaunt:** be gone. **minister:** servant. 49. **curst:** shrewish, bad-tempered. 54. **pattern:** example. 56. **bleed afresh:** It was popularly supposed that the wounds of a murdered man bled in the presence of the murderer. 58. **exhales:** draws out. 65. **quick:** aiive. 77. **By circumstance:** by relating the facts. 78. **defused:** diffused, confused. 84. **current:** genuine.

89. **Say:** suppose. 94. **falchion:** curved sword. 102. **hedgehog:** an insulting reference to Richard's crest of a wild boar. 107. **holp:** helped. 117. **timeless:** untimely. 120. **effect:** agent.

These nails should rend that beauty from my
    cheeks. 126
  GLO. These eyes could never endure sweet
    beauty's wreck.
You should not blemish it if I stood by.
As all the world is cheerèd by the sun,
So I by that. It is my day, my life. 130
  ANNE. Black night o'ershade thy day, and death
    thy life!
  GLO. Curse not thyself, fair creature — thou art
    both.
  ANNE. I would I were, to be revenged on thee.
  GLO. It is a quarrel most unnatural
To be revenged on him that loveth you. 135
  ANNE. It is a quarrel just and reasonable
To be revenged on him that slew my husband.
  GLO. He that bereft thee, lady, of thy husband,
Did it to help thee to a better husband. 139
  ANNE. His better doth not breathe upon the earth.
  GLO. He lives that loves thee better than he could.
  ANNE. Name him.
  GLO.   Plantagenet.
  ANNE.   Why, that was he.
  GLO. The selfsame name, but one of better nature.
  ANNE. Where is he?
  GLO.   Here. Why dost thou spit at me? 145
  ANNE. Would it were mortal poison, for thy sake!
  GLO. Never came poison from so sweet a place.
  ANNE. Never hung poison on a fouler toad.
Out of my sight! Thou dost infect my eyes. 149
  GLO. Thine eyes, sweet lady, have infected mine.
  ANNE. Would they were basilisks,° to strike thee
    dead!
  GLO. I would they were, that I might die at once,
For now they kill me with a living death.
Those eyes of thine from mine have drawn salt
    tears, 154
Shame their aspéct with store of childish drops.
These eyes, which never shed remorseful tear —
No, when my father York and Edward wept
To hear the piteous moan that Rutland made
When black-faced Clifford shook his sword at him;
Nor when thy warlike father, like a child, 160
Told the sad story of my father's death,
And twenty times made pause to sob and weep
That all the standers-by had wet their cheeks,
Like trees bedashed with rain — in that sad time
My manly eyes did scorn a humble tear. 165
And what these sorrows could not thence exhale,
Thy beauty hath, and made them blind with weep-
    ing.
I never sued to friend nor enemy,
My tongue could never learn sweet smoothing
    words,

But now thy beauty is proposed my fee,° 170
My proud heart sues, and prompts my tongue to
    speak.
Teach not thy lips such scorn, for they were made
For kissing, lady, not for such contempt.
If thy revengeful heart cannot forgive,
Lo, here I lend thee this sharp-pointed sword, 175
Which if thou please to hide in this true bosom
And let the soul forth that adoreth thee,
I lay it naked to the deadly stroke,
And humbly beg the death upon my knee.
Nay, do not pause, for I did kill King Henry. 180
But 'twas thy beauty that provokèd me.
Nay, now dispatch — 'twas I that stabbed young
    Edward,
But 'twas thy heavenly face that set me on.
Take up the sword again, or take up me.
  ANNE. Arise, dissembler.° Though I wish thy
    death, 185
I will not be the executioner.
  GLO. Then bid me kill myself, and I will do it.
  ANNE. I have already.
  GLO.   Tush, that was in thy rage.
Speak it again and, even with the word,
That hand which for thy love did kill thy love 190
Shall for thy love kill a far truer love.
To both their deaths shalt thou be accessory.
  ANNE. I would I knew thy heart.
  GLO. 'Tis figured in my tongue.
  ANNE. I fear me both are false. 195
  GLO. Then never man was true.
  ANNE. Well, well, put up your sword.
  GLO. Say, then, my peace is made.
  ANNE. That shall you know hereafter.
  GLO. But shall I live in hope? 200
  ANNE. All men, I hope, live so.
  GLO. Vouchsafe° to wear this ring.
  ANNE. To take is not to give.
  GLO. Look how this ring encompasseth thy finger,
Even so thy breast encloseth my poor heart. 205
Wear both of them, for both of them are thine.
And if thy poor devoted suppliant may
But beg one favor at thy gracious hand,
Thou dost confirm his happiness forever.
  ANNE. What is it? 210
  GLO. That it would please thee leave these sad
    designs
To him that hath more cause to be a mourner,
And presently° repair to Crosby Place,°
Where, after I have solemnly interrèd
At Chertsey monastery this noble King, 215
And wet his grave with my repentant tears,
I will with all expedient duty see you.

---

151. basilisk: an imaginary creature with a cock's head, an
animal's body, and a snake's tail, hatched out by a toad from a
cock's egg — a very deadly beast able to slay by its mere look.

170. thy . . . fee: when your beauty is the proposed reward.
185. dissembler: hypocrite. 202. Vouchsafe: grant, consent.
213. presently: immediately. Crosby Place: Richard's house in
London.

For divers unknown reasons, I beseech you
Grant me this boon.°
   ANNE. With all my heart, and much it joys me
      too   220
To see you are become so penitent.
Tressel and Berkeley, go along with me.
   GLO. Bid me farewell.
   ANNE.   'Tis more than you deserve.
But since you teach me how to flatter you,
Imagine I have said farewell already.   225
     [*Exeunt* LADY ANNE, TRESSEL, *and* BERKELEY.]
   GLO. Sirs, take up the corse.
   GENT.   Toward Chertsey, noble lord?
   GLO. No, to Whitefriars.° There attend° my com-
    ing.   [*Exeunt all but* GLOUCESTER.]
Was ever woman in this humor° wooed?
Was ever woman in this humor won?
I'll have her, but I will not keep her long.   230
What! I, that killed her husband and his father,
To take her in her heart's extremest hate,
With curses in her mouth, tears in her eyes,
The bleeding witness of her hatred by° —
Having God, her conscience, and these bars° against
   me,   235
And I nothing to back my suit at all
But the plain Devil and dissembling looks,
And yet to win her, all the world to nothing!°
Ha!
Hath she forgot already that brave Prince,   240
Edward, her lord, whom I, some three months
   since,
Stabbed in my angry mood at Tewksbury?
A sweeter and a lovelier gentleman,
Framed in the prodigality of nature,°   244
Young, valiant, wise, and no doubt right royal,
The spacious world cannot again afford.°
And will she yet debase her eyes on me,
That cropped the golden prime of this sweet Prince
And made her widow to a woeful bed?
On me, whose all not equals Edward's moiety?°
On me, that halt and am unshapen thus?   251
My dukedom to a beggarly denier,°
I do mistake my person all this while.
Upon my life, she finds, although I cannot,
Myself to be a marvelous proper° man.   255
I'll be at charges for° a looking-glass,
And entertain some score or two of tailors,
To study fashions to adorn my body.
Since I am crept in favor with myself,
I will maintain it with some little cost.   260
But first I'll turn yon fellow in° his grave,

---

219. boon: favor. 227. Whitefriars: a monastery in London.
attend: await. 228. humor: mood. 234. witness . . . by: i.e.,
the corpse of her father-in-law. 235. bars: hindrances. 238. all
. . . nothing: against all odds. 244. prodigality of nature: when
nature was most generous. 246. afford: produce. 250. moiety:
half. 252. denier: small copper coin. 255. proper: handsome.
256. be . . . for: buy. 261. turn . . . in: tip into.

And then return lamenting to my love.
Shine out, fair sun, till I have bought a glass,
That I may see my shadow as I pass.   [*Exit.*]

SCENE III. *The palace.*

[*Enter* QUEEN ELIZABETH, LORD RIVERS, *and*
    LORD GREY.]
   RIV. Have patience, madam. There's no doubt
   His Majesty
Will soon recover his accustomed health.
   GREY. In that you brook it ill, it makes him worse.
Therefore, for God's sake, entertain good comfort,
And cheer His Grace with quick and merry words.
   Q. ELIZ. If he were dead, what would betide of°
   me?   6
   RIV. No other harm but loss of such a lord.
   Q. ELIZ. The loss of such a lord includes all harm.
   GREY. The Heavens have blessed you with a
   goodly son
To be your comforter when he is gone.   10
   Q. ELIZ. Oh, he is young, and his minority
Is put unto the trust of Richard Gloucester,
A man that loves not me, nor none of you.
   RIV. Is it concluded he shall be Protector?
   Q. ELIZ. It is determined, not concluded° yet.   15
But so it must be if the King miscarry.
     [*Enter* BUCKINGHAM *and* DERBY.]
   GREY. Here come the Lords of Buckingham and
   Derby.
   BUCK. Good time of day unto your royal Grace!
   DER. God make your Majesty joyful as you have
   been!
   Q. ELIZ. The Countess Richmond, good my Lord
   of Derby,   20
To your good prayers will scarcely say amen.
Yet, Derby, notwithstanding she's your wife,
And loves not me, be you, good lord, assured
I hate not you for her proud arrogance.
   DER. I do beseech you, either not believe   25
The envious slanders of her false accusers,
Or if she be accused in true report,
Bear with her weakness, which I think proceeds
From wayward° sickness, and no grounded malice.
   RIV. Saw you the King today, my Lord of Derby?
   DER. But now the Duke of Buckingham and I
Are come from visiting His Majesty.   32
   Q. ELIZ. What likelihood of his amendment,
   lords?
   BUCK. Madam, good hope. His Grace speaks
   cheerfully.
   Q. ELIZ. God grant him health! Did you confer
   with him?   35

Sc. iii: 6. betide of: become of. 15. determined . . . concluded:
settled, but not formally ratified. 29. wayward: perverse.

BUCK. Madam, we did. He desires to make atonement°
Betwixt the Duke of Gloucester and your brothers,
And betwixt them and my Lord Chamberlain,°
And sent to warn° them to his royal presence.

Q. ELIZ. Would all were well! But that will never be.　　　40
I fear our happiness is at the highest.

[*Enter* GLOUCESTER, HASTINGS, *and* DORSET.]

GLO. They do me wrong, and I will not endure it.
Who are they that complain unto the King
That I, forsooth, am stern and love them not?
By holy Paul, they love His Grace but lightly　45
That fill his ears with such dissentious° rumors.
Because I cannot flatter and speak fair,
Smile in men's faces, smooth, deceive, and cog,°
Duck with French nods and apish courtesy,
I must be held a rancorous enemy.　　　50
Cannot a plain man live and think no harm
But thus his simple truth must be abused
By silken, sly, insinuating Jacks?°

RIV. To whom in all this presence speaks your Grace?　　　54

GLO. To thee, that hast nor honesty nor grace.
When have I injured thee? When done thee wrong?
Or thee? Or thee? Or any of your faction?
A plague upon you all! His royal person —
Whom God preserve better than you would wish! —
Cannot be quiet scarce a breathing-while　60
But you must trouble him with lewd° complaints.

Q. ELIZ. Brother of Gloucester, you mistake the matter.
The King, of his own royal disposition,
And not provoked by any suitor else —
Aiming, belike, at your interior hatred,　　65
Which in your outward actions shows itself
Against my kindred, brothers, and myself —
Makes him to send, that thereby he may gather
The ground of your ill will, and to remove it.

GLO. I cannot tell. The world is grown so bad　70
That wrens° make prey where eagles dare not perch.
Since every Jack became a gentleman,
There's many a gentle° person made a Jack.

Q. ELIZ. Come, come, we know your meaning, Brother Gloucester —
You envy my advancement and my friends'.　75
God grant we never may have need of you!

GLO. Meantime, God grants that we have need of you.
Our brother is imprisoned by your means,
Myself disgraced, and the nobility

Held in contempt, whilst many fair promotions　80
Are daily given to ennoble those
That scarce, some two days since, were worth a noble.°

Q. ELIZ. By Him that raised me to this careful° height
From that contented hap° which I enjoyed,
I never did incense His Majesty　　　85
Against the Duke of Clarence, but have been
An earnest advocate to plead for him.
My lord, you do me shameful injury
Falsely to draw° me in these vile suspécts.°

GLO. You may deny that you were not the cause
Of my Lord Hastings' late imprisonment.　91

RIV. She may, my lord, for ——

GLO. She may, Lord Rivers! Why, who knows not so?
She may do more, sir, than denying that —
She may help you to many fair preferments,　95
And then deny her aiding hand therein,
And lay those honors on your high deserts.
What may she not? She may, yea, marry,° may she ——

RIV. What, marry, may she?

GLO. What, marry, may she! Marry with a king,
A bachelor, a handsome stripling too.　　101
I wis° your grandam had a worser match.

Q. ELIZ. My Lord of Gloucester, I have too long borne
Your blunt upbraidings and your bitter scoffs.
By Heaven, I will acquaint His Majesty　105
With those gross taunts I often have endured.
I had rather be a country servant maid
Than a great queen, with this condition,
To be thus taunted, scorned, and baited at.°

[*Enter* QUEEN MARGARET,° *behind*.] Small joy have
I being England's Queen.　　　110

Q. MAR. And lessened be that small, God, I beseech Thee!
Thy honor, state, and seat is due to me.

GLO. What! Threat you me with telling of the King?
Tell him, and spare not. Look, what I have said
I will avouch in presence of the King.　　115
I dare adventure to be sent to the Tower.
'Tis time to speak, my pains° are quite forgot.

Q. MAR. Out, devil! I remember them too well.
Thou slewest my husband Henry in the Tower,
And Edward, my poor son, at Tewksbury.　120

GLO. Ere you were Queen, yea, or your husband King,

---

36. atonement: reconciliation.　38. Lord Chamberlain: Hastings.
39. warn: summon.　46. dissentious: troublemaking.　48. cog:
cheat.　53. Jacks: knaves.　61. lewd: vile.　71. wrens: the
smallest of English birds.　73. gentle: of gentle blood.

82. noble: 6s. 8d. See App. 27.　83. careful: full of care.
84. hap: good fortune.　89. draw: involve. suspects: suspicion.
98. marry: Mary, by the Virgin.　102. I wis: certainly.　109. baited
at: harrassed. See App. 5.　110 s.d., Queen Margaret: the
widow of King Henry VI. Her appearance here is quite unhistorical. She is a symbolical figure, the doom of the House of
York.　117. pains: labors.

I was a pack horse in his great affairs,
A weeder out of his proud adversaries,
A liberal rewarder of his friends.
To royalize his blood I spilt mine own.   125
   Q. MAR. Yea, and much better blood than his or
     thine.
   GLO. In all which time you and your husband
     Grey
Were factious° for the House of Lancaster.
And, Rivers, so were you. Was not your husband
In Margaret's battle at St. Albans° slain?   130
Let me put in your minds, if you forget,
What you have been ere now, and what you are;
Withal, what I have been, and what I am.
   Q. MAR. A murderous villain, and so still thou art.
   GLO. Poor Clarence did forsake his father, War-
     wick —   135
Yea, and forswore himself — which Jesu pardon! —
   Q. MAR. Which God revenge!
   GLO. —To fight on Edward's party for the
     crown.
And for his meed,° poor lord, he is mewed up.
I would to God my heart were flint, like Edward's,
Or Edward's soft and pitiful, like mine.   141
I am too childish-foolish for this world.
   Q. MAR. Hie thee to Hell for shame, and leave the
     world,
Thou cacodemon!° There thy kingdom is.   144
   RIV. My Lord of Gloucester, in those busy days
Which here you urge° to prove us enemies,
We followed then our lord, our lawful King.
So should we you, if you should be our king.
   GLO. If I should be! I had rather be a peddler.
Far be it from my heart, the thought of it!   150
   Q. ELIZ. As little joy, my lord, as you suppose
You should enjoy, were you this country's King,
As little joy may you suppose in me,
That I enjoy, being the queen thereof.
   Q. MAR. A little joy enjoys the Queen thereof,
For I am she, and altogether joyless.   156
I can no longer hold me patient.   [*Advancing.*]
Hear me, you wrangling pirates, that fall out
In sharing that which you have pilled° from me!
Which of you trembles not that looks on me?   160
If not that, I being Queen, you bow like subjects,
Yet that, by you deposed, you quake like rebels?
O gentle villain, do not turn away!
   GLO. Foul wrinkled witch, what mak'st thou in
     my sight?
   Q. MAR. But repetition of what thou hast marred,
That will I make before I let thee go.   166
   GLO. Wert thou not banishèd on pain of death?
   Q. MAR. I was, but I do find more pain in banish-
     ment

Than death can yield me here by my abode.
A husband and a son thou ow'st to me,   170
And thou a kingdom, all of you allegiance.
The sorrow that I have by right is yours,
And all the pleasures you usurp are mine.
   GLO. The curse my noble father laid on thee
When thou didst crown his warlike brows with
     paper,   175
And with thy scorns drew'st rivers from his eyes,
And then, to dry them, gav'st the Duke a clout°
Steeped in the faultless blood of pretty Rutland —
His curses, then from bitterness of soul   179
Denounced against thee, are all fall'n upon thee,
And God, not we, hath plagued thy bloody deed.
   Q. ELIZ. So just is God, to right the innocent.
   HAST. Oh, 'twas the foulest deed to slay that babe,°
And the most merciless, that e'er was heard of!
   RIV. Tyrants themselves wept when it was re-
     ported.   185
   DOR. No man but prophesied revenge for it.
   BUCK. Northumberland, then present, wept to see
     it.
   Q. MAR. What! Were you snarling all before I
     came,
Ready to catch each other by the throat,
And turn you all your hatred now on me?   190
Did York's dread curse prevail so much with
     Heaven
That Henry's death, my lovely Edward's death,
Their kingdom's loss, my woeful banishment,
Could all but answer for that peevish brat?   194
Can curses pierce the clouds and enter Heaven?
Why then, give way, dull clouds, to my quick
     curses!
If not by war, by surfeit° die your King,
As ours by murder, to make him a king!
Edward thy son, which now is Prince of Wales,
For Edward my son, which was Prince of Wales,
Die in his youth by like untimely violence!   201
Thyself a Queen, for me that was a Queen,
Outlive thy glory, like my wretched self!
Long mayst thou live to wail thy children's loss,
And see another, as I see thee now,   205
Decked in thy rights, as thou art stalled° in
     mine!
Long die thy happy days before thy death,
And after many lengthened hours of grief,
Die neither mother, wife, nor England's Queen!
Rivers and Dorset, you were standers-by,   210
And so wast thou, Lord Hastings, when my son
Was stabbed with bloody daggers. God, I pray Him
That none of you may live your natural age,
But by some unlooked accident cut off!
   GLO. Have done thy charm,° thou hateful with-
     ered hag!   215

---

128. **factious**: active partisans. 130. **Margaret's ... St. Albans:** the second Battle of St. Albans, where Margaret defeated the Yorkists in 1461. 139. **meed**: reward. 144. **cacodemon:** evil devil. 146. **urge**: put forward. 159. **pilled:** pillaged.

177. **clout:** cloth. 183. **that babe:** young Rutland. 197. **surfeit:** overindulgence. 206. **stalled:** installed. 215. **charm:** curse.

Q. MAR. And leave out thee? Stay, dog, for thou
  shalt hear me.
If Heaven have any grievous plague in store
Exceeding those that I can wish upon thee,
Oh, let them keep it till thy sins be ripe,
And then hurl down their indignation   220
On thee, the troubler of the poor world's peace!
The worm of conscience still beknaw thy soul!
Thy friends suspect for traitors while thou livest,
And take deep traitors for thy dearest friends!
No sleep close up that deadly eye of thine,   225
Unless it be whilst some tormenting dream
Affrights thee with a Hell of ugly devils!
Thou elvish-marked,° abortive, rooting hog!°
Thou that wast sealed in thy nativity
The slave of nature and the son of Hell!°   230
Thou slander of thy mother's heavy womb!
Thou loathèd issue of thy father's loins!
Thou rag of honor! Thou detested ——
  GLO. Margaret.
  Q. MAR.   Richard!
  GLO.   Ha!°
  Q. MAR.   I call thee not.   234
  GLO. I cry thee mercy, then, for I had thought
That thou hadst called me all these bitter names.
  Q. MAR. Why, so I did, but looked for no reply.
Oh, let me make the period° to my curse!
  GLO. 'Tis done by me, and ends in "Margaret."
  Q. ELIZ. Thus have you breathed your curse
  against yourself.   240
  Q. MAR. Poor painted° Queen, vain flourish° of
  my fortune!
Why strew'st thou sugar on that bottled° spider
Whose deadly web ensnareth thee about?
Fool, fool! Thou whet'st a knife to kill thyself.
The time will come that thou shalt wish for me
To help thee curse that poisonous bunchbacked°
  toad.   246
  HAST. False-boding° woman, end thy frantic
  curse,
Lest to thy harm thou move our patience.
  Q. MAR. Foul shame upon you! You have all
  moved mine.
  RIV. Were you well served, you would be taught
  your duty.   250
  Q. MAR. To serve me well, you all should do me
  duty,
Teach me to be your Queen, and you my subjects.
Oh, serve me well, and teach yourselves that duty!
  DOR. Dispute not with her, she is lunatic.

Q. MAR. Peace, Master Marquess, you are mala-
  pert.°   255
Your fire-new° stamp of honor is scarce current.
Oh, that your young nobility could judge
What 'twere to lose it, and be miserable!
They that stand high have many blasts to shake
  them,   259
And if they fall, they dash themselves to pieces.
  GLO. Good counsel, marry. Learn it, learn it,
  Marquess.
  DOR. It toucheth you, my lord, as much as me.
  GLO. Yea, and much more. But I was born so
  high,
Our aerie° buildeth in the cedar's top,
And dallies with the wind and scorns the sun.   265
  Q. MAR. And turns the sun to shade, alas! alas!
Witness my son, now in the shade of death,
Whose bright outshining beams thy cloudy wrath
Hath in eternal darkness folded up.
Your aerie buildeth in our aerie's nest.   270
O God, that seest it, do not suffer it.
As it was won with blood, lost be it so!
  BUCK. Have done! For shame, if not for charity.
  Q. MAR. Urge neither charity nor shame to me.
Uncharitably with me have you dealt,   275
And shamefully by you my hopes are butchered.
My charity is outrage, like my shame,
And in that shame still live my sorrow's rage!
  BUCK. Have done, have done.
  Q. MAR. O princely Buckingham, I'll kiss thy
  hand,   280
In sign of league and amity with thee.
Now fair befall° thee and thy noble house!
Thy garments are not spotted with our blood,
Nor thou within the compass of my curse.   284
  BUCK. Nor no one here, for curses never pass
The lips of those that breathe them in the air.
  Q. MAR. I'll not believe but they ascend the sky,
And there awake God's gentle-sleeping peace.
O Buckingham, take heed of yonder dog!   289
Look, when he fawns, he bites, and when he bites,
His venom tooth will rankle° to the death.
Have not to do with him, beware of him,
Sin, death, and Hell have set their marks on him,
And all their ministers attend on him.
  GLO. What doth she say, my Lord of Bucking-
  ham?   295
  BUCK. Nothing that I respect, my gracious lord.
  Q. MAR. What, dost thou scorn me for my gentle
  counsel?
And soothe the devil that I warn thee from?
Oh, but remember this another day
When he shall split thy very heart with sorrow,
And say poor Margaret was a prophetess.   301

228. elvish-marked: marked at birth by evil fairies. hog:
Richard's badge was a wild boar.   229–30. sealed . . . Hell: at
your birth nature marked you out as the slave of Hell by making
you deformed.   234. Ha!: i.e., you called me?   238. period:
end.   241. painted: imitation. vain flourish: queen merely in
show, as I was once.   242. bottled: shaped like a bottle. See
Pl. 2of.   246. bunch-backed: hunchbacked.   247. False-boding:
falsely prophesying.

255. malapert: impudent. 256. fire-new: newly minted.
264. aerie: the eagle's nest and brood. 282. fair befall: good
luck come to. 291. rankle: make fester.

Live each of you the subjects to his hate,
And he to yours, and all of you to God's! [*Exit.*]
    HAST. My hair doth stand on end to hear her
      curses.
    RIV. And so doth mine. I muse why she's at
      liberty.   305
    GLO. I cannot blame her. By God's holy Mother,
She hath had too much wrong, and I repent
My part thereof that I have done to her.
    Q. ELIZ. I never did her any, to my knowledge.
    GLO. But you have all the vantage of° her wrong.
I was too hot to do somebody good   311
That is too cold in thinking of it now.
Marry, as for Clarence, he is well repaid,
He is franked up° to fatting for his pains.
God pardon them that are the cause of it!   315
    RIV. A virtuous and a Christianlike conclusion,
To pray for them that have done scathe° to us.
    GLO. So do I ever — [*Aside*] being well advised.
For had I cursed now, I had cursed myself.
           [*Enter* CATESBY.]
    CAT. Madam, His Majesty doth call for you, 320
And for your Grace, and you, my noble lords.
    Q. ELIZ. Catesby, we come. Lords, will you go
      with us?
    RIV. Madam, we will attend your Grace.
           [*Exeunt all but* GLOUCESTER.]
    GLO. I do the wrong, and first begin to brawl.
The secret mischiefs that I set abroach°   325
I lay unto the grievous charge of others.
Clarence, whom I indeed have laid in darkness,
I do beweep to many simple gulls° —
Namely, to Hastings, Derby, Buckingham —
And say it is the Queen and her allies   330
That stir the King against the Duke my brother.
Now, they believe it, and withal whet me
To be revenged on Rivers, Vaughan, Grey.
But then I sigh, and with a piece of Scripture
Tell them that God bids us do good for evil. 335
And thus I clothe my naked villainy
With old odd ends stolen out of Holy Writ,
And seem a saint when most I play the devil.
[*Enter two* MURDERERS.] But, soft! Here come my
    executioners.
How now, my hardy stout resolvèd° mates!   340
Are you now going to dispatch this deed?
    I. MUR. We are, my lord, and come to have the
      warrant,
That we may be admitted where he is.
    GLO. Well thought upon — I have it here about
      me.   [*Gives the warrant.*]
When you have done, repair to Crosby Place. 345
But, sirs, be sudden in the execution,

Withal obdúrate° — do not hear him plead.
For Clarence is well spoken, and perhaps
May move your hearts to pity if you mark him.
    I. MUR. Tush!   350
Fear not, my lord, we will not stand to prate.
Talkers are no good doers. Be assured
We come to use our hands and not our tongues.
    GLO. Your eyes drop millstones when fools' eyes
      drop tears.
I like you, lads. About your business straight. 355
Go, go, dispatch.
    I. MUR. We will, my noble lord.   [*Exeunt.*]

SCENE IV. *London. The Tower.*

[*Enter* CLARENCE *and* BRAKENBURY.]
    BRAK. Why looks your Grace so heavily today?
    CLAR. Oh, I have passed a miserable night,
So full of ugly sights, of ghastly dreams,
That, as I am a Christian faithful man,
I would not spend another such a night   5
Though 'twere to buy a world of happy days,
So full of dismal terror was the time!
    BRAK. What was your dream? I long to hear you
      tell it.
    CLAR. Methought that I had broken from the
      Tower,
And was embarked to cross to Burgundy,   10
And in my company my brother Gloucester,
Who from my cabin tempted me to walk
Upon the hatches. Thence we looked toward Eng-
    land,
And cited up° a thousand fearful times
During the wars of York and Lancaster   15
That had befall'n us. As we paced along
Upon the giddy footing of the hatches,
Methought that Gloucester stumbled, and in falling
Struck me, that thought to stay° him, overboard,
Into the tumbling billows of the main.   20
Lord, Lord! Methought what pain it was to drown!
What dreadful noise of waters in mine ears!
What ugly sights of death within mine eyes!
Methought I saw a thousand fearful wrecks,
Ten thousand men that fishes gnawed upon,   25
Wedges of gold, great anchors, heaps of pearl,
Inestimable stones, unvalued jewels,
All scattered in the bottom of the sea.
Some lay in dead men's skulls, and in those holes
Where eyes did once inhabit there were crept, 30
As 'twere in scorn of eyes, reflecting gems,
Which wooed the slimy bottom of the deep
And mocked the dead bones that lay scattered by.
    BRAK. Had you such leisure in the time of death

---

310. vantage of: advantages derived from.   314. franked up:
shut up. A frank is a sty for fattening hogs.   317. scathe: harm.
325. set abroach: set going; lit., tapped, like a cask.   328. gulls:
fools.   340. resolved: resolute.

347. obdurate: hardhearted.
    Sc. iv: 14. cited up: called to mind   19. stay: stop.

To gaze upon the secrets of the deep?　　35
　CLAR. Methought I had, and often did I strive
To yield the ghost. But still the envious° flood
Kept in my soul, and would not let it forth
To seek the empty, vast, and wandering air,
But smothered it within my panting bulk,　　40
Which almost burst to belch it in the sea.
　BRAK. Awaked you not with this sore agony?
　CLAR. Oh no, my dream was lengthened after
life.
Oh, then began the tempest to my soul,
Who passed, methought, the melancholy flood,　45
With that grim ferryman° which poets write of,
Unto the kingdom of perpetual night.
The first that there did greet my stranger soul
Was my great father-in-law, renownèd Warwick,
Who cried aloud, "What scourge for perjury　50
Can this dark monarchy afford false Clarence?"
And so he vanished. Then came wandering by
A shadow like an angel, with bright hair
Dabbled in blood, and he squeaked out aloud,
"Clarence is come, false, fleeting, perjured Clar-
ence,　　55
That stabbed me in the field by Tewksbury.
Seize on him, Furies, take him to your torments!"
With that, methought a legion of foul fiends
Environed me about, and howlèd in mine ears
Such hideous cries that with the very noise　60
I trembling waked, and for a season after
Could not believe but that I was in Hell,
Such terrible impression made the dream.
　BRAK. No marvel, my lord, though it affrighted
you.
I promise you, I am afraid to hear you tell it.　65
　CLAR. O Brakenbury, I have done those things,
Which now bear evidence against my soul,
For Edward's sake — and see how he requites me!
O God! If my deep prayers cannot appease Thee,
But Thou wilt be avenged on my misdeeds,　70
Yet execute Thy wrath in me alone.
Oh, spare my guiltless wife and my poor children!
I pray thee, gentle keeper, stay by me.
My soul is heavy, and I fain would sleep.
　BRAK. I will, my lord. God give your Grace good
rest!　　　　　　　　[CLARENCE *sleeps*.]　75
Sorrow breaks seasons and reposing hours,
Makes the night morning and the noontide night.
Princes have but their titles for their glories,
An outward honor for an inward toil.
And, for unfelt imagination,　　80
They often feel a world of restless cares.°
So that, betwixt their titles and low names,
There's nothing differs but the outward fame.

[*Enter the two* MURDERERS.]
　1. MUR. Ho! Who's here?
　BRAK. In God's name, what are you, and how
came you hither?　　85
　1. MUR. I would speak with Clarence, and I came
hither on my legs.
　BRAK. Yea, are you so brief?
　2. MUR. O sir, it is better to be brief than tedious.
Show him our commission.° Talk no more.　91
　　　　　　　　　　[BRAKENBURY *reads it.*]
　BRAK. I am in this commanded to deliver
The noble Duke of Clarence to your hands.
I will not reason what is meant hereby,
Because I will be guiltless of the meaning.　95
Here are the keys, there sits the Duke asleep.
I'll to the King, and signify to him
That thus I have resigned my charge to you.
　1. MUR. Do so, it is a point of wisdom. Fare you
well.　　　　　　　　[*Exit* BRAKENBURY.]　99
　2. MUR. What, shall we stab him as he sleeps?
　1. MUR. No. Then he will say 'twas done cowardly, when he wakes.
　2. MUR. When he wakes! Why, fool, he shall
never wake till the Judgment Day.　　106
　1. MUR. Why, then he will say we stabbed him
sleeping.
　2. MUR. The urging of that word "judgment"
hath bred a kind of remorse in me.　　110
　1. MUR. What, art thou afraid?
　2. MUR. Not to kill him, having a warrant for
it, but to be damned for killing him, from which
no warrant can defend us.
　1. MUR. I thought thou hadst been resolute.　116
　2. MUR. So I am, to let him live.
　1. MUR. Back to the Duke of Gloucester — tell
him so.
　2. MUR. I pray thee stay a while. I hope my holy
humor° will change. 'Twas wont to hold me but
while one would tell° twenty.　　121
　1. MUR. How dost thou feel thyself now?
　2. MUR. Faith, some certain dregs of conscience
are yet within me.
　1. MUR. Remember our reward when the deed is
done.
　2. MUR. 'Zounds,° he dies. I had forgot the reward.
　1. MUR. Where is thy conscience now?　　130
　2. MUR. In the Duke of Gloucester's purse.
　1. MUR. So when he opens his purse to give us
our reward, thy conscience flies out.
　2. MUR. Let it go. There's few or none will entertain it.　　135
　1. MUR. How if it come to thee again?
　2. MUR. I'll not meddle with it. It is a dangerous
thing — it makes a man a coward. A man cannot

---

37. **envious:** malicious.　46. **grim ferryman:** Charon, who in
classical mythology ferried the souls of the dead across the river
Styx to the underworld.　80–81. **unfelt ... cares:** they endure
restless cares for the sake of an unreal glory.

91. **commission:** written instructions.　120. **humor:** mood.
121. **tell:** count.　129. **'Zounds:** by God's wounds.

steal but it accuseth him; he cannot swear but it
checks him; he cannot lie with his neighbor's   140
wife but it detects him. It is a blushing shamefast
spirit that mutinies in a man's bosom; it fills one
full of obstacles. It made me once restore a purse
of gold that I found; it beggars any man that keeps
it. It is turned out of all towns and cities for a   145
dangerous thing, and every man that means to live
well endeavors to trust to himself and to live without it.

    1. MUR. 'Zounds, it is even now at my elbow,
persuading me not to kill the Duke.   150

    2. MUR. Take the devil in thy mind, and believe
him not. He would insinuate with° thee but to
make thee sigh.

    1. MUR. Tut, I am strong-framed, he cannot pre-
vail with me, I warrant thee.   155

    2. MUR. Spoke like a tall° fellow that respects
his reputation. Come, shall we to this gear?°

    1. MUR. Take him over the costard° with the
hilts of thy sword, and then we will chop° him in
the malmsey butt° in the next room.   161

    2. MUR. Oh, excellent device! Make a sop of him.

    1. MUR. Hark! He stirs. Shall I strike?

    2. MUR. No, first let's reason with him.   165

    CLAR. Where art thou, keeper? Give me a cup
of wine.

    2. MUR. You shall have wine enough, my lord,
anon.

    CLAR. In God's name, what art thou?

    2. MUR. A man, as you are.   170

    CLAR. But not, as I am, royal.

    2. MUR. Nor you, as we are, loyal.

    CLAR. Thy voice is thunder, but thy looks are
humble.

    2. MUR. My voice is now the King's, my looks
mine own.

    CLAR. How darkly and how deadly dost thou
speak!   175
Your eyes do menace me. Why look you pale?
Who sent you hither? Wherefore do you come?

    BOTH. To, to, to——

    CLAR. To murder me?

    BOTH. Aye, aye.   179

    CLAR. You scarcely have the hearts to tell me so,
And therefore cannot have the hearts to do it.
Wherein, my friends, have I offended you?

    1. MUR. Offended us you have not, but the King.

    CLAR. I shall be reconciled to him again.

    2. MUR. Never, my lord. Therefore prepare to
die.   185

    CLAR. Are you called forth from out a world of
men

To slay the innocent? What is my offense?
Where are the evidence that do accuse me?
What lawful quest° have given their verdict up
Unto the frowning judge? Or who pronounced
The bitter sentence of poor Clarence' death?   191
Before I be convíct by course of law,
To threaten me with death is most unlawful.
I charge you, as you hope to have redemption
By Christ's dear blood shed for our grievous sins,
That you depart and lay no hands on me.   196
The deed you undertake is damnable.

    1. MUR. What we will do, we do upon command.

    2. MUR. And he that hath commanded is the
King.

    CLAR. Erroneous vassal!° The great King of
Kings   200
Hath in the tables of His law commanded
That thou shalt do no murder. And wilt thou then
Spurn at His edict, and fulfill a man's?
Take heed, for He holds vengeance in His hands,
To hurl upon their heads that break His law.   205

    2. MUR. And that same vengeance doth He hurl
on thee,
For false forswearing,° and for murder too.
Thou didst receive the holy sacrament,
To fight in quarrel of the House of Lancaster.

    1. MUR. And, like a traitor to the name of God,
Didst break that vow, and with thy treacherous
blade   211
Unrip'dst the bowels of thy sovereign's son.

    2. MUR. Whom thou wert sworn to cherish and
defend.

    1. MUR. How canst thou urge God's dreadful law
to us
When thou hast broke it in so dear° degree?   215

    CLAR. Alas! For whose sake did I that ill deed?
For Edward, for my brother, for his sake.
Why, sirs,
He sends ye not to murder me for this,
For in this sin he is as deep as I.   220
If God will be revengèd for this deed,
Oh, know you yet, He doth it publicly.
Take not the quarrel from His powerful arm;
He needs no indirect nor lawless course
To cut off those that have offended Him.   225

    1. MUR. Who made thee then a bloody minister
When gallant-springing° brave Plantagenet,
That princely novice,° was struck dead by thee?

    CLAR. My brother's love, the Devil, and my rage.

    1. MUR. Thy brother's love, our duty, and thy
fault   230
Provoke us hither now to slaughter thee.

    CLAR. Oh, if you love my brother, hate not me.
I am his brother, and I love him well.

---

152. insinuate with: worm his way into. 156. tall: fine. 157. gear:
job. 158. costard: lit., apple, "crack him on the nut." 160. chop:
clap, "chuck." 161. malmsey butt: barrel of malmsey, originally a Greek wine.

189. quest: jury. 200. vassal: slave. 207. forswearing: perjury.
215. dear: great. 227. gallant-springing: gallant and sprightly.
228. princely novice: young prince.

If you be hired for meed,° go back again,
And I will send you to my brother Gloucester,   235
Who shall reward you better for my life
Than Edward will for tidings of my death.
    2. MUR. You are deceived. Your brother Glou-
    cester hates you.
    CLAR. Oh no, he loves me, and he holds me dear.
Go you to him from me.
    BOTH.   Aye, so we will.   240
    CLAR. Tell him, when that our princely father
    York
Blessed his three sons with his victorious arm,
And charged us from his soul to love each other,
He little thought of this divided friendship.
Bid Gloucester think of this, and he will weep.   245
    1. MUR. Aye, millstones, as he lessoned° us to
    weep.
    CLAR. Oh, do not slander him, for he is kind.°
    1. MUR. Right,
As snow in harvest. Thou deceivest thyself.   249
'Tis he that sent us hither now to slaughter thee.
    CLAR. It cannot be, for when I parted with him,
He hugged me in his arms and swore, with sobs,
That he would labor° my delivery.
    2. MUR. Why, so he doth, now he delivers thee
From this world's thralldom to the joys of Heaven.
    1. MUR. Make peace with God, for you must die,
    my lord.   256
    CLAR. Hast thou that holy feeling in thy soul
To counsel me to make my peace with God,
And art thou yet to thy own soul so blind
That thou wilt war with God by murdering me?
Ah, sirs, consider, he that set you on   261
To do this deed will hate you for the deed.
    2. MUR. What shall we do?
    CLAR.   Relent, and save your souls.
    1. MUR. Relent! 'Tis cowardly and womanish.
    CLAR. Not to relent is beastly, savage, devilish.
Which of you, if you were a prince's son,   266
Being pent° from liberty, as I am now,
If two such murderers as yourselves came to you,
Would not entreat for life?
My friend, I spy some pity in thy looks.   270
Oh, if thine eye be not a flatterer,
Come thou on my side, and entreat for me,
As you would beg were you in my distress.
A begging prince what beggar pities not?
    2. MUR. Look behind you, my lord.   275
    1. MUR. Take that, and that. If all this will not
    do,   [Stabs him.]
I'll drown you in the malmsey butt within.
                   [Exit, with the body.]
    2. MUR. A bloody deed, and desperately dis-
    patched!
How fain, like Pilate, would I wash my hands

Of this most grievous guilty murder done!   280
           [Re-enter FIRST MURDERER.]
    1. MUR. How now! What mean'st thou that thou
    help'st me not?
By Heavens, the Duke shall know how slack thou
art!
    2. MUR. I would he knew that I had saved his
    brother!
Take thou the fee, and tell him what I say,
For I repent me that the Duke is slain.   285
                           [Exit.]
    1. MUR. So do not I. Go, coward as thou art.
Now must I hide his body in some hole
Until the Duke take order for his burial.
And when I have my meed, I must away,
For this will out,° and here I must not stay.   290
                           [Exit.]

Act II

SCENE I. *London. The palace.*

[*Flourish.*° *Enter* KING EDWARD *sick*, QUEEN
ELIZABETH, DORSET, RIVERS, HASTINGS,
BUCKINGHAM, GREY, *and others.*]
    K. EDW. Why, so. Now have I done a good day's
    work.
You peers, continue this united league.
I every day expect an embassage
From my Redeemer to redeem me hence,
And now in peace my soul shall part to Heaven,   5
Since I have set my friends at peace on earth.
Rivers and Hastings, take each other's hand —
Dissemble° not your hatred, swear your love.
    RIV. By Heaven, my heart is purged from grudg-
    ing hate,
And with my hand I seal my true heart's love.   10
    HAST. So thrive I as I truly swear the like!
    K. EDW. Take heed you dally° not before your
    King,
Lest He that is the supreme King of Kings
Confound your hidden falsehood, and award
Either of you to be the other's end.   15
    HAST. So prosper I as I swear perfect love!
    RIV. And I as I love Hastings with my heart!
    K. EDW. Madam, yourself are not exempt in this,
Nor your son Dorset — Buckingham, nor you.
You have been factious° one against the other.   20
Wife, love Lord Hastings, let him kiss your hand,
And what you do, do it unfeignedly.

---

290. will out: will be revealed.
    Act II, Sc. i: s.d., Flourish: trumpet call.   8. Dissemble:
falsely hide.   12. dally: trifle.   20. factious: plotting.

Q. ELIZ. Here, Hastings, I will never more re-
member
Our former hatred, so thrive I and mine!
K. EDW. Dorset, embrace him. Hastings, love
Lord Marquess.   25
DOR. This interchange of love I here protest
Upon my part shall be unviolable.
HAST. And so swear I, my lord.   [*They embrace.*]
K. EDW. Now, princely Buckingham, seal thou
this league
With thy embracements to my wife's allies,   30
And make me happy in your unity.
BUCK. [*To the* QUEEN] Whenever Buckingham
doth turn his hate
On you or yours, but with all duteous love
Doth cherish you and yours, God punish me
With hate in those where I expect most love!   35
When I have most need to employ a friend,
And most assurèd that he is a friend,
Deep, hollow, treacherous, and full of guile
Be he unto me! This do I beg of God
When I am cold in zeal to you or yours.   40
     [*They embrace.*]
K. EDW. A pleasing cordial, princely Buckingham,
Is this thy vow unto my sickly heart.
There wanteth now our brother Gloucester here,
To make the perfect period of this peace.
BUCK. And in good time here comes the noble
Duke.   45
     [*Enter* GLOUCESTER.]
GLO. Good morrow to my sovereign King and
Queen,
And, princely peers, a happy time of day!
K. EDW. Happy indeed, as we have spent the day.
Brother, we have done deeds of charity —
Made peace of enmity, fair love of hate,   50
Between these swelling wrong-incensèd peers.
GLO. A blessed labor, my most sovereign liege.
Amongst this princely heap,° if any here,
By false intelligence, or wrong surmise,
Hold me a foe —   55
If I unwittingly, or in my rage,
Have aught committed that is hardly borne°
By any in this presence — I desire
To reconcile me to his friendly peace.
'Tis death to me to be at enmity,   60
I hate it, and desire all good men's love.
First, madam, I entreat true peace of you,
Which I will purchase with my duteous service.
Of you, my noble cousin Buckingham,
If ever any grudge were lodged between us;   65
Of you, Lord Rivers, and, Lord Grey, of you,
That all without desert have frowned on me —
Dukes, earls, lords, gentlemen, indeed of all.
I do not know that Englishman alive
With whom my soul is any jot at odds   70

More than the infant that is born tonight.
I thank my God for my humility.
Q. ELIZ. A holy day shall this be kept hereafter.
I would to God all strifes were well compounded.°
My sovereign liege, I do beseech your Majesty   75
To take our brother Clarence to your grace.
GLO. Why, madam, have I offered love for this,
To be so flouted in this royal presence?
Who knows not that the noble Duke is dead?
     [*They all start.*]
You do him injury to scorn his corse.   80
RIV. Who knows not he is dead! Who knows he
is?
Q. ELIZ. All-seeing Heaven, what a world is this!
BUCK. Look I so pale, Lord Dorset, as the rest?
DOR. Aye, my good lord, and no one in this
presence
But his red color hath forsook his cheeks.   85
K. EDW. Is Clarence dead? The order was re-
versed.
GLO. But he, poor soul, by your first order died,
And that a wingèd Mercury° did bear.
Some tardy cripple bore the countermand,
That came too lag to see him burièd.   90
God grant that some, less noble and less loyal,
Nearer in bloody thoughts but not in blood,
Deserve not worse than wretched Clarence did,
And yet go current° from suspicion!
     [*Enter* DERBY.]
DER. A boon, my sovereign, for my service done!
K. EDW. I pray thee, peace. My soul is full of
sorrow.   96
DER. I will not rise unless your Highness grant.
K. EDW. Then speak at once what is it thou de-
mand'st.
DER. The forfeit, sovereign, of my servant's life,°
Who slew today a riotous gentleman   100
Lately attendant on the Duke of Norfolk.
K. EDW. Have I a tongue to doom my brother's
death
And shall the same give pardon to a slave?
My brother slew no man. His fault was thought,
And yet his punishment was cruel death.   105
Who sued to me for him? Who, in my rage,
Kneeled at my feet and bade me be advised?
Who spake of brotherhood? Who spake of love?
Who told me how the poor soul did forsake
The mighty Warwick, and did fight for me?   110
Who told me, in the field by Tewksbury,
When Oxford had me down, he rescued me,
And said "Dear brother, live and be a king"?
Who told me, when we both lay in the field
Frozen almost to death, how he did lap me   115

---

53. heap: gathering.   57. hardly borne: regarded as hard-dealing.   74. compounded: made up.   88. winged Mercury: the messenger of the gods, who wore winged sandals.   94. current: regarded as true.   99. forfeit . . . life: the life of my servant forfeited to the law.

Even in his own garments, and gave himself,
All thin and naked, to the numb cold night?
All this from my remembrance brutish wrath
Sinfully plucked, and not a man of you
Had so much grace to put it in my mind.   120
But when your carters or your waiting vassals
Have done a drunken slaughter, and defaced
The precious image of our dear Redeemer,
You straight are on your knees for pardon, pardon,
And I, unjustly too, must grant it you.   125
But for my brother not a man would speak,
Nor I, ungracious, speak unto myself
For him, poor soul. The proudest of you all
Have been beholding to him in his life,
Yet none of you would once plead for his life.   130
O God, I fear Thy justice will take hold
On me, and you, and mine, and yours for this!
Come, Hastings, help me to my closet.° Oh, poor
Clarence!   [*Exeunt some with* KING *and* QUEEN.]
    GLO. This is the fruit of rashness. Marked you not
How that the guilty kindred of the Queen   135
Looked pale when they did hear of Clarence'
death?
Oh, they did urge it still°unto the King!
God will revenge it. But come, let us in,
To comfort Edward with our company.
    BUCK. We wait upon your Grace.   140
                     [*Exeunt.*]

SCENE II. *The palace.*

[*Enter the* DUCHESS OF YORK, *with the two children
of* CLARENCE.]

    BOY. Tell me, good Grandam, is our father dead?
    DUCH. No, boy.
    BOY. Why do you wring your hands, and beat
your breast,
And cry "O Clarence, my unhappy son"?
    GIRL. Why do you look on us and shake your
head,   5
And call us wretches, orphans, castaways,
If that our noble father be alive?
    DUCH. My pretty cousins,° you mistake me much.
I do lament the sickness of the King,
As loathe to lose him — not your father's death.
It were lost sorrow to wail one that's lost.   11
    BOY. Then, Grandam, you conclude that he is
dead.
The King my uncle is to blame for this.
God will revenge it, Whom I will importune
With daily prayers all to that effect.   15

    GIRL. And so will I.
    DUCH. Peace, children, peace! The King doth love
you well.
Incapable° and shallow innocents,
You cannot guess who caused your father's death.
    BOY. Grandam, we can, for my good uncle Glou-
cester   20
Told me the King, provokèd by the Queen,
Devised impeachments° to imprison him.
And when my uncle told me so, he wept,
And hugged me in his arm, and kindly kissed my
cheek —
Bade me rely on him as on my father,   25
And he would love me dearly as his child.
    DUCH. Oh, that deceit should steal such gentle
shapes,
And with a virtuous vizard° hide foul guile!
He is my son — yea, and therein my shame —
Yet from my dugs he drew not this deceit.   30
    BOY. Think you my uncle did dissemble,
Grandam?
    DUCH. Aye, boy.
    BOY. I cannot think it. Hark! What noise is this?
[*Enter* QUEEN ELIZABETH, *with her hair about her
ears;* RIVERS *and* DORSET *after her.*]
    Q. ELIZ. Oh, who shall hinder me to wail and
weep,
To chide my fortune and torment myself?   35
I'll join with black despair against my soul,
And to myself become an enemy.
    DUCH. What means this scene of rude impatience?
    Q. ELIZ. To make an act° of tragic violence.
Edward, my lord, your son, our King, is dead.   40
Why grow the branches now the root is withered?
Why wither not the leaves, the sap being gone?
If you will live, lament; if die, be brief,
That our swift-wingèd souls may catch the King's,
Or, like obedient subjects, follow him   45
To his new kingdom of perpetual rest.
    DUCH. Ah, so much interest have I in thy sorrow
As I had title in thy noble husband!°
I have bewept a worthy husband's death,
And lived by looking on his images.°   50
But now two mirrors of his princely semblance°
Are cracked in pieces by malignant death,
And I for comfort have but one false glass,
Which grieves me when I see my shame in him.
Thou art a widow, yet thou art a mother,   55
And hast the comfort of thy children left thee.
But death hath snatched my husband from mine
arms,
And plucked two crutches from my feeble limbs,

---

133. closet: private room.   137. still: continually.
    Sc. ii: 8. cousins: kinsmen. The word is used of any blood rela-
tion.

18. Incapable: i.e., of understanding.   22. impeachments: accusations.   28. vizard: mask.   39. act: The Queen continues the
metaphor from drama: "This is an act in a tragedy of violent
deeds."   48. As . . . husband: as I had a claim in your husband
(who was my son).   50. images: i.e. children like himself.
51. semblance: likeness.

Edward and Clarence. Oh, what cause have I,
Thine being but a moiety° of my grief,   60
To overgo° thy plaints and drown thy cries!
    BOY. Good Aunt, you wept not for our father's
      death.
How can we aid you with our kindred tears?
    GIRL. Our fatherless distress was left unmoaned,
Your widow dolor likewise be unwept!   65
    Q. ELIZ. Give me no help in lamentation,°
I am not barren to bring forth complaints.
All springs reduce° their currents to mine eyes,
That I, being governed by the watery moon,
May send forth plenteous tears to drown the world!
Oh, for my husband, for my dear lord Edward!   71
    CHILDREN. Oh, for our father, for our dear lord
      Clarence!
    DUCH. Alas for both, both mine, Edward and
      Clarence!
    Q. ELIZ. What stay° had I but Edward? And he's
      gone.
    CHILDREN. What stay had we but Clarence? And
      he's gone.   75
    DUCH. What stays had I but they? And they are
      gone.
    Q. ELIZ. Was never widow had so dear a loss.
    CHILDREN. Were never orphans had so dear a loss.
    DUCH. Was never mother had so dear a loss.
Alas, I am the mother of these moans!   80
Their woes are parceled,° mine are general.
She for an Edward weeps, and so do I.
I for a Clarence weep, so doth not she.
These babes for Clarence weep, and so do I.
I for an Edward weep, so do not they.   85
Alas, you three, on me threefold distressed
Pour all your tears! I am your sorrow's nurse,
And I will pamper it with lamentations.
    DOR. Comfort, dear Mother. God is much dis-
      pleased
That you take with unthankfulness His doing.   90
In common worldly things, 'tis called ungrateful
With dull unwillingness to repay a debt
Which with a bounteous hand was kindly lent,
Much more to be thus opposite with Heaven,
For it requires the royal debt it lent you.°   95
    RIV. Madam, bethink you, like a careful mother,
Of the young Prince your son. Send straight for
      him.
Let him be crowned, in him your comfort lives.
Drown desperate sorrow in dead Edward's grave,
And plant your joys in living Edward's throne.
    [*Enter* GLOUCESTER, BUCKINGHAM, DERBY, HASTINGS,
        and RATCLIFF.]

    GLO. Madam, have comfort. All of us have cause
To wail the dimming of our shining star,   102
But none can cure their harms by wailing them.
Madam my mother, I do cry you mercy,
I did not see your Grace. Humbly on my knee   105
I crave your blessing.
    DUCH. God bless thee, and put meekness in thy
      mind,
Love, charity, obedience, and true duty!
    GLO. [*Aside*] Amen, and make me die a good
      old man!
That is the butt end of a mother's blessing.°   110
I marvel why her Grace did leave it out.
    BUCK. You cloudy princes and heart-sorrowing
      peers
That bear this mutual heavy load of moan,
Now cheer each other in each other's love.
Though we have spent° our harvest of this King,
We are to reap the harvest of his son.   116
The broken rancor of your high-swoln hearts,
But lately splintered, knit and joined together,
Must gently be preserved, cherished, and kept.
Meseemeth good° that, with some little train,°   120
Forthwith from Ludlow° the young Prince be
      fetched
Hither to London, to be crowned our King.
    RIV. Why with some little train, my Lord of
      Buckingham?
    BUCK. Marry, my lord, lest, by a multitude,
The new-healed wound of malice should break
      out.   125
Which would be so much the more dangerous
By how much the estate° is green° and yet ungov-
      erned.
Where every horse bears his commanding rein,
And may direct his course as please himself,
As well the fear of harm as harm apparent,   130
In my opinion, ought to be prevented.°
    GLO. I hope the King made peace with all of us,
And the compact is firm and true in me.
    RIV. And so in me. And so, I think, in all.
Yet, since it is but green, it should be put   135
To no apparent likelihood of breach,
Which haply° by much company might be urged.°
Therefore I say with noble Buckingham
That it is meet so few should fetch the Prince.
    HAST. And so say I.   140
    GLO. Then be it so, and go we to determine
Who they shall be that straight shall post° to
      Ludlow.
Madam, and you, my mother, will you go

---

60. moiety: share.   61. overgo: exceed.   66. Give . . . lamentation: i.e., I have sorrow enough of my own.   68. reduce: bring.
74. stay: support.   81. parceled: separate.   95. requires . . . you:
asks for the return of the King's life. It is a common idea in
Shakespeare's plays that life is a loan from God to be repaid
when He demands it.

110. butt . . . blessing: that is how a mother's blessing should
end.   115. spent: used up.   120. Meseemeth good: I think it good.
little train: few followers.   121. Ludlow: a castle in Shropshire,
and headquarters of the Lord President of Wales.   127. estate:
state. green: raw.   130–31. As . . . prevented: we should forestall suspected as well as obvious danger.   137. haply: by chance.
urged: provoked.   142. post: go in haste. See App. 17.

To give your censures° in this weighty business?

Q. ELIZ. & DUCH. With all our hearts.   145

[*Exeunt all but* BUCKINGHAM *and* GLOUCESTER.]

BUCK. My lord, whoever journeys to the Prince,

For God's sake, let not us two be behind.

For by the way I'll sort occasion,°

As index to the story we late talked of,

To part the Queen's proud kindred from the King.°

GLO. My other self, my counsel's consistory,°   151

My oracle, my prophet! — My dear cousin,

I, like a child, will go by thy direction.

Toward Ludlow then, for we'll not stay behind.

[*Exeunt.*]

SCENE III. *London. A street.*

[*Enter two* CITIZENS, *meeting.*]

1. CIT. Neighbor, well met. Whither away so fast?

2. CIT. I promise you I scarcely know myself.
Hear you the news abroad?

1. CIT.   Aye, that the King is dead.

2. CIT. Bad news, by 'r Lady, seldom comes the better.°

I fear, I fear, 'twill prove a troublous world.   5

[*Enter another* CITIZEN.]

3. CIT. Neighbors, Godspeed!

1. CIT.   Give you good morrow, sir.

3. CIT. Doth this news hold of good King Edward's death?

2. CIT. Aye, sir, it is too true, God help the while!°

3. CIT. Then, masters, look to see a troublous world.

1. CIT. No, no. By God's good grace his son shall reign.   10

3. CIT. Woe to that land that's governed by a child!

2. CIT. In him there is a hope of government,
That in his nonage Council under him,
And in his full and ripened years himself,
No doubt, shall then and till then govern well.°   15

1. CIT. So stood the state when Henry the Sixth
Was crowned in Paris but at nine months old.

3. CIT. Stood the state so? No, no, good friends, God wot,°

For then this land was famously enriched
With politic° grave counsel. Then the King   20
Had virtuous uncles to protect His Grace.

1. CIT. Why, so hath this, both by the father and mother.

3. CIT. Better it were they all came by the father,
Or by the father there were none at all,
For emulation° now, who shall be nearest,   25
Will touch us all too near if God prevent not.
Oh, full of danger is the Duke of Gloucester!
And the Queen's sons and brothers haught° and proud.
And were they to be ruled, and not to rule,
This sickly land might solace° as before.   30

1. CIT. Come, come, we fear the worst. All shall be well.

3. CIT. When clouds appear, wise men put on their cloaks.
When great leaves fall, the winter is at hand.
When the sun sets, who doth not look for night?
Untimely storms make men expect a dearth.   35
All may be well, but if God sort° it so,
'Tis more than we deserve, or I expect.

2. CIT. Truly, the souls of men are full of dread.
Ye cannot reason° almost with a man
That looks not heavily and full of fear.   40

3. CIT. Before the times of change,° still is it so.
By a divine instinct men's minds mistrust°
Ensuing dangers, as, by proof, we see
The waters swell before a boisterous storm.
But leave it all to God. Whither away?   45

2. CIT. Marry, we were sent for to the Justices.

3. CIT. And so was I. I'll bear you company.

[*Exeunt.*]

SCENE IV. *London. The palace.*

[*Enter the* ARCHBISHOP OF YORK, *the young* DUKE OF YORK, QUEEN ELIZABETH, *and the* DUCHESS OF YORK.]

ARCH. Last night, I hear, they lay at Northampton,
At Stony-Stratford will they be tonight.
Tomorrow, or next day, they will be here.

DUCH. I long with all my heart to see the Prince.
I hope he is much grown since last I saw him.   5

Q. ELIZ. But I hear no. They say my son of York°
Hath almost overta'en him in his growth.

YORK. Aye, Mother, but I would not have it so.

DUCH. Why, my young cousin, it is good to grow.

YORK. Grandam, one night, as we did sit at supper,
My uncle Rivers talked how I did grow   11
More than my brother. "Aye," quoth my uncle Gloucester,
"Small herbs have grace, great weeds do grow apace."

144. censures: opinions.   148. sort occasion: find opportunity.
150. To . . . King: i.e., to separate the widowed Queen's family
from the new boy King.   151. consistory: council chamber.
   Sc. iii: 4. seldom . . . better: a proverb, meaning "The new
king is usually worse than the old one."   8. God . . . while:
God help us now.   12–15. In . . . well: we may hope for good
government, for a Council will rule during his boyhood (*nonage*).
18. God wot: God knows.   20. politic: prudent.

25. emulation: rivalry.   28. haught: haughty.   30. solace: be
happy.   36. sort: choose.   39. reason: talk.   41. change: revolution.   42. mistrust: suspect.
   Sc. iv: 6. my . . . York: her younger son.

And since, methinks I would not grow so fast,
Because sweet flowers are slow and weeds make
    haste.   15
  DUCH. Good faith, good faith, the saying did not
    hold
In him that did object° the same to thee.
He was the wretched'st thing when he was young,
So long a-growing and so leisurely   19
That, if this rule were true, he should be gracious.
  ARCH. Why, madam, so no doubt he is.
  DUCH. I hope so too, but yet let mothers doubt.
  YORK. Now, by my troth,° if I had been remem-
    bered,°
I could have given my uncle's Grace° a flout,°   24
To touch his growth nearer than he touched mine.
  DUCH. How, my pretty York? I pray thee, let me
    hear it.
  YORK. Marry, they say my uncle grew so fast
That he could gnaw a crust at two hours old.
'Twas full two years ere I could get a tooth.
Grandam, this would have been a biting jest.   30
  DUCH. I pray thee, pretty York, who told thee this?
  YORK. Grandam, his nurse.
  DUCH. His nurse! Why, she was dead ere thou
    wert born.
  YORK. If 'twere not she, I cannot tell who told me.
  Q. ELIZ. A parlous° boy. Go to, you are too
    shrewd.°   35
  ARCH. Good madam, be not angry with the child.
  Q. ELIZ. Pitchers have ears.
             [*Enter a* MESSENGER.]
  ARCH. Here comes a messenger. What news?
  MESS. Such news, my lord, as grieves me to un-
    fold.
  Q. ELIZ. How fares the Prince?
  MESS.   Well, madam, and in health.   40
  DUCH. What is thy news, then?
  MESS. Lord Rivers and Lord Grey are sent to
    Pomfret,
With them Sir Thomas Vaughan, prisoners.
  DUCH. Who hath committed them?
  MESS.   The mighty Dukes
Gloucester and Buckingham.
  Q. ELIZ.   For what offense?   45
  MESS. The sum of all I can I have disclosed.
Why or for what these nobles were committed
Is all unknown to me, my gracious lady.
  Q. ELIZ. Ay me,° I see the downfall of our house!
The tiger now hath seized the gentle hind.°   50
Insulting tyranny begins to jet
Upon° the innocent and aweless° throne.
Welcome, destruction, death, and massacre!

I see, as in a map, the end of all.
  DUCH. Accursèd and unquiet wrangling days,   55
How many of you have mine eyes beheld!
My husband lost his life to get the crown,
And often up and down my sons were tossed,
For me to joy and weep their gain and loss.
And being seated, and domestic broils   60
Clean overblown, themselves, the conquerors,
Make war upon themselves, blood against blood,
Self against self. O preposterous
And frantic outrage, end thy damnèd spleen,°
Or let me die, to look on death no more!   65
  Q. ELIZ. Come, come, my boy, we will to sanctu-
    ary.°
Madam, farewell.
  DUCH.   I'll go along with you.
  Q. ELIZ. You have no cause.
  ARCH.   My gracious lady, go,
And thither bear your treasure and your goods.
For my part, I'll resign unto your Grace   70
The seal° I keep. And so betide° to me
As well I tender° you and all of yours!
Come, I'll conduct you to the sanctuary.   [*Exeunt.*]

Act III

SCENE I. *London. A street.*

[*The trumpets sound. Enter the young* PRINCE, *the*
DUKES OF GLOUCESTER *and* BUCKINGHAM, CARDINAL
    BOURCHIER, CATESBY, *and others.*]

  BUCK. Welcome, sweet Prince, to London, to your
    chamber.
  GLO. Welcome, dear Cousin, my thoughts' sov-
    ereign.°
The weary way hath made you melancholy.
  PRINCE. No, Uncle, but our crosses° on the way
Have made it tedious, wearisome, and heavy.   5
I want more uncles here to welcome me.
  GLO. Sweet Prince, the untainted virtue of your
    years
Hath not yet dived into the world's deceit.
Nor more can you distinguish of a man
Than of his outward show, which, God He knows,
Seldom or never jumpeth° with the heart.   11
Those uncles which you want° were dangerous;

---

17. **object:** apply.   23. **troth:** truth. **remembered:** reminded.
24. **uncle's Grace:** His Grace, my uncle. "Your Grace" is the
courtesy form of address to a Duke. **flout:** impudent reply.
35. **parlous:** "perilous," precocious. **shrewd:** bitter.   49. **Ay me:**
alas.   50. **hind:** female deer—a gentle creature.   51–52. **jet
Upon:** encroach upon. **aweless:** not provoking awe.

64. **spleen:** hatred.   66. **sanctuary:** the protection of the Church,
which claimed the right to give a place of refuge from pursuers
to any who entered a church.   71. **seal:** the Great Seal, without
which the highest acts of state cannot be formally ratified. See
Pl. 11b. **betide:** befall me.   72. **tender:** care for.
    Act III, Sc. i: 2. thoughts' sovereign: king of my thoughts.
4. **crosses:** difficulties.   11. **jumpeth:** agrees.   12. **want:** lack.
Gloucester, as so often, uses the word with double meaning.

Your Grace attended to their sugared words,
But looked not on the poison of their hearts.
God keep you from them, and from such false
    friends!   15
    PRINCE. God keep me from false friends! But they
were none.
    GLO. My lord, the Mayor of London comes to
greet you.
    [*Enter the* LORD MAYOR *and his train.*]
    MAY. God bless your Grace with health and
happy days!
    PRINCE. I thank you, good my lord, and thank
you all.
I thought my mother and my brother York   20
Would long ere this have met us on the way.
Fie, what a slug is Hastings, that he comes not
To tell us whether they will come or no!
    [*Enter* LORD HASTINGS.]
    BUCK. And in good time here comes the sweating
lord.
    PRINCE. Welcome, my lord. What, will our
mother come?   25
    HAST. On what occasion, God He knows, not I,
The Queen your mother and your brother York
Have taken sanctuary. The tender Prince
Would fain have come with me to meet your Grace,
But by his mother was perforce° withheld.   30
    BUCK. Fie, what an indirect° and peevish course
Is this of hers! Lord Cardinal, will your Grace
Persuade the Queen to send the Duke of York
Unto his princely brother presently?°
If she deny, Lord Hastings, go with him,   35
And from her jealous arms pluck him perforce.
    CARD. My Lord of Buckingham, if my weak
oratory
Can from his mother win the Duke of York,
Anon expect him here; but if she be obdúrate
To mild entreaties, God in Heaven forbid   40
We should infringe the holy privilege
Of blessèd sanctuary! Not for all this land
Would I be guilty of so deep a sin.
    BUCK. You are too senseless-obstinate,° my lord,
Too ceremonious° and traditional.   45
Weigh it but with the grossness of this age,
You break not sanctuary in seizing him.°
The benefit thereof is always granted
To those whose dealings have deserved the place,
And those who have the wit to claim the place. 50
This Prince hath neither claimed it nor deserved it,
And therefore, in mine opinion, cannot have it.
Then taking him from thence that is not there,
You break no privilege nor charter there.
Oft have I heard of sanctuary men,   55

But sanctuary children ne'er till now.
    CARD. My lord, you shall o'errule my mind for
once.
Come on, Lord Hastings, will you go with me?
    HAST. I go, my lord.
    PRINCE. Good lords, make all the speedy haste
you may. [*Exeunt* CARDINAL *and* HASTINGS.]   60
Say, Uncle Gloucester, if our brother come,
Where shall we sojourn till our coronation?
    GLO. Where it seems best unto your royal self.
If I may counsel you, some day or two
Your Highness shall repose you at the Tower.   65
Then where you please, and shall be thought most
fit
For your best health and recreation.
    PRINCE. I do not like the Tower, of any place.
Did Julius Caesar build that place,° my lord?
    BUCK. He did, my gracious lord, begin that
place,
Which since succeeding ages have re-edified.   71
    PRINCE. Is it upon recórd, or else reported
Successively from age to age, he built it?
    BUCK. Upon recórd, my gracious lord.
    PRINCE. But say, my lord, it were not registered,°
Methinks the truth should live from age to age   76
As 'twere retailed to all posterity,
Even to the general all-ending day.
    GLO. [*Aside*] So wise so young, they say, do
never live long.
    PRINCE. What say you, Uncle?   80
    GLO. I say, without characters,° fame lives long.
[*Aside*] Thus, like the formal vice Iniquity,
I moralize two meanings in one word.°
    PRINCE. That Julius Caesar was a famous man.
With what his valor did enrich his wit,   85
His wit set down to make his valor live.
Death makes no conquest of this conqueror,
For now he lives in fame, though not in life.
I'll tell you what, my cousin Buckingham ——
    BUCK. What, my gracious lord?   90
    PRINCE. An if° I live until I be a man,
I'll win our ancient right in France again,
Or die a soldier, as I lived a king.
    GLO. [*Aside*] Short summers lightly have a for-
ward spring.
    [*Enter young* YORK, HASTINGS, *and the* CARDINAL.]
    BUCK. Now, in good time, here comes the Duke
of York.   95
    PRINCE. Richard of York! How fares our loving
brother?

---

30. perforce: forcibly.   31. indirect: wrong.   34. presently: at
once.   44. senseless-obstinate: foolishly particular.   45. ceremonious: standing on ceremonies.   46–47. Weigh . . . him: when
you compare this deed with the general lack of morals in this
generation, it is no breach of sanctuary to seize him.

68–69. Tower . . . place: It was a general, but quite erroneous
belief, that the Tower was built by Julius Caesar. See Pl. 3a, and
Gen. Intro. p. 16a.   75. registered: formally recorded.   81. characters: (1) writing, (2) good character.   82–83. the . . . word:
thus like the character of the vice Iniquity in a morality play, I
use the word (character) with two meanings. Richard means: (1)
fame lives with written record, (2) fame lives when the character
(i.e., the man himself) is dead.   91. An if: if.

YORK. Well, my dread lord° — so must I call you
now.

PRINCE. Aye, Brother, to our grief, as it is yours.
Too late° he died that might have kept that title
Which by his death hath lost much majesty.   100

GLO. How fares our cousin, noble Lord of York?

YORK. I thank you, gentle Uncle. Oh, my lord,
You said that idle weeds are fast in growth.
The Prince my brother hath outgrown me far.

GLO. He hath, my lord.

YORK.   And therefore is he idle?

GLO. Oh, my fair cousin, I must not say so.   106

YORK. Then he is more beholding to you than I.

GLO. He may command me as my sovereign,
But you have power in me as in a kinsman.

YORK. I pray you, Uncle, give me this dagger.

GLO. My dagger, little Cousin? With all my
heart.   111

PRINCE. A beggar, brother?

YORK. Of my kind uncle, that I know will give,
And being but a toy,° which is no grief to give.

GLO. A greater gift than that I'll give my cousin.

YORK. A greater gift! Oh, that's the sword to it.°

GLO. Aye, gentle Cousin, were it light enough.

YORK. Oh, then I see you will part but with light
gifts.   118
In weightier things you'll say a beggar nay.

GLO. It is too heavy for your Grace to wear.

YORK. I weigh° it lightly, were it heavier.   121

GLO. What, would you have my weapon, little
lord?

YORK. I would, that I might thank you as you
call me.

GLO. How?

YORK. Little.   125

PRINCE. My Lord of York will still be cross° in
talk.
Uncle, your Grace knows how to bear with him.

YORK. You mean to bear me, not to bear with
me.
Uncle, my brother mocks both you and me.
Because that I am little, like an ape,   130
He thinks that you should bear me on your shoul-
ders.°

BUCK. With what a sharp-provided wit he rea-
sons!
To mitigate° the scorn he gives his uncle,
He prettily and aptly taunts himself.
So cunning and so young is wonderful.   135

GLO. My lord, will 't please you pass along?

Myself and my good cousin Buckingham
Will to your mother, to entreat of her
To meet you at the Tower and welcome you.

YORK. What, will you go unto the Tower, my
lord?   140

PRINCE. My Lord Protector needs will have it so.

YORK. I shall not sleep in quiet at the Tower.

GLO. Why, what should you fear?

YORK. Marry, my uncle Clarence' angry ghost.
My grandam told me he was murdered there.   145

PRINCE. I fear no uncles dead.

GLO. Nor none that live, I hope.

PRINCE. An if they live, I hope I need not fear.
But come, my lord, and with a heavy heart,
Thinking on them, go I unto the Tower.   150
[*A sennet.*]

[*Exeunt all but* GLOUCESTER, BUCKINGHAM
and CATESBY.]

BUCK. Think you, my lord, this little prating
York
Was not incensèd° by his subtle mother
To taunt and scorn you thus opprobiously?

GLO. No doubt, no doubt. Oh, 'tis a parlous boy —
Bold, quick, ingenious, forward, capable.°   155
He is all the mother's, from the top to toe.

BUCK. Well, let them rest. Come hither, Catesby.
Thou art sworn as deeply to effect what we intend
As closely to conceal what we impart.
Thou know'st our reasons urged upon the way,
What think'st thou? Is it not an easy matter   161
To make William Lord Hastings of our mind,
For the installment° of this noble Duke
In the seat royal of this famous isle?

CATE. He for his father's sake so loves the Prince
That he will not be won to aught against him. 166

BUCK. What think'st thou, then, of Stanley?
What will he?

CATE. He will do all in all as Hastings doth.

BUCK. Well, then, no more but this. Go, gentle
Catesby,
And, as it were far off, sound thou Lord Hastings,
How he doth stand affected° to our purpose,   171
And summon him tomorrow to the Tower,
To sit about° the coronation.
If thou dost find him tractable to us,
Encourage him, and show him all our reasons.   175
If he be leaden, icy-cold, unwilling,
Be thou so too, and so break off your talk,
And give us notice of his inclination.
For we tomorrow hold divided councils,°
Wherein thyself shalt highly be employed.   180

GLO. Commend me to Lord William. Tell him,
Catesby,

97. my . . . lord: now that young Edward is King, his little
brother must treat him respectfully.   99. late: lately.   114. toy:
trifle.   116. to it: to match it.   121. weigh: regard.   126. cross:
perverse.   131. bear . . . shoulders: The domestic fool employed
in a great house sometimes carried an ape on his shoulder.
The boy implies that his uncle is a fool.   133. mitigate: i.e.,
by calling himself ape he "gets away" with calling his uncle
fool.

152. incensed: set on.   155. capable: intelligent.   163. installment: enthroning.   171. affected: favorable.   173. sit about:
sit in council to discuss.   179. divided councils: separate councils.

His ancient knot° of dangerous adversaries
Tomorrow are let blood at Pomfret Castle.
And bid my friend, for joy of this good news,
Give Mistress Shore° one gentle kiss the more. 185
  BUCK. Good Catesby, go, effect this business
    soundly.
  CATE. My good lords both, with all the heed I
    may.
  GLO. Shall we hear from you, Catesby, ere we
    sleep?
  CATE. You shall, my lord.
  GLO. At Crosby Place, there shall you find us
    both.   [*Exit* CATESBY.] 190
  BUCK. Now, my lord, what shall we do if we
    perceive Lord
Hastings will not yield to our complots?°
  GLO. Chop off his head, man — somewhat we
    will do.
And look, when I am King, claim thou of me
The Earldom of Hereford, and the movables° 195
Whereof the King my brother stood possessed.
  BUCK. I'll claim that promise at your Grace's
    hands.
  GLO. And look to have it yielded with all willing-
    ness.
Come, let us sup betimes, that afterward
We may digest° our complots in some form. 200
                 [*Exeunt.*]

SCENE II. *Before* LORD HASTING'S *house.*

[*Enter a* MESSENGER.]
MESS. What ho! My lord!
HAST. [*Within*] Who knocks at the door?
MESS. A messenger from the Lord Stanley.
      [*Enter* LORD HASTINGS.]
HAST. What is 't o'clock?
MESS. Upon the stroke of four.   5
HAST. Cannot thy master sleep these tedious
    nights?
MESS. So it should seem by that I have to say.
First, he commends him to your noble lordship.
HAST. And then?
MESS. And then he sends you word   10
He dreamed tonight the boar° had razed his
    helm.°
Besides, he says there are two councils held,
And that may be determined at the one
Which may make you and him to rue° at the
    other.
Therefore he sends to know your lordship's
    pleasure,   15

If presently you will take horse with him,
And with all speed post with him toward the North,
To shun the danger that his soul divines.
  HAST. Go, fellow, go, return unto thy lord.
Bid him not fear the separated councils.   20
His honor and myself are at the one,
And at the other is my servant Catesby,
Where nothing can proceed that toucheth us
Whereof I shall not have intelligence.
Tell him his fears are shallow, wanting instance.°
And for his dreams, I wonder he is so fond° 26
To trust the mockery of unquiet slumbers.
To fly the boar before the boar pursues
Were to incense the boar to follow us,
And make pursuit where he did mean no chase. 30
Go, bid thy master rise and come to me,
And we will both together to the Tower,
Where he shall see the boar will use us kindly.
  MESS. My gracious lord, I'll tell him what you
    say.   [*Exit.*]
        [*Enter* CATESBY.]
  CATE. Many good morrows to my noble lord! 35
  HAST. Good morrow, Catesby. You are early
    stirring.
What news, what news, in this our tottering state?
  CATE. It is a reeling world indeed, my lord,
And I believe 'twill never stand upright
Till Richard wear the garland of the realm. 40
  HAST. How! Wear the garland! Dost thou mean
    the crown?
  CATE. Aye, my good lord.
  HAST. I'll have this crown of mine cut from my
    shoulders
Ere I will see the crown so foul misplaced.
But canst thou guess that he doth aim at it? 45
  CATE. Aye, on my life, and hopes to find you
    forward
Upon his party for the gain thereof.
And thereupon he sends you this good news,
That this same very day your enemies, 49
The kindred of the Queen, must die at Pomfret.
  HAST. Indeed I am no mourner for that news,
Because they have been still mine enemies,
But that I'll give my voice on Richard's side
To bar my master's heirs in true descent —
God knows I will not do it, to the death.° 55
  CATE. God keep your lordship in that gracious°
    mind!
  HAST. But I shall laugh at this a twelvemonth
    hence,
That they who brought me in my master's hate,
I live to look upon their tragedy.
I tell thee, Catesby ——   60
  CATE. What, my lord?
  HAST. Ere a fortnight make me elder,

---

182. knot: company. **185. Mistress Shore:** After the death of
Edward IV she had become Hastings' mistress. **192. complots:**
plots. **195. movables:** goods. **200. digest:** arrange.
  Sc. ii: 11. boar: i.e., Gloucester, whose crest was a boar.
razed . . . helm: shorn off his helmet. **14. rue:** be sorry.

25. instance: proof. **26. fond:** foolish. **55. to . . . death:** even
if I should die for it. **56. gracious:** holy.

I'll send some packing that yet think not on it.

CATE. 'Tis a vile thing to die, my gracious lord,
When men are unprepared and look not for it.   65
HAST. Oh, monstrous, monstrous! And so falls it
    out
With Rivers, Vaughan, Grey. And so 'twill do
With some men else who think themselves as safe
As thou and I — who, as thou know'st, are dear
To princely Richard and to Buckingham.   70
CATE. The Princes both make high account of
    you —
[*Aside*] For they account his head upon the
    Bridge.°
HAST. I know they do, and I have well deserved
    it.
[*Enter* LORD STANLEY.] Come on, come on, where
    is your boar spear, man?
Fear you the boar and go so unprovided?   75
STAN. My lord, good morrow. Good morrow,
    Catesby.
You may jest on, but, by the holy rood,°
I do not like these several° councils, I.
HAST. My lord,
I hold my life as dear as you do yours,   80
And never in my life, I do protest,
Was it more precious to me than 'tis now.
Think you, but that I know our state secure,°
I would be so triumphant as I am?
STAN. The lords at Pomfret, when they rode from
    London,   85
Were jocund and supposed their state was sure,
And they indeed had no cause to mistrust;
But yet you see how soon the day o'ercast.
This sudden stab of rancor° I misdoubt.
Pray God, I say, I prove a needless coward!   90
What, shall we toward the Tower? The day is
    spent.
HAST. Come, come, have with you. Wot you
    what, my lord?
Today the lords you talk of are beheaded.
STAN. They, for their truth, might better wear
    their heads
Than some that have accused them wear their
    hats.   95
But come, my lord, let us away.
            [*Enter a* PURSUIVANT.°]
HAST. Go on before. I'll talk with this good
    fellow.   [*Exeunt* STANLEY *and* CATESBY.]
How now, sirrah! How goes the world with thee?
PURS. The better that your lordship please to ask.
HAST. I tell thee, man, 'tis better with me now
Than when I met thee last where now we meet.

Then was I going prisoner to the Tower,   102
By the suggestion of the Queen's allies;
But now, I tell thee — keep it to thyself —
This day those enemies are put to death,   105
And I in better state than e'er I was.
PURS. God hold it, to your Honor's good con-
    tent!
HAST. Gramercy, fellow. There, drink that for
    me.   [*Throws him his purse.*]
PURS. God save your lordship.   [*Exit.*]
            [*Enter a* PRIEST.]
PR. Well met, my lord. I am glad to see your
    Honor.   110
HAST. I thank thee, good Sir John,° with all my
    heart.
I am in your debt for your last exercise.°
Come the next Sabbath, and I will content you.
            [*He whispers in his ear.*]
            [*Enter* BUCKINGHAM]
BUCK. What, talking with a priest, Lord Cham-
    berlain?
Your friends at Pomfret, they do need the priest.
Your Honor hath no shriving° work in hand.   116
HAST. Good faith, and when I met this holy man,
Those men you talk of came into my mind.
What, go you toward the Tower?
BUCK. I do, my lord, but long I shall not stay.
I shall return before your lordship thence.   121
HAST. 'Tis like enough, for I stay dinner there.
BUCK. [*Aside*] And supper too, although thou
    know'st it not.
Come, will you go?   124
HAST. I'll wait upon your lordship.   [*Exeunt.*]

SCENE III. *Pomfret° Castle.*

[*Enter* SIR RICHARD RATCLIFF, *with halberds,*°
    carrying RIVERS, GREY, *and* VAUGHAN
                to death.]

RAT. Come, bring forth the prisoners.
RIV. Sir Richard Ratcliff, let me tell thee this:
Today shalt thou behold a subject die
For truth, for duty, and for loyalty.
GREY. God keep the Prince from all the pack of
    you!   5
A knot you are of damnèd bloodsuckers.
VAUGH. You live that shall cry woe for this here-
    after.
RAT. Dispatch. The limit° of your lives is out.
RIV. O Pomfret, Pomfret! O thou bloody prison,
Fatal and ominous to noble peers!   10
Within the guilty closure of thy walls

72. account . . . Bridge: Traitors' heads were set up (over the
Bridge Gate) on London Bridge. See Pl. 3a.   77. rood: crucifix.
78. several: separate.   83. secure: Hastings means "safe," but
secure as often means "careless."   89. stab of rancor: premoni-
tion of hatred.   96. s.d., Pursuivant: officer attending on a
herald. See App. 9.

111. Sir John: the courtesy title of "Sir" was usually given
to priests; see *T Night*, IV.ii.20,n.   112. exercise: sermon.
116. shriving: confession and absolution.

        Sc. iii: Pomfret: also called Pontefract Castle. s.d., halberds:
See Pl. 21b.   8. limit: allotted time.

Richard the Second here was hacked to death;
And, for more slander to thy dismal seat,
We give thee up our guiltless blood to drink.
   GREY. Now Margaret's curse is fall'n upon our
     heads,   15
For standing by when Richard stabbed her son.
   RIV. Then cursed she Hastings, then cursed she
     Buckingham,
Then cursed she Richard. Oh, remember, God,
To hear her prayers for them, as now for us!
And for my sister and her princely sons,   20
Be satisfied, dear God, with our true blood,
Which, as thou know'st, unjustly must be spilt.
   RAT. Make haste. The hour of death is expiate.°
   RIV. Come, Grey, come, Vaughan, let us all em-
     brace,
And take our leave until we meet in Heaven. 25
                        [*Exeunt.*]

SCENE IV. *The Tower of London.*

[*Enter* BUCKINGHAM, DERBY, HASTINGS, *the* BISHOP OF
ELY, RATCLIFF, LOVEL, *with others, and take their
seats at a table.*]
   HAST. My lords, at once,° the cause why we are
     met
Is to determine of the coronation.
In God's name, speak. When is the royal day?
   BUCK. Are all things fitting for that royal time?
   DER. It is, and wants but nomination.°   5
   ELY. Tomorrow, then, I judge a happy day.
   BUCK. Who knows the Lord Protector's mind
     herein?
Who is most inward with the noble Duke?
   ELY. Your Grace, we think, should soonest know
     his mind.
   BUCK. Who, I, my lord! We know each other's
     faces,   10
But for our hearts, he knows no more of mine
Than I of yours —
Nor I no more of his than you of mine.
Lord Hastings, you and he are near in love.
   HAST. I thank His Grace, I know he loves me
     well.   15
But for his purpose in the coronation
I have not sounded him, nor he delivered
His gracious pleasure any way therein.
But you, my noble lords, may name the time,
And in the Duke's behalf I'll give my voice, 20
Which I presume he'll take in gentle part.
              [*Enter* GLOUCESTER.]
   ELY. Now in good time here comes the Duke
     himself.

   GLO. My noble lords and cousins all, good
     morrow.
I have been long a sleeper, but I hope
My absence doth neglect no great designs   25
Which by my presence might have been concluded.
   BUCK. Had not you come upon your cue, my
     lord,
William Lord Hastings had pronounced your
     part —
I mean, your voice — for crowning of the King.
   GLO. Than my Lord Hastings no man might be
     bolder.   30
His lordship knows me well, and loves me well.
   HAST. I thank your Grace.
   GLO.   My Lord of Ely!
   ELY.   My lord?
   GLO. When I was last in Holborn,°
I saw good strawberries in your garden there.
I do beseech you send for some of them.   35
   ELY. Marry, and will, my lord, with all my heart.
                        [*Exit.*]
   GLO. Cousin of Buckingham, a word with you.
            [*Drawing him aside.*]
Catesby hath sounded Hastings in our business,
And finds the testy gentleman so hot
As he will lose his head ere give consent   40
His master's son, as worshipful he terms it,
Shall lose the royalty of England's throne.
   BUCK. Withdraw you hence, my lord, I'll follow
     you. [*Exit* GLOUCESTER, BUCKINGHAM *following.*]
   DER. We have not yet set down this day of tri-
     umph.
Tomorrow, in mine opinion, is too sudden,   45
For I myself am not so well provided
As else I would be were the day prolonged.°
           [*Re-enter* BISHOP OF ELY.]
   ELY. Where is my Lord Protector? I have sent
     for these strawberries.
   HAST. His Grace looks cheerfully and smooth
     today.   50
There's some conceit° or other likes° him well
When he doth bid good morrow with such a spirit.
I think there's never a man in Christendom
That can less hide his love or hate than he,   54
For by his face straight shall you know his heart.
   DER. What of his heart perceive you in his face
By any likelihood he showed today?
   HAST. Marry, that with no man here he is of-
     fended,
For, were he, he had shown it in his looks.
   DER. I pray God he be not, I say.   60
     [*Re-enter* GLOUCESTER *and* BUCKINGHAM.]
   GLO. I pray you all, tell me what they deserve
That do conspire my death with devilish plots

---

23. **expiate:** fully come.
  Sc. iv: 1. at once: in a word. **5. nomination:** naming.

33. **Holborn:** district in London, where the Bishop of Ely had a
palace. **47. prolonged:** postponed. **51. conceit:** fancy. **likes:**
pleases.

Of damnèd witchcraft, and that have prevailed
Upon my body with their hellish charms?

HAST. The tender love I bear your Grace, my
    lord,   65
Makes me most forward in this noble presence
To doom the offenders, whatsoever they be.
I say, my lord, they have deservèd death.

GLO. Then be your eyes the witness of this ill.
See how I am bewitched. Behold, mine arm   70
Is like a blasted sapling, withered up.
And this is Edward's wife, that monstrous witch,
Consorted with that harlot strumpet Shore,
That by their witchcraft thus have markèd me.

HAST. If they have done this thing, my gracious
    lord ——   75

GLO. If! Thou protector of this damnèd strumpet,
Tellest thou me of "if"? Thou art a traitor.
Off with his head! Now, by Saint Paul I swear,
I will not dine until I see the same.
Lovel and Ratcliff, look that it be done.   80
The rest that love me, rise and follow me.
    [*Exeunt all but* HASTINGS, RATCLIFF, *and* LOVEL.]

HAST. Woe, woe for England! Not a whit for me,
For I, too fond, might have prevented this.
Stanley did dream the boar did raze his helm,
But I disdained it, and did scorn to fly.   85
Three times today my foot-cloth horse° did stum-
    ble,
And startled when he looked upon the Tower,
As loath to bear me to the slaughterhouse.
Oh, now I want the priest that spake to me.
I now repent I told the pursuivant,   90
As 'twere triumphing at mine enemies,
How they at Pomfret bloodily were butchered
And I myself secure in grace and favor.
O Margaret, Margaret, now thy heavy curse
Is lighted on poor Hastings' wretched head!   95

RAT. Dispatch, my lord. The Duke would be at
    dinner.
Make a short shrift.° He longs to see your head.

HAST. O momentary grace of mortal men,
Which we more hunt for than the grace of God!
Who builds his hopes in air of your good looks   100
Lives like a drunken sailor on a mast,
Ready, with every nod, to tumble down
Into the fatal bowels of the deep.

LOV. Come, come, dispatch. 'Tis bootless° to ex-
    claim.

HAST. O bloody Richard! Miserable England!
I prophesy the fearfull'st time to thee   106
That ever wretched age hath looked upon.
Come, lead me to the block, bear him my head.
They smile at me that shortly shall be dead.
    [*Exeunt.*]

---

86. **foot-cloth horse:** horse draped with an ornamental cloth which hung down to the ground on either side, used on ceremonial occasions. 97. **shrift:** confession in preparation for death. 104. **bootless:** vain.

SCENE V. *The Tower walls.*

[*Enter* GLOUCESTER *and* BUCKINGHAM, *in rotten
    armor, marvelous ill-favored.*]

GLO. Come, Cousin, canst thou quake, and change
    thy color,
Murder thy breath in middle of a word,
And then begin again, and stop again,
As if thou wert distraught and mad with terror?

BUCK. Tut, I can counterfeit the deep tragedian,°
Speak and look back, and pry on every side,   6
Tremble and start at wagging of a straw,
Intending° deep suspicion. Ghastly looks
Are at my service, like enforcèd smiles,
And both are ready in their offices°   10
At any time, to grace my stratagems.
But what, is Catesby gone?

GLO. He is, and see, he brings the Mayor along.
    [*Enter the* MAYOR *and* CATESBY.]

BUCK. Lord Mayor ——

GLO. Look to the drawbridge there!   15

BUCK. Hark! A drum.

GLO. Catesby, o'erlook the walls.

BUCK. Lord Mayor, the reason we have sent ——

GLO. Look back, defend thee — here are enemies.

BUCK. God and our innocency defend and guard
    us!   20

GLO. Be patient, they are friends, Ratcliff and
    Lovel.

[*Enter* LOVEL *and* RATCLIFF, *with* HASTINGS' *head.*]

LOV. Here is the head of that ignoble traitor,
The dangerous and unsuspected Hastings.

GLO. So dear I loved the man that I must weep.
I took him for the plainest harmless creature   25
That breathed upon this earth a Christian;
Made him my book, wherein my soul recorded
The history of all her secret thoughts.
So smooth he daubed° his vice with show of virtue
That, his apparent° open guilt omitted ——   30
I mean, his conversation° with Shore's wife ——
He lived from all attainder of suspéct.°

BUCK. Well, well, he was the covert'st sheltered°
    traitor
That ever lived.
Would you imagine, or almost believe,   35
Were 't not that, by great preservation,°
We live to tell it you, the subtle traitor
This day had plotted in the council house
To murder me and my good Lord of Gloucester?

MAY. What, had he so?   40

Sc. v: 5. **deep tragedian:** Shakespeare elsewhere criticizes "ham" acting. See *Haml.*, III.ii.1–40. 8. **Intending:** expressing. 10. **offices:** functions. 29. **daubed:** whitewashed. 30. **apparent:** well-known. 31. **conversation:** intercourse. 32. **from . . . suspect:** free from all suspicion of dishonor. 33. **covert'st sheltered:** most secret and hidden. 36. **preservation:** divine protection.

GLO. What, think you we are Turks° or infidels?
Or that we would, against the form of law,
Proceed thus rashly to the villain's death
But that the extreme peril of the case,
The peace of England and our persons' safety, 45
Enforced us to this execution?
    MAY. Now fair befall you! He deserved his death,
And you, my good lords both, have well proceeded,
To warn false traitors from the like attempts.
I never looked for better at his hands   50
After he once fell in with Mistress Shore.
    GLO. Yet had not we determined he should die
Until your lordship came to see his death,
Which now the loving haste of these our friends,
Somewhat against our meaning, have prevented.°
Because, my lord, we would have had you heard
The traitor speak and timorously confess   57
The manner and the purpose of his treason,
That you might well have signified the same
Unto the citizens, who haply may   60
Miscónstrue° us in him and wail his death.
    MAY. But, my good lord, your Grace's word shall
      serve
As well as I had seen and heard him speak.
And doubt you not, right noble Princes both,
But I'll acquaint our duteous citizens   65
With all your just proceedings in this cause.
    GLO. And to that end we wished your lordship
      here,
To avoid the carping censures of the world.
    BUCK. But since you come too late of our intents,
Yet witness what you hear we did intend.   70
And so, my good Lord Mayor, we bid farewell.
                          [*Exit* MAYOR.]
    GLO. Go, after, after, Cousin Buckingham.
The Mayor toward Guildhall hies° him in all post.
There, at your meet'st advantage° of the time,
Infer the bastardy° of Edward's children.   75
Tell them how Edward put to death a citizen
Only for saying he would make his son
Heir to the crown, meaning indeed his house,
Which, by the sign thereof, was termèd so.
Moreover, urge his hateful luxury°   80
And bestial appetite in change° of lust,
Which stretchèd to their servants, daughters, wives,
Even where his lustful eye or savage heart,
Without control, listed° to make his prey.
Nay, for a need, thus far come near my person. 85
Tell them, when that my mother went with child
Of that unsatiate Edward, noble York,
My princely father, then had wars in France;

And, by just computation of the time,
Found that the issue was not his begot,   90
Which well appearèd in his lineaments,
Being nothing like the noble Duke my father.
But touch this sparingly, as 'twere far off,
Because you know, my lord, my mother lives.
    BUCK. Fear not, my lord, I'll play the orator 95
As if the golden fee° for which I plead
Were for myself. And so, my lord, adieu.
    GLO. If you thrive well, bring them to Baynard's
      Castle,
Where you shall find me well accompanied   99
With reverend fathers and well-learnèd bishops.
    BUCK. I go, and toward three or four o'clock
Look for the news that the Guildhall affords.
                              [*Exit.*]
    GLO. Go, Lovel, with all speed to Doctor Shaw.
[*To* CATESBY] Go thou to Friar Penker. Bid them
    both
Meet me within this hour at Baynard's Castle.   105
                [*Exeunt all but* GLOUCESTER.]
Now will I in, to take some privy order
To draw the brats of Clarence out of sight,
And to give notice that no manner of person
At any time have recourse unto the Princes. [*Exit.*]

SCENE VI. *The same. A street.*

[*Enter a* SCRIVENER,° *with a paper in his hand.*]
    SCRIV. This is the indictment° of the good Lord
      Hastings,
Which in a set hand fairly is engrossed,°
That it may be this day read o'er in Paul's.
And mark how well the sequel hangs together.
Eleven hours I spent to write it over,   5
For yesternight by Catesby was it brought me.
The precedent° was full as long a-doing.
And yet within these five hours lived Lord Hast-
    ings,
Untainted,° unexamined, free, at liberty.
Here's a good world the while! Why, who's so
    gross°   10
That seeth not this palpable device?°
Yet who's so blind but says he sees it not?
Bad is the world, and all will come to naught
When such bad dealing must be seen in thought.°
                              [*Exit.*]

---

41. **Turks:** The Turks were regarded as the extreme example of tyrannical cruelty. 55. **prevented:** forestalled. 61. **Misconstrue:** misinterpret. 73. **hies:** hastens. 74. **meet'st advantage:** fittest opportunity. 75. **bastardy:** See III.vii.12. 80. **luxury:** lust. 81. **change:** i.e., always seeking a new mistress. 84. **listed:** chose.

96. **golden fee:** crown.
    Sc. vi: s.d., **Scrivener:** professional writer of legal documents. 1. **indictment:** formal condemnation. 2. **engrossed:** written out in legal form in a fair copy. 7. **precedent:** rough copy. 9. **Untainted:** free from taint, unsuspected. 10. **gross:** foolish. 11. **palpable device:** obvious plot; i.e., the condemnation was prepared before the trial. 14. **seen in thought:** kept quiet.

SCENE VII. *Baynard's Castle.*

[*Enter* GLOUCESTER *and* BUCKINGHAM, *at several*° *doors.*]

GLO. How now, my lord, what say the citizens?

BUCK. Now, by the holy Mother of Our Lord,
The citizens are mum, and speak not a word.

GLO. Touched you the bastardy of Edward's children?

BUCK. I did, with his contráct° with Lady Lucy,
And his contráct by deputy in France;   6
The insatiate greediness of his desires,
And his enforcement of the city wives;
His tyranny for trifles; his own bastardy,
As being got,° your father then in France,   10
And his resemblance, being not like the Duke.
Withal I did infer° your lineaments,°
Being the right idea° of your father,
Both in your form and nobleness of mind;
Laid open all your victories in Scotland;   15
Your discipline in war, wisdom in peace;
Your bounty, virtue, fair humility —
Indeed left nothing fitting for the purpose
Untouched or slightly handled in discourse.
And when mine oratory grew to an end,   20
I bid them that did love their country's good
Cry "God save Richard, England's royal King!"

GLO. Ah! And did they so?

BUCK. No, so God help me, they spake not a word,
But, like dumb statuas° or breathing stones,   25
Gazed each on other, and looked deadly pale.
Which when I saw, I reprehended them,
And asked the Mayor what meant this willful silence.
His answer was, the people were not wont
To be spoke to but by the Recorder.°   30
Then he was urged to tell my tale again —
"Thus saith the Duke, thus hath the Duke inferred," —
But nothing spake in warrant from himself.°
When he had done, some followers of mine own
At the lower end of the hall hurled up their caps,
And some ten voices cried, "God save King Richard!"   36
And thus I took the vantage° of those few —
"Thanks, gentle citizens and friends!" quoth I,
"This general applause and loving shout
Argues your wisdoms and your love to Richard" —
And even here brake off, and came away.   41

GLO. What tongueless blocks were they! Would they not speak?

BUCK. No, by my troth, my lord.

GLO. Will not the Mayor, then, and his brethren come?

BUCK. The Mayor is here at hand. Intend° some fear.   45
Be not you spoke with but by mighty suit.°
And look you get a prayer book in your hand,
And stand betwixt two churchmen, good my lord,
For on that ground I'll build a holy descant.°
And be not easily won to our request.   50
Play the maid's part — still answer nay, and take it.

GLO. I go, and if you plead as well for them
As I can say nay to thee for myself,
No doubt we'll bring it to a happy issue.

BUCK. Go, go up to the leads.° The Lord Mayor
knocks.   [*Exit* GLOUCESTER.]   55
[*Enter the* MAYOR *and* CITIZENS.]
Welcome, my lord. I dance attendance here.
I think the Duke will not be spoke withal.
[*Enter* CATESBY.]
Here comes his servant. How now, Catesby,
What says he?

CATE.   My lord, he doth entreat your Grace
To visit him tomorrow or next day.   60
He is within, with two right reverend Fathers,
Divinely bent to meditation,
And in no worldly suit would he be moved
To draw him from his holy exercise.

BUCK. Return, good Catesby, to thy lord again.
Tell him myself, the Mayor, and citizens,   66
In deep designs and matters of great moment,
No less importing° than our general good,
Are come to have some conference with His Grace.

CATE. I'll tell him what you say, my lord.   70
                        [*Exit.*]

BUCK. Ah, ha, my lord, this Prince is not an Edward!
He is not lolling on a lewd day bed,°
But on his knees at meditation;
Not dallying with a brace of courtesans,
But meditating with two deep divines;   75
Not sleeping, to engross° his idle body,
But praying, to enrich his watchful soul.
Happy were England would this gracious Prince
Take on himself the sovereignty thereof.
But sure, I fear we shall ne'er win him to it.   80

MAY. Marry, God forbid His Grace should say us nay!

BUCK. I fear he will.
[*Re-enter* CATESBY.]
How now, Catesby, what says your lord?

CATE.   My lord,
He wonders to what end you have assembled

Sc. vii: s.d., **several:** separate.   **5. contract:** betrothal. **10. got:** begotten. **12. infer:** remark upon. **lineaments:** features. **13. right idea:** very image. **25. statuas:** images. **30. Recorder:** the chief legal official of the City of London. **33. in . . . himself:** in his own authority. **37. vantage:** advantage.

45. Intend: pretend.   **46. mighty suit:** urgent petition.   **49. descant:** argument. See I.i.27,n.   **55. leads:** rooftop.   **68. No . . . importing:** concerned with nothing less.   **72. day bed:** couch. **76. engross:** make fat.

Such troops of citizens to speak with him,   85
His Grace not being warned thereof before.
My lord, he fears you mean no good to him.
    BUCK. Sorry I am my noble cousin should
Suspect me, that I mean no good to him.
By Heaven, I come in perfect love to him,   90
And so once more return and tell His Grace.
                                    [*Exit* CATESBY.]
When holy and devout religious men
Are at their beads, 'tis hard to draw them thence,
So sweet is zealous contemplation.
    [*Enter* GLOUCESTER *aloft, between two* BISHOPS.
        CATESBY *returns.*]
    MAY. See where he stands between two clergy-
        men!   95
    BUCK. Two props of virtue for a Christian Prince,
To stay° him from the fall of vanity.
And see, a book of prayer in his hand,
True ornaments to know a holy man.
Famous Plantagenet, most gracious Prince,   100
Lend favorable ears to our request,
And pardon us the interruption
Of thy devotion and right Christian zeal.
    GLO. My lord, there needs no such apology.
I rather do beseech you pardon me,   105
Who, earnest in the service of my God,
Neglect the visitation of my friends.
But, leaving this, what is your Grace's pleasure?
    BUCK. Even that, I hope, which pleaseth God
        above,
And all good men of this ungoverned isle.   110
    GLO. I do suspect I have done some offense
That seems disgracious° in the city's eyes,
And that you come to reprehend my ignorance.
    BUCK. You have, my lord. Would it might please
        your Grace,
At our entreaties, to amend that fault!   115
    GLO. Else wherefore breathe I in a Christian land?
    BUCK. Then know it is your fault that you resign
The supreme seat, the throne majestical,
The sceptered office of your ancestors,
Your state of fortune and your due of birth,°   120
The lineal° glory of your royal house,
To the corruption of a blemished stock
Whilst, in the mildness of your sleepy thoughts,
Which here we waken to our country's good,
This noble isle doth want her proper limbs —   125
Her face defaced with scars of infamy,
Her royal stock graft with ignoble plants,
And almost shouldered° in the swallowing gulf°
Of blind forgetfulness and dark oblivion.
Which to recure, we heartily solicit   130
Your gracious self to take on you the charge

And kingly government of this your land;
Not as Protector, steward, substitute,
Or lowly factor° for another's gain,
But as successively,° from blood to blood,   135
Your right of birth, your empery,° your own.
For this, consorted° with the citizens,
Your very worshipful and loving friends,
And by their vehement instigation,
In this just suit come I to move your Grace.   140
    GLO. I know not whether to depart in silence
Or bitterly to speak in your reproof
Best fitteth my degree° or your condition.°
If not to answer, you might haply think
Tongue-tied ambition, not replying, yielded   145
To bear the golden yoke of sovereignty
Which fondly you would here impose on me.
If to reprove you for this suit of yours,
So seasoned° with your faithful love to me,
Then, on the other side, I checked° my friends.   150
Therefore, to speak and to avoid the first,   151
And then in speaking not to incur the last,
Definitively° thus I answer you.
Your love deserves my thanks, but my desert
Unmeritable° shuns your high request.   155
First, if all obstacles were cut away
And that my path were even° to the crown
As my ripe revenue and due by birth,
Yet so much is my poverty of spirit,
So mighty and so many my defects,   160
As I had rather hide me from my greatness —
Being a bark° to brook° no mighty sea —
Than in my greatness covet to be hid
And in the vapor of my glory smothered.
But, God be thankéd, there's no need of me,   165
And much I need to help you, if need were.
The royal tree hath left us royal fruit,
Which, mellowed by the stealing hours of time,
Will well become the seat of majesty,
And make, no doubt, us happy by his reign.   170
On him I lay what you would lay on me,
The right and fortune of his happy stars,
Which God defend° that I should wring° from
        him!
    BUCK. My lord, this argues conscience in your
        Grace,
But the respects° thereof are nice° and trivial,   175
All circumstances well considered.
You say that Edward is your brother's son.
So say we too, but not by Edward's wife.
For first he was contráct° to Lady Lucy —

97. stay: prevent.   112. disgracious: disgraceful.   120. Your . . .
birth: the greatness which is yours through good fortune and
right of birth.   121. lineal: by right of descent.   128. shouldered: pushed over. gulf: whirlpool.

134. factor: agent.   135. successively: by right of succession.
136. empery: empire.   137. consorted: associated.   143. degree:
rank. condition: social position.   149. seasoned: flavored.
150. checked: rebuked.   153. Definitively: definitely.   155. Unmeritable: unworthy.   157. even: level, direct.   162. bark:
small ship. brook: endure.   173. defend: forbid. wring: wrest.
175. respects: considerations. nice: unimportant.   179. contract:
See Gen. Intro. p. 20a.

Your mother lives a witness to that vow —　　180
And afterward by substitute betrothed
To Bona, sister to the King of France.
These both put by, a poor petitioner,
A care-crazed mother of a many children,
A beauty-waning and distressèd widow,　　185
Even in the afternoon of her best days,
Made prize and purchase° of his lustful eye,
Seduced the pitch and height° of all his thoughts
To base declension° and loathed bigamy.
By her, in his unlawful bed, he got　　190
This Edward, whom our manners term the Prince.
More bitterly could I expostulate°
Save that, for reverence to some alive,
I give a sparing limit to my tongue.
Then, good my lord, take to your royal self　　195
This proffered benefit of dignity —
If not to bless us and the land withal,
Yet to draw forth° your noble ancestry
From the corruption of abusing times
Unto a lineal true-derivèd course.　　200
　　MAY. Do, good my lord. Your citizens entreat
　　you.
　　BUCK. Refuse not, mighty lord, this proffered
　　love.
　　CATE. Oh, make them joyful, grant their lawful
　　suit!
　　GLO. Alas, why would you heap these cares on
　　me?
I am unfit for state and majesty.　　205
I do beseech you, take it not amiss —
I cannot nor I will not yield to you.
　　BUCK. If you refuse it — as, in love and zeal,
Loath to depose the child, your brother's son,
As well we know your tenderness of heart　　210
And gentle, kind, effeminate remorse,°
Which we have noted in you to your kin,
And egally° indeed to all estates —
Yet whether you accept our suit or no,
Your brother's son shall never reign our King,　　215
But we will plant some other in the throne,
To the disgrace and downfall of your house.
And in this resolution here we leave you.
Come, citizens. 'Zounds! I'll entreat no more.　　219
　　GLO. Oh, do not swear, my Lord of Buckingham.
　　　　[*Exit* BUCKINGHAM *with the* CITIZENS.]
　　CATE. Call them again, my lord, and accept their
　　suit.
　　ANOTHER. Do, good my lord, lest all the land do
　　rue° it.
　　GLO. Would you enforce me to a world of care?
Well, call them again. I am not made of stones,

But penetrable to your kind entreats,°　　225
Albeit against my conscience and my soul.
　　[*Re-enter* BUCKINGHAM *and the rest.*] Cousin of
　　　　Buckingham, and you sage, grave men,
Since you will buckle fortune on my back
To bear her burden whether I will or no,
I must have patience to endure the load.　　230
But if black scandal or foul-faced reproach
Attend the sequel of your imposition,
Your mere enforcement shall acquittance° me
From all the impure blots and stains thereof;
For God He knows, and you may partly see,　　235
How far I am from the desire thereof.
　　MAY. God bless your Grace! We see it, and
　　will say it.
　　GLO. In saying so, you shall but say the truth.
　　BUCK. Then I salute you with this kingly title —
Long live Richard, England's royal King!　　240
　　MAY. & CITS. Amen.
　　BUCK. Tomorrow will it please you to be
　　crowned?
　　GLO. Even when you please, since you will have
　　it so.
　　BUCK. Tomorrow, then, we will attend your
　　Grace.
And so most joyfully we take our leave.　　245
　　GLO. Come, let us to our holy task again.
Farewell, good Cousin. Farewell, gentle friends.
　　　　　　　　　　　　　　　　　　　　　[*Exeunt.*]

Act IV

SCENE I. *Before the Tower.*

[*Enter, on one side,* QUEEN ELIZABETH, DUCHESS OF
YORK, *and* MARQUESS OF DORSET; *on the other,* ANNE,
DUCHESS OF GLOUCESTER, *leading* LADY MARGARET
PLANTAGENET, CLARENCE'S *young daughter.*]
　　DUCH. Who meets us here? My niece Plantagenet
Led in the hand of her kind aunt of Gloucester?
Now, for my life, she's wandering to the Tower,
On pure heart's love to greet the tender Princes.
Daughter, well met.
　　ANNE.　　　　　　God give your Graces both　　5
A happy and a joyful time of day!
　　Q. ELIZ. As much to you, good Sister! Whither
　　away?
　　ANNE. No farther than the Tower, and, as I
　　guess,
Upon the like devotion as yourselves,

---

187. purchase: in thieves' language, booty. 188. pitch . . .
height: high flight, a metaphor from the flight of the hawk.
See App. 26. 189. declension: lowering. 192. expostulate:
argue. 198. draw forth: restore. 211. effeminate remorse:
womanly pity. 213. egally: equally. 222. rue: regret.

225. entreats: entreaties. 233. acquittance: acquit.

To gratulate° the gentle Princes there.   10
  Q. ELIZ. Kind Sister, thanks. We'll enter all together.
[*Enter* BRAKENBURY.] And in good time here the Lieutenant comes.
Master Lieutenant, pray you, by your leave,
How doth the Prince, and my young son of York?
  BRAK. Right well, dear madam. By your patience,
I may not suffer you to visit them.   16
The King hath straitly charged the contrary.
  Q. ELIZ. The King! Why, who's that?
  BRAK. I cry you mercy. I mean the Lord Protector.
  Q. ELIZ. The Lord protect him from that kingly title!   20
Hath he set bounds betwixt their love and me?
I am their mother. Who should keep me from them?
  DUCH. I am their father's mother. I will see them.
  ANNE. Their aunt I am in law, in love their mother.
Then bring me to their sights. I'll bear thy blame,
And take thy office from thee,° on my peril.°   26
  BRAK. No, madam, no, I may not leave it so.
I am bound by oath, and therefore pardon me.
                          [*Exit.*]
        [*Enter* LORD STANLEY.]
  STAN. Let me but meet you, ladies, one hour hence,
And I'll salute your Grace of York as mother,   30
And reverend looker-on, of two fair Queens.
[*To* ANNE] Come, madam, you must straight to Westminster,
There to be crownèd Richard's royal Queen.
  Q. ELIZ. Oh, cut my lace° in sunder, that my pent heart
May have some scope to beat, or else I swoon   35
With this dead-killing news!
  ANNE. Despiteful° tidings! Oh, unpleasing news!
  DOR. Be of good cheer. Mother, how fares your Grace?
  Q. ELIZ. O Dorset, speak not to me, get thee hence!
Death and destruction dog thee at the heels.   40
Thy mother's name is ominous to children.
If thou wilt outstrip death, go cross the seas,
And live with Richmond, from° the reach of Hell.
Go, hie thee, hie thee from this slaughterhouse,
Lest thou increase the number of the dead,   45
And make me die the thrall° of Margaret's curse,
Nor mother, wife, nor England's counted Queen.

  STAN. Full of wise care is this your counsel, madam.
Take all the swift advantage of the hours.
You shall have letters from me to my son   50
To meet you on the way, and welcome you.
Be not ta'en tardy° by unwise delay.
  DUCH. Oh, ill-dispersing wind of misery!
O my accursèd womb, the bed of death,
A cockatrice° hast thou hatched to the world,   55
Whose unavoided° eye is murderous!
  STAN. Come, madam, come. I in all haste was sent.
  ANNE. And I in all unwillingness will go.
I would to God that the inclusive verge°
Of golden metal that must round my brow   60
Were red-hot steel, to sear me to the brain!
Anointed let me be with deadly venom,
And die ere men can say God save the Queen!
  Q. ELIZ. Go, go, poor soul, I envy not thy glory.
To feed my humor,° wish thyself no harm.   65
  ANNE. No! Why? When he that is my husband now
Came to me as I followed Henry's corse,
When scarce the blood was well washed from his hands
Which issued from my other angel husband,
And that dead saint which then I weeping followed —
Oh, when, I say, I looked on Richard's face,   71
This was my wish: " Be thou," quoth I, " accursed,
For making me, so young, so old a widow!
And when thou wed'st, let sorrow haunt thy bed,
And be thy wife — if any be so mad —   75
As miserable by the life of thee
As thou hast made me by my dear lord's death! "
Lo, ere I can repeat this curse again,
Even in so short a space, my woman's heart
Grossly grew captive to his honey words,   80
And proved the subject of my own soul's curse,
Which ever since hath kept my eyes from rest.
For never yet one hour in his bed
Have I enjoyed the golden dew of sleep,
But have been wakèd by his timorous dreams.   85
Besides, he hates me for my father Warwick,
And will, no doubt, shortly be rid of me.
  Q. ELIZ. Poor heart, adieu! I pity thy complaining.
  ANNE. No more than from my soul I mourn for yours.
  DOR. Farewell, thou woeful welcomer of glory!
  ANNE. Adieu, pour soul, that takest thy leave of it!   91
  DUCH. [*To* DORSET] Go thou to Richmond, and good fortune guide thee!

Act IV, Sc. i: **10. gratulate:** salute. **26. take ... thee:** relieve you of your duty. **on my peril:** a legal phrase meaning "I will pay all penalties." **34. cut my lace:** In Shakespeare's time ladies controlled their figures by tightly lacing themselves within busks or corsets made of whalebone, wood, or even iron. At moments of high emotion drastic relief was sometimes necessary. **37. Despiteful:** cruel. **43. from:** out of. **46. thrall:** slave.

52. ta'en tardy: taken because you are too late. **55. cockatrice:** basilisk. See I.ii.151,n. **56. unavoided:** if not avoided. **59. inclusive verge:** enclosing circle; i.e., the crown. **65. To ... humor:** to satisfy my mood.

[*To* ANNE] Go thou to Richard, and good angels
    guard thee!
[*To* QUEEN ELIZABETH] Go thou to sanctuary, and
    good thoughts possess thee!
I to my grave, where peace and rest lie with me!
Eighty odd years of sorrow have I seen,   96
And each hour's joy wrecked with a week of teen.°
    Q. ELIZ. Stay, yet look back with me unto the
    Tower.
Pity, you ancient stones, those tender babes
Whom envy hath immured° within your walls!
Rough cradle for such little pretty ones!   101
Rude ragged nurse, old sullen playfellow
For tender Princes, use my babies well!
So foolish sorrow bids your stones farewell.
                    [*Exeunt.*]

SCENE II. *London. The palace.*

[*Sennet.° Enter* RICHARD, *in pomp, crowned;*
BUCKINGHAM, CATESBY, A PAGE, *and others.*]
    K. RICH. Stand all apart. Cousin of Buckingham!
    BUCK. My gracious sovereign?
    K. RICH. Give me thy hand. [*Here he ascendeth
    the throne.*]   Thus high, by thy advice
And thy assistance, is King Richard seated.
But shall we wear these honors for a day?   5
Or shall they last, and we rejoice in them?
    BUCK. Still live they, and forever may they last!
    K. RICH. O Buckingham, now do I play the
    touch,°
To try if thou be current gold indeed.   9
Young Edward lives. Think now what I would say.
    BUCK. Say on, my loving lord.
    K. RICH. Why, Buckingham, I say I would be
    King.
    BUCK. Why, so you are, my thrice-renownèd
    liege.
    K. RICH. Ha! Am I King? 'Tis so, but Edward
    lives.   14
    BUCK. True, noble Prince.
    K. RICH.   Oh, bitter consequence,
That Edward still should live true noble Prince!°

97. each ... teen: for every hour of joy I have endured a week
of grief (*teen*). **100. immured:** walled in.
    Sc. ii: s.d., Sennet: trumpet call denoting the approach of a
procession. **8. play ... touch:** i.e., play the touchstone. A
touchstone was used by jewelers to ascertain the quality of a
piece of gold. The gold to be tested was rubbed on a stone. Another piece of gold of known quality was also rubbed on the
stone. Acid was then applied to both rubbings and the results
were compared. **15–16. Oh ... Prince:** This elaborate word
play is typical of Shakespeare's earlier style. At line 10 Richard says, "Young Edward lives," expecting Buckingham to
reply, "But not for long." Buckingham does not give the required answer. Richard repeats, "Edward lives." Buckingham
replies, "True, noble Prince." Richard retorts in effect, "That
is not the answer I expected. Now you are calling my rival a
true noble Prince."

Cousin, thou wert not wont to be so dull.
Shall I be plain? I wish the bastards dead,
And I would have it suddenly performed.
What sayest thou? Speak suddenly, be brief.   20
    BUCK. Your Grace may do your pleasure.
    K. RICH. Tut, tut, thou art all ice, thy kindness
    freezeth.
Say, have I thy consent that they shall die?
    BUCK. Give me some breath, some little pause,
    my lord,
Before I positively speak herein.   25
I will resolve° your Grace immediately.   [*Exit.*]
    CATE. [*Aside to a stander-by*] The King is angry,
    See, he bites the lip.
    K. RICH. I will converse with iron-witted fools
And unrespective° boys. None are for me
That look into me with considerate° eyes.   30
High-reaching Buckingham grows circumspect.
Boy!
    PAGE. My lord?
    K. RICH. Know'st thou not any whom corrupting
    gold
Would tempt unto a close exploit° of death?   35
    PAGE. My lord, I know a discontented gentleman
Whose humble means match not his haughty mind.
Gold were as good as twenty orators,
And will, no doubt, tempt him to anything.
    K. RICH. What is his name?
    PAGE.   His name, my lord, is Tyrrel. 40
    K. RICH. I partly know the man. Go, call him
    hither.   [*Exit* PAGE.]
The deep-revolving witty Buckingham
No more shall be the neighbor to my counsel.
Hath he so long held out° with me untired,
And stops he now for breath?   45
[*Enter* STANLEY] How now! What news with you?
    STAN. My lord, I hear the Marquis Dorset's fled
To Richmond, in those parts beyond the seas
Where he abides.   [*Stands apart.*] 49
    K. RICH. Catesby!
    CATE. My lord?
    K. RICH.   Rumor it abroad
That Anne, my wife, is sick and like to die.
I will take order for her keeping close.
Inquire me out some mean-born gentleman,
Whom I will marry straight to Clarence' daughter.
The boy is foolish, and I fear not him.   56
Look how thou dream'st!° I say again, give out
That Anne my wife is sick, and like to die.
About it, for it stands me much upon°
To stop all hopes whose growth may damage me.
                  [*Exit* CATESBY.]
I must be married to my brother's daughter,   61

26. resolve: give a definite answer to. **29. unrespective:** unobservant. **30. considerate:** understanding. **35. close exploit:**
secret deed. **44. held out:** kept up. **57. Look ... dream'st:** i.e.,
do not betray me in your sleep. **59. stands ... upon:** greatly
concerns me.

Or else my kingdom stands on brittle glass.
Murder her brothers, and then marry her!
Uncertain way of gain! But I am in
So far in blood that sin will pluck on sin. 65
Tear-falling pity dwells not in this eye.
[*Re-enter* PAGE, *with* TYRREL.] Is thy name Tyrrel?
TYR. James Tyrrel, and your most obedient sub-
    ject.
K. RICH. Art thou, indeed?
TYR.   Prove me, my gracious sovereign.
K. RICH. Dar'st thou resolve to kill a friend of
    mine? 70
TYR. Aye, my lord,
But I had rather kill two enemies.
K. RICH. Why, there thou hast it. Two deep ene-
    mies,
Foes to my rest and my sweet sleep's disturbers,
Are they that I would have thee deal upon. 75
Tyrrel, I mean those bastards in the Tower.
TYR. Let me have open means to come to them,
And soon I'll rid you from the fear of them.
K. RICH. Thou sing'st sweet music. Hark, come
    hither, Tyrrel.
Go, by this token. Rise, and lend thine ear. 80
                    [*Whispers.*]
There is no more but so. Say it is done,
And I will love thee, and prefer° thee too.
TYR. 'Tis done, my gracious lord.
K. RICH. Shall we hear from thee Tyrrel, ere we
    sleep?
TYR. Ye shall, my lord.   [*Exit.*] 85
      [*Re-enter* BUCKINGHAM.]
BUCK. My lord, I have considered in my mind
The late demand that you did sound me in.
K. RICH. Well, let that pass. Dorset is fled to Rich-
    mond.
BUCK. I hear that news, my lord.
K. RICH. Stanley, he is your wife's son. Well, look
    to it. 90
BUCK. My lord, I claim your gift, my due by
    promise,
For which your honor and your faith is pawned° —
The Earldom of Hereford and the movables
The which you promisèd I should possess.
K. RICH. Stanley, look to your wife. If she convey
Letters to Richmond, you shall answer it. 96
BUCK. What says your Highness to my just de-
    mand?
K. RICH. As I remember, Henry the Sixth
Did prophesy that Richmond should be King
When Richmond was a little peevish boy. 100
A king, perhaps, perhaps ——
BUCK. My lord!
K. RICH. How chance the prophet could not at
    that time
Have told me, I being by, that I should kill him?

    82. prefer: promote.   **92. pawned:** pledged.

BUCK. My lord, your promise for the earl-
    dom —— 105
K. RICH. Richmond! When last I was at Exeter,
The Mayor in courtesy showed me the castle,
And called it Rougemont. At which name I started,
Because a bard of Ireland told me once
I should not live long after I saw Richmond. 110
BUCK. My lord!
K. RICH. Aye, what's o'clock?
BUCK. I am thus bold to put your Grace in mind
Of what you promised me.
K. RICH.   Well, but what's o'clock?
BUCK. Upon the stroke of ten.
K. RICH.   Well, let it strike. 115
BUCK. Why let it strike?
K. RICH. Because that, like a Jack,° thou keep'st
    the stroke
Betwixt thy begging and my meditation.°
I am not in the giving vein today.
BUCK. Why, then resolve me whether you will or
    no. 120
K. RICH. Tut, tut,
Thou troublest me. I am not in the vein.
          [*Exeunt all but* BUCKINGHAM.]
BUCK. Is it even so? Rewards he my true service
With such deep contempt? Made I him King for
    this?
Oh, let me think on Hastings, and be gone 125
To Brecknock while my fearful° head is on!
                    [*Exit.*]

SCENE III. *The same.*

[*Enter* TYRREL.]
TYR. The tyrannous and bloody deed is done,
The most arch° act of piteous massacre
That ever yet this land was guilty of.
Dighton and Forrest, whom I did suborn°
To do this ruthless piece of butchery, 5
Although they were fleshed° villains, bloody dogs,
Melting with tenderness and kind compassion
Wept like two children in their deaths' sad stories.
"Lo, thus," quoth Dighton, "lay those tender
    babes."
"Thus, thus," quoth Forrest, "girdling one another
Within their innocent alabaster arms." 11
Their lips were four red roses on a stalk,
Which in their summer beauty kissed each other.
A book of prayers on their pillow lay,
"Which once," quoth Forrest, "almost changed my
    mind. 15

117. Jack: a figure on a clock which strikes the hours.
117–18. thou ... meditation: you keep on mechanically begging
and interrupting my thoughts, like a clock striking.   **126. fearful:** full of fear.
    Sc. iii: 2. most arch: supremest.   **4. suborn:** procure.
6. fleshed: blooded; i.e., who had previously committed murder.

But oh, the Devil " — there the villain stopped
Whilst Dighton thus told on: " We smothered
The most replenishèd° sweet work of nature
That from the prime creation e'er she framed."
Thus both are gone with conscience and remorse.
They could not speak, and so I left them both,   21
To bring this tidings to the bloody King.
And here he comes. [*Enter* KING RICHARD.] All hail,
   my sovereign liege!
  K. RICH. Kind Tyrrel, am I happy in thy news?
  TYR. If to have done the thing you gave in charge
Beget your happiness, be happy then,   26
For it is done, my lord.
  K. RICH.   But didst thou see them dead?
  TYR. I did, my lord.
  K. RICH.   And buried, gentle Tyrrel?
  TYR. The chaplain of the Tower hath buried
  them,
But how or in what place I do not know.   30
  K. RICH. Come to me, Tyrrel, soon at after supper,
And thou shalt tell the process of their death.
Meantime, but think how I may do thee good,
And be inheritor of thy desire.
Farewell till soon.   [*Exit* TYRREL.]   35
The son of Clarence have I pent up close,
His daughter meanly have I matched in marriage,
The sons of Edward sleep in Abraham's bosom,°
And Anne my wife hath bid the world good night.
Now, for I know the Breton Richmond aims   40
At young Elizabeth, my brother's daughter,
And, by that knot,° looks proudly o'er the crown,
To her I go, a jolly thriving wooer.
         [*Enter* CATESBY.]
  CATE. My lord!
  K. RICH. Good news or bad, that thou com'st in
  so bluntly?   45
  CATE. Bad news, my lord. Ely is fled to Rich-
  mond,
And Buckingham, backed with the hardy Welsh-
  men,
Is in the field, and still his power increaseth.
  K. RICH. Ely with Richmond troubles me more
  near
Than Buckingham and his rash-levied° army.   50
Come, I have heard that fearful commenting
Is leaden servitor to dull delay.°
Delay leads impotent and snail-paced beggary,°
Then fiery expedition° be my wing,
Jove's Mercury, and herald for a king!   55
Come, muster men. My counsel is my shield.°
We must be brief when traitors brave the field.
         [*Exeunt.*]

---

18. replenished: perfect.   38. Abraham's bosom: Paradise.
42. knot: marriage.   50. rash-levied: hastily collected.
51–52. fearful . . . delay: cowardly talk leads to stupid delay.
leaden servitor: heavy-footed servant.   53. Delay . . . beggary:
delay leads to poverty.   54. fiery expedition: hot haste.
56. counsel . . . shield: my shield is my councilor.

SCENE IV. *Before the palace.*

   [*Enter* QUEEN MARGARET.]
  Q. MAR. So now prosperity begins to mellow
And drop into the rotten mouth of death.
Here in these confines° slyly have I lurked,
To watch the waning of mine adversaries.
A dire induction° am I witness to,   5
And will to France, hoping the consequence
Will prove as bitter, black, and tragical.
Withdraw thee, wretched Margaret. Who comes
  here?
[*Enter* QUEEN ELIZABETH *and the* DUCHESS OF YORK.]
  Q. ELIZ. Ah, my young Princes! Ah, my tender
  babes!
My unblown° flowers, new-appearing sweets! 10
If yet your gentle souls fly in the air,
And be not fixed in doom perpetual,
Hover about me with your airy wings,
And hear your mother's lamentation!
  Q. MAR. Hover about her. Say that right for
  right°   15
Hath dimmed your infant morn to agèd night.
  DUCH. So many miseries have crazed° my voice
That my woe-wearied tongue is mute and dumb.
Edward Plantagenet, why art thou dead?
  Q. MAR. Plantagenet doth quit° Plantagenet,   20
Edward for Edward pays a dying debt.
  Q. ELIZ. Wilt thou, O God, fly from such gentle
  lambs,
And throw them in the entrails of the wolf?
When didst Thou sleep when such a deed was
  done?
  Q. MAR. When holy Harry died, and my sweet
  son.   25
  DUCH. Blind sight, dead life, poor mortal living
  ghost,
Woe's scene, world's shame, grave's due by life
  usurped,
Brief abstract and recórd of tedious days,
Rest thy unrest on England's lawful earth,
         [*Sitting down.*]
Unlawfully made drunk with innocents' blood! 30
  Q. ELIZ. Oh, that thou wouldst as well afford a
  grave
As thou canst yield a melancholy seat!
Then would I hide my bones, not rest them here.
Oh, who hath any cause to mourn but I?
         [*Sitting down by her.*]
  Q. MAR. If ancient sorrow be most reverend,   35
Give mine the benefit of seniory,°
And let my woes frown on the upper hand.

Sc. iv: 3. confines: regions.   5. induction: first step.   10. un-
blown: that never bloomed.   15. right . . . right: i.e., by the
murder of her children she is rightly served as I was.   17. crazed:
cracked.   20. quit: pay for, requite.   36. seniory: seniority.

If sorrow can admit society,°
[*Sitting down with them.*] Tell o'er your woes
   again by viewing mine.
I had an Edward — till a Richard killed him.   40
I had a Harry — till a Richard killed him.
Thou hadst an Edward — till a Richard killed him.
Thou hadst a Richard — till a Richard killed him.
   DUCH. I had a Richard too, and thou didst kill
   him.
I had a Rutland too, thou holp'st° to kill him.   45
   Q. MAR. Thou hadst a Clarence too, and Richard
   killed him.
From forth the kennel of thy womb hath crept
A hellhound that doth hunt us all to death.
That dog, that had his teeth before his eyes,
To worry lambs and lap their gentle blood,   50
That foul defacer of God's handiwork,
That excellent grand tyrant of the earth,
That reigns in gallèd° eyes of weeping souls,
Thy womb let loose, to chase us to our graves.
O upright, just, and true-disposing God,   55
How do I thank Thee that this carnal° cur
Preys on the issue of his mother's body,
And makes her pew fellow° with others' moan!
   DUCH. O Harry's wife, triumph not in my woes!
God witness with me, I have wept for thine.   60
   Q. MAR. Bear with me. I am hungry for revenge,
And now I cloy me with beholding it.
Thy Edward he is dead that stabbed my Edward;
Thy other Edward dead, to quit my Edward.
Young York he is but boot,° because both they   65
Match not the high perfection of my loss.
Thy Clarence he is dead that killed my Edward;
And the beholders of this tragic play,
The adulterate Hastings, Rivers, Vaughan, Grey,
Untimely smothered in their dusky graves.   70
Richard yet lives, Hell's black intelligencer,°
Only reserved their factor° to buy souls
And send them thither. But at hand, at hand,
Ensues his piteous and unpitied end.
Earth gapes, Hell burns, fiends roar, saints pray,
To have him suddenly conveyed away.   76
Cancel his bond° of life, dear God, I pray,
That I may live to say, "The dog is dead!"
   Q. ELIZ. Oh, thou didst prophesy the time would
   come
That I should wish for thee to help me curse   80
That bottled° spider, that foul bunch-backed toad!
   Q. MAR. I called thee then vain flourish of my
   fortune.
I called thee then poor shadow, painted Queen,
The presentation of but what I was,

The flattering index° of a direful pageant,   85
One heaved a-high to be hurled down below,
A mother only mocked with two sweet babes,
A dream of what thou wert, a breath, a bubble,
A sign of dignity, a garish° flag
To be the aim of every dangerous shot,   90
A queen in jest, only to fill the scene.
Where is thy husband now? Where be thy brothers?
Where are thy children? Wherein dost thou joy?
Who sues to thee, and cries "God save the
   Queen"?
Where be the bending peers that flattered thee?   95
Where be the thronging troops° that followed
   thee?
Decline all this, and see what now thou art —
For happy wife, a most distressèd widow,
For joyful mother, one that wails the name,
For Queen, a very caitiff° crowned with care,   100
For one being sued to, one that humbly sues,
For one that scorned at me, now scorned of me,
For one being feared of all, now fearing one,
For one commanding all, obeyed of none.
Thus hath the course of justice wheeled about,   105
And left thee but a very prey to time,
Having no more but thought of what thou wert
To torture thee the more, being what thou art.
Thou didst usurp my place, and dost thou not
Usurp the just proportion of my sorrow?   110
Now thy proud neck bears half my burdened°
   yoke,
From which even here I slip my weary neck,
And leave the burden of it all on thee.
Farewell, York's wife, and Queen of sad mischance.
These English woes will make me smile in France.
   Q. ELIZ. O thou well skilled in curses, stay awhile,
And teach me how to curse mine enemies!   117
   Q. MAR. Forbear to sleep the nights, and fast the
   days,
Compare dead happiness with living woe,
Think that thy babes were fairer than they were,
And he that slew them fouler than he is.   121
Bettering thy loss makes the bad causer worse.°
Revolving° this will teach thee how to curse.
   Q. ELIZ. My words are dull. Oh, quicken them
   with thine!
   Q. MAR. Thy woes will make them sharp, and
   pierce like mine.   [*Exit.*]   125
   DUCH. Why should calamity be full of words?
   Q. ELIZ. Windy attorneys to their client woes,
Airy succeeders of intestate joys,°

---

38. society: partnership. 45. holp'st: helped. 53. galled: sore.
56. carnal: flesh-eating. 58. pew fellow: companion on the same
bench. 65. boot: something given in addition, makeweight.
71. intelligencer: spy. 72. factor: agent; i.e., of Hell. 77. bond:
contract, lease. See II.ii.95,n. 81. bottled: shaped like a bottle.
See PL 2of.

85. index: lit., table of contents in the front of a book.
89. garish: gaudy. 96. troops: crowds. 100. caitiff: captive,
slave. 111. burdened: burdensome. 122. Bettering . . . worse:
i.e., by exaggerating your sorrows you may more heavily curse
the cause of them. 123. Revolving: meditating. 127–28. Windy
. . . joys: i.e., words are like pleaders who make windy speeches
on behalf of Woe, their client; words are children who succeed to
a worthless inheritance.

Poor breathing orators of miseries!
Let them have scope. Though what they do impart
Help not at all, yet do they ease the heart.   131
DUCH. If so, then be not tongue-tied. Go with
    me,
And in the breath of bitter words let's smother
My damnèd son, which thy two sweet sons smoth-
    ered.
I hear his drum. Be copious in exclaims.   135
[*Enter* KING RICHARD, *marching, with drums and
                    trumpets.*]
    K. RICH. Who intercepts my expedition?
    DUCH. Oh, she that might have intercepted thee,
By strangling thee in her accursèd womb,
From all the slaughters, wretch, that thou hast done!
    Q. ELIZ. Hidest thou that forehead with a golden
        crown   140
Where should be graven, if that right were right,
The slaughter of the Prince that owed° that crown,
And the dire death of my two sons and brothers?
Tell me, thou villain slave, where are my children?
    DUCH. Thou toad, thou toad, where is thy brother
        Clarence?   145
And little Ned Plantagenet, his son?
    Q. ELIZ. Where is kind Hastings, Rivers, Vaughan,
        Grey?
    K. RICH. A flourish, trumpets! Strike alarum,
        drums!
Let not the Heavens hear these telltale women
Rail on the Lord's anointed. Strike, I say!   150
                    [*Flourish. Alarums.*]
Either be patient, and entreat me fair,
Or with the clamorous report of war
Thus will I drown your exclamations.
    DUCH. Art thou my son?
    K. RICH. Aye, I thank God, my father, and your-
        self.   155
    DUCH. Then patiently hear my impatience.
    K. RICH. Madam, I have a touch of your condition,
Which cannot brook the accent of reproof.
    DUCH. Oh, let me speak!
    K. RICH.   Do then, but I'll not hear.
    DUCH. I will be mild and gentle in my speech.
    K. RICH. And brief, good Mother, for I am in
        haste.   161
    DUCH. Art thou so hasty? I have stayed for thee,
God knows, in anguish, pain, and agony.
    K. RICH. And came I not at last to comfort you?
    DUCH. No, by the holy rood, thou know'st it
        well,   165
Thou camest on earth to make the earth my Hell.
A grievous burden was thy birth to me,
Tetchy° and wayward was thy infancy,
Thy school days frightful, desperate. wild, and fu-
    rious,   169
Thy prime of manhood daring, bold, and venturous,

Thy age confirmed, proud, subtle, bloody, treacher-
    ous,
More mild, but yet more harmful, kind in hatred.
What comfortable hour canst thou name
That ever graced me in thy company?
    K. RICH. Faith, none but Humphrey Hour,° that
        called your Grace   175
To breakfast once forth of my company.
If I be so disgracious in your sight,
Let me march on, and not offend your Grace.
Strike up the drum.
    DUCH.   I prithee, hear me speak.
    K. RICH. You speak too bitterly.
    DUCH.   Hear me a word,
For I shall never speak to thee again.   181
    K. RICH. So.
    DUCH. Either thou wilt die, by God's just ordi-
        nance,
Ere from this war thou turn a conqueror,
Or I with grief and extreme age shall perish   185
And never look upon thy face again.
Therefore take with thee my most heavy curse,
Which in the day of battle tire thee more
Than all the complete armor that thou wear'st!
My prayers on the adverse party fight,   190
And there the little souls of Edward's children
Whisper the spirits of thine enemies
And promise them success and victory.
Bloody thou art, bloody will be thy end.   194
Shame serves° thy life and doth thy death attend.
                                    [*Exit.*]
    Q. ELIZ. Though far more cause, yet much less
        spirit to curse
Abides in me. I say amen to all.
    K. RICH. Stay, madam, I must speak a word with
        you.
    Q. ELIZ. I have no moe° sons of the royal blood
For thee to murder. For° my daughters, Richard,
They shall be praying nuns, not weeping queens,
And therefore level° not to hit their lives.   202
    K. RICH. You have a daughter called Elizabeth,
Virtuous and fair, royal and gracious.
    Q. ELIZ. And must she die for this? Oh, let her
        live,   205
And I'll corrupt her manners, stain her beauty,
Slander myself as false to Edward's bed,
Throw over her the veil of infamy.
So she may live unscarred of bleeding slaughter,
I will confess she was not Edward's daughter.   210
    K. RICH. Wrong not her birth, she is of royal blood.
    Q. ELIZ. To save her life, I'll say she is not so.
    K. RICH. Her life is only safest in her birth.
    Q. ELIZ. And only in that safety died her brothers.

---

142. owed: owned.   168. Tetchy: peevish.

175. Humphrey Hour: If the reading is correct, it means "dinnertime for the hungry" when needy gallants in Paul's hoped to
pick up a free meal. See Gen. Intro. p.17b.   195. serves: is servant
to.   199. moe: more.   200. For: as for.   202. level: aim.

K. RICH. Lo, at their births good stars were op-
posite.   215
Q. ELIZ. No, to their lives bad friends were con-
trary.
K. RICH. All unavoided° is the doom of destiny.
Q. ELIZ. True, when avoided grace makes destiny.
My babes were destined to a fairer death
If grace had blessed thee with a fairer life.   220
K. RICH. You speak as if that I had slain my cou-
sins.
Q. ELIZ. Cousins, indeed, and by their uncle coz-
ened°
Of comfort, kingdom, kindred, freedom, life.
Whose hand soever lanced their tender hearts,
Thy head, all indirectly, gave direction.   225
No doubt the murderous knife was dull and blunt
Till it was whetted on thy stone-hard heart,
To revel in the entrails of my lambs.
But that still° use of grief makes wild grief tame,
My tongue should to thy ears not name my boys
Till that my nails were anchored in thine eyes,   231
And I in such a desperate bay of death,
Like a poor bark, of sails and tackling reft,°
Rush all to pieces on thy rocky bosom.
K. RICH. Madam, so thrive I in my enterprise,
And dangerous success° of bloody wars,   236
As I intend more good to you and yours
Than ever you or yours were by me wronged!
Q. ELIZ. What good is covered with the face of
heaven,
To be discovered, that can do me good?   240
K. RICH. The advancement of your children, gen-
tle lady.
Q. ELIZ. Up to some scaffold, there to lose their
heads?
K. RICH. No, to the dignity and height of honor,
The high imperial type° of this earth's glory.
Q. ELIZ. Flatter my sorrows with report of it.   245
Tell me what state, what dignity, what honor,
Canst thou demise° to any child of mine?
K. RICH. Even all I have — yea, and myself and
all —
Will I withal endow a child of thine,
So in the Lethe° of thy angry soul   250
Thou drown the sad remembrance of those wrongs
Which thou supposest I have done to thee.
Q. ELIZ. Be brief, lest that the process of thy kind-
ness
Last longer telling than thy kindness' date.
K. RICH. Then know that from my soul I love thy
daughter.   255
Q. ELIZ. My daughter's mother thinks it with her
soul.

K. RICH. What do you think?
Q. ELIZ. That thou dost love my daughter from°
thy soul.
So from thy soul's love didst thou love her brothers,
And from my heart's love I do thank thee for it.   260
K. RICH. Be not so hasty to confound my meaning.
I mean that with my soul I love thy daughter,
And mean to make her Queen of England.
Q. ELIZ. Say then, who dost thou mean shall be
her King?
K. RICH. Even he that makes her Queen. Who
should be else?   265
Q. ELIZ. What, thou?
K. RICH. I, even I. What think you of it, madam?
Q. ELIZ. How canst thou woo her?
K. RICH.   That would I learn of you,
As one that are best acquainted with her humor.
Q. ELIZ. And wilt thou learn of me?
K. RICH.   Madam, with all my heart.   270
Q. ELIZ. Send to her, by the man that slew her
brothers,
A pair of bleeding hearts, thereon engrave
"Edward" and "York." Then haply she will weep.
Therefore present to her — as sometime Margaret
Did to thy father, steeped in Rutland's blood —   275
A handkerchief, which, say to her, did drain
The purple sap from her sweet brother's body,
And bid her dry her weeping eyes therewith.
If this inducement force her not to love,
Send her a story of thy noble acts.   280
Tell her thou madest away her Uncle Clarence,
Her uncle Rivers — yea, and, for her sake,
Madest quick conveyance° with her good aunt
Anne.
K. RICH. Come, come, you mock me. This is not
the way
To win your daughter.
Q. ELIZ.   There is no other way,   285
Unless thou couldst put on some other shape,
And not be Richard that hath done all this.
K. RICH. Say that I did all this for love of her.
Q. ELIZ. Nay, then indeed she cannot choose but
hate thee,
Having bought love with such a bloody spoil.°   290
K. RICH. Look, what is done cannot be now
amended.
Men shall deal unadvisedly° sometimes,
Which afterhours give leisure to repent.
If I did take the kingdom from your sons,
To make amends, I'll give it to your daughter.   295
If I have killed the issue of your womb,
To quicken your increase, I will beget
Mine issue of your blood upon your daughter.

---

217. **unavoided:** unavoidable.   222. **cozened:** cheated.
229. **still:** continual.   233. **reft:** bereft.   236. **success:** sequel.
244. **imperial type:** imperial badge; i.e., the crown.   247. **de-
mise:** convey, a legal phrase.   250. **Lethe:** river of forgetfulness in the underworld.

258. **from:** away from; i.e., you hate my daughter.   283. **conveyance:** removal.   290. **spoil:** used in a double sense, "plunder"
and "massacre."   292. **unadvisedly:** without stopping to consider.

A grandam's name is little less in love
Than is the doting title of a mother;   300
They are as children but one step below,
Even of your mettle,° of your very blood —
Of all one pain, save for a night of groans
Endured of her for whom you bid° like sorrow.
Your children were vexation to your youth,   305
But mine shall be a comfort to your age.
The loss you have is but a son being King,
And by that loss your daughter is made Queen.
I cannot make you what amends I would,
Therefore accept such kindness as I can.   310
Dorset your son, that with a fearful soul
Leads discontented steps in foreign soil,
This fair alliance quickly shall call home
To high promotions and great dignity.
The King that calls your beauteous daughter wife
Familiarly shall call thy Dorset brother.   316
Again shall you be mother to a king,
And all the ruins of distressful times
Repaired with double riches of content.
What! We have many goodly days to see.   320
The liquid drops of tears that you have shed
Shall come again, transformed to orient pearl,
Advantaging their loan with interest
Of ten times double gain of happiness.
Go then, my mother, to thy daughter go.   325
Make bold her bashful years with your experience,
Prepare her ears to hear a wooer's tale,
Put in her tender heart the aspiring flame°
Of golden sovereignty, acquaint the Princess
With the sweet silent hours of marriage joys.   330
And when this arm of mine hath chastised
The petty rebel, dull-brained Buckingham,
Bound with triumphant garlands will I come
And lead thy daughter to a conqueror's bed,
To whom I will retail my conquest won,   335
And she shall be sole victress, Caesar's Caesar.
    Q. ELIZ. What were I best to say? Her father's
brother
Would be her lord? Or shall I say her uncle?
Or he that slew her brothers and her uncles?
Under what title shall I woo for thee,   340
That God, the law, my honor, and her love
Can make seem pleasing to her tender years?
    K. RICH. Infer° fair England's peace by this alli-
ance.
    Q. ELIZ. Which she shall purchase with still lasting
war.
    K. RICH. Say that the King, which may command,
entreats.   345
    Q. ELIZ. That at her hands which the King's King
forbids.
    K. RICH. Say she shall be a high and mighty
Queen.

Q. ELIZ. To wail the title, as her mother doth.
K. RICH. Say I will love her everlastingly.   349
Q. ELIZ. But how long shall that title " ever " last?
K. RICH. Sweetly in force unto her fair life's end.
Q. ELIZ. But how long fairly shall her sweet life
last?
K. RICH. So long as Heaven and nature lengthens
it.
Q. ELIZ. So long as Hell and Richard likes of it.
K. RICH. Say I, her sovereign, am her subject
love.   355
Q. ELIZ. But she, your subject, loathes such sover-
eignty.
K. RICH. Be eloquent in my behalf to her.
Q. ELIZ. An honest tale speeds best being plainly
told.
K. RICH. Then in plain terms tell her my loving
tale.
Q. ELIZ. Plain and not honest is too harsh a style.
K. RICH. Your reasons are too shallow and too
quick.   361
Q. ELIZ. Oh no, my reasons are too deep and
dead —
Too deep and dead, poor infants, in their grave.
    K. RICH. Harp not on that string, madam. That is
past.
    Q. ELIZ. Harp on it still shall I till heartstrings
break.   365
    K. RICH. Now, by my George, my Garter,° and
my crown ——
    Q. ELIZ. Profaned, dishonored, and the third
usurped.
    K. RICH. I swear ——
    Q. ELIZ.   By nothing, for this is no oath.
The George, profaned, hath lost his holy honor.
The Garter, blemished, pawned his knightly virtue.
The crown, usurped, disgraced his kingly glory.
If something thou wilt swear to be believed,   372
Swear then by something that thou hast not
wronged.
    K. RICH. Now, by the world ——
    Q. ELIZ.   'Tis full of thy foul wrongs.
    K. RICH. My father's death ——
    Q. ELIZ.   Thy life hath that dishonored.   375
    K. RICH. Then, by myself ——
    Q. ELIZ.   Thyself thyself misusest.
    K. RICH. Why then, by God ——
    Q. ELIZ.   God's wrong is most of all.
If thou hadst feared to break an oath by Him,
The unity the King thy brother made
Had not been broken, nor my brother slain.   380
If thou hadst feared to break an oath by Him,
The imperial metal circling now thy brow

---

302. mettle: material.   304. bid: endured.   328. aspiring flame:
ambitious desire.   343. Infer: argue.

366. my . . . Garter: Knights of the Garter wore a collar with a
figure of Saint George, and an embroidered garter round the left
knee, with the motto: *Honi soit qui mal y pense* — "Evil be to
him who evil thinks." See Pl. 8d. 3b and App. 29.

Had graced the tender temples of my child,
And both the Princes had been breathing here,
Which now, two tender playfellows for dust,   385
Thy broken faith hath made a prey for worms.
What canst thou swear by now?

     K. RICH.   The time to come.

     Q. ELIZ. That thou hast wrongèd in the time
     o'erpast,

For I myself have many tears to wash   389
Hereafter time,° for time past wronged by thee.
The children live whose parents thou hast slaughtered,
Ungoverned youth,° to wail it in their age.
The parents live whose children thou hast butchered,
Old withered plants, to wail it with their age.
Swear not by time to come, for that thou hast   395
Misused ere used, by time misused o'erpast.

     K. RICH. As I intend to prosper and repent,
So thrive I in my dangerous attempt
Of hostile arms! Myself myself confound!
Heaven and fortune bar me happy hours!   400
Day, yield me not thy light, nor, night, thy rest!
Be opposite all planets of good luck
To my proceedings if with pure heart's love,
Immaculate devotion, holy thoughts,
I tender° not thy beauteous princely daughter!   405
In her consists my happiness and thine.
Without her, follows to this land and me,
To thee, herself, and many a Christian soul,
Death, desolation, ruin and decay.
It cannot be avoided but by this,   410
It will not be avoided but by this.
Therefore, good Mother — I must call you so —
Be the attorney of my love to her.
Plead what I will be, not what I have been —
Not my deserts, but what I will deserve.   415
Urge the necessity and state of times,
And be not peevish-fond° in great designs.

     Q. ELIZ. Shall I be tempted of the Devil thus?

     K. RICH. Aye, if the Devil tempt thee to do good.

     Q. ELIZ. Shall I forget myself to be myself?   420

     K. RICH. Aye, if yourself's remembrance wrong
     yourself.

     Q. ELIZ. But thou didst kill my children.

     K. RICH. But in your daughter's womb I bury
     them,

Where in that nest of spicery° they shall breed
Selves of themselves, to your recomforture.°   425

     Q. ELIZ. Shall I go win my daughter to thy will?

     K. RICH. And be a happy mother by the deed.

     Q. ELIZ. I go. Write to me very shortly,
And you shall understand from me her mind.

     K. RICH. Bear her my true love's kiss, and so farewell.   [*Exit* QUEEN ELIZABETH.]   430
Relenting fool, and shallow, changing woman!

[*Enter* RATCLIFF; CATESBY *following*.] How now!
     What news?

     RAT. My gracious sovereign, on the western coast
Rideth a puissant° navy; to the shore
Throng many doubtful hollow-hearted friends,   435
Unarmed, and unresolved to beat them back.
'Tis thought that Richmond is their admiral,
And there they hull,° expecting° but the aid
Of Buckingham to welcome them ashore.

     K. RICH. Some light-foot friend post to the Duke
of Norfolk —   440
Ratcliff, thyself, or Catesby — where is he?

     CATE. Here, my lord.

     K. RICH. Fly to the Duke. [*To* RATCLIFF] Post°
     thou to Salisbury.

When thou comest thither —— [*To* CATESBY]
     Dull unmindful villain,

Why stand'st thou still, and go'st not to the
     Duke?   445

     CATE. First, mighty sovereign, let me know your
     mind,

What from your Grace I shall deliver to him.

     K. RICH. O true, good Catesby, bid him levy
     straight

The greatest strength and power he can make,
And meet me presently° at Salisbury.   450

     CATE. I go.   [*Exit.*]

     RAT. What is't your Highness' pleasure I shall do
At Salisbury?

     K. RICH. Why, what wouldst thou do there before
I go?

     RAT. Your highness told me I should post before.

     K. RICH. My mind is changed, sir, my mind is
     changed.   456

[*Enter* LORD STANLEY.] How now, what news with
     you?

     STAN. None good, my lord, to please you with the
     hearing,

Nor none so bad but it may well be told.

     K. RICH. Hoyday,° a riddle! Neither good nor bad!
Why dost thou run so many mile about   461
When thou mayst tell thy tale a nearer way?
Once more, what news?

     STAN.   Richmond is on the seas.

     K. RICH. There let him sink, and be the seas on
him!

White-livered runagate,° what doth he there?   465

     STAN. I know not, mighty sovereign, but by guess.

     K. RICH. Well, sir, as you guess, as you guess?

     STAN. Stirred up by Dorset, Buckingham, and Ely,

---

390. **Hereafter time:** time to come.   392. **Ungoverned youth:** children without parents to control them.   405. **tender:** offer. 417. **peevish-fond:** obstinately foolish.   424. **nest of spicery:** the allusion is to the nest of spices which the phoenix made, which was both funeral pyre of the old phoenix and birthplace of the new. See *Temp*, III.iii.23,n.   425. **recomforture:** consolation.

434. **puissant:** powerful.   438. **hull:** float. **expecting:** awaiting. 443. **Post:** ride in haste. See App. 17.   450. **presently:** immediately.   460. **Hoyday:** exclamation of surprise.   465. **White-livered runagate:** cowardly traitor.

He makes for England, there to claim the crown.
  K. RICH. Is the chair empty? Is the sword un-
    swayed?   470
Is the King dead? The empire unpossessed?
What heir of York is there alive but we?
And who is England's King but great York's heir?
Then tell me, what doth he upon the sea?   474
  STAN. Unless for that, my liege, I cannot guess.
  K. RICH. Unless for that he comes to be your liege,
You cannot guess wherefore the Welshman comes.
Thou wilt revolt and fly to him, I fear.
  STAN. No, mighty liege, therefore mistrust me not.
  K. RICH. Where is thy power, then, to beat him
    back?   480
Where are thy tenants and thy followers?
Are they not now upon the western shore,
Safe-conducting the rebels from their ships?
  STAN. No, my good lord, my friends are in the
    North.
  K. RICH. Cold friends to Richard. What do they in
    the North   485
When they should serve their sovereign in the west?
  STAN. They have not been commanded, mighty
    sovereign.
Please it your Majesty to give me leave,
I'll muster up my friends, and meet your Grace
Where and what time your Majesty shall please.
  K. RICH. Aye, aye, thou wouldst be gone to join
    with Richmond.   491
I will not trust you, sir.
  STAN.   Most mighty sovereign,
You have no cause to hold my friendship doubtful.
I never was nor never will be false.
  K. RICH. Well,   495
Go muster men. But, hear you, leave behind
Your son, George Stanley. Look your faith be firm,
Or else his head's assurance is but frail.
  STAN. So deal with him as I prove true to you.
                                      [Exit.]

        [Enter a MESSENGER.]
  MESS. My gracious sovereign, now in Devonshire,
As I by friends am well advértisèd,   501
Sir Edward Courtney, and the haughty prelate
Bishop of Exeter, his brother there,
With many moe confederates, are in arms.
        [Enter another MESSENGER.]
  2. MESS. My liege, in Kent, the Guildfords are in
    arms,   505
And every hour more competitors°
Flock to their aid, and still their power increaseth.
        [Enter another MESSENGER.]
  3. MESS. My lord, the army of the Duke of Buck-
    ingham ——
  K. RICH. Out on you, owls! Nothing but songs of
    death?   [He strikes him.]
Take that, until thou bring me better news.   510

        506. competitors: conspirators.

  3. MESS. The news I have to tell your Majesty
Is that by sudden floods and fall of waters
Buckingham's army is dispersed and scattered,
And he himself wandered away alone,
No man knows whither.
  K. RICH.   I cry thee mercy.   515
There is my purse to cure that blow of thine.
Hath any well-advisèd° friend proclaimed
Reward to him that brings the traitor in?
  3. MESS. Such proclamation hath been made, my
    liege.
        [Enter another MESSENGER.]
  4. MESS. Sir Thomas Lovel and Lord Marquess
    Dorset,   520
'Tis said, my liege, in Yorkshire are in arms.
Yet this good comfort bring I to your Grace —
The Breton navy is dispersed by tempest.
Richmond, in Dorsetshire, sent out a boat
Unto the shore, to ask those on the banks   525
If they were his assistants, yea or no,
Who answered him they came from Buckingham
Upon his party. He, mistrusting them,
Hoised° sail and made away for Brittany.
  K. RICH. March on, march on, since we are up in
    arms,   530
If not to fight with foreign enemies,
Yet to beat down these rebels here at home.
        [Re-enter CATESBY.]
  CATE. My liege, the Duke of Buckingham is taken.
That is the best news. That the Earl of Richmond
Is with a mighty power° landed at Milford   535
Is colder tidings, yet they must be told.
  K. RICH. Away toward Salisbury! While we rea-
    son° here
A royal battle might be won and lost.
Someone take order Buckingham be brought
To Salisbury. The rest march on with me.   540
                            [Flourish. Exeunt.]

        SCENE V. LORD DERBY'S *house.*

    [*Enter* DERBY *and* SIR CHRISTOPHER URSWICK.]
  DER. Sir Christopher, tell Richmond this from me:
That in the sty of this most bloody boar
My son George Stanley is franked up in hold.°
If I revolt, off goes young George's head.
The fear of that withholds my present aid.   5
But, tell me, where is princely Richmond now?
  CHRIS. At Pembroke, or at Ha'rfordwest,° in
    Wales.   10
  DER. What men of name resort to him?

517. well-advised: thoughtful. 529. Hoised: hoisted. 535. power:
army. 537. reason: argue.
    Sc. v: 3. franked ... hold: confined in the boar's sty. See
I.iii.314,n. 10. Ha'rfordwest: Haverfordwest.

CHRIS. Sir Walter Herbert, a renownèd soldier,
Sir Gilbert Talbot, Sir William Stanley,
Oxford, redoubted Pembroke, Sir James Blunt,
And Rice ap° Thomas, with a valiant crew,   15
And many moe of noble fame and worth.
And toward London they do bend° their course,
If by the way they be not fought withal.
    DER. Return unto thy lord, commend me to him.
Tell him the Queen hath heartily consented
He shall espouse Elizabeth her daughter.
These letters will resolve him of my mind.   20
Farewell.   [*Exeunt.*]

Act V

SCENE I. *Salisbury. An open place.*

[*Enter the* SHERIFF, *and* BUCKINGHAM, *with halberds,
led to execution.*]

    BUCK. Will not King Richard let me speak with
      him?
    SHER. No, my good lord, therefore be patient.
    BUCK. Hastings, and Edward's children, Rivers,
      Grey,
Holy King Henry, and thy fair son Edward,
Vaughan, and all that have miscarried   5
By underhand corrupted foul injustice,
If that your moody discontented souls
Do through the clouds behold this present hour
Even for revenge mock my destruction!
This is All Souls' Day,° fellows, is it not?   10
    SHER. It is, my lord.
      BUCK. Why, then All Souls' Day is my body's
      Doomsday.
This is the day that, in King Edward's time,
I wished might fall on me° when I was found
False to his children or his wife's allies.   15
This is the day wherein I wished to fall
By the false faith of him I trusted most.
This, this All Souls' Day, to my fearful soul
Is the determined° respite° of my wrongs.
That high All-seer that I dallied° with   20
Hath turned my feigned prayer on my head,
And given in earnest what I begged in jest.
Thus doth He force the swords of wicked men
To turn their own points on their masters' bosoms.
Now Margaret's curse is fallen upon my head.   25
"When he," quoth she, "shall split thy heart with
    sorrow,

Remember Margaret was a prophetess."
Come, sirs, convey me to the block of shame,
Wrong hath but wrong, and blame the due of
    blame.   [*Exeunt.*]   30

SCENE II. *The camp near Tamworth.*

[*Enter* RICHMOND, OXFORD, BLUNT, HERBERT, *and
others, with drum and colors.*]

    RICHM. Fellows in arms, and my most loving
      friends,
Bruised underneath the yoke of tyranny,
Thus far into the bowels of the land
Have we marched on without impediment.
And here receive we from our father Stanley   5
Lines° of fair comfort and encouragement.
The wretched, bloody, and usurping boar
That spoiled your summer fields and fruitful vines
Swills your warm blood like wash, and makes his
    trough
In your emboweled° bosoms — this foul swine   10
Lies now even in the center of this isle,
Near to the town of Leicester, as we learn.
From Tamworth thither is but one day's march.
In God's name, cheerly on, courageous friends,
To reap the harvest of perpetual peace   15
By this one bloody trial of sharp war.
    OXF. Every man's conscience is a thousand swords,
To fight against that bloody homicide.
    HERB. I doubt not but his friends will fly to us.
    BLUNT. He hath no friends but who are friends for
      fear,   20
Which in his greatest need will shrink from him.
    RICHM. All for our vantage. Then, in God's name,
      march.
True hope is swift, and flies with swallow's wings,
Kings it makes gods, and meaner creatures kings.
        [*Exeunt.*]

SCENE III. *Bosworth Field.*

[*Enter* KING RICHARD *in arms with* NORFOLK, *the* EARL
OF SURREY, *and others.*]

    K. RICH. Here pitch our tents, even here in Bos-
      worth field.
My Lord of Surrey, why look you so sad?
    SUR. My heart is ten times lighter than my looks.
    K. RICH. My Lord of Norfolk ——
    NOR.   Here, most gracious liege.
    K. RICH. Norfolk, we must have knocks. Ha! Must
    we not?   5
    NOR. We must both give and take, my gracious
    lord.

---

15. ap: son of.   **17. bend:** direct.
    Act V, Sc. i: **10.** All Souls' Day: November 2.   **14.** I . . . me:
See II.i.32–40.   **19. determined:** foreordained. **respite:** day to
which something is postponed.   **20. dallied:** played the fool
with.

    Sc. ii: **6.** Lines: letters.   **10.** emboweled: ripped up.

K. RICH. Up with my tent there! Here will I lie
   tonight.
But where tomorrow? Well, all's one for that.
Who hath descried° the number of the foe?   9
  NOR. Six or seven thousand is their utmost power.
  K. RICH. Why, our battalion° trebles that account.
Besides, the King's name is a tower of strength,
Which they upon the adverse party want.
Up with my tent there! Valiant gentlemen,
Let us survey the vantage of the field,   15
Call for some men of sound direction.°
Let's want no discipline, make no delay,
For, lords, tomorrow is a busy day.   [*Exeunt.*]
[*Enter, on the other side of the field,* RICHMOND, SIR
   WILLIAM BRANDON, OXFORD, *and others. Some of
      the* SOLDIERS *pitch* RICHMOND's *tent.*]
  RICHM. The weary sun hath made a golden set,
And by the bright track of his fiery car°   20
Gives signal of a goodly day tomorrow.
Sir William Brandon, you shall bear my standard.
Give me some ink and paper in my tent —
I'll draw the form and model° of our battle,
Limit° each leader to his several° charge,   25
And part in just proportion our small strength.
My Lord of Oxford, you, Sir William Brandon,
And you, Sir Walter Herbert, stay with me.
The Earl of Pembroke keeps° his regiment.
Good Captain Blunt, bear my good night to him,
And by the second hour in the morning   31
Desire the Earl to see me in my tent.
Yet one thing more, good Blunt, before thou go'st —
Where is Lord Stanley quartered, dost thou know?
  BLUNT. Unless I have mista'en his colors much,
Which well I am assured I have not done,   36
His regiment lies half a mile at least
South from the mighty power of the King.
  RICHM. If without peril it be possible,
Good Captain Blunt, bear my good night to him,
And give him from me this most needful scroll.°   41
  BLUNT. Upon my life, my lord, I'll undertake it.
And so, God give you quiet rest tonight!
  RICHM. Good night, good Captain Blunt. Come,
   gentlemen,
Let us consult upon tomorrow's business.   45
In to our tent! The air is raw and cold.
          [*They withdraw into the tent.*]
[*Enter, to his tent,* KING RICHARD, NORFOLK, RATCLIFF,
   CATESBY, *and others.*]
  K. RICH. What is 't o'clock?
  CATE.   It's suppertime, my lord,
It's nine o'clock.
  K. RICH.   I will not sup tonight.
Give me some ink and paper.

What, is my beaver° easier than it was,   50
And all my armor laid into my tent?
  CATE. It is, my liege, and all things are in readi-
   ness.
  K. RICH. Good Norfolk, hie thee to thy charge.
Use careful watch, choose trusty sentinels.
  NOR. I go, my lord.   55
  K. RICH. Stir with the lark tomorrow, gentle Nor-
   folk.
  NOR. I warrant you, my lord.   [*Exit.*]
  K. RICH. Catesby!
  CATE. My lord?
  K. RICH.   Send out a pursuivant at arms°
To Stanley's regiment. Bid him bring his power 60
Before sunrising, lest his son George fall
Into the blind cave of eternal night. [*Exit* CATESBY.]
Fill me a bowl of wine. Give me a watch.°
Saddle white Surrey for the field tomorrow.
Look that my staves° be sound, and not too heavy.
Ratcliff!   66
  RAT. My lord?
  K. RICH. Saw'st thou the melancholy Lord North-
   umberland?
  RAT. Thomas the Earl of Surrey, and himself,
Much about cockshut time,° from troop to troop 70
Went through the army, cheering up the soldiers.
  K. RICH. So, I am satisfied. Give me a bowl of
  wine.
I have not that alacrity of spirit,
Nor cheer of mind, that I was wont to have.
Set it down. Is ink and paper ready?
  RAT.   It is, my lord. 75
  K. RICH. Bid my guard watch. Leave me. Ratcliff,
About the mid of night come to my tent
And help to arm me. Leave me, I say.
      [*Exeunt* RATCLIFF *and the other* ATTENDANTS.]
[*Enter* DERBY *to* RICHMOND *in his tent,* LORDS *and
        others attending.*]
  DER. Fortune and victory sit on thy helm!
  RICHM. All comfort that the dark night can afford
Be to thy person, noble father-in-law!   81
Tell me, how fares our loving mother?
  DER. I, by attorney,° bless thee from thy mother,
Who prays continually for Richmond's good.
So much for that. The silent hours steal on,   85
And flaky darkness breaks within the east.
In brief, for so the season bids us be,
Prepare thy battle early in the morning,
And put thy fortune to the arbitrament°
Of bloody strokes and mortal-staring° war.   90
I, as I may — that which I would I cannot —

Sc. iii: **9. descried:** spied. **11. battalion:** army. **16. sound
direction:** competent leadership. **20. fiery car:** i.e., the chariot
of the sun. **24. model:** plan. **25. Limit:** allot. **several:** separate,
individual. **29. keeps:** stays with. **41. needful scroll:** urgent
message.

50. beaver: face piece of the helmet. See Pl. 8a. **59. pursuivant
at arms:** herald's officer. **63. watch:** guard; or perhaps watch
light, a candle marked to show the time taken in burning.
65. staves: spears. **70. cockshut time:** twilight. **83. attorney:**
deputy. **89. arbitrament:** judgment. **90. mortal-staring:** with
deadly looks.

With best advantage will deceive the time,°
And aid thee in this doubtful shock of arms.
But on thy side I may not be too forward,
Lest, being seen, thy brother, tender George,   95
Be executed in his father's sight.
Farewell. The leisure and the fearful time
Cuts off the ceremonious vows° of love,
And ample interchange of sweet discourse,
Which so long sundered friends should dwell upon.
God give us leisure for these rites of love!   101
Once more, adieu. Be valiant, and speed well!
   RICHM. Good lords, conduct him to his regiment.
I'll strive, with troubled thoughts, to take a nap,
Lest leaden slumber peise° me down tomorrow   105
When I should mount with wings of victory.
Once more, good night, kind lords and gentlemen.
              [*Exeunt all but* RICHMOND.]
O Thou Whose captain I account myself,
Look on my forces with a gracious eye.
Put in their hands Thy bruising irons of wrath,   110
That they may crush down with a heavy fall
The usurping helmets of our adversaries!
Make us Thy ministers of chastisement,
That we may praise Thee in the victory!
To Thee I do commend my watchful soul   115
Ere I let fall the windows of mine eyes.
Sleeping and waking, oh, defend me still!   [*Sleeps.*]
[*Enter the* GHOST OF PRINCE EDWARD, *son to* HENRY *the Sixth.*]
   GHOST. [*To* RICHARD] Let me sit heavy on thy soul
     tomorrow!
Think how thou stab'dst me in my prime of youth
At Tewksbury. Despair, therefore, and die!   120
[*To* RICHARD] Be cheerful, Richmond, for the
    wrongèd souls
Of butchered princes fight in thy behalf.
King Henry's issue,° Richmond, comforts thee.
      [*Enter the* GHOST OF HENRY THE SIXTH.]
   GHOST. [*To* RICHARD] When I was mortal, my
    anointed body
By thee was punchèd full of deadly holes.   125
Think on the Tower and me. Despair, and die!
Harry the Sixth bids thee despair and die!
[*To* RICHARD] Virtuous and holy, be thou con-
    queror!
Harry, that prophesied thou shouldst be King,   129
Doth comfort thee in thy sleep. Live, and flourish!
        [*Enter the* GHOST OF CLARENCE.]
   GHOST. [*To* RICHARD] Let me sit heavy on thy soul
    tomorrow!
I that was washed to death with fulsome° wine,
Poor Clarence, by thy guile betrayed to death.
Tomorrow in the battle think on me,

And fall thy edgeless sword. Despair, and die!   135
[*To* RICHMOND] Thou offspring of the House of Lan-
    caster,
The wrongèd heirs of York do pray for thee.
Good angels guard thy battle! Live, and flourish!
   [*Enter the* GHOSTS OF RIVERS, GREY, *and* VAUGHAN.]
   GHOST OF RIV. [*To* RICHARD] Let me sit heavy on
    thy soul tomorrow,
Rivers, that died at Pomfret! Despair, and die!   140
   GHOST OF GREY. [*To* RICHARD] Think upon Grey,
    and let thy soul despair!
   GHOST OF VAUGHAN. [*To* RICHARD] Think upon
    Vaughan, and, with guilty fear,
Let fall thy lance. Despair, and die!
   ALL. [*To* RICHARD] Awake, and think our
    wrongs in Richard's bosom
Will conquer him! Awake, and win the day!   145
        [*Enter the* GHOST OF HASTINGS.]
   GHOST. [*To* RICHARD] Bloody and guilty, guiltily
    awake,
And in a bloody battle end thy days!
Think on Lord Hastings. Despair, and die!
[*To* RICHARD] Quiet untroubled soul, awake,
    awake!   149
Arm, fight, and conquer, for fair England's sake!
   [*Enter the* GHOSTS OF THE TWO YOUNG PRINCES.]
   GHOSTS. [*To* RICHARD] Dream on thy cousins
    smothered in the Tower.
Let us be lead within thy bosom, Richard,
And weigh thee down to ruin, shame, and death!
Thy nephews' souls bid thee despair and die!
[*To* RICHMOND] Sleep, Richmond, sleep in peace, and
    wake in joy.   155
Good angels guard thee from the boar's annoy!°
Live, and beget a happy race of kings!
Edward's unhappy sons do bid thee flourish.
    [*Enter the* GHOST OF LADY ANNE *his wife.*]
   GHOST. [*To* RICHARD] Richard, thy wife, that
    wretched Anne thy wife,
That never slept a quiet hour with thee,   160
Now fills thy sleep with perturbations.
Tomorrow in the battle think on me,
And fall thy edgeless sword. Despair, and die!
[*To* RICHMOND] Thou quiet soul, sleep thou a quiet
    sleep.
Dream of success and happy victory!   165
Thy adversary's wife doth pray for thee.
      [*Enter the* GHOST OF BUCKINGHAM.]
   GHOST. [*To* RICHARD] The first was I that helped
    thee to the crown,
The last was I that felt thy tyranny.
Oh, in the battle think on Buckingham,
And die in terror of thy guiltiness!   170
Dream on, dream on, of bloody deeds and death.
Fainting, despair; despairing, yield thy breath!

---

92. deceive . . . time: i.e., pretend to be loyal to Richard.
98. ceremonious vows: outward demonstrations of friendship.
105. peise: weigh down.   123. issue: child.   132. fulsome: nau-
seating.

156. annoy: hurt.

[*To* RICHMOND] I died for hope ere I could lend thee
    aid.
But cheer thy heart, and be thou not dismayed.
God and good angels fight on Richmond's side, 175
And Richard falls in height of all his pride.
[*The* GHOSTS *vanish.* KING RICHARD *starts out of his*
                        dream.]
    K. RICH. Give me another horse. Bind up my
        wounds.
Have mercy, Jesu! — Soft! I did but dream.
O coward conscience, how dost thou afflict me!
The lights burn blue. It is now dead midnight. 180
Cold fearful drops stand on my trembling flesh.
What do I fear? Myself? There's none else by.
Richard loves Richard; that is, I am I.
Is there a murderer here? No. Yes, I am.
Then fly. What, from myself? Great reason why —
Lest I revenge. What, myself upon myself? 186
Alack, I love myself. Wherefore? For any good
That I myself have done unto myself?
Oh no! Alas, I rather hate myself
For hateful deeds committed by myself! 190
I am a villain — yet I lie, I am not.
Fool, of thyself speak well. Fool, do not flatter.
My conscience hath a thousand several tongues,
And every tongue brings in a several tale,
And every tale condemns me for a villain. 195
Perjury, perjury, in the high'st degree,
Murder, stern murder, in the dir'st degree —
All several sins, all used in each degree,
Throng to the bar, crying all " Guilty, guilty! "
I shall despair. There is no creature loves me, 200
And if I die, no soul shall pity me.
Nay, wherefore should they, since that I myself
Find in myself no pity to myself?
Methought the souls of all that I had murdered
Came to my tent, and every one did threat 205
Tomorrow's vengeance on the head of Richard.
              [*Enter* RATCLIFF.]
    RAT. My lord!
    K. RICH. 'Zounds! Who is there?
    RAT. Ratcliff, my lord, 'tis I. The early village cock
Hath twice done salutation to the morn. 210
Your friends are up, and buckle on their armor.
    K. RICH. O Ratcliff, I have dreamed a fearful
        dream!
What thinkest thou, will our friends prove all true?
    RAT. No doubt, my lord.
    K. RICH.   O Ratcliff, I fear, I fear——
    RAT. Nay, good my lord, be not afraid of shadows.
    K. RICH. By the Apostle Paul, shadows tonight
Have struck more terror to the soul of Richard 217
Than can the substance of ten thousand soldiers
Armèd in proof,° and led by shallow Richmond.
It is not yet near day. Come, go with me. 220

    219. proof: armor that has been tested.

Under our tents I'll play the eavesdropper,
To see if any mean to shrink from me.   [*Exeunt.*]
[*Enter the* LORDS *to* RICHMOND, *sitting in his tent.*]
    LORDS. Good morrow, Richmond!
    RICHM. Cry mercy, lords and watchful gentlemen,
That you have ta'en a tardy sluggard here. 225
    LORDS. How have you slept, my lord?
    RICHM. The sweetest sleep and fairest-boding
        dreams
That ever entered in a drowsy head
Have I since your departure had, my lords.
Methought their souls whose bodies Richard mur-
    dered 230
Came to my tent, and cried on victory.
I promise you, my soul is very jocund
In the remembrance of so fair a dream.
How far into the morning is it, lords?
    LORDS. Upon the stroke of four. 235
    RICHM. Why, then 'tis time to arm and give di-
    rection.
          [*His oration to his* SOLDIERS.]
More than I have said, loving countrymen,
The leisure and enforcement of the time
Forbids to dwell upon. Yet remember this —
God and our good cause fight upon our side; 240
The prayers of holy saints and wrongèd souls,
Like high-reared bulwarks, stand before our faces.
Richard except, those whom we fight against
Had rather have us win than him they follow.
For what is he they follow? Truly, gentlemen, 245
A bloody tyrant and a homicide,
One raised in blood, and one in blood established,
One that made means to come by what he hath,
And slaughtered those that were the means to help
    him —
A base foul stone,° made precious by the foil° 250
Of England's chair,° where he is falsely set,
One that hath ever been God's enemy.
Then, if you fight against God's enemy,
God will in justice ward° you as His soldiers.
If you do sweat to put a tyrant down, 255
You sleep in peace, the tyrant being slain.
If you do fight against your country's foes,
Your country's fat shall pay your pains the hire.
If you do fight in safeguard of your wives,
Your wives shall welcome home the conquerors.
If you do free your children from the sword, 261
Your children's children quit it° in your age.
Then, in the name of God and all these rights,
Advance your standards, draw your willing swords.
For me, the ransom° of my bold attempt 265
Shall be this cold corpse on the earth's cold face.
But if I thrive, the gain of my attempt

  250. foul stone: valueless jewel. **foil:** tin foil, placed behind a
precious stone to increase its sparkle. **251. chair:** throne.
254. ward: guard. **262. quit it:** pay it back. **265. ransom:**
expiation.

The least of you shall share his part thereof.
Sound drums and trumpets boldly and cheerfully.
God and Saint George! Richmond and victory!   270
                                        [*Exeunt.*]
[*Re-enter* KING RICHARD, RATCLIFF, ATTENDANTS
                and FORCES.]

K. RICH. What said Northumberland as touching
        Richmond?
RAT. That he was never trainèd up in arms.
K. RICH. He said the truth. And what said Surrey
        then?
RAT. He smiled and said, " The better for our pur-
        pose."   274
K. RICH. He was in the right, and so indeed it is.
                                [*The clock strikes.*]
Tell° the clock there. Give me a calendar.
Who saw the sun today?
RAT.   Not I, my lord.
K. RICH. Then he disdains to shine, for by the
        book
He should have braved the east an hour ago.
A black day will it be to somebody.   280
Ratcliff!
RAT. My lord?
K. RICH.   The sun will not be seen today,
The sky doth frown and lour upon our army.
I would these dewy tears were from the ground.
Not shine today! Why, what is that to me   285
More than to Richmond? For the selfsame heaven
That frowns on me looks sadly upon him.
                        [*Re-enter* NORFOLK.]
NOR. Arm, arm, my lord, the foe vaunts in the
        field.
K. RICH. Come, bustle, bustle. Caparison° my
        horse.
Call up Lord Stanley, bid him bring his power.   290
I will lead forth my soldiers to the plain,
And thus my battle shall be ordered:
My foreward° shall be drawn out all in length,
Consisting equally of horse and foot,
Our archers shall be placèd in the midst.   295
John Duke of Norfolk, Thomas Earl of Surrey,
Shall have the leading of this foot and horse.
They thus directed, we will follow
In the main battle, whose puissance on either side
Shall be well wingèd with our chiefest horse.   300
This, and Saint George to boot! What think'st thou,
        Norfolk?
NOR. A good direction, warlike sovereign.
This found I on my tent this morning.
                        [*He showeth him a paper.*]
K. RICH. [*Reads.*] " Jockey of Norfolk, be not too
        bold,
For Dickon thy master is bought and sold."   305
A thing devisèd by the enemy.

Go, gentlemen, every man unto his charge.
Let not our babbling dreams affright our souls.
Conscience is but a word that cowards use,
Devised at first to keep the strong in awe.   310
Our strong arms be our conscience, swords our
        law.
March on, join bravely, let us to 't pell-mell —
If not to Heaven, then hand in hand to Hell.
                [*His oration to his* ARMY.]
What shall I say more than I have inferred?
Remember whom you are to cope withal —   315
A sort of vagabonds, rascals, and runaways,
A scum of Bretons,° and base lackey peasants,
Whom their o'ercloyed° country vomits forth
To desperate ventures and assured destruction.
You sleeping safe, they bring to you unrest.   320
You having lands and blest with beauteous wives,
They would restrain° the one, distain° the other.
And who doth lead them but a paltry fellow,
Long kept in Bretagne at our mother's cost?
A milksop, one that never in his life   325
Felt so much cold as over shoes in snow?
Let's whip these stragglers o'er the seas again,
Lash hence these overweening rags of France,
These famished beggars, weary of their lives,
Who, but for dreaming on this fond exploit,   330
For want of means, poor rats, had hanged them-
        selves.
If we be conquered, let men conquer us,
And not these bastard Bretons, whom our fathers
Have in their own land beaten, bobbed,° and
        thumped,
And in recórd° left them the heirs of shame.   335
Shall these enjoy our lands? Lie with our wives?
Ravish our daughters? [*Drum afar off.*] Hark! I
        hear their drum.
Fight, gentlemen of England! Fight, bold yeomen!
Draw, archers, draw your arrows to the head!
Spur your proud horses hard, and ride in blood.
Amaze the welkin° with your broken staves!   341
[*Enter a* MESSENGER.] What says Lord Stanley? Will
        he bring his power?
MESS. My lord, he doth deny to come.
K. RICH. Off with his son George's head!
NOR. My lord, the enemy is past the marsh.   345
After the battle let George Stanley die.
K. RICH. A thousand hearts are great within my
        bosom.
Advance our standards, set upon our foes.
Our ancient word of courage, fair Saint George,
Inspire us with the spleen° of fiery dragons!   350
Upon them! Victory sits on our helms.   [*Exeunt.*]

---

276. Tell: count.   289. Caparison: equip with battle harness.
293. foreward: front line.

317. Bretons: Richmond during his exile had lived in Brittany.
318. o'ercloyed: queasy with overfeeding.   322. restrain: seize.
distain: dishonor.   334. bobbed: banged.   335. in record: in
the history book.   341. Amaze ... welkin: frighten the sky.
350. spleen: wrath.

SCENE IV. *Another part of the field.*

[*Alarum:*° excursions.° *Enter* NORFOLK *and* FORCES *fighting; to him* CATESBY.]

CATE. Rescue, my Lord of Norfolk, rescue, rescue!
The King enacts more wonders than a man,
Daring an opposite to every danger.
His horse is slain, and all on foot he fights,
Seeking for Richmond in the throat of death.   5
Rescue, fair lord, or else the day is lost!
     [*Alarums. Enter* KING RICHARD.]
K. RICH. A horse! A horse! My kingdom for a horse!°
CATE. Withdraw, my lord. I'll help you to a horse.
K. RICH. Slave, I have set my life upon a cast,°
And I will stand the hazard° of the die.   10
I think there be six Richmonds in the field.
Five have I slain today instead of him.
A horse! A horse! My kingdom for a horse!
                  [*Exeunt.*]

SCENE V. *Another part of the field.*

[*Alarum. Enter* RICHARD *and* RICHMOND; *they fight.*
RICHARD *is slain. Retreat and flourish. Re-enter*
RICHMOND, DERBY *bearing the crown,
with divers other* LORDS.]

RICHM. God and your arms be praised, victorious friends!
The day is ours — the bloody dog is dead.
DER. Courageous Richmond, well hast thou acquit thee.°
Lo, here, this long usurpèd royalty°
From the dead temples of this bloody wretch   5
Have I plucked off, to grace thy brows withal.
Wear it, enjoy it, and make much of it.
RICHM. Great God of Heaven, say amen to all!
But tell me, is young George Stanley living?   9

DER. He is, my lord, and safe in Leicester town,
Whither, if it please you, we may now withdraw us.
RICHM. What men of name° are slain on either side?
DER. John Duke of Norfolk, Walter Lord Ferrers,
Sir Robert Brakenbury, and Sir William Brandon.
RICHM. Inter their bodies as becomes their births.
Proclaim a pardon to the soldiers fled   16
That in submission will return to us.
And then, as we have ta'en the sacrament,
We will unite the white rose and the red.°
Smile Heaven upon this fair conjunction,   20
That long have frowned upon their enmity!
What traitor hears me and says not amen?
England hath long been mad, and scarred herself —
The brother blindly shed the brother's blood,
The father rashly slaughtered his own son,   25
The son, compelled, been butcher to the sire.
All this divided York and Lancaster,
Divided in their dire division,
Oh, now let Richmond and Elizabeth,
The true succeeders of each royal house,   30
By God's fair ordinance conjoin together!
And let their heirs, God, if Thy will be so,
Enrich the time to come with smooth-faced peace,
With smiling plenty and fair prosperous days!
Abate° the edge of traitors, gracious Lord,   35
That would reduce° these bloody days again
And make poor England weep in streams of blood!
Let them not live to taste this land's increase
That would with treason wound this fair land's peace!
Now civil wounds are stopped, peace lives again.   40
That she may long live here, God say amen!
                  [*Exeunt.*]

---

12. name: high rank. **19. We . . . red:** i.e., the two warring sides of York (White Rose) and Lancaster (Red Rose), which was accomplished when Richmond, as Henry VII, married Elizabeth, daughter of Edward IV. See App. 28, Table C. **35–36. Abate . . . again:** The closing lines of this speech had special significance for their original audience. Queen Elizabeth was the granddaughter of Richmond and Elizabeth; but she had no heir, and to many it seemed only too likely that at her death the bloody story of the civil wars would be repeated. **reduce:** bring back.

Sc. iv: s.d., **Alarum:** trumpet call to arms. **excursion:** battle movements. **7. A . . . horse!:** This line was much admired, quoted, and imitated by Shakespeare's contemporaries. **9. cast:** throw of the dice. **10. hazard:** chance.
    Sc. v: **3. acquit thee:** given a good account of yourself. **4. royalty:** i.e., the crown.

THE COMEDY OF ERRORS

Introduction

The first definite mention of *The Comedy of Errors* occurs in an account of the elaborate revels given by the young law students of Gray's Inn during the Christmas holidays of 1594–95 (see pp. 31b–32a). This account, known as *Gesta Grayorum,* though written at the time, was not printed until 1688. According to it, so many illustrious spectators and others had been attracted by the reports of the first grand night of the revels that on the second grand night, which was fixed for Innocents' Day (December 28) 1594, all preparations were overwhelmed. The law students from the Temple who had been invited to attend were offended by the confusion and went home:

After their departure . . . a Comedy of Errors (like to Plautus his *Menechmus*) was played by the players. So that night was begun, and continued to the end, in nothing but confusion and errors; whereupon, it was ever afterwards called, *The Night of Errors.*

The Comedy of Errors is also to be found among the plays mentioned by Francis Meres in 1598 in the useful list inserted in *Palladis Tamia* (see pp. 11b–12a).

There are, moreover, certain topicalities in the play itself which point to the date 1592–93 as the time of its writing. They are:

1. III.ii.125–27. In his mock account of the peculiar shape of the kitchen wench, Dromio of Syracuse compares her with a globe of the world in which France is found "In her forehead, armed and reverted, making war against her heir." This is an obvious reference to the civil wars which raged in France from 1589 to 1593. In 1584 Henry III of France had declared Henry of Navarre his heir. In 1589 Henry III was assassinated, but Henry of Navarre, being then a Protestant, was opposed by the Catholic League (see p. 29a and *LLL* Intro. p. 395b). The war came to an end in 1593 when Henry became a Catholic and was reconciled to his enemies.

2. III.ii.137–41. "Oh, sir, upon her nose, all o'er embellished with rubies, carbuncles, sapphires, declining their rich aspect to the hot breath of Spain, who sent whole armadoes of carracks to be ballast at her nose." A carrack was a great merchant ship used to transport rich cargoes from South America to Spain. The English captured one of these carracks in September 1592. The booty was enormous and included such a quantity of pepper that it dislocated the pepper trade in London for several years.

Though none of these topicalities give a definite date, they support the general conclusion that *The Comedy of Errors* was not more than two or three years old at the time of its first performance during the Gray's Inn revels in 1594. Indeed, it is unlikely that before such an audience the players would have acted an old and out-of-date play.

The source of *The Comedy of Errors* is a Roman comedy by Plautus called *Menechmi — The Menechmus Twins.* Plautus's play, translated into English by W. W. (who has not been identified), was entered in the Stationers' Register on June 10, 1594, and was printed in 1595. A few verbal similarities between this translation and *The Comedy of Errors* suggest either that Shakespeare saw the English version in manuscript or, more probably, since Shakespeare had learned enough Latin at school to be able to read Plautus in the original, that W. W. knew Shakespeare's play.

The outline of the *Menechmi* as translated by W. W. is as follows:

Peniculus, a parasite, has attached himself to Menechmus, the citizen of Epidamnum, and so secures free meals and other benefits for himself. Menechmus comes on stage; he has filched a cloak belonging to his wife to bestow on his mistress, Erotium, who welcomes him eagerly, takes the cloak, and invites Menechmus and Peniculus to dinner. Thereafter Menechmus, trailed by Peniculus, goes off to do some business in the law courts while Erotium sends Cylindrus, her cook, to the market to buy the supplies.

The stage being cleared, Menechmus the traveler enters, accompanied by his servant Messenio and some sailors. Messenio grumbles that they have been searching for six years for Menechmus's lost brother.

While they talk, Cylindrus comes back from the market; he salutes the newly arrived Menechmus by name; but both men behave so oddly that each thinks the other is mad, and Messenio is suspicious that he and his master are being trapped by some courtesan. Then Erotium comes out and also mistakes Menechmus for his citizen brother; when she proceeds to relate some of his family history, Menechmus is persuaded to go in and eat her dinner.

Meanwhile Peniculus has been separated from his Menechmus in the crowd and arrives outside Erotium's house just as Menechmus the traveler is coming away from a very good dinner. Peniculus reproaches him and Menechmus answers so roughly that the parasite is annoyed and goes off to tell the whole story to Menechmus's wife. He has hardly gone when Erotium's maid appears; she gives the cloak and a gold chain to Menechmus the traveler with a request that he will take the cloak to the dyer's and the gold chain to the jeweler's to be remade with more gold. At this unexpected windfall, Menechmus thinks it is time he left Epidamnum lest his luck change. So off he goes to find Messenio.

Then enters the indignant wife of Menechmus the citizen, with the wheedling Peniculus at her heels, just as her real husband returns from the law courts where he has been detained by a long case. Menechmus, overcome by his wife's anger, promises to get the cloak back from Erotium. He goes over to her house and knocks on the door. Erotium replies that she has already given him the cloak as well as a chain; when he denies it, she slams the door in his face. Menechmus the citizen, very sorry for himself, goes away to ask advice from his friends.

Then Menechmus the traveler reappears, still carrying the cloak. He too is worried; Messenio, who has his purse with all his money, is nowhere to be found. The wife sees him, supposes him to be her real husband, and taunts him with his loose behavior. Menechmus is bewildered and indignantly denies her accusations. They are still wrangling when the wife's old father enters. At first he takes sides with his supposed son-in-law; but when Menechmus still protests that he knows neither of them, the old man is convinced that Menechmus is mad, and tells his daughter to run into the house for safety, while he goes to fetch a physician. Menechmus the traveler therefore makes off.

The father returns with the physician just as Menechmus the citizen comes back to his own house. When the physician asks the customary questions about his symptoms, Menechmus becomes so enraged that the father and the physician hasten away to get help. Menechmus is still more confused when Messenio comes in looking for his master, as the father returns with the physician and four porters to seize his son-in-law. Messenio rescues his supposed master and drives away his assailants; but Menech-

mus's bewilderment is further increased when Messenio promises to fetch his purse and goes off. Menechmus the citizen decides that he will make one more appeal to Erotium.

Then Menechmus the traveler enters with Messenio, whom he upbraids, but they are interrupted by the arrival of the other Menechmus. The long-separated brothers at last meet and recognize each other. Menechmus of Syracuse invites his brother of Epidamnum to go with him to Syracuse. Menechmus of Epidamnum agrees, and the play ends with Messenio making proclamation of the sale of his master's goods.

A comparison of *The Comedy of Errors* with the *Menechmi* shows how much Shakespeare owed to Plautus. He took the names of Syracuse and Epidamnum, the similarity of the twins, the shrill-voiced wife, the physician, and the courtesan; he dropped the old father-in-law and the parasite; he added Aegeon and the long-lost wife Aemilia (now an Abbess), the Duke, and Adriana's sister; and he gave to each twin brother a slave, conveniently born in the same hour and also identical to each other in looks, whereby the confusions are multiplied twofold.

The Comedy of Errors has all the signs of early work. The dramatic technique is elementary, especially in the long opening passage wherein Aegeon gives the audience the history of the twins in more than a hundred lines of almost uninterrupted autobiography. The diction in general is stiff, and speeches are seldom individual or alive, except when the "abbess" Aemilia denounces the scolding jealous wife (V.i.38–86). There is much rhyme, and a frequent use of the artificial stychomythia [1] of classical drama (e.g., II.i.10–15, 26–32). The variety of meter is unusual. In III.i., for instance, the scene begins with normal blank verse; at line 11 it changes to the rhymed "fourteener" which was popular in early sixteenth-century drama; at the beginning of the following scene (III.ii) the meter again changes to a lyric ten-syllable line with alternative rhymes. The wit is excessive and elaborate, especially in the passages of cross-talk between Dromio of Syracuse and his master (e.g., II.ii.34–110). Fine speech, however, is not necessary in a roaring farce. *The Comedy of Errors* is very good fun on the stage, but it is more suited for a New Year's Eve party than for a conference of critics.

[1] i.e., dialogue in which each speech is one full verse line.

The Comedy of Errors

DRAMATIS PERSONAE

SOLINUS, *Duke of Ephesus*
AEGEON, *a merchant of Syracuse*
ANTIPHOLUS OF EPHESUS } *twin brothers, and sons*
ANTIPHOLUS OF SYRACUSE } *to Aegeon and Aemilia*
DROMIO OF EPHESUS } *twin brothers, and attendants*
DROMIO OF SYRACUSE } *on the two Antipholuses*
BALTHAZAR, *a merchant*
ANGELO, *a goldsmith*
FIRST MERCHANT, *friend to Antipholus of Syracuse*
SECOND MERCHANT, *to whom Angelo is a debtor*

PINCH, *a schoolmaster*

AEMILIA, *wife to Aegeon, an abbess at Ephesus*
ADRIANA, *wife to Antipholus of Ephesus*
LUCIANA, *her sister*
LUCE, *servant to Adriana*
A COURTESAN

JAILER, OFFICERS, *and other* ATTENDANTS

SCENE — *Ephesus.*

Act I

SCENE I. *A hall in the* DUKE's *palace.*

[*Enter* DUKE, AEGEON, JAILER, OFFICERS, *and other*
ATTENDANTS.]

AEG. Proceed, Solinus, to procure my fall,
And by the doom° of death end woes and all.
DUKE. Merchant of Syracusa,° plead no more.
I am not partial to infringe° our laws.
The enmity and discord which of late   5
Sprung from the rancorous outrage of your Duke
To merchants, our well-dealing countrymen,
Who, wanting guilders° to redeem their lives,
Have sealed his rigorous statutes with their bloods,°
Excludes all pity from our threatening looks.   10
For, since the mortal and intestine jars°
'Twixt thy seditious countrymen and us,
It hath in solemn synods° been decreed,
Both by the Syracusians and ourselves,
To admit no traffic to our adverse° towns.   15
Nay, more,
If any born at Ephesus° be seen
At any Syracusian marts° and fairs —
Again, if any Syracusian born
Come to the bay of Ephesus — he dies,   20
His goods confiscate to the Duke's dispose,°
Unless a thousand marks° be levièd
To quit the penalty° and to ransom him.

Act I, Sc. i: 2. doom: judgment.   **3. Syracusa:** Syracuse is
on the east coast of Sicily.   **4. partial to infringe:** inclined to
break by lenience.   **8. guilders:** gold coins current in the Netherlands, but here used as a picturesque word for money.   **9. sealed
... bloods:** by death have confirmed the rigor of his laws.
11. intestine jars: deadly quarrels.   **13. synods:** councils.
15. adverse: hostile.   **17. Ephesus:** on the west coast of Asia
Minor.   **18. marts:** markets.   **21. dispose:** disposal.   **22. marks:**
worth 13s. 4d. See App. 24.   **23. quit ... penalty:** pay the
fine.

Thy substance, valued at the highest rate,
Cannot amount unto a hundred marks.   25
Therefore by law thou art condemned to die.
AEG. Yet this my comfort: When your words are
done,
My woes end likewise with the evening sun.
DUKE. Well, Syracusian, say in brief the cause
Why thou departed'st from thy native home,   30
And for what cause thou camest to Ephesus.
AEG. A heavier task could not have been imposed
Than I to speak my griefs unspeakable.
Yet, that the world may witness that my end
Was wrought by nature,° not by vile offense,   35
I'll utter what my sorrow gives me leave.
In Syracusa was I born, and wed
Unto a woman, happy but for me,°
And by me, had not our hap° been bad.
With her I lived in joy. Our wealth increased   40
By prosperous voyages I often made
To Epidamnum;° till my factor's° death,
And the great care of goods at random left,°
Drew me from kind embracements of my spouse,
From whom my absence was not six months old   45
Before herself, almost at fainting under
The pleasing punishment that women bear,°
Had made provision for her following me,
And soon and safe arrivèd where I was.
There had she not been long but° she became   50
A joyful mother of two goodly sons,
And, which was strange, the one so like the other
As could not be distinguished but by names.
That very hour, and in the self-same inn,

---

35. by nature: by the promptings of natural affection.
38. happy ... me: who would have been lucky, had I not brought
her bad luck.   **39. hap:** luck.   **42. Epidamnum:** correctly Epi-
damnus, a port on the eastern coast of the Adriatic Sea. **factor's:**
agent's.   **43. care ... left:** the anxiety caused by goods left
without proper supervision.   **46-47. almost ... bear:** i.e., she
was advanced in pregnancy.   **50. but:** before.

A meaner° woman was deliverèd   55
Of such a burden — male twins, both alike.
Those — for their parents were exceeding poor —
I bought, and brought up to attend° my sons.
My wife, not meanly° proud of two such boys,
Made daily motions for our home return.   60
Unwilling I agreed. Alas! Too soon
We came aboard.
A league° from Epidamnum had we sailed
Before the always-wind-obeying deep
Gave any tragic instance° of our harm.   65
But longer did we not retain much hope,
For what obscurèd light the heavens did grant
Did but convey unto our fearful minds
A doubtful warrant of immediate death;°   69
Which, though myself would gladly have embraced,
Yet the incessant weepings of my wife,
Weeping before for what she saw must come,
And piteous plainings° of the pretty babes,
That mourned for fashion,° ignorant what to fear,
Forced me to seek delays° for them and me.   75
And this it was, for other means was none.
The sailors sought for safety by our boat,°
And left the ship, then sinking-ripe,° to us.
My wife, more careful for the latter-born,
Had fastened him unto a small spare mast,   80
Such as seafaring men provide for storms.
To him one of the other twins was bound,
Whilst I had been like heedful of the other.
The children thus disposed, my wife and I,
Fixing our eyes on whom our care was fixed,   85
Fastened ourselves at either end the mast,
And, floating straight, obedient to the stream,
Was carried towards Corinth, as we thought.
At length the sun, gazing upon the earth,
Dispersed those vapors° that offended us,   90
And, by the benefit of his wished light,
The seas waxed calm, and we discoverèd
Two ships from far making amain° to us —
Of Corinth that, of Epidaurus this.
But ere they came — oh, let me say no more!   95
Gather the sequel by that° went before.
    DUKE. Nay, forward, old man. Do not break off
        so.
For we may pity, though not pardon thee.
    AEG. Oh, had the gods done so, I had not now
Worthily termed them merciless to us!   100
For, ere the ships could meet by twice five leagues,
We were encountered by a mighty rock,

Which being violently borne upon,
Our helpful ship was splittèd° in the midst,
So that, in this unjust divorce of us,   105
Fortune had left to both of us alike
What to delight in, what to sorrow for.
Her part, poor soul, seeming as burdened
With lesser weight — but not with lesser woe —
Was carried with more speed before the wind,   110
And in our sight they three were taken up
By fishermen of Corinth, as we thought.
At length, another ship had seized on us,
And, knowing whom it was their hap to save,
Gave healthful welcome to their shipwrecked
        guests,   115
And would have reft° the fishers of their prey,
Had not their bark been very slow of sail;
And therefore homeward did they bend their course.
Thus have you heard me severed from my bliss,
That by misfortunes was my life prolonged   120
To tell sad stories of my own mishaps.
    DUKE. And, for the sake of them thou sorrowest
        for,
Do me the favor to dilate° at full
What hath befallen of them and thee till now.
    AEG. My youngest boy, and yet my eldest care,
At eighteen years became inquisitive   126
After his brother, and importuned me
That his attendant — so his case was like,
Reft of his brother, but retained his name — °
Might bear him company in the quest of him,   130
Whom whilst I labored of a° love to see,
I hazarded the loss of whom I loved.
Five summers have I spent in farthest Greece,
Roaming clean° through the bounds of Asia,
And, coasting homeward, came to Ephesus,   135
Hopeless to find, yet loath to leave unsought
Or° that, or any place that harbors men.
But here must end the story of my life;
And happy were I in my timely death,
Could all my travels warrant° me they live.   140
    DUKE. Hapless Aegeon, whom the fates have
        marked
To bear the extremity of dire mishap!
Now, trust me, were it not against our laws,
Against my crown, my oath, my dignity,
Which princes, would they,° may not disannul,°
My soul should sue as advocate for thee.   146
But, though thou art adjudgèd to the death,
And passèd sentence may not be recalled
But to our honor's great disparagement,
Yet I will favor thee in what I can.   150
Therefore, merchant, I'll limit° thee this day

55. meaner: poorer.   **58. attend:** wait on.   **59. not meanly:** not slightly; i.e., greatly.   **63. league:** three miles.   **65. instance:** indication.   **69. doubtful . . . death:** warning that without doubt we should die immediately.   **73. plainings:** lamentations.   **74. for fashion:** i.e., like everyone else.   **75. delays:** means of postponing their deaths.   **77. boat:** Large ships towed a rowboat for use in emergency.   **78. sinking-ripe:** ready to sink.   **90. vapors:** mists.   **93. amain:** speedily.   **96. that:** what.

104. splitted: split in two.   **116. reft:** deprived by force.   **123. dilate:** expand.   **128–29. attendant . . . name:** his servant Dromio, who, too, had lost his twin brother, also called Dromio.   **131. of a:** out of.   **134. clean:** completely.   **137. Or:** either.   **140. warrant:** assure.   **145. would they:** even if they wished.   **disannul:** cancel.   **151. limit:** allot.

To seek thy help° by beneficial help.
Try all the friends thou hast in Ephesus.
Beg thou, or borrow, to make up the sum,
And live; if no, then thou art doomed to die.   155
Jailer, take him to thy custody.

    JAIL. I will, my lord.

    AEG. Hopeless and helpless doth Aegeon wend,
But to procrastinate his lifeless end.°   [*Exeunt.*]

SCENE II. *The Mart.*

[*Enter* ANTIPHOLUS OF SYRACUSE, DROMIO OF SYRACUSE
and FIRST MERCHANT.]

    I. MER. Therefore give out you are of Epidam-
num,
Lest that your goods too soon be confiscate.
This very day a Syracusian merchant
Is apprehended for arrival here,
And, not being able to buy out his life   5
According to the statute of the town,
Dies ere the weary sun set in the West.
There is your money that I had to keep.

    ANT. S. Go bear it to the Centaur,° where we
host,°
And stay there, Dromio, till I come to thee.   10
Within this hour it will be dinner time.
Till that, I'll view the manners of the town,
Peruse the traders, gaze upon the buildings,
And then return, and sleep within mine inn,
For with long travel I am stiff and weary.   15
Get thee away.

    DRO. S. Many a man would take you at your word,
And go indeed, having so good a mean.°   [*Exit.*]

    ANT. S. A trusty villain, sir, that very oft,
When I am dull with care and melancholy,   20
Lightens my humor° with his merry jests.
What, will you walk with me about the town,
And then go to my inn and dine with me?

    I. MER. I am invited, sir, to certain merchants,
Of whom I hope to make much benefit.   25
I crave your pardon. Soon at five o'clock,
Please you, I'll meet with you upon the mart,°
And afterward consort you° till bedtime
My present business calls me from you now.

    ANT. S. Farewell till then. I will go lose myself,
And wander up and down to view the city.   31

    I. MER. Sir, I commend you to your own content.
        [*Exit.*]

    ANT. S. He that commends me to mine own con-
tent
Commends me to the thing I cannot get.

I to the world am like a drop of water   35
That in the ocean seeks another drop,
Who, falling there to find his fellow forth,°
Unseen, inquisitive, confounds° himself.
So I, to find a mother and a brother,
In quest of them, unhappy, lose myself.   40
    [*Enter* DROMIO OF EPHESUS.]
Here comes the almanac of my true date.°
What now? How chance thou art returned so soon?

    DRO. E. Returned so soon! Rather approached too
late.
The capon burns, the pig falls from the spit.
The clock hath strucken twelve upon the bell;   45
My mistress° made it one upon my cheek.
She is so hot because the meat is cold;
The meat is cold because you come not home;
You come not home, because you have no stomach;°
You have no stomach, having broke your fast;   50
But we, that know what 'tis to fast and pray,
Are penitent for your default today.

    ANT. S. Stop in your wind,° sir! Tell me this, I
pray.
Where have you left the money that I gave you?

    DRO. E. Oh — sixpence, that I had o' Wednesday
last   55
To pay the saddler for my mistress' crupper?°
The saddler had it, sir; I kept it not.

    ANT. S. I am not in a sportive humor now.
Tell me, and dally not, where is the money?
We being strangers here, how darest thou trust   60
So great a charge from° thine own custody?

    DRO. E. I pray you, jest, sir, as you sit at dinner.
I from my mistress come to you in post.°
If I return, I shall be post° indeed,
For she will score your fault upon my pate.   65
Methinks your maw,° like mine, should be your
clock
And strike° you home without a messenger.

    ANT. S. Come, Dromio, come, these jests are out
of season.
Reserve them till a merrier hour than this.
Where is the gold I gave in charge to thee?   70

    DRO. E. To me, sir? Why, you gave no gold to me.

    ANT. S. Come on, sir knave, have done your fool-
ishness,
And tell me how thou hast disposed thy charge.°

    DRO. E. My charge was but to fetch you from the
mart

---

37. **find . . . forth:** i.e., discover his brother.   38. **confounds:**
loses.   41. **almanac . . . date:** i.e., he tells me how old I am because he was born in the same hour.   46. **mistress:** i.e., the wife
of Antipholus of Ephesus.   49. **stomach:** appetite.   53. **Stop
. . . wind:** stop chattering.   56. **crupper:** the loop passed round
a horse's tail and fastened to the saddle.   61. **from:** out of.
63. **post:** haste.   64. **post:** the pillar in a tavern on which accounts for drink were scored by chalk lines.   66. **maw:** stomach.
67. **strike:** summon by its striking the hours; i.e., by its intestinal
rumblings.   73. **thy charge:** the money entrusted to you.

---

152. **help:** relief, rescue.   159. **But . . . end:** merely to postpone
the end of his life.

    Sc. ii: 9. **Centaur:** the name of the inn. **host:** lodge.
18. **mean:** means; i.e., so much money.   21. **humor:** mood.
27. **mart:** exchange.   28. **consort you:** be your companion.

Home to your house, the Phoenix,° sir, to dinner.
My mistress and her sister stays for you.   76

ANT. S. Now, as I am a Christian, answer me
In what safe place you have bestowed my money,
Or I shall break that merry sconce° of yours,
That stands on tricks° when I am undisposed.   80
Where is the thousand marks thou had'st of me?

DRO. E. I have some marks of yours upon my pate,
Some of my mistress' marks upon my shoulders,
But not a thousand marks between you both.
If I should pay your worship those again,   85
Perchance you will not bear them patiently.

ANT. S. Thy mistress' marks? What mistress,
     slave, hast thou?

DRO. E. Your Worship's wife, my mistress at the
     Phoenix —
She that doth fast till you come home to dinner,
And prays that you will hie you° home to dinner.

ANT. S. What, wilt thou flout me thus unto my
     face,   91
Being forbid?° There, take you that, sir knave.

DRO. E. What mean you, sir? For God's sake, hold
     your hands!
Nay, an° you will not, sir, I'll take my heels. [*Exit.*]

ANT. S. Upon my life, by some device or other   95
The villain is o'erraught° of all my money.
They say this town is full of cozenage:°
As, nimble jugglers that deceive the eye,
Dark-working sorcerers that change the mind,
Soul-killing witches that deform the body,   100
Disguisèd cheaters, prating mountebanks,
And many such-like liberties of sin.°
If it prove so, I will be gone the sooner.
I'll to the Centaur to go seek this slave.   104
I greatly fear my money is not safe.   [*Exit.*]

Act II

SCENE I. *The house of* ANTIPHOLUS E.

[*Enter* ADRIANA *and* LUCIANA.]

ADR. Neither my husband nor the slave returned
That in such haste I sent to seek his master!
Sure, Luciana, it is two o'clock.

LUC. Perhaps some merchant hath invited him,
And from the mart he's somewhere gone to dinner.
Good Sister, let us dine, and never fret.   6
A man is master of his liberty.

Time is their master,° and when they see time,
They'll go or come. If so, be patient, Sister.   9

ADR. Why should their liberty than ours be more?

LUC. Because their business still° lies out o' door.

ADR. Look, when I serve him so, he takes it ill.

LUC. Oh, know he is the bridle of your will.

ADR. There's none but asses will be bridled so.

LUC. Why, headstrong liberty is lashed° with woe.
There's nothing situate under Heaven's eye   16
But hath his bound,° in earth, in sea, in sky.
The beasts, the fishes, and the wingèd fowls
Are their males' subjects and at their controls.
Men more divine, the masters of all these,   20
Lords of the wide world and wild watery seas,
Indued with intellectual sense and souls,
Or more pre-eminence than fish and fowls,
Are masters to their females, and their lords.°
Then let your will attend on their accords.   25

ADR. This servitude makes you to keep unwed.

LUC. Not this, but troubles of the marriage bed.

ADR. But, were you wedded, you would bear
     some sway.

LUC. Ere I learn love, I'll practice to obey.

ADR. How if your husband start some other
     where?°   30

LUC. Till he come home again, I would forbear.

ADR. Patience unmoved! No marvel, though, she
     pause.°
They can be meek that have no other cause.
A wretched soul, bruised with adversity,
We bid be quiet when we hear it cry;   35
But were we burdened with like weight of pain,
As much, or more, we should ourselves complain.
So thou, that hast no unkind mate to grieve thee,
With urging helpless patience wouldst relieve me.
But if thou live to see like right bereft,°   40
This fool-begged patience in thee will be left.°

LUC. Well, I will marry one day, but to try.
Here comes your man. Now is your husband nigh.

[*Enter* DROMIO E.]

ADR. Say, is your tardy master now at hand?

DRO. E. Nay, he's at two hands with me, and that
my two ears can witness.

ADR. Say, didst thou speak with him? Know'st
     thou his mind?

DRO. E. Aye, aye, he told his mind upon mine ear.
Beshrew° his hand, I scarce could understand it.

LUC. Spake he so doubtfully° thou couldst not
feel his meaning?   51

DRO. E. Nay, he struck so plainly I could too well

Act II, Sc. i: 8. Time . . . master: they serve their own time;
i.e., please themselves.   11. still: continually.   15. lashed:
punished.   17. bound: limit.   24. their lords: are their wives'
lords.   30. start . . . where: love elsewhere.   32. Patience . . .
pause: no one has tried her patience; no wonder she is so unmoved.   40. like . . . bereft: yourself treated as I am.   41. This
. . . left: you will soon drop this silly patience.   49. Beshrew:
ill luck to.   50. doubtfully: confusedly.

75. Phoenix: the name of the house. See App. 12.   79. sconce:
head (a slang word). See II.ii.34,n.   80. stands on tricks: plays
the fool.   90. hie you: hasten.   92. Being forbid: being told to
hold your tongue.   94. an: if.   96. o'erraught: overreached,
cheated.   97. cozenage: cheating.   102. liberties of sin: free
sinners.

feel his blows, and withal so doubtfully that I could
scarce understand° them.

    ADR. But say, I prithee, is he coming home? 55
It seems he hath great care to please his wife.

    DRO. E. Why, mistress, sure my master is horn-
    mad.°

    ADR. Horn-mad, thou villain!

    DRO. E.   I mean not cuckold-mad;
But, sure, he is stark mad.
When I desired him to come home to dinner, 60
He asked me for a thousand marks in gold.
" 'Tis dinnertime," quoth I. " My gold! " quoth he.
" Your meat doth burn," quoth I. " My gold! "
    quoth he.
" Will you come home? " quoth I. " My gold! "
    quoth he.
" Where is the thousand marks I gave thee, vil-
    lain? " 65
" The pig," quoth I, " is burned." " My gold! "
    quoth he.
" My mistress, sir," quoth I. " Hang up thy mistress!
I know not thy mistress; out on thy mistress! "

    LUC. Quoth who?

    DRO. E. Quoth my master. 70
" I know," quoth he, " no house, no wife, no mis-
    tress."
So that my errand, due unto my tongue,
I thank him, I bare home upon my shoulders;
For, in conclusion, he did beat me there.

    ADR. Go back again, thou slave, and fetch him
    home. 75

    DRO. E. Go back again, and be new beaten home?
For God's sake, send some other messenger.

    ADR. Back, slave, or I will break thy pate across.

    DRO. E. And he will bless° that cross with other
    beating.
Between you I shall have a holy head. 80

    ADR. Hence, prating peasant! Fetch thy master
    home.

    DRO. E. Am I so round° with you as you with me
That like a football you do spurn me thus? 83
You spurn me hence, and he will spurn me hither.
If I last in this service, you must case me in leather.
                      [Exit.]

    LUC. Fie, how impatience loureth° in your face!

    ADR. His company must do his minions grace,°
Whilst I at home starve for a merry look.
Hath homely age the alluring beauty took
From my poor cheek? Then he hath wasted it. 90
Are my discourses dull? Barren my wit?
If voluble and sharp discourse be marred,
Unkindness blunts it more than marble hard.

Do their gay vestments his affections bait?
That's not my fault; he's master of my state. 95
What ruins are in me that can be found,
By him not ruined? Then is he the ground
Of my defeatures.° My decayèd fair°
A sunny look of his would soon repair.
But, too unruly deer, he breaks the pale,° 100
And feeds from° home; poor I am but his stale.°

    LUC. Self-harming jealousy! Fie, beat it hence!

    ADR. Unfeeling fools can with such wrongs dis-
    pense.
I know his eye doth homage otherwhere,
Or else what lets° it but he would be here? 105
Sister, you know he promised me a chain.
Would that alone, alone he would detain,
So he would keep fair quarter with his bed!°
I see the jewel best enamelèd
Will lose his° beauty; yet the gold bides still 110
That others touch, and often touching° will
Wear gold: and no man that hath a name
By falsehood and corruption doth it shame.
Since that my beauty cannot please his eye,
I'll weep what's left away, and weeping die. 115

    LUC. How many fond° fools serve mad jealousy!
                      [Exeunt.]

SCENE II. *A public place.*

[*Enter* ANTIPHOLUS S.]

    ANT. S. The gold I gave to Dromio is laid up
Safe at the Centaur, and the heedful slave
Is wandered forth in care to seek me out,
By computation° and mine host's report.
I could not speak with Dromio since at first 5
I sent him from the mart. See, here he comes.
             [*Enter* DROMIO S.]
How now, sir! Is your merry humor altered?
As you love strokes, so jest with me again.
You know no Centaur? You received no gold?
Your mistress sent to have me home to dinner? 10
My house was at the Phoenix? Wast thou mad
That thus so madly thou didst answer me?

    DRO. S. What answer, sir? When spake I such a
    word?

    ANT. S. Even now, even here, not half an hour
    since.

    DRO. S. I did not see you since you sent me hence,
Home to the Centaur with the gold you gave me. 16

    ANT. S. Villain, thou didst deny the gold's receipt,
And told'st me of a mistress and a dinner,

---

54. understand: stand under, endure. **57. horn-mad:** like a mad bull; but Adriana naturally thinks that her husband is accusing her of infidelity. See App. 11. **79. bless:** make the sign of the cross on. **82. round:** straight, outspoken. **86. loureth:** threatens. **87. His . . . grace:** he must be kind to his darlings **by** staying with them.

98. defeatures: change of feature for the worse. **fair:** beauty. **100. pale:** fence. **101. from:** away from. **stale:** a thing cheaply regarded. **105. lets:** hinders. **107–08. Would . . . bed:** I wouldn't mind if he kept his chain, so long as he was faithful to me. **110. his:** its. **111. touch . . . touching:** testing by acid for purity. See *Rich III*, IV.ii.8,n. **116. fond:** foolish. **Sc. ii: 4. By computation:** as I suppose.

For which, I hope, thou felt'st I was displeased.

DRO. S. I am glad to see you in this merry vein. 20
What means this jest? I pray you, master, tell me.

ANT. S. Yea, dost thou jeer and flout me in the teeth?°
Think'st thou I jest? Hold, take thou that, and that.

[*Beating him.*]

DRO. S. Hold, sir, for God's sake! Now your jest is earnest.
Upon what bargain° do you give it me?   25

ANT. S. Because that I familiarly sometimes
Do use you for my fool, and chat with you,
Your sauciness will jest upon my love,
And make a common° of my serious hours.   29
When the sun shines, let foolish gnats make sport,
But creep in crannies when he hides his beams.
If you will jest with me, know my aspéct,°
And fashion your demeanor to my looks,
Or I will beat this method in your sconce.°   34

DRO. S. Sconce call you it? So° you would leave battering, I had rather have it a head. An° you use these blows long, I must get a sconce for my head, and insconce° it too; or else I shall seek my wit in my shoulders. But, I pray, sir, why am I beaten?   40

ANT. S. Dost thou not know?

DRO. S. Nothing, sir, but that I am beaten.

ANT. S. Shall I tell you why?

DRO. S. Aye, sir, and wherefore; for they say every why hath a wherefore.   45

ANT. S. Why, first — for flouting me; and then, wherefore —
For urging it the second time to me.

DRO. S. Was there ever any man thus beaten out of season,°
When in the why and the wherefore is neither rhyme nor reason?
Well, sir, I thank you.   50

ANT. S. Thank me, sir! For what?

DRO. S. Marry, sir, for this something that you gave me for nothing.

ANT. S. I'll make you amends next, to give you nothing for something. But say, sir, is it dinnertime?

DRO. S. No, sir. I think the meat wants that I have.

ANT. S. In good time, sir, what's that?

DRO. S. Basting.

ANT. S. Well, sir, then 'twill be dry.   60

DRO. S. If it be, sir, I pray you eat none of it.

ANT. S. Your reason?

DRO. S. Lest it make you choleric,° and purchase me another dry basting.°

ANT. S. Well, sir, learn to jest in good time. There's a time for all things.   66

DRO. S. I durst have denied that, before you were so choleric.

ANT. S. By what rule, sir?

DRO. S. Marry, sir, by a rule as plain as the plain bald pate of Father Time himself.   71

ANT. S. Let's hear it.

DRO. S. There's no time for a man to recover his hair that grows bald by nature.

ANT. S. May he not do it by fine and recovery?°   75

DRO. S. Yes, to pay a fine for a periwig, and recover the lost hair of another man.

ANT. S. Why is Time such a niggard of hair, being, as it is, so plentiful an excrement?°   79

DRO. S. Because it is a blessing that he bestows on beasts; and what he hath scanted men in hair, he hath given them in wit.

ANT. S. Why, but there's many a man hath more hair than wit.

DRO. S. Not° a man of those but he hath the wit to lose his hair.   86

ANT. S. Why, thou didst conclude hairy men plain dealers without wit.

DRO. S. The plainer dealer, the sooner lost; yet he loseth it in a kind of jollity.   90

ANT. S. For what reason?

DRO. S. For two, and sound ones, too.

ANT. S. Nay, not sound, I pray you.

DRO. S. Sure ones, then.

ANT. S. Nay, not sure, in a thing falsing.°   95

DRO. S. Certain ones, then.

ANT. S. Name them.

DRO. S. The one, to save the money that he spends in tiring;° the other, that at dinner they should not drop in his porridge.   100

ANT. S. You would all this time have proved there is no time for all things.

DRO. S. Marry, and I did, sir — namely, no time to recover hair lost by nature.

ANT. S. But your reason was not substantial, why there is no time to recover.

DRO. S. Thus I mend° it. Time himself is bald, and therefore to the world's end will have bald followers.

ANT. S. I knew 'twould be a bald conclusion.   110
But, soft! Who wafts° us yonder?

[*Enter* ADRIANA *and* LUCIANA.]

---

22. flout . . . teeth: mock me to my face.   **24–25. earnest . . . bargain:** *earnest* means (a) "serious," and (b) "money given on account of the main payment to come." **bargain:** purchase. **29. make a common:** treat as if they were public property. **32. aspect:** look. The word is used of a star which is favorable or otherwise. See *I Hen IV*, I.i.97,n, and App. I.   **34. sconce:** (a) a head; (b) a small military blockhouse or strong point. **35. So:** if only.   **36. An:** if.   **38. insconce:** seek protection within.   **48. out . . . season:** at the wrong time.

63. choleric: hot tempered.   **64. dry basting:** beating which does not break the skin.   **75. fine . . . recovery:** a legal phrase meaning "possession of property by means of an agreement approved in a court of law." This tedious cross-talk on hair continues to l. 110.   **79. excrement:** that which grows out of the body as hair, nails, etc.   **85–90. Not . . . jollity:** The reference is to the loss of hair caused by venereal disease.   **95. falsing:** deceptive.   **99. tiring:** wigs.   **108. mend:** improve.   **111. wafts:** waves to.

ADR. Aye, aye, Antipholus, look strange and
    frown.
Some other mistress hath thy sweet aspécts.°
I am not Adriana nor thy wife.
The time was once when thou unurged wouldst
    vow   115
That never words were music to thine ear,
That never object pleasing in thine eye,
That never touch well welcome to thy hand,
That never meat sweet-savored in thy taste,
Unless I spake, or looked, or touched, or carved to
    thee.   120
How comes it now, my Husband, oh, how comes it
That thou art then estrangèd from thyself?
Thyself I call it, being strange to me,°
That, undividable, incorporate,
Am better than thy dear self's better part.   125
Ah, do not tear away thyself from me!
For know, my love, as easy mayst thou fall°
A drop of water in the breaking gulf°
And take unmingled thence that drop again,
Without addition or diminishing,   130
As take from me thyself, and not me too.
How dearly would it touch thee to the quick,
Shouldst thou but hear I were licentious,
And that this body, consecrate to thee,
By ruffian lust should be contaminate!   135
Wouldst thou not spit at me and spurn at me,
And hurl the name of husband in my face,
And tear the stained skin off my harlot brow,
And from my false hand cut the wedding ring
And break it with a deep-divorcing vow?   140
I know thou canst, and therefore see thou do it.
I am possessed° with an adulterate blot.
My blood is mingled with the crime of lust.
For if we two be one, and thou play false,
I do digest the poison of thy flesh,   145
Being strumpeted by thy contagion.
Keep, then, fair league and truce with thy true bed.
I live distained, thou undishonorèd.°
    ANT. S. Plead you to me, fair dame? I know you
    not.
In Ephesus I am but two hours old,   150
As strange unto your town as to your talk,
Who, every word by all my wit being scanned,
Wants wit in all one word to understand.°
    LUC. Fie, Brother! How the world is changed with
    you!

When were you wont to use my sister thus?   155
She sent for you by Dromio home to dinner.
    ANT. S. By Dromio?
    DRO. S. By me?
    ADR. By thee; and this thou didst return from him,
That he did buffet thee, and, in his blows,   160
Denied my house for his, me for his wife.
    ANT. S. Did you converse, sir, with this gentle-
    woman?
What is the course and drift of your compact?°
    DRO. S. I, sir? I never saw her till this time.
    ANT. S. Villain, thou liest, for even her very words
Didst thou deliver to me on the mart.   166
    DRO. S. I never spake with her in all my life.
    ANT. S. How can she thus then call us by our
    names?
Unless it be by inspiration.°
    ADR. How ill agrees it with your gravity   170
To counterfeit° thus grossly with your slave,
Abetting him to thwart me in my mood!
Be it my wrong you are from me exempt,
But wrong not that wrong with a more contempt.°
Come, I will fasten on this sleeve of thine.   175
Thou art an elm, my Husband, I a vine,°
Whose weakness, married to thy stronger state,
Makes me with thy strength to communicate.
If aught possess thee from me,° it is dross,°
Usurping ivy, brier, or idle° moss,   180
Who, all for want of pruning, with intrusion
Infect thy sap, and live on thy confusion.°
    ANT. S. To me she speaks. She moves me for her
    theme.°
What, was I married to her in my dream?
Or sleep I now, and think I hear all this?   185
What error drives our eyes and ears amiss?
Until I know this sure uncertainty,°
I'll entertain the offered fallacy.°
    LUC. Dromio, go bid the servants spread for din-
    ner.
    DRO. S. Oh, for my beads!° I cross° me for a sin-
    ner.   190
This is the fairy land. Oh, spite of spites!
We talk with goblins, owls, and sprites.
If we obey them not, this will ensue —
They'll suck our breath, or pinch us black and
    blue.

113. aspects: see 32, n. 123. Thyself . . . me: It was a common fancy of a lover to regard the beloved as himself. Adriana (ll. 123–48) plays with this idea and elaborates it: "If I were to be unfaithful to you, you would be righteously angry; but seeing that you are myself, when you are faithless to me it is the same as if I were false to you." Later (III.ii.61–66) Antipholus makes love to Luciana in these terms. 127. fall: let fall. 128. breaking gulf: swirling whirlpool. 142. I am possessed: i.e., because you are. 148. I . . . undishonored: then I shall live without stain and you without dishonor. 153. Wants . . . understand: "can't make a word of sense in all your talk."

163. compact: agreement. 169. inspiration: supernatural means. 171. counterfeit: pretend. 173–74. Be . . . contempt: i.e., even if I am wronged because you cannot be controlled by me, yet do not make matters worse by despising me. 176. elm . . . vine: This is a common image in Latin poetry for the love of husband and wife, the grape vine being supported on a pollarded elm to which it clings. 179. possess . . . me: deprives me of possessing you. dross: something worthless. 180. idle: useless. 182. confusion: disorderly life. 183. moves . . . theme: is talking about me. 187. sure uncertainty: the truth of this mystery. 188. entertain . . . fallacy: accept the dream as if it were real. 190. Oh . . . beads: fetch me my rosary. Dromio thinks that they are in the power of evil spirits, and so needs the support of a holy object. cross: make the sign of the cross.

LUC. Why pratest thou to thyself and answer'st
     not?   195
Dromio, thou drone, thou snail, thou slug, thou sot!
     DRO. S. I am transformèd,° master, am not I?
     ANT. S. I think thou art in mind, and so am I.
     DRO. S. Nay, master, both in mind and in my
     shape.
     ANT. S. Thou hast thine own form.
     DRO. S.   No, I am an ape.   200
     LUC. If thou art changed to aught, 'tis to an ass.
     DRO. S. 'Tis true. She rides me, and I long for
     grass.
'Tis so, I am an ass, else it could never be
But I should know her as well as she knows me.
     ADR. Come, come, no longer will I be a fool   205
To put the finger in the eye and weep
Whilst man and master laughs my woes to scorn.
Come, sir, to dinner. Dromio, keep the gate.
Husband, I'll dine above with you today,
And shrive° you of a thousand idle pranks.   210
Sirrah,° if any ask you for your master,
Say he dines forth,° and let no creature enter.
Come, sister. Dromio, play the porter well.
     ANT. S. Am I in earth, in Heaven, or in Hell?
Sleeping or waking? Mad or well advised?°   215
Known unto these, and to myself disguised!
I'll say as they say, and perséver so,
And in this mist at all adventures go.°
     DRO. S. Master, shall I be porter at the gate?
     ADR. Aye, and let none enter, lest I break your
     pate.   220
     LUC. Come, come, Antipholus, we dine too late.
     [*Exeunt.*]

Act III

SCENE I. *Before the house of* ANTIPHOLUS E.

[*Enter* ANTIPHOLUS E., DROMIO E., ANGELO,
     and BALTHAZAR.]
     ANT. E. Good Signior Angelo, you must excuse us
     all.
My wife is shrewish when I keep not hours.
Say that I lingered with you at your shop
To see the making of her carcanet,°
And that tomorrow you will bring it home.   5
But here's a villain that would face me down°
He met me on the mart, and that I beat him,

And charged° him with a thousand marks in gold,
And that I did deny my wife and house.
Thou drunkard, thou, what didst thou mean by
     this?   10
     DRO. E. Say what you will, sir, but I know what
     I know.
That you beat me at the mart, I have your hand to
     show.
If the skin were parchment, and the blows you gave
     were ink,
Your own handwriting would tell you what I think.
     ANT. E. I think thou art an ass.
     DRO. E.   Marry, so it doth appear   15
By the wrongs I suffer and the blows I bear.
I should kick, being kicked, and, being at that pass,°
You would keep from my heels, and beware of an
     ass.
     ANT. E. You're sad, Signior Balthazar. Pray God
     our cheer
May answer my good will and your good welcome
     here.   20
     BAL. I hold your dainties cheap, sir, and your wel-
     come dear.
     ANT. E. Oh, Signior Balthazar, either at flesh or
     fish,
A table full of welcome makes scarce one dainty
     dish.
     BAL. Good meat, sir, is common; that every churl
     affords.
     ANT. E. And welcome more common; for that's
     nothing but words.   25
     BAL. Small cheer and great welcome makes a
     merry feast.
     ANT. E. Aye, to a niggardly host and more sparing
     guest.
But though my cates° be mean, take them in good
     part.
Better cheer may you have, but not with better
     heart.
But, soft! My door is locked. — Go bid them let us
     in.   30
     DRO. E. Maud, Bridget, Marian, Cicely, Gillian,
     Ginn!
     DRO. S. [*Within*] Mome,° malt-horse, capon, cox-
     comb, idiot, patch!°
Either get thee from the door, or sit down at the
     hatch.°
Dost thou conjure° for wenches, that thou call'st
     for such store,°
When one is one too many? Go get thee from the
     door.   35
     DRO. E. What patch is made our porter? My mas-
     ter stays in the street.

---

197. **transformed:** bewitched.   210. **shrive:** hear your confession
and forgive you.   211. **Sirrah:** term of address used to an inferior.   212. **forth:** away from home.   215. **well advised:** in
my right senses.   218. **at . . . go:** accept whatever may happen.

     Act III, Sc. i: 4. **carcanet:** collar of gold.   6. **face me down:**
tried to maintain against my sure knowledge that.

8. **charged:** entrusted.   17. **at . . . pass:** in that situation.
28. **cates:** delicacies.   32. **Mome:** blockhead. **patch:** fool.
33. **hatch:** the lower half of a divided door.   34. **conjure:** call
for by means of spells. **store:** quantity; i.e., of wenches.

DRO. S. [*Within*] Let him walk from whence he came, lest he catch cold on's feet.

ANT. E. Who talks within there? Ho, open the door!

DRO. S. [*Within*] Right, sir, I'll tell you when, an you'll tell me wherefore.

ANT. E. Wherefore? For my dinner. I have not dined today. 40

DRO. S. [*Within*] Nor today here you must not. Come again when you may.

ANT. E. What art thou that keepest me out from the house I owe?°

DRO. S. [*Within*] The porter for this time, sir, and my name is Dromio.

DRO. E. Oh, villain, thou hast stolen both mine office and my name!

The one ne'er got me credit, the other mickle° blame. 45

If thou hadst been Dromio today in my place,

Thou wouldst have changed thy face for a name, or thy name for an ass.°

LUCE. [*Within*] What a coil° is there, Dromio? Who are those at the gate?

DRO. E. Let my master in, Luce.

LUCE. [*Within*] 'Faith, no, he comes too late.

And so tell your master.

DRO. E. Oh, Lord, I must laugh! 50

Have at you° with a proverb —— Shall I set in my staff?°

LUCE. [*Within*] Have at you with another; that's —— When? Can you tell?°

DRO. S. [*Within*] If thy name be called Luce — Luce, thou hast answered him well.

ANT. E. Do you hear, you minion?° You'll let us in, I hope?

LUCE. [*Within*] I thought to have asked you.

DRO. S. [*Within*] And you said no. 55

DRO. E. So, come, help! Well struck! There was blow for blow.

ANT. E. Thou baggage, let me in.

LUCE. [*Within*] Can you tell for whose sake?

DRO. E. Master, knock the door hard.

LUCE. [*Within*] Let him knock till it ache.

ANT. E. You'll cry for this, minion, if I beat the door down.

LUCE. [*Within*] What needs all that, and a pair of stocks° in the town? 60

ADR. [*Within*]Who is that at the door that keeps° all this noise?

DRO. S. [*Within*] By my troth,° your town is

troubled with unruly boys.

ANT. E. Are you there, Wife? You might have come before.

ADR. [*Within*] Your wife, sir knave! Go get you from the door.

DRO. E. If you went in pain, master, this " knave " would go sore.° 65

ANG. Here is neither cheer, sir, nor welcome. We would fain° have either.

BAL. In debating which was best, we shall part with neither.

DRO. E. They stand at the door, master. Bid them welcome hither.

ANT. E. There is something in the wind, that we cannot get in.

DRO. E. You would say so, master, if your garments were thin. 70

Your cake here is warm within. You stand here in the cold.

It would make a man mad as a buck° to be so bought and sold.

ANT. E. Go fetch me something. I'll break ope the gate.

DRO. S. [*Within*] Break any breaking° here, and I'll break your knave's pate.

DRO. E. A man may break a word with you, sir, and words are but wind — 75

Aye, and break it in your face, so he break it not behind.

DRO. S. [*Within*] It seems thou want'st breaking. Out upon thee, hind!°

DRO. E. Here's too much " out upon thee! " I pray thee, let me in.

DRO. S. [*Within*] Aye, when fowls have no feathers, and fish have no fin. 79

ANT. E. Well, I'll break in. Go borrow me a crow.°

DRO. E. A crow without feather? Master, mean you so?

For a fish without a fin, there's a fowl without a feather.

If a crow help us in, sirrah, we'll pluck a crow° together.

ANT. E. Go get thee gone. Fetch me an iron crow.

BAL. Have patience, sir. Oh, let it not be so! 85

Herein you war against your reputation,

And draw within the compass of suspect°

The unviolated honor of your wife.

Once this° — your long experience of her wisdom,

Her sober virtue, years, and modesty, 90

Plead on her part° some cause to you unknown;

---

42. owe: own.   45. mickle: much.   47. Thou . . . ass: you would have assumed my name (but not my face) or else taken my name, which would cause you to be beaten as an ass. 48. coil: turmoil.   51. Have at you: I will throw a proverb at you. Shall . . . staff: a proverb meaning "make myself at home." 52. When . . . tell: a sarcastic saying — "I should like to know when." 54. minion: hussy.   60. stocks: See App. 10.   61. keeps: makes.   62. troth: truth.

65. If . . . sore: if you cared to take the trouble (*pain*), she would be well beaten for calling you knave.   66. fain: gladly. 72. buck: the male deer, notoriously fierce at the mating season. 74. Break . . . breaking: if anyone tries any breaking in. 77. hind: servant.   80. crow: crowbar.   83. pluck a crow: make a quarrel.   87. draw . . . suspect: cause to be suspected. 89. Once this: in a word.   91. Plead . . . part: are arguments for her of.

And doubt not, sir, but she will well excuse°
Why at this time the doors are made° against you.
Be ruled by me. Depart in patience,
And let us to the Tiger all to dinner;   95
And about evening come yourself alone
To know the reason of this strange restraint.
If by strong hand you offer to break in
Now in the stirring passage of the day,°
A vulgar comment will be made of it,   100
And that supposèd by the common rout
Against your yet ungallèd estimation,°
That may with foul intrusion enter in,
And dwell upon your grave when you are dead.
For slander lives upon succession,°   105
Forever housèd where it gets possession.
ANT. E. You have prevailed. I will depart in quiet,
And, in despite of mirth,° mean to be merry.
I know a wench of excellent discourse,
Pretty and witty, wild, and yet, too, gentle.   110
There will we dine. This woman that I mean,
My wife — but, I protest, without desert —
Hath oftentimes upbraided me withal.°
To her will we to dinner. [*To* ANGELO] Get you
          home,
And fetch the chain. By this° I know 'tis made.   115
Bring it, I pray you, to the Porpentine,°
For there's the house. That chain will I bestow —
Be it for nothing but to spite my wife —
Upon mine hostess there. Good sir, make haste.
Since mine own doors refuse to entertain me,   120
I'll knock elsewhere to see if they'll disdain me.
      ANG. I'll meet you at that place some hour hence.
      ANT. E. Do so. This jest shall cost me some ex-
          pense.   [*Exeunt.*]

SCENE II. *The same.*

[*Enter* LUCIANA, *with* ANTIPHOLUS s.]
LUC. And may it be that you have quite forgot
A husband's office? Shall, Antipholus,
Even in the spring of love, thy love-springs rot?
      Shall love, in building, grow so ruinous?
If you did wed my sister for her wealth,   5
      Then for her wealth's sake use her with more
          kindness.
Or if you like elsewhere, do it by stealth.
      Muffle your false love with some show of blind-
          ness;
Let not my sister read it in your eye.
      Be not thy tongue thy own shame's orator;   10
Look sweet, speak fair, become disloyalty;°

Apparel vice like virtue's harbinger;°
Bear a fair presence, though your heart be tainted;
      Teach sin the carriage of a holy saint;
Be secret-false. What need she be acquainted?   15
      What simple thief brags of his own attaint?°
'Tis double wrong to truant with your bed
      And let her read it in thy looks at board.°
Shame hath a bastard fame, well managèd;°
      Ill deeds are doubled with an evil word.   20
Alas, poor women! Make us but believe,
      Being compact of credit,° that you love us.
Though others have the arm, show us the sleeve.
      We in your motion turn,° and you may move us.
Then, gentle Brother, get you in again;   25
      Comfort my sister, cheer her, call her wife.
'Tis holy sport to be a little vain,°
      When the sweet breath of flattery conquers strife.
      ANT. S. Sweet mistress — what your name is else,
          I know not,
Nor by what wonder you do hit of° mine —   30
Less in your knowledge and your grace you show
          not
Than our earth's wonder, more than earth divine.
Teach me, dear creature, how to think and speak.
      Lay open to my earthly-gross conceit,°
Smothered in errors, feeble, shallow, weak,   35
      The folded° meaning of your words' deceit.
Against my soul's pure truth why labor you
      To make it wander in an unknown field?
Are you a god? Would you create me new?   39
      Transform me, then, and to your power I'll yield.
But if that I am I, then well I know
      Your weeping sister is no wife of mine,
Nor to her bed no homage do I owe.
      Far more, far more to you do I decline.°   44
Oh, train° me not, sweet mermaid, with thy note,°
      To drown me in thy sister's flood of tears.
Sing, siren,° for thyself, and I will dote.
      Spread o'er the silver waves thy golden hairs,
And as a bed I'll take them, and there lie,
      And, in that glorious supposition, think   50
He gains by death that hath such means to die.
      Let Love, being light, be drownèd if she sink!
      LUC. What, are you mad, that you do reason° so?
      ANT. S. Not mad, but mated;° how, I do not know.
      LUC. It is a fault that springeth from your eye.   55
      ANT. S. For gazing on your beams, fair sun, be-
          ing by.

spectable.   **12. harbinger:** a Court officer sent ahead to make
preparations when the king traveled.   **16. attaint:** crime.
18. board: table.   **19. Shame . . . managed:** a man who conceals his misdeeds at least keeps his good reputation.   **22. compact of credit:** utterly credulous.   **24. We . . . turn:** i.e., when
you turn, we turn.   **27. vain:** false.   **30. hit of:** guess.
34. earthly-gross conceit: stupid intelligence.   **36. folded:**
hidden.   **44. decline:** incline.   **45. train . . . note:** Mermaids,
like the sirens, were supposed to lure amorous mariners to destruction by their sweet singing.   **train:** allure.   **47. siren:**
See *T Andr*, II.i.23,n.   **53. reason:** talk.   **54. mated:** amazed.

92. excuse: explain.   **93. made:** shut.   **99. stirring . . . day:**
i.e., when the streets are crowded.   **102. yet . . . estimation:**
hitherto unblemished reputation.   **105. slander . . . succession:**
one slander follows another.   **108. in . . . mirth:** although they
mock me.   **113. withal:** therewith.   **115. By this:** by this time.
116. Porpentine: porcupine, the name of an inn.
      Sc. ii: 11. become disloyalty: make your disloyalty look re-

LUC. Gaze where you should, and that will clear your sight.

ANT. S. As good to wink,° sweet love, as look on night.

LUC. Why call you me love? Call my sister so.

ANT. S. Thy sister's sister.

LUC.   That's my sister.

ANT. S.   No, 60
It is thyself, mine own self's better part,°
Mine eye's clear eye, my dear heart's dearer heart,
My food, my fortune, and my sweet hope's aim,
My sole earth's Heaven, and my Heaven's claim.°

LUC. All this my sister is, or else should be.   65

ANT. S. Call thyself sister, sweet, for I am thee.
Thee will I love, and with thee lead my life.
Thou hast no husband yet, nor I no wife.
Give me thy hand.

LUC.   Oh, soft, sir! Hold you still.   69
I'll fetch my sister to get her good will.°   [Exit.]
                    [Enter DROMIO S.]

ANT. S. Why, how now, Dromio! Where runn'st thou so fast?

DRO. S. Do you know me, sir? Am I Dromio? Am I your man? Am I myself?

ANT. S. Thou art Dromio, thou art my man, thou art thyself.   75

DRO. S. I am an ass, I am a woman's man, and besides myself.

ANT. S. What woman's man? And how besides thyself?   80

DRO. S. Marry, sir, besides myself, I am due to a woman — one that claims me, one that haunts me, one that will have me.

ANT. S. What claim lays she to thee?   84

DRO. S. Marry, sir, such claim as you would lay to your horse; and she would have me as a beast. Not that, I being a beast, she would have me, but that she, being a very beastly creature, lays claim to me.

ANT. S. What is she?   90

DRO. S. A very reverent body; aye, such a one as a man may not speak of without he say Sir-reverence.° I have but lean luck in the match, and yet is she a wondrous fat° marriage.

ANT. S. How dost thou mean a fat marriage?   95

DRO. S. Marry, sir, she's the kitchen wench, and all grease; and I know not what use to put her to, but to make a lamp of her, and run from her by her own light. I warrant, her rags, and the tallow in them, will burn a Poland winter.° If she lives   100 till doomsday, she'll burn a week longer than the whole world.

ANT. S. What complexion is she of?

DRO. S. Swart,° like my shoe, but her face nothing like so clean kept. For why° she sweats, a man   105 may go over shoes in the grime of it.

ANT. S. That's a fault that water will mend.

DRO. S. No, sir, 'tis in grain.° Noah's flood could not do it.

ANT. S. What's her name?   110

DRO. S. Nell, sir; but her name and three quarters, that's an ell° and three quarters, will not measure her from hip to hip.

ANT. S. Then she bears some breadth?

DRO. S. No longer from head to foot than   115 from hip to hip. She is spherical, like a globe. I could find out countries in her.

ANT. S. In what part of her body stands Ireland?

DRO. S. Marry, sir, in her buttocks. I found it out by the bogs.   121

ANT. S. Where Scotland?

DRO. S. I found it by the barrenness — hard in the palm of the hand.

ANT. S. Where France?°   125

DRO. S. In her forehead, armed and reverted, making war against her heir.

ANT. S. Where England?

DRO. S. I looked for the chalky cliffs, but I could find no whiteness in them; but I guess it stood   130 in her chin, by the salt rheum° that ran between France and it.

ANT. S. Where Spain?

DRO. S. 'Faith, I saw it not, but I felt it hot in her breath.   135

ANT. S. Where America, the Indies?

DRO. S. Oh, sir, upon her nose, all o'er embellished with rubies, carbuncles,° sapphires, declining their rich aspect° to the hot breath of Spain, who sent whole armadoes of carracks° to be ballast° at her nose.   141

ANT. S. Where stood Belgia, the Netherlands?

DRO. S. Oh, sir, I did not look so low.° To conclude, this drudge, or diviner,° laid claim to me, called me Dromio, swore I was assured° to her,   145 told me what privy° marks I had about me, as, the mark of my shoulder, the mole in my neck, the great wart on my left arm, that I, amazed, ran from her as a witch.
And, I think, if my breast had not been made of faith, and my heart of steel,   150

---

58. wink: shut the eyes.   61. It . . . part: See II.ii.123,n.
64. My . . . claim: my right to go to Heaven.   70. good will:
assent — an excuse to escape.   92. Sir-reverence: for "saving
your reverence," an apology for an unpleasant fact or improper
remark.   94. fat: rich.   99. Poland winter: i.e., which lasts
till summer — a long time.

104. Swart: black.   105. For why: because.   108. in grain: in
the grain, natural color. See *T Night*, I.v.255.   112. ell: 45
inches. Nell is thus an outsize — nearly 80 inches in circumference.   125. Where France: See *Errors* Intro. p. 270a.
131. rheum: moisture.   138. carbuncles: means also "boils."
138-39. declining . . . aspect: looking downward.   140. armadoes
. . . carracks: fleets of great merchant ships. See *Errors* Intro.
p. 270a-b. ballast: laden, freighted.   142-43. Belgia . . . low:
Belgium and the Netherlands are known also as the Low Countries.   144. diviner: witch — because she seems to have a supernatural knowledge.   145. assured: betrothed.   146. privy: secret.

She had transformed me to a curtal° dog, and made
    me turn i' the wheel.°
ANT. s. Go hie° thee presently, post° to the road.°
An if° the wind blow any way from shore,
I will not harbor in this town tonight.
If any bark put forth, come to the mart,   155
Where I will walk till thou return to me.
If every one knows us, and we know none,
'Tis time, I think, to trudge, pack, and be gone.
    DRO. s. As from a bear a man would run for life,
So fly I from her that would be my wife.   [*Exit.*]
    ANT. s. There's none but witches do inhabit here,
And therefore 'tis high time that I were hence.   162
She that doth call me husband, even my soul
Doth for a wife abhor. But her fair sister,
Possessed with such a gentle sovereign grace,   165
Of such enchanting presence and discourse,
Hath almost made me traitor to myself.
But, lest myself be guilty to self-wrong,
I'll stop mine ears against the mermaid's song.
    [*Enter* ANGELO *with the chain.*]
    ANG. Master Antipholus ——
    ANT. s.   Aye, that's my name.   170
    ANG. I know it well, sir. Lo, here is the chain.
I thought to have ta'en° you at the Porpentine.
The chain unfinished made me stay thus long.
    ANT. s. What is your will that I shall do with this?
    ANG. What please yourself, sir. I have made it for
    you.   175
    ANT. s. Made it for me, sir! I bespoke° it not.
    ANG. Not once, nor twice, but twenty times you
    have.
Go home with it, and please your wife withal,
And soon at suppertime I'll visit you,
And then receive my money for the chain.   180
    ANT. s. I pray you, sir, receive the money now,
For fear you ne'er see chain nor money more.
    ANG. You are a merry man, sir. Fare you well.
                                   [*Exit.*]
    ANT. s. What I should think of this I cannot tell;
But this I think, there's no man is so vain°   185
That would refuse so fair an offered chain.
I see a man here needs not live by shifts,°
When in the streets he meets such golden gifts.
I'll to the mart, and there for Dromio stay.
If any ship put out, then straight away.   [*Exit.*]

---

151. **curtal**: with tail cut short. **turn ... wheel**: In large
kitchens small dogs were used to turn the cooking spits. 152. **hie**:
hasten. **post**: go quickly. **road**: harbor. 153. **An if**: if.
172. **ta'en**: met you at. 176. **bespoke**: ordered. 185. **vain**:
foolish. 187. **shifts**: dishonest means.

Act IV

SCENE I. *A public place.*

[*Enter* SECOND MERCHANT, ANGELO, *and an* OFFICER.]
    2. MER. You know since Pentecost the sum is due,
And since,° I have not much importuned you;
Nor now I had not, but that I am bound
To Persia, and want guilders for my voyage.
Therefore make present° satisfaction,   5
Or I'll attach° you by this officer.
    ANG. Even just the sum that I do owe to you
Is growing° to me by Antipholus,
And in the instant that I met with you
He had of me a chain. At five o'clock   10
I shall receive the money for the same.
Pleaseth you walk with me down to his house,
I will discharge my bond, and thank you too.
    [*Enter* ANTIPHOLUS E. *and* DROMIO E. *from the
        courtesan's.*]
    OFF. That labor may you save. See where he
    comes.
    ANT. E. While I go to the goldsmith's house, go
    thou   15
And buy a rope's end. That will I bestow
Among my wife and her confederates,
For locking me out of my doors by day.
But, soft! I see the goldsmith. Get thee gone.
Buy thou a rope, and bring it home to me.   20
    DRO. E. I buy a thousand pound a year. I buy a
    rope.°   [*Exit.*]
    ANT. E. A man is well holp° up that trusts to you.
I promisèd your presence and the chain,
But neither chain nor goldsmith came to me.
Belike you thought our love would last too long   25
If it were chained together, and therefore came not.
    ANG. Saving° your merry humor, here's the note
How much your chain weighs to the utmost carat,
The fineness of the gold, and chargeful fashion,°
Which doth amount to three odd ducats more   30
Than I stand debted to this gentleman.
I pray you see him presently discharged,
For he is bound to sea, and stays but for it.
    ANT. E. I am not furnished° with the present
    money.
Besides, I have some business in the town.   35
Good signior, take the stranger to my house,

Act IV, Sc. i: 2. **since**: since then. 5. **present**: immediate.
6. **attach**: arrest. 8. **growing**: becoming due. The financial
arrangements of this scene are typical of Shakespeare's England.
Payment by check was unknown, and few men could lay hands
on a large sum in ready coin. Hence these involved transactions.
Any man at any time was liable to arrest for debt. 21. **I ...
rope**: a much disputed sentence. Probably Dromio means: "I
shall be as glad to buy a rope for my master to use on his wife as I
would be to make a thousand a year." 22. **holp**: helped.
27. **Saving**: with all respect to. 29. **chargeful fashion**: expense
of making it. 34. **furnished**: provided.

And with you take the chain, and bid my wife
Disburse the sum on the receipt thereof.
Perchance I will be there as soon as you.
   ANG. Then you will bring the chain to her your-
     self?   40
   ANT. E. No. Bear it with you, lest I come not time
     enough.
   ANG. Well, sir, I will. Have you the chain about
     you?
   ANT. E. And if I have not, sir, I hope you have,
Or else you may return without your money.
   ANG. Nay, come, I pray you, sir, give me the
     chain.   45
Both wind and tide stays for this gentleman,
And I, to blame, have held him here too long.
   ANT. E. Good Lord! You use this dalliance° to ex-
     cuse
Your breach of promise to the Porpentine.
I should have chid you for not bringing it,   50
But, like a shrew, you first begin to brawl.
   2. MER. The hour steals on. I pray you, sir, dis-
     patch.
   ANG. You hear how he importunes me — the
     chain!
   ANT. E. Why, give it to my wife, and fetch your
     money.
   ANG. Come, come, you know I gave it you even
     now.   55
Either send the chain, or send me by some token.°
   ANT. E. Fie, now you run this humor out of
     breath.°
Come, where's the chain? I pray you let me see it.
   2. MER. My business cannot brook this dalliance.
Good sir, say whether you'll answer me or no.   60
If not, I'll leave him to the officer.
   ANT. E. I answer you! What should I answer you?
   ANG. The money that you owe me for the chain.
   ANT. E. I owe you none till I receive the chain.
   ANG. You know I gave it you half an hour since.
   ANT. E. You gave me none. You wrong me much
     to say so.   66
   ANG. You wrong me more, sir, in denying it.
Consider how it stands upon° my credit.
   2. MER. Well, Officer, arrest him at my suit.
   OFF. I do, and charge you in the Duke's name to
     obey me.   70
   ANG. This touches me in reputation.
Either consent to pay this sum for me,
Or I attach you by this officer.
   ANT. E. Consent to pay thee that I never had!
Arrest me, foolish fellow, if thou darest.   75
   ANG. Here is thy fee; arrest him, Officer.
I would not spare my brother in this case,
If he should scorn me so apparently.°

OFF. I do arrest you, sir. You hear the suit.
   ANT. E. I do obey thee till I give thee bail.   80
But, sirrah, you shall buy this sport as dear
As all the metal in your shop will answer.
   ANG. Sir, sir, I shall have law in Ephesus
To your notorious shame. I doubt it not.
     [Enter DROMIO S., from the bay.]
   DRO. S. Master, there is a bark of Epidamnum   85
That stays but till her owner comes aboard,
And then, sir, she bears away.° Our fraughtage,°
     sir,
I have conveyed aboard, and I have bought
The oil, the balsamum,° and aqua vitae.°
The ship is in her trim;° the merry wind   90
Blows fair from land. They stay for naught at all
But for their owner, master, and yourself.
   ANT. E. How now! A madman! Why, thou peev-
     ish sheep,
What ship° of Epidamnum stays for me?   94
   DRO. S. A ship you sent me to, to hire waftage.°
   ANT. E. Thou drunken slave, I sent thee for a
     rope,
And told thee to what purpose and what end.
   DRO. S. You sent me for a rope's end as soon.°
You sent me to the bay, sir, for a bark.
   ANT. E. I will debate this matter at more leisure,
And teach your ears to list me with more heed.   101
To Adriana, villain, hie thee straight.
Give her this key, and tell her, in the desk
That's covered o'er with Turkish tapestry
There is a purse of ducats. Let her send it.   105
Tell her I am arrested in the street,
And that shall bail me. Hie thee, slave, be gone!
On, Officer, to prison till it come.
     [Exeunt SECOND MERCHANT, ANGELO,
          OFFICER, and ANTIPHOLUS E.]
   DRO. S. To Adriana! That is where we dined,
Where Dowsabel° did claim me for her husband.
She is too big, I hope, for me to compass.°   111
Thither I must, although against my will,
For servants must their masters' minds fulfil. [Exit.]

SCENE II. *The house of* ANTIPHOLUS E.

     [Enter ADRIANA and LUCIANA.]
   ADR. Ah, Luciana, did he tempt thee so?
Mightst thou perceive austerely° in his eye
That he did plead in earnest? Yea or no?
   Looked he or° red or pale, or sad or merrily?
What observation madest thou, in this case,   5

---

48. **dalliance:** trifling. See *I Hen VI*, V.ii.5. 56. **send . . . token:** send some token (e.g., a seal ring) that I am entitled to have it. 57. **run . . . breath:** carry this joke too far. 68. **stands upon:** concerns. 78. **apparently:** flagrantly, openly.

87. **bears away:** hoists sail. **fraughtage:** baggage. 89. **balsamum:** balm, valuable resin. **aqua vitae:** spirits. 90. **in . . . trim:** ready for sea. 93–94. **sheep . . . ship:** pronounced alike — a common pun. 95. **waftage:** passage. 98. **You . . . soon:** i.e., you would as soon have me hanged. 110. **Dowsabel:** Sweet and Lovely (*douce et belle*). 111. **compass:** win — and "get my arms round."
     Sc. ii: 2. **austerely:** seriously. 4. **or:** either.

Of his heart's meteors tilting in his face?°
 LUC. First he denied you had in him no right.
 ADR. He meant he did me none — the more my
  spite.°
 LUC. Then swore he that he was a stranger here.
 ADR. And true he swore, though yet forsworn° he
  were.   10
 LUC. Then pleaded I for you.
 ADR.   And what said he?
 LUC. That love I begged for you he begged of me.
 ADR. With what persuasion did he tempt thy
  love?
 LUC. With words that in an honest suit might
  move.
First he did praise my beauty, then my speech. 15
 ADR. Didst speak him fair?
 LUC.   Have patience, I beseech.
 ADR. I cannot, nor I will not, hold me still.
My tongue, though not my heart, shall have his
 will.°
He is deformèd, crookèd, old, and sere,°
Ill-faced, worse-bodied, shapeless everywhere, 20
Vicious, ungentle, foolish, blunt, unkind,
Stigmatical in making,° worse in mind.
 LUC. Who would be jealous, then, of such a one?
No evil lost is wailed when it is gone.
 ADR. Ah, but I think him better than I say, 25
And yet would herein others' eyes were worse.
Far from her nest the lapwing° cries away.
 My heart prays for him, though my tongue do
 curse.
    [*Enter* DROMIO S.]
 DRO. S. Here! Go! The desk, the purse! Sweet,
  now, make haste.
 LUC. How hast thou lost thy breath?
 DRO S.   By running fast. 30
 ADR. Where is thy master, Dromio? Is he well?
 DRO. S. No, he's in Tartar Limbo,° worse than
  Hell.
A devil in an everlasting garment° hath him;
One whose hard heart is buttoned up with steel,
A fiend, a fury, pitiless and rough, 35
A wolf, nay, worse — a fellow all in buff,°
A backfriend,° a shoulder clapper,° one that coun-
 termands°

The passages of alleys, creeks, and narrow lands,
A hound that runs counter,° and yet draws dry-
 foot° well,
One that, before the Judgment, carries poor souls
 to Hell.   40
 ADR. Why, man, what is the matter?
 DRO. S. I do not know the matter. He is 'rested on
  the case.°
 ADR. What, is he arrested? Tell me at whose suit.
 DRO. S. I know not at whose suit he is arrested
  well,
But he's in a suit of buff which 'rested him, that can
 I tell.   45
Will you send him, mistress, redemption, the money
 in his desk?
 ADR. Go fetch it, Sister. [*Exit* LUCIANA.] This I
  wonder at,
That he, unknown to me, should be in debt.
Tell me, was he arrested on a band?°
 DRO. S. Not on a band, but on a stronger thing —
A chain, a chain! Do you not hear it ring? 51
 ADR. What, the chain?
 DRO. S. No, no, the bell. 'Tis time that I were
  gone.
It was two ere I left him, and now the clock strikes
 one.
 ADR. The hours come back! That did I never hear.
 DRO. S. Oh, yes. If any hour meet a sergeant, a'°
  turns back for very fear. 56
 ADR. As if Time were in debt! How fondly dost
  thou reason!
 DRO. S. Time is a very bankrupt, and owes more
  than he's worth to season.°
Nay, he's a thief too. Have you not heard men say
That Time comes stealing on by night and day? 60
If Time be in debt and theft, and a sergeant in the
 way,
Hath he not reason to turn back an hour in a day?
    [*Re-enter* LUCIANA *with a purse.*]
 ADR. Go, Dromio. There's the money; bear it
  straight,
And bring thy master home immediately. 64
Come, Sister. I am pressed down with conceit° —
Conceit, my comfort and my injury. [*Exeunt.*]

SCENE III. *A public place.*

[*Enter* ANTIPHOLUS S.]
 ANT. S. There's not a man I meet but doth salute
  me
As if I were their well-acquainted friend,

---

6. **heart's . . . face**: a difficult phrase. A meteor was regarded as a sign of disaster or wonder. Adriana means: "What signs of disastrous passion did you observe rushing in his face?" 8. **spite**: grief. 10. **forsworn**: perjured. 18. **his will**: its desire. 19. **sere**: dried up. 22. **Stigmatical in making**: deformed in body. 27. **lapwing**: called also the peewit or plover. It tries to distract attention from its nest in this way. 32. **Tartar Limbo**: Limbo is the place where the good but unbaptized souls remain; Tartar, in classical mythology, the place where the wicked are punished. 33. **everlasting garment**: leather coat, the uniform of the sergeant of the law. See *I Hen IV*, I.ii.48,49,n. 36. **buff**: leather. 37. **backfriend**: false friend; also one who approaches from behind. **shoulder clapper**: In making formal arrest, the sergeant claps a man on the shoulder. **countermands**: prohibits.

39. **counter**: the wrong way of the scent, with a pun on "Counter," one of the prisons in the City of London. **draws dry-foot**: hunts by the scent of the foot. 42. **on . . . case**: The phrase, as so often in Dromio's speeches, has more than one meaning — "in a lawsuit" and "on his skin." 49. **band**: bond. 56. **a'**: he. 58. **season**: keep in good condition. 65. **conceit**: imagination.

And every one doth call me by my name.
Some tender money to me; some invite me;
Some other give me thanks for kindnesses;5
Some offer me commodities to buy.
Even now a tailor called me in his shop,
And showed me silks that he had bought for me,
And therewithal took measure of my body.
Sure, these are but imaginary wiles,°10
And Lapland sorcerers° inhabit here.

[Enter DROMIO S.*]*

DRO. S. Master, here's the gold you sent me for.
What, have you got the picture of old Adam new-
appareled?°

ANT. S. What gold is this? What Adam dost thou
mean?15

DRO. S. Not that Adam that kept the Paradise, but
that Adam that keeps the prison: he that goes in the
calf's skin that was killed for the Prodigal;° he that
came behind you, sir, like an evil angel, and bid you
forsake your liberty.20

ANT. S. I understand thee not.

DRO. S. No? Why, 'tis a plain case. He that went,
like a bass viol, in a case of leather; the man, sir,
that, when gentlemen are tired, gives them a sob,°
and 'rests° them; he, sir, that takes pity on decayed
men, and gives them suits of durance;° he that26
sets up his rest° to do more exploits with his mace°
than a morris-pike.°

ANT. S. What, thou meanest an officer?

DRO. S. Aye, sir, the sergeant of the band; he30
that brings any man to answer it that breaks his
band; one that thinks a man always going to bed,
and says, "God give you good rest!"°

ANT. S. Well, sir, there rest in your foolery. Is
there any ship puts forth tonight? May we be35
gone?

DRO. S. Why, sir, I brought you word an hour
since, that the bark *Expedition* put forth tonight;
and then were you hindered by the sergeant to
tarry° for the hoy° *Delay.* Here are the angels°40
that you sent for to deliver you.

ANT. S. The fellow is distract, and so am I,
And here we wander in illusions.

Some blessed power deliver us from hence!

[Enter a COURTESAN.*]*

COUR. Well met, well met, Master Antipholus.
I see, sir, you have found the goldsmith now.46
Is that the chain you promised me today?

ANT. S. Satan, avoid!° I charge thee, tempt me
not.

DRO. S. Master, is this Mistress Satan?

ANT. S. It is the Devil.50

DRO. S. Nay, she is worse, she is the Devil's dam;°
and here she comes in the habit° of a light wench.
And thereof comes that the wenches say, "God
damn me." That's as much to say, "God make me
a light wench." It is written they appear to men55
like angels of light. Light is an effect° of fire, and
fire will burn; ergo, light wenches will burn. Come
not near her.

COUR. Your man and you are marvelous merry,
sir.
Will you go with me? We'll mend° our dinner
here?60

DRO. S. Master, if you do, expect spoon meat,° or
bespeak° a long spoon.°

ANT. S. Why, Dromio?

DRO. S. Marry, he must have a long spoon that
must eat with the Devil.65

ANT. S. Avoid then, fiend! What tell'st thou me of
supping?
Thou art, as you are all, a sorceress.
I conjure thee to leave me and be gone.

COUR. Give me the ring of mine you had at din-
ner,
Or, for my diamond, the chain you promised,70
And I'll be gone, sir, and not trouble you.

DRO. S. Some devils ask but the parings of one's
nail,
A rush, a hair, a drop of blood, a pin,
A nut, a cherry stone;°
But she, more covetous, would have a chain.75
Master, be wise. An if you give it her,
The Devil will shake her chain, and fright us with
it.

COUR. I pray you, sir, my ring, or else the chain.
I hope you do not mean to cheat me so.

ANT. S. Avaunt,° thou witch! Come, Dromio, let
us go.80

DRO. S. "Fly pride," says the peacock.° Mistress,
that you know.

[Exeunt ANTIPHOLUS S. *and* DROMIO S.*]*

COUR. Now, out of doubt Antipholus is mad,

Sc. iii: **10. imaginary wiles:** tricks that have no real existence.
11. Lapland sorcerers: Those who lived in the dark north were
regarded as creatures of darkness. **13. got . . . new-appareled:**
a much disputed and emended remark. Dromio probably
means: "Have you got out of your 'paradise,' like Adam when he
left the Garden of Eden newly clad in the skins of animals."
17–18. goes . . . Prodigal: who wears the skin of the calf killed
for the prodigal son; i.e., the sergeant. We do not get clear of the
joke about the sergeant's leather coat (see IV.ii.33,n) until l. 28.
24. sob: in some texts emended to *bob:* tap. **25. 'rests:** arrests.
26. suits of durance: suits that last forever; i.e., prison.
27. sets . . . rest: lit., plays a high stake, with a pun on "arrest."
mace: the staff of office carried by the sergeant. See *Caesar,*
IV.iii.268,n. **28. morris-pike:** Moorish pike: See Pl. 21d. **33. good
rest:** yet another pun on "arrest." **40. tarry:** wait. **hoy:**
small coasting vessel, the bark being a seagoing craft. **angels:**
worth 10*s.* See App. 27, and Pl. 10c.

48. avoid: be gone! **51. dam:** mother. **52. habit:** dress.
56. effect: result. **60. mend:** make up, get more. **61. spoon meat:**
pap. **62. bespeak:** order. **long spoon:** See *Temp,* II.ii.103,.n.
72–74: parings . . . cherry stone: Witches intending mischief required something belonging to the victim over which to conjure.
80. Avaunt: be off! **81. Fly . . . peacock:** The peacock is the
proudest of birds; for the peacock to decry pride is the greatest
hypocrisy.

Else would he never so demean himself.
A ring he hath of mine worth forty ducats,
And for the same he promised me a chain.   85
Both one and other he denies me now.
The reason that I gather he is mad,
Besides this present instance of his rage,
Is a mad tale he told today at dinner   89
Of his own doors being shut against his entrance.
Belike° his wife, acquainted with his fits,
On purpose shut the doors against his way.
My way is now to hie home to his house,
And tell his wife that, being lunatic,
He rushed into my house, and took perforce   95
My ring away. This course I fittest° choose;
For forty ducats is too much to lose.   [*Exit.*]

SCENE IV. *A street.*

[*Enter* ANTIPHOLUS E. *and the* OFFICER.]

ANT. E. Fear me not, man. I will not break away.
I'll give thee, ere I leave thee, so much money,
To warrant° thee, as I am 'rested for.
My wife is in a wayward mood today,
And will not lightly trust the messenger.   5
That I should be attached° in Ephesus,
I tell you, 'twill sound harshly in her ears.

[*Enter* DROMIO E. *with a rope's end.*]

Here comes my man. I think he brings the money.
How now, sir! Have you that I sent you for?

DRO. E. Here's that, I warrant you, will pay them
all.   10

ANT. E. But where's the money?

DRO. E. Why, sir, I gave the money for the rope.

ANT. E. Five hundred ducats, villain, for a rope?

DRO. E. I'll serve you, sir, five hundred at the
rate.°

ANT. E. To what end did I bid thee hie thee
home?   15

DRO. E. To a rope's end, sir, and to that end am I
returned.

ANT. E. And to that end, sir, I will welcome you.
[*Beating him.*]

OFF. Good sir, be patient.

DRO. E. Nay, 'tis for me to be patient. I am in   21
adversity.

OFF. Good now,° hold thy tongue.

DRO. E. Nay, rather persuade him to hold his
hands.

ANT. E. Thou whoreson,° senseless villain!   25

DRO. E. I would I were senseless, sir, that I might
not feel your blows.

ANT. E. Thou art sensible° in nothing but blows,
and so is an ass.

DRO. E. I am an ass, indeed. You may prove   30
it by my long ears. I have served him from the hour
of my nativity to this instant, and have nothing at
his hands for my service but blows. When I am
cold, he heats me with beating. When I am warm,
he cools me with beating. I am waked with it   35
when I sleep, raised with it when I sit, driven out of
doors with it when I go from home, welcomed
home with it when I return. Nay, I bear it on my
shoulders, as a beggar wont° her brat; and, I think,
when he hath lamed me, I shall beg with it from
door to door.   41

ANT. E. Come, go along. My wife is coming yonder.

[*Enter* ADRIANA, LUCIANA, *the* COURTESAN, *and*
PINCH.]

DRO. E. Mistress, *respice finem,* respect your end;
or rather, the prophecy like the parrot, " Beware
the rope's end."°   46

ANT. E. Wilt thou still talk?   [*Beating him.*]

COUR. How say you now? Is not your husband
mad?

ADR. His incivility° confirms no less.
Good Doctor Pinch, you are a conjurer.   50
Establish him in his true sense again,
And I will please you what you will demand.°

LUC. Alas, how fiery and how sharp he looks!

COUR. Mark how he trembles in his ecstasy!°

PINCH. Give me your hand, and let me feel your
pulse.   55

ANT. E. There is my hand, and let it feel your ear.
[*Striking him.*]

PINCH. I charge thee, Satan, housed within this
man,
To yield possession to my holy prayers,
And to thy state of darkness hie thee straight.
I conjure thee by all the saints in Heaven!   60

ANT. E. Peace, doting wizard, peace! I am not
mad.

ADR. Oh, that thou wert not, poor distressèd soul!

ANT. E. You minion, you, are these your custom-
ers?
Did this companion° with the saffron° face
Revel and feast it at my house today,   65
Whilst upon me the guilty doors were shut,
And I denied to enter in my house?

ADR. O Husband, God doth know you dined at
home,
Where would you had remained until this time,
Free from these slanders and this open shame!   70

---

91. Belike: probably.   96. fittest: most suitable.
Sc. iv: 3. warrant: give security.   6. attached: arrested.
14. at . . . rate: at that price.   22. Good now: my good man.
25. whoreson: lit., son of a whore, "son of a bitch."   28. sensible: able to feel.

39. wont: is accustomed to.   44–46. *respice . . . end:* a common pun. *Respice finem* means "remember the end" (i.e., your
eternal salvation); *respice funem* means "remember the rope"
(i.e., the reward for crime). *Respice finem* was one of the phrases
taught to parrots in the houses of the godly.   49. incivility:
wild behavior.   52. please . . . demand: pay whatever you ask.
54. ecstasy: fit of madness.   64. companion: fellow. saffron:
yellow

ANT. E. Dined at home! Thou villain, what sayest thou?

DRO. E. Sir, sooth to say,° you did not dine at
home.

ANT. E. Were not my doors locked up, and I shut
out?

DRO. E. Perdie,° your doors were locked, and you
shut out.   74

ANT. E. And did not she herself revile me there?

DRO. E. Sans fable,° she herself reviled you there.

ANT. E. Did not her kitchen maid rail, taunt, and
scorn me?

DRO. E. Certes,° she did. The kitchen vestal
scorned you.

ANT. E. And did not I in rage depart from thence?

DRO. E. In verity you did. My bones bear witness,
That since have felt the vigor of his rage.   81

ADR. Is 't good to soothe him in these contraries?

PINCH. It is no shame. The fellow finds his vein,°
And yielding to him humors well his frenzy.

ANT. E. Thou hast suborned° the goldsmith to arrest me.   85

ADR. Alas, I sent you money to redeem you
By Dromio here, who came in haste for it.

DRO. E. Money by me! Heart and good will you
might,
But surely, master, not a rag of money.

ANT. E. Went'st not thou to her for a purse of
ducats?   90

ADR. He came to me, and I delivered it.

LUC. And I am witness with her that she did.

DRO. E. God and the ropemaker bear me witness
That I was sent for nothing but a rope!

PINCH. Mistress, both man and master is pos-
sessed.   95
I know it by their pale and deadly looks.
They must be bound, and laid in some dark room.°

ANT. E. Say, wherefore didst thou lock me forth
today?
And why dost thou deny the bag of gold?   99

ADR. I did not, gentle Husband, lock thee forth.

DRO. E. And, gentle master, I received no gold,
But I confess, sir, that we were locked out.

ADR. Dissembling° villain, thou speakest false in
both.

ANT. E. Dissembling harlot, thou art false in all,
And art confederate with a damnèd pack   105
To make a loathsome abject scorn of me.
But with these nails I'll pluck out these false eyes
That would behold in me this shameful sport.

[*Enter three or four, and offer to bind him. He
strives.*]

ADR. Oh, bind him, bind him! Let him not come
near me.

PINCH. More company! The fiend is strong within
him.   110

LUC. Aye me, poor man, how pale and wan he
looks!

ANT. E. What, will you murder me? Thou jailer,
thou,
I am thy prisoner. Wilt thou suffer them
To make a rescue?

OFF.   Masters, let him go.
He is my prisoner, and you shall not have him.   115

PINCH. Go bind this man, for he is frantic too.

[*They offer to bind* DROMIO E.]

ADR. What wilt thou do, thou peevish Officer?
Hast thou delight to see a wretched man
Do outrage and displeasure to himself?

OFF. He is my prisoner. If I let him go,   120
The debt he owes will be required of me.

ADR. I will discharge thee° ere I go from thee.
Bear me forthwith unto his creditor,
And, knowing how the debt grows,° I will pay it.
Good Master Doctor, see him safe conveyed   125
Home to my house. Oh, most unhappy day!

ANT. E. Oh, most unhappy strumpet!

DRO. E. Master, I am here entered in bond for you.

ANT. E. Out on thee, villain! Wherefore dost thou
mad° me?   129

DRO. E. Will you be bound for nothing? Be mad,
good master. Cry, The Devil!

LUC. God help, poor souls, how idly do they talk!

ADR. Go bear him hence. Sister, go you with me.

[*Exeunt all but* ADRIANA, LUCIANA,
OFFICER, *and* COURTESAN.]

Say, now, whose suit is he arrested at?

OFF. One Angelo, a goldsmith. Do you know
him?   135

ADR. I know the man. What is the sum he owes?

OFF. Two hundred ducats.

ADR.   Say how grows it due?

OFF. Due for a chain your husband had of him.

ADR. He did bespeak a chain for me, but had it
not.   139

COUR. When as your husband, all in rage, today
Came to my house, and took away my ring —
The ring I saw upon his finger now —
Straight after did I meet him with a chain.

ADR. It may be so, but I did never see it.
Come, jailer, bring me where the goldsmith is.   145
I long to know the truth hereof at large.

[*Enter* ANTIPHOLUS S., *with his rapier drawn, and*
DROMIO S.]

LUC. God, for thy mercy! They are loose again.

ADR. And come with naked swords.
Let's call more help to have them bound again.

---

72. **sooth to say:** to tell the truth.   74. **Perdie:** by God.
76. **Sans fable:** no lying; i.e., you are speaking the truth.
78. **Certes:** for sure.   83. **vein:** mood.   85. **suborned:** instigated.   97. **bound . . . room:** This was the usual treatment for
lunatics. See *T Night*, IV.ii and V.i.348–50 for the treatment of
Malvolio's supposed lunacy.   103. **Dissembling:** cheating, false.

122. **discharge thee:** relieve you of the responsibility of the debt.
124. **grows:** is due.   129. **mad:** make mad.

OFF. Away! They'll kill us.   150
[*Exeunt all but* ANTIPHOLUS S. *and* DROMIO S.]
ANT. S. I see these witches are afraid of swords.
DRO. S. She that would be your wife now ran
    from you.
ANT. S. Come to the Centaur. Fetch our stuff
    from thence.
I long that we were safe and sound aboard.   154
    DRO. S. Faith, stay here this night. They will
surely do us no harm. You saw they speak us fair,
give us gold. Methinks they are such a gentle na-
tion that, but for the mountain of mad flesh that
claims marriage of me, I could find in my heart to
stay here still,° and turn witch.   160
    ANT. S. I will not stay tonight for all the town.
Therefore away, to get our stuff aboard. [*Exeunt.*]

Act V

SCENE I. *A street before a Priory.*

[*Enter* SECOND MERCHANT *and* ANGELO.]
    ANG. I am sorry, sir, that I have hindered you;
But, I protest, he had the chain of me,
Though most dishonestly he doth deny it.
    2. MER. How is the man esteemed here in the
    city?
    ANG. Of very reverent reputation, sir,   5
Of credit infinite, highly beloved,
Second to none that lives here in the city.
His word might bear my wealth° at any time.
    2. MER. Speak softly. Yonder, as I think, he walks.
[*Enter* ANTIPHOLUS S. *and* DROMIO S.]
    ANG. 'Tis so; and that self chain about his neck,
Which he forswore° most monstrously to have.   11
Good sir, draw near to me. I'll speak to him.
Signior Antipholus, I wonder much
That you would put me to this shame and trouble,
And, not without some scandal to yourself,   15
With circumstance° and oaths so to deny
This chain which now you wear so openly.
Beside the charge, the shame, imprisonment,
You have done wrong to this my honest friend,
Who, but for staying on our controversy,   20
Had hoisted sail and put to sea today.
This chain you had of me. Can you deny it?
    ANT. S. I think I had. I never did deny it.
    2. MER. Yes, that you did, sir, and forswore it too.
    ANT. S. Who heard me to deny it or forswear it?

    2. MER. These ears of mine, thou know'st, did
    hear thee.   26
Fie on thee, wretch! 'Tis pity that thou livest
To walk where any honest men resort.
    ANT. S. Thou are a villain to impeach° me thus.
I'll prove mine honor and mine honesty   30
Against thee presently,° if thou darest stand.°
    2. MER. I dare, and do defy thee for a villain.
                     [*They draw.*]
[*Enter* ADRIANA, LUCIANA, *the* COURTESAN, *and*
    OTHERS.]
    ADR. Hold, hurt him not, for God's sake! He is
    mad.
Some get within him,° take his sword away.
Bind Dromio too, and bear them to my house.   35
    DRO. S. Run, master, run; for God's sake, take° a
    house!
This is some priory. In, or we are spoiled!
[*Exeunt* ANTIPHOLUS S. *and* DROMIO S. *to the Priory.*]
    [*Enter* AEMILIA, *the Lady Abbess*]
    AEM. Be quiet, people. Wherefore throng you
    hither?
    ADR. To fetch my poor distracted husband hence.
Let us come in, that we may bind him fast,   40
And bear him home for his recovery.
    ANG. I knew he was not in his perfect wits.
    2. MER. I am sorry now that I did draw on him.
    AEM. How long hath this possession held the
    man?
    ADR. This week he hath been heavy, sour, sad,   45
And much different from the man he was,
But till this afternoon his passion
Ne'er brake into extremity of rage.
    AEM. Hath he not lost much wealth by wreck of
    sea?
Buried some dear friend? Hath not else his eye   50
Strayed his affection in unlawful love?
A sin prevailing much in youthful men,
Who give their eyes the liberty of gazing.
Which of these sorrows is he subject to?   54
    ADR. To none of these, except it be the last—
Namely, some love that drew him oft from home.
    AEM. You should for that have reprehended him.
    ADR. Why so I did.
    AEM.   Aye, but not rough enough.
    ADR. As roughly as my modesty would let me.
    AEM. Haply in private.
    ADR.   And in assemblies too.   60
    AEM. Aye, but not enough.
    ADR. It was the copy° of our conference.
In bed, he slept not for° my urging it;
At board, he fed not for my urging it;
Alone, it was the subject of my theme;   65
In company I often glanced° it;

---

160. still: always.
    Act V, Sc. i: 8. word ... wealth: I would have trusted him
with my wealth on his mere word.   11. forswore: denied an
oath.   16. circumstance: with detailed argument.

29. impeach: accuse.   31. presently: immediately. stand: i.e.,
fight.   34. within him: under his guard.   36. take: get inside.
62. copy: topic.   63. for: because of.   66. glanced: referred to.

Still did I tell him it was vile and bad.
AEM. And thereof came it that the man was mad.
The venom clamors of a jealous woman
Poisons more deadly than a mad dog's tooth.   70
It seems his sleeps were hindered by thy railing,
And thereof comes it that his head is light.
Thou say'st his meat was sauced with thy upbraidings;
Unquiet meals make ill digestions.
Thereof the raging fire of fever bred,   75
And what's a fever but a fit of madness?
Thou say'st his sports were hindered by thy brawls.
Sweet recreation barred, what doth ensue
But moody and dull Melancholy,
Kinsman to grim and comfortless Despair,   80
And at her heels a huge infectious troop
Of pale distemperatures° and foes to life?
In food, in sport, and life-preserving rest
To be disturbed, would mad or man or beast.
The consequence is, then, thy jealous fits   85
Have scared thy husband from the use of wits.
LUC. She never reprehended him but mildly,
When he demeaned himself rough, rude, and
    wildly.
Why bear you these rebukes, and answer not?
ADR. She did betray me to my own reproof.°   90
Good people, enter, and lay hold on him.
AEM. No, not a creature enters in my house.
ADR. Then let your servants bring my husband
    forth.
AEM. Neither. He took this place for sanctuary,
And it shall privilege him from your hands   95
Till I have brought him to his wits again,
Or lose my labor in assaying° it.
ADR. I will attend my husband, be his nurse,
Diet his sickness, for it is my office,
And will have no attorney° but myself;   100
And therefore let me have him home with me.
AEM. Be patient, for I will not let him stir
Till I have used the approvèd means I have,
With wholesome syrups, drugs, and holy prayers,
To make of him a formal° man again.   105
It is a branch and parcel of mine oath,
A charitable duty of my order.
Therefore depart, and leave him here with me.
ADR. I will not hence and leave my husband here.
And ill it doth beseem your Holiness   110
To separate the husband and the wife.
AEM. Be quiet and depart. Thou shalt not have
    him.   [Exit.]
LUC. Complain unto the Duke of this indignity.
ADR. Come, go. I will fall prostrate at his feet,
And never rise until my tears and prayers   115
Have won his Grace to come in person hither,

And take perforce my husband from the abbess.
2. MER. By this, I think, the dial° points at five.
Anon,° I'm sure, the Duke himself in person
Comes this way to the melancholy vale,   120
The place of death and sorry execution,
Behind the ditches of the abbey here.
ANG. Upon what cause?
2. MER. To see a reverend Syracusian merchant,
Who put unluckily into this bay   125
Against the laws and statutes of this town,
Beheaded publicly for his offense.
ANG. See where they come. We will behold his
    death.
LUC. Kneel to the Duke before he pass the abbey.
[Enter DUKE, attended, AEGEON bareheaded, with
    the HEADSMAN and other OFFICERS.]
DUKE. Yet once again proclaim it publicly,   130
If any friend will pay the sum for him,
He shall not die; so much we tender° him.
ADR. Justice, most sacred Duke, against the abbess!
DUKE. She is a virtuous and a reverend lady.
It cannot be that she hath done thee wrong.   135
ADR. May it please your Grace, Antipholus my
    husband —
Whom I made lord of me and all I had,
At your important° letters — this ill day
A most outrageous fit of madness took him,   139
That desperately he hurried through the street —
With him his bondman, all as mad as he —
Doing displeasure to the citizens
By rushing in their houses, bearing thence
Rings, jewels, anything his rage did like.   144
Once did I get him bound, and sent him home,
Whilst to take order for the wrongs I went,
That here and there his fury had committed.
Anon, I wot° not by what strong° escape,
He broke from those that had the guard of him,
And with his mad attendant and himself,   150
Each one with ireful passion, with drawn swords,
Met us again, and, madly bent on° us,
Chased us away; till, raising of more aid,
We came again to bind them. Then they fled
Into this abbey, whither we pursued them,   155
And here the abbess shuts the gates on us,
And will not suffer us to fetch him out,
Nor send him forth, that we may bear him hence.
Therefore, most gracious Duke, with thy command
Let him be brought forth, and borne hence for help.
DUKE. Long since thy husband served me in my
    wars,   161
And I to thee engaged a prince's word,
When thou didst make him master of thy bed,
To do him all the grace and good I could.

---

82. distemperatures: illnesses.   90. betray . . . reproof: she has made me confess that I was in the wrong.   97. assaying: attempting.   100. attorney: agent.   105. formal: normal.

118. dial: hand of the clock.   119. Anon: soon.   132. tender: allow.   138. important: of great weight, which had to be obeyed.   148. wot: know. strong: forcible.   152. bent on: threatened.

Go, some of you, knock at the abbey gate,   165
And bid the lady abbess come to me.
I will determine this before I stir.

[Enter a SERVANT.*]*

SERV. O mistress, mistress, shift and save your-
     self!
My master and his man are both broke loose,
Beaten the maids a-row,° and bound the doctor,
Whose beard they have singed off with brands of
     fire;   171
And ever, as it blazed, they threw on him
Great pails of puddled mire to quench the hair.
My master preaches patience to him, and the while
His man with scissors nicks him like a fool;°   175
And sure, unless you send some present° help,
Between them they will kill the conjurer.

ADR. Peace, fool! Thy master and his man are
     here;
And that is false thou dost report to us.

SERV. Mistress, upon my life, I tell you true.   180
I have not breathed almost since I did see it.
He cries for you, and vows, if he can take you,
To scorch your face and to disfigure you.

[Cry within.]

Hark, hark! I hear him, mistress. Fly, be gone!

DUKE. Come, stand by me. Fear nothing. Guard
     with halberds!°   185

ADR. Aye me, it is my husband! Witness you
That he is borne about invisible.
Even now we housed him in the abbey here,
And now he's there, past thought of human reason.

[Enter ANTIPHOLUS E. *and* DROMIO E.*]*

ANT. E. Justice, most gracious Duke, oh, grant me
     justice!   190
Even for the service that long since I did thee,
When I bestrid° thee in the wars and took
Deep scars to save thy life, even for the blood
That then I lost for thee, now grant me justice.

AEG. Unless the fear of death doth make me dote,
I see my son Antipholus, and Dromio.   196

ANT. E. Justice, sweet Prince, against that woman
     there!
She whom thou gavest to me to be my wife,
That hath abusèd and dishonored me
Even in the strength and height of injury.°   200
Beyond imagination is the wrong
That she this day hath shameless thrown on me.

DUKE. Discover° how, and thou shalt find me
     just.

ANT. E. This day, great Duke, she shut the doors
     upon me,
While she with harlots° feasted in my house.   205

170. **a-row:** all in a row, one after the other.   175. **nicks . . .
fool:** cuts his hair to make him look like a fool.   176. **present:**
immediate.   185. **halberds:** See Pl. 21b.   192. **bestrid:** stood
over when down. See *Cor,* II.ii.96–97.   200. **in . . . injury:** in
the most injurious manner.   203. **Discover:** reveal.   205. **harlots:** low companions.

DUKE. A grievous fault! Say, woman, didst thou
     so?

ADR. No, my good lord. Myself, he and my sister
Today did dine together. So befall my soul
As this is false he burdens me withal!

LUC. Ne'er may I look on day, nor sleep on night,
But she tells to your Highness simple truth!   211

ANG. Oh, perjured woman! They are both for-
     sworn.
In this the madman justly chargeth them.

ANT. E. My liege, I am advisèd what I say —
Neither disturbed with the effect of wine,   215
Nor heady-rash, provoked with raging ire,
Albeit my wrongs might make one wiser mad.
This woman locked me out this day from dinner.
That goldsmith there, were he not packed° with
     her,
Could witness it, for he was with me then,   220
Who parted with me to go fetch a chain,
Promising to bring it to the Porpentine,
Where Balthazar and I did dine together.
Our dinner done, and he not coming thither,
I went to seek him. In the street I met him,   225
And in his company, that gentleman.
There did this perjured goldsmith swear me down
That I this day of him received the chain,
Which, God He knows, I saw not; for the which
He did arrest me with an officer.   230
I did obey, and sent my peasant home
For certain ducats. He with none returned.
Then fairly I bespoke the officer
To go in person with me to my house.
By the way we met my wife, her sister, and a rab-
     ble more   235
Of vile confederates. Along with them
They brought one Pinch, a hungry° lean-faced vil-
     lain,
A mere anatomy,° a mountebank,
A threadbare juggler, and a fortuneteller,
A needy, hollow-eyed, sharp-looking wretch,   240
A living dead man. This pernicious slave,
Forsooth, took on him as a conjurer,
And, gazing in mine eyes, feeling my pulse,
And with no face, as 'twere, outfacing° me,
Cries out I was possessed. Then all together   245
They fell upon me, bound me, bore me thence,
And in a dark and dankish vault at home
There left me and my man, both bound together.
Till, gnawing with my teeth my bonds in sunder,
I gained my freedom, and immediately   250
Ran hither to your Grace, whom I beseech
To give me ample satisfaction
For these deep shames and great indignities.

219. **packed:** confederate.   237–41. **hungry . . . man:** Cf. description of the apothecary in *R & J,* V.i.37–75 and see Gen.
Intro. p. 60a.   238. **anatomy:** skeleton.   244. **outfacing:** staring
at, trying to intimidate.

ANG. My lord, in truth, thus far I witness with
    him,   254
That he dined not at home, but was locked out.
    DUKE. But had he such a chain of thee or no?
    ANG. He had, my lord, and when he ran in here,
These people saw the chain about his neck.
    2. MER. Besides, I will be sworn these ears of
    mine
Heard you confess you had the chain of him, 260
After you first forswore it on the mart.
And thereupon I drew my sword on you,
And then you fled into this abbey here,
From whence, I think, you are come by miracle.
    ANT. E. I never came within these abbey walls,
Nor ever didst thou draw thy sword on me. 266
I never saw the chain, so help me Heaven!
And this is false you burden me withal.
    DUKE. Why, what an intricate impeach° is this!
I think you all have drunk of Circe's cup.° 270
If here you housed him, here he would have been.
If he were mad, he would not plead so coldly.°
You say he dined at home. The goldsmith here
Denies that saying. Sirrah, what say you?
    DRO. E. Sir, he dined with her there, at the Por-
    pentine.   275
    COUR. He did, and from my finger snatched that
    ring.
    ANT. E. 'Tis true, my liege. This ring I had of her.
    DUKE. Saw'st thou him enter at the abbey here?
    COUR. As sure, my liege, as I do see your Grace.
    DUKE. Why, this is strange. Go call the abbess
    hither.   280
I think you are all mated,° or stark mad.
                [*Exit one to* AEMILIA.]
    AEG. Most mighty Duke, vouchsafe me speak a
    word.
Haply I see a friend will save my life,
And pay the sum that may deliver me. 284
    DUKE. Speak freely, Syracusian, what thou wilt.
    AEG. Is not your name, sir, called Antipholus?
And is not that your bondman, Dromio?
    DRO. E. Within this hour I was his bondman, sir,
But he, I thank him, gnawed in two my cords.
Now am I Dromio, and his man unbound. 290
    AEG. I am sure you both of you remember me.
    DRO. E. Ourselves we do remember, sir, by you,
For lately we were bound, as you are now.
You are not Pinch's patient, are you, sir?
    AEG. Why look you strange on me? You know
    me well.   295
    ANT. E. I never saw you in my life till now.
    AEG. Oh, grief hath changed me since you saw
    me last,
And careful° hours with Time's deformèd° hand

Have written strange defeatures° in my face;
But tell me yet, dost thou not know my voice? 300
    ANT. E. Neither.
    AEG. Dromio, nor thou?
    DRO. E.   No, trust me, sir, nor I.
    AEG. I am sure thou dost.
    DRO. E. Aye, sir, but I am sure I do not; and what-
soever a man denies, you are now bound to believe
him.   306
    AEG. Not know my voice! O Time's extremity,
Hast thou so cracked and splittèd my poor tongue
In seven short years that here my only son
Knows not my feeble key of untuned cares?° 310
Though now this grainèd° face of mine be hid
In sap-consuming winter's drizzled snow,
And all the conduits of my blood froze up,
Yet hath my night of life some memory,
My wasting lamps° some fading glimmer left, 315
My dull deaf ears a little use to hear.
All these old witnesses — I cannot err —
Tell me thou art my son Antipholus.
    ANT. E. I never saw my father in my life.
    AEG. But seven years since, in Syracusa, boy, 320
Thou know'st we parted. But perhaps, my son,
Thou shamest to acknowledge me in misery.
    ANT. E. The Duke and all that know me in the
    city
Can witness with me that it is not so.
I ne'er saw Syracusa in my life. 325
    DUKE. I tell thee, Syracusian, twenty years
Have I been patron to Antipholus,
During which time he ne'er saw Syracusa.
I see thy age and dangers make thee dote 329
    [*Re-enter* AEMILIA, *with* ANTIPHOLUS S.
              and DROMIO S.]
    AEM. Most mighty Duke, behold a man much
    wronged.   [*All gather to see them.*]
    ADR. I see two husbands, or mine eyes deceive me.
    DUKE. One of these men is Genius° to the other,
And so of these. Which is the natural man,
And which the spirit? Who deciphers them? 334
    DRO. S. I, sir, am Dromio. Command him away.
    DRO. E. I, sir, am Dromio. Pray, let me stay.
    ANT. S. Aegeon art thou not? Or else his ghost?
    DRO. S. Oh, my old master! Who hath bound him
    here?
    AEM. Whoever bound him, I will loose his bonds,
And gain a husband by his liberty. 340
Speak, old Aegeon, if thou be'st the man
That hadst a wife once called Aemilia,
That bore thee at a burden two fair sons.
Oh, if thou be'st the same Aegeon, speak,
And speak unto the same Aemilia! 345
    AEG. If I dream not, thou art Aemilia.

---

269. impeach: accusation.   270. Circe's cup: See *I Hen VI*,
V.iii.35,n.   272. coldly: rationally.   281. mated: bewildered.
298. careful: full of cares. deformed: deforming.

299. defeatures: changes of feature. 310. feeble . . . cares: my
voice made feeble by my sorrows. 311. grained: lined.
315. lamps: eyes. 332. Genius: guardian spirit.

If thou art she, tell me, where is that son
That floated with thee on the fatal raft?
  AEM. By men of Epidamnum he and I
And the twin Dromio, all were taken up.   350
But by and by rude fishermen of Corinth
By force took Dromio and my son from them,
And me they left with those of Epidamnum.
What then became of them I cannot tell;
I to this fortune that you see me in.   355
  DUKE. Why, here begins this morning story right.
These two Antipholuses, these two so like,
And these two Dromios, one in semblance —
Besides her urging° of her wreck at sea —
These are the parents to these children,°   360
Which accidentally are met together.
Antipholus, thou camest from Corinth first?
  ANT. S. No, sir, not I. I came from Syracuse.
  DUKE. Stay, stand apart. I know not which is
    which.
  ANT. E. I came from Corinth, my most gracious
    lord ——   365
  DRO. E. And I with him.
  ANT. E. Brought to this town by that most famous
    warrior,
Duke Menaphon, your most renownèd uncle.
  ADR. Which of you two did dine with me today?
  ANT. S. I, gentle mistress.
  ADR.   And are not you my husband?   370
  ANT. E. No. I say nay to that.
  ANT. S. And so do I; yet did she call me so.
And this fair gentlewoman, her sister here,
Did call me brother. [To LUCIANA] What I told you
    then,
I hope I shall have leisure to make good —   375
If this be not a dream I see and hear.
  ANG. That is the chain, sir, which you had of
    me.
  ANT. S. I think it be, sir. I deny it not.
  ANT. E. And you, sir, for this chain arrested me.
  ANG. I think I did, sir. I deny it not.   380
  ADR. I sent you money, sir, to be your bail,
By Dromio, but I think he brought it not.
  DRO. E. No, none by me.
  ANT. S. This purse of ducats I received from you,
And Dromio my man did bring them me.   385
I see we still did meet each other's man,
And I was ta'en for him, and he for me;
And thereupon these ERRORS are arose.
  ANT. E. These ducats pawn I for my father here.
  DUKE. It shall not need. Thy father hath his life.
  COUR. Sir, I must have that diamond from you.

  ANT. E. There, take it, and much thanks for my
    good cheer.   392
  AEM. Renownèd Duke, vouchsafe to take the
    pains
To go with us into the abbey here,
And hear at large discoursèd all our fortunes;   395
And all that are assembled in this place,
That by this sympathizèd° one day's error
Have suffered wrong, go keep us company,
And we shall make full satisfaction.
Thirty-three years have I but gone in travail   400
Of you, my sons, and till this present hour
My heavy burden ne'er deliverèd.
The Duke, my husband, and my children both,
And you the calendars of their nativity,°
Go to a gossips' feast,° and go with me.   405
After so long grief, such nativity!°
  DUKE. With all my heart, I'll gossip at this feast.
    [Exeunt all but ANTIPHOLUS S., ANTIPHOLUS E.,
              DROMIO S., and DROMIO E.]
  DRO. S. Master, shall I fetch your stuff from ship-
    board?
  ANT. E. Dromio, what stuff of mine hast thou em-
    barked?
  DRO. S. Your goods that lay at host,° sir, in the
    Centaur.   410
  ANT. S. He speaks to me. I am your master,
    Dromio.
Come, go with us. We'll look to that anon.
Embrace thy brother there. Rejoice with him.
    [Exeunt ANTIPHOLUS S. and ANTIPHOLUS E.]
  DRO. S. There is a fat friend at your master's
    house,
That kitchened me for you today at dinner.   415
She now shall be my sister, not my wife.
  DRO. E. Methinks you are my glass,° and not my
    brother.
I see by you I am a sweet-faced° youth.
Will you walk in to see their gossiping?
  DRO. S. Not I, sir. You are my elder.°   420
  DRO. E. That's a question. How shall we try it?
  DRO. S. We'll draw cuts° for the senior. Till then
    lead thou first.
  DRO. E. Nay, then, thus:
We came into the world like brother and brother,
And now let's go hand in hand, not one before
    another.   [Exeunt.]

397. sympathized: suffered by all.   404. calendars . . . nativity: i.e., the two Dromios. See I.ii.41.   405. gossips' feast:
christening feast.   406. nativity: birthday celebration.   410. at
host: in charge of the host.   417. glass: mirror, reflection.
418. sweet-faced: handsome.   420. elder: i.e., you should go in
first.   422. draw cuts: draw lots (by means of straws of unequal
lengths).

359. urging: mentioning.   360. children: pronounced childeren.

THE TRAGEDY OF TITUS ANDRONICUS

Introduction

Titus Andronicus is regarded by many critics as Shakespeare's worst play, and as a result ingenious attempts have been made to clear him of the charge of having written it. The history of *Titus Andronicus* is, however, fairly definite; and had the play been good, no one would ever have doubted either the facts or the authorship.

The first mention of *Titus Andronicus* occurs in Henslowe's *Diary* (see p. 38b). Between December 27, 1593, and February 6, 1594, the Earl of Sussex's Men acted at the Rose playhouse. On January 23, 1594, Henslowe records that they played as a new play "titus and ondronicus," for which he drew £3.8s as his share of the takings; this amount indicates that the playhouse was full. The play was again acted on January 28 and February 6, each performance producing for Henslowe 40s. Thereafter playing ceased in London for some months owing to an outbreak of the plague; but when at the beginning of June members of the Lord Admiral's and the Lord Chamberlain's companies acted together for ten days at the village of Newington, *Titus Andronicus* was presented twice. No further mention of the play appears in Henslowe's *Diary*; it now belonged to the Lord Chamberlain's men who began to act at the Theater (see p. 39b).

Some scholars are not satisfied with the note in Henslowe's *Diary* that *Titus Andronicus* was entirely a new play on January 23, 1594, and, observing that the *Diary* records another play called *Titus and Vespasian,* which was first acted by Lord Strange's Men on April 11, 1592, they consider that *Titus and Vespasian* was an earlier version of *Titus Andronicus*. This conclusion seems unlikely. Any play about Titus and Vespasian would presumably deal with the story of the Roman Emperor Vespasian and his son Titus, who captured and destroyed Jerusalem in A.D. 70, and *Titus Andronicus* has no connection either with Vespasian or his son or Jerusalem. Indeed, the story of the play is wholly romantic and is not based on any episode in Roman history.

Titus Andronicus was published very soon after the first performances. On February 6, 1594 — the day of the last performance by the Earl of Sussex's Men at the Rose — John Danter entered in the Stationers' Register (see pp. 65b–66a) "a booke intituled a Noble Roman Historye of Tytus Andronicus." At the same time he entered "the ballad thereof"; it was not uncommon for a printer in this way to secure his copyright of the ballad which appeared immediately following any notable event or popular play or book.

The play was printed in a quarto (Q1) with the title page: *The Most Lamentable Romaine Tragedie of Titus Andronicus: As it was Plaide by the Right Honourable the Earle of Darbie, Earle of Pembrooke, and Earle of Sussex their Seruants. London, Printed by Iohn Danter, and are to be sold by Edward White & Thomas Millington, at the little North doore of Paules at the signe of the Gunne. 1594.*

Quarto editions also exist dated 1600 and 1611; there may have been others of which no copy survives.

There is also a manuscript copy, dated 1595, of two passages — I.i.104–21 and V.i.125–44 — illustrated with a drawing of the scene in which Tamora pleads for the life of her son. This — the only contemporary illustration of any scene in Shakespeare's plays — is reproduced in Pl. 13a.

Titus Andronicus was included with the rest of the tragedies in the first folio (F1) of 1623. All the texts of this play are good, and there are few difficulties of reading, though the stage directions are sometimes obscure.

Titus Andronicus is one of the twelve plays named by Francis Meres in 1598 in his famous list (see pp. 11b–12a). Another reference was made to the play in 1604. A character in *Father Hubbard's Tale,* written by T.M., remarks "nevertheless for all my lamentable action of one arm, like old Titus Andronicus, I could purchase no more than one month's pay for ten months' pain and peril."

It follows that *Titus Andronicus* was a popular play; and apparently it was still being acted at least twenty years after its first performance. Indeed, Ben Jonson in 1614 coupled it with *The Spanish Tragedy* as a specimen of the kind of drama beloved by the old-fashioned playgoer. In the Induction to his play *Bartholomew Fair* Jonson makes a mock agreement between the author and the spectators, in which one of the clauses runs: "It is also agreed, that every man here exercise his own judgment, and not censure by contagion, or upon trust, from another's voice or face, that sits by him, be he never so first in the commission of wit; as also, that he be fixed and settled in his censure, that what he approves or not approves today, he will do the same tomorrow; and if tomorrow, the next day, and so the next week, if need be; and not to be brought about by any that sits on the bench with him, though they indict and arraign plays daily. He that will swear *Jeronimo* [*The Spanish Tragedy*] or *Andronicus* are the best plays yet, shall pass unexcepted at here, as a man whose judgment shows it is constant, and hath stood still these five-and-twenty or thirty years. Though it be an ignorance it is a virtuous and staid ignorance; and next to truth, a confirmed error does well; such a one the author knows where to find him."

Titus Andronicus is Shakespeare's first surviving tragedy. In his earliest attempts at writing plays, Shakespeare imitated the successes of those who had gone before him. In *Titus Andronicus* he was trying to rival Kyd's *Spanish Tragedy* (see pp. 36b–37a). This famous drama was the first conspicuously successful specimen of the gory revenge tragedies that were so lastingly popular on the Elizabethan stage.

In writing *The Spanish Tragedy* Kyd had found useful hints in the gruesome tragedies of the Roman playwright Seneca, particularly in *Thyestes. Thyestes* opens with the appearance of the Ghost of Tantalus, accompanied by the Fury Magaera. The two converse, and the Ghost is dispatched to stir up sinful madness in his old home, now the palace of Atreus. Atreus enters. He is thirsting for revenge on his exiled brother Thyestes. Thyestes had offended by stealing not only Atreus' wife but also a magic ram with a golden fleece which conferred royalty on its owner. Atreus, however, feigns forgiveness, and Thyestes, with his three sons, comes to visit him. Atreus seizes the boys, without the knowledge of their father, slays them, cuts off their heads and hands, and serves up portions of their bodies as food for the unhappy Thyestes. Hereafter, as was not surprising, the House of Atreus was devastated by an appalling succession of disasters. Kyd adopted Seneca's Ghost and Fury, and opened his play with the appearance of Revenge and the Ghost of Andrea, a Spanish gentleman who had been slain in battle. He also copied the device (which Shakespeare afterward used in Hamlet) of making the Ghost describe the underworld. He did, however, refrain from depicting the child-eating scene. Shakespeare also read *Thyestes;* but he spared his audience nothing.

In addition to *Thyestes,* Shakespeare used the old popular legend of the unhappy Philomela. This story probably came to his attention in Ovid's *Metamorphoses,* though there were English versions available, such as George Gascoigne's *Complaint of Philomene* (1576). According to the tale, Tereus, King of Thrace, married Procne, daughter of King Pandion of Athens, and much loved sister of Philomela. After a while Procne, wishing to hear news of Philomela, sent Tereus on a visit to his father-in-law, King Pandion. Tereus brought Philomela back with him, but the beauty of the girl so fired his passions that as soon as he reached his own country he ravished her. When she cried out that she would revenge her injury, he cut out her tongue and imprisoned her in a sheepcote with high walls. Then he went home and told Procne that Philomela was dead. But Philomela, though dumb, was still able to use her hands. She embroidered her tale on a garment which she caused to be sent to Procne. When Procne learned the truth, she swore vengeance for her sister. She slew Itys, her little son by Tereus, cooked the limbs and gave the unhallowed food to the father. Then — to quote from Gascoigne's version —

He knowing not their craft,
Sat down alone to eat,
And hungerly his own warm blood
Devourèd then for meat.

His oversight was such,
That he for Itys sent,
Whose murdered members in his maw,
He privily had pent.

No longer Procne then,
Her joy of grief could hide,

" The thing thou seekst, O wretch," quoth she,
" Within thee doth abide."

Wherewith he waxing wroth
And searching for his son,
Came forth at length, fair Philomene
By whom the grief begun,

And, cloaked in Bacchus' copes,
Wherewith she then was clad,
In father's bosom cast the head
Of Itys, silly [simple] lad.

Nor ever in her life
Had more desire to speak,
Than now, whereby her madding mood
Might all her malice wreak.

After this distressing affair, the gods intervened. Philomela was turned into a nightingale, Procne into a swallow, Tereus into a lapwing, and the boy Itys into a cock pheasant.

Another useful source of inspiration was Marlowe's sensational play *The Jew of Malta* (see p. 37b). Barabas the Jew is a perfect villain, a disciple of Machiavelli, who loves evil for its own sake, as he confides to his slave Ithamore:

As for myself, I walk abroad a-nights
And kill sick people groaning under walls;
Sometimes I go about and poison wells;
And now and then, to cherish Christian thieves,
I am content to lose some of my crowns,
That I may, walking in my gallery,
See 'em go pinioned along by my door.
Being young, I studied physic, and began
To practice first upon the Italian;
There I enriched the priests with burials,
And always kept the sextons' arms in ure [use]
With digging graves and ringing dead men's
    knells.
And after that was I an engineer,
And in the wars 'twixt France and Germany,
Under pretense of helping Charles the Fifth,
Slew friend and enemy with my stratagems.
Then after that was I an usurer,
And with extorting, cozening, forfeiting,
And tricks belonging unto brokery,
I filled the jails with bankrouts in a year,
And with young orphans planted hospitals,
And every moon made some or other mad,
And now and then one hang himself for grief,
Pinning upon his breast a long great scroll
How I with interest tormented him.

This speech, and the general air of implacable hate, Shakespeare copied into the character of Aaron the Moor, especially when, at the end of his career, Aaron taunts Lucius (V.i.61–150). Barabas, however, had some justification for his dislikes; Aaron is just maliciously wicked from a perverted sense of humor.

Few critics can seriously defend *Titus Andronicus;* but its failure is not solely due to a revolting and fantastic story. Modern playgoers may regard rape, mutilation, and severed heads and hands as unsuitable for stage presentation; yet there are scenes quite as painful in plays which are among the very greatest — the blinding of Gloucester in *Lear* for instance, or the conclusion of Sophocles' *Oedipus the King;* these are horrible but still justifiable in their contexts. The horrors in *Titus Andronicus* are too much; if ever presented on a modern stage they would move the audience not to shudders but to guffaws. Moreover, if a dramatist chooses to bring a drama of passion and revenge to a climax of horror when a parent unknowingly eats the flesh of his child, the episode should at least be adequately prepared and set off. In Seneca's *Thyestes,* as the wretched father takes his unholy meal, all heaven and earth tremble and quake, and Thyestes himself is seized with distressing convulsions in his entrails. In *Titus Andronicus,* no unusual signs or symptoms are noted when Tamora takes her first mouthful of Titus' pie.

The characterization too is inconsistent and badly motivated. At the beginning Saturninus, having decided to take Lavinia from his brother Bassianus, immediately rejects her in favor of the Gothic Queen. Titus Andronicus himself at his first entrance is the toughest of old warriors; he thinks nothing of slaying a son merely for standing up to him. Yet directly after this outburst of temper, he degenerates into a dotard so feeble that he grovels before the wretched Saturninus, whom he has just made Emperor. Nor can anyone defend such incidents as Lavinia carrying out Titus' severed hand in her teeth, because, poor girl, she has no hands; or the silly episode where Tamora and her sons pretend to be Revenge, Murder, and Rape.

Nevertheless, there are in *Titus Andronicus* dramatic speeches, individual lines, and passages of poetry as good as any that had been heard on English stages by 1594. Nor must it be forgotten that the play was a popular favorite with theatergoers.

Titus Andronicus

DRAMATIS PERSONAE

SATURNINUS, *son to the late Emperor of Rome, afterward emperor*

BASSIANUS, *brother to Saturninus*

TITUS ANDRONICUS, *a noble Roman*

MARCUS ANDRONICUS, *tribune of the people and brother to Titus*

LUCIUS
QUINTUS
MARTIUS > *sons to Titus Andronicus*
MUTIUS

YOUNG LUCIUS, *a boy, son to Lucius*

PUBLIUS, *son to Marcus Andronicus*

AEMILIUS, *a noble Roman*

ALARBUS
DEMETRIUS > *sons to Tamora*
CHIRON

AARON, *a Moor, beloved by Tamora*

A CAPTAIN, TRIBUNE, MESSENGER, *and* CLOWN; ROMANS *and* GOTHS

TAMORA, *Queen of the Goths*

LAVINIA, *daughter to Titus Andronicus*

A NURSE, *and a black Child*

KINSMEN *of Titus,* SENATORS, TRIBUNES, OFFICERS, SOLDIERS, *and* ATTENDANTS

SCENE — *Rome, and the country near it.*

Act I

SCENE I. *Rome. Before the Capitol, the tomb of the Andronici appearing.*

[*Flourish. Enter the* TRIBUNES *and* SENATORS *aloft. And then enter below,* SATURNINUS *and his* FOLLOWERS *from one side, and* BASSIANUS *and his* FOLLOWERS *from the other side, with drum and colors.*]

SAT. Noble patricians, patrons of my right,
Defend the justice of my cause with arms;
And, countrymen, my loving followers,
Plead my successive title° with your swords.
I am his first-born son, that was the last   5
That ware the imperial diadem of Rome.°
Then let my father's honors live in me,
Nor wrong mine age with this indignity.
  BAS. Romans, friends, followers, favorers of my
    right,
If ever Bassianus, Caesar's son,   10
Were gracious in the eyes of royal Rome,
Keep° then this passage to the Capitol;
And suffer not dishonor to approach
The imperial seat, to virtue consecrate,
To justice, continence° and nobility,   15
But let desért in pure election shine,
And, Romans, fight for freedom in your choice.
[*Enter* MARCUS ANDRONICUS, *aloft, with the crown.*]
  MARC. Princes, that strive by factions° and by
    friends
Ambitiously for rule and empery,°   19

Know that the people of Rome, for whom we stand
A special party, have by common voice,
In election for the Roman empery,
Chosen Andronicus, surnamed Pius
For many good and great deserts to Rome.
A nobler man, a braver warrior,   25
Lives not this day within the city walls.
He by the Senate is accited° home
From weary wars against the barbarous Goths,
That, with his sons — a terror to our foes — 29
Hath yoked a nation strong, trained up in arms.
Ten years are spent since first he undertook
This cause of Rome, and chastisèd with arms
Our enemies' pride. Five times he hath returned
Bleeding to Rome, bearing his valiant sons
In coffins from the field;   35
And now at last, laden with honor's spoils,
Returns the good Andronicus to Rome,
Renownèd Titus, flourishing in arms.
Let us entreat, by honor of his name,
Whom (worthily) you would have now succeed,
And in the Capitol and Senate's right,   41
Whom you pretend to honor and adore,
That you withdraw you and abate° your strength,
Dismiss your followers, and, as suitors should,
Plead your deserts in peace and humbleness.   45
  SAT. How fair the Tribune speaks to calm my
    thoughts!
  BAS. Marcus Andronicus, so I do affy°
In thy uprightness and integrity,
And so I love and honor thee and thine,
Thy noble brother Titus and his sons,   50
And her to whom my thoughts are humbled all,
Gracious Lavinia, Rome's rich ornament,
That I will here dismiss my loving friends,

Act I, Sc. i: **4. successive title:** right to succeed as Emperor. **5–6. first-born . . . Rome:** i.e., eldest son of the late Emperor. **12. Keep:** defend. **15. continence:** restraint. **18. factions:** parties. **19. empery:** empire.

27. accited: summoned. **43. abate:** make less. **47. affy:** trust.

And to my fortunes and the people's favor
Commit my cause in balance to be weighed.   55
> [*Exeunt the* FOLLOWERS OF BASSIANUS.]

SAT. Friends that have been thus forward in my
    right,
I thank you all and here dismiss you all,
And to the love and favor of my country
Commit myself, my person, and the cause.
> [*Exeunt the* FOLLOWERS OF SATURNINUS.]

Rome, be as just and gracious unto me   60
As I am confident° and kind to thee.
Open the gates and let me in.

BAS. Tribunes, and me, a poor competitor.
> [*Flourish.* SATURNINUS *and* BASSIANUS
> *go up into the Capitol.*]
> [*Enter a* CAPTAIN.]

CAP. Romans, make way. The good Andronicus,
Patron of virtue, Rome's best champion,   65
Successful in the battles that he fights,
With honor and with fortune is returned
From where he circumscribèd° with his sword,
And brought to yoke, the enemies of Rome.
> [*Drums and trumpets sounded. Enter* MARTIUS *and*
> MUTIUS; *after them, two* MEN *bearing a coffin cov-*
> *ered with black; then* LUCIUS *and* QUINTUS. *After*
> *them,* TITUS ANDRONICUS, *and then* TAMORA, QUEEN
> OF GOTHS, *with* ALARBUS, DEMETRIUS, CHIRON, AARON,
> *and other* GOTHS, *prisoners;* SOLDIERS *and* PEOPLE *fol-*
> *lowing. The* BEARERS *set down the coffin, and* TITUS
> *speaks.*]

TIT. Hail, Rome, victorious in thy mourning
    weeds!°   70
Lo, as the bark that hath discharged her fraught°
Returns with precious lading to the bay
From whence at first she weighed her anchorage,
Cometh Andronicus, bound with laurel boughs,°
To resalute his country with his tears,   75
Tears of true joy for his return to Rome.
Thou great defender° of this Capitol,
Stand gracious to the rites that we intend!
Romans, of five and twenty° valiant sons,
Half of the number that King Priam° had,   80
Behold the poor remains, alive and dead!
These that survive let Rome reward with love;
These that I bring unto their latest° home,
With burial amongst their ancestors.
Here Goths have given me leave to sheathe my
    sword.   85
Titus, unkind,° and careless of thine own,
Why suffer'st thou thy sons, unburied yet,

To hover on the dreadful shore of Styx?°
Make way to lay them by their brethren.
> [*They open the tomb.*]

There greet in silence, as the dead are wont,   90
And sleep in peace, slain in your country's wars!
O sacred receptacle of my joys,
Sweet cell of virtue and nobility,
How many sons hast thou of mine in store
That thou wilt never render° to me more!   95

LUC. Give us the proudest prisoner of the Goths,
That we may hew his limbs and on a pile
Ad manes fratrum° sacrifice his flesh
Before this earthy prison of their bones,
That so the shadows° be not unappeased,   100
Nor we disturbed with prodigies° on earth.

TIT. I give him you — the noblest that survives,
The eldest son of this distressèd Queen.

TAM. Stay,° Roman brethren! Gracious con-
    queror,
Victorious Titus, rue° the tears I shed,   105
A mother's tears in passion° for her son;
And if thy sons were ever dear to thee,
Oh, think my son to be as dear to me!
Sufficeth not that we are brought to Rome
To beautify thy triumphs and return,   110
Captive to thee and to thy Roman yoke;
But must my sons be slaughtered in the streets,
For valiant doings in their country's cause?
Oh, if to fight for king and commonweal
Were piety in thine, it is in these.   115
Andronicus, stain not thy tomb with blood.
Wilt° thou draw near the nature of the gods?
Draw near them then in being merciful.
Sweet mercy is nobility's true badge.
Thrice-noble Titus, spare my first-born son.   120

TIT. Patient° yourself, madam, and pardon me.
These are their brethren, whom you Goths beheld
Alive and dead, and for their brethren slain
Religiously they ask a sacrifice.
To this your son is marked, and die he must,   125
To appease their groaning shadows that are gone.

LUC. Away with him, and make a fire straight,
And with our swords, upon a pile of wood,
Let's hew his limbs till they be clean consumed.
> [*Exeunt the sons of* ANDRONICUS *with* ALARBUS.]

TAM. Oh, cruel, irreligious piety!   130

CHI. Was ever Scythia° half so barbarous?

DEM. Oppose° not Scythia to ambitious Rome.

---

61. **confident:** sure of my right.   68. **circumscribed:** encompassed, made to surrender.   70. **weeds:** garments.   71. **fraught:** freight, cargo.   74. **laurel boughs:** A laurel wreath was a sign of victory.   77. **Thou . . . defender:** i.e., the god Jupiter. 79. **five and twenty:** Titus has miscounted; later (III.i.10) he speaks of his two and twenty sons who died honorably. With the four who come into this scene, the total is twenty-six.   80. **King Priam:** King of Troy; he had fifty sons. See *Tr & Cr.*   83. **latest:** last.   86. **unkind:** unnatural.

88. **hover . . . Styx:** The Styx was one of the rivers that surrounded Hades. The souls of those whose bodies were still unburied were not allowed to cross.   95. **render:** give back.   98. *Ad . . . fratrum:* to the ghosts of our brothers.   100. **shadows:** ghosts.   101. **prodigies:** supernatural disturbances.   104. **Stay . . . :** For an Elizabethan drawing of this episode, see Pl. 13a. 105. **rue:** pity.   106. **passion:** grief.   117-19. **Wilt . . . badge:** Cf. *M of Ven,* IV.i.184-97.   121. **Patient:** make patient. 131. **Scythia:** South Russia, where the people were regarded as most savage.   See *Lear,* I.i.118.   132. **Oppose:** compare.

Alarbus goes to rest, and we survive
To tremble under Titus' threatening look. 134
Then, madam, stand resolved, but hope withal;
The self-same gods that armed the Queen of Troy
With opportunity of sharp revenge
Upon the Thracian tyrant in his tent°
May favor Tamora, the Queen of Goths
(When Goths were Goths and Tamora was queen),
To quit° the bloody wrongs upon her foes. 141
[*Re-enter the* SONS OF ANDRONICUS, *with their swords
bloody.*]
   LUC. See, lord and Father, how we have per-
     formed
Our Roman rites. Alarbus' limbs are lopped,
And entrails feed the sacrificing fire, 144
Whose smoke, like incense, doth perfume the sky.
Remaineth naught but to inter our brethren,
And with loud 'larums° welcome them to Rome.
   TIT. Let it be so; and let Andronicus
Make this his latest farewell to their souls.
[*Trumpets sounded, and the coffin
laid in the tomb.*]
In peace and honor rest you here, my sons. 150
Rome's readiest champions, repose you here in rest,
Secure from worldly chances and mishaps!
Here lurks no treason, here no envy swells,
Here grow no damnèd drugs; here are no storms,
No noise, but silence and eternal sleep. 155
In peace and honor rest you here, my sons!
[*Enter* LAVINIA.]
   LAV. In peace and honor live Lord Titus long;
My noble lord and Father, live in fame!
Lo, at this tomb my tributary° tears
I render for my brethren's obsequies,° 160
And at thy feet I kneel, with tears of joy
Shed on the earth, for thy return to Rome.
Oh, bless me here with thy victorious hand,
Whose fortunes Rome's best citizens applaud!
   TIT. Kind Rome, that hast thus lovingly reserved
The cordial° of mine age to glad my heart! 166
Lavinia, live; outlive thy father's days,
And fame's eternal date,° for virtue's praise!
[*Enter, below,* MARCUS ANDRONICUS *and* TRIBUNES.
Re-enter SATURNINUS *and* BASSIANUS, *attended.*]
   MARC. Long live Lord Titus, my belovèd brother,
Gracious triumpher in the eyes of Rome! 170
   TIT. Thanks, gentle Tribune, noble Brother Mar-
     cus.
   MARC. And welcome, Nephews, from successful
     wars,
You that survive, and you that sleep in fame!

Fair lords, your fortunes are alike in all, 174
That in your country's service drew your swords.
But° safer triumph is this funeral pomp
That hath aspired to Solon's happiness
And triumphs over chance in honor's bed.
Titus Andronicus, the people of Rome,
Whose friend in justice thou hast ever been, 180
Send thee by me, their Tribune and their trust,
This palliament° of white and spotless hue,
And name thee in election for the Empire,
With these our late-deceasèd Emperor's sons.
Be *candidatus*° then, and put it on, 185
And help to set a head on headless Rome.
   TIT. A better head her glorious body fits
Than his that shakes for age and feebleness.
What should I don this robe and trouble you?
Be chosen with proclamations today, 190
Tomorrow yield up rule, resign my life,
And set abroad new business for you all?
Rome, I have been thy soldier forty years,
And led my country's strength successfully,
And buried one and twenty° valiant sons, 195
Knighted in field, slain manfully in arms,
In right and service of their noble country.
Give me a staff of honor for mine age,
But not a scepter to control the world.
Upright he held it, lords, that held it last. 200
   MARC. Titus, thou shalt obtain and ask the em-
     pery.
   SAT. Proud and ambitious Tribune, canst thou
     tell?
   TIT. Patience, Prince Saturninus.
   SAT.   Romans, do me right.
Patricians, draw your swords, and sheathe them not
Till Saturninus be Rome's Emperor. 205
Andronicus, would thou wert shipped to Hell,
Rather than rob me of the people's hearts!
   LUC. Proud Saturnine, interrupter of the good
That noble-minded Titus means to thee!
   TIT. Content thee, Prince. I will restore to thee
The people's hearts, and wean them from them-
     selves.° 211
   BAS. Andronicus, I do not flatter thee,
But honor thee, and will do till I die.
My faction if thou strengthen with thy friends,
I will most thankful be; and thanks to men 215
Of noble minds is honorable meed.°
   TIT. People of Rome, and people's Tribunes here,
I ask your voices° and your suffrages.
Will you bestow them friendly on Andronicus?

136–38. Queen . . . tent: Hecuba, Queen of Troy, after the fall
of the city, was assigned as a slave to Polymnestor. In revenge
for the slaughter of her son Polydorus, she slew Polymnestor's
two sons and put out his eyes. 141. quit: repay. 147. 'larums:
alarums, warlike noises. 159. tributary: given as a tribute.
160. obsequies: funeral rites. 166. cordial: that which warms
my heart. 168. fame's . . . date: everlasting fame.

176–78. But . . . bed: i.e., it is better to be dead. Solon, the
Greek lawgiver and sage, observed: "Call no man happy until
he is dead." 182. palliament: ceremonial white gown. 185. candidatus: clad in white. Those who sought election as consul wore
a white cloak; hence the name "candidate." 195. one and
twenty: See l. 79. 211. wean . . . themselves: i.e., cause them
to change their minds and favor you for Emperor. 216. meed:
reward. 218. voices: approval.

TRIBUNES. To gratify the good Andronicus   220
And gratulate° his safe return to Rome,
The people will accept whom he admits.°
   TIT. Tribunes, I thank you; and this suit I make,
That you create your Emperor's eldest son,
Lord Saturnine, whose virtues will, I hope,   225
Reflect on Rome as Titan's° rays on earth
And ripen justice in this commonweal.
Then, if you will elect by my advice,
Crown him, and say, " Long live our Emperor! "
   MARC. With voices and applause of every sort,
Patricians and plebeians, we create   231
Lord Saturninus Rome's great Emperor,
And say, " Long live our Emperor Saturnine! "
      [*A long flourish° till they come down.*]
   SAT. Titus Andronicus, for thy favors done
To us in our election° this day,   235
I give thee thanks in part of thy deserts,
And will with deeds requite° thy gentleness.°
And, for an onset,° Titus, to advance
Thy name and honorable family,
Lavinia will I make my Empress,°   240
Rome's royal mistress, mistress of my heart,
And in the sacred Pantheon° her espouse.
Tell me, Andronicus, doth this motion please thee?
   TIT. It doth, my worthy lord; and in this match
I hold me highly honored of° your Grace.   245
And here, in sight of Rome, to Saturnine,
King and commander of our commonweal,
The wide world's Emperor, do I consecrate
My sword, my chariot, and my prisoners —
Presents well worthy Rome's imperious lord.   250
Receive them then, the tribute that I owe,
Mine honor's ensigns° humbled at thy feet.
   SAT. Thanks, noble Titus, father of my life!
How proud I am of thee and of thy gifts,
Rome shall record; and when I do forget   255
The least of these unspeakable deserts,
Romans, forget your fealty° to me.
   TIT. [*To* TAMORA] Now, madam, are you pris-
   oner to an emperor —
To him that, for your honor and your state,
Will use you nobly and your followers.   260
   SAT. A goodly lady, trust me, of the hue
That I would choose, were I to choose anew.
Clear up, fair Queen, that cloudy countenance.
Though chance of war hath wrought this change of
   cheer,°
Thou comest not to be made a scorn in Rome.   265
Princely shall be thy usage every way.
Rest on my word, and let not discontent

Daunt all your hopes. Madam, he° comforts you
Can make you greater than the Queen of Goths.
Lavinia, you are not displeased with this?   270
   LAV. Not I, my lord, sith° true nobility
Warrants these words in princely courtesy.
   SAT. Thanks, sweet Lavinia. Romans, let us go.
Ransomless here we set our prisoners free.   274
Proclaim our honors, lords, with trump and drum.
      [*Flourish.* SATURNINUS *courts* TAMORA
            in dumb show.°]
   BAS. [*Seizing* LAVINIA] Lord Titus, by your leave,
   this maid is mine.
   TIT. How, sir! Are you in earnest then, my lord?
   BAS. Aye, noble Titus, and resolved withal
To do myself this reason° and this right.
   MARC. *Suum cuique*° is our Roman justice.   280
This Prince in justice seizeth but his own.
   LUC. And that he will, and shall, if Lucius live.
   TIT. Traitors, avaunt!° Where is the Emperor's
   guard?
Treason, my lord! Lavinia is surprised!
   SAT. Surprised! By whom?
   BAS.   By him that justly may   285
Bear his betrothed from all the world away.
      [*Exeunt* BASSIANUS *and* MARCUS *with* LAVINIA.]
   MUT. Brothers, help to convey her hence away,
And with my sword I'll keep this door safe.
      [*Exeunt* LUCIUS, QUINTUS, *and* MARTIUS.]
   TIT. Follow, my lord, and I'll soon bring her back.
   MUT. My lord, you pass not here.
   TIT.   What, villain boy!   290
Barr'st me my way in Rome?   [*Stabbing* MUTIUS.]
   MUT.   Help, Lucius, help.   [*Dies.*]
[*During the fray,* SATURNINUS, TAMORA, DEMETRIUS,
CHIRON, *and* AARON *go out and re-enter above. Re-*
        enter LUCIUS.]
   LUC. My lord, you are unjust, and more than so;
In wrongful quarrel you have slain your son.
   TIT. Nor thou, nor he, are any sons of mine.
My sons would never so dishonor me.   295
Traitor, restore Lavinia to the Emperor.
   LUC. Dead, if you will; but not to be his wife
That is another's lawful promised love.   [*Exit.*]
   SAT. No, Titus, no. The Emperor needs her not,
Nor her, nor thee, nor any of thy stock.   300
I'll trust by leisure° him that mocks me once —
Thee never, nor thy traitorous haughty sons,
Confederates all thus to dishonor me.
Was none in Rome to make a stale°
But Saturnine? Full well, Andronicus,   305
Agree these deeds with that proud brag of thine
That saidst I begged the Empire at thy hands.

---

221. gratulate: express joy at.   222. admits: approves.   226. Titan: the sun god.   233. s.d., flourish: notes on the trumpet.
235. election: a four-syllable word.   237. requite: repay. gentleness: nobility.   238. onset: start.   240. Empress: pronounced
"empress."   242. Pantheon: the temple of all the gods.   245. of:
by.   252. honor's ensigns: emblems of the honors that I have
won.   257. fealty: loyalty.   264. cheer: frame of mind.

268. he: he who.   271. sith: since.   275. s.d., dumb show:
silent action.   279. reason: justice.   280. Suum cuique: his
own to each.   283. avaunt: be gone.   301. by leisure: barely.
304. stale: "sucker."

TIT. Oh, monstrous! What reproachful words are these?

SAT. But go thy ways. Go give that changing piece°
To him that flourished for her with his sword. 310
A valiant son-in-law thou shalt enjoy —
One fit to bandy° with thy lawless sons,
To ruffle° in the commonwealth of Rome.

TIT. These words are razors to my wounded heart.

SAT. And therefore, lovely Tamora, Queen of Goths, 315
That, like the stately Phoebe° 'mongst her nymphs,
Dost overshine the gallant'st dames of Rome,
If thou be pleased with this my sudden choice,
Behold, I choose thee, Tamora, for my bride,
And will create thee Empress of Rome. 320
Speak, Queen of Goths, dost thou applaud my choice?
And here I swear by all the Roman gods —
Sith priest and holy water are so near,
And tapers° burn so bright, and everything
In readiness for Hymenaeus° stand — 325
I will not resalute the streets of Rome,
Or climb my palace, till from forth this place
I lead espoused my bride along with me.

TAM. And here, in sight of Heaven, to Rome I swear,
If Saturnine advance the Queen of Goths, 330
She will a handmaid be to his desires,
A loving nurse, a mother to his youth.

SAT. Ascend, fair Queen, Pantheon. Lords, accompany
Your noble Emperor and his lovely bride,
Sent by the Heavens for Prince Saturnine, 335
Whose wisdom hath her fortune conquerèd.
There shall we consummate our spousal° rites.
[*Exeunt all but* TITUS.]

TIT. I am not bid to wait upon this bride.
Titus, when wert thou wont to walk alone,°
Dishonored thus and challengèd of wrongs? 340
[*Re-enter* MARCUS, LUCIUS, QUINTUS, *and* MARTIUS.]

MARC. O Titus, see, oh, see what thou hast done!
In a bad quarrel slain a virtuous son.

TIT. No, foolish Tribune, no! No son of mine —
Nor thou, nor these, confederates in the deed
That hath dishonored all our family. 345
Unworthy brother and unworthy sons!

LUC. But let us give him burial, as becomes;
Give Mutius burial with our brethren.

TIT. Traitors, away! He rests not in this tomb.
This monument five hundred years hath stood,
Which I have sumptuously re-edified.° 351

Here none but soldiers and Rome's servitors
Repose in fame — none basely slain in brawls.
Bury him where you can; he comes not here.

MARC. My lord, this is impiety in you. 355
My nephew Mutius' deeds do plead for him.
He must be buried with his brethren.

QUIN., MART. And shall, or him we will accompany.

TIT. And shall! What villain was it spake that word?

QUIN. He that would vouch° it in any place but here. 360

TIT. What, would you bury him in my despite?°

MARC. No, noble Titus, but entreat of thee
To pardon Mutius and to bury him.

TIT. Marcus, even thou hast struck upon my crest,°
And with these boys mine honor thou hast wounded. 365
My foes I do repute you every one,
So trouble me no more, but get you gone.

MART. He is not with himself.° Let us withdraw.

QUIN. Not I, till Mutius' bones be burièd.
[MARCUS *and the* SONS OF TITUS *kneel.*]

MARC. Brother, for in that name doth nature plead —— 370

QUIN. Father, and in that name doth nature speak ——

TIT. Speak thou no more, if all the rest will speed.°

MARC. Renownèd Titus, more than half my soul ——

LUC. Dear Father, soul and substance of us all ——

MARC. Suffer thy brother Marcus to inter 375
His noble nephew here in virtue's nest,°
That died in honor and Lavinia's cause.
Thou art a Roman; be not barbarous.
The Greeks upon advice° did bury Ajax
That slew himself, and wise Laertes' son° 380
Did graciously plead for his funerals.°
Let not young Mutius then, that was thy joy,
Be barred his entrance here.

TIT.   Rise, Marcus, rise.
The dismal'st day is this that e'er I saw,
To be dishonored by my sons in Rome! 385
Well, bury him, and bury me the next.
[MUTIUS *is put into the tomb.*]

309. changing piece: fickle creature. 312. bandy: squabble. 313. ruffle: brawl. 316. Phoebe: Diana. 324. tapers: candles, used ceremonially in Roman weddings. 325. Hymenaeus: the god of marriage. 337. spousal: bridal. 339. alone: i.e., without an escort of respectful servants. 351. re-edified: rebuilt.

360. vouch: stand by his word. 361. in my despite: in spite of me. 364. struck . . . crest: treated me dishonorably. 368. with himself: in his right mind. 372. if . . . speed: if you are going to say the same. 376. virtue's nest: the resting place of valor — a farfetched image. 379. upon advice: after careful consideration. 379–81. Ajax . . . funerals: After his death Achilles' armor was claimed by both Ajax and Ulysses. When the award went to Ulysses, Ajax became mad and slew a flock of sheep, supposing them to be the Greeks who had insulted him. When he recovered his senses, he committed suicide; but by the advice of Ulysses he was honorably buried. Laertes' son: Ulysses.

LUC. There lie thy bones, sweet Mutius, with thy friends,
Till we with trophies do adorn thy tomb.
    ALL. [*Kneeling*] No man shed tears for noble Mutius!
He lives in fame that died in virtue's cause. 390
    MARC. My lord, to step out of these dreary dumps,°
How comes it that the subtle Queen of Goths
Is of a sudden thus advanced in Rome?
    TIT. I know not, Marcus; but I know it is,
Whether by device° or no, the Heavens can tell.
Is she not then beholding° to the man 396
That brought her for this high good turn so far?
Yes, and will nobly him remunerate.
[*Flourish. Re-enter, from one side,* SATURNINUS *attended,* TAMORA, DEMETRIUS, CHIRON, *and* AARON; *from the other,* BASSIANUS, LAVINIA, *with others.*]
    SAT. So, Bassianus, you have played your prize.°
God give you joy, sir, of your gallant bride! 400
    BAS. And you of yours, my lord! I say no more,
Nor wish no less, and so I take my leave.
    SAT. Traitor, if Rome have law, or we have power,
Thou and thy faction shall repent this rape.
    BAS. Rape, call you it, my lord, to seize my own,
My true-betrothèd love, and now my wife? 406
But let the laws of Rome determine all.
Meanwhile I am possessed of that is mine.
    SAT. 'Tis good, sir. You are very short with us,
But, if we live, we'll be as sharp with you. 410
    BAS. My lord, what I have done, as best I may,
Answer I must, and shall do with my life.
Only thus much I give your Grace to know:
By all the duties that I owe to Rome,
This noble gentleman, Lord Titus here, 415
Is in opinion and in honor wronged,
That, in the rescue of Lavinia,
With his own hand did slay his youngest son,
In zeal to you and highly moved to wrath
To be controlled° in that he frankly gave. 420
Receive him then to favor, Saturnine,
That hath expressed himself in all his deeds
A father and a friend to thee and Rome.
    TIT. Prince Bassianus, leave° to plead my deeds.
'Tis thou, and those, that have dishonored me. 425
Rome and the righteous Heavens be my judge
How I have loved and honored Saturnine!
    TAM. My worthy lord, if ever Tamora
Were gracious in those princely eyes of thine,
Then hear me speak indifferently° for all, 430
And at my suit, sweet, pardon what is past.
    SAT. What, madam! Be dishonored openly,
And basely put it up° without revenge?

    TAM. Not so, my lord. The gods of Rome forfend°
I should be author to dishonor you! 435
But on mine honor dare I undertake
For good Lord Titus' innocence in all,
Whose fury not dissembled° speaks his griefs.
Then, at my suit, look graciously on him.
Lose not so noble a friend on vain suppose,° 440
Nor with sour looks afflict his gentle heart.
[*Aside to* SATURNINUS] My lord, be ruled by me, be won at last;
Dissemble all your griefs and discontents.
You are but newly planted in your throne.
Lest then the people, and patricians too, 445
Upon a just survey take Titus' part,
And so supplant° you for ingratitude,
Which Rome reputes to be a heinous° sin,
Yield at entreats, and then let me alone.
I'll find a day to massacre them all 450
And raze their faction and their family —
The cruel father and his traitorous sons
To whom I suèd for my dear son's life —
And make them know what 'tis to let a queen 454
Kneel in the streets and beg for grace in vain. —
Come, come, sweet Emperor — come, Andronicus —
Take up this good old man, and cheer the heart
That dies in tempest of thy angry frown.
    SAT. Rise, Titus, rise. My Empress hath prevailed.
    TIT. I thank your Majesty, and her, my lord. 460
These words, these looks, infuse new life in me.
    TAM. Titus, I am incorporate° in Rome,
A Roman now adopted happily,
And must advise the Emperor for his good.
This day all quarrels die, Andronicus. 465
And let it be mine honor, good my lord,
That I have reconciled your friends and you.
For you, Prince Bassianus, I have passed
My word and promise to the Emperor
That you will be more mild and tractable. 470
And fear not, lords, and you, Lavinia.
By my advice, all humbled on your knees,
You shall ask pardon of his Majesty.
    LUC. We do; and vow to Heaven, and to his Highness,
That what we did was mildly as we might,° 475
Tendering our sister's honor and our own.
    MARC. That, on mine honor, here I do protest.
    SAT. Away, and talk not. Trouble us no more.
    TAM. Nay, nay, sweet Emperor, we must all be friends.
The Tribune and his nephews kneel for grace. 480
I will not be denied. Sweetheart, look back.

---

391. dumps: melancholy.   395. device: plot.   396. beholding: indebted.   399. played . . . prize: won your match.   420. controlled: opposed, rebuked.   424. leave: cease.   430. indifferently: impartially.   433. put it up: put up with it.

434. forfend: forbid.   438. dissembled: disguised.   440. suppose: suspicion.   447. supplant: remove.   448. heinous: hateful.   462. incorporate: naturalized.   475. mildly . . . might: the least we could do.

SAT. Marcus, for thy sake and thy brother's here,
And at my lovely Tamora's entreats,
I do remit these young men's heinous faults.
Stand up.   485
Lavinia, though you left me like a churl,°
I found a friend; and sure as death I swore
I would not part a bachelor from the priest.
Come, if the Emperor's Court can feast two brides,
You are my guest, Lavinia, and your friends.   490
This day shall be a love-day, Tamora.

TIT. Tomorrow, an° it please your Majesty
To hunt the panther and the hart with me,
With horn and hound we'll give your Grace bon-
     jour.
SAT. Be it so, Titus, and gramercy° too.   495
                                        [Flourish. Exeunt.]

Act II

SCENE I. *Rome. Before the palace.*

[*Enter* AARON.]
AAR. Now climbeth Tamora Olympus'° top,
Safe out° of Fortune's shot, and sits aloft,
Secure of° thunder's crack or lightning flash,
Advanced above pale envy's threatening reach.
As when the golden sun salutes the morn,   5
And, having gilt the ocean with his beams,
Gallops the zodiac° in his glistering° coach,
And overlooks the highest-peering hills,
So Tamora.
Upon her wit doth earthly honor wait,   10
And virtue stoops and trembles at her frown.
Then, Aaron, arm thy heart, and fit thy thoughts,
To mount aloft with thy imperial mistress,
And mount her pitch,° whom thou in triumph long
Hast prisoner held, fettered in amorous chains,   15
And faster bound to Aaron's charming eyes
Than is Prometheus tied to Caucasus.°
Away with slavish weeds and servile thoughts!
I will be bright and shine in pearl and gold,
To wait upon this new-made Empress.   20
To wait, said I? To wanton with this Queen,
This goddess, this Semiramis,° this nymph,

This siren,° that will charm Rome's Saturnine,
And see his shipwreck and his commonweal's.
Holloa! What storm is this?   25
     [*Enter* DEMETRIUS *and* CHIRON, *braving.*°]
DEM. Chiron, thy years want wit, thy wit wants
     edge
And manners, to intrude where I am graced,°
And may, for aught thou know'st, affected° be.
CHI. Demetrius, thou dost overween° in all,
And so in this, to bear me down with braves.   30
'Tis not the difference of a year or two
Makes me less gracious, or thee more fortunate.
I am as able and as fit as thou
To serve, and to deserve my mistress' grace;
And that my sword upon thee shall approve,°   35
And plead my passions for Lavinia's love.
AAR. [*Aside*] Clubs, clubs!° These lovers will not
     keep the peace.
DEM. Why, boy,° although our mother, unad-
     vised,
Gave you a dancing-rapier° by your side,   39
Are you so desperate grown, to threat your friends?
Go to!° Have your lath° glued within your sheath
Till you know better how to handle it.
CHI. Meanwhile, sir, with the little skill I have,
Full well shalt thou perceive how much I dare.
DEM. Aye, boy, grow ye so brave? [*They draw.*]
AAR.   [*Coming forward*] Why, how now, lords!
So near the Emperor's palace dare you draw,   46
And maintain such a quarrel openly?
Full well I wot° the ground of all this grudge.
I would not for a million° of gold   49
The cause were known to them it most concerns;
Nor would your noble mother for much more
Be so dishonored in the Court of Rome.
For shame, put up!°
DEM.   Not I, till I have sheathed
My rapier in his bosom, and withal   54
Thrust those reproachful speeches down his throat
That he hath breathed in my dishonor here.
CHI. For that I am prepared and full resolved.
Foul-spoken coward, that thunder'st with thy
     tongue,
And with thy weapon nothing darest perform.
AAR. Away, I say!   60
Now, by the gods that warlike Goths adore,
This petty brabble° will undo us all.
Why, lords, and think you not how dangerous

486. like a churl: so rudely.   492. an: if.   495. gramercy:
thanks; lit., God reward you.
     Act II, Sc. i: 1. Olympus: the highest mountain in Greece,
and the home of the gods.   2. out: out of range.   3. of: from.
7. zodiac: the course of the sun. glistering: glistening.   14. mount
. . . pitch: soar to her height. pitch: See App. 26.   17. Prometheus . . . Caucasus: Prometheus stole fire from Heaven and
gave it to men. For this act he was punished by being chained in
the Caucasus where vultures daily tore out his liver, which was
renewed nightly.   22. Semiramis: wife of Ninus, mythological
founder of the Assyrian Empire, a type of magnificent and lustful
beauty.

23. siren: temptress. The sirens were beautiful maidens who
lurked on the shores of the Straits of Messina and lured mariners
to destruction by their singing.   25. s.d., braving: taunting each
other.   27. graced: favored.   28. affected: loved.   29. overween: behave arrogantly.   35. approve: prove.   37. clubs:
a riot. See *AYLI*, V.ii.45,n.   38. boy: a term of contempt.
39. dancing-rapier: ornamental sword, for show, not use.   41. Go
to: an expression of contempt or impatience. lath: wooden sword.
48. wot: know.   49. million: a three-syllable word.   53. put up:
sheathe your swords.   62. brabble: squabble.

It is to jet° upon a prince's right?
What, is Lavinia then become so loose, 65
Or Bassianus so degenerate,
That for her love such quarrels may be broached°
Without controlment, justice, or revenge?
Young lords, beware! An should the Empress know
This discord's ground, the music would not please.

CHI. I care not, I, knew she and all the world. 71
I love Lavinia more than all the world.

DEM. Youngling, learn thou to make some
    meaner choice.
Lavinia is thine elder brother's hope.

AAR. Why, are ye mad? Or know ye not, in Rome
How furious and impatient they be, 76
And cannot brook competitors in love?
I tell you, lords, you do but plot your deaths
By this device.

CHI.   Aaron, a thousand deaths
Would I propose to achieve° her whom I love. 80

AAR. To achieve her! How?

DEM.   Why makest thou it so strange?
She is a woman, therefore may be wooed;
She is a woman, therefore may be won;°
She is Lavinia, therefore must be loved.
What, man! More water glideth by the mill 85
Than wots the miller of; and easy it is
Of a cut loaf to steal a shive,° we know.
Though Bassianus be the Emperor's brother,
Better than he have worn Vulcan's badge.°

AAR. [Aside] Aye, and as good as Saturninus
    may. 90

DEM. Then why should he despair that knows to
    court it
With words, fair looks, and liberality?
What, hast not thou full often struck a doe
And borne her cleanly° by° the keeper's nose?

AAR. Why, then, it seems, some certain snatch° or
    so 95
Would serve your turns.

CHI.   Aye, so the turn were served.

DEM. Aaron, thou hast hit it.

AAR.   Would you had hit it, too!
Then should not we be tired with this ado.
Why, hark ye, hark ye! And are you such fools
To square° for this? Would it offend you, then,
That both should speed?° 101

CHI. Faith, not me.

DEM.   Nor me, so I were one.

AAR. For shame, be friends, and join for that you
    jar.°

'Tis policy and stratagem° must do
That° you affect; and so must you resolve 105
That what you cannot as you would achieve
You must perforce accomplish as you may.
Take this of me: Lucrece° was not more chaste
Than this Lavinia, Bassianus' love.
A speedier course than lingering languishment
Must we pursue, and I have found the path. 111
My lords, a solemn hunting is in hand.
There will the lovely Roman ladies troop.
The forest walks are wide and spacious,
And many unfrequented plots° there are, 115
Fitted by kind° for rape and villainy.
Single° you thither then this dainty doe,
And strike her home by force, if not by words.
This way, or not at all, stand you in hope.
Come, come, our Empress, with her sacred wit 120
To villainy and vengeance consecrate,
Will we acquaint with all that we intend;
And she shall file our engines with advice
That will not suffer you to square yourselves,°
But to your wishes' height advance you both. 125
The Emperor's Court is like the House of Fame,°
The palace full of tongues, of eyes and ears.
The woods are ruthless,° dreadful, deaf and dull.
There speak, and strike, brave boys, and take your
    turns;
There serve your lust, shadowed from Heaven's eye,
And revel in Lavinia's treasury. 131

CHI. Thy counsel, lad, smells of no cowardice.

DEM. Sit fas aut nefas,° till I find the stream
To cool this heat, a charm to calm these fits,
Per Styga, per manes vehor.°   [Exeunt.] 135

SCENE II. *A forest near Rome. Horns and cry
of hounds heard.*

[*Enter* TITUS ANDRONICUS, *with* HUNTERS, *&c.,*
MARCUS, LUCIUS, QUINTUS, *and* MARTIUS.]

TIT. The hunt is up,° the morn is bright and
    gray,°
The fields are fragrant, and the woods are green.
Uncouple° here, and let us make a bay,°
And wake the Emperor and his lovely bride,
And rouse the Prince, and ring a hunter's peal, 5

---

104. stratagem: cunning. **105. That:** what. **108. Lucrece:** the Roman lady, the pattern of chastity, whom Sextus Tarquinius ravished. Shakespeare told the story in *Lucrece.* **115. plots:** flat spaces. **116. kind:** nature. **117. Single:** separate. **123–24. And . . . yourselves:** "She will perfect (*file:* polish) our devices (*engines*), which you cannot adjust (*square*) by yourselves." **126. House of Fame:** i.e., a place where everything is known. **128. ruthless:** pitiless. **133. *Sit . . . nefas:*** be it right or wrong. **135. *Per . . . vehor:*** I am carried through the Styx and through the spirits of the dead; i.e., I will go through Hell to get what I want.

    Sc. ii: 1. hunt is up: the hunters and hounds are ready. **gray:** sometimes used for sky-blue. **3. Uncouple:** loose the hounds. **bay:** cry of hounds. See *MND,* IV.i.127,n and 128,n.

---

64. jet: encroach. **67. broached:** set flowing. **80. achieve:** win. **82–83. She . . . won:** See *I Hen VI,* V.iii.78 and *Rich III,* I.ii.228–29. **87. shive:** slice. **89. Vulcan's badge:** i.e., the marks of a deceived husband. Vulcan, the blacksmith of the gods, was married to Venus, who was constantly unfaithful. **94. cleanly:** neatly, without being discovered. **by:** under. **95. snatch:** taste, snack. **100. square:** quarrel. **101. speed:** have success. **103. join . . . jar:** unite to gain the object for which you are quarreling.

That all the Court may echo with the noise.
Sons, let it be your charge, as it is ours,
To attend the Emperor's person carefully.
I have been troubled in my sleep this night,
But dawning day new comfort hath inspired.   10
[A cry of hounds, and horns winded in a peal.°
Enter SATURNINUS, TAMORA, BASSIANUS, LAVINIA,
DEMETRIUS, CHIRON, *and their* ATTENDANTS.]
Many good morrows to your Majesty.
Madam, to you as many and as good.
I promisèd your Grace a hunter's peal.
  SAT. And you have rung it lustily, my lords,
Somewhat too early for new-married ladies.   15
  BAS. Lavinia, how say you?
  LAV.   I say no.
I have been broad awake two hours and more.
  SAT. Come on then. Horse and chariots let us
have,
And to our sport. [*To* TAMORA] Madam, now shall
ye see
Our Roman hunting.
  MARC.   I have dogs, my lord,   20
Will rouse the proudest panther in the chase
And climb the highest promontory top.
  TIT. And I have horse will follow where the
game
Makes way,° and run like swallows o'er the plain.
  DEM. Chiron, we hunt not, we, with horse nor
hound,   25
But hope to pluck a dainty doe to ground.
                              [*Exeunt.*]

SCENE III. *A lonely part of the forest.*

[*Enter* AARON, *with a bag of gold.*]
  AAR. He that had wit would think that I had
none,
To bury so much gold under a tree
And never after to inherit° it.
Let him that thinks of me so abjectly
Know that this gold must coin a stratagem,   5
Which, cunningly effected, will beget
A very excellent piece of villainy.
And so repose, sweet gold, for their unrest
                              [*Hides the gold.*]
That have their alms out of the Empress' chest.°
                      [*Enter* TAMORA.]
  TAM. My lovely Aaron, wherefore look'st thou
sad,   10
When everything doth make a gleeful boast?
The birds chant melody on every bush,
The snake lies rollèd° in the cheerful sun,
The green leaves quiver with the cooling wind

And make a checkered° shadow on the ground.
Under their sweet shade, Aaron, let us sit,   16
And, whilst the babbling echo mocks the hounds,
Replying shrilly to the well-tuned horns,
As if a double hunt were heard at once,
Let us sit down and mark their yellowing° noise;
And — after conflict such as was supposed   21
The° wandering Prince and Dido once enjoyed,
When with a happy storm they were surprised,
And curtained with a counsel-keeping cave —
We may, each wreathèd in the other's arms,   25
Our pastimes done, possess a golden slumber,
Whiles hounds and horns and sweet melodious birds
Be unto us as is a nurse's song
Of lullaby to bring her babe asleep.
  AAR. Madam, though Venus govern your desires,
Saturn is dominator° over mine.   31
What signifies my deadly-standing° eye,
My silence and my cloudy melancholy,
My fleece of woolly hair that now uncurls
Even as an adder when she doth unroll   35
To do some fatal execution?
No, madam, these are no venereal° signs.
Vengeance is in my heart, death in my hand;
Blood and revenge are hammering in my head.
Hark, Tamora, the Empress of my soul,   40
Which never hopes more Heaven than rests in
thee,
This is the day of doom for Bassianus.
His Philomel° must lose her tongue today,
Thy sons make pillage of her chastity,
And wash their hands in Bassianus' blood.   45
Seest thou this letter? Take it up, I pray thee,
And give the king this fatal-plotted° scroll.
Now question me no more; we are espied.
Here comes a parcel° of our hopeful booty,
Which dreads not yet their lives' destruction.   50
  TAM. Ah, my sweet Moor, sweeter to me than
life!
  AAR. No more, great Empress. Bassianus comes.
Be cross° with him, and I'll go fetch thy sons
To back thy quarrels, whatsoe'er they be. [*Exit.*]
                [*Enter* BASSIANUS *and* LAVINIA.]
  BAS. Who have we here? Rome's royal Empress,
Unfurnished° of her well-beseeming° troop?   56

---

10. s.d., winded . . . peal: blown in unison.   24. way: a path.
  Sc. iii: 3. inherit: possess.   9. That . . . chest: i.e., any of
the Andronici who is rewarded by the Empress will find that he
has only won trouble.   13. rolled: coiled.

15. checkered: light and dark.   20. yellowing: often emended
to "yelping."   22–24. The . . . cave: Aeneas, the Trojan Prince,
on his way from the sack of Troy, stayed at Carthage where
Dido, the widowed Queen, fell in love with him. Their passion
reached its climax when they were driven into a cave by a storm.
The story is told in Bk. I of Virgil's *Aeneid*. See *Temp*, II.i.76,n.
31. dominator: ruler. Those who were influenced by the planet
Saturn were grim and deadly. See App. I.   32. deadly-standing:
glaring and deadly.   37. venereal: of love.   43. Philomel: See
T Andr Intro. p. 295b.   47. fatal-plotted: planned for a deadly
purpose.   49. parcel: part, portion.   53. cross: perverse.
56. Unfurnished: unprovided. well-beseeming: appropriate.
Great persons never went abroad without a suitable escort.

Or is it Dian,° habited like her,
Who hath abandonèd her holy groves
To see the general hunting in this forest?
    TAM. Saucy controller° of my private steps!   60
Had I the power that some say Dian had,
Thy temples should be planted presently°
With horns, as was Actaeon's,° and the hounds
Should drive upon thy new-transformèd limbs,
Unmannerly intruder as thou art!   65
    LAV. Under your patience, gentle Empress,
'Tis thought you have a goodly gift in horning,°
And to be doubted° that your Moor and you
Are singled° forth to try experiments.   69
Jove shield your husband from his hounds today!
'Tis pity they should take him for a stag.
    BAS. Believe me, Queen, your swarth Cimmerian°
Doth make your honor of his body's hue,
Spotted,° detested, and abominable.
Why are you sequestered from all your train,   75
Dismounted from your snow-white goodly steed,
And wandered hither to an obscure plot,
Accompanied but with a barbarous Moor,
If foul desire had not conducted you?
    LAV. And, being intercepted in your sport,   80
Great reason that my noble lord be rated°
For sauciness — I pray you, let us hence,
And let her joy° her raven-colored love.
This valley fits the purpose passing° well.   84
    BAS. The King my brother shall have note of this.
    LAV. Aye, for these slips have made him noted°
    long.
Good King, to be so mightily abused!
    TAM. Why have I patience to endure all this?
        [*Enter* DEMETRIUS *and* CHIRON.]
    DEM. How now, dear sovereign, and our gracious
    Mother!
Why doth your Highness look so pale and wan?   90
    TAM. Have I not reason, think you, to look pale?
These two have ticed° me hither to this place.
A barren detested vale, you see it is —
The trees, though summer, yet forlorn and lean,
O'ercome with moss and baleful° mistletoe.   95
Here never shines the sun. Here nothing breeds,
Unless the nightly owl or fatal raven.
And when they showed me this abhorrèd pit,
They told me, here, at dead time of the night,°
A thousand fiends, a thousand hissing snakes,   100
Ten thousand swelling toads, as many urchins,°

Would make such fearful and confusèd cries
As any mortal body hearing it
Should straight fall mad, or else die suddenly.
No sooner had they told this hellish tale,   105
But straight they told me they would bind me here
Unto the body of a dismal yew,
And leave me to this miserable death;
And then they called me foul adulteress,
Lascivious Goth, and all the bitterest terms   110
That ever ear did hear to such effect.
And, had you not by wondrous fortune come,
This vengeance on me had they executed.
Revenge it, as you love your mother's life,
Or be ye not henceforth called my children.   115
    DEM. This is a witness that I am thy son.
        [*Stabs* BASSIANUS.]
    CHI. And this for me, struck home to show my
    strength.   [*Also stabs* BASSIANUS, *who dies.*]
    LAV. Aye, come, Semiramis — nay, barbarous
    Tamora!
For no name fits thy nature but thy own!
    TAM. Give me thy poniard.° You shall know, my
    boys,   120
Your mother's hand shall right your mother's
    wrong.
    DEM. Stay, madam. Here is more belongs to her.
First thrash the corn, then after burn the straw.
This minion° stood upon her chastity,
Upon her nuptial vow, her loyalty,   125
And with that painted° hope braves your mighti-
    ness.
And shall she carry this unto her grave?
    CHI. An if she do, I would I were a eunuch.
Drag hence her husband to some secret hole,
And make his dead trunk° pillow to our lust.   130
    TAM. But when ye have the honey ye desire,
Let not this wasp outlive us both to sting.
    CHI. I warrant you, madam, we will make that
    sure.
Come, mistress, now perforce we will enjoy
That nice-preservèd honesty° of yours.   135
    LAV. O Tamora! Thou bear'st a woman's
    face ——
    TAM. I will not hear her speak. Away with her!
    LAV. Sweet lords, entreat her hear me but a word.
    DEM. Listen, fair madam. Let it be your glory
To see her tears, but be your heart to them   140
As unrelenting flint to drops of rain.
    LAV. When did the tiger's young ones teach the
    dam?°
Oh, do not learn° her wrath; she taught it thee.
The milk thou suck'dst from her did turn to mar-
    ble;
Even at thy teat thou hadst thy tyranny.   145

---

57. **Dian:** Diana, the goddess of hunting and the moon. 60. **controller:** interfering critic.   62. **presently:** immediately.   63. **Actaeon:** Actaeon gazed on the goddess Diana while she and her nymphs were bathing. As a punishment he was turned into a stag which Diana's hounds tore to pieces.   67. **horning:** cuckolding. See App. 11.   68. **doubted:** suspected.   69. **singled:** separated.   72. **Cimmerian:** The Cimmerians lived in the dark North; so "black."   74. **Spotted:** infected.   81. **rated:** rebuked.   83. **joy:** enjoy.   84. **passing:** exceedingly.   86. **noted:** notorious.   92. **ticed:** enticed.   95. **baleful:** harmful.   99. **dead . . . night:** midnight.   101. **urchins:** hedgehogs.

120. **poniard:** dagger.   124. **minion:** darling — used contemptuously.   126. **painted:** i.e., unreal.   130. **trunk:** body.   135. **nicepreserved honesty:** prudishly guarded chastity.   142. **dam:** mother.   143. **learn:** teach.

Yet every mother breeds not sons alike.
[*To* CHIRON] Do thou entreat her show a woman's
pity.
CHI. What, wouldst thou have me prove myself
a bastard?
LAV. 'Tis true, the raven doth not hatch a lark.
Yet have I heard — Oh, could I find it now! — 150
The lion, moved with pity, did endure
To have his princely paws pared all away.
Some say that ravens foster forlorn children,
The whilst their own birds famish in their nests.
Oh, be to me, though thy hard heart say no, 155
Nothing so kind, but something pitiful!
TAM. I know not what it means. Away with her!
LAV. Oh, let me teach thee! For my father's sake,
That gave thee life when well he might have slain
thee,
Be not obdurate, open thy deaf ears. 160
TAM. Hadst thou in person ne'er offended me,
Even for his sake am I pitiless.
Remember, boys, I poured forth tears in vain
To save your brother from the sacrifice,
But fierce Andronicus would not relent. 165
Therefore, away with her, and use her as you will;
The worse to her, the better loved of me.
LAV. O Tamora, be called a gentle Queen,
And with thine own hands kill me in this place!
For 'tis not life that I have begged so long. 170
Poor I° was slain when Bassianus died.
TAM. What begg'st thou then? Fond° woman, let
me go.
LAV. 'Tis present death I beg; and one thing
more
That womanhood denies my tongue to tell.
Oh, keep me from their worse than killing lust,
And tumble me into some loathsome pit 176
Where never man's eye may behold my body.
Do this, and be a charitable murderer.
TAM. So should I rob my sweet sons of their fee.
No, let them satisfy their lust on thee. 180
DEM. Away! For thou hast stayed us here too
long.
LAV. No grace? No womanhood? Ah, beastly
creature!
The blot and enemy to our general name!
Confusion fall ——
CHI. Nay, then I'll stop your mouth. — Bring
thou her husband. 185
This is the hole where Aaron bid us hide him.
[DEMETRIUS *throws the body of* BASSIANUS
into the pit. Then exeunt DEMETRIUS *and*
CHIRON, *dragging off* LAVINIA.]
TAM. Farewell, my sons. See that you make her
sure.
Ne'er let my heart know merry cheer indeed,
Till all the Andronici be made away.

171. **Poor I**: I, poor woman. 172. **Fond**: foolish.

Now will I hence to seek my lovely Moor, 190
And let my spleenful sons this trull° deflower.
[*Exit.*]
[*Re-enter* AARON, *with* QUINTUS *and* MARTIUS.]
AAR. Come on, my lords, the better foot before.
Straight will I bring you to the loathsome pit
Where I espied the panther fast asleep. 194
QUIN. My sight is very dull, whate'er it bodes.°
MART. And mine, I promise you. Were it not for
shame,
Well could I leave our sport to sleep awhile.
[*Falls into the pit.*]
QUIN. What, art thou fall'n? What subtle hole is
this
Whose mouth is covered with rude-growing briers
Upon whose leaves are drops of new-shed blood
As fresh as morning dew distilled on flowers? 201
A very fatal place it seems to me.
Speak, Brother, hast thou hurt thee with the fall?
MART. O Brother, with the dismal'st object hurt
That ever eye with sight made heart lament! 205
AAR. [*Aside*] Now will I fetch the King to find
them here,
That he thereby may have a likely guess
How these were they that made away his brother.
[*Exit.*]
MART. Why dost not comfort me and help me out
From this unhallowed and blood-stainèd hole? 210
QUIN. I am surprisèd with an uncouth° fear;
A chilling sweat o'erruns my trembling joints;
My heart suspects more than mine eye can see.
MART. To prove thou hast a true-divining heart,
Aaron and thou look down into this den, 215
And see a fearful sight of blood and death.
QUIN. Aaron is gone, and my compassionate°
heart
Will not permit mine eyes once to behold
The thing whereat it trembles by surmise.
Oh, tell me how it is, for ne'er till now 220
Was I a child to fear I know not what.
MART. Lord Bassianus lies embrewèd° here,
All on a heap, like to a slaughtered lamb,
In this detested, dark, blood-drinking pit. 224
QUIN. If it be dark, how dost thou know 'tis he?
MART. Upon his bloody finger he doth wear
A precious ring, that lightens all the hole,
Which, like a taper in some monument,
Doth shine upon the dead man's earthy cheeks
And shows the ragged entrails° of the pit. 230
So pale did shine the moon on Pyramus°
When he by night lay bathed in maiden blood.
O Brother, help me with thy fainting hand —

191. **trull**: strumpet. 195. **My . . . bodes**: my eyesight grows
dim; I wonder what evil that signifies (*bodes*). 211. **uncouth**:
strange. 217. **compassionate**: sympathetic. 222. **embrewed**:
blood-stained. 230. **ragged entrails**: rough inside. 231. **Pyramus**: For the sad story of the suicide of Pyramus, see *MND*.
V.i.108–354.

If fear hath made thee faint, as me it hath —
Out of this fell° devouring receptacle,   235
As hateful as Cocytus'° misty mouth.
 QUIN. Reach me thy hand, that I may help thee
  out,
Or, wanting strength to do thee so much good,
I may be plucked into the swallowing womb
Of this deep pit, poor Bassianus' grave.   240
I have no strength to pluck thee to the brink.
 MART. Nor I no strength to climb without thy
  help.
 QUIN. Thy hand once more. I will not loose again
Till thou art here aloft, or I below.
Thou canst not come to me — I come to thee.   245
            [Falls in.]
  [Enter SATURNINUS with AARON.]
 SAT. Along with me. I'll see what hole is here,
And what he is that now is leaped into it.
Say, who art thou that lately didst descend
Into this gaping hollow of the earth?
 MART. The unhappy son of old Andronicus,   250
Brought hither in a most unlucky hour
To find thy brother Bassianus dead.
 SAT. My brother dead! I know thou dost but jest.
He and his lady both are at the lodge°
Upon the north side of this pleasant chase.°   255
'Tis not an hour since I left them there.
 MART. We know not where you left them all
  alive,
But, out, alas, here have we found him dead.
  [Re-enter TAMORA, with ATTENDANTS, TITUS
    ANDRONICUS, and LUCIUS.]
 TAM. Where is my lord the King?
 SAT. Here, Tamora, though grieved with killing
  grief.   260
 TAM. Where is thy brother Bassianus?
 SAT. Now to the bottom dost thou search my
  wound.
Poor Bassianus here lies murderèd.
 TAM. [Giving a letter] Then all too late I bring
  this fatal writ,
The complot° of this timeless° tragedy,   265
And wonder greatly that man's face can fold
In pleasing smiles such murderous tyranny.
 SAT. [Reads.] " An if° we miss to meet him hand-
  somely —
Sweet huntsman, Bassianus 'tis we mean —
Do thou so much as dig the grave for him.   270
Thou know'st our meaning. Look for thy reward
Among the nettles at the elder tree
Which overshades the mouth of that same pit
Where we decreed to bury Bassianus.
Do this and purchase us thy lasting friends."   275
O Tamora! Was ever heard the like?

This is the pit, and this the elder tree.
Look, sirs, if you can find the huntsman out
That should have murdered Bassianus here.   279
 AAR. My gracious lord, here is the bag of gold.
 SAT. [To TITUS] Two of thy whelps, fell curs of
  bloody kind,
Have here bereft my brother of his life.
Sirs, drag them from the pit unto the prison.
There let them bide until we have devised
Some never-heard-of torturing pain for them.   285
 TAM. What, are they in this pit? Oh, wondrous
  thing!
How easily murder is discoverèd!
 TIT. High Emperor, upon my feeble knee
I beg this boon, with tears not lightly shed,
That this fell fault of my accursèd sons,   290
Accursèd, if the fault be proved in them ——
 SAT. If it be proved! You see it is apparent.
Who found this letter? Tamora, was it you?
 TAM. Andronicus himself did take it up.
 TIT. I did, my lord. Yet let me be their bail.   295
For, by my fathers' reverend tomb, I vow
They shall be ready at your highness' will
To answer their suspicion° with their lives.
 SAT. Thou shalt not bail them. See thou follow
  me.
Some bring the murdered body, some the mur-
  derers.   300
Let them not speak a word; the guilt is plain.
For, by my soul, were there worse end than death,
That end upon them should be executed.
 TAM. Andronicus, I will entreat the king.
Fear not° thy sons. They shall do well enough.   305
 TIT. Come, Lucius, come! Stay not to talk with
  them.   [Exeunt.]

   SCENE IV. *Another part of the forest.*

  [Enter DEMETRIUS and CHIRON, with LAVINIA,
ravished, her hands cut off, and her tongue cut out.]
 DEM. So, now go tell, an if thy tongue can speak,
Who 'twas that cut thy tongue and ravished thee.
 CHI. Write down thy mind, bewray° thy mean-
  ing so,
An if thy stumps will let thee play the scribe.
 DEM. See how with signs and tokens she can
  scrowl.°   5
 CHI. Go home, call for sweet° water, wash thy
  hands.
 DEM. She hath no tongue to call, nor hands to
  wash;
And so let's leave her to her silent walks.

---

235. fell: terrible, cruel.   236. Cocytus: one of the rivers of
Hades.   254. lodge: hunting lodge.   255. chase: park.   265. complot: plot. timeless: untimely.   268. An if: if.

298. their suspicion: the charges of which they are suspected.
305. Fear not: do not fear for the safety of.
 Sc. iv: 3. bewray: reveal.   5. scrowl: scrawl, scribble.
6. sweet: perfumed.

CHI. An 'twere my case, I should go hang my-
   self.
DEM. If thou hadst hands to help thee knit° the
   cord.   [*Exeunt* DEMETRIUS *and* CHIRON.]   10
[*Horns winded within. Enter* MARCUS *from*
        hunting.]
MARC. Who is this? My niece that flies away so
   fast!
Cousin,° a word. Where is your husband?
If I do dream, would all my wealth would wake me!
If I do wake, some planet strike me down,
That I may slumber in eternal sleep!   15
Speak, gentle Niece. What stern ungentle hands
Have lopped and hewed and made thy body bare
Of her two branches, those sweet ornaments,
Whose circling shadows kings have sought to sleep
   in,
And might not gain so great a happiness   20
As have thy love? Why dost not speak to me?
Alas, a crimson river of warm blood,
Like to a bubbling fountain stirred with wind,
Doth rise and fall between thy rosèd lips,
Coming and going with thy honey breath.   25
But, sure, some Tereus° hath deflowered thee,
And, lest thou shouldst detect him, cut thy tongue.
Ah, now thou turnst away thy face for shame!
And, notwithstanding all this loss of blood,
As from a conduit° with three issuing spouts,   30
Yet do thy cheeks look red as Titan's° face
Blushing to be encountered with a cloud.
Shall I speak for thee? Shall I say 'tis so?
Oh, that I knew thy heart, and knew the beast,
That I might rail at him to ease my mind!   35
Sorrow concealèd, like an oven stopped,°
Doth burn the heart to cinders where it is.
Fair Philomel, why she but lost her tongue
And in a tedious° sampler° sewed her mind;
But, lovely Niece, that mean° is cut from thee. 40
A craftier Tereus, cousin, hast thou met,
And he hath cut those pretty fingers off
That could have better sewed than Philomel.
Oh, had the monster seen those lily hands
Tremble, like aspen leaves, upon a lute,°   45
And make the silken strings delight to kiss them,
He would not then have touched them for his life!
Or, had he heard the heavenly harmony
Which that sweet tongue hath made,   49
He would have dropped his knife and fell asleep,

As Cerberus at the Thracian poet's feet.°
Come, let us go and make thy father blind;
For such a sight will blind a father's eye.
One hour's storm will drown the fragrant meads;°
What will whole months of tears thy father's eyes?
Do not draw back, for we will mourn with thee. 56
Oh, could our mourning ease thy misery!
                            [*Exeunt.*]

Act III

SCENE I. *Rome. A street.*

[*Enter* JUDGES, SENATORS, *and* TRIBUNES, *with*
MARTIUS *and* QUINTUS, *bound, passing on to the*
place of execution; TITUS *going before, pleading.*]
TIT. Hear me, grave Fathers! Noble Tribunes,
   stay!
For pity of mine age, whose youth was spent
In dangerous wars, whilst you securely slept.
For all my blood in Rome's great quarrel shed,
For all the frosty nights that I have watched,   5
And for these bitter tears which now you see
Filling the agèd wrinkles in my cheeks,
Be pitiful to my condemnèd sons,
Whose souls are not corrupted as 'tis thought.
For two and twenty sons I never wept,   10
Because they died in Honor's lofty bed.
       [*Lieth down.° The* JUDGES, &c.
             pass by him and exeunt.]
For these, Tribunes, in the dust I write
My heart's deep languor° and my soul's sad tears.
Let my tears stanch the earth's dry appetite;   14
My sons' sweet blood will make it shame and blush.
O Earth, I will befriend thee more with rain
That shall distil from these two ancient urns°
Than youthful April shall with all his showers.
In summer's drought I'll drop upon thee still;
In winter with warm tears I'll melt the snow,   20
And keep eternal springtime on thy face,
So° thou refuse to drink my dear sons' blood.
      [*Enter* LUCIUS, *with his weapon drawn.*]
O reverend Tribunes! O gentle, aged men!
Unbind my sons, reverse the doom of death,
And let me say, that never wept before,   25
My tears are now prevailing orators.
LUC. O noble Father, you lament in vain.

---

10. **knit:** tie.   **12. Cousin:** kinswoman; the word is used of any near relation.   **26. Tereus:** See *T Andr* Intro. p. 295b.   **30. conduit:** fountain.   **31. Titan:** the sun.   **36. oven stopped:** The ancient oven was a cavity in brick or earth which was first heated by red hot charcoal. The charcoal was then raked out and the food to be cooked placed inside, the entrance being stopped by a turf or bricks. Unless the oven were opened at the proper time, the contents burned.   **39. tedious:** which took a long time. **sampler:** piece of embroidery. See *T Andr* Intro. p. 296a. **40. mean:** method.   **45. lute:** See Pl. 18d.

51. **Cerberus . . . feet:** Orpheus, the Thracian singer, sought his dead wife Eurydice among the dead. Such was the power of his music that he charmed even Cerberus, the three-headed dog, guarding the entrance of Hades.   **54. meads:** meadows.
   Act III, Sc. i: **11. s.d., Lieth down:** i.e., he throws himself prostrate on the ground.   **13. languor:** grief.   **17. urns:** i.e., his eyes.   **22. So:** so long as.

The Tribunes hear you not. No man is by,
And you recount your sorrows to a stone.   29
  TIT. Ah, Lucius, for thy brothers let me plead.
Grave Tribunes, once more I entreat of you ——
  LUC. My gracious lord, no tribune hears you
    speak.
  TIT. Why, 'tis no matter, man. If they did hear,
They would not mark me; or if they did mark,
They would not pity me. Yet plead I must,   35
And bootless° unto them.
Therefore I tell my sorrows to the stones;
Who, though they cannot answer my distress,
Yet in some sort they are better than the Tribunes,
For that they will not intercept° my tale.   40
When I do weep, they humbly at my feet
Receive my tears, and seem to weep with me;
And, were they but attirèd in grave weeds,°
Rome could afford no tribune like to these.
A stone is soft as wax, tribunes more hard than
    stones.   45
A stone is silent and offendeth not,
And tribunes with their tongues doom men to
    death.   [Rises.]
But wherefore stand'st thou with thy weapon
    drawn?
  LUC. To rescue my two brothers from their
    death —
For which attempt the judges have pronounced   50
My everlasting doom of banishment.
  TIT. Oh, happy man! They have befriended thee.
Why, foolish Lucius, dost thou not perceive
That Rome is but a wilderness of tigers?
Tigers must prey, and Rome affords no prey   55
But me and mine. How happy art thou, then,
From these devourers to be banishèd!
But who comes with our brother Marcus here?
    [Enter MARCUS and LAVINIA.]
  MARC. Titus, prepare thy aged eyes to weep,
Or, if not so, thy noble heart to break.   60
I bring consuming sorrow to thine age.
  TIT. Will it consume me? Let me see it then.
  MARC. This was thy daughter.
  TIT.   Why, Marcus, so she is.
  LUC. Aye me, this object kills me!
  TIT. Faint-hearted boy, arise, and look upon her.
Speak, Lavinia, what accursèd hand   66
Hath made thee handless in thy father's sight?
What fool hath added water to the sea,
Or brought a fagot to bright-burning Troy?
My grief was at the height before thou camest,   70
And now, like Nilus,° it disdaineth bounds.
Give me a sword! I'll chop off my hands, too.
For they have fought for Rome, and all in vain;
And they have nursed this woe in feeding life.
In bootless prayer have they been held up,   75

And they have served me to effectless° use.
Now all the service I require of them
Is that the one will help to cut the other.
'Tis well, Lavinia, that thou hast no hands,
For hands to do Rome service is but vain.   80
  LUC. Speak, gentle Sister, who hath martyred
    thee?
  MARC. Oh, that delightful engine° of her
    thoughts,
That blabbed them with such pleasing eloquence,
Is torn from forth that pretty hollow cage,
Where, like a sweet melodious bird, it sung   85
Sweet varied notes, enchanting every ear!
  LUC. Oh, say thou for her, who hath done this
    deed?
  MARC. Oh, thus I found her, straying in the park,
Seeking to hide herself, as doth the deer
That hath received some unrecuring° wound.   90
  TIT. It was my dear, and he that wounded her
Hath hurt me more than had he killed me dead.
For now I stand as one upon a rock,
Environed° with a wilderness of sea,   94
Who marks the waxing tide grow wave by wave,
Expecting ever when some envious surge
Will in his brinish bowels swallow him.
This way to death my wretched sons are gone.
Here stands my other son, a banished man,
And here my brother, weeping at my woes;   100
But that which gives my soul the greatest spurn°
Is dear Lavinia, dearer than my soul.
Had I but seen thy picture in this plight,
It would have madded me. What shall I do
Now I behold thy lively° body so?   105
Thou hast no hands to wipe away thy tears,
Nor tongue to tell me who hath martyred thee.
Thy husband he is dead; and for his death
Thy brothers are condemned, and dead by this.
Look, Marcus! Ah, Son Lucius, look on her!   110
When I did name her brothers, then fresh tears
Stood on her cheeks, as doth the honeydew
Upon a gathered lily almost withered.
  MARC. Perchance she weeps because they killed
    her husband,
Perchance because she knows them innocent.   115
  TIT. If they did kill thy husband, then be joyful,
Because the law hath ta'en revenge on them.
No, no, they would not do so foul a deed.
Witness the sorrow that their sister makes.
Gentle Lavinia, let me kiss thy lips;   120
Or make some sign how I may do thee ease.
Shall thy good uncle, and thy brother Lucius,
And thou, and I, sit round about some fountain,
Looking all downward, to behold our cheeks
How they are stained, as meadows yet not dry   125

---

36. bootless: in vain.   40. intercept: interrupt.   43. grave
weeds: solemn garments.   71. Nilus: the Nile.

76. effectless: ineffectual.   82. engine: instrument.   90. un-
recuring: uncurable.   94. Environed: surrounded.   101. spurn:
contemptuous blow.   105. lively: living.

With miry slime left on them by a flood?
And in the fountain shall we gaze so long
Till the fresh taste be taken from that clearness,
And made a brine pit with our bitter tears?
Or shall we cut away our hands, like thine?   130
Oh shall we bite our tongues, and in dumb shows°
Pass the remainder of our hateful days?
What shall we do? Let us, that have our tongues,
Plot some device of further misery
To make us wondered at in time to come.   135
    LUC. Sweet Father, cease your tears; for at your
      grief
See how my wretched sister sobs and weeps.
    MARC. Patience, dear Niece. Good Titus, dry
      thine eyes.
    TIT. Ah, Marcus, Marcus! Brother, well I wot
Thy napkin° cannot drink a tear of mine,   140
For thou, poor man, hast drowned it with thine
    own.
    LUC. Ah, my Lavinia, I will wipe thy cheeks.
    TIT. Mark, Marcus, mark! I understand her signs.
Had she a tongue to speak, now would she say
That to her brother which I said to thee.   145
His napkin, with his true tears all bewet,
Can do no service on her sorrowful cheeks.
Oh, what a sympathy of woe is this,
As far from help as Limbo° is from bliss!   149
      [*Enter* AARON.]
    AAR. Titus Andronicus, my lord the Emperor
Sends thee this word — that if thou love thy sons,
Let Marcus, Lucius, or thyself, old Titus,
Or anyone of you, chop off your hand
And send it to the King. He for the same
Will send thee hither both thy sons alive,   155
And that shall be the ransom for their fault.
    TIT. O gracious Emperor! O gentle Aaron!
Did ever raven sing so like a lark
That gives sweet tidings of the sun's uprise?
With all my heart I'll send the Emperor   160
My hand.
Good Aaron, wilt thou help to chop it off?
    LUC. Stay, Father! For that noble hand of thine,
That hath thrown down so many enemies,
Shall not be sent. My hand will serve the turn.   165
My youth can better spare my blood than you,
And therefore mine shall save my brothers' lives.
    MARC. Which of your hands hath not defended
    Rome,
And reared aloft the bloody battle-axe,
Writing destruction on the enemy's castle?   170
Oh, none of both but are of high desert.
My hand hath been but idle; let it serve
To ransom my two nephews from their death.
Then have I kept it to a worthy end.

    AAR. Nay, come, agree whose hand shall go
    along,   175
For fear they die before their pardon come.
    MARC. My hand shall go.
    LUC.   By Heaven, it shall not go!
    TIT. Sirs, strive no more. Such withered herbs as
    these
Are meet for plucking up, and therefore mine.
    LUC. Sweet Father, if I shall be thought thy son,
Let me redeem my brothers both from death.   181
    MARC. And for our father's sake and mother's
    care,
Now let me show a brother's love to thee.
    TIT. Agree between you. I will spare my hand.
    LUC. Then I'll go fetch an ax.   185
    MARC. But I will use the ax.
      [*Exeunt* LUCIUS *and* MARCUS.]
    TIT. Come hither, Aaron. I'll deceive them both.
Lend me thy hand, and I will give thee mine.
    AAR. [*Aside*] If that be call'd deceit, I will be
    honest,
And never, whilst I live, deceive men so.   190
But I'll deceive you in another sort,
And that you'll say, ere half an hour pass.
      [*Cuts off* TITUS's *hand.*]
      [*Re-enter* LUCIUS *and* MARCUS.]
    TIT. Now stay your strife. What shall be is
    dispatched.
Good Aaron, give his Majesty my hand.
Tell him it was a hand that warded° him   195
From thousand dangers; bid him bury it.
More hath it merited; that let it have.
As for my sons, say I account of them
As jewels purchased at an easy price,
And yet dear, too, because I bought mine own.   200
    AAR. I go, Andronicus; and for thy hand
Look by and by to have thy sons with thee.
[*Aside*] Their heads, I mean. Oh, how this villainy
Doth fat° me with the very thoughts of it!
Let fools do good, and fair men call for grace;   205
Aaron will have his soul black like his face.
                  [*Exit.*]
    TIT. Oh, here I lift this one hand up to Heaven,
And bow this feeble ruin to the earth.
If any power pities wretched tears,
To that I call! [*To* LAVINIA] What, wouldst thou
    kneel with me?   210
Do, then, dear heart, for Heaven shall hear our
    prayers,
Or with our sighs we'll breathe the welkin dim,°
And stain the sun with fog, as sometime clouds
When they do hug him in their melting bosoms.
    MARC. O Brother, speak with possibilities,   215
And do not break into these deep extremes.°

---

131. dumb shows: speechless signs. See *Haml*, III.ii.145.
140. napkin: handkerchief.   149. Limbo: the place of confinement for souls barred from Heaven.

195. warded: guarded.   204. fat: make me feel happy.
212. breathe . . . dim: make the sky (*welkin*) cloudy with our breath.   216. break . . . extremes: speak so extravagantly.

TIT. Is not my sorrow deep, having no bottom?
Then be my passions bottomless with them.
    MARC. But yet let reason govern thy lament.
    TIT. If there were reason for these miseries,   220
Then into limits° could I bind my woes.
When Heaven doth weep, doth not the earth o'er-
    flow?
If the winds rage, doth not the sea wax mad,
Threatening the welkin with his big-swoln face?
And wilt thou have a reason for this coil?°   225
I am the sea — hark, how her sighs do blow!
She is the weeping welkin, I the earth:
Then must my sea be movèd with her sighs;
Then must my earth with her continual tears
Become a deluge, overflowed and drowned,   230
For why° my bowels cannot hide her woes,
But like a drunkard must I vomit them.
Then give me leave, for losers will have leave
To ease their stomachs with their bitter tongues.
    [*Enter a* MESSENGER, *with two heads and a hand.*]
    MESS. Worthy Andronicus, ill art thou repaid
For that good hand thou sent'st the Emperor.   236
Here are the heads of thy two noble sons,
And here's thy hand, in scorn to thee sent back —
Thy griefs their sports, thy resolution mocked,
That woe is me to think upon thy woes,   240
More than remembrance of my father's death.
                [*Exit.*]
    MARC. Now let hot Aetna cool in Sicily,
And be my heart an ever-burning hell!
These miseries are more than may be borne.   244
To weep with them that weep doth ease some deal,
But sorrow flouted at is double death.
    LUC. Ah, that this sight should make so deep a
    wound,
And yet detested life not shrink thereat!
That ever death should let life bear his name,   249
Where life hath no more interest but to breathe!
           [LAVINIA *kisses* TITUS.]
    MARC. Alas, poor heart! That kiss is comfortless
As frozen water to a starvèd snake.
    TIT. When will this fearful slumber° have an
    end?
    MARC. Now farewell, flattery; die, Andronicus.
Thou dost not slumber. See, thy two sons' heads,
Thy warlike hand, thy mangled daughter here,   256
Thy other banished son with this dear sight
Struck pale and bloodless, and thy brother, I,
Even like a stony image, cold and numb.
Ah, now no more will I control thy griefs.   260
Rend off thy silver hair, thy other hand
Gnawing with thy teeth, and be this dismal sight
The closing up of our most wretched eyes.
Now is a time to storm. Why art thou still?

TIT. Ha, ha, ha!   265
    MARC. Why dost thou laugh? It fits not with this
    hour.
    TIT. Why, I have not another tear to shed.
Besides, this sorrow is an enemy,
And would usurp upon my watery eyes
And make them blind with tributary° tears.   270
Then which way shall I find Revenge's cave?
For these two heads do seem to speak to me,
And threat me I shall never come to bliss
Till all these mischiefs be returned° again
Even in their throats that have committed them.
Come, let me see what task I have to do.   276
You heavy° people, circle me about,
That I may turn me to each one of you,
And swear unto my soul to right your wrongs.
The vow is made. Come, Brother, take a head,   280
And in this hand the other will I bear.
Lavinia, thou shalt be employed in these things.
Bear thou my hand, sweet wench, between thy
    teeth.
As for thee, boy, go get thee from my sight.
Thou art an exile, and thou must not stay.   285
Hie° to the Goths, and raise an army there.
And, if you love me, as I think you do,
Let's kiss and part, for we have much to do.
           [*Exeunt all but* LUCIUS.]
    LUC. Farewell, Andronicus, my noble father,
The woeful'st man that ever lived in Rome.   290
Farewell, proud Rome; till Lucius come again,
He leaves his pledges dearer than his life.
Farewell, Lavinia, my noble sister.
Oh, would thou wert as thou tofore° hast been!
But now nor° Lucius nor Lavinia lives   295
But in oblivion° and hateful griefs.
If Lucius live, he will requite your wrongs,
And make proud Saturnine and his Empress
Beg at the gates, like Tarquin and his Queen.°
Now will I to the Goths and raise a power,   300
To be revenged on Rome and Saturnine.   [*Exit.*]

SCENE II. *A room in* TITUS's *house. A banquet
set out.*

[*Enter* TITUS, MARCUS, LAVINIA, *and young* LUCIUS,
a Boy.]
    TIT. So, so,° now sit; and, look you, eat no more
Than will preserve just so much strength in us
As will revenge these bitter woes of ours.

---

221. **into limits**: within boundaries.   225. **coil**: turmoil.   231. **For why**: because.   253. **fearful slumber**: i.e., life, which is now nothing but a nightmare.

270. **tributary**: which pay tribute to the enemy, sorrow.   274. **returned**: paid back.   277. **heavy**: sad.   286. **Hie**: hasten.   294. **tofore**: hitherto.   295. **nor**: neither.   296. **But in oblivion**: only in a state of complete despair.   299. **Tarquin . . . Queen**: After the outrage committed on Lucrece by his son Sextus (see II.i.108,n), Tarquin and his family were driven from Rome.
    Sc. ii: 1. **So, so**: In dialogue *so, so* indicates some action such as setting the stool ready for Lavinia. See *Lear*, III.vi.90.

Marcus, unknit that sorrow-wreathen knot.°   4
Thy niece and I, poor creatures, want our hands,
And cannot passionate° our tenfold grief
With folded arms. This poor right hand of mine
Is left to tyrannize upon my breast;
Who, when my heart, all mad with misery,
Beats in this hollow prison of my flesh,   10
Then thus I thump it down.
[*To* LAVINIA] Thou map of woe,° that thus dost
        talk in signs!
When thy poor heart beats with outrageous beat-
        ing,
Thou canst not strike it thus to make it still.
Wound it with sighing,° girl, kill it with groans,
Or get some little knife between thy teeth,   16
And just against thy heart make thou a hole,
That all the tears that thy poor eyes let fall
May run into that sink, and soaking in,
Drown the lamenting fool° in sea-salt tears.   20
        MARC. Fie, Brother, fie! Teach her not thus to lay
Such violent hands upon her tender life.
        TIT. How now! Has sorrow made thee dote al-
        ready?
Why, Marcus, no man should be mad but I.
What violent hands can she lay on her life?   25
Ah, wherefore dost thou urge the name of hands —
To bid Aeneas° tell the tale twice o'er,
How Troy was burnt and he made miserable?
Oh, handle not the theme, to talk of hands,
Lest we remember still that we have none.   30
Fie, fie, how franticly I square° my talk
As if we should forget we had no hands
If Marcus did not name the word of hands!
Come, let's fall to; and, gentle girl, eat this.
Here is no drink. Hark, Marcus, what she says.   35
I can interpret all her martyred signs.°
She say she drinks no other drink but tears,
Brewed with her sorrow, meshed° upon her cheeks.
Speechless complainer, I will learn thy thought.
In thy dumb action will I be as perfect   40
As begging hermits in their holy prayers.
Thou shalt not sigh, nor hold thy stumps to
        Heaven,
Nor wink, nor nod, nor kneel, nor make a sign,
But I of these will wrest an alphabet,   44

4. **unknit . . . knot:** Folded arms were a sign of grief, melancholy,
or perplexity. See *Haml,* I.v.174.   **6. passionate:** express
the strong emotion of.   **12. map of woe:** picture of sorrow.
15. Wound . . . sighing: It was supposed that sighs caused the
heart's blood to fail. If Lavinia sighs enough, she will kill herself.
See *Haml,* II.i.94–96.   **20. fool:** used sometimes as a term of
affection. See *Lear,* V.iii.305.   **27. Aeneas:** Virgil put the account of the destruction of Troy in the mouth of Aeneas, who
told the tale to Dido. See II.iii.22–24,n.   **31. square:** shape.
36. martyred signs: the signs of her martyrdom.   **38. meshed:**
for mashed, lit., brewed.

And by still° practice learn to know thy meaning.
        BOY. Good Grandsire, leave these bitter deep
        laments.
Make my aunt merry with some pleasing tale.
        MARC. Alas, the tender boy, in passion moved,
Doth weep to see his grandsire's heaviness.
        TIT. Peace, tender sapling! Thou art made of
        tears,   50
And tears will quickly melt thy life away.
        [MARCUS *strikes the dish with a knife.*]
What dost thou strike at, Marcus, with thy knife?
        MARC. At that that I have killed, my lord — a fly.
        TIT. Out on thee, murderer! Thou kill'st my
        heart.
Mine eyes are cloyed with view of tyranny.   55
A deed of death done on the innocent
Becomes not Titus' brother. Get thee gone!
I see thou art not for my company.
        MARC. Alas, my lord, I have but killed a fly.
        TIT. "But!" How if that fly had a father and
        mother?   60
How would he hang his slender gilded wings,
And buzz lamenting doings in the air!
Poor harmless fly,
That, with his pretty buzzing melody,
Came here to make us merry! And thou hast killed
        him.   65
        MARC. Pardon me, sir. It was a black ill-favored°
        fly,
Like to the Empress' Moor. Therefore I killed him.
        TIT. Oh, Oh, Oh,
Then pardon me for reprehending thee,
For thou hast done a charitable deed.   70
Give me thy knife, I will insult on° him,
Flattering myself as if it were the Moor
Come hither purposely to poison me.
There's for thyself, and that's for Tamora.
Ah, sirrah!°   75
Yet, I think, we are not brought so low,
But that between us we can kill a fly
That comes in likeness of a coal-black Moor.
        MARC. Alas, poor man, grief has so wrought on
        him,
He takes false shadows for true substances.   80
        TIT. Come, take away. Lavinia, go with me.
I'll to thy closet,° and go read with thee
Sad stories chancèd° in the times of old.
Come, boy, and go with me. Thy sight is young,   84
And thou shalt read when mine begin to dazzle.
        [*Exeunt.*]

45. still: continual.   **66. ill-favored:** ugly.   **71. insult on:** triumph over.   **75. sirrah:** used as a term of address to an inferior
or junior.   **82. closet:** private room.   **83. chanced:** which happened.

Act IV

SCENE I. *Rome.* TITUS's *garden.*

[*Enter young* LUCIUS *and* LAVINIA *running after him, and the* BOY *flies from her, with his books under his arm. Then enter* TITUS *and* MARCUS.]

BOY. Help, Grandsire, help! My Aunt Lavinia
Follows me everywhere, I know not why.
Good Uncle Marcus, see how swift she comes.
Alas, sweet Aunt, I know not what you mean.

MARC.   Stand by me, Lucius. Do not fear thine
    aunt.   5

TIT. She loves thee, boy, too well to do thee harm.

BOY. Aye, when my father was in Rome she did.

MARC. What means my Niece Lavinia by these
    signs?

TIT. Fear her not, Lucius. Somewhat doth she
    mean.
See, Lucius, see how much she makes of thee.   10
Somewhither would she have thee go with her.
Ah, boy, Cornelia° never with more care
Read to her sons than she hath read to thee
Sweet poetry and Tully's *Orator.*°

MARC.   Canst thou not guess wherefore she plies°
    thee thus?   15

BOY. My lord, I know not, I, nor can I guess,
Unless some fit or frenzy do possess her.
For I have heard my grandsire say full oft,
Extremity of griefs would make men mad,
And I have read that Hecuba° of Troy   20
Ran mad for sorrow. That made me to fear,
Although, my lord, I know my noble aunt
Loves me as dear as e'er my mother did,
And would not, but in fury,° fright my youth —
Which made me down to throw my books and fly,
Causeless perhaps. But pardon me, sweet Aunt.   26
And, madam, if my Uncle Marcus go,
I will most willingly attend° your ladyship.

MARC.   Lucius, I will. [LAVINIA *turns over with
her stumps the books which* LUCIUS *has let fall.*]

TIT. How now, Lavinia! Marcus, what means
    this?   30
Some book there is that she desires to see.
Which is it, girl, of these? Open them, boy.
But thou art deeper read, and better skilled.
Come, and take choice of all my library,
And so beguile thy sorrow till the Heavens   35
Reveal the damned contriver of this deed.
Why lifts she up her arms in sequence° thus?

MARC.   I think she means that there were more
    than one

Confederate in the fact.° Aye, more there was,
Or else to Heaven she heaves them for revenge.   40

TIT. Lucius, what book is that she tosseth° so?

BOY. Grandsire, 'tis Ovid's *Metamorphoses.*°
My mother gave it me.

MARC.   For love of her that's gone,
Perhaps she culled it from among the rest.

TIT. Soft! So busily she turns the leaves!   45
         [*Helping her.*]
What would she find? Lavinia, shall I read?
This is the tragic tale of Philomel,°
And treats of Tereus' treason and his rape;
And rape, I fear, was root of thine annoy.

MARC.   See, Brother, see! Note how she quotes°
    the leaves.   50

TIT. Lavinia, wert thou thus surprised, sweet girl,
Ravished and wronged, as Philomela was,
Forced in the ruthless, vast, and gloomy woods?
See, see!
Aye, such a place there is, where we did hunt —   55
Oh, had we never never hunted there! —
Patterned by that° the poet here describes,
By nature made for murders and for rapes.

MARC.   Oh, why should nature build so foul a den,
Unless the gods delight in tragedies?   60

TIT. Give signs, sweet girl — for here are none
    but friends —
What Roman lord it was durst do the deed.
Or slunk not Saturnine, as Tarquin erst,°
That left the camp to sin in Lucrece' bed?

MARC.   Sit down, sweet Niece. Brother, sit down
    by me.   65
Apollo, Pallas, Jove, or Mercury,°
Inspire me, that I may this treason find!
My lord, look here! Look here, Lavinia!
This sandy plot is plain.° Guide, if thou canst,
This after me. [*He writes his name with his staff,
    and guides it with feet and mouth.*] I have writ
    my name   70
Without the help of any hand at all.
Cursed be that heart that forced us to this shift!°
Write thou, good Niece, and here display at last
What God will have discovered for revenge.
Heaven guide thy pen to print thy sorrows plain,
That we may know the traitors and the truth!   76
    [*She takes the staff in her mouth, and guides it
               with her stumps, and writes.*]

TIT. Oh, do ye read, my lord, what she hath writ?
"STUPRUM.° CHIRON. DEMETRIUS."

MARC. What, what! The lustful sons of Tamora

---

39. **fact:** deed.   41. **tosseth:** turns over.   42. **Ovid's *Metamorphoses:*** a favorite and popular book, which tells the stories of those unhappy women of legend who, after many troubles, were transformed into other shapes.   47. **Philomel:** See *T Andr* Intro. p. 295b.   50. **quotes:** notes, points out.   57. **Patterned by that:** after the pattern that.   63. **erst:** once.   66. **Apollo . . . Mercury:** the most powerful of the Roman gods.   69. **plain:** flat.   72. **shift:** trick, device.   78. **STUPRUM:** rape.

Act IV, Sc. i: 12. Cornelia: a Roman matron, mother of the Gracchi, two famous political leaders. Her careful education of her sons was much admired.   14. **Tully's *Orator:*** Cicero's *De oratore.*   15. **plies:** keeps on worrying.   20. **Hecuba:** See *Haml,* II.ii.523–41.   24. **fury:** madness.   28. **attend:** wait on.   37. **in sequence:** one after the other.

Performers of this heinous, bloody deed?   80
  TIT. *Magni Dominator poli,*
Tam lentus audis scelera? Tam lentus vides?°
  MARC. Oh, calm thee, gentle lord, although I
    know
There is enough written upon this earth
To stir a mutiny in the mildest thoughts   85
And arm the minds of infants to exclaims.°
My lord, kneel down with me. Lavinia, kneel,
And kneel, sweet boy, the Roman Hector's hope.°
And swear with me — as, with the woeful fere°
And father of that chaste dishonored dame,   90
Lord Junius Brutus° sware for Lucrece' rape —
That we will prosecute by good advice°
Mortal revenge upon these traitorous Goths,
And see their blood or die with this reproach.
  TIT. 'Tis sure enough, an you knew how.   95
But if you hunt these bear whelps, then beware.
The dam will wake, and if she wind° you once,
She's with the lion deeply still in league
And lulls him whilst she playeth on her back,
And when he sleeps, will she do what she list.   100
You are a young huntsman, Marcus; let alone;
And come, I will go get a leaf° of brass,
And with a gad° of steel will write these words
And lay it by. The angry northern wind
Will blow these sands,° like Sibyl's leaves,°
  abroad,   105
And where's your lesson then? Boy, what say you?
  BOY. I say, my lord, that if I were a man,
Their mother's bedchamber should not be safe
For these bad bondmen to the yoke of Rome.°
  MARC. Aye, that's my boy! Thy father hath full
    oft   110
For his ungrateful country done the like.
  BOY. And, Uncle, so will I, an if I live.
  TIT. Come, go with me into mine armory.
Lucius, I'll fit thee, and withal, my boy
Shall carry from me to the Empress' sons   115
Presents that I intend to send them both.
Come, come! Thou'lt do thy message, wilt thou
  not?
  BOY. Aye, with my dagger in their bosoms,
    Grandsire.

  TIT. No, boy, not so. I'll teach thee another
  course.
Lavinia, come. Marcus, look to my house.   120
Lucius and I'll go brave it° at the Court.
Aye, marry,° will we, sir; and we'll be waited on.
    [*Exeunt* TITUS, LAVINIA, *and young* LUCIUS.]
  MARC. O Heavens, can you hear a good man
  groan,
And not relent, or not compassion° him?
Marcus, attend him in his ecstasy,°   125
That hath more scars of sorrow in his heart
Than foemen's marks upon his battered shield,
But yet so just that he will not revenge.
Revenge, ye Heavens, for old Andronicus! [*Exit.*]

SCENE II. *The same. A room in the palace.*

[*Enter* AARON, CHIRON, *and* DEMETRIUS *at one door;
and at another door, young* LUCIUS, *and an* ATTEND-
ANT, *with a bundle of weapons, and verses writ
upon them.*]

  CHI. Demetrius, here's the son of Lucius.
He hath some message to deliver us.
  AAR. Aye, some mad message from his mad
  grandfather.
  BOY. My lords, with all the humbleness I may,
I greet your honors from Andronicus.   5
  [*Aside*] And pray the Roman gods confound you
  both!
  DEM. Gramercy,° lovely Lucius. What's the
  news?
  BOY. [*Aside*] That you are both deciphered,°
  that's the news,
For villains marked with° rape. — May it please
  you,
My grandsire, well advised,° hath sent by me   10
The goodliest weapons of his armory
To gratify° your honorable youth,
The hope of Rome. For so he bid me say;
And so I do, and with his gifts present
Your lordships, that, whenever you have need,   15
You may be armèd and appointed° well.
And so I leave you both, [*Aside*] like bloody vil-
  lains.   [*Exeunt* BOY *and* ATTENDANT.]
  DEM. What's here? A scroll, and written round
  about!
Let's see.
[*Reads.*] " *Integer vitae, scelerisque purus,*   20
    Non eget Mauri jaculis, nec arcu."°

81–82. *Magni . . . vides:* ruler of the great Heavens, do you so
unconcernedly hear these crimes? So unconcernedly see them?
86. **exclaims:** exclamation. 88. **Roman . . . hope:** the hoped-
for champion to be — Hector was the champion of Troy. The
Romans regarded themselves as directly descended from the
Trojan heroes. 89. **fere:** spouse. 91. **Junius Brutus:** When
Tarquin's son violated Lucrece, it was Junius Brutus who led
the Romans to drive the Tarquin family out of Rome. 92. **by
. . . advice:** after careful thought. 97. **wind:** smell your scent.
102. **leaf:** sheet. 103. **gad:** point. 105. **sands:** i.e., the words
written by Lavinia in the sand. **Sibyl's leaves:** i.e., divine oracles.
The Sibyl was an ancient prophetess in Roman legend. She lived
in a cave at Cumae and delivered her prophecies by means of
leaves which she laid on the ground and which were scattered
by the wind. 109. **bondmen . . . Rome:** The sons of Tamora
were still nominally prisoners of the Romans.

121. **brave it:** swagger. 122. **marry:** Mary, by the Virgin.
124. **compassion:** pity. 125. **ecstasy:** fit of madness.
  Sc. ii. 7. **Gramercy:** thanks. See I.i.495,n. 8. **deciphered:**
revealed. 9. **marked with:** branded, known to have committed.
10. **well advised:** after careful thought. 12. **gratify:** honor.
16. **appointed:** equipped. 20–21. *Integer . . . arcu:* The opening lines of one of Horace's *Odes* (Bk.i.22) — "The man of upright life and clear from crime has no need of a Moor's javelins
or bow."

CHI. Oh, 'tis a verse in Horace. I know it well.
I read it in the grammar long ago.

AAR. Aye, just; a verse in Horace. Right, you
  have it.

[*Aside*] Now, what a thing it is to be an ass! 25
Here's no sound° jest. The old man hath found
  their guilt,
And sends them weapons wrapped about with lines
That wound, beyond their feeling, to the quick.°
But were our witty Empress well afoot,°
She would applaud Andronicus' conceit.°   30
But let her rest in her unrest awhile. —
And now, young lords, was 't not a happy star
Led us to Rome, strangers, and more than so,
Captives, to be advancèd to this height?
It did me good, before the palace gate   35
To brave° the Tribune in his brother's hearing.

DEM. But me more good to see so great a lord
Basely insinuate° and send us gifts.

AAR. Had he not reason, Lord Demetrius?
Did you not use his daughter very friendly?   40

DEM. I would we had a thousand Roman dames
At such a bay,° by turn to serve our lust.

CHI. A charitable wish and full of love.

AAR. Here lacks but your mother for to say
  amen.

CHI. And that would she for twenty thousand
  more.   45

DEM. Come, let us go and pray to all the gods
For our belovèd mother in her pains.

AAR. [*Aside*] Pray to the devils. The gods have
  given us over.°   [*Trumpets sound within.*]

DEM. Why do the Emperor's trumpets flourish
  thus?

CHI. Belike, for joy the Emperor hath a son.   50

DEM. Soft! Who comes here?

[*Enter* NURSE, *with a blackamoor* CHILD.]

NUR.   Good morrow, lords.
Oh, tell me, did you see Aaron the Moor?

AAR. Well, more or less, or ne'er a whit° at all,
Here Aaron is; and what with Aaron now?

NUR. O gentle Aaron, we are all undone!   55
Now help, or woe betide thee evermore!

AAR. Why, what a caterwauling dost thou keep!
What dost thou wrap and fumble in thine arms?

NUR. Oh, that which I would hide from Heaven's
  eye —
Our Empress' shame and stately Rome's disgrace!
She is delivered, lords, she is delivered.   61

AAR. To whom?

NUR.   I mean, she is brought abed.

AAR. Well, God give her good rest! What hath he
  sent her?

NUR. A devil.

AAR.   Why, then she is the devil's dam° —
A joyful issue.   65

NUR. A joyless, dismal, black and sorrowful issue.
Here is the babe, as loathsome as a toad
Amongst the fairest breeders° of our clime.
The Empress sends it thee, thy stamp, thy seal,   69
And bids thee christen it with thy dagger's point.

AAR. 'Zounds,° ye whore! Is black so base a hue?
Sweet blowse,° you are a beauteous blossom, sure.

DEM. Villain, what hast thou done?

AAR. That which thou canst not undo.

CHI. Thou hast undone our mother.   75

AAR. Villain, I have done thy mother.

DEM. And therein, hellish dog, thou hast undone
  her.
Woe to her chance,° and damned her loathèd
  choice!
Accursed the offspring of so foul a fiend!

CHI. It shall not live.   80

AAR. It shall not die.

NUR. Aaron, it must. The mother wills it so.

AAR. What, must it, Nurse? Then let no man
  but I
Do execution on my flesh and blood.

DEM. I'll broach° the tadpole on my rapier's
  point.   85
Nurse, give it me. My sword shall soon dispatch it.

AAR. Sooner this sword shall plow thy bowels up.
[*Takes the* CHILD *from the* NURSE, *and draws.*]
Stay, murderous villains! Will you kill your
  brother?
Now, by the burning tapers° of the sky,
That shone so brightly when this boy was got,   90
He dies upon my scimitar's° sharp point
That touches this my first-born son and heir!
I tell you, younglings, not Enceladus,°
With all his threatening band of Typhon's° brood,
Nor great Alcides,° nor the god of war,   95
Shall seize this prey out of his father's hands.
What, what, ye sanguine,° shallow-hearted boys!
Ye white-limed walls! Ye alehouse painted signs!°
Coal-black is better than another hue
In that it scorns to bear another hue;   100
For all the water in the ocean
Can never turn the swan's black legs to white,
Although she lave them hourly in the flood.

---

26. **sound**: wholesome. 28. **quick**: living flesh. 29. **well afoot**: well and on her feet. At this moment Tamora is in the throes of childbearing. 30. **conceit**: device. 36. **brave**: insult. 38. **insinuate**: flatter. 42. **At . . . bay**: i.e., brought to bay like a stag surrounded by the hounds. 48. **given us over**: abandoned us. 53. **a whit**: a bit.

64. **devil's dam**: the Devil's mother — because the newborn babe is black. The Devil was represented as black. 68. **breeders**: mothers. 71. **'Zounds**: by God's (Christ's) wounds. 72. **blowse**: slut. 78. **chance**: bad luck. 85. **broach**: spit, stick. 89. **tapers**: candles, i.e., stars. 91. **scimitar**: curved sword. 93–94. **Enceladus, Typhon**: mighty giants who made war on the gods. 95. **Alcides**: Hercules. 97. **sanguine**: cowardly. See *I Hen IV*, II.iv.268n. 98. **alehouse . . . signs**: bad paintings of real men.

Tell the Empress from me, I am of age
To keep mine own — excuse it how she can.   105
   DEM. Wilt thou betray thy noble mistress thus?
   AAR. My mistress is my mistress — this myself,
The vigor and the picture of my youth.
This before all the world do I prefer.
This mauger° all the world will I keep safe,   110
Or some of you shall smoke° for it in Rome.
   DEM. By this our mother is forever shamed.
   CHI. Rome will despise her for this foul escape.°
   NUR. The Emperor in his rage will doom her
     death.
   CHI. I blush to think upon this ignomy.°   115
   AAR. Why, there's the privilege your beauty bears.
Fie, treacherous hue, that will betray with blushing
The close enacts° and counsels of the heart!
Here's a young lad framed of another leer.°   119
Look how the black slave smiles upon the father,
As who should say, "Old lad, I am thine own."
He is your brother, lords, sensibly° fed
Of that self° blood that first gave life to you,
And from that womb where you imprisoned were
He is enfranchisèd° and come to light.   125
Nay, he is your brother by the surer side,°
Although my seal be stampèd in his face.
   NUR. Aaron, what shall I say unto the Empress?
   DEM. Advise thee, Aaron, what is to be done,
And we will all subscribe° to thy advice.   130
Save thou the child, so° we may all be safe.
   AAR. Then sit we down, and let us all consult.
My son and I will have the wind of you.°
Keep there. Now talk at pleasure of your safety.
                     [*They sit.*]
   DEM. How many women saw this child of his?
   AAR. Why, so, brave lords! When we join in
     league,   136
I am a lamb; but if you brave the Moor,
The chafèd° boar, the mountain lioness,
The ocean swells not so as Aaron storms.
But say, again, how many saw the child?   140
   NUR. Cornelia the midwife and myself,
And no one else but the delivered Empress.
   AAR. The Empress, the midwife, and yourself.
Two may keep counsel when the third's away.°
Go to the Empress, tell her this I said.   145
[*He kills the* NURSE.] Weke, weke!
So cries a pig preparèd to the spit.
   DEM. What mean'st thou, Aaron? Wherefore
     didst thou this?

   AAR. Oh, Lord, sir, 'tis a deed of policy.°
Shall she live to betray this guilt of ours —
A long-tongued babbling gossip? No, lords, no.
And now be it known to you my full intent.   151
Not far, one Muliteus, my countryman,
His wife but yesternight was brought to bed.
His child is like to her, fair as you are.
Go pack° with him, and give the mother gold,   155
And tell them both the circumstance of all;
And how by this their child shall be advanced
And be receivèd for the Emperor's heir,
And substituted in the place of mine,
To calm this tempest whirling in the Court;   160
And let the Emperor dandle him for his own.
Hark ye, lords. You see I have given her physic,°
              [*Pointing to the* NURSE]
And you must needs bestow° her funeral.
The fields are near, and you are gallant grooms.
This done, see that you take no longer days,°   165
But send the midwife presently to me.
The midwife and the nurse well made away,
Then let the ladies tattle what they please.
   CHI. Aaron, I see thou wilt not trust the air
With secrets.
   DEM.   For this care of Tamora.   170
Herself and hers are highly bound to thee.
     [*Exeunt,* DEMETRIUS *and* CHIRON *bearing off*
                the NURSE's *body.*]
   AAR. Now to the Goths, as swift as swallow flies,
There to dispose this treasure in mine arms,
And secretly to greet the Empress' friends.
Come on, you thick-lipped slave, I'll bear you
     hence,   175
For it is you that puts us to our shifts.°
I'll make you feed on berries and on roots,
And feed on curds and whey, and suck the goat,
And cabin° in a cave, and bring you up
To be a warrior and command a camp. [*Exit.*]   180

SCENE III. *The same. A public place.*

[*Enter* TITUS, *bearing arrows with letters at the
ends of them; with him,* MARCUS, *young* LUCIUS, *and
other* GENTLEMEN (PUBLIUS, SEMPRONIUS, *and*
CAIUS), *with bows.*]
   TIT. Come, Marcus, come. Kinsmen, this is the
     way.
Sir boy, let me see your archery.
Look ye draw home° enough, and 'tis there
     straight.

---

110. **mauger:** in spite of.   111. **smoke:** sweat; i.e., have a hot
time.   113. **escape:** escapade.   115. **ignomy:** ignominy, disgrace.   118. **enacts:** resolutions.   119. **leer:** complexion.
122. **sensibly:** as a creature of feeling, truly.   123. **self:** same.
125. **enfranchised:** set free.   126. **surer side:** i.e., the mother's.
130. **subscribe:** agree.   131. **so:** so that.   133. **wind of you:**
will keep upwind of you so that you do not surprise us. Aaron
suspects that the brothers will try to kill the babe by treachery.
138. **chafed:** angered.   144. **Two . . . away:** three people can
keep a secret so long as two of them don't know it.

148. **deed of policy:** cunning act.   155. **pack:** plot.   162. **physic:** medicine.   163. **bestow:** provide.   165. **see . . . days:** do
not delay.   176. **puts . . . shifts:** makes us scheme.   179. **cabin:**
live privately.

   Sc. iii: 3. **draw home:** i.e., shoot your arrow from a bow fully
drawn.

Terras Astraea reliquit.°   4
Be you remembered,° Marcus, she's gone, she's fled.
Sirs, take you to your tools. You, Cousins, shall
Go sound the ocean, and cast your nets.
Happily° you may catch her in the sea.
Yet there's as little justice as at land.
No! Publius and Sempronius, you must do it.   10
'Tis you must dig with mattock and with spade,
And pierce the inmost center of the earth.
Then, when you come to Pluto's° region,
I pray you deliver him this petition.
Tell him it is for justice and for aid,   15
And that it comes from old Andronicus,
Shaken with sorrows in ungrateful Rome.
Ah, Rome! Well, well, I made thee miserable
What time° I threw the people's suffrages°
On him that thus doth tyrannize o'er me.   20
Go get you gone; and pray be careful all,
And leave you not a man-of-war unsearched.
This wicked Emperor may have shipped her°
    hence,
And, kinsmen, then we may go pipe° for justice.
    MARC. O Publius, is not this a heavy case,   25
To see thy noble uncle thus distract?°
    PUB. Therefore, my lord, it highly us concerns
By day and night to attend him carefully
And feed his humor° kindly as we may,
Till time beget some careful° remedy.   30
    MARC. Kinsmen, his sorrows are past remedy.
Join with the Goths, and with revengeful war
Take wreak° on Rome for this ingratitude,
And vengeance on the traitor Saturnine.
    TIT. Publius, how now! How now, my masters!
What, have you met with her?   36
    PUB. No, my good lord, but Pluto sends you
    word,
If you will have Revenge from Hell, you shall.
Marry, for Justice, she is so employed,   39
He thinks, with Jove in Heaven, or somewhere else,
So that perforce you must needs stay a time.
    TIT. He doth me wrong to feed° me with delays.
I'll dive into the burning lake below
And pull her out of Acheron° by the heels.
Marcus, we are but shrubs, no cedars we,   45
No big-boned men framed of the Cyclops'° size,
But metal, Marcus, steel to the very back,
Yet wrung with wrongs more than our backs can
    bear.

And sith there's no justice in earth nor Hell,
We will solicit Heaven, and move the gods   50
To send down Justice for to wreak our wrongs.
Come, to this gear.° You are a good archer, Marcus.
    [*He gives them the arrows.*]
" *Ad°* Jovem," that's for you. Here, " *Ad Apolli-
    nem.*"
" *Ad Martem,*" that's for myself.
Here, boy, to Pallas.° Here, to Mercury.   55
To Saturn,° Caius, not to Saturnine.
You were as good to° shoot against the wind.
To it, boy! Marcus, loose° when I bid.
Of my word, I have written to effect.
There's not a god left unsolicited.   60
    MARC. Kinsmen, shoot all your shafts° into the
    Court.
We will afflict the Emperor in his pride.
    TIT. Now, masters, draw. [*They shoot.*] Oh, well
    said, Lucius!
Good boy, in Virgo's° lap. Give it Pallas.
    MARC. My lord, I aim a mile beyond the moon.°
Your letter is with Jupiter by this.   66
    TIT. Ha, ha!
Publius, Publius, what hast thou done?
See, see, thou hast shot off one of Taurus'° horns.
    MARC. This was the sport, my lord. When Publius
    shot,   70
The Bull,° being galled, gave Aries° such a knock
That down fell both the Ram's° horns in the Court.
And who should find them but the Empress' vil-
    lain?
She laughed, and told the Moor he should not
    choose
But give them to his master for a present.   75
    TIT. Why, there it goes. God give his lordship joy!
[*Enter a* CLOWN,° *with a basket, and two pigeons
    in it.*]
News, news from Heaven! Marcus, the post is
    come.
Sirrah, what tidings? Have you any letters?
Shall I have justice? What says Jupiter?
    CLO. Oh, the gibbet maker!° He says that he   80
hath taken them down again, for the man must not
be hanged till the next week.
    TIT. But what says Jupiter, I ask thee?
    CLO. Alas, sir, I know not Jupiter. I never drank
with him in all my life.   85

---

4. *Terras . . . reliquit:* Astraea has left the earth. She was goddess
of justice. During the age of innocence she lived among men, but
when men grew wicked she left the earth and became the star
Virgo.   **5.** remembered: reminded.   **8.** Happily: by good luck.
13. Pluto: the King of the Underworld.   **19.** What time: when.
suffrages: votes.   **23.** her: i.e., Justice.   **24.** pipe: whistle.
26. distract: insane.   **29.** feed . . . humor: humor him.   **30.** careful: healing.   **33.** wreak: vengeance.   **42.** feed: put me off.
44. Acheron: one of the rivers in Hades.   **46.** Cyclops: giants
who worked for Vulcan the blacksmith god.

52. gear: affair.   **53–56.** *Ad . . .* Saturn: See IV.i.66,n. *Ad:* to.
55. Pallas: Minerva (Pallas Athene among the Greeks), goddess
of the intellectual and moral side of life.   **56.** Saturn: father of
the god Jupiter.   **57.** You . . . to: you might as well.   **58.** loose:
shoot.   **61.** shafts: arrows.   **64.** Virgo: see l. 4.   **65.** aim . . .
moon: i.e., I shoot at impossibilities. Marcus is humoring the
old man in his ravings.   **69–72.** Taurus . . . Bull . . . Aries . . .
Ram: See App. 1. and App. 11.   **76. s.d.,** clown: countryman.
80. gibbet maker: like the rest of Shakespeare's clowns, he mistakes long words: he is more familiar with the *gibbet* than with
Jupiter.

TIT. Why, villain, art not thou the carrier?

CLO. Aye, of my pigeons, sir; nothing else.

TIT. Why, didst thou not come from Heaven? 88

CLO. From Heaven! Alas, sir, I never came there. God forbid I should be so bold to press to Heaven in my young days. Why, I am going with my pigeons to the Tribunal plebs° to take up a matter of brawl betwixt my uncle and one of the Emperial's° men. 94

MARC. Why, sir, that is as fit as can be to serve for your oration; and let him deliver the pigeons to the Emperor from you.

TIT. Tell me, can you deliver an oration to the Emperor with a grace?°

CLO. Nay, truly, sir, I could never say grace in all my life. 101

TIT. Sirrah, come hither. Make no more ado, But give your pigeons to the Emperor. By me thou shalt have justice at his hands. Hold, hold! Meanwhile here's money for thy charges. 105
Give me pen and ink.
Sirrah, can you with a grace deliver a supplication?°

CLO. Aye, sir.

TIT. Then here is a supplication for you. And when you come to him, at the first approach 110 you must kneel, then kiss his foot, then deliver up your pigeons, and then look for your reward. I'll be at hand, sir. See you do it bravely.

CLO. I warrant you, sir, let me alone.

TIT. Sirrah, hast thou a knife? Come, let me see it. 115
Here, Marcus, fold it in the oration,
For thou hast made it like an humble suppliant.
And when thou hast given it to the Emperor,
Knock at my door, and tell me what he says.

CLO. God be with you, sir, I will. [*Exit.*] 120

TIT. Come, Marcus, let us go. Publius, follow me.
[*Exeunt.*]

SCENE IV. *The same. Before the palace.*

[*Enter* SATURNINUS, TAMORA, CHIRON, DEMETRIUS, LORDS, *and others;* SATURNINUS *with the arrows in his hand that* TITUS *shot.*]

SAT. Why, lords, what wrongs are these! Was ever seen
An Emperor in Rome thus overborne,°
Troubled, confronted thus, and for the extent

Of egal° justice used in such contempt? 4
My lords, you know, as know the mightful gods,
However these disturbers of our peace
Buzz in the people's ears, there naught hath passed
But even with° law against the wilful sons
Of old Andronicus. And what an if°
His sorrows have so overwhelmed his wits, 10
Shall we be thus afflicted in his wreaks,
His fits, his frenzy, and his bitterness?
And now he writes to Heaven for his redress:
See, here's to Jove, and this to Mercury —
This to Apollo — this to the God of War. 15
Sweet scrolls to fly about the streets of Rome!
What's this but libeling against the Senate
And blazoning° our unjustice everywhere?
A goodly humor,° is it not, my lords?
As who would say, in Rome no justice were. 20
But if I live, his feignèd ecstasies°
Shall be no shelter to these outrages.
But he and his shall know that justice lives
In Saturninus' health; whom, if he sleep,
He'll so awake as he° in fury shall 25
Cut off the proud'st conspirator that lives.

TAM. My gracious lord, my lovely Saturnine,
Lord of my life, commander of my thoughts,
Calm thee, and bear the faults of Titus' age,
The effects of sorrow for his valiant sons, 30
Whose loss hath pierced him deep and scarred his heart;
And rather comfort his distressèd plight
Than prosecute the meanest or the best
For these contempts. [*Aside*] Why, thus it shall become
High-witted Tamora to gloze° with all. 35
But, Titus, I have touched thee to the quick,
Thy lifeblood out. If Aaron now be wise,
Then is all safe, the anchor in the port.
[*Enter* CLOWN.]
How now, good fellow! Wouldst thou speak with us?

CLO. Yea, forsooth, an your mistership be emperial. 40

TAM. Empress I am, but yonder sits the Emperor.

CLO. 'Tis he. God and Saint Stephen° give you godden.° I have brought you a letter and a couple of pigeons here. [SATURNINUS *reads the letter.*]

SAT. Go, take him away, and hang him presently.° 45

CLO. How much money must I have?

---

92. **Tribunal plebs:** for Tribune of the plebs.   93. **Emperial's:** for Emperor's.   99. **with a grace:** gracefully.   107. **supplication:** written petition.
   Sc. iv: 2. overborne: dominated.

4. **egal:** equal, impartial.   8. **even with:** just according to.   9. **an if:** if.   18. **blazoning:** advertising, lit., painting.   19. **humor:** whim.   21. **ecstasies:** lunacies.   24–25. **he . . . He . . . he:** i.e., Saturninus.   35. **gloze:** talk smoothly.   42. **Saint Stephen:** There is no known reason why the clown should invoke the first Christian martyr.   43. **godden:** good afternoon.   45. **presently:** immediately.

TAM. Come, sirrah, you must be hanged.

CLO. Hanged! By 'r Lady,° then I have brought
up a neck to a fair end. [*Exit, guarded*.]

SAT. Despiteful° and intolerable wrongs! 50
Shall I endure this monstrous villainy?
I know from whence this same device proceeds.
May this be borne? As if his traitorous sons
That died by law for murder of our brother
Have by my means been butchered wrongfully! 55
Go, drag the villain hither by the hair;
Nor age nor honor shall shape° privilege.
For this proud mock I'll be thy slaughterman,
Sly frantic wretch, that holp'st° to make me great
In hope thyself should govern Rome and me. 60
  [*Enter* AEMILIUS.]
What news with thee, Aemilius?

AEM. Arm, my lords! Rome never had more
  cause.
The Goths have gathered head,° and with a power
Of high-resolvèd men, bent to the spoil,
They hither march amain,° under conduct° 65
Of Lucius, son to old Andronicus,
Who threats, in course of this revenge, to do
As much as ever Coriolanus° did.

SAT. Is warlike Lucius General of the Goths?
These tidings nip me, and I hang the head 70
As flowers with frost or grass beat down with
  storms.
Aye, now begin our sorrows to approach.
'Tis he the common people love so much.
Myself hath often heard them say,
When I have walkèd like a private man, 75
That Lucius' banishment was wrongfully,
And they have wished that Lucius were their Em-
  peror.

TAM. Why should you fear? Is not your city
  strong?

SAT. Aye, but the citizens favor Lucius,
And will revolt from me to succor him. 80

TAM. King, be thy thoughts imperious, like thy
  name.
Is the sun dimmed, that gnats do fly in it?
The eagle suffers little birds to sing
And is not careful° what they mean thereby,
Knowing that with the shadow of his wings 85
He can at pleasure stint° their melody —
Even so mayst thou the giddy men of Rome.
Then cheer thy spirit; for know, thou Emperor,
I will enchant the old Andronicus 89
With words more sweet, and yet more dangerous,
Than baits to fish, or honey stalks° to sheep,
Whenas the one is wounded with the bait,
The other rotted with delicious feed.

SAT. But he will not entreat his son for us.

TAM. If Tamora entreat him, then he will; 95
For I can smooth, and fill his agèd ears
With golden promises, that, were his heart
Almost impregnable, his old ears deaf,
Yet should both ear and heart obey my tongue.
  [*To* AEMILIUS] Go thou before; be our ambassador.
Say that the Emperor requests a parley 101
Of warlike Lucius, and appoint the meeting
Even at his father's house, the old Andronicus.

SAT. Aemilius, do this message honorably;
And if he stand on hostage° for his safety, 105
Bid him demand what pledge will please him best.

AEM. Your bidding shall I do effectually. [*Exit.*]

TAM. Now will I to that old Andronicus
And temper° him with all the art I have, 109
To pluck proud Lucius from the warlike Goths.
And now, sweet Emperor, be blithe again,
And bury all thy fear in my devices.

SAT. Then go successantly,° and plead to him.
  [*Exeunt.*]

Act V

SCENE I. *Plains near Rome.*

[*Flourish. Enter* LUCIUS *and* GOTHS, *with drum and
  colors.*]

LUC. Approvèd warriors, and my faithful friends,
I have receivèd letters from great Rome
Which signify what hate they bear their Emperor
And how desirous of our sight they are.
Therefore, great lords, be, as your titles witness, 5
Imperious, and impatient of your wrongs;
And wherein Rome hath done you any scathe,°
Let him make treble satisfaction.

1. GOTH. Brave slip,° sprung from the great An-
  dronicus,
Whose name was once our terror, now our comfort,
Whose high exploits and honorable deeds 11
Ingrateful Rome requites with foul contempt,
Be bold in us. We'll follow where thou lead'st,
Like stinging bees in hottest summer's day,
Led by their master to the flowered fields, 15
And be avenged on cursèd Tamora.

ALL THE GOTHS. And as he saith, so say we all
  with him.

LUC. I humbly thank him, and I thank you all.
But who comes here, led by a lusty Goth?

---

48. **By 'r Lady:** by the Blessed Virgin. 50. **Despiteful:** spiteful.
57. **shape:** provide. 59. **holp'st:** didst help. 63. **gathered
head:** raised an army. 65. **amain:** with full force. **conduct:**
leadership. 68. **Coriolanus:** See *Cor,* IV.vi.64–68. 84. **careful:**
troubled. 86. **stint:** stop. 91. **honey stalks:** clover.

105. **stand on hostage:** demand hostages. 109. **temper:** make
him soft (like wax). 113. **successantly:** successfully.
  Act V, Sc. i: 7. **scathe:** harm. 9. **slip:** offshoot.

[Enter a GOTH, *leading* AARON *with his* CHILD *in his arms.]*

2. GOTH. Renownèd Lucius, from our troops I
    strayed   20
To gaze upon a ruinous monastery;
And, as I earnestly did fix mine eye
Upon the wasted building, suddenly
I heard a child cry underneath a wall.
I made unto the noise, when soon I heard   25
The crying babe controlled with this discourse:
"Peace, tawny° slave, half me and half thy dam!
Did not thy hue bewray whose brat thou art,
Had nature lent thee but thy mother's look,
Villain, thou mightst have been an Emperor;   30
But where the bull and cow are both milk-white,
They never do beget a coal-black calf.
Peace, villain, peace!"—even thus he rates° the
    babe—
"For I must bear thee to a trusty Goth,   34
Who, when he knows thou art the Empress' babe,
Will hold thee dearly for thy mother's sake."
With this, my weapon drawn, I rushed upon him,
Surprised him suddenly, and brought him hither
To use as you think needful of the man.   39
    LUC. O worthy Goth, this is the incarnate devil
That robbed Andronicus of his good hand.
This is the pearl that pleased your Empress' eye,
And here's the base fruit of his burning lust.
Say, wall-eyed° slave, whither wouldst thou convey
This growing image of thy fiend-like face?   45
Why dost not speak? What, deaf? Not a word?
A halter, soldiers! Hang him on this tree,
And by his side his fruit of bastardy.
    AAR. Touch not the boy. He is of royal blood.
    LUC. Too like the sire for ever being good.   50
First hang the child, that he may see it sprawl—
A sight to vex the father's soul withal.
Get me a ladder.
[A ladder brought, which AARON *is made to ascend.]*
    AAR.   Lucius, save the child,
And bear it from me to the Empress.
If thou do this, I'll show thee wondrous things   55
That highly may advantage thee to hear.
If thou wilt not, befall what may befall,°
I'll speak no more but "Vengeance rot you all!"
    LUC. Say on. An if it please me which thou
    speak'st,
Thy child shall live, and I will see it nourished. 60
    AAR. An if it please thee! Why, assure thee,
    Lucius,
'Twill vex thy soul to hear what I shall speak.
For I must talk of murders, rapes, and massacres,
Acts of black night, abominable deeds,
Complots of mischief, treason, villainies   65
Ruthful° to hear, yet piteously performed;

And this shall all be buried by my death
Unless thou swear to me my child shall live.
    LUC. Tell on thy mind. I say thy child shall live.
    AAR. Swear that he shall, and then I will begin.
    LUC. Who should I swear by? Thou believest no
    god.   71
That granted, how canst thou believe an oath?
    AAR. What if I do not? As, indeed, I do not.
Yet, for I know thou art religious,
And hast a thing within thee callèd conscience,   75
With twenty popish tricks and ceremonies
Which I have seen thee careful to observe,
Therefore I urge thy oath. For that I know
An idiot holds his bauble° for a god,   79
And keeps the oath which by that god he swears,
To that I'll urge him. Therefore thou shalt vow
By that same god, what god soe'er it be,
That thou adorest and hast in reverence,
To save my boy, to nourish and bring him up;
Or else I will discover naught to thee.   85
    LUC. Even by my god I swear to thee I will.
    AAR. First know thou, I begot him on the Em-
    press.
    LUC. Oh, most insatiate and luxurious° woman!
    AAR. Tut, Lucius, this was but a deed of charity
To that which thou shalt hear of me anon.   90
'Twas her two sons that murdered Bassianus.
They cut thy sister's tongue, and ravished her,
And cut her hands, and trimmed her as thou saw'st.
    LUC. Oh, detestable villain! Call'st thou that trim-
    ming?
    AAR. Why, she was washed and cut and trimmed,
    and 'twas   95
Trim sport for them that had the doing of it.
    LUC. Oh, barbarous, beastly villains, like thyself!
    AAR. Indeed, I was their tutor to instruct them.
That codding° spirit had they from their mother,
As sure a card as ever won the set.°   100
That bloody mind, I think, they learned of me,
As true a dog as ever fought at head.°
Well, let my deeds be witness of my worth.
I trained° thy brethren to that guileful° hole
Where the dead corpse of Bassianus lay.   105
I wrote the letter that thy father found,
And hid the gold within the letter mentioned,
Confederate with the Queen and her two sons.
And what not done that thou hast cause to rue,
Wherein I had no stroke of mischief in it?   110
I played the cheater for thy father's hand,
And, when I had it, drew myself apart,
And almost broke my heart with extreme laughter.
I pried me through the crevice of a wall
When for his hand he had his two sons' heads,   115

---

27. tawny: dusky.   33. rates: chides.   44. wall-eyed: glaring.
57. befall . . . befall: come what may.   66. Ruthful: pitiful.

79. bauble: headed stick carried by a fool. See Pl. 12f.   88. luxurious: lustful.   99. codding: lustful.   100. set: the number of
hands which make up the complete game, "rubber."   102. at
head: i.e., courageously, without turning tail.   104. trained:
lured. guileful: deceptive.

Beheld his tears, and laughed so heartily
That both mine eyes were rainy like to his.
And when I told the Empress of this sport,
She swounded° almost at my pleasing tale,
And for my tidings gave me twenty kisses.   120
  1. GOTH. What, canst thou say all this and never
    blush?
  AAR. Aye, like a black dog, as the saying is.
  LUC. Art thou not sorry for these heinous deeds?
  AAR. Aye, that I had not done a thousand more.
Even now I curse the day — and yet, I think,   125
Few come within the compass of my curse —
Wherein I did not some notorious ill:
As kill a man, or else devise his death;
Ravish a maid, or plot the way to do it;
Accuse some innocent, and forswear° myself;   130
Set deadly enmity between two friends;
Make poor men's cattle break their necks;
Set fire on barns and haystacks in the night,   133
And bid the owners quench them with their tears.
Oft have I digged up dead men from their graves
And set them upright at their dear friends' doors,
Even when their sorrows almost were forgot;
And on their skins, as on the bark of trees,
Have with my knife carvèd in Roman letters,
"Let not your sorrow die, though I am dead."   140
Tut, I have done a thousand dreadful things
As willingly as one would kill a fly,
And nothing grieves me heartily indeed,
But that I cannot do ten thousand more.
  LUC. Bring down the devil, for he must not die
So sweet a death as hanging presently.   146
  AAR. If there be devils, would I were a devil,
To live and burn in everlasting fire,
So I might have your company in Hell
But to torment you with my bitter tongue!   150
  LUC. Sirs, stop his mouth, and let him speak no
    more.
        [Enter a GOTH.*]*
  3. GOTH. My lord, there is a messenger from
    Rome
Desires to be admitted to your presence.
  LUC. Let him come near.   154
        [Enter AEMILIUS.*]*
Welcome, Aemilius. What's the news from Rome?
  AEM. Lord Lucius, and you Princes of the Goths,
The Roman Emperor greets you all by me;
And, for he understands you are in arms,
He craves a parley at your father's house,
Willing you to demand your hostages,   160
And they shall be immediately delivered.
  1. GOTH. What says our General?
  LUC. Aemilius, let the Emperor give his pledges
Unto my father and my uncle Marcus,
And we will come. March away.   165
        [Flourish. Exeunt.]

119. swounded: swooned.   130. forswear: perjure.

SCENE II. *Rome. Before* TITUS'S *house.*

[Enter TAMORA, DEMETRIUS, *and* CHIRON, *disguised.]*
  TAM. Thus, in this strange and sad habiliment,°
I will encounter with Andronicus
And say I am Revenge, sent from below
To join with him and right his heinous wrongs.
Knock at his study, where, they say, he keeps°   5
To ruminate strange plots of dire revenge.
Tell him Revenge is come to join with him,
And work confusion on his enemies.   *[Knock.]*
        [Enter TITUS, *above.]*
  TIT. Who doth molest my contemplation?
Is it your trick to make me ope° the door,   10
That so my sad decrees° may fly away
And all my study be to no effect?
You are deceived; for what I mean to do
See here in bloody lines I have set down,
And what is written shall be executed.   15
  TAM. Titus, I am come to talk with thee.
  TIT. No, not a word! How can I grace my talk,
Wanting a hand to give it action?
Thou hast the odds° of me; therefore no more.
  TAM. If thou didst know me, thou wouldst talk
    with me.   20
  TIT. I am not mad. I know thee well enough.
Witness this wretched stump, witness these crimson
    lines;
Witness these trenches° made by grief and care;
Witness the tiring day and heavy night;
Witness all sorrow, that I know thee well   25
For our proud Empress, mighty Tamora.
Is not thy coming for my other hand?
  TAM. Know, thou sad man, I am not Tamora.
She is thy enemy, and I thy friend.
I am Revenge, sent from the infernal kingdom   30
To ease the gnawing vulture° of thy mind
By working wreakful° vengeance on thy foes.
Come down and welcome me to this world's light.
Confer with me of murder and of death.
There's not a hollow cave or lurking place,   35
No vast obscurity or misty vale,
Where bloody murder or detested rape
Can couch° for fear, but I will find them out
And in their ears tell them my dreadful name,
Revenge, which makes the foul offender quake.   40
  TIT. Art thou Revenge? And art thou sent to me
To be a torment to mine enemies?
  TAM. I am. Therefore come down and welcome
    me.
  TIT. Do me some service ere I come to thee.
Lo, by thy side where Rape and Murder stands,   45

Sc. ii: 1. habiliment: garment.   5. keeps: lives.   10. ope:
open.   11. decrees: decisions — Titus is now feigning madness.
19. odds: advantage.   23. trenches: lines in his forehead.
31. vulture: i.e., torment. The image is from the torture of Prometheus. See II.i.17,n.   32. wreakful: revengeful.   38. couch:
crouch down.

Now give some surance° that thou art Revenge —
Stab them, or tear them on thy chariot wheels,
And then I'll come and be thy wagoner,°
And whirl along with thee about the globes.°
Provide thee two proper palfreys,° black as jet,   50
To hale° thy vengeful wagon swift away,
And find out murderers in their guilty caves.
And when thy car° is loaden° with their heads,
I will dismount and by the wagon wheel
Trot like a servile footman all day long,   55
Even from Hyperion's° rising in the East
Until his very downfall in the sea,
And day by day I'll do this heavy task,
So° thou destroy Rapine and Murder there.   59
  TAM. These are my ministers and come with me.
  TIT. Are these thy ministers? What are they
    called?
  TAM. Rapine and Murder — therefore callèd so,
'Cause they take vengeance of such kind of men.
  TIT. Good Lord, how like the Empress' sons they
    are,
And you the Empress! But we worldly men   65
Have miserable, mad, mistaking eyes.
O sweet Revenge, now do I come to thee,
And if one arm's embracement will content thee,
I will embrace thee in it by and by.   [*Exit above.*]
  TAM. This closing with° him fits his lunacy.   70
Whate'er I forge° to feed his brain-sick fits,
Do you uphold and maintain in your speeches,
For now he firmly takes me for Revenge.
And, being credulous in this mad thought,
I'll make him send for Lucius his son,   75
And, whilst I at a banquet hold him sure,
I'll find some cunning practice out of hand°
To scatter and disperse the giddy Goths,
Or at the least make them his enemies.
See, here he comes, and I must ply my theme.   80
    [*Enter* TITUS, *below.*]
  TIT. Long have I been forlorn, and all for thee.
Welcome, dread Fury, to my woeful house.
Rapine and Murder, you are welcome too.
How like the Empress and her sons you are!
Well are you fitted, had you but a Moor.   85
Could not all Hell afford you such a devil?
For well I wot the Empress never wags°
But in her company there is a Moor;
And would you represent our Queen aright,
It were convenient you had such a devil.   90
But welcome, as you are. What shall we do?
  TAM. What wouldst thou have us do, Androni-
    cus?
  DEM. Show me a murderer, I'll deal with him.

  CHI. Show me a villain that hath done a rape,
And I am sent to be revenged on him.   95
  TAM. Show me a thousand that have done thee
    wrong,
And I will be revengèd on them all.
  TIT. Look round about the wicked streets of
    Rome,
And when thou find'st a man that's like thyself,
Good Murder, stab him; he's a murderer.   100
Go thou with him, and when it is thy hap°
To find another that is like to thee,
Good Rapine, stab him; he's a ravisher.
Go thou with them; and in the Emperor's Court
There is a Queen, attended by a Moor.   105
Well mayst thou know her by thine own propor-
    tion,°
For up and down she doth resemble thee.
I pray thee, do on them some violent death.
They have been violent to me and mine.
  TAM. Well hast thou lessoned us. This shall we do.
But would it please thee, good Andronicus,   111
To send for Lucius, thy thrice valiant son,
Who leads toward Rome a band of warlike Goths,
And bid him come and banquet at thy house.
When he is here, even at thy solemn feast,   115
I will bring in the Empress and her sons,
The Emperor himself, and all thy foes;
And at thy mercy shall they stoop and kneel,
And on them shalt thou ease thy angry heart.
What says Andronicus to this device?   120
  TIT. Marcus, my Brother! 'Tis sad Titus calls.
    [*Enter* MARCUS.]
Go, gentle Marcus, to thy nephew Lucius.
Thou shalt inquire him out among the Goths.
Bid him repair° to me and bring with him
Some of the chiefest princes of the Goths.   125
Bid him encamp his soldiers where they are.
Tell him the Emperor, and the Empress, too,
Feast at my house, and he shall feast with them.
This do thou for my love, and so let him,
As he regards his agèd father's life.   130
  MARC. This will I do, and soon return again.
          [*Exit.*]
  TAM. Now will I hence about thy business,
And take my ministers along with me.
  TIT. Nay, nay, let Rape and Murder stay with
    me,
Or else I'll call my brother back again,   135
And cleave to no revenge but Lucius.
  TAM. [*Aside to her sons*] What say you, boys?
    Will you bide with him
Whiles° I go tell my lord the Emperor
How I have governed° our determined° jest?   139
Yield to his humor, smooth and speak him fair,

46. surance: assurance.   48. wagoner: coachman.   49. globes:
planets.   50. palfreys: horses; the word usually means "riding
horses."   51. hale: haul.   53. car: chariot. loaden: laden.
56. Hyperion: the sun.   59. So: so long as.   70. closing with:
embracing.   71. forge: invent.   77. out of hand: forthwith.
87. wags: moves.

101. hap: chance.   106. proportion: shape.   124. repair: come.
138. Whiles: while.   139. governed: managed. determined:
agreed upon.

And tarry with him till I turn again.

TIT. [*Aside*] I know them all, though they sup-
   pose me mad,
And will o'erreach them in their own devices —
A pair of cursèd hellhounds and their dam.   144

DEM. Madam, depart at pleasure. Leave us here.

TAM. Farewell, Andronicus. Revenge now goes
To lay a complot° to betray thy foes.

TIT. I know thou dost; and, sweet Revenge, farewell.   [*Exit* TAMORA.]

CHI. Tell us, old man, how shall we be employed?

TIT. Tut, I have work enough for you to do.   150
Publius, come hither, Caius, and Valentine!
       [*Enter* PUBLIUS *and others.*]

PUB. What is your will?

TIT. Know you these two?

PUB. The Empress' sons, I take them, Chiron and
Demetrius.   155

TIT. Fie, Publius, fie! Thou art too much de-
   ceived.
The one is Murder, Rape is the other's name;
And therefore bind them, gentle Publius.
Caius and Valentine, lay hands on them.
Oft have you heard me wish for such an hour,   160
And now I find it. Therefore bind them sure,
And stop their mouths, if they begin to cry.   [*Exit.*
    PUBLIUS, &c. *lay hold on* CHIRON *and* DEMETRIUS.]

CHI. Villains, forbear! We are the Empress' sons.

PUB. And therefore do we what we are com-
   manded.   164
Stop close their mouths, let them not speak a word.
Is he sure bound? Look that you bind them fast.
   [*Re-enter* TIT, *with* LAVINIA; *he bearing a knife,
     and she a basin.*]

TIT. Come, come, Lavinia; look, thy foes are
   bound.
Sirs, stop their mouths, let them not speak to me,
But let them hear what fearful words I utter.
O villains, Chiron and Demetrius!   170
Here stands the spring whom you have stained with
   mud,
This goodly summer with your winter mixed.
You killed her husband, and for that vile fault
Two of her brothers were condemned to death,
My hand cut off and made a merry jest;   175
Both her sweet hands, her tongue, and that more
   dear
Than hands or tongue, her spotless chastity,
Inhuman traitors, you constrained and forced.
What would you say if I should let you speak?
Villains, for shame you could not beg for grace!
Hark, wretches, how I mean to martyr you.   181
This one hand yet is left to cut your throats,
Whilst that Lavinia 'tween her stumps doth hold
The basin that receives your guilty blood.   184

You know your mother means to feast with me,
And calls herself Revenge, and thinks me mad.
Hark, villains! I will grind your bones to dust,
And with your blood and it I'll make a paste,
And of the paste a coffin° I will rear,
And make two pasties of your shameful heads;   190
And bid that strumpet, your unhallowed dam,
Like to the earth, swallow her own increase.°
This is the feast that I have bid her to,
And this the banquet she shall surfeit on;°
For worse than Philomel you used my daughter,
And worse than Progne° I will be revenged.   196
And now prepare your throats. Lavinia, come,
            [*He cuts their throats.*]
Receive the blood; and when that they are dead,
Let me go grind their bones to powder small,
And with this hateful liquor temper° it;   200
And in that paste let their vile heads be baked.
Come, come, be everyone officious°
To make this banquet, which I wish may prove
More stern and bloody than the Centaurs' Feast.°
So now bring them in, for I'll play the cook,   205
And see them ready against° their mother comes.
       [*Exeunt, bearing the dead bodies.*]

SCENE III. *Court of* TITUS's *house. A banquet
set out.*

[*Enter* LUCIUS, MARCUS, *and* GOTHS, *with* AARON,
    prisoner.]

LUC. Uncle Marcus, since it is my father's mind
That I repair to Rome, I am content.

1. GOTH. And ours with thine, befall what fortune will.

LUC. Good Uncle, take you in this barbarous
   Moor,
This ravenous tiger, this accursèd devil.   5
Let him receive no sustenance, fetter him,
Till he be brought unto the Empress' face
For testimony of her foul proceedings.
And see the ambush° of our friends be strong;
I fear the Emperor means no good to us.   10

AAR. Some devil whisper curses in mine ear,
And prompt me, that my tongue may utter forth
The venomous malice of my swelling heart!

LUC. Away, inhuman dog! Unhallowed slave!
Sirs, help our uncle to convey him in.   15
    [*Exeunt* GOTHS, *with* AARON. *Flourish within.*]

---

189. coffin: pie crust shaped like a box.   **192. increase:** offspring.
194. surfeit on: eat to excess.   **196. Progne:** See *T Andr* Intro.
p. 296a.   **200. temper:** mix.   **202. officious:** busy.   **204. Centaurs' Feast:** The centaurs were creatures half men and half
horses. When invited to the marriage feast of Pirithous (King of
the Lapithae) and Hippodamia, they attempted to carry off the
bride and other women. A bloody fight followed. The story is
told in Ovid's *Metamorphoses.*   **206. against:** by the time that.
Sc. iii: 9. ambush: hidden escort.

147. complot: plot.

The trumpets show the Emperor is at hand.

[*Enter* SATURNINUS *and* TAMORA, *with* AEMILIUS,
      TRIBUNES, SENATORS, *and others.*]

SAT. What, hath the firmament moe° suns than
      one?

LUC. What boots it° thee to call thyself a sun?

MARC. Rome's Emperor, and Nephew, break the
      parle.°

These quarrels must be quietly debated.   20
The feast is ready which the careful Titus
Hath ordained to an honorable end —
For peace, for love, for league° and good to Rome.
Please you, therefore, draw nigh, and take your
      places.   24

SAT. Marcus, we will. [*Hautboys° sound. The
            company sit down at table.*]

[*Enter* TITUS, *like a cook, placing the meat on the
table, and* LAVINIA *with a veil over her face, young*
      LUCIUS, *and others.*]

TIT. Welcome, my gracious lord; welcome, dread
      Queen;

Welcome, ye warlike Goths; welcome, Lucius;
And welcome, all. Although the cheer be poor,
'Twill fill your stomachs. Please you eat of it.

SAT. Why art thou thus attired, Andronicus?   30

TIT. Because I would be sure to have all well
To entertain your Highness and your Empress.

TAM. We are beholding° to you, good Androni-
      cus.

TIT. An if your Highness knew my heart, you
      were.

My lord the Emperor, resolve me° this: 35
Was it well done of rash Virginius
To slay his daughter with his own right hand°
Because she was enforced, stained, and deflowered?

SAT. It was, Andronicus.

TIT. Your reason, mighty lord?   40

SAT. Because the girl should not survive her
      shame

And by her presence still° renew his sorrows.

TIT. A reason mighty, strong and effectual,
A pattern, precedent, and lively warrant°
For me, most wretched, to perform the like.   45
Die, die, Lavinia, and thy shame with thee,
And with thy shame thy father's sorrow die!

                        [*Kills* LAVINIA.]

SAT. What hast thou done, unnatural and un-
      kind?

TIT. Killed her, for whom my tears have made
      me blind.

I am as woeful as Virginius was,   50
And have a thousand times more cause than he
To do this outrage; and it now is done.

SAT. What, was she ravished? Tell who did the
      deed.

TIT. Will 't please you eat? Will 't please your
      Highness feed?

TAM. Why hast thou slain thine only daughter
      thus?   55

TIT. Not I! 'Twas Chiron and Demetrius.
They ravished her, and cut away her tongue;
And they, 'twas they, that did her all this wrong.

SAT. Go fetch them hither to us presently.   59

TIT. Why, there they are both, baked in that pie,
Whereof their mother daintily hath fed,
Eating the flesh that she herself hath bred.
'Tis true, 'tis true; witness my knife's sharp point!

                        [*Kills* TAMORA.]

SAT. Die, frantic wretch, for this accursèd deed!

                        [*Kills* TITUS.]

LUC. Can the son's eye behold his father bleed?
There's meed for meed,° death for a deadly deed!

            [*Kills* SATURNINUS. *A great tumult.* LUCIUS,
            MARCUS, *and others go up into the balcony.*]

MARC. You sad-faced men, people and sons of
      Rome,   67
By uproars severed, as a flight of fowl
Scattered by winds and high tempestuous gusts,
Oh, let me teach you how to knit again   70
This scattered corn into one mutual° sheaf,
These broken limbs again into one body;
Lest Rome herself be bane° unto herself,
And she whom mighty kingdoms curtsy to,
Like a forlorn and desperate castaway,   75
Do shameful execution on herself.
But if my frosty signs and chaps° of age,
Grave witnesses of true experience,
Cannot induce you to attend my words —
[*To* LUCIUS] Speak, Rome's dear friend. As erst°
      our ancestor,   80
When with his solemn tongue he did discourse
To love-sick Dido's sad attending ear
The story of that baleful° burning night
When subtle Greeks surprised King Priam's Troy,
Tell us what Sinon° hath bewitched our ears,   85
Or who hath brought the fatal engine° in
That gives our Troy, our Rome, the civil wound.
My heart is not compact° of flint nor steel,
Nor can I utter all our bitter grief,
But floods of tears will drown my oratory   90
And break my utterance, even in the time
When it should move you to attend° me most,

---

17. moe: more. Saturninus means: "There is no room for two
emperors here."   18. boots it: what advantage is it, what right
have you to.   19. break . . . parle: cease this argument.
23. league: agreement.   25. s.d., Hautboys: oboes.   33. beholding: indebted.   35. resolve me: assure me of.   36–37. Virginius . . . hand: Virginius slew his daughter to save her from
the lust of Appius Claudius; she was not in fact *enforced*.   42. still:
continually.   44. warrant: justification.

66. meed . . . meed: measure for measure.   71. mutual: united.
73. bane: destruction.   77. chaps: lit., cracks in the skin, thus
wrinkles.   80. erst: formerly.   83. baleful: injurious.   85. Sinon: the Greek who persuaded the Trojans to admit the Wooden
Horse. See *III Hen VI*, III.ii.190,n.   86. fatal engine: i.e.,
the Horse.   88. compact: made.   92. attend: listen to.

Lending your kind commiseration.
Here is a captain, let him tell the tale.　94
Your hearts will throb and weep to hear him speak.
   LUC. Then, noble auditory,° be it known to you
That cursèd Chiron and Demetrius
Were they that murderèd our Emperor's brother,
And they it were that ravishèd our sister.　99
For their fell° faults our brothers were beheaded,
Our father's tears despised, and basely cozened°
Of that true hand that fought Rome's quarrel out
And sent her enemies unto the grave.
Lastly, myself unkindly banishèd,　104
The gates shut on me, and turned weeping out
To beg relief among Rome's enemies,
Who drowned their enmity in my true tears,
And oped° their arms to embrace me as a friend.
I am the turnèd forth, be it known to you,
That have preserved her welfare in my blood　110
And from her bosom took the enemy's point,
Sheathing the steel in my adventurous body.
Alas, you know I am no vaunter,° I.
My scars can witness, dumb although they are,
That my report is just and full of truth.　115
But, soft! Methinks I do digress too much,
Citing my worthless praise. Oh, pardon me;
For when no friends are by, men praise themselves.
   MARC. Now is my turn to speak. Behold the child.
       [*Pointing to the* CHILD *in the arms*
                of an ATTENDANT.]
Of this was Tamora deliverèd —　120
The issue of an irreligious Moor,
Chief architect and plotter of these woes.
The villain is alive in Titus' house,
And as he is, to witness this is true.
Now judge what cause had Titus to revenge　125
These wrongs, unspeakable, past patience,
Or more than any living man could bear.
Now you have heard the truth, what say you, Romans?
Have we done aught amiss, show us wherein;
And from the place where you behold us now,　130
The poor remainder of Andronici
Will, hand in hand, all headlong cast us down,
And on the ragged stones beat forth our brains,
And make a mutual closure° of our house.
Speak, Romans, speak, and if you say we shall,
Lo, hand in hand, Lucius and I will fall.　136
   AEM. Come, come, thou reverend man of Rome,
And bring our Emperor gently in thy hand —
Lucius our Emperor; for well I know
The common voice do cry it shall be so.　140
   ALL. Lucius, all hail, Rome's royal Emperor!
   MARC. Go, go into old Titus' sorrowful house,
                  [*To* ATTENDANTS]

And hither hale that misbelieving Moor,
To be adjudged some direful slaughtering death
As punishment for his most wicked life.　145
             [*Exeunt* ATTENDANTS.]
   [LUCIUS, MARCUS, *and the others descend.*]
   ALL. Lucius, all hail, Rome's gracious Governor!
   LUC. Thanks, gentle Romans. May I govern so,
To heal Rome's harms and wipe away her woe!
But, gentle people, give me aim° awhile,
For nature puts me to a heavy task.　150
Stand all aloof; but, Uncle, draw you near
To shed obsequious° tears upon this trunk.
Oh, take this warm kiss on thy pale cold lips,
               [*Kissing* TITUS.]
These sorrowful drops upon thy blood-stained face,
The last true duties of thy noble son!　155
   MARC. Tear for tear and loving kiss for kiss
Thy brother Marcus tenders on thy lips.
Oh, were the sum of these that I should pay
Countless and infinite, yet would I pay them!
   LUC. Come hither, boy. Come, come, and learn
   of us　160
To melt in showers. Thy gransire loved thee well.
Many a time he danced thee on his knee,
Sung thee asleep, his loving breast thy pillow.
Many a matter hath he told to thee,
Meet and agreeing with thine infancy.　165
In that respect then, like a loving child,
Shed yet some small drops from thy tender spring,
Because kind nature doth require it so.
Friends should associate friends in grief and woe.
Bid him farewell; commit him to the grave;　170
Do him that kindness, and take leave of him.
   BOY. O Grandsire, Grandsire! Even with all my
   heart
Would I were dead, so you did live again!
O Lord, I cannot speak to him for weeping.
My tears will choke me if I ope my mouth.　175
       [*Re-enter* ATTENDANTS *with* AARON.]
   A ROMAN. You, sad Andronici, have done with
   woes.
Give sentence on this execrable wretch,
That hath been breeder of these dire events.
   LUC. Set him breast-deep in earth and famish
   him.
There let him stand and rave and cry for food.　180
If anyone relieves or pities him,
For the offense he dies. This is our doom.
Some stay to see him fastened in the earth.
   AAR. Oh, why should wrath be mute, and fury
   dumb?
I am no baby, I, that with base prayers　185
I should repent the evils I have done.
Ten thousand worse than ever yet I did
Would I perform if I might have my will.

---

96. **auditory:** audience.　100. **fell:** cruel.　101. **cozened:**
cheated.　108. **oped:** opened.　113. **vaunter:** boaster.　134. **make
. . . closure:** agree to make an end.

149. **give me aim:** listen to me; unless *aim* is a misprint for "air."
152. **obsequious:** befitting a funeral. See *Haml.*, I.ii.92.

If one good deed in all my life I did,
I do repent it from my very soul.   190
  LUC. Some loving friends convey the Emperor
    hence,
And give him burial in his father's grave.
My father and Lavinia shall forthwith
Be closèd° in our household's monument.
As for that heinous tiger, Tamora,   195
No funeral rite, nor man in mourning weeds,

      194. closed: enclosed.

No mournful bell shall ring her burial;
But throw her forth to beasts and birds of prey.
Her life was beastly and devoid of pity,
And, being so, shall have like want of pity.   200
See justice done on Aaron, that damned Moor,
By whom our heavy haps had their beginning.
Then, afterward, to order well the state,
That like events may ne'er it ruinate.°   [*Exeunt.*]

      204. ruinate: ruin.

THE TAMING OF THE SHREW

Introduction

The Taming of the Shrew is one of Shakespeare's earlier plays, and there has been great controversy among scholars about its source, date, and composition. The undisputed facts are as follows:

1. In Henslowe's *Diary* there is the record that the Lord Admiral's Men and the Lord Chamberlain's Men combined for a few days in June 1594 (see Gen. Intro. p. 38b). Among the plays acted at that time was "the Tamynge of A shrowe," on June 11 (or 13).

2. The Stationers' Register on May 2, 1594, records the entry to Peter Short of "a booke intituled A plesant Conceyted historie called the Tayminge of a Shrowe."

3. The play thus entered appeared soon afterward with the title, *A Pleasant Conceited Historie, called The taming of a Shrew. As it was sundry times acted by the Right honorable the Earle of Pembrook his seruants. Printed at London by Peter Short and are to be sold by Cutbert Burbie, at his shop at the Royall Exchange. 1594.*

This play is very short, less than fourteen hundred lines. The text is slovenly and bears all the signs of being an unauthorized publication.

The Taming of a Shrew is not, however, Shakespeare's comedy, though there is obviously a close connection. The story is similar in many of its details, but the names of the characters are different and except for occasional lines the dialogue is different. The first problem, therefore, is whether Shakespeare rewrote *A Shrew* (as afterward he turned *The Troublesome Reign of King John* into *The Life and Death of King John;* see p. 542b) or whether *A Shrew* is in fact a pirated version of *The Shrew* put together in much the same way as the pirated versions of *II* and *III Henry VI, Hamlet, Henry V,* and *The Merry Wives of Windsor.* This problem has been hotly debated. The older theory — that *The Shrew* is a rewriting of *A Shrew* — is on the whole more likely because the differences in names and details between the two plays are considerable. With the other piracies the names of

the characters are usually the same and the dialogue, however garbled, bears close resemblance to the good copy.

4. Shakespeare's play, *The Taming of the Shrew,* was first printed in the folio of 1623. The text is good with few difficulties of reading, and the play is of average length, running to about 2650 lines.

The question of the date of *The Shrew* turns partly on the relationship between the two *Shrews.* If *A Shrew* is a piracy, then Shakespeare's play was written before May 1594. If *The Shrew* is the later play, it can be dated only by its style, for there is neither recognizable allusion to current events in it nor outside reference to it. It has the usual signs of early work — long explanatory speeches in stiff verse (e.g., Induction i.105–38, I.i.1–24) and much punning, especially between servant and master (e.g., I.ii.1–44, IV.i). On the grounds of style alone *The Taming of the Shrew* would seem to have been written at much the same time as *The Two Gentlemen of Verona,* or *The Comedy of Errors.* To add to the difficulty, some scholars believe that portions of *The Shrew* were written not by Shakespeare but by a collaborator. If so, style tests are even more unreliable than usual. However, despite the unsolved relationship between the two *Shrews,* it is still possible that Henslowe's entry refers to Shakespeare's play. If so, it was written before June 1594.

One topical passage is interesting. When Sly wakes up from his slumber, he cries out "Am not I Christopher Sly, old Sly's son of Burton Heath. . . . Ask Marian Hacket, the fat ale-wife of Wincot, if she know me not " (Ind. ii.18–24). There was a village called Barton about eight miles from Stratford, and another named Barton-on-the-Heath about sixteen miles away where Shakespeare's aunt lived, while Wincot was a hamlet four miles from Stratford and — as the parish register shows — some of its inhabitants were called Hacket.

The non-Shakespearean version of *The Taming of a Shrew* begins with the stage direction:

Enter a Tapster, beating out of his doores, Slie droonken. Slie lies down and sleeps. A nobleman and his men enter from hunting and find him. The lord orders his servants to carry Slie to his house, dress him in rich garments, and set him at a table in a chair. When the drunkard has been removed, two players and a boy enter and promise to perform the play of *The Taming of a Shrew.*

In the play that follows, the scene is set in Athens. A gentleman called Alfonso has three daughters, Kate (the eldest), Phylema, and Emelia; each of the younger daughters has a suitor who woos his lady in disguise. As in Shakespeare's play, the father refuses to allow a younger daughter to be married until a husband has been found for Kate the shrew. In *A Shrew* Kate's tamer is called Ferando. The motives of these two are made somewhat clearer than in Shakespeare's version. When Kate is first wooed by Ferando, she, in the words of the stage direction, *turns aside and speaks:*

But yet I will consent and marry him, —
For I methinks have lived too long a maid, —
And match him too, or else his manhood's good.

The disorderly wedding follows, and when Ferando brings his bride home, he behaves in the same boorish way as Shakespeare's Petruchio (see IV.i and " 3. FERANDO AND THE SHREW," p. 331b). Kate holds out for two scenes, but by the time Ferando is on his way back to Alfonso's house she is completely tamed.

The secondary plot, showing how the other daughters found husbands in Amelius and Polidor, is on much the same lines as in *The Shrew.* The plays ends with the three husbands betting on the obedience of their wives. The younger sisters refuse to come at the request of their husbands, but Kate obeys Ferando submissively and at his bidding she takes off her cap and treads on it. Then he tells her to fetch her sisters. She retires:

Enter Kate thrusting Phylema and Emelia before her, and makes them come unto their husbands call.

At Ferando's bidding Kate delivers a sermon on wifely obedience. He leads her away and the rest follow, leaving Polidor with his new wife Emelia. " How now, Polidor," says she, " in a dump, what sayest thou man? "

" I say thou art a shrew."
" That's better than a sheep."
" Well, since tis done let it go, come lets in."

And with this forbidding sentiment, *The Taming of a Shrew* ends.

As soon as the actors have left the stage, Slie, who in the course of the play has drunk himself into a coma, is carried in and left to come to his senses. The tapster emerges and rouses him. Slie sits up and finding himself no longer a lord concludes that he has been dreaming, rises and staggers homeward.

Other differences between the two versions of the story are that in the non-Shakespearean play there is no elderly suitor (to parallel Gremio); Emelia, the third sister, takes the place of Hortensio's widow; and the false father who backs up the story of Aurelius's wealth is a merchant called Phylotus, while the real father is called Duke of Cestos.

The differences and similarities in the dialogue are quite as marked, as some specimens will show.

1. THE OPENING SCENE OF THE INDUCTION (cf. Ind. I.i)

Enter a Tapster, beating out of his doores
Slie Droonken.
Tapster.
You whorson droonken slave, you had best be gone,
And empty your droonken panch some where else
For in this house thou shalt not rest to night.
Exit Tapster.
Slie. Tilly vally, by crisee Tapster Ile fese you
anon.
Fils the tother pot and alls paid for, looke you
I doo drinke it of mine owne Instegation,
Omne bene
Heere Ile lie a while, why Tapster I say,
Fils a fresh cushen heere.
Heigh ho, heers good warme lying.
He fals asleepe.
Enter a Noble man and his men
from hunting.
Lord. Now that the gloomie shaddow of the
night,
Longing to view Orions drisling lookes,
Leapes from th'antarticke World unto the skie
And dims the Welkin with her pitchie breath,
And darkesome night oreshades the christall
heavens,
Here breake we off our hunting for to night,
Cupple uppe the hounds and let us hie us home,

And bid the huntsman see them meated well,
For they have all deserv'd it well to daie,
But soft, what sleepie fellow is this lies heere?
Or is he dead, see one what he dooth lacke?

    Servingman. My lord, tis nothing but a drunken
    sleepe,
His head is too heavie for his bodie,
And he hath drunke so much that he can go no
    furder.

    Lord. Fie, how the slavish villaine stinkes of
    drinke.
Ho, sirha arise. What so sound asleepe?
Go take him uppe and beare him to my house,
And beare him easilie for feare he wake,
And in my fairest chamber make a fire,
And set a sumptuous banquet on the boord,
And put my richest garmentes on his backe,
Then set him at the Table in a chaire:
When that is doone against he shall awake,
Let heavenlie musicke play about him still,
Go two of you awaie and beare him hence,
And then Ile tell you what I have devisde,
But see in any case you wake him not.

          Exeunt two with *Slie.*
Now take my cloake and give me one of yours,
Al fellowes now, and see you take me so,
For we will waite upon this droonken man,
To see his countnance when he dooth awake
And finde himselfe clothed in such attire,
With heavenlie musicke sounding in his eares,
And such a banquet set before his eies,
The fellow sure will thinke he is in heaven,
But we will be about him when he wakes,
And see you call him Lord, at everie word,
And offer thou him his horse to ride abroad,
And thou his hawkes and houndes to hunt the
    deere,
And I will aske what sutes he meanes to weare,
And whatso ere he saith see you doo not laugh,
But still perswade him that he is a Lord.

          Enter one.
    Mes. And it please your honour your plaiers be
    com
And doo attend your honours pleasure here.

    Lord. The fittest time they could have chosen
    out,
Bid one or two of them come hither straight,
Now will I fit my selfe accordinglie,
For they shall play to him when he awakes.

      Enter two of the players with packs at their
          backs, and a boy.
Now sirs, what store of plaies have you?

    San. Marrie my lord you maie have a Tragicall
Or a comoditie, or what you will.

    The other. A Comedie thou shouldst say, souns
    thout shame us all.

    Lord. And whats the name of your Comedie?

    San. Marrie my lord tis calde The taming of a
    shrew:
Tis a good lesson for us my lord, for us y^t are
    maried men.

    Lord. The taming of a shrew, thats excellent sure,
Go see that you make you readie straight,
For you must play before a lord to night,
Say you are his men and I your fellow,
Hees something foolish, but what so ere he saies,
See that you be not dasht out of countenance.
And sirha go you make you ready straight,
And dresse your selfe like some lovelie ladie,
And when I call see that you come to me,
For I will say to him thou art his wife,
Dallie with him and hug him in thine armes,
And if he desire to goe to bed with thee,
Then faine some scuse and say thou wilt anon.
Be gone I say, and see thou doost it well.

    Boy. Feare not my Lord, Ile dandell him well
    enough
And make him thinke I love him mightilie.

                   Ex. boy.

    Lord. Now sirs go you and make you ready to,
For you must play assoone as he dooth wake.

    San. O brave, sirha Tom, we must play before
A foolish Lord, come lets go make us ready,
Go get a dishclout to make cleane your shooes,
And Ile speake for the properties, My Lord, we
    must
Have a shoulder of mutton for a propertie,
And a little vinegre to make our Divell rore.

    Lord. Very well: sirha see that they want
    nothing.   *Exeunt omnes.*

    2. THE OPENING SCENE OF THE COMEDY (cf. I.i)

      Enter two yoong Gentlemen, and a man
             and a boie.

    Pol. Welcome to *Athens* my beloved friend,
To *Platoes* schooles and *Aristotles* walkes,
Welcome from *Cestus* famous for the love
Of good *Leander* and his Tragedie,
For whom the *Helespont* weepes brinish teares,
The greatest griefe is I cannot as I would
Give entertainment to my deerest friend.

    Aurel. Thankes noble *Polidor* my second selfe,
The faithfull love which I have found in thee
Hath made me leave my fathers princelie court,
The Duke of *Cestus* thrice renowmed seate,
To come to *Athens* thus to find thee out,
Which since I have so happilie attaind,
My fortune now I doo account as great
As earst did *Casar* when he conquered most,
But tell me noble friend where shal we lodge,
For I am unacquainted in this place.

    Poli. My Lord if you vouchsafe of schollers fare,
My house, my selfe, and all is yours to use,

You and your men shall staie and lodge with me.
  Aurel. With all my hart, I will requite thy love.
        Enter *Simon, Alphonsus,* and his
              three daughters.
But staie; what dames are these so bright of hew
Whose eies are brighter than the lampes of heaven,
Fairer than rocks of pearle and pretious stone,
More lovelie farre then is the morning sunne,
When first she opes hir orientall gates.
  Alfon. Daughters be gone, and hie you to yᵉ
    church,
And I will hie me downe unto the key,
To see what Marchandise is come ashore.

3. FERANDO AND THE SHREW AT HOME (cf. IV.i)

      *Enter Sanders with two or three
            serving men*
  San. Come sirs provide all thinges as fast as you
    can,
For my Masters hard at hand and my new Mistris
And all, and he sent me before to see all thinges
    redy.
  Tom. Welcome home *Sander* sirra how lookes
    our
New Mistris they say she's a plagie shrew.
  San. I and that thou shalt find I can tell thee and
    thou
Dost not please her well, why my Maister
Has such a doo with hir as it passeth and he's even
like a madman.
  Will. Why *Sander* what dos he say.
  San. Why Ile tell you what: when they should
Go to church to be maried he puts on an olde
Jerkin and a paire of canvas breeches downe to the
Small of his legge and a red cap on his head and he
Lookes as thou wilt burst thy selfe with laffing
When thou seest him: he's ene as good as a
Foole for me: and then when they should go to
    dinner
He made me Saddle the horse and away he came.
And nere tarried for dinner and therefore you had
    best
Get supper reddy against they come, for
They be hard at hand I am sure by this time.
  Tom. Sounes see where they be all redy.
        Enter Ferando and Kate.
  Feran. Now welcome *Kate:* wher'es these villains
Here, what? not supper yet uppon the borde:
Nor table spred nor nothing don at all,
Wheres that villaine that I sent before.
  San. Now, *adsum,* sir.
  Feran. Come hether you villaine Ile cut your
    nose,
You Rogue: helpe me of with my bootes: wilt
    please
You to lay the cloth? sounes the villaine

Hurts my foote? pull easely I say; yet againe.
        He beates them all.
    They cover the bord and fetch in the meate.
Sounes? burnt and skorcht who drest this meate?
  Will. Forsouth John cooke.
        He throwes downe the table and meate
              and all, and beates them.
  Feran. Go you villaines bringe you me such
    meate,
Out of my sight I say and beare it hence,
Come *Kate* wele have other meate provided,
Is there a fire in my chamber sir?
  San. I forsooth.   *Exit Ferando and Kate.*
        Manent servingmen and eate up all the
              meate.
  Tom. Sounes? I thinke of my conscience my
    Masters
Mad since he was maried.
  Will. I laft what a boxe he gave *Sander*
For pulling of his bootes.
        Enter *Ferando* againe.
  San. I hurt his foote for the nonce man.
  Feran. Did you so you damned villaine.
        He beates them all out againe.
This humor must I holde me to a while,
To bridle and hold backe my headstrong wife,
With curbes of hunger: ease: and want of sleepe,
Nor sleepe nor meate shall she injoie to night,
Ile mew her up as men do mew their hawkes,
And make her gentlie come unto the lure,
Were she as stuborne or as full of strength
As were the *Thracian* horse *Alcides* tamde,
That King *Egeus* fed with flesh of men,
Yet would I pull her downe and make her come
As hungry hawkes do flie unto there lure.

Apart from *The Taming of a Shrew,* no close
parallel to Shakespeare's comedy in story or play
has been found, though there are resemblances
elsewhere to the various episodes. The trick
played on the drunken tinker is reported in several works of the sixteenth and seventeenth centuries and is thus summarized in Burton's *Anatomy of Melancholy:*

It is reported of *Philippus Bonus,* that Good
Duke of *Burgundy* (by *Lodovicus Vives in Epist.*
and *Pont. Heuter* in his history) that the said Duke,
at the marriage of *Eleonora,* sister to the King of
Portugal, at *Bruges* in *Flanders,* which was solem-
ized in the deep of Winter, when as by reason of
unseasonable weather he could neither hawk nor
hunt, and was now tired with cards, dice, &c. and
such other domestical sports, or to see Ladies dance,
with some of his Courtiers he would in the evening
walk disguised all about the Town. It so fortuned,
as he was walking late one night, he found a coun-

try-fellow dead drunk, snorting on a bulk [bench]; he caused his followers to bring him to his Palace, and there stripped him of his old clothes, and attiring him after the Court fashion, when he waked, he and they were ready to attend upon his Excellency, persuading him he was some great Duke. The poor fellow, admiring how he came there, was served in state all the day long; after supper he saw them dance, heard Musick, and the rest of those Court-like pleasures: but late at night, when he was well tippled, & again fast asleep, they put on his old robes, and so conveyed him to the place where they first found him. Now the fellow had not made them so good sport the day before, as he did when he returned to himself, all the jest was to see how he looked upon it. In conclusion, after some little admiration, the poor man told his friends he had seen a Vision, constantly believed it, would not otherwise be persuaded, and so the jest ended.

The wooing of Bianca by a suitor who changes places with his servant and pretends to be a tutor can be paralleled in an Italian play by Ariosto called *I Suppositi*. This play was translated and adapted for performance in English by George Gascoigne under the title *The Supposes,* and played at Gravesend in 1566. It was published in 1573. Such a device, however, in one form or another is not uncommon.

As for the taming of Katharine, there is a considerable collection of stories of strong-willed husbands who by a series of coarse or brutal tricks break the will of a bad-tempered or headstrong bride, but none is very close; and it is interesting to note, as perhaps indicating a change in general taste and in the attitude of men toward their womenfolk, that about twenty-five years after Shakespeare's play, John Fletcher wrote a sequel called *The Woman's Prize, or the Tamer Tamed.* This play opens with Kate dead and Petruchio a widower renowned for his ferocious bad temper. He marries as his second bride a young woman named Maria, who determines to vindicate her sex and who swears she will have nothing to do with her husband until she has " made him easy as a child and tame as fear." Petruchio, who loves her, is driven almost mad by her tricks until finally, as a last resort, he pretends to be dead and is carried into

her presence in a coffin. Maria utters such a plain-spoken homily of his faults that Petruchio is overcome with remorse and sits up penitent, whereupon Maria relents and all ends happily.

The Taming of the Shrew is often acted. It arouses a variety of feelings in spectators and in readers, for it can be regarded in many different lights. We can take the play at its face value as the story of an insensitive brute who marries a bad-tempered woman for the sake of her money and against her will, and then proceeds to starve and torture her until she is so broken that she can only echo her tamer. This is hardly an attitude that commends itself to modern notions, and such a story, regarded seriously, is no longer amusing. Or we can begin with the thought that surely Shakespeare never intended us to take delight in the torture of Kate but has an altogether different purpose in his play, that it is in fact a sort of allegory in extreme form of the eternal differences between the sexes.

However, one important factor in the drama is frequently overlooked. *The Taming of the Shrew* is not itself a play, but a play within a play. The real play, so slight and so soon forgotten, even by Shakespeare himself, is the trick played on the drunken tinker, recounted in what the editors call the Induction. Inductions were fairly common in Elizabethan plays. Kyd introduced *The Spanish Tragedy* with the appearance of Revenge and Don Andrea; Greene prefaced his romantic comedy *James IV* with a strange Induction of Bohun, a wild man who hides among the tombs, and Oberon, king of the fairies; Peele's *Old Wives' Tale* begins with the old wife telling a tale which comes to life in the play. This manner of presenting a play as part of a dream or story is a useful convention, especially when the theme of the play is to be wild and fantastic, for the Induction is a bridge between the fantasy and the hearer's sense of reality. It may be that the author of *The Taming of the Shrew* was saying in effect to the henpecked husbands in his audience: " A drunkard's dream, my friends — but don't you wish that it was true! "

The Taming of the Shrew°

DRAMATIS PERSONAE

A LORD
CHRISTOPHER SLY, *a tinker*   } *persons in the*
HOSTESS, PAGE, PLAYERS, HUNTSMEN, } *Induction*
  and SERVANTS
BAPTISTA, *a rich gentleman of Padua*
VINCENTO, *an old gentleman of Pisa*
LUCENTIO, *son to Vincentio, in love with Bianca*
PETRUCHIO, *a gentleman of Verona, a suitor to*
  Katharina
GREMIO   } *suitors to Bianca*
HORTENSIO
TRANIO   } *servants to Lucentio*
BIONDELLO

GRUMIO } *servants to Petruchio*
CURTIS
A PEDANT

KATHARINA, *the shrew* } *daughters to Baptista*
BIANCA
WIDOW

TAILOR, HABERDASHER, *and* SERVANTS *attending on*
  Baptista and Petruchio

SCENE — *Padua, and Petruchio's country house.*

INDUCTION

SCENE I. *Before an alehouse on a heath.*

[*Enter* HOSTESS *and* SLY.]
SLY. I'll pheeze° you, in faith.
HOST. A pair° of stocks,° you rogue!
SLY. Y'are a baggage. The Slys are no rogues.
Look in the Chronicles.° We came in with Richard
Conqueror.° Therefore *paucas pallabris.*° Let the
world slide. Sessa!°   6
HOST. You will not pay for the glasses you have
burst?
SLY. No, not a denier.° Go by, Jeronimy.° Go to
thy cold bed and warm thee.   10
HOST. I know my remedy. I must go fetch the
thirdborough.°   [*Exit.*]
SLY. Third, or fourth, or fifth borough, I'll answer
him by law.° I'll not budge an inch, boy. Let him
come, and kindly.   [*Falls asleep.*] 15
[*Horns winded.° Enter* A LORD *from hunting,*
  with his train.]
LORD. Huntsman, I charge thee, tender well my
  hounds.
Brach° Merriman, the poor cur, is embossed;°

And couple Clowder with the deep-mouthed brach.
Saw'st thou not, boy, how Silver made it good
At the hedge corner, in the coldest fault?°   20
I would not lose the dog for twenty pound.
  1. HUN. Why, Belman is as good as he, my lord.
He cried upon it at the merest loss°
And twice today picked out the dullest scent.
Trust me, I take him for the better dog.   25
  LORD. Thou art a fool. If Echo were as fleet,
I would esteem him worth a dozen such.
But sup them well and look unto them all.
Tomorrow I intend to hunt again.
  1. HUN. I will, my lord.   30
  LORD. What's here? One dead, or drunk? See,
    doth he breathe?
  2. HUN. He breathes, my lord. Were he not
    warmed with ale,
This were a bed but cold to sleep so soundly.
  LORD. Oh, monstrous beast! How like a swine he
    lies!
Grim Death, how foul and loathsome is thine
    image!°   35
Sirs, I will practice° on this drunken man.
What think you, if he were conveyed to bed,
Wrapped in sweet° clothes, rings put upon his
    fingers,
A most delicious banquet by his bed,
And brave° attendants near him when he wakes,
Would not the beggar then forget himself?   41
  1. HUN. Believe me, lord, I think he cannot
    choose.
  2. HUN. It would seem strange unto him when
    he waked.

Title: **Shrew:** As the rhyme at IV.i.210–11 indicates, the word
was pronounced "shrow." **Induction, Sc. i:** 1. **pheeze:** do for.
2. **pair of stocks:** See App. 10. **pair:** set.   4. **Chronicles:** history
book.   5. **Richard Conqueror:** for William the Conqueror. Those
who boasted of ancient blood claimed to have come over to England with William the Conqueror in 1066 — as certain ancient
families in the U.S. claim that their ancestors were passengers in
the *Mayflower*.   5. *paucas pallabris:* few words.   6. **Sessa:**
doubtfully explained; probably it means something like "what
the Hell!"   9. **denier:** a small worthless coin, "penny." **Go
by, Jeronimy:** a parody of a famous line in *The Spanish Tragedy:*
"Hieronimo beware; go by, go by." See Gen. Intro. p. 36b.
12. **thirdborough:** constable.   13–14. **I'll . . . law:** I'll insist on
my legal rights.   15. **s.d., winded:** sounded.   17. **Brach:** a
hound that hunts by scent. **embossed:** foaming at the mouth.

20. **coldest fault:** faintest scent.   23. **cried . . . loss:** gave tongue
when the scent was quite lost.   35. **image:** i.e., a man drunkenly asleep looks as if he were dead.   36. **practice:** play a trick.
38. **sweet:** perfumed.   40. **brave:** finely dressed.

LORD. Even as a flattering dream or worthless
　　fancy.
Then take him up and manage well the jest.　45
Carry him gently to my fairest chamber
And hang it round with all my wanton pictures.
Balm° his foul head in warm distillèd waters
And burn sweet wood to make the lodging sweet.
Procure me music ready when he wakes,　50
To make a dulcet° and a heavenly sound;
And if he chance to speak, be ready straight
And with a low submissive reverence
Say, "What is it your Honor will command? "
Let one attend him with a silver basin　55
Full of rose water and bestrewed with flowers;
Another bear the ewer, the third a diaper,°
And say, "Will't please your lordship cool your
　　hands? "
Some one be ready with a costly suit,
And ask him what apparel he will wear.　60
Another tell him of his hounds and horse,
And that his lady mourns at his disease.
Persuade him that he hath been lunatic,
And when he says he is,° say that he dreams,
For he is nothing but a mighty lord.　65
This do, and do it kindly,° gentle sirs.
It will be pastime passing° excellent
If it be husbanded with modesty.°
　　1. HUN. My lord, I warrant you we will play our
　　　part
As he shall think, by our true diligence,　70
He is no less than what we say he is.
　　LORD. Take him up gently, and to bed with him;
And each one to his office when he wakes.
　　　　　　[*Some bear out* SLY. *A trumpet sounds.*]
Sirrah,° go see what trumpet 'tis that sounds.
　　　　　　　　　　　　[*Exit* SERVINGMAN.]
Belike,° some noble gentleman that means,　75
Traveling some journey, to repose him here.
　　　　　　　　[*Re-enter* SERVINGMAN.]
How now! Who is it?
　　SERV.　　　　　An't° please your Honor, players
That offer service to your lordship.
　　LORD. Bid them come near.
　　　　　　　　　[*Enter* PLAYERS.]
　　　　　　　　Now, fellows, you are welcome.
　　PLAYERS. We thank your Honor.　80
　　LORD. Do you intend to stay with me tonight?
　　A PLAYER. So please your lordship to accept our
　　　duty.
　　LORD. With all my heart. This fellow I remember,
Since once he played a farmer's eldest son.
'Twas where you wooed the gentlewoman so well.
I have forgot your name, but, sure, that part　86

Was aptly fitted and naturally performed.
　　A PLAYER.° I think 'twas Soto that your Honor
　　means.
　　LORD. 'Tis very true. Thou didst it excellent.
Well, you are come to me in happy° time,　90
The rather for I have some sport in hand
Wherein your cunning° can assist me much.
There is a lord will hear you play tonight.
But I am doubtful of your modesties,
Lest overeyeing of his odd behavior —　95
For yet His Honor never heard a play —
You break into some merry passion°
And so offend him; for I tell you, sirs,
If you should smile, he grows impatient.
　　A PLAYER. Fear not my lord. We can contain our-
　　selves,　100
Were he the veriest antic° in the world.
　　LORD. Go, sirrah, take them to the buttery,°
And give them friendly welcome every one.
Let them want nothing that my house affords.
　　　　　　　　[*Exit one with the* PLAYERS.]
Sirrah, go you to Barthol'mew my page,　105
And see him dressed in all suits° like a lady.
That done, conduct him to the drunkard's cham-
　　ber,
And call him "madam," do him obeisance.
Tell him from me, as he will win my love,
He bear himself with honorable action　110
Such as he hath observed in noble ladies
Unto their lords by them accomplishèd.°
Such duty to the drunkard let him do
With soft low tongue and lowly courtesy,
And say, "What is 't your Honor will command,
Wherein your lady and your humble wife　116
May show her duty and make known her love? "
And then with kind embracements, tempting kisses,
And with declining head into his bosom,
Bid him shed tears, as being overjoyed　120
To see her noble lord restored to health,
Who for this seven years hath esteemed him
No better than a poor and loathsome beggar.
And if the boy have not a woman's gift
To rain a shower of commanded tears,　125
An onion° will do well for such a shift,°
Which, in a napkin being close° conveyed,
Shall in despite° enforce a watery eye.
See this dispatched with all the haste thou canst.
Anon I'll give thee more instructions.　130
　　　　　　　　[*Exit a* SERVINGMAN.]
I know the boy will well usurp the grace,

---

48. Balm: cleanse and anoint.　51. dulcet: sweet.　57. diaper:
towel.　64. says he is: i.e., a tinker.　66. kindly: naturally.
67. passing: exceedingly.　68. husbanded . . . modesty: carried
out without excess, not overdone.　74. Sirrah: term of address
used to an inferior.　75. Belike: probably.　77. An't: if it.

88. A player: F1 here prints "Sincklo," an actor in the Chamberlain's Company who is thrice mentioned elsewhere in stage directions.　90. happy: fortunate.　92. cunning: skill.　97. passion:
display of emotion.　101. antic: clown.　102. buttery: place
where the drink is kept, bar.　106. suits: details.　112. accomplished: performed.　126–28. onion . . . eye: See *Ant & Cleo*,
I.ii.176.　126. shift: purpose.　127. close: secretly.　128. in
despite: in spite of his reluctance to cry.

Voice, gait, and action of a gentlewoman.
I long to hear him call the drunkard husband,
And how my men will stay themselves from laughter
When they do homage to this simple peasant. 135
I'll in to counsel them. Haply my presence
May well abate the overmerry spleen°
Which otherwise would grow into extremes.

[*Exeunt.*]

SCENE II. *A bedchamber in the* LORD's *house.*

[*Enter aloft*° SLY, *with* ATTENDANTS, *some with apparel, others with basin and ewer and other appurtenances; and* LORD.]

SLY. For God's sake, a pot of small° ale.

1. SERV. Will't please your lordship drink a cup of sack?°

2. SERV. Will't please your Honor taste of these conserves?°

3. SERV. What raiment will your Honor wear today?

SLY. I am Christophero Sly. Call not me "Honor" nor "lordship." I ne'er drank sack in my life, 6
and if you give me any conserves, give me conserves of beef.° Ne'er ask me what raiment I'll wear, for
I have no more doublets° than backs, no more stockings than legs, nor no more shoes than 10
feet; nay, sometime more feet than shoes, or such shoes as my toes look through the overleather.

LORD. Heaven cease this idle humor° in your Honor!
Oh, that a mighty man of such descent, 15
Of such possessions and so high esteem,
Should be infusèd with so foul a spirit!

SLY. What, would you make me mad? Am not I
Christopher Sly, old Sly's son of Burton Heath,° by
birth a peddler, by education a card maker,° by 20
transmutation a bearherd,° and now by present
profession a tinker? Ask Marian Hacket, the fat ale-
wife of Wincot, if she know me not. If she say I
am not fourteen pence on the score° for sheer 25
ale,° score me up for the lyingest knave in Christendom. What! I am not bestraught.° Here's ——

3. SERV. Oh, this it is that makes your lady mourn!

2. SERV. Oh, this is it that makes your servants droop!

LORD. Hence comes it that your kindred shuns
your house, 30
As beaten hence by your strange lunacy.
O noble lord, bethink thee of thy birth,
Call home thy ancient thoughts from banishment,
And banish hence these abject lowly dreams.
Look how thy servants do attend on thee, 35
Each in his office ready at thy beck.
Wilt thou have music? Hark! Apollo° plays,

[*Music.*]

And twenty cagèd nightingales do sing.
Or wilt thou sleep? We'll have thee to a couch
Softer and sweeter than the lustful bed 40
On purpose trimmed up for Semiramis.°
Say thou wilt walk; we will bestrew° the ground.
Or wilt thou ride? Thy horses shall be trapped,°
Their harness studded all with gold and pearl.
Dost thou love hawking? Thou hast hawks will
soar 45
Above the morning lark. Or wilt thou hunt?
Thy hounds shall make the welkin° answer them
And fetch shrill echoes from the hollow earth.

1. SERV. Say thou wilt course.° Thy greyhounds
are as swift
As breathèd° stags, aye, fleeter than the roe. 50

2. SERV. Dost thou love pictures? We will fetch
thee straight
Adonis painted by a running brook,
And Cytherea° all in sedges° hid,
Which seem to move and wanton with her breath,
Even as the waving sedges play with wind. 55

LORD. We'll show thee Io° as she was a maid,
And how she was beguilèd and surprised,
As lively° painted as the deed was done.

3. SERV. Or Daphne° roaming through a thorny
wood, 59
Scratching her legs that one shall swear she bleeds,
And at that sight shall sad Apollo weep,
So workmanly the blood and tears are drawn.

LORD. Thou art a lord and nothing but a lord.
Thou hast a lady far more beautiful
Than any woman in this waning age. 65

1. SERV. And till the tears that she hath shed for
thee
Like envious° floods o'errun her lovely face,
She was the fairest creature in the world;
And yet she is inferior to none.

SLY. Am I a lord? And have I such a lady? 70
Or do I dream? Or have I dreamed till now?

---

137. **overmerry spleen:** excessive fit of laughter.
Sc. ii: s.d., **aloft:** i.e., on the upper stage. 1. **small:** weak;
i.e., the cheapest quality. 2. **sack:** wine from Spain — a gentleman's drink, beyond the means of such as Sly the tinker.
3. **conserves:** candied fruit. 7–8. **conserves of beef:** salt beef.
9. **doublets:** coats. 14. **humor:** obsession. See App. 3. 19. **Burton Heath:** See *Shrew* Intro. p. 328b. 20. **card maker:** a maker of the combs (*cards*) used in preparing wool for spinning. 21. **bearherd:** bear keeper. 25. **on ... score:** chalked up as owing.
25–26. **sheer ale:** pure beer. 27. **bestraught:** mad.

37. **Apollo:** god of music and the arts. 41. **Semiramis:** See *T Andr*, II.i.22n. 42. **bestrew:** spread carpets on. 43. **trapped:** adorned. 47. **welkin:** sky. 49. **course:** pursue the hare with greyhounds. 50. **breathed:** exercised, i.e., chased. 52–53. **Adonis ... Cytherea:** Adonis was a beautiful youth passionately beloved by the goddess Venus (*Cytherea*). Her vain love was the subject of Shakespeare's poem *Venus and Adonis*. See Pl. 7a. 53. **sedges:** water rushes. 56. **Io:** a maiden loved and pursued by the god Jupiter. 58. **lively:** realistically. 59. **Daphne:** a maiden loved and pursued by the god Apollo. 67. **envious:** hateful.

I do not sleep. I see, I hear, I speak.
I smell sweet savors, and I feel soft things.
Upon my life, I am a lord indeed,
And not a tinker nor Christophero Sly.　　75
Well, bring our lady hither to our sight;
And once again, a pot o' the smallest ale.

2. SERV. Will't please your Mightiness to wash
　　your hands?
Oh, how we joy to see your wit restored!
Oh, that once more you knew but what you are!　80
These fifteen years you have been in a dream,
Or when you waked, so waked as if you slept.

SLY. These fifteen years! By my fay,° a goodly
　　nap.
But did I never speak of all that time?

1. SERV. Oh, yes, my lord, but very idle words.
For though you lay here in this goodly chamber,　86
Yet would you say ye were beaten out of door,
And rail upon the hostess of the house,°
And say you would present her at the leet°
Because she brought stone° jugs and no sealed°
　　quarts.　　90
Sometimes you would call out for Cicely Hacket.

SLY. Aye, the woman's maid of the house.

3. SERV. Why, sir, you know no house nor no such
　　maid,
Nor no such men as you have reckoned up,
As Stephen Sly, and old John Naps of Greece,　95
And Peter Turph, and Henry Pimpernell,
And twenty more such names and men as these
Which never were nor no man ever saw.

SLY. Now Lord be thankèd for my good
　　amends!°

ALL. Amen.　　100

SLY. I thank thee. Thou shalt not lose by it.
　　[*Enter the* PAGE *as a lady, attended.*]

PAGE. How fares my noble lord?

SLY. Marry,° I fare well, for here is cheer enough.
Where is my wife?

PAGE. Here, noble lord. What is thy will with
　　her?　　105

SLY. Are you my wife, and will not call me hus-
　　band?
My men should call me "lord." I am your good-
　　man.°

PAGE. My Husband and my lord, my lord and
　　Husband,
I am your wife in all obedience.

SLY. I know it well. What must I call her?　110

LORD. Madam.

SLY. Al'ce madam, or Joan° madam?

LORD. "Madam" and nothing else. So lords call
　　ladies.

SLY. Madam Wife, they say that I have dreamed
And slept above some fifteen year or more.　115

PAGE. Aye, and the time seems thirty unto me,
Being all this time abandoned° from your bed.

SLY. 'Tis much. Servants, leave me and her alone.
Madam, undress you, and come now to bed.

PAGE. Thrice-noble lord, let me entreat of you
To pardon me yet for a night or two;　　121
Or, if not so, until the sun be set.
For your physicians have expressly charged,
In peril to incur your former malady,
That I should yet absent me from your bed.　125
I hope this reason stands for my excuse.

SLY. Aye, it stands so that I may hardly tarry so
long. But I would be loath to fall into my dreams
again. I will therefore tarry in despite of the flesh
and the blood.　　130
　　[*Enter a* MESSENGER.]

MESS. Your Honor's players, hearing your amend-
　　ment,
Are come to play a pleasant comedy;
For so your doctors hold it very meet,
Seeing too much sadness hath congealed your
　　blood,
And melancholy is the nurse of frenzy.°　135
Therefore they thought it good you hear a play
And frame your mind to mirth and merriment,
Which bars a thousand harms and lengthens life.

SLY. Marry, I will, let them play it. Is not a
comonty° a Christmas gambold° or a tumbling
trick?　　141

PAGE. No, my good lord. It is more pleasing stuff.

SLY. What, household stuff?

PAGE. It is a kind of history.°

SLY. Well, we'll see't. Come, Madam Wife, sit
by my side and let the world slip. We shall ne'er be
younger.°　　[*Flourish.*°]　147

Act I

SCENE I. *Padua. A public place.*

[*Enter* LUCENTIO *and his man* TRANIO.]

LUC. Tranio, since for the great desire I had
To see fair Padua, nursery of arts,

---

83. fay: faith.　88. house: inn.　89. leet: court held by the lord of the manor at which complaints of false measure were heard.　90. stone: earthenware. sealed: officially stamped as containing a quart　99. amends: recovery.　103. Marry: Mary, by the Virgin.　107. goodman: husband — a term used by persons of a lower class.　112. Al'ce ... Joan: Alice and Joan were at this time not used as upper-class names.

117. abandoned: banished.　135. melancholy ... frenzy: See App. 4. frenzy: madness.　140. comonty: for comedy. Sly is not acquainted with such upper-class entertainments as plays. gambold: frolic.　144. history: story.　146-47. We ... younger: a proverb meaning much the same as "Let us make hay while the sun shines."　147. s.d., Flourish: notes on the trumpet to draw attention to the entrance of the actors.

I am arrived for° fruitful Lombardy,
The pleasant garden of great Italy,
And by my father's love and leave am armed 5
With his good will and thy good company,
My trusty servant, well approved in all,
Here let us breathe° and haply institute
A course of learning and ingenious° studies.
Pisa, renownèd for grave citizens, 10
Gave me my being and my father first,°
A merchant of great traffic through the world,
Vincentio, come of the Bentivolii.
Vincentio's son brought up in Florence
It shall become to serve all hopes conceived,° 15
To deck his fortune with his virtuous deeds.
And therefore, Tranio, for the time I study,
Virtue and that part of philosophy
Will I apply that treats of happiness
By virtue specially to be achieved. 20
Tell me thy mind; for I have Pisa left
And am to Padua come, as he that leaves
A shallow plash° to plunge him in the deep
And with satiety seeks to quench his thirst.
  TRA. *Mi perdonato,*° gentle master mine, 25
I am in all affected° as yourself,
Glad that you thus continue your resolve
To suck the sweets of sweet philosophy.
Only, good master, while we do admire
This virtue and this moral discipline, 30
Let's be no stoics° nor no stocks,° I pray,
Or so devote to Aristotle's checks°
As Ovid° be° an outcast quite abjured.°
Balk logic with acquaintance° that you have,
And practice rhetoric in your common talk. 35
Music and poesy use to quicken° you.
The mathematics and the metaphysics
Fall to them as you find your stomach° serves you.
No profit grows where is no pleasure ta'en.
In brief, sir, study what you most affect.° 40
  LUC. Gramercies,° Tranio, well dost thou advise.
If, Biondello, thou wert come ashore,
We could at once put us in readiness
And take a lodging fit to entertain
Such friends as time in Padua shall beget. 45
But stay a while. What company is this?
  TRA. Master, some show to welcome us to town.
[*Enter* BAPTISTA, KATHARINA, BIANCA, GREMIO, *and*
HORTENSIO. LUCENTIO *and* TRANIO *stand by.*]

BAP. Gentlemen, importune me no farther,
For how I firmly am resolved you know;
That is, not to bestow my youngest daughter 50
Before I have a husband for the elder.
If either of you both love Katharina,
Because I know you well and love you well,
Leave shall you have to court her at your pleasure.
  GRE. [*Aside*] To cart° her rather. She's too
  rough for me. 55
There, there, Hortensio, will you any wife?
  KATH. I pray you, sir, is it your will
To make a stale° of me amongst these mates?°
  HOR. Mates, maid! How mean you that? No
  mates° for you,
Unless you were of gentler, milder mold. 60
  KATH. I'faith, sir, you shall never need to fear.
Iwis° it is not halfway to her heart,
But if it were, doubt not her care should be
To comb your noddle with a three-legged stool,
And paint your face, and use you like a fool. 65
  HOR. From all such devils, good Lord deliver us!
  GRE. And me too, good Lord!
  TRA. Husht, master! Here's some good pastime
  toward.
That wench is stark mad or wonderful froward.
  LUC. But in the other's silence do I see 70
Maid's mild behavior and sobriety.
Peace, Tranio!
  TRA. Well said, master. Mum, and gaze your fill.
  BAP. Gentlemen, that I may soon make good
What I have said — Bianca, get you in. 75
And let it not displease thee, good Bianca,
For I will love thee ne'er the less, my girl.
  KATH. A pretty peat!° It is best
Put finger in the eye, an° she knew why.°
  BIAN. Sister, content you in my discontent. 80
Sir, to your pleasure humbly I subscribe.°
My books and instruments shall be my company,
On them to look and practice by myself.
  LUC. Hark, Tranio! Thou may'st hear Minerva°
  speak.
  HOR. Signior Baptista, will you be so strange?°
Sorry am I that our good will effects° 86
Bianca's grief.
  GRE. Why will you mew° her up,
Signior Baptista, for this fiend of Hell,
And make her bear the penance of her° tongue?
  BAP. Gentlemen, content ye. I am resolved. 90
Go in, Bianca. [*Exit* BIANCA.]
And for I know she taketh most delight

Act I, sc. i: **3. for:** in. **8. breathe:** pause. **9. ingenious:** intellectual. **11. first:** before me. **14–15. Vincentio's . . . conceived:** it is right for Vincentio's son to fulfill the hopes of his family. **23. plash:** pool. **25.** *Mi perdonato:* pardon me. **26. affected:** inclined. **31. stoics:** The Stoics taught that men should cultivate wisdom and learn to control their desires and feelings. **stocks:** blocks, incapable of feeling. **32. checks:** restraints. **33. As . . . be:** as to make. **Ovid:** the Roman poet of love. **abjured:** sworn off. **34. Balk . . . acquaintance:** i.e., practice your logic on gay companions. **36. quicken:** enliven. **38. stomach:** appetite. **40. affect:** like. **41. Gramercies:** God have mercy — an expression of gratitude.

55. cart: punish as a prostitute. See App. 10. **58. To . . . stale:** make me cheap. **mates:** low persons, with a pun in the next line on *mates*, "companions," "equals." **62. Iwis:** assuredly. **78. peat:** little pet. **79. Put . . . why:** a nursery expression meaning "cry-baby." **an:** if. **81. subscribe:** agree. **84. Minerva:** goddess of wisdom and music. **85. strange:** unnatural. **86. effects:** causes. **87. mew:** shut — used of caging a hawk. **89: her . . . her:** Bianca . . . Katharine.

In music, instruments and poetry,
Schoolmasters will I keep within my house,
Fit to instruct her youth. If you, Hortensio,   95
Or Signior Gremio, you, know any such,
Prefer° them hither; for to cunning men
I will be very kind, and liberal
To mine own children in good bringing-up.
And so farewell. Katharina, you may stay;   100
For I have more to commune with Bianca. [*Exit.*]
     KATH. Why, and I trust I may go too, may I not?
What, shall I be appointed hours, as though, belike, I knew not what to take, and what to leave,
ha?   [*Exit.*]   105
     GRE. You may go to the Devil's dam.° Your gifts
are so good, here's none will hold you. Their love is
not so great, Hortensio, but we may blow our nails
together, and fast it fairly out.° Our cake's dough
on both sides.° Farewell. Yet, for the love I   110
bear my sweet Bianca, if I can by any means light on
a fit man to teach her that wherein she delights, I
will wish° him to her father.
     HOR. So will I, Signior Gremio; but a word,   115
I pray. Though the nature of our quarrel yet never
brooked parle,° know now, upon advice,° it toucheth us both — that we may yet again have access to
our fair mistress and be happy rivals in Bianca's love
— to labor and effect one thing specially.   121
     GRE. What's that, I pray?
     HOR. Marry, sir, to get a husband for her sister.
     GRE. A husband! A devil.   125
     HOR. I say a husband.
     GRE. I say a devil. Thinkest thou, Hortensio,
though her father be very rich, any man is so very
a fool to be married to Hell?
     HOR. Tush, Gremio, though it pass your patience
and mine to endure her loud alarums,° why,   131
man, there be good fellows in the world, an a man
could light on them, would take her with all faults,
and money enough.
     GRE. I cannot tell, but I had as lief° take her   135
dowry with this condition, to be whipped at the
high cross° every morning.
     HOR. Faith, as you say, there's small choice in
rotten apples. But come. Since this bar° in law
makes us friends, it shall be so far forth friendly
maintained till by helping Baptista's eldest   141
daughter to a husband we set his youngest free for
a husband, and then have to't° afresh. Sweet
Bianca! Happy man be his dole!° He that runs

fastest gets the ring. How say you, Signior Gremio?
     GRE. I am agreed, and would I had given   147
him the best horse in Padua to begin his wooing
that would thoroughly woo her, wed her, and bed
her, and rid the house of her! Come on.   150
                    [*Exeunt* GREMIO *and* HORTENSIO.]
     TRA. I pray, sir, tell me, is it possible
That love should of a sudden take such hold?
     LUC. O Tranio, till I found it to be true,
I never thought it possible or likely.
But see, while idly I stood looking on,   155
I found the effect of love in idleness,°
And now in plainness do confess to thee,
That art to me as secret and as dear
As Anna° to the Queen of Carthage was,
Tranio, I burn, I pine, I perish, Tranio,   160
If I achieve° not this young modest girl.
Counsel me, Tranio, for I know thou canst.
Assist me, Tranio, for I know thou wilt.
     TRA. Master, it is no time to chide you now.
Affection is not rated from the heart.°   165
If love have touched you, naught remains but so,
"*Redime te captum quam queas minimo.*"°
     LUC. Gramercies, lad, go forward. This contents.
The rest will comfort, for thy counsel's sound.   169
     TRA. Master, you looked so longly° on the maid,
Perhaps you marked° not what's the pith° of all.
     LUC. Oh, yes, I saw sweet beauty in her face,
Such as the daughter of Agenor° had,
That made great Jove to humble him to her hand
When with his knees he kissed the Cretan strand.°
     TRA. Saw you no more? Marked you not how her
sister   176
Began to scold and raise up such a storm
That mortal ears might hardly endure the din?
     LUC. Tranio, I saw her coral lips to move,
And with her breath she did perfume the air.   180
Sacred and sweet was all I saw in her.
     TRA. Nay, then, 'tis time to stir him from his
trance.
I pray, awake, sir. If you love the maid,
Bend thoughts and wits to achieve her. Thus it
stands:
Her elder sister is so curst° and shrewd°   185
That till the father rid his hands of her,
Master, your love must live a maid at home;
And therefore has he closely mewed her up,
Because she will not be annoyed with suitors.
     LUC. Ah, Tranio, what a cruel father's he!   190
But art thou not advised he took some care

---

97. Prefer: recommend.   106. dam: mother.   107–09. Their
. . . out: i.e., so far as their love is concerned, we may stand in
the cold and starve.   109–10. Our . . . sides: a proverb meaning "Our goose is cooked."   114. wish: commend.   117. brooked
parle: permitted negotiating; i.e., we have never discussed our
rivalry.   upon advice: after consideration.   131. alarums:
noises of battle.   135. lief: soon.   137. high cross: cross erected
at the center of a market place.   139. bar: impediment.
143. have to't: continue the fight.   144. Happy . . . dole: may
the lucky man have his reward.

156. I . . . idleness: i.e., like other men with nothing to do, I have
fallen in love.   159. Anna: sister of Dido, Queen of Carthage
and sharer of her secrets. See *Temp*, II.i.76,n.   161. achieve:
win.   165. Affection . . . heart: i.e., you can't rid a man of love
by chiding him.   167. Redime . . . minimo: i.e., buy yourself
out of captivity as cheaply as you can.   170. longly: for a long
time.   171. marked: observed. pith: i.e., most important point.
173. daughter of Agenor: i.e., Europa. See *M Ado*, V.iv.46,n.
175. strand: shore.   185. curst: bitter. shrewd: bad-tempered.

To get her cunning schoolmasters to instruct her?
  TRA. Aye, marry, am I, sir; and now 'tis plotted.°
  LUC. I have it, Tranio.
  TRA.   Master, for° my hand,
Both our inventions meet and jump° in one. 195
  LUC. Tell me thine first.
  TRA.   You will be schoolmaster
And undertake the teaching of the maid.
That's your device.
  LUC.   It is. May it be done?
  TRA. Not possible; for who shall bear your part
And be in Padua here Vincentio's son,   200
Keep house, and ply his book, welcome his friends,
Visit his countrymen and banquet them?
  LUC. Basta.° Content thee, for I have it full.°
We have not yet been seen in any house,
Nor can we be distinguished by our faces   205
For man or master. Then it follows thus:
Thou shalt be master. Tranio, in my stead,
Keep house, and port,° and servants, as I should.
I will some other be, some Florentine,
Some Neapolitan, or meaner man of Pisa.   210
'Tis hatched and shall be so. Tranio, at once
Uncase° thee. Take my colored hat and cloak.
When Biondello comes, he waits on thee,
But I will charm him first to keep his tongue.
  TRA. So had you need.   215
In brief, sir, sith° it your pleasure is,
And I am tied to be obedient —
For so your father charged me at our parting:
"Be serviceable to my son," quoth he,
Although I think 'twas in another sense —   220
I am content to be Lucentio.
Because so well I love Lucentio.
  LUC. Tranio, be so, because Lucentio loves.
And let me be a slave to achieve that maid
Whose sudden sight hath thralled° my wounded
    eye.   225
Here comes the rogue.
           [Enter BIONDELLO.]
           Sirrah, where have you been?
  BION. Where have I been! Nay, how now! Where
are you? Master, has my fellow Tranio stolen your
clothes? Or you stolen his? Or both? Pray, what's
the news?   230
  LUC. Sirrah, come hither. 'Tis no time to jest.
And therefore frame your manners to the time.
Your fellow Tranio here, to save my life,
Puts my apparel and my countenance on,
And I for my escape have put on his.   235
For in a quarrel since I came ashore,
I killed a man and fear I was descried.°
Wait you on him, I charge you, as becomes,

While I make way from hence to save my life.
You understand me?
  BION.   I, sir! Ne'er a whit.   240
  LUC. And not a jot° of Tranio in your mouth.
Tranio is changed into Lucentio.
  BION. The better for him. Would I were so too!
  TRA. So could I, faith, boy, to have the next wish
after,
That Lucentio indeed had Baptista's youngest
daughter.   245
But, sirrah, not for my sake, but your master's, I
advise
You use your manners discreetly in all kind of
companies.
When I am alone, why, then I am Tranio,
But in all places else your master Lucentio.   249
  LUC. Tranio, let's go. One thing more rests° that
thyself execute, to make one among these wooers.
If thou ask me why, sufficeth, my reasons are both
good and weighty.   [Exeunt.]
     [The presenters° above speak.]
  1. SERV. My lord, you nod. You do not mind the
play.
  SLY. Yes, by Saint Anne, do I. A good matter,
surely. Comes there any more of it?   256
  PAGE. My lord, 'tis but begun.
  SLY. 'Tis a very excellent piece of work, madam
lady. Would 'twere done!° [They sit and mark.°]

SCENE II. *Padua. Before* HORTENSIO's *house.*

    [Enter PETRUCHIO *and his man* GRUMIO.]
  PET. Verona, for a while I take my leave,
To see my friends in Padua, but of all
My best belovèd and approvèd friend,
Hortensio; and I trow° this is his house.
Here, sirrah Grumio. Knock, I say.   5
  GRU. Knock, sir. Whom should I knock? Is there
any man has rebused° your Worship?
  PET. Villain, I say, knock me° here soundly.
  GRU. Knock you here, sir! Why, sir, what am I,
sir, that I should knock you here, sir?   10
  PET. Villain, I say, knock me at this gate,
And rap me well, or I'll knock your knave's pate.
  GRU. My master is grown quarrelsome. I should
knock you first,
And then I know after who comes by the worst.°

193. plotted: planned; i.e., I have the idea.   **194. for:** by.
195. jump: agree.   **203. Basta:** enough. **have it full:** I see
the whole thing clearly.   **208. port:** style, manner of living.
212. Uncase: take off your outer garment.   **216. sith:** since.
225. thralled: enslaved.   **237. descried:** seen.

241. jot: smallest mention.   **250. rests:** remains.   **253. s.d.,
presenters:** The presenter (sometimes called the Chorus) was an
actor who explained or commented on the action of the play for
the benefit of the audience.   **259. 'twere done:** Hereafter in
Shakespeare's play Sly disappears. In the old play he opens an
eye from time to time and makes an occasional comment. **s.d.,
mark:** watch the play.
  Sc. ii: 4. trow: think.   **7. rebused:** for abused. Like others
of Shakespeare's simple servants, Grumio loves big words but
usually gets them wrong.   **8. me:** i.e., for me — as so often in
Elizabethan English.   **13–14. I . . . worst:** I should strike the
first blow, and then we'll see who comes off worst.

PET Will it not be?   15
Faith, sirrah, an you'll not knock, and I'll ring it.
I'll try how you can *sol, fa,* and sing it.
                    [*He wrings him by the ears.*]
GRU. Help, masters, help! My master is mad.
PET. Now, knock when I bid you, sirrah villain!
                    [*Enter* HORTENSIO.]
HOR. How now! What's the matter? My old   20
friend Grumio! And my good friend Petruchio!
How do you all at Verona?
  PET. Signior Hortensio, come you to part the
fray?
" Con tutto il core ben trovato,"° may I say.   24
  HOR. *" Alla nostra casa ben venuto, molto hon-*
orato signor mio Petruchio."°
Rise, Grumio, rise. We will compound° this quar-
rel.
  GRU. Nay, 'tis no matter, sir, what he 'leges° in
Latin. If this be not a lawful cause for me to leave
his service, look you, sir. He bid me knock him   30
and rap him soundly, sir. Well, was it fit for a serv-
ant to use his master so, being perhaps, for aught I
see, two and thirty, a pip out?°
Whom would to God I had well knocked at first,
Then had not Grumio come by the worst.   36
  PET. A senseless villain! Good Hortensio,
I bade the rascal knock upon your gate
And could not get him for my heart° to do it.
  GRU. Knock at the gate! Oh, heavens! Spake   40
you not these words plain: " Sirrah, knock me here,
rap me here, knock me well, and knock me sound-
ly "? And come you now with, " knocking at the
gate "?
  PET. Sirrah, be gone, or talk not, I advise you.
  HOR. Petruchio, patience. I am Grumio's pledge.
Why, this's a heavy chance° 'twixt him and you,
Your ancient, trusty, pleasant servant Grumio.   47
And tell me now, sweet friend, what happy gale
Blows you to Padua here from old Verona?
  PET. Such wind as scatters young men through
          the world   50
To seek their fortunes farther than at home,
Where small experience grows. But in a few,°
Signior Hortensio, thus it stands with me:
Antonio, my father, is deceased,
And I have thrust myself into this maze,°   55
Haply° to wive and thrive as best I may.
Crowns in my purse I have, and goods at home,
And so am come abroad to see the world.
  HOR. Petruchio, shall I then come roundly° to
          thee

And wish thee to a shrewd ill-favored° wife?   60
Thou'ldst thank me but a little for my counsel.
And yet I'll promise thee she shall be rich,
And very rich. But thou'rt too much my friend,
And I'll not wish thee to her.
  PET. Signior Hortensio, 'twixt such friends as we
Few words suffice. And therefore, if thou know   66
One rich enough to be Petruchio's wife,
As wealth is burden° of my wooing dance,
Be she as foul as was Florentius' love,°
As old as Sibyl,° and as curst and shrewd   70
As Socrates' Xanthippe,° or a worse,
She moves me not, or not removes, at least,
Affection's edge in me, were she as rough
As are the swelling Adriatic seas.
I come to wive it wealthily in Padua;   75
If wealthily, then happily in Padua.
  GRU. Nay, look you, sir, he tells you flatly what
his mind is. Why, give him gold enough and marry
him to a puppet or an aglet-baby,° or an old trot°
with ne'er a tooth in her head, though she have   80
as many diseases as two and fifty horses, why, noth-
ing comes amiss, so money comes withal.
  HOR. Petruchio, since we are stepped thus far in,
I will continue that° I broached in jest.
I can, Petruchio, help thee to a wife   85
With wealth enough and young and beauteous,
Brought up as best becomes a gentlewoman.
Her only fault, and that is faults enough,
Is that she is intolerable curst
And shrewd and froward, so beyond all measure
That, were my state far worser than it is,   91
I would not wed her for a mine of gold.
  PET. Hortensio, peace! Thou know'st not gold's
          effect.
Tell me her father's name and 'tis enough,
For I will board° her, though she chide as loud   95
As thunder when the clouds in autumn crack.
  HOR. Her father is Baptista Minola,
An affable and courteous gentleman.
Her name is Katharina Minola,
Renowned in Padua for her scolding tongue.   100
  PET. I know her father, though I know not her,
And he knew my deceasèd father well.
I will not sleep, Hortensio, till I see her;
And therefore let me be thus bold with you
To give you over° at this first encounter   105
Unless you will accompany me thither.
  GRU. I pray you, sir, let him go while the humor

60. **ill-favored:** homely.   68. **burden:** tune.   69. **foul . . . love:**
According to the story, Florentius was obliged to find the answer
to the riddle "What do women most desire?" An ugly old woman
promised to tell him on condition that he marry her. After they
were married she turned into a fair lady.   70. **Sibyl:** See *T Andr,*
IV.i.105,n.   71. **Xanthippe:** the wife of the philosopher Socrates,
and a notorious shrew.   79. **aglet-baby:** ornamental figure
fastened to the end of the points of laces used for tying the hose.
See p. 94a–b. **trot:** hag.   84. **that:** that which.   95. **board:**
assail.   105. **give . . . over:** desert; i.e., unless you help me I shall
no longer be your friend.

24. *Con . . . trovato:* with all my heart, well met.   25-26. *Alla . . .*
Petruchio: Welcome to our house, much honored Signior Petruchio.   27. **compound:** settle.   28. **'leges:** alleges.   33. **two . . .**
out: explained by editors as a reference to the card game of one
and thirty, and so perhaps meaning "a bit too much."   39. **heart:**
life.   46. **heavy chance:** sad misfortune.   52. **few:** few words.
55. **maze:** wandering.   56. **Haply:** perhaps.   59. **come roundly:**
speak plainly.

lasts. O' my word, an she knew him as well as
I do, she would think scolding would do little good
upon him. She may perhaps call him half a   110
score knaves or so. Why, that's nothing. An he
begin once, he'll rail in his rope tricks.° I'll tell you
what, sir, an she stand him but a little, he will
throw a figure° in her face and so disfigure her
with it that she shall have no more eyes to see
withal than a cat. You know him not, sir.   116

     HOR. Tarry, Petruchio, I must go with thee,
For in Baptista's keep my treasure is.
He hath the jewel of my life in hold,
His youngest daughter, beautiful Bianca,   120
And her withholds from me and other more,
Suitors to her and rivals in my love.
Supposing it a thing impossible,
For those defects I have before rehearsed,
That ever Katharina will be wooed,   125
Therefore this order hath Baptista ta'en:
That none shall have access unto Bianca
Till Katharine the Curst have got a husband.

     GRU. Katharine the Curst!
A title for a maid of all titles the worst.   130

     HOR. Now shall my friend Petruchio do me
       grace,°
And offer me, disguised in sober robes,
To old Baptista as a schoolmaster
Well seen° in music to instruct Bianca,
That so I may by this device at least   135
Have leave and leisure to make love to her
And, unsuspected, court her by herself.

     GRU. Here's no knavery! See, to beguile the old
folks, how the young folks lay their heads   140
together! [*Enter* GREMIO, *and* LUCENTIO *disguised.*]
Master, master, look about you. Who goes there,
ha?

     HOR. Peace, Grumio! It is the rival of my love.
Petruchio, stand by a while.

     GRU. A proper stripling, and an amorous!   144

     GRE. Oh, very well. I have perused the note.°
Hark you, sir, I'll have them very fairly bound.
All books of love, see that at any hand,°
And see you read no other lectures to her.
You understand me. Over and beside
Signior Baptista's liberality,   150
I'll mend° it with a largess.° Take your paper too,
And let me have them very well perfumed.
For she is sweeter than perfume itself
To whom they go to. What will you read to her?

     LUC. Whate'er I read to her, I'll plead for you
As for my patron, stand you so assured,   156
As firmly as yourself were still in place;
Yea, and perhaps with more successful words

Than you, unless you were a scholar, sir.

     GRE. Oh, this learning, what a thing it is!   160

     GRU. Oh, this woodcock,° what an ass it is!

     PET. Peace, sirrah!

     HOR. Grumio, mum! God save you, Signior
       Gremio.

     GRE. And you are well met, Signior Hortensio.
Trow° you whither I am going? To Baptista
       Minola.   165
I promised to inquire carefully
About a schoolmaster for the fair Bianca,
And by good fortune I have lighted well
On this young man, for learning and behavior
Fit for her turn, well read in poetry   170
And other books, good ones, I warrant ye.

     HOR. 'Tis well; and I have met a gentleman
Hath promised me to help me to another,
A fine musician to instruct our mistress.
So shall I no whit be behind in duty   175
To fair Bianca, so beloved of me.

     GRE. Beloved of me, and that my deeds shall
       prove.

     GRU. And that his bags° shall prove.

     HOR. Gremio, 'tis now no time to vent° our love.
Listen to me, and if you speak me fair,   180
I'll tell you news indifferent° good for either.
Here is a gentleman whom by chance I met,
Upon agreement from us to his liking,
Will undertake to woo curst Katharine,
Yea, and to marry her, if her dowry please.   185

     GRE. So said, so done, is well.
Hortensio, have you told him all her faults?

     PET. I know she is an irksome brawling scold.
If that be all, masters, I hear no harm.

     GRE. No, say'st me so, friend? What country-
       man?°   190

     PET. Born in Verona, old Antonio's son.
My father dead, my fortune lives for me,
And I do hope good days and long to see.

     GRE. O sir, such a life, with such a wife, were
       strange!
But if you have a stomach, to't i' God's name.   195
You shall have me assisting you in all.
But will you woo this wild cat?

     PET.   Will I live?°

     GRU. Will he woo her? Aye, or I'll hang her.

     PET. Why came I hither but to that intent?
Think you a little din can daunt mine ears?   200
Have I not in my time heard lions roar?
Have I not heard the sea, puffed up with winds,
Rage like an angry boar chafèd with sweat?
Have I not heard great ordnance in the field,
And Heaven's artillery thunder in the skies?   205
Have I not in a pitchèd battle heard

112. rope tricks: roguery; perhaps, however, Grumio's version of
"rhetoric."   114. throw a figure: use some rhetorical figure, i.e.,
striking expression.   131. grace: a favor.   134. Well seen:
expert.   145. note: list (of books).   147. at . . . hand: in any
case.   151. mend: increase. largess: gift of money.

161. woodcock: a very simple bird, easily deceived.   165. Trow:
know.   178. bags: money.   179. vent: utter. See *T Night,*
IV.i.10–17.   181. indifferent: equally.   190. What countryman: where do you come from.   197. Will I live: i.e., "You bet!"

Loud 'larums,° neighing steeds, and trumpets'
     clang?
And do you tell me of a woman's tongue,
That gives not half so great a blow to hear
As will a chestnut in a farmer's fire?   210
Tush, tush! Fear boys with bugs.°
   GRU.   For he fears none.
   GRE. Hortensio, hark.
This gentleman is happily arrived,
My mind presumes, for his own good and ours.
   HOR. I promised we would be contributors   215
And bear his charge of° wooing, whatsoe'er.
   GRE. And so we will, provided that he win her.
   GRU. I would I were as sure of a good dinner.

[*Enter* TRANIO *brave,*° *and* BIONDELLO.]

   TRA. Gentlemen, God save you. If I may be bold,
Tell me, I beseech you, which is the readiest way
To the house of Signior Baptista Minola?   221
   BION. He that has the two fair daughters. Is't he
you mean?
   TRA. Even he, Biondello.
   GRE. Hark you, sir. You mean not her to——
   TRA. Perhaps him and her, sir. What have you to
do?   226
   PET. Not her that chides, sir, at any hand, I pray.
   TRA. I love no chiders, sir. Biondello, let's away.
   LUC. Well begun, Tranio.
   HOR.   Sir, a word ere you go.
Are you a suitor to the maid you talk of, yea or no?
   TRA. And if I be, sir, is it any offense?   231
   GRE. No, if without more words you will get you
     hence.
   TRA. Why, sir, I pray, are not the streets as free
For me as for you?
   GRE.   But so is not she.
   TRA. For what reason, I beseech you?
   GRE.   For this reason, if you'll know,   235
That she's the choice love of Signior Gremio.
   HOR. That she's the chosen of Signior Hortensio.
   TRA. Softly, my masters! If you be gentlemen,
Do me this right. Hear me with patience.
Baptista is a noble gentleman   240
To whom my father is not all unknown,
And were his daughter fairer than she is,
She may more suitors have and me for one.
Fair Leda's daughter° had a thousand wooers;
Then well one more may fair Bianca have.   245
And so she shall. Lucentio shall make one,
Though Paris° came in hope to speed° alone.
   GRE. What, this gentleman will out talk us all!
   LUC. Sir, give him head. I know he'll prove a
     jade.°   249

   PET. Hortensio, to what end are all these words?
   HOR. Sir, let me be so bold as ask you,
Did you yet ever see Baptista's daughter?
   TRA. No, sir, but hear I do that he hath two,
The one as famous for a scolding tongue
As is the other for beauteous modesty.   255
   PET. Sir, sir, the first's for me. Let her go by.
   GRE. Yea, leave that labor to great Hercules,
And let it be more than Alcides'° twelve.
   PET. Sir, understand you this of me in sooth.°
The youngest daughter whom you hearken for
Her father keeps from all access of suitors   261
And will not promise her to any man
Until the elder sister first be wed.
The younger then is free, and not before.
   TRA. If it be so, sir, that you are the man   265
Must stead° us all and me amongst the rest;
And if you break the ice and do this feat,
Achieve the elder, set the younger free
For our access. Whose hap shall be to have her
Will not so graceless be to be ingrate.°   270
   HOR. Sir, you say well, and well you do conceive.
And since you do profess to be a suitor,
You must, as we do, gratify° this gentleman
To whom we all rest generally beholding.°
   TRA. Sir, I shall not be slack, in sign whereof,
Please ye, we may contrive° this afternoon,   276
And quaff carouses to our mistress' health,
And do as adversaries do in law,
Strive mightily, but eat and drink as friends.
   GRU., BION. Oh, excellent motion! Fellows, let's
     be gone.   280
   HOR. The motion's good indeed and be it so.
Petruchio, I shall be your *ben venuto.*°   [*Exeunt.*]

Act II

SCENE I. *Padua. A room in* BAPTISTA'S *house.*

[*Enter* KATHARINA *and* BIANCA.°]

   BIAN. Good Sister, wrong me not, nor wrong
     yourself,
To make a bondmaid and a slave of me;
That I disdain. But for these other gawds,°
Unbind my hands, I'll pull them off myself,
Yea, all my raiment, to my petticoat;   5
Or what you will command me will I do,
So well I know my duty to my elders.
   KATH. Of all thy suitors, here I charge thee tell

---

207. 'larums: alarums, sounds of battle.   211. Fear ... bugs:
frighten boys with tales of goblins.   216. charge of: expenses in.
218. s.d., brave: expensively dressed.   244. Leda's daughter:
Helen of Troy.   247. Paris: the young Trojan Prince who eloped
with Helen. speed: succeed.   249. jade: a horse in such poor
condition that it will soon tire.

258. Alcides: Hercules, who undertook twelve heroic labors.
259. sooth: truth.   266. stead: benefit.   270. ingrate: ungrateful.   273. gratify: reward.   274. beholding: indebted.   276. contrive: waste, spend.   282. *ben venuto:* welcome.
   Act II, Sc. i: s.d., Bianca: with her hands tied.   3. gawds:
trifles; i.e., articles of ornament.

Whom thou lovest best. See thou dissemble not.

BIAN. Believe me, Sister, of all the men alive 10
I never yet beheld that special face
Which I could fancy more than any other.

KATH. Minion,° thou liest. Is't not Hortensio?

BIAN. If you affect him, Sister, here I swear 14
I'll plead for you myself, but you shall have him.

KATH. Oh, then, belike, you fancy riches more.
You will have Gremio to keep you fair.

BIAN. Is it for him you do envy me so?
Nay then you jest, and now I well perceive
You have but jested with me all this while. 20
I prithee, Sister Kate, untie my hands.

KATH. If that be jest, then all the rest was so.
                                       [Strikes her.]

[Enter BAPTISTA.]

BAP. Why, how now, dame! Whence grows this
    insolence?
Bianca, stand aside. Poor girl! She weeps. —
Go ply thy needle. Meddle not with her — 25
For shame, thou hilding° of a devilish spirit!
Why dost thou wrong her that did ne'er wrong
    thee?
When did she cross thee with a bitter word?

KATH. Her silence flouts° me, and I'll be re-
    venged.   [Flies after BIANCA.]

BAP. What, in my sight? Bianca, get thee in. 30
                                 [Exit BIANCA.]

KATH. What, will you not suffer me? Nay, now
    I see
She is your treasure, she must have a husband.
I must dance barefoot° on her wedding day
And for your love to her lead apes in Hell.°
Talk not to me. I will go sit and weep 35
Till I can find occasion of revenge.   [Exit.]

BAP. Was ever gentleman thus grieved as I?
But who comes here?

*[Enter GREMIO, LUCENTIO in the habit of a mean
man;° PETRUCHIO, with HORTENSIO as a musician;
and TRANIO, with BIONDELLO bearing a lute° and
books.]*

GRE. Good morrow, Neighbor Baptista. 39

BAP. Good morrow, Neighbor Gremio. God save
you, gentlemen!

PET. And you, good sir. Pray have you not a
    daughter
Called Katharina, fair and virtuous?

BAP. I have a daughter, sir, called Katharina.

GRE. You are too blunt. Go to it orderly. 45

PET. You wrong me, Signior Gremio. Give me
    leave.
I am a gentleman of Verona, sir,

That, hearing of her beauty and her wit,
Her affability and bashful modesty,
Her wondrous qualities and mild behavior, 50
Am bold to show myself a forward guest
Within your house to make mine eye the witness
Of that report which I so oft have heard.
And, for an entrance° to my entertainment,°
I do present you with a man of mine, 55
                [Presenting HORTENSIO.]
Cunning in music and the mathematics,
To instruct her fully in those sciences
Whereof I know she is not ignorant.
Accept of him, or else you do me wrong.
His name is Licio, born in Mantua. 60

BAP. You're welcome, sir, and he, for your good
    sake.
But for my daughter Katharine, this I know,
She is not for your turn, the more my grief.

PET. I see you do not mean to part with her,
Or else you like not of my company. 65

BAP. Mistake me not. I speak but as I find.
Whence are you, sir? What may I call your name?

PET. Petruchio is my name, Antonio's son,
A man well known throughout all Italy.

BAP. I know him well. You are welcome for his
    sake. 70

GRE. Saving your tale, Petruchio, I pray,
Let us, that are poor petitioners,° speak too.
Baccarè!° You are marvelous forward.

PET. Oh, pardon me, Signior Gremio. I would
    fain be doing.

GRE. I doubt it not, sir, but you will curse your
    wooing. 75
Neighbor, this is a gift very grateful, I am sure of
it. To express the like kindness, myself, that have
been more kindly beholding to you than any, freely
give unto you this young scholar [presenting 79
LUCENTIO], that hath been long studying at Rheims,
as cunning in Greek, Latin, and other languages, as
the other in music and mathematics. His name is
Cambio. Pray accept his service.

BAP. A thousand thanks, Signior Gremio. 85
Welcome good Cambio. But, gentle sir [to TRANIO],
methinks you walk like a stranger. May I be so bold
to know the cause of your coming?

TRA. Pardon me, sir, the boldness is mine own,
That, being a stranger in this city here, 90
Do make myself a suitor to your daughter,
Unto Bianca, fair and virtuous.
Nor is your firm resolve unknown to me
In the preferment of the eldest sister.
This liberty is all that I request: 95
That, upon knowledge of my parentage,
I may have welcome 'mongst the rest that woo

---

13. Minion: hussy. 26. hilding: worthless creature. 29. flouts:
insults. 33. dance barefoot: It was an old (and humiliating)
custom for an elder unmarried sister to dance barefooted at the
wedding of her younger sister. 34. lead . . . Hell: This was the
alleged fate of old maids who died unwed. See *M Ado*, II.i.43.
38. s.d., mean man: person of humble position. lute: See Pl. 18d.

54. entrance: entrance fee, introduction. entertainment: welcome. 72. poor petitioners: humble suitors. 73. Baccarè:
back.

And free access and favor as the rest;
And, toward the education of your daughters,
I here bestow a simple instrument   100
And this small packet of Greek and Latin books.
If you accept them, then their worth is great.
   BAP. Lucentio is your name. Of whence, I pray?
   TRA. Of Pisa, sir, son to Vincentio.
   BAP. A mighty man of Pisa. By report   105
I know him well. You are very welcome, sir. —
Take you the lute, and you the set of books.
You shall go see your pupils presently.°
Holloa, within!
            [*Enter a* SERVANT.]
            Sirrah, lead these gentlemen
To my daughters, and tell them both   110
These are their tutors. Bid them use them well.
   [*Exit* SERVANT, *with* LUCENTIO *and* HORTENSIO,
                        BIONDELLO *following.*]
We will go walk a little in the orchard,
And then to dinner. You are passing welcome,
And so I pray you all to think yourself.
   PET. Signior Baptista, my business asketh haste,
And every day I cannot come to woo.   116
You knew my father well, and in him me,
Left solely heir to all his lands and goods,
Which I have bettered rather than decreased.
Then tell me, if I get your daughter's love,   120
What dowry shall I have with her to wife?
   BAP. After my death the one half of my lands,
And in possession° twenty thousand crowns.
   PET. And for that dowry I'll assure her of°
Her widowhood, be it that she survive me,   125
In all my lands and leases whatsoever.
Let specialties° be therefore drawn between us
That covenants° may be kept on either hand.
   BAP. Aye, when the special thing is well obtained,
That is, her love; for that is all in all.   130
   PET. Why, that is nothing. For I tell you, Father,
I am as péremptory° as she proud-minded,
And where two raging fires meet together,
They do consume the thing that feeds their fury.
Though little fire grows great with little wind,   135
Yet extreme gusts will blow out fire and all:
So I to her and so she yields to me,
For I am rough and woo not like a babe.
   BAP. Well mayst thou woo, and happy be thy
   speed!°
But be thou armed for some unhappy words.   140
   PET. Aye, to the proof, as mountains are for
   winds,
That shake not, though they blow perpetually.
   [*Re-enter* HORTENSIO, *with his head broke.*°]

   BAP. How now, my friend! Why dost thou look
   so pale?
   HOR. For fear, I promise you, if I look pale.
   BAP. What, will my daughter prove a good musi-
   cian?   145
   HOR. I think she'll sooner prove a soldier.
Iron may hold with her, but never lutes.
   BAP. Why, then thou canst not break her to the
   lute?
   HOR. Why, no, for she hath broke the lute to me.
I did but tell her she mistook her frets°   150
And bowed° her hand to teach her fingering,
When, with a most impatient devilish spirit,
"Frets, call you these?" quoth she. "I'll fume°
   with them!"
And with that word she struck me on the head,
And through the instrument my pate made way;
And there I stood amazèd for a while,   156
As on a pillory,° looking through the lute,
While she did call me rascal fiddler
And twangling Jack, with twenty such vile terms,
As had she studied to misuse me so.   160
   PET. Now, by the world, it is a lusty wench.
I love her ten times more than e'er I did.
Oh, how I long to have some chat with her!
   BAP. Well, go with me, and be not so discom-
   fited.
Proceed in practice with my younger daughter.   165
She's apt to learn and thankful for good turns.
Signior Petruchio, will you go with us,
Or shall I send my daughter Kate to you?
   PET. I pray you do. I will attend° her here
   [*Exeunt* BAPTISTA, GREMIO, TRANIO, *and* HORTENSIO.]
And woo her with some spirit when she comes.
Say that she rail; why, then I'll tell her plain   171
She sings as sweetly as a nightingale.
Say that she frown; I'll say she looks as clear
As morning roses newly washed with dew.
Say she be mute and will not speak a word;   175
Then I'll commend her volubility
And say she uttereth piercing eloquence.
If she do bid me pack,° I'll give her thanks
As though she bid me stay by her a week.
If she deny to wed, I'll crave the day   180
When I shall ask the banns° and when be married.
But here she comes; and now, Petruchio, speak.
            [*Enter* KATHARINA.]
Good morrow, Kate; for that's your name, I hear.
   KATH. Well have you heard, but something hard
   of hearing.
They call me Katharine° that do talk of me.   185

---

108. presently: immediately.   123. in possession: as an immediate gift.   124. assure . . . of: make a formal settlement for.
127. specialties: legal documents, detailing the sums.   128. covenants: agreements.   132. peremptory: short tempered.
139. speed: success.   142. s.d., broke: with the skin broken,
bleeding.

150. frets: rings of gut on the finger board to regulate the finger-
ing.   151. bowed: bent.   153. fume: steam — a pun on the
phrase "fret and fume" — be indignant.   157. pillory: See
App. 10.   169. attend: wait for.   178. pack: get out.   181. banns:
See App. 15.   185. call me Katharine: It is an impertinence for
Petruchio to call her Kate without previous introduction.

PET. You lie, in faith, for you are called plain
  Kate,
And bonny Kate, and sometimes Kate the Curst;
But Kate, the prettiest Kate in Christendom,
Kate of Kate-Hall, my superdainty Kate,
For dainties are all Kates° — and therefore, Kate,
Take this of me, Kate of my consolation: 191
Hearing thy mildness praised in every town,
Thy virtues spoke of, and thy beauty sounded,
Yet not so deeply as to thee belongs,
Myself am moved to woo thee for my wife.   195
  KATH. Moved! In good time. Let him that moved
    you hither
Remove you hence. I knew you at the first
You were a movable.°
  PET.   Why, what's a movable?
  KATH. A joined stool.°
  PET.   Thou hast hit it. Come sit on me.   199
  KATH. Asses are made to bear, and so are you.
  PET. Women are made to bear, and so are you.
  KATH. No such jade as you, if me you mean.
  PET. Alas, good Kate, I will not burden thee!
For, knowing thee to be but young and light ——
  KATH. Too light for such a swain° as you to
    catch,   205
And yet as heavy as my weight should be.
  PET. Should be! Should — buzz!°
  KATH.   Well ta'en, and like a buzzard.°
  PET. O slow-winged turtle!° Shall a buzzard take
    thee?
  KATH. Aye, for a turtle, as he takes a buzzard.°
  PET. Come, come, you wasp. I' faith, you are too
    angry.   210
  KATH. If I be waspish, best beware my sting.
  PET. My remedy is then to pluck it out.
  KATH. Aye, if the fool could find it where it lies.
  PET. Who knows not where a wasp does wear his
    sting?
In his tail.   215
  KATH. In his tongue.
  PET. Whose tongue?
  KATH. Yours, if you talk of tails; and so farewell.
  PET. What, with my tongue in your tail? Nay,
    come again.
Good Kate, I am a gentleman.
  KATH.   That I'll try.° [*She strikes him.*]   220
  PET. I swear I'll cuff you if you strike again.
  KATH. So may you lose your arms.°
If you strike me, you are no gentleman,

And if no gentleman, why then no arms.
  PET. A herald, Kate? Oh, put me in thy books!°
  KATH. What is your crest? A coxcomb?   226
  PET. A combless cock, so Kate will be my hen.
  KATH. No cock of mine. You crow too like a
    craven.°
  PET. Nay, come, Kate, come. You must not look
    so sour.
  KATH. It is my fashion when I see a crab.°   230
  PET. Why, here's no crab, and therefore look not
    sour.
  KATH. There is, there is.
  PET. Then show it me.
  KATH.   Had I a glass, I would.
  PET. What, you mean my face?   235
  KATH.   Well aimed of such a young° one.
  PET. Now, by Saint George, I am too young° for
    you.
  KATH. Yet you are withered.
  PET.   'Tis with cares.   240
  KATH.   I care not.
  PET. Nay, hear you, Kate. In sooth you scape not
    so.
  KATH. I chafe you if I tarry. Let me go.
  PET. No, not a whit. I find you passing gentle.
'Twas told me you were rough and coy and sullen,
And now I find report a very liar;   246
For thou art pleasant, gamesome, passing courteous,
But slow in speech, yet sweet as springtime flowers.
Thou canst not frown, thou canst not look
    askance,°
Nor bite the lip, as angry wenches will,   250
Nor hast thou pleasure to be cross in talk,
But thou with mildness entertain'st thy wooers,
With gentle conference, soft and affable.
Why does the world report that Kate doth limp?°
O slanderous world! Kate like the hazel twig   255
Is straight and slender, and as brown in hue
As hazel nuts, and sweeter than the kernels,
Oh, let me see thee walk. Thou dost not halt.°
  KATH. Go, fool, and whom thou keep'st com-
    mand.
  PET. Did ever Dian° so become a grove   260
As Kate this chamber with her princely gait?
Oh, be thou Dian, and let her be Kate,
And then let Kate be chaste and Dian sportful!
  KATH. Where did you study all this goodly
    speech?
  PET. It is extempore, from my mother wit.   265
  KATH. A witty mother! Witless else° her son.
  PET. Am I not wise?

190. dainties . . . Kates: with a pun on "cate" (dainty).
198. movable: piece of furniture. 199. joined stool: See Pl. 17a.
205. swain: country lover. 207. buzz: with a pun on the "be."
buzzard: (a) fool; (b) hawk of a kind unsuitable for hawking.
208. turtle: dove, the pattern of gentleness. 209. Aye . . . buzzard: i.e., I am as unlikely to choose you as a turtledove to
mate with a buzzard. 220. That . . . try: i.e., if he is a gentleman he will not strike back. 222. arms: coat of arms, and so
be degraded. See App. 9.

225. herald . . . books: See App. 9, paragraph 3. 228. craven:
a gamecock that will not fight. 230. crab: crab apple.
236. young: inexperienced. 237. young: agile. 249. askance:
scornfully. 254. doth limp: i.e., is deformed. 258. halt: limp.
260. Dian: Diana, the goddess of chastity and the chase.
266. Witless else: if your mother had not been witty you would
have been a fool.

KATH. Yes. Keep you warm.°

PET. Marry, so I mean, sweet Katharine, in thy bed.

And therefore, setting all this chat aside,   270
Thus in plain terms: Your father hath consented
That you shall be my wife, your dowry 'greed on,
And, will you, nill you,° I will marry you.
Now Kate, I am a husband for your turn.°
For, by this light whereby I see thy beauty,   275
Thy beauty, that doth make me like thee well,
Thou must be married to no man but me;
For I am he am born to tame you Kate,
And bring you from a wild Kate° to a Kate
Conformable as other household Kates.   280
Here comes your father. Never make denial.
I must and will have Katharine to my wife.

[Re-enter BAPTISTA, GREMIO, and TRANIO.]

BAP. Now, Signior Petruchio, how speed° you with my daughter?

PET. How but well, sir? How but well?
It were impossible I should speed amiss.   285

BAP. Why, how now, Daughter Katharine! In your dumps?

KATH. Call you me Daughter? Now, I promise you
You have showed a tender fatherly regard
To wish me wed to one half-lunatic,
A mad-cap ruffian and a swearing Jack   290
That thinks with oaths to face the matter out.

PET. Father, 'tis thus. Yourself and all the world
That talked of her have talked amiss of her.
If she be curst, it is for policy,°
For she's not froward, but modest as the dove.   295
She is not hot, but temperate as the morn.
For patience she will prove a second Grissel,°
And Roman Lucrece° for her chastity.
And to conclude, we have 'greed so well together
That upon Sunday is the wedding day.   300

KATH. I'll see thee hanged on Sunday first.

GRE. Hark, Petruchio, she says she'll see thee hanged first.

TRA. Is this your speeding? Nay, then, good night our part!

PET. Be patient, gentlemen. I choose her for my-self.
If she and I be pleased, what's that to you?   305
'Tis bargained 'twixt us twain, being alone,
That she shall still be curst in company.
I tell you, 'tis incredible to believe

How much she loves me. Oh, the kindest Kate!
She hung about my neck, and kiss on kiss   310
She vied° so fast, protesting oath on oath,
That in a twink she won me to her love.
Oh, you are novices! 'Tis a world to see
How tame, when men and women are alone,
A meacock° wretch can make the curstest shrew.
Give me thy hand, Kate. I will unto Venice   316
To buy apparel 'gainst° the wedding day.
Provide the feast, Father, and bid the guests.
I will be sure my Katharine shall be fine.

BAP. I know not what to say. But give me your hands.   320
God send you joy, Petruchio! 'Tis a match.

GRE., TRA. Amen, say we. We will be witnesses.

PET. Father, and Wife, and gentlemen, adieu.
I will to Venice. Sunday comes apace.
We will have rings, and things, and fine array;   325
And, kiss me, Kate! We will be married o' Sunday.

[Exeunt PETRUCHIO and KATHARINA severally.°]

GRE. Was ever match clapped up° so suddenly?

BAP. Faith, gentlemen, now I play a merchant's part
And venture madly on a desperate mart.°

TRA. 'Twas a commodity lay fretting° by you.
'Twill bring you gain or perish on the seas.   331

BAP. The gain I seek is quiet in the match.

GRE. No doubt but he hath got a quiet catch.
But now, Baptista, to your younger daughter.
Now is the day we long have looked for.   335
I am your neighbor and was suitor first.

TRA. And I am one that love Bianca more
Than words can witness or your thoughts can guess.

GRE. Youngling, thou canst not love so dear as I.

TRA. Greybeard, thy love doth freeze.

GRE.   But thine doth fry.   340
Skipper,° stand back. 'Tis age that nourisheth.

TRA. But youth in ladies' eyes that flourisheth.

BAP. Content you, gentlemen. I will compound° this strife.
'Tis deeds must win the prize, and he, of both,
That can assure my daughter greatest dower   345
Shall have my Bianca's love.
Say, Signior Gremio, what can you assure her?

GRE. First, as you know, my house within the city
Is richly furnishèd with plate and gold,
Basins and ewers to lave° her dainty hands,   350
My hangings all of Tyrian° tapestry.
In ivory coffers I have stuffed my crowns,°

268. Keep . . . warm: a reference to the proverb "He has wit enough to keep him warm."   273. will . . . you: willy-nilly, whether you want me or not.   274. for . . . turn: to suit you.   279. wild Kate: i.e., cat.   283. how speed: what progress are you making.   294. policy: cunning reasons.   297. Grissel: The famous story of Patient Griselda was told by the Clerk of Oxford in the Canterbury Tales. A lady of exemplary and incredible patience, she endured many insults and wrongs from her husband until he was reformed by her patience and goodness.   298. Roman Lucrece: See p. 1561.

311. vied: went one better — a term from card play.   315. meacock: milksop.   317. 'gainst: in anticipation of.   326. s.d., severally: by separate exits.   327. clapped up: arranged, lit., shaken hands upon. See W Tale, I.ii.104.   329. mart: bargain. 330. fretting: going to waste.   341. Skipper: playboy. See I Hen IV, III.ii.60.   343. compound: settle.   350. lave: wash 351. Tyrian: from Tyre, purple.   352. crowns: "dollars."

In cypress° chests my arras counterpoints,°
Costly apparel, tents,° and canopies,
Fine linen, Turkey cushions bossed° with pearl,
Valance° of Venice gold in needlework.   356
Pewter and brass, and all things that belong
To house or housekeeping. Then, at my farm
I have a hundred milch kine to the pail,
Sixscore fat oxen standing in my stalls,   360
And all things answerable to this portion.°
Myself am struck in years, I must confess,
And if I die tomorrow, this is hers
If whilst I live she will be only mine.
    TRA. That "only" came well in. Sir, list to me.
I am my father's heir and only son.   366
If I may have your daughter to my wife,
I'll leave her houses three or four as good
Within rich Pisa walls as any one
Old Signior Gremio has in Padua,   370
Besides two thousand ducats° by the year
Of fruitful land, all which shall be her jointure.°
What, have I pinched° you, Signior Gremio?
    GRE. Two thousand ducats by the year of land!
My land amounts not to so much in all.   375
That she shall have, besides an argosy°
That now is lying in Marseilles' road.°
What, have I choked you with an argosy?   378
    TRA. Gremio, 'tis known my father hath no less
Than three great argosies, besides two galliasses,°
And twelve tight galleys.° These I will assure her,
And twice as much, whate'er thou offer'st next.
    GRE. Nay, I have offered all, I have no more,
And she can have no more than all I have.
If you like me, she shall have me and mine.   385
    TRA. Why, then the maid is mine from all the
        world
By your firm promise. Gremio is outvied.°
    BAP. I must confess your offer is the best,
And, let your father make her the assurance,°
She is your own; else, you must pardon me,   390
If you should die before him, where's her dower?
    TRA. That's but a cavil.° He is old, I young.
    GRE. And may not young men die, as well as old?
    BAP. Well, gentlemen,
I am thus resolved. On Sunday next you know   395
My daughter Katharine is to be married.
Now, on the Sunday following shall Bianca
Be bride to you if you make this assurance;

If not, to Signior Gremio.
And so, I take leave and thank you both.   400
    GRE. Adieu, good Neighbor.   [*Exit* BAPTISTA.]
                    Now I fear thee not.
Sirrah young gamester,° your father were a fool
To give thee all, and in his waning age
Set foot under thy table.° Tut, a toy!   404
An old Italian fox is not so kind, my boy.° [*Exit.*]
    TRA. A vengeance on your crafty withered hide!
Yet I have faced it with a card of ten.°
'Tis in my head to do my master good.
I see no reason but supposed Lucentio
Must get a father, called — supposed Vincentio.
And that's a wonder. Fathers commonly   411
Do get their children, but in this case of wooing,
A child shall get a sire, if I fail not of my cunning.
                    [*Exit.*]

Act III

SCENE I. *Padua.* BAPTISTA'S *house.*

[*Enter* LUCENTIO, HORTENSIO,° *and* BIANCA.]
    LUC. Fiddler, forbear. You grow too forward, sir.
Have you so soon forgot the entertainment
Her sister Katharine welcomed you withal?°
    HOR. But, wrangling pedant, this is
The patroness of heavenly harmony.
Then give me leave to have prerogative,°   5
And when in music we have spent an hour,
Your lecture shall have leisure for as much.
    LUC. Preposterous ass, that never read so far
To know the cause why music was ordained!   10
Was it not to refresh the mind of man
After his studies or his usual pain?°
Then give me leave to read philosophy,
And while I pause, serve in your harmony.
    HOR. Sirrah, I will not bear these braves° of
        thine.   15
    BIAN. Why, gentlemen, you do me double wrong
To strive for that which resteth in my choice.
I am no breeching scholar° in the schools.
I'll not be tied to hours nor 'pointed° times,
But learn my lessons as I please myself.   20
And, to cut off all strife, here sit we down.

353. cypress: of cypress wood — a valuable and lasting material. **arras counterpoints:** tapestry counterpanes. **354. tents:** bed curtains. See Pl. 17b. **355. bossed:** embroidered. **356. Valance:** bed fringe. See Pl. 17b. **361. portion:** proportion, i.e., for such a great stock. **371. ducats:** worth about $1 each. **372. jointure:** marriage portion. **373. pinched:** made you squirm. **376. argosy:** a great merchant ship. See *M of Ven,* I.i.9–14. **377. road:** harbor. **380. galliasses:** fast merchant vessels used in the Mediterranean. **381. galleys:** fast vessels also used in the Mediterranean, propelled by oars manned by slaves. **387. outvied:** outbid. **389. make . . . assurance:** guarantee the settlement. **392. cavil:** quibble.

402. gamester: gambler. **404. Set . . . table:** i.e., become a pensioner in his son's house. **404–05. Tut . . . boy:** i.e., no Italian father will be such a fool as to give away all his wealth to his son. **407. faced . . . ten:** bluffed him by a high bid.
    Act III, Sc. i: s.d., Lucentio and Hortensio: They are still disguised as schoolmaster and musician. **3. welcomed . . . withal:** See II.i.142–60. **6. prerogative:** privilege (of starting first). **12. pain:** labor. **15. braves:** insults. **18. breeching scholar:** a young scholar of an age to be flogged. **19. 'pointed:** appointed.

Take you your instrument, play you the whiles.°
His lecture will be done ere you have tuned.

    HOR. You'll leave his lecture when I am in tune?

    LUC. That will be never. Tune your instrument.

    BIAN. Where left we last?   26

    LUC. Here, madam:

        " *Hic ibat Simois; hic est Sigeia tellus;*
          Hic steterat Priami regia celsa senis."°

    BIAN. Construe° them.   30

    LUC. " *Hic ibat,*" as I told you before, " *Simois,*"
I am Lucentio, " *hic est,*" son unto Vincentio of
Pisa, " *Sigeia tellus,*" disguised thus to get your
love; " *Hic steterat,*" and that Lucentio that comes
awooing, " *Priami,*" is my man Tranio, " *regia,*"   35
bearing my port,° " *celsa senis,*" that we might beguile the old pantaloon.°

    HOR. Madam, my instrument's in tune.

    BIAN. Let's hear. [*He plays.*] Oh fie! The treble
jars.

    LUC. Spit in the hole,° man, and tune again.   40

    BIAN. Now let me see if I can construe it.
" *Hic ibat Simois,*" I know you not, " *hic est Sigeia
tellus,*" I trust you not, " *Hic steterat Priami,*" take
heed he hear us not, " *regia,*" presume not, " *celsa
senis,*" despair not.   45

    HOR. Madam, 'tis now in tune.

    LUC.   All but the base.

    HOR. The base is right. 'Tis the base knave that
jars.

[*Aside*] How fiery and forward our pedant is!
Now, for my life, the knave doth court my love.
Pedascule,° I'll watch you better yet.   50

    BIAN. In time I may believe, yet I mistrust.

    LUC. Mistrust it not, for, sure, Aeacides
Was Ajax, called so from his grandfather.°

    BIAN. I must believe my master, else, I promise
you,
I should be arguing still upon that doubt.   55
But let it rest. Now, Licio, to you.
Good masters, take it not unkindly, pray,
That I have been thus pleasant with you both.

    HOR. You may go walk and give me leave a while.
My lessons° make° no music in three parts.°   60

    LUC. Are you so formal, sir? Well, I must wait,
[*Aside*] And watch withal; for, but° I be deceived,

Our fine musician groweth amorous.

    HOR. Madam, before you touch the instrument,
To learn the order of my fingering   65
I must begin with rudiments of art,
To teach you gamut° in a briefer sort,
More pleasant, pithy, and effectual,
Than hath been taught by any of my trade.
And there it is in writing, fairly drawn.   70

    BIAN. Why, I am past my gamut long ago.

    HOR. Yet read the gamut of Hortensio.

    BIAN. [*Reads.*]
    " ' Gamut ' I am, the ground° of all accord,°
       ' A re,' to plead Hortensio's passion.
    ' B mi,' Bianca, take him for thy lord,   75
       ' C fa ut,' that loves with all affection.
    ' D sol re,' one clef, two notes have I.
    ' E la mi,' show pity, or I die."
Call you this gamut? Tut, I like it not.
Old fashions please me best. I am not so nice°   80
To change true rules for old° inventions.

                [*Enter a* SERVANT.]

    SERV. Mistress, your father prays you leave your
books
And help to dress your sister's chamber up.
You know tomorrow is the wedding day.

    BIAN. Farewell, sweet masters both. I must be
gone.   [*Exeunt* BIANCA *and* SERVANT.]   85

    LUC. Faith, mistress, then I have no cause to stay.
                               [*Exit.*]

    HOR. But I have cause to pry into this pedant.
Methinks he looks as though he were in love.
Yet if thy thoughts, Bianca, be so humble°
To cast thy wandering eyes on every stale,°   90
Seize thee that list.° If once I find thee ranging,°
Hortensio will be quit with thee by changing.
                               [*Exit.*]

SCENE II. *Padua. Before* BAPTISTA'S *house.*

[*Enter* BAPTISTA, GREMIO, TRANIO, KATHARINA,
BIANCA, LUCENTIO, *and others,* ATTENDANTS.]

    BAP. Signior Lucentio [*To* TRANIO], this is the
'pointed day
That Katharine and Petruchio should be married,
And yet we hear not of our son-in-law.
What will be said? What mockery will it be,
To want° the bridegroom when the priest attends
To speak the ceremonial rites of marriage!   6
What says Lucentio to this shame of ours?

    KATH. No shame but mine. I must, forsooth, be
forced
To give my hand, opposed against my heart,

---

22. **the whiles:** meantime.   28–29. **Hic . . . senis:** Here ran the
River Simois; here is the land of Sigeia; here stood the high palace
of old Priam. The couplet is from Ovid's *Epistolae* i.33–34.
30. **Construe:** translate.   36. **bearing my port:** carrying himself
as if he were me.   37. **pantaloon:** silly old man, one of the stock
characters in the Italian comedy. See *AYLI*, II.vii.157–63.
40. **Spit . . . hole:** an insulting remark implying that Hortensio
is playing a mere pipe and not the more genteel lute.   50. **Pedascule:** pedant.   52–53. **Aeacides . . . grandfather:** This remark
is said aloud to deceive Hortensio into believing that the
Latin lesson is still in progress. Several of the Greek heroes were
descended from Aeacus.   60. **lessons:** music for practice. **make:**
is intended for. **three parts:** music for three different kinds of
voice. See *W Tale*, IV.iv.298–99.   62. **but:** unless.

67. **gamut:** the musical scale.   73. **ground:** lowest note. **accord:**
harmony.   80. **nice:** dainty.   81. **old:** "any old," strange.
89. **humble:** despicable.   90. **stale:** bait, decoy.   91. **Seize . . .
list:** let anyone who cares take you. **ranging:** straying.
    Sc. ii: 5. **want:** be without.

Unto a mad-brain rudesby,° full of spleen,° 10
Who wooed in haste and means to wed at leisure.
I told you, I, he was a frantic° fool,
Hiding his bitter jests in blunt behavior;
And to be noted for a merry man,
He'll woo a thousand, 'point the day of marriage,
Make friends, invite, and proclaim the banns,° 16
Yet never means to wed where he hath wooed.
Now must the world point at poor Katharine,
And say, " Lo, there is mad Petruchio's wife,
If it would please him come and marry her!" 20
    TRA. Patience, good Katharine, and Baptista too.
Upon my life, Petruchio means but well,
Whatever fortune stays him from his word.
Though he be blunt, I know him passing° wise.
Though he be merry, yet withal he's honest. 25
    KATH. Would Katharine had never seen him
      though!

        [*Exit weeping, followed by*
        BIANCA *and others.*]

    BAP. Go, girl. I cannot blame thee now to weep,
For such an injury would vex a very saint,
Much more a shrew of thy impatient humor.°

      [*Enter* BIONDELLO.]

    BION. Master, master! News, old° news, and such
news as you never heard of! 31
    BAP. Is it new and old too? How may that be?
    BION. Why, is it not news to hear of Petruchio's
coming?
    BAP. Is he come? 35
    BION. Why, no, sir.
    BAP. What then?
    BION. He is coming.
    BAP. When will he be here?
    BION. When he stands where I am and sees you
there. 41
    TRA. But say, what to thine old news?
    BION. Why, Petruchio is coming in a new hat and
an old jerkin;° a pair of old breeches thrice turned;°
a pair of boots that have been candle cases,° 45
one buckled, another laced; an old rusty sword ta'en
out of the town armory,° with a broken hilt, and
chapeless;° with two broken points;° his horse
hipped° with an old mothy saddle and stirrups 50

of no kindred, besides, possessed with the glanders
and like to mose in the chine, troubled with the
lampass, infected with the fashions, full of windgalls, sped with spavins, rayed with the yellows,
past cure of the fives, stark spoiled with the 55
staggers, begnawn with the bots, swayed in the
back and shoulder-shotten, near-legged before and
with a half-cheeked bit and a headstall of sheep's
leather which, being restrained to keep him from
stumbling, hath been often burst and now 60
repaired with knots, one girth six times pieced,°
and a woman's crupper of velure° which hath two
letters for her name fairly set down in studs and
here and there pieced° with pack-thread. 65
    BAP. Who comes with him?
    BION. Oh, sir, his lackey, for all the world ca-
parisoned like the horse, with a linen stock° on one
leg, and a kersey boothose° on the other, gartered
with a red and blue list,° an old hat, and " the 70
humor of forty fancies "° pricked° in't for a feather
—a monster, a very monster in apparel, and not
like a Christian footboy or a gentleman's lackey.
    TRA. 'Tis some odd humor° pricks° him to this
      fashion.
Yet oftentimes he goes but mean-appareled.
    BAP. I am glad he's come, howsoe'er he comes. 76
    BION. Why, sir, he comes not.
    BAP. Didst thou not say he comes?
    BION. Who? That Petruchio came?
    BAP. Aye, that Petruchio came. 80
    BION. No, sir. I say his horse comes, with him on
his back.
    BAP. Why, that's all one.
    BION. Nay,° by Saint Jamy,
I hold° you a penny, 85
A horse and a man
Is more than one,
And yet not many.

      [*Enter* PETRUCHIO *and* GRUMIO.]

    PET. Come, where be these gallants? Who's at
      home?

10. rudesby: ruffian. spleen: temper. 12. frantic: mad.
16. proclaim . . . banns: See App. 15. 24. passing: exceedingly.
29. humor: temper. 30. old: The word was first inserted by
Rowe in 1709 as required by the next speech. 44. jerkin: See
p. 93a. thrice turned: so old that they have been turned inside
out three times. 45. boots . . . cases: When the great thigh
boot (See Pl. 12c) worn by horsemen grew old and too stiff for
further use, a hole was cut in the side; it was then hung up as a
useful receptacle for candle ends and other oddments. 47. town
armory: Arms for emergencies were stored in each town, but they
were usually neglected and allowed to grow rusty. 48. chapeless:
The chape is the metal end at the bottom of a leather or velvet
scabbard. points: See p. 94a-b. 50–57. hipped . . . near-
legged: The many ailments of Petruchio's nag are: hipped, with
a strained hip; glanders, swelling under the neck; mose . . . chine,

discharge from the nostrils; lampass, swellings in the roof of the
mouth; fashions, small swellings in the body; windgalls, a disease
in the fetlocks; spavins, swelling on the joint of the hind leg;
rayed . . . yellows, afflicted with jaundice; fives, swellings behind
the ears; staggers, dizziness; bots, worms in the stomach; swayed
. . . back, sunk in the back; shoulder-shotten, dislocated in the
shoulders; near-legged, knock-kneed. 61. six . . . pieced: made
up of six pieces. 62. crupper of velure: The crupper is the
leather strap which passes under the tail to keep the saddle from
slipping forward. In a lady's saddle it was covered with velvet
(velure) with her initials inserted with metal studs. See Pl. 12c.
65. pieced: tied together. 68. stock: stocking. 69. kersey
boothose: overstockings made of coarse cloth. 70. list: the
strip of waste material at the end of a piece of weaving. 71. humor . . . fancies: i.e., a fantastic bundle of oddments. pricked:
pinned. 74. humor: whim. pricks: spurs, makes him choose.
84–88. Nay . . . many: The source of this little ditty written in
the style of Skelton is not known. 85. hold: bet.

BAP. You are welcome, sir.

PET.   And yet I come not well.   90

BAP. And yet you halt° not.

TRA.   Not so well appareled
As I wish you were.

PET. Were it better, I should rush in thus.°
But where is Kate? Where is my lovely bride?
How does my father? Gentles,° methinks you
    frown;   95
And wherefore gaze this goodly company
As if they saw some wondrous monument,
Some comet or unusual prodigy?°

BAP. Why, sir, you know this is your wedding
    day.
First were we sad, fearing you would not come;
Now sadder, that you come so unprovided.°   101
Fie, doff this habit, shame to your estate,°
An eyesore to our solemn festival!

TRA. And tell us what occasion of import°
Hath all so long detained you from your wife   105
And sent you hither to unlike yourself?

PET. Tedious it were to tell, and harsh to hear.
Sufficeth, I am come to keep my word,
Though in some part enforcèd to digress;
Which, at more leisure, I will so excuse   110
As you shall well be satisfied withal.
But where is Kate? I stay too long from her.
The morning wears, 'tis time we were at church.

TRA. See not your bride in these unreverent robes.
Go to my chamber. Put on clothes of mine.   115

PET. Not I, believe me. Thus I'll visit her.

BAP. But thus, I trust, you will not marry her.

PET. Good sooth, even thus; therefore ha' done
    with words.
To me she's married, not unto my clothes.
Could I repair what she will wear in me   120
As I can change these poor accouterments,
'Twere well for Kate and better for myself.
But what a fool am I to chat with you
When I should bid good morrow to my bride°
And seal the title with a lovely kiss!   125

            [Exeunt PETRUCHIO and GRUMIO.]

TRA. He hath some meaning in his mad attire.
We will persuade him, be it possible,
To put on better ere he go to church.

BAP. I'll after him, and see the event° of this.

            [Exeunt all but TRANIO and LUCENTIO.]

TRA. But to her love concerneth us to add   130

Her father's liking; which to bring to pass,
As I before imparted to your Worship,
I am to get a man — whate'er he be,
It skills° not much, we'll fit him to our turn —
And he shall be Vincentio of Pisa,   135
And make assurance here in Padua
Of greater sums than I have promisèd.
So shall you quietly enjoy your hope
And marry sweet Bianca with consent.

LUC. Were it not that my fellow schoolmaster
Doth watch Bianca's steps so narrowly,   141
'Twere good, methinks, to steal our marriage;°
Which once performed, let all the world say no,
I'll keep mine own, despite of all the world.

TRA. That by degrees we mean to look into,   145
And watch our vantage° in this business.
We'll overreach the greybeard, Gremio,
The narrow-prying father, Minola,
The quaint° musician, amorous Licio,
All for my master's sake, Lucentio.   150

            [Re-enter GREMIO.]

Signior Gremio, came you from the church?

GRE. As willingly as e'er I came from school.

TRA. And is the bride and bridegroom coming
    home?

GRE. A bridegroom say you? 'Tis a groom indeed,
A grumbling groom, and that the girl shall find.

TRA. Curster than she? Why, 'tis impossible.   156

GRE. Why, he's a devil, a devil, a very fiend.

TRA. Why, she's a devil, a devil, the Devil's dam.°

GRE. Tut, she's a lamb, a dove, a fool to° him!
I'll tell you, Sir Lucentio. When the priest   160
Should ask if Katharine should be his wife,
"Aye, by gogs-wouns,"° quoth he, and swore so
    loud
That, all amazed, the priest let fall the book,
And as he stooped again to take it up,   164
This mad-brained bridegroom took him such a cuff
That down fell priest and book, and book and
    priest.
"Now take them up," quoth he, "if any list."°

TRA. What said the wench when he rose again?

GRE. Trembled and shook; for-why he stamped
    and swore
As if the vicar meant to cozen° him.   170
But after many ceremonies done,
He calls for wine. "A health!" quoth he, as if
He had been aboard, carousing to his mates
After a storm, quaffed off the muscadel°
And threw the sops° all in the sexton's face,   175
Having no other reason

90–91. welcome . . . halt: a triple pun. To Baptista's cold wel-come Petruchio replies that he is clearly not well-come, which also means "does not walk well." Baptista caps this with halt not, i.e., do not limp.   93. Were . . . thus: even if it were better I should still be eager to greet my bride. See App. 15.   95. Gentles: gentlemen.   98. prodigy: terrifying and unnatural event. 101. unprovided: improperly prepared.   102. shame . . . estate: disgraceful to a man of your wealth.   104. import: importance. 124. morrow . . . bride: wake my bride — the first of the cere-monies in a wedding. See App. 15.   129. event: sequel, what happens next.

134. skills: matters.   142. steal . . . marriage: make a secret marriage.   146. vantage: advantage.   149. quaint: clever. 158. Devil's dam: See I.i.106,n.   159. to: compared with. 162. gogs-wouns: by God's (Christ's) wounds.   167. list: care. 170. cozen: cheat.   174. muscadel: a sweet wine, commonly used at weddings, with which groom and bride pledged each other It was customary to float sops of cake in the cup.

But that his beard grew thin and hungerly
And seemed to ask him° sops as he was drinking.
This done, he took the bride about the neck
And kissed her lips with such a clamorous smack
That at the parting all the church did echo.   181
And I, seeing this, came thence for very shame;
And after me, I know, the rout° is coming.
Such a mad marriage never was before.
Hark, hark! I hear the minstrels play. [*Music*]   185
[*Re-enter* PETRUCHIO, KATHARINA, BIANCA, BAPTISTA,
     HORTENSIO, GRUMIO, *and train.*]
     PET. Gentlemen and friends, I thank you for your
     pains.
I know you think to dine with me today
And have prepared great store of wedding cheer;
But so it is, my haste doth call me hence,
And therefore here I mean to take my leave.   190
     BAP. Is 't possible you will away tonight?
     PET. I must away today, before night come.
Make it no wonder. If you knew my business,
You would entreat me rather go than stay.
And, honest company, I thank you all,   195
That have beheld me give away myself
To this most patient, sweet, and virtuous wife.
Dine with my father,° drink a health to me,
For I must hence; and farewell to you all.
     TRA. Let us entreat you stay till after dinner.   200
     PET. It may not be.
     GRE.   Let me entreat you.
     PET. It cannot be.
     KATH.   Let me entreat you.
     PET. I am content.
     KATH.   Are you content to stay?
     PET. I am content you shall entreat me stay;
But yet not stay, entreat me how you can.   205
     KATH. Now, if you love me, stay.
     PET.   Grumio, my horse.
     GRU. Aye, sir, they be ready. The oats have eaten
the horses.°
     KATH. Nay, then,
Do what thou canst, I will not go today,   210
No, nor tomorrow, not till I please myself.
The door is open, sir. There lies your way.
You may be jogging whiles your boots are green.°
For me, I'll not be gone till I please myself.
'Tis like you'll prove a jolly° surly groom   215
That take it on you at the first so roundly.°
     PET. O Kate, content thee. Prithee be not angry.
     KATH. I will be angry. — What hast thou to do?°
Father, be quiet. He shall stay my leisure.
     GRE. Aye, marry, sir, now it begins to work.   220

     KATH. Gentlemen, forward to the bridal dinner.
I see a woman may be made a fool
If she had not a spirit to resist.
     PET. They shall go forward, Kate, at thy com-
     mand.
Obey the bride, you that attend on her.   225
Go to the feast, revel and domineer,°
Carouse full measure to her maidenhead,
Be mad and merry, or go hang yourselves.
But for my bonny Kate, she must with me.
Nay, look not big,° nor stamp, nor stare, nor fret.
I will be master of what is mine own.   231
She is my goods, my chattels;° she is my house,
My household stuff, my field, my barn,
My horse, my ox, my ass, my anything;
And here she stands, touch her whoever dare.   235
I'll bring mine action on the proudest he
That stops my way in Padua. Grumio,
Draw forth thy weapon, we are beset with thieves.
Rescue thy mistress if thou be a man.
Fear not, sweet wench, they shall not touch thee,
     Kate.   240
I'll buckler° thee against a million.
         [*Exeunt* PETRUCHIO, KATHARINA, *and* GRUMIO.]
     BAP. Nay, let them go, a couple of quiet ones.
     GRE. Went they not quickly, I should die with
     laughing.
     TRA. Of all mad matches never was the like.
     LUC. Mistress, what's your opinion of your sister?
     BIAN. That, being mad herself, she's madly
     mated.   246
     GRE. I warrant him, Petruchio is Kated.
     BAP. Neighbors and friends, though bride and
     bridegroom wants°
For to supply the places at the table,
You know there wants no junkets° at the feast.   250
Lucentio, you shall supply the bridegroom's place,
And let Bianca take her sister's room.
     TRA. Shall sweet Bianca practice how to bride it?
     BAP. She shall, Lucentio. Come, gentlemen, let's
go.   [*Exeunt.*]

Act IV

SCENE I. PETRUCHIO'S *country house.*

[*Enter* GRUMIO.]

     GRU. Fie, fie on all tired jades, on all mad mas-
ters, and all foul ways!° Was ever man so beaten?
Was ever man so rayed?° Was ever man so weary?
I am sent before to make a fire, and they are coming after to warm them. Now, were not I a   5

---

178. ask him: ask him for.   183. rout: crowd.   198. father:
i.e., my new father-in-law.   207–08. oats . . . horses: the horses
are already overfed.   213. whiles . . . green: a proverb meaning
"You may get going as soon as you like."   215. jolly: insolent.
216. That . . . roundly: since you presume at the beginning to
act so outrageously.   218. What . . . do: what business is it of
yours? — spoken to Baptista.

226. domineer: "have a good time."   230. big: threatening.
232. She . . . chattels: See Gen. Intro. pp. 19b–20a.   241. buckler: shield.   248. wants: are missing.   250. junkets: dainties.
     Act IV, Sc. i: 2. ways: roads.   3. rayed: dirtied.

little pot and soon not,° my very lips might freeze to my teeth, my tongue to the roof of my mouth, my heart in my belly, ere I should come by a fire to thaw me. But I, with blowing the fire, shall 10 warm myself, for, considering the weather, a taller man than I will take cold. Holloa, ho! Curtis!

[*Enter* CURTIS.]

CURT. Who is that calls so coldly?

GRU. A piece of ice. If thou doubt it, thou mayst slide from my shoulder to my heel with no 15 greater a run but my head and my neck. A fire, good Curtis.

CURT. Is my master and his wife coming, Grumio?

GRU. Oh, aye, Curtis, aye. And therefore fire, fire; cast on no water.° 21

CURT. Is she so hot a shrew as she's reported?

GRU. She was, good Curtis, before this frost. But thou knowest winter tames man, woman, and beast; for it hath tamed my old master, and my new mistress, and myself, fellow Curtis. 26

CURT. Away, you three-inch fool! I am no beast.

GRU. Am I but three inches? Why, thy horn is a foot, and so long am I at the least. But wilt 30 thou make a fire, or shall I complain on thee to our mistress, whose hand, she being now at hand, thou shalt soon feel, to thy cold comfort, for being slow in thy hot office?

CURT. I prithee, good Grumio, tell me how goes the world? 36

GRU. A cold world, Curtis, in every office but thine, and therefore fire. Do thy duty, and have thy duty,° for my master and mistress are almost frozen to death. 40

CURT. There's fire ready, and therefore, good Grumio, the news.

GRU. Why, "Jack, boy! Ho! Boy!"° and as much news as thou wilt.

CURT. Come, you are so full of cony-catching!°

GRU. Why, therefore fire, for I have caught 46 extreme cold. Where's° the cook? Is supper ready, the house trimmed, rushes strewed,° cobwebs swept; the servingmen in their new fustian,° their white stockings, and every officer his wedding garment on? Be the jacks° fair within, the jills° fair 51 without, the carpets laid,° and everything in order?

CURT. All ready, and therefore, I pray thee, news.

GRU. First, know my horse is tired, my master and mistress fallen out. 56

CURT. How?

GRU. Out of their saddles into the dirt, and thereby hangs a tale. 60

CURT. Let's ha't, good Grumio.

GRU. Lend thine ear.

CURT. Here.

GRU. There. [*Strikes him.*]

CURT. This is to feel a tale, not to hear a tale. 66

GRU. And therefore 'tis called a sensible° tale; and this cuff was but to knock at your ear and beseech listening. Now I begin: *Imprimis,*° we came down a foul hill, my master riding behind my mistress —— 70

CURT. Both of one horse?

GRU. What's that to thee?

CURT. Why, a horse.

GRU. Tell thou the tale. But hadst thou not crossed° me, thou shouldst have heard how her 75 horse fell and she under her horse. Thou shouldst have heard in how miry a place, how she was bemoiled,° how he left her with the horse upon her, how he beat me because her horse stumbled, how she waded through the dirt to pluck him off 80 me, how he swore, how she prayed, that never prayed before, how I cried, how the horses ran away, how her bridle was burst, how I lost my crupper, with many things of worthy memory which now shall die in oblivion and thou return unexperienced° to thy grave. 86

CURT. By this reckoning he is more shrew than she.

GRU. Aye, and that thou and the proudest of you all shall find when he comes home. But what 90 talk I of this? Call forth Nathaniel, Joseph, Nicholas, Philip, Walter, Sugarsop, and the rest. Let their heads be sleekly combed, their blue coats° brushed, and their garters of an indifferent knit.° Let 95 them curtsy with their left legs,° and not presume to touch a hair of my master's horse tail till they kiss their hands.° Are they all ready?

CURT. They are.

GRU. Call them forth.

CURT. Do you hear, ho? You must meet my master to countenance° my mistress! 101

GRU. Why, she hath a face of her own.

CURT. Who knows not that?

GRU. Thou, it seems, that calls for company to countenance her. 106

---

6. **little . . . hot:** a proverb — "a little pot soon boils"; i.e. small men are often hot tempered. Grumio is small. **20–21. fire . . . water:** another proverb. **39. duty:** due. **43. Jack . . . Boy:** a "catch" beginning "Jack boy, ho boy, news." See *T Night,* II.iii.18,n and 60,n. **45. cony-catching:** roguery. Technically cony-catching is cardsharping, but the word was applied to any form of cheating. See Gen. Intro. p. 28a. **47–52. Where's . . . order:** These were the normal preparations made when distinguished company was expected. **48. rushes strewed:** the floors covered with new rushes. **49. fustian:** coarse material from which liveries were made. **51. jack:** leather jug. **jill:** a measure for drink, half a pint — with a pun on Jacks and Jills (boys and girls). **52. carpets laid:** i.e., on the tables. Oriental carpets were used as tablecloths, not as floor coverings.

67. **sensible:** feeling. **69. *Imprimis:*** in the first place — the normal beginning of an inventory. **75. crossed:** interrupted. **78. bemoiled:** muddied. **86. unexperienced:** ignorant. **94. blue coats:** liveries. **95. indifferent knit:** reasonably well tied. **96. curtsy . . . legs:** See App. 7. **97. kiss . . . hands:** kiss the hands of master and mistress as a sign of respectful welcome. **101. countenance:** honor.

CURT. I call them forth to credit her.

GRU. Why, she comes to borrow nothing of them.

    [Enter four or five SERVINGMEN.*]*

NATH. Welcome home, Grumio!

PHIL. How now, Grumio! 110

JOS. What, Grumio!

NICH. Fellow Grumio!

NATH. How now, old lad?

GRU. Welcome, you; how now, you; what, you; fellow, you — and thus much for greeting. 115 Now, my spruce companions, is all ready, and all things neat?

NATH. All things is ready. How near is our master? 119

GRU. E'en at hand, alighted by this, and therefore be not — Cock's° passion, silence! I hear my master.

    [Enter PETRUCHIO *and* KATHARINA.*]*

PET. Where be these knaves? What, no man at door
To hold my stirrup nor to take my horse!
Where is Nathaniel, Gregory, Philip? 125

ALL SERV. Here, here, sir! Here, sir.

PET. Here, sir! Here, sir! Here, sir! Here, sir!
You logger-headed° and unpolished grooms!
What, no attendance? No regard?° No duty?
Where is the foolish knave I sent before? 130

GRU. Here, sir, as foolish as I was before.

PET. You peasant swain! You whoreson malt-horse drudge!°
Did I not bid thee meet me in the park
And bring along these rascal knaves with thee?

GRU. Nathaniel's coat, sir, was not fully made.
And Gabriel's pumps were all unpinked° i' the heel. 136
There was no link° to color Peter's hat,
And Walter's dagger was not come from sheathing.
There were none fine but Adam, Ralph, and Gregory.
The rest were ragged, old, and beggarly. 140
Yet, as they are, here are they come to meet you.

PET. Go, rascals, go, and fetch my supper in.

    [Exeunt SERVANTS.*]*

[Singing.] "Where is the life that late I led"——
Where are those — Sit down, Kate, and welcome. —
Soud, soud, soud, soud!° 145

    [Re-enter SERVANTS *with supper.]*

Why, when, I say? Nay, good sweet Kate, be merry.
Off with my boots, you rogues! You villains, when?
[Sings.] "It was the friar of orders gray,
    As he forth walkèd on his way"——
Out, you rogue! You pluck my foot awry. 150

Take that, and mend the plucking off the other.

    [Strikes him.]

Be merry, Kate. Some water, here. What ho!
Where's my spaniel Troilus? Sirrah, get you hence,
And bid my cousin Ferdinand come hither: —
One, Kate, that you must kiss and be acquainted with. 155
Where are my slippers? Shall I have some water?

    [Enter one with water.]

Come, Kate, and wash, and welcome heartily.
You whoreson villain! Will you let it fall?

    [Strikes him.]

KATH. Patience, I pray you. 'Twas a fault unwilling.

PET. A whoreson beetle-headed,° flap-eared knave! 160
Come, Kate, sit down. I know you have a stomach.
Will you give thanks, sweet Kate, or else shall I?
What's this? Mutton?

1. SERV.   Aye.

PET.   Who brought it?

PETER.   I.

PET. 'Tis burnt, and so is all the meat. 164
What dogs are these! Where is the rascal cook?
How durst you, villains, bring it from the dresser°
And serve it thus to me that love it not?
There, take it to you, trenchers,° cups, and all.

    [Throws the meat, &c. about the stage.]

You heedless joltheads° and unmannered slaves!
What, do you grumble? I'll be with you straight.

KATH. I pray you, Husband, be not so disquiet.
The meat was well if you were so contented.° 172

PET. I tell thee, Kate, 'twas burnt° and dried away,
And I expressly am forbid to touch it,
For it engenders choler, planteth anger, 175
And better 'twere that both of us did fast,
Since, of ourselves, ourselves are choleric,
Than feed it with such overroasted flesh.
Be patient. Tomorrow't shall be mended,
And, for this night, we'll fast for company. 180
Come, I will bring thee to thy bridal chamber.

    [Exeunt.]

    [Re-enter SERVANTS *severally.]*

NATH. Peter, didst ever see the like?

PETER. He kills her in her own humor.°

    [Re-enter CURTIS.*]*

GRU. Where is he?

CURT. In her chamber, making a sermon of continency to her; 186

---

121. **Cock's:** God's. 128. **logger-headed:** blockheaded. 129. **regard:** respect. 132. **malt-horse drudge:** horse which trudges round and round turning a grain mill. 136. **unpinked:** unready. Pinking is to make a pattern by pricking holes. 137. **link:** torch — the smoke from which was used to touch up a faded black hat. 145. **Soud . . . soud:** an ill-bred noise as he sinks into his chair.

160. **beetle-headed:** with a head like a wooden pile-driving hammer. 166. **dresser:** buffet. 168. **trenchers:** wooden plates. 169. **jolthead:** blockhead. 172. **if . . . contented:** if only you would be pleased to accept it. 173–78. **burnt . . . flesh:** See App. 3. Petruchio pretends that they are both suffering from an excess of the choleric humor. Diet was carefully considered in the treatment of all complaints caused by the humors. See *Errors*, II.ii.60–64. 183. **kills . . . humor:** i.e., he treats her as she has treated others, gives her tit for tat.

And rails, and swears, and rates, that she, poor soul,
Knows not which way to stand, to look, to speak,
And sits as one new-risen from a dream.
Away, away! For he is coming hither. [*Exeunt.*]
[*Re-enter* PETRUCHIO.]

PET. Thus have I politicly° begun my reign, 191
And 'tis my hope to end successfully.
My falcon° now is sharp and passing empty,
And till she stoop, she must not be full-gorged,
For then she never looks upon her lure. 195
Another way I have to man my haggard,
To make her come and know her keeper's call,
That is, to watch her, as we watch these kites
That bate, and beat, and will not be obedient.
She eat no meat today, nor none shall eat. 200
Last night she slept not, nor tonight she shall not.
As with the meat, some undeservèd fault
I'll find about the making of the bed,
And here I'll fling the pillow, there the bolster,
This way the coverlet, another way the sheets. 205
Aye, and amid this hurly° I intend°
That all is done in reverend care of her;
And in conclusion she shall watch all night.
And if she chance to nod, I'll rail and brawl,
And with the clamor keep her still° awake. 210
This is a way to kill a wife with kindness,°
And thus I'll curb her mad and headstrong humor.
He that knows better how to tame a shrew,
Now let him speak. 'Tis charity to show. [*Exit.*]

SCENE II. *Padua. Before* BAPTISTA'S *house.*

[*Enter* TRANIO *and* HORTENSIO.]

TRA. Is 't possible, friend Licio, that Mistress
Bianca
Doth fancy any other but Lucentio?°
I tell you, sir, she bears me fair in hand.°
HOR. Sir, to satisfy you in what I have said,
Stand by, and mark the manner of his teaching. 5
[*Enter* BIANCA *and* LUCENTIO.]
LUC. Now, mistress, profit you in what you
read?°
BIAN. What, master, read you? First resolve me
that.
LUC. I read that° I profess, the *Art to Love.*°
BIAN. And may you prove, sir, master of your art!
LUC. While you, sweet dear, prove mistress of my
heart! 10

HOR. Quick proceeders,° marry! Now, tell me, I
pray,
You that durst swear that your mistress Bianca
Loved none in the world so well as Lucentio.
TRA. Oh, despiteful° love! Unconstant woman-
kind!
I tell thee, Licio, this is wonderful. 15
HOR. Mistake no more. I am not Licio,
Nor a musician, as I seem to be,
But one that scorn° to live in this disguise
For such a one as leaves a gentleman
And makes a god of such a cullion.° 20
Know, sir, that I am called Hortensio.
TRA. Signior Hortensio, I have often heard
Of your entire affection to Bianca,
And since mine eyes are witness of her lightness,
I will with you, if you be so contented, 25
Forswear° Bianca and her love for ever.
HOR. See, how they kiss and court! Signior Lu-
centio,
Here is my hand, and here I firmly vow
Never to woo her more, but do forswear her
As one unworthy all the former favors 30
That I have fondly° flattered her withal.
TRA. And here I take the like unfeignèd oath,
Never to marry with her though she would entreat.
Fie on her! See how beastly° she doth court him!
HOR. Would all the world but he had quite for-
sworn! 35
For me, that I may surely keep mine oath,
I will be married to a wealthy widow,
Ere three days pass, which hath as long loved me
As I have loved this proud disdainful haggard.
And so farewell, Signior Lucentio. 40
Kindness in women, not their beauteous looks,
Shall win my love; and so I take my leave,
In resolution as I swore before. [*Exit.*]
TRA. Mistress Bianca, bless° you with such grace
As 'longeth to a lover's blessed case! 45
Nay, I have ta'en you napping, gentle love,
And have forsworn you with Hortensio.
BIAN. Tranio, you jest. But have you both for-
sworn me?
TRA. Mistress, we have.
LUC.   Then we are rid of Licio.
TRA. I' faith, he'll have a lusty widow now, 50
That shall be wooed and wedded in a day.
BIAN. God give him joy!
TRA. Aye, and he'll tame her.
BIAN.   He says so, Tranio.
TRA. Faith, he is gone unto the taming school.
BIAN. The taming school! What, is there such a
place? 55

191. **politicly:** cunningly, shrewdly. **193–99. falcon . . . obedient:** Petruchio thus tries to train Katharine as if she were a wild
hawk: *sharp*, keen with hunger; *watch*, keep awake; *kite*, inferior
hawk. For *stoop, lure, haggard, bate, beat*, and the method of
training, see App. 26. **206. hurly:** confusion. **intend:** pretend.
210. still: continuously. **211. kill . . . kindness:** a proverb
meaning to spoil with overindulgence.
Sc. ii: 2. Lucentio: Hortensio, of course, still takes the disguised Tranio for the real "Lucentio." **3. bears . . . hand:**
deceives with false hopes. **6. read:** study. **8. that:** that which.
Art to Love: a notorious book by Ovid.

11. **proceeders:** students, who in English academic language are
said to "proceed" to a degree. **14. despiteful:** spiteful. **18. scorn:**
scorns. **20. cullion:** low rogue. **26. Forswear:** swear to give
up. **31. fondly:** foolishly. **34. beastly:** in how beastly a way
44. bless: God bless.

TRA. Aye, mistress, and Petruchio is the master,
That teacheth tricks eleven and twenty long°
To tame a shrew and charm her chattering tongue.
                [*Enter* BIONDELLO.]
BION. Oh, master, master, I have watched so long
That I am dog-weary! But at last I spied   60
An ancient angel° coming down the hill
Will serve the turn.
TRA.   What is he, Biondello?
BION. Master, a mercatante,° or a pedant,
I know not what; but formal in apparel,
In gait and countenance surely like a father.   65
LUC. And what of him, Tranio?
TRA. If he be credulous and trust my tale,
I'll make him glad to seem Vincentio
And give assurance to Baptista Minola
As if he were the right° Vincentio.   70
Take in your love, and then let me alone.
         [*Exeunt* LUCENTIO *and* BIANCA.]
           [*Enter a* PEDANT.]
PED. God save you, sir!
TRA.   And you, sir! You are welcome.
Travel you far on, or are you at the farthest?°
PED. Sir, at the farthest for a week or two.
But then up farther, and as far as Rome,   75
And so to Tripoli, if God lend me life.
TRA. What countryman, I pray?
PED.   Of Mantua.
TRA. Of Mantua, sir? Marry, God forbid!
And come to Padua, careless of your life?
PED. My life, sir! How, I pray? For that goes
   hard.   80
TRA. 'Tis death for anyone in Mantua.
To come to Padua. Know you not the cause?
Your ships are stayed° at Venice, and the Duke,
For private quarrel 'twixt your Duke and him,
Hath published and proclaimed it openly.   85
'Tis marvel, but that you are but newly come,
You might have heard it else proclaimed about.
PED. Alas, sir, it is worse for me than so!
For I have bills for money by exchange°
From Florence, and must here deliver them.   90
TRA. Well, sir, to do you courtesy,
This will I do, and this I will advise you.
First, tell me, have you ever been at Pisa?
PED. Aye, sir, in Pisa have I often been,
Pisa renownèd for grave citizens.   95
TRA. Among them know you one Vincentio?
PED. I know him not, but I have heard of him;
A merchant of incomparable wealth.
TRA. He is my father, sir, and, sooth to say,
In countenance somewhat doth resemble you.   100

BION. [*Aside*] As much as an apple doth an oyster, and all one.
TRA. To save your life in this extremity,
This favor will I do you for his sake,
And think it not the worst of all your fortunes
That you are like to Sir Vincentio.   105
His name and credit shall you undertake,
And in my house you shall be friendly lodged.
Look that you take upon you° as you should.
You understand me, sir. So shall you stay
Till you have done your business in the city.   110
If this be courtesy, sir, accept of it.
PED. O sir, I do, and will repute you ever
The patron of my life and liberty.
TRA. Then go with me to make the matter good.
This, by the way, I let you understand.   115
My father is here looked for every day
To pass assurance of° a dower in marriage
'Twixt me and one Baptista's daughter here.
In all these circumstances I'll instruct you.
Go with me to clothe you as becomes you.   120
                    [*Exeunt.*]

SCENE III. *A room in* PETRUCHIO's *house.*

       [*Enter* KATHARINA *and* GRUMIO.]
GRU. No, no, forsooth. I dare not for my life.
KATH. The more my wrong, the more his spite
   appears.
What, did he marry me to famish me?
Beggars that come unto my father's door
Upon entreaty have a present° alms.   5
If not, elsewhere they meet with charity.
But I, who never knew how to entreat,
Nor never needed that I should entreat,
Am starved for meat, giddy for lack of sleep,
With oaths kept waking, and with brawling fed.   10
And that which spites me more than all these wants,
He does it under name of perfect love;
As who should say, if I should sleep or eat,
'Twere deadly sickness or else present death.
I prithee go and get me some repast.   15
I care not what, so it be wholesome food.
GRU. What say you to a neat's° foot?
KATH. 'Tis passing good. I prithee let me have it.
GRU. I fear it is too choleric° a meat.
How say you to a fat tripe finely broiled?   20
KATH. I like it well. Good Grumio, fetch it me.
GRU. I cannot tell. I fear 'tis choleric.
What say you to a piece of beef and mustard?
KATH. A dish that I do love to feed upon.
GRU. Aye, but the mustard is too hot a little.   25

KATH. Why then, the beef, and let the mustard
rest.°
GRU. Nay then, I will not. You shall have the
mustard,
Or else you get no beef of Grumio.
KATH. Then both, or one, or anything thou wilt.
GRU. Why then, the mustard without the beef.
KATH. Go, get thee gone, thou false deluding
slave,   [Beats him] 31
That feed'st me with the very name° of meat.
Sorrow on thee and all the pack of you
That triumph thus upon my misery!
Go, get thee gone, I say.   35
[Enter PETRUCHIO and HORTENSIO with meat.]
PET. How fares my Kate? What, sweeting,° all
amort?°
HOR. Mistress, what cheer?
KATH.   Faith, as cold as can be.
PET. Pluck up thy spirits. Look cheerfully upon
me.
Here, love, thou see'st how diligent I am
To dress° thy meat myself and bring it thee.   40
I am sure, sweet Kate, this kindness merits thanks.
What, not a word? Nay, then thou lovest it not,
And all my pains is sorted to no proof.°
Here, take away this dish.
KATH.   I pray you let it stand.
PET. The poorest service is repaid with thanks,
And so shall mine, before you touch the meat. 46
KATH. I thank you, sir.
HOR. Signior Petruchio, fie! You are to blame.
Come, Mistress Kate, I'll bear you company.
PET. [Aside] Eat it up all, Hortensio, if thou lov-
est me. —   50
Much good do it unto thy gentle heart!
Kate, eat apace;° and now, my honey love,
Will we return unto thy father's house
And revel it as bravely as the best,
With silken coats and caps and golden rings,   55
With ruffs and cuffs and fardingales° and things;
With scarfs and fans and double change of brav-
ery,°
With amber bracelets, beads and all this knavery.
What, hast thou dined? The tailor stays thy leisure
To deck thy body with his ruffling° treasure.   60
[Enter TAILOR.]
Come, tailor, let us see these ornaments.
Lay forth the gown.
[Enter HABERDASHER.]
What news with you, sir?
HAB. Here is the cap your Worship did bespeak.
PET. Why, this was molded on a porringer,°

A velvet dish. Fie, fie! 'Tis lewd and filthy.   65
Why, 'tis a cockle° or a walnut shell,
A knack, a toy, a trick, a baby's cap.
Away with it! Come, let me have a bigger.
KATH. I'll have no bigger. This doth fit the
time,°
And gentlewomen wear such caps as these.   70
PET. When you are gentle, you shall have one
too,
And not till then.
HOR. [Aside] That will not be in haste.
KATH. Why, sir, I trust I may have leave to
speak,
And speak I will. I am no child, no babe.
Your betters have endured me say my mind,   75
And if you cannot, best you stop your ears.
My tongue will tell the anger of my heart,
Or else my heart concealing it will break;
And rather than it shall, I will be free
Even to the uttermost, as I please, in words.   80
PET. Why, thou say'st true. It is a paltry cap,
A custard coffin,° a bauble, a silken pie.
I love thee well in that thou likest it not.
KATH. Love me or love me not, I like the cap,
And it I will have, or I will have none.   85
[Exit HABERDASHER.]
PET. Thy gown? Why, aye. Come, tailor, let us
see 't.
Oh, mercy, God! What masquing stuff° is here?
What's this? A sleeve?° 'Tis like a demicannon.°
What, up and down, carved like an apple tart?
Here's snip and nip and cut and slish and slash, 90
Like to a censer° in a barber's shop.
Why, what, i' Devil's name, tailor, call'st thou this?
HOR. [Aside] I see she's like to have neither cap
nor gown.
TAI. You bid me make it orderly and well,
According to the fashion and the time.   95
PET. Marry, and did; but if you be remembered,
I did not bid you mar it to the time.
Go, hop me over every kennel° home,
For you shall hop without my custom, sir.
I'll none of it. Hence! Make your best of it.   100
KATH. I never saw a better-fashioned gown,
More quaint,° more pleasing, nor more commend-
able.
Belike you mean to make a puppet° of me.
PET. Why, true. He means to make a puppet of
thee.
TAI. She says your Worship means to make a pup-
pet of her.   106

26. rest: remain, be left out.   32. very name: i.e., you only talk
about food.   36. sweeting: sweetheart, lit., a sweet apple. all
amort: sick to death, melancholy.   40. dress: prepare.   43. is
. . . proof: have produced no result.   52. apace: quickly.
56. ruffs . . . fardingales: See pp. 94b–95a.   57. bravery: fine
clothes.   60. ruffling: gay.   64. porringer: basin.

66. cockle: cockle shell.   69. fit . . . time: is fashionable.
82. custard coffin: custard pie.   87. masquing stuff: fancy dress
costume.   88. sleeve: See p. 95a. demicannon: large cannon.
The great sleeves worn by ladies could — not overfancifully —
be compared to a great cannon.   91. censer: pot with a per-
forated lid for burning perfume.   98. kennel: gutter.   102. quaint:
clever, smart.   103. puppet: plaything, doll.

PET. Oh, monstrous arrogance! Thou liest, thou thread, thou thimble,
Thou yard, three-quarters, half-yard, quarter, nail!°
Thou flea, thou nit, thou winter cricket° thou!   110
Braved° in mine own house with a skein of thread?
Away, thou rag, thou quantity,° thou remnant,
Or I shall so bemete° thee with thy yard
As thou shalt think on prating whilst thou livest!
I tell thee, I, that thou hast marred her gown.   115
   TAI. Your Worship is deceived. The gown is
      made
Just as my master had direction.
Grumio gave order how it should be done.
   GRU. I gave him no order. I gave him the stuff.
   TAI. But how did you desire it should be made?
   GRU. Marry, sir, with needle and thread.   121
   TAI. But did you not request to have it cut?
   GRU. Thou hast faced° many things.
   TAI. I have.
   GRU. Face not me. Thou hast braved° many   125
men. Brave not me. I will neither be faced nor
braved. I say unto thee I bid thy master cut out the
gown, but I did not bid him cut it to pieces. Ergo,
thou liest.   129
   TAI. Why, here is the note of the fashion to tes-
tify.
   PET. Read it.
   GRU. The note lies in's throat° if he say I said so.
   TAI. [*Reads.*] "*Imprimis*, a loose-bodied gown."
   GRU. Master, if ever I said loose-bodied   135
gown, sew me in the skirts of it, and beat me to
death with a bottom° of brown thread. I said a
gown.
   PET. Proceed.
   TAI. [*Reads.*] "With a small compassed° cape."
   GRU. I confess the cape.   141
   TAI. [*Reads.*] "With a trunk sleeve."°
   GRU. I confess two sleeves.
   TAI. [*Reads.*] "The sleeves curiously° cut."
   PET. Aye, there's the villainy.   145
   GRU. Error i' the bill,° sir; error i' the bill. I com-
manded the sleeves should be cut out and sewed up
again; and that I'll prove upon° thee, though thy
little finger be armed in a thimble.
   TAI. This is true that I say. An I had thee in place
where, thou shouldst know it.   151
   GRU. I am for thee straight.° Take thou the bill,

give me thy meteyard,° and spare not me.
   HOR. God-a-mercy, Grumio! Then he shall have
no odds.   155
   PET. Well, sir, in brief, the gown is not for me.
   GRU. You are i' the right, sir. 'Tis for my mis-
tress.
   PET. Go, take it up unto thy master's use.°
   GRU. Villain, not for thy life. Take up° my mis-
tress' gown for thy master's use!   161
   PET. Why, sir, what's your conceit° in that?
   GRU. Oh, sir, the conceit is deeper than you
      think for.
Take up my mistress' gown to his master's use!
Oh, fie, fie, fie!   165
   PET. [*Aside*] Hortensio, say thou wilt see the
      tailor paid. —
Go take it hence. Be gone, and say no more.
   HOR. Tailor, I'll pay thee for thy gown tomor-
      row.
Take no unkindness of his hasty words.
Away, I say! Commend me to thy master.   170
                                 [*Exit* TAILOR.]
   PET. Well, come, my Kate. We will unto your fa-
      ther's
Even in these honest mean habiliments.°
Our purses shall be proud, our garments poor,
For 'tis the mind that makes the body rich,
And as the sun breaks through the darkest clouds,
So honor peereth in the meanest habit.°   176
What,° is the jay more precious than the lark
Because his feathers are more beautiful?
Or is the adder better than the eel
Because his painted skin contents the eye?   180
Oh, no, good Kate. Neither art thou the worse
For this poor furniture and mean array.
If thou account'st it shame, lay it on me.
And therefore frolic. We will hence forthwith
To feast and sport us at thy father's house.   185
Go, call my men, and let us straight to him;
And bring our horses unto Long Lane end.
There will we mount and thither walk on foot.
Let's see. I think 'tis now some seven o'clock,°
And well we may come there by dinnertime.°   190
   KATH. I dare assure you, sir, 'tis almost two,
And 'twill be suppertime ere you come there.
   PET. It shall be seven ere I go to horse.
Look, what I speak, or do, or think to do,
You are still crossing it. Sirs, let 't alone.   195
I will not go today; and ere I do,
It shall be what o'clock I say it is.
   HOR. Why, so this gallant will command the sun.
                                       [*Exeunt.*]

---

109. **nail:** creature as small and thin as a nail.   110. **winter cricket:** i.e., starved and shriveled.   111. **Braved:** insulted.   112. **quantity:** piece of material.   113. **bemete:** measure; i.e., beat you with your yardstick.   123. **faced:** with double mean- ing, "made many facings" (decorations sewn onto a garment), and "outfaced."   125. **braved:** made fine and handsome. 133. **lies ... throat:** is a complete lie.   137. **bottom:** ball. 140. **compassed:** semicircular, as in Pl. 8b.   142. **trunk sleeve:** large at the shoulder and narrow at the wrist.   144. **curiously:** elaborately.   146. **Error ... bill:** i.e., a false indictment. 148. **prove upon:** fight to maintain.   152. **I ... straight:** I'm willing to fight you here and now.

153. **meteyard:** tailor's measuring yard.   159. **take ... use:** let your master have it back and make what use of it he can. 160. **Take up:** lift up.   162. **conceit:** idea.   172. **habiliments:** garments.   176. **habit:** clothes.   177. **What:** in what respect. 189. **seven o'clock:** i.e., 7 A.M.   190. **dinnertime:** about 11 A.M.

SCENE IV. *Padua. Before* BAPTISTA's *house.*

[*Enter* TRANIO, *and the* PEDANT
dressed like VINCENTIO.]

TRA. Sir, this is the house. Please it you that I call?
PED. Aye, what else? And but I be deceived,
Signior Baptista may remember me,
Near twenty years ago, in Genoa,
Where we were lodgers at the Pegasus.°   5
TRA. 'Tis well; and hold your own, in any case,
With such austerity as 'longeth to a father.
PED. I warrant you.
[*Enter* BIONDELLO.]
But, sir, here comes your boy.
'Twere good he were schooled.
TRA. Fear you not him. Sirrah Biondello,   10
Now do your duty throughly, I advise you.
Imagine 'twere the right Vincentio.
BION. Tut, fear not me.
TRA. But hast thou done thy errand to Baptista?
BION. I told him that your father was at Venice,
And that you looked for him this day in Padua.   16
TRA. Thou 'rt a tall° fellow. Hold thee that to
drink.°
Here comes Baptista. Set your countenance, sir.
[*Enter* BAPTISTA *and* LUCENTIO.]
Signior Baptista, you are happily° met.
[*To the* PEDANT] Sir, this is the gentleman I told
you of.   20
I pray you stand good father to me now,
Give me Bianca for my patrimony.
PED. Soft, son!
Sir, by your leave. Having come to Padua
To gather in some debts, my son Lucentio   25
Made me acquainted with a weighty cause
Of love between your daughter and himself;
And, for the good report I hear of you,
And for the love he beareth to your daughter
And she to him, to stay him° not too long,   30
I am content, in a good father's care,
To have him matched. And if you please to like
No worse than I, upon some agreement
Me shall you find ready and willing
With one consent to have her so bestowed;   35
For curious° I cannot be with you,
Signior Baptista, of whom I hear so well.
BAP. Sir, pardon me in what I have to say.
Your plainness and your shortness please me well.
Right true it is, your son Lucentio here   40
Doth love my daughter, and she loveth him,
Or both dissemble deeply their affections.
And therefore, if you say no more than this,
That like a father you will deal with him

And pass my daughter a sufficient dower,   45
The match is made, and all is done.
Your son shall have my daughter with consent.
TRA. I thank you, sir. Where then do you know
best
We be affied° and such assurance ta'en
As shall with either part's agreement stand?   50
BAP. Not in my house, Lucentio, for you know
Pitchers have ears, and I have many servants.
Besides, old Gremio is hearkening still,
And happily° we might be interrupted.
TRA. Then at my lodging, an it like you.   55
There doth my father lie, and there, this night,
We'll pass the business privately and well.
Send for your daughter by your servant here.
My boy shall fetch the scrivener° presently.
The worst is this, that at so slender warning   60
You are like to have a thin and slender pittance.°
BAP. It likes° me well. Cambio, hie you home,
And bid Bianca make her ready straight;
And, if you will, tell what hath happened:
Lucentio's father is arrived in Padua,   65
And how she's like to be Lucentio's wife.
BION. I pray the gods she may with all my heart!
TRA. Dally not with the gods, but get thee gone.
[*Exit* BIONDELLO.]
Signior Baptista, shall I lead the way?
Welcome! One mess° is like to be your cheer.   70
Come, sir, we will better it in Pisa.
BAP. I follow you.   [*Exeunt* TRANIO, PEDANT
and BAPTISTA.]
[*Re-enter* BIONDELLO.]
BION. Cambio.
LUC. What sayest thou, Biondello?
BION. You saw my master wink and laugh upon
you?   76
LUC. Biondello, what of that?
BION. Faith, nothing; but has left me here be-
hind to expound the meaning or moral° of his signs
and tokens.   80
LUC. I pray thee, moralize them.
BION. Then thus. Baptista is safe, talking with
the deceiving father of a deceitful son.
LUC. And what of him?
BION. His daughter is to be brought by you   86
to the supper.
LUC. And then?
BION. The old priest of Saint Luke's church is at
your command at all hours.
LUC. And what of all this?   90
BION. I cannot tell; except they are busied about
a counterfeit assurance. Take you assurance° of her,

Sc. iv: 5. **Pegasus:** the name of an inn. Pegasus was the winged horse of the hero Perseus.   17. **tall:** fine, brave. **Hold . . . drink:** i.e., he gives him a tip.   19. **happily:** in a lucky moment.   30. **stay him:** keep him waiting.   36. **curious:** over particular.

49. **affied:** betrothed before witnesses. See Gen. Intro. p. 20a and App. 15.   54. **happily:** perhaps.   59. **scrivener:** professional writer who prepared legal agreements.   61. **pittance:** allowance, scanty meal.   62. **likes:** pleases.   70. **mess:** dish, course.   79. **moral:** concluding intention.   92. **Take . . . assurance:** make sure of her.

cum privilegio ad imprimendum solum.° To the church. Take the priest, clerk, and some sufficient honest witnesses.   95
If this be not that you look for, I have no more to say,
But bid Bianca farewell for ever and a day.

LUC. Hearest thou, Biondello?

BION. I cannot tarry. I knew a wench married in an afternoon as she went to the garden for   100
parsley to stuff a rabbit, and so may you, sir. And so, adieu, sir. My master hath appointed me to go to Saint Luke's to bid the priest be ready to come against you come° with your appendix.° [*Exit.*]

LUC. I may, and will, if she be so contented.   106
She will be pleased. Then wherefore should I doubt?
Hap what hap may,° I'll roundly° go about her.
It shall go hard if Cambio go without her.   [*Exit.*]

SCENE V. *A public road.*

[*Enter* PETRUCHIO, KATHARINA, HORTENSIO, *and*
SERVANTS.*]

PET. Come on, i' God's name. Once more toward our father's.
Good Lord, how bright and goodly shines the moon!

KATH. The moon! The sun. It is not moonlight now.

PET. I say it is the moon that shines so bright.

KATH. I know it is the sun that shines so bright.

PET. Now, by my mother's son, and that's myself,   6
It shall be moon, or star, or what I list,
Or ere I journey to your father's house.
Go on, and fetch our horses back again.
Evermore crossed and crossed, nothing but crossed!

HOR. Say as he says, or we shall never go.   11

KATH. Forward, I pray since we have come so far,
And be it moon, or sun, or what you please.
An if you please to call it a rush candle,°
Henceforth I vow it shall be so for me.   15

PET. I say it is the moon.

KATH.   I know it is the moon.

PET. Nay, then you lie. It is the blessed sun.

KATH. Then, God be blessed, it is the blessed sun.
But sun it is not, when you say it is not,
And the moon changes even as your mind.   20
What you will have it named, even that it is,
And so it shall be so for Katharine.

HOR. Petruchio, go thy ways. The field is won.

PET. Well, forward, forward! Thus the bowl should run,
And not unluckily against the bias.°   25
But, soft! Company is coming here.
                [*Enter* VINCENTIO.]
[*To* VINCENTIO] Good morrow, gentle mistress. Where away?
Tell me, sweet Kate, and tell me truly too,
Hast thou beheld a fresher gentlewoman?
Such war of white and red within her cheeks!   30
What stars do spangle heaven with such beauty
As those two eyes become that heavenly face?
Fair lovely maid, once more good day to thee.
Sweet Kate, embrace her for her beauty's sake.

HOR. A' will make the man mad to make a woman of him.   36

KATH. Young budding virgin, fair and fresh and sweet,
Whither away, or where is thy abode?
Happy the parents of so fair a child;
Happier the man whom favorable stars   40
Allot thee for his lovely bedfellow!

PET. Why, how now, Kate! I hope thou art not mad.
This is a man, old, wrinkled, faded, withered,
And not a maiden, as thou say'st he is.

KATH. Pardon, old father, my mistaking eyes   45
That have been so bedazzled with the sun
That every thing I look on seemeth green.
Now I perceive thou art a reverend father.
Pardon, I pray thee, for my mad mistaking.

PET. Do, good old grandsire, and withal make known   50
Which way thou travelest. If along with us,
We shall be joyful of thy company.

VIN. Fair sir, and you my merry mistress,
That with your strange encounter° much amazed me,
My name is called Vincentio, my dwelling Pisa,   55
And bound I am to Padua, there to visit
A son of mine which long I have not seen.

PET. What is his name?

VIN.   Lucentio, gentle sir.

PET. Happily met, the happier for thy son.
And now by law, as well as reverend age,   60
I may entitle thee my loving father.
The sister to my wife, this gentlewoman,
Thy son by this° hath married. Wonder not,
Nor be not grieved. She is of good esteem,
Her dowry wealthy and of worthy birth;   65
Beside, so qualified° as may beseem
The spouse of any noble gentleman.
Let me embrace with old Vincentio,
And wander we to see they honest son,

---

93. cum . . . solum: lit., with the sole right to print — the legal phrase denoting that a printer had copyright of a particular book.   **103-04. come . . . come:** to meet you when you come.   **105. appendix:** with a pun on appendage.   **108. Hap . . . may:** whatever happens. **roundly:** straight.
  Sc. v: 14. rush candle: taper.

24-25. bowl . . . bias: See App. 13.   **54. encounter:** manner of greeting.   **63. by this:** by this time.   **66. qualified:** endowed with such qualities.

Who will of thy arrival be full joyous.   70
VIN. But is this true? Or is it else your pleasure,
Like pleasant travelers, to break a jest
Upon the company you overtake?
    HOR. I do assure thee, father, so it is.
    PET. Come, go along, and see the truth
        hereof,   75
For our first merriment hath made thee jealous.°
                        [*Exeunt all but* HORTENSIO.]
    HOR. Well, Petruchio, this has put me in heart.
Have to° my widow! And if she be froward,
Then hast thou taught Hortensio to be untoward.°
                                            [*Exit.*]

Act V

SCENE I. *Padua. Before* LUCENTIO's *house.*

[GREMIO *discovered.° Enter behind* BIONDELLO,
        LUCENTIO, *and* BIANCA.]
    BION. Softly and swiftly, sir, for the priest is
ready.
    LUC. I fly, Biondello. But they may chance to
need thee at home. Therefore leave us.
    BION. Nay, faith, I'll see the church o' your   5
back,° and then come back to my master's as soon
as I can.
        [*Exeunt* LUCENTIO, BIANCA, *and* BIONDELLO.]
    GRE. I marvel Cambio comes not all this while.
[*Enter* PETRUCHIO, KATHARINA, VINCENTO, GRUMIO,
        with ATTENDANTS.]
    PET. Sir, here's the door, this is Lucentio's house.
My father's° bears more° toward the market place.
Thither must I, and here I leave you, sir.   11
    VIN. You shall not choose but drink before you
        go.
I think I shall command your welcome here,
And, by all likelihood, some cheer is toward.
                                        [*Knocks.*]
    GRE. They're busy within. You were best knock
louder.   16
        [PEDANT *looks out of the window.*]
    PED. What's he that knocks as he would beat
down the gate?
    VIN. Is Signior Lucentio within, sir?
    PED. He's within, sir, but not to be spoken withal.
    VIN. What if a man bring him a hundred pound
or two to make merry withal?
    PED. Keep your hundred pounds to yourself. He
shall need none, so long as I live.   25

PET. Nay, I told you your son was well beloved
in Padua. Do you hear, sir? To leave frivolous circumstances, I pray you tell Signior Lucentio that his
father is come from Pisa and is here at the door to
speak with him.   30
    PED. Thou liest. His father has come from Padua,
and here looking out at the window.
    VIN. Art thou his father?
    PED. Aye, sir. So his mother says, if I may believe
her.   35
    PET. [*To* VINCENTIO] Why, how now, gentleman!
Why, this is flat knavery to take upon you another
man's name.
    PED. Lay hands on·the villain. I believe a' means
to cozen° somebody in this city under my counte-
nance.°   41
        [*Re-enter* BIONDELLO.]
    BION. I have seen them in the church together.
God send 'em good shipping!° But who is here?
Mine old master Vincentio! Now we are undone
and brought to nothing.   45
    VIN. [*Seeing* BIONDELLO] Come hither, crack-
hemp.°
    BION. I hope I may choose,° sir.
    VIN. Come hither, you rogue. What, have you
forgot me?   50
    BION. Forgot you! No, sir. I could not forget you,
for I never saw you before in all my life.
    VIN. What, you notorious villain, didst thou
never see thy master's father, Vincentio?   55
    BION. What, my old worshipful old master? Yes,
marry, sir. See where he looks out of the window.
    VIN. Is't so, indeed?   [*Beats* BIONDELLO.]
    BION. Help, help, help! Here's a madman will
murder me.   [*Exit.*]   61
    PED. Help, son! Help, Signior Baptista!
                            [*Exit from above.*]
    PET. Prithee, Kate, let's stand aside and see the
end of this controversy.   [*They retire.*]
        [*Re-enter* PEDANT *below;* TRANIO, BAPTISTA,
                and SERVANTS.]
    TRA. Sir, what are you, that offer to beat my
servant?   66
    VIN. What am I, sir! Nay, what are you, sir? Oh,
immortal gods! Oh, fine villain! A silken doublet!
A velvet hose! A scarlet cloak, and a copatain hat!°
Oh, I am undone! I am undone! While I play   70
the good husband° at home, my son and my servant
spend all at the university.
    TRA. How now! What's the matter?
    BAP. What, is the man lunatic?
    TRA. Sir, you seem a sober ancient gentleman   75

76. jealous: suspicious.   78. Have to: here's to.   79. untoward:
awkward, ill-mannered.
    Act V, Sc. i: s.d., discovered: on stage.   5–6. o' . . . back:
behind you; i.e., I'll see you safe in church.   10. father's: father-
in-law's. bears more: is nearer.

40. cozen: cheat.   40–41: under my countenance: disguised as
me.   43. good shipping: a good voyage together.   46. crack-
hemp: one who will stretch a rope, be hanged.   47. may choose:
i.e., I may please myself.   68–69. doublet . . . hat: See Notes
on Costume, p. 94a, and Pl. 8b.   71. husband: economical
householder.

by your habit, but your words show you a madman.
Why, sir, what 'cerns it you if I wear pearl and
gold? I thank my good father, I am able to maintain it.   79

VIN. Thy father! Oh villain! He is a sailmaker in
Bergamo.

BAP. You mistake, sir, you mistake, sir. Pray,
what do you think is his name?

VIN. His name! As if I knew not his name. I have
brought him up ever since he was three years old,
and his name is Tranio.   86

PED. Away, away, mad ass! His name is Lucentio, and he is mine only son, and heir to the lands
of me, Signior Vincentio.   89

VIN. Lucentio! Oh, he hath murdered his master!
Lay hold on him, I charge you, in the Duke's name.
Oh, my son, my son! Tell me, thou villain, where
is my son Lucentio?

TRA. Call forth an officer. [*Enter one with an officer.*] Carry this mad knave to the jail. Father Baptista, I charge you see that he be forthcoming.°   96

VIN. Carry me to the jail!

GRE. Stay, Officer. He shall not go to prison.

BAP. Talk not, Signior Gremio. I say he shall go
to prison.   100

GRE. Take heed, Signior Baptista, lest you be
cony-catched° in this business. I dare swear this is
the right Vincentio.

PED. Swear, if thou darest.

GRE. Nay, I dare not swear it.   105

TRA. Then thou wert best say that I am not Lucentio.

GRE. Yes, I know thee to be Signior Lucentio.

BAP. Away with the dotard! To the jail with him!

VIN. Thus strangers may be haled° and   111
abused. Oh, monstrous villain!

[*Re-enter* BIONDELLO, *with* LUCENTIO *and* BIANCA.]

BION. Oh, we are spoiled! And — yonder he is.
Deny him, forswear him, or else we are all un-
done.   115

LUC. [*Kneeling*] Pardon, sweet Father.

VIN.   Lives my sweet Son? [*Exeunt
BIONDELLO, TRANIO, and PEDANT, as fast as may be.*]

BIAN. Pardon, dear Father.

BAP.   How hast thou offended?
Where is Lucentio?

LUC.   Here's Lucentio,
Right son to the right Vincentio,   119
That have by marriage made thy daughter mine
While counterfeit supposes bleared thine eyne.°

GRE. Here's packing,° with a witness, to deceive
us all!

VIN. Where is that damned villain Tranio,

That faced and braved me in this matter so?

BAP. Why, tell me, is not this my Cambio?   125

BIAN. Cambio is changed into Lucentio.

LUC. Love wrought these miracles. Bianca's love
Made me exchange my state with Tranio,
While he did bear my countenance° in the town;
And happily I have arrivèd at the last   130
Unto the wishèd haven of my bliss.
What Tranio did, myself enforced him to.
Then pardon him, sweet Father, for my sake.

VIN. I'll slit the villain's nose, that would have
sent me to the jail.   135

BAP. But do you hear, sir? Have you married my
daughter without asking my good will?

VIN. Fear not, Baptista. We will content you,
go to.° But I will in, to be revenged for this villainy.   [*Exit.*]   140

BAP. And I, to sound the depth of this knavery.
[*Exit.*]

LUC. Look not pale, Bianca. Thy father will not
frown.   [*Exeunt* LUCENTIO *and* BIANCA.]

GRE. My cake is dough;° but I'll in among the
rest,   145
Out of hope of all but my share of the feast.
[*Exit.*]

KATH. Husband, let's follow to see the end of this
ado.

PET. First kiss me, Kate, and we will.

KATH. What, in the midst of the street?

PET. What, art thou ashamed of me?   150

KATH. No, sir, God forbid, but ashamed to kiss.

PET. Why, then let's home again. Come, sirrah,
let's away.

KATH. Nay, I will give thee a kiss. [*Kisses him.*]
Now pray thee, love, stay.

PET. Is not this well? Come, my sweet Kate.
Better once° than never, for never too late.°   155
[*Exeunt.*]

SCENE II. *Padua.* LUCENTIO's *house.*

[*Enter* BAPTISTA, VINCENTIO, GREMIO, *the* PEDANT,
LUCENTIO, BIANCA, PETRUCHIO, KATHARINA,
HORTENSIO, *and* WIDOW, TRANIO, BIONDELLO,
and GRUMIO; *the* SERVINGMEN *with* TRANIO
bringing in a banquet.°]

LUC. At last, though long, our jarring notes
agree.
And time it is, when raging war is done,
To smile at scapes and perils overblown.
My fair Bianca, bid my father welcome
While I with self-same kindness welcome thine.   5
Brother Petruchio, Sister Katharina,

---

96. forthcoming: i.e., to stand his trial.   102. cony-catched:
cheated.   111. haled: hauled, ill-treated.   121. counterfeit . . .
eyne: false substitutes deceived your eyes.   122. packing:
plotting.

129. bear my countenance: pretend to be me.   139. go to: an
expression of indignation.   145. cake is dough: i.e., I have no
luck. See I.i.109,n.   155. Better . . . late: i.e., "it's never too
late to mend." once: at some time or other.
Sc. ii: s.d., banquet: light refreshments after the main feast.

And thou, Hortensio, with thy loving widow,
Feast with the best, and welcome to my house.
My banquet is to close our stomachs up
After our great good cheer. Pray you, sit down,   10
For now we sit to chat, as well as eat.
     PET. Nothing but sit and sit, and eat and eat!
     BAP. Padua affords this kindness, Son Petruchio.
     PET. Padua affords nothing but what is kind.
     HOR. For both our sakes, I would that word were
       true.   15
     PET. Now, for my life, Hortensio fears° his
       widow.
     WID. Then never trust me, if I be afeard.
     PET. You are very sensible, and yet you miss my
       sense.
I mean, Hortensio is afeard of you.
     WID. He that is giddy thinks the world turns
       round.   20
     PET. Roundly replied.°
     KATH.   Mistress, how mean you that?
     WID. Thus I conceive by° him.
     PET. Conceives by° me! How likes Hortensio
       that?
     HOR. My widow says thus she conceives her tale.
     PET. Very well mended. Kiss him for that, good
       widow.   25
     KATH. "He that is giddy thinks the world turns
       round."
I pray you tell me what you meant by that.
     WID. Your husband, being troubled with a shrew,
Measures my husband's sorrow by his woe;
And now you know my meaning.   30
     KATH. A very mean meaning.
     WID.   Right, I mean you.
     KATH. And I am mean,° indeed, respecting you.
     PET. To her, Kate!
     HOR. To her, widow!
     PET. A hundred marks, my Kate does put her
       down.   35
     HOR. That's my office.
     PET. Spoke like an officer. Ha'° to thee, lad.
                  [*Drinks to* HORTENSIO.]
     BAP. How likes Gremio these quick-witted folks?
     GRE. Believe me, sir, they butt° together well.
     BIAN. Head and butt! A hasty-witted body   40
Would say your head and butt were head and
       horn.°
     VIN. Aye, Mistress Bride, hath that awakened
       you?
     BIAN. Aye, but not frighted me. Therefore I'll
       sleep again.

     PET. Nay, that you shall not. Since you have be-
       gun,
Have at° you for a bitter jest or two!   45
     BIAN. Am I your bird? I mean to shift my bush,
And then pursue me as you draw your bow.
You are welcome all.°
       [*Exeunt* BIANCA, KATHARINA, *and* WIDOW.]
     PET. She hath prevented° me. Here, Signior
       Tranio,
This bird you aimed at, though you hit her not.   50
Therefore a health to all that shot and missed.
     TRA. Oh, sir, Lucentio slipped° me like his grey-
       hound,
Which runs himself and catches for his master.
     PET. A good swift simile, but something currish.
     TRA. 'Tis well, sir, that you hunted for yourself.
'Tis thought your deer does hold you at a bay.°   56
     BAP. Oh, ho, Petruchio! Tranio hits you now.
     LUC. I thank thee for that gird,° good Tranio.
     HOR. Confess, confess, hath he not hit you here?
     PET. A' has a little galled° me, I confess;   60
And, as the jest did glance away from me,
'Tis ten to one it maimed you two outright.
     BAP. Now, in good sadness,° Son Petruchio,
I think thou hast the veriest shrew of all.
     PET. Well, I say no, and therefore for assurance
Let's each one send unto his wife,   66
And he whose wife is most obedient
To come at first when he doth send for her
Shall win the wager which we will propose.
     HOR. Content. What is the wager?
     LUC.   Twenty crowns.   70
     PET. Twenty crowns!
I'll venture so much of my hawk or hound,
But twenty times so much upon my wife.
     LUC. A hundred then.
     HOR.   Content.
     PET.   A match!° 'Tis done.
     HOR. Who shall begin?
     LUC.   That will I.   75
Go, Biondello, bid your mistress come to me.
     BION. I go.   [*Exit.*]
     BAP. Son, I'll be your half,° Bianca comes.
     LUC. I'll have no halves. I'll bear it all myself.
               [*Re-enter* BIONDELLO.]
How now! What news?
     BION.   Sir, my mistress sends you word   80
That she is busy and she cannot come.
     PET. How! She is busy, and she cannot come!
Is that an answer?

16–19. fears . . . afeard: fears means both "to scare" and "to be scared"; the Widow takes Petruchio's meaning in the first sense. 21. Roundly replied: a good straight answer. 22. conceive by: gather my meaning from. 23. Conceives by: is with child by. 32. am mean: think poorly. 37. Ha': have, here's to. 39. butt: clash — like goats fighting. F1, however, reads "they But." If this reading is correct, it means they argue back and forth. 41. head . . . horn: i.e., that you were a cuckold.

45. Have at: I will take a shot at. 48. You . . . all: With these words the ladies rise and go out, as the jesting is becoming too coarse for their liking. 49. prevented: forestalled. 52. slipped: released to pursue the game — a technical term in coursing. 56. hold . . . bay: turns to fight and so keeps the hounds baying at a distance. 58. gird: bitter jest. 60. galled: wounded. 63. sadness: seriousness. 74. match: bet. 78. your half: i.e., pay half the wager.

GRE.   Aye, and a kind one too.
Pray God, sir, your wife send you not a worse.
PET. I hope, better.   85
HOR. Sirrah Biondello, go and entreat my wife
To come to me forthwith.   [*Exit* BIONDELLO.]
PET.   Oh, ho! Entreat her!
Nay, then she must needs come.
HOR.   I am afraid, sir,
Do what you can, yours will not be entreated.
      [*Re-enter* BIONDELLO.]
Now, where's my wife?   90
BION. She says you have some goodly jest in hand.
She will not come; she bids you come to her.
PET. Worse and worse! She will not come! Oh vile,
Intolerable, not to be endured!
Sirrah Grumio, go to your mistress.   95
Say, I command her come to me.   [*Exit* GRUMIO.]
HOR. I know her answer.
PET.   What?
HOR.   She will not.
PET. The fouler fortune mine, and there an end.
BAP. Now, by my holidame,° here comes Katharina!
      [*Re-enter* KATHARINA.]
KATH. What is your will, sir, that you send for me?   100
PET. Where is your sister, and Hortensio's wife?
KATH. They sit conferring by the parlor fire.
PET. Go fetch them hither. If they deny to come,
Swinge° me them soundly forth unto their husbands.
Away, I say, and bring them hither straight.   105
            [*Exit* KATHARINA.]
LUC. Here is a wonder, if you talk of a wonder.
HOR. And so it is. I wonder what it bodes.
PET. Marry, peace it bodes, and love, and quiet life,
An awful rule,° and right supremacy;   109
And, to be short, what not that's sweet and happy?
BAP. Now, fair befall° thee, good Petruchio!
The wager thou hast won, and I will add
Unto their losses twenty thousand crowns —
Another dowry to another daughter,
For she is changed as she had never been.   115
PET. Nay, I will win my wager better yet
And show more sign of her obedience,
Her new-built virtue and obedience.
See where she comes and brings your froward wives
As prisoners to her womanly persuasion.   120
  [*Re-enter* KATHARINA, *with* BIANCA *and* WIDOW.]
Katharine, that cap of yours becomes you not.
Off with that bauble, throw it underfoot.

WID. Lord, let me never have a cause to sigh
Till I be brought to such a silly pass!°
BIAN. Fie, what a foolish duty call you this?   125
LUC. I would your duty were as foolish too.
The wisdom of your duty, fair Bianca,
Hath cost me an hundred crowns since suppertime.
BIAN. The more fool you, for laying° on my duty.
PET. Katharine, I charge thee tell these head-
    strong women   130
What duty they do owe their lords and husbands.
WID. Come, come, you're mocking. We will have
    no telling.
PET. Come on, I say, and first begin with her.
WID. She shall not.   134
PET. I say she shall — and first begin with her.
KATH. Fie, fie! Unknit that threatening unkind
    brows,
And dart not scornful glances from those eyes
To wound thy lord, thy king, thy governor.
It blots thy beauty as frosts do bite the meads,
Confounds thy fame° as whirlwinds shake fair
    buds,   140
And in no sense is meet or amiable.
A woman moved is like a fountain troubled,°
Muddy, ill-seeming, thick, bereft of beauty;
And while it is so, none so dry or thirsty
Will deign to sip or touch one drop of it.   145
Thy husband is thy lord, thy life, thy keeper,
Thy head, thy sovereign, one that cares for thee,
And for thy maintenance commits his body
To painful labor both by sea and land,
To watch the night in storms, the day in cold,   150
Whilst thou liest warm at home, secure,° and
    safe;
And craves no other tribute at thy hands
But love, fair looks and true obedience,
Too little payment for so great a debt.
Such duty as the subject owes the prince   155
Even such a woman oweth to her husband,
And when she is froward, peevish, sullen, sour,
And not obedient to his honest will,
What is she but a foul contending rebel
And graceless traitor to her loving lord?   160
I am ashamed that women are so simple
To offer war where they should kneel for peace,
Or seek for rule, supremacy, and sway,
When they are bound to serve, love, and obey.
Why are our bodies soft and weak and smooth,
Unapt to toil and trouble in the world,   166
But that our soft conditions° and our hearts
Should well agree with our external parts?
Come, come, you froward and unable° worms!
My mind hath been as big as one of yours,   170
My heart as great, my reason haply more,

---

99. holidame: either "holy dame" (Blessed Lady) or a variant of "halidom" (holy relic). See *R & J*, I.iii.43,n.   104. Swinge: beat.   109. awful rule: rule in which proper respect is paid to the head.   111. fair befall: good luck to.   124. pass: state of affairs.   129. laying: betting.   140. Confounds . . . fame: ruins your reputation.   142. troubled: stirred.   151. secure: without a care.   167. conditions: qualities.   169. unable: feeble.

To bandy° word for word and frown for frown;
But now I see our lances are but straws,
Our strength as weak, our weakness past compare,
That seeming to be most which we indeed least are.
Then vail your stomachs,° for it is no boot,°   176
And place your hands below your husband's foot;
In token of which duty, if he please,
My hand is ready, may it do him ease.

     PET. Why, there's a wench! Come on and kiss
        me, Kate.   180
     LUC. Well, go thy ways, old lad, for thou shalt
        ha't.
     VIN. 'Tis a good hearing when children are to-
        ward.
     LUC. But a harsh hearing when women are fro-
        ward.
     PET. Come, Kate, we'll to bed.
We three are married, but you two are sped.°   185
[*To* LUCENTIO] 'Twas I won the wager, though you
hit the white,°
And, being a winner, God give you good night!
               [*Exeunt* PETRUCHIO *and* KATHARINA.]

---

172. **bandy:** exchange — a term from tennis, meaning to hit the
ball to and fro.   176. **vail . . . stomachs:** lower your pride.
boot: advantage.   185. **sped:** done for.   187. **white:** center
of the target; but he puns on the name "Bianca," which means
white.

HOR. Now, go thy ways. Thou hast tamed a curst
     shrew.
'Tis a wonder, by your leave, she will be tamed so.
                                [*Exeunt.*]

The old play of *The Taming of a Shrew* ends thus:

     Then enter two bearing of *Slie* in his
     Own apparel again, and leaves him
     Where they found him, and then goes out.
     Then enter the *Tapster*.
Tapster. Now that the darksome night is overpast,
     And dawning day appears in crystal sky,
     Now must I haste abroad: but soft who's this?
     What *Slie* oh wondrous hath he lain here all night?
     I'll wake him, I think he's starved by this,
     But that his belly was so stuffed with ale,
     What now *Slie*, Awake for shame.
Slie. Sim gi's some more wine: what's all the
     Players gone: am not I a Lord?
Tapster. A Lord with a murrin: come, art thou drunken still?
Slie. Who's this? *Tapster*, oh Lord sirra, I have had
     The bravest dream tonight, that ever thou
     Heardest in all thy life.
Tapster. Ay marry but you had best get you home,
     For your wife will curse you for dreaming here tonight.
Slie. Will she? I know now how to tame a shrew.
     I dreamt upon it all this night till now,
     And thou hast waked me out of the best dream
     That ever I had in my life, but I'll to my
     Wife presently and tame her, too,
     And if she anger me.
Tapster. Nay tarry *Slie* for I'll go home with thee,
     And hear the rest that thou hast dreamt tonight.
                   Exeunt Omnes.

THE TWO GENTLEMEN OF VERONA

Introduction

The Two Gentlemen of Verona was first printed in the first folio of 1623 (F1). The text is fairly good, but there is some confusion in the names of places. At I.i.62, Valentine sets forth for *Milan*, but at II.v.1, his servant Speed welcomes Launce to *Padua;* while at III.i.81 the Duke speaks of a "lady in *Verona* here" and at V.iv.126–29 Valentine tells Thurio that if he mentions Silvia again, *Verona* shall not hold him. As with the F1 text of *The Winter's Tale,* the play is divided into acts and scenes but only those exits and entrances that occur at the beginning and the end of a scene are noted. Moreover, *The Two Gentlemen* (like *The Winter's Tale* and unlike most of the plays in F1) is provided with a list of "The names of all the actors." It is probable therefore that the copy was prepared for the press by a professional scribe, possibly the same scribe who prepared the copy for *The Tale.*

The Two Gentlemen of Verona seems never to have been popular. It is included among the twelve plays mentioned by Francis Meres in 1598 (see p. 12a), but otherwise no references, mentions, or quotations made during Shakespeare's lifetime have been discovered. There are, however, two possible allusions in the play to Marlowe's narrative poem *Hero and Leander:*

(a) VAL. And on a love-book pray for my success?
   PRO. Upon some book I love I'll pray for thee.
   VAL. That's on some shallow story of deep love,
   How young Leander crossed the Hellespont.
   (I.i.19–22)

(b) VAL. Why, then, a ladder quaintly made of cords,
   To cast up with a pair of anchoring hooks
   Would serve to scale another Hero's tower,
   So bold Leander would adventure it.
   (III.i.117–20)

Marlowe's poem was left unfinished at the time of his sensational death on May 30, 1593 (see Gen. Intro. p. 39a–b), but it may well have been circulated in manuscript; it was completed by George Chapman and first printed in 1598. Apart from these two passages, *The Two Gentlemen* can be dated only by the style, which has all the marks of early work — long explanatory speeches (III.i.1–50, IV.iii.11–36), elaborate, "poetical" language (II.vii, III.ii.73–87), playing with phrases (I.i.1–54), and excessive punning (I.i.72–158). The evidence, such as it is, suggests that the play was written about 1593.

In writing the play Shakespeare seems to have been considerably influenced by the work of John Lyly (see Gen. Intro. p. 36a–b). In Lyly's novel *Euphues,* the hero is introduced to his friend's betrothed Lucilla and falls in love with her, but Lucilla, unlike Silvia, returns his love. In this perplexity Lucilla laments to herself:

Ah wretched wench Lucilla, how art thou perplexed? what a doubtful fight dost thou feel betwixt faith and fancy? hope and fear? conscience and concupiscence? O my Euphues, little dost thou know the sudden sorrow that I sustain for thy sweet sake, whose wit hath bewitched me, whose rare qualities have deprived me of mine old quality, whose courteous behavior without curiosity, whose comely feature without fault, whose filed speech without fraud, hath wrapped me in this misfortune. And canst thou, Lucilla, be so light of love in forsaking Philautus to fly to Euphues? Canst thou prefer a stranger before thy countryman? A starter before thy companion? Why, Euphues doth perhaps desire my love, but Philautus hath deserved it. Why, Euphues' feature is worthy as good as I, but Philautus his faith is worthy a better. Ay, but the latter love is most fervent. Ay, but the first ought to be most faithful. Ay, but Euphues hath greater perfection. Ay, but Philautus hath deeper affection.

In Shakespeare's play, Proteus, likewise afflicted, reproaches himself in a similar vein (II.iv.192–214 and II.vi).

Lyly had followed his success as a novelist by writing plays which were performed by the boys of the Chapel Royal and St. Paul's before Queen Elizabeth and her courtiers in the 1580's. It is not likely that Shakespeare ever saw these performances, but several of the plays were published in 1591 and 1592, and in writing *Love's Labor's Lost* Shakespeare owed much to them.

The basic story of *The Two Gentlemen of Verona* is unusually simple and uncomplicated by any secondary plot. A similar tale, concerning the loves of Felix and Felismena, written in Spanish by Jorge de Montemayor and first printed in 1542, is often regarded as the ultimate source of the play; but the story of how a faithless companion made love to the betrothed of his sworn friend is one of the commonest plots of fiction and drama. It is not likely that Shakespeare could read Spanish. Moreover, the story seems already to have been dramatized in English; there is a record of a lost play called *Felix and Philiomena* being acted at Court in 1585.

The names of some of the characters in *The Two Gentlemen* have a significance. Valentine is true love; Proteus stands for fickleness; while Sir Eglamour — whose name suggests a lovesick fop — possibly derives from another fleet-footed knight in Malory's *Morte Darthur:*

And then Sir Arthur saw a rich pavilion: " What signifieth yonder pavilion? " " It is the knight's pavilion," said Merlin, " that ye fought with last, Sir Pellinore, but he is out, he is not there; he hath ado with a knight of yours, that hight Egglame, and they have fought together, but at the last Egglame fled, and else he had been dead, and he hath chased him even to Carlion, and we shall meet with him anon in the high way."

One passage has aroused amazed indignation — the rapid forgiveness of Proteus by Valentine at the end of the play (V.iv.19–83). Proteus, being repulsed by Silvia, who hotly scorns his love, threatens to force her; whereupon Valentine steps from the thicket and indignantly rebukes his friend. When Proteus promptly repents, Valentine replies:

> Then I am paid,
> And once again I do receive thee honest.
> Who by repentance is not satisfied
> Is nor of Heaven nor earth, for these are pleased.
> By penitence the Eternal's wrath's appeased.
> And, that my love may appear plain and free,
> All that was mine in Silvia I give thee.

Critics, disgusted by this easy forgiveness, have attempted to find various excuses for it; some have even suggested a corruption of the text. But the situation — supposing that Shakespeare intended it to be taken seriously — would not have unduly surprised Elizabethan playgoers. It was a common belief in Shakespeare's time that the love of a man for his friend, especially his " sworn brother," was stronger and nobler than the love of man for woman. Shakespeare himself, confronted with a similar situation when his own young friend had stolen his mistress, tried to console himself in Sonnet 42. The claims of friendship over love had already been strongly stated in Lyly's play *Endimion,* when Geron, the old man, thus addresses Endimion's friend Eumenides:

Eumenides, release Endimion, for all things (friendship excepted) are subject to fortune: love is but an eye-worm, which only tickleth the head with hopes, and wishes; friendship the image of eternity, in which there is nothing movable, nothing mischievous. As much difference as there is between beauty and virtue, bodies and shadows, colors and life, so great odds is there between love and friendship. Love is a chameleon, which draweth nothing into the mouth but air, and nourisheth nothing in the body but lungs. Believe me, Eumenides, desire dies in the same moment that beauty sickens, and beauty fadeth in the same instant that it flourisheth. When adversities flow, then love ebbs; but friendship standeth stiffly in storms. Time draweth wrinkles in a fair face, but addeth fresh colors to a fast friend, which neither heat, nor cold, nor misery, nor place, nor destiny, can alter or diminish. O friendship! of all things the most rare, and therefore most rare because most excellent, whose comforts in misery is always sweet, and whose counsels in prosperity are ever fortunate! Vain love, that only coming near to friendship in name, would seem to be the same, or better, in nature.

Shakespeare, however, does not seem to have taken the troubles of the lovers too deeply. Indeed in *The Two Gentlemen of Verona,* as in some of the other early comedies, *Love's Labor's Lost* or *A Midsummer Night's Dream,* for instance, there are touches of irony, as if Shakespeare were quietly mocking the whole convention of romantic love. *The Two Gentlemen of Verona* is far more amusing if taken as a burlesque than as serious comedy, and this may well have been Shakespeare's intention.

The Two Gentlemen of Verona

DRAMATIS PERSONAE

DUKE OF MILAN, *father to Silvia*
VALENTINE
PROTEUS } *the two gentlemen*
ANTONIO, *father to Proteus*
THURIO, *a foolish rival to Valentine*
EGLAMOUR, *agent for Silvia in her escape*
HOST, *where Julia lodges*
OUTLAWS, *with Valentine*
SPEED, *a clownish servant to Valentine*

LAUNCE, *the like to Proteus*
PANTHINO, *servant to Antonio*

JULIA, *beloved of Proteus*
SILVIA, *beloved of Valentine*
LUCETTA, *waiting woman to Julia*

SERVANTS, MUSICIANS

SCENE — *Verona; Milan; the frontiers of Mantua.*

Act I

SCENE I. *Verona. An open place.*

[*Enter* VALENTINE *and* PROTEUS.]

VAL. Cease to persuade, my loving Proteus.
Home-keeping° youth have ever homely wits.
Were 't not affection chains thy tender days
To the sweet glances of thy honored love,
I rather would entreat thy company   5
To see the wonders of the world abroad,
Than, living dully sluggardized° at home,
Wear out thy youth with shapeless° idleness.
But since thou lovest, love still, and thrive therein,
Even as I would when I to love begin.   10
  PRO. Wilt thou be gone? Sweet Valentine, adieu!
Think on thy Proteus when thou haply° seest
Some rare noteworthy object in thy travel.
Wish me partaker in thy happiness
When thou dost meet good hap,° and in thy dan-
      ger —   15
If ever danger do environ° thee —
Commend thy grievance to my holy prayers,
For I will be thy beadsman,° Valentine.
  VAL. And on a love-book° pray for my success?
  PRO. Upon some book I love I'll pray for thee.   20
  VAL. That's on some shallow story of deep love,
How young Leander crossed the Hellespont.°
  PRO. That's a deep story of a deeper love,
For he was more than over shoes in love.
  VAL. 'Tis true, for you are over boots in love,   25
And yet you never swum the Hellespont.
  PRO. Over the boots? Nay, give me not the
      boots.°

VAL. No, I will not, for it boots° thee not.
  PRO.   What?
VAL. To be in love, where scorn is bought with
      groans,
Coy looks with heart-sore sighs, one fading mo-
      ment's mirth   30
With twenty watchful, weary, tedious nights.
If haply won, perhaps a hapless° gain;
If lost, why then a grievous labor won;
However, but a folly bought with wit,
Or else a wit by folly vanquishèd.   35
  PRO. So, by your circumstance,° you call me fool.
  VAL. So, by your circumstance, I fear you'll prove.
  PRO. 'Tis love you cavil at.° I am not Love.
  VAL. Love is your master, for he masters you;
And he that is so yokèd by a fool,   40
Methinks, should not be chronicled° for wise.
  PRO. Yet writers say, as in the sweetest bud
The eating canker° dwells, so eating love
Inhabits in the finest wits of all.
  VAL. And writers say, as the most forward° bud
Is eaten by the canker ere it blow,°   46
Even so by love the young and tender wit
Is turned to folly, blasting° in the bud,
Losing his verdure even in the prime,°
And all the fair effects of future hopes.   50
But wherefore waste I time to counsel thee,
That art a votary° to fond desire?
Once more adieu! My father at the road°
Expects my coming, there to see me shipped.
  PRO. And thither will I bring thee, Valentine.   55
  VAL. Sweet Proteus, no. Now let us take our
      leave.
To Milan let me hear from thee by letters
Of thy success in love, and what news else

Betideth° here in absence of thy friend,
And I likewise will visit thee with mine.   60
   PRO. All happiness bechance° to thee in Milan!
   VAL. As much to you at home! And so, farewell.
                              [*Exit.*]
   PRO. He after honor hunts, I after love.
He leaves his friends to dignify° them more;
I leave myself, my friends, and all, for love.   65
Thou, Julia, thou hast metamorphosed° me,
Made me neglect my studies, lose my time,
War with good counsel,° set the world at naught,
Made wit with musing weak, heart sick with
    thought.
               [*Enter* SPEED.]
   SPEED. Sir Proteus, save you! Saw you my mas-
ter?   70
   PRO. But now° he parted hence to embark for
Milan.
   SPEED. Twenty to one, then, he is shipped already,
And I have played the sheep° in losing him.
   PRO. Indeed, a sheep doth very often stray,
An if° the shepherd be awhile away.   75
   SPEED. You conclude that my master is a shep-
herd, then, and I a sheep?
   PRO. I do.
   SPEED. Why then, my horns are his horns,°
whether I wake or sleep.   80
   PRO. A silly answer, and fitting well a sheep.
   SPEED. This proves me still a sheep.
   PRO. True, and thy master a shepherd.   84
   SPEED. Nay, that I can deny by a circumstance.°
   PRO. It shall go hard but° I'll prove it by another.
   SPEED. The shepherd seeks the sheep, and not the
sheep the shepherd; but I seek my master, and my
master seeks not me. Therefore I am no sheep.   91
   PRO. The sheep for fodder follow the shepherd;
the shepherd for food follows not the sheep. Thou
for wages followest thy master; thy master for   95
wages follows not thee. Therefore thou art a sheep.
   SPEED. Such another proof will make me cry
"baa."
   PRO. But, dost thou hear? Gavest thou my letter
to Julia?   100
   SPEED. Aye, sir. I, a lost mutton, gave your letter
to her, a laced mutton,° and she, a laced mutton,
gave me, a lost mutton, nothing for my labor.
   PRO. Here's too small a pasture for such store of
muttons.
   SPEED. If the ground be overcharged,° you were
best stick° her.

   PRO. Nay. In that you are astray, 'twere best
pound° you.   110
   SPEED. Nay, sir, less than a pound shall serve me
for carrying your letter.
   PRO. You mistake. I mean the pound — a pin-
fold.
   SPEED. From a pound to a pin? Fold it over and
    over,   115
'Tis threefold too little for carrying a letter to your
    lover.
   PRO. But what said she?
   SPEED. [*First nodding*] Aye.
   PRO. Nod — aye — why that's noddy.°
   SPEED. You mistook, sir. I say she did nod, and
you ask me if she did nod, and I say, "Aye."   121
   PRO. And that set together is noddy.
   SPEED. Now you have taken the pains to set it to-
gether, take it for your pains.
   PRO. No, no. You shall have it for bearing the
letter.   126
   SPEED. Well, I perceive I must be fain° to bear
with° you.
   PRO. Why, sir, how do you bear with me?
   SPEED. Marry, sir, the letter, very orderly, having
nothing but the word "noddy" for my pains.   131
   PRO. Beshrew° me, but you have a quick wit.
   SPEED. And yet it cannot overtake your slow
purse.
   PRO. Come, come, open the matter in brief. What
said she?   136
   SPEED. Open your purse, that the money and the
matter may be both at once delivered.
   PRO. Well, sir, here is for your pains.° What said
she?   140
   SPEED. Truly, sir, I think you'll hardly win her.
   PRO. Why, couldst thou perceive so much from
her?
   SPEED. Sir, I could perceive nothing at all from
her, no, not so much as a ducat° for delivering 145
your letter. And being so hard to me that brought
your mind, I fear she'll prove as hard to you in telling your mind. Give her no token° but stones,° for
she's as hard as steel.
   PRO. What said she? Nothing?   150
   SPEED. No, not so much as "Take this for thy
pains." To testify your bounty, I thank you, you
have testerned° me; in requital whereof, henceforth carry your letters yourself. And so, sir, I'll
commend you to my master.   155
   PRO. Go, go, be gone, to save your ship from
    wreck,

---

59. Betideth: happens. **61. bechance:** befall. **64. dignify:**
bring honor to. **66. metamorphosed:** changed into another
shape. **68. counsel:** advice. **71. But now:** just now.
73. sheep: with a pun on "ship." **75. An if:** if. **79. horns . . .
horns:** The joke is inexplicable. **85. circumstance:** deduction.
86. but: unless. **102. laced mutton:** prostitute. **107. overcharged:** overcrowded. **108. stick:** slaughter.

110. pound: shut up in the pound (sometimes called a *pinfold*),
with a pun on *pound* (£1) in l. 111. **119. noddy:** noodle.
127. fain: content. **127–28. bear with:** put up with. **132. Beshrew:** ill luck to. **139. pains:** labor — here Proteus hands over
the expected tip. **145. ducat:** worth about a dollar. **148. token:**
gift. **stones:** in the double sense of jewels and worthless gifts.
153. testerned: given me a testern (sixpence).

Which cannot perish having thee aboard,
Being destined to a drier death on shore.°

                              [*Exit* SPEED.]

I must go send some better messenger.
I fear my Julia would not deign my lines,   160
Receiving them from such a worthless post.°

                                    [*Exit.*]

SCENE II. *The same. Garden of* JULIA's *house.*

[*Enter* JULIA *and* LUCETTA.]

JUL. But say, Lucetta, now we are alone,
Wouldst thou, then, counsel me to fall in love?
  LUC. Aye, madam, so you stumble not unheed-
    fully.
  JUL. Of all the fair resort° of gentlemen
That every day with parle° encounter me,   5
In thy opinion which is worthiest love?
  LUC. Please you repeat their names, I'll show my
    mind
According to my shallow simple skill.
  JUL. What think'st thou of the fair Sir Egla-
    mour?°
  LUC. As of a knight well-spoken, neat and fine;
But, were I you, he never should be mine.   11
  JUL. What think'st thou of the rich Mercatio?
  LUC. Well of his wealth, but of himself, so so.
  JUL. What think'st thou of the gentle Proteus?
  LUC. Lord, Lord! To see what folly reigns in us!
  JUL. How now! What means this passion° at his
    name?   16
  LUC. Pardon, dear madam. 'Tis a passing shame
That I, unworthy body as I am,
Should censure° thus on lovely gentlemen.
  JUL. Why not on Proteus, as of all the rest? 20
  LUC. Then thus — of many good I think him
    best.
  JUL. Your reason?
  LUC. I have no other but a woman's reason.
I think him so, because I think him so.
  JUL. And wouldst thou have me cast my love on
    him?   25
  LUC. Aye, if you thought your love not cast away.
  JUL. Why, he, of all the rest, hath never moved°
    me.
  LUC. Yet he, of all the rest, I think, best loves ye.
  JUL. His little speaking shows his love but small.
  LUC. Fire that's closest kept burns most of all.
  JUL. They do not love that do not show their
    love.   31

  LUC. Oh, they love least that let men know their
    love.
  JUL. I would I knew his mind.
  LUC. Peruse this paper, madam.
  JUL. "To Julia." — Say, from whom?   35
  LUC. That the contents will show.
  JUL. Say, say, who gave it thee?
  LUC. Sir Valentine's page, and sent, I think,
    from Proteus.
He would have given it you, but I, being in the
    way,°
Did in your name receive it. Pardon the fault, I
    pray.   40
  JUL. Now, by my modesty, a goodly broker!°
Dare you presume to harbor wanton lines?
To whisper and conspire against my youth?
Now, trust me, 'tis an office of great worth,
And you an officer fit for the place.   45
There, take the paper. See it be returned,
Or else return no more into my sight.
  LUC. To plead for love deserves more fee than
    hate.
  JUL. Will ye be gone?
  LUC.   That you may ruminate. [*Exit.*]
  JUL. And yet I would I had o'erlooked° the
    letter.   50
It were a shame to call her back again,
And pray her to° a fault for which I chid her.
What fool is she, that knows I am a maid
And would not force the letter to my view!
Since maids, in modesty, say "no" to that   55
Which they would have the profferer construe°
    "aye."
Fie, fie, how wayward is this foolish love
That, like a testy babe, will scratch the nurse,
And presently,° all humbled, kiss the rod!
How churlishly I chid Lucetta hence,   60
When willingly I would have had her here!
How angerly I taught my brow to frown,
When inward joy enforced my heart to smile!
My penance is to call Lucetta back,
And ask remission for my folly past.   65
What ho! Lucetta!

                [*Re-enter* LUCETTA.]

  LUC.   What would your ladyship?
  JUL. Is 't near dinnertime?
  LUC.   I would it were,
That you might kill your stomach° on your meat,°
And not upon your maid.
  JUL. What is 't that you took up so gingerly? 70
  LUC. Nothing.
  JUL. Why didst thou stoop, then?

---

158. destined . . . shore: i.e., he that is born to be hanged will never be drowned.   161. post: messenger.
  Sc. ii: This scene should be compared with *M of Ven*, I.ii.
4. resort: party of visitors.   5. parle: talk.   9. Eglamour: Shakespeare gives the name again to Silvia's swift-footed escort. See *T Gent* Intro. p. 366a.   16. passion: emotion.   19. censure: criticize.   27. moved: conversed with.

39. being . . . way: meeting him.   41. broker: go-between. 50. o'erlooked: read.   52. pray . . . to: apologize for.   56. construe: translate.   59. presently: immediately.   68. stomach: in the double meaning of "anger" and "appetite." meat: pronounced, and punning on, "mate."

LUC. To take a paper up that I let fall.
JUL. And is that paper nothing?
LUC. Nothing concerning me.   75
JUL. Then let it lie for those that it concerns.
LUC. Madam, it will not lie where it concerns
Unless it have a false interpreter.
JUL. Some love of yours hath writ to you in
rhyme.
LUC. That I might sing it, madam, to a tune. 80
Give me a note. Your ladyship can set.°
JUL. As little by such toys° as may be possible.
Best sing it to the tune of " Light o' love."°
LUC. It is too heavy for so light a tune.   84
JUL. Heavy! Belike it hath some burden,° then?
LUC. Aye, and melodious were it, would you sing
it.
JUL. And why not you?
LUC.   I cannot reach so high.
JUL. Let's see your song. How now, minion!°
LUC. Keep tune there still, so you will sing it out;
And yet methinks I do not like this tune.   90
JUL. You do not?
LUC.   No, madam. It is too sharp.°
JUL. You, minion, are too saucy.
LUC. Nay, now you are too flat,
And mar the concord with too harsh a descant.°
There wanteth but a mean° to fill your song.   95
JUL. The mean is drowned with your unruly bass.
LUC. Indeed, I bid the base° for Proteus.
JUL. This babble shall not henceforth trouble me.
Here is a coil° with protestation! [*Tears the letter.*]
Go get you gone, and let the papers lie.   100
You would be fingering them to anger me.
LUC. She makes it strange, but she would be best
pleased
To be so angered with another letter.   [*Exit.*]
JUL. Nay, would I were so angered with the
same!
O hateful hands, to tear such loving words!   105
Injurious wasps, to feed on such sweet honey,
And kill the bees that yield it with your stings!
I'll kiss each several paper° for amends.
Look, here is writ " kind Julia." Unkind Julia!
As in revenge of thy ingratitude,   110
I throw thy name against the bruising stones,
Trampling contemptuously on thy disdain.
And here is writ " love-wounded Proteus."
Poor wounded name! My bosom, as a bed,
Shall lodge thee till thy wound be throughly healed,
And thus I search° it with a sovereign kiss.   116
But twice or thrice was " Proteus " written down.

Be calm, good wind, blow not a word away
Till I have found each letter in the letter,
Except mine own name. That some whirlwind
bear   120
Unto a ragged, fearful-hanging rock,
And throw it thence into the raging sea!
Lo, here in one line is his name twice writ,
" Poor forlorn Proteus, passionate Proteus,
To the sweet Julia." That I'll tear away;   125
And yet I will not, sith° so prettily
He couples it to his complaining names.
Thus will I fold them one upon another.
Now kiss, embrace, contend, do what you will.
       [*Re-enter* LUCETTA.]
LUC. Madam,   130
Dinner is ready, and your father stays.°
JUL. Well, let us go.
LUC. What, shall these papers lie like telltales
here?
JUL. If you respect them, best to take them up.
LUC. Nay, I was taken up° for laying them
down.   135
Yet here they shall not lie for catching cold.
JUL. I see you have a month's mind° to them.
LUC. Aye, madam, you may say what sights you
see.
I see things too, although you judge I wink.°
JUL. Come, come. Will 't please you go?   140
                        [*Exeunt.*]

SCENE III. *The same.* ANTONIO's *house.*

[*Enter* ANTONIO *and* PANTHINO.]
ANT. Tell me, Panthino, what sad° talk was that
Wherewith my brother held you in the cloister?
PAN. 'Twas of his nephew Proteus, your son.
ANT. Why, what of him?
PAN.   He wondered that your lordship
Would suffer him to spend his youth at home   5
While other men of slender reputation°
Put forth their sons to seek preferment° out:
Some to the wars to try their fortune there;
Some to discover islands far away;
Some to the studious universities.   10
For any, or for all these exercises,
He said that Proteus your son was meet,°
And did request me to importune you
To let him spend his time no more at home,
Which would be great impeachment° to his age
In having known no travel in his youth.   16
ANT. Nor need'st thou much importune me to
that

---

81. set: set it to music.   82. toys: trifles.   83. Light o' love: a
well known ditty.   85. burden: bass part.   88. minion: hussy.
91. sharp: bitter, with a pun on the musical meaning.   94. descant: harmony.   95. mean: tenor.   97. bid . . . base: Here
Lucetta drops the musical terms and continues in the metaphor
of the game of Prisoner's Base.   99. coil: fuss.   108. several
paper: separate piece.   116. search: probe.

126. sith: since.   131. stays: waits.   135. taken up: blamed
137. month's mind: longing.   139. wink: shut my eyes.
     Sc. iii: 1. sad: serious.   6. slender reputation: i.e., of far less
rank than yourself.   7. preferment: promotion.   12. meet:
fitted.   15. impeachment: detriment.

Whereon this month I have been hammering.°
I have considered well his loss of time,
And how he cannot be a perfect man,   20
Not being tried and tutored in the world.
Experience is by industry achieved,
And perfectèd by the swift course of time.
Then tell me, whither were I best to send him?
    PAN. I think your lordship is not ignorant   25
How his companion, youthful Valentine,
Attends° the Emperor in his royal Court.
    ANT. I know it well.
    PAN. 'Twere good, I think, your lordship sent him
      thither.
There shall he practice tilts and tournaments,°   30
Hear sweet discourse, converse with noblemen,
And be in eye° of every exercise
Worthy his youth and nobleness of birth.
    ANT. I like thy counsel. Well hast thou advised.
And that thou mayst perceive how well I like it   35
The execution of it shall make known.
Even with the speediest expedition°
I will dispatch him to the Emperor's Court.
    PAN. Tomorrow, may it please you, Don Al-
      phonso,
With other gentlemen of good esteem,   40
Are journeying to salute the Emperor,
And to commend their service to his will.
    ANT. Good company. With them shall Proteus go,
And—— In good time!° Now will we break with°
    him.
              [*Enter* PROTEUS.]
    PRO. Sweet love! Sweet lines! Sweet life!   45
Here is her hand, the agent of her heart;
Here is her oath for love, her honor's pawn.°
Oh, that our fathers would applaud our loves,
To seal° our happiness with their consents!
O heavenly Julia!   50
    ANT. How now! What letter are you reading
    there?
    PRO. May 't please your lordship, 'tis a word or
    two
Of commendations sent from Valentine,
Delivered by a friend that came from him.   54
    ANT. Lend me the letter. Let me see what news.
    PRO. There is no news, my lord, but that he writes
How happily he lives, how well beloved,
And daily gracèd by the Emperor,
Wishing me with him, partner of his fortune.
    ANT. And how stand you affected to° his wish?
    PRO. As one relying on your lordship's will,   61
And not depending on his friendly wish.

    ANT. My will is something sorted with° his wish.
Muse not that I thus suddenly proceed,
For what I will, I will, and there an end.   65
I am resolved that thou shalt spend some time
With Valentinus in the Emperor's Court.
What maintenance he from his friends receives,
Like exhibition° thou shalt have from me.
Tomorrow be in readiness to go.   70
Excuse it not, for I am péremptory.°
    PRO. My lord, I cannot be so soon provided.
Please you, deliberate a day or two.
    ANT. Look, what thou want'st shall be sent after
    thee.
No more of stay! Tomorrow thou must go.   75
Come on, Panthino. You shall be employed
To hasten on his expedition.
        [*Exeunt* ANTONIO *and* PANTHINO.]
    PRO. Thus have I shunned the fire for fear of
    burning,
And drenched me in the sea where I am drowned.
I feared to show my father Julia's letter,   80
Lest he should take exceptions to my love,
And with the vantage° of mine own excuse
Hath he excepted most against° my love.
Oh, how this spring of love resembleth
The uncertain glory of an April day,   85
Which now shows all the beauty of the sun,
And by and by a cloud takes all away!
           [*Re-enter* PANTHINO.]
    PAN. Sir Proteus, your father calls for you.
He is in haste. Therefore, I pray you, go.
    PRO. Why, this it is. My heart accords thereto,   90
And yet a thousand times it answers " no."
                    [*Exeunt.*]

Act II

SCENE I. *Milan. The* DUKE's *palace.*

        [*Enter* VALENTINE *and* SPEED.]
SPEED. Sir, your glove.
VAL.   Not mine. My gloves are on.
SPEED. Why, then, this may be yours, for this is
    but one.°
VAL. Ha! Let me see. Aye, give it me, it's mine.
Sweet ornament that decks a thing divine!
Ah, Silvia, Silvia!   5
SPEED. Madam Silvia! Madam Silvia!
VAL. How now, sirrah?°

---

18. hammering: pondering deeply.   27. Attends: waits on.
30. tilts . . . tournaments: courtly exercises in arms. In tilting
the two combatants, mounted and in full armor, charged at each
other with unpointed spears.   32. in eye: witness.   37. expedition: haste.   44. In . . . time: a phrase meaning "just when we
wanted him."   break with: tell.   47. pawn: pledge.   49. seal:
conclude. See *Ant & Cleo*, IV.xiv.49,n.   60. stand . . . to: like.

63. sorted with: of the same sort as.   69. exhibition: allowance
of money.   71. peremptory: determined.   82. vantage: i.e.,
having the advantage of my excuse.   83. excepted . . . against:
i.e., he has taken a practical way of stopping.

    Act II, Sc. i: 1–2. on . . . one: The two words were pronounced
almost alike.   7. sirrah: term of address used to an inferior.

SPEED. She is not within hearing, sir.

VAL. Why, sir, who bade you call her?

SPEED. Your Worship, sir, or else I mistook.   10

VAL. Well, you'll still° be too forward.

SPEED. And yet I was last chidden for being too slow.

VAL. Go to,° sir. Tell me, do you know Madam Silvia?   15

SPEED. She that your Worship loves?

VAL. Why, how know you that I am in love?

SPEED. Marry,° by these special marks. First, you have learned, like Sir Proteus, to wreathe° your arms like a malecontent, to relish a love song 20 like a robin redbreast, to walk alone like one that had the pestilence, to sigh like a schoolboy that had lost his A B C,° to weep like a young wench that had buried her grandam,° to fast like one that takes diet, to watch like one that fears robbing, to 25 speak puling like a beggar at Hallowmas.° You were wont, when you laughed, to crow like a cock; when you walked, to walk like one of the lions; when you fasted, it was presently° after dinner; when you looked sadly, it was for want of 30 money; and now you are metamorphosed with a mistress, that, when I look on you, I can hardly think you my master.

VAL. Are all these things perceived in me?

SPEED. They are all perceived without ye.   35

VAL. Without me? They cannot.

SPEED. Without you? Nay, that's certain, for without° you were so simple, none else would; but you are so without these follies that these follies are within you, and shine through you like the 40 water in an urinal,° that not an eye that sees you but is a physician to comment on your malady.

VAL. But tell me, dost thou know my lady Silvia?

SPEED. She that you gaze on so as she sits at supper?

VAL. Hast thou observed that? Even she, I mean.

SPEED. Why, sir, I know her not.   50

VAL. Dost thou know her by my gazing on her, and yet knowest her not?

SPEED. Is she not hard-favored,° sir?

VAL. Not so fair, boy, as well-favored.°

SPEED. Sir, I know that well enough.   55

VAL. What dost thou know?

SPEED. That she is not so fair as, of you, well-favored.

VAL. I mean that her beauty is exquisite, but her favor infinite.   60

SPEED. That's because the one is painted, and the other out of all count.°

VAL. How painted? And how out of count?

SPEED. Marry, sir, so painted, to make her fair, that no man counts of her beauty.   65

VAL. How esteemest thou me? I account of her beauty.

SPEED. You never saw her since she was deformed.°

VAL. How long hath she been deformed?   70

SPEED. Ever since you loved her.

VAL. I have loved her ever since I saw her, and still I see her beautiful.

SPEED. If you love her, you cannot see her.

VAL. Why?   75

SPEED. Because Love is blind. Oh, that you had mine eyes, or your own eyes had the lights they were wont to have when you chid at Sir Proteus for going ungartered!°

VAL. What should I see then?   80

SPEED. Your own present folly, and her passing° deformity; for he, being in love, could not see to garter his hose,° and you, being in love, cannot see to put on your hose.

VAL. Belike, boy, then, you are in love, for 85 last morning you could not see to wipe my shoes.

SPEED. True, sir, I was in love with my bed. I thank you, you swinged° me for my love, which makes me the bolder to chide you for yours.

VAL. In conclusion, I stand affected to her.   90

SPEED. I would you were set,° so your affection would cease.

VAL. Last night she enjoined me to write some lines to one she loves.

SPEED. And have you?   95

VAL. I have.

SPEED. Are they not lamely writ?

VAL. No, boy, but as well as I can do them. Peace! Here she comes.

SPEED. [*Aside*] Oh, excellent motion!° Oh,   100

---

11. **still:** always.   14. **Go to:** an exclamation of impatience. 18. **Marry:** Mary, by the Virgin.   19–26. **wreathe . . . Hallowmas:** Here Speed enumerates the well known signs of a melancholy lover. See App. 4.   23. **A B C:** Schoolboys learned to read from an Absey (or ABC) book. It was a single printed sheet covered with horn, pasted on a board with a handle, and containing the alphabet, the Lord's Prayer, and sometimes a short catechism. See *John*, I.i.196 and *LLL*, V.i.49.   24. **grandam:** grandmother.   26. **Hallowmas:** All Saints' Day (Nov. 1st) is the eve of All Souls' Day. It was a custom in some parts of England to beg for alms in return for which the recipient would pray for the souls of the giver's friends.   29. **presently:** immediately. 38. **without:** unless.   41. **water . . . urinal:** Inspection of the urine was a normal method of diagnosing an illness, used alike by quacks and qualified doctors. See *II Hen IV*, I.ii.1–6. 53. **hard-favored:** plain-faced, homely.

54. **well-favored:** good looking, with subsequent puns on *favored* (l. 58), meaning "liked," and *favor* (l. 60), meaning "kindness." Speed (l. 61) interprets the word as meaning "face."   61–62. **one . . . count:** i.e., her face (*the one*) is made up (*painted*), and her beauty (*the other*) cannot be reckoned (*out of count*).   69. **deformed:** transformed by love.   79. **ungartered:** See ll. 19–26, n. 81. **passing:** exceeding.   83. **hose:** See Note on Costume, p. 93a–b.   88. **swinged:** beat.   91. **set:** seated — as a contrast to *stand* in l. 90.   100. **motion:** He puns on *motion* (graceful movement) and *motion* (a puppet show). While the puppets went through their motions, the puppetmaster "interpreted" the action either by describing it or by providing voices.

exceeding puppet! Now will he interpret to her.

[*Enter* SILVIA.]

VAL. Madam and mistress, a thousand good morrows.

SPEED. [*Aside*] Oh, give ye good even! Here's a million of manners.°   105

SIL. Sir Valentine and servant, to you two thousand.

SPEED. [*Aside*] He should give her interest, and she gives it him.

VAL. As you enjoined me, I have writ your letter
Unto the secret nameless friend of yours,   111
Which I was much unwilling to proceed in,
But for my duty to your ladyship.

SIL. I thank you, gentle servant. 'Tis very clerkly°
done.

VAL. Now trust me, madam, it came hardly off,°
For, being ignorant to whom it goes,   116
I writ at random, very doubtfully.

SIL. Perchance you think too much of so much
pains?

VAL. No, madam. So it stead° you, I will write —
Please you command — a thousand times as much;
And yet ——   121

SIL. A pretty period!° Well, I guess the sequel,
And yet I will not name it — and yet I care not —
And yet take this again — and yet I thank you,
Meaning henceforth to trouble you no more.   125

SPEED. [*Aside*] And yet you will, and yet another " yet."

VAL. What means your ladyship? Do you not
like it?

SIL. Yes, yes. The lines are very quaintly° writ,
But since unwillingly, take them again.
Nay, take them.   130

VAL. Madam, they are for you.

SIL. Aye, aye. You writ them, sir, at my request,
But I will none of them. They are for you.
I would have had them writ more movingly.   134

VAL. Please you, I'll write your ladyship another.

SIL. And when it's writ, for my sake read it over,
And if it please you, so; if not, why, so.

VAL. If it please me, madam, what then?

SIL. Why, if it please you, take it for your labor.
And so, good morrow, servant.   [*Exit.*]   140

SPEED. Oh, jest unseen, inscrutable, invisible,
As a nose on a man's face, or a weathercock on a
steeple!°
My master sues to her, and she hath taught her
suitor,
He being her pupil, to become her tutor.   144
Oh, excellent device! Was there ever heard a better,

That my master, being scribe, to himself should
write the letter?

VAL. How now, sir? What are you reasoning°
with yourself?

SPEED. Nay, I was rhyming. 'Tis you that have
the reason.   150

VAL. To do what?

SPEED. To be a spokesman from Madam Silvia.

VAL. To whom?

SPEED. To yourself. Why, she woos you by a
figure.°   155

VAL. What figure?

SPEED. By a letter, I should say.

VAL. Why, she hath not writ to me?

SPEED. What need she, when she hath made you
write to yourself? Why, do you not perceive the
jest?   160

VAL. No, believe me.

SPEED. No believing you, indeed, sir. But did you
perceive her earnest?

VAL. She gave me none,° except an angry word.

SPEED. Why, she hath given you a letter.   165

VAL. That's the letter I writ to her friend.

SPEED. And that letter hath she delivered, and
there an end.

VAL. I would it were no worse.

SPEED. I'll warrant you, 'tis as well.   170
For often have you writ to her, and she, in modesty,
Or else for want of idle time, could not again reply;
Or fearing else some messenger that might her mind
discover°
Herself hath taught her love himself to write unto
her lover.
All this I speak in print,° for in print I found it.°
Why muse you, sir? 'Tis dinnertime.   176

VAL. I have dined.

SPEED. Aye, but hearken, sir. Though the chameleon° Love can feed on the air, I am one that am
nourished by my victuals and would fain° have
meat. Oh, be not like your mistress. Be moved, be
moved.   [*Exeunt.*]   182

SCENE II. *Verona.* JULIA'S *house.*

[*Enter* PROTEUS *and* JULIA.]

PRO. Have patience, gentle Julia.

JUL. I must, where is no remedy.

---

147. reasoning: talking about.   **155. by a figure:** figuratively, in this indirect way.   **163–64. earnest . . . none:** with a play on the various meanings of *earnest:* "truth" (as opposed to jest) and "money given on account of the main payment."   **173. discover:** reveal.   **175. All . . . it:** Speed presumably means that the previous lines (171–74), written in the old fashioned fourteener meter, are taken from some book; but if so, it has not been identified. **in print:** precisely.   **179. chameleon:** believed to be nourished on air. Since the chameleon changes its color to suit its background, it is used as a symbol for one who suits himself to his company and is always changing. See II.iv.26 and *Haml,* III.ii.98–100.   **180. fain:** gladly.

---

105. million of manners: such beautiful behavior.   **114. clerkly:** like a good scholar.   **115. came . . . oft:** caused me great difficulty.   **119. stead:** is of use to.   **122. period:** stop. **128. quaintly:** cleverly.   **141–42. Oh . . . steeple:** i.e., her intention is as plain as it can be.

PRO. When possibly I can, I will return.

JUL. If you turn not, you will return the sooner.
Keep this remembrance for thy Julia's sake.   5
    [Giving a ring.]

PRO. Why, then, we'll make exchange. Here, take
you this.

JUL. And seal the bargain with a holy kiss.

PRO. Here is my hand for my true constancy,
And when that hour o'erslips me in the day
Wherein I sigh not, Julia, for thy sake,   10
The next ensuing hour some foul mischance
Torment me for my love's forgetfulness!
My father stays° my coming; answer not.
The tide is now — nay, not thy tide of tears.
That tide will stay me longer than I should.   15
Julia, farewell! *[Exit JULIA.]* What, gone without a
word?
Aye, so true love should do. It cannot speak,
For truth hath better deeds than words to grace it.
    [Enter PANTHINO.]

PAN. Sir Proteus, you are stayed for.

PRO. Go. I come, I come.   20
Alas! This parting strikes poor lovers dumb.
    [Exeunt.]

SCENE III. *The same. A street.*

[Enter LAUNCE, leading a dog.]

LAUN. Nay, 'twill be this hour ere I have done
weeping. All the kind° of the Launces have this
very fault. I have received my proportion,° like the
prodigious° son, and am going with Sir Proteus to
the Imperial's° Court. I think Crab my dog be   5
the sourest-natured dog that lives. My mother weeping, my father wailing, my sister crying, our maid
howling, our cat wringing her hands, and all our
house in a great perplexity, yet did not this   10
cruel-hearted cur shed one tear. He is a stone, a very
pebble stone, and has no more pity in him than a
dog. A Jew would have wept to have seen our parting. Why, my grandam, having no eyes, look you,
wept herself blind at my parting. Nay, I'll show   15
you the manner of it. This shoe is my father. No,
this left shoe is my father. No, no, this left shoe
is my mother. Nay, that cannot be so neither. Yes,
it is so, it is so, it hath the worser sole. This shoe,
with the hole in it, is my mother, and this my   20
father — a vengeance on 't! There 'tis. Now, sir,
this staff is my sister, for, look you, she is as
white as a lily and as small as a wand. This hat is
Nan, our maid. I am the dog. No, the dog is   25
himself, and I am the dog — Oh! The dog is me,

and I am myself. Aye, so, so. Now come I to my
father. "Father, your blessing." Now should not
the shoe speak a word for weeping. Now should I
kiss my father. Well, he weeps on. Now come   30
I to my mother. Oh, that she could speak now
like a wood° woman! Well, I kiss her; why, there
'tis. Here's my mother's breath up and down. Now
come I to my sister. Mark the moan she makes.
Now the dog all this while sheds not a tear, nor
speaks a word; but see how I lay the dust with my
tears.   35
    [Enter PANTHINO.]

PAN. Launce, away, away, aboard! Thy master is
shipped,° and thou art to post after with oars.°
What's the matter? Why weepest thou, man?
Away, ass! You'll lose the tide if you tarry any
longer.   40

LAUN. It is no matter if the tied were lost, for it is
the unkindest tied that ever any man tied.

PAN. What's the unkindest tide?   44

LAUN. Why, he that's tied here — Crab, my dog.

PAN. Tut, man, I mean thou'lt lose the flood,°
and, in losing the flood, lose thy voyage, and, in
losing thy voyage, lose thy master, and, in losing
thy master, lose thy service, and, in losing thy service —— Why dost thou stop my mouth?   51

LAUN. For fear thou shouldst lose thy tongue.

PAN. Where should I lose my tongue?

LAUN. In thy tale.

PAN. In thy tail!   55

LAUN. Lose the tide, and the voyage, and the master, and the service, and the tied! Why, man, if the
river were dry, I am able to fill it with my tears. If
the wind were down, I could drive the boat with
my sighs.   60

PAN. Come, come away, man. I was sent to call
thee.

LAUN. Sir, call me what thou darest.

PAN. Wilt thou go?

LAUN. Well, I will go.   *[Exeunt.]*   65

SCENE IV. *Milan. The DUKE'S palace.*

[Enter SILVIA, VALENTINE, THURIO, and SPEED.]

SIL. Servant!

VAL. Mistress?

SPEED. Master, Sir Thurio frowns on you.

VAL. Aye, boy, it's for love.

SPEED. Not of you.   5

VAL. Of my mistress, then.

SPEED. 'Twere good you knocked **him**.   *[Exit.]*

SIL. Servant, you are sad.

VAL. Indeed, madam, I seem so.

Sc. ii: 13. **stays**: waits for.

Sc. iii: 2. **kind**: kindred, family.   3. **proportion**: for portion.
4. **prodigious**: for prodigal. For the Parable of the Prodigal Son,
see Luke 15:11–32.   5. **Imperial**: for "Emperor."

32. **wood**: mad.   37. **shipped**: on board. **post . . . oars**: follow
him in a rowboat, for Proteus's ship is anchored offshore in the
"road."   46. **flood**: full tide.

THU. Seem you that you are not?   10

VAL. Haply I do.

THU. So do counterfeits.

VAL. So do you.

THU. What seem I that I am not?

VAL. Wise.   15

THU. What instance of the contrary?

VAL. Your folly.

THU. And how quote° you my folly?

VAL. I quote it in your jerkin.

THU. My jerkin is a doublet.°   20

VAL. Well, then, I'll double your folly.

THU. How?

SIL. What, angry, Sir Thurio! Do you change color?

VAL. Give him leave, madam. He is a kind of chameleon.°   26

THU. That hath more mind to feed on your blood than live in your air.

VAL. You have said,° sir.

THU. Aye, sir, and done, too, for this time.   30

VAL. I know it well, sir. You always end ere you begin.

SIL. A fine volley of words, gentlemen, and quickly shot off.

VAL. 'Tis indeed, madam. We thank the giver.

SIL. Who is that, servant?   36

VAL. Yourself, sweet lady, for you gave the fire. Sir Thurio borrows his wit from your ladyship's looks, and spends what he borrows kindly in your company.   40

THU. Sir, if you spend word for word with me, I shall make your wit bankrupt.

VAL. I know it well, sir. You have an exchequer° of words and, I think, no other treasure to give your followers, for it appears by their bare° liveries that they live by your bare words.   46

SIL. No more, gentlemen, no more — here comes my father.

[*Enter* DUKE.]

DUKE. Now, daughter Silvia, you are hard beset.° Sir Valentine, your father's in good health.   50 What say you to a letter from your friends Of much good news?

VAL.   My lord, I will be thankful To any happy messenger from thence.

DUKE. Know ye Don Antonio, your countryman?

VAL. Aye, my good lord, I know the gentleman To be of worth and worthy estimation,   56 And not without desert so well reputed.

DUKE. Hath he not a son?

VAL. Aye, my good lord, a son that well deserves

The honor and regard of such a father.   60

DUKE. You know him well?

VAL. I know him as myself, for from our infancy We have conversed and spent our hours together. And though myself have been an idle truant, Omitting the sweet benefit of time   65 To clothe mine age with angel-like perfection, Yet hath Sir Proteus — for that's his name — Made use and fair advantage of his days; His years but young, but his experience old; His head unmellowed,° but his judgment ripe;   70 And, in a word, for far behind his worth Comes all the praises that I now bestow, He is complete in feature and in mind With all good grace to grace a gentleman.

DUKE. Beshrew me, sir, but if he make this good, He is as worthy for an empress' love   76 As meet° to be an emperor's counselor. Well, sir, this gentleman is come to me With commendation from great potentates, And here he means to spend his time awhile.   80 I think 'tis no unwelcome news to you.

VAL. Should I have wished a thing, it had been he.

DUKE. Welcome him, then, according to his worth. Silvia, I speak to you, and you, Sir Thurio, For Valentine, I need not cite° him to it.   85 I will send him hither to you presently.   [*Exit.*]

VAL. This is the gentleman I told your ladyship Had come along with me, but that his mistress Did hold his eyes locked in her crystal looks.   89

SIL. Belike that now she hath enfranchised° them Upon some other pawn for fealty.°

VAL. Nay, sure, I think she holds them prisoners still.

SIL. Nay, then, he should be blind, and, being blind, How could he see his way to seek out you?   94

VAL. Why, lady, Love hath twenty pair of eyes.

THU. They say that Love hath not an eye at all.

VAL. To see such lovers, Thurio, as yourself. Upon a homely object Love can wink.

SIL. Have done, have done. Here comes the gentleman.

[*Enter* PROTEUS.]

VAL. Welcome, dear Proteus! Mistress, I beseech you   100 Confirm his welcome with some special favor.

SIL. His worth is warrant for his welcome hither, If this be he you oft have wished to hear from.

VAL. Mistress, it is. Sweet lady, entertain° him To be my fellow servant to your ladyship.   105

Sc. iv: 18. **quote:** observe, pronounced "coat." **19–20. jerkin ... doublet:** See Note on Costume, p. 93a. **26. chameleon:** See II.i.179,n. **29. You ... said:** an ironical remark: "I can well believe it." **43. exchequer:** treasury. **45. bare:** threadbare. **49. hard beset:** attacked on all sides, i.e., you have eager suitors.

70. **unmellowed:** young, lit., unripe. **77. meet:** fit. **85. cite:** call. **90. enfranchised:** set at liberty. **91. pawn ... fealty:** pledge for loyalty, i.e., she has found another lover. **104. entertain:** engage as servant.

SIL. Too low a mistress for so high a servant.

PRO. Not so, sweet lady, but too mean a servant
To have a look of such a worthy mistress.

VAL. Leave off discourse of disability.°
Sweet lady, entertain him for your servant.   110

PRO. My duty will I boast of, nothing else.

SIL. And duty never yet did want his meed.°
Servant, you are welcome to a worthless mistress.

PRO. I'll die on him that says so but yourself.

SIL. That you are welcome?

PRO.   That you are worthless.   115
         [*Enter* SERVANT.]

SERV. Madam, my lord your father would speak
   with you.

SIL. I wait upon his pleasure. [*Exit* SERVANT.]
   Come, Sir Thurio,
Go with me. Once more, new servant, welcome.
I'll leave you to confer of home affairs.
When you have done, we look to hear from you.

PRO. We'll both attend upon your ladyship.   121
         [*Exeunt* SILVIA *and* THURIO.]

VAL. Now, tell me, how do all from whence you
   came?

PRO. Your friends are well, and have them much
   commended.

VAL. And how do yours?

PRO.   I left them all in health.

VAL. How does your lady? And how thrives your
   love?   125

PRO. My tales of love were wont to weary you.
I know you joy not in a love discourse.

VAL. Aye, Proteus, but that life is altered now.
I have done penance for contemning° Love,   129
Whose high imperious thoughts have punished me
With bitter fasts, with penitential groans,
With nightly tears, and daily heart-sore sighs;
For, in revenge of my contempt of love,
Love hath chased sleep from my enthrallèd° eyes,
And made them watchers of mine own heart's sor-
   row.   135
O gentle Proteus, Love's a mighty lord,
And hath so humbled me, as I confess
There is no woe to° his correction,°
Nor to his service no such joy on earth.
Now no discourse, except it be of love.   140
Now can I break my fast, dine, sup and sleep,
Upon the very naked name of love.

PRO. Enough. I read your fortune in your eye.
Was this the idol that you worship so?

VAL. Even she; and is she not a heavenly saint?

PRO. No, but she is an earthly paragon.   146

VAL. Call her divine.

PRO.   I will not flatter her.

VAL. Oh, flatter me, for love delights in praises.

PRO. When I was sick, you gave me bitter pills,
And I must minister the like to you.   150

VAL. Then speak the truth by her. If not divine,
Yet let her be a principality,°
Sovereign to all the creatures on the earth.

PRO. Except my mistress.

VAL.   Sweet, except not any,
Except thou wilt except against my love.°   155

PRO. Have I not reason to prefer mine own?

VAL. And I will help thee to prefer° her, too.
She shall be dignified with this high honor—
To bear my lady's train, lest the base earth
Should from her vesture chance to steal a kiss,   160
And, of so great a favor growing proud,
Disdain to root the summer-swelling flower,
And make rough winter everlastingly.

PRO. Why, Valentine, what braggardism° is this?

VAL. Pardon me, Proteus. All I can is nothing
To her, whose worth makes other worthies noth-
   ing.   166
She is alone.°

PRO.   Then let her alone.

VAL. Not for the world. Why, man, she is mine
   own,
And I as rich in having such a jewel
As twenty seas, if all their sand were pearl,   170
The water nectar,° and the rocks pure gold.
Forgive me, that I do not dream on thee,
Because thou seest me dote upon my love.
My foolish rival, that her father likes
Only for° his possessions are so huge,   175
Is gone with her along, and I must after,
For love, thou know'st, is full of jealousy.

PRO. But she loves you?

VAL. Aye, and we are betrothed. Nay, more, our
   marriage hour,
With all the cunning manner of our flight,   180
Determined of—how I must climb her window,
The ladder made of cords, and all the means
Plotted and 'greed on for my happiness.
Good Proteus, go with me to my chamber,
In these affairs to aid me with thy counsel.   185

PRO. Go on before. I shall inquire you forth.°
I must unto the road to disembark
Some necessaries that I needs must use,
And then I'll presently attend you.

VAL. Will you make haste?   190

PRO. I will.   [*Exit* VALENTINE.]
Even as one heat another heat expels,
Or as one nail by strength drives out another,

151–52. If . . . principality: i.e., if she is not a goddess at least call her an angel. *Principalities* are one of the orders of the angels. 154–55. except . . . love: without any exceptions, unless you will take exception to my love. 157. prefer: promote. 164. braggardism: silly boasting. 167. alone: incomparable, unique. 171. nectar: the drink of the gods. 175. for: because of. 186. inquire . . . forth: ask where you live.

109. Leave . . . disability: stop this mock modesty. 112. meed: reward. 129. contemning: despising. 134. enthralled: imprisoned. 138. to: compared with. correction: punishment.

So the remembrance of my former love
Is by a newer object quite forgotten.   195
Is it mine, or Valentine's praise,°
Her true perfection, or my false transgression,
That makes me reasonless to reason° thus?
She is fair; and so is Julia, that I love —
That I did love, for now my love is thawed,   200
Which, like a waxen image 'gainst a fire,
Bears no impression of the thing it was.
Methinks my zeal to Valentine is cold,
And that I love him not as I was wont.
Oh, but I love his lady too too much!   205
And that's the reason I love him so little.
How shall I dote on her with more advice,°
That thus without advice begin to love her!
'Tis but her picture° I have yet beheld,
And that hath dazzlèd my reason's light;   210
But when I look on her perfections,
There is no reason but° I shall be blind.
If I can check my erring love, I will;
If not, to compass° her I'll use my skill.   [*Exit.*]

SCENE V. *The same. A street.*

[*Enter* SPEED *and* LAUNCE *severally.*°]

SPEED. Launce! By mine honesty, welcome to Padua!°

LAUN. Forswear° not thyself, sweet youth, for I am not welcome. I reckon this always — that a man is never undone till he be hanged, nor never welcome to a place till some certain shot° be paid,   6
and the hostess say "Welcome!"

SPEED. Come on, you madcap, I'll to the alehouse with you presently, where, for one shot of five pence, thou shalt have five thousand welcomes.   10
But, sirrah, how did thy master part with Madam Julia?

LAUN. Marry, after they closed° in earnest, they parted very fairly in jest.

SPEED. But shall she marry him?   15

LAUN. No.

SPEED. How, then? Shall he marry her?

LAUN. No, neither.

SPEED. What, are they broken?

LAUN. No, they are both as whole as a fish.°   20

SPEED. Why, then, how stands the matter with them?

LAUN. Marry, thus. When it stands well with him, it stands well with her.

SPEED. What an ass art thou! I understand thee not.   26

LAUN. What a block art thou, that thou canst not! My staff understands me.

SPEED. What thou sayest?

LAUN. Aye, and what I do too. Look thee,   30
I'll but lean, and my staff understands me.

SPEED. It stands under thee, indeed.

LAUN. Why, stand-under and under-stand is all one.

SPEED. But tell me true, will 't be a match?   35

LAUN. Ask my dog. If he say aye, it will. If he say, no, it will. If he shake his tail and say nothing, it will.

SPEED. The conclusion is, then, that it will.

LAUN. Thou shalt never get such a secret from me but by a parable.   41

SPEED. 'Tis well that I get it so. But, Launce, how sayest thou, that my master is become a notable lover?

LAUN. I never knew him otherwise.   45

SPEED. Than how?

LAUN. A notable lubber, as thou reportest him to be.

SPEED. Why, thou whoreson° ass, thou mistakest me.   50

LAUN. Why fool, I meant not thee. I meant thy master.

SPEED. I tell thee, my master is become a hot lover.

LAUN. Why, I tell thee, I care not though he   55
burn himself in love. If thou wilt, go with me to the alehouse; if not, thou art an Hebrew, a Jew, and not worth the name of a Christian.

SPEED. Why?   59

LAUN. Because thou hast not so much charity in thee as to go to the ale° with a Christian. Wilt thou go?

SPEED. At thy service.   [*Exeunt.*]

SCENE VI. *The same. The* DUKE's *palace.*

[*Enter* PROTEUS.]

PRO. To leave my Julia, shall I be forsworn;
To love fair Silvia, shall I be forsworn;
To wrong my friend, I shall be much forsworn;
And even that power which gave me first my oath
Provokes me to this threefold perjury.   5
Love bade me swear, and Love bids me forswear.
O sweet-suggesting° Love, if thou hast sinned,

196. Is . . . praise: This line as it stands is two syllables short, and, moreover, Proteus had not praised her. Some such reading as "It is mine eye or Valentine his praise" is required.
198. reason: argue.   207. advice: mature thought.   209. picture: appearance.   212. reason but: doubt that I shall not; i.e., I certainly shall be.   214. compass: win.
  Sc. v: s.d., severally: by different doors.   2. Padua: Shakespeare has forgotten that the scene is Milan.   3. Forswear: perjure.   6. shot: payment, the cost of drinks.   13. closed: embraced.   20. whole . . . fish: a proverb like "as sound as a bell."

49. whoreson: "son of a bitch."   61. go . . . ale: It was a custom to raise money for church purposes by a community drinking party known as a church ale.
  Sc. vi: 7. sweet-suggesting: suggesting sweet thoughts.

Teach me, thy tempted subject, to excuse it!
At first I did adore a twinkling star,
But now I worship a celestial sun.   10
Unheedful° vows may heedfully° be broken,
And he wants° wit that wants resolvèd will
To learn° his wit to exchange the bad for better.
Fie, fie, unreverend tongue! To call her bad,
Whose sovereignty so oft thou hast preferred   15
With twenty thousand soul-confirming oaths.
I cannot leave to° love, and yet I do;
But there I leave to love where I should love.
Julia I lose, and Valentine I lose.
If I keep them, I needs must lose myself.   20
If I lose them, thus find I by their loss
For Valentine, myself, for Julia, Silvia.
I to myself am dearer than a friend,
For love is still most precious in itself;
And Silvia — witness Heaven, that made her
    fair! --   25
Shows Julia but a swarthy Ethiope.°
I will forget that Julia is alive,
Remembering that my love to her is dead,
And Valentine I'll hold an enemy,
Aiming at Silvia as a sweeter friend.   30
I cannot now prove constant to myself
Without some treachery used to Valentine.
This night he meaneth with a corded ladder
To climb celestial Silvia's chamber window,
Myself in counsel, his competitor.°   35
Now presently I'll give her father notice
Of their disguising and pretended° flight,
Who, all enraged, will banish Valentine;
For Thurio, he intends, shall wed his daughter.
But, Valentine being gone, I'll quickly cross   40
By some sly trick blunt° Thurio's dull proceeding.
Love, lend me wings to make my purpose swift,
As thou hast lent me wit to plot this drift!° [*Exit.*]

SCENE VII. *Verona.* JULIA'S *house.*

[*Enter* JULIA *and* LUCETTA.]
JUL. Counsel, Lucetta. Gentle girl, assist me.
And, even in kind love, I do conjure thee,
Who art the table° wherein all my thoughts
Are visibly charáctered° and engraved,
To lesson° me, and tell me some good mean°   5
How, with my honor,° I may undertake
A journey to my loving Protéus.
LUC. Alas, the way is wearisome and long!

JUL. A true-devoted pilgrim is not weary
To measure° kingdoms with his feeble steps;   10
Much less shall she that hath Love's wings to fly,
And when the flight is made to one so dear,
Of such divine perfection, as Sir Proteus.
    LUC. Better forbear till Proteus make return.
    JUL. Oh, know'st thou not, his looks are my
      soul's food?   15
Pity the dearth that I have pinèd in
By longing for that food so long a time.
Didst thou but know the inly° touch of love,
Thou wouldst as soon go kindle fire with snow
As seek to quench the fire of love with words.   20
    LUC. I do not seek to quench your love's hot fire,
But qualify° the fire's éxtreme rage,
Lest it should burn above the bounds of reason.
    JUL. The more thou damm'st it up, the more it
      burns.
The current that with gentle murmur glides,   25
Thou know'st, being stopped, impatiently doth
    rage;
But when his fair course is not hinderèd,
He makes sweet music with the enameled° stones,
Giving a gentle kiss to every sedge°
He overtaketh in his pilgrimage;   30
And so by many winding nooks he strays,
With willing sport, to the wild ocean.
Then let me go, and hinder not my course.
I'll be as patient as a gentle stream,
And make a pastime of each weary step,   35
Till the last step have brought me to my love;
And there I'll rest, as after much turmoil
A blessèd soul doth in Elysium.°
    LUC. But in what habit° will you go along?
    JUL. Not like a woman, for I would prevent   40
The loose encounters of lascivious men.
Gentle Lucetta, fit me with such weeds°
As may beseem some well-reputed page.
    LUC. Why, then, your ladyship must cut your
      hair.
    JUL. No, girl. I'll knit it up in silken strings   45
With twenty odd-conceited° true-love knots.°
To be fantastic may become a youth
Of greater time° than I shall show to be.
    LUC. What fashion, madam, shall I make your
      breeches?
    JUL. That fits as well as, "Tell me, good my
      lord,   50
What compass° will you wear your farthingale?"°

---

11. **Unheedful:** thoughtless. **heedfully:** after due thought.
12. **wants:** lacks. 13. **learn:** teach. 17. **leave to:** cease from.
26. **Ethiope:** Ethiopian. 35. **Myself . . . competitor:** i.e., he
has let me into his counsel as his partner (*competitor*). 37. **pretended:** intended. 41. **blunt:** stupid. 43. **drift:** idea, plan.
    Sc. vii: 3. **table:** notebook. 4. **charactered:** written.
5. **lesson:** teach. **mean:** means. 6. **with my honor:** without
losing my honor.

10. **measure:** pass through. 18. **inly:** inward. 22. **qualify:**
moderate. 28. **enameled:** shiny. 29. **sedge:** rush. 38. **Elysium:** Paradise. 39. **habit:** costume. 42. **weeds:** garments.
46. **odd-conceited:** fantastic. **true-love knots:** lovelocks. Young
men of fashion often wore their hair long and sometimes gathered
into a curl hanging by the ear. 48. **time:** age. 50–51. **That
. . . farthingale:** i.e., you might as well ask a man what sort of
petticoat he wants. **compass:** circumference. **farthingale:** See
p. 94b.

Why even what fashion thou best likest, Lucetta.

LUC. You must needs have them with a codpiece,
madam.

JUL. Out, out, Lucetta! That will be ill-favored.°

LUC. A round hose,° madam, now's not worth a
pin,   55
Unless you have a codpiece to stick pins on.

JUL. Lucetta, as thou lovest me, let me have
What thou think'st meet, and is most mannerly.
But tell me, wench, how will the world repute me
For undertaking so unstaid° a journey?   60
I fear me, it will make me scandalized.

LUC. If you think so, then stay at home, and go
not.

JUL. Nay, that I will not.

LUC. Then never dream on infamy, but go.
If Proteus like your journey when you come,   65
No matter who's displeased when you are gone.
I fear me, he will scarce be pleased withal.

JUL. That is the least, Lucetta, of my fear.
A thousand oaths, an ocean of his tears,
And instances of infinite of love,°   70
Warrant me welcome to my Proteus.

LUC. All these are servants to deceitful men.

JUL. Base men, that use them to so base effect!
But truer stars did govern° Proteus' birth.
His words are bonds, his oaths are oracles,   75
His love sincere, his thoughts immaculate,
His tears pure messengers sent from his heart,
His heart as far from fraud as Heaven from earth.

LUC. Pray Heaven he prove so when you come to
him!

JUL. Now, as thou lovest me, do him not that
wrong,   80
To bear a hard opinion of his truth.
Only deserve my love by loving him,
And presently go with me to my chamber
To take a note of what I stand in need of
To furnish me upon my longing° journey.   85
All that is mine I leave at thy dispose,°
My goods, my lands, my reputation.
Only, in lieu thereof,° dispatch me hence.
Come, answer not, but to it presently!
I am impatient of my tarriance.°   [*Exeunt.*]   90

53–55. codpiece ... hose: See Pl. 8c, Pl. 8b and p. 93b.   54. ill-
favored: ugly.   60. unstaid: unbecoming.   70. infinite of love:
the infinity of his love.   74. stars ... govern: See App. I.
85. longing: caused by longing.   86. dispose: disposal.   88. in
... thereof: in exchange.   90. tarriance: delay.

Act III

SCENE I. *Milan. Anteroom in the* DUKE's *palace.*

[*Enter* DUKE, THURIO, *and* PROTEUS.]

DUKE. Sir Thurio, give us leave,° I pray, awhile.
We have some secrets to confer about.
                [*Exit* THURIO.]
Now, tell me, Proteus, what's your will with me?

PRO. My gracious lord, that which I would dis-
cover°
The law of friendship bids me to conceal;   5
But when I call to mind your gracious favors
Done to me, undeserving as I am,
My duty pricks° me on to utter that
Which else no worldly good should draw from me.
Know, worthy Prince, Sir Valentine, my friend,   10
This night intends to steal away your daughter.
Myself am one made privy to° the plot.
I know you have determined to bestow her
On Thurio, whom your gentle daughter hates,
And should she thus be stol'n away from you,   15
It would be much vexation to your age.
Thus, for my duty's sake, I rather chose
To cross my friend in his intended drift
Than, by concealing it, heap on your head
A pack of sorrows which would press you down,
Being unprevented, to your timeless° grave.   21

DUKE. Proteus, I thank thee for thine honest
care,
Which to requite, command me while I live.
This love of theirs myself have often seen,
Haply when they have judged me fast asleep,   25
And oftentimes have purposed to forbid
Sir Valentine her company and my Court.
But, fearing lest my jealous aim° might err,
And so unworthily disgrace the man —
A rashness that I ever yet have shunned —   30
I gave him gentle looks, thereby to find
That which thyself hast now disclosed to me.
And, that thou mayst perceive my fear of this,
Knowing that tender youth is soon suggested,°
I nightly lodge her in an upper tower,   35
The key whereof myself have ever kept,
And thence she cannot be conveyed away.

PRO. Know, noble lord, they have devised a mean
How he her chamber window will ascend,
And with a corded ladder° fetch her down;   40
For which the youthful lover now is gone,
And this way comes he with it presently,
Where, if it please you, you may intercept him.

Act III, Sc. i: 1. give us leave: a polite way of saying leave us.
4. discover: reveal.   8. pricks: spurs.   12. privy to: in the
secret of.   21. timeless: untimely.   28. aim: guess, suspicion.
34. suggested: tempted.   40. corded ladder: ladder of cords.

But, good my lord, do it so cunningly
That my discovery be not aimed at;°   45
For, love of you, not hate unto my friend,
Hath made me publisher of this pretense.°
    DUKE. Upon mine honor, he shall never know
That I had any light from thee of this.
    PRO. Adieu, my lord. Sir Valentine is coming.
                                        [*Exit.*]

[*Enter* VALENTINE.]
    DUKE. Sir Valentine, whither away so fast?   51
    VAL. Please it your Grace, there is a messenger
That stays to bear my letters to my friends,
And I am going to deliver them.
    DUKE. Be they of much import?   55
    VAL. The tenor° of them doth but signify
My health and happy being at your Court.
    DUKE. Nay then, no matter. Stay with me awhile.
I am to break with thee of some affairs   59
That touch thee near, wherein thou must be secret.
'Tis not unknown to thee that I have sought
To match my friend Sir Thurio to my daughter.
    VAL. I know it well, my lord; and, sure, the
        match
Were rich and honorable. Besides, the gentleman
Is full of virtue, bounty, worth, and qualities   65
Beseeming such a wife as your fair daughter.
Cannot your Grace win her to fancy him?
    DUKE. No, trust me. She is peevish, sullen, fro-
        ward,
Proud, disobedient, stubborn, lacking duty,
Neither regarding that she is my child,   70
Nor fearing me as if I were her father.
And, may I say to thee, this pride of hers,
Upon advice,° hath drawn° my love from her;
And, where I thought the remnant of mine age   74
Should have been cherished by her childlike duty,
I now am full resolved to take a wife,
And turn her out to who will take her in.
Then let her beauty be her wedding dower.
For me and my possessions she esteems not.
    VAL. What would your Grace have me to do in
        this?   80
    DUKE. There is a lady in Verona° here
Whom I affect,° but she is nice and coy,°
And naught esteems my agèd eloquence.
Now, therefore, would I have thee to my tutor —
For long agone I have forgot to court;   85
Besides, the fashion of the time is changed —
How and which way I may bestow myself
To be regarded in her sun-bright eye.
    VAL. Win her with gifts, if she respect not words.
Dumb jewels often in their silent kind   90

More than quick words do move a woman's mind.
    DUKE. But she did scorn a present that I sent her.
    VAL. A woman sometime scorns° what best con-
        tents her.
Send her another. Never give her o'er,°
For scorn at first makes after-love the more.   95
If she do frown, 'tis not in hate of you,
But rather to beget more love in you.
If she do chide, 'tis not to have you gone;
For why,° the fools are mad, if left alone.
Take no repulse, whatever she doth say.   100
For "get you gone," she doth not mean "away!"
Flatter and praise, commend, extol their graces.
Though ne'er so black, say they have angels' faces.
That man that hath a tongue, I say, is no man
If with his tongue he cannot win a woman.   105
    DUKE. But she I mean is promised by her friends
Unto a youthful gentleman of worth,
And kept severely from resort of men,
That no man hath access by day to her.
    VAL. Why, then, I would resort to her by night.
    DUKE. Aye, but the doors be locked, and keys
        kept safe,   111
That no man hath recourse to her by night.
    VAL. What lets° but one may enter at her win-
        dow?
    DUKE. Her chamber is aloft, far from the ground,
And built so shelving that one cannot climb it   115
Without apparent° hazard of his life.
    VAL. Why, then, a ladder, quaintly made of
        cords,
To cast up with a pair of anchoring hooks
Would serve to scale another Hero's tower,
So bold Leander° would adventure it.   120
    DUKE. Now, as thou art a gentleman of blood,°
Advise me where I may have such a ladder.
    VAL. When would you use it? Pray, sir, tell me
        that.
    DUKE. This very night, for Love is like a child
That longs for everything that he can come by.
    VAL. By seven o'clock I'll get you such a ladder.
    DUKE. But, hark thee, I will go to her alone.   127
How shall I best convey the ladder thither?
    VAL. It will be light, my lord, that you may bear
        it
Under a cloak that is of any length.   130
    DUKE. A cloak as long as thine will serve the
        turn?
    VAL. Aye, my good lord.
    DUKE.   Then let me see thy cloak.
I'll get me one of such another length.
    VAL. Why, any cloak will serve the turn, my
        lord.

45. aimed at: guessed.   **47. pretense:** plot.   **56. tenor:** drift.
73. advice: consideration.   **drawn:** withdrawn, removed.
81. Verona: Shakespeare seems to have forgotten that his *Two Gentlemen* are now in Milan, not Verona.   **82. affect:** fancy. **nice . . . coy:** fastidious and shy.

93. scorns: pretends to dislike.   **94. give . . . o'er:** give up trying.   **99. For why:** because.   **113. lets:** hinders.   **116. apparent:** obvious.   **119–20. Hero . . . Leander:** See *T Gent* Intro. p. 365a.   **121. blood:** "courage" and "good family."

DUKE. How shall I fashion me° to wear a cloak?
I pray thee, let me feel thy cloak upon me.   136
What letter is this same? What's here? " To
    Silvia "!
And here an engine° fit for my proceeding!
I'll be so bold to break the seal for once.   [*Reads.*]
" My thoughts do harbor with my Silvia nightly,
   And slaves they are to me that send them flying.
Oh, could their master come and go as lightly,   142
   Himself would lodge where senseless they are
     lying!
My herald thoughts in thy pure bosom rest them,
   While I, their king, that thither them importune,
Do curse the grace that with such grace° hath
    blessed them,   146
   Because myself do want my servants' fortune.
I curse myself, for they are sent by me,
That they should harbor where their lord would
    be."
What's here?   150
   " Silvia, this night I will enfranchise thee."
'Tis so, and here's the ladder for the purpose.
Why, Phaethon° — for thou art Merops' son —
Wilt thou aspire to guide the heavenly car,°
And with thy daring folly burn the world?   155
Wilt thou reach stars because they shine on thee?
Go, base intruder. Overweening slave!
Bestow thy fawning smiles on equal mates,°
And think my patience, more than thy desert,
Is privilege for thy departure hence.   160
Thank me for this more than for all the favors
Which all too much I have bestowed on thee.
But if thou linger in my territories
Longer than swiftest expedition°
Will give thee time to leave our royal Court,   165
By Heaven, my wrath shall far exceed the love
I ever bore my daughter or thyself.
Be gone! I will not hear thy vain excuse;
But, as thou lovest thy life, make speed from hence.
                                   [*Exit.*]
VAL. And why not death rather than living tor-
   ment?   170
To die is to be banished from myself,
And Silvia is myself. Banished from her
Is self from self — a deadly banishment!
What light is light, if Silvia be not seen?
What joy is joy, if Silvia be not by?   175
Unless it be to think that she is by,

And feed upon the shadow° of perfection.
Except I be by Silvia in the night,
There is no music in the nightingale.
Unless I look on Silvia in the day,   180
There is no day for me to look upon.
She is my essence,° and I leave to be,
If I be not by her fair influence°
Fostered, illumined, cherished, kept alive.
I fly not death to fly his deadly doom.   185
Tarry I here, I but attend on death,
But fly I hence, I fly away from life.
         [*Enter* PROTEUS *and* LAUNCE.]
   PRO. Run, boy, run, run, and seek him out.
   LAUN. Soho,° soho!
   PRO. What seest thou?   190
   LAUN. Him we go to find. There's not a hair on's
head but 'tis a Valentine.°
   PRO. Valentine?
   VAL. No.
   PRO. Who then? His spirit?   195
   VAL. Neither.
   PRO. What then?
   VAL. Nothing.
   LAUN. Can nothing speak? Master, shall I strike?
   PRO. Who wouldst thou strike?   200
   LAUN. Nothing.
   PRO. Villain, forbear.
   LAUN. Why, sir, I'll strike nothing. I pray
   you ——
   PRO. Sirrah, I say, forbear. Friend Valentine, a
word.
   VAL. My ears are stopt, and cannot hear good
news,   205
So much of bad already hath possessed them.
   PRO. Then in dumb silence will I bury mine,
For they are harsh, untunable, and bad.
   VAL. Is Silvia dead?
   PRO. No, Valentine.   210
   VAL. No Valentine, indeed, for sacred Silvia.
Hath she forsworn me?
   PRO. No, Valentine.
   VAL. No Valentine, if Silvia have forsworn me.
What is your news?   215
   LAUN. Sir, there is a proclamation that you are
vanished.
   PRO. That thou art banishèd — oh, that's the
news! —
From hence, from Silvia, and from me thy friend.
   VAL. Oh, I have fed upon this woe already,
And now excess of it will make me surfeit.°   220
Doth Silvia know that I am banishèd?
   PRO. Aye, aye, and she hath offered to the
   doom —

---

135. **fashion me:** get used.   138. **engine:** device.   146. **grace**
. . . grace: gracious kindness . . . favor.   153–55. **Phaethon . . .**
world: Phaethon was the son of Helios the sun god by Clymene,
the wife of Merops. He asked to be allowed to drive his father's
chariot, but he was unable to control the horses and came so near
to burning up the world that Jupiter slew him with a thunderbolt.
Phaethon thus became the pattern of rash, presumptuous youth.
154. **car:** chariot.   158. **equal mates:** women of your own
humble rank. Mates is often used in a contemptuous sense. See
Shrew, I.i.58.   164. **expedition:** speed — a five-syllable word.

177. **shadow:** imitation, idea.   182. **essence:** concentration of
perfection.   183. **influence:** heavenly power. See App. 1.
189. **Soho:** a hunter's cry when following the hare.   192. **Valen-**
tine: i.e., true lover.   220. **surfeit:** feel sick.

Which, unreversed,° stands in effectual force —
A sea of melting pearl which some call tears.
Those at her father's churlish feet she tendered;
With them, upon her knees, her humble self,   226
Wringing her hands, whose whiteness so became them
As if but now they waxèd pale for woe.
But neither bended knees, pure hands held up,
Sad sighs, deep groans, nor silver-shedding tears,
Could penetrate her uncompassionate sire;   231
But Valentine, if he be ta'en, must die.
Besides, her intercession chafed him so,
When she for thy repeal° was suppliant,
That to close prison he commanded her   235
With many bitter threats of biding there.
    VAL. No more, unless the next word that thou speak'st
Have some malignant power upon my life.
If so, I pray thee, breathe it in mine ear,
As ending anthem° of my endless dolor.   240
    PRO. Cease to lament for that thou canst not help,
And study help for that which thou lament'st.
Time is the nurse and breeder of all good.
Here if thou stay, thou canst not see thy love.
Besides, thy staying will abridge thy life.   245
Hope is a lover's staff. Walk hence with that,
And manage it against despairing thoughts.
Thy letters may be here, though thou art hence,
Which, being writ to me, shall be delivered
Even in the milk-white bosom of thy love.   250
The time now serves not to expostulate.°
Come, I'll convey thee through the city gate,
And, ere I part with thee, confer at large
Of all that may concern thy love affairs.
As thou lovest Silvia, though not for thyself,   255
Regard thy danger, and along° with me!
    VAL. I pray thee, Launce, an if thou seest my boy,
Bid him make haste, and meet me at the North Gate.
    PRO. Go, sirrah, find him out. Come, Valentine.
    VAL. O my dear Silvia! Hapless Valentine!   260
    [Exeunt VALENTINE and PROTEUS.]
    LAUN. I am but a fool, look you, and yet I have
the wit to think my master is a kind of a knave.
But that's all one, if he be but one knave. He lives
not now that knows me to be in love, yet I am in
love. But a team of horse shall not pluck that   265
from me, nor who 'tis I love. And yet 'tis a woman,
but what woman, I will not tell myself. And yet 'tis
a milkmaid. Yet 'tis not a maid, for she hath had
gossips.° Yet 'tis a maid, for she is her master's
maid, and serves for wages. She hath more   270
qualities than a water spaniel — which is much in

a bare° Christian. [Pulling out a paper] Here is
the cate-log of her condition. "Imprimis,° she can
fetch and carry." Why, a horse can do no   275
more. Nay, a horse cannot fetch, but only carry;
therefore is she better than a jade.° "Item, she can
milk"; look you, a sweet virtue in a maid with
clean hands.
    [Enter SPEED.]
    SPEED. How now, Signior Launce! What news
with your mastership?   280
    LAUN. With my master's ship? Why, it is at sea.
    SPEED. Well, your old vice still; mistake the word.
What news, then, in your paper?
    LAUN. The blackest news that ever thou heard-
est.   286
    SPEED. Why, man, how black?
    LAUN. Why, as black as ink.
    SPEED. Let me read them.
    LAUN. Fie on thee, jolt-head!° Thou canst not
read.
    SPEED. Thou liest. I can.   292
    LAUN. I will try thee. Tell me this. Who begot
thee?
    SPEED. Marry, the son of my grandfather.
    LAUN. O illiterate loiterer! It was the son of thy
grandmother. This proves that thou canst not read.
    SPEED. Come, fool, come. Try me in thy paper.
    LAUN. There, and Saint Nicholas be thy speed!°
    SPEED. [Reads] "Imprimis, she can milk."   302
    LAUN. Aye, that she can.
    SPEED. "Item, she brews good ale."
    LAUN. And thereof comes the proverb:
"Blessing of your heart, you brew good ale."
    SPEED. "Item, she can sew."
    LAUN. That's as much as to say, "Can she so?"
    SPEED. "Item, she can knit."   310
    LAUN. What need a man care for a stock with a
wench when she can knit him a stock?°
    SPEED. "Item, she can wash and scour."
    LAUN. A special virtue, for then she need not be
washed and scoured.
    SPEED. "Item, she can spin."
    LAUN. Then may I set the world on wheels,°
when she can spin for her living.   319
    SPEED. "Item, she hath many nameless° virtues."
    LAUN. That's as much as to say bastard virtues,
that, indeed, know not their fathers, and therefore
have no names.
    SPEED. "Here follow her vices."
    LAUN. Close at the heels of her virtues.
    SPEED. "Item, she is not to be kissed fasting, in

223. unreversed: unless reversed.   234. repeal: recall from banishment.   240. ending anthem: funeral hymn, requiem.
251. expostulate: argue.   256. along: come along.   269. gossips:
godparents — for her bastards.

272. bare: simple.   274. Imprimis: firstly — the usual beginning
in an inventory. The clauses following begin with Item.
277. jade: third-rate horse.   290. jolt-head: blockhead.
301. speed: aid. St. Nicholas is the patron saint of young scholars.
311–12. stock . . . stock: dowry . . . stocking.   318. set . . .
wheels: have a roaring time.   320. nameless: too many to be
named.

respect of her breath."

LAUN. Well, that fault may be mended with a breakfast. Read on.

SPEED. "Item, she hath a sweet mouth."   330

LAUN. That makes amends for her sour breath.

SPEED. "Item, she doth talk in her sleep."

LAUN. It's no matter for that, so she sleep not in her talk.

SPEED. "Item, she is slow in words."

LAUN. O villain, that set this down among her vices! To be slow in words is a woman's only virtue. I pray thee out with 't, and place it for her chief virtue.   340

SPEED. "Item, she is proud."

LAUN. Out with that too. It was Eve's legacy, and cannot be ta'en from her.

SPEED. "Item, she hath no teeth."

LAUN. I care not for that neither, because I love crusts.

SPEED. "Item, she is curst."°   348

LAUN. Well, the best is, she hath no teeth to bite.

SPEED. "Item, she will often praise her liquor."

LAUN. If her liquor be good, she shall. If she will not, I will, for good things should be praised.

SPEED. "Item, she is too liberal."

LAUN. Of her tongue she cannot, for that's writ down she is slow of. Of her purse she shall not, for that I'll keep shut. Now of another thing she may, and that cannot I help. Well, proceed.   360

SPEED. "Item, she hath more hair than wit, and more faults than hairs, and more wealth than faults."

LAUN. Stop there. I'll have her. She was mine, and not mine, twice or thrice in that last article. Rehearse that once more.   366

SPEED. "Item, she hath more hair than wit "——

LAUN. More hair than wit? It may be. I'll prove it. The cover of the salt° hides the salt, and therefore it is more than the salt. The hair that 370 covers the wit is more than the wit, for the greater hides the less. What's next?

SPEED. "And more faults than hairs "——

LAUN. That's monstrous. Oh, that that were out!

SPEED. "And more wealth than faults."   376

LAUN. Why, that word makes the faults gracious. Well, I'll have her; and if it be a match, as nothing is impossible——

SPEED. What then?   380

LAUN. Why, then will I tell thee — that thy master stays for thee at the North Gate?

SPEED. For me?

LAUN. For thee! Aye, who art thou? He hath stayed for a better man than thee.

SPEED. And must I go to him?

LAUN. Thou must run to nim, for thou hast stayed so long that going° will scarce serve the turn.   389

SPEED. Why didst not tell me sooner? Pox° of your love letters!   [*Exit.*]

LAUN. Now will he be swinged for reading my letter — an unmannerly slave, that will thrust himself into secrets! I'll after, to rejoice in the boy's correction.   [*Exit.*]

SCENE II. *The same. The* DUKE's *palace.*

[*Enter* DUKE *and* THURIO.]

DUKE. Sir Thurio, fear not but that she will love you,
Now Valentine is banished from her sight.

THU. Since his exíle she hath despised me most,
Forsworn my company, and railed at me,
That I am desperate of obtaining her.   5

DUKE. This weak impréss of love is as a figure
Trenchèd° in ice, which with an hour's heat
Dissolves to water and doth lose his form.
A little time will melt her frozen thoughts,
And worthless Valentine shall be forgot.   10

[*Enter* PROTEUS.]

How now, Sir Proteus! Is your countryman,
According to our proclamation, gone?

PRO. Gone, my good lord.

DUKE. My daughter takes his going grievously.

PRO. A little time, my lord, will kill that grief.

DUKE. So I believe, but Thurio thinks not so.   16
Proteus, the good conceit° I hold of thee —
For thou hast shown some sign of good desert —
Makes me the better to confer with thee.

PRO. Longer than I prove loyal to your Grace   20
Let me not live to look upon your Grace.

DUKE. Thou know'st how willingly I would effect
The match between Sir Thurio and my daughter.

PRO. I do, my lord.

DUKE. And also, I think, thou art not ignorant
How she opposes her against my will.   26

PRO. She did, my lord, when Valentine was here.

DUKE. Aye, and perversely she persévers so.
What might we do to make the girl forget
The love of Valentine, and love Sir Thurio?   30

PRO. The best way is to slander Valentine
With falsehood, cowardice and poor descent,
Three things that women highly hold in hate.

DUKE. Aye, but she'll think that it is spoke in hate.

PRO. Aye, if his enemy deliver° it.   35
Therefore it must with circumstance° be spoken

---

348. **curst:** shrewish.   369. **salt:** salt cellar. The Elizabethan salt cellar was dignified with a cover and stood in the middle of the table.

388. **going:** walking.   390. **Pox:** plague, lit., venereal disease.
Sc. ii: 7. **Trenched:** cut, incised.   17. **conceit:** opinion.
35. **deliver:** utter.   36. **circumstance:** circumstantial evidence.

By one whom she esteemeth as his friend.
    DUKE. Then you must undertake to slander him.
    PRO. And that, my lord, I shall be loath to do.
'Tis an ill office for a gentleman,   40
Especially against his very friend.
    DUKE. Where your good word cannot advantage
      him,
Your slander never can endamage him.
Therefore the office is indifferent,°
Being entreated to it by your friend.   45
    PRO. You have prevailed, my lord. If I can do it
By aught that I can speak in his dispraise,
She shall not long continue love to him.
But say this weed her love from Valentine,°
It follows not that she will love Sir Thurio.   50
    THU. Therefore, as you unwind her love from
      him,
Lest it should ravel° and be good to none,
You must provide to bottom° it on me,
Which must be done by praising me as much
As you in worth dispraise Sir Valentine.   55
    DUKE. And, Proteus, we dare trust you in this
      kind,
Because we know, on Valentine's report,
You are already Love's firm votary,
And cannot soon revolt and change your mind.
Upon this warrant shall you have access   60
Where you with Silvia may confer at large.°
For she is lumpish, heavy, melancholy,
And, for your friend's sake, will be glad of you;
Where you may temper° her by your persuasion
To hate young Valentine and love my friend.   65
    PRO. As much as I can do, I will effect.
But you, Sir Thurio, are not sharp enough.
You must lay lime° to tangle her desires
By wailful sonnets, whose composèd° rhymes
Should be full fraught with serviceable vows.°   70
    DUKE. Aye,
Much is the force of heaven-bred poesy.
    PRO. Say that upon the altar of her beauty
You sacrifice your tears, your sighs, your heart.
Write till your ink be dry, and with your tears   75
Moist it again; and frame some feeling line
That may discover° such integrity.°
For Orpheus'° lute was strung with poets' sinews,
Whose golden touch could soften steel and stones,
Make tigers tame, and huge leviathans°   80
Forsake unsounded deeps to dance on sands.
After your dire-lamenting elegies,

Visit by night your lady's chamber window
With some sweet consort.° To their instruments
Tune a deploring dump.° The night's dead silence
Will well become such sweet-complaining griev-
    ance.   86
This, or else nothing, will inherit° her.
    DUKE. This discipline shows thou hast been in
      love.
    THU. And thy advice this night I'll put in prac-
      tice.
Therefore, sweet Proteus, my direction giver,   90
Let us into the city presently
To sort° some gentlemen well skilled in music.
I have a sonnet that will serve the turn
To give the onset° to thy good advice.
    DUKE. About it, gentlemen!   95
    PRO. We'll wait upon your Grace till after supper,
And afterward determine our proceedings.
    DUKE. Even now about it! I will pardon you.
                             [*Exeunt.*]

Act IV

SCENE I. *The frontiers of Mantua. A forest.*

[*Enter certain* OUTLAWS.]
    1. OUT. Fellows, stand fast. I see a passenger.°
    2. OUT. If there be ten, shrink not, but down with
      'em.
         [*Enter* VALENTINE *and* SPEED.]
    3. OUT. Stand, sir, and throw us that° you have
      about ye.
If not, we'll make you sit, and rifle you.
    SPEED. Sir, we are undone. These are the villains
That all the travelers do fear so much.   6
    VAL. My friends ——
    1. OUT. That's not so, sir. We are your enemies.
    2. OUT. Peace! We'll hear him.
    3. OUT. Aye, by my beard, will we, for he's a
      proper° man.   10
    VAL. Then know that I have little wealth to lose.
A man I am crossed with adversity.
My riches are these poor habiliments,°
Of which, if you should here disfurnish° me,
You take the sum and substance that I have.   15
    2. OUT. Whither travel you?
    VAL. To Verona.
    1. OUT. Whence came you?
    VAL. From Milan.
    3. OUT. Have you long sojourned there?   20

---

44. indifferent: neither good nor bad.   49. weed . . . Valentine: weed out her love for Valentine.   52. ravel: tangle.   53. bottom: tie. A *bottom* is a skein of thread; thus *to bottom* is to tie the end of the thread to the spool.   61. at large: freely.   64. temper: make soft (like wax), and so reshape.   68. lime: birdlime. 69. composed: elaborately written.   70. serviceable vows: vows that you are her servant.   77. discover: reveal. integrity: single-hearted devotion.   78. Orpheus: See *M of Ven*, V.i.80,n. 80. leviathans: whales.

84. consort: party of musicians. See *R & J*, III.i.48–52. 85. dump: doleful tune.   87. inherit: obtain.   92. sort: select. 94. give . . . onset: make a beginning.
    Act IV, Sc. i: 1. passenger: traveler on foot.   3. that: what, i.e., your money.   10. proper: fine, handsome.   13. habiliments: clothes.   14. disfurnish: deprive.

VAL. Some sixteen months, and longer might have
    stayed
If crookèd fortune had not thwarted me.
  1. OUT. What, were you banished thence?
  VAL. I was.
  2. OUT. For what offense?   25
  VAL. For that which now torments me to re-
    hearse.
I killed a man, whose death I much repent;
But yet I slew him manfully in fight,
Without false vantage° or base treachery.
  1. OUT. Why, ne'er repent it, if it were done so. 30
But were you banished for so small a fault?
  VAL. I was, and held me glad of such a doom.
  2. OUT. Have you the tongues?°
  VAL. My youthful travel therein made me happy,°
Or else I often had been miserable.   35
  3. OUT. By the bare scalp of Robin Hood's fat
    friar,°
This fellow were a king for our wild faction!°
  1. OUT. We'll have him. Sirs, a word.
  SPEED. Master, be one of them. It's an honorable
kind of thievery.   40
  VAL. Peace, villain!
  2. OUT. Tell us this. Have you anything to take
    to?
  VAL. Nothing but my fortune.
  3. OUT. Know, then, that some of us are gentle-
    men
Such as the fury of ungoverned° youth   45
Thrust from the company of awful° men.
Myself was from Verona banishèd
For practicing° to steal away a lady.
An heir, and near allied unto the Duke.
  2. OUT. And I from Mantua, for a gentleman 50
Who, in my mood,° I stabbed unto the heart.
  1. OUT. And I for° such like petty crimes as
    these.
But to the purpose — for we cite° our faults,
That they may hold excused our lawless lives;
And partly, seeing you are beautified   55
With goodly shape, and by your own report
A linguist, and a man of such perfection
As we do in our quality° much want——
  2. OUT. Indeed, because you are a banished man,
Therefore above the rest we parley to you. 60
Are you content to be our general?
To make a virtue of necessity,
And live, as we do, in this wilderness?
  3. OUT. What say'st thou? Wilt thou be of our
    consort?°

Say aye, and be the captain of us all.   65
We'll do thee homage and be ruled by thee,
Love thee as our commander and our king.
  1. OUT. But if thou scorn our courtesy, thou diest.
  2. OUT. Thou shalt not live to brag what we have
    offered.
  VAL. I take your offer, and will live with you, 70
Provided that you do no outrages
On silly° women or poor passengers.
  3. OUT. No, we detest such vile base practices.
Come, go with us, we'll bring thee to our crews,
And show thee all the treasure we have got,   75
Which, with ourselves, all rest at thy dispose.°
                            [Exeunt.]

SCENE II. *Milan. Outside the* DUKE'S *palace,
under* SILVIA'S *chamber.*

[Enter PROTEUS.*]*
  PRO. Already have I been false to Valentine,
And now I must be as unjust to Thurio.
Under the color° of commending him,
I have access my own love to prefer.
But Silvia is too fair, too true, too holy,   5
To be corrupted with my worthless gifts.
When I protest true loyalty to her,
She twits me with my falsehood to my friend.
When to her beauty I commend° my vows,
She bids me think how I have been forsworn 10
In breaking faith with Julia whom I loved;
And notwithstanding all her sudden quips,°
The least whereof would quell a lover's hope,
Yet, spaniel-like,° the more she spurns my love,
The more it grows, and fawneth on her still. 15
But here comes Thurio. Now must we to her win-
    dow,
And give some evening music to her ear.
      [Enter THURIO *and* MUSICIANS.*]*
  THU. How now, Sir Proteus, are you crept before
    us?
  PRO. Aye, gentle Thurio, for you know that love
Will creep in service where it cannot go.°   20
  THU. Aye, but I hope, sir, that you love not here.
  PRO. Sir, but I do, or else I would be hence.
  THU. Who? Silvia?
  PRO.   Aye, Silvia, for your sake.
  THU. I thank you for your own. Now, gentle-
    men,
Let's tune, and to it lustily awhile.   25
    [Enter, at a distance, HOST, *and* JULIA *in boy's
               clothes.]*

---

29. false vantage: unfair odds. **33. tongues:** knowledge of
languages. **34. happy:** fortunate. **36. Robin . . . friar:** Friar
Tuck. The outlaw naturally thinks of Robin Hood and his
company. **37. faction:** party, gang. **45. ungoverned:** lawless.
46. awful: respectable. **48. practicing:** plotting. **51. mood:**
moody fit. **52. for:** because of. **53. cite:** recite. **58. quality:**
profession. **64. consort:** company.

72. silly: simple. **76. dispose:** disposal.
  Sc. ii: 3. color: pretext. **9. commend:** recommend. **12. quips:**
taunts. **14. spaniel-like:** Shakespeare seems not to have liked
spaniels. See *MND,* II.i.203–07. **20. go:** walk briskly. See
Sonnets, 130:11.

HOST. Now, my young guest, methinks you're ally-cholly.° I pray you, why is it?

JUL. Marry, mine host, because I cannot be merry.

HOST. Come, we'll have you merry. I'll bring 30
you where you shall hear music, and see the gentleman that you asked for.

JUL. But shall I hear him speak?

HOST. Aye, that you shall.

JUL. That will be music.   [*Music plays.*] 35

HOST. Hark, hark!

JUL. Is he among these?

HOST. Aye, but, peace! Let's hear 'em.

SONG.

Who is Silvia? What is she,
  That all our swains° commend her? 40
Holy, fair, and wise is she;
  The Heaven such grace did lend her,
That she might admirèd be.

Is she kind as she is fair?
  For beauty lives with° kindness. 45
Love doth to her eyes repair
  To help him of his blindness,
And, being helped, inhabits there.

Then to Silvia let us sing,
  That Silvia is excelling; 50
She excels each mortal thing
  Upon the dull earth dwelling.
To her let us garlands bring.

HOST. How now! Are you sadder than you 55
were before? How do you, man? The music likes° you not.

JUL. You mistake. The musician likes me not.

HOST. Why, my pretty youth?

JUL. He plays false, Father.

HOST. How? Out of tune on the strings? 60

JUL. Not so, but yet so false that he grieves my very heartstrings.

HOST. You have a quick ear.

JUL. Aye, I would I were deaf. It makes me have a slow heart. 65

HOST. I perceive you delight not in music.

JUL. Not a whit, when it jars so.

HOST. Hark, what fine change° is in the music!

JUL. Aye, that change is the spite.

HOST. You would have them always play but one thing? 71

JUL. I would always have one play but one thing. But, host, doth this Sir Proteus that we talk on Often resort unto this gentlewoman?

HOST. I tell you what Launce, his man, told me —

he loved her out of all nick.° 75

JUL. Where is Launce?

HOST. Gone to seek his dog, which tomorrow, by his master's command, he must carry for a present to his lady. 80

JUL. Peace! Stand aside. The company parts.

PRO. Sir Thurio, fear not you. I will so plead That you shall say my cunning drift excels.

THU. Where meet we?

PRO.   At Saint Gregory's well.

THU.   Farewell.

[*Exeunt* THURIO *and* MUSICIANS.]
[*Enter* SILVIA *above.*]

PRO. Madam, good even to your ladyship. 85

SIL. I thank you for your music, gentlemen. Who is that that spake?

PRO. One, lady, if you knew his pure heart's truth,
You would quickly learn to know him by his voice.

SIL. Sir Proteus, as I take it. 90

PRO. Sir Proteus, gentle lady, and your servant.

SIL. What's your will?

PRO.   That I may compass° yours.

SIL. You have your wish. My will is even this:
That presently you hie° you home to bed.
Thou subtle, perjured, false, disloyal man! 95
Think'st thou I am so shallow, so conceitless,°
To be seducèd by thy flattery,
That hast deceived so many with thy vows?
Return, return, and make thy love amends.
For me — by this pale queen of night° I swear
I am so far from granting thy request 101
That I despise thee for thy wrongful suit,
And by and by intend to chide myself
Even for this time I spend in talking to thee.

PRO. I grant, sweet love, that I did love a lady,
But she is dead. 106

JUL. [*Aside*] 'Twere false, if I should speak it,
For I am sure she is not burièd.

SIL. Say that she be; yet Valentine thy friend
Survives, to whom, thyself art witness, 110
I am betrothed. And art thou not ashamed
To wrong him with thy importúnacy?

PRO. I likewise hear that Valentine is dead.

SIL. And so suppose am I, for in his grave
Assure thyself my love is burièd. 115

PRO. Sweet lady, let me rake it from the earth.

SIL. Go to thy lady's grave, and call hers thence;
Or, at the least, in hers sepúlcher thine.

JUL. [*Aside*] He heard° not that.

PRO. Madam, if your heart be so obdurate, 120
Vouchsafe me yet your picture for my love,
The picture that is hanging in your chamber.

---

27. **ally-cholly:** for "melancholy."   40. **swains:** young men.   45. **with:** by means of.   56. **likes:** pleases.   68. **change:** variety.   75. **nick:** reckoning — from the nick made in a tally. See *II Hen VI*, IV.vii.40,n.   92. **compass:** win.   94. **hie:** hasten.   96. **conceitless:** lacking in intelligence.   100. **pale . . . night:** Diana, the moon.   119. **heard:** took no notice of.

To that I'll speak, to that I'll sigh and weep.
For since the substance of your perfect self
Is else devoted,° I am but a shadow,°   125
And to your shadow will I make true love.

JUL. [*Aside*] If 'twere a substance, you would,
     sure, deceive it,
And make it but a shadow, as I am.

SIL. I am very loath to be your idol, sir,
But since your falsehood shall become you well   130
To worship shadows and adore false shapes,
Send to me in the morning, and I'll send it.
And so, good rest——

PRO.   As wretches have o'ernight
That wait for execution in the morn.
       [*Exeunt* PROTEUS *and* SILVIA *severally.*]

JUL. Host, will you go?   135

HOST. By my halidom,° I was fast asleep.

JUL. Pray you, where lies° Sir Proteus?

HOST. Marry, at my house. Trust me, I think 'tis
almost day.   139

JUL. Not so, but it hath been the longest night
That e'er I watched, and the most heaviest.
                     [*Exeunt.*]

SCENE III. *The same.*

[*Enter* EGLAMOUR.°]

EGL. This is the hour that Madam Silvia
Entreated me to call and know her mind.
There's some great matter she'd employ me in.
Madam, madam!

          [*Enter* SILVIA *above.*]

SIL. Who calls?

EGL.   Your servant and your friend.
One that attends your ladyship's command.   5

SIL. Sir Eglamour, a thousand times good mor-
     row.

EGL. As many, worthy lady, to yourself.
According to your ladyship's impose,°
I am thus early come to know what service
It is your pleasure to command me in.   10

SIL. O Eglamour, thou art a gentleman —
Think not I flatter, for I swear I do not —
Valiant, wise, remorseful,° well accomplished.
Thou art not ignorant what dear good will
I bear unto the banished Valentine,   15
Nor how my father would enforce me marry
Vain Thurio, whom my very soul abhors.
Thyself hast loved, and I have heard thee say
No grief did ever come so near thy heart
As when thy lady and thy true love died,   20

Upon whose grave thou vow'dst pure chastity.
Sir Eglamour, I would to° Valentine,
To Mantua, where I hear he makes abode,
And — for° the ways° are dangerous to pass —
I do desire thy worthy company,   25
Upon whose faith and honor I repose.
Urge not° my father's anger, Eglamour,
But think upon my grief, a lady's grief,
And on the justice of my flying hence
To keep me from a most unholy match,   30
Which Heaven and Fortune still rewards with
     plagues.
I do desire thee, even from a heart
As full of sorrows as the sea of sands,
To bear me company, and go with me;
If not, to hide what I have said to thee,   35
That I may venture to depart alone.

EGL. Madam, I pity much your grievances;
Which since I know they virtuously are placed,
I give consent to go along with you,
Recking as little what betideth me   40
As much I wish all good befortune° you.
When will you go?

SIL.   This evening coming.

EGL. Where shall I meet you?

SIL.   At Friar Patrick's cell,
Where I intend holy confession.

EGL. I will not fail your ladyship. Good morrow,
gentle lady.   45

SIL. Good morrow, kind Sir Eglamour.
               [*Exeunt severally.*]

SCENE IV. *The same.*

[*Enter* LAUNCE, *with his dog.*]

LAUN. When a man's servant shall play the cur
with him, look you, it goes hard: one that I brought
up of° a puppy; one that I saved from drowning
when three or four of his blind brothers and sisters
went to it! I have taught him, even as one would   5
say precisely, "thus I would teach a dog." I was
sent to deliver him as a present to Mistress Silvia
from my master, and I came no sooner into the dining chamber, but he steps me to her trencher°   10
and steals her capon's leg. Oh, 'tis a foul thing
when a cur cannot keep himself° in all companies!
I would have, as one should say, one that takes upon
him to be a dog indeed, to be, as it were, a dog at
all things. If I had not had more wit than he to   15
take a fault upon me that he did, I think verily he
had been hanged for 't. Sure as I live, he had suffered for 't. You shall judge. He thrusts me himself

125. devoted: vowed to another.   125–28. shadow . . . shadow
. . . shadow: inseparable follower . . . portrait . . . unreal nothing.   136. halidom: holy relic upon which an oath was sworn.
137. lies: lodges.
     Sc. iii: s.d., Eglamour: See *T Gent* Intro. p. 366a.   8. impose:
imposed command.   13. remorseful: full of pity.

22. to: go to.   24. for: because. ways: roads.   27. Urge not:
do not make an excuse of.   41. befortune: befall.
     Sc. iv: 3. of: from.   10. trencher: wooden plate.   12. keep
himself: hold himself in.

into the company of three or four gentlemanlike dogs under the Duke's table. He had not been 21 there — bless the mark!° — a pissing while,° but all the chamber smelt him. "Out with the dog!" says one. "What cur is that?" says another. "Whip him out," says the third. "Hang him up," says the Duke. I, having been acquainted with the smell 25 before, knew it was Crab, and goes me to the fellow that whips the dogs. "Friend," quoth I, "you mean to whip the dog?" "Aye, marry, do I," quoth he. "You do him the more wrong," 30 quoth I. "'Twas I did the thing you wot° of." He makes me no more ado, but whips me out of the chamber. How many masters would do this for his servant? Nay, I'll be sworn, I have sat in the stocks for puddings° he hath stolen, otherwise he 35 had been executed. I have stood on the pillory° for geese he hath killed, otherwise he had suffered for 't. — Thou thinkest not of this now. Nay, I remember the trick you served me when I took my leave of Madam Silvia. Did not I bid thee still 40 mark me and do as I do? When didst thou see me heave up my leg and make water against a gentlewoman's farthingale?° Didst thou ever see me do such a trick?

[*Enter* PROTEUS *and* JULIA.°]

PRO. Sebastian is thy name? I like thee well, And will employ thee in some service presently.

JUL. In what you please. I'll do what I can. 46

PRO. I hope thou wilt. [*To* LAUNCE] How now, you whoreson peasant!
Where have you been these two days loitering?

LAUN. Marry, sir, I carried Mistress Silvia the dog you bade me. 50

PRO. And what says she to my little jewel?°

LAUN. Marry, she says your dog was a cur, and tells you currish thanks is good enough for such a present.

PRO. But she received° my dog? 55

LAUN. No, indeed, did she not. Here have I brought him back again.

PRO. What, didst thou offer her this from me?

LAUN. Aye, sir. The other squirrel° was stolen from me by the hangman° boys in the market 60 place; and then I offered her mine own, who is a dog as big as ten of yours, and therefore the gift the greater.

PRO. Go get thee hence, and find my dog again, Or ne'er return again into my sight. 65

Away, I say! Stay'st thou to vex me here?

[*Exit* LAUNCE.]

A slave, that still an end° turns me to shame! Sebastian, I have entertained thee Partly that° I have need of such a youth That can with some discretion do my business — For 'tis no trusting to yond foolish lout — 71 But chiefly for thy face and thy behavior, Which, if my augury° deceive me not, Witness good bringing up, fortune, and truth. Therefore know thou, for this I entertain thee. 75 Go presently, and take this ring with thee. Deliver it to Madam Silvia.
She loved me well delivered° it to me.

JUL. It seems you loved not her to leave her token.
She is dead, belike?

PRO.   Not so. I think she lives. 80

JUL. Alas!

PRO. Why dost thou cry, "alas"?

JUL.   I cannot choose
But pity her.

PRO.   Wherefore shouldst thou pity her?

JUL. Because methinks that she loved you as well As you do love your lady Silvia. 85 She dreams on him that has forgot her love. You dote on her that cares not for your love. 'Tis pity love should be so contrary, And thinking on it makes me cry, "alas!"

PRO. Well, give her that ring, and therewithal This letter. That's her chamber. Tell my lady 91 I claim the promise for her heavenly picture. Your message done, hie home unto my chamber, Where thou shalt find me, sad and solitary. [*Exit.*]

JUL. How many women would do such a message? 95
Alas, poor Proteus! Thou hast entertained A fox to be the shepherd of thy lambs. Alas, poor fool! Why do I pity him That with his very heart despiseth me? Because he loves her, he despiseth me. 100 Because I love him, I must pity him. This ring I gave him when he parted from me To bind him to remember my good will, And now am I, unhappy messenger, To plead for that which I would not obtain, 105 To carry that which I would have refused, To praise his faith which I would have dispraised. I am my master's true-confirmèd° love, But cannot be true servant to my master Unless I prove false traitor to myself. 110 Yet will I woo for him, but yet so coldly, As, Heaven It knows, I would not have him speed.°

[*Enter* SILVIA, *attended.*]

22. bless . . . mark: a phrase used to apologize for some coarse word or regrettable action. while: time that it takes to. 31. wot: know.   34–36. stocks . . . pillory: See App. 10. 35. puddings: sausages.   43. farthingale: here used for petticoat. See p. 94b.   43. s.d., Julia: who is still disguised as a boy and remains so till the end of the play.   51. jewel: "precious." 55. received: accepted.   59. squirrel: little thing. The original and intended offering was a pretty little lap dog, not Launce's appalling cur.   60. hangman: emendation for "hangmans" in F1.

67. still an end: everlastingly.   69. that: because.   73. augury: ability to read signs.   78. delivered: i.e., who gave it. 108. true-confirmed: betrothed.   112. speed: succeed.

Gentlewoman, good day! I pray you be my mean
To bring me where to speak with Madam Silvia.
  SIL. What would you with her, if that I be she?
  JUL. If you be she, I do entreat your patience   116
To hear me speak the message I am sent on.
  SIL. From whom?
  JUL. From my master, Sir Proteus, madam.
  SIL. Oh, he sends you for a picture.   120
  JUL. Aye, madam.
  SIL. Ursula, bring my picture there.
                        [*She fetches the picture.*]
Go give your master this. Tell him from me:
One Julia, that his changing thoughts forget,   124
Would better fit his chamber than this shadow.°
  JUL. Madam, please you peruse this letter —
Pardon me, madam. I have unadvised
Delivered you a paper that I should not.
This is the letter to your ladyship.
  SIL. I pray thee let me look on that again.   130
  JUL. It may not be. Good madam, pardon me.
  SIL. There, hold!
I will not look upon your master's lines.
I know they are stuffed with protestations,
And full of new-found oaths which he will break
As easily as I do tear his paper.   136
  JUL. Madam, he sends your ladyship this ring.
  SIL. The more shame for him that he sends it me,
For I have heard him say a thousand times
His Julia gave it him at his departure.   140
Though his false finger have profaned the ring,
Mine shall not do his Julia so much wrong.
  JUL. She thanks you.
  SIL. What say'st thou?   144
  JUL. I thank you, madam, that you tender° her.
Poor gentlewoman! My master wrongs her much.
  SIL. Dost thou know her?
  JUL. Almost as well as I do know myself.
To think upon her woes I do protest
That I have wept a hundred several times.   150
  SIL. Belike she thinks that Proteus hath forsook
    her.
  JUL. I think she doth, and that's her cause of sor-
    row.
  SIL. Is she not passing° fair?
  JUL. She hath been fairer, madam, than she is.
When she did think my master loved her well,   155
She, in my judgment, was as fair as you;
But since she did neglect her looking glass
And threw her sun-expelling mask° away,
The air hath starved the roses in her cheeks
And pinched the lily tincture of her face,   160
That now she is become as black° as I.

  SIL. How tall was she?
  JUL. About my stature; for at Pentecost,
When all our pageants of delight were played,°
Our youth got me to play the woman's part,°   165
And I was trimmed° in Madam Julia's gown,
Which servèd me as fit, by all men's judgments,
As if the garment had been made for me.
Therefore I know she is about my height.
And at that time I made her weep agood,°   170
For I did play a lamentable part.
Madam 'twas Ariadne passioning°
For Theseus' perjury and unjust flight,°
Which I so lively acted with my tears
That my poor mistress, moved therewithal,   175
Wept bitterly; and would I might be dead,
If I in thought felt not her very sorrow!
  SIL. She is beholding° to thee, gentle youth.
Alas, poor lady, desolate and left!
I weep myself to think upon thy words.   180
Here, youth, there is my purse. I give thee this
For thy sweet mistress' sake, because thou lovest her.
Farewell.   [*Exit* SILVIA, *with attendants.*]
  JUL. And she shall thank you for 't, if e'er you
    know her.
A virtuous gentlewoman, mild and beautiful!   185
I hope my master's suit will be but cold,
Since she respects my mistress' love so much.
Alas, how love can trifle with itself!
Here is her picture. Let me see. I think,
If I had such a tire,° this face of mine   190
Were full as lovely as is this of hers.
And yet the painter flattered her a little,
Unless I flatter with myself too much.
Her hair is auburn, mine is perfect yellow.
If that be all the difference in his love,   195
I'll get me such a colored periwig.
Her eyes are gray° as glass, and so are mine.
Aye, but her forehead's low,° and mine's as high.
What should it be that he respects in her,
But I can make respective in myself°   200
If this fond° Love were not a blinded god?
Come, shadow, come, and take this shadow° up,

---

125. shadow: picture. See IV.ii.125–28.   145. tender: think kindly of.   153. passing: very.   158. sun-expelling mask: Fashionable ladies wore masks out of doors to protect their skins from sun tan and so preserve the roses-and-cream complexion which was greatly admired.   161. black: sunburned.

163–64. Pentecost . . . played: Miracle plays and other outdoor festivities were usually performed on Whitsunday (*Pentecost*), which falls in the early summer.   165. youth . . . part: Julia, whom Proteus takes to be a boy, would be a natural person to choose for a girl's part, since boys were chosen to take the parts of young women. See Gen. Intro. p. 59b.   166. trimmed: dressed up.   170. agood: plenty.   172–73. Ariadne . . . flight: Theseus went to Crete and there slew the monster Minotaur. Ariadne, the daughter of Minos, King of Crete, greatly aided him in the combat and afterward fled with him; but he left her asleep on the island of Naxos and sailed away without her. passioning: lamenting.   178. beholding: indebted.   190. tire: headdress.   197. gray: blue.   198. low: a low forehead was thought to denote lack of intelligence. See *Ant & Cleo*, III.iii. 36–37.   199–200. What . . . myself: i.e., what has she got that I have not?   201. fond: foolish.   202. shadow . . . shadow: shadow of what I was . . . picture — a repetition of IV.ii.125–26.

For 'tis thy rival. O thou senseless form,
Thou shalt be worshiped, kissed, loved, and
    adored!
And, were there sense in his idolatry,   205
My substance should be statue in thy stead.
I'll use thee kindly for thy mistress' sake,
That used me so; or else, by Jove I vow,
I should have scratched out your unseeing eyes 209
To make my master out of love with thee! [*Exit.*]

Act V

SCENE I. *Milan. An abbey.*

[*Enter* EGLAMOUR.]

EGL. The sun begins to gild the western sky,
And now it is about the very hour
That Silvia at Friar Patrick's cell should meet me.
She will not fail, for lovers break not hours
Unless it be to come before their time;   5
So much they spur their expedition.
See where she comes.
      [*Enter* SILVIA.]
             Lady, a happy evening!
SIL. Amen, amen! Go on, good Eglamour,
Out at the postern° by the abbey wall.
I fear I am attended° by some spies.   10
EGL. Fear not. The forest is not three leagues off.
If we recover° that, we are sure enough. [*Exeunt.*]

SCENE II. *The same. The* DUKE's *palace.*

[*Enter* THURIO, PROTEUS, *and* JULIA.]

THU. Sir Proteus, what says Silvia to my suit?
PRO. Oh, sir, I find her milder than she was,
And yet she takes exceptions° at your person.
THU. What, that my leg is too long?
PRO. No, that it is too little.   5
THU. I'll wear a boot to make it somewhat
    rounder.
JUL. [*Aside*] But love will not be spurred to what
    it loathes.
THU. What says she to my face?
PRO. She says it is a fair one.
THU. Nay then, the wanton lies. My face is
    black.   10
PRO. But pearls are fair, and the old saying is,
Black men are pearls in beauteous ladies' eyes.

JUL. [*Aside*] 'Tis true, such pearls as put out
    ladies' eyes,
For I had rather wink than look on them.
THU. How likes she my discourse?   15
PRO. Ill, when you talk of war.
THU. But well, when I discourse of love and
    peace?
JUL. [*Aside*] But better, indeed, when you hold
    your peace.
THU. What says she to my valor?
PRO. Oh, sir, she makes no doubt of that.   20
JUL. [*Aside*] She needs not, when she knows it
    cowardice.
THU. What says she to my birth?
PRO. That you are well derived.°
JUL. [*Aside*] True — from a gentleman to a fool.
THU. Considers she my possessions?   25
PRO. Oh, aye, and pities° them.
THU. Wherefore?
JUL. [*Aside*] That such an ass should owe°
  them.
PRO. That they are out by lease.°
JUL. Here comes the Duke.   30
      [*Enter* DUKE OF MILAN.]
DUKE. How now, Sir Proteus! How now, Thurio!
Which of you saw Sir Eglamour of late?
THU. Not I.
PRO.   Nor I.
DUKE.   Saw you my daughter?
PRO.   Neither.
DUKE. Why then,
She's fled unto that peasant Valentine,   35
And Eglamour is in her company.
'Tis true, for Friar Laurence met them both
As he in penance wandered through the forest.
Him he knew well, and guessed that it was she,
But, being masked, he was not sure of it.   40
Besides, she did intend confession
At Patrick's cell this even, and there she was not.
These likelihoods confirm her flight from hence.
Therefore, I pray you, stand not to discourse,
But mount you presently, and meet with me   45
Upon the rising of the mountain foot
That leads toward Mantua, whither they are fled.
Dispatch,° sweet gentlemen, and follow me.
                  [*Exit.*]
THU. Why, this it is to be a peevish° girl
That flies her fortune when it follows her.   50
I'll after, more to be revenged on Eglamour
Than for the love of reckless Silvia.   [*Exit.*]
PRO. And I will follow, more for Silvia's love
Than hate of Eglamour, that goes with her.   54
                  [*Exit.*]

Act V, Sc. i: **9. postern:** small door. **10. attended:** followed.
12. recover: reach.
    Sc. ii: **3. takes exceptions:** objects to.

23. well derived: come of a good family (but are a degenerate).
26. pities: despises. **28. owe:** own. **29. by lease:** i.e., in the
temporary possession of a fool. **48. Dispatch:** make haste.
49. peevish: foolish.

JUL. And I will follow, more to cross that love
Than hate for Silvia, that is gone for love. [*Exit.*]

SCENE III. *The frontiers of Mantua.*
The forest.

[*Enter* OUTLAWS *with* SILVIA.]

I. OUT. Come, come,
Be patient. We must bring you to our captain.
SIL. A thousand more mischances than this one
Have learned me how to brook° this patiently.
2. OUT. Come, bring her away.   5
I. OUT. Where is the gentleman that was with
   her?
3. OUT. Being nimble footed, he hath outrun us,
But Moyses and Valerius follow him.
Go thou with her to the west end of the wood. 9
There is our captain. We'll follow him that's fled.
The thicket is beset.° He cannot 'scape.
I. OUT. Come, I must bring you to our captain's
   cave.
Fear not. He bears an honorable mind,
And will not use a woman lawlessly.
SIL. O Valentine, this I endure for thee!   15
[*Exeunt.*]

SCENE IV. *Another part of the forest.*

[*Enter* VALENTINE.]

VAL. How use° doth breed a habit in a man!
This shadowy desert,° unfrequented woods,
I better brook than flourishing peopled towns.
Here can I sit alone, unseen of any,
And to the nightingale's complaining notes   5
Tune my distresses and record my woes.
O thou that dost inhabit in my breast,
Leave not the mansion so long tenantless,
Lest, growing ruinous, the building fall,
And leave no memory of what it was!   10
Repair° me with thy presence, Silvia;
Thou gentle nymph, cherish thy forlorn swain!
What hallooing and what stir is this today?
These are my mates, that make their wills their law,
Have some unhappy passenger in chase.   15
They love me well, yet I have much to do
To keep them from uncivil outrages.
Withdraw thee, Valentine. Who's this comes here?
[*He hides.*]

[*Enter* PROTEUS, SILVIA, *and* JULIA.]

PRO. Madam, this service I have done for you,
Though you respect not aught your servant doth
To hazard life and rescue you from him   21

That would have forced your honor and your love.
Vouchsafe me, for my meed, but one fair look.
A smaller boon than this I cannot beg,
And less than this, I am sure, you cannot give.   25
VAL. [*Aside*] How like a dream is this I see and
   hear!
Love, lend me patience to forbear awhile.
SIL. Oh, miserable, unhappy that I am!
PRO. Unhappy were you, madam, ere I came,
But by my coming I have made you happy.   30
SIL. By thy approach thou makest me most un-
   happy.
JUL. [*Aside*] And me, when he approacheth to
   your presence.
SIL. Had I been seizèd by a hungry lion,
I would have been a breakfast to the beast,
Rather than have false Proteus rescue me.   35
Oh, Heaven be judge how I love Valentine,
Whose life's as tender to me as my soul!
And full as much, for more there cannot be,
I do detest false perjured Proteus.
Therefore be gone. Solicit me no more.   40
PRO. What dangerous action, stood it next to
   death,
Would I not undergo for one calm look!
Oh, 'tis the curse in love, and still approved,°
When women cannot love where they're beloved!
SIL. When Proteus cannot love where he's be-
   loved.   45
Read over Julia's heart, thy first, best love,
For whose dear sake thou didst then rend thy faith
Into a thousand oaths; and all those oaths
Descended into perjury, to love me.   49
Thou hast no faith left now, unless thou'dst two,
And that's far worse than none. Better have none
Than plural faith which is too much by one.
Thou counterfeit to thy true friend!
PRO.   In love
Who respects friend?
SIL.   All men but Proteus.
PRO. Nay, if the gentle spirit of moving words
Can no way change you to a milder form,   56
I'll woo you like a soldier, at arms' end,
And love you 'gainst the nature of love — force ye.
SIL. Oh, Heaven!
PRO.   I'll force thee yield to my desire.
VAL. [*Coming forward.*] Ruffian, let go that rude
   uncivil touch,   60
Thou friend of an ill fashion!°
PRO.   Valentine!
VAL. Thou common° friend, that's without faith
   or love,
For such is a friend now. Treacherous man!
Thou hast beguiled my hopes. Naught but mine
   eye

Sc. iii: 4. **brook**: endure.   11. **beset**: surrounded.
Sc. iv: 1. **use**: custom. See *AYLI*, II.i.1–18.   2. **shadowy
desert**: deserted shade.   11. **Repair**: renew.

43. **approved**: proved true.   61. **of . . . fashion**: false.   62. **common**: cheap.

Could have persuaded me. Now I dare not say 65
I have one friend alive. Thou wouldst disprove me.
Who should be trusted now, when one's right hand
Is perjured to the bosom? Proteus,
I am sorry I must never trust thee more,
But count the world a stranger for thy sake. 70
The private° wound is deepest. Oh, time most accurst,
'Mongst all foes that a friend should be the worst!
    PRO. My shame and guilt confounds me.
Forgive me, Valentine. If hearty sorrow
Be a sufficient ransom for offense, 75
I tender° 't here. I do as truly suffer
As e'er I did commit.
    VAL.   Then I am paid,°
And once again I do receive thee honest.
Who by repentance is not satisfied
Is nor of Heaven nor earth, for these are pleased.
By penitence the Eternal's wrath's appeased. 81
And, that my love may appear plain and free,
All that was mine in Silvia I give thee.°
    JUL. O me unhappy!   [*Swoons.*]
    PRO. Look to the boy. 85
    VAL. Why, boy! Why, wag!° How now! What's
the matter? Look up. Speak.
    JUL. O good sir, my master charged me to deliver a ring to Madam Silvia, which, out of my
neglect, was never done. 90
    PRO. Where is that ring, boy?
    JUL.   Here 'tis. This is it.
    PRO. How! Let me see.
Why, this is the ring I gave to Julia.
    JUL. Oh, cry you mercy,° sir, I have mistook.
This is the ring you sent to Silvia. 95
    PRO. But how camest thou by this ring? At my
    depart
I gave this unto Julia.
    JUL. And Julia herself did give it me;
And Julia herself hath brought it hither.
    PRO. How! Julia! 100
    JUL. Behold her that gave aim to all thy oaths,
And entertained 'em deeply in her heart.
How oft hast thou with perjury cleft the root!°
O Proteus, let this habit make thee blush!
Be thou ashamed that I have took upon me 105
Such an immodest raiment, if shame live
In a disguise of love.
It is the lesser blot, modesty finds,
Women to change their shapes than men their
    minds.
    PRO. Than men their minds! 'Tis true. Oh,
    Heaven, were man 110
But constant, he were perfect! That one error

Fills him with faults, makes him run through all
    the sins.
Inconstancy falls off ere it begins.°
What is in Silvia's face, but I may spy
More fresh in Julia's with a constant eye? 115
    VAL. Come, come, a hand from either.
Let me be blest to make this happy close.°
'Twere pity two such friends should be long foes.
    PRO. Bear witness, Heaven, I have my wish for
    ever.
    JUL. And I mine. 120
[*Enter* OUTLAWS, *with* DUKE OF MILAN *and* THURIO.]
    OUTLAWS. A prize, a prize, a prize!
    VAL. Forbear, forbear, I say! It is my Lord the
    Duke.
Your Grace is welcome to a man disgraced,
Banished Valentine.
    DUKE.   Sir Valentine!
    THU. Yonder is Silvia, and Silvia's mine. 125
    VAL. Thurio, give back,° or else embrace thy
    death.
Come not within the measure of my wrath.
Do not name Silvia thine; if once again,
Verona shall not hold thee. Here she stands.
Take but possession of her with a touch. 130
I dare thee but to breathe upon my love.
    THU. Sir Valentine, I care not for her, I.
I hold him but a fool that will endanger
His body for a girl that loves him not.
I claim her not, and therefore she is thine. 135
    DUKE. The more degenerate and base art thou,
To make such means° for her as thou hast done,
And leave her on such slight conditions.°
Now, by the honor of my ancestry,
I do applaud thy spirit, Valentine, 140
And think thee worthy of an empress' love.
Know, then, I here forget all former griefs,°
Cancel all grudge, repeal thee home again,
Plead a new state° in thy unrivaled merit,
To which I thus subscribe. Sir Valentine, 145
Thou art a gentleman, and well derived.
Take thou thy Silvia, for thou hast deserved her.
    VAL. I thank your Grace. The gift hath made me
    happy.
I now beseech you, for your daughter's sake,
To grant one boon that I shall ask of you. 150
    DUKE. I grant it for thine own, whate'er it be.
    VAL. These banished men that I have kept
    withal°
Are men endued° with worthy qualities.

---

71. private: i.e., given by one's dearest friend. 76. tender: offer.
77. paid: satisfied. 83. All . . . thee: See *T Gent* Intro. p. 366a.
86. wag: merry lad. 94. cry . . . mercy: I beg your pardon.
103. cleft . . . root: i.e., of my heart.

113. Inconstancy . . . begins: an inconstant man quickly tires of
his new love. 117. close: conclusion. 126. give back: stand
back. 137. means: efforts. 138. on . . . conditions: so easily.
142. griefs: grievances. 144. Plead . . . state: make a fresh
start, i.e., from being a banished man you are now restored to
my favor. 152. kept withal: lived with. 153. endued: endowed.

Forgive them what they have committed here,
And let them be recalled from their exile.   155
They are reformèd, civil, full of good,
And fit for great employment, worthy lord.
   DUKE. Thou hast prevailed. I pardon them and
     thee.
Dispose of them as thou know'st their deserts.
Come, let us go. We will include all jars°   160
With triumphs,° mirth, and rare solemnity.
   VAL. And, as we walk along, I dare be bold
With our discourse to make your Grace to smile.
What think you of this page, my lord?

   DUKE. I think the boy hath grace in him. He
     blushes.   165
   VAL. I warrant you, my lord, more grace than
     boy.
   DUKE. What mean you by that saying?
   VAL. Please you, I'll tell you as we pass along,
That you will wonder what hath fortunèd.°
Come, Proteus. 'Tis your penance but° to hear   170
The story of your loves discoverèd.
That done, our day of marriage shall be yours,
One feast, one house, one mutual happiness.
                          [Exeunt.]

160. **include . . . jars:** conclude all differences.   161. **triumphs:** entertainments.   169. **fortuned:** happened.   170. **your . . . but:** your only penance will be.

LOVE'S LABOR'S LOST

Introduction

Love's Labor's Lost is at first sight a difficult play; it abounds in inexplicable lines, allusions, topicalities, jokes, and personalities so obscure and unintelligible that they bewilder even the most erudite of commentators. As a result critics tend to leave the play to those who are more interested in literary puzzles than in poetry. This is regrettable, for *Love's Labor's Lost* taken in the right spirit is a most amusing entertainment. It should not be judged according to any critical rules of comedy, or as the work of the sage philosopher who afterward wrote *Hamlet* or *Lear,* but rather as a musical comedy, a revue, a trifle for the amusement of a select audience at a Christmas house party. It is best to consider the play in this light first and the antiquarian matters later.

The theme of *Love's Labor's Lost* is Cupid's revenge, and it is composed in movements almost like an elaborate ballet. The first movement is the opening of the theme. Four normal, lusty, young men — Navarre, Berowne, Longaville, and Dumain — have quixotically agreed to the preposterous proposal that for three years they will forswear love and all earthly delights and devote themselves to study — the kind of resolution a student makes at the beginning of his final year and keeps for the first fortnight. But only Berowne realizes that the pact is impossible; he signs under protest. The first movement also introduces Costard the clown, who is Cupid's servant, since he is in love with Jaquenetta; and Armado, the fantastic Spaniard, who is also trying to resist Cupid.

The second movement opens with the arrival of the Princess of France and her ladies — Rosaline, Maria, and Katharine — escorted by Boyet, her chamberlain. They have come on an embassy to visit Navarre and all are ready to help Cupid; but the edict forbidding love thwarts them, and when Navarre inhospitably leaves them to encamp in the open, all four are eager to become instruments for Love's revenge. Love has already been at work. Berowne is the first traitor to his oath; he has fallen in love with Rosaline of the dark eyes. So he sends a note to his lady by Costard, who is already carrying another from Armado to Jaquenetta. In delivering them Costard mixes up the notes.

Then, before the third movement starts, comes the interlude of Holofernes the schoolmaster and Nathaniel the curate with their learned pleasantries. With the start of the third movement each of the students of philosophy has been caught. They come in one by one reading their love rhymes, each — as he thinks — hiding his shame from the others, until each in turn is betrayed and disgraced. Berowne is the last to be convicted when his letter to Rosaline falls into the hands of Navarre; but Berowne alone has the wit to see that perjury is a less dangerous offense than to deny Cupid's superior power. The new convert now hymns love in a magnificent paean of praise for his lady's eyes. He rallies the lovers, and all are now eager to enter the lists as Cupid's soldiers.

The fourth movement is prefaced by the second interlude of pedant and curate. Then follows a masque of Russians, when the four disguised lovers prepare to attack their ladies; but the women change their masks and confuse their adversaries. The movement is then repeated with a difference. The lovers return without their disguises and in their own persons; the ladies come back escorted by Boyet, and the attacks are resumed. Both groups now join to watch the presentation of the pageant of the Nine Worthies — a very human diversion. The fun is at its highest when there suddenly appears Mercade with the bad news that the King of France is dead. The laughter abruptly ceases, and just as each lover thinks that he has reached the goal, he is thwarted by the barrier of death.

So Cupid is revenged; a penance is laid on the lovers, and the gaiety becomes serious. But this would be too gloomy an ending for so light a play. The antic procession of the owl and the cuckoo, Winter and Spring, enters, and each sings his song. Armado leads his flock away and the sad lovers leave the stage empty. The ending has just that note of interrogation and seriousness with which sometimes Shakespeare ends even a most joyous comedy.

It is often forgotten that Shakespeare's plays as we read them in the text are but a small part of the original experience — the words only. The whole play was a combination of color, music, grouping, dancing, song, voice, and above all, movement. Only the words remain of *Love's Labor's Lost,* like an old record of some lavish opera. Shakespeare, though a poet of incomparable power, was primarily a man of the stage concerned with his plays as a fusion of dialogue and action. His lesser plays cannot be appreciated without action. *Love's Labor's Lost* is not a great play, but on the stage it has lasting qualities and great variety, and above all, poetry in abundance and great variety of meter — sonnets, lyrics, songs, the song of Winter and Spring, Berowne's tirade against learning and love, his praise of love and light, his alarm to Cupid's soldiers, his cameo portrait of Boyet; and with these too there are the humanity and the comedy.

Love's Labor's Lost would be better known if there were fewer difficulties for the ordinary reader. Indeed the problems are so many that the play is quite in a class by itself. Compared with other dramatists Shakespeare was usually sparing with direct topical allusions; *Love's Labor's Lost* abounds with them, but they are so obscure and intimate that nowadays most of them are quite inexplicable. It is thus probable that the play was originally written for a select audience rather than for the general public.

The first definite fact about *Love's Labor's Lost* is that an edition of the play was published in 1598 with the title page: *A Pleasant Conceited Comedie Called, Loues labors lost. As it was presented before her Highnes this last Christmas. Newly corrected and augmented By W. Shakespere. Imprinted at London by W.W. for Cutbert Burby. 1598.* This quarto may originally have been set from the original manuscript. It shows signs that in a few places speeches have been rewritten. The text in the first folio of 1623 was set from a copy of the quarto considerably revised. The words "newly corrected and augmented" on the title page imply that at least one earlier edition had appeared; but if so, no copy survives. A similar note occurs in the second quarto of *Romeo and Juliet,* which differed considerably from the first quarto. The second quarto of *I Henry IV* is also described as newly corrected, although the corrections are only of misprints; the third, fourth, and fifth quartos, though reprinted one from the other, were also described as newly corrected.

The date of *Love's Labor's Lost* is doubtful. The quarto establishes that it was written some time before 1598, but scholars are not generally agreed, and their guesses vary from 1588 to 1596. The style of the play — if style in a play so far out of the ordinary is any sure guide — would link it with the Sonnets and the earlier plays such as *Romeo and Juliet;* that is, before 1595. The guess which at present seems likeliest is that of the editors of the New Cambridge Shakespeare (A.T. Quiller Couch and J. Dover Wilson) who state that "in our opinion its first performance had Christmas 1593 for date and for place some great private house, possibly the Earl of Southampton's."

If this guess, and it can only be a guess, is correct, much will follow. In 1593 Shakespeare was twenty-nine. He had already experimented in various kinds of comedy, but in April 1593 his poem *Venus and Adonis* had appeared with a dedicatory letter to the Earl of Southampton. As a result of the poem, which was immediately successful, Shakespeare seems to have received many marks of favor from the young Earl (see Gen. Intro. page 10a–b). Moreover Southampton, to the surprise and annoyance of Lord Burghleigh, his guardian, refused to marry. It is therefore not improbable that love, or rather a disdain for love, was a theme which occupied the witty young men of Southampton's household. The theme of the four young men who despised love was thus ready to hand, and the names of these young men were in themselves topical. Many gallants had served in France with the forces which were aiding Henry of Navarre in 1591 and 1592; among the notable figures in the French campaign were the Marshal de Biron and the Duc de Longueville, two of Navarre's chief commanders, and the Duc de Mayne, his most powerful opponent. It was an amusing notion in itself to bring this ill-assorted company together to study philosophy and to avoid the society of women, especially as the real Navarre was himself a notorious philanderer constantly embarrassed by the demands of his various ladies.

Another topicality which can reasonably be identified occurs at IV.iii.254:

Oh, paradox! Black is the badge of Hell,
The hue of dungeons and the school of night.

In the early 1590's much scandal was caused in London by a coterie of intellectuals, of whom Sir Walter Ralegh was chief, who were accused of discussing obscure and forbidden topics. Other members of the group were Henry Percy, Earl of Northumberland, known as the Wizard Earl, a keen student of the sciences; Thomas Harriott, one of the greatest mathematicians of his age; Matthew Roydon, a minor man of letters; and the two poets Christopher Marlowe and George Chapman. The discussions of this group were much suspected; it was said that with Harriott as their schoolmaster a number of young noblemen were taught to jibe at the Scriptures, that such articles of faith as the immortality of the soul and the future life were ridiculed, and that scholars taught among other things to spell God backwards. In 1594 Chapman published an obscure poem called *The Shadow of Night,* which he dedicated to Roydon.

There are apparently other jibes at this group. Holofernes with his " foolish, extravagant spirit, full of forms, figures, shapes, objects, ideas, apprehensions, motions, revolutions" (IV.ii.67–69) would certainly have reminded the audience of the mathematician Harriott. Even Ralegh, who was no friend to the Southampton group, was, in the view of some scholars, caricatured under the fantastical Armado. Ralegh was much in the public eye at the time, but by 1592 he had fallen from grace. While still flattering the Queen as of old, he had seduced one of her maids of honor, whom he subsequently married. The Queen was so angry that she sent him to the Tower, where he lapsed into profound melancholy and wrote her fantastical letters.

However, such identifications can seldom be proved. Although from time to time characters utter remarks which would remind the audience of current gossip, it is rare, even in topical plays, that a character is a consistent caricature. The braggart, the pedant, and the witty boy have been stock figures in comedy from the days of Plautus and Terence. Such problems, however, have little to do with the poetical qualities of *Love's Labor's Lost* and cannot be briefly discussed. Those who wish to pursue them should consult the works of scholars.

The story of *Love's Labor's Lost* seems to be original, for no source has been discovered. But it is more than a coincidence that in 1592 three of Lyly's plays were published which gave Shakespeare a model for witty social comedy written for select audiences. The true source of *Love's Labor's Lost* is not, however, any book or play, but the lively, witty conversation of young men of high rank, education, and good breeding. The play is the work of a man who listened eagerly to good talk and reveled in its wit. We are apt to forget that conversation is the most potent of all literary influences.

In the study of most of Shakespeare's plays some knowledge of the background, source, and date is essential to full understanding. With *Love's Labor's Lost* it is almost the opposite. The student whose main interest is in drama and poetry should therefore ignore the obscure lines and the incomprehensible jokes. If he can regard the play as a lighthearted trifle he will find that it is still brimful of the finest poetry and very comical mirth.

Love's Labor's Lost

DRAMATIS PERSONAE

FERDINAND, *King of Navarre*
BEROWNE
LONGAVILLE } *lords attending on the King*
DUMAIN
BOYET
MERCADE } *lords attending on the Princess of France*
DON ADRIANO DE ARMADO, *a fantastical Spaniard*
SIR NATHANIEL, *a curate*
HOLOFERNES, *a schoolmaster*
DULL, *a constable*
COSTARD, *a clown*

MOTH, *page to Armado*
A FORESTER

THE PRINCESS *of France*
ROSALINE
MARIA } *ladies attending on the Princess*
KATHARINE
JAQUENETTA, *a country wench*

LORDS, ATTENDANTS, ETC.

SCENE — *Navarre.*

Act I

SCENE I. *The King of Navarre's park.*

[*Enter* FERDINAND, *King of Navarre,* BEROWNE,
LONGAVILLE, *and* DUMAIN.]

KING. Let fame, that all hunt after in their lives,
Live registered upon our brazen tombs,
And then grace us in the disgrace of death;
When, spite of cormorant° devouring Time,
The endeavor of this present breath may buy   5
That honor which shall bate° his scythe's keen edge,
And make us heirs of all eternity.
Therefore, brave conquerors — for so you are
That war against your own affections
And the huge army of the world's desires —   10
Our late edict shall strongly stand in force.
Navarre shall be the wonder of the world;
Our Court shall be a little Academe,°
Still and contemplative in living art.°
You three, Berowne, Dumain, and Longaville,   15
Have sworn for three years' term to live with me
My fellow scholars, and to keep those statutes
That are recorded in this schedule here.
Your oaths are passed, and now subscribe your
          names,
That his own hand may strike his honor down   20
That violates the smallest branch herein.
If you are armed° to do as sworn to do,
Subscribe to your deep oaths, and keep it too.
     LONG. I am resolved — 'tis but a three years' fast.
The mind shall banquet though the body pine.   25
Fat paunches have lean pates, and dainty bits
Make rich the ribs, but bankrupt quite the wits.

Act I, Sc. i: **4. cormorant:** a rapacious sea bird. **6. bate:** blunt. **13. Academe:** society of scholars, from the famous Athenian Academy at which Plato taught. **14. Still . . . art:** always pondering over the art of living, which was the main study of the Stoic philosophers. **22. armed:** resolved.

     DUM. My loving lord, Dumain is mortified.°
The grosser manner of these world's delights
He throws upon the gross world's baser slaves.   30
To love, to wealth, to pomp, I pine and die,
With all these living in philosophy.
     BER. I can but say their protestation over.°
So much, dear liege, I have already sworn;
That is, to live and study here three years.   35
But there are other strict observances —
As not to see a woman in that term,
Which I hope well is not enrollèd there;
And one day in a week to touch no food,
And but one meal on every day beside,   40
The which I hope is not enrollèd there;
And then, to sleep but three hours in the night,
And not be seen to wink of° all the day —
When I was wont to think no harm all night,
And make a dark night too of half the day —   45
Which I hope well is not enrollèd there.
Oh, these are barren tasks, too hard to keep:
Not to see ladies, study, fast, not sleep!
     KING. Your oath is passed to pass away from these.
     BER. Let me say no, my liege, an if° you please.
I only swore to study with your Grace,   51
And stay here in your Court for three years' space.
     LONG. You swore to that, Berowne, and to the rest.
     BER. By yea and nay,° sir, then I swore in jest.
What is the end of study? Let me know.   55
     KING. Why, that to know which else we should
          not know.
     BER. Things hid and barred, you mean, from com-
          mon sense?°
     KING. Aye, that is study's godlike recompense.
     BER. Come on, then, I will swear to study so,
To know the thing I am forbid to know.   60
As thus — to study where I well may dine

----

28. mortified: dead to fleshly delights. **33. say . . . over:** repeat. **43. wink of:** close the eyes during. **50. an if:** if. **54. By . . . nay:** assuredly. **57. common sense:** ordinary perception.

When I to feast expressly am forbid;
Or study where to meet some mistress fine
　When mistresses from common sense are hid;
Or, having sworn too hard a keeping oath,　　65
Study to break it and not break my troth.°
If study's gain be thus, and this be so,
Study knows that which yet it doth not know.
Swear me to this, and I will ne'er say no.
　KING. These be the stops that hinder study quite,
And train our intellects to vain delight.　　71
　BER. Why, all delights are vain, but that most vain
Which, with pain purchased, doth inherit pain° —
As painfully to pore upon a book
　To seek the light of truth, while truth the while
Doth falsely blind the eyesight of his look.　　76
　Light, seeking light, doth light of light beguile;°
So, ere you find where light in darkness lies,
Your light grows dark by losing of your eyes.
Study me how to please the eye indeed,　　80
　By fixing it upon a fairer eye,
Who dazzling so, that eye shall be his heed,
　And give him light that it was blinded by.°
Study is like the heaven's glorious sun,
　That will not be deep-searched with saucy looks.
Small have continual plodders ever won,　　86
　Save base authority from others' books.
These earthly godfathers of heaven's lights°
　That give a name to every fixèd star
Have no more profit of their shining nights　　90
　Than those that walk and wot° not what they are.
Too much to know is to know naught but fame,°
And every godfather can give a name.
　KING. How well he's read, to reason against read-
　　ing!
　DUM. Proceeded° well, to stop all good proceed-
　　ing!　　　　　　　　　　　　　　　　　　95
　LONG. He weeds the corn, and still lets grow the
　　weeding.°
　BER. The spring is near, when green geese° are
　　a-breeding.
　DUM. How follows that?
　BER.　　　　　　　　　　Fit in his place and time.
　DUM. In reason, nothing.
　BER.　　　　　　　Something, then, in rhyme.°
　KING. Berowne is like an envious sneaping° frost
That bites the first-born infants° of the spring.

66. troth: faith.　73. pain . . . pain: hard labor . . . discomfort.
77. beguile: cheat.　82–83. Who . . . by: i.e., the dazzling beauty
of his lady's eyes may blind him but they also give him light.
88. earthly . . . lights: i.e., astronomers who give names to the
stars.　91. wot: know.　92. fame: mere report.　95. Proceeded:
in the universities of Oxford and Cambridge the word means
"has taken his degree," i.e., shown himself a scholar.　96. weeding: that which was weeded out.　97. green geese: goslings.
98–99. How . . . rhyme: Dumain asks Berowne what he means.
Berowne replies that his words are quite suitable to such a goose
as Dumain. Dumain answers that it does not make sense; to
which Berowne retorts that if it is not reason, it is at least in
rhyme — a play on the common saying "neither rhyme nor
reason."　100. sneaping: nipping.　101. infants: buds.

　BER. Well, say I am. Why should proud summer
　　boast　　　　　　　　　　　　　　　　　　102
Before the birds have any cause to sing?
Why should I joy in any abortive birth?
At Christmas I no more desire a rose　　105
Than wish a snow in May's newfangled shows,
But like of each thing that in season grows.
So you, to study now it is too late,°
Climb o'er the house to unlock the little gate.
　KING. Well, sit you out. Go home, Berowne.
　　Adieu.　　　　　　　　　　　　　　　　　　110
　BER. No, my good lord, I have sworn to stay with
　　you.
And though I have for barbarism° spoke more
　Than for that angel knowledge you can say,
Yet confident I'll keep what I have swore,
　And bide the penance of each three years' day.
Give me the paper, let me read the same,　　116
And to the strict'st decrees I'll write my name.
　KING. How well this yielding rescues thee from
　　shame!
　BER. [*Reads.*] " Item, That no woman shall come
within a mile of my Court —— " Hath this been
proclaimed?　　　　　　　　　　　　　　　120
　LONG. Four days ago.
　BER. Let's see the penalty. [*Reads.*] " on pain of
losing her tongue." Who devised this penalty?　125
　LONG. Marry,° that did I.
　BER. Sweet lord, and why?
　LONG. To fright them hence with that dread pen-
　　alty.　　　　　　　　　　　　　　　　　　128
　BER. A dangerous law against gentility!° [*Reads.*]
" Item, If any man be seen to talk with a woman
within the term of three years, he shall endure such
public shame as the rest of the Court can possibly
devise."
This article, my liege, yourself must break;
　For well you know here comes in embassy　135
The French King's daughter with yourself to
　　speak —
　A maid of grace and complete majesty —
About surrender up of Aquitaine°
　To her decrepit, sick, and bedrid father.
Therefore this article is made in vain,　　140
　Or vainly comes the admirèd Princess hither.
　KING. What say you, lords? Why, this was quite
　　forgot.
　BER. So study evermore is overshot.°
While it doth study to have what it would,
It doth forget to do the thing it should;　　145
And when it hath the thing it hunteth most,
'Tis won as towns with fire, so won, so lost.°
　KING. We must of force dispense with this decree.

108. to . . . late: you are past the time for study.　112. barbarism: ignorance.　126. Marry: Mary, by the Virgin.　129. gentility: good manners.　138. Aquitaine: a province of France.
143. overshot: wide of the mark.　147. so . . . lost: i.e., like a
town captured after its destruction, not worth having.

She must lie° here on mere° necessity.

BER. Necessity will make us all forsworn°   150
Three thousand times within this three years'
   space;
For every man with his affects° is born,
   Not by might mastered, but by special grace.
If I break faith, this word shall speak for me,
I am forsworn on "mere necessity."   155
So to the laws at large I write my name. [*Subscribes.*]
   And he that breaks them in the least degree
Stands in attainder° of eternal shame.
   Suggestions° are to other as to me,
But I believe, although I seem so loath,   160
I am the last that will last keep his oath.
But is there no quick recreation° granted?

KING. Aye, that there is. Our Court, you know, is
   haunted
With a refinèd traveler of Spain —
A man in all the world's new fashion planted   165
   That hath a mint of phrases in his brain;
One whom the music of his own vain tongue
   Doth ravish like enchanting harmony;
A man of complements,° whom right and wrong
   Have chose as umpire of their mutiny.   170
This child of fancy, that Armado hight,°
   For interim° to our studies, shall relate,
In highborn words, the worth of many a knight
   From tawny Spain, lost in the world's debate.°
How you delight, my lords, I know not, I,   175
But I protest I love to hear him lie,
And I will use him for my minstrelsy.°

BER. Armado is a most illustrious wight,°
A man of fire-new° words, fashion's own knight.°

LONG. Costard the swain° and he shall be our
   sport,   180
And so to study three years is but short.

   [*Enter* DULL *with a letter, and* COSTARD.]

DULL. Which is the Duke's° own person?

BER. This, fellow. What wouldst?

DULL. I myself reprehend° his own person, for I
am His Grace's tharborough.° But I would see his
own person in flesh and blood.   186

BER. This is he.

DULL. Signior Arme — Arme — commends you.
There's villainy abroad. This letter will tell you
more.   190

COST. Sir, the contempts° thereof are as touching
me.

KING. A letter from the magnificent Armado.

BER. How low soever the matter, I hope in God
for high words.   195

LONG. A high hope for a low heaven. God grant
us patience!

BER. To hear? Or forbear laughing?

LONG. To hear meekly, sir, and to laugh moderately — or to forbear both.   200

BER. Well, sir, be it as the style shall give us cause
to climb in the merriness.

COST. The matter is to me, sir, as concerning
Jaquenetta. The matter of it is, I was taken with the
manner.°   205

BER. In what manner?

COST. In manner and form following, sir, all those
three: I was seen with her in the manor house, sitting
with her upon the form,° and taken following her
into the park; which, put together, is in manner and
form following. Now, sir, for the manner — it is the
manner of a man to speak to a woman. For the
form — in some form.   213

BER. For the following, sir?

COST. As it shall follow in my correction, and God
defend the right!

KING. Will you hear this letter with attention?

BER. As we would hear an oracle.

COST. Such is the simplicity of man to hearken
after the flesh.   220

KING. [*Reads.*] "Great deputy, the welkin's° vicegerent, and sole dominator° of Navarre, my soul's
earth's god, and body's fostering° patron." ——

COST. Not a word of Costard yet.

KING. [*Reads.*] "So it is" ——   225

COST. It may be so. But if he say it is so, he is, in
telling true, but so.

KING. Peace!

COST. Be to me, and every man that dares not
fight!   230

KING. No words!

COST. Of other men's secrets, I beseech you.

KING. [*Reads.*] "So it is, besieged with sable-
colored° melancholy, I did commend the black-
oppressing humor° to the most wholesome physic of
thy health-giving air; and, as I am a gentleman, betook myself to walk. The time when? About the
sixth hour, when beasts most graze, birds best peck,
and men sit down to that nourishment which is
called supper. So much for the time when. Now for
the ground which — which, I mean, I walked upon.
It is ycleped° thy park. Then for the place   240
where — where, I mean, I did encounter that obscene
and most preposterous event that draweth from my

149. lie: stay. mere: sheer.   150. forsworn: break our oath.
152. affects: natural inclinations.   158. attainder: condemnation.
159. Suggestions: temptations.   162. quick recreation: lively
sport.   169. complements: refined behavior.   171. hight: named.
172. interim: interlude, pastime.   174. debate: strife.   177. minstrelsy: band of musicians.   178. wight: man.   179. fire-new:
brand-new. fashion's . . . knight: It was the mark of the accomplished courtier to be able to discourse in the latest fashion of
vocabulary. Cf. Osric (*Haml.*, V.ii.81–195).   180. swain: countryman.   182. Duke: Ferdinand in this play is both Duke and
King.   184. reprehend: for "represent." Like other humble
characters in Shakespeare's plays, Costard loves long words but
is not always sure of their meanings.   185. tharborough: third
borough, constable.

191. contempts: for "contents."   204–05. with . . . manner: in
the act.   209. form: bench.   221. welkin: sky.   222. dominator:
ruler.   223. fostering: sustaining.   233. sable-colored: black.
234. humor: See App. 3 and 4.   240. ycleped: called.

snow-white pen the ebon-colored° ink which here thou viewest, beholdest, surveyest, or seest. But to the place where — it standeth north-northeast and by east from the west corner of thy curious-knotted° garden. There did I see that low-spirited swain, that base minnow of thy mirth —— "　　　　251

COST. Me?

KING. [*Reads.*] "that unlettered small-knowing soul —— "

COST. Me?　　　　255

KING. [*Reads.*] "that shallow vassal° —— "

COST. Still me?

KING. [*Reads.*] "which, as I remember, hight Costard —— "

COST. Oh, me!　　　　260

KING. [*Reads.*] "sorted and consorted, contrary to thy established proclaimed edict and continent canon,° which with — Oh, with — but with this I passion to say° wherewith —— "

COST. With a wench.　　　　265

KING. [*Reads.*] " with a child of our grandmother Eve, a female; or, for thy more sweet understanding, a woman. Him I, as my ever-esteemed duty pricks me on, have sent to thee to receive the meed° of punishment, by thy sweet Grace's officer, Anthony Dull, a man of good repute, carriage, bearing, and estimation."　　　　273

DULL. Me, an't° shall please you. I am Anthony Dull.

KING. [*Reads.*] "For Jaquenetta — so is the weaker vessel called which I apprehended with the aforesaid swain — I keep her as a vessel of thy law's fury; and shall, at the least of thy sweet notice, bring her to trial. Thine, in all compliments of devoted and heartburning heat of duty.

DON ADRIANO DE ARMADO."　　280

BER. This is not so well as I looked for, but the best that ever I heard.

KING. Aye, the best for the worst. But, sirrah, what say you to this?

COST. Sir, I confess the wench.　　　　285

KING. Did you hear the proclamation?

COST. I do confess much of the hearing it, but little of the marking of it.

KING. It was proclaimed a year's imprisonment to be taken with a wench.　　　　290

COST. I was taken with none, sir. I was taken with a damsel.

KING. Well, it was proclaimed damsel.

COST. This was no damsel neither, sir. She was a virgin.

KING. It is so varied too, for it was proclaimed virgin.　　　　295

COST. If it were, I deny her virginity. I was taken with a maid.

KING. This maid will not serve your turn,° sir.

COST. This maid will serve my turn, sir.　　301

KING. Sir, I will pronounce your sentence. You shall fast a week with bran and water.

COST. I had rather pray a month with mutton and porridge.　　　　305

KING. And Don Armado shall be your keeper. My Lord Berowne, see him delivered o'er. And go we, lords, to put in practice that Which each to other hath so strongly sworn.

[*Exeunt* KING, LONGAVILLE, *and* DUMAIN.]

BER. I'll lay° my head to any good man's hat,　310 These oaths and laws will prove an idle scorn. Sirrah,° come on.

COST. I suffer for the truth, sir; for true it is I was taken with Jaquenetta, and Jaquenetta is a true girl, and therefore welcome the sour cup of prosperity! Affliction may one day smile again, and till then, sit thee down, sorrow!　　　　[*Exeunt.*]

SCENE II. *The same.*

[*Enter* ARMADO *and* MOTH *his page.*]

ARM. Boy, what sign is it when a man of great spirit grows melancholy?

MOTH. A great sign, sir, that he will look sad.

ARM. Why, sadness is one and the selfsame thing, dear imp.　　　　5

MOTH. No, no, oh Lord, sir, no.

ARM. How canst thou part° sadness and melancholy, my tender juvenal?°

MOTH. By a familiar demonstration of the working, my tough senior.　　　　10

ARM. Why tough senior? Why tough senior?

MOTH. Why tender juvenal? Why tender juvenal?

ARM. I spoke it, tender juvenal, as a congruent epitheton° appertaining to thy young days, which we may nominate tender.

MOTH. And I, tough senior, as an appertinent title to your old time, which we may name tough.　18

ARM. Pretty and apt.

MOTH. How mean you, sir? I pretty, and my saying apt? Or I apt, and my saying pretty?

ARM. Thou pretty, because little.

MOTH. Little pretty, because little. Wherefore apt?

ARM. And therefore apt, because quick.　　25

MOTH. Speak you this in my praise, master?

ARM. In thy condign° praise.

MOTH. I will praise an eel with the same praise.

---

243. ebon-colored: black as ebony. **249. curious-knotted:** elaborately laid out with little borders of shrubs. See Pl. 16a. **256. vassal:** slave, with a pun on "vessel." **262–63. continent canon:** law ordaining continency. **264. passion to say:** say with grief. **269. meed:** reward. **274. an't:** if it.

300. serve . . . turn: help you. **310. lay:** wager. **312. Sirrah:** term of address used to an inferior.

Sc. ii: **7. part:** separate. **8. juvenal:** youth, juvenile. **13–14. congruent epitheton:** appropriate epithet. **27. condign:** worthily deserved.

ARM. What, that an eel is ingenious?

MOTH. That an eel is quick.   30

ARM. I do say thou art quick in answers. Thou heatest my blood.

MOTH. I am answered, sir.

ARM. I love not to be crossed.

MOTH. [*Aside*] He speaks the mere contrary — crosses° love not him.   36

ARM. I have promised to study three years with the Duke.

MOTH. You may do it in an hour, sir.

ARM. Impossible.   40

MOTH. How many is one thrice told?

ARM. I am ill at reckoning, it fitteth the spirit of a tapster.°   44

MOTH. You are a gentleman and a gamester, sir.

ARM. I confess both. They are both the varnish° of a complete man.

MOTH. Then I am sure you know how much the gross sum of deuce-ace° amounts to.

ARM. It doth amount to one more than two.   50

MOTH. Which the base vulgar do call three.

ARM. True.

MOTH. Why, sir, is this such a piece of study? Now here is three studied ere ye'll thrice wink. And how easy it is to put years to the word " three," and study three years in two words, the dancing horse° will tell you.

ARM. A most fine figure!

MOTH. To prove you a cipher.   59

ARM. I will hereupon confess I am in love; and as it is base for a soldier to love, so am I in love with a base wench. If drawing my sword against the humor of affection would deliver me from the reprobate thought of it, I would take Desire prisoner, and ransom him to any French courtier for a new-devised courtesy.° I think scorn to sigh — methinks I should outswear Cupid. Comfort me, boy. What great men have been in love?   68

MOTH. Hercules, master.

ARM. Most sweet Hercules! More authority, dear boy, name more. And, sweet my child, let them be men of good repute and carriage.

MOTH. Samson, master. He was a man of good carriage, great carriage, for he carried the town gates on his back like a porter° — and he was in love.   76

ARM. O well-knit Samson! Strong-jointed Samson! I do excel thee in my rapier as much as thou didst me in carrying gates. I am in love too. Who was Samson's love, my dear Moth?   80

MOTH. A woman, master.

ARM. Of what complexion?°

MOTH. Of all the four, or the three, or the two, or one of the four.

ARM. Tell me precisely of what complexion.   85

MOTH. Of the sea-water green,° sir.

ARM. Is that one of the four complexions?

MOTH. As I have read, sir, and the best of them too.

ARM. Green, indeed, is the color of lovers; but   90 to have a love of that color, methinks Samson had small reason for it. He surely affected° her for her wit.°

MOTH. It was so, sir, for she had a green° wit.   95

ARM. My love is most immaculate white and red.

MOTH. Most maculate° thoughts, master, are masked under such colors.

ARM. Define, define, well-educated infant.

MOTH. My father's wit, and my mother's tongue, assist me!   101

ARM. Sweet invocation of a child, most pretty and pathetical!

MOTH. If she be made of white and red,
    Her faults will ne'er be known;   105
  For blushing cheeks by faults are bred,
    And fears by pale white shown.
  Then if she fear, or be to blame,
    By this you shall not know;
  For still° her cheeks possess the same   110
    Which native° she doth owe.°

A dangerous rhyme, master, against the reason of white and red.

ARM. Is there not a ballad, boy, of " The King and the Beggar? "°   115

MOTH. The world was very guilty of such a ballad some three ages since, but I think now 'tis not to be found; or if it were, it would neither serve for the writing nor the tune.°   119

ARM. I will have that subject newly writ o'er, that I may example° my digression by some mighty precedent. Boy, I do love that country girl that I took in the park with the rational hind° Costard. She deserves well.

MOTH. [*Aside*] To be whipped, and yet a better love than my master.   126

ARM. Sing, boy, my spirit grows heavy in love.

MOTH. And that's great marvel, loving a light wench.

ARM. I say, sing.   130

82. **complexion**: i.e., humor. See App. 3. Moth however takes the word in its literal meaning of color in the face. 86. **sea-water green**: suffering from green sickness, a form of anemia common with teen-age girls. 92. **affected**: loved. 94. **wit**: intelligence. 95. **green**: raw, immature. 97. **maculate**: spotted, impure. 110. **still**: always. 111. **native**: naturally. **owe**: own. 114–15. **King . . . Beggar**: i.e., the story of King Cophetua who married a beggar maid. 118–19. **serve . . . tune**: i.e., it would not be suitable for your case. 121. **example**: find a precedent for. 123. **rational hind**: intelligent peasant.

36. **crosses**: money, so called because of the cross on the reverse side. See Pl. 10a. 44. **tapster**: bartender. 46. **varnish**: outward gloss. 49. **deuce-ace**: a throw of a pair of dice producing two and one. 57. **dancing horse**: a famous performing horse called Morocco, owned by a man called Bankes, which performed circus tricks, such as counting money. 65–66. **new-devised courtesy**: a new Court compliment. 75–76. **town . . . porter**: the story is told in Judges 16:1–3.

MOTH. Forbear till this company be past.

[*Enter* DULL, COSTARD, *and* JAQUENETTA.]

DULL. Sir, the Duke's pleasure is that you keep Costard safe. And you must suffer him to take no delight nor no penance; but a'° must fast three days a week. For this damsel, I must keep her at the 135 park. She is allowed for° the day woman.° Fare you well.

ARM. I do betray myself with blushing. Maid.

JAQ. Man.

ARM. I will visit thee at the lodge. 140

JAQ. That's hereby.

ARM. I know where it is situate.

JAQ. Lord, how wise you are!

ARM. I will tell thee wonders.

JAQ. With that face? 145

ARM. I love thee.

JAQ. So I heard you say.

ARM. And so farewell.

JAQ. Fair weather after you!

DULL. Come, Jaquenetta, away! 150

[*Exeunt* DULL *and* JAQUENETTA.]

ARM. Villain, thou shalt fast for thy offenses ere thou be pardoned.

COST. Well, sir, I hope when I do it I shall do it on a full stomach.

ARM. Thou shalt be heavily punished. 155

COST. I am more bound to you than your fellows, for they are but lightly rewarded.

ARM. Take away this villain. Shut him up.

MOTH. Come, you transgressing slave, away!

COST. Let me not be pent up, sir. I will fast, being loose. 161

MOTH. No, sir, that were fast and loose.° Thou shalt to prison.

COST. Well, if ever I do see the merry days of desolation that I have seen, some shall see. 165

MOTH. What shall some see?

COST. Nay, nothing, Master Moth, but what they look upon. It is not for prisoners to be too silent in their words, and therefore I will say nothing. I thank God I have as little patience as another man, and therefore I can be quiet. 171

[*Exeunt* MOTH *and* COSTARD.]

ARM. I do affect the very ground, which is base, where her shoe, which is baser, guided by her foot, which is basest, doth tread. I shall be forsworn, which is a great argument of falsehood, if I love. And how can that be true love which is falsely attempted? Love is a familiar,° Love is a devil. There is no evil angel but Love. Yet was Samson so tempted, and he had an excellent strength; yet was Solomon so seduced, and he had a very good wit. Cupid's 180 butt shaft° is too hard for Hercules' club, and there-

fore too much odds° for a Spaniard's rapier. The first and second cause° will not serve my turn; the passado° he respects not, the duello° he regards not. His disgrace is to be called boy,° but his glory is to subdue men. Adieu, valor! Rust, rapier! Be still, drum! For your manager is in love — yea, he loveth. Assist me, some extemporal god of rhyme, for I am sure I shall turn sonnet. Devise, wit; write, pen; for I am for whole volumes in folio.° [*Exit.*] 191

Act II

SCENE I. *The same.*

[*Enter the* PRINCESS OF FRANCE, ROSALINE, MARIA, KATHARINE, BOYET, LORDS, *and other* ATTENDANTS.]

BOYET. Now, madam, summon up your dearest°
  spirits.
Consider who the King your father sends,
To whom he sends, and what's his embassy.
Yourself, held precious in the world's esteem,
To parley with the sole inheritor 5
Of all perfections that a man may owe,
Matchless Navarre; the plea of no less weight
Than Aquitaine, a dowry for a queen.
Be now as prodigal of all dear grace
As Nature was in making graces dear° 10
When she did starve the general world beside,
And prodigally gave them all to you.

PRIN. Good Lord Boyet, my beauty, though but
  mean,
Needs not the painted° flourish of your praise.
Beauty is bought by judgment of the eye, 15
Not uttered° by base sale of chapmen's° tongues.
I am less proud to hear you tell my worth
Than you much willing to be counted wise
In spending your wit in the praise of mine.
But now to task the tasker. Good Boyet, 20
You are not ignorant, all-telling fame
Doth noise abroad, Navarre hath made a vow,
Till painful° study shall outwear three years,
No woman may approach his silent Court.
Therefore to's° seemeth it a needful course, 25
Before we enter his forbidden gates,
To know his pleasure; and in that behalf,

---

182. too . . . odds: too difficult. 183. first . . . cause: i.e., technical reasons for a duel. Among gentlemen of fashion the rules and vocabulary of honor were elaborate and exact. See *AYLI*, V.iv.50-108. 184. passado: thrust. duello: rules of dueling. 185. called boy: to call a man "boy" was to offer a gross insult. Cf. *M Ado*, V.i.79-91. 191. in folio: i.e., books of the largest size.

Act II, Sc. i: 1. dearest: best. 9-10. dear grace . . . graces dear: best charm . . . beauty scarce. 14. painted: artificial. 16. uttered: put up for sale. chapmen: salesmen. 23. painful: laborious. 25. to's: to us.

---

134. a': he. 136. allowed for: assigned to. day woman: dairy woman. 162. fast . . . loose: a cheating game. 177. familiar: attendant spirit. 181. butt shaft: arrow used for target practice.

Bold of° your worthiness, we single you
As our best-moving° fair solicitor.
Tell him the daughter of the King of France, 30
On serious business craving quick dispatch,
Importunes personal conference with His Grace.
Haste, signify so much while we attend,°
Like humble-visaged suitors, his high will.
    BOYET. Proud of employment, willingly I go. 35
    PRIN. All pride is willing pride, and yours is so.
                                        [*Exit* BOYET.]
Who are the votaries,° my loving lords,
That are vow fellows with this virtuous Duke?
    1. LORD. Lord Longaville is one.
    PRIN.   Know you the man?
    MAR. I know him, madam. At a marriage feast
Between Lord Perigort and the beauteous heir 41
Of Jacques Falconbridge, solemnized
In Normandy, saw I this Longaville.
A man of sovereign parts° he is esteemed,
Well fitted in arts, glorious in arms. 45
Nothing becomes him ill that he would° well.
The only soil of his fair virtue's gloss,
If virtue's gloss will stain with any soil,
Is a sharp wit matched with too blunt a will,
Whose edge hath power to cut, whose will still wills
It should none spare that come within his power. 51
    PRIN. Some merry mocking lord, belike, is't so?
    MAR. They say so most that most his humors°
    know.
    PRIN. Such short-lived wits do wither as they
    grow.
Who are the rest? 55
    KATH. The young Dumain, a well-accomplished
    youth,
Of all that virtue love for virtue loved.
Most power to do most harm, least knowing ill;
For he hath wit to make an ill shape good,
And shape to win grace though he had no wit. 60
I saw him at the Duke Alençon's once,
And much too little of that good I saw
Is my report to his great worthiness.
    ROS. Another of these students at that time
Was there with him, if I have heard a truth. 65
Berowne they call him, but a merrier man,
Within the limit of becoming mirth,
I never spent an hour's talk withal.
His eye begets occasion° for his wit,
For every object that the one doth catch 70
The other turns to a mirth-moving jest,
Which his fair tongue, conceit's expositor,°
Delivers in such apt and gracious words
That agèd ears play truant at his tales
And younger hearings are quite ravishèd, 75

So sweet and voluble is his discourse.
    PRIN. God bless my ladies! Are they all in love,
That every one her own hath garnishèd
With such bedecking ornaments of praise?
    1. LORD. Here comes Boyet.
                          [*Re-enter* BOYET.]
    PRIN.   Now, what admittance, lord? 80
    BOYET. Navarre had notice of your fair approach,
And he and his competitors° in oath
Were all addressed° to meet you, gentle lady,
Before I came. Marry, thus much I have learned:
He rather means to lodge° you in the field, 85
Like one that comes here to besiege his Court,
Than seek a dispensation for his oath
To let you enter his unpeopled house.
Here comes Navarre.
    [*Enter* KING, LONGAVILLE, DUMAIN, BEROWNE, *and*
                         ATTENDANTS.]
    KING. Fair Princess, welcome to the Court of
Navarre. 90
    PRIN. " Fair " I give you back again, and " wel-
come " I have not yet. The roof of this Court° is too
high to be yours, and welcome to the wide fields too
base to be mine.
    KING. You shall be welcome, madam, to my
    Court. 95
    PRIN. I will be welcome, then. Conduct me thither.
    KING. Hear me, dear lady, I have sworn an oath.
    PRIN. Our Lady help my lord! He'll be forsworn.
    KING. Not for the world, fair madam, by my will.
    PRIN. Why, will shall break it — will, and nothing
    else. 100
    KING. Your ladyship is ignorant what it is.
    PRIN. Were my lord so, his ignorance were wise,
Where now his knowledge must prove ignorance.
I hear your Grace hath sworn out housekeeping.°
'Tis deadly sin to keep that oath, my lord, 105
And sin to break it.
But pardon me, I am too sudden-bold —
To teach a teacher ill beseemeth me.
Vouchsafe to read the purpose of my coming,
And suddenly resolve me in° my suit. 110
    KING. Madam, I will, if suddenly I may.
    PRIN. You will the sooner, that I were away,
For you'll prove perjured if you make me stay.
    BER. Did not I dance with you in Brabant once?
    ROS. Did not I dance with you in Brabant once?
    BER. I know you did. 116
    ROS. How needless was it, then, to ask the ques-
tion!
    BER. You must not be so quick.
    ROS. 'Tis 'long of you° that spur me with such
    questions.

---

28. Bold of: confident in. **29. best-moving:** most persuasive.
33. attend: await. **37. votaries:** those who have sworn a vow.
44. sovereign parts: supreme qualities. **46. would:** would attempt. **53. humors:** whims. **69. begets occasion:** finds opportunity. **72. conceit's expositor:** commentator on wit.

82. competitors: fellows, partners. **83. addressed:** ready.
85. lodge: accommodate. **92. this Court:** i.e., the open sky.
104. housekeeping: hospitality. **110. suddenly . . . in:** give a
quick answer to. **119. long of you:** your fault.

BER. Your wit's too hot, it speeds too fast, 'twill
    tire.   120
ROS. Not till it leave the rider in the mire.
BER. What time o' day?
ROS. The hour that fools should ask.
BER. Now fair befall your mask!°
ROS. Fair fall° the face it covers!   125
BER. And send you many lovers!
ROS. Amen, so you be none.
BER. Nay, then will I be gone.
  KING. Madam, your father here doth intimate
The payment of a hundred thousand crowns,   130
Being but the one half of an entire sum
Disbursèd by my father in his wars.
But say that he or we, as neither have,
Received that sum, yet there remains unpaid
A hundred thousand more; in surety of the which,
One part of Aquitaine is bound to us,   136
Although not valued to the money's worth.
If, then, the King your father will restore
But that one half which is unsatisfied,
We will give up our right in Aquitaine,   140
And hold fair friendship with His Majesty.
But that, it seems, he little purposeth,
For here he doth demand to have repaid
A hundred thousand crowns; and not demands,
On payment of a hundred thousand crowns,   145
To have his title live in Aquitaine;
Which we much rather had depart withal,°
And have the money by our father lent
Than Aquitaine so gelded° as it is.
Dear Princess, were not his requests so far   150
From reason's yielding, your fair self should make
A yielding, 'gainst some reason, in my breast,
And go well satisfied to France again.
  PRIN. You do the King my father too much wrong,
And wrong the reputation of your name,   155
In so unseeming° to confess receipt
Of that which hath so faithfully been paid.
  KING. I do protest I never heard of it,
And if you prove it, I'll repay it back,
Or yield up Aquitaine.
  PRIN.   We arrest your word.°   160
Boyet, you can produce acquittances°
For such a sum from special officers
Of Charles his father.
  KING.   Satisfy me so.
  BOYET. So please your Grace, the packet is not
    come
Where that and other specialties° are bound.   165
Tomorrow you shall have a sight of them.
  KING. It shall suffice me. At which interview

All liberal reason I will yield unto.
Meantime receive such welcome at my hand
As honor, without breach of honor, may   170
Make tender of° to thy true worthiness.
You may not come, fair Princess, in my gates;
But here without you shall be so received
As you shall deem yourself lodged in my heart,
Though so denied fair harbor in my house.   175
Your own good thoughts excuse me, and farewell.
Tomorrow shall we visit you again.
  PRIN. Sweet health and fair desires consort° your
    Grace!
  KING. Thy own wish wish I thee in every place!
            [Exit.]
  BER. Lady, I will commend you to mine own
heart.   180
  ROS. Pray you, do my commendations. I would be
glad to see it.
  BER. I would you heard it groan.
  ROS. Is the fool sick?
  BER. Sick at the heart.   185
  ROS. Alack! let it blood.°
  BER. Would that do it good?
  ROS. My physic says " aye."
  BER. Will you prick't with your eye?
  ROS. No point, with my knife.   190
  BER. Now God save thy life!
  ROS. And yours from long living!
  BER. I cannot stay thanksgiving.   [Retiring.]
  DUM. Sir, I pray you a word. What lady is that
    same?   194
  BOYET. The heir of Alençon, Katharine her name.
  DUM. A gallant lady. Monsieur, fare you well.
            [Exit.]
  LONG. I beseech you a word. What is she in the
    white?
  BOYET. A woman sometimes, an° you saw her in
    the light.
  LONG. Perchance light in the light. I desire her
    name.
  BOYET. She hath but one for herself, to desire that
    were a shame.   200
  LONG. Pray you, sir, whose daughter?
  BOYET. Her mother's, I have heard.
  LONG. God's blessing on your beard!
  BOYET. Good sir, be not offended.
She is an heir of Falconbridge.   205
  LONG. Nay, my choler is ended.
She is a most sweet lady.
  BOYET. Not unlike, sir, that may be.
            [Exit LONGAVILLE.]
  BER. What's her name, in the cap?
  BOYET. Rosaline, by good hap.   210
  BER. Is she wedded or no?

---

124. mask: Fashionable ladies at this time often wore masks to
protect their skin from the sun. 125. Fair fall: good luck to.
147. depart withal: part with. 149. gelded: cut. 156. so unseem-
ing: appearing not. 160. arrest . . . word: formally take you
at your word. 161. acquittances: receipts. 165. specialties:
contracts.

171. Make . . . of: offer. 178. consort: accompany. 186. let it
blood: bleeding was a common remedy in many complaints.
108. an: if.

BOYET. To her will, sir, or so.

BER. You are welcome, sir. Adieu.

BOYET. Farewell to me, sir, and welcome to you.

[*Exit* BEROWNE.]

MAR. That last is Berowne, the merry madcap
lord —   215
Not a word with him but a jest.

BOYET.   And every jest but a word.°

PRIN. It was well done of you to take him at his
word.

BOYET. I was as willing to grapple as he was to
board.

MAR. Two hot sheeps, marry.

BOYET.   And wherefore not ships?°
No sheep, sweet lamb, unless we feed on your
lips.   220

MAR. You sheep, and I pasture. Shall that finish
the jest?

BOYET. So you grant pasture for me.

[*Offering to kiss her.*]

MAR.   Not so, gentle beast.
My lips are no common,° though several° they be.

BOYET. Belonging to whom?

MAR.   To my fortunes and me.

PRIN. Good wits will be jangling, but, gentles,
agree.   225
This civil war of wits were much better used
On Navarre and his bookmen, for here 'tis abused.

BOYET. If my observation, which very seldom lies,
By the heart's still rhetoric disclosèd with eyes,
Deceive me not now, Navarre is infected.   230

PRIN. With what?

BOYET. With that which we lovers entitle affected.°

PRIN. Your reason?

BOYET. Why, all his behaviors did make their re-
tire   234
To the court of his eye, peeping thorough° desire;
His heart, like an agate° with your print impressed;
Proud with his form, in his eye pride expressed.
His tongue, all impatient to speak and not see,
Did stumble with haste in his eyesight to be.
All senses to that sense did make their repair,   240
To feel only looking on fairest of fair.
Methought all his senses were locked in his eye,
As jewels in crystal for some prince to buy;
Who, tendering their own worth from where they
were glassed,°   244
Did point you to buy them, along as you passed.
His face's own margent° did quote° such amazes°
That all eyes saw his eyes enchanted with gazes.

I'll give you Aquitaine, and all that is his,
An you give him for my sake but one loving kiss.

PRIN. Come to our pavilion. Boyet is disposed.°

BOYET. But to speak that in words which his eye
hath disclosed.   251
I only have made a mouth of his eye
By adding a tongue which I know will not lie.

ROS. Thou art an old lovemonger, and speakest
skillfully.

MAR. He is Cupid's grandfather, and learns news
of him.   255

ROS. Then was Venus like her mother, for her
father° is but grim.

BOYET. Do you hear, my mad wenches?

MAR.   No.

BOYET.   What then, do you see?

ROS. Aye, our way to be gone.

BOYET.   You are too hard for me.   [*Exeunt.*]

Act III

SCENE I. *The same.*

[*Enter* ARMADO *and* MOTH.]

ARM. Warble, child, make passionate my sense of
hearing.

MOTH. [*Singing.*] " Concolinel ——— "°

ARM. Sweet air! Go, tenderness of years. Take this
key, give enlargement to the swain, bring him festi-
nately° hither. I must employ him in a letter to my
love.

MOTH. Master, will you win your love with a
French brawl?°   9

ARM. How meanest thou? Brawling in French?

MOTH. No, my complete master; but to jig off a
tune at the tongue's end, canary° to it with your feet,
humor it with turning up your eyelids, sigh a note
and sing a note, sometime through the throat   15
as if you swallowed love with singing love, sometime
through the nose as if you snuffed up love by smelling love; with your hat penthouse-like° o'er the shop
of your eyes; with your arms crossed on your thin-
belly doublet° like a rabbit on a spit; or your   20
hands in your pocket like a man after° the old paint-

---

216. but a word: i.e., and so worth little. 219. ships: a pun on
sheeps. 223. common: common pasture. several: a pun on
"separated" and "private property." 232. affected: in love.
235. thorough: through. 236. agate: engraved stone of a seal.
244. glassed: enclosed in glass. 246. margent: margin. quote:
note. The notes in learned works were commonly printed in the
margin. amazes: astonishment.

250. disposed: i.e., to mirth. 256. father: i.e., Jupiter.
  Act III, Sc. i: 2. Concolinel: probably the name of the song
which Moth sings. 5–6. festinately: hastily. 9. brawl: a French
dance. See App. 24. 13. canary: dance. 18. hat penthouse-like:
pulled down like a roof. To wear a wide-brimmed hat pulled down
over the eyebrows was one of the signs of a melancholy lover.
See App. 4. 19–20. thin-belly doublet: close fitting — without
the padding of the "great belly" doublet. See Pl. 8b, and comment on p. 93a. 21. after: i.e., in.

ing; and keep not too long in one tune, but a snip and away. These are complements,° these are humors. These betray nice wenches that would be betrayed without these, and make them men of note° — do you note me? — that most are affected to these.   26

ARM. How hast thou purchased this experience?

MOTH. By my penny of observation.

ARM. But oh — but oh ——

MOTH. " The hobbyhorse° is forgot."

ARM. Callest thou my love " hobbyhorse "?   30

MOTH. No, master, the hobbyhorse is but a colt, and your love perhaps a hackney.° But have you forgot your love?

ARM. Almost I had.   35

MOTH. Negligent student! Learn her by heart.

ARM. By heart and in heart, boy.

MOTH. And out of heart, master. All those three I will prove.

ARM. What wilt thou prove?   40

MOTH. A man, if I live; and this by, in, and without, upon the instant — by heart you love her, because your heart cannot come by her; in heart you love her, because your heart is in love with her; and out of heart you love her, being out of heart that you cannot enjoy her.   46

ARM. I am all these three.

MOTH. And three times as much more, and yet nothing at all.

ARM. Fetch hither the swain. He must carry me a letter.   51

MOTH. A message well sympathized° — a horse to be ambassador for an ass.

ARM. Ha, ha! What sayest thou?

MOTH. Marry, sir, you must send the ass upon the horse, for he is very slow-gaited. But I go.

ARM. The way is but short. Away!

MOTH. As swift as lead, sir.

ARM. The meaning, pretty ingenious?

Is not lead a metal heavy, dull, and slow?   60

MOTH. Minimè,° honest master — or rather, master, no.

ARM. I say lead is slow.

MOTH.   You are too swift, sir, to say so.

Is that lead slow which is fired from a gun?

ARM. Sweet smoke of rhetoric!

He reputes me a cannon, and the bullet, that's he.

I shoot thee at the swain.

MOTH.   Thump, then, and I flee. [Exit.]

ARM. A most acute juvenal, volable° and free of grace!   67

By thy favor, sweet welkin,° I must sigh in thy face.

Most rude melancholy, valor gives thee place.

My herald is returned.   70

[Re-enter MOTH with COSTARD.]

MOTH. A wonder, master! Here's a Costard° broken in a shin.°

ARM. Some enigma, some riddle. Come, thy l'envoy,° begin.

COST. No egma, no riddle, no l'envoy, no salve° in the mail,° sir. Oh, sir, plantain,° a plain plantain! No l'envoy, no l'envoy. No salve, sir, but a plantain!   76

ARM. By virtue, thou enforcest laughter, thy silly thought my spleen, the heaving of my lungs provokes me to ridiculous smiling. O pardon me, my stars! Doth the inconsiderate take salve for l'envoy, and the word " l'envoy " for a salve?   80

MOTH. Do the wise think them other? Is not l'envoy a salve?

ARM. No, page, it is an epilogue° or discourse, to make plain

Some obscure precedence that hath tofore been sain.°

I will example it:

The fox,° the ape, and the humblebee   85
Were still at odds, being but three.

There's the moral. Now the l'envoy.

MOTH. I will add the l'envoy. Say the moral again.

ARM. The fox, the ape, the humblebee   90
Were still at odds, being but three.

MOTH. Until the goose came out of door,
And stayed the odds° by adding° four.

Now will I begin your moral, and do you follow with my l'envoy.   95

The fox, the ape, and the humblebee,
Were still at odds, being but three.

ARM. Until the goose came out of door,
Staying the odds by adding four.

MOTH. A good l'envoy, ending in the goose.

Would you desire more?   101

COST. The boy hath sold him a bargain,° a goose, that's flat.

Sir, your pennyworth° is good, an your goose be fat.

To sell a bargain well is as cunning as fast and loose.°   104

Let me see, a fat l'envoy — aye, that's a fat goose.

ARM. Come hither, come hither. How did this argument begin?

MOTH. By saying that a Costard was broken in a shin.

Then called you for the l'envoy.

COST. True, and I for a plantain. Thus came your argument in.

22. complements: accompaniments.   24. of note: conspicuous.
29. hobbyhorse: See Haml, III.ii.144,n. The word also meant
"prostitute."   32. hackney: a horse available for common hire.
52. well sympathized: appropriately carried.   61. Minimè: not
in the least.   67. volable: quick-witted.   68. welkin: sky.

71. Costard: head; lit., apple.   broken . . . shin: with the skin of
the shin torn.   72. l'envoy: explained at ll. 82–83 below.   73. salve:
healing ointment.   74. mail: bag.   plantain: a broad-leafed weed
growing in grass, believed to be good for bruises.   82. epilogue:
conclusion.   83. sain: said.   85–98. The fox . . . four: These apparently
meaningless lines presumably a topical jest at some-
one's expense.   93. stayed . . . odds: i.e., turned them into evens.
adding: making up the total to.   102. bargain: bad bargain.
103. pennyworth: bargain.   104. fast . . . loose: See I.ii.162,n.

Then the boy's fat l'envoy, the goose that you
    bought,   110
And he ended the market.

ARM. But tell me, how was there a Costard broken
in a shin?

MOTH. I will tell you sensibly.°

COST. Thou hast no feeling of it, Moth. I will
speak that l'envoy.   115
I Costard, running out, that was safely within,
Fell over the threshold, and broke my shin.

ARM. We will talk no more of this matter.

COST. Till there be more matter in the shin.   120

ARM. Sirrah Costard, I will enfranchise° thee.

COST. Oh, marry me to one Frances. I smell some
l'envoy, some goose, in this.

ARM. By my sweet soul, I mean setting thee at
liberty, enfreedoming thy person. Thou wert   125
immured, restrained, captivated, bound.

COST. True, true, and now you will be my purgation, and let me loose.

ARM. I give thee thy liberty, set thee from durance;
and, in lieu thereof, impose on thee nothing but this:
Bear this significant [*Giving a letter.*] to the   130
country maid Jaquenetta. There is remuneration, for
the best ward° of mine honor is rewarding my
dependents. Moth, follow.   [*Exit.*]

MOTH. Like the sequel, I. Signor Costard, adieu.

COST. My sweet ounce of man's flesh! My incony°
Jew!   [*Exit* MOTH.] 136
Now will I look to° his remuneration. Remuneration! Oh, that's the Latin word for three farthings;
three farthings — remuneration. — "What's the
price of this inkle°?" — "One penny." — "No, I'll
give you a remuneration." Why, it carries it. 140
Remuneration! Why, it is a fairer name than French
crown. I will never buy and sell out of° this word.

             [*Enter* BEROWNE.]

BER. O my good knave Costard, exceedingly well
met!   145

COST. Pray you, sir, how much carnation° ribbon
may a man buy for a remuneration?

BER. What is a remuneration?

COST. Marry, sir, halfpenny farthing.

BER. Why, then, three-farthing worth of silk.   150

COST. I thank your Worship. God be wi' you!

BER. Stay, slave; I must employ thee.
As thou wilt win my favor, good my knave,
Do one thing for me that I shall entreat.

COST. When would you have it done, sir?   155

BER. This afternoon.

COST. Well, I will do it, sir. Fare you well.

BER. Thou knowest not what it is.

COST. I shall know, sir, when I have done it.

BER. Why, villain, thou must know first.   160

COST. I will come to your Worship tomorrow
morning.

BER. It must be done this afternoon. Hark, slave,
it is but this:
The Princess comes to hunt here in the park,   165
And in her train there is a gentle lady.
When tongues speak sweetly, then they name her
    name,
And Rosaline they call her. Ask for her,
And to her white hand see thou do commend   169
This sealed-up counsel.° There's thy guerdon.° Go.
              [*Giving him a shilling.*]

COST. Gardon, O sweet gardon! Better than remuneration, a 'levenpence farthing better. Most
sweet gardon! I will do it, sir, in print. Gardon!
Remuneration!   [*Exit.*]

BER. And I, forsooth, in love! I, that have been
love's whip —   175
A very beadle° to a humorous° sigh,
A critic, nay, a night-watch constable,
A domineering pedant o'er the boy,
Than whom no mortal so magnificent!   180
This wimpled,° whining, purblind, wayward boy,
This senior-junior, giant-dwarf, Dan Cupid,
Regent of love rhymes, lord of folded arms,
The anointed sovereign of sighs and groans,
Liege° of all loiterers and malcontents,   185
Dread prince of plackets,° king of codpieces,°
Sole imperator and great general
Of trotting 'paritors.° — Oh, my little heart! —
And I to be a corporal of his field,
And wear his colors like a tumbler's° hoop!   190
What! I love! I sue! I seek a wife!
A woman, that is like a German clock,
Still a-repairing,° ever out of frame,°
And never going aright, being a watch,
But being watched that it may still go right!   195
Nay, to be perjured, which is worst of all.
And, among three, to love the worst of all,
A whitely wanton with a velvet brow,
With two pitch balls stuck in her face for eyes —
Aye, and, by Heaven, one that will do the deed   200
Though Argus° were her eunuch° and her guard.
And I to sigh for her! To watch for her!
To pray for her! Go to, it is a plague
That Cupid will impose for my neglect
Of his almighty dreadful little might.   205
Well, I will love, write, sigh, pray, sue and groan.
Some men must love my lady, and some Joan.°
                        [*Exit.*]

170. counsel: secret communication. guerdon: reward. 176. beadle: parish officer who whipped offenders. humorous: melancholy. 181. wimpled: hooded. 185. Liege: lord. 186. placket:
opening in the petticoat. codpieces: See Pl. 8c and p. 93b.
188. 'paritors: apparitors, officers of the ecclesiastical court who
summoned offenders guilty of moral offenses. 190. tumbler: acro-
bat. 193. Still a-repairing: always needing repair. frame: setting.
201. Argus: the watchman of the gods, who had a hundred eyes.
eunuch: the guardian of a harem. 207. Joan: a country wench.

113. sensibly: feelingly. 121. enfranchise: liberate. 132. ward:
defense. 136. incony: fine. 137. to: at. 139. inkle: piece of
tape. 142. out of: without using. 146. carnation: red.

Act IV

SCENE I. *The same.*

[*Enter the* PRINCESS, *and her* TRAIN, *a* FORESTER,
BOYET, ROSALINE, MARIA, *and* KATHARINE.]

PRIN. Was that the King that spurred his horse so
   hard
Against the steep uprising of the hill?
  BOYET. I know not, but I think it was not he.
  PRIN. Whoe'er a' was, a' showed a mounting
   mind.°
Well, lords, today we shall have our dispatch. 5
On Saturday we will return to France.
Then, forester, my friend, where is the bush
That we must stand and play the murderer in?°
  FOR. Hereby, upon the edge of yonder coppice,
A stand where you may make the fairest shoot. 10
  PRIN. I thank my beauty, I am fair that shoot,
And thereupon thou speak'st the fairest shoot.
  FOR. Pardon me, madam, for I meant not so.
  PRIN. What, what? First praise me, and again say
   no?
Oh, short-lived pride! Not fair? Alack for woe! 15
  FOR. Yes, madam, fair.
  PRIN.   Nay, never paint me now.
Where fair is not, praise cannot mend the brow.
Here, good my glass,° take this for telling true.
Fair payment for foul words is more than due. 19
  FOR. Nothing but fair is that which you inherit.
  PRIN. See, see, my beauty will be saved by merit!
Oh, heresy in fair,° fit for these days!
A giving hand, though foul, shall have fair praise.
But come, the bow. Now mercy goes to kill,
And shooting well is then accounted ill. 25
Thus will I save my credit in the shoot —
Not wounding, pity would not let me do't.
If wounding, then it was to show my skill,
That more for praise than purpose meant to kill.
And, out of question, so it is sometimes 30
Glory grows guilty of detested crimes,
When, for fame's sake, for praise, an outward part,
We bend to that the working of the heart —
As I for praise alone now seek to spill 34
The poor deer's blood, that my heart means no ill.
  BOYET. Do not curst° wives hold that self-
   sovereignty
Only for praise sake, when they strive to be
Lords o'er their lords?
  PRIN. Only for praise. And praise we may afford

To any lady that subdues a lord. 40
  BOYET. Here comes a member of the commonwealth.

[*Enter* COSTARD.]

  COST. God dig-you-den° all! Pray you, which is the
head lady?
  PRIN. Thou shalt know her, fellow, by the rest that
have no heads. 45
  COST. Which is the greatest lady, the highest?
  PRIN. The thickest and the tallest.
  COST. The thickest and the tallest! It is so, truth **is**
   truth.
An your waist, mistress, were as slender as my wit,
One o' these maids' girdles for your waist should be
  fit. 50
Are not you the chief woman? You are the thickest
  here.
  PRIN. What's your will, sir? What's your will?
  COST. I have a letter from Monsieur Berowne to
  one Lady Rosaline.
  PRIN. Oh, thy letter, thy letter! He's a good friend
  of mine.
Stand aside, good bearer. Boyet, you can carve —
Break up° this capon. 56
  BOYET.   I am bound to serve.
This letter is mistook, it importeth none here,
It is writ to Jaquenetta.
  PRIN.   We will read it, I swear. 58
Break the neck of the wax, and everyone give ear.
  BOYET. [*Reads.*] " By Heaven, that thou art fair is
most infallible, true that thou art beauteous, truth
itself that thou art lovely. More fairer than fair, beautiful than beauteous, truer than truth itself, have
commiseration on thy heroical vassal! The magnanimous and most illustrate° King Cophetua set 65
eye upon the pernicious and indubitate beggar
Zenelophon; and he it was that might rightly say,
Veni, vidi, vici; which to annothanize° in the vul-
gar° — O base and obscure vulgar! — videlicet,° He
came, saw, and overcame: he came, one; saw, 70
two; overcame, three. Who came? The King. Why
did he come? To see. Why did he see? To overcome.
To whom came he? To the beggar. What saw he?
The beggar. Who overcame he? The beggar. The
conclusion is victory. On whose side? The King's.
The captive is enriched. On whose side? The 75
beggar's. The catastrophe° is a nuptial. On whose
side? The King's — no, on both in one, or one in
both. I am the King, for so stands the comparison,
thou the beggar, for so witnesseth thy lowliness.
Shall I command thy love? I may. Shall I en- 80
force thy love? I could. Shall I entreat thy love? I
will. What shalt thou exchange for rags? Robes. For

Act IV, Sc. i: **4. mounting mind:** lofty spirit. **7–8. bush . . .
in:** The Princess is about to hunt the deer in the manner practiced by Queen Elizabeth. The Queen and her ladies, armed
with bows and arrows, took up their stand and the deer were
driven past them well within range. **18. good my glass:** my
good mirror. **22. heresy in fair:** heresy against beauty. **36. curst:**
shrewish.

---

42. dig-you-den: give you a good evening. **56. Break up:** carve
(a chicken) or open (a letter). **65. illustrate:** illustrious.
68. annothanize: anatomize, dissect. **68–69. vulgar:** common
tongue. **69. videlicet:** viz., namely. **76. catastrophe:** conclusion.

tittles?° Titles. For thyself? Me. Thus, expecting thy
reply, I profane my lips on thy foot, my eyes on thy
picture, and my heart on thy every part. Thine,　85
in the dearest design of industry,°
　　　　　　" DON ADRIANO DE ARMADO "
Thus dost thou hear the Nemean lion° roar　　90
'Gainst thee, thou lamb, that standest as his prey.
Submissive fall his princely feet before,
　　And he from forage will incline to play.
But if thou strive, poor soul, what art thou then?
Food for his rage, repasture° for his den.　　95
PRIN. What plume of feathers° is he that indited
　　this letter?
What vane?° What weathercock? Did you ever hear
　　better?
BOYET. I am much deceived but I° remember the
　　style.
PRIN. Else your memory is bad, going o'er it ere-
　　while.°
BOYET. This Armado is a Spaniard that keeps here
　　in Court,　　　　　　　　　　　　　　　100
A phantasime,° a Monarcho,° and one that makes
　　sport
To the Prince and his bookmates.
PRIN.　　　　　　　　　Thou fellow, a word.
Who gave thee this letter?
COST.　　　　　　　I told you — my lord.
PRIN. To whom shouldst thou give it?
COST.　　　　　　　From my lord to my lady.
PRIN. From which lord to which lady?　　105
COST. From my lord Berowne, a good master of
　　mine,
To a lady of France that he called Rosaline.
PRIN. Thou hast mistaken his letter. Come, lords,
　　away.
[To ROSALINE] Here, sweet, put up this. 'Twill be
　　thine another day.
　　　　　　　　[Exeunt PRINCESS and TRAIN.]
BOYET. Who is the suitor?° Who is the suitor?
ROS.　　　　　　　Shall I teach you to know?　110
BOYET. Aye, my continent of beauty.
ROS.　　　　　　　Why, she that bears the bow.
Finely put off!°
BOYET. My lady goes to kill horns, but if thou
　　marry,
Hang me by the neck if horns that year miscarry.°
Finely put on!
ROS. Well then, I am the shooter.　　115
BOYET.　　　　　　　And who is your deer?

ROS. If we choose by the horns, yourself come not
　　near.
Finely put on, indeed!
MAR. You still wrangle with her, Boyet, and she
　　strikes at the brow.°
BOYET. But she herself is hit lower. Have I hit her
　　now?　　　　　　　　　　　　　　　120
ROS. Shall I come upon thee with an old saying
that was a man when King Pepin° of France was a
little boy, as touching the hit it?°
BOYET. So I may answer thee with one as old that
was a woman when Queen Guinever° of Britain was
a little wench, as touching the hit it.　　126
ROS. " Thou canst not hit it, hit it, hit it,
　　　Thou canst not hit it, my good man."
BOYET. " An I cannot, cannot, cannot,
　　　An I cannot, another can."　　130
　　　　　　　[Exeunt ROSALINE and KATHARINE.]
COST. By my troth, most pleasant. How both did
　　fit it!
MAR. A mark marvelous well shot, for they both
　　did hit it.
BOYET. A mark! Oh, mark but that mark! A mark,
　　says my lady!
Let the mark have a prick° in't, to mete° at, if it
　　may be.
MAR. Wide o' the bow hand!° I' faith, your hand
　　is out.　　　　　　　　　　　　　　135
COST. Indeed, a' must shoot nearer, or he'll ne'er
　　hit the clout.°
BOYET. An if my hand be out, then belike your
　　hand is in.
COST. Then will she get the upshoot° by cleaving
　　the pin.°
MAR. Come, come, you talk greasily,° your lips
　　grow foul.
COST. She's too hard for you at pricks, sir. Chal-
　　lenge her to bowl.　　　　　　　　140
BOYET. I fear too much rubbing.° Good night, my
　　good owl.　　　　[Exeunt BOYET and MARIA.]
COST. By my soul, a swain, a most simple clown!
Lord, Lord, how the ladies and I have put him
　　down!
O' my troth, most sweet jests, most incony vulgar
　　wit!
When it comes so smoothly off, so obscenely,° as it
　　were, so fit.　　　　　　　　　　　145
Armado o' th' one side — Oh, a most dainty man!
To see him walk before a lady and to bear her fan!

---

83. tittles: trifles.　86. industry: gallantry.　90. Nemean lion:
a fierce beast slain by Hercules.　95. repasture: food.　96. plume
of feathers: i.e., fantastical gallant.　97. vane: weathervane,
with a pun on "vain."　98. but I: if I do not.　99. going . . .
erewhile: if you have met it before.　101. phantasime: fantastic
ass. Monarcho: the name of a crazy Italian who haunted Queen
Elizabeth's Court.　110–11. suitor . . . bow: with a pun on
"shooter."　112. Finely . . . off: well answered.　114. if . . . miscarry: if horns go short; i.e., if someone is not made a cuckold. See App. 11.

119. strikes . . . brow: aims at your head.　122. Pepin: father
of Charlemagne; i.e., a very long time ago.　123. hit it: the
name of an old dance tune, given below.　125. Guinever: King
Arthur's Queen.　134. prick: center of the target. mete: aim.
135. Wide . . . hand: you're too far to the left.　136. clout:
cloth, bull's-eye.　138. get . . . upshoot: lit., be hailed as the
best shot. cleaving . . . pin: hitting the pin in the center of the
target.　139. greasily: indecently.　141. rubbing: lit., unevenness on the green.　145. obscenely: perhaps for "notoriously."

To see him kiss his hand! And how most sweetly a'
　　will swear!
And his page o' t' other side, that handful of wit!
Ah, Heavens, it is a most pathetical nit!°　　　150
Sola, sola!° [*Shout within. Exit* COSTARD, *running.*]

SCENE II.° *The same.*

[*Enter* HOLOFERNES, SIR NATHANIEL, *and* DULL.]

NATH. Very reverend sport, truly, and done in the
testimony of a good conscience.

HOL. The deer was, as you know, *sanguis,*° in
blood; ripe as the pomewater,° who now hangeth
like a jewel in the ear of *caelo,*° the sky, the wel- 5
kin, the heaven, and anon falleth like a crab° on the
face of *terra,* the soil, the land, the earth.

NATH. Truly, Master Holofernes, the epithets are
sweetly varied, like a scholar at the least. But, sir, I
assure ye it was a buck of the first head.°　　10

HOL. Sir Nathaniel, *haud credo.*

DULL. 'Twas not a *haud credo,* 'twas a pricket.°

HOL. Most barbarous intimation! Yet a kind of
insinuation, as it were, *in via,* in way, of explication;
facere, as it were, replication, or, rather, *osten-* 15
tare, to show, as it were, his inclination, after his undressed, unpolished, uneducated, unpruned, untrained, or rather unlettered, or ratherest unconfirmed fashion, to insert again my *haud credo* for a
deer.°　　　20

DULL. I said the deer was not a *haud credo,* 'twas
a pricket.

HOL. Twice-sod° simplicity, *bis coctus!*°
O thou monster Ignorance, how deformed dost thou
　　look!

NATH. Sir, he hath never fed of the dainties that
are bred in a book;　　　25
he hath not eat paper, as it were; he hath not drunk
ink. His intellect is not replenished, he is only an animal, only sensible in the duller parts.
And such barren plants are set before us that we
　　thankful should be,
Which we of taste and feeling are, for those parts
　　that do fructify in us more than he.　　30
For as it would ill become me to be vain, indiscreet,
　　or a fool,
So were there a patch set on learning° to see him in
　　a school.

But *omne bene,*° say I, being of an old father's mind,
Many can brook° the weather that love not the wind.

DULL. You two are bookmen. Can you tell me by
　　your wit　　　35
What was a month old at Cain's birth that's not five
　　weeks old as yet?

HOL. Dictynna,° goodman Dull. Dictynna, goodman Dull.

DULL. What is Dictynna?

NATH. A title to Phoebe, to Luna, to the moon.

HOL. The moon was a month old when Adam was
　　no more,　　　40
And raught° not to five weeks when he came to five-
　　score.
The allusion holds in the exchange.°

DULL. 'Tis true indeed, the collusion holds in the
　　exchange.

HOL. God comfort thy capacity! I say, the allusion
holds in the exchange.

DULL. And I say, the pollution holds in the exchange, for the moon is never but a month old. And
I say beside that 'twas a pricket that the Princess
killed.　　　49

HOL. Sir Nathaniel, will you hear an extemporal
epitaph on the death of the deer? And, to humor the
ignorant, call I the deer the Princess killed a pricket.

NATH. *Perge,*° good Master Holofernes, *perge,* so
it shall please you to abrogate° scurrility.　　55

HOL. I will something affect the letter,° for it
argues facility.
" The preyful Princess pierced and pricked a pretty
　　pleasing pricket,
　Some say a sore,° but not a sore till now made
　　sore with shooting.
The dogs did yell. But L° to sore, then sorel°
　　jumps from thicket,　　　60
　Or pricket sore, or else sorel; the people fall
　　a-hooting.
If sore be sore, then L to sore makes fifty sores one
　　sorel.
Of one sore I a hundred make by adding but one
　　more L."

NATH. A rare talent!　　　65

DULL. [*Aside*] If a talent° be a claw, look how he
claws° him with a talent.

HOL. This is a gift that I have, simple, simple; a
foolish extravagant spirit, full of forms, figures, 70
shapes, objects, ideas, apprehensions, motions, revolutions. These are begot in the ventricle° of memory,

nourished in the womb of pia mater,° and delivered upon the mellowing of occasion. But the gift is good in those in whom it is acute, and I am thankful for it.   75

NATH. Sir, I praise the Lord for you, and so may my parishioners; for their sons are well tutored by you, and their daughters profit very greatly under you. You are a good member of the commonwealth.   79

HOL. *Mehercle,*° if their sons be ingenuous,° they shall want no instruction; if their daughters be capable, I will put it to them. But *vir sapit qui pauca loquitur,*° a soul feminine saluteth us.

[*Enter* JAQUENETTA *and* COSTARD.]

JAQ. God give you good morrow, Master Parson.

HOL. Master Parson, *quasi* pers-on.° And if   85 one should be pierced,° which is the one?

COST. Marry, Master Schoolmaster, he that is likest to a hogshead.

HOL. Piercing a hogshead! A good luster of conceit in a turf of earth, fire enough for a flint, pearl enough for a swine — 'tis pretty, it is well.   90

JAQ. Good Master Parson, be so good as read me this letter. It was given me by Costard, and sent me from Don Armado. I beseech you read it.

HOL. *Fauste, precor gelida quando pecus omne sub umbra*   95
Ruminat° —

and so forth. Ah, good old Mantuan! I may speak of thee as the traveler doth of Venice:

Venetia, Venetia,
Chi non ti vede non ti pretia.°   100

Old Mantuan, old Mantuan, who understandeth thee not, loves thee not. Ut, re, sol, la, mi, fa.° Under pardon, sir, what are the contents? Or rather, as Horace says in his —— What, my soul, verses?   105

NATH. Aye, sir, and very learned.

HOL. Let me hear a staff,° a stanze, a verse. *Lege, domine.*°

NATH. [*Reads.*]

"If love make me forsworn, how shall I swear to love?
Ah, never faith could hold, if not to beauty vowed!   110
Though to myself forsworn, to thee I'll faithful prove;

Those thoughts to me were oaks, to thee like osiers° bowed.
Study his bias° leaves, and makes his book thine eyes,
Where all those pleasures live that art would comprehend.
If knowledge be the mark, to know thee shall suffice;   115
Well learned is that tongue that well can thee commend,
All ignorant that soul that sees thee without wonder,
Which is to me some praise that I thy parts admire.
Thy eye Jove's lightning bears, thy voice his dreadful thunder,
Which, not to anger bent, is music and sweet fire.   120
Celestial as thou art, oh, pardon love this wrong,
That sings Heaven's praise with such an earthly tongue."

HOL. You find not the apostrophas,° and so miss the accent. Let me supervise the canzonet.°   125 Here are only numbers ratified; but for the elegancy, facility, and golden cadence of poesy, *caret.*° Ovidius Naso was the man. And why, indeed, Naso, but for smelling out the odoriferous flowers of fancy, the jerks of invention? *Imitari* is nothing; so doth the hound his master, the ape his keeper, the tired horse his rider. But, damosella virgin, was this directed to you?   133

JAQ. Aye, sir, from one Monsieur Berowne, one of the strange Queen's lords.

HOL. I will overglance the superscript:° "To the snow-white hand of the most beauteous Lady Rosaline." I will look again on the intellect° of the letter, for the nomination of the party writing to the person written unto: "Your ladyship's in all desired employment, BEROWNE."   140 Sir Nathaniel, this Berowne is one of the votaries with the King. And here he hath framed a letter to a sequent° of the stranger Queen's, which accidentally, or by the way of progression, hath miscarried. Trip and go, my sweet. Deliver this paper into the royal hand of the King — it may concern much. Stay not° thy compliment,° I forgive thy duty.° Adieu.

JAQ. Good Costard, go with me. Sir, God save your life!   150

COST. Have with thee, my girl.

[*Exeunt* COSTARD *and* JAQUENETTA.]

---

73. **pia mater:** brain.   80. *Mehercle:* by Hercules. **ingenuous:** ingenious, quick-witted.   82–83. *vir . . . loquitur:* it's a wise man who speaks few words.   85. **quasi pers-on:** as if pronounced "perse one."   86. **pierced:** pronounced "persed."   95–96. *Fauste . . . Ruminat:* Faustus, I pray you when all your flock lies feeding under the cool shade — opening lines from the *Eclogues* of Battista Spagnuoli of Mantua which was a prescribed text for schoolboys in Shakespeare's day.   99–100. *Venetia . . . pretia:* Venice, Venice, who has not seen you does not prize you — an Italian proverb.   102. **Ut . . . fa:** Here he hums a scale.   107. **staff:** stanza.   107–108. *Lege, domine:* read, master.

112. **osiers:** willows.   113. **bias:** course; lit., of a bowl in the game of bowls.   123. **apostrophas:** apostrophes, poetic omission of a vowel.   125. **canzonet:** short song.   126–27. **Here . . . *caret*:** i.e., the verses do scan, but the poetry is wanting (*caret*).   136. **superscript:** address.   138. **intellect:** purport, meaning.   143. **sequent:** follower.   147. **Stay not:** do not wait for. **compliment:** curtsy.   148. **duty:** expression of respect.

NATH. Sir, you have done this in the fear of God, very religiously, and, as a certain father saith ——

HOL. Sir, tell me not of the father, I do fear colorable colors.° But to return to the verses. Did they please you, Sir Nathaniel?

NATH. Marvelous well for the pen.°   158

HOL. I do dine today at the father's of a certain pupil of mine, where, if before repast it shall please you to gratify the table with a grace, I will, on my privilege I have with the parents of the foresaid child or pupil, undertake your *benvenuto;*° where I will prove those verses to be very unlearned, neither   165 savoring of poetry, wit, nor invention. I beseech your society.

NATH. And thank you too; for society, saith the text, is the happiness of life.

HOL. And certes° the text most infallibly concludes it. [*To* DULL] Sir, I do invite you too, you shall not say me nay — *pauca verba.*° Away! The gentles are at their game, and we will to our recreation.   174

[*Exeunt.*]

SCENE III.° *The same.*

[*Enter* BEROWNE, *with a paper.*]

BER. The King he is hunting the deer, I am coursing° myself. They have pitched a toil,° I am toiling in a pitch — pitch that defiles. Defile! A foul word. Well, set thee down, sorrow! For so they say the   5 fool said, and so say I, and I the fool — well proved, wit! By the Lord, this love is as mad as Ajax.° It kills sheep, it kills me, I a sheep — well proved again o' my side! I will not love. If I do, hang me; i' faith, I will not. Oh, but her eye — by this light, but for her eye I would not love her; yes, for her two eyes. Well, I do nothing in the world but lie, and lie in my   12 throat.° By Heaven, I do love, and it hath taught me to rhyme, and to be melancholy; and here is part of my rhyme, and here my melancholy. Well, she hath one o' my sonnets already. The clown bore it, the fool sent it, and the lady hath it. Sweet clown, sweeter fool, sweetest lady! By the world, I would not care a pin if the other three were in.° Here comes one with a paper. God give him grace to groan! [*Stands aside.*]   21

[*Enter the* KING, *with a paper.*]

KING. Aye me!

BER. [*Aside*] Shot, by Heaven! Proceed, sweet Cupid. Thou hast thumped him with thy bird bolt° under the left pap. In faith, secrets!   25

KING. [*Reads.*]
" So sweet a kiss the golden sun gives not
    To those fresh morning drops upon the rose,
  As thy eye beams when their fresh rays have smote
    The night of dew that on my cheeks downflows.
  Nor shines the silver moon one half so bright   30
    Through the transparent bosom of the deep
  As doth thy face through tears of mine give light.
    Thou shinest in every tear that I do weep,
  No drop but as a coach doth carry thee,
    So ridest thou triumphing in my woe.   35
  Do but behold the tears that swell in me,
    And they thy glory through my grief will show.
  But do not love thyself — then thou wilt keep
  My tears for glasses,° and still make me weep.
  O queen of queens! How far dost thou excel   40
  No thought can think nor tongue of mortal tell."

How shall she know my griefs? I'll drop the paper.
Sweet leaves, shade folly. Who is he comes here?

[*Steps aside.*]

What, Longaville! And reading! Listen, ear.

BER. Now, in thy likeness, one more fool appear!

[*Enter* LONGAVILLE, *with a paper.*]

LONG. Aye me, I am forsworn!

BER. Why, he comes in like a perjure, wearing papers.°

KING. In love, I hope. Sweet fellowship in shame!

BER. One drunkard loves another of the name.   50

LONG. Am I the first that have been perjured so?

BER. I could put thee in comfort. Not by two that I know.
Thou makest the triumviry,° the cornercap° of society,
The shape of Love's Tyburn° that hangs up simplicity.°

LONG. I fear these stubborn lines lack power to move.   55
O sweet Maria, empress of my love!
These numbers° will I tear, and write in prose.

BER. Oh, rhymes are guards° on wanton Cupid's hose.
Disfigure not his slop.°

LONG.   This same shall go. [*Reads.*]
" Did not the heavenly rhetoric of thine eye,   60

154–155. colorable colors: plausible excuses.   158. pen: penmanship.   164. *benvenuto:* welcome.   171. certes: assuredly.   173. *pauca verba:* few words.

   Sc. iii: This scene is more entertaining to watch than to read. As each lover comes in and hides, he is unaware of the others who have come in before him, and — by stage convention — is supposed not to hear their sarcastic comments.   1–2. coursing: chasing.   2. pitched a toil: prepared a net.   7. Ajax: Ajax, disappointed that the shield of the dead Achilles was not awarded to him, went mad and slew a flock of sheep, supposing them to be his enemies.   12–13. lie . . . throat: the worst kind of lie.   19. in: i.e ., also in love.

24. bird bolt: short blunt arrow for shooting birds. See Pl. 22a.   39. glasses: eyes.   47–48. perjure . . . papers: Perjurors were condemned to stand in the pillory wearing a paper proclaiming their offense.   53. triumviry: party of three. cornercap: cap with three or four corners worn by graduates, judges, and divines.   54. Tyburn: the place of execution for London criminals where stood the permanent three-cornered gallows. simplicity: folly.   57. numbers: verses.   58. guards: ornamental strips of velvet or braid. See Pl. 9f and 9n, and comment on p. 94b.   59. slop: baggy breeches. See Pl. 8–Pl. 8c and comment on p. 93b.

'Gainst whom the world cannot hold argument,
Persuade my heart to this false perjury?
   Vows for thee broke deserve not punishment.
A woman I forswore, but I will prove,
   Thou being a goddess, I forswore not thee.   65
My vow was earthly, thou a heavenly love.
   Thy grace being gained cures all disgrace in me.
Vows are but breath, and breath a vapor is.
   Then thou, fair sun, which on my earth dost
       shine,
Exhalest this vapor vow; in thee it is.   70
   If broken then, it is no fault of mine.
If by me broke, what fool is not so wise
To lose an oath to win a paradise? "
   BER. This is the liver vein,° which makes flesh a
       deity,
A green goose a goddess — pure, pure idolatry.   75
God amend us, God amend! We are much out o'
   the way.°
   LONG. By whom shall I send this? — Company!
       Stay.   [*Steps aside.*]
   BER. All hid, all hid, an old infant play.
Like a demigod here sit I in the sky,
And wretched fools' secrets heedfully o'ereye.   80
More sacks to the mill! Oh, Heavens, I have my
   wish!
[*Enter* DUMAIN *with a paper.*] Dumain transformed!
   Four woodcocks° in a dish!
   DUM. O most divine Kate!
   BER. O most profane coxcomb!°
   DUM. By Heaven, the wonder in a mortal eye!   85
   BER. By earth, she is not, corporal,° there you lie.
   DUM. Her amber hairs for foul hath amber
       quoted.°
   BER. An amber-colored raven was well noted.
   DUM. As upright as the cedar.
   BER.   Stoop, I say.
Her shoulder is with child.°
   DUM.   As fair as day.   90
   BER. Aye, as some days, but then no sun must
       shine.
   DUM. Oh, that I had my wish!
   LONG.   And I had mine!
   KING. And I mine too, good Lord!
   BER. Amen, so I had mine. Is not that a good
       word?
   DUM. I would forget her, but a fever she   95
Reigns in my blood, and will remembered be.
   BER. A fever in your blood! Why, then incision°
Would let her out in saucers — sweet misprision!°

DUM. Once more I'll read the ode that I have writ.
BER. Once more I'll mark how love can vary
   wit.   100
DUM. [*Reads.*]
   "On a day — alack the day! —
      Love, whose month is ever May,
      Spied a blossom passing fair
      Playing in the wanton air.
   Through the velvet leaves the wind,   105
      All unseen, can passage find,
      That the lover, sick to death,
      Wish himself the heaven's breath.
   'Air,' quoth he, ' thy cheeks may blow.
      Air, would I might triumph so!   110
   But, alack, my hand is sworn
      Ne'er to pluck thee from thy thorn —
   Vow, alack, for youth unmeet,
      Youth so apt to pluck a sweet!
   Do not call it sin in me   115
      That I am forsworn for thee.
   Thou for whom Jove would swear
      Juno but an Ethiope° were,
   And deny himself for Jove,
      Turning mortal for thy love."   120
This will I send and something else more plain,
That shall express my true love's fasting pain.
Oh, would the King, Berowne, and Longaville
Were lovers too! Ill, to example ill,
Would from my forehead wipe a perjured note,   125
For none offend where all alike do dote.
   LONG. [*Advancing.*] Dumain, thy love is far from
       charity,
That in love's grief desirest society.
You may look pale, but I should blush, I know,
To be o'erheard and taken napping so.   130
   KING. [*Advancing.*] Come, sir, you blush, as his
       your case is such.
You chide at him, offending twice as much.
You do not love Maria, Longaville
Did never sonnet for her sake compile,
Nor never lay his wreathèd° arms athwart   135
His loving bosom, to keep down his heart.
I have been closely shrouded in this bush
And marked you both and for you both did blush.
I heard your guilty rhymes, observed your fashion,
Saw sighs reek° from you, noted well your passion.
" Aye me! " says one. " O Jove! " the other
   cries.   141
One, her hairs were gold, crystal the other's eyes.
[*To* LONGAVILLE] You would for paradise break faith
   and troth,
[*To* DUMAIN] And Jove, for your love, would in-
   fringe an oath.
What will Berowne say when that he shall hear   145
Faith so infringèd, which such zeal did swear?

---

74. **liver vein:** humor of a lover, the liver being regarded as the
seat of love.   76. **much . . . way:** i.e., we have erred and strayed.
82. **woodcocks:** i.e., fools.   84. **coxcomb:** fool.   86. **corporal:** an
appointment in a regiment corresponding to adjutant, with a pun
on "corporal," human.   87. **Her . . . quoted:** amber itself has
noted (*quoted*) that her hair is more amber than amber.   90. **with
child:** burdened; i.e., is not straight.   97. **incision:** cut for letting blood.   98. **misprision:** mistake.

118. **Ethiope:** Ethiopian.   135. **wreathed:** folded.   140. **reek:**
steam.

How will he scorn! How will he spend his wit!
How will he triumph, leap and laugh at it!
For all the wealth that ever I did see,
I would not have him know so much by° me.   150
    BER. [*Advancing.*] Now step I forth to whip
    hypocrisy.
Ah, good my liege, I pray thee pardon me!
Good heart, what grace hast thou, thus to reprove
These worms for loving, that art most in love?
Your eyes do make no coaches,° in your tears   155
There is no certain Princess that appears.
You'll not be perjured, 'tis a hateful thing —
Tush, none but minstrels like of sonneting!
But are you not ashamed? Nay, are you not,
All three of you, to be thus much o'ershot?°   160
You found his mote, the King your mote did see,
But I a beam° do find in each of three.
Oh, what a scene of foolery have I seen,
Of sighs, of groans, of sorrow and of teen!°
Oh me, with what strict patience have I sat   165
To see a king transformèd to a gnat!
To see great Hercules whipping a gig,°
And profound Solomon to tune a jig,
And Nestor° play at pushpin° with the boys,
And critic Timon° laugh at idle toys!°   170
Where lies thy grief, oh, tell me, good Dumain?
And, gentle Longaville, where lies thy pain?
And where my liege's? All about the breast.
A caudle,° ho!
    KING.   Too bitter is thy jest.
Are we betrayed thus to thy overview?   175
    BER. Not you to me, but I betrayed by you —
I, that am honest, I, that hold it sin
To break the vow I am engagèd in —
I am betrayed by keeping company
With men like you, men of inconstancy.   180
When shall you see me write a thing in rhyme?
Or groan for love? Or spend a minute's time
In pruning me?° When shall you hear that I
Will praise a hand, a foot, a face, an eye,
A gait, a state,° a brow, a breast, a waist,   185
A leg, a limb?
    KING.   Soft! Whither away so fast?
A true man or a thief that gallops so?
    BER. I post° from love. Good lover, let me go.
        [*Enter* JAQUENETTA *and* COSTARD.]
    JAQ. God bless the King!

    KING.   What present hast thou there?
    COST. Some certain treason.
    KING.   What makes treason here?   190
    COST. Nay, it makes nothing, sir.
    KING.   If it mar nothing neither,
The treason and you go in peace away together.
    JAQ. I beseech your Grace, let this letter be read.
Our parson misdoubts° it, 'twas treason, he said.
    KING. Berowne, read it over.   195
        [*Giving him the paper.*]
Where hadst thou it?
    JAQ. Of Costard.
    KING. Where hadst thou it?
    COST. Of Dun Adramadio, Dun Adramadio.
        [BEROWNE *tears the letter.*]
    KING. How now! What is in you? Why dost thou
    tear it?   200
    BER. A toy, my liege, a toy. Your Grace needs not
    fear it.
    LONG. It did move him to passion, and therefore
    let's hear it.
    DUM. [*Gathering up the pieces.*] It is Berowne's
    writing, and here is his name.
    BER. [*To* COSTARD] Ah, you whoreson logger-
    head!° You were born to do me shame.
Guilty, my lord, guilty! I confess, I confess.   205
    KING. What?
    BER. That you three fools lacked me fool to make
    up the mess.°
He, he, and you, and you, my liege, and I,
Are pickpurses in love, and we deserve to die.   209
Oh, dismiss this audience, and I shall tell you more.
    DUM. Now the number is even.
    BER.   True, true, we are four.
Will these turtles° be gone?
    KING.   Hence, sirs, away!
    COST. Walk aside the true folk, and let the traitors
    stay.   [*Exeunt* COSTARD *and* JAQUENETTA.]
    BER. Sweet lords, sweet lovers, oh, let us embrace!
As true we are as flesh and blood can be.   215
The sea will ebb and flow, Heaven show his face,
    Young blood doth not obey an old decree.
We cannot cross° the cause why we were born,
Therefore of all hands must we be forsworn.
    KING. What, did these rent lines show some love
    of thine?   220
    BER. Did they, quoth you? Who sees the heavenly
    Rosaline
That, like a rude and savage man of Ind,°
    At the first opening of the gorgeous east
Bows not his vassal head and stricken blind
    Kisses the base ground with obedient breast?   225
What peremptory eagle-sighted eye

---

150. **by:** concerning.   155. **coaches:** See l. 34 above.   160. **o'er-shot:** overshot, wide of the mark.   161–62. **mote . . . beam:** See Luke 6:41–42: "thou hypocrite, cast out first the beam out of thine own eye and then thou shalt see clearly to pull out the mote [speck of dust] that is in thy brother's eye."   164. **teen:** grief.   167. **gig:** spinning top rotated by whipping.   169. **Nestor:** the oldest and most experienced of the Greek generals. **pushpin:** a children's game in which each player pushes his pin to cross his opponent's.   170. **Timon:** the most bitter of all critics of human-ity. **toys:** trifles.   174. **caudle:** warm drink, especially for the sick suffering from heartburn.   183. **pruning me:** preening myself.   185. **state:** demeanor.   188. **post:** ride fast.

194. **misdoubts:** suspects.   204. **whoreson loggerhead:** bastardly blockhead.   206. **mess:** party of four at a table.   212. **turtles:** turtledoves; i.e., lovers.   218. **cross:** thwart.   222. **man of Ind:** Indian.

Dares look upon the heaven of her brow
That is not blinded by her majesty?
  KING. What zeal, what fury hath inspired thee
    now?
My love, her mistress, is a gracious moon,   230
  She an attending star, scarce seen a light.
  BER. My eyes are then no eyes, nor I Berowne.
Oh, but for my love, day would turn to night!
Of all complexions the culled sovereignty°
  Do meet, as at a fair, in her fair cheek,   235
Where several° worthies make one dignity,
  Where nothing wants that want itself doth seek.
Lend me the flourish of all gentle tongues —
  Fie, painted° rhetoric! Oh, she needs it not.
To things of sale a seller's praise belongs,   240
  She passes praise, then praise too short doth blot.
A withered hermit, fivescore winters worn,
  Might shake off fifty looking in her eye.
Beauty doth varnish age as if newborn,
  And gives the crutch the cradle's infancy.   245
Oh, 'tis the sun that maketh all things shine.
  KING. By Heaven, thy love is black as ebony.
  BER. Is ebony like her? O wood divine!
A wife of such wood were felicity.
Oh, who can give an oath? Where is a book?   250
  That I may swear beauty doth beauty lack
If that she learn not of her eye to look.
  No face is fair that is not full so black.
  KING. Oh, paradox! Black is the badge of Hell,
  The hue of dungeons and the school of night,°
And beauty's crest becomes the heavens well.   256
  BER. Devils soonest tempt, resembling spirits of
    light.
Oh, if in black my lady's brows be decked,
  It mourns that painting and usurping hair
Should ravish doters with a false aspect,°   260
  And therefore is she born to make black fair.
Her favor° turns the fashion of the days,
  For native blood° is counted painting now,
And therefore red, that would avoid dispraise,
  Paints itself black to imitate her brow.   265
  DUM. To look like her are chimney sweepers
    black.
  LONG. And since her time are colliers° counted
    bright.
  KING. And Ethiopes of their sweet complexion
    crack.
  DUM. Dark needs no candles now, for dark is
    light.   269
  BER. Your mistresses dare never come in rain,
  For fear their colors should be washed away.
  KING. 'Twere good yours did, for, sir, to tell you
    plain,

I'll find a fairer face not washed today.
  BER. I'll prove her fair, or talk till Doomsday here.
  KING. No devil° will fright thee then° so much as
    she.   275
  DUM. I never knew man hold vile stuff so dear.
  LONG. Look, here's thy love. My foot and her face
    see.
  BER. Oh, if the streets were pavèd with thine eyes,
  Her feet were much too dainty for such tread!
  DUM. O vile! Then, as she goes, what upward
    lies   280
  The street should see as she walked overhead.
  KING. But what of this? Are we not all in love?
  BER. Nothing so sure, and thereby all forsworn.
  KING. Then leave this chat, and, good Berowne,
    now prove
Our loving lawful, and our faith not torn.   285
  DUM. Aye, marry, there — some flattery for this
    evil.
  LONG. Oh, some authority how to proceed,
Some tricks, some quillets,° how to cheat the Devil.
  DUM. Some salve for perjury.
  BER.   'Tis more than need.
Have at you, then, affection's men-at-arms.°   290
Consider what you first did swear unto,
To fast, to study, and to see no woman —
Flat treason 'gainst the kingly state of youth.
Say, can you fast? Your stomachs are too young,
And abstinence engenders maladies.   295
And where that you have vowed to study, lords,
In that each of you have forsworn his book,
Can you still dream and pore and thereon look?
For when would you, my lord, or you, or you,
Have found the ground° of study's excellence   300
Without the beauty of a woman's face?
From women's eyes this doctrine I derive:
They are the ground, the books, the academes,
From whence doth spring the true Promethean° fire.
Why, universal plodding prisons up   305
The nimble spirits° in the arteries
As motion and long-during action tires
The sinewy vigor of the traveler.
Now, for not looking on a woman's face,
You have in that forsworn the use of eyes   310
And study too, the causer of your vow;
For where is any author in the world
Teaches such beauty as a woman's eye?
Learning is but an adjunct to ourself,
And where we are our learning likewise is.   315
Then when ourselves we see in ladies' eyes,
Do we not likewise see our learning there?
Oh, we have made a vow to study, lords,
And in that vow we have forsworn our books.

---

234. culled sovereignty: selected pre-eminence.   **236. several:** different.   **239. painted:** artificial, insincere.   **255. school of night:** See *LLL* Intro. p. 396a.   **260. aspect:** appearance. **262. favor:** complexion.   **263. native blood:** natural color. **267. colliers:** coal men.

275. No devil: the devil was believed to be black. **then:** i.e., at Doomsday.   **288. quillets:** subtleties.   **290. affection's men-at-arms:** love's bodyguard.   **300. ground:** foundation.   **304. Promethean:** heavenly. Prometheus stole fire from heaven and gave it to men.   **306. spirits:** vital energy.

For when would you, my liege, or you, or you,   320
In leaden° contemplation have found out
Such fiery numbers as the prompting eyes
Of beauty's tutors have enriched you with?
Other slow arts entirely keep° the brain,
And therefore, finding barren practicers,   325
Scarce show a harvest of their heavy toil.
But love, first learnèd in a lady's eyes,
Lives not alone immurèd in the brain,
But with the motion of all elements
Courses as swift as thought in every power,   330
And gives to every power a double power,
Above their functions and their offices.
It adds a precious seeing to the eye,
A lover's eyes will gaze an eagle blind.
A lover's ear will hear the lowest sound   335
When the suspicious head of theft° is stopped.
Love's feeling is more soft and sensible°
Than are the tender horns of cockled° snails.
Love's tongue proves dainty Bacchus gross in taste.
For valor, is not Love a Hercules,   340
Still climbing trees in the Hesperides?°
Subtle as Sphinx,° as sweet and musical
As bright Apollo's° lute, strung with his hair.
And when Love speaks, the voice of all the gods
Makes Heaven drowsy with the harmony.   345
Never durst poet touch a pen to write
Until his ink were tempered with Love's sighs.
Oh, then his lines would ravish savage ears,
And plant in tyrants mild humility.
From women's eyes this doctrine I derive: 350
They sparkle still the right Promethean fire;
They are the books, the arts, the academes,
That show, contain, and nourish all the world,
Else none at all in aught proves excellent.
Then fools you were these women to forswear,   355
Or keeping what is sworn, you will prove fools.
For wisdom's sake, a word that all men love —
Or for love's sake, a word that loves all men;
Or for men's sake, the authors of these women;
Or women's sake, by whom we men are men —
Let us once lose our oaths to find ourselves,   361
Or else we lose ourselves to keep our oaths.
It is religion to be thus forsworn,
For charity itself fulfills the law,
And who can sever love from charity?   365
     KING. Saint Cupid, then! And, soldiers, to the
       field!
     BER. Advance your standards, and upon them,
       lords,
Pell-mell, down with them! But be first advised

In conflict that you get the sun° of them.
     LONG. Now to plain dealing, lay these glozes° by.
Shall we resolve to woo these girls of France?   371
     KING. And win them too. Therefore let us devise
Some entertainment for them in their tents.
     BER. First, from the park let us conduct them
       thither,
Then homeward every man attach° the hand   375
Of his fair mistress. In the afternoon
We will with some strange pastime solace them,
Such as the shortness of the time can shape;
For revels, dances, masques,° and merry hours   379
Forerun fair Love, strewing her way with flowers.
     KING. Away, away! No time shall be omitted
That will betime, and may by us be fitted.
     BER. *Allons! Allons!* Sowed cockle reaped no
       corn,°
And justice always whirls in equal measure.   384
Light wenches may prove plagues to men forsworn;
   If so, our copper buys no better treasure.
                         [*Exeunt.*]

Act V

SCENE I. *The same.*

[*Enter* HOLOFERNES, SIR NATHANIEL, *and* DULL.]
HOL. *Satis quod sufficit.*°
     NATH. I praise God for you, sir. Your reasons° at
dinner have been sharp and sententious, pleasant
without scurrility, witty without affection,° audacious without impudency, learned without opinion,°
and strange without heresy. I did converse this
quondam° day with a companion of the King's who
is intituled, nominated, or called Don Adriano de
Armado.   9
     HOL. *Novi hominem tanquam te.*° His humor is
lofty, his discourse peremptory, his tongue filed,° his
eye ambitious, his gait majestical, and his general
behavior vain, ridiculous, and thrasonical.° He is
too picked, too spruce, too affected, too odd, as it
were, too peregrinate,° as I may call it.   16
     NATH. A most singular and choice epithet.
                [*Draws out his table book.*]
     HOL. He draweth out the thread of his verbosity

---

321. leaden: heavy.   324. keep: dwell in.   336. head of theft: A
much-disputed phrase, variously emended. If correct, it means
the hearing of a thief, who is naturally suspicious of every sound.
337. sensible: sensitive.   338. cockled: in shells.   341. Hesperides: where grew the golden apples which Hercules took.
342. Sphinx: a creature half woman, half lion which posed the
riddle to the people of Thebes.   343. Apollo: god of the arts.

369. get . . . sun: come at them when the sun is in their eyes.
370. glozes: pretenses.   375. attach: arrest, take hold of.
379. masques: courtly entertainments.   383. Sowed . . . corn: a
proverb, "If you sow weeds, you won't reap grain." cockle: a
weed which grows in wheat.
     Act V, Sc. i: 1. *Satis . . . sufficit:* what satisfies is enough.
2. reasons: discourses.   4. affection: affectation.   5. opinion:
arrogance.   7. quondam: former, bygone.   10. *Novi . . . te:* I
know the man as well as I know you.   11. filed: polished.
14. thrasonical: boastful.   16. peregrinate: foreign.

finer than the staple° of his argument. I abhor   20
such fanatical phantasimes, such insociable and
point-device° companions; such rackers of orthog-
raphy° as to speak dout, fine, when he should say
doubt; det, when he should pronounce debt, — d, e,
b, t, not d, e, t: he clepeth° a calf, cauf; half,   25
hauf; neighbor *vocatur*° nebour; neigh abbreviated
ne. This is abhominable — which he would call
abbominable. It insinuateth me of insanie° — *anne*
intelligis, domine?° To make frantic, lunatic.

NATH. *Laus Deo, bene intelligo.*°   30

HOL. *Bon, bon, fort bon!* Priscian a little
scratched,° 'twill serve.

NATH. *Videsne quis venit?*°

HOL. *Video, et gaudeo.*°

[*Enter* ARMADO, MOTH, *and* COSTARD.]

ARM. [*To* MOTH] Chirrah!   35

HOL. *Quare*° chirrah, not sirrah?

ARM. Men of peace, well encountered.

HOL. Most military sir, salutation.

MOTH. [*Aside to* COSTARD] They have been at a
great feast of languages, and stolen the scraps.   40

COST. Oh, they have lived long on the alms basket°
of words. I marvel thy master hath not eaten thee for
a word; for thou art not so long by the head as
honorificabilitudinitatibus.° Thou art easier swallowed than a flapdragon.°   45

MOTH. Peace! The peal begins.

ARM. [*To* HOLOFERNES] Monsieur, are you not let-
tered?

MOTH. Yes, yes, he teaches boys the hornbook.°
What is a, b, spelt backward, with the horn on   50
his head?

HOL. Ba, *pueritia,*° with a horn added.

MOTH. Ba, most silly sheep with a horn. You hear
his learning.

HOL. *Quis,*° quis, thou consonant?   55

MOTH. The third of the five vowels, if you repeat
them — or the fifth, if I.

HOL. I will repeat them — a, e, i ——

MOTH. The sheep. The other two concludes it —
o, u.   60

ARM. Now, by the salt wave of the Mediterraneum,
a sweet touch, a quick venue° of wit — snip, snap,
quick and home! It rejoiceth my intellect — true
wit!   64

MOTH. Offered by a child to an old man, which is
wit-old.°

HOL. What is the figure? What is the figure?

MOTH. Horns.

HOL. Thou disputest like an infant. Go, whip thy
gig.   70

MOTH. Lend me your horn to make one, and I will
whip about your infamy *circum circa*° — a gig of a
cuckold's horn.

COST. An I had but one penny in the world, thou
shouldst have it to buy gingerbread. Hold, there is
the very remuneration I had of thy master, thou
halfpenny purse of wit, thou pigeon egg° of discretion. Oh, an the heavens were so pleased that   78
thou wert but my bastard, what a joyful father
wouldst thou make me! Go to, thou hast it *ad* dunghill,° at the finger's ends, as they say.

HOL. Oh, I smell false Latin — dunghill for
unguem.

ARM. Artsman,° preambulate,° we will be sin-
guled° from the barbarous. Do you not educate
youth at the charge house on the top of the mountain?°   87

HOL. Or *mons,* the hill.

ARM. At your sweet pleasure, for the mountain.

HOL. I do, sans° question.

ARM. Sir, it is the King's most sweet pleasure and
affection to congratulate the Princess at her pavilion°
in the posteriors of this day, which the rude multitude call the afternoon.   95

HOL. The posterior of the day, most generous° sir,
is liable,° congruent, and measurable for the afternoon. The word is well culled, chose, sweet and apt,
I do assure you, sir, I do assure.   99

ARM. Sir, the King is a noble gentleman, and my
familiar,° I do assure ye, very good friend. For what
is inward° between us, let it pass. I do beseech thee
remember thy courtesy.° I beseech thee apparel thy
head. And among other important and most serious
designs, and of great import indeed too — but   105
let that pass; for I must tell thee it will please His

---

20. staple: lit., fiber of wool.   22. point-device: precise.
22–23. rackers of orthography: torturers of spelling.   25. clepeth:
calleth.   26. vocatur: is called.   28. insinuateth . . . insanie: to
me it suggests lunacy.   28–29. anne . . . domine: do you comprehend, master?   30. Laus . . . intelligo: praise be to God, I understand well.   31. Priscian . . . scratched: i.e., your Latin is not
too good. Priscian was a famous Latin grammarian about whom
there was a proverb "to break Priscian's head," meaning to
speak bad Latin.   33. Videsne . . . venit: do you see who comes?
34. Video . . . gaudeo: I see and rejoice.   36. Quare: why.
41. alms basket: a basket in which the scraps were collected for
distribution to the poor.   44. honorificabilitudinitatibus: The
word was a scholar's joke, as it was the longest word in the Latin
tongue; lit., "in the condition of being loaded with honors."
45. flapdragon: a lighted raisin floated on liquor which had to be
swallowed.   49. hornbook: the first reading book. It was printed
on a single sheet, mounted on a wooden handle, and protected
with transparent horn.   52. pueritia: childishness, my little one.
55. Quis: who.

62. venue: bout (of fencing).   66. wit-old: with a pun on "wittol," a complacent cuckold.   72. circum circa: round and round.
Theobald's emendation for *unum cita.*   77. pigeon egg: i.e.,
smooth little thing.   80–81. ad dunghill: for *ad unguem* — at the
fingernail; a schoolboy joke.   84. Artsman: scholar. preambulate: walk forth.   85. singuled: separated.   86–87. charge . . .
mountain: This is apparently another topical allusion, now lost.
charge house: probably a school at which a fee is charged (contrasted with a free-school).   91. sans: without.   93. pavilion:
tent.   96. generous: well-born.   97. liable: appropriate.
101. familiar: familiar friend.   102. inward: secret.   103. remember . . . courtesy: don't forget your manners; i.e., to take
off your hat in the presence of such an important person. But
as a gesture of politeness Armado immediately asks him to put
it on again. See App. 7.

Grace, by the world, sometime to lean upon my poor shoulder, and with his royal finger, thus, dally with my excrement,° with my mustachio — but, sweetheart, let that pass. By the world, I recount no   110 fable. Some certain special honors it pleaseth his greatness to impart to Armado, a soldier, a man of travel, that hath seen the world — but let that pass. The very all of all is — but, sweetheart, I do implore secrecy — that the King would have me pre-   116 sent the Princess, sweet chuck,° with some delightful ostentation, or show, or pageant, or antique,° or firework. Now, understanding that the curate and your sweet self are good at such eruptions and sudden breaking-out of mirth, as it were, I have acquainted you withal, to the end to crave your assistance.   123

HOL. Sir, you shall present before her the Nine Worthies.° Sir, as concerning some entertainment of time, some show in the posterior of this day, to be rendered by our assistants at the King's command, and this most gallant, illustrate,° and learned gentleman, before the Princess, I say none so fit as to present the Nine Worthies.   130

NATH. Where will you find men worthy enough to present them?

HOL. Joshua, yourself; myself and this gallant gentleman, Judas Maccabaeus. This swain, because of his great limb or joint, shall pass° Pompey the Great; the page, Hercules ——

ARM. Pardon, sir, error. He is not quantity enough for that Worthy's thumb. He is not so big as the end of his club.   139

HOL. Shall I have audience? He shall present Hercules in minority° — his enter and exit shall be strangling a snake,° and I will have an apology° for that purpose.

MOTH. An excellent device! So, if any of the audience hiss, you may cry, " Well done, Hercules! Now thou crushest the snake! " That is the way to make an offense gracious, though few have the grace to do it.

ARM. For the rest of the Worthies?

HOL. I will play three myself.   150

MOTH. Thrice-worthy gentleman!

ARM. Shall I tell you a thing?

HOL. We attend.

ARM. We will have, if this fadge° not, an antique. I beseech you, follow.   155

HOL. *Via,*° goodman Dull! Thou hast spoken no word all this while.

DULL. Nor understood none neither, sir.

HOL. *Allons!* We will employ thee.

DULL. I'll make one in a dance, or so, or I will play   160 On the tabor° to the Worthies and let them dance the hay.°

HOL. Most dull, honest Dull! To our sport, away!
[Exeunt.]

SCENE II. *The same.*

[Enter the PRINCESS, KATHARINE, ROSALINE, *and* MARIA.]

PRIN. Sweethearts, we shall be rich ere we depart
If fairings° come thus plentifully in,
A lady walled about with diamonds!°
Look you what I have from the loving King.

ROS. Madam, came nothing else along with that?

PRIN. Nothing but this! Yes, as much love in rhyme   6
As would be crammed up in a sheet of paper
Writ o' both sides the leaf, margent° and all,
That he was fain to seal on Cupid's name.

ROS. That was the way to make his godhead wax,
For he hath been five thousand years a boy.   11

KATH. Aye, and a shrewd unhappy gallows° too.

ROS. You'll ne'er be friends with him, A' killed your sister.

KATH. He made her melancholy, sad, and heavy,
And so she died. Had she been light,° like you,   15
Of such a merry, nimble, stirring spirit,
She might ha' been a grandam ere she died.
And so may you, for a light heart lives long.

ROS. What's your dark meaning, mouse, of this light word?

KATH. A light condition in a beauty dark.   20

ROS. We need more light to find your meaning out.

KATH. You'll mar the light by taking it in snuff,°
Therefore I'll darkly end the argument.

ROS. Look, what you do, you do it still i' th' dark.

KATH. So do not you, for you are a light wench.

ROS. Indeed I weigh° not you, and therefore light.°   26

KATH. You weigh me not? — Oh, that's you care not for me.

ROS. Great reason, for "past cure is still past
  care."
PRIN. Well bandied° both, a set of wit well played.
But, Rosaline, you have a favor° too.   30
Who sent it? And what is it?
ROS.   I would you knew.
And if my face were but as fair as yours,
My favor were as great — be witness this.
Nay, I have verses too, I thank Berowne,
The numbers true; and were the numbering° too,
I were the fairest goddess on the ground.   36
I am compared to twenty thousand fairs.
Oh, he hath drawn my picture in his letter!
  PRIN. Anything like?
  ROS. Much in the letters, nothing in the praise. 40
  PRIN. Beauteous as ink, a good conclusion.
  KATH. Fair as a text B° in a copybook.
  ROS. 'Ware pencils, ho! Let me not die your debtor,
My red dominical,° my golden letter.
Oh, that your face were not so full of O's!°   45
  KATH. A pox of that jest! And I beshrew° all
    shrows.°
  PRIN. But, Katharine, what was sent to you from
    fair Dumain?
  KATH. Madam, this glove.
  PRIN.   Did he not send you twain?
  KATH. Yes, madam, and moreover
Some thousand verses of a faithful lover,   50
A huge translation of hypocrisy,
Vilely compiled, profound simplicity.
  MAR. This and these pearls to me sent Longaville.
The letter is too long by half a mile.
  PRIN. I think no less. Dost thou not wish in heart
The chain were longer and the letter short?   56
  MAR. Aye, or I would these hands might never
    part.
  PRIN. We are wise girls to mock our lovers so.
  ROS. They are worse fools to purchase mocking so.
That same Berowne I'll torture ere I go.   60
Oh, that I knew he were but in by the week!°
How I would make him fawn, and beg, and seek,
And wait the season, and observe the times,
And spend his prodigal wits in bootless° rhymes,
And shape his service wholly to my hests,°   65
And make him proud to make me proud that jests.
So perttaunt-like° would I o'ersway his state

That he should be my fool, and I his fate.°
PRIN. None are so surely caught, when they are
  catched,
As wit turned fool. Folly, in wisdom hatched,   70
Hath wisdom's warrant and the help of school,
And wit's own grace to grace a learned fool.
  ROS. The blood of youth burns not with such
    excess
As gravity's revolt to wantonness.
  MAR. Folly in fools bears not so strong a note   75
As foolery in the wise when wit doth dote,
Since all the power thereof it doth apply
To prove, by wit, worth in simplicity.
  PRIN. Here comes Boyet, and mirth is in his face.
              [Enter BOYET.]
  BOYET. Oh, I am stabbed with laughter! Where's
    Her Grace?   80
  PRIN. Thy news, Boyet?
  BOYET.   Prepare, madam, prepare!
Arm, wenches, arm! Encounters mounted are°
Against your peace. Love doth approach disguised,
Armèd in arguments — you'll be surprised.
Muster your wits, stand in your own defense,   85
Or hide your heads like cowards and fly hence.
  PRIN. Saint Denis° to° Saint Cupid! What are
    they
That charge their breath against us? Say, scout, say.
  BOYET. Under the cool shade of a sycamore
I thought to close mine eyes some half an hour   90
When, lo! to interrupt my purposed rest,
Toward that shade I might behold addressed°
The King and his companions. Warily
I stole into a neighbor thicket by,
And overheard what you shall overhear —   95
That, by and by, disguised they will be here.
Their herald is a pretty knavish page
That well by heart hath conned° his embassage.
Action and accent did they teach him there —
"Thus must thou speak," and "thus thy body bear."
And ever and anon° they made° a doubt   101
Presence majestical would put him out;
"For," quoth the King, "an angel shalt thou see;
Yet fear not thou, but speak audaciously."
The boy replied, "An angel is not evil.   105
I should have feared her had she been a devil."
With that, all laughed, and clapped him on the
    shoulder,
Making the bold wag by their praises bolder.
One rubbed his elbow thus, and fleered° and swore
A better speech was never spoke before.   110
Another, with his finger and his thumb,
Cried, "Via! We will do't, come what will come";

---

29. bandied: exchanged; lit., the exchange of strokes in tennis.
30. favor: gift.   35. numbers . . . numbering: meter . . . estimation.   42. text B: an elaborate initial B. For specimens of
elaborate initial, see Pl. 11a, 11b.   44. red dominical: the red
letters used to mark Sundays in all almanacs, with a reference
to Katharine's golden hair. See App. 2. Red and gold were not
always distinguished in Shakespeare's time. Cf. *Macb*, II.iii.118.
45. O's: i.e., smallpox scars — a common disfigurement in the
sixteenth century.   46. beshrew: curse. shrows: shrews.   61. in
. . . week: a proverbial phrase meaning "completely caught."
64. bootless: vain.   65. hests: commands.   67. perttaunt-like:
this is the reading of Q and F and has never been explained,
though endlessly emended. It obviously means like a tyrant.

68. fate: destiny.   82. Encounters . . . are: attacks are prepared.
87. Saint Denis: patron saint of France. to: against.   92. addressed: directed.   98. conned: learned.   101. ever . . . anon:
from time to time. made: felt, expressed.   109. fleered: grinned
contemptuously.

The third he capered, and cried, " All goes well,"
The fourth turned on the toe, and down he fell.
With that, they all did tumble on the ground,   115
With such a zealous laughter, so profound,
That in this spleen° ridiculous appears,
To check their folly, passion's solemn tears.
 PRIN. But what, but what, come they to visit us?
 BOYET. They do, they do, and are appareled thus,
Like Muscovites or Russians, as I guess.   121
Their purpose is to parle,° to court and dance;
And everyone his love feat° will advance
Unto his several° mistress, which they'll know
By favors several° which they did bestow.   125
 PRIN. And will they so? The gallants shall be
  tasked;°
For, ladies, we will every one be masked,
And not a man of them shall have the grace,
Despite of suit,° to see a lady's face.
Hold, Rosaline, this favor thou shalt wear,   130
And then the King will court thee for his dear.
Hold, take thou this, my sweet, and give me thine,
So shall Berowne take me for Rosaline.
And change you favors too, so shall your loves
Woo contrary, deceived by these removes.°   135
 ROS. Come on, then. Wear the favors most in sight.
 KATH. But in this changing what is your intent?
 PRIN. The effect of my intent is to cross theirs.
They do it but in mocking merriment,
And mock for mock is only my intent.   140
Their several counsels° they unbosom shall
To loves mistook, and so be mocked withal
Upon the next occasion that we meet
With visages displayed, to talk and greet.   144
 ROS. But shall we dance, if they desire us to 't?
 PRIN. No, to the death, we will not move a foot.
Nor to their penned speech render we no grace,°
But while 'tis spoke each turn away her face.
 BOYET. Why, that contempt will kill the speaker's
  heart,
And quite divorce his memory from his part.   150
 PRIN. Therefore I do it, and I make no doubt
The rest will ne'er come in, if he be out.
There's no such sport as sport by sport o'erthrown,
To make theirs ours, and ours none but our own.
So shall we stay, mocking intended game,   155
And they, well mocked, depart away with shame.
     [*Trumpets sound within.*]
 BOYET. The trumpet sounds. Be masked. The
  maskers come.   [*The* LADIES *mask.*]
[*Enter* BLACKAMOORS *with music;* MOTH; *the* KING,
 BEROWNE, LONGAVILLE, *and* DUMAIN, *in Russian
  habits,° and masked.*]

 MOTH. " All hail, the richest beauties on the
  earth! "
 BOYET. Beauties no richer than rich taffeta.
 MOTH. " A holy parcel of the fairest dames   160
   [*The* LADIES *turn their backs to him.*]
That ever turned their — backs — to mortal views! "
 BER. [*Aside to* MOTH] Their eyes, villain, their
  eyes.
 MOTH. " That ever turned their eyes to mortal
  views!
Out —— "
 BOYET. True, out indeed.   165
 MOTH. " Out of your favors, heavenly spirits,
  vouchsafe
Not to behold —— "
 BER. [*Aside to* MOTH] Once to behold, rogue.
 MOTH. " Once to behold with your sun-beamèd
eyes — with your sun-beamèd eyes —— "
 BOYET. They will not answer to that epithet.   170
You were best call it " daughter-beamèd eyes."
 MOTH. They do not mark me, and that brings° me
  out.
 BER. Is this your perfectness? Be gone, you rogue!
           [*Exit* MOTH.]
 ROS. What would these strangers? Know their
  minds, Boyet.
If they do speak our language, 'tis our will   175
That some plain man recount their purposes.
Know what they would.
 BOYET. What would you with the Princess?
 BER. Nothing but peace and gentle visitation.
 ROS. What would they, say they?   180
 BOYET. Nothing but peace and gentle visitation.
 ROS. Why, that they have, and bid them so be
  gone.
 BOYET. She says you have it, and you may be gone.
 KING. Say to her we have measured many miles
To tread a measure° with her on this grass.   185
 BOYET. They say that they have measured many a
  mile
To tread a measure with you on this grass.
 ROS. It is not so. Ask them how many inches
Is in one mile. If they have measured many,
The measure then of one is easily told.   190
 BOYET. If to come hither you have measured miles,
And many miles, the Princess bids you tell
How many inches doth fill up one mile.
 BER. Tell her we measure them by weary steps.
 BOYET. She hears herself.   196
 ROS.   How many weary steps,
Of many weary miles you have o'ergone,
Are numbered in the travel of one mile?
 BER. We number nothing that we spend for you.
Our duty is so rich, so infinite,
That we may do it still without accompt.°   200

117. spleen: excess of mirth.   122. parle: converse.   123. love
feat: act of courting.   124. several: particular.   125. favors
several: the particular gifts.   126. tasked: tried.   129. Despite
of suit: in spite of their petition.   135. removes: changes.
141. counsels: secret thoughts.   147. grace: favor.   157. s.d.,
habits: costumes.

172. brings: puts.   185. tread a measure: dance. See App. 24.
200. accompt: reckoning.

Vouchsafe to show the sunshine of your face,
That we, like savages, may worship it.
   ROS. My face is but a moon, and clouded too.
   KING. Blessèd are clouds, to do as such clouds do!
Vouchsafe, bright moon, and these thy stars, to
    shine,   205
Those clouds removed, upon our watery eyne.°
   ROS. O vain petitioner! Beg a greater matter.
Thou now request'st but moonshine in the water.
   KING. Then in our measure do but vouchsafe one
    change.°   209
Thou bid'st me beg. This begging is not strange.
   ROS. Play, music, then! Nay, you must do it soon.
                                 [*Music plays.*]
Not yet! No dance! Thus change I like the moon.
   KING. Will you not dance? How come you thus
    estranged?
   ROS. You took the moon at full, but now she's
    changed.
   KING. Yet still she is the moon, and I the man.
The music plays, vouchsafe some motion to it.   216
   ROS. Our ears vouchsafe it.
   KING.   But your legs should do it.
   ROS. Since you are strangers, and come here by
    chance,
We'll not be nice. Take hands. We will not dance.
   KING. Why take we hands, then?
   ROS.   Only to part friends.   220
Curtsy, sweethearts, and so the measure ends.
   KING. More measure of this measure — be not
    nice.°
   ROS. We can afford no more at such a price.
   KING. Prize you yourselves. What buys your com-
    pany?
   ROS. Your absence only.
   KING.   That can never be.   225
   ROS. Then cannot we be bought, and so adieu —
Twice to your visor, and half once to you.
   KING. If you deny to dance, let's hold more chat.
   ROS. In private, then.
   KING. I am best pleased with that.
                            [*They converse apart.*]
   BER. White-handed mistress, one sweet word with
    thee.   230
   PRIN. Honey, and milk, and sugar — there is
    three.
   BER. Nay then, two treys,° an if you grow so nice,
Metheglin, wort, and malmsey.° Well run, dice!
There's half a dozen sweets.
   PRIN.   Seventh sweet, adieu.
Since you can cog,° I'll play no more with you.   235
   BER. One word in secret.
   PRIN.   Let it not be sweet.

   BER. Thou grievest my gall.°
   PRIN.   Gall! Bitter.
   BER.   Therefore meet. [*They converse apart.*]
   DUM. Will you vouchsafe with me to change a
    word?
   MAR. Name it.
   DUM.   Fair lady ——
   MAR.   Say you so? Fair lord ——
Take that for your fair lady.
   DUM.   Please it you,   240
As much in private, and I'll bid adieu.
                          [*They converse apart.*]
   KATH. What, was your vizard° made without a
    tongue?
   LONG. I know the reason, lady, why you ask.
   KATH. Oh, for your reason! Quickly, sir, I long.
   LONG. You have a double tongue within your
    mask,   245
And would afford my speechless vizard half.
   KATH. Veal, quoth the Dutchman.° Is not " veal "
    a calf?
   LONG. A calf, fair lady!
   KATH.   No, a fair lord calf.
   LONG. Let's part° the word.
   KATH.   No, I'll not be your half.
Take all, and wean it. It may prove an ox.   250
   LONG. Look how you butt yourself in these sharp
    mocks!
Will you give horns, chaste lady? Do not so.
   KATH. Then die a calf, before your horns do grow.
   LONG. One word in private with you, ere I die.
   KATH. Bleat softly, then. The butcher hears you
    cry.   [*They converse apart.*]   255
   BOYET. The tongues of mocking wenches are as
    keen
As is the razor's edge invisible,
Cutting a smaller hair than may be seen,
   Above the sense of sense. So sensible   259
Seemeth their conference, their conceits° have wings
Fleeter than arrows, bullets, wind, thought, swifter
    things.
   ROS. Not one word more, my maids. Break off,
    break off.
   BER. By Heaven, all dry-beaten° with pure scoff!
   KING. Farewell, mad wenches, you have simple
    wits.
   PRIN. Twenty adieus, my frozen Muscovits.   265
        [*Exeunt* KING, LORDS, *and* BLACKAMOORS.]
Are these the breed of wits so wondered at?
   BOYET. Tapers° they are, with your sweet breaths
    puffed out.
   ROS. Well-liking° wits they have — gross, gross;
    fat, fat.

---

206. eyne: eyes.   209. change: i.e., of time.   222. nice: dainty,
fussy.   232. treys: throws of three at dice.   233. Metheglin:
mead, a drink made with honey; wort: sweet unfermented beer;
malmsey: a sweet wine. I.e., Berowne replies with three more
"sweets."   235. cog: cheat.

237. gall: sore.   242. vizard: mask.   247. Veal . . . Dutchman:
i.e., the Dutchman's pronunciation of "well" followed by the
inevitable pun on *calf.*   249. part: divide.   260. conceits: witti-
cisms.   263. dry-beaten: beaten without breaking the skin.
267. Tapers: candles.   268. Well-liking: sleek.

PRIN. Oh, poverty in wit, kingly-poor° flout!°
Will they not, think you, hang themselves tonight?
Or ever, but in vizards, show their faces? 271
This pert Berowne was out of countenance quite.
ROS. Oh, they were all in lamentable cases!
The King was weeping-ripe° for a good° word. 274
  PRIN. Berowne did swear himself out of all suit.°
  MAR. Dumain was at my service, and his sword.
No point, quoth I. My servant straight was mute.
  KATH. Lord Longaville said I came o'er his heart,
And trow° you what he called me?
  PRIN.   Qualm,° perhaps.
  KATH. Yes, in good faith.
  PRIN.   Go, sickness as thou art!
  ROS. Well, better wits have worn plain statute
    caps.° 281
But will you hear? The King is my love sworn.
  PRIN. And quick Berowne hath plighted faith to
    me.
  KATH. And Longaville was for my service born.
  MAR. Dumain is mine, as sure as bark on tree.
  BOYET. Madam, and pretty mistresses, give ear.
Immediately they will again be here 287
In their own shapes; for it can never be
They will digest this harsh indignity.
  PRIN. Will they return?
  BOYET.   They will, they will, God knows, 290
And leap for joy, though they are lame with blows.
Therefore change favors, and when they repair,°
Blow° like sweet roses in this summer air.
  PRIN. How blow? How blow? Speak to be under
    stood.
  BOYET. Fair ladies masked are roses in their bud.
Dismasked, their damask° sweet commixture°
    shown, 296
Are angels vailing° clouds, or roses blown.
  PRIN. Avaunt, perplexity! What shall we do
If they return in their own shapes to woo? 299
  ROS. Good madam, if by me you'll be advised,
Let's mock them still, as well known as disguised.
Let us complain to them what fools were here,
Disguised like Muscovites in shapeless gear,°
And wonder what they were and to what end
Their shallow shows and prologue vilely penned,
And their rough carriage so ridiculous, 306
Should be presented at our tent to us.
  BOYET. Ladies, withdraw. The gallants are at
    hand.
  PRIN. Whip° to our tents, as roes run o'er land.
  [*Exeunt* PRINCESS, ROSALINE, KATHARINE, *and* MARIA.]

[*Re-enter the* KING, BEROWNE, LONGAVILLE, *and*
DUMAIN, *in their proper habits.*]

KING. Fair sir, God save you! Where's the Prin-
    cess? 310
  BOYET. Gone to her tent. Please it your Majesty
Command me any service to her thither?
  KING. That she vouchsafe me audience for one
    word.
  BOYET. I will, and so will she, I know, my lord.
                             [*Exit.*]
  BER. This fellow pecks up wit as pigeons peas,
And utters it again when God doth please. 316
He is wit's peddler, and retails his wares
At wakes and wassails,° meetings, markets, fairs.
And we that sell by gross, the Lord doth know,
Have not the grace to grace it with such show. 320
This gallant pins the wenches on his sleeve —
Had he been Adam, he had tempted Eve.
A' can carve° too, and lisp. Why, this is he
That kissed his hand away in courtesy;
This is the ape of form,° monsieur the nice, 325
That, when he plays at tables, chides the dice
In honorable terms. Nay, he can sing
A mean° most meanly, and in ushering,°
Mend° him who can. The ladies call him sweet,
The stairs as he treads on them kiss his feet. 330
This is the flower that smiles on everyone,
To show his teeth as white as whale's° bone;
And consciences that will not die in debt
Pay him the due of honey-tongued Boyet.
  KING. A blister on his sweet tongue, with my
    heart, 335
That put Armado's page out of his part!
  BER. See where it comes! Behavior, what wert thou
Till this madman showed thee? And what art thou
    now? 338
[*Re-enter the* PRINCESS, *ushered by* BOYET; ROSALINE,
MARIA, *and* KATHARINE.]

KING. All hail, sweet madam, and fair time of day!
  PRIN. " Fair " in " all hail " is foul, as I conceive.
  KING. Construe° my speeches better, if you may.
  PRIN. Then wish me better. I will give you leave.
  KING. We came to visit you, and purpose now
To lead you to our Court. Vouchsafe it, then.
  PRIN. This field shall hold me, and so hold your
    vow. 345
Nor God, nor I, delights in perjured men.
  KING. Rebuke me not for that which you provoke.
The virtue° of your eye must break my oath.
  PRIN. You nickname° virtue, vice you should have
    spoke,
For virtue's office never breaks men's troth. 350
Now by my maiden honor yet as pure

---

269. kingly-poor: a bad pun on *well-li-king* (l. 268). **flout:** jest.
274. weeping-ripe: on the point of bursting into tears. **good:**
kind. **275. out . . . suit:** out of court. **279. trow:** know. **Qualm:**
(pronounced calm), a feeling of sickness. **281. statute caps:** flat
woolen caps worn by citizens and apprentices. See Pl. 9l and p. 94a.
292. repair: come again. **293. Blow:** open like rosebuds; i.e., unmask. **296. damask . . . commixture:** pink-and-white complexion. **297. vailing:** lowering. **303. gear:** stuff. **309. Whip:** run.

318. wassails: feasts. **323. carve:** be affected. **325. ape of form:**
imitator of fashion. **328. mean:** tenor. **ushering:** escorting the
ladies. **329. Mend:** surpass. **332. whale's:** pronounced as two
syllables here. **341. Construe:** interpret. **348. virtue:** power.
349. nickname: mention mistakenly.

As the unsullied lily I protest
A world of torments though I should endure,
  I would not yield to be your house's guest,
So much I hate a breaking cause to be   355
Of heavenly oaths, vowed with integrity.
  KING. Oh, you have lived in desolation here,
Unseen, unvisited, much to our shame.
  PRIN. Not so, my lord; it is not so, I swear.
We have had pastimes here and pleasant game.
A mess° of Russians left us but of late.   361
  KING. How, madam! Russians!
  PRIN.   Aye, in truth, my lord,
Trim gallants, full of courtship and of state.
  ROS. Madam, speak true. It is not so, my lord.
My lady, to the manner of the days,   365
In courtesy gives undeserving praise.
We four indeed confronted were with four
In Russian habit. Here they stayed an hour,
And talked apace, and in that hour, my lord,
They did not bless us with one happy word.   370
I dare not call them fools, but this I think —
When they are thirsty, fools would fain have drink.
  BER. This jest is dry to me. Fair gentle sweet,
Your wit makes wise things foolish. When we
      greet,
With eyes best seeing, heaven's fiery eye,   375
By light we lose light.° Your capacity
Is of that nature that to your huge store
Wise things seem foolish and rich things but poor.
  ROS. This proves you wise and rich, for in my
      eye——
  BER. I am a fool, and full of poverty.   380
  ROS. But that you take what doth to you belong,
It were a fault to snatch words from my tongue.
  BER. Oh, I am yours, and all that I possess!
  ROS. All the fool mine?
  BER.   I cannot give you less.
  ROS. Which of the vizards was it that you wore?
  BER. Where? When? What vizard? Why demand
      you this?   386
  ROS. There, then, that vizard — that superfluous
      case
That hid the worse and showed the better face.
  KING. We are descried.° They'll mock us now
      downright.
  DUM. Let us confess, and turn it to a jest.   390
  PRIN. Amazed, my lord? Why looks your High-
      ness sad?
  ROS. Help, hold his brows! He'll swound! Why
      look you pale?
Seasick, I think, coming from Muscovy.
  BER. Thus pour the stars down plagues for per-
      jury.
Can any face of brass hold longer out?   395

Here stand I. Lady, dart thy skill at me,
  Bruise me with scorn, confound me with a flout,
Thrust thy sharp wit quite through my ignorance,
  Cut me to pieces with thy keen conceit,
And I will wish thee never more to dance,   400
  Nor never more in Russian habit wait.
Oh, never will I trust to speeches penned,
  Nor to the motion of a schoolboy's tongue,
Nor never come in vizard to my friend,
  Nor woo in rhyme, like a blind harper's song!°
Taffeta phrases, silken terms precise,   406
  Three-piled° hyperboles, spruce affectation,
Figures pedantical — these summer flies
  Have blown° me full of maggot ostentation.
I do forswear them, and I here protest,   410
  By this white glove — how white the hand, God
      knows! —
Henceforth my wooing mind shall be expressed
  In russet yeas and honest kersey° noes.
And, to begin, wench — so God help me, la! —
My love to thee is sound, sans° crack or flaw.   415
  ROS. Sans sans, I pray you.
  BER.   Yet I have a trick
Of the old rage.° — Bear with me, I am sick —
I'll leave it by degrees. Soft, let us see.
Write "Lord have mercy on us"° on those three.
They are infected, in their hearts it lies;   420
They have the plague, and caught it of your eyes.
These lords are visited, you are not free,
For the Lord's tokens° on you do I see.
  PRIN. No, they are free that gave these tokens to
      us.   424
  BER. Our states° are forfeit. Seek not to undo us.
  ROS. It is not so, for how can this be true,
That you stand forfeit, being those that sue?
  BER. Peace! For I will not have to do with you.
  ROS. Nor shall not, if I do as I intend.
  BER. Speak for yourselves. My wit is at an end.
  KING. Teach us, sweet madam, for our rude trans-
      gression   431
Some fair excuse.
  PRIN.   The fairest is confession.
Were not you here but even now disguised?
  KING. Madam, I was.
  PRIN.   And were you well advised?
  KING. I was, fair madam.
  PRIN.   When you then were here,   435
What did you whisper in your lady's ear?
  KING. That more than all the world I did respect
      her.

<hr>

405. **Nor . . . song**: i.e., the doggerel of a blind ballad singer. 407. **Three-piled**: the word is normally used for the thickest velvet. 409. **blown**: puffed. 413. **russet . . . kersey**: different kinds of coarse homespun cloth. 415. **sans**: without. 417. **rage**: poetic fury. 419. **Lord . . . us**: written over the doors of houses infected with the plague. 423. **Lord's tokens**: signs of the plague, and also the gifts of their lovers which the ladies are wearing. 425. **states**: estates.

<hr>

361. **mess**: party of four.   374–76. **when . . . light**: i.e., you are like the sun which blinds by excessive light.   389. **descried**: sighted, found out.

PRIN. When she shall challenge this, you will re-
ject her.   438
KING. Upon mine honor, no.
PRIN.   Peace, peace! Forbear.
Your oath once broke, you force not to° forswear.
KING. Despise me when I break this oath of mine.
PRIN. I will, and therefore keep it, Rosaline,
What did the Russian whisper in your ear?
ROS. Madam, he swore that he did hold me dear
As precious eyesight, and did value me   445
Above this world, adding thereto, moreover,
That he would wed me or else die my lover.
PRIN. God give thee joy of him! The noble lord
Most honorably doth uphold his word.
KING. What mean you, madam? By my life, my
troth,   450
I never swore this lady such an oath.
ROS. By Heaven, you did, and to confirm it plain,
You gave me this.° But take it, sir, again.
KING. My faith and this the Princess I did give.
I knew her by this jewel on her sleeve.   455
PRIN. Pardon me, sir, this jewel did she wear,
And Lord Berowne, I thank him, is my dear.
What, will you have me, or your pearl again?
BER. Neither of either, I remit both twain.
I see the trick on't. Here was a consent,   460
Knowing aforehand of our merriment,
To dash° it like a Christmas comedy.
Some carrytale, some pleaseman, some slight zany,°
Some mumblenews, some trencher knight,° some
Dick
That smiles his cheek in years,° and knows the trick
To make my lady laugh when she's disposed,   466
Told our intents before. Which once disclosed,
The ladies did change favors, and then we,
Following the signs, wooed but the sign° of she.
Now, to our perjury to add more terror,   470
We are again forsworn, in will and error.°
Much upon this° it is. [*To* BOYET] And might not
you
Forestall our sport, to make us thus untrue?
Do not you know my lady's foot by the squier,°
And laugh upon the apple of her eye?°   475
And stand between her back, sir, and the fire,
Holding a trencher,° jesting merrily?
You put our page out. Go, you are allowed.°
Die when you will, a smock° shall be your shroud.
You leer upon me, do you? There's an eye   480

Wounds like a leaden° sword.
BOYET.   Full merrily
Hath this brave manage,° this career,° been run.
BER. Lo, he is tilting straight! Peace! I have done.
[*Enter* COSTARD.] Welcome, pure wit! Thou part'st
a fair fray.
COST. Oh Lord, sir, they would know   485
Whether the three Worthies shall come in or no.
BER. What, are there but three?
COST.   No, sir, but it is vara fine,
For every one pursents three.
BER.   And three times thrice is nine.
COST. Not so, sir, under correction, sir, I hope it is
not so.
You cannot beg us,° sir, I can assure you, sir. We
know what we know.   490
I hope, sir, three times thrice, sir ——
BER. Is not nine.
COST. Under correction, sir, we know whereuntil°
it doth amount.
BER. By Jove, I always took three threes for nine.
COST. Oh Lord, sir, it were pity you should get
your living by reckoning, sir.
BER. How much is it?   499
COST. Oh Lord, sir, the parties themselves, the
actors, sir, will show whereuntil it doth amount. For
mine own part, I am, as they say, but to parfect° one
man in one poor man, Pompion° the Great, sir.
BER. Art thou one of the Worthies?   505
COST. It pleased them to think me worthy of
Pompion the Great. For mine own part, I know not
the degree° of the Worthy, but I am to stand for
him.
BER. Go, bid them prepare.   510
COST. We will turn it finely off, sir, we will take
some care.   [*Exit.*]
KING. Berowne, they will shame us. Let them not
approach.
BER. We are shameproof, my lord, and 'tis some
policy°
To have one show worse than the King's and his
company.
KING. I say they shall not come.   515
PRIN. Nay, my good lord, let me o'errule you now.
That sport best pleases that doth least know how,
Where zeal strives to content, and the contents
Dies in the zeal of that which it presents.   519
Their form confounded makes most form in mirth
When great things laboring perish in their birth.°

---

440. force . . . to: do not find it difficult to. **453. this:** i.e., the present originally sent by the King to the Princess. **462. dash:** make fun of. **463. pleaseman . . . zany:** yesman . . . stooge. **464. trencher knight:** hanger-on. **465. in years:** into wrinkles. **469. sign:** outward appearance. **471. will . . . error:** deliberately and by mistake. **472. upon this:** after this manner. **474. Do . . . squier:** i.e., know exactly how to please. **squier:** rule. **475. laugh . . . eye:** jest with her intimately. **477. trencher:** wooden plate. **478. allowed:** licensed; i.e., a privileged fool. **479. smock:** lady's nightdress.

481. leaden: i.e., incapable of wounding. **482. manage:** display of horsemanship in the tilting ground. **career:** charge. **490. beg us:** claim us as fools, from the legal procedure in the Court of Wards whereby interested parties begged the court for the custody of a minor or an idiot. **493. whereuntil:** whereunto. **502. parfect:** for "present." **504. Pompion:** pumpkin, for "Pompey." **508. degree:** rank. **513. policy:** wisdom. **518-21. Where . . . birth:** i.e., the unrehearsed results of a too ambitious play are the most amusing.

BER. A right description of our sport,° my lord.

[*Enter* ARMADO.]

ARM. Anointed, I implore so much expense of thy royal sweet breath as will utter a brace of words.   525

[*Converses apart with the* KING,
and delivers him a paper.]

PRIN. Doth this man serve God?

BER. Why ask you?   528

PRIN. He speaks not like a man of God's making.

ARM. That is all one, my fair, sweet, honey monarch; for I protest the schoolmaster is exceeding fantastical — too too vain, too too vain. But we will put it, as they say, to *fortuna de la guerra.*° I wish you the peace of mind, most royal couplement!°   535

[*Exit.*]

KING. Here is like to be a good presence of Worthies. He presents Hector of Troy; the swain, Pompey the Great; the parish curate, Alexander; Armado's page, Hercules; the pedant, Judas Maccabaeus.   540

And if these four Worthies in their first show thrive,
These four will change habits and present the other five.

BER. There is five in the first show.

KING. You are deceived, 'tis not so.

BER. The pedant, the braggart, the hedge priest,° the fool, and the boy.   546

Abate throw at novum,° and the whole world again
Cannot pick out five such, take each one in his vein.

KING. The ship is under sail, and here she comes amain.

[*Enter* COSTARD, *for* POMPEY.]

COS. "I Pompey am ——"

BOYET.   You lie, you are not he.   550

COS. "I Pompey am ——"

BOYET.   With libbard's° head on knee.

BER. Well said, old mocker. I must needs be friends with thee.

COS. "I Pompey am, Pompey surnamed the Big ——"

DUM. "The Great."

COS. It is "Great," sir.

                    "Pompey surnamed the Great,
That oft in field, with targe and shield, did make my foe to sweat.
And traveling along this coast, I here am come by chance,
And lay my arms before the legs of this sweet lass of France."

If your ladyship would say, "Thanks, Pompey," I had done.

PRIN. Great thanks, Great Pompey.   560

COST. 'Tis not so much worth, but I hope I was perfect. I made a little fault in "Great."

BER. My hat to a halfpenny, Pompey proves the best Worthy.

[*Enter* SIR NATHANIEL, *for* ALEXANDER.]

NATH. "When in the world I lived, I was the world's commander.   565
By east, west, north, and south, I spread my conquering might.
My scutcheon° plain declares that I am Alisander ——"

BOYET. Your nose says no, you are not, for it stands too right.°

BER. Your nose smells "no"° in this, most tender-smelling knight.

PRIN. The conqueror is dismayed. Proceed, good Alexander.   570

NATH. "When in the world I lived, I was the world's commander ——"

BOYET. Most true, 'tis right, you were so, Alisander.

BER. Pompey the Great ——

COST. Your servant, and Costard.

BER. Take away the conqueror, take away Alisander.

COST. [*To* SIR NATHANIEL] O sir, you have overthrown Alisander the conqueror! You will be scraped out of the painted cloth° for this. Your lion, that holds his poleax sitting on a close-stool, will be   580 given to Ajax:° he will be the ninth Worthy. A conqueror, and afeared to speak! Run away for shame, Alisander. [NATHANIEL *retires.*] There, an't shall please you, a foolish mild man — an honest man, look you, and soon dashed. He is a marvelous good neighbor, faith, and a very good bowler. But for Alisander — alas, you see how 'tis — a little o'erparted.° But there are Worthies a-coming will speak their mind in some other sort.   590

PRIN. Stand aside, good Pompey.

[*Enter* HOLOFERNES, *for* JUDAS; *and* MOTH, *for* HERCULES.]

HOL. "Great Hercules is presented by this imp,
Whose club killed Cerberus, that three-headed *canis.*°
And when he was a babe, a child, a shrimp,
Thus did he strangle serpents in his *manus.*°
Quoniam° he seemeth in minority,   596

---

522. our sport: i.e., our fiasco of the masque of the Muscovites. **534.** *fortuna . . . guerra:* the fortune of war. **535. couplement:** pair. **545. hedge priest:** low-grade, illiterate priest. **547. Abate . . . novum:** except for a throw at novum, a dice game at which the principal throws were five and nine. **551. libbard:** heraldic painting of a leopard or lion. The joke has not been satisfactorily explained, but presumably it refers to Pompey's symbolical costume or the coat of arms on his shield.

567. scutcheon: coat of arms. **568. too right:** Alexander's head was slightly twisted. **569. nose . . . 'no':** the real Alexander was said to have had a sweet smelling skin. **579. painted cloth:** See *I Hen IV,* IV.ii.27,n., and Pl. 6a. **579–81. Your . . . Ajax:** According to the heraldic experts of the day, the coat of arms of Alexander was a lion sitting in a chair and holding a battle-ax. Ajax was noted among the Greeks for his boasting; among the audience the name was inseparably connected with a privy. See App. 4. **588–89. little o'erparted:** hardly up to the part. **593. canis:** dog. **595. manus:** hand. **596. Quoniam:** since.

Ergo° I come with this apology."
Keep some state° in thy exit, and vanish.

[MOTH *retires*.]

"Judas I am —"

DUM. A Judas! 600

HOL. Not Iscariot, sir.

"Judas I am, ycliped° Maccabaeus."

DUM. Judas Maccabaeus clipped is plain Judas.

BER. A kissing traitor. How art thou proved
Judas?

HOL. "Judas I am ——" 605

DUM. The more shame for you, Judas.

HOL. What mean you, sir?

BOYET. To make Judas hang himself.

HOL. Begin, sir, you are my elder.°

BER. Well followed. Judas was hanged on an
elder. 610

HOL. I will not be put out of countenance.

BER. Because thou hast no face.

HOL. What is this?°

BOYET. A citternhead.°

DUM. The head of a bodkin.° 615

BER. A Death's face° in a ring.

LONG. The face of an old Roman coin, scarce seen.

BOYET. The pommel of Caesar's falchion.°

DUM. The carved-bone face on a flask.

BER. Saint George's half-cheek° in a brooch. 620

DUM. Aye, and in a brooch of lead.

BER. Aye, and worn in the cap of a toothdrawer.

And now forward, for we have put thee in countenance.

HOL. You have put me out of countenance.

BER. False. We have given thee faces. 625

HOL. But you have outfaced them all.

BER. An thou wert a lion, we would do so.

BOYET. Therefore, as he is an ass, let him go.

And so adieu, sweet Jude! Nay, why dost thou stay?

DUM. For the latter end of his name. 630

BER. For the ass to the Jude, give it him. — Jud-as,
away!

HOL. This is not generous,° not gentle, not humble.

BOYET. A light for Monsieur Judas! It grows dark,
he may stumble. [HOLOFERNES *retires*.]

PRIN. Alas, poor Maccabaeus, how hath he been
baited!° 634

[*Enter* ARMADO, *for* HECTOR.]

BER. Hide thy head, Achilles. Here comes Hector
in arms.

DUM. Though my mocks come home by me, I will
now be merry.

KING. Hector was but a Troyan° in respect of this.

BOYET. But is this Hector? 641

KING. I think Hector was not so clean-timbered.°

LONG. His leg is too big for Hector's.

DUM. More calf, certain. 645

BOYET. No, he is best indued in the small.°

BER. This cannot be Hector.

DUM. He's a god or a painter, for he makes faces.

ARM. "The armipotent° Mars, of lances the almighty, 651
Gave Hector a gift ——"

DUM. A gilt nutmeg.

BER. A lemon.

LONG. Stuck with cloves.

DUM. No, cloven. 655

ARM. Peace! —

"The armipotent Mars, of lances the almighty,
Gave Hector a gift, the heir of Ilion,
A man so breathed° that certain he would fight ye
From morn till night, out of his pavilion. 660
I am that flower ——"

DUM. That mint.

LONG. That columbine.

ARM. Sweet Lord Longaville, rein thy tongue.

LONG. I must rather give it the rein, for it runs
against Hector.

DUM. Aye, and Hector's a greyhound.° 665

ARM. The sweet warman is dead and rotten. Sweet
chucks, beat not the bones of the buried. When he
breathed, he was a man. But I will forward with my
device. [*To the* PRINCESS] Sweet royalty, bestow on
me the sense of hearing. 670

PRIN. Speak, brave Hector. We are much delighted.

ARM. I do adore thy sweet Grace's slipper. 674

BOYET. [*Aside to* DUMAIN] Loves her by the foot.

DUM. [*Aside to* BOYET] He may not by the yard.

ARM. "This Hector far surmounted Hannibal ——"

COST. The party° is gone, fellow Hector, she is
gone,° she is two months on her way.

ARM. What meanest thou? 680

COST. Faith, unless you play the honest Troyan,
the poor wench is cast away. She's quick, the child
brags in her belly already. 'Tis yours.

ARM. Dost thou infamonize° me among potentates? Thou shalt die. 685

COST. Then shall Hector be whipped for Jaquenetta that is quick by him, and hanged for Pompey
that is dead by him.

DUM. Most rare Pompey!

BOYET. Renowned Pompey! 690

---

597. *Ergo*: therefore. **598. state**: dignity. **602. ycliped**: called.
609. you ... elder: you seem to know more about it than I.
613. this: i.e., indicating his own face. **614. citternhead**: the
top of a cittern — a form of guitar. See Pl. 18b and c.
615. bodkin: dagger. **616. Death's face**: skull. **618. falchion**:
curved sword. **620. half-cheek**: side face. **632. generous**: noble.
634. baited: tormented.

640. Troyan: Trojan, gay lad. **642. clean-timbered**: clean-
limbed. **646. small**: lower part of the leg. **650. armipotent**:
powerful in arms. **659. so breathed**: with such good wind.
665. greyhound: i.e., a fast runner, as he showed when Achilles
ran after him. **678. The party**: i.e., Jaquenetta. **679. gone**:
ruined. **684. infamonize**: disgrace.

BER. Greater than great, great, great, great Pompey! Pompey the Huge!

DUM. Hector trembles.

BER. Pompey is moved. More Ates,° more Ates! Stir them on! Stir them on!   695

DUM. Hector will challenge him.

BER. Aye, if a' have no more man's blood in's belly than will sup a flea.

ARM. By the North Pole, I do challenge thee.

COST. I will not fight with a pole, like a Northern man, I'll slash, I'll do it by the sword. I bepray° 700 you let me borrow my arms again.

DUM. Room for the incensed Worthies!

COST. I'll do it in my shirt.

DUM. Most resolute Pompey!   705

MOTH. Master, let me take you a buttonhole lower.° Do you not see Pompey is uncasing° for the combat? What mean you? You will lose your reputation.

ARM. Gentlemen and soldiers, pardon me. I will not combat in my shirt.   710

DUM. You may not deny it. Pompey hath made the challenge.

ARM. Sweet bloods, I both may and will.

BER. What reason have you for't?   715

ARM. The naked truth of it is, I have no shirt.° I go woolward° for penance.

BOYET. True, and it was enjoined him in Rome for want of linen. Since when, I'll be sworn, he wore none but a dishclout° of Jaquenetta's, and that a' wears next his heart for a favor.°   722

[Enter MERCADE.*]*

MER. God save you, madam!

PRIN. Welcome, Mercade,
But that thou interrupt'st our merriment.   725

MER. I am sorry, madam, for the news I bring Is heavy in my tongue. The King your father——

PRIN. Dead, for my life!

MER. Even so. My tale is told.

BER. Worthies, away! The scene begins to cloud.

ARM. For mine own part, I breathe free breath. I have seen the day of wrong through the little hole of discretion, and I will right myself like a soldier.

[Exeunt WORTHIES.*]*

KING. How fares your Majesty?   736

PRIN. Boyet, prepare, I will away tonight.

KING. Madam, not so. I do beseech you, stay.

PRIN. Prepare, I say. I thank you, gracious lords, For all your fair endeavors, and entreat,   740 Out of a new-sad soul, that you vouchsafe In your rich wisdom to excuse, or hide, The liberal opposition of our spirits

If overboldly we have borne ourselves
In the converse of breath. Your gentleness   745
Was guilty of it. Farewell, worthy lord!
A heavy heart bears not a nimble tongue.
Excuse me so, coming too short of thanks
For my great suit so easily obtained.

KING. The extreme parts of time extremely forms
All causes to the purpose of his speed,°   751
And often, at his very loose,° decides
That which long process could not arbitrate.
And though the mourning brow of progeny
Forbid the smiling courtesy of love   755
The holy suit which fain it would convince,°
Yet, since love's argument was first on foot,
Let not the cloud of sorrow justle it
From what it purposed; since, to wail friends lost
Is not by much so wholesome-profitable   760
As to rejoice at friends but newly found.

PRIN. I understand you not. My griefs are double.

BER. Honest plain words best pierce the ear of grief,
And by these badges° understand the King.
For your fair sakes have we neglected time,   765
Played foul play with our oaths. Your beauty, ladies,
Hath much deformed us, fashioning our humors
Even to the opposèd end of our intents.
And what in us hath seemed ridiculous —
As love is full of unbefitting strains;   770
All wanton as a child, skipping, and vain;
Formed by the eye and therefore, like the eye,
Full of strange shapes, of habits and of forms,
Varying in subjects as the eye doth roll
To every varied object in his glance —   775
Which particoated° presence of loose love
Put on by us, if, in your heavenly eyes,
Have misbecomed our oaths and gravities,
Those heavenly eyes, that look into these faults,
Suggested° us to make. Therefore, ladies,   780
Our love being yours, the error that love makes
Is likewise yours. We to ourselves prove false
By being once false forever to be true
To those that make us both — fair ladies, you.
And even that falsehood, in itself a sin,   785
Thus purifies itself, and turns to grace.

PRIN. We have received your letters full of love,
Your favors, the ambassadors of love,
And in our maiden council rated them
At courtship, pleasant jest and courtesy,   790
As bombast° and as lining to the time.
But more devout° than this in our respects°
Have we not been, and therefore met your loves
In their own fashion, like a merriment.°

---

694. Ates: goddesses of mischief.   700. bepray: beseech. 706–07. take . . . lower: unbutton your doublet a buttonhole lower. uncasing: taking off his coat.   716. have no shirt: a confession of extreme poverty in a gallant. 717. go woolward: wear wool next my skin.   721. dishclout: dishcloth.   722. favor: love token.

750–51. The . . . speed: i.e., in extremity everything must be done speedily.   752. at . . . loose: quite at random.   756. convince: win.   764. badges: tokens.   776. particoated: wearing motley, the fool's dress. See Pl. 13c.   780. Suggested: prompted 791. bombast: padding.   792. devout: serious. respects: consideration, thoughts.   794. merriment: joke.

DUM. Our letters, madam, showed much more
    than jest.   795
  LONG. So did our looks.
  ROS.   We did not quote° them so.
  KING. Now, at the latest minute of the hour,
Grant us your loves.
    PRIN.   A time, methinks, too short
To make a world-without-end bargain in.
No, no, my lord, your Grace is perjured much,   800
Full of dear° guiltiness, and therefore this —
If for my love, as there is no such cause,
You will do aught, this shall you do for me.
Your oath I will not trust, but go with speed
To some forlorn and naked hermitage   805
Remote from all the pleasures of the world.
There stay until the twelve celestial signs
Have brought about the annual reckoning.°
If this austere insociable life
Change not your offer made in heat of blood;   810
If frosts and fasts, hard lodging and thin weeds°
Nip not the gaudy blossoms of your love,
But that it bear this trial, and last love —
Then, at the expiration of the year,
Come challenge me, challenge me by these deserts
And, by this virgin palm now kissing thine,   816
I will be thine, and till that instant shut
My woeful self up in a mourning house,
Raining the tears of lamentation
For the remembrance of my father's death.   820
If this thou do deny, let our hands part,
Neither entitled° in the other's heart.
    KING. If this, or more than this, I would deny,
    To flatter up these powers of mine with rest,
The sudden hand of death close up mine eye!   825
    Hence ever then my heart is in thy breast.
    BER. And what to me, my love? And what to me?
  ROS. You must be purgèd too, your sins are
    racked,°
You are attaint° with faults and perjury.
Therefore if you my favor mean to get,   830
A twelvemonth shall you spend, and never rest,
But seek the weary beds of people sick.
    DUM. But what to me, my love? But what to me?
  A wife?
    KATH. A beard,° fair health, and honesty.
With threefold love I wish you all these three.   835
    DUM. Oh, shall I say I thank you, gentle wife?
    KATH. Not so, my lord. A twelvemonth and a day
I'll mark no words that smooth-faced wooers say.
Come when the King doth to my lady come,
Then, if I have much love, I'll give you some.   840
    DUM. I'll serve thee true and faithfully till then.

    KATH. Yet swear not, lest ye be forsworn again.
  LONG. What says Maria?
  MAR.   At the twelvemonth's end
I'll change my black gown for a faithful friend.   844
  LONG. I'll stay with patience, but the time is long.
  MAR. The liker you.° Few taller are so young.
  BER. Studies my lady? Mistress, look on me.
Behold the window of my heart, mine eye,
What humble suit attends thy answer there.
Impose some service on me for thy love.   850
    ROS. Oft have I heard of you, my Lord Berowne,
Before I saw you, and the world's large tongue
Proclaims you for a man replete with mocks,°
Full of comparisons and wounding flouts,°
Which you on all estates° will execute   855
That lie within the mercy of your wit.
To weed this wormwood° from your fruitful brain,
And therewithal to win me, if you please —
Without the which I am not to be won —
You shall this twelvemonth term from day to day
Visit the speechless sick, and still° converse   861
With groaning wretches; and your task shall be
With all the fierce endeavor of your wit
To enforce the painèd impotent to smile.
    BER. To move wild laughter in the throat of
    death?   865
It cannot be, it is impossible.
Mirth cannot move a soul in agony.
    ROS. Why, that's the way to choke a gibing spirit
Whose influence is begot of that loose grace
Which shallow laughing hearers give to fools.   870
A jest's prosperity° lies in the ear
Of him that hears it, never in the tongue
Of him that makes it. Then, if sickly ears,
Deafed with the clamors of their own dear groans,
Will hear your idle scorns, continue then,   875
And I will have you and that fault withal.
But if they will not, throw away that spirit,
And I shall find you empty of that fault,
Right joyful of your reformation.
    BER. A twelvemonth! Well, befall what will be-
    fall,   880
I'll jest a twelvemonth in a hospital.
    PRIN. [To the KING] Aye, sweet my lord, and so I
    take my leave.
  KING. No, madam, we will bring you on your way.
  BER. Our wooing doth not end like an old play.
Jack hath not Jill. These ladies' courtesy°   885
Might well have made our sport a comedy.°
  KING. Come, sir, it wants a twelvemonth and a
    day,

---

796. **quote:** note, regard.   801. **dear:** with the double meaning of great and loving.   807–08. **twelve . . . reckoning:** i.e., a complete year. See App. 1.   811. **weeds:** garments.   822. **entitled:** having a claim.   828. **racked:** tortured.   829. **attaint:** charged. 834. **A beard:** i.e., a wish that you'll grow up.

846. **The . . . you:** like time, you are long; i.e., tall.   853. **replete . . . mocks:** full of mockery.   854. **wounding flouts:** bitter jokes which hurt.   855. **all estates:** men of all kinds.   857. **wormwood:** bitterness.   861. **still:** continuously.   871. **A . . . prosperity:** the success of a jest.   885. **These . . . courtesy:** i.e., if these ladies had been kind to us.   886. **comedy:** i.e., a play with a happy ending.

And then 'twill end.

BER.   That's too long for a play.
[*Re-enter* ARMADO.]

ARM. Sweet Majesty, vouchsafe me ——

PRIN. Was not that Hector?

DUM. The worthy knight of Troy.   890

ARM. I will kiss thy royal finger, and take leave. I am a votary, I have vowed to Jaquenetta to hold the plow for her sweet love three years. But, most esteemed greatness, will you hear the dialogue that the two learned men have compiled in praise of the owl and the cuckoo? It should have followed in the end of our show.

KING. Call them forth quickly. We will do so.

ARM. Holla! Approach. [*Re-enter* HOLOFERNES, NATHANIEL, MOTH, COSTARD, *and others.*] This   901
side is Hiems, Winter, this Ver, the Spring, the one maintained by the owl, the other by the cuckoo. Ver, begin.

THE SONG

SPRING.   When daisies pied° and violets blue
               And lady smocks all silver-white   905
           And cuckoo buds° of yellow hue
               Do paint the meadows with delight,
           The cuckoo° then, on every tree,
           Mocks married men; for thus sings he —
               Cuckoo,   910
           Cuckoo, cuckoo! Oh, word of fear,
           Unpleasing to a married ear!

           When shepherds pipe on oaten straws,
               And merry larks are plowmen's clocks,
           When turtles tread, and rooks, and daws,

And maidens bleach their summer
           smocks,   916
The cuckoo then, on every tree,
Mocks married men; for thus sings he —
           Cuckoo,
Cuckoo, cuckoo! Oh, word of fear,   920
Unpleasing to a married ear!

WINTER.   When icicles hang by the wall,
               And Dick the shepherd blows his nail,°
           And Tom bears logs into the hall,   924
               And milk comes frozen home in pail,
           When blood is nipped and ways be foul,
           Then nightly sings the staring owl —
               Tu-whit,
           Tu-who, a merry note,
           While greasy Joan doth keel° the pot.

           When all aloud the wind doth blow,   931
               And coughing drowns the parson's
               saw,°
           And birds sit brooding in the snow,
               And Marian's nose looks red and raw,
           When roasted crabs° hiss in the bowl,
           Then nightly sings the staring owl —   936
               Tu-whit,
           Tu-who, a merry note,
           While greasy Joan doth keel the pot.

ARM. The words of Mercury° are harsh after the songs of Apollo.° You that way — we this way.
                                              [*Exeunt.*]

923. blows . . . nail: i.e., to warm his fingers.   930. keel: cool.
932. saw: platitude, wise saying.   935. crabs: crab apples.
940. Mercury: the messenger of the gods.   941. Apollo: the god of the Arts.

904. pied: parti-colored.   905-06. lady smocks . . . cuckoo buds: wild flowers of the spring.   908. cuckoo: See App. 11.

The Tragedy of
KING RICHARD THE SECOND

Introduction[1]

The Tragedy of King Richard the Second was probably written in 1594 or 1595. There is no definite evidence, but the style is early, with regular rhythms, elaborate imagery, many conceits, and abundance of rhyme. The play was entered for publication in the Stationers' Register on August 29, 1597, to Andrew Wise, who in the same year brought out a Quarto (Q1) with the title *The Tragedie of King Richard the second. As it hath beene publikely acted by the right Honourable the Lorde Chamberlaine his Seruants.*

A second Quarto (Q2) and a third Quarto (Q3) appeared in 1598, with the added information " By William Shakespeare." None of these quartos included the deposition scene. No further quartos were published during Queen Elizabeth's reign. Shortly after her death the rights in the book were transferred to Matthew Law, but no new edition was published until 1608. This fourth quarto was the first to give the play complete, and in some copies the title page reads *The Tragedie of King Richard the Second: With the new additions of the Parliament Sceane, and the deposing of King Richard, As it hath been lately acted by the Kinges Majesties seruantes, at the Globe. By William Shake-speare.*

A fifth quarto was printed in 1615. The text in the first folio of 1623 was set up from one of the quartos which had been used in the playhouse.

The story of the play was taken mainly from the account of the reigns of Richard II and Henry IV in Raphael Holinshed's *Chronicles*. Richard's reign was so complex that the details needed to be much simplified to make it suitable for a drama. The play covers only the last three years of Richard's life, from which certain events leading to his deposition were selected and very freely adapted. The quarrel between Norfolk and Hereford, the scene at Coventry, York's desertion, the details of Richard's defeat, Carlisle's speech, and the murder of the King were mainly historical. The deposition scene was mostly in-

[1] See also App. 28.

vented, for there was in fact no public ceremony; Richard signed documents in the presence of attorneys. The deathbed speeches of Gaunt, the parting of Richard and his Queen, and Richard's soliloquy before his death were wholly unhistorical. Some extracts from the *Chronicles* will show how Shakespeare used his material.

1. THE QUARREL BETWEEN MOWBRAY AND HEREFORD (cf. 1.i)

Hereupon there were sundry of the nobles that lamented these mischiefs, and especially showed their griefs unto such by whose naughty counsel they understood the King to be misled; and this they did to the end that they being about him might either turn their copies and give him better counsel, or else he, having knowledge what evil report went of him, might mend his manners misliked of his nobles. But all was in vain, for so it fell out that in this Parliament holden at Shrewsbury Henry Duke of Hereford accused Thomas Mowbray Duke of Norfolk of certain words which he should utter in talk had betwixt them as they rode together lately before betwixt London and Brainford, sounding highly to the King's dishonor. And for further proof thereof he presented a supplication to the King, wherein he appealed the Duke of Norfolk in field of battle for a traitor, false and disloyal to the King, and enemy unto the realm. This supplication was read before both the Dukes in presence of the King; which done, the Duke of Norfolk took upon him to answer it, declaring that whatsoever the Duke of Hereford had said against him other than well, he lied falsely like an untrue knight as he was. And when the King asked of the Duke of Hereford what he said to it, he, taking his hood off his head, said: " My sovereign lord, even as the supplication which I took you importeth, right so I say for truth that Thomas Mowbray Duke of Norfolk is a traitor, false and disloyal to your loyal Majesty, your crown, and to all the states of your realm."

Then the Duke of Norfolk being asked what he said to this, he answered: " Right dear lord, with your favor that I make answer unto your cousin here, I say (your reverence saved) that Henry of Lancaster, Duke of Hereford, like a false and disloyal traitor as he is, doth lie, in that he hath or shall say of me otherwise than well." "No more," said the King, "we have heard enough"; and herewith commanded the Duke of Surrey, for that turn Marshal of England, to arrest in his name the two Dukes: the Duke of Lancaster, father to the Duke of Hereford, the Duke of York, the Duke of Aumerle, Constable of England, and the Duke of Surrey, Marshal of the realm, undertook as pledges body for body for the Duke of Hereford; but the Duke of Norfolk was not suffered to put in pledges, and so under arrest was led unto Windsor Castle, and there guarded with keepers that were appointed to see him safely kept.

2. NORFOLK'S DEFENSE (cf. I.i.83–151)

[On a later occasion both Dukes were brought before the King to justify their words. During the hearing:]

The King then demanded of the Duke of Norfolk if these were his words, and whether he had any more to say. The Duke of Norfolk then answered for himself: "Right dear sir, true it is that I have received so much gold to pay your people of the town of Calais; which I have done, and I do avouch that your town of Calais is as well kept at your commandment as ever it was at any time before, and that there never hath been by any of Calais any complaint made unto you of me. Right dear and my sovereign lord, for the voyage that I made unto France about your marriage I never received either gold or silver of you, nor yet for the voyage that the Duke of Aumerle and I made into Almagne, where we spent great treasure. Marry, true it is that once I laid an ambush to have slain the Duke of Lancaster that there sitteth; but nevertheless he hath pardoned me thereof, and there was good peace made betwixt us, for the which I yield him hearty thanks. This is that which I have to answer, and I am ready to defend myself against mine adversary. I beseech you therefore of right, and to have the battle against him in upright judgment."

3. THE BANISHMENT OF NORFOLK AND HEREFORD (cf. I.iii.117; I.iv.65)

The Duke of Hereford was quickly horsed, and closed his beaver, and cast his spear into the rest, and when the trumpets sounded set forward courageously towards his enemy six or seven paces. The Duke of Norfolk was not fully set forward when the King cast down his warder, and the heralds cried "Ho! ho!" Then the King caused their spears to be taken from them, and commanded them to repair again to their chairs, where they remained two long hours while the King and his Council deliberately consulted what order was best to be had in so weighty a cause. Finally, after they had devised and fully determined what should be done therein, the heralds cried silence; and Sir John Bushy, the King's secretary, read the sentence and determination of the King and his Council in a long roll, the effect whereof was that Henry Duke of Hereford should within fifteen days depart out of the realm, and not to return before the term of ten years were expired, except by the King he should be repealed again, and this upon pain of death; and that Thomas Mowbray Duke of Norfolk, because he had sown sedition in the realm by his words, should likewise avoid the realm, and never to return again into England, nor approach the borders or confines thereof upon pain of death; and that the King would stay the profits of his lands till he had levied thereof such sums of money as the Duke had taken up of the King's Treasurer for the wages of the garrison of Calais, which were still unpaid.

When these judgments were once read, the King called before him both the parties, and made them to swear that the one should never come in place where the other was willingly, nor keep any company together in any foreign region; which oath they both received humbly, and so went their ways. The Duke of Norfolk departed sorrowfully out of the realm into Almany, and at the last came to Venice, where he for thought and melancholy deceased; for he was in hope (as writers record) that he should have been borne out in the matter by the King, which when it fell out otherwise, it grieved him not a little. The Duke of Hereford took his leave of the King at Eltham, who there released four years of his banishment; so he took his journey over into Calais, and from thence went into France, where he remained. A wonder it was to see what number of people ran after him in every town and street where he came before he took the sea, lamenting and bewailing his departure, as who would say that when he departed, the only shield, defense, and comfort of the commonwealth was vaded and gone.

4. THE INSTRUMENT OF DEPOSITION TO WHICH RICHARD AGREED

[Shakespeare invented the scene of Richard's deposition but made use of this passage for Richard's speech of renunciation (cf. IV.i.201–20).]

The tenor of the instrument whereby King Richard resigneth the crown to the Duke of Lancaster

In the name of God, Amen: I, Richard by the grace of God King of Engand and of France, &c, Lord of Ireland, acquit and assoil all Archbishops, Bishops, and other prelates, secular or religious, of what dignity, degree, state, or condition soever they be; and also all Dukes, Marquesses, Earls, Barons, Lords, and all my liege men, both spiritual and secular, of what manner or degree they be, from their oath of fealty and homage and all other deeds and privileges made unto me, and from all manner bonds of allegiance, regality and lordship, in which they were or be bounden to me, or any otherwise constrained; and them, their heirs and successors forevermore, from the same bonds and oaths I release, deliver, and acquit, and set them for free, dissolved, and acquit, and to be harmless, for as much as longeth to my person by any manner, way or title of right that to me might follow of the foresaid things, or any of them. And also I resign all my kingly dignity, majesty, and crown, with all the lordships, power, and privileges, to the foresaid kingly dignity and crown belonging, and all other lordships and possessions to me in any manner of wise pertaining, of what name, title, quality, or condition soever they be, except the lands and possessions for me and mine obits purchased and bought. And I renounce all right and all manner of title of possession which I ever had or have in the same lordships and possessions, or any of them, with any manner of rights belonging or appertaining unto any part of them. And also the rule and governance of the same kingdom and lordships, with all ministrations of the same, and all things and every each of them that to the whole empire and jurisdictions of the same belongeth of right, or in any wise may belong. . . .

5. CARLISLE'S SPEECH (cf. iv.i.114–54)

[The speech was actually delivered after Richard's deposition.]

On Wednesday following request was made by the Commons that sith King Richard had resigned and was lawfully deposed from his royal dignity, he might have judgment decreed against him, so as the realm were not troubled by him, and that the causes of his deposing might be published through the realm for satisfying the people; which demand was granted. Whereupon the Bishop of Carlisle, a man both learned, wise, and stout of stomach, boldly showed forth his opinion concerning that demand, affirming that there was none amongst them worthy or meet to give judgment upon so noble a Prince as King Richard was, whom they had taken for their sovereign and liege lord by the space of two and twenty years or more. " And I assure you " (said he) " there is not so rank a traitor, nor so errant a thief, nor yet so cruel a murderer apprehended or detained in prison for his offense, but he shall be brought before the justice to hear his judgment; and will ye proceed to the judgment of an anointed King, hearing neither his answer nor excuse? I say, that the Duke of Lancaster whom you call King hath more trespassed to King Richard and his realm than King Richard hath done either to him or us; for it is

manifest and well known that the Duke was banished the realm by King Richard and his Council, and by the judgment of his own father, for the space of ten years, for what cause ye know, and yet without license of King Richard he is returned again into the realm, and (that is worse) hath taken upon him the name, title, and pre-eminence of King. And therefore I say that you have done manifest wrong to proceed in anything against King Richard without calling him openly to his answer and defense." As soon as the Bishop had ended this tale, he was attached by the Earl Marshal, and committed to ward in the Abbey of St. Albans.

In addition to Holinshed, Shakespeare had a model for his play in Marlowe's *The troublesome reign and lamentable death of Edward the Second,* entered for publication on July 3, 1593. Like Richard, Edward was a weakling who was compelled to abdicate, and who was afterward murdered. There is a general similarity in the speeches of Edward and of Richard when forced to resign the crown, particularly at the climax of Edward's grief:

LEICESTER. My lord, why waste you thus the time
   away?
They stay your answer. Will you yield your crown?
  KING EDWARD. Ah, Leicester, weigh how hardly I
   can brook
To lose my crown and kingdom without cause —
To give ambitious Mortimer my right,
That, like a mountain, overwhelms my bliss,
In which extreme my mind here murdered is!
But that the Heavens appoint I must obey.
Here, take my crown, the life of Edward too.
Two kings in England cannot reign at once.
But stay awhile. Let me be King till night,
That I may gaze upon this glittering crown.
So shall my eyes receive their last content,
My head, the latest honor due to it,
And jointly both yield up their wishèd right.
Continue ever, thou celestial sun,
Let never silent night possess this clime;
Stand still, you watches of the element —
All times and seasons, rest you at a stay,
That Edward may be still fair England's King!
But day's bright beams doth vanish fast away,
And needs I must resign my wishèd crown.
Inhuman creatures, nursed with tiger's milk,
Why gape you for your sovereign's overthrow?
My diadem, I mean, and guiltless life.
See, monsters, see! I'll wear my crown again.
What, fear you not the fury of your king?
But, hapless Edward, thou art fondly led;
They pass not for thy frowns as late they did,
But seek to make a new-elected King,

Which fills my mind with strange despairing
   thoughts,
Which thoughts are martyred with endless torments.
And in his torment comfort find I none
But that I feel the crown upon my head,
And therefore let me wear it yet awhile.
  TRUSSEL. My lord, the Parliament must have pres-
   ent news,
And therefore say, will you resign or no?
                  [*The King rageth.*]
  KING EDWARD. I'll not resign, but whil'st I live be
   King.
Traitors, be gone, and join you with Mortimer.
Elect, conspire, install, do what you will.
Their blood and yours shall seal these treacheries.

About the same time that Shakespeare wrote his play, Samuel Daniel brought out his narrative poem *Civil Wars between Lancaster and York*. Both Daniel and Shakespeare inserted quite unhistorical accounts of the parting of Richard and his Queen. Although there is little similarity between the two versions, it is likely that either one poet had seen the other's version or that both had seen still another version of the story, possibly a play that has not survived.

Contemporaries, especially followers of the Earl of Essex, saw in the play of *Richard II* certain topical parallels with their own times, which were much marked. As the Earl of Essex became more bitter and critical of Queen Elizabeth, he constantly complained that she was surrounded by evil counselors and refused to admit good advice, while Essex's enemies maintained that he was himself seeking to be a second Bolingbroke; and it is significant that in the quartos of the play published in 1597 and 1598 the deposition scene was omitted, although the deposition scene in Marlowe's *Edward II* had been freely printed in 1593. Essex's great quarrel with the Queen occurred in the summer of 1598; but an uneasy reconciliation was made, and by the end of the year Essex was preparing to take over a great army to quell the rebellion in Ireland. In February, 1599, a young lawyer called John Hayward published a prose history called *The First Part of the Life and Reign of King Henry IV*, which told of the events leading up to the deposition of Richard II. This book was dedicated to Essex in a Latin epistle which contained some curious and significant phrases: *Magnus siquidem es, et praesenti iudicio et futuri temporis expectatione* (You are indeed great, in present judgment and in the expectation of future time). The book further

included a preface signed A. P., pointing out that a study of history afforded " not only precepts but lively patterns both for private direction and for affairs of state." The Privy Council and the Queen herself were very suspicious of the book's inner meaning. Hayward and all concerned with the publication were closely examined, and Hayward was subsequently imprisoned in the Tower. The book itself was very popular, and is still one of the commonest Elizabethan books offered for sale by antiquarian booksellers.

The play of *Richard II* won further and unwelcome notoriety on February 7, 1601, when at the request of certain followers of the Earl of Essex the Chamberlain's Men foolishly revived it on the day before Essex's rebellion (see Gen. Intro. p. 45a).

Richard II had thus certain topical significances which are no longer obvious. The description of Bolingbroke going off to exile seemed at least to one writer to be a picture of Essex. Everard Guilpin, in a book of satires called *Skialethia*, written in 1597-98, imitated the passage with unmistakable and hostile reference to Essex:

For when great Felix passing through the street
Vaileth his cap to each one he doth meet,
And when no broom man that will pray for him
Shall have less truage [2] than his bonnet's brim,
Who would not think him perfect courtesy?
Or the honeysuckle of humility?
The Devil he is as soon. He is the Devil,
Brightly accoustred [3] to bemist [4] his evil.
Like a swartrutter's [5] hose his puff thoughts swell
With yeasty ambition: *Signor Machiavel*
Taught him this mumming [6] trick, with courtesy
To entrench himself with popularity,
And for a writhen [7] face, and body's move,
Be barricadoed in the people's love.

Richard II was the fifth play which Shakespeare wrote dealing with English history. In writing the first four — the three parts of *Henry VI* and *Richard III* — he had come to realize that all the horrors and treacheries of the long Wars of the Roses had their origin in the deposition of Richard II and the usurpation of the throne by Henry Bolingbroke. In *Richard II* Shakespeare went back to show how the story began and to tell how Richard II first wronged his cousin Henry Bolingbroke, who was led thereby to commit the greater wrong of usurping the throne.

In this play Shakespeare tried a new method of

---

[2] acknowledgment.   [3] accoutered.   [4] conceal.   [5] German mercenary.   [6] actor's.   [7] grimacing.

presenting history. The three parts of *Henry VI* were scenes from history. *Richard III* was the portrait of a remorseless, cynical Machiavellian, after the pattern of one of Marlowe's supermen. In *Richard II* Shakespeare presented history as the personal conflict of two individuals. The play is the drama of the failure and death of a King, but Richard's tragedy is not that he came to degradation, misery, and death, but that he wrought his own destruction. Two main causes brought about Richard's ruin: the first was his own character, the second was his cousin, Henry Bolingbroke. Shakespeare had now begun to realize that character is fate.

Richard himself has great charm, but he is weak, selfish, and unscrupulous and, like Narcissus, too easily attracted by his own reflection. He is forever posing. In the first scene he poses as a King who is a stern judge; " We were not born to sue but to command " (I.i.196), he says to Mowbray and Bolingbroke, but neither takes any notice of him. At the lists in Coventry he delights in the dramatic moment when he suddenly stops the combat and attracts attention away from the contestants to himself. He sees himself as the soldier king when he decides to take command of the expedition to Ireland; but in the presence of the dying Gaunt he appears merely mean, and his seizing of Bolingbroke's inheritance is an act of stupid tyranny. He next appears after his return from Ireland. He is now friendless and powerless, yet he takes a morbid delight in the sad spectacle of himself as a wronged and deserted monarch, and he does nothing to resist his enemies except to rant that God will provide angels to fight for him. In the last act of his reign, when he is summoned to make a formal resignation of the crown, he sees himself as a Christ deserted by a host of Judases, and he enjoys to the full the performance of his own tragedy. He keeps up this role in his parting from the Queen. Alone in prison, he plays with fancies of himself as beggar and King, but in the end he dies fighting.

Bolingbroke, Richard's opposite, has none of Richard's weaknesses and none of his charm. He is the strong, silent man of action; yet in the final contest between them, when Richard admits defeat by surrendering the crown, Bolingbroke is the artistic and moral loser. It is an emotional occasion when the plain man is self-conscious and ill at ease and the artist in his element. From his first entry, Richard dominates the scene. As he has nothing now to lose, he has no more to fear. His performance is magnificently dramatic. At the end of the scene, Richard is led away from the presence of the silent King, but he has left behind him the curse on the House of Lancaster.

The theme of the play is thus subtly conceived, and the best scenes — the opening, the lists at Coventry, and the deposition — are effectively planned; but the characterization and the dialogue, except for some high passages of poetry, fall far short.

Indeed, *Richard II* is not a great play. Some of the speeches — especially Gaunt's outburst on England (II.i), Richard's lamentations on his defeat (III.ii and III.iii), his surrender of the crown (IV.i), and his last musings (V.v) — are fine specimens of Shakespeare's earlier poetry. But the characterization is weak. The persons, even Richard himself and Bolingbroke, are not human beings, but mouthpieces for poetic sentiments. A comparison between Henry IV as he appears in Act V of *Richard II* and in Act I of the first part of *Henry IV* (written about two years later) will show how quickly Shakespeare's art of characterization developed. Some of the scenes, indeed, in *Richard II,* particularly those between York, his Duchess, and his son (V.ii.40–116; V.iii.45–146), are unintentionally comic. Nevertheless, in Shakespeare's development the play is important. It was the last of the plays in which he deliberately imitated a model or sacrificed drama to poetry.

Richard II

DRAMATIS PERSONAE

KING RICHARD *the Second*
JOHN OF GAUNT, *Duke of Lancaster* } *uncles to the*
EDMUND OF LANGLEY, *Duke of York* } *King*
HENRY, *surnamed* BOLINGBROKE, *Duke of Hereford,*
son to John of Gaunt; afterward KING HENRY IV
DUKE OF AUMERLE, *son to the Duke of York*
THOMAS MOWBRAY, *Duke of Norfolk*
DUKE OF SURREY
EARL OF SALISBURY
LORD BERKELEY
BUSHY }
BAGOT } *servants to King Richard*
GREEN }
EARL OF NORTHUMBERLAND
HENRY PERCY, *surnamed Hotspur, his son*
LORD ROSS
LORD WILLOUGHBY

LORD FITZWATER
BISHOP *of Carlisle*
ABBOT *of Westminster*
LORD MARSHAL
SIR STEPHEN SCROOP
SIR PIERCE OF EXTON
CAPTAIN *of a band of Welshmen*

QUEEN *to King Richard*
DUCHESS OF YORK
DUCHESS OF GLOUCESTER
LADY *attending on the Queen*

LORDS, HERALDS, OFFICERS, SOLDIERS, *two* GARDENERS,
KEEPER, MESSENGER, GROOM, *and other* ATTENDANTS

SCENE — *England and Wales.*

Act I

SCENE I. *London.* KING RICHARD's *palace.*

[*Enter* KING RICHARD, JOHN OF GAUNT, *with other*
NOBLES *and* ATTENDANTS.]
K. RICH. Old John of Gaunt, time-honored°
  Lancaster,
Hast thou, according to thy oath and band,°
Brought hither Henry Hereford, thy bold son,
Here to make good the boisterous late appeal° —
Which then our leisure would not let us hear — 5
Against the Duke of Norfolk, Thomas Mowbray?
  GAUNT. I have, my liege.
  K. RICH. Tell me, moreover, hast thou sounded
    him,
If he appeal the Duke on ancient malice,°
Or worthily, as a good subject should, 10
On some known ground of treachery in him?
  GAUNT. As near as I could sift him on that argu-
    ment,°
On some apparent° danger seen in him
Aimed at your Highness — no inveterate° malice.
  K. RICH. Then call them to our presence. Face to
    face, 15
And frowning brow to brow, ourselves will hear
The accuser and the accusèd freely speak.
High-stomached° are they both, and full of ire,

In rage deaf as the sea, hasty as fire.
[*Enter* BOLINGBROKE *and* MOWBRAY.]
  BOLING. Many years of happy days befall 20
My gracious sovereign, my most loving liege!
  MOW. Each day still better other's happiness,
Until the Heavens, envying earth's good hap,°
Add an immortal title to your crown!
  K. RICH. We thank you both. Yet one but flatters
    us, 25
As well appeareth by the cause you come;
Namely, to appeal each other of high treason.
Cousin of Hereford, what dost thou object
Against the Duke of Norfolk, Thomas Mowbray?
  BOLING. First — Heaven be the record of my
    speech — 30
In the devotion of a subject's love,
Tendering° the precious safety of my prince
And free from other misbegotten hate,
Come I appellant° to this princely presence.
Now, Thomas Mowbray, do I turn to thee, 35
And mark my greeting well, for what I speak
My body shall make good upon this earth
Or my divine soul answer it in Heaven.
Thou art a traitor and a miscreant,°
Too good to be so,° and too bad to live, 40
Since the more fair and crystal is the sky,
The uglier seem the clouds that in it fly.
Once more, the more to aggravate the note,°

Act I, Sc. i: **1. time-honored:** venerable. **2. band:** bond.
4. appeal: accusation which the accuser is prepared to justify
by mortal combat. **9. ancient malice:** long-standing hatred.
12. argument: matter, topic. **13. apparent:** open. **14. inveter-**
ate: long-established. **18. High-stomached:** haughty.

23. hap: luck. **32. Tendering:** caring for. **34. appellant:** one
accusing of treason. **39. miscreant:** lit., misbeliever, villain.
40. Too . . . so: of too high rank to be a traitor. **43. aggra-**
vate . . . note: make more conspicuous the disgrace.

With a foul traitor's name stuff I thy throat,°
And wish, so please my sovereign, ere I move,   45
What my tongue speaks my right drawn sword may
    prove.
    MOW. Let not my cold words here accuse my zeal.
'Tis not the trial of a woman's war,
The bitter clamor of two eager tongues,
Can arbitrate this cause betwixt us twain.   50
The blood is hot that must be cooled for this.
Yet can I not of such tame patience boast
As to be hushed and naught at all to say.
First, the fair reverence of your Highness curbs me
From giving reins and spurs to my free speech,   55
Which else would post° until it had returned
These terms of treason doubled down his throat.
Setting aside his high blood's royalty,°
And let him be no kinsman to my liege,°
I do defy him, and I spit at him,   60
Call him a slanderous coward and a villain.
Which to maintain I would allow him odds
And meet him, were I tied° to run afoot
Even to the frozen ridges of the Alps,
Or any other ground inhabitable,   65
Wherever Englishman durst set his foot.
Meantime let this° defend my loyalty —
By all my hopes, most falsely doth he lie.
    BOLING. Pale trembling coward, there I throw my
    gage,°
Disclaiming here the kindred of the King,   70
And lay aside my high blood's royalty,
Which fear, not reverence, makes thee to except.
If guilty dread have left thee so much strength
As to take up mine honor's pawn,° then stoop.
By that and all the rites of knighthood else,   75
Will I make good against thee, arm to arm,
What I have spoke, or thou canst worse devise.
    MOW. I take it up, and by that sword I swear
Which gently laid my knighthood on my shoulder,
I'll answer thee in any fair degree   80
Or chivalrous design of knightly trial.
And when I mount, alive may I not light
If I be traitor or unjustly fight!
    K. RICH. What doth our cousin lay to Mowbray's
    charge?
It must be great that can inherit us°   85
So much as of a thought of ill in him.
    BOLING. Look, what I speak, my life shall prove it
    true —
That Mowbray hath received eight thousand nobles°
In name of lendings for your Highness' soldiers,
The which he hath detained for lewd° employments,

Like a false traitor and injurious° villain.   91
Besides, I say and will in battle prove,
Or here or elsewhere to the furthest verge
That ever was surveyed by English eye,
That all the treasons for these eighteen years   95
Complotted and contrivèd in this land
Fetch° from false Mowbray their first head and
    spring.
Further I say, and further will maintain
Upon his bad life to make all this good,
That he did plot the Duke of Gloucester's death,°
Suggest° his soon-believing adversaries,   101
And consequently, like a traitor coward,
Sluiced out his innocent soul through streams of
    blood.
Which blood, like sacrificing Abel's, cries
Even from the tongueless caverns of the earth   105
To me for justice and rough chastisement.
And by the glorious worth of my descent,
This arm shall do it or this life be spent.
    K. RICH. How high a pitch° his resolution soars!
Thomas of Norfolk, what say'st thou to this?   110
    MOW. Oh, let my sovereign turn away his face,
And bid his ears a little while be deaf,
Till I have told this slander of° his blood
How God and good men hate so foul a liar.   114
    K. RICH. Mowbray, impartial are our eyes and ears.
Were he my brother — nay, my kingdom's heir —
As he is but my father's brother's son,
Now, by my scepter's awe, I make a vow,
Such neighbor nearness to our sacred blood
Should nothing privilege him, nor partialize°   120
The unstooping firmness of my upright soul.
He is our subject, Mowbray, so art thou.
Free speech and fearless I to thee allow.
    MOW. Then, Bolingbroke, as low as to thy heart,
Through the false passage of thy throat thou liest.
Three parts of that receipt I had for Calais   126
Disbursed I duly to His Highness' soldiers.
The other part reserved I by consent,
For that my sovereign liege was in my debt,
Upon remainder of a dear° account   130
Since last I went to France to fetch his Queen.
Now swallow down that lie. For Gloucester's death,
I slew him not, but to my own disgrace
Neglected my sworn duty in that case.
For you, my noble Lord of Lancaster,   135
The honorable father to my foe,
Once did I lay an ambush for your life —
A trespass that doth vex my grievèd soul.
But ere I last received the sacrament
I did confess it, and exactly° begged   140
Your Grace's pardon, and I hope I had it.

44. throat: To give a man "the lie in the throat" was the bitterest insult, which could only be answered by a fight to the death.
56. post: ride fast. See App. 17.   58. Setting . . . royalty: disregarding his royal blood. See App. 28.   59. liege: lord.   63. tied:
obliged.   67. let this: i.e., my sword.   69. gage: he throws down
a glove as pledge (gage) that he will fight.   74. pawn: pledge.
85. inherit us: make us become inheritor of.   88. nobles: gold
coins worth 6s 8d. See App. 27.   90. lewd: base.

91. injurious: insulting.   97. Fetch: derive.   100. Gloucester's
death: See App. 28.   101. Suggest: prompt.   109. pitch: lit., the
highest point in the flight of the hawk. See App. 26.   113. slander of: disgrace to.   120. partialize: make partial.   130. dear:
heavy.   140. exactly: in express terms.

This is my fault. As for the rest appealed,
It issues from the rancor of a villain,
A recreant° and most degenerate traitor.
Which in myself I boldly will defend,   145
And interchangeably° hurl down my gage
Upon this overweening traitor's foot,
To prove myself a loyal gentleman
Even in the best blood chambered in his bosom.
In haste whereof, most heartily I pray   150
Your Highness to assign our trial day.
    K. RICH. Wrath-kindled gentlemen, be ruled by
    me —
Let's purge° this choler without letting blood.
This we prescribe, though no physician.
Deep malice makes too deep incision.   155
Forget, forgive, conclude° and be agreed.   *RICH. CAN'T EVEN*
Our doctors say this is no month to bleed.   *MAKE THEM*
Good Uncle, let this end where it begun.   *PEACEFUL*
We'll calm the Duke of Norfolk, you your son.   159
    GAUNT. To be a make-peace shall become my age.
Throw down, my son, the Duke of Norfolk's gage.
    K. RICH. And, Norfolk, throw down his. *GAUNT BIDS*
    GAUNT.   When, Harry, when?   *HIS SON*
Obedience bids I should not bid again.   *TO CALL OFF*
    K. RICH. Norfolk, throw down, we bid. There is no   *THE*
    boot.°   *FIGHT- BUT*
    MOW. Myself I throw, dread sovereign, at thy   *NO*
    foot.   165 *CONTROL OF SON*
My life thou shalt command, but not my shame.
The one my duty owes, but my fair name,
Despite of death that lives upon my grave,
To dark dishonor's use thou shalt not have.   169
I am disgraced, impeached° and baffled° here,
Pierced to the soul with slander's venomed spear,
The which no balm can cure but his heartblood
Which breathed this poison.
    K. RICH.   Rage must be withstood.
Give me his gage. Lions° make leopards tame.
    MOW. Yea, but not change his spots. Take but my
    shame,   175
And I resign my gage. My dear dear lord,
The purest treasure mortal times afford
Is spotless reputation. That away,
Men are but gilded loam or painted clay.
A jewel in a ten-times-barred-up chest   180
Is a bold spirit in a loyal breast,
Mine honor is my life, both grow in one,

Take honor from me and my life is done.
Then, dear my liege, mine honor let me try.°
In that I live and for that will I die.   185
    K. RICH. Cousin, throw up your gage. Do you be-
    gin.
    BOLING. Oh, God defend my soul from such deep
    sin!
Shall I seem crestfallen in my father's sight?
Or with pale beggar-fear impeach my height   189
Before this outdared° dastard?° Ere my tongue
Shall wound my honor with such feeble wrong,
Or sound so base a parle,° my teeth shall tear
The slavish motive° of recanting fear
And spit it bleeding in his high disgrace
Where shame doth harbor, even in Mowbray's face.
                              [Exit GAUNT.] *RICH'S*
    K. RICH. ~~We were not born to sue, but to com-~~ *SILLY*
    mand,   196 *REMARK*
~~Which since we cannot do to make you friends,~~
Be ready, as your lives shall answer it,
At Coventry, upon Saint Lambert's Day.°
There shall your swords and lances arbitrate   200
The swelling difference of your settled hate.
Since we cannot atone° you, we shall see
Justice design the victor's chivalry.°
Lord Marshal, command our officers-at-arms°   204
Be ready to direct these home alarms.°   [Exeunt.]

SCENE II. *The* DUKE OF LANCASTER'S *palace.*
                         GAUNT EXCUSES HIMSELF FOR DOING
[Enter JOHN OF GAUNT *with the* DUCHESS OF *NOTHING —*
                    GLOUCESTER.]   *"DIVINE RIGHT"*
    GAUNT. Alas, the part I had in Woodstock's blood° *OF KINGS*
Doth more solicit me than your exclaims   *EXCUSE— POOR*
To stir against the butchers of his life!
But since correction lieth in those hands
Which made the fault that we cannot correct,   5
Put we our quarrel to the will of Heaven,
Who, when they see the hours ripe on earth,
Will rain hot vengeance on offenders' heads.
    DUCH. ~~Finds brotherhood in thee no sharper spur?~~
~~Hath love in thy old blood no living fire?~~   10
~~Edward's° seven sons, whereof thyself art one,~~ *BLOOD USED A LOT*
~~Were as seven vials of his sacred blood,~~
~~Or seven fair branches springing from one root,~~
~~Some of those seven are dried by nature's course,~~
~~Some of those branches by the Destinies cut.~~   15
~~But Thomas, my dear lord, my life, my Gloucester,~~
~~One vial full of Edward's sacred blood,~~

144. **recreant:** traitor.   146. **interchangeably:** in my turn.
153–57. **purge . . . bleed:** Richard indulges in an elaborate
metaphor taken from medicine. For many complaints the recognized treatment was bloodletting, for which certain days and
seasons (noted in the almanac) were considered more favorable
than others. **choler:** excess of bile, anger. See App. 2, 3. **incision:**
cut, the technical term for bloodletting.   156. **conclude:** come to
terms.   164. **boot:** help.   170. **impeached:** accused. **baffled:** disgraced. The term was used of the degradation of a knight found
guilty of breaking his oath. He was stripped of his armor, his
shield painted with his coat of arms was reversed, and his picture or effigy hung upside down.   174. **Lions:** The lion is the
symbol of the English Kings.

184. **try:** make trial of.   190. **outdared:** defied. **dastard:** coward.
192. **parle:** parley; i.e., proposal for peace.   193. **motive:** instrument; i.e., his tongue.   199. **Saint Lambert's Day:** September 17.
202. **atone:** reconcile.   203. **design . . . chivalry:** designate the
victorious champion; i.e., the man who has the just case.
204. **Lord . . . arms:** See App. 9.   205. **alarms:** disturbances.
    Sc. ii: 1. **part . . . blood:** i.e., my brotherhood. **part:** share.
Woodstock: Thomas of Woodstock, late Duke of Gloucester.
11. **Edward:** i.e., Edward III.

One flourishing branch of his most royal root,
Is cracked, and all the precious liquor spilt,
Is hacked down, and his summer leaves all faded,
By envy's hand and murder's bloody ax.   21
Ah, Gaunt, his blood was thine! That bed, that
    womb,
That metal, that self-mold,° that fashioned thee
Made him a man; and though thou livest and
    breathest,
Yet art thou slain in him. Thou dost consent   25
In some large measure to thy father's death
In that thou seest thy wretched brother die,
Who was the model° of thy father's life.
Call it not patience, Gaunt, it is despair.
In suffering thus thy brother to be slaughtered,   30
Thou showest the naked pathway to thy life,
Teaching stern murder how to butcher thee.
That which in mean men we entitle patience
Is pale cold cowardice in noble breasts.
What shall I say? To safeguard thine own life,   35
The best way is to venge my Gloucester's death.
    GAUNT. God's is the quarrel, for God's substitute,
His deputy anointed in His sight,
Hath caused his death.° The which if wrongfully,
Let Heaven revenge, for I may never lift   40
An angry arm against His minister.
    DUCH. Where then, alas, may I complain myself?
    GAUNT. To God, the widow's champion and de-
fense.
    DUCH. Why then, I will. Farewell, old Gaunt.
Thou goest to Coventry, there to behold   45
Our cousin Hereford and fell Mowbray fight.
Oh, sit my husband's wrongs on Hereford's spear,
That it may enter butcher Mowbray's breast!
Or if misfortune miss the first career,°
Be Mowbray's sins so heavy in his bosom   50
That they may break his foaming courser's back
And throw the rider headlong in the lists,
A caitiff° recreant to my cousin° Hereford!
Farewell, old Gaunt. Thy sometimes° brother's wife
With her companion grief must end her life.   55
    GAUNT. Sister, farewell. I must to Coventry.
As much good stay with thee as go with me!
    DUCH. Yet one word more. Grief boundeth where
    it falls,
Not with the empty hollowness, but weight.°
I take my leave before I have begun,   60
For sorrow ends not when it seemeth done.
Commend me to thy brother, Edmund York.
Lo, this is all. — Nay, yet depart not so.
Though this be all, do not so quickly go.

I shall remember more. Bid him — ah, what? —   65
With all good speed at Plashy visit me.
Alack, and what shall good old York there see
But empty lodgings and unfurnished walls,
Unpeopled offices, untrodden stones?   69
And what hear there for welcome but my groans?
Therefore commend me. Let him not come there
To seek out sorrow that dwells everywhere.
Desolate, desolate, will I hence and die.
The last leave of thee takes my weeping eye.
                           [*Exeunt.*]

SCENE III. *The lists° at Coventry.*

[*Enter the* LORD MARSHAL *and the* DUKE OF
            AUMERLE.]
    MAR. My Lord Aumerle, is Harry Hereford
    armed?
    AUM. Yea, at all points,° and longs to enter in.
    MAR. The Duke of Norfolk, sprightfully° and
    bold,
Stays but the summons of the appellant's° trumpet.
    AUM. Why, then, the champions are prepared, and
    stay   5
For nothing but His Majesty's approach.
[*The trumpets sound, and the* KING *enters with his
    nobles,* GAUNT, BUSHY, BAGOT, GREEN, *and others.
      When they are set, enter* MOWBRAY *in arms,
        defendant,° with a* HERALD.]
    K. RICH. Marshal, demand of yonder champion
The cause of his arrival here in arms.
Ask him his name, and orderly proceed
To swear him in the justice of his cause.   10
    MAR. In God's name and the King's, say who thou
    art,
And why thou comest thus knightly clad in arms,
Against what man thou comest, and what thy quar-
rel.
Speak truly, on thy knighthood and thy oath,
As so defend thee Heaven and thy valor!   15
    MOW. My name is Thomas Mowbray, Duke of
    Norfolk,
Who hither come engagèd by my oath —
Which God defend° a knight should violate! —
Both to defend my loyalty and truth
To God, my King, and my succeeding issue   20
Against the Duke of Hereford that appeals me,
And, by the grace of God and this mine arm,
To prove him, in defending of myself,
A traitor to my God, my King, and me.
And as I truly fight, defend me Heaven!   25
[*The trumpets sound. Enter* BOLINGBROKE, *appellant,
       in armor, with a* HERALD.]

---

23. self-mold: self-same mold. **28. model:** copy. **37-39. God's
. . . death:** i.e., since Gloucester's death was caused by the King
(*God's substitute*), it is God's business and not mine to punish
him. **49. career:** charge. **53. caitiff:** slave. **cousin:** kinsman;
the word is used of any relation by blood. **54. sometimes:**
former; i.e., dead. **58-59. Grief . . . weight:** my complaints rebound like a tennis ball from a wall; however, they are not light
like a ball, but heavy.

   Sc. iii: s.d., **lists:** combat ground enclosed by a palisade.
2. at . . . points: completely. **3. sprightfully:** full of spirit.
4. appellant: challenger. **6. s.d., defendant:** i.e., the challenged.
See Pl. 8a. **18. defend:** forbid.

K. RICH. Marshal, ask yonder knight in arms
Both who he is, and why he cometh hither
Thus plated° in habiliments of war,
And formally, according to our law,
Depose° him in the justice of his cause.   30
    MAR. What is thy name? And wherefore comest
        thou hither
Before King Richard in his royal lists?
Against whom comest thou? And what's thy quar-
    rel?
Speak like a true knight, so defend thee Heaven!
    BOLING. Harry of Hereford, Lancaster, and Derby
Am I, who ready here do stand in arms   36
To prove, by God's grace and my body's valor,
In lists, on Thomas Mowbray, Duke of Norfolk,
That he is a traitor foul and dangerous
To God of Heaven, King Richard, and to me.   40
And as I truly fight, defend me Heaven!
    MAR. On pain of death, no person be so bold
Or daring-hardy as to touch the lists,
Except the Marshal and such officers
Appointed to direct these fair designs.   45
    BOLING. Lord Marshal, let me kiss my sovereign's
        hand,
And bow my knee before His Majesty.
For Mowbray and myself are like two men
That vow a long and weary pilgrimage —
Then let us take a ceremonious leave   50
And loving farewell of our several friends.
    MAR. The appellant in all duty greets your High-
        ness,
And craves to kiss your hand and take his leave.
    K. RICH. We will descend and fold him in our
        arms.
Cousin of Hereford, as thy cause is right,   55
So be thy fortune in this royal fight!
Farewell, my blood, which if today thou shed,
Lament we may, but not revenge thee dead.
    BOLING. Oh, let no noble eye profane a tear°
For me if I be gored with Mowbray's spear.   60
As confident as is the falcon's flight
Against a bird do I with Mowbray fight.
My loving lord, I take my leave of you,
Of you, my noble cousin, Lord Aumerle —
Not sick, although I have to do with death,   65
But lusty, young, and cheerly° drawing breath.
Lo, as at English feasts, so I regreet°
The daintiest last, to make the end most sweet.
O thou, the earthly author of my blood,
Whose youthful spirit, in me regenerate,   70
Doth with a twofold vigor lift me up
To reach at victory above my head,
Add proof unto mine armor with thy prayers,
And with thy blessings steel my lance's point,

That it may enter Mowbray's waxen° coat   75
And furbish° new the name of John-a-Gaunt,
Even in the lusty havior of his son.
    GAUNT. God in thy good cause make thee prosper-
        ous!
Be swift like lightning in the execution,
And let thy blows, doubly redoubled,   80
Fall like amazing° thunder on the casque°
Of thy adverse pernicious enemy.
Rouse up thy youthful blood, be valiant and live.
    BOLING. Mine innocency and Saint George° to
        thrive!
    MOW. However God or fortune cast my lot,   85
There lives or dies, true to King Richard's throne,
A loyal, just, and upright gentleman.
Never did captive with a freer heart
Cast off his chains of bondage, and embrace
His golden uncontrolled enfranchisement,°   90
More than my dancing soul doth celebrate
This feast of battle with mine adversary.
Most mighty liege, and my companion peers,
Take from my mouth the wish of happy years.
As gentle and as jocund as to jest   95
Go I to fight. Truth hath a quiet breast.
    K. RICH. Farewell, my lord. Securely I espy
Virtue with valor couchèd in thine eye.
Order the trial, Marshal, and begin.
    MAR. Harry of Hereford, Lancaster, and Derby,
Receive thy lance, and God defend the right!   101
    BOLING. Strong as a tower in hope, I cry amen.
    MAR. Go bear this lance to Thomas, Duke of Nor-
        folk.
    1. HER. Harry of Hereford, Lancaster, and Derby,
Stands here for God, his sovereign, and himself,
On pain to be found false and recreant,   106
To prove the Duke of Norfolk, Thomas Mowbray,
A traitor to his God, his King, and him,
And dares him to set forward to the fight.
    2. HER. Here standeth Thomas Mowbray, Duke of
        Norfolk,   110
On pain to be found false and recreant,
Both to defend himself and to approve°
Henry of Hereford, Lancaster, and Derby
To God, his sovereign, and to him disloyal,
Courageously and with a free desire   115
Attending° but the signal to begin.
    MAR. Sound, trumpets, and set forward, combat-
        ants.   [*A charge sounded.*]
Stay, the King hath thrown his warder° down.
    K. RICH. Let them lay by their helmets and their
        spears,
And both return back to their chairs again.   120
Withdraw with us, and let the trumpets sound

---

28. **plated:** wearing armor. 30. **Depose:** cause to declare an oath.
59. **profane a tear:** make unholy lamentation — because if he is
killed it will show that he was a false traitor and so unworthy of
grief. 66. **cheerly:** cheerfully. 67. **regreet:** welcome.

75. **waxen:** as if it were soft as wax. 76. **furbish:** make
bright. 81. **amazing:** astounding. **casque:** helmet. 84. **Saint
George:** patron saint of England. 90. **enfranchisement:** liberty.
112. **approve:** prove. 116. **Attending:** awaiting. 118. **warder:**
staff.

While we return these Dukes what we decree.
                  [*A long flourish.*°]
Draw near,
And list what with our Council we have done.
For that our kingdom's earth should not be soiled
With that dear blood which it hath fostered,   126
And for our eyes do hate the dire aspéct
Of civil wounds plowed up with neighbors' sword,
And for we think the eagle-wingèd pride
Of sky-aspiring and ambitious thoughts,   130
With rival-hating envy, set on you
To wake our peace, which in our country's cradle
Draws the sweet infant breath of gentle sleep —
Which so roused up with boisterous untuned drums,
With harsh-resounding trumpets' dreadful bray,
And grating shock of wrathful iron arms,   136
Might from our quiet confines° fright fair peace,
And make us wade even in our kindred's blood.
Therefore we banish you our territories.
You, Cousin Hereford, upon pain of life,   140
Till twice five summers have enriched our fields
Shall not regreet our fair dominions,
But tread the stranger paths of banishment.
     BOLING. Your will be done. This must my comfort be,
That sun that warms you here shall shine on me,
And those his golden beams to you here lent   146
Shall point on me and gild my banishment.
     K. RICH. Norfolk, for thee remains a heavier doom,
Which I with some unwillingness pronounce.
The sly slow hours shall not determinate°   150
The dateless limit° of thy dear° exile.
The hopeless word of " never to return "
Breathe I against thee, upon pain of life.
     MOW. A heavy sentence, my most sovereign liege,
And all unlooked for from your Highness' mouth.
A dearer merit,° not so deep a maim°   156
As to be cast forth in the common air,
Have I deservèd at your Highness' hands.
The language I have learned these forty years,
My native English, now I must forgo.   160
And now my tongue's use is to me no more
Than an unstringed viol° or a harp,
Or like a cunning instrument cased up
Or, being open, put into his hands
That knows no touch to tune the harmony.   165
Within my mouth you have enjailed my tongue,
Doubly portcullised° with my teeth and lips.
And dull unfeeling barren ignorance
Is made my jailer to attend on me.
I am too old to fawn upon a nurse,   170

Too far in years to be a pupil now.
What is thy sentence, then, but speechless death,
Which robs my tongue from breathing native breath?
     K. RICH. It boots° thee not to be compassionate.°
After our sentence plaining° comes too late.   175
     MOW. Then thus I turn me from my country's light,
To dwell in solemn shades of endless night.
     K. RICH. Return° again, and take an oath with thee.
Lay on our royal sword your banished hands,
Swear by the duty that you owe to God —   180
Our part therein we banish with yourselves° —
To keep the oath that we administer.
You never shall, so help you truth and God!
Embrace each other's love in banishment —
Nor never look upon each other's face,   185
Nor never write, regreet, nor reconcile
This louring° tempest of your homebred hate,
Nor never by advisèd° purpose meet
To plot, contrive, or complot any ill
'Gainst us, our state, our subjects, or our land.   190
     BOLING. I swear.
     MOW. And I, to keep all this.
     BOLING. Norfolk, so far as to mine enemy.
By this time, had the King permitted us,
One of our souls had wandered in the air,   195
Banished this frail sepulcher of our flesh
As now our flesh is banished from this land.
Confess thy treasons ere thou fly the realm.
Since thou hast far to go, bear not along
The clogging burden of a guilty soul.   200
     MOW. No, Bolingbroke. If ever I were traitor,
My name be blotted from the book of life,
And I from Heaven banished as from hence!
But what thou art, God, thou, and I do know,
And all too soon, I fear, the King shall rue.   205
Farewell, my liege. Now no way can I stray —
Save back to England, all the world's my way.
                     [*Exit.*]
     K. RICH. Uncle, even in the glasses° of thine eyes
I see thy grievèd heart. Thy sad aspéct°
Hath from the number of his banished years   210
Plucked four away. [*To* BOLINGBROKE] Six frozen winters spent,
Return with welcome home from banishment.
     BOLING. How long a time lies in one little word!
Four lagging winters and four wanton springs
End in a word. Such is the breath of kings.   215
     GAUNT. I thank my liege, that in regard of me
He shortens four years of my son's exile.

---

122. s.d., flourish: a set of notes on the trumpet.   137. confines: territories.   150. determinate: end.   151. dateless limit: end to which no date is assigned. dear: i.e., heavy.   156. dearer merit: more valuable reward. maim: injury.   162. viol: six-stringed instrument of the cello type. See Pl. 18c.   167. portcullised: shut in. The portcullis was a heavy grating, sliding up and down in grooves, at the entrance to a castle.

174. boots: is of advantage. compassionate: piteous.   175. plaining: complaining.   178–90. Return . . . land: This speech is addressed to both combatants.   181. Our . . . yourselves: i.e., we absolve you from allegiance to us.   187. louring: threatening.   188. advised: deliberate.   208. glasses: lenses.   209. aspect: countenance.

GAUNT IS LIKE RICH. — GAUNT VOTES FOR OWN SON'S
(NEITHER GRASP THE SITUATION) EXILE — THEN TRIES TO MAKE EXILE
APPEAR AS A TRIP

But little vantage shall I reap thereby,
For ere the six years that he hath to spend
Can change their moons and bring their times
     about,   220
My oil-dried lamp and time-bewasted light
Shall be extinct with age and endless night.
My inch of taper° will be burnt and done,
And blindfold° death not let me see my son.
    K. RICH. Why, Uncle, thou hast many years to
     live.   225
    GAUNT. But not a minute, King, that thou canst
     give.
Shorten my days thou canst with sullen sorrow,
And pluck nights from me, but not lend a mor-
     row.
Thou canst help time to furrow me with age,
But stop no wrinkle in his pilgrimage.   230
Thy word is current° with him for my death,
But dead, thy kingdom cannot buy my breath.
    K. RICH. Thy son is banished upon good advice,
Whereto thy tongue a party verdict gave.°
Why at our justice seem'st thou then to lour?   235
    GAUNT. Things sweet to taste prove in digestion
     sour.
You urged me as a judge, but I had rather
You would have bid me argue like a father.
Oh, had it been a stranger, not my child,
To smooth his fault I should have been more mild.
A partial slander° ought I to avoid,   241
And in the sentence my own life destroyed.
Alas, I looked when some of you should say
I was too strict to make mine own away,
But you gave leave to my unwilling tongue   245
Against my will to do myself this wrong.
    K. RICH. Cousin, farewell, and, Uncle, bid him so.
Six years we banish him, and he shall go.
     [*Flourish. Exeunt* KING RICHARD *and* TRAIN.]
    AUM. Cousin, farewell. What presence must not
     know,°
From where you do remain let paper show.   250
    MAR. My lord, no leave take I, for I will ride,
As far as land will let me, by your side.
    GAUNT. Oh, to what purpose dost thou hoard thy
     words,
That thou return'st no greeting to thy friends?
    BOLING. I have too few to take my leave of you
When the tongue's office should be prodigal   256
To breathe the abundant dolor° of the heart.
    GAUNT. Thy grief is but thy absence for a time.
    BOLING. Joy absent, grief is present for that time.
    GAUNT. What is six winters? They are quickly
     gone.   260

    BOLING. To men in joy, but grief makes one hour
     ten.
    GAUNT. Call it a travel that thou takest for pleas-
     ure.
    BOLING. My heart will sigh when I miscall it so,
Which finds it an enforcèd pilgrimage.
    GAUNT. The sullen passage of thy weary steps
Esteem as foil° wherein thou art to set   266
The precious jewel of thy home return.
    BOLING. Nay, rather, every tedious stride I make
Will but remember me what a deal of world
I wander from the jewels that I love.   270
Must I not serve a long apprenticehood
To foreign passages,° and in the end,
Having my freedom, boast of nothing else
But that I was a journeyman° to grief?
    GAUNT. All places that the eye of Heaven° visits
Are to a wise man ports and happy havens.   276
Teach thy necessity to reason thus —
There is no virtue like necessity.
Think not the King did banish thee,
But thou the King. Woe doth the heavier sit   280
Where it perceives it is but faintly° borne.
Go, say I sent thee forth to purchase honor
And not the King exiled thee. Or suppose
Devouring pestilence hangs in our air
And thou art flying to a fresher clime.   285
Look, what thy soul holds dear, imagine it
To lie that way thou go'st, not whence thou comest
Suppose the singing birds musicians,
The grass whereon thou tread'st the presence°
     strewed,°
The flowers fair ladies, and thy steps no more   290
Than a delightful measure° or a dance.
For gnarling° sorrow hath less power to bite
The man that mocks at it and sets it light.
    BOLING. Oh, who can hold a fire in his hand
By thinking on the frosty Caucasus?   295
Or cloy the hungry edge of appetite
By bare imagination of a feast?
Or wallow naked in December snow
By thinking on fantastic summer's heat?
Oh no! The apprehension of the good   300
Gives but the greater feeling to the worse.
Fell sorrow's tooth doth never rankle° more
Than when he bites, but lanceth not the sore.
    GAUNT. Come, come, my son, I'll bring thee on thy
     way.
Had I thy youth and cause, I would not stay.   305
    BOLING. Then, England's ground, farewell. Sweet
     soil, adieu —

223. **taper**: candle.   224. **blindfold**: making blind.   231. **current**: valid; i.e., you can tell Death to take me, but you cannot buy me back from him.   234. **party . . . gave**: shared in giving the verdict.   241. **partial slander**: the slander of being partial to my own son.   249. **What . . . know**: i.e., what you cannot be present to say.   257. **dolor**: grief.

266. **foil**: See *Rich III*, V.iii.250,n.   272. **foreign passages**: wandering in foreign lands.   274. **journeyman**: hired worker.   275. **eye of Heaven**: the sun.   281. **faintly**: faintheartedly.   289. **presence**: the Presence Chamber where the courtiers assembled. **strewed**: covered with rushes.   291. **measure**: formal dance. See App. 24.   292. **gnarling**: growling.   302. **rankle**: make fester.

My mother, and my nurse, that bears me yet!
Where'er I wander, boast of this I can,
Though banished, yet a trueborn Englishman.

[*Exeunt.*]

SCENE IV. *The Court.*

[*Enter the* KING, *with* BAGOT *and* GREEN *at one door,
and the* DUKE OF AUMERLE *at another.*]

K. RICH. We did observe. Cousin Aumerle,
How far brought you high Hereford on his way?

AUM. I brought high Hereford, if you call him so,
But to the next highway, and there I left him.

K. RICH. And say, what store of parting tears were
shed? 5

AUM. Faith, none for me, except the northeast
wind,
Which then blew bitterly against our faces,
Awaked the sleeping rheum° and so by chance
Did grace our hollow parting with a tear.

K. RICH. What said our cousin when you parted
with him? 10

AUM. "Farewell."
And, for my heart disdainèd that my tongue
Should so profane the word, that taught me craft
To counterfeit oppression of such grief 14
That words seemed buried in my sorrow's grave.°
Marry, would the word "farewell" have lengthened
hours
And added years to his short banishment,
He should have had a volume of farewells.
But since it would not, he had none of me. 19

K. RICH. He is our cousin, Cousin; but 'tis doubt,
When time shall call him home from banishment,
Whether our kinsman come to see his friends.
Ourself and Bushy, Bagot here, and Green
Observed his courtship° to the common people —
How he did seem to dive into their hearts 25
With humble and familiar courtesy,°
What reverence he did throw away on slaves,
Wooing poor craftsmen with the craft of smiles
And patient underbearing° of his fortune,
As 'twere to banish their affects° with him. 30
Off goes his bonnet to an oyster wench.
A brace of draymen bid God speed him well
And had the tribute of his supple knee,
With "Thanks, my countrymen, my loving friends,"
As were our England in reversion° his, 35
And he our subjects' next degree in hope.

GREEN. Well, he is gone, and with him go these
thoughts.
Now for the rebels which stand out in Ireland,
Expedient manage° must be made, my liege,
Ere further leisure yield them further means 40
For their advantage and your Highness' loss.

K. RICH. We will ourself in person to this war.
And, for our coffers, with too great a Court°
And liberal largess,° are grown somewhat light,
We are enforced to farm° our royal realm, 45
The revenue whereof shall furnish us
For our affairs in hand. If that come short,
Our substitutes at home shall have blank charters,°
Whereto, when they shall know what men are rich,
They shall subscribe° them for large sums of gold
And send them after to supply our wants. 51
For we will make for Ireland presently.

[*Enter* BUSHY.] Bushy, what news?

BUSHY. Old John of Gaunt is grievous sick, my
lord,
Suddenly taken, and hath sent posthaste 55
To entreat your Majesty to visit him.

K. RICH. Where lies he?

BUSHY. At Ely House.°

K. RICH. Now put it, God, in the physician's mind
To help him to his grave immediately! 60
The lining of his coffers shall make coats
To deck our soldiers for these Irish wars.
Come, gentlemen, let's all go visit him.
Pray God we may make haste, and come too late!

ALL. Amen. [*Exeunt.*] 65

Act II

SCENE I. *Ely House.*

[*Enter* JOHN OF GAUNT *sick, with the* DUKE OF YORK,
etc.]

GAUNT. Will the King come, that I may breathe
my last
In wholesome counsel to his unstaid youth?

YORK. Vex not yourself, nor strive not with your
breath,
For all in vain comes counsel to his ear.

GAUNT. Oh, but they say the tongues of dying men
Enforce attention like deep harmony. 6

Sc. iv: **8. rheum:** moisture. **11–15.** "Farewell" . . . grave:
i.e., I did not wish him to "fare well," so I pretended that my
grief was too strong for words. **24–36. courtship . . . hope:**
There is some disturbance in the text here, which probably indicates that the passage is a later addition. See *Rich II* Intro.
p. 433b. **26. courtesy:** courtly behavior, bending the knee.
29. underbearing: supporting. **30. banish . . . affects:** carry
their affection with him into banishment. **35. in reversion:** by
right of legal succession.

39. Expedient manage: speedy arrangements. **43. too . . .
Court:** by maintaining too many courtiers. **44. largess:** presents
of money. **45. farm:** to let out. To raise ready money the King
took a payment in cash in return for the right to collect taxes.
48. blank charters: documents which rich men were compelled
to sign agreeing to pay the King certain sums of money, the
amount being left blank to be filled in by the King's officers.
50. subscribe: sign. **58. Ely House:** the Bishop of Ely's palace
in London.

[Handwritten annotations at top margin: "VIOLENT FIRES" / "IT IS UNREALISTIC THAT A DYING MAN WOULD SAY ALL THIS — THIS TALKING IS LIKE RICHARD (TAKES NO ACTION BUT TALKS)"]

Where words are scarce, they are seldom spent in
     vain,
For they breathe truth that breathe their words in
     pain.
He that no more must say is listened more
     Than they whom youth and ease have taught to
     glose.°   10
More are men's ends marked than their lives before.
     The setting sun, and music at the close,
As the last taste of sweets, is sweetest last,
Writ in remembrance more than things long past.
Though Richard my life's counsel would not hear,
My death's sad tale may yet undeaf his ear.   16
     YORK. No, it is stopped with other flattering
     sounds,
As praises, of whose taste the wise are fond,
Lascivious meters, to whose venom sound
The open ear of youth doth always listen —   20
Report of fashions in proud Italy,°
Whose manners still our tardy apish° nation
Limps after in base imitation.
Where doth the world thrust forth a vanity —
So it be° new, there's no respect° how vile —   25
That is not quickly buzzed into his ears?
Then all too late comes counsel to be heard
Where will° doth mutiny with wit's° regard.
Direct not him whose way himself will choose.
'Tis breath thou lack'st, and that breath wilt thou
     lose.   30

[Handwritten: "GAUNT MAKES SPEECH, BUT NOT WHILE"]

     GAUNT. Methinks I am a prophet new-inspired
And thus expiring do foretell of him.

[Handwritten: "RICH. IS THERE (SO FUTILE)"]

His rash fierce blaze of riot cannot last,
For violent fires soon burn out themselves —
Small showers last long, but sudden storms are short.
He tires betimes° that spurs too fast betimes,   36
With eager feeding food doth choke the feeder.
Light vanity, insatiate cormorant,°
Consuming means, soon preys upon itself.
This° royal throne of kings, this sceptered isle,   40
This earth of majesty, this seat of Mars,
This other Eden, demi-Paradise,
This fortress built by Nature for herself
Against infection° and the hand of war,
This happy breed of men, this little world,   45
This precious stone set in the silver sea,
Which serves it in the office of a wall
Or as a moat defensive to a house
Against the envy° of less happier lands —

[Handwritten: "FAMOUS SPEECH OF PATRIOTISM"]

This blessed plot, this earth, this realm, this Eng-
     land,   50
This nurse, this teeming womb of royal kings,
Feared by their breed and famous by their birth,
Renownèd for their deeds as far from home,
For Christian service and true chivalry,
As is the sepulcher in stubborn Jewry°   55
Of the world's ransom, blessèd Mary's Son —
This land of such dear souls, this dear dear land,
Dear for her reputation through the world,
Is now leased out,° I die pronouncing it,
Like to a tenement or pelting° farm.   60
England, bound in with the triumphant sea,
Whose rocky shore beats back the envious siege
Of watery Neptune, is now bound in with shame,
With inky blots and rotten parchment bonds.
That England, that was wont to conquer others,   65
Hath made a shameful conquest of itself.
Ah, would the scandal vanish with my life,
How happy then were my ensuing death!
     [*Enter* KING RICHARD *and* QUEEN, AUMERLE, BUSHY,
          GREEN, BAGOT, ROSS, *and* WILLOUGHBY.]
     YORK. The King is come. Deal mildly with his
     youth,
For young hot colts being raged° do rage the more.
     QUEEN. How fares our noble uncle Lancaster?   71
     K. RICH. What comfort, man? How is't with agèd
     Gaunt?
     GAUNT. Oh, how that name befits my composi-
     tion!°

[Handwritten: "GAUNT + RICH. PLAY WITH THEIR NAMES"]

Old Gaunt indeed, and gaunt in being old.
Within me grief hath kept a tedious fast,   75
And who abstains from meat that is not gaunt?
For sleeping England long time have I watched,
Watching breeds leanness, leanness is all gaunt.
The pleasure that some fathers feed upon
Is my strict fast — I mean my children's looks —   80
And therein fasting, hast thou made me gaunt.
Gaunt am I for the grave, gaunt as a grave,
Whose hollow womb inherits° naught but bones.
     K. RICH. Can sick men play so nicely with their
     names?
     GAUNT. No, misery makes sport to mock itself.
Since thou dost seek to kill my name in me,   86
I mock my name, great King, to flatter° thee.
     K. RICH. Should dying men flatter with those that
     live?
     GAUNT. No, no, men living flatter those that die.
     K. RICH. Thou, now a-dying, say'st thou flatterest
     me.   90
     GAUNT. Oh, no! Thou diest, though I the sicker be.
     K. RICH. I am in health, I breathe, and see thee ill.
     GAUNT. Now He that made me knows I see thee
     ill.

Act II, Sc. i: **10.** glose: flatter. **21.** proud Italy: It was a common complaint among moralists that young Englishmen who
went to Italy brought back nothing but vicious habits. Hence the
proverb "An Englishman italianate is a devil incarnate."
22. apish: imitating like an ape. **25.** So it be: so long as it is.
there's no respect: no matter. **28.** will: natural inclination. wit:
wisdom. **36.** betimes: soon, early. **38.** cormorant: a greedy sea
bird; i.e., a glutton. **40–56.** This . . . Son: a passage much admired by contemporaries and quoted in *England's Parnassus*
(1600), an anthology of English poetry. **44.** infection: the
plague. **49.** envy: malice.

55. the . . . Jewry: i.e., the Holy Sepulcher in Jerusalem.
59. leased out: i.e., because the King's revenues had been farmed
out. **60.** pelting: paltry. **70.** raged: enraged. **73.** composition:
frame, body. **83.** inherits: possesses. **87.** flatter: try to please.

Ill in myself to see, and in thee seeing ill.
Thy deathbed is no lesser than thy land, 95
Wherein thou liest in reputation sick.
And thou, too careless-patient as thou art,
Commit'st thy anointed body to the cure
Of those physicians that first wounded thee.
A thousand flatterers sit within thy crown, 100
Whose compass is no bigger than thy head,
And yet encagèd in so small a verge,°
The waste is no whit lesser than thy land.
Oh, had thy grandsire with a prophet's eye
Seen how his son's son should destroy his sons, 105
From forth thy reach he would have laid thy shame,
Deposing thee before thou wert possessed,
Which art possessed° now to depose thyself.
Why, Cousin, wert thou regent of the world,
It were a shame to let this land by lease; 110
But, for thy world enjoying but this land,
Is it not more than shame to shame it so?
Landlord° of England art thou now, not King.
Thy state of law is bondslave to the law,°
And thou ——
    K. RICH. A lunatic lean-witted fool, 115
Presuming on an ague's privilege,°
Darest with thy frozen admonition
Make pale our cheek, chasing the royal blood
With fury from his native residence.
Now, by my seat's right royal majesty, 120
Wert thou not brother to great Edward's son,
This tongue that runs so roundly° in thy head
Should run thy head from thy unreverent shoulders.
    GAUNT. Oh, spare me not, my brother Edward's son,
For that I was his father Edward's son. 125
That blood already, like the pelican,°
Hast thou tapped out and drunkenly caroused.
My brother Gloucester, plain well-meaning soul —
Whom fair befall° in Heaven 'mongst happy souls! —
May be a precedent and witness good 130
That thou respect'st not spilling Edward's blood.
Join with the present sickness that I have,
And thy unkindness be like crooked age,
To crop at once a too-long-withered flower.
Live in thy shame, but die not shame with thee!
These words hereafter thy tormentors be! 136
Convey me to my bed, then to my grave.
Love they to live that love and honor have.
    [*Exit, borne off by his* ATTENDANTS.]

    K. RICH. And let them die that age and sullens°
have,
For both hast thou, and both become the grave. 140
    YORK. I do beseech your Majesty, impute his words
To wayward sickliness and age in him.
He loves you, on my life, and holds you dear
As Harry Duke of Hereford, were he here.
    K. RICH. Right, you say true. As Hereford's love, so his. 145
As theirs, so mine, and all be as it is.
    [*Enter* NORTHUMBERLAND.]
    NORTH. My liege, old Gaunt commends him to your Majesty.
    K. RICH. What says he?
    NORTH.   Nay, nothing, all is said.
His tongue is now a stringless instrument.
Words, life, and all, old Lancaster hath spent. 150
    YORK. Be York the next that must be bankrupt so!
Though death be poor, it ends a mortal woe.
    K. RICH. The ripest fruit first falls, and so doth he.
His time is spent, our pilgrimage must be.
So much for that. Now for our Irish wars. 155
We must supplant those rough rugheaded° kerns°
Which live like venom where no venom else
But only they have privilege to live.
And for these great affairs do ask some charge,°
Toward our assistance we do seize to us 160
The plate, coin, revenues, and movables
Whereof our uncle Gaunt did stand possessed.
    YORK. How long shall I be patient? Ah, how long
Shall tender duty make me suffer wrong? 164
Not Gloucester's death, nor Hereford's banishment,
Not Gaunt's rebukes,° nor England's private wrongs,
Nor the prevention of poor Bolingbroke
About his marriage,° nor my own disgrace,
Have ever made me sour my patient cheek,
Or bend one wrinkle on my sovereign's face. 170
I am the last of noble Edward's sons,
Of whom thy father, Prince of Wales, was first.
In war was never lion raged more fierce,
In peace was never gentle lamb more mild,
Than was that young and princely gentleman. 175
His face thou hast, for even so looked he,
Accomplished with the number of thy hours.°
But when he frowned, it was against the French
And not against his friends. His noble hand
Did win what he did spend, and spent not that 180
Which his triumphant father's hand had won.
His hands were guilty of no kindred blood,°
But bloody with the enemies of his kin.

---

102. **verge:** compass. 107–08. **possessed . . . possessed:** in possession of . . . possessed by an evil spirit. 113. **Landlord:** i.e., because he has rented his kingdom. 114. **state . . . law:** you are now subject to the laws as a landlord, and no longer above the law as King. 116. **ague's privilege:** i.e., an invalid privileged to be peevish. **ague:** fever. 122. **roundly:** directly; i.e., impudently. 126. **pelican:** The pelican was believed to feed its young with blood from its breast, but when the young grew up they attacked the mother bird. 129. **fair befall:** may good come to.

139. **sullens:** sulks. 156. **rugheaded:** shaggy-headed. **kerns:** Irish foot soldiers. 159. **charge:** expense. 166. **Gaunt's rebukes:** the rebukes received by Gaunt. 167–68. **prevention . . . marriage:** There is nothing further in the play about this incident, which is mentioned by Holinshed. 177. **Accomplished . . . hours:** when he was your age. **Accomplished:** lit., "equipped." 182. **kindred blood:** blood of his kindred.

O Richard! York is too far gone with grief,
Or else he never would compare between.°   185
  K. RICH. Why, Uncle, what's the matter?
YORK.   O my liege,
Pardon me, if you please; if not, I, pleased
Not to be pardoned, am content withal.
Seek you to seize and gripe into your hands   189
The royalties° and rights of banished Hereford?
Is not Gaunt dead, and doth not Hereford live?
Was not Gaunt just, and is not Harry true?
Did not the one deserve to have an heir?
Is not his heir a well-deserving son?
Take Hereford's rights away, and take from Time
His charters and his customary rights,°   196
Let not tomorrow then ensue° today.
Be not thyself, for how art thou a king
But by fair sequence and succession?
Now, afore God — God forbid I say true! —   200
If you do wrongfully seize Hereford's rights,
Call in the letters° patents that he hath
By his attorneys general to sue
His livery, and deny his offered homage,
You pluck a thousand dangers on your head,   205
You lose a thousand well-disposèd hearts,
And prick my tender patience to those thoughts
Which honor and allegiance cannot think.
  K. RICH. Think what you will, we seize into our
    hands
His plate, his goods, his money, and his lands.   210
  YORK. I'll not be by the while. My liege, farewell.
What will ensue hereof, there's none can tell,
But by bad courses may be understood
That their events° can never fall out good. [*Exit.*]
  K. RICH. Go, Bushy, to the Earl of Wiltshire
    straight.   215
Bid him repair to us to Ely House
To see this business. Tomorrow next°
We will for Ireland — and 'tis time, I trow.°
And we create, in absence of ourself,
Our uncle York Lord Governor of England,   220
For he is just and always loved us well.
Come on, our Queen. Tomorrow must we part.
Be merry, for our time of stay is short.
    [*Flourish. Exeunt* KING, QUEEN, AUMERLE,
              BUSHY, GREEN, *and* BAGOT.]
  NORTH. Well, lords, the Duke of Lancaster is dead.
  ROSS. And living too, for now his son is Duke.

185. compare between: make such comparisons.   190. royalties:
rights belonging to a member of the royal family.   195–96. Take
. . . rights: i.e., if you take Hereford's inheritance you are de-
priving Time of his rights (viz., the natural law that the son inherits the father's wealth). charters: privileges.   197. ensue:
follow.   202–04. letters . . . homage: The lines are taken from
Holinshed. letters patent: a grant by the King of some right
or privilege. attorneys general: deputies. sue . . . livery: establish
his legal right to Gaunt's property. homage: formal acknowledge-
ment of allegiance to the King necessary before Bolingbroke could
assume possession.   214. events: sequels, results.   217. Tomorrow next: tomorrow.   218. trow: am sure.

  WILLO. Barely in title, not in revenues.   226
  NORTH. Richly in both, if justice had her right.
  ROSS. My heart is great,° but it must break with
    silence
Ere't be disburdened° with a liberal° tongue.
  NORTH. Nay, speak thy mind. And let him ne'er
    speak more   230
That speaks thy words again to do thee harm!
  WILLO. Tends° that thou wouldst speak to° the
    Duke of Hereford?
If it be so, out with it boldly, man.
Quick is mine ear to hear of good toward him.
  ROSS. No good at all that I can do for him,   235
Unless you call it good to pity him,
Bereft and gelded of his patrimony.
  NORTH. Now, afore God, 'tis shame such wrongs
    are borne
In him a royal prince and many moe°
Of noble blood in this declining land.   240
The King is not himself, but basely led
By flatterers. And what they will inform,
Merely in hate, 'gainst any of us all,
That will the King severely prosecute
'Gainst us, our lives, our children, and our heirs.
  ROSS. The commons hath he pilled° with grievous
    taxes,   246
And quite lost their hearts. The nobles hath he fined
For ancient quarrels, and quite lost their hearts.
  WILLO. And daily new exactions are devised,
As blanks,° benevolences,° and I wot° not what.
But what, o' God's name, doth become of this?   251
  NORTH. Wars have not wasted it, for warred he
    hath not,
But basely yielded upon compromise
That which his noble ancestors achieved with blows.
More hath he spent in peace than they in wars.   255
  ROSS. The Earl of Wiltshire hath the realm in
    farm.
  WILLO. The King's grown bankrupt, like a broken
    man.
  NORTH. Reproach and dissolution hangeth over
    him.
  ROSS. He hath not money for these Irish wars,
His burdenous taxations notwithstanding,   260
But by the robbing of the banished Duke.
  NORTH. His noble kinsman. Most degenerate
    King!
But, lords, we hear this fearful tempest sing,
Yet seek no shelter to avoid the storm.
We see the wind sit sore upon our sails,   265
And yet we strike not, but securely° perish.
  ROSS. We see the very wreck that we must suffer,

228. great: pregnant, heavy.   229. disburdened: relieved of its
burden. liberal: free.   232. Tends: is it your meaning? to:
concerning.   239. moe: more.   246. pilled: peeled, stripped.
250. blanks: See I.iv.48. benevolences: loans which the rich
were forced to give as "free" offerings. wot: know.   266. securely: overconfidently.

And unavoided° is the danger now
For suffering so the causes of our wreck.
    NORTH. Not so. Even through the hollow eyes of
      death   270
I spy life peering, but I dare not say
How near the tidings of our comfort is.
    WILLO. Nay, let us share thy thoughts, as thou dost
      ours.
    ROSS. Be confident to speak, Northumberland.
We three are but thyself, and, speaking so,   275
Thy words are but as thoughts. Therefore be bold.
    NORTH. Then thus. I have from Le Port Blanc, a
      bay
In Brittany, received intelligence°
That Harry Duke of Hereford, Rainold Lord Cob-
    ham,°   279
That late broke from the Duke of Exeter,
His brother, Archbishop late of Canterbury,
Sir Thomas Erpingham, Sir John Ramston,
Sir John Norbery, Sir Robert Waterton, and Francis
    Quoint —   284
All these well furnished by the Duke of Bretagne
With eight tall° ships, three thousand men of war —
Are making hither with all due expedience°
And shortly mean to touch our northern shore.
Perhaps they had ere this but that they stay
The first departing of the King for Ireland.   290
If then we shall shake off our slavish yoke,
Imp° out our drooping country's broken wing,
Redeem from broking pawn° the blemished crown,
Wipe off the dust that hides our scepter's gilt,
And make high majesty look like itself,   295
Away with me in post to Ravenspurgh.°
But if you faint, as fearing to do so,
Stay and be secret, and myself will go.
    ROSS. To horse, to horse! Urge doubts to them that
      fear.
    WILLO. Hold out my horse, and I will first be
      there.   [*Exeunt.*]   300

SCENE II. *Windsor Castle.*

[*Enter* QUEEN, BUSHY, *and* BAGOT.]
BUSHY. Madam, your Majesty is too much sad.
You promised, when you parted with the King,
To lay aside life-harming heaviness
And entertain a cheerful disposition.
    QUEEN. To please the King I did, to please myself

I cannot do it. Yet I know no cause   6
Why I should welcome such a guest as grief,
Save bidding farewell to so sweet a guest
As my sweet Richard. Yet again, methinks
Some unborn sorrow, ripe in fortune's womb,   10
Is coming toward me, and my inward soul
With nothing° trembles. At something it grieves
More than with parting from my lord the King.
    BUSHY. Each substance of a grief hath twenty
      shadows,
Which shows like grief itself, but is not so;   15
For sorrow's eye, glazèd with blinding tears,
Divides one thing entire to many objects° —
Like perspectives° which rightly gazed upon,
Show nothing but confusion, eyed awry
Distinguish form. So your sweet Majesty,   20
Looking awry upon your lord's departure,
Find shapes of grief, more than himself, to wail.
Which, looked on as it is, is naught but shadows
Of what it is not. Then, thrice-gracious Queen,
More than your lord's departure weep not. More's
    not seen,   25
Or if it be, 'tis with false sorrow's eye,
Which for things true weeps things imaginary.
    QUEEN. It may be so, but yet my inward soul
Persuades me it is otherwise. Howe'er it be,
I cannot but be sad, so heavy sad   30
As, though on thinking on no thought I think,
Makes me with heavy nothing faint and shrink.
    BUSHY. 'Tis nothing but conceit,° my gracious
      lady.
    QUEEN. 'Tis nothing less. Conceit is still° derived
From some forefather grief. Mine is not so,   35
For nothing hath begot my something grief,
Or something hath the nothing that I grieve.
'Tis in reversion° that I do possess,
But what it is, that is not yet known — what
I cannot name. 'Tis nameless woe, I wot.   40
         [*Enter* GREEN.]
    GREEN. God save your Majesty! And well met,
      gentlemen.
I hope the King is not yet shipped for Ireland.
    QUEEN. Why hopest thou so? 'Tis better hope he
      is,
For his designs crave haste, his haste good hope.
Then wherefore dost thou hope he is not shipped?
    GREEN. That he, our hope, might have retired° his
      power   46
And driven into despair an enemy's hope,
Who strongly hath set footing in this land.
The banished Bolingbroke repeals° himself,

---

268. **unavoided:** unavoidable. 277–78. **I . . . intelligence:** Note the compression of "real" time here. See App. 22. 279. **Cobham:** A line is apparently missing after *Cobham,* as is shown by the passage from Holinshed. He was a son of Richard Earl of Arundel, who broke from the Duke of Exeter. 286. **tall:** fine. 287. **expedience:** expedition, haste. 292. **Imp:** a metaphor from falconry; to *imp* is to graft new feathers into a broken wing. See App. 26. 293. **broking pawn:** the pawnbroker. 296. **Ravenspurgh:** in Yorkshire.

Sc. ii: 12. **With nothing:** at nothing. 16–17. **sorrow's . . . objects:** when the eye is blinded with tears single objects look double. 18. **perspectives:** ingenious pictures which when viewed from the front are meaningless, but when seen foreshortened from the side are clear. 33. **conceit:** imagination. 34. **still:** continually. 38. **reversion:** destined to be mine later. See I.iv.35. 46. **retired:** withdrawn. 49. **repeals:** recalls.

And with uplifted arms is safe arrived   50
At Ravenspurgh.
    QUEEN.   Now God in Heaven forbid!
    GREEN. Ah, madam, 'tis too true. And that is
      worse,
The Lord Northumberland, his son young Henry
    Percy,
The Lords of Ross, Beaumond, and Willoughby,
With all their powerful friends, are fled to him.   55
    BUSHY. Why have you not proclaimed Northum-
    berland
And all the rest revolted faction traitors?°
    GREEN. We have. Whereupon the Earl of Wor-
    cester
Hath broke his staff,° resigned his stewardship,
And all the household servants fled with him   60
To Bolingbroke.
    QUEEN. So, Green, thou art the midwife to my
    woe,
And Bolingbroke my sorrow's dismal heir.
Now hath my soul brought forth her prodigy,°
And I, a gasping new-delivered mother,   65
Have woe to woe, sorrow to sorrow, joined.
    BUSHY. Despair not, madam.
    QUEEN.   Who shall hinder me?
I will despair, and be at enmity
With cozening° hope. He is a flatterer,
A parasite, a keeper-back of death,   70
Who gently would dissolve the bands of life,
Which false hope lingers° in extremity.
          [Enter YORK.]
    GREEN. Here comes the Duke of York.
    QUEEN. With signs of war° about his aged neck.
Oh, full of careful° business are his looks!   75
Uncle, for God's sake, speak comfortable words.
    YORK. Should I do so, I should belie my thoughts.
Comfort's in Heaven, and we are on the earth,
Where nothing lives but crosses, cares, and grief.
Your husband, he is gone to save far off   80
Whilst others come to make him lose at home.
Here am I left to underprop his land,
Who, weak with age, cannot support myself.
Now comes the sick hour that his surfeit° made,
Now shall he try° his friends that flattered him. 85
          [Enter a SERVANT.]
    SERV. My lord, your son was gone before I came.
    YORK. He was? Why, so! Go all which way it will!
The nobles they are fled, the commons they are cold,
And will, I fear, revolt on Hereford's side.
Sirrah, get thee to Plashy, to my sister Gloucester.
Bid her send me presently° a thousand pound.   91

Hold, take my ring.
    SERV. My lord, I had forgot to tell your lordship,
Today, as I came by, I called there —
But I shall grieve you to report the rest.   95
    YORK. What is't, knave?
    SERV. An hour before I came, the Duchess died.
    YORK. God for His mercy! What a tide of woes
Comes rushing on this woeful land at once!
I know not what to do. I would to God,   100
So my untruth° had not provoked him to it,
The King had cut off my head with my brother's.
What, are there no posts dispatched for Ireland?
How shall we do for money for these wars?
Come, Sister — Cousin, I would say — pray pardon
    me.   105
Go, fellow, get thee home, provide some carts
And bring away the armor that is there.
          [Exit SERVANT.]
Gentlemen, will you go muster men?
If I know how or which way to order these affairs
Thus thrust disorderly into my hands,   110
Never believe me. Both are my kinsmen.
The one is my sovereign, whom both my oath
And duty bids defend. The other again
Is my kinsman, whom the King hath wronged,
Whom conscience and my kindred bids to right.
Well, somewhat we must do. Come, Cousin, I'll
Dispose of you.   117
Gentlemen, go, muster up your men,
And meet me presently at Berkeley.
I should to Plashy too,   120
But time will not permit. All is uneven,
And everything is left at six and seven.°
          [Exeunt YORK *and* QUEEN.]
    BUSHY. The wind sits fair for news to go to Ire-
    land,
But none returns.° For us to levy power
Proportionable to the enemy   125
Is all unpossible.
    GREEN. Besides, our nearness to the King in love
Is near the hate of those love not the King.
    BAGOT. And that's the wavering commons. For
    their love
Lies in their purses, and whoso empties them   130
By so much fills their hearts with deadly hate.
    BUSHY. Wherein the King stands generally con-
    demned.
    BAGOT. If judgment lie in them, then so do we,°
Because we ever have been near the King.
    GREEN. Well, I will for refuge straight to Bristol
    Castle.   135
The Earl of Wiltshire is already there.

---

57. **revolted . . . traitors:** traitors belonging to a conspiracy of
rebels. 59. **broke . . . staff:** Court officials carried a white staff
as sign of office. At resignation or the death of the sovereign
the staff was broken. See Pl. 8d. 64. **prodigy:** monster.
69. **cozening:** cheating. 72. **lingers:** makes to linger. 74. **signs
of war:** armor. 75. **careful:** anxious. 84. **surfeit:** excess.
85. **try:** test. 91. **presently:** immediately.

101. **So my untruth:** so long as it was not disloyalty that.
122. **six . . . seven:** sixes and sevens, in confusion. 124. **none
returns:** At times the wind blew so continuously from the east
that sailing ships could not make the passage from Ireland to
England for several weeks. 133. **If . . . we:** i.e., if the commons
condemn the King, they condemn us too.

BUSHY. Thither will I with you, for little office
The hateful commons will perform for us
Except like curs to tear us all to pieces.
Will you go along with us?　　　　　　　　　140
　　BAGOT. No, I will to Ireland to His Majesty.
Farewell. If heart's presages° be not vain,
We three here part that ne'er shall meet again.
　　BUSHY. That's as York thrives to beat back Boling-
　　broke.
　　GREEN. Alas, poor Duke! The task he undertakes
Is numbering sands and drinking oceans dry.　146
Where one on his side fights, thousand will fly.
Farewell at once, for once, for all, and ever.
　　BUSHY. Well, we may meet again.
　　BAGOT.　　　　　　　I fear me never.　[*Exeunt.*]

SCENE III. *Wilds in Gloucestershire.*

[*Enter* BOLINGBROKE *and* NORTHUMBERLAND,
with Forces.]

　　BOLING. How far is it, my lord, to Berkeley now?
　　NORTH. Believe me, noble lord,
I am a stranger here in Gloucestershire.
These high wild hills and rough uneven ways
Draws out our miles, and makes them wearisome,
And yet your fair discourse hath been as sugar,　6
Making the hard way sweet and delectable.
But I bethink me what a weary way
From Ravenspurgh to Cotswold will be found
In Ross and Willoughby, wanting your company,°
Which, I protest, hath very much beguiled　11
The tediousness and process of my travel.
But theirs is sweetened with the hope to have
The present benefit which I possess,
And hope to joy is little less in joy　　　15
Than hope enjoyed. By this the weary lords
Shall make their way seem short, as mine hath done
By sight of what I have, your noble company.
　　BOLING. Of much less value is my company
Than your good words. But who comes here?　20
[*Enter* HENRY PERCY.]
　　NORTH. It is my son, young Harry Percy,°
Sent from my brother Worcester, whencesoever.°
Harry, how fares your uncle?
　　H. PERCY. I had thought, my lord, to have learned
　　his health of you.
　　NORTH. Why, is he not with the Queen?　25
　　H. PERCY. No, my good lord. He hath forsook the
　　Court,
Broken his staff of office, and dispersed
The household of the King.
　　NORTH.　　　　　　　What was his reason?

He was not so resolved when last we spake together.
　　H. PERCY. Because your lordship was proclaimèd
　　traitor.　　　　　　　　　　　　30
But he, my lord, is gone to Ravenspurgh,
To offer service to the Duke of Hereford,
And sent me over by Berkeley, to discover
What power the Duke of York had levied there,
Then with directions to repair to Ravenspurgh.　35
　　NORTH. Have you forgot the Duke of Hereford,
　　boy?
　　H. PERCY. No, my good lord, for that is not forgot
Which ne'er I did remember. To my knowledge,
I never in my life did look on him.
　　NORTH. Then learn to know him now. This is the
　　Duke.　　　　　　　　　　　　40
　　H. PERCY. My gracious lord, I tender you my serv-
　　ice,
Such as it is, being tender, raw, and young —
Which elder days shall ripen and confirm
To more approvèd° service and desert.
　　BOLING. I thank thee, gentle Percy, and be sure
I count myself in nothing else so happy　　46
As in a soul remembering my good friends.
And as my fortune ripens with thy love,
It shall be still thy true love's recompense.°
My heart this covenant makes, my hand thus seals
it.　　　　　　　　　　　　　　50
　　NORTH. How far is it to Berkeley? And what stir
Keeps good old York there with his men of war?
　　H. PERCY. There stands the castle, by yon tuft of
　　trees,
Manned with three hundred men, as I have heard,
And in it are the Lords of York, Berkeley, and Sey-
　　mour —　　　　　　　　　　　55
None else of name and noble estimate.
[*Enter* ROSS *and* WILLOUGHBY.]
　　NORTH. Here come the Lords of Ross and Wil-
　　loughby,
Bloody with spurring, fiery-red with haste.
　　BOLING. Welcome, my lords. I wot your love pur-
　　sues
A banished traitor. All my treasury　　　60
Is yet but unfelt° thanks, which more enriched
Shall be your love and labor's recompense.
　　ROSS. Your presence makes us rich, most noble
　　lord.
　　WILLO. And far surmounts our labor to attain it.
　　BOLING. Evermore thanks, the exchequer of the
　　poor,°　　　　　　　　　　　65
Which, till my infant fortune comes to years,
Stands for my bounty. But who comes here?
[*Enter* BERKELEY.]
　　NORTH. It is my Lord of Berkeley, as I guess.

142. presages: forebodings.
　　Sc. iii: 8–10. weary . . . company: i.e., without your company
this will be a very tedious journey for Ross and Willoughby.
21. young . . . Percy: See *I Hen IV*, I.i.92,n. 22. whencesoever: from wherever he may be.

44. approved: tested. 48–49. fortune . . . recompense: as my
fortunes improve, your love shall be rewarded. 61. unfelt: in-
tangible. 65. thanks . . . poor: the poor can repay only with
thanks.

BERK. My Lord of Hereford, my message is to you.
BOLING. My lord, my answer is — to Lancaster,°
And I am come to seek that name in England,   71
And I must find that title in your tongue
Before I make reply to aught you say.
    BERK. Mistake me not, my lord. 'Tis not my meaning
To rase° one title of your honor out.   75
To you, my lord, I come, what lord you will,
From the most gracious Regent of this land,
The Duke of York, to know what pricks you on
To take advantage of the absent time°
And fright our native peace with self-born° arms.
    [*Enter* YORK *attended.*]
    BOLING. I shall not need transport my words by
        you.   81
Here comes His Grace in person. My noble uncle!
    [*Kneels.*]
    YORK. Show me thy humble heart, and not thy
        knee,
Whose duty° is deceivable° and false.
    BOLING. My gracious uncle!   85
    YORK. Tut, tut!
Grace me no grace,° nor uncle me no uncle:
I am no traitor's uncle, and that word " grace "°
In an ungracious mouth is but profane.
Why have those banished and forbidden legs   90
Dared once to touch a dust of England's ground?
But then more " why? " Why have they dared to
        march
So many miles upon her peaceful bosom,
Frighting her pale-faced villages with war
And ostentation° of despisèd° arms?   95
Comest thou because the anointed King is hence?
Why, foolish boy, the King is left behind,
And in my loyal bosom lies his power.
Were I but now the lord of such hot youth
As when brave Gaunt, thy father, and myself   100
Rescued the Black Prince, that young Mars of men,
From forth the ranks of many thousand French,
Oh, then how quickly should this arm of mine,
Now prisoner to the palsy, chastise thee
And minister correction to thy fault!   105
    BOLING. My gracious uncle, let me know my fault.
On what condition stands it, and wherein?
    YORK. Even in condition of the worst degree,
In gross rebellion and detested treason.
Thou art a banished man, and here art come   110
Before the expiration of thy time
In braving arms against thy sovereign.

    BOLING. As I was banished, I was banished Hereford,
But as I come, I come for Lancaster.
And, noble Uncle, I beseech your Grace   115
Look on my wrongs with an indifferent° eye.
You are my father, for methinks in you
I see old Gaunt alive. Oh, then, my father,
Will you permit that I shall stand condemned   119
A wandering vagabond, my rights and royalties
Plucked from my arms perforce and given away
To upstart unthrifts?° Wherefore was I born?
If that my cousin king be King of England,
It must be granted I am Duke of Lancaster.
You have a son, Aumerle, my noble cousin.   125
Had you first died, and he been thus trod down,
He should have found his uncle Gaunt a father,
To rouse his wrongs and chase them to the bay.°
I am denied to sue my livery° here,
And yet my letters patent give me leave.   130
My father's goods are all distrained and sold,
And these and all are all amiss employed.
What would you have me do? I am a subject,
And I challenge law. Attorneys are denied me,
And therefore personally I lay my claim   135
To my inheritance of free descent.
    NORTH. The noble Duke hath been too much
        abused.
    ROSS. It stands your Grace upon° to do him right.
    WILLO. Base men by his endowments° are made
        great.
    YORK. My lords of England, let me tell you this.
I have had feeling of my cousin's wrongs   141
And labored all I could to do him right.
But in this kind to come, in braving arms,
Be his own carver and cut out his way,
To find out right with wrong, it may not be.   145
And you that do abet him in this kind
Cherish rebellion and are rebels all.
    NORTH. The noble Duke hath sworn his coming is
But for his own, and for the right of that
We all have strongly sworn to give him aid,   150
And let him ne'er see joy that breaks that oath!
    YORK. Well, well, I see the issue of these arms.
I cannot mend it, I must needs confess,
Because my power is weak and all ill left.
But if I could, by Him that gave me life   155
I would attach° you all and make you stoop
Unto the sovereign mercy of the King.
But since I cannot, be it known to you
I do remain as neuter. So fare you well —
Unless you please to enter in the castle   160
And there repose you for this night.
    BOLING. An offer, Uncle, that we will accept.

---

70. **Lancaster:** because he is now Duke of Lancaster. **75. rase:** erase, omit. **79. absent time:** time of the King's absence. **80. self-born:** i.e., born by native Englishmen and not by foreigners. **84. duty:** act of kneeling. **deceivable:** full of deceit. **87. Grace . . . grace:** A common kind of idiom. See *R & J*, III. v.153. **88. grace:** York puns on "grace," a state of grace, and "grace," the courtesy title of a Duke. **95. ostentation:** display. **despised:** despicable.

116. **indifferent:** impartial. **122. unthrifts:** spendthrifts. **128. to . . . bay:** to the death. The bay is the death of a deer in the hunt. **129. sue my livery:** See II.i.203–04. **138. stands . . . upon:** it rests with your Grace. **139. his endowments:** i.e., Bolingbroke's possessions. **156. attach:** arrest.

But we must win your Grace to go with us
To Bristol Castle, which they say is held
By Bushy, Bagot, and their complices,   165
The caterpillars of the commonwealth,°
Which I have sworn to weed and pluck away.
    YORK. It may be I will go with you. But yet I'll pause,
For I am loath to break our country's laws.
Nor friends nor foes, to me welcome you are.   170
Things past redress are now with me past care.
                        [*Exeunt.*]

SCENE IV. *A camp in Wales.*

[*Enter* SALISBURY *and a Welsh* CAPTAIN.]
    CAP. My Lord of Salisbury, we have stayed ten days
And hardly kept our countrymen together,
And yet we hear no tidings from the King.
Therefore we will disperse ourselves. Farewell.   4
    SAL. Stay yet another day, thou trusty Welshman.
The King reposeth all his confidence in thee.
    CAP. 'Tis thought the King is dead. We will not stay.
The bay trees in our country are all withered,
And meteors fright the fixèd stars of heaven.   9
The pale-faced moon looks bloody on the earth,°
And lean-looked prophets whisper fearful change.°
Rich men look sad and ruffians dance and leap,
The one in fear to lose what they enjoy,
The other to enjoy by rage and war.
These signs forerun the death or fall of kings.   15
Farewell. Our countrymen are gone and fled,
As well assured Richard their King is dead.   [*Exit.*]
    SAL. Ah, Richard, with the eyes of heavy mind
I see thy glory like a shooting star
Fall to the base earth from the firmament.   20
Thy sun sets weeping in the lowly west,
Witnessing storms to come, woe and unrest.
Thy friends are fled to wait upon thy foes,
And crossly° to thy good all fortune goes.   [*Exit.*]

Act III

SCENE I. *Bristol. Before the Castle.*

[*Enter* BOLINGBROKE, YORK, NORTHUMBERLAND, ROSS,
PERCY, WILLOUGHBY, *with* BUSHY *and* GREEN,
prisoners.]
    BOLING. Bring forth these men.
Bushy and Green, I will not vex your souls —

---

166. caterpillars . . . commonwealth: a common Elizabethan metaphor for those who prey on the state, "grafters."
    Sc. iv: 8–10. The . . . earth: all these events were regarded by the superstitious as omens of disaster. 11. change: revolution. 24. crossly: adversely.

Since presently your souls must part your bodies —
With too much urging° your pernicious lives,
For 'twere no charity. Yet, to wash your blood   5
From off my hands, here in the view of men
I will unfold some causes of your deaths.
You have misled a prince, a royal King,
A happy gentleman in blood and lineaments,°
By you unhappied and disfigured clean.°   10
You have in manner with your sinful hours°
Made a divorce betwixt his Queen and him,
Broke the possession of a royal bed
And stained the beauty of a fair Queen's cheeks
With tears drawn from her eyes by your foul
      wrongs.
Myself, a prince by fortune of my birth,   16
Near to the King in blood, and near in love
Till you did make him misinterpret me,
Have stooped my neck under your injuries,
And sighed my English breath in foreign clouds,
Eating the bitter bread of banishment,   21
Whilst you have fed upon my signories,°
Disparked° my parks and felled my forest woods,
From my own windows torn my household coat,°
Razed out my imprese,° leaving me no sign   25
Save men's opinions and my living blood
To show the world I am a gentleman.
This and much more, much more than twice all
      this,
Condemns you to the death. See them delivered
      over
To execution and the hand of death.   30
    BUSHY. More welcome is the stroke of death to me
Than Bolingbroke to England. Lords, farewell.
    GREEN. My comfort is that Heaven will take our souls
And plague injustice with the pains of Hell.
    BOLING. My Lord Northumberland, see them dispatched.   35
           [*Exeunt* NORTHUMBERLAND *and others,*
                       with the prisoners.]
Uncle, you say the Queen is at your house.
For God's sake, fairly let her be entreated.°
Tell her I send to her my kind commends.°
Take special care my greetings be delivered.
    YORK. A gentleman of mine I have dispatched   40
With letters of your love to her at large.°
    BOLING. Thanks, gentle Uncle. Come, lords, away,
To fight with Glendower and his complices.
Awhile to work, and after holiday.   [*Exeunt.*]

Act III, Sc. i: 4. urging: stressing. 9. happy . . . lineaments: fortunate in his descent and personal appearance. 10. clean: completely. 11. in . . . hours: because of your sinful way of life. 22. signories: manors. 23. Disparked: broken-down the enclosures of. 24. household coat: coat of arms in stained glass. 25. imprese: heraldic device. 37. entreated: treated. 38. commends: commendations. 41. at large: at length, fully.

SCENE II. *The coast of Wales. A castle in view.*

[*Drums: flourish and colors.° Enter* KING RICHARD, *the* BISHOP OF CARLISLE, AUMERLE, *and Soldiers.*]

K. RICH. Barkloughly° Castle call they this at
   hand?
AUM. Yea, my lord. How brooks° your Grace the
   air
After your late tossing on the breaking seas?
K. RICH. Needs must I like it well. I weep for joy
To stand upon my kingdom once again.   5
Dear earth, I do salute thee with my hand,
Though rebels wound thee with their horses' hoofs.
As a long-parted mother with her child
Plays fondly with her tears and smiles in meeting,
So, weeping, smiling, greet I thee, my earth, 10
And do thee favors° with my royal hands.
Feed not thy sovereign's foe, my gentle earth,
Nor with thy sweets comfort his ravenous° sense;°
But let thy spiders, that suck up thy venom,
And heavy-gaited° toads° lie in their way, 15
Doing annoyance° to the treacherous feet
Which with usurping steps do trample thee.
Yield stinging nettles to mine enemies,
And when they from thy bosom pluck a flower,
Guard it, I pray thee, with a lurking adder, 20
Whose double tongue° may with a mortal° touch
Throw death upon thy sovereign's enemies.
Mock not my senseless conjuration,° lords.
This earth shall have a feeling and these stones
Prove armèd soldiers ere her native King 25
Shall falter under foul rebellion's arms.
CAR. Fear not, my lord. That Power that made you
   King
Hath power to keep you King in spite of all.
The means that Heaven yields must be embraced,
And not neglected; else, if Heaven would 30
And we will not, Heaven's offer we refuse,
The proffered means of succor and redress.
AUM. He means, my lord, that we are too remiss,
Whilst Bolingbroke, through our security,°
Grows strong and great in substance and in power.
K. RICH. Discomfortable° Cousin! Know'st thou
   not 36
That when the searching eye of Heaven is hid

[Handwritten annotations: "DIVINE RIGHT IDEA — THAT NOT ONLY ANGELS BUT NATURE LOVES THE KING" ; "CARLISLE AGREES WITH RICHARD'S RIGHT — BUT THEY MUST DO SOMETHING"]

Behind the globe that lights the lower world,°
Then thieves and robbers range abroad unseen
In murders and in outrage, boldly here; 40
But when from under this terrestrial ball
He fires the proud tops of the eastern pines
And darts his light through every guilty hole,
Then murders, treasons, and detested sins,
The cloak of night being plucked from off their
   backs, 45
Stand bare and naked, trembling at themselves?
So when this thief, this traitor, Bolingbroke,
Who all this while hath reveled in the night
Whilst we were wandering with the Antipodes,°
Shall see us rising in our throne, the east, 50
His treasons will sit blushing in his face,
Not able to endure the sight of day,
But self-affrighted tremble at his sin.
Not all the water in the rough rude sea
Can wash the balm° off from an anointed king. 55
The breath of worldly men cannot depose
The deputy elected by the Lord.
For every man that Bolingbroke hath pressed°
To lift shrewd° steel against our golden crown,
God for His Richard hath in heavenly pay 60
A glorious angel. Then, if angels fight,
Weak men must fall, for Heaven still guards the
   right.
[*Enter* SALISBURY.] Welcome, my lord. How far off
   lies your power?°
SAL. Nor near° nor farther off, my gracious lord,
Than this weak arm. Discomfort guides my tongue
And bids me speak of nothing but despair. 66
One day too late, I fear me, noble lord,
Hath clouded all thy happy days on earth.
Oh, call back yesterday, bid time return,
And thou shalt have twelve thousand fighting
   men!
Today, today, unhappy day, too late, 71
O'erthrows thy joys, friends, fortune, and thy state.
For all the Welshmen, hearing thou wert dead,
Are gone to Bolingbroke, dispersed, and fled.
AUM. Comfort, my liege. Why looks your Grace
   so pale? 75
K. RICH. But now° the blood of twenty thousand
   men
Did triumph in my face, and they are fled.
And till so much blood thither come again,
Have I not reason to look pale and dead?
All souls that will be safe, fly from my side, 80
For time hath set a blot upon my pride.
AUM. Comfort, my liege. Remember who you are.

[Handwritten annotation: "RICHARD IS GOING EAST TO WALES + LEAVING IRELAND"]

Sc. ii: s.d., colors: i.e., a soldier carrying a flag. 1. Barkloughly: The name comes from Holinshed, and is probably a misprint for Harlech, a castle in Wales. 2. brooks: endures, enjoys. 11. favors: Richard is saluting the earth by touching it. 13. ravenous: gluttonous, like a beast of prey. sense: nature. 15. heavy-gaited: heavy-footed, lumbering. toads: toads and spiders were considered poisonous. 16. annoyance: hurt. 21. double tongue: forked tongue. Adders were believed to sting with the tongue. mortal: deadly. 23. senseless conjuration: attempt to conjure things that have no feeling. 34. security: lack of care. 36. Discomfortable: causing discomfort.

37–38. eye . . . world: i.e., when the sun (*eye of Heaven*) which lights the world passes behind the earth (*globe*). 49. Antipodes: the other side of the earth. 55. balm: consecrated oil used in anointing a king. 58. pressed: conscripted. 59. shrewd: malicious. 63. power: army. 64. near: nearer. 76. But now: a moment ago.

K. RICH. I had forgot myself.° Am I not King?
Awake, thou coward Majesty! Thou sleepest.
Is not the King's name twenty thousand names?   85
Arm, arm, my name! A puny subject strikes
At thy great glory. Look not to the ground,
Ye favorites of a King. Are we not high?
High be our thoughts. I know my uncle York
Hath power enough to serve our turn. But who
    comes here?   90

           [*Enter* SCROOP.]

SCROOP. More health and happiness betide° my
    liege
Than can my care-tunèd tongue deliver him!
    K. RICH. Mine ear is open and my heart prepared.
The worst is worldly loss thou canst unfold.
Say, is my kingdom lost? Why, 'twas my care,   95
And what loss is it to be rid of care?°
Strives Bolingbroke to be as great as we?
Greater he shall not be. If he serve God,
We'll serve Him too and be his fellow so.
Revolt our subjects? That we cannot mend.   100
They break their faith to God as well as us.
Cry woe, destruction, ruin, and decay —
The worst is death, and death will have his day.
    SCROOP. Glad am I that your Highness is so armed
To bear the tidings of calamity.   105
Like an unseasonable stormy day,
Which makes the silver rivers drown their shores
As if the world were all dissolved to tears,
So high above his limits° swells the rage
Of Bolingbroke, covering your fearful° land   110
With hard bright steel and hearts harder than steel.
Whitebeards have armed their thin and hairless
      scalps°
Against thy Majesty. Boys with women's voices
Strive to speak big and clap their female joints
In stiff unwieldy arms against thy crown.   115
Thy very beadsmen° learn to bend their bows
Of double-fatal° yew against thy state.
Yea, distaff women° manage° rusty bills°
Against thy seat.° Both young and old rebel,
And all goes worse than I have power to tell.   120
    K. RICH. Too well, too well thou tell'st a tale so ill.
Where is the Earl of Wiltshire? Where is Bagot?
What is become of Bushy? Where is Green?
That they have let the dangerous enemy
Measure° our confines with such peaceful steps?
If we prevail, their heads shall pay for it.   126

83. I . . . myself: This constant change of mood in Richard was
imitated from Marlowe's *Edward II*. See *Rich II* Intro. p. 432b.
91. betide: befall.   95-96. care . . . care: responsibility . . .
trouble.   109. limits: boundaries.   110. fearful: full of fear.
112. Whitebeards . . . scalps: even the most aged have covered
their thinning or bald heads with helmets.   116. beadsmen: old
men pensioned to pray for their benefactor.   117. double-fatal:
because the yew is poisonous to cattle and also used for deadly
bows.   118. distaff women: women who spin; the *distaff* is a
staff used in spinning.   manage: wield.   bills: See Pl. 21c.
119. seat: throne.   125. Measure: pace out.

I warrant they have made peace with Bolingbroke.
    SCROOP. Peace have they made with him indeed,
      my lord.
      K. RICH. Oh, villains, vipers, damned without re-
      demption!
Dogs, easily won to fawn on any man!   130
Snakes, in my heartblood warmed, that sting my
    heart!
Three Judases, each one thrice worse than Judas!
Would they make peace? Terrible Hell make war
Upon their spotted souls for this offense!
    SCROOP. Sweet love, I see, changing his property,°
Turns to the sourest and most deadly hate.   136
Again uncurse their souls. Their peace is made
With heads and not with hands. Those whom you
    curse
Have felt the worst of death's destroying wound,
And lie full low, graved in the hollow ground.   140
    AUM. Is Bushy, Green, and the Earl of Wiltshire
      dead?
    SCROOP. Aye, all of them at Bristol lost their heads.
    AUM. Where is the Duke my father with his
      power?
    K. RICH. No matter where, of comfort no man
      speak.
Let's talk of graves, of worms and epitaphs,   145
Make dust our paper and with rainy eyes
Write sorrow on the bosom of the earth.
Let's choose executors and talk of wills.
And yet not so, for what can we bequeath
Save our deposèd bodies to the ground?   150
Our lands, our lives, and all are Bolingbroke's,
And nothing can we call our own but death
And that small model° of the barren earth
Which serves as paste° and cover to our bones.
For God's sake, let us sit upon the ground   155
And tell sad stories of the death of kings —
How some have been deposed, some slain in war,
Some haunted by the ghosts they have deposed,°
Some poisoned by their wives, some sleeping killed,
All murdered. For within the hollow crown   160
That rounds the mortal temples of a king
Keeps Death his Court, and there the antic° sits,
Scoffing his state and grinning at his pomp,
Allowing him a breath, a little scene,
To monarchize,° be feared, and kill with looks,   165
Infusing him with self and vain conceit,°
As if this flesh which walls about our life
Were brass impregnable, and humored thus
Comes at the last and with a little pin   169
Bores through his castle wall, and farewell King!

135. property: natural quality.   153. model: mold, shape; i.e.,
the earthly body.   154. paste: covering like piecrust.   158. ghosts
. . . deposed: i.e., those whom they have deposed and turned
into ghosts by murdering them.   162. antic: buffoon, because
Death is represented as a grinning skull. See Pl. 12f.   165. monarchize: play the monarch.   166. self . . . conceit: vain self-con-
ceit.

Cover your heads° and mock not flesh and blood
With solemn reverence. Throw away respect,
Tradition, form, and ceremonious duty,
For you have but mistook me all this while.
I live with bread like you, feel want,   175
Taste grief, need friends. Subjected° thus,
How can you say to me I am a king?
    CAR. My lord, wise men ne'er sit and wail their
      woes,
But presently prevent the ways to wail.°
To fear the foe, since fear oppresseth strength,   180
Gives in your weakness strength unto your foe,
And so your follies fight against yourself.
Fear, and be slain. No worse can come to fight.
And fight and die is death destroying death,   184
Where° fearing dying pays death servile breath.
    AUM. My father hath a power. Inquire of him,
And learn to make a body of a limb.
    K. RICH. Thou chidest me well. Proud Boling-
      broke, I come
To change blows with thee for our day of doom.
This ague fit of fear is overblown —   190
An easy task it is to win our own.
Say, Scroop, where lies our uncle with his power?
Speak sweetly, man, although thy looks be sour.
    SCROOP. Men judge by the complexion of the sky
The state and inclination of the day.   195
So may you by my dull and heavy eye —
    My tongue hath but a heavier tale to say.
I play the torturer, by small and small
To lengthen out the worst that must be spoken.
Your uncle York is joined with Bolingbroke,   200
And all your northern castles yielded up,
And all your southern gentlemen in arms
Upon his party.
    K. RICH. Thou hast said enough.
[*To* AUMERLE] Beshrew° thee, Cousin, which didst
    lead me forth
Of that sweet way I was in to despair!°   205
What say you now? What comfort have we now?
By Heaven, I'll hate him everlastingly
That bids me be of comfort any more.
Go to Flint Castle. There I'll pine away.
A king, woe's slave, shall kingly woe obey.   210
That power I have, discharge, and let them go
To ear° the land that hath some hope to grow,
For I have none. Let no man speak again
To alter this, for counsel is but vain.
    AUM. My liege, one word.
    K. RICH.   He does me double wrong 215
That wounds me with the flatteries of his tongue.

Discharge my followers. Let them hence away,
From Richard's night to Bolingbroke's fair day.
                   [*Exeunt.*]

SCENF III. *Wales. Before Flint Castle.*

[*Enter, with drum and colors,* BOLINGBROKE, YORK
    NORTHUMBERLAND, *Attendants, and Forces.*]
    BOLING. So that by this intelligence we learn
The Welshmen are dispersed, and Salisbury
Is gone to meet the King, who lately landed
With some few private friends upon this coast.
    NORTH. The news is very fair and good, my lord.
Richard not far from hence hath hid his head.   6
    YORK. It would beseem the Lord Northumberland
To say "King Richard." Alack the heavy day
When such a sacred king should hide his head!
    NORTH. Your Grace mistakes. Only to be brief   10
Left I his title out.
    YORK.   The time hath been,
Would you have been so brief with him, he would
Have been so brief with you, to shorten you,
For taking so the head,° your whole head's length.
    BOLING. Mistake not, Uncle, further than you
    should.   15
    YORK. Take not, good Cousin, further than you
    should,
Lest you mistake the heavens are o'er our heads.
    BOLING. I know it, Uncle, and oppose not myself
Against their will. But who comes here?
[*Enter* HENRY PERCY.] Welcome, Harry. What, will
not this castle yield?   20
    H. PERCY. The castle royally is manned, my lord,
Against thy entrance.
    BOLING. Royally!
Why, it contains no king?
    H. PERCY.   Yes, my good lord,
It doth contain a king. King Richard lies   25
Within the limits of yon lime and stone.
And with him are the Lord Aumerle, Lord Salis-
    bury,
Sir Stephen Scroop, besides a clergyman
Of holy reverence, who, I cannot learn.
    NORTH. Oh, belike it is the Bishop of Carlisle. 30
    BOLING. Noble lords,
Go to the rude ribs° of that ancient castle.
Through brazen trumpet send the breath of parley°
Into his ruined ears, and thus deliver.
Henry Bolingbroke   35
On both his knees doth kiss King Richard's hand
And sends allegiance and true faith of heart
To his most royal person, hither come
Even at his feet to lay my arms and power

[handwritten margin note: YORK IS PICKY— SHOWS HIS REVERENCE TO KING]

Handwritten margin note (top left): BOLING. USES FLATTERING MEANS BUSINESS — WORDS BUT WILL KILL RICHARD IF HE DOESN'T DO AS THEY WISH

Provided that my banishment repealed°
And lands restored again be ~~freely granted.~~
If not, I'll use the advantage of my power
And ~~lay the summer's dust with showers of blood~~
~~Rained from the wounds of slaughtered English-~~
~~men.~~
The which, how far off from the mind of Boling-
broke   45
It is such crimson tempest should bedrench
The fresh green lap of fair King Richard's land,
My stooping duty° tenderly shall show.
Go, signify as much while here we march
Upon the grassy carpet of this plain.   50
Let's march without the noise of threatening drum,
That from this castle's tattered° battlements
Our fair appointments° may be well perused.
Methinks King Richard and myself should meet
With no less terror than the elements   55
Of fire and water° when their thundering shock
At meeting tears the cloudy cheeks of heaven.
Be he the fire, I'll be the yielding water.
The rage be his, whilst on the earth I rain
My waters — on the earth, and not on him.   60
March on, and mark King Richard how he looks.
[*Parle° without, and answer within. Then a flourish.*
    Enter on the walls, KING RICHARD, *the* BISHOP OF
        CARLISLE, AUMERLE, SCROOP, *and* SALISBURY.]
See, see, ~~King Richard doth himself appear,~~
~~As doth the blushing discontented sun~~
From out the fiery portal of the east
When he perceives the envious clouds are bent   65
To dim his glory and to stain the track
Of his bright passage to the Occident.
    YORK. Yet looks he like a king. Behold, his eye,
As bright as is the eagle's, lightens forth
Controlling majesty.° Alack, alack, for woe,   70
That any harm should stain so fair a show!
    K. RICH. [*To* NORTHUMBERLAND] We° are amazed,
        and thus long have we stood
To watch the fearful bending of thy knee,
Because we thought ourself thy lawful king.
And if we be, how dare thy joints forget   75
To pay their awful° duty to our presence?
If we be not, show us the hand of God
That hath dismissed us from our stewardship;
For well we know no hand of blood and bone
Can gripe° the sacred handle of our scepter   80
Unless he do profane, steal, or usurp.
And though you think that all, as you have done,
Have torn their souls° by turning them from us,

Handwritten margin note: RICHARD COMPARES HIMSELF TO SUN

Handwritten margin note (left): YORK NOTES RICH'S KINGLY PRESENCE

And we are barren and bereft of friends,
Yet know my master, God Omnipotent,   85
Is mustering in His clouds on our behalf
Armies of pestilence; and they shall strike
Your children yet unborn and unbegot,
That lift your vassal° hands against my head
And threat the glory of my precious crown.   90
Tell Bolingbroke — for yond methinks he stands —
That every stride he makes upon my land
Is dangerous treason. He is come to open
The purple testament of bleeding war.°
But ere the crown he looks for live in peace,   95
Ten thousand bloody crowns of mothers' sons
Shall ill become the flower of England's face,
Change the complexion of her maid-pale peace
To scarlet indignation, and bedew
Her pastures' grass with faithful English blood.
    NORTH. The King of Heaven forbid our lord the
        King   101
Should so with civil° and uncivil° arms
Be rushed upon! Thy thrice noble cousin
Harry Bolingbroke doth humbly kiss thy hand.
And by the honorable tomb he swears   105
That stands upon your royal grandsire's bones,
And by the royalties of both your bloods,
Currents that spring from one most gracious head,
And by the buried hand of warlike Gaunt,
And by the worth and honor of himself,   110
Comprising all that may be sworn or said,
His coming hither hath no further scope
Than for his lineal royalties,° and to beg
Enfranchisement° immediate on his knees.
Which on thy royal party granted once,   115
His glittering arms he will commend° to rust,
His barbèd° steeds to stables, and his heart
To faithful service of your Majesty.
This swears he, as he is a prince, is just.
And as I am a gentleman, I credit him.   120
    K. RICH. Northumberland, say thus the King re-
        turns:
His noble cousin is right welcome hither,
And all the number of his fair demands
Shall be accomplished without contradiction.
With all the gracious utterance thou hast,   125
Speak to his gentle hearing kind commends.°
[*To* AUMERLE] We do debase ourselves, Cousin, do
        we not,
To look so poorly and to speak so fair?
Shall we call back Northumberland and send
Defiance to the traitor, and so die?   130

Handwritten margin notes (right): RICH'S TRUE PROPHECY — RICH. UTTERS OWN DEATH — KNOW WHAT HE'S DOING

---

40. **repealed:** recalled, canceled.   48. **stooping duty:** kneeling as an outward sign of respect.   52. **tattered:** ragged, because battlements have a "torn" appearance.   53. **appointments:** equipment.   55–56. **elements . . . water:** i.e., when fire strikes a cloud — the old explanation of thunder.   61. **s.d., Parle:** a trumpet call summoning to parley.   69–70. **lightens . . . majesty:** flashes out a look of authority.   72. **We:** the royal "we," used by kings when speaking officially.   76. **awful:** full of awe.   80. **gripe:** grip.   83. **torn . . . souls:** violated their faith.

89. **vassal:** base.   93–94. **open . . . war:** to give effect to the bloodshed bequeathed by war — a far-fetched metaphor. War is regarded as a testator, bequeathing blood; to open the testament is the first stage in carrying out the testator's will.   102. **civil:** in civil war. **uncivil:** rude.   113. **lineal royalties:** rights descending to him through his royal blood.   114. **Enfranchisement:** freedom; i.e., cancelation of banishment.   116. **commend:** deliver.   117. **barbed:** armed.   126. **commends:** commendations.

AUM. No, good my lord, let's fight with gentle
  words
Till time lend friends and friends their helpful
  swords.
    K. RICH. Oh, God, oh, God, that e'er this tongue of
  mine,
That laid the sentence of dread banishment
On yon proud man, should take it off again   135
With words of sooth!° Oh, that I were as great
As is my grief, or lesser than my name!
Or that I could forget what I have been,
Or not remember what I must be now!
Swell'st thou, proud heart? I'll give thee scope° to
  beat,   140
Since foes have scope to beat both thee and me.
    AUM. Northumberland comes back from Boling-
  broke. *ARTISTIC EVEN AT TIME OF BEING DEPOSED*
    K. RICH. What must the King do now? Must he
  submit?
The King shall do it. Must he be deposed?
The King shall be contented. Must he lose   145
The name of king? O' God's name, let it go.
I'll give my jewels for a set of beads,°
My gorgeous palace for a hermitage,
My gay apparel for an almsman's° gown,
My figured° goblets for a dish of wood,   150
My scepter for a palmer's° walking-staff,
My subjects for a pair of carvèd saints,
And my large kingdom for a little grave,
A little little grave, an obscure grave.
Or I'll be buried in the King's highway,   155
Some way of common trade,° where subjects' feet
May hourly trample on their sovereign's head;
For on my heart they tread now whilst I live,
And buried once, why not upon my head?
Aumerle, thou weep'st, my tender-hearted cousin!
We'll make foul weather with despisèd tears,   161
Our sighs and they shall lodge° the summer corn
And make a dearth in this revolting land.
Or shall we play the wantons° with our woes,
And make some pretty match° with shedding tears?
As thus, to drop them still° upon one place   166
Till they have fretted° us a pair of graves
Within the earth, and, therein laid — there lies
Two kinsmen digged their graves with weeping
  eyes.
Would not this ill do well? Well, well, I see   170
I talk but idly, and you laugh at me.
Most mighty prince, my Lord Northumberland,
What says King Bolingbroke? Will His Majesty
Give Richard leave to live till Richard die?

You make a leg,° and Bolingbroke says aye.   175
    NORTH. My lord, in the base° court he doth at-
  tend°
To speak with you. May it please you to come down.
    K. RICH. Down, down I come, like glistering
  Phaëton,°
Wanting the manage° of unruly jades.°
In the base court? Base court, where kings grow
  base,   180
To come at traitors' calls and do them grace.
In the base court? Come down? Down, court!
  Down, King!
For night owls shriek where mounting larks should
  sing.   [Exeunt from above.]
    BOLING. What says His Majesty?
    NORTH.   Sorrow and grief of heart
Makes him speak fondly,° like a frantic man,   185
Yet he is come.
    [Enter KING RICHARD and his attendants below.]
    BOLING. Stand all apart,
And show fair duty to His Majesty.
                        [He kneels down.]
My gracious lord ——
    K. RICH. Fair Cousin, you debase your princely
  knee   190
To make the base earth proud with kissing it.
Me rather had° my heart might feel your love
Than my unpleasèd eye see your courtesy.
Up, Cousin, up. Your heart is up, I know,
Thus high at least, although your knee be low.   195
    BOLING. My gracious lord, I come but for mine
  own.
    K. RICH. Your own is yours, and I am yours, and
  all.
    BOLING. So far be mine, my most redoubted
  lord,
As my true service shall deserve your love.
    K. RICH. Well you deserve. They well deserve to
  have   200
That know the strong'st and surest way to get.
Uncle, give me your hands. Nay, dry your eyes.
Tears show their love, but want their remedies.°
Cousin, I am too young to be your father,
Though you are old enough to be my heir.   205
What you will have, I'll give, and willing too,
For do we must what force will have us do.
Set on toward London, Cousin, is it so?
    BOLING. Yea, my good lord.
    K. RICH.   Then I must not say no.
                        [Flourish. Exeunt.]

---

136. sooth: flattery.   140. scope: freedom. Here Richard plucks
open his garment.   147. set of beads: rosary.   149. almsman:
poor man living on charity.   150. figured: ornamented. See Pl.
20h.   151. palmer: pilgrim.   156. trade: tread.   162. lodge: beat
flat.   164. play . . . wantons: play frivolous tricks.   165. match:
competition.   166. still: continuously.   167. fretted: worn.

175. make a leg: curtsy.   176. base: lower or outer. attend:
wait.   178. Phaëton: the son of the sun. He tried to drive his
father's chariot, but the horses were too fierce for him and he was
thrown out.   179. Wanting . . . manage: lacking control. jades:
horses bad-tempered or in poor condition.   185. fondly: foolishly.
192. Me . . . had: I would rather.   203. want . . . remedies: cannot remedy.

[Handwritten at top: IN THIS SCENE, BOTH FRUIT TREES & FLOWERS — OF CONCERN]

SCENE IV. *Langley. The* DUKE OF YORK'S *garden.*

[*Enter the* QUEEN *and two* LADIES.]

QUEEN. What sport shall we devise here in this garden
To drive away the heavy thought of care?
LADY. Madam, we'll play at bowls.°
QUEEN. 'Twill make me think the world is full of rubs,
And that my fortune runs against the bias. 5
LADY. Madam, we'll dance.
QUEEN. My legs can keep no measure in delight
When my poor heart no measure° keeps in grief.
Therefore no dancing, girl, some other sport.
LADY. Madam, we'll tell tales. 10
QUEEN. Of sorrow or of joy?
LADY.   Of either, madam.
QUEEN. Of neither, girl.
For if of joy, being altogether wanting,
It doth remember° me the more of sorrow.
Or if of grief, being altogether had, 15
It adds more sorrow to my want of joy.
For what I have I need not to repeat,
And what I want it boots° not to complain.
LADY. Madam, I'll sing.
QUEEN.   'Tis well that thou hast cause.
But thou shouldst please me better wouldst thou weep. 20
LADY. I could weep, madam, would it do you good.
QUEEN. And I could sing would weeping do me good,
And never borrow any tear of thee.

[Handwritten left margin: START HERE]

[*Enter a* GARDENER, *and two* SERVANTS.] But stay, here come the gardeners.
Let's step into the shadow of these trees. 25
My wretchedness unto a row of pins,°
They'll talk of state,° for everyone doth so
Against a change.° Woe is forerun with woe.

[Handwritten right margin: WHY DOES QUEEN? HIDE?]

[QUEEN *and* LADIES *retire.*]
GARD. Go, bind thou up yon dangling apricocks,°
Which, like unruly children, make their sire 30
Stoop with oppression of their prodigal° weight.
Give some supportance to the bending twigs.
Go thou, and like an executioner,
Cut off the heads of too-fast-growing sprays°
That look too lofty in our commonwealth. 35
All must be even° in our government.
You thus employed, I will go root away
The noisome weeds which without profit suck

[Handwritten right margin: A MOTIVE; IS HER WANTING TO HEAR OF STATE — A TOUCH OF REALITY]

[Handwritten left margin: COMPARING RUNNING OF GARDEN TO THE MANAGEMENT OF A KINGDOM; APPROPRIATE SINCE THEY SPEAK OF FAMILY TREE]

The soil's fertility from wholesome flowers.
SERV. Why should we in the compass of a pale°
Keep law and form and due proportion, 41
Showing, as in a model, our firm estate,
When our sea-wallèd garden, the whole land,
Is full of weeds, her fairest flowers choked up,
Her fruit trees all unpruned, her hedges ruined, 45
Her knots° disordered, and her wholesome herbs
Swarming with caterpillars?
GARD.   Hold thy peace.
He that hath suffered° this disordered spring
Hath now himself met with the fall of leaf.
The weeds which his broad-spreading leaves did shelter, 50
That seemed in eating him to hold him up,
Are plucked up root and all by Bolingbroke.
I mean the Earl of Wiltshire, Bushy, Green.
SERV. What, are they dead?
GARD.   They are, and Bolingbroke
Hath seized the wasteful King. Oh, what pity is it
That he had not so trimmed and dressed his land
As we this garden! We at time of year 57
Do wound the bark, the skin of our fruit trees,
Lest, being overproud° in sap and blood,
With too much riches it confound° itself. 60
Had he done so to great and growing men,
They might have lived to bear and he to taste
Their fruits of duty. Superfluous branches
We lop away, that bearing boughs may live.
Had he done so, himself had borne the crown 65
Which waste of idle hours hath quite thrown down.
SERV. What, think you then the King shall be deposed?
GARD. Depressed° he is already, and deposed
'Tis doubt° he will be. Letters came last night
To a dear friend of the good Duke of York's 70
That tell black tidings.
QUEEN. Oh, I am pressed to death° through want of speaking! [*Coming forward.*]
Thou, old Adam's° likeness, set to dress this garden,
How dares thy harsh rude tongue sound this unpleasing news?
What Eve, what serpent, hath suggested° thee 75
To make a second fall of cursèd man?
Why dost thou say King Richard is deposed?
Darest thou, thou little better thing than earth,
Divine° his downfall? Say where, when, and how
Camest thou by this ill tidings? Speak, thou wretch.
GARD. Pardon me, madam. Little joy have I 81
To breathe this news, yet what I say is true.

[Handwritten right margin, near 72-79: RICHARD ACTS AS IF HE'S IN A GARDEN OR PART OF A TAPESTRY; GARDEN IS LIKE A TAPESTRY (IMAGE OF PLUM)]

Sc. iv: 3–5. bowls...rubs...bias: See App. 13. 7–8. measure...measure: formal dance...limit. 14. remember: remind. 18. boots: is of advantage. 26. My...pins: i.e., I'll wager my misery against a trifle. 27. talk of state: discuss politics. 28. Against a change: in anticipation of revolution. 29. apricocks: apricots. 31. prodigal: extravagant. 34. sprays: sprigs. 36. even: level, tidy.

40. compass...pale: limits of an enclosed park or garden. 46. knots: flowerbeds, often laid out in "knots" or fancy shapes. See Pl. 16a. 48. suffered: allowed. 59. overproud: luxuriant. 60. confound: destroy. 68. Depressed: humbled. 69. 'Tis doubt: no doubt. 72. pressed to death: See Gen. Intro. p. 27b. 73. old Adam: for Adam was the first gardener, as the Gravedigger observed. See *Haml*, V.i.33–44. 75. suggested: prompted. 79. Divine: foretell by divination.

King Richard, he is in the mighty hold°
Of Bolingbroke. Their fortunes both are weighed.
In your lord's scale is nothing but himself,   85
And some few vanities that make him light;
But in the balance of great Bolingbroke,
Besides himself, are all the English peers,
And with that odds he weighs King Richard down.
Post you to London, and you will find it so.   90
I speak no more than everyone doth know.
    QUEEN. Nimble mischance, that art so light of
        foot,
Doth not thy embassage belong to me,°
And am I last that knows it? Oh, thou think'st
To serve me last, that I may longest keep   95
Thy sorrow in my breast. Come, ladies, go,
To meet at London London's King in woe.
What, was I born to this, that my sad look
Should grace the triumph of great Bolingbroke?
Gardener, for telling me these news of woe,   100
Pray God the plants thou graft'st may never grow.
                    [*Exeunt* QUEEN *and* LADIES.]
    GARD. Poor Queen! So that thy state might be no
        worse,
I would my skill were subject to thy curse.
Here did she fall° a tear; here in this place
I'll set a bank of rue,° sour herb of grace.   105
Rue, even for ruth,° here shortly shall be seen,
In the remembrance of a weeping Queen.
                                            [*Exeunt.*]

Act IV

SCENE I. *Westminster Hall.*

[*Enter as to the Parliament,* BOLINGBROKE, AUMERLE,
NORTHUMBERLAND, PERCY, FITZWATER, SURREY, *the*
BISHOP OF CARLISLE, *the* ABBOT OF WESTMINSTER, *and
another* LORD, HERALD, OFFICERS, *and* BAGOT.]
    BOLING. Call forth Bagot.   *shows Boling's*
Now, Bagot, freely speak thy mind. —   *direct*
                                        approach
What thou dost know of noble Gloucester's death,
Who wrought it with° the King, and who per-
        formed
The bloody office of his timeless° end.   5
    BAGOT. Then set before my face the Lord Aumerle.
    BOLING. Cousin, stand forth, and look upon that
        man.
    BAGOT. My Lord Aumerle, I know your daring
        tongue

Scorns to unsay what once it hath delivered.
In that dead° time when Gloucester's death was
        plotted,   10
I heard you say, "Is not my arm of length,
That reacheth from the restful° English Court
As far as Calais, to mine uncle's head?"
Amongst much other talk, that very time,
I heard you say that you had rather refuse   15
The offer of a hundred thousand crowns
Than Bolingbroke's return° to England,
Adding withal, how blest this land would be
In this your cousin's death.
    AUM.   Princes and noble lords,
What answer shall I make to this base man?   20
Shall I so much dishonor my fair stars°
On equal terms to give him chastisement?
Either I must, or have mine honor soiled
With the attainder° of his slanderous lips.
There is my gage,° the manual seal° of death   25
That marks thee out for Hell. I say thou liest,
And will maintain what thou hast said is false
In thy heartblood, though being° all too base
To stain the temper° of my knightly sword.   29
    BOLING. Bagot, forbear. Thou shalt not take it up.
    AUM. Excepting one,° I would he were the best
In all this presence that hath moved me so.
    FITZ. If that thy valor stand on sympathy,°
There is my gage, Aumerle, in gage to thine.
By that fair sun which shows me where thou stand'st
I heard thee say, and vauntingly thou spakest it,   36
That thou wert cause of noble Gloucester's death.
If thou deny'st it twenty times, thou liest.
And I will turn thy falsehood to thy heart,
Where it was forgèd, with my rapier's point.   40
    AUM. Thou darest not, coward, live to see that day.
    FITZ. Now, by my soul, I would it were this hour.
    AUM. Fitzwater, thou art damned to Hell for this.
    H. PERCY. Aumerle, thou liest. His honor is as true
In this appeal as thou art all unjust.   45
And that thou art so, there I throw my gage,
To prove it on thee to the extremest point
Of mortal breathing.° Seize it, if thou darest.
    AUM. An if I do not, may my hands rot off
And never brandish more revengeful steel   50
Over the glittering helmet of my foe!
    LORD. I task the earth to the like,° forsworn
        Aumerle,
And spur thee on with full as many lies
As may be holloed in thy treacherous ear

---

83. hold: grasp. 93. embassage . . . me: should not your message have been delivered to me. 104. fall: let fall. 105. rue:
called also "herb of grace," because *rue* means "repent."
106. ruth: pity.
    Act IV, Sc. i: 4. wrought it with: persuaded. 5. timeless: un-
timely.

10. dead: deadly. 12. restful: peaceful. 17. Than . . . return:
than have Bolingbroke return. 21. fair stars: good fortune.
24. attainder: dishonorable accusation. 25. gage: pledge; i.e.,
glove. See I.i.67–74. manual seal: sealed warrant. 28. though
being: although you are. 29. temper: lit., hardness. 31. Excepting one: with one exception; i.e., Bolingbroke. 33. If . . .
sympathy: if you are so proud that you will only fight with an
equal. sympathy: equality. 47–48. to . . . breathing: to your last
breath. 52. I . . . like: I charge the earth to bear my gage too.

From sun to sun. There is my honor's pawn.° 55
Engage it° to the trial, if thou darest.
   AUM. Who sets° me else? By Heaven, I'll throw
    at all.
I have a thousand spirits in one breast,
To answer twenty thousand such as you.
   SURREY. My Lord Fitzwater, I do remember well
The very time Aumerle and you did talk. 61
   FITZ. 'Tis very true. You were in presence° then,
And you can witness with me this is true.
   SURREY. As false, by Heaven, as Heaven itself is
    true.
   FITZ. Surrey, thou liest.
   SURREY.   Dishonorable boy! 65
That lie shall lie so heavy on my sword
That it shall render vengeance and revenge
Till thou the lie-giver and that lie do lie
In earth as quiet as thy father's skull.
In proof whereof, there is my honor's pawn. 70
Engage it to the trial, if thou darest.
   FITZ. How fondly dost thou spur a forward horse!
If I dare eat, or drink, or breathe, or live,
I dare meet Surrey in a wilderness,°
And spit upon him whilst I say he lies, 75
And lies, and lies. There is my bond of faith,°
To tie thee to my strong correction.
As I intend to thrive in this new world,°
Aumerle is guilty of my true appeal.°
Besides, I heard the banished Norfolk say 80
That thou, Aumerle, didst send two of thy men
To execute the noble Duke at Calais.
   AUM. Some honest Christian trust me with a gage
That Norfolk lies. Here do I throw down this,
If he may be repealed,° to try his honor. 85
   BOLING. These differences shall all rest under gage
Till Norfolk be repealed. Repealed he shall be
And, though mine enemy, restored again
To all his lands and signories. When he's returned,
Against Aumerle we will enforce his trial. 90
   CAR. That honorable day shall ne'er be seen.
Many a time hath banished Norfolk fought
For Jesu Christ in glorious Christian field,
Streaming the ensign° of the Christian cross
Against black pagans, Turks, and Saracens; 95
And toiled° with works of war, retired himself
To Italy, and there at Venice gave
His body to that pleasant country's earth
And his pure soul unto his captain Christ,
Under whose colors he had fought so long. 100
   BOLING. Why, Bishop, is Norfolk dead?

   CAR. As surely as I live, my lord.
   BOLING. Sweet peace conduct his sweet soul to the
    bosom
Of good old Abraham!° Lords appellants,°
Your differences shall all rest under gage 105
Till we assign you to your days of trial.
    [*Enter* YORK, *attended.*]
   YORK. Great Duke of Lancaster, I come to thee
From plume-plucked° Richard, who with willing
    soul
Adopts thee heir, and his high scepter yields
To the possession of thy royal hand. 110
Ascend his throne, descending now from him,
And long live Henry, fourth of that name!
   BOLING. In God's name, I'll ascend the regal
    throne.
   CAR. Marry,° God forbid!
Worst in this royal presence may I speak,° 115
Yet best beseeming me to speak the truth.
Would God that any in this noble presence
Were enough noble to be upright judge
Of noble Richard! Then true noblesse would
Learn him forbearance from so foul a wrong. 120
What subject can give sentence on his king?
And who sits here that is not Richard's subject?
Thieves are not judged but they are by to hear,
Although apparent° guilt be seen in them.
And shall the figure of God's majesty, 125
His captain, steward, deputy elect,
Anointed, crowned, planted many years,
Be judged by subject and inferior breath,
And he himself not present? Oh, forfend° it, God,
That in a Christian climate souls refined 130
Should show so heinous, black, obscene a deed!
I speak to subjects, and a subject speaks,
Stirred up by God, thus boldly for his King.
My Lord of Hereford° here, whom you call King,
Is a foul traitor to proud Hereford's King.° 135
And if you crown him, let me prophesy,°
The blood of English shall manure the ground
And future ages groan for this foul act.
Peace shall go sleep with Turks and infidels,
And in this seat of peace tumultuous wars 140
Shall kin with kin and kind with kind° confound.

103–04. bosom ... Abraham: i.e., Paradise. The phrase is from the parable of Dives and Lazarus (Luke 16:22): "And it came to pass that the beggar died, and was carried by the angels into Abraham's bosom." 104. Lords appellants: accusing lords. 108. plume-plucked: crestfallen. 114. Marry: Mary, by the Virgin. 115. Worst ... speak: I am the worst speaker in this royal assembly. 124. apparent: open. 129. forfend: forbid. 134. Hereford: i.e., Bolingbroke. 135. proud ... King: i.e., Richard, the true King. 136. let me prophesy: Carlisle expresses the theme of the whole series of Shakespeare's history plays from *Richard II* to *Richard III*: that by wrongfully seizing the throne of England the House of Lancaster caused civil war in England for nearly a century. 141. kin ... kind: both words mean much the same, but puns on *kin* (of the same family) and *kind* (nature) are common.

55. honor's pawn: pledge of my honor. 56. Engage it: make a gage of it; i.e., accept it as a token of challenge. 57. sets: challenges. 62. in presence: in Court. See I.iii.289. 74. in a wilderness: i.e., a place where there is no escape. 76. bond of faith: pledge. 78. new world: i.e., under Bolingbroke my new King. 79. appeal: accusation. 85. repealed: called back from banishment. 94. Streaming ... ensign: flying the flag. 96. toiled: overwearied.

Disorder, horror, fear, and mutiny
Shall here inhabit, and this land be called
The field of Golgotha° and dead men's skulls.
Oh, if you raise this house against this house,   145
It will the woefulest division prove
That ever fell upon this cursèd earth.
Prevent it, resist it, let it not be so,
Lest child, child's children, cry against you " Woe "!
  NORTH. Well have you argued, sir, and, for your
    pains,   150
Of capital treason° we arrest you here.
My Lord of Westminster, be it your charge
To keep him safely till his day of trial.
May it please you, lords, to grant the commons' suit?
  BOLING. Fetch hither Richard, that in common
    view   155
He may surrender. So we shall proceed
Without suspicion.
  YORK.   I will be his conduct.   [*Exit.*]
  BOLING. Lords, you that here are under our arrest,
Procure your sureties° for your days of answer.
Little are we beholding to your love,   160
And little looked for at your helping hands.
[*Re-enter* YORK, *with* RICHARD, *and* OFFICERS *bearing*
    the regalia.]
  K. RICH. Alack, why am I sent for to a king
Before I have shook off the regal thoughts
Wherewith I reigned? I hardly yet have learned
To insinuate, flatter, bow, and bend my limbs.   165
Give sorrow leave awhile to tutor me
To this submission. Yet I well remember
The favors° of these men. Were they not mine?
Did they not sometime° cry " All hail! " to me?
So Judas did to Christ. But He in twelve   170
Found truth in all but one, I in twelve thousand,
    none.
God save the King! Will no man say amen?
Am I both priest and clerk?° Well then, amen.
God save the King! although I be not he,
And yet, amen if Heaven do think him me.   175
To do what service am I sent for hither?
  YORK. To do that office of thine own goodwill
Which tired majesty° did make thee offer,
The resignation of thy state and crown
To Henry Bolingbroke.   180
  K. RICH. Give me the crown. Here, Cousin, seize
    the crown.
Here, Cousin —
On this side my hand, and on that side yours.
Now is this golden crown like a deep well
That owes° two buckets, filling one another,   185

The emptier ever dancing in the air,
The other down, unseen and full of water.
That bucket down and full of tears am I,
Drinking my griefs whilst you mount up on high.
  BOLING. I thought you had been willing to resign.
  K. RICH. My crown I am, but still my griefs are
    mine.   191
You may my glories and my state depose.
But not my griefs. Still am I king of those.
  BOLING. Part of your cares you give me with your
    crown.
  K. RICH. Your cares° set up do not pluck my cares
    down.   195
My care is loss of care, by old care done.
Your care is gain of care, by new care won.
The cares I give I have, though given away.
They tend° the crown, yet still with me they stay.
  BOLING. Are you contented to resign the crown?
  K. RICH. Aye, no — no, aye, for I° must nothing
    be,   201
Therefore no no, for I resign to thee.
Now mark me how I will undo myself.
I give this heavy weight from off my head
And this unwieldy scepter from my hand,   205
The pride of kingly sway from out my heart.
With mine own tears I wash away my balm,
With mine own hands I give away my crown,
With mine own tongue deny my sacred state,
With mine own breath release all duty's rites.°   210
All pomp and majesty I do forswear,
My manors, rents, revénues I forgo,
My acts, decrees, and statutes I deny.
God pardon all oaths that are broke to me!
God keep all vows unbroke that swear to thee!   215
Make me, that nothing have, with nothing grieved,
And thou with all pleased, that hast all achieved!
Long mayst thou live in Richard's seat to sit,
And soon lie Richard in an earthy pit!
God save King Harry, unkinged Richard says,   220
And send him many years of sunshine days!
What more remains?
  NORTH. No more, but that you read
These accusations and these grievous crimes
Committed by your person and your followers
Against the state° and profit of this land,   225
That, by confessing them, the souls of men
May deem that you are worthily deposed.
  K. RICH. Must I do so? And must I ravel out°
My weaved-up folly? Gentle Northumberland,
If thy offenses were upon recórd,   230
Would it not shame thee in so fair a troop
To read a lecture of them? If thou wouldst,

---

144. **Golgotha:** the "Place of a Skull," the scene of the Crucifixion. 151. **capital treason:** treason which carries a death penalty. 159. **sureties:** bail. 168. **favors:** faces. 169. **sometime:**
once. 173. **priest . . . clerk:** In services in the Church of England the priest read out the prayers and the clerk pronounced the
"Amen" at the end. 178. **tired majesty:** weariness of ruling.
185. **owes: owns.**

195–98. **cares . . . cares:** Richard plays on the various meanings
of *care* — responsibility, duty, sorrow, anxiety. 199. **tend:** attend, wait on. 201. **Aye . . . I:** Puns on *aye* and *I* are common,
and more marked in the early texts, where both are spelt "I."
210. **duty's rites:** signs of respect to a King. 225. **state:** settled
order. 228. **ravel out:** unweave.

There shouldst thou find one heinous article,
Containing the deposing of a king
And cracking the strong warrant of an oath,   235
Marked with a blot, damned in the book of Heaven.
Nay, all of you that stand and look upon
Whilst that my wretchedness doth bait° myself,
Though some of you with Pilate wash your hands,°
Showing an outward pity, yet you Pilates   240
Have here delivered me to my sour cross,
And water cannot wash away your sin.

NORTH. My lord, dispatch.° Read o'er these articles.

K. RICH. Mine eyes are full of tears, I cannot see.
And yet salt water blinds them not so much   245
But they can see a sort° of traitors here.
Nay, if I turn mine eyes upon myself,
I find myself a traitor with the rest;
For I have given here my soul's consent
To undeck the pompous body of a king,   250
Made glory base and sovereignty a slave,
Proud majesty a subject, state a peasant.

NORTH. My lord ——

K. RICH. No lord of thine, thou haught° insulting man,
Nor no man's lord. I have no name, no title,   255
No, not that name was given me at the font,
But 'tis usurped. Alack the heavy day,
That I have worn so many winters out
And know not now what name to call myself!
Oh, that I were a mockery king of snow,   260
Standing before the sun of Bolingbroke
To melt myself away in water drops!
Good King, great King, and yet not greatly good,
An if my word be sterling° yet in England,
Let it command a mirror hither straight,   265
That it may show me what a face I have,
Since it is bankrupt of his majesty.

BOLING. Go some of you and fetch a looking-glass.
[*Exit an* ATTENDANT.]

NORTH. Read o'er this paper while° the glass doth come.

K. RICH. Fiend, thou torment'st me ere I come to Hell!   270

BOLING. Urge it no more, my Lord Northumberland.

NORTH. The commons will not then be satisfied.

K. RICH. They shall be satisfied. I'll read enough
When I do see the very book indeed
Where all my sins are writ, and that's myself.   275
[*Re-enter* ATTENDANT, *with a glass.*] Give me the glass, and therein will I read.
No deeper wrinkles yet? Hath sorrow struck
So many blows upon this face of mine
And made no deeper wounds? O flattering glass,

Like to my followers in prosperity,   280
Thou dost beguile me! Was this face the face°
That every day under his household roof
Did keep ten thousand men? Was this the face
That, like the sun, did make beholders wink?
Was this the face that faced so many follies,   285
And was at last outfaced by Bolingbroke?
A brittle glory shineth in this face —
As brittle as the glory is the face.
[*Dashes the glass against the ground.*]
For there it is, cracked in a hundred shivers.°
Mark, silent King, the moral of this sport,°   290
How soon my sorrow hath destroyed my face.

BOLING. The shadow° of your sorrow hath destroyed
The shadow of your face.

K. RICH.   Say that again.
The shadow of my sorrow! Ha! Let's see.
'Tis very true, my grief lies all within.   295
And these external manners of laments
Are merely shadows to the unseen grief
That swells with silence in the tortured soul.
There lies the substance, and I thank thee, King,
For thy great bounty, that not only givest   300
Me cause to wail, but teachest me the way
How to lament the cause. I'll beg one boon,°
And then be gone and trouble you no more.
Shall I obtain it?

BOLING.   Name it, fair Cousin.

K. RICH. "Fair Cousin"? I am greater than a king.   305
For when I was a king, my flatterers
Were then but subjects. Being now a subject,
I have a King here to my flatterer.
Being so great, I have no need to beg.

BOLING. Yet ask.   310

K. RICH. And shall I have?

BOLING. You shall.

K. RICH. Then give me leave to go.

BOLING. Whither?

K. RICH. Whither you will, so I were from your sights.   315

BOLING. Go, some of you convey° him to the Tower.

K. RICH. Oh, good! Convey? Conveyers are you all
That rise thus nimbly by a true king's fall.
[*Exeunt* KING RICHARD, *some* LORDS, *and a* GUARD.]

BOLING. On Wednesday next we solemnly set down
Our coronation. Lords, prepare yourselves.   320
[*Exeunt all except the* BISHOP OF CARLISLE,
the ABBOT OF WESTMINSTER, *and* AUMERLE.]

---

238. bait: worry.   239. with ... hands: See Matthew 27:24–25. 243. dispatch: make haste.   246. sort: gang.   254. haught: haughty.   264. sterling: current.   269. while: until.

281. Was ... face: imitated from the famous line in Marlowe's *Dr. Faustus*, "Was this the face that launched a thousand ships?" 289. shivers: splinters.   290. moral ... sport: inner meaning of this byplay.   292. shadow: reflection.   302. boon: favor. 316. convey: escort; but Richard (l. 317) puns on the slang meaning of *convey* — steal.

ABBOT. A woeful pageant have we here beheld.
CAR. The woe's to come. The children yet unborn
Shall feel this day as sharp to them as thorn.
AUM. You holy clergymen, is there no plot
To rid the realm of this pernicious blot?   325
ABBOT. My lord,
Before I freely speak my mind herein,
You shall not only take the sacrament
To bury mine intents,° but also to effect
Whatever I shall happen to devise.   330
I see your brows are full of discontent,
Your hearts of sorrow and your eyes of tears.
Come home with me to supper, and I'll lay
A plot shall show us all a merry day.   [*Exeunt.*]

Act V

SCENE I. *London. A street leading to the Tower.*

[*Enter* QUEEN *and* LADIES.]

QUEEN. This way the King will come. This is the
    way
To Julius Caesar's ill-erected tower,°
To whose flint bosom my condemnèd lord
Is doomed a prisoner by proud Bolingbroke.
Here let us rest, if this rebellious earth   5
Have any resting for her true king's queen.

[*Enter* RICHARD *and* GUARD.]

But soft, but see, or rather do not see,
My fair rose° wither. Yet look up, behold,
That you in pity may dissolve to dew
And wash him fresh again with truelove tears.   10
Ah, thou the model where old Troy did stand,°
Thou map of honor, thou King Richard's tomb,
And not King Richard, thou most beauteous inn,
Why should hard-favored grief be lodged in thee
When triumph is become an alehouse° guest?   15
K. RICH. Join not with grief, fair woman, do not so,
To make my end too sudden. Learn, good soul,
To think our former state a happy dream,
From which awaked, the truth of what we are
Shows us but this. I am sworn brother,° sweet,   20
To grim Necessity, and he and I

329. bury . . . intents: conceal my intentions.
    Act V, Sc. i: 2. Julius . . . tower: See *Rich III*, III.i.68,n;
Gen. Intro. p. 16a; and Pl. 3a. ill-erected: erected for evil.
8. rose: addressed to Richard. The rose is often used as an emblem of beauty. See *Haml*, III.i.160 and *I Hen IV*, I.iii.175.
11. model . . . stand: a ruin, like Troy after the sack. model: pattern. 13–15. beauteous . . . alehouse: In this extravagant parallel she means that Richard is like an expensive hotel that entertains Sorrow, while Bolingbroke, though a mere beer parlor, entertains Triumph. 20. sworn brother: Knights about to undertake some perilous enterprise often swore to share everything alike.

Will keep a league till death. Hie thee to France
And cloister° thee in some religious house.
Our holy lives must win a new world's° crown,
Which our profane° hours here have stricken down.
QUEEN. What, is my Richard both in shape and
    mind
Transformed and weakened? Hath Bolingbroke de-
    posed
Thine intellect? Hath he been in thy heart?
The lion dying thrusteth forth his paw
And wounds the earth, if nothing else, with rage
To be o'erpowered. And wilt thou, pupil-like,   31
Take thy correction mildly, kiss the rod,
And fawn on rage with base humility,
Which art a lion and a king of beasts?
K. RICH. A king of beasts, indeed. If aught but
    beasts,   35
I had been still a happy king of men.
Good sometime Queen, prepare thee hence for
    France.
Think I am dead, and that even here thou takest,
As from my deathbed, thy last living leave.
In winter's tedious nights sit by the fire   40
With good old folks, and let them tell thee tales
Of woeful ages long ago betid.°
And ere thou bid good night, to quit their griefs,°
Tell thou the lamentable tale of me,
And send the hearers weeping to their beds.   45
For why,° the senseless brands° will sympathize°
The heavy accent of thy moving tongue,
And in compassion weep the fire out;
And some will mourn in ashes, some coal-black,
For the deposing of a rightful king.   50

[*Enter* NORTHUMBERLAND *and others.*]

NORTH. My lord, the mind of Bolingbroke is
    changed.
You must to Pomfret,° not unto the Tower.
And, madam, there is order ta'en for you.
With all swift speed you must away to France.
K. RICH. Northumberland, thou ladder where-
    withal   55
The mounting Bolingbroke ascends my throne,
The time shall not be many hours of age
More than it is, ere foul sin gathering head°
Shall break into corruption. Thou shalt think,
Though he divide the realm and give thee half,   60
It is too little, helping him to all.
And he shall think that thou, which know'st the way
To plant unrightful kings, wilt know again,
Being ne'er so little urged,° another way
To pluck him headlong from the usurped throne.

23. cloister: become a nun. 24. new world's: i.e., heavenly.
25. profane: worldly. 42. betid: befallen. 43. to . . . griefs: to recompense them for their sad tales. 46. For why: because. senseless brands: logs that have no feeling. sympathize: feel for. 52. Pomfret: Pontefract Castle, near York. See *Rich III*, III.iii.9–14. 58. gathering head: i.e., like a boil about to burst. 64. urged: encouraged.

The love of wicked men converts° to fear,   66
That fear to hate, and hate turns one or both
To worthy danger and deservèd death.
    NORTH. My guilt be on my head, and there an end.
Take leave and part, for you must part forthwith.
    K. RICH. <u>Doubly divorced! Bad men, you violate</u>
<u>A twofold marriage — 'twixt my crown and me,</u>
<u>And then betwixt me and my married wife.</u>
Let me unkiss the oath 'twixt thee and me.°
And yet not so, for with a kiss 'twas made.   75
Part us, Northumberland, I toward the north,
Where shivering cold and sickness pines the clime,
My wife to France, from whence, set forth in pomp,
She came adornèd hither like sweet May,
Sent back like Hallowmas° or short'st of day.   80
    QUEEN. And must we be divided? Must we part?
    K. RICH. Aye, hand from hand, my love, and heart
      from heart.
    QUEEN. Banish us both and send the King with
      me.   83
    NORTH. That were some love but little policy.°
    QUEEN. Then whither he goes, thither let me go.
    K. RICH. So two, together weeping, make one
      woe.
Weep thou for me in France, I for thee here.
Better far off than near, be ne'er the near.°
Go, count thy way with sighs, I mine with groans.
    QUEEN. So longest way shall have the longest
      moans.   90
    K. RICH. Twice for one step I'll groan, the way
      being short,
And piece the way out with a heavy heart.
Come, come, in wooing sorrow let's be brief,
Since, wedding it, there is such length in grief.
One kiss shall stop our mouths, and dumbly part.
Thus give I mine, and thus take I thy heart.   96
    QUEEN. Give me mine own again. 'Twere no good
      part
To take on me to keep and kill thy heart.
So, now I have mine own again, be gone,
That I may strive to kill it with a groan.   100
    K. RICH. We make woe wanton° with this fond
      delay.
Once more, adieu. The rest let sorrow say.
                         [Exeunt.]

      SCENE II. *The* DUKE OF YORK'S *palace.*
    [*Enter* YORK *and his* DUCHESS.]
    DUCH. My lord, you told me you would tell the
      rest,

[handwritten margin notes: CAPABLE OF ACTION WITH STRONG HAND OF HIS BOSS BOLINGBROKE — EFFICIENT WITH PROPERLY DIRECTED]

When weeping made you break the story off
Of our two cousins coming into London.
    YORK. Where did I leave?
    DUCH.   At that sad stop, my lord,
Where rude misgoverned° hands from windows'
    tops   5
Threw dust and rubbish on King Richard's head.
    YORK. Then, as I said, the Duke, great Boling-
      broke,
Mounted upon a hot and fiery steed
Which his aspiring° rider seemed to know,
With slow but stately pace kept on his course   10
Whilst all tongues cried "God save thee, Boling-
    broke!"
You would have thought the very windows spake,
So many greedy looks of young and old
Through casements darted their desiring eyes
Upon his visage, and that all the walls   15
With painted imagery had said at once°
"Jesu preserve thee! Welcome, Bolingbroke!"
Whilst he, from the one side to the other turning,
Bareheaded, lower than his proud steed's neck,
Bespake them thus; "I thank you, countrymen."
And thus still doing, thus he passed along.   21
    DUCH. Alack, poor Richard! Where rode he the
      whilst?
    YORK. As in a theater the eyes of men
After a well-graced actor leaves the stage
Are idly bent on him that enters next,   25
Thinking his prattle to be tedious,
Even so, or with much more contempt, men's eyes
Did scowl on gentle Richard. No man cried "God
    save him!"
No joyful tongue gave him his welcome home.
But dust was thrown upon his sacred head,   30
Which with such gentle sorrow he shook off,
His face still combating with tears and smiles,
The badges° of his grief and patience,
That had not God, for some strong purpose,
    steeled
The hearts of men, they must perforce have melted,
And barbarism itself° have pitied him.   36
But Heaven hath a hand in these events,
To whose high will we bound our calm contents.°
To Bolingbroke are we sworn subjects now,
Whose state and honor I for aye allow.   40
    DUCH. Here comes my son Aumerle.
    YORK.   Aumerle that was,
But that is lost for being Richard's friend,
And, madam, you must call him Rutland now.
I am in Parliament pledge for his truth
And lasting fealty to the new-made King.   45

---

66. converts: changes. 74. unkiss . . . me: unmake our marriage vow. 80. Hallowmas: All Saints' Day, November 1. 84. policy: political wisdom. 88. Better . . . near: better be widely separated, if we cannot be nearer to each other. 101. wanton: frivolous. See III.iii.164.

Sc. ii: 5. misgoverned: ill-behaved. 9. aspiring: ambitious. 15–16. all . . . once: as if the walls had been covered with painted figures that cried out. 33. badges: tokens. 36. barbarism itself: even barbarians. 38. bound . . . contents: we force ourselves to be calmly contented.

[*Enter* AUMERLE.]

DUCH. Welcome, my son. Who are the violets° now

That strew the green lap of the new-come spring?

AUM. Madam, I know not, nor I greatly care not.

God knows I had as lief be none as one.

YORK. Well, bear you well in this new spring of time,   50

Lest you be cropped before you come to prime.

What news from Oxford? Hold those justs° and tri-umphs?

AUM. For aught I know, my lord, they do.

YORK. You will be there, I know.

AUM. If God prevent not, I purpose so.   55

YORK. What seal is that that hangs without thy bosom?

Yea, look'st thou pale? Let me see the writing.

AUM. My lord, 'tis nothing.

YORK.   No matter, then, who see it.

I will be satisfied. Let me see the writing.

AUM. I do beseech your Grace to pardon me.   60

It is a matter of small consequence,

Which for some reasons I would not have seen.

YORK. Which for some reasons, sir, I mean to see.

I fear, I fear ——

DUCH.   What should you fear?

'Tis nothing but some bond that he is entered into°

For gay apparel 'gainst° the triumph day.   66

YORK. Bound to himself! What doth he with a bond

That he is bound to? Wife, thou art a fool.

Boy, let me see the writing.

AUM. I do beseech you pardon me, I may not show it.   70

YORK. I will be satisfied. Let me see it, I say.

[*He plucks it out of his bosom and reads it.*]

Treason! Foul treason! Villain! Traitor! Slave!

DUCH. What is the matter, my lord?

YORK. Ho! Who is within there?

[*Enter a* SERVANT.] Saddle my horse.

God for His mercy, what treachery is here!   75

DUCH. Why, what is it, my lord?

YORK. Give me my boots, I say, saddle my horse.

[*Exit* SERVANT.]

Now, by mine honor, by my life, by my troth,

I will appeach° the villain.

DUCH.   What is the matter?

YORK. Peace, foolish woman.   80

DUCH. I will not peace. What is the matter, Au-merle?

AUM. Good Mother, be content. It is no more

Than my poor life must answer.

DUCH.   Thy life answer!

YORK. Bring me my boots. I will unto the King.

[*Re-enter* SERVANT *with boots.*]

DUCH. Strike him, Aumerle. Poor boy, thou art amazed.°   85

Hence, villain! Never more come in my sight.

YORK. Give me my boots, I say.

DUCH. Why, York, what wilt thou do?

Wilt thou not hide the trespass of thine own?°

Have we more sons? Or are we like to have?   90

Is not my teeming date° drunk up with time?

And wilt thou pluck my fair son from mine age

And rob me of a happy mother's name?

Is he not like thee? Is he not thine own?

YORK. Thou fond mad woman,   95

Wilt thou conceal this dark conspiracy?

A dozen of them here have ta'en the sacrament,

And interchangeably set down their hands,°

To kill the King at Oxford.

DUCH.   He shall be none.

We'll keep him here. Then what is that to him?

YORK. Away, fond woman! Were he twenty times my son,   101

I would appeach him.

DUCH.   Hadst thou groaned for him

As I have done, thou wouldst be more pitiful.°

But now I know thy mind. Thou dost suspect

That I have been disloyal to thy bed,   105

And that he is a bastard, not thy son.

Sweet York, sweet husband, be not of that mind.

He is as like thee as a man may be,

Not like to me, or any of my kin,

And yet I love him.

YORK. Make way, unruly woman! [*Exit.*] 110

DUCH. After, Aumerle! Mount thee upon his horse,

Spur post,° and get before him to the King

And beg thy pardon ere he do accuse thee.

I'll not be long behind. Though I be old,

I doubt not but to ride as fast as York.   115

And never will I rise up from the ground

Till Bolingbroke have pardoned thee. Away, be gone!   [*Exeunt.*]

SCENE III. *Windsor Castle.*

[*Enter* BOLINGBROKE, HENRY PERCY, *and other* LORDS.]

BOLING. Can no man tell me of my unthrifty son?°

'Tis full three months since I did see him last.

If any plague hang over us, 'tis he.

I would to God, my lords, he might be found.

Inquire at London, 'mongst the taverns there,   5

---

46. violets: i.e., Court favorites.   **52.** justs: tournaments.
65. entered into: i.e., that he has signed to borrow money.
66. 'gainst: against, in anticipation of.   **79.** appeach: accuse.

85. amazed: bewildered.   **89.** trespass . . . own: sin committed by your own son.   **91.** teeming date: period of childbearing.
98. interchangeably . . . hands: i.e., each party of the conspiracy holds a document signed by all the others. See App. 6 and Pl. 11a.
103. pitiful: full of pity.   **112.** Spur post: ride fast. See App. 17.
    Sc. iii: **1.** unthrifty son: prodigal son; i.e., Prince Henry, after-ward Henry V.

For there, they say, he daily doth frequent
With unrestrainèd loose companions,°
Even such, they say, as stand in narrow lanes
And beat our watch° and rob our passengers.°
Which he, young wanton and effeminate° boy,   10
Takes on the° point of honor to support
So dissolute a crew.
   H. PERCY. My lord, some two days since I saw the
     Prince
And told him of those triumphs held at Oxford.
   BOLING. And what said the gallant?   15
   H. PERCY. His answer was, he would unto the
     stews,°
And from the common'st creature pluck a glove
And wear it as a favor, and with that
He would unhorse the lustiest challenger.
   BOLING. As dissolute as desperate, yet through
     both   20
I see some sparks of better hope, which elder years
May happily bring forth. But who comes here?
            [Enter AUMERLE.]
   AUM. Where is the King?
   BOLING. What means our cousin, that he stares
     and looks
So wildly?   25
   AUM. God save your Grace! I do beseech your
     Majesty
To have some conference with your Grace alone.
   BOLING. Withdraw yourselves, and leave us here
     alone.   [Exeunt PERCY and LORDS.]
What is the matter with our cousin now?
   AUM. Forever may my knees grow to the earth,
My tongue cleave to my roof within my mouth,   31
Unless a pardon ere I rise or speak.
   BOLING. Intended or committed was this fault?
If on the first,° how heinous e'er it be,
To win thy after-love I pardon thee.   35
   AUM. Then give me leave that I may turn the key,
That no man enter till my tale be done.
   BOLING. Have thy desire.
   YORK. [Within.°] My liege, beware, look to thy-
     self.
Thou hast a traitor in thy presence there.   40
   BOLING. Villain, I'll make thee safe.   [Drawing.]
   AUM. Stay thy revengeful hand. Thou hast no
     cause to fear.
   YORK. [Within.] Open the door, secure,° fool-
     hardy King.
Shall I for love speak treason° to thy face?
Open the door, or I will break it open.   45
           [Enter YORK.]
   BOLING. What is the matter, Uncle? Speak.
Recover breath, tell us how near is danger,

That we may arm us to encounter it.
   YORK. Peruse this writing here and thou shalt
     know
The treason that my haste forbids me show.   50
   AUM. Remember, as thou read'st, thy promise
     passed.
I do repent me. Read not my name there,
My heart is not confederate° with my hand.
   YORK. It was, villain, ere thy hand did set it down.
I tore it from the traitor's bosom, King.   55
Fear, and not love, begets his penitence.
Forget to pity him, lest thy pity prove
A serpent that will sting thee to the heart.
   BOLING. Oh, heinous, strong, and bold conspiracy!
Oh, loyal father of a treacherous son!   60
Thou sheer, immaculate, and silver fountain
From whence this stream through muddy passages
Hath held his current and defiled himself!
Thy overflow of good converts to bad,
And thy abundant goodness shall excuse   65
This deadly blot in thy digressing° son.
   YORK. So shall my virtue be his vice's bawd,
And he shall spend mine honor with his shame
As thriftless sons their scraping fathers' gold.
Mine honor lives when his dishonor dies,   70
Or my shamed life in his dishonor lies.
Thou kill'st me in his life. Giving him breath,
The traitor lives, the true man's put to death.
   DUCH. [Within.] What ho, my liege! For God's
     sake, let me in.
   BOLING. What shrill-voiced suppliant makes this
     eager cry?   75
   DUCH. A woman, and thy aunt, great King — 'tis
     I.
Speak with me, pity me, open the door.
A beggar begs that never begged before.
   BOLING. Our scene is altered from a serious thing,
And now changed to " The Beggar and the King."°
My dangerous cousin, let your mother in.   81
I know she is come to pray for your foul sin.
   YORK. If thou do pardon, whosoever pray,
More sins for this forgiveness prosper may.
This festered joint cut off, the rest rest sound,   85
This let alone will all the rest confound.
         [Enter DUCHESS OF YORK.]
   DUCH. O King, believe not this hardhearted man!
Love loving not itself none other can.°
   YORK. Thou frantic woman, what dost thou
     make° here?
Shall thy old dugs once more a traitor rear?   90
   DUCH. Sweet York, be patient. Hear me, gentle
     liege.   [Kneels.]

---

7. loose companions: low company. 9. watch: See Gen. Intro.
p. 18a. passengers: passers-by. 10. effeminate: self-indulgent.
11. Takes on the: regards it as a. 16. stews: brothels. 34. If
... first: i.e., intended. 39. s.d., within: off stage. 43. secure:
careless. 44. speak treason: i.e., by calling you a fool.

53. confederate: fellow conspirator with. 66. digressing: erring.
79-80. Our ... King: the tragedy is now turning into comedy
and should be called The Beggar and the King. 88. Love ...
can: a man who cannot love his own son cannot love anyone
else. 89. make: do.

BOLING. Rise up, good Aunt.

DUCH.   Not yet, I thee beseech.
Forever will I walk upon my knees,
And never see day that the happy sees
Till thou give joy — until thou bid me joy   95
By pardoning Rutland, my transgressing boy.

AUM. Unto my mother's prayers I bend my knee.
                   [*Kneels.*]

YORK. Against them both my true joints bended
be.   [*Kneels.*]
Ill mayst thou thrive if thou grant any grace!   99

DUCH. Pleads he in earnest? Look upon his face.
His eyes do drop no tears, his prayers are in jest,
His words come from his mouth, ours from our
    breast.
He prays but faintly and would be denied,
We pray with heart and soul and all beside.
His weary joints would gladly rise, I know,   105
Our knees shall kneel till to the ground they grow.
His prayers are full of false hypocrisy,
Ours of true zeal and deep integrity.
Our prayers do outpray his, then let them have
That mercy which true prayer ought to have.   110

BOLING. Good Aunt, stand up.

DUCH.   Nay, do not say " Stand up,"
Say " Pardon " first, and afterward " Stand up."
An if I were thy nurse, thy tongue to teach,
" Pardon " should be the first word of thy speech.
I never longed to hear a word till now.   115
Say " Pardon," King, let pity teach thee how.
The word is short, but not so short as sweet;
No word like " pardon " for kings' mouths so meet.

YORK. Speak it in French, king, say, " *Pardonne-
moi.*"°

DUCH. Dost thou teach pardon pardon to destroy?
Ah, my sour husband, my hardhearted lord,   121
That set'st the word itself against the word!
Speak " pardon " as 'tis current in our land,°
The chopping° French we do not understand.
Thine eye begins to speak, set thy tongue there.   125
Or in thy piteous heart plant thou thine ear,
That hearing how our plaints and prayers do pierce,
Pity may move thee " pardon " to rehearse.°

BOLING. Good Aunt, stand up.

DUCH.   I do not sue to stand.
Pardon is all the suit I have in hand.   130

BOLING. I pardon him, as God shall pardon me.

DUCH. Oh, happy vantage° of a kneeling knee!
Yet am I sick for fear. Speak it again.
Twice saying " pardon " doth not pardon twain,
But makes one pardon strong.

BOLING.   With all my heart   135
I pardon him.

DUCH.   A god on earth thou art.

BOLING. But for our trusty brother-in-law, and the
    Abbot,
With all the rest of that consorted crew,°
Destruction straight shall dog them at the heels.
Good Uncle, help to order several powers°   140
To Oxford, or where'er these traitors are.
They shall not live within this world, I swear,
But I will have them, if I once know where.
Uncle, farewell, and Cousin too, adieu.   144
Your mother well hath prayed, and prove you true.°

DUCH. Come, my old son. I pray God make thee
new.   [*Exeunt.*]

SCENE IV. *The same.*

[*Enter* EXTON *and* SERVANT.]

EXTON. Didst thou not mark the King, what
    words he spake —
" Have I no friend will rid me of this living fear? "
Was it not so?

SERV.   These were his very words.

EXTON. " Have I no friend? " quoth he. He spake
    it twice,
And urged it twice together, did he not?   5

SERV. He did.

EXTON. And speaking it, he wistly° looked on me,
As who should say, " I would thou wert the man
That would divorce this terror from my heart,"
Meaning the King at Pomfret. Come, let's go.   10
I am the King's friend, and will rid his foe.
                  [*Exeunt.*]

SCENE V. *Pomfret Castle.*

[*Enter* KING RICHARD.] EVEN WHEN ALONE/R.
                                 IS
K. RICH. I have been studying how I may compare
                               DRAMATIC
This prison where I live unto the world.
And for because the world is populous,
And here is not a creature but myself,
I cannot do it, yet I'll hammer it out.   5
My brain I'll prove the female to my soul,
My soul the father, and these two beget
A generation of still breeding° thoughts,
And these same thoughts people this little world
In humors° like the people of this world,   10
For no thought is contented. The better sort,
As thoughts of things divine, are intermixed
With scruples,° and do set the word itself
Against the word.

---

138. consorted crew: crew of conspirators.   140. powers: forces.
145. prove . . . true: may you prove true.
    Sc. iv: 7. wistly: wistfully.
    Sc. v: 8. still breeding: ever breeding.   10. humors: varieties
of temperament. See App. 3.   13. scruples: religious doubts.

119. Pardonne-moi: excuse me; *moi* was pronounced "moy."
123. current . . . land: i.e., with the English meaning.   124. chop-
ping: changing the meaning.   128. rehearse: repeat.   132. vantage: superior position, advantage.

As thus, "Come, little ones," and then again,   15
"It is as hard to come as for a camel
To thread the postern° of a small needle's eye."
Thoughts tending to ambition, they do plot
Unlikely wonders — how these vain weak nails
May tear a passage through the flinty ribs   20
Of this hard world, my ragged° prison walls,
And, for they cannot, die in their own pride.
Thoughts tending to content flatter themselves
That they are not the first of fortune's slaves,°
Nor shall not be the last, like silly beggars   25
Who sitting in the stocks° refuge their shame,°
That many have and others must sit there.
And in this thought they find a kind of ease,
Bearing their own misfortunes on the back
Of such as have before endured the like.   30
Thus play I in one person many people,
And none contented. Sometimes am I King,
Then treasons make me wish myself a beggar,
And so I am. Then crushing penury
Persuades me I was better when a king.   35
Then am I kinged again. And by and by
Think that I am unkinged by Bolingbroke,
And straight am nothing. But whate'er I be,
Nor I nor any man that but man is
With nothing shall be pleased till he be eased   40
With being nothing. Music do I hear? [Music.]
Ha, ha! Keep time. How sour sweet music is
When time is broke and no proportion° kept!
So is it in the music of men's lives.
And here have I the daintiness of ear   45
To check time broke in a disordered string,°
But for the concord of my state and time
Had not an ear to hear my true time broke.
I wasted time, and now doth time waste me.   49
For now hath Time made me his numbering° clock.
My thoughts are minutes, and with sighs they jar°
Their watches on unto mine eyes, the outward
    watch,
Whereto my finger, like a dial's point,
Is pointing still, in cleansing them from tears.
Now, sir, the sound that tells what hour it is   55
Are clamorous groans, which strike upon my heart,
Which is the bell. So sighs and tears and groans
Show minutes, times, and hours. But my time
Runs posting on in Bolingbroke's proud joy
While I stand fooling here, his Jack-o'-the-clock.°
This music mads me, let it sound no more,   61
For though it have holp° madmen to their wits,°
In me it seems it will make wise men mad.

Yet blessing on his heart that gives it me!
For 'tis a sign of love, and love to Richard   65
Is a strange brooch° in this all-hating world.
    [Enter a GROOM OF THE STABLE.]
GROOM. Hail, royal Prince!
K. RICH.   Thanks, noble peer.°
The cheapest of us is ten groats too dear.°
What art thou? And how comest thou hither,
Where no man never comes but that sad dog   70
That brings me food to make misfortune live?
  GROOM. I was a poor groom of thy stable, King,
When thou wert king, who, traveling toward York,
With much ado at length have gotten leave
To look upon my sometimes royal master's face.   75
Oh, how it yearned° my heart when I beheld
In London streets, that coronation day,
When Bolingbroke rode on roan Barbary,
That horse that thou so often hast bestrid,
That horse that I so carefully have dressed!   80
  K. RICH. Rode he on Barbary? Tell me, gentle
    friend,
How went he under him?
  GROOM. So proudly as if he disdained the ground.
  K. RICH. So proud that Bolingbroke was on his
    back!
That jade° hath eat bread from my royal hand,   85
This hand hath made him proud with clapping
    him.
Would he not stumble? Would he not fall down,
Since pride must have a fall, and break the neck
Of that proud man that did usurp his back?
Forgiveness, horse! Why do I rail on thee,   90
Since thou, created to be awed by man,
Wast born to bear? I was not made a horse,
And yet I bear a burden like an ass,
Spurred, galled, and tired by jauncing° Bolingbroke.
    [Enter KEEPER, with a dish.]
  KEEP. Fellow, give place. Here is no longer stay.
  K. RICH. If thou love me, 'tis time thou wert away.
  GROOM. What my tongue dares not, that my heart
    shall say.   [Exit.]
  KEEP. My lord, will't please you to fall to?
  K. RICH. Taste of it first, as thou art wont to do.   99
  KEEP. My lord, I dare not. Sir Pierce of Exton,
who lately came from the King, commands the contrary.
  K. RICH. The Devil take Henry of Lancaster and
    thee!
Patience is stale, and I am weary of it.
    [Beats the KEEPER.]
  KEEP. Help, help, help!   105

---

17. postern: small door. 21. ragged: rough. 24. slaves: i.e.,
victims. 26. stocks: a form of punishment for minor offenses,
the offender having his legs padlocked in the holes of a board.
refuge . . . shame: excuse their disgrace. 43. proportion: harmony. 46. check . . . string: trouble about music played out of
tune. 50. numbering: telling the time. 51. jar: tick. 60. Jack-
o'-the-clock: See Rich III, IV.ii.117. 62. holp: helped. madmen . . . wits: The Greeks used music as a remedy for certain
kinds of madness.

66. brooch: ornament; i.e., kindness. 67. noble peer: Richard
replies ironically to "royal Prince" by calling the groom a noble
peer (lit., equal). 68. ten . . . dear: a royal or rose noble was a
gold coin of Edward II worth 10s; the noble was worth 6s 8d —
less by ten groats (4d). 76. yearned: grieved. 85. jade: See
III.iii.179. 94. jauncing: stirring up his horse to restless prancing.

[*Enter* EXTON *and* SERVANTS, *armed.*]
K. RICH. How now! What means death in this
    rude assault?
Villain, thy own hand yields thy death's instrument.
    [*Snatching an ax from a* SERVANT *and killing him.*]
Go thou, and fill another room in Hell.
    [*He kills another. Then* EXTON *strikes him down.*]
That hand shall burn in never-quenching fire
That staggers° thus my person. Exton, thy fierce
    hand   110
Hath with the King's blood stained the King's own
    land.   *STILL POETIC*
Mount, mount, my soul! Thy seat is up on high,   *TO*
Whilst my gross flesh sinks downward, here to die.*END*
                                            [*Dies.*]
    EXTON. As full of valor as of royal blood.
Both have I spilled — oh, would the deed were
    good!   *ANTICIPATES BOLING'S ANGER*   115
For now the Devil, that told me I did well,
Says that this deed is chronicled in Hell.
This dead King to the living King I'll bear.
Take hence the rest, and give them burial here.
                                        [*Exeunt.*]

SCENE VI. *Windsor Castle.*

[*Flourish. Enter* BOLINGBROKE, YORK, *with other*
    LORDS, *and* ATTENDANTS.]
    BOLING. Kind Uncle York, the latest news we hear
Is that the rebels have consumed with fire
Our town of Cicester° in Gloucestershire,
But whether they be ta'en or slain we hear not.
[*Enter* NORTHUMBERLAND.] Welcome, my lord.
    What is the news?   5
    NORTH. First, to thy sacred state wish I all happi-
        ness.
The next news is, I have to London sent
The heads of Oxford, Salisbury, Blunt, and Kent.
The manner of their taking may appear
At large discoursèd in this paper here.   10
    BOLING. We thank thee, gentle Percy, for thy
        pains,
And to thy worth will add right worthy gains.

110. staggers: makes stagger.
    Sc. vi: 3. Cicester: local pronunciation of Cirencester, an an-
cient town in Gloucestershire.

[*Enter* FITZWATER.]
    FITZ. My lord, I have from Oxford sent to London
The heads of Brocas and Sir Bennet Seely,
Two of the dangerous consorted traitors   15
That sought at Oxford thy dire overthrow.
    BOLING. Thy pains, Fitzwater, shall not be forgot,
Right noble is thy merit, well I wot.
[*Enter* HENRY PERCY, *and the* BISHOP OF CARLISLE.]
    H. PERCY. The grand conspirator, Abbot of West-
        minster,
With clog° of conscience and sour melancholy   20
Hath yielded up his body to the grave.
But here is Carlisle living, to abide
Thy kingly doom and sentence of his pride. *CARLISLE*
    BOLING. Carlisle, this is your doom. *IS SPARED*
Choose out some secret place, some reverend room,°
More than thou hast, and with it joy° thy life.   26
So as thou livest in peace, die free from strife.
For though mine enemy thou hast ever been,
High sparks of honor in thee have I seen.
    [*Enter* EXTON, *with persons bearing a coffin.*]
    EXTON. Great King, within this coffin I present
Thy buried fear. Herein all breathless lies   31
The mightiest of thy greatest enemies,
Richard of Bordeaux, by me hither brought.
    BOLING. Exton, I thank thee not, for thou hast
        wrought
A deed of slander with thy fatal hand   35
Upon my head and all this famous land.
    EXTON. From your own mouth, my lord, did I this
        deed.
    BOLING. They love not poison that do poison need,
Nor do I thee. Though I did wish him dead,
I hate the murderer, love him murderèd.   40
The guilt of conscience take thou for thy labor,
But neither my good word nor princely favor.
With Cain go wander thorough° shades of night,
And never show thy head by day nor light.
Lords, I protest, my soul is full of woe   45
That blood should sprinkle me to make me grow.
Come, mourn with me for that I do lament,
And put on sullen black incontinent.°
I'll make a voyage to the Holy Land
To wash this blood off from my guilty hand.   50
March sadly after, grace my mournings here
In weeping after this untimely bier.   [*Exeunt.*]

20. clog: weight.   25. reverend room: place respected.   26. joy
enjoy.   43. thorough: through.   48. incontinent: forthwith.

THE TRAGEDY OF ROMEO AND JULIET

Introduction

The Tragedy of Romeo and Juliet was probably written in 1594 or 1595. There is no precise evidence of date and nothing in the play which can be identified as a topical allusion except that the Nurse when trying to establish the time of Juliet's weaning says: " 'Tis since the earthquake now eleven years" (I.iii.23). Earthquakes are so rare in England as to be notable, and there was an earthquake, well remembered, on April 6, 1580; but it would be rash to assume that the play was written in 1591; the reminiscences of this scatter-brained old woman are hardly good enough evidence for anything. The style, however, is unmistakably early, and the play was written when Shakespeare was still an admirer and an imitator of Marlowe. References to *Romeo and Juliet* begin early, the first occurring in 1595.

The story of Romeo and Juliet was well known, and had been told in Italian, French, and English; but the play was based on an English poem by Arthur Brooke called *The Tragical History of Romeus and Juliet,* printed in 1562. Brooke stated in his preface, " I saw the same argument lately set forth on stage with more commendation than I can look for," and it is probable that there were other stage versions between 1562 and 1595.

The story as told by Brooke ran to more than three thousand lines, but is much simpler than in Shakespeare's play. It begins by describing the feud between the Capilets and Montagues, and may be summarized as follows:

Romeus is a beautiful youth passionately in love with a lady who gives him no encouragement. Being reduced to utter misery, he is advised by one of his trustiest friends to choose another love. At Christmas time, Romeus and five friends go masked to the Capilets' banquet. He falls in love at first sight with Juliet, and she with him, and they declare their love. They then learn each other's names. Juliet is greatly disturbed, but resolves that she will serve him if he will make her his lawful wedded wife:

> For so perchance this new
> alliance may procure
> Unto our houses such a peace
> as ever shall endure.

Romeus constantly passes by Juliet's window, and at last on a moonlit night she leans out of the window and sees him. She promises to follow him if he will marry her. Romeus goes at once to Friar Lawrence, who is persuaded to marry them. Juliet sends her nurse to Romeus; the meeting is arranged and the lovers are married. Romeus gives the Nurse a ladder of cord and when night is come he climbs up to Juliet's bedroom. For the next month or two Romeus continues to visit her by night. On Easter Monday, Tybalt, Juliet's cousin, leads out a party to fight with the Montagues. Romeus tries to stop the fight, but is insulted by Tybalt. They fight and Tybalt is killed. The Capilets denounce Romeus, and the Prince condemns him to exile. Juliet is overwhelmed by distress, but the Nurse offers to go to Romeus, who is hiding in the Friar's cell. Meantime the Friar has learned of the sentence of banishment. Romeus becomes frantic with grief, but the Friar restores him to reason, and advises him to visit his lady. He goes, and they spend the night together. They part at dawn, and Romeus, having promised to keep her informed of his fortunes through the Friar, sets out for Mantua.

Juliet pines in his absence. Her mother perceives the change, and tells old Capilet that Juliet is pining because most of her friends are married, and she needs a husband. Suitors are encouraged and especially the County Paris. Juliet's mother commends the young man, but Juliet will have none of him. Lady Capilet tells her husband, who sends for Juliet. He threatens to cast her out if she disobeys. Juliet goes again to Friar Lawrence and declares that she will kill herself. The Friar tells Juliet of his skill in drugs and gives her a potion which will make her appear dead, promising that when she awakes in the tomb he and Romeus will take her away. Juliet goes back and tells her mother that she is ready to obey their command to marry Paris. Old Capilet is greatly pleased. Great preparations are made for the wedding, Juliet all the while deceiving her parents and the Nurse. The night before the wedding Juliet prepares the potion and drinks it. Next morning the Nurse finds her apparently dead. The family assemble and lament her untimely death. Meantime the Friar has sent Friar John to Mantua with a letter for Romeus, but Friar John, entering a religious house to find a companion for his journey, is detained because one of the brethren has died of the plague.

Peter, Romeus's servant, sees the funeral of Juliet, and hastens to Mantua to tell his master. Romeus buys poison of an apothecary. He writes a letter to his father, telling the whole story, and by night returns to Verona. With the aid of Peter he breaks open the tomb and laments over Juliet's body. Then he takes the poison and dies by her side. The Friar, alarmed that he has received no answer to his letter, goes to the tomb and finds Romeus dead. Juliet awakes, but when she sees Romeus, refuses to leave him. The Friar and Peter, alarmed by a noise, run away. Juliet stabs herself with Romeus's dagger. The watch, seeing lights in the tomb, raise the alarm and discover the bodies. They find the Friar and the servant and arrest them. Next day they inform the Prince. Everyone hurries to the tomb and the whole story is revealed. The Capilets and Montagues are reconciled and the two bodies are buried in a stately monument.

Brooke, though his verse was usually crude and very long-winded, had some sense of character, which Shakespeare found helpful and adapted closely. Three examples from Brooke will show what Shakespeare found and what he added for himself.

1. ROMEUS TELLS THE NURSE OF HIS PLAN TO MARRY JULIET (cf. I.iii.1–62; II.iv.180–232)

"On Saturday," quoth he,
  "if Juliet come to shrift,
She shall be shrived and married;
  how like you, Nurse, this drift?"
"Now, by my troth," quoth she,
  "God's blessing have your heart,
For yet in all my life I have
  not heard of such a part.
Lord, how you young men can
  such crafty wiles devise,
If that you love the daughter well,
  to blear the mother's eyes.
An easy thing it is,
  with cloak of holiness,
To mock the silly mother that
  suspecteth nothing less.
But that it pleasèd you
  to tell me of the case,
For all my many years perhaps
  I should have found it scarce.
Now for the rest let me
  and Juliet alone;
To get her leave, some feat [1] excuse
  I will devise anon:
For that her golden locks
  by sloth have been unkempt,
Or for unwares some wanton dream
  the youthful damsel dreamt,
Or for in thoughts of love
  her idle time she spent,

[1] neat.

Or otherwise within her heart
  deservèd to be shent.
I know her mother will
  in no case say her nay,
I warrant you she shall not fail
  to come on Saturday."
And then she swears to him,
  the mother loves her well;
And how she gave her suck in youth
  she leaveth not to tell.
"A pretty babe," quoth she,
  "it was when it was young;
Lord, how it could full prettily
  have prated with its tongue!
A thousand times and more
  I laid her on my lap,
And clapped her on the buttock soft,
  and kissed where I did clap.
And gladder then was I
  of such a kiss forsooth,
Than I had been to have a kiss
  of some old lecher's mouth."
And thus of Juliet's youth
  began this prating nurse,
And of her present state to make
  a tedious long discourse.
For though he pleasure took
  in hearing of his love,
The message answer seemed him
  to be of more behoove.
But when these beldams sit
  at ease upon their tale,
The day and eke the candlelight
  before their talk shall fail,
And part they say is true,
  and part they do devise,
Yet boldly do they that of both
  when no man checks their lies.
Then he six crowns of gold
  out of his pocket drew,
And gave them her, "A slight reward,"
  quoth he, "and so, adieu."

2. OLD CAPILET'S ANGER WITH JULIET
  (cf. III.iv.126–97)

The sire, whose swelling wrath
  her tears could not assuage,
With fiery eyes and scarlet cheeks
  thus spake her in his rage,
Whilst ruthfully stood by
  the maiden's mother mild.
"Listen," quoth he, "unthankful
  and thou disobedient child.
Hast thou so soon let slip
  out of thy mind the word
That thou so oftentimes hast heard
  rehearsèd at my board.

How much the Roman youth
 of parents stood in awe,
And eke what power upon their seed
 the fathers had by law?
Whom they not only might
 pledge, alienate, and sell,
(When so they stood in need) but more,
 if children did rebel,
The parents had the power
 of life and sudden death.
What if those goodmen should again
 receive the living breath,
In how straight bonds would they
 thy stubborn body bind?
What weapons would they seek for thee?
 What torments would they find
To chasten (if they saw)
 the lewdness of thy life,
Thy great unthankfulness to me,
 and shameful sturdy strife?
Such care thy mother had,
 so dear thou wert to me,
That I with long and earnest suit
 provided have for thee
One of the greatest lords,
 that wonnes [2] about this town,
And for his many virtues' sake
 a man of great renown.
Of whom both thou and I
 unworthy are too much,
So rich ere long he shall be left,
 his father's wealth is such,
Such is the nobleness
 and honour of the race
From whence his father came. And yet
 thou playest in this case
The dainty fool and stubborn girl;
 for want of skill
Thou dost refuse thy offered weal,
 and disobey my will.
Even by His strength I swear
 that first did give me life,
And gave me in my youth the strength
 to get thee on my wife,
Unless by Wednesday next
 thou bend as I am bent,
And at our castle called Freetown
 thou freely do assent
To County Paris' suit,
 and promise to agree
To whatsoever then shall pass
 'twixt him, my wife, and me,
Not only will I give
 all that I have away
From thee to those that shall me love,
 me honor and obey,

     [2] dwells.

But also to so close
 and to so hard a jail
I shall thee wed for all thy life
 that sure thou shalt not fail
A thousand times a day
 to wish for sudden death,
And curse the day and hour when first
 thy lungs did give thee breath.
Advise thee well and say
 that thou art warnèd now,
And think not that I speak in sport,
 or mind to break my vow.
For were it not that I
 to County Paris gave
My faith, which I must keep unfalsed,
 my honor so to save,
Ere thou go hence myself
 would see thee chastened so
That thou should'st once for all be taught
 thy duty how to know,
And what revenge of old
 these angry sires did find
Against their children that rebelled
 and showed themselves unkind."
These said, the old man straight
 is gone in haste away,
Ne for his daughter's answer would
 the testy father stay.

3. JULIET'S SOLILOQUY BEFORE TAKING THE POTION
 (cf. IV.iii.14–58)

 " What do I know," quoth she,
  " if that this powder shall
Sooner or later than it should
 or else not work at all?
And then, my craft descried
 as open as the day,
The peoples' tale and laughingstock
 shall I remain for aye.
And what know I," quoth she,
  " if serpents odious,
And other beasts and worms that are
 of nature venomous,
That wonted are to lurk
 in dark caves underground,
And commonly, as I have heard,
 in dead men's tombs are found,
Shall harm me yea or nay,
 where I shall lie as dead?
Or how shall I that always have
 in so fresh air been bred
Endure the loathsome stink
 of such a heapèd store
Of carcasses not yet consumed,
 and bones that long before
Entombèd were, where I
 my sleeping place shall have

Where all my ancestors do rest,
  my kindred's common grave?
Shall not the friar and my
  Romeus, when they come,
Find me, if I awake before,
  ystifled in the tomb? "
And whilst she in these thoughts
  doth dwell somewhat too long,
The force of her imagining
  anon did wax so strong
That she surmised she saw
  out of the hollow vault,
A grisly thing to look upon,
  the carcass of Tybalt,
Right in the selfsame sort
  that she few days before
Had seen him in his blood embrewed,
  to death eke wounded sore.
And then when she again
  within herself had weighed
That quick she should be buried there,
  and by his side be laid,
All comfortless, for she
  shall living fere [3] have none
But many a rotten carcass and
  full many a naked bone,
Her dainty tender parts
  'gan shiver all for dread,
Her golden hairs did stand upright
  upon her childish head.
Then, pressèd with the fear
  that she there livèd in,
A sweat as cold as mountain ice
  pierced through her tender skin,
That with the moisture hath
  wet every part of hers.
And more besides she vainly thinks
  whilst vainly thus she fears;
A thousand bodies dead
  have compassed her about,
And lest they will dismember her
  she greatly stands in doubt.
But when she felt her strength
  began to wear away
By little and little, and in her heart
  her fear increasèd aye,
Dreading that weakness might
  or foolish cowardice
Hinder the execution of
  the purposed enterprise,
As she had frantic been,
  in haste the glass she caught,
And up she drank the mixture quite,
  withouten farther thought.
Then on her breast she crossed
  her arms long and small,

[3] companion.

And so, her senses failing her,
  into a trance did fall.

Romeo and Juliet was first published in 1597, when a quarto (Q1) appeared entitled: *An Excellent conceited Tragedie of Romeo and Iuliet. As it hath been often (with great applause) plaid publiquely, by the right Honourable the L. of Hunsdon* [4] *his Seruants.* A second quarto (Q2) was printed in 1599 with the title page: *The Most Excellent and lamentable Tragedie, of Romeo and Iuliet. Newly corrected, augmented, and amended, by the right Honourable the Lord Chamberlaine his Seruants.* There are great differences between the two quartos. Q1 is one of the pirated quartos of Shakespeare's plays, set up from a copy obtained by some underhand means, and giving a very corrupt version (see Gen. Intro. p. 66b). Q2 was set up either from Shakespeare's original manuscript or from the playhouse copy. It shows signs of revision and rewriting (see pp. 64b–65a), and in places the prompter's notes have crept in. Thus at IV.v.102, instead of *Enter Peter* Q2 reads *Enter Will Kempe* — the clown of the company.

Q1 is seven hundred lines shorter than Q2. In the early scenes it follows Q2 closely; in later scenes there are considerable differences. It is a far better production than the other pirated quartos, and was certainly used in printing Q2, as there are some striking similarities; the speeches of the Nurse in I.iii for some unexplained reason are printed in italics in both versions. At times its readings are so much better that mistakes in Q2 can be corrected by it.

A third quarto (Q3), printed in 1609, was ultimately used as copy for the first folio (F1) in 1623. There are two other quartos, one undated and the other printed in 1637. Editors usually base the text on Q2, but use readings from Q1 and F1 when thought preferable.

A comparison of Brooke's *Romeus and Juliet* with the play shows how skillfully Shakespeare wrote *Romeo and Juliet*. Brooke told the story of a love intrigue which lasted for nine months and then ended unhappily; Shakespeare compressed his play into five days' crescendo of passion and disaster. In the poem, Romeus and Juliet enjoyed their secret love for several weeks before the death of Tybalt caused Romeus to be banished; Shakespeare set the death of Tybalt and Romeo's

[4] See Gen. Intro. p. 39b.

sentence of banishment between the morning of the marriage of Romeo and Juliet and their wedding night. The pace of the play throughout is quick and exciting.

The plot is superb. Each scene leads up naturally to the next to develop a theme which is stated in the Prologue:

A pair of star-crossed lovers take their life,
    Whose misadventured piteous overthrows
Doth with their death bury their parents' strife.

Romeo and Juliet is indeed a story of ill luck. Everything at first seems hopeful until some unforeseen mischance spoils the best-laid plans and the best intentions. By chance Romeo is present at the Capulets' feast and there sees Juliet and falls in love with her. To the Friar, who stands apart from the interminable feud of the Capulets and the Montagues, the marriage seems the luckiest of accidents:

For this alliance may so happy prove,
    To turn your households' rancor to pure love.

But the same chance which caused Romeo to meet Juliet also brought the quarrelsome Tybalt to oversee their meeting, to swear to kill Romeo, and to seek him on his return from his secret wedding. Chance again causes Mercutio to take on the quarrel, and, by sheer ill luck, in trying to part the combatants, Romeo causes Mercutio to miss his parry of Tybalt's thrust. The fatal duel between Romeo and Tybalt is the inevitable sequel, and one more death is added to the score of the family feud. Even so there might have been an ultimate reconciliation but for old Capulet's well-meaning plan to console Juliet by hastening on her wedding with Paris.

The final tragedy might still have been averted, for the Friar's desperate plan to save Juliet's honor by giving her the sleeping potion has every chance of success; but again chance interferes. The letter, which was to tell Romeo to rescue his wife, miscarries by unforeseeable accident, and the Friar reaches the vault just too late. The whole play is a succession of unlucky mischances, but Shakespeare has told his tale so well that at no time do any of the accidents seem in any way strained or unnatural. The actions of Tybalt, old Capulet, Romeo, and Juliet are entirely true to life and to their own individual natures; the characterization of the play is thus as skillful as its plotting.

Character in drama is shown in various ways: by a person's action; by his words, and not less by the way in which he expresses himself; and by what others say of him. All the characters in *Romeo and Juliet* are fully drawn. Thus in creating Romeo, Shakespeare before first bringing him onto the stage shows the anxiety of his parents at his moody behavior. Then Romeo himself appears and in his talk with Benvolio reveals his excess of emotion; in his love for the inaccessible Rosaline he is moody, distracted, and unbalanced. He continues in this mood until he has seen Juliet, and then his lethargy disappears; he rises to a lyric ecstasy and the old gay Romeo returns. Marriage makes him suddenly serious; he is even ready, contrary to his nature, to return fair words to the insolent Tybalt. But with the death of Mercutio he is forced into the duel with Tybalt, and his new happiness falls into ruin. In the Friar's cell he is reduced to a misery even more distracted than before, from which suicide seems the only way of escape. He revives at the prospect of being reunited to Juliet, but when the news reaches him that she is dead, self-slaughter is the natural answer and end to the turmoil of his emotions.

The other characters are as skillfully created. Juliet begins as a demure girl who is prepared to listen respectfully to the advice of her mother. When she has fallen in love, she becomes suddenly a woman of great courage and resource, who will face even death and fantastic horror to regain her husband.

It was perhaps less difficult for Shakespeare to create the older characters, such as the Nurse or old Capulet, but even these are fully shown; they are living people and not merely caricatures of testy elders. The old father is as quick-tempered as the rest of the family, whether toward a Montague or toward a daughter who is inclined to be a chop-logic; but in his own house at ease with his guests he will have no disorder, and he can even speak a word in praise of Romeo.

The most skillful, though not the most obvious, triumph of characterization is shown in the contrast between the five young men — Romeo, Benvolio, Paris, Mercutio, and Tybalt — for these are all young men of the same age and class, and yet each is distinct and individual.

Nevertheless, *Romeo and Juliet* was written when Shakespeare was still more of a poet than a dramatist. Again and again he holds up the action for a poetic speech or an exchange of word play. At its best, as in the love duet between Romeo and Juliet (II.ii) or in Juliet's soliloquy when waiting for Romeo (III.ii.1–31), the poetry is lyrical and lovely. At its worst, as in Lady Capulet's long description of Paris as a suitable "book" for Juliet (I.iii.81–94) or in Romeo's list of the bitter-sweetnesses of love (I.i.197–201), it verges on the absurd. The excessive wit, the puns, and the double and triple meanings with which the play abounds were pleasant enough to a generation nurtured on Lyly's *Euphues* or devoted to the conceits of the sonnet, but this style of writing soon went out of fashion as poets and dramatists became more interested in human beings and their problems and less fascinated by the game of playing with words.

With Shakespeare much wit is always a sign of an early play. *Romeo and Juliet* lacks the depth of the later tragedies, partly because Shakespeare's skill had not yet matured, partly because the theme itself is pathetic rather than essentially tragic. To effect that utter purging of the emotions which comes with the greatest tragedies there is needed a maturity in the victims and a magnitude in the theme. Neither Romeo nor Juliet has that greatness which is essential in the victim of deep tragedy; they suffer for the stupidity of their parents, and their fate is pathetic and accidental rather than truly tragic. Nevertheless *Romeo and Juliet* remains Shakespeare's first great play, which must have shown to the discerning playgoer that something was happening in the English theater.

Romeo and Juliet

DRAMATIS PERSONAE

ESCALUS, *Prince of Verona*
PARIS, *a young nobleman, kinsman to the Prince*
MONTAGUE } *heads of two houses at variance with*
CAPULET } *each other*
AN OLD MAN, *of the Capulet family*
ROMEO, *son to Montague*
MERCUTIO, *kinsman to the Prince, and friend to Romeo*
BENVOLIO, *nephew to Montague, and friend to Romeo*
TYBALT, *nephew to Lady Capulet*
FRIAR LAURENCE, *a Franciscan*
FRIAR JOHN, *of the same order*
BALTHASAR, *servant to Romeo*
SAMPSON } *servants to Capulet*
GREGORY }

PETER, *servant to Juliet's nurse*
ABRAHAM, *servant to Montague*
AN APOTHECARY
THREE MUSICIANS
PAGE *to Paris; another* PAGE; *an* OFFICER

LADY MONTAGUE, *wife to Montague*
LADY CAPULET, *wife to Capulet*
JULIET, *daughter to Capulet*
NURSE *to Juliet*

CITIZENS *of Verona:* KINSFOLK *of both houses;* MASKERS, GUARDS, WATCHMEN, *and* ATTENDANTS

CHORUS

SCENE — *Verona; Mantua.*

PROLOGUE

[*Enter* CHORUS.°]
CHOR. Two households, both alike in dignity,
  In fair Verona, where we lay our scene,
From ancient grudge break to new mutiny,°
  Where civil blood makes civil hands unclean.
From forth the fatal loins of these two foes   5
  A pair of star-crossed° lovers take their life,
Whose misadventured piteous overthrows
  Do with their death bury their parents' strife.
The fearful passage of their death-marked love,
  And the continuance of their parents' rage,   10
Which, but their children's end, naught could remove,
  Is now the two hours'° traffic° of our stage;
The which if you with patient ears attend,
What here shall miss, our toil shall strive to mend.°

For an analysis of the original staging of *R & J* see Gen. Intro. p. 56a–58b.
  Prologue: Chorus. A Chorus or Prologue was seldom used by Shakespeare to introduce and explain the action of a play, but it was usual with the other dramatists. **3. mutiny:** quarrel. **6. star-crossed:** thwarted by evil stars. See App. 1. **12. two hours:** the normal time taken for a performance in the Elizabethan playhouse, where there was no scenery to change and the actors spoke rapidly. **traffic:** business. **14. What ... mend:** i.e., if you find shortcomings in our play, we will try to set them right.
  Act I, Sc. i: s.d., **swords and bucklers:** See Pl. 22i, 22j. **1. carry coals:** do dirty work, be put upon. **2. colliers:** coal-

Act I

SCENE I. *Verona. A public place.*

[*Enter* SAMPSON *and* GREGORY, *of the House of Capulet, with swords and bucklers.*°]
SAM. Gregory, on my word, we'll not carry coals.°
GRE. No, for then we should be colliers.°
SAM. I mean, an° we be in choler,° we'll draw.   5
GRE. Aye, while you live, draw your neck out o' the collar.°
SAM. I strike quickly, being moved.
GRE. But thou art not quickly moved to strike.
SAM. A dog of the house of Montague moves me.
GRE. To move is to stir, and to be valiant is to   11 stand. Therefore if thou art moved, thou runn'st away.
SAM. A dog of that house shall move me to stand. I will take the wall° of any man or maid of Montague's.   16
GRE. That shows thee a weak slave, for the weakest goes to the wall.°
SAM. 'Tis true, and therefore women, being the

dealers, notorious for their dirty tricks. **5. an:** if. **5–7. choler ... collar:** puns on "collier," "choler" (wrath), and "collar" (halter) are common. **15. take ... wall:** go on the inside of the sidewalk, where the ground was higher and less muddy, and so show superiority. **17–18. weakest ...wall:** Gregory retorts with another proverb.

weaker vessels, are ever thrust to the wall. Therefore
I will push Montague's men from the wall and thrust
his maids to the wall.   22

GRE. The quarrel is between our masters and us
their men.

SAM. 'Tis all one, I will show myself a tyrant.
When I have fought with the men, I will be cruel
with the maids. I will cut off their heads.   28

GRE. The heads of the maids?

SAM. Aye, the heads of the maids, or their maidenheads — take it in what sense thou wilt.

GRE. They must take it in sense that feel it.

SAM. Me they shall feel while I am able to stand.
And 'tis known I am a pretty piece of flesh.   35

GRE. 'Tis well thou art not fish. If thou hadst, thou
hadst been poor John.° Draw thy tool. Here comes
two of the house of Montagues.

    [*Enter* ABRAHAM *and* BALTHASAR.]

SAM. My naked weapon is out. Quarrel — I will
back thee.

GRE. How! Turn thy back and run?   41

SAM. Fear me not.

GRE. No, marry,° I fear thee!

SAM. Let us take the law of our sides. Let them
begin.   45

GRE. I will frown as I pass by, and let them take it
as they list.

SAM. Nay, as they dare. I will bite my thumb° at
them, which is a disgrace to them, if they bear it.   50

ABR. Do you bite your thumb at us, sir?

SAM. I do bite my thumb, sir.

ABR. Do you bite your thumb at us, sir?

SAM. [*Aside to* GREGORY] Is the law of our side, if I
say aye?

GRE. No.   56

SAM. No, sir, I do not bite my thumb at you, sir;
but I bite my thumb, sir.

GRE. Do you quarrel, sir?

ABR. Quarrel, sir! No, sir.   60

SAM. But if you do, sir, I am for you. I serve as
good a man as you.

ABR. No better.

SAM. Well, sir.

    [*Enter* BENVOLIO.]

GRE. [*Aside to* SAMPSON] Say "Better." Here
comes one of my master's kinsmen.   66

SAM. Yes, better, sir.

ABR. You lie.

SAM. Draw, if you be men. Gregory, remember
thy swashing° blow.   70
                                            [*They fight.*]

BEN. Part, fools! [*Beating down their weapons.*]
Put up your swords. You know not what you do.

    [*Enter* TYBALT.]

TYB. What, art thou drawn among these heartless
    hinds°?
Turn thee, Benvolio, look upon thy death.

BEN. I do but keep the peace. Put up thy sword,
Or manage it to part these men with me.   76

TYB. What, drawn, and talk of peace! I hate the
    word
As I hate Hell, all Montagues, and thee.
Have at thee, coward!   [*They fight.*]
[*Enter several of both houses, who join the fray; then
    enter* CITIZENS *and* PEACE OFFICERS, *with clubs.*]

1. OFF. Clubs, bills, and partisans°! Strike! Beat
    them down!   80
Down with the Capulets! Down with the Monta-
    gues!

[*Enter old* CAPULET *in his gown, and* LADY CAPULET.]

CAP. What noise is this? Give me my long sword,°
    ho!

LADY CAP. A crutch, a crutch! Why call you for a
    sword?

CAP. My sword, I say! Old Montague is come,
And flourishes his blade in spite of° me.   85

    [*Enter old* MONTAGUE *and* LADY MONTAGUE.]

MON. Thou villain Capulet! — Hold me not, let
    me go.

LADY MON. Thou shalt not stir one foot to seek a
    foe.

    [*Enter* PRINCE ESCALUS, *with his train.*]

PRIN. Rebellious subjects, enemies to peace,
Profaners of this neighbor-stainèd steel° —   89
Will they not hear? What ho! You men, you beasts,
That quench the fire of your pernicious rage
With purple fountains issuing from your veins,
On pain of torture, from those bloody hands
Throw your mistempered° weapons to the ground,
And hear the sentence of your movèd prince.   95
Three civil brawls, bred of an airy° word,
By thee, old Capulet and Montague,
Have thrice disturbed the quiet of our streets,
And made Verona's ancient citizens
Cast by their grave beseeming ornaments°   100
To wield old partisans, in hands as old,
Cankered with peace, to part your cankered° hate.
If ever you disturb our streets again,
Your lives shall pay the forfeit of the peace.

73. **heartless hinds:** a fourfold pun; *hind* means "servant" and
"female deer," and *heartless* "without feelings" and "without
harts" (male deer). This play is packed with phrases that carry
two or more meanings, often bawdy. 80. **bills ... partisans:**
See Pl. 21c, 21a. 82. **long sword:** The old English long sword
was rapidly giving place to the rapier, introduced from the Continent. Capulet naturally calls for the old-fashioned weapon.
See Pl. 22i. 85. **in ... of:** to show his contempt for. 89. **Profaners ... steel:** who profane (disgrace) your swords by staining
them with the blood of your neighbors. 94. **mistempered:**
"wrathful" and "made for a bad purpose." 96. **airy:** light as
air. 100. **Cast ... ornaments:** i.e., throw off the ornaments of
peace which are suitable to sober, aged citizens. 102. **Cankered
... cankered:** corroded ... malignant.

37. **poor John:** dried salted hake, a cheap food. 43. **marry:**
Mary, by the Virgin Mary. 49. **bite my thumb:** an insulting
gesture, made by snicking the thumbnail on the upper teeth.
70. **swashing:** smashing.

For this time, all the rest depart away.   105
You, Capulet, shall go along with me,
And, Montague, come you this afternoon,
To know our further pleasure in this case,
To old Freetown,° our common judgment place.
Once more, on pain° of death, all men depart.   110
                    [*Exeunt all but* MONTAGUE, LADY
                         MONTAGUE, *and* BENVOLIO.]
    MON. Who set this ancient quarrel new abroach°?
Speak, Nephew, were you by when it began?
    BEN. Here were the servants of your adversary
And yours close fighting ere I did approach.
I drew to part them. In the instant came   115
The fiery Tybalt, with his sword prepared,
Which as he breathed defiance to my ears,
He swung about his head and cut the winds,
Who, nothing hurt withal, hissed him in scorn.
While we were interchanging thrusts and blows,
Came more and more, and fought on part and part
Till the Prince came, who parted either part.   122
    LADY MON. Oh, where is Romeo? Saw you him to-
    day?
Right glad I am he was not at this fray.
    BEN. Madam, an hour before the worshiped sun
Peered forth the golden window of the east,   126
A troubled mind drave me to walk abroad,
Where, underneath the grove of sycamore
That westward rooteth from the city's side,
So early walking did I see your son.   130
Towards him I made; but he was ware° of me,
And stole into the covert of the wood.
I, measuring his affections by my own,
That most are busied when they're most alone,
Being one too many by my weary self,
Pursued my humor,° not pursuing his,   135
And gladly shunned who gladly fled from me.
    MON. Many a morning hath he there been seen,
With tears augmenting the fresh morning's dew,
Adding to clouds more clouds with his deep sighs.
But all so soon as the all-cheering sun   140
Should in the farthest east begin to draw
The shady curtains from Aurora's° bed,
Away from light steals home my heavy son,
And private in his chamber pens himself,
Shuts up his windows, locks fair daylight out, 145
And makes himself an artificial night.
Black and portentous must this humor prove
Unless good counsel may the cause remove.
    BEN. My noble uncle, do you know the cause?
    MON. I neither know it nor can learn of him.   150
    BEN. Have you impórtuned° him by any means?
    MON. Both by myself and many other friends.
But he, his own affections' counselor,
Is to himself — I will not say how true —

But to himself so secret and so close,   155
So far from sounding and discovery,
As is the bud bit with an envious° worm
Ere he can spread his sweet leaves to the air,
Or dedicate his beauty to the sun.
Could we but learn from whence his sorrows grow,
We would as willingly give cure as know.   161
                    [*Enter* ROMEO.]
    BEN. See where he comes. So please you, step aside.
I'll know his grievance, or be much denied.
    MON. I would thou wert so happy° by thy stay
To hear true shrift.° Come, madam, let's away. 165
                    [*Exeunt* MONTAGUE *and* LADY.]
    BEN. Good morrow, Cousin.
    ROM.   Is the day so young?
    BEN. But new struck nine.
    ROM.   Aye me, sad hours seem long!
Was that my father that went hence so fast?
    BEN. It was. What sadness lengthens Romeo's
    hours?
    ROM. Not having that which, having, makes them
    short.   170
    BEN. In love?
    ROM. Out ——
    BEN. Of love?
    ROM. Out of her favor where I am in love.
    BEN. Alas that love, so gentle in his view,°   175
Should be so tyrannous and rough in proof!°
    ROM. Alas that love, whose view is muffled still,°
Should without eyes see pathways to his will!
Where shall we dine? Oh me! What fray was here?
Yet tell me not, for I have heard it all.   180
Here's much to do with hate, but more with love.
Why then, O brawling love! O loving hate!
O anything, of nothing first create!
O heavy lightness! Serious vanity!
Misshapen chaos of well-seeming forms!   185
Feather of lead, bright smoke, cold fire, sick health!
Still-waking° sleep, that is not what it is!
This love feel I, that feel no love in this.
Dost thou not laugh?
    BEN.   No, Coz,° I rather weep.
    ROM. Good heart, at what?
    BEN.   At thy good heart's oppression. 190
    ROM. Why, such is love's transgression.
Griefs of mine own lie heavy in my breast,
Which thou wilt propagate,° to have it pressed°
With more of thine. This love that thou hast shown
Doth add more grief to too much of mine own.   195
Love is a smoke raised with the fume° of sighs;
Being purged, a fire sparkling in lovers' eyes;
Being vexed, a sea nourished with lovers' tears.
What is it else? A madness most discreet,

---

109. **Freetown**: a misunderstanding of a line in *Romeus and Juliet*.
See *R & J* Intro. p. 470a. 110. **pain**: penalty. 111. **abroach**:
on foot. 131. **ware**: aware. 135. **humor**: mood. 142. **Aurora's**:
of the dawn. 151. **importuned**: asked repeatedly.

157. **envious**: hateful. 164. **happy**: fortunate. 165. **shrift**: confession. 175. **view**: appearance. 176. **in proof**: i.e., when experienced. 177. **view . . . still**: sight is blindfolded always.
187. **Still-waking**: ever watchful. 189. **Coz**: cousin. 193. **propagate**: increase. **pressed**: weighed down. 196. **fume**: mist.

A choking gall and a preserving sweet.   200
Farewell, my coz.
   BEN.   Soft! I will go along.
And if you leave me so, you do me wrong.
   ROM. Tut, I have lost myself, I am not here.
This is not Romeo, he's some other where.
   BEN. Tell me in sadness,° who is that you love?
   ROM. What, shall I groan and tell thee?   206
   BEN.   Groan! Why, no,
But sadly tell me who.
   ROM. Bid a sick man in sadness make his will.
Ah, word ill urged to one that is so ill!
In sadness, Cousin, I do love a woman.   210
   BEN. I aimed so near when I supposed you loved.
   ROM. A right good mark-man!° And she's fair I
    love.
   BEN. A right fair mark, fair Coz, is soonest hit.
   ROM. Well, in that hit you miss. She'll not be hit
With Cupid's arrow. She hath Dian's° wit,   215
And in strong proof° of chastity well armed,
From love's weak childish bow she lives unharmed.
She will not stay the siege of loving terms,
Nor bide the encounter of assailing eyes,
Nor ope her lap to saint-seducing gold.   220
Oh, she is rich in beauty, only poor
That when she dies, with beauty dies her store.°
   BEN. Then she hath sworn that she will still live
    chaste?
   ROM. She hath, and in that sparing makes huge
    waste;
For beauty, starved with her severity,   225
Cuts beauty off from all posterity.
She is too fair, too wise, wisely too fair,
To merit bliss by making me despair.°
She hath forsworn° to love, and in that vow
Do I live dead, that live to tell it now.   230
   BEN. Be ruled by me, forget to think of her.
   ROM. Oh, teach me how I should forget to think.
   BEN. By giving liberty unto thine eyes.
Examine other beauties.
   ROM.   'Tis the way
To call hers exquisite, in question more.°   235
These happy masks° that kiss fair ladies' brows,
Being black, put us in mind they hide the fair.
He that is stricken blind cannot forget
The precious treasure of his eyesight lost.
Show me a mistress that is passing° fair,   240

What doth her beauty serve but as a note
Where I may read who passed° that passing fair?
Farewell. Thou canst not teach me to forget.
   BEN. I'll pay that doctrine,° or else die in debt.
                       [*Exeunt.*]

SCENE II. *A street.*

[*Enter* CAPULET, PARIS, *and* SERVANT.]
   CAP. But Montague is bound° as well as I,
In penalty alike, and 'tis not hard, I think,
For men so old as we to keep the peace.
   PAR. Of honorable reckoning° are you both,
And pity 'tis you lived at odds so long.   5
But now, my lord, what say you to my suit?
   CAP. But saying o'er what I have said before.
My child is yet a stranger in the world —
She hath not seen the change of fourteen years.
Let two more summers wither in their pride   10
Ere we may think her ripe to be a bride.
   PAR. Younger than she are happy mothers made.
   CAP. And too soon marred are those so early made.
The earth hath swallowed all my hopes but she,
She is the hopeful lady of my earth.°   15
But woo her, gentle Paris, get her heart.
My will to her consent is but a part;
An she agree, within her scope of choice°
Lies my consent and fair according° voice.
This night I hold an old accustomed feast,   20
Whereto I have invited many a guest
Such as I love, and you among the store,
One more, most welcome, makes my number more
At my poor house look to behold this night
Earth-treading stars that make dark heaven light.
Such comfort as do lusty young men feel   26
When well-appareled April on the heel
Of limping winter treads, even such delight
Among fresh female buds shall you this night
Inherit at my house. Hear all, all see,   30
And like her most whose merit most shall be.
Which on more view, of many mine, being one,
May stand in number, though in reckoning none.°
Come, go with me. [*To* SERVANT, *giving a paper*]
    Go, sirrah,° trudge about
Through fair Verona. Find those persons out   35
Whose names are written there, and to them say

---

205. in sadness: seriously.   212. mark-man: marksman.
216. Dian: Diana, the Virgin huntress goddess, was not interested
in men.   217. proof: armor.   222. with . . . store: i.e., she will
leave no offspring to carry on her beauty. Cf. Sonnet 4.
228. To . . . despair: to make me desperate while she earns her
heavenly reward for keeping her vow of chastity.   229. forsworn: sworn that she will not.   234–35. 'Tis . . . more: to examine their beauty is the way to realize her greater beauty.
235. masks: Elizabethan ladies, admiring an ivory complexion,
wore masks in the open air to preserve their faces from the
sun. These masks were usually black, but sometimes colored.
240. passing: exceedingly.

241–42. note . . . passed: the beauty of any other mistress reminds me of the surpassing beauty of my own.   244. I'll . . .
doctrine: I will pay for that teaching; i.e., I will have you convinced that you are wrong.
   Sc. ii: 1. bound: i.e., to keep peace.   4. Of . . . reckoning:
reckoned honorable.   15. hopeful . . . earth: i.e., the only hope
left of my posterity. earth: body. See II.i.2.   18. scope of choice:
range of choice; i.e., if she chooses suitably.   19. fair according:
readily agreeing.   32–33. Which . . . none: i.e., my daughter will
be one amongst the beauties whom you will see, but none will
be worth more.   34. sirrah: spoken to his servant, a term used
for inferiors.

My house and welcome on their pleasure stay.

[*Exeunt* CAPULET *and* PARIS.]

SERV. Find them out whose names are written here!
It is written that the shoemaker should meddle with
his yard° and the tailor with his last, the fisher   40
with his pencil and the painter with his nets; but I
am sent to find those persons whose names are here
writ, and can never find what names the writing person hath here writ. I must to the learned. In good
time.°   45

[*Enter* BENVOLIO *and* ROMEO.]

BEN. Tut, man, one fire burns out another's burning,

One pain is lessened by another's anguish.
Turn giddy, and be holp° by backward turning,
One desperate grief cures with another's languish.
Take thou some new infection to thy eye,   50
And the rank poison of the old will die.

ROM. Your plantain° leaf is excellent for that.

BEN. For what, I pray thee?

ROM.   For your broken° shin.

BEN. Why, Romeo, art thou mad?

ROM. Not mad, but bound more than a madman
is,   55
Shut up in prison, kept without my food,
Whipped and tormented° and —— Godden,° good
fellow.

SERV. God gi' godden. I pray, sir, can you read?

ROM. Aye, mine own fortune in my misery.   60

SERV. Perhaps you have learned it without book,
but I pray, can you read anything you see?

ROM. Aye, if I know the letters and the language.

SERV. Ye say honestly. Rest you merry!°

ROM. Stay, fellow, I can read. [*Reads.*]   66
"Signior Martino and his wife and daughters;
County° Anselme and his beauteous sisters; the lady
widow of Vitruvio; Signior Placentio and his lovely
nieces; Mercutio and his brother Valentine; mine
uncle Capulet, his wife, and daughters; my fair niece
Rosaline; Livia; Signior Valentio and his cousin
Tybalt; Lucio and the lively Helena."   74
A fair assembly. Whither should they come?

SERV. Up.

ROM. Whither?

SERV. To supper, to our house.

ROM. Whose house?

SERV. My master's.   80

ROM. Indeed I should have asked you that before.

SERV. Now I'll tell you without asking. My master
is the great rich Capulet, and if you be not of the

House of Montagues, I pray come and crush° a cup
of wine. Rest you merry!   [*Exit.*]   86

BEN. At this same ancient feast of Capulet's
Sups the fair Rosaline whom thou so lovest,
With all the admirèd beauties of Verona.
Go thither, and with unattainted° eye   90
Compare her face with some that I shall show,
And I will make thee think thy swan a crow.

ROM. When the devout religion of mine eye
Maintains such falsehood, then turn tears to fires,
And these, who, often drowned, could never die,   95
Transparent° heretics, be burned for liars!
One fairer than my love! The all-seeing sun
Ne'er saw her match since first the world begun.

BEN. Tut, you saw her fair, none else being by,
Herself poised° with herself in either eye.   100
But in that crystal scales let there be weighed
Your lady's love against some other maid
That I will show you shining at this feast,
And she shall scant° show well that now seems best.

ROM. I'll go along, no such sight to be shown,   105
But to rejoice in splendor of mine own.   [*Exeunt.*]

SCENE III. *A room in* CAPULET's *house.*

[*Enter* LADY CAPULET *and* NURSE.]

LADY CAP. Nurse, where's my daughter? Call her
forth to me.

NURSE. Now, by my maidenhead at twelve year
old,
I bade her come. What, lamb! What, ladybird!° —
God forbid! — Where's this girl? What, Juliet!

[*Enter* JULIET.]

JUL. How now! Who calls?

NURSE. Your mother.

JUL. Madam, I am here. What is your will?   6

LADY CAP. This is the matter. Nurse, give leave
awhile,
We must talk in secret. — Nurse, come back again,
I have remembered me, thou'st° hear our counsel.
Thou know'st my daughter's of a pretty age.   10

NURSE. Faith, I can tell her age unto an hour.

LADY CAP. She's not fourteen.

NURSE.   I'll lay fourteen of my teeth —
And yet, to my teen° be it spoken, I have but four —
She is not fourteen. How long is it now
To Lammastide?°

LADY CAP.   A fortnight and odd days.   15

39–40. **shoemaker ... yard:** He mixes his metaphors, as is
common with servants in Shakespeare's plays. **yard:** measure.
44–45. **In ... time:** what a lucky chance; i.e., the arrival of the
two gentlemen. 48. **holp:** helped. 52. **plaintain:** a weed with
broad flat leaves, a popular remedy for bruises and nettle stings.
53. **broken:** with the skin broken. 55–57. **bound ... tormented:** the usual treatment for lunatics. **Godden:** good evening, a form of greeting used in the afternoon. 65. **Rest ...
merry:** God keep you merry. 68. **County:** Count.

85. **crush:** quaff. 90. **unattainted:** unbiased. 96. **Transparent:**
bright. 100. **poised:** balanced. 104. **scant:** scarcely.

Sc. iii: 3. **ladybird:** lit., a small round insect with bright red
spots; a pretty little thing. It also has a bad meaning, "tart."
The Nurse, realizing that she has used the wrong word, continues
abruptly: "God forbid!" 9. **thou's:** thou shalt. 13. **teen:**
sorrow. 15. **Lammastide:** August 1. Shakespeare deliberately
sets the story in the hot season, when "the mad blood is stirring." See III.i.3–4. In *Romeus and Juliet* the incident occurred on Easter Sunday.

NURSE. Even or odd, of all days in the year,
Come Lammas Eve at night shall she be fourteen.
Susan and she — God rest all Christian souls! —
Were of an age. Well, Susan is with God.
She was too good for me. — But, as I said,   20
On Lammas Eve at night shall she be fourteen.
That shall she, marry, I remember it well.
'Tis since the earthquake now eleven years,°
And she was weaned — I never shall forget it —
Of all the days of the year, upon that day.   25
For I had then laid wormwood to my dug,
Sitting in the sun under the dovehouse wall;
My lord and you were then at Mantua. —
Nay, I do bear a brain.° — But, as I said,
When it did taste the wormwood on the nipple   30
Of my dug, and felt it bitter, pretty fool,
To see it tetchy,° and fall out with the dug!
Shake, quoth the dovehouse.° 'Twas no need, I
     trow,°
To bid me trudge.
And since that time it is eleven years;   35
For then she could stand high-lone° — nay, by the
     rood,°
She could have run and waddled all about,
For even the day before, she broke° her brow,
And then my husband — God be with his soul!
A'° was a merry man — took up the child.   40
"Yea," quoth he, "dost thou fall upon thy face?
Thou wilt fall backward when thou hast more wit,
Wilt thou not, Jule?" And, by my holidame,°
The pretty wretch left crying, and said "Aye."
To see now how a jest shall come about!   45
I warrant an I should live a thousand years,
I never should forget it. "Wilt thou not, Jule?"
     quoth he,
And, pretty fool, it stinted,° and said "Aye."
     LADY CAP. Enough of this. I pray thee hold thy
     peace.
NURSE. Yes, madam, yet I cannot choose but laugh
To think it should leave crying, and say "Aye."   51
And yet, I warrant, it had upon its brow
A bump as big as a young cockerel's stone,°
A perilous° knock, and it cried bitterly.   54
"Yea," quoth my husband, "fall'st upon thy face?
Thou wilt fall backward when thou comest to age,
Wilt thou not, Jule?" It stinted, and said "Aye."
     JUL. And stint thou too, I pray thee, Nurse, say I.
     NURSE. Peace, I have done. God mark° thee to His
     grace!

Thou wast the prettiest babe that e'er I nursed.   60
An I might live to see thee married once,
I have my wish.
     LADY CAP. Marry, that "marry" is the very theme
I came to talk of. Tell me, daughter Juliet,
How stands your disposition to be married?   65
     JUL. It is an honor that I dream not of.
     NURSE. An honor! Were not I thine only nurse,
I would say thou hadst sucked wisdom from thy teat.
     LADY CAP. Well, think of marriage now. Younger
     than you
Here in Verona, ladies of esteem,   70
Are made already mothers. By my count,
I was your mother much upon these years
That you are now a maid. Thus then in brief —
The valiant Paris seeks you for his love.
     NURSE. A man, young lady! Lady, such a man   75
As all the world —— Why, he's a man of wax.°
     LADY CAP. Verona's summer hath not such a
     flower.
     NURSE. Nay, he's a flower, in faith, a very flower.
     LADY CAP. What say you? Can you love the gentle-
     man?
This night you shall behold him at our feast.   80
Read o'er the volume° of young Paris' face,
And find delight writ there with beauty's pen.
Examine every married lineament,°
And see how one another lends content,
And what obscured in this fair volume lies   85
Find written in the margent° of his eyes.
This precious book of love, this unbound lover,
To beautify him, only lacks a cover.
The fish lives in the sea, and 'tis much pride
For fair without the fair within to hide.°   90
That book in many's eyes doth share the glory
That in gold clasps locks in the golden story.
So shall you share all that he doth possess,
By having him making yourself no less.
     NURSE. No less! Nay, bigger. Women grow by
     men.   95
     LADY CAP. Speak briefly. Can you like of Paris'
     love?
     JUL. I'll look to like, if looking liking move.°
But no more deep will I endart mine eye   98
Than your consent° gives strength to make it fly.
          [*Enter a* SERVINGMAN.]
     SERV. Madam, the guests are come, supper served
up, you called, my young lady asked for, the nurse
cursed in the pantry, and everything in extremity. I
must hence to wait. I beseech you, follow straight.°

23. 'Tis . . . years: See *R & J* Intro. p. 468a. 29. I . . . brain: I
have a head. 32. tetchy: peevish. 33. Shake . . . dovehouse:
This phrase has not been satisfactorily explained, but a dovehouse is a dovecote, where the lord of the manor bred pigeons
for his own table. trow: guess. 36. high-lone: quite alone.
rood: crucifix. 38. broke: broke the skin of. 40. A': he.
43. holidame: halidom, holy relic, upon which an oath was
sworn. 48. stinted: stopped. 53. stone: testicle. 54. perilous: grievous. 59. mark: select.

76. man of wax: like a model in wax; i.e., perfect. 81-92. volume . . . story: The elaborate metaphor of Paris as a book is
continued throughout these lines. 83. married lineament: perfectly united part. 86. margent: margin. 90. For . . . hide: i.e.,
for a fair outside to cover a fair mind. 97. I'll . . . move: I'll
look at him if that will make me love him. 99. your consent:
This was the correct attitude of an Elizabethan maiden nicely
brought up. See Gen. Intro. p. 20a–b. 103. straight: at once,
straightway.

LADY CAP. We follow thee.   [*Exit* SERVINGMAN.]
    Juliet, the County stays.°   105
NURSE. Go, girl, seek happy nights to happy days.
                        [*Exeunt.*]

SCENE IV. *A street.*

[*Enter* ROMEO, MERCUTIO, BENVOLIO, *with five or six
    other* MASKERS, *and* TORCHBEARERS]
    ROM. What, shall this speech be spoke for our ex-
      cuse?
Or shall we on without apology?
    BEN. The date is out of such prolixity.°
We'll have no Cupid hoodwinked° with a scarf,
Bearing a Tartar's painted bow of lath,°   5
Scaring the ladies like a crow-keeper;°
Nor no without-book prologue, faintly spoke
After the prompter, for our entrance.
But let them measure us by what they will,
We'll measure° them a measure, and be gone.   10
    ROM. Give me a torch. I am not for this am-
      bling.°
Being but heavy,° I will bear the light.
    MER. Nay, gentle Romeo, we must have you
      dance.
    ROM. Not I, believe me. You have dancing shoes
With nimble soles. I have a soul of lead   15
So stakes me to the ground I cannot move.
    MER. You are a lover. Borrow Cupid's wings,
And soar with them above a common bound.°
    ROM. I am too sore enpiercèd with his shaft
To soar with his light feathers, and so bound,   20
I cannot bound a pitch° above dull woe.
Under love's heavy burden do I sink.
    MER. And to sink in it, should you burden love,
Too great oppression for a tender thing.
    ROM. Is love a tender thing? It is too rough,   25
Too rude, too boisterous, and it pricks like thorn.
    MER. If love be rough with you, be rough with
      love.
Prick love for pricking, and you beat love down.
Give me a case to put my visage° in.
A visor for a visor!° What care I   30
What curious eye doth quote° deformities?

Here are the beetle° brows shall blush for me.
    BEN. Come, knock and enter, and no sooner in
But every man betake him to his legs.
    ROM. A torch for me. Let wantons light of heart
Tickle the senseless rushes° with their heels,   36
For I am proverbed with a grandsire phrase.°
I'll be a candleholder,° and look on.
The game was ne'er so fair, and I am done.°
    MER. Tut, dun's° the mouse, the constable's own
      word.°   40
If thou art dun, we'll draw thee from the mire
Of this sir-reverence° love wherein thou stick'st
Up to the ears. Come, we burn daylight,° ho.
    ROM. Nay, that's not so.
    MER.   I mean, sir, in delay
We waste our lights in vain, like lamps by day.   45
Take our good meaning, for our judgment sits
Five times in that ere once in our five wits.°
    ROM. And we mean well in going to this mask,
But 'tis no wit to go.
    MER.   Why, may one ask?
    ROM. I dreamed a dream tonight.
    MER.   And so did I.   50
    ROM. Well, what was yours?
    MER.   That dreamers often lie.
    ROM. In bed asleep, while they do dream things
      true.
    MER. Oh then, I see Queen Mab° hath been with
      you.
She is the fairies' midwife, and she comes
In shape no bigger than an agate stone°   55
On the forefinger of an alderman,
Drawn with a team of little atomies°
Athwart men's noses as they lie asleep —
Her wagon spokes made of long spinners'° legs;
The cover, of the wings of grasshoppers;   60
Her traces,° of the smallest spider's web;
Her collars, of the moonshine's watery beams;
Her whip, of cricket's bone; the lash, of film;°
Her wagoner, a small gray-coated gnat
Not half so big as a round little worm   65
Pricked from the lazy finger of a maid.°

Her chariot is an empty hazelnut,
Made by the joiner squirrel or old grub,
Time out o' mind the fairies' coachmakers.
And in this state she gallops night by night   70
Through lovers' brains, and then they dream of
     love;
O'er courtiers' knees, that dream on curtseys
     straight;
O'er lawyers' fingers, who straight dream on fees;
O'er ladies' lips, who straight on kisses dream,
Which oft the angry Mab with blisters plagues   75
Because their breaths with sweetmeats tainted are.
Sometime she gallops o'er a courtier's nose,
And then dreams he of smelling out a suit.°
And sometime comes she with a tithe pig's° tail
Tickling a parson's nose as a' lies asleep,   80
Then dreams he of another benefice.
Sometime she driveth o'er a soldier's neck,
And then dreams he of cutting foreign throats,
Of breaches, ambuscadoes, Spanish blades,
Of healths five fathom deep; and then anon   85
Drums in his ear, at which he starts and wakes,
And being thus frighted swears a prayer or two,
And sleeps again. This is that very Mab
That plaits the manes of horses in the night,
And bakes the elflocks° in foul sluttish hairs,   90
Which once untangled much misfortune bodes.
This is the hag,° when maids lie on their backs,
That presses them and learns them first to bear,
Making them women of good carriage.
This is she ——
     ROM.   Peace, peace, Mercutio, peace!   95
Thou talk'st of nothing.
     MER.   True, I talk of dreams,
Which are the children of an idle brain,
Begot of nothing but vain fantasy,°
Which is as thin of substance as the air
And more inconstant than the wind, who woos
Even now the frozen bosom of the North,   101
And, being angered, puffs away from thence,
Turning his face to the dew-dropping South.
     BEN. This wind you talk of blows us from our-
     selves.
Supper is done, and we shall come too late.   105
     ROM. I fear, too early. For my mind misgives
Some consequence, yet hanging in the stars,
Shall bitterly begin his fearful date°
With this night's revels, and expire the term
Of a despisèd life° closed in my breast   110

By some vile forfeit of untimely death.
But He that hath the steerage of my course
Direct my sail! On, lusty gentlemen.
     BEN. Strike, drum.   [*Exeunt.*]

SCENE V. *A hall in* CAPULET's *house.*

[MUSICIANS *waiting. Enter* SERVINGMEN, *with
napkins.*]
     I. SERV. Where's Potpan, that he helps not to take
away? He shift a trencher!° He scrape a trencher!
     2. SERV. When good manners shall lie all in one or
two men's hands, and they unwashed too, 'tis a foul
thing.   6
     I. SERV. Away with the joint stools,° remove the
court cupboard,° look to the plate.° Good thou,
save me a piece of marchpane.° And, as thou lovest
me, let the porter let in Susan Grindstone and Nell.
Antony, and Potpan!   11
     2. SERV. Aye, boy, ready.
     I. SERV. You are looked for and called for, asked
for and sought for, in the great chamber.°
     3. SERV. We cannot be here and there too. Cheerly,
boys. Be brisk a while, and the longer liver take all.°
                       [*They retire behind.*]
[*Enter* CAPULET, *with* JULIET *and others of his house,
meeting the* GUESTS *and* MASKERS.]
     CAP. Welcome, gentlemen! Ladies that have their
     toes
Unplagued with corns will have a bout with you.
Ah ha, my mistresses! Which of you all   20
Will now deny to dance? She that makes dainty,°
She, I'll swear, hath corns — am I come near ye
     now?°
Welcome, gentlemen! I have seen the day
That I have worn a visor,° and could tell
A whispering tale in a fair lady's ear   25
Such as would please. 'Tis gone, 'tis gone, 'tis gone.
You are welcome, gentlemen! Come, musicians,
     play.
A hall, a hall°! Give room! And foot it, girls.
            [*Music plays, and they dance.*]
More light, you knaves, and turn the tables up,
And quench the fire, the room is grown too hot.   30
Ah, sirrah, this unlooked-for sport comes well.
Nay, sit, nay, sit, good Cousin Capulet,

Sc. v: 2. trencher: wooden platter. **7. joint stools:** stools
made of joiners' work. See Pl. 17a. **8. court cupboard:** side-
board. See Pl. 20a. **plate:** silver plate. **9. marchpane:** marzipan,
a mixture made of almond paste, often in an elaborate shape.
14. great chamber: Elizabethan great houses had a great chamber used for dining and social occasions. After dinner the tables
were pushed to one side, turned up (i.e., on their sides), and a
space cleared for dancing. **16. longer . . . all:** i.e., the last survivor takes all. **21. makes dainty:** pretends to be shy. **22. am
. . . now:** i.e., do I touch a tender spot? **24. worn a visor:**
i.e., been a dancer. **28. a hall, a hall!:** i.e., clear the hall for
dancing.

---

78. suit: with the double meaning of "fine clothes" and "petition
for favor," a common pun. **79. tithe pig's:** The parson was
entitled to a tithe or tenth of the produce of his parishioners, which he often took in kind. See Gen. Intro. p. 19a.
90. elflocks: The knots in the manes of horses and uncombed
human hair were sometimes attributed to mischievous fairies.
92. hag: nightmare. **98. fantasy:** fancy. **108. date:** period.
109-10. expire . . . life: cause the lease of my life to come to an
end.

For you and I are past our dancing days.
How long is 't now since last yourself and I
Were in a mask?

   2. CAP.   By 'r Lady, thirty years.　　35
   CAP. What, man! 'Tis not so much, 'tis not so
     much.
'Tis since the nuptial of Lucentio,
Come Pentecost as quickly as it will,
Some five and twenty years, and then we masked.
   2. CAP. 'Tis more, 'tis more. His son is elder, sir,
His son is thirty.
   CAP.   Will you tell me that?　　41
His son was but a ward° two years ago.
   ROM. [*To a* SERVINGMAN] What lady's that which
     doth enrich the hand
Of yonder knight?
   SERV. I know not, sir.　　45
   ROM. Oh, she doth teach the torches to burn
     bright!
It seems she hangs upon the cheek of night
Like a rich jewel in an Ethiop's ear —
Beauty too rich for use, for earth too dear!
So shows a snowy dove trooping with crows　　50
As yonder lady o'er her fellows shows.
The measure done, I'll watch her place of stand,
And, touching hers, make blessèd my rude hand.
Did my heart love till now? Forswear it, sight!
For I ne'er saw true beauty till this night.　　55
   TYB. This, by his voice, should be a Montague.
Fetch me my rapier, boy. What dares the slave
Come hither, covered with an antic face,°
To fleer° and scorn at our solemnity?
Now, by the stock and honor of my kin,　　60
To strike him dead I hold it not a sin.
   CAP. Why, how now, kinsman! Wherefore storm
     you so?
   TYB. Uncle, this is a Montague, our foe,
A villain, that is hither come in spite
To scorn at our solemnity this night.　　65
   CAP. Young Romeo, is it?
   TYB.   'Tis he, that villain
     Romeo.
   CAP. Content thee, gentle Coz, let him alone,
He bears him like a portly° gentleman.
And, to say truth, Verona brags of him
To be a virtuous and well-governed youth.　　70
I would not for the wealth of all this town
Here in my house do him disparagement.
Therefore be patient, take no note of him.
It is my will, the which if thou respect,
Show a fair presence and put off these frowns,　　75
An ill-beseeming semblance° for a feast.
   TYB. It fits when such a villain is a guest.
I'll not endure him.

   CAP.   He shall be endured.
What, goodman boy° I say he shall. Go to,　　80
Am I the master here, or you? Go to.
You'll not endure him! God shall mend my soul,
You'll make a mutiny among my guests!
You will set cock-a-hoop!° You'll be the man!
   TYB. Why, Uncle, 'tis a shame.
   CAP.   Go to, go to,
You are a saucy boy. Is't so, indeed?　　85
This trick° may chance to scathe° you, I know what.
You must contrary me! Marry, 'tis time.
Well said, my hearts! You are a princox,° go.
Be quiet, or —— More light, more light! For shame!
I'll make you quiet. What, cheerly, my hearts!　　90
   TYB. Patience perforce with willful choler meeting
Makes my flesh tremble in their different greeting.
I will withdraw. But this intrusion shall,
Now seeming sweet, convert to bitterest gall.
                  [*Exit.*]
   ROM. [*To* JULIET] If I profane with my unworthi-
     est hand　　95
This holy shrine, the gentle fine° is this,
My lips, two blushing pilgrims, ready stand
   To smooth that rough touch with a tender kiss.
   JUL. Good° pilgrim, you do wrong your hand too
     much,
   Which mannerly devotion° shows in this;　　100
For saints have hands that pilgrims' hands do touch,
   And palm to palm is holy palmers'° kiss.
   ROM. Have not saints lips, and holy palmers too?
   JUL. Aye, pilgrim, lips that they must use in
     prayer.
   ROM. Oh then, dear saint, let lips do what hands
     do.　　105
They pray. Grant thou, lest faith turn to despair.
   JUL. Saints do not move, though grant for pray-
     ers' sake.
   ROM. Then move not while my prayer's effect I
     take.
Thus from my lips by thine my sin is purged.
               [*Kissing her.*]
   JUL. Then have my lips the sin that they have
     took.　　110
   ROM. Sin from my lips? Oh, trespass sweetly
     urged!°

80. goodman boy: a contemptuous phrase. *Goodman* indicated a man under the rank of gentleman, but above that of a laborer; *boy*, a youngster, an insulting term. See III.i.69. **84. cock-a-hoop:** an ancient phrase of doubtful origin. In the sixteenth century it meant "to take the spigot out of the barrel, and so let the liquor flow without interruption," hence "be utterly reckless." Today it means "boastfully triumphant." Capulet means "You want to start a roughhouse." **86. trick:** habit, i.e., of quarreling. **scathe:** injure. **88. princox:** conceited boy. **96. fine:** punishment. **99–102. Good . . . kiss:** Juliet takes up Romeo's metaphor of "pilgrim," and for the next ten lines they follow it up with an elaborate play on religious imagery. **100. devotion:** the pilgrim's vow. **102. palmer:** a pilgrim who carried a palm leaf as a sign that he had made the journey to the Holy Land. **111. urged:** argued.

42. ward: a minor in charge of a guardian. **58. antic face:** grotesque mask. **59. fleer:** sneer. **68. portly:** dignified. **76. semblance:** appearance.

Give me my sin again.

JUL.   You kiss by the book.°

NURSE Madam, your mother craves a word with
    you.

ROM. What is her mother?

NURSE.   Marry, bachelor,
Her mother is the lady of the house,   115
And a good lady, and a wise and virtuous.
I nursed her daughter, that you talked withal.
I tell you, he that can lay hold of her
Shall have the chinks.°

ROM.   Is she a Capulet?

Oh, dear° account! My life is my foe's debt.°   120

BEN. Away, be gone. The sport is at the best.

ROM. Aye, so I fear. The more is my unrest.

CAP. Nay, gentlemen, prepare not to be gone,
We have a trifling foolish banquet° toward.
Is it e'en so? Why then, I thank you all,   125
I thank you, honest gentlemen. Good night.
More torches here! Come on, then, let's to bed.
Ah, sirrah, by my fay,° it waxes late.
I'll to my rest.   [*Exeunt all but* JULIET *and* NURSE.]

JUL. Come hither, Nurse. What is yond gentle-
    man?   130

NURSE. The son and heir of old Tiberio.

JUL. What's he that now is going out of door?

NURSE. Marry, that, I think, be young Petruchio.

JUL. What's he that follows there, that would not
    dance?

NURSE. I know not.   135

JUL. Go ask his name. If he be marrièd,
My grave is like to be my wedding bed.

NURSE. His name is Romeo, and a Montague,
The only son of your great enemy.   139

JUL. My only love sprung from my only hate!
Too early seen unknown, and known too late!
Prodigious° birth of love it is to me,
That I must love a loathèd enemy.

NURSE. What's this? What's this?

JUL.   A rhyme I learned even now
Of one I danced withal. [*One calls within,* "Juliet."]

NURSE.   Anon, anon!   145
Come, let's away, the strangers all are gone.
                    [*Exeunt.*]

---

112. by ... book: according to the book of instructions; i.e.,
you are merely being gallant. 119. chinks: cash. 120. dear:
in the double meaning of "costly" and "beloved." foe's debt:
owed to my foe. 124. banquet: light refreshments. 128. fay:
faith. 142. Prodigious: monstrous, unnatural.

Act II

PROLOGUE

[*Enter* CHORUS]

CHOR. Now old desire° doth in his deathbed lie,
    And young affection gapes to be his heir.
That fair for which love groaned for and would die,
    With tender Juliet matched, is now not fair.
Now Romeo is beloved and loves again,   5
    Alike° bewitchèd by the charm of looks,
But to his foe supposed he must complain,
    And she steal love's sweet bait from fearful hooks.
Being held a foe, he may not have access
    To breathe such vows as lovers use to swear,   10
And she as much in love, her means much less
    To meet her new belovèd anywhere.
But passion lends them power, time means, to meet,
Tempering extremities° with extreme sweet. [*Exit.*]

SCENE I. *A lane by the wall of* CAPULET's
                    orchard.

[*Enter* ROMEO, *alone.*]

ROM. Can I go forward when my heart is here?
Turn back, dull earth,° and find thy center° out.
                            [*Exit.*]

[*Enter* BENVOLIO *with* MERCUTIO.]

BEN. Romeo! My cousin Romeo!

MER.   He is wise,
And, on my life, hath stol'n him home to bed.

BEN. He ran this way, and leaped this orchard
    wall.   5
Call, good Mercutio.

MER.   Nay, I'll conjure° too.
Romeo! Humors! Madman! Passion! Lover!
Appear thou in the likeness of a sigh.
Speak but one rhyme, and I am satisfied,
Cry but " aye me! " pronounce but " love " and
    " dove,"   10
Speak to my gossip° Venus one fair word,
One nickname for her purblind° son and heir,
Young Adam Cupid, he that shot so trim°
When King Cophetua° loved the beggar maid!
He heareth not, he stirreth not, he moveth not.   15

Act II, Pro.: 1. old desire: i.e., Romeo's love for Rosaline.
6. Alike: equally. 14. Tempering extremities: moderating extreme difficulties.

Sc. i: 2. dull earth: i.e., my body. center: the absolute center
of the universe; i.e., Juliet. See App. 1. 6. conjure: call up a
spirit. 11. gossip: friend with whom one exchanges confidences
and scandal. 12. purblind: dim-sighted. 13. Young ... trim:
This is a much disputed line; Q1 and Q2 read "Young Abraham: Cupid he ..." F1 reads: "Young Abraham Cupid." Most
editors emend to "Adam Cupid." Adam was a name given to
good archers, after Adam Bell, a famous one. See *M Ado,* I.i.261.
14. King Cophetua: the hero of a popular ballad; he fell in love
with a beggar maid, whom he married.

The ape is dead, and I must conjure him.
I conjure thee by Rosaline's bright eyes,
By her high forehead and her scarlet lip,
By her fine foot, straight leg, and quivering thigh,
And the demesnes° that there adjacent lie,   20
That in thy likeness thou appear to us!
    BEN. An if he hear thee, thou wilt anger him.
    MER. This cannot anger him. 'Twould anger him
To raise a spirit in his mistress' circle
Of some strange nature, letting it there stand   25
Till she had laid it and conjured it down.
That were some spite.° My invocation
Is fair and honest, and in his mistress' name
I conjure only but to raise up him.   29
    BEN. Come, he hath hid himself among these trees,
To be consorted° with the humorous° night.
Blind is his love, and best befits the dark.
    MER. If love be blind, love cannot hit the mark.
Now will he sit under a medlar° tree,
And wish his mistress were that kind of fruit   35
As maids call medlars when they laugh alone.
Oh, Romeo, that she were, Oh, that she were
An open et cetera,° thou a poperin° pear!
Romeo, good night. I'll to my truckle bed,°
This field bed is too cold for me to sleep.   40
Come, shall we go?
    BEN.   Go then, for 'tis in vain
To seek him here that means not to be found.
                           [*Exeunt.*]

SCENE II.° CAPULET's *orchard.*

[*Enter* ROMEO.]
    ROM. He jests at scars that never felt a wound.
            [JULIET *appears above at a window.*]
But, soft! What light through yonder window
    breaks?
It is the east, and Juliet is the sun!
Arise, fair sun, and kill the envious moon,°
Who is already sick and pale with grief   5
That thou her maid art far more fair than she.
Be not her maid, since she is envious.
Her vestal° livery is but sick and green,
And none but fools do wear it. Cast it off.
It is my lady, oh, it is my love!   10

Oh, that she knew she were!
She speaks, yet she says nothing. What of that?
Her eye discourses, I will answer it.
I am too bold, 'tis not to me she speaks.
Two of the fairest stars in all the heaven,   15
Having some business, do entreat her eyes
To twinkle in their spheres° till they return.
What if her eyes were there, they in her head?
The brightness of her cheek would shame those stars
As daylight doth a lamp; her eyes in heaven   20
Would through the airy region stream so bright
That birds would sing and think it were not night.
See how she leans her cheek upon her hand!
Oh, that I were a glove upon that hand,
That I might touch that cheek!
    JUL.   Aye me!
    ROM.   She speaks.
Oh, speak again, bright angel! For thou art   26
As glorious to this night, being o'er my head,
As is a wingèd messenger of Heaven
Unto the white-upturnèd wondering eyes
Of mortals that fall back to gaze on him   30
When he bestrides the lazy-pacing clouds
And sails upon the bosom of the air.
    JUL. O Romeo, Romeo, wherefore **art thou**
      Romeo?
Deny thy father and refuse thy name,
Or, if thou wilt not, be but sworn my love   35
And I'll no longer be a Capulet.
    ROM. [*Aside*] Shall I hear more, or shall I speak
      at this?
    JUL. 'Tis but thy name that is my enemy.
Thou art thyself, though not a Montague.
What's Montague? It is nor hand, nor foot,   40
Nor arm, nor face, nor any other part
Belonging to a man. Oh, be some other name!
What's in a name? That which we call a rose
By any other name would smell as sweet.
So Romeo would, were he not Romeo called,   45
Retain that dear perfection which he owes°
Without that title. Romeo, doff thy name,
And for thy name, which is no part of thee,
Take all myself.
    ROM.   I take thee at thy word.
Call me but love, and I'll be new baptized.   50
Henceforth I never will be Romeo.
    JUL. What man art thou that, thus bescreened in
      night,
So stumblest on my counsel?
    ROM.   By a name
I know not how to tell thee who I am.
My name, dear saint, is hateful to myself   55
Because it is an enemy to thee.
Had I it written, I would tear the word.
    JUL. My ears have yet not drunk a hundred words
Of thy tongue's uttering, yet I know the sound.

---

20. demesnes: domains.   27. spite: outrage.   31. consorted:
associated. humorous: moody.   34. medlar: a tree which produces a fruit like a small brown apple, only eaten when it has
grown soft; used here with a quibble on "meddler." See *AYLI*,
III.ii.124.   38. et cetera: often used (like "so-and-so") as a
nice substitute for a nasty word. poperin: lit., a pear from
Poperinghe in Flanders, but used obscenely for the male parts.
39. truckle bed: trundle bed, a bed on casters, pushed under the
great bed in the daytime.
    Sc. ii: This division is not in the original play but has been
made by editors. See Gen. Intro. pp. 56b–57a.   4. envious
moon: the moon is also Diana, the virgin goddess.   8. vestal:
virgin.

17. spheres: See App. I.   46. owes: owns.

Art thou not Romeo, and a Montague?   60
  ROM. Neither, fair saint, if either thee dislike.°
  JUL. How camest thou hither, tell me, and where-
    fore?
The orchard walls are high and hard to climb,
And the place death, considering who thou art,
If any of my kinsmen find thee here.   65
  ROM. With love's light wings did I o'erperch°
    these walls,
For stony limits cannot hold love out.
And what love can do, that dares love attempt,
Therefore thy kinsmen are no let° to me.
  JUL. If they do see thee, they will murder thee.   70
  ROM. Alack, there lies more peril in thine eye
Than twenty of their swords. Look thou but sweet,
And I am proof° against their enmity.
  JUL. I would not for the world they saw thee here.
  ROM. I have night's cloak to hide me from their
    eyes,   75
And but° thou love me, let them find me here.
My life were better ended by their hate
Than death prorogued,° wanting of thy love.
  JUL. By whose direction found'st thou out this
    place?
  ROM. By love, that first did prompt me to inquire.
He lent me counsel, and I lent him eyes.   81
I am no pilot, yet wert thou as far
As that vast shore washed with the farthest sea,
I would adventure for such merchandise.
  JUL. Thou know'st the mask of night is on my
    face,   85
Else would a maiden blush bepaint my cheek
For that which thou hast heard me speak tonight.
Fain would I dwell on form,° fain, fain deny
What I have spoke. But farewell compliment!°
Dost thou love me? I know thou wilt say "Aye,"   90
And I will take thy word. Yet if thou swear'st,
Thou mayst prove false. At lovers' perjuries
They say Jove laughs. O gentle Romeo,
If thou dost love, pronounce it faithfully.
Or if thou think'st I am too quickly won,   95
I'll frown and be perverse and say thee nay,
So thou wilt woo; but else, not for the world.
In truth, fair Montague, I am too fond,
And therefore thou mayst think my 'havior light.
But trust me, gentleman, I'll prove more true   100
Than those that have more cunning to be strange.°
I should have been more strange, I must confess,
But that thou overheard'st, ere I was ware,
My true love's passion. Therefore pardon me,
And not impute this yielding to light love,   105
Which the dark night hath so discovered.
  ROM. Lady, by yonder blessed moon I swear,

That tips with silver all these fruit-tree tops ——
  JUL. Oh, swear not by the moon, th' inconstant
    moon,
That monthly changes in her circled orb,   110
Lest that thy love prove likewise variable.
  ROM. What shall I swear by?
  JUL.   Do not swear at all.
Or, if thou wilt, swear by thy gracious self,
Which is the god of my idolatry,
And I'll believe thee.
  ROM.   If my heart's dear love ——
  JUL. Well, do not swear. Although I joy in thee,
I have no joy of this contráct° tonight.   117
It is too rash, too unadvised, too sudden,
Too like the lightning, which doth cease to be
Ere one can say "It lightens." Sweet, good night!
This bud of love, by summer's ripening breath,   121
May prove a beauteous flower when next we meet.
Good night, good night! As sweet repose and rest
Come to thy heart as that within my breast!
  ROM. Oh, wilt thou leave me so unsatisfied?   125
  JUL. What satisfaction canst thou have tonight?
  ROM. The exchange of thy love's faithful vow for
    mine.
  JUL. I gave thee mine before thou didst request it,
And yet I would it were to give again.
  ROM. Wouldst thou withdraw it? For what pur-
    pose, love?   130
  JUL. But to be frank, and give it thee again.
And yet I wish but for the thing I have.
My bounty is as boundless as the sea,
My love as deep; the more I give to thee,
The more I have, for both are infinite.   135
I hear some noise within. Dear love, adieu!
                      [NURSE *calls within.*°]
Anon,° good Nurse! Sweet Montague, be true.
Stay but a little, I will come again.   [*Exit.*]
  ROM. Oh, blessed, blessed night! I am afeard,
Being in night, all this is but a dream,   140
Too flattering-sweet to be substantial.
           [*Re-enter* JULIET, *above.*]
  JUL. Three words, dear Romeo, and good night
    indeed.
If that thy bent° of love be honorable,
Thy purpose marriage, send me word tomorrow
By one that I'll procure to come to thee,   145
Where and what time thou wilt perform the rite,
And all my fortunes at thy foot I'll lay,
And follow thee my lord throughout the world.
  NURSE. [*Within*] Madam!
  JUL. I come, anon. — But if thou mean'st not
    well, I do beseech thee ——   151
  NURSE. [*Within*] Madam!
  JUL.   By and by, I come —
To cease thy suit, and leave me to my grief.

---

61. **dislike**: displease.   66. **o'erperch**: fly over.   69. **let**: hindrance.   73. **proof**: armored.   76. **And but**: if only.   78. **prorogued**: postponed.   88. **dwell on form**: behave according to
convention.   89. **compliment**: polite behavior.   98. **fond**: foolishly affectionate.   101. **strange**: outwardly cold.

117. **contract**: betrothal.   136. **s.d., within**: off stage.   137. **Anon:**
by and by, in a moment.   143. **bent**: intention.

Tomorrow will I send.

ROM.　　　　　　So thrive my soul ——

JUL. A thousand times good night!　　　[*Exit.*]

ROM. A thousand times the worse, to want thy
　　light.　　　　　　　　　　　　　　　155

Love goes toward love as schoolboys from their
　books,

But love from love toward school with heavy looks.
　　　　　　　　　　　　　[*Retiring slowly.*]
　　　　　　[*Re-enter* JULIET, *above.*]

JUL. Hist! Romeo, hist! — Oh, for a falconer's°
　voice,

To lure this tassel-gentle° back again!　　160

Bondage is hoarse,° and may not speak aloud,

Else would I tear the cave where Echo lies

And make her airy tongue more hoarse than mine

With repetition of my Romeo's name.

ROM. It is my soul that calls upon my name.　165

How silver-sweet sound lovers' tongues by night,

Like softest music to attending ears!

JUL. Romeo!

ROM.　　　My dear?°

JUL.　　　　　　At what o'clock tomorrow

Shall I send to thee?

ROM.　　　　　At the hour of nine.

JUL. I will not fail. 'Tis twenty years till then.

I have forgot why I did call thee back.　　171

ROM. Let me stand here till thou remember it.

JUL. I shall forget, to have thee still stand there,

Remembering how I love thy company.

ROM. And I'll still stay, to have thee still forget,

Forgetting any other home but this.　　176

JUL. 'Tis almost morning. I would have thee
　　gone,

And yet no farther than a wanton's° bird,

Who lets it hop a little from her hand,

Like a poor prisoner in his twisted gyves,°　180

And with a silk thread plucks it back again,

So loving-jealous of his liberty.

ROM. I would I were thy bird.

JUL.　　　　　　Sweet, so would I.

Yet I should kill thee with much cherishing.

Good night, good night! Parting is such sweet sor-
　row　　　　　　　　　　　　　　185

That I shall say good night till it be morrow.

　　　　　　　　　　　　　　　[*Exit.*]

ROM. Sleep dwell upon thine eyes, peace in thy
　　breast!

Would I were sleep and peace, so sweet to rest!

Hence will I to my ghostly° father's cell,　189

His help to crave and my dear hap° to tell.　[*Exit.*]

SCENE III. FRIAR LAURENCE'S *cell.*

[*Enter* FRIAR LAURENCE, *with a basket.*]

FRI. L. The gray-eyed morn smiles on the frown-
　ing night,

Checkering° the eastern clouds with streaks of light,

And fleckèd° darkness like a drunkard reels

From forth day's path and Titan's° fiery wheels.

Now, ere the sun advance his burning eye,　　5

The day to cheer and night's dank dew to dry,

I must upfill° this osier cage° of ours

With baleful weeds and precious-juicèd flowers.

The earth that's Nature's mother is her tomb,

What is her burying grave, that is her womb.　10

And from her womb children of divers kind

We sucking on her natural bosom find,

Many for many virtues excellent,

None but for some, and yet all different.

Oh, mickle° is the powerful grace that lies　15

In herbs, plants, stones, and their true qualities.

For naught so vile that on the earth doth live,

But to the earth some special good doth give;

Nor aught so good but, strained from that fair use,

Revolts from true birth, stumbling on abuse.°　20

Virtue itself turns vice, being misapplied,

And vice sometime's by action dignified.

Within the infant rind of this small flower

Poison hath residence, and medicine power.

For this, being smelt, with that part cheers each
　part,　　　　　　　　　　　　　　25

Being tasted, slays all senses with the heart.

Two such opposèd kings encamp them still°

In man as well as herbs, grace° and rude will°;

And where the worser is predominant,

Full soon the canker° death eats up that plant.　30

　　　　　　　　　　　[*Enter* ROMEO.]

ROM. Good morrow, Father.

FRI. L.　　　　　　　　Benedicite!

What early tongue so sweet saluteth me?

Young son, it argues a distempered° head

So soon to bid good morrow to thy bed.

Care keeps his watch in every old man's eye,　35

And where care lodges, sleep will never lie;

But where unbruisèd youth with unstuffed brain

Doth couch his limbs, there golden sleep doth reign.

Therefore thy earliness doth me assure

Thou art uproused by some distemperature.　40

Or if not so, then here I hit it right,

Our Romeo hath not been in bed tonight.

ROM. That last is true. The sweeter rest was mine.

FRI. L. God pardon sin! Wast thou with Rosaline?

ROM. With Rosaline, my ghostly father? No.　45

---

159. falconer: keeper of hawks.　160. tassel-gentle: male pere-
grine falcon.　161. Bondage is hoarse: i.e., being under the
control of my parents, I can only whisper.　168. My dear: In
Elizabethan times this was a phrase of tenderest affection.
178. wanton: spoiled child.　180. gyves: fetters.　189. ghostly:
spiritual.　190. hap: luck.

Sc. iii: 2. Checkering: variegating.　3. flecked: dappled.
4. Titan: the sun.　7. upfill: fill up. osier cage: wicker basket.
15. mickle: mighty.　20. abuse: misuse.　27. still: always.
28. grace: the power of goodness. rude will: man's natural desire
for evil.　30. canker: cankerworm.　33. distempered: disturbed.

I have forgot that name and that name's woe.

FRI. L. That's my good son. But where hast thou
    been, then?

ROM. I'll tell thee ere thou ask it me again.
I have been feasting with mine enemy,
Where on a sudden one hath wounded me   50
That's by me wounded. Both our remedies
Within thy help and holy physic° lies.
I bear no hatred, blessed man, for, lo,
My intercession likewise steads° my foe.

FRI. L. Be plain, good son, and homely° in thy
    drift.   55
Riddling confession finds but riddling shrift.°

ROM. Then plainly know my heart's dear love is
    set
On the fair daughter of rich Capulet.
As mine on hers, so hers is set on mine,
And all combined° save what thou must combine
By holy marriage. When, and where, and how, 61
We met, we wooed and made exchange of vow,
I'll tell thee as we pass; but this I pray,
That thou consent to marry us today.

FRI. L. Holy Saint Francis, what a change is here!
Is Rosaline, that thou didst love so dear,   66
So soon forsaken? Young men's love then lies
Not truly in their hearts, but in their eyes.
Jesu Maria, what a deal of brine
Hath washed thy sallow cheeks for Rosaline!   70
How much salt water thrown away in waste,
To season° love, that of it doth not taste!
The sun not yet thy sighs from heaven clears,
Thy old groans ring yet in mine ancient ears.
Lo, here upon thy cheek the stain doth sit   75
Of an old tear that is not washed off yet.
If e'er thou wast thyself and these woes thine,
Thou and these woes were all for Rosaline.
And art thou changed? Pronounce this sentence°
    then ――   79
Women may fall when there's no strength in men.

ROM. Thou chid'st me oft for loving Rosaline.

FRI. L. For doting, not for loving, pupil mine.

ROM. And bad'st me bury love.

FRI. L.   Not in a grave
To lay one in, another out to have.

ROM. I pray thee, chide not. She whom I love now
Doth grace for grace and love for love allow.   86
The other did not so.

FRI. L.   Oh, she knew well
Thy love did read by rote and could not spell.°
But come, young waverer, come, go with me,
In one respect I'll thy assistant be;   90
For this alliance may so happy prove,

To turn your households' rancor to pure love.

ROM. Oh, let us hence. I stand on sudden haste.°

FRI. L. Wisely and slow. They stumble that run
    fast.   [*Exeunt.*]

SCENE IV. *A street.*

[*Enter* BENVOLIO *and* MERCUTIO.]

MER. Where the devil should this Romeo be?
Came he not home tonight?

BEN. Not to his father's, I spoke with his man.

MER. Ah, that same pale hardhearted wench, that
    Rosaline,
Torments him so that he will sure run mad.   5

BEN. Tybalt, the kinsman of old Capulet,
Hath sent a letter to his father's house.

MER. A challenge, on my life.

BEN. Romeo will answer it.

MER. Any man that can write may answer a let-
    ter.   10

BEN. Nay, he will answer the letter's master, how
he dares, being dared.

MER. Alas, poor Romeo, he is already dead!
Stabbed with a white wench's black eye, shot thorough the ear with a love song, the very pin° of his
heart cleft with the blind bowboy's butt shaft.° And
is he a man to encounter Tybalt?   17

BEN. Why, what is Tybalt?

MER. More than Prince of Cats,° I can tell you.
Oh, he's the courageous captain of compliments.° He
fights as you sing prick song,° keeps time, distance,
and proportion; rests me his minim° rest, one, 22
two, and the third in your bosom. The very butcher
of a silk button, a duelist, a duelist, a gentleman of
the very first house,° of the first and second cause.°
Ah, the immortal passado! The punto reverso! The
hai!°

BEN. The what?   28

MER. The pox of such antic, lisping, affecting fantasticoes,° these new tuners of accents! " By Jesu, a
very good blade! A very tall° man! A very good
whore! " Why, is not this a lamentable thing, Grand-

---

93. Oh . . . haste: let us go quickly, for I am impatient.
    Sc. iv: 15. pin: center of the target. 16. butt shaft: un-
pointed arrow, used for target practice. 19. Prince of Cats: In
the tale of Reynard the Fox, Tibert (or Tybalt) is Prince of
Cats. 20. captain of compliments: expert in the niceties of
fashionable behavior. 21. prick song: melody accompanying a
song. 22. minim: the shortest note in music. 23–27. butcher
. . . hai: A professional fencer would undertake to touch his opponent on any button of his doublet. Mercutio mocks Tybalt
because he is an expert with the new-fashioned rapier. See Pl.
22l. Dueling with the rapier had its own ritual and vocabulary,
such as *passado*, lunge; *punto reverso*, a backhanded stroke; and
hai, the cry as the fencer thrusts home. 25. first house: finest
school. first . . . cause: the reasons which (according to the exact rules of honor) caused a gentleman to issue a challenge.
See *AYLI*, V.iv.48–108. 30. fantasticoes: fantastical fellows.
31. tall: brave.

52. physic: remedy. 54. steads: benefits. 55. homely: simple.
56. shrift: absolution. 60. combined: united. 72. season: keep
fresh, as meat is kept wholesome by salt. 79. sentence:
proverb. 88. love . . . spell: your love was merely repeating
phrases by heart (*by rote*), like a child that pretends to read
because it knows the words.

sire, that we should be thus afflicted with these strange flies, these fashionmongers, these perdona-mi's,° who stand so much on the new form that they cannot sit at ease on the old bench? Oh, their bones,° their bones!   37

[Enter ROMEO.]

BEN. Here comes Romeo, here comes Romeo.

MER. Without his roe, like a dried herring. Oh, flesh, flesh, how art thou fishified! Now is he for the numbers° that Petrarch flowed in. Laura° to his lady was but a kitchen wench — marry, she had a better love to berhyme her — Dido,° a dowdy;° Cleo-   43 patra, a gypsy;° Helen and Hero, hildings° and har-lots; Thisbe, a gray eye or so, but not to the purpose. Signior Romeo, *bon jour!* — there's a French saluta-tion to your French slop.° You gave us the counter-feit° fairly last night.

ROM. Good morrow to you both. What counterfeit did I give you?   50

MER. The slip, sir, the slip. Can you not conceive?

ROM. Pardon, good Mercutio, my business was great, and in such a case as mine a man may strain courtesy.   55

MER. That's as much as to say, Such a case as yours constrains a man to bow in the hams.

ROM. Meaning, to curtsy.

MER. Thou hast most kindly hit it.

ROM. A most courteous exposition.   60

MER. Nay, I am the very pink of courtesy.

ROM. Pink for flower.

MER. Right.

ROM. Why, then is my pump well flowered.°   64

MER. Well said. Follow me this jest now till thou hast worn out thy pump, that, when the single sole of it is worn, the jest may remain, after the wearing, solely singular.

ROM. Oh, single-soled jest, solely singular for the singleness!   70

MER. Come between us, good Benvolio. My wits faint.

ROM. Switch and spurs,° switch and spurs, or I'll cry a match.°   74

MER. Nay, if thy wits run the wild-goose chase,° I have done; for thou hast more of the wild goose in

one of thy wits than, I am sure, I have in my whole five. Was I with you there for the goose?°   80

ROM. Thou wast never with me for anything when thou wast not there for the goose.

MER. I will bite thee by the ear for that jest.

ROM. Nay, good goose, bite not.

MER. Thy wit is a very bitter sweeting, it is a most sharp sauce.   85

ROM. And is it not well served in to a sweet goose?

MER. Oh, here's a wit of cheveril,° that stretches from an inch narrow to an ell broad!

ROM. I stretch it out for that word "broad," which, added to the goose, proves thee far and wide a broad goose.   91

MER. Why, is not this better now than groaning for love? Now art thou sociable,° now art thou Romeo; now art thou what thou art, by art as well as by nature. For this driveling love is like a great natu-ral° that runs lolling up and down to hide his bau-ble° in a hole.   97

BEN. Stop there, stop there.

MER. Thou desirest me to stop in my tale against the hair.°

BEN. Thou wouldst else have made thy tale large.°   102

MER. Oh, thou art deceived — I would have made it short. For I was come to the whole depth of my tale, and meant indeed to occupy the argument no longer.   106

ROM. Here's goodly gear!°

[Enter NURSE *and* PETER.]

MER. A sail, a sail!

BEN. Two, two — a shirt and a smock.°

NURSE. Peter!   110

PET. Anon?

NURSE. My fan, Peter.

MER. Good Peter, to hide her face, for her fan's the fairer face.

NURSE. God ye good morrow, gentlemen.   115

MER. God ye good-den, fair gentlewoman.

NURSE. Is it good-den?°

MER. 'Tis no less, I tell you, for the bawdy hand of the dial is now upon the prick° of noon.

NURSE. Out upon you! What a man are you!   120

ROM. One, gentlewoman, that God hath made himself to mar.

NURSE. By my troth, it is well said. "For himself to mar," quoth a'? Gentlemen, can any of you tell me where I may find the young Romeo?   125

34–35. perdona-mi's: Italian for "pardon me." The man of fash-ion affected foreign languages.   **36. bones:** with a pun on the French *bon.*   **41. numbers:** verses.   **Laura:** Petrarch's love, to whom he wrote his sonnets.   **43–45. Dido . . . Thisbe:** all beau-tiful heroines of famous tragic stories.   **dowdy:** slut.   **gypsy:** Egyptian and so dusky.   **hildings:** good-for-nothings.   **47. slop:** baggy breeches. See Pl. 8c and p. 93a.   **47–51. counterfeit . . . slip:** a counterfeit coin was called a slip.   **64. pump . . . flowered:** my shoe is pinked (punched) with a pattern of flowers. See Pl. 8c. This kind of verbal wit, when every phrase has two or more meanings, was fashionable at this time, particularly among young gallants.   **73. Switch . . . spurs:** at full gallop — urge your wit on.   **74. match:** wager. Romeo means: If you can't keep up this wit contest, I claim the wager.   **75. wild-goose chase:** a race where the second horseman must follow the first wherever he goes.

80. Was . . . goose: have I proved you to be a goose?   **87. chev-eril:** kid skin.   **93. sociable:** i.e., Romeo, to Mercutio's delight, has now recovered his spirits.   **96. natural:** fool.   **97. bauble:** the fool's stick, ornamented with a doll's head. See Pl. 12f.   **99–100. against . . . hair:** contrary to the natural life of the hair, as when one strokes a cat from the tail forward.   **102. large:** licentious.   **107. gear:** stuff.   **109. shirt . . . smock:** man and a woman.   **117. Is it good-den:** is it afternoon?   **119. prick:** point.

ROM. I can tell you, but young Romeo will be older when you have found him than he was when you sought him. I am the youngest of that name, for fault of a worse.

NURSE. You say well.   130

MER. Yea, is the worst well? Very well took,° i' faith — wisely, wisely.

NURSE. If you be he, sir, I desire some confidence° with you.

BEN. She will indite° him to some supper.   135

MER. A bawd, a bawd, a bawd! So ho!°

ROM. What hast thou found?

MER. No° hare,° sir, unless a hare, sir, in a lenten pie, that is something stale and hoar° ere it be spent. [*Sings.*]   140

> " An old hare hoar,
>   And an old hare hoar,
> Is very good meat in Lent.
>   But a hare that is hoar,
>   Is too much for a score   145
> When it hoars ere it be spent."

Romeo, will you come to your father's? We'll to dinner thither.

ROM. I will follow you.

MER. Farewell, ancient lady, farewell [*Singing*], " lady, lady, lady."   151

[*Exeunt* MERCUTIO *and* BENVOLIO.]

NURSE. Marry, farewell! I pray you, sir, what saucy merchant was this, that was so full of his ropery?°

ROM. A gentleman, Nurse, that loves to hear himself talk, and will speak more in a minute than he will stand to in a month.   157

NURSE. An a' speak anything against me, I'll take him down, an a' were lustier than he is, and twenty such Jacks;° and if I cannot, I'll find those that shall. Scurvy knave! I am none of his flirt-gills,° I am none of his skainsmates.° [*Turning to* PETER] And thou must stand by too, and suffer every knave to use me at his pleasure?   164

PET. I saw no man use you at his pleasure. If I had, my weapon should quickly have been out, I warrant you. I dare draw as soon as another man, if I see occasion in a good quarrel and the law on my side.   169

NURSE. Now, afore God, I am so vexed that every part about me quivers. Scurvy knave! Pray you, sir, a word. And as I told you, my young lady bade me inquire you out — what she bade me say, I will keep to myself. But first let me tell ye, if ye should lead her into a fool's paradise, as they say, it were a   175 very gross kind of behavior, as they say. For the gentlewoman is young, and therefore if you should deal double with her, truly it were an ill thing to be offered to any gentlewoman, and very weak dealing.   181

ROM. Nurse, commend me to thy lady and mistress. I protest° unto thee ——

NURSE. Good heart, and, i' faith, I will tell her as much. Lord, Lord, she will be a joyful woman.   186

ROM. What wilt thou tell her, Nurse? Thou dost not mark° me.

NURSE. I will tell her, sir, that you do protest, which, as I take it, is a gentlemanlike offer.   190

ROM. Bid her devise
Some means to come to shrift this afternoon,
And there she shall at Friar Laurence' cell
Be shrived and married. Here is for thy pains.

NURSE. No, truly, sir, not a penny.   195

ROM. Go to, I say you shall.

NURSE. This afternoon, sir? Well, she shall be there.

ROM. And stay, good Nurse, behind the abbey wall.
Within this hour my man shall be with thee,   200
And bring thee cords made like a tackled stair,°
Which to the high topgallant° of my joy
Must be my convoy in the secret night.
Farewell. Be trusty, and I'll quit thy pains.°
Farewell, commend me to thy mistress.   205

NURSE. Now God in Heaven bless thee! Hark you, sir.

ROM. What say'st thou, my dear nurse?

NURSE. Is your man secret? Did you ne'er hear say Two may keep counsel, putting one away?°   209

ROM. I warrant thee, my man's as true as steel.

NURSE. Well, sir, my mistress is the sweetest lady — Lord, Lord, when 'twas a litle prating thing —— Oh, there is a nobleman in town, one Paris, that would fain lay knife aboard;° but she, good soul, had as lieve° see a toad, a very toad, as see him. I   215 anger her sometimes, and tell her that Paris is the properer° man. But I'll warrant you, when I say so, she looks as pale as any clout° in the versal world.° Doth not rosemary and Romeo begin both with a letter?   220

ROM. Aye, Nurse, what of that? Both with an R.

NURSE. Ah, mocker! That's the dog's name.° R is for the —— No, I know it begins with some other

---

131. **took:** understood.   133. **confidence:** for "conference." The old Nurse loves long words, but is not always sure of their meaning.   135. **indite:** for "invite."   136. **So ho!:** the hunter's cry signifying he has spied game.   138–51. **No . . . lady:** Mercutio, as usual, is mocking, to the great annoyance of the Nurse, who realizes that he is insulting her but cannot understand what he is saying.   138. **hare:** prostitute.   139. **hoar:** moldy.   153. **ropery:** for "roguery."   160. **Jacks:** knaves.   161. **flirt-gills:** loose women.   162. **skainsmates:** gangsters.

183. **protest:** declare.   188. **mark:** pay attention to.   201. **tackled stair:** rope ladder, as on a sailing ship.   202. **topgallant:** small mast fixed to the top of the mainmast.   204. **quit . . . pains:** reward your trouble.   209. **putting . . . away:** i.e., two can keep a secret only when but one of them knows it.   214. **lay . . . aboard:** get her for himself.   215. **lieve:** soon.   217. **properer:** more handsome.   218. **clout:** cloth. **versal world:** universe.   222. **dog's name:** the letter R was called the dog's letter because it makes a growling sound.

letter — and she hath the prettiest sententious° of it,
of you and rosemary, that it would do you good to
hear it.　　　　　　　　　　　　　　　　　　227
　　ROM. Commend me to thy lady.
　　NURSE. Aye, a thousand times. [*Exit* ROMEO.]
Peter!
　　PET. Anon?
　　NURSE. Peter, take my fan, and go before, and
apace.°　　　　　　　　　　　　　　[*Exeunt.*] 232

SCENE V. CAPULET's *orchard.*

[*Enter* JULIET.]

　　JUL. The clock struck nine when I did send the
　　　nurse.
In half an hour she promised to return.
Perchance she cannot meet him. That's not so.
Oh, she is lame! Love's heralds should be thoughts,
Which ten times faster glide than the sun's beams,
Driving back shadows over lowering° hills.　　6
Therefore do nimble-pinioned° doves draw love,
And therefore hath the wind-swift Cupid wings.
Now is the sun upon the highmost hill
Of this day's journey, and from nine till twelve　10
Is three long hours; yet she is not come.
Had she affections and warm youthful blood,
She would be as swift in motion as a ball,
My words would bandy° her to my sweet love,
And his to me.　　　　　　　　　　　　15
But old folks, many feign as they were dead,
Unwieldy, slow, heavy and pale as lead.
[*Enter* NURSE, *with* PETER.] Oh, God, she comes! O
　　honey Nurse, what news?
Hast thou met with him? Send thy man away.　19
　　NURSE. Peter, stay at the gate.　　[*Exit* PETER.]
　　JUL. Now, good sweet Nurse —— Oh, Lord, why
　　　look'st thou sad?
Though news be sad, yet tell them merrily;
If good, thou shamest the music of sweet news
By playing it to me with so sour a face.
　　NURSE. I am aweary, give me leave° a while.　25
Fie, how my bones ache! What a jaunce° have I had!
　　JUL. I would thou hadst my bones and I thy news.
Nay, come, I pray thee, speak, good, good Nurse,
　　speak.
　　NURSE. Jesu, what haste? Can you not stay a
　　　while?
Do you not see that I am out of breath?　　30
　　JUL. How art thou out of breath when thou hast
　　　breath
To say to me that thou art out of breath?
The excuse that thou dost make in this delay

Is longer than the tale thou dost excuse.
Is thy news good, or bad? Answer to that.　　35
Say either, and I'll stay the circumstance.°
Let me be satisfied, is 't good or bad?
　　NURSE. Well, you have made a simple choice. You
know not how to choose a man. Romeo! No, not he,
though his face be better than any man's, yet his　40
leg excels all men's; and for a hand, and a foot, and a
body, though they be not to be talked on, yet they
are past compare. He is not the flower of courtesy,°
but, I'll warrant him, as gentle as a lamb. Go thy
ways, wench, serve God. What, have you dined at
home?　　　　　　　　　　　　　　　46
　　JUL. No, no. But all this did I know before.
What says he of our marriage? What of that?
　　NURSE. Lord, how my head aches! What a head
have I!
It beats as it would fall in twenty pieces.　　50
My back o' t' other side — ah, my back, my back!
Beshrew° your heart for sending me about
To catch my death with jauncing up and down!
　　JUL. I' faith, I am sorry that thou art not well.
Sweet, sweet, sweet Nurse, tell me, what says my
　　love?　　　　　　　　　　　　　　55
　　NURSE. Your love says, like an honest gentleman,
and a courteous, and a kind, and a handsome, and, I
warrant, a virtuous —— Where is your mother?
　　JUL. Where is my mother! Why, she is within,
Where should she be? How oddly thou repliest!　61
" Your love says, like an honest gentleman,
Where is your mother? "
　　NURSE.　　　　　　　Oh, God's Lady dear!°
Are you so hot°? Marry, come up,° I trow.
Is this the poultice for my aching bones?　　65
Henceforward do your messages yourself.
　　JUL. Here's such a coil!° Come, what says
　　　Romeo?
　　NURSE. Have you got leave to go to shrift today?
　　JUL. I have.
　　NURSE. Then hie° you hence to Friar Laurence'
　　　cell,　　　　　　　　　　　　　　70
There stays a husband to make you a wife.
Now comes the wanton blood up in your cheeks,
They'll be in scarlet straight at any news.
Hie you to church, I must another way,
To fetch a ladder by the which your love　　75
Must climb a bird's nest soon when it is dark.
I am the drudge, and toil in your delight,
But you shall bear the burden soon at night.
Go, I'll to dinner, hie you to the cell.
　　JUL. Hie to high fortune! Honest Nurse, fare-
　　　well.　　　　　　　　　　　　　80
　　　　　　　　　　　　　　　　[*Exeunt.*]

---

225. **sententious:** for "sentence" — proverb.　**232. apace:**
quickly.
　Sc. v: **6. lowering:** frowning.　**7. nimble-pinioned:** swift-
winged.　**14. bandy:** hit back, as a tennis ball.　**25. give . . .
leave:** let me alone.　**26. jaunce:** running to and fro.

36. stay . . . circumstance: wait for details.　**43. flower of courtesy:** perfect gentleman.　**52. Beshrew:** plague on.　**63. God's
. . . dear:** by God's dear Mother; i.e., the Virgin Mary.　**64. hot:**
eager.　**Marry . . . up:** An expression of angry impatience.
67. coil: fuss.　**70. hie:** hasten.

SCENE VI. FRIAR LAURENCE's *cell.*

[*Enter* FRIAR LAURENCE *and* ROMEO.]
FRI. L. So smile the Heavens upon this holy act
That afterhours with sorrow chide us not!
ROM. Amen, amen! But come what sorrow can,
It cannot countervail° the exchange of joy
That one short minute gives me in her sight.   5
Do thou but close our hands with holy words,
Then love-devouring death do what he dare,
It is enough I may but call her mine.
FRI. L. These violent delights have violent ends,
And in their triumph die, like fire and powder°   10
Which as they kiss consume. The sweetest honey
Is loathsome in his own deliciousness,
And in the taste confounds the appetite.
Therefore, love moderately, long love doth so,
Too swift arrives as tardy as too slow.   15
[*Enter* JULIET.] Here comes the lady. Oh, so light a foot
Will ne'er wear out the everlasting flint.
A lover may bestride the gossamer°
That idles in the wanton summer air,
And yet not fall, so light is vanity.°   20
JUL. Good even to my ghostly confessor.
FRI. L. Romeo shall thank thee, daughter, for us both.
JUL. As much to him, else is his thanks too much.°
ROM. Ah, Juliet, if the measure of thy joy
Be heaped like mine, and that thy skill be more   25
To blazon° it, then sweeten with thy breath
This neighbor air, and let rich music's tongue
Unfold the imagined happiness that both
Receive in either by this dear encounter.
JUL. Conceit,° more rich in matter than in words,
Brags of his substance, not of ornament.   31
They are but beggars that can count their worth,
But my true love is grown to such excess,
I cannot sum up sum of half my wealth.
FRI. L. Come, come with me, and we will make
     short work,   35
For, by your leaves, you shall not stay alone
Till Holy Church incorporate two in one. [*Exeunt.*]

Sc. vi: **4. countervail:** counterbalance. **10. fire . . . powder:** Elizabethan cannon were discharged by applying a lighted match to loose gunpowder. See Pl. 12a. **18. gossamer:** a small spider's web that floats in the wind. **20. vanity:** unreality. **23. As . . . much:** may it be an evening good to him also, or else he has small cause for thanks. **26. blazon:** describe, a herald's word for the technical description or painting of a coat of arms. **30. Conceit:** understanding.

Act III

SCENE I. *A public place.*

[*Enter* MERCUTIO, BENVOLIO, PAGE, *and* SERVANTS.]
BEN. I pray thee, good Mercutio, let's retire.
The day is hot, the Capulets abroad,
And if we meet, we shall not 'scape a brawl;
For now these hot days is the mad blood stirring.   4
MER. Thou art like one of those fellows that when he enters the confines of a tavern claps me his sword upon the table and says, "God send me no need of thee!" and by the operation of the second cup draws it on the drawer,° when indeed there is no need.   10
BEN. Am I like such a fellow?
MER. Come, come, thou art as hot a Jack in thy mood as any in Italy, and as soon moved to be moody, and as soon moody to be moved.
BEN. And what to?   15
MER. Nay, an there were two such, we should have none shortly, for one would kill the other. Thou! Why, thou wilt quarrel with a man that hath a hair more, or a hair less, in his beard than thou hast. Thou wilt quarrel with a man for cracking nuts,   20 having no other reason but because thou hast hazel eyes. What eye but such an eye would spy out such a quarrel? Thy head is as full of quarrels as an egg is full of meat, and yet thy head hath been beaten as addle as an egg for quarreling. Thou hast quar-   25 reled with a man for coughing in the street, because he hath wakened thy dog that hath lain asleep in the sun. Didst thou not fall out with a tailor for wearing his new doublet° before Easter? With another   30 for tying his new shoes with old ribbon? And yet thou wilt tutor me from quarreling!°
BEN. An I were so apt to quarrel as thou art, any man should buy the fee simple° of my life for an hour and a quarter.   36
MER. The fee simple! Oh, simple!
[*Enter* TYBALT *and others.*]
BEN. By my head, here come the Capulets.
MER. By my heel, I care not.
TYB. Follow me close, for I will speak to them. Gentlemen, good-den — a word with one of you.   41
MER. And but one word with one of us? Couple it with something — make it a word and a blow.
TYB. You shall find me apt enough to that, sir, an you will give me occasion.
MER. Could you not take some occasion without giving?   47
TYB. Mercutio, thou consort'st° with Romeo ——

Act III, Sc. i: 10. drawer: potboy who fetches the drinks in a tavern. **30. doublet:** See Pl. 8b and p. 93a. **32. tutor . . . quarreling:** instruct me how to avoid quarreling. **35. fee simple:** absolute possession, a legal phrase meaning "holding in perpetuity." **48. consort'st:** you are a companion of. Mercutio takes up the other meaning of "consort" — a party of musicians playing different instruments.

MER. Consort! What, dost thou make us minstrels? An thou make minstrels of us, look to hear nothing but discords. Here's my fiddlestick,° here's that shall make you dance. 'Zounds,° consort! 52

BEN. We talk here in the public haunt of men. Either withdraw unto some private place, 55
And reason coldly of your grievances,
Or else depart. Here all eyes gaze on us.

MER. Men's eyes were made to look, and let them gaze.
I will not budge for no man's pleasure, I.

[*Enter* ROMEO.]

TYB. Well, peace be with you, sir. Here comes my man.° 59

MER. But I'll be hanged, sir, if he wear your livery. Marry, go before to field,° he'll be your follower. Your worship in that sense may call him man.

TYB. Romeo, the hate I bear thee can afford
No better term than this — thou art a villain. 64

ROM. Tybalt, the reason that I have to love thee
Doth much excuse the appertaining rage
To such a greeting. Villain am I none,
Therefore farewell. I see thou know'st me not.°

TYB. Boy,° this shall not excuse the injuries 69
That thou hast done me, therefore turn and draw.

ROM. I do protest I never injured thee,
But love thee better than thou canst devise°
Till thou shalt know the reason of my love.
And so, good Capulet — which name I tender°
As dearly as mine own — be satisfied. 75

MER. Oh, calm, dishonorable, vile submission!
Alla stoccata° carries it away. [*Draws.*]
Tybalt, you ratcatcher, will you walk?

TYB. What wouldst thou have with me? 79

MER. Good King of Cats,° nothing but one of your nine lives, that I mean to make bold withal, and, as you shall use me hereafter, dry-beat° the rest of the eight. Will you pluck your sword out of his pilcher° by the ears? Make haste, lest mine be about your ears ere it be out. 85

TYB. I am for you. [*Drawing.*]

ROM. Gentle Mercutio, put thy rapier up.

MER. Come, sir, your passado.° [*They fight.*]

ROM. Draw, Benvolio, beat down their weapons.
Gentlemen, for shame, forbear this outrage! 90
Tybalt, Mercutio, the Prince expressly hath
Forbid this bandying° in Verona streets.

Hold, Tybalt, good Mercutio!

[TYBALT *under* ROMEO's *arm stabs* MERCUTIO *and flies with his followers.*]

MER.   I am hurt.
A plague o' both your houses! I am sped.°
Is he gone, and hath nothing?

BEN.   What, art thou hurt?

MER. Aye, aye, a scratch, a scratch — marry, 'tis enough. 96
Where is my page? Go, villain, fetch a surgeon.

[*Exit* PAGE.]

ROM. Courage, man, the hurt cannot be much.

MER. No, 'tis not so deep as a well nor so wide as a church door, but 'tis enough, 'twill serve. Ask for me tomorrow and you shall find me a grave 101 man.° I am peppered, I warrant, for this world. A plague o' both your houses! 'Zounds, a dog, a rat, a mouse, a cat, to scratch a man to death! A braggart, a rogue, a villain, that fights by the book of arithmetic!° Why the devil came you between us! I was hurt under your arm. 108

ROM. I thought all for the best.

MER. Help me into some house, Benvolio,
Or I shall faint. A plague o' both your houses!
They have made worms' meat of me. I have it,
And soundly too — your houses! 113

[*Exeunt* MERCUTIO *and* BENVOLIO.]

ROM. This gentleman, the Prince's near ally,
My very friend, hath got his mortal hurt
In my behalf, my reputation stained
With Tybalt's slander — Tybalt, that an hour
Hath been my kinsman. O sweet Juliet,
Thy beauty hath made me effeminate,
And in my temper softened valor's steel! 120

[*Re-enter* BENVOLIO.]

BEN. O Romeo, Romeo, brave Mercutio's dead!
That gallant spirit hath aspired° the clouds,
Which too untimely here did scorn the earth.

ROM. This day's black fate on more days doth depend,°
This but begins the woe others must end. 125

[*Re-enter* TYBALT.]

BEN. Here comes the furious Tybalt back again.

ROM. Alive, in triumph! And Mercutio slain!
Away to Heaven, respective lenity,°
And fire-eyed fury be my conduct° now!
Now, Tybalt, take the "villain" back again 130
That late thou gavest me; for Mercutio's soul
Is but a little way above our heads,
Staying for thine to keep him company.
Either thou, or I, or both, must go with him.

---

51. **fiddlestick:** i.e., rapier.   52. **'Zounds:** by God's wounds, a common oath.   59. **my man:** i.e., the man I want. Mercutio chooses to interpret the word in the other sense of "my servant."   61. **field:** a place convenient for a duel.   68. **know'st me not:** i.e., that by my marriage with Juliet I am now your kinsman.   69. **Boy:** See I.v.80,n.   72. **devise:** think.   74. **tender:** regard.   77. **Alla stoccata:** a thrust. Mercutio thinks that Tybalt with his newfangled skill with the rapier has terrified Romeo into behaving like a coward.   80. **King of Cats:** See II.iv.19,n.   82. **dry-beat:** bruise, beat without drawing blood.   84. **pilcher:** scabbard; lit., leather coat.   88. **passado:** See II.iv.27,n.   92. **bandying:** quarreling.

94. **sped:** done for.   101–02. **grave man:** Mercutio's last pun.   106–07. **book of arithmetic:** exact rules of fencing.   122. **aspired:** soared to.   124. **This . . . depend:** i.e., this day is but the beginning of many more fatal days.   128. **respective lenity:** considerate mercy; i.e., I will no longer make allowances for Tybalt as Juliet's kinsman.   129. **conduct:** guide.

TYB. Thou, wretched boy, that didst consort him
    here,   135
Shalt with him hence.
    ROM.   This shall determine that.
                     [They fight; TYBALT falls.]
BEN. Romeo, away, be gone!
The citizens are up, and Tybalt slain.
Stand not amazed. The Prince will doom thee death
If thou art taken. Hence, be gone, away!   140
ROM. Oh, I am fortune's fool!°
    BEN.   Why dost thou stay?   *[Exit ROMEO.]*
                [Enter CITIZENS, etc.]
    1. CIT. Which way ran he that killed Mercutio?
Tybalt, that murderer, which way ran he?
    BEN. There lies that Tybalt.
    1. CIT.   Up, sir, go with me.
I charge thee in the Prince's name, obey.   145
[Enter PRINCE, attended; MONTAGUE, CAPULET, their
              WIVES, and others.]
    PRIN. Where are the vile beginners of this fray?
    BEN. O noble Prince, I can discover° all
The unlucky manage° of this fatal brawl.
There lies the man, slain by young Romeo,
That slew thy kinsman, brave Mercutio.   150
    LADY CAP. Tybalt, my cousin! Oh, my brother's
    child!
O Prince! O Cousin! Husband! Oh, the blood is spilt
Of my dear kinsman! Prince, as thou art true,
For blood of ours shed blood of Montague.
O Cousin, Cousin!   155
    PRIN. Benvolio, who began this bloody fray?
    BEN. Tybalt, here slain, whom Romeo's hand did
    slay —
Romeo that spoke him fair, bade him bethink
How nice° the quarrel was, and urged withal
Your high displeasure. All this uttered   160
With gentle breath, calm look, knees humbly bowed,
Could not take truce with the unruly spleen°
Of Tybalt deaf to peace, but that he tilts
With piercing steel at bold Mercutio's breast,
Who, all as hot, turns deadly point to point,   165
And, with a martial scorn, with one hand beats
Cold death aside and with the other sends
It back to Tybalt, whose dexterity
Retorts it. Romeo, he cries aloud,
" Hold, friends! Friends, part! " and, swifter than his
    tongue,   170
His agile arm beats down their fatal points,
And 'twixt them rushes. Underneath whose arm
An envious° thrust from Tybalt hit the life
Of stout Mercutio, and then Tybalt fled,
But by and by comes back to Romeo,   175
Who had but newly entertained revenge,
And to 't they go like lightning. For ere I

Could draw to part them was stout Tybalt slain,
And as he fell, did Romeo turn and fly.
This is the truth, or let Benvolio die.   180
    LADY CAP. He is a kinsman to the Montague,
Affection makes him false, he speaks not true.
Some twenty of them fought in this black strife,
And all those twenty could but kill one life.
I beg for justice, which thou, Prince, must give.   185
Romeo slew Tybalt, Romeo must not live.
    PRIN. Romeo slew him, he slew Mercutio.
Who now the price of his dear blood doth owe?
    MON. Not Romeo, Prince, he was Mercutio's
    friend.   189
His fault concludes but what the law should end,
The life of Tybalt.
    PRIN.   And for that offense
Immediately we do exile him hence.
I have an interest° in your hate's proceeding,
My blood for your rude brawls doth lie a-bleeding.
But I'll amerce° you with so strong a fine   195
That you shall all repent the loss of mine.
I will be deaf to pleading and excuses,
Nor tears nor prayers shall purchase out° abuses.
Therefore use none. Let Romeo hence in haste,
Else, when he's found, that hour is his last.   200
Bear hence this body, and attend our will.°
Mercy but murders, pardoning those that kill.
                            [Exeunt.]

SCENE II. CAPULET'S *orchard*.

[Enter JULIET.]

    JUL. Gallop apace, you fiery-footed steeds,
Toward Phoebus'° lodging. Such a wagoner
As Phaëton° would whip you to the west,
And bring in cloudy night immediately.
Spread thy close curtain, love-performing night,   5
That runaways' eyes° may wink, and Romeo
Leap to these arms, untalked of and unseen.
Lovers can see to do their amorous rites
By their own beauties; or, if love be blind,
It best agrees with night. Come, civil° night,   10
Thou sober-suited matron, all in black,
And learn me how to lose a winning match
Played for a pair of stainless maidenhoods.
Hood my unmanned blood bating° in my cheeks

193. an interest: i.e., Mercutio was my kinsman. 195. amerce:
punish. 198. purchase out: pay for. 201. attend . . . will: come
to receive my judgment.
    Sc. ii: 2. Phoebus: Phoebus, the sun, was daily drawn across
the sky in his chariot. 3. Phaëton: the sun god's son, who
tried to drive his father's chariot, but the horses bolted.
6. runaways' eyes: There has been much controversy about this
line, whether Phoebus or night is the runaway. Cf. *M of Ven,*
II.vi.47. 10. civil: respectable. 14. Hood . . . bating: images
from falconry. See App. 26. Hood: the hawk's head was covered
with a hood to keep it quiet. unmanned: untrained, and so
wild. bating: fluttering.

141. fortune's fool: fooled by fortune. 147. discover: reveal.
148. manage: management, circumstances. 159. nice: trifling.
162. spleen: fiery temper. 173. envious: hateful.

With thy black mantle, till strange love grown bold
Think true love acted simple modesty.　　　　16
Come, night, come, Romeo, come, thou day in
　　night,
For thou wilt lie upon the wings of night
Whiter than new snow on a raven's back.
Come, gentle night, come, loving, black-browed
　　night,　　　　　　　　　　　　　　　　　20
Give me my Romeo; and when he shall die,
Take him and cut him out in little stars,
And he will make the face of heaven so fine
That all the world will be in love with night,
And pay no worship to the garish° sun.　　　25
Oh, I have bought the mansion of a love,
But not possessed it, and though I am sold,
Not yet enjoyed. So tedious is this day
As is the night before some festival
To an impatient child that hath new robes　　30
And may not wear them. Oh, here comes my
　　nurse,
And she brings news, and every tongue that speaks
But Romeo's name speaks heavenly eloquence.
[*Enter* NURSE, *with cords.*] Now, Nurse, what news?
What hast thou there? The cords
That Romeo bid thee fetch?
　　NURSE. Aye, aye, the cords. [*Throws them down.*]
　　JUL. Aye me! What news? Why dost thou wring
　　　thy hands?
　　NURSE. Ah, welladay! He's dead, he's dead, he's
　　　dead.
We are undone, lady, we are undone.
Alack the day! He's gone, he's killed, he's dead.
　　JUL. Can Heaven be so envious?
　　NURSE.　　　　　　　　　　　Romeo can,　40
Though Heaven cannot. O Romeo, Romeo!
Who ever would have thought it? Romeo!
　　JUL. What devil art thou that dost torment me
　　　thus?
This torture should be roared in dismal Hell.
Hath Romeo slain himself? Say thou but " I,"°　45
And that bare vowel " I " shall poison more
Than the death-darting eye of cockatrice.°
I am not I, if there be such an I,
Or those eyes shut, that make thee answer " I."
If he be slain, say " I," or if not, no.　　　50
Brief sounds determine° of my weal or woe.
　　NURSE. I saw the wound, I saw it with mine
　　　eyes —
God save the mark! — here on his manly breast.
A piteous corse,° a bloody piteous corse,
Pale, pale as ashes, all bedaubed in blood,　　55
All in gore blood. I swounded at the sight.
　　JUL. Oh, break, my heart! Poor bankrupt, break
　　　at once!

To prison, eyes, ne'er look on liberty!
Vile earth to earth resign, end motion here,
And thou and Romeo press one heavy bier!　　60
　　NURSE. O Tybalt, Tybalt, the best friend I had!
O courteous Tybalt! Honest gentleman!
That ever I should live to see thee dead!
　　JUL. What storm is this that blows so contrary?
Is Romeo slaughtered, and is Tybalt dead?　　65
My dear-loved cousin, and my dearer lord?
Then, dreadful trumpet, sound the general doom!°
For who is living if those two are gone?
　　NURSE. Tybalt is gone, and Romeo banishèd —
Romeo that killed him, he is banishèd.　　　70
　　JUL. Oh, God! Did Romeo's hand shed Tybalt's
　　　blood?
　　NURSE. It did, it did. Alas the day, it did!
　　JUL. Oh, serpent heart, hid with a flowering
　　　face!
Did ever dragon keep so fair a cave?
Beautiful tyrant! Fiend angelical!　　　　75
Dove-feathered raven! Wolvish-ravening lamb!°
Despisèd substance of divinest show!
Just opposite to what thou justly seem'st,
A damnèd saint, an honorable villain!
O Nature, what hadst thou to do in Hell　　80
When thou didst bower° the spirit of a fiend
In mortal paradise of such sweet flesh?
Was ever book containing such vile matter
So fairly bound? Oh, that deceit should dwell
In such a gorgeous palace!
　　NURSE.　　　　　　　　　There's no trust,　85
No faith, no honesty in men — all perjured,
All forsworn, all naught, all dissemblers.°
Ah, where's my man? Give me some aqua vitae.°
These griefs, these woes, these sorrows, make me old.
Shame come to Romeo!
　　JUL.　　　　　　　　Blistered be thy tongue　90
For such a wish! He was not born to shame.
Upon his brow shame is ashamed to sit,
For 'tis a throne where honor may be crowned
Sole monarch of the universal earth.
Oh, what a beast was I to chide at him!　　95
　　NURSE. Will you speak well of him that killed
　　　your cousin?
　　JUL. Shall I speak ill of him that is my husband?
Ah, poor my lord, what tongue shall smooth thy
　　name
When I, thy three-hours wife, have mangled it?　99
But wherefore, villain, didst thou kill my cousin?
That villain cousin would have killed my husband.
Back, foolish tears, back to your native spring,
Your tributary drops belong to woe
Which you mistaking offer up to joy.　　　104

---

25. garish: gaudy.　**45. Say ... "I":** Puns on "aye" and "I"
are common.　**47. cockatrice:** a fabulous serpent so deadly that
it could slay by its mere glance.　**51. determine:** decide.
54. corse: corpse.

67. general doom: Day of Judgment.　**73–76. Oh ... lamb:**
This elaborate series of oxymoron (bitter-sweet) images is typical
of early Elizabethan dramatic poetry.　**81. bower:** embower.
87. dissemblers: hypocrites.　**88. aqua vitae:** spirits.

My husband lives, that Tybalt would have slain,
And Tybalt's dead, that would have slain my hus-
     band.
All this is comfort, wherefore weep I, then?
Some word there was, worser than Tybalt's death,
That murdered me. I would forget it fain,
But, oh, it presses to my memory   110
Like damnèd guilty deeds to sinners' minds.
" Tybalt is dead, and Romeo banishèd."
That " banishèd," that one word " banishèd,"
Hath slain ten thousand Tybalts. Tybalt's death
Was woe enough if it had ended there.   115
Or, if sour woe delights in fellowship,
And needly° will be ranked with other griefs,
Why followed not, when she said " Tybalt's dead,"
Thy father, or thy mother, nay, or both,
Which modern° lamentation might have moved?
But with a rearward following Tybalt's death,   121
" Romeo is banishèd." To speak that word
Is father, mother, Tybalt, Romeo, Juliet,
All slain, all dead. " Romeo is banishèd."
There is no end, no limit, measure, bound,   125
In that word's death; no words can that woe
     sound.
Where is my father, and my mother, Nurse?
     NURSE. Weeping and wailing over Tybalt's corse.
Will you go to them? I will bring you thither.
     JUL. Wash they his wounds with tears. Mine shall
     be spent,   130
When theirs are dry, for Romeo's banishment.
Take up those cords. Poor ropes, you are beguiled,
Both you and I, for Romeo is exiled.
He made you for a highway to my bed,
But I, a maid, die maiden-widowèd.   135
Come, cords, come, Nurse, I'll to my wedding bed,
And death, not Romeo, take my maidenhead!
     NURSE. Hie to your chamber. I'll find Romeo
To comfort you. I wot° well where he is.
Hark ye, your Romeo will be here at night.   140
I'll to him — he is hid at Laurence' cell.
     JUL. Oh, find him! Give this ring to my true
     knight,
And bid him come to take his last farewell.
                                   [*Exeunt.*]

SCENE III. FRIAR LAURENCE'S *cell.*

[*Enter* FRIAR LAURENCE.]
     FRI. L. Romeo, come forth, come forth, thou fear-
     ful° man.
Affliction is enamored of thy parts,°
And thou art wedded to calamity.

[*Enter* ROMEO.]
     ROM. Father, what news? What is the Prince's
     doom?°
What sorrow craves acquaintance at my hand   5
That I yet know not?
     FRI. L.   Too familiar
Is my dear son with such sour company.
I bring thee tidings of the Prince's doom.
     ROM. What less than Doomsday is the Prince's
     doom?
     FRI. L. A gentler judgment vanished° from his
     lips,   10
Not body's death, but body's banishment.
     ROM. Ha, banishment! Be merciful, say " death,"
For exile hath more terror in his look,
Much more, than death. Do not say " banishment."
     FRI. L. Hence from Verona art thou banishèd.   15
Be patient, for the world is broad and wide.
     ROM. There is no world without° Verona walls,
But Purgatory, torture, Hell itself.
Hence banishèd is banished from the world,
And world's exile is death. Then " banishèd "   20
Is death mistermed. Calling death " banishèd,"
Thou cut'st my head off with a golden ax,
And smilest upon the stroke that murders me.
     FRI. L. Oh, deadly sin! Oh, rude unthankfulness!
Thy fault our law calls death, but the kind Prince,
Taking thy part, hath rushed° aside the law,   26
And turned that black word " death " to " banish-
     ment."
This is dear mercy, and thou seest it not.
     ROM. 'Tis torture, and not mercy. Heaven is
     here,
Where Juliet lives, and every cat and dog   30
And little mouse, every unworthy thing,
Live here in Heaven and may look on her,
But Romeo may not. More validity,
More honorable state, more courtship, lives
In carrion flies than Romeo. They may seize   35
On the white wonder of dear Juliet's hand,
And steal immortal blessing from her lips,
Who, even in pure and vestal modesty,
Still blush, as thinking their own kisses sin.
But Romeo may not, he is banishèd.   40
This may flies do, but I from this must fly.
They are free men, but I am banishèd.
And say'st thou yet that exile is not death?
Hadst thou no poison mixed, no sharp-ground knife,
No sudden mean of death, though ne'er so mean,
But " banishèd " to kill me? — " Banishèd "?   46
O Friar, the damnèd use that word in Hell,
Howling attends it. How hast thou the heart,
Being a divine, a ghostly confessor,
A sin-absolver, and my friend professed,   50
To mangle me with that word " banishèd "?

---

117. needly: necessarily.   120. modern: ordinary.   139. wot:
know.
  Sc. iii: 1. fearful: full of fear.   2. Affliction . . . parts: sorrow
has fallen in love with your good qualities.
4. doom: decree, punishment.   10. vanished: escaped from.
17. without: outside.   26. rushed: brushed.

FRI. L. Thou fond° madman, hear me but speak a
   word.

ROM. Oh, thou wilt speak again of banishment.

FRI. L. I'll give thee armor to keep off that word,
Adversity's sweet milk, philosophy,   55
To comfort thee, though thou art banishèd.

ROM. Yet "banishèd"? Hang up philosophy!
Unless philosophy can make a Juliet,
Displant° a town, reverse a Prince's doom,
It helps not, it prevails not. Talk no more.   60

FRI. L. Oh, then I see that madmen have no ears.

ROM. How should they when that wise men have
   no eyes?

FRI. L. Let me dispute° with thee of thy estate.°

ROM. Thou canst not speak of that thou dost not
   feel.
Wert thou as young as I, Juliet thy love,   65
An hour but married, Tybalt murderèd,
Doting like me, and like me banishèd,
Then mightst thou speak, then mightst thou tear thy
   hair
And fall upon the ground, as I do now,
Taking the measure of an unmade grave.   70
                 [Knocking within.]

FRI. L. Arise, one knocks. Good Romeo, hide thyself.

ROM. Not I, unless the breath of heartsick groans
Mistlike enfold me from the search of eyes.
                      [Knocking.]

FRI. L. Hark how they knock! Who's there?
   Romeo, arise,
Thou wilt be taken. — Stay awhile! — Stand up,
                      [Knocking.]
Run to my study. — By and by!° — God's will,   76
What simpleness is this! — I come, I come!
                      [Knocking.]
Who knocks so hard? Whence come you? What's
   your will?

NURSE. [Within] Let me come in, and you shall
   know my errand.
I come from Lady Juliet.

FRI. L.   Welcome, then.   80
               [Enter NURSE.]

NURSE. O holy Friar, oh, tell me, holy Friar,
Where is my lady's lord, where's Romeo?

FRI. L. There on the ground, with his own tears
   made drunk.

NURSE. Oh, he is even in my mistress' case,
Just in her case!

FRI. L.   Oh, woeful sympathy!   85
Piteous predicament!

NURSE.   Even so lies she,
Blubbering and weeping, weeping and blubbering.
Stand up, stand up, stand, an you be a man.
For Juliet's sake, for her sake, rise and stand.

Why should you fall into so deep an O?°   90

ROM. Nurse!

NURSE. Ah sir, ah sir! Well, death's the end of all.

ROM. Spakest thou of Juliet? How is it with her?
Doth she not think me an old° murderer,
Now I have stained the childhood of our joy   95
With blood removed but little from her own?
Where is she? And how doth she? And what says
My concealed lady to our canceled love?

NURSE. Oh, she says nothing, sir, but weeps and
   weeps,
And now falls on her bed, and then starts up   100
And Tybalt calls, and then on Romeo cries,
And then down falls again.

ROM.   As if that name,
Shot from the deadly level° of a gun,
Did murder her, as that name's cursèd hand
Murdered her kinsman. Oh, tell me, Friar, tell me,
In what vile part of this anatomy°   106
Doth my name lodge? Tell me, that I may sack
The hateful mansion.   [Drawing his dagger.]

FRI. L.   Hold thy desperate hand.
Art thou a man? Thy form cries out thou art.
Thy tears are womanish, thy wild acts denote   110
The unreasonable fury of a beast.
Unseemly woman in a seeming man!
Or ill-beseeming beast in seeming both!°
Thou hast amazed me. By my holy order,
I thought thy disposition better tempered.°   115
Hast thou slain Tybalt? Wilt thou slay thyself?
And slay thy lady too that lives in thee,
By doing damnèd hate upon thyself?   118
Why rail'st thou on thy birth, the Heaven and earth?
Since birth and Heaven and earth all three do meet
In thee at once, which thou at once wouldst lose.
Fie, fie, thou shamest thy shape, thy love, thy wit,
Which, like a usurer,° abound'st in all,
And usest none in that true use indeed   124
Which should bedeck thy shape, thy love, thy wit.
Thy noble shape is but a form of wax,°
Digressing° from the valor of a man;
Thy dear love sworn, but hollow perjury,
Killing that love which thou hast vowed to cherish;
Thy wit, that ornament to shape and love,   130
Misshapen in the conduct of them both,
Like powder in a skill-less soldier's flask,
Is set afire by thine own ignorance,
And thou dismembered with thine own defense.°
What, rouse thee, man! Thy Juliet is alive,   135
For whose dear sake thou wast but lately dead.
There art thou happy. Tybalt would kill thee,
But thou slew'st Tybalt. There art thou happy too.

---

52. fond: foolish.   59. Displant: remove.   63. dispute: discuss.
estate: circumstances.   76. By . . . by: wait a moment.

90. an O: a great sigh.   94. old: veritable; lit., experienced.
103. level: aim.   106. anatomy: body.   113. Or . . . both: a
shameful beast, for you are neither man nor woman.   115. tempered: mixed.   123. usurer: miser.   126. form of wax: i.e., a
mere dummy.   127. Digressing: differing.   134. dismembered
. . . defense: blown to pieces by your own weapon.

The law, that threatened death, becomes thy friend
And turns it to exile. There art thou happy.   140
A pack of blessings lights upon thy back,
Happiness courts thee in her best array;
But, like a misbehaved and sullen wench,
Thou pout'st upon thy fortune and thy love.
Take heed, take heed, for such die miserable.   145
Go, get thee to thy love, as was decreed,
Ascend her chamber — hence and comfort her.
But look thou stay not till the watch be set,°
For then thou canst not pass to Mantua,
Where thou shalt live till we can find a time   150
To blaze° your marriage, reconcile your friends,
Beg pardon of the Prince, and call thee back
With twenty hundred thousand times more joy
Than thou went'st forth in lamentation.
Go before, Nurse. Commend me to thy lady,   155
And bid her hasten all the house to bed,
Which heavy sorrow makes them apt unto.
Romeo is coming.
   NURSE. Oh Lord, I could have stayed here all the
   night
To hear good counsel. Oh, what learning is!   160
My lord, I'll tell my lady you will come.
   ROM. Do so, and bid my sweet prepare to chide.
   NURSE. Here, sir, a ring she bid me give you, sir.
Hie you, make haste, for it grows very late. [*Exit.*]
   ROM. How well my comfort is revived by this!
   FRI. L. Go hence, good night, and here stands all
   your state.   166
Either be gone before the watch be set,
Or by the break of day disguised from hence.
Sojourn in Mantua. I'll find out your man,
And he shall signify from time to time   170
Every good hap to you that chances here.
Give me thy hand, 'tis late. Farewell, good night.
   ROM. But that a joy past joy calls out on me,
It were a grief so brief to part with thee.   174
Farewell.   [*Exeunt.*]

SCENE IV. *A room in* CAPULET'S *house.*

[*Enter* CAPULET, LADY CAPULET, *and* PARIS.]
   CAP. Things have fall'n out, sir, so unluckily,
That we have had no time to move° our daughter.
Look you, she loved her kinsman Tybalt dearly,
And so did I. Well, we were born to die.
'Tis very late, she'll not come down tonight.   5
I promise you, but for your company
I would have been abed an hour ago.
   PAR. These times of woe afford no time to woo.
Madam, good night. Commend me to your daugh-
   ter.

   LADY CAP. I will, and know her mind early tomor-
   row;   10
Tonight she's mewed° up to her heaviness.
   CAP. Sir Paris, I will make a desperate tender°
Of my child's love. I think she will be ruled
In all respects by me —— nay, more, I doubt it not.
Wife, go you to her ere you go to bed,   15
Acquaint her here of my son° Paris' love,
And bid her, mark you me, on Wednesday next ——
But, soft! what day is this?
   PAR.   Monday, my lord.
   CAP. Monday! Ha, ha! Well, Wednesday is too
   soon.
O' Thursday let it be. O' Thursday, tell her,   20
She shall be married to this noble Earl.
Will you be ready? Do you like this haste?
We'll keep no great ado, a friend or two;
For, hark you, Tybalt being slain so late,
It may be thought we held him carelessly,   25
Being our kinsman, if we revel much.
Therefore we'll have some half a dozen friends,
And there an end. But what say you to Thursday?
   PAR. My lord, I would that Thursday were tomor-
   row.
   CAP. Well, get you gone. O' Thursday be it, then.
Go you to Juliet ere you go to bed,   31
Prepare her, wife, against° this wedding day.
Farewell, my lord. Light to my chamber, ho!
Afore me,° it is so very very late
That we may call it early by and by.   35
Good night.   [*Exeunt.*]

SCENE V. CAPULET'S *orchard.*

[*Enter* ROMEO *and* JULIET, *above, at the window*.]
   JUL. Wilt thou be gone? It is not yet near day.
It was the nightingale, and not the lark,
That pierced the fearful hollow of thine ear.
Nightly she sings on yond pomegranate tree.
Believe me, love, it was the nightingale.   5
   ROM. It was the lark, the herald of the morn,
No nightingale. Look, love, what envious streaks
Do lace° the severing clouds in yonder east.
Night's candles are burnt out, and jocund day
Stands tiptoe on the misty mountaintops.   10
I must be gone and live, or stay and die.
   JUL. Yond light is not daylight, I know it, I.
It is some meteor that the sun exhales,°
To be to thee this night a torchbearer
And light thee on thy way to Mantua.   15
Therefore stay yet — thou need'st not to be gone.

---

148. **watch be set:** The watch go on duty at the gates for the
night. See Gen. Intro. p. 18a.   151. **blaze:** make public.
   Sc. iv: 2. **move:** make the proposal to.

11. **mewed:** lit., caged like a hawk.   12. **desperate tender:** bold
offer.   16. **son:** i.e., intended son-in-law.   32. **against:** in readiness for.   34. **Afore me:** an oath meaning "before God."
   Sc. v: 8. **lace:** cover with stripes.   13. **exhales:** draws out.
Cf. *I Hen IV,* V.i.19.

ROM. Let me be ta'en, let me be put to death,
I am content, so thou wilt have it so.
I'll say yon gray is not the morning's eye,
'Tis but the pale reflex° of Cynthia's° brow;   20
Nor that is not the lark whose notes do beat
The vaulty heaven so high above our heads.
I have more care to stay than will to go.
Come, death, and welcome! Juliet wills it so.
How is 't, my soul? Let's talk. It is not day.   25
    JUL. It is, it is. Hie hence, be gone, away!
It is the lark that sings so out of tune,
Straining harsh discords and unpleasing sharps.
Some say the lark makes sweet division.°
This doth not so, for she divideth us.   30
Some say the lark and loathèd toad change eyes.°
Oh, now I would they had changed voices too!
Since arm from arm that voice doth us affray,°
Hunting thee hence with hunt's-up° to the day.
Oh, now be gone, more light and light it grows.   35
    ROM. More light and light. More dark and dark
      our woes!
        [*Enter* NURSE, *to the chamber.*]
    NURSE. Madam!
    JUL. Nurse?
    NURSE. Your lady mother is coming to your cham-
      ber.   39
The day is broke, be wary, look about.   [*Exit.*]
    JUL. Then, window, let day in, and let life out.
    ROM. Farewell, farewell! One kiss, and I'll de-
      scend.   [*Descends.*]
    JUL. Art thou gone so? Love, lord, ay, husband,
      friend!
I must hear from thee every day in the hour,
For in a minute there are many days.   45
Oh, by this count I shall be much in years
Ere I again behold my Romeo!
    ROM. Farewell!
I will omit no opportunity
That may convey my greetings, love, to thee.   50
    JUL. Oh, think'st thou we shall ever meet again?
    ROM. I doubt it not, and all these woes shall serve
For sweet discourses in our time to come.
    JUL. Oh God! I have an ill-divining soul.
Methinks I see thee, now thou art below,   55
As one dead in the bottom of a tomb.
Either my eyesight fails or thou look'st pale.
    ROM. And trust me, love, in my eye so do you.
Dry sorrow drinks our blood.° Adieu, adieu!
                                            [*Exit.*]
    JUL. O Fortune, Fortune, all men call thee fickle.
If thou art fickle, what dost thou with him   61
That is renowned for faith? Be fickle, Fortune,

For then, I hope, thou wilt not keep him long,
But send him back.   64
    LADY CAP. [*Within*] Ho, daughter! Are you up?
    JUL. Who is 't that calls? It is my lady mother!
Is she not down so late, or up so early?
What unaccustomed cause procures her hither?
                          [*Enter* LADY CAPULET.]
    LADY CAP. Why, how now, Juliet!
    JUL.   Madam, I am not well.
    LADY CAP. Evermore weeping for your cousin's
      death?   70
What, wilt thou wash him from his grave with
      tears?
And if thou couldst, thou couldst not make him live,
Therefore have done. Some grief shows much of
      love,
But much of grief shows still some want of wit.
    JUL. Yet let me weep for such a feeling° loss.   75
    LADY CAP. So shall you feel the loss, but not the
      friend
Which you weep for.
    JUL.   Feeling so the loss,
I cannot choose but ever weep the friend.
    LADY CAP. Well, girl, thou weep'st not so much for
      his death
As that the villain lives which slaughtered him.   80
    JUL. What villain, madam?
    LADY CAP.   That same villain, Romeo.
    JUL. [*Aside*] Villain and he be many miles
      asunder.
God pardon him! I do, with all my heart,
And yet no man like he doth grieve my heart.
    LADY CAP. That is because the traitor murderer
      lives.   85
    JUL. Aye, madam, from the reach of these my
      hands.
Would none but I might venge my cousin's death!
    LADY CAP. We will have vengeance for it, fear
      thou not.
Then weep no more. I'll send to one in Mantua,
Where that same banished runagate° doth live,   90
Shall give him such an unaccustomed dram°
That he shall soon keep Tybalt company.
And then I hope thou wilt be satisfied.
    JUL. Indeed I never shall be satisfied
With Romeo till I behold him — dead —   95
Is my poor heart so for a kinsman vexed.
Madam, if you could find out but a man
To bear a poison, I would temper° it,
That Romeo should, upon receipt thereof,
Soon sleep in quiet. Oh, how my heart abhors   100
To hear him named and cannot come to him,
To wreak° the love I bore my cousin
Upon his body that hath slaughtered him!

---

20. **reflex:** reflection. **Cynthia's:** the moon's. 29. **division:** melody. 31. **change eyes:** The toad has bright eyes and a harsh
croak, the lark dull eyes but a lovely voice. 33. **affray:** frighten.
34. **hunt's-up:** song played or sung in the early morning to arouse
the hunters. 59. **Dry . . . blood:** Sighing was supposed to consume the heart's blood, hence Juliet's pallor.

75. **feeling:** deeply felt. 90. **runagate:** runaway. 91. **unaccustomed dram:** unexpected dose. 98. **temper:** mix. 102. **wreak:**
revenge.

LADY CAP. Find thou the means, and I'll find such
  a man.
But now I'll tell thee joyful tidings, girl.   105
  JUL. And joy comes well in such a needy time.
What are they, I beseech your ladyship?
  LADY CAP. Well, well, thou hast a careful father,
  child,
One who, to put thee from thy heaviness,
Hath sorted° out a sudden day of joy,   110
That thou expect'st not, nor I looked not for.
  JUL. Madam, in happy time,° what day is that?
  LADY CAP. Marry, my child, early next Thursday
  morn,
The gallant, young, and noble gentleman,
The County Paris, at Saint Peter's Church,   115
Shall happily make thee there a joyful bride.
  JUL. Now, by Saint Peter's Church, and Peter
  too,
He shall not make me there a joyful bride.
I wonder at this haste, that I must wed
Ere he that should be husband comes to woo.   120
I pray you tell my lord and father, madam,
I will not marry yet. And when I do, I swear
It shall be Romeo, whom you know I hate,
Rather than Paris. These are news indeed!
  LADY CAP. Here comes your father, tell him so
  yourself   125
And see how he will take it at your hands.
                    [*Enter* CAPULET *and* NURSE.]
  CAP. When the sun sets, the air doth drizzle dew,
But for the sunset of my brother's son
It rains downright.
How now! A conduit,° girl? What, still in tears?
Evermore showering? In one little body   131
Thou counterfeit'st° a bark,° a sea, a wind.
For still thy eyes, which I may call the sea,
Do ebb and flow with tears; the bark thy body is,
Sailing in this salt flood; the winds, thy sighs,   135
Who raging with thy tears, and they with them,
Without a sudden calm will overset
Thy tempest-tossed body. How now, wife!
Have you delivered to her our decree?
  LADY CAP. Aye, sir, but she will none, she gives
  you thanks.   140
I would the fool were married to her grave!
  CAP. Soft! Take me with you, take me with you,°
  wife.
How! Will she none? Doth she not give us thanks?
Is she not proud? Doth she not count her blest,
Unworthy as she is, that we have wrought   145
So worthy a gentleman to be her bridegroom?
  JUL. Not proud you have, but thankful that you
  have.
Proud can I never be of what I hate,
But thankful even for hate that is meant love.

  CAP. How, how! How, how! Chop-logic!° What
  is this?   150
"Proud," and "I thank you," and "I thank you
  not,"
And yet "not proud." Mistress minion,° you,
Thank me no thankings, nor proud me no prouds,
But fettle° your fine joints 'gainst Thursday next,
To go with Paris to Saint Peter's Church,   155
Or I will drag thee on a hurdle° thither.
Out, you green-sickness carrion!° Out, you baggage!
You tallow-face!
  LADY CAP.   Fie, fie! What, are you mad?
  JUL. Good Father, I beseech you on my knees,
Hear me with patience but to speak a word.   160
  CAP. Hang thee, young baggage! Disobedient
  wretch!
I tell thee what. Get thee to church o' Thursday
Or never after look me in the face.
Speak not, reply not, do not answer me.
My fingers itch. Wife, we scarce thought us blest
That God had lent us but this only child,   166
But now I see this one is one too much,
And that we have a curse in having her.
Out on her, hilding!
  NURSE.   God in Heaven bless her!
You are to blame, my lord, to rate° her so.   170
  CAP. And why, my lady wisdom? Hold your
  tongue,
Good prudence. Smatter° with your gossips, go.
  NURSE. I speak no treason.
  CAP.   Oh, God ye godden.
  NURSE. May not one speak?
  CAP.   Peace, you mumbling fool!
Utter your gravity o'er a gossip's bowl,   175
For here we need it not.
  LADY CAP.   You are too hot.
  CAP. God's bread! It makes me mad.
Day, night, hour, tide, time, work, play,
Alone, in company, still° my care hath been
To have her matched. And having now provided
A gentleman of noble parentage,   181
Of fair demesnes, youthful, and nobly trained,
Stuffed,° as they say, with honorable parts,°
Proportioned as one's thought would wish a man —
And then to have a wretched puling° fool,   185
A whining mammet,° in her fortune's tender,°
To answer "I'll not wed, I cannot love,
I am too young, I pray you, pardon me."
But an you will not wed, I'll pardon you.
Graze where you will, you shall not house with me.

Look to 't, think on 't, I do not use to jest.   191
Thursday is near. Lay hand on heart, advise.°
An you be mine, I'll give you to my friend.
An you be not, hang, beg, starve, die in the streets,
For, by my soul, I'll ne'er acknowledge thee,   195
Nor what is mine shall never do thee good —
Trust to 't, bethink you, I'll not be forsworn.°
                                        [*Exit.*]
JUL. Is there no pity sitting in the clouds
That sees into the bottom of my grief?
O sweet my mother, cast me not away!   200
Delay this marriage for a month, a week;
Or, if you do not, make the bridal bed
In that dim monument where Tybalt lies.
    LADY CAP. Talk not to me, for I'll not speak a
    word.   204
Do as thou wilt, for I have done with thee.   [*Exit.*]
    JUL. Oh, God! — O Nurse, how shall this be pre-
    vented?
My husband is on earth, my faith in Heaven.
How shall that faith return again to earth
Unless that husband send it me from Heaven
By leaving earth? Comfort me, counsel me.   210
Alack, alack, that Heaven should practice strata-
    gems°
Upon so soft a subject as myself!
What say'st thou? Hast thou not a word of joy?
Some comfort, Nurse.
    NURSE.   Faith, here it is.   214
Romeo is banished, and all the world to nothing°
That he dares ne'er come back to challenge° you;
Or if he do, it needs must be by stealth.
Then, since the case so stands as now it doth,
I think it best you married with the County.
Oh, he's a lovely gentleman!   220
Romeo's a dishclout to him. An eagle, madam,
Hath not so green, so quick, so fair an eye
As Paris hath. Beshrew my very heart,
I think you are happy in this second match,
For it excels your first. Or if it did not,   225
Your first is dead, or 'twere as good he were
As living here and you no use of him.
    JUL. Speakest thou from thy heart?
    NURSE. And from my soul too, else beshrew them
    both.
    JUL. Amen!
    NURSE. What?
    JUL. Well, thou hast comforted me marvelous
    much.   230
Go in, and tell my lady I am gone,
Having displeased my father, to Laurence' cell,
To make confession and to be absolved.
    NURSE. Marry, I will, and this is wisely done.
                                        [*Exit.*]

JUL. Ancient damnation!° Oh, most wicked
    fiend!   235
Is it more sin to wish me thus forsworn,
Or to dispraise my lord with that same tongue
Which she hath praised him with above compare
So many thousand times? Go, counselor.
Thou and my bosom henceforth shall be twain.   240
I'll to the Friar, to know his remedy.
If all else fail, myself have power to die.   [*Exit.*]

Act IV

SCENE I. FRIAR LAURENCE'S *cell*.

[*Enter* FRIAR LAURENCE *and* PARIS.]
    FRI. L. On Thursday, sir? The time is very short.
    PAR. My father° Capulet will have it so,
And I am nothing slow to slack his haste.°
    FRI. L. You say you do not know the lady's mind.
Uneven is the course,° I like it not.   5
    PAR. Immoderately she weeps for Tybalt's death,
And therefore have I little talked of love,
For Venus smiles not in a house of tears.
Now, sir, her father counts it dangerous
That she doth give her sorrow so much sway,   10
And in his wisdom hastes our marriage,
To stop the inundation of her tears,
Which, too much minded by herself alone,
May be put from her by society.
Now do you know the reason of this haste.   15
    FRI. L. [*Aside*] I would I knew not why it should
    be slowed.
Look, sir, here comes the lady toward my cell.
                            [*Enter* JULIET.]
    PAR. Happily met, my lady and my wife!
    JUL. That may be, sir, when I may be a wife.
    PAR. That may be must be, love, on Thursday
    next.   20
    JUL. What must be shall be.
    FRI. L.   That's a certain text.
    PAR. Come you to make confession to this Father?
    JUL. To answer that, I should confess to you.
    PAR. Do not deny to him that you love me.
    JUL. I will confess to you that I love him.   25
    PAR. So will ye, I am sure, that you love me.
    JUL. If I do so, it will be of more price
Being spoke behind your back than to your face.
    PAR. Poor soul, thy face is much abused with tears.
    JUL. The tears have got small victory by that,   30

---

192. advise: be advised.   **197. be forsworn:** break my oath.
211. stratagems: violent deeds.   **215. all . . . nothing:** there is
no chance.   **216. challenge:** claim.

235. Ancient damnation: damnable old woman.
    Act IV, Sc. i: **2. father:** i.e., intended father-in-law.   **3. And
. . . haste:** I am as eager as he to push on the marriage.
5. Uneven . . . course: a rough proceeding; i.e., to marry Juliet
before you have asked her consent.

For it was bad enough before their spite.°
 PAR. Thou wrong'st it more than tears with that
  report.
 JUL. That is no slander, sir, which is a truth,
And what I spake, I spake it to my face.
 PAR. Thy face is mine, and thou hast slandered it.
 JUL. It may be so, for it is not mine own. 36
Are you at leisure, holy Father, now,
Or shall I come to you at evening mass?
 FRI. L. My leisure serves me, pensive daughter,
  now.
My lord, we must entreat the time alone. 40
 PAR. God shield° I should disturb devotion!
Juliet, on Thursday early will I rouse ye.
Till then, adieu, and keep this holy kiss. [*Exit.*]
 JUL. Oh, shut the door, and when thou hast done
  so,
Come weep with me — past hope, past cure, past
  help! 45
 FRI. L. Ah, Juliet, I already know thy grief,
It strains me past the compass° of my wits.
I hear thou must, and nothing may prorogue it,
On Thursday next be married to this County.
 JUL. Tell me not, Friar, that thou hear'st of
  this, 50
Unless thou tell me how I may prevent it.
If in thy wisdom thou canst give no help,
Do thou but call my resolution wise,
And with this knife I'll help it presently.°
God joined my heart and Romeo's, thou our hands,
And ere this hand, by thee to Romeo's sealed, 56
Shall be the label to another deed,°
Or my true heart with treacherous revolt
Turn to another, this shall slay them both.
Therefore, out of thy long-experienced time, 60
Give me some present counsel; or, behold,
'Twixt my extremes and me this bloody knife
Shall play the umpire, arbitrating that
Which the commission° of thy years and art
Could to no issue of true honor bring. 65
Be not so long to speak, I long to die
If what thou speak'st speak not of remedy.
 FRI. L. Hold, daughter. I do spy a kind of hope,
Which craves as desperate an execution
As that is desperate which we would prevent. 70
If, rather than to marry County Paris,
Thou hast the strength of will to slay thyself,
Then is it likely thou wilt undertake
A thing like death to chide away this shame,
That copest° with death himself to 'scape from it.
And, if thou darest, I'll give thee remedy. 76
 JUL. Oh, bid me leap, rather than marry Paris,
From off the battlements of yonder tower;

Or walk in thievish ways; or bid me lurk
Where serpents are; chain me with roaring bears;
Or shut me nightly in a charnel house,° 81
O'ercover'd quite with dead men's rattling bones,
With reeky° shanks and yellow chapless° skulls;
Or bid me go into a new-made grave,
And hide me with a dead man in his shroud — 85
Things that to hear them told have made me
  tremble —
And I will do it without fear or doubt,
To live an unstained wife to my sweet love.
 FRI. L. Hold, then, go home, be merry, give con-
  sent
To marry Paris. Wednesday is tomorrow. 90
Tomorrow night look that thou lie alone,
Let not thy nurse lie with thee in thy chamber.
Take thou this vial, being then in bed,
And this distillèd liquor drink thou off,
When presently through all thy veins shall run 95
A cold and drowsy humor;° for no pulse
Shall keep his native progress, but surcease.°
No warmth, no breath, shall testify thou livest.
The roses in thy lips and cheeks shall fade
To paly ashes, thy eyes' windows fall, 100
Like death when he shuts up the day of life.
Each part, deprived of supple government,
Shall, stiff and stark and cold, appear like death.
And in this borrowed likeness of shrunk death
Thou shalt continue two and forty hours, 105
And then awake as from a pleasant sleep.
Now, when the bridegroom in the morning comes
To rouse thee from thy bed, there art thou dead.
Then, as the manner of our country is,
In thy best robes uncovered on the bier 110
Thou shalt be borne to that same ancient vault
Where all the kindred of the Capulets lie.
In the meantime, against thou shalt awake,
Shall Romeo by my letters know our drift,°
And hither shall he come, and he and I 115
Will watch thy waking, and that very night
Shall Romeo bear thee hence to Mantua.
And this shall free thee from this present shame,
If no inconstant toy° nor womanish fear
Abate thy valor in the acting it. 120
 JUL. Give me, give me! Oh, tell not me of fear!
 FRI. L. Hold, get you gone, be strong and prosper-
  ous
In this resolve. I'll send a friar with speed
To Mantua, with my letters to thy lord.
 JUL. Love give me strength! And strength shall
  help afford. 125
Farewell, dear Father! [*Exeunt.*]

---

31. **spite:** injury. 41. **shield:** forbid. 47. **compass:** reach.
54. **presently:** immediately. 56–57. **ere . . . deed:** before my
hand consents to another contract. **label:** the strip of parchment
on which the seal is fixed. See Pl. 11a and App. 6. 64. **commission:** authority. 75. **copest:** encounterest.

81. **charnel house:** bone shed. In Shakespeare's time the churchyard was used again and again; bones disinterred in making a
new grave were thrown into the charnel house. See App. 16.
83. **reeky:** stinking. **chapless:** without jaws. 96. **humor:** moisture. 97. **surcease:** cease. 114. **drift:** intention. 119. **inconstant toy:** fickle fancy.

SCENE II. *Hall in* CAPULET'S *house.*

[*Enter* CAPULET, LADY CAPULET, NURSE, *and two*
SERVINGMEN.]

CAP. So many guests invite as here are writ.

[*Exit* FIRST SERVANT.]

Sirrah, go hire me twenty cunning cooks.

2. SERV. You shall have none ill, sir, for I'll try if
they can lick their fingers.

CAP. How canst thou try them so?   5

2. SERV. Marry, sir, 'tis an ill cook that cannot lick
his own fingers. Therefore he that cannot lick his
fingers goes not with me.

CAP. Go, be gone.   [*Exit* SECOND SERVANT.]
We shall be much unfurnished° for this time.   10
What, is my daughter gone to Friar Laurence?

NURSE. Aye, forsooth.

CAP. Well, he may chance to do some good on her.
A peevish self-willed harlotry° it is.

[*Enter* JULIET.]

NURSE. See where she comes from shrift with
merry look.   15

CAP. How now, my headstrong! Where have you
been gadding?

JUL. Where I have learned me to repent the sin
Of disobedient opposition
To you and your behests, and am enjoined
By holy Laurence to fall prostrate here,   20
To beg your pardon. Pardon, I beseech you!
Henceforward I am ever ruled by you.

CAP. Send for the County, go tell him of this.
I'll have this knot knit up tomorrow morning.

JUL. I met the youthful lord at Laurence' cell,   25
And gave him what becomèd° love I might,
Not stepping o'er the bounds of modesty.

CAP. Why, I am glad on 't, this is well. Stand up.
This is as 't should be. Let me see the County.
Aye, marry, go, I say, and fetch him hither.   30
Now, afore God, this reverend holy Friar,
All our whole city is much bound to him.

JUL. Nurse, will you go with me into my closet,
To help me sort° such needful ornaments
As you think fit to furnish me tomorrow?   35

LADY CAP. No, not till Thursday, there is time
enough.

CAP. Go, Nurse, go with her. We'll to church tomorrow.   [*Exeunt* JULIET *and* NURSE.]

LADY CAP. We shall be short in our provision.
'Tis now near night.

CAP.   Tush, I will stir about,
And all things shall be well, I warrant thee, wife.
Go thou to Juliet, help to deck up her.   41
I'll not to bed tonight, let me alone,
I'll play the housewife for this once. What ho!
They are all forth. Well, I will walk myself

To County Paris, to prepare him up   45
Against tomorrow. My heart is wondrous light
Since this same wayward girl is so reclaimed.

[*Exeunt.*]

SCENE III. JULIET'S *chamber.*

[*Enter* JULIET *and* NURSE.]

JUL. Aye, those attires are best. But, gentle Nurse,
I pray thee leave me to myself tonight;
For I have need of many orisons°
To move the Heavens to smile upon my state,   4
Which, well thou know'st, is cross° and full of sin.

[*Enter* LADY CAPULET.]

LADY CAP. What, are you busy, ho? Need you my
help?

JUL. No, madam, we have culled° such necessar-
ies
As are behooveful° for our state° tomorrow.
So please you, let me now be left alone,
And let the nurse this night sit up with you,   10
For I am sure you have your hands full all
In this so sudden business.

LADY CAP.   Goodnight.
Get thee to bed and rest, for thou hast need.

[*Exeunt* LADY CAPULET *and* NURSE.]

JUL. Farewell! God knows when we shall meet
again.
I have a faint cold fear thrills through my veins   15
That almost freezes up the heat of life.
I'll call them back again to comfort me.
Nurse! — What should she do here?
My dismal scene I needs must act alone.
Come, vial.   20
What if this mixture do not work at all?
Shall I be married then tomorrow morning?
No, no, this shall forbid it. Lie thou there.

[*Laying down a dagger.*]

What if it be a poison which the Friar
Subtly hath ministered° to have me dead,   25
Lest in this marriage he should be dishonored
Because he married me before to Romeo?
I fear it is. And yet methinks it should not,
For he hath still been tried° a holy man.
How if, when I am laid into the tomb,   30
I wake before the time that Romeo
Come to redeem me? There's a fearful point.
Shall I not then be stifled in the vault,
To whose foul mouth no healthsome air breathes in,
And there die strangled ere my Romeo comes?   35
Or if I live, is it not very like,
The horrible conceit° of death and night,

Sc. ii: 10. unfurnished: unprovided.   14. harlotry: hussy.
26. becomed: suitable.   34. sort: select.

Sc. iii: 3. orisons: prayers.   5. cross: thwarted.   7. culled:
selected.   8. behooveful: fit. state: position.   25. ministered:
administered, provided.   29. still . . . tried: always been proved.
37. conceit: idea.

Together with the terror of the place,
As in a vault, an ancient receptacle,
Where for this many hundred years the bones   40
Of all my buried ancestors are packed;
Where bloody Tybalt, yet but green in earth,
Lies festering in his shroud; where, as they say,
At some hours in the night spirits resort —
Alack, alack, is it not like that I   45
So early waking, what with loathsome smells
And shrieks like mandrakes'° torn out of the earth,
That living mortals hearing them run mad?
Oh, if I wake, shall I not be distraught,
Environèd with all these hideous fears,   50
And madly play with my forefathers' joints,
And pluck the mangled Tybalt from his shroud,
And in this rage, with some great kinsman's bone,
As with a club, dash out my desperate brains?
Oh, look! Methinks I see my cousin's ghost   55
Seeking out Romeo, that did spit his body
Upon a rapier's point. Stay, Tybalt, stay!
Romeo, I come! This do I drink to thee.
  [*She falls upon her bed, within the curtains.*]

SCENE IV. *Hall in* CAPULET'S *house.*

[*Enter* LADY CAPULET *and* NURSE.]
LADY CAP. Hold, take these keys, and fetch more
 spices, Nurse.
NURSE. They call for dates and quinces in the
 pastry.°
  [*Enter* CAPULET.]
CAP. Come, stir, stir, stir! The second cock hath
 crowed,
The curfew bell hath rung, 'tis three o'clock.
Look to the baked meats, good Angelica.   5
Spare not for cost.
NURSE. Go, you cotquean,° go,
Get you to bed. Faith, you'll be sick tomorrow
For this night's watching.
CAP. No, not a whit. What! I have watched ere
 now
All night for lesser cause, and ne'er been sick.   10
LADY CAP. Aye, you have been a mousehunt° in
 your time,
But I will watch you from such watching now.
  [*Exeunt* LADY CAPULET *and* NURSE.]
CAP. A jealoushood,° a jealoushood!
[*Enter three or four* SERVINGMEN, *with spits, and
 logs, and baskets.*] Now, fellow,
What's there?
 1. SERV. Things for the cook, sir, but I know not
 what.

CAP. Make haste, make haste. [*Exit* FIRST SERVING-
 MAN.] Sirrah, fetch drier logs.   15
Call Peter, he will show thee where they are.
 2. SERV. I have a head, sir, that will find out logs
And never trouble Peter for the matter.
 CAP. Mass,° and well said, a merry whoreson,° ha!
Thou shalt be loggerhead. [*Exit* SECOND SERVING-
 MAN.] Good faith, 'tis day.   20
The County will be here with music straight,
For so he said he would. [*Music within.*] I hear him
 near.
Nurse! Wife! What ho! What, Nurse, I say!
[*Re-enter* NURSE.] Go waken Juliet, go and trim her
 up.
I'll go and chat with Paris. Hie, make haste,   25
Make haste. The bridegroom he is come already.°
Make haste, I say. [*Exeunt.*]

SCENE V. JULIET'S *chamber.*

[*Enter* NURSE.]
NURSE. Mistress! What, mistress! Juliet! Fast, I
 warrant her, she.
Why, lamb! Why, lady! Fie, you slugabed!
Why, love, I say! Madam! Sweetheart! Why, **bride!**
What, not a word? You take your pennyworths
 now,
Sleep for a week; for the next night, I warrant,   5
The County Paris hath set up his rest°
That you shall rest but little. God forgive me,
Marry and amen, how sound is she asleep!
I needs must wake her. Madam, madam, madam!
Aye, let the County take you in your bed,   10
He'll fright you up, i' faith. Will it not be?
  [*Undraws the curtains.*]
What, dressed! And in your clothes! And down
 again!
I must needs wake you. Lady, lady, lady!
Alas, alas! Help, help! My lady's dead!
Oh, welladay that ever I was born!   15
Some aqua vitae, ho! My lord! My lady!°
  [*Enter* LADY CAPULET.]
LADY CAP. What noise is here?
NURSE. Oh, lamentable day!
LADY CAP. What is the matter?
NURSE. Look, look! Oh, heavy day!
LADY CAP. Oh me, oh me! My child, my only life.
Revive, look up, or I will die with thee.   20
Help! help! Call help.
  [*Enter* CAPULET.]
CAP. For shame, bring Juliet forth, her lord is
 come.

---

47. **mandrakes:** mandragora, a narcotic root. See Pl. 12e.
 Sc. iv: 2. **pastry:** bakehouse. 6. **cotquean:** a man who med-
dles with women's affairs. 11. **mousehunt:** one who follows
the girls; in today's slang "a wolf." 13. **jealoushood:** "Mrs.
Jealousy."

19. **Mass:** by the mass. **whoreson:** lit., bastard, but not used
seriously. 26. **The ... already:** See App. 15.
 Sc. v: 6. **set ... rest:** to hold one's hand, a metaphor from
primero, a card game; hence, "to be determined."

NURSE. She's dead, deceased, she's dead, alack the
　　day!
LADY CAP. Alack the day, she's dead, she's dead,
　　she's dead!
CAP. Ha! Let me see her. Out, alas! She's cold.　25
Her blood is settled and her joints are stiff.
Life and these lips have long been separated.
Death lies on her like an untimely frost
Upon the sweetest flower of all the field.
　NURSE. Oh, lamentable day!
LADY CAP. 　　　　　　　　Oh, woeful time!　30
　CAP. Death, that hath ta'en her hence to make me
　　wail,
Ties up my tongue and will not let me speak.
[*Enter* FRIAR LAURENCE *and* PARIS, *with* MUSICIANS.]
　FRI. L. Come, is the bride ready to go to church?
　CAP. Ready to go, but never to return.
O son, the night before thy wedding day　35
Hath death lain with thy wife. See, there she lies,
Flower as she was, deflowerèd by him.
Death is my son-in-law, Death is my heir,
My daughter he hath wedded. I will die,
And leave him all — life, living, all is Death's.　40
　PAR. Have I thought long to see this morning's
　　face
And doth it give me such a sight as this?
　LADY CAP. Accurst, unhappy, wretched, hateful
　　day!
Most miserable hour that e'er time saw
In lasting labor of his pilgrimage!　45
But one, poor one, one poor and loving child,
But one thing to rejoice and solace in,
And cruel death hath catched it from my sight!
　NURSE. Oh, woe! Oh, woeful, woeful, woeful day!
Most lamentable day, most woeful day,　50
That ever, ever, I did yet behold!
Oh, day, oh, day, oh, day! Oh, hateful day!
Never was seen so black a day as this.
Oh, woeful day, oh, woeful day!
　PAR. Beguiled, divorced, wronged, spited, slain!
Most detestable death, by thee beguiled,　56
By cruel cruel thee quite overthrown!
Oh, love! Oh, life! Not life, but love in death!
　CAP. Despised, distressed, hated, martyred, killed!
Uncomfortable time, why camest thou now　60
To murder, murder our solemnity?
O child! O child! My soul, and not my child!
Dead art thou! Alack, my child is dead,
And with my child my joys are burièd!
　FRI. L. Peace ho, for shame! Confusion's cure lives
　　not　65
In these confusions. Heaven and yourself
Had part in this fair maid, now Heaven hath all,
And all the better is it for the maid.
Your part in her you could not keep from death,
But Heaven keeps his part in eternal life.　70
The most you sought was her promotion,

For 'twas your heaven she should be advanced.
And weep ye now, seeing she is advanced
Above the clouds, as high as Heaven itself?
Oh, in this love, you love your child so ill　75
That you run mad, seeing that she is well.
She's not well married that lives married long,
But she's best married that dies married young.
Dry up your tears, and stick your rosemary°
On this fair corse, and, as the custom is,　80
In all her best array bear her to church.
For though fond nature bids us all lament,
Yet nature's tears are reason's merriment.°
　CAP. All things that we ordainèd festival
Turn from their office to black funeral.　85
Our instruments to melancholy bells,
Our wedding cheer to a sad burial feast,
Our solemn hymns to sullen dirges change,
Our bridal flowers serve for a buried corse,
And all things change them to the contrary.　90
　FRI. L. Sir, go you in, and, madam, go with him.
And go, Sir Paris, everyone prepare
To follow this fair corse unto her grave.
The Heavens do lour upon you for some ill;
Move them no more by crossing their high will.　95
[*Exeunt* CAPULET, LADY CAPULET, PARIS, *and* FRIAR.]
　1. MUS. Faith, we may put up our pipes, and be
gone.
　NURSE. Honest good fellows, ah, put up, put up,
For well you know this is a pitiful case.　[*Exit.*]
　2. MUS. Aye, by my troth, the case° may be
amended.　101
　　　　　　[*Enter* PETER.°]
　PET. Musicians, oh, musicians, "Heart's ease,°
heart's ease." Oh, an you will have me live, play
"Heart's ease."
　1. MUS. Why "Heart's ease"?　105
　PET. Oh, musicians, because my heart itself plays
"My heart is full of woe." Oh, play me some merry
dump,° to comfort me.
　1. MUS. Not a dump we, 'tis no time to play
now.　110
　PET. You will not, then?
　1. MUS. No.
　PET. I will then give it you soundly.
　1. MUS. What will you give us?
　PET. No money, on my faith, but the gleek.° I
will give you the minstrel.°　116
　1. MUS. Then will I give you the serving creature.
　PET. Then will I lay the serving creature's dagger

79. **rosemary**: rosemary was carried both for weddings and
funerals.　83. **nature's . . . merriment**: though it is natural to
weep, it is reasonable to rejoice because she has gone to a better place.　100–01. **case . . . case**: a pun on *case* — "affair" and
case — "instrument box."　102. s.d., **Enter Peter**: Q2 has *Enter
Will Kempe*, the company's clown. See Gen. Intro. p. 60a. The
tedious foolery which follows is a specimen of one of his turns;
Kempe may perhaps have made it funny. **Heart's ease**: a popular song of the time.　108. **dump**: doleful ditty.　115. **gleek**:
mock.　116. **I . . . minstrel**: i.e., I'll beat you.

on your pate. I will carry no crotchets.° I'll re you,
I'll fa you, do you note me?   121

1. MUS. An you re us and fa us, you note us.

2. MUS. Pray you put up your dagger, and put out
your wit.

PET. Then have at you with my wit! I will dry-
beat you with an iron wit, and put up my iron dagger. Answer me like men: 127

 " When griping grief the heart doth wound
   And doleful dumps the mind oppress,
 Then music with her silver sound —— "   130
Why " silver sound "? Why " music with her silver
sound "? — What say you, Simon Catling?°

1. MUS. Marry, sir, because silver hath a sweet
sound.

PET. Pretty! What say you, Hugh Rebeck?°   135

2. MUS. I say " silver sound " because musicians
sound for silver.

PET. Pretty too! What say you, James Soundpost?°

3. MUS. Faith, I know not what to say.   140

PET. Oh, I cry you mercy, you are the singer.° I
will say for you. It is " music with her silver sound "
because musicians have no gold for sounding.

 " Then music with her silver sound   145
   With speedy help doth lend redress." [*Exit.*]

1. MUS. What a pestilent knave is this same!

2. MUS. Hang him, Jack! Come, we'll in here.
Tarry for the mourners, and stay° dinner.   150
                                        [*Exeunt.*]

Act V

SCENE I. *Mantua. A street.*

[*Enter* ROMEO.]

ROM. If I may trust the flattering truth of sleep,°
My dreams presage some joyful news at hand.
My bosom's lord° sits lightly in his throne,
And all this day an unaccustomed spirit
Lifts me above the ground with cheerful thoughts.
I dreamed my lady came and found me dead —   6
Strange dream, that gives a dead man leave to
   think! —
And breathed such life with kisses in my lips
That I revived and was an emperor.
Ah me, how sweet is love itself possessed   10
When but love's shadows are so rich in joy!

[*Enter* BALTHASAR, *booted.*°] News from Verona!
   How now, Balthasar!
Dost thou not bring me letters from the Friar?
How doth my lady? Is my father well?
How fares my Juliet? That I ask again;   15
For nothing can be ill if she be well.

BAL. Then she is well, and nothing can be ill.
Her body sleeps in Capels' monument,
And her immortal part with angels lives.
I saw her laid low in her kindred's vault,   20
And presently took post° to tell it you.
Oh, pardon me for bringing these ill news,
Since you did leave it for my office, sir.

ROM. Is it e'en so? Then I defy you, stars!°
Thou know'st my lodging. Get me ink and paper,
And hire post horses.° I will hence tonight.   26

BAL. I do beseech you, sir, have patience.
Your looks are pale and wild, and do import
Some misadventure.

ROM.   Tush, thou art deceived.
Leave me, and do the thing I bid thee do.   30
Hast thou no letters to me from the Friar?

BAL. No, my good lord.

ROM.   No matter. Get thee gone,
And hire those horses. I'll be with thee straight.
                                  [*Exit* BALTHASAR.]

Well, Juliet, I will lie with thee tonight.
Let's see for means.— O mischief, thou art swift 35
To enter in the thoughts of desperate men!
I do remember an apothecary,
And hereabouts he dwells, which late I noted
In tattered weeds,° with overwhelming° brows,
Culling of simples.° Meager were his looks,   40
Sharp misery had worn him to the bones.
And in his needy shop a tortoise hung,
An alligator stuffed and other skins
Of ill-shaped fishes; and about his shelves
A beggarly account° of empty boxes,   45
Green earthen pots, bladders, and musty seeds,
Remnants of packthread and old cakes of roses,°
Were thinly scattered, to make up a show.
Noting this penury, to myself I said,
" An if a man did need a poison now,   50
Whose sale is present death in Mantua,
Here lives a caitiff° wretch would sell it him."
Oh, this same thought did but forerun my need,
And this same needy man must sell it me.
As I remember, this should be the house.   55
Being holiday, the beggar's shop is shut.
What ho! Apothecary!

---

120. **carry no crotchets:** not put up with your whims. **133. Cat-**
ling: catgut fiddle string. **135. Rebeck:** a three-stringed fiddle.
See Pl. 19a. **139. Soundpost:** part of a violin. **141. I . . .**
singer: I ask your pardon, you're just a dumb singer. **150. stay:**
wait for.

Act V, Sc. i: **1. flattering . . . sleep:** sleep that lies like truth.
3. bosom's lord: heart.

12. **s.d., booted:** wearing riding boots, an indication that he has
ridden far. **21. took post:** rode fast. **24. defy . . . stars:**
Romeo throughout has been star-crossed by malignant fate.
Now he finally defies fate to do him any worse injury. **26. post**
horses: See App. 17. **39. weeds:** garments. **overwhelming:** overhanging. **40. simples:** herbs. **45. account:** number. **47. cakes**
of roses: dried rose leaves compressed into a cake, used as a
perfume. **52. caitiff:** miserable creature.

[*Enter* APOTHECARY.]

AP.　　　　　　　　　Who calls so loud?

ROM. Come hither, man. I see that thou art poor.
Hold, there is forty ducats. Let me have
A dram of poison, such soon-speeding gear°　　60
As will disperse itself through all the veins,
That the life-weary taker may fall dead,
And that the trunk° may be discharged of breath
As violently as hasty powder fired
Doth hurry from the fatal cannon's womb.　　65

AP. Such mortal drugs I have, but Mantua's law
Is death to any he that utters° them.

ROM. Art thou so bare and full of wretchedness,
And fear'st to die? Famine is in thy cheeks,
Need and oppression starveth in thy eyes,　　70
Contempt and beggary hangs upon thy back,
The world is not thy friend, nor the world's law.
The world affords no law to make thee rich,
Then be not poor, but break it, and take this.

AP. My poverty, but not my will, consents.　　75

ROM. I pay thy poverty and not thy will.

AP. Put this in any liquid thing you will,
And drink it off, and if you had the strength
Of twenty men, it would dispatch you straight.

ROM. There is thy gold, worse poison to men's
　　souls,　　　　　　　　　　　　　　　　80
Doing more murder in this loathsome world
Than these poor compounds that thou mayst not sell.
I sell thee poison, thou hast sold me none.
Farewell. Buy food, and get thyself in flesh.
Come, cordial and not poison, go with me　　85
To Juliet's grave, for there must I use thee.

[*Exeunt.*]

SCENE II. FRIAR LAURENCE'S *cell.*

[*Enter* FRIAR JOHN.]

FRI. J. Holy Franciscan friar! Brother, ho!

[*Enter* FRIAR LAURENCE.]

FRI. L. This same should be the voice of Friar
John.
Welcome from Mantua. What says Romeo?
Or if his mind be writ, give me his letter.

FRI. J. Going to find a barefoot brother out,　　5
One of our order, to associate° me
Here in this city visiting the sick,
And finding him, the searchers of the town,
Suspecting that we both were in a house
Where the infectious pestilence° did reign,　　10
Sealed up the doors and would not let us forth,
So that my speed to Mantua there was stayed.

FRI. L. Who bare my letter, then, to Romeo?

FRI. J. I could not send it — here it is again —

Nor get a messenger to bring it thee,　　15
So fearful were they of infection.

FRI. L. Unhappy fortune! By my brotherhood,
The letter was not nice,° but full of charge°
Of dear import,° and the neglecting it
May do much danger. Friar John, go hence.　　20
Get me an iron crow° and bring it straight
Unto my cell.

FRI. J. Brother, I'll go and bring it thee.　　[*Exit.*]

FRI. L. Now must I to the monument alone.
Within this three hours will fair Juliet wake.　　25
She will beshrew° me much that Romeo
Hath had no notice of these accidents.
But I will write again to Mantua,
And keep her at my cell till Romeo come.
Poor living corse, closed in a dead man's tomb!　　30

[*Exit.*]

SCENE III. *A churchyard; in it a monument belonging to the* CAPULETS.

[*Enter* PARIS *and his* PAGE, *bearing flowers and a torch.*]

PAR. Give me thy torch, boy. Hence, and stand
aloof.
Yet put it out, for I would not be seen.
Under yond yew trees lay thee all along,°
Holding thine ear close to the hollow ground.
So shall no foot upon the churchyard tread,　　5
Being loose, unfirm, with digging up of graves,
But thou shalt hear it. Whistle then to me,
As signal that thou hear'st something approach.
Give me those flowers. Do as I bid thee, go.

PAGE. [*Aside*] I am almost afraid to stand alone
Here in the churchyard, yet I will adventure.　　11

[*Retires.*]

PAR. Sweet flower, with flowers thy bridal bed I
strew —
Oh, woe! Thy canopy is dust and stones —
Which with sweet water nightly I will dew,　　14
Or, wanting that, with tears distilled by moans.
The obsequies° that I for thee will keep
Nightly shall be to strew thy grave and weep.

[*The* PAGE *whistles.*]

The boy gives warning something doth approach.
What cursèd foot wanders this way tonight,
To cross° my obsequies and true love's rite?　　20
What, with a torch! Muffle° me, night, awhile.

[*Retires.*]

[*Enter* ROMEO *and* BALTHASAR, *with a torch, mattock,° etc.*]

---

60. **gear:** stuff.　63. **trunk:** body.　67. **utters:** sells.
Sc. ii: 6. **associate:** accompany.　10. **pestilence:** the plague.
See Gen. Intro. p. 18a–b.

18. **nice:** trifling. **full of charge:** weighty.　19. **dear import:** great
importance.　21. **crow:** crowbar.　26. **beshrew:** blame.
Sc. iii: 3. **all along:** at full length.　16. **obsequies:** funeral
rites.　20. **cross:** thwart.　21. **Muffle:** conceal.　22. s.d., **mattock:** a tool like a pick, but with a broad end.

ROM. Give me that mattock and the wrenching
    iron.
Hold, take this letter. Early in the morning
See thou deliver it to my lord and father.
Give me the light. Upon thy life, I charge thee,   25
Whate'er thou hear'st or seest, stand all aloof,
And do not interrupt me in my course.
Why I descend into this bed of death
Is partly to behold my lady's face,
But chiefly to take thence from her dead finger   30
A precious ring, a ring that I must use
In dear employment. Therefore hence, be gone.
But if thou, jealous,° dost return to pry
In what I farther shall intend to do,
By Heaven, I will tear thee joint by joint   35
And strew this hungry churchyard with thy limbs.
The time and my intents are savage-wild,
More fierce and more inexorable far
Than empty° tigers or the roaring sea.
    BAL. I will be gone, sir, and not trouble you.   40
    ROM. So shalt thou show me friendship. Take
        thou that.
Live, and be prosperous, and farewell, good fellow.
    BAL. [*Aside*] For all this same, I'll hide me here-
        about.
His looks I fear, and his intents I doubt.   [*Retires.*]
    ROM. Thou detestable maw,° thou womb of death,
Gorged with the dearest morsel of the earth,   46
Thus I enforce thy rotten jaws to open,
And in despite° I'll cram thee with more food.
                            [*Opens the tomb.*]
    PAR. This is that banished haughty Montague
That murdered my love's cousin, with which grief
It is supposèd the fair creature died,   51
And here is come to do some villainous shame°
To the dead bodies. I will apprehend him.
                            [*Comes forward.*]
Stop thy unhallowed toil, vile Montague!
Can vengeance be pursued further than death?   55
Condemnèd villain, I do apprehend thee.
Obey, and go with me, for thou must die.
    ROM. I must indeed, and therefore came I hither.
Good gentle youth, tempt not a desperate man.
Fly hence and leave me. Think upon these gone,   60
Let them affright thee. I beseech thee, youth,
Put not another sin upon my head,
By urging me to fury. Oh, be gone!
By Heaven, I love thee better than myself,
For I come hither armed against myself.   65
Stay not, be gone. Live, and hereafter say
A madman's mercy bid thee run away.
    PAR. I do defy thy conjurations
And apprehend thee for a felon here.   69

ROM. Wilt thou provoke me? Then have at thee,
    boy!   [*They fight.*]
    PAGE. Oh, Lord, they fight! I will go call the
        watch.   [*Exit.*]
    PAR. Oh, I am slain! [*Falls.*] If thou be merciful,
Open the tomb, lay me with Juliet.   [*Dies.*]
    ROM. In faith, I will. Let me peruse this face.
Mercutio's kinsman, noble County Paris!   75
What said my man, when my betossèd soul
Did not attend° him as we rode? I think
He told me Paris should have married Juliet.
Said he not so? Or did I dream it so?
Or am I mad, hearing him talk of Juliet,   80
To think it was so? Oh, give me thy hand,
One writ with me in sour misfortune's book!
I'll bury thee in a triumphant grave —
A grave? Oh, no, a lantern,° slaughtered youth;
For here lies Juliet, and her beauty makes   85
This vault a feasting presence° full of light.
Death, lie thou there, by a dead man interred.
                [*Laying* PARIS *in the monument.*]
How oft when men are at the point of death
Have they been merry! Which their keepers call
A lightning before death. Oh, how may I   90
Call this a lightning? O my love! My wife!
Death, that hath sucked the honey of thy breath,
Hath had no power yet upon thy beauty.
Thou art not conquered; beauty's ensign yet
Is crimson in thy lips and in thy cheeks,   95
And death's pale flag is not advancèd there.
Tybalt, liest thou there in thy bloody sheet?
Oh, what more favor can I do to thee
Than with that hand that cut thy youth in twain
To sunder his that was thine enemy?   100
Forgive me, Cousin! Ah, dear Juliet,
Why art thou yet so fair? Shall I believe
That unsubstantial death is amorous,
And that the lean abhorrèd monster keeps
Thee here in dark to be his paramour?   105
For fear of that, I still will stay with thee,
And never from this palace of dim night
Depart again. Here, here will I remain
With worms that are thy chambermaids. Oh, here
Will I set up my everlasting rest,°   110
And shake the yoke of inauspicious stars
From this world-wearied flesh. Eyes, look your last!
Arms, take your last embrace! And lips, O you
The doors of breath, seal with a righteous kiss
A dateless bargain to engrossing death!°   115
Come, bitter conduct,° come, unsavory guide!

---

33. **jealous:** curious.   39. **empty:** hungry.   45. **maw:** stomach.
48. **despite:** scorn.   52. **villainous shame:** Paris suspects that
Romeo has come to steal some parts of the dead bodies from the
tomb of the Capulets to work spells against them by necromancy.

77. **attend:** listen to.   84. **lantern:** dome or small turret with
windows, set in the roof of a hall to give additional light.
86. **presence:** Presence Chamber, where the Queen held public
court.   110. **set . . . rest:** lit., stake all, with a pun on *rest* —
death. A metaphor from primero, a card game in which a stake
was reserved. When this was won, the game ended.   115. **dateless . . . death:** an everlasting agreement with death, which
gains sole possession of everything.   116. **conduct:** guide.

Thou desperate pilot, now at once run on
The dashing rocks thy seasick weary bark.
Here's to my love! [*Drinks.*] O true apothecary!
Thy drugs are quick. Thus with a kiss I die. [*Dies.*]
    [*Enter, at the other end of the churchyard,* FRIAR
    LAURENCE, *with a lantern, crow, and spade.*]
    FRI. L. Saint Francis be my speed!° How oft to-
      night   121
Have my old feet stumbled° at graves! Who's there?
    BAL. Here's one a friend, and one that knows you
      well.
    FRI. L. Bliss be upon you! Tell me, good my
      friend,
What torch is yond that vainly lends his light   125
To grubs and eyeless skulls? As I discern,
It burneth in the Capel's monument.
    BAL. It doth so, holy sir, and there's my master,
One that you love.
    FRI. L.   Who is it?
    BAL.   Romeo.
    FRI. L. How long hath he been there?
    BAL.   Full half an hour.   130
    FRI. L. Go with me to the vault.
    BAL.   I dare not, sir.
My master knows not but I am gone hence,
And fearfully did menace me with death
If I did stay to look on his intents.
    FRI. L. Stay, then, I'll go alone. Fear comes upon
      me —   135
Oh, much I fear some ill unlucky thing.
    BAL. As I did sleep under this yew tree here,
I dreamed my master and another fought,
And that my master slew him.
    FRI. L.   Romeo! [*Advances.*]
Alack, alack, what blood is this which stains   140
The stony entrance of this sepulcher?
What mean these masterless and gory swords
To lie discolored by this place of peace?
[*Enters the tomb.*] Romeo! Oh, pale! Who else?
    What, Paris too?
And steeped in blood? Ah, what an unkind hour
Is guilty of this lamentable chance!   146
The lady stirs.   [JULIET *wakes.*]
    JUL. O comfortable° Friar! Where is my lord?
I do remember well where I should be,
And there I am. Where is my Romeo?   150
                    [*Noise within.*]
    FRI. L. I hear some noise. Lady, come from that
      nest
Of death, contagion, and unnatural sleep.
A greater power than we can contradict
Hath thwarted our intents. Come, come away.
Thy husband in thy bosom there lies dead,   155
And Paris too. Come, I'll dispose of thee
Among a sisterhood of holy nuns.

Stay not to question, for the watch is coming.
Come, go, good Juliet, I dare no longer stay.
    JUL. Go, get thee hence, for I will not away.   160
                  [*Exit* FRIAR LAURENCE.]
What's here? A cup, closed in my true love's hand?
Poison, I see, hath been his timeless° end.
O churl! Drunk all, and left no friendly drop
To help me after? I will kiss thy lips —
Haply° some poison yet doth hang on them   165
To make me die with a restorative.   [*Kisses him.*]
Thy lips are warm.
    1. WATCH. [*Within*] Lead, boy. Which way?
    JUL. Yea, noise? Then I'll be brief. O happy dag-
      ger!   [*Snatching* ROMEO'S *dagger.*]
This is thy sheath. [*Stabs herself.*] There rust, and
    let me die.   [*Falls on* ROMEO'S *body, and dies.*]
    [*Enter* WATCH, *with the* PAGE *of* PARIS.]
    PAGE. This is the place — there, where the torch
    doth burn.   171
    1. WATCH. The ground is bloody. Search about
    the churchyard.
Go, some of you, whoe'er you find attach.°
Pitiful sight! Here lies the County slain,
And Juliet bleeding, warm, and newly dead,   175
Who here hath lain this two days buried.
Go tell the Prince. Run to the Capulets,
Raise up the Montagues. Some others search.
We see the ground whereon these woes do lie,
But the true ground of all these piteous woes   180
We cannot without circumstance° descry.
    [*Re-enter some of the* WATCH, *with* BALTHASAR.]
    2. WATCH. Here's Romeo's man. We found him in
    the churchyard.
    1. WATCH. Hold him in safety till the Prince come
    hither.
[*Re-enter* FRIAR LAURENCE, *and another* WATCHMAN.]
    3. WATCH. Here is a friar that trembles, sighs, and
    weeps.
We took this mattock and this spade from him   185
As he was coming from this churchyard's side.
    1. WATCH. A great suspicion. Stay the friar too.
    [*Enter the* PRINCE *and* ATTENDANTS.]
    PRIN. What misadventure is so early up
That calls our person from our morning rest?
    [*Enter* CAPULET, LADY CAPULET, *and others.*]
    CAP. What should it be that they so shriek
    abroad?   190
    LADY CAP. The people in the street cry Romeo,
Some Juliet, and some Paris, and all run
With open outcry toward our monument.
    PRIN. What fear is this which startles in our ears?
    1. WATCH. Sovereign, here lies the County Paris
    slain,   195
And Romeo dead, and Juliet, dead before,
Warm and new-killed.

---

121. **speed:** aid.   122. **stumbled:** Stumbling was regarded as an evil omen.   148. **comfortable:** bringing comfort.

162. **timeless:** untimely.   165. **Haply:** perhaps.   173. **attach:** arrest.   181. **circumstance:** knowledge of facts.

PRIN. Search, seek, and know how this foul murder comes.

1. WATCH. Here is a friar, and slaughtered
Romeo's man,
With instruments upon them fit to open   200
These dead men's tombs.

CAP. Oh, heavens! O wife, look how our daughter
bleeds!
This dagger hath mista'en, for, lo, his house°
Is empty on the back of Montague,
And it missheathèd in my daughter's bosom!   205

LADY CAP. Oh me! This sight of death is as a bell°
That warns my old age to a sepulcher.

[*Enter* MONTAGUE *and others.*]

PRIN. Come, Montague, for thou art early up,
To see thy son and heir more early down.

MON. Alas, my liege, my wife is dead tonight,
Grief of my son's exile hath stopped her breath.   211
What further woe conspires against mine age?

PRIN. Look, and thou shalt see.

MON. O thou untaught! What manners is in this,
To press before thy father to a grave?   215

PRIN. Seal up the mouth of outrage° for a while
Till we can clear these ambiguities
And know their spring, their head, their true de-
scent.
And then will I be general of your woes,
And lead you even to death. Meantime forbear,   220
And let mischance be slave to patience.
Bring forth the parties of suspicion.°

FRI. L. I am the greatest, able to do least,
Yet most suspected, as the time and place
Doth make against me, of this direful murder.   225
And here I stand, both to impeach° and purge°
Myself condemnèd and myself excused.

PRIN. Then say at once what thou dost know in
this.

FRI. L. I will be brief, for my short date of breath°
Is not so long as is a tedious tale.   230
Romeo, there dead, was husband to that Juliet,
And she, there dead, that Romeo's faithful wife.
I married them, and their stol'n marriage day
Was Tybalt's doomsday, whose untimely death
Banished the new-made bridegroom from this city,
For whom, and not for Tybalt, Juliet pined.   236
You, to remove that siege of grief from her,
Betrothed and would have married her perforce
To County Paris. Then comes she to me,
And with wild looks bid me devise some mean   240
To rid her from this second marriage,
Or in my cell there would she kill herself.
Then gave I her, so tutored by my art,

A sleeping potion, which so took effect
As I intended, for it wrought on her   245
The form of death. Meantime I writ to Romeo
That he should hither come as this dire night,
To help to take her from her borrowed grave,
Being the time the potion's force should cease.
But he which bore my letter, Friar John,   250
Was stayed by accident, and yesternight
Returned my letter back. Then all alone
At the prefixèd hour of her waking
Came I to take her from her kindred's vault,
Meaning to keep her closely° at my cell   255
Till I conveniently could send to Romeo.
But when I came, some minute ere the time
Of her awaking, here untimely lay
The noble Paris and true Romeo dead.
She wakes, and I entreated her come forth,   260
And bear this work of Heaven with patience.
But then a noise did scare me from the tomb,
And she too desperate would not go with me,
But, as it seems, did violence on herself.
All this I know, and to the marriage   265
Her nurse is privy.° And if aught in this
Miscarried by my fault, let my old life
Be sacrificed some hour before his time
Unto the rigor of severest law.   269

PRIN. We still° have known thee for a holy man.
Where's Romeo's man? What can he say in this?

BAL. I brought my master news of Juliet's death,
And then in post he came from Mantua
To this same place, to this same monument.
This letter he early bid me give his father,   275
And threatened me with death, going in the vault,
If I departed not and left him there.

PRIN. Give me the letter, I will look on it.
Where is the County's page, that raised the watch?
Sirrah, what made° your master in this place?   280

PAGE. He came with flowers to strew his lady's
grave,
And bid me stand aloof, and so I did.
Anon comes one with light to ope the tomb,
And by and by my master drew on him,
And then I ran away to call the watch.   285

PRIN. This letter doth make good the Friar's
words,
Their course of love, the tidings of her death.
And here he writes that he did buy a poison
Of a poor 'pothecary, and therewithal
Came to this vault to die and lie with Juliet.   290
Where be these enemies? Capulet! Montague!
See what a scourge is laid upon your hate
That Heaven finds means to kill your joys with love!
And I, for winking at your discords too,
Have lost a brace of kinsmen. All are punished.   295

CAP. O Brother Montague, give me thy hand.

---

203. **house:** i.e., scabbard.   206. **bell:** i.e., passing bell. See App. 19.   216. **Seal ... outrage:** At these words the curtains at the back of the stage are closed to conceal the three bodies. **outrage:** violent deeds.   222. **parties of suspicion:** suspected parties.   226. **impeach:** accuse. **purge:** clear.   229. **short ... breath:** the little life still left to me.

255. **closely:** secretly.   266. **is privy:** shares the secret.   270. **still:** always.   280. **made:** did.

This is my daughter's jointure,° for no more
Can I demand.
    MON.   But I can give thee more.
For I will raise her statue in pure gold,
That whiles Verona by that name is known   300
There shall no figure at such rate° be set
As that of true and faithful Juliet.

    297. jointure: dowry. 301. rate: value.

    CAP. As rich shall Romeo's by his lady's lie,
Poor sacrifices of our enmity!
    PRIN. A glooming peace this morning with it
      brings,   305
The sun for sorrow will not show his head.
Go hence, to have more talk of these sad things.
    Some shall be pardoned and some punishèd.
For never was a story of more woe   309
Than this of Juliet and her Romeo.   [*Exeunt.*]

A MIDSUMMER NIGHT'S DREAM

Introduction

A Midsummer Night's Dream was probably written late in 1594 or early in 1595. There are a few topical allusions which can be identified.

1. Titania's speech (II.i.87–117) on the evil weather was presumably inspired by the excessively bad summer of 1594, which caused a failure of the harvest and much distress. There are several contemporary records of the disaster. Thus John Stow, in his *Annals*:

This year in the month of May, fell many great showers of rain, but in the months of June and July, much more; for it commonly rained every day, or night, till St. James's Day, and two days after together most extremely, all which, notwithstanding in the month of August there followed a fair harvest, but in the month of September fell great rains, which raised high waters, such as stayed the carriages, and bare down bridges, at Cambridge, Ware and elsewhere, in many places. Also the price of grain grew to be such as a strike or bushel of rye was sold for five shillings, a bushel of wheat for six, seven, or eight shillings, &c, for still it rose in price, which dearth happened (after the common opinion) more by means of overmuch transporting by our own merchants for their private gain, than through the unseasonableness of the weather passed.

2. In the rehearsal, Bottom warns his fellow actors (III.i.30):

Masters, you ought to consider with yourselves. To bring in — God shield us! — a lion among ladies is a most dreadful thing; for there is not a more fearful wildfowl than your lion living, and we ought to look to it.

On August 30, 1594, the infant son of King James VI of Scotland was baptized in Edinburgh. Queen Elizabeth was the godmother, and she sent a party of courtiers to Scotland to represent her at the ceremony. It is likely that those present, used to a far higher standard of courtly comforts and entertainments, brought back amusing accounts of the affair, especially of the grand dinner. The whole ceremony was described in a contemporary pamphlet which recorded that during the state banquet a chariot appeared, drawn by a blackamoor, wherein stood Ceres, Fecundity, Faith, Concord, Liberality, and Perseverance. "The chariot was to have been drawn in by a lion, but because his presence might have brought some fears to the nearest, or the sights of the lights and the torches might have commoved his tameness, it was thought meet that the Moor should supply that room."

There are other obviously topical allusions in the play, but as these have not been certainly identified, they do not throw much light on the date of writing. The most important is at V.i.52:

The thrice three Muses mourning for the death
Of Learning, late deceased in beggary.

That is some satire, keen and critical,
Not sorting with a nuptial ceremony.

on Robert Greene's death

If these words were written in 1594 or 1595, they would most probably refer to the death, in poverty, of Robert Greene on September 2, 1592 (see Gen. Intro. p. 39a). Greene's death was echoed for some years in pamphlets which could quite accurately be called "keen and critical." If the lines were written in 1599 for a revival of the play, then they may refer to the death of Edmund Spenser in January, 1599.

There is some evidence that the play has in parts been rewritten. Professor Dover Wilson in his edition notes that in the first 184 lines of Act V, the printer of the quarto has made several mistakes in dividing the lines of verse, and that these mistakes occur in passages where the rhythm of the verse is freer than in the rest of the play. For example, he printed the famous passage (ll. 11–18) thus:

The Poet's eye, in a fine frenzy, rolling, doth glance
From heaven to earth, from earth to heaven. And as
Imagination bodies forth the forms of things
Unknown: the Poet's pen turns them to shapes,
And gives too airy nothing, a local habitation,
And a name. Such tricks hath strong imagination.

Professor Dover Wilson guessed that these passages were later additions, written on the margin of the manuscript in such space as could be found, and that they baffled the compositor.

There is no record of early performance, but the play is so full of marriage preparations that most critics believe that it was composed for some particular wedding. Of the possible society weddings, that of William Stanley, Earl of Derby (and brother of a former patron of the Chamberlain's Men) with the Lady Elizabeth Vere, granddaughter of Lord Burghley, on January 26, 1595, best fits the probable date of writing; but there is no evidence, and the title page of the quarto definitely states that the play was " sundry times publicly acted."

A Midsummer Night's Dream was entered in the Stationers' Register on October 8, 1600, to Thomas Fisher. A first quarto appeared in 1600 with the title: *A Midsommer nights dreame. As it hath beene sundry times publickely acted, by the Right honourable, the Lord Chamberlaine his seruants. Written by William Shakespeare.* A second quarto, falsely dated 1600, was printed in 1619, and based on the first. The text printed in the first folio in 1623 was printed from a revised copy of the second quarto.

The plot of *A Midsummer Night's Dream* as a whole was Shakespeare's invention, but some of the details he took from Chaucer, Plutarch's " Life of Theseus," Ovid, folklore, and his own plays.

The situation at the opening of the play when " Duke " Theseus is about to wed the Amazon Queen Hippolyta may have been suggested by the opening lines of the *Knight's Tale* in the *Canterbury Tales*.

> Whilom, as oldë stories tellen us,
> There was a Duke that hightë Theseus;
> Of Athenes he was lord and governour,
> And in his timë such a conqueror,
> That greater was there none under the sun.
> Full many a richë country had he won;
> That with his wisdom and his chivalry
> He conquered all the regne of Femyny,
> That whilom was y-cleped Scythia;
> And weddedë the Queen Hippolita,
> And brought her home with him in his country
> With muchel glory and great solemnity.

The rest of the *Knight's Tale* has no connection with the play, but there are occasional phrases

and suggestions, such as that Theseus was a mighty hunter.

> This mean I now by mighty Theseus
> That for to hunten is so desirous,
> And namely the great hart in May,
> That in his bed there daweth him no day,
> That he nis [is not] clad, and ready for to ride
> With hunt and horn, and houndës him beside.
> For in his hunting hath he such delight,
> That it is all his joy and appetite
> To been himself the great hartë's bane,
> For after Mars he serveth now Diane.

Shakespeare seems also to have read the " Life of Theseus " in *Plutarch's Lives,* from which he took an occasional line or idea, including the name of Egeus.

The story of Pyramus and Thisbe was well known. It had been told by Ovid — Shakespeare's favorite Latin author — in the *Metamorphoses, Book IV.* Of this work an English translation by Arthur Golding, printed in 1567 in a long fourteen-syllable line, was almost as crude as Quince's version of the tragedy. The main parts of the story were thus Englished by Golding:

> Within the town (of whose huge walls
>   so monstrous high and thick
> The fame is given Semiramis
>   for making them of brick)
> Dwelt hard together two young folk
>   in houses joined so near
> That under all one roof well nigh
>   both two twain conveyèd were. . . .
> The wall that parted house from house
>   had riven therein a cranny
> Which shrunk at making of the wall;
>   this fault not marked of any
> Of many hundred years before
>   (what doth not love espy?)
> These lovers first of all found out,
>   and made a way whereby
> To talk together secretly,
>   and through the same did go
> Their loving whisperings very light
>   and safely to and fro.
> Now as at one side Pyramus
>   and Thisbe on the other
> Stood often drawing one of them
>   the pleasant breath from other,
> " O thou envious wall," they said,
>   " why let'st thou lovers thus?
> What matter were it if that thou
>   permitted both of us

In arms each other to embrace?
  Or if thou think that this
Were overmuch, yet mightest thou
  at least make room to kiss.
And yet thou shalt not find us churls:
  we think ourselves in debt
For this same piece of courtesy,
  in vouching safe to let
Our sayings to our friendly ears
  thus freely come and go."
Thus having where they stood in vain
  complainèd of their woe,
When night drew near, they bade adieu
  and each gave kisses sweet
Unto the parget [plaster] on their side,
  the which did never meet.
Next morning with her cheerful light
  had driven the stars aside
And Phoebus with his burning beams
  the dewy grass had dried.
These lovers at their wonted place
  by fore-appointment met.
Whereafter much complaint and moan
  they cov'nanted to get
Away from such as watchèd them,
  and in the evening late
To steal out of their fathers' house
  and eke the city gate.
And to th' intent that in the fields
  they strayed not up and down
They did agree at Ninus' tomb
  to meet without the town,
And tarry underneath a tree
  that by the same did grow
Which was a fair high mulberry
  with fruit as white as snow,
Hard by a cool and trickling spring.
  This bargain pleased them both
And so daylight (which to their thought
  away but slowly goeth)
Did in the ocean fall to rest,
  and night from thence doth rise.
As soon as darkness once was come,
  straight Thisbe did devise
A shift to wind her out of doors,
  that none that were within
Perceivèd her. And muffling her
  with clothes about her chin,
That no man might discern her face,
  to Ninus' tomb she came
Unto the tree, and sat her down
  there underneath the same.
Love made her bold. But see the chance,
  there comes besmeared with blood
About the chaps a lioness
  all foaming from the wood
From slaughter lately made of kine

to staunch [quench] her bloody thirst
With water of the foresaid spring.
  Whom Thisbe spying first
Afar by moonlight, thereupon
  with fearful steps gan fly
And in a dark and irksome cave
  did hide herself thereby.
And as she fled away for haste
  she let her mantle fall
The which for fear she left behind,
  not looking back at all.
Now when the cruel lioness
  her thirst had staunchèd well,
In going to the wood she found
  the slender weed that fell
From Thisbe, which with bloody teeth
  in pieces she did tear.
The night was somewhat further spent
  ere Pyramus came there,
Who seeing in the subtle sand
  the print of lion's paw
Waxed pale for fear. But when also
  the bloody cloak he saw
All rent and torn, " One night," he said,
  " shall lovers two confound,
Of which long life deservèd she
  of all that live on ground.
My soul deserves of this mischance
  the peril for to bear.
I wretch have been the death of thee,
  which to this place of fear
Did cause thee in the night to come,
  and came not here before.
My wicked limbs and wretched guts
  with cruel teeth therefore
Devour ye, O ye lions all,
  that in this rock do dwell."
But cowards use to wish for death.
  The slender weed that fell
From Thisbe up he takes, and straight
  does bear it to the tree,
Which was appointed erst [formerly] the place
  of meeting for to be.
And when he had bewept and kissed
  the garment which he knew,
" Receive thou my blood too," quoth he,
  and therewithal he drew
His sword, the which among his guts
  he thrust, and by and by
Did draw it from the bleeding wound
  beginning for to die,
And cast himself upon his back.
  The blood did spin on high
As when a conduit pipe is cracked,
  the water bursting out
Does shoot itself a great way off
  and pierce the air about.

Then Thisbe comes out from her hiding place, sees her lover "beweltred in his blood," and laments at great length.

> This said, she took the sword yet warm
>   with slaughter of her love
> And setting it beneath her breast,
>   did to her heart it shove.

The Fairies came partly from folklore, partly from literature. Oberon, King of the Fairies, had appeared not long before in Greene's play *King James the Fourth.* Titania was a title of the goddess Diana, used by Ovid, but not by Golding in his translation. Belief in fairies, which had been fairly strong some generations before, was dying out except among the ignorant. This trend was thus summarized by King James VI of Scotland in his *Daemonology* (1597):

That fourth kind of spirits, which by the Gentiles was called Diana and her wandering Court, and amongst us was called the Phairy (as I told you), or our good neighbors, was one of the sorts of illusions that was rifest in the time of Papistry; for although it was holden odious to prophesy by the Devil, yet whom these kind of spirits carried away and informed, they were thought to be sonsiest and of best life. To speak of the many vain trattles [gossip] founded upon that illusion: how there was a King and Queen of Phairy, of such a jolly Court and train as they had, how they had a teind [tithe] and duty, as it were, of all goods; how they naturally rode and went, ate and drank, and did all other actions like natural men and women — I think it liker Virgil's *Campi Elysii* nor anything that ought to be believed by Christians, except in general, that as I spake sundry times before, the Devil illuded the senses of sundry simple creatures in making them believe that they saw and heard such things as were nothing so indeed.

Among educated men and women fairies had become a picturesque fancy, and a topic for pretty verse and Courtly entertainment.

Puck the mischief-maker was perhaps more credited than the King of the Fairies. He was known as Robin Goodfellow to country gossips. Thomas Nashe in *Terrors of the Night* (1593) had thus described him and his like:

In the time of infidelity, when spirits were so familiar with men that they called them *Dii Penates,* their household gods or their *lares,* they never sacrificed to them till sunsetting. The Robin Goodfellows, elves, fairies, hobgoblins of our latter age,

which idolatrous former days and the fantastical world of Greece ycleped fawns, satyrs, dryads, and hamadryads, did most of their merry pranks in the night. Then ground they malt, and had hempen shirts for their labors, danced in rounds in green meadows, pinched maids in their sleep that swept not their houses clean, and led poor travelers out of their way notoriously.

Shakespeare was apparently the first to give the name of Puck (the pook or spirit) to Robin. The name may have been appropriately taken from Spenser's *Epithalamium* — the wedding song which he composed for his own wedding, and which appeared in the early weeks of 1595. In one of the later stanzas Spenser prayed that his wedding night might be free from alarms:

> Let no lamenting cries, nor doleful tears,
> Be heard all night, within nor yet without:
> Ne let false whispers, breeding hidden fears,
> Break gentle sleep with misconceivèd doubt.
> Let no deluding dreams, nor dreadful sights
> Make sudden sad affrights;
> Ne let house fires, nor lightnings' helpless harms,
> Ne let the Pook, nor other evil sprites,
> Ne let mischievous witches with their charms,
> Ne let hobgoblins, names whose sense we see not,
> Fray us with things that be not.

Other incidents Shakespeare took from his own plays. *Two Gentlemen of Verona* had told of the cross-wooing of two pairs of lovers whose affections had become mixed. In *Love's Labor's Lost* he had parodied the efforts of amateurs to produce a drama for a royal visitor. In *Romeo and Juliet,* Mercutio's outburst on Queen Mab (I.iv. 53–94) was the first sketch of fairy pranks.

A Midsummer Night's Dream aptly describes the play. Midsummer's Day was traditionally a general holiday and a time of merrymaking; Midsummer Night was the grand festival of witches and fairies. In a Midsummer Night's dream anything might happen. As is common in Elizabethan plays, there are three stories: the complex love affairs of Demetrius and Lysander, Hermia and Helena; the casting, rehearsal, and performance of the comical tragedy of Pyramus and Thisbe by the workingmen of Athens; and the troubles in fairyland between Oberon and Titania. Each plot is connected with the others, and all center in the wedding of Theseus and Hippolyta.

The play begins on solid earth. The final preparations for Theseus' wedding are being made when Egeus bursts in to demand his right as a father to bestow his daughter in marriage on the man of his choosing. The second scene introduces the Athenian workingmen and shows the casting of their play with Quince as director, Bottom as star performer, and the rest merely apprehensive amateurs. So long as daylight holds mortals are in control and the fairies lie hidden. But once the moon is up things of common day fade and the woods near Athens become the domain of the fairies, into which mortals trespass at their peril. In the third scene (II.i) we are introduced to Puck, the mischief-maker, Oberon, King of the Fairies, and Titania, his Queen. When Demetrius crashes into fairyland pursued by the clinging Helena, the dream begins and reality ends.

The characterization in the play is varied. The lovers are not very interesting if taken or played seriously, but if their speeches are regarded as a parody on romantic stories and the parts are played with a touch of burlesque they become amusingly comic. Theseus and Hippolyta, so far as their small parts allow, are distinct. Theseus has already had considerable experience as a lover and a soldier, and he has ceased to be romantic. When Hippolyta tells him of the strange experiences of the lovers in the woods, he tolerantly answers that

> The lunatic, the lover, and the poet
> Are of imagination all compact.

This is hardly a gallant speech from a bridegroom on his wedding day, but the marriage itself was not a love match. Hippolyta too has character; she is an Amazon, a haughty, muscular lady with no patience for the crude efforts of Bottom and his fellow players. The contrast between Hippolyta and her husband is well shown during the play. The lady is bored and contemptuous, but Theseus remains gracious and encouraging to the least of his subjects.

All the workingmen are cunningly drawn.

Quince seems to be the oldest of the party, and there are hints that he is something of a poet—at least Bottom thinks he ought to write a ballad. Furthermore, Quince is a man of great tact; no one else, not even the Duke, can control Bottom. Snout and Starveling are the difficulty-makers who exist in every amateur dramatic society; "You can *never* bring in a wall," cries Snout triumphantly. But all are surpassed by Bottom, the weaver, who is magnificently stolid, unimaginative and imperturbable, yet a considerable wag in his own crude way. He alone remains calm before a jeering audience, and he subdues it to silence when lesser men such as the miserable Snout are put out of their parts and give up in despair. He keeps his head, even though it be an asshead, when the Fairy Queen falls demonstratively in love with him.

The third set of characters are the fairies. They are presented as little folk, and their size is constantly stressed. The cowslips are the bodyguard of the Fairy Queen, and a snake skin is

> Weed wide enough to wrap a fairy in,

yet their loves and passions are as intense as those of the humans.

The dream ends with dawn when everything has been restored: Demetrius has Helena, Lysander has Hermia, Bottom has his own natural face, and Oberon his Indian boy. When Theseus and Hippolyta come upon the sleeping lovers, the fairies have vanished and mortals are again in control. Then night returns; Bottom and his company present their play, a very human performance; the lovers go bedward; and the lights are put out in the great chamber. Once more the fairies swarm out, and in the end we are left doubting where reality began and dreaming ended.

Fantasy to be successful calls for a certain delicacy of imagination in the spectators. Shakespeare was lucky in the versatility of an audience which could pass from the bloody melodrama of *Richard III* and the tragedy of *Romeo and Juliet* to this delicate mixture of farce and fancy.

A Midsummer Night's Dream

[handwritten: suggests madness]
[handwritten: a fantasy]
[handwritten: Implies a piece of utter fantasy.]

DRAMATIS PERSONAE

THESEUS, *Duke of Athens*
EGEUS, *father to Hermia*
LYSANDER
DEMETRIUS } *in love with Hermia*
PHILOSTRATE, *master of the revels to Theseus*
QUINCE, *a carpenter*
SNUG, *a joiner*
BOTTOM, *a weaver*
FLUTE, *a bellows-mender*
SNOUT, *a tinker*
STARVELING, *a tailor*

HIPPOLYTA, *queen of the Amazons, betrothed to Theseus*

HERMIA, *daughter to Egeus, in love with Lysander*
HELENA, *in love with Demetrius*

OBERON, *king of the fairies*
TITANIA, *queen of the fairies*
PUCK, *or Robin Goodfellow* *[handwritten: (spirit)]*
PEASEBLOSSOM
COBWEB
MOTH } *fairies*
MUSTARDSEED
OTHER FAIRIES *attending their King and Queen.*
Attendants on Theseus and Hippolyta

SCENE — *Athens, and a wood near it.*

[handwritten: 1st subplot of love betwee well-born Athens]

Act I

[handwritten: Theseus-Hippolyta story is the frame story for the play]

SCENE I. *Athens. The palace of Theseus.*

[Enter THESEUS, HIPPOLYTA, PHILOSTRATE, *and Attendants.]*

[handwritten: MOON CONNECTED WITH LOVE + MARRIAGE HERE]
[handwritten: MOON STAGS AT PYRAMUS + THISBES LOVE]

THE. Now, fair Hippolyta,° our nuptial hour
Draws on apace;° four happy days bring in *[handwritten: WITNESS]*
Another moon. But oh, methinks, how slow *[handwritten: 2]*
This old moon wanes! She lingers° my desires,
Like to a stepdame, or a dowager, *[handwritten: HAS TO DO WITH THIS 5 MARRIAGE]*
Long withering out a young man's revenue.
HIP. Four days will quickly steep° themselves in
    night,
Four nights will quickly dream away the time,
And then the moon, like to a silver bow
New-bent in heaven, shall behold the night   10
Of our solemnities.
THE.   Go, Philostrate,
Stir up the Athenian youth to merriments,
Awake the pert° and nimble spirit of mirth.
Turn melancholy forth to funerals.
The pale companion° is not for our pomp.   15
                 [Exit PHILOSTRATE.]
Hippolyta, I wooed thee with my sword,
And won thy love, doing thee injuries;
But I will wed thee in another key,
With pomp, with triumph, and with reveling.

[Enter EGEUS, HERMIA, LYSANDER, *and* DEMETRIUS.]
EGE. Happy be Theseus, our renownèd Duke!   20
THE. Thanks, good Egëus. What's the news with
    thee?
EGE. Full of vexation come I, with complaint
Against my child, my daughter Hermia.
Stand forth, Demetrius. My noble lord, *[handwritten: WITNESS 1.]*
This man hath my consent to marry her.   25
Stand forth, Lysander. And, my gracious Duke,
This man hath bewitched the bosom of my child.
Thou, thou, Lysander, thou hast given her rhymes,
And interchanged love tokens with my child.
Thou hast by moonlight at her window sung,   30
With feigning° voice, verses of feigning love;
And stolen the impression of her fantasy°
With bracelets of thy hair, rings, gawds,° conceits,°
Knacks,° trifles, nosegays,° sweetmeats, messengers
Of strong prevailment in unhardened youth.   35
With cunning hast thou filched my daughter's heart,
Turned her obedience, which is due to me,
To stubborn harshness. And, my gracious Duke,
Be it so° she will not here before your Grace
Consent to marry with Demetrius,   40
I beg the ancient privilege of Athens,
As she is mine, I may dispose of her,
Which shall be either to this gentleman
Or to her death, according to our law
Immediately° provided in that case.   45
THE. What say you, Hermia? Be advised,° fair
    maid,

[handwritten: WITNESS 2]

Act I, Sc. i: **1. Hippolyta:** Queen of the Amazons, a legendary race of female warriors who lived in South Russia. Theseus had defeated them in battle. **2. apace:** quickly. **4. lingers:** delays. **5-6. Like . . . revenue:** i.e., like a stepmother or a widowed mother (*dowager*) who has to be provided with an annuity. **withering out:** making to dwindle. **7. steep:** turn into. **13. pert:** lively. **15. pale companion:** i.e., melancholy. **companion:** fellow.

31. feigning: deceptive. **32. stolen . . . fantasy:** made a false impression on her imagination. **33. gawds:** trifles. **conceits:** pretty compliments. **34. Knacks:** knickknacks. **nosegays:** bunches of flowers. **39. Be it so:** if. **45. Immediately:** expressly. **46. Be advised:** consider.

[handwritten: LAW IS PRECISE + BINDING]
[handwritten: LOVE IS WILD + FREE]
[handwritten: WHILE]

To you your father should be as a god,
One that composed° your beauties — yea, and one
To whom you are but as a form° in wax
By him imprinted and within his power   50
To leave the figure or disfigure it.
Demetrius is a worthy gentleman.

HER. So is Lysander.

THE.   In himself he is;
But in this kind,° wanting° your father's voice,
The other must be held the worthier.   55

HER. I would my father looked but with my eyes.

THE. Rather your eyes must with his judgment
look.

HER. I do entreat your Grace to pardon me.
I know not by what power I am made bold,
Nor how it may concern my modesty,°   60
In such a presence here to plead my thoughts;
But I beseech your Grace that I may know
The worst that may befall me in this case
If I refuse to wed Demetrius.

THE. Either to die the death,° or to abjure   65
Forever the society of men.
Therefore, fair Hermia, question your desires.
Know of° your youth, examine well your blood,
Whether, if you yield not to your father's choice,
You can endure the livery of a nun —   70
For aye° to be in shady cloister mewed,°
To live a barren sister all your life,
Chanting faint hymns to the cold fruitless moon.
Thrice blessèd they that master so their blood,
To undergo such maiden pilgrimage;   75
But earthlier happy° is the rose distilled,°
Than that which, withering on the virgin thorn,
Grows, lives, and dies in single blessedness.

HER. So will I grow, so live, so die, my lord,
Ere I will yield my virgin patent° up   80
Unto his lordship, whose unwishèd yoke
My soul consents not to give sovereignty.

THE. Take time to pause; and by the next new
moon —
The sealing day betwixt my love and me,
For everlasting bond of fellowship° —   85
Upon that day either prepare to die
For disobedience to your father's will,
Or else to wed Demetrius, as he would,
Or on Diana's altar to protest°
For aye austerity and single life.   90

DEM. Relent, sweet Hermia. And, Lysander, yield

Thy crazèd title° to my certain right.

LYS. You have her father's love, Demetrius,
Let me have Hermia's. Do you marry him.

EGE. Scornful Lysander! True, he hath my love,
And what is mine my love shall render° him.   96
And she is mine, and all my right of her
I do estate° unto Demetrius.

LYS. I am, my lord, as well derived as he,
As well possessed;° my love is more than his;   100
My fortunes every way as fairly ranked,
If not with vantage,° as Demetrius'.
And, which is more than all these boasts can be,
I am beloved of beauteous Hermia.
Why should not I then prosecute my right?   105
Demetrius, I'll avouch it to his head,°
Made love to Nedar's daughter, Helena,
And won her soul, and she, sweet lady, dotes,
Devoutly dotes, dotes in idolatry,
Upon this spotted° and inconstant man.   110

THE. I must confess that I have heard so much,
And with Demetrius thought to have spoke thereof;
But, being overfull of self-affairs,
My mind did lose it. But, Demetrius, come,
And come, Egëus. You shall go with me.   115
I have some private schooling° for you both.
For you, fair Hermia, look you arm yourself
To fit your fancies° to your father's will,
Or else the law of Athens yields you up —
Which by no means we may extenuate —   120
To death, or to a vow of single life.
Come, my Hippolyta. What cheer, my love?
Demetrius and Egëus, go along.
I must employ you in some business
Against° our nuptial, and confer with you   125
Of something nearly° that concerns yourselves.

EGE. With duty and desire we follow you.

[Exeunt all but LYSANDER *and* HERMIA.*]*

LYS. How now, my love! Why is your cheek so
pale?
How chance the roses there do fade so fast?

HER. Belike for want of rain, which I could well
Beteem° them from the tempest of my eyes.   131

LYS. Aye me! for aught that I could ever read,
Could ever hear by tale or history,
The course of true love never did run smooth,
But either it was different in blood ——   135

HER. Oh, cross!° Too high to be enthralled° to
low.°

LYS. Or else misgraffèd° in respect of years ——

---

48. composed: formed.   49. form: shape.   54. in . . . kind: in
this case; i.e., the marriage. wanting: being without.   60. how
. . . modesty: whether it may make me appear immodest.
65. die . . . death: to be put to death by the law.   68. Know of:
remember.   71. aye: ever. mewed: caged.   73. moon: i.e.,
Diana, goddess of chastity and single life.   76. earthlier happy:
happier on earth. distilled: which sheds its essence on another.
80. virgin patent: privilege of my virginity.   84–85. sealing . . .
fellowship: the day when we conclude our marriage.   89. protest: vow.

92. crazed title: flawed claim.   96. render: give up to.   98. estate: transfer.   99–100. derived . . . possessed: of as good birth
and wealth.   102. vantage: advantage, superiority.   110. avouch
. . . head: declare it to his face.   110. spotted: stained.
116. schooling: advice.   118. fit . . . fancies: suit your ideas of
love.   125. Against: in anticipation of.   126. nearly: closely.
131. Beteem: bring forth.   136. cross: perversity. enthralled:
made servant to. low: one of low birth.   137. misgraffed: ill-
grafted.

HER. Oh, spite! Too old to be engaged to young.

LYS. Or else it stood upon the choice of
    friends ——

HER. Oh, Hell! To choose love by another's eyes.

LYS. Or, if there were a sympathy in choice,   141
War, death, or sickness did lay siege to it,
Making it momentany° as a sound,
Swift as a shadow, short as any dream;
Brief as the lightning in the collied° night,   145
That, in a spleen,° unfolds both heaven and earth,
And ere a man hath power to say " Behold! "
The jaws of darkness do devour it up.
So quick bright things come to confusion.°

HER. If then true lovers have been ever crossed,°
It stands as an edíct in destiny.°   151
Then let us teach our trial patience,
Because it is a customary cross, *ALMOST A LAW*
As due to love as thoughts and dreams and sighs,
Wishes and tears, poor fancy's° followers.   155

LYS. A good persuasion. Therefore hear me,
    Hermia.

LYS. GETS LOST ON WAY TO AUNT'S HOUSE — PECULIAR

I have a widow aunt, a dowager
Of great revénue, and she hath no child. *3 mi.*
From Athens is her house remote seven leagues;°
And she respects° me as her only son.   160
There, gentle Hermia, may I marry thee,
And to that place the sharp Athenian law
Cannot pursue us. If thou lovest me, then,
Steal forth thy father's house tomorrow night,
And in the wood, a league without the town,   165
Where I did meet thee once with Helena
To do observance to a morn of May,°
There will I stay for thee.

HER.   My good Lysander!
I swear to thee, by Cupid's strongest bow,
By his best arrow with the golden head,°   170
By the simplicity of Venus' doves,°
By that which knitteth souls and prospers loves,
And by that fire which burned the Carthage Queen°
When the false Troyan under sail was seen ——
By all the vows that ever men have broke,   175
In number more than ever women spoke,
In that same place thou hast appointed me,
Tomorrow truly will I meet with thee.

LYS. Keep promise, love. Look, here comes Hel-
    ena.

143. momentany: momentary.   145. collied: coal-black.
146. spleen: flash of wrath.   149. confusion: pronounced as four
syllables.   150. crossed: thwarted.   151. edict in destiny: decree
of fate.   155. fancy: love.   159. league: three miles.   160. respects: regards.   167. do . . . May: observe May Day.
170. golden head: Cupid has two kinds of arrows, the leaden
causes dislike, the golden, love.   171. Venus' doves: Doves were
sacred to Venus, the goddess of love.   173. Carthage Queen:
Dido, Queen of Carthage, fell in love with Aeneas when he
visited her after his escape from Troy. Aeneas deserted her,
whereupon she mounted a funeral pyre and killed herself in
the flames.

[*Enter* HELENA.]

HER. Godspeed, fair Helena! Whither away?

HEL. Call you me fair? That fair again unsay.
Demetrius loves your fair. O happy fair!   182
Your eyes are lodestars,° and your tongue's sweet air
More tunable than lark to shepherd's ear
When wheat is green, when hawthorn buds appear.
Sickness is catching. Oh, were favor° so,   186
Yours would I catch, fair Hermia, ere I go.
My ear should catch your voice, my eye your eye,
My tongue should catch your tongue's sweet melody.
Were the world mine, Demetrius being bated,°   190
The rest I'd give to be to you translated.°
Oh, teach me how you look, and with what art
You sway the motion° of Demetrius' heart!

HER. I frown upon him, yet he loves me still.

HEL. Oh, that your frowns would teach my smiles
    such skill!   195

HER. I give him curses, yet he gives me love.

HEL. Oh, that my prayers could such affection
    move!

HER. The more I hate, the more he follows me.

HEL. The more I love, the more he hateth me.

HER. His folly, Helena, is no fault of mine.   200

HEL. None but your beauty. Would that fault
    were mine!

HER. Take comfort. He no more shall see my face.
Lysander and myself will fly this place.
Before the time I did Lysander see,
Seemed Athens as a paradise to me.   205
Oh then, what graces in my love do dwell,
That he hath turned a Heaven unto a Hell!

LYS. Helen, to you our minds we will unfold.
Tomorrow night, when Phoebe° doth behold
Her silver visage in the watery glass,°   210
Decking with liquid pearl the bladed grass,
A time that lovers' flights doth still° conceal,
Through Athens' gates have we devised to steal.

HER. And in the wood, where often you and I
Upon faint primrose beds were wont to lie,   215
Emptying our bosoms of their counsel sweet,
There my Lysander and myself shall meet,
And thence from Athens turn away our eyes,
To seek new friends and stranger companies.
Farewell, sweet playfellow. Pray thou for us,   220
And good luck grant thee thy Demetrius!
Keep word, Lysander. We must starve our sight
From lovers' food till morrow deep midnight.

LYS. I will, my Hermia. [*Exit* HERMIA.] Helena,
    adieu.   224
As you on him, Demetrius dote on you!   [*Exit.*]

HEL. How happy some o'er other some° can be!

183. lodestars: guiding stars.   186. favor: with double meaning,
"beauty" and "affection."   190. bated: excepted.   191. translated: transformed.   193. motion: inclination.   209. Phoebe:
Diana, the moon.   210. watery glass: i.e., reflected in the
water.   212. still: always.   226. o'er . . . some: compared with
some others.

[handwritten: 3rd plot → a burlesque version of love; parody of love]

Through Athens I am thought as fair as she.
But what of that? Demetrius thinks not so,
He will not know what all but he do know.
And as he errs, doting on Hermia's eyes,   230
So I, admiring of his qualities.
Things base and vile, holding no quantity,°
Love can transpose to form and dignity.
Love looks not with the eyes, but with the mind;
And therefore is winged Cupid painted blind.   235
Nor hath Love's mind of any judgment taste;°
Wings, and no eyes, figure unheedy haste.
And therefore is Love said to be a child,
Because in choice he is so oft beguiled.
As waggish° boys in game themselves forswear,
So the boy Love is perjured everywhere: 241
For ere Demetrius looked on Hermia's eyne,°
He hailed down oaths that he was only mine;
And when this hail some heat from Hermia felt,
So he dissolved, and showers of oaths did melt.   245
I will go tell him of fair Hermia's flight. *[handwritten: Helena is so mad in love she will tell Demetrius]*
Then to the wood will he tomorrow night
Pursue her; and for this intelligence°
If I have thanks, it is a dear expense.°
But herein mean I to enrich° my pain,   250
To have his sight thither and back again.   [*Exit.*]

[handwritten: ← 2nd subplot MADE TO APPEAR RIDICULOUS]

SCENE II. *The same.* QUINCE'S *house.*

[*Enter* QUINCE, SNUG, BOTTOM, FLUTE, SNOUT,
       and STARVELING.]

QUIN. Is all our company here?
BOT. You were best to call them generally,° man
by man, according to the scrip.°
QUIN. Here is the scroll of every man's name
which is thought fit, through all Athens, to play in
our interlude° before the Duke and the Duchess on
his wedding day at night.   7
BOT. First, good Peter Quince, say what the play
treats on. Then read the names of the actors, and so
grow to a point.°   10
QUIN. Marry,° our play is, *The most lamentable
comedy, and most cruel death of Pyramus and
Thisby.*
BOT. A very good piece of work, I assure you, and
a merry. Now, good Peter Quince, call forth   15
your actors by the scroll. Masters, spread yourselves.
QUIN. Answer as I call you. Nick Bottom, the
weaver.

---

232. **quantity:** proportion.   236. **Nor . . . taste:** i.e., Love has
no judgment.   240. **waggish:** frolicsome.   242. **eyne:** eyes.
248. **intelligence:** information.   249. **dear expense:** something
that costs one dear.   250. **enrich:** make rich — by the pleasure
of seeing him.
   Sc. ii: 2. **generally:** Bottom loves a long word, but usually
gets it wrong. Here he means "severally"; i.e., separately.
3. **scrip:** list.   6. **interlude:** play.   10. **grow . . . point:** come to
a conclusion.   11. **Marry:** Mary, by the Virgin.

BOT. Ready. Name what part I am for, and pro-
ceed.   21
QUIN. You, Nick Bottom, are set down for Pyra-
mus.
BOT. What is Pyramus? A lover, or a tyrant?
QUIN. A lover, that kills himself most gallant for
love.   26
BOT. That will ask some tears in the true performing of it. If I do it, let the audience look to their eyes.
I will move storms, I will condole° in some measure.
To the rest. Yet my chief humor° is for a tyrant. I
could play Ercles° rarely, or a part to tear a cat° in,
to make all split.   32
        " The raging rocks
           And shivering shocks
         Shall break the locks   35
           Of prison gates.
         And Phibbus'° car°
           Shall shine from far,
         And make and mar
           The foolish Fates."   40
This was lofty! Now name the rest of the players.
This is Ercles' vein, a tyrant's vein. A lover is more
condoling.
QUIN. Francis Flute, the bellows-mender.
FLU. Here, Peter Quince.   45
QUIN. Flute, you must take Thisby on you.
FLU. What is Thisby? A wandering knight?
QUIN. It is the lady that Pyramus must love.
FLU. Nay, faith, let not me play a woman. I have a
beard coming.   50
QUIN. That's all one. You shall play it in a mask,
and you may speak as small° as you will.
BOT. An° I may hide my face, let me play Thisby
too. I'll speak in a monstrous little voice, " Thisne,
Thisne." " Ah Pyramus, my lover dear! Thy Thisby
dear, and lady dear! "   56
QUIN. No, no. You must play Pyramus, and Flute,
you Thisby.
BOT. Well, proceed.
QUIN. Robin Starveling, the tailor.   60
STAR. Here, Peter Quince.
QUIN. Robin Starveling, you must play Thisby's
mother. Tom Snout, the tinker. *[handwritten: — PLAYS PYRAMUS' FATHER]*
SNOUT. Here, Peter Quince.
QUIN. You, Pyramus' father. Myself, Thisby's   65
father. Snug, the joiner, you, the lion's part. And, I
hope, here is a play fitted.
SNUG. Have you the lion's part written? Pray you,
if it be, give it me, for I am slow of study.
QUIN. You may do it extempore, for it is nothing
but roaring.   71
BOT. Let me play the lion too. I will roar that I will

---

29. **condole:** lit., sympathize; Bottom means "lament."   30. **humor:** whim.   31. **Ercles:** Hercules, a roaring figure in the old
drama. **tear a cat:** proverbial expression for ham acting.
37. **Phibbus:** for "Phoebus." **car:** chariot.   52. **small:** shrilly.
53. **An:** if.

do any man's heart good to hear me; I will roar that
I will make the Duke say, "Let him roar again, let
him roar again."   75

QUIN. An you should do it too terribly, you would
fright the Duchess and the ladies, that they would
shriek; and that were enough to hang us all.

ALL. That would hang us, every mother's son.   80

BOT. I grant you, friends, if you should fright the
ladies out of their wits, they would have no more discretion but to hang us. But I will aggravate° my
voice so that I will roar you as gently as any sucking
dove, I will roar you an 'twere any nightingale. 85

QUIN. You can play no part but Pyramus; for
Pyramus is a sweet-faced man, a proper° man as one
shall see in a summer's day, a most lovely, gentlemanlike man. Therefore you must needs play Pyramus.   90

BOT. Well, I will undertake it. What beard were I
best to play it in?

QUIN. Why, what you will.

BOT. I will discharge it in either your straw- 95
color beard, your orange-tawny beard, your purple-
in-grain° beard, or your French-crown-color beard,
your perfect yellow.

QUIN. Some of your French crowns have no hair
at all,° and then you will play barefaced. But, 100
masters, here are your parts. And I am to entreat
you, request you, and desire you, to con° them by tomorrow night; and meet me in the palace wood, a
mile without the town, by moonlight. There will we
rehearse, for if we meet in the city, we shall be
dogged with company, and our devices known. 106
In the meantime I will draw a bill of properties such
as our play wants. I pray you, fail me not.

BOT. We will meet, and there we may rehearse
most obscenely° and courageously. Take pains, be
perfect. Adieu.   111

QUIN. At the Duke's Oak we meet.

BOT. Enough. Hold or cut bowstrings.°

[*Exeunt.*]

Act II

SCENE I. *A wood near Athens.*

[*Enter, from opposite sides, a* FAIRY, *and* PUCK.]

PUCK. How now, spirit! Whither wander you?

FAI.   Over hill, over dale,

Love Fight Among Fairies

Thorough° bush, thorough brier,
Over park, over pale,°
    Thorough flood, thorough fire,   5
I do wander everywhere,
Swifter than the moon's sphere.
And I serve the Fairy Queen,
To dew her orbs° upon the green.
The cowslips° tall her pensioners° be.   10
    In their gold coats spots you see;
    Those be rubies, fairy favors,
    In those freckles live their savors.
I must go seek some dewdrops here,
And hang a pearl in every cowslip's ear.   15
Farewell, thou lob° of spirits, I'll be gone.
Our Queen and all her elves come here anon.

PUCK. The King doth keep his revels here tonight.
Take heed the Queen come not within his sight;
For Oberon is passing° fell° and wrath,   20
Because that she as her attendant hath
A lovely boy, stolen from an Indian king.
She never had so sweet a changeling,°
And jealous Oberon would have the child
Knight of his train,° to trace° the forests wild;   25
But she perforce withholds the lovèd boy,
Crowns him with flowers, and makes him all her joy.
And now they never meet in grove or green,
By fountain clear or spangled starlight sheen,
But they do square,° that all their elves for fear   30
Creep into acorn cups and hide them there.

FAI. Either I mistake your shape and making
    quite,
Or else you are that shrewd and knavish sprite
Called Robin Goodfellow.° Are not you he
That frights the maidens of the villagery;   35
Skim milk, and sometimes labor in the quern,°
And bootless° make the breathless housewife churn;
And sometime make the drink to bear no barm;°
Mislead night wanderers, laughing at their harm?
Those that Hobgoblin call you, and sweet Puck,   40
You do their work, and they shall have good luck.
Are not you he?

PUCK.   Thou speak'st aright.
I am that merry wanderer of the night.
I jest to Oberon, and make him smile,
When I a fat and bean-fed horse beguile,   45

Act II, Sc. i: 3. Thorough: through. **4. pale:** fence. **9. orbs:**
fairy rings; circles of dark grass common in English meadows.
10. cowslips: a wild plant which grows in meadows, with clusters
of small yellow-orange flowers on a stem about eight to nine
inches tall. **pensioners:** the Queen's personal bodyguard, all
young men of fine physique and good family. **16. lob:** lubber,
lout. **20. passing:** exceedingly. **fell:** fierce. **23. changeling:**
child exchanged by fairies. It was a country superstition that
the fairies sometimes stole a beautiful child and left an ugly one
in its place; here the changeling is the stolen child. **25. train:**
following. **trace:** follow the tracks in. **30. square:** quarrel.
34. Robin Goodfellow: See *MND* Intro. p. 514a–b. **36. quern:**
handmill for grinding wheat. **37. bootless:** vainly. **38. barm:**
yeast.

83. aggravate: for "moderate." **87. proper:** handsome.
96–97. purple-in-grain: dyed purple. **99–100. French . . . all:**
Loss of hair was one of the results of venereal or "French"
disease. **102. con:** learn by heart. **110. obscenely:** for "obscurely." **113. Hold . . . bowstrings:** a proverbial phrase, of
which the origin is not satisfactorily explained, meaning come
what may.

Neighing in likeness of a filly foal.
And sometime lurk I in a gossip's° bowl,
In very likeness of a roasted crab;°
And when she drinks, against her lips I bob
And on her withered dewlap° pour the ale. 50
The wisest aunt, telling the saddest tale,
Sometime for three-foot stool mistaketh me;
Then slip I from her bum, down topples she,
And " tailor "° cries, and falls into a cough,
And then the whole quire° hold their hips and
    laugh, 55
And waxen in their mirth, and neeze,° and swear
A merrier hour was never wasted there.
But, room, fairy! Here comes Oberon.
    FAI. And here my mistress. Would that he were
      gone!
[*Enter, from one side,* OBERON, *with his train; from
     the other,* TITANIA, *with hers.*]
    OBE. Ill met by moonlight,° proud Titania. 60
    TITA. What, jealous Oberon! Fairies, skip hence.
I have forsworn° his bed and company.
    OBE. Tarry, rash wanton. Am not I thy lord?
    TITA. Then I must be thy lady. But I know
When thou hast stolen away from fairyland, 65
And in the shape of Corin sat all day,
Playing on pipes of corn,° and versing love
To amorous Phillida.° Why art thou here,
Come from the farthest steppe of India
But that, forsooth, the bouncing Amazon, 70
Your buskined° mistress and your warrior love,
To Theseus must be wedded, and you come
To give their bed joy and prosperity?
    OBE. How canst thou thus for shame, Titania,
Glance at my credit° with Hippolyta, 75
Knowing I know thy love to Theseus?
Didst thou not lead him through the glimmering
    night
From Perigenia, whom he ravishèd?
And make him with fair Aegle break his faith,
With Ariadne and Antiopa?° 80
    TITA. These are the forgeries° of jealousy.
And never, since the middle summer's spring,
Met we on hill, in dale, forest, or mead,
By pavèd fountain or by rushy brook,

Or in the beachèd margent° of the sea, 85
To dance our ringlets° to the whistling wind,
But with thy brawls thou hast disturbed our sport.
Therefore° the winds, piping to us in vain,
As in revenge, have sucked up from the sea
Contagious fogs, which, falling in the land, 90
Have every pelting° river made so proud
That they have overborne their continents.°
The ox hath therefore stretched his yoke in vain,
The plowman lost his sweat, and the green corn°
Hath rotted ere his youth attained a beard. 95
The fold° stands empty in the drownèd field,
And crows are fatted with the murrion° flock.
The nine men's morris° is filled up with mud;
And the quaint° mazes° in the wanton° green,
For lack of tread, are undistinguishable. 100
The human mortals want° their winter here.
No night is now with hymn or carol blest.
Therefore the moon, the governess of floods,
Pale in her anger, washes all the air,
That rhéumatic diseases do abound. 105
And thorough this distemperature° we see
The seasons alter. Hoary-headed frosts
Fall in the fresh lap of the crimson rose,
And on old Hiems'° thin and icy crown
An odorous chaplet of sweet summer buds 110
Is, as in mockery, set. The spring, the summer,
The childing° autumn, angry winter, change
Their wonted liveries, and the mazed° world,
By their increase, now knows not which is which.
And this same progeny of evils comes 115
From our debate, from our dissension.
We are their parents and original.
    OBE. Do you amend it, then. It lies in you.
Why should Titania cross her Oberon?
I do but beg a little changeling boy, 120
To be my henchman.°
    TITA.   Set your heart at rest.
The fairyland buys not the child of me.

[Handwritten marginalia: "THEY ACCUSE EACH OTHER OF DOING OLD THINGS"; "OBERON WANTS CHANGELING BOY OF TITANIA"; "SERVANT"; "INDIAN"]

85. margent: margin. 86. ringlets: round dances. 88–114. Therefore ... which: See *MND* Intro. p. 511a. 91. pelting: paltry.
92. continents: banks. 94. corn: wheat, oats, barley, rye, but
not maize. 96. fold: sheep-pen. 97. murrion: plague-stricken.
98. nine ... morris: "Merels was a game for two players or
parties, each of whom had the same number of pebbles, disks,
pegs, or pins. It was also known as Nine Men's Morris, Five-
penny Morris, and Three Men's Morris, according to the number of 'men' used. The usual form of the diagram on which it is
played is a square with one or more squares inside it. The pegs
or stones placed at set points are moved by one side so as to take
up the men of the other." (*Shakespeare's England*, II.467.)
99. quaint: curious. maze: a set of elaborate and intricate paths
leading (or misleading) to a center. Those who know the secret
can find their way; those who do not are baffled at every turn.
To preserve the pattern in a village green, the paths must be
re-trod every year. At Hampton Court there is an ancient
maze with high yew hedges in which it is easy to be lost for
hours. wanton: luxuriant. 101. want: lack; i.e., are without the
usual winter feasting. 106. distemperature: disorder in nature. 109. Hiems: Winter. 112. childing: pregnant, fertile.
113. mazed: bewildered. 121. henchman: servant.

47. gossip: goodwife (by nature given to gossiping). 48. crab:
crab apple. Roasted apples were sometimes floated in drinks to
give flavor. 50. dewlap: loose skin under the chin. 54. tailor:
Nobody has as yet explained convincingly why she should cry
"tailor." 55. quire: company. 56. neeze: sneeze. 60. moonlight: The constant suggestion of moonlight throughout Acts
II, III, and IV is worth noting. 62. forsworn: sworn to avoid.
66–68. shape ... Phillida: i.e., becoming an idle shepherd
making love to a shepherdess. Corin and Phillida are typical
names in pastoral verse. 67. pipes of corn: oaten straws, a favorite musical instrument of pastoral shepherds. 71. buskined:
wearing hunting boots. See Pl. 13a. 75. credit: reputation.
78–80. Perigenia ... Antiopa: These details of Theseus's love
life Shakespeare found in Plutarch. See *MND* Intro. p. 512b.
81. forgeries: false inventions.

His mother was a votaress° of my order.
And in the spicèd Indian air, by night,
Full often hath she gossiped by my side;   125
And sat with me on Neptune's yellow sands,
Marking the embarkèd traders° on the flood,
When we have laughed to see the sails conceive
And grow big-bellied with the wanton wind,
Which she, with pretty and with swimming gait
Following — her womb then rich with my young
    squire —   131
Would imitate, and sail upon the land,
To fetch me trifles, and return again
As from a voyage, rich with merchandise.
But she, being mortal, of that boy did die,   135
And for her sake do I rear up her boy,
And for her sake I will not part with him.
   OBE. How long within this wood intend you stay?
   TITA. Perchance till after Theseus' wedding day.
If you will patiently dance in our round,   140
And see our moonlight revels, go with us;
If not, shun me, and I will spare° your haunts.
   OBE. Give me that boy, and I will go with thee.
   TITA. Not for thy fairy kingdom. Fairies, away!
We shall chide downright, if I longer stay.   145
      [*Exit* TITANIA *with her train.*]
   OBE. Well, go thy way. Thou shalt not from this
    grove
Till I torment thee for this injury.
My gentle Puck, come hither. Thou rememberest
Since once I sat upon a promontory
And heard a mermaid,° on a dolphin's back,   150
Uttering such dulcet and harmonious breath
That the rude sea grew civil at her song,
And certain stars shot madly from their spheres°
To hear the sea maid's music.
   PUCK.   I remember.
   OBE. That very time I saw, but thou couldst not,
Flying between the cold moon and the earth,   156
Cupid all armed. A certain aim he took
At a fair° vestal thronèd by the west,
And loosed his love shaft smartly from his bow,
As it should pierce a hundred thousand hearts.   160
But I might see young Cupid's fiery shaft
Quenched in the chaste beams of the watery moon,
And the imperial votaress passed on,
In maiden meditation, fancy-free.
Yet marked I where the bolt° of Cupid fell.   165
It fell upon a little western flower,
Before milk-white, now purple with love's wound,

And maidens call it love-in-idleness.°
Fetch me that flower, the herb I showed thee
   once.
The juice of it on sleeping eyelids laid   170
Will make or man or woman madly dote
Upon the next live creature that it sees.
Fetch me this herb, and be thou here again
Ere the leviathan° can swim a league.
   PUCK. I'll put a girdle round about the earth°
In forty minutes.   [*Exit.*]
   OBE.   Having once this juice,   176
I'll watch Titania when she is asleep
And drop the liquor of it in her eyes.
The next thing then she waking looks upon,
Be it on lion, bear, or wolf, or bull,   180
On meddling monkey or on busy ape,
She shall pursue it with the soul of love.
And ere I take this charm from off her sight,
As I can take it with another herb,
I'll make her render up her page to me.   185
But who comes here? I am invisible,°
And I will overhear their conference.
      [*Enter* DEMETRIUS, HELENA *following him.*]
   DEM. I love thee not, therefore pursue me not.
Where is Lysander and fair Hermia?
The one I'll slay, the other slayeth me.   190
Thou told'st me they were stolen unto this wood,
And here am I, and wode° within this wood,
Because I cannot meet my Hermia.
Hence, get thee gone, and follow me no more.
   HEL. You draw me, you hardhearted adamant.°
But yet you draw not iron, for my heart   196
Is true as steel. Leave you° your power to draw,
And I shall have no power to follow you.
   DEM. Do I entice you? Do I speak you fair?
Or, rather, do I not in plainest truth   200
Tell you I do not nor I cannot love you?
   HEL. And even for that do I love you the more.
I am your spaniel, and, Demetrius,
The more you beat me, I will fawn on you.
Use me but as your spaniel, spurn me, strike me,
Neglect me, lose me — only give me leave,   206
Unworthy as I am, to follow you.
What worser place can I beg in your love —
And yet a place of high respect with me —
Than to be usèd as you use your dog?   210
   DEM. Tempt not too much the hatred of my spirit,
For I am sick when I do look on thee.
   HEL. And I am sick when I look not on you.
   DEM. You do impeach° your modesty too much,

---

123. votaress: devoted follower.   **127. embarked traders:** merchant ships.   **142. spare:** avoid.   **150. heard a mermaid:** probably an allusion to one of the elaborate entertainments prepared for Queen Elizabeth.   **153. spheres:** courses. See App. 1. **158–64. fair . . . fancy-free:** a tactful and complimentary allusion to Queen Elizabeth, the Virgin Queen, whose bosom was impenetrable to Cupid's arrows. **vestal:** one vowed to virginity. **votaress:** one who has made a vow. **fancy-free:** not caught by love. **165. bolt:** arrow.

168. love-in-idleness: wild pansy.   **174. leviathan:** whale. **175. I'll . . . earth:** I'll fly round the earth. **186. I am invisible:** Presumably Oberon here puts on a cloak to symbolize invisibility. Henslowe in his *Diary* noted that the Admiral's Men in 1598 bought "a robe for to go invisible."   **192. wode:** mad. **195. adamant:** lodestone, a very hard magnetic stone. **197. Leave you:** if you will leave off.   **214. impeach:** discredit.

To leave the city, and commit yourself   215
Into the hands of one that loves you not;
To trust the opportunity of night
And the ill counsel of a desert place
With the rich worth of your virginity.

HEL. Your virtue is my privilege. For that   220
It is not night when I do see your face,
Therefore I think I am not in the night.
Nor doth this wood lack worlds of company,
For you in my respect° are all the world.
Then how can it be said I am alone   225
When all the world is here to look on me?

DEM. I'll run from thee and hide me in the
    brakes,°
And leave thee to the mercy of wild beasts.

HEL. The wildest hath not such a heart as you.
Run when you will, the story shall be changed.   230
Apollo flies, and Daphne holds the chase;°
The dove pursues the griffin;° the mild hind
Makes speed to catch the tiger — bootless° speed
When cowardice pursues, and valor flies.

DEM. I will not stay thy questions, let me go.   235
Or, if thou follow me, do not believe
But I shall do thee mischief in the wood.

HEL. Aye, in the temple, in the town, the field,
You do me mischief. Fie, Demetrius!
Your wrongs do set a scandal on my sex.   240
We cannot fight for love, as men may do;
We should be wooed, and were not made to woo.
                    [*Exit* DEMETRIUS.]
I'll follow thee, and make a Heaven of Hell,
To die upon the hand I love so well.   [*Exit.*]

OBE. Fare thee well, nymph. Ere he do leave this
    grove,   245
Thou shalt fly him, and he shall seek thy love.
[*Re-enter* PUCK.] Hast thou the flower there?
    Welcome, wanderer.

PUCK. Aye, there it is.

OBE.   I pray thee, give it me.
I know a bank where the wild thyme blows,
Where oxlips° and the nodding violet grows;   250
Quite overcanopied with luscious woodbine,°
With sweet musk roses, and with eglantine.°
There sleeps Titania sometime of the night,
Lulled in these flowers with dances and delight.
And there the snake throws her enameled° skin,
Weed° wide enough to wrap a fairy in.   256
And with the juice of this I'll streak her eyes,
And make her full of hateful fantasies.
Take thou some of it, and seek through this grove.

A sweet Athenian lady is in love   260
With a disdainful youth. Anoint his eyes;
But do it when the next thing he espies
May be the lady. Thou shalt know the man
By the Athenian garments he hath on.
Effect it with some care, that he may prove   265
More fond° on her than she upon her love.
And look thou meet me ere the first cock crow.

PUCK. Fear not, my lord, your servant shall do so.
                                        [*Exeunt.*]

SCENE II. *Another part of the wood.*

[*Enter* TITANIA, *with her train.*]

TITA. Come, now a roundel° and a fairy song,
Then, for the third part of a minute, hence —
Some to kill cankers° in the musk-rose buds,
Some war with reremice° for their leathern wings,
To make my small elves coats, and some keep back
The clamorous owl that nightly hoots and wonders
At our quaint spirits. Sing me now asleep,   7
Then to your offices, and let me rest.
                        [*The fairies sing.*]

1. FAI. You spotted snakes with double tongue,
        Thorny hedgehogs, be not seen.   10
    Newts and blindworms,° do no wrong,
        Come not near our fairy Queen.

CHORUS. Philomel,° with melody
        Sing in our sweet lullaby;
    Lulla, lulla, lullaby, lulla, lulla, lullaby.   15
        Never harm,
        Nor spell, nor charm,
        Come our lovely lady nigh.
        So, good night, with lullaby.

1. FAI. Weaving spiders, come not here.   20
        Hence, you long-legged spinners, hence!
    Beetles black, approach not near.
        Worm nor snail, do no offense.

CHORUS. Philomel, with melody
        Sing in our sweet lullaby;   25
    Lulla, lulla, lullaby, lulla, lulla, lullaby.
        Never harm,
        Nor spell, nor charm,
        Come our lovely lady nigh.
        So, good night, with lullaby.

2. FAI. Hence, away! Now all is well.
        One aloof stand sentinel.
            [*Exeunt* FAIRIES. TITANIA *sleeps.*]
[*Enter* OBERON, *and squeezes the flower on*
            TITANIA'S *eyelids.*]

OBE. What thou seest when thou dost wake,

---

224. respect: estimation. 227. brakes: bushes. 231. Apollo . . .
chase: The natural order is reversed; the meek pursues the
strong. According to the legend, Apollo pursued Daphne,
who was turned into a laurel bush.   232. griffin: a fabulous
beast, eagle in front and lion behind.   233. bootless: vain.
250. oxlips: cross between the primrose and the cowslip.
251. woodbine: honeysuckle.   252. eglantine: sweetbrier.
255. enameled: shiny.   256. Weed: garment.

266. fond: foolishly doting.
    Sc. ii: 1. roundel: round dance. 3. cankers: cankerworms.
4. reremice: bats. 11. blindworm: slow worm, a small harmless
snakelike creature (actually a legless lizard), common in the
English countryside. 13. Philomel: the nightingale.

Do it for thy truelove take,
Love and languish for his sake.
Be it ounce,° or cat, or bear,   30
Pard,° or boar with bristled hair,
In thy eye that shall appear
When thou wakest, it is thy dear.
Wake when some vile thing is near.   [*Exit.*]

    [*Enter* LYSANDER *and* HERMIA.]

    LYS. Fair love, you faint with wandering in the
      wood,   35
And to speak troth,° I have forgot our way.
We'll rest us, Hermia, if you think it good,
    And tarry for the comfort of the day.
    HER. Be it so, Lysander. Find you out a bed,
For I upon this bank will rest my head.   40
    LYS. One turf shall serve as pillow for us both —
One heart, one bed, two bosoms, and one troth.
    HER. Nay, good Lysander, for my sake, my dear,
Lie further off yet, do not lie so near.
    LYS. Oh, take the sense, sweet, of my innocence!
Love takes the meaning in love's conference.   46
I mean that my heart unto yours is knit
So that but one heart we can make of it.
Two bosoms interchainèd with an oath,
So then two bosoms and a single troth.   50
Then by your side no bedroom me deny
For lying so, Hermia, I do not lie.
    HER. Lysander riddles very prettily.
Now much beshrew° my manners and my pride,
If Hermia meant to say Lysander lied.   55
But, gentle friend, for love and courtesy
Lie further off; in human modesty,
Such separation as may well be said
Becomes a virtuous bachelor and a maid,
So far be distant. And good night, sweet friend.   60
Thy love ne'er alter till thy sweet life end!
    LYS. Amen, amen, to that fair prayer say I,
And then end life when I end loyalty!
Here is my bed. Sleep give thee all his rest!   64
    HER. With half that wish the wisher's eye be
      pressed!   [*They sleep.*]

      [*Enter* PUCK.]

    PUCK. Through the forest have I gone,
But Athenian found I none
On whose eyes I might approve°
This flower's force in stirring love.
Night and silence. — Who is here?   70
Weeds of Athens he doth wear.
This is he, my master said,
Despisèd the Athenian maid,
And here the maiden, sleeping sound
On the dank and dirty ground.   75
Pretty soul! She durst not lie
Near this lacklove, this kill-courtesy.
Churl,° upon thy eyes I throw

All the power this charm doth owe.
When thou wakest, let love forbid   80
Sleep his seat on thy eyelid.
So awake when I am gone,
For I must now to Oberon.   [*Exit.*]

    [*Enter* DEMETRIUS *and* HELENA, *running.*]

    HEL. Stay, though thou kill me, sweet Demetrius.
    DEM. I charge thee, hence, and do not haunt me
      thus.   85
    HEL. Oh, wilt thou darkling° leave me? Do not so.
    DEM. Stay, on thy peril.° I alone will go.   [*Exit.*]
    HEL. Oh, I am out of breath in this fond° chase!
The more my prayer, the lesser is my grace.
Happy is Hermia, wheresoe'er she lies,   90
For she hath blessèd and attractive eyes.
How came her eyes so bright? Not with salt tears;
If so, my eyes are oftener washed than hers.
No, no, I am as ugly as a bear,
For beasts that meet me run away for fear.   95
Therefore no marvel though Demetrius
Do, as a monster, fly my presence thus.
What wicked and dissembling° glass of mine
Made me compare with Hermia's sphery° eyne?
But who is here? Lysander! On the ground!   100
Dead? Or asleep? I see no blood, no wound.
Lysander, if you live, good sir, awake.
    LYS. [*Awaking*] And run through fire I will for
      thy sweet sake.
Transparent° Helena! Nature shows art,
That through thy bosom makes me see thy heart.
Where is Demetrius? Oh, how fit a word   106
Is that vile name to perish on my sword!
    HEL. Do not say so, Lysander, say not so.
What though he love your Hermia? Lord, what
      though?
Yet Hermia still loves you. Then be content.   110
    LYS. Content with Hermia! No, I do repent
The tedious minutes I with her have spent.
Not Hermia but Helena I love.
Who will not change a raven for a dove?
The will of man is by his reason swayed,   115
And reason says you are the worthier maid.
Things growing are not ripe until their season.
So I, being young, till now ripe not to reason;
And touching now the point° of human skill,
Reason becomes the marshal° to my will,°   120
And leads me to your eyes, where I o'erlook
Love's stories, written in love's richest book.
    HEL. Wherefore was I to this keen mockery born?
When at your hands did I deserve this scorn?
Is't not enough, is't not enough, young man,   125
That I did never, no, nor never can,
Deserve a sweet look from Demetrius' eye,

---

86. darkling: in the dark.   87. on . . . peril: i.e., or harm will come to you.   88. fond: foolish.   98. dissembling: deceiving. 99. sphery: starlike.   104. Transparent: i.e., because her heart is visible.   119. point: high spot.   120. marshal: director. will: passion.

---

30. ounce: lynx.   31. Pard: leopard.   36. troth: truth.   54. beshrew: plague on.   68. approve: test.   78. Churl: boor.

But you must flout my insufficiency?
Good troth, you do me wrong, good sooth,° you
    do,
In such disdainful manner me to woo.   130
But fare you well. Perforce I must confess
I thought you lord of more true gentleness.
Oh, that a lady, of one man refused,
Should of another therefore be abused!   [*Exit.*]
  LYS. She sees not Hermia. Hermia, sleep thou
    there.   135
And never mayst thou come Lysander near!
For as a surfeit of the sweetest things
The deepest loathing to the stomach brings,
Or as the heresies that men do leave
Are hated most of those they did deceive,   140
So thou, my surfeit and my heresy,
Of all be hated, but the most of me!
And, all my powers, address your love and might
To honor Helen and to be her knight!   [*Exit.*]
  HER. [*Awaking*] Help me, Lysander, help me! Do
    thy best   145
To pluck this crawling serpent from my breast!
Aye me, for pity! What a dream was here!
Lysander, look how I do quake with fear.
Methought a serpent eat my heart away,
And you sat smiling at his cruel prey.   150
Lysander! What, removed? Lysander! Lord!
What, out of hearing? Gone? No sound, no word?
Alack, where are you? Speak, an if you hear,
Speak, of all loves! I swoon almost with fear.
No? Then I well perceive you are not nigh.   155
Either death or you I'll find immediately.   [*Exit.*]

Act III

SCENE I. *The wood.* TITANIA *lying asleep.*

[*Enter* QUINCE, SNUG, BOTTOM, FLUTE, SNOUT, *and*
    STARVELING.]

  BOT. Are we all met?
  QUIN. Pat, pat, and here's a marvelous convenient
place for our rehearsal. This green plot shall be our
stage, this hawthorn brake° our tiring-house;° and
we will do it in action as we will do it before the
Duke.   6
  BOT. Peter Quince——
  QUIN. What sayest thou, bully Bottom?
  BOT. There are things in this comedy of Pyramus
and Thisby that will never please. First, Pyra-   10
mus must draw a sword to kill himself, which the
ladies cannot abide. How answer you that?

  SNOUT. By'r lakin,° a parlous fear.
  STAR. I believe we must leave the killing out, when
all is done.   16
  BOT. Not a whit. I have a device to make all well.
Write me a prologue, and let the prologue seem to
say we will do no harm with our swords, and that
Pyramus is not killed indeed. And, for the more   20
better assurance, tell them that I Pyramus am not
Pyramus, but Bottom the weaver. This will put them
out of fear.
  QUIN. Well, we will have such a prologue, and it
shall be written in eight and six.°   25
  BOT. No, make it two more. Let it be written in
eight and eight.
  SNOUT. Will not the ladies be afeard of the lion?
  STAR. I fear it, I promise you.
  BOT. Masters, you ought to consider with   30
yourselves. To bring in — God shield us! — a lion
among ladies° is a most dreadful thing; for there is
not a more fearful wildfowl than your lion living,
and we ought to look to 't.
  SNOUT. Therefore another prologue must tell he is
not a lion.   36
  BOT. Nay, you must name his name, and half his
face must be seen through the lion's neck. And he
himself must speak through, saying thus, or to the
same defect° — " Ladies " — or " Fair ladies —   40
I would wish you " — or " I would request you " —
or " I would entreat you — not to fear, not to tremble. My life for yours. If you think I come hither as a
lion, it were pity of my life. No, I am no such thing,
I am a man as other men are." And there indeed   45
let him name his name, and tell them plainly he is
Snug the joiner.
  QUIN. Well, it shall be so. But there is two hard
things: that is, to bring the moonlight into a chamber, for you know Pyramus and Thisby meet by
moonlight.   51
  SNOUT. Doth the moon shine that night we play
our play?
  BOT. A calendar, a calendar! Look in the almanac.° Find out moonshine, find out moonshine.
  QUIN. Yes, it doth shine that night.   56
  BOT. Why, then may you leave a casement° of the
great-chamber° window, where we play, open, and
the moon may shine in at the casement.
  QUIN. Aye, or else one must come in with a   60
bush of thorns and a lantern,° and say he comes to
disfigure,° or to present, the person of moonshine.
Then, there is another thing. We must have a wall in

129. sooth: truth.
Act III, Sc. i: 4. brake: thicket. tiring-house: dressing room.

14. By'r lakin: by our little lady; i.e., the Virgin Mary.
25. eight . . . six: the common ballad meter of alternate lines of
six and eight syllables. 31–32. lion . . . ladies: See *MND* Intro.
p. 511a–b. 40. defect: for "effect." 55. almanac: See App. 2.
57. casement: window opening on a hinge. 58. great-chamber:
hall of a great house. See Pl. 4b. 61. bush . . . lantern: supposedly carried by the man in the moon. 62. disfigure: for
"prefigure."

the great chamber, for Pyramus and Thisby, says the
story, did talk through the chink of a wall.   66

SNOUT. You can never bring in a wall. What say
you, Bottom?

BOT. Some man or other must present wall. And
let him have some plaster, or some loam,° or some
roughcast° about him, to signify wall. And let   71
him hold his fingers thus, and through that cranny
shall Pyramus and Thisby whisper.

QUIN. If that may be, then all is well. Come, sit
down, every mother's son, and rehearse your   75
parts. Pyramus, you begin. When you have spoken
your speech, enter into that brake. And so every one
according to his cue.

     [*Enter* PUCK *behind.*]

PUCK. What hempen homespuns° have we swag-
gering here,
So near the cradle of the Fairy Queen?   80
What, a play toward!° I'll be an auditor —
An actor too perhaps, if I see cause.

QUIN. Speak, Pyramus. Thisby, stand forth.

BOT. " Thisby, the flowers of odious savors
sweet —— "

QUIN. Odors, odors.   85

BOT. " —— odors savors sweet.
So hath thy breath, my dearest Thisby dear.
But hark, a voice! Stay thou but here awhile,
And by and by I will to thee appear."   [*Exit.*]

PUCK. A stranger Pyramus than e'er played here.
     [*Exit.*]

FLU. Must I speak now?   91

QUIN. Aye, marry must you, for you must understand he goes but to see a noise that he heard, and is
to come again.

FLU. " Most radiant Pyramus, most lily-white of
hue,   95
Of color like the red rose on triumphant brier,
Most briskly juvenal,° and eke° most lovely Jew,
As true as truest horse, that yet would never tire,
I'll meet thee, Pyramus, at Ninny's tomb."   99

QUIN. " Ninus' tomb," man. Why, you must not
speak that yet. That you answer to Pyramus. You
speak all your part at once, cues and all. Pyramus
enter. Your cue is past. It is " never tire."   105

FLU. Oh — " As true as truest horse, that yet
would never tire."

     [*Re-enter* PUCK, *and* BOTTOM *with an ass's head.*]

BOT. " If I were fair, Thisby, I were only thine."

QUIN. Oh, monstrous! Oh, strange! We are
haunted. Pray, masters! Fly, masters! Help!

     [*Exeunt* QUINCE, SNUG, FLUTE, SNOUT, *and*
           STARVELING.]

PUCK. I'll follow you, I'll lead you about a round,°

Through bog, through bush, through brake,
through brier.   110
Sometime a horse I'll be, sometime a hound,
A hog, a headless bear, sometime a fire,
And neigh, and bark, and grunt, and roar, and
burn,
Like horse, hound, hog, bear, fire, at every turn.
     [*Exit.*]

BOT. Why do they run away? This is a knavery of
them to make me afeard.   116

     [*Re-enter* SNOUT.]

SNOUT. O Bottom, thou art changed! What do I
see on thee?

BOT. What do you see? You see an asshead of your
own, do you?   120

     [*Exit* SNOUT.]

     [*Re-enter* QUINCE.]

QUIN. Bless thee, Bottom! Bless thee! Thou art
translated.°   [*Exit.*]

BOT. I see their knavery. This is to make an ass of
me, to fright me, if they could. But I will not stir
from this place, do what they can. I will walk   125
up and down here, and I will sing, that they shall
hear I am not afraid. [*Sings.*]
   " The ousel° cock so black of hue,
      With orange-tawny bill,
     The throstle° with his note so true,   130
      The wren° with little quill;° "

TITA. [*Awaking*] What angel wakes me from my
flowery bed?

BOT. [*Sings.*]
   " The finch, the sparrow, and the lark,
      The plainsong° cuckoo gray,
     Whose note full many a man doth mark,   135
      And dares not answer nay° — "
for indeed who would set his wit to° so foolish a
bird? Who would give a bird the lie, though he cry
" cuckoo " never so?

TITA. I pray thee, gentle mortal, sing again.   140
Mine ear is much enamored of thy note,
So is mine eye enthrallèd° to thy shape.
And thy fair virtue's force perforce doth move me
On the first view to say, to swear, I love thee.

BOT. Methinks, mistress, you should have   145
little reason for that. And yet, to say the truth, reason and love keep little company together nowadays;
the more the pity, that some honest neighbors will
not make them friends. Nay, I can gleek° upon occasion.   150

TITA. Thou art as wise as thou art beautiful.

BOT. Not so, neither. But if I had wit enough to
get out of this wood, I have enough to serve mine
own turn.

---

70. loam: preparation of clay used for covering walls.   71. roughcast: rough plaster.   79. hempen homespuns: coarse clothing
spun at home; i.e., country clowns.   81. toward: in hand.
97. juvenal: youth. eke: also.   109. about a round: roundabout.

122. translated: transformed.   128. ousel: blackbird.   130. throstle: thrush.   131. wren: the smallest of English birds. quill:
feather.   134. plainsong: singing a simple melody.
135–36. Whose . . . nay: See App. II.   137. set . . . to: try to
answer.   142. enthralled: enslaved.   149. gleek: wisecrack.

TITA. Out of this wood do not desire to go. 155
Thou shalt remain here, whether thou wilt or no.
I am a spirit of no common rate.
The summer still° doth tend° upon my state;
And I do love thee. Therefore go with me.
I'll give thee fairies to attend on thee, 160
And they shall fetch thee jewels from the deep,
And sing while thou on pressèd flowers dost sleep.
And I will purge thy mortal grossness so
That thou shalt like an airy spirit go. 164
Peaseblossom! Cobweb! Moth! And Mustardseed!

[*Enter* PEASEBLOSSOM, COBWEB, MOTH, *and*
MUSTARDSEED.]

1. FAI. Ready.
2. FAI.   And I.
3. FAI.   And I.
4. FAI.   And I.
ALL.   Where shall we go?
TITA. Be kind and courteous to this gentleman.
Hop in his walks, and gambol° in his eyes.
Feed him with apricocks° and dewberries,°
With purple grapes, green figs, and mulberries. 170
The honey bags steal from the humblebees,
And for night tapers crop their waxen thighs,
And light them at the fiery glowworm's eyes,
To have my love to bed and to arise.
And pluck the wings from painted butterflies, 175
To fan the moonbeams from his sleeping eyes.
Nod to him, elves, and do him courtesies.

1. FAI. Hail, mortal!
2. FAI. Hail!
3. FAI. Hail! 180
4. FAI. Hail!
BOT. I cry your Worship's mercy,° heartily. I beseech your Worship's name.
COB. Cobweb.
BOT. I shall desire you of more acquaintance, 185
good Master Cobweb. If I cut my finger, I shall make
bold with you.° Your name, honest gentleman?
PEAS. Peaseblossom.°
BOT. I pray you, commend me to Mistress 190
Squash,° your mother, and to Master Peascod,°
your father. Good Master Peaseblossom, I shall desire you of more acquaintance too. Your name, I beseech you, sir?
MUS. Mustardseed. 195
BOT. Good Master Mustardseed, I know your patience well. That same cowardly, giantlike ox beef
hath devoured many a gentleman of your house. I
promise you your kindred hath made my eyes water
ere now. I desire your more acquaintance, good
Master Mustardseed. 201

158. still: always. tend: attend.   168. gambol: caper.   169. apricocks: apricots. dewberries: blackberries.   182. I . . . mercy:
I beg your pardon.   186–87. Cobweb . . . you: an ancient means
of first aid for a cut finger.   189. Peaseblossom: the blossom
of a garden pea.   191. Squash: the unripe peapod. Peascod:
the full pod.

TITA. Come, wait upon him; lead him to my
bower.
The moon methinks looks with a watery eye,
And when she weeps, weeps every little flower,
Lamenting some enforcèd chastity. 205
Tie up my love's tongue, bring him silently.

[*Exeunt.*]

SCENE II. *Another part of the wood.*

[*Enter* OBERON.]

OBE. I wonder if Titania be awaked,
Then, what it was that next came in her eye,
Which she must dote on in extremity.
[*Enter* PUCK.] Here comes my messenger.
                                        How now, mad spirit!
What night rule° now about this haunted grove? 5
PUCK. My mistress with a monster is in love.
Near to her close and consecrated bower,
While she was in her dull and sleeping hour,
A crew of patches,° rude mechanicals,°
That work for bread upon Athenian stalls,° 10
Were met together to rehearse a play,
Intended for great Theseus' nuptial day.
The shallowest thickskin of that barren° sort,
Who Pyramus presented,° in their sport
Forsook his scene, and entered in a brake, 15
When I did him at this advantage take,
An ass's nole° I fixèd on his head.
Anon his Thisbe must be answerèd,
And forth my mimic° comes. When they him spy,
As wild geese that the creeping fowler eye, 20
Or russet-pated choughs,° many in sort,
Rising and cawing at the gun's report,
Sever themselves and madly sweep the sky,
So at his sight away his fellows fly.
And, at our stamp, here o'er and o'er one falls, 25
He murder cries, and help from Athens calls.
Their sense thus weak, lost with their fears thus
   strong,
Made senseless things begin to do them wrong;
For briers and thorns at their apparel snatch,
Some sleeves, some hats, from yielders all things
   catch. 30
I led them on in this distracted fear,
And left sweet Pyramus translated there,
When in that moment, so it came to pass,
Titania waked, and straightway loved an ass.
OBE. This falls out better than I could devise. 35
But hast thou yet latched° the Athenian's eyes
With the love juice, as I did bid thee do?

Sc. ii: 5. night rule: mischief.   9. patches: clowns. mechanicals: workingmen.   10. stalls: shops.   13. barren: empty-headed.
14. presented: represented.   17. nole: noddle, head.   19. mimic:
actor.   21. russet-pated choughs: gray-headed jackdaws.
36. latched: caught; i.e., charmed.

PUCK. I took him sleeping — that is finished
  too —
And the Athenian woman by his side,
That, when he waked, of force she must be eyed. 40
  [*Enter* HERMIA *and* DEMETRIUS.]
OBE. Stand close. This is the same Athenian.
PUCK. This is the woman, but not this the man.
DEM. Oh, why rebuke you him that loves you so?
Lay breath so bitter on your bitter foe.
  HER. Now I but chide, but I should use thee
    worse,   45
For thou, I fear, hast given me cause to curse.
If thou hast slain Lysander in his sleep,
Being o'er shoes in blood, plunge in the deep,
And kill me too.
The sun was not so true unto the day   50
As he to me. Would he have stolen away
From sleeping Hermia? I'll believe as soon
This whole earth may be bored, and that the moon
May through the center° creep, and so displease
Her brother's noontide with the Antipodes.°   55
It cannot be but thou hast murdered him.
So should a murderer look, so dead,° so grim.
  DEM. So should the murdered look, and so
    should I,
Pierced through the heart with your stern cruelty.
Yet you, the murderer, look as bright, as clear, 60
As yonder Venus° in her glimmering sphere.
  HER. What's this to my Lysander? Where is he?
Ah, good Demetrius, wilt thou give him me?
  DEM. I had rather give his carcass to my hounds.
  HER. Out, dog! Out, cur! Thou drivest me past the
    bounds   65
Of maiden's patience. Hast thou slain him, then?
Henceforth be never numbered among men!
Oh, once tell true, tell true, even for my sake!
Durst thou have looked upon him being awake,
And hast thou killed him sleeping? Oh, brave
  touch.°   70
Could not a worm, an adder, do so much?
An adder did it, for with doubler tongue
Than thine, thou serpent, never adder stung.
  DEM. You spend your passion on a misprised°
    mood.
I am not guilty of Lysander's blood,   75
Nor is he dead, for aught that I can tell.
  HER. I pray thee, tell me then that he is well.
  DEM. An if I could, what should I get therefore?
  HER. A privilege never to see me more.
And from thy hated presence part I so.   80
See me no more, whether he be dead or no. [*Exit.*]
  DEM. There is no following her in this fierce vein.

Here therefore for a while I will remain.
So sorrow's heaviness doth heavier grow
For debt that bankrupt sleep doth sorrow owe,° 85
Which now in some slight measure it will pay
If for his tender° here I make some stay.
  [*Lies down and sleeps.*]
OBE. What hast thou done? Thou hast mistaken
  quite,
And laid the love juice on some truelove's sight,
Of thy misprision° must perforce ensue   90
Some true love turned, and not a false turned true.
  PUCK. Then fate o'errules, that, one man holding
    troth,
A million fail, confounding oath on oath.°
OBE. About the wood go swifter than the wind,
And Helena of Athens look thou find.   95
All fancy-sick° she is and pale of cheer,°
With sighs of love that costs the fresh blood° dear.
By some illusion° see thou bring her here.
I'll charm his eyes against° she do appear.
  PUCK. I go, I go, look how I go,   100
Swifter than arrow from the Tartar's° bow. [*Exit.*]
OBE. Flower of this purple dye,
Hit with Cupid's archery,
Sink in apple of his eye.
When his love he doth espy,   105
Let her shine as gloriously
As the Venus of the sky.
When thou wakest, if she be by,
Beg of her for remedy.
  [*Re-enter* PUCK.]
PUCK. Captain of our fairy band,   110
Helena is here at hand,
And the youth, mistook by me,
Pleading for a lover's fee.
Shall we their fond pageant see?
Lord, what fools these mortals be!   115
  OBE. Stand aside. The noise they make
Will cause Demetrius to awake.
  PUCK. Then will two at once woo one,
That must needs be sport alone.
And those things do best please me   120
That befall preposterously.
  [*Enter* LYSANDER *and* HELENA.]
LYS. Why should you think that I should woo in
  scorn?
Scorn and derision never come in tears.
Look, when I vow, I weep, and vows so born
  In their nativity all truth appears.   125

---

54. center: i.e., of the earth. See App. 1.   54–55. so . . . Antipodes: i.e., the moon will pass through the earth and appear
at the other side, to the annoyance of the sun who is shining
there.   57. dead: deadly.   61. Venus: i.e., the star.   70. touch:
feat.   74. misprised: mistaken.

84–85. So . . . owe: a man in sorrow cannot sleep; sleep's debt
to sorrow thus becomes heavier.   87. tender: offer; i.e., sleep.
90. misprision: mistake.   92–93. Then . . . oath: then fate over-
rules his efforts, for one man true in love, a million are false,
breaking oath after oath.   96. fancy-sick: lovesick. cheer: face.
97. sighs . . . blood: It was believed that sighs consumed the
heart's blood.   98. illusion: deception.   99. against: by the time
that.   101. Tartar: the Tartars, who live in Siberia, were
famous bowmen.

How can these things in me seem scorn to you,
Bearing the badge of faith to prove them true?
  HEL. You do advance your cunning more and
    more.
  When truth kills truth, oh, devilish-holy fray!
These vows are Hermia's. Will you give her o'er?
  Weigh oath with oath, and you will nothing
    weigh.   131
Your vows to her and me, put in two scales,
Will even weigh — and both as light as tales.
  LYS. I had no judgment when to her I swore.
  HEL. Nor none, in my mind, now you give her
    o'er.   135
  LYS. Demetrius loves her, and he loves not you.
  DEM. [*Awaking.*] O Helen, goddess, nymph, per-
    fect, divine!
To what, my love, shall I compare thine eyne?
Crystal is muddy. Oh, how ripe in show   139
Thy lips, those kissing cherries, tempting grow!
That pure congealèd white, high Taurus'° snow,
Fanned with the eastern wind, turns to a crow
When thou hold'st up thy hand. Oh, let me kiss
This princess of pure white, this seal° of bliss!
  HEL. Oh, spite! Oh, Hell! I see you all are bent
To set against me for your merriment.   146
If you were civil and knew courtesy,
You would not do me thus much injury.
Can you not hate me, as I know you do,
But you must join in souls to mock me too?   150
If you were men, as men you are in show,
You would not use a gentle lady so —
To vow, and swear, and superpraise my parts,
When I am sure you hate me with your hearts.
You both are rivals, and love Hermia,   155
And now both rivals, to mock Helena.
A trim° exploit, a manly enterprise,
To conjure tears up in a poor maid's eyes
With your derision! None of noble sort
Would so offend a virgin, and extort   160
A poor soul's patience, all to make you sport.
  LYS. You are unkind, Demetrius. Be not so;
For you love Hermia — this you know I know.
And here, with all goodwill, with all my heart,
In Hermia's love I yield you up my part.   165
And yours of Helena to me bequeath,
Whom I do love, and will do till my death.
  HEL. Never did mockers waste more idle breath.
  DEM. Lysander, keep thy Hermia. I will none.
If e'er I loved her, all that love is gone.   170
My heart to her but as guest-wise sojourned,°
And now to Helen is it home returned,
There to remain.
  LYS.   Helen, it is not so.
  DEM. Disparage not the faith thou dost not know,

Lest, to thy peril, thou aby° it dear.   175
Look where thy love comes — yonder is thy dear.
        [*Re-enter* HERMIA.]
  HER. Dark night, that from the eye his function
    takes,
The ear more quick of apprehension makes.
Wherein it doth impair the seeing sense,
It pays the hearing double recompense.   180
Thou art not by mine eye, Lysander, found;
Mine ear, I thank it, brought me to thy sound.
But why unkindly didst thou leave me so?
  LYS. Why should he stay whom love doth press to
    go?
  HER. What love could press Lysander from my
    side?   185
  LYS. Lysander's love, that would not let him bide
Fair Helena, who more engilds the night
Than all yon fiery oes° and eyes of light.
Why seek'st thou me? Could not this make thee
    know,
The hate I bare thee made me leave thee so?   190
  HER. You speak not as you think. It cannot be.
  HEL. Lo, she is one of this confederacy!
Now I perceive they have conjoined all three
To fashion this false sport, in spite of me.°
Injurious Hermia! Most ungrateful maid!   195
Have you conspired, have you with these contrived°
To bait° me with this foul derision?
Is all the counsel that we two have shared,
The sister's vows, the hours that we have spent,
When we have chid the hasty-footed time   200
For parting us — Oh, is it all forgot?
All school days' friendship, childhood innocence?
We, Hermia, like two artificial° gods,
Have with our needles created both one flower,
Both on one sampler,° sitting on one cushion,   205
Both warbling of one song, both in one key —
As if our hands, our sides, voices, and minds
Had been incorporate.° So we grew together,
Like to a double cherry, seeming parted
But yet a union in partition —   210
Two lovely berries molded on one stem.
So, with two seeming bodies, but one heart,
Two of the first, like coats in heraldry,
Due but to one, and crownèd with one crest.°
And will you rent our ancient love asunder,   215
To join with men in scorning your poor friend?
It is not friendly, 'tis not maidenly.
Our sex, as well as I, may chide you for it,
Though I alone do feel the injury.

175. aby: abide, pay for.   188. oes: circles; i.e., stars, with a
pun on "o" and "i."   194. in . . . me: to spite me.   196. contrived: devised, plotted.   197. bait: taunt.   203. artificial:
creative.   205. sampler: piece of embroidery.   208. incorporate:
in one body.   213–14. Two . . . crest: i.e., two bodies with a
single heart — an elaborate metaphor from heraldry. After marriage the coats of arms of husband and wife are united in one
coat under one crest. See App. 9.

141. Taurus: a range of mountains in Asia Minor.   144. seal:
guarantee.   157. trim: fine.   171. guest-wise sojourned: made
a short stay.

HER. I am amazèd at your passionate words.   220
I scorn you not. It seems that you scorn me.
HEL. Have you not set Lysander, as in scorn,
To follow me and praise my eyes and face?
And made your other love, Demetrius,
Who even but now did spurn me with his foot,   225
To call me goddess, nymph, divine and rare,
Precious, celestial? Wherefore speaks he this
To her he hates? And wherefore doth Lysander
Deny your love, so rich within his soul,
And tender me, forsooth, affection,   230
But by your setting on, by your consent?
What though I be not so in grace as you,
So hung upon with love, so fortunate,
But miserable most, to love unloved?
This you should pity rather than despise.   235
HER. I understand not what you mean by this.
HEL. Aye, do, persever,° counterfeit sad looks,
Make mouths upon me when I turn my back,
Wink each at other, hold the sweet jest up.
This sport, well carried, shall be chronicled.°   240
If you have any pity, grace, or manners,
You would not make me such an argument.°
But fare ye well. 'Tis partly my own fault,
Which death or absence soon shall remedy.
LYS. Stay, gentle Helena, hear my excuse.   245
My love, my life, my soul, fair Helena!
HEL. Oh, excellent!
HER.   Sweet, do not scorn her so.
DEM. If she cannot entreat, I can compel.
LYS. Thou canst compel no more than she entreat.
Thy threats have no more strength than her weak
    prayers.   250
Helen, I love thee, by my life, I do.
I swear by that which I will lose for thee,
To prove him false that says I love thee not.
DEM. I say I love thee more than he can do.   254
LYS. If thou say so, withdraw, and prove it too.
DEM. Quick, come!
HER.   Lysander, whereto tends all this?
LYS. Away, you Ethiope!°
DEM.   No, no, he'll ——
Seem to break loose,° take on as you would fol-
    low,
But yet come not. You are a tame man, go!
LYS. Hang off, thou cat, thou bur! Vile thing, let
    loose,   260
Or I will shake thee from me like a serpent!

HER. Why are you grown so rude? What change is
    this?
Sweet love ——
LYS.   Thy love! Out, tawny° Tartar, out!
Out, loathèd medicine! Hated potion, hence!   264
HER. Do you not jest?
HEL.   Yes, sooth, and so do you.
LYS. Demetrius, I will keep my word with thee.
DEM. I would I had your bond,° for I perceive
A weak bond° holds you. I'll not trust your word.
LYS. What, should I hurt her, strike her, kill her
    dead?
Although I hate her, I'll not harm her so.   270
HER. What, can you do me greater harm than
    hate?
Hate me! Wherefore? Oh, me! What news, my love!
Am not I Hermia? Are not you Lysander?
I am as fair now as I was erewhile.°
Since night you loved me, yet since night you left
    me.   275
Why, then you left me — Oh, the gods forbid! —
In earnest, shall I say?
LYS.   Aye, by my life,
And never did desire to see thee more.
Therefore be out of hope, of question, of doubt;
Be certain, nothing truer. 'Tis no jest   280
That I do hate thee, and love Helena.
HER. Oh, me! You juggler! You canker blossom!°
You thief of love! What, have you come by night
And stolen my love's heart from him?
HEL.   Fine, i'faith!
Have you no modesty, no maiden shame,   285
No touch of bashfulness? What, will you tear
Impatient answers from my gentle tongue?
Fie, fie! You counterfeit, you puppet,° you!
HER. Puppet? Why so? Aye, that way goes the
    game.
Now I perceive that she hath made compare   290
Between our statures, she hath urged her height.
And with her personage, her tall personage,
Her height, forsooth, she hath prevailed with him.
And are you grown so high in his esteem
Because I am so dwarfish and so low?   295
How low am I, thou painted maypole?° Speak —
How low am I? I am not yet so low
But that my nails can reach unto thine eyes.
HEL. I pray you, though you mock me, gentlemen,
Let her not hurt me. I was never curst,°   300
I have no gift at all in shrewishness.
I am a right maid° for my cowardice.
Let her not strike me. You perhaps may think,
Because she is something lower than myself,

237. persever: keep it up.   240. chronicled: recorded in the history book.   242. argument: subject for a story.   257. Ethiope:
Ethiopian. From the number of references to the dark complexion of different women in Shakespeare's plays it is evident
that one of the boy actors was dark-skinned. See Gen. Intro.
p. 58b.   257–58. No . . . loose: There is a difficulty of reading
here. Q1 reads "No, no: heele, Seeme to breake loose." The
Folio reads: "No, no, Sir, seem to breake loose." This makes
sense. Hermia is clutching Lysander; Demetrius taunts him
saying that he pretends to want a fight, but is in reality willing enough to be held back by a woman.

263. tawny: dark-skinned.   267. bond: written agreement.
268. weak bond: i.e., Hermia.   274. erewhile: a short while ago.
282. canker blossom: worm in the bud.   288. puppet: doll.
296. maypole: because compared to Hermia she is tall and thin.
300. curst: bad-tempered.   302. right maid: truly feminine.

That I can match her.

HER.   Lower! Hark again.   305

HEL. Good Hermia, do not be so bitter with me.
I evermore did love you, Hermia,
Did ever keep your counsels, never wronged you,
Save that, in love unto Demetrius,
I told him of your stealth unto this wood.   310
He followed you, for love I followed him;
But he hath chid° me hence, and threatened me
To strike me, spurn me, nay, to kill me too.
And now, so you will let me quiet go,
To Athens will I bear my folly back,   315
And follow you no further. Let me go.
You see how simple and how fond I am.

HER. Why, get you gone. Who is't that hinders
you?

HEL. A foolish heart, that I leave here behind.

HER. What, with Lysander?

HEL.   With Demetrius.

LYS. Be not afraid. She shall not harm thee, Helena.   321

DEM. No, sir, she shall not, though you take her
part.

HEL. Oh, when she's angry, she is keen and
shrewd!°
She was a vixen when she went to school,
And though she be but little, she is fierce.   325

HER. Little again! Nothing but low and little!
Why will you suffer her to flout me thus?
Let me come to her.

LYS.   Get you gone, you dwarf,
You minimus,° of hindering knotgrass° made,
You bead, you acorn.

DEM.   You are too officious   330
In her behalf that scorns your services.
Let her alone. Speak not of Helena,
Take not her part; for if thou dost intend
Never so little show of love to her,
Thou shalt aby it.

LYS.   Now she holds me not.   335
Now follow, if thou darest, to try whose right,
Of thine or mine, is most in Helena.

DEM. Follow! Nay, I'll go with thee, cheek by
jole.° [*Exeunt* LYSANDER *and* DEMETRIUS.]

HER. You, mistress, all this coil° is 'long of you.
Nay, go not back.

HEL.   I will not trust you, I,   340
Nor longer stay in your curst company.
Your hands than mine are quicker for a fray,
My legs are longer though, to run away. [*Exit.*]

HER. I am amazed, and know not what to say.
[*Exit.*]

OBE. This is thy negligence. Still thou mistakest,

Or else committ'st thy knaveries willfully.   346

PUCK. Believe me, King of Shadows, I mistook.
Did not you tell me I should know the man
By the Athenian garments he had on?
And so far blameless proves my enterprise   350
That I have 'nointed an Athenian's eyes.
And so far am I glad it so did sort,
As this their jangling° I esteem a sport.

OBE. Thou see'st these lovers seek a place to fight.
Hie° therefore, Robin, overcast the night.   355
The starry welkin° cover thou anon°
With drooping fog, as black as Acheron,°
And lead these testy rivals so astray
As one come not within another's way.
Like to Lysander sometime frame thy tongue,   360
Then stir Demetrius up with bitter wrong.
And sometime rail thou like Demetrius,
And from each other look thou lead them thus
Till o'er their brows death-counterfeiting sleep
With leaden° legs and batty wings doth creep.   365
Then crush this herb into Lysander's eye,
Whose liquor hath this virtuous property,
To take from thence all error with his might,
And make his eyeballs roll with wonted sight.
When they next wake, all this derision°   370
Shall seem a dream and fruitless vision,
And back to Athens shall the lovers wend,
With league whose date till death shall never end.°
Whiles I in this affair do thee employ,
I'll to my Queen and beg her Indian boy.   375
And then I will her charmèd eye release
From monster's view, and all things shall be peace.

PUCK. My fairy lord, this must be done with haste,
For night's swift dragons° cut the clouds full fast,
And yonder shines Aurora's° harbinger,°   380
At whose approach, ghosts, wandering here and
there,
Troop home to churchyards. Damnèd spirits all,
That in crossways° and floods have burial,
Already to their wormy beds are gone.
For fear lest day should look their shames upon,
They willfully themselves exíle from light,   386
And must for aye° consort with black-browed
night.

OBE. But we are spirits of another sort.°
I with the morning's love have oft made sport,
And, like a forester, the groves may tread   390
Even till the eastern gate, all fiery-red,
Opening on Neptune with fair blessèd beams,
Turns into yellow gold his salt green streams.

---

312. chid: scolded.   323. shrewd: a shrew.   329. minimus:
littlest thing. hindering knotgrass: believed to stunt growth; it
is a clinging weed.   338. cheek by jole: lit., cheek by jaw.
339. coil: tumult.

353. jangling: wrangling.   355. Hie: hasten.   356. welkin:
sky. anon: at once.   357. Acheron: river of the underworld.
365. leaden: heavy.   370. derision: mockery.   373. With . . .
end: united everlastingly.   379. night's . . . dragons: the dragons which draw the chariot of Night.   380. Aurora: the dawn.
harbinger: forerunner. See *Macb*, I.iv.44, and *Haml*, I.i.149–56.
383. crossways: suicides were buried at crossroads.   387. aye:
ever.   388. another sort: i.e., not damned or infernal, and so
able to endure daylight.

But, notwithstanding, haste. Make no delay.   394
We may effect this business yet ere day.   [*Exit.*]
  PUCK. Up and down, up and down,
I will lead them up and down.
I am feared in field and town.
Goblin, lead them up and down.
Here comes one.   400
          [*Re-enter* LYSANDER.]
    LYS. Where art thou, proud Demetrius? Speak
      thou now.
    PUCK. Here, villain, drawn° and ready. Where art
      thou?
    LYS. I will be with thee straight.
    PUCK.   Follow me, then,
To plainer° ground.
          [*Exit* LYSANDER, *as following the voice.*]
              [*Re-enter* DEMETRIUS.]
    DEM.   Lysander! Speak again.
Thou runaway, thou coward, art thou fled?   405
Speak! In some bush? Where dost thou hide thy
      head?
    PUCK. Thou coward, art thou bragging to the
      stars,
Telling the bushes that thou look'st for wars,
And wilt not come? Come, recreant.° Come, thou
      child,
I'll whip thee with a rod. He is defiled   410
That draws a sword on thee.
    DEM.   Yea, art thou there?
    PUCK. Follow my voice. We'll try no manhood
      here.°   [*Exeunt.*]
          [*Re-enter* LYSANDER.]
    LYS. He goes before me and still dares me on.
When I come where he calls, then he is gone.
The villain is much lighter-heeled than I,   415
I followed fast, but faster he did fly,
That fallen am I in dark uneven way,
And here will rest me. [*Lies down.*] Come, thou
      gentle day!
For if but once thou show me thy gray light,   419
I'll find Demetrius, and revenge this spite. [*Sleeps.*]
          [*Re-enter* PUCK *and* DEMETRIUS.]
    PUCK. Ho, ho, ho! Coward, why comest thou
      not?
    DEM. Abide° me, if thou darest, for well I wot°
Thou runn'st before me, shifting every place,
And darest not stand, nor look me in the face.
Where art thou now?
    PUCK.   Come hither. I am here.   425
    DEM. Nay, then, thou mock'st me. Thou shalt buy
      this dear
If ever I thy face by daylight see.
Now, go thy way. Faintness constraineth me
To measure out my length on this cold bed.

By day's approach look to be visited.   430
              [*Lies down and sleeps.*]
          [*Re-enter* HELENA.]
    HEL. O weary night, O long and tedious night,
      Abate° thy hours! Shine comforts from the east,
That I may back to Athens by daylight,
      From these that my poor company detest.
And sleep, that sometimes shuts up sorrow's eye,
Steal me awhile from mine own company.   436
              [*Lies down and sleeps.*]
    PUCK. Yet but three? Come one more,
Two of both kinds makes up four.
Here she comes, curst and sad.
Cupid is a knavish lad,   440
Thus to make poor females mad.
          [*Re-enter* HERMIA.]
    HER. Never so weary, never so in woe,
      Bedabbled with the dew, and torn with briers,
I can no further crawl, no further go,
      My legs can keep no pace with my desires.   445
Here will I rest me till the break of day.
Heavens shield Lysander, if they mean a fray!
              [*Lies down and sleeps.*]
    PUCK. On the ground
        Sleep sound.
      I'll apply   450
        To your eye,
    Gentle lover, remedy.
        [*Squeezing the juice on* LYSANDER'*s eye.*]
      When thou wakest,
      Thou takest
      True delight   455
      In the sight
    Of thy former lady's eye.
    And the country proverb known,
    That every man should take his own,
    In your waking shall be shown.   460
        Jack shall have Jill,
        Nought shall go ill,
The man shall have his mare again, and all shall be
      well.   [*Exit.*]

Act IV

SCENE I. *The same.* LYSANDER, DEMETRIUS,
    HELENA, *and* HERMIA, *lying asleep.*

[*Enter* TITANIA *and* BOTTOM; PEASEBLOSSOM, COBWEB,
MOTH, MUSTARDSEED, *and other* FAIRIES *attending;*
          OBERON *behind unseen.*]
    TITA. Come, sit thee down upon this flowery bed,
      While I thy amiable cheeks do coy,°

---

402. drawn: with a sword drawn.   404. plainer: flatter.
409. recreant: traitor.   412. We'll . . . here: we will not make
trial of your courage here.   422. Abide: wait for. wot: know.

432. Abate: shorten.
Act IV, Sc. i: 2. coy: caress.

And stick musk roses in thy sleek smooth head,
And kiss thy fair large ears, my gentle joy.
BOT. Where's Peaseblossom?   5
PEAS. Ready.
BOT. Scratch my head, Peaseblossom. Where's
Mounsieur Cobweb?
COB. Ready.
BOT. Mounsieur Cobweb, good mounsieur, get
you your weapons in your hand, and kill me a   11
red-hipped humblebee on the top of a thistle, and,
good mounsieur, bring me the honey bag. Do not
fret yourself too much in the action, mounsieur, and,
good mounsieur, have a care the honey bag break
not. I would be loath to have you overflown with   16
a honey bag, signior. Where's Mounsieur Mustardseed?
MUS. Ready.   19
BOT. Give me your neaf,° Mounsieur Mustardseed. Pray you, leave your courtesy,° good mounsieur.
MUS. What's your will?
BOT. Nothing, good mounsieur, but to help Caval-
ery° Cobweb to scratch. I must to the barber's,   25
mounsieur, for methinks I am marvelous hairy
about the face, and I am such a tender ass, if my hair
do but tickle me, I must scratch.
TITA. What, wilt thou hear some music, my sweet
love?
BOT. I have a reasonable good ear in music.   30
Let's have the tongs and the bones.
TITA. Or say, sweet love, what thou desirest to eat.
BOT. Truly, a peck of provender. I could munch
your good dry oats. Methinks I have a great desire to
a bottle° of hay. Good hay, sweet hay, hath no   35
fellow.°
TITA. I have a venturous fairy that shall seek
The squirrel's hoard, and fetch thee new nuts.
BOT. I had rather have a handful or two of dried
peas. But I pray you let none of your people stir   40
me. I have an exposition° of sleep come upon me.
TITA. Sleep thou, and I will wind thee in my arms.
Fairies, be gone, and be all ways away.
        [*Exeunt* FAIRIES.]
So doth the woodbine the sweet honeysuckle   45
Gently entwist, the female ivy so
Enrings the barky fingers of the elm.
Oh, how I love thee! How I dote on thee!
        [*They sleep.*]
        [*Enter* PUCK.]
OBE. [*Advancing*] Welcome, good Robin. See'st
thou this sweet sight?
Her dotage now I do begin to pity.   50
For, meeting her of late behind the wood,
Seeking sweet favors for this hateful fool,

I did upbraid her, and fall out with her;
For she his hairy temples then had rounded
With coronet of fresh and fragrant flowers,   55
And that same dew, which sometime on the buds
Was wont to swell, like round and orient pearls,
Stood now within the pretty flowerets' eyes
Like tears that did their own disgrace bewail.
When I had at my pleasure taunted her,   60
And she in mild terms begged my patience,
I then did ask of her her changeling child,
Which straight she gave me, and her fairy sent
To bear him to my bower in fairyland.
And now I have the boy, I will undo   65
This hateful imperfection of her eyes.
And, gentle Puck, take this transformèd scalp
From off the head of this Athenian swain,
That, he awaking when the other do,
May all to Athens back again repair,°   70
And think no more of this night's accidents
But as the fierce vexation of a dream.
But first I will release the Fairy Queen.
        Be as thou wast wont to be,
        See as thou wast wont to see.   75
        Dian's° bud o'er Cupid's flower
        Hath such force and blessèd power.
Now, my Titania, wake you, my sweet Queen.
TITA. My Oberon! What visions have I seen!
Methought I was enamored of an ass.   80
OBE. There lies your love.
TITA.   How came these things to pass?
Oh, how mine eyes do loathe his visage now!
OBE. Silence awhile. Robin, take off this head.
Titania, music call, and strike more dead
Than common sleep of all these five the sense.°   85
TITA. Music, ho! Music, such as charmeth sleep!
        [*Music, still.*]
PUCK. Now, when thou wakest, with thine own
        fool's eyes peep.
OBE. Sound, music! Come, my Queen, take hands
        with me,
And rock the ground whereon these sleepers be.   90
Now thou and I are new in amity,
And will tomorrow midnight solemnly
Dance in Duke Theseus' house triumphantly,
And bless it to all fair prosperity.
There shall the pairs of faithful lovers be   95
Wedded, with Theseus, all in jollity.
PUCK. Fairy King, attend, and mark.
I do hear the morning lark.
OBE. Then, my Queen, in silence sad,°
Trip we after night's shade.   100
We the globe can compass soon,
Swifter than the wandering moon.
TITA. Come, my lord, and in our flight,

20. neaf: fist.   21. leave . . . courtesy: i.e., there's no need to
bow.   23–24. Cavalery: cavaleiro, a gallant soldier.   35. bottle:
bundle.   36. fellow: equal.   41. exposition: for "disposition."

70. repair: return.   76. Dian: Diana. See I.i.73.   84–85. strike
. . . sense: make them more dead asleep than normal. these
five: i.e., Bottom, Demetrius, Lysander, Hermia, and Helena.
99. sad: serious.

Tell me how it came this night
That I sleeping here was found　　　105
With these mortals on the ground.　　　[*Exeunt.*]
[*Horns winded° within. Enter* THESEUS,
HIPPOLYTA, EGEUS, *and train.*]
THE. Go, one of you, find out the forester,
For now our observation° is performed.
And since we have the vaward° of the day,
My love shall hear the music of my hounds.°　　　110
Uncouple in the western valley, let them go.
Dispatch, I say, and find the forester.
　　　　　　　　[*Exit an* ATTENDANT.]
We will, fair Queen, up to the mountain's top,
And mark the musical confusion
Of hounds and echo in conjunction.　　　115
HIP. I was with Hercules and Cadmus once
When in a wood of Crete they bayed° the bear
With hounds of Sparta. Never did I hear
Such gallant chiding;° for, besides the groves,
The skies, the fountains, every region near　　　120
Seemed all one mutual cry. I never heard
So musical a discord, such sweet thunder.
THE. My hounds are bred out of the Spartan
　　　kind,
So flewed,° so sanded;° and their heads are hung
With ears that sweep away the morning dew;　　　125
Crook-kneed, and dewlapped° like Thessalian
　　　bulls;
Slow in pursuit, but matched in mouth like bells,°
Each under each.° A cry° more tunable
Was never holloed to, nor cheered with horn,
In Crete, in Sparta, nor in Thessaly.　　　130
Judge when you hear. But, soft! What nymphs are
　　　these?
EGE. My lord, this is my daughter here asleep.
And this, Lysander. This Demetrius is,
This Helena, old Nedar's Helena.
I wonder of their being here together.　　　135
THE. No doubt they rose up early to observe
The rite of May, and, hearing our intent,
Came here in grace of° our solemnity.°
But speak, Egeus, is not this the day　　　139
That Hermia should give answer of her choice?
EGE. It is, my lord.
THE. Go, bid the huntsmen wake them with their
　　　horns.
[*Horns and shout within.° * LYSANDER, DEMETRIUS,
HELENA, *and* HERMIA, *wake and start up.*]

Good morrow, friends. Saint Valentine° is past.
Begin these wood birds but to couple now?
LYS. Pardon, my lord.
THE.　　　　　　　I pray you all, stand up.
I know you two are rival enemies.　　　146
How comes this gentle concord in the world,
That hatred is so far from jealousy,
To sleep by hate, and fear no enmity?
LYS. My lord, I shall reply amazedly,　　　150
Half sleep, half waking. But as yet, I swear,
I cannot truly say how I came here,
But, as I think — for truly would I speak,
And now I do bethink me, so it is —
I came with Hermia hither. Our intent　　　155
Was to be gone from Athens, where we might,
Without the peril° of the Athenian law —
EGE. Enough, enough, my lord, you have enough.
I beg the law, the law, upon his head.
They would have stolen away. They would, Deme-
　　　trius,　　　160
Thereby to have defeated you and me,
You of your wife and me of my consent —
Of my consent that she should be your wife.
DEM. My lord, fair Helen told me of their stealth,
Of this their purpose hither to this wood.　　　165
And I in fury hither followed them,
Fair Helena in fancy° following me.
But, my good lord, I wot not by what power —
But by some power it is — my love to Hermia,
Melted as the snow, seems to me now　　　170
As the remembrance of an idle gaud°
Which in my childhood I did dote upon.
And all the faith, the virtue of my heart,
The object and the pleasure of mine eye,
Is only Helena. To her, my lord,　　　175
Was I betrothed ere I saw Hermia.
But, like in sickness, did I loathe this food,
But, as in health, come to my natural taste,
Now I do wish it, love it, long for it,
And will forevermore be true to it.　　　180
THE. Fair lovers, you are fortunately met.
Of this discourse we more will hear anon.
Egeus, I will overbear your will,
For in the temple, by and by, with us
These couples shall eternally be knit.　　　185
And, for° the morning now is something worn,
Our purposed hunting shall be set aside.
Away with us to Athens! Three and three,°
We'll hold a feast in great solemnity.
Come, Hippolyta.　　　190
　　　[*Exeunt* THESEUS, HIPPOLYTA, EGEUS, *and train.*]
DEM. These things seem small and undistinguish-
　　　able,

Like far-off mountains turnèd into clouds.

HER. Methinks I see these things with parted eye,
When everything seems double.

HEL.   So methinks.
And I have found Demetrius like a jewel,   195
Mine own, and not mine own.

DEM.   Are you sure
That we are awake? It seems to me
That yet we sleep, we dream. Do not you think
The Duke was here, and bid us follow him?

HER. Yea, and my father.

HEL.   And Hippolyta.   200

LYS. And he did bid us follow to the temple.

DEM. Why, then, we are awake. Let's follow him,
And by the way let us recount our dreams.
                                   [*Exeunt.*]

BOT. [*Awaking*] When my cue comes, call me,
and I will answer. My next is "Most fair Pyra-   205
mus." Heigh-ho! Peter Quince! Flute, the bellows-
mender! Snout, the tinker! Starveling! God's my life,
stolen hence, and left me asleep! I have had a most
rare vision. I have had a dream past the wit of man to
say what dream it was. Man is but an ass if he   211
go about to expound this dream. Methought I was —
there is no man can tell what. Methought I was —
and methought I had — but man is but a patched°
fool if he will offer to say what methought I   215
had. The eye of man hath not heard, the ear of man
hath not seen, man's hand is not able to taste, his
tongue to conceive, nor his heart to report, what my
dream was. I will get Peter Quince to write a ballad°
of this dream. It shall be called Bottom's Dream,   220
because it hath no bottom, and I will sing it in the
latter end of a play, before the Duke. Peradventure,°
to make it the more gracious, I shall sing it at her
death.°   [*Exit.*]

SCENE II. *Athens.* QUINCE's *house.*

[*Enter* QUINCE, FLUTE, SNOUT, *and* STARVELING.]

QUIN. Have you sent to Bottom's house? Is he
come home yet?

STAR. He cannot be heard of. Out of doubt he is
transported.°

FLU. If he come not, then the play is marred. It
goes not forward, doth it?   6

QUIN. It is not possible. You have not a man in all
Athens able to discharge Pyramus but he.

FLU. No, he hath simply the best wit of any handi-
craft man in Athens.   10

QUIN. Yea, and the best person too, and he is a very
paramour for a sweet voice.

FLU. You must say "paragon." A paramour is,
God bless us, a thing of naught.°

[*Enter* SNUG.]

SNUG. Masters, the Duke is coming from the   15
temple, and there is two or three lords and ladies
more married. If our sport had gone forward, we
had all been made men.

FLU. Oh, sweet bully Bottom! Thus hath he lost
sixpence a day during his life;° he could not   20
have scaped sixpence a day. An the Duke had not
given him sixpence a day for playing Pyramus, I'll
be hanged. He would have deserved it. Sixpence a
day in Pyramus, or nothing.

[*Enter* BOTTOM.]

BOT. Where are these lads? Where are these
hearts?   26

QUIN. Bottom! Oh, most courageous day! Oh,
most happy hour!

BOT. Masters, I am to discourse wonders. But ask
me not what, for if I tell you I am no true Athe-   30
nian. I will tell you everything, right as it fell out.

QUIN. Let us hear, sweet Bottom.

BOT. Not a word of me. All that I will tell you is
that the Duke hath dined. Get your apparel to-   35
gether, good strings° to your beards, new ribbons to
your pumps.° Meet presently° at the palace. Every
man look o'er his part, for the short and the long is,
our play is preferred.° In any case, let Thisby have
clean linen, and let not him that plays the lion   40
pare his nails, for they shall hang out for the lion's
claws. And, most dear actors, eat no onions nor garlic, for we are to utter sweet breath, and I do not
doubt but to hear them say it is a sweet comedy.   45
No more words. Away! Go, away!   [*Exeunt.*]

Act V

SCENE I. *Athens. The palace of* THESEUS.

[*Enter* THESEUS, HIPPOLYTA, PHILOSTRATE, LORDS,
               and ATTENDANTS.]

HIP. 'Tis strange, my Theseus, that these lovers
   speak of.

THE. More strange than true. I never may believe
These antique fables, nor these fairy toys.°
Lovers and madmen have such seething brains,
Such shaping fantasies,° that apprehend   5
More than cool reason ever comprehends.
The lunatic, the lover, and the poet

---

214. patched: wearing a particolored coat, the regular costume
of a professional fool.   219. ballad: See App. 8.   222. Peradventure: perchance.   224–25. at . . . death: i.e., Thisby's at the
end of the play.

Sc. ii: 4. transported: carried off.

14. naught: wickedness.   20. sixpence . . . life: i.e., a royal
pension of sixpence a day for life.   36. strings: i.e., for tying
them on.   37. pumps: shoes. presently: immediately.   39. preferred: accepted.

Act V, Sc. i: 3. fairy toys: trifling tales about fairies.   5. fantasies: fancies.

Are of imagination all compact.°
One sees more devils than vast Hell can hold,
That is the madman. The lover, all as frantic,   10
Sees Helen's beauty in a brow of Egypt.°
The poet's eye, in a fine frenzy rolling,
Doth glance from heaven to earth, from earth to
    heaven,
And as imagination bodies forth
The forms of things unknown, the poet's pen   15
Turns them to shapes, and gives to airy nothing
A local habitation and a name.
Such tricks hath strong imagination
That if it would but apprehend some joy,
It comprehends some bringer of that joy;   20
Or in the night, imagining some fear,
How easy is a bush supposed a bear!
    HIP. But all the story of the night told over,
And all their minds transfigured° so together,
More witnesseth than fancy's images,   25
And grows to something of great constancy,°
But, howsoever, strange and admirable.°
    THE. Here come the lovers, full of joy and mirth.
[Enter LYSANDER, DEMETRIUS, HERMIA, and HELENA.]
Joy, gentle friends! Joy and fresh days of love
Accompany your hearts!
    LYS.   More than to us   30
Wait in your royal walks, your board, your bed!
    THE. Come now, what masques,° what dances
    shall we have
To wear away this long age of three hours
Between our after-supper and bedtime?
Where is our usual manager of mirth?   35
What revels are in hand? Is there no play
To ease the anguish of a torturing hour?
Call Philostrate.
    PHILOST.   Here, mighty Theseus.
    THE. Say, what abridgment° have you for this eve-
    ning?
What masque? What music? How shall we beguile
The lazy time, if not with some delight?   41
    PHILOST. There is a brief° how many sports are
    ripe.°
Make choice of which your Highness will see first.
                        [Giving a paper.]
    THE. [Reads.]
    "The battle with the Centaurs,° to be sung
        By an Athenian eunuch to the harp."   45
We'll none of that. That have I told my love,
In glory of my kinsman Hercules.

"The riot of the tipsy Bacchanals,
    Tearing the Thracian singer in their rage."°
That is an old device, and it was played   50
When I from Thebes came last a conqueror.
    "The thrice three Muses mourning for the death
        Of Learning,° late deceased in beggary."
That is some satire, keen and critical,
Not sorting with a nuptial ceremony.   55
    "A tedious brief scene of young Pyramus
        And his love Thisbe, very tragical mirth."
Merry and tragical! Tedious and brief!
That is, hot ice and wondrous strange snow.
How shall we find the concord of this discord?   60
    PHILOST. A play there is, my lord, some ten words
    long,
Which is as brief as I have known a play.
But by ten words, my lord, it is too long,
Which makes it tedious; for in all the play
There is not one word apt, one player fitted.   65
And tragical, my noble lord, it is,
For Pyramus therein doth kill himself.
Which, when I saw rehearsed, I must confess
Made mine eyes water, but more merry tears
The passion of loud laughter never shed.   70
    THE. What are they that do play it?
    PHILOST. Hardhanded men that work in Athens
    here,
Which never labored in their minds till now,
And now have toiled their unbreathed° memories
With this same play, against° your nuptial.   75
    THE. And we will hear it.
    PHILOST.   No, my noble lord,
It is not for you. I have heard it over,
And it is nothing, nothing in the world —
Unless you can find sport in their intents,°   79
Extremely stretched° and conned with cruel pain,°
To do you service.
    THE.   I will hear that play,
For never anything can be amiss,
When simpleness and duty tender it.
Go, bring them in, and take your places, ladies.
                        [Exit PHILOSTRATE.]
    HIP. I love not to see wretchedness o'ercharged,°
And duty in his service perishing.°   86
    THE. Why, gentle sweet, you shall see no such
    thing.
    HIP. He says they can do nothing in this kind.°
    THE. The kinder we, to give them thanks for
    nothing.
Our sport shall be to take what they mistake.   90

---

8. Are . . . compact: wholly composed of imagination — which in Shakespeare's time meant the "power of seeing things." 11. Sees . . . Egypt: i.e., to the lover a gypsy is as beautiful as Helen of Troy. Gypsies were supposed to be Egyptians. 24. transfigured: excited.   26. constancy: consistency; i.e., the fact that they are all excited shows that something strange has happened to them.   27. admirable: marvelous.   32. masques: courtly entertainments.   39. abridgment: pastime, entertainment.   42. brief: list. ripe: ready.   44. Centaurs: creatures half man, half horse.

48–49. riot . . . rage: the story of how Orpheus the singer was torn in pieces by the frenzied women worshippers of Bacchus. 52–53. death . . . Learning: See MND Intro. p. 511b.   74. unbreathed: unpracticed.   75. against: in anticipation of.   79. intents: intentions.   80. Extremely stretched: overreaching themselves. pain: labor.   85. wretchedness o'ercharged: poor men trying to do too much.   86. duty . . . perishing: a subject ruining himself through excess of zeal.   88. kind: i.e., acting.

And what poor duty cannot do, noble respect
Takes it in might, not merit.°
Where I have come, great clerks° have purposed
To greet me with premeditated welcomes,
Where I have seen them shiver and look pale,   95
Make periods in the midst of sentences,
Throttle their practiced accent in their fears,
And, in conclusion, dumbly have broke off,
Not paying me a welcome. Trust me, sweet,
Out of this silence yet I picked a welcome,   100
And in the modesty of fearful° duty
I read as much as from the rattling tongue
Of saucy and audacious eloquence.
Love, therefore, and tongue-tied simplicity
In least speak most, to my capacity.°   105

[*Re-enter* PHILOSTRATE.]

PHILOST. So please your Grace, the Prologue is addressed.°

THE. Let him approach.

[*Flourish of trumpets. Enter* QUINCE *for the*
PROLOGUE.]

PROL. If° we offend, it is with our goodwill.
That you should think, we come not to offend,
But with goodwill. To show our simple skill,   110
That is the true beginning of our end.
Consider, then, we come but in despite.°
We do not come, as minding to content you,
Our true intent is. All for your delight,
We are not here. That you should here repent you,
The actors are at hand, and, by their show,   116
You shall know all, that you are like to know.

THE. This fellow doth not stand upon points.°

LYS. He hath rid his prologue like a rough colt, he
knows not the stop. A good moral, my lord. It is not
enough to speak, but to speak true.   121

HIP. Indeed he hath played on his prologue like a
child on a recorder° — a sound, but not in government.°

THE. His speech was like a tangled chain —   125
nothing impaired, but all disordered. Who is next?

[*Enter* PYRAMUS *and* THISBE, WALL, MOONSHINE, *and*
LION.]

PROL. Gentles, perchance you wonder at this show,
But wonder on, till truth make all things plain.
This man is Pyramus, if you would know.   130
This beauteous lady Thisby is certain.
This man, with lime and roughcast, doth present
Wall, that vile Wall which did these lovers sunder,
And through Wall's chink, poor souls, they are content   134

To whisper. At the which let no man wonder.
This man, with lanthorn,° dog, and bush of thorn,
Presenteth Moonshine; for, if you will know,
By moonshine did these lovers think no scorn
To meet at Ninus' tomb, there, there to woo.
This grisly beast, which Lion hight° by name,   140
The trusty Thisby, coming first by night,
Did scare away, or rather did affright.
And, as she fled, her mantle she did fall,°
Which Lion vile with bloody mouth did stain.
Anon comes Pyramus, sweet youth and tall,   145
And finds his trusty Thisby's mantle slain.
Whereat, with blade, with bloody blameful blade,
He bravely broached his boiling bloody breast.
And Thisby, tarrying in mulberry shade,
His dagger drew, and died. For all the rest,   150
Let Lion, Moonshine, Wall, and lovers twain
At large discourse, while here they do remain.

[*Exeunt* PROLOGUE, PYRAMUS, THISBE, LION,
and MOONSHINE.]

THE. I wonder if the lion be to speak.

DEM. No wonder, my lord. One lion may when
many asses do.   155

WALL. In this same interlude it doth befall
That I, one Snout by name, present a wall,
And such a wall, as I would have you think,
That had in it a crannied° hole or chink,
Through which the lovers, Pyramus and Thisby,
Did whisper often very secretly.   161
This loam, this roughcast, and this stone doth show
That I am that same wall. The truth is so.
And this the cranny is, right and sinister,°   164
Through which the fearful lovers are to whisper.

THE. Would you desire lime and hair to speak
better?

DEM. It is the wittiest partition that ever I heard
discourse, my lord.

THE. Pyramus draws near the wall. Silence!   170

[*Re-enter* PYRAMUS.]

PYR. O grim-looked night! O night with hue so
black!
O night, which ever art when day is not!
O night, O night! alack, alack, alack,
I fear my Thisby's promise is forgot!
And thou, O wall, O sweet, O lovely wall,   175
That stand'st between her father's ground and
mine!
Thou wall, O wall, O sweet and lovely wall,
Show me thy chink, to blink through with mine
eyne!   [WALL *holds up his fingers.*]
Thanks, courteous wall. Jove shield thee well for
this!
But what see I? No Thisby do I see.   180
O wicked wall, through whom I see no bliss!
Cursed be thy stones for thus deceiving me!

91–92. noble . . . merit: i.e., a noble mind accepts the good intention for the bad performance.   93. great clerks: learned scholars.   101. fearful: full of fear.   105. capacity: understanding.   106. addressed: ready.   108–17. If . . . know: Quince, by mistaking his punctuation, makes woeful sense of his words.   112. despite: ill will.   118. stand . . . points: observe his punctuation marks.   123. recorder: See Pl. 19b.   123–24. government: control.

136. lanthorn: lantern with horn sides.   140. hight: called.   143. fall: let fall.   159. crannied: cracked.   164. sinister: left-handed.

THE. The wall, methinks, being sensible,° should curse again.   184

PYR. No, in truth, sir, he should not. " Deceiving me " is Thisby's cue. She is to enter now, and I am to spy her through the wall. You shall see, it will fall pat as I told you. Yonder she comes.

[*Re-enter* THISBE.]

THIS. O wall, full often hast thou heard my moans,
For parting my fair Pyramus and me!   191
My cherry lips have often kissed thy stones,
    Thy stones with lime and hair knit up in thee.

PYR. I see a voice. Now will I to the chink,
To spy an I can hear my Thisby's face.   195
Thisby!

THIS. My love thou art, my love I think.

PYR. Think what thou wilt, I am thy lover's grace;
And, like Limander,° am I trusty still.   199

THIS. And I like Helen,° till the Fates me kill.

PYR. Not Shafalus to Procrus° was so true.

THIS. As Shafalus to Procrus, I to you.

PYR. Oh, kiss me through the hole of this vile wall!

THIS. I kiss the wall's hole, not your lips at all.

PYR. Wilt thou at Ninny's tomb meet me straight-way?   205

THIS. 'Tide life, 'tide death, I come without delay.
[*Exeunt* PYRAMUS *and* THISBE.]

WALL. Thus have I, wall, my part dischargèd so;
And, being done, thus wall away doth go. [*Exit.*]

THE. Now is the mural° down between the two neighbors.

DEM. No remedy, my lord, when walls are so will-ful to hear without warning.   212

HIP. This is the silliest stuff that ever I heard.

THE. The best in this kind are but shadows,° and the worst are no worse if imagination amend them.

HIP. It must be your imagination, then, and   216
not theirs.

THE. If we imagine no worse of them than they of themselves, they may pass for excellent men. Here come two noble beasts in, a man and a lion.   221

[*Re-enter* LION *and* MOONSHINE.]

LION. You, ladies, you, whose gentle hearts do fear
The smallest monstrous mouse that creeps on floor,
May now perchance both quake and tremble here,
    When lion rough in wildest rage doth roar. 225
Then know that I, one Snug the joiner, am
A lion fell,° nor else no lion's dam;
For, if I should as lion come in strife
Into this place, 'twere pity on my life.°

THE. A very gentle beast, and of a good con-science.   231

DEM. The very best at a beast, my lord, that e'er I saw.

LYS. This lion is a very fox for his valor.

THE. True, and a goose for his discretion.   235

DEM. Not so, my lord, for his valor cannot carry his discretion, and the fox carries the goose.

THE. His discretion, I am sure, cannot carry his valor, for the goose carries not the fox. It is   240
well. Leave it to his discretion, and let us listen to the moon.

MOON. This lanthorn doth the hornèd moon pre-sent ——

DEM. He should have worn the horns on his head.

THE. He is no crescent, and his horns are invisible within the circumference.   247

MOON. This lanthorn doth the hornèd moon pre-sent,
Myself the man i' the moon do seem to be.

THE. This is the greatest error of all the rest.   250
The man should be put into the lantern. How is it else the man i' the moon?

DEM. He dares not come there for the candle, for you see it is already in snuff.°   254

HIP. I am aweary of this moon. Would he would change!

THE. It appears, by his small light of discretion, that he is in the wane. But yet, in courtesy, in all rea-son, we must stay the time.°

LYS. Proceed, Moon.   260

MOON. All that I have to say is, to tell you that the lanthorn is the moon; I, the man i' the moon; this thornbush, my thornbush; and this dog, my dog.

DEM. Why, all these should be in the lantern,   265
for all these are in the moon. But, silence! Here comes Thisbe.

[*Re-enter* THISBE.]

THIS. This is old Ninny's tomb. Where is my love?

LION. [*Roaring*] Oh ——   [THISBE *runs off.*]

DEM. Well roared, Lion.   270

THE. Well run, Thisbe.

HIP. Well shone, Moon. Truly, the moon shines with a good grace.

[*The* LION *shakes* THISBE's *mantle, and exit.*]

THE. Well moused,° Lion.

LYS. And so the lion vanished.   275

DEM. And then came Pyramus.

[*Re-enter* PYRAMUS.]

PYR. Sweet Moon, I thank thee for thy sunny beams,
I thank thee, Moon, for shining now so bright.
For, by thy gracious, golden, glittering gleams,
    I trust to take of truest Thisby sight.   280
        But stay, oh, spite!
        But mark, poor knight,

---

183. being sensible: having feeling. 199. Limander: for "Leander." 200. Helen: for "Hero," Leander's love. 201. Shafalus to Procrus: Cephalus to Procris. 209. mural: wall. 214. shadows: things of no substance. 227. fell: fierce. 229. pity . . . life: i.e., I should be hanged for it

254. in snuff: smoking. Before self-consuming wicks were in-vented for candles, wicks had to be snuffed (cut) constantly or they would smoke foully. 259. stay . . . time: see it out. 273. moused: torn as a cat tears a mouse.

What dreadful dole° is here!
 Eyes, do you see?
 How can it be?   285
Oh, dainty duck! Oh, dear!
 Thy mantle good,
 What, stained with blood!
Approach, ye Furies fell!
 O Fates, come, come,   290
 Cut thread and thrum,°
Quail,° crush, conclude, and quell!°

THE. This passion, and the death of a dear friend,
would go near to make a man look sad.

HIP. Beshrew my heart, but I pity the man.   295

PYR. O wherefore, Nature, didst thou lions frame?
Since lion vile hath here deflowered my dear,
Which is — no, no — which was the fairest dame
That lived, that loved, that liked, that looked with
 cheer.
  Come, tears, confound.   300
  Out, sword, and wound
The pap of Pyramus.
 Aye, that left pap,
 Where heart doth hop.   [*Stabs himself.*]
Thus die I, thus, thus, thus.   305
 Now am I dead,
 Now am I fled,
My soul is in the sky.
 Tongue, lose thy light,   309
 Moon, take thy flight,   [*Exit* MOONSHINE.]
Now die, die, die, die, die.   [*Dies.*]

DEM. No die, but an ace, for him,° for he is but
one.

LYS. Less than an ace, man, for he is dead, he is
nothing.   315

THE. With the help of a surgeon he might yet
recover, and prove an ass.

HIP. How chance Moonshine is gone before
Thisbe comes back and finds her lover?

THE. She will find him by starlight. Here she
comes, and her passion ends the play.   321

   [*Re-enter* THISBE.]

HIP. Methinks she should not use a long one for
such a Pyramus. I hope she will be brief.

DEM. A mote° will turn the balance, which Pyramus, which Thisbe, is the better — he for a   325
man, God warrant us, she for a woman, God bless us.

LYS. She hath spied him already with those sweet
eyes.

DEM. And thus she means, videlicet:°   330

THIS. Asleep, my love?
  What, dead, my dove?
  O Pyramus, arise!

Speak, speak. Quite dumb?
Dead, dead? A tomb   335
Must cover thy sweet eyes.
 These lily lips,
 This cherry nose,
These yellow cowslip cheeks,
 Are gone, are gone.   340
 Lovers, make moan.
His eyes were green as leeks.
 O Sisters Three,°
 Come, come to me,
With hands as pale as milk,   345
 Lay them in gore,
 Since you have shore
With shears his thread of silk.
 Tongue, not a word.
 Come, trusty sword,   350
Come, blade, my breast imbrue.°
     [*Stabs herself.*]
 And, farewell, friends.
 Thus Thisby ends.
 Adieu, adieu, adieu.   [*Dies.*]

THE. Moonshine and Lion are left to bury the
dead.   356

DEM. Aye, and Wall too.

BOT. [*Starting up*] No, I assure you the wall is
down that parted their fathers. Will it please you to
see the epilogue, or to hear a Bergomask° dance between two of our company?   361

THE. No epilogue, I pray you, for your play needs
no excuse. Never excuse, for when the players are all
dead, there need none to be blamed. Marry, if he
that writ it had played Pyramus and hanged   365
himself in Thisbe's garter, it would have been a fine
tragedy. And so it is, truly, and very notably dis-
charged. But, come, your Bergomask. Let your epi-
logue alone.   [*A dance.*]
The iron tongue of midnight hath told twelve.   370
Lovers, to bed, 'tis almost fairy time.
I fear we shall outsleep the coming morn
As much as we this night have overwatched.
This palpable-gross° play hath well beguiled
The heavy gait of night. Sweet friends, to bed. 375
A fortnight hold we this solemnity,
In nightly revels and new jollity.   [*Exeunt.*]
    [*Enter* PUCK.]

PUCK. Now the hungry lion roars,
 And the wolf behowls the moon,
Whilst the heavy plowman snores,   380
 All with weary task fordone.°
Now the wasted brands° do glow,
 Whilst the screech owl, screeching loud,

---

283. dole: dolor, grief.   291. thrum: lit., the end of the thread
in a piece of weaving. So *cut thread and thrum* means "destroy
everything."   292. Quail: overwhelm. quell: slay.   312. No . . .
him: Demetrius makes a poor pun on *die* (perish) and *die* (singular of "dice"). ace: throw of one.   324. mote: speck of dust.
330. videlicet: namely, "viz."

343. Sisters Three: the three Fates who sit spinning man's destiny.   351. imbrue: make bloody.   360. Bergomask: a rough
country-dance, named after the province of Bergamo in Italy,
whose people were noted for their rustic manners.   374. palpable-
gross: crudely gross.   381. fordone: overcome.   382. brands: firebrands.

Puts the wretch that lies in woe
  In remembrance of a shroud.   385
Now it is the time of night
  That the graves, all gaping wide,
Every one lets forth his sprite,
  In the churchway paths to glide.
And we fairies, that do run   390
  By the triple Hecate's° team,
From the presence of the sun,
  Following darkness like a dream,
Now are frolic. Not a mouse
Shall disturb this hallowed house.   395
I am sent with broom before,
To sweep the dust behind the door.

[*Enter* OBERON *and* TITANIA *with their train.*]

OBE. Through the house give glimmering light,
  By the dead and drowsy fire.
Every elf and fairy sprite   400
  Hop as light as bird from brier,
And this ditty, after me,
Sing, and dance it trippingly.

TITA. First, rehearse your song by rote,
To each word a warbling note.   405
Hand in hand, with fairy grace,
Will we sing, and bless this place.

[*Song and dance.*]

OBE. Now, until the break of day,
Through this house each fairy stray.
To the best bridebed will we,   410
Which by us shall blessèd be,
And the issue there create
Ever shall be fortunate.

So shall all the couples three
Ever true in loving be,   415
And the blots of Nature's hand
Shall not in their issue stand—
Never mole, harelip, nor scar,
Nor mark prodigious,° such as are
Despisèd in nativity,   420
Shall upon their children be.
With this field dew consecrate,
Every fairy take his gait,
And each several° chamber bless,
Through this palace, with sweet peace,   425
And the owner of it blest,
Ever shall in safety rest.
Trip away, make no stay,
Meet me all by break of day.

[*Exeunt* OBERON, TITANIA, *and train.*]

PUCK. If we shadows have offended,   430
Think but this, and all is mended,
That you have but slumbered here
While these visions did appear,
And this weak and idle theme,
No more yielding but a dream,   435
Gentles, do not reprehend.
If you pardon, we will mend.
And, as I am an honest Puck,
If we have unearnèd luck
Now to scape the serpent's tongue,°   440
We will make amends ere long,
Else the Puck a liar call.
So, good night unto you all.
Give me your hands,° if we be friends,   444
And Robin shall restore amends.   [*Exit.*]

---

391. triple Hecate: The goddess Diana is sometimes referred to as three-formed, because she was worshiped as Luna (or Cynthia), the Moon, in Heaven; Diana on earth; and Proserpine (or *Hecate*) in Hades.

419. prodigious: unnatural.   424. several: separate.   440. serpent's tongue: i.e., hissing.   444. Give . . . hands: clap.

THE LIFE AND DEATH OF KING JOHN

Introduction[1]

The Life and Death of King John was first printed in the F1 of 1623. The text is good and offers few serious difficulties. *King John* is one of the twelve plays noted by Francis Meres in the list given in *Palladis Tamia* in 1598 (see p. 12a) and was therefore written before that date. Apart from Meres' reference there is no other extant mention of the play by any of Shakespeare's contemporaries, and no fact by which the play can be certainly dated. Scholars have suggested for its writing a number of dates from 1589 to 1597. The only evidence is the style, and that, without some external corroboration, is unreliable, especially as there are notable differences of style within the play itself. Some speeches, such as the Bastard's soliloquy on his new promotion (I.i.182–216), or on the advantages of "Commodity" (II.i.561–98), are written with mature ease; but other passages, such as the citizen's proposal that Blanch shall marry Lewis (II.i.423–55) or Pandulph's opening speech (III.i.136–46) or his argument to persuade Philip to desert John (III.i.263–97) are in a more turgid, involved, and elaborate manner. If these differences are significant, they show either that Shakespeare himself revised the play or that he had a collaborator. There is a competence about the best passages that is not to be found in any other of Shakespeare's plays written earlier than *The Merchant of Venice* (circa 1596).

If the summer of 1596 was indeed the date of the composition of the play in its present form, it follows that certain passages would have had a topical significance for the original audience. From the summer of 1595 to the summer of 1596 there was a feeling of acute anxiety among Englishmen. It was known that a new and even greater Armada was being prepared in Spain, and there was a general sense of national disunity. This feeling is expressed in several other works in terms very similar to some of the sentiments uttered in the closing lines of *King John*. Thus in William Covell's *Polimanteia, or the means lawful and unlawful, to judge of the fall of a Commonwealth against the frivolous and foolish conjectures of this age* (1595), England laments that she is torn in pieces by her own inhabitants, and, Covell comments in the margin, "England cannot perish but by Englishmen." Similarly in a *Watchword for War,* entered in the Stationers' Register in January 1596, the author declares, "If we be true within ourselves, we need not care or fear the enemy."

Furthermore, relations between England and France were becoming strained as the French King, Henry IV, grew more and more dissatisfied with the help given him by the English against the Spaniards; and there were many murmurs in London that the French were about to desert their allies by making a separate peace with the enemy. The dangers became increasingly acute when the Spaniards suddenly attacked and captured Calais in April 1596. These alarming events naturally led to panic and excitement in England. In April, John Norden entered for publication *A Christian and familiar comfort and encouragement unto all English subjects,* in which he warned magistrates to beware of sudden and indiscreet hurly-burlies, for it was a policy of the enemy to cause panic by sudden reports, dangerous bruits, and open "hoobubs."

Audiences at the Theater, to whom these events were fresh and disturbing, could hardly have missed a significance in such speeches as the Bastard's words on French perfidy,

> And this same bias, this Commodity,
> This bawd, this broker, this all-changing word,
> Clapped on the outward eye of fickle France,
> Hath drawn him from his own determined aid,
> From a resolved and honorable war
> To a most base and vile-concluded peace.
> (II.i.581–86)

Or in the accounts of the rumors and murmurs in the streets:

> But as I traveled hither through the land,
> I find the people strangely fantasied,
> Possessed with rumors, full of idle dreams,
> Not knowing what they fear, but full of fear.
> (IV.ii.142–46)

[1] See also App. 28.

and

> Old men and beldams in the streets
> Do prophesy upon it dangerously.
> Young Arthur's death is common in their
> 　　mouths,
> And when they talk of him, they shake their
> 　　heads
> And whisper one another in the ear;
> And he that speaks doth gripe the hearer's wrist,
> Whilst he that hears makes fearful action
> With wrinkled brows, with nods, with rolling
> 　　eyes.
> I saw a smith stand with his hammer, thus,
> The whilst his iron did on the anvil cool,
> With open mouth swallowing a tailor's news;
> Who, with his shears and measure in his hand,
> Standing on slippers, which his nimble haste
> Had falsely thrust upon contrary feet,
> Told of a many thousand warlike French
> That were embattailèd and ranked in Kent.
> Another lean unwashed artificer
> Cuts off his tale and talks of Arthur's death.
> 　　　　　　　　　　　　(IV.ii.185–202)

And the final appeal for national unity carried a message that was intended more for Shakespeare's audience than for the subjects of King John's successor:

> This England never did, nor never shall,
> Lie at the proud foot of a conqueror
> But when it first did help to wound itself.
> Now these her princes are come home again,
> Come the three corners of the world in arms,
> And we shall shock them. Naught shall make us
> 　　rue,
> If England to itself do rest but true.
> 　　　　　　　　　　　　(V.vii.112–18)

The national danger lifted during the summer. A great expedition was collected at Plymouth and was joined by a number of young men of wealth and good family. There would seem to be a glance at this gallant assembly in the speech of Chatillon:

> And all the unsettled humors of the land,
> Rash, inconsiderate, fiery voluntaries,
> With ladies' faces and fierce dragons' spleens,
> Have sold their fortunes at their native homes,
> Bearing their birthrights proudly on their backs
> To make a hazard of new fortunes here.
> In brief, a braver choice of dauntless spirits
> Than now the English bottoms have waft o'er
> Did never float upon the swelling tide
> To do offense and scath in Christendom.
> 　　　　　　　　　　　　(II.i.66–75)

Sir Anthony Standen, who went with the expedition, wrote from Plymouth on May 30, "By Monday at night we hope to be under sail, if the wind serve, which must be a northeast or north, and a little of the west. We have 300 greenheaded youths covered with feathers, gold and silver lace, at the least ten thousand soldiers, as tall handsome men, as ever I cast eye on, who being conducted by a lion must work [a] lion's effects. Our navy in this port beautiful to behold, about 150 sail, whereof 18 of her Majesty's own, since her reign never so many before." [2]

The source of *King John* is an earlier play in two parts, both printed in 1591, and entitled: *The Troublesome Raigne of Iohn King of England, with the discouerie of King Richard Cordelions Base sonne (vulgarly named, The Bastard Fawconbridge): also the death of King Iohn at Swinstead Abbey. As it was (sundry times) publikely acted by the Queenes Maiesties Players, in the honourable Citie of London.* And *The Second part of the troublesome Raigne of King Iohn, conteining the death of Arthur Plantaginet, the landing of Lewes, and the poysning of King Iohn at Swinstead Abbey. As it was (sundry times) publikely acted by the Queenes Maiesties Players, in the honourable Citie of London.* The Queen's Company of players had flourished during the 1580's. They were founded in 1583 and dissolved in 1594. In 1611 *The Troublesome Reign* was reprinted with the addition of the words "Written by W. Sh."—a dishonest attempt to pass it off as Shakespeare's work.

In rewriting *The Troublesome Reign*, Shakespeare changed the dialogue entirely, with the exception of a few phrases and one solitary line—

> For that my grandsire was an Englishman
> 　　　　　　　　　　　　(V.v.42)

but he followed the plot very closely and for the most part repeated the episodes in the same order. Some extracts from the old play will show the differences between the two versions.

1. HUBERT AND ARTHUR (cf. IV.i)

Enter *Hubert de Burgh* with three men.

Hubert My masters, I haue shewed you what warrant I haue for this attempt; I perceive by your heauie countenances, you had rather be otherwise imployed, and for my owne part, I would the King had made choyce of some other executioner: onely this is my comfort, that a King commaunds, whose precepts neglected or omitted, threatneth torture for the default. Therefore in briefe, leaue me, and be readie to attend the aduenture: stay within that entry, and when you heare me crie, *God saue the King,* issue sodainly foorth, lay handes on *Arthur,* set him in this chayre, wherin (once fast bound) leaue him with me to finish the rest.

Attendants We goe, though loath. *Exeunt.*
Hubert My Lord, will it please your Honour to take the benefite of the faire euening?

Enter *Arthur* to *Hubert de Burgh.*
Arthur Gramercie *Hubert* for thy care of me,
In or to whom restraint is newly knowen,
The ioy of walking is small benefit,
Yet will I take thy offer with small thankes,
I would not loose the pleasure of the eye.
But tell me curteous keeper if you can,
How long the King will haue me tarrie heere.
  Hubert I know not Prince, but as I gesse not long.
God send you freedome, and *God saue the King,*
  They issue forth.
  Arthur Why how naw sirs, what may this outrage meane?
O helpe me *Hubert,* gentle keeper helpe:
God send this sodaine mutinous approach
Tend not to reaue a wretched guiltles life.
  Hubert So sirs, depart, and leaue the rest for me.
  Arthur Then *Arthur* yeeld, death frowneth in thy face,
What meaneth this? Good *Hubert* plead the case.
  Hubert Patience yong Lord, and listen words of woe,
Harmfull and harsh, hells horror to be heard:
A dismall tale fit for a furies tongue.
I faint to tell, deepe sorrow is the sound.
  Arthur What, must I die?
  Hubert No newes of death, but tidings of more hate,
A wrathfull doome, and most unluckie fate:
Deaths dish were daintie at so fell a feast,
Be deafe, heare not, its hell to tell the rest.
  Arthur Alas thou wrongst my youth with words of feare,
Tis hell, tis horror, not for one to heare:
What is it man if it must needes be don,
Act it, and end it, that the paine were gon.
  Hubert I will not chaunt such dolour with my tongue,
Yet must I act the outrage with my hand.
My heart my head, and all my powers beside,
To aide the office haue at once denide.
Peruse this letter, lines of treble woe,
Read ore my charge, and pardon when you know.

Hubert these are to commaund thee, as thou tendrest our quiet in minde and the estate of our person, that presently vpon the receipt of our commaund, thou put out the eyes of *Arthur Plantaginet.*

  Arthur Ah monstrous damned man, his very breath infects the elements.
Contagious venyme dwelleth in his heart,
Effecting meanes to poyson all the world.
Unreuerent may I be to blame the heauens
Of great iniustice, that the miscreant
Lives to oppresse the innocents with wrong.
Ah *Hubert,* makes he thee his instrument
To sound the tromp that causeth hell triumph?
Heauen weepes, the Saints doo shed celestiall teares,
They feare thy fall, and cyte thee with remorse,
They knock thy conscience, moouing pitie there,
Willing to fence thee from the rage of hell:
Hell *Hubert,* trust me all the plagues of hell
Hangs on performance of this damned deede.
This seale, the warrant of the bodies blisse,
Ensureth Satan chieftaine of thy soule:
Subscribe not *Hubert,* giue not Gods part away.
I speake not onely for eyes priuiledge,
The chiefe exterior that I would enioy:
But for thy perill, farre beyond my paine,
Thy sweete soules losse, more than my eyes vaine lack;
A cause internall, and eternall too.
Aduise thee *Hubert,* for the case is hard,
To loose saluation for a Kings reward.
  Hubert My Lord, a subiect dwelling in the land
Is tyed to execute the Kings commaund.
  Arthur Yet God commands, whose power reacheth further,
That no commaund should stand in force to murther.
  Hubert But that same Essence hath ordaind a law,
A death for guilt, to keepe the world in awe.
  Arthur I plead not guiltie, treasonles and free.
  Hubert But that appeale my Lord concernes not me.
  Arthur Why, thou art he that maist omit the perill.
  Hubert I, if my Soueraigne would remit his quarrell.
  Arthur His quarrell is unhallowed false and wrong.
  Hubert Then be the blame to whom it doth belong.
  Arthur Why thats to thee if thou as they proceede,
Conclude their iudgement with so vile a deede.
  Hubert Why then no execution can be lawfull,
If Iudges doomes must be reputed doubtfull.

Arthur Yes where in forme of Lawe in place and time,
The offender is convicted of the crime.
   Hubert My Lord, my Lord, this long expostulation,
Heapes up more griefe, than promise of redresse;
For this I know, and so resolude I end,
That subjects liues on Kings commaunds depend.
I must not reason why he is your foe,
But doo his charge since he commaunds it so.
   Arthur Then doo thy charge, and charged be thy soule
With wrongfull persecution done this day.
You rowling eyes, whose superficies yet
I doo behold with eyes that Nature lent:
Send foorth the terror of your Moovers frowne,
To wreake my wrong vpon the murtherers
That rob me of your faire reflecting view:
Let hell to them (as earth they wish to mee)
Be darke and direfull guerdon for their guylt,
And let the black tormenters of deepe *Tartary*
Upbraide them with this damned enterprise,
Inflicting change of tortures on their soules.
Delay not *Hubert,* my orisons are ended,
Began I pray thee, reaue me of my sight:
But to performe a tragedie indeede,
Conclude the period with a mortall stab.
Constance farewell, tormentor come away,
Make my dispatch the Tirants feasting day.
   Hubert I faint, I feare, my conscience bids desist:
Faint did I say, feare was it that I named?
My King commaunds, that warrant sets me free:
But God forbids, and he commaundeth Kings,
That great Commaunder counterchecks my charge,
He stays my hand, he maketh soft my heart,
Goe cursed tooles, your office is exempt,
Cheere thee yong Lord, thou shalt not loose an eye,
Though I should purchase it with losse of life.
Ile to the King, and say his will is done,
And of the langor tell him thou art dead,
Goe in with me, for *Hubert* was not borne
To blinde those lampes that Nature pollisht so,
   Arthur Hubert, if euer *Arthur* be in state,
Looke for amends of this received gift
I tooke my eysight by thy curtesie,
Thou lentst them me, I will not be ingrate.
But now procrastination may offend
The issue that thy kindnes undertakes:
Depart we *Hubert* to preuent the worst.   *Exeunt.*

2. THE DEATH OF KING JOHN (cf. V.vii.27–66)

Iohn Me thinks I see a cattalogue of sinne
Wrote by a fiend in Marble characters,
The least enough to loose my part in heauen.
Me thinks the Deuill whispers in mine eares
And tels me tis in vayne to hope for grace,
I must be damnd for *Arthurs* sodaine death.

I see I see a thousand thousand men
Come to accuse me for my wrong on earth,
And there is none so mercifull a God
That will forgiue the number of my sinnes.
How haue I liud, but by anothers losse?
What haue I loud [loved] but wrack of others weale?
When haue I vowd, and not infringd mine oath?
Where haue I done a deede deseruing well?
How, what, when, and where, haue I bestowd a day
That tended not to some notorious ill.
My life repleat with rage and tyranie,
Craues little pittie for so strange a death.
Or who will say that *Iohn* disceasd too soone,
Who will not say he rather liud too long.
Dishonor did attaynt me in my life,
And shame attendeth *Iohn* vnto his death.
Why did I scape the fury of the French,
And dyde not by the temper of their swords?
Shamelesse my life, and shamefully it ends,
Scornd by my foes, disdained of my friends.
   Bastard Forgiue the world and all your earthly foes,
And call on Christ, who is your latest friend.
   Iohn My tongue doth falter: *Philip,* I tell thee man,
Since *Iohn* did yeeld vnto the Priest of *Rome,*
Nor he nor his haue prospred on the earth:
Curst are his blessings, and his curse is blisse.
But in the spirit I cry vnto my God,
As did the Kingly Prophet *Dauid* cry,
(Whose hands, as mine, with murder were attaint)
I am not he shall buyld the Lord a house,
Or roote these Locusts from the face of earth:
But if my dying heart deceaue me not,
From out these loynes shall spring a Kingly braunch
Whose armes shall reach vnto the gates of *Rome,*
And with his feete treads downe the Strumpets pride,
That sits vpon the chaire of *Babylon.*
Philip, my heart strings breake, the poysons flame
Hath ouercome in me weake Natures power,
And in the faith of Jesu *Iohn* doth dye.
   Bastard See how he striues for life, unhappy Lord,
Whose bowells are deuided in themselves.
This is the fruite of Poperie, when true Kings
Are slaine and shouldred out by Monkes and Friers.

   There is, however, one very noticeable difference between *The Troublesome Reign* and *King John.* The older play was violent in its anti-papal propaganda, and every chance was taken to abuse the Pope and the Catholic Church. When Pandulph demands John's reasons for refusing to admit Stephen Langton as Archbishop of Canterbury, John replies:

And what hast thou or the Pope thy maister to doo to demaund of me, how I employ mine owne? Know sir Priest as I honour the Church and holy Churchmen, so I scorne to be subiect to the greatest Prelate in the world. Tell thy Maister so from me, and say, *Iohn* of *England* said it, that neuer an Italian Priest of them all, shall either haue tythe, tole, or poling penie out of *England,* but as I am King, so wil I raigne next vnder God, supreame head both ouer spirituall and temporall: and hee that contradicts me in this, Ile make him hoppe headlesse.

Later, the Bastard's methods of raising money from the monks are shown in a ribald scene where Philip in opening a treasure chest discovers a hidden nun. Again at the end of the play, the episode of the poisoning of King John is given in detail, and the monk who commits the deed is so zealous that he persuades the King to drink by first swallowing a draught of the poison himself. In his *King John,* Shakespeare turned John's speech into verse (III.i.147–60), but he omitted the other episodes altogether.

In filling his play with anti-Catholic propaganda the author of *The Troublesome Reign* was following a point of view which had already been expressed by Bishop John Bale in a manuscript morality play called *Kyng Johan,* written in the first half of the sixteenth century. Bale by straining history made John an early champion of Protestantism and even a martyr for the cause. *The Troublesome Reign,* like so many of the Chronicle plays, was based on the chronicles of Halle and Holinshed (see p. 105a), but they were used with great freedom. The doings of the Bastard Faulconbridge, for instance, are quite unhistorical and are based on a single observation of Holinshed:

Philip, bastard son to King Richard, to whom his father had given the castle and honor of Coinack, killed the Viscount of Limoges in revenge of his father's death.

However, Shakespeare seems not to have gone much further than the old play for the story of his *King John.*

Historical events can be presented on the stage in a variety of ways. In his earliest history plays — the three parts of *Henry VI* — Shakespeare was still following the older and rather naïve method of introducing a handful of persons with historical names who harangue each other in stiff, high-sounding verse and from time to time fight, stab, rush about the stage, or expire. This kind of drama suited a simple-minded audience. However, by the time he had concluded the series with *Richard III,* Shakespeare had advanced to a more subtle conception of the history play. *Richard III* is not so much a play of clashing events as a drama of fate and retribution. Richard himself is a man of evil destiny, but evil brings its own retribution on the wrongdoer; and the significance of the lesson is constantly expressed by means of prophecy and proverbial " sentences." There is thus a good deal of symbolism in *Richard III.* Later, in his mature history plays — the two parts of *Henry IV* — Shakespeare abandoned symbolism and showed history as the clash of personality between Henry IV, Prince Hal, and Hotspur in the First Part, and between father and son in the Second. Henry and Hotspur are not so much symbolical figures representing Unscrupulous Tyranny and Headstrong Nobility as two men with human frailties and virtues.

King John comes between the early *Henry VI* cycle and the later, mature *Henry IV* cycle. It is not one of Shakespeare's more successful plays, for he was unsure of his plan. At one time the characters are alive and interesting as human beings; and then for long passages and scenes the history is stiffened into a kind of symbolic action.

Thus the breaking of faith between King Philip and King John at the instigation of the Papal Legate — which in real life would be a matter of private discussion or committee meetings — is shown symbolically when Philip, who has been holding John's hand, drops it at the bidding of the Legate (III.i.262).

The opening scene of the play is good. In his first speeches John shows himself a brave, vigorous, and almost heroic king. He answers threats with threats, and keeps his word; for he arrives in France on the heels of the French ambassador, complete with his family (his mother and his niece) and with his army ready for immediate battle. In these first episodes John's energy may be due to his doughty mother, the dowager Queen Elinor; certainly when she disappears he collapses. This theme — the influence of a domineering mother — might well have been developed; years later Shakespeare made much of it in *Coriolanus*. Instead, in the long second act the action becomes almost a symbolic mime, wholly unrealistic, as in one single scene Philip and his followers besiege Angiers; Chatillon returns from England; John and his followers invade France; the two kings wrangle; they summon Angiers to surrender; they withdraw their armies to fight an indecisive battle; the heralds of the two kings return and call on the town to surrender; the two armies return and are ready for another battle; the Bastard suggests that the kings should unite against the men of Angiers, who thereupon suggest that Lewis and Blanch should be matched; the two young people come forward, look at each other, fall in love; and all go off to the wedding.

Such a method of dramatizing history makes no attempt at realism; the dramatist puts high-sounding speeches into the mouths of puppets who comment on history in much the same way as the historian writes a chapter entitled " Arthur's legal claims."

This method has some advantages, but it must be carried out consistently; Shakespeare drops the symbolical manner whenever the irrepressible Bastard appears. The Bastard in a far-off way is an ancestor of Edmund in *Lear* (another bastard, but a far more ruthless devotee of " Commodity ") and of Falstaff, whose irreverent comments also from time to time liven the solemnity of high events; he is an important character in the development of Shakespeare's art. Hitherto Shakespeare had treated history very seriously. There were no deliberate laughs either in *Richard III* or *Richard II;* and though there were a few low comedy scenes in the three parts of *Henry VI,* they were distinct and separate from the scenes concerning high personages. In *King John* Shakespeare deliberately and successfully thrusts a comic character into the highest scenes of the play.

The symbolic vein is maintained from the beginning of II.i to III.iii, when John is about to go home to England; and then once more Shakespeare makes John a human being, or at least an interesting specimen of stage villain, as he plans to have his nephew Arthur murdered. So nasty a proposal requires nice wording, and Hubert in spite of his ugly face is rather stupid; but at last he gets the idea and prepares to carry it out. The scene between Hubert and little Arthur has been much admired, especially by critics in the nineteenth century; modern readers find the pathos excessive, for the child is too eloquent and too noble in his pleadings; but the scene is at least highly emotional and moving by contrast with the heavy wordiness of what has gone before.

From this point on the character of John changes almost abruptly. Hitherto, though an unpleasant villain, he has been bold and vigorous. Henceforth he collapses and makes a pitiable show before his nobles, and an abject contrast to his nephew the Bastard. When Hubert returns with false news that Arthur is dead and that the people are on the verge of rebellion, John rounds on him in terror (IV.ii.182–248). This passage is perhaps the finest piece of psychological insight in the play.

With the degeneration of the King, the Bastard also changes. He ceases to be the unscrupulous wag and becomes instead the fire-eating son of Richard the Lion-hearted; to him are given the best serious speeches of the last part of the play. After the death of Arthur, a few more scenes of historical events follow, and then John dies, with less eloquence than might have been expected.

King John has its interesting moments, but it is not a great play; for indeed the reign of John Plantagenet, though exceedingly troublesome, was not well suited for a play of any kind.

King John

DRAMATIS PERSONAE

KING JOHN
PRINCE HENRY, *son to the King*
ARTHUR, *Duke of Bretagne, nephew to the King*
THE EARL OF PEMBROKE
THE EARL OF ESSEX
THE EARL OF SALISBURY
THE LORD BIGOT
HUBERT DE BURGH
ROBERT FAULCONBRIDGE, *son to Sir Robert Faulconbridge*
PHILIP THE BASTARD, *his half brother*
JAMES GURNEY, *servant to Lady Faulconbridge*
PETER OF POMFRET, *a prophet*
PHILIP, *King of France*
LEWIS, *the Dauphin*

LYMOGES, *Duke of Austria*
CARDINAL PANDULPH, *the Pope's legate*
MELUN, *a French lord*
CHATILLON, *ambassador from France to King John*

QUEEN ELINOR, *mother to King John*
CONSTANCE, *mother to Arthur*
BLANCH *of Spain, niece to King John*
LADY FAULCONBRIDGE

LORDS, CITIZENS *of Angiers,* SHERIFF, HERALDS, OFFICERS, SOLDIERS, MESSENGERS, *and other* ATTENDANTS

SCENE — *Partly in England, and partly in France.*

Act I

SCENE I. KING JOHN'S *palace.*

[*Enter* KING JOHN, QUEEN ELINOR, PEMBROKE, ESSEX, SALISBURY, *and others, with* CHATILLON.]

K. JOHN. Now, say, Chatillon, what would
 France with us?
CHAT. Thus, after greeting, speaks the King of
 France
In my behavior° to the Majesty,
The borrowed Majesty,° of England here.   4
 EL. A strange beginning: "Borrowed Majesty!"
 K. JOHN. Silence, good Mother. Hear the embassy.
 CHAT. Philip of France, in right and true behalf
Of thy deceasèd brother Geffrey's son,
Arthur Plantagenet, lays most lawful claim
To this fair island and the territories,   10
To Ireland, Poictiers, Anjou, Touraine, Maine,°
Desiring thee to lay aside the sword
Which sways usurpingly these several titles
And put the same into young Arthur's hand,
Thy nephew and right royal sovereign.   15
 K. JOHN. What follows if we disallow of° this?
 CHAT. The proud control° of fierce and bloody
 war
To enforce these rights so forcibly withheld.
 K. JOHN. Here have we war for war and blood
 for blood,

Controlment for controlment. So answer France.
 CHAT. Then take my King's defiance from my
 mouth,   21
The farthest° limit of my embassy.
 K. JOHN. Bear mine to him, and so depart in
 peace.
Be thou as lightning in the eyes of France,
For ere thou canst report I will be there,   25
The thunder of my cannon° shall be heard.
So hence! Be thou the trumpet of our wrath
And sullen presage° of your own decay.
An honorable conduct° let him have.
Pembroke, look to 't. Farewell, Chatillon.   30
     [*Exeunt* CHATILLON *and* PEMBROKE.]
 EL. What now, my Son! Have I not ever said
How that ambitious Constance would not cease
Till she had kindled France and all the world,
Upon the right and party of her son?
This might have been prevented and made whole
With very easy arguments of love,°   36
Which now the manage° of two kingdoms must
With fearful bloody issue arbitrate.
 K. JOHN. Our strong possession and our right
 for us.
 EL. Your strong possession much more than your
 right,   40
Or else it must go wrong with you and me.
So much my conscience whispers in your ear,

---

22. **farthest:** extreme; i.e., my last word.   26. **cannon:** an anachronism, for cannon were not used for at least another century.   28. **sullen presage:** grim foretelling.   29. **conduct:** escort.   35–36. **This . . . love:** i.e., if Constance had been reasonable, this matter might have been settled amicably.   37. **manage:** management, i.e., the rulers.

Act I. Sc. i: 3. **In my behavior:** in my person.   4. **borrowed Majesty:** i.e., because John is a usurper. See App. 28, King John. 11. **Poictiers . . . Maine:** French territories at this time in English possession.   16. **disallow of:** refuse.   17. **control:** force.

Which none but Heaven and you and I shall hear.
                    [*Enter a* SHERIFF.]
ESS. My liege,° here is the strangest controversy
Come from the country to be judged by you   45
That e'er I heard. Shall I produce the men?
    K. JOHN. Let them approach.
Our abbeys and our priories shall pay
This expedition's charge.
        [*Enter* ROBERT FAULCONBRIDGE, *and* PHILIP *his
                bastard brother.*]
                        What men are you?
    BAST. Your faithful subject I, a gentleman   50
Born in Northamptonshire, and eldest son,
As I suppose, to Robert Faulconbridge,
A soldier, by the honor-giving hand
Of Coeur-de-lion° knighted in the field.
    K. JOHN. What art thou?   55
    ROB. The son and heir to that same Faulcon-
        bridge.
    K. JOHN. Is that the elder, and art thou the heir?
You came not of one mother then, it seems.
    BAST. Most certain of one mother, mighty
        King —
That is well known — and, as I think, one father.
But for the certain knowledge of that truth   61
I put you o'er° to Heaven and to my mother.
Of that I doubt,° as all men's children may.
    EL. Out on thee, rude man! Thou dost shame
        thy mother
And wound her honor with this diffidence.°   65
    BAST. I, madam? No, I have no reason for it.
That is my brother's plea and none of mine;
The which if he can prove, a'° pops me out
At least from fair five hundred pound a year.   69
Heaven guard my mother's honor and my land!
    K. JOHN. A good blunt fellow. Why, being
        younger born,
Doth he lay claim to thine inheritance?
    BAST. I know not why, except to get the land;
But once he slandered me with bastardy.
But whether I be as true begot or no,   75
That still I lay upon my mother's head;°
But that I am as well begot, my liege —
Fair fall° the bones that took the pains for me! —
Compare our faces, and be judge yourself.
If old Sir Robert did beget us both   80
And were our father and this son like him,
O old Sir Robert, Father, on my knee
I give Heaven thanks I was not like to thee!
    K. JOHN. Why, what a madcap hath Heaven lent
        us here!
    EL. He hath a trick° of Coeur-de-lion's face.   85

The accent of his tongue affecteth° him.
Do you not read some tokens of my son
In the large composition° of this man?
    K. JOHN. Mine eye hath well examinèd his parts
And finds them perfect Richard. Sirrah,° speak   90
What doth move you to claim your brother's land?
    BAST. Because he hath a half-face,° like my father.
With half that face would he have all my land.
A half-faced groat° five hundred pound a year!
    ROB. My gracious liege, when that my father
        lived,   95
Your brother did employ my father much ——
    BAST. Well, sir, by this you cannot get my land.
Your tale must be how he employed my mother.
    ROB. And once dispatched him in an embassy
To Germany, there with the Emperor   100
To treat of high affairs touching° that time.
The advantage of his absence took the King
And in the meantime sojourned at my father's;
Where how he did prevail I shame to speak,
But truth is truth. Large lengths of seas and shores
Between my father and my mother lay,   106
As I have heard my father speak himself,
When this same lusty gentleman was got.°
Upon his deathbed he by will bequeathed
His lands to me and took it on his death°   110
That this my mother's son was none of his;
And if he were, he came into the world
Full fourteen weeks before the course of time.
Then, good my liege, let me have what is mine,
My father's land, as was my father's will.   115
    K. JOHN. Sirrah, your brother is legitimate.
Your father's wife did after wedlock bear him,
And if she did play false, the fault was hers;
Which fault lies on the hazards of all husbands°
That marry wives. Tell me, how if my brother,   120
Who, as you say, took pains to get this son,
Had of your father claimed this son for his?
In° sooth,° good friend, your father might have
        kept
This calf, bred from his cow, from all the world.
In sooth he might. Then, if he were my brother's,
My brother might not claim him, nor your father,
Being none of his, refuse him. This concludes: 127
My mother's son did get your father's heir;
Your father's heir must have your father's land.
    ROB. Shall then my father's will be of no force
To dispossess that child which is not his?   131

86. affecteth: is like.   88. composition: frame.   90. Sirrah:
term of address used to an inferior.   92. half-face: thin face.
See *II Hen IV*, III.ii.283.   94. groat: silver coin worth 4*d*.
101. touching: that concerned.   108. got: begotten.   110. took
... death: swore most solemnly, as he was on his deathbed.
119. lies ... husbands: is a risk that all husbands must face.
123–29. In ... land: The King is stating the normal laws of
legitimacy, which presume that the husband is the father of his
wife's children. Unless there is absolute proof to the contrary,
he may not disclaim paternity, nor may any other man claim it.
123. sooth: truth.

44. liege: lord.   54. Coeur-de-lion: Richard I, the Lionheart.
See App. 28, King John.   62. put ... o'er: refer you.   63. doubt:
suspect.   65. diffidence: distrust, suspicion.   68. a': he.
76. lay ... head: that is for my mother to declare.   78. Fair
fall: good luck to.   85. trick: expression.

BAST. Of no more force to dispossess me, sir,
Than was his will to get me, as I think.
   EL. Whether hadst thou° rather be a Faulcon-
     bridge,
And like thy brother, to enjoy thy land,   135
Or the reputed son of Coeur-de-lion,
Lord of thy presence° and no land beside?
   BAST. Madam, an if° my brother had my shape,
And I had his, Sir Robert's his,° like him,
And if my legs were two such riding rods,°   140
My arms such eel skins stuffed, my face so thin
That in mine ear I durst not stick a rose
Lest men should say, "Look, where three farthings
     goes!"°
And, to his shape,° were heir to all this land,
Would I might never stir from off this place,   145
I would give it every foot to have this face.
I would not be Sir Nob° in any case.
   EL. I like thee well. Wilt thou forsake thy for-
     tune,
Bequeath thy land to him, and follow me?
I am a soldier and now bound to France.   150
   BAST. Brother, take you my land, I'll take my
     chance.
Your face hath got five hundred pound a year,
Yet sell your face for five pence and 'tis dear.
Madam, I'll follow you unto the death.   154
   EL. Nay, I would have you go before me thither.
   BAST. Our country manners give our betters way.
   K. JOHN. What is thy name?
   BAST. Philip, my liege, so is my name begun;°
Philip, good old Sir Robert's wife's eldest son.
   K. JOHN. From henceforth bear his name whose
     form thou bear'st.   160
Kneel thou down Philip, but rise more great;
Arise Sir Richard and Plantagenet.°
   BAST. Brother by the mother's side, give me your
     hand.
My father gave me honor, yours gave land.
Now blessèd be the hour, by night or day,   165
When I was got, Sir Robert was away!
   EL. The very spirit of Plantagenet!
I am thy grandam, Richard. Call me so.
   BAST. Madam, by chance but not by truth;° what
     though?
Something about,° a little from the right,   170

In at the window, or else o'er the hatch.°
Who dares not stir by day must walk by night,
And have is have, however men do catch.
Near or far off, well won is still well shot,
And I am I, howe'er I was begot.   175
   K. JOHN. Go, Faulconbridge. Now hast thou thy
     desire.
A landless knight makes thee a landed squire.
Come, madam, and come, Richard, we must speed
For France, for France, for it is more than need.°
   BAST. Brother, adieu. Good fortune come to
     thee!   180
For thou wast got i' the way of honesty.
                  [*Exeunt all but* BASTARD.]
A foot of honor° better than I was,
But many a many foot of land the worse.
Well, now can I make any Joan° a lady.
"Good den,° Sir Richard!" — "God-a-mercy, fel-
     low!" —   185
And if his name be George, I'll call him Peter,
For new-made honor doth forget men's names.°
'Tis too respective° and too sociable
For your conversion.° Now° your traveler,
He and his toothpick° at my Worship's mess,°   190
And when my knightly stomach is sufficed,
Why then I suck my teeth and catechize
My picked° man of countries. "My dear sir,"
Thus, leaning on mine elbow, I begin,
"I shall beseech you" — that is Question now;   195
And then comes Answer like an Absey° book.
"O sir," says Answer, "at your best command;
At your employment; at your service, sir."
"No, sir," says Question, "I, sweet sir, at yours."
And so, ere Answer knows what Question would —
Saving° in dialogue of compliment,   201
And talking of the Alps and Apennines,
The Pyrenean and the River Po —
It draws toward supper in conclusion so.
But this is worshipful society   205
And fits the mounting spirit like myself;°
For he is but a bastard to the time°
That doth not smack of observation.°

134. **Whether . . . thou:** would you. 137. **presence:** the shape that you possess (from your real father). 138. **an if:** if. 139. **Sir . . . his:** a double genitive, i.e., Sir Robert's. 140. **riding rods:** switches. 143. **three . . . goes:** The three-farthing coin was small and thin, and distinguished from the silver penny by a rose behind the Queen's head. 144. **And . . . shape:** and as well as having Sir Robert's likeness. 147. **Sir Nob:** Sir Bob. 158. **begun:** i.e., I don't own the surname of my "father," Faulconbridge. 161-62. **Kneel . . . Plantagenet:** i.e., the King formally bestows knighthood on the Bastard. See *II Hen VI*, IV.ii.127–28,n. 169. **by . . . truth:** i.e., as it happens I am your grandson, but illegitimately. 170. **Something about:** indirectly.

171. **hatch:** half-door; i.e., I am a Plantagenet, even though I got the title by an indirect route. 179. **more . . . need:** i.e., we are already late. 182. **A . . . honor:** i.e., I now have a title. 184. **Joan:** country girl. See *LLL*, III.i.207. 185. **Good den:** good afternoon. 187. **new-made . . . names:** it is the mark of a man newly promoted to forget his old acquaintance. 188. **too respective:** not superior enough. 189. **For . . . conversion:** for one who has been suddenly promoted. 189–204. **Now . . . so:** The Bastard here imagines himself behaving like some great gentleman full of courtly affectations of phrase and deportment as he entertains a distinguished traveler. 190. **toothpick:** At this time the toothpick was considered an affected foreign device. **mess:** table. 193. **picked:** select, refined. 196. **Absey:** See *T Gent*, II.i.23,n. 201. **Saving:** only. They spend the first hour in polite conversation. 206. **mounting . . . myself:** one who is as ambitious as I am. 207. **bastard . . . time:** no true son of this age. 208. **smack of observation:** does not watch how the tide runs; is not a "yes-man."

And° so am I, whether I smack or no,
And not alone in habit and device,°   210
Exterior form, outward accouterment,
But from the inward motion to deliver
Sweet, sweet, sweet poison for the age's tooth;
Which, though I will not practice to deceive,
Yet, to avoid deceit, I mean to learn,   215
For it shall strew the footsteps of my rising.
But who comes in such haste in riding robes?
What woman-post° is this? Hath she no husband
That will take pains to blow a horn before her?

[*Enter* LADY FAULCONBRIDGE *and* JAMES GURNEY.]

Oh, me! It is my mother. How now, good lady?
What brings you here to Court so hastily?   221
    LADY F. Where is that slave, thy brother? Where
       is he,
That holds in chase° mine honor up and down?
    BAST. My brother Robert? Old Sir Robert's son?
Colbrand° the giant, that same mighty man?   225
Is it Sir Robert's son that you seek so?
    LADY F. Sir Robert's son! Aye, thou unreverend
      boy,
Sir Robert's son. Why scorn'st thou at Sir Robert?
He is Sir Robert's son, and so art thou.
    BAST. James Gurney, wilt thou give us leave
      awhile?   230
    GUR. Good leave, good Philip.
    BAST.   Philip! Sparrow!° James,
There's toys abroad.° Anon° I'll tell thee more.
                          [*Exit* GURNEY.]

Madam, I was not old Sir Robert's son.
Sir Robert might have eat his part in me
Upon Good Friday and ne'er broke his fast.   235
Sir Robert could do well; marry,° to confess,
Could he get me? Sir Robert could not do it.
We know his handiwork. Therefore, good Mother,
To whom am I beholding for these limbs?
Sir Robert never holp° to make this leg.   240
    LADY F. Hast thou conspirèd with thy brother,
      too,
That for thine own gain shouldst defend mine
    honor?
What means this scorn, thou most untoward knave?
    BAST. Knight, knight, good Mother, Basilisco-
      like.°

What! I am dubbed!° I have it on my shoulder.
But, Mother, I am not Sir Robert's son.   246
I have disclaimed Sir Robert and my land.
Legitimation, name, and all is gone.
Then, good my Mother, let me know my father.
Some proper° man, I hope. Who was it, Mother?
    LADY F. Hast thou denied thyself a Faulcon-
      bridge?   251
    BAST. As faithfully as I deny the Devil.
    LADY F. King Richard Coeur-de-lion was thy
      father.
By long and vehement suit I was seduced
To make room for him in my husband's bed.   255
Heaven lay not my transgression to my charge!
Thou art the issue of my dear° offense,
Which was so strongly urged past my defense.
    BAST. Now, by this light, were I to get again,
Madam, I would not wish a better father.   260
Some sins do bear their privilege° on earth,
And so doth yours. Your fault was not your folly.
Needs must you lay your heart at his dispose,
Subjected tribute to commanding love,
Against whose fury and unmatchèd force   265
The aweless° lion could not wage the fight,
Nor keep his princely heart from Richard's hand.°
He that perforce robs lions of their hearts
May easily win a woman's. Aye, my Mother,
With all my heart I thank thee for my father!   270
Who lives and dares but say thou didst not well
When I was got, I'll send his soul to Hell.
Come, lady, I will show thee to my kin;
    And they shall say, when Richard me begot,
If thou hadst said him nay, it had been sin.   275
    Who says it was, he lies. I say 'twas not.
                             [*Exeunt.*]

Act II

SCENE I. *France. Before Angiers.*

[*Enter* AUSTRIA *and forces, drums, etc. on one side;
on the other* KING PHILIP *of France and his power,*
LEWIS, ARTHUR, CONSTANCE, *and* ATTENDANTS.]
    LEW. Before Angiers well met, brave Austria.
Arthur, that great forerunner of thy blood,
Richard, that robbed the lion of his heart
And fought the holy wars in Palestine,
By this brave Duke° came early to his grave.   5

209–16. **And . . . rising:** i.e., and I am a real bastard anyhow, whether I am obsequious or not; and I will deceive my contemporaries not only in my outward appearance but also from my mind (*inward motion*). Though I will not deliberately deceive, yet I'll learn how, lest I be deceived myself; for many will try to deceive me as I rise. **210. device:** coat of arms. **218. woman-post:** woman riding hastily. See App. 17. **223. holds in chase:** pursues to destroy. **225. Colbrand:** a giant in popular fairy tales, slain by Guy of Warwick. **231. Philip! Sparrow:** Sparrows were called Philip (pronounced Phip) from their peep. **232. There's . . . abroad:** some odd things have been happening hereabout. **Anon:** by and by. **236. marry:** Mary, by the Virgin. **240. holp:** helped. **244. Basilisco-like:** Basilisco was the braggart knight in the play of *Soliman and Perseda* by Kyd.

245. dubbed: ceremoniously knighted. See ll. 161–62. **250. proper:** handsome. **257. dear:** grievous. **261. bear . . . privilege:** are to be allowed. **266–67. The . . . hand:** See App. 28, King John. **266. aweless:** fearless.

Act II, Sc. i: **5. By . . . Duke:** See App. 28, King John.

And for amends to his posterity,
At our importance° hither is he come
To spread his colors,° boy, in thy behalf,
And to rebuke the usurpation
Of thy unnatural uncle, English John.   10
Embrace him, love him, give him welcome hither.
  ART. God shall forgive you Coeur-de-lion's death
The rather that you give his offspring life,
Shadowing their right under your wings of war.
I give you welcome with a powerless hand,   15
But with a heart full of unstainèd love.
Welcome before the gates of Angiers, Duke.
  LEW. A noble boy! Who would not do thee right?
  AUST. Upon thy cheek lay I this zealous kiss
As seal to this indenture° of my love: 20
That to my home I will no more return
Till Angiers and the right thou hast in France,
Together with that pale, that white-faced° shore,
Whose foot spurns back the ocean's roaring tides
And coops from other lands her islanders,   25
Even till that England, hedged in with the main,°
That water-wallèd bulwark, still secure°
And confident from foreign purposes,
Even till that utmost corner of the West
Salute thee for her King; till then, fair boy,   30
Will I not think of home, but follow arms.
  CON. Oh, take his mother's thanks, a widow's
      thanks,
Till your strong hand shall help to give him
      strength
To make a more° requital to your love!
  AUST. The peace of Heaven is theirs that lift their
      swords   35
In such a just and charitable war.
  K. PHI. Well then, to work. Our cannon shall be
      bent°
Against the brows of this resisting town.
Call for our chiefest men of discipline
To cull the plots of best advantages.°   40
We'll lay before this town our royal bones,
Wade to the market place in Frenchmen's blood,
But° we will make it subject to this boy.
  CON. Stay for an answer to your embassy,
Lest, unadvised, you stain your swords with blood.
My Lord Chatillon may from England bring   46
That right in peace which here we urge in war,
And then we shall repent each drop of blood
That hot rash haste so indirectly° shed.
      [*Enter* CHATILLON.]
  K. PHI. A wonder, lady! Lo, upon thy wish,   50
Our messenger Chatillon is arrived!

What England says, say briefly, gentle lord.
We coldly pause° for thee. Chatillon, speak.
  CHAT. Then turn your forces from this paltry
      siege
And stir them up against a mightier task.   55
England, impatient° of your just demands,
Hath put himself in arms. The adverse winds,
Whose leisure I have stayed, have given him time
To land his legions all as soon as I.
His marches are expedient° to this town,   60
His forces strong, his soldiers confident.
With him along is come the Mother-Queen,
An Até,° stirring him to blood and strife;
With her her niece, the Lady Blanch of Spain;
With them a bastard of the King's deceased.°   65
And all the unsettled humors° of the land,
Rash, inconsiderate, fiery voluntaries,°
With ladies' faces and fierce dragons' spleens,°
Have sold their fortunes at their native homes,
Bearing their birthrights proudly on their backs°
To make a hazard of new fortunes here.   71
In brief, a braver choice of dauntless spirits
Than now the English bottoms° have waft° o'er
Did never float upon the swelling tide
To do offense and scath° in Christendom.   75
                                    [*Drum beats.*]
The interruption of their churlish drums
Cuts off more circumstance.° They are at hand
To parley or to fight. Therefore prepare.
  K. PHI. How much unlooked for is this expedi-
      tion!°
  AUST. By how much unexpected, by so much   80
We must awake endeavor for defense,
For courage mounteth with occasion.°
Let them be welcome then. We are prepared.
[*Enter* KING JOHN, ELINOR, BLANCH, *the* BASTARD,
      LORDS, *and* FORCES.]
  K. JOHN. Peace be to France, if France in peace
      permit
Our just and lineal entrance° to our own.   85
If not, bleed France, and Peace ascend to Heaven,
Whiles we, God's wrathful agent, do correct°
Their proud contempt that beats His peace to
      Heaven.
  K. PHI. Peace be to England, if that War return
From France to England, there to live in peace.   90
England we love, and for that England's sake
With burden of our armor here we sweat.
This toil of ours should be a work of thine;

But thou from loving England art so far
That thou hast underwrought° his lawful King,   95
Cut off the sequence of posterity,°
Outfacèd infant state,° and done a rape
Upon the maiden virtue of the Crown.
Look here upon thy brother Geffrey's face.
These eyes, these brows, were molded out of his.
This little abstract doth contain that large   101
Which died in Geffrey, and the hand of time
Shall draw this brief into as huge a volume.°
That Geffrey was thy elder brother born,
And this his son; England was Geffrey's right,   105
And this is Geffrey's.° In the name of God
How comes it then that thou art called a King,
When living blood doth in these temples beat
Which owe° the crown that thou o'ermasterest?°
   K. JOHN. From whom hast thou this great com-
     mission, France,   110
To draw my answer from thy articles?°
   K. PHI. From that Supernal° Judge that stirs
     good thoughts
In any breast of strong authority
To look into the blots and stains of right.   114
That Judge hath made me guardian to this boy,
Under whose warrant I impeach° thy wrong,
And by whose help I mean to chastise it.
   K. JOHN. Alack, thou dost usurp authority.   118
   K. PHI. Excuse — it is to beat usurping down.
   EL. Who is it thou dost call usurper, France?
   CON. Let me make answer. Thy usurping son.
   EL. Out, insolent! Thy bastard shall be King,
That thou mayst be a Queen and check° the world!
   CON. My bed was ever to thy son as true
As thine was to thy husband, and this boy   125
Liker in feature to his father Geffrey
Than thou and John in manners, being as like
As rain to water, or Devil to his dam.°
My boy a bastard! By my soul, I think
His father never was so true begot.   130
It cannot be, an if thou wert his mother.
   EL. There's a good mother, boy, that blots° thy
     father.
   CON. There's a good grandam, boy, that would
     blot thee.
   AUST. Peace!
   BAST.   Hear the crier.
   AUST.   What the Devil art thou?

   BAST. One that will play the Devil, sir, with you,
An a' may catch your hide° and you alone.   136
You are the hare of whom the proverb goes,
Whose valor plucks dead lions by the beard.
I'll smoke° your skin coat, an I catch you right.
Sirrah, look to 't. I' faith, I will, i' faith.   140
   BLAN. Oh, well did he become that lion's robe
That did disrobe the lion of that robe!
   BAST. It lies as sightly° on the back of him
As great Alcides'° shows upon an ass.
But, ass, I'll take that burden from your back,   145
Or lay on that shall make your shoulders crack.
   AUST. What cracker° is this same that deafs our
     ears
With this abundance of superfluous breath?
King Philip, determine what we shall do straight.
   K. PHI. Women and fools, break off your confer-
     ence.   150
King John, this is the very sum of all:
England and Ireland, Anjou, Touraine, Maine,
In right of Arthur do I claim of them.
Wilt thou resign them, and lay down thy arms?
   K. JOHN. My life as soon. I do defy thee, France.
Arthur of Bretagne, yield thee to my hand,   156
And out of my dear love I'll give thee more
Than e'er the coward hand of France can win.
Submit thee, boy.
   EL.   Come to thy grandam, child.
   CON. Do, child, go to it° grandam, child.   160
Give grandam kingdom, and it grandam will
Give it a plum, a cherry, and a fig.
There's a good grandam.
   ART.   Good my Mother, peace!
I would that I were low laid in my grave.
I am not worth this coil° that's made for me.   165
   EL. His mother shames him so, poor boy, he
     weeps.
   CON. Now shame upon you, whether she does or
     no!
His grandam's wrongs,° and not his mother's
     shames,
Draws those heaven-moving pearls from his poor
     eyes,
Which Heaven shall take in nature of a fee.   170
Aye, with these crystal beads Heaven shall be
     bribed
To do him justice and revenge on you.
   EL. Thou monstrous slanderer of Heaven and
     earth!
   CON. Thou monstrous injurer of Heaven and
     earth!
Call not me slanderer. Thou and thine usurp   175

---

95. **underwrought:** undermined.   96. **sequence of posterity:** the proper succession by right of birth.   97. **Outfaced . . . state:** intimidated an infant King.   101–03. **abstract . . . volume:** i.e., Arthur is a shorter edition of the larger volume, his father, and in time this little synopsis (*abstract*) will also become a complete volume.   106. **this is Geffrey's:** Here he points to the crown that John is wearing.   109. **owe:** are true owners of. **o'ermasterest:** usurpest.   111. **draw . . . articles:** to make answers for me to the charges which you are laying against me.   112. **Supernal:** heavenly.   116. **impeach:** accuse.   123. **check:** control.   128. **dam:** mother.   132. **blots:** dishonors.

136. **hide:** Austria wears the famous lion skin. See App. 28, King John and I.i.266–67.   139. **smoke:** make the dust fly in.   143. **sightly:** appropriately.   144. **Alcides:** Hercules, who wore the skin of the fierce Nemean lion which he had slain.   147. **cracker:** boaster.   160. **it:** its.   165. **coil:** fuss.   168. **grandam's wrongs:** wrongs committed by his grandmother.

The dominations,° royalties, and rights
Of this oppressèd boy. This is thy eld'st son's son,
Infortunate° in nothing but in thee.
Thy sins are visited in this poor child.
The canon° of the law is laid on him,   180
Being but the second generation
Removèd from thy sin-conceiving womb.
    K. JOHN. Bedlam,° have done.
    CON.   I have but this to say:
That he is not only plaguèd for her sin,
But God hath made her sin and her the plague
On this removèd issue,° plagued for her   186
And with her plague; her sin his injury,
Her injury the beadle° to her sin,
All punished in the person of this child,
And all for her. A plague upon her!   190
    EL. Thou unadvisèd° scold, I can produce
A will that bars the title of thy son.
    CON. Aye, who doubts that? A will! A wicked
    will.
A woman's will; a cankered° grandam's will!
    K. PHI. Peace, lady! Pause, or be more temperate.
It ill beseems this presence to cry aim°   196
To these ill-tunèd repetitions.
Some trumpet summon hither to the walls
These men of Angiers. Let us hear them speak
Whose title they admit, Arthur's or John's.   200
[*Trumpet sounds. Enter certain* CITIZENS *upon the
walls.*]
    I. CIT. Who is it that hath warned° us to the
    walls?
    K. PHI. 'Tis France, for England.
    K. JOHN.   England, for itself.
You men of Angiers, and my loving subjects ——
    K. PHI. You loving men of Angiers, Arthur's sub-
jects,   204
Our trumpet called you to this gentle parle° ——
    K. JOHN. For our advantage. Therefore hear us
    first.
These flags of France, that are advancèd° here
Before the eye and prospect° of your town,
Have hither marched to your endamagement.
The cannons have their bowels full of wrath,   210
And ready mounted are they to spit forth
Their iron indignation 'gainst your walls.
All preparation for a bloody siege
And merciless proceeding by these French   214
Confronts your city's eyes, your winking° gates,

And but for our approach, those sleeping stones
That as a waist° doth girdle you about,
By the compulsion of their ordinance°
By this time from their fixèd beds of lime
Had been dishabited,° and wide havoc made   220
For bloody power to rush upon your peace.
But on the sight of us, your lawful King,
Who painfully° with much expedient march
Have brought a countercheck° before your gates
To save unscratched your city's threatened cheeks,
Behold, the French, amazed, vouchsafe a parle.
And now, instead of bullets wrapped in fire   227
To make a shaking fever in your walls,
They shoot but calm words folded up in smoke
To make a faithless° error in your ears.   230
Which trust accordingly, kind citizens,
And let us in, your King, whose labored spirits,
Forwearied in this action of swift speed,
Crave harborage within your city walls.
    K. PHI. When I have said, make answer to us
    both.   235
Lo, in this right hand, whose protection
Is most divinely vowed upon the right
Of him it holds, stands young Plantagenet,
Son to the elder brother of this man,
And King o'er him and all that he enjoys.   240
For this downtrodden equity,° we tread
In warlike march these greens° before your town,
Being no further enemy to you
Than the constraint of hospitable zeal
In the relief of this oppressèd child   245
Religiously provokes. Be pleasèd then
To pay that duty which you truly owe
To him that owes° it, namely this young Prince;
And then our arms, like to a muzzled bear,
Save in aspèct,° hath all offense sealed up.   250
Our cannons' malice vainly shall be spent
Against the invulnerable clouds of Heaven,
And with a blessèd and unvexed retire,°
With unhacked swords and helmets all unbruised,
We will bear home that lusty blood again   255
Which here we came to spout against your town,
And leave your children, wives, and you in peace.
But if you fondly pass° our proffered offer,
'Tis not the roundure° of your old-faced walls
Can hide you from our messengers of war,   260
Though all these English and their discipline
Were harbored in their rude circumference.
Then tell us, shall your city call us lord
In that behalf which we have challenged it?
Or shall we give the signal to our rage   265
And stalk in blood to our possession?

---

176. **dominations:** sovereignty.   178. **Infortunate:** unfortunate.
180. **canon:** the divine law — that the sins of the fathers shall
be visited upon the children to the third and fourth generation.
183. **Bedlam:** lunatic.   186. **removed issue:** distant descendant,
i.e., grandchild.   188. **beadle:** parish officer who inflicted punishment on prostitutes and rogues.   191. **unadvised:** unthinking.
194. **cankered:** malignant.   196. **cry aim:** encourage — from
the custom of encouraging archers in a match to aim well.
201. **warned:** summoned.   205. **parle:** parley, conference.
207. **advanced:** raised.   208. **prospect:** view.   215. **winking:**
shut.

217. **waist:** belt.   218. **ordinance:** ordnance, cannon.   220. **dishabited:** dislodged.   223. **painfully:** laboriously.   224. **countercheck:** sharp reply.   230. **faithless:** false, perfidious.   241. **equity:**
right.   242. **greens:** lawns.   248. **owes:** owns.   250. **aspect:**
appearance.   253. **retire:** withdrawal.   258. **fondly pass:** foolishly neglect.   259. **roundure:** circumference.

1. CIT. In brief, we are the King of England's sub-
jects.
For him, and in his right, we hold this town.
  K. JOHN. Acknowledge then the King, and let me
in.
  1. CIT. That can we not; but he that proves the
King,   270
To him will we prove loyal. Till that time
Have we rammed up our gates against the world.
  K. JOHN. Doth not the crown of England prove
the King?
And if not that, I bring you witnesses,
Twice fifteen thousand hearts of England's
breed ——   275
  BAST. Bastards, and else.°
  K. JOHN. To verify our title with their lives.
  K. PHI. As many and as well-born bloods as
those ——
  BAST. Some bastards too.
  K. PHI. —— Stand in his face to contradict his
claim.   280
  1. CIT. Till you compound° whose right is worthi-
est,
We for the worthiest hold the right from both.
  K. JOHN. Then God forgive the sin of all those
souls
That to their everlasting residence,
Before the dew of evening fall, shall fleet   285
In dreadful trial of our kingdom's King!
  K. PHI. Amen, amen! Mount, chevaliers! To
arms!
  BAST. Saint George, that swinged° the dragon,
and e'er since
Sits on his horse back at mine hostess' door,°
Teach us some fence!° [*To* AUSTRIA] Sirrah, were I
at home,   290
At your den, sirrah, with your lioness,
I would set an oxhead to your lion's hide
And make a monster of you.
  AUST.   Peace! No more.
  BAST. Oh, tremble, for you hear the lion roar.
  K. JOHN. Up higher to the plain, where we'll set
forth   295
In best appointment all our regiments.
  BAST. Speed then, to take advantage of the field.
  K. PHI. It shall be so; and at the other hill
Command the rest to stand. God and our right!
                                               [*Exeunt.*]
    [*Here, after excursions,° enter the* HERALD
    of France, with trumpets, to the gates.]
  F. HER. You men of Angiers, open wide your
gates,   300

And let young Arthur, Duke of Bretagne, in,
Who by the hand of France this day hath made
Much work for tears in many an English mother,
Whose sons lie scattered on the bleeding ground.
Many a widow's husband groveling lies,   305
Coldly embracing the discolored earth,
And victory, with little loss, doth play
Upon the dancing banners of the French,
Who are at hand, triumphantly displayed,
To enter conquerors, and to proclaim   310
Arthur of Bretagne England's King and yours.
    [*Enter* ENGLISH HERALD, *with trumpet.*]
  E. HER. Rejoice, you men of Angiers, ring your
bells.
King John, your King and England's, doth ap-
proach,
Commander of this hot malicious day.   314
Their armors, that marched hence so silver-bright,
Hither return all gilt° with Frenchmen's blood.
There stuck no plume in any English crest
That is removèd by a staff° of France.
Our colors do return in those same hands   319
That did display them when we first marched forth;
And, like a jolly troop of huntsmen, come
Our lusty English, all with purpled hands,
Dyed in the dying slaughter of their foes.
Open your gates, and give the victors way.
  1. CIT.° Heralds, from off our towers we might
behold,   325
From first to last, the onset and retire
Of both your armies, whose equality
By our best eyes cannot be censurèd.°
Blood hath bought blood, and blows have an-
swered blows,
Strength matched with strength, and power con-
fronted power.   330
Both are alike, and both alike we like.
One must prove greatest. While they weigh so
even,
We hold our town for neither, yet for both.
    [*Re-enter the two* KINGS, *with their powers,
    severally.°*]
  K. JOHN. France, hast thou yet more blood to cast
away?
Say, shall the current of our right run on?   335
Whose passage, vexed with thy impediment,
Shall leave his native channel and o'erswell
With course disturbed even thy confining shores
Unless thou let his silver° water keep
A peaceful progress to the ocean.   340
  K. PHI. England, thou hast not saved one drop of
blood

---

276. and else: included.   281. compound: agree.   288. swinged:
beat up.   289. Sits . . . door: St. George and the Dragon was a
common inn-sign. See App. 12.   290. fence: fencing, how to
fight.   299. s.d., excursions: rapid entrances and exits of soldiers
to indicate a battle.

316. gilt: reddened. In Shakespeare's day gold and red were often
regarded as the same color. See *Macb*, II.ii.56,n.   318. staff:
spear.   325. 1. cit.: In F1 this speech is given to "Hubert."
328. censured: judged.   333. s.d., severally: by different doors.
339. silver: clear.

In this hot trial more than we of France —
Rather, lost more. And by this hand I swear,
That sways the earth this climate overlooks,°
Before we will lay down our just-borne arms,   345
We'll put thee down, 'gainst whom these arms we
      bear,
Or add a royal number to the dead,
Gracing the scroll that tells of this war's loss
With slaughter coupled to the name of Kings.°
BAST. Ha, Majesty! How high thy glory towers
When the rich blood of Kings is set on fire!   351
Oh, now doth Death line his dead chaps° with steel.
The swords of soldiers are his teeth, his fangs,
And now he feasts, mousing° the flesh of men,
In undetermined differences° of Kings.   355
Why stand these royal fronts° amazèd thus?
Cry " Havoc,"° Kings. Back to the stainèd field,
You equal potents,° fiery kindled spirits!
Then let confusion of one part confirm°
The other's peace. Till then, blows, blood, and
      death!   360
    K. JOHN. Whose party do the townsmen yet° ad-
    mit?
    K. PHI. Speak, citizens, for England. Who's your
    King?
    I. CIT. The King of England, when we know the
    King.
    K. PHI. Know him in us, that here hold up his
    right.
    K. JOHN. In us, that are our own great deputy
And bear possession of our person here,   366
Lord of our presence,° Angiers, and of you.
    I. CIT. A greater power than we denies all this;
And till it be undoubted, we do lock
Our former scruple° in our strong-barred gates,
Kinged of° our fears, until our fears, resolved,   371
Be by some certain king purged and deposed.
    BAST. By Heaven, these scroyles° of Angiers flout
      you, Kings,
And stand securely on their battlements,
As in a theater, whence they gape and point   375
At your industrious scenes and acts of death.
Your royal presences be ruled by me.
Do like the mutines° of Jerusalem,°
Be friends awhile and both conjointly bend
Your sharpest deeds of malice on this town.   380

By east and west let France and England mount
Their battering cannon, chargèd to the mouths,
Till their soul-fearing° clamors have brawled down
The flinty ribs of this contemptuous city.
I'd play incessantly upon these jades,°   385
Even till unfenced desolation°
Leave them as naked as the vulgar air.
That done, dissever° your united strengths,
And part your mingled colors once again.
Turn face to face and bloody point to point.   390
Then, in a moment, Fortune shall cull forth
Out of one side her happy minion,°
To whom in favor she shall give the day
And kiss him with a glorious victory.
How like you this wild counsel, mighty States?°
Smacks it not something of the policy?°   396
    K. JOHN. Now, by the sky that hangs above our
      heads,
I like it well. France, shall we knit our powers
And lay this Angiers even with the ground;
Then after fight who shall be King of it?   400
    BAST. An if thou hast the mettle of a king,
Being wronged as we are by this peevish town,
Turn thou the mouth of thy artillery,
As we will ours, against these saucy walls;
And when that we have dashed them to the ground,
Why then defy each other, and pell-mell°   406
Make work upon ourselves, for Heaven or Hell.
    K. PHI. Let it be so. Say, where will you assault?
    K. JOHN. We from the west will send destruction
Into this city's bosom.   410
    AUST. I from the north.
    K. PHI.   Our thunder from the south
Shall rain their drift° of bullets on this town.
    BAST. [*Aside*] Oh, prudent discipline!° From
      north to south!
Austria and France shoot in each other's mouth.
I'll stir them to it. Come, away, away!   415
    I. CIT. Hear us, great Kings. Vouchsafe awhile to
    stay,
And I shall show you peace and fair-faced league.°
Win you this city without stroke or wound.
Rescue those breathing lives to die in beds°
That here come sacrifices° for the field.   420
Perséver not,° but hear me, mighty Kings.
    K. JOHN. Speak on with favor.° We are bent° to
    hear.

---

344. **That . . . overlooks:** that rules the land beneath this sky.
348–49: **Gracing . . . Kings:** honoring the casualty lists with the
names of the Kings that will be killed in the war.   352. **chaps:**
cheeks.   354. **mousing:** tearing.   355. **undetermined differences:** unsettled quarrels.   356. **fronts:** lit., foreheads, persons.
357. **Cry "Havoc":** no prisoners! See *Caesar*, III.i.270–75.
358. **potents:** powers.   359. **confirm:** establish (by victory).
361. **yet:** now.   367. **Lord . . . presence:** King by my own right.
370. **scruple:** doubt.   371. **Kinged of:** ruled by.   373. **scroyles:**
scabs.   378. **mutines:** mutineers. **Jerusalem:** During the siege
of Jerusalem by the Roman general Titus, two warring factions
of the Jews agreed to sink their differences and join against the
common enemy.

383. **soul-fearing:** frightening.   385. **jades:** lit., poor nags.
386. **unfenced desolation:** their walls laid flat.   388. **dissever:** separate.   392. **minion:** darling.   395. **States:** Kings.
396. **Smacks . . . policy:** does it not taste like good political
sense? The Bastard is very pleased with himself at being able to
play the politician.   406. **pell-mell:** all in a heap.   412. **drift:**
shower.   413. **discipline:** tactics.   417. **fair-faced league:**
beautiful agreement.   419. **Rescue . . . beds:** i.e., save these
living soldiers to die naturally of old age.   420. **sacrifices:** i.e.,
doomed to die.   421. **Persever not:** do not continue with your
plan.   422. **favor:** my approval. **bent:** inclined.

1. CIT. That daughter there of Spain, the Lady
     Blanch,
Is niece to England. Look upon the years
Of Lewis the Dauphin and that lovely maid.   425
If lusty love should go in quest of beauty,
Where should he find it fairer than in Blanch?
If zealous love should go in search of virtue,
Where should he find it purer than in Blanch?
If love ambitious sought a match of birth,   430
Whose veins bound° richer blood than Lady
     Blanch?
Such° as she is, in beauty, virtue, birth,
Is the young Dauphin every way complete —
If not complete of, say he is not she;°
And she again wants nothing, to name want,   435
If want it be not that she is not he.
He is the half part of a blessèd man
Left to be finishèd by such as she;
And she a fair divided excellence
Whose fullness of perfection lies in him.   440
Oh, two such silver currents, when they join,
Do glorify the banks that bound them in;
And two such shores to two such streams made one,
Two such controlling bounds, shall you be, Kings,
To these two princes if you marry them.   445
This union shall do more than battery can
To our fast-closèd gates; for at this match,°
With swifter spleen° than powder can enforce,
The mouth of passage shall we fling wide ope
And give you entrance. But without this match,
The sea enragèd is not half so deaf,   451
Lions more confident, mountains and rocks
More free from motion — no, not Death himself
In mortal fury half so peremptory° —
As we to keep this city.
     BAST.   Here's a stay   455
That shakes the rotten carcass of old Death
Out of his rags!° Here's a large mouth, indeed,
That spits forth death and mountains, rocks and
     seas,
Talks as familiarly of roaring lions
As maids of thirteen do of puppy dogs!   460
What cannoneer begot this lusty blood?
He speaks plain cannon fire, and smoke, and
     bounce;°
He gives the bastinado° with his tongue.
Our ears are cudgeled. Not a word of his
But buffets better than a fist of France.   465
Zounds!° I was never so bethumped with words

Since I first called my brother's father dad.
     EL. Son, list to this conjunction,° make this
     match.
Give with our niece a dowry large enough;
For by this knot thou shalt so surely tie   470
Thy now unsured assurance° to the crown
That yon green boy shall have no sun to ripe
The bloom that promiseth a mighty fruit.
I see a yielding in the looks of France.
Mark, how they whisper. Urge them while their
     souls   475
Are capable of this ambition,°
Lest zeal,° now melted by the windy breath
Of soft petitions, pity and remorse,
Cool and congeal again to what it was.
     1. CIT. Why answer not the double Majesties
This friendly treaty of our threatened town?   481
     K. PHI. Speak England first, that hath been for-
     ward first
To speak unto this city. What say you?
     K. JOHN. If that the Dauphin there, thy princely
     son,
Can in this book of beauty read "I love,"   485
Her dowry shall weigh equal with a queen.
For Anjou, and fair Touraine, Maine, Poictiers,
And all that we upon this side the sea,
Except this city now by us besieged,
Find liable° to our crown and dignity   490
Shall gild her bridal bed and make her rich
In titles, honors, and promotions,°
As she in beauty, education, blood,
Holds hand with any princess of the world.
     K. PHI. What say'st thou, boy? Look in the lady's
     face.   495
     LEW. I do, my lord; and in her eye I find
A wonder, or a wondrous miracle,
The shadow of myself formed in her eye;
Which, being but the shadow of your son,
Becomes a sun and makes your son a shadow.   500
I do protest I never loved myself
Till now infixèd I beheld myself
Drawn in the flattering table° of her eye.
                       [*Whispers with* BLANCH.]
     BAST. Drawn° in the flattering table of her eye!
Hanged in the frowning wrinkle of her brow!
And quartered in her heart! He doth espy   506
     Himself love's traitor. This is pity now
That, hanged and drawn and quartered, there
     should be
In such a love so vile a lout as he.

---

431. **bound**: contain.   432–40. **Such . . . him**: i.e., these two young people need each other to make each other perfect. This is one of many verbose passages in this play. See *John* Intro. p. 541a.   434. **If . . . she**: i.e., she is the only thing he wants. 447. **match**: in the double sense of the marriage and the gunner's match which fires the cannon.   448. **spleen**: wrath.   454. **peremptory**: absolute.   455–57. **Here's . . . rags**: here is a sudden stop which shakes Death up; i.e., Death will be disappointed by this sudden end to the war.   462. **bounce**: bang.   463. **bastinado**: thrashing.   466. **Zounds**: by God's wounds.

468. **list . . . conjunction**: listen to this proposed agreement. 471. **unsured assurance**: uncertain claim.   476. **ambition**: desire — to come to terms.   477. **zeal**: i.e., for Arthur's cause, as in l. 565.   490. **liable**: subject.   492. **promotions**: dignities. 503. **table**: flat surface on which a picture is painted. 504. **Drawn**: the Bastard mocks Lewis's *drawn* by punning on "hung, drawn, and quartered" — the death of a traitor. See Gen. Intro. p. 27b.

BLAN. My° uncle's will in this respect is mine.
If he see aught in you that makes him like,   511
That anything he sees which moves his liking
I can with ease translate it to my will;
Or if you will, to speak more properly,
I will enforce it easily to my love.   515
Further I will not flatter you, my lord,
That all I see in you is worthy love
Than this — that nothing do I see in you,
Though churlish° thoughts themselves should be
    your judge,
That I can find should merit any hate.   520
    K. JOHN. What say these young ones? What say
    you, my Niece?
BLAN. That she is bound in honor still° to do
What you in wisdom still vouchsafe to say.
    K. JOHN. Speak then, Prince Dauphin. Can you
    love this lady?
    LEW. Nay, ask me if I can refrain from love,
For I do love her most unfeignedly.   526
    JOHN. Then do I give Volquessen,° Touraine,
    Maine,
Poictiers, and Anjou, these five provinces,
With her to thee; and this addition more,
Full thirty thousand marks° of English coin.   530
Philip of France, if thou be pleased withal,
Command thy son and daughter to join hands.
    K. PHI. It likes° us well. Young Princes, close
    your hands.
    AUST. And your lips too, for I am well assured
That I did so when I was first assured.°   535
    K. PHI. Now, citizens of Angiers, ope your gates,
Let in that amity which you have made.
For at Saint Mary's chapel presently°
The rites of marriage shall be solemnized.
Is not the Lady Constance in this troop?°   540
I know she is not, for this match made up
Her presence would have interrupted much.°
Where is she and her son? Tell me, who knows.
    LEW. She is sad and passionate° at your High-
    ness' tent.
    K. PHI. And, by my faith, this league that we
    have made   545
Will give her sadness very little cure.
Brother of England, how may we content
This widow lady? In her right we came;
Which we, God knows, have turned another way
To our own vantage.
    K. JOHN.   We will heal up all,   550
For we'll create young Arthur Duke of Bretagne
And Earl of Richmond, and this rich fair town
We make him lord of. Call the Lady Constance.

510-20. My . . . hate: Blanch speaks these words to Lewis only.
519. churlish: surly.   522. still: always.   527. Volquessen:
the district round Rouen.   530. mark: two-thirds of a pound,
13s. 4d.   533. likes: pleases.   535. assured: betrothed.   538. presently: immediately.   540. troop: party.   541–42. for . . . much:
if she had been here, she would have loudly interrupted this
proposal.   544. passionate: in a state of violent emotion.

Some speedy messenger bid her repair°
To our solemnity.° I trust we shall,   555
If not fill up the measure of her will,
Yet in some measure satisfy her so
That we shall stop her exclamation.
Go we as well as haste will suffer us
To this unlooked for, unprepared pomp.   560
            [*Exeunt all but the* BASTARD.]
    BAST. Mad world! Mad Kings! Mad composi-
    tion!°
John, to stop Arthur's title in the whole,
Hath willingly departed with° a part.
And France, whose armor Conscience buckled on,
Whom Zeal and Charity brought to the field   565
As God's own soldier, rounded in the ear
With that same purpose changer,° that sly Devil,
That broker that still breaks the pate of faith,
That daily break-vow — he that wins of all,
Of kings, of beggars, old men, young men, maids,
Who, having no external thing to lose   571
But the word " maid," cheats the poor maid of
    that —
That smooth-faced gentleman, tickling° Commod-
    ity,°
Commodity, the bias° of the world —
The world, who of itself is peisèd° well,   575
Made to run even upon even ground,
Till this advantage,° this vile-drawing bias,
This sway of motion, this Commodity,
Makes it take head from all indifferency,°
From all direction, purpose, course, intent —   580
And this same bias, this Commodity,
This bawd, this broker, this all-changing word,
Clapped on° the outward eye of fickle France,
Hath drawn him from his own determined aid,
From a resolved and honorable war   585
To a most base and vile-concluded peace.
And why rail I on this Commodity?
But for° because he hath not wooed me yet.
Not that I have the power to clutch my hand
When his fair angels° would salute my palm,   590
But for my hand, as unattempted yet,
Like a poor beggar raileth on the rich.
Well, whiles I am a beggar, I will rail
And say there is no sin but to be rich;
And being rich, my virtue then shall be   595
To say there is no vice but beggary.
Since kings break faith upon commodity,
Gain, be my lord,° for I will worship thee. [*Exit.*]

554. repair: come.   555. solemnity: marriage.   561. composition: agreement.   563. departed with: relinquished.   566–
67. rounded . . . changer: into whose ear that same corrupter
of morals has whispered.   573. tickling: flattering. Commodity:
self-interest.   574. bias: the weight in a bowling ball which
makes it take a curved course. See App. 13.   575. peised:
balanced, poised.   577. advantage: profitable deal.   579. indifference: impartiality.   583. Clapped on: blinding.   588. But
for: because.   590. angels: money, the angel being worth 10s.
See Pl. 10c.   598. Gain . . . lord: i.e., I will serve my own profit.

Act III

SCENE I. *The* FRENCH KING's *pavilion.*

[*Enter* CONSTANCE, ARTHUR, *and* SALISBURY.]

CON. Gone to be married! Gone to swear a peace!
False blood to false blood joined! Gone to be
   friends!
Shall Lewis have Blanch, and Blanch those prov-
   inces?
It is not so. Thou hast misspoke, misheard.
Be well advised,° tell o'er thy tale again.   5
It cannot be. Thou dost but say 'tis so.
I trust I may not trust thee, for thy word
Is but the vain breath of a common man.
Believe me, I do not believe thee, man.
I have a King's oath to the contrary.   10
Thou shalt be punished for thus frighting me,
For I am sick and capable of° fears,
Oppressed with wrongs and therefore full of fears,
A widow, husbandless, subject to fears,
A woman, naturally born to fears;   15
And though thou now confess thou didst but jest,
With my vexed spirits I cannot take a truce,
But they will quake and tremble all this day.
What dost thou mean by shaking of thy head?
Why dost thou look so sadly on my son?   20
What means that hand upon that breast of thine?
Why holds thine eye that lamentable rheum,°
Like a proud river peering o'er his bounds?°
Be these sad signs confirmers of thy words?
Then speak again — not all thy former tale,   25
But this one word, whether thy tale be true.
   SAL. As true as I believe you think them false
That give you cause to prove my saying true.
   CON. Oh, if thou teach me to believe this sorrow,
Teach thou this sorrow how to make me die,   30
And let belief and life encounter so
As doth the fury of two desperate men
Which in the very meeting fall and die.
Lewis marry Blanch! O boy, then where art thou?
France friend with England, what becomes of me?
Fellow, be gone. I cannot brook° thy sight.   36
This news hath made thee a most ugly man.
   SAL. What other harm have I, good lady, done,
But spoke the harm that is by others done?
   CON. Which harm within itself so heinous° is   40
As it makes harmful all that speak of it.
   ART. I do beseech you, madam, be content.
   CON. If thou, that bid'st me be content, wert
   grim,
Ugly, and slanderous to thy mother's womb,

Full of unpleasing blots and sightless° stains,   45
Lame, foolish, crookèd, swart,° prodigious,°
Patched with foul moles and eye-offending marks,
I would not care, I then would be content,
For then I should not love thee, no, nor thou
Become thy great birth nor deserve a crown.   50
But thou art fair, and at thy birth, dear boy,
Nature and Fortune joined to make thee great.°
Of Nature's gifts thou mayst with lilies boast,
And with the half-blown° rose. But Fortune, oh,
She is corrupted, changed, and won from thee.   55
She adulterates° hourly with thine uncle John,
And with her golden hand hath plucked on°
   France
To tread down fair respect of sovereignty,°
And made His Majesty the bawd to theirs.
France is a bawd to Fortune and King John —   60
That strumpet Fortune, that usurping John!
Tell me, thou fellow, is not France forsworn?°
Envenom° him with words, or get thee gone,
And leave those woes alone which I alone
Am bound to underbear.
   SAL.   Pardon me, madam,   65
I may not go without you to the Kings.
   CON. Thou mayst, thou shalt. I will not go with
   thee.
I will instruct my sorrows to be proud.
For Grief is proud and makes his owner stoop.
To me and to the state of my great grief   70
Let Kings assemble; for my grief's so great
That no supporter but the huge firm earth
Can hold it up. Here I and Sorrows sit.
Here is my throne; bid Kings come bow to it.
   [*Seats herself on the ground.*]
[*Enter* KING JOHN, KING PHILIP, LEWIS, BLANCH,
ELINOR, *the* BASTARD, AUSTRIA, *and* ATTENDANTS.]
   K. PHI. 'Tis true, fair Daughter; and this blessèd
   day   75
Ever in France shall be kept festival.
To solemnize this day the glorious sun
Stays in his course and plays the alchemist,
Turning with splendor of his precious eye
The meager cloddy earth to glittering gold.°   80
The yearly course that brings this day about
Shall never see it but a holiday.
   CON. A wicked day, and not a holy day!
   [*Rising.*]
What hath this day deserved? What hath it done
That it in golden° letters should be set   85
Among the high tides° in the calendar?

---

45. **sightless**: unsightly.   46. **swart**: black. **prodigious**: monstrous, unnatural.   52. **Nature . . . great**: See App. 18.   54. **half-blown**: half opened, and so at its most attractive.   56. **adulterates**: plays the harlot.   57. **plucked on**: encouraged.   58. **To . . . sovereignty**: to disgrace the honor of a King.   62. **forsworn**: perjured.   63. **Envenom**: poison.   78–80. **alchemist . . . gold**: See App. 21.   85. **golden**: red. See II.i.316,n and App. 2.   86. **high tides**: great festivals.

Act III, Sc. i: 5. **well advised**: very cautious.   12. **capable of**: liable to.   22. **rheum**: moisture.   23. **bounds**: banks.   36. **brook**: endure.   40. **heinous**: hateful.

Nay, rather turn this day out of the week,
This day of shame, oppression, perjury.
Or, if it must stand still, let wives with child
Pray that their burdens may not fall this day,   90
Lest that their hopes prodigiously° be crossed.
But on this day let seamen fear no wreck.
No bargains break that are not this day made.
This day, all things begun come to ill end,
Yea, faith itself to hollow falsehood change!   95
    K. PHI. By Heaven, lady, you shall have no
       cause
To curse the fair proceedings of this day.
Have I not pawned° to you my majesty?
    CON. You have beguiled me with a counterfeit
Resembling majesty, which, being touched° and
       tried,   100
Proves valueless. You are forsworn, forsworn.
You came in arms to spill mine enemies' blood,
But now in arms you strengthen it with yours.
The grappling vigor and rough frown of war
Is cold in amity° and painted° peace,   105
And our oppression° hath made up this league.
Arm, arm, you Heavens, against these perjured
       Kings!
A widow cries. Be husband to me, Heavens!
Let not the hours of this ungodly day
Wear out the day in peace, but, ere sunset,   110
Set arměd Discord 'twixt these perjured Kings!
Hear me, oh, hear me!
    AUST.   Lady Constance, peace!
    CON. War! War! No peace! Peace is to me a war.
O Lymoges!° O Austria! Thou dost shame
That bloody spoil.° Thou slave, thou wretch, thou
       coward!   115
Thou little valiant, great in villainy!
Thou ever strong upon the stronger side!
Thou Fortune's champion, that dost never fight
But when her humorous° ladyship is by
To teach thee safety! Thou art perjured too,   120
And soothest up° greatness. What a fool art thou,
A ramping° fool, to brag and stamp and swear
Upon my party!° Thou cold-blooded slave,
Hast thou not spoke like thunder on my side,
Been sworn my soldier, bidding me depend   125
Upon thy stars, thy fortune, and thy strength,
And dost thou now fall over° to my foes?
Thou wear a lion's hide! Doff it for shame,
And hang a calf's skin on those recreant° limbs.

AUST. Oh, that a man should speak those words
       to me!   130
    BAST. And hang a calf's skin on those recreant
       limbs.
    AUST. Thou darest not say so, villain, for thy life.
    BAST. And hang a calf's skin on those recreant
       limbs.
    K. JOHN. We like not this. Thou dost forget thy-
       self.   134
      [*Enter* PANDULPH.]
    K. PHI. Here comes the holy legate of the Pope.
    PAN. Hail, you anointed deputies of Heaven!°
To thee, King John, my holy errand is.
I, Pandulph, of fair Mílan Cardinal,
And from Pope Innocent the legate here,
Do in his name religiously demand   140
Why thou against the Church, our holy mother,
So willfully dost spurn;° and force perforce°
Keep Stephen Langton, chosen Archbishop
Of Canterbury, from that holy see.
This, in our aforesaid Holy Father's name,   145
Pope Innocent, I do demand of thee.
    K. JOHN. What earthy name to interrogatories°
Can task the free breath of a sacred king?°
Thou canst not, Cardinal, devise a name
So slight, unworthy, and ridiculous   150
To charge me to an answer, as the Pope.
Tell him this tale; and from the mouth of England
Add thus much more: that no Italian priest
Shall tithe or toll in our dominions,
But as we, under Heaven, are supreme head,   155
So under Him that great supremacy,
Where we do reign, we will alone uphold
Without the assistance of a mortal hand.
So tell the Pope, all reverence set apart
To him and his usurped authority.°   160
    K. PHI. Brother of England, you blaspheme in
       this.
    K. JOHN. Though you and all the kings of Chris-
       tendom
Are led so grossly by this meddling priest,
Dreading the curse that money may buy out,
And by the merit of vile gold, dross, dust,   165
Purchase corrupted pardon of a man
Who in that sale sells pardon from himself,
Though you and all the rest so grossly led
This juggling witchcraft with revénue cherish,
Yet I alone, alone do me oppose   170
Against the Pope and count his friends my foes.
    PAN. Then, by the lawful power that I have,

---

91. **prodigiously:** unnaturally. See l. 46.   98. **pawned:** pledged.
100. **touched:** tested. See *Rich III*, IV.ii.8,n.   105. **Is . . .
amity:** has grown cold in friendship. **painted:** false.   106. **our
oppression:** the oppression of us.   114. **Lymoges:** actually
Lymoges was *not* Austria. See App. 28.   115. **bloody spoil:**
i.e., the lion skin. See II.i.136.   119. **humorous:** changeable.
121. **soothest up:** dost flatter.   122. **ramping:** wild, lit., like a
beast rearing on its hind legs.   123. **Upon my party:** that he
was on my side.   127. **fall over:** go over, desert.   129. **recreant:**
cowardly.

136. **deputies of Heaven:** Kings were regarded as God's vice-
regents on earth. See *Rich II*, IV.i.125–29 and Gen. Intro. p. 20b.
142. **spurn:** kick contemptuously. **force perforce:** by forcible
means.   147–48. **What . . . king:** what mortal man can compel
a sacred king to answer questions.   147. **interrogatories:** questions put, usually on oath, in a legal examination. See *John*
Intro. p. 545a.   159–60. **all . . . authority:** i.e., since I have
no respect for him or for his authority which he falsely claims.

Thou shalt stand cursed and excommunicate.
And blessèd shall he be that doth revolt
From his allegiance to an heretic;   175
And meritorious shall that hand be called,
Canónizèd and worshipped as a saint,
That takes away by any secret course
Thy hateful life.
CON.   Oh, lawful let it be
That I have room with Rome° to curse awhile!
Good Father Cardinal, cry thou amen   181
To my keen curses, for without my wrong
There is no tongue hath power to curse him right.
PAN. There's law and warrant, lady, for my curse.
CON. And for mine too. When° law can do no
right,   185
Let it be lawful that law bar no wrong.
Law cannot give my child his kingdom here,
For he that holds his kingdom holds the law.
Therefore, since law itself is perfect wrong,
How can the law forbid my tongue to curse?   190
PAN. Philip of France, on peril of a curse,
Let go the hand of that archheretic,
And raise the power of France upon° his head
Unless he do submit himself to Rome.
EL. Look'st thou pale, France? Do not let go thy
hand.   195
CON. Look to that, Devil, lest that France repent,
And, by disjoining hands, Hell lose a soul.
AUST. King Philip, listen to the Cardinal.
BAST. And hang a calf's skin on his recreant
limbs.
AUST. Well, ruffian, I must pocket up° these
wrongs,   200
Because——
BAST. Your breeches best may carry them.
K. JOHN. Philip, what say'st thou to the Cardinal?
CON. What should he say, but as the Cardinal?
LEW. Bethink you, Father; for the difference
Is purchase of a heavy curse from Rome,   205
Or the light° loss of England for a friend.
Forgo° the easier.
BLAN.   That's the curse of Rome.
CON. O Lewis, stand fast! The Devil tempts thee
here
In likeness of a new untrimmèd° bride.
BLAN. The Lady Constance speaks not from her
faith,   210
But from her need.
CON.   Oh,° if thou grant my need,

Which only lives but by the death of faith,
That need must needs infer this principle——
That faith would live again by death of need.
Oh, then, tread down my need, and faith mounts
up;   215
Keep my need up, and faith is trodden down!
K. JOHN. The King is moved, and answers not to
this.
CON. Oh, be removed from him, and answer well!
AUST. Do so, King Philip. Hang no more in
doubt.
BAST. Hang nothing but a calf's skin, most sweet
lout.   220
K. PHI. I am perplexed, and know not what to
say.
PAN. What canst thou say but will perplex thee
more
If thou stand excommunicate and cursed?
K. PHI. Good Reverend Father, make my person
yours,
And tell me how you would bestow yourself.   225
This royal hand and mine are newly knit,
And the conjunction of our inward souls
Married in league, coupled and linked together
With all religious strength of sacred vows.
The latest breath that gave the sound of words
Was deep-sworn faith, peace, amity, true love 231
Between our kingdoms and our royal selves,
And even before this truce, but new before,°
No longer than we well could wash our hands
To clap° this royal bargain up of peace,   235
Heaven knows they were besmeared and overstained
With Slaughter's pencil,° where Revenge did paint
The fearful difference of incensèd Kings.
And shall these hands, so lately purged of blood,
So newly joined in love, so strong in both,   240
Unyoke this seizure and this kind regreet?°
Play fast and loose with faith? So jest with Heaven,
Make such unconstant children of ourselves
As now again to snatch our palm from palm,
Unswear faith sworn, and on the marriage bed
Of smiling Peace to march a bloody host   246
And make a riot on the gentle brow
Of true Sincerity? O holy sir,
My Reverend Father, let it not be so!
Out of your grace, devise, ordain, impose   250
Some gentle order, and then we shall be blest
To do your pleasure and continue friends.
PAN. All form is formless, order orderless,
Save what is opposite to England's love.   254
Therefore to arms! Be champion of our Church,
Or let the Church, our mother, breathe her curse,

180. room . . . Rome: The pun is used again in *Caesar*, I.ii.156.
185–90. When . . . curse: when the law is corrupt, it cannot
prevent wrong. The law cannot give my child his rightful kingdom because the law is controlled by the usurper who withholds
his kingdom. Therefore, since the law itself is corrupt, how can
it forbid me to curse? 193. upon: against. 200. pocket up:
submit to. 206. light: unimportant. 207. Forgo: relinquish.
209. untrimmed: still a virgin. 211–14. Oh . . . need: if you give
me what I need (i.e., just treatment)—for I lack justice because

of your lack of faith in dealing with me—that very lack of justice proves that if the lack was satisfied, then I should no longer
need justice. 233. but . . . before: only made just before.
235. clap: shake hands upon. 237. pencil: paint brush. 241. regreet: renewal of peace.

A mother's curse, on her revolting son.
France, thou mayst hold a serpent by the tongue,
A chafèd° lion by the mortal° paw,
A fasting tiger safer by the tooth,   260
Than keep in peace that hand which thou dost hold.
  K. PHI. I may disjoin my hand, but not my faith.
  PAN. So° makest thou faith an enemy to faith,
And like a civil war set'st oath to oath,   264
Thy tongue against thy tongue. Oh, let thy vow
First made to Heaven, first be to Heaven per-
    formed;
That is, to be the champion of our Church.
What since thou sworest is sworn against thyself,
And may not be performèd by thyself;
For that which thou hast sworn to do amiss   270
Is not amiss when it is truly done,
And being not done, where doing tends to ill,
The truth is then most done not doing it.
The better act of purposes mistook
Is to mistake again; though indirect,   275
Yet indirection thereby grows direct,
And falsehood falsehood cures, as fire cools fire
Within the scorchèd veins of one new-burned.
It is religion that doth make vows kept,
But thou hast sworn against religion   280
By what thou swear'st against the thing thou
    swear'st,
And makest an oath the surety for thy truth
Against an oath. The truth thou art unsure
To swear, swears only not to be forsworn;
Else what a mockery should it be to swear!   285
But thou dost swear only to be forsworn;
And most forsworn, to keep what thou dost swear.
Therefore thy later vows against thy first
Is in thyself rebellion to thyself,
And better conquest never canst thou make   290
Than arm thy constant and thy nobler parts
Against these giddy loose suggestions;
Upon which better part our prayers come in,
If thou vouchsafe them. But if not, then know
The peril of our curses light on thee   295
So heavy as thou shalt not shake them off,
But in despair die under their black weight.
  AUST. Rebellion, flat rebellion!
  BAST.   Will 't not be?
Will not a calf's skin stop that mouth of thine?

  LEW. Father, to arms!
  BLAN.   Upon thy wedding day?   300
Against the blood that thou hast married?
What, shall our feast be kept with slaughtered
    men?
Shall braying trumpets and loud churlish drums,
Clamors of Hell, be measures° to our pomp?°
O Husband, hear me! Aye, alack, how new   305
Is husband in my mouth! Even for that name
Which till this time my tongue did ne'er pronounce
Upon my knee I beg, go not to arms
Against mine uncle.
  CON.   Oh, upon my knee,
Made hard with kneeling, I do pray to thee,   310
Thou virtuous Dauphin, alter not the doom
Forethought° by Heaven!
  BLAN. Now shall I see thy love. What motive may
Be stronger with thee than the name of wife?
  CON. That which upholdeth him that thee up-
    holds,   315
His honor. Oh, thine honor, Lewis, thine honor!
  LEW. I muse° your Majesty doth seem so cold
When such profound respects° do pull you on.
  PAN. I will denounce a curse upon his head.
  K. PHI. Thou shalt not need. England, I will fall
    from thee.   320
  CON. Oh, fair return of banished majesty!
  EL. Oh, foul revolt of French inconstancy!°
  K. JOHN. France, thou shalt rue this hour within
    this hour.
  BAST. Old Time the clock setter, that bald sexton°
    Time,
Is it as he will?° Well then, France shall rue.   325
  BLAN. The sun's o'ercast with blood. Fair day,
    adieu!
Which is the side that I must go withal?
I am with both. Each army hath a hand,
And in their rage, I having hold of both,
They whirl asunder and dismember me.   330
Husband, I cannot pray that thou mayst win.
Uncle, I needs must pray that thou mayst lose.
Father, I may not wish the fortune thine.
Grandam, I will not wish thy wishes thrive.
Whoever wins, on that side shall I lose;   335
Assurèd loss before the match be played.
  LEW. Lady, with me, with me thy fortune lies.
  BLAN. There where my fortune lives, there my
    life dies.
  K. JOHN. Cousin,° go draw our puissance° to-
    gether.   [*Exit* BASTARD.]

---

259. **chafed**: irritated. **mortal**: deadly.   263–89. **So . . . thyself:**
This long and somewhat quibbling argument may be thus paraphrased: "By keeping your faith you are an enemy to the Faith,
and therefore guilty of rebellion. Your first duty is to the Church.
What you have sworn just now is contrary to your duty and
therefore may not be performed, since an oath to commit wrong
is not wrongfully broken when that wrong is not committed.
The best way to set a mistake right is to make a second mistake.
A falsehood committed against falsehood sets a crooked path
straight. Religion gives sanctity to an oath, but if you offend
against religion in an oath, then that oath demands to be broken;
or else it would be a mockery ever to make an oath. It follows
that your latest oath is a perjury of your former oaths."

304. **measures**: wedding dances. See App. 24. **pomp**: solemnity.
312. **Forethought**: predestined.   317. **muse**: wonder why.
318. **respects**: considerations.   322. **French inconstancy**: See
John Intro. p. 541b. 324. **bald sexton**: Time is so called because
the sexton is responsible for the clock on the tower of the village
church.   325. **Is . . . will**: i.e., time will show the future.
339. **Cousin**: kinsman. The word is used of any near relation.
puissance: power, army.

France, I am burned up with inflaming wrath,   340
A rage whose heat hath this condition,
That nothing can allay, nothing but blood,
The blood, and dearest-valued blood, of France.
  K. PHI. Thy rage shall burn thee up, and thou
    shalt turn
To ashes, ere our blood shall quench that fire.   345
Look to thyself, thou art in jeopardy.
  K. JOHN. No more than he that threats. To arms
    let's hie!°   [*Exeunt.*]

SCENE II. *The same. Plains near Angiers.*

[*Alarums, excursions. Enter the* BASTARD,
with AUSTRIA'S *head.*]

BAST. Now, by my life, this day grows wondrous
  hot.
Some airy devil hovers in the sky
And pours down mischief. Austria's head lie there
While Philip breathes.°
  [*Enter* KING JOHN, ARTHUR, *and* HUBERT.]
  K. JOHN. Hubert, keep this boy. Philip, make
    up.°   5
My mother is assailèd in our tent
And ta'en, I fear.
  BAST.   My lord, I rescued her.
Her Highness is in safety, fear you not.
But on, my liege, for very little pains
Will bring this labor to an happy end. [*Exeunt.*] 10

SCENE III. *The same.*

[*Alarums, excursions, retreat.° Enter* KING JOHN,
ELINOR, ARTHUR, *the* BASTARD, HUBERT, *and* LORDS.]
  K. JOHN. [*To* ELINOR] So shall it be. Your Grace
    shall stay behind
So strongly guarded. [*To* ARTHUR] Cousin, look not
    sad.
Thy grandam loves thee, and thy uncle will
As dear be to thee as thy father was.
  ART. Oh, this will make my mother die with
    grief!   5
  K. JOHN. [*To the* BASTARD] Cousin, away for
    England! Haste before.
And, ere° our coming, see thou shake the bags
Of hoarding abbots; imprisoned angels°
Set at liberty. The fat ribs of peace
Must by the hungry now be fed upon.   10
Use our commission in his utmost force.°

BAST. Bell, book, and candle° shall not drive me
  back
When gold and silver becks° me to come on.
I leave your Highness. Grandam, I will pray,
If ever I remember to be holy,   15
For your fair safety; so, I kiss your hand.
  EL. Farewell, gentle Cousin.
  K. JOHN.   Coz,° farewell. [*Exit* BASTARD.]
  EL. Come hither, little kinsman. Hark, a word.
  K. JOHN. Come hither, Hubert. O my gentle Hu-
    bert,
We owe thee much! Within this wall of flesh   20
There is a soul counts thee her creditor
And with advantage° means to pay thy love.
And, my good friend, thy voluntary oath
Lives in this bosom, dearly cherishèd.
Give me thy hand. I had a thing to say,   25
But I will fit it with some better time.
By Heaven, Hubert, I am almost ashamed
To say what good respect° I have of thee.
  HUB. I am much bounden° to your Majesty.
  K. JOHN. Good friend, thou hast no cause to say
    so yet,   30
But thou shalt have; and creep time ne'er so slow,
Yet it shall come for me to do thee good.
I had a thing to say, but let it go.
The sun is in the heaven, and the proud day,
Attended with the pleasures of the world,   35
Is all too wanton and too full of gawds°
To give me audience. If the midnight bell
Did with his iron tongue and brazen mouth
Sound on into the drowsy ear of night;
If this same were a churchyard where we stand,   40
And thou possessèd with a thousand wrongs;
Or if that surly spirit, melancholy,
Had baked thy blood and made it heavy-thick,
Which else runs tickling up and down the veins,
Making that idiot, Laughter, keep men's eyes   45
And strain their cheeks to idle merriment,
A passion hateful to my purposes;
Or if that thou couldst see me without eyes,
Hear me without thine ears, and make reply
Without a tongue, using conceit° alone,   50
Without eyes, ears, and harmful sound of words;
Then, in despite° of brooded° watchful day,
I would into thy bosom pour my thoughts.
But, ah, I will not! Yet I love thee well,
And, by my troth,° I think thou lovest me well. 55
  HUB. So well that what you bid me undertake,
Though that my death were adjunct° to my act,
By Heaven, I would do it.
  K. JOHN.   Do not I know thou wouldst?

---

347. hie: hasten.
  Sc. ii: 4. breathes: rests.   5. make up: go up to the front
line.
  Sc. iii: s.d., Alarums . . . retreat: noises of trumpet and drum
indicating battle.   7. ere: before.   8. angels: i.e., coins worth
10s. See Pl. 10c.   11. Use . . . force: use the powers that I have
given you to the utmost.

12. Bell . . . candle: used in the ceremonial of solemn excommunication.   13. becks: beckons.   17. Coz: cousin, kinsman.
22. advantage: interest.   28. respect: opinion.   29. bounden:
bound, indebted to.   36. gawds: frivolous trifles.   50. conceit:
imagination.   52. despite: spite. brooded: brooding.   55. troth:
truth.   57. adjunct: fixed to, followed on.

Good Hubert, Hubert, Hubert, throw thine eye
On yon young boy. I'll tell thee what, my friend,
He is a very serpent in my way,   61
And wheresoe'er this foot of mine doth tread,
He lies before me. Dost thou understand me?
Thou art his keeper.
HUB.   And I'll keep him so
That he shall not offend your Majesty.
K. JOHN.   Death. 65
HUB. My lord?
K. JOHN.   A grave.
HUB.   He shall not live.
K. JOHN.   Enough.
I could be merry now. Hubert, I love thee.
Well, I'll not say what I intend for thee.
Remember. Madam, fare you well.
I'll send those powers o'er to your Majesty.   70
EL. My blessing go with thee!
K. JOHN.   For England, Cousin, go.
Hubert shall be your man, attend on you
With all true duty. On toward Calais, ho! [*Exeunt.*]

SCENE IV. *The same. The* FRENCH KING'S *tent.*

[*Enter* KING PHILIP, LEWIS, PANDULPH, *and*
ATTENDANTS.]
K. PHI. So, by a roaring tempest on the flood,
A whole armado° of convicted sail°
Is scattered and disjoined from fellowship.
PAN. Courage and comfort! All shall yet go well.
K. PHI. What can go well when we have run so
ill?   5
Are we not beaten? Is not Angiers lost?
Arthur ta'en prisoner? Divers dear friends slain?
And bloody England into England gone,
O'erbearing interruption,° spite of France?
LEW. What° he hath won, that hath he fortified.
So hot a speed with such advice disposed,   11
Such temperate order in so fierce a cause,
Doth want example. Who hath read or heard
Of any kindred action like to this?
K. PHI. Well could I bear that England had this
praise,   15
So we could find some pattern of our shame.°
[*Enter* CONSTANCE.]
Look, who comes here! A grave unto a soul,°
Holding the eternal spirit against her will
In the vile prison of afflicted breath.°

I prithee, lady, go away with me.   20
CON. Lo, now! Now see the issue° of your peace.
K. PHI. Patience, good lady! Comfort, gentle Con-
stance!
CON. No, I defy all counsel, all redress,
But that which ends all counsel, true redress,
Death, Death. O amiable lovely Death!   25
Thou odoriferous stench! Sound rottenness!
Arise forth from the couch of lasting night,
Thou hate and terror to prosperity,
And I will kiss thy détestable bones,°
And put my eyeballs in thy vaulty brows,   30
And ring these fingers with thy household worms,
And stop this gap of breadth with fulsome dust,
And be a carrion monster° like thyself.
Come, grin on me, and I will think thou smilest
And buss° thee as thy wife. Misery's love,   35
Oh, come to me!
K. PHI.   O fair affliction, peace!
CON. No, no, I will not, having breath to cry.
Oh, that my tongue were in the thunder's mouth!
Then with a passion would I shake the world,
And rouse from sleep that fell anatomy°   40
Which cannot hear a lady's feeble voice,
Which scorns a modern° invocation.
PAN. Lady, you utter madness, and not sorrow.
CON. Thou art not holy to belie me so.
I am not mad. This hair I tear is mine.   45
My name is Constance. I was Geffrey's wife.
Young Arthur is my son, and he is lost.
I am not mad. I would to Heaven I were!
For then, 'tis like I should forget myself.
Oh, if I could, what grief should I forget!   50
Preach some philosophy to make me mad,
And thou shalt be canónized, Cardinal;
For, being not mad, but sensible of grief,
My reasonable part produces reason
How I may be delivered of these woes,   55
And teaches me to kill or hang myself.
If I were mad, I should forget my son
Or madly think a babe of clouts° were he.
I am not mad. Too well, too well I feel
The different plague of each calamity.   60
K. PHI. Bind up those tresses. Oh, what love I
note
In the fair multitude of those her hairs!
Where° but by chance a silver drop hath fallen,
Even to that drop ten thousand wiry° friends
Do glue themselves in sociable grief,   65
Like true, inseparable, faithful loves
Sticking together in calamity.

Sc. iv: 2. **armado:** fleet. **convicted sail:** overwhelmed ships.
9. **interruption:** attempts to stop him.   10–13. **What . . . example:** John has put the places he has won into a state of defense.
The speed of his victories and the skill that he has shown in this
fierce war are without precedent.   16. **So . . . shame:** if I
could find some instance of another nation similarly disgraced.
17. **grave . . . soul:** i.e., one unwilling to live.   18–19. **Holding
. . . breath:** so long as she is alive, her soul is kept unwillingly in
the prison of flesh.

21. **issue:** result, sequel.   29. **bones:** Death is imagined as a
skeleton. See Pl. 12f.   33. **carrion monster:** loathsome carcass.
35. **buss:** kiss.   40. **anatomy:** skeleton.   42. **modern:** slight,
commonplace.   58. **babe of clouts:** rag doll.   63–65. **Where
. . . grief:** where a tear has dropped among her disheveled hairs,
they cling together as if sharing her grief.   64. **wiry:** Hairs are
often compared to wires by Elizabethan poets. See Sonnet 130:4.

CON. To England, if you will.

K. PHI.   Bind up your hairs.

CON. Yes, that I will, and wherefore will I do it?
I tore them from their bonds and cried aloud,   70
" Oh, that these hands could so redeem my son
As they have given these hairs their liberty!"
But now I envy at° their liberty
And will again commit them to their bonds
Because my poor child is a prisoner.   75
And, Father Cardinal, I have heard you say
That we shall see and know our friends in Heaven.
If that be true, I shall see my boy again;
For since the birth of Cain, the first male child,
To him that did but yesterday suspire,°   80
There was not such a gracious creature born.
But now will canker° sorrow eat my bud
And chase the native beauty from his cheek,
And he will look as hollow as a ghost,
As dim and meager as an ague's fit,   85
And so he'll die; and, rising so again,
When I shall meet him in the Court of Heaven,
I shall not know him. Therefore never, never
Must I behold my pretty Arthur more.   89

PAN. You hold too heinous a respect of grief.°

CON. He talks to me that never had a son.

K. PHI. You are as fond of grief as of your child.

CON. Grief fills the room up of my absent child,
Lies in his bed, walks up and down with me,
Puts on his pretty looks, repeats his words,   95
Remembers° me of all his gracious parts,
Stuffs out his vacant garments with his form;
Then have I reason to be fond of Grief.
Fare you well. Had you such a loss as I,
I could give better comfort than you do.   100
I will not keep this form° upon my head
When there is such disorder in my wit.
O Lord! My boy, my Arthur, my fair son!
My life, my joy, my food, my all the world!   104
My widow-comfort, and my sorrows' cure! [*Exit.*]

K. PHI. I fear some outrage, and I'll follow her.
                                          [*Exit.*]

LEW. There's nothing in this world can make me
   joy.
Life is as tedious as a twice-told tale
Vexing the dull ear of a drowsy man,
And bitter shame hath spoiled the sweet world's
   taste,   110
That it yields naught but shame and bitterness.

PAN. Before the curing of a strong disease,
Even in the instant of repair and health,
The fit is strongest. Evils that take leave,
On their departure most of all show evil.   115
What have you lost by losing of this day?

LEW. All days of glory, joy, and happiness.

PAN. If you had won it, certainly you had.°
No, no; when Fortune means to men most good,
She looks upon them with a threatening eye.   120
'Tis strange to think how much King John hath lost
In this which he accounts so clearly won.
Are not you grieved that Arthur is his prisoner?

LEW. As heartily as he is glad he hath him.

PAN. Your mind is all as youthful as your blood.
Now hear me speak with a prophetic spirit;   126
For even the breath of what I mean to speak
Shall blow each dust, each straw, each little rub,°
Out of the path which shall directly lead
Thy foot to England's throne. And therefore mark:
John hath seized Arthur, and it cannot be   131
That, whiles warm life plays in that infant's veins,
The misplaced John should entertain an hour,
One minute, nay, one quiet breath of rest.
A scepter snatched with an unruly hand   135
Must be as boisterously° maintained as gained,
And he that stands upon a slippery place
Makes nice of no vile hold to stay him up.°
That John may stand, then Arthur needs must
   fall.
So be it, for it cannot be but so.   140

LEW. But what shall I gain by young Arthur's
   fall?

PAN. You, in the right of Lady Blanch, your wife,
May then make all the claim that Arthur did.

LEW. And lose it, life and all, as Arthur did.

PAN. How green you are and fresh in this old
   world!   145
John lays you plots.° The times conspire with you.
For he that steeps his safety in true blood
Shall find but bloody safety and untrue.°
This act so evilly born shall cool the hearts
Of all his people and freeze up their zeal,   150
That none so small advantage shall step forth
To check his reign,° but they will cherish it;
No natural exhalation° in the sky,
No scope of nature,° no distempered° day,
No common wind, no customèd event,   155
But they will pluck away° his natural cause
And call them meteors,° prodigies, and signs,
Abortives,° presages, and tongues of Heaven,
Plainly denouncing vengeance upon John.

---

73. **envy at:** hate.   80. **suspire:** draw breath.   82. **canker:**
maggot.   90. **You . . . grief:** you take too hateful a view of
sorrow.   96. **Remembers:** reminds.   101. **form:** order.

118. **If . . . had:** i.e., you would be unlucky if you had won
this war. Pandulph explains this cryptic remark in ll. 125–80.
128. **rub:** impediment.   136. **boisterously:** violently.   138. **Makes
. . . up:** is not particular what means he uses to keep his hold.
146. **John . . . plots:** the plots which John makes are for your
advantage.   147–48. **For . . . untrue:** the man who makes himself safe by shedding the blood of the true King (Arthur) will
find that his safety is bloody and false.   151–52. **That . . . reign:**
his people will take every opportunity (*advantage*) to end (*check*)
his rule.   153. **exhalation:** meteor.   154. **scope of nature:**
natural occurrence. **distempered:** stormy.   156. **pluck away:**
misinterpret.   157. **meteors:** comets, always regarded as signs
of disaster.   158. **Abortives:** unnatural births (as of two-headed
calves).

LEW. May be he will not touch young Arthur's
   life,   160
But hold himself safe in his prisonment.
   PAN. Oh, sir, when he shall hear of your ap-
     proach,
If that young Arthur be not gone already,
Even at that news he dies; and then the hearts
Of all his people shall revolt from him   165
And kiss the lips of unacquainted change,°
And pick strong matter of revolt and wrath
Out of the bloody fingers' ends of John.
Methinks I see this hurly° all on foot.
And, oh, what better matter breeds° for you   170
Than I have named! The bastard Faulconbridge
Is now in England, ransacking the Church,
Offending charity. If but a dozen French
Were there in arms, they would be as a call°
To train° ten thousand English to their side,   175
Or as a little snow, tumbled about,
Anon becomes a mountain. O noble Dauphin,
Go with me to the King. 'Tis wonderful
What may be wrought out of their discontent
Now that their souls are topful of offense.°   180
For England go. I will whet on the King.
   LEW. Strong reasons make strong actions. Let us
     go.
If you say aye, the King will not say no. [*Exeunt.*]

Act IV

SCENE I. *A room in a castle.*

[*Enter* HUBERT *and* EXECUTIONERS.]
   HUB. Heat me these irons hot, and look thou
     stand
Within the arras.° When I strike my foot
Upon the bosom of the ground, rush forth,
And bind the boy which you shall find with me
Fast to the chair. Be heedful. Hence, and watch. 5
   I. EX. I hope your warrant° will bear out° the
     deed.
   HUB. Uncleanly scruples! Fear not you. Look to 't.
                       [*Exeunt* EXECUTIONERS.]
Young lad, come forth. I have to say with° you.
                    [*Enter* ARTHUR.]
   ART. Good morrow, Hubert.

   HUB.   Good morrow, little Prince.
   ART. As little Prince, having so great a title   10
To be more Prince, as may be.° You are sad.
   HUB. Indeed, I have been merrier.
   ART.   Mercy on me!
Methinks no body should be sad but I.
Yet I remember, when I was in France,
Young gentlemen would be as sad as night   15
Only for wantonness.° By my Christendom,°
So° I were out of prison and kept sheep,
I should be as merry as the day is long;
And so I would be here, but that I doubt°
My uncle practices° more harm to me.   20
He is afraid of me, and I of him.
Is it my fault that I was Geffrey's son?
No, indeed, is't not, and I would to Heaven
I were your son, so you would love me, Hubert.
   HUB. [*Aside*] If I talk to him, with his innocent
     prate   25
He will awake my mercy, which lies dead.
Therefore I will be sudden, and dispatch.
   ART. Are you sick, Hubert? You look pale today.
In sooth, I would you were a little sick
That I might sit all night and watch with you.   30
I warrant I love you more than you do me.
   HUB. [*Aside*] His words do take possession of my
     bosom.
Read here, young Arthur.   [*Showing a paper.*]
[*Aside*]   How now, foolish rheum!
Turning dispiteous° torture out of door!
I must be brief, lest resolution drop   35
Out at mine eyes in tender womanish tears. —
Can you not read it? Is it not fair writ?
   ART. Too fairly, Hubert, for so foul effect.
Must you with hot irons burn out both mine eyes?
   HUB. Young boy, I must.
   ART.   And will you?
   HUB.   And I will.   40
   ART. Have you the heart? When your head did
     but ache,
I knit my handkerchief about your brows —
The best I had, a Princess wrought it me° —
And I did never ask it you again;
And with my hand at midnight held your head,   45
And like the watchful minutes to the hour,
Still and anon° cheered up the heavy time,
Saying, "What lack you?" and "Where lies your
     grief?"°
Or "What good love may I perform for you?"
Many a poor man's son would have lien° still   50

---

166. kiss . . . change: gladly welcome a new order.   169. hurly:
turmoil.   170. breeds: is ripening.   174. call: decoy bird.
175. train: allure.   180. topful of offense: full of grievances.
   Act IV, Sc. i: 2. Within . . . arras: behind the curtains.
6. warrant: written orders. bear out: justify.   8. to . . . with:
something to say to.

10–11. As . . . be: although I should rightfully be a great Prince,
I am as little a Prince as can be.   16. wantonness: affectation.
See App. 4. Christendom: faith as a Christian.   17. So: if only.
19. doubt: suspect.   20. practices: plots.   34. dispiteous:
pitiless.   43. wrought it me: made it for me.   47. Still . . .
anon: continually from time to time.   48. grief: pain.   50. lien:
lain.

And ne'er have spoke a loving word to you;
But you at your sick service° had a Prince.
Nay, you may think my love was crafty love,
And call it cunning. Do, an if you will.
If Heaven be pleased that you must use me ill,   55
Why then you must. Will you put out mine eyes?
These eyes that never did nor never shall
So much as frown on you?
    HUB.   I have sworn to do it,
And with hot irons must I burn them out.
    ART. Ah, none but in this iron age would do it!
The iron of itself, though heat red-hot,   61
Approaching near these eyes, would drink my tears
And quench his fiery indignation
Even in the matter° of mine innocence —
Nay, after that, consume away in rust,   65
But for containing fire to harm mine eye.
Are you more stubborn-hard than hammered iron?°
An if an angel should have come to me
And told me Hubert should put out mine eyes,
I would not have believed him — no tongue but
    Hubert's.   70
    HUB. Come forth.   [Stamps.]
[Re-enter EXECUTIONERS, with a cord, irons, &c.]
Do as I bid you do.
    ART. Oh, save me, Hubert, save me! My eyes are
    out
Even with the fierce looks of these bloody men.   74
    HUB. Give me the iron, I say, and bind him here.
    ART. Alas, what need you be so boisterous-rough?
I will not struggle, I will stand stone-still.
For Heaven sake, Hubert, let me not be bound!
Nay, hear me, Hubert, drive these men away,
And I will sit as quiet as a lamb.   80
I will not stir, nor wince, nor speak a word,
Nor look upon the iron angerly.
Thrust but these men away, and I'll forgive you,
Whatever torment you do put me to.   84
    HUB. Go, stand within. Let me alone with him.
    I. EX. I am best pleased to be from° such a deed.
                          [Exeunt EXECUTIONERS.]
    ART. Alas, I then have chid away my friend!
He hath a stern look, but a gentle heart.
Let him come back, that his compassion may
Give life to yours.
    HUB.   Come, boy, prepare yourself.   90
    ART. Is there no remedy?
    HUB.   None, but to lose your eyes.
    ART. Oh, Heaven, that there were but a mote° in
    yours,
A grain, a dust, a gnat, a wandering hair,
Any annoyance in that precious sense!°

Then, feeling what small things are boisterous
    there,   95
Your vile intent must needs seem horrible.
    HUB. Is this your promise? Go to, hold your
    tongue.
    ART. Hubert, the utterance of a brace of tongues
Must needs want pleading for a pair of eyes.°
Let me not hold my tongue, let me not, Hubert;
Or, Hubert, if you will, cut out my tongue,   101
So I may keep mine eyes. Oh, spare mine eyes,
Though to no use but still to look on you!
Lo, by my troth, the instrument is cold
And would not harm me.
    HUB.   I can heat it, boy.   105
    ART. No, in good sooth. The fire is dead with
    grief,
Being create for comfort, to be used
In undeserved extremes.° See else yourself.
There is no malice in this burning coal.
The breath of Heaven hath blown his spirit out
And strewed repentant ashes on his head.   111
    HUB. But with my breath I can revive it, boy.
    ART. An if you do, you will but make it blush
And glow with shame of your proceedings, Hubert.
Nay, it perchance will sparkle in your eyes,   115
And, like a dog that is compelled to fight,
Snatch at his master that doth tarre° him on.
All things that you should use to do me wrong
Deny their office. Only you do lack
That mercy which fierce fire and iron extends,   120
Creatures of note for mercy-lacking uses.°
    HUB. Well, see to live. I will not touch thine eye
For all the treasure that thine uncle owes.°
Yet am I sworn, and I did purpose, boy,
With this same very iron to burn them out.   125
    ART. Oh, now you look like Hubert! All this
    while
You were disguised.
    HUB.   Peace. No more. Adieu.
Your uncle must not know but° you are dead.
I'll fill these doggèd° spies with false reports.
And, pretty child, sleep doubtless and secure°   130
That Hubert, for the wealth of all the world,
Will not offend thee.
    ART.   Oh, Heaven! I thank you, Hubert.
    HUB. Silence. No more. Go closely° in with me.
Much danger do I undergo for thee.   [Exeunt.]

98–99. the . . . eyes: even if I had two tongues, they could not
plead eloquently enough for two eyes.   108. undeserved extremes: extreme and undeserved cruelty.   117. tarre: encourage
to fight.   119–21. Only . . . uses: you alone are without the
mercy to be found in fire and iron (because even they have gone
cold rather than hurt me), and they are well known for the cruel
uses to which they are put.   123. owes: owns.   128. but:
otherwise than that.   129. dogged: doglike, cruel.   130. doubtless . . . secure: without anxiety and care.   133. closely:
secretly.

52. at . . . service: at your service when you were sick.   64. matter: substance, i.e., tears.   67. hammered iron: iron beaten into
an instrument of torture.   86. to be from: to be free from.
92. mote: speck of dust.   94. sense: i.e., sight, eyes.

SCENE II. KING JOHN's *palace.*

[*Enter* KING JOHN, PEMBROKE, SALISBURY,
and other LORDS.]

K. JOHN. Here once again we sit, once again
crowned,
And looked upon, I hope, with cheerful eyes.
PEM. This " once again," but that your High-
ness pleased,
Was once° superfluous. You were crowned before,
And that high royalty was ne'er plucked off,　　5
The faiths of men ne'er stainèd with revolt.
Fresh expectation troubled not the land
With any longed-for change or better state.
SAL. Therefore, to be possessed with double
pomp,°
To guard° a title that was rich before,　　　　10
To gild refinèd gold, to paint the lily,
To throw a perfume on the violet,
To smooth the ice, or add another hue
Unto the rainbow, or with taper light°
To seek the beauteous eye of Heaven to garnish　15
Is wasteful and ridiculous excess.
PEM. But that your royal pleasure must be done,
This act is as an ancient tale new told
And in the last repeating troublesome,
Being urgèd° at a time unseasonable.　　　　20
SAL. In this the antique and well noted face
Of plain old form is much disfigurèd,
And, like a shifted wind unto a sail,
It makes the course of thoughts to fetch about,°
Startles and frights consideration,°　　　　　25
Makes sound opinion sick and truth suspected
For putting on so new a fashioned robe.
PEM. When workmen strive to do better than
well,
They do confound their skill in covetousness,°
And oftentimes excusing of a fault　　　　　30
Doth make the fault the worse by the excuse,
As patches set upon a little breach°
Discredit more in hiding of the fault
Than did the fault before it was so patched.
SAL. To this effect, before you were new crowned,
We breathed our counsel; but it pleased your High-
ness　　　　　　　　　　　　　　　　　36
To overbear it, and we are all well pleased,
Since all and every part of what we would　　38
Doth make a stand at what your Highness will.°
K. JOHN. Some reasons of this double coronation

I have possessed you with° and think them strong;
And more, more strong (then lesser is my fear),
I shall indue you with.° Meantime but ask
What you would have reformed that is not well,
And well shall you perceive how willingly　　45
I will both hear and grant you your requests.
PEM. Then I — as one that am the tongue of
these
To sound the purposes of all their hearts,
Both for myself and them, but, chief of all,
Your safety, for the which myself and them　　50
Bend their best studies — heartily request
The enfranchisement° of Arthur, whose restraint
Doth move the murmuring lips of discontent
To break into this dangerous argument:
If° what in rest you have in right you hold,　　55
Why then your fears, which, as they say, attend
The steps of wrong, should move you to mew up
Your tender kinsman, and to choke his days
With barbarous ignorance and deny his youth
The rich advantage of good exercise.°　　　　60
That the time's enemies may not have this
To grace occasions,° let it be our suit
That you have bid us ask his liberty,°
Which for our goods we do no further ask
Then whereupon our weal,° on you depending,
Counts it your weal he have his liberty.　　　66
[*Enter* HUBERT.]
K. JOHN. Let it be so. I do commit his youth
To your direction. Hubert, what news with you?
[*Taking him apart.*]
PEM. This is the man should do the bloody deed.
He showed his warrant to a friend of mine.　　70
The image° of a wicked heinous fault
Lives in his eye. That close aspect° of his
Does show the mood of a much troubled breast,
And I do fearfully believe 'tis done,
What we so feared he had a charge to do.　　75
SAL. The color of the King doth come and go
Between his purpose and his conscience,
Like heralds 'twixt two dreadful battles° set.
His passion° is so ripe it needs must break.

Sc. ii: **4. once:** i.e., once was enough.　**9. possessed . . .
pomp:** to be given solemn possession of your crown twice over.
10. guard: ornament. See *M of Ven.*, II.ii.164,n.　**14. taper light:**
the light of a candle.　**20. urged:** insisted on.　**24. fetch about:**
change direction.　**25. consideration:** thought.　**29. confound
. . . covetousness:** spoil what they have done well through excessive ambition.　**32. breach:** hole.　**38–39. Since . . . will:**
since our desires in the matter are halted by your commands.

41. possessed . . . with: informed you about.　**42–43. And . . .
with:** The interpretation of these lines has caused much discussion. The simplest explanation is probably to take *then lesser
is my fear* as an aside, and to paraphrase: "And I will acquaint
you with other reasons far more weighty (and which will relieve
my mind by removing my fears), namely, the death of Arthur."
52. enfranchisement: setting at liberty.　**55–58. If . . . kinsman:** if you hold rightfully what you possess peaceably, why
then do fears, which are said only to accompany wrongdoing,
cause you to cage up (*mew*) your nephew?　**60. exercise:**
education.　**61–62. That . . . occasions:** in order that the enemies of the present state of things may not have this complaint
to use to suit their purposes (*occasions*).　**62–63. let . . . liberty:**
let it be our petition (*suit*) that you have asked us to request that
he shall be set free.　**65. weal:** welfare.　**71. image:** reflection.
72. close aspect: suspicious look.　**78. battles:** armies.　**79. passion:** emotion.

PEM. And when it breaks,° I fear will issue
   thence   80
The foul corruption of a sweet child's death.
  K. JOHN. We cannot hold mortality's strong
   hand.°
Good lords, although my will to give is living,
The suit which you demand is gone and dead.
He tells us Arthur is deceased tonight.   85
  SAL. Indeed we feared his sickness was past cure.
  PEM. Indeed we heard how near his death he was
Before the child himself felt he was sick.
This must be answered either here or hence.
  K. JOHN. Why do you bend such solemn brows
   on me?   90
Think you I bear the shears of destiny?
Have I commandment on the pulse of life?
  SAL. It is apparent foul play, and 'tis shame
That greatness should so grossly offer it.
So thrive it in your game!° And so, farewell.   95
  PEM. Stay yet, Lord Salisbury. I'll go with thee
And find the inheritance of this poor child,
His little kingdom of a forcèd grave.
That blood which owed the breadth of all this isle
Three foot of it doth hold. Bad world the while!°
This must not be thus borne. This will break out
To all our sorrows, and ere long I doubt.   102
                  [*Exeunt* LORDS.]
  K. JOHN. They burn in indignation. I repent.
There is no sure foundation set on blood,
No certain life achieved by others' death.   105
           [*Enter a* MESSENGER.]
A fearful° eye thou hast. Where is that blood
That I have seen inhabit in those cheeks?
So foul a sky clears not without a storm.
Pour down thy weather. How goes all in France?
  MESS. From France to England. Never such a
   power   110
For any foreign preparation
Was levied in the body of a land.
The copy of your speed is learned by them,°
For when you should be told they do prepare,
The tidings comes that they are all arrived.   115
  K. JOHN. Oh, where hath our intelligence° been
   drunk?
Where hath it slept? Where is my mother's care,
That such an army could be drawn in France
And she not hear of it?
  MESS.   My liege, her ear
Is stopped with dust. The first of April died   120

Your noble mother. And, as I hear, my lord,
The Lady Constance in a frenzy° died
Three days before. But this from Rumor's tongue
I idly heard. If true or false, I know not.
  K. JOHN. Withhold thy speed, dreadful Occa-
   sion!°   125
Oh, make a league with me till I have pleased
My discontented peers! What! Mother dead!
How wildly then walks my estate in France!
Under whose conduct° came those powers of
  France
That thou for truth givest out are landed here?   130
  MESS. Under the Dauphin.
  K. JOHN.   Thou hast made me giddy
With these ill tidings.
    [*Enter the* BASTARD *and* PETER *of Pomfret.*]
            Now, what says the world
To your proceedings? Do not seek to stuff
My head with more ill news, for it is full.
  BAST. But if you be afeard to hear the worst,   135
Then let the worst unheard fall on your head.
  K. JOHN. Bear with me, Cousin, for I was amazed
Under the tide. But now I breathe again
Aloft the flood and can give audience
To any tongue, speak it of what it will.   140
  BAST. How I have sped° among the clergymen
The sums I have collected shall express.°
But as I traveled hither through the land,
I find the people strangely fantasied,°
Possessed with rumors, full of idle dreams,   145
Not knowing what they fear, but full of fear.
And here's a prophet that I brought with me
From forth the streets of Pomfret, whom I found
With many hundreds treading on his heels,
To whom he sung, in rude harsh-sounding rhymes,
That, ere the next Ascension day at noon,   151
Your Highness should deliver up your crown.
  K. JOHN. Thou idle dreamer, wherefore didst
   thou so?
  PETER. Foreknowing that the truth will fall out
   so.
  K. JOHN. Hubert, away with him. Imprison him,
And on that day at noon whereon he says   156
I shall yield up my crown, let him be hanged.
Deliver him to safety,° and return,
For I must use thee. [*Exit* HUBERT *with* PETER.] O
  my gentle Cousin,
Hear'st thou the news abroad who are arrived?
  BAST. The French, my lord. Men's mouths are
   full of it.   161
Besides, I met Lord Bigot and Lord Salisbury,
With eyes as red as new-enkindled fire,
And others more, going to seek the grave

---

80. **breaks:** i.e., like a bursting boil.   **82. We . . . hand:** we cannot hold back death.   **93–95. It . . . game:** this is clearly foul play, and it is a shame that a king (*greatness*) should act so flagrantly (*grossly*). May you get the reward of one who cheats at his game!   **100. Bad . . . while:** it is a bad world in which such things can happen.   **106. fearful:** frightened.   **113. The . . . them:** they have learned to imitate your speed. See III.iv.10–14.   **116. intelligence:** military intelligence, spies.

122. **frenzy:** fit of madness.   **125. Occasion:** course of events, luck.   **129. conduct:** command.   **141. sped:** succeeded. **142. express:** show.   **144. strangely fantasied:** full of strange notions.   **158. safety:** safekeeping.

Of Arthur, whom they say is killed tonight   165
On your suggestion.
    K. JOHN.   Gentle kinsman, go,
And thrust thyself into their companies.
I have a way° to win their loves again.
Bring them before me.
    BAST.   I will seek them out.
    K. JOHN. Nay, but make haste! The better foot
before.°   170
Oh, let me have no subject enemies
When adverse° foreigners affright my towns
With dreadful pomp of stout invasion!
Be Mercury,° set feathers to thy heels,
And fly like thought from them to me again.   175
    BAST. The spirit of the time shall teach me speed.
                          [*Exit.*]
    K. JOHN. Spoke like a sprightful° noble gentle-
man.
Go after him, for he perhaps shall need
Some messenger betwixt me and the peers;
And be thou he.
    MESS.   With all my heart, my liege. [*Exit.*]
    K. JOHN. My mother dead!   181
            [*Re-enter* HUBERT.]
    HUB. My lord, they say five moons were seen
tonight —
Four fixèd, and the fifth did whirl about
The other four in wondrous motion.
    K. JOHN. Five moons!
    HUB.   Old men and beldams° in the streets
Do prophesy upon it dangerously.   186
Young Arthur's death is common in their mouths,
And when they talk of him, they shake their heads
And whisper one another in the ear;
And he that speaks doth gripe the hearer's wrist,
Whilst he that hears makes fearful action°   191
With wrinkled brows, with nods, with rolling eyes.
I saw a smith stand with his hammer, thus,
The whilst his iron did on the anvil cool,
With open mouth swallowing a tailor's news;   195
Who, with his shears and measure in his hand,
Standing on slippers, which his nimble haste
Had falsely thrust upon contrary feet,
Told of a many thousand warlike French
That were embattailèd° and ranked in Kent.   200
Another lean unwashed artificer°
Cuts off his tale and talks of Arthur's death.
    K. JOHN. Why seek'st thou to possess me with
these fears?
Why urgest thou so oft young Arthur's death?
Thy hand hath murdered him. I had a mighty
cause   205

To wish him dead, but thou hadst none to kill him.
    HUB. No had, my lord! Why, did you not pro-
voke° me?
    K. JOHN. It is the curse of kings to be attended°
By slaves that take their humors° for a warrant
To break within the bloody house of life,   210
And on the winking of authority°
To understand a law; to know the meaning
Of dangerous majesty when perchance it frowns
More upon humor than advised respect.°   214
    HUB. Here is your hand and seal for what I did.
    K. JOHN. Oh, when the last account 'twixt Heaven
and earth
Is to be made, then shall this hand and seal
Witness against us to damnation!
How oft the sight of means to do ill deeds
Make deeds ill done! Hadst not thou been by,   220
A fellow by the hand of nature marked,
Quoted,° and signed° to do a deed of shame,
This murder had not come into my mind.
But taking note of thy abhorred aspéct,°
Finding thee fit for bloody villainy,   225
Apt, liable to be employed in danger,
I faintly broke with° thee of Arthur's death,
And thou, to be endearèd to a King,
Made it no conscience to destroy a Prince.
    HUB. My lord——   230
    K. JOHN. Hadst thou but shook thy head or made
a pause
When I spake darkly what I purposèd,
Or turned an eye of doubt upon my face,
As bid me tell my tale in express words,°
Deep shame had struck me dumb, made me break
off,   235
And those thy fears might have wrought fears in
me.
But thou didst understand me by my signs
And didst in signs again parley with sin;
Yea, without stop, didst let thy heart consent,
And consequently thy rude hand to act   240
The deed which both our tongues held vile to
name.
Out of my sight, and never see me more!
My nobles leave me, and my state is braved°
Even at my gates with ranks of foreign powers.
Nay, in the body of this fleshly land,°   245
This kingdom, this confine of blood and breath,
Hostility and civil tumult reigns
Between my conscience and my cousin's death.

207. **provoke:** encourage.   208. **attended:** waited on.   209. **humors:** whims.   211. **winking of authority:** when a king shuts his eyes.   214. **advised respect:** decision carefully thought out.   222. **Quoted:** specially noted. **signed:** designated.   224. **abhorred aspect:** horrible looks.   227. **faintly . . . with:** vaguely hinted to. See III.iii.19–69.   243. **state is braved:** kingdom is insulted.   245. **this . . . land:** i.e., my own body, often compared to a microcosm (or little universe). See *Caesar*, II.i.63–69.

168. **have a way:** know how.   170. **better . . . before:** put your best foot foremost.   172. **adverse:** hostile.   174. **Mercury:** the messenger of the gods, who wore winged sandals.   177. **sprightful:** spirited.   185. **beldams:** old hags.   191. **fearful action:** expresses his fear in his gestures.   200. **embattailed:** ready for battle.   201. **artificer:** workman.

HUB. Arm you against your other enemies —
I'll make a peace between your soul and you.   250
Young Arthur is alive. This hand of mine
Is yet a maiden and an innocent hand,
Not painted with the crimson spots of blood.
Within this bosom never entered yet
The dreadful motion of a murderous thought,   255
And you have slandered nature in my form,°
Which, howsoever rude exteriorly,
Is yet the cover of a fairer mind
Than to be butcher of an innocent child.
  K. JOHN. Doth Arthur live? Oh, haste thee to the
    peers,   260
Throw this report on their incensèd rage,
And make them tame to their obedience!
Forgive the comment that my passion made
Upon thy feature; for my rage was blind,
And foul imaginary eyes of blood°   265
Presented thee more hideous than thou art.
Oh, answer not, but to my closet° bring
The angry lords with all expedient haste.
I conjure° thee but slowly. Run more fast.
                       [*Exeunt.*]

SCENE III. *Before the castle.*

[*Enter* ARTHUR, *on the walls.*]

ART. The wall is high, and yet will I leap down.
Good ground, be pitiful and hurt me not!
There's few or none do know me. If they did,
This shipboy's semblance° hath disguised me quite.
I am afraid; and yet I'll venture it.   5
If I get down, and do not break my limbs,
I'll find a thousand shifts° to get away.
As good to die and go, as die and stay.
                      [*Leaps down.*]
Oh, me! My uncle's spirit is in these stones.   9
Heaven take my soul, and England keep my bones!
                         [*Dies.*]

[*Enter* PEMBROKE, SALISBURY, *and* BIGOT.]

SAL. Lords, I will meet him at Saint Edmunds-
    bury.
It is our safety, and we must embrace
This gentle offer of the perilous time.   13
  PEM. Who brought that letter from the Cardinal?
  SAL. The Count Melun, a noble lord of France,
Whose private° with me of the Dauphin's love
Is much more general° than these lines import.
  BIG. Tomorrow morning let us meet him, then.
  SAL. Or rather, then set forward; for 'twill be
Two long days' journey, lords, or ere° we meet.   20

[*Enter the* BASTARD.]

BAST. Once more today well met, distempered°
    lords!
The King by me requests your presence straight.°
  SAL. The King hath dispossessed himself of us.
We will not line his thin bestainèd° cloak
With our pure honors, nor attend the foot   25
That leaves the print of blood where'er it walks.
Return and tell him so. We know the worst.
  BAST. Whate'er you think, good words, I think,
    were best.
  SAL. Our griefs, and not our manners, reason°
    now.
  BAST. But there is little reason in your grief.   30
Therefore 'twere reason you had manners now.
  PEM. Sir, sir, impatience hath his privilege,°
  BAST. 'Tis true — to hurt his master, no man else.
  SAL. This is the prison. What is he lies here?
                  [*Seeing* ARTHUR.]
  PEM. O Death, made proud with pure and
    princely beauty!   35
The earth had not a hole to hide this deed.
  SAL. Murder, as hating what himself hath done,
Doth lay it open to urge on revenge.
  BIG. Or, when he doomed this beauty to a grave,
Found it too precious-princely for a grave.   40
  SAL. Sir Richard, what think you? Have you be-
    held,
Or have you read or heard? Or could you think?
Or do you almost think, although you see,
That you do see? Could thought, without this ob-
    ject,
Form such another? This is the very top,   45
The height, the crest, or crest unto the crest,
Of murder's arms. This is the bloodiest shame,
The wildest savagery, the vilest stroke,
That ever wall-eyed° wrath or staring rage
Presented to the tears of soft remorse.°   50
  PEM. All murders past do stand excused in this.
And this, so sole and so unmatchable,
Shall give a holiness, a purity,
To the yet unbegotten sin of times,°
And prove a deadly bloodshed but a jest,   55
Exampled by this heinous spectacle.
  BAST. It is a damnèd and a bloody work,
The graceless action of a heavy hand,
If that it be the work of any hand.
  SAL. If that it be the work of any hand!   60
We had a kind of light what would ensue.
It is the shameful work of Hubert's hand,
The practice and the purpose of the King;
From whose obedience I forbid my soul,

---

256. form: outward appearance.   265. imaginary . . . blood:
your eyes, which seemed to be full of blood.   267. closet:
private room.   269. conjure: solemnly commend.
  Sc. iii: 4. semblance: appearance.   7. shifts: devices.
16. private: private conversation.   17. general: far-reaching.
20. or ere: before.

21. distempered: disgruntled.   22. straight: at once.   24. thin
bestained: rotten and dirty.   29. reason: are talking.   32. impatience . . . privilege: an impatient man can be excused for
bad manners. See *Lear*, II.ii.76.   49. wall-eyed: glaring.
50. remorse: pity.   54. times: ages yet unborn.

Kneeling before this ruin of sweet life,   65
And breathing to his breathless excellence
The incense of a vow, a holy vow,
Never to taste the pleasures of the world,
Never to be infected with delight
Nor conversant with ease and idleness   70
Till I have set a glory to this hand
By giving it the worship° of revenge.
  PEM., BIG. Our souls religiously confirm thy
    words.
        [*Enter* HUBERT.]
  HUB. Lords, I am hot with haste in seeking you.
Arthur doth live. The King hath sent for you.   75
  SAL. Oh, he is bold and blushes not at death.
Avaunt,° thou hateful villain, get thee gone!
  HUB. I am no villain.
  SAL.   Must I rob the law? [*Drawing his sword.*]
  BAST. Your sword is bright, sir. Put it up again.
  SAL. Not till I sheathe it in a murderer's skin.   80
  HUB. Stand back, Lord Salisbury, stand back, I
    say.
By Heaven, I think my sword's as sharp as yours.
I would not have you, lord, forget yourself,
Nor tempt the danger of my true defense,
Lest I, by marking° of your rage, forget   85
Your worth, your greatness, and nobility.
  BIG. Out, dunghill! Darest thou brave° a noble-
    man?
  HUB. Not for my life; but yet I dare defend
My innocent life against an emperor.
  SAL. Thou art a murderer.
  HUB.   Do not prove me so.°   90
Yet I am none. Whose tongue soe'er speaks false,
Not truly speaks. Who speaks not truly, lies.
  PEM. Cut him to pieces.
  BAST.   Keep the peace, I say.
  SAL. Stand by, or I shall gall° you, Faulconbridge.
  BAST. Thou wert better gall the Devil, Salisbury.
If thou but frown on me, or stir thy foot,   96
Or teach thy hasty spleen° to do me shame,
I'll strike thee dead. Put up thy sword betime,°
Or I'll so maul you and your toasting-iron   99
That you shall think the Devil is come from Hell.
  BIG. What wilt thou do, renownèd Faulcon-
    bridge?
Second a villain and a murderer?
  HUB. Lord Bigot, I am none.
  BIG.   Who killed this Prince?
  HUB. 'Tis not an hour since I left him well.
I honored him, I loved him, and will weep   105
My date of life° out for his sweet life's loss.
  SAL. Trust not those cunning waters of his eyes,

For villainy is not without such rheum,
And he, long traded° in it, makes it seem
Like rivers of remorse and innocency.   110
Away with me, all you whose souls abhor
The uncleanly savors° of a slaughterhouse,
For I am stifled with this smell of sin.
  BIG. Away toward Bury, to the Dauphin there!
  PEM. There tell the King he may inquire us out.
                              [*Exeunt* LORDS.]
  BAST. Here's a good world! Knew you of this fair
    work?   116
Beyond the infinite and boundless reach
Of mercy, if thou didst this deed of death,
Art thou damned, Hubert.
  HUB.   Do but hear me, sir.
  BAST. Ha! I'll tell thee what.   120
Thou'rt damned as black° — nay, nothing is so
    black.
Thou art more deep damned than Prince Lucifer.
There is not yet so ugly a fiend of Hell
As thou shalt be if thou didst kill this child.
  HUB. Upon my soul ——
  BAST.   If thou didst but consent   125
To this most cruel act, do but despair;
And if thou want'st a cord, the smallest thread
That ever spider twisted from her womb
Will serve to strangle thee. A rush° will be a beam
To hang thee on; or wouldst thou drown thyself,
Put but a little water in a spoon,   131
And it shall be as all the ocean,
Enough to stifle such a villain up.
I do suspect thee very grievously.
  HUB. If I in act, consent, or sin of thought,   135
Be guilty of the stealing that sweet breath
Which was embounded in this beauteous clay,°
Let Hell want pains enough to torture me.
I left him well.
  BAST.   Go, bear him in thine arms.
I am amazed,° methinks, and lose my way   140
Among the thorns and dangers of this world.
How easy dost thou take all England up!
From forth this morsel of dead royalty,
The life, the right and truth of all this realm
Is fled to Heaven, and England now is left   145
To tug and scamble,° and to part by the teeth
The unowed° interest of proud-swelling state.
Now for the bare-picked bone of majesty
Doth doggèd War bristle his angry crest
And snarleth in the gentle eyes of Peace.   150
Now powers from° home and discontents at home
Meet in one line, and vast confusion waits,

72. worship: honorable ceremony; i.e., my hand will be honored
when it takes vengeance on this King.   77. Avaunt: away!
85. marking: taking notice of.   87. brave: insult.   90. Do . . .
so: i.e., by forcing me to kill you.   94. gall: wound.   97. spleen:
wrath.   98. betime: quickly.   106. date of life: the length of
my life.

109. long traded: i.e., used to such hypocrisy.   112. savors:
odors.   121. damned as black: Damned souls were painted
black in the old religious paintings. See *Haml*, III.iii.94–95.
129. rush: reed.   137. embounded . . . clay: enclosed within
this lovely body.   140. amazed: lost as in a maze.   146. scamble:
scramble for.   147. unowed: unowned — because the possession
of the crown is in dispute.   151. from: away from; i.e., foreign.

As doth a raven on a sick-fallen beast,
The imminent decay of wrested pomp.°
Now happy he whose cloak and cincture° can   155
Hold out this tempest. Bear away that child,
And follow me with speed. I'll to the King.
A thousand businesses are brief in hand,°
And Heaven itself doth frown upon the land.

                                    [*Exeunt.*]

Act V

SCENE I. KING JOHN'S *palace.*

[*Enter* KING JOHN, PANDULPH, *and* ATTENDANTS.]

K. JOHN. Thus have I yielded up into your hand
The circle of my glory.   [*Giving the crown.*]
PAN.   Take again°
From this my hand, as holding of the Pope
Your sovereign greatness and authority.
    K. JOHN. Now keep your holy word. Go meet the
    French,   5
And from His Holiness use all your power
To stop their marches 'fore we are inflamed.
Our discontented counties do revolt.
Our people quarrel with obedience,
Swearing allegiance and the love of soul°   10
To stranger blood, to foreign royalty.
This inundation of mistempered humor°
Rests by you only to be qualified.°
Then pause not, for the present time's so sick
That present° medicine must be ministered,   15
Or overthrow incurable ensues.
    PAN. It was my breath that blew this tempest up,
Upon your stubborn usage of the Pope;
But since you are a gentle convertite,°
My tongue shall hush again this storm of war   20
And make fair weather in your blustering land.
On this Ascension Day, remember well,
Upon your oath of service to the Pope,
Go I to make the French lay down their arms.
                                    [*Exit.*]
    K. JOHN. Is this Ascension Day? Did not the
    prophet   25
Say that before Ascension Day at noon
My crown I should give off? Even so I have
I did suppose it should be on constraint,

But, Heaven be thanked, it is but voluntary.
                [*Enter the* BASTARD.]
BAST. All Kent hath yielded. Nothing there holds
    out   30
But Dover Castle. London hath received,
Like a kind host, the Dauphin and his powers.
Your nobles will not hear you, but are gone
To offer service to your enemy,
And wild amazement hurries up and down   35
The little number of your doubtful friends.
    K. JOHN. Would not my lords return to me again
After they heard young Arthur was alive?
    BAST. They found him dead and cast into the
    streets —
An empty casket where the jewel of life   40
By some damned hand was robbed and ta'en away.
    K. JOHN. That villain Hubert told me he did live.
    BAST. So, on my soul, he did, for aught he knew.
But wherefore do you droop? Why look you sad?
Be great in act, as you have been in thought.   45
Let not the world see fear and sad distrust
Govern the motion of a kingly eye.
Be stirring as the time. Be fire with fire.
Threaten the threatener, and outface the brow
Of bragging Horror. So shall inferior eyes,   50
That borrow their behaviors from the great,
Grow great by your example and put on
The dauntless spirit of resolution.
Away, and glister° like the God of War
When he intendeth to become° the field.   55
Show boldness and aspiring confidence.
What, shall they seek the lion in his den
And fright him there? And make him tremble
    there?
Oh, let it not be said. Forage,° and run
To meet displeasure farther from the doors,   60
And grapple with him ere he come so nigh.
    K. JOHN. The legate of the Pope hath been with
    me,
And I have made a happy peace with him;
And he hath promised to dismiss the powers
Led by the Dauphin.
    BAST.   Oh, inglorious league!   65
Shall we, upon the footing of our land,°
Send fair-play orders and make compromise,
Insinuation, parley, and base truce
To arms invasive? Shall a beardless boy,
A cockered° silken wanton, brave° our fields   70
And flesh° his spirit in a warlike soil,
Mocking the air with colors idly spread,°
And find no check?° Let us, my liege, to arms.

---

154. wrested pomp: usurped power.   **155. cincture:** belt. F1
reads "center."   **158. brief in hand:** need immediate attention.
    Act V, Sc. i: 2. Take again . . . : The Cardinal gives back
the crown, indicating that John holds his throne only by permission of the Pope.   **10. love of soul:** loyalty.   **12. mistempered humor:** excess of discontent. See App. 3.   **13. Rests
. . . qualified:** can only be lessened by you.   **15. present:** immediate.   **19. convertite:** convert.

54. glister: shine in your armor.   **55. become:** show himself in
his might in.   **59. Forage:** ravage.   **66. upon . . . land:** on our
own land; i.e., while the enemy is still on our own ground.
70. cockered: spoilt.   **brave:** insult.   **71. flesh:** get his first taste
of blood. See *I Hen IV,* V.iv.133–34.   **72. Mocking . . .
spread:** insult us by freely flying his colors.   **73. And . . . check:**
without hindrance.

Perchance the Cardinal cannot make your peace.
Or if he do, let it at least be said   75
They saw we had a purpose of defense.

   K. JOHN. Have thou the ordering of this present
     time.
   BAST. Away, then, with good courage! Yet, I
     know,
Our party may well meet a prouder foe.° [*Exeunt.*]

SCENE II. *The* DAUPHIN's *camp
at St. Edmundsbury.*

[*Enter, in arms,* LEWIS, SALISBURY, MELUN,
PEMBROKE, BIGOT, *and* SOLDIERS.]

   LEW. My Lord Melun, let this° be copied out,
And keep it safe for our remembrance.
Return the precedent° to these lords again,
That, having our fair order written down,
Both they and we, perusing o'er these notes,   5
May know wherefore we took the sacrament
And keep our faiths firm and inviolable.

   SAL. Upon our sides it never shall be broken.
And, noble Dauphin, albeit we swear
A voluntary zeal and an unurged° faith   10
To your proceedings, yet believe me, Prince,
I am not glad that such a sore of time
Should seek a plaster° by contemned° revolt
And heal the inveterate canker° of one wound
By making many. Oh, it grieves my soul   15
That I must draw this metal from my side
To be a widow maker! Oh, and there
Where honorable rescue and defense
Cries out upon the name of Salisbury!
But such is the infection of the time   20
That, for the health and physic of our right,
We cannot deal but with the very hand
Of stern injustice and confusèd wrong.
And is 't not pity, O my grievèd friends,
That we, the sons and children of this isle,   25
Were born to see so sad an hour as this,
Wherein we step after° a stranger, march
Upon her gentle bosom, and fill up
Her enemies' ranks — I must withdraw and weep
Upon the spot of this enforcèd cause° —   30
To grace the gentry° of a land remote
And follow unacquainted° colors here?
What, here? O nation, that thou couldst remove!°
That Neptune's arms, who clippeth° thee about,
Would bear thee from the knowledge of thyself   35

And grapple thee unto a pagan shore,
Where these two Christian armies might combine
The blood of malice in a vein of league,
And not to spend it so unneighborly!

   LEW. A noble temper dost thou show in this,   40
And great affections wrestling in thy bosom
Doth make an earthquake of nobility.
Oh, what a noble combat hast thou fought
Between compulsion and a brave respect!°
Let me wipe off this honorable dew   45
That silvery doth progress on thy cheeks.
My heart hath melted at a lady's tears,
Being an ordinary inundation,
But this effusion of such manly drops,
This shower, blown up by tempest of the soul,   50
Startles mine eyes and makes me more amazed
Than had I seen the vaulty top of heaven
Figured° quite o'er with burning meteors.
Lift up thy brow, renownèd Salisbury,
And with a great heart heave away this storm.   55
Commend these waters to those baby eyes
That never saw the giant world enraged,
Nor met with fortune other than at feasts,
Full of warm blood, of mirth, of gossiping.
Come, come; for thou shalt thrust thy hand as
     deep   60
Into the purse of rich prosperity
As Lewis himself. So, nobles, shall you all
That knit your sinews to the strength of mine.
And even there, methinks, an angel spake.°

       [*Enter* PANDULPH.]
Look, where the holy legate comes apace   65
To give us warrant from the hand of Heaven
And on our actions set the name of right
With holy breath.

   PAN.   Hail, noble Prince of France!
The next is this: King John hath reconciled
Himself to Rome. His spirit is come in   70
That so stood out against the holy Church,
The great metropolis and See of Rome.
Therefore thy threatening colors now wind up,°
And tame the savage spirit of wild War,
That, like a lion fostered up at° hand,   75
It may lie gently at the foot of Peace
And be no further harmful than in show.

   LEW. Your Grace shall pardon me, I will not
     back.
I am too high-born to be propertied,°
To be a secondary at control,°   80
Or useful servingman and instrument
To any sovereign state throughout the world.

---

79. Our . . . foe: we can beat a far stronger enemy.
   Sc. ii: **1.** this: i.e., the signed agreement. **3.** precedent:
original agreement. **10.** unurged: uncompelled. **13.** plaster:
poultice, healing remedy. contemned: despised, dishonorable.
14. inveterate canker: chronic sore. **27.** step after: are followers
of. **30.** spot . . . cause: this dishonor which is forced upon us.
31. grace . . . gentry: honor the gentlemen. **32.** unacquainted:
unfamiliar. **33.** remove: change. **34.** clippeth: embraceth.

44. compulsion . . . respect: between what you are forced to do
and your honor. **53.** Figured: decorated. **64.** And . . . spake:
i.e., this trumpet call — the flourish announcing the approach
of Pandulph — is like the call of the angel to the Last Judgment.
73. wind up: put away. **75.** fostered up at: brought up by.
79. propertied: treated like a property, "pushed around."
80. secondary at control: controlled by someone else.

Your breath first kindled the dead coal of wars
Between this chastisèd kingdom and myself
And brought in matter that should feed this fire;
And now 'tis far too huge to be blown out　　86
With that same weak wind which enkindled it.
You taught me how to know the face of right,
Acquainted me with interest to this land,°
Yea, thrust this enterprise into my heart.　　90
And come ye now to tell me John hath made
His peace with Rome? What is that peace to me?
I, by the honor of my marriage bed,
After young Arthur, claim this land for mine;
And, now it is half-conquered, must I back　　95
Because that John hath made his peace with Rome?
Am I Rome's slave? What penny hath Rome borne,
What men provided, what munition sent
To underprop this action? Is 't not I
That undergo this charge? Who else but I　　100
And such as to my claim are liable°
Sweat in this business and maintain this war?
Have I not heard these islanders shout out
"Vive le Roi!" as I have banked° their towns?
Have I not here the best cards for the game　　105
To win this easy match played for a crown?
And shall I now give o'er the yielded set?°
No, no, on my soul, it never shall be said.

PAN. You look but on the outside of this work.

LEW. Outside or inside, I will not return　　110
Till my attempt so much be glorified
As to my ample hope was promisèd
Before I drew this gallant head of war°
And culled° these fiery spirits from the world
To outlook° conquest and to win renown　　115
Even in the jaws of danger and of death.

　　　　　　　　　　　　　[Trumpet sounds.]
What lusty trumpet thus doth summon us?

　　　　　　[Enter the BASTARD, *attended.]*
BAST. According to the fair play of the world,
Let me have audience. I am sent to speak.
My holy Lord of Milan, from the King　　120
I come to learn how you have dealt for him;
And, as you answer, I do know the scope
And warrant limited unto my tongue.°

PAN. The Dauphin is too willful-opposite.
And will not temporize° with my entreaties.　　125
He flatly says he'll not lay down his arms.

BAST. By all the blood that ever fury breathed,
The youth says well. Now hear our English King;
For thus his royalty doth speak in me.
He is prepared, and reason too° he should.　　130

This apish° and unmannerly approach,
This harnessed masque and unadvisèd revel,°
This unhaired° sauciness and boyish troops,
The King doth smile at, and is well prepared
To whip this dwarfish war, these pigmy arms,　　135
From out the circle of his territories.
That hand which had the strength, even at your
　　door,
To cudgel you and make you take the hatch,°
To dive like buckets in concealèd wells,
To crouch in litter of your stable planks,　　140
To lie like pawns° locked up in chests and trunks,
To hug with swine, to seek sweet safety out
In vaults and prisons, and to thrill and shake
Even at the crying of your nation's crow,
Thinking his voice an armèd Englishman;　　145
Shall that victorious hand be feebled here
That in your chambers gave you chastisement?
No. Know the gallant monarch is in arms
And like an eagle o'er his aery towers
To souse° annoyance° that comes near his nest.
And you degenerate, you ingrate revolts,°　　151
You bloody Neroes, ripping up the womb
Of your dear mother° England, blush for shame.
For your own ladies and pale-visaged maids,
Like Amazons,° come tripping after drums,　　155
Their thimbles into armèd gauntlets change,
Their needles° to lances, and their gentle hearts
To fierce and bloody inclination.

LEW. There end thy brave,° and turn thy face in
　　peace.
We grant thou canst outscold us. Fare thee well.
We hold our time too precious to be spent　　161
With such a brabbler.°

PAN.　　　　　　　　Give me leave to speak.

BAST. No, I will speak.

LEW.　　　　　　　　We will attend to neither.
Strike up the drums, and let the tongue of war
Plead for our interest and our being here.　　165

BAST. Indeed, your drums, being beaten, will cry
　　out,
And so shall you, being beaten. Do but start
An echo with the clamor of thy drum,
And even at hand a drum is ready braced°

131. apish: apelike, frivolous.　132. harnessed . . . revel: this masque in armor and foolish show. The Bastard treats the Dauphin as if he were the leader of a fancy-dress army of boys. 133. unhaired: beardless, youthful.　138. take . . . hatch: take a short cut by leaping over the half-door without stopping to open it.　141. pawns: pledges.　150. souse: swoop down on. The word is used of an attack of a bird of prey. annoyance: a threat.　151. ingrate revolts: ungrateful rebels.　152–53. Neroes . . . mother: It was said that the Roman emperor Nero, having murdered his mother, caused her body to be opened so that he might see the womb in which he had been conceived.　155. Amazons: fierce female warriors; see *MND*, I.i.1,n.　157. needles: pronounced "needls."　159. brave: bragging.　162. brabbler: boaster.　169. braced: taut, tuned for playing.

89. Acquainted . . . land: showed me that I have a claim on this land.　101. liable: supporters.　104. banked: passed close by. 107. And . . . set: shall I abandon the game now that I have won the rubber?　113. gallant . . . war: this army of young gallants. 114. culled: collected.　115. outlook: stare down.　123. warrant . . . tongue: what my tongue shall be directed to say. 125. temporize: come to terms.　130. reason too: it is right that.

That shall reverberate all as loud as thine.   170
Sound but another, and another shall
As loud as thine rattle the welkin's° ear
And mock the deep-mouthed thunder. For at hand,
Not trusting to this halting legate here,
Whom he hath used rather for sport than need,
Is warlike John; and in his forehead sits   176
A bare-ribbed Death,° whose office is this day
To feast upon whole thousands of the French.
  LEW. Strike up our drums to find this danger
    out.
  BAST. And thou shalt find it, Dauphin, do not
    doubt.   [*Exeunt.*] 180

SCENE III. *The field of battle.*

[*Alarums. Enter* KING JOHN *and* HUBERT.]
  K. JOHN. How goes the day with us? Oh, tell me,
    Hubert.
  HUB. Badly, I fear. How fares your Majesty?
  K. JOHN. This fever that hath troubled me so
    long
Lies heavy on me. Oh, my heart is sick!
          [*Enter a* MESSENGER.]
  MESS. My lord, your valiant kinsman, Faulcon-
    bridge,   5
Desires your Majesty to leave the field
And send him word by me which way you go.
  K. JOHN. Tell him, toward Swinstead, to the
    abbey there.
  MESS. Be of good comfort, for the great supply°
That was expected by the Dauphin here   10
Are wrecked three nights ago on Goodwin Sands.
This news was brought to Richard but even now.
The French fight coldly° and retire themselves.
  K. JOHN. Aye me! This tyrant fever burns me up,
And will not let me welcome this good news.   15
Set on toward Swinstead. To my litter straight.
Weakness possesseth me, and I am faint. [*Exeunt.*]

SCENE IV. *Another part of the field.*

[*Enter* SALISBURY, PEMBROKE, *and* BIGOT.]
  SAL. I did not think the King so stored with
    friends.
  PEM. Up once again. Put spirit in the French.
If they miscarry, we miscarry too.
  SAL. That misbegotten devil, Faulconbridge,
In spite of spite,° alone upholds the day.   5
  PEM. They say King John sore sick hath left the
    field.

[*Enter* MELUN, *wounded.*]
  MEL. Lead me to the revolts° of England here.
  SAL. When we were happy, we had other names.
  PEM. It is the Count Melun.
  SAL.   Wounded to death.
  MEL. Fly, noble English, you are bought and sold.
Unthread the rude eye of rebellion,°   11
And welcome home again discarded faith.
Seek out King John, and fall before his feet.
For if the French be lords of this loud day,
He° means to recompense the pains you take   15
By cutting off your heads. Thus hath he sworn,
And I with him, and many moe° with me,
Upon the altar at Saint Edmundsbury,
Even on that altar where we swore to you
Dear amity and everlasting love.   20
  SAL. May this be possible? May this be true?
  MEL. Have I not hideous death within my view,
Retaining but a quantity of life,
Which bleeds away, even as a form of wax
Resolveth from his figure° 'gainst the fire?   25
What in the world should make me now deceive,
Since I must lose the use of all deceit?
Why should I then be false, since it is true
That I must die here and live hence by truth?°
I say again, if Lewis do win the day,   30
He is forsworn° if e'er those eyes of yours
Behold another day break in the East.
But even this night, whose black contagious breath
Already smokes about the burning crest
Of the old, feeble, and day-wearied sun,   35
Even this ill night, your breathing shall expire,
Paying the fine of rated treachery°
Even with a treacherous fine° of all your lives,
If Lewis by your assistance win the day.
Commend me to one Hubert with your King.   40
The love of him, and this respect besides,°
For that my grandsire was an Englishman,
Awakes my conscience to confess all this.
In lieu° whereof, I pray you bear me hence
From forth the noise and rumor° of the field,   45
Where I may think the remnant of my thoughts
In peace and part this body and my soul
With contemplation and devout desires.
  SAL. We do believe thee; and beshrew° my soul
But I do love the favor and the form   50
Of this most fair occasion, by the which
We will untread° the steps of damnèd flight,
And, like a bated° and retirèd flood,

172. **welkin:** sky.   177. **bare-ribbed Death:** skeleton death. See Pl. 12f.
Sc. iii. 9. **supply:** reinforcement.   13. **coldly:** without enthusiasm.
Sc. iv: 5. **In . . . spite:** in spite of anything we can do.

7. **revolts:** rebels.   11. **Unthread . . . rebellion:** withdraw yourselves from your rebellion. The image is that of withdrawing the thread from a needle.   15. **He:** i.e., Lewis.   17. **moe:** more.   25. **Resolveth . . . figure:** loses its shape.   29. **live . . . truth:** i.e., my hope of Heaven depends on my telling the truth now.   31. **forsworn:** perjured.   37. **fine . . . treachery:** penalty for treachery at its full value.   38. **fine:** end.   41. **this . . . besides:** this consideration also.   44. **lieu:** recompense.   45. **rumor:** uproar.   49. **beshrew:** evil take.   52. **untread:** retrace.   53. **bated:** abated.

Leaving our rankness° and irregular course,
Stoop low within those bounds we have o'erlooked°
And calmly run on in obedience   56
Even to our ocean, to our great King John.
My arm shall give thee help to bear thee hence,
For I do see the cruel pangs of death
Right in thine eye. Away, my friends! New flight;
And happy newness, that intends old right.   61

[*Exeunt, leading off* MELUN.]

SCENE V. *The French camp.*

[*Enter* LEWIS *and his train.*]

LEW. The sun of heaven methought was loath to
   set,
But stayed and made the western welkin blush
When English measure backward their own ground
In faint retire. Oh, bravely came we off
When with a volley of our needless° shot,   5
After such bloody toil, we bid good night
And wound our tottering° colors clearly°up,°
Last in the field, and almost lords of it!

[*Enter a* MESSENGER.]

MESS. Where is my Prince, the Dauphin?
LEW.   Here. What news?
MESS. The Count Melun is slain. The English
   lords   10
By his persuasion are again fallen off,
And your supply which you have wished so long
Are cast away and sunk on Goodwin Sands.
LEW. Ah, foul shrewd° news! Beshrew thy very
   heart!
I did not think to be so sad tonight   15
As this hath made me. Who was he that said
King John did fly an hour or two before
The stumbling° night did part our weary powers?
MESS. Whoever spoke it, it is true, my lord.
LEW. Well, keep good quarter° and good care to-
   night.
                                                 20
The day shall not be up so soon as I
To try the fair adventure of tomorrow. [*Exeunt.*]

SCENE VI. *An open place in the neighborhood
       of Swinstead Abbey.*

[*Enter the* BASTARD *and* HUBERT, *severally.*]

HUB. Who's there? Speak, ho! Speak quickly, or
   I shoot.
BAST. A friend. What art thou?
HUB.   Of the part of England.
BAST. Whither dost thou go?

HUB. What's that to thee? Why may not I de-
   mand
Of thine affairs as well as thou of mine?   5
BAST. Hubert, I think.
HUB.   Thou hast a perfect thought.
I will upon all hazards well believe
Thou art my friend that know'st my tongue so well.
Who art thou?
BAST.   Who thou wilt; and if thou please,
Thou mayst befriend me so much as to think   10
I come one way of the Plantagenets.
HUB. Unkind remembrance!° Thou and eyeless
   night
Have done me shame. Brave soldier, pardon me,
That any accent breaking from thy tongue
Should 'scape the true acquaintance of mine ear.°
BAST. Come, come. Sans° compliment, what news
   abroad?   16
HUB. Why, here walk I in the black brow of
   night
To find you out.
BAST.   Brief, then; and what's the news?
HUB. Oh, my sweet sir, news fitting to the
   night —
Black, fearful, comfortless and horrible.   20
BAST. Show me the very wound of this ill news.
I am no woman, I'll not swoon at it.
HUB. The King, I fear, is poisoned by a monk.
I left him almost speechless and broke out
To acquaint you with this evil, that you might   25
The better arm you to the sudden time
Than if you had at leisure known of this.°
BAST. How did he take it? Who did taste to him?
HUB. A monk, I tell you, a resolvèd° villain,
Whose bowels suddenly burst out.° The King   30
Yet speaks and peradventure° may recover.
BAST. Who didst thou leave to tend° His Majesty?
HUB. Why, know you not? The lords are all
   come back
And brought Prince Henry in their company;
At whose request the King hath pardoned them,
And they are all about His Majesty.   36
BAST. Withhold thine indignation, mighty
   Heaven,
And tempt us not to bear above our power!°
I'll tell thee, Hubert, half my power° this night,
Passing these flats,° are taken by the tide.   40
These Lincoln Washes have devoured them.

---

54. **rankness:** excessive growth.   55. **o'erlooked:** overflowed.

Sc. v: 5. **volley . . . needless:** needless volley of. *Shot* is an anachronism. See I.i.26,n.   7. **wound . . . up:** i.e., came off in good order. **tottering:** tattered. **clearly:** cleanly, neatly.   14. **shrewd:** bitter.   18. **stumbling:** which causes to stumble.   20. **quarter:** watch.

Sc. vi: 12. **Unkind remembrance:** forgive my bad memory.   14–15. **That . . . ear:** that I should not recognize your voice.   16. **Sans:** without.   26–27. **The . . . this:** that you might be better prepared for this emergency than if you had learned of it later.   28–30. **taste . . . out:** It was the custom that all dishes offered to a king be inspected by a taster to detect poison. The monk who poisoned King John thus sacrificed his life to ensure that the King should take the poison.   29. **resolved:** resolute, desperate.   31. **peradventure:** perhaps.   32. **tend:** care for.   38. **tempt . . . power:** do not try us more than we can bear.   39. **power:** army.   40. **flats:** low-lying land near the sea.

Myself, well mounted, hardly have escaped.
Away before. Conduct me to the King.
I doubt° he will be dead or ere I come.   [*Exeunt.*]

SCENE VII. *The orchard at Swinstead Abbey.*

[*Enter* PRINCE HENRY, SALISBURY, *and* BIGOT.]
P. HEN. It is too late. The life of all his blood
Is touched corruptibly, and his pure brain,
Which some suppose the soul's frail dwelling house,
Doth by the idle comments that it makes
Foretell the ending of mortality.°   5
       [*Enter* PEMBROKE.]
PEM. His Highness yet doth speak, and holds be-
    lief
That, being brought into the open air,
It would allay the burning quality
Of that fell° poison which assaileth him.
P. HEN. Let him be brought into the orchard
    here.   10
Doth he still rage?   [*Exit* BIGOT.]
PEM.   He is more patient
Than when you left him. Even now he sung.
P. HEN. Oh, vanity of sickness! Fierce extremes
In their continuance will not feel themselves.
Death, having preyed upon the outward parts,   15
Leaves them invisible,° and his siege is now
Against the mind,° the which he pricks and
    wounds
With many legions of strange fantasies,
Which, in their throng and press to that last hold,
Confound themselves.° 'Tis strange that Death
    should sing.   20
I am the cygnet° to this pale faint swan,
Who chants a doleful hymn to his own death°
And from the organ pipe of frailty° sings
His soul and body to their lasting rest.
SAL. Be of good comfort, Prince, for you are born
To set a form upon that indigest°   26
Which he hath left so shapeless and so rude.
[*Enter* ATTENDANTS, *and* BIGOT, *carrying* KING JOHN
    in a chair.]
K. JOHN. Aye, marry, now my soul hath elbow-
    room.
It would not out at windows nor at doors.°
There is so hot a summer in my bosom   30

That all my bowels crumble up to dust.
I am a scribbled form, drawn with a pen
Upon a parchment, and against this fire
Do I shrink up.
P. HEN.   How fares your Majesty?
K. JOHN. Poisoned — ill fare — dead, forsook,
    cast off.   35
And none of you will bid the winter come
To thrust his icy fingers in my maw,°
Nor let my kingdom's rivers take their course
Through my burned bosom, nor entreat the North
To make his bleak winds kiss my parchèd lips   40
And comfort me with cold. I do not ask you much.
I beg cold comfort; and you are so strait°
And so ingrateful, you deny me that.
P. HEN. Oh, that there were some virtue in my
    tears
That might relieve you!
K. JOHN.   The salt in them is hot.   45
Within me is a Hell, and there the poison
Is as a fiend confined to tyrannize
On unreprievable° condemnèd blood.
       [*Enter the* BASTARD.]
BAST. Oh, I am scalded with my violent motion°
And spleen of speed° to see your Majesty!   50
K. JOHN. O Cousin, thou art come to set° mine
    eye.
The tackle° of my heart is cracked and burned,
And all the shrouds° wherewith my life should sail
Are turnèd to one thread, one little hair.
My heart hath one poor string to stay° it by,   55
Which holds but till thy news be uttered;
And then all this thou seest is but a clod
And module of confounded royalty.°
BAST. The Dauphin is preparing hitherward,
Where Heaven He knows how we shall answer
    him,   60
For in a night the best part of my power,
As I upon advantage° did remove,
Were in the Washes all unwarily
Devourèd by the unexpected flood. [*The* KING *dies.*]
SAL. You breathe these dead news in as dead an
    ear.   65
My liege! My lord! But now a King, now thus.
P. HEN. Even so must I run on, and even so stop.
What surety of the world, what hope, what stay,
When this was now a King and now is clay?
BAST. Art thou gone so? I do but stay behind   70
To do the office for thee of revenge,
And then my soul shall wait on thee to Heaven,
As it on earth hath been thy servant still.°

---

44. doubt: fear.
   Sc. vii: 5. mortality: life.   9. fell: fearful.   15–17. Death
. . . mind: Death, having first attacked the visible parts of the
body, now leaves them and strikes inward; i.e., there are now no
outward symptoms of sickness, but his brain is affected.   16. invisible: i.e., without any outward symptom.   19–20. Which
. . . themselves: i.e., his delirious ravings, crowding in upon his
mind, which is the last stronghold of life, contradict themselves.
21. cygnet: young swan, heir.   22. chants . . . death. It was a
popular belief that swans sing only once, just before death.
23. organ . . . frailty: frail mortal voice.   26. indigest: state of
confusion.   29. It . . . doors: I could not die indoors.

37. maw: stomach.   42. strait: mean.   48. unreprievable: beyond reprieve.   49. scalded . . . motion: boiling with heat, I
have come so fast.   50. spleen of speed: eager haste. See
II.i.448.   51. set: close.   52. tackle: rigging.   53. shrouds:
sails.   55. stay: hold.   58. module . . . royalty: specimen of a
dead king.   62. upon advantage: seeing a favorable opportunity.   73. still: always.

Now, now, you stars that move in your right
    spheres,°
Where be your powers? Show now your mended
    faiths, 75
And instantly return with me again
To push destruction and perpetual shame
Out of the weak door of our fainting land.
Straight let us seek, or straight we shall be sought.
The Dauphin rages at our very heels. 80
    SAL. It seems you know not, then, so much as we.
The Cardinal Pandulph is within at rest,
Who half an hour since came from the Dauphin
And brings from him such offers of our peace
As we with honor and respect° may take, 85
With purpose presently° to leave this war.
    BAST. He will the rather do it when he sees
Ourselves well sinewèd° to our defense.
    SAL. Nay, it is in a manner done already,
For many carriages he hath dispatched 90
To the seaside and put his cause and quarrel
To the disposing of the Cardinal;
With whom yourself, myself, and other lords,
If you think meet, this afternoon will post°
To consummate this business happily. 95
    BAST. Let it be so. And you, my noble Prince,

With other princes that may best be spared,
Shall wait upon your father's funeral.
    P. HEN. At Worcester must his body be interred,
For so he willed it.
    BAST.   Thither shall it then. 100
And happily may your sweet self put on
The lineal state° and glory of the land!
To whom, with all submission, on my knee
I do bequeath my faithful services
And true subjection everlastingly. 105
    SAL. And the like tender° of our love we make,
To rest without a spot for evermore.°
    P. HEN. I have a kind soul that would give you
    thanks
And knows not how to do it but with tears.
    BAST. Oh, let us pay the time but needful woe,
Since it hath been beforehand with our griefs.° 111
This England° never did, nor never shall,
Lie at the proud foot of a conqueror
But when it first did help to wound itself.
Now these her princes are come home again, 115
Come the three corners of the world in arms,
And we shall shock them. Naught shall make us
    rue
If England to itself do rest but true.   [*Exeunt.*]

---

74. **stars . . . spheres:** i.e., you noblemen who have returned to your proper loyalty. See App. 1.   **85. respect:** good reputation. **86. presently:** immediately.   **88. sinewed:** united.   **94. post:** hasten.

102. **lineal state:** kingdom due to you by right of birth.   **106. tender:** offer.   **107. To . . . evermore:** i.e., to be loyal forever.   **110–11. Oh . . . griefs:** let us not grieve more than is necessary, since we have already had our fill of troubles.   **112. This England . . . :** See *John* Intro. p. 542.

THE MERCHANT OF VENICE

Introduction

The Merchant of Venice was probably written in 1595 or 1596, but there is no definite evidence of date. The style is maturer than that of *Romeo and Juliet* (*c.* 1594) and less mature than that of *II Henry IV* (*c.* 1598). The earliest recorded performance was in 1605, when the play was acted at Court before King James I on Shrove Sunday, February 10. It pleased the King so much that he ordered a second performance on the twelfth.

The play itself contains two possible topical allusions to events in 1594.

1.   . . . music is
  Even as the flourish when true subjects bow
  To a new-crowned monarch.

These lines (III.ii.48–50) may be a reflection of the coronation of Henry IV of France on February 27, 1594 — an event which caused considerable interest in England.

2. In the trial scene Gratiano says to Shylock:

Thou almost makest me waver in my faith,
To hold opinion with Pythagoras
That souls of animals infuse themselves
Into the trunks of men. Thy currish spirit
Governed a wolf who, hanged for human
  slaughter,
Even from the gallows did his fell soul fleet,
And whilst thou lay'st in thy unhallowed dam
Infused itself in thee, for thy desires
Are wolvish, bloody, starved, and ravenous.

This passage (IV.i.130–38) is a probable echo of the famous case of Dr. Roderigo Lopez, who was executed for high treason on June 7, 1594. Lopez was a Jewish physician who had come to England as a refugee from Portugal in 1559. In time he established a considerable practice at the Court and was appointed physician to the Queen. He also acted as an agent for the many spies who carried information between Spain and England. Early in 1594, the Earl of Essex, who had cause to dislike Lopez, thought that he had discovered a Spanish plot. Lopez, who was now an old man, was arrested, and while under examination told varying tales. He was accused of having taken bribes from the King of Spain to poison Queen Elizabeth. It seems likely that Lopez double-crossed the King by taking the money without any intention of fulfilling the bargain. But with other alleged accomplices he was tried and found guilty. The Queen was at first unwilling to believe in his guilt, but after long delays he was hanged and quartered as a traitor. On the scaffold Lopez protested that he was innocent and declared that he " loved the Queen as well as he loved Jesus Christ." This remark coming from a known Jew "made no small laughter in the standers-by." As Lopez was sometimes called Lopus (or "wolf") by contemporaries, Gratiano's remark is probably topical.

There are two main stories in *The Merchant of Venice*. The first tells how Portia was to be wedded to the suitor who made the right choice of three caskets; the second shows how a cruel Jew agreed to lend a Christian a sum of money on the condition that if the debt was not repaid by a certain date the debtor should forfeit a pound of his flesh, and how when the case came to trial the Jew was outwitted.

There are many versions of both stories in different languages. The direct source of *The Merchant of Venice* was probably a play which has not survived. A play on the subject apparently existed in 1570.

One version of the story of the caskets, found in the medieval collection of tales known as the *Gesta Romanorum,* may be summarized as follows:

It was agreed that the daughter of the King of Ampluy should marry the son of the Emperor of Rome. The lady set out in a fair ship with a goodly company, but on the way the ship was wrecked and all were drowned but the lady; she was swallowed by a whale. When she found herself inside the whale's belly, she kindled a fire and used her knife so effectively that the whale, according to his nature, made for land, where a party which came down to take the whale rescued the lady. On her telling her story, she was conveyed to the Emperor, who had great compassion for her; but before giving her in marriage to his son he first desired to make proof that she was worthy. He therefore commanded three metal vessels to be brought forth. The first was made of gold set with precious stones, but within were dead men's bones; it bore the words "Whoso chooseth me shall find what he deserveth." The second vessel was made of fine silver, but filled with earth and worms, and bore the words "Whoso chooseth me shall find what his nature desireth." The third vessel was made of lead, but within it was full of precious stones, and it bore the words "Whoso chooseth me shall find that God hath disposed to him." So the maiden, having prayed to God, looked first on the vessel of gold; but when she saw the words she said, "Though this vessel be full precious and made of pure gold, nevertheless I know not what is within, therefore, my dear Lord, this vessel will I not choose." Then she looked at the vessel of silver and having read the superscription, she said, "If I choose this vessel, what is within I know not, but well I wot there shall I find what my nature desireth, and my nature desireth the lust of the flesh, therefore this vessel will I not choose." Then she looked at the third vessel, the vessel of lead, and she thought that though the vessel was neither rich nor precious, yet the words said "'Whoso chooseth me shall find that God hath disposed,' and without doubt God never disposeth any harm, therefore will I now choose this vessel by the leave of God." So she chose the vessel of lead and thus won both the precious jewels and the son of the Emperor.

Of the various versions of the story of the pound of flesh, the nearest is an Italian tale called *Il Pecorone,* written by Ser Giovanni in 1378 and printed in 1558. It was not printed in English in Shakespeare's time. The outline of the story is as follows:

Giannetto was the youngest son of a merchant of Florence called Bindo. The merchant, being at point of death, told his youngest son to go to Venice to his godfather, Ansaldo, who was childless. Ansaldo received his godson with great joy and encouraged him to lead a pleasant life. After a while it seemed good that Giannetto should see the world, so Ansaldo fitted out a ship full of rich merchandise to voyage to Alexandria and trade there. Giannetto set out, but on the way he came to a port called Belmonte, which was ruled by a rich and beautiful widow who had ruined many gentlemen, for she made a law that whosoever came to Belmonte should be her wooer. If he could win her love, he should become the lord of the country, but if he failed, then he should lose all that he possessed. Giannetto determined to try his luck. The lady received him most courteously. They spent the day in feasting, and in the evening when they were about to go to bed wine and sweetmeats were offered to Giannetto, who ate and drank; but the wine was drugged with a sleeping potion and Giannetto fell asleep. The lady at once took away his ship and all the merchandise, and the next day sent him away.

When he returned to Venice Giannetto pretended to his godfather that he had been shipwrecked. After a while he became very downcast, and Ansaldo fitted out a second ship, even richer than the first. Giannetto, however, had no thought of making good the losses of Ansaldo; his one desire was again to try his luck with the lady of Belmonte. As before, the lady received him courteously and entertained him even more lavishly; but again the wine and the sweetmeats were brought, and Giannetto again fell asleep before he could win the love of the lady. So once more he returned penniless to Venice. Nevertheless Ansaldo forgave him for the second time, and when he saw that Giannetto could never be happy without the lady who had already cost him so dear, he sold most of his goods and even borrowed 10,000 ducats from a Jew on the condition that if the ducats were not repaid on the Feast of St. John, the Jew might cut a pound of his flesh from any part of his body.

Thus newly equipped, Giannetto for the third time returned to Belmonte. A great tournament was held in his honor at which he distinguished himself so greatly that the whole Court wished to have him for their lord. When the time came for Giannetto and the lady to go to bed, a damsel whispered to him to beware of the wine. Giannetto therefore only pretended to drink and feigned sleep, but when the lady was about to rise and command that his ship should be confiscated, he opened his eyes and cried out that he had won the trial and now she must marry him. So the wedding was lavishly celebrated, and Giannetto ruled excellently, so engrossed in his happiness that he forgot about his godfather. But when at length the Feast of St. John came, Giannetto suddenly remembered that on that very day Ansaldo's bond to the Jew would be forfeited. Thereupon he confessed all to his lady, who forthwith sent him back to Venice to aid Ansaldo. The Jew had at least shown so much mercy that he refrained from demanding his forfeit until Ansaldo had been given an opportunity of embracing his godson before he died. Giannetto at once offered the Jew the payment of his debt, and even as much as 100,000 ducats; but the Jew was obdurate, and, though the whole city of Venice was incensed against him, he would accept no other payment than his pound of flesh.

Meanwhile the lady had herself come to Venice in the guise of a Doctor of Law of Bologna, accompanied by two servants. Giannetto and the Jew went to this Doctor, who first strongly urged the Jew to have mercy, and to accept the 100,000 ducats; but as the Jew still refused, they appealed to the tribunal of Venice for judgment, which could only be that the Jew should have his bond. All things were made ready. The Jew ordered that Ansaldo should be stripped naked. He took in his hand the razor which he had caused to be made especially for the purpose. But at this moment the Doctor interrupted him, saying: " Take heed what you do, for if you take more or less than one pound, your head will be struck off; and if you shed only one drop of blood, you shall die too." And further, the Doctor caused the executioner to bring the block and the ax. Then the Jew was bidden to proceed; but he thought better of it and replied that he would take the 100,000 ducats. But now the Doctor of Law in turn proved inflexible, and did not cease until the Jew in fury tore up the bond. Giannetto was overjoyed, and carried the ducats to the inn where the Doctor lodged to give them as a present; but the Doctor would not accept the money and asked only for the ring which Giannetto was wearing. Giannetto replied that this ring had been given him by his lady, whom he loved more than anything in this world; but at length he was moved by gratitude to part with his ring to the Doctor.

When Giannetto returned to Belmonte his lady had already reached home and resumed her woman's clothes, declaring that she had spent the time of her husband's absence at the baths. She received Ansaldo kindly, but to her husband she gave a cold welcome. He asked her why she was so cold to him. She answered that she did not want his kisses, which he must surely have been bestowing on his former mistresses in Venice. When he hotly denied the charge, she asked for her ring, and refused to believe his oath that he had given it to the Doctor. She swore moreover that he had given it to a woman. The tears began to rise in Giannetto's eyes, and then the lady could not keep up her pretense any longer. She embraced him, showed him the ring, and told him the whole story. So they came to love each other even more than before. As for Ansaldo, Giannetto called the damsel who had given him the good advice about the wine and married her to Ansaldo. So they all spent the rest of their lives in great felicity and contentment.

In writing or rewriting *The Merchant of Venice* Shakespeare had before him a recent and most successful play which also told of a Jew who hated all Christians. This was Marlowe's tragedy *The Jew of Malta,* which was one of Edward Alleyn's more successful parts and was still being played at the Rose playhouse. Barabas, the Jew of Malta, like Shylock had an only daughter and many ducats, but he was altogether a more monstrous and far less credible character than Shylock. In a few passages Shakespeare owed something to Marlowe in portraying Shylock as remorseless and vindictive; but Barabas was a monster of hate who did not hesitate to poison a whole nunnery because it contained the daughter who had offended him. In comparison Shylock is a mild-mannered simpleton.

The Merchant of Venice was entered in the Stationers' Register on July 22, 1598, to James Roberts as " a booke of the Marchaunt of Venyce, or otherwise called the Jewe of Venyce, Provided that yt bee not prynted by the said James Robertes or anye other whatsoever without lycence first had from the Right honorable the lord Chamberlen." This was apparently a blocking entry intended to prevent publication (see Gen. Intro. p. 66a). On October 28, 1600, Roberts transferred his rights in the play to Thomas Hayes, who shortly afterward produced a quarto (Q1) with the title: *The most excellent Historie of the Merchant of Venice. With the extreame crueltie of Shylocke the Iewe towards the sayd Merchant, in cutting a iust pound of his flesh: and the obtayning of Portia by the choyse of three chests. As it hath beene diuers times acted by the Lord Chamberlaine his Seruants. Written by William Shakespeare.* (See Pl. 14b).

The Merchant of Venice is the first play of Shakespeare's maturity. Hitherto he had been rather a poet using drama as a vessel for poetry, always ready to hold up the play so that a character might utter a poem or draw out the varieties of meaning of a phrase or a word for a dozen lines on end. Hereafter even the most lyrical of his speeches is an essential part of the action, so that in the later plays there are less fine writing and fewer ornate passages which can be extracted for an anthology; but withal he gained a greater power of statement and a deeper sense of human character. *The Merchant of Venice* is by far the most competent play that Shakespeare had yet written, in plot, situation, character, and dialogue.

Much of the success of the play is due to a well-knit plot which is worth studying in detail. It begins with Antonio the merchant, melancholy he knows not why, and unable to shake off the mood; and then, in the quiet that follows the departure of his noisy acquaintances, Bassanio, his young friend for whom he will sacrifice all, asks his help in the romantic gamble for Portia. The next scene gives a glimpse of Portia at home, bound by the strange condition of her father's will. With the third scene the play gains speed. It opens with mature ease. Bassanio enters in conversation with Shylock, and in thirty lines without preliminaries or explanation the whole situation and the characters of the two men are firmly shown: Bassanio overanxious for his loan, Shylock, the hardheaded businessman, coldly weighing the risk, and yet excited by the chance of a deal which may bring ruin on his old enemy Antonio. There are wrongs on both sides. Antonio may rightly hate Shylock's methods, but Shylock has every reason to resent Antonio's arrogant assumption of greater moral worth. The instinctive hatred of these two flares up and results in the monstrous proposal that Shylock lend the money gratis but that Antonio risk his life for the loan. The scene ends with Bassanio's foreboding that somehow the Jew will get his pound of flesh.

Shakespeare then quickens the excitement and shows the advance of the fortunes of the chief characters by a succession of ten short scenes: Belmont, where the Prince of Morocco has come to make his choice; Venice, with Launcelot Gobbo leaving the Jew to take service with Bassanio, Lorenzo eloping with Jessica, Shylock's worthless little daughter, and Bassanio setting out for Belmont; Belmont, where the Prince of Morocco reveals to himself the contents of the gold casket; Venice, where the news of Antonio's misfortunes is beginning to come through; Belmont, to see the Prince of Aragon open the silver casket and, as he departs crestfallen, the coming of Bassanio to try his luck; Venice, where Shylock's rage against Antonio has now ripened into implacable hate.

After these quick movements and the growing sense of doom, there follows the long, leisurely scene where Bassanio makes his choice of the caskets and wins the prize. The scene is deliberately drawn out, and the lyric moment enhanced by music until Portia with a free conscience can give herself to the man whom she would herself have chosen. Then, when everyone is still in the happy mood of congratulation, comes the sudden reversal for which the audience has been so well prepared: Antonio is bankrupt and the Jew will take his revenge. Two short scenes lead up to the

trial of the case of Shylock *versus* Antonio; it is still an exciting trial even to an audience long familiar with the old story. It is also a sign of Shakespeare's increasing skill as a dramatist that the great speech on the quality of mercy is not only entirely appropriate in its context, but is no longer than twenty-one lines.

In the final act Shakespeare returns to the mood of lyric love, and he creates by sheer poetry, and without any help from the electrician, the atmosphere of romantic moonlight on a warm summer's night passing gradually to dawn as the lovers all return to Belmont.

The characterization is as good as the plot; for the people are human, each with his faults and virtues. Antonio is an honest merchant, a friend to the death, but his treatment of Shylock is narrow-minded and self-righteous. Bassanio is a gay young spendthrift, but is forgiven much as an ardent lover. Portia is witty, attractive, courageous, intelligent, but nevertheless feline in her treatment of Shylock and of her husband over the ring. As for Shylock, opinion has changed during the centuries. In Shakespeare's time a Jew, especially on the stage, was a monster, capable of any cruelty toward a Christian; yet Shakespeare made him a man with real and bitter grievances enough to sour a saint. When the play was first acted there was little sympathy for him, and some surprise that he was let off so lightly. In more recent times, star actors who have taken the part have rather stressed the pathos in the Jew, so that in spite of his vindictiveness, Shylock often seems to stand out as the only man of worth in a worthless society.

The Merchant of Venice is not, however, one of Shakespeare's finest achievements. It should be compared rather with what had gone before than with the later plays. It lacks the sincerity and the depth of the greater comedies; at no time does Shakespeare tear the heart of the spectator, who is never seriously disturbed lest Bassanio choose the silver casket or Antonio bleed to death before his eyes. The play is a good tale admirably told, but no more.

The Merchant of Venice

DRAMATIS PERSONAE

THE DUKE OF VENICE
THE PRINCE OF MOROCCO ⎱ *suitors to Portia*
THE PRINCE OF ARAGON ⎰
ANTONIO, *a merchant of Venice*
BASSANIO, *his friend, suitor likewise to Portia*
SALANIO ⎱
SALARINO ⎰ *friends to Antonio and Bassanio*
GRATIANO ⎰
SALERIO ⎰
LORENZO, *in love with Jessica*
SHYLOCK, *a rich Jew*
TUBAL, *a Jew, his friend*
LAUNCELOT GOBBO, *the clown, servant to Shylock*
OLD GOBBO, *father to Launcelot*

LEONARDO, *servant to Bassanio*
BALTHASAR ⎱ *servants to Portia*
STEPHANO ⎰

PORTIA, *a rich heiress*
NERISSA, *her waiting-maid*
JESSICA, *daughter to Shylock*

MAGNIFICOES *of* Venice, OFFICERS *of the Court of* Justice, JAILER, SERVANTS *to Portia, and other* ATTENDANTS

SCENE — *Partly at Venice, and partly at Belmont, the seat of Portia, on the Continent.*

Act I

SCENE I. *Venice. A street.*

[*Enter* ANTONIO, SALARINO, *and* SALANIO.]
ANT. In sooth, I know not why I am so sad.
It wearies me, you say it wearies you;
But how I caught it, found it, or came by it,
What stuff 'tis made of, whereof it is born,
I am to° learn. 5
And such a want-wit sadness makes of me
That I have much ado to know myself.
    SALAR. Your mind is tossing on the ocean —
There where your argosies° with portly° sail,
Like signiors and rich burghers° on the flood, 10
Or, as it were, the pageants° of the sea,
Do overpeer° the petty traffickers
That curtsy to them, do them reverence,
As they fly by them with their woven wings.°
    SALAN. Believe me, sir, had I such venture forth,
The better part of my affections would 16
Be with my hopes abroad. I should be still°
Plucking the grass to know where sits the wind,
Peering in maps for ports, and piers, and roads.°
And every object that might make me fear 20
Misfortune to my ventures, out of doubt
Would make me sad.
    SALAR.   My wind, cooling my broth,
Would blow me to an ague° when I thought

What harm a wind too great at sea might do.
I should not see the sandy hourglass run 25
But I should think of shallows and of flats,°
And see my wealthy *Andrew*° docked in sand
Vailing° her high top lower than her ribs
To kiss her burial. Should I go to church
And see the holy edifice of stone, 30
And not bethink me straight of dangerous rocks,
Which touching but my gentle vessel's side
Would scatter all her spices on the stream,
Enrobe the roaring waters with my silks —
And, in a word, but even now worth this, 35
And now worth nothing? Shall I have the thought
To think on this, and shall I lack the thought
That such a thing bechanced would make me sad?
But tell not me — I know Antonio
Is sad to think upon his merchandise. 40
    ANT. Believe me, no. I thank my fortune for it,
My ventures are not in one bottom trusted,
Nor to one place, nor is my whole estate
Upon the fortune of this present year.
Therefore my merchandise makes me not sad. 45
    SALAR. Why, then you are in love.
    ANT.   Fie, fie!
    SALAR. Not in love neither? Then let us say you are sad
Because you are not merry; and 'twere as easy
For you to laugh, and leap, and say you are merry
Because you are not sad. Now, by two-headed
    Janus,° 50

Act I, Sc. i: **5. am to:** have yet to. **9. argosies:** An argosy is a great merchant ship, sometimes called a carrack. **portly:** swelling. **10. burghers:** citizens, businessmen. **11. pageants:** elaborate spectacles, such as are shown on floats. **12. overpeer:** look down on. **14. woven wings:** i.e., sails. **17. still:** always. **19. roads:** anchorages. **23. ague:** fever.

26. flats: sandbanks. **27. Andrew:** the name of a ship. Probably Shakespeare has in mind the great carrack *St. Andrew* brought home to England after the capture of Cadiz in the summer of 1596. See Gen. Intro. p. 29b. **28. Vailing:** lowering. **50. Janus:** a Roman god with two faces, the one smiling, the other frowning.

Nature hath framed strange fellows in her time —
Some that will evermore peep through their eyes,
And laugh like parrots at a bagpiper,
And other of such vinegar aspéct
That they'll not show their teeth in way of smile   55
Though Nestor° swear the jest be laughable.

     [*Enter* BASSANIO, LORENZO, *and* GRATIANO.]

     SALAN. Here comes Bassanio, your most noble
     kinsman,
Gratiano, and Lorenzo. Fare ye well.
We leave you now with better company.

     SALAR. I would have stayed till I had made you
     merry   60
If worthier friends had not prevented° me.

     ANT. Your worth is very dear in my regard.
I take it, your own business calls on you,
And you embrace the occasion to depart.

     SALAR. Good morrow, my good lords.   65

     BASS. Good signiors both, when shall we laugh?
     Say, when?
You grow exceeding strange. Must it be so?

     SALAR. We'll make our leisures to attend on yours.

         [*Exeunt* SALARINO *and* SALANIO.]

     LOR. My Lord Bassanio, since you have found An-
     tonio,
We two will leave you. But at dinnertime   70
I pray you have in mind where we must meet.

     BASS. I will not fail you.

     GRA. You look not well, Signior Antonio.
You have too much respect upon° the world.
They lose it that do buy it with much care.   75
Believe me, you are marvelously° changed.

     ANT. I hold the world but as the world, Gra-
     tiano —
A stage where every man must play a part,
And mine a sad one.

     GRA.   Let me play the fool.
With mirth and laughter let old wrinkles come,   80
And let my liver° rather heat with wine
Than my heart cool with mortifying° groans.
Why should a man whose blood is warm within
Sit like his grandsire cut in alabaster?°
Sleep when he wakes, and creep into the jaundice°
By being peevish? I tell thee what, Antonio —   86
I love thee, and it is my love that speaks —
There are a sort of men whose visages
Do cream and mantle° like a standing pond,
And do a willful stillness entertain,°   90

With purpose to be dressed in an opinion°
Of wisdom, gravity, profound conceit,°
As who should say, "I am Sir Oracle,
And when I ope my lips, let no dog bark!"
O my Antonio, I do know of these,   95
That therefore only are reputed wise
For saying nothing; when, I am very sure,
If they should speak, would almost damn those ears
Which, hearing them, would call their brothers
     fools.°
I'll tell thee more of this another time.   100
But fish not with this melancholy bait°
For this fool gudgeon,° this opinion.
Come, good Lorenzo. Fare ye well awhile.
I'll end my exhortation after dinner.

     LOR. Well, we will leave you, then, till dinnertime.
I must be one of these same dumb wise men,   106
For Gratiano never lets me speak.

     GRA. Well, keep me company but two years moe,°
Thou shalt not know the sound of thine own tongue.

     ANT. Farewell. I'll grow a talker for this gear.°

     GRA. Thanks, i'faith, for silence is only commend-
     able   111
In a neat's tongue° dried and a maid not vendible.°

         [*Exeunt* GRATIANO *and* LORENZO.]

     ANT. Is that anything now?

     BASS. Gratiano speaks an infinite deal of nothing,
more than any man in all Venice. His reasons° are as
two grains of wheat hid in two bushels of chaff.   116
You shall seek all day ere you find them, and when
you have them, they are not worth the search.

     ANT. Well, tell me now, what lady is the same
To whom you swore a secret pilgrimage   120
That you today promised to tell me of?

     BASS. 'Tis not unknown to you, Antonio,
How much I have disabled mine estate
By something° showing a more swelling port°
Than my faint means would grant continuance.
Nor do I now make moan to be abridged°   126
From such a noble rate; but my chief care
Is to come fairly off from the great debts
Wherein my time, something too prodigal,
Hath left me gaged.° To you, Antonio,   130
I owe the most, in money and in love.
And from your love I have a warranty

---

56. Nestor: the old veteran in the Greek army that went against Troy. Anything that Nestor guaranteed must be good. See *Tr & Cr.*   **61. prevented:** forestalled.   **74. respect upon:** respect for.   **76. marvelously:** exceedingly.   **81. liver:** regarded as the seat of the passions.   **82. mortifying:** deadly.   **84. grandsire . . . alabaster:** like the alabaster image of his grandfather. Alabaster was much used for monuments of the dead in English churches of the type shown in Pl. 2b.   **85. jaundice:** disorder in the bile, caused by, and causing, intense depression.   **89. cream . . . mantle:** cover with a thick motionless scum.   **90. entertain:** affect.

91. dressed . . . opinion: get a reputation for.   **92. conceit:** thought. **98–99. If . . . fools:** if they should say anything which would make their brothers fools and so be damned — a reminiscence of Matthew 5:22: "But I say unto you, that whosoever is angry with his brother without a cause shall be in danger of the judgment . . . but whosoever shall say, Thou fool, shall be in danger of hell fire."   **101. melancholy bait:** bait which causes melancholy, for *opinion* (reputation) is not worth having.   **102. gudgeon:** a small fish easily caught.   **108. moe:** more.   **110. gear:** stuff, chatter; *gear* is one of those words used vaguely like "case" or "lot." **112. neat's tongue:** ox tongue. **vendible:** marketable.   **115. reasons:** intelligent remarks.   **124. something:** somewhat. **swelling port:** extravagant living; i.e., by being too much of a "playboy."   **126. abridged:** cut down.   **130. gaged:** pledged, in debt.

To unburden all my plots° and purposes
How to get clear of all the debts I owe.
    ANT. I pray you, good Bassanio, let me know it.
And if it stand, as you yourself still do,   136
Within the eye of honor,° be assured
My purse, my person, my extremest means,
Lie all unlocked to your occasions.°
    BASS. In my school days, when I had lost one
    shaft,°   140
I shot his fellow of the selfsame flight°
The selfsame way with more advisèd° watch,
To find the other forth, and by adventuring both,
I oft found both. I urge this childhood proof°
Because what follows is pure innocence.   145
I owe you much, and, like a willful youth,
That which I owe is lost. But if you please
To shoot another arrow that self way
Which you did shoot the first, I do not doubt,
As I will watch the aim, or° to find both   150
Or bring your latter hazard° back again,
And thankfully rest debtor for the first.
    ANT. You know me well, and herein spend but
    time
To wind about my love with circumstance.°
And out of doubt you do me now more wrong   155
In making question of my uttermost°
Than if you had made waste of all I have.
Then do but say to me what I should do
That in your knowledge may by me be done,
And I am prest° unto it. Therefore, speak.   160
    BASS. In Belmont is a lady richly left,°
And she is fair and, fairer than that word,
Of wondrous virtues. Sometimes from her eyes
I did receive fair speechless messages.
Her name is Portia, nothing undervalued   165
To Cato's daughter, Brutus' Portia.°
Nor is the wide world ignorant of her worth,
For the four winds blow in from every coast
Renownèd suitors. And her sunny locks
Hang on her temples like a golden fleece,   170
Which makes her seat of Belmont Colchos' strond,
And many Jasons come in quest of her.°
O my Antonio, had I but the means
To hold a rival place with one of them,
I have a mind presages° me such thrift°   175
That I should questionless be fortunate!
    ANT. Thou know'st that all my fortunes are at sea,
Neither have I money nor commodity

To raise a present° sum. Therefore go forth,
Try what my credit can in Venice do.   180
That shall be racked,° even to the uttermost,
To furnish thee to Belmont, to fair Portia.
Go, presently inquire, and so will I,
Where money is, and I no question make   184
To have it of my trust,° or for my sake.   [*Exeunt.*]

SCENE II. *Belmont. A room in* PORTIA'S *house.*

[*Enter* PORTIA *and* NERISSA.]

    POR. By my troth,° Nerissa, my little body is
aweary of this great world.
    NER. You would be, sweet madam, if your mis-
eries were in the same abundance as your good fortunes are. And yet, for aught I see, they are as   5
sick that surfeit° with too much as they that starve
with nothing. It is no mean happiness, therefore, to
be seated in the mean. Superfluity comes sooner by
white hairs,° but competency° lives longer.   10
    POR. Good sentences,° and well pronounced.
    NER. They would be better if well followed.
    POR. If to do were as easy as to know what were
good to do, chapels had been churches and poor
men's cottages princes' palaces. It is a good di-   15
vine° that follows his own instructions. I can easier
teach twenty what were good to be done than be one
of the twenty to follow mine own teaching. The brain
may devise laws for the blood, but a hot temper leaps
o'er a cold decree. Such a hare is madness the   20
youth, to skip o'er the meshes° of good counsel the
cripple. But this reasoning° is not in the fashion° to
choose me a husband. Oh, me, the word " choose." I
may neither choose whom I would nor refuse whom
I dislike. So is the will of a living daughter   25
curbed by the will° of a dead father. Is it not hard,
Nerissa, that I cannot choose one, nor refuse none?
    NER. Your father was ever virtuous, and holy   30
men at their death have good inspirations. Therefore
the lottery° that he hath devised in these three chests
of gold, silver, and lead — whereof who chooses his
meaning chooses you — will, no doubt, never be
chosen by any rightly but one who shall rightly   35
love. But what warmth is there in your affection
toward any of these princely suitors that are already
come?
    POR. I pray thee, overname° them, and as thou

---

133. plots: plans. 136–37. stand . . . honor: i.e., is honorable.
139. occasions: needs. 140. shaft: arrow. 141. flight: batch of
arrows. 142. advised: careful. 144. proof: experience. 150. or:
either. 151. hazard: risk, speculation. 153–54. spend . . . circumstance: you need not waste time by this indirect approach.
156. In . . . uttermost: in questioning whether I shall help you
to the uttermost. 160. prest: ready. 161. richly left: with a
rich legacy. 166. Brutus' Portia: See *Caesar*, II.i.233, etc.
171–72. Colchos' . . . her: Jason sailed to Colchos in the *Argo*
to fetch away the Golden Fleece. strond: strand, shore. 175. presages: foretells. thrift: profit.

179. present: immediate. 181. racked: stretched. 185. trust:
credit.
Sc. ii: 1. troth: faith. 6. surfeit: gorge themselves.
9–10. Superfluity . . . hairs: a man who has too much ages
quickest. 10. competency: modest means. 11. sentences: proverbs. 15–16. divine: preacher. 21. meshes: net. 22. reasoning: arguing. fashion: manner, way. 25–26. will . . . will: desire . . . testament. 32. lottery: lucky draw. 39. overname:
repeat the names of.

namest them I will describe them, and according   40
to my description, level° at my affection.

NER. First, there is the Neapolitan Prince.

POR. Aye, that's a colt indeed, for he doth nothing
but talk of his horse, and he makes it a great   45
appropriation° to his own good parts that he can
shoe him himself. I am much afeard my lady his
mother played false with a smith.

NER. Then there is the County° Palatine.

POR. He doth nothing but frown, as who   50
should say, "If you will not have me, choose." He
hears merry tales and smiles not. I fear he will prove
the weeping philosopher° when he grows old, being
so full of unmannerly sadness in his youth. I had
rather be married to a death's-head° with a bone   55
in his mouth than to either of these. God defend me
from these two!

NER. How say you by the French lord, Monsieur
Le Bon?

POR. God made him, and therefore let him   60
pass for a man. In truth, I know it is a sin to be a
mocker, but he! — Why, he hath a horse better than
the Neapolitan's, a better bad habit of frowning than
the Count Palatine. He is every man in no man. If a
throstle° sing, he falls straight a-capering. He   65
will fence with his own shadow. If I should marry
him, I should marry twenty husbands. If he would
despise me, I would forgive him, for if he love me to
madness, I shall never requite him.   70

NER. What say you, then, to Falconbridge, the
young baron of England?

POR. You know I say nothing to him, for he
understands not me, nor I him. He hath neither
Latin, French, nor Italian, and you will come   75
into the court and swear that I have a poor pennyworth in the English. He is a proper° man's picture,
but, alas! who can converse with a dumb show?°
How oddly he is suited! I think he bought his
doublet° in Italy, his round hose° in France,   80
his bonnet in Germany, and his behavior everywhere.°

NER. What think you of the Scottish lord, his
neighbor?

POR. That he hath a neighborly charity in   85
him, for he borrowed° a box of the ear of the Englishman and swore he would pay him again when he

was able. I think the Frenchman became his surety,
and sealed under° for another.

NER. How like you the young German, the Duke
of Saxony's nephew?   91

POR. Very vilely in the morning, when he is sober,
and most vilely in the afternoon, when he is drunk.
When he is best, he is a little worse than a man, and
when he is worst, he is little better than a beast.   95
An° the worst fall that ever fell, I hope I shall make
shift° to go without him.

NER. If he should offer to choose and choose
the right casket, you should refuse to perform
your father's will if you should refuse to accept
him.   102

POR. Therefore, for fear of the worst, I pray thee
set a deep glass of Rhenish° wine on the contrary°
casket, for if the Devil be within and that temptation
without, I know he will choose it. I will do   106
anything, Nerissa, ere I'll be married to a sponge.

NER. You need not fear, lady, the having any of
these lords. They have acquainted me with   110
their determinations, which is, indeed, to return to
their home and to trouble you with no more suit unless you may be won by some other sort° than your
father's imposition, depending on the caskets.   115

POR. If I live to be as old as Sibylla,° I will die as
chaste as Diana° unless I be obtained by the manner
of my father's will. I am glad this parcel of wooers
are so reasonable, for there is not one among them
but I dote on his very absence, and I pray God grant
them a fair departure.   121

NER. Do you not remember, lady, in your father's
time, a Venetian, a scholar and a soldier, that came
hither in company of the Marquis of Montferrat?

POR. Yes, yes, it was Bassanio, as I think he was so
called.

NER. True, madam. He of all the men that ever
my foolish eyes looked upon was the best deserving
a fair lady.   131

POR. I remember him well, and I remember him
worthy of thy praise. [*Enter a* SERVINGMAN.] How
now! What news?

SERV. The four strangers seek for you, madam, to
take their leave. And there is a forerunner   136
come from a fifth, the Prince of Morocco, who brings
word the Prince his master will be here tonight.

POR. If I could bid the fifth welcome with so good
a heart as I can bid the other four farewell, I should
be glad of his approach. If he have the condition of a

---

41. **level**: guess.   46. **appropriation**: special addition.   49. **County**: Count.   53. **weeping philosopher**: Heraclitus, who wept over the follies of mankind.   55. **death's-head**: skull.   65. **throstle**: thrush.   77. **proper**: handsome.   78. **dumb show**: In some plays the action is first symbolized by a pantomime in which the actors say nothing. For a specimen see *Haml*, III.ii.145.   80. **doublet**: coat. **round hose**: short breeches. See Pl. 8b and comment on p. 93a–b.   71–82. **What . . . everywhere**: These were common criticisms of the English — that they knew no language but their own and borrowed their fashions from every nation at once.   86. **borrowed**: received.

89. **sealed under**: agreed to be his surety. Before England and Scotland were united in 1603, the French and the Scots were close allies.   96. **An**: if.   96–97. **make shift**: contrive.   104. **Rhenish**: Rhine. **contrary**: opposite.   113. **sort**: manner.   116. **Sibylla**: the ancient prophetess to whom Apollo promised that her years should be as many as the grains of sand which she held in her hand.   117. **Diana**: virgin goddess of chastity.

saint and the complexion of a devil,° I had rather he
should shrive° me than wive me.   145
Come, Nerissa. Sirrah,° go before.
Whiles we shut the gates upon one wooer, another
    knocks at the door.   [*Exeunt.*]

SCENE III. *Venice. A public place.*

[*Enter* BASSANIO *and* SHYLOCK.]

SHY. Three thousand ducats.° Well.
BASS. Aye, sir, for three months.
SHY. For three months. Well.
BASS. For the which, as I told you, Antonio shall
be bound.   5
SHY. Antonio shall become bound. Well.
BASS. May you stead° me? Will you pleasure me?
Shall I know your answer?
SHY. Three thousand ducats for three months, and
Antonio bound.   10
BASS. Your answer to that.
SHY. Antonio is a good man.
BASS. Have you heard any imputation to the con-
trary?
SHY. Oh, no, no, no, no. My meaning in say- 15
ing he is a good man is to have you understand me
that he is sufficient.° Yet his means are in supposi-
tion.° He hath an argosy bound to Tripolis, another
to the Indies. I understand, moreover, upon the
Rialto,° he hath a third at Mexico, a fourth for 20
England, and other ventures he hath, squandered
abroad. But ships are but boards, sailors but men.
There be land rats and water rats, water thieves and
land thieves — I mean pirates. And then there is the
peril of waters, winds, and rocks. The man is, 25
notwithstanding, sufficient. Three thousand ducats.
I think I may take his bond.
BASS. Be assured you may.
SHY. I will be assured I may, and that I may 30
be assured, I will bethink me. May I speak with
Antonio?
BASS. If it please you to dine with us.
SHY. Yes, to smell pork, to eat of the habitation
which your prophet the Nazarite conjured the 35
devil into.° I will buy with you, sell with you, talk
with you, walk with you, and so following; but I will
not eat with you, drink with you, nor pray with you.
What news on the Rialto? Who is he comes here?

[*Enter* ANTONIO.]

BASS. This is Signior Antonio.   41
SHY. [*Aside*] How like a fawning publican° he
    looks!
I hate him for he is a Christian,
But more for that in low simplicity
He lends out money gratis and brings down   45
The rate of usance° here with us in Venice.
If I can catch him once upon the hip,
I will feed fat the ancient grudge I bear him.
He hates our sacred nation, and he rails,
Even there where merchants most do congregate,
On me, my bargains, and my well-won thrift,° 51
Which he calls interest. Cursed be my tribe
If I forgive him!
BASS.   Shylock, do you hear?
SHY. I am debating of my present store,
And by the near guess of my memory,   55
I cannot instantly raise up the gross°
Of full three thousand ducats. What of that?
Tubal, a wealthy Hebrew of my tribe,
Will furnish me. But soft! How many months
Do you desire? [*To* ANTONIO] Rest you fair, good
    signior.   60
Your Worship was the last man in our mouths.
ANT. Shylock, although I neither lend nor borrow,
By taking nor by giving of excess,°
Yet to supply the ripe° wants of my friend
I'll break a custom. [*To* BASSANIO] Is he yet pos-
    sessed°   65
How much ye would?
SHY.   Aye, aye, three thousand ducats.
ANT. And for three months.
SHY. I had forgot — three months, you told me so.
Well, then, your bond, and let me see. But hear you,
Methought you said you neither lend nor borrow
Upon advantage.
ANT.   I do never use it.   71
SHY. When Jacob grazed his uncle Laban's°
    sheep —
This Jacob from our holy Abram was,
As his wise mother wrought in his behalf,
The third possessor — aye, he was the third° ——
ANT. And what of him? Did he take interest? 76

42. fawning publican: The publicans were collectors of taxes for
the Romans. To a strict Jew *publican* was a term of bitter abuse,
as in the parable of the Pharisee and the publican, "The Pharisee
stood and prayed thus with himself, 'God, I thank thee, that I
am not as other men are . . . or even as this publican.'" Luke
18:11.   46. usance: usury. Usury is the taking of excessive interest, and so exploiting the needy; but in Shakespeare's time
even a moderate rate of interest was in theory regarded as
immoral, for Christians should help one another. In practice 10%
was allowed. Usury was one of the greatest abuses of the time.
See *M for Meas*, IV.iii.4–12.   51. thrift: profit.   56. gross: full
sum.   63. excess: interest; i.e., more than the original loan.
64. ripe: needing immediate help.   65. possessed: informed.
72. Jacob . . . Laban's: The story is told in Genesis 30:27–43.
74–75. wise . . . third: Jacob's mother by fraud persuaded Isaac
to bless his younger son. See Genesis 27.

144. complexion . . . devil: the Devil was black.   145. shrive:
give absolution.   146. Sirrah: form of address used to an
inferior.
    Sc. iii: 1. ducat: worth about $2.   7. stead: help.   17. suffi-
cient: solvent. supposition: doubt.   20. Rialto: the Merchants'
Exchange, where businessmen met twice daily to make deals
and exchange news.   35–36. conjured . . . into: i.e., the swine
into which entered the devils cast out of the man of the
tombs in the country of the Gadarenes. See Mark 5:1–17.

SHY. No, not take interest, not, as you would say,
Directly interest. Mark what Jacob did.
When Laban and himself were compromised°
That all the eanlings° which were streaked and
    pied°   80
Should fall as Jacob's hire, the ewes, being rank,°
In the end of autumn turned to the rams.
And when the work of generation was
Between these woolly breeders in the act,
The skillful shepherd peeled me certain wands 85
And, in the doing of the deed of kind,°
He stuck them up before the fulsome° ewes,
Who, then conceiving, did in eaning time°
Fall° particolored lambs, and those were Jacob's.
This was a way to thrive, and he was blest.   90
And thrift is blessing, if men steal it not.
    ANT. This was a venture, sir, that Jacob served for,
A thing not in his power to bring to pass,
But swayed and fashioned by the hand of Heaven.
Was this inserted to make interest good?   95
Or is your gold and silver ewes and rams?
    SHY. I cannot tell. I make it breed as fast.
But note me, signior.
    ANT.   Mark you this, Bassanio,
The Devil can cite Scripture for his purpose.
An evil soul producing holy witness   100
Is like a villain with a smiling cheek,
A goodly apple rotten at the heart.
Oh, what a goodly outside falsehood hath!
    SHY. Three thousand ducats. 'Tis a good round
    sum.
Three months from twelve — then, let me see, the
    rate ——   105
    ANT. Well, Shylock, shall we be beholding to you?
    SHY. Signior Antonio, many a time and oft
In the Rialto you have rated° me
About my moneys and my usances.
Still have I borne it with a patient shrug,   110
For sufferance° is the badge of all our tribe.
You call me misbeliever, cutthroat dog,
And spit upon my Jewish gaberdine,°
And all for use of that which is mine own.
Well, then, it now appears you need my help.   115
Go to, then, you come to me and you say
"Shylock, we would have moneys." You say so,
You that did void your rheum° upon my beard
And foot me as you spurn a stranger cur
Over your threshold. Moneys is your suit.   120
What should I say to you? Should I not say,
"Hath a dog money? Is it possible
A cur can lend three thousand ducats?" Or
Shall I bend low and in a bondman's° key,

With bated breath and whispering humbleness,   125
Say this —
"Fair sir, you spit on me on Wednesday last,
You spurned me such a day, another time
You called me dog, and for these courtesies
I'll lend you thus much moneys"?   130
    ANT. I am as like to call thee so again,
To spit on thee again, to spurn thee too.
If thou wilt lend this money, lend it not
As to thy friends, for when did friendship take
A breed° for barren metal of his friend?   135
But lend it rather to thine enemy,
Who if he break,° thou mayst with better face
Exact the penalty.
    SHY.   Why, look you how you storm!
I would be friends with you, and have your love,
Forget the shames that you have stained me with,
Supply your present wants, and take no doit°   141
Of usance for my moneys, and you'll not hear me.
This is kind I offer.
    BASS. This were kindness.
    SHY.   This kindness will I show.
Go with me to a notary, seal me there   145
Your single bond.° And, in a merry sport,
If you repay me not on such a day,
In such a place, such sum or sums as are
Expressed in the condition, let the forfeit
Be nominated for an equal° pound   150
Of your fair flesh, to be cut off and taken
In what part of your body pleaseth me.
    ANT. Content, i' faith. I'll seal to such a bond,
And say there is much kindness in the Jew.
    BASS. You shall not seal to such a bond for me.
I'll rather dwell in my necessity.   156
    ANT. Why, fear not, man, I will not forfeit it.
Within these two months — that's a month before
This bond expires — I do expect return
Of thrice three times the value of this bond.   160
    SHY. O Father Abram, what these Christians are,
Whose own hard dealings teaches them suspect
The thoughts of others! Pray you, tell me this.
If he should break his day, what should I gain
By the exaction of the forfeiture?   165
A pound of man's flesh taken from a man
Is not so estimable, profitable neither,
As flesh of muttons, beefs, or goats. I say
To buy his favor I extend this friendship.
If he will take it, so; if not, adieu.   170
And, for my love, I pray you wrong me not.
    ANT. Yes, Shylock, I will seal unto this bond.
    SHY. Then meet me forthwith at the notary's.
Give him direction for this merry bond,
And I will go and purse the ducats straight,   175
See to my house, left in the fearful° guard

---

79. compromised: agreed. 80. eanlings: lambs. streaked . . .
pied: striped . . . particolored, or as in Genesis, "ringstraked and
spotted." 81. rank: in heat. 86. kind: nature. 87. fulsome:
fat. 88. eaning time: lambing season. 89. Fall: give birth to.
108. rated: abused. 111. sufferance: patience. 113. gaberdine:
cloak. 118. void . . . rheum: spit. 124. bondman: slave.

135. breed: increase. 137. break: go bankrupt. 141. doit: small
Dutch coin, "cent." 146. single bond: i.e., without any second
security. 150. equal: exact. 176. fearful: to be feared.

Of an unthrifty knave, and presently
I will be with you.
    ANT.   Hie thee, gentle Jew.   [*Exit* SHYLOCK.]
The Hebrew will turn Christian. He grows kind.
    BASS. I like not fair terms and a villain's mind.
    ANT. Come on. In this there can be no dismay.
My ships come home a month before the day.   182
                        [*Exeunt.*]

Act II

SCENE I. *Belmont. A room in* PORTIA'S *house.*

[*Flourish of cornets.° Enter the* PRINCE OF MOROCCO
and his train; PORTIA, NERISSA, *and others attending.*]
    MOR. Mislike me not for my complexion,
The shadowed° livery of the burnished sun,
To whom I am a neighbor and near bred.
Bring me the fairest creature northward born,
Where Phoebus'° fire scarce thaws the icicles,   5
And let us make incision for your love,
To prove whose blood is reddest,° his or mine.
I tell thee, lady, this aspéct° of mine
Hath feared° the valiant. By my love, I swear
The best-regarded virgins of our clime   10
Have loved it too. I would not change this hue,
Except to steal your thoughts, my gentle Queen.
    POR. In terms of choice I am not solely led
By nice direction of a maiden's eyes.°
Besides, the lottery of my destiny   15
Bars me the right of voluntary choosing.
But if my father had not scanted° me
And hedged me by his wit, to yield myself
His wife who wins me by that means I told you,
Yourself, renownèd Prince, then stood as fair   20
As any comer I have looked on yet
For my affection.
    MOR.   Even for that I thank you.
Therefore I pray you lead me to the caskets,
To try my fortune. By this scimitar°
That slew the Sophy° and a Persian prince   25
That won three fields° of Sultan Solyman,°
I would outstare the sternest eyes that look,
Outbrave the heart most daring on the earth,
Pluck the young sucking cubs from the she-bear,
Yea, mock the lion when he roars for prey,   30

To win thee, lady. But, alas the while!
If Hercules and Lichas° play at dice
Which is the better man, the greater throw
May turn by fortune from the weaker hand.
So is Alcides° beaten by his page,   35
And so may I, blind fortune leading me,
Miss that which one unworthier may attain,
And die with grieving.
    POR.   You must take your chance,
And either not attempt to choose at all
Or swear before you choose, if you choose wrong,
Never to speak to lady afterward   41
In way of marriage. Therefore be advised.
    MOR. Nor will not. Come, bring me unto my
    chance.
    POR. First, forward to the temple. After dinner
Your hazard shall be made.
    MOR.   Good fortune, then!   45
To make me blest or cursed'st among men.
                  [*Cornets, and exeunt.*]

SCENE II. *Venice. A street.*

[*Enter* LAUNCELOT GOBBO.]
    LAUN. Certainly my conscience will serve me to
run from this Jew my master. The fiend is at mine
elbow and tempts me, saying to me, "Gobbo,
Launcelot Gobbo, good Launcelot," or "good
Gobbo," or "good Launcelot Gobbo, use your legs,
take the start, run away." My conscience says,   5
"No, take heed, honest Launcelot, take heed, honest
Gobbo," or, as aforesaid, "honest Launcelot Gobbo,
do not run, scorn running with thy heels." Well, the
most courageous fiend bids me pack.° "Via!"° says
the fiend, "away!" says the fiend, "for the   10
heavens,° rouse up a brave mind," says the fiend,
"and run." Well, my conscience, hanging about the
neck of my heart, says very wisely to me, "My honest
friend Launcelot, being an honest man's son" — or
rather an honest woman's son, for indeed my   15
father did something smack, something grow to, he
had a kind of taste° — well, my conscience says,
"Launcelot, budge not." "Budge," says the fiend.
"Budge not," says my conscience. "Conscience,"
say I, "you counsel well." "Fiend," say I,   21
"you counsel well." To be ruled by my conscience,
I should stay with the Jew my master, who, God
bless the mark,° is a kind of devil; and to run away
from the Jew, I should be ruled by the fiend,   26

Act II, Sc. i: s.d., **Flourish of cornets:** fanfare to announce
the approach of a royal person. See Pl. 19c. **2. shadowed:** black;
my black skin shows that I am the servant of the sun. **5. Phoebus:** the sun god. **7. reddest:** i.e., bravest. **8. aspect:** face.
9. feared: frightened. **13–14. In . . . eyes:** I do not choose only
by delicate ladylike distinctions of appearance. **17. scanted:**
restricted. **24. scimitar:** curved sword. **25. Sophy:** Shah of
Persia. **26. fields:** battles. **Sultan Solyman:** the Turkish Emperor.

32. Lichas: the page of Hercules. **35. Alcides:** Hercules.
    Sc. ii: **9. pack:** get going. **Via:** get on. **10–11. for . . . heav-
ens:** for heavens' sake. **16–17. something . . . taste:** my father
was not too honest, there was a sort of burnt taste about him.
Launcelot's remarks are at times more allusive than clear.
smack: taste. **grow to:** a phrase used of milk burned in the pan.
23–24. God . . . mark: one of those meaningless phrases used as
apology before an unpleasant remark.

who, saving your reverence,° is the Devil himself. Certainly the Jew is the very Devil incarnal,° and, in my conscience, my conscience is but a kind of hard conscience to offer to counsel me to stay with the Jew. The fiend gives the more friendly counsel. 31 I will run, fiend, my heels are at your command. I will run.

[*Enter* OLD GOBBO, *with a basket.*]

GOB. Master young man, you, I pray you which is the way to Master Jew's? 35

LAUN. [*Aside*] Oh heavens, this is my true-begotten father! Who, being more than sand-blind,° high-gravel blind, knows me not. I will try confusions° with him.

GOB. Master young gentleman, I pray you which is the way to Master Jew's? 41

LAUN. Turn up on your right hand at the next turning, but at the next turning of all, on your left; marry,° at the very next turning, turn of no hand, but turn down indirectly to the Jew's house. 46

GOB. By God's sonties,° 'twill be a hard way to hit. Can you tell me whether one Launcelot, that dwells with him, dwell with him or no?

LAUN. Talk you of young Master Launcelot? 50 [*Aside*] Mark me now, now will I raise the waters. Talk you of young Master Launcelot?°

GOB. No master, sir, but a poor man's son. His father, though I say it, is an honest exceeding° poor man, and, God be thanked, well to live.° 55

LAUN. Well, let his father be what 'a will, we talk of young Master Launcelot.

GOB. Your Worship's friend, and Launcelot,° sir.

LAUN. But I pray you, ergo,° old man, ergo, I beseech you, talk you of young Master Launcelot? 60

GOB. Of Launcelot, an't please your mastership.

LAUN. Ergo, Master Launcelot. Talk not of Master Launcelot, Father, for the young gentleman, according to Fates and Destinies and such odd 65 sayings, the Sisters Three° and such branches of learning, is indeed deceased, or as you would say in plain terms, gone to Heaven.

GOB. Marry, God forbid! The boy was the very staff of my age, my very prop. 70

LAUN. Do I look like a cudgel or a hovel post,° a staff or a prop? Do you know me, Father?

GOB. Alack the day, I know you not, young gentleman: but I pray you tell me, is my boy, God rest his soul, alive or dead? 75

LAUN. Do you not know me, Father?

GOB. Alack, sir, I am sand-blind. I know you not.

LAUN. Nay, indeed, if you had your eyes, you might fail of the knowing me. It is a wise father 80 that knows his own child. Well, old man, I will tell you news of your son. Give me your blessing. Truth will come to light, murder cannot be hid long, a man's son may, but at the length truth will out. 85

GOB. Pray you, sir, stand up. I am sure you are not Launcelot, my boy.

LAUN. Pray you let's have no more fooling about it, but give me your blessing. I am Launcelot, your boy that was, your son that is, your child that shall be.

GOB. I cannot think you are my son. 92

LAUN. I know not what I shall think of that, but I am Launcelot, the Jew's man, and I am sure Margery your wife is my mother. 95

GOB. Her name is Margery, indeed. I'll be sworn, if thou be Launcelot, thou art mine own flesh and blood. Lord worshiped might He be! What a beard hast thou got! Thou hast got more hair on thy chin than Dobbin my fill horse° has on his tail. 101

LAUN. It should seem, then, that Dobbin's tail grows backward. I am sure he had more hair of his tail than I have of my face when I last saw him. 105

GOB. Lord, how art thou changed! How dost thou and thy master agree? I have brought him a present. How 'gree you now?

LAUN. Well, well, but, for mine own part, as I have set up my rest° to run away, so I will not 110 rest till I have run some ground. My master's a very Jew. Give him a present! Give him a halter. I am famished in his service, you may tell every finger I have with my ribs. Father, I am glad you are come. Give me your present to one Master Bassanio, 115 who indeed gives rare new liveries. If I serve not him, I will run as far as God has any ground. Oh, rare fortune! Here comes the man. To him, Father, for I am a Jew if I serve the Jew any longer. 120

[*Enter* BASSANIO, *with* LEONARDO *and other followers.*]

BASS. You may do so, but let it be so hasted that supper be ready at the farthest by five of the clock. See these letters delivered, put the liveries to making, and desire Gratiano to come anon° to my lodging.

[*Exit a* SERVANT.]

LAUN. To him, Father.

GOB. God bless your Worship!

BASS. Gramercy!° Wouldst thou aught with me?

GOB. Here's my son, sir, a poor boy —— 129

27. saving . . . reverence: with apologies for the remark, used like "God save the mark"; see l. 23 above. **28. incarnal:** for "incarnate." Launcelot loves big words, which he often gets wrong. **37. sand-blind:** nearsighted; but as Old Gobbo is nearly blind, Launcelot infers that he has gravel, not sand, in his eyes. **39. confusions:** for "conclusions." **43. marry:** Mary, by the Virgin. **47. By . . . sonties:** by God's saints. **52. Master Launcelot:** *Master* was the proper title for a gentleman. Launcelot to fool his father pretends that he has gone up in the world. **54. exceeding:** exceedingly. **55. well to live:** who lives a good life; i.e., "poor but honest." **58. and Launcelot:** i.e., plain Launcelot, not Master Launcelot. **59. ergo:** therefore. **66. Sisters Three:** the three Sisters of Destiny. Launcelot has picked up some literary jargon from his betters. **71. hovel post:** post supporting a hovel.

101. fill horse: cart horse. **110. set . . . rest:** determined to stake all; a metaphor from the card game of primero. See *R & J*, V.iii.110. **124. anon:** at once. **128. Gramercy:** God have mercy, a form of thanks.

LAUN. Not a poor boy, sir, but the rich Jew's man,
that would, sir — as my father shall specify ——

GOB. He hath a great infection,° sir, as one would
say, to serve ——   134

LAUN. Indeed, the short and the long is, I serve
the Jew, and have a desire — as my father shall
specify ——

GOB. His master and he, saving your Worship's
reverence, are scarce cater-cousins° ——   139

LAUN. To be brief, the very truth is that the Jew,
having done me wrong, doth cause me — as my
father, being, I hope, an old man, shall frutify° unto
you ——

GOB. I have here a dish of doves that I would bestow upon your Worship, and my suit is ——   145

LAUN. In very brief, the suit is impertinent° to
myself, as your Worship shall know by this honest
old man, and though I say it, though old man, yet
poor man, my father.

BASS. One speak for both. What would you?   150

LAUN. Serve you, sir.

GOB. That is the very defect° of the matter, sir.

BASS. I know thee well, thou hast obtained thy suit.
Shylock thy master spoke with me this day,
And hath preferred° thee, if it be preferment   155
To leave a rich Jew's service to become
The follower of so poor a gentleman.

LAUN. The old proverb is very well parted° between my master Shylock and you, sir. You have the
grace of God, sir, and he hath enough.°   160

BASS. Thou speak'st it well. Go, Father, with thy
son.
Take leave of thy old master and inquire
My lodging out. Give him a livery
More guarded° than his fellows'. See it done.   164

LAUN. Father, in. I cannot get a service, no, I have
ne'er a tongue in my head. Well, if any man in Italy
have a fairer table° which doth offer to swear upon
a book, I shall have good fortune. Go to, here's a
simple line of life. Here's a small trifle of wives —
alas, fifteen wives is nothing! A'leven widows   170
and nine maids is a simple coming-in for one man.
And then to 'scape drowning thrice, and to be in
peril of my life with the edge of a feather bed° —
here are simple scapes. Well, if Fortune be a woman,
she's a good wench for this gear.° Father,   175
come. I'll take my leave of the Jew in the twinkling
of an eye.   [*Exeunt* LAUNCELOT *and* OLD GOBBO.]

BASS. I pray thee, good Leonardo, think on this.

These things being bought and orderly bestowed,
Return in haste, for I do feast tonight
My best-esteemed acquaintance. Hie° thee, go.   180

LEON. My best endeavors shall be done herein.
          [*Enter* GRATIANO.]

GRA. Where is your master?

LEON.   Yonder, sir, he walks. [*Exit.*]

GRA. Signior Bassanio ——

BASS.   Gratiano!   185

GRA. I have a suit to you.

BASS.   You have obtained it.

GRA. You must not deny me. I must go with you to
Belmont.

BASS. Why, then you must. But hear thee, Gra-
tiano.
Thou art too wild, too rude, and bold of voice —
Parts that become thee happily enough,   191
And in such eyes as ours appear not faults,
But where thou art not known, why, there they show
Something too liberal.° Pray thee, take pain
To allay° with some cold drops of modesty   195
Thy skipping spirit, lest through thy wild behavior
I be misconstrued° in the place I go to,
And lose my hopes.

GRA.   Signior Bassanio, hear me.
If I do not put on a sober habit,   199
Talk with respect,° and swear but now and then,
Wear prayer books in my pocket, look demurely —
Nay more, while grace is saying, hood mine eyes
Thus with my hat, and sigh, and say " Amen " —
Use all the observance of civility,°
Like one well studied in a sad ostent°   205
To please his grandam, never trust me more.

BASS. Well, we shall see your bearing.

GRA. Nay, but I bar tonight. You shall not gauge°
me
By what we do tonight.

BASS.   No, that were pity.
I would entreat you rather to put on   210
Your boldest suit of mirth, for we have friends
That purpose merriment. But fare you well.
I have some business.

GRA. And I must to Lorenzo and the rest,   214
But we will visit you at suppertime.   [*Exeunt.*]

SCENE III. *The same. A room in* SHYLOCK'S
house.

[*Enter* JESSICA *and* LAUNCELOT GOBBO.]

JES. I am sorry thou wilt leave my father so.
Our house is hell, and thou, a merry devil,
Didst rob it of some taste of tediousness.

---

133. infection: for "affection." 139. cater-cousins: good friends.
142. frutify: for "certify." 146. impertinent: for "pertinent."
152. defect: for "effect." 155. preferred: promoted, recommended. 158. parted: divided. 159–60. You . . . enough: the
old proverb is "He that hath the grace of God hath enough."
164. guarded: ornamented with strips of braid. See Pl. 9n and
comment on p. 94b. 167. table: palm of the hand. Here Launcelot indulges in some palmistry on his own hand. 173. with
. . . bed: i.e., smothering. 175. gear: sort of thing. See I.i.110,n.

181. Hie: hasten. 194. liberal: free. 195. allay: dilute.
197. misconstrued: misinterpreted. 200. respect: respectability.
204. observance of civility: polite behavior. 205. sad ostent:
solemn face. 208. gauge: measure.

But fare thee well. There is a ducat for thee.
And, Launcelot, soon at supper shalt thou see   5
Lorenzo, who is thy new master's guest.
Give him this letter, do it secretly,
And so farewell. I would not have my father
See me in talk with thee.   9
 LAUN. Adieu! Tears exhibit° my tongue. Most
beautiful pagan, most sweet Jew! If a Christian did
not play the knave and get° thee, I am much de-
ceived. But, adieu. These foolish drops do something
drown my manly spirit. Adieu.
 JES. Farewell, good Launcelot.   15
      [*Exit* LAUNCELOT GOBBO.]
Alack, what heinous sin is it in me
To be ashamed to be my father's child!
But though I am a daughter to his blood,
I am not to his manners. O Lorenzo,
If thou keep promise, I shall end this strife,   20
Become a Christian, and thy loving wife.   [*Exit.*]

SCENE IV. *The same. A street.*

[*Enter* GRATIANO, LORENZO, SALARINO, *and* SALANIO.]
 LOR. Nay, we will slink away in suppertime,
Disguise° us at my lodging, and return
All in an hour.
 GRA. We have not made good preparation.   4
 SALAR. We have not spoke us° yet of torchbearers.
 SALAN. 'Tis vile unless it may be quaintly° or-
  dered,
And better in my mind not undertook.
 LOR. 'Tis now but four o'clock. We have two
  hours
To furnish us.
[*Enter* LAUNCELOT GOBBO, *with a letter.*] Friend
  Launcelot, what's the news?
 LAUN. An it shall please you to break up° this, it
shall seem to signify.   11
 LOR. I know the hand — in faith, 'tis a fair hand,
And whiter than the paper it writ on
Is the fair hand that writ.
 GRA.   Love news, in faith.
 LAUN. By your leave, sir.   15
 LOR. Whither goest thou?
 LAUN. Marry, sir, to bid my old master the Jew to
sup tonight with my new master the Christian.
 LOR. Hold here, take this. Tell gentle Jessica   20
I will not fail her — speak it privately.
Go, gentlemen,   [*Exit* LAUNCELOT GOBBO.]
Will you prepare you for this masque° tonight?
I am provided of a torchbearer.   24

 SALAR. Aye, marry, I'll be gone about it straight.
 SALAN. And so will I.
 LOR.   Meet me and Gratiano
At Gratiano's lodging some hour hence.
 SALAR. 'Tis good we do so.
    [*Exeunt* SALARINO *and* SALANIO.]
 GRA. Was not that letter from fair Jessica?
 LOR. I must needs tell thee all. She hath directed
How I shall take her from her father's house,   31
What gold and jewels she is furnished with,
What page's suit she hath in readiness.
If e'er the Jew her father come to Heaven,
It will be for his gentle daughter's sake.   35
And never dare misfortune cross her foot
Unless she do it under this excuse,
That she is issue to a faithless Jew.°
Come, go with me. Peruse this as thou goest.   39
Fair Jessica shall be my torchbearer.   [*Exeunt.*]

SCENE V. *The same. Before* SHYLOCK's *house.*

[*Enter* SHYLOCK *and* LAUNCELOT GOBBO.]
 SHY. Well, thou shalt see, thy eyes shall be thy
  judge,
The difference of old Shylock and Bassanio. —
What, Jessica! — Thou shalt not gormandize,
As thou hast done with me. — What, Jessica! —
And sleep and snore, and rend apparel out. —   5
Why, Jessica, I say!
 LAUN.   Why, Jessica!
 SHY. Who bids thee call? I do not bid thee call.
 LAUN. Your Worship was wont to tell me that I
could do nothing without bidding.
    [*Enter* JESSICA.]
 JES. Call you? What is your will?   10
 SHY. I am bid forth to supper, Jessica.
There are my keys. But wherefore should I go?
I am not bid for love, they flatter me.
But yet I'll go in hate, to feed upon
The prodigal Christian. Jessica, my girl,   15
Look to my house. I am right loath to go.
There is some ill abrewing toward my rest,
For I did dream of moneybags tonight.
 LAUN. I beseech you, sir, go. My young master
doth expect your reproach.°   20
 SHY. So do I his.
 LAUN. And they have conspired together, I will
not say you shall see a masque; but if you do, then
it was not for nothing that my nose fell ableeding on
Black Monday° last at six o'clock i' the morn-   25

ing, falling out that year on Ash Wednesday was
four year, in the afternoon.°

SHY. What, are there masques? Hear you me,
　Jessica.
Lock up my doors, and when you hear the drum
And the vile squealing of the wry-necked° fife,　30
Clamber not you up to the casements° then,
Nor thrust your head into the public street
To gaze on Christian fools with varnished° faces,
But stop my house's ears, I mean my casements.
Let not the sound of shallow foppery enter　　35
My sober house. By Jacob's staff, I swear
I have no mind of feasting forth tonight,
But I will go. Go you before me, sirrah.
Say I will come.

LAUN. I will go before, sir. Mistress, look out at
window, for all this.　　　　　　　　　41
There will come a Christian by
Will be worth a Jewess' eye.　　　　　*[Exit.]*

SHY. What says that fool of Hagar's offspring,°
　ha?

JES. His words were, "Farewell, mistress," noth-
　ing else.　　　　　　　　　　　　45

SHY. The patch° is kind enough, but a huge
　feeder,
Snail-slow in profit, and he sleeps by day
More than the wildcat. Drones hive not with me,
Therefore I part with him, and part with him
To one that I would have him help to waste　50
His borrowed purse. Well, Jessica, go in.
Perhaps I will return immediately.
Do as I bid you, shut doors after you.
Fast bind, fast find,　　　　　　　　54
A proverb never stale in thrifty mind.　*[Exit.]*

JES. Farewell, and if my fortune be not crost,
I have a father, you a daughter, lost.　*[Exit.]*

SCENE VI. *The same.*

[Enter GRATIANO and SALARINO, masked.]

GRA. This is the penthouse° under which Lorenzo
Desired us to make stand.

SALAR.　　　　　　　His hour is almost past.

GRA. And it is marvel he outdwells his hour,
For lovers ever run before the clock.

SALAR. Oh, ten times faster Venus' pigeons fly　5
To seal love's bonds new-made than they are wont
To keep obligèd faith unforfeited!°

GRA. That ever holds. Who riseth from a feast
With that keen appetite that he sits down?
Where is the horse that doth untread° again　10
His tedious measures° with the unbated fire
That he did pace them first? All things that are,
Are with more spirit chasèd than enjoyed.
How like a younker° or a prodigal
The scarfèd° bark puts from her native bay,　15
Hugged and embracèd by the strumpet wind!
How like the prodigal doth she return,
With overweathered ribs and ragged sails,
Lean, rent, and beggared by the strumpet wind!

SALAR. Here comes Lorenzo. More of this here-
　after.　　　　　　　　　　　　20

[Enter LORENZO.]

LOR. Sweet friends, your patience for my long
　abode.
Not I, but my affairs, have made you wait.
When you shall please to play the thieves for wives,
I'll watch as long for you then. Approach,
Here dwells my father Jew. Ho! Who's within?　25

[Enter JESSICA, above, in boy's clothes.]

JES. Who are you? Tell me, for more certainty,
Albeit° I'll swear that I do know your tongue.

LOR. Lorenzo, and thy love.

JES. Lorenzo certain, and my love indeed,
For who love I so much? And now who knows　30
But you, Lorenzo, whether I am yours?

LOR. Heaven and thy thoughts are witness that
　thou art.

JES. Here, catch this casket, it is worth the pains.
I am glad 'tis night, you do not look on me,
For I am much ashamed of my exchange.°　35
But love is blind, and lovers cannot see
The pretty follies that themselves commit,
For if they could, Cupid himself would blush
To see me thus transformèd to a boy.　　39

LOR. Descend, for you must be my torchbearer.

JES. What, must I hold a candle to my shames?
They in themselves, good sooth, are too too light.
Why, 'tis an office of discovery,° love,
And I should be obscured.

LOR.　　　　　　So are you, sweet,
Even in the lovely garnish° of a boy.　　45
But come at once,
For the close night doth play the runaway,
And we are stayed° for at Bassanio's feast.　48

JES. I will make fast the doors, and gild myself
With some more ducats, and be with you straight.

[Exit above.]

GRA. Now, by my hood, a Gentile, and no Jew.

LOR. Beshrew° me but I love her heartily,

26–27. falling ... afternoon: Launcelot is talking deliberate
nonsense, for Ash Wednesday is the first day of Lent. **30. wry-
necked:** making the player twist his neck. **31. casements:**
windows that open on hinges. **33. varnished:** wearing painted
masks. **44. Hagar's offspring:** Ishmaelite; i.e., vagabond. See
Genesis 15. **46. patch:** fool.

Sc. vi: 1. penthouse: projecting eaves. **5–7. Oh ... unforfeited:** i.e., a lover runs far quicker to win a new love than to
keep faith with an old. **pigeons:** doves which draw the chariot
of Venus, the goddess of love. **obliged:** already pledged.

10. untread: retrace. **11. measures:** paces. **14. younker:** gay
youth. **15. scarfed:** decked out with flags. See Pl. 7b.
27. Albeit: although. **35. exchange:** i.e., of boy's for girl's
clothes. **43. office of discovery:** task which will reveal me.
45. garnish: ornament, dress. **48. stayed:** waited. **52. Beshrew:**
plague on.

For she is wise, if I can judge of her.
And fair she is, if that mine eyes be true.
And true she is, as she hath proved herself,   55
And therefore, like herself, wise, fair, and true,
Shall she be placèd in my constant soul.
[*Enter* JESSICA, *below.*] What, art thou come? On,
  gentlemen, away!
Our masquing mates by this time for us stay.
                    [*Exit with* JESSICA *and* SALARINO.]
                    [*Enter* ANTONIO.]
  ANT. Who's there?   60
  GRA. Signior Antonio!
  ANT. Fie, fie, Gratiano, where are all the rest?
'Tis nine o'clock. Our friends all stay for you.
No masque tonight. The wind is come about,
Bassanio presently° will go aboard.   65
I have sent twenty out to seek for you.
  GRA. I am glad on't. I desire no more delight
Than to be under sail and gone tonight.   [*Exeunt.*]

SCENE VII. *Belmont. A room in* PORTIA'S
              house.

[*Flourish of cornets. Enter* PORTIA, *with the* PRINCE
    OF MOROCCO, *and their trains.*]
  POR. Go draw aside the curtains, and discover°
The several caskets to this noble Prince.
Now make your choice.
  MOR. The first, of gold, who this inscription bears,
" Who chooseth me shall gain what many men de-
  sire."   5
The second, silver, which this promise carries,
" Who chooseth me shall get as much as he de-
  serves."
This third, dull lead, with warning all as blunt,
" Who chooseth me must give and hazard all he
  hath."
How shall I know if I do choose the right?   10
  POR. The one of them contains my picture, Prince.
If you choose that, then I am yours withal.
  MOR. Some god direct my judgment! Let me see,
I will survey the inscriptions back again.
What says this leaden casket?   15
" Who chooseth me must give and hazard all he
  hath."
Must give — for what? For lead? Hazard for lead?
This casket threatens. Men that hazard all
Do it in hope of fair advantages.
A golden mind stoops not to shows of dross,°   20
I'll then nor give nor hazard aught for lead.
What says the silver with her virgin° hue?
" Who chooseth me shall get as much as he de-
  serves."

As much as he deserves! Pause there, Morocco,
And weigh thy value with an even hand.   25
If thou be'st rated by thy estimation,°
Thou dost deserve enough, and yet enough
May not extend so far as to the lady.
And yet to be afeard of my deserving
Were but a weak disabling of myself.   30
As much as I deserve! Why, that's the lady.
I do in birth deserve her, and in fortunes,
In graces and in qualities of breeding.
But more than these, in love I do deserve.
What if I strayed no further, but chose here?   35
Let's see once more this saying graved in gold:
" Who chooseth me shall gain what many men de-
  sire."
Why, that's the lady. All the world desires her.
From the four corners of the earth they come
To kiss this shrine, this mortal-breathing saint.   40
The Hyrcanian° deserts and the vasty wilds
Of wide Arabia are as throughfares° now
For princes to come view fair Portia.
The watery kingdom,° whose ambitious head
Spits in the face of heaven, is no bar   45
To stop the foreign spirits, but they come,
As o'er a brook, to see fair Portia.
One of these three contains her heavenly picture.
Is't like that lead contains her? 'Twere damnation
To think so base a thought. It were too gross   50
To rib her cerecloth° in the obscure grave.
Or shall I think in silver she's immured,°
Being ten times undervalued to tried gold?
Oh, sinful thought! Never so rich a gem
Was set in worse than gold. They have in England
A coin that bears the figure of an angel°   56
Stamped in gold, but that's insculped upon,
But here an angel in a golden bed
Lies all within. Deliver me the key.
Here do I choose, and thrive I as I may!   60
  POR. There, take it, Prince, and if my form lie
    there,
Then I am yours.   [*He unlocks the golden casket.*]
  MOR.   O Hell! What have we here?
A carrion Death,° within whose empty eye
There is a written scroll! I'll read the writing.
[*Reads.*] " All that glisters is not gold,   65
      Often have you heard that told.
      Many a man his life hath sold
      But my outside to behold.
      Gilded tombs do worms infold.
      Had you been as wise as bold,   70
      Young in limbs, in judgment old,

65. presently: immediately.
    Sc. vii: 1. discover: reveal, disclose. 20. dross: scum thrown
off in smelting. 22. virgin: i.e., white.

26. estimation: worth. 41. Hyrcanian: wild country south of
the Caspian Sea. 42. throughfares: thoroughfares. 44. watery
kingdom: ocean. 51. rib . . . cerecloth: enclose her shroud.
The *cerecloth* was a wax covering used in embalming the illustrious dead. 52. immured: walled in. 56. angel: gold coin
worth 10s. See Pl. 10c and App. 27. 63. Death: skull.
See Pl. 12f.

Your answer had not been enscrolled.°
Fare you well. Your suit is cold."
Cold, indeed, and labor lost.
Then, farewell, heat, and welcome, frost!   75
Portia, adieu. I have too grieved a heart
To take a tedious leave. Thus losers part.
            [Exit with his train. Flourish of cornets.]
POR. A gentle riddance. Draw the curtains, go.
Let all of his complexion choose me so.   *[Exeunt.]*

SCENE VIII. *Venice. A street.*

[Enter SALARINO *and* SALANIO.*]*
SALAR. Why, man, I saw Bassanio under sail.
With him is Gratiano gone along,
And in their ship I am sure Lorenzo is not.
  SALAN. The villain Jew with outcries raised the
    Duke,
Who went with him to search Bassanio's ship.   5
  SALAR. He came too late, the ship was under sail.
But there the Duke was given to understand
That in a gondola were seen together
Lorenzo and his amorous Jessica.
Besides, Antonio certified the Duke   10
They were not with Bassanio in his ship.
  SALAN. I never heard a passion so confused,
So strange, outrageous, and so variable,
As the dog Jew did utter in the streets:
"My daughter! Oh, my ducats! Oh, my daughter!
Fled with a Christian! Oh, my Christian ducats!   16
Justice! The law! My ducats, and my daughter!
A sealed bag, two sealed bags of ducats,
Of double ducats, stolen from me by my daughter!
And jewels, two stones, two rich and precious stones,
Stolen by my daughter! Justice! Find the girl!   21
She hath the stones upon her, and the ducats!"
  SALAR. Why, all the boys in Venice follow him
Crying his stones, his daughter, and his ducats.
  SALAN. Let good Antonio look he keep his day,
Or he shall pay for this.
  SALAR.   Marry, well remembered.   26
I reasoned° with a Frenchman yesterday
Who told me, in the narrow seas that part
The French and English, there miscarried
A vessel of our country richly fraught.°   30
I thought upon Antonio when he told me,
And wished in silence that it were not his.
  SALAN. You were best to tell Antonio what you
    hear,
Yet do not suddenly, for it may grieve him.
  SALAR. A kinder gentleman treads not the earth.
I saw Bassanio and Antonio part.   36
Bassanio told him he would make some speed
Of his return. He answered, "Do not so.

Slubber° not business for my sake, Bassanio,
But stay the very riping of the time.   40
And for the Jew's bond which he hath of me,
Let it not enter in your mind of love.
Be merry, and employ your chiefest thoughts
To courtship, and such fair ostents° of love
As shall conveniently become you there."   45
And even there, his eye being big with tears,
Turning his face, he put his hand behind him,
And with affection wondrous sensible°
He wrung Bassanio's hand, and so they parted.
  SALAN. I think he only loves the world for him.
I pray thee, let us go and find him out   51
And quicken his embracèd heaviness
With some delight or other.
  SALAR.   Do we so.   *[Exeunt.]*

SCENE IX. *Belmont. A room in* PORTIA'S
house.

[Enter NERISSA *and a* SERVITOR.*]*
NER. Quick, quick, I pray thee. Draw the curtain
    straight.
The Prince of Aragon hath ta'en his oath,
And comes to his election° presently.
[Flourish of cornets. Enter the PRINCE OF ARAGON,
PORTIA, and their trains.]
  POR. Behold, there stand the caskets, noble Prince.
If you choose that wherein I am contained,   5
Straight shall our nuptial rites be solemnized.
But if you fail, without more speech, my lord,
You must be gone from hence immediately.
  AR. I am enjoined by oath to observe three things.
First, never to unfold to anyone   10
Which casket 'twas I chose. Next, if I fail
Of the right casket, never in my life
To woo a maid in way of marriage.
Lastly,
If I do fail in fortune of my choice,   15
Immediately to leave you and be gone.
  POR. To these injunctions everyone doth swear
That comes to hazard for my worthless self.
  AR. And so have I addressed me.° Fortune now
To my heart's hope! Gold, silver, and base lead.   20
"Who chooseth me must give and hazard all he
    hath."
You shall look fairer ere I give or hazard.
What says the golden chest? Ha! Let me see:
"Who chooseth me shall gain what many men de-
    sire."
What many men desire! That "many" may be
    meant   25

---

72. enscrolled: inscribed, recorded.
  Sc. viii: 27. reasoned: conversed. 30. fraught: laden.

39. Slubber: be slovenly with.   44. ostents: outward shows.
48. wondrous sensible: wonderfully full of feeling.
  Sc. ix: 3. election: choice.   19. addressed me: prepared
myself.

By the fool multitude, that choose by show,
Not learning more than the fond° eye doth teach,
Which pries not to the interior but, like the martlet,°
Builds in the weather on the outward wall,
Even in the force and road of casualty.°   30
I will not choose what many men desire,
Because I will not jump° with common spirits
And rank me with the barbarous multitudes.
Why, then to thee, thou silver treasure house.
Tell me once more what title thou dost bear: 35
"Who chooseth me shall get as much as he de-
    serves."
And well said too, for who shall go about
To cozen° fortune, and be honorable
Without the stamp of merit?° Let none presume
To wear an undeservèd dignity.   40
Oh, that estates, degrees, and offices
Were not derived corruptly, and that clear honor
Were purchased by the merit of the wearer!
How many then should cover° that stand bare!
How many be commanded that command!   45
How much low peasantry would then be gleaned°
From the true seed of honor! And how much honor
Picked from the chaff and ruin of the times,
To be new-varnished!° Well, but to my choice.
"Who chooseth me shall get as much as he de-
    serves."   50
I will assume desert. Give me a key for this,
And instantly unlock my fortunes here.
                         [*He opens the silver casket.*]
    POR. [*Aside*] Too long a pause for that which you
        find there.
    AR. What's here? The portrait of a blinking idiot,
Presenting me a schedule!° I will read it.   55
How much unlike art thou to Portia!
How much unlike my hopes and my deservings!
"Who chooseth me shall have as much as he de-
    serves."
Did I deserve no more than a fool's head?
Is that my prize? Are my deserts no better?   60
    POR. To offend and judge are distinct offices,
And of opposèd natures.
    AR.   What is here?
[*Reads.*] " The fire seven times trièd this.
            Seven times tried that judgment is
            That did never choose amiss.   65
            Some there be that shadows kiss.
            Such have but a shadow's bliss.
            There be fools alive, I wis,°
            Silvered o'er, and so was this.

Take what wife you will to bed,   70
I will ever be your head.
So be gone. You are sped."°
Still more fool I shall appear
By the time I linger here.
With one fool's head I came to woo,   75
But I go away with two.
Sweet, adieu. I'll keep my oath,
Patiently to bear my wroth.°
                  [*Exeunt* ARAGON *and train.*]
    POR. Thus hath the candle singed the moth.
Oh, these deliberate° fools! When they do choose,
They have the wisdom by their wit to lose.   81
    NER. The ancient saying is no heresy,
Hanging and wiving goes by destiny.
    POR. Come, draw the curtain, Nerissa.
                         [*Enter a* SERVANT.]
    SERV. Where is my lady?
    POR.   Here. What would my lord?   85
    SERV. Madam, there is alighted at your gate
A young Venetian, one that comes before
To signify the approaching of his lord,
From whom he bringeth sensible regreets,°
To wit, besides commends° and courteous breath,
Gifts of rich value. Yet I have not seen   91
So likely° an ambassador of love.
A day in April never came so sweet,
To show how costly summer was at hand,
As this forespurrer° comes before his lord.   95
    POR. No more, I pray thee. I am half-afeard
Thou wilt say anon he is some kin to thee,
Thou spend'st such high-day wit° in praising him.
Come, come, Nerissa, for I long to see
Quick Cupid's post° that comes so mannerly.   100
    NER. Bassanio, Lord Love, if thy will it be!
                                         [*Exeunt.*]

Act III

SCENE I. *Venice. A street.*

[*Enter* SALANIO *and* SALARINO.]
    SALAN. Now, what news on the Rialto?
    SALAR. Why, yet it lives there unchecked that An-
tonio hath a ship of rich lading wrecked on the narrow seas° — the Goodwins,° I think they call the
place, a very dangerous flat and fatal, where the carcasses of many a tall ship lie buried, as they say,   5

---

27. **fond:** foolish. 28. **martlet:** martin, a bird of the swallow species. 30. **casualty:** mischance. 32. **jump:** agree. 38. **cozen:** cheat. 39. **stamp of merit:** seal certifying genuineness. 44. **cover:** wear their hats. See App. 7. 46. **gleaned:** plucked. 47–49. **honor . . . new-varnished:** how many men of noble family now ruined and living in poverty would be newly restored to their former glory. **new-varnished:** freshly painted. 55. **schedule:** writing. 68. **I wis:** assuredly.

72. **sped:** done for. 78. **wroth:** ruth, calamity. 80. **deliberate:** calculating. 89. **sensible regreets:** salutations full of feeling. 90. **commends:** salutations. 92. **likely:** handsome. 95. **forespurrer:** forerunner. 98. **high-day wit:** gay expressions. 100. **post:** messenger.

   Act III, Sc. 1: 3. **narrow seas:** English Channel. **Goodwins:** Goodwin Sands, off the coast of Kent, a treacherous spot.

if my gossip Report be an honest woman of her word.

SALAN. I would she were as lying a gossip in that as ever knapped° ginger, or made her neighbors 10 believe she wept for the death of a third husband. But it is true, without any slips of prolixity,° or crossing the plain highway of talk,° that the good Antonio, the honest Antonio —— Oh, that I had a title good enough to keep his name company! — 16

SALAR. Come, the full stop.°

SALAN. Ha! What sayest thou? Why, the end is, he hath lost a ship.

SALAR. I would it might prove the end of his losses. 21

SALAN. Let me say "Amen" betimes, lest the Devil cross° my prayer, for here he comes in the likeness of a Jew. [*Enter* SHYLOCK.] How now, Shylock! What news among the merchants? 26

SHY. You knew, none so well, none so well as you, of my daughter's flight.

SALAR. That's certain. I, for my part, knew the tailor that made the wings she flew withal. 30

SALAN. And Shylock, for his own part, knew the bird was fledged,° and then it is the complexion° of them all to leave the dam.

SHY. She is damned for it.

SALAR. That's certain, if the Devil may be her judge. 36

SHY. My own flesh and blood to rebel!

SALAN. Out upon it, old carrion! Rebels it at these years?

SHY. I say, my daughter is my flesh and blood. 40

SALAR. There is more difference between thy flesh and hers than between jet and ivory, more between your bloods than there is between red wine and Rhenish.° But tell us, do you hear whether Antonio have had any loss at sea or no? 45

SHY. There I have another bad match° — a bankrupt, a prodigal, who dare scarce show his head on the Rialto, a beggar that was used to come so smug° upon the mart.° Let him look to his bond. He was wont to call me usurer — let him look to his 50 bond. He was wont to lend money for a Christian courtesy — let him look to his bond.

SALAR. Why, I am sure if he forfeit, thou wilt not take his flesh. What's that good for?

SHY. To bait fish withal. If it will feed noth- 55 ing else, it will feed my revenge. He hath disgraced me, and hindered° me half a million, laughed at my losses, mocked at my gains, scorned my nation, thwarted my bargains, cooled my friends, heated

mine enemies. And what's his reason? I am a 60 Jew. Hath not a Jew eyes? Hath not a Jew hands, organs, dimensions, senses, affections, passions? Fed with the same food, hurt with the same weapons, subject to the same diseases, healed by the same means, warmed and cooled by the same winter 65 and summer as a Christian is? If you prick us, do we not bleed? If you tickle us, do we not laugh? If you poison us, do we not die? And if you wrong us, shall we not revenge? If we are like you in the rest, we will resemble you in that. If a Jew wrong a 70 Christian, what is his humility?° Revenge. If a Christian wrong a Jew, what should his sufferance be by Christian example? Why, revenge. The villainy you teach me I will execute, and it shall go hard but° I will better the instruction. 76

[*Enter a* SERVANT.]

SERV. Gentlemen, my master Antonio is at his house, and desires to speak with you both.

SALAR. We have been up and down to seek him.

[*Enter* TUBAL.]

SALAR. Here comes another of the tribe. A 80 third cannot be matched, unless the Devil himself turn Jew.

[*Exeunt* SALANIO, SALARINO, *and* SERVANT.]

SHY. How now, Tubal! What news from Genoa? Hast thou found my daughter?

TUB. I often came where I did hear of her, but cannot find her. 86

SHY. Why, there, there, there, there! A diamond gone, cost me two thousand ducats in Frankfort!° The curse never fell upon our nation till now, I never felt it till now. Two thousand ducats in 90 that, and other precious, precious jewels. I would my daughter were dead at my foot, and the jewels in her ear! Would she were hearsed° at my foot, and the ducats in her coffin! No news of them? Why, so. — And I know not what's spent in the search. 95 Why, thou loss upon loss! The thief gone with so much, and so much to find the thief, and no satisfaction, no revenge. Nor no ill luck stirring but what lights on my shoulders, no sighs but of my breathing, no tears but of my shedding. 101

TUB. Yes, other men have ill luck too. Antonio, as I heard in Genoa ——

SHY. What, what, what? Ill luck, ill luck?

TUB. Hath an argosy cast away, coming from Tripolis. 106

SHY. I thank God, I thank God! Is't true, is't true?

TUB. I spoke with some of the sailors that escaped the wreck. 110

SHY. I thank thee, good Tubal. Good news, good news! Ha, ha! Where? In Genoa?

---

10. knapped: chewed.   12. slips of prolixity: slipping into tedious talk.   12–13. crossing . . . talk: leaving plain speech.
17. full stop: i.e., cease this roundabout talk and come to the point.   23. cross: hinder.   32. fledged: ready to leave the nest. complexion: nature.   43. Rhenish: Rhine (white wine).
46. match: bargain.   48. smug: neatly dressed.   49. mart: market place.   57. hindered: prevented me from making.

71. what . . . humility: in what way does he show Christian forbearance?   75–76. it . . . but: unless something prevents.
88. Frankfort: famous for its fairs, at which fine jewelry was sold.   93. hearsed: on her bier.

TUB. Your daughter spent in Genoa, as I heard, in one night fourscore ducats.

SHY. Thou stick'st a dagger in me. I shall 115 never see my gold again. Fourscore ducats at a sitting! Fourscore ducats!

TUB. There came divers° of Antonio's creditors in my company to Venice that swear he cannot choose but break.° 120

SHY. I am very glad of it. I'll plague him, I'll torture him. I am glad of it.

TUB. One of them showed me a ring that he had of your daughter for a monkey.

SHY. Out upon her! Thou torturest me, 125 Tubal. It was my turquoise, I had it of Leah when I was a bachelor. I would not have given it for a wilderness of monkeys.

TUB. But Antonio is certainly undone.

SHY. Nay, that's true, that's very true. Go, 130 Tubal, fee me° an officer.° Bespeak° him a fortnight before. I will have the heart of him if he forfeit, for were he out of Venice, I can make what merchandise° I will. Go, go, Tubal, and meet me at our synagogue. Go, good Tubal, at our synagogue, 135 Tubal. [*Exeunt.*]

SCENE II. *Belmont. A room in* PORTIA's *house.*

[*Enter* BASSANIO, PORTIA, GRATIANO, NERISSA, *and* ATTENDANTS.]

POR. I pray you tarry. Pause a day or two
Before you hazard, for in choosing wrong
I lose your company. Therefore forbear awhile.
There's something tells me, but it is not love,
I would not lose you, and you know yourself, 5
Hate counsels not in such a quality.°
But lest you should not understand me well —
And yet a maiden hath no tongue but thought —
I would detain you here some month or two
Before you venture for me. I could teach you 10
How to choose right, but I am then forsworn.°
So will I never be. So may you miss me.
But if you do, you'll make me wish a sin —
That I had been forsworn. Beshrew your eyes,
They have o'erlooked° me, and divided me. 15
One half of me is yours, the other half yours,
Mine own, I would say, but if mine, then yours,
And so all yours! Oh, these naughty° times
Put bars between the owners and their rights!
And so, though yours, not yours. Prove it so, 20
Let fortune go to Hell for it, not I.

I speak too long, but 'tis to peize° the time,
To eke° it and to draw it out in length,
To stay you from election.

BASS.   Let me choose,
For as I am, I live upon the rack.° 25

POR. Upon the rack, Bassanio! Then confess
What treason° there is mingled with your love.

BASS. None but that ugly treason of mistrust
Which makes me fear the enjoying of my love.
There may as well be amity and life 30
'Tween snow and fire as treason and my love.

POR. Aye, but I fear you speak upon the rack,
Where men enforcèd do speak anything.

BASS. Promise me life, and I'll confess the truth.

POR. Well, then, confess and live.

BASS.   "Confess" and "love" 35
Had been the very sum of my confession.
Oh, happy torment when my torturer
Doth teach me answers for deliverance!
But let me to my fortune and the caskets.

POR. Away, then! I am locked in one of them. 40
If you do love me, you will find me out.
Nerissa and the rest, stand all aloof.
Let music sound while he doth make his choice,
Then, if he lose, he makes a swanlike end,°
Fading in music. That the comparison 45
May stand more proper, my eye shall be the stream
And watery deathbed for him. He may win,
And what is music then? Then music is
Even as the flourish° when true subjects bow
To a new-crowned monarch. Such it is 50
As are those dulcet sounds in break of day
That creep into the dreaming bridegroom's ear
And summon him to marriage. Now he goes,
With no less presence, but with much more love,
Than young Alcides° when he did redeem 55
The virgin tribute paid by howling Troy
To the sea monster. I stand for sacrifice.
The rest aloof are the Dardanian° wives,
With bleared visages,° come forth to view
The issue° of the exploit. Go, Hercules! 60
Live thou, I live. With much much more dismay
I view the fight than thou that makest the fray.
[*A song, whilst* BASSANIO *comments on the caskets to himself.*]
        "Tell me where is fancy° bred,
            Or in the heart or in the head?
            How begot, how nourishèd? 65
                Reply, reply.
            It is engendered in the eyes,

---

118. divers: various.   120. break: go bankrupt.   131. fee me: hire. officer: sergeant of the law, who made arrests for debt. See *II Hen IV*, II.i for the officer at work. Bespeak: order, reserve.

Sc. ii: 6. quality: manner.   11. forsworn: perjured.   15. o'erlooked: bewitched.   18. naughty: wicked.

---

22. peize: retard.   23. eke: increase.   25. rack: in torment. See App. 10.   27. treason: Portia continues the image, for the rack was used only to extract confessions of treason.   44. swanlike end: Swans were supposed to sing once only, just before death.   49. flourish: fanfare of trumpets.   55. Alcides: Hercules, who rescued the daughter of the Trojan King from being sacrificed to a sea monster.   58. Dardanian: Trojan.   59. bleared visages: tear-stained faces.   60. issue: result.   63. fancy: love.

With gazing fed, and fancy dies
In the cradle where it lies.
    Let us all ring fancy's knell.   70
    I'll begin it. — Ding, dong, bell."
ALL. " Ding, dong, bell."
BASS. So may the outward shows be least them-
    selves.
The world is still° deceived with ornament.
In law, what plea so tainted and corrupt   75
But, being seasoned° with a gracious voice,
Obscures the show of evil? In religion,
What damnèd error but some sober brow
Will bless it, and approve° it with a text,
Hiding the grossness with fair ornament?   80
There is no vice so simple° but assumes
Some mark of virtue on his outward parts.
How many cowards whose hearts are all as false
As stairs of sand wear yet upon their chins
The beards of Hercules and frowning Mars,   85
Who, inward searched, have livers° white as milk.
And these assume but valor's excrement°
To render them redoubted!° Look on beauty
And you shall see 'tis purchased by the weight,
Which therein works a miracle in nature,   90
Making them lightest that wear most of it.
So are those crispèd snaky golden locks
Which make such wanton gambols with the wind
Upon supposèd fairness, often known
To be the dowry of a second head,   95
The skull that bred them in the sepulcher.°
Thus ornament is but the guilèd° shore
To a most dangerous sea, the beauteous scarf
Veiling an Indian° beauty — in a word,
The seeming truth which cunning times put on   100
To entrap the wisest. Therefore, thou gaudy gold,
Hard food for Midas,° I will none of thee.
Nor none of thee, thou pale and common drudge°
'Tween man and man. But thou, thou meager lead,
Which rather threatenest than dost promise aught,
Thy paleness moves me more than eloquence,   106
And here choose I. Joy be the consequence!
    POR. [Aside] How all the other passions fleet to
    air,
As doubtful thoughts, and rash-embraced despair,
And shuddering fear, and green-eyed jealousy!   110

O love, be moderate, allay thy ecstasy,
In measure rain thy joy, scant° this excess!
I feel too much thy blessing. Make it less,
For fear I surfeit!°
    BASS.   What find I here?   115
                [Opening the leaden casket.]
Fair Portia's counterfeit!° What demigod
Hath come so near creation? Move these eyes?
Or whether, riding on the balls of mine,
Seem they in motion? Here are severed lips,
Parted with sugar breath. So sweet a bar°   120
Should sunder such sweet friends. Here in her hairs
The painter plays the spider, and hath woven
A golden mesh to entrap the hearts of men
Faster than gnats in cobwebs. But her eyes —
How could he see to do them? Having made one,
Methinks it should have power to steal both his   126
And leave itself unfurnished.° Yet look how far
The substance of my praise doth wrong this shadow
In underprizing° it, so far this shadow
Doth limp behind the substance. Here's the scroll,
The continent° and summary of my fortune.   131
[Reads.] " You that choose not by the view,
    Chance as fair, and choose as true!
    Since this fortune falls to you,
    Be content and seek no new.   135
    If you be well pleased with this,
    And hold your fortune for your bliss,
    Turn you where your lady is
    And claim her with a loving kiss. "
A gentle scroll. Fair lady, by your leave,   140
I come by note,° to give and to receive.
Like one of two contending in a prize
That thinks he hath done well in people's eyes,
Hearing applause and universal shout,
Giddy in spirit, still gazing in a doubt   145
Whether those peals of praise be his or no.
So, thrice-fair lady, stand I, even so,
As doubtful whether what I see be true,
Until confirmed, signed, ratified by you.
    POR. You see me, Lord Bassanio, where I stand,
Such as I am. Though for myself alone   151
I would not be ambitious in my wish,
To wish myself much better; yet for you
I would be trebled twenty times myself —
A thousand times more fair, ten thousand times
More rich —   156
That only to stand high in your account,°
I might in virtues, beauties, livings,° friends,
Exceed account. But the full sum of me
Is sum of something which, to term in gross,   160
Is an unlessoned girl, unschooled, unpracticed,

---

74. still: always.   **75–76. tainted . . . seasoned:** as bad food is concealed by a strong sauce.   **79. approve:** prove.   **81. simple:** unmixed (with good).   **86. livers:** the liver was the seat of passion and emotion, and especially of courage; a coward's liver was therefore white and bloodless.   **87. excrement:** that which grows out of a man, such as hair or nails. Here *valor's excrement* is a fine manly beard.   **88. redoubted:** redoubtable, formidable.   **92–96. crisped . . . sepulcher:** i.e., curly golden hair is often borrowed, its true owner being a corpse.   **97. guiled:** beguiling.   **99. Indian:** dark, which was not considered beautiful. See Sonnet 127.   **102. Midas:** Midas, King of Phrygia, was granted his hasty wish that everything which he touched might be turned into gold. He forgot to except food.   **103. common drudge:** i.e., silver, because used for common trade.

112. scant: make less.   **115. surfeit:** sicken from excess.   **116. counterfeit:** portrait.   **120. So . . . bar:** i.e., sweet breath should naturally come between upper and lower lip.   **127. unfurnished:** without a companion.   **129. underprizing:** undervaluing.   **131. continent:** that which contains.   **141. by note:** as instructed.   **157. account:** estimation.   **158. livings:** possessions.

Happy in this, she is not yet so old
But she may learn. Happier than this,
She is not bred so dull but she can learn.
Happiest of all is that her gentle spirit   165
Commits itself to yours to be directed,
As from her lord, her governor, her king.
Myself and what is mine to you and yours
Is now converted.° But now I was the lord
Of this fair mansion, master of my servants,   170
Queen o'er myself. And even now, but now,
This house, these servants, and this same myself
Are yours, my lord. I give them with this ring,
Which when you part from, lose, or give away,
Let it presage the ruin of your love,   175
And be my vantage° to exclaim on° you.
    BASS. Madam, you have bereft me of all words.
Only my blood speaks to you in my veins,
And there is such confusion in my powers
As after some oration fairly spoke   180
By a belovèd prince, there doth appear
Among the buzzing pleasèd multitude,
Where every something, being blent together,
Turns to a wild of nothing, save of joy,   184
Expressed and not expressed. But when this ring
Parts from this finger, then parts life from hence.
Oh, then be bold to say Bassanio's dead!
    NER. My lord and lady, it is now our time
That have stood by and seen our wishes prosper
To cry, good joy. Good joy, my lord and lady!   190
    GRA. My Lord Bassanio and my gentle lady,
I wish you all the joy that you can wish,
For I am sure you can wish none from me.
And when your Honors mean to solemnize
The bargain of your faith, I do beseech you,   195
Even at that time I may be married too.
    BASS. With all my heart, so thou canst get a wife.
    GRA. I thank your lordship, you have got me
        one.
My eyes, my lord, can look as swift as yours.
You saw the mistress, I beheld the maid,   200
You loved, I loved for intermission.°
No more pertains to me, my lord, than you.
Your fortune stood upon the casket there,
And so did mine too, as the matter falls;
For wooing here until I sweat again,   205
And swearing till my very roof° was dry
With oaths of love, at last, if promise last,
I got a promise of this fair one here
To have her love provided that your fortune
Achieved° her mistress.
    POR.   Is this true, Nerissa?   210
    NER. Madam, it is, so you stand pleased withal.
    BASS. And do you, Gratiano, mean good faith?
    GRA. Yes, faith, my lord.

    BASS. Our feast shall be much honored in your
marriage.   215
    GRA. We'll play with them the first boy for a thou-
sand ducats.
    NER. What, and stake down?°
    GRA. No. We shall ne'er win at that sport, and
stake down.   220
But who comes here? Lorenzo and his infidel?
What, and my old Venetian friend Salerio?
    [Enter LORENZO, JESSICA, and SALERIO, a messenger
                    from Venice.]
    BASS. Lorenzo and Salerio, welcome hither,
If that the youth of my new interest° here
Have power to bid you welcome. By your leave,
I bid my very friends and countrymen,   226
Sweet Portia, welcome.
    POR.   So do I, my lord.
They are entirely welcome.
    LOR. I thank your Honor. For my part, my lord,
My purpose was not to have seen you here,   230
But meeting with Salerio by the way,
He did entreat me, past all saying nay,
To come with him along.
    SALER.   I did, my lord,
And I have reason for it. Signior Antonio
Commends him to you.   [Gives BASSANIO a letter.]
    BASS.   Ere I ope his letter,   235
I pray you tell me how my good friend doth.
    SALER. Not sick, my lord, unless it be in mind,
Nor well, unless in mind. His letter there
Will show you his estate.
    GRA. Nerissa, cheer yon stranger, bid her wel-
        come.   240
Your hand, Salerio. What's the news from Venice?
How doth that royal merchant, good Antonio?
I know he will be glad of our success.
We are the Jasons,° we have won the fleece.
    SALER. I would you had won the fleece that he hath
lost.   245
    POR. There are some shrewd° contents in yon
        same paper
That steals the color from Bassanio's cheek.
Some dear friend dead, else nothing in the world
Could turn so much the constitution
Of any constant° man. What, worse and worse!   250
With leave, Bassanio, I am half yourself,
And I must freely have the half of anything
That this same paper brings you.
    BASS.   O sweet Portia,
Here are a few of the unpleasant'st words
That ever blotted paper! Gentle lady,   255
When I did first impart my love to you,
I freely told you all the wealth I had
Ran in my veins, I was a gentleman,

___

169. converted: transferred. 176. vantage: opportunity. exclaim
on: reproach. 201. intermission: to fill in the time. 206. roof:
i.e., of the mouth. 210. Achieved: won.

219. stake down: spot cash. 224. youth ... interest: i.e., if
one so new to this house. 244. We ... Jasons: See I.i.171,n.
246. shrewd: bitter. 250. constant: well-balanced.

And then I told you true. And yet, dear lady,
Rating myself at nothing, you shall see   260
How much I was a braggart. When I told you
My state was nothing, I should then have told you
That I was worse than nothing; for, indeed,
I have engaged° myself to a dear friend,
Engaged my friend to his mere° enemy,   265
To feed my means. Here is a letter, lady,
The paper as the body of my friend
And every word in it a gaping wound,
Issuing lifeblood. But is it true, Salerio?
Have all his ventures failed? What, not one hit?
From Tripolis, from Mexico, and England,   271
From Lisbon, Barbary, and India?
And not one vessel scape the dreadful touch
Of merchant-marring rocks?

SALER.   Not one, my lord.
Besides, it should appear that if he had   275
The present money to discharge the Jew,
He would not take it. Never did I know
A creature that did bear the shape of man
So keen and greedy to confound a man.
He plies the Duke at morning and at night,   280
And doth impeach° the freedom of the state
If they deny him justice. Twenty merchants,
The Duke himself, and the magnificoes°
Of greatest port° have all persuaded with him,
But none can drive him from the envious° plea   285
Of forfeiture, of justice, and his bond.

JES. When I was with him I have heard him swear
To Tubal and to Chus, his countrymen,
That he would rather have Antonio's flesh
Than twenty times the value of the sum   290
That he did owe him. And I know, my lord,
If law, authority, and power deny not,
It will go hard with poor Antonio.

POR. Is it your dear friend that is thus in trouble?
BASS. The dearest friend to me, the kindest man,
The best-conditioned and unwearied spirit   296
In doing courtesies, and one in whom
The ancient Roman honor more appears
Than any that draws breath in Italy.
POR. What sum owes he the Jew?   300
BASS. For me, three thousand ducats.
POR.   What, no more?
Pay him six thousand, and deface° the bond —
Double six thousand, and then treble that,
Before a friend of this description
Shall lose a hair through Bassanio's fault.   305
First go with me to church and call me wife,
And then away to Venice to your friend,
For never shall you lie by Portia's side
With an unquiet soul. You shall have gold
To pay the petty debt twenty times over.   310

When it is paid, bring your true friend along.
My maid Nerissa and myself meantime
Will live as maids and widows. Come, away!
For you shall hence upon your wedding day.
Bid your friends welcome, show a merry cheer.°
Since you are dear-bought, I will love you dear.   316
But let me hear the letter of your friend.
BASS. [Reads.] " Sweet Bassanio, my ships have all
miscarried, my creditors grow cruel, my estate is very
low, my bond to the Jew is forfeit. And since in pay-
ing it it is impossible I should live, all debts are   321
cleared between you and I, if I might but see you at
my death. Notwithstanding, use your pleasure. If
your love do not persuade you to come, let not my
letter."   325
POR. O love, dispatch all business, and be gone!
BASS. Since I have your good leave to go away,
I will make haste. But till I come again
No bed shall e'er be guilty of my stay,   329
No rest be interposer 'twixt us twain. [Exeunt.]

SCENE III. *Venice. A street.*

[*Enter* SHYLOCK, SALARINO, ANTONIO, *and* JAILER.]
SHY. Jailer, look to him. Tell not me of mercy.
This is the fool that lent out money gratis.
Jailer, look to him.
ANT.   Hear me yet, good Shylock.
SHY. I'll have my bond, speak not against my bond.   5
I have sworn an oath that I will have my bond.
Thou call'dst me dog before thou hadst a cause,
But since I am a dog, beware my fangs.
The Duke shall grant me justice. I do wonder,
Thou naughty jailer, that thou art so fond°
To come abroad with him at his request.   10
ANT. I pray thee, hear me speak.
SHY. I'll have my bond, I will not hear thee speak.
I'll have my bond, and therefore speak no more.
I'll not be made a soft and dull-eyed fool,
To shake the head, relent, and sigh, and yield   15
To Christian intercessors. Follow not,
I'll have no speaking. I will have my bond. [Exit.]
SALAR. It is the most impenetrable cur
That ever kept° with men.
ANT.   Let him alone.
I'll follow him no more with bootless° prayers.   20
He seeks my life — his reason well I know.
I oft delivered from his forfeitures
Many that have at times made moan to me,
Therefore he hates me.
SALAR.   I am sure the Duke
Will never grant this forfeiture to hold.   25
ANT. The Duke cannot deny the course of law.

---

264. **engaged**: pledged.   265. **mere**: sheer, entire.   281. **impeach**: accuse.   283. **magnificoes**: chief men of Venice.   284. **port**: dignity.   285. **envious**: spiteful.   302. **deface**: cancel.

315. **merry cheer**: cheerful face.
Sc. iii: 9. **fond**: foolish.   19. **kept**: lived.   20. **bootless**: vain.

For the commodity° that strangers have
With us in Venice, if it be denied,
Will much impeach the justice of his state,
Since that the trade and profit of the city   30
Consisteth of all nations. Therefore go.
These griefs and losses have so bated° me
That I shall hardly spare a pound of flesh
Tomorrow to my bloody creditor.
Well, jailer, on. Pray God Bassanio come   35
To see me pay his debt, and then I care not!
                                        [*Exeunt.*]

SCENE IV. *Belmont. A room in* PORTIA's
                        house.

[*Enter* PORTIA, NERISSA, LORENZO, JESSICA, *and*
                        BALTHASAR.]
    LOR. Madam, although I speak it in your presence,
You have a noble and a true conceit
Of godlike amity,° which appears most strongly
In bearing thus the absence of your lord.
But if you knew to whom you show this honor, 5
How true a gentleman you send relief,
How dear a lover of my lord your husband,
I know you would be prouder of the work
Than customary bounty° can enforce you.
    POR. I never did repent for doing good,   10
Nor shall not now. For in companions
That do converse and waste the time together,
Whose souls do bear an equal yoke of love,
There must be needs a like proportion
Of lineaments, of manners, and of spirit.   15
Which makes me think that this Antonio,
Being the bosom lover of my lord,
Must needs be like my lord. If it be so,
How little is the cost I have bestowed
In purchasing the semblance° of my soul°   20
From out the state of hellish misery!
This comes too near the praising of myself,
Therefore no more of it. Hear other things.
Lorenzo, I commit into your hands
The husbandry° and manage of my house   25
Until my lord's return. For mine own part,
I have toward Heaven breathed a secret vow
To live in prayer and contemplation,
Only attended by Nerissa here,
Until her husband and my lord's return.   30
There is a monastery two miles off,
And there will we abide. I do desire you
Not to deny this imposition,°
The which my love and some necessity

Now lays upon you.
    LOR.   Madam, with all my heart. 35
I shall obey you in all fair commands.
    POR. My people do already know my mind,
And will acknowledge you and Jessica
In place of Lord Bassanio and myself.
And so farewell till we shall meet again.   40
    LOR. Fair thoughts and happy hours attend on
        you!
    JES. I wish your ladyship all heart's content.
    POR. I thank you for your wish, and am well
        pleased
To wish it back on you. Fare you well, Jessica.
                [*Exeunt* JESSICA *and* LORENZO.]
Now, Balthasar,   45
As I have ever found thee honest-true,
So let me find thee still. Take this same letter,
And use thou all the endeavor of a man
In speed to Padua. See thou render this
Into my cousin's hand, Doctor Bellario.   50
And look, what notes and garments he doth give
        thee
Bring them, I pray thee, with imagined speed°
Unto the tranect,° to the common ferry
Which trades to Venice. Waste no time in words,
But get thee gone. I shall be there before thee. 55
    BALTH. Madam, I go with all convenient speed.
                                        [*Exit.*]
    POR. Come on, Nerissa, I have work in hand
That you yet know not of. We'll see our husbands
Before they think of us.
    NER.   Shall they see us?
    POR. They shall, Nerissa, but in such a habit° 60
That they shall think we are accomplishèd°
With that we lack.° I'll hold thee any wager,
When we are both accoutered like young men,
I'll prove the prettier fellow of the two,
And wear my dagger with the braver grace,   65
And speak between the change of man and boy
With a reed° voice, and turn two mincing steps
Into a manly stride, and speak of frays
Like a fine bragging youth. And tell quaint lies,
How honorable ladies sought my love,   70
Which I denying, they fell sick and died,
I could not do withal.° Then I'll repent,
And wish, for all that, that I had not killed them.
And twenty of these puny lies I'll tell,
That men shall swear I have discontinued school
Above a twelvemonth. I have within my mind 76
A thousand raw° tricks of these bragging Jacks,°
Which I will practice.
    NER.   Why, shall we turn to men?

27. **commodity:** privilege. 32. **bated:** made thin.
    Sc. iv: 2–3. **true . . . amity:** you truly understand the mean-
ing of great friendship. 9. **customary bounty:** ordinary kindness. 20. **the semblance:** i.e., a man like. **my soul:** my soul's
mate. 25. **husbandry:** housekeeping. 33. **imposition:** task imposed.

52. **imagined speed:** quick as thought. 53. **tranect:** a word
otherwise unknown, possibly the Italian *traghetto*, ferry.
60. **habit:** costume. 61. **accomplished:** equipped. 62. **we lack:**
i.e., manhood. 67. **reed:** reedy, piping. 72. **I . . . withal:** I
couldn't help it. 77. **raw:** adolescent, sophomoric. **Jacks:**
knaves.

POR. Fie, what a question's that
If thou wert near a lewd interpreter!°   80
But come, I'll tell thee all my whole device
When I am in my coach, which stays for us
At the park gate, and therefore haste away,
For we must measure twenty miles today. [*Exeunt.*]

SCENE V. *The same. A garden.*

[*Enter* LAUNCELOT GOBBO *and* JESSICA.]

LAUN. Yes, truly, for, look you, the sins of the
father are to be laid upon the children. Therefore I
promise ye I fear you.° I was always plain with you,
and so now I speak my agitation° of the matter.
Therefore be of good cheer, for truly I think you   5
are damned. There is but one hope in it that can do
you any good, and that is but a kind of bastard hope
neither.

JES. And what hope is that, I pray thee?   10

LAUN. Marry, you may partly hope that your
father got you not, that you are not the Jew's daughter.

JES. That were a kind of bastard hope, indeed. So
the sins of my mother should be visited upon me.   16

LAUN. Truly, then, I fear you are damned both by
father and mother. Thus when I shun Scylla, your
father, I fall into Charybdis,° your mother. Well,
you are gone both ways.   20

JES. I shall be saved by my husband. He hath
made me a Christian.

LAUN. Truly, the more to blame he. We were
Christians enow° before, e'en as many as could well
live, one by another. This making of Christians   25
will raise the price of hogs. If we grow all to be pork-
eaters, we shall not shortly have a rasher on the coals
for money.

[*Enter* LORENZO.]

JES. I'll tell my husband, Launcelot, what you say.
Here he comes.   30

LOR. I shall grow jealous of you shortly, Launcelot, if you thus get my wife into corners.

JES. Nay, you need not fear us, Lorenzo. Launcelot and I are out.° He tells me flatly there is no mercy
for me in Heaven, because I am a Jew's daugh-   35
ter. And he says you are no good member of the
commonwealth, for in converting Jews to Christians
you raise the price of pork.   39

LOR. I shall answer that better to the commonwealth than you can the getting-up of the Negro's
belly. The Moor° is with child by you, Launcelot.

LAUN. It is much that the Moor should be more
than reason, but if she be less than an honest woman,
she is indeed more than I took her for.   47

LOR. How every fool can play upon the word! I
think the best grace of wit will shortly turn into
silence, and discourse grow commendable in none
only but parrots. Go in, sirrah. Bid them prepare for
dinner.   52

LAUN. That is done, sir. They have all stomachs.

LOR. Goodly Lord, what a wit-snapper are you!
Then bid them prepare dinner.   56

LAUN. That is done too, sir, only "cover" is the
word.

LOR. Will you cover,° then, sir?

LAUN. Not so, sir, neither. I know my duty.   59

LOR. Yet more quarreling with occasion!° Wilt
thou show the whole wealth of thy wit in an instant?
I pray thee understand a plain man in his plain
meaning. Go to thy fellows, bid them cover the table,
serve in the meat, and we will come in to dinner.   65

LAUN. For the table, sir, it shall be served in. For
the meat, sir, it shall be covered. For your coming in
to dinner, sir, why, let it be as humors and conceits°
shall govern.   [*Exit.*]

LOR. Oh, dear discretion, how his words are
suited!°   70
The fool hath planted in his memory
An army of good words, and I do know
A many fools that stand in better place
Garnished° like him, that for a tricksy° word
Defy the matter. How cheer'st thou, Jessica?   75
And now, good sweet, say thy opinion.
How dost thou like the Lord Bassanio's wife?

JES. Past all expressing. It is very meet
The Lord Bassanio live an upright life,
For having such a blessing in his lady,   80
He finds the joys of Heaven here on earth.
And if on earth he do not mean it,° then
In reason he should never come to Heaven.
Why, if two gods should play some heavenly match
And on the wager lay two earthly women,   85
And Portia one, there must be something else
Pawned° with the other, for the poor rude world
Hath not her fellow.

LOR.   Even such a husband
Hast thou of me as she is for a wife.

JES. Nay, but ask my opinion too of that.   90

LOR. I will anon. First, let us go to dinner.

JES. Nay, let me praise you while I have a stomach.°

---

80. lewd interpreter: someone who saw a lewd meaning in your
words.

Sc. v: 3. I . . . you: fear for you.   4. agitation: for "cogitation."   18–19. Scylla . . . Charybdis: legendary sea monsters
who waited for mariners on either side of the Strait of Messina. Those who escaped the one were destroyed by the other.
24. enow: enough.   34. are out: have fallen out.   42. The Moor:
The scandal is obviously topical but cannot be explained.

57–58. cover . . . cover: lay the table . . . put on your hat (as in
the presence of an equal).   60. quarreling . . . occasion: quibbling at every opportunity.   68. humors . . . conceits: whims
and fancies.   70. suited: how he makes words suit his
purpose!   74. Garnished: furnished. tricksy: smart.   82. do
. . . it: i.e., to live an upright life.   87. Pawned: pledged; i.e.,
the other woman would need something extra to make her
equal the value of Portia.   92. stomach: appetite.

LOR. No, pray thee, let it serve for table talk.
Then, howsoe'er thou speak'st, 'mong other things
I shall digest it.   94
      JES.   Well, I'll set you forth.   [*Exeunt.*]

Act IV

SCENE I. *Venice. A court of justice.*

[*Enter the* DUKE, *the* MAGNIFICOES, ANTONIO,
    BASSANIO, GRATIANO, SALERIO, *and others.*]
DUKE. What, is Antonio here?
ANT. Ready, so please your Grace.
DUKE. I am sorry for thee. Thou art come to an-
swer
A stony adversary, an inhuman wretch
Uncapable of pity, void and empty   5
From any dram of mercy.
      ANT.   I have heard
Your Grace hath ta'en great pains to qualify°
His rigorous course. But since he stands obdúrate,
And that no lawful means can carry me
Out of his envy's reach, I do oppose   10
My patience to his fury, and am armed
To suffer, with a quietness of spirit,
The very tyranny and rage of his.
    DUKE. Go one, and call the Jew into the court.
    SALER. He is ready at the door. He comes, my
      lord.   15
             [*Enter* SHYLOCK.]
    DUKE. Make room, and let him stand before our
      face.
Shylock, the world thinks, and I think so too,
That thou but lead'st this fashion° of thy malice
To the last hour of act. And then 'tis thought
Thou'lt show thy mercy and remorse° more strange
Than is thy strange apparent cruelty,   21
And where thou now exact'st the penalty,
Which is a pound of this poor merchant's flesh,
Thou wilt not only loose° the forfeiture,
But, touched with human gentleness and love, 25
Forgive a moiety° of the principal,
Glancing an eye of pity on his losses
That have of late so huddled on his back,
Enow to press a royal merchant down
And pluck commiseration of his state   30
From brassy bosoms and rough hearts of flint,
From stubborn Turks and Tartars, never trained
To offices° of tender courtesy.
We all expect a gentle answer, Jew.

Act IV. Sc. i: **7. qualify**: moderate. **18. fashion**: appearance.
20. remorse: pity.   **24. loose**: release.   **26. moiety**: part.
33. offices: actions.

SHY. I have possessed° your Grace of what I pur-
      pose,   35
And by our holy Sabbath have I sworn
To have the due and forfeit of my bond.
If you deny it, let the danger light
Upon your charter° and your city's freedom.
You'll ask me why I rather choose to have   40
A weight of carrion flesh than to receive
Three thousand ducats. I'll not answer that,
But say it is my humor° — is it answered?
What if my house be troubled with a rat,
And I be pleased to give ten thousand ducats   45
To have it baned?° What, are you answered yet?
Some men there are love not a gaping pig,°
Some that are mad if they behold a cat,
And others when the bagpipe sings i' the nose
Cannot contain their urine. For affection,°   50
Mistress of passion, sways it to the mood
Of what it likes or loathes. Now for your answer.
As there is no firm reason to be rendered
Why he cannot abide a gaping pig,
Why he, a harmless necessary cat,   55
Why he, a woolen bagpipe,° but of force
Must yield to such inevitable shame
As to offend, himself being offended,
So can I give no reason, nor I will not,
More than a lodgèd° hate and a certain loathing 60
I bear Antonio, that I follow thus
A losing° suit against him. Are you answered?
    BASS. This is no answer, thou unfeeling man,
To excuse the current of thy cruelty.
    SHY. I am not bound to please thee with my an-
      swers.   65
    BASS. Do all men kill the things they do not love?
    SHY. Hates any man the thing he would not kill?
    BASS. Every offense is not a hate at first.
    SHY. What, wouldst thou have a serpent sting thee
      twice?
    ANT. I pray you, think you question with the Jew.°
You may as well go stand upon the beach   71
And bid the main flood° bate° his usual height,
You may as well use question with the wolf
Why he hath made the ewe bleat for the lamb,
You may as well forbid the mountain pines   75
To wag their high tops and to make no noise
When they are fretten° with the gusts of heaven,
You may as well do anything most hard
As seek to soften that — than which what's
      harder? —

---

35. possessed: informed.   **39. charter**: English cities were
granted royal charters by the sovereign which gave them
certain rights and privileges, but which could be revoked.
43. humor: whim. **46. baned**: poisoned. **47. gaping pig**: roasted
porker with a lemon in its mouth. **50. affection**: natural disposition. **56. woolen bagpipe**: bagpipe in a woolen cover. See Pl. 19C.
60. lodged: deep-seated. **62. losing**: unprofitable. **70. I . . .
Jew**: i.e., with one naturally hardhearted. **72. main flood**:
ocean. **bate**: abate, lessen. **77. fretten**: fretted, tormented.

His Jewish heart. Therefore, I do beseech you   80
Make no more offers, use no farther means,
But with all brief and plain conveniency
Let me have judgment and the Jew his will.

BASS. For thy three thousand ducats here is six.

SHY. If every ducat in six thousand ducats   85
Were in six parts and every part a ducat,
I would not draw° them. I would have my bond.

DUKE. How shalt thou hope for mercy, rendering none?

SHY. What judgment shall I dread, doing no wrong?
You have among you many a purchased slave   90
Which, like your asses and your dogs and mules,
You use in abject and in slavish parts°
Because you bought them. Shall I say to you,
Let them be free, marry them to your heirs?
Why sweat they under burdens? Let their beds   95
Be made as soft as yours, and let their palates
Be seasoned° with such viands? You will answer
" The slaves are ours." So do I answer you.
The pound of flesh which I demand of him
Is dearly bought. 'Tis mine, and I will have it.   100
If you deny me, fie upon your law!
There is no force in the decrees of Venice.
I stand for judgment. Answer — shall I have it?

DUKE. Upon my power I may dismiss this court
Unless Bellario, a learned Doctor   105
Whom I have sent for to determine this
Come here today.

SALER.   My lord, here stays without
A messenger with letters from the Doctor,
New-come from Padua.   109

DUKE. Bring us the letters. Call the messenger.

BASS. Good cheer, Antonio! What, man, courage yet!
The Jew shall have my flesh, blood, bones, and all
Ere thou shalt lose for me one drop of blood.

ANT. I am a tainted° wether of the flock,
Meetest for death. The weakest kind of fruit   115
Drops earliest to the ground, and so let me.
You cannot better be employed, Bassanio,
Than to live still and write mine epitaph.

[*Enter* NERISSA, *dressed like a lawyer's clerk.*]

DUKE. Came you from Padua, from Bellario?

NER. From both, my lord. Bellario greets your
Grace.   [*Presenting a letter.*]

BASS. Why dost thou whet thy knife so earnestly?

SHY. To cut the forfeiture from that bankrupt there.   122

GRA. Not on thy sole,° but on thy soul, harsh Jew,
Thou makest thy knife keen. But no metal can —
No, not the hangman's ax — bear half the keenness
Of thy sharp envy. Can no prayers pierce thee?   126

SHY. No, none that thou hast wit enough to make.

GRA. Oh, be thou damned, inexecrable° dog!
And for thy life let justice be accused.°
Thou almost makest me waver in my faith,   130
To hold opinion with Pythagoras°
That souls of animals infuse themselves
Into the trunks of men. Thy currish spirit
Governed a wolf° who, hanged for human slaughter,
Even from the gallows did his fell° soul fleet,°   135
And whilst thou lay'st in thy unhallowed dam
Infused itself in thee, for thy desires
Are wolvish, bloody, starved, and ravenous.

SHY. Till thou canst rail the seal from off my bond,
Thou but offend'st° thy lungs to speak so loud.   140
Repair thy wit, good youth, or it will fall
To cureless ruin. I stand here for law.

DUKE. This letter from Bellario doth commend
A young and learnèd Doctor to our court.
Where is he?

NER.   He attendeth here hard by   145
To know your answer, whether you'll admit him.

DUKE. With all my heart. Some three or four of you
Go give him courteous conduct° to this place.
Meantime the court shall hear Bellario's letter.   149

CLERK. [*Reads.*] " Your Grace shall understand
that at the receipt of your letter I am very sick. But
in the instant that your messenger came, in loving
visitation was with me a young Doctor of Rome. His
name is Balthasar. I acquainted him with the cause
in controversy between the Jew and Antonio   155
the merchant. We turned o'er many books together.
He is furnished with my opinion, which, bettered
with his own learning — the greatness whereof I cannot enough commend — comes with him, at my importunity,° to fill up your Grace's request in   160
my stead. I beseech you let his lack of years be no
impediment to let him lack a reverend estimation,°
for I never knew so young a body with so old a head.
I leave him to your gracious acceptance, whose trial
shall better publish his commendation."°   166

DUKE. You hear the learnèd Bellario, what he writes.
And here, I take it, is the Doctor come.

[*Enter* PORTIA *for* BALTHASAR.] Give me your hand.
Come you from old Bellario?   169

POR. I did, my lord.

DUKE.   You are welcome. Take your place.
Are you acquainted with the difference
That holds this present question in the court?

---

128. inexecrable: merciless.   129. And . . . accused: i.e., if you
are spared, justice itself commits a crime.   131. Pythagoras:
the Greek philosopher who taught the doctrine of the transmigration of souls.   134. Governed a wolf: See *M of Ven* Intro.
p. 579a–b.   135. fell: cruel. fleet: lose.   140. offend'st: dost
injure.   148. conduct: escort.   159–160. importunity: urgent
persuasion.   162. reverend estimation: respect due to one older.
165–66. trial . . . commendation: worth shall be demonstrated
when tested.

POR. I am informèd throughly° of the cause.   173
Which is the merchant here, and which the Jew?
DUKE. Antonio and old Shylock, both stand forth.
POR. Is your name Shylock?
SHY.   Shylock is my name.
POR. Of a strange nature is the suit you follow,
Yet in such rule that the Venetian law
Cannot impugn° you as you do proceed.
[*To* ANTONIO.] You stand within his danger,° do you
    not?   180
ANT. Aye, so he says.
POR.   Do you confess the bond?
ANT. I do.
POR.   Then must the Jew be merciful.
SHY. On what compulsion must I? Tell me that.
POR. The quality° of mercy is not strained,°
It droppeth as the gentle rain from heaven   185
Upon the place beneath. It is twice blest;
It blesseth him that gives and him that takes.
'Tis mightiest in the mightiest. It becomes
The thronèd monarch better than his crown.
His scepter shows the force of temporal power,   190
The attribute to awe and majesty
Wherein doth sit the dread and fear of kings.
But mercy is above this sceptered sway,
It is enthronèd in the hearts of kings,
It is an attribute to God himself,   195
And earthly power doth then show likest God's
When mercy seasons° justice. Therefore, Jew,
Though justice be thy plea, consider this,
That in the course of justice none of us
Should see salvation. We do pray for mercy,   200
And that same prayer doth teach us all to render°
The deeds of mercy. I have spoke thus much
To mitigate the justice of thy plea,   203
Which if thou follow, this strict court of Venice
Must needs give sentence 'gainst the merchant there.
SHY. My deeds upon my head! I crave the law,
The penalty and forfeit of my bond.
POR. Is he not able to discharge the money?
BASS. Yes, here I tender° it for him in the court,
Yea, twice the sum. If that will not suffice,   210
I will be bound to pay it ten times o'er
On forfeit of my hands, my head, my heart.
If this will not suffice, it must appear
That malice bears down truth. And I beseech you
Wrest° once the law to your authority.   215
To do a great right, do a little wrong,
And curb this cruel devil of his will.
POR. It must not be. There is no power in Venice
Can alter a decree established.
'Twill be recorded for a precedent,   220
And many an error, by the same example,

Will rush into the state. It cannot be.
SHY. A Daniel° come to judgment! Yea, a Daniel!
O wise young judge, how I do honor thee!
POR. I pray you let me look upon the bond.   225
SHY. Here 'tis, most reverend Doctor, here it is.
POR. Shylock, there's thrice thy money offered
    thee.
SHY. An oath, an oath, I have an oath in Heaven.
Shall I lay perjury upon my soul?
No, not for Venice.
POR.   Why, this bond is forfeit,°   230
And lawfully by this the Jew may claim
A pound of flesh, to be by him cut off
Nearest the merchant's heart. Be merciful.
Take thrice thy money, bid me tear the bond.
SHY. When it is paid according to the tenor.°   235
It doth appear you are a worthy judge,
You know the law, your exposition
Hath been most sound. I charge you by the law,
Whereof you are a well-deserving pillar,
Proceed to judgment. By my soul I swear   240
There is no power in the tongue of man
To alter me. I stay here on my bond.
ANT. Most heartily I do beseech the court
To give the judgment.
POR.   Why then, thus it is.
You must prepare your bosom for his knife.   245
SHY. O noble judge! O excellent young man!
POR. For the intent and purpose of the law
Hath full relation° to the penalty
Which here appeareth due upon the bond.
SHY. 'Tis very true. O wise and upright judge!
How much more elder art thou than thy looks!   251
POR. Therefore lay bare your bosom.
SHY.   Aye, his breast.
So says the bond — doth it not, noble judge? —
"Nearest his heart." Those are the very words.
POR. It is so. Are there balance here to weigh   255
The flesh?
SHY.   I have them ready.
POR. Have by some surgeon, Shylock, on your
    charge,
To stop his wounds, lest he do bleed to death.
SHY. Is it so nominated in the bond?
POR. It is not so expressed, but what of that?   260
'Twere good you do so much for charity.
SHY. I cannot find it. 'Tis not in the bond.
POR. You, merchant, have you anything to say?
ANT. But little. I am armed and well prepared.
Give me your hand, Bassanio. Fare you well!   265
Grieve not that I am fallen to this for you,

173. throughly: thoroughly.   179. impugn: call in question.
180. within . . . danger: in his power to exact a penalty.
184. quality: nature. strained: forced; i.e., mercy must be given
freely.   197. seasons: is mixed with.   201. render: pay back.
209. tender: offer.   215. Wrest: wrench.

223. Daniel: In the History of Susanna in the Apocrypha,
Susanna was falsely accused of adultery by two elders, and
condemned to death; but Daniel, a wise young man, by questioning the elders separately revealed their false testimony.
230. bond is forfeit: i.e., the defendant must pay the forfeit
demanded.   235. tenor: intention.   248. Hath . . . relation: is
fully in accord with.

For herein Fortune shows herself more kind
Than is her custom. It is still° her use
To let the wretched man outlive his wealth,
To view with hollow eye and wrinkled brow   270
An age of poverty, from which lingering penance
Of such misery doth she cut me off.
Commend me to your honorable wife.
Tell her the process of Antonio's end,
Say how I loved you, speak me fair in death,   275
And when the tale is told, bid her be judge
Whether Bassanio had not once a love.
Repent but you that you shall lose your friend,
And he repents not that he pays your debt,
For if the Jew do cut but deep enough,   280
I'll pay it presently with all my heart.
BASS. Antonio, I am married to a wife
Which is as dear to me as life itself,
But life itself, my wife, and all the world
Are not with me esteemed above thy life.   285
I would lose all, aye, sacrifice them all
Here to this devil, to deliver you.
   POR. Your wife would give you little thanks for
     that
If she were by to hear you make the offer.
   GRA. I have a wife whom, I protest, I love.   290
I would she were in Heaven so she could
Entreat some power to change this currish Jew.
   NER. 'Tis well you offer it behind her back.
The wish would make else an unquiet house.
   SHY. [*Aside*] These be the Christian husbands. I
     have a daughter.   295
Would any of the stock of Barrabas°
Had been her husband rather than a Christian!
[*To Portia.*] We trifle time. I pray thee, pursue
     sentence.
   POR. A pound of that same merchant's flesh is
     thine.
The court awards it, and the law doth give it.   300
   SHY. Most rightful judge!
   POR. And you must cut this flesh from off his
     breast.
The law allows it, and the court awards it.
   SHY. Most learned judge! A sentence! Come, pre-
     pare!
   POR. Tarry a little. There is something else.   305
This bond doth give thee here no jot of blood.
The words expressly are " a pound of flesh."
Take then thy bond, take thou thy pound of flesh,
But in the cutting it if thou dost shed
One drop of Christian blood, thy lands and goods
Are, by the laws of Venice, confiscate   311
Unto the state of Venice.
   GRA. O upright judge! Mark, Jew. O learnèd
     judge!

   SHY. Is that the law?
   POR.   Thyself shalt see the act.
For, as thou urgest justice, be assured   315
Thou shalt have justice, more than thou desirest.
   GRA. O learnèd judge! Mark, Jew, a learnèd judge!
   SHY. I take this offer, then. Pay the bond thrice
And let the Christian go.
   BASS.   Here is the money.
   POR. Soft!°   320
The Jew shall have all justice. Soft! No haste.
He shall have nothing but the penalty.
   GRA. O Jew! An upright judge, a learnèd judge!
   POR. Therefore prepare thee to cut off the flesh.
Shed thou no blood, nor cut thou less nor more   325
But just a pound of flesh. If thou cut'st more
Or less than a just° pound, be it but so much
As makes it light or heavy in the substance,
Or the division of the twentieth part
Of one poor scruple° — nay, if the scale do turn
But in the estimation of a hair —   331
Thou diest and all thy goods are confiscate.
   GRA. A second Daniel, a Daniel, Jew!
Now, infidel, I have you on the hip.°
   POR. Why doth the Jew pause? Take thy forfei-
     ture.   335
   SHY. Give me my principal and let me go.
   BASS. I have it ready for thee. Here it is.
   POR. He hath refused it in the open court.
He shall have merely justice and his bond.
   GRA. A Daniel, still say I, a second Daniel!   340
I thank thee, Jew, for teaching me that word.
   SHY. Shall I not have barely my principal?
   POR. Thou shalt have nothing but the forfeiture,
To be so taken at thy peril, Jew.
   SHY. Why, then the Devil give him good of it!
I'll stay no longer question.
   POR.   Tarry, Jew.   346
The law hath yet another hold on you.
It is enacted in the laws of Venice,
If it be proved against an alien
That by direct or indirect attempts   350
He seek the life of any citizen,
The party 'gainst the which he doth contrive°
Shall seize one half his goods. The other half
Comes to the privy coffer° of the state.
And the offender's life lies in the mercy   355
Of the Duke only, 'gainst all other voice.
In which predicament, I say, thou stand'st,
For it appears, by manifest proceeding,
That indirectly, and directly too,
Thou hast contrived against the very life   360
Of the defendant, and thou hast incurred

---

268. **still:** continually.   296. **Barrabas:** either Barabbas the
robber whom the Jews preferred to Jesus (see Luke 23:18–19)
or Barabas the Jew of Malta (see *M of Ven* Intro. p. 581a–b and
Gen. Intro. p. 37b), who was better known to playgoers.

320. **Soft:** pause a little.   327. **just:** exact.   330. **scruple:** minute
portion (actually, 20 grains).   334. **on . . . hip:** at a disadvantage.
352. **contrive:** plot.   354. **privy coffer:** privy purse. Shakespeare
is thinking rather of English finance at the time. Fines of this
kind were paid into the privy purse; i.e., the Sovereign's personal income.

The danger formerly by me rehearsed.
Down, therefore, and beg mercy of the Duke.
   GRA. Beg that thou mayst have leave to hang thyself.
And yet, thy wealth being forfeit to the state,   365
Thou hast not left the value of a cord,
Therefore thou must be hanged at the state's charge.
   DUKE. That thou shalt see the difference of our
     spirits,
I pardon thee thy life before thou ask it.
For half thy wealth, it is Antonio's.   370
The other half comes to the general state,
Which humbleness may drive unto a fine.°
   POR. Aye, for the state, not for Antonio.
   SHY. Nay, take my life and all — pardon not that.
You take my house when you do take the prop   375
That doth sustain my house. You take my life
When you do take the means whereby I live.
   POR. What mercy can you render him, Antonio?
   GRA. A halter gratis. Nothing else, for God's sake.
   ANT. So please my lord the Duke and all the
     court,   380
To quit° the fine for one half of his goods,
I am content, so he will let me have
The other half in use, to render it,
Upon his death, unto the gentleman
That lately stole his daughter.   385
Two things provided more, that, for this favor,
He presently become a Christian.
The other, that he do record a gift,
Here in the court, of all he dies possessed
Unto his son Lorenzo and his daughter.   390
   DUKE. He shall do this, or else I do recant
The pardon that I late pronouncèd here.
   POR. Art thou contented, Jew? What dost thou
     say?
   SHY. I am content.
   POR.   Clerk, draw a deed of gift.
   SHY. I pray you give me leave to go from hence.
I am not well. Send the deed after me   396
And I will sign it.
   DUKE.   Get thee gone, but do it.
   GRA. In christening shalt thou have two godfathers.
Had I been judge, thou shouldst have had ten more,°
To bring thee to the gallows, not the font.   400
                        [*Exit* SHYLOCK.]
   DUKE. Sir, I entreat you home with me to dinner.
   POR. I humbly do desire your Grace of pardon.
I must away this night toward Padua,
And it is meet° I presently set forth.
   DUKE. I am sorry that your leisure serves you not.
Antonio, gratify° this gentleman,   406
For, in my mind, you are much bound to him.
              [*Exeunt* DUKE *and his train.*]

   BASS. Most worthy gentleman, I and my friend
Have by your wisdom been this day acquitted
Of grievous penalties, in lieu whereof,   410
Three thousand ducats, due unto the Jew,
We freely cope° your courteous pains° withal.
   ANT. And stand indebted, over and above,
In love and service to you evermore.
   POR. He is well paid that is well satisfied,   415
And I, delivering you, am satisfied,
And therein do account myself well paid.
My mind was never yet more mercenary.
I pray you, know me when we meet again.°
I wish you well, and so I take my leave.   420
   BASS. Dear sir, of force I must attempt you
     further.
Take some remembrance of us — as a tribute,
Not as a fee. Grant me two things, I pray you —
Not to deny me, and to pardon me.   424
   POR. You press me far, and therefore I will yield.
[*To* ANTONIO] Give me your gloves, I'll wear them
     for your sake.
[*To* BASSANIO] And, for your love,° I'll take this ring
     from you.
Do not draw back your hand. I'll take no more,
And you in love shall not deny me this.
   BASS. This ring, good sir, alas! it is a trifle.   430
I will not shame myself to give you this.
   POR. I will have nothing else but only this,
And now methinks I have a mind to it.
   BASS. There's more depends on this than on the
     value.
The dearest ring in Venice will I give you,   435
And find it out by proclamation.
Only for this, I pray you pardon me.
   POR. I see, sir, you are liberal in offers.
You taught me first to beg, and now methinks   439
You teach me how a beggar should be answered.
   BASS. Good sir, this ring was given me by my wife,
And when she put it on, she made me vow
That I should neither sell nor give nor lose it.
   POR. That 'scuse serves many men to save their
     gifts.
An° if your wife be not a madwoman,   445
And know how well I have deserved the ring,
She would not hold out enemy forever
For giving it to me. Well, peace be with you!
              [*Exeunt* PORTIA *and* NERISSA.]
   ANT. My Lord Bassanio, let him have the ring.
Let his deservings and my love withal   450
Be valued 'gainst your wife's commandment.
   BASS. Go, Gratiano, run and overtake him.
Give him the ring, and bring him, if thou canst,
Unto Antonio's house. Away! Make haste.
                     [*Exit* GRATIANO.]

---

372. fine: a lesser penalty. **381. quit:** remit. **399. ten more:** i.e., a jury of twelve to bring in a verdict of guilty. **404. meet:** fit. **406. gratify:** pay the fee of.

412. cope: meet, requite. **pains:** trouble. **419. know ... again:** a polite phrase meaning "I hope we shall see more of each other"; but Portia uses it ironically. **427. for ... love:** as a keepsake. **445. An:** if.

Come, you and I will thither presently,   455
And in the morning early will we both
Fly toward Belmont. Come, Antonio.   *[Exeunt.]*

SCENE II. *The same. A street.*

[Enter PORTIA *and* NERISSA.*]*
POR. Inquire the Jew's house out, give him this
    deed
And let him sign it. We'll away tonight
And be a day before our husbands home.
This deed will be well welcome to Lorenzo.
        [Enter GRATIANO.*]*
GRA. Fair sir, you are well o'erta'en.   5
My Lord Bassanio upon more advice°
Hath sent you here this ring, and doth entreat
Your company at dinner.
POR.   That cannot be.
His ring I do accept most thankfully,
And so I pray you tell him. Furthermore,   10
I pray you show my youth old Shylock's house.
GRA. That will I do.
NER.   Sir, I would speak with you.
[Aside to PORTIA*]* I'll see if I can get my husband's
    ring,
Which I did make him swear to keep forever.
POR. *[Aside to* NERISSA*]* Thou mayst, I warrant.
    We shall have old° swearing   15
That they did give the rings away to men,
But we'll outface them, and outswear them too.
[Aloud] Away! Make haste. Thou know'st where I
    will tarry.
NER. Come, good sir, will you show me to this
    house?   *[Exeunt.]*

Act V

SCENE I. *Belmont. Avenue to* PORTIA'*s house.*

[Enter LORENZO *and* JESSICA.*]*
LOR. The moon shines bright. In such a night as
    this,
When the sweet wind did gently kiss the trees
And they did make no noise, in such a night
Troilus° methinks mounted the Troyan walls,
And sighed his soul towárd the Grecian tents,   5
Where Cressid lay that night.
JES.   In such a night

Did Thisbe° fearfully o'ertrip° the dew,
And saw the lion's shadow ere himself,°
And ran dismayed away.
LOR.   In such a night
Stood Dido° with a willow° in her hand   10
Upon the wild sea banks and waft° her love
To come again to Carthage.
JES.   In such a night
Medea° gathered the enchanted herbs
That did renew old Aeson.
LOR.   In such a night
Did Jessica steal from the wealthy Jew,   15
And with an unthrift° love did run from Venice
As far as Belmont.
JES.   In such a night
Did young Lorenzo swear he loved her well,
Stealing her soul with many vows of faith
And ne'er a true one.
LOR.   In such a night   20
Did pretty Jessica, like a little shrew,
Slander her love, and he forgave it her.
JES. I would outnight you did nobody come.
But hark, I hear the footing of a man.
        [Enter STEPHANO.*]*
LOR. Who comes so fast in silence of the night?
STEPH. A friend.   26
LOR. A friend! What friend? Your name, I pray
    you, friend?
STEPH. Stephano is my name, and I bring word
My mistress will before the break of day
Be here at Belmont. She doth stray about   30
By holy crosses, where she kneels and prays
For happy wedlock hours.
LOR.   Who comes with her?
STEPH. None but a holy hermit° and her maid.
I pray you, is my master yet returned?
LOR. He is not, nor we have not heard from him.
But go we in, I pray thee, Jessica,   36
And ceremoniously let us prepare
Some welcome for the mistress of the house.
        [Enter LAUNCELOT GOBBO.*]*
LAUN. Sola,° sola! Wo ha, ho! Sola, sola!
LOR. Who calls?   40
LAUN. Sola! Did you see Master Lorenzo? Master
Lorenzo, sola, sola!
LOR. Leave holloaing, man. Here.
LAUN. Sola! Where? Where?
LOR. Here.   45

7. **Thisbe:** For the sad story of Pyramus and Thisbe see *MND,* V.i.108–354. **o'ertrip:** run trippingly over. 8. **himself:** i.e., Pyramus. 10. **Dido:** the widowed queen of Carthage, whom Aeneas loved and deserted. **willow:** the sign of a deserted lover. 11. **waft:** waved to. 13. **Medea:** the sorceress who helped Jason to fetch away the Golden Fleece and afterward refused to leave him. *Aeson* was Jason's father. 16. **unthrift:** spendthrift. 33. **holy hermit:** This good man does not appear for he has no existence in fact. He is part of the feigned excuse for Portia's absence from home. See III.iv.30. 39. **Sola:** Launcelot imitates the sound of the postboy's horn. See App. 17.

Sc. ii: 6. **advice:** consideration. 15. **old:** any amount of.
Act V, Sc. i: 4. **Troilus:** Troilus the Trojan was deprived of his love Cressida, who was taken away to the Greek camp. See *Tr & Cr,* IV.ii. etc.

LAUN. Tell him there's a post come from my master, with his horn full of good news. My master will be here ere morning. [*Exit.*]

LOR. Sweet soul, let's in, and there expect° their
coming.
And yet no matter. Why should we go in?   50
My friend Stephano, signify, I pray you,
Within the house, your mistress is at hand,
And bring your music forth into the air.
[*Exit* STEPHANO.]
How sweet the moonlight sleeps upon this bank!
Here will we sit and let the sounds of music   55
Creep in our ears. Soft stillness and the night
Become the touches of sweet harmony.
Sit, Jessica. Look how the floor of heaven
Is thick inlaid with patines° of bright gold.
There's not the smallest orb which thou behold'st
But in his motion° like an angel sings,   61
Still quiring° to the young-eyed cherubins.
Such harmony is in immortal souls,
But whilst this muddy vesture of decay°
Doth grossly close it in, we cannot hear it.   65
[*Enter* MUSICIANS.] Come, ho! and wake Diana°
with a hymn!
With sweetest touches pierce your mistress' ear,
And draw her home with music. [*Music.*]

JES. I am never merry when I hear sweet music.

LOR. The reason is, your spirits are attentive.   70
For do but note a wild and wanton herd,
Or race of youthful and unhandled colts,
Fetching mad bounds, bellowing, and neighing loud,
Which is the hot condition of their blood.
If they but hear perchance a trumpet sound,   75
Or any air of music touch their ears,
You shall perceive them make a mutual stand,
Their savage eyes turned to a modest gaze
By the sweet power of music. Therefore the poet
Did feign that Orpheus° drew trees, stones, and
floods,   80
Since naught so stockish,° hard, and full of rage
But music for the time doth change his nature.
The man that hath no music in himself,
Nor is not moved with concord of sweet sounds,
Is fit for treasons, stratagems,° and spoils.   85
The motions of his spirit are dull as night,
And his affections dark as Erebus.°
Let no such man be trusted. Mark the music.
[*Enter* PORTIA *and* NERISSA.]

POR. That light we see is burning in my hall.
How far that little candle throws his beams!   90

So shines a good deed in a naughty world.

NER. When the moon shone, we did not see the
candle.

POR. So doth the greater glory dim the less.
A substitute shines brightly as a king
Until a king be by, and then his state   95
Empties itself, as doth an inland brook
Into the main of waters. Music! Hark!

NER. It is your music, madam, of the house.

POR. Nothing is good, I see, without respect.°
Methinks it sounds much sweeter than by day.   100

NER. Silence bestows that virtue on it, madam.

POR. The crow doth sing as sweetly as the lark
When neither is attended,° and I think
The nightingale if she should sing by day,
When every goose is cackling, would be thought
No better a musician than the wren.   106
How many things by season seasoned are°
To their right praise and true perfection!
Peace, ho! The moon sleeps with Endymion,°
And would not be awaked. [*Music ceases.*]

LOR.   That is the voice,   110
Or I am much deceived, of Portia.

POR. He knows me as the blind man knows the
cuckoo,
By the bad voice.

LOR.   Dear lady, welcome home.

POR. We have been praying for our husbands'
healths,   114
Which speed,° we hope, the better for our words.
Are they returned?

LOR.   Madam, they are not yet,
But there is come a messenger before
To signify their coming.

POR.   Go in, Nerissa.
Give order to my servants that they take
No note at all of our being absent hence —   120
Nor you, Lorenzo, Jessica, nor you.
[*A tucket° sounds.*]

LOR. Your husband is at hand, I hear his trumpet.
We are no telltales, madam, fear you not.

POR. This night methinks is but the daylight sick,
It looks a little paler. 'Tis a day   125
Such as the day is when the sun is hid.
[*Enter* BASSANIO, ANTONIO, GRATIANO, *and their
followers.*]

BASS. We should hold day with the Antipodes
If you would walk in absence of the sun.°

POR. Let me give light, but let me not be light,
For a light wife doth make a heavy husband,   130

---

49. expect: await.   **59. patines:** plates.   **61. in . . . motion:** See App. 1.   **62. quiring:** singing.   **64. muddy . . . decay:** i.e., the mortal earthly body. So long as we are mortal we cannot hear immortal music.   **66. wake Diana:** the goddess Diana is also the moon; she loved a mortal shepherd called Endymion.   **80. Orpheus:** The musician of Thrace was so skillful that even the trees bent to listen to him.   **81. stockish:** like an unfeeling block.   **85. stratagems:** deeds of violence.   **87. Erebus:** Hell.

99. without respect: without reference to circumstances; i.e., in itself.   **103. attended:** listened to.   **107. by . . . are:** give a pleasant taste by appearing at the right time.   **109. Endymion:** See l. 66 above.   **115. speed:** prosper.   **121. s.d., tucket:** a short trumpet fanfare.   **127–28. We . . . sun:** if you always chose to walk in the dark it would be daylight with us at the same time as on the opposite side of the globe; i.e., your presence makes darkness light.

And never be Bassanio so for me.
But God sort° all! You are welcome home, my lord.
   BASS. I thank you, madam. Give welcome to my
      friend.
This is the man, this is Antonio,
To whom I am so infinitely bound.   135
   POR. You should in all sense be much bound to
      him,
For, as I hear, he was much bound for you.
   ANT. No more than I am well acquitted of.°
   POR. Sir, you are very welcome to our house.
It must appear in other ways than words,   140
Therefore I scant this breathing courtesy.°
   GRA. [To NERISSA] By yonder moon I swear you do
      me wrong.
In faith, I gave it to the judge's clerk.
Would he were gelt° that had it, for my part,
Since you do take it, love, so much at heart.   145
   POR. A quarrel, ho! Already! What's the matter?
   GRA. About a hoop of gold, a paltry ring
That she did give me, whose posy° was
For all the world like cutler's poetry
Upon a knife, " Love me, and leave me not."   150
   NER. What talk you of the posy or the value?
You swore to me when I did give it you
That you would wear it till your hour of death,
And that it should lie with you in your grave.   154
Though not for me, yet for your vehement oaths,
You should have been respective,° and have kept it.
Gave it a judge's clerk! No, God's my judge,
The clerk will ne'er wear hair on's face that had it.
   GRA. He will an if he live to be a man.
   NER. Aye, if a woman live to be a man.   160
   GRA. Now, by this hand, I gave it to a youth,
A kind of boy, a little scrubbèd° boy,
No higher than thyself, the judge's clerk,
A prating boy that begged it as a fee.
I could not for my heart deny it him.   165
   POR. You were to blame, I must be plain with you,
To part so slightly with your wife's first gift —
A thing stuck on with oaths upon your finger
And so riveted with faith unto your flesh.
I gave my love a ring and made him swear   170
Never to part with it, and here he stands.
I dare be sworn for him he would not leave it,
Nor pluck it from his finger, for the wealth
That the world masters. Now, in faith, Gratiano,
You give your wife too unkind a cause of grief.   175
An 'twere to me, I should be mad at it.
   BASS. [Aside] Why, I were best to cut my left
      hand off,
And swear I lost the ring defending it.
   GRA. My Lord Bassanio gave his ring away
Unto the judge that begged it, and indeed   180

Deserved it too. And then the boy, his clerk,
That took some pains in writing, he begged mine,
And neither man nor master would take aught
But the two rings.
   POR.   What ring gave you, my lord?
Not that, I hope, which you received of me.   185
   BASS. If I could add a lie unto a fault,
I would deny it, but you see my finger
Hath not the ring upon it. It is gone.
   POR. Even so void is your false heart of truth.
By Heaven, I will ne'er come in your bed   190
Until I see the ring.
   NER.   Nor I in yours
Till I again see mine.
   BASS.   Sweet Portia,
If you did know to whom I gave the ring,
If you did know for whom I gave the ring,
And would conceive° for what I gave the ring,
And how unwillingly I left the ring,   196
When naught would be accepted but the ring,
You would abate the strength of your displeasure.
   POR. If you had known the virtue of the ring,
Or half her worthiness that gave the ring,   200
Or your own honor to contain the ring,
You would not then have parted with the ring.
What man is there so much unreasonable,
If you had pleased to have defended it
With any terms of zeal, wanted the modesty   205
To urge the thing held as a ceremony?°
Nerissa teaches me what to believe.
I'll die for't but some woman had the ring.
   BASS. No, by my honor, madam, by my soul,
No woman had it, but a civil Doctor,°   210
Which did refuse three thousand ducats of me,
And begged the ring, the which I did deny him,
And suffered him to go displeased away,
Even he that did uphold the very life
Of my dear friend. What should I say, sweet lady?
I was enforced to send it after him,   216
I was beset with shame and courtesy,
My honor would not let ingratitude
So much besmear it. Pardon me, good lady,
For by these blessed candles of the night,   220
Had you been there, I think you would have begged
The ring of me to give the worthy Doctor.
   POR. Let not that Doctor e'er come near my house.
Since he hath got the jewel that I loved,
And that which you did swear to keep for me,   225
I will become as liberal as you.
I'll not deny him anything I have,
No, not my body nor my husband's bed.
Know him I shall, I am well sure of it.
Lie not a night from home, watch me like Argus.°
If you do not, if I be left alone,   231

---

132. sort: dispose of.   138. acquitted of: paid for.   141. scant
. . . courtesy: cut short this welcome of mere words.   144. gelt:
gelded.   148. posy: motto engraved inside a ring.   156. respective: careful.   162. scrubbed: scrubby.

195. conceive: imagine.   206. ceremony: something sacred.
210. civil Doctor: Doctor of Civil Law.   230. Argus: who had a
hundred eyes.

Now, by mine honor, which is yet mine own,
I'll have that Doctor for my bedfellow.

  NER. And I his clerk, therefore be well advised
How you do leave me to mine own protection.   235

  GRA. Well, do you so. Let not me take him, then,
For if I do, I'll mar the young clerk's pen.

  ANT. I am the unhappy subject of these quarrels.

  POR. Sir, grieve not you. You are welcome notwithstanding.

  BASS. Portia, forgive me this enforcèd wrong,
And in the hearing of these many friends   241
I swear to thee, even by thine own fair eyes,
Wherein I see myself——

  POR.   Mark you but that!
In both my eyes he doubly sees himself —
In each eye, one. Swear by your double self,   245
And there's an oath of credit.

  BASS.   Nay, but hear me.
Pardon this fault and by my soul I swear
I never more will break an oath with thee.

  ANT. I once did lend my body for his wealth,
Which, but for him that had your husband's ring,
Had quite miscarried. I dare be bound again,   251
My soul upon the forfeit, that your lord
Will never more break faith advisedly.°

  POR. Then you shall be his surety. Give him this,
And bid him keep it better than the other.   255

  ANT. Here, Lord Bassanio, swear to keep this ring.

  BASS. By Heaven, it is the same I gave the Doctor!

  POR. I had it of him. Pardon me, Bassanio,
For, by this ring, the Doctor lay with me.

  NER. And pardon me, my gentle Gratiano,   260
For that same scrubbèd boy, the Doctor's clerk,
In lieu of° this last night did lie with me.

  GRA. Why, this is like the mending of highways
In summer, where the ways are fair enough.   264
What, are we cuckolds° ere we have deserved it?

  POR. Speak not so grossly. You are all amazed.
Here is a letter, read it at your leisure.
It comes from Padua, from Bellario.
There you shall find that Portia was the Doctor,
Nerissa there her clerk. Lorenzo here   270
Shall witness I set forth as soon as you,

And even but now returned. I have not yet
Entered my house. Antonio, you are welcome,
And I have better news in store for you
Than you expect. Unseal this letter soon.   275
There you shall find three of your argosies
Are richly come to harbor suddenly.
You shall not know by what strange accident
I chancèd on this letter.

  ANT.   I am dumb.   279

  BASS. Were you the Doctor and I knew you not?

  GRA. Were you the clerk that is to make me cuckold?

  NER. Aye, but the clerk that never means to do it
Unless he live until he be a man.

  BASS. Sweet Doctor, you shall be my bedfellow.
When I am absent, then lie with my wife.   285

  ANT. Sweet lady, you have given me life and living,
For here I read for certain that my ships
Are safely come to road.

  POR.   How now, Lorenzo!
My clerk hath some good comforts too for you.

  NER. Aye, and I'll give them him without a fee.
There do I give to you and Jessica,   291
From the rich Jew, a special deed of gift,
After his death, of all he dies possessed of.

  LOR. Fair ladies, you drop manna in the way
Of starvèd people.

  POR.   It is almost morning,   295
And yet I am sure you are not satisfied
Of these events at full. Let us go in.
And charge us there upon inter'gatories,°
And we will answer all things faithfully.

  GRA. Let it be so. The first inter'gatory   300
That my Nerissa shall be sworn on is
Whether till the next night she had rather stay,
Or go to bed now, being two hours to day.
But were the day come, I should wish it dark,
That I were couching with the Doctor's clerk.   305
Well, while I live I'll fear no other thing
So sore as keeping safe Nerissa's ring.   [*Exeunt.*]

---

253. **advisedly:** deliberately.   262. **In lieu of:** in return for.
265. **cuckolds:** deceived by our wives.

298. **inter'gatories:** interrogatories, a list of questions on oath put to a suspected person or witness in the enquiry preliminary to a trial.

The First Part of
KING HENRY THE FOURTH

Introduction[1]

The First Part of King Henry the Fourth was probably written in the autumn of 1597. The play is a sequel to *Richard II,* which had been published in the late summer of 1597 and was selling well, particularly because the followers of the Earl of Essex were finding certain parallels between that story and their own times (see *Rich II* Intro. p. 433a–b). In writing *I Henry IV* Shakespeare began the story at the point where *Richard II* ended, but his method of writing the sequel was quite different. Hitherto his history plays had been mostly serious; he certainly shaped historical facts and dates to suit his own purposes, but he seldom digressed. There was no clowning or laughter either in *Richard III* or in *Richard II.* In *Henry IV* half the play is occupied with the riotous and quite unhistorical low comedy of Sir John Falstaff and his gang. As a result there was less room for history, and Shakespeare reduced the historical plot to a series of simple scenes.

For his historical facts, Shakespeare went, as before, to Holinshed's *Chronicles,* from which he extracted and adapted ten episodes: 1. News is brought to the King that the Percies of Northumberland are growing troublesome (I.i). 2. The Percies come to Court and quarrel with the King (I.iii). 3. Hotspur, at home with his wife, prepares for his campaign against the King (II.ii). 4. Hotspur and Worcester, having joined with the Welsh Prince, Owen Glendower, agree on the terms of their alliance (III.i). 5. The King rebukes Prince Hal for his unprincely life (III.ii). 6. Hotspur, Worcester, and their friends prepare to give battle to the King's forces (IV.i). 7. The King's messenger proposes a parley (IV.iii). 8. Worcester and Vernon parley with the King, who offers terms (V.i). 9. Worcester falsely reports the King's offer and the battle begins (V.ii). 10. Hotspur is slain and the rebels are defeated at the Battle of Shrewsbury (V.iii, iv, v).

Some specimens will show how Shakespeare used his Holinshed:

1. THE QUARREL BETWEEN THE KING AND THE PERCIES (cf. I.i AND iii)

Henry Earl of Northumberland, with his brother Thomas Earl of Worcester, and his son the Lord Henry Percy, surnamed Hotspur, which were to King Henry in the beginning of his reign both faithful friends and earnest aiders, began now to envy his wealth and felicity; and especially they were grieved because the King demanded of the Earl and his son such Scottish prisoners as were taken at Holmedon and Nesbit; for of all the captives which were taken in the conflicts foughten in those two places, there was delivered to the King's possession only Mordake Earl of Fife, the Duke of Albany's son; though the King did divers and sundry times require deliverance of the residue, and that with great threatenings, wherewith the Percies being sore offended (for that they claimed them as their own proper prisoners, and their peculiar preys), by the counsel of the Lord Thomas Percy, Earl of Worcester, whose study was ever (as some write) to procure malice and set things in a broil, came to the King unto Windsor (upon a purpose to prove him), and there required of him that either by ransom or otherwise he would cause to be delivered out of prison Edmund Mortimer Earl of March, their cousin german, whom (as they reported) Owen Glendower kept in filthy prison, shackled with irons, only for that he took his part, and was to him faithful and true.

The King began not a little to muse at this request, and not without cause; for indeed it touched him somewhat near, sith this Edmund was son to Roger Earl of March, son to the Lady Philip, daughter of Lionel Duke of Clarence, the third son of King Edward the Third; which Edmund, at King Richard's going into Ireland, was proclaimed heir apparent to the crown and realm; whose aunt, called Eleanor, the Lord Henry Percy had married; and therefore King Henry could not well bear that any man should be earnest about the advancement of that lineage. The King, when he had studied on the matter, made answer that the Earl of March was not taken prisoner for his cause, nor in his service, but willingly suffered himself to be taken, because he would not withstand the attempts of Owen Glendower and his complices, and therefore he would neither ransom him nor relieve him.

The Percies with this answer and fraudulent excuse were not a little fumed, insomuch that Henry Hotspur said openly: " Behold, the heir of the realm is robbed of his right, and yet the robber with his own will not redeem him! " So in this fury the Percies departed, minding nothing more than to depose King Henry from the high type of his royalty, and to place in his seat their cousin Edmund Earl of March, whom they did not only deliver out of captivity, but also (to the high displeasure of King Henry) entered in league with the foresaid Glendower.

2. THE SUSPICIONS OF THE KING AGAINST PRINCE HENRY (cf. III.ii)

Lord Henry, Prince of Wales, eldest son to King Henry, got knowledge that certain of his father's servants were busy to give informations against him, whereby discord might arise betwixt him and his father; for they put into the King's head not only what evil rule (according to the course of youth) the Prince kept, to the offense of many, but also what great resort of people came to his house; so that the Court was nothing furnished with such a train as daily followed the Prince. These tales brought no small suspicion into the King's head, lest his son would presume to usurp the crown, he being yet alive; through which suspicious jealousy it was perceived that he favored not his son, as in times past he had done.

The Prince (sore offended with such persons as by slanderous reports sought not only to spot his good name abroad in the realm, but to sow discord also betwixt him and his father) wrote his letters into every part of the realm, to reprove all such slanderous devices of those that sought his discredit. And to clear himself the better (that the world might understand what wrong he had to be slandered in such wise), about the feast of Peter and Paul — to wit, the nine and twentieth day of June — he came to the Court with such a number of noblemen and other his friends that wished him well as the like train had been seldom seen repairing to the Court at any one time in those days. . . .

Thus were the father and the son reconciled, betwixt whom the said pickthanks had sown division, insomuch that the son, upon a vehement conceit of unkindness sprung in the father, was in the way to be worn out of favor. Which was the more likely to come to pass by their informations that privily charged him with riot and other uncivil demeanor unseemly for a Prince. Indeed he was youthfully given, grown to audacity, and had chosen him companions agreeable to his age, with whom he spent the time in such recreations, exercises, and delights as he fancied. But yet (it should seem by the report of some writers) that his behavior was not offensive or at least tending to the damage of anybody; sith he had a care to avoid doing of wrong, and to tether his affections within the tract of virtue, whereby he opened unto himself a ready passage of good liking among the prudent sort, and was beloved of such as could discern his disposition, which was in no degree so excessive as that he deserved in such vehement manner to be suspected.

The adventures of Sir John Falstaff and Prince Hal are wholly fictitious and mostly Shakespeare's own inventing, though the Prince's wild behavior had long become a stage tradition and had been shown in at least one play which still survives in print. This was a crude piece called *The famous victories of Henry the Fifth,* which crams into a succession of short scenes the more popular episodes of the King's life. This play had been acted by the now defunct company of the Queen's Men. It was entered for publication in 1594, though the earliest surviving copy is dated 1598. The main episodes in *The Famous Victories* are a robbery by the Prince and his companions on Gadshill, but the details differ from those of the incident in *I Henry IV;* a riot committed by the Prince and his followers, who are sent to prison; a courthouse scene where a thief is sentenced by the judge, whereupon the Prince gives the judge a box on the ear and is himself sent to prison; the sickness of King Henry IV; the reconciliation between father and son; a second scene of the King's sickness when the Prince, thinking that his father is dead, takes the crown but is recalled and again rebuked by the King, who dies directly after a further reconciliation; the new King Henry V on coming from his coronation dismisses his former companions, and immediately asks the Archbishop of Canterbury to expound his right to the French crown; the visit of the French King's ambassador, who presents a tun of tennis balls as a present from the Dauphin; the reconciliation of the King with the Lord Chief Justice; the enrollment of recruits; the news of the English advance received at the French Court; a scene in the French camp; Henry's orders for the battle; a brief battle scene (mostly indicated by noises behind the stage); the French offer of submission; the severe terms proposed by Henry; Henry's wooing of the French Princess Katharine; the French King's agreement to Henry's terms; and the final reconciliation. As well as the historical episodes, there are a number of passages of poor low comedy.

Shakespeare took little from this primitive drama. There is an occasional echo of a line, and while in *The Famous Victories* one of the Prince's wanton companions is called Sir John Oldcastle, alias Jockey, he not only has a very small part, appearing only twice, but he is undistinguished either for wit, bulk, or cowardice. In the first version of Shakespeare's *Henry IV,* the fat knight was called Oldcastle. The real Sir John Oldcastle was a very different person, of whom Holinshed wrote:

Also in this first year of this King's [Henry V's] reign Sir John Oldcastle, which by his wife was called Lord Cobham, a valiant captain and a hardy gentleman, was accused to the Archbishop of Canterbury of certain points of heresy, who, knowing him to be highly in the King's favor, declared to His Highness the whole accusation. The King first, having compassion of the nobleman, required the prelates that if he were a strayed sheep, rather by gentleness than by rigor to reduce him to the fold. And after this, he himself sent for him, and right earnestly exhorted him, and lovingly admonished him to reconcile himself to God and to His laws. The Lord Cobham not only thanked him for his most favorable clemency, but also declared first to him by word of mouth, and afterward by writing, the foundation of his faith and the ground of his belief, affirming His Grace to be his supreme head and competent judge, and none other person, offering a hundred knights and esquires to come to his purgation, or else to fight in open lists in defense of his just cause.

Oldcastle was nevertheless tried by a spiritual court, and found guilty of heresy. He was sent to the Tower to await the King's decision, but made his escape to Wales. For some years he lay in hiding, but was ultimately captured and brought to London, where he was condemned to death and burned as a heretic. He thus won a place in Fox's *Book of Martyrs* with others who suffered for their anti-Catholic opinions. Except for a somewhat profane habit of misquoting Scripture and parodying the Puritans, Shakespeare's fat knight has few of the marks of a Protestant martyr.

The name Oldcastle caused Shakespeare considerable trouble. In 1597 the title of Lord Cobham had recently passed to a nobleman called Henry Brooke, an unpleasant young man inclined to puritanism, and with a very good opinion of himself. He was so greatly offended that his predecessor should be presented on a public stage in such a disreputable guise that Shakespeare was obliged to alter the name. The fat knight was therefore renamed Falstaff, after Sir John Fastolfe, who had already made a brief but discreditable appearance in *I Henry VI.* The real Fastolfe was a distinguished though unlucky commander in the French wars after Henry V's death. A few traces of the old name remain. The speech heading *Old.* (for *Fal.*) occurs once in the original quarto of the second part of *Henry IV,* and the epilogue refers to the scandal.

There was also some topicality in *I Henry IV.* The competition between the Chamberlain's and the Admiral's Men was growing acute, and in the scene where Falstaff plays the heavy father to Prince Hal (II.iv.311–527), Shakespeare parodied the pompous style of plays popular at the Rose playhouse and the tragic manner of Edward Alleyn (see Gen. Intro. pp. 36b–37b).

The play was printed very soon after its first performance. This was unusual, as the players, whenever possible, held back a popular play; they may however have been influenced by a desire to show the public that the change from Oldcastle to Falstaff had indeed been made. The play was entered for printing on February 26, 1598, to Andrew Wise as "The historye of Henry the iiiith with his battaile of Shrewsburye against Henry Hotspurre of the Northe with the conceipted mirthe of Sir John Falstoff." It appeared soon after with the title: *The History of Henrie the Fourth; With the battell at Shrewsburie, betweene the King and Lord Henry Percy, surnamed Henrie Hotspur of the North. With the humorous conceits of Sir John Falstalffe.* There is no suggestion in this title page that any second part had as yet been acted or planned. The quarto was reprinted in 1599 as "newly corrected by William Shakespeare," but this statement is untrue, as there are only minute differences between the first and second quartos. Other editions appeared in 1604, 1608, 1613, and 1622. The text printed in the first folio was set up from one of the quartos, from which the profane oaths have been carefully removed. Falstaff, it may be noted, was the most popular of all Shakespeare's characters and was more mentioned and quoted by contemporaries than any other.

In *I Henry IV* Shakespeare first reached complete maturity as a dramatist. In *Richard II* the characters lacked life. Richard himself was a picturesque and pathetic embodiment of sentimental poetry, but few of the others were interesting as individuals. The persons in *I Henry IV* are alive from the first; Shakespeare took elaborate care in creating his characters, especially Hotspur. In his first appearance (I.iii) Hotspur reveals his fiery and impatient mind, always darting away as a new thought appears, obsessed with a zeal for military honor which is not far from vanity, roused at a word, which makes him an easy victim for the King and his crafty uncle Worcester. Having drawn this side of his nature, Shakespeare next shows him (II.iii) in a charming little episode at home with his young wife; and to give added point to this episode has Prince Hal in the next scene briefly sum him up:

. . . the Hotspur of the North, he that kills me some six or seven dozen of Scots at a breakfast, washes his hands, and says to his wife, " Fie upon this quiet life! I want work." " O my sweet Harry," says she, " how many hast thou killed today? " " Give my roan horse a drench," says he, and answers, " Some fourteen," an hour after — " a trifle, a trifle."

It is cruel parody, but a sign that Shakespeare was now sure of himself, for only an artist who has complete self-confidence dares to make fun of his own serious efforts. Hotspur is next shown in conference with Glendower, Worcester, and Mortimer, and the contrast between these four very different characters is cleverly drawn. Hotspur has no patience with the Welshman's solemn claims to be extraordinary, is too impetuous to conceal his boredom, and mocks him beyond endurance; it is a tribute to Hotspur's personality, and a piece of subtle artistry, that such a man as Glendower should twice swallow his anger and give way. Hotspur is a blunt and practical young man with no use for poetry or art, natural or supernatural, insisting on his own way until it is given him and then yielding at once, and very fond of his wife in his own bluff way. He is a perfect specimen of the romantic soldier who filled Shakespeare with admiration and amusement, for he was careful to set Falstaff beside Hotspur. Falstaff's brief catechism on honor is a mocking echo of Hotspur's heroics. Hotspur dies at the hands of the Prince whom he had despised, lamenting not so much the loss of his hopes as of his honor as a soldier, and when he is dead his body is dishonorably prodded by the live Falstaff. Hotspur is the first of the full-length, elaborate studies of character which afterward abound in Shakespeare's plays.

Yet the most notable person in *I Henry IV* is Sir John Falstaff. In creating Falstaff Shakespeare used principally his own eyes and ears. Falstaff is the gross incarnation of a type of soldier found in any army, and there were many such — though on a lower level of greatness — swarming in London in the autumn of 1597, spending the profits of the campaign in taverns, brothels, and playhouses while they intrigued for a new command in the next season's campaign. Some of these captains were men of good family and education, younger sons who had no hope of an inheritance, and who preferred the excitements and loot of the wars to such a life as Justice Shallow lived in the country. Many were rogues who cheated the Government and their own men. Some ran to fat. Captain Nicholas Dawtrey, for instance, who was one of Edmund Spenser's acquaintances in Dublin, was so bulky that when he was wounded in battle it took eight men to shift him to the rear.[2] Moreover at all times military men have been noted for blustering ways and rich vocabularies.

There is no need to debate whether Falstaff was a coward. His philosophy — as is that of many a better man — was simple: " The better part of valor is discretion " (V.iv.120), and " Honor is a mere scutcheon " (V.i.142). " Give me life," he comments on the dead Blunt, " which if I can save, so; if not, honor comes unlooked for, and there's an end " (V.iii.63–65). He is quite out of place on any serious occasion, but for a rowdy evening a superb good companion. It is as well not to take Falstaff too seriously.

As for Prince Henry, he is shown as a young man who is deliberately posing as a waster so that when the time comes he may the more effectively confound the prophets and begin his reign by surprising his subjects. Herein he is as politic and crafty as his father. Henry IV had deliberately affected modesty, humility, and sobriety in contrast to his cousin, the shallow, pleasure-loving Richard II. The Prince purposely mixes with low company to contrast with his father; if his companions do not realize their part in this plan, the misfortune is theirs. In battle he shows himself the superior of Hotspur, not only as a soldier but in his complete understanding of men. This calculating self-control in all companies may not make him an amiable man, but it is preparing him to become a ruthlessly efficient ruler.

[2] See *The Falstaff Saga* by J. Dawtrey.

Henry IV, Part I

DRAMATIS PERSONAE

KING HENRY *the Fourth*
HENRY, *Prince of Wales*
JOHN *of Lancaster* } *sons to the King*
EARL OF WESTMORELAND

SIR WALTER BLUNT
THOMAS PERCY, *Earl of Worcester*
HENRY PERCY, *Earl of Northumberland*
HENRY PERCY, *surnamed* HOTSPUR, *his son*
EDMUND MORTIMER, *Earl of March*
RICHARD SCROOP, *Archbishop of York*
ARCHIBALD, *Earl of Douglas*
OWEN GLENDOWER
SIR RICHARD VERNON
SIR JOHN FALSTAFF
SIR MICHAEL, *a friend to the Archbishop of York*

POINS
GADSHILL
PETO
BARDOLPH

LADY PERCY, *wife to Hotspur and sister to Mortimer*
LADY MORTIMER, *daughter to Glendower and wife to Mortimer*
MISTRESS QUICKLY, *hostess of a tavern in Eastcheap*

LORDS, OFFICERS, SHERIFF, VINTNER, CHAMBERLAIN, DRAWERS, *two* CARRIERS, TRAVELERS, *and* ATTENDANTS

SCENE — *England and Wales.*

Act I

SCENE I. *London. The palace.*

[*Enter* KING HENRY, LORD JOHN OF LANCASTER, *the* EARL OF WESTMORELAND, SIR WALTER BLUNT, *and others.*]

KING. So shaken as we are, so wan with care,
Find we° a time for frighted peace to pant,
And breathe short-winded accents of new broils
To be commenced in stronds° afar remote.
No more the thirsty entrance of this soil   5
Shall daub her lips with her own children's blood.
No more shall trenching war° channel her fields,
Nor bruise her flowerets° with the armèd hoofs
Of hostile paces. Those opposèd eyes,
Which, like the meteors° of a troubled heaven,   10
All of one nature, of one substance bred,
Did lately meet in the intestine shock°
And furious close° of civil butchery,
Shall now, in mutual well-beseeming° ranks,
March all one way, and be no more opposed   15
Against acquaintance, kindred, and allies.
The edge of war, like an ill-sheathèd knife,
No more shall cut his master. Therefore, friends,
As far as to the sepulcher of Christ,
Whose soldier now, under whose blessèd cross   20
We are impressèd° and engaged to fight,

Forthwith a power of English shall we levy,
Whose arms were molded in their mothers' womb
To chase these pagans in those holy fields
Over whose acres walked those blessed feet   25
Which fourteen hundred years ago were nailed
For our advantage on the bitter cross.
But this our purpose now is twelvemonth old,
And bootless 'tis to tell you we will go.
Therefore we meet not now.° Then let me hear   30
Of you, my gentle cousin° Westmoreland,
What yesternight our Council did decree
In forwarding this dear expedience.°

WEST. My liege, this haste was hot in question,°
And many limits of the charge° set down   35
But yesternight, when all athwart° there came
A post° from Wales loaden° with heavy news,
Whose worst was that the noble Mortimer,°
Leading the men of Herefordshire to fight
Against the irregular° and wild Glendower,   40
Was by the rude hands of that Welshman taken,
A thousand of his people butchered.
Upon whose dead corpse there was such misuse,
Such beastly shameless transformation,
By those Welshwomen done as may not be   45
Without much shame retold or spoken of.

KING. It seems then that the tidings of this broil
Brake off our business for the Holy Land.

Act I, Sc. i: **2. Find we:** let us find. **4. stronds:** strands, shores. **7. trenching war:** trench warfare. **8. flowerets:** little flowers. **10. meteors:** comets or shooting stars, regarded as terrifying omens. **12. intestine shock:** clash of civil war. **13. close:** hand-to-hand battle. **14. well-beseeming:** seemly. **21. impressed:** enlisted.

29-30. bootless . . . now: i.e., there is no need to tell you of my decision, which has long been made. Our present meeting is to consider the details. **bootless:** vain. **31. cousin:** kinsman, used of any near relation. **33. dear expedience:** urgent enterprise, dear to me. **34. hot in question:** under eager discussion. **35. limits . . . charge:** estimates of the cost. **36. athwart:** cutting across. **37. post:** messenger. See App. 17. **loaden:** laden. **38. Mortimer:** See App. 28 and *I Hen IV* Intro. p. 613b. **40. irregular:** unruly.

WEST. This matched with other did, my gracious
    lord;
For more uneven° and unwelcome news   50
Came from the north and thus it did import:
On Holyrood Day,° the gallant Hotspur there,
Young Harry Percy, and brave Archibald,
That ever valiant and approved° Scot,
At Holmedon° met,   55
Where they did spend a sad and bloody hour,
As by discharge of their artillery,
And shape of likelihood,° the news was told.
For he that brought them, in the very heat
And pride of their contention° did take horse,   60
Uncertain of the issue° any way.
    KING. Here is a dear, a true industrious friend,
Sir Walter Blunt, new-lighted from his horse,
Stained with the variation of each soil
Betwixt that Holmedon and this seat of ours,   65
And he hath brought us smooth and welcome news.
The Earl of Douglas is discomfited.
Ten thousand bold Scots, two and twenty knights,
Balked° in their own blood did Sir Walter see
On Holmedon's plains. Of prisoners, Hotspur took
Mordake the Earl of Fife, and eldest son   71
To beaten Douglas; and the Earl of Athol,
Of Murray, Angus, and Menteith.
And is not this an honorable spoil?
A gallant prize? Ha, Cousin, is it not?   75
    WEST. In faith,
It is a conquest for a prince to boast of.
    KING. Yea, there thou makest me sad and makest
    me sin
In envy that my Lord Northumberland
Should be the father to so blest a son —   80
A son who is the theme of honor's tongue,
Amongst a grove, the very straightest plant,
Who is sweet Fortune's minion° and her pride —
Whilst I, by looking on the praise of him,
See riot and dishonor stain the brow   85
Of my young Harry. Oh, that it could be proved
That some night-tripping fairy° had exchanged
In cradle clothes our children where they lay,
And called mine Percy, his Plantagenet!
Then would I have his Harry, and he mine.   90
But let him from my thoughts. What think you,
    Coz,°
Of this young Percy's° pride? The prisoners
Which he in this adventure hath surprised

To his own use he keeps, and sends me word
I shall have none but Mordake Earl of Fife.   95
    WEST. This is his uncle's teaching. This is Wor-
    cester,
Malevolent° to you in all aspécts,
Which makes him prune° himself, and bristle up
The crest of youth against your dignity.
    KING. But I have sent for him to answer this,   100
And for this cause awhile we must neglect
Our holy purpose to Jerusalem.
Cousin, on Wednesday next our Council we
Will hold at Windsor. So inform the lords,
But come yourself with speed to us again,   105
For more is to be said and to be done
Than out of anger° can be uttered.
    WEST. I will, my liege.   [Exeunt.]

SCENE II. *London. An apartment of the
Prince's.*

[*Enter the* PRINCE OF WALES *and* FALSTAFF.]

FAL. Now, Hal, what time of day is it, lad?
PRINCE. Thou art so fat-witted, with drinking of
old sack° and unbuttoning thee after supper and
sleeping upon benches after noon, that thou hast forgotten to demand that truly which thou wouldst   5
truly know. What a devil hast thou to do with the
time of the day? Unless hours were cups of sack, and
minutes capons, and clocks the tongues of bawds,
and dials the signs of leaping houses,° and the
blessed sun himself a fair hot wench in flame-colored
taffeta,° I see no reason why thou shouldst be so
superfluous to demand the time of the day.   13
FAL. Indeed, you come near me now, Hal; for we
that take purses go by the moon and the seven stars,
and not by Phoebus,° he, " that wandering knight so
fair." And I prithee, sweet wag, when thou art King,
as, God save thy Grace — Majesty I should say, for
grace thou wilt have none ——   20
PRINCE. What, none?
FAL. No, by my troth,° not so much as will serve
to be prologue to an egg and butter.   24
PRINCE. Well, how then? Come, roundly, roundly.
FAL. Marry, then, sweet wag, when thou art King,
let not us that are squires of the night's body be
called thieves of the day's beauty.° Let us be Diana's

---

50. **uneven:** rough. 52. **Holyrood Day:** September 14. 54. **approved:** tried. 55. **Holmedon:** in Northumberland, near the Scottish border. 58. **shape of likelihood:** what was likely to happen. 60. **pride . . . contention:** height of battle. 61. **issue:** result. 69. **Balked:** laid in ridges. 83. **minion:** darling. 87. **night-tripping fairy:** a fairy coming by night. The fairies, so some believed, used sometimes to steal a beautiful child and to leave a changeling in its place. 91. **Coz:** cousin. 92. **young Percy:** Shakespeare depicts Hotspur as a rash youth of about the same age as Prince Hal. Actually at the battle of Shrewsbury (1403) the Prince was barely 14 years old and Percy was 39.

97. **Malevolent:** boding evil, like a planet that brings disaster. 98. **prune:** preen, like a hawk in good condition trimming its feathers. 107. **out of anger:** from an angry heart. Sc. ii: 3. **sack:** Spanish dry white wine. 10. **leaping houses:** brothels. 11–12. **flame-colored taffeta:** bright red silk — the color flaunted by harlots. 16. **Phoebus:** the sun, with a pun on the Knight of the Sun, hero of a chivalric romance. 22. **troth:** truth. 27–28. **let . . . beauty:** i.e., do not let us who are gentlemen of the dark (i.e., highwaymen) be called *thieves of the day's beauty* (i.e., loafers) — with a pun on "beauty" and "booty."

foresters,° gentlemen of the shade, minions of the moon. And let men say we be men of good government,° being governed, as the sea is, by our noble and chaste mistress the moon, under whose countenance we steal. 　　　　　　　　　　　　　　　　33

PRINCE. Thou sayest well, and it holds well too; for the fortune of us that are the moon's men doth ebb and flow like the sea, being governed, as the sea is, by the moon. As for proof, now — a purse of gold most resolutely snatched on Monday night and 39 most dissolutely spent on Tuesday morning; got with swearing "Lay by"° and spent with crying "Bring in"° — now in as low an ebb as the foot of the ladder,° and by and by in as high a flow as the ridge of the gallows.

FAL. By the Lord, thou sayest true, lad. And is not my hostess of the tavern a most sweet wench? 　　46

PRINCE. As the honey of Hybla,° my old lad of the castle.° And is not a buff jerkin° a most sweet robe of durance?°

FAL. How now, how now, mad wag! What, in thy quips° and thy quiddities?° What a plague have I to do with a buff jerkin? 　　　　　　　　　　52

PRINCE. Why, what a pox have I to do with my hostess of the tavern?

FAL. Well, thou hast called her to a reckoning many a time and oft.

PRINCE. Did I ever call for thee to pay thy part?

FAL. No. I'll give thee thy due, thou hast paid all there. 　　　　　　　　　　　　　　　　　60

PRINCE. Yea, and elsewhere, so far as my coin would stretch. And where it would not, I have used my credit. 　　　　　　　　　　　　　　　　63

FAL. Yea, and so used it that, were it not here apparent that thou art heir° apparent—— But I prithee, sweet wag, shall there be gallows standing in England when thou art King? And resolution° thus fobbed° as it is with the rusty curb of old Father Antic° the law? Do not thou, when thou art King, hang a thief. 　　　　　　　　　　　70

PRINCE. No, thou shalt.

FAL. Shall I? Oh, rare! By the Lord, I'll be a brave judge.

PRINCE. Thou judgest false already. I mean thou shalt have the hanging of the thieves and so become a rare hangman. 　　　　　　　　　　　　76

FAL. Well, Hal, well, and in some sort it jumps° with my humor° as well as waiting in the court, I can tell you.

PRINCE. For obtaining of suits? 　　　　　　80

FAL. Yea, for obtaining of suits,° whereof the hangman° hath no lean wardrobe. 'Sblood,° I am as melancholy as a gib-cat° or a lugged bear.°

PRINCE. Or an old lion, or a lover's lute. 　　84

FAL. Yea, or the drone of a Lincolnshire bagpipe.

PRINCE. What sayest thou to a hare,° or the melancholy of Moorditch?° 　　　　　　　　　88

FAL. Thou hast the most unsavory similes, and art indeed the most comparative,° rascaliest, sweet young Prince. But, Hal, I prithee trouble me no more with vanity. I would to God thou and I knew where a commodity° of good names were to be bought. An old lord of the Council rated° me the other day 94 in the street about you, sir, but I marked him not; and yet he talked very wisely, but I regarded him not; and yet he talked wisely, and in the street too.

PRINCE. Thou didst well, for wisdom cries out in the streets, and no man regards it.° 　　　　100

FAL. Oh, thou hast damnable iteration,° and art indeed able to corrupt a saint. Thou hast done much harm upon me, Hal. God forgive thee for it! Before I knew thee, Hal, I knew nothing; and now am I, if a man should speak truly, little better than one 105 of the wicked. I must give over this life, and I will give it over. By the Lord, an° I do not, I am a villain. I'll be damned for never a king's son in Christendom.

PRINCE. Where shall we take a purse tomorrow, Jack? 　　　　　　　　　　　　　　　111

FAL. 'Zounds,° where thou wilt, lad. I'll make one. An I do not, call me villain and baffle° me.

PRINCE. I see a good amendment of life in thee — from praying to purse-taking.

FAL. Why, Hal, 'tis my vocation, Hal. 'Tis no sin for a man to labor in his vocation. 　　　　　117

[Enter POINS.] Poins! Now shall we know if Gadshill have set a match.° Oh, if men were to be saved by merit, what hole in Hell were hot enough for him? This is the most omnipotent villain that ever cried "Stand" to a true man.

PRINCE. Good morrow, Ned. 　　　　　　123

POINS. Good morrow, sweet Hal. What says Mon-

28–29. Diana's foresters: thieves who rob by night. *Diana*: the moon. 30–31. good government: well-behaved. 41. Lay by: i.e., "stick 'em up." 42. Bring in: i.e., the drink. 43. ladder: from which a condemned man was thrust off the gallows into space. See Gen. Intro. p. 27b. 47. Hybla: in Sicily, famous for its honey. 47–48. old . . . castle: roisterer, with a pun on Falstaff's original name of Oldcastle. 48. buff jerkin: leather coat worn by the sheriff's sergeant. 49. robe of durance: coat that endures (wears well) and that takes you to *durance* (prison). 51. quips: wisecracks. quiddities: quibbles. 64–65. here . . . heir: a pun, *heir* being pronounced as "hair." 67. resolution: a stout heart. 68. fobbed: fubbed, cheated. 69. Father Antic: i.e., Daddy Buffoon.

77. jumps: agrees. 78. humor: whim. 81. obtaining of suits: with a pun on *suit* — "petitions to the sovereign for favor" and "clothes." 82. hangman: The clothes of the executed were the hangman's perquisite. 'Sblood: by God's blood. 83. gib-cat: tomcat. lugged bear: bear torn by the dogs. See App. 5. 87. hare: regarded as a melancholy creature. 88. melancholy of Moorditch: Moorditch was one of the open sewers of the City of London, proverbial for its stink. See App. 4. 90. comparative: quick at making comparisons. 93. commodity: parcel. 94. rated: rebuked. 99–100. wisdom . . . it: quoted loosely from Proverbs 1:20–24. 101. iteration: ability to quote. 107. an: if. 112. 'Zounds: by God's Wounds. 113. baffle: disgrace. See *Rich II*. I.i.170,n. 119. set a match: "framed a holdup."

sieur Remorse? What says Sir John Sack and Sugar?
Jack! How agrees the Devil and thee about thy soul,
that thou soldest him on Good Friday last for a cup
of Madeira and a cold capon's leg?°   129

PRINCE. Sir John stands to his word, the Devil
shall have his bargain, for he was never yet a breaker
of proverbs.° He will give the Devil his due.

POINS. Then art thou damned for keeping thy
word with the Devil.   135

PRINCE. Else he had been damned for cozening°
the Devil.

POINS. But, my lads, my lads, tomorrow morning,
by four o'clock, early at Gadshill!° There are pilgrims going to Canterbury with rich offer-   140
ings,° and traders riding to London with fat purses.
I have vizards° for you all, you have horses for yourselves. Gadshill lies tonight in Rochester. I have be-
spoke° supper tomorrow night in Eastcheap. We
may do it as secure as sleep. If you will go, I   145
will stuff your purses full of crowns. If you will not,
tarry at home and be hanged.

FAL. Hear ye, Yedward,° if I tarry at home and go
not, I'll hang you for going.   150

POINS. You will, chops?

FAL. Hal, wilt thou make one?

PRINCE. Who, I rob? I a thief? Not I, by my faith.

FAL. There's neither honesty, manhood, nor good
fellowship in thee, nor thou camest not of the blood
royal, if thou darest not stand for ten shillings.°

PRINCE. Well then, once in my days I'll be a madcap.   160

FAL. Why, that's well said.

PRINCE. Well, come what will, I'll tarry at home.

FAL. By the Lord, I'll be a traitor then, when thou
art King.   165

PRINCE. I care not.

POINS. Sir John, I prithee, leave the Prince and me
alone. I will lay him down such reasons for this adventure that he shall go.   169

FAL. Well, God give thee the spirit of persuasion
and him the ears of profiting, that what thou speakest may move and what he hears may be believed,°
that the true Prince may, for recreation sake, prove a
false thief; for the poor abuses of the time want
countenance.° Farewell. You shall find me in Eastcheap.   176

PRINCE. Farewell, thou latter spring!° Farewell,
Allhallown summer!°   [*Exit* FALSTAFF.]

POINS. Now, my good sweet honey lord, ride with
us tomorrow. I have a jest to execute that I can-   180
not manage alone. Falstaff, Bardolph, Peto, and
Gadshill shall rob those men that we have already
waylaid. Yourself and I will not be there, and when
they have the booty, if you and I do not rob them,
cut this head off from my shoulders.

PRINCE. How shall we part with them in setting
forth?   188

POINS. Why, we will set forth before or after them,
and appoint them a place of meeting, wherein it is at
our pleasure to fail, and then will they adventure
upon the exploit themselves; which they shall have
no sooner achieved but we'll set upon them.   194

PRINCE. Yea, but 'tis like that they will know us
by our horses, by our habits,° and by every other
appointment,° to be ourselves.

POINS. Tut! Our horses they shall not see, I'll tie
them in the wood. Our vizards we will change after
we leave them. And, sirrah, I have cases of buck-
ram° for the nonce,° to immask our noted outward
garments.   202

PRINCE. Yea, but I doubt they will be too hard for
us.

POINS. Well, for two of them, I know them to be
as true-bred cowards as ever turned back; and for
the third, if he fight longer than he sees rea-   207
son,° I'll forswear arms. The virtue of this jest will
be the incomprehensible lies that this same fat rogue
will tell us when we meet at supper — how thirty, at
least, he fought with; what wards,° what blows,
what extremities he endured. And in the reproof° of
this lies the jest.   213

PRINCE. Well, I'll go with thee. Provide us all
things necessary and meet me tomorrow night in
Eastcheap. There I'll sup. Farewell.

POINS. Farewell, my lord.   [*Exit.*]

PRINCE. I know you all,° and will a while uphold°
The unyoked humor° of your idleness.
Yet herein will I imitate the sun,   220
Who doth permit the base contagious° clouds
To smother up his beauty from the world,
That, when he please again to be himself,
Being wanted, he may be more wondered at
By breaking through the foul and ugly mists   225
Of vapors that did seem to strangle him.

128–29. Good . . . leg: Good Friday being the Church's most
solemn fast day, to drink Madeira and eat chicken was a damnable sin.   131–32. breaker of proverbs: one to prove proverbs false.
136. cozening: cheating.   139. Gadshill: near Rochester in Kent.
Some slight confusion is caused as the same name is used for
one of the gang. See l. 118, and II.i. 36–106.   140–41. rich
offerings: i.e., for the shrine of Saint Thomas à Becket at Canterbury.   142. vizards: masks.   144. bespoke: ordered.   149. Yedward: a form of Edward, Poins's first name.   157–58. blood . . .
shillings: pun on *royal*, a coin worth 10s.   170–72. God . . .
believed: Falstaff constantly drops into the pious jargon of
professional preachers.   174–75. want countenance: need encouragement.

177. latter spring: late spring; i.e., green autumn.   178. Allhallown summer: Indian summer. Allhallown (All Saints' Day) is
on November 1.   196. habits: clothes.   197. appointment: accouterment.   200–01. cases of buckram: overalls of coarse linen.
201. nonce: occasion.   207–08. fight . . . reason: This is Falstaff's
avowed rule of life. See later V.iv.120.   211. wards: defense.
See II.iv.215.   212. reproof: rebuttal.   218. I . . . all: This
soliloquy is important for the understanding of the Prince's
later treatment of Falstaff and the gang. uphold: tolerate.
219. unyoked humor: unrestrained behavior.   221. contagious:
poisonous.

If all the year were playing holidays,
To sport would be as tedious as to work.
But when they seldom come, they wished-for come,
And nothing pleaseth but rare accidents.   230
So, when this loose behavior I throw off
And pay the debt I never promisèd,
By how much better than my word I am,
By so much shall I falsify men's hopes.
And like bright metal on a sullen° ground,   235
My reformation, glittering o'er my fault,
Shall show more goodly and attract more eyes
Than that which hath no foil° to set it off.
I'll so offend, to make offense a skill,°
Redeeming time° when men think least I will.   240
                              [*Exit.*]

SCENE III. *London. The palace.*

[*Enter the* KING, NORTHUMBERLAND, WORCESTER, HOTSPUR, SIR WALTER BLUNT, *with others.*]

KING. My blood hath been too cold and temperate,
Unapt to stir at these indignities,
And you have found me;° for accordingly
You tread upon my patience. But be sure
I will from henceforth rather be myself,°   5
Mighty and to be feared, than my condition,°
Which hath been smooth as oil, soft as young down,
And therefore lost that title of respect°
Which the proud soul ne'er pays but to the proud.
   WOR. Our house, my sovereign liege, little de-
       serves   10
The scourge of greatness to be used on it,
And that same greatness too which our own hands
Have holp° to make so portly.°
   NORTH. My lord——
   KING. Worcester, get thee gone, for I do see   15
Danger and disobedience in thine eye.
O sir, your presence is too bold and peremptory,
And Majesty might never yet endure
The moody frontier of a servant brow.°
You have good leave to leave us.° When we need
Your use and counsel, we shall send for you.   21
                       [*Exit* WORCESTER.]
[*To* NORTHUMBERLAND] You were about to speak.
   NORTH.   Yea, my good lord.
Those prisoners in your Highness' name demanded,°

Which Harry Percy here at Holmedon took,
Were, as he says, not with such strength denied   25
As is delivered to your Majesty.
Either envy,° therefore, or misprision°
Is guilty of this fault, and not my son.
   HOT. My liege, I did deny no prisoners.
But I remember, when the fight was done,   30
When I was dry with rage and éxtreme toil,
Breathless and faint, leaning upon my sword,
Came there a certain lord, neat, and trimly dressed,
Fresh as a bridegroom, and his chin new-reaped°
Showed like a stubble land at harvest home.   35
He was perfumèd like a milliner,
And 'twixt his finger and his thumb he held
A pouncet box,° which ever and anon
He gave his nose and took 't away again;
Who therewith angry, when it next came there,   40
Took it in snuff.° And still he smiled and talked,
And as the soldiers bore dead bodies by,
He called them untaught knaves, unmannerly,
To bring a slovenly unhandsome corse°
Betwixt the wind and his nobility.   45
With many holiday and lady terms°
He questioned me, amongst the rest, demanded
My prisoners in your Majesty's behalf.
I then, all smarting with my wounds being cold,
To be so pestered with a popinjay,°   50
Out of my grief° and my impatience
Answered neglectingly I know not what,
He should, or he should not; for he made me mad
To see him shine so brisk, and smell so sweet,
And talk so like a waiting gentlewoman°   55
Of guns and drums and wounds — God save the
       mark! —°
And telling me the sovereign'st° thing on earth
Was parmaceti° for an inward bruise;
And that it was great pity, so it was,
This villainous saltpeter should be digged   60
Out of the bowels of the harmless earth,
Which many a good tall° fellow had destroyed
So cowardly; and but for these vile guns,
He would himself have been a soldier.
This bald unjointed chat° of his, my lord,   65
I answered indirectly, as I said.
And I beseech you, let not his report
Come current° for an accusation

---

235. **sullen:** dull.   238. **foil:** See *Rich III*, V.iii.250,n.   239. **skill:** art.   240. **Redeeming time:** making up for the time I have lost.   Sc. iii: 3. **found me:** found me out.   5. **myself:** i.e., King. 6. **than my condition:** than my naturally mild disposition.   8. **title of respect:** claim to be respected.   13. **holp:** helped. **portly:** magnificent.   19. **frontier... brow:** frowning look on a servant's brow. 20. **leave ... us:** a polite phrase of dismissal.   23. **prisoners ... demanded:** In earlier times a prisoner became the property of his captor, who released him on payment of a ransom according to his rank and wealth.

27. **envy:** malice — of Hotspur's enemies. **misprision:** misunderstanding.   34. **chin new-reaped:** beard closely cut.   38. **pouncet box:** small box containing perfume, which the fastidious sniffed to counteract foul smells.   41. **Took ... snuff:** sniffed, with a pun on the idiomatic meaning "resented."   44. **corse:** corpse.   46. **holiday ... terms:** fancy phrases, as opposed to "working-day" or plain English.   50. **popinjay:** parrot.   51. **grief:** smart (of my wounds).   55. **waiting gentlewoman:** lady in waiting, the essence of fancy femininity.   56. **God ... mark:** an impatient apology for a coarse remark.   57. **sovereign'st:** most excellent.   58. **parmaceti:** spermaceti, a fatty substance found in the whale and used as an ointment.   62. **tall:** brave.   65. **bald ... chat:** slight disconnected chatter.   68. **Come current:** be regarded as valid.

Betwixt my love and your high Majesty.
    BLUNT. The circumstance considered, good my
      lord,   70
Whate'er Lord Harry Percy then had said
To such a person and in such a place,
At such a time, with all the rest retold,
May reasonably die and never rise
To do him wrong, or any way impeach°   75
What then he said, so he unsay it now.
    KING. Why, yet° he doth deny his prisoners,
But with proviso° and exception,
That we at our own charge shall ransom straight
His brother-in-law, the foolish Mortimer,   80
Who, on my soul, hath willfully betrayed
The lives of those that he did lead to fight
Against that great magician,° damned Glendower,
Whose daughter, as we hear, the Earl of March
Hath lately married. Shall our coffers, then, 85
Be emptied to redeem a traitor home?
Shall we buy treason, and indent° with fears,
When they have lost and forfeited themselves?
No, on the barren mountains let him starve.
For I shall never hold that man my friend   90
Whose tongue shall ask me for one penny cost
To ransom home revolted Mortimer.
    HOT. Revolted Mortimer!
He never did fall off,° my sovereign liege,
But by the chance of war. To prove that true 95
Needs no more but one tongue for all those wounds,
Those mouthèd° wounds, which valiantly he took
When on the gentle Severn's sedgy° bank,
In single opposition, hand to hand,
He did confound° the best part of an hour   100
In changing hardiment° with great Glendower.
Three times they breathed and three times did they
    drink,
Upon agreement, of swift Severn's flood;
Who then, affrighted with their bloody looks,
Ran fearfully among the trembling reeds,   105
And hid his crisp head in the hollow bank
Bloodstainèd with these valiant combatants.
Never did base and rotten policy°
Color her working° with such deadly wounds;
Nor never could the noble Mortimer   110
Receive so many, and all willingly.
Then let not him be slandered with revolt.
    KING. Thou dost belie him,° Percy, thou dost belie
    him.
He never did encounter with Glendower.
I tell thee,   115
He durst as well have met the Devil alone

As Owen Glendower for an enemy.
Art thou not ashamed? But, sirrah,° henceforth
Let me not hear you speak of Mortimer.
Send me your prisoners with the speediest means,
Or you shall hear in such a kind from me   121
As will displease you. My Lord Northumberland,
We license your departure with your son.
Send us your prisoners, or you will hear of it.
    [*Exeunt* KING HENRY, BLUNT, *and train.*]
    HOT. An if the Devil come and roar for them,
I will not send them. I will after straight   126
And tell him so, for I will ease my heart,
Albeit I make a hazard° of my head.
    NORTH. What, drunk with choler?° Stay and
    pause awhile.
Here comes your uncle.
    [*Re-enter* WORCESTER.]
    HOT.   Speak of Mortimer!   130
'Zounds, I will speak of him, and let my soul
Want mercy if I do not join with him.
Yea, on his part I'll empty all these veins,
And shed my dear blood drop by drop in the dust,
But I will lift the downtrod Mortimer   135
As high in the air as this unthankful King,
As this ingrate and cankered° Bolingbroke.
    NORTH. Brother, the King hath made your nephew
    mad.
    WOR. Who struck this heat up after I was gone?
    HOT. He will, forsooth, have all my prisoners.
And when I urged the ransom once again   141
Of my wife's brother, then his cheek looked pale,
And on my face he turned an eye of death,
Trembling even at the name of Mortimer.
    WOR. I cannot blame him. Was not he proclaimed
By Richard that dead is the next of blood?   146
    NORTH. He was, I heard the proclamation.
And then it was when the unhappy King —
Whose wrongs in us God pardon!° — did set forth
Upon his Irish expedition,   150
From whence he intercepted° did return
To be deposed and shortly° murderèd.
    WOR. And for whose death we in the world's wide
    mouth
Live scandalized and foully spoken of.
    HOT. But, soft, I pray you. Did King Richard
    then   155
Proclaim my brother° Edmund Mortimer
Heir to the crown?
    NORTH.   He did, myself did hear it.
    HOT. Nay, then I cannot blame his cousin King,
That wished him on the barren mountains starve.
But shall it be that you, that set the crown 160

---

75. impeach: accuse, call in question.   77. yet: still, after all.
78. proviso: stipulation.   83. magician: See III.i.36–49.   87. indent: make an agreement. See App. 6.   94. fall off: desert.
97. mouthed: looking like a mouth.   98. sedgy: reedy.   100. confound: consume.   101. changing hardiment: exchanging blows.
108. policy: cunning.   109. Color . . . working: disguise its real
intention.   113. belie him: lie about him.

118. sirrah: a form of address used to an inferior, here deliberately
insulting.   128. hazard: risk.   129. choler: wrath.   137. cankered: malignant.   149. Whose . . . pardon: may God forgive
the wrongs committed by us against him.   151. intercepted:
being hindered.   152. shortly: in a short time.   156. brother:
brother-in-law.

Upon the head of this forgetful man,
And for his sake wear the detested blot
Of murderous subornation,° shall it be
That you a world of curses undergo,
Being the agents, or base second means,°   165
The cords, the ladder, or the hangman rather?
Oh, pardon me that I descend so low,
To show the line° and the predicament°
Wherein you range° under this subtle King.
Shall it for shame be spoken in these days,   170
Or fill up chronicles in time to come,
That men of your nobility and power
Did gage° them both in an unjust behalf,
As both of you — God pardon it! — have done,
To put down Richard, that sweet lovely rose,   175
And plant this thorn, this canker,° Bolingbroke?
And shall it in more shame be further spoken,
That you are fooled, discarded, and shook off
By him for whom these shames ye underwent?
No, yet time serves wherein you may redeem   180
Your banished honors, and restore yourselves
Into the good thoughts of the world again,
Revenge the jeering and disdained° contempt
Of this proud King, who studies day and night
To answer all the debt he owes to you   185
Even with the bloody payment of your deaths.
Therefore, I say ——
   WOR.   Peace, Cousin, say no more.
And now I will unclasp a secret book,
And to your quick-conceiving° discontents
I'll read you matter deep and dangerous,   190
As full of peril and adventurous spirit
As to o'erwalk a current roaring loud
On the unsteadfast footing of a spear.°
   HOT. If he fall in, good night! Or sink or swim.
Send danger from the east unto the west,   195
So honor cross it from the north to south,
And let them grapple. Oh, the blood more stirs
To rouse a lion than to start a hare!
   NORTH. Imagination of some great exploit
Drives him beyond the bounds of patience.°   200
   HOT. By Heaven, methinks it were an easy leap,
To pluck bright honor from the pale-faced moon,
Or dive into the bottom of the deep,
Where fathom line could never touch the ground,
And pluck up drownèd honor by the locks,   205
So he that doth redeem her thence might wear
Without corrival° all her dignities.
But out upon this half-faced fellowship!°

   WOR. He apprehends a world of figures here,°
But not the form of what he should attend.   210
Good Cousin, give me audience for a while.
   HOT. I cry you mercy.
   WOR.   Those same noble Scots
That are your prisoners ——
   HOT.   I'll keep them all.
By God, he shall not have a Scot of them.
No, if a Scot would save his soul, he shall not.   215
I'll keep them, by this hand.
   WOR.   You start away
And lend no ear unto my purposes.
Those prisoners you shall keep.
   HOT.   Nay, I will, that's flat.
He said he would not ransom Mortimer,
Forbade my tongue to speak of Mortimer.   220
But I will find him when he lies asleep,
And in his ear I'll holloa " Mortimer! "
Nay,
I'll have a starling° shall be taught to speak
Nothing but " Mortimer," and give it him,   225
To keep his anger still in motion.
   WOR. Hear you, Cousin, a word.
   HOT. All studies here I solemnly defy,
Save how to gall° and pinch this Bolingbroke.
And that same sword-and-buckler° Prince of
   Wales,
But that I think his father loves him not   231
And would be glad he met with some mischance,
I would have him poisoned with a pot of ale.
   WOR. Farewell, kinsman. I'll talk to you
When you are better tempered to attend.   235
   NORTH. Why, what a wasp-stung and impatient
   fool
Art thou to break into this woman's mood,
Tying thine ear to no tongue but thine own!
   HOT. Why, look you, I am whipped and scourged
   with rods,
Nettled,° and stung with pismires,° when I hear
Of this vile politician,° Bolingbroke.   241
In Richard's time — what do you call the place? —
A plague upon it, it is in Gloucestershire,
'Twas where the madcap Duke his uncle kept,
His uncle York, where I first bowed my knee   245
Unto this king of smiles, this Bolingbroke —
'Sblood! —
When you and he came back from Ravenspurgh.
   NORTH. At Berkeley Castle.°
   HOT. You say true.   250
Why, what a candy deal° of courtesy

162–63. wear ... subornation: wear the mark of shame as accessories to murder. subornation: procuring someone to commit a crime. 165. second means: assistants. 168. line: disgrace. predicament: class, category. 169. range: rank. 173. gage: pledge, engage. 176. canker: wild rose, contrasted with the garden rose. 183. disdained: disdainful. 189. quick-conceiving: quick-witted. 193. unsteadfast ... spear: with a spear as unsteady bridge. 200. patience: self-control. 207. corrival: partner. 208. half-faced fellowship: starving partnership; i.e., sharing of honor which is insufficient for two to share.

209. apprehends ... here: i.e., he is entirely carried away by his imagination. figures: shapes, fantasies. 224. starling: The starling, like the jackdaw and the parrot, can be taught to mimic sound. 229. gall: make sore. 230. sword-and-buckler: swashbuckler. 240. Nettled: whipped with nettles. pismires: ants. 241. politician: schemer. 249. Berkeley Castle: For this episode see *Rich II*, II.iii.41–50. 251. candy deal: deal of candy, i.e., hypocritical.

This fawning greyhound then did proffer me!
Look, " when his infant fortune came to age,"
And " gentle Harry Percy," and " kind Cousin."
Oh, the devil take such cozeners! God forgive me!
Good Uncle, tell your tale, I have done.　　　256
　　WOR. Nay, if you have not, to it again.
We will stay° your leisure.
　　HOT.　　　　　　　I have done, i' faith.
　　WOR. Then once more to your Scottish prisoners.
Deliver them up without their ransom straight,　260
And make the Douglas' son your only mean°
For powers° in Scotland; which, for divers reasons
Which I shall send you written, be assured
Will easily be granted. [*To* NORTHUMBERLAND] You,
　　my lord,
Your son in Scotland being thus employed,　　265
Shall secretly into the bosom creep
Of that same noble prelate, well beloved,
The Archbishop.
　　HOT. Of York, is it not?
　　WOR. True, who bears hard°　　　　　　270
His brother's death at Bristol, the Lord Scroop.
I speak not this in estimation,°
As what I think might be, but what I know
Is ruminated,° plotted, and set down,
And only stays but to behold the face　　275
Of that occasion that shall bring it on.
　　HOT. I smell it. Upon my life, it will do well.
　　NORTH. Before the game is afoot, thou still° let'st
　　slip.°
　　HOT. Why, it cannot choose but be a noble plot.
And then the power of Scotland and of York,　280
To join with Mortimer, ha?
　　WOR.　　　　　　And so they shall.
　　HOT. In faith, it is exceedingly well aimed.
　　WOR. And 'tis no little reason bids us speed,
To save our heads by raising of a head;°
For, bear ourselves as even as we can,°　　285
The King will always think him in our debt,
And think we think ourselves unsatisfied,
Till he hath found a time to pay us home.
And see already how he doth begin
To make us strangers to his looks of love.　290
　　HOT. He does, he does. We'll be revenged on him.
　　WOR. Cousin, farewell. No further go in this
Than I by letters shall direct your course.
When time is ripe, which will be suddenly,
I'll steal to Glendower and Lord Mortimer,　295
Where you and Douglas and our powers at once,
As I will fashion° it, shall happily meet,
To bear our fortunes in our own strong arms,

Which now we hold at much uncertainty.
　　NORTH. Farewell, good Brother. We shall thrive,
　　I trust.　　　　　　　　　　　　300
　　HOT. Uncle, adieu. Oh, let the hours be short
Till fields and blows and groans applaud our sport!
　　　　　　　　　　　　　[*Exeunt.*]

Act II

SCENE I. *Rochester. An innyard.*

[*Enter a* CARRIER *with a lantern in his hand*.]

　1. CAR. Heigh-ho! An it be not four by the day, I'll
be hanged. Charles's Wain° is over the new chimney, and yet our horse not packed.° What, ostler!　4
　OSTLER. [*Within*] Anon, anon.
　1. CAR. I prithee, Tom, beat° Cut's° saddle, put a
few flocks° in the point.° Poor jade,° is wrung° in
the withers° out of all cess.°　　　　　　8
　　　　　　[*Enter another* CARRIER.]
　2. CAR. Peas and beans are as dank here as a dog,
and that is the next way to give poor jades the bots.°
This house is turned upside down since Robin Ostler
died.
　1. CAR. Poor fellow, never joyed since the price of
oats rose. It was the death of him.　　　14
　2. CAR. I think this be the most villainous house in
all London road for fleas. I am stung like a tench.°
　1. CAR. Like a tench! By the mass, there is ne'er a
king Christen° could be better bit than I have been
since the first cock.　　　　　　　20
　2. CAR. Why, they will allow us ne'er a jordan,°
and then we leak in your chimney, and your chamber lye° breeds fleas like a loach.
　1. CAR. What, ostler! Come away and be hanged!
Come away.　　　　　　　　　25
　2. CAR. I have a gammon of bacon° and two razes°
of ginger, to be delivered as far as Charing Cross.
　1. CAR. God's body! The turkeys in my pannier°
are quite starved. What, ostler! A plague on thee!
Hast thou never an eye in thy head? Canst not hear?
An 'twere not as good deed as drink to break the pate

---

258. stay: await.　261. mean: means.　262. powers: forces, armies.　270. bears hard: takes hardly.　272. in estimation:
as a guess.　274. ruminated: considered.　278. still: continuously. let'st slip: let loose the greyhound.　284. head: armed
force.　285. bear . . . can: however discreetly we may behave.
297. fashion: contrive.

Act II, Sc. i: 2. Charles's Wain: Charles's Wagon, the constellation of the Great Bear, called also the Great Dipper.
4. horse . . . packed: Carriers at this time used pack horses for
transport.　6. beat: i.e., to make the padding more even. Cut:
name of a horse with a docked tail.　7. flocks: tufts of wool. point:
pommel. jade: horse in poor condition. wrung: galled.　8. withers:
point of the shoulder. out . . . cess: excessively.　10. bots: worms.
16. tench: The tench and the loach (fresh-water fish) are sometimes infested with a form of louse.　19. Christen: Christian.
21. jordan: chamber pot.　23. chamber lye: urine. Elizabethan
sanitary arrangements and domestic habits were crude.　26. gammon of bacon: cured ham. razes: roots.　28. pannier: basket.

on thee, I am a very villain. Come, and be hanged!
Hast no faith in thee?　　　　　　　　　　　　　35

[*Enter* GADSHILL.]

GADS. Good morrow, carriers. What's o'clock?

1. CAR. I think it be two o'clock.

GADS. I prithee lend me thy lantern, to see my gelding in the stable.　　　　　　　　　　　39

1. CAR. Nay, by God, soft,° I know a trick worth two of that, i' faith.

GADS. I pray thee, lend me thine.

2. CAR. Aye, when? Canst tell?° Lend me thy lantern, quoth he? Marry, I'll see thee hanged first.

GADS. Sirrah carrier, what time do you mean to come to London?　　　　　　　　　　　46

2. CAR. Time enough to go to bed with a candle, I warrant thee. Come, Neighbor Mugs, we'll call up the gentlemen. They will along with company, for they have great charge.°　　　[*Exeunt* CARRIERS.]

GADS. What ho! Chamberlain!°　　　　　　52

CHAM. [*Within*] At hand, quoth pickpurse.

GADS. That's even as fair as — at hand, quoth the chamberlain; for thou variest no more from picking of purses than giving direction doth from laboring. Thou layest the plot° how.　　　　　　　57

[*Enter* CHAMBERLAIN.]

CHAM. Good morrow, Master Gadshill. It holds current that I told you yesternight. There's a franklin° in the wild° of Kent hath brought three hundred marks° with him in gold. I heard him tell it to one of his company last night at supper — a kind of auditor, one that hath abundance of charge too, God knows what. They are up already, and call for eggs and butter. They will away presently.　　　66

GADS. Sirrah, if they meet not with Saint Nicholas' clerks,° I'll give thee this neck.

CHAM. No, I'll none of it. I pray thee, keep that for the hangman, for I know thou worshipest Saint Nicholas as truly as a man of falsehood may.　　72

GADS. What talkest thou to me of the hangman? If I hang, I'll make a fat pair of gallows; for if I hang, old Sir John hangs with me, and thou knowest he is no starveling. Tut! There are other Trojans° that thou dreamest not of, the which for sport sake　77 are content to do the profession some grace; that would, if matters should be looked into, for their own credit sake, make all whole. I am joined with no foot landrakers,° no long-staff sixpenny strikers,°

none of these mad mustachio purple-hued maltworms;° but with nobility and tranquility, burgomasters and great oneyers,° such as can hold in,° such as will strike sooner than speak, and speak　85 sooner than drink, and drink sooner than pray. And yet, 'zounds, I lie; for they pray continually to their saint, the commonwealth; or rather, not pray to her, but prey on her, for they ride up and down on her and make her their boots.°　　　　　　　91

CHAM. What, the commonwealth their boots? Will she hold out water in foul way?

GADS. She will, she will — justice hath liquored° her. We steal as in a castle, cocksure. We have the receipt° of fern seed,° we walk invisible.　　96

CHAM. Nay, by my faith, I think you are more beholding to the night than to fern seed for your walking invisible.

GADS. Give me thy hand. Thou shalt have a share in our purchase,° as I am a true man.　　　101

CHAM. Nay, rather let me have it, as you are a false thief.

GADS. Go to. "Homo" is a common name to all men. Bid the ostler bring my gelding out of　105 the stable. Farewell, you muddy° knave.　[*Exeunt.*]

SCENE II. *The highway, near* GADSHILL.

[*Enter* PRINCE HENRY *and* POINS.]

POINS. Come, shelter, shelter. I have removed Falstaff's horse, and he frets like a gummed velvet.°

PRINCE. Stand close.

[*Enter* FALSTAFF.]

FAL. Poins! Poins, and be hanged! Poins!　　4

PRINCE. Peace, ye fat-kidneyed rascal! What a brawling dost thou keep!

FAL. Where's Poins, Hal?

PRINCE. He is walked up to the top of the hill. I'll go seek him.　　　　　　　　　　　　9

FAL. I am accursed to rob in that thief's company. The rascal hath removed my horse, and tied him I know not where. If I travel but four foot by the squier° further afoot, I shall break my wind. Well, I doubt not but to die a fair death for all this, if I 'scape hanging for killing that rogue. I have forsworn°　16 his company hourly any time this two and twenty years, and yet I am bewitched with the rogue's

---

40. **soft:** go easy.　43. **Canst tell:** i.e., "says you!"　51. **great charge:** much money.　52. **Chamberlain:** man in charge of the bedrooms at an inn.　57. **layest . . . plot:** It was a common complaint that the chamberlains of inns were in league with highwaymen.　60. **franklin:** rich farmer. **wild:** weald; the hilly district in Kent and adjoining counties.　61. **mark:** 13s 4d (⅔ of a pound). See App. 27.　67–68. **Saint Nicholas' clerks:** thieves, Saint Nicholas being their patron saint.　76. **Trojans:** good lads.　81. **foot landrakers:** roving footpads; i.e., thieves so poor that they go on foot. **long-staff . . . strikers:** robbers who use a long staff and will hold a man up for a pittance.

82–83. **mustachio . . . maltworms:** red-faced tipplers with great mustaches.　84. **oneyers:** ones. **hold in:** keep their mouths shut.　91. **boots:** booty. The chamberlain caps his remark with a pun on leather boots.　94. **liquored:** greased.　96. **receipt:** directions for using, recipe. **fern seed:** The seed of the fern is so small that it was said to be invisible, and if found on Saint John's Day, to confer invisibility on the finder.　101. **purchase:** in thieves' language, plunder.　106. **muddy:** muddleheaded.

Sc. ii: 2. **gummed velvet:** Cheap velvet (as well as taffeta) was sometimes treated with gum to give it stiffening, but it frayed sooner.　13. **squier:** square, rule.　16. **forsworn:** sworn off.

company. If the rascal have not given me medicines°
to make me love him, I'll be hanged; it could not be
else, I have drunk medicines. Poins! Hal! A   21
plague upon you both! Bardolph! Peto! I'll starve ere
I'll rob a foot further. An 'twere not as good a deed
as drink, to turn true man and to leave these rogues,
I am the veriest varlet° that ever chewed with a   25
tooth. Eight yards of uneven ground is threescore
and ten miles afoot with me, and the stony-hearted
villains know it well enough. A plague upon it when
thieves cannot be true one to another! [*They*   30
whistle.] Whew! A plague upon you all! Give me
my horse, you rogues, give me my horse, and be
hanged!

PRINCE. Peace, ye fat-guts! Lie down, lay thine ear
close to the ground and list if thou canst hear the
tread of travelers.   35

FAL. Have you any levers to lift me up again,
being down? 'Sblood, I'll not bear mine own flesh so
far afoot again for all the coin in thy father's exchequer. What a plague mean ye to colt° me thus?

PRINCE. Thou liest. Thou art not colted, thou art
uncolted.   42

FAL. I prithee, good Prince Hal, help me to my
horse, good king's son.

PRINCE. Out, ye rogue! Shall I be your ostler?   45

FAL. Go hang thyself in thine own heir-apparent
garters! If I be ta'en, I'll peach for this. An I have
not ballads° made on you all and sung to filthy tunes,
let a cup of sack be my poison. When a jest is so forward, and afoot too! I hate it.   50

[*Enter* GADSHILL, BARDOLPH *and* PETO *with him.*]

GADS. Stand.

FAL. So I do, against my will.

POINS. Oh, 'tis our setter.° I know his voice. Bardolph, what news?   54

BARD. Case° ye, case ye, on with your vizards.
There's money of the King's coming down the hill,
'tis going to the King's exchequer.

FAL. You lie, ye rogue, 'tis going to the King's
tavern.

GADS. There's enough to make us all.   60

FAL. To be hanged.

PRINCE. Sirs, you four shall front them in the narrow lane, Ned Poins and I will walk lower. If they
'scape from your encounter, then they light on us.

PETO. How many be there of them?   66

GADS. Some eight or ten.

FAL. 'Zounds, will they not rob us?

PRINCE. What, a coward, Sir John Paunch?

FAL. Indeed I am not John of Gaunt, your grandfather, but yet no coward, Hal.   71

PRINCE. Well, we leave that to the proof.

POINS. Sirrah Jack, thy horse stands behind the

hedge. When thou needest him, there thou shalt find
him. Farewell, and stand fast.   75

FAL. Now cannot I strike him, if I should be
hanged.

PRINCE. Ned, where are our disguises?

POINS. Here, hard by. Stand close.

[*Exeunt* PRINCE *and* POINS.]

FAL. Now, my masters, happy man be his dole,°
say I. Every man to his business.   81

[*Enter the* TRAVELERS.]

1. TRAV. Come, neighbor. The boy shall lead our
horses down the hill. We'll walk afoot awhile, and
ease our legs.

THIEVES. Stand!

TRAVS. Jesus bless us!   86

FAL. Strike, down with them, cut the villains'
throats! Ah, whoreson° caterpillars,° bacon-fed
knaves! They hate us youth. Down with them, fleece
them.

TRAVS. Oh, we are undone, both we and ours forever!   92

FAL. Hang ye, gorbellied° knaves, are ye undone?
No, ye fat chuffs,° I would your store were here!°
On, bacons,° on! What, ye knaves! Young men must
live. You are grand jurors,° are ye? We'll jure ye,
'faith.   97

[*Here they rob them and bind them. Exeunt.*]

[*Re-enter* PRINCE HENRY *and* POINS *disguised.*]

PRINCE. The thieves have bound the true men.
Now could thou and I rob the thieves and go merrily to London, it would be argument° for a week,
laughter for a month, and a good jest forever.

POINS. Stand close. I hear them coming.   103

[*Enter the* THIEVES *again.*]

FAL. Come, my masters, let us share, and then to
horse before day. An the Prince and Poins be not
two arrant° cowards, there's no equity stirring.°
There's no more valor in that Poins than in a wild
duck.   108

PRINCE. Your money!

POINS. Villains! [*As they are sharing, the* PRINCE
and POINS *set upon them; they all run away; and* FAL-
STAFF, *after a blow or two, runs away too, leaving the
booty behind them.*]

PRINCE. Got with much ease. Now merrily to
horse.
The thieves are all scattered and possessed with fear
So strongly that they dare not meet each other.
Each takes his fellow for an officer.
Away, good Ned. Falstaff sweats to death,   115
And lards the lean earth as he walks along.

---

80. happy . . . dole: i.e., here's luck; lit., may the lucky man have
his reward.   88. whoreson: bastard. caterpillars: See *Rich II*,
II.iii.166,n.   93. gorbellied: big-bellied.   94. chuffs: mean
misers. were here: i.e., in your bellies.   95. bacons: fat pigs.
96. grand jurors: i.e., men of highest respectability.   101. argument: matter for talk.   106. arrant: complete. no . . . stirring:
no sound judgment in the world.

---

19. medicines: love potions.   25. varlet: knave.   40. colt: trick.
48. ballads: See App. 8.   53. setter: the accomplice who brings
the victim in.   55. Case: mask.

Were't not for laughing, I should pity him.

POINS. How the rogue roared!   [*Exeunt.*]

SCENE III. *Warkworth Castle.*

[*Enter HOTSPUR alone, reading a letter.*]

HOT. "But, for mine own part, my lord, I could be well contented to be there, in respect of the love I bear your house." He could be contented. Why is he not, then? In respect of the love he bears our house. He shows in this he loves his own barn better 5 than he loves our house. Let me see some more. "The purpose you undertake is dangerous"—why, that's certain. 'Tis dangerous to take a cold, to sleep, to drink; but I tell you, my lord fool, out of this nettle danger we pluck this flower safety. "The purpose you undertake is dangerous; the friends you 10 have named uncertain; the time itself unsorted;° and your whole plot too light for the counterpoise of so great an opposition." Say you so, say you so? I say unto you again, you are a shallow cowardly 15 hind,° and you lie. What a lackbrain is this! By the Lord, our plot is a good plot as ever was laid, our friends true and constant—a good plot, good friends, and full of expectation. An excellent plot, very good friends. What a frosty-spirited rogue 20 is this! Why, my Lord of York° commends the plot and the general course of the action. 'Zounds, an I were now by this rascal, I could brain him with his lady's fan. Is there not my father, my uncle, and myself? Lord Edmund Mortimer, my Lord of 25 York, and Owen Glendower? Is there not besides the Douglas? Have I not all their letters to meet me in arms by the ninth of the next month? And are they not some of them set forward already? What a pagan rascal is this, an infidel! Ha! You shall see 30 now in very sincerity of fear and cold heart, will he to the King, and lay open all our proceedings. Oh, I could divide myself, and go to buffets,° for moving° such a dish of skim milk with so honorable an 35 action! Hang him! Let him tell the King. We are prepared. I will set forward tonight.

[*Enter LADY PERCY.*] How now, Kate! I must leave
   you within these two hours.

LADY P. O my good lord, why are you thus alone? For what offense have I this fortnight been 41 A banished woman from my Harry's bed? Tell me, sweet lord, what is't that takes from thee Thy stomach,° pleasure, and thy golden sleep? Why dost thou bend thine eyes upon the earth, 45 And start so often when thou sit'st alone? Why hast thou lost the fresh blood in thy cheeks,

And given my treasures° and my rights of thee To thick-eyed° musing and cursed melancholy? In thy faint slumbers I by thee have watched, 50 And heard thee murmur tales of iron wars, Speak terms of manage° to thy bounding steed, Cry "Courage! To the field!" And thou hast talked Of sallies and retires,° of trenches, tents, Of palisadoes,° frontiers,° parapets, 55 Of basilisks, of cannon, culverin,° Of prisoners' ransom, and of soldiers slain, And all the currents° of a heady° fight. Thy spirit within thee hath been so at war And thus hath so bestirred thee in thy sleep 60 That beads of sweat have stood upon thy brow, Like bubbles in a late-disturbèd stream. And in thy face strange motions have appeared, Such as we see when men restrain their breath On some great sudden hest.° Oh, what portènts are
   these? 65 Some heavy business hath my lord in hand, And I must know it, else he loves me not.

HOT. What ho! [*Enter SERVANT.*] Is Gilliams with
   the packet gone?

SERV. He is, my lord, an hour ago.

HOT. Hath Butler brought those horses from the
   sheriff? 70

SERV. One horse, my lord, he brought even now.

HOT. What horse? A roan, a crop-ear,° is it not?

SERV. It is, my lord.

HOT.   That roan shall be my throne. Well, I will back him straight. Oh, Esperance!° Bid Butler lead him forth into the park. 75
   [*Exit SERVANT.*]

LADY P. But hear you, my lord.

HOT. What say'st thou, my lady?

LADY P. What is it carries you away?

HOT. Why, my horse, my love, my horse.

LADY P. Out, you mad-headed ape! 80 A weasel hath not such a deal of spleen° As you are tossed with. In faith, I'll know your business, Harry, that I will. I fear my brother Mortimer doth stir About his title, and hath sent for you 85 To line° his enterprise. But if you go——

HOT. So far afoot, I shall be weary, love.

LADY P. Come, come, you paraquito,° answer me

---

48. treasures: i.e., that ought to be mine.   49. thick-eyed: dull-sighted, because he sees nothing.   52. manage: horsemanship.   54. sallies . . . retires: raids and retreats.   55 palisadoes: defensive protection of pointed stakes. See Pl. 12a. frontiers: barricades.   56. basilisks . . . culverin: the heavier pieces of artillery. The basilisk was of 5-inch caliber and fired a shot of $15\frac{1}{2}$ lbs., the cannon of 8-inch caliber with a 60-lb. shot, the culverin of $5\frac{1}{2}$-inch caliber with a 17-lb. shot. Shakespeare is thinking of Elizabethan ordnance rather than the cannon used in 1400.   58. currents: courses, rapid movement. heady: fierce.   65. hest: command, action.   72. crop-ear: with short ears.   74. Esperance: hope— the battle cry of the Percies.   81. spleen: anger, passion.   86. line: strengthen.   88. paraquito: parrot.

Sc. iii: 11. unsorted: ill-chosen.   16. hind: female deer, the essence of timidity.   21. Lord of York: Richard Scroop, Archbishop of York.   34. go to buffets: come to blows. moving: trying to move.   44. stomach: appetite.

Directly unto this question that I ask.
In faith, I'll break thy little finger, Harry,   90
An if thou wilt not tell me all things true.
    HOT. Away,
Away, you trifler! Love! I love thee not,
I care not for thee, Kate. This is no world
To play with mammets° and to tilt with lips.°   95
We must have bloody noses and cracked crowns,
And pass them current° too. God's me, my horse!
What say'st thou, Kate? What wouldst thou have
    with me?
    LADY P. Do you not love me? Do you not, indeed?
Well, do not, then, for since you love me not,   100
I will not love myself. Do you not love me?
Nay, tell me if you speak in jest or no.
    HOT. Come, wilt thou see me ride?
And when I am o' horseback, I will swear
I love thee infinitely. But hark you, Kate,   105
I must not have you henceforth question me
Whither I go, nor reason whereabout.
Whither I must, I must. And, to conclude,
This evening must I leave you, gentle Kate.
I know you wise, but yet no farther wise   110
Than Harry Percy's wife. Constant you are,
But yet a woman. And for secrecy,
No lady closer, for I well believe
Thou wilt not utter what thou dost not know,
And so far will I trust thee, gentle Kate.   115
    LADY P. How! So far?
    HOT. Not an inch further. But hark you, Kate,
Whither I go, thither shall you go too;
Today will I set forth, tomorrow you.   119
Will this content you, Kate?
    LADY P.   It must of force. [*Exeunt.*]

SCENE IV. *The Boar's Head Tavern in Eastcheap.*

[*Enter the* PRINCE, *and* POINS.]
    PRINCE. Ned, prithee come out of that fat° room,
and lend me thy hand to laugh a little.
    POINS. Where hast been, Hal?
    PRINCE. With three or four loggerheads° amongst
three or fourscore hogsheads.° I have sounded   5
the very base string of humility.° Sirrah, I am sworn
brother to a leash° of drawers, and can call them all
by their Christen names, as Tom, Dick, and Francis.
They take it already upon their salvation that though
I be but Prince of Wales, yet I am the king of   10
courtesy; and tell me flatly I am no proud Jack, like

Falstaff, but a Corinthian,° a lad of mettle, a good
boy, by the Lord, so they call me, and when I am
King of England, I shall command all the good lads
in Eastcheap. They call drinking deep, dyeing   15
scarlet, and when you breathe in your watering,°
they cry " hem! "° and bid you play it off.° To conclude, I am so good a proficient in one quarter of an
hour that I can drink with any tinker in his own   20
language during my life. I tell thee, Ned, thou hast
lost much honor that thou wert not with me in this
action. But, sweet Ned — to sweeten which name of
Ned, I give thee this pennyworth of sugar, clapped
even now into my hand by an underskinker,°   25
one that never spake other English in his life than
" Eight shillings and sixpence," and " You are welcome," with this shrill addition, " Anon,° anon, sir!
Score° a pint of bastard° in the Half-Moon,"° or so.
But, Ned, to drive away the time till Falstaff   30
come, I prithee do thou stand in some by-room while
I question my puny° drawer to what end he gave me
the sugar. And do thou never leave calling " Francis," that his tale to me may be nothing but   35
" Anon." Step aside, and I'll show thee a precedent.°
    POINS. Francis!
    PRINCE. Thou art perfect.
    POINS. Francis!   [*Exit* POINS.]
            [*Enter* FRANCIS.]
    FRAN. Anon, anon, sir. Look down into the Pom-
garnet,° Ralph.
    PRINCE. Come hither, Francis.
    FRAN. My lord?
    PRINCE. How long hast thou to serve, Francis?°   44
    FRAN. Forsooth, five years, and as much as to ——
    POINS. [*Within*] Francis!
    FRAN. Anon, anon, sir.   49
    PRINCE. Five year! By'r Lady, a long lease for the
clinking of pewter. But, Francis, darest thou be so
valiant as to play the coward with thy indenture°
and show it a fair pair of heels and run from it?   54
    FRAN. Oh, Lord, sir, I'll be sworn upon all the
books in England I could find in my heart.°
    POINS. [*Within*] Francis!
    FRAN. Anon, sir.
    PRINCE. How old art thou, Francis?
    FRAN. Let me see — about Michaelmas next I shall
be ——   61

---

95. mammets: dolls. tilt . . . lips: kiss. 97. current: with a pun
on *cracked crowns;* i.e., broken heads, and crown pieces, cracked
and so not current.
    Sc. iv: 1. fat: stuffy. 4. loggerheads: blockheads. 5. hogs-
heads: casks. 5–6. sounded . . . humility: i.e., have sunk to
the lowest depth. 7. leash: set of three, properly used of a
leash of greyhounds.

12. Corinthian: a gay lad. 16. watering: drinking. 17. cry
" hem ": one of those exclamations made by topers, like "Here's
how." play it off: get it down. 25. underskinker: assistant bartender. 28. Anon: at once or by and by. the drawer's cry,
"Coming, sir." 29. Score: chalk up, the method of recording
a debt for drink still used in English public houses. bastard:
a sweet white wine. Half-Moon: Each room in an inn or a tavern had its own name. 32. puny: freshman. 36. precedent:
specimen. 42. Pomgarnet: Pomegranate — another room.
45. How . . . Francis: i.e., how many years of your apprenticeship still remain. As Francis has only served two of his seven
years, he is sixteen. 53. indenture: agreement of apprenticeship.
See App. 6. 56. could . . . heart: i.e., very willingly.

POINS. [*Within*] Francis!

FRAN. Anon, sir. Pray stay a little, my lord.

PRINCE. Nay, but hark you, Francis. For the sugar thou gavest me, 'twas a pennyworth, was't not?   66

FRAN. Oh, Lord, I would it had been two!

PRINCE. I will give thee for it a thousand pound. Ask me when thou wilt, and thou shalt have it.   70

POINS. [*Within*] Francis!

FRAN. Anon, anon.

PRINCE. Anon, Francis? No, Francis, but tomorrow, Francis; or, Francis, o' Thursday; or indeed, Francis, when thou wilt. But Francis!

FRAN. My lord?   76

PRINCE. Wilt thou rob this leathern-jerkin, crystal-button, not-pated, agate-ring, puke-stocking, caddis-garter, smooth-tongue, Spanish-pouch ——°   80

FRAN. Oh, Lord, sir, who do you mean?

PRINCE. Why, then, your brown bastard is your only drink, for look you, Francis, your white canvas doublet will sully. In Barbary,° sir, it cannot come to so much.

FRAN. What, sir?   86

POINS. [*Within*] Francis!

PRINCE. Away, you rogue! Dost thou not hear them call? [*Here they both call him; the* DRAWER *stands amazed, not knowing which way to go.*]

[*Enter* VINTNER.]

VINT. What, standest thou still, and hearest such a calling? Look to the guests within. [*Exit* FRANCIS.] My lord, old Sir John, with half-a-dozen more, are at the door. Shall I let them in?   94

PRINCE. Let them alone awhile, and then open the door. [*Exit* VINTNER.] Poins!

[*Re-enter* POINS.]

POINS. Anon, anon, sir.

PRINCE. Sirrah, Falstaff and the rest of the thieves are at the door. Shall we be merry?   99

POINS. As merry as crickets, my lad. But hark ye, what cunning match° have you made with this jest of the drawer? Come, what's the issue?°   103

PRINCE. I am now of all humors° that have showed themselves humors since the old days of Goodman Adam to the pupilage° of this present twelve o'clock at midnight.

[*Re-enter* FRANCIS.] What's o'clock, Francis?   108

FRAN. Anon, anon, sir.   [*Exit.*]

PRINCE. That ever this fellow should have fewer words than a parrot, and yet the son of a woman! His industry is upstairs and downstairs, his elo-

quence the parcel° of a reckoning. I am not yet of Percy's mind, the Hotspur of the North, he that kills me some six or seven dozen of Scots at a break-   115 fast, washes his hands, and says to his wife, "Fie upon this quiet life! I want work." "O my sweet Harry," says she, "how many hast thou killed today?" "Give my roan horse a drench,"° says he, and answers "Some fourteen" an hour after   120 — "a trifle, a trifle." I prithee call in Falstaff. I'll play Percy, and that damned brawn° shall play Dame Mortimer his wife. "Rivo!"° says the drunkard. Call in ribs, call in tallow.   125

[*Enter* FALSTAFF, GADSHILL, BARDOLPH, *and* PETO; FRANCIS *following with wine.*]

POINS. Welcome, Jack. Where hast thou been?

FAL. A plague of all cowards, I say, and a vengeance too! Marry, and amen! Give me a cup of sack, boy. Ere I lead this life long, I'll sew netherstocks° and mend them and foot them too. A plague of all cowards! Give me a cup of sack, rogue. Is there   131 no virtue extant?°   [*He drinks.*]

PRINCE. Didst thou never see Titan° kiss a dish of butter? Pitiful-hearted Titan, that melted° at the sweet tale of the sun's! If thou didst, then behold that compound.   136

FAL. You rogue, here's lime° in this sack too. There is nothing but roguery to be found in villainous man. Yet a coward is worse than a cup of sack with lime in it. A villainous coward! Go thy   140 ways, old Jack, die when thou wilt. If manhood, good manhood, be not forgot upon the face of the earth, then am I a shotten° herring. There live not three good men unhanged in England, and one of them is fat, and grows old. God help the while!° A bad world, I say. I would I were a weaver, I   146 could sing psalms° or anything. A plague of all cowards, I say still.

PRINCE. How now, woolsack! What mutter you?

FAL. A king's son! If I do not beat thee out of thy kingdom with a dagger of lath,° and drive all thy subjects afore thee like a flock of wild geese, I'll never wear hair on my face more. You Prince of Wales!   154

PRINCE. Why, you whoreson round man, what's the matter?

FAL. Are not you a coward? Answer me to that. And Poins there?

POINS. 'Zounds, ye fat paunch, an ye call me coward, by the Lord, I'll stab thee.   160

77–80. leathern-jerkin . . . Spanish-pouch: This list gives the outward characteristics of a prosperous innkeeper: leather coat (*jerkin*) with crystal buttons, close-cropped head (*not-pated*), large ring, gray (*puke*) stockings, worsted (*caddis*) garters, a *smooth tongue*, and a *pouch* of *Spanish* leather. **84. In Barbary:** in North Africa — but the Prince's words have passed beyond location. **101. what . . . match:** what is the game. **103. issue:** result. **104. of . . . humors:** i.e., will match my mood with any man's. **106. pupilage:** boyhood.

113. parcel: items. **119. drench:** purge. **122. brawn:** fat pig. **124. Rivo:** another drinkers' exclamation. See l. 17. **129. netherstocks:** stockings, at this time cut out of material and sewed, not knitted. See comment on p. 93b. **132. virtue extant:** manhood in existence. **133. Titan:** the sun. **134. that melted:** i.e., the butter. **137. lime:** used to adulterate wine by giving it a better color and taste. **143. shotten:** without its roe. **145. God . . . while:** God help these times. **146–47. weaver . . . psalms:** See *T Night*, II.iii.61,n. **151. dagger of lath:** wooden dagger.

FAL. I call thee coward! I'll see thee damned ere I call thee coward. But I would give a thousand pound I could run as fast as thou canst. You are straight enough in the shoulders, you care not who sees your back. Call you that backing of your friends? A plague upon such backing! Give me them that will face me. Give me a cup of sack. I am a rogue if I drunk today.   169

PRINCE. O villain! Thy lips are scarce wiped since thou drunkest last.

FAL. All's one for that. [*He drinks.*] A plague of all cowards, still say I.

PRINCE. What's the matter?   174

FAL. What's the matter! There be four of us here have ta'en a thousand pound this day morning.

PRINCE. Where is it, Jack? Where is it?

FAL. Where is it! Taken from us it is — a hundred upon poor four of us.   180

PRINCE. What, a hundred, man?

FAL. I am a rogue if I were not at half-sword° with a dozen of them two hours together. I have 'scaped by miracle. I am eight times thrust through the doublet,° four through the hose;° my buckler°   185 cut through and through; my sword hacked like a handsaw — *ecce signum!*° I never dealt° better since I was a man. All would not do. A plague of all cowards! Let them speak. If they speak more or less than truth, they are villains and the sons of darkness.   191

PRINCE. Speak, sirs, how was it?

GADS. We four set upon some dozen ——

FAL. Sixteen at least, my lord.

GADS. And bound them.   195

PETO. No, no, they were not bound.

FAL. You rogue, they were bound, every man of them, or I am a Jew else, an Ebrew° Jew.

GADS. As we were sharing, some six or seven fresh men set upon us ——   200

FAL. And unbound the rest, and then come in the other.

PRINCE. What, fought you with them all?   203

FAL. All! I know not what you call all, but if I fought not with fifty of them, I am a bunch of radish. If there were not two or three and fifty upon poor old Jack, then am I no two-legged creature.

PRINCE. Pray God you have not murdered some of them.   210

FAL. Nay, that's past praying for. I have peppered two of them — two I am sure I have paid,° two rogues in buckram suits. I tell thee what, Hal, if I tell thee a lie, spit in my face, call me horse.° Thou knowest my old ward.° Here I lay, and thus I bore

my point. Four rogues in buckram let drive at me ——   217

PRINCE. What, four? Thou saidst but two even now.

FAL. Four, Hal, I told thee four.

POINS. Aye, aye, he said four.   221

FAL. These four came all afront, and mainly° thrust at me. I made me no more ado, but took all their seven points in my target, thus.

PRINCE. Seven? Why, there were but four even now.   226

FAL. In buckram?

POINS. Aye, four, in buckram suits.

FAL. Seven, by these hilts,° or I am a villain else.

PRINCE. Prithee let him alone. We shall have more anon.

FAL. Dost thou hear me, Hal?

PRINCE. Aye, and mark thee too, Jack.   234

FAL. Do so, for it is worth the listening to. These nine in buckram that I told thee of ——

PRINCE. So, two more already.

FAL. Their points being broken ——

POINS. Down fell their hose.°   239

FAL. Began to give me ground. But I followed me close, came in foot and hand, and with a thought seven of the eleven I paid.

PRINCE. Oh, monstrous! Eleven buckram men grown out of two!   244

FAL. But, as the Devil would have it, three misbegotten knaves in Kendal green° came at my back and let drive at me; for it was so dark, Hal, that thou couldst not see thy hand.   248

PRINCE. These lies are like their father that begets them — gross as a mountain, open, palpable. Why, thou clay-brained guts, thou knotty-pated° fool, thou whoreson, obscene, greasy tallow catch ——°   253

FAL. What, art thou mad? Art thou mad? Is not the truth the truth?

PRINCE. Why, how couldst thou know these men in Kendal green when it was so dark thou couldst not see thy hand? Come, tell us your reason. What sayest thou to this?   259

POINS. Come, your reason, Jack, your reason.

FAL. What, upon compulsion? 'Zounds, an I were at the strappado, or all the racks° in the world, I would not tell you on compulsion. Give you a reason

---

182. at half-sword: within half a sword's length. A cautious fighter kept at greater distance. **185. doublet:** coat. **hose:** breeches. See Pl. 8b and comment on p. 93a-b. **buckler:** small shield. See Pls. 9 and 21i. **187. ecce signum:** behold the sign. **dealt:** fought. **198. Ebrew:** Hebrew. **212. paid:** paid home, done for. **214. horse:** Like the ass, the horse was regarded as stupid. **215. ward:** stance, position of guard. Here Falstaff re-enacts his heroic exploit.

222. mainly: violently. **229. hilts:** sword hilt. **238-39. Their . . . hose:** Poins puns on the other meaning of *points*, laces tying the hose to the doublet. See p. 94a-b. **246. Kendal green:** cloth made (originally at Kendal in Westmoreland) of the poorest-quality wool, and used by woodmen and servants. **252. knotty-pated:** blockhead. **253. tallow catch:** the word is variously emended and interpreted. Johnson suggested "keech" — a lump of fat prepared by the butcher for the candlemaker. A *tallow catch* would naturally be "a thing for catching tallow"; i.e., the rim on the candlestick which, when piled up with the drippings of wax, is no bad image for Falstaff. **262. strappado . . . racks:** forms of torture. See App. 10.

on compulsion! If reasons were as plentiful as 264
blackberries, I would give no man a reason upon
compulsion, I.

PRINCE. I'll be no longer guilty of this sin — this
sanguine° coward, this bed-presser, this horseback-
breaker, this huge hill of flesh —— 269

FAL. 'Sblood, you starveling,° you elf skin,° you
dried neat's tongue,° you bull's pizzle,° you stockfish!° Oh, for breath to utter what is like thee! You
tailor's yard, you sheath, you bow case, you vile
standing tuck ——° 274

PRINCE. Well, breathe a while, and then to it
again, and when thou hast tired thyself in base comparisons, hear me speak but this.

POINS. Mark, Jack. 278

PRINCE. We two saw you four set on four and
bound them, and were masters of their wealth. Mark
now, how a plain tale shall put you down. Then did
we two set on you four; and, with a word, outfaced
you from your prize, and have it; yea, and can show
it you here in the house. And, Falstaff, you carried
your guts away as nimbly, with as quick dex- 285
terity, and roared for mercy, and still run and roared,
as ever I heard bull calf. What a slave art thou, to
hack thy sword as thou hast done, and then say it
was in fight! What trick, what device, what starting
hole,° canst thou now find out to hide thee from this
open and apparent shame? 292

POINS. Come, let's hear, Jack. What trick hast thou
now?

FAL. By the Lord, I knew ye as well as he that
made ye. Why, hear you, my masters. Was it for me
to kill the heir apparent? Should I turn upon the true
Prince? Why, thou knowest I am as valiant as Hercules. But beware instinct, the lion will not touch the
true prince.° Instinct is a great matter, I was now a
coward on instinct. I shall think the better of 300
myself and thee during my life, I for a valiant lion,
and thou for a true Prince. But, by the Lord, lads, I
am glad you have the money. Hostess, clap to the
doors. Watch tonight, pray tomorrow. Gal- 305
lants, lads, boys, hearts of gold, all the titles of good
fellowship come to you! What, shall we be merry?
Shall we have a play extempore?

PRINCE. Content, and the argument° shall be thy
running away. 311

FAL. Ah, no more of that, Hal, an thou lovest me!

[*Enter* HOSTESS.]

HOSTESS. O Jesu, my lord the Prince!

PRINCE. How now, my lady the hostess! What sayest thou to me? 316

HOSTESS. Marry, my lord, there is a nobleman of
the Court at door would speak with you. He says he
comes from your father.

PRINCE. Give him as much as will make him a
royal man,° and send him back again to my mother.

FAL. What manner of man is he? 323

HOSTESS. An old man.

FAL. What doth gravity out of his bed at midnight? Shall I give him his answer? 326

PRINCE. Prithee do, Jack.

FAL. Faith, and I'll send him packing. [*Exit.*]

PRINCE. Now, sirs. By'r Lady, you fought fair; so
did you, Peto; so did you, Bardolph. You are lions
too, you ran away upon instinct, you will not touch
the true prince — no, fie! 332

BARD. Faith, I ran when I saw others run.

PRINCE. Faith, tell me now in earnest, how came
Falstaff's sword so hacked?

PETO. Why, he hacked it with his dagger, and said
he would swear truth out of England but he would
make you believe it was done in fight, and persuaded
us to do the like. 339

BARD. Yea, and to tickle our noses with speargrass
to make them bleed, and then to beslubber° our garments with it and swear it was the blood of true
men. I did that I did not this seven year before, I
blushed to hear his monstrous devices. 344

PRINCE. O villain, thou stolest a cup of sack eighteen years ago, and wert taken with the manner,° and
ever since thou hast blushed° extempore. Thou hadst
fire and sword on thy side, and yet thou rannest
away. What instinct hadst thou for it? 350

BARD. My lord, do you see these meteors? Do you
behold these exhalations?°

PRINCE. I do.

BARD. What think you they portend?

PRINCE. Hot livers and cold purses. 355

BARD. Choler,° my lord, if rightly taken.

PRINCE. No, if rightly taken, halter.

[*Re-enter* FALSTAFF.] Here comes lean Jack, here
comes barebone. How now, my sweet creature of
bombast!° How long is't ago, Jack, since thou sawest
thine own knee? 361

---

268. **sanguine:** one suffering from an excess of the sanguine humor. See App. 3. 270. **you starveling:** Falstaff, being thoroughly roused, retorts with a string of images expressing the thinness of the Prince. **elf skin:** sometimes emended to eelskin, but probably it meant snakeskin, which, as Oberon observed, was "Weed wide enough to wrap a fairy in." (*MND*, II.i.256). 271. **neat's tongue:** ox tongue. **bull's pizzle:** This portion of the bull's anatomy was dried and used as a whip. 272. **stockfish:** dried codfish. 274. **standing tuck:** a rapier stuck in the ground. 290–91. **starting hole:** a hole into which a rabbit bolts for safety. 298–99. **lion ... prince:** This was very generally believed. 310. **argument:** plot.

321–22. **as ... man:** i.e., 3s 4d, which is the difference between a *royal* (10s) and a noble (6s 8d). See App. 27. It is a sign of Prince Hal's low behavior that he should make such jokes about a nobleman of the Court. 341. **beslubber:** smear. 346. **with ... manner:** in the act. 347. **blushed:** For Bardolph's permanent blush see III,iii.27–55 and *Hen V*, III.vi.108. 351–52. **meteors ... exhalations:** Bardolph indicates his own fiery face which, he claims, is proof that he is a man of wrath. **exhalations:** meteors. 356. **Choler:** anger; pronounced in the same way as "collar," and so puns on the two words are common. See *T Night*, I.v.6,n. 360. **bombast:** cotton batting, used to stuff garments to make them appear baggy.

FAL. My own knee! When I was about thy years, Hal, I was not an eagle's talon in the waist, I could have crept into any alderman's thumb ring.° A plague of sighing and grief! It blows a man up like a bladder. There's villainous news abroad. Here 366 was Sir John Bracy from your father; you must to the Court in the morning. That same mad fellow of the North, Percy, and he of Wales, that gave Amamon° the bastinado° and made Lucifer cuckold,° and swore the Devil his true liegeman° upon the cross of a Welsh hook — what a plague call you him? 372

POINS. O, Glendower.°

FAL. Owen, Owen, the same. And his son-in-law Mortimer, and old Northumberland, and that sprightly Scot of Scots, Douglas, that runs o' horseback up a hill perpendicular ——

PRINCE. He that rides at high speed and with his pistol kills a sparrow flying. 380

FAL. You have hit it.

PRINCE. So did he never the sparrow.

FAL. Well, that rascal hath good mettle° in him. He will not run. 384

PRINCE. Why, what a rascal art thou then, to praise him so for running!

FAL. O' horseback, ye cuckoo, but afoot he will not budge a foot.

PRINCE. Yes, Jack, upon instinct. 389

FAL. I grant ye, upon instinct. Well, he is there too, and one Mordake, and a thousand bluecaps° more. Worcester is stolen away tonight; thy father's beard is turned white with the news. You may buy land now as cheap as stinking mackerel. 395

PRINCE. Why, then, it is like, if there come a hot June and this civil buffeting hold, we shall buy maidenheads as they buy hobnails, by the hundreds.

FAL. By the mass, lad, thou sayest true; it is like we shall have good trading that way. But tell me, Hal, art not thou horrible afeard? Thou being heir apparent, could the world pick thee out three such enemies again as that fiend Douglas, that spirit Percy, and that devil Glendower? Art thou not horribly afraid? Doth not thy blood thrill at it? 407

PRINCE. Not a whit, i' faith. I lack some of thy instinct.

FAL. Well, thou wilt be horribly chid tomorrow when thou comest to thy father. If thou love me, practice an answer. 412

PRINCE. Do thou stand for° my father, and examine me upon the particulars of my life.

FAL. Shall I? Content. This chair shall be my state,° this dagger my scepter, and this cushion my crown. 417

PRINCE. Thy state is taken for a joined stool,° thy golden scepter for a leaden° dagger, and thy precious rich crown for a pitiful bald crown! 420

FAL. Well, an the fire of grace be not quite out of thee, now shalt thou be moved. Give me a cup of sack to make my eyes look red, that it may be thought I have wept; for I must speak in passion, and I will do it in King Cambyses'° vein. 426

PRINCE. Well, here is my leg.°

FAL. And here is my speech. Stand aside, nobility.

HOSTESS. Oh Jesu, this is excellent sport, i' faith!

FAL. Weep° not, sweet queen, for trickling tears are vain. 430

HOSTESS. Oh, the father,° how he holds his countenance!°

FAL. For God's sake, lords, convey my tristful° queen,
For tears do stop the floodgates of her eyes. 435

HOSTESS. Oh Jesu, he doth it as like one of these harlotry players° as ever I see!

FAL. Peace, good pint pot; peace, good ticklebrain. Harry, I do not only marvel where thou spendest thy time, but also how thou art accompanied.° For 440 though the camomile,° the more it is trodden on, the faster it grows, yet youth, the more it is wasted, the sooner it wears. That thou art my son, I have partly thy mother's word, partly my own opinion, but chiefly a villainous trick° of thine eye, and a 445 foolish hanging of thy nether° lip, that doth warrant° me. If then thou be son to me, here lies the point; why, being son to me, art thou so pointed at? Shall the blessed sun of heaven prove a micher° 450 and eat blackberries? A question not to be asked. Shall the son of England prove a thief and take purses? A question to be asked. There is a thing, Harry, which thou hast often heard of, and it is known to many in our land by the name of pitch. This pitch, as ancient writers do report, doth 455 defile; so doth the company thou keepest. For, Harry, now I do not speak to thee in drink but in tears, not in pleasure but in passion, not in words only, but in

---

364. thumb ring: large seal ring, especially common on the thumbs of businessmen. **369. Amamon:** the name of a fiend. **370. bastinado:** thrashing. **cuckold:** a man deceived by his wife. See App. II. **371. liegeman:** subject. **373. O, Glendower:** probably Shakespeare wrote *O* in his manuscript as abbreviation for Owen, which the printer mistook for an exclamation. **383. mettle:** matter, material. **391. bluecaps:** Scots. **413. stand for:** represent.

416. state: throne. **418. joined stool:** wooden stool made by a joiner. See Pl. 17a. **419. leaden:** blunt. **426. King Cambyses':** the chief character in an early drama which still survives; it is a marvelous specimen of ridiculous rant. **427. my leg:** my curtsy. **430–35: Weep . . . eyes:** Falstaff begins in the artificial style of earlier plays, of the kind still being acted by the rival company at the Rose. See Gen. Intro. p. 41b. **431. Oh . . . father:** by God the Father. **holds . . . countenance:** keeps a straight face. **434. tristful:** sad, a poetical word. **437. harlotry players:** worthless players. As the Admiral's Men were the only other company then playing in London, the parody of their heavy style was obvious. **440. how . . . accompanied:** what company you keep. **441. For . . . camomile:** The whole of this passage is a parody of the elaborate style of Lyly's *Euphues*. The *camomile* is a small creeping aromatic plant with a flower like a daisy. **445. trick:** habit. **446. nether:** lower. **447. warrant:** guarantee. **450. micher:** a truant.

woes also. And yet there is a virtuous man whom I
have often noted in thy company, but I know not his
name.   461

PRINCE. What manner of man, an it like your
Majesty?

FAL. A goodly portly° man, i' faith, and a corpulent; of a cheerful look, a pleasing eye, and a   465
most noble carriage. And, as I think, his age some
fifty, or, by'r Lady, inclining to threescore. And now
I remember me, his name is Falstaff. If that man
should be lewdly given, he deceiveth me, for, Harry,
I see virtue in his looks. If then the tree may be   470
known by the fruit, as the fruit by the tree, then,
peremptorily° I speak it, there is virtue in that Falstaff. Him keep with, the rest banish. And tell me
now, thou naughty varlet, tell me, where hast thou
been this month?   475

PRINCE. Dost thou speak like a king? Do thou
stand for me, and I'll play my father.

FAL. Depose me? If thou dost it half so gravely, so
majestically, both in word and matter, hang me up
by the heels for a rabbit-sucker° or a poulter's° hare.

PRINCE. Well, here I am set.   482

FAL. And here I stand. Judge, my masters.

PRINCE. Now, Harry, whence come you?

FAL. My noble lord, from Eastcheap.   485

PRINCE. The complaints I hear of thee are grievous.

FAL. 'Sblood, my lord, they are false. Nay, I'll
tickle ye° for a young Prince, i' faith.   489

PRINCE. Swearest thou, ungracious° boy? Henceforth ne'er look on me. Thou art violently carried
away from grace. There is a devil haunts thee in the
likeness of an old fat man, a tun° of man is thy companion. Why dost thou converse with that trunk of
humors,° that bolting hutch° of beastliness,   495
that swollen parcel of dropsies, that huge bombard°
of sack, that stuffed cloak bag° of guts, that roasted
Manningtree° ox with the pudding in his belly, that
reverend vice,° that gray iniquity, that father ruffian, that vanity in years? Wherein is he good,   500
but to taste sack and drink it? Wherein neat and
cleanly,° but to carve a capon and eat it? Wherein
cunning,° but in craft? Wherein crafty,° but in
villainy? Wherein villainous, but in all things?
Wherein worthy, but in nothing?   505

FAL. I would your Grace would take me with
you.° Whom means your Grace?

PRINCE. That villainous abominable misleader of
youth, Falstaff, that old white-bearded Satan.

FAL. My lord, the man I know.   510

PRINCE. I know thou dost.

FAL. But to say I know more harm in him than in
myself were to say more than I know. That he is old,
the more the pity, his white hairs do witness it; but
that he is, saving your reverence, a whore-   515
master, that I utterly deny. If sack and sugar be a
fault, God help the wicked! If to be old and merry be
a sin, then many an old host that I know is damned.
If to be fat be to be hated, then Pharaoh's lean kine
are to be loved. No, my good lord. Banish Peto,   520
banish Bardolph, banish Poins. But for sweet Jack
Falstaff, kind Jack Falstaff, true Jack Falstaff, valiant
Jack Falstaff, and therefore more valiant, being, as he
is, old Jack Falstaff, banish not him thy Harry's company, banish not him thy Harry's company.   525
Banish plump Jack, and banish all the world.

PRINCE. I do, I will.   [*A knocking heard.*
      Exeunt HOSTESS, FRANCIS, *and* BARDOLPH.]
      [*Re-enter* BARDOLPH, *running.*]

BARD. Oh, my lord, my lord! The sheriff with a
most monstrous watch° is at the door.   530

FAL. Out, ye rogue! Play out the play. I have much
to say in the behalf of that Falstaff.

      [*Re-enter the* HOSTESS.]

HOSTESS. Oh Jesu, my lord, my lord! —

PRINCE. Heigh, heigh! The Devil rides upon a
fiddlestick.° What's the matter?   535

HOSTESS. The sheriff and all the watch are at the
door. They are come to search the house. Shall I let
them in?

FAL. Dost thou hear, Hal? Never call a true piece
of gold a counterfeit. Thou art essentially mad, without seeming so.   541

PRINCE. And thou a natural coward, without instinct.

FAL. I deny your major.° If you will deny the
sheriff, so; if not, let him enter. If I become not a
cart° as well as another man, a plague on my bringing up! I hope I shall as soon be strangled with a
halter as another.   548

PRINCE. Go, hide thee behind the arras,° the rest
walk up above. Now, my masters, for a true face and
good conscience.

FAL. Both which I have had; but their date is out,°
and therefore I'll hide me.   553

PRINCE. Call in the sheriff.

      [*Exeunt all except the* PRINCE *and* PETO.]

[*Enter* SHERIFF *and the* CARRIER.]

Now, Master Sheriff, what is your will with me?

SHER. First, pardon me, my lord. A hue and
　　cry°
Hath followed certain men unto this house.

PRINCE. What men?

SHER. One of them is well known, my gracious
　　lord,
A gross fat man.

CAR.　　　　　As fat as butter.　　　　　560

PRINCE. The man, I do assure you, is not here,
For I myself at this time have employed him.
And, sheriff, I will engage my word to thee
That I will, by tomorrow dinnertime,
Send him to answer thee, or any man,　　　565
For anything he shall be charged withal.
And so let me entreat you leave the house.

SHER. I will, my lord. There are two gentlemen
Have in this robbery lost three hundred marks.

PRINCE. It may be so. If he have robbed these
　　men,　　　　　　　　　　　　　　　570
He shall be answerable. And so farewell.

SHER. Good night, my noble lord.

PRINCE. I think it is good morrow, is it not?

SHER. Indeed, my lord, I think it be two o'clock.
　　　　　　　[*Exeunt* SHERIFF *and* CARRIER.]

PRINCE. This oily rascal is known as well as　575
Paul's.° Go, call him forth.

PETO. Falstaff! — Fast asleep behind the arras, and
snorting like a horse.

PRINCE. Hark how hard he fetches breath. Search
his pockets. [*He searcheth his pockets, and findeth
certain papers.*] What hast thou found?　　582

PETO. Nothing but papers, my lord.

PRINCE. Let's see what they be. Read them.

PETO. [*Reads.*]

"Item, A capon,　. . . . . . .　2s. 2d.
Item, Sauce, ...　4d.
Item, Sack, two gallons,　. . . .　5s. 8d.
Item, Anchovies and sack after supper, 2s. 6d.
Item, Bread, ...　ob.°"

PRINCE. Oh, monstrous! But one halfpenny-　591
worth of bread to this intolerable deal of sack! What
there is else, keep close, we'll read it at more advantage. There let him sleep till day. I'll to the Court in
the morning. We must all to the wars, and thy　595
place shall be honorable. I'll procure this fat rogue a
charge of foot,° and I know his death will be a march
of twelvescore.° The money shall be paid back again
with advantage.° Be with me betimes in the morning. And so good morrow, Peto.　　　　600

PETO. Good morrow, good my lord.　[*Exeunt.*]

---

556. hue . . . cry: See Gen. Intro. p. 28a.　576. Paul's: St. Paul's
Church. See Gen. Intro. p. 17a and Pl. 2a.　590. ob: one halfpenny.　597. charge of foot: commission as commander of a
company of infantry.　598. twelvescore: i.e. paces. The pace
was 60 inches.　599. advantage: interest.

Act III

SCENE I. *Bangor. The* ARCHDEACON's *house.*

[*Enter* HOTSPUR, WORCESTER, MORTIMER, *and*
GLENDOWER.]

MORT. These promises are fair, the parties sure,
And our induction° full of prosperous hope.

HOT. Lord Mortimer, and Cousin Glendower,
Will you sit down?
And Uncle Worcester. A plague upon it!　　　5
I have forgot the map.

GLEND.　　　　　No, here it is.
Sit, Cousin Percy. Sit, good Cousin Hotspur,
For by that name as oft as Lancaster
Doth speak of you, his cheek looks pale, and with
A rising sigh he wisheth you in Heaven.　　　10

HOT. And you in Hell, as oft as he hears Owen
　　Glendower spoke of.

GLEND. I cannot blame him. At my nativity°
The front° of heaven was full of fiery shapes,
Of burning cressets;° and at my birth　　　15
The frame and huge foundation of the earth
Shaked like a coward.

HOT. Why, so it would have done at the same season if your mother's cat had but kittened, though
yourself had never been born.　　　　　20

GLEND. I say the earth did shake when I was born.

HOT. And I say the earth was not of my mind
If you suppose as fearing you it shook.

GLEND. The heavens were all on fire, the earth did
tremble.

HOT. Oh, then the earth shook to see the heavens
　　on fire,　　　　　　　　　　　　　　25
And not in fear of your nativity.
Diseasèd nature oftentimes breaks forth
In strange eruptions; oft the teeming° earth
Is with a kind of colic pinched and vexed
By the imprisoning of unruly wind　　　30
Within her womb; which, for enlargement striving,
Shakes the old beldam° earth and topples down
Steeples and moss-grown towers. At your birth
Our grandam earth, having this distemperature,°
In passion° shook.

GLEND.　　　　　Cousin,° of many men　35
I do not bear these crossings.° Give me leave
To tell you once again that at my birth
The front of heaven was full of fiery shapes,
The goats ran from the mountains, and the herds

Act III, Sc. i: 2. induction: opening.　12. nativity: moment
of birth. See App. 1.　14. front: forehead.　15. burning cressets:
stars blazing like beacons.　28. teeming: pregnant. This theory
of earthquakes — that they were caused by the expulsion of
wind from within the earth — was generally believed.　32. beldam: grandmother.　34. distemperature: disorder.　35. passion:
agitation. Cousin: kinsman; used of any relation. Hotspur
is remotely related to Glendower through Lady Percy. See
App. 28.　36. crossings: opposition.

Were strangely clamorous to the frighted fields. 40
These signs have marked me extraordinary,
And all the courses of my life do show
I am not in the roll of common men.
Where is he living, clipped in° with the sea
That chides° the banks of England, Scotland, Wales,
Which calls me pupil,° or hath read to me?° 46
And bring him out that is but woman's son
Can trace° me in the tedious ways of art,°
And hold me pace° in deep experiments.

  HOT. I think there's no man speaks better Welsh.
I'll to dinner. 51

  MORT. Peace, Cousin Percy, you will make him
    mad.

  GLEND. I can call spirits from the vasty deep.

  HOT. Why, so can I, or so can any man;
But will they come when you do call for them? 55

  GLEND. Why, I can teach you, Cousin, to command
The Devil.

  HOT. And I can teach thee, Coz, to shame the
    Devil°
By telling truth. Tell truth, and shame the Devil. 59
If thou have power to raise him, bring him hither,
And I'll be sworn I have power to shame him hence.
Oh, while you live, tell truth, and shame the Devil!

  MORT. Come, come, no more of this unprofitable
    chat.

  GLEND. Three times hath Henry Bolingbroke
    made head°
Against my power. Thrice from the banks of Wye
And sandy-bottomed Severn have I sent him 66
Bootless° home and weather-beaten back.

  HOT. Home without boots, and in foul weather
    too!
How 'scapes he agues,° in the Devil's name?

  GLEND. Come, here's the map. Shall we divide our
    right 70
According to our threefold order° ta'en?

  MORT. The Archdeacon hath divided it
Into three limits° very equally.
England, from Trent and Severn hitherto,
By south and east is to my part assigned. 75
All westward, Wales beyond the Severn shore,
And all the fertile land within that bound,
To Owen Glendower. And, dear Coz, to you
The remnant northward, lying off from Trent.
And our indentures tripartite° are drawn; 80
Which being sealed interchangeably,°
A business that this night may execute,

Tomorrow, Cousin Percy, you and I
And my good Lord of Worcester will set forth
To meet your father and the Scottish power, 85
As is appointed us, at Shrewsbury.
My father° Glendower is not ready yet,
Nor shall we need his help these fourteen days.
Within that space you may have drawn together 89
Your tenants, friends, and neighboring gentlemen.

  GLEND. A shorter time shall send me to you, lords.
And in my conduct shall your ladies come,
From whom you now must steal and take no leave;
For there will be a world of water shed
Upon the parting of your wives and you. 95

  HOT. Methinks my moiety,° north from Burton
    here,
In quantity equals not one of yours.
See how this river comes me cranking in,°
And cuts me from the best of all my land
A huge half-moon, a monstrous cantle° out. 100
I'll have the current in this place dammed up,
And here the smug° and silver Trent shall run
In a new channel, fair and evenly.
It shall not wind with such a deep indent,°
To rob me of so rich a bottom° here. 105

  GLEND. Not wind? It shall, it must. You see it
    doth.

  MORT. Yea, but
Mark how he bears his course, and runs me up
With like advantage on the other side,
Gelding the opposèd continent° as much 110
As on the other side it takes from you.

  WOR. Yea, but a little charge° will trench him
    here
And on this north side win this cape of land,
And then he runs straight and even.

  HOT. I'll have it so. A little charge will do it. 115

  GLEND. I'll not have it altered.

  HOT.   Will not you?

  GLEND. No, nor you shall not.

  HOT.   Who shall say me nay?

  GLEND. Why, that will I.

  HOT. Let me not understand you, then. Speak it in
    Welsh. 120

  GLEND. I can speak English, lord, as well as you;
For I was trained up in the English Court,
Where, being but young, I framèd to the harp
Many an English ditty lovely well,
And gave the tongue a helpful ornament,° 125
A virtue that was never seen in you.

  HOT. Marry,°
And I am glad of it with all my heart.

---

44. **clipped in:** encircled. 45. **chides:** roars against. 46. **calls me pupil:** i.e., is my master. **hath . . . me:** has been my tutor. 48. **trace:** follow. **tedious . . . art:** difficult course of magic. 49. **hold me pace:** keep pace with me. 58. **shame . . . Devil:** because he is the father of lies. 64. **made head:** advanced. 67. **Bootless:** profitless. 69. **agues:** fever. 71. **our . . . order:** agreement made between us three. 73. **limits:** divisions. 80. **indentures tripartite:** See App. 6 and Pl. 11a. 81. **sealed interchangeably:** each party sealing each copy of the agreement.

87. **father:** i.e., father-in-law. 96. **moiety:** share. 98. **me . . . in:** comes winding into my part. 100. **cantle:** slice. 102. **smug:** smooth. 104. **indent:** indentation. 105. **bottom:** valley. 110. **opposed continent:** opposite bank. 112. **charge:** cost. 125. **helpful ornament:** i.e., musical accompaniment. 127. **Marry:** Mary, by the Virgin.

I had rather be a kitten and cry mew
Than one of these same meter balladmongers.°   130
I had rather hear a brazen canstick turned,°
Or a dry wheel grate on the axletree;
And that would set my teeth nothing on edge,
Nothing so much as mincing poetry.
'Tis like the forced gait of a shuffling nag.   135
    GLEND. Come, you shall have Trent turned.
    HOT. I do not care. I'll give thrice so much
      land
To any well-deserving friend.
But in the way of bargain, mark ye me,
I'll cavil° on the ninth part of a hair.   140
Are the indentures drawn? Shall we be gone?
    GLEND. The moon shines fair, you may away by
      night.
I'll haste the writer, and withal
Break with° your wives of your departure hence.
I am afraid my daughter will run mad,   145
So much she doteth on her Mortimer.   [*Exit.*]
    MORT. Fie, Cousin Percy! How you cross my
      father!
    HOT. I cannot choose. Sometime he angers me
With telling me of the moldwarp° and the ant,
Of the dreamer Merlin° and his prophecies,   150
And° of a dragon and a finless fish,
A clip-winged griffin° and a molten raven,
A couching lion and a ramping° cat,
And such a deal of skimble-skamble° stuff
As puts me from my faith. I tell you what —   155
He held me last night at least nine hours
In reckoning up the several° devils' names
That were his lackeys. I cried " hum," and " well, go
      to,"
But marked him not a word. Oh, he is as tedious
As a tired horse, a railing wife,   160
Worse than a smoky house. I had rather live
With cheese and garlic in a windmill, far,
Than feed on cates° and have him talk to me
In any summerhouse° in Christendom.
    MORT. In faith, he is a worthy gentleman,   165
Exceedingly well read, and profited
In strange concealments;° valiant as a lion,
And wondrous affable, and as bountiful
As mines of India. Shall I tell you, Cousin?
He holds your temper° in a high respect,   170
And curbs himself even of his natural scope

When you come 'cross his humor; faith, he does.
I warrant you that man is not alive
Might so have tempted him as you have done
Without the taste of danger and reproof.   175
But do not use it oft, let me entreat you.
    WOR. In faith, my lord, you are too willful-
      blame;°
And since your coming hither have done enough
To put him quite beside his patience.
You must needs learn, lord, to amend this fault.   180
Though sometimes it show greatness, courage,
      blood —
And that's the dearest° grace it renders you —
Yet oftentimes it doth present harsh rage,
Defect of manners, want of government,°
Pride, haughtiness, opinion,° and disdain;   185
The least of which haunting a nobleman
Loseth men's hearts, and leaves behind a stain
Upon the beauty of all parts besides,
Beguiling° them of commendation.
    HOT. Well, I am schooled. Good manners be your
      speed!°   190
Here come our wives, and let us take our leave.
      [*Re-enter* GLENDOWER *with the* LADIES.]
    MORT. This is the deadly spite° that angers me —
My wife can speak no English, I no Welsh.
    GLEND. My daughter weeps. She will not part with
      you.
She'll be a soldier too, she'll to the wars.   195
    MORT. Good Father, tell her that she and my aunt
      Percy
Shall follow in your conduct speedily.
      [GLENDOWER *speaks to* LADY MORTIMER *in Welsh,
      and she answers him in the same.*]
    GLEND. She is desperate here, a peevish self-willed
harlotry,° one that no persuasion can do good   199
upon.
      [LADY MORTIMER *speaks in Welsh.*]
    MORT. I understand thy looks. That pretty Welsh°
Which thou pour'st down from these swelling
      heavens°
I am too perfect in; and but for shame,
In such a parley° should I answer thee.
      [LADY MORTIMER *speaks again in Welsh.*]
I understand thy kisses and thou mine,   205
And that's a feeling disputation.°
But I will never be a truant, love,
Till I have learned thy language; for thy tongue
Makes Welsh as sweet as ditties highly penned,
Sung by a fair queen in a summer's bower,   210

---

130. **meter balladmongers:** doggerel rhymesters. 131. **brazen . . . turned:** brass candlestick being cut out on the lathe. 140. **cavil:** raise objections. 144. **Break with:** break the news to. 149. **moldwarp:** mole. 150. **Merlin:** the old magician at King Arthur's Court. As the Welsh were (more or less) descendants of Arthur's British countrymen, Merlin's prophecies would appeal to Glendower. 151–53. **And . . . cat:** These beasts occur as symbols in ancient prophecies. **griffin:** fabulous beast — half lion, half eagle. 153. **ramping:** on its hind legs. 154. **skimble-skamble:** rambling. 157. **several:** separate, different. 163. **cates:** delicacies. 164. **summerhouse:** country house. 166–67. **profited . . . concealments:** expert in strange mysteries. 170. **temper:** character.

177. **willful-blame:** to be blamed for willfulness. 182. **dearest:** most valuable. 184. **government:** self-control. 185. **opinion:** conceit. 189. **Beguiling:** causing to lose. 190. **Good . . . speed:** may good manners bring you luck. 192. **spite:** vexation. 199. **harlotry:** silly girl. 201. **pretty Welsh:** i.e., tears. 202. **swelling heavens:** i.e., eyes full of tears. 204. **parley:** manner of speech. 206. **feeling disputation:** conversation by touch.

With ravishing division,° to her lute.
    GLEND. Nay, if you melt, then will she run mad.
        [LADY MORTIMER *speaks again in Welsh.*]
    MORT. Oh, I am ignorance itself in this!
    GLEND. She bids you on the wanton° rushes° lay
      you down
And rest your gentle head upon her lap,   215
And she will sing the song that pleaseth you
And on your eyelids crown the god of sleep,
Charming your blood with pleasing heaviness,°
Making such difference 'twixt wake and sleep
As is the difference betwixt day and night   220
The hour before the heavenly-harnessed team°
Begins his golden progress in the east.
    MORT. With all my heart I'll sit and hear her sing.
By that time will our book,° I think, be drawn.
    GLEND. Do so,   225
And those musicians that shall play to you
Hang in the air a thousand leagues from hence,
And straight they shall be here. Sit, and attend.
    HOT. Come, Kate, thou art perfect in lying down.
Come, quick, quick, that I may lay my head in thy
lap.   231
    LADY P. Go, ye giddy goose.   [*The music plays.*]
    HOT. Now I perceive the Devil understands
    Welsh,
And 'tis no marvel he is so humorous.°
By'r Lady, he is a good musician.   235
    LADY P. Then should you be nothing but musical,
for you are altogether governed by humors. Lie still,
ye thief, and hear the lady sing in Welsh.
    HOT. I had rather hear Lady, my brach,° howl in
Irish.   241
    LADY P. Wouldst thou have thy head broken?
    HOT. No.
    LADY P. Then be still.
    HOT. Neither — 'tis a woman's fault.   245
    LADY P. Now God help thee!
    HOT. To the Welsh lady's bed.
    LADY P. What's that?
    HOT. Peace! She sings.
    [*Here* LADY MORTIMER *sings a Welsh song.*]
Come, Kate, I'll have your song too.   250
    LADY P. Not mine, in good sooth.°
    HOT. Not yours, in good sooth! Heart! You swear
like a comfit-maker's° wife. "Not you, in good
sooth," and "as true as I live," and "as God shall
mend me," and "as sure as day,"   255
And givest such sarcenet surety for thy oaths°
As if thou never walk'st further than Finsbury.°
Swear me, Kate, like a lady as thou art,

211. **division:** melody. 214. **wanton:** luxuriant. **rushes:** used to
cover floors. 218. **heaviness:** drowsiness. 221. **team:** i.e., the
horses of the sun. 224. **book:** agreement. 234. **humorous:** full
of whims. 240. **brach:** bitch. 251. **sooth:** truth. 253. **comfit-
maker:** candymaker. 256. **sarcenet . . . oaths:** you swear by
such soft things. **sarcenet:** fine silk. 257. **Finsbury:** Finsbury
fields, whither London citizens took their Sunday-afternoon walk.

A good mouth-filling oath, and leave "in sooth"
And such protest of pepper gingerbread°   260
To velvet guards° and Sunday citizens.°
Come, sing.
    LADY P. I will not sing.
    HOT. 'Tis the next way to turn tailor,° or be red-
breast teacher.° An the indentures be drawn, 265
I'll away within these two hours, and so come in
when ye will.   [*Exit.*]
    GLEND. Come, come, Lord Mortimer, you are as
    slow
As hot Lord Percy is on fire to go.
By this our book is drawn. We'll but seal, 270
And then to horse immediately.
    MORT.   With all my heart. [*Exeunt.*]

SCENE II. *London. The palace.*

[*Enter the* KING, PRINCE OF WALES, *and others.*]
    KING. Lords, give us leave. The Prince of Wales
    and I
Must have some private conference. But be near at
    hand,
For we shall presently have need of you.
                  [*Exeunt* LORDS.]
I know not whether God will have it so,
For some displeasing service I have done,   5
That, in his secret doom,° out of my blood°
He'll breed revengement and a scourge for me;
But thou dost in thy passages of life
Make me believe that thou art only marked
For the hot vengeance and the rod of Heaven 10
To punish my misreadings. Tell me else,
Could such inordinate° and low desires,
Such poor, such bare, such lewd,° such mean at-
    tempts,
Such barren pleasures, rude society,
As thou art matched withal and grafted to,   15
Accompany the greatness of thy blood,
And hold their level with thy princely heart?
    PRINCE. So please your Majesty, I would I could
Quit° all offenses with as clear excuse
As well as I am doubtless I can purge   20
Myself of many I am charged withal.
Yet such extenuation let me beg
As, in reproof° of many tales devised,
Which oft the ear of greatness needs must hear,

260. **pepper gingerbread:** a very mild form of heat. 261. **velvet
guards:** literally bands of velvet used to ornament a gown (and
still used on the gown of a Ph.D.). See Pl. 9f and comment on
p. 94b. **Sunday citizens:** citizens in their Sunday best. 264. **turn
tailor:** Tailors (before the invention of the sewing machine) used
to sing at their work as they sat cross-legged. 265. **redbreast
teacher:** one who teaches caged birds to sing. The little English
robin was highly valued as a songbird.
Sc. ii: 6. **doom:** judgment. **out . . . blood:** through one of my
children. 12. **inordinate:** intemperate. 13. **lewd:** low. 19. **Quit:**
acquit myself of. 23. **reproof:** rebuttal.

By smiling pickthanks° and base newsmongers, 25
I may for some things true wherein my youth
Hath faulty wandered and irregular
Find pardon on my true submission.
 KING. God pardon thee! Yet let me wonder, Harry,
At thy affections, which do hold a wing 30
Quite from the flight° of all thy ancestors.
Thy place in Council thou hast rudely lost,
Which by thy younger brother is supplied,
And art almost an alien to the hearts
Of all the Court and princes of my blood. 35
The hope and expectation of thy time°
Is ruined, and the soul of every man
Prophetically doth forethink thy fall.
Had I so lavish of my presence been,
So common-hackneyed° in the eyes of men, 40
So stale and cheap to vulgar company,
Opinion,° that did help me to the crown,
Had still kept loyal to possession,°
And left me in reputeless banishment,
A fellow of no mark nor likelihood. 45
By being seldom seen, I could not stir
But like a comet I was wondered at,
That men would tell their children " This is he."
Others would say, " Where, which is Bolingbroke? "
And then I stole all courtesy from Heaven, 50
And dressed myself in such humility
That I did pluck allegiance from men's hearts,
Loud shouts and salutations from their mouths,
Even in the presence of the crownèd King.
Thus did I keep my person fresh and new, 55
My presence, like a robe pontifical,°
Ne'er seen but wondered at. And so my state,
Seldom but sumptuous, showed like a feast,
And won by rareness such solemnity.
The skipping° King, he ambled up and down, 60
With shallow jesters and rash bavin° wits,
Soon kindled and soon burnt; carded° his state,
Mingled his royalty with capering fools,
Had his great name profanèd with their scorns,
And gave his countenance, against his name,° 65
To laugh at gibing° boys and stand the push°
Of every beardless vain comparative,°
Grew a companion to the common streets,
Enfeoffed° himself to popularity,°

That, being daily swallowed by men's eyes, 70
They surfeited with honey and began
To loathe the taste of sweetness, whereof a little
More than a little is by much too much.
So when he had occasion to be seen,
He was but as the cuckoo is in June,° 75
Heard, not regarded; seen, but with such eyes
As, sick and blunted with community,°
Afford no extraordinary gaze,
Such as is bent on sunlike majesty
When it shines seldom in admiring eyes; 80
But rather drowsed and hung their eyelids down,
Slept in his face° and rendered such aspèct°
As cloudy° men use to their adversaries,
Being with his presence glutted, gorged, and full.
And in that very line,° Harry, standest thou; 85
For thou hast lost thy princely privilege
With vile participation.° Not an eye
But is aweary of thy common sight,
Save mine, which hath desired to see thee more,
Which now doth that I would not have it do — 90
Make blind itself with foolish tenderness.
 PRINCE. I shall hereafter, my thrice gracious lord,
Be more myself.
 KING.   For all the world
As thou art to this hour° was Richard then
When I from France set foot at Ravenspurgh, 95
And even as I was then is Percy now.
Now, by my scepter and my soul to boot,
He hath more worthy interest to the state
Than thou the shadow of succession;°
For of no right,° nor color like to right, 100
He doth fill fields with harness° in the realm,
Turns head against the lion's armèd jaws,
And being no more in debt to years than thou,°
Leads ancient lords and reverend bishops on
To bloody battles and to bruising arms. 105
What never-dying honor hath he got
Against renownèd Douglas! — whose high deeds,
Whose hot incursions° and great name in arms
Holds from all soldiers chief majority
And military title capital° 110
Through all the kingdoms that acknowledge Christ.
Thrice hath this Hotspur, Mars in swathling° clothes,
This infant warrior, in his enterprises
Discomfited great Douglas, ta'en him once,
Enlarged him, and made a friend of him, 115

---

25. pickthanks: men who curry favor by telling tales. 30–31. affections . . . flight: desires, natural inclinations . . . fly a different course. 36. time: lifetime. 40. common-hackneyed: at every man's call. A hackney is a hired horse. 42. Opinion: popular opinion. 43. loyal to possession: loyal to the possessor; i.e., Richard II. 56. robe pontifical: a bishop's robe. 60. skipping: frivolous. 61. bavin: brushwood for kindling, worthless and easily broken. 62. carded: adulterated. 65. against . . . name: contrary to the interest of his reputation. 66. gibing: mocking. stand . . . push: endure the sallies of. 67. beardless . . . comparative: every boy who cared to make jokes at his expense. 69. Enfeoffed: conveyed, made himself over to. popularity: low company, common people.

75. cuckoo . . . June: See App. II. 77. community: that which is common. 82. in . . . face: in his presence — a gross insult. aspect: look. 83. cloudy: sullen. 85. line: class. 87. vile participation: mixing with low company. 94. to . . . hour: up to now. 99. shadow of succession: shadowy right of succession. 100. of no right: with no right. 101. harness: armor. 103. no . . . thou: See I.i.92,n. 108. incursions: raids. 109–10. Holds . . . capital: keeps from all other soldiers the claim to be considered the greatest. 112. swathling: swaddling.

To fill the mouth of deep defiance up°
And shake the peace and safety of our throne.
And what say you to this? Percy, Northumberland,
The Archbishop's Grace of York, Douglas, Morti-
   mer,
Capitulate° against us and are up.   120
But wherefore do I tell these news to thee?
Why, Harry, do I tell thee of my foes,
Which art my near'st and dearest enemy?
Thou that art like enough through vassal° fear,
Base inclination, and the start of spleen°   125
To fight against me under Percy's pay,
To dog his heels and curtsy at his frowns,
To show how much thou art degenerate.
    PRINCE. Do not think so, you shall not find it so.
And God forgive them that so much have swayed
Your Majesty's good thoughts away from me!   131
I will redeem all this on Percy's head,
And in the closing of some glorious day
Be bold to tell you that I am your son;
When I will wear a garment all of blood,   135
And stain my favors° in a bloody mask
Which, washed away, shall scour my shame with it.
And that shall be the day, whene'er it lights,
That this same child of honor and renown,
This gallant Hotspur, this all-praisèd knight,   140
And your unthought-of Harry chance to meet.
For every honor sitting on his helm,
Would they were multitudes, and on my head
My shames redoubled! For the time will come
That I shall make this Northern youth exchange
His glorious deeds for my indignities.   146
Percy is but my factor,° good my lord,
To engross° up glorious deeds on my behalf.
And I will call him to so strict account
That he shall render every glory up —   150
Yea, even the slightest worship° of his time —
Or I will tear the reckoning from his heart.
This, in the name of God, I promise here.
The which if He be pleased I shall perform,
I do beseech your Majesty may salve°   155
The long-grown wounds of my intemperance.
If not, the end of life cancels all bands,°
And I will die a hundred thousand deaths
Ere break the smallest parcel° of this vow.
    KING. A hundred thousand rebels die in this.   160
Thou shalt have charge and sovereign trust herein.
[*Enter* BLUNT.] How now, good Blunt? Thy looks
   are full of speed.
    BLUNT. So hath the business that I come to speak
   of.
Lord Mortimer of Scotland hath sent word

That Douglas and the English rebels met   165
The eleventh of this month at Shrewsbury.
A mighty and a fearful head° they are,
If promises be kept on every hand,
As ever offered foul play in a state.
    KING. The Earl of Westmoreland set forth today,
With him my son, Lord John of Lancaster;   171
For this advértisement is five days old.
On Wednesday next, Harry, you shall set forward,
On Thursday we ourselves will march. Our meeting
Is Bridgenorth. And, Harry, you shall march   175
Through Gloucestershire, by which account,
Our business valued,° some twelve days hence
Our general forces at Bridgenorth shall meet.
Our hands are full of business. Let's away.
Advantage feeds him fat° while men delay.   180
                           [*Exeunt.*]

SCENE III. *Boar's Head Tavern in Eastcheap.*

[*Enter* FALSTAFF *and* BARDOLPH.]
    FAL. Bardolph, am I not fallen away vilely since
this last action?° Do I not bate?° Do I not dwindle?
Why, my skin hangs about me like an old lady's
loose gown,° I am withered like an old applejohn.°
Well, I'll repent, and that suddenly, while I am in   5
some liking.° I shall be out of heart° shortly, and
then I shall have no strength to repent. An I have not
forgotten what the inside of a church is made of, I
am a peppercorn, a brewer's horse° — the inside of a
church! Company, villainous company, hath been
the spoil of me.   11
    BARD. Sir John, you are so fretful you cannot live
long.
    FAL. Why, there is it. Come sing me a bawdy song,
make me merry. I was as virtuously given as a gentleman need to be — virtuous enough; swore little;
diced not above seven times a week; went to a
bawdyhouse not above once in a quarter — of an
hour; paid money that I borrowed, three or four   20
times; lived well, and in good compass.° And now I
live out of all order, out of all compass.
    BARD. Why, you are so fat, Sir John, that you must
needs be out of all compass, out of all reasonable
compass, Sir John.   26
    FAL. Do thou amend thy face, and I'll amend my
life. Thou art our admiral,° thou bearest the lantern

---

167. head: force.   177. Our . . . valued: considering how much
we have to do.   180. Advantage . . . fat: advantage makes the
most of his opportunities.
    Sc. iii: 2. last action: i.e., the Gadshill affair. bate: grow thin.
4. loose gown: See Pl. 9m. applejohn: withered apple, long kept.
6. in . . . liking: in good condition. out of heart: have no heart
for it.   9. brewer's horse: i.e., old and decrepit.   21. compass:
(lit., circumference) limits, with a pun on Falstaff's girth.   28. admiral: the admiral's ship, which led the way and carried a lighted
lantern by night so that the fleet should keep together.

---

116. To . . . up: so that defiance may speak with a loud mouth.
120. Capitulate: make agreement.   124. vassal: slavish.   125. start
of spleen: impulse of bad temper.   136. favors: features, face.
147. factor: agent, buyer.   148. engross: buy up wholesale.
151. worship: honor.   155. salve: heal.   157. bands: bonds,
debts.   159. parcel: portion.

in the poop,° but 'tis in the nose of thee. Thou art
the Knight of the Burning Lamp.   30
BARD. Why, Sir John, my face does you no harm.
FAL. No, I'll be sworn, I make as good use of it as
many a man doth of a death's-head° or a memento
mori.° I never see thy face but I think upon   35
Hell-fire and Dives° that lived in purple, for there he
is in his robes, burning, burning. If thou wert anyway given to virtue, I would swear by thy face; my
oath should be " By this fire, that's God's angel."°
But thou art altogether given over, and wert in-   40
deed, but for the light in thy face, the son of utter
darkness. When thou rannest up Gadshill in the
night to catch my horse, if I did not think thou hadst
been an ignis fatuus° or a ball of wildfire,° there's no
purchase in money. Oh, thou art a perpetual tri-   45
umph,° an everlasting bonfire light! Thou hast
saved me a thousand marks in links° and torches,
walking with thee in the night betwixt tavern and
tavern. But the sack that thou hast drunk me would
have bought me lights as good cheap at the dear-   51
est chandler's° in Europe. I have maintained that
salamander° of yours with fire any time this two and
thirty years, God reward me for it!   55
BARD. 'Sblood, I would my face were in your
belly!
FAL. God-a-mercy! So should I be sure to be heartburned. [*Enter* HOSTESS.] How now, Dame Partlet
the hen!° Have you inquired yet who picked my
pocket?   61
HOSTESS. Why, Sir John, what do you think, Sir
John? Do you think I keep thieves in my house? I
have searched, I have inquired, so has my husband,
man by man, boy by boy, servant by servant.   65
The tithe° of a hair was never lost in my house
before.
FAL. Ye lie, hostess. Bardolph was shaved° and
lost many a hair, and I'll be sworn my pocket was
picked. Go to, you are a woman, go.   70
HOSTESS. Who, I? No, I defy thee. God's light, I
was never called so in mine own house before!
FAL. Go to, I know you well enough.
HOSTESS. No, Sir John, you do not know me, Sir
John. I know you, Sir John. You owe me money,   75
Sir John, and now you pick a quarrel to beguile me
of it. I bought you a dozen of shirts to your back.
FAL. Dowlas,° filthy dowlas. I have given them

away to bakers' wives, and they have made bolters°
of them.   81
HOSTESS. Now, as I am a true woman, holland° of
eight shillings an ell.° You owe money here besides,
Sir John, for your diet and by-drinkings,° and
money lent you, four and twenty pound.   86
FAL. He had his part of it. Let him pay.
HOSTESS. He? Alas, he is poor, he hath nothing.
FAL. How! Poor? Look upon his face — what call
you rich? Let them coin his nose, let them coin   90
his cheeks. I'll not pay a denier.° What, will you
make a younker° of me? Shall I not take mine ease
in mine inn but I shall have my pocket picked? I
have lost a seal ring of my grandfather's worth forty
mark.   95
HOSTESS. Oh Jesu, I have heard the Prince tell
him, I know not how oft, that that ring was copper!°
FAL. How! The Prince is a Jack,° a sneak-cup.°
'Sblood, an he were here, I would cudgel him like a
dog if he would say so.   101
[*Enter the* PRINCE *and* PETO, *marching, and* FALSTAFF
meets them playing on his truncheon like a fife.]
How now, lad! Is the wind in that door, i' faith?
Must we all march?
BARD. Yea, two and two, Newgate fashion.°
HOSTESS. My lord, I pray you hear me.   105
PRINCE. What sayest thou, Mistress Quickly? How
doth thy husband? I love him well, he is an honest
man.
HOSTESS. Good my lord, hear me.
FAL. Prithee let her alone, and list to me.   110
PRINCE. What sayest thou, Jack?
FAL. The other night I fell asleep here behind the
arras, and had my pocket picked. This house is
turned bawdyhouse; they pick pockets.
PRINCE. What didst thou lose, Jack?   115
FAL. Wilt thou believe me, Hal? Three or four
bonds of forty pound apiece, and a seal ring of my
grandfather's.
PRINCE. A trifle, some eightpenny matter.
HOSTESS. So I told him, my lord, and I said I   120
heard your Grace say so. And, my lord, he speaks
most vilely of you, like a foul-mouthed man as he is,
and said he would cudgel° you.
PRINCE. What! He did not?
HOSTESS. There's neither faith, truth, nor womanhood in me else.   126
FAL. There's no more faith in thee than in a
stewed prune, nor no more truth in thee than in a

---

29. poop: stern.   34. death's-head: skull.   34–35. memento
mori: reminder of death.   36. Dives: the rich man in the parable of Dives and Lazarus. See Luke 16:19–31.   39. By . . .
angel: a parody of a line in Chapman's *Blind Beggar of
Alexandria*, a recent and popular play at the Rose Theater.
44. ignis fatuus: will-o'-the-wisp. wildfire: firework.   46. triumph: rejoicing, celebrated with torches and bonfires.   47. links:
torches used to light the way on a dark night.   52. chandler:
seller of candles.   54. salamander: a kind of lizard, believed to
enjoy fire.   59–60. Dame . . . hen: the wife of Chanticleer the
cock in the story of Reynard the Fox.   66. tithe: tenth part.
68. shaved: caught venereal disease.   78. Dowlas: coarse linen.

80. bolters: sieves for sifting flour from bran.   82. holland: fine
linen.   83. ell: 45 inches.   85. by-drinkings: drinks between
meals.   91. denier: the smallest English coin, worth 1/10d.
92. younker: "sucker."   97. copper: copper-gilt was the cheapest kind of imitation gold.   99. Jack: knave. sneak-cup: one
who steals cups from taverns, the lowest kind of theft.
104. Newgate fashion: i.e., like the chain gang. Newgate: the
London prison for felons.   123. cudgel: beat.

drawn fox,° and for womanhood, Maid Marian may be the deputy's wife of the ward to thee.° Go, you thing, go.   131

HOSTESS. Say, what thing? What thing?

FAL. What thing! Why, a thing to thank God on.

HOSTESS. I am no thing to thank God on, I   135
would thou shouldst know it. I am an honest man's wife. And, setting thy knighthood aside, thou art a knave to call me so.

FAL. Setting thy womanhood aside, thou art a beast to say otherwise.   140

HOSTESS. Say, what beast, thou knave, thou?

FAL. What beast! Why, an otter.

PRINCE. An otter, Sir John! Why an otter?

FAL. Why, she's neither fish nor flesh. A man knows not where to have her.   145

HOSTESS. Thou art an unjust man in saying so. Thou or any man knows where to have me, thou knave, thou!

PRINCE. Thou sayest true, hostess, and he slanders thee most grossly.   150

HOSTESS. So he doth you, my lord, and said this other day you ought° him a thousand pound.

PRINCE. Sirrah, do I owe you a thousand pound?

FAL. A thousand pound, Hal! A million!   155
Thy love is worth a million. Thou owest me thy love.

HOSTESS. Nay, my lord, he called you Jack, and said he would cudgel you.

FAL. Did I, Bardolph?   160

BARD. Indeed, Sir John, you said so.

FAL. Yea, if he said° my ring was copper.

PRINCE. I say 'tis copper.° Darest thou be as good as thy word now?   164

FAL. Why, Hal, thou knowest, as thou art but man, I dare; but as thou art Prince, I fear thee as I fear the roaring of the lion's whelp.

PRINCE. And why not as the lion?

FAL. The King himself is to be feared as the lion. Dost thou think I'll fear thee as I fear thy   170
father? Nay, an I do, I pray God my girdle break.

PRINCE. Oh, if it should, how would thy guts fall about thy knees! But, sirrah, there's no room for faith, truth, nor honesty in this bosom of thine; it is all filled up with guts and midriff. Charge an   175
honest woman with picking thy pocket! Why, thou whoreson, impudent, embossed° rascal, if there were anything in thy pocket but tavern reckonings, memorandums of bawdyhouses, and one poor penny-

worth of sugar candy to make thee long-   180
winded, if thy pocket were enriched with any other injuries° but these, I am a villain. And yet you will stand to it, you will not pocket up wrong. Art thou not ashamed?   184

FAL. Dost thou hear, Hal? Thou knowest in the state of innocency Adam fell, and what should poor Jack Falstaff do in the days of villainy?° Thou seest I have more flesh than another man, and therefore more frailty. You confess, then, you picked my pocket?   190

PRINCE. It appears so by the story.

FAL. Hostess, I forgive thee. Go, make ready breakfast. Love thy husband, look to thy servants, cherish thy guests. Thou shalt find me tractable° to any honest reason. Thou seest I am pacified   195
still.° Nay, prithee be gone. [*Exit* HOSTESS.] Now, Hal, to the news at Court. For the robbery, lad, how is that answered?

PRINCE. Oh, my sweet beef,° I must still be good angel to thee. The money is paid back again.   200

FAL. Oh, I do not like that paying back. 'Tis a double labor.

PRINCE. I am good friends with my father, and may do anything.   204

FAL. Rob me the exchequer the first thing thou doest, and do it with unwashed hands° too.

BARD. Do, my lord.

PRINCE. I have procured thee, Jack, a charge of foot.   209

FAL. I would it had been of horse. Where shall I find one that can steal well? Oh for a fine thief, of the age of two and twenty or thereabouts! I am heinously° unprovided. Well, God be thanked for these rebels, they offend none but the virtuous. I laud them, I praise them.   215

PRINCE. Bardolph!

BARD. My lord?

PRINCE. Go bear this letter to Lord John of Lancaster, to my brother John; this to my Lord of Westmoreland. [*Exit* BARDOLPH.] Go, Peto, to horse,   220
to horse, for thou and I have thirty miles to ride yet ere dinnertime. [*Exit* PETO.] Jack, meet me tomorrow in the Temple Hall at two o'clock in the afternoon.
There shalt thou know thy charge, and there receive Money and order for their furniture.°   226
The land is burning, Percy stands on high,
And either we or they must lower lie.   [*Exit.*]

FAL. Rare words! Brave world! Hostess, my
    breakfast, come!
Oh, I could wish this tavern were my drum! [*Exit.*]

---

129. **drawn fox**: fox driven out from cover, and so cunning. 129–30. **Maid . . . thee**: Maid Marian, the woman in Robin Hood's gang, was a character in a morris dance (see App. 24). She was played by a man as lumpish and awkward. The wife of the deputy of the ward was likely to give herself airs of dignity. Falstaff means "you are more lumpish than Maid Marian compared with a most stately matron." 152. **ought**: owed. 162. **if he said**: See Touchstone on the virtue of "if" as a means of making a safe threat (*AYLI*, V.iv.100–08). 163. **I . . . copper**: Here Falstaff gets the "lie direct." 177. **embossed**: swollen.

181–82. **pocket . . . injuries**: a pun on the phrase "to pocket up injuries." 187. **days of villainy**: these wicked times. 194. **tractable**: agreeable. 196. **still**: always. 199. **beef**: ox. 206. **unwashed hands**: without stopping to wash your hands. 212. **heinously**: atrociously. 226. **furniture**: equipment.

Act IV

SCENE I. *The rebel camp near Shrewsbury.*

[*Enter* HOTSPUR, WORCESTER, *and* DOUGLAS.]

HOT. Well said, my noble Scot. If speaking truth
In this fine age were not thought flattery,
Such attribution° should the Douglas have
As not a soldier of this season's stamp°
Should go so general current through the world. 5
By God, I cannot flatter, I do defy
The tongues of soothers;° but a braver place
In my heart's love hath no man than yourself.
Nay, task me to my word.° Approve° me, lord.
DOUG. Thou art the king of honor. 10
No man so potent breathes upon the ground
But I will beard° him.
HOT.　　　　Do so, and 'tis well.
[*Enter a* MESSENGER *with letters.*]
What letters hast thou there? —I can but thank
　you.
MESS. These letters come from your father.
HOT. Letters from him! Why comes he not him-
　self? 15
MESS. He cannot come, my lord, he is grievous
　sick.
HOT. 'Zounds! How has he the leisure to be sick
In such a justling° time? Who leads his power?
Under whose government come they along?
MESS. His letters bear his mind, not I, my lord.
WOR. I prithee tell me, doth he keep his bed? 21
MESS. He did, my lord, four days ere I set forth,
And at the time of my departure thence
He was much feared by his physicians.
WOR. I would the state of time had first been
　whole°
Ere he by sickness had been visited. 25
His health was never better worth° than now.
HOT. Sick now! Droop now! This sickness doth
　infect
The very lifeblood of our enterprise.
'Tis catching hither, even to our camp. 30
He writes me here that inward sickness —
And that his friends by deputation° could not
So soon be drawn,° nor did he think it meet
To lay so dangerous and dear° a trust
On any soul removed but on his own. 35

Yet doth he give us bold advértisement°
That with our small conjunction° we should on,
To see how fortune is disposed to us;
For, as he writes, there is no quailing now,
Because the King is certainly possessed° 40
Of all our purposes. What say you to it?
WOR. Your father's sickness is a maim to us.
HOT. A perilous gash, a very limb lopped off.
And yet, in faith, it is not; his present want°
Seems more than we shall find it. Were it good 45
To set° the exact° wealth of all our states
All at one cast?° To set so rich a main°
On the nice hazard° of one doubtful hour?
It were not good, for therein should we read
The very bottom and the soul of hope, 50
The very list,° the very utmost bound°
Of all our fortunes.
DOUG.　　　Faith, and so we should,
Where now remains a sweet reversion.°
We may boldly spend upon the hope of what
Is to come in. 55
A comfort of retirement° lives in this.
HOT. A rendezvous, a home to fly unto,
If that the Devil and mischance look big°
Upon the maidenhead of our affairs.
WOR. But yet I would your father had been here.
The quality and hair° of our attempt 61
Brooks no division. It will be thought
By some, that know not why he is away,
That wisdom, loyalty, and mere dislike
Of our proceedings kept the Earl from hence. 65
And think how such an apprehension
May turn the tide of fearful faction,°
And breed a kind of question in our cause;
For well you know we of the offering° side
Must keep aloof from strict arbitrament,° 70
And stop all sight holes, every loop from whence
The eye of reason may pry in upon us.
This absence of your father's draws° a curtain
That shows the ignorant a kind of fear
Before not dreamed of.
HOT.　　　You strain too far. 75
I rather of his absence make this use.
It lends a luster and more great opinion,
A larger dare to our great enterprise,
Than if the Earl were here; for men must think
If we without his help can make a head° 80
To push against a kingdom, with his help

<hr>

36. **advertisement:** advice.　37. **conjunction:** forces that have joined.　40. **possessed:** informed.　44. **his ... want:** the need of him at this present time.　46. **set:** hazard. **exact:** entire. 47. **cast:** throw of the dice. **main:** stake.　48. **nice hazard:** delicate chance.　51. **list:** limit. **bound:** boundary.　53. **reversion:** portion yet to come.　56. **comfort of retirement:** a place to which we can retire for comfort.　58. **look big:** threaten. 61. **hair:** nature.　67. **fearful faction:** timid rebellion.　69. **offering:** challenging.　70. **strict arbitrament:** exact judgment. 73. **draws:** draws back.　80. **make a head:** raise an army. See I.iii.284.

<hr>

Act IV, Sc. i: 3. **attribution:** citation of merits.　4. **season's stamp:** of this year's minting. The idea is that Douglas is like a new coin, acceptable (*current*) everywhere as valuable. 7. **soothers:** flatterers.　9. **task ... word:** cause me to make my word good. **Approve:** put to the proof.　12. **beard:** dare; lit., pull by the beard.　18. **justling:** jostling, disturbed.　25. **I ... whole:** I wish the times themselves had first been healthy. 27. **better worth:** worth more.　32. **deputation:** deputy; i.e., he could not send anyone else.　33. **drawn:** drawn together. 34. **dear:** important.

We shall o'erturn it topsy-turvy down.
Yet all goes well, yet all our joints are whole.

DOUG. As heart can think. There is not such a word
Spoke of in Scotland as this term of fear.   85

[*Enter* SIR RICHARD VERNON.]

HOT. My cousin Vernon! Welcome, by my soul.

VER. Pray God my news be worth a welcome, lord.
The Earl of Westmoreland, seven thousand strong,
Is marching hitherward; with him Prince John.

HOT. No harm. What more?

VER.   And further, I have learned,   90
The King himself in person is set forth,
Or hitherward intended speedily,
With strong and mighty preparation.

HOT. He shall be welcome too. Where is his son,
The nimble-footed madcap Prince of Wales,   95
And his comrades, that daffed° the world aside
And bid it pass?°

VER.   All furnished,° all in arms;
All plumed like estriches that with the wind
Bated like eagles having lately bathed;°
Glittering in golden coats, like images;°   100
As full of spirit as the month of May,
And gorgeous as the sun at midsummer;
Wanton° as youthful goats, wild as young bulls.
I saw young Harry, with his beaver° on,
His cuisses° on his thighs, gallantly armed,   105
Rise from the ground like feathered Mercury,°
And vaulted with such ease into his seat
As if an angel dropped down from the clouds
To turn and wind a fiery Pegasus,°   109
And witch° the world with noble horsemanship.

HOT. No more, no more. Worse than the sun in
   March,
This praise doth nourish agues. Let them come.
They come like sacrifices in their trim,°
And to the fire-eyed maid of smoky war
All hot and bleeding will we offer them.   115
The mailèd Mars° shall on his altar sit
Up to the ears in blood. I am on fire
To hear this rich reprisal° is so nigh
And yet not ours. Come, let me taste my horse,
Who is to bear me like a thunderbolt   120
Against the bosom of the Prince of Wales.
Harry to Harry shall, hot horse to horse,

Meet and ne'er part till one drop down a corse.
Oh that Glendower were come!

VER.   There is more news.
I learned in Worcester, as I rode along,   125
He cannot draw his power this fourteen days.

DOUG. That's the worst tidings that I hear of yet.

WOR. Aye, by my faith, that bears a frosty sound.

HOT. What may the King's whole battle° reach
   unto?

VER. To thirty thousand.

HOT.   Forty let it be.   130
My father and Glendower being both away,
The powers of us may serve so great a day.
Come, let us take a muster speedily.
Doomsday is near. Die all, die merrily.

DOUG. Talk not of dying. I am out of° fear   135
Of death or death's hand for this one half-year.

[*Exeunt.*]

SCENE II. *A public road near Coventry.*

[*Enter* FALSTAFF *and* BARDOLPH.]

FAL. Bardolph, get thee before to Coventry, fill me
a bottle of sack. Our soldiers shall march through,
we'll to Sutton Co'fil'° tonight.

BARD. Will you give me money, Captain?

FAL. Lay out,° lay out.   5

BARD. This bottle makes an angel.°

FAL. An if it do, take it for thy labor. And if it
make twenty, take them all, I'll answer the coinage.°
Bid my Lieutenant Peto meet me at town's end.   10

BARD. I will, Captain. Farewell.   [*Exit.*]

FAL. If I be not ashamed of my soldiers,° I am a
soused gurnet.° I have misused the King's press°
damnably. I have got, in exchange of a hundred and
fifty soldiers, three hundred and odd pounds. I   15
press me none but good householders, yeomen's°
sons; inquire me out contracted bachelors,° such as
had been asked twice on the banns; such a commod-
ity° of warm slaves as had as lieve° hear the Devil as
a drum; such as fear the report of a caliver°   20
worse than a struck fowl or a hurt wild duck. I
pressed me none but such toasts-and-butter, with

---

129. battle: main army.   135. out of: free from.
Sc. ii: 3. Sutton Co'fil': Sutton Coldfield, a town in Warwickshire.   5. Lay out: pay for it.   6. makes an angel: comes
to an angel (10s) which you owe me. See Pl. 10c.   7–9. take . . .
coinage: Falstaff deliberately misunderstands Bardolph's
"make" — "if the bottle will make angels, I'll guarantee the
coins."   12. If . . . soldiers: Falstaff (see following to l. 52) was
typical of many dishonest captains in the 1590's. His methods
of levying recruits are further shown in *II Hen IV*, III.ii. See
Gen. Intro. p. 30b–31a.   13. soused gurnet: pickled gurnet (sea
fish with a large head). King's press: the right to conscript
soldiers granted by the King's commission.   16. yeomen: wealthy
farmers.   17. contracted bachelors: bachelors engaged to be
married in a short time.   19. commodity: parcel. lieve: soon
20. caliver: lighter form of musket or harquebus, used by the
infantry. See Pl. 22f.

---

96. daffed: waved.   97. bid it pass: cried "let the world pass";
i.e., "who cares a damn?" furnished: in full armor.   97–99. All
. . . bathed: These lines are much annotated. As they stand they
mean: "All wearing plumes like ostriches that flap their wings
(*bate*) in the wind like eagles that have lately bathed." But the
comparison seems hardly apt. Either a line has been omitted
after *wind*, or *with* is a misprint of some such verb as
"wing."   100. images: i.e., of the saints in a Catholic church
103. Wanton: lusty.   104. beaver: visor of the helmet. See Pl. 8a.
105. cuisses: thigh pieces.   106. feathered Mercury: Mercury,
the messenger of the gods, wore winged sandals.   109. Pegasus:
Perseus's winged horse.   110. witch: bewitch.   113. in . . . trim:
dressed up.   116. mailed Mars: the god of war in his armor.
118. reprisal: prize.

hearts in their bellies no bigger than pins' heads, and they have bought out their services. And now my whole charge consists of ancients, corporals, 25 lieutenants, gentlemen of companies,° slaves as ragged as Lazarus in the painted cloth° where the glutton's dogs licked his sores; and such as indeed were never soldiers, but discarded unjust serv- 30 ingmen,° younger sons to younger brothers,° re- volted tapsters, and ostlers trade-fallen;° the cank- ers of a calm world and a long peace, ten times more dishonorable ragged than an old-faced ancient. And such have I to fill up the rooms of them that 35 have bought out their services that you would think that I had a hundred and fifty tattered prodigals lately come from swine-keeping, from eating draff and husks.° A mad fellow° met me on the way and told me I had unloaded all the gibbets° and 40 pressed the dead bodies. No eye hath seen such scarecrows. I'll not march through Coventry with them, that's flat. Nay, and the villains march wide betwixt the legs, as if they had gyves° on, for indeed I had the most of them out of prison. There's but a shirt and a half in all my company; and the half- 46 shirt is two napkins tacked together and thrown over the shoulders like a herald's coat° without sleeves; and the shirt, to say the truth, stolen from my host at St. Alban's, or the red-nose innkeeper of Daven- 50 try. But that's all one. They'll find linen enough on every hedge.°

[*Enter the* PRINCE *and* WESTMORELAND.]

PRINCE. How now, blown° Jack! How now, quilt! 54

FAL. What, Hal! How now, mad wag! What a devil dost thou in Warwickshire? My good Lord of Westmoreland, I cry you mercy. I thought your honor had already been at Shrewsbury. 59

WEST. Faith, Sir John, 'tis more than time that I were there, and you too; but my powers are there al- ready. The King, I can tell you, looks for us all. We must away all night.

FAL. Tut, never fear me. I am as vigilant as a cat to steal cream. 65

PRINCE. I think to steal cream indeed, for thy theft hath already made thee butter. But tell me, Jack, whose fellows are these that come after?

FAL. Mine, Hal, mine.

PRINCE. I did never see such pitiful rascals. 70

FAL. Tut, tut, good enough to toss,° food for pow- der, food for powder. They'll fill a pit as well as bet- ter. Tush, man, mortal men, mortal men.

WEST. Aye, but, Sir John, methinks they are ex- ceeding poor and bare, too beggarly. 75

FAL. Faith, for their poverty, I know not where they had that; and for their bareness, I am sure they never learned that of me.

PRINCE. No, I'll be sworn, unless you call three fingers° on the ribs bare. But, sirrah, make haste. Percy is already in the field. 81

FAL. What, is the King encamped?

WEST. He is, Sir John. I fear we shall stay too long.

FAL. Well,
To the latter end of a fray and the beginning of a feast 85
Fits a dull fighter and a keen guest.   [*Exeunt.*]

SCENE III. *The rebel camp near Shrewsbury.*

[*Enter* HOTSPUR, WORCESTER, DOUGLAS, *and* VERNON.]

HOT. We'll fight with him tonight.

WOR.   It may not be.

DOUG. You give him then advantage.

VER.   Not a whit.

HOT. Why say you so? Looks he not for supply?°

VER. So do we.

HOT.   His is certain, ours is doubtful.

WOR. Good Cousin, be advised, stir not tonight. 5

VER. Do not, my lord.

DOUG.   You do not counsel well.
You speak it out of fear and cold heart.

VER. Do me no slander, Douglas. By my life,
And I dare well maintain it with my life,
If well-respected° honor bid me on, 10
I hold as little counsel with weak fear
As you, my lord, or any Scot that this day lives.
Let it be seen tomorrow in the battle
Which of us fears.

DOUG.   Yea, or tonight.

VER.   Content.

HOT. Tonight, say I. 15

VER. Come, come, it may not be. I wonder much,
Being men of such great leading° as you are,
That you foresee not what impediments
Drag back our expedition.° Certain horse°
Of my cousin Vernon's are not yet come up. 20

25–26. **charge . . . companies:** Falstaff has picked up a selection of veterans of various ranks. **ancients:** ensigns, second lieu- tenants. **gentlemen of companies:** gentlemen of good family who served in the ranks of the companies of noblemen. 27. **Lazarus . . . cloth:** In taverns and less wealthy houses painted cloths showing scenes from Scripture and classical legend were hung on the walls instead of the more costly tapestry. See Pl. 6a. 31. **servingmen:** servants from some great household. See App. 14. **younger . . . brothers:** young gentlemen who had no hope of an allowance or a legacy. 32. **ostlers trade-fallen:** unemployed grooms. 39. **draff . . . husks:** offal and husks, like the Prodigal Son in the parable who "would fain have filled his belly with the husks that the swine did eat" (Luke, 15:11–32). **mad fellow:** wit. 40. **unloaded . . . gibbets:** The bodies of executed felons were often hung up in iron cages near the scene of the crime until they rotted. 44. **gyves:** fetters on the legs. 48. **herald's coat:** a sleeveless coat embroidered with the royal coat of arms. 51–52. **linen . . . hedge:** The washing was laid on the hedges to dry and air. See *W Tale,* IV.iii.23–24. 53. **blown:** inflated.

71. **good . . . toss:** i.e., on pikes; "good enough for cannon fod- der." 79–80. **three fingers:** i.e., three fingers' thickness of fat.
Sc. iii: 3. **supply:** reinforcements. 10. **well-respected:** well- considered (not foolhardy). 17. **leading:** experience in leader- ship. 19. **expedition:** haste. **horse:** cavalry.

Your uncle Worcester's horse came but today,
And now their pride and mettle° is asleep,
Their courage with hard labor tame and dull,
That not a horse is half the half of himself.

HOT. So are the horses of the enemy   25
In general, journey-bated° and brought low.
The better part of ours are full of rest.

WOR. The number of the King exceedeth ours.
For God's sake, Cousin, stay till all come in.
    [*The trumpet sounds a parley.*]
    [*Enter* SIR WALTER BLUNT.]

BLUNT. I come with gracious offers from the King,
If you vouchsafe me hearing and respect.   31

HOT. Welcome, Sir Walter Blunt, and would to
    God
You were of our determination!°
Some of us love you well, and even those some
Envy your great deservings and good name   35
Because you are not of our quality,°
But stand against us like an enemy.

BLUNT. And God defend° but still I should stand
    so
So long as out of limit and true rule
You stand against anointed Majesty.   40
But to my charge.° The King hath sent to know
The nature of your griefs, and whereupon
You conjure from the breast of civil peace
Such bold hostility, teaching his duteous land
Audacious cruelty. If that the King   45
Have any way your good deserts forgot,
Which he confesseth to be manifold,
He bids you name your griefs, and with all speed
You shall have your desires with interest,
And pardon absolute for yourself and these   50
Herein misled by your suggestion.°

HOT. The King is kind, and well we know the
    King
Knows at what time to promise, when to pay.
My father and my uncle and myself
Did give him that same royalty he wears.   55
And when he was not six and twenty strong,
Sick in the world's regard,° wretched and low,
A poor unminded outlaw sneaking home,
My father gave him welcome to the shore.
And when he heard him swear and vow to God   60
He came but to be Duke of Lancaster,
To sue his livery° and beg his peace
With tears of innocency and terms of zeal,°
My father, in kind heart and pity moved,
Swore him assistance, and performed it too.   65
Now when the lords and barons of the realm

Perceived Northumberland did lean to him,
The more and less came in with cap and knee —
Met him in boroughs, cities, villages,
Attended him on bridges, stood in lanes,   70
Laid gifts before him, proffered him their oaths,
Gave him their heirs as pages, followed him
Even at the heels in golden° multitudes.
He presently, as greatness knows itself,
Steps me a little higher than his vow   75
Made to my father while his blood was poor,
Upon the naked shore at Ravenspurgh;
And now, forsooth, takes on him to reform
Some certain edicts and some strait° decrees
That lie too heavy on the commonwealth,   80
Cries out upon abuses, seems to weep
Over his country's wrongs. And by this face,
This seeming brow of justice, did he win
The hearts of all that he did angle for —
Proceeded further, cut me off the heads   85
Of all the favorites that the absent King
In deputation° left behind him here
When he was personal° in the Irish war.

BLUNT. Tut, I came not to hear this.

HOT.   Then to the point.
In short time after, he deposed the King,   90
Soon after that, deprived him of his life.
And in the neck° of that, tasked° the whole state.
To make that worse, suffered his kinsman March,
Who is, if every owner were well placed,
Indeed his king, to be engaged° in Wales,   95
There without ransom to lie forfeited;
Disgraced me in my happy victories,
Sought to entrap me by intelligence;°
Rated° mine uncle from the Council board,
In rage dismissed my father from the Court;   100
Broke oath on oath, committed wrong on wrong;
And in conclusion drove us to seek out
This head of safety,° and withal to pry
Into his title, the which we find
Too indirect° for long continuance.   105

BLUNT. Shall I return this answer to the King?

HOT. Not so, Sir Walter. We'll withdraw a
    while.
Go to the King, and let there be impawned°
Some surety for a safe return again,
And in the morning early shall mine uncle   110
Bring him our purposes. And so farewell.

BLUNT. I would you would accept of grace and
    love.

HOT. And maybe so we shall.

BLUNT.   Pray God you do. [*Exeunt.*]

---

22. mettle: ardor.   **26. journey-bated:** tired by the journey.
33. determination: mind.   **36. quality:** fellowship, party. **38. defend:** forbid.   **41. my charge:** what I have been instructed (*charged*) to say.   **51. suggestion:** temptation.   **57. Sick . . . regard:** poorly regarded by the world. **62. sue . . . livery:** claim his inheritance. See *Rich II*, II.i.203; II.iii.129. **63. terms of zeal:** protestations of loyalty.

73. golden: wearing their richest clothes.   **79. strait:** strict.
87. In deputation: as his deputies.   **88. was personal:** went in person. **92. in . . . neck:** on top of. **tasked:** taxed. **95. engaged:** held as pledge, hostage. **98. intelligence:** spies. **99. Rated:** dismissed with abuse.   **103. head of safety:** armed force to keep us safe.   **105. indirect:** not in the straight line of descent. **108. impawned:** kept as hostage.

SCENE IV. *York. The* ARCHBISHOP'S *palace.*

[*Enter the* ARCHBISHOP OF YORK *and* SIR MICHAEL.°]
ARCH. Hie, good Sir Michael, bear this sealèd
    brief°
With wingèd haste to the Lord Marshal,
This to my cousin Scroop, and all the rest
To whom they are directed. If you knew   4
How much they do import, you would make haste.
    SIR M. My good lord,
I guess their tenor.°
    ARCH.   Like enough you do.
Tomorrow, good Sir Michael, is a day
Wherein the fortune of ten thousand men
Must bide the touch;° for, sir, at Shrewsbury,   10
As I am truly given to understand,
The King with mighty and quick-raisèd power
Meets with Lord Harry. And I fear, Sir Michael —
What with the sickness of Northumberland,
Whose power was in the first proportion,°   15
And what with Owen Glendower's absence thence,
Who with them was a rated sinew° too
And comes not in, o'er-ruled by prophecies —
I fear the power of Percy is too weak
To wage an instant° trial with the King.   20
    SIR M. Why, my good lord, you need not fear.
There is Douglas and Lord Mortimer.
    ARCH. No, Mortimer is not there.
    SIR M. But there is Mordake, Vernon, Lord Harry
    Percy,
And there is my Lord of Worcester and a head   25
Of gallant warriors, noble gentlemen.
    ARCH. And so there is. But yet the King hath
    drawn
The special head° of all the land together —
The Prince of Wales, Lord John of Lancaster,
The noble Westmoreland and warlike Blunt,   30
And many mo° corrivals° and dear men
Of estimation° and command in arms.
    SIR M. Doubt not, my lord, they shall be well op-
    posed.
    ARCH. I hope no less, yet needful 'tis to fear,
And, to prevent° the worst, Sir Michael, speed.   35
For if Lord Percy thrive not ere the King
Dismiss his power, he means to visit us,°
For he hath heard of our confederacy,°
And 'tis but wisdom to make strong against him.
Therefore make haste. I must go write again   40
To other friends. And so farewell, Sir Michael.
                  [*Exeunt.*]

Sc. iv: s.d., Sir Michael: He has not been identified, presumably a priest or knight in the Archbishop's service. **1. brief:**
letter. **7. tenor:** import. **10. bide . . . touch:** be put to the
test. **15. in . . . proportion:** the largest part. **17. rated sinew:**
strength highly valued. **20. instant:** immediate. **28. special
head:** crack troops, "shock troops." **31. mo:** more. **corrivals:**
supporters. **31–32. dear . . . estimation:** men highly regarded.
35. prevent: forestall. **37. visit us:** come our way. **38. confederacy:** conspiracy.

Act V

SCENE I. *The* KING'S *camp near Shrewsbury.*

[*Enter the* KING, PRINCE OF WALES, LORD JOHN OF
    LANCASTER, SIR WALTER BLUNT, *and* FALSTAFF.°]
KING. How bloodily the sun begins to peer
Above yon busky° hill! The day looks pale
At his distemperature.°
    PRINCE.   The southern wind
Doth play the trumpet° to his purposes,
And by his hollow whistling in the leaves   5
Foretells a tempest and a blustering day.
    KING. Then with the losers let it sympathize,
For nothing can seem foul to those that win.
    [*The trumpet sounds. Enter* WORCESTER
           and VERNON.]
How now, my Lord of Worcester! 'Tis not well
That you and I should meet upon such terms   10
As now we meet. You have deceived our trust,
And made us doff our easy robes of peace
To crush our old limbs in ungentle steel.
This is not well, my lord, this is not well.
What say you to it? Will you again unknit   15
This churlish knot° of all-abhorrèd war?
And move in that obedient orb° again
Where you did give a fair and natural light,
And be no more an exhaled meteor,°
A prodigy of fear,° and a portent   20
Of broachèd° mischief to the unborn times?
    WOR. Hear me, my liege.
For mine own part, I could be well content
To entertain the lag end of my life
With quiet hours, for I do protest   25
I have not sought the day of this dislike.
    KING. You have not sought it! How comes it,
    then?
    FAL. Rebellion lay in his way, and he found it.
    PRINCE. Peace, chewet,° peace!
    WOR. It pleased your Majesty to turn your looks
Of favor from myself and all our house.   31
And yet I must remember° you, my lord,
We were the first and dearest of your friends.
For you my staff of office° did I break
In Richard's time, and posted° day and night   35
To meet you on the way, and kiss your hand,
When yet you were in place and in account

Act V, Sc. i: s.d., Falstaff: It is worth noting that Shakespeare
places Falstaff in immediate attendance on the King. **2. busky:**
bushy. **3. distemperature:** sickness. **4. play . . . trumpet:** like
the trumpeter blowing an introductory flourish. **16. churlish
knot:** knot which unites men for a brutal purpose. **17. obedient
orb:** sphere of obedience, like a planet taking its natural course.
See App. I. **19. exhaled meteor:** meteor created of vapor drawn
up by the sun. **20. prodigy of fear:** a fearful sign of disaster.
21. broached: set loose; lit., tapped (like a cask). **29. chewet:**
jackdaw. **32. remember:** remind. **34. staff of office:** See *Rich
II*, II.iii.26–28 and Pl. 8d. **35. posted:** rode hastily.

Nothing so strong and fortunate as I.
It was myself, my brother, and his son
That brought you home, and boldly did outdare   40
The dangers of the time. You swore to us,
And you did swear that oath at Doncaster,
That you did nothing purpose 'gainst the state,
Nor claim no further than your new-fall'n right,°
The seat of Gaunt, Dukedom of Lancaster.   45
To this we swore our aid. But in short space
It rained down fortune showering on your head;
And such a flood of greatness fell on you,
What with our help, what with the absent King,
What with the injuries of a wanton° time,   50
The seeming sufferances° that you had borne,
And the contrarious winds that held the King
So long in his unlucky Irish wars
That all in England did repute him dead.
And from this swarm of fair advantages   55
You took occasion to be quickly wooed
To gripe° the general sway° into your hand;
Forgot your oath to us at Doncaster;
And being fed by us you used us so
As that ungentle gull,° the cuckoo's bird,°   60
Useth the sparrow — did oppress our nest;
Grew by our feeding to so great a bulk
That even our love durst not come near your sight
For fear of swallowing, but with nimble wing
We were enforced, for safety sake, to fly   65
Out of your sight and raise this present head.
Whereby we stand opposèd by such means
As you yourself have forged against yourself,
By unkind usage, dangerous countenance,°
And violation of all faith and troth°   70
Sworn to us in your younger enterprise.
    KING. These things indeed you have articulate,°
Proclaimed at market crosses, read in churches,
To face° the garment of rebellion
With some fine color that may please the eye   75
Of fickle changelings° and poor discontents,
Which gape and rub the elbow at the news
Of hurly-burly innovation.°
And never yet did insurrection want
Such water colors to impaint his cause,   80
Nor moody beggars, starving for a time
Of pell-mell havoc° and confusion.
    PRINCE. In both your armies there is many a soul
Shall pay full dearly for this encounter
If once they join in trial. Tell your nephew,   85
The Prince of Wales doth join with all the world
In praise of Henry Percy. By my hopes,

This present enterprise set off his head,°
I do not think a braver gentleman,
More active-valiant or more valiant-young,   90
More daring or more bold, is now alive
To grace this latter age with noble deeds.
For my part, I may speak it to my shame,
I have a truant been to chivalry,°
And so I hear he doth account me too.   95
Yet this before my father's majesty —
I am content that he shall take the odds°
Of his great name and estimation,
And will, to save the blood on either side,
Try fortune with him in a single fight.   100
    KING. And, Prince of Wales, so dare we venture thee,
Albeit considerations infinite
Do make against it. No, good Worcester, no,
We love our people well, even those we love
That are misled upon your cousin's part.   105
And, will they take the offer of our grace,
Both he and they and you — yea, every man —
Shall be my friend again and I'll be his.
So tell your cousin, and bring me word
What he will do. But if he will not yield,   110
Rebuke and dread correction wait on us°
And they shall do their office. So, be gone.
We will not now be troubled with reply.
We offer fair, take it advisedly.
                    [*Exeunt* WORCESTER *and* VERNON.]
    PRINCE. It will not be accepted, on my life.   115
The Douglas and the Hotspur both together
Are confident against the world in arms.
    KING. Hence, therefore, every leader to his charge,°
For on their answer will we set on them.
And God befriend us as our cause is just!   120
    [*Exeunt all but the* PRINCE OF WALES *and* FALSTAFF.]
    FAL. Hal, if thou see me down in the battle, and
bestride me so, 'tis a point of friendship.
    PRINCE. Nothing but a colossus° can do thee that
friendship. Say thy prayers, and farewell.   124
    FAL. I would 'twere bedtime, Hal, and all well.
    PRINCE. Why, thou owest God a death.   [*Exit.*]
    FAL. 'Tis not due yet, I would be loath to pay Him
before his day. What need I be so forward with him
that calls not on me? Well, 'tis no matter.   130
Honor pricks me on.° Yea, but how if honor prick
me off° when I come on? How then? Can honor set
to° a leg? No. Or an arm? No. Or take away the
grief of a wound? No. Honor hath no skill in surgery, then? No. What is honor? A word. What   135
is in that word honor? What is that honor? Air. A

44. **new-fall'n right:** inheritance which had recently come.
50. **wanton:** wild.   51. **sufferances:** injuries.   57. **gripe:** grip.
general sway: rule of the whole state.   60. **gull:** nestling.
cuckoo's bird: See App. II.   69. **dangerous countenance:**
threatening looks.   70. **troth:** truth.   72. **articulate:** drawn
up in schedules.   74. **face:** trim.   76. **changelings:** turncoats.
78. **hurly-burly innovation:** confusion and revolution.   82. **havoc:**
slaughter.

88. **set . . . head:** being excepted.   94. **chivalry:** knightly deeds.
97. **take . . . odds:** have the advantage.   111. **wait on us:** are
our servants.   118. **charge:** command.   123. **colossus:** See
Caesar, I.ii.135–38.   131. **Honor . . . on:** honor spurs me forward
to heroism.   131–32. **prick me off:** mark me down on the casualty list.   132–33. **set to:** mend.

trim° reckoning! Who hath it? He that died o' Wednesday. Doth he feel it? No. Doth he hear it? No.
'Tis insensible, then? Yea, to the dead. But will   140
it not live with the living? No. Why? Detraction°
will not suffer it. Therefore I'll none of it. Honor is
a mere scutcheon.° And so ends my catechism.

[*Exit.*]

SCENE II. *The rebel camp.*

[*Enter* WORCESTER *and* VERNON.]

WOR. Oh, no, my nephew must not know, Sir
Richard,
The liberal and kind offer of the King.
VER. 'Twere best he did.
WOR.   Then are we all undone.
It is not possible, it cannot be
The King should keep his word in loving us.   5
He will suspect us still, and find a time
To punish this offense in other faults.
Suspicion all our lives shall be stuck full of eyes;
For treason is but trusted like the fox,
Who, ne'er so tame, so cherished and locked up,   10
Will have a wild trick° of his ancestors.
Look how we can, or° sad or merrily,
Interpretation will misquote° our looks,
And we shall feed like oxen at a stall,
The better cherished, still the nearer death.   15
My nephew's trespass may be well forgot.
It hath the excuse of youth and heat of blood,
And an adopted name of privilege,°
A harebrained Hotspur, governed by a spleen.°
All his offenses live upon my head   20
And on his father's. We did train° him on,
And, his corruption being ta'en from us,
We, as the spring of all, shall pay for all.
Therefore, good Cousin, let not Harry know,
In any case, the offer of the King.   25
VER. Deliver° what you will, I'll say 'tis so.
Here comes your cousin.

[*Enter* HOTSPUR *and* DOUGLAS.]

HOT. My uncle is returned.
Deliver up° my Lord of Westmoreland.
Uncle, what news?   30
WOR. The King will bid you battle presently.°
DOUG. Defy him by the Lord of Westmoreland.
HOT. Lord Douglas, go you and tell him so.
DOUG. Marry, and shall, and very willingly.

[*Exit.*]

WOR. There is no seeming mercy in the King.   35
HOT. Did you beg any? God forbid!
WOR. I told him gently of our grievances,
Of his oath-breaking, which he mended thus,
By now forswearing° that he is forsworn.
He calls us rebels, traitors, and will scourge   40
With haughty arms this hateful name in us.

[*Re-enter* DOUGLAS.]

DOUG. Arm, gentlemen, to arms! For I have
thrown
A brave defiance in King Henry's teeth —
And Westmoreland, that was engaged,° did bear
it —
Which cannot choose but bring him quickly on.   45
WOR. The Prince of Wales stepped forth before
the King
And, Nephew, challenged you to single fight.
HOT. Oh, would the quarrel lay upon our heads,
And that no man might draw short breath° today
But I and Harry Monmouth! Tell me, tell me,   50
How showed his tasking?° Seem'd it in contempt?
VER. No, by my soul. I never in my life
Did hear a challenge urged° more modestly,
Unless a brother should a brother dare
To gentle exercise and proof of arms.   55
He gave you all the duties of° a man,
Trimmed up your praises with a princely tongue,
Spoke your deservings like a chronicle,
Making you ever better than his praise
By still dispraising praise valued with you.°   60
And, which became him like a prince indeed,
He made a blushing cital° of himself,
And chid his truant youth with such a grace
As if he mastered there a double spirit
Of teaching and of learning instantly.   65
There did he pause. But let me tell the world,
If he outlive the envy° of this day,
England did never owe° so sweet a hope,
So much misconstrued in his wantonness.
HOT. Cousin, I think thou art enamored   70
On his follies. Never did I hear
Of any prince so wild a libertine.
But be he as he will, yet once ere night
I will embrace him with a soldier's arm,
That he shall shrink under my courtesy.   75
Arm, arm with speed. And, fellows, soldiers, friends,
Better consider what you have to do
Than I, that have not well the gift of tongue,
Can lift your blood up with persuasion.

[*Enter a* MESSENGER.]

MESS. My lord, here are letters for you.   80
HOT. I cannot read them now.
O gentlemen, the time of life is short!

---

137. **trim**: neat. 141. **Detraction**: slander. 143. **scutcheon**: coat
of arms, painted on boards or cloth, carried in the funeral of a
gentleman and afterward hung up in the church.

Sc. ii: 11. **wild trick**: wild habits. 12. **or**: either. 13. **Interpretation . . . misquote**: men will deliberately misinterpret.
18. **adopted . . . privilege**: his nickname Hotspur will be his
excuse. 19. **spleen**: impetuosity. 21. **train**: lure. 26. **Deliver**:
report. 29. **Deliver up**: release. Westmoreland had been hostage
for Worcester's safe return. 31. **presently**: immediately.

39. **forswearing**: falsely denying an oath. 44. **engaged**: pledged
as hostage. 49. **draw . . . breath**: i.e., in fighting. 51. **tasking**:
challenge. 53. **urged**: put forward. 56. **duties of**: respect due to.
60. **By . . . you**: by continuously saying that your praise was
undervalued. 62. **cital**: recital. 68. **envy**: malice. 69. **owe**: own.

To spend that shortness basely were too long
If life did ride upon a dial's point,°
Still° ending at the arrival of an hour.   85
An if we live, we live to tread on kings;
If die, brave death when princes die with us!
Now, for our consciences, the arms are fair
When the intent° of bearing them is just.

[*Enter another* MESSENGER.]

MESS. My lord, prepare. The King comes on
apace.   90
HOT. I thank him, that he cuts me from my tale,
For I profess not talking, only this —
Let each man do his best. And here draw I
A sword whose temper° I intend to stain
With the best blood that I can meet withal   95
In the adventure of this perilous day.
Now, Esperance! Percy! and set on.
Sound all the lofty instruments of war,
And by that music let us all embrace;
For, heaven to earth, some of us never shall   100
A second time do such a courtesy.

[*The trumpets sound. They embrace, and exeunt.*]

SCENE III. *Plain between the camps.*

[*The* KING *enters with his power. Alarum to the battle.*° *Then enter* DOUGLAS *and* SIR WALTER BLUNT.]

BLUNT. What is thy name, that in the battle thus
Thou crossest me? What honor dost thou seek
Upon my head?
DOUG.   Know then, my name is Douglas,
And I do haunt thee in the battle thus
Because some tell me that thou art a King.   5
BLUNT. They tell thee true.
DOUG. The Lord of Stafford dear today hath
bought
Thy likeness; for instead of thee, King Harry,°
This sword hath ended him. So shall it thee
Unless thou yield thee as my prisoner.   10
BLUNT. I was not born a yielder, thou proud Scot,
And thou shalt find a King that will revenge
Lord Stafford's death.

[*They fight.* DOUGLAS *kills* BLUNT. *Enter* HOTSPUR.]

HOT. O Douglas, hadst thou fought at Holmedon
thus,   15
I never had triumphed upon a Scot.
DOUG. All's done, all's won. Here breathless lies
the King.
HOT. Where?
DOUG. Here.
HOT. This, Douglas? No. I know this face full
well.

A gallant knight he was, his name was Blunt,   20
Semblably furnished° like the King himself.
DOUG. A fool go with thy soul° whither it goes!
A borrowed title hast thou bought too dear.
Why didst thou tell me that thou wert a king?   24
HOT. The King hath many marching in his coats.°
DOUG. Now, by my sword, I will kill all his coats.
I'll murder all his wardrobe, piece by piece,
Until I meet the King.
HOT.   Up, and away!   28
Our soldiers stand full fairly for the day.° [*Exeunt.*]

[*Alarum. Enter* FALSTAFF, *alone.*]

FAL. Though I could 'scape shot-free° at London,
I fear the shot here. Here's no scoring but upon the
pate. Soft! Who are you? Sir Walter Blunt. There's
honor for you! Here's no vanity!° I am as hot as
molten lead, and as heavy too. God keep lead out of
me! I need no more weight than mine own   35
bowels. I have led my ragamuffins where they are
peppered.° There's not three of my hundred and
fifty left alive, and they are for the town's end, to beg
during life. But who comes here?   40

[*Enter the* PRINCE.]

PRINCE. What, stand'st thou idle here? Lend me
thy sword.
Many a nobleman lies stark and stiff
Under the hoofs of vaunting enemies
Whose deaths are yet unrevenged. I prithee lend me
thy sword.   44
FAL. O Hal, I prithee give me leave to breathe a
while. Turk Gregory° never did such deeds in arms
as I have done this day. I have paid Percy, I have
made him sure.
PRINCE. He is, indeed, and living to kill thee. I
prithee lend me thy sword.   50
FAL. Nay, before God, Hal, if Percy be alive, thou
get'st not my sword. But take my pistol, if thou wilt.
PRINCE. Give it me. What, is it in the case?
FAL. Aye, Hal, 'tis hot, 'tis hot. There's that will
sack a city.   56

[*The* PRINCE *draws it out, and finds it
to be a bottle of sack.*]

PRINCE. What, is it a time to jest and dally now?

[*He throws the bottle at him. Exit.*]

FAL. Well, if Percy be alive, I'll pierce° him. If he
do come in my way, so. If he do not, if I come in   60
his willingly, let him make a carbonado° of me. I

84. dial's point: hand of a clock.   85. Still: always.   89. intent:
cause.   94. temper: lit., hardness, quality.
Sc. iii: s.d., Alarum . . . battle: battle noises.   8. thee . . .
Harry: Blunt is wearing the King's coat of arms and not his
own, and so is mistaken by Douglas for the King.

21. Semblably furnished: wearing similar armor.   22. A . . .
soul: a proverbial phrase, "you foolish soul."   25. coats: coats
of arms.   29. full . . . day: i.e., are full of fight.   30. shot-free:
without paying the *shot* (the tavern bill) which had been
scored up against him.   33. no vanity: spoken ironically. "Who
said honor was not a vain thing?"   36–37. where . . . peppered:
Falstaff's heroism has a base motive. Until the army is remustered
he will pocket the pay of his dead soldiers.   46. Turk Gregory:
Pope Gregory VII, who had a reputation for ferocity. The Turk
was proverbial for cruelty.   59. pierce: pronounced "perse," a
pun on "Percy."   61. carbonado: piece of meat slashed for
broiling.

like not such grinning honor as Sir Walter hath.
Give me life, which if I can save, so; if not, honor
comes unlooked-for, and there's an end.　　　[*Exit.*]

SCENE IV. *Another part of the field.*

[*Alarum. Excursions.*° *Enter the* KING, *the* PRINCE,
LORD JOHN OF LANCASTER, *and*
EARL OF WESTMORELAND.]

KING. I prithee
Harry, withdraw thyself, thou bleed'st too much.
Lord John of Lancaster, go you with him.
　　LANC. Not I, my lord, unless I did bleed too.
　　PRINCE. I beseech your Majesty, make up,°　　5
Lest your retirement do amaze° your friends.
　　KING. I will do so.
My Lord of Westmoreland, lead him to his tent.
　　WEST. Come, my lord, I'll lead you to your tent.
　　PRINCE. Lead me, my lord? I do not need your
　　help.　　10
And God forbid a shallow scratch should drive
The Prince of Wales from such a field as this,
Where stained° nobility lies trodden on
And rebels' arms triumph in massacres!
　　LANC. We breathe° too long. Come, Cousin West-
　　moreland,　　15
Our duty this way lies. For God's sake, come.
　　　　　[*Exeunt* PRINCE JOHN *and* WESTMORELAND.]
　　PRINCE. By God, thou hast deceived me, Lan-
　　caster,
I did not think thee lord of such a spirit.
Before, I loved thee as a brother, John,
But now I do respect thee as my soul.　　20
　　KING. I saw him hold Lord Percy at the point
With lustier maintenance than I did look for
Of such an ungrown warrior.
　　PRINCE.　　　　　　　　Oh, this boy
Lends mettle° to us all!　　　　　[*Exit.*]
　　　　　　　[*Enter* DOUGLAS.]
　　DOUG. Another King! They grow like Hydra's
　　heads.°　　25
I am the Douglas, fatal to all those
That wear those colors on them. What art thou,
That counterfeit'st the person of a king?
　　KING. The King himself, who, Douglas, grieves at
　　heart
So many of his shadows° thou hast met　　30
And not the very King. I have two boys
Seek Percy and thyself about the field.
But, seeing thou fall'st on me so luckily,

I will assay° thee. So defend thyself.
　　DOUG. I fear thou art another counterfeit,　　35
And yet, in faith, thou bear'st thee like a king.
But mine I am sure thou art, whoe'er thou be,
And thus I win thee.
　[*They fight; the* KING *being in danger, re-enter*
　　　　　　　PRINCE OF WALES.]
　　PRINCE. Hold up thy head, vile Scot, or thou art
　　like
Never to hold it up again! The spirits　　40
Of valiant Shirley, Stafford, Blunt,° are in my arms.
It is the Prince of Wales that threatens thee,
Who never promiseth but he means to pay.
　　　　　　　　[*They fight:* DOUGLAS *flies.*]
Cheerly, my lord. How fares your Grace?
Sir Nicholas Gawsey hath for succor sent,　　45
And so hath Clifton. I'll to Clifton straight.
　　KING. Stay, and breathe a while.
Thou hast redeemed thy lost opinion,°
And showed thou makest some tender° of my life,
In this fair rescue thou hast brought to me.　　50
　　PRINCE. Oh God! They did me too much injury
That ever said I hearkened for° your death.
If it were so, I might have let alone
The insulting° hand of Douglas over you,
Which would have been as speedy in your end　　55
As all the poisonous potions in the world,
And saved the treacherous labor of your son.
　　KING. Make up to Clifton. I'll to Sir Nicholas
　　Gawsey.　　　　　　　　　[*Exit.*]
　　　　　　　[*Enter* HOTSPUR.]
　　HOT. If I mistake not, thou art Harry Monmouth.
　　PRINCE. Thou speak'st as if I would deny my
　　name.　　60
　　HOT. My name is Harry Percy.
　　PRINCE.　　　　　　　　Why, then I see
A very valiant rebel of the name.
I am the Prince of Wales. And think not, Percy,
To share with me in glory any more.
Two stars keep not their motion in one sphere,　　65
Nor can one England brook a double reign
Of Harry Percy and the Prince of Wales.
　　HOT. Nor shall it, Harry, for the hour is come
To end the one of us. And would to God
Thy name in arms were now as great as mine!　　70
　　PRINCE. I'll make it greater ere I part from thee,
And all the budding honors on thy crest
I'll crop, to make a garland for my head.
　　HOT. I can no longer brook thy vanities.
　　　　　　　　　　　　　　[*They fight.*]
　　　　　　　[*Enter* FALSTAFF.]
　　FAL. Well said, Hal! To it, Hal! Nay, you shall
find no boy's play here, I can tell you.　　76

Sc. iv: s.d., **Excursions:** noises to indicate rapid movements
in battle.　**5. make up:** go up to the front line.　**6. amaze:** fill
with dismay.　**13. stained:** bloodstained.　**15. breathe:** rest.
24. mettle: courage.　**25. Hydra's heads:** Hydra was a many-
headed monster slain by Hercules. As soon as one head was cut
off, two others grew in its place.　**30. shadows:** imitations.

34. assay: challenge.　**41. Shirley . . . Blunt:** who have all fallen
in the battle.　**48. opinion:** reputation.　**49. makest . . . tender:**
hast some regard for.　**52. hearkened for:** desired.　**54. insulting:** triumphing.

[*Re-enter* DOUGLAS; *he fights with* FALSTAFF, *who falls down as if he were dead, and exit* DOUGLAS. HOTSPUR *is wounded, and falls.*]

HOT. O Harry, thou hast robbed me of my youth!
I better brook the loss of brittle life
Than those proud titles thou hast won of me.
They wound my thoughts worse than thy sword my
    flesh.   80
But thought's the slave of life, and life Time's fool,
And Time, that takes survèy of all the world,
Must have a stop.° Oh, I could prophesy,
But that the earthy and cold hand of death
Lies on my tongue. No, Percy, thou art dust,   85
And food for ——   [*Dies.*]
    PRINCE. For worms, brave Percy. Fare thee well,
        great heart!
Ill-weaved ambition, how much art thou shrunk!
When that this body did contain a spirit,
A kingdom for it was too small a bound,°   90
But now two paces of the vilest earth
Is room enough. This earth that bears thee dead
Bears not alive so stout a gentleman.
If thou wert sensible° of courtesy,
I should not make so dear a show of zeal.°   95
But let my favors° hide thy mangled face,
And, even in thy behalf, I'll thank myself
For doing these fair rites of tenderness.
Adieu, and take thy praise with thee to Heaven!
Thy ignominy sleep with thee in the grave,   100
But not remembered in thy epitaph!
                    [*He spieth* FALSTAFF *on the ground.*]
What, old acquaintance! Could not all this flesh
Keep in a little life? Poor Jack, farewell!
I could have better spared a better man.
Oh, I should have a heavy miss of thee   105
If I were much in love with vanity!°
Death hath not struck so fat a deer today,
Though many dearer, in this bloody fray.
Emboweled° will I see thee by and by.   109
Till then in blood by noble Percy lie.   [*Exit.*]
    FAL. [*Rising up*] Emboweled! If thou embowel
me today, I'll give you leave to powder° me and eat
me too tomorrow. 'Sblood, 'twas time to counterfeit,
or that hot termagant° Scot had paid me scot and
lot° too. Counterfeit? I lie, I am no counterfeit. 115
To die is to be a counterfeit, for he is but the counterfeit of a man who hath not the life of a man. But to
counterfeit dying when a man thereby liveth is to be

no counterfeit, but the true an[...]
indeed. The better part of valo[...]
the which better part I have s[...]
I am afraid of this gunpowde[...]
dead. How if he should counte[...]
my faith, I am afraid he would[...]
counterfeit. Therefore I'll mak[...]
I'll swear I killed him. Why m[...]
as I? Nothing confutes me but[...]
me. Therefore, sirrah [*Stabbing him*], with a   130
new wound in your thigh, come you along with me.
                    [*Takes up* HOTSPUR *on his back.*]
            [*Re-enter the* PRINCE OF WALES *and* LORD JOHN
                    OF LANCASTER.]
    PRINCE. Come, Brother John, full bravely hast
        thou fleshed
Thy maiden sword.°
    LANC.   But, soft! Whom have we here?
Did you not tell me this fat man was dead?   135
    PRINCE. I did, I saw him dead,
Breathless and bleeding on the ground. Art thou
    alive?
Or is it fantasy° that plays upon our eyesight?
I prithee, speak, we will not trust our eyes   139
Without our ears. Thou art not what thou seem'st.
    FAL. No, that's certain, I am not a double° man.
But if I be not Jack Falstaff, then am I a Jack. There
is Percy [*Throwing the body down*]. If your father
will do me any honor, so; if not, let him kill the next
Percy himself. I look to be either earl or duke, I can
assure you.   146
    PRINCE. Why, Percy I killed myself, and saw thee
        dead.
    FAL. Didst thou? Lord, Lord, how this world is
given to lying! I grant you I was down and out of
breath, and so was he. But we rose both at an   150
instant, and fought a long hour by Shrewsbury
clock. If I may be believed, so; if not, let them that
should reward valor bear the sin upon their own
heads. I'll take it upon my death, I gave him this
wound in the thigh. If the man were alive, and   155
would deny it, 'zounds, I would make him eat a
piece of my sword.
    LANC. This is the strangest tale that ever I heard.
    PRINCE. This is the strangest fellow, Brother John.
Come, bring your luggage nobly on your back.   160
For my part, if a lie may do thee grace,
I'll gild it with the happiest terms° I have.
                        [*A retreat is sounded.*]
The trumpet sounds retreat,° the day is ours.
Come, Brother, let us to the highest° of the field,
To see what friends are living, who are dead.   165
            [*Exeunt* PRINCE OF WALES *and* LANCASTER.]

81–83. **thought's . . . stop:** thought can only exist while there is life, but life is treated like a fool by Time, and Time itself will end — a thought in one form or another constantly recurring in Shakespeare's plays. 90. **bound:** boundary. 94. **sensible:** able to feel. 95. **show of zeal:** mark of respect. 96. **favors:** scarf or handkerchief given to a knight by his lady. 106. **vanity:** folly. 109. **Emboweled:** disemboweled. He carries on the metaphor and pun of deer (l. 107), for the last act in the hunt was the disemboweling of the slain deer. 112. **powder:** pickle. 114. **termagant:** ferocious. 114–15. **paid . . . lot:** paid all dues.

133–34. **fleshed . . . sword:** you have fought bravely in your first action. 138. **fantasy:** imagination, illusion. 141. **double:** i.e., a double of myself. 162. **happiest terms:** best phrases. 163. **trumpet . . . retreat:** i.e., to recall the troops from the pursuit. 164. **highest:** i.e., ground.

...l follow, as they say, for reward. He that
...s me, God reward him! If I do grow great, I'll
...w less; for I'll purge, and leave sack, and live
...leanly as a nobleman should do. [*Exit.*]

SCENE V. *Another part of the field.*

[*The trumpets sound. Enter the* KING, PRINCE
OF WALES, LORD JOHN OF LANCASTER, EARL
OF WESTMORELAND, *with* WORCESTER *and*
VERNON *prisoners.*]

KING. Thus ever did rebellion find rebuke.
Ill-spirited° Worcester! Did not we send grace,
Pardon, and terms of love to all of you?
And wouldst thou turn our offers contrary,
Misuse the tenor of thy kinsman's trust?   5
Three knights upon our party slain today,
A noble Earl and many a creature else
Had been alive this hour
If like a Christian thou hadst truly borne
Betwixt our armies true intelligence.   10
  WOR. What I have done my safety urged me to.
And I embrace this fortune patiently,
Since not to be avoided it falls on me.
  KING. Bear Worcester to the death, and Vernon
    too.
Other offenders we will pause upon.   15
        [*Exeunt* WORCESTER *and* VERNON, *guarded.*]
How goes the field?
  PRINCE. The noble Scot, Lord Douglas, when he
    saw

Sc. v: 2. Ill-spirited: evil-spirited.

The fortune of the day quite turned from him,
The noble Percy slain, and all his men
Upon the foot of fear, fled with the rest;   20
And falling from a hill, he was so bruised
That the pursuers took him. At my tent
The Douglas is, and I beseech your Grace
I may dispose of him.
      KING.   With all my heart.
  PRINCE. Then, Brother John of Lancaster, to you
This honorable bounty shall belong.   26
Go to the Douglas, and deliver him
Up to his pleasure, ransomless and free.
His valor shown upon our crests today
Hath taught us how to cherish such high deeds   30
Even in the bosom of our adversaries.
  LANC. I thank your Grace for this high courtesy,
Which I shall give away immediately.
  KING. Then this remains, that we divide our
    power.
You, Son John, and my cousin Westmoreland   35
Toward York shall bend you with your dearest°
    speed,
To meet Northumberland and the prelate Scroop,
Who, as we hear, are busily in arms.
Myself and you, Son Harry, will toward Wales,
To fight with Glendower and the Earl of March.   40
Rebellion in this land shall lose his sway,
Meeting the check° of such another day.
And since this business so fair is done,
Let us not leave till all our own be won. [*Exeunt.*]

36. dearest: best.   42. Meeting ... check: incurring such a
disaster.

The Second Part of
KING HENRY THE FOURTH

Introduction[1]

The *Second Part of King Henry the Fourth* was probably written in the spring of 1598, soon after the *First Part* was printed. It continues the story where the *First Part* ended.

The play was entered for publication to Andrew Wise and William Aspley on August 23, 1600, and a first quarto was published soon afterward with the title: *The Second part of Henrie the fourth, continuing to his death, and coronation of Henrie the fift. With the humours of sir Iohn Falstaffe, and swaggering Pistoll. As it hath been sundrie times publikely acted by the right honourable, the Lord Chamberlaine his seruants. Written by William Shakespeare. London. Printed by V. S. for Andrew Wise, and William Aspley. 1600.* The play was not again printed until the first folio of 1623.

The quarto of 1600 is a fairly good text, possibly set up from Shakespeare's own manuscript, but it omits several striking passages which first appeared in the folio. The more important of these are Morton's speech to Northumberland (I.i.166–79); Lord Bardolph's speech on plotting a rebellion (I.iii.35–55); the Archbishop's speech on the fickleness of the mob (I.iii.85–108); Lady Percy's speech in memory of her dead husband (II.iii.23–45); the Archbishop's speech on the grievances of his party (IV.i.55–79); and the passage between Mowbray and Westmoreland (IV.i. 103–39). The reason for these omissions is clear. At a time when readers and playgoers were oversensitive to possible political allusions, and especially after the troubles caused by Hayward's *Life of Henry the Fourth* (see Gen. Intro. p. 45a, and *Rich II* Intro. p. 433a–b), it was but common prudence to omit any lines which might arouse the suspicions of the Council. By August 1600 Essex was in disgrace, but he had many sympathizers, and it would not have been difficult for a zealous informer to have found some parallel between Essex and Hotspur or between Essex's grievances

and those put out in the play by the party of the Archbishop of York.

The folio text was carefully revised and prepared for the press, but certain changes were made. In 1606 an Act of Parliament had been passed ordaining that anyone who in a stage play used the name of God, or of Christ Jesus, or of the Holy Ghost or the Trinity, should be fined £10 for each offense. As a result, the loose conversation of Falstaff and his friends was carefully purged; "Heaven" was substituted for "God," "in good earnest" for "God save me," "what" for "God's light"; even so mild a remark as "i' faith" was omitted.

In *II Henry IV* the Falstaff scenes were entirely Shakespeare's own invention, though some of the characters, such as Justice Shallow or Silence, may well have been portraits of worthies whom Shakespeare knew in his own home country. For his history, Shakespeare went as before to Holinshed's *Chronicle,* which gave him the necessary facts for the more serious scenes; but the events of the later part of the reign of Henry IV were not particularly dramatic, and Shakespeare contented himself with selecting a series of episodes to bridge the gap between the death of Hotspur at the Battle of Shrewsbury (which concluded Part I), and the accession of Prince Hal as King Henry V, which ends Part II. *II Henry IV* is thus rather a link between *I Henry IV* and *Henry V* than a drama complete and coherent in itself. Moreover, Holinshed's narrative was less colorful than usual, as some extracts will show:

1. THE REBELLION IN THE NORTH (cf. IV.i, ii, AND iii)

But at the same time, to his further disquieting, there was a conspiracy put in practice against him at home by the Earl of Northumberland, who had conspired with Richard Scroop, Archbishop of York, Thomas Mowbray, Earl Marshal, son to Thomas Duke of Norfolk (who for the quarrel betwixt him and King Henry had been banished, as ye have heard), the Lords Hastings, Faulconbridge, Bardolf, and divers others. It was appointed that they should meet all together with their whole power upon Yorkswold, at a day assigned, and that the Earl of Northumberland should be chieftain, promising to bring with him a great number of Scots. The Archbishop, accompanied with the Earl Marshal, devised certain articles of such matters as it was supposed that not only the commonalty of the realm, but also the nobility, found themselves grieved with; which articles they showed first unto such of their adherents as were near about them, and after sent them abroad to their friends further off; assuring them that for redress of such oppressions they would shed the last drop of blood in their bodies, if need were.

The Archbishop, not meaning to stay after he saw himself accompanied with a great number of men that came flocking to York to take his part in this quarrel, forthwith discovered his enterprise, causing the articles aforesaid to be set up in the public streets of the city of York, and upon the gates of the monasteries, that each man might understand the cause that moved him to rise in arms against the King, the reforming whereof did not yet appertain unto him. Hereupon, knights, esquires, gentlemen, yeomen, and other of the commons, as well as of the city, towns, and countries about, being allured either for desire of change or else for desire to see a reformation in such things as were mentioned in the articles, assembled together in great numbers; and the Archbishop, coming forth amongst them clad in armor, encouraged, exhorted, and (by all means he could) pricked them forth to take the enterprise in hand, and manfully to continue in their begun purpose, promising forgiveness of sins to all them whose hap it was to die in the quarrel. And thus not only all the citizens of York, but all other in the countries about, that were able to bear weapon came to the Archbishop and the Earl Marshal. Indeed, the respect that men had to the Archbishop caused them to like the better of the cause, since the gravity of his age, his integrity of life, and incomparable learning, with the reverend aspect of his amiable personage, moved all men to have him in no small estimation.

The King, advertised of these matters, meaning to prevent them, left his journey into Wales and marched with all speed toward the north parts. Also Ralph Neville, Earl of Westmoreland, that was not far off, together with the Lord John of Lancaster, the King's son, being informed of this rebellious attempt, assembled together such power as they might make, and, together with those which were appointed to attend on the said Lord John to defend the borders against the Scots (as the Lord Henry Fitzhugh, the Lord Ralph Ewers, the Lord Robert Umfreville, and others), made forward against the rebels and, coming into a plain within the forest of Gaultree, caused their standards to be pitched down in like sort as the Archbishop had pitched his over against them, being far stronger in number of people than the other; for (as some write) there were of the rebels at least twenty thousand men.

When the Earl of Westmoreland perceived the force of the adversaries, and that they lay still, and attempted not to come forward upon him, he subtly devised how to quail [quell] their purpose; and forthwith dispatched messengers unto the Archbishop to understand the cause as it were of that great assembly, and for what cause (contrary to the King's peace) they came so in armor. The Archbishop answered that he took nothing in hand against the King's peace, but that whatsoever he did tended rather to advance the peace and quiet of the commonwealth than otherwise; and where he and his company were in arms, it was for fear of the King, to whom he could have no free access by reason of such a multitude of flatterers as were about him; and therefore he maintained that his purpose to be good and profitable, as well for the King himself as for the realm, if men were willing to understand a truth. And herewith he showed forth a scroll, in which the articles were written whereof before ye have heard.

The messengers, returning to the Earl of Westmoreland, showed him what they had heard and brought from the Archbishop. When he had read the articles, he showed in word and countenance outwardly that he liked of the Archbishop's holy and virtuous intent and purpose, promising that he and his would prosecute the same in assisting the Archbishop, who, rejoicing hereat, gave credit to the Earl, and persuaded the Earl Marshal (against his will as it were) to go with him to a place appointed for them to commune together. Here, when they were met with like number on either part, the articles were read over, and without any more ado, the Earl of Westmoreland and those that were with him agreed to do their best to see that a reformation might be had according to the same.

The Earl of Westmoreland, using more policy than the rest, " Well," said he, " then our travail is come to the wished end; and where our people have been long in armor, let them depart home to their wonted trades and occupations. In the meantime let us drink together in sign of agreement, that the people on both sides may see it and know that it is true that we be light [agreed] at a point." They had no sooner shaken hands together but that a knight was sent straightway from the Archbishop to bring word to the people that there was peace concluded, commanding each man to lay aside his arms and to resort home to their houses. The people, beholding such tokens of peace as shaking of hands and drinking together of the Lords in loving manner.

they being already wearied with the unaccustomed travail of war, brake up their field and returned homeward. But in the meantime whilst the people of the Archbishop's side withdrew away, the number on the contrary part increased according to order given by the Earl of Westmoreland; and yet the Archbishop perceived not that he was deceived until the Earl of Westmoreland arrested both him and the Earl Marshal, with divers other.

2. THE DEATH OF HENRY IV (cf. IV.iv; v)

The morrow after Candlemas Day began a Parliament which he [King Henry IV] had called at London, but he departed this life before the same Parliament was ended; for now that his provisions were ready, and that he was furnished with sufficient treasure, soldiers, captains, victuals, munitions, tall ships, strong galleys, and all things necessary for such a royal journey as he pretended [intended] to take into the Holy Land, he was eftsoons taken with a sore sickness, which was not a leprosy, stricken by the hand of God (saith Master Hall) as foolish friars imagined, but a very apoplexy of the which he languished till his appointed hour, and had none other grief nor malady. So that what man ordaineth, God altereth at His good will and pleasure, not giving place more to the Prince than to the poorest creature living when He seeeth his time to dispose of him this way or that, as to His omnipotent power and divine providence seemeth expedient. During this his last sickness he caused his crown (as some write) to be set on a pillow at his bed's head, and suddenly his pangs so sore troubled him that he lay as though all his vital spirits had been from him departed. Such as were about him, thinking verily that he had been departed, covered his face with a linen cloth.

The Prince his son, being hereof advertised, entered into the chamber, took away the crown, and departed. The father, being suddenly revived out of that trance, quickly perceived the lack of his crown, and having knowledge that the Prince his son had taken it away, caused him to come before his presence, requiring of him what he meant so to misuse himself. The Prince with a good audacity answered: "Sir, to mine and all men's judgment you seemed dead in this world, wherefore I, as your next heir apparent, took that as mine own, and not as yours." "Well, fair son," said the King with a great sigh, "what right I had to it, God knoweth." "Well," said the Prince, "if you die King, I will have the garland and trust to keep it with the sword against all mine enemies, as you have done." Then said the King, "I commit all to God, and remember you to do well." With that he turned himself in his bed, and shortly after departed to God in a chamber of the Abbots of Westminster called Jerusalem, the twentieth day of March, in the year 1413, and in the year of his age forty-six, when he had reigned thirteen years, five months, and odd days, in great perplexity and little pleasure (or fourteen years, as some have noted, who name not the disease whereof he died, but refer it to sickness absolutely, whereby his time of departure did approach and fetch him out of the world) . . .

3. THE REFORMATION OF THE NEW KING (cf. v.ii; v)

Such great hope and good expectation was had of this man's [Henry V's] fortunate success to follow that within three days after his father's decease divers noblemen and honorable personages did to him homage and swore to him due obedience, which had not been seen done to any of his predecessors Kings of this realm till they had been possessed of the crown. He was crowned the ninth of April, being Passion Sunday, which was a sore, ruggy, and tempestuous day with wind, snow, and sleet, that men greatly marveled thereat, making divers interpretations what the same might signify. But this King even at first appointing with himself to show that in his person princely honors should change public manners, he determined to put on him the shape of a new man. For whereas aforetime he had made himself a companion unto misruly mates of dissolute order and life, he now banished them all from his presence (but not unrewarded or else unpreferred), inhibiting them upon a great pain [penalty] not once to approach, lodge, or sojourn within ten miles of his Court or presence. And in their places he chose men of gravity, wit, and high policy, by whose wise counsel he might at all times rule to his honor and dignity, calling to mind how once to the high offense of the King his father he had with his fist stricken the Chief Justice for sending one of his minions (upon desert) to prison, when the Justice stoutly commanded himself also straight to ward, and he (then Prince) obeyed. The King after expelled him out of his Privy Council, banished him the Court, and made the Duke of Clarence (his younger brother) president of Council in his stead.

II Henry IV thus shows many signs of being an afterthought, a sequel written when the first part—especially the Falstaff scenes—had proved successful beyond all expectation. When the two parts are compared, it is clear that several of the persons and episodes in Part II are expansions of persons or ideas which were more slightly sketched in Part I. The Hostess, who made only a brief appearance in Part I, has developed into Mistress Quickly; the parodies of Alleyn's tragic style in the play scene (*I Hen IV*, II.iv) are embodied in a complete character in Ancient Pistol; Falstaff's account of how he had collected recruits for his company (*I Hen IV*, IV.ii.12–52) is expanded into a long scene with Justice Shallow (*II Hen IV*, III.ii). Indeed Falstaff, who began as the stooge of Prince Hal in Part I, in Part II has become the major and dominating character.

These developments are signs that to meet popular demand Shakespeare sacrificed history to fiction. In Part I 1,501 lines were given to the historical scenes, and 1,539 lines to the comic plot; in Part II 1,370 lines were given to history, but 1,991 lines to the Falstaff story. The historical plot of Part I is a coherent whole; in Part II it consists simply of nine scenes from history. Of these, three are given to the remnants of the Percy family, three to the dying King, two to the rebellion in the North, and one to the new King's first acts on succeeding his father. King Henry IV is indeed almost a minor character in his own play. He is shown paying the last of the debts for his usurpation of the throne. At his first appearance he is worn out with care and utters the finest of many Elizabethan apostrophes to sleep; in his last scene, after rebuking the prodigal son whom he still misunderstands, he supplements the account of his own methods of winning the crown (*I Hen IV*, III.ii) with cynical advice on how his son should keep it. Shakespeare indeed in his plays from time to time expressed the most devoted sentiments for the divinity of kingship, but he had no illusions about the frailty of kings. The play also shows the final development of Prince Hal from the wild playboy of Part I to the stern King who emerges at the end of Part II.

Nevertheless, in Part II far more even than in Part I, Falstaff and his gang are the main interest. They have also increased in stature. Mrs Quickly is now a voluble gossip, with a wonderful flow of chatter which gushes out in a continuous and illogical torrent. Her husband has disappeared, and she is completely dominated by Falstaff, who sponges on her shamelessly. Bardolph's nose is as red as ever, and there are three newcomers — Doll Tearsheet, a professional lady who includes Falstaff among her most distinguished customers; Falstaff's boy; and above all Ancient Pistol, who is a living parody of the rival

acting company, for he struts about the stage in Alleyn's best manner, Tamburlaine style, his vocabulary made up of scraps and misquotations of the wilder melodramas then in the repertory of the Rose playhouse.

Falstaff himself has gained in bulk and in wit; his scenes of low comedy with Mrs Quickly and Doll Tearsheet are wilder, funnier, and much lower than anything in Part I, and the scenes with Justice Shallow are perfect. Yet Falstaff steadily degenerates, and his fall is as tremendous as his bulk. It has been a fashion among critics to exalt Falstaff and to denounce Prince Hal for so ruthlessly rejecting him. There is little to commend this view. The truth is that Falstaff, although a lovable and infinitely witty rogue, has become repulsive by the end of the play. Falstaff is a perpetual joke, but a joke must never go stale or take itself too seriously. The friendship between royalty and a private man, even if wholly respectable, calls for infinite tact; between Falstaff and the Prince it can exist only so long as Prince Hal has no serious responsibilities. Immediately the position changes, Falstaff must gracefully retire to his tavern to tell tall stories of the gay days when he was the Prince's favorite. When Falstaff fails to realize the change, he loses that sense of humor which is his one redeeming quality. His comedy turns to tragedy, for he commits the unforgivable sin against friendship of forcing his old friend into an intolerable position when he must choose between the claims of friendship and of duty.

With Pistol and Justice Shallow, Falstaff has ridden from Gloucestershire, and arrives in London as King Henry V is coming from his coronation. At this most embarrassing and public moment the King is confronted by the sins of his youth incarnate in this gross bodily form. Everyone is watching to see what he will do; in that instant Henry must choose between his past and his future, and as Falstaff should have known long since, the King will not hesitate. So Falstaff's bubble is pricked and he shrinks away. His end is regrettable but inevitable, for Sir John — not Henry V — has been false to himself.

Henry IV, Part II

DRAMATIS PERSONAE

RUMOR, *the Presenter*
KING HENRY *the Fourth*
HENRY, PRINCE OF WALES, *after-*
ward King Henry V
THOMAS, DUKE OF CLARENCE ⎫ *his sons*
PRINCE JOHN OF LANCASTER ⎬
PRINCE HUMPHREY OF GLOUCESTER ⎭
EARL OF WARWICK
EARL OF WESTMORELAND
EARL OF SURREY
GOWER
HARCOURT
BLUNT
LORD CHIEF JUSTICE *of the King's Bench*
A SERVANT *of the Chief Justice*
EARL OF NORTHUMBERLAND
SCROOP, *Archbishop of York*
LORD MOWBRAY
LORD HASTINGS
LORD BARDOLPH
SIR JOHN COLEVILE
TRAVERS *and* MORTON, *retainers of Northumberland*

SIR JOHN FALSTAFF
HIS PAGE
BARDOLPH
PISTOL
POINS
PETO
SHALLOW ⎫ *country justices*
SILENCE ⎬
DAVY, *servant to Shallow*
MOULDY, SHADOW, WART, FEEBLE, *and* BULLCALF, *re-*
cruits
FANG *and* SNARE, *sheriff's officers*

LADY NORTHUMBERLAND
LADY PERCY
MISTRESS QUICKLY, *hostess of a tavern in Eastcheap*
DOLL TEARSHEET

LORDS *and* ATTENDANTS; PORTER, DRAWERS, BEADLES,
GROOMS, &c. A DANCER, *speaker of the epilogue*

SCENE — *England.*

INDUCTION°

Warkworth.° Before the castle.

[*Enter* RUMOR, *painted full of tongues.°*]
RUM. Open your ears, for which of you will stop
The vent° of hearing when loud Rumor speaks?
I, from the Orient to the drooping West,
Making the wind my post horse,° still° unfold
The acts commencèd on this ball of earth.   5
Upon my tongues continual slanders ride,
The which in every language I pronounce,
Stuffing the ears of men with false reports.
I speak of peace while covert° enmity
Under the smile of safety wounds the world.   10
And who but Rumor, who but only I,
Make fearful musters° and prepared defense
Whiles the big year, swoln° with some other grief,
Is thought with child by the stern tyrant war,
And no such matter? Rumor is a pipe°   15
Blown by surmises, jealousies, conjectures,
And of so easy and so plain a stop°
That the blunt monster with uncounted heads,
The still-discordant° wavering multitude,
Can play upon it. But what need I thus   20
My well-known body to anatomize°
Among my household?° Why is Rumor here?
I run before King Harry's victory,
Who in a bloody field by Shrewsbury
Hath beaten down young Hotspur and his troops,
Quenching the flame of bold rebellion   26
Even with the rebels' blood. But what mean I
To speak so true at first? My office is
To noise abroad that Harry Monmouth fell
Under the wrath of noble Hotspur's sword,   30
And that the King before the Douglas' rage
Stooped his anointed head as low as death.
This have I rumored through the peasant towns
Between that royal field of Shrewsbury
And this worm-eaten hold° of ragged° stone,   35
Where Hotspur's father, old Northumberland,

Induction: introduction. Shakespeare seldom used any introduction, but with other dramatists it was common at this time
for plays to be introduced by a short prologue spoken by a
Chorus, or Presenter. **s.d., Warkworth:** in Northumberland.
s.d., Rumor . . . tongues: wearing a robe decorated with tongues.
2. vent: passage. **4. post horse:** See App. **17. still:** always, continually. **9. covert:** secret. **12. Make . . . musters:** Shakespeare
had in mind his own times. During the 1590's there were
continual rumors of invasions and preparations. See Gen. Intro.
pp. 28b–31a. **13. swoln:** swollen.

15. pipe: i.e., musical instrument. **17. plain a stop:** i.e., easy to
play. **19. still-discordant:** always jarring; i.e., disagreeing.
21. anatomize: analyze. **22. Among my household:** i.e., this
crowded playhouse. **35. hold:** fortress. **ragged:** rough.

Lies crafty-sick.° The posts come tiring on,
And not a man of them brings other news
Than they have learned of me. From Rumor's
    tongues   39
They bring smooth comforts false, worse than true
    wrongs.   [*Exit.*]

Act I

SCENE I. *The same.*

[*Enter* LORD BARDOLPH.]

L. BARD. Who keeps the gate here, ho? [*The* POR-
TER *opens the gate.*] Where is the Earl?
POR. What shall I say you are?
L. BARD.   Tell thou the Earl
That the Lord Bardolph doth attend° him here.
    POR. His lordship is walked forth into the orchard.
Please it your Honor, knock but at the gate   5
And he himself will answer.
    [*Enter* NORTHUMBERLAND.]
L. BARD.   Here comes the Earl. [*Exit* PORTER.]
NORTH. What news, Lord Bardolph? Every min-
    ute now
Should be the father of some stratagem.°
The times are wild. Contention, like a horse
Full of high feeding, madly hath broke loose   10
And bears down all before him.
    L. BARD.   Noble Earl,
I bring you certain° news from Shrewsbury.
    NORTH. Good, an° God will!
    L. BARD.   As good as heart can wish.
The King is almost wounded to the death,
And in the fortune° of my lord your son,   15
Prince Harry slain outright, and both the Blunts
Killed by the hand of Douglas. Young Prince John
And Westmoreland and Stafford fled the field,
And Harry Monmouth's brawn, the hulk Sir John,°
Is prisoner to your son. Oh, such a day,   20
So fought, so followed, and so fairly won,
Came not till now to dignify the times
Since Caesar's fortunes!
    NORTH.   How is this derived?
Saw you the field? Came you from Shrewsbury?
    L. BARD. I spake with one, my lord, that came from
    thence,   25
A gentleman well bred and of good name,

That freely rendered me these news for true.
    NORTH. Here comes my servant Travers, whom I
    sent
On Tuesday last to listen after news.
    [*Enter* TRAVERS.]
L. BARD. My lord, I overrode° him on the way,
And he is furnished with no certainties   31
More than he haply may retail from me.
    NORTH. Now, Travers, what good tidings comes
    with you?
    TRA. My lord, Sir John Umfrevile turned me back
With joyful tidings, and, being better horsed,   35
Outrode me. After him came spurring hard
A gentleman, almost forspent° with speed,
That stopped by me to breathe° his bloodied horse.
He asked the way to Chester, and of him
I did demand what news from Shrewsbury.   40
He told me that rebellion had bad luck,
And that young Harry Percy's spur was cold.
With that, he gave his able° horse the head,
And bending forward struck his armèd heels
Against the panting sides of his poor jade°   45
Up to the rowelhead,° and starting so
He seemed in running to devour the way,
Staying no longer question.
    NORTH.   Ha! Again.
Said he young Harry Percy's spur was cold?
Of Hotspur Coldspur? That rebellion   50
Had met ill luck?
    L. BARD.   My lord, I'll tell you what—
If my young lord your son have not the day,
Upon mine honor, for a silken point°
I'll give my barony. Never talk of it.
    NORTH. Why should that gentleman that rode by
    Travers   55
Give then such instances of loss?
    L. BARD.   Who, he?
He was some hilding° fellow that had stolen
The horse he rode on, and, upon my life,
Spoke at a venture. Look, here comes more news.
    [*Enter* MORTON.]
    NORTH. Yea, this man's brow, like to a title leaf,
Foretells the nature of a tragic volume.°   61
So looks the strond° whereon the imperious flood
Hath left a witnessed usurpation.°
Say, Morton, didst thou come from Shrewsbury?
    MOR. I ran from Shrewsbury, my noble lord,   65
Where hateful death put on his ugliest mask
To fright our party.
    NORTH.   How doth my son and brother?

---

37. crafty-sick: pretending to be sick. See *I Hen IV*, IV.i.13–42.
    Act I, Sc. i: 3. attend: wait on. **8. stratagem:** deed of violence.
12. certain: sure. **13. an:** if. **15. in . . . fortune:** by the good
fortune. **19. brawn . . . John:** It is worth noting that Sir John
Falstaff is quite seriously regarded as one of the principal supporters of the King. **brawn:** fat pig. **hulk:** large cargo ship, and
so a man of immense bulk.

30. overrode: overtook. **37. forspent:** utterly exhausted.
38. breathe: rest. **43. able:** strong. **45. jade:** horse in poor condition or vicious. **46. rowelhead:** prick of the spur. **53. silken
point:** silk lace for tying the doublet to the hose, so a thing of no
value; e.g., "shoestring." **57. hilding:** worthless. **60–61. title
. . . volume:** like the title page of a tragedy. For a specimen,
see Pl. 14a. **62. strond:** shore. **62–63. imperious . . . usurpation:** like the desolate wreckage left on the shore after a high
flood.

Thou tremblest, and the whiteness in thy cheek
Is apter than thy tongue to tell thy errand.
Even such a man, so faint, so spiritless,   70
So dull, so dead in look, so woebegone,
Drew Priam's° curtain in the dead of night
And would have told him half his Troy was burned.
But Priam found the fire ere he his tongue,
And I my Percy's death ere thou report'st it.   75
This thou wouldst say, "Your son did thus and thus,
Your brother thus. So fought the noble Douglas"—
Stopping my greedy ear with their bold deeds.
But in the end, to stop my ear indeed,
Thou hast a sigh to blow away this praise,   80
Ending with "Brother, son, and all are dead."
     MOR. Douglas is living, and your brother, yet,
But for my lord your son——
     NORTH.   Why, he is dead.
See what a ready tongue suspicion hath!
He that but fears the thing he would not know   85
Hath by instinct knowledge from others' eyes
That what he feared is chanced.° Yet speak, Morton.
Tell thou an earl his divination° lies,
And I will take it as a sweet disgrace,
And make thee rich for doing me such wrong.   90
     MOR. You are too great to be by me gainsaid.°
Your spirit is too true, your fears too certain.
     NORTH. Yet, for all this, say not that Percy's dead.
I see a strange° confession in thine eye.
Thou shakest thy head, and hold'st it fear or sin 95
To speak a truth. If he be slain, say so.
The tongue offends not that reports his death.
And he doth sin that doth belie° the dead,
Not he which says the dead is not alive.
Yet the first bringer of unwelcome news   100
Hath but a losing office,° and his tongue
Sounds ever after as a sullen bell
Remembered tolling a departing friend.°
     L. BARD. I cannot think, my lord, your son is dead.
     MOR. I am sorry I should force you to believe 105
That which I would to God I had not seen.
But these mine eyes saw him in bloody state,
Rendering faint quittance,° wearied and out-
     breathed,
To Harry Monmouth, whose swift wrath beat down
The never-daunted Percy to the earth,   110
From whence with life he never more sprung up.
In few,° his death, whose spirit lent a fire
Even to the dullest peasant in his camp,
Being bruited° once, took fire and heat away
From the best-tempered° courage in his troops.   115

For from his metal was his party steeled,
Which once in him abated,° all the rest
Turned on themselves, like dull and heavy lead.
And as the thing that's heavy in itself
Upon enforcement° flies with greatest speed,   120
So did our men, heavy in Hotspur's loss,
Lend to this weight such lightness with their fear
That arrows fled not swifter toward their aim
Than did our soldiers, aiming at their safety,
Fly from the field. Then was that noble Worcester
Too soon ta'en prisoner. And that furious Scot,   126
The bloody Douglas, whose well-laboring sword
Had three times slain the appearance° of the King,
'Gan° vail his stomach° and did grace° the shame
Of those that turned their backs, and in his flight,
Stumbling in fear, was took. The sum of all   131
Is that the King hath won, and hath sent out
A speedy power° to encounter you, my lord,
Under the conduct° of young Lancaster
And Westmoreland. This is the news at full.   135
     NORTH. For this I shall have time enough to
         mourn.
In poison there is physic, and these news,
Having been well, that would have made me sick,
Being sick, have in some measure made me well.
And as the wretch whose fever-weakened joints,
Like strengthless hinges, buckle under life,   141
Impatient of his fit, breaks like a fire
Out of his keeper's° arms, even so my limbs,
Weakened with grief, being now enraged with
         grief,
Are thrice themselves. Hence, therefore, thou nice°
         crutch!   145
A scaly gauntlet° now with joints of steel
Must glove this hand. And hence, thou sickly quoif!°
Thou art a guard too wanton° for the head
Which princes, fleshed° with conquest, aim to hit.
Now bind my brows with iron, and approach   150
The ragged'st hour that time and spite dare bring
To frown upon the enraged Northumberland!
Let Heaven kiss earth! Now let not Nature's hand
Keep the wild flood confined! Let order die!
And let this world no longer be a stage   155
To feed contention in a lingering act,°
But let one spirit of the firstborn Cain°
Reign in all bosoms, that, each heart being set
On bloody courses, the rude scene may end,
And darkness be the burier of the dead!   160

---

72. **Priam:** King of Troy, which after ten years' siege was sacked by the Greeks. See *Haml*, II.ii.472–541.   87. **is chanced:** has happened.   88. **divination:** prophecy, intuition of disaster.   91. **gainsaid:** denied.   94. **strange:** uneasy.   98. **belie:** lie about.   101. **losing office:** duty which brings him loss.   103. **tolling . . . friend:** See App. 19.   108. **quittance:** payment, return of blows.   112. **few:** few words.   114. **bruited:** rumored.   115. **best-tempered:** of the finest quality of steel.

117. **abated:** brought low.   120. **Upon enforcement:** when forced into motion.   128. **slain . . . appearance:** See *I Hen IV*, V.iii.& 129. **'Gan:** began. **vail . . . stomach:** lower his courage. **grace:** do grace to, justify.   133. **power:** force.   134. **conduct:** leadership.   143. **keeper:** nurse.   145. **nice:** delicate.   146. **scaly gauntlet:** steel glove. See Pl. 8a.   147. **quoif:** cap to keep the head warm.   148. **wanton:** frivolous.   149. **fleshed:** eager to taste blood.   156. **To . . . act:** to maintain strife in an act which seems never-ending; i.e., let the present strife be brought to a swift, bloody conclusion.   157. **firstborn Cain:** i.e., the first murderer.

TRA. This strainèd° passion doth you wrong, my
    lord.

L. BARD. Sweet Earl, divorce not wisdom from
    your honor.

MOR. The lives of all your loving complices°
Lean on your health, the which if you give o'er
To stormy passion must perforce decay.   165
You cast the event° of war, my noble lord,
And summed the account of chance, before you said
"Let us make head."° It was your presurmise
That, in the dole° of blows, your son might drop.
You knew he walked o'er perils, on an edge,   170
More likely to fall in than to get o'er.
You were advised his flesh was capable
Of wounds and scars, and that his forward spirit
Would lift him where most trade° of danger ranged,
Yet did you say "Go forth." And none of this,   175
Though strongly apprehended, could restrain
The stiff-borne° action. What hath then befallen,
Or what hath this bold enterprise brought forth,
More than that being which was like to be?

L. BARD. We all that are engagèd to° this loss   180
Knew that we ventured on such dangerous seas
That if we wrought out° life 'twas ten to one.
And yet we ventured, for the gain proposed
Choked the respect° of likely peril feared.
And since we are o'erset, venture again.   185
Come, we will all put forth, body and goods.

MOR. 'Tis more than time. And, my most noble
    lord,
I hear for certain, and do speak the truth,
The gentle Archbishop of York is up°
With well-appointed powers. He is a man   190
Who with a double surety° binds his followers.
My lord your son had only but the corpse,
But shadows and the shows of men, to fight.
For that same word, "rebellion," did divide
The action of their bodies from their souls,   195
And they did fight with queasiness,° constrained,
As men drink potions, that their weapons only
Seemed on our side. But for their spirits and souls,
This word, "rebellion," it had froze them up
As fish are in a pond. But now the Bishop   200
Turns insurrection to religion.
Supposed sincere and holy in his thoughts,
He's followed both with body and with mind,
And doth enlarge his rising with the blood
Of fair King Richard,° scraped from Pomfret°
    stones;   205

Derives from heaven his quarrel and his cause;
Tells them he doth bestride a bleeding land,
Gasping for life under great Bolingbroke;
And more and less° do flock to follow him.   209

NORTH. I knew of this before, but, to speak truth,
This present grief had wiped it from my mind.
Go in with me, and counsel every man
The aptest° way for safety and revenge.   213
Get posts and letters, and make friends with speed.
Never so few, and never yet more need.   [*Exeunt.*]

SCENE II. *London. A street.*

[*Enter* FALSTAFF, *with his* PAGE *bearing his
sword and buckler.*]

FAL. Sirrah, you giant,° what says the doctor to
my water?°

PAGE. He said, sir, the water itself was a good
healthy water, but for the party that owed° it, he
might have moe° diseases than he knew for.   6

FAL. Men of all sorts take a pride to gird° at me.
The brain of this foolish-compounded clay, man, is
not able to invent anything that tends to laughter
more than I invent or is invented on me. I am   10
not only witty in myself, but the cause that wit is in
other men. I do here walk before thee like a sow that
hath overwhelmed all her litter but one. If the Prince
put thee into my service for any other reason than
to set me off,° why, then I have no judgment.   15
Thou whoreson° mandrake,° thou art fitter to be
worn in my cap than to wait at my heels. I was never
manned° with an agate° till now. But I will inset
you neither in gold nor silver, but in vile ap-   20
parel, and send you back again to your master, for a
jewel — the juvenal,° the Prince your master, whose
chin is not yet fledged.° I will sooner have a beard
grow in the palm of my hand than he shall get one
on his cheek, and yet he will not stick to say his   25
face is a face royal.° God may finish it when He will,
'tis not a hair amiss yet. He may keep it still at a face
royal, for a barber shall never earn sixpence out of it,
and yet he'll be crowing as if he had writ man° ever
since his father was a bachelor.° He may keep   30

---

161. **strained:** unnatural, excessive.   163. **complices:** accomplices.
166. **cast . . . event:** reckoned up the chances.   168. **make head:**
raise a force.   169. **dole:** distribution.   174. **trade:** traffic, resort.
177. **stiff-borne:** hard-fought.   180. **engaged to:** pledged to
endure.   182. **wrought out:** won through with.   184. **respect:**
consideration.   189. **up:** i.e., in arms.   191. **double surety:**
twofold pledge.   196. **queasiness:** nausea, sick hearts.   204–05. **enlarge . . . Richard:** make his rising more powerful by exhibiting
the blood of the murdered Richard.   205. **Pomfret:** Pontefract
Castle, where Richard II was murdered.

209. **more . . . less:** greatest and least, men of all classes.
213. **aptest:** fittest.
    Sc. ii: 1. **you giant:** It seems likely that about the beginning
of 1598 the Lord Chamberlain's Company acquired a small boy
actor who was a considerable success. See Gen. Intro. p. 59b. For
the boy carrying his master's sword and buckler, see Pl. 9a; also
Pl. 22i, j.   1–2. **doctor . . . water:** Inspection of the urine was
a common method of arriving at a diagnosis.   5. **owed:** owned.
6. **moe:** more.   7. **gird:** gibe.   15. **set me off:** be a contrast to
me.   17. **whoreson:** bastard. **mandrake:** a forked root resembling a man in shape. See Pl. 12e.   19. **manned:** waited on.
agate: small figure cut in an agate.   22. **juvenal:** young man.
23. **fledged:** covered with down; lit., out of the nest.   26. **face
royal:** i.e., worth a royal — 10s. See App. 27.   29. **writ man:**
described himself as a man.   30. **bachelor:** young man.

his own grace, but he's almost out of mine, I can assure him. What said Master Dombledon about the satin for my short cloak and my slops?°　　34

PAGE. He said, sir, you should procure him better assurance° than Bardolph. He would not take his band° and yours, he liked not the security.　　38

FAL. Let him be damned, like the glutton!° Pray God his tongue be hotter! A whoreson Achitophel!° A rascally yea-forsooth knave! To bear a gentleman in hand,° and then stand upon security! The whoreson smoothpates° do now wear nothing but high shoes, and bunches of keys at their girdles. And if a man is through with them in honest taking-up,° 45 then they must stand upon security. I had as lief they would put ratsbane° in my mouth as offer to stop it with security. I looked a'° should have sent me two and twenty yards of satin, as I am a true knight, and he sends me security. Well, he may sleep in se- 50 curity,° for he hath the horn of abundance, and the lightness of his wife shines through it. And yet cannot he see, though he have his own lantern to light him.° Where's Bardolph?

PAGE. He's gone into Smithfield to buy your Worship a horse.　　57

FAL. I bought him in Paul's,° and he'll buy me a horse in Smithfield.° An I could get me but a wife in the stews,° I were manned, horsed, and wived.

[*Enter the* LORD CHIEF JUSTICE *and* SERVANT.]

PAGE. Sir, here comes the nobleman that committed° the Prince for striking him about Bardolph.

FAL. Wait close.° I will not see him.　　65

CH. JUST. What's he that goes there?

SERV. Falstaff, an 't please your lordship.

CH. JUST. He that was in question for the robbery?　　69

SERV. He, my lord. But he hath since done good service at Shrewsbury, and, as I hear, is now going with some charge° to the Lord John of Lancaster.

CH. JUST. What, to York? Call him back again.

SERV. Sir John Falstaff!　　76

FAL. Boy, tell him I am deaf.

PAGE. You must speak louder. My master is deaf.

CH. JUST. I am sure he is, to the hearing of anything good. Go, pluck him by the elbow. I must speak with him.

SERV. Sir John!　　83

FAL. What! A young knave, and begging! Is there not wars? Is there not employment? Doth not the King lack subjects? Do not the rebels need soldiers? Though it be a shame to be on any side but one, it is worse shame to beg than to be on the worst side, were it worse than the name of rebellion can tell how to make it.　　90

SERV. You mistake me, sir.

FAL. Why, sir, did I say you were an honest man? Setting my knighthood and my soldiership aside,° I had lied in my throat if I had said so.　　94

SERV. I pray you, sir, then set your knighthood and your soldiership aside and give me leave to tell you you lie in your throat° if you say I am any other than an honest man.　　98

FAL. I give thee leave to tell me so! I lay aside that which grows to me!° If thou gettest any leave of me, hang me. If thou takest leave, thou wert better be hanged. You hunt counter.° Hence! Avaunt!° 103

SERV. Sir, my lord would speak with you.

CH. JUST. Sir John Falstaff, a word with you.

FAL. My good lord! God give your lordship good time of day.° I am glad to see your lordship abroad. I heard say your lordship was sick. I hope your 108 lordship goes abroad° by advice. Your lordship, though not clean past your youth, hath yet some smack° of age in you, some relish of the saltness° of time, and I most humbly beseech your lordship to have a reverend care of your health.　　114

CH. JUST. Sir John, I sent for you before your expedition to Shrewsbury.

FAL. An 't please your lordship, I hear His Majesty is returned with some discomfort° from Wales. 119

CH. JUST. I talk not of His Majesty. You would not come when I sent for you.

FAL. And I hear, moreover, His Highness is fallen into this same whoreson apoplexy.°

CH. JUST. Well, God mend him! I pray you let me speak with you.　　126

FAL. This apoplexy is, as I take it, a kind of lethargy, an 't please your lordship, a kind of sleeping in the blood, a whoreson tingling.

CH. JUST. What tell you me of it? Be it as it is.

FAL. It hath its original from much grief, from study and perturbation of the brain. I have read

---

34. slops: wide breeches. See Pl. 8c and comment on p. 93b. **37. assurance:** guarantee. **38. band:** bond. **39. the glutton:** i.e., Dives in the parable of Dives and Lazarus. **40. Achitophel:** the counselor who advised Absalom, King David's rebellious son. See II Samuel 16. The parallel is not particularly apt. **41. bear . . . hand:** delude with false hope. **43. smoothpates:** smoothheaded citizens. **45. taking-up:** obtaining on credit. **47. ratsbane:** rat poison. **48. a':** he. **51. security:** carelessness. **51–54. horn . . . him:** Falstaff puns on three meanings of horn: (a) the cornucopia or horn of abundance, the mythological symbol of a horn overflowing with fruits; (b) the cuckold's horn, supposed to be worn by every husband deceived by his wife; (c) the horn sides (horn being used before glass) of a lantern. See App. 11. **58. bought . . . Paul's:** See Gen. Intro. p. 17a. **59. Smithfield:** the London cattle market. **60. stews:** brothels. **64. committed:** sent to prison. See *I Hen IV*, Intro. p. 614b. **65. Wait close:** stand close by me. **72. charge:** command.

93. Setting . . . aside: forgetting for a moment that I am a knight and a soldier. **97. lie . . . throat:** the worst kind of lie; to accuse a man of uttering it was a mortal offense. **100. grows to me:** is part of me. **103. hunt counter:** i.e., off the scent. **Avaunt:** be off. **106–07. good . . . day:** a form of polite salutation. **109. abroad:** out of doors. **112. smack:** taste. **saltness:** probably the "saltness of age" as contrasted with the "freshness of youth." **119. discomfort:** indisposition. **124. apoplexy:** paralysis.

the cause of his effects in Galen.° It is a kind of deafness. 134

CH. JUST. I think you are fallen into the disease, for you hear not what I say to you.

FAL. Very well, my lord, very well. Rather, an 't please you, it is the disease of not listening, the malady of not marking, that I am troubled withal. 140

CH. JUST. To punish you by the heels° would amend the attention of your ears, and I care not if I do become your physician. 143

FAL. I am as poor as Job, my lord, but not so patient. Your lordship may minister the potion of imprisonment to me in respect of poverty, but how I should be your patient to follow your prescriptions, the wise may make some dram of a scruple,° or indeed a scruple itself. 149

CH. JUST. I sent for you when there were matters against you for your life, to come speak with me.

FAL. As I was then advised by my learnèd counsel in the laws of this land service,° I did not come. 155

CH. JUST. Well, the truth is, Sir John, you live in great infamy.

FAL. He that buckles him in my belt cannot live in less.

CH. JUST. Your means are very slender and your waste is great. 161

FAL. I would it were otherwise. I would my means were greater and my waist slenderer.

CH. JUST. You have misled the youthful Prince.

FAL. The young Prince hath misled me. I am the fellow with the great belly, and he my dog. 166

CH. JUST. Well, I am loath to gall° a new-healed wound. Your day's service at Shrewsbury hath a little gilded over your night's exploit on Gadshill. You may thank the unquiet time for your quiet o'erposting° that action. 171

FAL. My lord?

CH. JUST. But since all is well, keep it so. Wake not a sleeping wolf.

FAL. To wake a wolf is as bad as to smell a fox.

CH. JUST. What! You are as a candle, the better part burned out.

FAL. A wassail candle,° my lord, all tallow. If I did say of wax,° my growth would approve the truth. 181

CH. JUST. There is not a white hair on your face but should have his effect of gravity.

FAL. His effect of gravy, gravy, gravy.

CH. JUST. You follow the young Prince up and down like his ill angel. 186

FAL. Not so, my lord. Your ill angel is light,° but I hope he that looks upon me will take me without weighing. And yet, in some respects, I grant I cannot go. I cannot tell. Virtue is of so little regard 190 in these costermonger times° that true valor is turned bearherd.° Pregnancy° is made a tapster, and hath his quick wit wasted in giving reckonings. All the other gifts appertinent to man, as the malice of this age shapes them, are not worth a goose- 195 berry. You that are old consider not the capacities of us that are young, you do measure the heat of our livers with the bitterness of your galls. And we that are in the vaward° of our youth, I must confess, are wags° too. 200

CH. JUST. Do you set down your name in the scroll of youth, that are written down old with all the characters° of age? Have you not a moist eye? A dry hand? A yellow cheek? A white beard? A decreasing leg? An increasing belly? Is not your voice 205 broken? Your wind short? Your chin double? Your wit single?° And every part about you blasted with antiquity? And will you yet call yourself young? Fie, fie, fie, Sir John! 209

FAL. My lord, I was born about three of the clock in the afternoon, with a white head and something° a round belly. For my voice, I have lost it with hallooing and singing of anthems. To approve° my youth further, I will not. The truth is, I am only old in judgment and understanding. And he that 215 will caper with me for a thousand marks,° let him lend me the money, and have at him. For the box of the ear that the Prince gave you, he gave it like a rude prince, and you took it like a sensible lord. I have checked him for it, and the young lion repents — marry,° not in ashes and sackcloth, but in new silk and old sack.° 222

CH. JUST. Well, God send the Prince a better companion!

FAL. God send the companion a better Prince! I cannot rid my hands of him. 226

CH. JUST. Well, the King hath severed you and Prince Harry. I hear you are going with Lord John of Lancaster against the Archbishop and the Earl of Northumberland. 230

FAL. Yea, I thank your pretty sweet wit for it. But look you, pray, all you that kiss my lady Peace at home, that our armies join not in a hot day. For, by the Lord, I take but two shirts out with me, and I mean not to sweat extraordinarily. If it be a hot 235 day, and I brandish anything but a bottle, I would I

134. Galen: a Greek physician (died A.D. 201), and a writer of medical textbooks, still much studied in Shakespeare's time. 141. by . . . heels: by putting you in the stocks. 148. dram . . . scruple: a minute portion of a minute quantity. 155. laws . . . service: laws of military service. 167. gall: irritate. 170–71. quiet o'erposting: peaceful escape from. 179. wassail candle: a thick candle used at feasts. 180. wax: with a pun on *wax*, meaning grow greater.

187. ill . . . light: with the common pun on *angel* — a gold coin worth 6s.8d. See App. 27 and Pl. 10c. 191. costermonger times: i.e., when everything is reckoned by its cash value. 192. bearherd: leader of a tame bear. Pregnancy: quick wit. 199. vaward: vanguard. 200. wags: gay lads. 203. characters: signs. 207. single: feeble. 211. something: somewhat. 213. approve: demonstrate. 216. marks: 13s.4d. 221. marry: Mary, by the Virgin. 222. sack: Spanish wine. See IV.iii.102–35.

might never spit white° again. There is not a dangerous action can peep out his head but I am thrust
upon it. Well, I cannot last ever. But it was alway
yet the trick of our English nation, if they have   240
a good thing, to make it too common. If ye will needs
say I am an old man, you should give me rest. I
would to God my name were not so terrible to the
enemy as it is. I were better to be eaten to death with
a rust than to be scoured° to nothing with perpetual
motion.   247

CH. JUST. Well, be honest, be honest, and God
bless your expedition!

FAL. Will your lordship lend me a thousand pound
to furnish° me forth?

CH. JUST. Not a penny, not a penny. You are too
impatient to bear crosses.° Fare you well. Commend
me to my cousin Westmoreland.   254

[*Exeunt* CHIEF JUSTICE *and* SERVANT.]

FAL. If I do, fillip° me with a three-man beetle.° A
man can no more separate age and covetousness than
a' can part young limbs and lechery. But the gout
galls the one and the pox pinches the other, and so
both the degrees° prevent° my curses. Boy!   260

PAGE. Sir?

FAL. What money is in my purse?

PAGE. Seven groats° and twopence.   263

FAL. I can get no remedy against this consumption
of the purse. Borrowing only lingers and lingers it
out, but the disease is incurable. Go bear this letter to
my Lord of Lancaster, this to the Prince, this to the
Earl of Westmoreland. And this to old Mistress
Ursula, whom I have weekly sworn to marry since I
perceived the first white hair on my chin.   270
About it. You know where to find me. [*Exit* PAGE]
A pox of this gout! Or a gout of this pox! For the one
or the other plays the rogue with my great toe. 'Tis
no matter if I do halt.° I have the wars for my
color,° and my pension shall seem the more reasonable. A good wit will make use of anything. I   277
will turn diseases to commodity.°   [*Exit.*]

SCENE III. *York. The* ARCHBISHOP'S *palace.*

[*Enter the* ARCHBISHOP, *the* LORDS HASTINGS,
MOWBRAY, *and* BARDOLPH.]

ARCH. Thus have you heard our cause and known
our means.

And, my most noble friends, I pray you all
Speak plainly your opinions of our hopes.
And first, Lord Marshal, what say you to it?

MOWB. I well allow the occasion of° our arms,   5
But gladly would be better satisfied
How in° our means we should advance ourselves
To look with forehead bold and big enough
Upon the power and puissance° of the King.

HAST. Our present musters grow upon the file°
To five and twenty thousand men of choice,°   11
And our supplies° live largely in the hope
Of great Northumberland, whose bosom burns
With an incensèd fire of injuries.

L. BARD. The question then, Lord Hastings, stand-
eth thus: 15
Whether our present five and twenty thousand
May hold up head without Northumberland?

HAST. With him, we may.

L. BARD.   Yea, marry, there's the point.
But if without him we be thought too feeble,
My judgment is, we should not step too far   20
Till we had his assistance by the hand.°
For in a theme° so bloody-faced as this
Conjecture, expectation, and surmise
Of aids incertain should not be admitted.

ARCH. 'Tis very true, Lord Bardolph, for indeed
It was young Hotspur's case at Shrewsbury.   26

L. BARD. It was, my lord, who lined° himself with
hope,
Eating the air on promise of supply,
Flattering himself in project of a power
Much smaller than the smallest of his thoughts.°   30
And so, with great imagination°
Proper to madmen, led his powers to death,
And winking° leaped into destruction.

HAST. But, by your leave, it never yet did hurt
To lay down likelihoods and forms of hope.   35

L. BARD. Yes, if this present quality of war,
Indeed the instant action,° a cause on foot,
Lives so in hope as in an early spring
We see the appearing buds, which to prove fruit,
Hope gives not so much warrant as despair   40
That frosts will bite them.° When we mean to build,
We first survey the plot,° then draw the model.°
And when we see the figure° of the house,
Then must we rate the cost of the erection,

237. **spit white:** not satisfactorily explained; perhaps a sign that
a man has drunk well, or "spit clean" — a sign of good health.
246. **scoured:** rubbed. 251. **furnish:** equip. 253. **bear crosses:**
a common pun. The phrase means (a) to endure disappointment,
and (b) to carry money — so called from the cross on the coin.
See Pl. 10a. 255. **fillip:** flip. **three-man beetle:** heavy hammer wielded by three men, and used for pile-driving. 260. **both
...degrees:** i.e., youth and age. **prevent:** forestall; i.e., both
youth and age have their own curses already. 263. **groats:**
worth 4*d.* 275. **halt:** limp. 276. **color:** excuse. 278. **commodity:** advantage.

Sc. iii: 5. **occasion of:** reason for. 7. **in:** with. 9. **puissance:**
might. 10. **file:** roster. 11. **men of choice:** picked men. 12. **supplies:** reinforcements. 21. **by...hand:** at hand. 22. **theme:**
problem. 27. **lined:** strengthened. 29–30. **in...thoughts:** in
expectation of a force that turned out to be far less than he
had imagined. 31. **imagination:** i.e., lack of a sense of reality.
33. **winking:** with his eyes shut. 36–37. **Yes...action:** A
much-debated passage; possibly a line has been omitted. The
general meaning is that it is harmful to be optimistic when it
is a case of immediate war. 37–41. **a...them:** when a project for war is set on foot, the promoter's hopes are like buds
in early spring. We may hope that they will become fruit, but
should fear that the frost will destroy them; i.e., "safety first."
42. **plot:** ground. **model:** plan. 43. **figure:** design.

Which if we find outweighs ability,   45
What do we then but draw anew the model
In fewer offices,° or at last desist
To build at all? Much more, in this great work,
Which is almost to pluck a kingdom down
And set another up, should we survey   50
The plot of situation and the model,
Consent° upon a sure foundation,
Question surveyors, know our own estate,
How able such a work to undergo
To weigh against his opposite.° Or else   55
We fortify in paper° and in figures,
Using the names of men instead of men —
Like one that draws the model of a house
Beyond his power to build it, who, half through,
Gives o'er and leaves his part-created cost°   60
A naked subject to the weeping clouds,
And waste for churlish° winter's tyranny.
    HAST. Grant that our hopes, yet likely of fair birth,
Should be stillborn, and that we now possessed
The utmost man of expectation,°   65
I think we are a body strong enough,
Even as we are, to equal with the King.
      L. BARD. What, is the King but five and twenty
      thousand?
    HAST. To us° no more — nay, not so much, Lord
    Bardolph.
For his divisions, as the times do brawl,   70
Are in three heads: one power against the French,
And one against Glendower, perforce a third
Must take up us. So is the unfirm King
In three divided, and his coffers sound°
With hollow poverty and emptiness.   75
    ARCH. That he should draw his several° strengths
    together
And come against us in full puissance
Need not be dreaded.
    HAST.   If he should do so,
He leaves his back unarmed, the French and Welsh
Baying° him at the heels. Never fear that.   80
      L. BARD. Who is it like should lead his forces
      hither?
    HAST. The Duke of Lancaster and Westmoreland.
Against the Welsh, himself and Harry Monmouth.
But who is substituted° 'gainst the French,
I have no certain notice.
      ARCH.   Let us on,   85
And publish the occasion of our arms.
The commonwealth is sick of their own choice,
Their overgreedy love hath surfeited.°
A habitation giddy and unsure

Hath he that buildeth on the vulgar heart.°   90
O thou fond many,° with what loud applause
Didst thou beat Heaven with blessing Bolingbroke
Before he was what thou wouldst have him be!
And being now trimmed in thine own desires,°
Thou, beastly feeder, art so full of him   95
That thou provokest thyself to cast him up.
So, so, thou common dog, didst thou disgorge
Thy glutton bosom of the royal Richard.
And now thou wouldst eat thy dead vomit up,
And howl'st to find it.° What trust is in these
    times?   100
They that when Richard lived would have him die
Are now become enamored on his grave.
Thou° that threw'st dust° upon his goodly head
When through proud London he came sighing on
After the admirèd heels of Bolingbroke,   105
Criest now " O earth, yield us that king again,
And take thou this! " Oh, thoughts of men accursed!
Past and to come seems best, things present, worst.
    MOWB. Shall we go draw our numbers and set on?
    HAST. We are time's subjects, and time bids be
    gone.   [*Exeunt.*]

Act II

SCENE I. *London. A street.*

[*Enter* HOSTESS, FANG *and his* BOY *with her, and*
SNARE *following.*]

    HOST. Master Fang,° have you entered the ac-
tion?°
    FANG. It is entered.
    HOST. Where's your yeoman?° Is't a lusty yeo-
man? Will a' stand to 't?   5
    FANG. Sirrah, where's Snare?
    HOST. Oh Lord, aye! Good Master Snare.
    SNARE. Here, here.
    FANG. Snare, we must arrest Sir John Falstaff.
    HOST. Yea, good Master Snare. I have entered him
and all.   11
    SNARE. It may chance cost some of us our lives, for
he will stab.
    HOST. Alas the day! Take heed of him. He stabbed
me in mine own house, and that most beastly. In   15
good faith, he cares not what mischief he does, if his

---

47. **offices:** rooms.   52. **Consent:** agree.   55. **his opposite:** i.e.,
the cost.   56. **fortify in paper:** our plans are but paper.   60. **part-
created cost:** costly undertaking but half finished.   62. **churlish:**
rough.   65. **utmost . . . expectation:** every man that we could
hope for.   69. **To us:** so far as we are concerned.   74. **sound:**
echo.   76. **several:** separate.   80. **Baying:** barking.   84. **substituted:** sent as deputy.   88. **surfeited:** overeaten.

90. **vulgar heart:** the love of the people.   91. **fond many:** foolish
multitude.   94. **trimmed . . . desires:** decked out as you wished
him to be.   100. **howl'st . . . it:** howl because you cannot find it.
103. **Thou:** i.e., the common people. **threw'st dust:** See *Rich II*,
V.ii.23–38.
    Act II, Sc. i: 1. **Master Fang:** the sheriff's sergeant.   1–2. **en-
tered . . . action:** given notice of the action.   4. **yeoman:** the
sergeant's man.

weapon be out. He will foin° like any devil, he will
spare neither man, woman, nor child.   19

FANG. If I can close with him, I care not for his
thrust.

HOST. No, nor I neither. I'll be at your elbow.

FANG. An I but fist him once, an a' come but
within my vice° ——   24

HOST. I am undone by his going. I warrant you,
he's an infinitive° thing upon my score.° Good Master Fang, hold him sure. Good Master Snare, let him
not 'scape. A' comes continuantly to Pie Corner —
saving your manhoods° — to buy a saddle, and he is
indited° to dinner to the Lubber's Head° in   30
Lumbert° Street, to Master Smooth's the silkman.
I pray ye, since my exion° is entered and my case so
openly known to the world, let him be brought in°
to his answer. A hundred mark is a long one for a
poor lone woman to bear. And I have borne, and   35
borne, and borne, and have been fubbed off,° and
fubbed off, and fubbed off, from this day to that day,
that it is a shame to be thought on. There is no
honesty in such dealing, unless a woman should   40
be made an ass and a beast, to bear every knave's
wrong. Yonder he comes, and that arrant° malmsey-
nose° knave Bardolph with him. Do your offices, do
your offices. Master Fang and Master Snare, do me,
do me, do me your offices.   45

[*Enter* FALSTAFF, PAGE, *and* BARDOLPH.]

FAL. How now! Whose mare's dead?° What's the
matter?

FANG. Sir John, I arrest you at the suit of Mistress
Quickly.

FAL. Away, varlets!° Draw, Bardolph. Cut me off
the villain's head. Throw the quean° in the channel.°   52

HOST. Throw me in the channel! I'll throw thee in
the channel. Wilt thou? Wilt thou? Thou bastardly
rogue! Murder, murder! Ah, thou honeysuckle° villain! Wilt thou kill God's officers and the King's?
Ah, thou honey-seed rogue! Thou art a honey-seed,
a man-queller,° and a woman-queller.   59

FAL. Keep them off, Bardolph.

FANG. A rescue!° A rescue!

HOST. Good people, bring a rescue or two. Thou
wo't, wo't thou? Thou wo't, wo't ta? Do, do, thou
rogue! Do, thou hempseed!°   64

PAGE. Away, you scullion!° You rampallian!° You
fustilarian!° I'll tickle your catastrophe.°

[*Enter the* LORD CHIEF JUSTICE, *and his men.*]

CH. JUST. What is the matter? Keep the peace
here, ho!

HOST. Good my lord, be good to me. I beseech you,
stand to me.   70

CH. JUST. How now, Sir John! What are you
brawling here?
Doth this become your place, your time and business?
You should have been well on your way to York.
Stand from him, fellow. Wherefore hang'st upon
him?   74

HOST. O my most worshipful lord, an 't please
your Grace, I am a poor widow of Eastcheap, and he
is arrested at my suit.

CH. JUST. For what sum?   78

HOST. It is more than for some, my lord, it is for
all, all I have. He hath eaten me out of house and
home, he hath put all my substance into that fat belly
of his. But I will have some of it out again, or I will
ride thee o' nights like the mare.°   83

FAL. I think I am as like to ride the mare, if I
have any vantage of ground° to get up.

CH. JUST. How comes this, Sir John? Fie! What
man of good temper° would endure this tempest of
exclamation? Are you not ashamed to enforce a poor
widow to so rough a course to come by her own?   90

FAL. What is the gross sum that I owe thee?

HOST. Marry, if thou wert an honest man, thyself
and the money too. Thou didst swear to me upon a
parcel-gilt° goblet, sitting in my Dolphin Chamber,°
at the round table, by a sea-coal° fire, upon Wed-   95
nesday in Wheeson° week, when the Prince broke
thy head for liking° his father to a singing man° of
Windsor — thou didst swear to me then, as I was
washing thy wound, to marry me and make me my
lady thy wife. Canst thou deny it? Did not   100
goodwife Keech, the butcher's wife, come in then
and call me Gossip° Quickly? Coming in to borrow

---

18. foin: thrust.   **24. vice:** grip.   **26. infinitive:** Like many
other characters of her social standing in Shakespeare's plays,
Mrs. Quickly loves long words but does not always get them
right; she means "infinite." **score:** tavern account.   **29. saving
. . . manhoods:** a phrase of apology, usually for an improper
remark.   **30. indited:** for "invited." **Lubber's Head:** for Libbard's
(Leopard's) Head.   **31. Lumbert:** Lombard. See App. 12.   **32. ex-
ion:** for "action."   **33. brought in:** i.e., to court.   **36. fubbed
off:** put off.   **42. arrant:** out-and-out; lit., "errant" — vagabond.
43. malmsey-nose: For Bardolph's nose, see *I Hen IV*, III.iii.
27-55. **malmsey:** a sweet red wine.   **46. Whose . . . dead:** what's
all the fuss?   **50. varlets:** knaves.   **51. quean:** slut.   **52. channel:**
gutter.   **55. honeysuckle:** apparently for "homicidal," as "honey-
seed" (l. 58) is "homicide."   **59. man-queller:** man-killer.
61. A rescue: a call to passers-by to come to the help of the
officers (or their victim).

64. hempseed: gallows bird.   **65. scullion:** slavey, dishwasher.
rampallian: rascal.   **66. fustilarian:** stinker — from "fustilugs,"
a fat, frowsy woman. **catastrophe:** in modern slang, "fanny."
83. mare: nightmare, believed to be a spirit which bestrode those
who slept on their backs. See *R & J*, I.iv.92–94.   **85. vantage
of ground:** higher ground. Men of Falstaff's bulk need assistance
in getting their legs over the saddle.   **88. temper:** disposition.
94. parcel-gilt: partly gilt. **Dolphin Chamber:** Rooms in taverns
were named. See *I Hen IV*, II.iv.41.   **95. sea-coal:** coal from
mines transported by sea from Newcastle to London; *coal* usually
means "charcoal."   **96. Wheeson:** Whitsun, the seventh Sunday
after Easter; Pentecost.   **97. liking:** likening, comparing. **singing man:** singer in the choir. The insult was the suggestion that
the King and the chorister had the same father.   **102. Gossip:** a
name used by middle-class women in talking of each other.

a mess° of vinegar, telling us she had a good dish of
prawns, whereby thou didst desire to eat some,
whereby I told thee they were ill for a green°   105
wound? And didst thou not, when she was gone
downstairs, desire me to be no more so familiarity
with such poor people, saying that ere long they
should call me madam? And didst thou not kiss me
and bid me fetch thee thirty shillings? I put thee
now to thy book oath. Deny it, if thou canst.   112

FAL. My lord, this is a poor mad soul, and she says
up and down the town that her eldest son is like
you.° She hath been in good case,° and the truth is,
poverty hath distracted° her. But for these foolish
officers, I beseech you I may have redress against
them.   118

CH. JUST. Sir John, Sir John, I am well acquainted
with your manner of wrenching the true cause the
false way. It is not a confident brow, nor the throng
of words that come with such more than impudent
sauciness from you, can thrust me from a level°
consideration. You have, as it appears to me,   123
practiced upon° the easy-yielding spirit of this
woman, and made her serve your uses both in purse
and in person.

HOST. Yea, in truth, my lord.   128

CH. JUST. Pray thee, peace. Pay her the debt you
owe her, and unpay the villainy you have done her.
The one you may do with sterling money, and the
other with current° repentance.   132

FAL. My lord, I will not undergo this sneap° without reply. You call honorable boldness impudent
sauciness. If a man will make courtesy° and say
nothing, he is virtuous. No, my lord, my humble
duty remembered,° I will not be your suitor.° I say
to you I do desire deliverance from these officers,
being upon hasty employment in the King's affairs.   140

CH. JUST. You speak as having power to do wrong.
But answer in the effect of your reputation,° and
satisfy the poor woman.

FAL. Come hither, Hostess.   144

[*Enter* GOWER.]

CH. JUST. Now, Master Gower, what news?

GOW. The King, my lord, and Harry Prince of
Wales
Are near at hand. The rest the paper tells.

FAL. As I am a gentleman.

HOST. Faith, you said so before.   149

FAL. As I am a gentleman. Come, no more words
of it.

HOST. By this heavenly ground I tread on, I must
be fain° to pawn both my plate and the tapestry of
my dining chambers.   155

FAL. Glasses, glasses, is the only drinking.° And
for thy walls, a pretty slight drollery,° or the story of
the Prodigal, or the German hunting° in water
work,° is worth a thousand of these bed hangings
and these fly-bitten tapestries.° Let it be ten pound,
if thou canst. Come, an 'twere not for thy hu-   161
mors,° there's not a better wench in England. Go,
wash thy face, and draw° the action. Come, thou
must not be in this humor with me, dost not know
me? Come, come, I know thou wast set onto this.

HOST. Pray thee, Sir John, let it be but twenty
nobles.° I' faith, I am loath to pawn my plate, so
God save me, la!

FAL. Let it alone, I'll make other shift.° You'll be
a fool still.   170

HOST. Well, you shall have it, though I pawn my
gown. I hope you'll come to supper. You'll pay me
all together?

FAL. Will I live? [*To* BARDOLPH] Go, with her,
with her. Hook on,° hook on.   175

HOST. Will you have Doll Tearsheet meet you at
supper?

FAL. No more words. Let's have her.

[*Exeunt* HOSTESS, BARDOLPH, OFFICERS, *and* BOY.]

CH. JUST. I have heard better news.

FAL. What's the news, my lord?   180

CH. JUST. Where lay the King last night?

GOW. At Basingstoke, my lord.

FAL. I hope, my lord, all's well. What is the news,
my lord?

CH. JUST. Come all his forces back?   185

GOW. No. Fifteen hundred foot, five hundred
horse,
Are marched up to my Lord of Lancaster,
Against Northumberland and the Archbishop.

FAL. Comes the King back from Wales, my noble
lord?

CH. JUST. You shall have letters of me presently.
Come, go along with me, good Master Gower.   191

FAL. My lord!

CH. JUST. What's the matter?

---

103. **mess:** quantity.   105. **green:** raw.   114–15. **eldest . . . you:**
i.e., that the Chief Justice is his father.   115. **in . . . case:** in
good circumstances.   116. **distracted:** made mad.   122. **level:**
unbiased.   124. **practiced upon:** tricked, taken advantage of.
131–32. **sterling . . . current:** sterling money (i.e., sound money)
is current (i.e., negotiable). Even the Chief Justice takes every
chance of making a pun, which moves Falstaff to answer him
with real irritation.   133. **sneap:** rebuke.   135. **make courtesy:**
curtsy, show signs of respect.   136–37. **my . . . remembered:**
with all due respects.   137. **be . . . suitor:** ask favors of you.
142. in . . . reputation: as becomes a man of your reputation.

154. **fain:** pleased, obliged.   156. **Glasses . . . drinking:** to be
in fashion one must have glasses, not metal cups.   157. **drollery:**
comic picture.   158. **German hunting:** a hunting scene painted
in Germany.   158–59. **water work:** distemper. For a specimen,
see Pl. 6a.   160. **tapestries:** Woven or embroidered tapestries
were expensive and high class, and Mrs. Quickly is naturally
proud of her furnishings. Falstaff proposes that she shall substitute for them cheap new painted cloths.   162. **humors:** whims.
163. **draw:** withdraw.   167. **nobles:** coins worth 6s.8d. See App.
27.   169. **make . . . shift:** manage in some other way.   175. **Hook
on:** i.e., don't let her change her mind.

FAL. Master Gower, shall I entreat you with me to dinner? 195

GOW. I must wait upon my good lord here, I thank you, good Sir John.

CH. JUST. Sir John, you loiter here too long, being° you are to take soldiers up in counties as you go.

FAL. Will you sup with me, Master Gower? 201

CH. JUST. What foolish master taught you these manners, Sir John?

FAL. Master Gower, if they become me not, he was a fool that taught them me.° This is the right fencing grace, my lord — tap for tap, and so part fair.° 207

CH. JUST. Now the Lord lighten° thee! Thou art a great fool. [*Exeunt.*]

SCENE II. *London. Another street.*

[*Enter* PRINCE HENRY *and* POINS.]

PRINCE. Before God, I am exceeding weary.

POINS. Is 't come to that? I had thought weariness durst not have attached° one of so high blood. 3

PRINCE. Faith, it does me, though it discolors the complexion° of my greatness to acknowledge it. Doth it not show vilely in me to desire small° beer? 8

POINS. Why, a prince should not be so loosely studied° as to remember so weak a composition.°

PRINCE. Belike then my appetite was not princely got, for, by my troth, I do now remember the poor creature, small beer. But indeed these humble considerations make me out of love with my greatness. What a disgrace is it to me to remember thy 15 name! Or to know thy face tomorrow! Or to take note how many pair of silk stockings thou hast; viz., these, and those that were thy peach-colored ones! Or to bear the inventory of thy shirts, as one for superfluity° and another for use! But that the tennis-court keeper knows better than I. For it is a 20 low ebb of linen with thee when thou keepest not racket there,° as thou hast not done a great while be-

cause the rest of thy low countries have made a shift to eat up thy holland.° And God knows whether those that bawl out the ruins of thy linen shall 25 inherit His kingdom.° But the midwives say the children are not in the fault, whereupon the world increases, and kindreds are mightily strengthened.

POINS. How ill it follows, after you have la- 31 bored so hard, you should talk so idly! Tell me, how many good young princes would do so, their fathers being so sick as yours at this time is?

PRINCE. Shall I tell thee one thing, Poins? 35

POINS. Yes, faith, and let it be an excellent good thing.

PRINCE. It shall serve among wits of no higher breeding than thine.°

POINS. Go to. I stand the push° of your one thing that you will tell. 41

PRINCE. Marry, I tell thee it is not meet that I should be sad, now my father is sick. Albeit I could tell to thee, as to one it pleases me, for fault of a better, to call my friend, I could be sad, and sad indeed too.

POINS. Very hardly upon such a subject.° 47

PRINCE. By this hand, thou thinkest me as far in the Devil's book° as thou and Falstaff for obduracy° and persistency. Let the end try the man.° But I tell thee, my heart bleeds inwardly that my father is so sick. And keeping such vile company as thou art hath in reason taken from me all ostentation° of sorrow. 54

POINS. The reason?

PRINCE. What wouldst thou think of me if I should weep?

POINS. I would think thee a most princely hypocrite. 59

PRINCE. It would be every man's thought, and thou art a blessed fellow to think as every man thinks. Never a man's thought in the world keeps the roadway better than thine.° Every man would think me a hypocrite indeed. And what accites° your most worshipful thought to think so? 65

POINS. Why, because you have been so lewd,° and so much engraffed to° Falstaff.

PRINCE. And to thee. 68

199. being: since. **204–05. he . . . me:** i.e., I am behaving as the Chief Justice taught me. If you don't like my manners, my master must have been a fool. **205–07. This . . . fair:** This is good fencing, to give thrust for thrust, and so end all square on both sides. **208. lighten:** enlighten.

　Sc. ii: **3. attached:** arrested, seized on. **4–5. discolors . . . complexion:** makes me change color. **6. small:** weak. **9–10. so . . . studied:** such a slack student. **10. weak a composition:** i.e., small beer. This enigmatic backchat is not easy to follow; like most specimens of wit, the more up to date it is at the moment of writing, the sooner it becomes outmoded and incomprehensible. Poins means that a prince with a proper sense of his duties and dignities would not condescend to remember small beer. The Prince continues the idea with a little lecture on the poor memories of great men, especially for names and faces. For a similar and more elaborate discourse, see *King John,* I.i.181–200. **19. for superfluity:** to spare. **21–22. low . . . there:** Tennis was much played by courtiers, who continuously changed their shirts as they sweated. Poins, being now reduced to one spare shirt, is ashamed to reveal his poverty on the tennis court.

23–24. rest . . . holland: an elaborate series of puns. **low countries:** tail end, and also the Netherlands. **made a shift:** contrived, with a pun on *shift,* meaning shirt. **holland:** the best linen. **24–26. God . . . kingdom:** *bawl* is an emendation for "bal" of the quarto; the passage is omitted from the folio. If correct, the sentence apparently means "your crying bastards use your old shirts as diapers." **38–39. It . . . thine:** it will be good enough for intelligences no better than yours. **40. push:** attack. **47. Very . . . subject:** Poins cynically comments that the Prince's grief at his father's death would hardly be very deep. **49. book:** record. **obduracy:** impenitence. **50. Let . . . man:** i.e., the outcome will show the man's worth — a hint of the serious purpose behind the Prince's behavior. **53. ostentation:** outward show. **62–63. Never . . . thine:** i.e., you are a perfect specimen of a commonplace mind. **64. accites:** excites. **66. lewd:** low. **67. engraffed to:** grafted with, close to.

POINS. By this light, I am well spoke on, I can hear it with mine own ears. The worst that they can say of me is that I am a second brother° and that I am a proper fellow of my hands,° and those two things I confess I cannot help. By the mass, here comes Bardolph. 74

[*Enter* BARDOLPH *and* PAGE.]

PRINCE. And the boy that I gave Falstaff. A' had him from me Christian, and look if the fat villain have not transformed him ape.

BARD. God save your Grace!

PRINCE. And yours, most noble Bardolph! 79

BARD. Come, you virtuous ass, you bashful fool, must you be blushing? Wherefore blush you now? What a maidenly man-at-arms are you become! Is 't such a matter to get a pottle pot's° maidenhead? 84

PAGE. A' calls me e'en now, my lord, through a red lattice,° and I could discern no part of his face from the window.° At last I spied his eyes, and methought he had made two holes in the alewife's new petticoat and so peeped through.

PRINCE. Has not the boy profited?

BARD. Away, you whoreson upright rabbit, away!

PAGE. Away, you rascally Althaea's dream,° away! 94

PRINCE. Instruct us, boy. What dream, boy?

PAGE. Marry, my lord, Althaea dreamed she was delivered of a firebrand, and therefore I call him her dream.

PRINCE. A crown's worth of good interpretation. There 'tis, boy. 100

POINS. Oh, that this good blossom could be kept from cankers!° Well, there is sixpence to preserve thee.

BARD. An you do not make him hanged among you, the gallows shall have wrong. 105

PRINCE. And how doth thy master, Bardolph?

BARD. Well, my lord. He heard of your Grace's coming to town. There's a letter for you.

POINS. Delivered with good respect.° And how doth the martlemas,° your master? 110

BARD. In bodily health, sir.

POINS. Marry, the immortal part needs a physician, but that moves not him. Though that be sick, it dies not. 114

PRINCE. I do allow this wen° to be as familiar with me as my dog, and he holds his place, for look you how he writes. 117

POINS. [*Reads*] "John Falstaff, knight"—every man must know that, as oft as he has occasion to name himself. Even like those that are kin to the King, for they never prick their finger but they say "There's some of the King's blood spilt." "How comes that?" says he that takes upon him not to conceive.° The answer is as ready as a borrow- 125 er's cap, "I am the King's poor cousin, sir."

PRINCE. Nay, they will be kin to us or they will fetch it from Japhet.° But to the letter. 128

POINS. [*Reads*] "Sir John Falstaff, knight, to the son of the King, nearest his father, Harry Prince of Wales, greeting." Why, this is a certificate.°

PRINCE. Peace! 133

POINS. [*Reads*] "I will imitate the honorable Romans in brevity." He sure means brevity in breath, short-winded. "I commend me to thee, I commend thee, and I leave thee. Be not too familiar with Poins, for he misuses thy favors so much that he swears thou art to marry his sister Nell. Repent at idle times as thou mayest, and so farewell. 141

"Thine, by yea and no, which is as much as to say, as thou usest him, Jack Falstaff with my familiars, John with my brothers and sisters, and Sir John with all Europe."

My lord, I'll steep this letter in sack and make him eat it.

PRINCE. That's to make him eat twenty of his words. But do you use me thus, Ned? Must I marry your sister? 151

POINS. God send the wench no worse fortune! But I never said so.

PRINCE. Well, thus we play the fools with the time, and the spirits of the wise sit in the clouds and mock us. Is your master here in London? 157

BARD. Yea, my lord.

PRINCE. Where sups he? Doth the old boar feed in the old frank?°

BARD. At the old place, my lord, in Eastcheap.

PRINCE. What company?

PAGE. Ephesians,° my lord, of the old Church.

PRINCE. Sup any women with him?

PAGE. None, my lord, but old Mistress Quickly and Mistress Doll Tearsheet. 167

PRINCE. What pagan may that be?

PAGE. A proper gentlewoman, sir, and a kinswoman of my master's.

PRINCE. Even such kin as the parish heifers are to the town bull. Shall we steal upon them, Ned, at supper?

POINS. I am your shadow, my lord, I'll follow you.

---

71. second brother: i.e., without an inheritance. **72. proper . . . hands:** fine fighter. **84. pottle pot:** tankard holding two quarts. **85–86. red lattice:** The lattice windows of taverns were painted red. **86–87. discern . . . window:** because the red lattice was perfect camouflage for Bardolph's face. **93. Althaea's dream:** i.e., that she had given birth to a firebrand. Actually, the boy was mistaken, for it was Hecuba's dream. **102. cankers:** cankerworms. **109. good respect:** nice manners — ironically said, for Bardolph is no courtier. **110. martlemas:** Martinmas, "St. Martin's summer," a patch of fine weather that sometimes comes late in fall; Indian summer. **115. wen:** tumor.

125. conceive: understand. **128. fetch . . . Japhet:** i.e., if they cannot claim nearer kinship, they will go back to Noah. Japhet was the one of Noah's sons from whom the white races are supposed to be descended. **132. certificate:** formal document, which often begins with a recital of the titles of the giver. **160. frank:** sty. **164. Ephesians:** like Trojans, Corinthians, etc., means gay lads, "the gang."

PRINCE. Sirrah,° you boy, and Bardolph, no word
to your master that I am yet come to town. There's
for your silence.　　　　　　　　　　　　178

BARD. I have no tongue, sir.

PAGE. And for mine, sir, I will govern it.

PRINCE. Fare you well, go.
　　　　　　　　　　[*Exeunt* BARDOLPH *and* PAGE.]

This Doll Tearsheet should be some road.°　183

POINS. I warrant you as common as the way between St. Albans and London.

PRINCE. How might we see Falstaff bestow° himself tonight in his true colors and not ourselves be
seen?　　　　　　　　　　　　　　188

POINS. Put on two leathern jerkins° and aprons,
and wait upon him at his table as drawers.°

PRINCE. From a god to a bull? A heavy descension!° It was Jove's case.° From a prince to a prentice? A low transformation! That shall be mine, for
in everything the purpose must weigh with°　195
the folly. Follow me, Ned.　　　　　[*Exeunt.*]

SCENE III. *Warkworth. Before the castle.*

[*Enter* NORTHUMBERLAND, LADY NORTHUMBERLAND,
　　　　　　and LADY PERCY.]

NORTH. I pray thee, loving wife and gentle daugh-
　　ter,
Give even way° unto my rough affairs.
Put not you on the visage of the times,
And be like them to Percy troublesome.

LADY N. I have given over, I will speak no more.
Do what you will, your wisdom be your guide.　6

NORTH. Alas, sweet wife, my honor is at pawn,
And, but my going,° nothing can redeem it.

LADY P. Oh, yet, for God's sake, go not to these
　　wars!　　　　　　　　　　　　9
The time was, Father, that you broke your word
When you were more endeared to it° than now —
When your own Percy, when my heart's dear
　　Harry,
Threw many a northward look to see his father
Bring up his powers, but he did long in vain.
Who then persuaded you to stay at home?　15
There were two honors lost, yours and your son's.
For yours, the God of Heaven brighten it!
For his, it stuck upon him as the sun
In the gray° vault of heaven, and by his light
Did all the chivalry of England move　　20

To do brave acts. He was indeed the glass
Wherein the noble youth did dress themselves.
He had no legs that practiced not his gait,
And speaking thick,° which nature made his blem-
　　ish,
Became the accents of the valiant,　　　25
For those that could speak low and tardily
Would turn their own perfection to abuse,
To seem like him. So that in speech, in gait,
In diet, in affections of delight,°
In military rules, humors of blood,°　　　30
He was the mark and glass, copy° and book,°
That fashioned others. And him — oh, wondrous
　　him!
Oh, miracle of men! — him did you leave,
Second to none, unseconded by you,
To look upon the hideous god of war　　35
In disadvantage, to abide a field°
Where nothing but the sound of Hotspur's name
Did seem defensible.° So you left him.
Never, oh, never, do his ghost the wrong
To hold your honor more precise and nice°　40
With others than with him! Let them alone.
The Marshal and the Archbishop are strong.
Had my sweet Harry had but half their numbers,
Today might I, hanging on Hotspur's neck,
Have talked of Monmouth's° grave.

NORTH.　　　　　　　　Beshrew° your heart,　45
Fair Daughter, you do draw my spirits from me
With new lamenting ancient oversights.
But I must go and meet with danger there,
Or it will seek me in another place
And find me worse provided.°

LADY N.　　　　　　　Oh, fly to Scotland,　50
Till that the nobles and the armèd commons
Have of their puissance° made a little taste.

LADY P. If they get ground and vantage of the
　　King,
Then join you with them, like a rib of steel,
To make strength stronger. But, for all our loves,
First let them try themselves. So did your son,　56
He was so suffered. So came I a widow,
And never shall have length of life enough
To rain upon remembrance with mine eyes,
That it may grow and sprout as high as heaven,　60
For recordation° to my noble husband.

NORTH. Come, come, go in with me. 'Tis with my
　　mind
As with the tide swelled up unto his height,
That makes a stillstand,° running neither way.

---

176. Sirrah: term of address used to inferiors.　183. road: i.e.,
available for all comers.　186. bestow: behave.　189. jerkins:
jackets.　190. drawers: waiters.　193. descension: descent in
the social scale. Jove's case: in order to get the love of Europa,
Jupiter transformed himself into a bull.　195. weigh with: corre-
spond to.

Sc. iii: 2. Give . . . way: make the way smooth.　8. but my
going: unless I go.　11. more . . . it: had dearer reasons for keeping it.　19. gray: Elizabethan writers did not always distinguish
between gray and sky-blue.

24. thick: fast.　29. affections of delight: in the things in which
he took pleasure.　30. humors of blood: natural inclination. See
App. 3.　31. copy: pattern. book: book of manners.　36. abide
a field: fight a battle.　38. defensible: able to put up a defense.
40. precise . . . nice: exact and particular.　45. Monmouth: i.e.,
Prince Henry. Beshrew: plague on.　50. provided: prepared.
52. puissance: might.　61. recordation: memorial.　64. stillstand: standstill.

Fain would I go to meet the Archbishop,   65
But many thousand reasons hold me back.
I will resolve for Scotland. There am I
Till time and vantage° crave my company.
                              [*Exeunt.*]

SCENE IV. *London. The Boar's Head Tavern
          in Eastcheap.*

[*Enter two* DRAWERS.]

1. DRAW. What the devil hast thou brought there?
Applejohns?° Thou knowest Sir John cannot endure
an applejohn.   3

2. DRAW. Mass, thou sayest true. The Prince once
set a dish of applejohns before him, and told him
there were five more Sir Johns and, putting off his
hat, said " I will now take my leave of these six dry,
round, old, withered knights." It angered him to the
heart. But he hath forgot that.   10

1. DRAW. Why, then, cover, and set them down.°
And see if thou canst find out Sneak's noise,° Mistress Tearsheet would fain hear some music. Dispatch. The room where they supped is too hot, they'll
come in straight.   15

2. DRAW. Sirrah, here will be the Prince and Master Poins anon, and they will put on two of our
jerkins and aprons, and Sir John must not know of
it. Bardolph hath brought word.   20

1. DRAW. By the mass, here will be old utis.° It
will be an excellent stratagem.

2. DRAW. I'll see if I can find out Sneak. [*Exit.*]

[*Enter* HOSTESS *and* DOLL TEARSHEET.]

HOST. I' faith, sweetheart, methinks now you are
in an excellent good temperality.° Your pulsidge°
beats as extraordinarily as heart would desire,   26
and your color, I warrant you, is as red as any rose,
in good truth, la! But, i' faith, you have drunk too
much canaries,° and that's a marvelous searching°
wine, and it perfumes the blood ere one can say
" What's this? " How do you now?   32

DOLL. Better than I was. Hem!

HOST. Why, that's well said. A good heart's worth
gold. Lo, here comes Sir John.   35

[*Enter* FALSTAFF.]

FAL. [*Singing*] " When Arthur° first in court " —
Empty the jordan.° [*Exit* FIRST DRAWER.] — [*Sing-*

ing] " And was a worthy king." How now, Mistress
Doll!

HOST. Sick of a calm,° yea, good faith.   40

FAL. So is all her sect. An they be once in a calm,
they are sick.

DOLL. You muddy° rascal, is that all the comfort
you give me?

FAL. You make fat rascals,° Mistress Doll.   45

DOLL. I make them! Gluttony and diseases make
them, I make them not.

FAL. If the cook help to make the gluttony, you
help to make the diseases, Doll. We catch of you,
Doll, we catch of you. Grant that, my poor virtue,
grant that.   51

DOLL. Yea, joy, our chains and our jewels.°

FAL. " Your brooches, pearls, and ouches."° For
to serve bravely is to come halting off, you know; to
come off the breach with his pike bent bravely, and
to surgery bravely; to venture upon the charged
chambers° bravely ——   57

DOLL. Hang yourself, you muddy conger,° hang
yourself!

HOST. By my troth, this is the old fashion. You
two never meet but you fall to some discord. You are
both, i' good truth, as rheumatic° as two dry toasts.
You cannot one bear with another's confirmi-   62
ties.° What the goodyear!° One must bear, and that
must be you. You are the weaker vessel, as they say,
the emptier vessel.   66

DOLL. Can a weak empty vessel bear such a huge
full hogshead? There's a whole merchant's venture
of Bordeaux stuff° in him, you have not seen a
hulk° better stuffed in the hold. Come, I'll be friends
with thee, Jack. Thou art going to the wars, and
whether I shall ever see thee again or no, there is
nobody cares.   73

[*Re-enter* FIRST DRAWER.]

1. DRAW. Sir, Ancient° Pistol's below and would
speak with you.

DOLL. Hang him, swaggering rascal! Let him not
come hither. It is the foul-mouthedst rogue in England.   78

HOST. If he swagger, let him not come here — no,
by my faith. I must live among my neighbors, I'll
no swaggerers. I am in good name and fame with
the very best. Shut the door, there comes no swag-

---

68. vantage: advantage.

Sc. iv: 2. Applejohns: a variety of apple which kept well, but
whose skin was liable to shrivel.   11. cover . . . down: put on
the cloth and lay the table.   12. noise: band of musicians.
21. old utis: rare fun.   25. temperality: Mrs. Quickly may mean
"temper" or may have mixed "temporal" with "spirits." pul-
sidge: pulse.   30. canaries: wine from the Canaries. searching:
that reaches the spot quickly, intoxicating.   36. When Arthur:
the first lines of a popular ballad of Sir Lancelot.   37. jordan:
chamber pot. Elizabethan conveniences were primitive.

40. calm: qualm, feeling of queasiness.   43. muddy: dirty.
45. rascals: with a pun on *rascal*, meaning a deer in poor condition.   52. our . . . jewels: because old ruffians, like Falstaff,
wheedle the jewels out of Doll and her professional sisters.
53. Your . . . ouches: another line from a ballad. ouch: carbuncle.   56–57. charged chambers: loaded cannon.   58. conger:
conger eel.   61. rheumatic: Mrs. Quickly mixes *rheumatic*, damp,
with "choleric," hot-tempered.   63. confirmities: for "infirmities."   What . . . goodyear: meaningless phrase, like "what
the deuce." Its origin is obscure.   68–69. merchant's . . .
stuff: whole cargo of Bordeaux wine.   70. hulk: trading ship.
74. Ancient: ensign, second lieutenant. The Ancient carried the
company ensign

gerers here. I have not lived all this while to have swaggering now. Shut the door, I pray you.   85

FAL. Dost thou hear, Hostess?

HOST. Pray ye, pacify yourself, Sir John. There comes no swaggerers here.

FAL. Dost thou hear? It is mine Ancient.   89

HOST. Tilly-fally,° Sir John, ne'er tell me. Your ancient swaggerer comes not in my doors. I was before Master Tisick, the debuty,° t' other day, and as he said to me, 'twas no longer ago than Wednesday last, "I' good faith, Neighbor Quickly," says he — Master Dumbe, our minister, was by then —   95 "Neighbor Quickly," says he, "receive those that are civil, for," said he, "you are in an ill name." Now a' said so, I can tell whereupon. "For," says he, "you are an honest woman, and well thought on, therefore take heed what guests you receive.   100 Receive," says he, "no swaggering companions."° There comes none here. You would bless you to hear what he said. No, I'll no swaggerers.   104

FAL. He's no swaggerer, Hostess, a tame cheater,° i' faith. You may stroke him as gently as a puppy greyhound. He'll not swagger with a Barbary hen° if her feathers turn back in any show of resistance. Call him up, drawer.   [*Exit* FIRST DRAWER.]

HOST. Cheater, call you him? I will bar no honest man my house, nor no cheater. But I do not love swaggering, by my troth. I am the worse when one says swagger. Feel, masters, how I shake, look you, I warrant you.   114

DOLL. So you do, Hostess.

HOST. Do I? Yea, in very truth do I, an 'twere an aspen leaf. I cannot abide swaggerers.

[*Enter* PISTOL, BARDOLPH, *and* PAGE.]

PIST. God save you, Sir John!   119

FAL. Welcome, Ancient Pistol. Here, Pistol, I charge you° with a cup of sack. Do you discharge° upon mine hostess.

PIST. I will discharge upon her, Sir John, with two bullets.   124

FAL. She is pistolproof, sir, you shall hardly offend° her.

HOST. Come, I'll drink no proofs nor no bullets. I'll drink no more than will do me good, for no man's pleasure, I.   129

PIST. Then to you, Mistress Dorothy. I will charge you.

DOLL. Charge me! I scorn you, scurvy companion. What! You poor, base, rascally, cheating, lack-linen mate! Away, you moldy rogue, away! I am meat for your master.   135

PIST. I know you, Mistress Dorothy.

DOLL. Away, you cutpurse rascal! You filthy bung,° away! By this wine, I'll thrust my knife in your moldy chaps° an you play the saucy cuttle° with me. Away, you bottle-ale rascal! You baskethilt stale juggler,° you! Since when, I pray you, sir? God's light, with two points° on your shoulder? Much!   143

PIST. God let me not live but I will murder your ruff° for this.

FAL. No more, Pistol, I would not have you go off here. Discharge yourself of our company, Pistol.

HOST. No, good Captain Pistol, not here, sweet Captain.   150

DOLL. Captain! Thou abominable damned cheater, art thou not ashamed to be called captain? An captains were of my mind, they would truncheon° you out for taking their names upon you before you have earned them. You a captain! You slave,   155 for what? For tearing a poor whore's ruff in a bawdy house? He a captain! Hang him, rogue! He lives upon moldy stewed prunes and dried cakes. A captain! God's light, these villains will make the word as odious as the word "occupy,"° which   160 was an excellent good word before it was ill sorted,° therefore captains had need look to 't.

BARD. Pray thee go down, good Ancient.

FAL. Hark thee hither, Mistress Doll.   165

PIST. Not I. I tell thee what, Corporal Bardolph, I could tear her. I'll be revenged of her.

PAGE. Pray thee go down.

PIST. I'll see her damned first, to Pluto's damned lake,° by this hand, to the infernal deep, with Erebus° and tortures vile also. Hold hook and line, say I. Down, down, dogs! Down, faitors!° Have we not Hiren here?°   173

HOST. Good Captain Peesel, be quiet, 'tis very late, i' faith. I beseek you now, aggravate your choler.

PIST. These be good humors, indeed! Shall pack horses,
And hollow pampered jades of Asia,
Which cannot go but thirty mile a day,°   179

138. bung: purse (in thieves' language); but Doll is too angry to talk exact sense.   **139. chaps:** cheeks. **cuttle:** lit., the knife used by a cutpurse.   **141. basket-hilt . . . juggler:** one who shows off ancient tricks with an old sword.   **142. points:** laces (for fastening the breastplate to the shoulders).   **145. ruff:** See Pl. 13C and note on p. 95a.   **153. truncheon:** beat with their truncheons. A *truncheon* is a staff carried by officers and officials.   **160. occupy:** like "intercourse," the word had various meanings.   **161. ill sorted:** ill-used.   **169–70. Pluto's . . . lake:** Ancient Pistol loves to talk in a jargon collected from the more extravagant plays of the Admiral's Men at the Rose Theater. He was thus a living parody of the great actor Alleyn. See Gen. Intro. pp. 36b and 41b. **Pluto:** king of the underworld.   **171. Erebus:** Hell.   **172–73. faitors:** cheaters. **Have . . . here:** a much-parodied line from a play (now lost) by Peele.   **177–79. Shall . . . day:** misquotation of a famous line in Marlowe's *Tamburlaine, Part II*, where Tamburlaine enters in a chariot drawn by captive kings and cries: "Holla, ye pampered jades of Asia, What! Can you draw but twenty miles a day?"

90. Tilly-fally: an indignant exclamation.   **92. debuty:** deputy, the representative of the alderman, and responsible for order in his ward.   **101. companions:** ruffians.   **105. cheater:** the confidence man who brings the victim along, naturally smooth-tongued and nice-mannered.   **107. Barbary hen:** guinea fowl.   **121. charge you:** give you a toast. **discharge:** give a toast to.   **126. offend:** hurt.

Compare with Caesars, and with Cannibals,°
And Trojan Greeks? Nay, rather damn them with
King Cerberus,° and let the welkin° roar.
Shall we fall foul for toys?°

HOST. By my troth, Captain, these are very bitter
words.   185

BARD. Be gone, good Ancient. This will grow to
a brawl anon.

PIST. Die men like dogs! Give crowns like pins!
Have we not Hiren here?   189

HOST. O' my word, Captain, there's none such
here. What the goodyear! Do you think I would
deny her? For God's sake, be quiet.

PIST. Then feed, and be fat, my fair Calipolis.°
Come, give's some sack.   194
" Si fortune me tormente, sperato me contento."°
Fear we broadsides? No, let the fiend give fire.
Give me some sack. And, sweetheart, lie thou there.°
                                        [Laying down his sword.]
Come we to full points° here, and are etceteras
    nothing?

FAL. Pistol, I would be quiet.   199

PIST. Sweet knight. I kiss thy neaf.° What! We
have seen the seven stars.°

DOLL. For God's sake, thrust him downstairs. I
cannot endure such a fustian° rascal.

PIST. Thrust him downstairs! Know we not Gallo-
way nags?°   205

FAL. Quoit° him down, Bardolph, like a shovegroat shilling.° Nay, an a' do nothing but speak
nothing, a' shall be nothing here.

BARD. Come, get you downstairs.

PIST. What! Shall we have incision?° Shall we
imbrue?°   [Snatching up his sword.]   210
Then death rock me asleep, abridge° my doleful
    days!
Why then, let grievous, ghastly, gaping wounds
Untwine the Sisters Three!° Come, Atropos, I
    say!

HOST. Here's goodly stuff toward!°

FAL. Give me my rapier, boy.   215

DOLL. I pray thee, Jack, I pray thee do not draw.

FAL. Get you downstairs.
                        [Drawing, and driving PISTOL out.]

HOST. Here's a goodly tumult! I'll forswear   219
keeping house afore I'll be in these tirrits° and
frights. So, murder, I warrant now. Alas, alas! Put
up your naked weapons, put up your naked   222
weapons.   [Exeunt PISTOL and BARDOLPH.]

DOLL. I pray thee, Jack, be quiet. The rascal's
gone. Ah, you whoreson little valiant villain you!

HOST. Are you not hurt i' the groin? Methought
a' made a shrewd thrust at your belly.   228
                        [Re-enter BARDOLPH.]

FAL. Have you turned him out o' doors?

BARD. Yea, sir. The rascal's drunk. You have hurt
him, sir, i' the shoulder.

FAL. A rascal! To brave me!   232

DOLL. Ah, you sweet little rogue you! Alas, poor
ape, how thou sweatest! Come, let me wipe thy face,
come on, you whoreson chops. Ah, rogue! i' faith,
I love thee. Thou art as valorous as Hector of Troy,
worth five of Agamemnon, and ten times better than
the Nine Worthies.° Ah, villain!   239

FAL. A rascally slave! I will toss the rogue in a
blanket.

DOLL. Do, an thou darest for thy heart. An thou
dost, I'll canvass° thee between a pair of sheets.   244
                        [Enter Music.°]

PAGE. The music is come, sir.

FAL. Let them play. Play, sirs. Sit on my knee,
Doll. A rascal bragging slave! The rogue fled from
me like quicksilver.   248

DOLL. I' faith, and thou followedst him like a
church. Thou whoreson little tidy Bartholomew
boar pig,° when wilt thou leave fighting o' days
and foining° o' nights, and begin to patch up thine
old body for Heaven?   253
[Enter, behind, PRINCE HENRY and POINS, disguised
                        as drawers.]

FAL. Peace, good Doll! Do not speak like a death's-
head.° Do not bid me remember mine end.

DOLL. Sirrah, what humor's° the Prince of?

FAL. A good shallow young fellow. A' would have
made a good pantler,° a' would ha' chipped bread
well.°   259

DOLL. They say Poins has a good wit.

FAL. He a good wit? Hang him, baboon! His wit's

---

180. **Cannibals:** for "Hannibals."   182. **King Cerberus:** Cerberus was actually the three-headed dog which guarded the
entrance to Hades. **welkin:** sky.   183. **toys:** trifles.   193. **Then
... Calipolis:** a quotation from Peele's *Battle of Alcazar,*
where the heroic Moor, Muly Mahomet, enters with a lump of
the flesh of a lioness on his sword's point to sustain his starving
wife Calipolis.   195. **Si ... contento:** Pistol's version of an Italian
proverb meaning "If Fortune torments me, Hope contents me."
197. **sweetheart ... there:** To clap his sword noisily on the
table was a common trick of the tavern bully. Cf. *R & J,* III.i.
5–10.   198. **full points:** periods. Pistol has now strayed into
metaphors from writing.   200. **neaf:** fist.   201. **have ... stars:**
i.e., made a night of it.   203. **fustian:** ranting, lit., coarse cloth.
205. **Galloway nags:** Irish horses of poor quality.   206. **Quoit:**
chuck.   207. **shovegroat shilling:** *Shovegroat* (now called shovehalf-
penny) is still played in English public houses. A smooth coin
is slid along the table into a numbered space.   210. **incision:**
bloodletting. **imbrue:** dye our swords with blood.   211. **abridge:**
cut off.   213. **Sisters Three:** The Three Sisters of Destiny who
spin man's fate, of whom Atropos was one.   214. **goodly ... toward:** here's a fine to-do.

220. **tirrits:** twitters.   239. **Nine Worthies:** the great heroes of
legend. See *LLL,* V.i. 130–50; V.ii.536–722.   244. **canvass:** Doll
answers with a pun on canvass, meaning toss in a blanket, and
encourage, have intercourse with. s.d., **Enter Music:** i.e., musicians.   250–51. **Bartholomew ... pig:** Roast pig was one of the
special attractions at St. Bartholomew's Fair, held in London
on August 24.   252. **foining:** thrusting.   255. **death's-head:**
skull, carved on memorials and elsewhere to remind the beholder of his own end. See Pl. 12f.   256. **humor:** character.
See App. 3.   258. **pantler:** pantryman.   258–59. **chipped ...
well:** chipped off the crust, one of the pantryman's jobs.

as thick as Tewksbury mustard.° There's no more conceit° in him than is in a mallet. 263

DOLL. Why does the Prince love him so, then?

FAL. Because their legs are both of a bigness; and a' plays at quoits well; and eats conger and fennel;° and drinks off candles' ends for flapdragons;° and rides the wild mare° with the boys; and jumps upon joined stools;° and swears with a good grace; and wears his boots very smooth, like unto the sign 270 of the leg;° and breeds no bate with telling of discreet stories;° and such other gambol faculties a' has that show a weak mind and an able body, for the which the Prince admits him. For the Prince himself is such another, the weight of a hair will turn the scales between their avoirdupois. 277

PRINCE. Would not this nave of a wheel° have his ears cut off?

POINS. Let's beat him before his whore.

PRINCE. Look whether the withered elder hath not his poll clawed like a parrot.° 282

POINS. Is it not strange that desire should so many years outlive performance?

FAL. Kiss me, Doll.

PRINCE. Saturn° and Venus this year in conjunction! What says the almanac to that? 287

POINS. And look whether the fiery Trigon,° his man, be not lisping to his master's old tables,° his notebook, his counsel-keeper.

FAL. Thou dost give me flattering busses.°

DOLL. By my troth, I kiss thee with a most constant° heart.

FAL. I am old, I am old. 294

DOLL. I love thee better than I love e'er a scurvy young boy of them all.

FAL. What stuff wilt have a kirtle° of? I shall receive money o' Thursday. Shalt have a cap tomorrow. A merry song, come. It grows late, we'll to bed. Thou'lt forget me when I am gone. 300

DOLL. By my troth, thou'lt set me a-weeping an thou sayest so. Prove that ever I dress myself handsome till thy return. Well, hearken at the end.°

FAL. Some sack, Francis. 305

PRINCE & POINS. Anon, anon, sir.

[*Coming forward.*]

FAL. Ha! A bastard son of the King's? And art not thou Poins his brother?

PRINCE. Why, thou globe of sinful continents,° what a life dost thou lead! 310

FAL. A better than thou. I am a gentleman, thou art a drawer.

PRINCE. Very true, sir, and I come to draw you out by the ears. 314

HOST. Oh, the Lord preserve thy good Grace! By my troth, welcome to London. Now, the Lord bless that sweet face of thine! O Jesu, are you come from Wales?

FAL. Thou whoreson mad compound° of majesty, by this light flesh and corrupt blood, thou art welcome. 321

DOLL. How, you fat fool! I scorn you.

POINS. My lord, he will drive you out of your revenge and turn all to a merriment if you take not the heat.° 325

PRINCE. You whoreson candle mine° you, how vilely did you speak of me even now before this honest, virtuous, civil gentlewoman!

HOST. God's blessing of your good heart! And so she is, by my troth. 330

FAL. Didst thou hear me?

PRINCE. Yea, and you knew me, as you did when you ran away by Gadshill. You knew I was at your back, and spoke it on purpose to try my patience.

FAL. No, no, no, not so. I did not think thou wast within hearing. 337

PRINCE. I shall drive you then to confess the willful abuse, and then I know how to handle you.

FAL. No abuse, Hal, o' mine honor, no abuse. 340

PRINCE. Not to dispraise me, and call me pantler and bread-chipper and I know not what?

FAL. No abuse, Hal.

POINS. No abuse? 344

FAL. No abuse, Ned, i' the world. Honest Ned, none. I dispraised him before the wicked, that the wicked might not fall in love with him. In which doing, I have done the part of a careful friend and a true subject, and thy father is to give me thanks for it. No abuse, Hal. None, Ned, none. No, faith, boys, none. 351

PRINCE. See now whether pure fear and entire cowardice doth not make thee wrong this virtuous gentlewoman to close with° us. Is she of the wicked? Is thine hostess here of the wicked? Or is thy boy of the wicked? Or honest Bardolph, whose zeal burns in his nose, of the wicked? 357

---

262. **Tewksbury mustard:** Tewksbury is not far from Stratford-on-Avon, and its mustard balls were famous. 263. **conceit:** inventive wit. 266. **conger . . . fennel:** conger eel flavored with fennel sauce — the kind of dish eaten only by the young and hearty. 267. **flapdragons:** lighted candles floated in a glass of drink. The drinker must drink without burning himself. 268. **rides . . . mare:** plays wild games. 269. **joined stools:** See Pl. 17a. 270–71. **sign . . . leg:** picture of a perfect leg. See App. 12. 271–72. **breeds . . . stories:** causes no trouble by telling discreet tales; i.e., all his tales are indiscreet. 278. **nave . . . wheel:** i.e., the huge round center of the wheel of a country cart. 282. **poll . . . parrot:** Doll is on Falstaff's knee, ruffling his hair. 286. **Saturn:** the father of Jupiter, and so elderly. See App. 1 and 2. 288. **fiery Trigon:** The Zodiac was divided into four trigons; the fiery trigon consisted of the fiery signs, Aries, Leo, and Sagittarius. 289. **tables:** notebook; i.e., Mrs. Quickly. 291. **busses:** kisses. 293. **constant:** faithful. 297. **kirtle:** skirt. See Pl. 9i and k and comment on p. 94b. 304. **hearken . . . end:** a form of the proverb *respice finem:* look at the end; i.e., the end will show.

309. **sinful continents:** a triple pun on the five continents, on contents, and on continence. 319. **compound:** lump. 324–25. **if . . . heat:** if you don't strike while the iron is hot. 326. **candle mine:** mass of tallow. 354. **close with:** come to terms.

POINS. Answer, thou dead elm,° answer.

FAL. The Fiend hath pricked down Bardolph irrecoverable, and his face is Lucifer's privy° kitchen, where he doth nothing but roast maltworms. For the boy, there is a good angel about him, but the Devil outbids him too.   363

PRINCE. For the women?

FAL. For one of them, she is in Hell already, and burns° poor souls. For the other, I owe her money, and whether she be damned for that I know not.

HOST. No, I warrant you.   369

FAL. No, I think thou art not, I think thou art quit° for that. Marry, there is another indictment upon thee, for suffering flesh to be eaten in thy house contrary to the law,° for the which I think thou wilt howl.   374

HOST. All victualers do so. What's a joint of mutton or two in a whole Lent?

PRINCE. You, gentlewoman——

DOLL. What says your Grace?

FAL. His Grace° says that which his flesh rebels against.   [*Knocking within*]   380

HOST. Who knocks so loud at door? Look to the door there, Francis.

[*Enter* PETO.]

PRINCE. Peto, how now! What news?

PETO. The King your father is at Westminster, And there are twenty weak and wearied posts°   385 Come from the North. And as I came along, I met and overtook a dozen captains, Bareheaded, sweating, knocking at the taverns, And asking every one for Sir John Falstaff.

PRINCE. By Heaven, Poins, I feel me much to blame,   390 So idly to profane the precious time, When tempest of commotion, like the south° Borne with black vapor, doth begin to melt And drop upon our bare unarmèd heads.   394 Give me my sword and cloak. Falstaff, good night.

[*Exeunt* PRINCE HENRY, POINS, PETO, *and* BARDOLPH.]

FAL. Now comes in the sweetest morsel of the night, and we must hence and leave it unpicked. [*Knocking within*] More knocking at the door! [*Re-enter* BARDOLPH.] How now! What's the matter?

BARD. You must away to court, sir, presently.° A dozen captains stay at door for you.   402

FAL. [*To the* PAGE] Pay the musicians, sirrah. Farewell, hostess. Farewell, Doll. You see, my good wenches, how men of merit are sought after. The undeserver may sleep when the man of action is called on. Farewell, good wenches. If I be not sent away post,° I will see you again ere I go.   408

DOLL. I cannot speak, if my heart be not ready to burst——Well, sweet Jack, have a care of thyself.

FAL. Farewell, farewell.

[*Exeunt* FALSTAFF *and* BARDOLPH.]

HOST. Well, fare thee well. I have known thee these twenty-nine years come peascod time,° but an honester and truer-hearted man——Well, fare thee well.   415

BARD. [*Within*] Mistress Tearsheet!

HOST. What's the matter?

BARD. [*Within*] Bid Mistress Tearsheet come to my master.   419

HOST. Oh, run, Doll, run. Run, good Doll. Come. [*She comes blubbered.*°] Yea, will you come, Doll?

[*Exeunt.*]

Act III

SCENE I. *Westminster. The palace.*

[*Enter* KING HENRY *in his nightgown,*° *with a* PAGE.]

K. HEN. Go call the Earls of Surrey and of Warwick. But ere they come bid them o'erread these letters, And well consider of them. Make good speed.

[*Exit* PAGE.]

How many thousand of my poorest subjects Are at this hour asleep! O Sleep, O gentle Sleep,   5 Nature's soft nurse, how have I frighted thee, That thou no more wilt weigh my eyelids down And steep my senses in forgetfulness? Why rather, Sleep, liest thou in smoky cribs,° Upon uneasy° pallets° stretching thee,   10 And hushed with buzzing night flies to thy slumber, Than in the perfumed chambers of the great, Under the canopies of costly state° And lulled with sound of sweetest melody? O thou dull god, why liest thou with the vile   15 In loathsome beds and leavest the kingly couch A watch case° or a common 'larum bell?° Wilt thou upon the high and giddy mast Seal up the ship boy's eyes, and rock his brains

---

358. **dead elm**: rotten dead tree. Next to the oak, the elm is the largest in girth of English trees. 360. **privy**: private. 367. **burns**: infects. 371. **quit**: forgiven. 372–73. **flesh . . . law**: See Gen. Intro. pp. 17b–18a. 379. **His Grace**: with a pun on "grace" in the theological sense of "state of grace." 385. **posts**: messengers. See App. 17. 392. **south**: Winds from the south brought **rain.** 401. **presently**: immediately.

408. **post**: posthaste. 413. **peascod time**: when the peas are in pod; early summer. 421. **s.d., blubbered**: weeping. The real emotion of the two women at Falstaff's departure is to be noted.
Act III, Sc. i: s.d., nightgown: dressing gown. 9. **cribs**: huts. 10. **uneasy**: uncomfortable. **pallets**: mattresses. 13. **state**: pomposity. See Pl. 17b. 17. **watch case**: interpreted as (a) sentry box or (b) case of a watch—a good image, as the sleepless King is like a watch which never stops working. **'larum bell**: either (a) a bell used for sounding alarms or (b) the bell of a clock or watch.

In cradle of the rude imperious surge   20
And in the visitation of the winds,
Who take the ruffian billows by the top,
Curling their monstrous heads and hanging them
With deafening clamor in the slippery clouds,
That, with the hurly,° death itself awakes?   25
Canst thou, O partial° Sleep, give thy repose
To the wet sea boy in an hour so rude,
And in the calmest and most stillest night,
With all appliances and means to boot,°
Deny it to a king? Then happy low,° lie down!   30
Uneasy lies the head that wears a crown.
        [Enter WARWICK *and* SURREY.*]*
  WAR. Many good morrows to your Majesty!
  K. HEN. Is it good morrow, lords?
  WAR. 'Tis one o'clock, and past.
  K. HEN. Why, then, good morrow to you all, my
    lords.   35
Have you read o'er the letters that I sent you?
  WAR. We have, my liege.
  K. HEN. Then you perceive the body of our king-
    dom
How foul it is, what rank diseases grow,
And with what danger, near the heart of it.   40
  WAR. It is but as a body yet distempered,°
Which to his former strength may be restored
With good advice and little medicine.
My Lord Northumberland will soon be cooled.
  K. HEN. Oh God! that one might read the book
    of fate,   45
And see the revolution of the times
Make mountains level, and the continent,°
Weary of solid firmness, melt itself
Into the sea! And other times to see
The beachy girdle of the ocean   50
Too wide for Neptune's hips, how chances mock,
And changes fill the cup of alteration
With divers liquors! Oh, if this were seen,
The happiest youth, viewing his progress through,
What perils past, what crosses° to ensue,   55
Would shut the book, and sit him down and die.
'Tis not ten years gone
Since Richard and Northumberland, great friends,
Did feast together, and in two years after
Were they at wars. It is but eight years since   60
This Percy was the man nearest my soul,
Who like a brother toiled in my affairs,
And laid his love and life under my foot —
Yea, for my sake, even to the eyes of Richard
Gave him defiance. But which of you was by —   65

[To WARWICK*]* You, Cousin Nevil,° as I may re-
    member —
When Richard, with his eye brimful of tears,
Then checked and rated° by Northumberland,
Did speak these words, now proved a prophecy?
"Northumberland, thou ladder by the which   70
My cousin Bolingbroke ascends my throne"° —
Though then, God knows, I had no such intent,
But that necessity so bowed the state°
That I and greatness were compelled to kiss —
"The time shall come," thus did he follow it,   75
"The time will come that foul sin, gathering
    head,
Shall break into corruption." So went on
Foretelling this same time's condition,
And the division of our amity.
  WAR. There° is a history in all men's lives,   80
Figuring the nature of the times deceased.°
The which observed, a man may prophesy,
With a near aim, of the main chance of things
As yet not come to life, which in their seeds
And weak beginnings lie intreasured.   85
Such things become the hatch and brood of time,
And by the necessary form of this
King Richard might create a perfect guess
That great Northumberland, then false to him,
Would of that seed grow to a greater falseness,   90
Which should not find a ground to root upon,
Unless on you.
  K. HEN.   Are these things then necessities?
Then let us meet them like necessities.
And that same word even now cries out on us.
They say the Bishop and Northumberland   95
Are fifty thousand strong.
  WAR.   It cannot be, my lord.
Rumor doth double, like the voice and echo,
The numbers of the feared. Please it your Grace
To go to bed. Upon my soul, my lord,
The powers that you already have sent forth   100
Shall bring this prize in very easily.
To comfort you the more, I have received
A certain instance° that Glendower is dead.
Your Majesty hath been this fortnight ill,   104
And these unseasoned° hours perforce must add
Unto your sickness.
  K. HEN.   I will take your counsel.
And were these inward° wars once out of hand,
We would, dear lords, unto the Holy Land.
                        [Exeunt.]

---

25. hurly: tumult.   **26. partial:** having favorites.   **29. means to boot:** means of helping sleep — as detailed in Sir Philip Sidney's famous sonnet. "Take thou of me smooth pillows, sweetest bed, /A chamber deaf to noise and blind to light,/A rosy garland and a weary head." In this soliloquy Shakespeare makes his contribution to the large collection of Elizabethan invocations to sleep. See also *Macb*, II.ii.35–43.   **30. low:** men of lowly rank. **41. distempered:** sick, but not fatally.   **47. continent:** land, shore. **55. crosses:** difficulties.

66. Nevil: This is an anachronism. The title of Earl of Warwick in Henry IV's time was held by the Beauchamp family. **68. rated:** abused.   **70–71. Northumberland . . . throne:** See *Rich II*, V.i.55–68.   **73. bowed . . . state:** weighed down the nation.   **80–92. There . . . you:** i.e., a man's past shows what he will be in the future. Richard could guess that as Northumberland was false to him, so would he be to you.   **81. Figuring . . . deceased:** setting out the past.   **103. instance:** proof.   **105. unseasoned:** unseasonable, late.   **107. inward:** at home.

SCENE II. *Gloucestershire. Before* JUSTICE SHALLOW's *house*

[*Enter* SHALLOW *and* SILENCE, *meeting;* MOULDY, SHADOW, WART, FEEBLE, BULLCALF, *a* SERVANT *or two with them.*]

SHAL. Come on, come on, come on, sir. Give me your hand, sir, give me your hand, sir. An early stirrer, by the rood!° And how doth my good cousin Silence?

SIL. Good morrow, good Cousin Shallow.   5

SHAL. And how doth my cousin your bedfellow? And your fairest daughter and mine, my goddaughter Ellen?

SIL. Alas, a black ousel,° Cousin Shallow!   9

SHAL. By yea and nay, sir, I dare say my cousin William is become a good scholar. He is at Oxford still, is he not?

SIL. Indeed, sir, to my cost.   13

SHAL. A' must, then, to the Inns o' Court° shortly. I was once of Clement's Inn, where I think they will talk of mad Shallow yet.   16

SIL. You were called "lusty Shallow" then, Cousin.

SHAL. By the mass, I was called anything, and I would have done anything indeed too, and roundly° too. There was I, and little John Doit of Staffordshire, and black George Barnes, and Francis Pickbone, and Will Squele, a Cotswold man, — you had not four such swingebucklers° in all Inns o' Court again. And I may say to you we knew where   25 the bona robas° were, and had the best of them all at commandment.° Then was Jack Falstaff, now Sir John, a boy, and page to Thomas Mowbray, Duke of Norfolk.

SIL. This Sir John, Cousin, that comes hither anon about soldiers?   31

SHAL. The same Sir John, the very same. I see him break Skogan's head at the court gate when a' was a crack° not thus high. And the very same day did I fight with one Sampson Stockfish, a fruiterer, behind Gray's Inn. Jesu, Jesu, the mad days that I have spent! And to see how many of my old acquaintance are dead!   38

SIL. We shall all follow, Cousin.

SHAL. Certain, 'tis certain, very sure, very sure. Death, as the Psalmist saith, is certain to all, all shall die. How° a good yoke of bullocks at Stamford° fair?   43

SIL. By my troth, I was not there.

SHAL. Death is certain. Is old Double of your town living yet?

SIL. Dead, sir.   47

SHAL. Jesu, Jesu, dead! A' drew a good bow, and dead! A' shot a fine shoot. John a Gaunt° loved him well, and betted much money on his head. Dead! A' would have clapped i' the clout° at twelvescore,° and carried you a forehand shaft° a fourteen and fourteen and a half, that it would have done a man's heart good to see. How a score of ewes now?   55

SIL. Thereafter as they be. A score of good ewes may be worth ten pounds.

SHAL. And is old Double dead?

SIL. Here come two of Sir John Falstaff's men, as I think.   60

[*Enter* BARDOLPH, *and one with him.*]

BARD. Good morrow, honest gentlemen. I beseech you, which is Justice Shallow?

SHAL. I am Robert Shallow, sir, a poor esquire° of this county, and one of the King's Justices of the Peace. What is your good pleasure with me?   65

BARD. My captain, sir, commends him to you, my captain, Sir John Falstaff, a tall° gentleman, by Heaven, and a most gallant leader.

SHAL. He greets me well, sir. I knew him a good backsword man.° How doth the good knight? May I ask how my lady his wife doth?   71

BARD. Sir, pardon, a soldier is better accommodated° than with a wife.

SHAL. It is well said, in faith, sir, and it is well said indeed too. Better accommodated! It is good, yea, indeed is it. Good phrases are surely, and ever were, very commendable. Accommodated! It comes of *accommodo.*° Very good, a good phrase.

BARD. Pardon me, sir, I have heard the word.   80 Phrase call you it? By this good day, I know not the phrase, but I will maintain the word with my sword to be a soldierlike word, and a word of exceeding good command,° by Heaven. Accommodated; that is, when a man is, as they say, accommodated;   85 or when a man is, being, whereby a' may be thought to be accommodated. Which is an excellent thing.

SHAL. It is very just.°

[*Enter* FALSTAFF.]

Look, here comes good Sir John. Give me your good hand, give me your Worship's good hand. By   90 my troth, you like well° and bear your years very well. Welcome, good Sir John.

FAL. I am glad to see you well, good Master Robert Shallow. Master Surecard, as I think?   95

Sc. ii: **3. rood:** crucifix.   **9. ousel:** blackbird.   **14. Inns o' Court:** See Gen. Intro. p. 31b.   **20. roundly:** "made a good job of it."   **24. swingebucklers:** swashbucklers.   **26. bona robas:** showy girls.   **27. at commandment:** when we wanted.   **34. crack:** small boy.   **42. How:** how much.   **43. Stamford:** an ancient town in Northamptonshire.

49. John a Gaunt: father of Henry IV. See *Rich II.*   **52. clapped . . . clout:** smacked it in the center of the target. **clout:** piece of cloth used for the bull's-eye. **twelvescore:** i.e., 240 yards. **53. forehand shaft:** heavy arrow for long-range shooting. **63. esquire:** gentleman of superior rank, rating immediately below a knight.   **67. tall:** valiant.   **70. backsword man:** expert at singlestick. A singlestick is a stick with a basketwork protection for the hand.   **73. accommodated:** provided — at this time regarded as rather a precious word.   **79. accommodo:** i.e., I provide. **83–84. word . . . command:** an exceedingly good military term. **88. just:** justly said.   **91. like well:** look well, thrive.

SHAL. No, Sir John, it is my cousin Silence, in commission with me.°

FAL. Good Master Silence, it well befits you should be of the peace.

SIL. Your good Worship is welcome.   100

FAL. Fie! This is hot weather, gentlemen. Have you provided me here half a dozen sufficient° men?

SHAL. Marry, have we,° sir. Will you sit?

FAL. Let me see them, I beseech you.   105

SHAL. Where's the roll? Where's the roll? Where's the roll? Let me see, let me see, let me see. So, so, so,° so, so, so, so. Yea, marry, sir. Ralph Mouldy! Let them appear as I call, let them do so, let them do so. Let me see, where is Mouldy?   111

MOUL. Here, an 't please you.

SHAL. What think you, Sir John? A good-limbed fellow, young, strong, and of good friends.°

FAL. Is thy name Mouldy?   115

MOUL. Yea, an 't please you.

FAL. 'Tis the more time thou wert used.

SHAL. Ha, ha, ha! Most excellent, i' faith! Things that are moldy lack use. Very singular good! In faith, well said, Sir John, very well said.   120

FAL. Prick° him.

MOUL. I was pricked well enough before, an you could have let me alone. My old dame° will be undone now for one to do her husbandry° and her drudgery. You need not to have pricked me, there are other men fitter to go out than I.   126

FAL. Go to. Peace, Mouldy. You shall go. Mouldy, it is time you were spent.

MOUL. Spent!

SHAL. Peace, fellow, peace, stand aside. Know you where you are? For the other, Sir John. Let me see. Simon Shadow!°   132

FAL. Yea, marry, let me have him to sit under. He's like to be a cold° soldier.

SHAL. Where's Shadow?

SHAD. Here, sir.

FAL. Shadow, whose son art thou?   137

SHAD. My mother's son, sir.

FAL. Thy mother's son! Like enough, and thy father's shadow. So the son of the female is the shadow of the male. It is often so, indeed, but much° of the father's substance!   142

SHAL. Do you like him, Sir John?

FAL. Shadow will serve for summer. Prick him, for we have a number of shadows to fill up the muster book.°   146

SHAL. Thomas Wart!

FAL. Where's he?

WART. Here, sir.

FAL. Is thy name Wart?   150

WART. Yea, sir.

FAL. Thou art a very ragged wart.

SHAL. Shall I prick him down, Sir John?

FAL. It were superfluous, for his apparel is built upon his back, and the whole frame stands upon pins. Prick him no more.   156

SHAL. Ha, ha, ha! You can do it,° sir, you can do it. I commend you well. Francis Feeble!

FEE. Here, sir.

SHAL. What trade art thou, Feeble?   160

FEE. A woman's tailor,° sir.

SHAL. Shall I prick him, sir?

FAL. You may. But if he had been a man's tailor, he'd ha' pricked you. Wilt thou make as many holes in an enemy's battle as thou hast done in a woman's petticoat?   166

FEE. I will do my goodwill, sir. You can have no more.

FAL. Well said, good woman's tailor! Well said, courageous Feeble! Thou wilt be as valiant as the wrathful dove or most magnanimous mouse. Prick the woman's tailor. Well, Master Shallow, deep, Master Shallow.   173

FEE. I would Wart might have gone, sir.

FAL. I would thou wert a man's tailor, that thou mightst mend him and make him fit to go. I cannot put him to a private soldier that is the leader of so many thousands.° Let that suffice, most forcible Feeble.

FEE. It shall suffice, sir.   180

FAL. I am bound to thee, reverend Feeble. Who is next?

SHAL. Peter Bullcalf o' the green!

FAL. Yea, marry, let's see Bullcalf.

BULL. Here, sir.   185

FAL. 'Fore God, a likely fellow! Come, prick me Bullcalf till he roar again.

BULL. Oh Lord! Good my lord Captain ——

FAL. What, dost thou roar before thou art pricked?

BULL. Oh Lord, sir! I am a diseased man.   191

FAL. What disease hast thou?

BULL. A whoreson cold, sir, a cough, sir, which I caught with ringing in the King's affairs upon his coronation day,° sir.   195

FAL. Come, thou shalt go to the wars in a gown, we will have away thy cold, and I will take such order that thy friends shall ring for thee. Is here all?   199

SHAL. Here is two more called than your number.

97. in . . . me: he also holds a commission of the peace; i.e., is a magistrate. **102. sufficient:** fit. **104. have we:** we certainly have. **109. So . . . so:** *So* used thus in dialogue usually indicates action or gesture. Shallow checks off the recruits from their names on the roll. **114. of . . . friends:** i.e., comes of decent family. **121. Prick:** mark him down on the list. The names of those selected from a list were actually pricked with a pin. **123. dame:** mother. **124. husbandry:** farm work. **132. Shadow:** See Gen. Intro. p. 30b. **134. cold:** with a pun on *cold*, meaning unwilling. **141. much:** not much. **146. muster book:** nominal roll.

157. You . . . it: you are a wit. **161. woman's tailor:** Like modern male designers of women's wear, often a feeble specimen of manhood. **178. many thousands:** i.e., lice. **195. coronation day:** accession day, observed as an annual holiday. See App. 19.

You must have but four here, sir. And so I pray you go in with me to dinner.

FAL. Come, I will go drink with you, but I cannot tarry dinner. I am glad to see you, by my troth, Master Shallow. 205

SHAL. Oh, Sir John, do you remember since we lay all night in the windmill in Saint George's field?°

FAL. No more of that, good Master Shallow, no more of that.

SHAL. Ha! 'Twas a merry night. And is Jane Nightwork alive? 211

FAL. She lives, Master Shallow.

SHAL. She never could away with° me.

FAL. Never, never. She would always say she could not abide Master Shallow. 215

SHAL. By the mass, I could anger her to the heart. She was then a bona roba. Doth she hold her own well?

FAL. Old, old, Master Shallow. 219

SHAL. Nay, she must be old, she cannot choose but be old, certain she's old, and had Robin Nightwork by old Nightwork before I came to Clement's Inn.

SIL. That's fifty-five year ago. 224

SHAL. Ha, Cousin Silence, that thou hadst seen that that this knight and I have seen! Ha, Sir John, said I well?

FAL. We have heard the chimes at midnight, Master Shallow. 229

SHAL. That we have, that we have, that we have — in faith, Sir John, we have. Our watchword was "Hem boys!"° Come, let's to dinner, come, let's to dinner. Jesus, the days that we have seen! Come, come. [*Exeunt* FALSTAFF *and the* JUSTICES.] 234

BULL. Good Master Corporate° Bardolph, stand my friend, and here's four Harry ten shillings in French crowns° for you. In very truth, sir, I had as lief° be hanged, sir, as go. And yet, for mine own part, sir, I do not care, but rather because I am 240 unwilling, and, for mine own part, have a desire to stay with my friends. Else, sir, I did not care, for mine own part, so much.

BARD. Go to, stand aside. 243

MOUL. And, good Master Corporal Captain, for my old dame's sake, stand my friend. She has nobody to do anything about her when I am gone, and she is old and cannot help herself. You shall have forty,° sir.

BARD. Go to, stand aside. 249

FEE. By my troth, I care not, a man can die but once. We owe God a death. I'll ne'er bear a base

mind. An 't° be my destiny, so; an 't be not, so. No man's too good to serve 's prince, and let it go which way it will, he that dies this year is quit° for the next. 255

BARD. Well said. Thou'rt a good fellow.

FEE. Faith, I'll bear no base mind.

[*Re-enter* FALSTAFF *and the* JUSTICES.]

FAL. Come, sir, which men shall I have?

SHAL. Four of which you please.

BARD. Sir, a word with you. I have three pound to free Mouldy and Bullcalf. 261

FAL. Go to. Well.

SHAL. Come, Sir John, which four will you have?

FAL. Do you choose for me.

SHAL. Marry, then, Mouldy, Bullcalf, Feeble, and Shadow. 267

FAL. Mouldy and Bullcalf. For you, Mouldy, stay at home till you are past service. And for your part, Bullcalf, grow till you come unto it. I will none of you.

SHAL. Sir John, Sir John, do not yourself wrong. They are your likeliest men, and I would have you served with the best. 274

FAL. Will you tell me, Master Shallow, how to choose a man? Care I for the limb, the thews,° the stature, bulk, and big assemblance° of a man! Give me the spirit, Master Shallow. Here's Wart. You see what a ragged appearance it is. A' shall charge you and discharge° you with the motion of a 280 pewterer's hammer,° come off and on swifter than he that gibbets on the brewer's bucket.° And this same half-faced° fellow, Shadow. Give me this man. He presents no mark to the enemy, the foeman may with as great aim level at the edge of a pen- 285 knife. And for a retreat, how swiftly will this Feeble the woman's tailor run off! Oh, give me the spare men, and spare me the great ones. Put me a caliver° into Wart's hand, Bardolph. 290

BARD. Hold, Wart, traverse.° Thus, thus, thus.

FAL. Come, manage me your caliver. So. Very well. Go to. Very good, exceeding good. Oh, give me always a little, lean, old, chapped,° bald shot. Well said, i' faith, Wart, thou'rt a good scab. Hold, there's a tester° for thee. 296

SHAL. He is not his craft's master, he doth not do it right. I remember at Mile End Green, when I lay at Clement's Inn — I was then Sir Dagonet in Ar-

---

207. Saint . . . field: an open district west of Southwark in London — a low neighborhood.　213. could . . . with: could endure.　232. Hem boys: one of those meaningless convivial cries, like "Here's how."　235. Corporate: corporal.　236–37. Harry . . . crowns: When Shakespeare wrote the play a Henry VII ten shillings was worth 5s, and a French crown 4s. Bullcalf's contribution was in all worth £1.　239. lief: soon.　247. forty: i.e., shillings.

252. An't: if it.　254. quit: exempt.　276. thews: sinews.　277. assemblance: composition, frame.　279–80. charge . . . discharge: load and fire. See Pl. 22f, and p. 99a.　281. pewterer's hammer: when pewter is handwrought with a hammer, the pewterer keeps up a quick, even beat.　282. gibbets . . . bucket: The brewer's man was equipped with a wooden yoke on his shoulder; at either end hung a chain and hook to which he attached a bucket. gibbets: hangs.　283. half-faced: thinfaced.　289. caliver: light musket used by the infantry. See Pl. 22f.　291. traverse: quick march. Here Wart is put through the drill by Bardolph and Falstaff.　294. chapped: dry-skinned.　296. tester: sixpence.

thur's show° — there was a little quiver° fel- 300
low, and a' would manage you his piece thus, and a'
would about and about, and come you in and come
you in. " Rah, tah, tah,"° would a' say, " Bounce "°
would a' say, and away again would a' go, and again
would a' come. I shall ne'er see such a fellow.   306

FAL. These fellows will do well, Master Shallow.
God keep you, Master Silence. I will not use many
words with you. Fare you well, gentlemen both. I
thank you. I must a dozen mile tonight. Bardolph,
give the soldiers coats.   311

SHAL. Sir John, the Lord bless you! God prosper
your affairs! God send us peace! At your return visit
our house, let our old acquaintance be renewed.
Peradventure I will with ye to the court.   316

FAL. 'Fore God, I would you would, Master
Shallow.

SHAL. Go to, I have spoke at a word.° God keep
you.   320

FAL. Fare you well, gentle gentlemen. [*Exeunt*
JUSTICES.] On, Bardolph, lead the men away.
[*Exeunt* BARDOLPH, RECRUITS, *etc.*] As I return, I
will fetch off° these Justices. I do see the bottom of
Justice Shallow. Lord, Lord, how subject we 325
old men are to this vice of lying! This same starved
Justice hath done nothing but prate to me of the
wildness of his youth, and the feats he hath done
about Turnbull Street,° and every third word a lie,
duer° paid to the hearer than the Turk's trib- 330
ute.° I do remember him at Clement's Inn like a
man made after supper of a cheeseparing. When a'
was naked, he was for all the world like a forked
radish, with a head fantastically carved upon it with
a knife. A' was so forlorn that his dimensions 335
to any thick° sight were invisible. A' was the very
genius of famine, yet lecherous as a monkey, and
the whores called him mandrake.° A' came ever in
the rearward of the fashion, and sung those tunes
to the overscutched° huswives that he heard 340
the carmen whistle, and sware they were his fancies
or his good nights.° And now is this Vice's dagger°
become a squire, and talks as familiarly of John a
Gaunt as if he had been sworn brother to him, and

I'll be sworn a' ne'er saw him but once in the 345
tiltyard and then he burst his head for crowding
among the Marshal's men.° I saw it, and told John
a Gaunt he beat his own name, for you might have
thrust him and all his apparel into an eelskin, the
case of a treble hautboy° was a mansion for 350
him, a court. And now has he land and beefs. Well,
I'll be acquainted with him if I return, and it shall
go hard but I will make him a philosopher's two
stones° to me. If the young dace° be a bait for the
old pike, I see no reason in the law of nature 355
but I may snap at him. Let time shape, and there an
end.   [*Exit.*]

Act IV

SCENE I. *Yorkshire. Gaultree Forest.*

[*Enter the* ARCHBISHOP OF YORK, MOWBRAY,
HASTINGS, *and others.*]

ARCH. What is this forest called?

HAST. 'Tis Gaultree Forest, an 't shall please your
Grace.

ARCH. Here stand, my lords, and send discover-
ers° forth
To know the numbers of our enemies.

HAST. We have sent forth already.

ARCH.   'Tis well done.
My friends and brethren in these great affairs,   6
I must acquaint you that I have received
New-dated letters from Northumberland,
Their cold intent, tenor and substance, thus:
Here doth he wish his person, with such powers 10
As might hold sortance with his quality,°
The which he could not levy, whereupon
He is retired, to ripe° his growing fortunes,
To Scotland. And concludes in hearty prayers
That your attempts may overlive° the hazard 15
And fearful meeting of their opposite.°

MOWB. Thus do the hopes we have in him touch
ground
And dash themselves to pieces.

[*Enter a* MESSENGER.]

HAST.   Now, what news?

---

300. **Arthur's show:** an archery club in which each of the members
took the name of one of King Arthur's knights. Dagonet was
Arthur's fool. **quiver:** nimble.   304. **Rah . . . tah:** imitation of
drumbeats. The drum was used to give commands to the infantry. **Bounce:** bang! The description of the action of the
shot is accurate. The front rank of marksmen came forward
with their pieces loaded, fired, and then withdrew to the rear to
reload.   319. **spoke . . . word:** mean what I say.   324. **fetch off:**
get the better of.   329. **Turnbull Street:** a red-light district.
330. **duer:** more promptly when due.   330–31. **Turk's tribute:**
The Turks were greatly feared by the peoples of the Mediterranean, and tribute demanded by the Turks was promptly
paid.   336. **thick:** near.   338. **mandrake:** See I.ii.17n.   340. **over-
scutched:** often whipped — because they had played the whore.
342. **fancies . . . nights:** his love songs or his lullabies. **Vice's
dagger:** wooden dagger — thin and harmless. See *T Night*, IV.ii.
134–41,n.

347. **Marshal's men:** The Knight Marshal was the Court official
directly responsible for keeping order in the Court and its precincts.   350. **hautboy:** oboe, a long narrow wind instrument.
353–54. **philosopher's . . . stones:** i.e., the notions of transmuting
base metal into gold and of compounding the elixir of life which
would give perpetual youth. See App. 21.   354. **dace:** small fish
used as live bait for pike.

Act IV, Sc. i: 3. **discoverers:** scouts.   11. **hold . . . quality:**
be suitable to his rank.   13. **ripe:** make ripe.   15. **overlive:**
survive.   16. **opposite:** opponent.

MESS. West of this forest, scarcely off a mile,
In goodly form° comes on the enemy,   20
And by the ground they hide I judge their number
Upon or near the rate of thirty thousand.
　　MOWB. The just proportion° that we gave them
　　out.°
Let us sway° on and face them in the field.
　　ARCH. What well-appointed° leader fronts us
　　here?   25

　　　　　　[Enter WESTMORELAND.]

　　MOWB. I think it is my Lord of Westmoreland.
　　WEST. Health and fair greeting from our general,
The Prince, Lord John and Duke of Lancaster.
　　ARCH. Say on, my Lord of Westmoreland, in
　　peace.
What doth concern your coming?
　　WEST.　　　　　　Then, my lord,   30
Unto your Grace do I in chief address
The substance of my speech. If that rebellion
Came like itself, in base and abject routs,°
Led on by bloody youth, guarded° with rags,
And countenanced° by boys and beggary —   35
I say if damned commotion° so appeared,
In his true, native, and most proper shape,
You, Reverend Father, and these noble lords
Had not been here, to dress the ugly form
Of base and bloody insurrection   40
With your fair honors. You, Lord Archbishop,
Whose see° is by a civil° peace maintained,
Whose beard the silver hand of peace hath touched,
Whose learning and good letters° peace hath tu-
　　tored,
Whose white investments° figure innocence,   45
The dove and very blessed spirit of peace,
Wherefore do you so ill translate yourself
Out of the speech of peace that bears such grace
Into the harsh and boisterous tongue of war,
Turning your books to graves, your ink to blood,   50
Your pens to lances, and your tongue divine
To a loud trumpet and a point° of war?
　　ARCH. Wherefore do I this? So the question
　　stands.
Briefly to this end: We are all diseased,
And with our surfeiting and wanton° hours   55
Have brought ourselves into a burning fever,
And we must bleed° for it. Of which disease
Our late King, Richard, being infected, died.
But,° my most noble Lord of Westmoreland,

I take not on me here as a physician,   60
Nor do I as an enemy to peace
Troop in the throngs of military men,
But rather show awhile like fearful war,
To diet rank° minds sick of happiness
And purge the obstructions which begin to stop   65
Our very veins of life. Hear me more plainly.
I have in equal° balance justly weighed
What wrongs our arms may do, what wrongs we
　　suffer,
And find our griefs° heavier than our offenses.
We see which way the stream of time doth run,   70
And are enforced from our most quiet there
By the rough torrent of occasion,°
And have the summary of all our griefs,
When time shall serve, to show in articles,°
Which long ere this we offered to the King,   75
And might by no suit° gain our audience.°
When we are wronged and would unfold our
　　griefs,
We are denied access unto his person
Even by those men that most have done us wrong.
The dangers of the days but newly gone,   80
Whose memory is written on the earth
With yet appearing blood, and the examples
Of every minute's instance,° present now,
Hath put us in these ill-beseeming° arms,
Not to break peace or any branch of it,   85
But to establish here a peace indeed,
Concurring both in name and quality.°
　　WEST. When ever yet was your appeal denied?
Wherein have you been gallèd° by the King?
What peer hath been suborned° to grate on° you,
That you should seal this lawless bloody book   91
Of forged rebellion with a seal divine,°
And consecrate commotion's bitter edge?°
　　ARCH. My brother general, the commonwealth,
To brother born a household cruelty,   95
I make my quarrel in particular.°
　　WEST. There is no need of any such redress,
Or if there were, it not belongs to you.
　　MOWB. Why not to him in part, and to us all
That feel the bruises of the days before,   100
And suffer the condition of these times

64. rank: a medical term meaning in a condition requiring blood-letting. 67. equal: exact. 69. griefs: grievances. 72. occasion: circumstances. 74. in articles: detailed in a schedule. 76. suit: petition. audience: personal hearing. 82–83. examples . . . in-stance: examples of which each minute gives fresh instances. 84. ill-beseeming: unseemly. 87. Concurring . . . quality: which shall agree in name and nature; i.e., be a genuine peace. 89. galled: made sore. 90. suborned: procured. grate on: annoy. 91–92. you . . . divine: you should fix your divine seal as guaran-teeing the forged deed of rebellion. book: deed, document. 93. edge: sword. 94–96. My . . . particular: These difficult lines have been much annotated. As they stand, they are unintel-ligible. Most commentators suspect that something has been left out. Dr. Johnson, who amended *brother* in l. 94 to *quarrel*, ex-plained *brother* in l. 95 as a reference to the Archbishop's own brother put to death by the King. See *I Hen IV*, I.iii.270.

20. form: formation. 23. just proportion: exact estimate. gave . . . out: reported. 24. sway: push. 25. well-appointed: well-armed. 33. routs: mobs. 34. guarded: adorned, ornamented. 35. countenanced: supported. 36. commotion: riot. 42. see: the ecclesiastical district controlled by the Archbishop. civil: well-ordered. 44. good letters: wide reading. 45. investments: vestments. 52. point: trumpet call. 55. surfeiting . . . wanton: gluttonous and frivolous. 57. bleed: be let blood, a normal treatment for fever. 59–66. But . . . life: i.e., but I do not intend to be a physician and cure by bleeding, but rather by wholesome diet and purges.

To lay a heavy and unequal° hand
Upon our honors?
   WEST.   Oh, my good Lord Mowbray,
Construe the times to their necessities,°
And you shall say indeed it is the time,   105
And not the King, that doth you injuries.
Yet for your part, it not appears to me
Either from the King or in the present time
That you should have an inch of any ground
To build a grief on. Were you not restored   110
To all the Duke of Norfolk's signories,°
Your noble and right well remembered father's?
   MOWB. What thing, in honor, had my father lost
That need to be revived and breathed in me?   114
The King that loved him, as the state stood then,
Was force perforce° compelled to banish him.
And then that Henry Bolingbroke° and he,
Being mounted and both rousèd in their seats,°
Their neighing coursers daring° of the spur, 119
Their armèd staves in charge,° their beavers° down,
Their eyes of fire sparkling through sights of
    steel
And the loud trumpet blowing them together —
Then, then, when there was nothing could have
    stayed
My father from the breast of Bolingbroke,
Oh, when the King did throw his warder° down,
His own life hung upon the staff he threw.   126
Then threw he down himself and all their lives
That by indictment° and by dint° of sword
Have since miscarried under Bolingbroke.
   WEST. You speak, Lord Mowbray, now you know
    not what.   130
The Earl of Hereford was reputed then
In England the most valiant gentleman.
Who knows on whom fortune would then have
    smiled?
But if your father had been victor there,
He ne'er had borne it out° of Coventry.   135
For all the country in a general voice
Cried hate upon him, and all their prayers and
    love
Were set on Hereford, whom they doted on
And blessed and graced° indeed, more than the
    King.
But this is mere digression from my purpose. 140
Here come I from our princely General
To know your griefs, to tell you from His Grace
That he will give you audience, and wherein

It shall appear that your demands are just,
You shall enjoy them, everything set off°   145
That might so much as think you enemies.
   MOWB. But he hath forced us to compel this offer,
And it proceeds from policy,° not love.
   WEST. Mowbray, you overween° to take it so.
This offer comes from mercy, not from fear. 150
For, lo! within a ken° our army lies,
Upon mine honor, all too confident
To give admittance to a thought of fear.
Our battle° is more full of names° than yours,
Our men more perfect in the use of arms,   155
Our armor all as strong, our cause the best.
Then reason will our hearts should be as good.
Say you not then our offer is compelled.
   MOWB. Well, by my will we shall admit no parley.
   WEST. That argues but the shame of your offense.
A rotten case abides no handling.   161
   HAST. Hath the Prince John a full commission,°
In very ample virtue° of his father,
To hear and absolutely to determine
Of what conditions we shall stand upon?   165
   WEST. That is intended in the General's name.°
I muse° you make so slight a question.
   ARCH. Then take, my Lord of Westmoreland, this
    schedule,
For this contains our general grievances.
Each° several article herein redressed,   170
All members of our cause, both here and hence,
That are insinewed to this action,
Acquitted by a true substantial form,
And present execution of our wills
To us and to our purposes confined,   175
We come within our awful banks again,
And knit our powers to the arm of peace.
   WEST. This will I show the General. Please you,
    lords,
In sight of both our battles we may meet,
And either end in peace — which God so frame!° —
Or to the place of difference° call the swords 181
Which must decide it.
   ARCH.   My lord, we will do so.
                      [*Exit* WESTMORELAND.]
   MOWB. There is a thing within my bosom tells me

102. **unequal:** unjust.   104. **Construe . . . necessities:** remember that in these lawless times injustices must often be committed. **construe:** interpret.   111. **signories:** estates.   116. **force perforce:** forced by necessity, willy-nilly.   117. **And . . . Bolingbroke:** For this episode, see *Rich II*, I.iii. 100–18.   118. **roused . . . seats:** raised in their saddles.   119. **daring:** not afraid, eager for.   120. **staves in charge:** lances leveled in readiness. **beaver:** visor, face piece of the helmet. See Pl. 8a.   125. **warder:** staff. 128. **indictment:** legal accusation. **dint:** stroke.   135. **ne'er . . . out:** would not have got out alive.   139. **graced:** favored.

145. **set off:** laid aside, forgotten.   148. **policy:** cunning. 149. **overween:** presume.   151. **ken:** lit., the limit of sight, 20 miles.   154. **battle:** army drawn up for battle. **names:** distinguished leaders.   162. **commission:** written authority signed by the King.   163. **virtue:** power.   166. **intended . . . name:** naturally included as part of a general's powers.   167. **muse:** marvel. 170–77. **Each . . . peace:** when each separate (*several*) article of this schedule has been redressed, and when all the members who have made common cause with us, be they here or elsewhere (*hence*), that are joined by strong sinews (*insinewed*) to this action, and when each have been acquitted of any crime in proper legal form, and when our desires (*wills*) have been immediately satisfied (*executed*) but confined to what we intended, then will we return to the limits of due obedience (*awful banks*), and restore our army to peaceful labor.   180. **frame:** fashion, accomplish.   181. **difference:** dispute, battle.

That no conditions of our peace can stand.

HAST. Fear you not that. If we can make our
    peace   185
Upon such large terms and so absolute
As our conditions shall consist upon,
Our peace shall stand as firm as rocky mountains.

MOWB. Yea, but our valuation° shall be such
That every slight and false-derivèd cause —   190
Yea, every idle,° nice° and wanton° reason —
Shall to the King taste° of this action,
That, were our royal faiths martyrs in love,°
We shall be winnowed with so rough a wind
That even our corn shall seem as light as chaff 195
And good from bad find no partition.°

ARCH. No, no, my lord. Note this. The King is
    weary
Of dainty° and such picking° grievances.
For he hath found to end one doubt by death
Revives two greater in the heirs of life,°   200
And therefore will he wipe his tables° clean,
And keep no telltale to his memory
That may repeat and history his loss
To new remembrance. For full well he knows
He cannot so precisely weed this land   205
As his misdoubts present occasion.°
His foes are so enrooted with his friends
That, plucking to unfix an enemy,
He doth unfasten so and shake a friend.
So that this land, like an offensive wife   210
That hath enraged him on to offer strokes,
As he is striking, holds his infant up,
And hangs resolved correction° in the arm
That was upreared to execution.

HAST. Besides, the King hath wasted all his rods
On late offenders, that he now doth lack   216
The very instruments of chastisement.
So that his power, like to a fangless lion,
May offer,° but not hold.

ARCH.   'Tis very true.
And therefore be assured, my good Lord Marshal,
If we do now make our atonement° well,   221
Our peace will, like a broken limb united,
Grow stronger for the breaking.

MOWB.   Be it so.
Here is returned my Lord of Westmoreland.
    [*Re-enter* WESTMORELAND.]

WEST. The Prince is here at hand. Pleaseth your
    lordship   225

To meet His Grace just° distance 'tween our armies.

MOWB. Your Grace of York, in God's name, then,
    set forward.

ARCH. Before, and greet His Grace. My lord, we
    come.   [*Exeunt.*]

SCENE II. *Another part of the forest.*

[*Enter, from one side,* MOWBRAY, *attended; afterward, the* ARCHBISHOP, HASTINGS, *and others; from
the other side,* PRINCE JOHN OF LANCASTER, *and*
WESTMORELAND; OFFICERS, *and others with them.*]

LANC. You are well encountered here, my Cousin
    Mowbray.
Good day to you, gentle Lord Archbishop,
And so to you, Lord Hastings, and to all.
My Lord of York, it better showed with you
When that your flock, assembled by the bell,   5
Encircled you to hear with reverence
Your exposition on the holy text
Than now to see you here an iron man,°
Cheering a rout of rebels with your drum,
Turning the word to sword and life to death.   10
That man that sits within a monarch's heart,
And ripens in the sunshine of his favor,
Would he abuse the countenance of the King,
Alack, what mischiefs might he set abroach°
In shadow of such greatness! With you, Lord Bishop,
It is even so. Who hath not heard it spoken   16
How deep you were within the books of God?
To us the Speaker in His parliament,
To us the imagined voice of God Himself,
The very opener and intelligencer°   20
Between the grace, the sanctities of Heaven
And our dull workings.° Oh, who shall believe
But you misuse the reverence of your place,
Employ the countenance and grace of Heaven
As a false favorite doth his Prince's name,   **25**
In deeds dishonorable? You have ta'en up,
Under the counterfeited zeal of God,
The subjects of His substitute,° my father,
And both against the peace of Heaven and him
Have here upswarmed° them.

ARCH.   Good my Lord of Lancaster,   30
I am not here against your father's peace,
But, as I told my Lord of Westmoreland,
The time misordered doth, in common sense,
Crowd us and crush° us to this monstrous° form,
To hold our safety up.° I sent your Grace   35
The parcels° and particulars of our grief,

The which hath been with scorn shoved from the
    Court,
Whereon this Hydra° son of war is born,
Whose dangerous eyes may well be charmed asleep
With grant of our most just and right desires,   40
And true obedience, of this madness cured,
Stoop tamely to the foot of majesty.
    MOWB. If not, we ready are to try our fortunes
To the last man.
    HAST.   And though we here fall down,
We have supplies° to second° our attempt.   45
If they miscarry, theirs shall second them,
And so success of mischief° shall be born,
And heir from heir shall hold this quarrel up
Whiles England shall have generation.
    LANC. You are too shallow, Hastings, much too
    shallow,   50
To sound° the bottom of the aftertimes.
    WEST. Pleaseth your Grace to answer them di-
    rectly
How far forth you do like their articles.
    LANC. I like them all, and do allow them well,
And swear here, by the honor of my blood,   55
My father's purposes have been mistook,
And some about him have too lavishly
Wrested° his meaning and authority.
My lord, these griefs shall be with speed redressed,
Upon my soul, they shall. If this may please you,   60
Discharge your powers unto their several counties,
As we will ours. And here between the armies
Let's drink together friendly and embrace,
That all their eyes may bear those tokens home°
Of our restorèd love and amity.   65
    ARCH. I take your princely word for these re-
    dresses.
    LANC. I give it you, and will maintain my word.
And thereupon I drink unto your Grace.
    HAST. Go, Captain, and deliver to the army   69
This news of peace. Let them have pay, and part.
I know it will well please them. Hie thee,° Captain.
                    [Exit OFFICER.]
    ARCH. To you, my noble Lord of Westmoreland.
    WEST. I pledge your Grace, and, if you knew what
    pains
I have bestowed to breed this present peace,
You would drink freely. But my love to ye   75
Shall show itself more openly hereafter.
    ARCH. I do not doubt you.
    WEST.   I am glad of it.
Health to my lord and gentle Cousin Mowbray.
    MOWB. You wish me health in very happy season,
For I am, on the sudden, something ill.   80

    ARCH. Against ill chances men are ever merry,
But heaviness foreruns the good event.°
    WEST. Therefore be merry, Coz, since sudden
    sorrow
Serves to say thus, " Some good thing comes to-
    morrow."   84
    ARCH. Believe me, I am passing° light in spirit.
    MOWB. So much the worse, if your own rule be
    true.   *[Shouts within]*
    LANC. The word of peace is rendered. Hark how
    they shout!
    MOWB. This had been cheerful after victory.
    ARCH. A peace is of the nature of a conquest,
For then both parties nobly are subdued,   90
And neither party loser.
    LANC.   Go, my lord,
And let our army be dischargèd too.
                    [Exit WESTMORELAND.]
And, good my lord, so please you, let our trains°
March by us, that we may peruse the men
We should have coped° withal.
    ARCH.   Go, good Lord Hastings,   95
And ere they be dismissed let them march by.
                         [Exit HASTINGS.]
    LANC. I trust, lords, we shall lie tonight together.
[Re-enter WESTMORELAND.] Now, Cousin, wherefore
    stands our army still?
    WEST. The leaders, having charge from you to
    stand,
Will not go off until they hear you speak.   100
    LANC. They know their duties.
                 [Re-enter HASTINGS.]
    HAST. My lord, our army is dispersed already.
Like youthful steers unyoked, they take their courses
East, west, north, south, or, like a school broke up,
Each hurries toward his home and sporting place.°
    WEST. Good tidings, my Lord Hastings, for the
    which   106
I do arrest thee, traitor, of high treason.
And you, Lord Archbishop, and you, Lord Mow-
    bray.
Of capital° treason I attach° you both.
    MOWB. Is this proceeding just and honorable?
    WEST. Is your assembly so?   111
    ARCH. Will you thus break your faith?
    LANC.   I pawned° thee none.
I promised you redress of these same grievances
Whereof you did complain, which, by mine honor,
I will perform with a most Christian care.   115
But for you, rebels, look to taste the due
Meet for rebellion and such acts as yours.
Most shallowly did you these arms commence,
Fondly° brought here, and foolishly sent hence.
Strike up our drums, pursue the scattered stray.°

---

38. **Hydra:** a many-headed monster slain by Hercules. 45. **supplies:** reinforcements. **second:** support. 47. **success of mischief:**
succession of mischief; i.e., son following father. 51. **sound:** to
discover the depth by sounding. 58. **Wrested:** wrenched.
64. **bear. . . home:** carry home the report of our pledges (*tokens*)
of reconciliation. 71. **Hie thee:** hasten.

82. **event:** sequel. 85. **passing:** exceedingly. 93. **trains:** followers. 95. **coped:** encountered. 105. **sporting place:** playground.
109. **capital:** deserving death. **attach:** arrest. 112. **pawned:**
pledged. 119. **Fondly:** foolishly. 120. **stray:** stragglers.

God, and not we, hath safely fought today.   121
Some guard these traitors to the block of death,
Treason's true bed and yielder-up of breath.

[*Exeunt.*]

SCENE III. *Another part of the forest.*

[*Alarum. Excursions.° Enter* FALSTAFF *and*
COLEVILE, *meeting.*]

FAL. What's your name, sir? Of what condition°
are you, and of what place, I pray?

COLE. I am a knight, sir, and my name is Colevile of the Dale.   4

FAL. Well, then, Colevile is your name, a knight
is your degree, and your place the dale. Colevile
shall be still your name, a traitor your degree, and
the dungeon your place, a place deep enough, so
shall you be still Colevile of the Dale.   10

COLE. Are not you Sir John Falstaff?

FAL. As good a man as he, sir, whoe'er I am. Do
ye yield, sir? Or shall I sweat for you? If I do sweat,
they are the drops° of thy lovers, and they weep for
thy death. Therefore rouse up fear and trembling,
and do observance to my mercy.   17

COLE. I think you are Sir John Falstaff, and in
that thought yield me.

FAL. I have a whole school° of tongues in this
belly of mine, and not a tongue of them all speaks
any other word but my name. An I had but a belly
of any indifferency,° I were simply the most   23
active fellow in Europe. My womb,° my womb, my
womb undoes me. Here comes our General.

[*Enter* PRINCE JOHN OF LANCASTER, WESTMORELAND,
BLUNT, *and others.*]

LANC. The heat° is past, follow no further now.
Call in the powers, good Cousin Westmoreland.   28

[*Exit* WESTMORELAND.]

Now, Falstaff, where have you been all this while?
When everything is ended, then you come.
These tardy tricks of yours will, on my life,
One time or other break some gallows' back.   32

FAL. I would be sorry, my lord, but it should be
thus. I never knew yet but rebuke and check was the
reward of valor. Do you think me a swallow, an arrow, or a bullet? Have I, in my poor and old   36
motion, the expedition° of thought? I have speeded
hither with the very extremest inch of possibility, I
have foundered ninescore and odd posts.° And here,
travel-tainted as I am, have, in my pure and immaculate valor, taken Sir John Colevile of the Dale,
a most furious knight and valorous enemy. But   42

Sc. iii: s.d., Alarum. Excursions: noises indicating the call
to arms and battle.   1. condition: rank.   15. drops: tears.
20. school: shoal.   23. indifferency: normal size.   24. womb:
belly.   27. heat: i.e., of battle.   37. expedition: speed.   39. posts:
post horses.

what of that? He saw me, and yielded, that I may
justly say, with the hook-nosed fellow of Rome,°
"I came, saw, and overcame."

LANC. It was more of his courtesy than your deserving.   48

FAL. I know not. Here he is, and here I yield him,
And I beseech your Grace let it be booked with the
rest of this day's deeds, or, by the Lord, I will have
it in a particular ballad° else, with mine own picture
on the top on 't, Colevile kissing my foot. To the
which course if I be enforced, if you do not all show
like gilt twopences to me, and I in the clear sky   55
of fame o'ershine you as much as the full moon doth
the cinders of the element,° which show like pins'
heads to her, believe not the word of the noble.
Therefore let me have right, and let desert mount.

LANC. Thine's too heavy to mount.   62

FAL. Let it shine, then.

LANC. Thine's too thick to shine.

FAL. Let it do something, my good lord, that may
do me good, and call it what you will.   66

LANC. Is thy name Colevile?

COLE. It is, my lord.

LANC. A famous rebel art thou, Colevile.

FAL. And a famous true subject took him.   70

COLE. I am, my lord, but as my betters are
That led me hither. Had they been ruled by me,
You should have won them dearer than you have.

FAL. I know not how they sold themselves. But
thou, like a kind fellow, gavest thyself away gratis,
and I thank thee for thee.   76

[*Re-enter* WESTMORELAND.]

LANC. Now, have you left pursuit?

WEST. Retreat is made and execution° stayed.°

LANC. Send Colevile with his confederates
To York, to present° execution.   80
Blunt, lead him hence, and see you guard him
     sure.

[*Exeunt* BLUNT *and others with* COLEVILE.]

And now dispatch we toward the Court, my lords.
I hear the King my father is sore sick.
Our news shall go before us to His Majesty,
Which, Cousin, you shall bear to comfort him,   85
And we with sober speed will follow you.

FAL. My lord, I beseech you give me leave to go
Through Gloucestershire. And when you come to
     Court,
Stand my good lord, pray, in your good report.   89

LANC. Fare you well, Falstaff. I, in my condition,°
Shall better speak of you than you deserve.

[*Exeunt all except* FALSTAFF.]

FAL. I would you had but the wit. 'Twere better
than your dukedom. Good faith, this same young

44. hook-nosed . . . Rome: Julius Caesar, who reported his
victory over the King of Pontus in the words "Veni, vidi, vici."
52. ballad: See App. 8.   57. cinders . . . element: i.e., the stars.
78. execution: slaughter. stayed: stopped.   80. present: immediate.   90. condition: i.e., as commander.

sober-blooded boy doth not love me, nor a man cannot make him laugh — but that's no marvel,   95
he drinks no wine. There's never none of these demure boys come to any proof,° for thin drink doth
so overcool their blood, and making many fish meals,
that they fall into a kind of male greensickness,°
and then when they marry, they get° wenches.   100
They are generally fools and cowards, which some
of us should be too but for inflammation.° A good
sherris sack° hath a twofold operation in it. It ascends me into the brain, dries me there all the foolish and dull and crudy° vapors which environ   105
it, makes it apprehensive,° quick, forgetive,° full of
nimble, fiery, and delectable shapes — which, delivered o'er to the voice, the tongue, which is the
birth, becomes excellent wit. The second prop-   110
erty of your excellent sherris is the warming of the
blood, which, before cold and settled, left the liver°
white and pale, which is the badge of pusillanimity
and cowardice. But the sherris warms it and makes
it course from the inwards to the parts extreme.   115
It illumineth the face, which as a beacon° gives
warning to all the rest of this little kingdom, man,
to arm. And then the vital commoners and inland
petty spirits muster me all to their captain, the   120
heart, who, great and puffed up with this retinue,
doth any deed of courage, and this valor comes of
sherris. So that skill in the weapon is nothing without sack, for that sets it awork, and learning a mere
hoard of gold kept by a devil till sack com-   125
mences° it and sets it in act and use. Hereof comes
it that Prince Harry is valiant, for the cold blood he
did naturally inherit of his father he hath, like lean
sterile and bare land, manured, husbanded,° and
tilled with excellent endeavor of drinking good   130
and good store of fertile sherris, that he is become
very hot and valiant. If I had a thousand sons, the
first humane principle I would teach them should be
to forswear thin potations, and to addict themselves
to sack.   135

[*Enter* BARDOLPH.] How now, Bardolph?

BARD. The army is discharged all and gone.

FAL. Let them go. I'll through Gloucestershire,
and there will I visit Master Robert Shallow, Es-

quire. I have him already tempering° between my
finger and my thumb, and shortly will I seal   141
with him. Come away.   [*Exeunt.*]

SCENE IV. *Westminster. The Jerusalem
Chamber.*

[*Enter* KING HENRY, *the* PRINCES THOMAS OF
CLARENCE *and* HUMPHREY OF GLOUCESTER,
WARWICK, *and others.*]

K. HEN. Now, lords, if God doth give successful
end
To this debate° that bleedeth at our doors,
We will our youth lead on to higher fields
And draw no swords but what are sanctified.°
Our navy is addressed,° our power collected,   5
Our substitutes in absence° well invested,°
And everything lies level° to our wish.
Only, we want a little personal strength,
And pause us till these rebels, now afoot,
Come underneath the yoke of government.   10

WAR. Both which we doubt not but your Majesty
Shall soon enjoy.

K. HEN.   Humphrey, my son of Gloucester,
Where is the Prince your brother?

GLO. I think he's gone to hunt, my lord, at Windsor.

K. HEN. And how accompanied?

GLO.   I do not know, my lord.   15

K. HEN. Is not his brother, Thomas of Clarence,
with him?

GLO. No, my good lord, he is in presence° here.

CLA. What would my lord and father?

K. HEN. Nothing but well to thee, Thomas of
Clarence.
How chance thou art not with the Prince thy
brother?   20
He loves thee, and thou dost neglect him, Thomas.
Thou hast a better place in his affection
Than all thy brothers. Cherish it, my boy,
And noble offices thou mayest effect
Of mediation, after I am dead,   25
Between his greatness and thy other brethren.
Therefore omit° him not, blunt not his love,
Nor lose the good advantage of his grace
By seeming cold or careless of his will.
For he is gracious if he be observed.°   30

97. come . . . proof: stand the test. 99. greensickness: a kind
of anemia from which unmarried girls suffered. 100. get: beget.
102. inflammation: the heating effects of liquor. 103. sherris
sack: a Spanish wine; sherry. 105. crudy: crude. 106. apprehensive: lively. forgetive: quick to invent. 112. liver: The liver
was regarded as the seat of the passions, and especially of courage.
See *T Night*, III.ii.65–67, for Sir Andrew Aguecheek's liver.
116. beacon: During the wars with Spain beacons were continually left ready on all high points and watched, so that warning of invasion could immediately be given. The beacons were
lit several times, notably in 1588 to give warning of the
Spanish Armada. 126. commences: gives it its degree. "Commencement" is the term used in the universities of Oxford and
Cambridge for permission to graduate. 129. husbanded: cultivated.

140. tempering: softening. The wax used for sealing documents
was made of beeswax and was softened, and not (like modern
shellac sealing wax) melted.
    Sc. iv: 2. debate: dispute. 3–4. We . . . sanctified: The King
reverts to his old desire to lead a crusade to the Holy Land. See
I Hen IV, I.i.18–30. 5. addressed: ready. 6. substitutes in
absence: those who will be deputies in our absence. invested:
properly appointed. 7. level: ready. 17. in presence: in the
Court. 27. omit: neglect. 30. observed: humored.

He hath a tear for pity, and a hand
Open as day for melting charity.
Yet notwithstanding, being incensed, he's flint,
As humorous° as winter, and as sudden
As flaws congealèd° in the spring of day.   35
His temper, therefore, must be well observed.
Chide him for faults, and do it reverently,
When you perceive his blood inclined to mirth.
But, being moody, give him line and scope
Till that his passions, like a whale on ground,   40
Confound° themselves with working.° Learn this,
    Thomas,
And thou shalt prove a shelter to thy friends,
A hoop of gold to bind thy brothers in,
That the united vessel of their blood,
Mingled with venom of suggestion —   45
As, force perforce, the age will pour it in —
Shall never leak,° though it do work as strong
As aconitum° or rash gunpowder.
    CLA. I shall observe him with all care and love.
    K. HEN. Why art thou not at Windsor with him,
    Thomas?   50
    CLA. He is not there today. He dines in London.
    K. HEN. And how accompanied? Canst thou tell
    that?
    CLA. With Poins, and other his continual fol-
    lowers.
    K. HEN. Most subject is the fattest° soil to weeds,
And he, the noble image of my youth,   55
Is overspread with them. Therefore my grief
Stretches itself beyond the hour of death.
The blood weeps from my heart when I do shape,
In forms imaginary, the unguided days
And rotten times that you shall look upon   60
When I am sleeping with my ancestors.
For when his headstrong riot hath no curb,
When rage and hot blood are his councilors,
When means and lavish manners° meet together,
Oh, with what wings shall his affections fly   65
Toward fronting° peril and opposed decay!°
    WAR. My gracious lord, you look beyond° him
    quite.
The Prince but studies his companions
Like a strange tongue, wherein, to gain the language,
'Tis needful that the most immodest word   70
Be looked upon and learned, which once attained,
Your Highness knows, comes to no further use
But to be known and hated. So, like gross terms,°

---

34. **humorous:** capricious.   35. **flaws congealed:** snow flurries.
41. **Confound:** wear out. **working:** thrashing around. 43–47. **hoop
. . . leak:** The image is that of a cask, made of several staves
and held together by the hoops, which will hold any liquid,
no matter how penetrating. Thomas is the hoop, his brothers
the staves, and the cask will be tested by malicious tales.
48. **aconitum:** aconite, a poison extracted from the monkshood
(or wolfsbane).   54. **fattest:** richest.   64. **means . . . manners:**
opportunity and vicious ways. 66. **fronting:** opposing. **opposed
decay:** ruin which is standing ready like an enemy.   67. **look
beyond:** mistake.   73. **gross terms:** filthy words.

The Prince will in the perfectness of time
Cast off his followers, and their memory   75
Shall as a pattern° or a measure live,
By which His Grace must mete° the lives of others,
Turning past evils to advantages.
    K. HEN. 'Tis seldom when the bee doth leave her
    comb
In the dead carrion.°
[*Enter* WESTMORELAND.]   Who's here? Westmore-
    land?   80
    WEST. Health to my sovereign, and new happiness
Added to that that I am to deliver!
Prince John your son doth kiss your Grace's hand.
Mowbray, the Bishop Scroop, Hastings, and all
Are brought to the correction of your law.   85
There is not now a rebel's sword unsheathed,
But Peace puts forth her olive everywhere.
The manner how this action hath been borne
Here at more leisure may your Highness read,
With every course° in his particular.   90
    K. HEN. O Westmoreland, thou art a summer bird
Which ever in the haunch of winter sings
The lifting-up of day.°
[*Enter* HARCOURT.]   Look, here's more news.
    HAR. From enemies Heaven keep your Majesty,
And when they stand against you, may they fall   95
As those that I am come to tell you of!
The Earl Northumberland and the Lord Bardolph,
With a great power of English and of Scots,
Are by the Sheriff of Yorkshire overthrown.
The manner and true order of the fight,   100
This packet, please it you, contains at large.
    K. HEN. And wherefore should these good news
    make me sick?
Will Fortune never come with both hands full,
But write her fair words still in foulest letters?
She either gives a stomach and no food —   105
Such are the poor, in health — or else a feast
And takes away the stomach — such are the rich
That have abundance and enjoy it not.
I should rejoice now at this happy news,
And now my sight fails, and my brain is giddy.   110
Oh me! Come near me. Now I am much ill.
    GLO. Comfort, your Majesty!
    CLA.   O my royal Father!
    WEST. My sovereign lord, cheer up yourself, look
    up.
    WAR. Be patient, Princes. You do know these fits
Are with His Highness very ordinary.   115
Stand from him, give him air, he'll straight be well.
    CLA. No, no, he cannot long hold out these pangs.
The incessant care and labor of his mind
Hath wrought the mure° that should confine it in

---

76. **pattern:** example.   77. **mete:** measure.   79–80. **'Tis . . . carrion:** the bees which have built in a dead carcass will seldom
leave it.   90. **course:** event.   92–93. **in . . . day:** at the latter
end (*haunch*) of winter sings to welcome the longer days.
119. **wrought . . . mure:** worn the wall thin.

So thin that life looks through and will break out.
GLO. The people fear me,° for they do observe
Unfathered° heirs and loathly° births of nature.
The seasons change their manners, as° the year   123
Had found some months asleep and leaped them
   over.
CLA. The river° hath thrice flowed,° no ebb be-
   tween,   125
And the old folk, time's doting chronicles,
Say it did so a little time before
That our great-grandsire, Edward, sicked and died.
WAR. Speak lower, Princes, for the King recovers.
GLO. This apoplexy will certain be his end.   130
K. HEN. I pray you take me up and bear me hence
Into some other chamber. Softly, pray.   [*Exeunt.*]

SCENE V.° *Another chamber.*

[KING HENRY *lying on a bed:* CLARENCE, GLOUCESTER,
   WARWICK, *and others in attendance.*]

K. HEN. Let there be no noise made, my gentle
   friends,
Unless some dull° and favorable° hand
Will whisper music to my weary spirit.
WAR. Call for the music in the other room.
K. HEN. Set me the crown upon my pillow here.   5
CLA. His eye is hollow, and he changes much.
WAR. Less noise, less noise!
         [*Enter* PRINCE HENRY.]
PRINCE.   Who saw the Duke of Clarence?
CLA. I am here, Brother, full of heaviness.
PRINCE. How now! Rain within doors,° and none
   abroad!
How doth the King?   10
GLO. Exceeding ill.
PRINCE.   Heard he the good news yet?
Tell it him.
GLO. He altered much upon the hearing it.
PRINCE. If he be sick with joy, he'll recover with-
   out physic.   15
WAR. Not so much noise, my lords. Sweet Prince,
   speak low.
The King your father is disposed to sleep.
CLA. Let us withdraw into the other room.

121. fear me: make me fearful.   122. Unfathered: i.e., unnatural. loathly: loathsome. Unnatural births, such as calves with
two heads, were regarded as portents of evil.   123. as: as if.
125. river: i.e., the Thames. thrice flowed: i.e., the tide rose
thrice without any intervening low tide. The Thames is a tidal
river. On very rare occasions the tide fails either to rise or to fall.
The phenomenon of no high tide occurred in Shakespeare's time
on September 6, 1592. The phenomenon was recorded by Holinshed as having also occurred on October 12, 1411.
   Sc. v: In the original texts no change of scene was marked or
intended. The King was carried either to the back of the stage
or to the chamber aloft (where the bed was already in position)
and the curtains were opened. See Gen. Intro. p. 55b and Pl. 5b.
2. dull: drowsy. favorable: kindly.   9. Rain . . . doors: i.e., why
do you all look so gloomy?

WAR. Will 't please your Grace to go along with
   us?   19
PRINCE. No, I will sit and watch here by the King.
         [*Exeunt all except the* PRINCE.]
Why doth the crown lie there upon his pillow,
Being so troublesome a bedfellow?
Oh, polished perturbation!° Golden care!
That keep'st the ports° of slumber open wide
To many a watchful night! Sleep with it now!   25
Yet not so sound and half so deeply sweet
As he whose brow with homely biggen° bound
Snores out the watch of night. O majesty!
When thou dost pinch thy bearer, thou dost sit
Like a rich armor worn in heat of day,   30
That scalds with safety.° By his gates of breath°
There lies a downy feather which stirs not.
Did he suspire,° that light and weightless down
Perforce must move. My gracious lord! My father!
This sleep is sound indeed, this is a sleep,   35
That from this golden rigol° hath divorced
So many English kings. Thy due from me
Is tears and heavy sorrows of the blood,°
Which nature, love, and filial tenderness
Shall, O dear Father, pay thee plenteously.   40
My due from thee is this imperial crown,
Which, as immediate from thy place and blood,
Derives° itself to me. Lo, here it sits,°
Which God shall guard. And put the world's whole
   strength°
Into one giant arm, it shall not force   45
This lineal° honor from me. This from thee
Will I to mine leave, as 'tis left to me.   [*Exit.*]
K. HEN. Warwick! Gloucester! Clarence!
         [*Re-enter* WARWICK, GLOUCESTER, CLARENCE,
                  and the rest.]
CLA. Doth the King call?
WAR. What would your Majesty? How fares your
   Grace?   50
K. HEN. Why did you leave me here alone, my
   lords?
CLA. We left the Prince my brother here, my
   liege,
Who undertook to sit and watch by you.
K. HEN. The Prince of Wales! Where is he? Let
   me see him.
He is not here.   55
WAR. This door is open, he is gone this way.
GLO. He came not through the chamber where
   we stayed.
K. HEN. Where is the crown? Who took it from
   my pillow?

23. perturbation: cause of anxiety.   24. ports: gates.   27. biggen:
coarse linen cloth tied round the head as a nightcap.   31. scalds
. . . safety: burns while it protects. gates of breath: nostrils.
33. suspire: breathe.   36. rigol: circle.   38. blood: heart.
43. Derives: comes by descent. here it sits: The Prince sets the
crown on his own head.   44. And . . . strength: even if the whole
strength of the world be put.   46. lineal: descending by right of
birth.

WAR. When we withdrew, my liege, we left it
    here.
    K. HEN. The Prince hath ta'en it hence. Go, seek
    him out.   60
Is he so hasty that he doth suppose
My sleep my death?
Find him, my Lord of Warwick, chide him hither.
                        [*Exit* WARWICK.]
This part° of his conjoins° with my disease,
And helps to end me. See, Sons, what things you
    are!   65
How quickly nature falls into revolt
When gold becomes her object!
For this the foolish overcareful fathers
Have broke their sleep with thoughts, their brains
    with care,
Their bones with industry.   70
For this they have engrossed° and pilèd up
The cankered° heaps of strange-achievèd° gold.
For this they have been thoughtful to invest°
Their sons with arts° and martial exercises.
When, like the bee, culling from every flower   75
The virtuous sweets,
Our thighs packed with wax, our mouths with
    honey,
We bring it to the hive, and, like the bees,
Are murdered for our pains. This bitter taste
Yield his engrossments° to the ending father.   80
[*Re-enter* WARWICK.] Now, where is he that will not
    stay so long
Till his friend sickness hath determined° me?
    WAR. My lord, I found the Prince in the next
    room,
Washing with kindly tears his gentle cheeks,
With such a deep demeanor° in great sorrow   85
That tyranny, which never quaffed but blood,°
Would, by beholding him, have washed his knife
With gentle eyedrops. He is coming hither.
    K. HEN. But wherefore did he take away the
    crown?
[*Re-enter* PRINCE HENRY.] Lo where he comes. Come
    hither to me, Harry.   90
Depart the chamber, leave us here alone.
              [*Exeunt* WARWICK *and the rest.*]
    PRINCE. I never thought to hear you speak again.
    K. HEN. Thy wish was father, Harry, to that
    thought.
I stay too long by thee, I weary thee.
Dost thou so hunger for mine empty chair   95
That thou wilt needs invest thee with my honors
Before thy hour be ripe? O foolish youth!
Thou seek'st the greatness that will overwhelm thee.

Stay but a little, for my cloud of dignity
Is held from falling with so weak a wind   100
That it will quickly drop. My day is dim.
Thou hast stolen that which after some few hours
Were thine without offense, and at my death
Thou hast sealed up° my expectation.
Thy life did manifest thou lovedst me not,   105
And thou wilt have me die assured of it.
Thou hidest a thousand daggers in thy thoughts,
Which thou hast whetted on thy stony heart
To stab at half an hour of my life.
What! Canst thou not forbear me half an hour?
Then get thee gone and dig my grave thyself,   111
And bid the merry bells° ring to thine ear
That thou art crowned, not that I am dead.
Let all the tears that should bedew my hearse
Be drops of balm° to sanctify thy head.   115
Only compound° me with forgotten dust,
Give that which gave thee life unto the worms.
Pluck down my officers, break my decrees,
For now a time is come to mock at form.°
Harry the Fifth is crowned. Up, vanity!   120
Down, royal state!° All you sage counselors, hence!
And to the English Court assemble now,
From every region, apes of idleness!
Now, neighbor confines,° purge you of your scum.
Have you a ruffian that will swear, drink, dance,
Revel the night, rob, murder, and commit   126
The oldest sins the newest kind of ways?
Be happy, he will trouble you no more.
England shall double-gild his treble guilt,°
England shall give him office, honor, might.   130
For the fifth Harry from curbed license° plucks
The muzzle of restraint, and the wild dog
Shall flesh° his tooth on every innocent.
O my poor kingdom, sick with civil blows!°
When that my care could not withhold thy riots,
What wilt thou do when riot is thy care?°   136
Oh, thou wilt be a wilderness again,
Peopled with wolves, thy old inhabitants!
    PRINCE. Oh, pardon me, my liege! But for my
    tears,
The moist impediments unto my speech,   140
I had forestalled this dear and deep rebuke
Ere you with grief had spoke and I had heard
The course of it so far. There is your crown,
And He that wears the crown immortally
Long guard it yours! If I affect° it more   145
Than as your honor and as your renown,

---

64. **part**: action. **conjoins**: joins. 71. **engrossed**: bought up
wholesale. 72. **cankered**: rusted. **strange-achieved**: won in
strange ways. 73. **invest**: equip. 74. **arts**: learning. 79–80. This
... **engrossments**: his hoarding brings a bitter taste. 82. **deter-**
mined: ended. 85. **deep demeanor**: sad countenance. 86. **That**
... **blood**: that even a tyrant who drank nothing but blood.

104. **sealed up**: finally confirmed. See App. 6.   112. **bells**: See
App. 19.   115. **balm**: the sacred oil used in anointing a King.
116. **compound**: mix.   119. **form**: order.   121. **state**: dignity.
124. **confines**: countries. 129. **double-gild ... guilt**: Shakespeare
repeated this pun in *Hen V*, II, Chorus, l. 26, and *Macb*, II.ii.55.
131. **curbed license**: restrained vice.   133. **flesh**: stain with
blood.   134. **civil blows**: the wounds of civil war. 135–36. **care**
... **care**: anxious watch ... concern.   145. **affect**: desire.

Let me no more from this obedience° rise,
Which my most inward true and duteous spirit
Teacheth, this prostrate and exterior bending.
God witness with me, when I here came in   150
And found no course of breath within your Majesty,
How cold it struck my heart! If I do feign,
Oh, let me in my present wildness die,
And never live to show the incredulous world
The noble change that I have purposèd!   155
Coming to look on you, thinking you dead,
And dead almost, my liege, to think you were,
I spake unto this crown as having sense,
And thus upbraided it: " The care on thee depend-
       ing
Hath fed upon the body of my father,   160
Therefore thou best of gold art worst of gold.
Other, less fine in carat, is more precious,
Preserving life in medicine potable.°
But thou, most fine, most honored, most renowned,
Hast eat thy bearer up." Thus, my most royal liege,
Accusing it, I put it on my head,   166
To try with it, as with an enemy
That had before my face murdered my father,
The quarrel of a true inheritor.
But if it did infect my blood with joy,   170
Or swell my thoughts to any strain of pride,
If any rebel or vain spirit of mine
Did with the least affection of a welcome
Give entertainment to the might of it,
Let God forever keep it from my head,   175
And make me as the poorest vassal° is
That doth with awe and terror kneel to it!
       K. HEN. O my son,
God put it in thy mind to take it hence,
That thou mightst win the more thy father's love
Pleading so wisely in excuse of it!   181
Come hither, Harry, sit thou by my bed,
And hear, I think, the very latest° counsel
That ever I shall breathe. God knows, my son,
By what bypaths and indirect° crooked ways   185
I met this crown, and I myself know well
How troublesome it sat upon my head.
To thee it shall descend with better quiet,
Better opinion,° better confirmation.°
For all the soil of the achievement° goes   190
With me into the earth. It seemed in me
But as an honor snatched with boisterous° hand,
And I had many living to upbraid
My gain of it by their assistances,
Which daily grew to quarrel and to bloodshed,   195
Wounding supposèd° peace. All these bold fears
Thou see'st with peril I have answered,

For all my reign hath been but as a scene
Acting that argument.° And now my death
Changes the mode,° for what in me was pur-
       chased°   200
Falls upon thee in a more fairer sort,
So° thou the garland° wear'st successively.°
Yet, though thou stand'st more sure than I could do,
Thou art not firm enough, since griefs are green.°
And all my friends, which thou must make thy
       friends,   205
Have but their stings and teeth newly ta'en out,
By whose fell working° I was first advanced
And by whose power I well might lodge a fear
To be again displaced. Which to avoid,
I cut them off, and had a purpose now   210
To lead out many to the Holy Land,
Lest rest and lying still might make them look
Too near unto my state.° Therefore, my Harry,
Be it thy course to busy giddy minds
With foreign quarrels, that action, hence borne
       out,°
May waste° the memory of the former days.   216
More would I, but my lungs are wasted so
That strength of speech is utterly denied me.
How I came by the crown, O God, forgive,
And grant it may with thee in true peace live!   220
       PRINCE. My gracious liege,
You won it, wore it, kept it, gave it me.
Then plain and right must my possession be,
Which I with more than with a common pain°
'Gainst all the world will rightfully maintain.   225
       [*Enter* LORD JOHN OF LANCASTER.]
   K. HEN. Look, look, here comes my John of Lan-
       caster.
   LANC. Health, peace, and happiness to my royal
       father!
   K. HEN. Thou bring'st me happiness and peace,
       Son John,
But health, alack, with youthful wings is flown
From this bare withered trunk. Upon thy sight   230
My worldly business makes a period.°
Where is my Lord of Warwick?
   PRINCE.   My Lord of Warwick!
       [*Re-enter* WARWICK, *and others.*]
   K. HEN. Doth any name particular belong
Unto the lodging where I first did swoon?
   WAR. 'Tis called Jerusalem, my noble lord.   235
   K. HEN. Laud° be to God! Even there my life must
       end.
It hath been prophesied to me many years

147. obedience: act of obedience; i.e., kneeling.   163. medicine potable: gold in solution, called *aurum potabile* and regarded as a medicine of great worth. See App. 21.   176. vassal: slave.   183. latest: last.   185. indirect: devious.   189. opinion: reputation. confirmation: approval.   190. soil . . . achievement: infamy of the winning.   192. boisterous: violent.   196. supposed: unreal.   199. argument: plot (of a play).   200. mode: mood, musical key, "tune." purchased: acquired.   202. So: since. garland: crown. successively: by right of succession.   204. griefs . . . green: grievances are fresh.   207. fell working: fierce labors.   212–13. look . . . state: examine my claims to the throne too closely.   215. hence . . . out: i.e., in foreign lands.   216. waste: wear away.   224. pain: labor.   231. period: full stop.   236. Laud: praise.

I should not die but in Jerusalem,
Which vainly I supposed the Holy Land.
But bear me to that chamber, there I'll lie,   240
In that Jerusalem shall Harry die.   [*Exeunt.*]

Act V

SCENE I. *Gloucestershire.* SHALLOW's *house.*

[*Enter* SHALLOW, FALSTAFF, BARDOLPH, *and* PAGE.]
SHAL. By cock and pie,° sir, you shall not away
tonight. What, Davy, I say!
FAL. You must excuse me, Master Robert Shallow.
SHAL. I will not excuse you, you shall not be ex-   5
cused, excuses shall not be admitted, there is no ex-
cuse shall serve, you shall not be excused. Why,
Davy!

[*Enter* DAVY.]
DAVY. Here, sir.
SHAL. Davy, Davy, Davy, Davy, let me see, Davy.
Let me see, Davy, let me see. Yea, marry, William
cook, bid him come hither. Sir John, you shall not
be excused.
DAVY. Marry, sir, thus, those precepts° cannot be
served. And, again, sir, shall we sow the headland
with wheat?   16
SHAL. With red wheat, Davy. But for William
cook — are there no young pigeons?
DAVY. Yes, sir. Here is now the smith's note for
shoeing and plow irons.   20
SHAL. Let it be cast° and paid. Sir John, you shall
not be excused.
DAVY. Now, sir, a new link to the bucket must
needs be had. And, sir, do you mean to stop any of
William's wages about the sack he lost the other day
at Hinckley fair?   26
SHAL. A' shall answer it. Some pigeons, Davy, a
couple of short-legged hens, a joint of mutton, and
any pretty little tiny kickshaws,° tell William cook.
DAVY. Doth the man of war stay all night, sir?   31
SHAL. Yea, Davy. I will use him well. A friend i'
the Court is better than a penny in purse. Use his
men well, Davy, for they are arrant knaves, and will
backbite.
DAVY. No worse than they are backbitten, sir, for
they have marvelous foul linen.
SHAL. Well conceited,° Davy. About thy business,
Davy.   40

DAVY. I beseech you, sir, to countenance° William
Visor of Woncot against Clement Perkes o' the hill.
SHAL. There is many complaints, Davy, against
that Visor. That Visor is an arrant knave, on my
knowledge.   46
DAVY. I grant your Worship that he is a knave,
sir. But yet, God forbid, sir, but a knave should have
some countenance at his friend's request. An honest
man, sir, is able to speak for himself when a knave is
not. I have served your Worship truly, sir, this   51
eight years, and if I cannot once or twice in a quarter
bear out° a knave against an honest man, I have but
a very little credit with your Worship. The knave is
mine honest friend, sir, therefore I beseech your
Worship let him be countenanced.   57
SHAL. Go to, I say he shall have no wrong. Look
about,° Davy. [*Exit* DAVY.] Where are you, Sir
John? Come, come, come, off with your boots. Give
me your hand, Master Bardolph.
BARD. I am glad to see your Worship.
SHAL. I thank thee with all my heart, kind Master
Bardolph. [*To the* PAGE] And welcome, my tall fellow. Come, Sir John.   66
FAL. I'll follow you, good Master Robert Shallow.
[*Exit* SHALLOW.] Bardolph, look to our horses.
[*Exeunt* BARDOLPH *and* PAGE.] If I were sawed into
quantities,° I should make four dozen of such   70
bearded hermits' staves° as Master Shallow. It is a
wonderful thing to see the semblable coherence° of
his men's spirits and his. They, by observing of him,
do bear themselves like foolish Justices; he, by conversing with them, is turned into a Justicelike   75
servingman. Their spirits are so married in conjunction with the participation of society° that they flock
together in consent,° like so many wild geese. If I
had a suit to Master Shallow, I would humor his
men with the imputation of being near° their   80
master. If to his men, I would curry with Master
Shallow that no man could better command his
servants. It is certain that either wise bearing or ignorant carriage° is caught, as men take diseases, one
of another. Therefore let men take heed of their   85
company. I will devise matter enough out of this
Shallow to keep Prince Harry in continual laughter
the wearing-out of six fashions, which is four terms,°
or two actions,° and a' shall laugh without intervallums.° Oh, it is much that a lie with a slight   90

41. countenance: favor—when his case comes up for trial. There
is a good deal of local color in these Gloucestershire scenes.
Woncot (spelled Woodmancote) is a village in Gloucestershire,
and in Shakespeare's time there were Visors and Perkes living
thereabouts.   53. bear out: support.   58–59. Look about: get
moving.   70. quantities: lengths.   71. staves: staffs.   72. semblable coherence: close likeness.   76–77. so . . . society: so
united by sharing the company of each other.   78. in consent:
by fellow feeling.   80. near: in the favor of.   84. ignorant
carriage: boorish behavior.   88. four terms: There were four
law terms in the year.   89. actions: lawsuits.   90. intervallums:
intermissions.

Act V, Sc. i: 1. cock . . . pie: an innocent rustic oath. Editors
dispute whether it means simply by cock and magpie, or is a
perversion of something stronger, as moderns use "Gee" and
"Jeez" for God and Jesus.   14. precepts: orders.   21. cast:
added up.   30. kickshaws: trifles, fancy dishes.   39. Well
conceited: very clever.

oath and a jest with a sad° brow will do with a fellow
that never had the ache in his shoulders!° Oh, you
shall see him laugh till his face be like a wet cloak
ill laid up!   95

SHAL. [*Within*] Sir John!

FAL. I come, Master Shallow, I come, Master Shal-
low.   [*Exit.*]

SCENE II. *Westminster. The palace.*

[*Enter* WARWICK *and the* LORD CHIEF JUSTICE,
meeting.]

WAR. How now, my Lord Chief Justice! Whither
away?

CH. JUST. How doth the King?

WAR. Exceeding well. His cares are now all ended.

CH. JUST. I hope, not dead.

WAR.   He's walked the way of nature,
And to our purposes he lives no more.   5

CH. JUST. I would His Majesty had called me with
him.
The service that I truly did his life
Hath left me open to all injuries.

WAR. Indeed I think the young King loves you
not.

CH. JUST. I know he doth not, and do arm myself
To welcome the condition of the time,   11
Which cannot look more hideously upon me
Than I have drawn it in my fantasy.°

[*Enter* LANCASTER, CLARENCE, GLOUCESTER,
WESTMORELAND, *and others.*]

WAR. Here come the heavy issue° of dead Harry.
Oh, that the living Harry had the temper   15
Of him, the worst of these three gentlemen!
How many nobles then should hold their places
That must strike sail° to spirits of vile sort!

CH. JUST. Oh God, I fear all will be overturned!

LANC. Good morrow, Cousin Warwick, good mor-
row.   20

GLO. & CLA. Good morrow, Cousin.

LANC. We meet like men that had forgot to speak.

WAR. We do remember, but our argument°
Is all too heavy to admit much talk.

LANC. Well, peace be with him that hath made
us heavy!   25

CH. JUST. Peace be with us, lest we be heavier!

GLO. Oh, good my lord, you have lost a friend
indeed,
And I dare swear you borrow not that face
Of seeming sorrow, it is sure your own.

LANC. Though no man be assured what grace to
find,°   30

91. sad: solemn.   92. ache . . . shoulders: i.e., rheumatism.
   Sc. ii: 13. fantasy: imagination.   14. heavy issue: sad sons.
18. strike sail: i.e., as a ship lowers its sails in sign of submission.
23. argument: topic for conversation.   30. be . . . find: is sure
what treatment to expect from the new King.

You stand in coldest° expectation.
I am the sorrier. Would 'twere otherwise.

CLA. Well, you must now speak Sir John Falstaff
fair,
Which swims against your stream of quality.°

CH. JUST. Sweet Princes, what I did, I did in
honor,   35
Led by the impartial conduct of my soul,
And never shall you see that I will beg
A ragged and forestalled remission.°
If truth and upright innocency fail me,
I'll to the King my master that is dead,   40
And tell him who hath sent me after him.

WAR. Here comes the Prince.

[*Enter* KING HENRY *the Fifth, attended.*]

CH. JUST. Good morrow, and God save your Majesty!

K. HEN. V. This new and gorgeous garment, ma-
jesty,
Sits not so easy on me as you think.   45
Brothers, you mix your sadness with some fear.
This is the English, not the Turkish Court.
Not Amurath an Amurath succeeds,°
But Harry Harry. Yet be sad, good Brothers,
For, by my faith, it very well becomes you.   50
Sorrow so royally in you appears
That I will deeply put the fashion on,
And wear it in my heart. Why then, be sad,
But entertain no more of it, good Brothers,
Than a joint burden laid upon us all.   55
For me, by Heaven, I bid you be assured
I'll be your father and your brother too.
Let me but bear your love, I'll bear your cares.
Yet weep that Harry's dead, and so will I,
But Harry lives, that shall convert those tears 60
By number into hours of happiness.

PRINCES. We hope no other from your Majesty.

K. HEN. V. You all look strangely on me. And you
most.
You are, I think, assured I love you not.

CH. JUST. I am assured, if I be measured rightly,
Your Majesty hath no just cause to hate me.   66

K. HEN. V. No?
How might a prince of my great hopes forget
So great indignities you laid upon me?
What! Rate,° rebuke, and roughly send to prison
The immediate heir of England! Was this easy? 71
May this be washed in Lethe,° and forgotten?

CH. JUST. I then did use the person of your father,
The image of his power lay then in me.
And in the administration of his law,

31. coldest: least favorable.   34. swims . . . quality: which goes
against the inclination of a man of your quality.   38. ragged
. . . remission: beggarly pardon, asked for before an offense has
been committed.   48. Amurath . . . succeeds: In 1574 the
Sultan Amurath on succeeding to the throne had all his brothers
strangled, as also did his son in 1598.   70. Rate: scold.
72. Lethe: the river of forgetfulness.

Whiles I was busy for the commonwealth,
Your Highness pleasèd to forget my place,
The majesty and power of law and justice,
The image° of the King whom I presented,°
And struck me in my very seat of judgment.　80
Whereon, as an offender to your father,
I gave bold way to my authority,
And did commit you. If the deed were ill,
Be you contented, wearing now the garland,°
To have a son set your decrees at naught,　85
To pluck down justice from your awful bench,
To trip the course of law and blunt the sword
That guards the peace and safety of your person —
Nay, more, to spurn at your most royal image
And mock your workings in a second body.°　90
Question your royal thoughts, make the case yours.
Be now the father and propose a son,
Hear your own dignity so much profaned,
See your most dreadful laws so loosely slighted,
Behold yourself so by a son disdained.　95
And then imagine me taking your part,
And in your power soft-silencing your son.
After this cold considerance,° sentence me,
And, as you are a king, speak in your state°
What I have done that misbecame my place,　100
My person, or my liege's sovereignty.
　　K. HEN. V. You are right, Justice, and you weigh
　　　this well,
Therefore still bear the balance° and the sword.
And I do wish your honors may increase
Till you do live to see a son of mine　105
Offend you, and obey you, as I did.
So shall I live to speak my father's words:
" Happy am I that have a man so bold
That dares do justice on my proper° son,
And not less happy, having such a son,　110
That would deliver up his greatness so
Into the hands of justice." You did commit me.
For which, I do commit into your hand
The unstained sword that you have used° to bear —
With this remembrance, that you use the same　115
With the like bold, just, and impartial spirit
As you have done 'gainst me. There is my hand.
You shall be as a father to my youth.
My voice shall sound as you do prompt mine ear,
And I will stoop and humble my intents　120
To your well-practiced wise directions.
And, Princes all, believe me, I beseech you,
My father is gone wild° into his grave,
For in his tomb lie my affections.°
And with his spirit sadly I survive,　125

To mock the expectation of the world,
To frustrate prophecies, and to raze out
Rotten opinion,° who hath writ me down
After my seeming.° The tide of blood in me
Hath proudly flowed in vanity° till now.　130
Now doth it turn and ebb back to the sea,
Where it shall mingle with the state of floods
And flow henceforth in formal majesty.°
Now call we our high court of Parliament.
And let us choose such limbs of noble counsel　135
That the great body of our state may go
In equal rank with the best-governed nation,
That war, or peace, or both at once, may be
As things acquainted° and familiar to us.　139
In which you, Father, shall have foremost hand.
Our coronation done, we will accite,°
As I before remembered, all our state.°
And, God consigning° to my good intents,
No Prince nor peer shall have just cause to say,　144
God shorten Harry's happy life one day!　[*Exeunt.*]

SCENE III. *Gloucestershire.* SHALLOW'S *orchard.*

[*Enter* FALSTAFF, SHALLOW, SILENCE, DAVY, BARDOLPH, *and the* PAGE.]

　SHAL. Nay, you shall see my orchard, where in
an arbor we will eat a last year's pippin of my own
graffing,° with a dish of caraways,° and so forth.
Come, Cousin Silence. And then to bed.
　FAL. 'Fore God, you have here a goodly dwelling
and a rich.
　SHAL. Barren, barren, barren, beggars all, beggars
all, Sir John. Marry, good air. Spread, Davy, spread,
Davy. Well said, Davy.　10
　FAL. This Davy serves you for good uses. He is
your servingman and your husband.°
　SHAL. A good varlet,° a good varlet, a very good
varlet, Sir John. By the mass, I have drunk too much
sack at supper. A good varlet. Now sit down, now
sit down. Come, Cousin.　16
　SIL. Ah, sirrah! quoth a',° we shall [*Singing*]
　" Do nothing but eat, and make good cheer,
　　And praise God for the merry year,
　　When flesh° is cheap and females dear,　20

---

79. **image:** likeness, representation. **presented:** represented.
84. **garland:** crown. 90. **second body:** deputy. 98. **cold considerance:** impartial consideration. 99. **your state:** i.e., as King and not as vengeful individual. 103. **balance:** the symbol of impartial justice. 109. **proper:** own. 114. **used:** been accustomed. 123. **gone wild:** because he takes the Prince's wildness with him. 124. **affections:** lusts.

128. **Rotten opinion:** the opinion that I was rotten. 129. **my seeming:** what I seemed to be. 130. **vanity:** frivolity. 133. **formal majesty:** kingly dignity. 139. **acquainted:** well known. 141. **accite:** summon. 142. **all . . . state:** i.e., the three estates of the realm — Lords, Bishops, Commons — which made up the Parliament. 143. **consigning:** agreeing.
Sc. iii: 3. **graffing:** grafting. **caraways:** caraway seeds, eaten with apples to counteract wind. 12. **husband:** husbandman; i.e., he looks after the farm. 13. **varlet:** servant. 17. **quoth a':** says he. Silence is another advertisement for the effects of sack; it moves him to song. 20. **flesh:** meat.

And lusty lads roam here and there
　　　So merrily,
　And ever among so merrily."
FAL. There's a merry heart! Good Master Silence,
I'll give you a health° for that anon.   25
SHAL. Give Master Bardolph some wine, Davy.
DAVY. Sweet sir, sit, I'll be with you anon. Most
sweet sir, sit. Master Page, good Master Page, sit.
Proface!° What you want in meat we'll have in   30
drink. But you must bear,° the heart's° all. [*Exit.*]
SHAL. Be merry, Master Bardolph, and, my little
soldier there, be merry.
　SIL. [*Singing*]
　"Be merry, be merry, my wife has all,   35
　　For women are shrews, both short and tall.
　'Tis merry in hall when beards wag all,°
　　And welcome merry Shrovetide.°
　Be merry, be merry."   39
FAL. I did not think Master Silence had been a
man of this mettle.
SIL. Who, I? I have been merry twice and once
ere now.
　　　　　[*Re-enter* DAVY.]
DAVY. [*To* BARDOLPH] There's a dish of leather-
coats° for you.
SHAL. Davy!   45
DAVY. Your Worship! [*To* BARDOLPH] I'll be with
you straight. A cup of wine, sir?
　SIL. [*Singing*]
　"A cup of wine that's brisk and fine,
　　And drink unto the leman° mine,
　　And a merry heart lives long-a."   50
FAL. Well said, Master Silence.
SIL. An we shall be merry, now comes in the
sweet o' the night.   54
FAL. Health and long life to you, Master Silence.
　SIL. [*Singing.*]
　"Fill the cup, and let it come.
　　I'll pledge you a mile to the bottom."
SHAL. Honest Bardolph, welcome. If thou wantest
anything, and wilt not call, beshrew thy heart. Wel-
come, my little tiny thief [*To the* PAGE], and wel-
come indeed too. I'll drink to Master Bardolph, and
to all the cavaleros° about London.   63
DAVY. I hope to see London once ere I die.
BARD. An I might see you there, Davy——
SHAL. By the mass, you'll crack a quart together,
ha! Will you not, Master Bardolph?
BARD. Yea, sir, in a pottle pot.°   68
SHAL. By God's liggens,° I thank thee. The knave

will stick by thee, I can assure thee that. A' will not
out,° he is true-bred.
BARD. And I'll stick by him, sir.   72
SHAL. Why, there spoke a king. Lack nothing. Be
merry. [*Knocking within*] Look who's at door 74
there, ho! Who knocks?   [*Exit* DAVY.]
FAL. [*To* SILENCE, *seeing him take off a bumper*]
Why, now you have done me right.°
　SIL. [*Singing*]
　　"Do me right,
　　　And dub me knight.
　　　　Samingo."
Is 't not so?   80
FAL. 'Tis so.
SIL. Is 't so? Why then, say an old man can do
somewhat.
　　　　　[*Re-enter* DAVY.]
DAVY. An 't please your Worship, there's one Pistol
come from the Court with news.   85
FAL. From the Court! Let him come in. [*Enter*
PISTOL.] How now, Pistol!
PIST. Sir John, God save you!
FAL. What wind blew you hither, Pistol?   89
PIST. Not the ill wind which blows no man to
good. Sweet knight, thou art now one of the great-
est men in this realm.
SIL. By 'r lady, I think a' be, but° Goodman° Puff
of Barson.
PIST. Puff!   95
Puff in thy teeth, most recreant° coward base!
Sir John, I am thy Pistol and thy friend,
And helter-skelter have I rode to thee,
And tidings do I bring and lucky joys
And golden times and happy news of price.   100
FAL. I pray thee, now, deliver them like a man of
this world.
PIST. A foutre° for the world and worldlings
base!
I speak of Africa and golden joys.
FAL. O base Assyrian knight, what is thy news?
Let King Cophetua° know the truth thereof.   106
SIL. [*Singing*] "And Robin Hood, Scarlet, and
John."
PIST. Shall dunghill curs confront the Helicons?°
And shall good news be baffled?°
Then, Pistol, lay thy head in Furies' lap.   110
SHAL. Honest gentleman, I know not your breed-
ing.°
PIST. Why then, lament therefore.
SHAL. Give me pardon, sir. If, sir, you come with
news from the Court, I take it there's but two ways,

---

25. **give . . . health**: drink to your health.   30. **Proface**: set to.
31. **bear**: be patient, a polite apology for the fare provided. **heart**:
good intention.   37. **beards . . . all**: i.e., in animated chatter.
38. **Shrovetide**: the days, usually three, before the beginning of
Lent, when men let themselves go in anticipation of the lean days
to follow.   44. **leathercoats**: russet apples.   49. **leman**: sweetheart.   63. **cavaleros**: gallants.   68. **pottle pot**: See II.ii.84.
69. **liggens**: probably "little legs" — but Shallow has passed beyond coherence.

70–71. **A' . . . out**: he won't pass out; i.e., can hold a skinful.
76. **done me right**: drank as deep a health to me as I to you.
93. **but**: except for. **Goodman**: a title given to those beneath the
rank of gentleman.   96. **recreant**: traitor.   103. **foutre**: a word of
contempt.   106. **King Cophetua**: who married a begger maid; Falstaff lapses into Pistol's manner of speech.   108. **Helicons**: Pistol
means Muses.   109. **baffled**: disgraced.   111. **breeding**: origin.

either to utter them or to conceal them. I am, sir, under the King, in some authority.   118

PIST. Under which King, Besonian?° Speak, or die.

SHAL. Under King Harry.

PIST.   Harry the Fourth? Or Fifth? 120

SHAL. Harry the Fourth.

PIST.   A foutre for thine office! Sir John, thy tender lambkin now is King, Harry the Fifth's the man. I speak the truth. When Pistol lies, do this,° and fig me,° like The bragging Spaniard.

FAL. What, is the old King dead?   126

PIST. As nail in door. The things I speak are just.

FAL. Away, Bardolph! Saddle my horse. Master Robert Shallow, choose what office thou wilt in the land, 'tis thine. Pistol, I will double-charge thee with dignities.   131

BARD. Oh joyful day! I would not take a knighthood for my fortune.

PIST. What! I do bring good news.   134

FAL. Carry Master Silence to bed. Master Shallow, my Lord Shallow — be what thou wilt, I am fortune's steward° — get on thy boots.° We'll ride all night. O sweet Pistol! Away, Bardolph! [Exit BARDOLPH.] Come, Pistol, utter more to me, and withal devise something to do thyself good. Boot, boot, Master Shallow! I know the young King is sick 141 for me. Let us take any man's horses, the laws of England are at my commandment. Blessed are they that have been my friends, and woe to my Lord Chief Justice!   145

PIST. Let vultures vile seize on his lungs also! "Where is the life that late I led?" say they. Why, here it is. Welcome these pleasant days!

                              [Exeunt.]

SCENE IV. *London. A street.*

[Enter BEADLES, *dragging in* HOSTESS QUICKLY *and* DOLL TEARSHEET.]

HOST. No, thou arrant knave, I would to God that I might die, that I might have thee hanged. Thou hast drawn my shoulder out of joint.

I. BEAD. The constables have delivered her over to me, and she shall have whipping cheer° enough, I warrant her. There hath been a man or two lately killed about her.   7

DOLL. Nuthook,° nuthook, you lie. Come on, I'll

tell thee what, thou damned tripe-visaged° rascal, an the child I now go with do miscarry, thou wert better thou hadst struck thy mother, thou paper-faced villain.   12

HOST. Oh the Lord, that Sir John were come! He would make this a bloody day to somebody. But I pray God the fruit of her womb miscarry!

I. BEAD. If it do, you shall have a dozen of cushions again. You have but eleven now.° Come, I charge you both go with me, for the man is dead that you and Pistol beat amongst you.   19

DOLL. I'll tell you what, you thin man in a censer,° I will have you as soundly swinged° for this — you bluebottle° rogue, you filthy famished correctioner,° if you be not swinged, I'll forswear half-kirtles.° 24

I. BEAD. Come, come, you she knight errant,° come.

HOST. Oh God, that right should thus overcome might! Well, of sufferance comes ease.

DOLL. Come, you rogue, come, bring me to a Justice.   30

HOST. Aye, come, you starved bloodhound.

DOLL. Goodman death, goodman bones!

HOST. Thou atomy° thou!

DOLL. Come, you thin thing, come, you rascal.

I. BEAD. Very well.   [Exeunt.]

SCENE V. *A public place near Westminster Abbey.*

[Enter two GROOMS, *strewing rushes.*°]

I. GROOM. More rushes, more rushes.

2. GROOM. The trumpets have sounded twice.

I. GROOM. 'Twill be two o'clock ere they come from the coronation. Dispatch, dispatch. [Exeunt.]
[Enter FALSTAFF, SHALLOW, PISTOL, BARDOLPH, *and* PAGE.]

FAL. Stand here by me, Master Robert Shallow, I will make the King do you grace.° I will leer° upon him as a' comes by, and do but mark the countenance that he will give me.   8

PIST. God bless thy lungs, good knight.

FAL. Come here, Pistol, stand behind me. Oh, if I had had time to have made new liveries, I would have bestowed the thousand pound I borrowed of you. But 'tis no matter, this poor show doth better. This doth infer the zeal I had to see him.   15

---

119. Besonian: recruit, "rookie."   124. do this: Here he makes some expressive gesture. fig me: the sign of the fig (an insult of immemorial antiquity) is made by thrusting the thumb between the fore and middle fingers.   137. steward: and so able to be generous with his mistress's goods. boots: large heavy boots used by riders.

Sc. iv: 5. whipping cheer: a taste of the whip. Convicted whores were publicly whipped.   8. Nuthook: lit., a hooked stick for pulling down nuts, so one who grabs.

9. tripe-visaged: with a pale pock-marked face, like tripe.   17. eleven now: i.e., to stuff herself out, as if pregnant.   20. thin . . . censer: a *censer* is a pot with a lid in which perfume or incense is burned, but the exact meaning of Doll's abuse has not been found.   21. swinged: thrashed.   23. bluebottle: because he wore a blue coat. correctioner: beadle, who administered correction.   24. half-kirtles: skirts.   25. she . . . errant: female nightwalker.   33. atomy: for "anatomy," living skeleton.

Sc. v: s.d., strewing rushes: strewn as a mark of respect for the occasion.   6. grace: favor. leer: look lovingly.

SHAL. It doth so.

FAL. It shows my earnestness of affection ——

SHAL. It doth so.

FAL. My devotion ——

SHAL. It doth, it doth, it doth.   20

FAL. As it were, to ride day and night, and not to
deliberate, not to remember, not to have patience to
shift me° ——

SHAL. It is best, certain.   24

FAL. But to stand stained with travel, and sweating with desire to see him, thinking of nothing else,
putting all affairs else in oblivion, as if there were
nothing else to be done but to see him.   29

PIST. 'Tis " *semper idem,*" for " *absque hoc nihil
est.*"° 'Tis all in every part.

SHAL. 'Tis so, indeed.

PIST. My knight, I will inflame thy noble liver,
And make thee rage.

Thy Doll, and Helen° of thy noble thoughts,   35
Is in base durance and contagious° prison,
Haled thither
By most mechanical° and dirty hand.
Rouse up revenge from ebon° den with fell Alecto's°
        snake,
For Doll is in. Pistol speaks naught but truth.   40

FAL. I will deliver her.

        [*Shouts within, and the trumpets sound.*]

PIST. There roared the sea, and trumpet clangor
        sounds.

[*Enter* KING HENRY V *and his train, the* LORD CHIEF
                JUSTICE *among them.*]

FAL. God save thy Grace, King Hal! My royal
Hal!   44

PIST. The Heavens thee guard and keep, most
royal imp° of fame!

FAL. God save thee, my sweet boy!

K. HEN. V. My Lord Chief Justice, speak to that
        vain man.

CH. JUST. Have you your wits? Know you what
'tis you speak?   49

FAL. My King! My Jove! I speak to thee, my heart!

K. HEN. V. I know thee not, old man. Fall to thy
        prayers.

How ill white hairs become a fool and jester!
I have long dreamed of such a kind of man,
So surfeit-swelled,° so old, and so profane,
But, being awaked, I do despise my dream.   55
Make less thy body hence, and more thy grace.
Leave gormandizing. Know the grave doth gape
For thee thrice wider than for other men.
Reply not to me with a fool-born jest.

Presume not that I am the thing I was,   60
For God doth know, so shall the world perceive,
That I have turned away my former self,
So will I those that kept me company.
When thou dost hear I am as I have been,
Approach me, and thou shalt be as thou wast,   65
The tutor and the feeder of my riots.
Till then, I banish thee, on pain of death,
As I have done the rest of my misleaders,
Not to come near our person by ten mile.
For competence of life° I will allow you,   70
That lack of means enforce you not to evil.
And as we hear you do reform yourselves,
We will, according to your strength and qualities,
Give you advancement. Be it your charge, my
        lord,
To see performed the tenor° of our word.   75
Set on.   [*Exeunt* KING, *etc.*]

FAL. Master Shallow, I owe you a thousand pound.

SHAL. Yea, marry, Sir John, which I beseech you
to let me have home with me.   80

FAL. That can hardly be, Master Shallow. Do not
you grieve at this. I shall be sent for in private to
him. Look you, he must seem thus to the world.
Fear not your advancements, I will be the man yet
that shall make you great.   85

SHAL. I cannot well perceive how, unless you
should give me your doublet° and stuff me out with
straw. I beseech you, good Sir John, let me have five
hundred of my thousand.

FAL. Sir, I will be as good as my word. This that
you heard was but a color.°   91

SHAL. A color° that I fear you will die in, Sir John.

FAL. Fear no colors.° Go with me to dinner. Come,
Lieutenant Pistol, come, Bardolph. I shall be sent
for soon at night.°   96

[*Re-enter* PRINCE JOHN, *and the* LORD CHIEF JUSTICE;
                OFFICERS *with them.*]

CH. JUST. Go, carry Sir John Falstaff to the Fleet.°
Take all his company along with him.

FAL. My lord, my lord ——

CH. JUST. I cannot now speak. I will hear you
        soon.   100
Take them away.

PIST. *Si fortuna me tormenta, spero contenta.*°

[*Exeunt all but* PRINCE JOHN *and the* CHIEF JUSTICE.]

LANC. I like this fair proceeding of the King's.
He hath intent his wonted followers
Shall all be very well provided for,   105
But all are banished till their conversations
Appear more wise and modest to the world.

---

23. shift me: change my shirt. **30–31. semper . . . est:** always
the same, for apart from this there is nothing. **35. Helen:** the
ideal of all beautiful mistresses. **36. contagious:** infectious.
London prisons were notoriously unsanitary. **38. mechanical:**
workingman's. **39. ebon:** black. Alecto: one of the Furies.
46. imp: little lad. **54. surfeit-swelled:** swollen through over-
eating.

70. competence of life: means to live. **75. tenor:** purpose.
87. doublet: jacket. See Pl. 8b and comment on p. 93a. **91. color:**
pretense. **92. color:** with a pun on "collar" — halter. **93. Fear
no colors:** a proverbial phrase meaning "fear no one." See *T
Night,* I.v.6. **96. at night:** i.e., for a private interview "after
office hours." **97. Fleet:** a London prison. **102. Si . . . contenta.**
See II.iv.195,n.

CH. JUST. And so they are.

LANC. The King hath called his Parliament, my
lord.

CH. JUST. He hath.   110

LANC. I will lay odds that ere this year expire
We bear our civil swords° and native fire
As far as France. I heard a bird so sing,   113
Whose music, to my thinking, pleased the King.
Come, will you hence?   [*Exeunt.*]

EPILOGUE°

[*Spoken by a* DANCER.]

First my fear,° then my curtsy, last my speech.
My fear is, your displeasure; my curtsy, my duty;
and my speech, to beg your pardons. If you look for
a good speech now, you undo me. For what I have
to say is of mine own making, and what indeed I   5
should say will, I doubt, prove mine own marring.
But to the purpose, and so to the venture. Be it
known to you, as it is very well, I was lately here in
the end of a displeasing play, to pray your patience
for it and to promise you a better. I meant in-   10

112. **civil swords:** the swords lately used in civil war.

Epilogue: Epilogues are common in the plays of other dramatists but occur only in seven other Shakespearian plays. They
usually appeal for the approval or applause of the audience.
This Epilogue was evidently written for the first performance,
by way of apology for some play now unknown which had caused
displeasure, and for the scandal caused by the Oldcastle affair.
See *I Hen IV* Intro. p. 615a–b.   **1. fear:** lest you be displeased.

deed to pay you with this, which, if like an ill venture it come unluckily home, I break,° and you, my
gentle creditors, lose. Here I promised you I would
be, and here I commit my body to your mercies.   14
Bate me° some, and I will pay you some, and, as
most debtors do, promise you infinitely.

If my tongue cannot entreat you to acquit° me,
will you command me to use my legs? And yet that
were but light payment, to dance out of your debt.
But a good conscience will make any possible   20
satisfaction, and so would I. All the gentlewomen
here have forgiven me. If the gentlemen will not,
then the gentlemen do not agree with the gentlewomen, which was never seen before in such an assembly.   26

One word more, I beseech you. If you be not too
much cloyed with fat meat, our humble author will
continue the story, with Sir John in it,° and make
you merry with fair Katharine of France. Where,
for anything I know, Falstaff shall die of a   31
sweat, unless already a' be killed with your hard
opinions, for Oldcastle died a martyr, and this is not
the man. My tongue is weary. When my legs are
too, I will bid you good night, and so kneel   35
down before you, but indeed to pray for the Queen.°

12. **break:** go bankrupt.   15. **Bate me:** let me off.   17. **acquit:**
release from a debt.   28–29. **will . . . it:** It is clear from this un-
fulfilled promise that Shakespeare had not yet started either to
plan or to write *Henry V*.   36. **pray . . . Queen:** This pious custom
still persists in the English theater, where a few bars of "God
Save the King" are played before or after the performance.

MUCH ADO ABOUT NOTHING

Introduction

Much Ado about Nothing was probably written in 1598. The first definite record of its existence occurs in the Stationers' Register, where there is a casual note, dated August 4, 1600, that four plays belonging to the Lord Chamberlain's Company are " to be staied " — that is, are not to be printed. The plays were: *As You Like It, Henry V,* Ben Jonson's *Every Man in His Humor,* and *Much Ado about Nothing.* Nevertheless, on August 23 the play was entered for printing in the normal way, together with *II Henry IV,* as the property of the printers Andrew Wise and William Aspley. Soon afterward a quarto appeared with the title page: *Much adoe about Nothing. As it hath been sundrie times publikely acted by the right honourable, the Lord Chamberlaine his seruants. Written by William Shakespeare. London. Printed by V.S. for Andrew Wise, and William Aspley. 1600.* This quarto is quite well printed and there are few serious difficulties in the text. There are, however, no divisions into acts and scenes; several notes of exit and entrance have been omitted; and the speakers' names are often confused. Thus Antonio, Leonato's brother, appears sometimes as " Old " (old man) or " Brother "; Don Pedro is " Pedro " and " Prince." The most interesting confusion is in the names of Dogberry and Verges, who in IV.ii become " Kempe " and " Cowley " — the actors who took the parts. These inconsistencies suggest that the printer was using the original manuscript of an author writing for his own company.

The plot is compounded of several incidents. The main story tells how Claudio, having fallen in love with Hero, is persuaded to believe that he has seen her talking with a lover at her bedroom window on the night before the wedding, and is thus led to repudiate her. This plot, in various forms, is not uncommon in tales of the sixteenth century; one version is told by Spenser in *The Faerie Queene,* Book II, Canto IV. The version nearest to that in *Much Ado* is to be found in a story by Matteo Bandello in an Italian novel published in 1554. The outline of Bandello's story is as follows:

In the year 1283, King Pedro of Aragon seized the Island of Sicily. While his Court was being held at Messina, one of his knights, Don Timbreo di Cardona, fell in love with a young lady called Fenicia, who was the daughter of Lionato de Lionati. The wedding day was appointed; but another knight, Signor Girondo Olerio Valentiano, had also fallen in love with Fenicia and wished to prevent the marriage. He therefore caused a young man to tell Don Timbreo that Fenicia had a lover who visited her secretly. So Don Timbreo hid in Lionato's garden, and there saw a young gentleman with two companions carrying a ladder. The ladder was placed against the wall, and one of the men climbed up and entered a window. Next morning Don Timbreo sent a messenger to Lionato to declare that with his own eyes he had perceived that Fenicia was disloyal to him and she could therefore find herself another husband. Fenicia was so dismayed by this unjust accusation that she fell into a deep swoon and even the physicians believed her to be dead. It was not until her mother began to prepare the body for burial that she opened her eyes. Thereupon Lionato was summoned, and they agreed that while the funeral ceremonies should proceed, Fenicia should meanwhile be sent away secretly into the country.

The report of Fenicia's death caused great sorrow in Messina, for when the case was examined the evidence on which she had been condemned appeared very slight. Don Timbreo was thus filled with remorse, as was Signor Girondo, who confessed his treacherous trick. The two men therefore came to Lionato, and Timbreo declared that he would recompense the injured father by obeying any command that might be laid on him. Lionato replied that since Don Timbreo wished to marry, he must take the lady whom he would offer, and to this Timbreo agreed.

A year had now passed. Fenicia was living under the name of Lucilla and her health had so greatly improved in the country that she was hardly recognizable. So Lionato arranged that Don Timbreo, accompanied by Signor Girondo and his friends, should attend mass at a village outside Messina, where he should meet the lady chosen for his bride. The mass being finished, Lucilla was brought out and the marriage was performed. At the marriage feast which followed all was revealed and the lovers were happily reconciled. Girondo humbly begged Fenicia's pardon, and the day's festivities were symmetrically completed by Girondo's betrothal to Fenicia's sister.

There is obviously some connection between this story and the play in the coincidence of the names Don Pedro, Lionato, and Messina, but the details vary considerably, and it is quite likely that the direct source of *Much Ado about Nothing* was some play that has now been lost.

There are indeed a few traces of apparent alteration in the play itself. In the quarto text, the opening stage direction reads: "*Enter Leonato, Governor of Messina, Innogen his wife, Hero his daughter, and Beatrice his niece, with a messenger.*" The wife reappears in a stage direction at the beginning of II.i, but she has no part in the play and is always omitted by modern editors.

There are other inconsistencies. The devices by which Borachio persuaded Margaret to impersonate Hero and Hero to sleep in another room are never satisfactorily explained in the play. It is possible, therefore, that *Much Ado about Nothing* is a play in two strata, the earlier being the Hero-Claudio story. When Shakespeare came to rewrite it, he expanded the story of Benedick and Beatrice, which is entirely his own invention, and in order to keep the play at the right length he was obliged to cut out much of the Hero-Claudio plot. As a result, some necessary explanations are missing. Moreover, it is noticeable that much of the Hero-Claudio story is written in the verse of Shakespeare's earlier style, while the Benedick-Beatrice story is mostly in prose.

There are other critical problems in *Much Ado about Nothing*. These are not noticeable on the stage, but they certainly obtrude when the play is read. The plot is complex, with three stories running parallel; these are the love affair of Hero and Claudio, which leads to disaster; the trap set to persuade Benedick and Beatrice to fall in love; and the plot of Don John, which is foiled by Dogberry and his Watch. The Hero-Claudio story again subdivides into three parts — the proxy wooing, the repudiation, and Hero's final restoration. This part of the play is on the whole weak, melodramatic, and to modern readers almost offensive, because after his outrageous conduct, Claudio's undeserved reward affronts the sense of justice.

The play begins with the return of Don Pedro, Prince of Aragon, with his officers from the wars, a scene which would have reminded Shakespeare's audience of a similar return from the wars after the successful expedition to Cadiz two years before (see Gen. Intro. p. 29b). Among the party are Claudio and Benedick. They are welcomed by Leonato, Governor of Messina, and by Hero his daughter and Beatrice his niece. Claudio, who had been attracted before the campaign, now falls in love with Hero and asks the Prince to negotiate the marriage for him. Then follows a masked dance. Don John, the Prince's bastard brother, a warped villain, persuades Claudio that the Prince is wooing Hero for himself. When Don Pedro, Leonato, Hero, and Claudio next meet, the Prince, to Claudio's amazement, explains that all is well. Leonato gladly consents to the wedding, Hero says nothing, and the two are betrothed. Thus ends the first scene of the second act. Shakespeare had therefore spent a whole act in tying up a tangle which falls apart at once. Why, ask the critics, these unnecessary complications? So far as the Hero and Claudio story is concerned, Shakespeare has now to go back and start again. Moreover, the modern reader is from this point alienated from Claudio. Since Don John had deceived him once, surely he might be more careful next time.

Nevertheless, against the objections of critics, it should be noted that *Much Ado about Nothing* is one of the best acting plays that Shakespeare ever wrote. Much of the success of this first act, and indeed of the whole Hero-Claudio story, depends on the actor taking the part of Don John. He is more important in person than in dialogue. He is a man of few words and therefore in the reading we are likely to overlook him. But when the play is adequately acted, with Don John malevolently brooding in the background, conspicuous and sinister in his silence, the story becomes far more effective.

Villainy has been foiled at the first attempt, but it is not vanquished. At this point Shakespeare begins to make the Benedick-Beatrice story move. Claudio and his friends plot to bring about the mating of Benedick and Beatrice by persuading each that the other is in love. A moment of high comedy is thus promised and foreshadowed. Immediately afterward another incident follows, which may be disastrous. Don John will try again. At the suggestion of one of his precious pair of villains, Borachio, he will endeavor to convince Claudio and Don Pedro that Hero is faithless. At this point we are told in detail what is about to happen. With the information firmly fixed in our minds, we are taken back to the other story. Both Benedick and Beatrice are to be deceived by overheard conversations. These developments are shown in two successive episodes, which, though divided into scenes by modern editors, are in fact one continuous scene.

The two episodes are carefully contrasted. First Benedick comes on alone, walks forward to the edge of the stage, and chats with the audience about love, and especially Claudio in love. He is thus much occupied with love thoughts, though not consciously for himself. Don Pedro and his fellow conspirators appear. Benedick hides and overhears the conversation that has been prepared for him. Benedick is then left alone to his own thoughts, and once more he soliloquizes. In the development of Shakespeare's dramatic art this is an interesting soliloquy, for it is the first of the more subtle, psychological revelations in which a mental process is laid bare before us. Benedick, like others before and since, has to make a complete reversal of his hitherto loudly proclaimed principles, and he must justify his inconsistency on the highest moral grounds. Then, as a man will, he immediately sees confirmation of his own happy thoughts in the plain and unfriendly words of Beatrice, who is still untouched. The whole of this scene is in prose. The next is a verse scene. Hero, accompanied by Margaret and Ursula, comes into the garden. Beatrice hides, and also overhears. Then the change is shown. The Beatrice whom we had hitherto seen was very much a speaker of bitter prose. Once she believes herself to be in love, she breaks out, almost spontaneously, into a sonnet. It may be, of course, that this rhymed passage is another outcrop of the old play, but if so why does Shakespeare leave this one speech and not the others? It is not an accident, but a most effective way of showing that Beatrice's mannishness, like armor, is the defense of a sensitive girl who is really afraid of losing control of her emotions.

The two avowed haters are now separately in love with each other, and the grand joke will be to see them meet for the first time. But at this point Shakespeare suspends the Benedick-Beatrice plot entirely; the joke will be the better for keeping. We are taken back to the story of Hero. Don John tells Claudio and Don Pedro of Hero's alleged behavior, but the window episode is not shown. Shakespeare was right to keep this in the background. If he had shown it, the deception would have been either so palpable that no excuse could be found for Claudio or so realistic that every excuse could be found for him. It is right, therefore, to keep it vague. To do this, and to surprise the audience and to show the passing of time, a new set of characters are now introduced — Dogberry, Verges, and the Watch. This admirable low comedy makes us for the moment entirely forget the others. Obviously it is nighttime, for the Watch come out only in the evening. Then Conrade and Borachio, Don John's agents in villainy, wander by. Borachio's plot has succeeded. He has received his reward, has spent some of it in the tavern, and is now confidentially drunk. Quite naturally, therefore, he tells Conrade what has happened. And quite naturally the Watch, who is standing by, overhears. From his words we realize that it was too dark to see, too far away to hear, and yet Claudio had believed. After this dramatic recital the villains are arrested by the Watch, and now the excitement begins. Will the truth come out before the wedding, or will Hero be falsely accused and vilely shamed?

This situation and its handling is a good illustration of a fundamental principle of Shakespeare's dramatic art.

There are two main ways of telling a story of misunderstanding. The first is to deceive the audience and the characters and then to spring a surprise and a reversal of the situation at the end. The second is to show the audience step by step what is happening, but to deceive the characters. Shakespeare prefers this method, whereby he achieves the effect of dramatic irony, which is always much deeper than surprise. Henceforward, in this part of the play every speech has two meanings. We are far more deeply moved by Hero's misfortunes when we can see them approaching than if they came suddenly and unexpectedly. Horror and the kindred feelings are always worse when the disaster can be foreseen as unavoidable.

The story now approaches tragedy. Hero dresses for her wedding. The bridegroom arrives. Then Dogberry enters. He has the news which will save everyone, if only he can tell it to Leonato; but both old men are pompous and foolish, each in his own way. Dogberry is too crass to tell his tale plainly, Leonato too fussy to realize that the constable has something important to say. Disaster is now inevitable, and we can only wait for it. The family assemble. Claudio carries out his threat and withdraws with his friends, leaving Hero apparently dead. Most of the party believe Hero to be guilty; only Beatrice instinctively, and the Friar by observation, believe in her innocence. Benedick at least will suspend judgment until he has heard the evidence more fully.

Throughout all this excitement we have forgotten the grand climax of the other plot — the moment when Benedick and Beatrice should next be alone together. Shakespeare has kept their declaration of love until there is no audience of tittering conspirators to jeer at their embarrassment. But once that moment is reached, the dialogue which follows is most moving — all the more because it is so genuine and so terse after the windy, theatrical rhetoric of Claudio and Leonato. Benedick, transformed for the moment into the " knight errant," must demand that his lady lay on him a task. He has asked for it; and the answer is right — " kill Claudio." Thus Benedick is presented with a knotty little problem in knight errantry: he must choose between love and friendship. The true knight would prefer his sworn brother before all others, man or woman; but the command of his newly won lady is also of great power, and Benedick, overcome rather than convinced by her torrential indignation, agrees and goes off to kill Claudio.

At this point the play is in some danger. Both plots have reached a moment of high tension; considerable adroitness will be needed to avoid either a flat conclusion or one of those interminable last acts which are all explanation. Shakespeare therefore cleans the slate and brings back Dogberry and Verges. One of the great advantages of the Elizabethan method of mixing clowns in more majestical matters is that it allowed a contrast and variety of emotions. The laughter which follows tears is heartier than the laughter of continuous farce. So the scene begins in low comedy with the pompous Dogberry examining the prisoners, which results in the Sexton's extracting the essential evidence to vindicate Hero.

We are now ready for the end, but Shakespeare raises the tension once more. Leonato and his old brother, vastly grieving, encounter Don Pedro and Claudio. Benedick accosts them and issues his challenge, but they refuse to take him seriously. Then comes the complete reversal. The prisoners are led in, Borachio confesses, and Claudio apologizes. Modern readers, however, find some difficulty in accepting what follows: Leonato's proposal that, since Hero is dead, Claudio shall marry another member of his family. After what has happened, it is hard to imagine that Leonato still regards this young man as a suitable husband for his only daughter. But to an Elizabethan the proposal would have seemed less astonishing. Marriage between great families was not an affair of love. Hero had moral and legal claims on Claudio; Claudio had promised to marry her and now rightly he must be made to fulfill his promise. As the favorite of his Prince, Claudio is such a very desirable match that much might be forgiven.

A few other matters have still to be disentangled. Benedick is shown briefly as a lover, and his halting efforts at love-making are much more agreeable than Claudio's more voluble protestations. And then, finally, the last surprise is disclosed when Hero is shown to be alive, and the whole story dissolves into merriment and dancing.

The play should not be taken too seriously. Shakespeare is providing entertainment for two hours, very varied and agreeable, but for all that, as it turns out, " much ado about nothing."

Much Ado about Nothing

DRAMATIS PERSONAE

DON PEDRO, *Prince of Aragon*
DON JOHN, *his bastard brother*
CLAUDIO, *a young lord of Florence*
BENEDICK, *a young lord of Padua*
LEONATO, *Governor of Messina*
ANTONIO, *his brother*
BALTHASAR, *attendant on Don Pedro*
CONRADE } *followers of Don John*
BORACHIO }
FRIAR FRANCIS
DOGBERRY, *a constable*

VERGES, *a headborough*
A SEXTON
A BOY

HERO, *daughter to Leonato*
BEATRICE, *niece to Leonato*
MARGARET } *gentlewomen attending on Hero*
URSULA }

MESSENGERS, WATCH, ATTENDANTS, ETC.

SCENE — *Messina.*

Act I

SCENE I. *Before* LEONATO's *house.*

[*Enter* LEONATO, HERO, *and* BEATRICE,
with a MESSENGER.]

LEON. I learn in this letter that Don Pedro of Aragon comes this night to Messina.

MESS. He is very near by this.° He was not three leagues off when I left him.

LEON. How many gentlemen have you lost in this action? 6

MESS. But few of any sort,° and none of name.°

LEON. A victory is twice itself when the achiever brings home full numbers. I find here that Don Pedro hath bestowed much honor on a young Florentine called Claudio. 11

MESS. Much deserved on his part, and equally remembered by Don Pedro. He hath borne himself beyond the promise of his age, doing in the figure of a lamb the feats of a lion. He hath indeed better bettered expectation than you must expect of me to tell you how. 17

LEON. He hath an uncle here in Messina will be very much glad of it.

MESS. I have already delivered him letters, and there appears much joy in him, even so much that joy could not show itself modest enough without a badge of bitterness.°

LEON. Did he break out into tears?

MESS. In great measure. 25

LEON. A kind° overflow of kindness.° There are no faces truer than those that are so washed. How much better is it to weep at joy than to joy at weeping!

BEAT. I pray you, is Signior Mountanto° returned from the wars, or no? 31

MESS. I know none of that name, lady. There was none such in the army of any sort.

LEON. What is he that you ask for, Niece?

HERO. My cousin means Signior Benedick of Padua. 36

MESS. Oh, he's returned, and as pleasant as ever he was.

BEAT. He° set up his bills° here in Messina and challenged Cupid at the flight;° and my uncle's 40 fool, reading the challenge, subscribed° for Cupid and challenged him at the bird bolt.° I pray you, how many hath he killed and eaten in these wars? But how many hath he killed? For indeed I promised to eat all of his killing. 45

LEON. Faith, Niece, you tax° Signior Benedick too much. But he'll be meet° with you, I doubt it not.

MESS. He hath done good service, lady, in these wars.

BEAT. You had musty victual, and he hath 50 holp° to eat it. He is a very valiant trencherman,° he hath an excellent stomach.

30. **Signior Mountanto:** "Signior Thruster." In fencing terms *montanto* was a thrust. 39–42. **He . . . bolt:** The point of Beatrice's elaborate jest is obscure. It may be paraphrased: Benedick challenged Cupid as an archer at the most difficult kind of shooting; my uncle's fool accepted, and challenged him to short-range competition with harmless arrows; i.e., Benedick is not the sort of man to cause a woman to fall in love. 39. **set . . . bills:** hung up a poster. 40. **flight:** arrow used for long-range shooting. 41. **subscribed:** signed underneath; i.e., accepted the challenge. 42. **bird bolt:** short blunt arrow, used for shooting small birds — a harmless missile. See Pl. 22a. 46. **tax:** censure, satirize. 47. **meet:** even. 51. **holp:** helped. **trencherman:** eater.

Act I, Sc. i: 3. [**by this:** by this time. 7. **sort:** rank. **name:** i.e., great family. 23. **badge of bitterness:** a sign that joy is servant to sorrow; i.e. if he had not wept, his joy would have appeared immodest. **badge:** a metal plate bearing the master's coat of arms, worn by a servant. 26. **kind:** natural. **kindness:** affection.

MESS. And a good soldier too, lady.

BEAT. And a good soldier to a lady, but what is
he to a lord?   55

MESS. A lord to a lord, a man to a man, stuffed°
with all honorable virtues.

BEAT. It is so indeed, he is no less than a stuffed
man. But for the stuffing — well, we are all mortal.

LEON. You must not, sir, mistake my niece.   61
There is a kind of merry war betwixt Signior Benedick and her. They never meet but there's a skirmish
of wit between them.   64

BEAT. Alas! he gets nothing by that. In our last
conflict four of his five wits° went halting° off, and
now is the whole man governed with one. So that
if he have wit enough to keep himself warm, let him
bear it for a difference° between himself and his
horse; for it is all the wealth that he hath left,   70
to be known a reasonable creature.° Who is his companion now? He hath every month a new sworn
brother.°

MESS. Is 't possible?   74

BEAT. Very easily possible. He wears his faith but
as the fashion of his hat, it ever changes with the
next block.°

MESS. I see, lady, the gentleman is not in your
books.°

BEAT. No, an° he were, I would burn my   80
study. But I pray you who is his companion? Is
there no young squarer° now that will make a voyage with him to the Devil?

MESS. He is most in the company of the right
noble Claudio.   85

BEAT. Oh Lord, he will hang upon him like a
disease. He is sooner caught than the pestilence, and
the taker runs presently° mad. God help the noble
Claudio! If he have caught the Benedick, it will cost
him a thousand pound° ere a' be cured.   90

MESS. I will hold friends° with you, lady.

BEAT. Do, good friend.

LEON. You will never run mad,° Niece.

BEAT. No, not till a hot January.

MESS. Don Pedro is approached.   95

[*Enter* DON PEDRO, DON JOHN, CLAUDIO, BENEDICK,
and BALTHASAR.]

D. PEDRO. Good Signior Leonato, you are come to
meet your trouble. The fashion of the world is to
avoid cost, and you encounter it.

LEON. Never came trouble to my house in the
likeness of your Grace; for trouble being gone,   100
comfort should remain, but when you depart from
me, sorrow abides and happiness takes his leave.

D. PEDRO. You embrace your charge too willingly.
I think this is your daughter.   104

LEON. Her mother hath many times told me so.

BENE. Were you in doubt, sir, that you asked her?

LEON. Signior Benedick, no, for then were you a
child.   109

D. PEDRO. You have it full, Benedick. We may
guess by this what you are, being a man.° Truly, the
lady fathers herself.° Be happy, lady, for you are
like an honorable father.

BENE. If Signior Leonato be her father, she would
not have his head on her shoulders for all Messina,
as like him as she is.   116

BEAT. I wonder that you will still be talking, Signior Benedick. Nobody marks you.

BENE. What, my dear Lady Disdain! Are you yet
living?   120

BEAT. Is it possible Disdain should die while she
hath such meet° food to feed it as Signior Benedick?
Courtesy itself must convert to disdain if you come
in her presence.   124

BENE. Then is courtesy a turncoat. But it is certain I am loved of all ladies, only you excepted. And
I would I could find in my heart that I had not a
hard heart, for truly I love none.

BEAT. A dear happiness° to women. They would
else have been troubled with a pernicious suitor. I
thank God and my cold blood I am of your hu-   131
mor° for that. I had rather hear my dog bark at a
crow than a man swear he loves me.

BENE. God keep your ladyship still in that mind!
So some gentleman or other shall 'scape a predesti-
nate° scratched face.   136

BEAT. Scratching could not make it worse an
'twere such a face as yours were.

BENE. Well, you are a rare parrot-teacher.

BEAT. A bird of my tongue is better than a beast
of yours.   141

BENE. I would my horse had the speed of your
tongue, and so good a continuer. But keep your way,
i' God's name. I have done.

BEAT. You always end with a jade's trick.° I know
you of old.   146

D. PEDRO. That is the sum of all, Leonato. Signior
Claudio and Signior Benedick, my dear friend Leonato hath invited you all. I tell him we shall stay here
at the least a month, and he heartily prays   150

56. stuffed: The word is used with various meanings. The messenger means "crammed full"; Beatrice (l. 59) means "stuffed
with straw." See III.iv.65.   66. five wits: i.e., common wit,
imagination, fantasy, estimation, memory. halting: limping.
69. difference: an heraldic term — a slight difference in the coat
of arms borne by different members of one family. See App.
9.   71. reasonable creature: man — and not quite a beast.
72–73. sworn brother: knights who had formed a romantic
friendship for each other swore brotherhood that they would
share good and evil fortune alike.   77. block: the wooden mold
on which a felt hat is shaped.   78–79. in . . . books: in your
good books; i.e., the list of your friends.   80. an: if.   82. squarer:
quarreler.   88. presently: immediately.   90. thousand pound:
See App. 27.   91. hold friends: be careful to keep friendly.
93. never . . . mad: i.e., "catch the Benedick." See l. 89 above.

111. being a man: i.e., you are known to be a dangerous man
among the ladies.   112. fathers herself: is like her father.
122. meet: suitable.   129. dear happiness: rare good luck.
132. humor: mood.   136. predestinate: predestinated, fated.
145. jade's trick: dirty trick. A *jade* is a bad-tempered horse.

some occasion may detain us longer. I dare swear he is no hypocrite, but prays from his heart.

LEON. If you swear, my lord, you shall not be forsworn.° [*To* DON JOHN] Let me bid you 155 welcome, my lord. Being reconciled to the Prince your brother, I owe you all duty.

D. JOHN. I thank you. I am not of many words, but I thank you.

LEON. Please it your Grace lead on? 160

D. PEDRO. Your hand, Leonato. We will go together. [*Exeunt all except* BENEDICK *and* CLAUDIO.]

CLAUD. Benedick, didst thou note the daughter of Signior Leonato?

BENE. I noted her° not, but I looked on her. 165

CLAUD. Is she not a modest young lady?

BENE. Do you question me, as an honest man should do, for my simple true judgment? Or would you have me speak after my custom, as being a professed tyrant to their sex? 170

CLAUD. No, I pray thee speak in sober judgment.

BENE. Why, i' faith, methinks she's too low for a high praise, too brown for a fair praise, and too little for a great praise. Only this commendation I 175 can afford her, that were she other than she is, she were unhandsome; and being no other but as she is, I do not like her.

CLAUD. Thou thinkest I am in sport. I pray thee tell me truly how thou likest her. 180

BENE. Would you buy her, that you inquire after her?

CLAUD. Can the world buy such a jewel?

BENE. Yea, and a case to put it into. But speak you this with a sad brow?° Or do you play the 185 flouting Jack,° to tell us Cupid is a good hare-finder° and Vulcan° a rare° carpenter? Come, in what key shall a man take you, to go in the song?°

CLAUD. In mine eye she is the sweetest lady that ever I looked on. 190

BENE. I can see yet without spectacles, and I see no such matter. There's her cousin, an she were not possessed with a fury, exceeds her as much in beauty as the first of May doth the last of December. But I hope you have no intent to turn husband, have 196 you?

CLAUD. I would scarce trust myself, though I had sworn the contrary, if Hero would be my wife.

BENE. Is 't come to this? In faith, hath not the world one man but he will wear his cap with 200 suspicion?° Shall I never see a bachelor of threescore again? Go to, i' faith. An thou wilt needs thrust thy neck into a yoke, wear the print° of it, and sigh away Sundays.° Look, Don Pedro is returned to seek you. 205

[*Re-enter* DON PEDRO.]

D. PEDRO. What secret hath held you here, that you followed not to Leonato's?

BENE. I would your Grace would constrain me to tell.

D. PEDRO. I charge thee on thy allegiance.° 210

BENE. You hear, Count Claudio. I can be secret as a dumb man, I would have you think so, but, on my allegiance, mark you this, on my allegiance. He is in love. With who? Now that is your Grace's part. Mark how short his answer is — with Hero, Leonato's short daughter. 216

CLAUD. If this were so, so were it uttered.

BENE. Like the old tale, my lord: "It is not so, nor 'twas not so, but, indeed, God forbid it should be so." 220

CLAUD. If my passion change not shortly, God forbid it should be otherwise.

D. PEDRO. Amen, if you love her, for the lady is very well worthy.

CLAUD. You speak this to fetch me in,° my lord.

D. PEDRO. By my troth, I speak my thought. 226

CLAUD. And in faith, my lord, I spoke mine.

BENE. And by my two faiths and troths, my lord, I spoke mine.

CLAUD. That I love her, I feel. 230

D. PEDRO. That she is worthy, I know.

BENE. That I neither feel how she should be loved, nor know how she should be worthy, is the opinion that fire cannot melt out of me. I will die in it at the stake. 235

D. PEDRO. Thou wast ever an obstinate heretic in the despite of° beauty.

CLAUD. And never could maintain his part but in the force of his will.° 239

BENE. That a woman conceived me, I thank her; that she brought me up, I likewise give her most humble thanks. But that I will have a recheat° winded° in my forehead, or hang my bugle in an invisible baldric,° all women shall pardon me. Because I will not do them the wrong to mistrust any, 245 I will do myself the right to trust none, and the fine° is, for the which I may go the finer, I will live a bachelor.

D. PEDRO. I shall see thee, ere I die, look pale with love. 250

BENE. With anger, with sickness, or with hunger,

---

155. be forsworn: break your oath. See *M Ado* Intro. p. 698b. **165. noted her:** made careful notes on her. **185. sad brow:** sober countenance. **186. flouting Jack:** mocking knave. Cupid ... **hare-finder:** Cupid, the blind god, is so keen-sighted that he can see a crouching hare. **187. Vulcan:** the blacksmith god. **rare:** skillful. **187–88. Come ... song:** i.e., how shall I answer to fit your mood? **200–01. cap ... suspicion:** i.e., not suspect that he is a cuckold. See App. 11.

203. print: impression. **203–04. sigh ... Sundays:** spend tedious weekends at home. **210. on ... allegiance:** the most solemn form of command, for to disobey was high treason. **225. fetch me in:** make me give myself away. **236–37. in ... of:** in being spiteful about. **238–39. in ... will:** by sheer willfulness. **242. recheat:** a call on the hunting horn, with the usual joke on the cuckold's horn. **243. winded:** sounded. **244. baldric:** the belt, slung across the chest, by which the hunter's horn was carried. **246. fine:** conclusion.

my lord, not with love. Prove that ever I lose more
blood with love than I will get again with drinking,
pick out mine eyes with a ballad-maker's pen,° and
hang me up at the door of a brothel house for the
sign of blind Cupid.°   256

D. PEDRO. Well, if ever thou dost fall from this
faith, thou wilt prove a notable argument.

BENE. If I do, hang me in a bottle like a cat° and
shoot at me, and he that hits me, let him be clapped
on the shoulder and called Adam.°   261

D. PEDRO. Well, as time shall try.°
"In time the savage bull doth bear the yoke."°

BENE. The savage bull may, but if ever the sen-
sible° Benedick bear it, pluck off the bull's   265
horns and set them in my forehead. And let me be
vilely painted, and in such great letters as they write
"Here is good horse to hire" let them signify under
my sign "Here you may see Benedick the married
man."   270

CLAUD. If this should ever happen, thou wouldst
be horn-mad.°

D. PEDRO. Nay, if Cupid have not spent all his
quiver in Venice,° thou wilt quake for this shortly.

BENE. I look for an earthquake too, then.   275

D. PEDRO. Well, you will temporize with the
hours.° In the meantime, good Signior Benedick, repair to Leonato's. Commend me to him, and tell him
I will not fail him at supper, for indeed he hath made
great preparation.   280

BENE. I have almost matter enough in me for such
an embassage, and so I commit you° ——

CLAUD. To the tuition of God. From my house,
if I had it ——

D. PEDRO. The sixth of July. Your loving friend,
Benedick.   286

BENE. Nay, mock not, mock not. The body of
your discourse is sometime guarded° with fragments, and the guards° are but slightly basted° on
neither. Ere you flout old ends° any further, examine
your conscience. And so I leave you. [Exit.]   291

CLAUD. My liege, your Highness now may do me
good.

D. PEDRO. My love is thine to teach. Teach it but
how

And thou shalt see how apt it is to learn
Any hard lesson that may do thee good.   295

CLAUD. Hath° Leonato any son, my lord?

D. PEDRO. No child but Hero, she's his only heir.
Dost thou affect° her, Claudio?

CLAUD.   Oh, my lord,
When you went onward on this ended action,
I looked upon her with a soldier's eye,   300
That liked but had a rougher task in hand
Than to drive liking to the name of love.
But now I am returned and that war thoughts
Have left their places vacant, in their rooms
Come thronging soft and delicate desires,   305
All prompting me how fair young Hero is,
Saying I liked her ere I went to wars.

D. PEDRO. Thou wilt be like a lover presently,
And tire the hearer with a book of words.
If thou dost love fair Hero, cherish it,   310
And I will break with her° and with her father,
And thou shalt have her. Was 't not to this end
That thou began'st to twist so fine a story?

CLAUD. How sweetly you do minister to love,
That know love's grief by his complexion!°   315
But lest my liking might too sudden seem,
I would have salved° it with a longer treatise.

D. PEDRO. What need the bridge much broader
than the flood?
The fairest grant is the necessity.°
Look, what will serve is fit. 'Tis once° thou lovest,
And I will fit thee with the remedy.   321
I know we shall have reveling tonight.
I will assume thy part in some disguise,
And tell fair Hero I am Claudio;
And in her bosom I'll unclasp my heart,   325
And take her hearing prisoner with the force
And strong encounter of my amorous tale.
Then after to her father will I break,
And the conclusion is, she shall be thine.
In practice let us put it presently.   [*Exeunt.*]

SCENE II. *A room in* LEONATO'S *house.*

[*Enter* LEONATO *and* ANTONIO, *meeting.*]

LEON. How now, Brother! Where is my cousin,°
your son? Hath he provided this music?

ANT. He is very busy about it. But, Brother, I can
tell you strange news, that you yet yet dreamed not of.

254. ballad-maker's pen: See App. 8. 256. sign . . . Cupid: the
usual sign hung before a brothel. See App. 12. 259. bottle . . .
cat: A live cat in a wicker bottle was sometimes used as a target for archery. 261. called Adam: probably "hailed as a
champion," from Adam Bell, a famous archer. 262. try: prove
true. 263. In . . . yoke: a quotation from *The Spanish Tragedy*,
the most famous of all Elizabethan plays. See Gen. Intro. pp.
36b–37a. 265. sensible: rational. 272. horn-mad: mad with
jealousy. 273–74. spent . . . Venice: Venice in Shakespeare's
day, like Paris in modern times, was notable for the splendor
and number of its courtesans. 276–77. temporize . . . hours:
come to terms with love in time. 282. I . . . you: Benedick in
taking his leave begins with the words of formal close to a letter.
288. guarded: with the double meaning of "ornamented" and
"protected." 289. guards: ornamental braid. basted: stitched.
290. old ends: old scraps of wit.

296–312. Hath . . . her: Claudio is a prudent suitor. He begins
by inquiring after Hero's financial prospects, and then asks Don
Pedro to put in a good word for him with her father. This was
the normal procedure in negotiating a marriage in Shakespeare's
time. 298. affect: feel affection for. 311. break . . . her: broach
the subject, discover her feelings. 315. complexion: bodily appearance. 317. salved: soothed; i.e., made less abrupt.
319. fairest . . . necessity: the greatest favor is that which
satisfies a need. 320. 'Tis once: in a word.
Sc. ii: 1. cousin: used of any close relation; here nephew.

LEON. Are they good?   6

ANT. As the event stamps them.° But they have a good cover,° they show well outward. The Prince° and Count Claudio, walking in a thick-pleached alley° in mine orchard, were thus much over-   10 heard by a man of mine. The Prince discovered° to Claudio that he loved my niece your daughter, and meant to acknowledge it this night in a dance; and if he found her accordant,° he meant to take the present time by the top,° and instantly break with you of it.   16

LEON. Hath the fellow any wit that told you this?

ANT. A good sharp fellow. I will send for him, and question him yourself.   20

LEON. No, no, we will hold it as a dream till it appear itself. But I will acquaint my daughter withal, that she may be the better prepared for an answer if peradventure this be true. Go you and tell her of it. [*Enter* ATTENDANTS.] Cousins, you know what you have to do. Oh, I cry you mercy,° friend   26 — go you with me, and I will use your skill. Good Cousin, have a care this busy time.   [*Exeunt.*]

SCENE III. *The same.*

[*Enter* DON JOHN *and* CONRADE.]

CON. What the goodyear,° my lord! Why are you thus out of measure sad?

D. JOHN. There is no measure in the occasion that breeds,° therefore the sadness is without limit.   5

CON. You should hear reason.

D. JOHN. And when I have heard it, what blessing brings it?

CON. If not a present remedy, at least a patient sufferance.°   10

D. JOHN. I wonder that thou, being (as thou sayest thou art) born under Saturn,° goest about to apply a moral medicine to a mortifying° mischief.° I cannot hide what I am.° I must be sad when I have cause, and smile at no man's jests; eat when I   15 have stomach, and wait for no man's leisure; sleep when I am drowsy, and tend on no man's business; laugh when I am merry, and claw° no man in his humor.   19

CON. Yea, but you must not make the full show of this till you may do it without controlment. You have of late stood out against your brother, and he hath ta'en you newly into his grace, where it is impossible you should take true root but by the fair weather that you make yourself. It is needful   25 that you frame the season° for your own harvest.

D. JOHN. I had rather be a canker° in a hedge than a rose in his grace, and it better fits my blood to be disdained of all than to fashion a carriage°   30 to rob love from any. In this, though I cannot be said to be a flattering honest man, it must not be denied but I am a plain-dealing villain. I am trusted with a muzzle, and enfranchised with a clog;° therefore I have decreed not to sing in my cage.° If I   35 had my mouth, I would bite; if I had my liberty, I would do my liking. In the meantime let me be that I am, and seek not to alter me.

CON. Can you make no use of your discontent?

D. JOHN. I make all use of it, for I use it only.   41 Who comes here? [*Enter* BORACHIO.] What news, Borachio?

BORA. I came yonder from a great supper.   43 The Prince your brother is royally entertained by Leonato, and I can give you intelligence° of an intended marriage.

D. JOHN. Will it serve for any model° to build mischief on? What is he for a fool that betroths himself to unquietness?   50

BORA. Marry, it is your brother's right hand.

D. JOHN. Who? The most exquisite Claudio?

BORA. Even he.

D. JOHN. A proper squire! And who, and who? Which way looks he?   55

BORA. Marry, on Hero, the daughter and heir of Leonato.

D. JOHN. A very forward March chick!° How came you to this?   59

BORA. Being entertained° for a perfumer, as I was smoking° a musty room comes me the Prince and Claudio, hand in hand, in sad° conference. I whipped me behind the arras,° and there heard it agreed upon that the Prince should woo Hero for himself, and having obtained her, give her to Count Claudio.   66

D. JOHN. Come, come, let us thither. This may prove food to my displeasure. That young start-up hath all the glory of my overthrow. If I can cross° him any way, I bless myself every way. You are both sure, and will assist me?   71

7. As . . . them: it depends on how things turn out.   8. cover: outward appearance.   8–16. The Prince . . . it: This is another of the misunderstandings which are never explained. See *M Ado* Intro. p. 698a–b.   9–10. thick-pleached alley: garden walk, sheltered by thick interlocked boughs, common in Old World gardens. See Pl. 16a.   11. discovered: revealed.   14. accordant: agreeable.   14–15. take . . . top: take time by the forelock.   26. cry . . . mercy: beg your pardon.

Sc. iii: 1. What . . . goodyear: a phrase whose origin has not been satisfactorily explained; probably something like "what the deuce."   4–5. no . . . breeds: the cause of my discontent is immeasurable.   10. sufferance: endurance.   12. born . . . Saturn: i.e., therefore grim and saturnine. See App. 2.   13. mortifying: killing. mischief: disease.   14. what I am: i.e., a royal bastard. 18. claw: stroke, flatter.

26. frame . . . season: contrive the proper occasion.   27. canker: wild rose.   30. fashion a carriage: force myself to behave politely. 34. enfranchised . . . clog: made free with a weight round my leg; i.e., I am treated like a fierce dog, trusted only when muzzled and chained.   35. decreed . . . cage: I will not sing like an imprisoned songbird.   45. intelligence: information.   48. model: ground plan.   58. forward . . . chick: i.e., precocious youngster. 60. entertained: employed.   61. smoking: burning perfume in. 62. sad: serious.   63. arras: tapestry hangings.   69. cross: thwart.

CON. To the death, my lord.

D. JOHN. Let us to the great supper. Their cheer is the greater that I am subdued. Would the cook were of my mind!° Shall we go prove° what's to be done?   76

BORA. We'll wait upon your lordship. [*Exeunt.*]

Act II

SCENE I. *A hall in* LEONATO'S *house.*

[*Enter* LEONATO, ANTONIO, HERO, BEATRICE, *and others.*]

LEON. Was not Count John here at supper?

ANT. I saw him not.

BEAT. How tartly that gentleman looks! I never can see him but I am heartburned° an hour after. 5

HERO. He is of a very melancholy disposition.

BEAT. He were an excellent man that were made just in the midway between him and Benedick. The one is too like an image and says nothing, and the other too like my lady's eldest son, evermore tattling.   11

LEON. Then half Signior Benedick's tongue in Count John's mouth, and half Count John's melancholy in Signior Benedick's face ——   14

BEAT. With a good leg and a good foot, Uncle, and money enough in his purse, such a man would win any woman in the world, if a'° could get her goodwill.

LEON. By my troth, Niece, thou wilt never get thee a husband if thou be so shrewd of° thy tongue.

ANT. In faith, she's too cursed.°   22

BEAT. Too cursed is more than cursed. I shall lessen God's sending that way, for it is said "God sends a cursed cow short horns,"° but to a cow too cursed he sends none.   26

LEON. So, by being too cursed, God will send you no horns.

BEAT. Just,° if he send me no husband, for the which blessing I am at him upon my knees 30 every morning and evening. Lord, I could not endure a husband with a beard on his face. I had rather lie in the woolen.°

LEON. You may light on a husband that hath no beard.   35

BEAT. What should I do with him? Dress him in my apparel and make him my waiting gentlewoman? He that hath a beard is more than a youth, and he that hath no beard is less than a man. And he that is more than a youth is not for me, and he 40 that is less than a man, I am not for him. Therefore I will even take sixpence in earnest° of the bearward,° and lead his apes into Hell.°

LEON. Well, then, go you into Hell?   44

BEAT. No, but to the gate, and there will the Devil meet me, like an old cuckold, with horns on his head, and say "Get you to Heaven, Beatrice, get you to Heaven. Here's no place for you maids." So deliver I up my apes, and away to Saint Peter for the Heavens. He shows me where the bachelors sit, and there live we as merry as the day is long.   52

ANT. [*To* HERO] Well, Niece, I trust you will be ruled by your father.

BEAT. Yes, faith, it is my cousin's duty to make curtsy and say, "Father, as it please you." But yet for all that, Cousin, let him be a handsome fellow, or else make another curtsy and say, "Father, as it please me."   59

LEON. Well, Niece, I hope to see you one day fitted with a husband.

BEAT. Not till God make men of some other metal° than earth. Would it not grieve a woman to be overmastered with a piece of valiant dust? To make an account of her life to a clod of way- 65 ward marl?° No, Uncle, I'll none. Adam's sons are my brethren, and truly, I hold it a sin to match in my kindred.°

LEON. Daughter, remember what I told you. If the Prince do solicit you in that kind, you know your answer.   71

BEAT. The fault will be in the music, Cousin, if you be not wooed in good time. If the Prince be too important,° tell him there is measure in everything, and so dance out the answer. For, hear me, 75 Hero. Wooing, wedding, and repenting is as a Scotch jig,° a measure,° and a cinquepace.° The first suit is hot and hasty, like a Scotch jig, and full as fantastical; the wedding, mannerly modest, as a measure full of state and anciently;° and then 80 comes repentance, and, with his bad legs, falls into the cinquepace faster and faster till he sink into his grave.

LEON. Cousin, you apprehend passing° shrewdly.

BEAT. I have a good eye, Uncle, I can see a church by daylight.   86

74–75. Would . . . mind: i.e., he would then poison them all. **75. prove:** see for ourselves.

Act II, Sc. i: 5. am heartburned: suffer from indigestion. **17. a':** he. **21. shrewd of:** shrewish. **22. cursed:** bitter. **24–25. God . . . horns:** a common proverb, meaning that a badtempered cow has least power to hurt — with the inevitable joke on cuckold's horns. **29. Just:** just so. **33. lie . . . woolen:** i.e., without sheets, and so be tickled by the blankets.

42. in earnest: on account of service to be rendered. **43. bearward:** keeper of bears and monkeys. See App. 5. **lead . . . Hell:** this was the proverbial fate of old maids who died unwed. **63. metal:** material. **66. marl:** clay. **67–68. match . . . kindred:** marry a relative. **74. important:** importunate. **77. Scotch jig:** a lively, violent dance. **measure:** a stately formal dance. **cinquepace:** first five steps of the galliard, a quick, elaborate dance. See App. 24. **80. state . . . anciently:** formality and oldfashioned courtliness. **84. passing:** exceedingly.

LEON. The revelers are entering, Brother. Make good room.   [*All put on their masks.*]

Enter DON PEDRO, CLAUDIO, BENEDICK, BALTHASAR, DON JOHN, BORACHIO, MARGARET, URSULA, *and others, masked.*]

D. PEDRO. Lady, will you walk about° with your friend?   90

HERO. So you walk softly, and look sweetly, and say nothing, I am yours for the walk — and especially when I walk away.

D. PEDRO. With me in your company?

HERO. I may say so, when I please.   95

D. PEDRO. And when please you to say so?

HERO. When I like your favor,° for God defend° the lute should be like the case!°

D. PEDRO. My visor° is Philemon's roof.° Within the house is Jove.   100

HERO. Why, then, your visor should be thatched.

D. PEDRO. [*Drawing her aside*] Speak low, if you speak love.

BALTH. Well, I would you did like me.   104

MARG. So would not I, for your own sake, for I have many ill qualities.

BALTH. Which is one?

MARG. I say my prayers aloud.

BALTH. I love you the better. The hearers may cry "Amen."   110

MARG. God match me with a good dancer!

BALTH. Amen.

MARG. And God keep him out of my sight when the dance is done! Answer, clerk.°   114

BALTH. No more words. The clerk is answered.

URS. I know you well enough. You are Signior Antonio.

ANT. At a word, I am not.

URS. I know you by the waggling of your head.

ANT. To tell you true, I counterfeit him.   121

URS. You could never do him so ill-well unless you were the very man. Here's his dry hand up and down. You are he, you are he.

ANT. At a word, I am not.   125

URS. Come, come, do you think I do not know you by your excellent wit? Can virtue hide itself? Go to, mum, you are he. Graces will appear, and there's an end.

BEAT. Will you not tell me who told you so?   130

BENE. No, you shall pardon me.

BEAT. Nor will you not tell me who you are?

BENE. Not now.

BEAT. That I was disdainful, and that I had my good wit out of the *Hundred Merry Tales*° — well, this was Signior Benedick that said so.   136

BENE. What's he?

BEAT. I am sure you know him well enough.

BENE. Not I, believe me.

BEAT. Did he never make you laugh?   140

BENE. I pray you, what is he?

BEAT. Why, he is the Prince's jester — a very dull fool, only his gift is in devising impossible slanders. None but libertines delight in him, and the commendation is not in his wit, but in his villainy;   145 for he both pleases men and angers them, and then they laugh at him and beat him. I am sure he is in the fleet.° I would he had boarded me.

BENE. When I know the gentleman, I'll tell him what you say.   151

BEAT. Do, do. He'll but break a comparison or two on me, which, peradventure not marked or not laughed at, strikes him into melancholy — and then there's a partridge wing saved, for the fool will   155 eat no supper that night. [*Music*] We must follow the leaders.

BENE. In every good thing.

BEAT. Nay, if they lead to any ill, I will leave them at the next turning. [*Dance. Then exeunt all except* DON JOHN, BORACHIO, *and* CLAUDIO.]

D. JOHN. Sure my brother is amorous on Hero, and hath withdrawn her father to break with him about it. The ladies follow her, and but one visor remains.

BORA. And this is Claudio. I know him by his bearing.   166

D. JOHN. Are not you Signior Benedick?

CLAUD. You know me well. I am he.

D. JOHN. Signior, you are very near my brother in his love. He is enamored on Hero. I pray you, dissuade him from her. She is no equal for his   171 birth. You may do the part of an honest man in it.

CLAUD. How know you he loves her?

D. JOHN. I heard him swear his affection.   175

BORA. So did I too, and he swore he would marry her tonight.

D. JOHN. Come, let us to the banquet.°

    [*Exeunt* DON JOHN *and* BORACHIO.]

CLAUD. Thus answer I in name of Benedick, But hear these ill news with the ears of Claudio. 'Tis certain so. The Prince woos for himself.   181 Friendship is constant in all other things Save in the office° and affairs of love; Therefore all hearts in love use their own tongues, Let every eye negotiate for itself,   185 And trust no agent, for beauty is a witch Against whose charms faith melteth into blood.°

---

89. walk about: dance a measure. See App. 24.   **97. favor:** face. **defend:** forbid.   **98. lute ... case:** the instrument should be as ugly as its case, for Don Pedro is wearing a grotesque mask. **99. visor:** mask. **Philemon's roof:** Philemon and Baucis were a good old couple who unawares gave hospitality in their cottage to the gods Jupiter and Mercury.   **114. Answer, clerk:** In services in the Church of England the parson used to read the prayers and versicles, while the clerk led the congregation in the amens and responses.

135. *Hundred ... Tales:* a popular book of jokes, first published in 1526.   **147–48. in ... fleet:** i.e., among the returned soldiers. **178. banquet:** light refreshments given at an evening entertainment.   **183. office:** business.   **187. blood:** passion.

This is an accident of hourly proof,°
Which I mistrusted° not. Farewell, therefore, Hero!

[Re-enter BENEDICK.*]*

BENE. Count Claudio?   190
CLAUD. Yea, the same.
BENE. Come, will you go with me?
CLAUD. Whither?
BENE. Even to the next willow, about your own business, County.° What fashion will you wear   195
the garland of? About your neck, like a usurer's chain?° Or under your arm, like a lieutenant's scarf? You must wear it one way, for the Prince hath got your Hero.
CLAUD. I wish him joy of her.   200
BENE. Why, that's spoken like an honest drovier.° So they sell bullocks. But did you think the Prince would have served you thus?
CLAUD. I pray you, leave me.   204
BENE. Ho! Now you strike like the blind man. 'Twas the boy that stole your meat, and you'll beat the post.
CLAUD. If it will not be, I'll leave you.   *[Exit.]*
BENE. Alas, poor hurt fowl! Now will he creep into sedges.° But that my Lady Beatrice should know me and not know me! The Prince's fool!   210
Ha? It may be I go under that title because I am merry. Yea, but so I am apt to do myself wrong, I am not so reputed. It is the base, though bitter, disposition of Beatrice that puts the world into her   215
person, and so gives me out.° Well, I'll be revenged as I may.

[Re-enter DON PEDRO.*]*

D. PEDRO. Now, signior, where's the Count? Did you see him?   219
BENE. Troth, my lord, I have played the part of Lady Fame. I found him here as melancholy as a lodge in a warren.° I told him, and I think I told him true, that your Grace had got the goodwill of this young lady. And I offered him my company to a willow tree,° either to make him a garland,   225
as being forsaken, or to bind him up a rod, as being worthy to be whipped.
D. PEDRO. To be whipped! What's his fault?
BENE. The flat transgression of a schoolboy who, being overjoyed with finding a bird's nest, shows it his companion, and he steals it.   231
D. PEDRO. Wilt thou make a trust a transgression? The transgression is in the stealer.
BENE. Yet it had not been amiss the rod had been made, and the garland too; for the garland he   235

might have worn himself, and the rod he might have bestowed on you, who, as I take it, have stolen his birds' nest.
D. PEDRO. I will but teach them to sing and restore them to the owner.   240
BENE. If their singing answer your saying, by my faith, you say honestly.
D. PEDRO. The Lady Beatrice hath a quarrel to you. The gentleman that danced with her told her she is much wronged by you.   245
BENE. Oh, she misused me past the endurance of a block! An oak but with one green leaf on it would have answered her. My very visor began to assume life and scold with her. She told me, not thinking I had been myself, that I was the Prince's jester,   250
that I was duller than a great thaw, huddling jest upon jest with such impossible conveyance° upon me that I stood like a man at a mark,° with a whole army shooting at me. She speaks poniards,° and every word stabs. If her breath were as terrible   255
as her terminations,° there were no living near her. She would infect to the North Star. I would not marry her though she were endowed with all that Adam had left him before he transgressed. She would have made Hercules have turned spit,°   260
yea, and have cleft his club to make the fire, too. Come, talk not of her. You shall find her the infernal Ate° in good apparel. I would to God some scholar would conjure her;° for certainly while she is here a man may live as quiet in Hell as in a sanctu-   265
ary, and people sin upon purpose because they would go thither. So, indeed, all disquiet, horror, and perturbation follows her.
D. PEDRO. Look, here she comes.   270

[Re-enter CLAUDIO, BEATRICE, HERO,
and LEONATO.*]*

BENE. Will your Grace command me any service to the world's end? I will go on the slightest errand now to the Antipodes° that you can devise to send me on. I will fetch you a toothpicker° now from the furthest inch of Asia, bring you the length of   275
Prester John's° foot, fetch you a hair off the great Cham's° beard, do you any embassage to the Pigmies,° rather than hold three words' conference with this harpy. You have no employment for me?
D. PEDRO. None but to desire your good company.
BENE. Oh, God, sir, here's a dish I love not.   282
I cannot endure my Lady Tongue.   *[Exit.]*

---

188. accident . . . proof: common occurrence.   189. mistrusted: suspected.   195. County: count.   196–97. usurer's chain: Men of wealth used to advertise their importance by wearing long gold chains — as a modern money lender often sports a large diamond ring.   201. drovier: cattle-driver.   209. sedges: reeds. 215–16. puts . . . out: claims to know what everyone is saying and describes me thus.   222. lodge . . . warren: a gamekeeper's hut, a lonely, melancholy place.   225. willow tree: the emblem of a forlorn lover.

252. conveyance: jugglery, trickery.   253. mark: target.   254. poniards: daggers.   256. terminations: expressions.   260. turned spit: Turning the spit on which meat was roasted was the most menial of tasks in the kitchen.   263. Ate: the goddess of strife. 263–64. scholar . . . her: as evil spirits were exorcised in Latin, a scholar was necessary. See *Haml.*, I.i.42.   273. Antipodes: the other end of the earth. Benedick will undertake any distant voyage to get away from his tormentor.   274. toothpicker: toothpick.   276. Prester John: fabled King of Abyssinia and the strange parts beyond.   276–77. great Cham: the Mongol Emperor.   278. Pigmies: another distant and romantic race.

D. PEDRO. Come, lady, come, you have lost the heart of Signior Benedick. 286

BEAT. Indeed, my lord, he lent it me awhile, and I gave him use for it, a double heart for his single one. Marry, once before he won it of me with false dice, therefore your Grace may well say I have lost it.° 291

D. PEDRO. You have put him down, lady, you have put him down.

BEAT. So I would not he should do me, my lord, lest I should prove the mother of fools. I have brought Count Claudio, whom you sent me to seek. 297

D. PEDRO. Why, how now, Count! Wherefore are you sad?

CLAUD. Not sad, my lord. 300

D. PEDRO. How then? Sick?

CLAUD. Neither, my lord.

BEAT. The Count is neither sad, nor sick, nor merry, nor well, but civil Count, civil as an 305 orange,° and something of that jealous complexion.

D. PEDRO. I' faith, lady, I think your blazon° to be true, though I'll be sworn, if he be so, his conceit° is false. Here, Claudio, I have wooed in thy name, and fair Hero is won. I have broke with her father, and his goodwill obtained. Name the day of marriage, and God give thee joy! 312

LEON. Count, take of me my daughter, and with her my fortunes. His Grace hath made the match, and all grace say " Amen " to it. 315

BEAT. Speak, Count, 'tis your cue.

CLAUD. Silence is the perfectest herald of joy. I were but little happy if I could say how much. Lady, as you are mine, I am yours. I give away myself for you, and dote upon the exchange. 320

BEAT. Speak, Cousin, or if you cannot, stop his mouth with a kiss, and let not him speak neither.

D. PEDRO. In faith, lady, you have a merry heart.

BEAT. Yea, my lord, I thank it, poor fool — it keeps on the windy side of care. My cousin tells him in his ear that he is in her heart.

CLAUD. And so she doth, Cousin. 329

BEAT. Good Lord, for alliance!° Thus goes everyone to the world but I, and I am sunburned,° I may sit in a corner and cry heigh-ho for a husband!

D. PEDRO. Lady Beatrice, I will get you one.

BEAT. I would rather have one of your father's getting.° Hath your Grace ne'er a brother like 335 you? Your father got excellent husbands, if a maid could come by them.

D. PEDRO. Will you have me, lady?

BEAT. No, my lord, unless I might have an- 340 other for working days. Your Grace is too costly to wear every day. But I beseech your Grace pardon me. I was born to speak all mirth and no matter. 344

D. PEDRO. Your silence most offends me, and to be merry best becomes you, for, out of question, you were born in a merry hour.

BEAT. No, sure, my lord, my mother cried; but then there was a star danced, and under that was I born. Cousins, God give you joy! 350

LEON. Niece, will you look to those things I told you of?

BEAT. I cry you mercy, Uncle. By your Grace's pardon. [*Exit.*]

D. PEDRO. By my troth, a pleasant-spirited lady.

LEON. There's little of the melancholy ele- 357 ment° in her, my lord. She is never sad but when she sleeps, and not ever sad then, for I have heard my daughter say she hath often dreamed of unhappiness and waked herself with laughing. 361

D. PEDRO. She cannot endure to hear tell of a husband.

LEON. Oh, by no means. She mocks all her wooers out of suit. 365

D. PEDRO. She were an excellent wife for Benedick.

LEON. Oh Lord, my lord, if they were but a week married they would talk themselves mad.

D. PEDRO. County Claudio, when mean you to go to church? 371

CLAUD. Tomorrow, my lord. Time goes on crutches till love have all his rites.

LEON. Not till Monday, my dear son, which is hence a just sevennight,° and a time too brief, too, to have all things answer my mind. 376

D. PEDRO. Come, you shake the head at so long a breathing.° But I warrant thee, Claudio, the time shall not go dully by us. I will, in the interim, undertake one of Hercules' labors, which is to bring 380 Signior Benedick and the Lady Beatrice into a mountain of affection the one with the other. I would fain have it a match, and I doubt not but to fashion it if you three will but minister such assistance as I shall give you direction. 386

LEON. My lord, I am for you, though it cost me ten nights' watchings.

CLAUD. And I, my lord.

D. PEDRO. And you too, gentle Hero?

HERO. I will do any modest office, my lord, to help my cousin to a good husband. 391

D. PEDRO. And Benedick is not the unhopefulest husband that I know. Thus far can I praise him. He is of a noble strain, of approved° valor and confirmed honesty. I will teach you how to humor 395

287–91. Indeed . . . it: This passage has not been satisfactorily explained, but when Beatrice is being sarcastic, she is liable to become cryptic. 305–06. civil . . . orange: with a pun on Seville oranges and their yellow color, which was the sign of jealousy. 307. blazon: description, originally a heraldic term. 308. conceit: imagination. 330. Good . . . alliance: Good Lord, what a thing this marrying is! 331. sunburned: no fine lady, for an ivory complexion was most admired. 335. getting: begetting.

357–58. melancholy element: See App. 3. 375. a . . . sevennight: exactly a week. 378. breathing: pause. 394. approved: proved.

your cousin that she shall fall in love with Benedick. And I, with your two helps, will so practice on Benedick that, in despite of his quick wit and his queasy° stomach, he shall fall in love with Beatrice. If we can do this, Cupid is no longer an archer. 400 His glory shall be ours, for we are the only love gods. Go in with me, and I will tell you my drift.°

[*Exeunt.*]

SCENE II. *The same.*

[*Enter* DON JOHN *and* BORACHIO.]

D. JOHN. It is so. The Count Claudio shall marry the daughter of Leonato.

BORA. Yea, my lord, but I can cross it. 3

D. JOHN. Any bar, any cross,° any impediment will be medicinable° to me. I am sick in displeasure to him, and whatsoever comes athwart his affection° ranges evenly° with mine. How canst thou cross this marriage? 8

BORA. Not honestly, my lord, but so covertly that no dishonesty shall appear in me.

D. JOHN. Show me briefly how.

BORA. I think I told your lordship, a year since, how much I am in the favor of Margaret, the waiting gentlewoman to Hero.

D. JOHN. I remember. 15

BORA. I can, at any unseasonable instant of the night, appoint her to look out at her lady's chamber window.

D. JOHN. What life is in that, to be the death of this marriage? 20

BORA. The poison of that lies in you to temper.° Go you to the Prince your brother. Spare not to tell him that he hath wronged his honor in marrying the renowned Claudio — whose estimation do you mightily hold up — to a contaminated stale,° such a one as Hero. 26

D. JOHN. What proof shall I make of° that?

BORA. Proof enough to misuse° the Prince, to vex Claudio, to undo Hero, and kill Leonato. Look you for any other issue? 30

D. JOHN. Only to despite° them I will endeavor anything.

BORA. Go, then. Find me a meet° hour to draw Don Pedro and the Count Claudio alone. Tell them that you know that Hero loves me, intend a 35 kind of zeal both to the Prince and Claudio, as — in love of your brother's honor, who hath made this match, and his friend's reputation, who is thus like to be cozened° with the semblance° of a maid —

that you have discovered thus. They will scarcely 40 believe this without trial. Offer them instances,° which shall bear no less likelihood than to see me at her chamber window, hear me call Margaret Hero, hear Margaret term me Claudio,° and bring them to see this the very night before the in- 45 tended wedding — for in the meantime I will so fashion the matter that Hero shall be absent. And there shall appear such seeming truth of Hero's disloyalty that jealousy shall be called assurance° and all the preparation overthrown. 51

D. JOHN. Grow this to what adverse issue it can, I will put it in practice. Be cunning in the working this and thy fee is a thousand ducats.°

BORA. Be you constant in the accusation and my cunning shall not shame me. 56

D. JOHN. I will presently go learn their day of marriage. [*Exeunt.*]

SCENE III. LEONATO's *orchard.*

[*Enter* BENEDICK.]

BENE. Boy!

[*Enter* BOY.]

BOY. Signior?

BENE. In my chamber window lies a book. Bring it hither to me in the orchard.

BOY. I am here already, sir. 5

BENE. I know that, but I would have thee hence, and here again. [*Exit* BOY.] I do much wonder that one man, seeing how much another man is a fool when he dedicates his behaviors to love, will, after he hath laughed at such shallow follies in others, 10 become the argument of his own scorn by falling in love — and such a man is Claudio. I have known when there was no music with him but the drum and the fife, and now had he rather hear the tabor and the pipe.° I have known when he would 15 have walked ten mile afoot to see a good armor,° and now will he lie ten nights awake carving the fashion of a new doublet.° He was wont to speak plain and to the purpose, like an honest man and a soldier, and now is he turned orthography,° his 20 words are a very fantastical banquet — just so many strange dishes. May I be so converted, and see with these eyes? I cannot tell, I think not. I will not be sworn but love may transform me to an oyster, 25

41. instances: proofs.   43–44. hear . . . Claudio: if Claudio had heard the supposed Hero call someone else Claudio, he would surely have guessed that there was a mistake. See *M Ado* Intro. p. 698a.   50. assurance: certainty.   54. ducat: Italian coin worth about $2.25.

   Sc. iii: 14–15. tabor . . . pipe: the musical instruments of shepherds and other men of peace. See Pl. 13d. tabor: small drum. pipe: wind instrument made of a single pipe of wood.   16. armor: suit of armor.   18. doublet: jacket, often elaborately cut and embroidered. See Pl. 8b and p. 93a.   20. orthography: phrase maker.

399. queasy: delicate, particular.   402. drift: idea.
   Sc. ii: 4. cross: obstacle. medicinable: healing medicine. 6. affection: liking.   7. ranges evenly: runs parallel.   21. temper: mix.   25. stale: whore.   27. make of: offer for.   28. misuse: deceive.   31. despite: spite.   33. meet: fit.   39. cozened: cheated. semblance: appearance.

but I'll take my oath on it till he have made an
oyster of me he shall never make me such a fool.
One woman is fair, yet I am well; another is wise,
yet I am well; another virtuous, yet I am well. But
till all graces be in one woman, one woman 30
shall not come in my grace. Rich she shall be, that's
certain; wise, or I'll none; virtuous, or I'll never
cheapen° her; fair, or I'll never look on her; mild,
or come not near me; noble,° or not I for an angel;°
of good discourse, an excellent musician; and 35
her hair shall be of what color it please God. Ha!
The Prince and Monsieur Love! I will hide me in
the arbor.   [*Withdraws.*]

[*Enter* DON PEDRO, CLAUDIO, LEONATO,
and BALTHASAR.°]

D. PEDRO. Come, shall we hear this music?
CLAUD. Yea, my good lord. How still the evening
  is,   40
As hushed on purpose to grace harmony!
D. PEDRO. See you where Benedick hath hid him-
  self?
CLAUD. Oh, very well, my lord. The music ended,
We'll fit the kid fox with a pennyworth.°
D. PEDRO. Come, Balthasar, we'll hear that song
  again.   45
BALTH. Oh, good my lord, tax° not so bad a voice
To slander music any more than once.
D. PEDRO. It is the witness still° of excellency
To put a strange face° on his own perfection.
I pray thee, sing, and let me woo no more.   50
BALTH. Because you talk of wooing, I will sing.
Since many a wooer doth commence his suit
To her he thinks not worthy, yet he woos,
Yet will he swear he loves.
D. PEDRO.   Nay, pray thee, come.
Or if thou wilt hold longer argument,   55
Do it in notes.
BALTH.   Note this before my notes,
There's not a note of mine that's worth the noting.
D. PEDRO. Why, these are very crotchets that he
  speaks —
Note, notes, forsooth, and nothing.°
                        [*Plays the tune.*]
BENE. Now, divine air!° Now is his soul rav- 60
ished! Is it not strange that sheep's guts° should hale
souls out of men's bodies? Well, a horn for my
money, when all's done.

---

33. cheapen: bargain for.   **34. noble:** 6s 8d. **angel:** 10s. Puns
on these coins are common. See Pl. 10, and App. 27.   **38. s.d.,**
Balthasar: F1 prints "Jack Wilson," a singer who once took the
part.   **44. fit . . . pennyworth:** "we'll give him something for
his money." The *kid fox* is a reference to the fable of the Kid and
the Fox, told, for instance, in Spenser's *Shepherd's Calendar*, V.
The kid thought itself clever, but was carried off by the fox.
46. tax: censure.   **48. still:** always.   **49. strange face:** assumed
appearance.   **59. nothing:** a pun on noting.   **60. air:** tune.
61. sheep's guts: from which strings for musical instruments
were made. Benedick is no lover of chamber music.

BALTH. [*Sings.*]
  Sigh no more, ladies, sigh no more,
    Men were deceivers ever,   65
  One foot in sea and one on shore,
    To one thing constant never.
  Then sigh not so, but let them go,
    And be you blithe and bonny,
  Converting all your sounds of woe   70
    Into Hey nonny, nonny.

  Sing no more ditties, sing no moe°
    Of dumps° so dull and heavy.
  The fraud of men was ever so,
    Since summer first was leavy.   75
  Then sigh not so, but let them go,
    And be you blithe and bonny,
  Converting all your sounds of woe
    Into Hey nonny, nonny.
D. PEDRO. By my troth, a good song.
BALTH. And an ill singer, my lord.
D. PEDRO. Ha, no, no, faith, thou singest well
enough for a shift.°   80
BENE. An he had been a dog that should have
howled thus, they would have hanged him. And I
pray God his bad voice bode no mischief. I had as lief
have heard the night raven,° come what plague
could have come after it.   85
D. PEDRO. Yea, marry, dost thou hear, Balthasar? I
pray thee get us some excellent music, for tomorrow
night we would have it at the Lady Hero's chamber
window.
BALTH. The best I can, my lord.   90
D. PEDRO. Do so. Farewell.   [*Exit* BALTHASAR.]
Come hither, Leonato. What was it you told me of
today — that your niece Beatrice was in love with
Signior Benedick?
CLAUD. Oh, aye. Stalk on, stalk on, the fowl sits.
I did never think that lady would have loved any
man.   97
LEON. No, nor I neither. But most wonderful that
she should so dote on Signior Benedick, whom she
hath in all outward behaviors seemed ever to abhor.
BENE. Is 't possible? Sits the wind in that corner?
LEON. By my troth, my lord, I cannot tell   102
what to think of it but that she loves him with an
enraged° affection. It is past the infinite of thought.°
D. PEDRO. Maybe she doth but counterfeit.
CLAUD. Faith, like enough.
LEON. Oh, God, counterfeit! There was never
counterfeit of passion came so near the life of pas-
sion as she discovers it.   111
D. PEDRO. Why, what effects of passion shows she?
CLAUD. Bait the hook well — this fish will bite.
LEON. What effects, my lord? She will sit you,
you heard my daughter tell you how.   116

---

72. moe: more.   **73. dumps:** melancholy.   **80. shift:** makeshift.
84. night raven: i.e., a bird of ill-omen.   **104. enraged:** furious.
infinite of thought: i.e., unimaginable.

CLAUD. She did, indeed.

D. PEDRO. How, how, I pray you? You amaze me. I would have thought her spirit had been invincible against all assaults of affection.   120

LEON. I would have sworn it had, my lord, especially against Benedick.

BENE. I should think this a gull° but that the white-bearded fellow speaks it. Knavery cannot, sure, hide himself in such reverence.   125

CLAUD. He hath ta'en the infection. Hold it up.°

D. PEDRO. Hath she made her affection known to Benedick?

LEON. No, and swears she never will. That's her torment.   130

CLAUD. 'Tis true indeed, so your daughter says. " Shall I," says she, " that have so oft encountered him with scorn, write to him that I love him? "

LEON. This says she now when she is begin-   135 ning to write to him; for she'll be up twenty times a night, and there will she sit in her smock° till she have writ a sheet of paper. My daughter tells us all.

CLAUD. Now you talk of a sheet of paper, I remember a pretty jest your daughter told us of.

LEON. Oh, when she had writ it, and was reading it over, she found Benedick and Beatrice between the sheet?

CLAUD. That.   145

LEON. Oh, she tore the letter into a thousand half-pence, railed at herself that she should be so immodest to write to one that she knew would flout her. " I measure him," says she, " by my own spirit, for I should flout him if he writ to me — yea, though I love him, I should."   151

CLAUD. Then down upon her knees she falls, weeps, sobs, beats her heart, tears her hair, prays, curses. " O sweet Benedick! God give me patience! "

LEON. She doth indeed, my daughter says   156 so. And the ecstasy° hath so much overborne° her that my daughter is sometime afeard she will do a desperate outrage to herself. It is very true.

D. PEDRO. It were good that Benedick knew of it by some other, if she will not discover it.   161

CLAUD. To what end? He would make but a sport of it, and torment the poor lady worse.

D. PEDRO. An he should, it were an alms° to hang him. She's an excellent sweet lady, and out of all suspicion she is virtuous.   166

CLAUD. And she is exceeding wise.

D. PEDRO. In everything but in loving Benedick.

LEON. Oh, my lord, wisdom and blood combating in so tender a body, we have ten proofs to one that blood hath the victory. I am sorry for her, as I have just cause, being her uncle and her guardian.   174

D. PEDRO. I would she had bestowed this dotage

on me. I would have daffed all other respects° and made her half myself. I pray you tell Benedick of it and hear what a' will say.

LEON. Were it good, think you?   179

CLAUD. Hero thinks surely she will die; for she says she will die if he love her not, and she will die ere she make her love known, and she will die if he woo her rather than she will bate° one breath of her accustomed crossness.   183

D. PEDRO. She doth well. If she should make tender° of her love, 'tis very possible he'll scorn it, for the man, as you know all, hath a contemptible° spirit.

CLAUD. He is a very proper° man.

D. PEDRO. He hath indeed a good outward happiness.   190

CLAUD. Before God! And in my mind, very wise.

D. PEDRO. He doth indeed show some sparks that are like wit.

CLAUD. And I take him to be valiant.   194

D. PEDRO. As Hector, I assure you. And in the managing of quarrels you may say he is wise, for either he avoids them with great discretion or undertakes them with a most Christianlike fear.   200

LEON. If he do fear God, a' must necessarily keep peace. If he break the peace, he ought to enter into a quarrel with fear and trembling.

D. PEDRO. And so will he do, for the man doth fear God, howsoever it seems not in him by   205 some large jests he will make. Well, I am sorry for your niece. Shall we go seek Benedick, and tell him of her love?

CLAUD. Never tell him, my lord. Let her wear it out with good counsel.°   210

LEON. Nay, that's impossible. She may wear her heart out first.

D. PEDRO. Well, we will hear further of it by your daughter. Let it cool the while. I love Benedick well, and I could wish he would modestly ex-   215 amine himself to see how much he is unworthy so good a lady.

LEON. My lord, will you walk? Dinner is ready.

CLAUD. If he do not dote on her upon this, I will never trust my expectation.   220

D. PEDRO. Let there be the same net spread for her and that must your daughter and her gentlewomen carry. The sport will be when they hold one an opinion of another's dotage, and no such matter. That's the scene that I would see, which will   225 be merely a dumb show.° Let us send her to call him in to dinner.

[*Exeunt* DON PEDRO, CLAUDIO, *and* LEONATO.]

BENE. [*Coming forward*] This can be no trick.

176. daffed . . . respects: pushed aside all other considerations.
183. bate: abate.   186. tender: offer.   187. contemptible: contemptuous.   189. proper: handsome.   209–10. wear counsel: get over it by good advice.   226. dumb show: See *Haml*, III.ii.146,n.

123. gull: trick.   126. Hold it up: keep the joke going.
137. smock: nightdress.   157. ecstasy: excess of emotion. overborne: overcome.   164. an alms: a good deed.

The conference was sadly borne.° They have the
truth of this from Hero. They seem to pity the   230
lady. It seems her affections have their full bent.°
Love me! Why, it must be requited. I hear how I am
censured.° They say I will bear myself proudly if I
perceive the love come from her. They say too   234
that she will rather die than give any sign of affection. I did never think to marry. I must not seem
proud. Happy are they that hear their detractions
and can put them to mending. They say the lady
is fair — 'tis a truth, I can bear them witness;   239
and virtuous — 'tis so, I cannot reprove° it; and wise,
but for loving me — by my troth, it is no addition
to her wit, nor no great argument of her folly, for
I will be horribly in love with her. I may chance
have some odd quirks° and remnants of wit   244
broken on me because I have railed so long against
marriage. But doth not the appetite alter? A man
loves the meat in his youth that he cannot endure in
his age. Shall quips° and sentences° and these
paper bullets° of the brain awe a man from the
career of his humor?° No, the world must be   250
peopled. When I said I would die a bachelor, I did
not think I should live till I were married. Here
comes Beatrice. By this day, she's a fair lady! I do
spy some marks of love in her.   255

[*Enter* BEATRICE.]

BEAT. Against my will I am sent to bid you come
in to dinner.

BENE. Fair Beatrice, I thank you for your pains.

BEAT. I took no more pains for those thanks than
you take pains to thank me. If it had been painful, I
would not have come.   261

BENE. You take pleasure, then, in the message?

BEAT. Yea, just so much as you may take upon a
knife's point and choke a daw° withal. You   264
have no stomach, signior. Fare you well.   [*Exit.*]

BENE. Ha! "Against my will I am sent to bid you
come in to dinner." There's a double meaning in
that. "I took no more pains for those thanks than
you took pains to thank me." That's as much as to
say, "Any pains that I take for you is as easy   270
as thanks." If I do not take pity of her, I am a villain; if I do not love her, I am a Jew.° I will go get
her picture.   [*Exit.*]

229. **sadly borne:** seriously maintained. ❘ 231. **full bent:** are
tightly stretched, like a strung bow.   233. **censured:** judged.
240. **reprove:** disprove.   244. **quirks:** wisecracks.   248. **quips:**
jokes. **sentences:** proverbs, wise sayings.   249. **paper bullets:**
i.e., light and harmless.   250. **career . . . humor:** course of his
inclination. See V.i.135.   264. **daw:** jackdaw, a foolish bird.
272. **Jew:** i.e., an unbeliever.

Act III

SCENE I. LEONATO'S *orchard.*

[*Enter* HERO, MARGARET, *and* URSULA.]

HERO. Good Margaret, run thee to the parlor.
There shalt thou find my cousin Beatrice
Proposing° with the Prince and Claudio.
Whisper her ear and tell her I and Ursula
Walk in the orchard, and our whole discourse   5
Is all of her — say that thou overheard'st us.
And bid her steal into the pleachèd° bower
Where honeysuckles, ripened by the sun,
Forbid the sun to enter, like favorites°
Made proud by princes, that advance their pride   10
Against that power that bred it. There will she hide
     her,
To listen our propose. This is thy office.°
Bear thee well in it, and leave us alone.

MARG. I'll make her come, I warrant you, pres-
     ently.°   [*Exit.*]

HERO. Now, Ursula, when Beatrice doth come,
As we do trace° this alley up and down   16
Our talk must only be of Benedick.
When I do name him, let it be thy part
To praise him more than ever man did merit.
My talk to thee must be how Benedick   20
Is sick in love with Beatrice. Of this matter
Is little Cupid's crafty arrow made,
That only wounds by hearsay.

[*Enter* BEATRICE, *behind.*]   Now begin,
For look where Beatrice, like a lapwing,° runs
Close by the ground to hear our conference.   25

URS. The pleasant'st angling is to see the fish
Cut with her golden oars° the silver stream,
And greedily devour the treacherous bait.
So angle we for Beatrice, who even now
Is couchèd in the woodbine coverture.°   30
Fear you not my part of the dialogue.

HERO. Then go we near her, that her ear lose
     nothing
Of the false sweet bait that we lay for it.
         [*Approaching the bower*]
No, truly, Ursula, she is too disdainful.
I know her spirits are as coy and wild   35
As haggards° of the rock.

Act III, Sc. i: 3. **Proposing:** conversing.   7. **pleached:** covered
with branches. See I.ii.9.   9. **like favorites:** This sudden simile
could not have failed to remind original spectators of the Earl
of Essex, who had quarreled violently with Queen Elizabeth in
June 1598 and was in disgrace from September 1599 until his
execution on February 25, 1601. See Gen. Intro. p. 23b.   12. **office:**
duty.   14. **presently:** immediately.   16. **trace:** traverse.
24. **lapwing:** The lapwing, like the partridge, runs swiftly and
close to the ground.   27. **golden oars:** i.e., red fins. Some English
fresh-water fish, such as roach and perch, have conspicuously red
fins.   30. **woodbine coverture:** honeysuckle thicket, hiding place.
36. **haggards:** female wild hawks. See App. 26.

URS.   But are you sure
That Benedick loves Beatrice so entirely?
   HERO. So says the Prince and my new-trothèd°
   lord.
   URS. And did they bid you tell her of it, madam?
   HERO. They did entreat me to acquaint her of it.
But I persuaded them, if they loved Benedick, 41
To wish him wrestle with affection
And never to let Beatrice know of it.
   URS. Why did you so? Doth not the gentleman
Deserve as full as fortunate a bed   45
As ever Beatrice shall couch upon?
   HERO. Oh god of love! I know he doth deserve
As much as may be yielded to a man.
But Nature never framed a woman's heart
Of prouder stuff than that of Beatrice.   50
Disdain and scorn ride sparkling in her eyes,
Misprizing° what they look on, and her wit
Values itself so highly that to her
All matter else seems weak. She cannot love,
Nor take no shape nor project of affection,° 55
She is so self-endeared.°
   URS.   Sure, I think so,
And therefore certainly it were not good
She knew his love, lest she make sport at it. 58
   HERO. Why, you speak truth. I never yet saw man,
How wise, how noble, young, how rarely featured,
But she would spell him backward.° If fair-faced,
She would swear the gentleman should be her sister;
If black, why, Nature, drawing of an antique,°
Made a foul blot; if tall, a lance ill-headed,
If low, an agate° very vilely cut;   65
If speaking, why, a vane blown with all winds,
If silent, why, a block movèd with none.
So turns she every man the wrong side out,
And never gives to truth and virtue that
Which simpleness and merit purchaseth.   70
   URS. Sure, sure, such carping is not commendable.
   HERO. No, not to be so odd and from all fashions°
As Beatrice is cannot be commendable.
But who dare tell her so? If I should speak,
She would mock me into air. Oh, she would laugh
   me   75
Out of myself, press me to death° with wit!
Therefore let Benedick, like covered fire,
Consume away in sighs, waste inwardly.
It were a better death than die with mocks,
Which is as bad as die with tickling.   80
   URS. Yet tell her of it. Hear what she will say.
   HERO. No, rather I will go to Benedick
And counsel him to fight against his passion.

And truly I'll devise some honest slanders
To stain my cousin with. One doth not know   85
How much an ill word may empoison liking.
   URS. Oh, do not do your cousin such a wrong!
She cannot be so much without true judgment —
Having so swift and excellent a wit
As she is prized to have — as to refuse   90
So rare a gentleman as Signior Benedick.
   HERO. He is the only° man of Italy,
Always excepted my dear Claudio.
   URS. I pray you be not angry with me, madam,
Speaking my fancy. Signior Benedick,   95
For shape, for bearing, argument,° and valor,
Goes foremost in report through Italy.
   HERO. Indeed he hath an excellent good name.
   URS. His excellence did earn it ere he had it.
When are you married, madam?   100
   HERO. Why, every day, tomorrow. Come, go in.
I'll show thee some attires, and have thy counsel
Which is the best to furnish° me tomorrow.
   URS. She's limed,° I warrant you. We have caught
   her, madam.
   HERO. If it prove so, then loving goes by haps.°
Some Cupid kills with arrows, some with traps. 106
           [*Exeunt* HERO *and* URSULA.]
   BEAT. [*Coming forward*] What° fire is in mine
   ears? Can this be true?
Stand I condemned for pride and scorn so much?
Contempt, farewell, and maiden pride, adieu!
No glory lives behind the back of such.   110
And, Benedick, love on, I will requite thee,
   Taming my wild heart to thy loving hand.
If thou dost love, my kindness shall incite thee
   To bind our loves up in a holy band,
For others say thou dost deserve and I   115
Believe it better than reportingly.°   [*Exit.*]

SCENE II. *A room in* LEONATO'S *house.*

[*Enter* DON PEDRO, CLAUDIO, BENEDICK, *and* LEONATO.]
   D. PEDRO. I do but stay till your marriage be consummate, and then go I toward Aragon.
   CLAUD. I'll bring you thither, my lord, if you'll vouchsafe me.   4
   D. PEDRO. Nay, that would be as great a soil in the new gloss of your marriage as to show a child his new coat and forbid him to wear it. I will only be bold with° Benedick for his company, for from the crown of his head to the sole of his foot he is all mirth. He hath twice or thrice cut Cupid's bow- 10
string, and the little hangman° dare not shoot at him. He hath a heart as sound as a bell, and his

---

38. **new-trothed:** newly betrothed.   52. **Misprizing:** despising.
55. **take . . . affection:** accept any form or idea of love for another.   56. **self-endeared:** fond of herself.   61. **spell . . . backward:** "turn him inside out."   63. **antique:** grotesque.
65. **agate:** a little figure cut in a seal ring. See *II Hen IV,* I.ii.19.   72. **from . . . fashions:** so contrary.   76. **press . . . death:** See Gen. Intro. p. 27b.

92. **only:** one and only, foremost.   96. **argument:** intelligent conversation.   103. **furnish:** dress.   104. **limed:** caught in birdlime.
105. **haps:** chance.   107–16. **What . . . reportingly:** See *M Ado* Intro. p. 699a. **reportingly:** by the reports of others.
Sc. ii: 7–8. **be . . . with:** be so bold as to ask.   11. **hangman:** executioner.

tongue is the clapper, for what his heart thinks his tongue speaks.

BENE. Gallants, I am not as I have been.   15

LEON. So say I. Methinks you are sadder.

CLAUD. I hope he be in love.

D. PEDRO. Hang him, truant! There's no true drop of blood in him to be truly touched with love. If he be sad, he wants money.   20

BENE. I have the toothache.

D. PEDRO. Draw it.

BENE. Hang it!

CLAUD. You must hang it first and draw it afterward.   25

D. PEDRO. What! Sigh for the toothache?

LEON. Where is but a humor or a worm.°

BENE. Well, everyone can master a grief° but he that has it.

CLAUD. Yet say I he is in love.   30

D. PEDRO. There is no appearance of fancy° in him, unless it be a fancy that he hath to strange disguises° — as to be a Dutchman today, a Frenchman tomorrow; or in the shape of two countries at once — as a German from the waist downward, all slops,° and a Spaniard from the hip upward, no doublet. Unless he have a fancy to this foolery, as it appears he hath, he is no fool for fancy, as you would have it appear he is.   39

CLAUD. If he be not in love with some woman, there is no believing old signs. A' brushes his hat o' mornings. What should that bode?

D. PEDRO. Hath any man seen him at the barber's?

CLAUD. No, but the barber's man hath been   45 seen with him, and the old ornament of his cheek° hath already stuffed tennis balls.°

LEON. Indeed, he looks younger than he did by the loss of a beard.

D. PEDRO. Nay, a' rubs himself with civet.° Can you smell him out by that?   51

CLAUD. That's as much as to say the sweet youth's in love.

D. PEDRO. The greatest note of it is his melancholy.°

CLAUD. And when was he wont to wash his face?°

D. PEDRO. Yea, or to paint himself? For the which, I hear what they say of him.   59

CLAUD. Nay, but his jesting spirit, which is now crept into a lute string and now governed by stops.°

D. PEDRO. Indeed that tells a heavy tale for him. Conclude, conclude he is in love.

CLAUD. Nay, but I know who loves him.   65

D. PEDRO. That would I know too. I warrant one that knows him not.

CLAUD. Yes, and his ill conditions,° and, in despite° of all, dies for him.

D. PEDRO. She shall be buried with her face upward.°   71

BENE. Yet is this no charm for the toothache. Old signior, walk aside with me. I have studied eight or nine wise words to speak to you, which these hobbyhorses° must not hear.

[*Exeunt* BENEDICK *and* LEONATO.]

D. PEDRO. For my life, to break with him about Beatrice.

CLAUD. 'Tis even so. Hero and Margaret have by this played their parts with Beatrice, and then the two bears will not bite one another when they meet.

[*Enter* DON JOHN.]

D. JOHN. My lord and brother, God save you!   82

D. PEDRO. Good-den,° Brother.

D. JOHN. If your leisure served, I would speak with you.   85

D. PEDRO. In private?

D. JOHN. If it please you. Yet Count Claudio may hear, for what I would speak of concerns him.

D. PEDRO. What's the matter?   90

D. JOHN. [*To* CLAUDIO] Means your lordship to be married tomorrow?

D. PEDRO. You know he does.

D. JOHN. I know not that, when he knows what I know.   95

CLAUD. If there be any impediment, I pray you discover it.

D. JOHN. You may think I love you not. Let that appear hereafter, and aim better at me by that I now will manifest. For my brother, I think he holds you well, and in dearness of heart hath holp to effect your ensuing marriage — surely suit ill spent and labor ill bestowed.

D. PEDRO. Why, what's the matter?   104

D. JOHN. I came hither to tell you, and, circumstances shortened, for she has been too long a-talking of, the lady is disloyal.

CLAUD. Who, Hero?

D. JOHN. Even she, Leonato's Hero, your Hero, every man's Hero.   110

CLAUD. Disloyal?

D. JOHN. The word is too good to paint out her

27. humor . . . worm: These were recognized causes of toothache. humor: cold.   28. grief: pain.   31. fancy: love.   32. strange disguises: It was a common criticism of Elizabethan gallants that they wore a fantastical mixture of foreign fashions. See *M of Ven*, II.ii.79.   35. slops: baggy breeches. See Pl. 8c and comment on p. 93b.   46. old . . . cheek: Benedick at his first entrance wore a large beard; now he is neatly trimmed and hides the change by holding a handkerchief to his cheek.   47. tennis balls: made of leather, stuffed with hair.   50. civet: a perfume, much favored by gallants, made from a glandular secretion of the civet cat.   55. melancholy: Benedick as the complete lover is showing some of the outward signs. For Rosalind's description of the symptoms see *AYLI*, III.ii.392–403. See App. 4.   56. wash . . . face: i.e., with cosmetics. The fashionable gallant used make-up.

61. crept . . . stops: shrank to the size of a string on a lover's lute, and is controlled by *stops* — the frets on the finger board by which the tone is controlled. See Pl. 18d.   68. ill conditions: bad qualities.   69. despite: spite.   70–71. buried . . . upward: another version of Margaret's remark at III.iv.26.   74–75. hobbyhorses: buffoons.   83. Good-den: good afternoon.

wickedness, I could say she were worse. Think you of a worse title and I will fit her to it. Wonder not till further warrant. Go but with me tonight, you shall see her chamber window entered, even the night before her wedding day. If you love her then, tomorrow wed her, but it would better fit your honor to change your mind.

CLAUD. May this be so? 120

D. PEDRO. I will not think it.

D. JOHN. If you dare not trust that you see, confess not that you know. If you will follow me, I will show you enough, and when you have seen more, and heard more, proceed accordingly. 125

CLAUD. If I see anything tonight why I should not marry her tomorrow, in the congregation where I should wed there will I shame her.

D. PEDRO. And as I wooed for thee to obtain her, I will join with thee to disgrace her. 130

D. JOHN. I will disparage her no farther till you are my witnesses. Bear it coldly° but till midnight, and let the issue show itself.

D. PEDRO. Oh, day untowardly turned!

CLAUD. Oh, mischief strangely thwarting! 135

D. JOHN. Oh, plague right well prevented! So will you say when you have seen the sequel. [*Exeunt.*]

SCENE III. *A street.*

[*Enter* DOGBERRY *and* VERGES *with the* WATCH.°]

DOGB. Are you good men and true?

VERG. Yea, or else it were pity but they should suffer salvation,° body and soul.

DOGB. Nay, there were a punishment too good for them, if they should have any allegiance° in them, being chosen for the Prince's watch. 6

VERG. Well, give them their charge,° Neighbor Dogberry.

DOGB. First, who think you the most desartless° man to be constable? 10

FIRST WATCH. Hugh Otecake, sir, or George Seacole, for they can write and read.

DOGB. Come hither, Neighbor Seacole. God hath blessed you with a good name. To be a well-favored° man is the gift of fortune, but to write and read comes by nature.° 16

SEC. WATCH. Both which, Master Constable ——

DOGB. You have. I knew it would be your answer.

Well, for your favor, sir, why, give God thanks and make no boast of it. And for your writing and 20 reading, let that appear when there is no need of such vanity. You are thought here to be the most senseless° and fit man for the constable of the watch, therefore bear you the lantern. This is your charge. You shall comprehend° all vagrom° men. You are to bid any man stand, in the Prince's name. 26

SEC. WATCH. How if a' will not stand?

DOGB. Why, then take no note of him, but let him go, and presently call the rest of the watch together and thank God you are rid of a knave. 31

VERG. If he will not stand when he is bidden, he is none of the Prince's subjects.

DOGB. True, and they are to meddle with none but the Prince's subjects. You shall also make no 35 noise in the streets, for for the watch to babble and to talk is most tolerable° and not to be endured.

WATCH. We will rather sleep than talk. We know what belongs to° a watch. 40

DOGB. Why, you speak like an ancient and most quiet watchman, for I cannot see how sleeping should offend. Only have a care that your bills° be not stolen. Well, you are to call at all the alehouses and bid those that are drunk get them to bed. 46

WATCH. How if they will not?

DOGB. Why, then let them alone till they are sober. If they make you not then the better answer, you may say they are not the men you took them for. 51

WATCH. Well, sir.

DOGB. If you meet a thief, you may suspect him, by virtue of your office, to be no true man. And for such kind of men, the less you meddle or make with them, why, the more is for your honesty. 56

WATCH. If we know him to be a thief, shall we not lay hands on him?

DOGB. Truly, by your office you may, but I think they that touch pitch will be defiled. The most 60 peaceable way for you, if you do take a thief, is to let him show himself what he is and steal out of your company.

VERG. You have been always called a merciful man, partner. 65

DOGB. Truly, I would not hang a dog by my will, much more a man who hath any honesty in him.

VERG. If you hear a child cry in the night, you must call to the nurse and bid her still it. 70

WATCH. How if the nurse be asleep and will not hear us?

DOGB. Why, then depart in peace and let the child wake her with crying; for the ewe that will not hear her lamb when it baas will never answer a calf when he bleats. 76

VERG. 'Tis very true.

132. coldly: patiently.

Sc. iii: s.d., with . . . Watch: See Gen. Intro. p. 18a. **3. salvation:** for "damnation." Shakespeare's humbler characters often have an excessive love of long words which they misuse. **5. allegiance:** loyalty, but Dogberry supposes it to mean "treachery." **7. charge:** instructions. **9. desartless:** for "deserving." **14. well-favored:** handsome. **14–16. To . . . nature:** Dogberry is mistaken. Beauty is a gift of Nature; Fortune gives such attainments as wealth and learning. For a discussion of this question on a higher plane, see *AYLI*, I.ii.34–57, and App. 18.

23. senseless: for "sensible." **25. comprehend:** for "apprehend." **vagrom:** vagabond. See *M Ado* Intro. p. 699b. **37. tolerable:** for "intolerable." **40. what . . . to:** the duties of. **44. bills:** the watchmen's weapon. See Pl. 21c.

DOGB. This is the end of the charge: You, Constable, are to present° the Prince's own person. If you meet the Prince in the night, you may stay him.   81

VERG. Nay, by 'r Lady, that I think a' cannot.

DOGB. Five shillings to one on 't, with any man that knows the statues,° he may stay him. Marry, not without the Prince be willing, for indeed the watch ought to offend no man, and it is an offense to stay a man against his will.

VERG. By 'r Lady, I think it be so.   89

DOGB. Ha, ah, ha! Well, masters, good night. An there be any matter of weight chances, call up me. Keep your fellows' counsels and your own, and good night. Come, neighbor.

WATCH. Well, masters, we hear our charge. Let us go sit here upon the church bench till two, and then all to bed.   96

DOGB. One word more, honest neighbors. I pray you watch about Signior Leonato's door, for the wedding being there tomorrow, there is a great coil° tonight. Adieu. Be vigitant,° I beseech you.

[*Exeunt* DOGBERRY *and* VERGES.]
[*Enter* BORACHIO *and* CONRADE.°]

BORA. What, Conrade!   102

WATCH. [*Aside*] Peace! Stir not.

BORA. Conrade, I say!

CON. Here, man, I am at thy elbow.

BORA. Mass,° and my elbow itched. I thought there would a scab° follow.

CON. I will owe thee an answer for that. And now forward with thy tale.   109

BORA. Stand thee close, then, under this penthouse,° for it drizzles rain, and I will, like a true drunkard, utter all to thee.

WATCH. [*Aside*] Some treason, masters. Yet stand close.

BORA. Therefore know I have earned of Don John a thousand ducats.   116

CON. Is it possible that any villainy should be so dear?

BORA. Thou shouldst rather ask if it were possible any villainy should be so rich, for when rich villains have need of poor ones, poor ones may make what price they will.   122

CON. I wonder at it.

BORA. That shows thou art unconfirmed.° Thou knowest that the fashion of a doublet, or a hat, or a cloak, is nothing to a man.°

CON. Yes, it is apparel.

BORA. I mean, the fashion.

CON. Yes, the fashion is the fashion.   129

BORA. Tush! I may as well say the fool's the fool. But seest thou not what a deformed thief this fashion is?

WATCH. [*Aside*] I know that Deformed, a' has been a vile thief this seven year, a' goes up and down like a gentleman. I remember his name.   136

BORA. Didst thou not hear somebody?

CON. No, 'twas the vane on the house.

BORA. Seest thou not, I say, what a deformed thief this fashion is? How giddily a' turns about all the hot bloods between fourteen and five and thirty? Sometimes fashioning them like Pharaoh's soldiers in the reechy° painting, sometime like god Bel's° priests in the old church window, sometime like the shaven Hercules in the smirched° worm-eaten   145 tapestry, where his codpiece° seems as massy as his club?

CON. All this I see, and I see that the fashion wears out more apparel than the man. But art not thou thyself giddy with the fashion too, that thou hast shifted out of thy tale into telling me of the fashion?   152

BORA. Not so, neither. But know that I° have tonight wooed Margaret, the Lady Hero's gentlewoman, by the name of Hero. She leans me out at her mistress' chamber window, bids me a thousand times good night. —I tell this tale vilely. I should first tell thee how the Prince, Claudio and my master, planted and placed and possessed° by my master Don John, saw afar off in the orchard this amiable encounter.   161

CON. And thought they Margaret was Hero?

BORA. Two of them did, the Prince and Claudio, but the Devil my master knew she was Mar-   165 garet. And partly by his oaths, which first possessed them, partly by the dark night, which did deceive them, but chiefly by my villainy, which did confirm any slander that Don John had made, away went Claudio enraged, swore he would meet her, as he was appointed, next morning at the temple and there before the whole congregation shame her with what he saw o'ernight, and send her home again without a husband.   175

FIRST WATCH. We charge you, in the Prince's name, stand!

SEC. WATCH. Call up the right master constable. We have here recovered° the most dangerous piece of lechery° that was known in the commonwealth.   181

---

80. present: represent.   84. statues: for "statutes."   99. coil: turmoil.   100. vigitant: for "vigilant."   101. s.d., Enter . . . Conrade: See *M Ado* Intro. p. 699b.   106. Mass: by the mass. 107. scab: with a pun on the two meanings of "blister" and "low fellow."   111. penthouse: overhanging roof of a shed or porch. See Gen. Intro. p. 56a.   124. unconfirmed: inexperienced. 126. is . . . man: is as nothing when compared to. Borachio (whose name means drunkard) is very fuddled. The thought at the back of his mind is that a man changes the fashion of his clothes, but that his character remains the same.

143. reechy: begrimed with smoke. Bel: from the story of *Bel and the Dragon* in the Apocrypha.   145. smirched: dirty. 146. codpiece: See Pl. 8c and comment on p. 93b.   153–75. I . . . husband: See *M Ado* Intro. p. 699b.   159. possessed: informed. 179. recovered: for "discovered."   180. lechery: for "treachery."

FIRST WATCH. And one Deformed is one of them. I know him, a' wears a lock.°

CON. Masters, masters ——

SEC. WATCH. You'll be made bring Deformed forth, I warrant you.   186

CON. Masters ——

FIRST WATCH. Never speak. We charge you let us obey° you to go with us.

BORA. We are like to prove a goodly commodity, being taken up of these men's bills.°   191

CON. A commodity in question, I warrant you. Come, we'll obey you.   [*Exeunt.*]

SCENE IV. HERO's *apartment.*

[*Enter* HERO, MARGARET, *and* URSULA.]

HERO. Good Ursula, wake my cousin Beatrice and desire her to rise.

URS. I will, lady.

HERO. And bid her come hither.   4

URS. Well.   [*Exit.*]

MARG. Troth, I think your other rebato° were better.

HERO. No, pray thee, good Meg, I'll wear this.

MARG. By my troth 's not so good, and I warrant your cousin will say so.   10

HERO. My cousin's a fool, and thou art another. I'll wear none but this.

MARG. I like the new tire° within excellently, if the hair were a thought browner, and your gown's a most rare fashion, i' faith. I saw the Duchess of Milan's gown that they praise so.   16

HERO. Oh, that exceeds, they say.

MARG. By my troth 's but a nightgown° in respect of yours, — cloth o' gold, and cuts,° and laced with silver, set with pearls, down sleeves,° side   20 sleeves,° and skirts round underborne° with a bluish tinsel. But for a fine, quaint, graceful, and excellent fashion, yours is worth ten on 't.

HERO. God give me joy to wear it! For my heart is exceeding heavy.   25

MARG. 'Twill be heavier soon by the weight of a man.

HERO. Fie upon thee! Art not ashamed?

MARG. Of what, lady? Of speaking honorably? Is

not marriage honorable in a beggar? Is not   3 your lord honorable without marriage? I think yo would have me say, " saving your reverence, a hus band."° An bad thinking do not wrest true speak ing, I'll offend nobody. Is there any harm in " th heavier for a husband "? None, I think, an it be th right husband and the right wife; otherwise 'ti light, and not heavy. Ask my Lady Beatrice else — here she comes.

[*Enter* BEATRICE.]

HERO. Good morrow, Coz.

BEAT. Good morrow, sweet Hero.   4

HERO. Why, how now? Do you speak in the sic tune?°

BEAT. I am out of all other tune, methinks.

MARG. Clap 's° into " Light-o'-love."° That goe without a burden.° Do you sing it, and I'll dance it

BEAT. Ye light-o'-love, with your heels! Then,   4 if your husband have stables enough, you'll see h shall lack no barns.°

MARG. Oh, illegitimate construction! I scorn tha with my heels.   5

BEAT. 'Tis almost five o'clock, Cousin, 'tis tim you were ready. By my troth, I am exceeding ill Heigh-ho!

MARG. For a hawk, a horse, or a husband?   5

BEAT. For the letter that begins them all, H.°

MARG. Well, an you be not turned Turk,° there' no more sailing by the star.

BEAT. What means the fool, trow?°

MARG. Nothing I, but God send everyone thei heart's desire!   6

HERO. These gloves the Count sent me. They ar an excellent perfume.

BEAT. I am stuffed,° Cousin, I cannot smell.

MARG. A maid, and stuffed! There's goodly catch ing of cold.   6

BEAT. Oh, God help me! God help me! How lon have you professed apprehension?°

MARG. Ever since you left it. Doth not my wit be come me rarely?   7

BEAT. It is not seen enough, you should wear it i your cap. By my troth, I am sick.

MARG. Get you some of this distilled Carduu Benedictus,° and lay it to your heart. It is the onl thing for a qualm.°   7

HERO. There thou prickest her with a thistle.

---

183. lock: lovelock, a curl of hair hanging by the ear.   **189. obey:** for " command."   **190–91. prove . . . bills:** Borachio puns on the double meaning of bill, " weapon " and " acknowledgment of debt." **commodity:** goods. **taken up:** obtained on credit. **bills:** bonds guaranteeing payment on the terms agreed.

Sc. iv: **6. rebato:** high collar or wire frame supporting the ruff. See Pl. 2b and comment on p. 95a.   **13. tire:** headdress. **18. nightgown:** dressing gown, " house coat."   **19. cuts:** embroidered squares inserted in places where the material had been cut away.   **20. down sleeves:** long sleeves to the wrist. **20–21. side sleeves:** hanging sleeves from the shoulder. See Pl. 7a and comment on p. 95a.   **21. underborne:** worn over or lined.

32–33. saving . . . husband: you seem to regard *husband* as a improper word. **saving . . . reverence:** often contracted to " sir reverence," a phrase apologizing for an improper word or remark **41–42. in . . . tune:** i.e., as if you were unwell.   **45. Clap:** brea into a song. **Light-o'-love:** a well-known ditty.   **46. burden** chorus.   **49. barns:** with a pun on " bairns."   **56. H:** " H " and " ache " were pronounced alike.   **57. turned Turk:** become a heathen; i.e., have deserted your old faith.   **59. trow:** I wonder **64. am stuffed:** have a cold.   **68. apprehension:** sharp wit **73–74. Carduus Benedictus:** blessed thistle, a herb often and highly recommended as a cure for various complaints.   **75. qualm** feeling of sickness.

BEAT. Benedictus! Why Benedictus? You have some moral° in this Benedictus.

MARG. Moral! No, by my troth, I have no moral meaning, I meant plain holy thistle. You may 80 think perchance that I think you are in love. Nay, by 'r Lady, I am not such a fool to think what I list; nor I list not to think what I can; nor, indeed, I cannot think, if I would think my heart out of thinking, that you are in love, or that you will be in love, 85 or that you can be in love. Yet Benedick was such another, and now is he become a man. He swore he would never marry, and yet now, in despite of his heart, he eats his meat without grudging. And how you may be converted, I know not, but methinks you look with your eyes as other women do.

BEAT. What pace is this that thy tongue keeps?

MARG. Not a false gallop.°   94

[*Re-enter* URSULA.]

URS. Madam, withdraw. The Prince, the Count, Signior Benedick, Don John, and all the gallants of the town, are come to fetch you to church.

HERO. Help to dress me, good Coz, good Meg, good Ursula.   [*Exeunt.*]

SCENE V. *Another room in* LEONATO'S *house.*

[*Enter* LEONATO, *with* DOGBERRY *and* VERGES.]

LEON. What would you with me, honest neighbor?

DOGB. Marry, sir, I would have some confidence° with you that decerns° you nearly.

LEON. Brief, I pray you, for you see it is a busy time with me.   6

DOGB. Marry, this it is, sir.

VERG. Yes, in truth it is, sir.

LEON. What is it, my good friends?   9

DOGB. Goodman Verges, sir, speaks a little off the matter — an old man, sir, and his wits are not so blunt° as, God help, I would desire they were, but, in faith, honest as the skin between his brows.

VERG. Yes, I thank God I am as honest as any man living that is an old man and no honester than I. 17

DOGB. Comparisons are odorous° — *palabras,°* neighbor Verges.

LEON. Neighbors, you are tedious.   20

DOGB. It pleases your Worship to say so, but we are the poor Duke's officers.° But truly, for mine own part, if I were as tedious° as a king, I could find in my heart to bestow it all of your Worship. 25

LEON. All thy tediousness on me, ah?

DOGB. Yea, an 'twere a thousand pound more than 'tis, for I hear as good exclamation on your Worship as of any man in the city, and though I be but a poor man, I am glad to hear it.   30

VERG. And so am I.

LEON. I would fain know what you have to say.

VERG. Marry, sir, our watch tonight, excepting your Worship's presence, ha' ta'en a couple of as arrant° knaves as any in Messina.   35

DOGB. A good old man, sir — he will be talking. As they say, "When the age is in, the wit is out." God help us! It is a world to see. Well said, i' faith, neighbor Verges. Well, God's a good man. An two men ride of a horse, one must ride behind. An 40 honest soul, i' faith, sir, by my troth he is, as ever broke bread. But God is to be worshiped, all men are not alike, alas, good neighbor!

LEON. Indeed, neighbor, he comes too short of you.   46

DOGB. Gifts that God gives.

LEON. I must leave you.

DOGB. One word, sir. Our watch, sir, have indeed comprehended° two aspicious° persons, and we would have them this morning examined before your Worship.   52

LEON. Take their examination yourself, and bring it me. I am now in great haste, as it may appear unto you.

DOGB. It shall be suffigance.°

LEON. Drink some wine ere you go. Fare you well.

[*Enter a* MESSENGER.]

MESS. My lord, they stay for you to give your daughter to her husband.   60

LEON. I'll wait upon them. I am ready.

[*Exeunt* LEONATO *and* MESSENGER.]

DOGB. Go, good partner, go, get you to Francis Seacole. Bid him bring his pen and inkhorn to the jail. We are now to examination these men.

VERG. And we must do it wisely.   65

DOGB. We will spare for no wit, I warrant you, here's that shall drive some of them to a noncome.° Only get the learned writer to set down our excommunication,° and meet me at the jail.   [*Exeunt.*]

Act IV

SCENE I. *A church.*

[*Enter* DON PEDRO, DON JOHN, LEONATO,
FRIAR FRANCIS, CLAUDIO, BENEDICK, HERO,
BEATRICE, *and attendants.*]

LEON. Come, Friar Francis, be brief — only to the plain form of marriage, and you shall recount their particular duties afterward.

---

78. moral: i.e., hidden meaning.   94. false gallop: canter.

Sc. v: 3. confidence: for "conference."   4. decerns: for "concerns."   12. blunt: for "sharp."   18. odorous: for "odious." palabras: for *pocas palabras*; i.e., few words.   22. poor . . . officers: the Duke's poor officers.   24. tedious: Dogberry supposes the word to be complimentary.

35. arrant: out-and-out.   50. comprehended: for "apprehended." aspicious: for "suspicious."   55. suffigance: for "sufficient." 67. noncome: for *non plus*, state of confusion.   69. excommunication: for "examination."

FRIAR. You come hither, my lord, to marry this
lady.   5

CLAUD. No.

LEON. To be married to her. Friar, you come to
marry her.

FRIAR. Lady, you come hither to be married to this
Count.   10

HERO. I do.

FRIAR. If either of you know any inward impediment why you should not be conjoined, I charge
you, on your souls, to utter it.

CLAUD. Know you any, Hero?   15

HERO. None, my lord.

FRIAR. Know you any, Count?

LEON. I dare make his answer, none.

CLAUD. Oh, what men dare do! What men may
do! What men daily do, not knowing what they do!

BENE. How now! Interjections? Why, then,   22
some be of laughing, as, ah, ha, he!

CLAUD. Stand thee by, Friar. Father, by your
leave,
Will you with free and unconstrainèd soul   25
Give me this maid, your daughter?

LEON. As freely, son, as God did give her me.

CLAUD. And what have I to give you back whose
worth
May counterpoise this rich and precious gift?

D. PEDRO. Nothing, unless you render her again.

CLAUD. Sweet Prince, you learn° me noble thank-
fulness.   31
There, Leonato, take her back again.
Give not this rotten orange to your friend,
She's but the sign and semblance of her honor.
Behold how like a maid she blushes here!   35
Oh, what authority and show of truth
Can cunning sin cover itself withal!
Comes not that blood as modest evidence
To witness simple virtue? Would you not swear,
All you that see her, that she were a maid,   40
By these exterior shows? But she is none.
She knows the heat of a luxurious° bed.
Her blush is guiltiness, not modesty.

LEON. What do you mean, my lord?

CLAUD.   Not to be married,
Not to knit my soul to an approved° wanton.   45

LEON. Dear my lord, if you, in your own proof,°
Have vanquished the resistance of her youth,
And made defeat of her virginity ——

CLAUD. I know what you would say. If I have
known her,
You will say she did embrace me as a husband,   50
And so extenuate the 'forehand sin.°
No, Leonato,

I never tempted her with word too large,°
But, as a brother to his sister, showed
Bashful sincerity and comely love.   5

HERO. And seemed I ever otherwise to you?

CLAUD. Out on thee! Seeming! I will write
against it.
You seem to me as Dian° in her orb,°
As chaste as is the bud ere it be blown,°
But you are more intemperate in your blood   6
Than Venus, or those pampered animals
That rage in savage sensuality.

HERO. Is my lord well, that he doth speak so
wide?°

LEON. Sweet Prince, why speak not you?

D. PEDRO.   What should I speak.
I stand dishonored, that have gone about   6
To link my dear friend to a common stale.

LEON. Are these things spoken, or do I but dream

D. JOHN. Sir, they are spoken, and these things are
true.

BENE. This looks not like a nuptial.

HERO.   True! O God

CLAUD. Leonato, stand I here?   7
Is this the Prince? Is this the Prince's brother?
Is this face Hero's? Are our eyes our own?

LEON. All this is so, but what of this, my lord?

CLAUD. Let me but move one question to your
daughter,
And by that fatherly and kindly power   7
That you have in her, bid her answer truly.

LEON. I charge thee do so, as thou art my child.

HERO. Oh, God defend me! How am I beset!°
What kind of catechizing call you this?

CLAUD. To make you answer truly to your name

HERO. Is it not Hero? Who can blot that name   8
With any just reproach?

CLAUD.   Marry, that can Hero.
Hero itself can blot out Hero's virtue.
What man was he talked with you yesternight
Out at your window betwixt twelve and one?   8
Now, if you are a maid, answer to this.

HERO. I talked with no man at that hour, my lord

D. PEDRO. Why, then are you no maiden. Leonato
I am sorry you must hear. Upon mine honor,
Myself, my brother, and this grievèd Count   9
Did see her, hear her, at that hour last night
Talk with a ruffian at her chamber window,
Who hath indeed, most like a liberal° villain,
Confessed the vile encounters they have had
A thousand times in secret.   9

D. JOHN. Fie, fie! They are not to be named, my
lord,
Not to be spoke of,

Act IV, Sc. i: **31. learn:** teach.   **42. luxurious:** lustful.
45. approved: proved.   **46. in . . . proof:** by putting her resistance to the test.   **51. 'forehand sin:** the sin of mating before
marriage, which could be partially excused since Claudio and
Hero were already betrothed. See Gen. Intro. p. 20a.

53. large: unrestrained.   **58. Dian:** Diana, goddess of chastity
orb: sphere; i.e., the moon, for Diana was also Luna, the moon
See *MND*, IV.i.76.   **59. blown:** fully opened.   **63. so wide:** i.e.
so far from the truth.   **78. beset:** set upon.   **93. liberal:** gross

There is not chastity enough in language
Without offense to utter them. Thus, pretty lady,
I am sorry for thy much misgovernment.°   100
   CLAUD. O Hero, what a Hero hadst thou been
If half thy outward graces had been placed
About thy thoughts and counsels of thy heart!
But fare thee well, most foul, most fair! Farewell,
Thou pure impiety and impious purity!   105
For thee I'll lock up all the gates of love,
And on my eyelids shall conjecture hang
To turn all beauty into thoughts of harm,°
And never shall it more be gracious.   109
   LEON. Hath no man's dagger here a point for me?
                         [HERO *swoons.*]
   BEAT. Why, how now, Cousin! Wherefore sink
   you down?
   D. JOHN. Come, let us go. These things, come thus
   to light,
Smother her spirits up.
    [*Exeunt* DON PEDRO, DON JOHN, *and* CLAUDIO.]
   BENE. How doth the lady?
   BEAT.   Dead, I think. Help, Uncle!
Hero! Why, Hero! Uncle! Signior Benedick! Friar!
   LEON. O Fate! Take not away thy heavy hand.
Death is the fairest cover for her shame   117
That may be wished for.
   BEAT.   How now, Cousin Hero!
   FRIAR. Have comfort, lady.
   LEON. Dost thou look up?   120
   FRIAR. Yea, wherefore should she not?
   LEON. Wherefore! Why, doth not every earthly
   thing
Cry shame upon her? Could she here deny
The story that is printed in her blood?°
Do not live, Hero, do not ope thine eyes.   125
For did I think thou wouldst not quickly die,
Thought I thy spirits were stronger than thy shames,
Myself would, on the rearward of reproaches,
Strike at thy life.° Grieved I, I had but one?
Chid I for that at frugal Nature's frame?   130
Oh, one too much by thee! Why had I one?
Why ever wast thou lovely in my eyes?
Why had I not with charitable hand
Took up a beggar's issue at my gates,
Who, smirchèd thus and mired with infamy,   135
I might have said, " No part of it is mine,
This shame derives itself from unknown loins "?
But mine, and mine I loved, and mine I praised,
And mine that I was proud on, mine so much
That I myself was to myself not mine,   140
Valuing of her — why, she, oh, she is fallen
Into a pit of ink, that the wide sea
Hath drops too few to wash her clean again,

And salt too little which may season° give
To her foul-tainted flesh!
   BENE.   Sir, sir, be patient.   145
For my part, I am so attired in wonder
I know not what to say.
   BEAT. Oh, on my soul, my cousin is belied!°
   BENE. Lady, were you her bedfellow last night?
   BEAT. No, truly not, although until last night   150
I have this twelvemonth been her bedfellow.
   LEON. Confirmed, confirmed! Oh, that is stronger
   made
Which was before barred up with ribs of iron!
Would the two Princes lie, and Claudio lie,   154
Who loved her so, that, speaking of her foulness,
Washed it with tears? Hence from her! Let her die.
   FRIAR. Hear me a little,
For I have only been silent so long
And given way unto this course of fortune
By noting of the lady.° I have marked   160
A thousand blushing apparitions
To start into her face, a thousand innocent shames
In angel whiteness beat away those blushes.
And in her eye there hath appeared a fire
To burn the errors that these Princes hold   165
Against her maiden truth. Call me a fool,
Trust not my reading nor my observations,
Which with experimental seal doth warrant
The tenor of my book° — trust not my age,
My reverence, calling, nor divinity —   170
If this sweet lady lie not guiltless here
Under some biting error.
   LEON.   Friar, it cannot be.
Thou seest that all the grace that she hath left
Is that she will not add to her damnation
A sin of perjury. She not denies it.   175
Why seek'st thou, then, to cover with excuse
That which appears in proper nakedness?
   FRIAR. Lady, what man is he you are accused of?
   HERO. They know that do accuse me, I know none.
If I know more of any man alive   180
Than that which maiden modesty doth warrant,
Let all my sins lack mercy! O my father,
Prove you that any man with me conversed
At hours unmeet, or that I yesternight
Maintained the change° of words with any creature,
Refuse me, hate me, torture me to death!   186
   FRIAR. There is some strange misprision° in the
   Princes.
   BENE. Two of them have the very bent° of honor,

---

144. season: freshness.   148. belied: has had lies told about her.
157–60. Hear . . . lady: If the punctuation of these lines is correct, the Friar means that he has kept silence because he has been
fully occupied in closely observing the lady.   167–69. observations . . . book: my observation of life, which sets the seal of
practical experience on what I have learned from books. warrant:
guarantee. tenor: purport.   185. Maintained . . . change: exchanged.   187. misprision: misunderstanding.   188. beat:
natural inclination.

---

100. misgovernment: evil conduct.   107–08. And . . . harm:
hereafter whenever I see any beautiful woman I shall suspect
her.   124. blood: blushes.   128–29. rearward . . . life: i.e.,
would kill you after this shame.

And if their wisdoms be misled in this,
The practice° of it lives in John the bastard,   190
Whose spirits toil in frame of° villainies.
   LEON. I know not. If they speak but truth of her,
These hands shall tear her. If they wrong her honor,
The proudest of them shall well hear of it.
Time hath not yet so dried this blood of mine,   195
Nor age so eat up my invention,°
Nor fortune made such havoc of my means,
Nor my bad life reft me so much of friends,
But they shall find, awaked in such a kind,
Both strength of limb and policy of mind,   200
Ability in means and choice of friends,
To quit me° of them throughly.°
   FRIAR.   Pause awhile,
And let my counsel sway you in this case.
Your daughter here the Princes left for dead.
Let her awhile be secretly kept in,   205
And publish it that she is dead indeed.
Maintain a mourning ostentation,°
And on your family's old monument
Hang mournful epitaphs,° and do all rites
That appertain unto a burial.   210
   LEON. What shall become of this? What will this
    do?
   FRIAR. Marry, this, well carried,° shall on her be-
    half
Change slander to remorse° — that is some good.
But not for that dream I on this strange course,
But on this travail look for greater birth.   215
She dying, as it must be so maintained,
Upon the instant that she was accused,
Shall be lamented, pitied, and excused
Of every hearer. For it so falls out,
That what we have we prize not to the worth   220
Whiles we enjoy it; but being lacked and lost,
Why, then we rack° the value, then we find
The virtue that possession would not show us
Whiles it was ours. So will it fare with Claudio.
When he shall hear she died upon his words,   225
The idea of her life shall sweetly creep
Into his study of imagination;°
And every lovely organ of her life
Shall come appareled in more precious habit,
More moving-delicate and full of life,   230
Into the eye and prospect of his soul
Than when she lived indeed. Then shall he mourn,
If ever love had interest in his liver,°
And wish he had not so accused her,

No, though he thought his accusation true.   235
Let this be so, and doubt not but success
Will fashion the event in better shape
Than I can lay it down in likelihood.
But if all aim but this be leveled false,
The supposition of the lady's death   240
Will quench the wonder of her infamy.°
And if it sort not° well, you may conceal her,
As best befits her wounded reputation,
In some reclusive° and religious life,
Out of all eyes, tongues, minds, and injuries.   245
   BENE. Signior Leonato, let the Friar advise you.
And though you know my inwardness and love°
Is very much unto the Prince and Claudio,
Yet, by mine honor, I will deal in this
As secretly and justly as your soul   250
Should with your body.
   LEON.   Being that° I flow in grief,
The smallest twine may lead me.
   FRIAR. 'Tis well consented. Presently away,
For to strange sores strangely they strain the cure.
Come, lady, die to live. This wedding day   255
Perhaps is but prolonged. Have patience and en-
    dure. [*Exeunt all but* BENEDICK *and* BEATRICE.°]
   BENE. Lady Beatrice, have you wept all this while?
   BEAT. Yea, and I will weep awhile longer.
   BENE. I will not desire that.
   BEAT. You have no reason, I do it freely.°   260
   BENE. Surely I do believe your fair cousin is
wronged.
   BEAT. Ah, how much might the man deserve of
me that would right her!
   BENE. Is there any way to show such friendship?
   BEAT. A very even° way, but no such friend.   265
   BENE. May a man do it?
   BEAT. It is a man's office, but not yours.
   BENE. I do love nothing in the world so well as
you. Is not that strange?   270
   BEAT. As strange as the thing I know not. It were
as possible for me to say I loved nothing so well as
you. But believe me not, and yet I lie not, I confess
nothing, nor I deny nothing. I am sorry for my
cousin.   275
   BENE. By my sword, Beatrice, thou lovest me.
   BEAT. Do not swear, and eat it.
   BENE. I will swear by it that you love me, and I
will make him eat it that says I love not you.
   BEAT. Will you not eat your word?   280
   BENE. With no sauce that can be devised to it. I
protest I love thee.
   BEAT. Why, then, God forgive me!

---

190. **practice:** plotting.   191. **toil . . . of:** labor to contrive.
196. **invention:** intellect.   202. **quit me:** pay back, avenge.
throughly: thoroughly.   207. **Maintain . . . ostentation:** perform
the outward shows of mourning, which in a noble family were
elaborate. See App. 9.   209. **epitaphs:** memorial verses.
212. **carried:** managed.   213. **remorse:** pity.   222. **rack:** stretch
out.   227. **study of imagination:** contemplation.   233. **liver:**
supposed to be the seat of the emotions, especially love.

236–41. **Let . . . infamy:** do this, and without doubt the result
will be even better than I can suggest; even if we fail in our aim,
her shame will be forgotten in her supposed death.   242. **sort
not:** does not turn out.   244. **reclusive:** retired.   247. **inwardness
. . . love:** intimate affection.   251. **Being that:** since.   256. **s.d.
Benedick . . . Beatrice:** See *M Ado* Intro. p. 700a.   260. **freely:**
i.e., without your asking.   265. **even:** straight.

BENE. What offense, sweet Beatrice?

BEAT. You have stayed° me in a happy hour. I was about to protest I loved you.   286

BENE. And do it with all thy heart.

BEAT. I love you with so much of my heart that none is left to protest.

BENE. Come, bid me do anything for thee.   290

BEAT. Kill Claudio.

BENE. Ha! Not for the wide world.

BEAT. You kill me to deny it. Farewell.

BENE. Tarry, sweet Beatrice.

BEAT. I am gone, though I am here. There is no love in you. Nay, I pray you let me go.   296

BENE. Beatrice——

BEAT. In faith, I will go.

BENE. We'll be friends first.

BEAT. You dare easier be friends with me than fight with mine enemy.   301

BENE. Is Claudio thine enemy?

BEAT. Is he not approved° in the height° a villain that hath slandered, scorned, dishonored my kinswoman? Oh, that I were a man! What, bear her in hand° until they come to take hands, and then,   306 with public accusation, uncovered slander, unmitigated rancor—— Oh, God, that I were a man! I would eat his heart in the market place.

BENE. Hear me, Beatrice——   310

BEAT. Talk with a man out at a window! A proper saying!

BENE. Nay, but, Beatrice——

BEAT. Sweet Hero! She is wronged, she is slandered, she is undone.   315

BENE. Beat——

BEAT. Princes and Counties! Surely, a princely testimony, a goodly Count, Count Comfect,° a sweet gallant, surely! Oh, that I were a man for his sake! Or that I had any friend would be a man for   320 my sake! But manhood is melted into courtesies, valor into compliment, and men are only turned into tongue, and trim ones too. He is now as valiant as Hercules that only tells a lie, and swears it. I cannot be a man with wishing, therefore I will die a woman with grieving.   326

BENE. Tarry, good Beatrice. By this hand, I love thee.

BEAT. Use it for my love some other way than swearing by it.   330

BENE. Think you in your soul the Count Claudio hath wronged Hero?

BEAT. Yea, as sure as I have a thought or a soul.

BENE. Enough, I am engaged,° I will challenge him. I will kiss your hand, and so I leave you. By this hand, Claudio shall render me a dear account.°

---

285. stayed: stopped.   303. approved: proved. in . . . height: in the highest degree.   305–06. bear . . . hand: delude her. 318. Count Comfect: "Count Candy."   334. engaged: pledged. 336. render . . . account: shall pay me dearly for it.

As you hear of me, so think of me. Go, comfort your cousin. I must say she is dead. And so farewell.

[*Exeunt.*]   338

SCENE II.° *A prison.*

[*Enter* DOGBERRY, VERGES, *and* SEXTON, *in gowns; and the* WATCH, *with* CONRADE *and* BORACHIO.]

DOGB. Is our whole dissembly° appeared?

VERG. Oh, a stool and a cushion° for the sexton.

SEXTON. Which be the malefactors?

DOGB. Marry, that am I and my partner.

VERG. Nay, that's certain, we have the exhibition° to examine.   6

SEXTON. But which are the offenders that are to be examined? Let them come before Master Constable.

DOGB. Yea, marry, let them come before me. What is your name, friend?   11

BORA. Borachio.

DOGB. Pray write down Borachio. Yours, sirrah?

CON. I am a gentleman, sir, and my name is Conrade.   16

DOGB. Write down master gentleman Conrade. Masters, do you serve God?

CON. & BORA. Yea, sir, we hope.

DOGB. Write down that they hope they serve God. And write God first, for God defend° but God should go before such villains! Masters, it is proved already that you are little better than false knaves, and it will go near to be thought so shortly. How answer you for yourselves?   25

CON. Marry, sir, we say we are none.

DOGB. A marvelous witty fellow, I assure you, but I will go about with him.° Come you hither, sirrah, a word in your ear. Sir, I say to you, it is thought you are false knaves.   30

BORA. Sir, I say to you we are none.

DOGB. Well, stand aside. 'Fore God, they are both in a tale.° Have you writ down that they are none?

SEXTON. Master Constable, you go not the   35 way to examine. You must call forth the watch that are their accusers.

DOGB. Yea, marry, that's the eftest° way. Let the watch come forth. Masters, I charge you, in the Prince's name, accuse these men.   40

FIRST WATCH. This man said, sir, that Don John, the Prince's brother, was a villain.

Sc. ii: In the Q speech headings for this scene Dogberry's lines are marked "Kempe" and Verges' "Cowley"—the actors who first took the parts. For Kempe, see Gen. Intro. p. 44a–b. 1. dissembly: for "assembly."   2. cushion: a mark of respect, due to one who can read and write.   5. exhibition: Verges gives the word a new meaning. Knowing that the legal word "inhibition" means "prohibition," he supposes that "instruction to proceed" should be "exhibition."   21. defend: forbid.   28. go . . . him: get around him.   33–34. both . . . tale: have agreed to tell the same story.   38. eftest: neatest; apparently the word was coined by Dogberry.

DOGB. Write down Prince John a villain. Why, this is flat perjury, to call a Prince's brother villain.

BORA. Master Constable ——   45

DOGB. Pray thee, fellow, peace. I do not like thy look, I promise thee.

SEXTON. What heard you him say else?

SEC. WATCH. Marry, that he had received a thousand ducats of Don John for accusing the Lady Hero wrongfully.   51

DOGB. Flat burglary as ever was committed.

VERG. Yea, by mass, that it is.

SEXTON. What else, fellow?

FIRST WATCH. And that Count Claudio did mean, upon his words, to disgrace Hero before the whole assembly and not marry her.

DOGB. O villain! Thou wilt be condemned into everlasting redemption° for this.

SEXTON. What else?   60

WATCH. This is all.

SEXTON. And this is more, masters, than you can deny. Prince John is this morning secretly stolen away. Hero was in this manner accused, in this very manner refused, and upon the grief of this sud- 65 denly died. Master Constable, let these men be bound and brought to Leonato's. I will go before and show him their examination.   [*Exit.*]

DOGB. Come, let them be opinioned.°

VERG. Let them be in the hands ——   70

CON. Off, coxcomb!°

DOGB. God's my life, where's the sexton? Let him write down the Prince's officer, coxcomb. Come, bind them. Thou naughty varlet!°

CON. Away! You are an ass, you are an ass.   75

DOGB. Dost thou not suspect° my place? Dost thou not suspect my years! Oh, that he were here to write me down an ass! But, masters, remember that I am an ass, though it be not written down, yet forget not that I am an ass. No, thou villain, thou art full 80 of piety,° as shall be proved upon thee by good witness. I am a wise fellow, and, which is more, an officer; and, which is more, a householder; and, which is more, as pretty a piece of flesh° as any is in Messina; and one that knows the law, go to; and a rich fellow enough, go to; and a fellow that hath had losses;° and one that hath two gowns, and everything handsome about him. Bring him away. 89 Oh, that I had been writ down an ass!   [*Exeunt.*]

---

59. **redemption:** for "damnation."   69. **opinioned:** pinioned. 71. **coxcomb:** fool, from the fool's cap. See *Lear*, I.iv.105–22, and Pl. 12f and 13c.   74. **varlet:** knave.   76. **suspect:** for "respect."   81. **piety:** for "impiety."   84. **piece of flesh:** creature. 87–88. **hath . . . losses:** i.e., been an even greater man than he is now.

Act V

SCENE I. *Before* LEONATO'*s house.*

[*Enter* LEONATO *and* ANTONIO.]

ANT. If you go on thus, you will kill yourself,
And 'tis not wisdom thus to second° grief
Against yourself.

LEON.   I pray thee, cease thy counsel,
Which falls into mine ears as profitless
As water in a sieve. Give not me counsel,   5
Nor let no comforter delight mine ear
But such a one whose wrongs do suit with° mine.
Bring me a father that so loved his child,
Whose joy of her is overwhelmed like mine,
And bid him speak of patience.   10
Measure his woe the length and breadth of mine,
And let it answer every strain° for strain,
As thus for thus, and such a grief for such,
In every lineament,° branch, shape, and form.
If such a one will smile and stroke his beard,   15
Bid sorrow wag, cry "hem!" when he should groan,
Patch° grief with proverbs, make misfortune drunk
With candlewasters,° bring him yet to me,
And I of him will gather patience.
But there is no such man. For, Brother, men   20
Can counsel and speak comfort to that grief
Which they themselves not feel; but, tasting it,
Their counsel turns to passion,° which before
Would give preceptial medicine to rage,°
Fetter strong madness in a silken thread,   25
Charm ache with air, and agony with words.
No, no, 'tis all men's office to speak patience
To those that wring° under the load of sorrow,
But no man's virtue nor sufficiency
To be so moral° when he shall endure   30
The like himself. Therefore give me no counsel.
My griefs cry louder than advértisement.°

ANT. Therein do men from children nothing differ.

LEON. I pray thee, peace. I will be flesh and blood.
For there was never yet philosopher   35
That could endure the toothache patiently,

Act V, Sc. i: 2. **second:** assist.   7. **suit with:** match with. 12. **strain:** used in the musical sense — let him match his song of woe with mine.   14. **lineament:** feature.   16. **Bid . . . groan:** This is a much-disputed line. As it stands in the Globe text it means: "Tell sorrow to be cheery when he should groan." **wag:** wag the beard in gay chatter, as in the song "'Tis merry in hall when beards wag all." See *II Hen IV*, V.iii.37. **hem:** a drinker's exclamation, like "Here's how." Q and F read "And sorrow, wagge, crie hem."   17. **Patch:** cover.   18. **candlewasters:** those who sit up late.   23. **Their . . . passion:** their good advice becomes strong emotion.   24. **preceptial . . . rage:** would try to cure rage by healing advice.   28. **wring:** suffer torture. 30. **moral:** full of fine sentiment.   32. **cry . . . advertisement:** are too great to be consoled by good advice.

However they have writ the style of gods
And made a push° at chance° and sufferance.°
  ANT. Yet bend not all the harm upon yourself.
Make those that do offend you suffer too.   40
  LEON. There thou speak'st reason. Nay, I will do
so.
My soul doth tell me Hero is belied,
And that shall Claudio know, so shall the Prince,
And all of them that thus dishonor her.   44
  ANT. Here comes the Prince and Claudio hastily.
      [*Enter* DON PEDRO *and* CLAUDIO.]
  D. PEDRO. Good-den, good-den.
  CLAUD.   Good day to both of you.
  LEON. Hear you, my lords——
  D. PEDRO. We have some haste, Leonato.
  LEON. Some haste, my lord! Well, fare you well,
my lord.
Are you so hasty now? Well, all is one.
  D. PEDRO. Nay, do not quarrel with us, good old
man.   50
  ANT. If he could right himself with quarreling,
Some of us would lie low.
  CLAUD.   Who wrongs him?
  LEON. Marry, thou dost wrong me, thou dissem-
bler, thou.——
Nay, never lay thy hand upon thy sword.
I fear thee not.
  CLAUD.   Marry,° beshrew° my hand   55
If it should give your age such cause of fear.
In faith, my hand meant nothing to my sword.
  LEON. Tush, tush, man, never fleer° and jest at
me.
I speak not like a dotard nor a fool,
As, under privilege of age, to brag   60
What I have done being young, or what would do
Were I not old. Know, Claudio, to thy head,
Thou hast so wronged mine innocent child and me
That I am forced to lay my reverence by,
And, with gray hairs and bruise of many days,   65
Do challenge thee to trial of a man.
I say thou hast belied mine innocent child.
Thy slander hath gone through and through her
heart,
And she lies buried with her ancestors,
Oh, in a tomb where never scandal slept   70
Save this of hers, framed by thy villainy!
  CLAUD. My villainy?
  LEON.   Thine, Claudio, thine, I say.
  D. PEDRO. You say not right, old man.
  LEON.   My lord, my lord,
I'll prove it on his body, if he dare,
Despite his nice fence° and his active practice, 75

His May of youth° and bloom of lustihood.°
  CLAUD. Away! I will not have to do with you.
  LEON. Canst thou so daff° me? Thou hast killed
my child.
If thou kill'st me, boy,° thou shalt kill a man.
  ANT. He shall kill two of us, and men indeed.   80
But that's no matter, let him kill one first,
Win me and wear me. Let him answer me.
Come, follow me, boy, come, sir boy, come, follow
me.
Sir boy, I'll whip you from your foining° fence,
Nay, as I am a gentleman, I will.   85
  LEON. Brother——
  ANT. Content yourself. God knows I loved my
niece,
And she is dead, slandered to death by villains
That dare as well answer a man indeed
As I dare take a serpent by the tongue.   90
Boys, apes, braggarts, Jacks,° milksops!
  LEON. Brother Antony——
  ANT. Hold you content. What, man! I know
them, yea,
And what they weigh, even to the utmost scruple°——
Scambling,° outfacing,° fashion-monging° boys
That lie, and cog,° and flout, deprave° and slander,
Go antiquely° and show outward hideousness,   96
And speak off half a dozen dangerous words,
How they might hurt their enemies if they durst——
And this is all.
  LEON. But, Brother Antony——
  ANT.   Come, 'tis no matter.   100
Do not you meddle, let me deal in this.
  D. PEDRO. Gentlemen both, we will not wake° your
patience.
My heart is sorry for your daughter's death.
But, on my honor, she was charged with nothing
But what was true, and very full of proof.   105
  LEON. My lord, my lord——
  D. PEDRO. I will not hear you.
  LEON. No? Come, Brother, away! I will be heard.
  ANT. And shall, or some of us will smart for it.
            [*Exeunt* LEONATO *and* ANTONIO.]
  D. PEDRO. See, see, here comes the man we went
to seek.   110
      [*Enter* BENEDICK.]
  CLAUD. Now, signior, what news?
  BENE. Good day, my lord.
  D. PEDRO. Welcome, signior. You are almost come
to part almost a fray.   114
  CLAUD. We had like to have had our two noses
snapped off with two old men without teeth.

38. **made a push:** made a brave show against. **chance:** misfortune. **sufferance:** pain.   55. **Marry:** Mary, by the Virgin
Mary. **beshrew:** plague on.   58. **fleer:** sneer.   75. **fence:**
fencing. Leonato as one of the older generation who used the
long sword despises the new-fashioned fencing with the rapier.
See Pl. 22j and comment.

76. **May of youth:** youth in full bloom. **lustihood:** manhood.
78. **daff:** put aside.   79. **boy:** a deliberate and deadly insult. Cf.
Cor, V.vi.101.   84. **foining:** thrusting.   91. **Jacks:** knaves.
93. **scruple:** minutest weight.   94. **Scambling:** pushing, quarrelsome. **outfacing:** swaggering. **fashion-monging:** dressed in
the latest fashion.   95. **cog:** cheat. **deprave:** slander.   96. **an-
tiquely:** like buffoons.   102. **wake:** disturb

D. PEDRO. Leonato and his brother. What thinkest thou? Had we fought, I doubt we should have been too young for them.

BENE. In a false quarrel there is no true valor. I came to seek you both.   121

CLAUD. We have been up and down to seek thee, for we are high-proof° melancholy and would fain have it beaten away. Wilt thou use thy wit?

BENE. It is in my scabbard. Shall I draw it?   125

D. PEDRO. Dost thou wear thy wit by thy side?

CLAUD. Never any did so, though very many have been beside their wit. I will bid thee draw° as we do the minstrels, draw to pleasure us.

D. PEDRO. As I am an honest man, he looks pale. Art thou sick, or angry?   131

CLAUD. What, courage, man! What though care killed a cat, thou hast mettle enough in thee to kill care.

BENE. Sir, I shall meet your wit in the career,° an you charge it against me. I pray you choose another subject.   137

CLAUD. Nay, then, give him another staff.° This last was broke cross.°

D. PEDRO. By this light, he changes more and more. I think he be angry indeed.   141

CLAUD. If he be, he knows how to turn his girdle.°

BENE. Shall I speak a word in your ear?

CLAUD. God bless° me from a challenge!   144

BENE. [*Aside to* CLAUDIO] You are a villain. I jest not. I will make it good how you dare, with what you dare, and when you dare. Do me right, or I will protest° your cowardice. You have killed a sweet lady, and her death shall fall heavy on you. Let me hear from you.   151

CLAUD. Well, I will meet you, so I may have good cheer.°

D. PEDRO. What, a feast, a feast?

CLAUD. I' faith, I thank him. He hath bid me to a calf's head and a capon, the which if I do not carve most curiously,° say my knife's naught. Shall I not find a woodcock° too?

BENE. Sir, your wit ambles well, it goes easily.   159

D. PEDRO. I'll tell thee how Beatrice praised thy wit the other day. I said thou hadst a fine wit. "True," said she, "a fine little one." "No," said I, "a great wit." "Right," says she, "a great gross one." "Nay," said I, "a good wit." "Just," said she, "it hurts no-

body." "Nay," said I, "the gentleman is wise." "Certain," said she, "a wise gentleman." "Nay," said I, "he hath the tongues."° "That I be-   165 lieve," said she, "for he swore a thing to me on Monday night which he forswore on Tuesday morning. There's a double tongue, there's two tongues." Thus did she, an hour together, transshape° thy particular virtues. Yet at last she concluded, with a sigh, thou wast the properest man in Italy.   174

CLAUD. For the which she wept heartily, and said she cared not.

D. PEDRO. Yea, that she did, but yet, for all that, an if she did not hate him deadly, she would love him dearly. The old man's daughter told us all.   180

CLAUD. All, all, and, moreover, God saw him when he was hid in the garden.

D. PEDRO. But when shall we set the savage bull's horns° on the sensible Benedick's head?

CLAUD. Yea, and text underneath, "Here dwells Benedick the married man"?   186

BENE. Fare you well, boy. You know my mind. I will leave you now to your gossiplike° humor. You break jests as braggarts do their blades, which, God be thanked, hurt not. My lord, for your many   190 courtesies I thank you. I must discontinue your company. Your brother the bastard is fled from Messina. You have among you killed a sweet and innocent lady. For my Lord Lackbeard there, he and I shall meet, and till then peace be with him.   [*Exit.*]

D. PEDRO. He is in earnest.   197

CLAUD. In most profound earnest, and I'll warrant you for the love of Beatrice.

D. PEDRO. And hath challenged thee.   200

CLAUD. Most sincerely.

D. PEDRO. What a pretty thing man is when he goes in his doublet and hose° and leaves off his wit!

CLAUD. He is then a giant to an ape, but then is an ape a doctor to such a man.°   206

D. PEDRO. But, soft you, let me be. Pluck up, my heart, and be sad.° Did he not say my brother was fled?

[*Enter* DOGBERRY, VERGES, *and the* WATCH, *with* CONRADE *and* BORACHIO.]

DOGB. Come, you, sir. If justice cannot tame you, she shall ne'er weigh more reasons in her balance. Nay, an you be a cursing hypocrite once, you must be looked to.

D. PEDRO. How now? Two of my brother's men bound! Borachio one!   215

CLAUD. Hearken after their offense, my lord.

---

123. high-proof: in the highest degree.   128. draw: start playing; i.e., draw the fiddle bow across the strings.   135. career: charge in a tilting match.   138. staff: tilting spear.   139. broke cross: In tilting the skillful rider broke his staff full on his opponent's shield. The novice who flinched from the impact broke his staff across it.   142. turn . . . girdle: a proverb used to describe an angry man; the origin and meaning are uncertain.   144. bless: preserve.   149. protest: proclaim.   153. cheer: entertainment.   156–57. carve . . . curiously: Carving was still part of a gentleman's education, as it had been in Chaucer's time. See the *Prologue* to the *Canterbury Tales*, l. 100.   158. woodcock: a foolish bird.

165. hath . . . tongues: can speak foreign languages.   172. transshape: transform.   183–84. savage . . . horns: See I.i.263–66.   188. gossiplike: tattling.   202–03. goes . . . hose: i.e., a man is a fine thing in his clothes (but without them, as Lear put it, he is no more than "a poor, bare, forked animal" — *Lear*, III.iv. 112).   205–06. He . . . man: clothed man is a much better thing than an ape, yet an ape is a learned man compared with such a fool.   208. sad: serious.

D. PEDRO. Officers, what offense have these men done?

DOGB. Marry, sir, they have committed false report; moreover, they have spoken untruths; secondarily, they are slanders; sixth and lastly, they have belied a lady; thirdly, they have verified unjust things; and, to conclude, they are lying knaves. 224

D. PEDRO. First, I ask thee what they have done; thirdly, I ask thee what's their offense; sixth and lastly, why they are committed; and, to conclude, what you lay to their charge.

CLAUD. Rightly reasoned, and in his own division,° and, by my troth, there's one meaning well suited.°   231

D. PEDRO. Who have you offended, masters, that you are thus bound to your answer? This learned constable is too cunning to be understood. What's your offense?   235

BORA. Sweet Prince, let me go no farther to mine answer. Do you hear me, and let this Count kill me. I have deceived even your very eyes. What your wisdoms could not discover, these shallow fools have brought to light, who in the night overheard 240 me confessing to this man how Don John your brother incensed me to slander the Lady Hero; how you were brought into the orchard and saw me court Margaret in Hero's garments; how you disgraced her, when you should marry her. My 245 villainy they have upon record, which I had rather seal with my death than repeat over to my shame. The lady is dead upon mine and my master's false accusation, and, briefly, I desire nothing but the reward of a villain.   251

D. PEDRO. Runs not this speech like iron through your blood?

CLAUD. I have drunk poison whiles he uttered it.

D. PEDRO. But did my brother set thee onto this?

BORA. Yea, and paid me richly for the practice of it.

D. PEDRO. He is composed and framed of treachery,
And fled he is upon this villainy.

CLAUD. Sweet Hero! Now thy image doth appear
In the rare semblance that I loved it first.   260

DOGB. Come, bring away the plaintiffs.° By this time our sexton hath reformed° Signior Leonato of the matter. And, masters, do not forget to specify, when time and place shall serve, that I am an ass.

VERG. Here, here comes Master Signior Leonato, and the sexton too.

[*Re-enter* LEONATO *and* ANTONIO, *with the* SEXTON.]

LEON. Which is the villain? Let me see his eyes,
That when I note another man like him, 270
I may avoid him. Which of these is he?

BORA. If you would know your wronger, look on me.

LEON. Art thou the slave that with thy breath hast killed
Mine innocent child?

BORA.   Yea, even I alone.

LEON. No, not so, villain, thou beliest thyself.
Here stand a pair of honorable men,   276
A third is fled that had a hand in it.
I thank you, Princes, for my daughter's death.
Record it with your high and worthy deeds.
'Twas bravely done, if you bethink you of it.   280

CLAUD. I know not how to pray your patience,
Yet I must speak. Choose your revenge yourself,
Impose me to what penance your invention°
Can lay upon my sin. Yet sinned I not
But in mistaking.

D. PEDRO.   By my soul, nor I.   285
And yet to satisfy this good old man
I would bend under any heavy weight
That he'll enjoin me to.

LEON. I cannot bid you bid my daughter live,
That were impossible. But I pray you both   290
Possess° the people in Messina here
How innocent she died, and if your love
Can labor aught in sad invention,°
Hang her an epitaph upon her tomb,
And sing it to her bones, sing it tonight.   295
Tomorrow morning come you to my house,
And since you could not be my son-in-law,
Be yet my nephew.° My brother hath a daughter,
Almost the copy of my child that's dead,
And she alone is heir to both of us.   300
Give her the right you should have given her cousin,
And so dies my revenge.

CLAUD.   O noble sir,
Your overkindness doth wring tears from me!
I do embrace your offer, and dispose
For henceforth of poor Claudio.   305

LEON. Tomorrow, then, I will expect your coming,
Tonight I take my leave. This naughty man
Shall face to face be brought to Margaret,
Who I believe was packed° in all this wrong,
Hired to it by your brother.

BORA.   No, by my soul, she was not,   310
Nor knew not what she did when she spoke to me,
But always hath been just and virtuous
In anything that I do know by her.

DOGB. Moreover, sir, which indeed is not under white and black, this plaintiff here, the of- 315 fender, did call me ass. I beseech you, let it be remembered in his punishment. And also, the watch heard them talk of one Deformed. They say he wears a key in his ear, and a lock hanging by it, and bor-

---

230. division: categories.   230–31. one . . . suited: one meaning dressed up in several different ways.   261. plaintiffs: for "defendants."   262. reformed: for "informed."   283. invention: imagination.   291. Possess: inform.   293. invention: work of imagination; i.e., funeral poem.   297–98. And . . . nephew: See *M Ado* Intro. p. 700b.   309. packed: an accomplice, one of the pack.

rows money in God's name, the which he hath　320
used so long and never paid that now men grow
hardhearted and will lend nothing for God's sake.
Pray you examine him upon that point.

LEON. I thank thee for thy care and honest pains.

DOGB. Your Worship speaks like a most thankful
and reverend youth, and I praise God for you.

LEON. There's for thy pains.　327

DOGB. God save the foundation!°

LEON. Go. I discharge thee of thy prisoner, and I
thank thee.　330

DOGB. I leave an arrant knave with your Worship,
which I beseech your Worship to correct yourself,
for the example of others. God keep your Worship!
I wish your Worship well. God restore you to health!
I humbly give you leave to depart, and if a merry
meeting may be wished, God prohibit° it!　336
Come, neighbor.　[*Exeunt* DOGBERRY *and* VERGES.]

LEON. Until tomorrow morning, lords, farewell.

ANT. Farewell, my lords. We look for you tomorrow.

D. PEDRO. We will not fail.

CLAUD.　　　　　　　Tonight I'll mourn with Hero.

LEON. [*To the* WATCH] Bring you these fellows on.
We'll talk with Margaret,　341
How her acquaintance grew with this lewd° fellow.
　　　　　　　　　　　　　　[*Exeunt, severally.*]

SCENE II. LEONATO'S *garden.*

[*Enter* BENEDICK *and* MARGARET, *meeting.*]

BENE. Pray thee, sweet Mistress Margaret, deserve well at my hand by helping me to the speech
of Beatrice.

MARG. Will you, then, write me a sonnet in praise
of my beauty?　5

BENE. In so high a style, Margaret, that no man
living shall come over° it, for, in most comely truth,
thou deservest it.

MARG. To have no man come over me! Why, shall
I always keep belowstairs?°　10

BENE. Thy wit is as quick as the greyhound's
mouth. It catches.

MARG. And yours as blunt as the fencer's foils,
which hit but hurt not.　14

BENE. A most manly wit, Margaret. It will not
hurt a woman. And so, I pray thee call Beatrice. I
give thee the bucklers.°

MARG. Give us the swords, we have bucklers of our
own.　19

BENE. If you use them, Margaret, you must put in

the pikes° with a vice,° and they are dangerous
weapons for maids.

MARG. Well, I will call Beatrice to you, who I
think hath legs.　24

BENE. And therefore will come.

　　　　　　　　　　　　　　[*Exit* MARGARET.]

[*Sings.*]　　　" The god of love,
　　　　　　　　That sits above,
　　　　And knows me, and knows me,
　　　　　　How pitiful I deserve——"　29
I mean in singing, but in loving, Leander the good
swimmer, Troilus° the first employer of panders,
and a whole bookful of these quondam° carpetmon-
gers° whose names yet run smoothly in the even
road of a blank verse, why, they were never so truly
turned over and over as my poor self in love. Marry,
I cannot show it in rhyme. I have tried. I can　36
find out no rhyme to " lady " but " baby," an innocent rhyme; for " scorn," " horn," a hard rhyme; for
" school," " fool," a babbling rhyme — very ominous endings. No, I was not born under a rhyming
planet, nor I cannot woo in festival terms.　41
[*Enter* BEATRICE.] Sweet Beatrice, wouldst thou come
when I called thee?

BEAT. Yea, signior, and depart when you bid me.

BENE. Oh, stay but till then!　45

BEAT. " Then " is spoken, fare you well now. And
yet ere I go let me go with that I came, which is,
with knowing what hath passed between you and
Claudio.

BENE. Only foul words, and thereupon I will kiss
thee.　51

BEAT. Foul words is but foul wind, and foul wind
is but foul breath, and foul breath is noisome. Therefore I will depart unkissed.

BENE. Thou hast frighted the word out of his right
sense, so forcible is thy wit. But I must tell thee
plainly, Claudio undergoes° my challenge, and
either I must shortly hear from him or I will sub-
scribe° him a coward. And I pray thee now, tell me
for which of my bad parts didst thou first fall in love
with me?　61

BEAT. For them all together, which maintained so
politic a state° of evil that they will not admit any
good part to intermingle with them. But for which
of my good parts did you first suffer love for me?　66

BENE. Suffer love — a good epithet! I do suffer
love indeed, for I love thee against my will.

---

328. foundation: i.e., this noble house.　**336. prohibit:** for
"grant."　**342. lewd:** wicked.
　Sc. ii: 7. come over: overcome, with a pun on "stile."
10. belowstairs: i.e., with the servants.　**17. give . . . bucklers:**
yield you the victory. **buckler:** small shield. See Pl. 9 and 21i.

21. pikes: spikes. The buckler was sometimes equipped with a
spike which could be pushed into the opponent's face. **vice:** screw.
30–31. Leander . . . Troilus: supreme specimens of lovesick
wooers. Marlowe's poem *Hero and Leander* had been published in
1598. For Troilus and his pander see *Tr & Cr.*　**32. quondam:**
former.　**33. carpetmongers:** "armchair generals," who have
distinguished themselves on the carpet and not on the field of
battle.　**57. undergoes:** endures; i.e., has received.　**59. subscribe:** publicly proclaim. See I.i.41.　**63. politic a state:** well-
ordered community.

BEAT. In spite of your heart, I think — alas, poor heart! If you spite it for my sake, I will spite it for yours, for I will never love that which my friend hates.   72

BENE. Thou and I are too wise to woo peaceably.

BEAT. It appears not in this confession. There's not one wise man among twenty that will praise himself.   77

BENE. An old, an old instance, Beatrice, that lived in the time of good neighbors. If a man do not erect in this age his own tomb ere he dies, he shall live no longer in monument than the bell rings and the widow weeps.°   82

BEAT. And how long is that, think you?

BENE. Question. Why, an hour in clamor° and a quarter in rheum.° Therefore is it most expedient for the wise, if Don Worm, his conscience, find no impediment to the contrary, to be the trumpet of his own virtues, as I am to myself. So much for praising myself, who, I myself will bear witness, is praiseworthy. And now tell me, how doth your cousin?

BEAT. Very ill.   92

BENE. And how do you?

BEAT. Very ill too.

BENE. Serve God, love me, and mend. There will I leave you too, for here comes one in haste.   96

[*Enter* URSULA.]

URS. Madam, you must come to your uncle. Yonder's old coil° at home. It is proved my Lady Hero hath been falsely accused, the Prince and Claudio mightily abused. And Don John is the author of all, who is fled and gone. Will you come presently?   102

BEAT. Will you go hear this news, signior?

BENE. I will live in thy heart, die in thy lap, and be buried in thy eyes, and moreover I will go with thee to thy uncle's.   [*Exeunt.*]

SCENE III. *A church.*

[*Enter* DON PEDRO, CLAUDIO, *and three or four with tapers.*]

CLAUD. Is this the monument of Leonato?

A LORD. It is, my lord.

CLAUD. [*Reading out of a scroll.*]

  "Done to death by slanderous **tongues**
        Was the Hero that here lies.
  Death, in guerdon° of her wrongs,   5
        Gives her fame which never dies.
  So the life that died with shame
  Lives in death with glorious fame."

  Hang thou there upon the tomb,
        Praising her when I am dumb.   10
Now, music, sound, and sing your solemn hymn.

SONG

  Pardon, goddess of the night,°
  Those that slew thy virgin knight,°
  For the which, with songs of woe,
  Round about her tomb they go.   15
        Midnight, assist our moan,
        Help us to sigh and groan,
            Heavily, heavily.
        Graves, yawn, and yield your dead,
        Till death be utterèd,   20
            Heavily, heavily.°

CLAUD. Now, unto thy bones good night!
Yearly will I do this rite.

D. PEDRO. Good morrow, masters. Put your
  torches out.
The wolves have preyed, and look, the gentle day,
Before the wheels of Phoebus,° round about   26
Dapples the drowsy east with spots of gray.
Thanks to you all, and leave us. Fare you well.

CLAUD. Good morrow, masters. Each his several
  way.

D. PEDRO. Come, let us hence and put on other
  weeds,°   30
And then to Leonato's we will go.

CLAUD. And Hymen° now with luckier issue
  speed 's
Than this for whom we rendered up this woe.

                                                [*Exeunt.*]

SCENE IV. *A room in* LEONATO'S *house.*

[*Enter* LEONATO, ANTONIO, BENEDICK, BEATRICE, MARGARET, URSULA, FRIAR FRANCIS, *and* HERO.]

FRIAR. Did I not tell you she was innocent?

LEON. So are the Prince and Claudio, who accused
  her
Upon the error that you heard debated.
But Margaret was in some fault for this,
Although against her will,° as it appears   5
In the true course of all the question.°

ANT. Well, I am glad that all things sort° so well.

BENE. And so am I, being else by faith enforced
To call young Claudio to a reckoning for it.

LEON. Well, Daughter, and you gentlewomen all,
Withdraw into a chamber by yourselves,   11

79–82. **If . . . weeps:** The short memories of Elizabethan widows were notorious. For this reason most of the elaborate Elizabethan tombs were erected by the occupants for themselves. See Gen. Intro. p. 20a.   84. **clamor:** noisy grief.   85. **rheum:** moisture.   98. **old coil:** a great to-do.
Sc. iii: 5. **guerdon:** reward.

12. **goddess . . . night:** Diana, goddess of chastity.   13. **virgin knight:** i.e., Hero.   19–21. **Graves . . . heavily:** These lines do not make sense, unless the meaning is that the dead are to come up to listen to the dirge. The "sad inventions" of Claudio have indeed been "labored."   26. **wheels of Phoebus:** wheels of the sun god's chariot.   30. **weeds:** garments.   32. **Hymen:** god of marriage.
    Sc. iv: 5. **will:** intention.   6. **question:** examination.   7. **sort:** turn out.

And when I send for you, come hither masked.
                    [*Exeunt* LADIES.]
The Prince and Claudio promised by this hour
To visit me. You know your office, Brother.
You must be father to your brother's daughter,   15
And give her to young Claudio.
    ANT. Which I will do with confirmed counte-
nance.°
    BENE. Friar, I must entreat your pains, I think.
    FRIAR. To do what, signior?
    BENE. To bind me, or undo me, one of them.   20
Signior Leonato, truth it is, good signior,
Your niece regards me with an eye of favor.
    LEON. That eye my daughter lent her — 'tis most
true.
    BENE. And I do with an eye of love requite her.
    LEON. The sight whereof I think you had from
me,   25
From Claudio, and the Prince. But what's your will?
    BENE. Your answer, sir, is enigmatical.
But, for my will, my will is, your goodwill
May stand with ours, this day to be conjoined
In the state of honorable marriage.   30
In which, good Friar, I shall desire your help.
    LEON. My heart is with your liking.
    FRIAR.   And my help.
Here comes the Prince and Claudio.
[*Enter* DON PEDRO *and* CLAUDIO, *and two or three
                    others.*]
    D. PEDRO. Good morrow to this fair assembly.
    LEON. Good morrow, Prince. Good morrow,
Claudio.   35
We here attend° you. Are you yet° determined
Today to marry with my brother's daughter?
    CLAUD. I'll hold my mind, were she an Ethiope.°
    LEON. Call her forth, Brother, here's the Friar
ready.   [*Exit* ANTONIO.]
    D. PEDRO. Good morrow, Benedick. Why, what's
the matter   40
That you have such a February face,
So full of frost, of storm, and cloudiness?
    CLAUD. I think he thinks upon the savage bull.°
Tush, fear not, man, we'll tip thy horns with gold,
And all Europa° shall rejoice at thee   45
As once Europa° did at lusty Jove
When he would play the noble beast in love.
    BENE. Bull Jove, sir, had an amiable low,
And some such strange bull leaped your father's cow
And got a calf in that same noble feat   50
Much like to you, for you have just his bleat.
    CLAUD. For this I owe you.° Here comes other
reckonings.°

17. confirmed countenance: straight face.   36. attend: wait
for. yet: still.   38. Ethiope: Ethiopian.   43. savage bull: See
I.i.263–66, and V.i.183.   45. Europa: Europe.   46. Europa: a
maiden loved by Jupiter, who transformed himself into a white
bull to get her.   52. owe you: i.e., will pay you back. reckonings: matters.

[*Re-enter* ANTONIO, *with the* LADIES *masked.*] Which
is the lady I must seize upon?
    ANT. This same is she, and I do give you her.
    CLAUD. Why, then she's mine. Sweet, let me see
your face.   55
    LEON. No, that you shall not till you take her hand
Before this Friar and swear to marry her.
    CLAUD. Give me your hand. Before this holy Friar,
I am your husband, if you like of me.   59
    HERO. And when I lived, I was your other wife,
                    [*Unmasking*]
And when you loved, you were my other husband.
    CLAUD. Another Hero!
    HERO.   Nothing certainer.
One Hero died defiled, but I do live,
And surely as I live, I am a maid.   64
    D. PEDRO. The former Hero! Hero that is dead!
    LEON. She died, my lord, but whiles° her slander
lived.
    FRIAR. All this amazement can I qualify.°
When after that the holy rites are ended,
I'll tell you largely° of fair Hero's death.
Meantime let wonder seem familiar,°   70
And to the chapel let us presently.
    BENE. Soft and fair, Friar. Which is Beatrice?
    BEAT. [*Unmasking*] I answer to that name. What
is your will?
    BENE. Do not you love me?
    BEAT.   Why, no, no more than reason.
    BENE. Why, then your uncle, and the Prince, and
Claudio   75
Have been deceived. They swore you did.
    BEAT. Do not you love me?
    BENE.   Troth, no, no more than reason.
    BEAT. Why, then my cousin, Margaret, and Ursula
Are much deceived, for they did swear you did.
    BENE. They swore that you were almost sick for me.
    BEAT. They swore that you were well-nigh dead
for me.   81
    BENE. 'Tis no such matter. Then you do not love
me?
    BEAT. No, truly, but in friendly recompense.
    LEON. Come, Cousin, I am sure you love the gen-
tleman.
    CLAUD. And I'll be sworn upon 't that he loves her,
For here's a paper, written in his hand,   86
A halting° sonnet of his own pure brain,
Fashioned to Beatrice.
    HERO.   And here's another,
Writ in my cousin's hand, stolen from her pocket,
Containing her affection unto Benedick.   90
    BENE. A miracle! Here's our own hands against
our hearts. Come, I will have thee, but, by this light,
I take thee for pity.

66. but whiles: only so long as.   67. qualify: moderate.
69. largely: fully.   70. wonder . . . familiar: strange things seem
normal.   87. halting: lame.

BEAT. I would not deny you, but, by this good day,
I yield upon great persuasion, and partly to save   95
your life, for I was told you were in a consumption.

BENE. Peace! I will stop your mouth.

                      [*Kissing her*]

D. PEDRO. How dost thou, Benedick the married
man?   99

BENE. I'll tell thee what, Prince, a college of wit-
crackers cannot flout me out of my humor.° Dost
thou think I care for a satire or an epigram? No. If
a man will be beaten with brains, a' shall wear nothing handsome about him.° In brief, since I do pur-   105
pose to marry, I will think nothing to any purpose that the world can say against it; and therefore
never flout at me for what I have said against it, for
man is a giddy thing, and this is my conclusion. For
thy part, Claudio, I did think to have beaten   110
thee, but in that thou art like to be my kinsman, live
unbruised, and love my cousin.

CLAUD. I had well hoped thou wouldst have denied Beatrice, that I might have cudgeled thee out
of thy single life, to make thee a double-dealer,   116
which, out of question, thou wilt be if my cousin do
not look exceeding narrowly to thee.

BENE. Come, come, we are friends. Let's have a
dance ere we are married, that we may lighten our
own hearts and our wives' heels.   121

LEON. We'll have dancing afterward.

BENE. First, of my word, therefore play, music.
Prince, thou art sad. Get thee a wife, get thee a wife.
There is no staff° more reverend than one tipped
with horn.°   126

              [*Enter a* MESSENGER.]

MESS. My lord, your brother John is ta'en in flight,
And brought with armed men back to Messina.

BENE. Think not on him till tomorrow. I'll devise
thee brave punishments for him. Strike up,   130
pipers!   [*Dance. Exeunt.*]

---

101. humor: inclination.   102–04. If . . . him: a man who is
afraid of what others say will never be distinguished.

125. staff: walking stick used by the elderly and respectable.
125–6. tipped . . . horn: the usual joke about cuckolds. Benedick
thus gets the last word, for the Prince is at least half in love with
Beatrice.

THE LIFE OF KING HENRY THE FIFTH

Introduction[1]

The Life of King Henry the Fifth can be dated with some accuracy. In the Chorus before Act V (lines 28–34) there is an unmistakable reference to the Earl of Essex's triumphal departure for Ireland on March 29, 1599 (see Gen. Intro. p. 23b). By the early summer rumors were circulating in London that Essex had failed, and on September 28 he returned to London, and was thenceforward in disgrace. The complimentary lines in the Chorus would thus have been topical only for a few weeks in the spring of 1599.

Henry V is a continuation of *II Henry IV,* which had been produced about a year before. At the end of that play Shakespeare promised:

If you be not too much cloyed with fat meat, our humble author will continue the story, with Sir John in it, and make you merry with fair Katharine of France. Where, for anything I know, Falstaff shall die of a sweat, unless already a' be killed with your hard opinions, for Oldcastle died a martyr, and this is not the man.

The promise was not kept. Although the rest of the gang reappear, with a newcomer in Corporal Nym, Falstaff is not seen, though his death is reported in II.iii. It is not known why Falstaff thus vanished, but it would certainly have been difficult, after his devastating rejection (*II Hen IV,* V.v), for Shakespeare to bring him again into the presence of Henry V. It may be, as some critics maintain, that Shakespeare felt that Falstaff would overshadow the King and so spoil the play. It may be that Shakespeare himself had lost the knack of creating Falstaff; when Falstaff reappeared in *The Merry Wives of Windsor* only his bulk remained; his wit and his humor had woefully diminished. Or there may have been some quite practical reason, such as the departure of the actor who originally created the part. Whatever the explanation, the whole balance and structure of comedy and history in *Henry V* is different from that in *Henry IV*.

In writing the serious scenes Shakespeare, as in the other History Plays, again followed Holinshed's *Chronicle,* at times so closely that he did

1 See also App. 28.

little more than turn Holinshed's prose into blank verse. The long lecture on the Salic law delivered by the Archbishop (I.ii.35–100) is a transcript, phrase for phrase, from the *Chronicle,* as is also the list of French casualties (IV.viii.81–110). Some extracts will show what Shakespeare owed to his source:

I. THE CHARACTER OF HENRY V

This Henry was a king of life without spot; a prince whom all men loved, and of none disdained; a captain against whom fortune never frowned, nor mischance once spurned; whose people him so severe a justicer both loved and obeyed, and so humane withal that he left no offense unpunished, nor friendship unrewarded; a terror to rebels, and suppressor of sedition; his virtues notable, his qualities most praiseworthy.

In strength and nimbleness of body from his youth few to him comparable; for in wrestling, leaping, and running, no man well able to compare. In casting of great iron bars and heavy stones he excelled commonly all men, never shrinking at cold, nor slothful for heat; and when he most labored, his head commonly uncovered; no more weary of harness [armor] than a light cloak; very valiantly abiding at needs both hunger and thirst; so manful of mind as never seen to quinch at a wound, or to smart at the pain; to turn his nose from evil savor, or to close his eyes from smoke or dust; no man more moderate in eating and drinking, with diet not delicate, but rather more meet for men of war than for princes or tender stomachs. Every honest person was permitted to come to him sitting at meal, where either secretly or openly to declare his mind. High and weighty causes, as well between men of war and other, he would gladly hear; and either determined them himself or else for end committed them to others. He slept very little, but that very soundly, insomuch that when his soldiers sang at night, or minstrels played, he then slept fastest; of courage invincible, of purpose unmutable; so wisehardy always as fear was banished from him; at every alarum he first in armor, and foremost in ordering. In time of war such was his providence, bounty, and hap as he had true intelligence not only what his enemies did, but what they said and intended. Of his devices and purposes, few, before the thing was at the point to be done, should be made privy.

2. THE ARCHBISHOP'S ARGUMENT (cf. i.ii.35–100)

[The Archbishop spoke] against the surmised and false feigned law Salic, which the Frenchmen allege ever against the Kings of England in bar of their just title to the crown of France. The very words of that supposed law are these: "*In terram Salicam mulieres ne succedant*"; that is to say, "Into the Salic land let not women succeed." Which the French glossers expound to be the realm of France, and that this law was made by King Pharamond; whereas yet their own authors affirm that the land Salic is in Germany, between the rivers of Elbe and Sala; and that when Charles the Great had overcome the Saxons, he placed there certain Frenchmen, which having in disdain the dishonest manners of the German women, made a law that the females should not succeed to any inheritance within that land, which at this day is called Meisen. So that, if this be true, this law was not made for the realm of France, nor the Frenchmen possessed the land Salic, till four hundred and one and twenty years after the death of Pharamond, the supposed maker of this Salic law; for this Pharamond deceased in the year 426 and Charles the Great subdued the Saxons, and placed the Frenchmen in those parts beyond the river of Sala, in the year 805.

Moreover, it appeareth by their own writers that King Pepin, which deposed Childeric, claimed the crown of France as heir general, for that he was descended of Blithild, daughter to King Clothair the First. Hugh Capet also (who usurped the crown upon Charles Duke of Loraine, the sole heir male of the line and stock of Charles the Great), to make his title seem true, and appear good (though indeed it was stark naught), conveyed himself as heir to the Lady Lingard, daughter to King Charlemagne, son to Lewis the Emperor, that was son to Charles the Great. King Lewis also, the Tenth (otherwise called Saint Lewis), being very heir to the said usurper Hugh Capet, could never be satisfied in his conscience how he might justly keep and possess the crown of France till he was persuaded and fully instructed that Queen Isabel his grandmother was lineally descended of the Lady Ermengard, daughter and heir to the above named Charles Duke of Loraine; by the which marriage, the blood and line of Charles the Great was again united and restored to the crown and scepter of France. So that more clear than the sun it openly appeareth that the title of King Pepin, the claim of Hugh Capet, the possession of Lewis — yea, and the French Kings to this day — are derived and conveyed from the heir female, though they would, under the color of such a feigned law, bar the Kings and Princes of this realm of England of their right and lawful inheritance.

The Archbishop further alleged out of the Book of Numbers this saying: "When a man dieth without a son, let the inheritance descend to his daughter."

3. THE KING'S WORDS BEFORE THE BATTLE (cf. iv.iii.21–67)

It is said that as he heard one of the host utter his wish to another thus: "I would to God there were with us now so many good soldiers as are at this hour within England!" the King answered: "I would not wish a man more here than I have. We are indeed in comparison to the enemies but a few, but if God of His clemency do favor us and our just cause (as I trust He will), we shall speed well enough. But let no man ascribe victory to our own strength and might, but only to God's assistance, to Whom I have no doubt we shall worthily have cause to give thanks therefore. And if so be that for our offenses' sakes we shall be delivered into the hands of our enemies, the less number we be, the less damage shall the realm of England sustain. But if we should fight in trust of multitude of men, and so get the victory (our minds being prone to pride), we should thereupon peradventure ascribe the victory not so much to the gift of God as to our own puissance, and thereby provoke His high indignation and displeasure against us. And if the enemy get the upper hand, then should our realm and country suffer more damage and stand in further danger. But be you of good comfort, and show yourselves valiant! God and our just quarrel shall defend us and deliver these our proud adversaries with all the multitude of them which you see (or at the least the most of them) into our hands."

Apart from the records in the *Chronicle,* several other dramatists had written plays about Henry V, who, like other national heroes, had become a legendary figure. A playgoer therefore expected some scenes showing the King's wild youth, his habit of passing disguised amongst common men, and his blunt wooing of French Kate. These were available to Shakespeare in the old play of *The Famous Victories of Henry the Fifth,* which had been printed in 1598 (see *I Hen IV* Intro. p. 614b).

The full version of *Henry V* was not printed until it appeared in the first folio in 1623. A casual note in the Stationers' Register, dated August 4, 1600, records that *Henry V, Much Ado about Nothing, As You Like It,* and Jonson's *Every Man out of His Humor* were to be "staied"; that is, not licensed for printing. Nevertheless in 1600 a pirated edition of *Henry V* appeared with the title: *The Chronicle History of Henry the fift, With his battel fought at Agin Court in*

France. Togither with Auncient Pistoll. As it hath bene sundry times playd by the Right honorable the Lord Chamberlaine his seruants. London. Printed by Thomas Creede, for Tho. Millington, and Iohn Busby. And are to be sold at his house in Carter Lane, next the Powle head. 1600. The text of this edition is incredibly bad and was reproduced from a version taken down by shorthand or else put together from memory. It is about a thousand lines shorter than the correct text, omits the Choruses and many speeches, and feebly paraphrases the rest. This quarto was reprinted in 1602 and in 1619. The text in the folio is fairly well printed, but the printer mistook a number of words and made woeful confusion of the passages in French.

An interval of about a year separated the writing of *Henry V* from the writing of *II Henry IV*. Much had happened in the London theaters during these months, particularly the success of Ben Jonson's *Every Man in His Humor*. In the rewritten version of that play, printed in 1616, there appears a prologue in which Jonson sneered at the usual methods of the actors who

>   with three rusty swords,
> And help of some few foot and half-foot words,
> Fight over York and Lancaster's long jars,
> And in the tiring-house bring wounds to scars.

This prologue can hardly have been used at the original production of *Every Man in His Humor* by Shakespeare's company in 1598, but it certainly expressed the views of Jonson, and those who agreed with him, in demanding that the stage should present life realistically. Indeed Shakespeare seems to have been on the defensive in writing *Henry V,* for he prefaced the play with an apologetic Chorus to answer those critics who mocked at the absurdity of trying to show great events on a bare platform. A history play, Shakespeare claimed, did not attempt to be realistic; its aim was rather to stimulate the imagination of the spectator.

The feelings of critics toward *Henry V* differ according to the times. In moments of crisis or national peril, when patriotism is aglow, the play is a trumpet call to heroic action; in more pacific times it seems somewhat brassy for everyday enjoyment. In other ways *Henry V* is less satisfying than either part of *Henry IV*. There is not enough conflict or balance in the story. Henry himself is

too perfect. And except for his one soliloquy and his prayer before Agincourt, he is seen only on the outside, as a king and not as a man. His enemies, the French, are too worthless, too obviously self-doomed, to be worthy opponents. The subplot also is uneven. The incidents, such as the moving account of the death of Falstaff, or Fluellen's beating of Pistol, are good in themselves, but they lack the coherence of the *Henry IV* plays. Shakespeare indeed relied rather on rhetoric than on a well-constructed plot; still, the rhetoric is magnificent, particularly in Henry's speeches to the conspirators (II.ii), or before Harfleur (III.i), his soliloquy in the night before the battle (IV.i.247–301), and his speech to Westmoreland (IV.iii.19–67).

Henry V is often spoken of as Shakespeare's ideal king. It may be so; but Shakespeare had no illusions about either Henry V or his father, Henry IV, who on his own confession was a scheming hypocrite and an unscrupulous liar, and whose last advice to his son was "to busy giddy minds With foreign quarrels." There is thus little glamor about the true motives for the French war; it is calculated policy. The clergy support it in the hope that it may distract attention from an embarrassing proposal to cut off their revenues. The nobles are eager for a fight, and the profits which may follow. Pistol expresses it most crudely and frankly:

>   Yokefellows in arms,
> Let us to France, like horseleeches, my boys,
> To suck, to suck, the very blood to suck!

Yet even if Shakespeare may have felt little sentimentality about his hero, Henry V may still have been his ideal king, for Shakespeare realized that those qualities which make an ideal king are not the same as those which make a good companion. Henry is brutal and ruthless; he demands discipline in others and himself; he knows when to be stern and when to unbend; he can stir the hearts of his subjects; he has an overwhelming sense of his own responsibility. He is, above all things, efficient, and in practical matters the efficiency of Henry in his Council or on the battlefield is to be preferred to the humor of Falstaff in the tavern. Those critics who condemn Henry V for casting off his old companions are themselves guilty of a lack of humor.

Henry V

DRAMATIS PERSONAE

KING HENRY *the Fifth*
DUKE OF GLOUCESTER ⎱ *brothers to the King*
DUKE OF BEDFORD ⎰
DUKE OF EXETER, *uncle to the King*
DUKE OF YORK, *cousin to the King*
EARLS OF SALISBURY, WESTMORELAND, *and* WARWICK
ARCHBISHOP OF CANTERBURY
BISHOP OF ELY
EARL OF CAMBRIDGE
LORD SCROOP
SIR THOMAS GREY
SIR THOMAS ERPINGHAM, GOWER, FLUELLEN,
  MACMORRIS, JAMY, *officers in King Henry's army*
BATES, COURT, WILLIAMS, *soldiers in the same*
PISTOL, NYM, BARDOLPH
BOY
A HERALD
CHARLES *the Sixth, King of France*

LEWIS, *the Dauphin*
DUKES OF BURGUNDY, ORLEANS, *and* BOURBON
THE CONSTABLE *of France*
RAMBURES *and* GRANDPRÉ, *French lords*
GOVERNOR *of Harfleur*
MONTJOY, *a French herald*
AMBASSADORS *to the King of England*

ISABEL, *Queen of France*
KATHARINE, *daughter to Charles and Isabel*
ALICE, *a lady attending on her*
HOSTESS *of a tavern in Eastcheap, formerly Mistress*
  Quickly, and now married to Pistol

LORDS, LADIES, OFFICERS, SOLDIERS, CITIZENS,
  MESSENGERS, *and* ATTENDANTS

CHORUS

SCENE — *England; afterward France.*

PROLOGUE

[*Enter* CHORUS.°]
CHOR. O for a Muse of fire,° that would ascend
The brightest heaven of invention,°
A kingdom for a stage, princes to act
And monarchs to behold the swelling scene!
Then should the warlike Harry, like himself,   5
Assume the port° of Mars, and at his heels,
Leashed in like hounds, should famine, sword, and
    fire
Crouch° for employment. But pardon, gentles° all,
The flat unraisèd° spirits that have dared
On this unworthy scaffold to bring forth   10
So great an object. Can this cockpit° hold
The vasty fields of France? Or may we cram
Within this wooden O° the very casques°
That did affright the air at Agincourt?
Oh, pardon! Since a crooked figure may   15
Attest° in little place a million,
And let us, ciphers to this great accompt,°
On your imaginary forces° work.
Suppose within the girdle of these walls

Are now confined two mighty monarchies,   20
Whose high uprearèd and abutting° fronts
The perilous narrow ocean° parts asunder.
Piece out our imperfections with your thoughts.
Into a thousand parts divide one man,
And make imaginary puissance.°   25
Think when we talk of horses that you see them
Printing their proud hoofs i' the receiving earth.
For 'tis your thoughts that now must deck our kings,
Carry them here and there, jumping o'er times,
Turning the accomplishment of many years   30
Into an hourglass. For the which supply,
Admit me Chorus to this history,
Who prologue-like your humble patience pray
Gently to hear, kindly to judge, our play. [*Exit.*]

Act I

SCENE I. *London. An antechamber in the*
KING's palace.

[*Enter the* ARCHBISHOP OF CANTERBURY, *and the*
BISHOP OF ELY.]
CANT. My lord, I'll tell you — that self° bill is
urged
Which in the eleventh year of the last King's° reign

Prologue. Chorus: See *Hen V*, Intro. p. 734a.   **1. Muse of fire:** i.e., burning inspiration to kindle this audience.   **1–2. that . . . invention:** that would reach the topmost height of inspiration. **invention:** artistic invention.   **6. port:** bearing.   **8. Crouch:** ready to spring.   **gentles:** gentle spectators.   **9. unraised:** uninspired.   **11. cockpit:** i.e., playhouse.   **13. wooden O:** i.e., the Curtain Playhouse, which was a round frame building. See Gen. Intro. pp. 36a and 41b.   **very casques:** even the actual helmets. **16. Attest:** stand for.   **17. accompt:** reckoning.   **18. imaginary forces:** powers of imagination.

21. abutting: neighboring.   **22. narrow ocean:** i.e., English Channel.   **25. puissance:** might.
  Act I, Sc. i: **1. self:** same.   **2. last King:** i.e., Henry IV.

Was like° and had indeed against us passed
But that the scambling° and unquiet time
Did push it out of farther question.   5
    ELY. But how, my lord, shall we resist it now?
    CANT. It must be thought on. If it pass against
us,
We lose the better half of our possession.
For all the temporal° lands which men devout
By testament have given to the Church   10
Would they strip from us, being valued thus:
As much as would maintain, to the King's honor,
Full fifteen earls and fifteen hundred knights,
Six thousand and two hundred good esquires,
And, to relief of lazars° and weak age,   15
Of indigent faint souls past corporal toil,
A hundred almshouses right well supplied.
And to the coffers of the King beside,
A thousand pounds by the year. Thus runs the
   bill.
    ELY. This would drink deep.
    CANT.   'Twould drink the cup and all.   20
    ELY. But what prevention?
    CANT. The King is full of grace and fair regard.
    ELY. And a true lover of the Holy Church.
    CANT. The courses of his youth promised it not.
The breath no sooner left his father's body   25
But that his wildness, mortified° in him,
Seemed to die too. Yea, at that very moment,
Consideration° like an angel came
And whipped the offending Adam° out of him,
Leaving his body as a paradise   30
To envelop and contain celestial spirits.
Never was such a sudden scholar made,
Never came reformation in a flood
With such a heady currance,° scouring faults.
Nor never Hydra-headed° willfulness   35
So soon did lose his seat, and all at once,
As in this King.
    ELY.   We are blessed in the change.
    CANT. Hear him but reason° in divinity,
And all-admiring with an inward wish
You would desire the King were made a prelate.   40
Hear him debate of commonwealth affairs,
You would say it hath been all in all his study.
List° his discourse of war, and you shall hear
A fearful battle rendered you in music.
Turn him to any cause of policy,°   45

The Gordian knot° of it he will unloose,
Familiar as his garter — that, when he speaks,
The air, a chartered libertine,° is still,
And the mute wonder lurketh in men's ears,
To steal his sweet and honeyed sentences.°   50
So that the art and practic part of life
Must be the mistress° to this theoric.°
Which is a wonder how His Grace should glean it,
Since his addiction was to courses vain,
His companies° unlettered, rude, and shallow,   55
His hours filled up with riots, banquets, sports,
And never noted in him any study,
Any retirement, any sequestration°
From open haunts and popularity.
    ELY. The strawberry grows underneath the nettle,
And wholesome berries thrive and ripen best   61
Neighbored by fruit of baser quality.
And so the Prince obscured his contemplation
Under the veil of wildness, which no doubt
Grew like the summer grass, fastest by night,   65
Unseen, yet crescive in his faculty.°
    CANT. It must be so, for miracles are ceased,
And therefore we must needs admit the means°
How things are pérfected.
    ELY.   But, my good lord,
How now for mitigation° of this bill   70
Urged by the Commons? Doth His Majesty
Incline to it, or no?
    CANT.   He seems indifferent,°
Or rather swaying more upon our part
Than cherishing the exhibiters° against us.
For I have made an offer to His Majesty,   75
Upon° our spiritual convocation
And in regard of causes now in hand,
Which I have opened to His Grace at large,°
As touching France, to give a greater sum
Than ever at one time the clergy yet   80
Did to his predecessors part withal.
    ELY. How did this offer seem received, my lord?
    CANT. With good acceptance of His Majesty,
Save that there was not time enough to hear,
As I perceived His Grace would fain have done,   85
The severals and unhidden passages°
Of his true titles to some certain dukedoms,
And generally to the crown and seat of France,

3. **like:** likely.   4. **scambling:** contentious.   9. **temporal:** i.e., belonging to laymen.   15. **lazars:** beggars; lit., lepers.   26. **mortified:** killed.   28. **Consideration:** serious thoughtfulness. 29. **whipped ... Adam:** drove out the natural sinful spirit. Lunatics were sometimes whipped to drive out the evil spirit with which they were possessed. **Adam:** i.e., original sin. 34. **heady currance:** violent flood. The allusion is to Hercules' method of cleansing the foul Augean stables, which he accomplished by turning a river through them.   35. **Hydra-headed:** Hydra was a many-headed monster killed by Hercules. 38. **reason:** debate.   43. **List:** listen to.   45. **cause of policy:** political problem.

46. **Gordian knot:** When Alexander the Great in his conquests reached Gordium, he was told that the man who could untie the knot which bound the pole to the yoke of the wagon of King Gordius should be King of Asia. Alexander cut the knot with his sword.   48. **chartered libertine:** privileged to be free.   50. **sentences:** wise sayings.   51–52. **art ... theoric:** his theories of life must have been founded on his practical experience. **art:** craftsmanship. **practic:** practical.   52. **mistress:** i.e., superior to. 55. **companies:** companions.   58. **sequestration:** separation. 66. **crescive ... faculty:** growing by its own natural power. 68. **admit ... means:** accept the natural cause.   70. **mitigation:** moderating.   72. **indifferent:** impartial.   74. **exhibiters:** promoters of the bill.   76. **Upon:** as a result of.   78. **opened ... large:** explained fully to His Majesty.   86. **severals ... passages:** the particular and clear sources.

Derived from Edward,° his great-grandfather.
  ELY. What was the impediment that broke this
    off?   90
  CANT. The French Ambassador upon that instant
Craved audience, and the hour I think is come
To give him hearing. Is it four o'clock?
  ELY. It is.
  CANT. Then go we in, to know his embassy,   95
Which I could with a ready guess declare
Before the Frenchman speak a word of it.
  ELY. I'll wait upon you, and I long to hear it.
                                    [Exeunt.]

SCENE II. *The same. The Presence Chamber.*°

[Enter KING HENRY, GLOUCESTER, BEDFORD, EXETER,
  WARWICK, WESTMORELAND, *and* ATTENDANTS.]
  K. HEN. Where is my gracious Lord of Canter-
    bury?
  EXE. Not here in presence.
  K. HEN.   Send for him, good Uncle.
  WEST. Shall we call in the Ambassador, my liege?
  K. HEN. Not yet, my cousin. We° would be re-
    solved,
Before we hear him, of some things of weight   5
That task° our thoughts, concerning us and France.
    [Enter the ARCHBISHOP OF CANTERBURY
         and the BISHOP OF ELY.]
  CANT. God and His angels guard your sacred
    throne,
And make you long become it!
  K. HEN.   Sure we thank you.
My learnèd lord, we pray you to proceed
And justly and religiously unfold   10
Why the law Salic° that they have in France
Or° should, or should not, bar us in our claim.
And God forbid, my dear and faithful lord,
That you should fashion, wrest,° or bow° your
    reading,
Or nicely° charge your understanding° soul   15
With opening titles miscreate,° whose right
Suits not in native colors with the truth.°
For God doth know how many now in health
Shall drop their blood in approbation°
Of what your Reverence shall incite us to.   20
Therefore take heed how you impawn° our person,
How you awake our sleeping sword of war.

We charge you, in the name of God, take heed.
For never two such kingdoms did contend
Without much fall of blood, whose guiltless drops
Are every one a woe, a sore complaint   26
'Gainst him whose wrongs give edge unto the swords
That make such waste in brief mortality.°
Under this conjuration° speak, my lord,
For we will hear, note, and believe in heart   30
That what you speak is in your conscience washed
As pure as sin with baptism.
  CANT. Then hear me, gracious Sovereign, and you
    peers,
That owe yourselves, your lives and services,
To this imperial throne. There° is no bar   35
To make against your Highness' claim to France
But this, which they produce from Pharamond,
"In terram Salicam mulieres ne succedant" —
"No woman shall succeed in Salic land."
Which Salic land the French unjustly gloze°   40
To be the realm of France, and Pharamond
The founder of this law and female bar.
Yet their own authors faithfully affirm
That the land Salic is in Germany,
Between the floods° of Sala and of Elbe,   45
Where Charles the Great, having subdued the
    Saxons,
There left behind and settled certain French.
Who, holding in disdain the German women
For some dishonest manners° of their life,
Established then this law: to wit, no female   50
Should be inheritrix in Salic land.
Which Salic, as I said, twixt Elbe and Sala,
Is at this day in Germany called Meisen.
Then doth it well appear the Salic law
Was not devisèd for the realm of France.   55
Nor did the French possess the Salic land
Until four hundred one and twenty years
After defunction° of King Pharamond,
Idly supposed the founder of this law,
Who died within the year of our redemption   60
Four hundred twenty-six. And Charles the Great
Subdued the Saxons, and did seat the French
Beyond the river Sala, in the year
Eight hundred five. Besides, their writers say,
King Pepin, which deposèd Childeric,   65
Did, as heir general, being descended
Of Blithild, which was daughter to King Clothair,
Make claim and title to the crown of France.
Hugh Capet also, who usurped the crown
Of Charles the Duke of Lorraine, sole heir male 70
Of the true line and stock of Charles the Great,
To find his title with some shows of truth —

---

89. **Edward:** i.e., Edward III.
  Sc. ii: s.d., Presence Chamber: the place where the King
gave public audiences. **4. We:** the royal "we," used when a
King is speaking officially. **6. task:** fully occupy. **11. law
Salic:** the Salic law which forbade a woman's succeeding to the
throne, explained later, ll. 35–95. **12. Or:** either. **14. wrest:**
wrench. **bow:** bend. **15. nicely:** unscrupulously. **understanding:**
i.e., that knows the truth to be otherwise. **16. opening . . .
miscreate:** making claims falsely based. **17. Suits . . . truth:**
does not match the natural color of truth. **19. approbation:**
putting to the test. **21. impawn:** pledge.

28. waste . . . mortality: destruction of brief lives. **29. conjuration:** solemn appeal. **35–100. There . . . daughter:** The whole
of this long speech is taken almost verbatim from Holinshed.
See *Hen V* Intro. p. 733a. **40. gloze:** gloss; i.e., interpret.
45. floods: waters. **49. dishonest manners:** loose conduct.
58. defunction: decease.

Though, in pure truth, it was corrupt and naught —
Conveyed° himself as heir to the Lady Lingare,
Daughter to Charlemagne, who was the son   75
To Lewis the Emperor, and Lewis the son
Of Charles the Great. Also King Lewis the Tenth,
Who was sole heir to the usurper Capet,
Could not keep quiet in his conscience,
Wearing the crown of France, till satisfied   80
That fair Queen Isabel, his grandmother,
Was lineal of° the Lady Ermengare,
Daughter to Charles the foresaid Duke of Lorraine.
By the which marriage the line of Charles the Great
Was reunited to the crown of France.   85
So that, as clear as is the summer's sun,
King Pepin's title and Hugh Capet's claim,
King Lewis his satisfaction, all appear
To hold in right and title of the female.
So do the Kings of France unto this day,   90
Howbeit they would hold up this Salic law
To bar your Highness claiming from the female,
And rather choose to hide them in a net°
Than amply to imbar° their crooked° titles
Usurped from you and your progenitors.   95
  K. HEN. May I with right and conscience make
    this claim?
  CANT. The sin upon my head, dread Sovereign!
For in the Book of Numbers° is it writ,
When the man dies, let the inheritance
Descend unto the daughter. Gracious lord,   100
Stand for your own, unwind your bloody flag,
Look back into your mighty ancestors.
Go, my dread lord, to your great-grandsire's tomb,
From whom you claim, invoke his warlike spirit,
And your great-uncle's, Edward the Black Prince,
Who on the French ground played a tragedy,°   106
Making defeat on the full power of France
Whiles his most mighty father on a hill
Stood smiling to behold his lion's whelp
Forage° in blood of French nobility.   110
Oh, noble English, that could entertain
With half their forces the full pride of France
And let another half stand laughing by,
All out of work and cold for action!
  ELY. Awake remembrance of these valiant dead,
And with your puissant° arm renew their feats.   116
You are their heir, you sit upon their throne.
The blood and courage that renownèd them
Runs in your veins, and my thrice-puissant liege
Is in the very May morn of his youth,   120
Ripe for exploits and mighty enterprises.

EXE. Your brother kings and monarchs of the
    earth
Do all expect that you should rouse yourself,
As did the former lions of your blood.
  WEST. They know your Grace hath cause and
    means and might.   125
So hath your Highness. Never King of England
Had nobles richer and more loyal subjects,
Whose hearts have left their bodies here in England
And lie pavilioned° in the fields of France.   129
  CANT. Oh, let their bodies follow, my dear liege,
With blood and sword and fire to win your right.
In aid whereof we of the spiritualty
Will raise your Highness such a mighty sum
As never did the clergy at one time
Bring in to any of your ancestors.   135
  K. HEN. We must not only arm to invade the
    French,
But lay down our proportions° to defend
Against the Scot, who will make road° upon us
With all advantages.°
  CANT. They of those marches,° gracious sovereign,
Shall be a wall sufficient to defend   141
Our inland from the pilfering borderers.°
  K. HEN. We do not mean the coursing snatchers°
    only,
But fear the main intendment° of the Scot,
Who hath been still° a giddy° neighbor to us.   145
For you shall read that my great-grandfather
Never went with his forces into France
But that the Scot on his unfurnished kingdom
Came pouring, like the tide into a breach,
With ample and brim fullness of his force,   150
Galling the gleanèd land° with hot assays,°
Girding with grievous siege castles and towns,
That England, being empty of defense,
Hath shook and trembled at the ill neighborhood.
  CANT. She hath been then more feared° than
    harmed, my liege,   155
For hear her but exampled by herself.
When all her chivalry hath been in France,
And she a mourning widow of her nobles,
She hath herself not only well defended,
But taken and impounded° as a stray°   160
The King of Scots,° whom she did send to France,
To fill King Edward's fame with prisoner kings

---

74. Conveyed: falsely claimed. **82. lineal of:** descended from.
93. net: i.e., a flimsy and ridiculous excuse. **94. imbar:** secure.
crooked: false. **98. Book of Numbers:** "If a man die, and
have no son, then shall ye cause his inheritance to pass to his
daughter." (27:8) **106. played a tragedy:** i.e., the Battle of
Crécy (1346), when Edward III defeated the French. His son
Edward, the Black Prince, then a youth of sixteen, greatly distinguished himself. **110. Forage:** seek his prey. **116. puissant:**
mighty.

129. pavilioned: in their tents. **137. proportions:** estimates of
the forces required. **138. make road:** invade. **139. With . . .
advantages:** explained in ll. 169–73. **140. marches:** borders.
142. pilfering borderers: thieves living on the border. In the
fourteenth and fifteenth centuries there was a constant state of
war on the border between England and Scotland. **143. coursing snatchers:** raiding thieves. **144. intendment:** design.
145. still: always. **giddy:** unreliable. **151. gleanèd land:** i.e.,
when the men of war were away. **assays:** attempts. **155. feared:**
frightened. **160. impounded:** shut up in the village pound.
stray: a stray beast. **161. King of Scots:** David II, who was
taken while Edward III was absent on his Crécy campaign.
Actually he was sent to London, not to France.

And make her chronicle as rich with praise
As is the ooze and bottom of the sea
With sunken wreck and sumless° treasures.   165
   WEST. But there's a saying very old and true —
     " If that you will France win,
      Then with Scotland first begin."
For once the eagle England being in prey,°
To her unguarded nest the weasel Scot   170
Comes sneaking, and so sucks her princely eggs,
Playing the mouse in absence of the cat,
To tear and havoc° more than she can eat.
   EXE. It follows then the cat must stay at home.
Yet that is but a crushed° necessity,   175
Since we have locks to safeguard necessaries,
And pretty traps to catch the petty thieves.
While that the armèd hand doth fight abroad,
The advisèd° head defends itself at home.
For government, though high and low and lower,
Put into parts,° doth keep in one consent,°   181
Congreeing° in a full and natural close,°
Like music.
   CANT.   Therefore doth Heaven divide
The state of man in divers functions,
Setting endeavor in continual motion.   185
To which is fixèd, as an aim or butt,°
Obedience. For so work the honeybees,°
Creatures that by a rule in nature teach
The act of order to a peopled kingdom.
They have a King and officers of sorts,°   190
Where some, like magistrates, correct at home,
Others, like merchants, venture trade abroad,
Others, like soldiers, armèd in their stings,
Make boot° upon the summer's velvet buds,
Which pillage they with merry march bring home
To the tent royal of their Emperor.   196
Who, busied in his majesty, surveys
The singing masons building roofs of gold,
The civil citizens kneading up the honey,
The poor mechanic porters crowding in   200
Their heavy burdens at his narrow gate,
The sad-eyed Justice, with his surly hum,
Delivering o'er to executors° pale
The lazy yawning drone. I this infer,
That many things, having full reference   205
To one consent, may work contrariously.
As many arrows, loosed several ways,°
Come to one mark; as many ways meet in one town;

As many fresh streams meet in one salt sea;
As many lines close in the dial's center —   210
So may a thousand actions, once afoot,
End in one purpose, and be all well borne
Without defeat. Therefore to France, my liege.
Divide your happy England into four,
Whereof take you one quarter into France,   215
And you withal shall make all Gallia shake.
If we, with thrice such powers° left at home,
Cannot defend our own doors from the dog,
Let us be worried and our nation lose
The name of hardiness and policy.°   220
   K. HEN. Call in the messengers sent from the
    Dauphin.°   [*Exeunt some* ATTENDANTS.]
Now are we well resolved, and, by God's help,
And yours, the noble sinews° of our power,
France being ours, we'll bend it to our awe
Or break it all to pieces. Or there we'll sit,   225
Ruling in large and ample empery°
O'er France and all her almost kingly dukedoms,
Or lay these bones in an unworthy urn,
Tombless, with no remembrance over them.
Either our history shall with full mouth   230
Speak freely of our acts, or else our grave,
Like Turkish mute, shall have a tongueless mouth,
Not worshiped° with a waxen° epitaph.
[*Enter* AMBASSADORS *of France.*] Now are we well
    prepared to know the pleasure
Of our fair cousin° Dauphin, for we hear   235
Your greeting is from him, not from the King.
   1. AMB. May't please your Majesty to give us leave
Freely to render° what we have in charge,°
Or shall we sparingly show you far off
The Dauphin's meaning and our embassy?   240
   K. HEN. We are no tyrant, but a Christian king,
Unto whose grace our passion is as subject
As are our wretches fettered in our prisons.
Therefore with frank and with uncurbed plainness
Tell us the Dauphin's mind.
   1. AMB.   Thus, then, in few.°   245
Your Highness, lately sending into France,
Did claim some certain dukedoms, in the right
Of your great predecessor, King Edward the Third.
In answer of which claim, the Prince our master
Says that you savor too much of your youth,   250
And bids you be advised there's naught in France
That can be with a nimble galliard° won.
You cannot revel into dukedoms there.
He therefore sends you, meeter° for your spirit,
This tun° of treasure, and, in lieu of this,   255

165. sumless: countless.   169. in prey: seeking her prey.
173. havoc: rend in pieces.   175. crushed: forced.   179. advised:
thoughtful.   181. Put . . . parts: i.e., divided among Ministers,
as the various parts of music among the musicians. consent:
harmony.   182. Congreeing: harmonizing. close: cadence.
186. butt: target.   187–204. honeybees . . . drone: This elaborate parallel between a kingdom and a hive is found also in
Lyly's *Euphues*, but it is fairly common. It was used before
Queen Elizabeth by the Speaker in the Parliament of 1593.
190. of sorts: of different ranks.   194. boot: plunder.   203. executors: executioners.   207. loosed . . . ways: shot from different directions.

217. powers: forces.   220. policy: statesmanship.   221. Dauphin:
The title given to the eldest son of the King of France; in
Shakespeare's time (and in F1) called "Dolphin."   223. sinews:
supports.   226. empery: rule.   233. worshiped: honored. waxen:
i.e., not enduring.   235. cousin: used of any relation, but in
Courtly etiquette all kings were related.   238. render: declare.
have in charge: have been commanded to say.   245. in few:
i.e., words.   252. galliard: a lively dance. See App. 24.
254. meeter: fitter.   255. tun: barrel.

Desires you let the dukedoms that you claim
Hear no more of you. This the Dauphin speaks.
    K. HEN. What treasure, Uncle?
    EXE.   Tennis balls,° my liege.
    K. HEN. We are glad the Dauphin is so pleasant
      with us.
His present and your pains we thank you for.   260
When° we have matched our rackets to these balls,
We will in France, by God's grace, play a set
Shall strike his father's crown into the hazard.°
Tell him he hath made a match with such a wran-
    gler°
That all the courts of France will be disturbed   265
With chaces.° And we understand him well,
How he comes o'er us with° our wilder days,
Not measuring what use we made of them.
We never valued this poor seat of England,
And therefore, living hence, did give ourself   270
To barbarous license — as 'tis ever common
That men are merriest when they are from home.
But tell the Dauphin I will keep my state,°
Be like a king and show my sail of greatness,°
When I do rouse me in my throne of France.   275
For that I have laid by my majesty,
And plodded like a man for working days.
But I will rise there with so full a glory
That I will dazzle all the eyes of France —
Yea, strike the Dauphin blind to look on us.   280
And tell the pleasant Prince this mock of his
Hath turned his balls to gunstones,° and his soul
Shall stand sore chargèd for the wasteful vengeance
That shall fly with them. For many a thousand wid-
    ows   284
Shall this his mock mock out of their dear husbands,
Mock mothers from their sons, mock castles down;
And some are yet ungotten° and unborn
That shall have cause to curse the Dauphin's scorn.
But this lies all within the will of God,
To Whom I do appeal, and in Whose name   290
Tell you the Dauphin I am coming on,
To venge me° as I may and to put forth
My rightful hand in a well-hallowed cause.
So get you hence in peace, and tell the Dauphin
His jest will savor but of shallow wit   295
When thousands weep more than did laugh at it.
Convey them with safe conduct. Fare you well.
                        [*Exeunt* AMBASSADORS.]

258. Tennis balls: made of leather stuffed with hair.
261–66. When . . . chaces: The King replies to the Ambassador
in a series of elaborate metaphors taken from tennis, which in
Shakespeare's time was played in a court surrounded on three
sides by walls. The game was a cross between the modern squash
rackets and lawn tennis, as both wall and floor were used.
263. hazard: a hole in the wall. If the ball is sent into the
hazard, the opponent cannot return it, and so loses his point.
264. wrangler: opponent.   266. chaces: second bounces, a missed
return.   267. comes . . . with: reminds us of.   273. state:
dignity.   274. show . . . greatness: will show full sail.   282. gunstones: cannon balls, originally made of stone.   287. ungotten:
unbegotten.   292. venge me: take my revenge.

    EXE. This was a merry message.
    K. HEN. We hope to make the sender blush at it.
Therefore, my lords, omit no happy° hour   300
That may give furtherance to our expedition.
For we have now no thought in us but France,
Save those to God, that run before our business.
Therefore let our proportions° for these wars
Be soon collected, and all things thought upon   305
That may with reasonable swiftness add
More feathers to our wings. For, God before,°
We'll chide this Dauphin at his father's door.
Therefore let every man now task his thought,°
That this fair action may on foot be brought.   310
                      [*Exeunt. Flourish.*]

Act II

PROLOGUE

[*Enter* CHORUS.]
    CHOR. Now all the youth of England are on fire,
And silken dalliance° in the wardrobe lies.
Now thrive the armorers, and honor's thought°
Reigns solely in the breast of every man.
They sell the pasture now to buy the horse,   5
Following the mirror° of all Christian kings
With wingèd heels, as English Mercuries.°
For now sits Expectation in the air,
And hides a sword from hilts unto the point
With crowns imperial, crowns and coronets,   10
Promised to Harry and his followers.
The French, advised by good intelligence
Of this most dreadful preparation,
Shake in their fear and with pale° policy°
Seek to divert the English purposes.   15
O England! Model to thy inward greatness,
Like little body with a mighty heart,
What mightst thou do that honor would thee do
Were all thy children kind° and natural!
But see thy fault! France hath in thee found out   20
A nest of hollow bosoms, which he fills
With treacherous crowns. And three corrupted men,
One, Richard Earl of Cambridge, and the second,
Henry Lord Scroop of Masham, and the third,
Sir Thomas Grey, knight, of Northumberland,   25
Have, for the gilt of France — oh, guilt° indeed! —

300. happy: favorable.   304. proportions: forces.   307. God before: before God.   309. task . . . thought: take careful thought.
    Act II. Prologue: 2. silken dalliance: silk clothes suitable for
flirtations.   3. honor's thought: thoughts of honor to be won.
6. mirror: perfect pattern.   7. winged . . . Mercuries: Mercury,
the messenger of the gods, wore winged sandals.   14. pale:
frightened. policy: cunning.   19. kind: showing natural love.
26. gilt . . . guilt: The pun is common in Shakespeare.

Confirmed° conspiracy with fearful France.
And by their hands this grace of kings must die,
If Hell and treason hold their promises,
Ere he take ship for France, and in Southampton.
Linger your patience on, and we'll digest   31
The abuse of distance, force a play.°
The sum is paid, the traitors are agreed,
The King is set from London, and the scene
Is now transported, gentles, to Southampton.   35
There is the playhouse now, there must you sit.
And thence to France shall we convey you safe,
And bring you back, charming the narrow seas
To give you gentle pass. For, if we may,
We'll not offend one stomach° with our play.   40
But till the King come forth, and not till then,
Unto Southampton do we shift our scene.   [*Exit.*]

SCENE I. *London. A street.*

[*Enter* CORPORAL NYM *and* LIEUTENANT BARDOLPH.]

BARD. Well met, Corporal Nym.°
NYM. Good morrow, Lieutenant Bardolph.°
BARD. What, are Ancient° Pistol and you friends yet?   4
NYM. For my part, I care not. I say little, but when time shall serve, there shall be smiles — but that shall be as it may. I dare not fight, but I will wink° and hold out mine iron. It is a simple one, but what though? It will toast cheese, and it will endure cold as another man's sword will. And there's an end.   11
BARD. I will bestow a breakfast to make you friends, and we'll be all three sworn brothers° to France. Let it be so, good Corporal Nym.
NYM. Faith, I will live so long as I may, that's the certain of it. And when I cannot live any longer, I will do as I may. That is my rest,° that is the rendezvous° of it.
BARD. It is certain, Corporal, that he is married to Nell Quickly. And certainly she did you wrong, for you were trothplight° to her.   21
NYM. I cannot tell. Things must be as they may. Men may sleep, and they may have their throats about them at that time, and some say knives have edges. It must be as it may. Though patience be a tired mare, yet she will plod. There must be conclusions. Well, I cannot tell.   27

[*Enter* PISTOL *and* HOSTESS.]

BARD. Here comes Ancient Pistol and his wife. Good Corporal, be patient here. How now, mine host Pistol!
PIST. Base tike,° call'st thou me host?° Now, by this hand, I swear I scorn the term, Nor shall my Nell keep lodgers.   33
HOST. No, by my troth, not long, for we cannot lodge and board a dozen or fourteen gentlewomen that live honestly by the prick of their needles but it will be thought we keep a bawdy house straight. [NYM *and* PISTOL *draw.*] Oh, welladay. Lady,° if he be not drawn now! We shall see willful adultery and murder committed.   40
BARD. Good Lieutenant! Good Corporal! Offer nothing here.
NYM. Pish!
PIST. Pish for thee, Iceland dog! Thou prick-eared° cur of Iceland!°
HOST. Good Corporal Nym, show thy valor, and put up your sword.   46
NYM. Will you shog off?° I would have you solus.°
PIST. "Solus," egregious dog? O viper vile! The "solus" in thy most mervailous° face,   50
The "solus" in thy teeth, and in thy throat, And in thy hateful lungs — yea, in thy maw,° perdy,°
And, which is worse, within thy nasty mouth! I do retort the "solus" in thy bowels, For I can take,° and Pistol's cock° is up,   55
And flashing fire will follow.
NYM. I am not Barbason,° you cannot conjure me. I have a humor° to knock you indifferently well. If you grow foul with me, Pistol, I will scour you with my rapier, as I may, in fair terms. If you would walk off, I would prick your guts a little, in good terms, as I may. And that's the humor of it.   63
PIST. O braggart vile, and damnèd furious wight!° The grave doth gape, and doting death is near, Therefore exhale.
BARD. Hear me, hear me what I say. He that strikes the first stroke, I'll run him up to the hilts, as I am a soldier.   [*Draws.*]

27. Confirmed: agreed to.   31–32. digest . . . play: i.e., we shall accept the difficulty of presenting different places on one stage, and by sheer imagination create our play. Some editors emend "we'll" to "well."   40. one stomach: anyone's critical taste.
Sc. i: 1. Corporal Nym: This worthy is a newcomer to the gang attached to Falstaff, who have already appeared in the two parts of *Hen IV*. His name means "steal." See *Hen V* Intro. p. 732a.   2. Lieutenant Bardolph: Bardolph has been promoted; he was only a corporal in *II Hen IV*.   3. Ancient: Ensign, Second Lieutenant.   8. wink: close an eye.   13. sworn brothers: Knights bent on heroic adventure sometimes swore brotherhood to each other, that they would share ill and good alike.   17. rest: last throw. See *R & J*, V.iii.110,n.   18. rendezvous: meeting place, perhaps "last resort," but Nym uses words with meanings peculiar to himself.   21. trothplight: See Gen. Intro. p. 20a.

31. tike: cur. host: tavernkeeper. By marrying Mistress Quickly, Pistol takes over her business, but as a soldier he scorns to be considered a tradesman.   38. Lady: by Our Lady; i.e., the Virgin.   44. prick-eared: with straight erect ears. cur of Iceland: Iceland dogs were rough-haired and quarrelsome.   47. shog off: move off. A modern Nym would say "scram."   48. solus: alone.   50. mervailous: marvelous.   52. maw: stomach. perdy: by God.   55. take: catch fire, be offended. cock: see Pl. 22g.   57. Barbason: the name of a fiend, invented by Nym.   58. humor: See App. 3.   64. wight: man, a poetical word.   66. exhale: draw your last breath.

PIST. An oath of mickle° might, and fury shall
    abate.   70
Give me thy fist, thy forefoot to me give.
Thy spirits are most tall.°
    NYM. I will cut thy throat, one time or other, in
fair terms. That is the humor of it.
    PIST. "Couple a gorge!"°   75
That is the word. I thee defy again.
O hound of Crete, think'st thou my spouse to get?
No, to the spital° go,
And from the powdering tub° of infamy
Fetch forth the lazar kite of Cressid's kind,°   80
Doll Tearsheet° she by name, and her espouse.
I have, and I will hold, the quondam° Quickly
For the only she, and — *pauca,*° there's enough.
Go to.   84
                      [*Enter the* BOY.]
    BOY. Mine host Pistol, you must come to my mas-
ter, and you, Hostess. He is very sick, and would
to bed. Good Bardolph, put thy face between his
sheets and do the office of a warming pan.° Faith,
he's very ill.
    BARD. Away, you rogue!   90
    HOST. By my troth, he'll yield the crow a pud-
ding° one of these days. The King has killed his
heart.° Good Husband, come home presently.°
                [*Exeunt* HOSTESS *and* BOY.]
    BARD. Come, shall I make you two friends? We
must to France together. Why the devil should we
keep knives to cut one another's throats?   96
    PIST. Let floods o'erswell, and fiends for food
    howl on!
    NYM. You'll pay me the eight shillings I won of
you at betting?
    PIST. Base is the slave that pays.   100
    NYM. That now I will have. That's the humor of it.
    PIST. As manhood shall compound.° Push home.
                       [*They draw.*]
    BARD. By this sword, he that makes the first thrust,
I'll kill him — by this sword, I will.   105
    PIST. Sword is an oath, and oaths must have their
course.
    BARD. Corporal Nym, an° thou wilt be friends, be
friends. An thou wilt not, why, then enemies with
me too. Prithee, put up.
    NYM. I shall have my eight shillings I won of you
at betting?   111

PIST. A noble° shalt thou have, and present pay,
And liquor likewise will I give to thee,
And friendship shall combine, and brotherhood.
I'll live by Nym, and Nym shall live by me.   115
Is not this just? For I shall sutler° be
Unto the camp, and profits will accrue.
Give me thy hand.
    NYM. I shall have my noble?
    PIST. In cash most justly paid.   120
    NYM. Well, then, that's the humor of 't.
             [*Re-enter* HOSTESS.]
    HOST. As ever you came of women, come in
quickly to Sir John. Ah, poor heart! He is so shaked
of a burning quotidian tertian° that it is most lamentable to behold. Sweet men, come to him.   126
    NYM. The King hath run bad humors on the
knight. That's the even of it.
    PIST. Nym, thou hast spoke the right,
His heart is fracted° and corroborate.°   130
    NYM. The King is a good King. But it must be as
it may, he passes some humors and careers.°
    PIST. Let us condole the knight, for, lambkins, we
will live.

SCENE II. *Southampton. A council chamber.*

[*Enter* EXETER, BEDFORD, *and* WESTMORELAND.]
    BED. 'Fore God, His Grace is bold, to trust these
    traitors.
    EXE. They shall be apprehended by and by.
    WEST. How smooth and even they do bear them-
    selves!
As if allegiance in their bosoms sat,
Crownèd with faith and constant loyalty.   5
    BED. The King hath note of all that they intend,
By interception which they dream not of.
    EXE. Nay, but the man that was his bedfellow,
Whom he hath dulled and cloyed° with gracious
    favors,
That he should, for a foreign purse, so sell   10
His sovereign's life to death and treachery.
    [*Trumpets sound. Enter* KING HENRY, SCROOP,
      CAMBRIDGE, GREY, *and* ATTENDANTS.]
    K. HEN. Now sits the wind fair, and we will
    aboard.
My Lord of Cambridge, and my kind Lord of Ma-
    sham,
And you, my gentle knight, give me your thoughts.

---

70. mickle: mighty.   72. tall: valiant.   75. Couple a gorge: Elizabethan soldiers' French for "slit a throat."   78. spital: hospital.   79. powdering tub: tub used for the cure of venereal disease by sweating.   80. lazar . . . kind: Cressida, the pattern of loose woman, ended her days in the hospital for venereal disease. lazar: beggar. kite: bird of prey.   81. Doll Tearsheet: See *II Hen IV*.   82. quondam: former. She is now Mistress Pistol. 83. pauca: few words.   87–88. face . . . pan: for Bardolph's face see *I Hen IV*, III.iii. 26–55.   91–92. yield . . . pudding: i.e., be hanged and devoured by the crows. The Hostess is referring to the boy.   92–93. his heart: i.e., Falstaff's.   93. presently: immediately.   103. compound: come to terms.   107. an: if.

112. noble: 6s 8d — i.e., a reduction for cash payment. 116. sutler: canteen man.   125. quotidian tertian: The Hostess is mixed in her medical terms; a *quotidian* is a fever which recurs daily, a *tertian* recurs every third day.   130. fracted: cracked. corroborate: the kind of high-sounding word which appeals to Pistol, who apparently thinks that it means "split." 132. careers: lit., a short gallop at full speed, so headstrong whim.   Sc. ii: 9. dulled . . . cloyed: made tired and overfull.

Think you not that the powers we bear with us   15
Will cut their passage through the force of France,
Doing the execution and the act
For which we have in head° assembled them?
   SCROOP. No doubt, my liege, if each man do his
     best.
   K. HEN. I doubt not that, since we are well per-
     suaded   20
We carry not a heart with us from hence
That grows not in a fair consent with ours,
Nor leave not one behind that doth not wish
Success and conquest to attend on us.   24
   CAM. Never was monarch better feared and loved
Than is your Majesty. There's not, I think, a subject
That sits in heartgrief and uneasiness
Under the sweet shade of your government.
   GREY. True. Those that were your father's enemies
Have steeped their galls° in honey, and do serve you
With hearts create° of duty and of zeal.   31
   K. HEN. We therefore have great cause of thank-
     fulness,
And shall forget the office° of our hand
Sooner than quittance° of desert and merit
According to the weight and worthiness.   35
   SCROOP. So service shall with steelèd sinews toil,
And labor shall refresh itself with hope,
To do your Grace incessant services.
   K. HEN. We judge no less. Uncle of Exeter,
Enlarge° the man committed yesterday   40
That railed against our person. We consider
It was excess of wine that set him on,
And on his more advice° we pardon him.
   SCROOP. That's mercy, but too much security.°
Let him be punished, Sovereign, lest example   45
Breed, by his sufferance,° more of such a kind.
   K. HEN. Oh, let us yet be merciful.
   CAM. So may your Highness, and yet punish too.
   GREY. Sir,
You show great mercy if you give him life,   50
After the taste of much correction.
   K. HEN. Alas, your too much love and care of me
Are heavy orisons° 'gainst this poor wretch!
If little faults, proceeding on distemper,°   54
Shall not be winked at, how shall we stretch our eye
When capital crimes, chewed, swallowed, and di-
     gested,
Appear before us? We'll yet enlarge that man,
Though Cambridge, Scroop, and Grey, in their dear
     care
And tender preservation of our person,
Would have him punished. And now to our French
     causes.   60

Who are the late commissioners?
   CAM. I one, my lord.
Your Highness bade me ask for it° today.
   SCROOP. So did you me, my liege.
   GREY. And I, my royal sovereign.   65
   K. HEN. Then, Richard Earl of Cambridge, there
     is yours,
There yours, Lord Scroop of Masham, and, sir
     knight,
Grey of Northumberland, this same is yours.
Read them, and know I know your worthiness.
My Lord of Westmoreland, and Uncle Exeter,   70
We will aboard tonight. Why, how now, gentlemen!
What see you in those papers that you lose
So much complexion? Look ye how they change!
Their cheeks are paper. Why, what read you there
That hath so cowarded° and chased your blood   75
Out of appearance?
   CAM.   I do confess my fault,
And do submit me to your Highness' mercy.
   GREY & SCROOP. To which we all appeal.
   K. HEN. The mercy that was quick° in us but late,
By your own counsel is suppressed and killed.   80
You must not dare, for shame, to talk of mercy,
For your own reasons° turn into your bosoms,
As dogs upon their masters, worrying you.
See you, my Princes and my noble peers,
These English monsters! My Lord of Cambridge
     here,   85
You know how apt our love was to accord
To furnish him with all appertinents°
Belonging to his honor. And this man
Hath, for a few light crowns, lightly conspired,
And sworn unto the practices° of France,   90
To kill us here in Hampton. To the which
This knight, no less for bounty bound to us
Than Cambridge is, hath likewise sworn. But, oh,
What shall I say to thee, Lord Scroop? Thou cruel,
Ingrateful, savage, and inhuman creature!   95
Thou that didst bear the key of all my counsels,
That knew'st the very bottom of my soul,
That almost mightst have coined me into gold
Wouldst thou have practiced on me for thy use,
May it be possible that foreign hire   100
Could out of thee extract one spark of evil
That might annoy° my finger? 'Tis so strange
That, though the truth of it stands off as gross°
As black and white, my eye will scarcely see it.
Treason° and murder ever kept together,   105
As two yoke devils sworn to either's purpose,
Working so grossly in a natural cause

---

18. in head: as an armed force.   30. galls: bitterness.   31. create:
made of.   33. office: use.   34. quittance: payment.   40. Enlarge:
set free.   43. on . . . advice: since he has a chance to reflect.
44. security: carelessness, lack of precaution.   46. his sufferance: by making allowance for him.   53. orisons: prayers.
54. distemper: drunkenness.

63. it: i.e., the document appointing him commissioner.   75. cow-
arded: made a coward.   79. quick: living.   82. reasons: arguments.   87. appertinents: appurtenances, things pertaining to.
90. practices: plots.   102. annoy: hurt.   103. gross: plain, obvious.
105–08. Treason . . . them: usually treason and murder work together and have some cause or excuse for their action which seems
so natural that no one is surprised.

That admiration° did not hoop° at them.
But thou, 'gainst all proportion, didst bring in
Wonder to wait on treason and on murder.   110
And whatsoever cunning fiend it was
That wrought upon thee so preposterously
Hath got the voice° in Hell for excellence.
All other devils that suggest by treasons
Do botch and bungle up damnation   115
With patches, colors, and with forms being fetched
From glistering° semblances of piety.°
But he that tempered° thee bade thee stand up,°
Gave thee no instance° why thou shouldst do treason,
Unless to dub° thee with the name of traitor.   120
If that same demon that hath gulled° thee thus
Should with his lion gait° walk the whole world,
He might return to vasty Tartar° back,
And tell the legions "I can never win
A soul so easy as that Englishman's."   125
Oh, how hast thou with jealousy infected
The sweetness of affiance!° Show men dutiful?
Why, so didst thou. Seem they grave and learned?
Why, so didst thou. Come they of noble family?
Why, so didst thou. Seem they religious?   130
Why, so didst thou. Or are they spare in diet,
Free from gross passion or of mirth or anger,
Constant in spirit, not swerving with the blood,°
Garnished and decked in modest complement,°
Not working with the eye without the ear,   135
And but in purged° judgment trusting neither?
Such and so finely bolted° didst thou seem.
And thus thy fall hath left a kind of blot,
To mark the full-fraught° man and best indued°
With some suspicion. I will weep for thee,   140
For this revolt of thine, methinks, is like
Another fall of man. Their faults are open.
Arrest them to the answer of the law,
And God acquit them of their practices!
EXE.   I arrest thee of high treason, by the name of
Richard Earl of Cambridge.   146
I arrest thee of high treason, by the name of Henry
Lord Scroop of Masham.
I arrest thee of high treason, by the name of Thomas
Grey, knight, of Northumberland.   150
SCROOP.   Our purposes God justly hath discovered,
And I repent my fault more than my death,
Which I beseech your Highness to forgive,
Although my body pay the price of it.

CAM.   For me, the gold of France did not seduce,
Although I did admit it as a motive   156
The sooner to effect what I intended.
But God be thankèd for prevention,
Which I in sufferance heartily will rejoice,
Beseeching God and you to pardon me.   160
GREY.   Never did faithful subject more rejoice
At the discovery of most dangerous treason
Than I do at this hour joy o'er myself,
Prevented from a damnèd enterprise.
My fault, but not my body, pardon, Sovereign. 165
K. HEN.   God quit° you in his mercy! Hear your sentence.
You have conspired against our royal person,
Joined with an enemy proclaimed, and from his coffers
Received the golden earnest° of our death.
Wherein you would have sold your King to slaughter,   170
His Princes and his peers to servitude,
His subjects to oppression and contempt,
And his whole kingdom into desolation.
Touching our person seek we no revenge,
But we our kingdom's safety must so tender,°   175
Whose ruin you have sought, that to her laws
We do deliver you. Get you therefore hence,
Poor miserable wretches, to your death.
The taste whereof, God of his mercy give
You patience to endure, and true repentance   180
Of all your dear offenses! Bear them hence.
[*Exeunt* CAMBRIDGE, SCROOP, *and* GREY, *guarded.*]
Now, lords, for France, the enterprise whereof
Shall be to you, as us, like glorious.
We doubt not of a fair° and lucky war,
Since God so graciously hath brought to light 185
This dangerous treason lurking in our way
To hinder our beginnings. We doubt not now
But every rub° is smoothèd on our way.
Then forth, dear countrymen. Let us deliver
Our puissance into the hand of God,   190
Putting it straight in expedition.°
Cheerly to sea. The signs° of war advance.
No King of England if not King of France.
[*Exeunt.*]

SCENE III. *London. Before a tavern.*

[*Enter* PISTOL, HOSTESS, NYM, BARDOLPH, *and* BOY.]
HOST.   Prithee, honeysweet Husband, let me bring
thee to Staines.°

---

108. **admiration:** wonder. **hoop:** whoop, cry out.   113. **voice:** vote.   116–17. **forms . . . piety:** outward appearances of a religious motive.   117. **glistering:** falsely glittering.   118. **tempered:** molded. **stand up:** i.e., as a finished work of art.   119. **instance:** reason.   120. **dub:** lit., confer the title of knight on.   121. **gulled:** cheated.   122. **lion gait:** walking about like a lion.   123. **Tartar:** Tartarus, Hell.   127. **affiance:** trust, loyalty.   133. **blood:** passion, lust.   134. **complement:** the outward signs of a noble man.   136. **purged:** free from partiality.   137. **bolted:** sifted, like fine flour sifted from the bran.   139. **full-fraught:** lit., fully laden. **indued:** endowed.

166. **quit:** acquit, forgive.   169. **earnest:** money given on account of services to be rendered.   175. **tender:** care for.   184. **fair:** fortunate.   188. **rub:** impediment. See App. 13.   191. **expedition:** motion.   192. **signs:** standards.
Sc. iii: 2. **Staines:** a town on the Thames, on the road to Southampton.

PIST. No, for my manly heart doth yearn.°
Bardolph, be blithe. Nym, rouse thy vaunting veins.
Boy, bristle thy courage up, for Falstaff he is dead,
And we must yearn therefore.   6

BARD. Would I were with him, wheresome'er he
is, either in Heaven or in Hell!

HOST. Nay, sure he's not in Hell. He's in Arthur's
bosom,° if ever man went to Arthur's bosom. A'°
made a finer end and went away an it had been any
christom child.° A' parted even just between twelve
and one, even at the turning o' the tide. For after I
saw him fumble with the sheets, and play with flowers, and smile upon his fingers' ends, I knew   16
there was but one way. For his nose was as sharp as
a pen, and a' babbled° of green fields. " How now,
Sir John! " quoth I. " What, man! Be o' good cheer."
So a' cried out " God, God, God! " three or four   20
times. Now I, to comfort him, bid him a' should not
think of God, I hoped there was no need to trouble
himself with any such thoughts yet. So a' bade me
lay more clothes on his feet. I put my hand into the
bed and felt them, and they were as cold as any   25
stone. Then I felt to his knees, and they were as cold
as any stone, and so upward and upward, and all
was as cold as any stone.

NYM. They say he cried out of sack.°

HOST. Aye, that a' did.   30

BARD. And of women.

HOST. Nay, that a' did not.

BOY. Yes, that a' did, and said they were devils
incarnate.

HOST. A' could never abide carnation.° 'Twas a
color he never liked.   36

BOY. A' said once, the Devil would have him
about women.

HOST. A' did in some sort, indeed, handle women,
but then he was rheumatic, and talked of the whore
of Babylon.   41

BOY. Do you not remember, a' saw a flea stick
upon Bardolph's nose, and a' said it was a black soul
burning in hell-fire?   44

BARD. Well, the fuel is gone that maintained that
fire. That's all the riches I got in his service.

NYM. Shall we shog? The King will be gone from
Southampton.

PIST. Come, let's away. My love, give me thy lips.
Look to my chattels and my movables.   50

Let senses rule, the word is " Pitch and Pay." °
Trust none,
For oaths are straws, men's faiths are wafer cakes,
And holdfast is the only dog, my duck.
Therefore, Caveto° be thy counselor.   55
Go, clear thy crystals.° Yokefellows in arms,
Let us to France, like horseleeches, my boys,
To suck, to suck, the very blood to suck!

BOY. And that's but unwholesome food, they say.

PIST. Touch her soft mouth, and march.   61

BARD. Farewell, Hostess.   [*Kissing her.*]

NYM. I cannot kiss. That is the humor of it. But
adieu.

PIST. Let housewifery° appear. Keep close, I thee
command.   65

HOST. Farewell, adieu.   [*Exeunt.*]

SCENE IV. *France. The* KING'S *palace.*

[*Flourish.° Enter the* FRENCH KING, *the* DAUPHIN,
DUKES OF BERRI *and* BRETAGNE, *the* CONSTABLE,°
and OTHERS.]

FR. KING. Thus comes the English with full power
upon us,
And more than carefully it us concerns
To answer royally in our defenses.
Therefore the Dukes of Berri and of Bretagne,
Of Brabant and of Orleans, shall make forth,   5
And you, Prince Dauphin, with all swift dispatch,
To line and new-repair our towns of war
With men of courage and with means defendant.°
For England his approaches makes as fierce
As waters to the sucking of a gulf.°   10
It fits us then to be as provident
As fear may teach us out of late examples°
Left by the fatal and neglected English
Upon our fields.

DAU.   My most redoubted father,
It is most meet we arm us 'gainst the foe,   15
For peace itself should not so dull a kingdom,
Though war nor no known quarrel were in question,
But that defenses, musters, preparations,
Should be maintained, assembled, and collected
As were a war in expectation.   20
Therefore I say 'tis meet we all go forth
To view the sick and feeble parts of France.
And let us do it with no show of fear —
No, with no more than if we heard that England
Were busied with a Whitsun morris dance.°   25

---

3. yearn: grieve.   9–10. Arthur's bosom: the Hostess's version
of "Abraham's bosom"; i.e., Heaven.   10. A': he.   13. christom
child: a child in its christening robe, so a perfect innocent.
18. babbled: The original folio reading is "and a Table of greene
fields." The emendation "babbled" was suggested by Theobald in
1726 and is generally regarded as one of the most brilliant of all
corrections. The likelier reading is "talk" (spelt "talke") — a
misprint for "table" (and vice versa), which I have thrice met in
my own proofs. The quarto reads "when I saw him fumble with
the sheets and talk of floures."   29. sack: Falstaff's favorite
drink. See *II Hen IV*, IV.iii.103–35.   35. carnation: flesh-
color.

51. Pitch . . . Pay: cash down, no credit.   55. Caveto: caution.
56. crystals: eyes.   65. housewifery: good management.
Sc. iv: s.d., Flourish: trumpet fanfare.   Constable: a principal
officer in the royal household.   8. means defendant: means of
defense.   10. gulf: whirlpool.   12. late examples: See later ll.
53–64.   25. Whitsun . . . dance: i.e., innocent gaiety. Folk dancing in the open was a usual pastime in the Whitsun holidays,
which fall in early summer. See App. 24.

For, my good liege, she is so idly kinged,°
Her scepter so fantastically borne
By a vain, giddy, shallow, humorous° youth,
That fear attends her not.
CON.   Oh, peace, Prince Dauphin!
You are too much mistaken in this King.   30
Question your Grace the late ambassadors,
With what great state he heard their embassy,
How well supplied with noble councilors,
How modest in exception,° and withal
How terrible in constant resolution,   35
And you shall find his vanities forespent°
Were but the outside of the Roman Brutus,°
Covering discretion with a coat of folly —
As gardeners do with ordure° hide those roots
That shall first spring and be most delicate.   40
DAU. Well, 'tis not so, my Lord High Constable,
But though we think it so, it is no matter.
In cases of defense 'tis best to weigh
The enemy more mighty than he seems.
So the proportions of defense are filled,°   45
Which of a weak and niggardly projection°
Doth, like a miser, spoil his coat with scanting
A little cloth.
FR. KING. Think we King Harry strong,
And, Princes, look you strongly arm to meet him.
The kindred of him hath been fleshed° upon us,   50
And he is bred out of that bloody strain
That haunted us in our familiar paths.
Witness our too much memorable shame
When Crécy battle fatally was struck,
And all our Princes captived by the hand   55
Of that black name, Edward, Black Prince of Wales,
Whiles that his mountain sire, on mountain stand-
ing,
Up in the air, crowned with the golden sun,
Saw his heroical seed, and smiled to see him,
Mangle the work of nature and deface   60
The patterns that by God and by French fathers
Had twenty years been made. This is a stem
Of that victorious stock, and let us fear
The native mightiness and fate of him.
[*Enter a* MESSENGER.]
MESS. Ambassadors from Harry King of England
Do crave admittance to your Majesty.   66
FR. KING. We'll give them present° audience. Go,
and bring them.
[*Exeunt* MESSENGER *and certain* LORDS.]
You see this chase is hotly followed, friends.
DAU. Turn head, and stop pursuit, for coward
dogs

Most spend their mouths° when what they seem to
threaten   70
Runs far before them. Good my sovereign,
Take up the English short, and let them know
Of what a monarchy you are the head.
Self-love, my liege, is not so vile a sin
As self-neglecting.
[*Re-enter* LORDS, *with* EXETER *and train.*]
FR. KING.   From our brother England?   75
EXE. From him, and thus he greets your Majesty.
He wills you, in the name of God Almighty,
That you divest yourself, and lay apart
The borrowed glories that by gift of Heaven,
By law of nature and of nations, 'long°   80
To him and to his heirs; namely, the crown
And all wide-stretchèd honors that pertain
By custom and the ordinance of times
Unto the crown of France. That you may know
'Tis no siníster° nor no awkward claim,   85
Picked from the wormholes of long-vanished days,
Nor from the dust of old oblivion raked,
He sends you this most memorable line,°
In every branch truly demonstrative,
Willing you overlook this pedigree.   90
And when you find him evenly° derived
From his most famed of famous ancestors,
Edward the Third, he bids you then resign
Your crown and kingdom, indirectly° held
From him the native and true challenger.°   95
FR. KING. Or else what follows?
EXE. Bloody constraint,° for if you hide the crown
Even in your hearts, there will he rake for it.
Therefore in fierce tempest is he coming,
In thunder and in earthquake, like a Jove,   100
That, if requiring° fail, he will compel.
And bids you, in the bowels° of the Lord,
Deliver up the crown, and to take mercy
On the poor souls for whom this hungry war
Opens his vasty° jaws; and on your head   105
Turning the widows' tears, the orphans' cries,
The dead men's blood, the pining maidens' groans
For husbands, fathers, and betrothèd lovers
That shall be swallowed in this controversy.
This is his claim, his threatening, and my message —
Unless the Dauphin be in presence here,   111
To whom expressly I bring greeting too.
FR. KING. For us, we will consider of this further.
Tomorrow shall you bear our full intent
Back to our brother England.
DAU.   For the Dauphin,   115
I stand here for him. What to him from England?
EXE. Scorn and defiance, slight regard, contempt,
And anything that may not misbecome

26. idly kinged: has such a frivolous king.   28. humorous: whimsical.   34. exception: disagreement.   36. forespent: former.   37. Roman Brutus: Lucius Junius Brutus (ancestor of Marcus Brutus), who drove out Tarquin, pretended to be a simpleton.   39. ordure: manure.   45. So . . . filled: so long as the proper measures of defense are taken.   46. of . . . projection: if too meanly estimated.   50. fleshed: excited by the taste of first blood.   67. present: immediate.

70. spend . . . mouths: bark.   80. 'long: belong.   85. sinister: left-hand, irregular.   88. line: pedigree.   91. evenly: directly.   94. indirectly: not in the direct line of descent.   95. challenger: claimant.   97. constraint: force.   101. requiring: asking.   102. bowels: i.e., mercy.   105. vasty: vast.

The mighty sender, doth he prize you at.
Thus says my King. An if your father's Highness
Do not, in grant of all demands at large,   121
Sweeten the bitter mock you sent His Majesty,
He'll call you to so hot an answer of it
That caves and womby vaultages° of France
Shall chide your trespass, and return your mock
In second accent° of his ordnance.°   126

DAU. Say if my father render fair return,
It is against my will, for I desire
Nothing but odds° with England. To that end,
As matching to his youth and vanity,   130
I did present him with the Paris balls.°

EXE. He'll make your Paris Louvre° shake for it,
Were it the mistress Court of mighty Europe.
And be assured you'll find a difference,
As we his subjects have in wonder found,   135
Between the promise of his greener° days
And these he masters now. Now he weighs time°
Even to the utmost grain. That you shall read
In your own losses, if he stay in France.

FR. KING. Tomorrow shall you know our mind at
    full.   140

EXE. Dispatch us with all speed, lest that our King
Come here himself to question our delay,
For he is footed in this land already.

FR. KING. You shall be soon dispatched with fair
    conditions.
A night is but small breath and little pause   145
To answer matters of this consequence.

         [*Flourish. Exeunt.*]

Act III

PROLOGUE

[*Enter* CHORUS.]

CHOR. Thus with imagined wing° our swift scene
    flies
In motion of no less celerity
Than that of thought. Suppose that you have seen
The well-appointed King at Hampton pier
Embark his royalty, and his brave° fleet   5
With silken streamers the young Phoebus° fan-
    ning.
Play with your fancies, and in them behold
Upon the hempen tackle ship boys climbing.
Hear the shrill whistle which doth order give

To sounds confused. Behold the threaden° sails,   10
Borne with the invisible and creeping wind,
Draw the huge bottoms through the furrowed sea,
Breasting the lofty surge. Oh, do but think
You stand upon the rivage° and behold
A city on the inconstant billows dancing,   15
For so appears this fleet majestical,
Holding due course to Harfleur.° Follow, follow.
Grapple your minds to sternage° of this navy,
And leave your England, as dead midnight still,
Guarded with grandsires, babies, and old women,
Either past or not arrived to pith° and puissance.
For who is he whose chin is but enriched   22
With one appearing hair that will not follow
These culled° and choice-drawn° cavaliers to
    France?
Work, work your thoughts, and therein see a siege.
Behold the ordnance on their carriages,   26
With fatal mouths gaping on girded° Harfleur.
Suppose the Ambassador from the French comes
    back,
Tells Harry that the King doth offer him
Katharine his daughter, and with her, to dowry,   30
Some petty and unprofitable dukedoms.
The offer likes° not. And the nimble gunner
With linstock° now the devilish cannon touches,
         [*Alarum, and chambers go off.*°]
And down goes all before them. Still be kind,   34
And eke out° our performance with your mind.
         [*Exit.*]

SCENE I. *France. Before Harfleur.*

[*Alarum.*° *Enter* KING HENRY, EXETER, BEDFORD,
GLOUCESTER, *and* SOLDIERS, *with scaling ladders.*°]

K. HEN. Once more unto the breach, dear friends,
    once more,
Or close the wall up with our English dead.
In peace there's nothing so becomes a man
As modest stillness and humility.
But when the blast of war blows in our ears,   5
Then imitate the action of the tiger,
Stiffen the sinews, summon up the blood,
Disguise fair nature with hard-favored° rage.
Then lend the eye a terrible aspéct,
Let it pry through the portage° of the head   10
Like the brass cannon. Let the brow o'erwhelm it
As fearfully as doth a gallèd° rock

---

124. **vaultages:** hollow places.   126. **In . . . accent:** i.e., to the echo. **ordnance:** cannon.   129. **odds:** disagreement.   131. **Paris balls:** i.e., the tennis balls from Paris.   132. **Louvre:** the royal palace in Paris.   136. **greener:** rawer, younger.   137. **weighs time:** i.e., no longer wastes it.

    Act III. Prologue: 1. imagined wing: on the wing of imagination.   5. **brave:** splendid.   6. **Phoebus:** the sun.

10. **threaden:** linen.   14. **rivage:** shore.   17. **Harfleur:** opposite Le Havre at the mouth of the Seine.   18. **sternage:** the stern. 21. **pith:** strength.   24. **culled:** selected. **choice-drawn:** carefully chosen.   27. **girded:** surrounded.   32. **likes:** pleases.   33. **linstock:** the gunner's staff holding the match. See Pl. 12a. s.d., **chambers go off:** small cannon discharged. See Gen. Intro. p. 51b.   35. **eke out:** supplement.

    Sc. i: s.d., Alarum: trumpet call to arms. **scaling ladders:** See Pl. 12a.   8. **hard-favored:** grim-faced.   10. **portage:** porthole.   12. **galled:** worn by the sea.

O'erhang and jutty° his confounded° base,
Swilled with the wild and wasteful ocean.
Now set the teeth and stretch the nostril wide,   15
Hold hard the breath, and bend up every spirit
To his full height. On, on, you noblest English,
Whose blood is fet° from fathers of war proof!°
Fathers that, like so many Alexanders,
Have in these parts from morn till even fought,   20
And sheathed their swords for lack of argument.°
Dishonor not your mothers. Now attest
That those whom you called fathers did beget
   you.
Be copy now to men of grosser blood,
And teach them how to war. And you, good yeo-
   men,°   25
Whose limbs were made in England, show us here
The mettle of your pasture. Let us swear
That you are worth your breeding, which I doubt
   not,
For there is none of you so mean and base
That hath not noble luster in your eyes.   30
I see you stand like greyhounds in the slips,°
Straining upon the start. The game's afoot.
Follow your spirit, and upon this charge
Cry " God for Harry, England, and Saint George! "°
     [*Exeunt. Alarum, and chambers go off.*]

SCENE II. *The same.*

[*Enter* NYM, BARDOLPH, PISTOL, *and* BOY.]

BARD. On, on, on, on, on! To the breach, to the
breach!

NYM. Pray thee, Corporal, stay. The knocks are
too hot, and, for mine own part, I have not a case°
of lives. The humor of it is too hot, that is the very
plainsong° of it.   6

PIST. The plainsong is most just, for humors do
abound:
" Knocks go and come, God's vassals drop and die,
     And sword and shield,
       In bloody field,   10
     Doth win immortal fame."

BOY. Would I were in an alehouse in London! I
would give all my fame for a pot of ale and safety.

PIST. And I: 15
     " If wishes would prevail with me,
       My purpose should not fail with me,
         But thither would I hie."°

BOY. " As duly, but not as truly,
       As bird doth sing on bough."   20

[*Enter* FLUELLEN.]

FLU. Up to the breach, you dogs! Avaunt,° you
cullions!°   [*Driving them forward.*]

PIST. Be merciful, great Duke, to men of mold.°
Abate thy rage, abate thy manly rage,
Abate thy rage, great Duke!   25
Good bawcock,° bate thy rage. Use lenity, sweet
   chuck!°

NYM. These be good humors! Your Honor wins
bad humors.   [*Exeunt all but* BOY.]

BOY. As young as I am, I have observed these three
swashers.° I am boy to them all three. But all   30
they three, though they would serve me, could not be
man to me, for indeed three such antics° do not
amount to a man. For Bardolph, he is white-livered°
and red-faced, by the means whereof a' faces it out
but fights not. For Pistol, he hath a killing   35
tongue and a quiet sword, by the means whereof a'
breaks words and keeps whole weapons. For Nym,
he hath heard that men of few words are the best
men, and therefore he scorns to say his prayers lest
a' should be thought a coward. But his few bad   40
words are matched with as few good deeds, for a'
never broke any man's head but his own, and that
was against a post when he was drunk. They will
steal anything and call it purchase.° Bardolph stole
a lute case, bore it twelve leagues, and sold it for   45
three halfpence. Nym and Bardolph are sworn brothers in filching, and in Calais they stole a fire shovel.
I knew by that piece of service the men would carry
coals.° They would have me as familiar with men's
pockets as their gloves or their handkerchers.   50
Which makes much against my manhood, if I should
take from another's pocket to put into mine, for it is
plain pocketing-up° of wrongs. I must leave them,
and seek some better service. Their villainy goes   55
against my weak stomach, and therefore I must cast
it up.   [*Exit.*]

[*Re-enter* FLUELLEN, GOWER *following.*]

GOW. Captain Fluellen, you must come presently
to the mines.° The Duke of Gloucester would speak
with you.   60

FLU. To the mines! Tell you the Duke it is not so
good to come to the mines. For look you, the mines
is not according to the disciplines of the war.° The
concavities of it is not sufficient. For look you, th'
athversary, you may discuss unto the Duke, look
you, is digt himself four yard under the counter-
mines. By Cheshu, I think a' will plow° up all if
there is not better directions.   68

21. **Avaunt:** be off.   22. **cullions:** base fellows.   23. **mold:** earth;
i.e., mortal men.   26. **bawcock:** fine cock. **chuck:** chick.
30. **swashers:** swaggerers.   32. **antics:** clowns, fantastics.
33. **white-livered:** i.e., cowardly.   44. **purchase:** thieves' word
for booty.   48–49. **would . . . coals:** do dirty work.   54. **pocket-
ing-up:** with a pun on the idiomatic meaning of *putting up with.*
59. **mines:** i.e., dug under the enemy's walls.   63. **disciplines
. . . war:** military science.   67. **plow:** blow. The Welshman when
talking English has some difficulty with the letters *b* and *v.*

13. **jutty:** jut over. **confounded:** worn.   18. **fet:** fetched. **war-
proof:** proved in war.   21. **argument:** matter for dispute.
25. **yeomen:** men from the country, who formed the bulk of the
archers.   31. **slips:** collar, quickly released, by which greyhounds
are held.   34. **Saint George:** patron saint of England.
    Sc. ii: 4. **case:** set.   6. **plainsong:** simple tune.   18. **hie:**
hasten.

GOW. The Duke of Gloucester, to whom the order of the siege is given, is altogether directed by an Irishman, a very valiant gentleman, i' faith.

FLU. It is Captain Macmorris, is it not?

GOW. I think it be. 73

FLU. By Cheshu, he is an ass, as in the world. I will verify as much in his beard. He has no more directions in the true disciplines of the wars, look you, of the Roman disciplines, than is a puppy dog.

[*Enter* MACMORRIS *and* CAPTAIN JAMY.°]

GOW. Here a' comes, and the Scots captain, Captain Jamy, with him. 80

FLU. Captain Jamy is a marvelous falorous gentleman, that is certain, and of great expedition and knowledge in th' aunchient wars, upon my particular knowledge of his directions. By Cheshu, he will maintain his argument as well as any military man in the world, in the disciplines of the pristine° wars of the Romans. 87

JAMY. I say gud day, Captain Fluellen.

FLU. Godden° to your Worship, good Captain James.

GOW. How now, Captain Macmorris! Have you quit the mines? Have the pioners° given o'er? 92

MAC. By Chrish, la! Tish ill done. The work ish give over, the trumpet sound the retreat. By my hand, I swear, and my father's soul, the work ish ill done, it ish give over. I would have blowed up the town, so Chrish save me, la! in an hour. Oh, tish ill done, tish ill done, by my hand, tish ill done! 99

FLU. Captain Macmorris, I beseech you now will you vouchsafe me, look you, a few disputations with you, as partly touching or concerning the disciplines of the war, the Roman wars, in the way of argument, look you, and friendly communication — partly to satisfy my opinion, and partly for the satisfaction, look you, of my mind, as touching the direction of the military discipline. That is the point. 108

JAMY. It sall be vary gud, gud feith, gud Captains bath. And I sall quit° you with gud leve, as I may pick occasion. That sall I, marry.

MAC. It is no time to discourse, so Chrish save me. The day is hot, and the weather, and the wars, and the King, and the Dukes. It is no time to discourse. The town is beseeched,° and the trumpet call 115 us to the breach, and we talk and, be Chrish, do nothing. 'Tis shame for us all. So God sa' me, 'tis shame to stand still. It is shame, by my hand. And there is throats to be cut, and works to be done, and there ish nothing done, so Chrish sa' me, la! 121

JAMY. By the mess,° ere theise eyes of mine take

themselves to slomber, ay'll de gud service, or ay'll lig° i' the grund for it — aye, or go to death. And ay'll pay 't as valorously as I may, that sall I suerly do, that is the breff and the long. Marry, I wad full fain hear some question 'tween you tway.° 128

FLU. Captain Macmorris, I think, look you, under your correction, there is not many of your nation ——

MAC. Of my nation!° What ish my nation? Ish a villain, and a bastard, and a knave, and a rascal. What ish my nation? Who talks of my nation? 135

FLU. Look you, if you take the matter otherwise than is meant, Captain Macmorris, peradventure I shall think you do not use me with that affability as in discretion you ought to use me, look you, being as good a man as yourself, both in the disciplines of war and in the derivation of my birth and in other particularities. 142

MAC. I do not know you so good a man as myself. So Chrish save me, I will cut off your head.

GOW. Gentlemen both, you will mistake each other.

JAMY. A! That's a foul fault.

[*A parley° sounded.*]

GOW. The town sounds a parley. 149

FLU. Captain Macmorris, when there is more better opportunity to be required, look you, I will be so bold as to tell you I know the disciplines of war. And there is an end. [*Exeunt.*]

SCENE III. *The Same. Before the Gates.*

[*The* GOVERNOR *and some* CITIZENS *on the walls; the English forces below. Enter* KING HENRY *and his train.*]

K. HEN. How yet resolves the governor of the town?

This is the latest parle° we will admit,
Therefore to our best mercy give yourselves,
Or like to men proud of destruction
Defy us to our worst. For, as I am a soldier — 5
A name that in my thoughts becomes me best —
If I begin the battery once again,
I will not leave the half-achieved° Harfleur
Till in her ashes she lie buried.
The gates of mercy shall be all shut up, 10
And the fleshed° soldier, rough and hard of heart,
In liberty of bloody hand shall range°
With conscience wide as Hell, mowing like grass

78. s.d., Macmorris . . . Jamy: There is no trace in the quarto of this passage between the Welshman, the Irishman, and the Scot, each speaking with his native accent. 86. pristine: ancient. 89. Godden: good afternoon. 92. pioners: pioneers, one of whose tasks was to construct mines (i.e., tunnels). 110. quit: requite; i.e., return your favors. 115. beseeched: besieged. 122. mess: mass.

124. lig: lie. 128. tway: two. 133. Of my nation: Macmorris is spoiling for a fight, and ready to interpret any remark as an insult to Ireland. 148. s.d., parley: trumpet call, summoning to parley.
Sc. iii: 2. latest parle: last parley. 8. half-achieved: half-won. 11. fleshed: See II.iv.50. 12. In . . . range: shall wander in search of plunder without restraint. If a city refused to yield and was afterward taken, the victorious soldiers were given free leave to ravage and plunder.

Your fresh-fair virgins and your flowering infants.
What is it then to me if impious war,   15
Arrayed in flames like to the Prince of Fiends,
Do, with his smirched° complexion, all fell feats°
Enlinked to waste and desolation?
What is 't to me, when you yourselves are cause,
If your pure maidens fall into the hand   20
Of hot and forcing violation?
What rein can hold licentious wickedness
When down the hill he holds his fierce career?
We may as bootless° spend our vain command
Upon the enraged soldiers in their spoil   25
As send precepts to the leviathan°
To come ashore. Therefore, you men of Harfleur,
Take pity of your town and of your people
Whiles yet my soldiers are in my command,
Whiles yet the cool and temperate wind of grace   30
O'erblows the filthy and contagious clouds
Of heady° murder, spoil, and villainy.
If not, why, in a moment look to see
The blind and bloody soldier with foul hand
Defile the locks of your shrill-shrieking daughters,
Your fathers taken by the silver beards   36
And their most reverend heads dashed to the walls,
Your naked infants spitted upon pikes
Whiles the mad mothers with their howls confused
Do break the clouds, as did the wives of Jewry   40
At Herod's bloody-hunting slaughtermen.°
What say you? Will you yield, and this avoid,
Or, guilty in defense, be thus destroyed?
GOV. Our expectation° hath this day an end.
The Dauphin, whom of succors we entreated,   45
Returns us that his powers are yet not ready
To raise so great a siege. Therefore, great King,
We yield our town and lives to thy soft mercy.
Enter our gates, dispose of us and ours,
For we no longer are defensible.   50
K. HEN. Open your gates. Come, Uncle Exeter,
Go you and enter Harfleur. There remain,
And fortify it strongly 'gainst the French.
Use mercy to them all. For us, dear Uncle,
The winter coming on, and sickness growing   55
Upon our soldiers, we will retire to Calais.
Tonight in Harfleur will we be your guest,
Tomorrow for the march are we addressed.°
[*Flourish. The* KING *and his train enter the town.*]

SCENE IV.° *The* FRENCH KING's *palace.*

[*Enter* KATHARINE *and* ALICE.]
KATH. Alice, tu as été en Angleterre, et tu parles
bien le langage.

17. smirched: stained with smoke. fell feats: terrible deeds.
24. bootless: vainly. 26. leviathan: whale. 32. heady: violent.
41. slaughtermen: i.e., at the Massacre of the Innocents. See
Matthew 2: 16–18. 44. expectation: hope. 58. addressed: ready.
   Sc. iv: The printer of the folio made sad havoc of the French
in this scene, which has been put right by editors. About 1602–04

ALICE. Un peu, madame.
KATH. Je te prie, m'enseignez. Il faut que j'ap-
prenne à parler. Comment appelez-vous la main en
Anglais?   6
ALICE. La main? Elle est appelée de hand.
KATH. De hand. Et les doigts?
ALICE. Les doigts? Ma foi, j'oublie les doigts, mais
je me souviendrai. Les doigts? Je pense qu'ils sont
appelés de fingres — oui, de fingres.   11
KATH. La main, de hand, les doigts, de fingres. Je
pense que je suis le bon écolier. J'ai gagné deux mots
d'Anglais vîtement. Comment appelez-vous les
ongles?   15
ALICE. Les ongles? Nous les appelons de nails.
KATH. De nails. Ecoutez. Dites-moi si je parle
bien: de hand, de fingres, et de nails.
ALICE. C'est bien dit, madame, il est fort bon   20
Anglais.
KATH. Dites-moi l'Anglais pour le bras.
ALICE. De arm, madame.
KATH. Et le coude.
ALICE. De elbow.   24
KATH. De elbow. Je m'en fais la répétition de tous
les mots que vous m'avez appris dès à présent.
ALICE. Il est trop difficile, madame, comme je
pense.
KATH. Excusez-moi, Alice, écoutez: de hand, de
fingres, de nails, de arma, de bilbow.   31
ALICE. De elbow, madame.
KATH. Oh, Seigneur Dieu, je m'en oublie! De
elbow. Comment appelez-vous le col?
ALICE. De neck, madame.   35
KATH. De nick. Et le menton?
ALICE. De chin.
KATH. De sin. Le col, de nick, le menton, de sin.
ALICE. Oui. Sauf votre honneur, en vérité, vous
prononcez les mots aussi droit que les natifs d'An-
gleterre.
KATH. Je ne doute point d'apprendre, par la grace
de Dieu, et en peu de temps.   44
ALICE. N'avez vous pas déjà oublié ce que je vous
ai enseigné?
KATH. Non, je réciterai à vous promptement: de
hand, de fingres, de mails ——
ALICE. De nails, madame.
KATH. De nails, de arm, de ilbow.   50
ALICE. Sauf votre honneur, de elbow.
KATH. Ainsi dis-je: de elbow, de nick, et de sin.
Comment appelez-vous le pied et la robe?
ALICE. De foot, madame, et de coun.   54

Shakespeare was lodging in London with a Huguenot family
called Mountjoy, and took some interest in the affairs of Mary
Mountjoy, the daughter of the house. (See Gen. Intro. p. 14b.)
Some commentators find pleasure in the thought that she may
have taught Shakespeare the French words for this play. Presumably they do not realize that the plain purpose of the scene
is to get some low amusement from the fact that certain words
which sound innocent in one language are indecent in the other.

KATH. De foot et de coun! Oh, Seigneur Dieu! Ce sont mots de son mauvais, corruptible, gros, et impudique, et non pour les dames d'honneur d'user. Je ne voudrais prononcer ces mots devant les seigneurs de France pour tout le monde. Foh! Le foot et le coun! Néanmoins, je réciterai une autre fois 60 ma leçon ensemble: de hand, de fingres, de nails, de arm, de elbow, de nick, de sin, de foot, de coun.

ALICE. Excellent, madame!

KATH. C'est assez pour une fois. Allons-nous à 64 dîner.   [*Exeunt*]

SCENE V. *The same.*

[*Enter the* KING OF FRANCE, *the* DAUPHIN, *the* DUKE OF BOURBON, *the* CONSTABLE OF FRANCE, *and others.*]

FR. KING. 'Tis certain he hath passed the river Somme.

CON. And if he be not fought withal, my lord, Let us not live in France, let us quit all, And give our vineyards to a barbarous people.

DAU. Oh, *Dieu vivant!* Shall a few sprays of us, 5 The emptying of our fathers' luxury, Our scions, put in wild and savage stock, Spurt up so suddenly into the clouds, And overlook their grafters?°

BOUR. Normans, but bastard Normans, Norman bastards!   10 *Mort de ma vie!* If they march along Unfought withal, but I will sell my dukedom To buy a slobbery° and a dirty farm In that nook-shotten° isle of Albion.

CON. *Dieu de batailles!* Where have they this mettle?°   15 Is not their climate foggy, raw, and dull, On whom, as in despite,° the sun looks pale, Killing their fruit with frowns? Can sodden water,° A drench for surreined° jades,° their barley broth, Decoct° their cold blood to such valiant heat? 20 And shall our quick blood, spirited with wine, Seem frosty? Oh, for honor of our land, Let us not hang like roping° icicles Upon our houses' thatch whiles a more frosty people

Sweat drops of gallant youth in our rich fields! — Poor we may call them in their native lords.° 26

DAU. By faith and honor, Our madams mock at us, and plainly say Our mettle is bred out, and they will give Their bodies to the lust of English youth,   30 To new-store France with bastard warriors.

BOUR. They bid us to the English dancing schools, And teach lavoltas° high and swift corantos,° Saying our grace is only in our heels, And that we are most lofty runaways.   35

FR. KING. Where is Montjoy the herald? Speed him hence. Let him greet England with our sharp defiance. Up, Princes! and, with spirit of honor edged More sharper than your swords, hie to the field. Charles Delabreth, High Constable of France, 40 You Dukes of Orleans, Bourbon, and of Berri, Alençon, Brabant, Bar, and Burgundy, Jaques Chatillon, Rambures, Vaudemont, Beaumont, Grandpré, Roussi, and Fauconberg, Foix, Lestrale, Bouciqualt, and Charolois° — 45 High Dukes, great Princes, barons, lords, and knights, For your great seats° now quit you° of great shames. Bar° Harry England, that sweeps through our land With pennons painted in the blood of Harfleur. Rush on his host as doth the melted snow   50 Upon the valleys whose low vassal seat The Alps doth spit and void his rheum° upon. Go down upon him; you have power enough, And in a captive chariot into Rouen Bring him our prisoner.

CON.   This becomes the great. 55 Sorry am I his numbers are so few, His soldiers sick and famished in their march. For I am sure when he shall see our army, He'll drop his heart into the sink of fear And for achievement° offer us his ransom.   60

FR. KING. Therefore, Lord Constable, haste on Montjoy, And let him say to England that we send To know what willing ransom he will give. Prince Dauphin, you shall stay with us in Rouen.

DAU. Not so, I do beseech your Majesty.   65

FR. KING. Be patient, for you shall remain with us. Now forth, Lord Constable and Princes all, And quickly bring us word of England's fall.
                                      [*Exeunt.*]

Sc. v: 5–9. Shall . . . grafters: shall some sprigs (*sprays*) of us French — bastards begotten by the lust (*luxury*) of our ancestors — be like slips for grafting (*scions*) which, when set in a wild tree, grow great so suddenly and overtop the original tree from which the slips were taken (*grafters*)? By this elaborate image from the process of grafting cultivated slips onto a wild stock (as is the custom of gardeners with fruit trees) the Dauphin is reminding his party that many of the English nobility were descended from the followers of William the Norman, who conquered Saxon England in 1066. 13. slobbery: muddy, sloppy. 14. nook-shotten: pushed in a corner; i.e., remote and barbarous. 15. mettle: material, courage. 17. despite: spite. 18. sodden water: water boiled with slops. 19. surreined: overridden. jades: horses in poor condition. 20. Decoct: warm up. 23. roping: dangling.

26. Poor . . . lords: even their noblemen are a poor set. 33. lavolta: a high jumping dance performed by two dancers with arms intertwined. coranto: a quick sliding dance with unexpected movements. See App. 24. 40–45. Charles . . . Charolois: this catalogue of names was taken direct from Holinshed. 47. seats: estates. quit you: rid yourselves. 48. Bar: stop. 52. void . . . rheum: spit. 60. for achievement: instead of victory.

SCENE VI. *The English camp in Picardy.*

[*Enter* GOWER *and* FLUELLEN, *meeting.*]

GOW. How now, Captain Fluellen! Come you from the bridge?

FLU. I assure you there is very excellent services committed at the bridge.

GOW. Is the Duke of Exeter safe?   5

FLU. The Duke of Exeter is as magnanimous as Agamemnon,° and a man that I love and honor with my soul, and my heart, and my duty, and my life, and my living, and my uttermost power. He is not — God be praised and blessed! — any hurt in the world, but keeps the bridge most valiantly, with excellent discipline. There is an Aunchient Lieutenant there at the pridge, I think in my very conscience he is as valiant a man as Mark Antony, and he is a man of no estimation in the world, but I did see him do as gallant service.   15

GOW. What do you call him?

FLU. He is called Aunchient Pistol.

GOW. I know him not.   20

[*Enter* PISTOL.]

FLU. Here is the man.

PIST. Captain, I thee beseech to do me favors. The Duke of Exeter doth love thee well.

FLU. Aye, I praise God, and I have merited some love at his hands.   25

PIST. Bardolph, a soldier, firm and sound of heart, And of buxom° valor, hath, by cruel fate And giddy Fortune's furious fickle wheel, That goddess blind That stands upon the rolling restless stone ——   30

FLU. By your patience, Aunchient Pistol. Fortune is painted blind, with a muffler afore her eyes, to signify to you that Fortune is blind. And she is painted also with a wheel to signify to you, which is the moral of it, that she is turning, and in-   35 constant, and mutability, and variation. And her foot, look you, is fixed upon a spherical stone, which rolls, and rolls, and rolls. In good truth, the poet makes a most excellent description of it. Fortune is an excellent moral.   40

PIST. Fortune is Bardolph's foe, and frowns on him, For he hath stolen a pax,° and hanged must a' be. A damnèd death!

Let gallows gape for dog, let man go free And let not hemp his windpipe suffocate. But Exeter hath given the doom of death   45 For pax of little price. Therefore, go speak, the Duke will hear thy voice, And let not Bardolph's vital thread be cut With edge of penny cord and vile reproach.   50 Speak, Captain, for his life, and I will thee require.

FLU. Aunchient Pistol, I do partly understand your meaning.

PIST. Why then, rejoice therefore.

FLU. Certainly, Aunchient, it is not a thing to rejoice at. For if, look you, he were my brother, I would desire the Duke to use his good pleasure and put him to execution, for discipline ought to be used.

PIST. Die and be damned! And figo° for thy friendship!   59

FLU. It is well.

PIST. The fig of Spain!   [*Exit.*]

FLU. Very good.

GOW. Why, this is an arrant° counterfeit rascal. I remember him now — a bawd, a cutpurse.   65

FLU. I'll assure you a' uttered as prave words at the pridge as you shall see in a summer's day. But it is very well. What he has spoke to me, that is well, I warrant you, when time is serve.   69

GOW. Why, 'tis a gull,° a fool, a rogue, that now and then goes to the wars, to grace himself at his return into London under the form of a soldier. And such fellows are perfect in the great commanders' names. And they will learn you by rote where services were done — at such and such a sconce,°   75 at such a breach, at such a convoy; who came off bravely, who was shot, who disgraced, what terms the enemy stood on. And this they con° perfectly in the phrase of war, which they trick up with new-tuned oaths. And what a beard of the general's cut° and a horrid suit of the camp will do among foaming bottles and ale-washed wits is wonderful to be thought on. But you must learn to know such slanders of the age,° or else you may be marvelously mistook.   85

FLU. I tell you what, Captain Gower, I do perceive he is not the man that he would gladly make show to the world he is. If I find a hole in his coat, I will tell him my mind. [*Drum heard*] Hark you, the King is coming, and I must speak with him   91 from the pridge. [*Drum and Colors.*° *Enter* KING HENRY, GLOUCESTER, *and* SOLDIERS.] God pless your Majesty!

Sc. vi: **7. Agamemnon:** general of the Greek forces that besieged Troy. **27. buxom:** lively. **42. pax:** The actual incident is from Holinshed: "Yet in this great necessity the poor people of the country were not spoiled, nor anything taken of them without payment, nor any outrage or offense done by the Englishmen, except one, which was that a soldier took a pyx out of a church, for which he was apprehended, and the King not once removed till the box was restored, and the offender strangled." A *pyx* is the vessel in which the consecrated wafer is kept; a *pax* is a plate stamped with the figure of a crucifix, kissed first by the priest and then by the laity.

59. figo: fig, an insulting gesture made by thrusting the thumb between the first and second fingers. **64. arrant:** out-and-out. **70. gull:** simpleton. **75. sconce:** strong point, blockhouse. **78. con:** learn by heart. **80. beard . . . cut:** After the Cádiz expedition Essex grew a great beard, which was much imitated by his followers. **84. slanders . . . age:** abuses of our time. **92. s.d., Drum . . . colors:** a drummer and a soldier carrying a flag.

K. HEN. How now, Fluellen! Camest thou from the bridge?

FLU. Aye, so please your Majesty. The Duke of Exeter has very gallantly maintained the pridge. 95 The French is gone off, look you, and there is gallant and most prave passages. Marry, th' athversary was have possession of the pridge, but he is enforced to retire, and the Duke of Exeter is master of the pridge. I can tell your Majesty, the Duke is a prave man. 101

K. HEN. What men have you lost, Fluellen?

FLU. The perdition° of th' athversary hath been very great, reasonable great. Marry, for my part, I think the Duke hath lost never a man but one that is like to be executed for robbing a church, one Bardolph, if your Majesty know the man. His face is all bubukles,° and whelks,° and knobs, and flames o' fire. And his lips blows at his nose, and it is like a coal of fire, sometimes plue and sometimes red, but his nose is executed, and his fire's out. 112

K. HEN. We would have all such offenders so cut off. And we give express charge that in our marches through the country there be nothing compelled° from the villages, nothing taken but paid for, none of the French upbraided or abused in disdainful language. For when lenity and cruelty play for a kingdom, the gentler gamester is the soonest winner. 120

[*Tucket. Enter* MONTJOY.]

MONT. You know me by my habit.°

K. HEN. Well then, I know thee. What shall I know of thee?

MONT. My master's mind.

K. HEN. Unfold it. 124

MONT. Thus says my King: " Say thou to Harry of England: ' Though we seemed dead, we did but sleep. Advantage° is a better soldier than rashness.' Tell him we could have rebuked him at Harfleur, but that we thought not good to bruise an injury till it were full ripe.° Now we speak upon our 130 cue,° and our voice is imperial. England shall repent his folly, see his weakness, and admire° our sufferance.° Bid him therefore consider of his ransom, which must proportion the losses we have borne, the subjects we have lost, the disgrace we have di- 135 gested; which in weight to reanswer, his pettiness would bow under.° For our losses, his exchequer is too poor. For the effusion of our blood, the muster of his kingdom too faint a number. And for our disgrace, his own person, kneeling at our feet, but 140

a weak and worthless satisfaction. To this add defiance. And tell him, for conclusion, he hath betrayed his followers, whose condemnation is pronounced." So far my King and master, so much my office. 145

K. HEN. What is thy name? I know thy quality.°

MONT. Montjoy.

K. HEN. Thou dost thy office fairly. Turn thee back,
And tell thy King I do not seek him now,
But could be willing to march on to Calais 150
Without impeachment.° For to say the sooth,
Though 'tis no wisdom to confess so much
Unto an enemy of craft and vantage,°
My people are with sickness much enfeebled,
My numbers lessened, and those few I have 155
Almost no better than so many French.
Who when they were in health, I tell thee, herald,
I thought upon one pair of English legs
Did march three Frenchmen. Yet, forgive me, God,
That I do brag thus! This your air of France 160
Hath blown that vice in me. I must repent.
Go, therefore, tell thy master here I am.
My ransom is this frail and worthless trunk,
My army but a weak and sickly guard,
Yet, God before, tell him we will come on 165
Though France himself and such another neighbor
Stand in our way. There's for thy labor, Montjoy.
Go, bid thy master well advise himself.°
If we may pass, we will. If we be hindered,
We shall your tawny° ground with your red blood
Discolor. And so, Montjoy, fare you well. 171
The sum of all our answer is but this:
We would not seek a battle as we are,
Nor, as we are, we say we will not shun it.
So tell your master. 175

MONT. I shall deliver so. Thanks to your Highness.
[*Exit.*]

GLO. I hope they will not come upon us now.

K. HEN. We are in God's hand, Brother, not in theirs.
March to the bridge, it now draws toward night.
Beyond the river we'll encamp ourselves, 180
And on tomorrow bid them march away. [*Exeunt.*]

SCENE VII. *The French camp, near Agincourt.*

[*Enter the* CONSTABLE *of France, the* LORD RAMBURES,
ORLEANS, DAUPHIN, *with others.*]

CON. Tut! I have the best armor° of the world.
Would it were day!

ORL. You have an excellent armor, but let my horse have his due.

CON. It is the best horse of Europe. 5

ORL. Will it never be morning?

103. perdition: loss.   109. bubukles: large boils — a word coined by Fluellen from "bubo" and "carbuncles." whelks: pimples. 115. compelled: forced.   121. habit: garment; i.e., his herald's coat.   127. Advantage: profit; i.e., by waiting we win. 129–30. bruise . . . ripe: to burst the boil before it was ripe. 130–31. upon . . . cue: i.e., when it is the proper time. 132. admire: be astonished at.   133. sufferance: patience. 136–37. which . . . under: our injuries are so heavy that so slight a man must bend under the weight in attempting to repay them.

146. quality: profession; i.e., herald.   151. impeachment: prevention.   153. of . . . vantage: who is clever and has the advantage. 168. well . . . himself: think carefully.   170. tawny: yellow. Sc. vii: 1. armor: suit of armor.

DAU. My Lord of Orleans, and my Lord High Constable, you talk of horse and armor?

ORL. You are as well provided of both as any prince in the world. 10

DAU. What a long night is this! I will not change my horse with any that treads but on four pasterns.° Ca, ha! He bounds from the earth as if his entrails were hairs, *le cheval volant,* the Pegasus, *chez les narines de feu!°* When I bestride him, I soar, I am a hawk. He trots the air, the earth sings when he touches it, the basest horn of his hoof is more musical than the pipe of Hermes. 19

ORL. He's of the color of the nutmeg.

DAU. And of the heat of the ginger. It is a beast for Perseus. He is pure air and fire, and the dull elements of earth and water° never appear in him but only in patient stillness while his rider mounts him. He is indeed a horse, and all other jades you may call beasts. 26

CON. Indeed, my lord, it is a most absolute and excellent horse.

DAU. It is the prince of palfreys.° His neigh is like the bidding of a monarch, and his countenance enforces homage. 31

ORL. No more, Cousin.

DAU. Nay, the man hath no wit that cannot, from the rising of the lark to the lodging° of the lamb, vary deserved praise on my palfrey. It is a theme as fluent as the sea. Turn the sands into eloquent tongues and my horse is argument for them all. 'Tis a subject for a sovereign to reason on, and for a sovereign's sovereign to ride on, and for the world, familiar to us and unknown, to lay apart their particular functions and wonder at him. I once writ a sonnet in his praise, and began thus: "Wonder of nature —— " 40

ORL. I have heard a sonnet begin so to one's mistress. 45

DAU. Then did they imitate that which I composed to my courser, for my horse is my mistress.

ORL. Your mistress bears well.

DAU. Me well, which is the prescript° praise and perfection of a good and particular mistress. 50

CON. Nay, for methought yesterday your mistress shrewdly shook your back.

DAU. So perhaps did yours.

CON. Mine was not bridled.

DAU. Oh, then belike she was old and gentle, and you rode like a kern° of Ireland, your French hose° off and in your strait strossers.° 57

CON. You have good judgment in horsemanship.

DAU. Be warned by me, then. They that ride so and ride not warily fall into foul bogs. I had rather have my horse to my mistress.

CON. I had as lief have my mistress a jade.

DAU. I tell thee, Constable, my mistress wears his own hair. 65

CON. I could make as true a boast as that if I had a sow to my mistress.

DAU. *"Le chien est retourné à son propre vomissement, et la truie lavée au bourbier."°* Thou makest use of anything. 70

CON. Yet do I not use my horse for my mistress, or any such proverb so little kin to the purpose.

RAM. My Lord Constable, the armor that I saw in your tent tonight, are those stars or suns upon it?

CON. Stars, my lord. 76

DAU. Some of them will fall tomorrow, I hope.

CON. And yet my sky shall not want.

DAU. That may be, for you bear a many superfluously, and 'twere more honor some were away. 81

CON. Even as your horse bears your praises, who would trot as well were some of your brags dismounted.

DAU. Would I were able to load him with his desert! Will it never be day? I will trot tomorrow a mile, and my way shall be paved with English faces.

CON. I will not say so, for fear I should be 89 faced out of my way. But I would it were morning, for I would fain be about the ears of the English.

RAM. Who will go to hazard° with me for twenty prisoners?

CON. You must first go yourself to hazard ere you have them. 96

DAU. 'Tis midnight, I'll go arm myself. [*Exit.*]

ORL. The Dauphin longs for morning.

RAM. He longs to eat the English.

CON. I think he will eat all he kills. 100

ORL. By the white hand of my lady, he's a gallant Prince.

CON. Swear by her foot, that she may tread out the oath.°

ORL. He is simply the most active gentleman of France. 106

CON. Doing his activity,° and he will still be doing.

ORL. He never did harm that I heard of.

CON. Nor will do none tomorrow. He will keep that good name still. 111

ORL. I know him to be valiant.

CON. I was told that by one that knows him better than you.

ORL. What's he?

---

12. **pastern:** the part of a horse's leg between hoof and fetlock. 14–15. **le . . . feu:** the flying horse, the Pegasus, with nostrils of fire. **Pegasus:** the winged horse of the Greek hero Perseus, who saved Andromache from the monster. 22–23. **air . . . water:** See App. 3. 29. **palfrey:** saddle horse. 34. **lodging:** lying down. 49. **prescript:** prescribed. 56. **kern:** Irish foot soldier. **French hose:** baggy breeches. See Pl. 8b and comment on p. 93a–b. **57. strait strossers:** underpants.

68–69. **Le . . . bourbier:** the dog is turned to his own vomit again, and the sow that was washed to her wallowing in the mire. See II Peter 2 : 22. 92. **go to hazard:** play craps. 104. **tread . . . oath:** fulfill his oath by dancing. 107. **Doing . . . activity:** i.e., playing the fool.

CON. Marry, he told me so himself, and he said he
cared not who knew it.   118

ORL. He needs not. It is no hidden virtue in him.

CON. By my faith, sir, but it is. Never anybody
saw it but his lackey. 'Tis a hooded valor, and when
it appears, it will bate.°

ORL. Ill will never said well.

CON. I will cap that proverb with " There is flattery in friendship."   125

ORL. And I will take up that with " Give the Devil
his due."

CON. Well placed. There stands your friend for
the Devil. Have at the very eye of that proverb with
" A pox of the Devil."   130

ORL. You are the better at proverbs, by how much
" A fool's bolt° is soon shot."

CON. You have shot over.°

ORL. 'Tis not the first time you were overshot.°

[Enter a MESSENGER.]

MESS. My Lord High Constable, the English lie
within fifteen hundred paces of your tents.   136

CON. Who hath measured the ground?

MESS. The Lord Grandpré.

CON. A valiant and most expert gentleman. Would
it were day! Alas, poor Harry of England! He longs
not for the dawning as we do.   141

ORL. What a wretched and peevish° fellow is this
King of England, to mope with his fatbrained° followers so far out of his knowledge!°

CON. If the English had any apprehension,° they
would run away.   146

ORL. That they lack, for if their heads had any
intellectual armor, they could never wear such heavy
headpieces.

RAM. That island of England breeds very valiant
creatures. Their mastiffs° are of unmatchable courage.   152

ORL. Foolish curs, that run winking into the
mouth of a Russian bear and have their heads
crushed like rotten apples! You may as well say that's
a valiant flea that dare eat his breakfast on the lip
of a lion.   157

CON. Just, just, and the men do sympathize with
the mastiffs in robustious° and rough coming-on,
leaving their wits with their wives. And then give
them great meals of beef, and iron and steel, they
will eat like wolves, and fight like devils.   162

ORL. Aye, but these English are shrewdly out of
beef.°

CON. Then shall we find tomorrow they have only
stomachs to eat and none to fight. Now is it time to
arm. Come, shall we about it?   167

ORL. It is now two o'clock. But let me see, by ten
We shall have each a hundred Englishmen.

[Exeunt.]

Act IV

PROLOGUE

[Enter CHORUS.]

CHOR. Now entertain conjecture° of a time
When creeping murmur and the poring° dark
Fills the wide vessel of the universe.
From camp to camp through the foul womb of
      night
The hum of either army stilly° sounds,   5
That the fixed sentinels almost receive
The secret whispers of each other's watch.
Fire answers fire, and through their paly° flames
Each battle° sees the other's umbered° face.
Steed threatens steed, in high and boastful neighs
Piercing the night's dull ear. And from the tents 11
The armorers, accomplishing° the knights,
With busy hammers closing rivets up
Give dreadful note of preparation.
The country cocks do crow, the clocks do toll,   15
And the third hour of drowsy morning name.
Proud of their numbers and secure° in soul,
The confident and overlusty French
Do the low-rated° English play at dice,
And chide the cripple tardy-gaited° Night   20
Who, like a foul and ugly witch, doth limp
So tediously away. The poor condemnèd English,
Like sacrifices, by their watchful fires
Sit patiently and inly° ruminate
The morning's danger, and their gesture sad   25
Investing lank-lean cheeks and war-worn coats
Presenteth them unto the gazing moon
So many horrid ghosts. Oh, now who will behold
The royal captain of this ruined band
Walking from watch to watch, from tent to tent,   30
Let him cry " Praise and glory on his head! "
For forth he goes and visits all his host,
Bids them good morrow with a modest smile,
And calls them brothers, friends, and countrymen.

121–22. hooded . . . bate: a metaphor from hawking. See *R & J*,
III.ii.14 and App. 26.   132. bolt: arrow.   133. shot over: i.e.,
missed the target.   134. overshot: outshot.   142. peevish:
foolish.   143. fatbrained: fatheaded.   144. out . . . knowledge:
in actions which he does not understand.   145. apprehension:
intelligence, sense.   151. mastiffs: dogs bred particularly for
baiting bears and bulls. See App. 5.   159. robustious: violent.
163–64. shrewdly . . . beef: The English were reputed to lose
heart if deprived of beef. shrewdly: grievously.

Act IV. Prologue: 1. entertain conjecture: imagine.   2. poring:
peering.   5. stilly: i.e., in the still night.   8. paly: pale.
9. battle: army. umbered: dark brown.   12. accomplishing:
fixing on the equipment. A knight fully armored was actually
riveted into his armor and could not get out of it without help.
See Pl. 8a.   17. secure: careless, overconfident.   19. low-rated:
valued at a low price.   20. tardy-gaited: slow-stepping.   24. inly:
inwardly.

Upon his royal face there is no note   35
How dread an army hath enrounded him.
Nor doth he dedicate one jot of color
Unto the weary and all-watchèd night,
But freshly looks and overbears attaint°
With cheerful semblance and sweet majesty,   40
That every wretch, pining and pale before,
Beholding him, plucks comfort from his looks.
A largess° universal like the sun
His liberal eye doth give to every one,
Thawing cold fear, that mean and gentle° all   45
Behold, as may unworthiness define,°
A little touch° of Harry in the night.
And so our scene must to the battle fly,
Where — oh, for pity! — we shall much disgrace
With four or five most vile and ragged foils,°   50
Right ill-disposed in brawl ridiculous,
The name of Agincourt. Yet sit and see,
Minding° true things by what their mockeries° be.
                                          [*Exit.*]

SCENE I. *The English camp at Agincourt.*

[*Enter* KING HENRY, BEDFORD, *and* GLOUCESTER.]
  K. HEN. Gloucester, 'tis true that we are in great
    danger.
The greater therefore should our courage be.
Good morrow, Brother Bedford. God Almighty!
There is some soul of goodness in things evil,
Would men observingly° distill° it out.   5
For our bad neighbor makes us early stirrers,
Which is both healthful and good husbandry.°
Besides, they are our outward consciences,
And preachers to us all, admonishing
That we should dress us fairly for our end.   10
Thus may we gather honey from the weed,
And make a moral of° the Devil himself.
[*Enter* ERPINGHAM.] Good morrow, old Sir Thomas
    Erpingham.
A good soft pillow for that good white head
Were better than a churlish turf of France.   15
  ERP. Not so, my liege. This lodging likes° me
    better,
Since I may say " Now lie I like a king."
  K. HEN. 'Tis good for men to love their present
    pains
Upon example, so the spirit is eased.
And when the mind is quickened, out of doubt,   20

The organs, though defunct and dead before,
Break up their drowsy grave and newly move,
With casted slough° and fresh legerity.°
Lend me thy cloak, Sir Thomas. Brothers both,
Commend me to the Princes in our camp,   25
Do my good morrow to them, and anon
Desire them all to my pavilion.
  GLO. We shall, my liege.
  ERP. Shall I attend your Grace?
  K. HEN.   No, my good knight,
Go with my brothers to my lords of England.   30
I and my bosom must debate a while,
And then I would no other company.
  ERP. The Lord in Heaven bless thee, noble Harry!
                              [*Exeunt all but* KING.]
  K. HEN. God-a-mercy, old heart! Thou speak'st
    cheerfully.
                              [*Enter* PISTOL.]
  PIST. *Qui va là?*°   35
  K. HEN. A friend.
  PIST. Discuss unto me, art thou officer?
Or art thou base, common, and popular?°
  K. HEN. I am a gentleman of a company.°
  PIST. Trail'st thou the puissant° pike?°   40
  K. HEN. Even so. What are you?
  PIST. As good a gentleman as the Emperor.
  K. HEN. Then you are a better than the King.
  PIST. The King's a bawcock, and a heart of gold,
A lad of life, an imp° of fame,   45
Of parents good, of fist most valiant.
I kiss his dirty shoe, and from heartstring
I love the lovely bully. What is thy name?
  K. HEN. Harry le Roy.
  PIST. Le Roy! A Cornish name. Art thou of Cor-
    nish crew?   50
  K. HEN. No, I am a Welshman.
  PIST. Know'st thou Fluellen?
  K. HEN. Yes.
  PIST. Tell him I'll knock his leek° about his pate
Upon Saint Davy's day.   55
  K. HEN. Do not you wear your dagger in your cap
that day, lest he knock that about yours.
  PIST. Art thou his friend?
  K. HEN. And his kinsman too.
  PIST. The figo for thee, then!   60
  K. HEN. I thank you. God be with you!
  PIST. My name is Pistol called.   [*Exit.*]
  K. HEN. It sorts well with your fierceness.
                              [*Enter* FLUELLEN *and* GOWER.]
  GOW. Captain Fluellen!   64
  FLU. So! In the name of Jesu Christ, speak lower.
It is the greatest admiration° in the universal world

---

39. overbears attaint: overcomes the stain of fear.   43. largess:
money freely given.   45. mean . . . gentle: poor men and gentlemen.   46. as . . . define: so far as the author's poor ability can
show.   47. little touch: glimpse.   50. foils: rapiers. See *Hen V*
Intro. p. 734a.   53. Minding: bearing in mind. mockeries: poor
imitations.
    Sc. i: 5. observingly: by careful observation. distill: extract.
7. husbandry: economy.   12. make . . . of: find a moral lesson
in.   16. likes: pleases.

23. slough: skin. legerity: light spirits.   35. Qui va là: who goes
there?   38. popular: one who mixes in low company.   39. gentleman . . . company: gentleman volunteer. See Gen. Intro. p. 31a.
40. puissant: powerful. pike: See Pl. 21d.   45. imp: child.
54. leek: the national emblem of the Welsh.   66. admiration:
wonder.

when the true and aunchient prerogatifes° and laws
of the wars is not kept. If you would take the pains
but to examine the wars of Pompey the Great, you
shall find, I warrant you, that there is no tiddle- 70
taddle nor pibble-pabble in Pompey's camp. I warrant you you shall find the ceremonies of the wars,
and the cares of it, and the forms of it, and the sobriety of it, and the modesty of it, to be otherwise. 75

GOW. Why, the enemy is loud. You hear him all
night.

FLU. If the enemy is an ass and a fool and a prating
coxcomb, is it meet, think you, that we should also,
look you, be an ass and a fool and a prating coxcomb? In your own conscience, now? 81

GOW. I will speak lower.

FLU. I pray you and beseech you that you will.

        [*Exeunt* GOWER *and* FLUELLEN.]

K. HEN. Though it appear a little out of fashion,
There is much care and valor in this Welshman. 86
[*Enter three soldiers,* JOHN BATES, ALEXANDER COURT,
      and MICHAEL WILLIAMS.]

COURT. Brother John Bates, is not that the morning which breaks yonder?

BATES. I think it be. But we have no great cause
to desire the approach of day. 90

WILL. We see yonder the beginning of the day,
but I think we shall never see the end of it. Who
goes there?

K. HEN. A friend.

WILL. Under what captain serve you? 95

K. HEN. Under Sir Thomas Erpingham.

WILL. A good old commander and a most kind
gentlemen. I pray you, what thinks he of our estate?

K. HEN. Even as men wrecked upon a sand, that
look to be washed off the next tide.

BATES. He hath not told his thought to the King?

K. HEN. No, nor is it not meet° he should. For,
though I speak it to you, I think the King is 105
but a man, as I am. The violet smells to him as it
doth to me, the element° shows to him as it doth to
me, all his senses have but human conditions. His
ceremonies laid by, in his nakedness he appears but
a man, and though his affections° are higher 110
mounted than ours, yet when they stoop,° they stoop
with the like wing. Therefore when he sees reason
of fears as we do, his fears, out of doubt, be of the
same relish° as ours are. Yet, in reason, no man
should possess him with any appearance of fear, lest
he, by showing it, should dishearten his army. 117

BATES. He may show what outward courage he
will, but I believe, as cold a night as 'tis, he could
wish himself in Thames up to the neck. And so I

would he were, and I by him, at all adventures,° so
we were quit° here. 122

K. HEN. By my troth, I will speak my conscience°
of the King. I think he would not wish himself anywhere but where he is.

BATES. Then I would he were here alone. So
should he be sure to be ransomed, and a many poor
men's lives saved. 128

K. HEN. I dare say you love him not so ill, to wish
him here alone, howsoever you speak this to feel
other men's minds. Methinks I could not die anywhere so contented as in the King's company, his
cause being just and his quarrel honorable. 134

WILL. That's more than we know.

BATES. Aye, or more than we should seek after.
For we know enough if we know we are the King's
subjects. If his cause be wrong, our obedience to the
King wipes the crime of it out of us. 139

WILL. But if the cause be not good, the King himself hath a heavy reckoning to make when all those
legs and arms and heads chopped off in a battle shall
join together at the latter day and cry all " We died
at such a place " — some swearing, some crying for
a surgeon, some upon their wives left poor be- 145
hind them, some upon the debts they owe, some
upon their children rawly° left. I am afeard there
are few die well that die in a battle, for how can
they charitably dispose of anything when blood is
their argument? Now if these men do not die well,
it will be a black matter for the King that led them
to it, whom to disobey were against all proportion
of subjection.° 153

K. HEN. So, if a son that is by his father sent about
merchandise do sinfully miscarry° upon the sea, the
imputation of his wickedness, by your rule, should
be imposed upon his father that sent him. Or if a
servant under his master's command transporting
a sum of money be assailed by robbers and die in
many irreconciled° iniquities, you may call the 160
business of the master the author of the servant's
damnation. But this is not so. The King is not bound
to answer the particular endings of his soldiers, the
father of his son, nor the master of his servant. For
they purpose not their death when they pur- 165
pose their services. Besides, there is no king, be his
cause never so spotless, if it come to the arbiterment°
of swords, can try it out with all unspotted soldiers.
Some peradventure have on them the guilt of premeditated and contrived murder; some, of be- 170
guiling virgins with the broken seals of perjury;
some, making the wars their bulwark, that have
before gored the gentle bosom of peace with pillage
and robbery. Now if these men have defeated the

---

67. **prerogatifes:** prerogatives, ordinances.   104. **meet:** fit.
107. **element:** sky.   110. **affections:** desires.   111. **stoop:** swoop
down.   114–15. **of . . . relish:** taste the same.

121. **at . . . adventures:** at all risks.   122. **quit:** rid of it.
123. **conscience:** innermost thought.   147. **rawly:** poorly provided.   152–53. **proportion of subjection:** proper behavior of a
subject.   155. **sinfully miscarry:** die in his sins.   160. **irrecon-
ciled:** not confessed and absolved.   167. **arbiterment:** decision.

law and outrun native punishment,° though 175
they can outstrip men, they have no wings to fly from
God. War is His beadle,° war is His vengeance, so
that here men are punished for before-breach of the
King's laws in now the King's quarrel. Where they
feared the death, they have borne life away, 180
and where they would be safe, they perish. Then if
they die unprovided, no more is the King guilty of
their damnation than he was before guilty of those
impieties for the which they are now visited. Every
subject's duty is the King's, but every subject's 185
soul is his own. Therefore should every soldier in the
wars do as every sick man in his bed, wash every
mote° out of his conscience. And dying so, death is
to him advantage, or not dying, the time was 190
blessedly lost wherein such preparation was gained.
And in him that escapes, it were not sin to think
that, making God so free an offer, He let him outlive that day to see His greatness and to teach others
how they should prepare. 196

WILL. 'Tis certain every man that dies ill, the ill
upon his own head, the King is not to answer it.

BATES. I do not desire he should answer for me,
and yet I determine to fight lustily for him. 201

K. HEN. I myself heard the King say he would not
be ransomed.

WILL. Aye, he said so to make us fight cheerfully.
But when our throats are cut, he may be ransomed
and we ne'er the wiser.

K. HEN. If I live to see it, I will never trust his
word after. 208

WILL. You pay him, then. That's a perilous shot
out of an elder-gun, that a poor and a private displeasure can do against a monarch!° You may as
well go about to turn the sun to ice with fanning in
his face with a peacock's feather. You'll never trust
his word after! Come, 'tis a foolish saying. 215

K. HEN. Your reproof is something too round.° I
should be angry with you if the time were convenient.

WILL. Let it be a quarrel between us if you live.

K. HEN. I embrace it. 221

WILL. How shall I know thee again?

K. HEN. Give me any gage° of thine, and I will
wear it in my bonnet. Then, if ever thou darest acknowledge it, I will make it my quarrel. 225

WILL. Here's my glove. Give me another of thine.

K. HEN. There.

WILL. This will I also wear in my cap. If ever thou
come to me and say, after tomorrow, "This is my
glove," by this hand, I will take° thee a box on the
ear. 232

K. HEN. If ever I live to see it, I will challenge it.

WILL. Thou darest as well be hanged.

K. HEN. Well, I will do it, though I take thee in
the King's company. 237

WILL. Keep thy word. Fare thee well.

BATES. Be friends, you English fools, be friends.
We have French quarrels enow,° if you could tell
how to reckon. 241

K. HEN. Indeed, the French may lay twenty French
crowns to one they will beat us, for they bear them
on their shoulders. But it is no English treason to
cut French crowns, and tomorrow the King 245
himself will be a clipper.° [*Exeunt* SOLDIERS.]
Upon° the King! Let us our lives, our souls,
Our debts, our careful° wives,
Our children, and our sins lay on the King!
We must bear all. Oh, hard condition, 250
Twin-born with greatness, subject to the breath
Of every fool, whose sense no more can feel
But his own wringing!° What infinite heartsease
Must kings neglect that private men enjoy!
And what have kings that privates have not too,
Save ceremony,° save general ceremony? 256
And what art thou, thou idol ceremony?
What kind of god art thou, that suffer'st more
Of mortal griefs than do thy worshipers?
What are thy rents?° What are thy comings-in?
O Ceremony, show me but thy worth! 261
What is thy soul of adoration?°
Art thou aught else but place, degree, and form,
Creating awe and fear in other men?
Wherein thou art less happy being feared 265
Than they in fearing.
What drink'st thou oft, instead of homage sweet,
But poisoned flattery? Oh, be sick, great greatness,
And bid thy ceremony give thee cure!
Think'st thou the fiery fever will go out 270
With titles blown from adulation?°
Will it give place to flexure° and low bending?
Canst thou, when thou command'st the beggar's
 knee,
Command the health of it? No, thou proud dream,
That play'st so subtly with a king's repose, 275
I am a king that find thee, and I know

240. enow: enough. 242–46. Indeed . . . clipper: The King puns
on double meanings of crown: "coin" and "head." "The French
may bet twenty to one they will beat us, for there are twenty
of them to our one; but it's no treason for an Englishman to
cut a French crown." As money at this time was stamped out
with an irregular rim, it was possible to clip pieces off. This
was a capital offense. See App. 27 and Pl. 10. 247–301. Upon
. . . advantages: This is the first time in the play that a glimpse
has been given of Henry's personal feelings. Hitherto he has
been the personification of official majesty. 248. careful: anxious. 253. wringing: suffering. 256. ceremony: outward pomp,
here pronounced "seer'mony." 260. rents: profits. 262. soul
of adoration: the essential cause why you should be adored.
270–71. Think'st . . . adulation: can flattery with its empty
titles blow out the fire of a fever? 272. flexure: bending of the
knee.

175. outrun . . . punishment: escaped punishment at home.
177. beadle: the parish officer who administered punishment.
189. mote: speck. 209–11. That's . . . monarch: that's a silly
remark; what's the good of being annoyed with a king. elder-
gun: popgun. 216. round: direct. 223. gage: pledge, token.
231. take: give.

'Tis not the balm,° the scepter° and the ball,°
The sword, the mace,° the crown imperial,
The intertissued° robe of gold and pearl,
The farcèd° title running 'fore the king,   280
The throne he sits on, nor the tide of pomp
That beats upon the high shore of this world —
No, not all these, thrice-gorgeous ceremony,
Not all these, laid in bed majestical,
Can sleep so soundly as the wretched slave   285
Who with a body filled and vacant mind
Gets him to rest crammed with distressful bread,
Never sees horrid night, the child of Hell,
But, like a lackey, from the rise to set
Sweats in the eye of Phoebus° and all night   290
Sleeps in Elysium.° Next day after dawn,
Doth rise and help Hyperion° to his horse,
And follows so the ever-running year,
With profitable labor, to his grave.
And, but for ceremony, such a wretch,   295
Winding up° days with toil and nights with sleep,
Had the forehand and vantage of a king.
The slave, a member of the country's peace,°
Enjoys it, but in gross brain little wots°   299
What watch the King keeps to maintain the peace,
Whose hours the peasant best advantages.°

[*Re-enter* ERPINGHAM.]

ERP. My lord, your nobles, jealous of° your ab-
    sence,
Seek through your camp to find you.
K. HEN.   Good old knight,
Collect them all together at my tent.   304
I'll be before thee.
ERP.   I shall do 't, my lord.   [*Exit.*]
K. HEN. O God of battles, steel my soldiers'
    hearts!
Possess them not with fear, take from them now
The sense of reckoning if the opposèd numbers
Pluck their hearts from them. Not° today, O Lord,
Oh, not today, think not upon the fault   310
My father made in compassing the crown!
I Richard's body have interrèd new,
And on it have bestowed more contrite tears
Than from it issued forcèd drops of blood.
Five hundred poor I have in yearly pay,   315
Who twice a day their withered hands hold up
Toward Heaven, to pardon blood, and I have built

Two chantries° where the sad and solemn priests
Sing still° for Richard's soul. More will I do,
Though all that I can do is nothing worth,   320
Since that my penitence comes after all,
Imploring pardon.

[*Re-enter* GLOUCESTER.]

GLO. My liege!
K. HEN.   My brother Gloucester's voice? Aye,
I know thy errand, I will go with thee.   325
The day, my friends, and all things stay for me.

[*Exeunt.*]

SCENE II. *The French camp.*

[*Enter the* DAUPHIN, ORLEANS, RAMBURES,
and others.]

ORL. The sun doth gild our armor. Up, my lords!
DAU. *Montez à cheval!* My horse! Varlet!
    Laquais!° Ha!
ORL. O brave spirit!
DAU. *Via! Les eaux et la terre.*
ORL. *Rien puis? L'air et le feu.*   5
DAU. *Ciel,* Cousin Orleans.

[*Enter* CONSTABLE.]

Now, my Lord Constable!
CON. Hark how our steeds for present° service
    neigh!
DAU. Mount them, and make incision in their
    hides,
That their hot blood may spin in English eyes   10
And dout° them with superfluous courage, ha!
RAM. What, will you have them weep our horses'
    blood?
How shall we then behold their natural tears?

[*Enter* MESSENGER.]

MESS. The English are embattled, you French
    peers.
CON. To horse, you gallant Princes! Straight to
    horse!   15
Do but behold yon poor and starvèd band
And your fair show shall suck away their souls,
Leaving them but the shales° and husks of men.
There is not work enough for all our hands,
Scarce blood enough in all their sickly veins   20
To give each naked curtal ax° a stain,
That our French gallants shall today draw out
And sheathe for lack of sport. Let us but blow on
    them,
The vapor of our valor will o'erturn them.
'Tis positive 'gainst all exceptions, lords,   25
That our superfluous lackeys and our peasants,

---

277. **balm:** holy oil with which a king is anointed. **scepter:** the golden rod held by a king. **ball:** a symbol of office. See Pl. 2b. 278. **mace:** a symbol of the power to strike down offenders. See Pl. 22h. 279. **intertissued:** interwoven. 280. **farced:** stuffed with pompous phrases. 290. **Phoebus:** the sun. 291. **Elysium:** Paradise. 292. **Hyperion:** the sun. 296. **Winding up:** completing. 298. **member . . . peace:** a citizen living in peace. 299. **wots:** knows. 301. **best advantages:** has the greatest advantage of; i.e., the days bring profit to the poor man but only anxiety to the King. 302. **jealous of:** suspicious — lest harm should have befallen. 309–22. **Not . . . pardon:** Henry never forgets that he and his father are usurpers on the English throne. See *II Hen IV*, IV.v.184–220.

318. **chantries:** chapels where priests sing Masses for the repose of the souls of the dead. 319. **still:** continuously.

Sc. ii: 2. **Laquais:** lackey, servant. 8. **present:** immediate. 11. **dout:** put out. 18. **shales:** shells. 21. **curtal ax:** cutlass, sword used by a horseman when the lance has been broken.

Who in unnecessary action swarm
About our squares of battle, were enow
To purge this field of such a hilding° foe,
Though we upon this mountain's basis by   30
Took stand for idle speculation.°
But that our honors must not. What's to say?
A very little little let us do,
And all is done. Then let the trumpets sound
The tucket sonance° and the note to mount,   35
For our approach shall so much dare° the field
That England shall couch down in fear and yield.

[*Enter* GRANDPRÉ.]

GRAND. Why do you stay so long, my lords of
France?
Yon island carrions,° desperate of their bones,
Ill-favoredly° become the morning field.   40
Their ragged curtains° poorly are let loose,
And our air shakes them passing scornfully.
Big Mars seems bankrupt in their beggared host
And faintly through a rusty beaver° peeps.
The horsemen sit like fixèd candlesticks,°   45
With torch staves in their hand. And their poor
jades
Lob down° their heads, dropping the hides and hips,
The gum down-roping° from their pale-dead eyes,
And in their pale dull mouths the gimmal° bit
Lies foul with chewed grass, still and motionless.
And their executors,° the knavish crows,   51
Fly o'er them, all impatient for their hour.
Description cannot suit itself in words
To demonstrate the life of such a battle
In life so lifeless as it shows itself.   55

CON. They have said their prayers, and they stay
for death.
DAU. Shall we go send them dinners and fresh
suits,
And give their fasting horses provender,
And after fight with them?
CON. I stay but for my guidon.° To the field!   60
I will the banner from a trumpet take,
And use it for my haste. Come, come, away!
The sun is high, and we outwear° the day.

[*Exeunt.*]

SCENE III. *The English camp.*

[*Enter* GLOUCESTER, BEDFORD, EXETER, ERPINGHAM,
with all his host; SALISBURY *and* WESTMORELAND.]
GLO. Where is the King?

29. hilding: worthless.   **31. speculation:** looking on.   **35. tucket**
sonance: trumpet call.   **36. dare:** dazzle, fascinate; the word
is used of catching larks.   **39. carrions:** carcasses.   **40. Ill-fa-**
voredly: leanly, uglily.   **41. curtains:** i.e., flags.   **44. beaver:** the
facepiece of the helmet. See Pl. 8a.   **45. fixed candlesticks:** like
ornamental figures on a candlestick.   **47. Lob down:** hang down.
48. down-roping: dangling down.   **49. gimmal:** jointed.   **51. ex-**
ecutors: i.e., those who will succeed to what is left of their bodies.
60. guidon: standard.   **63. outwear:** wear out, waste.

BED. The King himself is rode to view their battle.
WEST. Of fighting men they have full threescore
thousand.
EXE. There's five to one. Besides, they all are fresh.
SAL. God's arm strike with us! 'Tis a fearful odds.
God be wi' you, Princes all. I'll to my charge.°   6
If we no more meet till we meet in Heaven,
Then, joyfully, my noble Lord of Bedford,
My dear Lord Gloucester, and my good Lord
Exeter,
And my kind kinsman, warriors all, adieu!   10

BED. Farewell, good Salisbury, and good luck go
with thee!
EXE. Farewell, kind lord. Fight valiantly today.
And yet I do thee wrong to mind° thee of it,
For thou art framed° of the firm truth of valor.

[*Exit* SALISBURY.]

BED. He is as full of valor as of kindness,   15
Princely in both.

[*Enter the* KING.]

WEST.   Oh, that we now had here
But one ten thousand of those men in England
That do no work today!
K. HEN.   What's he that wishes so?
My cousin Westmoreland? No, my fair cousin.
If we are marked to die, we are enow   20
To do our country loss, and if to live,
The fewer men, the greater share of honor.
God's will! I pray thee wish not one man more.
By Jove, I am not covetous for gold,
Nor care I who doth feed upon° my cost.   25
It yearns° me not if men my garments wear,
Such outward things dwell not in my desires.
But if it be a sin to covet honor,
I am the most offending soul alive.
No, faith, my coz,° wish not a man from England.
God's peace! I would not lose so great an honor   31
As one man more, methinks, would share from me
For the best hope I have. Oh, do not wish one more!
Rather proclaim it, Westmoreland, through my
host,
That he which hath no stomach to this fight,   35
Let him depart. His passport shall be made
And crowns for convoy put into his purse.
We would not die in that man's company
That fears his fellowship to die with us.°
This day is called the feast of Crispian.°   40
He that outlives this day and comes safe home
Will stand a-tiptoe when this day is named
And rouse him at the name of Crispian.
He that shall live this day and see old age
Will yearly on the vigil feast his neighbors   45

Sc. iii: 6. charge: command.   **13. mind:** remind.   **14. framed:**
made.   **25. upon:** at.   **26. yearns:** grieves.   **30. coz:** cousin,
but used of any relation.   **39. fears . . . us:** is afraid to share
death with us.   **40. Crispian:** Crispin and Crispian were both
martyred at Soissons in A.D. 287. They became the patron saints
of shoemakers. Their day is October 25.

And say, " Tomorrow is Saint Crispian."
Then will he strip his sleeve and show his scars,
And say " These wounds I had on Crispin's Day."
Old men forget, yet all shall be forgot,
But he'll remember with advantages°   50
What feats he did that day. Then shall our names,
Familiar in his mouth as household words,
Harry the King, Bedford and Exeter,
Warwick and Talbot, Salisbury and Gloucester,
Be in their flowing cups freshly remembered.   55
This story shall the good man teach his son,
And Crispin Crispian shall ne'er go by,
From this day to the ending of the world,
But we in it shall be remembered —
We few, we happy few, we band of brothers.   60
For he today that sheds his blood with me
Shall be my brother. Be he ne'er so vile,
This day shall gentle his condition.°
And gentlemen in England now abed   64
Shall think themselves accursed they were not here,
And hold their manhoods cheap whiles any speaks
That fought with us upon Saint Crispin's Day.

[Re-enter SALISBURY.]

SAL. My sovereign lord, bestow° yourself with
   speed.
The French are bravely in their battles° set,
And will with all expedience° charge on us.   70
K. HEN. All things are ready, if our minds be so.
WEST. Perish the man whose mind is backward
   now!
K. HEN. Thou dost not wish more help from Eng-
   land, Coz?
WEST. God's will! My liege, would you and I
   alone,
Without more help, could fight this royal battle!   75
K. HEN. Why, now thou hast unwished five thou-
   sand men,
Which likes me better than to wish us one.
You know your places. God be with you all!

[Tucket. Enter MONTJOY.]

MONT. Once more I come to know of thee, King
   Harry,
If for thy ransom thou wilt now compound°   80
Before thy most assurèd overthrow.
For certainly thou art so near the gulf,°
Thou needs must be englutted.° Besides, in mercy,
The Constable desires thee thou wilt mind
Thy followers of repentance, that their souls   85
May make a peaceful and a sweet retire
From off these fields, where, wretches, their poor
   bodies
Must lie and fester.

K. HEN.   Who hath sent thee now?
MONT. The Constable of France.
K. HEN. I pray thee, bear my former answer back.
Bid them achieve° me and then sell my bones.   91
Good God! Why should they mock poor fellows
   thus?
The man that once did sell the lion's skin
While the beast lived was killed with hunting him.
A many of our bodies shall no doubt   95
Find native° graves, upon the which, I trust,
Shall witness live in brass° of this day's work.
And those that leave their valiant bones in France,
Dying like men, though buried in your dunghills,
They shall be famed. For there the sun shall greet
   them   100
And draw their honors reeking° up to Heaven,
Leaving their earthly parts to choke your clime,
The smell whereof shall breed a plague in France.
Mark then abounding valor in our English,
That being dead, like to the bullet's grazing,   105
Break out into a second course of mischief,
Killing in relapse of mortality.°
Let me speak proudly. Tell the Constable
We are but warriors for the working day.°
Our gayness and our gilt are all besmirched   110
With rainy marching in the painful field.
There's not a piece of feather° in our host —
Good argument, I hope, we will not fly —
And time hath worn us into slovenry.
But, by the mass, our hearts are in the trim,   115
And my poor soldiers tell me yet ere night
They'll be in fresher robes, or they will pluck
The gay new coats o'er the French soldiers' heads
And turn them out of service.° If they do this —
As, if God please, they shall — my ransom then   120
Will soon be levied. Herald, save thou thy labor.
Come thou no more for ransom, gentle herald.
They shall have none, I swear, but these my joints,
Which if they have as I will leave 'em them,
Shall yield them little, tell the Constable.   125
MONT. I shall, King Harry. And so fare thee well.
Thou never shalt hear herald any more.   *[Exit.]*
K. HEN. I fear thou'lt once more come again for
   ransom.

[Enter YORK.]

YORK. My lord, most humbly on my knee I beg
The leading of the vaward.°   130

91. achieve: win, kill. 96. native: i.e., in England. 97. in brass:
i.e., a brass memorial tablet, of which there are many in English
churches set up in the fifteenth, sixteenth, and seventeenth centuries.   101. reeking: rising up like mist.   107. relapse of
mortality: deadly rebound, or renewed deadliness.   109. working
day: in our working clothes; i.e., not much to look at.
112. feather: Knights and officers in Shakespeare's time used to
deck their helmets with gay plumes. Henry's army is too bedraggled for any finery.   117–19. they . . . service: A servant
on appointment was given a new livery; if dismissed, it was
taken from him. See *M of Ven*, II.ii.161–64.   130. vaward: vanguard.

50. with advantages: i.e., the story will gain in telling. 63. gentle
. . . condition: make him a gentleman.   68. bestow: move.
69. battles: order of battle.   70. expedience: haste.   80. compound: offer terms.   82. gulf: whirlpool.   83. englutted: swallowed.

K. HEN. Take it, brave York. Now, soldiers, march
away.
And how Thou pleasest, God, dispose the day!
                        [*Exeunt.*]

SCENE IV.° *The field of battle.*

[*Alarum. Excursions. Enter* PISTOL, FRENCH SOLDIER,
and BOY.]

PIST. Yield, cur!

FR. SOL. *Je pense que vous êtes gentilhomme de
bonne qualité.*

PIST. Qualtitie calmie custure me!° Art thou a
gentleman? What is thy name? Discuss.   5

FR. SOL. *O Seigneur Dieu!*

PIST. O Signieur Dew should be a gentleman.
Perpend° my words, O Signieur Dew, and mark.
O Signieur Dew, thou diest on point of fox,°
Except, O signieur, thou do give to me   10
Egregious° ransom.

FR. SOL. *Oh, prenez miséricorde! Ayez pitié de
moi!°*

PIST. Moy shall not serve, I will have forty moys,
Or I will fetch thy rim° out at thy throat   15
In drops of crimson blood.

FR. SOL. *Est-il impossible d'échapper la force de
ton bras?*

PIST. Brass, cur!
Thou damned and luxurious° mountain goat,   20
Offer'st me brass?

FR. SOL. *Oh, pardonnez-moi!*

PIST. Say'st thou me so? Is that a ton of moys?
Come hither, boy. Ask me this slave in French
What is his name.   25

BOY. *Ecoutez. Comment êtes-vous appelé?*

FR. SOL. Monsieur le Fer.

BOY. He says his name is Master Fer.

PIST. Master Fer! I'll fer him, and firk° him, and
ferret° him. Discuss the same in French unto
him.

BOY. I do not know the French for fer, and ferret,
and firk.

PIST. Bid him prepare, for I will cut his throat.

FR. SOL. *Que dit-il, monsieur?*   35

BOY. *Il me commande de vous dire que vous faites
vous prêt, car ce soldat ici est disposé tout à cette
heure de couper votre gorge.*

PIST. Owy, cuppele gorge, permafoy.°

Sc. iv: As in III.iv, the French has been restored to sense by
editors.   **4. Qualtitie . . . me:** Pistol's attempt at a French
phrase, which has not been explained.   **8. Perpend:** observe.
9. fox: sword.   **11. Egregious:** enormous.   **13. moi:** pronounced
moy.   **15. rim:** lit., diaphragm, but Pistol is being picturesque.
20. luxurious: lustful.   **29. firk:** beat.   **30. ferret:** worry.
39. cuppele . . . permafoy: Elizabethan soldiers who served in
France had their own versions of French phrases, of which these
are two. The "trays beans" and "mercy bowcups" of American
soldiers during World War II are comparable.

Peasant, unless thou give me crowns, brave crowns,
Or mangled shalt thou be by this my sword.   41

FR. SOL. *Oh, je vous supplie, pour l'amour de Dieu,
me pardonner! Je suis gentilhomme de bonne
maison. Gardez ma vie, et je vous donnerai deux
cents écus.*

PIST. What are his words?   46

BOY. He prays you to save his life. He is a gentleman of a good house, and for his ransom he will
give you two hundred crowns.

PIST. Tell him my fury shall abate, and I   50
The crowns will take.

FR. SOL. *Petit monsieur, que dit-il?*

BOY. *Encore qu'il est contre son jurement de pardonner aucun prisonnier; néanmoins, pour les écus
que vous l'avez promis, il est content de vous donner
la liberté, le franchisement.*   56

FR. SOL. *Sur mes genoux je vous donne mille re-
mercîmens, et je m'estime heureux que je suis tombé
entre les mains d'un chevalier, je pense, le plus brave,
vaillant, et très distingué seigneur d'Angleterre.*   61

PIST. Expound unto me, boy.

BOY. He gives you, upon his knees, a thousand
thanks, and he esteems himself happy that he hath
fallen into the hands of one, as he thinks, the most
brave, valorous, and thrice-worthy signieur of England.

PIST. As I suck blood, I will some mercy show.
Follow me!   69

BOY. *Suivez-vous le grand capitaine.* [*Exeunt*
PISTOL, *and* FRENCH SOLDIER.] I did never know so
full a voice issue from so empty a heart. But the saying is true, "The empty vessel makes the greatest
sound." Bardolph and Nym had ten times more
valor than this roaring devil i' the old play, that   75
everyone may pare his nails with a wooden dagger,°
and they are both hanged. And so would this be if
he durst steal anything adventurously. I must stay
with the lackeys, with the luggage of our camp. The
French might have a good prey of us if he knew
of it, for there is none to guard it but boys.   [*Exit.*]

SCENE V. *Another part of the field.*

[*Enter* CONSTABLE, ORLEANS, BOURBON, DAUPHIN,
and RAMBURES.]

CON. O diable!

ORL. *O Seigneur! Le jour est perdu, tout est perdu!*

DAU. *Mort de ma vie!* All is confounded, all!
Reproach and everlasting shame
Sits mocking in our plumes. *O méchante fortune!*   5
Do not run away.   [*A short alarum.*]

CON.   Why, all our ranks are broke.

75–76. roaring . . . dagger: In the old miracle plays the Devil
was a popular character; he came in roaring and carried a wooden
sword. Cf. *T Night,* IV.ii.130–141.

DAU. Oh, perdurable° shame! Let's stab ourselves.
Be these the wretches that we played at dice for?
   ORL. Is this the King we sent to for his ransom?
   BOUR. Shame and eternal shame, nothing but
     shame!   10
Let us die in honor. Once more back again,
And he that will not follow Bourbon now,
Let him go hence, and with his cap in hand,
Like a base pander,° hold the chamber door
Whilst by a slave, no gentler than my dog,   15
His fairest daughter is contaminated.
   CON. Disorder, that hath spoiled us, friend° us
     now!
Let us on heaps go offer up our lives.
   ORL. We are enow yet living in the field
To smother up the English in our throngs,°   20
If any order might be thought upon.
   BOUR. The devil take order now! I'll to the throng.
Let life be short, else shame will be too long.
                    [*Exeunt.*]

SCENE VI. *Another part of the field.*

[*Alarum. Enter* KING HENRY *and forces,* EXETER, *and
         others.*]

   K. HEN. Well have we done, thrice valiant coun-
     trymen.
But all's not done. Yet keep the French the field.
   EXE. The Duke of York commends him to your
     Majesty.
   K. HEN. Lives he, good Uncle? Thrice within this
     hour
I saw him down, thrice up again, and fighting.   5
From helmet to the spur all blood he was.
   EXE. In which array, brave soldier, doth he lie,
Larding° the plain, and by his bloody side,
Yokefellow to his honor-owing° wounds,
The noble Earl of Suffolk also lies.   10
Suffolk first died. And York, all haggled° over,
Comes to him, where in gore he lay insteeped,°
And takes him by the beard, kisses the gashes
That bloodily did yawn upon his face,
And cries aloud " Tarry, dear Cousin Suffolk!   15
My soul shall thine keep company to Heaven.
Tarry, sweet soul, for mine, then fly abreast,
As in this glorious and well-foughten field
We kept together in our chivalry! "
Upon these words I came and cheered him up.   20
He smiled me in the face, raught° me his hand,
And, with a feeble gripe,° says, " Dear my lord,
Commend my service to my sovereign."

So did he turn, and over Suffolk's neck
He threw his wounded arm and kissed his lips,   25
And so espoused to death, with blood he sealed
A testament° of noble-ending love.
The pretty and sweet manner of it forced
Those waters from me which I would have stopped.
But I had not so much of man in me,   30
And all my mother came into mine eyes
And gave me up to tears.
   K. HEN.   I blame you not,
For, hearing this, I must perforce compound°
With mistful eyes, or they will issue too.   [*Alarum.*]
But hark! What new alarum is this same?   35
The French have reinforced their scattered men.
Then every soldier kill his prisoners.°
Give the word through.   [*Exeunt.*]

SCENE VII. *Another part of the field.*

[*Enter* FLUELLEN *and* GOWER.]

   FLU. Kill the poys and the luggage! 'Tis expressly
against the law of arms. 'Tis as arrant a piece of
knavery, mark you now, as can be offer't. In your
conscience, now, is it not?   4
   GOW. 'Tis certain there's not a boy left alive, and
the cowardly rascals that ran from the battle ha'
done this slaughter. Besides, they have burned and
carried away all that was in the King's tent, wherefore the King, most worthily, hath caused every
soldier to cut his prisoner's throat. Oh, 'tis a gallant
King!   11
   FLU. Aye, he was porn at Monmouth, Captain
Gower. What call you the town's name where
Alexander the Pig was born?
   GOW. Alexander the Great.   15
   FLU. Why, I pray you, is not pig great? The pig,
or the great, or the mighty, or the huge, or the
magnanimous, are all one reckonings, save the
phrase is a little variations.   19
   GOW. I think Alexander the Great was born in
Macedon. His father was called Philip of Macedon,
as I take it.
   FLU. I think it is in Macedon where Alexander is
porn. I tell you, Captain, if you look in the maps of
the 'orld, I warrant you sall find, in the com-   25
parisons between Macedon and Monmouth, that the
situations, look you, is both alike. There is a river
in Macedon, and there is also moreover a river at
Monmouth. It is called Wye at Monmouth, but it is
out of my prains what is the name of the other
river. But 'tis all one, 'tis alike as my fingers is   31
to my fingers, and there is salmons in both. If you
mark Alexander's life well, Harry of Monmouth's

Sc. v: 7. **perdurable**: enduring.   **14. pander**: one who introduces the customer to a harlot.   **17. friend**: befriend.
20. throngs: numbers, crowd.
   Sc. vi: **8. Larding**: making rich.   **9. honor-owing**: owning
honor, honorable.   **11. haggled**: hacked.   **12. insteeped**:
stained.   **21. raught**: reached.   **22. gripe**: grip.

27. testament: last will.   **33. compound**: come to terms.
37. kill . . . prisoners: i.e., lest the prisoners should turn on their
captors.

life is come after it indifferent° well, for there is
figures° in all things. Alexander, God knows,   35
and you know, in his rages, and his furies, and his
wraths, and his cholers, and his moods, and his displeasures, and his indignations, and also being a
little intoxicates in his prains, did, in his ales and
his angers, look you, kill his best friend, Cleitus.   41

GOW. Our King is not like him in that. He never
killed any of his friends.

FLU. It is not well done, mark you now, to take
the tales out of my mouth ere it is made and   45
finished. I speak but in the figures and comparisons
of it. As Alexander killed his friend Cleitus, being
in his ales and his cups, so also Harry Monmouth,
being in his right wits and his good judgments,
turned away the fat knight with the great-belly   50
doublet.° He was full of jests, and gipes,° and
knaveries, and mocks. I have forgot his name.

GOW. Sir John Falstaff.

FLU. That is he. I'll tell you there is good men
porn at Monmouth.   56

GOW. Here comes His Majesty.

[*Alarum. Enter* KING HENRY *and forces;* WARWICK,
GLOUCESTER, EXETER, *and others.*]

K. HEN. I was not angry since I came to France
Until this instant. Take a trumpet, herald.
Ride thou unto the horsemen on yon hill.   60
If they will fight with us, bid them come down,
Or void the field. They do offend our sight.
If they'll do neither, we will come to them,
And make them skirr° away as swift as stones
Enforcèd from the old Assyrian slings.   65
Besides, we'll cut the throats of those we have,
And not a man of them that we shall take
Shall taste our mercy. Go and tell them so.

[*Enter* MONTJOY.]

EXE. Here comes the herald of the French, my
liege.   69

GLO. His eyes are humbler than they used to be.

K. HEN. How now! What means this, herald?
Know'st thou not
That I have fined° these bones of mine for ransom?
Comest thou again for ransom?

MONT.   No, great King.
I come to thee for charitable license,
That we may wander o'er this bloody field   75
To book° our dead, and then to bury them,
To sort our nobles from our common men.
For many of our Princes — woe the while! —
Lie drowned and soaked in mercenary blood.
So do our vulgar drench their peasant limbs   80
In blood of Princes, and their wounded steeds
Fret° fetlock-deep in gore, and with wild rage

Yerk° out their armèd heels at their dead masters,
Killing them twice. Oh, give us leave, great King,
To view the field in safety and dispose   85
Of their dead bodies!

K. HEN.   I tell thee truly, herald,
I know not if the day be ours or no,
For yet a many of your horsemen peer°
And gallop o'er the field.

MONT.   The days is yours.

K. HEN. Praisèd be God, and not our strength,
for it!   90
What is this castle called that stands hard by?

MONT. They call it Agincourt.

K. HEN. Then call we this the field of Agincourt,
Fought on the day of Crispin Crispianus.

FLU. Your grandfather of famous memory,   95
an 't please your Majesty, and your great-uncle
Edward the Plack Prince of Wales, as I have read
in the chronicles, fought a most prave pattle here
in France.

K. HEN. They did, Fluellen.   100

FLU. Your Majesty says very true. If your Majesties is remembered of it, the Welshmen did good
service in a garden where leeks did grow, wearing
leeks in their Monmouth caps,° which, your
Majesty know, to this hour is an honorable badge of
the service. And I do believe your Majesty takes no
scorn to wear the leek upon Saint Tavy's Day.°   108

K. HEN. I wear it for a memorable honor,
For I am Welsh, you know, good countryman.

FLU. All the water in Wye cannot wash your
Majesty's Welsh plood out of your pody, I can tell
you that. God pless it and preserve it, as long as
it pleases His grace, and His majesty too!

K. HEN. Thanks, good my countryman.   115

FLU. By Jeshu, I am your Majesty's countryman,
I care not who know it, I will confess it to all the
'orld. I need not to be ashamed of your Majesty,
praised be God, so long as your Majesty is an honest
man.   120

K. HEN. God keep me so! Our heralds go with
him.
Bring me just° notice of the numbers dead
On both our parts. Call yonder fellow hither.

[*Points to* WILLIAMS. *Exeunt* HERALDS
with MONTJOY.]

EXE. Soldier, you must come to the King.   124

K. HEN. Soldier, why wearest thou that glove in
thy cap?

WILL. An 't please your Majesty, 'tis the gage of
one that I should fight withal, if he be alive.

K. HEN. An Englishman?   129

WILL. An 't please your Majesty, a rascal that

Sc. vii: **34. indifferent:** fairly.   **35. figures:** significance.
50-51. great-belly doublet: In this form of doublet the front part
hung forward in the shape of a peapod. See Pl. 8d.   **51. gipes:**
jibes.   **64. skirr:** scurry.   **72. fined:** reserved as a fine.
76. book: make a list of.   **82. Fret:** plunge wildly.

83. Yerk: kick.   **88. peer:** appear.   **102-04. Welshmen . . .
caps:** This incident is otherwise unrecorded, nor is the origin
known of the Welsh custom of wearing leeks on St. David's Day.
108. Saint Tavy's Day: March 1. *Tavy* (David) was the patron
saint of Wales.   **122. just:** exact.

swaggered with me last night, who, if alive and ever dare to challenge this glove, I have sworn to take him a box o' th' ear. Or if I can see my glove in his cap, which he swore as he was a soldier he would wear if alive, I will strike it out soundly.   136

K. HEN. What think you, Captain Fluellen? Is it fit this soldier keep his oath?

FLU. He is a craven and a villain else, an 't please your Majesty, in my conscience.   140

K. HEN. It may be his enemy is a gentleman of great sort, quite from the answer of his degree.°

FLU. Though he be as good a gentleman as the Devil is, as Lucifer and Belzebub himself, it is necessary, look your Grace, that he keep his vow and his oath. If he be perjured, see you now, his reputation is as arrant a villain and a Jacksauce° as ever his black shoe trod upon God's ground and his earth, in my conscience, la!   150

K. HEN. Then keep thy vow, sirrah, when thou meetest the fellow.

WILL. So I will, my liege, as I live.

K. HEN. Who servest thou under?

WILL. Under Captain Gower, my liege.   155

FLU. Gower is a good captain, and is good knowledge and literatured in the wars.

K. HEN. Call him hither to me, soldier.   158

WILL. I will, my liege.   [Exit.]

K. HEN. Here, Fluellen, wear thou this favor for me and stick it in thy cap. When Alençon and myself were down together,° I plucked this glove from his helm. If any man challenge this, he is a friend to Alençon and an enemy to our person. If thou encounter any such, apprehend him, an thou dost me love.   166

FLU. Your Grace doo's me as great honors as can be desired in the hearts of his subjects. I would fain see the man that has but two legs that shall find himself aggriefed at this glove, that is all, but I would fain see it once, an 't please God of His grace that I might see.   172

K. HEN. Knowest thou Gower?

FLU. He is my dear friend, an 't please you.

K. HEN. Pray thee, go seek him, and bring him to my tent.

FLU. I will fetch him.   [Exit.]

K. HEN. My Lord of Warwick, and my brother Gloucester,
Follow Fluellen closely at the heels.
The glove which I have given him for a favor   180
May haply purchase him a box o' th' ear.

It is the soldier's. I by bargain should
Wear it myself. Follow, good Cousin Warwick.
If that the soldier strike him, as I judge
By his blunt bearing he will keep his word,   185
Some sudden mischief may arise of it.
For I do know Fluellen valiant
And, touched with choler,° hot as gunpowder,
And quickly will return an injury.   189
Follow, and see there be no harm between them.
Go you with me, Uncle of Exeter.   [Exeunt.]

SCENE VIII. Before KING HENRY's pavilion.

[Enter GOWER and WILLIAMS.]

WILL. I warrant it is to knight you, Captain.

[Enter FLUELLEN.]

FLU. God's will and His pleasure, Captain, I beseech you now, come apace° to the King. There is more good toward you peradventure than is in your knowledge to dream of.   5

WILL. Sir, know you this glove?

FLU. Know the glove! I know the glove is a glove.

WILL. I know this, and thus I challenge it.

[Strikes him.]

FLU. 'Sblood!° An arrant traitor as any is in the universal world, or in France, or in England!   11

GOW. How now, sir! You villain!

WILL. Do you think I'll be forsworn?°

FLU. Stand away, Captain Gower. I will give treason his payment into plows, I warrant you.   15

WILL. I am no traitor.

FLU. That's a lie in thy throat.° I charge you in His Majesty's name, apprehend him. He's a friend of the Duke Alençon's.   19

[Enter WARWICK and GLOUCESTER.]

WAR. How now, how now! What's the matter?

FLU. My Lord of Warwick, here is — praised be God for it! — a most contagious treason come to light, look you, as you shall desire in a summer's day. Here is His Majesty.

[Enter KING HENRY and EXETER.]

K. HEN. How now! What's the matter?   25

FLU. My liege, here is a villain and a traitor that, look your Grace, has struck the glove which your Majesty is take out of the helmet of Alençon.

WILL. My liege, this was my glove, here is the fellow of it. And he that I gave it to in change° promised to wear it in his cap. I promised to strike him if he did. I met this man with my glove in his cap, and I have been as good as my word.   34

FLU. Your Majesty hear now, saving your Maj-

142. quite . . . degree: far above his rank and therefore not required to answer.   148. Jacksauce: saucy knave.   161–62. Alençon . . . together: Holinshed records: "The King that day showed himself a valiant knight, albeit almost felled by the Duke of Alençon; yet with plain strength he slew two of the Duke's company, and felled the Duke himself, whom, when he would have yielded, the King's Guard, contrary to his mind, slew out of hand."

188. choler: temper.
          Sc. viii: 3. apace: quickly.   10. 'Sblood: by God's blood.
13. be forsworn: break my oath.   17. lie . . . throat: the most deadly insult, which could only be repaid by mortal combat.
31. change: exchange.

esty's manhood, what an arrant, rascally, beggarly, lousy knave it is. I hope your Majesty is pear me testimony and witness, and will avouchment,° that this is the glove of Alençon that your Majesty is give me. In your conscience, now.

K. HEN. Give me thy glove, soldier. Look, here is the fellow of it.   42
'Twas I, indeed, thou promised'st to strike, And thou hast given me most bitter terms.°

FLU. An 't° please your Majesty, let his neck answer for it, if there is any martial law in the world.

K. HEN. How canst thou make me satisfaction?

WILL. All offenses, my lord, come from the heart. Never came any from mine that might offend your Majesty.   51

WILL. Your Majesty came not like yourself. You appeared to me but as a common man — witness the night, your garments, your lowliness. And 55 what your Highness suffered under that shape, I beseech you to take it for your own fault and not mine. For had you been as I took you for, I made no offense. Therefore I beseech your Highness pardon me.   60

K. HEN. Here, Uncle Exeter, fill this glove with crowns
And give it to this fellow. Keep it, fellow, And wear it for an honor in thy cap Till I do challenge it. Give him the crowns.   65
And, Captain, you must needs be friends with him.

FLU. By this day and this light, the fellow has mettle enough in his belly. Hold, there is twelve-pence for you, and I pray you to serve God, and keep you out of prawls, and prabbles,° and quarrels, and dissensions, and I warrant you it is the better for you.

WILL. I will none of your money.   72

FLU. It is with a good will, I can tell you, it will serve you to mend your shoes. Come, wherefore should you be so pashful? Your shoes is not so good. 'Tis a good silling, I warrant you, or I will change it.

[*Enter an* ENGLISH HERALD.]

K. HEN. Now, herald, are the dead numbered?

HER. Here is the number of the slaughtered French.

K. HEN. What prisoners of good sort° are taken, Uncle?   80

EXE. Charles° Duke of Orleans, nephew to the King,
John Duke of Bourbon, and Lord Bouciqualt. Of other lords and barons, knights and squires, Full fifteen hundred, besides common men.

K. HEN. This note doth tell me of ten thousand French   85

38. avouchment: certify.   44. bitter terms: insults.   45. An 't:
if it.   70. prabbles: brabbles, quarrels.   80. sort: rank.
81–111. Charles . . . twenty: This casualty list is taken directly
from Holinshed.

That in the field lie slain. Of Princes in this number, And nobles bearing banners,° there lie dead One hundred twenty-six. Added to these, Of knights, esquires, and gallant gentlemen, Eight thousand and four hundred, of the which 90 Five hundred were but yesterday dubbed knights. So that in these ten thousand they have lost There are but sixteen hundred mercenaries. The rest are Princes, barons, lords, knights, squires, And gentlemen of blood and quality.   95
The names of those their nobles that lie dead: Charles Delabreth, High Constable of France, Jaques of Chatillon, Admiral of France, The master of the crossbows, Lord Rambures, Great Master of France, the brave Sir Guichard
     Dolphin,   100
John Duke of Alençon, Anthony Duke of Brabant, The brother to the Duke of Burgundy, And Edward Duke of Bar. Of lusty earls, Grandpré and Roussi, Fauconberg and Foix, 104
Beaumont and Marle, Vaudemont and Lestrale. Here was a royal fellowship° of death! Where is the number of our English dead?

[HERALD *shows him another paper.*]
Edward the Duke of York, the Earl of Suffolk, Sir Richard Ketly, Davy Gam, esquire. None else of name, and of all other men   110
But five and twenty.° O God, Thy arm was here, And not to us, but to Thy arm alone, Ascribe we all! When, without stratagem, But in plain shock and even play of battle, Was ever known so great and little loss   115
On one part and on th' other? Take it, God, For it is none but Thine!

EXE.   'Tis wonderful!

K. HEN. Come, go we in procession to the village. And be it death proclaimed through our host To boast of this or take that praise from God   120
Which is His only.

FLU. Is it not lawful, an 't please your Majesty, to tell how many is killed?

K. HEN. Yes, Captain, but with this acknowledgment,
That God fought for us.   125

FLU. Yes, my conscience, He did us great good.

K. HEN. Do we all holy rites.
Let there be sung "*Non nobis*" and "*Te Deum*," The dead with charity enclosed in clay. And then to Calais, and to England then,   130
Where ne'er from France arrived more happy men.
[*Exeunt.*]

87. bearing banners: i.e., displaying their coats of arms.
106. fellowship: partnership.   111. But . . . twenty: The English
losses, though not so low as given by Shakespeare, have been
variously estimated from 100 to 600 killed. The French lost over
10,000 killed through their insane tactics of charging in full
armor through boggy ground against archers protected by a
palisade of sharpened stakes.

Act V

PROLOGUE

[*Enter* CHORUS.]

CHOR. Vouchsafe to those that have not read the
  story
That I may prompt them. And of such as have,
I humbly pray them to admit the excuse
Of time, of numbers, and due course of things
Which cannot in their huge and proper life   5
Be here presented. Now we bear the King
Toward Calais. Grant him there. There seen,
Heave him away upon your wingèd thoughts
Athwart the sea. Behold, the English beach
Pales in° the flood with men, with wives and boys,
Whose shouts and claps outvoice the deep-mouthed
  sea,   11
Which like a mighty whiffler° 'fore the King
Seems to prepare his way. So let him land,
And solemnly see him set on to London.
So swift a pace hath thought that even now   15
You may imagine him upon Blackheath,°
Where that his lords desire him to have borne
His bruisèd helmet and his bended sword
Before him through the city. He forbids it,
Being free from vainness and self-glorious pride,
Giving full trophy,° signal,° and ostent°   21
Quite from himself to God. But now behold,
In the quick forge and working house° of thought,
How London doth pour out her citizens!
The mayor and all his brethren in best sort,°   25
Like to the Senators of the antique Rome,
With the plebeians swarming at their heels,
Go forth and fetch their conquering Caesar in.°
As, by a lower but loving likelihood,°
Were° now the General of our gracious Empress,
As in good time he may, from Ireland coming,   31
Bringing rebellion broachèd° on his sword,
How many would the peaceful city quit,
To welcome him! Much more, and much more
  cause,
Did they this Harry. Now in London place him.
As yet the lamentation of the French   36
Invites the King of England's stay at home.
The Emperor's° coming in behalf of France,

To order peace between them. And omit
All the occurrences, whatever chanced,   40
Till Harry's back return again to France.
There must we bring him, and myself have played
The interim,° by remembering° you 'tis past. 43
Then brook abridgment,° and your eyes advance,
After your thoughts, straight back again to France.
                                              [*Exit.*]

SCENE I. *France. The English camp.*

[*Enter* FLUELLEN *and* GOWER.]

GOW. Nay, that's right, but why wear you your
leek today? Saint Davy's Day is past.

FLU. There is occasions and causes why and
wherefore in all things. I will tell you, asse my
friend, Captain Gower. The rascally, scald,°   5
beggarly, lousy, pragging knave Pistol, which you
and yourself and all the world know to be no petter
than a fellow, look you now, of no merits, he is
come to me and prings me pread and salt yesterday,
look you, and bid me eat my leek. It was in a   10
place where I could not breed no contention° with
him, but I will be so bold as to wear it in my cap till
I see him once again, and then I will tell him a little
piece of my desires.

[*Enter* PISTOL.]

GOW. Why, here he comes, swelling like a turkey
cock.   16

FLU. 'Tis no matter for his swellings nor his
turkeycocks. God pless you, Aunchient Pistol! You
scurvy, lousy knave, God pless you.

PIST. Ha! Art thou bedlam?° Dost thou thirst,
  base Trojan,°   20
To have me fold up Parca's fatal web?°
Hence! I am qualmish° at the smell of leek.

FLU. I peseech you heartily, scurvy, lousy knave,
at my desires, and my requests, and my petitions,
to eat, look you, this leek. Because, look you,   25
you do not love it, nor your affections and your
appetites and your digestions doo's not agree with
it, I would desire you to eat it.

PIST. Not for Cadwallader° and all his goats.

FLU. There is one goat for you. [*Strikes him.*]
Will you be so good, scald knave, as eat it?   31

PIST. Base Trojan, thou shalt die.

FLU. You say very true, scald knave, when God's
will is. I will desire you to live in the meantime, and
eat your victuals. Come, there is sauce for it.
[*Strikes him.*] You called me yesterday mountain

Act V. Prologue: 10. Pales in: encircles.   12. whiffler: an
officer who makes way for a royal procession.   16. Blackheath:
district south of London.   21. trophy: lit., pile of arms of the
defeated set up in triumph. signal: sign. ostent: display.
23. working house: workshop.   25. in . . . sort: in their best
clothes.   27–28. With . . . in: This incident forms the first two
scenes of *Julius Caesar*, which was first staged a few weeks after
the first performance of *Henry V*.   29. loving likelihood: much-
desired probability.   30–34. Were . . . him: See *Hen V* Intro.
p. 732a.   32. broached: stuck as on a spit, impaled.   38. Emperor: i.e., Sigismund, who came over to England in 1416 to
negotiate between Henry and the French King.

42–43. myself . . . interim: i.e., I have related all that is supposed
to have happened between Acts IV and V.   43. remembering:
reminding.   44. brook abridgment: endure the omission.
  Sc. i: 5. scald: scaly, scabby.   11. breed no contention: start
a quarrel.   20. bedlam: lunatic. Trojan: in Pistol's romantic
imagination a term of abuse.   21. fold . . . web: cut short the
thread of your fate (*Parca*).   22. am qualmish: feel sick.
29. Cadwallader: a Welsh Prince.

squire,° but I will make you today a squire of low
degree.° I pray you fall to. If you can mock a leek,
you can eat a leek.   39

GOW. Enough, Captain. You have astonished
him.

FLU. I say I will make him eat some part of my
leek or I will peat his pate four days. Bite, I pray
you. It is good for your green wound and your
ploody coxcomb.   45

PIST. Must I bite?

FLU. Yes, certainly, and out of doubt and out of
question too, and ambiguities.

PIST. By this leek, I will most horribly revenge.
I eat and eat, I swear ——   50

FLU. Eat, I pray you. Will you have some more
sauce to your leek? There is not enough leek to
swear by.

PIST. Quiet thy cudgel. Thou dost see I eat.   54

FLU. Much good do you, scald knave, heartily.
Nay, pray you throw none away, the skin is good
for your broken coxcomb. When you take occasions
to see leeks hereafter, I pray you mock at 'em. That
is all.

PIST. Good.   60

FLU. Aye, leeks is good. Hold you, there is a
groat° to heal your pate.

PIST. Me a groat!

FLU. Yes, verily and in truth you shall take it, or
I have another leek in my pocket which you shall
eat.   66

PIST. I take thy groat in earnest° of revenge.

FLU. If I owe you anything, I will pay you in
cudgels. You shall be a woodmonger,° and buy
nothing of me but cudgels. God b' wi' you, and   70
keep you, and heal your pate.   [*Exit.*]

PIST. All Hell shall stir for this.

GOW. Go, go. You are a counterfeit cowardly
knave. Will you mock at an ancient tradition, begun
upon an honorable respect and worn as a memorable trophy of predeceased° valor, and dare not   75
avouch° in your deeds any of your words? I have
seen you gleeking° and galling° at this gentleman
twice or thrice. You thought because he could not
speak English in the native garb° he could not   80
therefore handle an English cudgel. You find it
otherwise, and henceforth let a Welsh correction
teach you a good English condition. Fare ye well.
                                              [*Exit.*]

PIST. Doth Fortune play the huswife° with me
now?   85

News have I that my Doll° is dead i' the spital
Of malady of France,°
And there my rendezvous is quite cut off.
Old I do wax, and from my weary limbs
Honor is cudgeled. Well, bawd° I'll turn,   90
And something lean to cutpurse of quick hand.°
To England will I steal, and there I'll steal.
And patches will I get unto these cudgeled scars,
And swear I got them in the Gallia wars.   [*Exit.*]

SCENE II. *France. A royal palace.*

[*Enter, at one door,* KING HENRY, EXETER, BEDFORD,
GLOUCESTER, WARWICK, WESTMORELAND, *and other*
LORDS; *at another, the* FRENCH KING,° QUEEN ISABEL,
the PRINCESS KATHARINE, ALICE *and other* LADIES; *the*
DUKE OF BURGUNDY, *and his train.*]

K. HEN. Peace to this meeting, wherefore we are
met!
Unto our brother France, and to our sister,
Health and fair time of day. Joy and good wishes
To our most fair and princely cousin Katharine.
And, as a branch and member of this royalty°   5
By whom this great assembly is contrived,°
We do salute you, Duke of Burgundy.
And, Princes French, and peers, health to you all!

FR. KING. Right joyous are we to behold your face,
Most worthy Brother England, fairly met.   10
So are you, Princes English, every one.

Q. ISA. So happy be the issue, Brother England,
Of this good day and of this gracious meeting
As we are now glad to behold your eyes —
Your eyes, which hitherto have borne in them   15
Against the French, that met them in their bent,
The fatal balls of murdering basilisks.°
The venom of such looks, we fairly hope,
Have lost their quality, and that this day
Shall change all griefs and quarrels into love.   20

K. HEN. To cry amen to that, thus we appear.

Q. ISA. You English Princes all, I do salute you.

BUR. My duty to you both, on equal love,
Great Kings of France and England! That I have
labored,
With all my wits, my pains and strong endeavors,

---

86. Doll: She was called Nell in II.i.33, and many texts are
amended accordingly. It is possible that Shakespeare forgot that
Pistol had married the quondam Mrs. Quickly and not Doll
Tearsheet, who was last heard of as being treated in the hospital
(II.i.78–81). "Doll," however, is commonly used for any woman
of easy virtue.   87. malady of France: venereal disease.
90. bawd: brothel-keeper.   91. cutpurse . . . hand: See *W Tale,*
IV.iv.682–87, and Gen. Intro. p. 28a.
     Sc. ii: s.d., French King: Actually the French King was in-
sane at this time and the Duke of Burgundy acted for him.
5. royalty: royal family.   6. contrived: arranged.   17. balls . . .
basilisks: a double pun, *balls* being eyeballs and cannon balls
and *basilisk* large cannon and a fierce kind of serpent capable
of killing by its very look.

36–37. mountain squire: i.e., poor Welshman.   37–38. squire
. . . degree: as contrasted with a mountain squire. *The Squire
of Low Degree* was a popular romance.   62. groat: fourpence.
67. in earnest: as payment on account.   69. woodmonger:
dealer in wood.   75. predeceased: long since dead.   76. avouch:
certify.   77. gleeking: mocking. galling: annoying.   80. garb:
garment, fashion.   85. huswife: hussy.

To bring your most imperial Majesties   26
Unto this bar° and royal interview,
Your Mightiness on both parts best can witness.
Since then my office hath so far prevailed
That, face to face and royal eye to eye,   30
You have congreeted,° let it not disgrace me
If I demand, before this royal view,
What rub° or what impediment there is
Why that the naked, poor, and mangled Peace,
Dear nurse of arts, plenties, and joyful births,   35
Should not in this best garden of the world,
Our fertile France, put up her lovely visage?°
Alas, she hath from France too long been chased,
And all her husbandry° doth lie on heaps,
Corrupting in it° own fertility.   40
Her vine, the merry cheerer of the heart,
Unprunèd dies. Her hedges even-pleached,°
Like prisoners wildly overgrown with hair,
Put forth disordered twigs. Her fallow leas°
The darnel, hemlock, and rank fumitory°   45
Doth root upon while that the colter° rusts
That should deracinate° such savagery.
The even mead,° that erst brought sweetly forth
The freckled cowslip, burnet,° and green clover,
Wanting the scythe, all uncorrected, rank,   50
Conceives by idleness, and nothing teems
But hateful docks, rough thistles, kecksies,° burrs,
Losing both beauty and utility.
And as our vineyards, fallows, meads, and hedges,
Defective in their natures, grow to wildness,   55
Even so our houses and ourselves and children
Have lost, or do not learn for want of time,
The sciences that should become our country,
But grow like savages — as soldiers will
That nothing do but meditate on blood —   60
To swearing and stern looks, diffused° attire,
And everything that seems unnatural.
Which to reduce into our former favor
You are assembled. And my speech entreats
That I may know the let° why gentle Peace   65
Should not expel these inconveniences
And bless us with her former qualities.
    K. HEN. If, Duke of Burgundy, you would the peace,
Whose want gives growth to the imperfections
Which you have cited, you must buy that peace   70
With full accord to all our just demands,
Whose tenors° and particular effects
You have enscheduled° briefly in your hands.

    BUR. The King hath heard them, to the which as yet
There is no answer made.
    K. HEN.   Well then, the peace,   75
Which you before so urged, lies in his answer.
    FR. KING. I have but with a cursorary° eye
O'erglanced the articles. Pleaseth your Grace
To appoint some of your Council presently
To sit with us once more, with better heed   80
To resurvey them, we will suddenly
Pass our accept° and peremptory° answer.
    K. HEN. Brother, we shall. Go, Uncle Exeter,
And Brother Clarence, and you, Brother Gloucester,
Warwick and Huntingdon, go with the King.   85
And take with you free power to ratify,
Augment, or alter, as your wisdoms best
Shall see advantageable for our dignity,
Anything in or out of our demands,
And we'll consign° thereto. Will you, fair Sister,   90
Go with the Princes, or stay here with us?
    Q. ISA. Our gracious brother, I will go with them.
Haply a woman's voice may do some good
When articles too nicely° urged be stood on.
    K. HEN. Yet leave our cousin Katharine here with us.   95
She is our capital° demand, comprised
Within the forerank of our articles.
    Q. ISA. She hath good leave.
    [*Exeunt all except* HENRY, KATHARINE, *and* ALICE.]
    K. HEN.   Fair Katharine, and most fair,
Will you vouchsafe to teach a soldier terms°
Such as will enter at a lady's ear   100
And plead his love suit to her gentle heart?
    KATH. Your Majesty shall mock at me. I cannot
speak your England.
    K. HEN. O fair Katharine, if you will love me
soundly with your French heart, I will be glad to
hear you confess it brokenly with your English
tongue. Do you like me, Kate?   107
    KATH. *Pardonnez-moi,* I cannot tell vat is " like
me."
    K. HEN. An angel is like you, Kate, and you are
like an angel.   111
    KATH. *Que dit-il? Que je suis semblable à les
anges?*
    ALICE. *Oui, vraiment, sauf votre grace, ainsi dit-il.*
    K. HEN. I said so, dear Katharine, and I must not
blush to affirm it.   117
    KATH. *O bon Dieu! Les langues des hommes sont
pleines de tromperies.*
    K. HEN. What says she, fair one? That the tongues
of men are full of deceits?
    ALICE. Oui, dat de tongues of de mans is be full of
deceits. Dat is de Princess.   123

---

27. bar: court.   31. congreeted: met harmoniously.   33. rub: obstruction. See App. 13.   37. put . . . visage: raise her fair face. 39. husbandry: agriculture.   40. it: its.   42. even-pleached: thick and even.   44. leas: open land.   45. darnel . . . fumitory: European weeds which grow in plowed fields.   46. colter: blade of the plowshare.   47. deracinate: uproot.   48. even mead: level meadow.   49. burnet: a weed with a brown flower.   52. docks . . . kecksies: weeds that grow in neglected meadows.   61. diffused: slovenly.   65. let: hindrance.   72. tenors: general intention.   73. enscheduled: listed.

77. cursorary: cursory, casual.   82. accept: acceptance. peremptory: final.   90. consign: agree.   94. nicely: precisely. 96. capital: chief.   99. terms: phrases.

K. HEN. The Princess is the better Englishwoman. I' faith, Kate, my wooing is fit for thy understanding. I am glad thou canst speak no better English, for if thou couldst, thou wouldst find me such a plain king that thou wouldst think I had sold my farm to buy my crown. I know no ways to mince it° in love, but directly to say "I love you." 130 Then if you urge me farther than to say "Do you in faith?" I wear out my suit.° Give me your answer, i' faith, do. And so clap° hands and a bargain. How say you, lady? 135

KATH. *Sauf votre honneur,* me understand vell.

K. HEN. Marry, if you would put me to verses or to dance for your sake, Kate, why, you undid me. For the one, I have neither words nor measure,° and for the other, I have no strength in measure, 140 yet a reasonable measure in strength. If I could win a lady at leapfrog, or by vaulting into my saddle with my armor on my back, under the correction of° bragging be it spoken, I should quickly leap into a wife. Or if I might buffet for my love, or 145 bound° my horse for her favors, I could lay on like a butcher and sit like a jackanapes,° never off. But, before God, Kate, I cannot look greenly° nor gasp out my eloquence, nor I have no cunning in protestation — only downright oaths, which I never 150 use till urged, nor never break for urging. If thou canst love a fellow of this temper, Kate, whose face is not worth sunburning, that never looks in his glass for love of anything he sees there, let thine eye be thy cook.° I speak to thee plain soldier. If 155 thou canst love me for this, take me; if not, to say to thee that I shall die is true, but for thy love, by the Lord, no. Yet I love thee too. And while thou livest, dear Kate, take a fellow of plain and uncoined constancy,° for he perforce must do thee right, 160 because he hath not the gift to woo in other places. For these fellows of infinite tongue that can rhyme themselves into ladies' favors, they do always reason themselves out again. What! A speaker is but 165 a prater, a rhyme is but a ballad.° A good leg will fall, a straight back will stoop, a black beard will turn white, a curled pate will grow bald, a fair face will wither, a full eye will wax hollow. But a good heart, Kate, is the sun and the moon — or 170 rather the sun and not the moon, for it shines bright and never changes, but keeps his course truly. If thou would have such a one, take me. And take me, take a soldier. Take a soldier, take a king. And what

sayest thou then to my love? Speak, my fair, and fairly, I pray thee. 177

KATH. Is it possible dat I sould love de enemy of France?

K. HEN. No, it is not possible you should love the enemy of France, Kate. But in loving me you should love the friend of France, for I love France so well that I will not part with a village of it, I will have it all mine. And, Kate, when France is mine and I am yours, then yours is France and you are mine. 186

KATH. I cannot tell vat is dat.

K. HEN. No, Kate? I will tell thee in French, which I am sure will hang upon my tongue like a new-married wife about her husband's neck, 190 hardly to be shook off. *Je quand sur le possession de France, et quand vous avez le possession de moi* — let me see, what then? Saint Denis° be my speed! — *donc votre est France et vous êtes mienne.* It is as easy for me, Kate, to conquer the kingdom as 195 to speak so much more French. I shall never move thee in French, unless it be to laugh at me.

KATH. *Sauf votre honneur, le Français que vous parlez, il est meilleur que l'Anglais lequel je parle.*

K. HEN. No, faith, is 't not, Kate. But thy 202 speaking of my tongue, and I thine, most truly-falsely, must needs be granted to be much at one. But, Kate, dost thou understand thus much English — canst thou love me?

KATH. I cannot tell. 207

K. HEN. Can any of your neighbors tell, Kate? I'll ask them. Come, I know thou lovest me. And at night, when you come into your closet, you'll 210 question this gentlewoman about me. And I know, Kate, you will to her dispraise those parts in me that you love with your heart. But, good Kate, mock me mercifully, the rather, gentle Princess, because I love thee cruelly. If ever thou beest mine, Kate, as 215 I have a saving faith within me tells me thou shalt, I get thee with scambling,° and thou must therefore needs prove a good soldier-breeder. Shall not thou and I, between Saint Denis and Saint George, 220 compound a boy, half French, half English, that shall go to Constantinople and take the Turk by the beard?° Shall we not? What sayest thou, my fair flower-de-luce?°

KATH. I do not know dat. 225

K. HEN. No, 'tis hereafter to know, but now to promise. Do but now promise, Kate, you will endeavor for your French part of such a boy, and for my English moiety° take the word of a king and a bachelor. How answer you, *la plus belle Katharine du monde, mon très cher et divine déesse?* 232

129–30. **mince it:** talk in a fancy way. 132. **wear . . . suit:** i.e., go dumb, with a pun on the double meaning of *suit* — "petition" and "clothes." 134. **clap:** clasp. 139–41. **measure . . . measure:** meter . . . dancing . . . amount. 143. **under . . . of:** with apologies for. 146. **bound:** make prance. 147. **jackanapes:** monkey. See App. 5. 148. **greenly:** like an inexperienced youth. 154–55. **let . . . cook:** i.e., convert my plainness into something fancy and delectable. 159–60. **uncoined constancy:** genuine loyalty. 166. **ballad:** i.e., doggerel. See App. 8.

193. **Saint Denis:** patron saint of France. 217. **scambling:** scuffling. 222–23. **Constantinople . . . beard:** i.e., do romantic and heroic deeds. Actually the boy was Henry VI, a saintly innocent. 224. **flower-de-luce:** fleur-de-lis, wild iris, the emblem of the French kings. 230. **moiety:** share.

KATH. Your majestee ave *fausse* French enough to deceive de most *sage demoiselle* dat is *en France.*

K. HEN. Now, fie upon my false French! By mine honor, in true English, I love thee, Kate. By which honor I dare not swear thou lovest me, yet my blood begins to flatter me that thou dost, notwithstanding the poor and untempering° effect of my visage. 240 Now, beshrew° my father's ambition! He was thinking of civil wars when he got° me. Therefore was I created with a stubborn outside, with an aspect of iron, that when I come to woo ladies, I fright 245 them. But, in faith, Kate, the elder I wax, the better I shall appear. My comfort is that old age, that ill layer-up of beauty, can do no more spoil upon my face. Thou hast me, if thou hast me, at the worst, and thou shalt wear me, if thou wear me, bet- 250 ter and better. And therefore tell me, most fair Katharine, will you have me? Put off your maiden blushes, avouch the thoughts of your heart with the looks of an empress. Take me by the hand, and say " Harry of England, I am thine." Which word 255 thou shalt no sooner bless mine ear withal but I will tell thee aloud " England is thine, Ireland is thine, France is thine, and Henry Plantagenet is thine "— who, though I speak it before his face, if he be not fellow with the best king, thou shalt find the 260 best king of good fellows. Come, your answer in broken music,° for thy voice is music and thy English broken. Therefore, queen of all, Katharine, break thy mind to me in broken English — wilt thou have me? 266

KATH. Dat is as it sall please de *roi mon père.*

K. HEN. Nay, it will please him well, Kate, it shall please him, Kate.

KATH. Den it sall also content me. 270

K. HEN. Upon that I kiss your hand, and I call you my Queen.

KATH. *Laissez, mon seigneur, laissez, laissez. Ma foi, je ne veux point que vous abaissez votre grandeur en baisant la main d'une de votre seigneurie indigne serviteur. Excusez-moi, je vous supplie, mon très-puissant seigneur.* 277

K. HEN. Then I will kiss your lips, Kate.

KATH. *Les dames et demoiselles pour être baisées devant leur noces, il n'est pas la coutume de France.* 282

K. HEN. Madam my interpreter, what says she?

ALICE. Dat it is not be de fashion pour les ladies of France, — I cannot tell vat is *baiser* en Anglish.

K. HEN. To kiss. 287

ALICE. Your Majesty *entendre* bettre *que moi.*

K. HEN. It is not a fashion for the maids in France to kiss before they are married, would she say? 291

ALICE. *Oui, vraiment.*

K. HEN. O Kate, nice customs courtesy° to great kings. Dear Kate, you and I cannot be confined within the weak list° of a country's fashion. 295 We are the makers of manners, Kate, and the liberty that follows our places stops the mouth of all find-faults — as I will do yours, for upholding the nice° fashion of your country in denying me a kiss. Therefore, patiently and yielding. [*Kissing her*] You 300 have witchcraft in your lips, Kate. There is more eloquence in a sugar touch of them than in the tongues of the French Council, and they should sooner persuade Harry of England than a general petition of monarchs. Here comes your father. 306

[*Re-enter the* FRENCH KING *and his* QUEEN, BURGUNDY, *and other* LORDS.]

BUR. God save your Majesty! My royal cousin, teach you our Princess English?

K. HEN. I would have her learn, my fair cousin, how perfectly I love her, and that is good English.

BUR. Is she not apt? 312

K. HEN. Our tongue is rough, Coz, and my condition° is not smooth. So that, having neither the voice nor the heart of flattery about me, I cannot so conjure up the spirit of love in her that he will appear in his true likeness. 317

BUR. Pardon the frankness of my mirth if I answer you for that. If you would conjure in her, you must make a circle; if conjure up love in her in his true likeness, he must appear naked and blind. Can you blame her, then, being a maid yet rosed over with the virgin crimson of modesty, if she deny the appearance of a naked blind boy in her naked seeing self? It were, my lord, a hard condition for a maid to consign to. 326

K. HEN. Yet they do wink and yield, as love is blind and enforces.

BUR. They are then excused, my lord, when they see not what they do.

K. HEN. Then, good my lord, teach your cousin to consent winking. 332

BUR. I will wink on her to consent, my lord, if you will teach her to know my meaning. For maids well summered and warm kept are like flies at Bartholomewtide,° blind, though they have their eyes. And then they will endure handling, which before would not abide looking on. 338

K. HEN. This moral° ties me over to time and a hot summer, and so I shall catch the fly, your cousin, in the latter end, and she must be blind too.

BUR. As love is, my lord, before it loves. 342

K. HEN. It is so. And you may, some of you, thank love for my blindness, who cannot see many a fair

French city for one fair French maid that stands in
my way.

FR. KING. Yes, my lord, you see them perspectively,° the cities turned into a maid, for they are
all girdled with maiden walls that war hath never
entered.   350

K. HEN. Shall Kate be my wife?

FR. KING. So please you.

K. HEN. I am content, so° the maiden cities you
talk of may wait on her. So the maid that stood in
the way for my wish shall show me the way to my
will.°   356

FR. KING. We have consented to all terms of reason.

K. HEN. Is 't so, my lords of England?

WEST. The King hath granted every article.
His daughter first, and then in sequel all,
According to their firm proposèd natures.   362

EXE. Only he hath not yet subscribed this:
Where your Majesty demands that the King of
France, having any occasion to write for matter of
grant,° shall name your Highness in this form and
with this addition, in French, *Notre très-cher fils
Henri, Roi d'Angleterre, Héritier de France;* and
thus in Latin, *Praeclarissimus filius noster Henricus,
Rex Angliae, et Haeres Franciae.*   370

FR. KING. Nor this I have not, Brother, so denied,
But your request shall make me let it pass.

K. HEN. I pray you, then, in love and dear alli-
ance,
Let that one article rank with the rest,
And thereupon give me your daughter.   375

FR. KING. Take her, fair son, and from her blood
raise up
Issue to me, that the contending kingdoms
Of France and England, whose very shores look pale
With envy of each other's happiness,   379
May cease their hatred, and this dear conjunction°
Plant neighborhood and Christianlike accord
In their sweet bosoms, that never war advance
His bleeding sword 'twixt England and fair France.

ALL. Amen!

K. HEN. Now welcome, Kate. And bear me wit-
ness all,   385

That here I kiss her as my sovereign Queen.
[*Flourish.*]

Q. ISA. God, the best maker of all marriages,
Combine your hearts in one, your realms in one!
As man and wife, being two, are one in love,
So be there 'twixt your kingdoms such a spousal°
That never may ill office, or fell° jealousy,   391
Which troubles oft the bed of blessèd marriage,
Thrust in between the paction° of these kingdoms
To make divorce of their incorporate league —
That English may as French, French Englishmen,
Receive each other. God speak this Amen!   396

ALL. Amen!

K. HEN. Prepare we for our marriage. On which
day,
My Lord of Burgundy, we'll take your oath,
And all the peers', for surety° of our leagues.   400
Then shall I swear to Kate, and you to me.
And may our oaths well kept and prosperous be!
[*Sennet. Exeunt.*]

EPILOGUE

[*Enter* CHORUS.]

CHOR. Thus far, with rough and all-unable pen,
Our bending° author hath pursued the story,
In little room confining mighty men,
Mangling by starts° the full course of their glory.
Small time, but in that small most greatly lived   5
This star of England. Fortune made his sword,
By which the world's best garden he achieved,°
And of it left his son imperial lord.
Henry the Sixth, in infant bands° crowned King
Of France and England, did this King succeed,
Whose state so many had the managing   11
That they lost France and made his England
bleed.
Which oft our stage hath shown,° and, for their sake
In your fair minds let this acceptance take.° [*Exit.*]

348. perspectively: as through a "perspective" — a glass which
makes images distorted.   353. so: so long as.   356. will:
desire.   365–66. to . . . grant: i.e., in formal documents.
380. conjunction: union.

390. spousal: marriage.   391. fell: fierce.   393. paction: agreement.   400. surety: ratification.
Epilogue: 2. bending: bowing.   4. Mangling by starts: marring the story by telling it in fragments.   7. achieved: won.
9. infant bands: swaddling clothes. bands: bonds.   13. oft . . .
shown, i.e., in the three parts of *Henry VI.*   14. let . . . take:
receive this.

AS YOU LIKE IT

Introduction

As You Like It was first published in the first folio in 1623. The text is well printed and there are few misprints or difficulties of reading. The play was certainly written before August 1600, because there is a note in the Stationers' Register dated August 4, 1600, that *As You Like It* with three other plays was to be "staied," i.e., not printed (see Gen. Intro. pp. 65b–66a). Other evidence suggests that it was written after June 1599. Celia remarks (I.ii.94), ". . . since the little wit that fools have was silenced, the little foolery that wise men have makes a great show." This is probably a topical reference to the order of the Privy Council issued in June 1599, that certain of the more notorious books of satires should be collected and burned.

Jaques's famous speech on the seven ages of man beginning (II.vii.139),

> All the world's a stage
> And all the men and women merely players

was probably inspired by the motto of the new Globe Theater — *Totus mundus agit histrionem* (the whole world plays the actor). The Globe playhouse was completed and first occupied in the summer of 1599. There is also a direct quotation from Marlowe's *Hero and Leander* in the second of the lines (III.v.81):

> Dead shepherd, now I find thy saw of might —
> Whoever loved that loved not at first sight?

Hero and Leander was left unfinished at Marlowe's death on May 31, 1593. It was first published in 1598.

Shakespeare took the story of *As You Like It* from a novel called *Rosalynde* written by Thomas Lodge during a voyage to the Canaries and first published in 1590. *Rosalynde* was the most popular and one of the best of the pastoral romantic tales which were the fashion in the early 1590's. By 1598 the book was in its fourth edition. The story was thus likely to be well known to many in the original audience. Shakespeare followed his source fairly closely, though he added some characters of his own and changed most of the names. In *Rosalynde* the usurping Duke is called Torismond and the banished Duke Gerismond; the hero is Rosader (Orlando) and the wicked brother Saladyne (Oliver); the two girls are Rosalynde and Alinda (Celia); the faithful servant is Adam Spencer, Phebe's swain is called Montanus (Sylvius), and the old shepherd Coridon (Corin).

Rosalynde was written in the elaborate leisurely style popularized by Lyly in *Euphues*. Indeed, to attract the reader Lodge gave his book the subtitle *Euphues' Golden Legacy. Found after his death in his cell at Silexedra. Bequeathed to Philautus's sons, nursed up with their father in England.* The outline of Lodge's tale runs as follows:

Old Sir John of Bordeaux lay dying. On his deathbed he bestowed legacies and much advice on his three sons Saladyne, the eldest, Fernandine, and Rosader, his youngest and favorite. As soon as his father was dead Saladyne began to meditate how he might rob his brothers, so he sent Fernandine away to study and made Rosader his footboy. As Rosader grew up he began to resent this treatment:

". . . why should I, that am a gentleman born, pass my time in such unnatural drudgery? Were it not better either in Paris to become a scholar, or in the Court a courtier, or in the field a soldier, than to live a footboy to my own brother? Nature hath lent me wit to conceive, but my brother denied me art to contemplate. I have strength to perform any honorable exploit, but no liberty to accomplish my virtuous endeavors. Those good parts that God hath bestowed upon me the envy of my brother doth smother in obscurity, the harder is my fortune, and the more his frowardness." (Cf. *AYLI*, I.i.1–26.)

At this moment Saladyne and his servants appeared and the brothers began to quarrel. Rosader seized a garden rake, dispersed the servants, and chased Saladyne into a loft. Saladyne promised redress, but learning that Torismond (who had banished the rightful king, Gerismond, and had usurped the throne of France) was holding a tournament at which a Norman wrestler was to challenge all comers, he persuaded Rosader to fight the wrestler and secretly bribed the wrestler to kill Rosader. So the latter appeared at the tournament, and there he began to cast eyes at Rosalynde, daughter of the banished King, as well he might,

". . . for upon her cheeks there seemed a battle between the graces, who should bestow most favors to make her excellent. The blush that gloried Luna when she kissed the shepherd on the hills of Latmos was not tainted with such a pleasant dye as the vermilion flourished on the silver hue of Rosalynde's countenance. Her eyes were like those lamps that make the wealthy covert of the heavens more gorgeous, sparkling favor and disdain, courteous and yet coy, as if in them Venus had placed all her amorets, and Diana all her chastity. The trammels of her hair, folded in a caul of gold, so far surpassed the burnished glister of the metal as the sun doth the meanest star in brightness. The tresses that folds in the brows of Apollo were not half so rich to the sight, for in her hairs it seemed Love had laid herself in ambush, to entrap the proudest eye that durst gaze upon their excellence. What should I need to decipher her particular beauties, when by the censure of all she was the paragon of all earthly perfection?"

Rosalynde was likewise attracted by Rosader and gave him such a loving look that he threw the wrestler and broke his neck. So Rosader, accompanied by a number of young gentlemen, returned home in triumph, to the surprise and disgust of Saladyne.

Soon afterward Torismond determined to banish Rosalynde in spite of the protests of her dear friend and cousin Alinda. So the two cousins decided to run away, though Alinda was fearful because there would be no man in their company. Rosalynde therefore disguised herself as a page and changed her name to Ganymede, Alinda changed hers to Aliena, and off they set. After a long journey they reached the Forest of Arden and there they came upon some verses which had been carved on the bark of a tree by a lovesick shepherd called Montanus. On they went, and by and by they encountered an old shepherd called Coridon. Aliena asked Coridon where they could find shelter, and he replied that his landlord was ready to sell both farm and stock. So Aliena agreed to buy the farm and to retain Coridon as her overseer.

Meanwhile Saladyne was again plotting to kill Rosader. Very early one morning with some of his servants he entered his brother's chamber, bound him, and chained him to a post in the hall, where he remained for three days without food, until Adam Spencer, a faithful old servant of Sir John, secretly released him. Rosader, however, pretended still to be bound until Saladyne and his guests were at dinner, when he ran among them with a poleax and put them to flight. Thereupon Saladyne and the survivors complained to the sheriff, who came to take Rosader. But Rosader and Adam broke through the sheriff's party and escaped to the Forest of Arden. The hard journey was almost too much for old Adam, who lay down ready to die. So Rosader went forth to seek food, and by chance lighted on the

exiled King Gerismond, who with his outlaws was dining at a long table under the shade of some lemon trees. Rosader challenged any of the company to fight with him, but Gerismond courteously invited him to share the meal. Then Rosader went to fetch Adam, and as soon as he had revealed his name he was eagerly welcomed by the banished King.

Meanwhile Rosalynde in her disguise as Ganymede had encountered Rosader (who did not recognize the pretty youth) and learned of certain verses which he had made in honor of his love. So Ganymede pretended to rail at all women, but when she was alone she grew very sorry for herself. Next day the two girls again encountered Rosader, whose talk was still of the excellencies of his Rosalynde. Ganymede, to persuade him to stay longer, pretended to be Rosalynde and encouraged Rosader to woo her, and finally to carry the pretense still further Aliena said:

" 'I'll play the priest. From this day forth Ganymede shall call thee husband, and thou shall call Ganymede wife, and so we'll have a marriage.'

" 'Content,' quoth Rosader, and laughed.

" 'Content,' quoth Ganymede, and changed as red as a rose. And so with a smile and a blush, they made up this jesting match, that after proved to a marriage in earnest, Rosader full little thinking he had wooed and won his Rosalynde."

In the meantime Torismond had begun to covet Saladyne's wealth, and first put him in prison, then banished him from the land. So Saladyne too made his way to the Forest of Arden, where in great weariness he lay down and fell asleep. While he was thus senseless a hungry lion came upon him and waited for him to move. At this moment Rosader passed by. He recognized his unkind brother, and after a struggle in his own mind whether or not he should leave him to his fate, he suddenly charged the lion with his boar spear and slew it. Saladyne woke up but at first did not recognize Rosader. When he realized how nobly Rosader had behaved, he begged his forgiveness and the two brothers were reconciled. Rosader thereupon took Saladyne and presented him to Gerismond.

All this while Rosader had neglected Ganymede, but by and by he returned to visit the two girls. As he was talking to Aliena certain rascals who prowled in the forest thought to kidnap her and carry her off to her father. Rosader fought valiantly, but was sorely wounded; Saladyne, attracted by the struggle, came to his rescue and together they drove off the enemy. As a result Aliena fell violently in love with Saladyne and he with her. Soon after this Coridon took the two girls to watch the behavior of Phoebe, the disdainful shepherdess loved by Montanus. Phoebe treated her swain with such bitter words that Ganymede started out from her hiding place and rebuked her hotly; but Phoebe was so greatly stirred by the beauty of Ganymede that she immediately fell in love. Saladyne now declared his love for Aliena and asked her to marry him:

"At the word 'marriage' Aliena stood in a maze what to answer, fearing that if she were too coy, to drive him away with her disdain, and if she were too courteous, to discover the heat of her desires."

So Aliena consented and Ganymede sent Saladyne to find Rosader.

Phoebe by this time was so much in love with Ganymede that she was almost dead. She therefore wrote Ganymede a letter, which she sent by Montanus. When Ganymede received the letter, she fell into a great laughter, but she went with Montanus to see Phoebe, and there she made Phoebe promise that if she could be persuaded to cease loving Ganymede she would marry Montanus, to which Phoebe agreed.

Then the preparations for the wedding of Saladyne and Aliena went forward with great joy. By and by Montanus came in dressed like a forsaken lover, and when King Gerismond heard his tale he sent for Phoebe and asked her why she was so disdainful of Montanus' love. She replied that she was in love with Ganymede. Gerismond then sent for Ganymede, whose face somehow reminded him of his daughter Rosalynde, but when he mentioned Rosalynde's name Rosader sighed deeply and told Gerismond that he loved her. Gerismond replied that if Rosalynde were there, he would give her to Rosader for his wife, at which Aliena was so amused that she could hardly keep countenance. Then Ganymede answered:

"'If I should affect the fair Phoebe, I should offer poor Montanus great wrong to win that from him in a moment that he hath labored for so many months. Yet have I promised to the beautiful shepherdess to wed myself never to woman except unto her — but with this promise, that if I can by reason suppress Phoebe's love toward me, she shall like of none but of Montanus.'

"'To that,' quoth Phoebe, 'I stand, for my love is so far beyond reason as will admit no persuasion of reason.'

"'For justice,' quoth he, 'I appeal to Gerismond.'

"'And to his censure will I stand,' quoth Phoebe.

"'And in your victory,' quoth Montanus, 'stands the hazard of my fortunes. For if Ganymede go away with conquest, Montanus is in conceit love's monarch. If Phoebe win, then am I in effect most miserable.'

"'We will see this controversy,' quoth Gerismond, 'and then we will to church. Therefore, Ganymede, let us hear your argument.'

"'Nay, pardon my absence a while,' quoth she, 'and you shall see one in store.'

"In went Ganymede and dressed herself in woman's attire, having on a gown of green, with kirtle of rich sendal, so quaint that she seemed Diana triumphing in the forest. Upon her head she wore a chaplet of roses, which gave her such a grace that she looked like Flora perked in the pride of all her flowers. Thus attired came Rosalynde in, and presented herself at her father's feet, with her eyes full of tears, craving his blessing and discoursing unto him all her fortunes, how she was banished by Torismond, and how ever since she lived in that country disguised."

So the weddings of all three pairs of lovers were celebrated, but hardly had they sat down to dinner when suddenly Fernandine (the second son of old Sir John) appeared in the forest and desired to speak with them. He told them that Torismond was approaching with an army to give battle with the twelve peers of France who had taken up arms to restore Gerismond to his kingdom. So Gerismond rose up, and Saladyne and Rosader seized their weapons, and thus leaving their brides they went off to do battle. Torismond's army was put to flight and he himself slain. Then Gerismond, the true King, returned to Paris, where he was received with great joy, and there he sent for Alinda and Rosalynde. He created Rosader heir to his kingdom, restored Saladyne to his lands, and suitably promoted the others.

Such was the story which Shakespeare turned into his comedy. He followed Lodge very closely for the major incidents, compressing a little and making some minor alterations. In the play, for instance, Orlando (Rosader) is wounded by the lioness and not by the kidnappers. *Rosalynde,* though a lighthearted tale, was for the most part seriously written; Shakespeare's *As You Like It* is full of little touches of parody and satire. And he added much of his own — in particular the genial Touchstone, fool by profession, cynic philosopher by nature; William and the underwashed Audrey, two real yokels to contrast with the pretty ladies and gentlemen playing at being foresters and shepherdesses; and above all Jaques, the melancholy intellectual.

When Shakespeare wrote this play, the vogue for satire was at its height, and Jonson's *Every Man in His Humor* (see Gen. Intro. p. 42a–b) was the success of the season with the Chamberlain's Men. It is therefore hardly likely that in 1599 Shakespeare could have seriously intended *As You Like It* to be nothing more than an old-fashioned pastoral romance. Moreover, though the play was far from being a comedy of humors, yet Shakespeare was to some extent influenced by the new fashion of elaborately depicting realistic characters. Indeed for the next few years his manner of writing plays changed. Hitherto he had balanced plot and character. Henceforward he was more interested in character, and he tended to pick out one or two persons in a play and to show their characters from every angle by bringing them into contact with a variety of persons and situations.

Jaques is the first notable example of this change. He exists simply as a study of character for its own sake. He has no essential part in the plot — indeed *As You Like It* could be acted without him — but he is nevertheless the most interesting and vivid of all the company in the Forest of Arden. We see more of him than of any of the other characters. He is not even allowed to appear until his entrance has been carefully prepared by an account of his moods and his moralizings. He is given the best speeches, even the speech on the seven ages of man. He is Shakespeare's picture — the first of several — of the melancholic humor (see App. 4.), but it is a special kind of melancholy " compounded of many simples, extracted from many objects, and indeed the sundry contemplation of my travels, in which my often rumination wraps me in a most humorous sadness."

As You Like It is also to some extent a satire on the pastoral ideals and conventions. The forest lovers behave according to their kind. Orlando woos his Rosalind in verses; but they are very poor verses, a very false gallop of verse. Ganymede (alias Rosalind) is moved momentarily to self-pity at the sorrows of the lovelorn Silvius; but Touchstone mocks her with his account of how he wooed Jane Smile and how he kissed her batlet and the cow's dugs that her pretty chapped hands had milked. Old Corin grows eloquent about the joys of the shepherd's life; but Touchstone overwhelms him with his courtly wit. The exiled courtiers hymn the pure joys of life under the greenwood tree; but Jaques caps their verses with some of his own —

> Here shall he see
> Gross fools as he,
> An if he will come to me.

But there is no need to take *As You Like It* too seriously. It is a lighthearted comedy which appeals to readers at all stages and in all lighter moods. It pleases some by its idyllic romance, others by its optimistic philosophy of simple goodness, and yet others by its cynical irony. Indeed, you can take this play just as you like it.

As You Like It

DRAMATIS PERSONAE

DUKE, *living in banishment*
FREDERICK, *his brother, and usurper of his dominions*
AMIENS ⎫
JAQUES ⎭ *lords attending on the banished Duke*
LE BEAU, *a courtier attending upon Frederick*
CHARLES, *wrestler to Frederick*
OLIVER ⎫
JAQUES ⎬ *sons of Sir Rowland de Boys*
ORLANDO ⎭
ADAM ⎫
DENNIS ⎭ *servants to Oliver*
TOUCHSTONE, *a clown*
SIR OLIVER MARTEXT, *a vicar*

CORIN ⎫
SILVIUS ⎭ *shepherds*
WILLIAM, *a country fellow, in love with Audrey*
A person representing Hymen

ROSALIND, *daughter to the banished Duke*
CELIA, *daughter to Frederick*
PHEBE, *a shepherdess*
AUDREY, *a country wench*

LORDS, PAGES, *and* ATTENDANTS, &c.

SCENE — *Oliver's house; Duke Frederick's court; and the Forest of Arden.*

Act I

SCENE I. *Orchard of* OLIVER'S *house.*

[*Enter* ORLANDO *and* ADAM.]

ORL. As I remember it, Adam, it was upon this fashion: Bequeathed° me by will but poor a° thousand crowns, and, as thou sayest, charged my brother, on his blessing,° to breed° me well — and there begins my sadness. My brother Jaques he 5 keeps at school, and report speaks goldenly of his profit; for my part, he keeps me rustically at home, or, to speak more properly, stays me° here at home unkept. For call you that keeping for a gentleman of my birth that differs not from the stalling of 10 an ox? His horses are bred better, for besides that they are fair with their feeding, they are taught their manage,° and to that end riders dearly° hired. But I, his brother, gain nothing under him but growth, for the which his animals on his dunghills are 15 as much bound to° him as I. Besides this nothing that he so plentifully gives me, the something that nature gave me his countenance seems to take from me.° He lets me feed with his hinds,° bars me° the place of a brother, and, as much as in him lies, 20 mines my gentility with my education.° This is it,

Adam, that grieves me, and the spirit of my father, which I think is within me, begins to mutiny against this servitude. I will no longer endure it, though yet I know no wise remedy how to avoid it. 26
ADAM. Yonder comes my master, your brother.
ORL. Go apart, Adam, and thou shalt hear how he will shake me up.° 30
[*Enter* OLIVER.]
OLI. Now, sir! What make you here?
ORL. Nothing. I am not taught to make anything.
OLI. What mar you then, sir?
ORL. Marry,° sir, I am helping you to mar that which God made, a poor unworthy brother of yours, with idleness.
OLI. Marry, sir, be better employed, and be naught awhile.° 39
ORL. Shall I keep your hogs and eat husks with them? What prodigal portion° have I spent that I should come to such penury?
OLI. Know you where you are, sir?
ORL. Oh, sir, very well, here in your orchard.
OLI. Know you before whom, sir? 45
ORL. Aye, better than him I am before knows me. I know you are my eldest brother, and, in the gentle condition of blood, you should so know me.° The courtesy of nations° allows you my better, in that you are the firstborn. But the same tradition 50 takes not away my blood, were there twenty brothers betwixt us. I have as much of my father in me as

Act I, Sc. i: 2. **Bequeathed:** i.e., my father bequeathed. **poor a:** a poor; i.e., only. 4. **on . . . blessing:** if he wished to receive his blessing. **breed:** educate. 8. **stays me:** forces me to stay. 13. **manage:** training. **dearly:** at great cost. 16. **bound to:** owe him as much gratitude; i.e., nothing. 17–19. **something . . . me:** even the natural claims that I have of him as my brother he denies by his unfriendly treatment. **countenance:** lit., face, so kindly (or unkindly) looks. 19. **hinds:** laborers. **bars me:** prevents me from holding. 21. **mines . . . education:** undermines my gentle birth by lack of education.

30. **shake me up:** treat me violently. 34. **Marry:** Mary, by the Virgin. 38–39. **be . . . awhile:** make yourself scarce. 41. **prodigal portion:** i.e., I have not wasted my portion like the Prodigal Son. See Luke 15: 11–32. 47–48. **in . . . me:** if you were a true gentleman you would treat me as one. 49. **courtesy of nations:** the custom of civilized society.

you, albeit I confess your coming before me is nearer
to his reverence.°

OLI. What, boy!°   55

ORL. Come, come, elder brother, you are too young
in this.

OLI. Wilt thou lay hands on me, villain?

ORL. I am no villain. I am the youngest son of Sir
Rowland de Boys; he was my father, and he is   60
thrice a villain that says such a father begot villains.
Wert thou not my brother, I would not take this
hand from thy throat till this other had pulled out
thy tongue for saying so. Thou hast railed on° thyself.   65

ADAM. Sweet masters, be patient. For your father's
remembrance, be at accord.

OLI. Let me go, I say.

ORL. I will not, till I please. You shall hear me.
My father charged you in his will to give me   70
good education. You have trained me like a peasant,
obscuring and hiding from me all gentlemanlike
qualities. The spirit of my father grows strong in
me, and I will no longer endure it. Therefore allow
me such exercises° as may become a gentleman,   75
or give me the poor allottery° my father left me by
testament. With that I will go buy my fortunes.

OLI. And what wilt thou do? Beg, when that is
spent? Well, sir, get you in. I will not long be troubled with you, you shall have some part of your
will.° I pray you leave me.   82

ORL. I will no further offend you than becomes
me for my good.

OLI. Get you with him, you old dog.

ADAM. Is "old dog" my reward? Most true, I   88
have lost my teeth in your service. God be with
my old master! He would not have spoke such a
word.   [*Exeunt* ORLANDO *and* ADAM.]

OLI. Is it even so? Begin you to grow upon° me?
I will physic your rankness,° and yet give no thousand crowns neither. Holla, Dennis!

[*Enter* DENNIS.]

DEN. Calls your Worship?

OLI. Was not Charles, the Duke's wrestler, here
to speak with me?   95

DEN. So please you, he is here at the door and importunes access° to you.

OLI. Call him in. [*Exit* DENNIS.] 'Twill be a good
way, and tomorrow the wrestling is.

[*Enter* CHARLES.]

CHA. Good morrow to your Worship.   100

OLI. Good Monsieur Charles, what's the **new**
news at the new Court?

CHA. There's no news at the Court, sir, but the
old news; that is, the old Duke is banished by his
younger brother the new Duke, and three or   105
four loving lords have put themselves into voluntary exile with him, whose lands and revenues enrich the new Duke; therefore he gives them good
leave to wander.

OLI. Can you tell if Rosalind, the Duke's daughter, be banished with her father?   111

CHA. Oh no, for the Duke's daughter, her cousin,
so loves her, being ever from their cradles bred together, that she would have followed her exile or
have died to stay behind her. She is at the Court and
no less beloved of her uncle than his own daughter,
and never two ladies loved as they do.

OLI. Where will the old Duke live?   119

CHA. They say he is already in the Forest of Arden,° and a many merry men with him, and there
they live like the old Robin Hood° of England.
They say many young gentlemen flock to him every
day, and fleet° the time carelessly,° as they did in
the golden world.°   125

OLI. What, you wrestle tomorrow before the new
Duke?

CHA. Marry do I, sir, and I came to acquaint you
with a matter. I am given, sir, secretly to understand
that your younger brother, Orlando, hath a   130
disposition to come in disguised against me to try a
fall.° Tomorrow, sir, I wrestle for my credit, and
he that escapes me without some broken limb shall
acquit° him well. Your brother is but young and
tender, and, for your love, I would be loath to   135
foil° him, as I must for my own honor if he come
in. Therefore, out of my love to you, I came hither
to acquaint you withal, that either you might stay
him from his intendment or brook° such disgrace
well as he shall run into, in that it is a thing of his
own search, and altogether against my will.   142

OLI. Charles, I thank thee for thy love to me,
which thou shalt find I will most kindly requite. I
had myself notice of my brother's purpose herein,
and have by underhand means labored to dissuade
him from it, but he is resolute. I'll tell thee, Charles
— it is the stubbornest young fellow of France, full
of ambition, an envious emulator° of every man's
good parts, a secret and villainous contriver°   150
against me his natural brother. Therefore use thy
discretion. I had as lief thou didst break his neck as
his finger. And thou wert best look to 't, for if thou

53–54. **is . . . reverence:** gives you a greater claim to be highly
regarded as he was.   55. **What, boy:** Here Oliver strikes Orlando.
64. **railed on:** abused.   75. **exercises:** training.   76. **allottery:**
portion.   81–82. **your will:** your legacy, and what you desire.
91. **grow upon:** become troublesome to.   92. **physic . . . rankness:** cure your excess of blood. Rankness was a medical term for
a condition requiring the letting of blood. See *Caesar*, III.i.152.
97. **importunes access:** asks for permission to see you on an
urgent matter.

121. **Arden:** the Ardennes, in Belgium.   122. **Robin Hood:** the
famous English outlaw of legend and ballad.   124. **fleet:** spend.
carelessly: without a care.   125. **golden world:** the mythical
good old days, before men learned to be wicked.   132. **fall:** i.e.,
in wrestling.   134. **acquit:** distinguish; lit., get a favorable verdict.   136. **foil:** overthrow.   140. **brook:** endure.   149. **envious
emulator:** jealous hater.   150. **contriver:** plotter.

dost him any slight disgrace, or if he do not mightily grace himself on thee,° he will practice°　155
against thee by poison, entrap thee by some treacherous device, and never leave thee till he hath ta'en thy
life by some indirect means or other. For I assure
thee, and almost with tears I speak it, there is not
one so young and so villainous this day living. I
speak but brotherly of him, but should I anatomize°
him to thee as he is, I must blush and weep, and
thou must look pale and wonder.　　　　164

CHA. I am heartily glad I came hither to you. If
he come tomorrow, I'll give him his payment. If
ever he go alone° again, I'll never wrestle for prize
more. And so, God keep your Worship!　　168

OLI. Farewell, good Charles. [*Exit* CHARLES.]
Now will I stir this gamester. I hope I shall see an
end of him, for my soul, yet I know not why, hates
nothing more than he. Yet he's gentle,° never
schooled, and yet learned, full of noble device,° of
all sorts enchantingly beloved, and indeed so much
in the heart of the world, and especially of my　175
own people, who best know him, that I am altogether misprized.° But it shall not be so long, this
wrestler shall clear all. Nothing remains but that I
kindle° the boy thither, which now I'll go　179
about.　　　　　　　　　　　　　　　[*Exit.*]

SCENE II. *Lawn before the* DUKE'S *palace.*

[*Enter* ROSALIND *and* CELIA.]

CEL. I pray thee, Rosalind, sweet my coz,° be
merry.

ROS. Dear Celia, I show more mirth than I am
mistress of, and would you yet I were merrier? Unless you could teach me to forget a banished　5
father, you must not learn° me how to remember
any extraordinary pleasure.

CEL. Herein I see thou lovest me not with the full
weight that I love thee. If my uncle, thy banished
father, had banished thy uncle, the Duke my　10
father, so thou hadst been still with me I could have
taught my love to take thy father for mine. So
wouldst thou if the truth of thy love to me were so
righteously tempered° as mine is to thee.　　15

ROS. Well, I will forget the condition of my estate,
to rejoice in yours.

CEL. You know my father hath no child but I,
nor none is like to have. And truly, when he dies,
thou shalt be his heir, for what he hath taken away
from thy father perforce, I will render thee again in

affection. By mine honor, I will, and when I break
that oath, let me turn monster. Therefore, my sweet
Rose, my dear Rose, be merry.　　　　25

ROS. From henceforth I will, Coz, and devise
sports. Let me see, what think you of falling in love?

CEL. Marry, I prithee do, to make sport withal.
But love no man in good earnest, nor no further in
sport neither than with safety of a pure blush thou
mayst in honor come off again.　　　　32

ROS. What shall be our sport, then?

CEL. Let us sit and mock the good housewife Fortune from her wheel,° that her gifts may henceforth
be bestowed equally.

ROS. I would we could do so, for her benefits are
mightily misplaced, and the bountiful blind woman
doth most mistake in her gifts to women.　　39

CEL. 'Tis true, for those that she makes fair she
scarce° makes honest,° and those that she makes
honest she makes very ill-favoredly.°

ROS. Nay, now thou goest from Fortune's office to
Nature's. Fortune reigns in gifts of the world, not in
the lineaments° of Nature.　　　　45

[*Enter* TOUCHSTONE.]

CEL. No? When Nature hath made a fair creature, may she not by Fortune fall into the fire?
Though Nature hath given us wit to flout° at Fortune, hath not Fortune sent in this fool to cut off the
argument?　　　　　　　　　　　50

ROS. Indeed, there is Fortune too hard for Nature,
when Fortune makes Nature's natural° the cutter-
off of Nature's wit.

CEL. Peradventure this is not Fortune's work
neither, but Nature's, who perceiveth our natural
wits too dull to reason of such goddesses, and　55
hath sent this natural for our whetstone; for always
the dullness of the fool is the whetstone of the wits.
How now, wit! Whither wander you?°

TOUCH. Mistress, you must come away to your
father.　　　　　　　　　　　　61

CEL. Were you made the messenger?

TOUCH. No, by mine honor, but I was bid to come
for you.

ROS. Where learned you that oath, fool?　　65

TOUCH. Of a certain knight that swore by his
honor they were good pancakes, and swore by his
honor the mustard was naught.° Now I'll stand to
it the pancakes were naught and the mustard was
good, and yet was not the knight forsworn.°　71

---

155. grace . . . thee: distinguish himself at your expense. practice: plot.　162. anatomize: dissect, analyze.　167. alone: i.e.,
without support.　172. gentle: a natural gentleman.　173. noble
device: noble thoughts.　177. misprized: considered worthless,
despised.　179. kindle: incite.

Sc. ii: 1. coz: cousin.　6. learn: teach.　15. tempered: compounded.

35. Fortune . . . wheel: Fortune was personified as a blind woman
spinning men's fortunes at a spinning wheel. For Fluellen's
learned discourse on this symbolism, see *Hen V*, III.vi.31–40.
See also App. 18.　41. scarce: seldom. honest: chaste.　42. ill-
favoredly: ugly.　45. lineaments: characteristics; i.e., features.
48. flout: mock.　52. natural: fool, one who is by nature an idiot.
Touchstone, however, hardly comes into this category of fools;
he is rather the professional jester.　59. wit . . . you: a variant
form of the saying "wit, whither wilt?" Cf. IV.i.168.　69. naught:
bad.　71. forsworn: false in his oath.

CEL. How prove you that, in the great heap of your knowledge?

ROS. Aye, marry, now unmuzzle your wisdom.

TOUCH. Stand you both forth now. Stroke your chins, and swear by your beards that I am a knave.

CEL. By our beards, if we had them, thou art. 79

TOUCH. By my knavery, if I had it, then I were. But if you swear by that that is not, you are not forsworn. No more was this knight swearing by his honor, for he never had any, or if he had, he had sworn it away before ever he saw those pancakes or that mustard. 85

CEL. Prithee who is 't that thou meanest?

TOUCH. One that old Frederick, your father, loves.

CEL. My father's love is enough to honor him. Enough! Speak no more of him, you'll be whipped for taxation° one of these days. 91

TOUCH. The more pity that fools may not speak wisely what wise men do foolishly.

CEL. By my troth, thou sayest true, for since the little wit that fools have was silenced, the little foolery that wise men have makes a great show.° Here comes Monsieur Le Beau. 97

ROS. With his mouth full of news.

CEL. Which he will put on us, as pigeons feed their young.° 100

ROS. Then shall we be news-crammed.

CEL. All the better. We shall be the more marketable. [*Enter* LE BEAU.] *Bon jour,* Monsieur Le Beau. What's the news?

LE BEAU. Fair Princess, you have lost much good sport. 106

CEL. Sport! Of what color?°

LE BEAU. What color, madam! How shall I answer you?

ROS. As wit and fortune will. 110

TOUCH. Or as the Destinies decree.

CEL. Well said. That was laid on with a trowel.°

TOUCH. Nay, if I keep not my rank ——

ROS. Thou losest thy old smell.°

LE BEAU. You amaze me, ladies. I would 115 have told you of good wrestling which you have lost the sight of.

ROS. Yet tell us the manner of the wrestling.

LE BEAU. I will tell you the beginning, and if it please your ladyships, you may see the end; for 120 the best is yet to do, and here where you are they are coming to perform it.

CEL. Well, the beginning, that is dead and buried.°

LE BEAU. There comes an old man and his three sons —— 126

CEL. I could match this beginning with an old tale.°

LE BEAU. Three proper° young men, of excellent growth and presence.° 130

ROS. With bills on their necks, " Be it known unto all men by these presents."°

LE BEAU. The eldest of the three wrestled with Charles, the Duke's wrestler, which Charles in a moment threw him, and broke three of his 135 ribs, that there is little hope of life in him. So he served the second, and so the third. Yonder they lie, the poor old man, their father, making such pitiful dole° over them that all the beholders take his part with weeping. 140

ROS. Alas!

TOUCH. But what is the sport, monsieur, that the ladies have lost?

LE BEAU. Why, this that I speak of. 144

TOUCH. Thus men may grow wiser every day. It is the first time that ever I heard breaking of ribs was sport for ladies.

CEL. Or I, I promise thee.

ROS. But is there any else longs to see this broken music° in his sides? Is there yet another dotes upon rib-breaking? Shall we see this wrestling, Cousin? 152

LE BEAU. You must if you stay here, for here is the place appointed for the wrestling, and they are ready to perform it. 155

CEL. Yonder, sure, they are coming. Let us now stay and see it.

[*Flourish.*° *Enter* DUKE FREDERICK, LORDS, ORLANDO, CHARLES, *and* ATTENDANTS.]

DUKE F. Come on. Since the youth will not be entreated, his own peril° on his forwardness.

ROS. Is yonder the man? 160

LE BEAU. Even he, madam.

CEL. Alas, he is too young! Yet he looks successfully.°

DUKE F. How now, Daughter and Cousin!° Are you crept hither to see the wrestling? 165

ROS. Aye, my liege, so please you give us leave.

DUKE F. You will take little delight in it, I can tell you, there is such odds in the man.° In pity of the challenger's youth I would fain° dissuade him, 170

---

91. taxation: satire.   94–96. since . . . show: See *AYLI* Intro. p. 773a.   99–100. pigeons . . . young: Pigeons thrust the food into the mouths of their young.   107. Sport . . . color: Celia pretends that Le Beau had said "spot," the two words, in Shakespeare's time, being pronounced alike.   112. laid . . . trowel: i.e., as a bricklayer slaps down the mortar.   113–14. rank . . . smell: position as a professional fool; but Celia pretends that it means highly scented — like a fox.   123–24. the . . . buried: i.e., tell the beginning that is now past history.

127–28. I . . . tale: your words sound like the beginning of an old tale.   129. proper: handsome.   130. presence: appearance.   131–32. With . . . presents: Rosalind makes a far-fetched pun. Le Beau's "presence" reminds her of "presents" as it occurs in the common formula at the beginning of many legal documents: "Know all men by these presents" — *noverint universi per praesentes.* bills: advertisements.   139. dole: lamentation.   149–50. broken music: lit., music performed by different kinds of instruments.   157. s.d., Flourish: fanfare of trumpets.   159. his . . . peril: i.e., he does it at his own risk.   163. successfully: as if he would succeed.   164. Cousin: used of any near relation.   169. such . . . man: the odds on Charles are so great.   170. fain: gladly.

but he will not be entreated. Speak to him, ladies, see if you can move him.

CEL. Call him hither, good Monsieur Le Beau.

DUKE F. Do so. I'll not be by.   174

LE BEAU. Monsieur the challenger, the Princess calls for you.

ORL. I attend° them with all respect and duty.

ROS. Young man, have you challenged Charles the wrestler?   179

ORL. No, fair Princess, he is the general challenger. I come but in, as others do, to try with him the strength of my youth.

CEL. Young gentleman, your spirits are too bold for your years. You have seen cruel proof of this man's strength. If you saw yourself with your   185 eyes, or knew yourself with your judgment, the fear of your adventure would counsel you to a more equal enterprise. We pray you, for your own sake, to embrace your own safety and give over this attempt.   190

ROS. Do, young sir, your reputation shall not therefore be misprized. We will make it our suit to the Duke that the wrestling might not go forward.

ORL. I beseech you punish me not with your hard thoughts, wherein I confess me much guilty, to deny so fair and excellent ladies anything. But let your fair eyes and gentle wishes go with me to my trial. Wherein if I be foiled, there is but one shamed that was never gracious; if killed, but one dead that   200 is willing to be so. I shall do my friends no wrong, for I have none to lament me; the world no injury, for in it I have nothing. Only in the world I fill up a place which may be better supplied when I have made it empty.   205

ROS. The little strength that I have, I would it were with you.

CEL. And mine, to eke out hers.

ROS. Fare you well. Pray Heaven I be deceived in you!   210

CEL. Your heart's desires be with you!

CHA. Come, where is this young gallant that is so desirous to lie with his mother earth?

ORL. Ready, sir, but his will hath in it a more modest working.°   215

DUKE F. You shall try but one fall.

CHA. No, I warrant your Grace, you shall not entreat him to a second, that have so mightily persuaded him from a first.   219

ORL. You mean to mock me after, you should not have mocked me before. But come your ways.°

ROS. Now Hercules be thy speed,° young man!

CEL. I would I were invisible, to catch the strong fellow by the leg.   [*They wrestle.*]

ROS. Oh, excellent young man!   225

CEL. If I had a thunderbolt in mine eye, I can tell who should down.   [*Shout.* CHARLES *is thrown.*]

DUKE F. No more, no more.

ORL. Yes, I beseech your Grace. I am not yet well breathed.°   230

DUKE F. How dost thou, Charles?

LE BEAU. He cannot speak, my lord.

DUKE F. Bear him away. What is thy name, young man?

ORL. Orlando, my liege, the youngest son of Sir Rowland de Boys.   235

DUKE F. I would thou hadst been son to some man else.
The world esteemed thy father honorable,
But I did find him still° mine enemy.
Thou shouldst have better pleased me with this deed
Hadst thou descended from another house.   240
But fare thee well, thou art a gallant youth.
I would thou hadst told me of another father.
      [*Exeunt* DUKE FREDERICK, *train, and* LE BEAU.]

CEL. Were I my father, Coz, would I do this?

ORL. I am more proud to be Sir Rowland's son,
His youngest son, and would not change that calling°   245
To be adopted heir to Frederick.

ROS. My father loved Sir Rowland as his soul,
And all the world was of my father's mind.
Had I before known this young man his son,
I should have given him tears unto° entreaties   250
Ere he should thus have ventured.

CEL.   Gentle Cousin,
Let us go thank him and encourage him.
My father's rough and envious disposition
Sticks me at heart.° Sir, you have well deserved.
If you do keep your promises in love   255
But justly, as you have exceeded all promise,
Your mistress shall be happy.

ROS.   Gentleman,
      [*Giving him a chain from her neck*]
Wear this for me, one out of suits° with Fortune,
That could° give more but that her hand lacks means.
Shall we go, Coz?

CEL.   Aye. Fare you well, fair gentleman.   260

ORL. Can I not say I thank you? My better parts
Are all thrown down,° and that which here stands up
Is but a quintain,° a mere lifeless block.

ROS. He calls us back. My pride fell with my fortunes,
I'll ask him what he would. Did you call, sir?   265
Sir, you have wrestled well and overthrown

---

177. attend: wait on.   214–15. more . . . working: i.e., I do not intend to do anything so improper.   221. come . . . ways: i.e. come on.   222. speed: aid.

230. breathed: exercised.   238. still: always.   245. calling: name.   250. unto: added to.   254. Sticks . . . heart: pierces me to the heart.   258. out of suits: not in the service of, not favored by.   259. could: would if she could.   261–62. My . . . down: i.e., I am behaving as if I had no manners.   263. quintain: a block, shaped like a man, used for tilting practice.

More than your enemies.°
CEL.   Will you go, Coz?
ROS. Have with you. Fare you well.
                    [*Exeunt* ROSALIND *and* CELIA.]
ORL. What passion hangs these weights upon my
     tongue?   269
I cannot speak to her, yet she urged conference.°
O poor Orlando, thou art overthrown!
Or Charles or something weaker masters thee.
                    [*Re-enter* LE BEAU.]
LE BEAU. Good sir, I do in friendship counsel you
To leave this place. Albeit you have deserved
High commendation, true applause, and love, 275
Yet such is now the Duke's condition
That he miscónstrues all that you have done.
The Duke is humorous.° What he is, indeed,
More suits you to conceive° than I to speak of.
     ORL. I thank you, sir. And pray you tell me
this: 280
Which of the two was daughter of the Duke
That here was at the wrestling?
     LE BEAU. Neither his daughter, if we judge by
          manners;
But yet indeed the lesser° is his daughter.
The other is daughter to the banished Duke, 285
And here detained by her usurping uncle,
To keep his daughter company, whose loves
Are dearer than the natural bond of sisters.
But I can tell you that of late this Duke
Hath ta'en displeasure 'gainst his gentle niece, 290
Grounded upon no other argument
But that the people praise her for her virtues
And pity her for her good father's sake.
And, on my life, his malice 'gainst the lady
Will suddenly break forth. Sir, fare you well. 295
Hereafter, in a better world than this,
I shall desire more love and knowledge of you.
     ORL. I rest much bounden to you. Fare you well.
                    [*Exit* LE BEAU.]
Thus must I from the smoke into the smother,°
From tyrant Duke unto a tyrant brother.   300
But heavenly Rosalind!   [*Exit.*]

SCENE III. *A room in the palace.*

[*Enter* CELIA *and* ROSALIND.]
CEL. Why, Cousin! Why, Rosalind! Cupid have
mercy! Not a word?
ROS. Not one to throw at a dog.
CEL. No, thy words are too precious to be cast

away upon curs, throw some of them at me. Come,
lame me with reasons.°   6
     ROS. Then there were two cousins laid up, when
the one should be lamed with reasons and the other
mad without any.
     CEL. But is all this for your father?   10
     ROS. No, some of it is for my child's father. Oh,
how full of briers is this working-day world!
     CEL. They are but burrs, Cousin, thrown upon
thee in holiday foolery. If we walk not in the trodden paths, our very petticoats will catch them. 15
     ROS. I could shake them off my coat. These burrs
are in my heart.
     CEL. Hem° them away.   19
     ROS. I would try if I could cry hem and have him.
     CEL. Come, come, wrestle with thy affections.
     ROS. Oh, they take the part of a better wrestler
than myself!
     CEL. Oh, a good wish upon you! You will try in
time, in despite° of a fall. But, turning these 25
jests out of service, let us talk in good earnest. Is it
possible, on such a sudden, you should fall into so
strong a liking with old Sir Rowland's youngest
son?   30
     ROS. The Duke my father loved his father dearly.
     CEL. Doth it therefore ensue that you should love
his son dearly? By this kind of chase,° I should hate
him, for my father hated his father dearly, yet I
hate not Orlando.   35
     ROS. No, faith, hate him not, for my sake.
     CEL. Why should I not? Doth he not deserve
well?
     ROS. Let me love him for that, and do you love
him because I do. Look, here comes the Duke. 41
     CEL. With his eyes full of anger.
                    [*Enter* DUKE FREDERICK, *with* LORDS.]
DUKE F. Mistress, dispatch you with your safest
          haste°
And get you from our Court.
ROS.   Me, Uncle?
DUKE F.   You, Cousin.
Within these ten days if that thou be'st found 45
So near our public Court as twenty miles,
Thou diest for it.
ROS.   I do beseech your Grace,
Let me the knowledge of my fault bear with me.
If with myself I hold intelligence,°
Or have acquaintance with mine own desires, 50
If that I do not dream, or be not frantic° —
As I do trust I am not — then, dear Uncle,
Never so much as in a thought unborn
Did I offend your Highness.

267. **More . . . enemies:** i.e., my heart. 270. **urged conference:** invited me to talk. 278. **humorous:** moody, touchy. 279. **conceive:** imagine. 284. **lesser:** the F1 reads "taller," but later (IV. iii.86–89) Rosalind is described as the taller. 299. **smother:** thick smoke—a phrase like "out of the frying pan into the fire."

Sc. iii: 6. **lame . . . reasons:** make me lame by throwing arguments at me. 19. **Hem:** i.e., cough them up. 25. **despite:** spite. 33. **By . . . chase:** by chasing after that kind of argument. 43. **safest haste:** i.e., the quicker you go, the safer for you. 49. **If . . . intelligence:** if I understood my own thoughts. 51. **frantic:** mad.

DUKE F.   Thus do all traitors.
If their purgation° did consist in words,   55
They are as innocent as grace° itself.
Let it suffice thee that I trust thee not.
   ROS. Yet your mistrust cannot make me a traitor.
Tell me whereon the likelihood depends.
   DUKE F. Thou art thy father's daughter, there's
     enough.   60
   ROS. So was I when your Highness took his duke-
dom,
So was I when your Highness banished him.
Treason is not inherited, my lord,
Or if we did derive° it from our friends,°
What's that to me? My father was no traitor.   65
Then, good my liege, mistake me not so much
To think my poverty is treacherous.
   CEL. Dear sovereign, hear me speak.
   DUKE F. Aye, Celia, we stayed her for your sake,
Else had she with her father ranged along.°   70
   CEL. I did not then entreat to have her stay,
It was your pleasure and your own remorse.°
I was too young that time to value her,
But now I know her. If she be a traitor,
Why so am I. We still have slept together,   75
Rose at an instant, learned, played, eat together,
And wheresoe'er we went, like Juno's swans,°
Still we went coupled and inseparable.
   DUKE F. She is too subtle for thee, and her smooth-
     ness,
Her very silence and her patience,   80
Speak to the people, and they pity her.
Thou art a fool. She robs thee of thy name,
And thou wilt show more bright and seem more
     virtuous
When she is gone. Then open not thy lips.
Firm and irrevocable is my doom   85
Which I have passed upon her, she is banished.
   CEL. Pronounce that sentence then on me, my
     liege.
I cannot live out of her company.
   DUKE F. You are a fool. You, Niece, provide your-
     self.
If you outstay the time, upon mine honor,   90
And in the greatness of my word, you die.
            [*Exeunt* DUKE FREDERICK *and* LORDS.]
   CEL. O my poor Rosalind, whither wilt thou go?
Wilt thou change fathers? I will give thee mine.
I charge thee, be not thou more grieved than I am.
   ROS. I have more cause.
   CEL.   Thou hast not, Cousin.   95

Prithee, be cheerful. Know'st thou not the Duke
Hath banished me, his daughter?
   ROS.   That he hath not.
   CEL. No, hath not? Rosalind lacks then the love
Which teacheth thee that thou and I am one.   99
Shall we be sundered? Shall we part, sweet girl?
No. Let my father seek another heir.
Therefore devise with me how we may fly,
Whither to go and what to bear with us.
And do not seek to take your change upon you,°
To bear your griefs yourself and leave me out;   105
For, by this Heaven, now at our sorrows pale,
Say what thou canst, I'll go along with thee.
   ROS. Why, whither shall we go?
   CEL. To seek my uncle in the forest of Arden.
   ROS. Alas, what danger will it be to us,   110
Maids as we are, to travel forth so far!
Beauty provoketh thieves sooner than gold.
   CEL. I'll put myself in poor and mean attire
And with a kind of umber smirch my face.°
The like do you. So shall we pass along   115
And never stir assailants.
   ROS.   Were it not better,
Because that I am more than common tall,
That I did suit me° all points° like a man?
A gallant curtal ax° upon my thigh,
A boar spear° in my hand, and — in my heart   120
Lie there what hidden woman's fear there will —
We'll have a swashing° and a martial outside,
As many other mannish cowards have
That do outface it with their semblances.°   124
   CEL. What shall I call thee when thou art a man?
   ROS. I'll have no worse a name than Jove's own
     page,
And therefore look you call me Ganymede.
But what will you be called?
   CEL. Something that hath a reference to my state,
No longer Celia, but Aliena.°   130
   ROS. But, Cousin, what if we assayed° to steal
The clownish fool out of your father's Court?
Would he not be a comfort to our travel?
   CEL. He'll go along o'er the wide world with me,
Leave me alone to woo him. Let's away   135
And get our jewels and our wealth together,
Devise the fittest time and safest way
To hide us from pursuit that will be made
After my flight. Now go we in content   139
To liberty and not to banishment.   [*Exeunt.*]

104. take . . . you: bear your changed fortunes alone.   **114. um-ber . . . face:** Elizabethan ladies regarded an ivory complexion as beautiful. The pale complexions of the two girls would have made them conspicuous among countryfolk.   **118. suit me:** dress myself. **all points:** in every detail.   **119. curtal ax:** cutlass. **120. boar spear:** See Pl. 7a.   **122. swashing:** swaggering. **124. semblances:** outward appearances.   **130. Aliena:** i.e., the alien, stranger. **131. assayed:** attempted.

55. purgation: proof of innocence.   **56. grace:** i.e., divine grace. **64. derive:** acquire by descent. **friends:** relations.   **70. ranged along:** wandered in his company.   **72. remorse:** pity.   **77. Juno's swans:** Editors have pointed out that Venus was the goddess who possessed a chariot drawn by swans.

Act II

SCENE I. *The Forest of Arden.*

[*Enter* DUKE Senior, AMIENS, *and two or three* LORDS, *like foresters.*]

DUKE S. Now, my comates and brothers in exíle,
Hath not old custom° made this life more sweet
Than that of painted° pomp? Are not these woods
More free from peril than the envious Court?
Here feel we but the penalty of Adam,°   5
The seasons' difference, as the icy fang
And churlish chiding of the winter's wind,
Which, when it bites and blows upon my body,
Even till I shrink with cold, I smile and say
" This is no flattery. These are councilors   10
That feelingly° persuade me what I am."
Sweet are the uses° of adversity,
Which, like the toad, ugly and venomous,
Wears yet a precious jewel in his head.°
And this our life exempt from public haunt°   15
Finds tongues in trees, books in the running brooks,
Sermons in stones, and good in everything.°
I would not change it.

AMI.   Happy is your Grace,
That can translate the stubbornness of fortune
Into so quiet and so sweet a style.   20

DUKE S. Come, shall we go and kill us venison?
And yet it irks me the poor dappled fools,
Being native burghers° of this desert city,
Should in their own confines° with forkèd heads°
Have their round haunches gored.

I. LORD.   Indeed, my lord,
The melancholy Jaques grieves at that,   26
And, in that kind,° swears you do more usurp
Than doth your brother that hath banished you.
Today my Lord of Amiens and myself
Did steal behind him as he lay along°   30
Under an oak whose antique root peeps out
Upon the brook that brawls along this wood.
To the which place a poor sequestered° stag,
That from the hunter's aim had ta'en a hurt,
Did come to languish, and indeed, my lord,   35
The wretched animal heaved forth such groans
That their discharge did stretch his leathern coat
Almost to bursting, and the big round tears
Coursed one another down his innocent nose

In piteous chase. And thus the hairy fool,   40
Much markèd of the melancholy Jaques,
Stood on the extremest verge of the swift brook,
Augmenting it with tears.

DUKE S.   But what said Jaques?
Did he not moralize° this spectacle?

I. LORD. Oh yes, into a thousand similes.   45
First, for his weeping into the needless stream,
" Poor deer," quoth he, " thou makest a testament
As worldlings do, giving thy sum of more°
To that which had too much." Then, being there
alone,
Left and abandoned of his velvet° friends,   50
" 'Tis right," quoth he. " Thus misery doth part
The flux° of company." Anon a careless herd,
Full of the pasture, jumps along by him
And never stays to greet him. " Aye," quoth Jaques
" Sweep on, you fat and greasy citizens,   55
'Tis just the fashion. Wherefore do you look
Upon that poor and broken bankrupt there? "
Thus most invectively° he pierceth through
The body of the country, city, Court,
Yea, and of this our life, swearing that we   60
Are mere usurpers, tyrants, and what's worse,
To fright the animals and to kill them up
In their assigned and native dwelling-place.

DUKE S. And did you leave him in this contemplation?

2. LORD. We did, my lord, weeping and commenting   65
Upon the sobbing deer.

DUKE S.   Show me the place.
I love to cope° him in these sullen° fits,
For then he's full of matter.°

I. LORD. I'll bring you to him straight. [*Exeunt.*]

SCENE II. *A room in the palace.*

[*Enter* DUKE FREDERICK, *with* LORDS.]

DUKE F. Can it be possible that no man saw them?
It cannot be. Some villains of my Court
Are of consent and sufferance° in this.

I. LORD. I cannot hear of any that did see her.
The ladies, her attendants of her chamber,   5
Saw her abed, and in the morning early
They found the bed untreasured of their mistress.

2. LORD. My lord, the roynish° clown at whom so
oft
Your Grace was wont to laugh is also missing.
Hisperia, the Princess' gentlewoman,   10

Act II, Sc. i: 2. old custom: long experience. 3. painted: artificial. 5. but . . . Adam: only the penalty laid on man; i.e., to feel the cold. "But" is an emendation for the F1 reading "not." 11. feelingly: i.e., through my feelings. 12. uses: advantages. 13–14. toad . . . head: This was a common belief. 15. exempt . . . haunt: free from crowds. 16–17. Finds . . . everything: i.e., that there is everywhere a lesson in nature. 23. burghers: citizens. 24. confines: territories. forked heads: i.e., arrows. See Pl. 22a. 27. kind: manner; i.e., hunting the deer. 30. lay along: stretched at full length. 33. sequestered: separated from the others.

44. moralize: make moral comments on. 48. sum of more: i.e., adding your tears to the water. 50. velvet: velvet-coated, sleek. 52. flux: flow, crowd. 58. invectively: with bitter satire. 67. cope: encounter. sullen: moody. 68. matter: good sense.
Sc. ii: 3. of . . . sufferance: willing accomplices. 8. roynish: scurvy.

Confesses that she secretly o'erheard
Your daughter and her cousin much commend
The parts and graces of the wrestler
That did but lately foil the sinewy Charles,
And she believes, wherever they are gone,   15
That youth is surely in their company.
    DUKE F. Send to his brother, fetch that gallant
     hither.
If he be absent, bring his brother to me.
I'll make him find him. Do this suddenly,
And let not search and inquisition° quail°   20
To bring again these foolish runaways.   [*Exeunt.*]

SCENE III. *Before* OLIVER'*s house.*

[*Enter* ORLANDO *and* ADAM, *meeting.*]
    ORL. Who's there?
    ADAM. What, my young master? O my gentle
     master!
O my sweet master! O you memory
Of old Sir Rowland! Why, what make° you here?
Why are you virtuous? Why do people love you?   5
And wherefore are you gentle, strong, and valiant?
Why would you be so fond° to overcome
The bonny prizer° of the humorous Duke?
Your praise is come too swiftly home before you.
Know you not, master, to some kind of men   10
Their graces serve them but as enemies?
No more do yours. Your virtues, gentle master,
Are sanctified and holy traitors° to you.
Oh, what a world is this when what is comely
Envenoms° him that bears it!   15
    ORL. Why, what's the matter?
    ADAM.   O unhappy youth!
Come not within these doors, within this roof
The enemy of all your graces lives.
Your brother — no, no brother, yet the son —
Yet not the son, I will not call him son   20
Of him I was about to call his father —
Hath heard your praises, and this night he means
To burn the lodging where you use to lie
And you within it. If he fail of that,
He will have other means to cut you off.   25
I overheard him and his practices.°
This is no place, this house is but a butchery.
Abhor it, fear it, do not enter it.
    ORL. Why, whither, Adam, wouldst thou have me
     go?   29
    ADAM. No matter whither so you come not here.
    ORL. What, wouldst thou have me go and beg my
     food?
Or with a base and boisterous° sword enforce

A thievish living on the common road?
This I must do, or know not what to do.
Yet this I will not do, do how I can.
I rather will subject me° to the malice   35
Of a diverted blood° and bloody brother.
    ADAM. But do not so. I have five hundred crowns,
The thrifty hire° I saved under your father,
Which I did store to be my foster nurse   40
When service should in my old limbs lie lame,
And unregarded age in corners thrown.
Take that, and He that doth the ravens feed,
Yea, providently caters for the sparrow,
Be comfort to my age! Here is the gold,   45
All this I give you. Let me be your servant.
Though I look old, yet I am strong and lusty,
For in my youth I never did apply
Hot and rebellious liquors in my blood,
Nor did not with unbashful forehead° woo   50
The means of° weakness and debility;
Therefore my age is as a lusty winter,
Frosty, but kindly. Let me go with you,
I'll do the service of a younger man
In all your business and necessities.   55
    ORL. O good old man, how well in thee appears
The constant° service of the antique° world,
When service sweat for duty, not for meed!°
Thou art not for the fashion of these times,
Where none will sweat but for promotion,   60
And having that do choke their service up
Even with the having.° It is not so with thee.
But, poor old man, thou prunest a rotten tree
That cannot so much as a blossom yield
In lieu of all thy pains and husbandry.°   65
But come thy ways, we'll go along together,
And ere we have thy youthful wages spent
We'll light upon some settled low content.°
    ADAM. Master, go on, and I will follow thee
To the last gasp, with truth and loyalty.   70
From seventeen years till now almost fourscore
Here livèd I, but now live here no more.
At seventeen years many their fortunes seek,
But at fourscore it is too late a week.°
Yet fortune cannot recompense me better   75
Than to die well and not my master's debtor.
                        [*Exeunt.*]

---

36. subject me: submit.   **37. diverted blood:** i.e., one whose natural feelings have been turned aside.   **39. thrifty hire:** saved-up pay.   **50. unbashful forehead:** vicious boldness.   **51. means of:** i.e., pleasures that bring.   **57. constant:** faithful. **antique:** ancient, "good old."   **58. meed:** reward.   **61–62. having . . . having:** and as soon as they have their reward cease to give good service.   **65. husbandry:** economy.   **68. settled . . . content:** humble but contented way of living.   **74. too . . . week:** a week too late.

---

20. inquisition: inquiry. **quail:** slacken.
    Sc. iii: **4. make:** do.   **7. fond:** foolish.   **8. prizer:** prize fighter.
13. sanctified . . . traitors: traitors who appear pious and holy.
15. Envenoms: poisons.   **26. practices:** plots.   **32. boisterous:** threatening.

SCENE IV. *The* FOREST *of Arden.*

[*Enter* ROSALIND *disguised as* GANYMEDE, CELIA
disguised as ALIENA, *and* TOUCHSTONE.]

ROS. Oh, Jupiter, how weary are my spirits!

TOUCH. I care not for my spirits if my legs were not weary.

ROS. I could find in my heart to disgrace my man's apparel and to cry like a woman. But I must com- 5
fort the weaker vessel, as doublet and hose° ought to show itself courageous to petticoat, therefore, courage, good Aliena.

CEL. I pray you bear with me, I cannot go no further. 10

TOUCH. For my part, I had rather bear with you than bear you. Yet I should bear no cross° if I did bear you, for I think you have no money in your purse.

ROS. Well, this is the forest of Arden. 15

TOUCH. Aye, now am I in Arden, the more fool I. When I was at home, I was in a better place. But travelers must be content.

ROS. Aye, be so, good Touchstone.

[*Enter* CORIN *and* SILVIUS.] Look you who comes here, a young man and an old in solemn talk. 21

COR. That is the way to make her scorn you still.

SIL. Oh, Corin, that thou knew'st how I do love her!

COR. I partly guess, for I have loved ere now.

SIL. No, Corin, being old, thou canst not guess,
Though in thy youth thou wast as true a lover 26
As ever sighed upon a midnight pillow.
But if thy love were ever like to mine —
As sure I think did never man love so —
How many actions most ridiculous 30
Hast thou been drawn to by thy fantasy?°

COR. Into a thousand that I have forgotten.

SIL. Oh, thou didst then ne'er love so heartily!
If thou remember'st not the slightest folly
That ever love did make thee run into, 35
Thou hast not loved.
Or if thou hast not sat as I do now,
Wearing° thy hearer in° thy mistress' praise,
Thou hast not loved.
Or if thou hast not broke from company 40
Abruptly, as my passion now makes me,
Thou hast not loved.
Oh, Phebe, Phebe, Phebe! [*Exit.*]

ROS. Alas, poor shepherd! Searching of thy wound,°
I have by hard adventure° found mine own. 45

TOUCH. And I mine. I remember when I was in love I broke my sword upon a stone and bid him take that for coming a-night to Jane Smile. And I remember the kissing of her batlet° and the cow's dugs that her pretty chopt° hands had milked. 50
And I remember the wooing of a peascod° instead of her, from whom I took two cods° and, giving her them again, said with weeping tears, " Wear these for my sake." We that are truelovers run into strange capers, but as all is mortal in nature, so is all nature in love mortal in folly.° 56

ROS. Thou speakest wiser than thou art ware of.

TOUCH. Nay, I shall ne'er be ware of mine own wit till I break my shins against it. 60

ROS.   Jove, Jove! This shepherd's passion
      Is much upon my fashion.

TOUCH. And mine, but it grows something stale with me.

CEL. I pray you, one of you question yon man
If he for gold will give us any food. 65
I faint almost to death.

TOUCH. Holloa, you clown!°

ROS. Peace, fool. He's not thy kinsman.

COR.   Who calls?

TOUCH. Your betters, sir.

COR.   Else are they very wretched.

ROS. Peace, I say. Good even to you, friend.

COR. And to you, gentle sir, and to you all. 70

ROS. I prithee, shepherd, if that love or gold
Can in this desert place buy entertainment,°
Bring us where we may rest ourselves and feed.
Here's a young maid with travel much oppressed
And faints for succor.

COR.   Fair sir, I pity her, 75
And wish, for her sake more than for mine own,
My fortunes were more able to relieve her.
But I am shepherd to another man
And do not shear the fleeces that I graze.°
My master is of churlish disposition 80
And little recks° to find the way to Heaven
By doing deeds of hospitality.
Besides, his cote,° his flocks and bounds of feed,°
Are now on sale, and at our sheepcote now,
By reason of his absence, there is nothing 85
That you will feed on. But what is, come see,
And in my voice most welcome shall you be.

ROS. What is he that shall buy his flock and pasture?

COR. That young swain° that you saw here but erewhile,

Sc. iv: 6. doublet . . . hose: i.e., man's attire, for Rosalind is now dressed as Ganymede. See Pl. 8b and comment on p. 93a-b. 12. bear no cross: lit., endure no misfortune; but it also meant "have no money," as Elizabethan money had a cross on the reverse side. See Pl. 10a. 31. fantasy: fancy, love. 38. Wearing: wearing out. in: with. 44. Searching . . . wound: i.e., listening to you probing your wound. 45. hard adventure: painful chance. 49. batlet: bat used for beating clothes during washing. 50. chopt: chapped. 51. peascod: usually peapod, but here the whole plant. 52. cods: pods. 56. mortal in folly: deadly silly. 67. clown: rustic. 72. entertainment: accommodation. 79. do . . . graze: do not sell the wool of the sheep I feed—because he is a hired shepherd and not the owner. 81. recks: cares. 83. cote: cottage. bounds of feed: pastures. 89. swain: a poetic word, usually implying a young man in love.

That little cares for buying anything.   90
  ROS. I pray thee, if it stand with honesty,
Buy thou the cottage, pasture, and the flock,
And thou shalt have to pay for it of us.
  CEL. And we will mend° thy wages. I like this
    place,
And willingly could waste my time in it.   95
  COR. Assuredly the thing is to be sold.
Go with me. If you like upon report
The soil, the profit, and this kind of life,
I will your very faithful feeder be
And buy it with your gold right suddenly.   100
                      [Exeunt.]

SCENE V. *The forest.*

[Enter AMIENS, JAQUES, *and others.]*
  AMI. *[Sings.]*
        Under the greenwood tree
        Who loves to lie with me,
        And turn° his merry note
        Unto the sweet bird's throat,
    Come hither, come hither, come hither.   5
        Here shall he see
        No enemy
      But winter and rough weather.
  JAQ. More, more, I prithee, more.
  AMI. It will make you melancholy, Monsieur
Jaques.   11
  JAQ. I thank it. More, I prithee, more. I can suck
melancholy out of a song as a weasel sucks eggs.
More, I prithee, more.
  AMI. My voice is ragged. I know I cannot please
you.   16
  JAQ. I do not desire you to please me, I do desire
you to sing. Come, more, another stanzo.° Call you
'em stanzos?
  AMI. What you will, Monsieur Jaques.
  JAQ. Nay, I care not for their names, they owe me
nothing.° Will you sing?   23
  AMI. More at your request than to please myself.
  JAQ. Well then, if ever I thank any man, I'll
thank you. But that they call compliment is like the
encounter of two dog apes,° and when a man thanks
me heartily, methinks I have given him a penny and
he renders me the beggarly thanks.° Come, sing,
and you that will not, hold your tongues.   31
  AMI. Well, I'll end the song. Sirs, cover° the
while.° The Duke will drink under this tree. He
hath been all this day to look you.
  JAQ. And I have been all this day to avoid him.

He is too disputable° for my company. I think of as
many matters as he, but I give Heaven thanks, and
make no boast of them. Come, warble, come.   38
        SONG. *[All together here.]*
        Who doth ambition shun,
        And loves to live i' the sun,
        Seeking the food he eats,
        And pleased with what he gets,
    Come hither, come hither, come hither.
        Here shall he see   45
        No enemy
      But winter and rough weather.
  JAQ. I'll give you a verse to this note,° that I made
yesterday in despite of my invention.°
  AMI. And I'll sing it.   50
  JAQ. Thus it goes:
        If it do come to pass
        That any man turn ass,
        Leaving his wealth and ease
        A stubborn will to please,   55
    Ducdame,° ducdame, ducdame.
        Here shall he see
        Gross fools as he,
        An if he will come to me.
  AMI. What's that " ducdame? "   60
  JAQ. 'Tis a Greek invocation to call fools into a
circle. I'll go sleep, if I can. If I cannot, I'll rail
against all the firstborn of Egypt.   63
  AMI. And I'll go seek the Duke. His banquet is
prepared.   *[Exeunt. severally.°]*

SCENE VI. *The forest.*

[Enter ORLANDO *and* ADAM.]
  ADAM. Dear master, I can go no further. Oh, I die
for food. Here lie I down, and measure out° my
grave. Farewell, kind master.
  ORL. Why, how now, Adam! No greater heart in
thee? Live a little, comfort a little, cheer thyself   5
a little. If this uncouth forest yield anything savage,
I will either be food for it or bring it for food to thee.
Thy conceit° is nearer death than thy powers.° For
my sake be comfortable,° hold death awhile at the
arm's end. I will here be with thee presently,°   10
and if I bring thee not something to eat, I will give

---

94. mend: improve.
  Sc. v: 3. turn: harmonize. Some editors read "tune."
18. stanzo: stanza; lit., a stand or set. 22–23. owe me nothing:
i.e., and so mean nothing to me. 28. dog apes: male baboons.
30. beggarly thanks: i.e., effusively like a beggar. 32. cover:
lay the table. 33. the while: in the meanwhile.

36. disputable: argumentative. 48. to . . . note: to go with this
tune. 49. despite . . . invention: i.e., although I am no good
at this sort of thing. in despite: in spite of. invention: the
creative faculty. 56. Ducdame: a three-syllable word. Many
commentators have tried to trace the origin of this word. It is
most probably one of the many meaningless syllables—like
"hey nonny no"—so often used to fill out the line of a song.
Jaques' own explanation (l. 61) is that it is a Greek invocation
to call fools into a circle (i.e., set them gossiping). It has greatly
stimulated scholars to make learned guesses. 65. s.d., severally:
by different exits.
  Sc. vi: 2. measure out: i.e., the length of. 8. conceit: imagination. powers: strength. 9. comfortable: comforted. 10. presently: immediately.

thee leave to die. But if thou diest before I come, thou
art a mocker of my labor. Well said! Thou lookest
cheerly, and I'll be with thee quickly. Yet thou liest
in the bleak air. Come, I will bear thee to some   15
shelter, and thou shalt not die for lack of a dinner
if there live anything in this desert. Cheerly, good
Adam!   [*Exeunt.*]

SCENE VII. *The forest.*

[*A table set out. Enter* DUKE *Senior,* AMIENS, *and*
LORDS *like outlaws.*]

DUKE S. I think he be transformed into a beast,
For I can nowhere find him like a° man.
  1. LORD. My lord, he is but even now gone hence.
Here was he merry, hearing of a song.
  DUKE S. If he, compact of jars,° grow musical,   5
We shall have shortly discord in the spheres.°
Go, seek him. Tell him I would speak with him.
                [*Enter* JAQUES.]
  1. LORD. He saves my labor by his own approach.
  DUKE S. Why, how now, monsieur! What a life is
    this
That your poor friends must woo your company?
What, you look merrily!   11
  JAQ. A fool, a fool! I met a fool i' the forest,
A motley fool,° a miserable world!
As I do live by food, I met a fool,
Who laid him down and basked him in the sun,   15
And railed on Lady Fortune in good terms,
In good set terms,° and yet a motley fool.
" Good morrow, fool," quoth I. " No, sir," quoth
    he.
" Call me not fool till Heaven hath sent me fortune."
And then he drew a dial° from his poke,°   20
And looking on it with lackluster eye,
Says very wisely, " It is ten o'clock.
Thus we may see," quoth he, " how the world wags.
'Tis but an hour ago since it was nine,
And after one hour more 'twill be eleven,   25
And so, from hour to hour, we ripe and ripe,
And then, from hour to hour, we rot and rot,
And thereby hangs a tale." When I did hear
The motley fool thus moral on the time,
My lungs began to crow like chanticleer,°   30
That fools should be so deep-contemplative,°
And I did laugh sans° intermission
An hour by his dial. Oh, noble fool!
A worthy fool! Motley's the only wear.
  DUKE S. What fool is this?   35

JAQ. Oh, worthy fool! One that hath been a cour
    tier,
And says if ladies be but young and fair,
They have the gift to know it. And in his brain,
Which is as dry as the remainder° biscuit
After a voyage, he hath strange places crammed   40
With observation, the which he vents°
In mangled forms.° Oh, that I were a fool!
I am ambitious for a motley coat.
  DUKE S. Thou shalt have one.
  JAQ.   It is my only suit,°
Provided that you weed your better judgments   45
Of all opinion that grows rank° in them
That I am wise. I must have liberty
Withal, as large a charter° as the wind
To blow on° whom I please. For so fools have,
And they that are most gallèd° with my folly,   50
They most must laugh. And why, sir, must they so?
The " why " is plain as way to parish church.
He that a fool doth very wisely hit
Doth very foolishly, although he smart,
Not to seem senseless of the bob.° If not,   55
The wise man's folly is anatomized°
Even by the squandering° glances of the fool.
Invest° me in my motley, give me leave
To speak my mind, and I will through and through
Cleanse the foul body of the infected world,   60
If they will patiently receive my medicine.
  DUKE S. Fie on thee! I can tell what thou wouldst
    do.
  JAQ. What, for a counter,° would I do but good?
  DUKE S. Most mischievous foul sin, in chiding sin.
For thou thyself hast been a libertine   65
As sensual as the brutish sting° itself,
And all the embossèd sores and headed evils
That thou with license of free foot° hast caught
Wouldst thou disgorge into the general world.
  JAQ. Why, who cries out on pride   70
That can therein tax any private party?°
Doth it not flow as hugely as the sea
Till that the weary very means do ebb?°
What woman in the city do I name
When that I say the city woman bears   75
The cost of princes on unworthy shoulders?
Who can come in and say that I mean her

Sc. vii: 2. **like a**: in the shape of.   5. **compact of jars**: made
of discords.   6. **discord . . . spheres**: See App. 1.   13. **motley
fool**: i.e., a professional fool. *Motley* was the particolored dress
worn by court jesters. See Pl. 12f, 13c.   17. **set terms**: phrases
carefully composed.   20. **dial**: watch. **poke**: pocket.   30. **chanticleer**: the cock.   31. **deep-contemplative**: profoundly thoughtful.   32. **sans**: without.

39. **remainder**: leftover.   41. **vents**: utters.   42. **mangled
forms**: quaint phrases.   44. **suit**: with a pun on suit, meaning
petition and suit of clothes.   46. **rank**: abundantly, like weeds
in a garden.   48. **large a charter**: as free a privilege.   49. **blow
on**: censure.   50. **galled**: rubbed sore.   55. **Not . . . bob**: not
to pretend that he has not been hurt. **bob**: blow.   56. **anatomized**: dissected.   57. **squandering**: scattered far and wide.
58. **Invest**: robe.   63. **counter**: a valueless token.   66. **brutish
sting**: i.e., lust.   67–68. **embossed . . . foot**: carbuncles and boils
that result from licentious living.   70–71. **who . . . party**: who is
attacking any particular person when he denounces pride?
Satirists of the time, when rebuked for attacking individuals,
usually replied that they were denouncing the sin and not individual sinners.   73. **weary . . . ebb**: i.e., until the means of pride
(i.e., wealth) grow tired and ebb away.

When such a one as she such is her neighbor?
Or what is he of basest function°
That says his bravery is not on my cost,°   80
Thinking that I mean him, but therein suits°
His folly to the mettle° of my speech?
There then, how then? What then? Let me see
      wherein
My tongue hath wronged him. If it do him right,°
Then he hath wronged himself. If he be free,°   85
Why then my taxing like a wild goose flies,
Unclaimed of any man. But who comes here?
      [*Enter* ORLANDO, *with his sword drawn.*]
ORL. Forbear, and eat no more.
JAQ.   Why, I have eat none yet.
ORL. Nor shalt not, till necessity° be served.
JAQ. Of what kind should this cock come of?   90
DUKE S. Art thou thus boldened, man, by thy dis-
      tress?
Or else a rude despiser of good manners,
That in civility° thou seem'st so empty?
      ORL. You touched my vein at first.° The thorny
      point°
Of bare distress hath ta'en from me the show   95
Of smooth civility. Yet am I inland-bred°
And know some nurture. But forbear, I say.
He dies that touches any of this fruit
Till I and my affairs are answered.
      JAQ. An° you will not be answered with reason,
I must die.   101
DUKE S. What would you have? Your gentleness
      shall force
More than your force move us to gentleness.
      ORL. I almost die for food, and let me have it.
DUKE S. Sit down and feed, and welcome to our
      table.   105
ORL. Speak you so gently? Pardon me, I pray you.
I thought that all things had been savage here,
And therefore put I on the countenance
Of stern commandment. But whate'er you are
That in this desert inaccessible,   110
Under the shade of melancholy boughs,
Lose and neglect the creeping hours of time,
If ever you have looked on better days,
If ever been where bells have knolled° to church,
If ever sat at any good man's feast,   115
If ever from your eyelids wiped a tear
And know what 'tis to pity and be pitied,
Let gentleness my strong enforcement° be.
In the which hope I blush, and hide my sword.   119

DUKE S. True is it that we have seen better days,
And have with holy bell been knolled to church,
And sat at good men's feasts, and wiped our eyes
Of drops that sacred pity hath engendered.
And therefore sit you down in gentleness
And take upon command° what help we have   125
That to your wanting may be ministered.
ORL. Then but forbear your food a little while
Whiles, like a doe, I go to find my fawn
And give it food. There is an old poor man
Who after me hath many a weary step   130
Limped in pure love. Till he be first sufficed,°
Oppressed with two weak evils, age and hunger,
I will not touch a bit.
DUKE S.   Go find him out,
And we will nothing waste till you return.   134
ORL. I thank ye, and be blest for your good com-
      fort!   [*Exit.*]
DUKE S. Thou seest we are not all alone unhappy.
This wide and universal theater
Presents more woeful pageants than the scene
Wherein we play in.
JAQ.   All the world's a stage,°
And all the men and women merely players.   140
They have their exits and their entrances,
And one man in his time plays many parts,
His acts being seven ages. At first the infant,
Mewling° and puking in the nurse's arms.
Then the whining schoolboy, with his satchel   145
And shining morning face, creeping like snail
Unwillingly to school. And then the lover,
Sighing like furnace, with a woeful ballad°
Made to his mistress' eyebrow. Then a soldier,   149
Full of strange oaths and bearded like the pard,°
Jealous in honor,° sudden and quick in quarrel,
Seeking the bubble reputation°
Even in the cannon's mouth. And then the justice,
In fair round belly with good capon lined,°
With eyes severe and beard of formal cut,°   155
Full of wise saws° and modern instances,°
And so he plays his part. The sixth age shifts
Into the lean and slippered Pantaloon°
With spectacles on nose and pouch on side,   159
His youthful hose, well saved, a world too wide
For his shrunk shank, and his big manly voice,
Turning again toward childish treble, pipes
And whistles in his sound. Last scene of all,

---

79. **basest function:** most degraded kind of employment.
80. **bravery . . . cost:** his fine clothes have not cost me anything.
81. **suits:** fits.   82. **mettle:** material; i.e., his protest shows that
my words have fitted him.   84. **do . . . right:** if my charges are
just.   85. **free:** guiltless.   89. **necessity:** i.e., those who must
have food.   93. **civility:** civilized behavior.   94. **touched . . .
first:** i.e., your first guess is right; I am indeed desperate. **vein:**
disposition. **thorny point:** acuteness.   96. **inland-bred:** one who
knows civilization. See III.ii.363.   100. **An:** if.   114. **knolled:**
tolled.   118. **enforcement:** means of forcing.

125. **upon command:** as you may choose to order.   131. **sufficed:**
satisfied.   139. **All . . . stage:** See *AYLI* Intro. p. 773a.   144. **Mew-
ling:** whimpering.   148. **ballad:** poem.   150. **pard:** leopard.
151. **Jealous in honor:** sensitive about his honor.   152. **bubble
reputation:** fame as quickly burst as a bubble.   154. **good . . .
lined:** bribed with the present of a fat chicken. It was a common
complaint that those who wished for justice from country magistrates had to bring presents with them. Such magistrates were
known as "basket justices."   155. **formal cut:** of severe pattern,
trim.   156. **saws:** sayings. **modern instances:** commonplace
illustrations.   158. **Pantaloon:** the foolish old man of Italian
comedy.

That ends this strange eventful history,
Is second childishness and mere oblivion,   165
Sans teeth, sans eyes, sans taste, sans everything.
       [*Re-enter* ORLANDO, *with* ADAM.]
    DUKE S. Welcome. Set down your venerable bur-
    then,
And let him feed.
    ORL. I thank you most for him.
    ADAM.   So had you need.
I scarce can speak to thank you for myself.   170
    DUKE S. Welcome. Fall to. I will not trouble you
As yet, to question you about your fortunes.
Give us some music, and, good Cousin, sing.
    AMI. [*Sings.*]
      Blow, blow, thou winter wind.
      Thou art not so unkind   175
        As man's ingratitude.
      Thy tooth is not so keen,
      Because thou art not seen,
        Although thy breath be rude.
Heigh-ho! Sing, heigh-ho! unto the green holly.   180
Most friendship is feigning, most loving mere folly.
      Then, heigh-ho, the holly!
       This life is most jolly.

      Freeze, freeze, thou bitter sky,
      That dost not bite so nigh   185
        As benefits forgot.
      Though thou the waters warp,°
      Thy sting is not so sharp
        As friend remembered not.
Heigh-ho! Sing, heigh-ho! unto the green holly.
Most friendship is feigning, most loving mere folly.
      Then, heigh-ho, the holly!
       This life is most jolly.
    DUKE S. If that you were the good Sir Rowland's
    son,
As you have whispered faithfully you were,
And as mine eye doth his effigies° witness
Most truly limned° and living in your face,
Be truly welcome hither. I am the Duke   195
That loved your father. The residue of your for-
    tune,°
Go to my cave and tell me. Good old man,
Thou art right welcome, as thy master is.
Support him by the arm. Give me your hand,
And let me all your fortunes understand. [*Exeunt.*]

187. warp: freeze. 193. effigies: image. 194. limned: painted.
196. residue ... fortune: the rest of the story of your life.

Act III

SCENE I. *A room in the palace.*

[*Enter* DUKE FREDERICK, LORDS, *and* OLIVER.]
    DUKE F. Not see him since? Sir, sir, that cannot be.
But were I not the better part made mercy,
I should not seek an absent argument
Of my revenge, thou present.° But look to it.
Find out thy brother, wheresoe'er he is.   5
Seek him with candle, bring him dead or living
Within this twelvemonth, or turn thou no more
To seek a living in our territory.
Thy lands and all things that thou dost call thine
Worth seizure do we seize into our hands   10
Till thou canst quit° thee by thy brother's mouth
Of what we think against thee.
    OLI. Oh, that your Highness knew my heart in
    this!
I never loved my brother in my life.
    DUKE F. More villain thou. Well, push him out of
    doors,   15
And let my officers of such a nature
Make an extent upon° his house and lands.
Do this expediently° and turn him going.
                           [*Exeunt.*]

SCENE II. *The forest.*

[*Enter* ORLANDO, *with a paper.*]
    ORL. "Hang there, my verse, in witness of my
    love.
And thou, thrice-crownèd queen° of night, survey
With thy chaste eye, from thy pale sphere° above,
    Thy huntress' name that my full life doth sway.
O Rosalind! These trees shall be my books   5
    And in their barks my thoughts I'll character,°
That every eye which in this forest looks
    Shall see thy virtue witnessed° everywhere.
Run, run, Orlando, carve on every tree
The fair, the chaste, and unexpressive° she."   10
                               [*Exit.*]
    [*Enter* CORIN *and* TOUCHSTONE.]
    COR. And how like you this shepherd's life, Mas-
    ter Touchstone?
    TOUCH. Truly, shepherd, in respect of itself, it is
a good life; but in respect that it is a shepherd's life,
it is naught.° In respect that it is solitary, I like   15

Act III, Sc. i: 3–4. I ... present: I should not look for your
brother, but take vengeance on you. 11. quit: acquit. 17. **Make
... upon**: seize upon. 18. expediently: expeditiously.
    Sc. ii: 2. thrice-crowned queen: the goddess Diana, so called
on earth; in Heaven she was Luna, the Moon, and in the underworld, Persephone. 3. pale sphere: i.e., the moon. 6. character:
inscribe. 8. witnessed: borne witness to. 10. unexpressive: in-
expressible, beyond description. 15. naught: worthless.

it very well; but in respect that it is private,° it is a
very vile life. Now, in respect it is in the fields, it
pleaseth me well; but in respect it is not in the Court,
it is tedious. As it is a spare° life, look you, it fits my
humor well; but as there is no more plenty in it,   20
it goes much against my stomach. Hast any philosophy in thee, shepherd?

COR. No° more but that I know the more one
sickens, the worse at ease he is; and that he that   25
wants money, means, and content is without three
good friends; that the property of rain is to wet and
fire to burn; that good pasture makes fat sheep, and
that a great cause of the night is lack of the sun; that
he that hath learned no wit by nature nor art°   30
may complain of good breeding or comes of a very
dull kindred.

TOUCH. Such a one is a natural° philosopher.
Wast ever in Court, shepherd?

COR. No, truly.   35

TOUCH. Then thou art damned.

COR. Nay, I hope.

TOUCH. Truly, thou art damned, like an ill-roasted
egg all on one side.

COR. For not being at Court? Your reason.   40

TOUCH. Why, if thou never wast at Court, thou
never sawest good manners.° If thou never sawest
good manners, then thy manners must be wicked,
and wickedness is sin, and sin is damnation. Thou
art in a parlous° state, shepherd.   45

COR. Not a whit, Touchstone. Those that are good
manners at the Court are as ridiculous in the country as the behavior of the country is most mockable
at the Court. You told me you salute not at the Court,
but you kiss your hands. That courtesy would be uncleanly if courtiers were shepherds.   52

TOUCH. Instance,° briefly, come, instance.

COR. Why, we are still handling our ewes, and
their fells,° you know, are greasy.   55

TOUCH. Why, do not your courtier's hands sweat?
And is not the grease of a mutton as wholesome as
the sweat of a man? Shallow, shallow. A better instance, I say, come.

COR. Besides, our hands are hard.   60

TOUCH. Your lips will feel them the sooner. Shallow again. A more sounder instance, come.

COR. And they are often tarred over with the surgery of our sheep, and would you have us kiss tar?
The courtier's hands are perfumed with civet.°   66

TOUCH. Most shallow man! Thou wormsmeat in

respect of a good piece of flesh indeed! Learn of the
wise, and perpend.° Civet is of a baser birth than tar,
the very uncleanly flux of a cat. Mend the instance,
shepherd.   71

COR. You have too Courtly a wit for me. I'll rest.

TOUCH. Wilt thou rest damned? God help thee,
shallow man! God make incision° in thee! Thou art
raw.°   76

COR. Sir, I am a true laborer. I earn that I eat, get
that I wear, owe no man hate, envy no man's happiness, glad of other men's good, content with my
harm,° and the greatest of my pride is to see my
ewes graze and my lambs suck.   81

TOUCH. That is another simple sin in you, to bring
the ewes and the rams together and to offer to get
your living by the copulation of cattle; to be bawd°
to a bellwether, and to betray a she-lamb of a   85
twelvemonth to a crooked-pated, old, cuckoldy°
ram, out of all reasonable match.° If thou beest
not damned for this, the Devil himself will have
no shepherds. I cannot see else how thou shouldst
'scape.   90

COR. Here comes young Master Ganymede, my
new mistress's brother.

[*Enter* ROSALIND, *with a paper, reading.*]

ROS. "From the east to western Ind,°
      No jewel is like Rosalind.   94
      Her worth, being mounted on the wind,°
      Through all the world bears Rosalind.
      All the pictures fairest lined°
      Are but black to Rosalind.
      Let no face be kept in mind
      But the fair of Rosalind."   100

TOUCH. I'll rhyme you so eight years together,
dinners and suppers and sleeping hours excepted.
It is the right butterwomen's rank to market.°

ROS. Out, fool!   105

TOUCH. For a taste:
      If a hart do lack a hind,°
      Let him seek out Rosalind.
      If the cat will after kind,
      So be sure will Rosalind.   110
      Winter garments must be lined,
      So must slender Rosalind.
      They that reap must sheaf and bind,
      Then to cart with Rosalind.
      Sweetest nut hath sourest rind,   115
      Such a nut is Rosalind.
      He that sweetest rose will find
      Must find love's prick and Rosalind.

---

16. private: solitary. Touchstone as a frequenter of the court
prefers a public kind of life.   **19. spare:** frugal.   **24–32. No . . .
kindred:** Corin answers Touchstone's Court wit with a selection
of rustic wisdom.   **30. nature . . . art:** See App. 18.   **33. natural:**
with a pun on *natural*, meaning fool.   **42. good manners:** with
double meaning -- polite behavior and a moral life.   **45. parlous:**
perilous.   **53. Instance:** give an example.   **55. fells:** fleeces.
66. civet: perfume obtained from glandular secretions of the
civet cat.

69. perpend: consider.   **75. make incision:** cut to let blood — a
common treatment for many complaints.   **76. raw:** unripe,
"green."   **79–80. content . . . harm:** content to bear my own
troubles.   **84. bawd:** go-between.   **86. cuckoldy:** lecherous.
87. match: mating.   **93. Ind:** India.   **95. mounted . . . wind:**
blown about by the wind.   **97. lined:** drawn.   **104. right . . .
market:** i.e., like a lot of old countrywomen ambling along to
market.   **107. hart . . . hind:** male and female deer.

This is the very false gallop° of verses. Why do you infect yourself with them?   120

ros. Peace, you dull fool! I found them on a tree.

touch. Truly, the tree yields bad fruit.

ros. I'll graff° it with you, and then I shall graff it with a medlar.° Then it will be the earliest fruit i' the country, for you'll be rotten ere you be half ripe, and that's the right virtue of the medlar.

touch. You have said, but whether wisely or no, let the forest judge.   130

[*Enter* CELIA, *with a writing.*]

ros. Peace!

Here comes my sister, reading. Stand aside.

cel. [*Reads.*]

" Why should this a desert be?
    For it is unpeopled? No,
Tongues I'll hang on every tree,   135
    That shall civil° sayings show
Some, how brief the life of man
    Runs his erring° pilgrimage,
That the stretching of a span°
    Buckles in his sum of age;   140
Some, of violated vows
    'Twixt the souls of friend and friend.
But upon the fairest boughs,
    Or at every sentence end,
Will I Rosalinda write,   145
    Teaching all that read to know
The quintessence° of every sprite
    Heaven would in little show.
Therefore Heaven Nature charged
    That one body should be filled   150
With all graces wide-enlarged.
    Nature presently distilled
Helen's cheek, but not her heart,
    Cleopatra's majesty,
Atalanta's better part,   155
    Sad Lucretia's modesty.°
Thus Rosalind of many parts
    By heavenly synod° was devised,
Of many faces, eyes, and hearts,
    To have the touches dearest prized.   160
Heaven would that she these gifts should have,
And I to live and die her slave."

ros. O most gentle pulpiter!° What tedious

homily° of love have you wearied your parishioners withal, and never cried "Have patience, good people!"   166

cel. How now! Back, friends! Shepherd, go off a little. Go with him, sirrah.

touch. Come, shepherd, let us make an honorable retreat, though not with bag and baggage, yet with scrip° and scrippage.°   171

[*Exeunt* CORIN *and* TOUCHSTONE.]

cel. Didst thou hear these verses?

ros. Oh, yes, I heard them all, and more too, for some of them had in them more feet than the verses would bear.   175

cel. That's no matter. The feet might bear the verses.

ros. Aye, but the feet were lame and could not bear themselves without the verse and therefore stood lamely in the verse.   180

cel. But didst thou hear without wondering how thy name should be hanged and carved upon these trees?

ros. I was seven of the nine days° out of the wonder before you came; for look here what I found on a palm tree. I was never so berhymed° since Pythagoras'° time, that I was an Irish rat, which I can hardly remember.   188

cel. Trow° you who hath done this?

ros. Is it a man?

cel. And a chain that you once wore about his neck. Change you color?

ros. I prithee — who?

cel. Oh Lord, Lord! It is a hard matter for friends to meet, but mountains may be removed with earthquakes and so encounter.   196

ros. Nay, but who is it?

cel. Is it possible?

ros. Nay, I prithee now with most petitionary vehemence,° tell me who it is.   200

cel. Oh, wonderful, wonderful, and most wonderful wonderful! And yet again wonderful, and after that, out of all hooping!°

ros. Good my complexion! Dost thou think though I am caparisoned° like a man, I have a   205 doublet and hose in my disposition?° One inch of delay more is a South Sea of discovery.° I prithee tell me who is it quickly, and speak apace. I would

---

119. false gallop: canter. The rolling motion of a canter is like the even stress of Orlando's bad verses.   123. graff: graft. 124. medlar: a fruit resembling a small brown apple, but not eaten until it has grown soft.   136. civil: civilized.   138. erring: wandering.   139. span: the distance between the thumb and forefinger of the stretched hand; about 9 inches.   147. quintessence: fifth essence, that which remains when the four elements have been taken away.   153–56. Helen's . . . modesty: Rosalind has the good parts of four famous women of story. Helen was divinely fair but unfaithful, Cleopatra, a Queen most royal but unchaste, Atalanta, a swift runner but led aside by cupidity, Lucretia, a model wife but betrayed.   158. synod: assembly. 163. pulpiter: preacher, an emendation for the F1 reading "Jupiter."

164. homily: sermon.   171. scrip: the shepherd's wallet. scrippage: a word invented by Touchstone to balance baggage. 184. seven . . . days: i.e., I have endured almost a nine days' wonder.   186. berhymed: rhymed to death. It was believed that in Ireland rats could be destroyed by incantation in rhyme.   187. Pythagoras: He taught the doctrine of the transmigration of souls — that the human soul after death passed into the body of an animal.   189. Trow: know. 199–200. petitionary vehemence: pleading emphasis.   203. out . . . hooping: beyond any cry of wonder.   205. caparisoned: decked out.   206. disposition: nature.   206–07. One . . . discovery: i.e., the slightest delay in telling me makes your story seem as endless as the South Sea to a voyager.

thou couldst stammer, that thou mightst pour this concealed man out of thy mouth as wine 210 comes out of a narrow-mouthed bottle, either too much at once or none at all. I prithee take the cork out of thy mouth that I may drink thy tidings.

CEL. So you may put a man in your belly. 215

ROS. Is he of God's making? What manner of man? Is his head worth a hat? Or his chin worth a beard?

CEL. Nay, he hath but a little beard.

ROS. Why, God will send more, if the man will be thankful. Let me stay the growth of his beard if thou delay me not the knowledge of his chin.° 222

CEL. It is young Orlando, that tripped up the wrestler's heels and your heart both in an instant.

ROS. Nay, but the devil take mocking. Speak, sad brow° and true maid.

CEL. I' faith, Coz, 'tis he.

ROS. Orlando?

CEL. Orlando. 230

ROS. Alas the day! What shall I do with my doublet and hose? What did he when thou sawest him? What said he? How looked he? Wherein went he? What makes he here? Did he ask for me? Where remains he? How parted he with thee? And 235 when shalt thou see him again? Answer me in one word.

CEL. You must borrow me Gargantua's° mouth first. 'Tis a word too great for any mouth of this age's size. To say aye and no to these particulars is more than to answer in a catechism. 241

ROS. But doth he know that I am in this forest and in man's apparel? Looks he as freshly as he did the day he wrestled? 244

CEL. It is as easy to count atomies° as to resolve the propositions of a lover,° but take a taste of my finding him,° and relish it with good observance. I found him under a tree, like a dropped acorn.

ROS. It may well be called Jove's tree when it drops forth such fruit. 250

CEL. Give me audience, good madam.

ROS. Proceed.

CEL. There lay he, stretched along° like a wounded knight.

ROS. Though it be pity to see such a sight, it well becomes the ground. 256

CEL. Cry "holloa"° to thy tongue, I prithee, it curvets° unseasonably. He was furnished° like a hunter.

ROS. Oh, ominous! He comes to kill my heart.

CEL. I would sing my song without a burden. Thou bringest me out of tune. 263

ROS. Do you not know I am a woman? When I think, I must speak. Sweet, say on.

CEL. You bring me out. Soft! Comes he not here?

[Enter ORLANDO and JAQUES.]

ROS. 'Tis he. Slink by, and note him.

JAQ. I thank you for your company, but, good faith, I had as lief have been myself alone. 270

ORL. And so had I, but yet, for fashion sake, I thank you too for your society.

JAQ. God buy you.° Let's meet as little as we can.

ORL. I do desire we may be better strangers. 275

JAQ. I pray you mar no more trees with writing love songs in their barks.

ORL. I pray you mar no moe° of my verses with reading them ill-favoredly.°

JAQ. Rosalind is your love's name? 280

ORL. Yes, just.°

JAQ. I do not like her name.

ORL. There was no thought of pleasing you when she was christened.

JAQ. What stature is she of? 285

ORL. Just as high as my heart.

JAQ. You are full of pretty answers. Have you not been acquainted with goldsmiths' wives, and conned them out of rings?° 289

ORL. Not so, but I answer you right painted cloth,° from whence you have studied your questions.

JAQ. You have a nimble wit. I think 'twas made of Atalanta's° heels. Will you sit down with me? And we two will rail against our mistress the world, and all our misery. 296

ORL. I will chide no breather° in the world but myself, against whom I know most faults.

JAQ. The worst fault you have is to be in love.

ORL. 'Tis a fault I will not change for your best virtue. I am weary of you. 302

JAQ. By my troth, I was seeking for a fool when I found you.

ORL. He is drowned in the brook. Look but in and you shall see him. 306

JAQ. There I shall see mine own figure.

ORL. Which I take to be either a fool or a cipher.

JAQ. I'll tarry no longer with you. Farewell, good Signior Love. 310

ORL. I am glad of your departure. Adieu, good Monsieur Melancholy. *[Exit JAQUES.]*

221-22. let . . . chin: I can wait for his beard to grow, so long as you tell me whose chin it is.   225-26. sad brow: in sober earnest.   238. Gargantua: the enormous giant of Rabelais' satirical tale.   245. atomies: motes in a sunbeam.   245-46. resolve . . . lover: solve a lover's problems.   246-47. taste . . . him: i.e., to whet your appetite for my tale.   253. along: at full length.   257. holloa: hold up! whoa!   258. curvets: prances. furnished: equipped.

262. burden: refrain.   274. God . . . you: God be with you.   278. moe: more.   279. ill-favoredly: with a wry face.   281. just: exactly.   289. out of rings: Rings were often inscribed with "posies" — pretty little sentences or mottoes.   290-91. painted cloth: In taverns and other rooms for which genuine tapestry was too costly, coarse cloths painted with Scriptural or classical scenes were used to cover the walls. The figures were sometimes painted with texts or labels issuing from their mouths with suitable remarks. See Pl. 6a.   294. Atalanta: See l. 155, n.   297. breather: living creature.

ROS. [*Aside to* CELIA] I will speak to him like a saucy lackey,° and under that habit play the knave with him. Do you hear, forester?   315

ORL. Very well. What would you?

ROS. I pray you, what is 't o' clock?

ORL. You should ask me what time o' day. There's no clock in the forest.   319

ROS. Then there is no truelover in the forest, else sighing every minute and groaning every hour would detect the lazy foot of Time as well as a clock.°

ORL. And why not the swift foot of Time? Had not that been as proper?   325

ROS. By no means, sir. Time travels in divers° paces with divers persons. I'll tell you who Time ambles withal, who Time trots withal, who Time gallops withal, and who he stands still withal.

ORL. I prithee who doth he trot withal?   330

ROS. Marry, he trots hard with a young maid between the contract° of her marriage and the day it is solemnized. If the interim be but a sennight,° Time's pace is so hard that it seems the length of seven year.   335

ORL. Who ambles Time withal?

ROS. With a priest that lacks Latin and a rich man that hath not the gout; for the one sleeps easily because he cannot study, and the other lives merrily because he feels no pain, the one lacking the burden of lean and wasteful learning, the other knowing no burden of heavy tedious penury. These Time ambles withal.

ORL. Who doth he gallop withal?   344

ROS. With a thief to the gallows, for though he go as softly as foot can fall, he thinks himself too soon there.

ORL. Who stays it still withal?

ROS. With lawyers in the vacation, for they sleep between term and term and then they perceive not how Time moves.   351

ORL. Where dwell you, pretty youth?

ROS. With this shepherdess, my sister. Here in the skirts° of the forest, like fringe upon a petticoat.

ORL. Are you native of this place?   356

ROS. As the cony° that you see dwell where she is kindled.°

ORL. Your accent is something finer than you could purchase in so removed° a dwelling.   360

ROS. I have been told so of many. But indeed an old religious° uncle of mine taught me to speak, who was in his youth an inland man,° one that

knew courtship too well, for there he fell in love. I have heard him read many lectures against it, and I thank God I am not a woman, to be touched with so many giddy offenses as he hath generally taxed their whole sex withal.   368

ORL. Can you remember any of the principal evils that he laid to the charge of women?

ROS. There were none principal, they were all like one another as halfpence are, every one fault seeming monstrous till his fellow fault came to match it.

ORL. I prithee recount some of them.   375

ROS. No, I will not cast away my physic but on those that are sick. There is a man haunts the forest that abuses our young plants with carving "Rosalind" on their barks, hangs odes upon hawthorns and elegies on brambles — all, forsooth, deify- 380 ing the name of Rosalind. If I could meet that fancy-monger,° I would give him some good counsel, for he seems to have the quotidian° of love upon him.

ORL. I am he that is so love-shaked. I pray you tell me your remedy.   386

ROS. There is none of my uncle's marks upon you. He taught me how to know a man in love, in which cage of rushes° I am sure you are not prisoner.   390

ORL. What were his marks?

ROS. A lean cheek, which you have not; a blue eye° and sunken, which you have not; an unquestionable° spirit, which you have not; a beard neglected, which you have not — but I pardon you 395 for that, for simply your having in beard is a younger brother's revenue.° Then your hose should be ungartered, your bonnet° unbanded,° your sleeve unbuttoned, your shoe untied, and everything about you demonstrating a careless desolation. But 400 you are no such man, you are rather point-device° in your accouterments,° as loving yourself than seeming the lover of any other.

ORL. Fair youth, I would I could make thee believe I love.   405

ROS. Me believe it! You may as soon make her that you love believe it, which, I warrant, she is apter to do than to confess she does. That is one of the points in the which women still give the lie to their consciences. But, in good sooth, are you he that hangs the verses on the trees wherein Rosalind is so admired?   412

ORL. I swear to thee, youth, by the white hand of Rosalind, I am that he, that unfortunate he.

ROS. But are you so much in love as your rhymes speak?

---

314. lackey: servant.   **320–23. else . . . clock:** by giving a sigh at each minute and a groan at each hour you would discover the slow passage of Time as clearly as if you had a clock. **326. divers:** different.   **332. contract:** formal betrothal.   See Gen. Intro. p. 20a, and App. 15.   **333. sennight:** week. **355. skirts:** outskirts.   **357. cony:** rabbit.   **358. kindled:** brought forth.   **360. removed:** remote.   **362. religious:** i.e., a hermit.   **363. inland man:** city dweller.

381–82. fancymonger: trader in love.   **383. quotidian:** fever which recurs daily.   **390. cage of rushes:** cage of reed made for little birds.   **392–93. blue eye:** with dark rings under the eye. See App. 4.   **394. unquestionable:** glum.   **396–97. having . . . revenue:** your beard anyhow is a poor thing like the income of a younger brother.   **398. bonnet:** hat. **unbanded:** without a band.   **401. point-device:** very neat.   **402. accouterments:** equipment.

ORL. Neither rhyme nor reason can express how much. 419

ROS. Love is merely a madness, and I tell you deserves as well a dark house and a whip as madmen do.° And the reason why they are not so punished and cured is that the lunacy is so ordinary that the whippers are in love too. Yet I profess curing it by counsel. 425

ORL. Did you ever cure any so?

ROS. Yes, one, and in this manner. He was to imagine me his love, his mistress, and I set him every day to woo me. At which time would I, being but a moonish° youth, grieve, be effeminate, 430 changeable, longing and liking, proud, fantastical, apish, shallow, inconstant, full of tears, full of smiles, for every passion something and for no passion truly anything, as boys and women are for the most part cattle of this color. Would now like 435 him, now loathe him; then entertain him, then forswear° him; now weep for him, then spit at him; that I drave my suitor from his mad humor° of love to a living humor of madness, which was to forswear the full stream of the world° and to live in a 440 nook merely monastic.° And thus I cured him, and this way will I take upon me to wash your liver° as clean as a sound sheep's heart, that there shall not be one spot of love in 't.

ORL. I would not be cured, youth. 446

ROS. I would cure you if you would but call me Rosalind and come every day to my cote and woo me.

ORL. Now, by the faith of my love, I will. Tell me where it is. 451

ROS. Go with me to it and I'll show it you. And by the way you shall tell me where in the forest you live. Will you go?

ORL. With all my heart, good youth. 455

ROS. Nay, you must call me Rosalind. Come, Sister, will you go? [*Exeunt.*]

SCENE III. *The forest.*

[*Enter* TOUCHSTONE *and* AUDREY; JAQUES *behind.*]

TOUCH. Come apace,° good Audrey. I will fetch up your goats, Audrey. And how, Audrey? Am I the man yet? Doth my simple feature content you?

AUD. Your features! Lord warrant us! What features? 6

TOUCH. I am here with thee and thy goats, as the most capricious° poet, honest Ovid, was among the Goths.°

JAQ. [*Aside*] Oh, knowledge ill-inhabited, worse than Jove in a thatched house!° 11

TOUCH. When° a man's verses cannot be understood, nor a man's good wit seconded° with the forward child understanding, it strikes a man more dead than a great reckoning in a little room.° Truly, I would the gods had made thee poetical. 16

AUD. I do not know what " poetical " is. Is it honest in deed and word? Is it a true thing?

TOUCH. No, truly, for the truest poetry is the most feigning, and lovers are given to poetry, and what they swear in poetry may be said as lovers they do feign. 22

AUD. Do you wish, then, that the gods had made me poetical?

TOUCH. I do, truly, for thou swearest to me thou art honest.° Now if thou wert a poet, I might have some hope thou didst feign. 27

AUD. Would you not have me honest?

TOUCH. No, truly, unless thou wert hard-favored,° for honesty coupled to beauty is to have honey a sauce to sugar.

JAQ. [*Aside*] A material° fool!

AUD. Well, I am not fair, and therefore I pray the gods make me honest. 34

TOUCH. Truly, and to cast away honesty upon a foul slut were to put good meat into an unclean dish.

AUD. I am not a slut, though I thank the gods I am foul. 39

TOUCH. Well, praised be the gods for thy foulness! Sluttishness may come hereafter. But be it as it may be, I will marry thee, and to that end I have been with Sir Oliver Martext,° the vicar of the next village, who hath promised to meet me in this place of the forest and to couple us. 45

JAQ. [*Aside*] I would fain see this meeting.

AUD. Well, the gods give us joy!

TOUCH. Amen. A man may, if he were of a fearful heart, stagger° in this attempt; for here we have no temple but the wood, no assembly but horn 50 beasts. But what though? Courage! As horns° are odious, they are necessary. It is said, " Many a man knows no end of his goods." Right, many a man has

---

8. capricious: with a pun on *caper*: a goat, a most lascivious beast.   8–9. Ovid . . . Goths: Ovid was banished from Rome for an intrigue with the daughter of the Emperor Augustus and forced to live with the Getae (*Goths*). There is a second pun on Goths and goats.   11. Jove . . . house: i.e., a god living in a cottage. 12–15. When . . . room: This cryptic remark is probably topical, but the allusion is lost. seconded: supported. great . . . room: i.e., a huge bill for a private dinner party.   26. honest: chaste. 29. hard-favored: plain-faced, homely.   32. material: full of matter.   43. Sir . . . Martext: A minister of the church was often a Bachelor of Arts, and so entitled "dominus," which was translated "sir." Oliver, however, is not a properly ordained minister but a local preacher who mars texts by his misinterpretations.   49. stagger: tremble.   51. horns: the inevitable joke about the cuckold's horn. See App. 11.

421–22. dark . . . do: This was the common treatment given to lunatics.   430. moonish: fickle, changeable as the moon. 437. forswear: deny with an oath.   438. humor: mood. 440. full . . . world: i.e., a full life.   441. merely monastic: an absolute monk.   442. liver: the seat of the passions.

Sc. iii: 1. apace: quickly.

good horns and knows no end of them. Well, that is the dowry of his wife, 'tis none of his own 55 getting. Horns? — Even so. — Poor men alone? No, no, the noblest deer hath them as huge as the rascal.° Is the single man therefore blessed? No. As a walled town is more worthier than a village, so is the forehead of a married man more honorable 60 than the bare brow of a bachelor; and by how much defense is better than no skill, by so much is a horn° more precious than to want. Here comes Sir Oliver. [*Enter* SIR OLIVER MARTEXT.] Sir Oliver Martext, you are well met. Will you dispatch us here under this tree, or shall we go with you to your chapel? 67

SIR OLI. Is there none here to give the woman?

TOUCH. I will not take her on gift of any man.

SIR OLI. Truly, she must be given° or the marriage is not lawful.

JAQ. Proceed, proceed. I'll give her. 72

TOUCH. Good even, good Master What-ye-call't. How do you, sir? You are very well met. God 'ild° you for your last company. I am very glad to see you. Even a toy° in hand here, sir. Nay, pray be covered.°

JAQ. Will you be married, Motley? 79

TOUCH. As the ox hath his bow,° sir, the horse his curb, and the falcon her bells, so man hath his desires; and as pigeons bill, so wedlock would be nibbling.°

JAQ. And will you, being a man of your breeding, be married under a bush like a beggar? Get you 85 to church, and have a good priest that can tell you what marriage is. This fellow will but join you together as they join wainscot;° then one of you will prove a shrunk panel, and like green timber warp, warp. 90

TOUCH. [*Aside*] I am not in the mind, but I were better to be married of him than of another. For he is not like to marry me well, and not being well married, it will be a good excuse for me hereafter to leave my wife. 95

JAQ. Go thou with me, and let me counsel thee.

TOUCH. Come, sweet Audrey.
We must be married or we must live in bawdry.
Farewell, good Master Oliver: not — 100
     "O sweet Oliver,
       O brave Oliver,
       Leave me not behind thee — "
but —
     "Wind° away, 105
       Begone, I say,

I will not to wedding with thee."

[*Exeunt* JAQUES, TOUCHSTONE *and* AUDREY.]

SIR OLI. 'Tis no matter. Ne'er a fantastical knave of them all shall flout° me out of my calling. 109
[*Exit.*]

SCENE IV. *The forest.*

[*Enter* ROSALIND *and* CELIA.]

ROS. Never talk to me, I will weep.

CEL. Do, I prithee, but yet have the grace to consider that tears do not become a man.

ROS. But have I not cause to weep? 4

CEL. As good cause as one would desire, therefore weep.

ROS. His very hair is of the dissembling° color.

CEL. Something browner than Judas's.° Marry, his kisses are Judas's own children. 10

ROS. I'faith, his hair is of a good color.

CEL. An excellent color. Your chestnut was ever the only color.

ROS. And his kissing is as full of sanctity as the touch of holy bread. 15

CEL. He hath bought a pair of cast° lips of Diana.° A nun of winter's sisterhood kisses not more religiously, the very ice of chastity is in them.

ROS. But why did he swear he would come this morning and comes not? 21

CEL. Nay, certainly there is no truth in him.

ROS. Do you think so?

CEL. Yes, I think he is not a pickpurse nor a horse-stealer; but for his verity in love, I do think him as concave as a covered goblet° or a worm-eaten nut.

ROS. Not true in love? 29

CEL. Yes, when he is in, but I think he is not in.

ROS. You have heard him swear downright he was.

CEL. "Was" is not "is." Besides, the oath of a lover is no stronger than the word of a tapster;° they are both the confirmer of false reckonings. He attends here in the forest on the Duke your father. 37

ROS. I met the Duke yesterday and had much question° with him. He asked me of what parentage I was. I told him of as good as he, so he laughed and let me go. But what talk we of fathers when there is such a man as Orlando? 42

CEL. Oh, that's a brave man! He writes brave verses, speaks brave words, swears brave oaths and breaks them bravely, quite traverse, athwart° the heart of his lover — as a puisny° tilter that spurs his

---

58. **rascal:** a young lean deer in poor condition.   62. **horn:** with a pun on the cornucopia or horn of plenty.   70. **given:** a woman was, in theory, the possession of her father until marriage, when he gave her away to her husband. This notion is still symbolized in the marriage service of the Church of England.   74. **God 'ild:** God reward.   77. **toy:** trifle.   77–78. **be covered:** put your hat on.   80. **bow:** yoke.   83. **nibbling:** i.e., getting at a man. 88. **wainscot:** wooden paneling. See Pl. 17.   105. **Wind:** turn.

109. **flout:** mock.

Sc. iv: 8. **dissembling:** cheating.   9. **browner . . . Judas's:** Judas Iscariot, the traitor, was portrayed with red hair.   16. **cast:** cast off. Some editors read "chaste."   17. **Diana:** the goddess of chastity.   28. **concave . . . goblet:** as hollow as a drinking cup with a cover. See Pl. 20h.   35. **tapster:** the potboy in a tavern who brings the drinks.   39. **question:** conversation.   45. **quite . . . athwart:** i.e., the glancing blow of one who is afraid to ride "full tilt" at his opponent.   46. **puisny:** inexperienced, paltry.

horse but on one side breaks his staff like a noble
goose. But all's brave that youth mounts and folly
guides. Who comes here?   49

[*Enter* CORIN.]

COR. Mistress and master, you have oft inquired
After the shepherd that complained of love
Who you saw sitting by me on the turf
Praising the proud disdainful shepherdess
That was his mistress.

CEL.   Well, and what of him?

COR. If you will see a pageant° truly played   55
Between the pale complexion of true love
And the red glow of scorn and proud disdain,
Go hence a little and I shall conduct you,
If you will mark it.

ROS.   Oh, come, let us remove.
The sight of lovers feedeth those in love.   60
Bring us to this sight and you shall say
I'll prove a busy actor in their play.   [*Exeunt.*]

SCENE V. *Another part of the forest.*

[*Enter* SILVIUS *and* PHEBE.]

SIL. Sweet Phebe, do not scorn me, do not, Phebe.
Say that you love me not, but say not so
In bitterness. The common executioner,
Whose heart the accustomed sight of death makes
      hard,
Falls° not the ax upon the humbled neck   5
But first begs pardon. Will you sterner be
Than he that dies and lives by bloody drops?

[*Enter* ROSALIND, CELIA, *and* CORIN, *behind.*]

PHE. I would not be thy executioner.
I fly thee, for I would not injure thee.
Thou tell'st me there is murder in mine eye.   10
'Tis pretty,° sure, and very probable,
That eyes, that are the frail'st and softest things,
Who shut their coward gates on atomies,°
Should be called tyrants, butchers, murderers!
Now I do frown on thee with all my heart,   15
And if mine eyes can wound, now let them kill thee.
Now counterfeit° to swoon, why, now fall down.
Or if thou canst not, oh, for shame, for shame,
Lie not, to say mine eyes are murderers!   19
Now show the wound mine eye hath made in thee.
Scratch thee but with a pin and there remains
Some scar of it. Lean but upon a rush,
The cicatrice° and capable impressure°
Thy palm some moment keeps. But now mine eyes,
Which I have darted at thee, hurt thee not,   25
Nor, I am sure, there is no force in eyes

That can do hurt.

SIL.   O dear Phebe,
If ever — as that ever may be near —
You meet in some fresh cheek the power of fancy,°
Then shall you know the wounds invisible   30
That love's keen arrows make.

PHE.   But till that time
Come not thou near me. And when that time comes,
Afflict me with thy mocks, pity me not,
As till that time I shall not pity thee.

ROS. And why, I pray you? Who might be your
      mother   35
That you insult, exult, and all at once
Over the wretched? What though you have no
      beauty —
As, by my faith, I see no more in you
Than without candle may go dark to bed° —
Must you be therefore proud and pitiless?   40
Why, what means this? Why do you look on me?
I see no more in you than in the ordinary
Of nature's salework.° 'Od's my little life,°
I think she means to tangle my eyes too!
No, faith, proud mistress, hope not after it.   45
'Tis not your inky brows, your black silk hair,°
Your bugle° eyeballs, nor your cheek of cream,
That can entame my spirits to your worship.
You foolish shepherd, wherefore do you follow her
Like foggy south,° puffing with wind and rain?   50
You are a thousand times a properer° man
Than she a woman. 'Tis such fools as you
That makes the world full of ill-favored children.
'Tis not her glass, but you, that flatters her,
And out of you she sees herself more proper   55
Than any of her lineaments° can show her.
But, mistress, know yourself. Down on your knees
And thank Heaven, fasting, for a good man's love.
For I must tell you friendly in your ear,
Sell when you can. You are not for all markets.   60
Cry the man mercy,° love him, take his offer.
Foul is most foul, being foul to be a scoffer.°
So take her to thee, shepherd. Fare you well.

PHE. Sweet youth, I pray you, chide a year to-
      gether.
I had rather hear you chide than this man woo.   65

ROS. He's fallen in love with your foulness and
she'll fall in love with my anger. If it be so, as fast as
she answers thee with frowning looks, I'll sauce her
with bitter words. Why look you so upon me?   70

PHE. For no ill will I bear you.

---

55. pageant: play.
     Sc. v: 5. Falls: lets fall.   11. pretty: a pretty notion.
13. atomies: the smallest particles. See III.ii.245,n.   17. counterfeit: pretend.   23. cicatrice: scar. capable impressure: imprint
retained.

29. fancy: love.   39. without . . . bed: i.e., you're not so brilliant
that you can go to bed by your own light.   42–43. ordinary . . .
salework: no extraordinary piece of goods.   43. 'Od's . . . life:
a mild oath, "bless us."   46. black . . . hair: Black was not considered beautiful. See Sonnet 130.   47. bugle: beady.   50. foggy
south: The south wind brought fogs and illness.   51. properer:
more handsome.   56. lineaments: features.   61. Cry . . . mercy:
ask his pardon.   62. Foul . . . scoffer: i.e., you are ugly anyway,
and uglier when you are disdainful.

ROS. I pray you do not fall in love with me,
For I am falser than vows made in wine.
Besides, I like you not. If you will know my house,
'Tis at the tuft° of olives here hard by.   75
Will you go, Sister? Shepherd, ply° her hard.
Come, Sister. Shepherdess, look on him better,
And be not proud. Though all the world could see,
None could be so abused in sight as he.
Come, to our flock.   80

          [*Exeunt* ROSALIND, CELIA *and* CORIN.]

PHE. Dead shepherd, now I find thy saw of
          might —
"Who ever loved that loved not at first sight?"°
SIL. Sweet Phebe ——
PHE.   Ha, what say'st thou, Silvius?
SIL. Sweet Phebe, pity me.
PHE. Why, I am sorry for thee, gentle Silvius.   85
SIL. Wherever sorrow is, relief would be.
If you do sorrow at my grief in love,
By giving love your sorrow and my grief
Were both extermined.   89
PHE. Thou hast my love. Is not that neighborly?
SIL. I would have you.
PHE.   Why, that were covetousness.
Silvius, the time was that I hated thee,
And yet it is not that I bear thee love.
But since that thou canst talk of love so well,
Thy company, which erst° was irksome to me,   95
I will endure, and I'll employ thee too.
But do not look for further recompense
Than thine own gladness that thou art employed.
SIL. So holy and so perfect is my love,
And I in such a poverty of grace,°   100
That I shall think it a most plenteous crop
To glean the broken ears after the man
That the main harvest reaps. Loose now and then
A scattered smile, and that I'll live upon.
PHE. Know'st thou the youth that spoke to me ere-
          while?°   105
SIL. Not very well, but I have met him oft,
And he hath bought the cottage and the bounds
That the old carlot° once was master of.
PHE. Think not I love him, though I ask for him.
'Tis but a peevish° boy, yet he talks well.   110
But what care I for words? Yet words do well
When he that speaks them pleases those that hear.
It is a pretty youth — not very pretty —
But, sure, he's proud, and yet his pride becomes him.
He'll make a proper man. The best thing in him
Is his complexion, and faster than his tongue   116
Did make offense his eye did heal it up.
He is not very tall, yet for his years he's tall.
His leg is but soso, and yet 'tis well.

There was a pretty redness in his lip,   120
A little riper and more lusty red
Than that mixed in his cheek, 'twas just the differ-
          ence
Betwixt the constant red and mingled damask.°
There be some women, Silvius, had they marked
          him
In parcels° as I did, would have gone near   125
To fall in love with him. But for my part,
I love him not nor hate him not, and yet
I have more cause to hate him than to love him.
For what had he to do to chide at me?   129
He said mine eyes were black and my hair black,
And, now I am remembered, scorned at me.
I marvel why I answered not again.
But that's all one, omittance is no quittance.°
I'll write to him a very taunting letter,
And thou shalt bear it. Wilt thou, Silvius?   135
SIL. Phebe, with all my heart.
PHE.   I'll write it straight,
The matter's in my head and in my heart.
I will be bitter with him and passing° short.
Go with me, Silvius.   [*Exeunt.*]

Act IV

SCENE I. *The forest.*

[*Enter* ROSALIND, CELIA, *and* JAQUES.]

JAQ. I prithee, pretty youth, let me be better ac-
quainted with thee.
ROS. They say you are a melancholy fellow.
JAQ. I am so, I do love it better than laughing.   4
ROS. Those that are in extremity of either are
abominable fellows, and betray themselves to every
modern censure° worse than drunkards.
JAQ. Why, 'tis good to be sad and say nothing.
ROS. Why, then 'tis good to be a post.   9
JAQ. I have neither the scholar's melancholy,
which is emulation;° nor the musician's, which is
fantastical; nor the courtier's, which is proud; nor
the soldier's, which is ambitious; nor the lawyer's,
which is politic;° nor the lady's, which is nice; nor
the lover's, which is all these. But it is a melan-   15
choly of mine own, compounded of many simples,°
extracted from many objects, and indeed the sundry

---

75. **tuft:** clump.   76. **ply:** press, work at.   81–82. **Dead . . .
sight:** See *AYLI* Intro. p. 773a.   95. **erst:** erstwhile, formerly.
100. **poverty of grace:** poor favor.   105. **erewhile:** just now.
108. **carlot:** carl, peasant. See II.iv.75–87.   110. **peevish:** perverse, silly.

123. **mingled damask:** blended pink (the color of damask roses).
125. **In parcels:** in parts, each part separately.   133. **omittance
. . . quittance:** i.e., because I let him off now, that does not mean
that he will get off altogether.   138. **passing:** exceedingly.

          Act IV, Sc. i: 7. **modern censure:** trifling criticism.   11. **emu-
lation:** jealous rivalry.   14. **politic:** put on for crafty ends.
16. **simples:** drugs, ingredients.

contemplation of my travels, in which my often rumination wraps me in a most humorous sadness.° 20

ROS. A traveler!° By my faith, you have great reason to be sad. I fear you have sold your own lands to see other men's; then, to have seen much and to have nothing is to have rich eyes and poor hands. 25

JAQ. Yes, I have gained my experience.

ROS. And your experience makes you sad. I had rather have a fool to make me merry than experience to make me sad — and to travel for it too!

[*Enter* ORLANDO.]

ORL. Good day and happiness, dear Rosalind! 30

JAQ. Nay, then, God buy you° an you talk in blank verse. [*Exit.*]

ROS. Farewell, Monsieur Traveler. Look you lisp° and wear strange suits. Disable° all the benefits of your own country, be out of love with your 35 nativity° and almost chide God for making you that countenance° you are, or I will scarce think you have swam in a gondola.° Why, how now, Orlando! Where have you been all this while? You a lover! An you serve me such another trick, never come in my sight more. 41

ORL. My fair Rosalind, I come within an hour of my promise.

ROS. Break an hour's promise in love! He that will divide a minute into a thousand parts and 45 break but a part of the thousandth part of a minute in the affairs of love, it may be said of him that Cupid hath clapped him o' the shoulder,° but I'll warrant him heart-whole.

ORL. Pardon me, dear Rosalind. 50

ROS. Nay, an you be so tardy, come no more in my sight. I had as lief be wooed of a snail.

ORL. Of a snail?

ROS. Aye, of a snail, for though he comes slowly, he carries his house on his head — a better jointure,° I think, than you make a woman. Besides, he brings his destiny with him. 57

ORL. What's that?

ROS. Why, horns,° which such as you are fain to be beholding to your wives for. But he comes armed in his fortune and prevents the slander of his wife.°

ORL. Virtue is no hornmaker, and my Rosalind is virtuous.

ROS. And I am your Rosalind. 65

CEL. It pleases him to call you so, but he hath a Rosalind of a better leer° than you.

ROS. Come, woo me, woo me, for now I am in a holiday° humor and like enough to consent. What would you say to me now an I were your very very Rosalind? 71

ORL. I would kiss before I spoke.

ROS. Nay, you were better speak first, and when you were graveled° for lack of matter, you might take occasion to kiss. Very good orators, when 75 they are out, they will spit, and for lovers lacking — God warn° us! — matter, the cleanliest shift° is to kiss.

ORL. How if the kiss be denied?

ROS. Then she puts you to entreaty and there begins new matter. 81

ORL. Who could be out, being before his beloved mistress?

ROS. Marry, that should you if I were your mistress, or I should think my honesty ranker° than my wit. 86

ORL. What, of my suit?

ROS. Not out of your apparel, and yet out of your suit.° Am not I your Rosalind?

ORL. I take some joy to say you are, because I would be talking of her. 91

ROS. Well, in her person° I say I will not have you.

ORL. Then in mine own person I die.

ROS. No, faith, die by attorney.° The poor world is almost six thousand years old, and in all this time there was not any man died in his own person, 96 videlicet,° in a love cause. Troilus had his brains dashed out with a Grecian club, yet he did what he could to die before, and he is one of the patterns of love. Leander, he would have lived many a fair 100 year, though Hero had turned nun, if it had not been for a hot midsummer night; for, good youth, he went but forth to wash him in the Hellespont and being taken with the cramp was drowned. And the foolish chroniclers of that age found it was 105 "Hero of Sestos."° But these are all lies. Men have died from time to time and worms have eaten them, but not for love.

ORL. I would not have my right Rosalind of this mind, for I protest her frown might kill me. 110

ROS. By this hand, it will not kill a fly. But come,

18–20. my . . . sadness: by often ruminating on my experiences I am filled with moody sadness. 21. A traveler: Jibes at Englishmen' who had traveled were common. 31. God . . . you: God be with you. 33. lisp: affect a foreign accent. 34. Disable: make slighting remarks about. 36. nativity: place and moment of birth. 37. countenance: natural face. 38. swam . . . gondola: i.e., visited Venice, which (like Paris for the modern American) was the goal of all travelers. 48. clapped . . . shoulder: arrested him, made him prisoner. 55. jointure: marriage portion. 59. horns: See App. 11. 60–62. he . . . wife: i.e., the snail has his horns before marriage and so forestalls (*prevents*) the slanders which his wife will bring him.

67. leer: look. 69. holiday: i.e., gay. 74. graveled: run aground. 77. warn: colloquial for "warrant." cleanliest shift: the cleanest way of getting round the difficulty. 85. ranker: fouler. 89. suit: the same pun as in II.vii.44. 92. in . . . person: as her representative. 94. by attorney: by proxy. 97. videlicet: namely, "viz." 97–106. Troilus . . . Sestos: No one, says Rosalind, has really died for love, not even the great lovers of legend, such as Troilus, who was madly in love with Cressida, or Leander who used to swim over the Hellespont to visit Hero of Sestos and was drowned; historians in those days said that his death was caused by Hero, but in truth it was the cramp.

now I will be your Rosalind in a more coming-on° disposition, and ask me what you will, I will grant it.

ORL. Then love me, Rosalind. 115

ROS. Yes, faith, will I, Fridays and Saturdays and all.

ORL. And wilt thou have me?

ROS. Aye, and twenty such.

ORL. What sayest thou? 120

ROS. Are you not good?

ORL. I hope so.

ROS. Why then, can one desire too much of a good thing? Come, Sister, you shall be the priest and marry us. Give me your hand, Orlando. What do you say, Sister? 126

ORL. Pray thee, marry us.

CEL. I cannot say the words.

ROS. You must begin, " Will you, Orlando ———"

CEL. Go to. Will you, Orlando, have to wife this Rosalind? 131

ORL. I will.

ROS. Aye, but when?

ORL. Why now, as fast as she can marry us. 134

ROS. Then you must say " I take thee, Rosalind, for wife."

ORL. I take thee, Rosalind, for wife.

ROS. I might ask you for your commission,° but I do take thee, Orlando, for my husband. There's a girl goes before the priest,° and certainly a woman's thought runs before her actions. 141

ORL. So do all thoughts, they are winged.

ROS. Now tell me how long you would have her after you have possessed her.

ORL. Forever and a day. 145

ROS. Say " a day," without the " ever." No, no, Orlando. Men are April when they woo, December when they wed. Maids are May when they are maids, but the sky changes when they are wives. I will be more jealous of thee than a Barbary cock pi- 150 geon over his hen, more clamorous than a parrot against° rain, more newfangled° than an ape, more giddy in my desires than a monkey. I will weep for nothing, like Diana in the fountain,° and I will do that when you are disposed to be merry. I will laugh like a hyen,° and that when thou art inclined to sleep. 157

ORL. But will my Rosalind do so?

ROS. By my life, she will do as I do.

ORL. Oh, but she is wise.

ROS. Or else she could not have the wit to do this. The wiser, the waywarder.° Make° the doors upon a woman's wit and it will out at the casement.° Shut

that and 'twill out at the keyhole. Stop that, 'twill fly with the smoke out at the chimney. 166

ORL. A man that had a wife with such a wit, he might say " Wit, whither wilt? " °

ROS. Nay, you might keep that check° for it till you met your wife's wit going to your neighbor's bed. 171

ORL. And what wit could wit have to excuse that?

ROS. Marry, to say she came to seek you there. You shall never take her without her answer, unless you take her without her tongue. Oh, that woman that cannot make her fault her husband's occasion,° let her never nurse her child herself, for she will breed it like a fool! 179

ORL. For these two hours, Rosalind, I will leave thee.

ROS. Alas, dear love, I cannot lack thee two hours!

ORL. I must attend the Duke at dinner. By two o'clock I will be with thee again. 185

ROS. Aye, go your ways, go your ways, I knew what you would prove. My friends told me as much, and I thought no less. That flattering tongue of yours won me. 'Tis but one cast away,° and so come, death! Two o'clock is your hour? 190

ORL. Aye, sweet Rosalind.

ROS. By my troth,° and in good earnest, and so God mend me, and by all pretty oaths that are not dangerous, if you break one jot of your promise or come one minute behind your hour, I will 195 think you the most pathetical break-promise, and the most hollow lover, and the most unworthy of her you call Rosalind, that may be chosen out of the gross band° of the unfaithful. Therefore beware my censure and keep your promise. 200

ORL. With no less religion than if thou wert indeed my Rosalind. So adieu.

ROS. Well, Time is the old justice that examines all such offenders, and let Time try. Adieu. 204
[*Exit* ORLANDO.]

CEL. You have simply misused our sex in your love prate. We must have your doublet and hose plucked over your head, and show the world what the bird hath done to her own nest.° 208

ROS. O Coz, Coz, Coz, my pretty little coz, that thou didst know how many fathom deep I am in love! But it cannot be sounded. My affection hath an unknown bottom,° like the bay of Portugal.

CEL. Or rather, bottomless, that as fast as you pour affection in, it runs out. 215

ROS. No, that same wicked bastard of Venus° that was begot of thought, conceived of spleen, and born

---

112. **coming-on:** encouraging.   **138. commission:** i.e., authority.   **140. girl . . . priest:** i.e., anticipates the priest's words, because she is so eager.   **152. against:** in anticipation of. **newfangled:** eager for novelties.   **154. Diana . . . fountain:** i.e., like a fountain with the figure of Diana, always dripping.   **156. hyen:** hyena.   **163. waywarder:** more capricious. **Make:** shut.   **164. casement:** window that opens on hinges.

168. **Wit . . . wilt:** a proverb — "Wit [*intelligence*], where are you going? "   **169. check:** rebuke.   **176–77. that . . . occasion:** that cannot blame her husband as the cause of her own faults. **occasion:** that which causes.   **189. cast away:** abandoned. **192. troth:** truth.   **199. gross band:** vile company.   **208. done . . . nest:** i.e., fouled it.   **213. unknown bottom:** i.e., too deep to be measured.   **216. bastard of Venus:** i.e., Cupid.

of madness, that blind rascally boy that abuses everyone's eyes because his own are out, let him be judge
how deep I am in love. I'll tell thee, Aliena, I cannot be out of the sight of Orlando. I'll go find a
shadow and sigh till he come.   222
CEL. And I'll sleep.   [*Exeunt.*]

SCENE II. *The forest.*

[*Enter* JAQUES, LORDS, *and* FORESTERS.]
JAQ. Which is he that killed the deer?
A LORD. Sir, it was I.
JAQ. Let's present him to the Duke, like a Roman
conqueror, and it would do well to set the deer's
horns upon his head for a branch of victory. Have
you no song, forester, for this purpose?   7
FOR. Yes, sir.
JAQ. Sing it. 'Tis no matter how it be in tune so
it make noise enough.
FOR. [*Sings.*]
  What shall he have that killed the deer?
  His leather skin and horns to wear.
     Then sing him home.
          [*The rest shall bear this burden.*]
  Take thou no scorn to wear the horn,
  It was a crest ere thou wast born.   15
     Thy father's father wore it,
     And thy father bore it.
  The horn, the horn, the lusty horn
  Is not a thing to laugh to scorn.   [*Exeunt.*]

SCENE III. *The forest.*

[*Enter* ROSALIND *and* CELIA.]
ROS. How say you now? Is it not past two o'clock?
And here much° Orlando!
CEL. I warrant you with pure love and troubled
brain he hath ta'en his bow and arrows and is gone
forth to sleep. Look who comes here.   5
          [*Enter* SILVIUS.]
SIL. My errand is to you, fair youth,
My gentle Phebe bid me give you this.
I know not the contents, but as I guess
By the stern brow and waspish action
Which she did use as she was writing of it,   10
It bears an angry tenor.° Pardon me,
I am but as a guiltless messenger.
ROS. Patience herself would startle at this letter
And play the swaggerer — bear this, bear all.°
She says I am not fair, that I lack manners,   15
She calls me proud, and that she could not love me
Were man as rare as phoenix.° 'Od's my will!

Her love is not the hare that I do hunt.
Why writes she so to me? Well, shepherd, well,
This is a letter of your own device.   20
SIL. No, I protest I know not the contents.
Phebe did write it.
ROS.   Come, come, you are a fool,
And turned into the extremity of love.
I saw her hand. She has a leathern° hand,
A freestone-colored° hand. I verily did think   25
That her old gloves were on, but 'twas her hands.
She has a huswife's hand, but that's no matter.
I say she never did invent this letter.
This is a man's invention and his hand.
SIL. Sure, it is hers.   30
ROS. Why, 'tis a boisterous° and a cruel style,
A style for challengers. Why, she defies me,
Like Turk to Christian. Women's gentle brain
Could not drop forth such giant-rude invention,
Such Ethiope° words, blacker in their effect°   35
Than in their countenance.° Will you hear the let-
  ter?
SIL. So please you, for I never heard it yet,
Yet heard too much of Phebe's cruelty.
ROS. She Phebes me. Mark how the tyrant writes.
[*Reads.*] "Art thou god to shepherd turned   40
          That a maiden's heart hath burned?"
Can a woman rail thus?
SIL. Call you this railing?
ROS. [*Reads.*]
  "Why, thy godhead laid apart,°
     Warr'st thou with a woman's heart?"   45
Did you ever hear such railing?
  "Whiles the eye of man did woo me,
     That could do no vengeance to me."
Meaning me a beast.
  "If the scorn of your bright eyne°   50
  Have power to raise such love in mine,
  Alack, in me what strange effect
  Would they work in mild aspéct!°
  Whiles you chid me, I did love,
  How then might your prayers move!   55
  He that brings this love to thee
  Little knows this love in me.
  And by him seal up thy mind,°
  Whether that thy youth and kind°
  Will the faithful offer take   60
  Of me and all that I can make,
  Or else by him my love deny,
  And then I'll study how to die."
SIL. Call you this chiding?
CEL. Alas, poor shepherd!   65

---

24. leathern: i.e., the hand of a workingwoman, not of a lady.
25. freestone-colored: of the color of Bath brick; i.e., yellow-
brown.   31. boisterous: violent.   35. Ethiope: i.e., black. effect:
intention.   36. countenance: appearance.   44. thy . . . apart:
why do you, a god, become man?   50. eyne: eyes.   53. mild
aspect: gentle looks.   58. seal . . . mind: write your answer and
send it by him.   59. kind: nature.

Sc. iii: 2. here much: i.e., a fine lot of.   11. tenor: intention.
14. bear . . . all: a person who could endure this would bear
anything.   17. phoenix: See *Temp,* III.iii.23,n.

ROS. Do you pity him? No, he deserves no pity.
Wilt thou love such a woman? What, to make thee
an instrument and play false strains upon thee!
Not to be endured! Well, go your way to her, for I
see love hath made thee a tame snake, and say   70
this to her: That if she loves me, I charge her to love
thee. If she will not, I will never have her unless
thou entreat for her. If you be a truelover, hence,
and not a word, for here comes more company.   75

[*Exit* SILVIUS.]

[*Enter* OLIVER.]

OLI. Good morrow, fair ones. Pray you, if you
know,
Where in the purlieus° of this forest stands
A sheepcote fenced about with olive trees?
CEL. West of this place, down in the neighbor bottom.
The rank° of osiers° by the murmuring stream   80
Left on your right hand brings you to the place.
But at this hour the house doth keep itself,
There's none within.
OLI. If that an eye may profit by a tongue,
Then should I know you by description,   85
Such garments and such years. " The boy is fair,
Of female favor,° and bestows himself°
Like a ripe sister,° the woman low,
And browner than her brother." Are not you
The owner of the house I did inquire for?   90
CEL. It is no boast, being asked, to say we are.
OLI. Orlando doth commend him to you both,
And to that youth he calls his Rosalind
He sends this bloody napkin. Are you he?
ROS. I am. What must we understand by this?   95
OLI. Some of my shame, if you will know of me
What man I am, and how, and why, and where
This handkercher was stained.
CEL.   I pray you tell it.
OLI. When last the young Orlando parted from
you
He left a promise to return again   100
Within an hour, and pacing through the forest,
Chewing the food of sweet and bitter fancy,°
Lo, what befell! He threw his eye aside,
And mark what object did present itself.
Under an oak whose boughs were mossed with age
And high top bald with dry antiquity,   106
A wretched ragged man, o'ergrown with hair,
Lay sleeping on his back. About his neck
A green and gilded snake had wreathed itself,
Who with her head nimble in threats approached
The opening of his mouth. But suddenly,   111
Seeing Orlando, it unlinked itself
And with indented glides° did slip away

Into a bush, under which bush's shade
A lioness, with udders all drawn dry,°   115
Lay couching, head on ground, with catlike watch,
When that the sleeping man should stir. For 'tis
The royal disposition of that beast
To prey on nothing that doth seem as dead.
This seen, Orlando did approach the man   120
And found it was his brother, his elder brother.
CEL. Oh, I have heard him speak of that same
brother,
And he did render° him the most unnatural
That lived amongst men.
OLI.   And well he might so do,
For well I know he was unnatural.   125
ROS. But to Orlando. Did he leave him there,
Food to the sucked and hungry lioness?
OLI. Twice did he turn his back and purposed so.
But kindness,° nobler ever than revenge,
And nature, stronger than his just occasion,°   130
Made him give battle to the lioness,
Who quickly fell before him. In which hurtling°
From miserable slumber I awaked.
CEL. Are you his brother?
ROS.   Was 't you he rescued?
CEL. Was 't you that did so oft contrive to kill
him?   135
OLI. 'Twas I, but 'tis not I. I do not shame
To tell you what I was, since my conversion
So sweetly tastes, being the thing I am.
ROS. But — for the bloody napkin?
OLI.   By and by.
When from the first to last betwixt us two   140
Tears our recountments° had most kindly bathed,
As how I came into that desert place,
In brief, he led me to the gentle Duke,
Who gave me fresh array and entertainment,°
Committing me unto my brother's love.   145
Who led me instantly unto his cave,
There stripped himself, and here upon his arm
The lioness had torn some flesh away,
Which all this while had bled, and now he fainted
And cried, in fainting, upon Rosalind.   150
Brief, I recovered him, bound up his wound,
And after some small space, being strong at heart,
He sent me hither, stranger as I am,
To tell this story, that you might excuse
His broken promise, and to give this napkin,   155
Dyed in his blood, unto the shepherd youth
That he in sport doth call his Rosalind.

[ROSALIND *swoons*.]

CEL. Why, how now, Ganymede! Sweet Ganymede!

---

77. purlieus: boundaries.   **80. rank:** row. **osiers:** willows, of the kind used for making baskets.   **87. female favor:** girlish face. **bestows himself:** behaves.   **88. Like . . . sister:** like an elder sister.   **102. fancy:** love.   **113. indented glides:** wavy motion.

115. udders . . . dry: i.e., hungry and fierce.   **123. render:** describe.   **129. kindness:** natural affection.   **130. just occasion:** i.e., his opportunity for getting even with his wicked brother. **132. hurtling:** noise of battle.   **141. recountments:** accounts of our adventures.   **144. entertainment:** good treatment.

OLI. Many will swoon when they do look on blood.

CEL. There is more in it. Cousin Ganymede! 160

OLI. Look, he recovers.

ROS. I would I were at home.

CEL.   We'll lead you thither.
I pray you, will you take him by the arm?

OLI. Be of good cheer, youth. You a man! You
lack a man's heart. 165

ROS. I do so, I confess it. Ah, sirrah, a body would
think this was well counterfeited!° I pray you tell
your brother how well I counterfeited. Heigh-ho!

OLI. This was not counterfeit. There is too great
testimony in your complexion that it was a passion
of earnest.° 172

ROS. Counterfeit, I assure you.

OLI. Well then, take a good heart and counterfeit
to be a man.

ROS. So I do. But, i' faith, I should have been a
woman by right.

CEL. Come, you look paler and paler. Pray you
draw homeward. Good sir, go with us.

OLI. That will I, for I must bear answer back 180
How you excuse my brother, Rosalind.

ROS. I shall devise something. But I pray you commend my counterfeiting to him. Will you go?
[Exeunt.]

Act V

SCENE I. *The forest.*

[Enter TOUCHSTONE *and* AUDREY.*]*

TOUCH. We shall find a time, Audrey. Patience,
gentle Audrey.

AUD. Faith, the priest was good enough, for all the
old gentleman's saying. 4

TOUCH. A most wicked Sir Oliver, Audrey, a most
vile Martext. But, Audrey, there is a youth here in
the forest lays claim to you.

AUD. Aye, I know who 'tis. He hath no interest in
me in the world. Here comes the man you mean. 10

TOUCH. It is meat and drink to me to see a clown.
By my troth, we that have good wits have much to
answer for — we shall be flouting,° we cannot hold.

[Enter WILLIAM.*]*

WILL. Good even, Audrey. 15

AUD. God ye good even, William.

WILL. And good even to you, sir.

TOUCH. Good even, gentle friend. Cover thy head,
cover thy head, nay, prithee be covered. How old
are you, friend? 20

WILL. Five and twenty, sir.

TOUCH. A ripe age. Is thy name William?

WILL. William, sir.

TOUCH. A fair name. Wast born i' the forest here?

WILL. Aye, sir, I thank God. 26

TOUCH. "Thank God," a good answer. Art rich?

WILL. Faith, sir, soso.

TOUCH. "Soso" is good, very good, very excellent
good. And yet it is not, it is but soso. Art thou wise?

WILL. Aye, sir, I have a pretty wit. 32

TOUCH. Why, thou sayest well. I do now remember a saying, "The fool doth think he is wise, but
the wise man knows himself to be a fool." The 35
heathen philosopher, when he had a desire to eat a
grape, would open his lips when he put it into his
mouth, meaning thereby that grapes were made to
eat and lips to open. You do love this maid? 40

WILL. I do, sir.

TOUCH. Give me your hand. Art thou learned?

WILL. No, sir.

TOUCH. Then learn this of me: To have is to have;
for it is a figure in rhetoric that drink, being 45
poured out of a cup into a glass, by filling the one
doth empty the other, for all your writers do consent
that *ipse*° is he. Now you are not *ipse,* for I am he.

WILL. Which he, sir? 50

TOUCH. He, sir, that must marry this woman.
Therefore, you clown, abandon — which is in the
vulgar° leave, — the society — which in the boorish
is company — of this female — which in the common is woman. Which together is, abandon the 55
society of this female, or, clown, thou perishest; or,
to thy better understanding, diest; or, to wit, I kill
thee, make thee away, translate thy life into death,
thy liberty into bondage. I will deal in poison with
thee, or in bastinado,° or in steel, I will bandy 60
with thee in faction,° I will o'errun thee with policy,° I will kill thee a hundred and fifty ways. Therefore tremble, and depart.

AUD. Do, good William. 64

WILL. God rest you merry sir. *[Exit.]*
[Enter CORIN.*]*

COR. Our master and mistress seek you. Come,
away, away!

TOUCH. Trip, Audrey! Trip, Audrey! I attend, I attend. *[Exeunt.]*

SCENE II. *The forest.*

[Enter ORLANDO *and* OLIVER.*]*

ORL. Is 't possible that on so little acquaintance you
should like her? That but seeing you should love
her? And, loving, woo? And, wooing, she should
grant? And will you persever to enjoy her? 5

---

167. counterfeited: imitated, pretended.   171–72. passion of
earnest: genuine emotion.

Act V, Sc. i: 14. flouting: jesting.

49. ipse: himself.   53. vulgar: common tongue.   60. bastinado:
a thrashing.   60–61. bandy . . . faction: strive with you by intrigue.   61–62. o'errun . . . policy: overcome you by some crafty
device.

OLI. Neither call the giddiness° of it in question, the poverty of her, the small acquaintance, my sudden wooing, nor her sudden consenting; but say with me, I love Aliena, say with her that she loves me, consent with both that we may enjoy each other. It shall be to your good, for my father's house and all the revenue that was old Sir Rowland's will I estate° upon you, and here live and die a shepherd. 14

ORL. You have my consent. Let your wedding be tomorrow. Thither will I invite the Duke and all 's contented followers. Go you and prepare Aliena, for look you, here comes my Rosalind.

[*Enter* ROSALIND.]

ROS. God save you, Brother. 20
OLI. And you, fair Sister. [*Exit.*]
ROS. O my dear Orlando, how it grieves me to see thee wear thy heart in a scarf!
ORL. It is my arm.
ROS. I thought thy heart had been wounded with the claws of a lion. 26
ORL. Wounded it is, but with the eyes of a lady.
ROS. Did your brother tell you how I counterfeited to swoon when he showed me your handkercher? 30
ORL. Aye, and greater wonders than that.
ROS. Oh, I know where you are. Nay, 'tis true. There was never anything so sudden but the fight of two rams, and Caesar's thrasonical° brag of " I came, saw, and overcame."° For your brother and my sister no sooner met but they looked, no sooner looked 35 but they loved, no sooner loved but they sighed, no sooner sighed but they asked one another the reason, no sooner knew the reason but they sought the remedy. And in these degrees have they made a pair 40 of stairs to marriage which they will climb incontinent, or else be incontinent before marriage. They are in the very wrath° of love and they will together, clubs cannot part them.° 45
ORL. They shall be married tomorrow, and I will bid the Duke to the nuptial. But oh, how bitter a thing it is to look into happiness through another man's eyes! By so much the more shall I tomorrow be at the height of heart-heaviness, by how 50 much I shall think my brother happy in having what he wishes for.
ROS. Why then, tomorrow I cannot serve your turn for Rosalind?
ORL. I can live no longer by thinking.° 55
ROS. I will weary you then no longer with idle talking. Know of me then, for now I speak to some

purpose, that I know you are a gentleman of good conceit.° I speak not this that you should bear a good opinion of my knowledge, insomuch I say 60 I know you are. Neither do I labor for a greater esteem than may in some little measure draw a belief from you to do yourself good and not to grace me. Believe then, if you please, that I can do strange things. I have, since I was three year old, con- 65 versed with a magician most profound in his art and yet not damnable.° If you do love Rosalind so near the heart as your gesture cries it out, when your brother marries Aliena, shall you marry her. I know into what straits of fortune° she is driven, and 70 it is not impossible to me, if it appear not inconvenient to you, to set her before your eyes tomorrow human as she is and without any danger.

ORL. Speakest thou in sober meanings? 76
ROS. By my life, I do, which I tender° dearly, though I say I am a magician. Therefore put you in your best array, bid your friends, for if you will be married tomorrow, you shall, and to Rosalind if you will. [*Enter* SILVIUS *and* PHEBE.] Look, here 81 comes a lover of mine and a lover of hers.
PHE. Youth, you have done me much ungentleness°
To show the letter that I writ to you.
ROS. I care not if I have. It is my study° 85
To seem despiteful and ungentle to you.
You are there followed by a faithful shepherd.
Look upon him, love him, he worships you.
PHE. Good shepherd, tell this youth what 'tis to love.
SIL. It is to be all made of sighs and tears, 90
And so am I for Phebe.
PHE. And I for Ganymede.
ORL. And I for Rosalind.
ROS. And I for no woman.
SIL. It is to be all made of faith and service, 95
And so am I for Phebe.
PHE. And I for Ganymede.
ORL. And I for Rosalind.
ROS. And I for no woman.
SIL. It is to be all made of fantasy,° 100
All made of passion, and all made of wishes,
All adoration, duty, and observance,
All humbleness, all patience and impatience,
All purity, all trial,° all observance,°
And so am I for Phebe. 105
PHE. And so am I for Ganymede.
ORL. And so am I for Rosalind.
ROS. And so am I for no woman. 109
PHE. If this be so, why blame you me to love you?

Sc. ii: 6. **giddiness:** rashness. 13. **estate:** settle. 33. **thrasonical:** boastful. 33–34. **I . . . overcame:** Julius Caesar after his victory over the King of Pontus reported to the Senate in three words: *Veni, vidi, vici.* 44. **wrath:** passion. 45. **clubs . . . them:** When a brawl was started in London streets, there was a cry of "Clubs." Thereupon the apprentices in the shops seized their clubs and swarmed out to separate the parties. 55. **thinking:** i.e., pretense.

59. **conceit:** intelligence. 67. **not damnable:** i.e., his magic was used to good and not wicked ends. 70. **straits of fortune:** difficult situation. 77. **tender:** regard. 83. **done . . . ungentleness:** you have not behaved like a gentleman toward me. 85. **study:** deliberate purpose. 100. **fantasy:** imagination. 104. **all trial:** enduring any trial. **observance:** devotion.

SIL. If this be so, why blame you me to love you?
ORL. If this be so, why blame you me to love you?
ROS. Why do you speak too, "Why blame you me
to love you?"   116
ORL. To her that is not here, nor doth not hear.
ROS. Pray you, no more of this, 'tis like the howling of Irish wolves against the moon. [*To* SILVIUS]
I will help you if I can. [*To* PHEBE] I would   120
love you if I could. Tomorrow meet me all together.
[*To* PHEBE] I will marry you if ever I marry woman,
and I'll be married tomorrow. [*To* ORLANDO] I will
satisfy you if ever I satisfied man, and you shall be
married tomorrow. [*To* SILVIUS] I will content   125
you if what pleases you contents you, and you shall
be married tomorrow. [*To* ORLANDO] As you love
Rosalind, meet. [*To* SILVIUS] As you love Phebe,
meet. And as I love no woman, I'll meet. So, fare
you well. I have left you commands.   131
SIL. I'll not fail, if I live.
PHE. Nor I.
ORL. Nor I.   [*Exeunt.*]

SCENE III. *The forest.*

[*Enter* TOUCHSTONE *and* AUDREY.]
TOUCH. Tomorrow is the joyful day, Audrey, tomorrow will we be married.
AUD. I do desire it with all my heart, and I hope
it is no dishonest° desire to desire to be a woman of
the world. Here come two of the banished Duke's
pages.   6
                  [*Enter two* PAGES.]
I. PAGE. Well met, honest gentleman.
TOUCH. By my troth, well met. Come, sit, sit, and
a song.
2. PAGE. We are for you. Sit i' the middle.   10
I. PAGE. Shall we clap into 't° roundly, without
hawking° or spitting or saying we are hoarse, which
are the only prologues° to a bad voice?
2. PAGE. I' faith, i' faith, and both in a tune, like
two gypsies on a horse.
                        SONG
It was a lover and his lass,
   With a hey, and a ho, and a hey nonino,
That o'er the green cornfield did pass
   In the springtime, the only pretty ringtime,°   20
When birds do sing, hey ding a ding, ding.
Sweet lovers love the spring.

Between the acres of the rye,
   With a hey, and a ho, and a hey nonino,
These pretty country folks would lie,   25

In the springtime, the only pretty ringtime,
When birds do sing, hey ding a ding, ding.
Sweet lovers love the spring.

This carol they began that hour,
   With a hey, and a ho, and a hey nonino,
How that a life was but a flower
   In the springtime, the only pretty ringtime,   30
When birds do sing, hey ding a ding, ding.
Sweet lovers love the spring.

And therefore take the present time,
   With a hey, and a ho, and a hey nonino,
For love is crownèd with the prime°
   In the springtime, the only pretty ringtime,   34
When birds do sing, hey ding a ding, ding.
Sweet lovers love the spring.
TOUCH. Truly, young gentlemen, though there
was no great matter in the ditty, yet the note was
very untunable.
I. PAGE. You are deceived, sir. We kept time, we
lost not our time.   39
TOUCH. By my troth, yes. I count it but time lost
to hear such a foolish song. God buy you, and God
mend your voices! Come, Audrey.   [*Exeunt.*]

SCENE IV. *The forest.*

[*Enter* DUKE *Senior,* AMIENS, JAQUES, ORLANDO,
                OLIVER, *and* CELIA.]
DUKE S. Dost thou believe, Orlando, that the boy
Can do all this that he hath promised?
ORL. I sometimes do believe, and sometimes do
   not,
As those that fear they hope and know they fear.
        [*Enter* ROSALIND, SILVIUS, *and* PHEBE.]
ROS. Patience once more, whiles our compact is
   urged.°   5
You say if I bring in your Rosalind,
You will bestow her on Orlando here?
DUKE S. That would I had I kingdoms to give
   with her.
ROS. And you say you will have her when I bring
   her?   9
ORL. That would I were I of all kingdoms king.
ROS. You say you'll marry me if I be willing?
PHE. That will I, should I die the hour after.
ROS. But if you do refuse to marry me,
You'll give yourself to this most faithful shepherd?
PHE. So is the bargain.   15
ROS. You say that you'll have Phebe if she will?
SIL. Though to have her and death were both one
   thing.

Sc. iii: **4. dishonest:** unchaste.   **11. clap into 't:** get down to
it.   **12. hawking:** clearing the throat.   **13. only prologues:** usual
apologies.   **20. ringtime:** i.e., the time for wedding bells.

33. prime: perfection.
Sc. iv: **5. compact is urged:** agreement is repeated.

ROS. I have promised to make all this matter
   even.°
Keep you your word, O Duke, to give your daugh-
   ter,
You yours, Orlando, to receive his daughter.   20
Keep your word, Phebe, that you'll marry me
Or else, refusing me, to wed this shepherd.
Keep your word, Silvius, that you'll marry her
If she refuse me. And from hence I go
To make these doubts all even.   25

[Exeunt ROSALIND *and* CELIA.]

DUKE S. I do remember in this shepherd boy
Some lively touches of my daughter's favor.°
ORL. My lord, the first time that I ever saw him
Methought he was a brother to your daughter.
But, my good lord, this boy is forest-born,   30
And hath been tutored in the rudiments
Of many desperate studies by his uncle,
Whom he reports to be a great magician
Obscurèd° in the circle of this forest.   34

[Enter TOUCHSTONE *and* AUDREY.]

JAQ. There is, sure, another flood toward, and
these couples are coming to the ark. Here comes a
pair of very strange beasts, which in all tongues are
called fools.
TOUCH. Salutation and greeting to you all!   39
JAQ. Good my lord, bid him welcome. This is the
motley-minded gentleman that I have so often met
in the forest. He hath been a courtier, he swears.
TOUCH. If any man doubt that, let him put me to
my purgation.° I have trod a measure.° I have   45
flattered a lady. I have been politic° with my friend,
smooth with mine enemy. I have undone three
tailors.° I have had four quarrels, and like to have
fought one.
JAQ. And how was that ta'en up?   50
TOUCH. Faith, we met, and found the quarrel was
upon the seventh cause.
JAQ. How seventh cause? Good my lord, like this
fellow.
DUKE S. I like him very well.   55
TOUCH. God 'ild° you, sir, I desire you of the like.
I press in here, sir, amongst the rest of the country
copulatives,° to swear and to forswear, according as
marriage binds and blood breaks. A poor virgin, sir,
an ill-favored thing, sir, but mine own. A poor humor of mine, sir, to take that that no man else will.
Rich honesty dwells like a miser, sir, in a poor house,
as your pearl in your foul oyster.   64
DUKE S. By my faith, he is very swift and sententious.°

TOUCH. According to the fool's bolt,° sir, and such
dulcet diseases.°
JAQ. But for the seventh cause, how did you find
the quarrel on the seventh cause?   70
TOUCH. Upon a lie seven times removed — Bear
your body more seeming, Audrey — as thus, sir. I
did dislike the cut of a certain courtier's beard. He
sent me word if I said his beard was not cut well, he
was in the mind it was. This is called the Retort   75
Courteous. If I sent him word again "it was not
well cut," he would send me word he cut it to please
himself. This is called the Quip Modest. If again "it
was not well cut," he disabled my judgment.° This
is called the Reply Churlish. If again "it was   80
not well cut," he would answer I spake not true.
This is called the Reproof Valiant. If again "it was
not well cut," he would say I lie. This is called the
Countercheck Quarrelsome. And so to the Lie Cir-
cumstantial° and the Lie Direct.°   86
JAQ. And how oft did you say his beard was not
well cut?
TOUCH. I durst go no further than the Lie Circumstantial, nor he durst not give me the Lie Direct,
and so we measured swords and parted.
JAQ. Can you nominate in order now the degrees
of the lie?   94
TOUCH. Oh, sir, we quarrel in print,° by the book,
as you have books for good manners. I will name
you the degrees. The first, the Retort Courteous; the
second, the Quip Modest; the third, the Reply Churlish; the fourth, the Reproof Valiant; the fifth, the
Countercheck Quarrelsome; the sixth, the Lie with
Circumstance; the seventh, the Lie Direct. All   101
these you may avoid but the Lie Direct, and you may
avoid that too, with an "If." I knew when seven justices could not take up° a quarrel, but when the
parties were met themselves, one of them thought
but of an "If," as, "If you said so, then I said   106
so," and they shook hands and swore brothers. Your
"If" is the only peacemaker, much virtue in "If."
JAQ. Is not this a rare fellow, my lord? He's as
good at anything and yet a fool.   110
DUKE S. He uses his folly like a stalking-horse,°
and under the presentation of that he shoots his wit.

[Enter HYMEN,° ROSALIND, *and* CELIA. *Still*° *music.*]

HYM. Then is there mirth in Heaven
When earthly things made even   115
Atone° together.

Good Duke, receive thy daughter.
Hymen from Heaven brought her,
  Yea, brought her hither,
That thou mightst join her hand with his   120
Whose heart within his bosom is.
  ROS. [*To* DUKE S.] To you I give myself, for I am
    yours.
[*To* ORLANDO] To you I give myself, for I am yours.
  DUKE S. If there be truth in sight, you are my
    daughter.
  ORL. If there be truth in sight, you are my Rosa-
    lind.   125
  PHE. If sight and shape be true,
Why then, my love adieu!
  ROS. I'll have no father, if you be not he.
I'll have no husband, if you be not he.
Nor ne'er wed woman, if you be not she.   130
  HYM. Peace, ho! I bar confusion.
'Tis I must make conclusion
  Of these most strange events.
Here's eight that must take hands
To join in Hymen's bands   135
  If truth holds true contents.
You and you no cross° shall part.
You and you are heart in heart.
You to his love must accord
Or have a woman to your lord.   140
You and you are sure together,
As the winter to foul weather.
Whiles a wedlock hymn we sing
Feed yourselves with questioning,
That reason wonder may diminish,   145
How thus we met, and these things finish.
SONG
  Wedding is great Juno's crown.
    Oh, blessed bond of board and bed!
  'Tis Hymen peoples every town.
    High wedlock then be honorèd.   150
  Honor, high honor and renown,
    To Hymen, god of every town!
  DUKE S. O my dear niece, welcome thou art to me!
Even Daughter, welcome, in no less degree.   154
  PHE. I will not eat my word now thou art **mine**,
Thy faith my fancy to thee doth combine.
[*Enter* JAQUES DE BOYS.]
  JAQ. DE B. Let me have audience for a word **or**
    two.
I am the second son of old Sir Rowland
That bring these tidings to this fair assembly.
Duke Frederick, hearing how that every day   160
Men of great worth resorted to this forest,
Addressed° a mighty power,° which were on foot,
In his own conduct,° purposely to take
His brother here and put him to the sword.
And to the skirts of this wild wood he came,   165

Where meeting with an old religious man,°
After some question with him, was converted
Both from his enterprise and from the world,
His crown bequeathing to his banished brother,
And all their lands restored to them again   170
That were with him exiled. This to be true
I do engage° my life.
  DUKE S.   Welcome, young man,
Thou offer'st° fairly to thy brothers' wedding.
To one his lands withheld, and to the other
A land itself at large, a potent dukedom.   175
First, in this forest let us do those ends
That here were well begun and well begot.
And after, every of this happy number
That have endured shrewd° days and nights with us
Shall share the good of our returnèd fortune   180
According to the measure of their states.
Meantime, forget this new-fallen dignity,
And fall into our rustic revelry.   183
Play, music! And you, brides and bridegrooms all,
With measure heaped in joy, to the measures° fall.
  JAQ. Sir, by your patience. If I heard you rightly,
The Duke hath put on a religious life
And thrown into neglect the pompous Court?
  JAQ. DE B. He hath.
  JAQ. To him will I. Out of these convertites° 190
There is much matter to be heard and learned.
[*To* DUKE] You to your former honor I bequeath,
Your patience and your virtue well deserves it.
[*To* ORLANDO] You to a love that your true faith doth
    merit.
[*To* OLIVER] You to your land, and love, and great
    allies.   195
[*To* SILVIUS] You to a long and well-deservèd bed.
[*To* TOUCHSTONE] And you to wrangling, for thy
    loving voyage
Is but for two months victualed.° So, to your pleas-
    ures.
I am for other than for dancing measures.
  DUKE S. Stay, Jaques, stay.   200
  JAQ. To see no pastime I. What you would have
I'll stay to know at your abandoned cave.   [*Exit.*]
  DUKE S. Proceed, proceed. We will begin these
    rites,
As we do trust they'll end, in true delights.
[*A dance.*]

EPILOGUE

  ROS. It is not the fashion to see the lady the epilogue, but it is no more unhandsome than to see the
lord the prologue. If it be true that good wine needs

---

137. cross: trouble.   162. Addressed: prepared. **power**: army.
163. In . . . conduct: under his own command.

166. religious man: hermit.   172. engage: pledge.   173. **Thou offer'st**: you make a good present.   179. shrewd: bitter.
185. **measures**: dances.   190. **convertites**: converts to the religious life.   198. victualed: provisioned.

no bush,° 'tis true that a good play needs no epilogue. Yet to good wine they do use good bushes, 5
and good plays prove the better by the help of good epilogues. What a case am I in then, that am neither a good epilogue nor cannot insinuate° with you in the behalf of a good play! I am not furnished° like a beggar, therefore to beg will not become me. 10
My way is to conjure° you, and I'll begin with the women. I charge you, O women, for the love you bear to men, to like as much of this play as please you. And I charge you, O men, for the love you bear to women — as I perceive by your simpering 15
none of you hates them — that between you and the women the play may please. If I were a woman° I would kiss as many of you as had beards that pleased me, complexions that liked° me, and breaths that I defied not. And I am sure as many as have good 20
beards or good faces or sweet breaths will, for my kind offer, when I make curtsy bid me farewell.

                                         [*Exeunt.*]

Epilogue: 3–4. good . . . bush: good wine needs no advertisement, an old proverb arising from the custom of vintners of hanging up a bush as a sign of their trade.   **8. insinuate:** ingratiate myself.   **9. furnished:** dressed.   **11. conjure:** win you over by magic.

17. If . . . woman: In the play the part of Rosalind was acted by a boy.   **19. liked:** pleased.

THE TRAGEDY OF JULIUS CAESAR

Introduction

The Tragedy of Julius Caesar was first printed in the first folio (F1) in 1623; the text is good and there are few difficulties. The play was written in 1599. There are several pieces of evidence for this date.

1. Thomas Platter, a German traveler, noted in his diary for the year 1599:

After dinner on the 21st of September, at about two o'clock, I went with my companions over the water, and in the strewn roof-house [the playhouse with a thatched roof] saw the tragedy of the first Emperor Julius with at least fifteen characters very well acted. At the end of the comedy they danced according to their custom with extreme elegance. Two men in men's clothes and two in women's gave this performance, in wonderful combination with each other.[1]

2. John Weever in *The Mirror for Martyrs, or the Life and Death of Sir John Oldcastle,* printed in 1601 but composed, as the author states, two years before, wrote:

The many-headed multitude were drawn
By Brutus' speech, that Caesar was ambitious.
When eloquent Mark Antony had shown
His virtues, who but Brutus then was vicious?

3. Ben Jonson in *Every Man out of His Humour,* printed in 1600, after Jonson had quarreled with the Chamberlain's Men, in a satirical passage made Clove begin a speech (III.i): "Then coming to the pretty animal, as reason long since is fled to animals, you know." This is a fairly clear sneer at Antony's words:

O judgment, thou art fled to brutish beasts,
And men have lost their reason! (III.ii.109)

Jonson commented unfavorably on *Julius Caesar* elsewhere. In the collection of jottings published posthumously in 1641 under the title *Timber or Discoveries* there appeared a critical note on Shakespeare, in which he wrote: "Many times he fell into those things which could not escape laughter, as when he said in the person of Caesar, one speaking to him: 'Caesar, thou dost me

wrong.' He replied: 'Caesar never did wrong but with just cause,' and suchlike, which were ridiculous." The passage in *Julius Caesar* now reads:

Know, Caesar doth not wrong, nor without cause
Will he be satisfied. (III.i.47)

Presumably Shakespeare altered the offending line.

4. Shakespeare himself, when writing the Chorus to the last act of *Henry the Fifth* in the early months of 1599, had the theme of *Julius Caesar* in mind:

Like to the Senators of the antique Rome,
With the plebeians swarming at their heels,
Go forth and fetch their conquering Caesar in.

The story of Julius Caesar had often been retold in story, poem, and play before Shakespeare's time, but the direct sources of the play were the lives of Julius Caesar, Marcus Brutus, and Marcus Antonius in Sir Thomas North's translation of *The Lives of the Noble Grecians and Romans by that eminent historiographer and philosopher, Plutarch of Chaeronea.*

Plutarch was a Greek born in A.D. 46. He was educated at Athens, and became what would now be called a professor of philosophy. He lectured at Rome, and left a large collection of essays and learned articles called the *Morals* — once much read — as well as the famous *Lives*. These were a series of parallel biographies of eminent Greeks and Romans. Plutarch wrote forty-eight of these parallels, adding to most of them a brief comparison.

The *Lives* are not formal biographies, giving dates, places, and facts, but rather biographical and psychological studies of great men. Plutarch assumed that his readers were already familiar with the facts, and his intention was to portray character. He consulted the best authorities, and preferably those who could provide anecdotes and sayings, for, as he wrote, " the noblest deeds do not always show men's virtues and vices, but oftentimes a light occasion, a word, or some sport, makes men's natural dispositions and manners appear more plain than the famous battles

---

[1] Quoted by E. K. Chambers, *The Elizabethan Stage,* Vol. II, pp. 364–65.

wherein are slain ten thousand men or the great armies or cities won by siege or assault."

The *Lives* reached English readers in the translation made by Sir Thomas North and printed in 1579. North, however, went not to the Greek but to a French translation made from the Latin by Jacques Amyot and published in 1559 and 1565. A second edition of North's translation was printed in 1595 by Richard Field, who was also the printer of Shakespeare's *Venus and Adonis* and *The Rape of Lucrece*. "North's Plutarch" is a great book, a fine specimen of vigorous Elizabethan prose, for North himself was a man of very varied experience, with a lively mind and a superb mastery of words. There is no richer collection of historical material for a dramatist.

Nevertheless, to make a coherent play Shakespeare had to simplify vastly the history of events between Caesar's return to Rome in September 45 B.C. and the Second Battle of Philippi, two years later. Moreover, he did not choose to follow the common pattern of historical-biographical plays, which usually ended with the death of the hero in Act V. Instead he set the murder of Caesar in the third act, and in the last two acts showed how the murderers came to destruction. For this Plutarch was partly responsible, for *Julius Caesar* is based rather on his "Life of Brutus" than on that of Caesar.

Plutarch gave all the details of the story, and, equally important, some valuable indications of character. He summed up the difference between Brutus and Cassius thus:

And surely, in my opinion, I am persuaded that Brutus might indeed have come to have been the chiefest man of Rome if he could have contented himself for a time to have been next unto Caesar, and to have suffered his glory and authority, which he had gotten by his great victories, to consume with time. But Cassius being a choleric man, and hating Caesar privately more than he did the tyranny openly, he incensed Brutus against him. It was also reported that Brutus could evil away with the tyranny, and that Cassius hated the tyrant.

Shakespeare used his sources freely. His methods can best be seen by comparing a section of the play with Plutarch's narrative. In *Julius Caesar* the death and funeral of Caesar are shown in the third act. These events were thus described in the "Life of Brutus":

Now it was reported that Caesar was coming in his litter; for he determined not to stay in the Senate all that day (because he was afraid of the unlucky signs of the sacrifices), but to adjourn matters of importance unto the next session and council holden, feigning himself not to be well at ease. When Caesar came out of his litter, Popillius Laenas, that had talked before with Brutus and Cassius, and had prayed the gods they might bring this enterprise to pass, went unto Caesar, and kept him a long time with a talk. Caesar gave good ear unto him. Wherefore the conspirators (if so they should be called), not hearing what he said to Caesar, but conjecturing by that he had told them a little before that his talk was none other but the very discovery of their conspiracy, they were afraid every man of them, and one looking in another's face, it was easy to see that they all were of a mind that it was no tarrying for them till they were apprehended, but rather that they should kill themselves with their own hands.

And when Cassius and certain others clapped their hands on their swords under their gowns to draw them, Brutus marking the countenance and gesture of Laenas and considering that he did use himself rather like a humble and earnest suitor than like an accuser, he said nothing to his companions (because there were many among them that were not of the conspiracy), but with a pleasant countenance encouraged Cassius. And immediately after, Laenas went from Caesar and kissed his hand, which showed plainly that it was for some matter concerning himself that he had held him so long in talk. Now all the Senators being entered first into this place or chapter house where the council should be kept, all the other conspirators straight stood about Caesar's chair, as if they had something to have said to him. And some say that Cassius, casting his eyes upon Pompey's image, made his prayer unto it as if it had been alive. Trebonius, on the other side, drew Antonius aside as he came into the house where the Senate sat, and held him with a long talk without.

When Caesar was come into the house, all the Senate rose to honor him at his coming in. So when he was set, the conspirators flocked about him, and among them they presented one Tillius Cimber, who made humble suit for the calling-home again of his brother that was banished. They all made as though they were intercessors for him, and took him by the hands, and kissed his head and breast. Caesar at the first simply refused their kindness and entreaties; but afterward, perceiving they still pressed on him, he violently thrust them from him. Then Cimber with both his hands plucked Caesar's gown over his shoulders, and Casca that stood behind him drew his dagger first and struck Caesar upon the shoulder, but gave him no great wound. Caesar, feeling himself hurt, took him straight by the hand he held his dagger in, and cried out in Latin: O traitor Casca, what doest thou? Casca on the other side cried in Greek, and called his brother to help him.

So, divers running on a heap together to fly upon Caesar, he, looking about him to have fled, saw Brutus with a sword drawn in his hand ready to strike at him. Then he let Casca's hand go, and casting his gown over his face, suffered every man to strike at him that would. Then the conspirators, thronging one upon another because every man was desirous to have a cut at him, so many swords and daggers lighting upon one body, one of them hurt another, and among them Brutus caught a blow on his hand, because he would make one in murdering of him, and all the rest also were every man of them bloodied. Caesar being slain in this manner, Brutus, standing in the midst of the house, would have spoken and stayed the other Senators that were not of the conspiracy, to have told them the reason why they had done this fact. But they, as men both affrayed and amazed, fled one upon another's neck in haste to get out at the door, and no man followed them. For it was set down and agreed between them that they should kill no man but Caesar only, and should entreat all the rest to defend their liberty.

All the conspirators but Brutus, determining upon this matter, thought it good also to kill Antonius, because he was a wicked man, and that in nature favored tyranny; besides also, for that he was in great estimation with soldiers, having been conversant of long time amongst them, and specially having a mind bent to great enterprises, he was also of great authority at that time, being Consul with Caesar. But Brutus would not agree to it. First, for that he said it was not honest; secondly, because he told them there was hope of change in him. For he did not mistrust but that Antonius, being a nobleminded and courageous man, (when he should know that Caesar was dead) would willingly help his country to recover her liberty, having then an example unto him, to follow their courage and virtue. So Brutus by this means saved Antonius' life, who at that present time disguised himself, and stole away. But Brutus and his consorts, having their swords bloody in their hands, went straight to the Capitol, persuading the Romans as they went to take their liberty again.

Now at the first time when the murder was newly done, there were sudden outcries of people that ran up and down the city, the which indeed did the more increase the fear and tumult. But when they saw they slew no man, neither did spoil or make havoc of anything, then certain of the Senators, and many of the people, emboldening themselves, went to the Capitol unto them. There a great number of men being assembled together one after another, Brutus made an oration unto them to win the favor of the people, and to justify that they had done. All those that were by said they had done well, and cried unto them that they should boldly come down from the Capitol. Whereupon Brutus and his companions came boldly down into the market place. The rest followed in troop, but Brutus went foremost, very honorably compassed in round about with the noblest men of the city, which brought him from the Capitol, through the market place, to the pulpit for orations.

When the people saw him in the pulpit, although they were a multitude of rakehells of all sorts, and had a good will to make some stir, yet being ashamed to do it for the reverence they bore unto Brutus, they kept silence, to hear what he would say. When Brutus began to speak, they gave him quiet audience. Howbeit, immediately after they showed that they were not all contented with the murder. For when another called Cinna would have spoken and began to accuse Caesar, they fell into a great uproar among them, and marvelously reviled him. Insomuch that the conspirators again returned into the Capitol. There Brutus, being affrayed to be besieged, sent back again the noblemen that came hither with him, thinking it no reason that they which were no partakers of the murder should be partakers of the danger.

Then the next morning, the Senate being assembled and holden within the temple of the goddess Tellus — to wit, the Earth — and Antonius, Plancus, and Cicero having made a motion to the Senate in that assembly that they should take an order to pardon and forget all that was past, and to establish friendship and peace again, it was decreed that they should not only be pardoned, but also that the Consuls should refer it to the Senate what honors should be appointed unto them. This being agreed upon, the Senate broke up, and Antonius the Consul, to put them in heart that were in the Capitol, sent them his son for a pledge. Upon this assurance, Brutus and his companions came down from the Capitol, where every man saluted and embraced each other, among the which Antonius himself did bid Cassius to supper to him, and Lepidus also bade Brutus, and so one bade another as they had friendship and acquaintance together.

The next day following, the Senate, being called again to council, did first of all commend Antonius for that he had wisely stayed and quenched the beginning of a civil war. Then they also gave Brutus and his consorts great praises, and lastly they appointed them several governments of provinces. For unto Brutus they appointed Crete; Africa unto Cassius; Asia unto Trebonius; Bithynia unto Cimber; and unto the other Decius Brutus Albinus, Gaul on this side the Alps. When this was done, they came to talk of Caesar's will and testament, and of his funerals and tomb. Then Antonius, thinking good his testament should be read openly, and also that his body should be honorably buried, and not in hugger-mugger, lest the people might thereby take occasion to be worse offended if they did otherwise, Cassius stoutly spoke against it.

But Brutus went with the motion, and agreed unto it, wherein it seemeth he committed a second fault. For the first fault he did was when he would not consent to his fellow conspirators that Antonius should be slain. And therefore he was justly accused that thereby he had saved and strengthened a strong and grievous enemy of their conspiracy. The second fault was when he agreed that Caesar's funerals should be as Antonius would have them, the which indeed marred all. For first of all, when Caesar's testament was openly read among them, whereby it appeared that he bequeathed unto every citizen of Rome seventy-five drachmas a man, and that he left his gardens and arbors unto the people — which he had on this side of the river of Tiber in the place where now the Temple of Fortune is built — the people then loved him, and were marvelous sorry for him.

Afterward when Caesar's body was brought into the market place, Antonius making his funeral oration in praise of the dead, according to the ancient custom of Rome, and perceiving that his words moved the common people to compassion, he framed his eloquence to make their hearts yearn the more, and taking Caesar's gown all bloody in his hand, he laid it open to the sight of them all, showing what a number of cuts and holes it had upon it. Therewithal the people fell presently into such a rage and mutiny that there was no more order kept amongst the common people. For some of them cried out, "Kill the murderers!" Others plucked up forms, tables, and stalls about the market place, as they had done before at the funerals of Clodius, and having laid them all on a heap together, they set them on fire, and thereupon did put the body of Caesar, and burned it in the midst of the most holy places. And furthermore, when the fire was thoroughly kindled, some here, some there, took burning firebrands and ran with them to the murderers' houses that had killed him, to set them afire. Howbeit, the conspirators, foreseeing the danger before, had wisely provided for themselves, and fled.

The account given in the "Life of Antonius" differs very little, but there are a few additional details in the "Life of Caesar":

So, Caesar coming into the [Senate] house, all the Senate stood up on their feet to do him honor. Then part of Brutus's company and confederates stood round about Caesar's chair, and part of them came also toward him, as though they made suit with

Metellus Cimber, to call home his brother again from banishment. And thus, prosecuting still their suit, they followed Caesar till he was set in his chair. Who denying their petitions and being offended with them one after another, because the more they were denied, the more they pressed upon him and were the earnester with him, Metellus at length, taking the gown with both his hands, pulled it over his neck, which was the sign given the confederates to set upon him.

Then Casca behind him strake him in the neck with his sword. Howbeit, the wound was not great nor mortal, because, it seemed, the fear of such a devilish attempt did amaze him, and take his strength from him, that he killed him not at the first blow. But Caesar, turning straight unto him, caught hold of his sword and held it hard, and they both cried out, Caesar in Latin: "O vile traitor Casca, what doest thou?" And Casca in Greek to his brother, "Brother, help me." At the beginning of this stir, they that were present, not knowing of the conspiracy, were so amazed with the horrible sight they saw they had no power to fly, neither to help him, not so much as once to make any outcry. They on the other side that had conspired his death compassed him in on every side with their swords drawn in their hands, that Caesar turned him nowhere but he was stricken at by some, and still had naked swords in his face, and was hacked and mangled among them, as a wild beast taken of hunters. For it was agreed among them that every man should give him a wound, because all their parts should be in this murder. And then Brutus himself gave him one wound about his privities.

Men report also that Caesar did still defend himself against the rest, running every way with his body. But when he saw Brutus with his sword drawn in his hand, then he pulled his gown over his head and made no more resistance, and was driven either casually, or purposely by the counsel of the conspirators, against the base whereupon Pompey's image stood, which ran all of a gore blood till he was slain. Thus it seemed that the image took just revenge of Pompey's enemy, being thrown down on the ground at his feet, and yielding up his ghost there, for the number of wounds he had upon him. For it is reported that he had three-and-twenty wounds upon his body. And divers of the conspirators did hurt themselves, striking one body with so many blows.

Shakespeare thus studied all three versions. He kept closely to the account of Caesar's death, but added the incident of the murderers bathing their hands in Caesar's blood. He omitted all suggestion of the events in the Senate House on the day after the murder, and moved the reconciliation of Antony with the conspirators back to the time of the murder. Brutus's speech to the crowd was actually given on the day of the murder; Shakespeare made it a prelude to Antony's speech at the funeral. Brutus's words were Shakespeare's own, but the clipped style was suggested by an earlier passage in the " Life of Brutus ":

He was properly learned in the Latin tongue, and was able to make long discourse in it, besides that he could also plead very well in Latin. But for the Greek tongue, they do note in some of his epistles that he counterfeited that brief compendious manner of speech of the Lacedaemonians. As when the war was begun, he wrote unto the Pergamenians in this sort; " I understand you have given Dolabella money. If you have done it willingly, you confess you have offended me; if against your wills, show it then by giving me willingly." Another time again unto the Samians: "Your counsels be long, your doings be slow, consider the end." . . . These were Brutus's manner of letters, which were honored for their briefness.

Antony's magnificent speech, except for the bare hints given by Plutarch, was entirely Shakespeare's own devising. Much as he owed to Plutarch, the play was even more his own making.

The real Caesar had a curious career. In his early forties he was well known in Rome as a dangerously attractive vicious playboy. He owed more money than any Roman had ever owed before, and he was an expert racketeer, his particular line being elections; he controlled the toughest gangs who beat up the opposition voters. He then offered himself as a candidate for office, and as a result became military governor of Spain, which was one of the unruly provinces. This taste of political and military power seems to have excited him. Two years later, by a bargain with Crassus, the richest of the Roman capitalists, and Pompey, the most experienced of Roman generals, he became Consul; and then, to the surprise of all who knew him, he went off as commander of the Roman Army in Gaul on a five-year appointment, which was afterward extended by another five years. During this time he showed that he was a superb general, of the kind whose men will follow anywhere.

In 49 B.C. Caesar decided that politics in Rome were in such chaos that it was time for him to go back. So he set out, but with his army. The Senate was alarmed, it debated, it passed resolutions,

it adjourned. Still Caesar came on. Then the Senate ordered Pompey to go out and deal with him, but instead Caesar dealt with Pompey so effectively that he chased him out of Italy and over the Mediterranean to Egypt, where he was murdered. Caesar stayed in Egypt for a year. He was fascinated with the country and with its young Queen, Cleopatra. Then he came back to Rome in the autumn of 45 B.C. with his head full of schemes for the reorganization of the civilized world. For the next six months he put through many reforms, and then on the ides of March 44 B.C. he was murdered in the Senate House, and chaos came back.

In some ways *Julius Caesar* marks a change in Shakespeare's development as a dramatist. In the earlier tragedies he was concerned more with the interplay of events; in *Julius Caesar* he was interested rather in the motives of the protagonists, so that the theme of the play is not so much the life and death of a dictator as the mind and motives of Caesar's murderers. It seems clear that Shakespeare was more concerned with Brutus and Cassius than with Caesar. The portrait of Caesar is unsympathetic; he is a pompous tyrant, and though he commits no action that justifies murder, he has that insufferable sense of superiority which infuriates lesser men such as Cassius. This view of Caesar has been much criticized, but dramatically it is right. Had Caesar been shown as a noble and sympathetic patriot, there could have been no justification for the murder and no sympathy with Brutus and the rest.

In real life the events which are called history are very complex. In a play they must be shown in two or at most three hours. The dramatist must therefore compress, choosing one incident as typical of many and vastly simplifying the story. Shakespeare begins by showing how Caesar has made enemies of different kinds. First the tribunes of the people; they hate him because he has come back in triumph over Pompey, a Roman and their friend; they know that if Caesar remains dictator that will be the end of their power as leaders of the people. Then there is Cassius. He hates Caesar as a man. Caesar and he went to school together, and now Cassius must bow if Caesar even looks his way. Cassius is madly jealous of Caesar, and he first starts the conspiracy, but he knows that it will not sound convincing unless he can persuade others that there is some lofty motive behind it, or can find some better man than himself to lead and make the affair respectable. Brutus is his man.

In some ways the play is about Brutus rather than Caesar. Brutus is universally admired, for he is a genuine idealist. Five centuries before, his ancestor Lucius Junius Brutus led the revolt which drove out Tarquin, the last King of Rome. Once Brutus can be persuaded that Caesar is another Tarquin, Brutus will do anything. Brutus is thus faced with an insoluble problem: to live under the tyranny of Caesar is to allow a wrong; to kill Caesar is to commit a wrong. After a long struggle in his own mind he ultimately decides that the murder of Caesar is a holy duty. But a high-minded idealist is not the right man to lead a revolution which begins with murder. As soon as Cassius has made Brutus the leader of the movement, he has put himself into second place, and he must now obey his leader.

Up to the moment when Caesar is killed all goes well with the conspirators; but as soon as Caesar is dead fate turns against them. While the conspiracy was being planned, Cassius had warned Brutus against Antony, but Brutus despises Antony because he is not like himself, an austere, abstemious man. Thenceforward it be-

comes a contest between these two. At first the odds are against Antony; but by superior knowledge of human nature he overcomes Brutus and obtains leave to make the funeral speech over Caesar's body. Here is his chance. He understands crowds, and Brutus does not. Brutus thinks that it is only necessary to tell the crowd why he killed Caesar and they will at once fall into orderly democratic ways. Antony knows better, and by a magnificent piece of oratory he so turns the crowd against the conspirators that they flee for their lives. They had killed Caesar's body, but they had forgotten Caesar's spirit.

The story is resumed a few months later. Brutus and Cassius have fled to Greece, where they gather armies to meet Antony, who is now combined with Lepidus and young Octavius Caesar. Everything goes wrong, and the two leaders are openly squabbling. Both have degenerated, and there is little left now of the high ideals which began the business.

In the battle which follows their ill luck continues. Cassius kills himself through a misunderstanding, and Brutus is left alone with a few faithful followers, to surrender or to kill himself. Caesar's spirit has won.

Julius Caesar

DRAMATIS PERSONAE

JULIUS CAESAR
OCTAVIUS CAESAR } *triumvirs after the death of*
MARCUS ANTONIUS } *Julius Caesar*
M. AEMIL. LEPIDUS }

CICERO   }
PUBLIUS   } *Senators*
POPILIUS LENA }

MARCUS BRUTUS
CASSIUS
CASCA
TREBONIUS   } *conspirators against Julius*
LIGARIUS   } *Caesar*
DECIUS BRUTUS
METELLUS CIMBER
CINNA

FLAVIUS *and* MARULLUS, *tribunes*
ARTEMIDORUS *of Cnidos, a teacher of rhetoric*
A SOOTHSAYER
CINNA, *a poet*
ANOTHER POET

LUCILIUS   }
TITINIUS   }
MESSALA   } *friends to Brutus and Cassius*
YOUNG CATO   }
VOLUMNIUS   }

VARRO   }
CLITUS   }
CLAUDIUS   }
STRATO   } *servants to Brutus*
LUCIUS   }
DARDANIUS }

PINDARUS, *servant to Cassius*

CALPURNIA, *wife to Caesar*
PORTIA, *wife to Brutus*

SENATORS, CITIZENS, GUARDS, ATTENDANTS, &c.

SCENE — *Rome; the neighborhood of Sardis; the neighborhood of Philippi.*

Act I

SCENE I. *Rome. A street.*

[*Enter* FLAVIUS, MARULLUS, *and certain* COMMONERS.]

FLA. Hence! Home, you idle creatures, get you
    home.
Is this a holiday? What! Know you not,
Being mechanical,° you ought not walk
Upon a laboring day without the sign°
Of your profession? Speak, what trade art thou? 5
1. COM. Why, sir, a carpenter.
MAR. Where is thy leather apron and thy rule?
What dost thou with thy best apparel on?
You, sir, what trade are you?
2. COM. Truly, sir, in respect of a fine workman,°
I am but, as you would say, a cobbler. 11
MAR. But what trade art thou? Answer me directly.°
2. COM. A trade, sir, that I hope I may use with
a safe conscience, which is indeed, sir, a mender of
bad soles.° 15
MAR. What trade, thou knave? Thou naughty
knave, what trade?

2. COM. Nay, I beseech you, sir, be not out° with
me. Yet if you be out, sir, I can mend you.
MAR. What mean'st thou by that? Mend me, thou
saucy fellow! 21
2. COM. Why, sir, cobble you.
FLA. Thou art a cobbler, art thou?
2. COM. Truly, sir, all that I live by is with the
awl. I meddle with no tradesman's matters, nor 25
women's matters, but with awl. I am indeed, sir, a
surgeon to old shoes. When they are in great danger, I re-cover them. As proper° men as ever trod
upon neat's leather° have gone upon my handiwork.
FLA. But wherefore art not in thy shop today? 31
Why dost thou lead these men about the streets?
2. COM. Truly, sir, to wear out their shoes, to get
myself into more work. But indeed, sir, we 35
make holiday, to see Caesar and to rejoice in his triumph.°
MAR. Wherefore rejoice? What conquest brings
    he home?
What tributaries° follow him to Rome,
To grace in captive bonds his chariot wheels?
You blocks, you stones, you worse than senseless
    things! 40
O you hard hearts, you cruel men of Rome,

Act I, Sc. i: **3. mechanical:** workingmen.   **4. sign:** i.e., tools
and working clothes.   **10. in . . . workman:** so far as fine work
is concerned.   **12. directly:** without quibbling.   **15. soles:** puns
on "sole" and "soul" are inevitable. Cf. *M of Ven*, IV.i.123.

18. out: angry.   **28. proper:** handsome.   **29. neat's leather:**
oxhide.   **36. in his triumph:** Roman generals after a victorious
campaign entered Rome in a triumphal procession. Caesar's triumph, however, is over another Roman, Pompey.   **38. tributaries:** captives.

Knew you not Pompey? Many a time and oft
Have you climbed up to walls and battlements,
To towers and windows, yea, to chimney tops,°
Your infants in your arms, and there have sat   45
The livelong day with patient expectation
To see great Pompey pass the streets of Rome.
And when you saw his chariot but appear,
Have you not made a universal shout,
That Tiber trembled underneath her banks   50
To hear the replication° of your sounds
Made in her concave shores?
And do you now put on your best attire?
And do you now cull out° a holiday?
And do you now strew flowers in his way   55
That comes in triumph over Pompey's blood?
Be gone!
Run to your houses, fall upon your knees,
Pray to the gods to intermit° the plague
That needs must light on this ingratitude.   60
   FLA. Go, go, good countrymen, and for this fault
Assemble all the poor men of your sort.
Draw them to Tiber banks and weep your tears
Into the channel till the lowest stream
Do kiss the most exalted shores of all.   65
                    [*Exeunt all the* COMMONERS.]
See whether their basest metal° be not moved.
They vanish tongue-tied in their guiltiness.
Go you down that way toward the Capitol,
This way will I. Disrobe the images°
If you do find them decked with ceremonies.°   70
   MAR. May we do so?
You know it is the feast of Lupercal.°
   FLA. It is no matter. Let no images
Be hung with Caesar's trophies. I'll about,
And drive away the vulgar from the streets.   75
So do you too, where you perceive them thick.
These growing feathers plucked from Caesar's wing
Will make him fly an ordinary pitch,°
Who else would soar above the view of men
And keep us all in servile fearfulness. [*Exeunt.*]   80

SCENE II. *A public place.*

[*Flourish. Enter* CAESAR; ANTONY, *for the course;*°
CALPURNIA, PORTIA, DECIUS, CICERO, BRUTUS, CASSIUS,
and CASCA; *a great crowd following, among them
a* SOOTHSAYER.]

CAE. Calpurnia!
CASC.   Peace, ho! Caesar speaks.
CAE.   [*Music ceases.*] Calpurnia!
CAL. Here, my lord.
CAE. Stand you directly in Antonius' way
When he doth run his course.° Antonius!
ANT. Caesar, my lord?   5
CAE. Forget not, in your speed, Antonius,
To touch Calpurnia, for our elders say
The barren, touchèd in this holy chase,
Shake off their sterile curse.
ANT.   I shall remember:
When Caesar says " Do this," it is performed.   10
CAE. Set on, and leave no ceremony out.
                    [*Flourish.*]
SOOTH. Caesar!
CAE. Ha! Who calls?
CASC. Bid every noise be still — peace yet again!
CAE. Who is it in the press° that calls on me?   15
I hear a tongue, shriller than all the music,
Cry " Caesar." Speak. Caesar is turned to hear.
SOOTH. Beware the ides of March.°
CAE.   What man is that?
BRU. A soothsayer bids you beware the ides of
   March.
CAE. Set him before me. Let me see his face.   20
CASS. Fellow, come from the throng. Look upon
   Caesar.
CAE. What say'st thou to me now? Speak once
   again.
SOOTH. Beware the ides of March.
CAE. He is a dreamer. Let us leave him — pass.
   [*Sennet.° Exeunt all but* BRUTUS *and* CASSIUS.]
CASS. Will you go see the order of the course?   25
BRU. Not I.
CASS. I pray you, do.
BRU. I am not gamesome. I do lack some part
Of that quick spirit that is in Antony.
Let me not hinder, Cassius, your desires.   30
I'll leave you.
CASS. Brutus, I do observe you now of late.
I have not from your eyes that gentleness
And show of love as I was wont to have.
You bear too stubborn and too strange a hand°   35
Over your friend that loves you.

44. chimney tops: Throughout the play Shakespeare has in mind rather his own London than Rome. Such a sight as this was familiar. Cf. the funeral of Queen Elizabeth, described in App. 16. 51. replication: echo.   54. cull out: choose to take.   59. intermit: omit, leave out.   66. metal: material, stuff of which they are made; "metal" and "mettle" were the same in Shakespeare's time.   69. Disrobe . . . images: strip the statues.   70. ceremonies: decorations.   72. Lupercal: Lupercalia, celebrated on February 15. See I.ii.4,n.   78. pitch: flight. See App. 26.
   Sc. ii: s.d., for the course: stripped for running.

4. run his course: At the feast of the Lupercalia "divers noblemen's sons, young men (and some of them magistrates themselves that govern them) . . . run naked through the city, striking in sport them they meet in their way with leather thongs, hair and all on, to make them give place. And many noblewomen and gentlewomen also go of purpose to stand in their way, and do put forth their hands to be stricken as scholars hold them out to their schoolmaster to be stricken, with the ferula (rod), persuading themselves that, being with child, they shall have good delivery, and so, being barren, that it will make them conceive with child." (North's Plutarch.)   15. press: crowd.   18. ides of March: March 15.   24. s.d., Sennet: trumpet call.   35. bear . . . hand: your behavior toward your friend is too rough and unkind.

BRU.   Cassius,
Be not deceived. If I have veiled my look,
I turn the trouble of my countenance
Merely upon myself. Vexèd I am
Of late with passions of some difference,°   40
Conceptions only proper to myself,
Which give some soil° perhaps to my behaviors.
But let not therefore my good friends be grieved —
Among which number, Cassius, be you one —
Nor cónstrue° any further my neglect   45
Than that poor Brutus, with himself at war,
Forgets the shows° of love to other men.
    CASS. Then, Brutus, I have much mistook your
       passion,
By means whereof this breast of mine hath buried
Thoughts of great value, worthy cogitations.   50
Tell me, good Brutus, can you see your face?
    BRU. No, Cassius, for the eye sees not itself
But by reflection, by some other things.
    CASS. 'Tis just.
And it is very much lamented, Brutus,   55
That you have no such mirrors as will turn°
Your hidden worthiness into your eye,
That you might see your shadow.° I have heard
Where many of the best respect in Rome,
Except immortal Caesar,° speaking of Brutus,   60
And groaning underneath this age's yoke,°
Have wished that noble Brutus had his eyes.
    BRU. Into what dangers would you lead me, Cas-
       sius,
That you would have me seek into myself
For that which is not in me?   65
    CASS. Therefore, good Brutus, be prepared to hear.
And since you know you cannot see yourself
So well as by reflection, I your glass
Will modestly discover to yourself
That of yourself which you yet know not of.   70
And be not jealous on° me, gentle Brutus.
Were I a common laugher,° or did use
To stale° with ordinary oaths my love
To every new protester;° if you know
That I do fawn on men and hug them hard,   75
And after scandal° them; or if you know
That I profess° myself in banqueting
To all the rout° — then hold me dangerous.
                [*Flourish*° *and shout.*]
    BRU. What means this shouting? I do fear the
       people
Choose Caesar for their king.

    CASS.   Aye, do you fear it?   80
Then must I think you would not have it so.
    BRU. I would not, Cassius, yet I love him well.
But wherefore do you hold me here so long?
What is it that you would impart to me?
If it be aught towárd the general good,   85
Set honor in one eye and death i' the other,
And I will look on both indifferently;°
For let the gods so speed° me as I love
The name of honor more than I fear death.
    CASS. I know that virtue to be in you, Brutus,   90
As well as I do know your outward favor.°
Well, honor is the subject of my story.
I cannot tell what you and other men
Think of this life, but for my single self
I had as lief° not be as live to be   95
In awe of such a thing as I myself.°
I was born free as Caesar; so were you.
We both have fed as well, and we can both
Endure the winter's cold as well as he.
For once, upon a raw and gusty day,   100
The troubled Tiber chafing with her shores,
Caesar said to me " Darest thou, Cassius, now
Leap in with me into this angry flood
And swim to yonder point? " Upon the word,
Accoutered° as I was, I plungèd in   105
And bade him follow. So indeed he did.
The torrent roared, and we did buffet it
With lusty sinews,° throwing it aside
And stemming it with hearts of controversy.°
But ere we could arrive the point proposed,   110
Caesar cried, " Help me, Cassius, or I sink! "
I, as Aeneas° our great ancestor
Did from the flames of Troy upon his shoulder
The old Anchises bear, so from the waves of Tiber
Did I the tired Caesar — and this man   115
Is now become a god, and Cassius is
A wretched creature, and must bend his body
If Caesar carelessly but nod on him.
He had a fever when he was in Spain,
And when the fit was on him, I did mark   120
How he did shake. 'Tis true, this god did shake.
His coward lips did from their color fly,°
And that same eye whose bend° doth awe the world
Did lose his° luster. I did hear him groan.   124
Aye, and that tongue of his that bade the Romans
Mark him and write his speeches in their books,
Alas, it cried, " Give me some drink, Titinius,"

---

40. passions . . . difference: conflicting emotions.   42. soil:
blemish.   45. construe: interpret.   47. shows: outward appearances.   56. turn: reflect.   58. shadow: reflection.   60. immortal Caesar: spoken with great bitterness.   61. age's
yoke: burdens of these times.   71. jealous on: suspicious of.
72. laugher: jester.   73. stale: make common.   74. protester:
one who makes solemn protestations.   76. scandal: speak scandal of.   77. profess: publicize.   78. rout: rabble.   78. s.d., Flourish: a long trumpet call to announce the appearance of an
important person.

87. indifferently: unconcernedly.   88. speed: give good fortune to.   91. favor: face.   95. lief: soon.   96. In . . . myself:
afraid of a mere mortal like myself.   105. Accoutered: fully
armed.   108. sinews: muscles.   109. hearts . . . controversy:
eager rivalry.   112. Aeneas: Aeneas was one of the few Trojans
who escaped the sack of Troy. He carried off his old father
Anchises, and with his company sailed away to Italy, where, according to legend, he became the founder of the Roman race.
Aeneas's adventures are the subject of Virgil's *Aeneid*.   122. His
. . . fly: the color fled from his cowardly lips.   123. bend: sway.
124. his: its.

As a sick girl. Ye gods! It doth amaze me
A man of such a feeble temper should
So get the start° of the majestic world   130
And bear the palm° alone.   [*Shout. Flourish.*]
   BRU. Another general shout!
I do believe that these applauses are
For some new honors that are heaped on Caesar.
   CASS. Why, man, he doth bestride the narrow
   world   135
Like a Colossus,° and we petty men
Walk under his huge legs and peep about
To find ourselves dishonorable graves.
Men at some time are masters of their fates.
The fault, dear Brutus, is not in our stars,°   140
But in ourselves, that we are underlings.°
Brutus, and Caesar. What should be in that Caesar?
Why should that name be sounded more than
   yours?
Write them together, yours is as fair a name.
Sound them, it doth become the mouth as well.   145
Weigh them, it is as heavy. Conjure° with 'em,
Brutus will start a spirit as soon as Caesar.
Now, in the names of all the gods at once,
Upon what meat doth this our Caesar feed   149
That he is grown so great? Age, thou art shamed!
Rome, thou hast lost the breed of noble bloods!
When went there by an age, since the great flood,
But it was famed with more than with one man?
When could they say till now that talked of Rome
That her wide walls encompassed but one man?
Now is it Rome indeed, and room° enough,   156
When there is in it but one only man.
Oh, you and I have heard our fathers say
There was a Brutus° once that would have brooked°
The eternal Devil to keep his state in Rome   160
As easily as a king.
   BRU. That you do love me, I am nothing jealous.
What you would work me to, I have some aim.
How I have thought of this and of these times,
I shall recount hereafter; for this present,   165
I would not, so with love I might entreat you,
Be any further moved. What you have said
I will consider. What you have to say
I will with patience hear, and find a time
Both meet° to hear and answer such high things.
Till then, my noble friend, chew upon this: 171
Brutus had rather be a villager

Than to repute himself a son of Rome
Under these hard conditions as this time
Is like to lay upon us.   175
   CASS. I am glad that my weak words
Have struck but thus much show of fire from Bru-
   tus.
   BRU. The games are done, and Caesar is return-
   ing.
   CASS. As they pass by, pluck Casca by the sleeve,
And he will, after his sour fashion, tell you   180
What hath proceeded worthy note today.
      [*Re-enter* CAESAR *and his train.*]
   BRU. I will do so. But look you, Cassius,
The angry spot doth glow on Caesar's brow,
And all the rest look like a chidden train.°
Calpurnia's cheek is pale, and Cicero   185
Looks with such ferret° and such fiery eyes
As we have seen him in the Capitol,
Being crossed in conference° by some Senators.
   CASS. Casca will tell us what the matter is.
   CAE. Antonius!   190
   ANT. Caesar?
   CAE. Let me have men about me that are fat,
Sleek-headed men, and such as sleep o' nights.
Yond Cassius has a lean and hungry look.
He thinks too much, such men are dangerous.   195
   ANT. Fear him not, Caesar. He's not dangerous,
He is a noble Roman, and well given.°
   CAE. Would he were fatter! But I fear him not.
Yet if my name were liable to fear,
I do not know the man I should avoid   200
So soon as that spare Cassius. He reads much,
He is a great observer, and he looks
Quite through the deeds of men. He loves no plays
As thou dost, Antony; he hears no music.
Seldom he smiles, and smiles in such a sort   205
As if he mocked himself, and scorned his spirit
That could be moved to smile at anything.
Such men as he be never at heart's ease
While they behold a greater than themselves,
And therefore are they very dangerous.   210
I rather tell thee what is to be feared
Than what I fear, for always I am Caesar.
Come on my right hand, for this ear is deaf,
And tell me truly what thou think'st of him.
[*Sennet. Exeunt* CAESAR *and all his train but* CASCA.]
   CASC. You pulled me by the cloak. Would you
   speak with me?   215
   BRU. Aye, Casca. Tell us what hath chanced today
That Caesar looks so sad.
   CASC. Why, you were with him, were you not?
   BRU. I should not then ask Casca what had
   chanced.   219
   CASC. Why, there was a crown offered him; and

---

130. get the start: become the leader.   **131. palm:** prize, sign of victory.   **136. Colossus:** the Colossus of Rhodes (an island in the Aegean Sea) was one of the seven wonders of the ancient world. It was a great bronze statue straddling the entrance to the harbor, beneath which ships passed.   **140. stars:** many still believed that a man's fate was governed by the stars. See App. 1.   **141. underlings:** inferior beings.   **146. Conjure:** use as an incantation to summon up spirits.   **156. Rome . . . room:** both words were pronounced and often spelled alike.   **159. Brutus:** Lucius Junius Brutus was chiefly responsible for the expulsion of Tarquin, the last King of Rome. Marcus Brutus claimed descent from him. **brooked:** endured.   **170. meet:** fit.

184. chidden train: scolded retinue.   **186. ferret:** ferrets have little red eyes.   **188. crossed . . . conference:** opposed in debate.   **197. well given:** well disposed.

being offered him, he put it by with the back of his hand, thus. And then the people fell a-shouting.

BRU. What was the second noise for?

CASC. Why, for that too.   225

CASS. They shouted thrice. What was the last cry for?

CASC. Why, for that too.

BRU. Was the crown offered him thrice?

CASC. Aye, marry,° was 't, and he put it by thrice, every time gentler than other. And at every   230 putting-by mine honest neighbors shouted.

CASS. Who offered him the crown?

CASC. Why, Antony.

BRU. Tell us the manner of it, gentle Casca.

CASC. I can as well be hanged as tell the man-   235 ner of it.° It was mere foolery — I did not mark it. I saw Mark Antony offer him a crown, yet 'twas not a crown neither, 'twas one of these coronets;° and, as I told you, he put it by once. But for all that, to my thinking, he would fain° have had it. Then   240 he offered it to him again, then he put it by again. But, to my thinking, he was very loath to lay his fingers off it. And then he offered it the third time, he put it the third time by. And still as he refused it the rabblement hooted and clapped their chopped°   245 hands and threw up their sweaty nightcaps° and uttered such a deal of stinking breath because Caesar refused the crown that it had almost choked Caesar; for he swounded° and fell down at it. And for mine own part, I durst not laugh, for fear of opening my lips and receiving the bad air.   252

CASS. But, soft, I pray you. What, did Caesar swound?

CASC. He fell down in the market place and foamed at mouth and was speechless.   255

BRU. 'Tis very like — he hath the falling sickness.°

CASS. No, Caesar hath it not. But you, and I, And honest Casca, we have the falling sickness.

CASC. I know not what you mean by that,   260 but I am sure Caesar fell down. If the tagrag people did not clap him and hiss him according as he pleased and displeased them, as they use to do the players in the theater, I am no true man.

BRU. What said he when he came unto himself?

CASC. Marry, before he fell down, when he   265 perceived the common herd was glad he refused the crown, he plucked me ope° his doublet° and offered them his throat to cut. An° I had been a man of any occupation,° if I would not have taken him at a

word, I would I might go to Hell among the   270 rogues. And so he fell. When he came to himself again, he said if he had done or said anything amiss, he desired Their Worships to think it was his   273 infirmity. Three or four wenches where I stood cried, "Alas, good soul!" and forgave him with all their hearts: but there's no heed to be taken of them. If Caesar had stabbed their mothers, they would have done no less.

BRU. And after that, he came, thus sad, away?

CASC. Aye.   280

CASS. Did Cicero say anything?

CASC. Aye, he spoke Greek.

CASS. To what effect?   283

CASC. Nay, an I tell you that, I'll ne'er look you i' the face again. But those that understood him smiled at one another and shook their heads — but for mine own part, it was Greek to me. I could tell you more news too. Marullus and Flavius, for   288 pulling scarfs° off Caesar's images, are put to silence. Fare you well. There was more foolery yet, if I could remember it.

CASS. Will you sup with me tonight, Casca?

CASC. No, I am promised forth.

CASS. Will you dine with me tomorrow?

CASC. Aye, if I be alive, and your mind hold, and your dinner worth the eating.   295

CASS. Good. I will expect you.

CASC. Do so. Farewell, both.   [*Exit.*]

BRU. What a blunt fellow is this grown to be! He was quick mettle° when he went to school.   300

CASS. So is he now in execution
Of any bold or noble enterprise,
However he puts on this tardy° form.
This rudeness is a sauce to his good wit,
Which gives men stomach to digest his words   305
With better appetite.

BRU. And so it is. For this time I will leave you.
Tomorrow, if you please to speak with me,
I will come home to you, or, if you will,
Come home to me and I will wait for you.   310

CASS. I will do so. Till then, think of the world.

[*Exit* BRUTUS.]

Well, Brutus, thou art noble. Yet I see
Thy honorable mettle may be wrought
From that it is disposed.° Therefore it is meet
That noble minds keep ever with their likes,   315
For who so firm that cannot be seduced?
Caesar doth bear me hard,° but he loves Brutus.
If I were Brutus now and he were Cassius,
He should not humor° me. I will this night,
In several hands,° in at his windows throw,   320
As if they came from several citizens,

229. marry: Mary, by the Virgin.   235–36. I . . . it: I'll be hanged if I can tell.   238. coronets: little crowns worn by those of lesser rank than king.   240. fain: gladly.   245. chopped: chapped, toil-worn.   246. nightcaps: close-fitting caps. 250. swounded: swooned.   256. falling-sickness: epilepsy. 267. ope: open. doublet: short coat. See Pl. 8b and p. 93a. 268. An: if.   269. occupation: trade, and therefore provided with tools.

289. scarfs: decorations.   300. mettle: temperament, material. See I.i.66,n.   303. tardy: sluggish.   314. From . . . disposed: from its natural quality.   317. bear me hard: dislike me. 319. humor: influence.   320. several hands: different handwritings.

Writings, all tending to the great opinion
That Rome holds of his name, wherein obscurely
Caesar's ambition shall be glancèd at.
And after this let Caesar seat him° sure,   325
For we will shake him, or worse days endure.
                                        [*Exit.*]

SCENE III. *A street.*

[*Thunder and lightning. Enter, from opposite sides,*
CASCA, *with his sword drawn, and* CICERO.]
  CIC. Good even, Casca. Brought you Caesar
home?
Why are you breathless? And why stare you so?
  CASC. Are not you moved, when all the sway° of
earth
Shakes like a thing unfirm? O Cicero,
I have seen tempests when the scolding winds   5
Have rived° the knotty oaks, and I have seen
The ambitious ocean swell and rage and foam,
To be exalted° with the threatening clouds.
But never till tonight, never till now,
Did I go through a tempest dropping fire.   10
Either there is a civil strife in Heaven,
Or else the world too saucy with the gods
Incenses them to send destruction.
  CIC. Why, saw you anything more wonderful?
  CASC. A common slave — you know him well by
sight —   15
Held up his left hand, which did flame and burn
Like twenty torches joined, and yet his hand,
Not sensible of° fire, remained unscorched.
Besides — I ha' not since put up my sword —
Against° the Capitol I met a lion,°   20
Who glazed° upon me and went surly by
Without annoying me. And there were drawn
Upon a heap a hundred ghastly women
Transformèd with their fear, who swore they saw
Men all in fire walk up and down the streets.   25
And yesterday the bird of night° did sit
Even at noonday upon the market place,
Hooting and shrieking. When these prodigies
Do so conjointly meet, let not men say
" These are their reasons, they are natural."°   30
For I believe they are portentous things
Unto the climate that they point upon.°
  CIC. Indeed, it is a strange-disposèd time.
But men may cónstrue things after their fashion,

Clean from the purpose of the things themselves.
Comes Caesar to the Capitol tomorrow?   36
  CASC. He doth, for he did bid Antonius
Send word to you he would be there tomorrow.
  CIC. Good night then, Casca. This disturbèd sky
Is not to walk in.
  CASC.   Farewell, Cicero. [*Exit* CICERO.] 40
              [*Enter* CASSIUS.]
  CASS. Who's there?
  CASC.   A Roman.
  CASS.   Casca, by your voice.
  CASC. Your ear is good. Cassius, what night is
this!
  CASS. A very pleasing night to honest men.
  CASC. Who ever knew the heavens menace so?
  CASS. Those that have known the earth so full of
faults.   45
For my part, I have walked about the streets,
Submitting me unto the perilous night,
And thus unbraced,° Casca, as you see,
Have bared my bosom to the thunder stone.°
And when the cross° blue lightning seemed to open
The breast of Heaven, I did present myself   51
Even in the aim and very flash of it.
  CASC. But wherefore did you so much tempt the
heavens?
It is the part of° men to fear and tremble
When the most mighty gods by tokens send   55
Such dreadful heralds to astonish us.
  CASS. You are dull, Casca, and those sparks of life
That should be in a Roman you do want,°
Or else you use not. You look pale and gaze
And put on fear and cast yourself in wonder,°   60
To see the strange impatience of the heavens.
But if you would consider the true cause
Why all these fires, why all these gliding ghosts,
Why birds and beasts from quality and kind,°
Why old men fool and children calculate,°   65
Why all these things change from their ordinance,°
Their natures and preformèd faculties,
To monstrous° quality, why, you shall find
That Heaven hath infused them with these spirits
To make them instruments of fear and warning   70
Unto some monstrous state.
Now could I, Casca, name to thee a man
Most like this dreadful night
That thunders, lightens, opens graves, and roars
As doth the lion in the Capitol° —   75
A man no mightier than thyself or me
In personal action, yet prodigious grown
And fearful,° as these strange eruptions are.

325. him: himself.
      Sc. iii: 3. sway: settled order. 6. rived: split. 8. exalted:
lifted high. 18. sensible of: sensitive to. 20. Against: beside. Capitol . . . lion: Shakespeare thought of the Capitol as if it
were the Tower of London. Here were kept the lions which were
among the sights of London. See Gen. Intro. p. 16a and Pl. 3a.
21. glazed: glared. 26. bird of night: screech owl. 30. These
. . . natural: this is the scientific explanation. 31–32. portentous
. . . upon: they are omens of disaster toward the country which
they threaten.

48. unbraced: with the doublet loose. See comment on p. 94a–b.
49. thunder stone: thunderbolt. 50. cross: zigzag. 54. part of:
natural to. 58. want: lack. 60. cast . . . wonder: are amazed.
64. from . . . kind: contrary to their natural disposition. 65. calculate: prophesy. 66. ordinance: natural order. 68. monstrous: unnatural. 75. lion . . . Capitol: See note on l. 20.
78. fearful: causing fear.

CASC. 'Tis Caesar that you mean, is it not, Cassius?

CASS. Let it be who it is. For Romans now   80
Have thews° and limbs like to their ancestors.
But, woe the while!° our fathers' minds are dead,
And we are governed with our mothers' spirits,
Our yoke and sufferance° show us womanish.

CASC. Indeed they say the Senators tomorrow   85
Mean to establish Caesar as a king,
And he shall wear his crown by sea and land
In every place save here in Italy.

CASS. I know where I will wear this dagger then.
Cassius from bondage will deliver Cassius.   90
Therein, ye gods, you make the weak most strong.
Therein, ye gods, you tyrants do defeat.
Nor stony tower, nor walls of beaten brass,
Nor airless dungeon, nor strong links of iron,
Can be retentive to the strength of spirit;   95
But life, being weary of these worldly bars,
Never lacks power to dismiss itself.
If I know this, know all the world besides,
That part of tyranny that I do bear
I can shake off at pleasure.   [*Thunder still.*]

CASC.   So can I.   100
So every bondman in his own hand bears
The power to cancel his captivity.

CASS. And why should Caesar be a tyrant, then?
Poor man! I know he would not be a wolf
But that he sees the Romans are but sheep.   105
He were no lion were not Romans hinds.°
Those that with haste will make a mighty fire
Begin it with weak straws. What trash° is Rome,
What rubbish and what offal, when it serves
For the base matter to illuminate°   110
So vile a thing as Caesar! But, O Grief,
Where hast thou led me? I perhaps speak this
Before a willing bondman; then I know
My answer must be made. But I am armed,
And dangers are to me indifferent.°   115

CASC. You speak to Casca, and to such a man
That is no fleering° telltale. Hold, my hand
Be factious° for redress of all these griefs,
And I will set this foot of mine as far
As who goes farthest.

CASS.   There's a bargain made.   120
Now know you, Casca, I have moved already
Some certain of the noblest-minded Romans
To undergo with me an enterprise

Of honorable-dangerous consequence.
And I do know, by this they stay° for me   125
In Pompey's porch;° for now, this fearful night,
There is no stir or walking in the streets,
And the complexion of the element°
In favor's° like the work we have in hand,
Most bloody, fiery, and most terrible.   130
                                   [*Enter* CINNA.]

CASC. Stand close° awhile, for here comes one in haste.

CASS. 'Tis Cinna, I do know him by his gait—
He is a friend. Cinna, where haste you so?

CIN. To find out you. Who's that? Metellus Cimber?

CASS. No, it is Casca, one incorporate   135
To our attempts.° Am I not stayed for, Cinna?

CIN. I am glad on 't. What a fearful night is this!
There's two or three of us have seen strange sights.

CASS. Am I not stayed for? Tell me.

CIN.   Yes, you are.
O Cassius, if you could   140
But win the noble Brutus to our party——

CASS. Be you content. Good Cinna, take this paper,
And look you lay it in the praetor's° chair,
Where Brutus may but find it, and throw this
In at his window; set this up with wax   145
Upon old Brutus'° statue. All this done,
Repair to Pompey's porch, where you shall find us.
Is Decius Brutus and Trebonius there?

CIN. All but Metellus Cimber, and he's gone
To seek you at your house. Well, I will hie,   150
And so bestow these papers as you bade me.

CASS. That done, repair to Pompey's theater.
                                     [*Exit* CINNA.]
Come, Casca, you and I will yet ere day
See Brutus at his house. Three parts of him
Is ours already, and the man entire   155
Upon the next encounter yields him ours.

CASC. Oh, he sits high in all the people's hearts,
And that which would appear offense in us
His countenance, like richest alchemy,°
Will change to virtue and to worthiness.   160

CASS. Him and his worth and our great need of him
You have right well conceited.° Let us go,
For it is after midnight, and ere day
We will awake him and be sure of him.   [*Exeunt.*]

---

81. **thews:** sinews, strength.   82. **woe the while:** alas for the time.   84. **Our . . . sufferance:** our enduring this slavery.   106. **hinds:** female deer, the gentlest of creatures.   108. **trash:** twigs.   110. **base . . . illuminate:** the rubbish from which the light is kindled.   115. **indifferent:** a matter of indifference.   117. **fleering:** sneering.   118. **factious:** partisan.   125. **stay:** wait.   126. **Pompey's porch:** the portico, part of the theater Pompey had built.   128. **element:** sky.   129. **favor:** face, appearance.   131. **Stand close:** hide yourself.   135–36. **incorporate . . . attempts:** i.e., one of our conspiracy.   143. **praetor:** a Roman official next in rank to the consul, the highest official in Rome.   146. **old Brutus:** See I.ii.159,n.   159. **alchemy:** See App. 21.   162. **conceited:** perceived.

Act II

SCENE I. *Rome.* BRUTUS's *orchard.*

[*Enter* BRUTUS.]

BRU. What, Lucius, ho!
I cannot, by the progress of the stars,
Give guess how near to day. Lucius, I say!
I would it were my fault to sleep so soundly. 4
When, Lucius, when? Awake, I say! What, Lucius!

[*Enter* LUCIUS.]

LUC. Called you, my lord?
BRU. Get me a taper° in my study, Lucius.
When it is lighted, come and call me here.
LUC. I will, my lord.   [*Exit.*]
BRU. It must be by his death° and for my part 10
I know no personal cause to spurn at him,
But for the general.° He would be crowned.
How that might change his nature, there's the question.
It is the bright day that brings forth the adder,
And that craves° wary walking. Crown him? —
That — 15
And then, I grant, we put a sting in him,
That at his will he may do danger with.
The abuse of greatness is when it disjoins
Remorse° from power; and to speak truth of Caesar,
I have not known when his affections° swayed 20
More than his reason. But 'tis a common proof°
That lowliness is young ambition's ladder,
Whereto the climber-upward turns his face.
But when he once attains the upmost round,
He then unto the ladder turns his back, 25
Looks in the clouds, scorning the base degrees°
By which he did ascend. So Caesar may.
Then, lest he may, prevent.° And since the quarrel
Will bear no color° for the thing he is,
Fashion it thus:° that what he is, augmented, 30
Would run to these and these extremities.
And therefore think him as a serpent's egg
Which hatched would as his kind grow mischievous,
And kill him in the shell.

[*Re-enter* LUCIUS.]

LUC. The taper burneth in your closet,° sir. 35
Searching the window for a flint,° I found
This paper thus sealed up, and I am sure
It did not lie there when I went to bed.

[*Gives him the letter.*]

BRU. Get you to bed again. It is not day.
Is not tomorrow, boy, the ides of March? 40
LUC. I know not, sir.
BRU. Look in the calendar and bring me word.

Act II, Sc. i: **7. taper:** candle. **10. his death:** i.e., Caesar's. **12. general:** general good. **15. craves:** demands. **19. Remorse:** pity. **20. affections:** feelings. **21. proof:** experience. **26. degrees:** steps. **28. prevent:** forestall. **29. bear . . . color:** cannot be justified. **30. Fashion . . . thus:** regard it in this way. **35. closet:** small private room. **36. flint:** used to make a light.

LUC. I will, sir.   [*Exit.*]
BRU. The exhalations° whizzing in the air
Give so much light that I may read by them. 45

[*Opens the letter and reads.*]

" Brutus, thou sleep'st. Awake and see thyself.
Shall Rome, &c.° Speak, strike, redress."
" Brutus, thou sleep'st. Awake."
Such instigations have been often dropped
Where I have took them up. 50
" Shall Rome, &c." Thus must I piece it out —
Shall Rome stand under one man's awe? What, Rome?
My ancestors did from the streets of Rome
The Tarquin drive, when he was called a king.
" Speak, strike, redress." Am I entreated 55
To speak and strike? O Rome, I make thee promise,
If the redress will follow, thou receivest
Thy full petition at the hand of Brutus!

[*Re-enter* LUCIUS.]

LUC. Sir, March is wasted fifteen days. 59

[*Knocking within.*]

BRU. 'Tis good. Go to the gate. Somebody knocks.

[*Exit* LUCIUS.]

Since Cassius first did whet me against Caesar
I have not slept.
Between the acting of a dreadful thing
And the first motion, all the interim is
Like a phantasma or a hideous dream.° 65
The Genius and the mortal instruments
Are then in council, and the state of man,
Like to a little kingdom, suffers then
The nature of an insurrection.°

[*Re-enter* LUCIUS.]

LUC. Sir, 'tis your brother° Cassius at the door,
Who doth desire to see you.
BRU.   Is he alone? 71
LUC. No, sir, there are moe° with him.
BRU.   Do you know them?
LUC. No, sir. Their hats° are plucked about their ears,
And half their faces buried in their cloaks,
That by no means I may discover them 75
By any mark of favor.
BRU.   Let 'em enter. [*Exit* LUCIUS.]
They are the faction.° O Conspiracy,
Shamest thou to show thy dangerous brow by night,
When evils are most free? Oh, then by day

---

44. exhalations: meteors. **47. Rome, &c.:** as the actor would be supplied with the letter from which he reads, there was no need for Shakespeare to include it in the manuscript. **63–65. Between . . . dream:** the interval between the first idea and the dreadful deed itself is like a hideous apparition or a nightmare. **66–69. Genius . . . insurrection:** the mind (*genius*) and body (*mortal instruments*), and a man's whole nature, are then like a kingdom in a state of civil war. **70. brother:** brother-in-law. **72. moe:** more. **73. hats:** Caesar's Romans in this play all wear Elizabethan costumes — doublets, nightgowns, cloaks, and wide-brimmed hats. This is one of several anachronisms in the play. **77. the faction:** of the party.

Where wilt thou find a cavern dark enough   80
To mask thy monstrous visage? Seek none, Con-
    spiracy —
Hide it in smiles and affability.
For if thou path, thy native semblance **on**,°
Not Erebus° itself were dim enough
To hide thee from prevention.°   85
  [*Enter the conspirators,* CASSIUS, CASCA, DECIUS,
    CINNA, METELLUS CIMBER, *and* TREBONIUS.]
  CASS. I think we are too bold upon your rest.
Good morrow, Brutus. Do we trouble you?
  BRU. I have been up this hour, awake all night.
Know I these men that come along with you?
  CASS. Yes, every man of them, and no man here
But honors you, and every one doth wish   91
You had but that opinion of yourself
Which every noble Roman bears of you.
This is Trebonius.
  BRU.   He is welcome hither.
  CASS. This, Decius Brutus.
  BRU.   He is welcome too. 95
  CASS. This, Casca, this, Cinna, and this, Metellus
    Cimber.
  BRU. They are all welcome.
What watchful cares do interpose themselves
Betwixt your eyes and night?   99
  CASS. Shall I entreat a word?   [*They whisper.*]
  DEC. Here lies the east. Doth not the day break
    here?
  CASC. No.
  CIN. Oh, pardon, sir, it doth, and yon gray lines
That fret° the clouds are messengers of day.
  CASC. You shall confess that you are both de-
    ceived.
Here, as I point my sword, the sun arises,   106
Which is a great way growing on the south,
Weighing the youthful season of the year.°
Some two months hence up higher toward the north
He first presents his fire, and the high° east   110
Stands as the Capitol,° directly here.
  BRU. Give me your hands all over, one by one.
  CASS. And let us swear our resolution.
  BRU. No, not an oath. If not the face of men,
The sufferance° of our souls, the time's abuse —
If these be motives weak, break off betimes,°   116
And every man hence to his idle bed.
So let high-sighted° tyranny range on°
Till each man drop by lottery.° But if these,
As I am sure they do, bear fire enough   120
To kindle cowards and to steel with valor

The melting spirits of women, then, countrymen,
What need we any spur but our own cause
To prick° us to redress? What other bond
Than secret Romans that have spoke the word,   125
And will not palter?° And what other oath
Than honesty to honesty engaged°
That this shall be or we will fall for it?
Swear priests and cowards and men cautelous,°
Old feeble carrions° and such suffering souls   130
That welcome wrongs; unto bad causes swear
Such creatures as men doubt; but do not stain
The even° virtue of our enterprise,
Nor the insuppressive mettle of our spirits,
To think that or our cause or° our performance
Did need an oath when every drop of blood   136
That every Roman bears, and nobly bears,
Is guilty of a several bastardy
If he do break the smallest particle
Of any promise that hath passed from him.   140
  CASS. But what of Cicero? Shall we sound him?
I think he will stand very strong with us.
  CASC. Let us not leave him out.
  CIN.   No, by no means.
  MET. Oh, let us have him, for his silver hairs
Will purchase us a good opinion,   145
And buy men's voices to commend our deeds.
It shall be said his judgment ruled our hands.
Our youths and wildness shall no whit appear,
But all be buried in his gravity.
  BRU. Oh, name him not. Let us not break with
    him,°   150
For he will never follow anything
That other men begin.
  CASS.   Then leave him **out**.
  CASC. Indeed he is not fit.
  DEC. Shall no man else be touched but only Cae-
    sar?
  CASS. Decius, well urged.° I think it is not meet
Mark Antony, so well beloved of Caesar,   156
Should outlive Caesar. We shall find of him
A shrewd contriver;° and you know his means,
If he improve them, may well stretch so far
As to annoy° us all. Which to prevent,   160
Let Antony and Caesar fall together.
  BRU. Our course will seem too bloody, Caius Cas-
    sius,
To cut the head off and then hack the limbs,
Like wrath in death and envy° afterward.
For Antony is but a limb of Caesar.   165
Let us be sacrificers, but not butchers, Caius.
We all stand up against the spirit of Caesar,
And in the spirit of men there is no blood.

---

83. path . . . on: walk openly in your natural guise. **84. Erebus:**
Hell. **85. prevention:** premature discovery. **104. fret:** ornament. **107–08. great . . . year:** in the first quarter of the year
the sun rises south of true east. **110. high:** true. **111. Capitol:**
See I.iii.20,n. The Tower of London also lay due east of the
city. **115. sufferance:** suffering. **116. betimes:** in good time.
118. high-sighted: with proud looks. **range on:** go in search of
prey. **119. lottery:** turn.

124. prick: spur. **126. palter:** play false. **127. engaged:**
pledged. **129. cautelous:** crafty. **130. carrions:** carcasses.
133. even: steadfast. **135. or . . . or:** either . . . or. **150. break
with him:** disclose our plot to him. **155. urged:** brought forward. **158. shrewd contriver:** cunning plotter. **160. annoy:**
harm. **164. envy:** hatred.

Oh, that we then could come by Caesar's spirit,
And not dismember Caesar! But, alas,   170
Caesar must bleed for it! And, gentle friends,
Let's kill him boldly, but not wrathfully.
Let's carve him as a dish fit for the gods,
Not hew him as a carcass fit for hounds.
And let our hearts, as subtle masters do,   175
Stir up their servants to an act of rage
And after seem to chide 'em.° This shall make
Our purpose necessary and not envious,
Which so appearing to the common eyes,
We shall be called purgers, not murderers.   180
And for Mark Antony, think not of him,
For he can do no more than Caesar's arm
When Caesar's head is off.

CASS.   Yet I fear him,°
For in the ingrafted love he bears to Caesar ——

BRU. Alas, good Cassius, do not think of him.
If he love Caesar, all that he can do   186
Is to himself, take thought and die for Caesar.
And that were much he should, for he is given
To sports, to wildness and much company.

TRE. There is no fear° in him. Let him not die,
For he will live and laugh at this hereafter.   191
                              [*Clock strikes.*]

BRU. Peace! Count the clock.°

CASS.   The clock hath stricken three.

TRE. 'Tis time to part.

CASS.   But it is doubtful yet
Whether Caesar will come forth today or no,
For he is superstitious grown of late,   195
Quite from the main° opinion he held once
Of fantasy, of dreams and ceremonies.
It may be these apparent prodigies,°
The unaccustomed terror of this night
And the persuasion of his augurers,°   200
May hold him from the Capitol today.

DEC. Never fear that. If he be so resolved,
I can o'ersway him. For he loves to hear
That unicorns° may be betrayed with trees
And bears with glasses,° elephants with holes,°
Lions with toils° and men with flatterers ——   206
But when I tell him he hates flatterers,
He says he does, being then most flattered.
Let me work,

For I can give his humor the true bent,°   210
And I will bring him to the Capitol.

CASS. Nay, we will all of us be there to fetch him.

BRU. By the eighth hour.° Is that the uttermost?

CIN. Be that the uttermost, and fail not then.

MET. Caius Ligarius doth bear Caesar hard,   215
Who rated° him for speaking well of Pompey.
I wonder none of you have thought of him.

BRU. Now, good Metellus, go along by him.
He loves me well, and I have given him reasons.
Send him but hither and I'll fashion° him.   220

CASS. The morning comes upon 's. We'll leave
you, Brutus.
And friends, disperse yourselves, but all remember
What you have said, and show yourselves true Romans.

BRU. Good gentlemen, look fresh and merrily.
Let not our looks put on our purposes,   225
But bear it as our Roman actors do,
With untired spirits and formal constancy.°
And so, good morrow to you every one.
                              [*Exeunt all but* BRUTUS.]
Boy! Lucius! Fast asleep! It is no matter.
Enjoy the honey-heavy dew of slumber.   230
Thou hast no figures° nor no fantasies
Which busy care draws in the brains of men,
Therefore thou sleep'st so sound.
                              [*Enter* PORTIA.]

POR.   Brutus, my lord!

BRU. Portia, what mean you? Wherefore rise you
now?
It is not for your health thus to commit   235
Your weak condition to the raw cold morning.

POR. Nor for yours neither. You've ungently, Bru-
tus,
Stole from my bed. And yesternight at supper
You suddenly arose and walked about,
Musing and sighing, with your arms across.   240
And when I asked you what the matter was,
You stared upon me with ungentle looks.
I urged you further, then you scratched your head,
And too impatiently stamped with your foot.
Yet I insisted, yet you answered not,   245
But with an angry wafture° of your hand
Gave sign for me to leave you. So I did,
Fearing to strengthen that impatience
Which seemed too much enkindled, and withal
Hoping it was but an effect of humor,°   250
Which sometime hath his hour with every man.
It will not let you eat, nor talk, nor sleep,
And, could it work so much upon your shape
As it hath much prevailed on your condition,

175–77. as . . . 'em: like some masters who first stir up their servants to commit some violence against an enemy and afterward
pretend to be angry.   183. Yet . . . him: It is part of the tragedy of Cassius that he always knows what should be done, but
allows himself to be overruled by Brutus.   190. fear: cause for
fear.   192. clock: There were in fact no striking clocks in
Caesar's time.   196. main: general.   198. apparent prodigies:
evident signs of disaster.   200. augurers: professional interpreters of omens.   204. unicorns: It was believed by some natural historians that the lion defeated the mythical unicorn by
guile. It would stand in front of a tree to provoke the unicorn
to charge, and then slip aside. The unicorn, impaled by its own
horn, thus became an easy prey.   205. glasses: mirrors; i.e.,
the bear, a vain creature, was led into a trap by its desire to look
at itself. holes: pits.   206. toils: nets.

210. give . . . bent: bend his inclination in the right direction.
213. eighth hour: the normal time for starting business in
Shakespeare's London.   216. rated: rebuked.   220. fashion:
mold.   227. formal constancy: outward appearance of stead-
fastness.   231. figures: specters of the imagination.   246. waf-
ture: wave.   250. humor: moodiness.

I should not know you, Brutus. Dear my lord,   255
Make me acquainted with your cause of grief.
  BRU. I am not well in health, and that is all.
  POR. Brutus is wise, and were he not in health,
He would embrace the means to come by it.
  BRU. Why, so I do. Good Portia, go to bed.   260
  POR. Is Brutus sick, and is it physical°
To walk unbraced° and suck up the humors
Of the dank° morning? What, is Brutus sick,
And will he steal out of his wholesome bed
To dare the vile contagion of the night,   265
And tempt the rheumy° and unpurgèd air
To add unto his sickness? No, my Brutus;
You have some sick offense within your mind,
Which by the right and virtue of my place
I ought to know of. And, upon my knees,   270
I charm° you, by my once commended beauty,
By all your vows of love and that great vow
Which did incorporate and make us one,
That you unfold to me, yourself, your half,
Why you are heavy, and what men tonight   275
Have had resort to you; for here have been
Some six or seven who did hide their faces
Even from darkness.
  BRU.   Kneel not, gentle Portia.
  POR. I should not need if you were gentle Brutus.
Within the bond of marriage, tell me, Brutus,   280
Is it excepted I should know no secrets
That appertain to you? Am I yourself
But, as it were, in sort or limitation,°
To keep with you at meals, comfort your bed,
And talk to you sometimes? Dwell I but in the sub-
    urbs°   285
Of your good pleasure? If it be no more,
Portia is Brutus' harlot,° not his wife.
  BRU. You are my true and honorable wife,
As dear to me as are the ruddy drops°
That visit my sad heart.   290
  POR. If this were true, then should I know this
    secret.
I grant I am a woman, but withal
A woman that Lord Brutus took to wife.
I grant I am a woman, but withal
A woman well reputed, Cato's° daughter.   295
Think you I am no stronger than my sex,
Being so fathered and so husbanded?
Tell me your counsels, I will not disclose 'em.
I have made strong proof of my constancy,°
Giving myself a voluntary wound   300

261. physical: good for your health.   262. unbraced: with
your coat open.   263. dank: damp air was believed to be a
cause of sickness.   266. rheumy: liable to cause rheumatism.
271. charm: adjure.   282–83. Am ... limitation: am I your wife
only in a limited way?   285. suburbs: outskirts.   287. harlot:
the London brothels were situated in the suburbs.   289. ruddy
drops: blood.   295. Cato: Marcus Porcius Cato, a man of unusual political honesty, had consistently opposed Caesar. When
Caesar had finally defeated Pompey's armies, Cato killed himself
rather than live under a tyrant.   299. constancy: firmness.

Here in the thigh. Can I bear that with patience
And not my husband's secrets?
  BRU.   O ye gods.
Render me worthy of this noble wife!
                      [*Knocking within.*]
Hark, hark! One knocks. Portia, go in a while,
And by and by thy bosom shall partake   305
The secrets of my heart.
All my engagements I will construe to thee,
All the cháractery° of my sad brows.
Leave me with haste. [*Exit* PORTIA.] Lucius, who's
    that knocks?
       [*Re-enter* LUCIUS *with* LIGARIUS.]
  LUC. Here is a sick man that would speak with
    you.   310
  BRU. Caius Ligarius, that Metellus spake of.
Boy, stand aside. Caius Ligarius! How?
  LIG. Vouchsafe good morrow from a feeble
    tongue.
  BRU. Oh, what a time have you chose out, brave
    Caius,
To wear a kerchief!° Would you were not sick!   315
  LIG. I am not sick if Brutus have in hand
Any exploit worthy the name of honor.
  BRU. Such an exploit have I in hand, Ligarius,
Had you a healthful ear to hear of it.
  LIG. By all the gods that Romans bow before,
I here discard my sickness! Soul of Rome!   321
Brave son, derived from honorable loins!
Thou, like an exorcist,° hast conjured up
My mortified° spirit. Now bid me run,
And I will strive with things impossible,   325
Yea, get the better of them. What's to do?
  BRU. A piece of work that will make sick men
    whole.
  LIG. But are not some whole that we must make
    sick?
  BRU. That must we also. What it is, my Caius,
I shall unfold to thee as we are going   330
To whom it must be done.
  LIG.   Set on your foot,
And with a heart new-fired I follow you,
To do I know not what, but it sufficeth
That Brutus leads me on.
  BRU.   Follow me, then.   [*Exeunt.*]

SCENE II. CAESAR'S *house.*

[*Thunder and lightning. Enter* CAESAR, *in his nightgown.*°]

  CAE. Nor Heaven nor earth have been at peace to-
    night.
Thrice hath Calpurnia in her sleep cried out,

308. cháractery: that which is written in my face.   315. kerchief: muffler, as worn by an invalid.   323. exorcist: one who
summons the spirits of the dead.   324. mortified: dead.
    Sc. ii: s.d., nightgown: dressing gown.

" Help, ho! They murder Caesar! " Who's within?
　　　　　[*Enter a* SERVANT.]
SERV. My lord?
CAE. Go bid the priests do present° sacrifice,　5
And bring me their opinions of success.
SERV. I will, my lord.　　　　　　　[*Exit.*]
　　　　　[*Enter* CALPURNIA.]
CAL. What mean you, Caesar? Think you to walk
　forth?
You shall not stir out of your house today.
CAE. Caesar shall forth.° The things that threat-
　ened me　　　　　　　　　　　　　10
Ne'er looked but on my back. When they shall see
The face of Caesar, they are vanishèd.
CAL. Caesar, I never stood on ceremonies,°
Yet now they fright me. There is one within,
Besides the things that we have heard and seen,　15
Recounts most horrid sights seen by the watch.°
A lioness hath whelpèd° in the streets.
And graves have yawned and yielded up their dead.
Fierce fiery warriors fight upon the clouds,
In ranks and squadrons and right form of war,　20
Which drizzled blood upon the Capitol.
The noise of battle hurtled in the air,
Horses did neigh and dying men did groan,
And ghosts did shriek and squeal about the streets.
O Caesar! these things are beyond all use,°　25
And I do fear them.
CAE.　　　　　　What can be avoided
Whose end is purposed by the mighty gods?
Yet Caesar shall go forth, for these predictions
Are to the world in general as to Caesar.　29
CAL. When beggars die, there are no comets° seen.
The heavens themselves blaze forth the death of
　princes.
CAE. Cowards die many times before their deaths,
The valiant never taste of death but once.
Of all the wonders that I yet have heard,
It seems to me most strange that men should fear,
Seeing that death, a necessary end,
Will come when it will come.　　　　　36
　　　　　[*Re-enter* SERVANT.]
　　　　　　　What say the augurers?
SERV. They would not have you to stir forth to-
　day.
Plucking the entrails of an offering° forth,
They could not find a heart within the beast.　40
CAE. The gods do this in shame of cowardice.
Caesar should be a beast without a heart

If he should stay at home today for fear.
No, Caesar shall not. Danger knows full well
That Caesar is more dangerous than he.　　45
We are two lions littered in one day,
And I the elder and more terrible.
And Caesar shall go forth.
CAL.　　　　　　　　Alas, my lord,
Your wisdom is consumed in confidence.°
Do not go forth today. Call it my fear　　50
That keeps you in the house, and not your own.
We'll send Mark Antony to the Senate House,
And he shall say you are not well today.
Let me, upon my knee, prevail in this.
CAE. Mark Antony shall say I am not well,　55
And, for thy humor,° I will stay at home.
　　　　　[*Enter* DECIUS.]
Here's Decius Brutus. He shall tell them so.
DEC. Caesar, all hail! Good morrow, worthy Cae-
　sar.
I come to fetch you to the Senate House.
CAE. And you are come in very happy time,　60
To bear my greeting to the Senators
And tell them that I will not come today.
Cannot is false, and that I dare not, falser —
I will not come today. Tell them so, Decius.
CAL. Say he is sick.
CAE.　　　　　　Shall Caesar send a lie?　65
Have I in conquest stretched mine arm so far,
To be afeared to tell graybeards the truth?
Decius, go tell them Caesar will not come.
DEC. Most mighty Caesar, let me know some
　cause,
Lest I be laughed at when I tell them so.　70
CAE. The cause is in my will — I will not come.
That is enough to satisfy the Senate.
But, for your private satisfaction,
Because I love you, I will let you know.
Calpurnia here, my wife, stays me at home.　75
She dreamt tonight she saw my statuë,°
Which like a fountain with a hundred spouts
Did run pure blood, and many lusty Romans
Came smiling and did bathe their hands in it.
And these does she apply for warnings and portents
And evils imminent, and on her knee　　81
Hath begged that I will stay at home today.
DEC. This dream is all amiss interpreted.
It was a vision fair and fortunate.
Your statue spouting blood in many pipes,　85
In which so many smiling Romans bathed,
Signifies that from you great Rome shall suck
Reviving blood, and that great men shall press
For tinctures, stains, relics, and cognizance.°

---

5. present: immediate.　10. Caesar . . . forth: It was typical of
stage tyrants in Elizabethan drama to talk pompously of themselves in the third person.　13. stood . . . ceremonies: paid much
attention to omens.　16. watch: See Gen. Intro. p. 18a.
17. whelped: dropped its young.　25. use: custom.　30. comets:
comets were always regarded as portents of great disasters.
39. offering: sacrifice. Roman augurers had several methods of
divining the future. Any abnormality in the beast killed for sacrifice was regarded as highly significant.

49. confidence: overconfidence.　56. humor: whim.　76. statue:
here pronounced as three syllables.　88–89. great . . . cognizance: Decius interprets the dream in a double sense. To Caesar
he implies that men shall seek honors from him in the form of
coats of arms and badges signifying that they are his personal
servants. To the audience the meaning of his speech is that men

This by Calpurnia's dream is signified.   90
  CAE. And this way have you well expounded it.
  DEC. I have, when you have heard what I can say.
And know it now — the Senate have concluded
To give this day a crown to mighty Caesar.
If you shall send them word you will not come,   95
Their minds may change. Besides, it were a mock
Apt to be rendered,° for someone to say
" Break up the Senate till another time,
When Caesar's wife shall meet with better dreams."
If Caesar hide himself, shall they not whisper   100
" Lo, Caesar is afraid "?
Pardon me, Caesar, for my dear dear love
To your proceeding bids me tell you this,
And reason to my love is liable.
  CAE. How foolish do your fears seem now, Cal-
    purnia!   105
I am ashamèd I did yield to them.
Give me my robe, for I will go.
[*Enter* PUBLIUS, BRUTUS, LIGARIUS, METELLUS, CASCA,
    TREBONIUS, *and* CINNA.]
And look where Publius is come to fetch me.
  PUB. Good morrow, Caesar.
  CAE.   Welcome, Publius.
What, Brutus, are you stirred so early too?   110
Good morrow, Casca. Caius Ligarius,
Caesar was ne'er so much your enemy
As that same ague which hath made you lean.
What is 't o'clock?
  BRU.   Caesar, 'tis strucken° eight.
  CAE. I thank you for your pains and courtesy.
             [*Enter* ANTONY.]
See! Antony, that revels long o' nights,   116
Is notwithstanding up. Good morrow, Antony.
  ANT. So to most noble Caesar.
  CAE.   Bid them prepare within.
I am to blame to be thus waited for.
Now, Cinna, now, Metellus. What, Trebonius!
I have an hour's talk in store for you.   121
Remember that you call on me today.
Be near me, that I may remember you.
  TRE. Caesar, I will. [*Aside*] And so near will I be
That your best friends shall wish I had been fur-
    ther.   125
  CAE. Good friends, go in and taste some wine
    with me,
And we like friends will straightway go together.
  BRU. [*Aside*] That every like is not the same, O
    Caesar,
The heart of Brutus yearns° to think upon!
                  [*Exeunt.*]

SCENE III. *A street near the Capitol.*

      [*Enter* ARTEMIDORUS, *reading a paper.*]
  ART. " Caesar, beware of Brutus; take heed of Cas-
sius; come not near Casca; have an eye to Cinna;
trust not Trebonius; mark well Metellus Cimber;
Decius Brutus loves thee not; thou hast wronged
Caius Ligarius. There is but one mind in all   5
these men, and it is bent against Caesar. If thou be-
est not immortal, look about you. Security° gives
way to conspiracy. The mighty gods defend thee!
          " Thy lover, ARTEMIDORUS."
Here will I stand till Caesar pass along,   11
And as a suitor° will I give him this.
My heart laments that virtue cannot live
Out of the teeth of emulation.°
If thou read this, O Caesar, thou mayst live;   15
If not, the Fates with traitors do contrive.°   [*Exit.*]

SCENE IV. *Another part of the same street,
before the house of* BRUTUS.

    [*Enter* PORTIA *and* LUCIUS.]
  POR. I prithee, boy, run to the Senate House.
Stay not to answer me, but get thee gone.
Why dost thou stay?
  LUC.   To know my errand, madam.
  POR. I would have had thee there, and here again,
Ere I can tell thee what thou shouldst do there.   5
O Constancy, be strong upon my side!
Set a huge mountain 'tween my heart and tongue!
I have a man's mind, but a woman's might.
How hard it is for women to keep counsel!
Art thou here yet?
  LUC.   Madam, what should I do?   10
Run to the Capitol, and nothing else?
And so return to you, and nothing else?
  POR. Yes, bring me word, boy, if thy lord look
    well,
For he went sickly forth. And take good note
What Caesar doth, what suitors press to him.   15
Hark, boy! What noise is that?
  LUC. I hear none, madam.
  POR.   Prithee,° listen well.
I heard a bustling rumor° like a fray,
And the wind brings it from the Capitol.
  LUC. Sooth, madam, I hear nothing.
         [*Enter the* SOOTHSAYER.]
  POR.   Come hither, fellow.   20
Which way hast thou been?
  SOOTH.   At mine own house, good lady.

---

will preserve relics of his death. It was a custom to dip handker-
chiefs in the blood of those executed for their religious principles.
These relics were highly valued. **tincture:** stain, but in heraldic
language a coat of arms. **cognizance:** badge worn by a great
man's servant; also "token." **96–97. mock . . . rendered:** jibe
likely to be made. **114. strucken:** struck. **129. yearns:** grieves.
    Sc. iii: 7. Security: carelessness.   **12. suitor:** petitioner.
13–14. virtue . . . emulation: i.e., envy (*emulation*) always gets
its teeth into goodness.   **16. contrive:** plot.
    Sc. iv: 17. Prithee: I pray thee.   **18. bustling rumor:** indis-
tinct noise.

POR. What is 't o'clock?

SOOTH.   About the ninth hour, lady.

POR. Is Caesar yet gone to the Capitol?

SOOTH. Madam, not yet. I go to take my stand   25
To see him pass on to the Capitol.

POR. Thou hast some suit to Caesar, hast thou
    not?

SOOTH. That I have, lady. If it will please Caesar
To be so good to Caesar as to hear me,
I shall beseech him to befriend himself.   30

POR. Why, know'st thou any harm's intended to-
    ward him?

SOOTH. None that I know will be, much that I
    fear may chance.
Good morrow to you. Here the street is narrow,
The throng that follows Caesar at the heels,
Of Senators, of praetors, common suitors,   35
Will crowd a feeble man almost to death.
I'll get me to a place more void,° and there
Speak to great Caesar as he comes along.   [*Exit.*]

POR. I must go in. Aye me, how weak a thing
The heart of women is! O Brutus,   40
The heavens speed° thee in thine enterprise!
Sure, the boy heard me. Brutus hath a suit
That Caesar will not grant. Oh, I grow faint.
Run, Lucius, and commend me to my lord.
Say I am merry. Come to me again,   45
And bring me word what he doth say to thee.

                    [*Exeunt severally.*°]

Act III

SCENE I. *Rome. Before the Capitol; the Senate sitting above.*

[*A crowd of people; among them* ARTEMIDORUS *and
the* SOOTHSAYER. *Flourish. Enter* CAESAR, BRUTUS, CAS-
SIUS, CASCA, DECIUS, METELLUS, TREBONIUS, CINNA;
ANTONY, LEPIDUS, POPILIUS, PUBLIUS, *and others.*]

CAE. The ides of March are come.

SOOTH. Aye, Caesar, but not gone.

ART. Hail, Caesar! Read this schedule.°

DEC. Trebonius doth desire you to o'erread,
At your best leisure, this his humble suit.   5

ART. O Caesar, read mine first, for mine's a suit
That touches Caesar nearer. Read it, great Caesar.

CAE. What touches us ourself shall be last served.

ART. Delay not, Caesar. Read it instantly.

CAE. What, is the fellow mad?

PUB.   Sirrah,° give place.   10

CASS. What, urge you your petitions in the street?
Come to the Capitol.

[*Caesar goes up to the Senate House, the rest following.*]

POP. I wish your enterprise today may thrive.

CASS. What enterprise, Popilius?

POP.   Fare you well. [*Advances to* CAESAR.]

BRU. What said Popilius Lena?   15

CASS. He wished today our enterprise might
    thrive.
I fear our purpose is discovered.

BRU. Look how he makes to° Caesar. Mark him.

CASS.   Casca,
Be sudden, for we fear prevention.
Brutus, what shall be done? If this be known,   20
Cassius or Caesar never shall turn back,
For I will slay myself.

BRU.   Cassius, be constant.
Popilius Lena speaks not of our purposes,
For look, he smiles and Caesar doth not change.

CASS. Trebonius knows his time, for look you,
    Brutus,   25
He draws Mark Antony out of the way.

                    [*Exeunt* ANTONY *and* TREBONIUS.]

DEC. Where is Metellus Cimber? Let him go,
And presently prefer his suit to Caesar.

BRU. He is addressed. Press near and second him.

CIN. Casca, you are the first that rears your hand.

CAE. Are we all ready? What is now amiss   31
That Caesar and his Senate must redress?

MET. Most high, most mighty, and most puissant
    Caesar,
Metellus Cimber throws before thy seat
A humble heart ——   [*Kneeling.*]

CAE.   I must prevent thee, Cimber.   35
These couchings° and these lowly° courtesies
Might fire the blood of ordinary men,
And turn preordinance and first decree
Into the law of children.° Be not fond,°
To think that Caesar bears such rebel blood   40
That will be thawed from the true quality
With that which melteth fools — I mean sweet
    words,
Low-crookèd° curtsies, and base spaniel fawning.
Thy brother by decree is banished.
If thou dost bend and pray and fawn for him,   45
I spurn thee like a cur out of my way.
Know, Caesar doth not wrong, nor without cause
Will he be satisfied.

MET. Is there no voice more worthy than my own,
To sound more sweetly in great Caesar's ear   50
For the repealing° of my banished brother?

BRU. I kiss thy hand, but not in flattery, Caesar,

---

37. void: empty.   41. speed: help.   46. s.d., severally: by
different exits.

Act III, Sc. i: 3. schedule: paper.   10. Sirrah: term of address
used to an inferior.

18. makes to: goes toward.   36. couchings: low bowings. lowly:
humble.   38–39. And . . . children: i.e., my will has the force of
that which was ordained from the first, and does not change
capriciously, like the will of a child.   39. fond: foolish.
43. Low-crooked: bending low.   51. repealing: recalling.

Desiring thee that Publius Cimber may
Have an immediate freedom of repeal.

CAE. What, Brutus!

CASS.   Pardon, Caesar, Caesar, pardon.   55
As low as to thy foot doth Cassius fall,
To beg enfranchisement° for Publius Cimber.

CAE. I could be well moved, if I were as you.
If I could pray to move, prayers would move me;
But I am constant as the Northern Star.   60
Of whose true-fixed and resting quality
There is no fellow° in the firmament.
The skies are painted with unnumbered° sparks,
They are all fire, and every one doth shine,
But there's but one in all doth hold his place.   65
So in the world. 'Tis furnished well with men,
And men are flesh and blood, and apprehensive;°
Yet in the number I do know but one
That unassailable holds on his rank,
Unshaked of motion. And that I am he,   70
Let me a little show it, even in this,
That I was constant Cimber should be banished,
And constant do remain to keep him so.

CIN. O Caesar ——

CAE.   Hence! Wilt thou lift up Olympus?

DEC. Great Caesar ——

CAE.   Doth not Brutus bootless° kneel?   75

CASC. Speak, hands, for me!

    [CASCA *first, then the other conspira-
    tors and* MARCUS BRUTUS *stab* CAESAR.]

CAE. *Et tu, Brute?* Then fall, Caesar!   [*Dies.*]

CIN. Liberty! Freedom! Tyranny is dead!
Run hence, proclaim, cry it about the streets.

CASS. Some to the common pulpits, and cry out
" Liberty, freedom, and enfranchisement! "   81

BRU. People, and Senators, be not affrighted.
Fly not, stand still. Ambition's debt is paid.

CASC. Go to the pulpit, Brutus.

DEC.   And Cassius too.

BRU. Where's Publius?   85

CIN. Here, quite confounded with this mutiny.

MET. Stand fast together, lest some friend of Cae-
    sar's

Should chance ——

BRU. Talk not of standing. Publius, good cheer.
There is no harm intended to your person,   90
Nor to no Roman else. So tell them, Publius.

CASS. And leave us, Publius, lest that the people
Rushing on us should do your age some mischief.

BRU. Do so, and let no man abide° this deed
But we the doers.

    [*Re-enter* TREBONIUS.]

CASS.   Where is Antony?   95

TRE. Fled to his house amazed.
Men, wives, and children stare, cry out, and run

As it were Doomsday.°

BRU.   Fates, we will know your pleasures.
That we shall die, we know; 'tis but the time,
And drawing days out, that men stand upon.°   100

CASC. Why, he that cuts off twenty years of life
Cuts off so many years of fearing death.

BRU. Grant that, and then is death a benefit.
So are we Caesar's friends that have abridged
His time of fearing death. Stoop, Romans, stoop,
And let us bathe our hands in Caesar's blood   106
Up to the elbows, and besmear our swords.
Then walk we forth, even to the market place,
And waving our red weapons o'er our heads,
Let's all cry " Peace, freedom, and liberty! "   110

CASS. Stoop then, and wash. How many ages hence
Shall this our lofty scene be acted over
In states unborn and accents yet unknown!

BRU. How many times shall Caesar bleed in
    sport,°
That now on Pompey's basis° lies along°   115
No worthier than the dust!

CASS.   So oft as that shall be,
So often shall the knot° of us be called
The men that gave their country liberty.

DEC. What, shall we forth?

CASS.   Aye, every man away.
Brutus shall lead, and we will grace his heels   120
With the most boldest and best hearts of Rome.

    [*Enter a* SERVANT.]

BRU. Soft! Who comes here? A friend of An-
    tony's.

SERV. Thus, Brutus, did my master bid me kneel,
Thus did Mark Antony bid me fall down,
And, being prostrate, thus he bade me say: 125
Brutus is noble, wise, valiant, and honest,
Caesar was mighty, bold, royal, and loving.
Say I love Brutus and I honor him,
Say I feared Caesar, honored him, and loved him.
If Brutus will vouchsafe that Antony   130
May safely come to him and be resolved°
How Caesar hath deserved to lie in death,
Mark Antony shall not love Caesar dead
So well as Brutus living, but will follow
The fortunes and affairs of noble Brutus   135
Thorough° the hazards of this untrod state°
With all true faith. So says my master Antony.

BRU. Thy master is a wise and valiant Roman —
I never thought him worse.
Tell him, so please him come unto this place,   140
He shall be satisfied and, by my honor,
Depart untouched.

SERV.   I'll fetch him presently.°   [*Exit.*]

98. Doomsday: the Day of Judgment.   100. stand upon: trouble
themselves with.   114. in sport: for entertainment, i.e., in
dramas.   115. Pompey's basis: the base of Pompey's statue.
along: stretched out.   117. knot: bunch, party.   131. resolved:
freed from doubts.   136. Thorough: through. untrod state:
uncertain future.   142. presently: immediately.

57. enfranchisement: release.   62. fellow: equal.   63. unnumbered: innumerable.   67. apprehensive: quick-witted.   75. bootless: in vain.   94. abide: pay the penalty for.

BRU. I know that we shall have him well to
friend.°
CASS. I wish we may, but yet have I a mind
That fears him much, and my misgiving still   145
Falls shrewdly to the purpose.°
              [*Re-enter* ANTONY.]
   BRU. But here comes Antony. Welcome, Mark
Antony.
   ANT. O mighty Caesar, dost thou lie so low?
Are all thy conquests, glories, triumphs, spoils,
Shrunk to this little measure? Fare thee well.   150
I know not, gentlemen, what you intend,
Who else must be let blood, who else is rank.°
If I myself, there is no hour so fit
As Caesar's death's hour, nor no instrument
Of half that worth as those your swords, made rich
With the most noble blood of all this world.   156
I do beseech ye, if you bear me hard,
Now, whilst your purpled hands do reek° and
smoke,
Fulfill your pleasure. Live a thousand years,
I shall not find myself so apt to die.   160
No place will please me so, no mean° of death,
As here by Caesar, and by you cut off,
The choice and master spirits of this age.
   BRU. O Antony, beg not your death of us.
Though now we must appear bloody and cruel,
As by our hands and this our present act   166
You see we do. Yet see you but our hands
And this the bleeding business they have done.
Our hearts you see not. They are pitiful,
And pity to the general wrong of Rome —   170
As fire drives out fire, so pity pity —
Hath done this deed on Caesar. For your part,
To you our swords have leaden° points, Mark An-
tony.
Our arms in strength of malice,° and our hearts
Of brothers' temper, do receive you in   175
With all kind love, good thoughts, and reverence.
   CASS. Your voice shall be as strong as any man's
In the disposing of new dignities.°
   BRU. Only be patient till we have appeased
The multitude, beside themselves with fear,   180
And then we will deliver you the cause
Why I, that did love Caesar when I struck him,
Have thus proceeded.
   ANT.   I doubt not of your wisdom.
Let each man render° me his bloody hand.
First, Marcus Brutus, will I shake with you.   185

Next, Caius Cassius, do I take your hand.
Now, Decius Brutus, yours, now yours, Metellus;
Yours, Cinna, and, my valiant Casca, yours —
Though last, not least in love, yours, good Trebo-
nius.
Gentlemen all — alas, what shall I say?   190
My credit now stands on such slippery ground
That one of two bad ways you must conceit° me,
Either a coward or a flatterer.
That I did love thee, Caesar, oh, 'tis true.
If then thy spirit look upon us now,   195
Shall it not grieve thee dearer than thy death
To see thy Antony making his peace,
Shaking the bloody fingers of thy foes,
Most noble! in the presence of thy corse?°
Had I as many eyes as thou hast wounds,   200
Weeping as fast as they stream forth thy blood,
It would become me better than to close
In terms of friendship with thine enemies.
Pardon me, Julius! Here wast thou bayed,° brave
hart,   204
Here didst thou fall, and here thy hunters stand,
Signed in thy spoil° and crimsoned in thy lethe.°
O world, thou wast the forest to this hart,
And this, indeed, O world, the heart of thee.
How like a deer strucken by many princes
Dost thou here lie!   210
   CASS. Mark Antony ——
   ANT.   Pardon me, Caius Cassius.
The enemies of Caesar shall say this;
Then, in a friend, it is cold modesty.
   CASS. I blame you not for praising Caesar so,
But what compact mean you to have with us?   215
Will you be pricked in number° of our friends,
Or shall we on, and not depend on you?
   ANT. Therefore I took your hands, but was indeed
Swayed from the point by looking down on Caesar.
Friends am I with you all and love you all,   220
Upon this hope that you shall give me reasons
Why and wherein Caesar was dangerous.
   BRU. Or else were this a savage spectacle.
Our reasons are so full of good regard
That were you, Antony, the son of Caesar,   225
You should be satisfied.
   ANT.   That's all I seek.
And am moreover suitor that I may
Produce his body to the market place,
And in the pulpit, as becomes a friend,
Speak in the order of his funeral.   230
   BRU. You shall, Mark Antony.
   CASS.   Brutus, a word with you.
[*Aside to* BRUTUS] You know not what you do. Do
not consent

---

143. well . . . friend: as a good friend.   **146. Falls . . . purpose:**
I am highly (*shrewdly*) disturbed at your proposal.   **152. rank:**
medical term, meaning in a state requiring bloodletting. Period-
ical bloodletting was considered good for the general health.
158. reek: steam.   **161. mean:** means.   **173. leaden:** blunt.
174. in . . . malice: having the power to do harm.   **178. disposing . . . dignities:** Brutus offers Antony fine sentiments. Cassius,
knowing his man better, proposes a share in the loot.   **184. render:** offer.

192. conceit: conceive, imagine.   **199. corse:** corpse.   **204. bayed:**
brought to bay; i.e., surrounded by baying hounds and unable
to escape. Antony uses the metaphors of hunting the deer.
206. Signed . . . spoil: stained with your slaughter (*spoil*). **lethe:**
blood.   **216. pricked . . . number:** marked in the list.

That Antony speak in his funeral.
Know you how much the people may be moved
By that which he will utter?
    BRU.   By your pardon,   235
I will myself into the pulpit first,
And show the reason of our Caesar's death.
What Antony shall speak, I will protest
He speaks by leave and by permission,
And that we are contented Caesar shall   240
Have all true rites and lawful ceremonies.
It shall advantage more than do us wrong.
    CASS. I know not what may fall. I like it not.
    BRU. Mark Antony, here, take you Caesar's body.
You shall not in your funeral speech blame us,   245
But speak all good you can devise of Caesar,
And say you do 't by our permission,
Else shall you not have any hand at all
About his funeral. And you shall speak
In the same pulpit whereto I am going —   250
After my speech is ended.
    ANT.   Be it so.
I do desire no more.
    BRU. Prepare the body then, and follow us.
                      [*Exeunt all but* ANTONY.]
    ANT. O, pardon me, thou bleeding piece of earth,
That I am meek and gentle with these butchers!
Thou art the ruins of the noblest man   256
That ever livèd in the tide of times.
Woe to the hand that shed this costly blood!
Over thy wounds now do I prophesy,
Which like dumb mouths do ope° their ruby lips
To beg the voice and utterance of my tongue,   261
A curse shall light upon the limbs of men.
Domestic fury and fierce civil strife
Shall cumber all the parts of Italy.
Blood and destruction shall be so in use,   265
And dreadful objects so familiar,
That mothers shall but smile when they behold
Their infants quartered with° the hands of war,
All pity choked with custom of fell deeds.°
And Caesar's spirit ranging° for revenge,   270
With Até° by his side come hot from Hell,
Shall in these confines° with a monarch's voice
Cry " Havoc,"° and let slip the dogs of war,
That this foul deed shall smell above the earth
With carrion men, groaning for burial.   275
                 [*Enter a* SERVANT.]
You serve Octavius Caesar,° do you not?
    SERV. I do, Mark Antony.
    ANT. Caesar did write for him to come to Rome.
    SERV. He did receive his letters, and is coming,

And bid me say to you by word of mouth ——   280
[*Seeing the body*] O Caesar!
    ANT. Thy heart is big.° Get thee apart and weep.
Passion,° I see, is catching, for mine eyes,
Seeing those beads of sorrow stand in thine,
Began to water. Is thy master coming?   285
    SERV. He lies tonight within seven leagues of
    Rome.
    ANT. Post back with speed, and tell him what
    hath chanced.
Here is a mourning Rome, a dangerous Rome,
No Rome of safety for Octavius yet.
Hie hence, and tell him so. Yet stay awhile.   290
Thou shalt not back till I have borne this corse
Into the market place. There shall I try,°
In my oration, how the people take
The cruel issue° of these bloody men,
According to the which, thou shalt discourse   295
To young Octavius of the state of things.
Lend me your hand.   [*Exeunt with* CAESAR's *body.*]

SCENE II. *The Forum.*

[*Enter* BRUTUS *and* CASSIUS, *and a throng of*
CITIZENS.]
    CITS. We will be satisfied. Let us be satisfied.
    BRU. Then follow me, and give me audience,
    friends.
Cassius, go you into the other street,
And part° the numbers.
Those that will hear me speak, let 'em stay here,   5
Those that will follow Cassius, go with him,
And public reasons shall be rendered
Of Caesar's death.
    1. CIT.   I will hear Brutus speak.
    2. CIT. I will hear Cassius, and compare their rea-
    sons
When severally we hear them rendered.   10
         [*Exit* CASSIUS, *with some of the* CITIZENS.]
         [BRUTUS *goes into the pulpit.*]
    3. CIT. The noble Brutus is ascended. Silence!
    BRU. Be patient till the last.
Romans, countrymen,° and lovers! Hear me for my
cause, and be silent, that you may hear. Believe me
for mine honor, and have respect to mine honor,   15
that you may believe. Censure° me in your wisdom,
and awake your senses, that you may the better
judge. If there be any in this assembly, any dear
friend of Caesar's, to him I say that Brutus' love to

---

260. ope: open.   268. quartered with: cut in pieces by.   269. All
... deeds: i.e., cruel (*fell*) deeds will be so common that men
will no longer feel pity.   270. ranging: roaming like a beast of
prey.   271. Até: goddess of mischief.   272. confines: boundaries; i.e., this country.   273. Cry "Havoc": no quarter! — no
prisoners will be taken.   276. Octavius Caesar: Octavius, who
ultimately became the Emperor Augustus, was the grandson of

Julius Caesar's sister Julia and was adopted by Caesar as his
heir.   282. big: swollen with emotion.   283. Passion: emotion.
292. try: test.   294. issue: action.
Sc. ii: 4. part: divide.   13. Romans, countrymen: See *Caesar*
Intro. p. 813a. Shakespeare uses prose for Brutus's speech to denote his "dry" style of speaking. Verse is the natural medium
for Antony's emotional outburst.   16. Censure: judge.

Caesar was no less than his. If then that friend   20
demand why Brutus rose against Caesar, this is my
answer — not that I loved Caesar less, but that I
loved Rome more. Had you rather Caesar were living, and die all slaves, than that Caesar were dead,
to live all freemen? As Caesar loved me, I weep   25
for him; as he was fortunate, I rejoice at it; as he was
valiant, I honor him. But as he was ambitious, I slew
him. There is tears for his love, joy for his fortune,
honor for his valor, and death for his ambition. Who
is here so base that would be a bondman? If   31
any, speak, for him have I offended. Who is here so
rude° that would not be a Roman? If any, speak,
for him have I offended. Who is here so vile that
will not love his country? If any, speak, for him
have I offended. I pause for a reply.   37

ALL. None, Brutus, none.

BRU. Then none have I offended. I have done no
more to Caesar than you shall do to Brutus. The
question of his death is enrolled° in the Capitol, his
glory not extenuated, wherein he was worthy,   42
nor his offenses enforced,° for which he suffered
death.

[*Enter* ANTONY *and others, with* CAESAR's *body.*]
Here comes his body, mourned by Mark Antony,
who, though he had no hand in his death, shall receive the benefit of his dying, a place in the   47
commonwealth — as which of you shall not? With
this I depart — that, as I slew my best lover for the
good of Rome, I have the same dagger for myself
when it shall please my country to need my death.

ALL. Live, Brutus! Live, live!   53

1. CIT. Bring him with triumph home unto his
house.

2. CIT. Give him a statue with his ancestors.

3. CIT. Let him be Caesar.

4. CIT.   Caesar's better parts
Shall be crowned in Brutus.

1. CIT. We'll bring him to his house with shouts
and clamors.   58

BRU. My countrymen ——

2. CIT.   Peace! Silence! Brutus speaks.

1. CIT. Peace, ho!

BRU. Good countrymen, let me depart alone,
And, for my sake, stay here with Antony.   61
Do grace to Caesar's corpse, and grace his speech
Tending to Caesar's glories, which Mark Antony
By our permission is allowed to make.
I do entreat you, not a man depart,   65
Save I alone, till Antony have spoke.   [*Exit.*]

1. CIT. Stay, ho, and let us hear Mark Antony!

3. CIT. Let him go up into the public chair.
We'll hear him. Noble Antony, go up.   69

ANT. For Brutus' sake, I am beholding to you.
[*Goes into the pulpit.*]

4. CIT. What does he say of Brutus?

3. CIT.   He says, for Brutus' sake,
He finds himself beholding to us all.

4. CIT. 'Twere best he speak no harm of Brutus
here.

1. CIT. This Caesar was a tyrant.

3. CIT.   Nay, that's certain.
We are blest that Rome is rid of him.   75

2. CIT. Peace! Let us hear what Antony can say.

ANT. You gentle Romans ——

ALL.   Peace, ho! Let us hear him.

ANT. Friends, Romans, countrymen, lend me your
ears.
I come to bury Caesar, not to praise him.
The evil that men do lives after them,   80
The good is oft interrèd with their bones.
So let it be with Caesar. The noble Brutus
Hath told you Caesar was ambitious.
If it were so, it was a grievous fault,
And grievously hath Caesar answered it.   85
Here, under leave of Brutus and the rest —
For Brutus is an honorable man,
So are they all, all honorable men —
Come I to speak in Caesar's funeral.
He was my friend, faithful and just to me.   90
But Brutus says he was ambitious,
And Brutus is an honorable man.
He hath brought many captives home to Rome,
Whose ransoms did the general coffers° fill.
Did this in Caesar seem ambitious?   95
When that the poor have cried, Caesar hath wept —
Ambition should be made of sterner stuff.
Yet Brutus says he was ambitious,
And Brutus is an honorable man.
You all did see that on the Lupercal   100
I thrice presented him a kingly crown,
Which he did thrice refuse. Was this ambition?
Yet Brutus says he was ambitious,
And, sure, he is an honorable man.
I speak not to disprove what Brutus spoke,   105
But here I am to speak what I do know.
You all did love him once, not without cause.
What cause withholds you then to mourn for him?
O judgment, thou art fled to brutish beasts,
And men have lost their reason! Bear with me,°
My heart is in the coffin there with Caesar,   111
And I must pause till it come back to me.

1. CIT. Methinks there is much reason in his sayings.

2. CIT. If thou consider rightly of the matter,
Caesar has had great wrong.

3. CIT.   Has he, masters?   115
I fear there will a worse come in his place.

4. CIT. Marked ye his words? He would not take
the crown,

---

33. rude: barbarous.   **41. enrolled:** preserved among the records.
43. enforced: stressed.

94. general coffers: public treasury; lit., treasure chests.
110. Bear with me: be patient with me.

Therefore 'tis certain he was not ambitious.
  1. CIT. If it be found so, some will dear abide° it.
  2. CIT. Poor soul! His eyes are red as fire with
    weeping.   120
  3. CIT. There's not a nobler man in Rome than
    Antony.
  4. CIT. Now mark him, he begins again to speak.
  ANT. But yesterday the word of Caesar might
Have stood against the world. Now lies he there,
And none so poor to do him reverence.   125
O masters, if I were disposed to stir
Your hearts and minds to mutiny and rage,
I should do Brutus wrong and Cassius wrong,
Who, you all know, are honorable men.
I will not do them wrong; I rather choose   130
To wrong the dead, to wrong myself and you,
Than I will wrong such honorable men.
But here's a parchment with the seal of Caesar —
I found it in his closet — 'tis his will.
Let but the commons° hear this testament —   135
Which, pardon me, I do not mean to read —
And they would go and kiss dead Caesar's wounds
And dip their napkins in his sacred blood,°
Yea, beg a hair of him for memory,
And, dying, mention it within their wills,   140
Bequeathing it as a rich legacy
Unto their issue.
  4. CIT. We'll hear the will. Read it, Mark Antony.
  ALL. The will, the will! We will hear Caesar's
    will.
  ANT. Have patience, gentle friends. I must not
    read it.   145
It is not meet you know how Caesar loved you.
You are not wood, you are not stones, but men;
And, being men, hearing the will of Caesar,
It will inflame you, it will make you mad.
'Tis good you know not that you are his heirs,   150
For if you should, oh, what would come of it!
  4. CIT. Read the will. We'll hear it, Antony.
You shall read us the will, Caesar's will.
  ANT. Will you be patient? Will you stay awhile?
I have o'ershot myself to tell you of it.   155
I fear I wrong the honorable men
Whose daggers have stabbed Caesar. I do fear it.
  4. CIT. They were traitors — honorable men!
  ALL. The will! The testament!
  2. CIT. They were villains, murderers. The will!
    Read the will.   160
  ANT. You will compel me then to read the will?
Then make a ring about the corpse of Caesar,
And let me show you him that made the will.
Shall I descend? And will you give me leave?
  ALL. Come down.   165
  2. CIT. Descend.
      [He comes down from the pulpit.]

  3. CIT. You shall have leave.
  4. CIT. A ring. Stand round.
  1. CIT. Stand from the hearse, stand from the
    body.   169
  2. CIT. Room for Antony, most noble Antony.
  ANT. Nay, press not so upon me. Stand far off.
  ALL. Stand back. Room! Bear back.
  ANT. If you have tears, prepare to shed them now.
You all do know this mantle. I remember
The first time ever Caesar put it on.   175
'Twas on a summer's evening, in his tent,
That day he overcame the Nervii.
Look, in this place ran Cassius' dagger through.
See what a rent the envious Casca made.
Through this the well-belovèd Brutus stabbed,   180
And as he plucked his cursèd steel away,
Mark how the blood of Caesar followed it,
As rushing out of doors, to be resolved
If Brutus so unkindly knocked, or no.
For Brutus, as you know, was Caesar's angel.   185
Judge, O you gods, how dearly Caesar loved him!
This was the most unkindest cut of all,
For when the noble Caesar saw him stab,
Ingratitude, more strong than traitors' arms,
Quite vanquished him. Then burst his mighty heart,
And, in his mantle muffling up his face,   191
Even at the base of Pompey's statuë,
Which all the while ran blood, great Caesar fell.
Oh, what a fall was there, my countrymen!
Then I, and you, and all of us fell down,   195
Whilst bloody treason flourished over us.
Oh, now you weep, and I perceive you feel
The dint° of pity. These are gracious drops.   198
Kind souls, what weep you when you but behold
Our Caesar's vesture° wounded? Look you here —
Here is himself, marred, as you see, with traitors.
  1. CIT. Oh, piteous spectacle!
  2. CIT. Oh, noble Caesar!
  3. CIT. Oh, woeful day!
  4. CIT. Oh, traitors, villains!   205
  1. CIT. Oh, most bloody sight!
  2. CIT. We will be revenged.
  ALL. Revenge! About! Seek! Burn! Fire! Kill!
    Slay!
Let not a traitor live!
  ANT. Stay, countrymen.   210
  1. CIT. Peace there! Hear the noble Antony.
  2. CIT. We'll hear him, we'll follow him, we'll die
    with him.
  ANT. Good friends, sweet friends, let me not stir
    you up
To such a sudden flood of mutiny.   215
They that have done this deed are honorable.
What private griefs they have, alas, I know not,
That made them do it. They are wise and honorable,
And will, no doubt, with reasons answer you.

---

119. dear abide: See III.i.94.   **135. commons:** common people.
138. dip . . . blood: See II.ii.88–89,n.   **198. dint:** stroke.   **200. vesture:** clothing.

I come not, friends, to steal away your hearts.　220
I am no orator, as Brutus is,
But, as you know me all, a plain blunt man
That love my friend; and that they know full well
That gave me public leave to speak of him.
For I have neither wit, nor words, nor worth,　225
Action, nor utterance, nor the power of speech,
To stir men's blood. I only speak right on,
I tell you that which you yourselves do know,
Show you sweet Caesar's wounds, poor poor dumb
　　mouths,
And bid them speak for me. But were I Brutus,　230
And Brutus Antony, there were an Antony
Would ruffle up your spirits, and put a tongue
In every wound of Caesar that should move
The stones of Rome to rise and mutiny.
　ALL. We'll mutiny.　　　　　　　　　　235
　I. CIT. We'll burn the house of Brutus.
　3. CIT. Away, then! Come, seek the conspirators.
　ANT. Yet hear me, countrymen, yet hear me
　　speak.
　ALL. Peace, ho! Hear Antony. Most noble An-
　　tony!
　ANT. Why, friends, you go to do you know not
　　what.　　　　　　　　　　　　　240
Wherein hath Caesar thus deserved your loves?
Alas, you know not. I must tell you, then —
You have forgot the will I told you of.
　ALL. Most true, the will! Let's stay and hear the
　　will.　　　　　　　　　　　　　244
　ANT. Here is the will, and under Caesar's seal.
To every Roman citizen he gives,
To every several° man, seventy-five drachmas.
　2. CIT. Most noble Caesar! We'll revenge his
　　death.
　3. CIT. Oh, royal Caesar!
　ANT. Hear me with patience.　　　　　250
　ALL. Peace, ho!
　ANT. Moreover, he hath left you all his walks,
His private arbors and new-planted orchards,
On this side Tiber. He hath left them you,
And to your heirs forever—common pleasures,　255
To walk abroad and recreate yourselves.
Here was a Caesar! When comes such another?
　I. CIT. Never, never. Come, away, away!
We'll burn his body in the holy place,
And with the brands fire the traitors' houses.　260
Take up the body.
　2. CIT. Go fetch fire.
　3. CIT. Pluck down benches.
　4. CIT. Pluck down forms,° windows, anything.
　　　　　[*Exeunt* CITIZENS *with the body.*]
　ANT. Now let it work. Mischief, thou art afoot,
Take thou what course thou wilt.　　　266
[*Enter a* SERVANT.]　　　　How now, fellow?
　SERV. Sir, Octavius is already come to Rome.

247. **several**: individual.　264. **forms**: benches.

　ANT. Where is he?
　SERV. He and Lepidus° are at Caesar's house.
　ANT. And thither will I straight to visit him.　270
He comes upon a wish.° Fortune is merry,
And in this mood will give us anything.
　SERV. I heard him say Brutus and Cassius
Are rid like madmen through the gates of Rome.
　ANT. Belike they had some notice of the people,
How I had moved them. Bring me to Octavius.
　　　　　　　　　　　　　　[*Exeunt.*]

SCENE III. *A street.*

[*Enter* CINNA *the poet.*]
　CIN. I dreamt tonight that I did feast with Caesar,
And things unluckily charge my fantasy.°
I have no will to wander forth of doors,
Yet something leads me forth.
　　　　　　　　[*Enter* CITIZENS.]
　I. CIT. What is your name?　　　　　5
　2. CIT. Whither are you going?
　3. CIT. Where do you dwell?
　4. CIT. Are you a married man or a bachelor?
　2. CIT. Answer every man directly.
　I. CIT. Aye, and briefly.　　　　　10
　4. CIT. Aye, and wisely.
　3. CIT. Aye, and truly, you were best.
　CIN. What is my name? Whither am I going?
Where do I dwell? Am I a married man or a bachelor? Then, to answer every man directly and　14
briefly, wisely and truly, wisely I say I am a bachelor.
　2. CIT. That's as much as to say they are fools
that marry. You'll bear me a bang° for that, I fear.
Proceed, directly.
　CIN. Directly, I am going to Caesar's funeral.　22
　I. CIT. As a friend or an enemy?
　CIN. As a friend.
　2. CIT. That matter is answered directly.　　25
　4. CIT. For your dwelling, briefly.
　CIN. Briefly, I dwell by the Capitol.
　3. CIT. Your name, sir, truly.
　CIN. Truly, my name is Cinna.　　　　30
　I. CIT. Tear him to pieces. He's a conspirator.
　CIN. I am Cinna the poet, I am Cinna the poet.
　4. CIT. Tear him for his bad verses, tear him for
his bad verses.　　　　　　　　　35
　CIN. I am not Cinna the conspirator.
　4. CIT. It is no matter, his name's Cinna. Pluck
but his name out of his heart, and turn him going.
　3. CIT. Tear him, tear him! Come, brands.　40
Ho, firebrands — to Brutus', to Cassius'! Burn all.
Some to Decius' house, and some to Casca's, some
to Ligarius'. Away, go!　　　　　[*Exeunt.*]

269. **Lepidus**: afterward one of the Big Three, with Antony and
Octavius. See IV.i.　271. **He . . . wish**: just when I wanted him.
　Sc. iii: 2. unluckily . . . fantasy: my imagination is burdened
with thoughts of bad luck.　20. **bear . . . bang**: owe me a blow;
i.e., I'll strike you.

Act IV

SCENE I. *A house in Rome.*

[ANTONY, OCTAVIUS, *and* LEPIDUS, *seated at a table.*]

ANT. These many then shall die, their names are
    pricked.°
OCT. Your brother too must die. Consent you,
    Lepidus?
LEP. I do consent.
OCT.   Prick him down, Antony.
LEP. Upon condition Publius shall not live,
Who is your sister's son, Mark Antony.   5
  ANT. He shall not live. Look, with a spot I damn°
    him.
But, Lepidus, go you to Caesar's house.
Fetch the will hither, and we shall determine
How to cut off some charge in legacies.°
  LEP. What, shall I find you here?   10
  OCT. Or here or at the Capitol.   [*Exit* LEPIDUS.]
  ANT. This is a slight unmeritable° man,
Meet to be sent on errands. Is it fit,
The threefold world divided, he should stand
One of the three to share it?
  OCT.   So you thought him,°   15
And took his voice who should be pricked to die
In our black sentence° and proscription.°
  ANT. Octavius, I have seen more days than you.
And though we lay these honors on this man,
To ease ourselves of divers slanderous loads,°   20
He shall but bear them as the ass bears gold,
To groan and sweat under the business,
Either led or driven, as we point the way.
And having brought our treasure where we will,
Then take we down his load and turn him off,   25
Like to the empty ass, to shake his ears
And graze in commons.°
  OCT.   You may do your will.
But he's a tried and valiant soldier.
  ANT. So is my horse, Octavius, and for that
I do appoint him store of provender.°   30
It is a creature that I teach to fight,
To wind,° to stop, to run directly on,
His corporal motion° governed by my spirit.
And, in some taste,° is Lepidus but so.
He must be taught, and trained, and bid go forth,
A barren-spirited fellow, one that feeds   36

On abjects,° orts,° and imitations,
Which, out of use and staled by other men,
Begin his fashion.° Do not talk of him
But as a property.° And now, Octavius,   40
Listen great things. Brutus and Cassius
Are levying powers.° We must straight make
    head.°
Therefore let our alliance be combined,
Our best friends made, our means stretched,
And let us presently go sit in council   45
How covert matters° may be best disclosed,
And open perils surest answered.
  OCT. Let us do so, for we are at the stake,°
And bayed about with many enemies.
And some that smile have in their hearts, I fear,   50
Millions of mischiefs.   [*Exeunt.*]

SCENE II. *Camp near Sardis.° Before* BRUTUS's *tent.*

[*Drum. Enter* BRUTUS, LUCILIUS, LUCIUS, *and* SOL-
    DIERS; TITINIUS *and* PINDARUS *meet them.*]

BRU. Stand, ho!
LUCIL. Give the word, ho, and stand!
BRU. What now, Lucilius! Is Cassius near?
LUCIL. He is at hand, and Pindarus is come
To do you salutation from his master.   5
  BRU. He greets me well. Your master, Pindarus,
In his own change,° or by ill officers,
Hath given me some worthy cause to wish
Things done undone. But if he be at hand,
I shall be satisfied.
  PIN.   I do not doubt   10
But that my noble master will appear
Such as he is, full of regard° and honor.
  BRU. He is not doubted. A word, Lucilius,
How he received you. Let me be resolved.
  LUCIL. With courtesy and with respect enough,
But not with such familiar instances,°   16
Nor with such free and friendly conference,°
As he hath used of old.
  BRU.   Thou hast described
A hot friend cooling. Ever note, Lucilius,
When love begins to sicken and decay,   20
It useth an enforcèd ceremony.°
There are no tricks in plain and simple faith.

Act IV, Sc. i: 1. **pricked:** See III.i.216,n.   6. **damn:** condemn.   9. **cut . . . legacies:** avoid paying some of the legacies. 12. **unmeritable:** without merit.   15. **So . . . him:** i.e., when you made him a partner in our triumvirate (rule of three).   17. **black sentence:** sentence of death. **proscription:** after a successful revolution, lists were published of those "proscribed," who could then be killed as public enemies.   20. **slanderous loads:** the burden of slander.   27. **graze . . . commons:** in English villages there was usually a common grazing ground where the villagers turned out their beasts to feed.   30. **provender:** fodder.   32. **wind:** turn.   33. **corporal motion:** bodily action.   34. **in . . . taste:** in some measure.

37. **abjects:** worthless things. **orts:** scraps of food.   **38–39. Which . . . fashion:** which he begins to use when they have ceased to be fashionable with other men.   40. **property:** a thing to be pushed around.   42. **powers:** armies. **make head:** gather forces. 46. **covert matters:** things hid.   48. **at . . . stake:** like a bear surrounded by hounds. See App. 5.
  Sc. ii: s.d., **Sardis:** in Lydia. Brutus and Cassius fled to the East and returned to Greece to meet the army of Antony and Octavius.   7. **In . . . change:** because he has changed his nature.   12. **full . . . regard:** worthy of respect.   16. **familiar instances:** friendly behavior.   17. **conference:** talk.   21. **enforced ceremony:** forced politeness.

But hollow men, like horses hot at hand,°
Make gallant show and promise of their mettle,
But when they should endure the bloody spur,   25
They fall their crests° and like deceitful jades°
Sink in the trial. Comes his army on?
 LUCIL. They mean this night in Sardis to be quartered.
The greater part, the horse in general,°
Are come with Cassius. [*Low march within.*]
 BRU.   Hark! He is arrived.   30
March gently on to meet him.
   [*Enter* CASSIUS *and his powers.*]
 CASS. Stand, ho!
 BRU. Stand, ho! Speak the word along.
 1. SOL. Stand!
 2. SOL. Stand!   35
 3. SOL. Stand!
 CASS. Most noble brother, you have done me wrong.
 BRU. Judge me, you gods! Wrong I mine enemies?
And if not so, how should I wrong a brother?
 CASS. Brutus, this sober° form of yours hides wrongs,   40
And when you do them ——
 BRU.   Cassius, be content,
Speak your griefs softly. I do know you well.
Before the eyes of both our armies here,
Which should perceive nothing but love from us,
Let us not wrangle. Bid them move away,   45
Then in my tent, Cassius, enlarge your griefs,°
And I will give you audience.
 CASS.   Pindarus,
Bid our commanders lead their charges° off
A little from this ground.   49
 BRU. Lucilius, do you the like, and let no man
Come to our tent till we have done our conference.
Let Lucius and Titinius guard our door. [*Exeunt.*]

SCENE III. BRUTUS's *tent.*

[*Enter* BRUTUS *and* CASSIUS.]
 CASS. That you have wronged me doth appear in this:
You have condemned and noted° Lucius Pella
For taking bribes here of the Sardians,
Wherein my letters, praying on his side,
Because I knew the man, were slighted off.°   5
 BRU. You wronged yourself to write in such a case.
 CASS. In such a time as this it is not meet

That every nice° offense should bear his comment.°
 BRU. Let me tell you, Cassius, you yourself
Are much condemned to have an itching palm,°
To sell and mart° your offices for gold   11
To undeservers.
 CASS. I an itching palm!
You know that you are Brutus that speaks this,
Or, by the gods, this speech were else your last.
 BRU. The name of Cassius honors this corruption,
And chastisement doth therefore hide his head.   16
 CASS. Chastisement!
 BRU. Remember March, the ides of March remember.
Did not great Julius bleed for justice' sake?
What villain touched his body that did stab,   20
And not for justice? What, shall one of us,
That struck the foremost man of all this world
But for supporting robbers, shall we now
Contaminate our fingers with base bribes,
And sell the mighty space of our large honors   25
For so much trash as may be graspèd thus?
I had rather be a dog and bay the moon
Than such a Roman.
 CASS. Brutus, bait not me,°
I'll not endure it. You forget yourself,
To hedge me in.° I am a soldier, I,   30
Older in practice, abler than yourself
To make conditions.°
 BRU. Go to. You are not, Cassius.
 CASS. I am.
 BRU. I say you are not.
 CASS. Urge me no more, I shall forget myself.   35
Have mind upon your health,° tempt me no farther.
 BRU. Away, slight man!
 CASS. Is 't possible?
 BRU. Hear me, for I will speak.
Must I give way and room to your rash choler?°
Shall I be frighted when a madman stares?   40
 CASS. O ye gods, ye gods! Must I endure all this?
 BRU. All this! Aye, more. Fret till your proud heart break.
Go show your slaves how choleric you are,
And make your bondmen° tremble. Must I budge?
Must I observe you? Must I stand and crouch   45
Under your testy humor?° By the gods,
You shall digest the venom of your spleen,
Though it do split you; for, from this day forth,
I'll use you for my mirth, yea, for my laughter,
When you are waspish.
 CASS. Is it come to this?   50
 BRU. You say you are a better soldier.

---

23. hot . . . hand: restless when the rider wishes them to stand.
26. fall . . . crests: become crestfallen, spiritless. jades: poor-spirited nags.   29. horse . . . general: all the cavalry.   40. sober: composed.   46. griefs: grievances.   48. charges: commands.
 Sc. iii: 2. noted: censured.   5. slighted off: treated slightingly.

8. nice: petty. bear . . . comment: be carefully noted.   10. itching palm: a hand always eager for bribes.   11. mart: trade.
28. bait . . . me: do not bark at me as though I were a bear.
30. hedge . . . in: control me.   32. make conditions: decide upon what conditions a man shall be appointed to office.   36. health: welfare.   39. choler: wrath.   44. bondmen: slaves.   46. testy humor: peevish temper.

Let it appear so, make your vaunting true
And it shall please me well. For mine own part,
I shall be glad to learn of noble men.
    CASS. You wrong me every way, you wrong me,
      Brutus.   55
I said an elder soldier, not a better.
Did I say better?
    BRU.   If you did, I care not.
    CASS. When Caesar lived, he durst not thus have
      moved me.
    BRU. Peace, peace! You durst not so have tempted
      him.
    CASS. I durst not!   60
    BRU. No.
    CASS. What, durst not tempt him!
    BRU.   For your life you durst not.
    CASS. Do not presume too much upon my love.
I may do that I shall be sorry for.
    BRU. You have done that you should be sorry for.
There is no terror, Cassius, in your threats,   66
For I am armed so strong in honesty
That they pass by me as the idle wind
Which I respect not. I did send to you
For certain sums of gold, which you denied me.   70
For I can raise no money by vile means —
By heaven, I had rather coin my heart,
And drop my blood for drachmas,° than to wring
From the hard hands of peasants their vile trash
By any indirection.° I did send   75
To you for gold to pay my legions,
Which you denied me. Was that done like Cassius?
Should I have answered Caius Cassius so?
When Marcus Brutus grows so covetous,
To lock such rascal counters° from his friends,   80
Be ready, gods, with all your thunderbolts,
Dash him to pieces!
    CASS.   I denied you not.
    BRU. You did.
    CASS.   I did not. He was but a fool
That brought my answer back. Brutus hath rived°
    my heart.   85
A friend should bear his friend's infirmities,
But Brutus makes mine greater than they are.
    BRU. I do not, till you practice them on me.
    CASS. You love me not.
    BRU.   I do not like your faults.
    CASS. A friendly eye could never see such faults.
    BRU. A flatterer's would not, though they do ap-
    pear   91
As huge as high Olympus.°
    CASS. Come, Antony, and young Octavius, come,
Revenge yourselves alone on Cassius,
For Cassius is aweary of the world —   95
Hated by one he loves, braved° by his brother,

Checked° like a bondman, all his faults observed,
Set in a notebook, learned and conned by rote,°
To cast into my teeth. Oh, I could weep
My spirit from mine eyes! There is my dagger,   100
And here my naked breast; within, a heart
Dearer than Plutus'° mine, richer than gold.
If that thou be'st a Roman, take it forth,
I, that denied thee gold, will give my heart.
Strike, as thou didst at Caesar; for I know   105
When thou didst hate him worst, thou lovedst him
    better
Than ever thou lovedst Cassius.
    BRU.   Sheathe your dagger.
Be angry when you will, it shall have scope;°
Do what you will, dishonor shall be humor.°
O Cassius, you are yokèd with a lamb   110
That carries anger as the flint bears fire,
Who, much enforcèd, shows a hasty spark
And straight is cold again.
    CASS.   Hath Cassius lived
To be but mirth and laughter to his Brutus,   114
When grief and blood ill-tempered vexeth him?
    BRU. When I spoke that, I was ill-tempered too.
    CASS. Do you confess so much? Give me your
    hand.
    BRU. And my heart too.
    CASS.   O Brutus!
    BRU.   What's the matter?
    CASS. Have not you love enough to bear with me
When that rash humor which my mother gave me
Makes me forgetful?
    BRU.   Yes, Cassius, and from henceforth,   121
When you are overearnest with your Brutus,
He'll think your mother chides, and leave you so.
    POET. [*Within*] Let me go in to see the generals.
There is some grudge between 'em, 'tis not meet
They be alone.   126
    LUCIL. [*Within*] You shall not come to them.
    POET. [*Within*] Nothing but death shall stay me.
    [*Enter* POET, *followed by* LUCILIUS, TITINIUS, *and*
                LUCIUS.]
    CASS. How now! What's the matter?
    POET. For shame, you generals! What do you
    mean?   130
Love and be friends, as two such men should be,
For I have seen more years, I'm sure, than ye.
    CASS. Ha, ha! How vilely doth this cynic° rhyme!
    BRU. Get you hence, sirrah. Saucy fellow, hence!
    CASS. Bear with him, Brutus. 'Tis his fashion.
    BRU. I'll know his humor when he knows his
    time.°   136

---

73. **drachmas:** Greek coins.   75. **indirection:** crooked means.
80. **rascal counters:** wretched tokens.   85. **rived:** split.
92. **Olympus:** the highest mountain in Thessaly and the home
of the gods.   96. **braved:** taunted.

97. **Checked:** rebuked.   98. **conned by rote:** learned by heart.
102. **Plutus:** for Pluto, the god of riches.   108. **scope:** free play.
109. **dishonor . . . humor:** dishonorable conduct shall be regarded
as just your "humor." See App. 3.   133. **cynic:** rude fellow.
Cynic philosophers, of whom Diogenes was the most memorable,
scorned easy living and polite manners.   136. **I'll . . . time:** I will
be patient with his whims if he displays them at the proper time.

What should the wars do with these jigging fools?
Companion,° hence!
    CASS.   Away, away, be gone! [*Exit* POET.]
    BRU. Lucilius and Titinius, bid the commanders
Prepare to lodge their companies tonight.   140
    CASS. And come yourselves, and bring Messala
    with you
Immediately to us. [*Exeunt* LUCILIUS *and* TITINIUS.]
    BRU.   Lucius, a bowl of wine! [*Exit* LUCIUS.]
    CASS. I did not think you could have been so
    angry.
    BRU. O Cassius, I am sick of many griefs.
    CASS. Of your philosophy you make no use   145
If you give place to accidental evils.
    BRU. No man bears sorrow better. Portia is dead.
    CASS. Ha! Portia!
    BRU. She is dead.
    CASS. How 'scaped I killing when I crossed you
    so?   150
Oh, insupportable and touching loss!
Upon what sickness?
    BRU.   Impatient of my absence,
And grief that young Octavius with Mark Antony
Have made themselves so strong — for with her
    death
That tidings came — with this she fell distract,°
And, her attendants absent, swallowed fire.   156
    CASS. And died so?
    BRU.   Even so.
    CASS.   O ye immortal gods!
    [*Re-enter* LUCIUS, *with wine and taper.*]
    BRU. Speak no more of her. Give me a bowl of
    wine.
In this I bury all unkindness, Cassius.   [*Drinks.*]
    CASS. My heart is thirsty for that noble pledge.
Fill, Lucius, till the wine o'erswell the cup.   161
I cannot drink too much of Brutus' love. [*Drinks.*]
    BRU. Come in, Titinius!   [*Exit* LUCIUS.]
    [*Re-enter* TITINIUS, *with* MESSALA.]
             Welcome, good Messala.
Now sit we close about this taper here,
And call in question° our necessities.   165
    CASS. Portia, art thou gone?
    BRU.   No more, I pray you.
Messala, I have here receivèd letters
That young Octavius and Mark Antony
Come down upon us with a mighty power,
Bending their expedition toward Philippi.°   170
    MES. Myself have letters of the selfsame tenor.
    BRU. With what addition?
    MES. That by proscription and bills of outlawry
Octavius, Antony, and Lepidus
Have put to death a hundred Senators.   175
    BRU. Therein our letters do not well agree.

Mine speak of seventy Senators that died
By their proscriptions, Cicero being one.
    CASS. Cicero one!
    MES.   Cicero is dead,
And by that order of proscription.   180
Had you your letters from your wife, my lord?
    BRU. No, Messala.
    MES. Nor nothing in your letters writ of her?
    BRU. Nothing, Messala.
    MES.   That, methinks, is strange.
    BRU. Why ask you? Hear you aught of her in
    yours?   185
    MES. No, my lord.
    BRU. Now, as you are a Roman, tell me true.
    MES. Then like a Roman bear the truth I tell —
For certain she is dead,° and by strange manner.
    BRU. Why, farewell, Portia. We must die, Mes-
    sala.   190
With meditating that she must die once
I have the patience to endure it now.
    MES. Even so great men great losses should en-
    dure.
    CASS. I have as much of this in art as you,
But yet my nature° could not bear it so.   195
    BRU. Well, to our work alive. What do you think
Of marching to Philippi presently?
    CASS. I do not think it good.
    BRU.   Your reason?
    CASS.   This it is:
'Tis better that the enemy seek us.
So shall he waste his means, weary his soldiers,   200
Doing himself offense,° whilst we lying still
Are full of rest, defense, and nimbleness.
    BRU. Good reasons must of force give place to
    better.
The people 'twixt Philippi and this ground
Do stand but in a forced affection,   205
For they have grudged us contribution.
The enemy, marching along by them,
By them shall make a fuller number up,
Come on refreshed, new-added, and encouraged.
From which advantage shall we cut him off   210
If at Philippi we do face him there,
These people at our back.
    CASS.   Hear me, good brother ——
    BRU. Under your pardon. You must note beside
That we have tried the utmost of our friends,
Our legions are brimful, our cause is ripe.   215
The enemy increaseth every day,
We, at the height, are ready to decline.
There is a tide in the affairs of men

---

138. **Companion:** fellow, used as a word of contempt.   155. **distract:** distraught.   165. **call ... question:** consider.   170. **Philippi:** a city in Macedon. where the decisive battles between the two forces were fought.

189. **certain ... dead:** There seems to be a discrepancy in this passage, for Brutus has already told Cassius of Portia's death. Either the scene was rewritten and, as sometimes happened in the printing of Shakespeare's plays, both the original and the revised passage have been left, or else Shakespeare wished to exhibit Brutus displaying stoic calm.   194–95. **art ... nature:** See App. 18.   201. **offense:** harm.

Which taken at the flood leads on to fortune;
Omitted, all the voyage of their life   220
Is bound in shallows and in miseries.
On such a full sea are we now afloat,
And we must take the current when it serves,
Or lose our ventures.
    CASS.   Then, with your will, go on.   224
We'll along ourselves and meet them at Philippi.
    BRU. The deep of night is crept upon our talk,
And nature must obey necessity,
Which we will niggard° with a little rest.
There is no more to say?
    CASS.   No more. Good night.
Early tomorrow will we rise and hence.   230
    BRU. Lucius! [*Re-enter* LUCIUS.] My gown.°
                    [*Exit* LUCIUS.]
                Farewell, good Messala.
Good night, Titinius. Noble, noble Cassius,
Good night, and good repose.
    CASS.   O my dear brother!
This was an ill beginning of the night.
Never come such division 'tween our souls!   235
Let it not, Brutus.
    BRU.   Everything is well.
    CASS. Good night, my lord.
    BRU.   Good night, good brother.
    TIT. *and* MES. Good night, Lord Brutus.
    BRU. Farewell, everyone. [*Exeunt all but* BRUTUS.]
    [*Re-enter* LUCIUS, *with the gown.*]
Give me the gown. Where is thy instrument?
    LUC. Here in the tent.
    BRU.   What, thou speak'st drowsily?   240
Poor knave, I blame thee not, thou art o'erwatched.°
Call Claudius and some other of my men.
I'll have them sleep on cushions in my tent.
    LUC. Varro and Claudius!
    [*Enter* VARRO *and* CLAUDIUS.]
    VAR. Calls my lord?   245
    BRU. I pray you, sirs, lie in my tent and sleep.
It may be I shall raise you by and by
On business to my brother Cassius.
    VAR. So please you, we will stand and watch your
      pleasure.
    BRU. I will not have it so. Lie down, good sirs.
It may be I shall otherwise bethink me.   251
Look, Lucius, here's the book I sought for so,
I put it in the pocket of my gown.
            [VARRO *and* CLAUDIUS *lie down.*]
    LUC. I was sure your lordship did not give it me.
    BRU. Bear with me,° good boy, I am much forget-
    ful.   255
Canst thou hold up thy heavy eyes awhile,
And touch thy instrument a strain or two?
    LUC. Aye, my lord, an 't please you.

    BRU.   It does, my boy.
I trouble thee too much, but thou art willing.
    LUC. It is my duty, sir.   260
    BRU. I should not urge thy duty past thy might —
I know young bloods look for a time of rest.
    LUC. I have slept, my lord, already.
    BRU. It was well done, and thou shalt sleep again,
I will not hold thee long. If I do live,   265
I will be good to thee.   [*Music, and a song.*]
This is a sleepy tune. O murderous° slumber,
Lay'st thou thy leaden mace° upon my boy,
That plays thee music? Gentle knave, good night.
I will not do thee so much wrong to wake thee.   270
If thou dost nod, thou break'st thy instrument,
I'll take it from thee, and, good boy, good night.
Let me see, let me see, is not the leaf turned down
Where I left reading? Here it is, I think.
                     [*Sits down.*]
    [*Enter the* GHOST OF CAESAR.]
How ill this taper burns! Ha! Who comes here?
I think it is the weakness of mine eyes   276
That shapes this monstrous apparition.
It comes upon me. Art thou anything?
Art thou some god, some angel, or some devil,
That makest my blood cold, and my hair to stare?
Speak to me what thou art.   281
    GHOST. Thy evil spirit, Brutus.
    BRU.   Why comest thou?
    GHOST. To tell thee thou shalt see me at Philippi.
    BRU. Well, then I shall see thee again?
    GHOST. Ay, at Philippi.   285
    BRU. Why, I will see thee at Philippi then.
                    [*Exit* GHOST.]
Now I have taken heart, thou vanishest.
Ill spirit, I would hold more talk with thee.
Boy, Lucius! Varro! Claudius! Sirs, awake!
Claudius!   290
    LUC. The strings, my lord, are false.
    BRU. He thinks he still is at his instrument.
Lucius, awake!
    LUC. My lord?   295
    BRU. Didst thou dream, Lucius, that thou so
    criedst out?
    LUC. My lord, I do not know that I did cry.
    BRU. Yes, that thou didst. Didst thou see any-
    thing?
    LUC. Nothing, my lord.
    BRU. Sleep again, Lucius. Sirrah Claudius!   300
[*To* VARRO] Fellow thou, awake!
    VAR. My lord?
    CLAU. My lord?
    BRU. Why did you so cry out, sirs, in your sleep?

228. niggard: satisfy grudgingly.   **231. gown:** nightgown, a garment like the modern dressing gown; another instance of Elizabethan costume.   **241. o'erwatched:** weary with too much
watchfulness.   **255. Bear ... me:** See III.ii.110,n.

267. murderous: i.e., because it deprives men of sense. **268. lead-
en mace:** The metaphor is of the officer laying his mace upon a
prisoner whom he is arresting; "leaden" is often applied to sleep
because it is heavy and overwhelming. **mace:** See Pl. 22h. Officers
of the law carried a small mace as sign of office, as a modern
policeman wears the star badge.

VAR. *and* CLAU. Did we, my lord?

BRU.   Aye. Saw you anything?   305

VAR. No, my lord, I saw nothing.

CLAU.   Nor I, my lord.

BRU. Go and commend me to my brother Cassius.
Bid him set on his powers betimes before,°
And we will follow.

VAR. *and* CLAU. It shall be done, my lord. [*Exeunt.*]

Act V

SCENE I. *The plains of Philippi.*

[*Enter* OCTAVIUS, ANTONY, *and their* ARMY.]

OCT. Now, Antony, our hopes are answerèd.
You said the enemy would not come down,
But keep the hills and upper regions.
It proves not so, their battles° are at hand,
They mean to warn us at Philippi here,   5
Answering before we do demand of them.

ANT. Tut, I am in their bosoms,° and I know
Wherefore they do it. They could be content
To visit other places,° and come down
With fearful° bravery,° thinking by this face   10
To fasten in our thoughts that they have courage.
But 'tis not so.

[*Enter a* MESSENGER.]

MESS.   Prepare you, generals.
The enemy comes on in gallant show.
Their bloody sign of battle° is hung out,
And something to be done immediately.   15

ANT. Octavius, lead your battle softly on,
Upon the left hand of the even field.°

OCT. Upon the right hand I. Keep thou the left.

ANT. Why do you cross me in this exigent?°

OCT. I do not cross you, but I will do so.   20

[*March. Drum. Enter* BRUTUS, CASSIUS, *and their*
ARMY; LUCILIUS, TITINIUS, MESSALA, *and others.*]

BRU. They stand, and would have parley.

CASS. Stand fast, Titinius. We must out and talk.

OCT. Mark Antony, shall we give sign of battle?

ANT. No, Caesar, we will answer on their charge.
Make forth, the generals would have some words.

OCT. Stir not until the signal.   26

BRU. Words before blows. Is it so, countrymen?

OCT. Not that we love words better, as you do.

BRU. Good words are better than bad strokes, Octavius.

ANT. In your bad strokes, Brutus, you give good
words.   30
Witness the hole you made in Caesar's heart,
Crying " Long live! Hail, Caesar! "

CASS.   Antony,
The posture° of your blows are yet unknown,
But for your words, they rob the Hybla° bees,
And leave them honeyless.

ANT.   Not stingless too.   35

BRU. Oh, yes, and soundless too,
For you have stol'n their buzzing, Antony,
And very wisely threat before you sting.

ANT. Villains, you did not so when your vile dag-
gers
Hacked one another in the sides of Caesar.   40
You showed your teeth like apes, and fawned like
hounds,
And bowed like bondmen, kissing Caesar's feet,
Whilst damnèd Casca, like a cur, behind
Struck Caesar on the neck. O you flatterers!

CASS. Flatterers! Now, Brutus, thank yourself.
This tongue had not offended so today   46
If Cassius might have ruled.

OCT. Come, come, the cause. If arguing make us
sweat,
The proof of it will turn to redder drops.
Look,   50
I draw a sword against conspirators.
When think you that the sword goes up° again?
Never, till Caesar's three and thirty wounds
Be well avenged, or till another Caesar
Have added slaughter to the sword of traitors.   55

BRU. Caesar, thou canst not die by traitors' hands,
Unless thou bring'st them with thee.

OCT.   So I hope.
I was not born to die on Brutus' sword.

BRU. Oh, if thou wert the noblest of thy strain,
Young man, thou couldst not die more honorable.

CASS. A peevish° schoolboy, worthless of such
honor,   61
Joined with a masker° and a reveler!

ANT. Old Cassius still!

OCT.   Come, Antony, away!
Defiance, traitors, hurl we in your teeth.
If you dare fight today, come to the field;   65
If not, when you have stomachs.°

[*Exeunt* OCTAVIUS, ANTONY, *and their* ARMY.]

CASS. Why, now, blow wind, swell billow, and
swim bark!°
The storm is up, and all is on the hazard.

BRU. Ho, Lucilius! Hark, a word with you.

LUCIL.   [*Standing forth*] My lord?

[BRUTUS *and* LUCILIUS *converse apart.*]

---

308. set . . . before: lead on his army ahead of ours in good time.
Act V, Sc. i: 4. battles: armies drawn up ready for battle.
7. in . . . bosoms: in the secrets of their hearts. **8–9. They . . .
places:** i.e., they would prefer to be anywhere but here. **10. fearful:** full of fear. **bravery:** brave show. **14. bloody . . . battle:** red
flag of defiance. **17. even field:** level ground. **19. exigent:**
critical moment.

33. posture: quality. **34. Hybla:** a mountain in Sicily famous
for the honey produced there. **52. goes up:** returns to the scabbard. **61. peevish:** silly. **62. masker:** one who spends his time
in masques and night life. See I.ii.203–04; II.ii.116. **66. stomachs:** appetites. **67. bark:** ship.

CASS. Messala!

MES. [*Standing forth*] What says my general?

CASS. Messala,   71
This is my birthday, as° this very day
Was Cassius born. Give me thy hand, Messala.
Be thou my witness that, against my will,
As Pompey was, am I compelled to set   75
Upon one battle all our liberties.
You know that I held Epicurus strong,°
And his opinion. Now I change my mind,
And partly credit things that do presage.°
Coming from Sardis, on our former° ensign°   80
Two mighty eagles fell, and there they perched,
Gorging and feeding from our soldiers' hands,
Who to Philippi here consorted° us.
This morning are they fled away and gone,
And in their steads do ravens, crows, and kites 85
Fly o'er our heads and downward look on us,
As we were sickly prey. Their shadows seem
A canopy most fatal, under which
Our army lies, ready to give up the ghost.

MES. Believe not so.

CASS.   I but believe it partly,   90
For I am fresh of spirit and resolved
To meet all perils very constantly.

BRU. Even so, Lucilius.

CASS.   Now, most noble Brutus,
The gods today stand friendly, that we may,
Lovers in peace, lead on our days to age!   95
But since the affairs of men rest still° incertain,
Let's reason with° the worst that may befall.
If we do lose this battle, then is this
The very last time we shall speak together.
What are you then determinèd to do?   100

BRU. Even by the rule of that philosophy
By which I did blame Cato for the death
Which he did give himself° — I know not how,
But I do find it cowardly and vile,
For fear of what might fall, so to prevent   105
The time of life° — arming myself with patience
To stay° the providence of some high powers
That govern us below.

CASS.   Then, if we lose this battle,
You are contented to be led in triumph
Thorough the streets of Rome?   110

BRU. No, Cassius, no. Think not, thou noble Ro-
man,
That ever Brutus will go bound to Rome.
He bears too great a mind. But this same day

Must end that work the ides of March begun,
And whether we shall meet again I know not. 115
Therefore our everlasting farewell take.
Forever and forever, farewell, Cassius!
If we do meet again, why, we shall smile;
If not, why then this parting was well made.

CASS. Forever and forever farewell, Brutus!   120
If we do meet again, we'll smile indeed;
If not, 'tis true this parting was well made.

BRU. Why then, lead on. Oh, that a man might
know
The end of this day's business ere it come!
But it sufficeth that the day will end,   125
And then the end is known. Come, ho! Away!
[*Exeunt.*]

SCENE II. *The field of battle.*

[*Alarum. Enter* BRUTUS *and* MESSALA.]

BRU. Ride, ride, Messala, ride, and give these bills[1]
Unto the legions on the other side. [*Loud alarum.*]
Let them set on at once, for I perceive
But cold demeanor° in Octavius' wing.
And sudden push gives them the overthrow.   5
Ride, ride, Messala. Let them all come down.
[*Exeunt.*]

SCENE III. *Another part of the field.*

[*Alarums. Enter* CASSIUS *and* TITINIUS.]

CASS. Oh, look, Titinius, look, the villains fly!
Myself have to mine own turned enemy.°
This ensign° here of mine was turning back.
I slew the coward, and did take it from him.

TIT. O Cassius, Brutus gave the word too early,
Who, having some advantage on Octavius,   6
Took it too eagerly. His soldiers fell to spoil
Whilst we by Antony are all enclosed.

[*Enter* PINDARUS.]

PIN. Fly further off, my lord, fly further off.
Mark Antony is in your tents, my lord.   10
Fly, therefore, noble Cassius, fly far off.

CASS. This hill is far enough. Look, look, Titinius,
Are those my tents where I perceive the fire?

TIT. They are, my lord.

CASS.   Titinius, if thou lovest me,
Mount thou my horse and hide thy spurs in him
Till he have brought thee up to yonder troops   16
And here again, that I may rest assured

---

72. **as:** on.   77. **held . . . strong:** was a firm believer in Epicurus, a Greek philosopher who taught his followers that the gods, if they existed, were not interested in man, and that they should therefore despise all superstition.   79. **presage:** foretell.   80. **former:** foremost.   **ensign:** the colors carried by a company. 83. **consorted:** accompanied.   96. **still:** always.   97. **reason with:** consider.   101–03: **Even . . . himself:** i.e., according to my rule of life suicide is a cowardly way out of difficulties. **Cato:** See II. ii.295,n.   105–06. **prevent . . . life:** forestall the natural end of life.   107. **stay:** await.

Sc. ii: 1. **bills:** written messages.   4. **cold demeanor:** lack of offensive spirit.
Sc. iii: 2. **Myself . . . enemy:** i.e., I am now the enemy of my own men because they have become cowards.   3. **ensign:** used both for the company's colors and for the junior officer who carried them.

Whether yond troops are friend or enemy.
TIT. I will be here again, even with a thought.
[*Exit.*]
CASS. Go, Pindarus, get higher on that hill — 20
My sight was ever thick.° Regard° Titinius,
And tell me what thou notest about the field.
[PINDARUS *ascends the hill.*]
This day I breathèd first. Time is come round,
And where I did begin, there shall I end,
My life is run his compass. Sirrah, what news? 25
PIN. [*Above*] O my lord!
CASS. What news?
PIN. [*Above*] Titinius is enclosèd round about
With horsemen that make to him on the spur,
Yet he spurs on. Now they are almost on him. 30
Now, Titinius! Now some light.° Oh, he lights too.
He's ta'en. [*Shout.*] And, hark! They shout for joy.
CASS. Come down, behold no more.
Oh, coward that I am, to live so long,
To see my best friend ta'en before my face! 35
[PINDARUS *descends.*]
Come hither, sirrah.
In Parthia did I take thee prisoner,
And then I swore thee, saving of thy life,
That whatsoever I did bid thee do
Thou shouldst attempt it. Come now, keep thine
oath. 40
Now be a free man, and with this good sword,
That ran through Caesar's bowels, search this
bosom.
Stand not to answer. Here, take thou the hilts,
And when my face is covered, as 'tis now,
Guide thou the sword. [PINDARUS *stabs him*] Cae-
sar, thou art revenged, 45
Even with the sword that killed thee. [*Dies.*]
PIN. So, I am free, yet would not so have been,
Durst I have done my will. O Cassius!
Far from this country Pindarus shall run,
Where never Roman shall take note of him. [*Exit.*]
[*Re-enter* TITINIUS *with* MESSALA.]
MES. It is but change,° Titinius, for Octavius 51
Is overthrown by noble Brutus' power,
As Cassius' legions are by Antony.
TIT. These tidings will well comfort Cassius.
MES. Where did you leave him?
TIT. All disconsolate, 55
With Pindarus his bondman, on this hill.
MES. Is not that he that lies upon the ground?
TIT. He lies not like the living. Oh, my heart!
MES. Is not that he?
TIT. No, this was he, Messala,
But Cassius is no more. O setting sun, 60
As in thy red rays thou dost sink to night,
So in his red blood Cassius' day is set,
The sun of Rome is set! Our day is gone,

Clouds, dews, and dangers come. Our deeds are
done!
Mistrust of my success hath done this deed. 65
MES. Mistrust of good success hath done this
deed.
O hateful error, melancholy's child,°
Why dost thou show to the apt° thoughts of men
The things that are not? O error, soon conceived,
Thou never comest unto a happy birth, 70
But kill'st the mother that engendered° thee!
TIT. What, Pindarus! Where art thou, Pindarus?
MES. Seek him, Titinius, whilst I go to meet
The noble Brutus, thrusting this report
Into his ears. I may say " thrusting " it, 75
For piercing steel and darts envenomèd
Shall be as welcome to the ears of Brutus
As tidings of this sight.
TIT. Hie you, Messala,
And I will seek for Pindarus the while.
[*Exit* MESSALA.]
Why didst thou send me forth, brave Cassius? 80
Did I not meet thy friends? And did not they
Put on my brows this wreath of victory,
And bid me give it thee? Didst thou not hear their
shouts?
Alas, thou hast miscónstrued everything!
But hold thee, take this garland on thy brow. 85
Thy Brutus bid me give it thee, and I
Will do his bidding. Brutus, come apace,
And see how I regarded Caius Cassius.
By your leave, gods, this is a Roman's part.
Come, Cassius' sword, and find Titinius' heart. 90
[*Kills himself.*]
[*Alarum. Re-enter* MESSALA, *with* BRUTUS, *young*
CATO, *and others.*]
BRU. Where, where, Messala, doth his body lie?
MES. Lo, yonder, and Titinius mourning it.
BRU. Titinius' face is upward.
CATO. He is slain.
BRU. O Julius Caesar, thou art mighty yet!
Thy spirit walks abroad, and turns our swords 95
In our own proper° entrails. [*Low alarums.*]
CATO. Brave Titinius!
Look whether he have not crowned dead Cassius!
BRU. Are yet two Romans living such as these?
The last of all the Romans, fare thee well!
It is impossible that ever Rome 100
Should breed thy fellow. Friends, I owe moe tears
To this dead man than you shall see me pay.
I shall find time, Cassius, I shall find time.
Come therefore, and to Thasos send his body.
His funerals shall not be in our camp, 105
Lest it discomfort us. Lucilius, come,
And come, young Cato. Let us to the field.
Labeo and Flavius, set our battles on.

---

21. thick: short. Regard: watch.   31. light: alight, descend.
51. change: exchange.

67. melancholy's child: See App. 4.   68. apt: ready to be
deceived.   71. engendered: conceived.   96. proper: own.

'Tis three o'clock, and, Romans' yet ere night   109
We shall try fortune in a second fight.°   [*Exeunt.*]

SCENE IV. *Another part of the field.*

[*Alarum. Enter, fighting,* SOLDIERS *of both armies;
then* BRUTUS, *young* CATO, LUCILIUS, *and others.*]
  BRU. Yet, countrymen, oh, yet hold up your
    heads!
  CATO. What bastard doth not? Who will go with
    me?
I will proclaim my name about the field.
I am the son of Marcus Cato, ho! —
A foe to tyrants, and my country's friend.   5
I am the son of Marcus Cato, ho!
  BRU. And I am Brutus, Marcus Brutus, I —
Brutus, my country's friend. Know me for Brutus!
                  [*Exit.*]
  LUCIL. O young and noble Cato, art thou down?
Why, now thou diest as bravely as Titinius,   10
And mayst be honored, being Cato's son.
  1. SOL. Yield, or thou diest.
  LUCIL.   Only I yield to die.
[*Offering money*] There is so much that thou wilt
    kill me straight.
Kill Brutus, and be honored in his death.
  1. SOL. We must not. A noble prisoner!   15
  2. SOL. Room, ho! Tell Antony, Brutus is ta'en.
  1. SOL. I'll tell the news. Here comes the general.
            [*Enter* ANTONY.]
Brutus is ta'en, Brutus is ta'en, my lord.
  ANT. Where is he?
  LUCIL. Safe, Antony, Brutus is safe enough.   20
I dare assure thee that no enemy
Shall ever take alive the noble Brutus.
The gods defend him from so great a shame!
When you do find him, or alive or dead,
He will be found like Brutus, like himself.   25
  ANT. This is not Brutus, friend, but, I assure you,
A prize no less in worth. Keep this man safe,
Give him all kindness. I had rather have
Such men my friends than enemies. Go on,
And see whether Brutus be alive or dead,   30
And bring us word unto Octavius' tent
How everything is chanced.   [*Exeunt.*]

SCENE V. *Another part of the field.*

[*Enter* BRUTUS, DARDANIUS, CLITUS, STRATO, *and*
VOLUMNIUS.]
  BRU. Come, poor remains of friends, rest on this
    rock.

110. **second fight:** There were two battles at Philippi; the second
actually occurred twenty days after the first and not (as in the
play) on the same day.

  CLI. Statilius showed the torchlight, but, my lord,
He came not back. He is or ta'en or slain.
  BRU. Sit thee down, Clitus. Slaying is the word,
It is a deed in fashion. Hark thee, Clitus.   5
                [*Whispering.*]
  CLI. What, I, my lord? No, not for all the world.
  BRU. Peace then, no words.
  CLI.   I'll rather kill myself.
  BRU. Hark thee, Dardanius.   [*Whispering.*]
  DAR.   Shall I do such a deed?
  CLI. O Dardanius!
  DAR. O Clitus!   10
  CLI. What ill request did Brutus make to thee?
  DAR. To kill him, Clitus. Look, he meditates.
  CLI. Now is that noble vessel full of grief,
That it runs over even at his eyes.
  BRU. Come hither, good Volumnius, list a word.
  VOL. What says my lord?
  BRU.   Why, this, Volumnius.   16
The ghost of Caesar hath appeared to me
Two several° times by night — at Sardis once,
And this last night here in Philippi fields.
I know my hour is come.
  VOL.   Not so, my lord.   20
  BRU. Nay, I am sure it is, Volumnius.
Thou seest the world, Volumnius, how it goes,
Our enemies have beat us to the pit. [*Low alarums.*]
It is more worthy to leap in ourselves
Than tarry till they push us. Good Volumnius,   25
Thou know'st that we two went to school together.
Even for that our love of old, I prithee
Hold thou my sword hilts whilst I run on it.
  VOL. That's not an office for a friend, my lord
                [*Alarum still.*]
  CLI. Fly, fly, my lord, there is no tarrying here.
  BRU. Farewell to you, and you, and you, Volum-
    nius.   31
Strato, thou hast been all this while asleep —
Farewell to thee too, Strato. Countrymen,
My heart doth joy that yet in all my life
I found no man but he was true to me.   35
I shall have glory by this losing day,
More than Octavius and Mark Antony
By this vile conquest shall attain unto.
So, fare you well at once, for Brutus' tongue
Hath almost ended his life's history.   40
Night hangs upon mine eyes, my bones would rest
That have but labored to attain this hour.
      [*Alarum. Cry within,* "Fly, fly, fly!"]
  CLI. Fly, my lord, fly!
  BRU.   Hence! I will follow.
    [*Exeunt* CLITUS, DARDANIUS, *and* VOLUMNIUS.]
I prithee, Strato, stay thou by thy lord.
Thou art a fellow of a good respect,°   45
Thy life hath had some smatch° of honor in it.

Sc. v: 18. **several:** separate.   45. **good respect:** worthy of respect.   46. **smatch:** taste.

Hold then my sword, and turn away thy face
While I do run upon it. Wilt thou, Strato?
    STRA. Give me your hand first. Fare you well, my
      lord.
    BRU. Farewell, good Strato. [*Runs on his sword.*]
      Caesar, now be still.   50
I killed not thee with half so good a will.   [*Dies.*]
[*Alarum. Retreat. Enter* OCTAVIUS, ANTONY, MESSALA,
        LUCILIUS, *and the* ARMY.]
    OCT. What man is that?
    MES. My master's man. Strato, where is thy mas-
      ter?
    STRA. Free from the bondage you are in, Messala.
The conquerors can but make a fire of him,   55
For Brutus only overcame himself,
And no man else hath honor by his death.
    LUCIL. So Brutus should be found. I thank thee,
      Brutus,
That thou hast proved Lucilius' saying true.
    OCT. All that served Brutus, I will entertain°
      them.   60
Fellow, wilt thou bestow thy time with me?

60. entertain: take into service.

    STRA. Aye, if Messala will prefer° me to you.
    OCT. Do so, good Messala.
    MES. How died my master, Strato?
    STRA. I held the sword, and he did run on it.   65
    MES. Octavius, then take him to follow thee
That did the latest° service to my master.
    ANT. This was the noblest Roman of them all.
All the conspirators, save only he,
Did that they did in envy of great Caesar.   70
He only, in a general honest thought
And common good to all, made one of them.
His life was gentle,° and the elements
So mixed in him° that Nature might stand up
And say to all the world, " This was a man."   75
    OCT. According to his virtue let us use him,
With all respect and rites of burial.
Within my tent his bones tonight shall lie,
Most like a soldier, ordered honorably.
So call the field to rest, and let's away,   80
To part° the glories of this happy day.   [*Exeunt.*]

62. prefer: recommend.   67. latest: last.   73. gentle: noble.
73–74. elements . . . him: i.e., he was a man perfectly balanced
See App. 3.   81. part: share.

TWELFTH NIGHT
or What You Will

Introduction

Twelfth Night,[1] *or What You Will* was first printed in the folio of 1623; the text is good and presents few difficulties. The play was probably written in 1600 or 1601; there are a number of topical passages glancing at events in those years:

1. Maria says of Malvolio, " He does smile his face into more lines than is in the new map with the augmentation of the Indies " (III.ii.84). This map appeared in 1600. It was drawn by Edward Wright and was the first English map on the principle of Mercator's projection (see Pl. 1a).

2. " I will not give my part of this sport for a pension of thousands to be paid from the Sophy " (II.v.196). In 1597 Sir Anthony Shirley, a well-known adventurer and a close follower of the Earl of Essex, set out with his brother Robert and a party of Englishmen on a mission to the Sophy (Shah) of Persia. After many adventures they arrived safely, were kindly received, and handsomely rewarded. Some of the party returned by way of the Caspian Sea, Russia, and Archangel, and reached London in September 1600. Shirley himself was suspected of disloyalty and never came back to England. An account of the journey was quickly printed, but on October 2 it was suppressed by order of the Council, and all copies seized and burnt. A longer account was written by William Parry, one of the party, and entered for publication on November 11, 1601. Shirley's adventures caused much comment.

3. Viola comments on the fool (III.i.67):

This fellow is wise enough to play the fool,
And to do that well craves a kind of wit.
He must observe their mood on whom he jests,
The quality of persons, and the time,
And, like the haggard, check at every feather
That comes before his eye. This is a practice
As full of labor as a wise man's art.
For folly that he wisely shows is fit,
But wise men, folly fall'n, quite taint their wit.

Robert Armin, who in 1600 succeeded Will Kempe as the clown of the Lord Chamberlain's Company, was expert at composing verses extempore. He would ask someone in the audience to suggest a topic and would then produce a poem out of his head. Late in 1600 or early in 1601 he printed a collection of these trifles called *Quips upon Questions.* One of the subjects was " He Plays the Fool," of which the first two of five stanzas run:

True it is, he plays the fool indeed,
But in the play, he plays it as he must;
Yet when the play is ended, then his speed
Is better than the pleasure of thy trust.
    For he shall have what thou that time has spent,
    Playing the fool, thy folly to content.

He plays the wise man then, and not the fool
That wisely for his living can do so.
So doth the carpenter with his sharp tool,
Cut his own finger oft, yet lives by 't too.
    He is a fool to cut his limb, say I,
    But not so with his tool to live thereby.

To this poem he added a " Quip ":

A merry man is often thought unwise,
Yet mirth in modesty's loved of the wise.
Then say, should he for a fool go
When he's a more fool that accounts him so?
Many men descant on another's wit
When they have less themselves in doing it.

Shakespeare at greater leisure rewrote this effort of the Company's new clown.

4. In a conversation between the Clown and Cesario (i.e., Viola in disguise) the Clown says (III.i.19):

CLO. I would, therefore, my sister had had no name, sir.
VIO. Why, man?
CLO. Why, sir, her name's a word, and to dally with that word might make my sister wanton. But indeed words are very rascals since bonds disgrace them.

The reference was probably to a scandalous case tried in the Star Chamber on June 12, 1600.

[1] January 6, the twelfth day after Christmas and the last and gayest night of the winter holidays. The title thus indicates a merry tale.

Mistress Mall Fowler, a woman of notoriously loose life, fell in love with one William Haynes. The two plotted to get rid of the woman's husband by accusing him of high treason, but the plot came to light after Fowler had been imprisoned in the Tower for some months. Haynes was condemned to pay a fine of £200, to stand in the pillory, and to have both his ears cut off; Mall Fowler was to be whipped and imprisoned perpetually; but the greatest disgust was expressed at the conduct of her brother, Henry Boughton, because he had been bawd and pander to his own sister. It is possible that in the passage quoted " bond " should read " bawd " (spelt " baud "); a similar misreading occurs in *Hamlet* I.iii.130.

5. In describing the shipwreck in *Twelfth Night* the Captain says (I.ii.10):

When you and those poor number saved with you
Hung on our driving boat, I saw your brother,
Most provident in peril, bind himself,
Courage and hope both teaching him the practice,
To a strong mast that lived upon the sea.

This passage was probably suggested to Shakespeare by an incident in a news pamphlet called *News from Ostend,* entered for publication on August 5, 1601. It records the miraculous escape in a sea fight of a man who " committed himself to the mercy of God and the merciless seas upon a piece of a mast rather than that he would fall into the hands of his bloody enemies. After he had so floated upon the waves of the sea an hour or two he was taken up by another ship which had spied the man driving on the water."

The earliest note of a performance of *Twelfth Night* occurs in the diary of John Manningham, a barrister of the Middle Temple, under the date February 2, 1602:

At our feast we had a play called *Twelve Night; or, What You Will,* much like *The Comedy of Errors,* or *Menaechmi* in Plautus, but most like and near to that in Italian called *Inganni.* A good practice in it to make the steward believe his lady widow was in love with him, by counterfeiting a letter as from his lady in general terms, telling him what she liked best in him, and prescribing his gesture in smiling, his apparel, etc., and then when he came to practice making him believe they took him to be mad.

As for the source of *Twelfth Night,* the resemblances noted by Manningham to *The Com-*

edy of Errors, the *Menaechmi,* and two Italian plays called *Inganni* are not very close, though in each there are mistakes caused by the likeness of twins. Indeed about a dozen different stories could possibly have been used by Shakespeare. The nearest and likeliest is the tale of *Apolonius and Silla,* included by Barnabe Riche in a collection called *Riche His Farewell to the Military Profession* (1581). The outline of the story of *Apolonius and Silla* is as follows:

Apolonius, the young Duke of Constantinople, after a campaign against the Turks was driven by tempest to take refuge with his ships in Cyprus. Here he was entertained by Pontus the Governor, who had twin children, Silvio, a son, and Silla, a daughter. Silla fell in love with Apolonius and gave him every encouragement, but the young Duke was too much occupied with warlike thoughts to notice her, and after a time he sailed home. Silla decided to follow him. She persuaded her servant Pedro to pass her off as his sister, and together they took passage in a galley bound for Constantinople. At sea the captain of the ship began to make violent love to the girl; but a lucky storm arose, and the galley was driven ashore and broken to pieces. Most of the company were drowned, but Silla floated to shore on a chest which contained clothes and money belonging to the captain. She therefore dressed herself in man's clothes and, presenting herself at the Duke's palace under the name of " Silvio," was given employment by the Duke as a servingman.

By this time Apolonius himself had fallen in love with a young, beautiful, and wealthy widow named Julina. So " Silvio " was sent to carry his messages and love gifts, with the result that Julina fell violently in love with the supposed young gentleman. Meanwhile the real Silvio, suspecting that his sister had run off with Pedro, set out to pursue them, and in due course came to Constantinople. Here by chance the widow Julina met him, and calling him by name, asked him to supper the next night. Silvio was surprised but attracted. He accepted the invitation, and spent the night with his hostess. Next morning, realizing that some mistake had been made, he decided that it would be wisest to continue his travels.

Soon afterward, Julina went to the Duke to ask his permission to marry the man of her own choice, to which at first he consented; but when his servants told him that his own servingman had put his nose out of joint, he was so angry that he caused " Silvio " to be thrust into a dungeon. Julina, finding that " Silvio " no longer came to visit her, was much disturbed, and especially as she now realized that she was pregnant. So she came again to Apolonius, told her tale, and begged that " Silvio " might be released. Thereupon " Silvio " was brought before the Duke and Julina, but denied hotly being the father of Julina's child. This moved Julina to tears and protestations and the Duke to great wrath until " Silvio," seeing no other remedy, led Julina aside and revealed that she was indeed a woman. Thereupon the Duke, deeply touched by Silla's devotion to himself, married her with great solemnity. But Julina was now in a worse case than ever, for she did not know whom to claim as the father of her child. Such strange events, however, soon came to the ears of the true Silvio, who hastened back to Constantinople, married Julina, and was reunited with his sister.

If indeed Riche's story was the direct source of the main plot of *Twelfth Night,* Shakespeare took only the main outline and certain incidents. He made far less of the wooing of the Countess by the Duke, and he stressed the love of brother and sister. Moreover Olivia is not a widow, but — like Viola — a young woman mourning the loss of a brother. Shakespeare found nothing of the rescue of Sebastian or of the adventures of Antonio in *Apolonius and Silla,* nor any hint for the story of Toby, Maria, Andrew, and Malvolio.

In plotting the secondary scenes of lower comedy, Shakespeare borrowed some ideas from the new comedy of humors (see Gen. Intro. p. 42a). Andrew is a foolish gentleman of the same kindred as Ben Jonson's Matthew or Stephen, Maria is the witty servant who plots the mischief, Malvolio is the Puritan. But, as usual, Shakespeare refrained from elaborate and exact caricature of individuals or contemporary types. Though Malvolio is an essential killjoy, he neither sings psalms down the nose nor talks in a Scriptural jargon.

" Puritan " would have reminded Shakespeare of a notable case of a particular Puritan which had roused considerable controversy and inspired several pamphlets between 1596 and 1602. In 1596 John Darrell, a Puritan preacher, began to win a reputation as an exorcist who could drive out evil spirits from those possessed. His first case was that of Thomas Darling, the " Boy of Burton," who was taken with strange fits and hallucinations. Darrell was called in, and after a lengthy exercise of prayer the evil spirit was expelled. In 1597 Darrell and another preacher called George More were summoned to deal with seven persons in the house of Master Nicholas Starkey of Cleworth in Lancashire. Darrell was

again successful. After a bout of prayer wherein the preachers tried to pray down the crying of the spirits, which lasted continuously from seven in the morning till three in the afternoon, the possessed persons were at last relieved. In the following November Darrell was called to deal with the case of a boy called Somers at Nottingham. Unfortunately, soon afterward Somers confessed that he was a fraud, and a bitter controversy raged between the Puritans who believed in Darrell and the officials of the Church of England who were eager to see him discredited. Eventually Darrell and his fellow preacher were brought before the ecclesiastical commissioners for examination, and for several months they were kept in prison in London. Meanwhile the Bishop of London instructed his chaplain, the Reverend Samuel Harsnett, to write a book against Darrell. Darrell's friends retorted with pamphlets in his defense, which in their turn were counterattacked. Of the pro-Darrell pamphlets the most interesting was More's detailed account of the Starkey case, printed in 1600. More noted that soon after the arrival of the preachers, when they called for a Bible, the possessed children fell into laughter and cried out, " Reach them the bibble babble, bibble babble," which Sir Topas seems to echo (IV.ii.105). There was thus considerable topical significance for the original audience in the scenes of the Puritan Malvolio's supposed possession.

The general tone of *Twelfth Night* is musical-melancholy, and the play opens with a passage of music which creates the atmosphere for what is to follow. The first scene shows Orsino, Duke of Illyria. He is suffering from lover's melancholy in its milder form, and he is in love with love rather than with the Countess Olivia whom he is wooing. The second scene shows Viola newly rescued from shipwreck and about to drown her sorrows for her supposedly dead brother in adventure. The third scene, as is usual in Elizabethan drama, introduces the third set of characters — the household of Olivia, which includes Maria, her waiting gentlewoman; Sir Toby, her disreputable kinsman; Sir Andrew, the silly gentleman. All three scenes are in deliberate contrast of tone: the sentimental melancholy of the Duke, the practical energy of Viola, and the low comedy of Sir Toby and Sir Andrew.

Thus the three threads of the plot are displayed, and the play is ready to move. A short interval of time passes. Viola has now been transformed into "Cesario," the Duke's gentleman, and is already in high favor. "Cesario" is accordingly sent as the Duke's messenger to Olivia. The fifth scene will naturally show the delivery of this message. It begins with the entry of Maria and the Clown. At last Olivia herself appears, accompanied by her solemn steward Malvolio (see App. 14). The Clown comes forward to meet her. The Clown is an important person in the plot, for he connects the three threads of the story. He is moreover the direct cause of the downfall of Malvolio, for Malvolio's sneer that he is a barren rascal moves him to a spiteful revenge and begins the feud between them. Then "Cesario" enters as Orsino's messenger. The two women are here contrasted. Both are mourning the loss of a brother. "Cesario" is gay and excited in spite of her troubles, Olivia is listlessly enjoying her sorrow. She is always extravagant in her emotions, whether of sorrow or of love, and she would have made herself entirely ridiculous but for the tact of Viola — though Viola, being already in love with the Duke, is not a little jealous of her rival and is amused rather than sympathetic when she finds that she has roused a hopeless passion in Olivia. Olivia at the beginning of the interview is cold and dignified, but she soon unbends, and the ensuing conversation of these two is a good specimen of Elizabethan Court wit at its best. So "Cesario" departs, having fired the affections of Olivia, and the plot begins to gain speed.

The next scene (II.i) introduces the supposedly drowned Sebastian. As usual in planning a comedy of mistaken identities, Shakespeare lets the audience into the secret early, and thereby creates dramatic irony. We know that the real Sebastian is at hand, and that sooner or later brother and sister must meet. We see also from the close resemblance between them that some very pretty complications will arise. Moreover, brother and sister have that curious physiological and psychological affinity that sometimes occurs with identical twins. To underline the resemblance, in the next scene we have another look at "Cesario," when Malvolio gives her Olivia's ring.

Thus several events are pending: Olivia is in love with "Cesario," "Cesario" is in love with Orsino, and other complications are arising. Time, or rather the illusion of time, is now needed for their ripening. Shakespeare therefore inserts the drinking scene of Sir Toby, Sir Andrew, the Clown, and Maria, with its noisy revelry which brings down Malvolio, and thereby starts the plot for his downfall. The noise and low comedy in this scene (II.iii.) is in deliberate contrast to the quiet romantic beauty of the next, when directly after the Clown's song Viola in the safety of disguise discloses her love for Orsino.

In the next scene (II.v) we are taken back to Malvolio and to the finding and reading of the letter, an episode whose comic intensity is enhanced by its following hard upon the lyric mood of the preceding scene. After this "Cesario" comes again to Olivia, thereby provoking the peevishness of Sir Andrew. Then, both to separate Malvolio's love-making from the letter scene, and also to bring the reunion of brother and sister nearer, we have another brief glimpse of Sebastian and his adoring rescuer Antonio (III.iii).

The mood then changes again to low comedy when Malvolio makes his fantastic declaration of love to Olivia. She supposes that he is mad and gives him into Toby's charge to be confined as a lunatic. This is followed by Sir Andrew's saucy challenge and the mock duel between Sir Andrew and "Cesario," which again brings home to Viola the many inconveniences of disguise. The duel is interrupted by the quite natural appearance of Antonio, who is immediately arrested by the Duke's officers. At the end of this scene Viola, who is naturally quick-witted, realizes from Antonio's bitter words that Sebastian must be alive, and she goes off much excited. Sebastian himself then appears. At first he is mistaken by the Clown for "Cesario," and then set upon by two men who are complete strangers to him, so that in a moment he is involved in a fight with Toby. Hereupon, to complete the misunderstandings, the beautiful Countess comes out and invites him into her house.

After this — to give Sebastian time for his dinner, and to remind us of Malvolio — there follows a scene (IV.ii) where the Clown disguised as the curate comes to give spiritual consolation to Malvolio in his prison. This scene has the effect of bringing the sympathy back to Malvolio, for he has been overpunished. Sebastian now comes out of the house very bewildered, and the more so when a few moments later Olivia appears with a priest, and demands that he shall immediately plight troth with her. Sebastian's acquiescence is perhaps surprising, but he has endured such a series of shocks that he is not sure whether he is mad or dreaming, and anyhow Olivia is a very charming kind of delusion.

The plot is now ready for all the stories to be combined into one ending. Up to this point Shakespeare has given an air of unreality to Orsino's love by keeping him separate from Olivia, and of reality to Viola's love by setting her alongside Orsino. To unite all three threads of the story, Shakespeare now moves the Duke and his followers over to Olivia's house, thereby concentrating all the characters in one place. There for a moment the play becomes serious. " Cesario " is claimed as husband by Olivia and angrily discarded by Orsino, but before anything further can be said or done, Sir Toby and Sir Andrew — both much battered — wander in, thus distracting the attention from " Cesario." They are escorted away, and at this point, to everyone's astonishment, the real Sebastian enters.

Here is the true climax and high moment of the play — the recognition and the reunion of brother and sister. Viola knows that Sebastian is alive, Sebastian thinks that she is dead. His gradual realization that the impossible is true is exquisitely wrought. Here is the real ending, but Shakespeare never ends his plays at the height of emotion; he always slackens the tension before he dismisses his audience.

There are still two outstanding matters to be cleared up. First Orsino transfers his affections to Viola, who is incidentally the only person in the play who marries her original choice. Orsino's action is not so surprising as it might seem, for his real need has been not Olivia but a mate; from the first he has been attracted by Viola, and he is humbled by the realization that she could, while loving him, woo another for him. There is one other matter to be cleared up — Malvolio is still in prison. He is brought in and the trickery is explained, but when he realizes how he has been fooled, he rushes away in vengeful rage, and finally forfeits all sympathy. So the lovers and the rest go into the house, leaving only the Clown. He brings the play to an end with an ironic, melancholy little ditty which gives that suggestion of pathos and questioning with which Shakespeare sometimes ends a comedy — the feeling that perhaps nothing very much matters after all.

Twelfth Night is deservedly the most popular of all Shakespeare's romantic comedies, and the most often acted. It is a perfect play for the stage; each player in turn has his moment and no one overshadows the rest. The plot is superbly planned, and each of the characters is completely formed.

The characterization is as good as the plot. Each person has enough character for his place in the play and no more. It is worth remembering that when Shakespeare wrote this play the vogue for the realistic comedy of humors was at its height (see Gen. Intro. p. 42a). The story of *Twelfth Night* is highly romantic; though it could not possibly have happened in real life, yet it remains alive long after more realistic comedies — actual transcripts from contemporary life — have faded into merely antiquarian curiosities. This is a paradox of literary art. Shakespeare realized, as Ben Jonson did not, that to hold the mirror up to nature a play needs to be something more than an exact reflection of contemporary manners. Shakespeare's scenes may be romantic and impossible, but his characters are human beings with the permanent characteristics of humanity, which survive long after passing fashions have been forgotten.

The design of *Twelfth Night* is beautifully proportioned and subtle. It is the most musical of all Shakespeare's plays. It not only begins with music, the whole play is an elaborate composition. Indeed, perhaps the best single word to describe *Twelfth Night* is " symphony," which according to the definition of the dictionary is " an elaborate orchestral composition of several contrasted but closely related movements."

Twelfth Night

DRAMATIS PERSONAE

ORSINO, *Duke of Illyria*
SEBASTIAN, *brother to Viola*
ANTONIO, *a sea captain, friend to Sebastian*
A SEA CAPTAIN, *friend to Viola*
VALENTINE ⎫
CURIO ⎭ *gentlemen attending on the Duke*
SIR TOBY BELCH, *uncle to Olivia*
SIR ANDREW AGUECHEEK
MALVOLIO, *steward to Olivia*

FABIAN ⎫
FESTE, *a clown* ⎭ *servants to Olivia*

OLIVIA
VIOLA
MARIA, *Olivia's woman*

LORDS, PRIESTS, SAILORS, OFFICERS, MUSICIANS, *and other* ATTENDANTS

SCENE — *A city in Illyria, and the seacoast near it.*

Act I

SCENE I. *An apartment in the* DUKE's *palace.*

[*Enter* DUKE, CURIO, *and other* LORDS; MUSICIANS *attending.*]
DUKE. If music be the food of love, play on.
Give me excess of it, that, surfeiting,°
The appetite may sicken, and so die.
That strain again! It had a dying fall.°
Oh, it came o'er my ear like the sweet sound   5
That breathes upon a bank of violets,
Stealing and giving odor! Enough, no more.
'Tis not so sweet now as it was before.
O spirit of love, how quick and fresh art thou!
That, notwithstanding thy capacity   10
Receiveth as the sea, naught enters there,
Of what validity and pitch soe'er,
But falls into abatement and low price,
Even in a minute!° So full of shapes is fancy
That it alone is high fantastical.°   15
    CUR. Will you go hunt, my lord?
    DUKE.   What, Curio?
    CUR. The hart.
    DUKE. Why, so I do, the noblest that I have.
Oh, when mine eyes did see Olivia first,
Methought she purged the air of pestilence!°   20
That instant was I turned into a hart,
And my desires, like fell° and cruel hounds,
E'er since pursue me.
[*Enter* VALENTINE.] How now! What news from her?

VAL. So please my lord, I might not be admitted,
But from her handmaid do return this answer: 25
The element° itself, till seven years' heat,°
Shall not behold her face at ample view;°
But, like a cloistress,° she will veilèd walk
And water once a day her chamber round
With eye-offending brine — all this to season°   30
A brother's dead love, which she would keep fresh
And lasting in her sad remembrance.
    DUKE. Oh, she that hath a heart of that fine frame
To pay this debt of love but to a brother,
How will she love when the rich golden shaft°   35
Hath killed the flock of all affections° else
That live in her; when liver, brain, and heart,°
These sovereign thrones, are all supplied, and filled
Her sweet perfections with one self king!°
Away before me to sweet beds of flowers.   40
Love thoughts lie rich when canopied with bowers.
                              [*Exeunt.*]

SCENE II. *The seacoast.*

[*Enter* VIOLA, *a* CAPTAIN, *and* SAILORS.]
VIO. What country, friends, is this?
CAP. This is Illyria,° lady.
VIO. And what should I do in Illyria?
My brother he is in Elysium.°
Perchance he is not drowned. What think you, sailors?   5
CAP. It is perchance that you yourself were saved.
VIO. Oh, my poor brother! And so perchance may he be.

Act I, Sc. i: 2. surfeiting: being overfull.   4. dying fall: cadence which falls away.   10–14. capacity . . . minute: i.e., though the spirit of love is as wide and deep as the sea, yet whatever falls into it, no matter how valuable and lofty, becomes worthless in a moment. pitch: lit., the soaring flight of a hawk.   14–15. So . . . fantastical: love (*fancy*) is so full of imagination (*shapes*) that above all others (*alone*) it is overflowing with fantasies (*high fantastical*).   20. purged . . . pestilence: The plague was believed by many to be caused by foul air.   22. fell: fierce.

26. element: sky. seven . . . heat: till seven years have passed.   27. ample view: fully.   28. cloistress: nun in a cloister.   30. season: keep fresh.   35. golden shaft: Cupid has two arrows; the golden causes love, the leaden dislike.   36. affections: desires.   37. liver . . . heart: These parts were believed to be the seat of the passions, intelligence, and affection.   39. self king: sole object of adoration.
    Sc. ii: 2. Illyria: actually on the east coast of the Adriatic sea, but Shakespeare has in fact chosen a picturesque name for an imaginary kingdom.   4. Elysium: Paradise.

CAP. True, madam. And to comfort you with chance,
Assure yourself, after our ship did split,   9
When you and those poor number saved with you
Hung on our driving° boat, I saw your brother,
Most provident in peril, bind himself,
Courage and hope both teaching him the practice,
To a strong mast that lived upon the sea;
Where, like Arion° on the dolphin's back,   15
I saw him hold acquaintance with the waves
So long as I could see.

VIO. For saying so, there's gold.
Mine own escape unfoldeth to my hope,
Whereto thy speech serves for authority,   20
The like of him.° Know'st thou this country?

CAP. Aye, madam, well, for I was bred and born
Not three hours' travel from this very place.

VIO. Who governs here?

CAP. A noble Duke, in nature as in name.   25

VIO. What is his name?

CAP. Orsino.

VIO. Orsino! I have heard my father name him.
He was a bachelor then.

CAP. And so is now, or was so very late.   30
For but a month ago I went from hence,
And then 'twas fresh in murmur — as, you know,
What great ones do the less will prattle of —
That he did seek the love of fair Olivia.

VIO. What's she?   35

CAP. A virtuous maid, the daughter of a Count
That died some twelvemonth since, then leaving her
In the protection of his son, her brother,
Who shortly also died. For whose dear love,
They say, she hath abjured the company   40
And sight of men.

VIO.   Oh, that I served that lady,
And might not be delivered to the world
Till I had made mine own occasion mellow,
What my estate is!°

CAP.   That were hard to compass,
Because she will admit no kind of suit,   45
No, not the Duke's.

VIO. There is a fair behavior in thee, Captain.
And though that Nature with a beauteous wall
Doth oft close in pollution, yet of thee
I will believe thou hast a mind that suits   50
With this thy fair and outward character.°
I prithee, and I'll pay thee bounteously,
Conceal me what I am, and be my aid
For such disguise as haply shall become

The form of my intent. I'll serve this Duke.   55
Thou shalt present me as a eunuch° to him.
It may be worth thy pains, for I can sing,°
And speak to him in many sorts of music,
That will allow me very worth his service.°
What else may hap to time I will commit,   60
Only shape thou thy silence to my wit.

CAP. Be you his eunuch, and your mute I'll be.
When my tongue blabs, then let mine eyes not see.

VIO. I thank thee. Lead me on.   [*Exeunt.*]

SCENE III. OLIVIA's *house.*

[*Enter* SIR TOBY BELCH *and* MARIA.]

SIR TO. What a plague means my niece, to take the death of her brother thus? I am sure care's an enemy to life.

MAR. By my troth, Sir Toby, you must come in earlier o' nights. Your cousin, my lady, takes great exceptions to your ill hours.   5

SIR TO. Why, let her except, before excepted.°

MAR. Aye, but you must confine yourself within the modest limits of order.   9

SIR TO. Confine! I'll confine myself no finer than I am. These clothes are good enough to drink in, and so be these boots too. An° they be not, let them hang themselves in their own straps.   13

MAR. That quaffing and drinking will undo you. I heard my lady talk of it yesterday, and of a foolish knight that you brought in one night here to be her wooer.

SIR TO. Who, Sir Andrew Aguecheek?

MAR. Aye, he.

SIR TO. He's as tall° a man as any 's in Illyria.   20

MAR. What's that to the purpose?

SIR TO. Why, he has three thousand ducats a year.

MAR. Aye, but he'll have but a year in all these ducats. He's a very fool and a prodigal.   25

SIR TO. Fie that you'll say so! He plays o' the viol de gamboys,° and speaks three or four languages word for word without book, and hath all the good gifts of nature.   29

MAR. He hath indeed, almost natural,° for besides that he's a fool, he's a great quarreler. And but that he hath the gift of a coward to allay the gust° he

56. eunuch: boy singer.   **57. I . . . sing:** The part of Viola was originally written for a boy with a good voice, but later small alterations were made and the songs were given to the Clown.   **59. allow . . . service:** approve me as worth employing.
Sc. iii: 6. except . . . excepted: Toby caps Maria's "exception" with a common legal phrase *exceptis excipiendis* (with the exceptions already excepted).   **12. An:** if.   **20. tall:** Andrew is tall and thin, but Toby implies that he is also "tall" in the common meaning of "brave."   **26–27. viol de gamboys:** bass viol, viola da gamba, so called because it was held between the legs. See Pl. 18a.   **30. natural:** with a pun on "natural," meaning born fool.   **33. allay . . . gust:** water down the taste.

11. driving: driven before the wind.   **15. Arion:** for the F1 reading "Orion." Arion was a singer. He was captured by pirates who were about to kill him. He asked to be allowed to sing for the last time. Then he jumped into the sea, where a dolphin, charmed by his song, carried him safe to land.   **19–21. Mine . . . him:** i.e., my escape and your speech give me hope that he is still alive.   **43–44. mine . . . is:** i.e., until the time is ripe for me to reveal my own affairs.   **51. character:** face — an outward indication of the nature within.

hath in quarreling, 'tis thought among the prudent he would quickly have the gift of a grave. 35

SIR TO. By this hand, they are scoundrels and sub-stractors° that say so of him. Who are they?

MAR. They that add, moreover, he's drunk nightly in your company. 39

SIR TO. With drinking healths to my niece. I'll drink to her as long as there is a passage in my throat and drink in Illyria. He's a coward and a coys-trill° that will not drink to my niece till his brains turn o' the toe like a parish top.° What, wench! *Cas-tiliano vulgo;°* for here comes Sir Andrew Ague-face. 46

[*Enter* SIR ANDREW AGUECHEEK.]

SIR AND. Sir Toby Belch! How now, Sir Toby Belch!

SIR TO. Sweet Sir Andrew!

SIR AND. Bless you, fair shrew. 50

MAR. And you too, sir.

SIR TO. Accost, Sir Andrew, accost.°

SIR AND. What's that?

SIR TO. My niece's chambermaid.

SIR AND. Good Mistress Accost, I desire better ac-quaintance. 56

MAR. My name is Mary, sir.

SIR AND. Good Mistress Mary Accost——

SIR TO. You mistake, knight. "Accost" is front her, board her, woo her, assail her. 60

SIR AND. By my troth, I would not undertake her in this company. Is that the meaning of "accost"?

MAR. Fare you well, gentlemen.

SIR TO. An thou let part so, Sir Andrew, would thou mightst never draw sword again. 66

SIR AND. An you part so, mistress, I would I might never draw sword again. Fair lady, do you think you have fools in hand?

MAR. Sir, I have not you by the hand. 70

SIR AND. Marry,° but you shall have, and here's my hand.

MAR. Now, sir, "thought is free." I pray you, bring your hand to the buttery bar° and let it drink.

SIR AND. Wherefore, sweetheart? What's your metaphor? 76

MAR. It's dry,° sir.

SIR AND. Why, I think so. I am not such an ass but I can keep my hand dry. But what's your jest? 80

MAR. A dry jest, sir.

SIR AND. Are you full of them?

MAR. Aye, sir, I have them at my fingers' ends. Marry, now I let go your hand, I am barren. [*Exit.*]

SIR TO. O knight, thou lackest a cup of canary.° When did I see thee so put down? 86

SIR AND. Never in your life, I think, unless you see canary put me down. Methinks sometimes I have no more wit than a Christian or an ordinary man has. But I am a great eater of beef° and I believe that does harm to my wit. 91

SIR TO. No question.

SIR AND. An I thought that, I'd forswear it. I'll ride home tomorrow, Sir Toby.

SIR TO. *Pourquoi,°* my dear knight? 95

SIR AND. What is "*pourquoi*"? Do or not do? I would I had bestowed that time in the tongues that I have in fencing, dancing and bearbaiting. Oh, had I but followed the arts!

SIR TO. Then hadst thou had an excellent head of hair. 101

SIR AND. Why, would that have mended my hair?

SIR TO. Past question, for thou seest it will not curl by nature.° 105

SIR AND. But it becomes me well enough, does 't not?

SIR TO. Excellent. It hangs like flax on a distaff,° and I hope to see a housewife take thee between her legs and spin it off.° 110

SIR AND. Faith, I'll home tomorrow, Sir Toby. Your niece will not be seen, or if she be, it's four to one she'll none of me. The Count himself here hard by woos her. 114

SIR TO. She'll none o' the Count. She'll not match above her degree,° neither in estate, years, nor wit. I have heard her swear 't. Tut, there's life in 't, man.

SIR AND. I'll stay a month longer. I am a fellow o' the strangest mind i' the world. I delight in masques and revels° sometimes altogether. 121

SIR TO. Art thou good at these kickshawses,° knight?

SIR AND. As any man in Illyria, whatsoever he be, under the degree of my betters. And yet I will not compare with an old man.° 126

SIR TO. What is thy excellence in a galliard,° knight?

SIR AND. Faith, I can cut a caper.°

SIR TO. And I can cut the mutton° to 't. 130

SIR AND. And I think I have the backtrick° simply as strong as any man in Illyria.

---

37. substractors: detractors.   **43. coystrill:** knave.   **44. parish top:** a large spinning top used by villagers on frosty days when it was too cold to work.   **45. Castiliano vulgo:** i.e., keep a straight face; lit., a Castilian face. The origin of the phrase is disputed.   **52. accost:** introduce yourself.   **71. Marry:** Mary, by the Virgin.   **74. buttery bar:** ledge on the half-door of the buttery on which tankards were rested. "Bar" is still used in this sense in "cocktail bar." The phrase "bring your hand to the buttery bar" is an invitation to a flirtation which Andrew is too simple to understand.   **77. dry:** A dry hand denoted lack of generosity and desire.

85. canary: wine from the Canary Isles.   **90. eater of beef:** Diet was believed to have considerable influence on bodily and mental health.   **95. Pourquoi:** why.   **104–05. curl by nature:** emendation for the F1 reading "cool my nature."   **108. distaff:** used in spinning.   **110. spin it off:** cause you to lose your hair as a result of venereal disease.   **116. degree:** rank.   **120–21. masques . . . revels:** Courtly entertainments. See Gen. Intro. p. 32a.   **122. kickshawses:** trifles.   **126. old man:** expert.   **127. galliard:** a quick, lively dance. See App. 24.   **129. caper:** jump into the air.   **130. cut . . . mutton:** Mutton was often served with caper sauce.   **131. backtrick:** a movement in dancing.

SIR TO. Wherefore are these things hid? Wherefore have these gifts a curtain before 'em? Are they like to take dust, like Mistress Mall's picture?° 135 Why dost thou not go to church in a galliard and come home in a coranto?° My very walk should be a jig,° I would not so much as make water but in a sinkapace.° What dost thou mean? Is it a world to hide virtues in? I did think, by the excellent constitution of thy leg, it was formed under the star 141 of a galliard.

SIR AND. Aye, 'tis strong, and it does indifferent well in a flame-colored stock. Shall we set about some revels? 145

SIR TO. What shall we do else? Were we not born under Taurus?°

SIR AND. Taurus! That's sides and heart.

SIR TO. No, sir, it is legs and thighs. Let me see thee caper. Ha! higher. Ha, ha! excellent! 150

[*Exeunt.*]

SCENE IV. *The* DUKE's *palace.*

[*Enter* VALENTINE, *and* VIOLA *in man's attire.*]

VAL. If the Duke continue these favors toward you, Cesario, you are like to be much advanced. He hath known you but three days, and already you are no stranger. 4

VIO. You either fear his humor° or my negligence, that you call in question the continuance of his love. Is he inconstant, sir, in his favors?

VAL. No, believe me.

VIO. I thank you. Here comes the Count.

[*Enter* DUKE, CURIO, *and* ATTENDANTS.]

DUKE. Who saw Cesario, ho? 10

VIO. On your attendance, my lord. Here.

DUKE. Stand you a while aloof. Cesario, Thou know'st no less but all. I have unclasped To thee the book even of my secret soul. 14 Therefore, good youth, address thy gait unto her. Be not denied access, stand at her doors, And tell them there thy fixèd foot shall grow Till thou have audience.

VIO.   Sure, my noble lord, If she be so abandoned to her sorrow As it is spoke, she never will admit me. 20

DUKE. Be clamorous and leap all civil bounds° Rather than make unprofited return.

VIO. Say I do speak with her, my lord, what then?

DUKE. Oh, then unfold the passion of my love, Surprise her with discourse of my dear faith. 25 It shall become thee well to act my woes. She will attend it better in thy youth Than in a nuncio's° of more grave aspéct.°

VIO. I think not so, my lord.

DUKE.   Dear lad, believe it, For they shall yet belie thy happy years 30 That say thou art a man. Diana's lip Is not more smooth and rubious;° thy small pipe° Is as the maiden's organ, shrill and sound, And all is semblative° a woman's part. I know thy constellation is right apt° 35 For this affair. Some four or five attend him, All, if you will; for I myself am best When least in company. Prosper well in this, And thou shalt live as freely as thy lord, To call his fortunes thine.

VIO.   I'll do my best 40 To woo your lady. [*Aside*] Yet, a barful° strife! Whoe'er I woo, myself would be his wife. [*Exeunt.*]

SCENE V. OLIVIA's *house.*

[*Enter* MARIA *and* CLOWN.]

MAR. Nay, either tell me where thou hast been, or I will not open my lips so wide as a bristle may enter in way of thy excuse. My lady will hang thee for thy absence.

CLO. Let her hang me. He that is well hanged in this world needs to fear no colors.° 6

MAR. Make that good.°

CLO. He shall see none to fear.

MAR. A good lenten° answer. I can tell thee where that saying was born, of "I fear no colors." 10

CLO. Where, good Mistress Mary?

MAR. In the wars, and that may you be bold to say in your foolery. 14

CLO. Well, God give them wisdom that have it, and those that are fools, let them use their talents.

MAR. Yet you will be hanged for being so long absent — or to be turned away, is not that as good as a hanging to you?

CLO. Many a good hanging prevents a bad 20 marriage, and for turning away, let summer bear it out.°

MAR. You are resolute, then?

135. **Mistress . . . picture:** a topical allusion now lost. Mall or Moll was a common nickname for a prostitute. This Mall may have been the notorious Mall Newberry. See *T Night* Intro. p. 846a. 137. **coranto:** a running dance. 138. **jig:** a lively dance. 139. **sinkapace:** "cinque pace," a dance of five steps. 146–47. **born . . . Taurus:** The common penny almanac of the time printed the figure of a naked man surrounded by the signs of the zodiac with lines pointing to the parts of the body governed by each. Both Andrew and Toby are wrong, as Taurus governed the neck and throat.

Sc. iv: 5. **humor:** whim, inclination. See App. 3. 21. **civil bounds:** restraints of good manners.

28. **nuncio:** messenger. **grave aspect:** sober countenance. 32. **rubious:** ruby-red. **small pipe:** little throat. 34. **semblative:** resembling. 35. **constellation . . . apt:** you are born under a lucky star. 41. **barful:** full of bars, impediments.

Sc. v: 6. **fear no colors:** proverbial phrase meaning "I dare anyone." Since "collar," "color," and "choler" were pronounced alike, puns on these words were endless. 7. **Make . . . good:** prove it. 9. **lenten:** fasting, lean. 21–22. **let . . . out:** have the upper hand; i.e., if I have to go, I hope it's good weather.

CLO. Not so, neither, but I am resolved on two
points.°   25
MAR. That if one break, the other will hold, or if
both break, your gaskins° fall.
CLO. Apt, in good faith, very apt. Well, go thy
way. If Sir Toby would leave drinking, thou wert as
witty a piece of Eve's flesh° as any in Illyria.   31
MAR. Peace, you rogue, no more o' that. Here
comes my lady. Make your excuse wisely, you   33
were best.   [*Exit.*]
CLO. Wit, an 't be thy will, put me into good fooling! Those wits that think they have thee do very
oft prove fools, and I that am sure I lack thee may
pass for a wise man. For what says Quinapalus?°
" Better a witty fool than a foolish wit."   40
[*Enter* LADY OLIVIA *with* MALVOLIO.] God bless thee,
lady!
OLI. Take the fool away.
CLO. Do you not hear, fellows? Take away the
lady.
OLI. Go to, you're a dry fool, I'll no more of you.
Besides, you grow dishonest.   46
CLO. Two faults,° madonna, that drink and good
counsel will amend. For give the dry fool drink,
then is the fool not dry. Bid the dishonest man mend
himself; if he mend, he is no longer dishonest;   50
if he cannot, let the botcher° mend him. Anything
that's mended is but patched. Virtue that trans-
gresses is but patched with sin, and sin that amends
is but patched with virtue. If that this simple syllo-
gism° will serve, so. If it will not, what rem-   55
edy? As there is no true cuckold° but calamity,
so beauty's a flower. The lady bade take away the
fool, therefore I say again, take her away.
OLI. Sir, I bade them take away you.   60
CLO. Misprision° in the highest degree! Lady,
cucullus non facit monachum.° That's as much to
say as I wear not motley° in my brain. Good madonna, give me leave to prove you a fool.
OLI. Can you do it?   65
CLO. Dexteriously, good madonna.
OLI. Make your proof.
CLO. I must catechize you for it, madonna. Good
my mouse° of virtue, answer me.
OLI. Well, sir, for want of other idleness, I'll bide
your proof.   71
CLO. Good madonna, why mournest thou?

OLI. Good fool, for my brother's death.
CLO. I think his soul is in Hell, madonna.
OLI. I know his soul is in Heaven, fool.   75
CLO. The more fool, madonna, to mourn for your
brother's soul being in Heaven. Take away the fool,
gentlemen.
OLI. What think you of this fool, Malvolio? Doth
he not mend?   80
MAL. Yes, and shall do till the pangs of death
shake him. Infirmity, that decays the wise, doth
ever make the better fool.
CLO. God send you, sir, a speedy infirmity, for the
better increasing your folly! Sir Toby will be sworn
that I am no fox, but he will not pass his word for
twopence that you are no fool.   86
OLI. How say you to that, Malvolio?
MAL. I marvel your ladyship takes delight in such
a barren rascal.° I saw him put down the other day
with an ordinary fool that has no more brain   90
than a stone. Look you now, he's out of his guard already. Unless you laugh and minister occasion° to
him, he is gagged. I protest, I take these wise men
that crow so at these set kind of fools no better than
the fools' zanies.°   96
OLI. Oh, you are sick of self-love, Malvolio, and
taste with a distempered appetite. To be generous,
guiltless, and of free° disposition is to take those
things for bird bolts° that you deem cannon   100
bullets. There is no slander in an allowed° fool,
though he do nothing but rail; nor no railing in a
known discreet man, though he do nothing but reprove.
CLO. Now Mercury° endue thee with leasing,°
for thou speakest well of fools!   106
[*Re-enter* MARIA.]
MAR. Madam, there is at the gate a young gentleman much desires to speak with you.
OLI. From the Count Orsino, is it?
MAR. I know not, madam. 'Tis a fair young man,
and well attended.   111
OLI. Who of my people hold him in delay?
MAR. Sir Toby, madam, your kinsman.
OLI. Fetch him off, I pray you. He speaks nothing
but madman, fie on him! [*Exit* MARIA.] Go you,
Malvolio. If it be a suit from the Count, I am   116
sick, or not at home — what you will, to dismiss it.
[*Exit* MALVOLIO.] Now you see, sir, how your fool-
ing grows old, and people dislike it.   119
CLO. Thou hast spoke for us, madonna, as if thy
eldest son should be a fool, whose skull Jove cram

---

25. **points:** laces used to attach the hose to the doublet.
27. **gaskins:** breeches.   31. **Eve's flesh:** erring woman — the
first hint that there is something between Toby and Maria.
39. **Quinapalus:** a character invented by Rabelais. The clown
specializes in mock learning.   47. **Two faults:** The fool is in disgrace and to cajole Olivia into good humor rattles out mock
learned nonsense. 51. **botcher:** an unskillful mender of old
garments. 55. **syllogism:** learned argument. 56. **cuckold:** husband deceived by his wife. 61. **Misprision:** error. 62. **cucullus
. . . monachum:** a cowl does not make a monk. 63. **motley:** the
fool's particolored costume. See Pl. 12f, 13c. 69. **mouse:** a term
of endearment, like "duck."

89. **barren rascal:** By this remark Malvolio rouses the malice
of the fool, and so ultimately brings about his own downfall.
92. **minister occasion:** i.e., give him a lead. 96. **zanies:** stooges;
the zany was the clown's assistant who tried to copy his tricks.
99. **free:** innocent. 100. **bird bolts:** short, blunt headed arrows
used in a crossbow for killing small birds. See Pl. 22a. 101. **allowed:** licensed.   105. **Mercury:** the god of thieves and rascals.
endue . . . leasing: endow you with lying.

with brains! for — here he comes° — one of thy kin has a most weak pia mater.°

[*Enter* SIR TOBY.]

OLI. By mine honor, half-drunk. What is he at the gate, Cousin?   125

SIR TO. A gentleman.

OLI. A gentleman! What gentleman?

SIR TO. 'Tis a gentleman here — a plague o' these pickle-herring!° How now, sot!

CLO. Good Sir Toby!   130

OLI. Cousin, Cousin, how have you come so early by this lethargy?°

SIR TO. Lechery! I defy lechery. There's one at the gate.

OLI. Aye, marry, what is he?   135

SIR TO. Let him be the Devil an he will, I care not. Give me faith, say I. Well, it's all one.   [*Exit.*]

OLI. What's a drunken man like, fool?

CLO. Like a drowned man, a fool, and a madman. One draught above heat makes him a fool, the second mads him, and a third drowns him.   141

OLI. Go thou and seek the crowner,° and let him sit o' my coz,° for he's in the third degree of drink, he's drowned. Go look after him.   144

CLO. He is but mad yet, madonna, and the fool shall look to the madman.   [*Exit.*]

[*Re-enter* MALVOLIO.]

MAL. Madam, yond young fellow swears he will speak with you. I told him you were sick; he takes on him to understand so much, and therefore   150 comes to speak with you. I told him you were asleep; he seems to have a foreknowledge of that too, and therefore comes to speak with you. What is to be said to him, lady? He's fortified against any denial.

OLI. Tell him he shall not speak with me.   155

MAL. Has been told so, and he says he'll stand at your door like a sheriff's post,° and be the supporter° to a bench, but he'll speak with you.

OLI. What kind o' man is he?

MAL. Why, of mankind.   160

OLI. What manner of man?

MAL. Of very ill manner. He'll speak with you, will you or no.

OLI. Of what personage and years is he?   164

MAL. Not yet old enough for a man, nor young enough for a boy, as a squash° is before 'tis a peascod, or a codling when 'tis almost an apple. 'Tis with him in standing water,° between boy and man.

He is very well-favored° and he speaks very shrewishly.° One would think his mother's milk were scarce out of him.   171

OLI. Let him approach. Call in my gentlewoman.

MAL. Gentlewoman, my lady calls.   [*Exit.*]

[*Re-enter* MARIA.]

OLI. Give me my veil. Come, throw it o'er   175 my face. We'll once more hear Orsino's embassy.

[*Enter* VIOLA *and* ATTENDANTS.]

VIO. The honorable lady of the house, which is she?

OLI. Speak to me, I shall answer for her. Your will?   180

VIO. Most radiant, exquisite, and unmatchable beauty, I pray you tell me if this be the lady of the house, for I never saw her. I would be loath to cast away my speech, for besides that it is excellently well penned, I have taken great pains to con°   185 it. Good beauties, let me sustain no scorn. I am very comptible,° even to the least sinister° usage.

OLI. Whence came you, sir?

VIO. I can say little more than I have studied, and that question's out of my part. Good gentle one, give me modest assurance if you be the lady of the house, that I may proceed in my speech.   192

OLI. Are you a comedian?°

VIO. No, my profound heart. And yet, by the very fangs of malice I swear, I am not that I play.° Are you the lady of the house?

OLI. If I do not usurp myself, I am.

VIO. Most certain, if you are she, you do usurp yourself; for what is yours to bestow is not yours to reserve. But this is from my commission.° I   200 will on with my speech in your praise, and then show you the heart of my message.

OLI. Come to what is important in 't. I forgive you the praise.   205

VIO. Alas, I took great pains to study it, and 'tis poetical.

OLI. It is the more like to be feigned. I pray you keep it in. I heard you were saucy at my gates, and allowed your approach rather to wonder° at you than to hear you. If you be not mad, be gone. If   211 you have reason, be brief. 'Tis not that time of moon° with me to make one in so skipping° a dialogue.

MAR. Will you hoist sail, sir? Here lies your way.

VIO. No, good swabber,° I am to hull° here a little

<hr />

122. **here he comes**: i.e., Toby. This is the usual phrase to draw attention to a character entering at the back of the stage. See Gen. Intro. p. 56b.   123. **pia mater**: brain.   129. **pickle-herring**: very salt and indigestible, and so causing thirst and wind.   132. **lethargy**: lack of sense.   142. **crowner**: coroner, whose function is to hold an inquest on the bodies of those who die unnaturally.   143. **coz**: cousin — used for any near relation.   157. **sheriff's post**: painted post set up before the house of the sheriff as a sign of office.   158. **supporter**: support.   166. **squash**: unripe peapod.   168. **standing water**: the moment at the change of the tide when the water neither ebbs nor flows.

169. **well-favored**: good-looking.   170. **shrewishly**: like a shrew, shrill.   185. **con**: learn by heart.   187. **comptible**: susceptible. **sinister**: left-handed, unkind.   193. **comedian**: actor.   195. **that I play**: i.e., the part I act, that of a man.   200. **from my commission**: not included in my instructions.   210. **allowed . . . wonder**: I allowed you to come in so that I might look at you — not to listen to your prepared speeches.   212-13. **time of moon**: lucky end of the month.   213. **skipping**: frivolous.   218. **swabber**: one who swabs the decks. Viola retorts to Maria's "hoist sail" with a series of nautical metaphors. **hull**: lie at anchor.

longer. Some mollification for your giant,° sweet
lady. Tell me your mind. I am a messenger.   220

OLI. Sure, you have some hideous matter to deliver when the courtesy of it is so fearful.° Speak
your office.

VIO. It alone concerns your ear. I bring no over-
ture° of war, no taxation of° homage. I hold   225
the olive in my hand, my words are as full of peace
as matter.

OLI. Yet you began rudely. What are you? What
would you?   229

VIO. The rudeness that hath appeared in me have
I learned from my entertainment. What I am, and
what I would, are as secret as maidenhead — to your
ears, divinity; to any other's, profanation.   234

OLI. Give us the place alone. We will hear this
divinity.° [*Exeunt* MARIA *and* ATTENDANTS.] Now,
sir, what is your text?

VIO. Most sweet lady——

OLI. A comfortable doctrine, and much may be
said of it. Where lies your text?   240

VIO. In Orsino's bosom.

OLI. In his bosom! In what chapter of his
bosom?

VIO. To answer by the method,° in the first of his
heart.   245

OLI. Oh, I have read it. It is heresy. Have you no
more to say?

VIO. Good madam, let me see your face.

OLI. Have you any commission from your lord to
negotiate with my face? You are now out of   250
your text. But we will draw the curtain and show
you the picture. Look you, sir, [*Unveiling*] such a
one I was this present° — is 't not well done?

VIO. Excellently done, if God did all.

OLI. 'Tis in grain,° sir, 'twill endure wind and
weather.   256

VIO. 'Tis beauty truly blent,° whose red and white
Nature's own sweet and cunning hand laid on.
Lady, you are the cruel'st she alive
If you will lead these graces to the grave   260
And leave the world no copy.°

OLI. Oh, sir, I will not be so hardhearted, I will
give out divers schedules of my beauty. It shall be
inventoried, and every particle and utensil labeled
to my will — as, item, two lips, indifferent red;   265

item, two gray eyes, with lids to them; item, one
neck, one chin, and so forth. Were you sent hither
to praise me?

VIO. I see what you are, you are too proud;
But if you were the Devil, you are fair.   270
My lord and master loves you. Oh, such love
Could be but recompensed, though you were
     crowned
The nonpareil° of beauty!

OLI.   How does he love me?

VIO. With adorations, fertile tears,   274
With groans that thunder love, with sighs of fire.

OLI. Your lord does know my mind. I cannot love
     him.
Yet I suppose him virtuous, know him noble,
Of great estate, of fresh and stainless youth;
In voices well divulged,° free, learned, and valiant;
And in dimension° and the shape of nature   280
A gracious person. But yet I cannot love him.
He might have took his answer long ago.

VIO. If I did love you in my master's flame,
With such a suffering, such a deadly life,
In your denial I would find no sense.   285
I would not understand it.

OLI.   Why, what would you?

VIO. Make me a willow cabin° at your gate,
And call upon my soul within the house;
Write loyal cantons° of contemnèd° love
And sing them loud even in the dead of night;   290
Halloo your name to the reverberate hills,
And make the babbling gossip of the air
Cry out "Olivia!" Oh, you should not rest
Between the elements of air and earth,
But you should pity me!

OLI.   You might do much.   295
What is your parentage?

VIO. Above my fortunes, yet my state is well.
I am a gentleman.

OLI.   Get you to your lord.
I cannot love him. Let him send no more,
Unless, perchance, you come to me again   300
To tell me how he takes it. Fare you well.
I thank you for your pains. Spend this for me.

VIO. I am no fee'd post,° lady, keep your purse.
My master, not myself, lacks recompense.
Love make his heart of flint that you shall love;   305
And let your fervor, like my master's, be
Placed in contempt! Farewell, fair cruelty. [*Exit.*]

OLI. "What is your parentage?"
"Above my fortunes, yet my state is well.
I am a gentleman." I'll be sworn thou art.   310
Thy tongue, thy face, thy limbs, actions, and spirit,

219. mollification . . . giant: Viola apologizes to Olivia for the
interruption — "I had to pacify your little lady." Maria's smallness is emphasized. See Gen. Intro. pp. 59b–60a.   **222. courtesy
. . . fearful:** you must have some dreadful message to deliver if
it need such elaborate introduction.   **225. overture:** declaration. **taxation of:** demand for.   **236. divinity:** Olivia takes up
Viola's *divinity*, and the two follow up the metaphor in their
conversation.   **244. To . . . method:** to keep up the metaphor.
252–53. such . . . present: This is the F₁ reading, and has been
much emended. The general meaning is "This is what I really
am."   **255. in grain:** i.e., the colors are fast, they will not wash
out.   **257. blent:** blended.   **261. leave . . . copy:** die without
children to carry on the pattern. Cf. Sonnets 1–17.

273. nonpareil: without an equal.   **279. voices . . . divulged:**
spoken well of.   **280. dimension:** bodily form.   **287. willow
cabin:** an arbor of willow — the unhappy lover's tree.   **289. can-
tons:** songs. **contemned:** despised.   **303. fee'd post:** paid messenger.

Do give thee fivefold blazon.° Not too fast. Soft,
    soft!
Unless the master were the man. How now!
Even so quickly may one catch the plague?
Methinks I feel this youth's perfections   315
With an invisible and subtle stealth
To creep in at mine eyes. Well, let it be.
What ho, Malvolio!

      [Re-enter MALVOLIO.*]*

MAL.   Here, madam, at your service.
OLI. Run after that same peevish messenger,   319
The County's° man. He left this ring behind him,
Would I or not. Tell him I'll none of it.
Desire him not to flatter with his lord,
Nor hold him up with hopes. I am not for him.
If that the youth will come this way tomorrow,
I'll give him reasons for 't. Hie thee,° Malvolio.   325
MAL. Madam, I will.   *[Exit.]*
OLI. I do I know not what, and fear to find
Mine eye too great a flatterer for my mind.   328
Fate, show thy force, ourselves we do not owe.°
What is decreed must be, and be this so.   *[Exit.]*

Act II

SCENE I. *The seacoast.*

[Enter ANTONIO *and* SEBASTIAN.*]*

ANT. Will you stay no longer? Nor will you not
that I go with you?
SEB. By your patience, no. My stars shine darkly
over me. The malignancy° of my fate might perhaps
distemper° yours, therefore I shall crave of you   5
your leave that I may bear my evils alone. It were
a bad recompense for your love to lay any of them
on you.
ANT. Let me yet know of you whither you are
bound.   10
SEB. No, sooth, sir. My determinate voyage is
mere extravagancy.° But I perceive in you so excellent a touch of modesty that you will not extort from
me what I am willing to keep in; therefore it charges
me in manners the rather to express myself.°   15
You must know of me then, Antonio, my name is
Sebastian, which I called Roderigo.° My father was
that Sebastian of Messaline° whom I know you have

heard of. He left behind him myself and a sister,
both born in an hour. If the Heavens had been   20
pleased, would we had so ended! But you, sir, altered
that, for some hour before you took me from the
breach° of the sea was my sister drowned.
ANT. Alas the day!   25
SEB. A lady, sir, though it was said she much resembled me, was yet of many accounted beautiful.
But though I could not with such estimable won-
der° overfar believe that, yet thus far I will boldly
publish° her — she bore a mind that envy could   30
not but call fair. She is drowned already, sir, with
salt water, though I seem to drown her remembrance again with more.   33
ANT. Pardon me, sir, your bad entertainment.°
SEB. O good Antonio, forgive me your trouble.
ANT. If you will not murder me for my love, let
me be your servant.
SEB. If you will not undo what you have done —
that is, kill him whom you have recovered — desire
it not. Fare ye well at once. My bosom is full of   40
kindness,° and I am yet so near the manners of my
mother that upon the least occasion more mine eyes
will tell tales of me. I am bound to the Count Or-
sino's Court. Farewell.   *[Exit.]*
ANT. The gentleness of all the gods go with
    thee!   45
I have many enemies in Orsino's Court,
Else would I very shortly see thee there.
But, come what may, I do adore thee so
That danger shall seem sport, and I will go.
          [Exit.]

SCENE II. *A street.*

[Enter VIOLA, MALVOLIO *following.]*

MAL. Were not you even now with the Countess
Olivia?
VIO. Even now, sir. On a moderate pace I have
since arrived but hither.   4
MAL. She returns this ring to you, sir. You might
have saved me my pains, to have taken it away yourself. She adds, moreover, that you should put your
lord into a desperate assurance° she will none of
him. And one thing more, that you be never so
hardy to come again in his affairs, unless it be to report your lord's taking of this. Receive it so.   12
VIO. She took the ring of me. I'll none of it.
MAL. Come, sir, you peevishly threw it to her; and
her will is, it should be so returned. If it be worth
stooping for, there it lies in your eye. If not, be it his
that finds it.   *[Exit.]*

---

312. **blazon:** coat of arms denoting a gentleman.   320. **County:**
Count.   325. **Hie thee:** hasten.   329. **owe:** own.
Act II, Sc. i: 4. **malignancy:** evil disposition. See App. 1.
5. **distemper:** disturb.   11–12. **determinate . . . extravagancy:**
the journey I have determined is mere wandering. There is a
touch of affectation in Sebastian's language.   14–15. **it . . . myself:** good manners demand that I tell you who I am.   17. **I
. . . Roderigo:** hitherto I have pretended that my name was
Roderigo.   18. **Messaline:** Messina in Sicily.

24. **breach:** where the waves break.   28–29. **estimable wonder:**
admiring judgment.   30. **publish:** proclaim.   34. **your . . . entertainment:** looking after you so badly.   41. **kindness:** tender
feeling.
Sc. ii: 9. **desperate assurance:** certainty that there is no hope.

vio. I left no ring with her. What means this
lady?
Fortune forbid my outside have not charmed her!
She made good view of me;° indeed, so much   20
That sure methought her eyes had lost her tongue,
For she did speak in starts distractedly.
She loves me, sure, the cunning of her passion
Invites me in this churlish messenger.
None of my lord's ring! Why, he sent her none.   25
I am the man. If it be so, as 'tis,
Poor lady, she were better love a dream.
Disguise, I see thou art a wickedness,
Wherein the pregnant° enemy does much.
How easy is it for the proper-false°   30
In women's waxen hearts to set their forms!
Alas, our frailty is the cause, not we!
For such as we are made of, such we be.
How will this fadge?° My master loves her dearly;
And I, poor monster, fond as much on him,   35
And she, mistaken, seems to dote on me.
What will become of this? As I am man,
My state is desperate for my master's love;
As I am woman — now alas the day! —
What thriftless° sighs shall poor Olivia breathe!   40
O Time, thou must untangle this, not I!
It is too hard a knot for me to untie!   [*Exit.*]

SCENE III. OLIVIA's *house.*

[*Enter* SIR TOBY *and* SIR ANDREW.]

SIR TO. Approach, Sir Andrew. Not to be abed
after midnight is to be up betimes; and "*diluculo
surgere,*"° thou know'st ——
SIR AND. Nay, by my troth,° I know not. But I
know to be up late is to be up late.   5
SIR TO. A false conclusion. I hate it as an unfilled
can.° To be up after midnight, and to go to bed
then, is early, so that to go to bed after midnight is
to go to bed betimes. Does not our life consist of the
four elements?°   10
SIR AND. Faith, so they say, but I think it rather
consists of eating and drinking.
SIR TO. Thou 'rt a scholar. Let us therefore eat and
drink. Marian, I say, a stoup° of wine!
[*Enter* CLOWN.]
SIR AND. Here comes the fool, i' faith.   15
CLO. How now, my hearts! Did you never see the
picture of " we three "?°
SIR TO. Welcome, ass. Now let's have a catch.°

SIR AND. By my troth, the fool has an excellent
breast.° I had rather than forty shillings I had   20
such a leg, and so sweet a breath to sing, as the fool
has. In sooth, thou wast in very gracious fooling last
night, when thou spokest of Pigrogromitus, of the
Vapians passing the equinoctial of Queubus.° 'Twas
very good, i' faith. I sent thee sixpence for thy
leman.° Hadst it?   26
CLO. I did impeticos thy gratillity,° for Malvolio's
nose is no whipstock. My lady has a white hand, and
the Myrmidons are no bottle-ale houses.
SIR AND. Excellent! Why, this is the best fooling,
when all is done. Now, a song.   31
SIR TO. Come on, there is sixpence for you — let's
have a song.
SIR AND. There's a testril° of me too. If one knight
give a ——   35
CLO. Would you have a love song, or a song of
good life?
SIR TO. A love song, a love song.
SIR AND. Aye, aye. I care not for good life.
CLO. [*Sings.*]
O mistress mine, where are you roaming?   40
Oh, stay and hear, your truelove's coming,
That can sing both high and low.
Trip no further, pretty sweeting,
Journeys end in lovers meeting,
Every wise man's son doth know.   45
SIR AND. Excellent good, i' faith.
SIR TO. Good, good.
CLO. [*Sings.*]
What is love? 'Tis not hereafter,
Present mirth hath present laughter,
What's to come is still unsure.   50
In delay there lies no plenty,
Then come kiss me, sweet and twenty,°
Youth's a stuff will not endure.
SIR AND. A mellifluous° voice, as I am a true
knight.   55
SIR TO. A contagious breath.
SIR AND. Very sweet and contagious, i' faith.
SIR TO. To hear by the nose, it is dulcet in con-
tagion.° But shall we make the welkin° dance in-
deed? Shall we rouse the night owl in a catch°   60
that will draw three souls out of one weaver?° Shall
we do that?

20. made . . . me: took a good look at me.   29. pregnant: re-
sourceful.   30. proper-false: men who are handsome but deceitful.   34. fadge: turn out.   40. thriftless: useless.
Sc. iii: 2–3. diluculo surgere: early to rise — a tag from the
schoolboy's Latin grammar.   4. troth: truth.   7. can: pot.
10. four elements: See App. 3.   14. stoup: large drinking pot.
See Pl. 20e and g.   17. we three: a picture of two asses, the
spectator being the third.   18. catch: rowdy song, where each
singer in turn catches up the song a few words after the others.

20. breast: voice.   23–24. Pigrogromitus . . . Queubus: more
mock learned foolery.   26. leman: sweetheart.   27. impeticos
. . . gratillity: pocket your tip. The rest of the fool's profundity
is unexplained; but as both knights are growing more and more
fuddled, it is not important.   34. testril: coin worth sixpence.
52. sweet . . . twenty: gay girl.   54. mellifluous: honey-sweet.
58–59. dulcet in contagion: sweetly catching.   59. welkin: sky.
60. catch: See l. 18, n. The words of the catch which they sing
at l. 75 are "Hold thy peace, thou knave."   61. three . . .
weaver: Weavers, mostly Puritan refugees from the Netherlands, were noted psalm singers. It will need a powerful song to
draw out three souls.

SIR AND. An you love me, let's do 't. I am dog at a catch. 64

CLO. By 'r lady, sir, and some dogs will catch well.

SIR AND. Most certain. Let our catch be " Thou knave."

CLO. " Hold thy peace, thou knave," knight? 69 I shall be constrained in 't to call thee knave, knight.

SIR AND. 'Tis not the first time I have constrained one to call me knave. Begin, fool. It begins " Hold thy peace."

CLO. I shall never begin if I hold my peace.

SIR AND. Good, i' faith. Come, begin. 75
[*Catch sung.*]

[*Enter* MARIA.]

MAR. What a caterwauling do you keep here! If my lady have not called up her steward Malvolio and bid him turn you out of doors, never trust me. 79

SIR TO. My lady's a Cataian,° we are politicians,° Malvolio's a Peg-a-Ramsey,° and " Three merry men be we." Am not I consanguineous?° Am I not of her blood? Tillyvally.° Lady! [*Sings.*] " There dwelt a man in Babylon, lady, lady! " 84

CLO. Beshrew me,° the knight's in admirable fooling.

SIR AND. Aye, he does well enough if he be disposed, and so do I too. He does it with a better grace, but I do it more natural. 89

SIR TO. [*Sings.*] " Oh, the twelfth day of December "——

MAR. For the love o' God, peace!

[*Enter* MALVOLIO.]

MAL. My masters, are you mad? Or what are you? Have you no wit, manners, nor honesty, but to gabble like tinkers at this time of night? Do ye make an alehouse of my lady's house, that ye squeak 95 out your coziers'° catches without any mitigation or remorse of voice? Is there no respect of place, persons, nor time in you? 99

SIR TO. We did keep time, sir, in our catches. Sneck up!°

MAL. Sir Toby, I must be round° with you. My lady bade me tell you that though she harbors you as her kinsman, she's nothing allied to your disorders. If you can separate yourself and your 105 misdemeanors, you are welcome to the house. If not, an it would please you to take leave of her, she is very willing to bid you farewell.

SIR TO. " Farewell,° dear heart, since I must needs be gone." 110

MAR. Nay, good Sir Toby.

CLO. " His eyes do show his days are almost done."

MAL. Is't even so?

SIR TO. " But I will never die." 115

CLO. Sir Toby, there you lie.

MAL. This is much credit to you.

SIR TO. " Shall I bid him go? "

CLO. " What an if you do? "

SIR TO. " Shall I bid him go, and spare not? " 120

CLO. " Oh, no, no, no, no, you dare not."

SIR TO. Out o' tune, sir. Ye lie. Art any more than a steward? Dost thou think because thou art virtuous, there shall be no more cakes and ale? 125

CLO. Yes, by Saint Anne, and ginger shall be hot i' the mouth too.

SIR TO. Thou 'rt i' the right. Go, sir, rub your chain° with crumbs.° A stoup of wine, Maria!

MAL. Mistress Mary, if you prized my lady's 130 favor at anything more than contempt, you would not give means for this uncivil rule.° She shall know of it, by this hand. [*Exit.*]

MAR. Go shake your ears. 134

SIR AND. 'Twere as good a deed as to drink when a man's a-hungry, to challenge him the field, and then to break promise with him and make a fool of him.

SIR TO. Do 't, knight. I'll write thee a challenge, or I'll deliver thy indignation to him by word of mouth.

MAR. Sweet Sir Toby, be patient for tonight. 142 Since the youth of the Count's was today with my lady, she is much out of quiet. For Monsieur Malvolio, let me alone with him. If I do not gull 145 him into a nayword,° and make him a common recreation,° do not think I have wit enough to lie straight in my bed. I know I can do it.

SIR TO. Possess us, possess us. Tell us something of him. 150

MAR. Marry, sir, sometimes he is a kind of Puritan.

SIR AND. Oh, if I thought that, I'd beat him like a dog!

SIR TO. What, for being a Puritan? Thy exquisite reason, dear knight? 156

SIR AND. I have no exquisite reason for 't, but I have reason good enough.

MAR. The devil a Puritan that he is, or anything constantly, but a timepleaser;° an affectioned° 160 ass, that cons state° without book and utters it by great swarths — the best persuaded of himself, so crammed, as he thinks, with excellencies, that it is his grounds of faith that all that look on him love him. And on that vice in him will my revenge find notable cause to work. 166

---

80. Cataian: Chinaman. **politicians:** deep ones. **81. Peg-a-Ramsey:** It is not known who this lady was or why Malvolio resembled her. **82. consanguineous:** related by blood. Toby's mind has now strayed to Olivia. **83. Tillyvally:** "hoity-toity." **85. Beshrew me:** lit., ill luck take me. **96. coziers:** cobblers. **101. Sneck up:** be hanged. **102. round:** direct. **109–21. Farewell . . . not:** Toby and the Clown here indulge in an impromptu duet.

129. chain: i.e., of office as a steward. **with crumbs:** used for polishing silver. **132. uncivil rule:** disorderly conduct. **146. nayword:** byword. **146–47. common recreation:** general laughingstock. **160. timepleaser:** one who suits his behavior to his own advantage. **affectioned:** affected. **161. cons state:** learns courtly behavior by heart.

SIR TO. What wilt thou do?

MAR. I will drop in his way some obscure epistles of love, wherein, by the color of his beard, the shape of his leg, the manner of his gait, the expres- 170 sure of his eye, forehead, and complexion, he shall find himself most feelingly° personated. I can write very like my lady your niece. On a forgotten matter we can hardly make distinction of our hands. 175

SIR TO. Excellent! I smell a device.

SIR AND. I have 't in my nose too.

SIR TO. He shall think, by the letters that thou wilt drop, that they come from my niece, and that she's in love with him. 180

MAR. My purpose is indeed a horse of that color.

SIR AND. And your horse now would make him an ass.

MAR. Ass, I doubt not. 185

SIR AND. Oh, 'twill be admirable!

MAR. Sport royal, I warrant you. I know my physic will work with him. I will plant you two, and let the fool make a third, where he shall find the letter. Observe his construction of it. For 190 this night, to bed, and dream on the event. Farewell.
[*Exit.*]

SIR TO. Good night, Penthesilea.°

SIR AND. Before me, she's a good wench.

SIR TO. She's a beagle,° true-bred, and one that adores me. What o' that? 196

SIR AND. I was adored once too.

SIR TO. Let's to bed, knight. Thou hadst need send for more money.

SIR AND. If I cannot recover° your niece, I am a foul way out.° 201

SIR TO. Send for money, knight. If thou hast her not i' the end, call me cut.°

SIR AND. If I do not, never trust me, take it how you will. 205

SIR TO. Come, come, I'll go burn some sack.° 'Tis too late to go to bed now. Come, knight, come, knight.
[*Exeunt.*]

SCENE IV. *The* DUKE'S *palace.*

[*Enter* DUKE, VIOLA, CURIO, *and others.*]

DUKE. Give me some music. Now, good morrow, friends.
Now, good Cesario, but that piece of song,°

That old and antique song we heard last night.
Methought it did relieve my passion much,
More than light airs and recollected terms° 5
Of these most brisk and giddy-paced° times.
Come, but one verse.

CUR. He is not here, so please your lordship, that should sing it.

DUKE. Who was it? 10

CUR. Feste, the jester, my lord, a fool that the Lady Olivia's father took much delight in. He is about the house.

DUKE. Seek him out, and play the tune the while.
[*Exit* CURIO. *Music plays.*]
Come hither, boy. If ever thou shalt love, 15
In the sweet pangs of it remember me;
For such as I am all truelovers are,
Unstaid and skittish in all motions else
Save in the constant image of the creature
That is beloved. How dost thou like this tune? 20

VIO. It gives a very echo to the seat
Where Love is throned.

DUKE.   Thou dost speak masterly.
My life upon 't, young though thou art, thine eye
Hath stayed upon some favor° that it loves. 25
Hath it not, boy?

VIO.   A little, by your favor.

DUKE. What kind of woman is 't?

VIO.   Of your complexion.

DUKE. She is not worth thee, then. What years, i' faith?

VIO. About your years, my lord.

DUKE. Too old, by Heaven. Let still° the woman take 30
An elder than herself, so wears she to him,
So sways she level in her husband's heart.
For, boy, however we do praise ourselves,
Our fancies are more giddy and unfirm,
More longing, wavering, sooner lost and worn, 35
Than women's are.

VIO.   I think it well, my lord.

DUKE. Then let thy love be younger than thyself,
Or thy affection cannot hold the bent.°
For women are as roses, whose fair flower
Being once displayed, doth fall that very hour. 40

VIO. And so they are. Alas, that they are so —
To die, even when they to perfection grow!
[*Re-enter* CURIO *and* CLOWN.]

DUKE. Oh, fellow, come, the song we had last night.
Mark it, Cesario, it is old and plain.
The spinsters and the knitters in the sun 45

---

172. **feelingly:** exactly. 192. **Penthesilea:** Queen of the Amazons, a large, muscular lady — an ironical description of the little gentlewoman. 195. **beagle:** a small hound. 200. **recover:** win. 201. **foul . . . out:** have wasted a lot of money. 203. **cut:** gelded. 206. **burn . . . sack:** warm some sack. Sack (Falstaff's favorite drink; see *II Hen IV*, IV.iii.103–35) was a Spanish wine. It was sometimes sweetened and drunk warm.

Sc. iv: 2. **piece of song:** another indication that Viola was originally intended to be the singer. See I.ii.57,n.

5. **recollected terms:** artificial phrases. 6. **giddy-paced:** frivolous. 25. **favor:** face. Viola (l. 26) in the safety of disguise takes up the word "by your favor," which Orsino interprets as "by your leave." 30. **still:** always. 38. **hold . . . bent:** keep the tension; the image is of a strung bow.

And the free maids that weave their thread with
    bones°
Do use to chant it. It is silly sooth,°
And dallies with the innocence of love,
Like the old age.

CLO. Are you ready, sir?   50
DUKE. Aye, prithee sing.   [*Music.*]
CLO. [*Sings.*]
Come away, come away, death,
    And in sad cypress° let me be laid.
Fly away, fly away, breath,
    I am slain by a fair cruel maid.   55
My shroud° of white, stuck all with yew,
    Oh, prepare it!
My part of death, no one so true
    Did share it!

Not a flower, not a flower sweet,   60
    On my black coffin let there be strown.
Not a friend, not a friend greet
    My poor corpse, where my bones shall be thrown.
A thousand thousand sighs to save,
    Lay me, oh, where
Sad truelover never find my grave,
    To weep there!
DUKE. There's for thy pains.   69
CLO. No pains, sir. I take pleasure in singing, sir.
DUKE. I'll pay thy pleasure then.
CLO. Truly, sir, and pleasure will be paid, one
time or another.
DUKE. Give me now leave to leave thee.   74
CLO. Now, the melancholy god protect thee, and
the tailor make thy doublet° of changeable° taffeta,
for thy mind is a very opal. I would have men of
such constancy° put to sea, that their business might
be everything and their intent everywhere; for that's
it that always makes a good voyage of nothing.   80
Farewell.   [*Exit.*]
DUKE. Let all the rest give place.
            [CURIO *and* ATTENDANTS *retire.*]
                   Once more, Cesario,
Get thee to yond same sovereign cruelty.
Tell her my love, more noble than the world,
Prizes not quantity of dirty lands.   85
The parts° that fortune hath bestowed upon her,
Tell her I hold as giddily as fortune.°
But 'tis that miracle and queen of gems
That nature pranks° her in attracts my soul.
VIO. But if she cannot love you, sir?   90
DUKE. I cannot be so answered.
VIO.   Sooth, but you must.

Say that some lady, as perhaps there is,
Hath for your love as great a pang of heart
As you have for Olivia. You cannot love her,
You tell her so. Must she not then be answered?   95
DUKE. There is no woman's sides
Can bide the beating of so strong a passion
As love doth give my heart, no woman's heart
So big to hold so much. They lack retention.
Alas, their love may be called appetite —   100
No motion of the liver,° but the palate —
That suffer surfeit, cloyment, and revolt;
But mine is all as hungry as the sea,
And can digest as much. Make no compare
Between that love a woman can bear me   105
And that I owe Olivia.
VIO.   Aye, but I know ——
DUKE. What dost thou know?
VIO. Too well what love women to men may owe.
In faith, they are as true of heart as we.
My father had a daughter loved a man,   110
As it might be, perhaps, were I a woman,
I should your lordship.
DUKE.   And what's her history?
VIO. A blank, my lord. She never told her love,
But let concealment, like a worm i' the bud,
Feed on her damask° cheek. She pined in thought,
And with a green and yellow melancholy   116
She sat like Patience on a monument,°
Smiling at grief. Was not this love indeed?
We men may say more, swear more, but indeed
Our shows are more than will,° for still we prove
Much in our vows, but little in our love.   121
DUKE. But died thy sister of her love, my boy?
VIO. I am all the daughters of my father's house,
And all the brothers too. And yet I know not.
Sir, shall I to this lady?
DUKE.   Aye, that's the theme.   125
To her in haste. Give her this jewel. Say
My love can give no place, bide no denay.°
                          [*Exeunt.*]

SCENE V. OLIVIA'S *garden.*

[*Enter* SIR TOBY, SIR ANDREW, *and* FABIAN.]
SIR TO. Come thy ways, Signior Fabian.
FAB. Nay, I'll come. If I lose a scruple° of this
sport, let me be boiled to death with melancholy.
SIR TO. Wouldst thou not be glad to have the nig-
gardly rascally sheepbiter° come by some notable
shame?   6
FAB. I would exult, man. You know he brought

---

46. weave . . . bones: i.e., make lace with bone bobbins.
47. silly sooth: simple truth.   **53. cypress:** coffin of cypress
wood.   **56. shroud:** See App. 16.   **76. doublet:** jacket. See Pl.
8b and comment on p. 93a. **changeable:** changing its color as
the light falls. **78. such constancy:** The fool is ironical, for
Orsino hitherto has been "to one thing constant never."
86. parts: wealth.   **87. giddily as fortune:** i.e., I am not interested in her wealth.   **89. pranks:** adorns.

101. liver: true passion, as in I.i.37.   **115. damask:** color of the
damask rose, pink and white.   **117. Patience . . . monument:** a
statue of Patience.   **120. Our . . . will:** our outward appearances
are greater than our feelings.   **127. denay:** denial.
Sc. v: 2. scruple: minute part.   **5. sheepbiter:** sheepstealer.

me out o' favor with my lady about a bearbaiting°
here.   10

SIR TO. To anger him we'll have the bear again,
and we will fool him black and blue. Shall we not,
Sir Andrew?

SIR AND. An we do not, it is pity of our lives.   15

SIR TO. Here comes the little villain. [*Enter* MARIA.]
How now, my metal of India!°

MAR. Get ye all three into the box tree.° Malvolio's
coming down this walk. He has been yonder i' the
sun practicing behavior to his own shadow this   20
half-hour. Observe him, for the love of mockery, for
I know this letter will make a contemplative idiot°
of him. Close, in the name of jesting! Lie thou there,
[*Throws down a letter*] for here comes the   25
trout that must be caught with tickling.°   [*Exit.*]
[*Enter* MALVOLIO.]

MAL. 'Tis but fortune, all is fortune. Maria once
told me she did affect me.° And I have heard herself come thus near, that, should she fancy, it should
be one of my complexion. Besides, she uses me   30
with a more exalted respect than anyone else that
follows her. What should I think on 't?

SIR TO. Here's an overweening rogue!   34

FAB. Oh, peace! Contemplation makes a rare tur-
keycock of him. How he jets under his advanced
plumes!°

SIR AND. 'Slight,° I could so beat the rogue!

SIR TO. Peace, I say.

MAL. To be Count Malvolio!   40

SIR TO. Ah, rogue!

SIR AND. Pistol him, pistol him.

SIR TO. Peace, peace!

MAL. There is example for 't. The lady of the
Strachy° married the yeoman of the wardrobe.°   45

SIR AND. Fie on him, Jezebel!°

FAB. Oh, peace! Now he's deeply in. Look how
imagination blows him.

MAL. Having been three months married to her,
sitting in my state° ——   50

SIR TO. Oh, for a stonebow,° to hit him in the eye!

MAL. Calling my officers about me, in my
branched° velvet gown, having come from a day
bed,° where I have left Olivia sleeping ——   55

SIR TO. Fire and brimstone!

FAB. Oh, peace, peace!

MAL. And then to have the humor of state.° And
after a demure travel of regard,° telling them I know
my place as I would they should do theirs, to ask for
my kinsman Toby ——   61

SIR TO. Bolts and shackles!

FAB. Oh, peace, peace, peace! Now, now.

MAL. Seven of my people, with an obedient start,
make out for him. I frown the while, and per-   65
chance wind up my watch, or play with my — some
rich jewel.° Toby approaches, curtsies there to
me ——

SIR TO. Shall this fellow live?

FAB. Though our silence be drawn from us with
cars,° yet peace.   71

MAL. I extend my hand to him thus, quenching
my familiar smile with an austere regard of con-
trol° ——

SIR TO. And does not Toby take you a blow o' the
lips then?   76

MAL. Saying, "Cousin Toby, my fortunes having
cast me on your niece, give me this prerogative° of
speech ——"

SIR TO. What, what?   80

MAL. "You must amend your drunkenness."

SIR TO. Out, scab!

FAB. Nay, patience, or we break the sinews of our
plot.

MAL. "Besides, you waste the treasure of your
time with a foolish knight ——"   86

SIR AND. That's me, I warrant you.

MAL. "One Sir Andrew ——"

SIR AND. I knew 'twas I, for many do call me fool.

MAL. What employment have we here?   91
[*Taking up the letter.*]

FAB. Now is the woodcock° near the gin.°

SIR TO. Oh, peace! And the spirit of humors° intimate reading aloud to him!   94

MAL. By my life, this is my lady's hand. These be
her very C's, her U's, and her T's; and thus makes
she her great P's. It is, in contempt of question,° her
hand.

SIR AND. Her C's, her U's and her T's. Why
that?   100

MAL. [*Reads.*] "To the unknown beloved, this,
and my good wishes: —" Her very phrases! By your
leave, wax.° Soft, and the impressure her Lucrece,°

---

9. **bearbaiting**: a popular sport, detested by the Puritans. See
App. 5.   17. **metal of India**: fine gold.   18. **box tree**: an evergreen shrub much used by Elizabethan gardeners for ornamental
hedges.   22. **contemplative idiot**: pompous ass.   26. **caught . . .
tickling**: a poacher's method of catching trout with the bare
hand.   28. **she . . . me**: Olivia liked me.   36–37. **jets . . .
plumes**: struts with his tail feathers up.   38. **'Slight**: by God's
light.   44–45. **lady . . . Strachy**: She has not been identified.
45. **yeoman . . . wardrobe**: in a great household each department was under the control of a *yeoman*, or upper servant, and a
"gentleman." See App. 14.   46. **Jezebel**: Andrew's knowledge
of the Bible is weak, but at least he does know that Jezebel was
a shameless person.   50. **state**: chair of state.   51. **stonebow**:
crossbow for shooting stones. See Pl. 22c.   54. **branched**: embroidered with a pattern of leaves and branches. See Pl. 8b.
55. **day bed**: couch.

58. **humor of state**: dignified manner of some statesman.   59. **demure . . . regard**: glancing gravely from one to the other.
66–67. **my — some rich jewel**: Malvolio inadvertently touches
his steward's chain.   70–71. **drawn . . . cars**: though we should
be torn to pieces by chariots and wild horses.   73–74. **austere
. . . control**: severe look of authority.   78. **prerogative**: privilege.
92. **woodcock**: regarded as a very simple bird. **gin**: trap.
93. **spirit of humors**: i.e., of mockery, as in a comedy of humors.
See Gen. Intro. p. 42a and App. 3.   97. **contempt of question**:
without any doubt.   103. **wax**: See App. 6. **her Lucrece**: the
head of Lucrece, the device on her seal.

with which she uses to seal. 'Tis my lady. To whom
should this be?   105

FAB. This wins, him, liver and all.

MAL. [*Reads.*] " Jove knows I love.
         But who?
         Lips, do not move.
         No man must know."   110
" No man must know." What follows? The num-
bers° altered! " No man must know." If this should
be thee, Malvolio?

SIR TO. Marry, hang thee, brock!°

MAL. [*Reads.*]
   " I may command where I adore,   115
     But silence, like a Lucrece knife,°
   With bloodless stroke my heart doth gore.
   M, O, A, I, doth sway my life."

FAB. A fustian° riddle!

SIR TO. Excellent wench, say I.   120

MAL. " M, O, A, I, doth sway my life." Nay, but
first, let me see, let me see, let me see.

FAB. What dish o' poison has she dressed him!

SIR TO. And with what wing the staniel° checks
at it!   125

MAL. " I may command where I adore." Why, she
may command me. I serve her, she is my lady. Why,
this is evident to any formal capacity,° there is no obstruction in this. And the end — what should that
alphabetical position portend? If I could make   130
that resemble something in me —— Softly! M, O, A,
I ——

SIR TO. Oh, aye, make up that. He is now at a cold
scent.

FAB. Sowter° will cry upon 't for all this, though
it be as rank as a fox.°   136

MAL. M — Malvolio. M — why, that begins my
name.

FAB. Did not I say he would work it out? The cur
is excellent at faults.°   140

MAL. M — but then there is no consonancy° in
the sequel, that suffers under probation.° A should
follow, but O does.

FAB. And O shall end, I hope.

SIR TO. Aye, or I'll cudgel him and make him cry
O!   146

MAL. And then I comes behind.

FAB. Aye, an you had any eye behind you, you
might see more detraction at your heels than fortunes before you.   150

MAL. M, O, A, I. This simulation° is not as the
former. And yet, to crush° this a little, it would bow
to me,° for every one of these letters are in my name.
Soft! Here follows prose. [*Reads.*]   154

" If this fall into thy hand, revolve.° In my stars°
I am above thee; but be not afraid of greatness. Some
are born great, some achieve greatness, and some
have greatness thrust upon 'em. Thy Fates open
their hands. Let thy blood and spirit embrace them,
and to inure thyself to what thou art like to be,   160
cast thy humble slough° and appear fresh. Be opposite with a kinsman, surly with servants, let thy
tongue tang° arguments of state, put thyself into the
trick of singularity.° She thus advises thee that sighs
for thee. Remember who commended thy yel-   165
low stockings, and wished to see thee ever cross-
gartered.° I say, remember. Go to, thou art made,
if thou desirest to be so. If not, let me see thee a
steward still, the fellow of servants, and not worthy
to touch Fortune's fingers. Farewell. She that   170
would alter services with thee,
      " THE FORTUNATE-UNHAPPY "

Daylight and champain° discovers not more. This is
open. I will be proud, I will read politic au-   175
thors,° I will baffle° Sir Toby, I will wash off gross
acquaintance, I will be point-device° the very man. I
do not now fool myself, to let imagination jade me,°
for every reason excites to this, that my lady loves
me. She did commend my yellow stockings of   180
late, she did praise my leg being cross-gartered; and
in this she manifests herself to my love, and with a
kind of injunction drives me to these habits of her
liking. I thank my stars I am happy. I will be
strange,° stout,° in yellow stockings, and cross-   185
gartered, even with the swiftness of putting on. Jove
and my stars be praised! Here is yet a postscript.
                          [*Reads.*]

" Thou canst not choose but know who I am. If
thou entertainest my love, let it appear in thy   190
smiling. Thy smiles become thee well, therefore in
my presence still smile, dear my sweet, I prithee."

Jove, I thank thee. I will smile, I will do every-   194
thing that thou wilt have me.   [*Exit.*]

FAB. I will not give my part of this sport for a
pension of thousands to be paid from the Sophy.°

SIR TO. I could marry this wench for this device ——   200

---

112. numbers: meter.   **114.** brock: badger.   **116. Lucrece knife:**
the knife with which Lucrece killed herself.   **119. fustian:** coarse
cloth, so "common."   **124. staniel:** kestrel, an inferior kind of
hawk. See App. 26.   **128. formal capacity:** normal intelligence.
135. Sowter: lit., cobbler, nickname for a clumsy hound.
135–36. cry . . . fox: he'll make a great cry, and follow it up, for
the scent is as strong as a fox's.   **140. excellent at faults:** will
follow the scent, however bad. **fault:** a break in a scent.   **141. consonancy:** consistency.   **142. suffers . . . probation:** fails when
tested.   **151. simulation:** disguised meaning.

152. crush: force.   **152–53. bow . . . me:** incline my way.   **155. revolve:** ponder. **stars:** fate.   **161. slough:** snakeskin.   **163. tang:**
resound.   **164. trick of singularity:** unusual behavior.
166–67. cross-gartered: See Pl. 8c and comment on p. 93b.
174. champain: open country.   **175–76. politic authors:** books on
statecraft.   **176. baffle:** bring into disgrace. See *Rich II*, I.i.170,n.
177. point-device: exactly.   **178. jade me:** play me a dirty trick.
185. strange: distant. **stout:** haughty.   **198. Sophy:** Shah of
Persia. See *T Night* Intro. p. 845a.

SIR AND. So could I too.

SIR TO. And ask no other dowry with her but such another jest.

SIR AND. Nor I neither.

FAB. Here comes my noble gull-catcher.°   205

[*Re-enter* MARIA.]

SIR TO. Wilt thou set thy foot o' my neck?

SIR AND. Or o' mine either?

SIR TO. Shall I play my freedom at trey-trip,° and become thy bondslave?

SIR AND. I' faith, or I either?   210

SIR TO. Why, thou hast put him in such a dream that when the image of it leaves him he must run mad.

MAR. Nay, but say true. Does it work upon him?

SIR TO. Like aqua vitae° with a midwife.   216

MAR. If you will then see the fruits of the sport, mark his first approach before my lady. He will come to her in yellow stockings, and 'tis a color she abhors, and cross-gartered, a fashion she detests.   220 And he will smile upon her, which will now be so unsuitable to her disposition, being addicted to a melancholy as she is, that it cannot but turn him into a notable contempt. If you will see it, follow me.   225

SIR TO. To the gates of Tartar, thou most excellent devil of wit!

SIR AND. I'll make one too.   [*Exeunt.*]

Act III

SCENE I. OLIVIA'S *garden.*

[*Enter* VIOLA, *and* CLOWN *with a tabor.*°]

VIO. Save thee, friend, and thy music. Dost thou live by thy tabor?

CLO. No, sir, I live by the church.

VIO. Art thou a churchman?°   4

CLO. No such matter, sir. I do live by the church, for I do live at my house, and my house doth stand by° the church.

VIO. So thou mayst say the King lies by a beggar, if a beggar dwell near him, or the church stands by thy tabor, if thy tabor stand by the church.   11

CLO. You have said, sir. To see this age! A sentence is but a cheveril° glove to a good wit. How quickly the wrong side may be turned outward!   15

VIO. Nay, that's certain. They that dally° nicely with words may quickly make them wanton.

CLO. I would, therefore, my sister had had no name, sir.   20

VIO. Why, man?

CLO. Why, sir, her name's a word, and to dally with that word might make my sister wanton. But indeed words are very rascals since bonds disgraced them.°   25

VIO. Thy reason, man?

CLO. Troth, sir, I can yield you none without words, and words are grown so false I am loath to prove reason with them.   29

VIO. I warrant thou art a merry fellow and carest for nothing.

CLO. Not so, sir. I do care for something, but in my conscience, sir, I do not care for you. If that be to care for nothing, sir, I would it would make you invisible.   35

VIO. Art not thou the Lady Olivia's fool?

CLO. No indeed, sir. The Lady Olivia has no folly. She will keep no fool, sir, till she be married, and fools are as like husbands as pilchards° are to herrings — the husband's the bigger. I am indeed not her fool, but her corrupter of words.   41

VIO. I saw thee late at the Count Orsino's.

CLO. Foolery, sir, does walk about the orb like the sun. It shines everywhere. I would be sorry, sir, but the fool should be as oft with your master as with my mistress. I think I saw your wisdom there.   47

VIO. Nay, an thou pass upon° me. I'll no more with thee. Hold, there's expenses for thee.

CLO. Now Jove, in his next commodity° of hair, send thee a beard!   51

VIO. By my troth, I'll tell thee, I am almost sick for one — [*Aside*] though I would not have it grow on my chin. Is thy lady within?

CLO. Would not a pair of these° have bred, sir?

VIO. Yes, being kept together and put to use.   56

CLO. I would play Lord Pandarus° of Phrygia,° sir, to bring a Cressida to this Troilus.

VIO. I understand you, sir. 'Tis well begged.   60

CLO. The matter, I hope, is not great, sir, begging but a beggar.° Cressida was a beggar. My lady is within, sir. I will construe to them whence you come, who you are and what you would are out of my welkin — I might say " element,"° but the word   65 is overworn.   [*Exit.*]

16. dally: play.   23–25. sister . . . them: See *T Night* Intro. p. 845b.   39. pilchard: a smaller variety of herring.   48. pass upon: make a thrust at.   50. commodity: consignment. 55. pair of these: i.e., wouldn't you like to give me another coin? 57. Pandarus: the go-between in the love affair of Cressida and Troilus. See *Tr & Cr.* Phrygia: the district of Asia Minor in which Troy stood.   61–62. The . . . beggar: the Clown is himself an incorrigible beggar. See V.i.31–42.   65. welkin . . . element: both words mean sky. *Element* is still overworn by writers of textbooks who cannot avoid the "supernatural element," the "pastoral element," etc.

205. gull-catcher: fool-catcher.   208. trey-trip: game played with cards and dice.   216. aqua vitae: spirits especially favored by old women such as Juliet's Nurse. See *R & J*, IV.v.16.

Act III, Sc. i: s.d., tabor: small drum. See Pl. 13d. 4. churchman: cleric.   7. by: near.   14. cheveril: kidskin.

VIO. This fellow° is wise enough to play the fool,
And to do that well craves° a kind of wit.
He must observe their mood on whom he jests,
The quality of persons, and the time,　　　70
And, like the haggard,° check at° every feather
That comes before his eye. This is a practice
As full of labor as a wise man's art.
For folly that he wisely shows is fit,
But wise men, folly-fall'n, quite taint their wit.　75
　　　[Enter SIR TOBY, and SIR ANDREW.]
SIR TO. Save° you, gentleman.
VIO. And you, sir.
SIR AND. Dieu vous garde, monsieur.
VIO. Et vous aussi. Votre serviteur.
SIR AND. I hope, sir, you are, and I am yours.　81
SIR TO. Will you encounter° the house? My niece
is desirous you should enter, if your trade be to her.
VIO. I am bound to your niece, sir. I mean she is
the list° of my voyage.　　　86
SIR TO. Taste your legs, sir, put them to motion.
VIO. My legs do better understand me, sir, than I
understand what you mean by bidding me taste my
legs.　　　91
SIR TO. I mean to go, sir, to enter.
VIO. I will answer you with gait and entrance. But
we are prevented.° [Enter OLIVIA and MARIA.] Most
excellent accomplished lady, the heavens rain odors
on you!　　　96
SIR AND. That youth's a rare courtier. "Rain
odors," well.
VIO. My matter hath no voice, lady, but to your
own most pregnant° and vouchsafed° ear.　　100
SIR AND. "Odors," "pregnant," and "vouch-
safed." I'll get 'em all three all ready.
OLI. Let the garden door be shut, and leave me to
my hearing. [Exeunt SIR TOBY, SIR ANDREW, and
MARIA.] Give me your hand, sir.　　　105
VIO. My duty, madam, and most humble service.
OLI. What is your name?
VIO. Cesario is your servant's name, fair Princess.
OLI. My servant, sir! 'Twas never merry world
Since lowly feigning was called compliment.　110
You're servant to the Count Orsino, youth.
VIO. And he is yours, and his must needs be yours.
Your servant's servant is your servant, madam.
OLI. For him, I think not on him. For his
　thoughts,
Would they were blanks rather than filled with me!
VIO. Madam, I come to whet your gentle thoughts
On his behalf.　　　117

OLI.　　　　　Oh, by your leave, I pray you,
I bade you never speak again of him.
But would you undertake another suit,
I had rather hear you to solicit that　　　120
Than music from the spheres.°
VIO.　　　　　Dear lady——
OLI. Give me leave, beseech you. I did send,
After the last enchantment you did here,
A ring in chase of you. So did I abuse°
Myself, my servant, and, I fear me, you.　　125
Under your hard construction° must I sit,
To force that on you, in a shameful cunning,
Which you knew none of yours. What might you
　think?
Have you not set mine honor at the stake
And baited it with all the unmuzzled thoughts°
That tyrannous heart can think? To one of your re-
　ceiving°　　　131
Enough is shown. A cypress,° not a bosom,
Hides my heart. So let me hear you speak.
VIO. I pity you.
OLI.　　　　　That's a degree to love.
VIO. No, not a grize,° for 'tis a vulgar proof°
That very oft we pity enemies.　　　136
OLI. Why, then, methinks 'tis time to smile again.
O world, how apt the poor are to be proud!
If one should be a prey, how much the better
To fall before the lion than the wolf!　　　140
　　　[Clock strikes.]
The clock upbraids me with the waste of time.
Be not afraid, good youth, I will not have you.
And yet, when wit and youth is come to harvest,
Your wife is like to reap a proper man.
There lies your way, due west.
VIO.　　　　　Then westward ho!°　145
Grace and good disposition attend your ladyship!
You'll nothing, madam, to my lord by me?
OLI. Stay.
I prithee tell me what thou think'st of me.　　150
VIO. That you do think you are not what you are.
OLI. If I think so, I think the same of you.
VIO. Then think you right. I am not what I am.
OLI. I would you were as I would have you be!
VIO. Would it be better, madam, than I am?　155
I wish it might, for now I am your fool.
OLI. Oh, what a deal of scorn looks beautiful
In the contempt and anger of his lip!
A murderous guilt shows not itself more soon
Than love that would seem hid. Love's night is
　noon.　　　160
Cesario, by the roses of the spring,

---

67. This fellow: See T Night Intro. p. 845a–b.　68. craves: calls
for.　71. haggard: wild hawk. As this line seems to contradict the preceding, some editors emend "And" to "But." check
at: go after.　76. Save: God save.　82. encounter: lit., go to
meet. Toby addresses this young courtier with the extravagant
terms fashionable at the time.　86. list: boundary, objective.
94. prevented: forestalled.　100. pregnant: receptive. vouchsafed: condescending.

121. music . . . spheres: See App. 1, and M of Ven, V.i.60.
124. abuse: wrong.　126. construction: interpretation, judgment.　129. at . . . thoughts: An image from bearbaiting. See
App. 5.　131. receiving: understanding.　132. cypress: a sheer
material.　135. grize: step. vulgar proof: common experience.
145. westward ho: the Thames waterman's cry. See Gen. Intro.
p. 16b.

By maidhood, honor, truth, and everything,
I love thee so, that, mauger° all thy pride,
Nor wit nor reason can my passion hide.
Do not extort thy reasons from this clause, 165
For that I woo, thou therefore hast no cause,
But rather reason thus with reason fetter,
Love sought is good, but given unsought is better.°
   VIO. By innocence I swear, and by my youth,
I have one heart, one bosom, and one truth, 170
And that no woman has; nor never none
Shall mistress be of it, save I alone.
And so adieu, good madam. Nevermore
Will I my master's tears to you deplore.
   OLI. Yet come again, for thou perhaps mayst
     move 175
That heart which now abhors to like his love.
                             [Exeunt.]

SCENE II. OLIVIA'S *house.*

[Enter SIR TOBY, SIR ANDREW, *and* FABIAN.]
   SIR AND. No, faith, I'll not stay a jot longer.
   SIR TO. Thy reason, dear venom,° give thy reason.
   FAB. You must needs yield your reason, Sir Andrew. 5
   SIR AND. Marry, I saw your niece do more favors
to the Count's servingman° than ever she bestowed
upon me. I saw 't i' the orchard.
   SIR TO. Did she see thee the while, old boy? Tell
me that. 10
   SIR AND. As plain as I see you now.
   FAB. This was a great argument of love in her toward you.
   SIR AND. 'Slight, will you make an ass o' me?
   FAB. I will prove it legitimate, sir, upon the oaths
of judgment and reason. 16
   SIR TO. And they have been grand jurymen° since
before Noah was a sailor.
   FAB. She did show favor to the youth in your sight
only to exasperate you, to awake your dormouse 20
valor, to put fire in your heart and brimstone in your
liver. You should then have accosted her, and with
some excellent jests, fire-new from the mint,° you
should have banged the youth into dumbness. This
was looked for at your hand, and this was 25
balked. The double gilt° of this opportunity you

let time wash off, and you are now sailed into the
north of my lady's opinion, where you will hang like
an icicle on a Dutchman's beard unless you do redeem it by some laudable attempt either of valor or
policy. 31
   SIR AND. An 't be any way, it must be with valor,
for policy I hate. I had as lief be a Brownist° as a
politician. 34
   SIR TO. Why then, build me thy fortunes upon the
basis of valor. Challenge me the Count's youth to
fight with him. Hurt him in eleven places. My niece
shall take note of it, and assure thyself there is no
love broker° in the world can more prevail in
man's commendation with woman than report of
valor. 41
   FAB. There is no way but this, Sir Andrew.
   SIR AND. Will either of you bear me a challenge to
him?
   SIR TO. Go, write it in a martial hand. Be 45
curst° and brief. It is no matter how witty, so it be
eloquent and full of invention.° Taunt him with the
license of ink. If thou thou'st° him some thrice, it
shall not be amiss. And as many lies as will lie 49
in thy sheet of paper, although the sheet were big
enough for the bed of Ware° in England, set 'em
down. Go, about it. Let there be gall° enough in thy
ink, though thou write with a goose pen,° no matter.
About it.
   SIR AND. Where shall I find you? 55
   SIR TO. We'll call thee at the cubiculo.° Go.
                         [Exit SIR ANDREW.]
   FAB. This is a dear manikin to you, Sir Toby.
   SIR TO. I have been dear to him, lad, some two
thousand strong, or so.°
   FAB. We shall have a rare letter from him. But
you'll not deliver 't? 61
   SIR TO. Never trust me, then, and by all means
stir on the youth to an answer. I think oxen and
wainropes° cannot hale them together. For Andrew,
if he were opened and you find so much blood in his
liver as will clog the foot of a flea, I'll eat the rest of
the anatomy. 67
   FAB. And his opposite, the youth, bears in his visage no great presage of cruelty.

---

163. mauger: in spite of. 165–68. Do . . . better: i.e., do not
argue to yourself that because I (the woman) am the wooer, you
should therefore have no reason to return my love; rather rebut
that argument by this — it is good for a man to ask for a
woman's love, but better still to receive it without asking.
   Sc. ii: 2. venom: poison, because Andrew is full of hate.
7. servingman: See App. 14. 17. grand juryman: The grand
jury was chosen from the most respectable citizens. Fabian
means "Judgment and Reason have been a most highly respected pair since the Flood." 23. fire-new . . . mint: i.e., as
bright as new pennies. 26. double gilt: The best gold plate

was twice dipped. Fabian amuses himself and Toby by puzzling
Andrew with this metaphorical talk. 33. Brownist: The
Brownists were one of the most extreme sects of Puritans.
39. love broker: go-between in making a marriage, an important
office when marriages were arranged. 46. curst: vicious. 47. invention: wit. 48. thou thou'st: to call a stranger "thou" was
a considerable insult, as it implied that he was an inferior.
51. bed of Ware: a famous bed, made after the pattern of the
bed illustrated in Pl. 17b. It could hold 7 couples at a time. It is
now in the Victoria and Albert Museum in London. 52. gall:
"oak apple," produced in the branches of an oak by a parasite,
and used for making ink. Toby puns on "gall," meaning bitterness. 53. goose pen: the pen used at this time was made of a
goose quill. 56. cubiculo: bedchamber. 58–59. I . . . so: I've
cost him some 2,000 ducats. 64. wainropes: cart ropes.

[*Enter* MARIA.]

SIR TO. Look where the youngest wren of nine° comes. 71

MAR. If you desire the spleen, and will laugh yourself into stitches, follow me. Yond gull Malvolio is turned heathen, a very renegado,° for there is no Christian that means to be saved by believing 75 rightly can ever believe such impossible passages of grossness. He's in yellow stockings.

SIR TO. And cross-gartered? 79

MAR. Most villainously, like a pedant that keeps a school i' the church. I have dogged him like his murderer. He does obey every point of the letter that I dropped to betray him. He does smile his face into more lines than is in the new map° with the augmentation of the Indies. You have not seen such 85 a thing as 'tis. I can hardly forbear hurling things at him. I know my lady will strike him. If she do, he'll smile and take 't for a great favor.

SIR TO. Come, bring us, bring us where he is. 90
[*Exeunt.*]

SCENE III. *A street.*

[*Enter* SEBASTIAN *and* ANTONIO.]

SEB. I would not by my will have troubled you,
But since you make your pleasure of your pains,
I will no further chide you.

ANT. I could not stay behind you. My desire,
More sharp than filèd steel, did spur me forth; 5
And not all love to see you, though so much
As might have drawn one to a longer voyage,
But jealousy what might befall your travel,
Being skill-less in these parts, which to a stranger,
Unguided and unfriended, often prove 10
Rough and unhospitable. My willing love,
The rather by these arguments of fear,
Set forth in your pursuit.

SEB.   My kind Antonio,
I can no other answer make but thanks,
And thanks, and everoft° good turns 15
Are shuffled off with such uncurrent° pay.
But were my worth as is my conscience firm,
You should find better dealing. What's to do?
Shall we go see the reliques° of this town?

ANT. Tomorrow, sir. Best first go see your lodging. 20

SEB. I am not weary, and 'tis long to night.
I pray you, let us satisfy our eyes
With the memorials and the things of fame
That do renown this city.

ANT.   Would you'd pardon me.
I do not without danger walk these streets. 25
Once, in a sea fight, 'gainst the Count his galleys
I did some service, of such note indeed
That were I ta'en here it would scarce be answered.

SEB. Belike you slew great number of his people.

ANT. The offense is not of such a bloody nature,
Albeit the quality° of the time and quarrel 31
Might well have given us bloody argument.
It might have since been answered in repaying
What we took from them, which, for traffic's sake,°
Most of our city did. Only myself stood out, 35
For which, if I be lapsèd° in this place,
I shall pay dear.

SEB.   Do not then walk too open.

ANT. It doth not fit me. Hold, sir, here's my purse.
In the south suburbs, at the Elephant,°
Is best to lodge. I will bespeak our diet° 40
While you beguile the time and feed your knowledge
With viewing of the town. There shall you have me.

SEB. Why I your purse?

ANT. Haply° your eye shall light upon some toy°
You have desire to purchase, and your store, 45
I think, is not for idle markets,° sir.

SEB. I'll be your purse bearer and leave you
For an hour.

ANT.   To the Elephant.

SEB. I do remember.   [*Exeunt.*]

SCENE IV. OLIVIA's *garden.*

[*Enter* OLIVIA *and* MARIA.]

OLI. I have sent after him. He says he'll come.
How shall I feast him? What bestow of him?°
For youth is bought more oft than begged or borrowed.
I speak too loud.
Where is Malvolio? He is sad and civil,° 5
And suits well for a servant with my fortunes.
Where is Malvolio?

MAR. He's coming, madam, but in very strange manner. He is sure possessed,° madam.

OLI. Why, what's the matter? Does he rave? 10

MAR. No, madam, he does nothing but smile. Your ladyship were best to have some guard about you if he come, for sure the man is tainted in 's wits.

OLI. Go call him hither. [*Exit* MARIA.] I am as mad as he, 15
If sad and merry madness equal be.

70. youngest ... nine: the youngest of the brood, sometimes called the "rickling," is often smaller than the rest. The wren is the smallest of English birds.   74. renegado: Christian turned heathen.   84. new map: See *T Night* Intro. p. 845a, and Pl. 1a.
    Sc. iii: 15. and ... oft: Two words have apparently been omitted in this line. Some editors read "ever *thanks, and* oft."
16. uncurrent: worthless.   19. reliques: antiquities.

31. quality: nature.   34. traffic's sake: for the sake of business. 36. lapsed: taken.   39. Elephant: There was a famous London Inn of this name on the south side of the Thames; it is now known as the Elephant and Castle.   40. bespeak ... diet: order our dinner.   44. Haply: perchance. toy: trifle.   46. idle markets: unnecessary purchases.
    Sc. iv: 2. of him: on him.   5. civil: sober, serious.   9. possessed: i.e., with an evil spirit. See *T Night* Intro. p. 847a-b.

[Re-enter MARIA, *with* MALVOLIO.] How now, Malvolio!

MAL. Sweet lady, ho, ho.

OLI. Smilest thou?
I sent for thee upon a sad occasion.   20

MAL. Sad, lady? I could be sad. This does make some obstruction in the blood, this cross-gartering, but what of that? If it please the eye of one, it is with me as the very true sonnet is, " Please one, and please all."°   25

OLI. Why, how dost thou, man? What is the matter with thee?

MAL. Not black in my mind, though yellow in my legs. It did come to his hands, and commands shall be executed. I think we do know the sweet Roman hand.°   31

OLI. Wilt thou go to bed, Malvolio?

MAL. To bed! Aye, sweetheart, and I'll come to thee.

OLI. God comfort thee! Why dost thou smile so and kiss thy hand so oft?   36

MAR. How do you, Malvolio?

MAL. At your request! Yes, nightingales answer daws.°

MAR. Why appear you with this ridiculous boldness before my lady?   41

MAL. " Be not afraid of greatness." 'Twas well writ.

OLI. What meanest thou by that, Malvolio?

MAL. " Some are born great——"   45

OLI. Ha!

MAL. " Some achieve greatness——"

OLI. What sayest thou?

MAL. " And some have greatness thrust upon them."   50

OLI. Heaven restore thee!

MAL. " Remember who commended thy yellow stockings."

OLI. Thy yellow stockings!

MAL. " And wished to see thee cross-gartered."

OLI. Cross-gartered!   56

MAL. " Go to, thou art made, if thou desirest to be so."

OLI. Am I made?   59

MAL. " If not, let me see thee a servant still."

OLI. Why, this is very midsummer madness.

[Enter SERVANT.]

SERV. Madam, the young gentleman of the Count Orsino's is returned. I could hardly entreat him back. He attends your ladyship's pleasure.   65

OLI. I'll come to him. *[Exit* SERVANT.] Good

Maria, let this fellow be looked to. Where's my cousin Toby? Let some of my people have a special care of him. I would not have him miscarry° for the   69
half of my dowry.   *[Exeunt* OLIVIA *and* MARIA.]

MAL. Oh, ho! Do you come near me now? No worse man than Sir Toby to look to me! This concurs directly with the letter. She sends him on purpose, that I may appear stubborn to him, for she incites me to that in the letter. " Cast thy humble   75
slough," says she. " Be opposite with a kinsman, surly with servants, let thy tongue tang with arguments of state, put thyself into the trick of singularity "— and consequently sets down the manner how, as a sad face, a reverend carriage, a slow tongue,   80
in the habit of some sir of note,° and so forth. I have limed° her, but it is Jove's doing, and Jove make me thankful! And when she went away now, " Let this fellow be looked to." Fellow! Not Malvolio, nor   85
after my degree, but fellow.° Why, everything adheres together, that no dram of a scruple,° no scruple of a scruple, no obstacle, no incredulous or unsafe circumstance —— What can be said? Nothing that can be can come between me and the full pros-   90
pect of my hopes. Well, Jove, not I, is the doer of this, and he is to be thanked.

[Re-enter MARIA, *with* SIR TOBY *and* FABIAN.]

SIR TO. Which way is he, in the name of sanctity? If all the devils of Hell be drawn in little,° and Legion himself° possessed him, yet I'll speak to him.   96

FAB. Here he is, here he is. How is 't with you, sir? How is 't with you, man?

MAL. Go off, I discard you. Let me enjoy my private. Go off.   100

MAR. Lo, how hollow the fiend speaks within him! Did not I tell you? Sir Toby, my lady prays you to have a care of him.

MAL. Ah, ha! Does she so?   104

SIR TO. Go to, go to; peace, peace. We must deal gently with him. Let me alone. How do you, Malvolio? How is 't with you? What, man! defy the Devil. Consider, he's an enemy to mankind.

MAL. Do you know what you say?   110

MAR. La you, an you speak ill of the Devil, how he takes it at heart! Pray God he be not bewitched!

FAB. Carry his water° to the wise woman.   114

24–25. Please . . . all: The ditty is not a sonnet but a ballad, called "The crow sits upon the wall, Please one and please all." It was not at all the kind of song suitable for Malvolio. 31. Roman hand: The Italian handwriting (from which modern handwriting and *italic* type derives) was coming into fashion among aristocratic writers, and superseding the old English "Court" or "secretary" hand. 38–39. nightingales . . . daws: songbirds answer jackdaws.

69. miscarry: come to harm.   81. sir of note: great man. 82. limed: caught, as with birdlime.   86. fellow: the word has a double meaning. The fellow of a college or learned society is a man of dignity; the word is also used of an inferior.   87. dram . . . scruple: minutest part.   94. in little: into a small space. 95. Legion himself: the name given to the devils cast out of the man from the tombs (Mark 5: 1–19). Toby pretends that Malvolio is possessed and treats him accordingly. Witches (who could be of either sex) were often accused of causing possession. See *T Night* Intro. p. 847a–b.   114. his water: diagnosis of diseases by inspection of the urine was practiced by qualified doctors as well as by quacks. Cf. the gloomy report on Falstaff's health (*II Hen IV*, I.ii.1–6).

MAR. Marry, and it shall be done tomorrow morning, if I live. My lady would not lose him for more than I'll say.

MAL. How now, mistress!

MAR. Oh Lord! 119

SIR TO. Prithee, hold thy peace, this is not the way. Do you not see you move him? Let me alone with him.

FAB. No way but gentleness — gently, gently. The fiend is rough, and will not be roughly used.

SIR TO. Why, how now, my bawcock!° How dost thou, chuck?° 126

MAL. Sir!

SIR TO. Aye, biddy,° come with me. What, man! 'Tis not for gravity to play at cherry pit° with Satan. Hang him, foul collier!° 130

MAR. Get him to say his prayers, good Sir Toby, get him to pray.

MAL. My prayers, minx!

MAR. No, I warrant you, he will not hear of godliness.° 135

MAL. Go, hang yourselves all! You are idle shallow things. I am not of your element. You shall know more hereafter. [*Exit.*]

SIR TO. Is 't possible?

FAB. If this were played upon a stage now, I could condemn it as an improbable fiction. 141

SIR TO. His very genius° hath taken the infection° of the device,° man.

MAR. Nay, pursue him now, lest the device take air and taint.° 145

FAB. Why, we shall make him mad indeed.

MAR. The house will be the quieter.

SIR TO. Come, we'll have him in a dark room and bound. My niece is already in the belief that he's mad. We may carry it thus, for our pleasure 150 and his penance, till our very pastime, tired out of breath, prompt us to have mercy on him, at which time we will bring the device to the bar° and crown thee for a finder of madmen. But see, but see. 155

[*Enter* SIR ANDREW.]

FAB. More matter for a May morning.°

SIR AND. Here's the challenge, read it. I warrant there's vinegar and pepper in 't.

FAB. Is 't so saucy? 159

SIR AND. Aye, is 't, I warrant him. Do but read.

SIR TO. Give me. [*Reads.*] "Youth, whatsoever thou art, thou art but a scurvy fellow."

FAB. Good, and valiant. 163

SIR TO. [*Reads.*] "Wonder not, nor admire° not in thy mind, why I do call thee so, for I will show thee no reason for 't."

FAB. A good note. That keeps you from the blow of the law. 169

SIR TO. [*Reads.*] "Thou comest to the Lady Olivia, and in my sight she uses thee kindly; but thou liest in thy throat.° That is not the matter I challenge thee for."

FAB. Very brief, and to exceeding good sense — less. 175

SIR TO. [*Reads.*] "I will waylay thee going home, where if it be thy chance to kill me ——"

FAB. Good.

SIR TO. [*Reads.*] "Thou killest me like a rogue and a villain." 180

FAB. Still you keep o' the windy side° of the law. Good.

SIR TO. [*Reads.*] "Fare thee well, and God have mercy upon one of our souls! He may have mercy upon mine, but my hope is better, and so look to thyself. Thy friend, as thou usest him, and thy sworn enemy,   ANDREW AGUECHEEK." If this letter move him not, his legs cannot. I'll give 't him. 189

MAR. You may have very fit occasion for 't. He is now in some commerce with my lady, and will by and by depart.

SIR TO. Go, Sir Andrew. Scout me for him at the corner of the orchard like a bumbaily.° So 195 soon as ever thou seest him, draw, and, as thou drawest, swear horrible; for it comes to pass oft that a terrible oath, with a swaggering accent sharply twanged off, gives manhood more approbation than ever proof itself would have earned him. Away!

SIR AND. Nay, let me alone for swearing.° [*Exit.*]

SIR TO. Now will not I deliver his letter, for the behavior of the young gentleman gives him out to be of good capacity and breeding. His employment between his lord and my niece confirms no 205 less. Therefore this letter, being so excellently ignorant, will breed no terror in the youth. He will find it comes from a clodpole.° But, sir, I will deliver his challenge by word of mouth, set upon Aguecheek a notable report of valor, and drive the gentle- 210 man, as I know his youth will aptly receive it, into a most hideous opinion of his rage, skill, fury, and impetuosity. This will so fright them both that they will kill one another by the look, like cockatrices.° 215

---

125. **bawcock:** fine fellow. Toby humors Malvolio by talking baby talk to him.   126. **chuck:** chick.   128. **biddy:** child's name for a chick.   129. **cherry pit:** a game of throwing cherry stones into a hole.   130. **foul collier:** The Devil is a collier (coalman) because he is black.   134-35. **will . . . godliness:** One of the tests usually applied to a witch was to ask him to say the Lord's Prayer. If he could not, or would not, it was a most suspicious sign of guilt.   142. **genius:** guardian angel. **taken . . . infection:** caught the plague.   143. **device:** plan.   144-45. **take . . . taint:** be spoiled and go bad.   154. **device . . . bar:** bring to public trial.   156. **May morning:** Mayday was a general holiday.

164. **admire:** be amazed.   171-72. **liest . . . throat:** This was the bitterest insult possible.   181. **windy side:** safe side.   195. **bumbaily:** sheriff's officer who made arrests for debt.   201. **let . . . swearing:** i.e., I'm an expert at swearing.   208. **clodpole:** blockhead.   215. **cockatrice:** a fabulous serpent, able to kill by its mere look. See *Rich III*, I.ii.151n.

[*Re-enter* OLIVIA, *with* VIOLA.]

FAB. Here he comes with your niece. Give them way till he take leave, and presently after him.

SIR TO. I will meditate the while upon some horrid message for a challenge. 220

[*Exeunt* SIR TOBY, FABIAN, *and* MARIA.]

OLI. I have said too much unto a heart of stone,
And laid mine honor too unchary° out.
There's something in me that reproves my fault,
But such a headstrong potent fault it is
That it but mocks reproof. 225

VIO. With the same 'havior that your passion bears
Goes on my master's grief.

OLI. Here, wear this jewel for me, 'tis my picture.
Refuse it not, it hath no tongue to vex you.
And I beseech you come again tomorrow. 230
What shall you ask of me that I'll deny,
That honor saved may upon asking give?

VIO. Nothing but this — your true love for my master.

OLI. How with mine honor may I give him that
Which I have given to you?

VIO. I will acquit° you. 235

OLI. Well, come again tomorrow. Fare thee well.
A fiend like thee might bear my soul to Hell. [*Exit.*]

[*Re-enter* SIR TOBY *and* FABIAN.]

SIR TO. Gentleman, God save thee.

VIO. And you, sir. 239

SIR TO. That defense thou hast, betake thee to 't. Of what nature the wrongs are thou hast done him, I know not, but thy interceptor, full of despite,° bloody as the hunter, attends thee at the orchard end. Dismount thy tuck,° be yare° in thy preparation, for thy assailant is quick, skillful, and deadly. 246

VIO. You mistake, sir. I am sure no man hath any quarrel to me. My remembrance is very free and clear from any image of offense done to any man. 250

SIR TO. You'll find it otherwise, I assure you. Therefore, if you hold your life at any price, betake you to your guard; for your opposite hath in him what youth, strength, skill, and wrath can furnish man withal. 255

VIO. I pray you, sir, what is he?

SIR TO. He is knight, dubbed° with unhatched° rapier and on carpet consideration,° but he is a devil in private brawl. Souls and bodies hath he divorced three, and his incensement at this moment is 260 so implacable that satisfaction can be none but by pangs of death and sepulcher. Hob, nob,° is his word, give 't or take 't.

VIO. I will return again into the house and desire some conduct of the lady. I am no fighter. I 265 have heard of some kind of men that put quarrels purposely on others, to taste their valor. Belike this is a man of that quirk.°

SIR TO. Sir, no, his indignation derives itself out of a very competent° injury. Therefore get you 270 on and give him his desire. Back you shall not to the house, unless you undertake that with me which with as much safety you might answer him. Therefore on, or strip your sword stark-naked, for meddle you must, that's certain, or forswear° to wear iron about you. 276

VIO. This is as uncivil as strange. I beseech you, do me this courteous office, as to know of the knight what my offense to him is. It is something of my negligence, nothing of my purpose. 280

SIR TO. I will do so. Signior Fabian, stay you by this gentleman till my return. [*Exit.*]

VIO. Pray you, sir, do you know of this matter?

FAB. I know the knight is incensed against 285 you, even to a mortal arbitrament,° but nothing of the circumstance more.

VIO. I beseech you, what manner of man is he?

FAB. Nothing of that wonderful promise, to 290 read him by his form, as you are like to find him in the proof of his valor. He is, indeed, sir, the most skillful, bloody, and fatal opposite that you could possibly have found in any part of Illyria. Will you walk toward him? I will make your peace with him if I can.

VIO. I shall be much bound to you for 't. I am one that had rather go with sir priest° than sir knight. I care not who knows so much of my 299 mettle. [*Exeunt.*]

[*Re-enter* SIR TOBY, *with* SIR ANDREW.]

SIR TO. Why, man, he's a very devil. I have not seen such a firago.° I had a pass with him, rapier, scabbard, and all, and he gives me the stuck-in° with such a mortal motion that it is inevitable; and on the answer, he pays you as surely as your feet 305 hit the ground they step on. They say he has been fencer to the Sophy.

SIR AND. Pox on 't, I'll not meddle with him.

SIR TO. Aye, but he will not now be pacified. Fabian can scarce hold him yonder. 310

SIR AND. Plague on 't, an I thought he had been valiant and so cunning in fence, I'd have seen him damned ere I'd have challenged him. Let him let the matter slip, and I'll give him my horse, gray Capilet. 315

222. unchary: heedlessly. 235. acquit: release from a payment. 243. despite: spite. 244. tuck: sword. yare: handy. 257. dubbed: knighted. unhatched: unhacked, not dented by use in battle. 258. carpet consideration: kneeling on a carpet, and not on the battlefield. 262. Hob, nob: hit or miss.

268. quirk: whim. 270. competent: considerable. 275. forswear: swear not to. 286. mortal arbitrament: decision by deadly combat. 298. sir priest: a Bachelor of Arts was termed "Dominus" (= Sir); in the class lists at Cambridge University the B.A.'s are still noted as "Ds." As most priests were graduates, they were called "Sir." 302. firago: for virago, a mannish woman. 303. stuck-in: thrust.

SIR TO. I'll make the motion. Stand here, make a good show on 't. This shall end without the perdition of souls. [*Aside*] Marry, I'll ride your horse as well as I ride you.   319

[*Re-enter* FABIAN *and* VIOLA.]

[*To* FABIAN] I have his horse to take up the quarrel. I have persuaded him the youth's a devil.

FAB. He is as horribly conceited° of him, and pants and looks pale, as if a bear were at his heels.   324

SIR TO. [*To* VIOLA] There's no remedy, sir, he will fight with you for 's oath sake. Marry, he hath better bethought him of his quarrel, and he finds that now scarce to be worth talking of. Therefore draw, for the supportance of his vow. He protests he will not hurt you.   330

VIO. [*Aside*] Pray God defend me! A little thing would make me tell them how much I lack of a man.

FAB. Give ground, if you see him furious.   334

SIR TO. Come, Sir Andrew, there's no remedy. The gentleman will, for his honor's sake, have one bout with you. He cannot by the duello° avoid it. But he has promised me, as he is a gentleman and a soldier, he will not hurt you. Come on — to 't.   340

SIR AND. Pray God he keep his oath!

VIO. I do assure you 'tis against my will.

[*They draw.*]

[*Enter* ANTONIO.]

ANT. Put up your sword. If this young gentleman Have done offense, I take the fault on me. If you offend him, I for him defy you.   345

SIR TO. You, sir! Why, what are you?

ANT. One, sir, that for his love dares yet do more Than you have heard him brag to you he will.

SIR TO. Nay, if you be an undertaker,° I am   349 for you.   [*They draw.*]

[*Enter* OFFICERS.]

FAB. O good Sir Toby, hold! Here come the officers.

SIR TO. I'll be with you anon.

VIO. Pray, sir, put your sword up, if you please.

SIR AND. Marry will I, sir, and, for that I   356 promised you, I'll be as good as my word. He will bear you easily and reins well.

1. OFF. This is the man. Do thy office.

2. OFF. Antonio, I arrest thee at the suit of Count Orsino.   361

ANT. You do mistake me, sir.

1. OFF. No, sir, no jot. I know your favor° well, Though now you have no sea cap on your head. Take him away. He knows I know him well.   365

ANT. I must obey. [*To* VIOLA] This comes with seeking you. But there's no remedy, I shall answer it. What will you do, now my necessity

Makes me to ask you for my purse? It grieves me Much more for what I cannot do for you   370 Than what befalls myself. You stand amazed, But be of comfort.

2. OFF. Come, sir, away.

ANT. I must entreat of you some of that money.

VIO. What money, sir?   375 For the fair kindness you have showed me here, And, part, being prompted by your present trouble, Out of my lean and low ability° I'll lend you something. My having is not much; I'll make division of my present° with you.   380 Hold, there's half my coffer.°

ANT.   Will you deny me now? Is 't possible that my deserts to you Can lack persuasion? Do not tempt my misery, Lest that it make me so unsound a man As to upbraid you with those kindnesses   385 That I have done for you.

VIO.   I know of none, Nor know I you by voice or any feature. I hate ingratitude more in a man Than lying vainness, babbling drunkenness, Or any taint of vice whose strong corruption   390 Inhabits our frail blood.

ANT.   Oh, Heavens themselves!

2. OFF. Come, sir, I pray you, go.

ANT. Let me speak a little. This youth that you see here I snatched one half out of the jaws of death, Relieved him with such sanctity of love,   395 And to his image, which methought did promise Most venerable worth, did I devotion.

1. OFF. What's that to us? The time goes by — away!

ANT. But oh, how vile an idol proves this god! Thou hast, Sebastian, done good feature shame. In nature there's no blemish but the mind;   401 None can be called deformed but the unkind. Virtue is beauty, but the beauteous evil Are empty trunks, o'erflourished by the Devil.°

1. OFF. The man grows mad. Away with him! Come, come, sir.   405

ANT. Lead me on.   [*Exit with* OFFICERS.]

VIO. Methinks his words do from such passion fly That he believes himself. So do not I. Prove true, imagination,° oh, prove true, That I, dear brother, be now ta'en for you!   410

SIR TO. Come hither, knight, come hither, Fabian. We'll whisper o'er a couplet or two of most sage saws.°

---

323. **as . . . conceited:** has as horrible ideas of.   338. **duello:** the rules of duelling, a matter of great importance to a man of honor.
349. **undertaker:** meddler.   363. **favor:** face.

378. **low ability:** small means.   380. **my present:** what I have at present.   381. **coffer:** purse, lit., chest.   404. **empty . . . Devil:** over-elaborately carved chests which have nothing inside. See Pl. 17c.   409. **Prove . . . imagination:** Viola has never given up hope. Now she realizes from Antonio's words that Sebastian is not only alive but near.   413. **saws:** wise sayings.

vio. He named Sebastian. I my brother know
Yet living in my glass, even such and so   415
In favor was my brother, and he went
Still in this fashion, color, ornament,
For him I imitate. Oh, if it prove,
Tempests are kind and salt waves fresh in love!°
                                        [*Exit.*]
  sir to. A very dishonest paltry boy, and   420
more a coward than a hare. His dishonesty appears
in leaving his friend here in necessity and denying
him, and for his cowardship, ask Fabian.
  fab. A coward, a most devout coward, religious
in it.   425
  sir and. 'Slid,° I'll after him again and beat him.
  sir to. Do. Cuff him soundly, but never draw thy
sword.
  sir and. An I do not——   [*Exit.*]
  fab. Come, let's see the event.
  sir to. I dare lay any money 'twill be nothing yet.
                                        [*Exeunt.*]

Act IV

SCENE I. *Before* olivia's *house.*

[*Enter* sebastian *and* clown.]

  clo. Will you make me believe that I am not sent
for you?
  seb. Go to, go to, thou art a foolish fellow. Let me
be clear of thee.
  clo. Well held out, i' faith! No, I do not   5
know you; nor I am not sent to you by my lady, to
bid you come speak with her; nor your name is not
Master Cesario; nor this is not my nose neither.
Nothing that is so is so.
  seb. I prithee, vent° thy folly somewhere else.
Thou know'st not me.   11
  clo. Vent my folly! He has heard that word of
some great man and now applies it to a fool. Vent
my folly! I am afraid this great lubber, the world,
will prove a cockney.° I prithee now, ungird   15
thy strangeness and tell me what I shall vent to my
lady. Shall I vent to her that thou art coming?
  seb. I prithee, foolish Greek,° depart from me.
There's money for thee. If you tarry longer, I   20
shall give worse payment.

<hr>

419. salt . . . love: i.e., the sea has been kind, with a play of
words on "salt" and "fresh" = good, unsalted, and recent.
426. 'Slid: by God's eyelid.
  Act IV, Sc. i: 10. vent: utter. 14–15. lubber . . . cockney: a
much-disputed passage. The fool when posing as a philosopher
is not always very clear. As it stands, the passage means "this
great clumsy world will turn out to be a spoiled child (*cockney*)."
19. foolish Greek: foolish jester. The Greeks were considered
empty-headed and merry folk.

  clo. By my troth, thou hast an open hand. These
wise men that give fools money get themselves a
good report — after fourteen years' purchase.°   25
  [*Enter* sir andrew, sir toby, *and* fabian.]
  sir and. Now, sir, have I met you again? There's
for you.
  seb. Why, there's for thee, and there, and there.
Are all the people mad?   29
  sir to. Hold, sir, or I'll throw your dagger o'er the
house.
  clo. This will I tell my lady straight. I would not
be in some of your coats for twopence.   [*Exit.*]
  sir to. Come on, sir, hold.   34
  sir and. Nay, let him alone. I'll go another way to
work with him. I'll have an action of battery against
him, if there be any law in Illyria. Though I struck
him first, yet it's no matter for that.
  seb. Let go thy hand.   39
  sir to. Come, sir, I will not let you go. Come,
my young soldier, put up your iron. You are well
fleshed.° Come on.
  seb. I will be free from thee. What wouldst thou
now?   44
If thou darest tempt me further, draw thy sword.
  sir to. What, what? Nay, then I must have an
ounce or two of this malapert° blood from you.
              [*Enter* olivia.]
  oli. Hold, Toby. On thy life, I charge thee, hold!
  sir to. Madam!   50
  oli. Will it be ever thus? Ungracious wretch,
Fit for the mountains and the barbarous caves,
Where manners ne'er were preached! Out of my
    sight!
Be not offended, dear Cesario.
Rudesby,° be gone!
      [*Exeunt* sir toby, sir andrew, *and* fabian.]
                  I prithee, gentle friend,   55
Let thy fair wisdom, not thy passion, sway
In this uncivil and unjust extent°
Against thy peace. Go with me to my house,
And hear thou there how many fruitless pranks   59
This ruffian hath botched° up, that thou thereby
Mayst smile at this. Thou shalt not choose but go.
Do not deny. Beshrew his soul for me,
He started one poor heart of mine in thee.
  seb. What relish is in this? How runs the stream?
Or I am mad, or else this is a dream.   65
Let fancy still my sense in Lethe° steep.
If it be thus to dream, still let me sleep!
  oli. Nay, come, I prithee. Would thou'dst be
    ruled by me!

<hr>

25. fourteen . . . purchase: the value of land was reckoned to be
twelve times the annual rent, so this is a high rate. 42–43. well
fleshed: lit., you have shown courage in your first action; i.e.,
you've had enough fighting for the present. Cf. *I Hen IV*,
V.iv.133. 48. malapert: saucy. 55. Rudesby: ruffian. 57. extent: attack. 60. botched: patched. 66. Lethe: the river of
forgetfulness in the underworld.

SEB. Madam, I will.

OLI. Oh, say so, and so be! [*Exeunt.*]

SCENE II. OLIVIA'S *house.*

[*Enter* MARIA *and* CLOWN.]

MAR. Nay, I prithee put on this gown and this beard. Make him believe thou art Sir Topas° the curate. Do it quickly. I'll call Sir Toby the whilst. [*Exit.*]

CLO. Well, I'll put it on, and I will dissemble° my- 5 self in 't, and I would I were the first that ever dissembled in such a gown. I am not tall enough to become the function well, nor lean enough to be thought a good student, but to be said an honest man and a good housekeeper goes as fairly as to say 10 a careful man and a great scholar. The competitors° enter.

[*Enter* SIR TOBY *and* MARIA.]

SIR TO. Jove bless thee, Master Parson.

CLO. *Bonos dies,* Sir Toby. For, as the old hermit of Prague, that never saw pen and ink, very 15 wittily said to a niece of King Gorboduc,° "That that is is," so I, being Master Parson, am Master Parson; for what is "that" but "that," and "is" but "is"?

SIR TO. To him, Sir Topas. 20

CLO. What ho,° I say! Peace in this prison!

SIR TO. The knave counterfeits well—a good knave.

MAL. [*Within*] Who calls there?

CLO. Sir Topas the curate, who comes to visit Malvolio the lunatic. 26

MAL. Sir Topas, Sir Topas, good Sir Topas, go to my lady.

CLO. Out, hyperbolical° fiend! How vexest thou this man! Talkest thou nothing but of ladies? 30

SIR TO. Well said, Master Parson.

MAL. Sir Topas, never was man thus wronged. Good Sir Topas, do not think I am mad. They have laid me here in hideous darkness. 34

CLO. Fie, thou dishonest Satan! I call thee by the most modest terms, for I am one of those gentle ones that will use the Devil himself with courtesy. Sayest thou that house is dark?

MAL. As Hell, Sir Topas. 39

CLO. Why, it hath bay windows transparent as barricadoes,° and the clerestories° toward the south-north are as lustrous as ebony—and yet complainest thou of obstruction?

MAL. I am not mad, Sir Topas. I say to you, this house is dark. 45

CLO. Madman, thou errest. I say, there is no darkness but ignorance, in which thou art more puzzled than the Egyptians in their fog.°

MAL. I say, this house is as dark as ignorance, though ignorance were as dark as Hell. And I 50 say there was never man thus abused. I am no more mad than you are. Make the trial of it in any constant question.°

CLO. What is the opinion of Pythagoras° concerning wild fowl? 55

MAL. That the soul of our grandam might haply inhabit a bird.

CLO. What thinkest thou of his opinion?

MAL. I think nobly of the soul, and no way approve his opinion. 60

CLO. Fare thee well. Remain thou still in darkness. Thou shalt hold the opinion of Pythagoras ere I will allow of thy wits, and fear to kill a woodcock° lest thou dispossess the soul of thy grandam. Fare thee well. 65

MAL. Sir Topas, Sir Topas!

SIR TO. My most exquisite Sir Topas!

CLO. Nay, I am for all waters.°

MAR. Thou mightst have done this without thy beard and gown. He sees thee not. 70

SIR TO. To him in thine own voice, and bring me word how thou findest him. I would we were well rid of this knavery. If he may be conveniently delivered, I would he were, for I am now so far in offense with my niece that I cannot pursue with 75 any safety this sport to the upshot.° Come by and by to my chamber. [*Exeunt* SIR TOBY *and* MARIA.]

CLO. [*Sings.*]
Hey, Robin, jolly Robin,
Tell me how thy lady does. 9

MAL. Fool——

CLO. "My lady is unkind, perdy."°

MAL. Fool——

CLO. "Alas, why is she so?"

MAL. Fool, I say—— 84

CLO. "She loves another——" Who calls, ha?

MAL. Good fool, as ever thou wilt deserve well at my hand, help me to a candle, and pen, ink, and paper. As I am a gentleman, I will live to be thankful to thee for 't.

CLO. Master Malvolio! 90

MAL. Aye, good fool.

Sc. ii: 2. Sir Topas: See III.iv.298,n. 4. dissemble: disguise. 11. competitors: conspirators. 16. King Gorboduc: one of the legendary kings invented by early chroniclers to fill the gaps in English history before records began; but the Clown as usual introduces the name to give an air of learning to his nonsense. 21. What ho: Here the fool assumes a ministerial voice. 29. hyperbolical: extravagant. 41. barricadoes: barricades. clerestories: the upper part of the inner wall of a church above the arches, containing a row of windows.

48. fog: darkness; i.e., the ninth of the plagues of Egypt. See Exodus 10: 21–23. 52–53. constant question: coherent argument. 54. Pythagoras: Pythagoras held that the human soul after death could pass into a beast or a bird. 63. woodcock: regarded as a foolish bird. 68. for . . . waters: i.e., can turn my hand to anything. 76. upshot: conclusion. 81. perdy: by God.

CLO. Alas, sir, how fell you besides your five wits?°

MAL. Fool, there was never man so notoriously abused. I am as well in my wits, fool, as thou art. 96

CLO. But as well? Then you are mad indeed, if you be no better in your wits than a fool.

MAL. They have here propertied° me, keep me in darkness, send ministers to me, asses, and do all they can to face me out of my wits. 101

CLO. Advise you what you say. The minister is here. Malvolio, Malvolio, thy wits the Heavens restore! Endeavor thyself to sleep, and leave thy vain bibble-babble. 105

MAL. Sir Topas——

CLO. Maintain no words° with him, good fellow. Who, I, sir? Not I, sir. God be wi' you, good Sir Topas. Marry, amen. I will, sir, I will.

MAL. Fool, fool, fool, I say—— 110

CLO. Alas, sir, be patient. What say you, sir? I am shent° for speaking to you.

MAL. Good fool, help me to some light and some paper. I tell thee I am as well in my wits as any man in Illyria. 115

CLO. Welladay° that you were, sir!

MAL. By this hand, I am. Good fool, some ink, paper, and light; and convey what I will set down to my lady. It shall advantage thee more than ever the bearing of letter did. 120

CLO. I will help you to 't. But tell me true, are you not mad indeed? Or do you but counterfeit?

MAL. Believe me, I am not, I tell thee true.

CLO. Nay, I'll ne'er believe a madman till I see his brains. I will fetch you light and paper and ink. 127

MAL. Fool, I'll requite it in the highest degree. I prithee be gone.

CLO. [*Sings.*]

    I am gone, sir,   130
      And anon, sir,
    I'll be with you again,
      In a trice,
      Like to the old vice,
    Your need to sustain,   135
    Who, with dagger of lath,°
    In his rage and his wrath,
      Cries, ah, ha! to the Devil.
    Like a mad lad,
    Pare thy nails, dad.   140
    Adieu, Goodman Devil.   [*Exit.*]

92–93. five wits: i.e., full possession of your senses. The five were common wit, imagination, fantasy, estimation, and memory. **99. propertied:** treated like a property; i.e., "thrust me into the attic." **107. Maintain no words:** Here the fool resumes his assumed voice as he keeps up a dialogue with himself as Sir Topas addressing the Clown. **112. shent:** rebuked. **116. Welladay:** alas. **134–36. vice . . . lath:** the clown's part in the old Morality plays. He was armed with a wooden dagger (*dagger of lath*), with which he attacked the Devil and tried to cut his nails.

SCENE III. OLIVIA's *garden.*

[*Enter* SEBASTIAN.]

SEB. This is the air, that is the glorious sun,
This pearl she gave me, I do feel 't and see 't.
And though 'tis wonder that enwraps me thus,
Yet 'tis not madness. Where's Antonio, then?
I could not find him at the Elephant.   5
Yet there he was, and there I found this credit,°
That he did range° the town to seek me out.
His counsel now might do me golden service.
For though my soul disputes well with my sense,
That this may be some error, but no madness,   10
Yet doth this accident and flood of fortune
So far exceed all instance,° all discourse,
That I am ready to distrust mine eyes
And wrangle with my reason, that persuades me
To any other trust but that I am mad,   15
Or else the lady's mad — yet, if 'twere so,
She could not sway her house, command her followers,
Take and give back affairs and their dispatch
With such a smooth, discreet, and stable bearing
As I perceive she does. There's something in 't   20
That is deceivable.° But here the lady comes.

[*Enter* OLIVIA *and* PRIEST.]

OLI. Blame not this haste of mine. If you mean well,
Now go with me and with this holy man
Into the chantry° by. There, before him,
And underneath that consecrated roof,   25
Plight° me the full assurance of your faith,
That my most jealous and too doubtful soul
May live at peace. He shall conceal it
While you are willing it shall come to note,
What time we will our celebration keep   30
According to my birth. What do you say?

SEB. I'll follow this good man, and go with you,
And, having sworn truth, ever will be true.

OLI. Then lead the way, good Father, and Heavens so shine,
That they may fairly note this act of mine!   35

[*Exeunt.*]

Act V

SCENE I. *Before* OLIVIA's *house.*

[*Enter* CLOWN *and* FABIAN.]

FAB. Now, as thou lovest me, let me see his letter.

CLO. Good Master Fabian, grant me another request.

Sc. iii: 6. credit: report. **7. range:** traverse. **12. exceed . . . instance:** go beyond anything recorded. **21. deceivable:** deceptive. **24. chantry:** chapel. **26. Plight:** promise. Olivia is proposing not full marriage but formal betrothal, which will legally bind Sebastian. See Gen. Intro. p. 20a.

FAB. Anything.   5

CLO. Do not desire to see this letter.

FAB. This is to give a dog,° and in recompense desire my dog again.

[*Enter* DUKE, VIOLA, CURIO, *and* LORDS.]

DUKE. Belong you to the Lady Olivia, friends?

CLO. Aye, sir, we are some of her trappings.°   10

DUKE. I know thee well. How dost thou, my good fellow?

CLO. Truly, sir, the better for my foes and the worse for my friends.

DUKE. Just the contrary—the better for thy friends.   16

CLO. No, sir, the worse.

DUKE. How can that be?

CLO. Marry, sir, they praise me and make an ass of me. Now my foes tell me plainly I am an ass,   20 so that by my foes, sir, I profit in the knowledge of myself, and by my friends I am abused. So that, conclusions to be as kisses,° if your four negatives make your two affirmatives, why then, the worse for my friends, and the better for my foes.   26

DUKE. Why, this is excellent.

CLO. By my troth, sir, no, though it please you to be one of my friends.

DUKE. Thou shalt not be the worse for me. There's gold.   31

CLO. But that it would be double-dealing,° sir, I would you could make it another.

DUKE. Oh, you give me ill counsel.

CLO. Put your grace in your pocket,° sir, for this once, and let your flesh and blood obey it.   36

DUKE. Well, I will be so much a sinner, to be a double-dealer. There's another.

CLO. Primo, secundo, tertio, is a good play, and the old saying is, the third pays for all. The   40 triplex, sir, is a good tripping measure, or the bells of Saint Bennet,° sir, may put you in mind—one, two, three.

DUKE. You can fool no more money out of me at this throw. If you will let your lady know I am   45 here to speak with her, and bring her along with you, it may awake my bounty further.

CLO. Marry, sir, lullaby to your bounty till I come again. I go, sir, but I would not have you to think that my desire of having is the sin of covetous-   50

ness. But, as you say, sir, let your bounty take a nap. I will awake it anon.   [*Exit.*]

VIO. Here comes the man, sir, that did rescue me.

[*Enter* ANTONIO *and* OFFICERS.]

DUKE. That face of his I do remember well,
Yet when I saw it last it was besmeared   55
As black as Vulcan° in the smoke of war.
A bawbling° vessel was he captain of,
For shallow draught and bulk unprizable,°
With which such scathful grapple° did he make
With the most noble bottom° of our fleet   60
That very envy and the tongue of loss
Cried fame and honor on him. What's the matter?

1. OFF. Orsino, this is that Antonio
That took the *Phoenix* and her fraught° from
    Candy,°
And this is he that did the *Tiger* board,   65
When your young nephew Titus lost his leg.
Here in the streets, desperate° of shame and state,°
In private brabble° did we apprehend him.

VIO. He did me kindness, sir, drew on my side,
But in conclusion put strange speech upon me.   70
I know not what 'twas but distraction.°

DUKE. Notable pirate! Thou salt-water thief!
What foolish boldness brought thee to their mercies
Whom thou, in terms so bloody and so dear,
Hast made thine enemies?

ANT.   Orsino, noble sir,   75
Be pleased that I shake off these names you give
    me.
Antonio never yet was thief or pirate,
Though I confess, on base and ground enough,
Orsino's enemy. A witchcraft drew me hither.
That most ingrateful boy there by your side   80
From the rude sea's enragèd and foamy mouth
Did I redeem—a wreck past hope he was.
His life I gave him and did thereto add
My love, without retention or restraint,
All his in dedication. For his sake   85
Did I expose myself, pure for his love,
Into the danger of this adverse° town,
Drew to defend him when he was beset,
Where being apprehended, his false cunning,
Not meaning to partake with me in danger,   90
Taught him to face me out of his acquaintance,
And grew a twenty years' removèd thing
While one would wink—denied me mine own
    purse,
Which I had recommended to his use
Not half an hour before.

VIO.   How can this be?   95

DUKE. When came he to this town?

Act V, Sc. i: 7. give a dog: This was a contemporary anecdote recorded in Manningham's diary: "Dr. Bullein, the Queen's kinsman, had a dog which he doted on, so much that the Queen understanding of it requested he would grant her one desire, and he should have whatsoever he should ask. She demanded his dog; he gave it, and, 'Now, Madam,' quoth he, 'you promised to give me my desire.' 'I will,' quoth she. 'Then I pray you give me my dog again.'"   **10. trappings:** ornamental accessories. **22–23. conclusions . . . kisses:** as a kiss stops all lovers' arguments.   **32. double-dealing:** The Clown is trying to extract another coin from the Duke.   **35. Put . . . pocket:** forget your respectability.   **42. Saint Bennet:** St. Benedict, a London church.

56. Vulcan: the blacksmith god.   **57. bawbling:** trifling.   **58. unprizable:** not worth taking as a prize.   **59. scathful grapple:** destructive attack.   **60. bottom:** vessel.   **64. fraught:** cargo. **Candy:** Crete.   **67. desperate:** utterly regardless. **state:** civil behavior. **68. brabble:** brawl.   **71. distraction:** madness.   **87. adverse:** hostile.

ANT. Today, my lord, and for three months before,
No interim, not a minute's vacancy,
Both day and night did we keep company.
    [*Enter* OLIVIA *and* ATTENDANTS.]
DUKE. Here comes the Countess. Now Heaven
walks on earth.   100
But for thee, fellow — fellow, thy words are madness.
Three months this youth hath tended upon me.
But more of that anon. Take him aside.
  OLI. What would my lord, but that he may not
have,
Wherein Olivia may seem serviceable?   105
Cesario, you do not keep promise with me.
  VIO. Madam!
  DUKE. Gracious Olivia ——
  OLI. What do you say, Cesario? Good my
lord ——
  VIO. My lord would speak, my duty hushes me.
  OLI. If it be aught to the old tune, my lord,   111
It is as fat° and fulsome° to mine ear
As howling after music.
  DUKE.   Still so cruel?
  OLI. Still so constant, lord.
  DUKE. What, to perverseness? You uncivil lady,
To whose ingrate° and unauspicious altars   116
My soul the faithful'st offerings hath breathed out
That e'er devotion tendered! What shall I do?
  OLI. Even what it please my lord that shall become
him.
  DUKE. Why should I not, had I the heart to do it,
Like to the Egyptian thief° at point of death,   121
Kill what I love? — A savage jealousy
That sometime savors nobly. But hear me this.
Since you to nonregardance cast my faith,
And that I partly know the instrument   125
That screws° me from my true place in your favor,
Live you the marble-breasted tyrant still.
But this your minion,° whom I know you love,
And whom, by Heaven I swear, I tender dearly,
Him will I tear out of that cruel eye,   130
Where he sits crownèd in his master's spite.°
Come, boy, with me. My thoughts are ripe in mischief.
I'll sacrifice the lamb that I do love,
To spite a raven's heart within a dove.
  VIO. And I, most jocund, apt, and willingly,   135
To do you rest, a thousand deaths would die.
  OLI. Where goes Cesario?
  VIO.   After him I love
More than I love these eyes, more than my life,

More, by all mores, than e'er I shall love wife.
If I do feign, you witnesses above   140
Punish my life for tainting of my love!
  OLI. Aye me, detested! How am I beguiled!
  VIO. Who does beguile you? Who does do you
wrong?
  OLI. Hast thou forgot thyself? Is it so long?
Call forth the holy Father.
  DUKE.   Come, away!   145
  OLI. Whither, my lord? Cesario, husband, stay.
  DUKE. Husband!
  OLI.   Aye, husband. Can he that deny?
  DUKE. Her husband, sirrah!
  VIO.   No, my lord, not I.
  OLI. Alas, it is the baseness of thy fear
That makes thee strangle thy propriety.°   150
Fear not, Cesario. Take thy fortunes up.
Be that thou know'st thou art, and then thou art
As great as that thou fear'st.
  [*Enter* PRIEST.]   Oh, welcome, Father!
Father, I charge thee, by thy reverence,
Here to unfold, though lately we intended   155
To keep in darkness what occasion now
Reveals before 'tis ripe, what thou dost know
Hath newly passed between this youth and me.
  PRIEST. A contract of eternal bond of love,
Confirmed by mutual joinder of your hands,   160
Attested by the holy close of lips,
Strengthened by interchangement of your rings.
And all the ceremony of this compáct°
Sealed in my function, by my testimony.
Since when, my watch hath told me, toward my
grave   165
I have traveled but two hours.
  DUKE. O thou dissembling cub! What wilt thou be
When time hath sowed a grizzle on thy case?°
Or will not else thy craft so quickly grow
That thine own trip shall be thine overthrow?°   170
Farewell, and take her, but direct thy feet
Where thou and I henceforth may never meet.
  VIO. My lord, I do protest ——
  OLI.   Oh, do not swear!
Hold little faith, though thou hast too much fear.
          [*Enter* SIR ANDREW.]
  SIR AND. For the love of God, a surgeon! Send one
presently° to Sir Toby.   176
  OLI. What's the matter?
  SIR AND. He has broke my head across and has
given Sir Toby a bloody coxcomb° too. For the love
of God, your help! I had rather than forty pound I
were at home.   181
  OLI. Who has done this, Sir Andrew?
  SIR AND. The Count's gentleman, one Cesario. We

---

112. fat: gross. fulsome: nauseous.   116. ingrate: ungrateful.
121. Egyptian thief: Thyamis, an Egyptian robber, captured
Chariclea and shut her in a cave. Being attacked by other robbers, he rushed into the cave intending to slay her rather than
that she should fall into other hands.   125–26. instrument . . .
screws: a jack that forces.   128. minion: darling.   131. in . . .
spite: to the vexation of his master.

150. strangle . . . propriety: lit., choke your proper self; i.e., behave like a coward.   163. compact: agreement.   168. hath . . .
case: has brought you gray hairs.   170. thine . . . overthrow:
your trickery will overthrow you.   176. presently: immediately.
179. bloody coxcomb: broken head.

took him for a coward, but he's the very Devil incardinate.°   185

DUKE. My gentleman, Cesario?

SIR AND. 'Od's lifelings,° here he is! You broke
my head for nothing, and that that I did, I was set
on to do 't by Sir Toby.

VIO. Why do you speak to me? I never hurt you.
You drew your sword upon me without cause,   191
But I bespake you fair, and hurt you not.

SIR AND. If a bloody coxcomb be a hurt, you have
hurt me. I think you set nothing by a bloody coxcomb. [*Enter* SIR TOBY *and* CLOWN.]   Here comes
Sir Toby halting.° You shall hear more. But if   195
he had not been in drink, he would have tickled you
othergates° than he did.

DUKE. How now, gentleman! How is 't with
you?   200

SIR TO. That's all one. Has hurt me, and there's
the end on 't. Sot, didst see Dick surgeon, sot?

CLO. Oh, he's drunk, Sir Toby, an hour agone. His
eyes were set at eight i' the morning.°   205

SIR TO. Then he's a rogue, and a passy measures
pavin.° I hate a drunken rogue.

OLI. Away with him! Who hath made this havoc
with them?

SIR AND. I'll help you, Sir Toby, because we'll be
dressed together.   211

SIR TO. Will you help? An asshead and a coxcomb
and a knave, a thin-faced knave, a gull!

OLI. Get him to bed, and let his hurt be looked to.
[*Exeunt* CLOWN, FABIAN, SIR TOBY, *and* SIR ANDREW.]
[*Enter* SEBASTIAN.]

SEB. I am sorry, madam, I have hurt your kins-
     man,
But had it been the brother of my blood,
I must have done no less with wit and safety.
You throw a strange regard° upon me, and by that
I do perceive it hath offended you.   220
Pardon me, sweet one, even for the vows
We made each other but so late ago.

DUKE. One face, one voice, one habit, and two
     persons,
A natural perspective,° that is and is not!

SEB. Antonio, O my dear Antonio!   225
How have the hours racked and tortured me
Since I have lost thee!

ANT. Sebastian are you?

SEB.   Fear'st thou that, Antonio?

ANT. How have you made division of yourself?
An apple, cleft in two, is not more twin   230
Than these two creatures. Which is Sebastian?

OLI. Most wonderful!

SEB. Do I stand there? I never had a brother,
Nor can there be that deity in my nature,
Of here and everywhere.° I had a sister,   235
Whom the blind waves and surges have devoured.
Of charity, what kin are you to me?
What countryman? What name? What parentage?

VIO. Of Messaline. Sebastian was my father.
Such a Sebastian was my brother too,   240
So went he suited° to his watery tomb.
If spirits can assume both form and suit,
You come to fright us.

SEB.   A spirit I am indeed,
But am in that dimension grossly clad°
Which from the womb I did participate.   245
Were you a woman, as the rest goes even,
I should my tears let fall upon your cheek,
And say " Thrice welcome, drownèd Viola! "

VIO. My father had a mole upon his brow.

SEB. And so had mine.   250

VIO. And died that day when Viola from her birth
Had numbered thirteen years.

SEB. Oh, that recórd is lively in my soul!
He finishèd indeed his mortal act
That day that made my sister thirteen years.   255

VIO. If nothing lets° to make us happy both
But this my masculine usurped attire,
Do not embrace me till each circumstance
Of place, time, fortune, do cohere and jump°
That I am Viola. Which to confirm,   260
I'll bring you to a captain in this town,
Where lie my maiden weeds,° by whose gentle help
I was preserved to serve this noble Count.
All the occurrence of my fortune since
Hath been between this lady and this lord.   265

SEB. [*To* OLIVIA] So comes it, lady, you have been
     mistook.
But nature to her bias° drew in that.
You would have been contracted to a maid,
Nor are you therein, by my life, deceived,
You are betrothed both to a maid and man.   270

DUKE. Be not amazed. Right noble is his blood.
If this be so, as yet the glass° seems true,
I shall have share in this most happy wreck.
[*To* VIOLA] Boy, thou hast said to me a thousand
     times
Thou never shouldst love woman like to me.   275

VIO. And all those sayings will I overswear,
And all those swearings keep as true in soul

---

185. incardinate: incarnate.   187. 'Od's lifelings: by God's little
life.   195. halting: limping.   196–97. othergates: otherwise.
205. Set . . . morning: dimmed by drink (*set*) since eight in the
morning.   206–07. passy . . . pavin: The folio reads "passy
measures panyn" (misprint for "pauyn"). Toby is very drunk.
The fool's words "set at eight" stir in his fuddled head the
memory that there were eight strains in the "passa measures
pavan," a slow, stately dance. See App. 24.   219. regard: look.
224. perspective: a picture which shows one image when seen in
front and another when viewed from an angle. See *Rich II*,
II.ii.18–20.

234–35. Nor . . . everywhere: I cannot be a god to be in two
places at once.   241. suited: clothed.   244. in . . . clad:
enclosed in bodily form.   256. lets: hinders.   259. jump:
agree.   262. weeds: garments.   267. bias: natural inclination.
272. glass: reflection.

As doth that orbèd continent the fire°
That severs day from night.
   DUKE.   Give me thy hand,
And let me see thee in thy woman's weeds.   280
   VIO. The captain that did bring me first on shore
Hath my maid's garments. He upon some action
Is now in durance,° at Malvolio's suit,
A gentleman, and follower of my lady's.
   OLI. He shall enlarge him. Fetch Malvolio hither.
And yet, alas, now I remember me,   286
They say, poor gentleman, he's much distract.
     [*Re-enter* CLOWN *with a letter, and* FABIAN.]
A most extracting frenzy° of mine own
From my remembrance clearly banished his.
How does he, sirrah?   290
   CLO. Truly, madam, he holds Belzebub at the
stave's end° as well as a man in his case may do.
Has here writ a letter to you. I should have given 't
you today morning, but as a madman's epistles are
no gospels, so it skills° not much when they are de-
livered.   296
   OLI. Open 't, and read it.
   CLO. Look then to be well edified when the fool
delivers° the madman. [*Reads.*] " By the Lord,
madam " ——   300
   OLI. How now! Art thou mad?
   CLO. No, madam, I do but read madness. An your
ladyship will have it as it ought to be, you must allow Vox.°
   OLI. Prithee, read i' thy right wits.   305
   CLO. So I do, madonna, but to read his right wits
is to read thus. Therefore perpend,° my Princess,
and give ear.
   OLI. [*To* FABIAN] Read it you, sirrah.   309
   FAB. [*Reads.*] " By the Lord, madam, you wrong
me, and the world shall know it. Though you have
put me into darkness and given your drunken
cousin rule over me, yet have I the benefit of my
senses as well as your ladyship. I have your own letter that induced me to the semblance I put on, with
the which I doubt not but to do myself much right,
or you much shame. Think of me as you please. I
leave my duty a little unthought-of,° and speak out
of my injury.
     " THE MADLY USED MALVOLIO "
   OLI. Did he write this?   320
   CLO. Aye, madam.
   DUKE. This savors not much of distraction.
   OLI. See him delivered, Fabian. Bring him hither.
     [*Exit* FABIAN.]

My lord, so please you, these things further thought
   on,
To think me as well a sister as a wife,   325
One day shall crown the alliance on 't, so please you,
Here at my house and at my proper° cost.
   DUKE. Madam, I am most apt to embrace your
   offer.
   [*To* VIOLA] Your master quits° you, and for your
   service done him,
So much against the mettle° of your sex,   330
So far beneath your soft and tender breeding,
And since you called me master for so long,
Here is my hand. You shall from this time be
Your master's mistress.
   OLI.   A sister! You are she.
     [*Re-enter* FABIAN, *with* MALVOLIO.]
   DUKE. Is this the madman?   335
   OLI.   Aye, my lord, this same.
How now, Malvolio!
   MAL.   Madam, you have done me wrong,
Notorious wrong.
   OLI.   Have I, Malvolio? No.
   MAL. Lady, you have. Pray you peruse that letter.
You must not now deny it is your hand.
Write from° it, if you can, in hand or phrase,   340
Or say 'tis not your seal, not your invention.
You can say none of this. Well, grant it then
And tell me, in the modesty of honor,
Why you have given me such clear lights of favor,
Bade me come smiling and cross-gartered to you,
To put on yellow stockings and to frown   346
Upon Sir Toby and the lighter people.
And, acting this in an obedient hope,
Why have you suffered me to be imprisoned,
Kept in a dark house, visited by the priest,   350
And made the most notorious geck° and gull
That e'er invention played on? Tell me why.
   OLI. Alas, Malvolio, this is not my writing,
Though, I confess, much like the character.°
But out of question 'tis Maria's hand.   355
And now I do bethink me it was she
First told me thou wast mad, then camest in smiling.
And in such forms which here were presupposed
Upon thee in the letter. Prithee, be content.   359
This practice° hath most shrewdly passed upon thee,
But when we know the grounds and authors of it,
Thou shalt be both the plaintiff and the judge
Of thine own cause.
   FAB.   Good madam, hear me speak,
And let no quarrel nor no brawl to come
Taint the condition° of this present hour,   365
Which I have wondered at. In hope it shall not,
Most freely I confess, myself and Toby

---

278. orbed . . . fire: the sun.   283. durance: confinement.
288. frenzy: madness.   291-92. holds . . . end: he keeps the
fiend at bay; i.e., he is putting up a fight against Belzebub, who
possesses him.   295. skills: makes little difference.   299. delivers: utters the words of.   304. allow Vox: the proper tone of
voice.   307. perpend: consider.   318. duty . . . unthought-of:
i.e., I do not write with the formal phrases that a steward
should use to his mistress.

327. proper: own.   329. quits: releases.   330. mettle: material,
nature.   340. Write from: deny.   351. geck: fool.   354. character: handwriting.   360. practice: plot.   365. Taint . . . condition: spoil the harmony.

Set this device against Malvolio here,
Upon some stubborn and uncourteous parts
We had conceived° against him. Maria writ   370
The letter at Sir Toby's great importance,°
In recompense whereof he hath married her.
How with a sportful malice it was followed
May rather pluck on laughter than revenge,
If that the injuries be justly weighed   375
That have on both sides passed.

   OLI. Alas, poor fool, how have they baffled° thee!

   CLO. Why, "some are born great, some achieve
greatness, and some have greatness thrown upon
them." I was one, sir, in this interlude; one Sir   380
Topas, sir. But that's all one. "By the Lord, fool, I
am not mad." But do you remember? "Madam,
why laugh you at such a barren rascal? An you
smile not, he's gagged." And thus the whirligig of
time brings in his revenges.°   385

   MAL. I'll be revenged on the whole pack of you.
                                 [Exit.]

   OLI. He hath been most notoriously abused.

   DUKE. Pursue him, and entreat him to a peace.
He hath not told us of the captain yet.   390
When that is known, and golden time convents,°
A solemn combination shall be made
Of our dear souls. Meantime, sweet sister,
We will not part from hence. Cesario, come —
For so you shall be, while you are a man,   395

But when in other habits you are seen,
Orsino's mistress and his fancy's Queen.
              [Exeunt all, except CLOWN.]

   CLO. *[Sings.]*
    When that I was and a little tiny boy,
      With hey, ho, the wind and the rain,
    A foolish thing was but a toy,   400
      For the rain it raineth every day.

    But when I came to man's estate,
      With hey, ho, the wind and the rain,
    'Gainst knaves and thieves men shut their gate,
      For the rain it raineth every day.   405

    But when I came, alas! to wive,
      With hey, ho, the wind and the rain,
    By swaggering could I never thrive,
      For the rain it raineth every day.

    But when I came unto my beds,°   410
      With hey, ho, the wind and the rain,
    With tosspots° still had drunken heads,
      For the rain it raineth every day.

    A great while ago the world begun,
      With hey, ho, the wind and the rain,   415
    But that's all one, our play is done,
      And we'll strive to please you every day.
                       [Exit.]

---

370. conceived: perceived.   **371. importance:** importunity, insistence.   **377. baffled:** disgraced.   **385. brings . . . revenges:** i.e., now I have my own back. See I.v.88.   **391. golden . . . convents:** happy time summons.

410. unto my beds: a difficult phrase, meaning probably "when I came to the end of my life."   **412. tosspots:** drunkards.

The Tragedy of
HAMLET, PRINCE OF DENMARK

Read

Introduction

Hamlet is in every way the most interesting play ever written. Apart from the fascination of Hamlet's character, it has a long and intricate history as a drama; the text is full of problems for the scholar; it teems with allusions for the antiquarian. For the last hundred and fifty years critics have competed in offering their key to the heart of Hamlet's mystery. It is the final ambition of every actor to give the part his own interpretation, and even the doctors, especially the psychiatrists, have taken Hamlet into the laboratory and examined his inhibitions.

The story of Hamlet in some form is at least seven hundred years old. Hamlet appears first as Amlethus in the *Historia Danica,* written by Saxo Grammaticus in the twelfth century. The original source of the English play is a French story told in the *Histoires tragiques* of François de Belleforest, published in Paris in 1576. The outline of Belleforest's story follows:

In pre-Christian times there was a Danish Prince called Horvendile, who was married to Queen Geruth. Their son was named Hamlet. Prince Horvendile was murdered by his brother Fengon, who thereupon married Queen Geruth. In order to escape from the tyranny of his uncle, Prince Hamlet pretended to be mad. Fengon was suspicious and tried to get at the truth by sending a harlot to tempt Hamlet, but Hamlet was forewarned. Then Fengon sent one of his councilors to hide secretly behind the arras in the Queen's chamber, so that he might overhear Hamlet's conversation with his mother. Hamlet came into the chamber, pretending in his madness to be a cock, and beating with his arms upon the arras he felt the eavesdropper. He slew him with his sword, cut the body in pieces, boiled them, and fed them to the hogs.

Fengon then sent Hamlet to the King of England, with sealed letters commanding that he should be put to death. On the voyage Hamlet read the letters and exchanged them for others in which it was ordered that the bearer should be hanged and he himself should be married to the daughter of the King of England. So Hamlet came back into Denmark, where he found that his supposed death was being celebrated in a mighty funeral feast. He waited until the guests were dead-drunk, and then set fire to the hall and burned them all. After this he went up to his uncle's bedchamber and, after delivering a speech on the duty of revenging his dead father, he cut off his uncle's head.

Hamlet now abandoned all pretense that he was mad. He summoned the Danes and made an oration in which he told the whole story, at which they were so moved that they proclaimed him King. After his coronation, he went back to England to fetch his wife. The King of England would have murdered him, but again he escaped. Then the Queen of Scots, whose name was Hermetrude, fell in love with him and insisted on marrying him. So Hamlet returned once more to Denmark with his two wives. But Hermetrude soon tired of him; she fell in love with Wiglerus, another of his uncles, and caused Hamlet to be murdered.

The Hamlet story appeared in England as a play at some time before 1589. In that year Thomas Nashe wrote a preface for Robert Greene's novel *Menaphon,* in which he satirized a number of contemporary writers. In this preface, Nashe wrote:

It is a common practice nowadays amongst a sort of shifting [1] companions, that run through every art and thrive by none, to leave the trade of *Noverint* [2] whereto they were born, and busy themselves with the endeavors of art, that could scarcely Latinize their neck verse [3] if they should have need. Yet English Seneca read by candlelight yields many good sentences as 'Blood is a beggar,' and so forth, and if you entreat him fair in a frosty morning, he will afford you whole Hamlets, I should say handfuls of tragical speeches.

Nashe was a very young man and loved clever obscure writing; but it seems likely that he was here referring to Thomas Kyd, the author of *The Spanish Tragedy,* which was then a fairly new play. *The Spanish Tragedy* told how old Hieronimo took vengeance on the murderers of his son

---

[1] shiftless.   [2] scrivener; see Gen. Intro. p. 37a.   [3] The verses read when a man pleaded "benefit of clergy." See Gen. Intro. p. 28a.

Horatio. If this passage indeed refers to Kyd, it seems likely that Kyd had followed up the success of *The Spanish Tragedy* with another story of revenge telling how the young Prince Hamlet took vengeance for his murdered father.

The first actual record of a play of *Hamlet* is in the summer of 1594. During the few days that the Lord Chamberlain's and the Lord Admiral's players acted together (see Gen. Intro. p. 39b), Henslowe noted that on June 11 they put on a play called *Hamlet*.

The next reference to *Hamlet* is in 1596, when Thomas Lodge wrote a book called *Wit's Misery*, in which he described allegorically various contemporary types. Among others was the Devil, Hate-Virtue, who could be known by this: " He walks for the most part in black under color of gravity, and looks as pale as the vizard of the ghost which cried so miserably at the Theater like an oyster wife, *Hamlet, revenge.*" As the Lord Chamberlain's Company was acting at the Theater at that time, Lodge's remarks show that *Hamlet* was one of the plays in their repertory. There was thus a *Hamlet* play in existence and popular between 1589 and 1596. It is not likely that this was Shakespeare's play as it is now known. The style is too mature for it to have been one of his early works, and in its printed version *Hamlet* includes a number of topical allusions which can certainly be referred to the years 1600 and 1601. These, however, may have been later additions.

The definite history of Shakespeare's *Hamlet* began in 1602. On July 26, James Roberts, the printer, entered in the Stationers' Register a " booke called the Revenge of Hamlett, Prince Denmarke, as yt was latelie Acted by the Lord Chamberleyne his servantes." This entry was probably intended to block publication (see Gen. Intro. p. 66a). Nevertheless, in 1603 there appeared the first version of Shakespeare's *Hamlet*, a quarto (Q1) with the title page: *The Tragicall Historie of Hamlet Prince of Denmarke. By William Shake-speare. As it hath beene diuerse times acted by his Highnesse seruants in the Cittie of London: as also in the two Vniuersities of Cambridge and Oxford, and else-where.* Since the Company are called " his Highnesse seruants," it is clear that Q1 was issued after May 19, when the Lord Chamberlain's Men became the King's Players. Q1 is a very garbled version of Shakespeare's play and obviously was a piracy. It is about seventeen hundred lines shorter than the

true play and differs in a number of details. The old councilor is called Corambis, not Polonius; the arrangement of the scenes is different; and there are important differences in the closet scene. More than two hundred and forty lines in Q1 did not appear in any form in the other versions, and much of the verse is in an early stiff style. Several different theories have been put forward to explain how Q1 was put together, but it is generally agreed that it was founded on the part of the actor who played Marcellus, for the scenes in which Marcellus appears are accurately reproduced. For the rest, it may either have been gathered by shorthand from an actual performance or vamped up by one of the minor actors who wrote down what he remembered of the play. Q1 has little value as a text, but some of the stage directions show what actually happened at a performance and are most interesting. It may indeed represent a version of the play in a transition stage before Shakespeare had completely rewritten the old *Hamlet*.

Among the interesting stage directions in Q1 the following are worth noting:

(a) *Enter in a Dumbe Shew, the King and the Queene, he sits downe in an Arbor, she leaues him: Then enters Lucianus with poyson in a Viall, and powres it in his ears, and goes away: Then the Queene commeth and findes him dead: and goes away with the other.* (III.ii.145)

(b) *Enter the ghost in his night gowne.* (III.iv.102)

(c) *Enter Ofelia playing on a Lute, and her haire downe singing.* (IV.v.20)

(d) *Enter King and Queene, Leartes, and other lordes, with a Priest after the coffin.* (V.i.240)

(e) *Enter a Bragart Gentleman.* (V.ii.80)

(f) *They catch one anothers Rapiers, and both are wounded, Leartes falles downe, the Queene falles downe and dies.* (V.ii.313)

Some of the differences between the first and second Quartos are shown in the General Introduction (pp. 61–2). Another illustration of the shortcomings of the compiler of Q1 occurs in his version of the famous " To be or not to be " speech (see III.i.56), which runs in Q1 thus:

To be, or not to be, I there's the point,
To Die, to sleepe, is that all? I all:
No, to sleepe, to dreame, I mary there it goes,
For in that dreame of death, when wee awake,
And borne before an euerlasting Judge,
From whence no passenger euer retur'nd,

The vndiscouered country, at whose sight
The happy smile, and the accursed damn'd.
But for this, the joyfull hope of this,
Whol'd beare the scornes and flattery of the world,
Scorned by the right rich, the rich curssed of the
    poore?
The widow being oppressed, the orphan wrong'd,
The taste of hunger, or a tirants raigne,
And thousand more calamities besides,
To grunt and sweate under this weary life,
When that he may his full *Quietus* make,
With a bare bodkin, who would this indure,
But for a hope of something after death?
Which pusles the braine, and doth confound the
    sence.
Which makes us rather beare those euilles we haue,
Than flie to others that we know not of.
I that, O this conscience makes cowardes of us all,
Lady in thy orizons, be all my sinnes remembred.

About a year later a new edition of the play
came out. This is known as the second quarto
(Q2). Its title page runs: *The Tragicall Historie
of Hamlet, Prince of Denmarke. By William
Shakespeare. Newly imprinted and enlarged to
almost as much againe as it was, according to the
true and perfect Coppie* (see Pl. 14d). Q2 gives
the fullest text of the play. It was probably set up
directly from Shakespeare's own manuscript, but
it is very carelessly printed and full of mistakes.
Q2 was reprinted in 1607 and 1611.

Hamlet was again printed in the first folio
(F1), in 1623. There are many differences between Q2 and F1. Some of the passages amount-
ing to more than two hundred lines in Q2 are
omitted, some new passages are added. The text
in F1 is much more carefully printed than in Q2
and many of the mistakes have been corrected.
On the other hand, F1 has many mistakes of its
own. In Q2 there is no division into acts or scenes;
in F1 the acts and scenes are marked down to the
beginning of Act II, Scene ii, but thereafter
omitted. The general opinion held by modern
scholars is that F1 was set up from a copy of the
play as later used in the playhouse. The problems
of the text of *Hamlet* are thus very complicated.
In modern texts, editors combine Q2 and F1 and
print all the passages. Where there is a difference
in reading, the editors either choose that which
seems to them best or else emend the text. The
study of the text of *Hamlet* indeed requires a
large volume to itself.

There has been so much critical interpretation
of *Hamlet* that a student should form his own impression of the play before listening to any of the
arguments of the various sects of critics. It is as
well to remember as an elementary fact, too often
forgotten — that *Hamlet* is an Elizabethan play
and not a Victorian treatise on philosophy or psychology, and that it was written to be acted in the
Globe Theater about 1600. *Hamlet* belongs to a
well-known type of drama, the "revenge" play.
In such plays, there was a regular set of conventions. Vengeance, at least on the stage, was a
pious duty laid on the next of kin. It was, in Bacon's words, "wild justice" — but something
more than justice, for a credit balance was necessary. The Old Law claimed "an eye for an eye
and a tooth for a tooth"; vengeance required
both eyes, a jaw full of teeth, and above all that
its victim, after exquisite torment of body and
mind, should burn everlastingly in hell-fire. A
perfect vengeance, therefore, demanded great
artistry.

Most revenge plays were written according to a
common pattern. They required a crime, invariably murder, whereby the duty of vengeance was
laid on the next of kin; the discovery of the murderer by the avenger, usually a matter of some
difficulty; the impediments to revenge; and finally, the triumphant conclusion in which the
murderer was appropriately destroyed. And,
since playgoers liked gore, the avenger and half
a dozen others must perish in one red ruin in
the last act, and it was usual to include at least
one ghost and a mad scene. The pattern had
been set in Kyd's *Spanish Tragedy*.

An example of satisfactory vengeance is to be
found in Thomas Nashe's novel *Jack Wilton, the
Unfortunate Traveller* (1594). Cutwolf, wishing
to exact vengeance on Esdras (who had murdered his brother) corners his victim. Esdras in
despair promises to commit any desperate action
to save his own life, whereupon Cutwolf, who is
telling the story, demands:

First and foremost, he should renounce God and
His laws, and utterly disclaim the whole title or interest he had in any covenant of salvation. Next, he
should curse Him to His face, as Job was willed by
his wife, and write an absolute firm obligation of
his soul to the Devil, without condition or exception.
Thirdly and lastly (having done this), he should
pray to God fervently never to have mercy upon him,
or pardon him. . . . These fearful ceremonies
brought to an end, I bade him ope his mouth and
gape wide. He did so (as what will not slaves do for

fear?); therewith made I no more ado, but shot him full into the throat with my pistol. No more spake he after, so did I shoot him that he might never speak after, or repent him. His body being dead looked as black as a toad. The Devil presently branded it for his own.

Revenges almost as extravagant occur in such plays as Kyd's *The Spanish Tragedy,* Marston's *Antonio's Revenge* (which is contemporary with *Hamlet*), and later in the tragedies of Webster and Tourneur. The reasons Hamlet gives for sparing his uncle (III.iii.74–95) would have been regarded as normal by any Elizabethan playgoer. In writing *Hamlet,* Shakespeare began with one advantage. The audience knew the story. There was therefore no need to start with an explanation. Instead, in the first scene of the play Shakespeare set about creating atmosphere; and he put the playgoer in the right mood with a sense of foreboding that something indeed was "rotten in the state of Denmark." In the second scene, the plot begins to move. King Claudius is shown holding his first council. The King dispatches the various items of official business on the agenda, in the course of which the state of affairs in Denmark is fully revealed.

Hamlet is then left alone, and his first soliloquy reveals certain matters that are pressing on his mind. His mother, with indecent haste, has married the brother of her late husband. According to canon law, she has therefore committed incest, for in early Christian times the command that man and wife should be one flesh was taken so literally that all the wife's relations became the husband's and vice versa. Shakespeare next shows a scene of the Polonius family and the increasing difficulties of Ophelia's position. After this domestic scene of pure comedy, the action returns to the battlements. The ghost appears, leads Hamlet away, tells him the whole story of the murder in the orchard, and demands revenge. Thus ends the first part of the play, which shows how murder was revealed and the duty of vengeance laid on Prince Hamlet.

At this point, critics become indignant with Hamlet and ask why he did not at once kill his uncle; to which there is the common-sense answer that the word of a ghost seen alone at midnight is hardly good enough evidence to kill anyone. Moreover, according to contemporary theological notions, a Christian knew that the appearance of a spirit or wraith in the shade of a person newly dead might be evil. As King James expressed it in his *Daemonology:*

> Amongst the Gentiles, the Devil used that much to make them believe that it was some good spirit that appeared to them then, either to forewarn them of the death of their friend, or else to discover unto them the will of the defunct, or what was the way of his slaughter. . . . And this way he easily deceived the Gentiles, because they knew not God. And to that same effect is it that he now appears in that manner to some ignorant Christians. For he dare not so illude any that knoweth that neither can the spirit of the defunct return to his friend, or yet an angel use such forms.

The second part of the play starts some weeks later. In this part we are shown how Hamlet proved his uncle guilty. To indicate the passage of time, the play begins with Polonius sending his man Reynaldo to Paris with the next installment of Laertes' allowance. It shows also Hamlet's reaction to Ophelia's refusal to have anything more to do with him. For Hamlet the situation is even worse than at the beginning of the play, for he is now burdened with the horrible suspicion that as yet he can neither verify nor disprove. When Rosencrantz and Guildenstern tell him of the players, he sees his chance of proving once and for all the truth of the midnight revelation. His soliloquy at the end of Act II (ii.575–634) concludes with the words:

> The spirit that I have seen
> May be the Devil, and the Devil hath power
> To assume a pleasing shape. Yea, and perhaps
> Out of my weakness and my melancholy,
> As he is very potent with such spirits,
> Abuses me to damn me. I'll have grounds
> More relative than this. The play's the thing
> Wherein I'll catch the conscience of the King.

This emphasis on the Devil and on melancholy is a literal statement of scientific fact as it was believed by Shakespeare's contemporaries. Melancholy in its extremest forms was the cause of all kinds of mental aberration, including delusion and hallucination. Hamlet, therefore, anticipating modern scientists by some centuries, decides to apply an elementary form of lie detector to his uncle. In the play scene, Claudius reveals his guilt beyond any possible doubt. Now Hamlet knows for certain that it was a true ghost and not a figment of his melancholy imagination.

At this point the whole direction of the play changes. In the act of proving for certain the guilt of his uncle Hamlet has revealed to Claudius that he knows all. The initiative passes to Claudius, and he can take action against his nephew. As Claudius tries to pray, Hamlet passes by on his way to his mother. This is the only time in the play that Claudius is alone or that Claudius and Hamlet are alone together. But the opportunity for vengeance is unsuitable. Again the words of Hamlet's soliloquy (III.iii.74–95) should be taken literally. Revenge demanded hell-fire for the victim and at this moment Claudius was apparently in a state of grace. So Hamlet passes into his mother's chamber, and there kills Polonius.

The third part of the play then begins. Hamlet himself has committed a murder, and the duty of vengeance is laid on Laertes. Soon afterward, Hamlet goes on his way to England and disappears for a long while. During his absence the second revenge story — the revenge of Laertes for his father Polonius — is set in motion. Ophelia meanwhile has gone mad. Laertes returns, leading a revolution, but the King overcomes him by superior will power and the two plot Hamlet's death. When Hamlet unexpectedly returns, destruction awaits him.

At this crisis Shakespeare deliberately holds back the final catastrophe. He introduces two new characters, the Gravediggers. The gravedigging scene has several dramatic purposes. It gives emotional relief, and it is a cynical contrast to Hamlet's lofty philosophy. Hamlet had brooded much over man and mortality; here in common life are the two who have the last word with man. Then comes the funeral of Ophelia, simple, almost sordid, and the sudden ferocity of the fight at the open grave. The excitement is growing, but once more Shakespeare holds us back. He introduces Osric, the fashionable courtier, with nothing to recommend him but his wealth, his clothes, and his pretty manners. He is, in fact, another of the " humor " types so common on the stage in these years. The audience is now ready for the final catastrophe, when both vengeances are consummated and all the guilty punished in one bloody ending.

When the play is viewed as a tragedy of the Elizabethan and not the Romantic era, many of its problems disappear. Nevertheless, there are other problems in *Hamlet*. Shakespeare took this old story of blood and revenge and made it modern — that is, modern to his generation. For some reason it seems to have been his favorite play. When he wrote it, he was, with all thinking men of his age, in a period of profound disillusionment and pessimism, and he made it the vessel into which he poured his thoughts on all kinds of problems: on fathers and children, on sex, on drunkenness, on suicide, on mortality and corruption, on ingratitude and loyalty, on acting, on handwriting even, on fate, on man and the universe. There is more of Shakespeare himself in this play than in any of his others.

Hamlet

DRAMATIS PERSONAE

CLAUDIUS, *King of Denmark*
HAMLET, *son to the late, and nephew to the present King*
POLONIUS, *Lord Chamberlain*
HORATIO, *friend to Hamlet*
LAERTES, *son to Polonius*
VOLTIMAND
CORNELIUS
ROSENCRANTZ
GUILDENSTERN } *courtiers*
OSRIC
A GENTLEMAN
A PRIEST
MARCELLUS } *officers*
BERNARDO
FRANCISCO, *a soldier*

REYNALDO, *servant to Polonius*
PLAYERS
TWO CLOWNS, *gravediggers*
FORTINBRAS, *Prince of Norway*
A CAPTAIN
ENGLISH AMBASSADORS

GERTRUDE, *Queen of Denmark, and mother to Hamlet*

OPHELIA, *daughter to Polonius*
LORDS, LADIES, OFFICERS, SOLDIERS, SAILORS, MESSENGERS, *and other* ATTENDANTS

GHOST *of Hamlet's father*

SCENE — *Denmark.*

Act I

SCENE I. *Elsinore. A platform° before the castle.*

[FRANCISCO *at his post. Enter to him* BERNARDO.]
BER. Who's there?
FRAN. Nay, answer me. Stand, and unfold yourself.°
BER. Long live the King!°
FRAN. Bernardo?
BER. He.   5
FRAN. You come most carefully upon your hour.
BER. 'Tis now struck twelve. Get thee to bed, Francisco.
FRAN. For this relief much thanks. 'Tis bitter cold, *MUST BE WINTER (REST OF*
And I am sick at heart. *PLAY IN SUMMER)*
BER. Have you had quiet guard?
FRAN.   Not a mouse stirring. 10
BER. Well, good night.
If you do meet Horatio and Marcellus,
The rivals° of my watch, bid them make haste.
FRAN. I think I hear them. Stand, ho! Who is there?
[*Enter* HORATIO *and* MARCELLUS.]
HOR. Friends to this ground.
MAR.   And liegemen° to the Dane. 15
FRAN. Give you good night.

MAR.   Oh, farewell, honest soldier.
Who hath relieved you?
FRAN.   Bernardo hath my place.
Give you good night.   [*Exit.*]
MAR.   Holloa! Bernardo!
BER.   Say,
What, is Horatio there?
HOR.   A piece of him.
BER. Welcome, Horatio. Welcome, good Marcellus.   20
MAR. What, has this thing appeared again tonight?
BER. I have seen nothing.
MAR. Horatio says 'tis but our fantasy,°
And will not let belief take hold of him
Touching this dreaded sight twice seen of us. 25
Therefore I have entreated him along
With us to watch the minutes of this night,
That if again this apparition come,
He may approve our eyes° and speak to it.
HOR. Tush, tush, 'twill not appear.
BER.   Sit down awhile, 30
And let us once again assail your ears,
That are so fortified against our story,
What we have two nights seen.
HOR.   Well, sit we down,
And let us hear Bernardo speak of this.
BER. Last night of all,   35
When yond same star that's westward from the pole°
Had made his course to illume° that part of heaven

Act I, Sc. i: s.d., **platform:** the level place on the ramparts where the cannon were mounted.   2. **unfold yourself:** reveal who you are.   3. **Long . . . King:** probably the password for the night.   13. **rivals:** partners.   15. **liegemen:** loyal subjects.   23. **fantasy:** imagination.   29. **approve our eyes:** verify what we have seen.   36. **pole:** Polestar.   37. **illume:** light.

Where now it burns, Marcellus and myself,
The bell then beating one ——
         [*Enter* GHOST.]
MAR. Peace, break thee off. Look where it comes
   again!   40
BER. In the same figure, like the King that's
   dead.
MAR. Thou art a scholar.° Speak to it, Horatio.
BER. Looks it not like the King? Mark it, Horatio.
HOR. Most like. It harrows° me with fear and
   wonder.
BER. It would be spoke to.
MAR.   Question it, Horatio.   45
HOR. What art thou that usurp'st this time of
   night,
Together with° that fair and warlike form
In which the majesty of buried Denmark°
Did sometimes march? By Heaven I charge thee,
   speak!
MAR. It is offended.
BER.   See, it stalks away!   50
HOR. Stay! Speak, speak! I charge thee, speak!
                 [*Exit* GHOST.]
MAR. 'Tis gone, and will not answer.
BER. How now, Horatio! You tremble and look
   pale.
Is not this something more than fantasy?
What think you on 't?   55
HOR. Before my God, I might not this believe
Without the sensible and true avouch
Of mine own eyes.°
MAR.   Is it not like the King?
HOR. As thou art to thyself.
Such was the very armor he had on   60
When he the ambitious Norway combated.
So frowned he once when, in an angry parle,°
He smote the sledded Polacks° on the ice.
'Tis strange.
MAR. Thus twice before, and jump at this dead
   hour,°   65
With martial stalk hath he gone by our watch.
HOR. In what particular thought to work I know
   not,
But in the gross and scope° of my opinion
This bodes some strange eruption° to our state.

MAR. Good now, sit down and tell me, he that
   knows,   70
Why this same strict and most observant watch
So nightly toils° the subject° of the land;
And why such daily cast of brazen cannon
And foreign mart° for implements of war;
Why° such impress° of shipwrights, whose sore
   task   75
Does not divide the Sunday from the week;
What might be toward,° that this sweaty haste
Doth make the night joint laborer with the day.
Who is 't that can inform me?
HOR.   That can I,
At least the whisper goes so. Our last King,   80
Whose image even but now appeared to us,
Was, as you know, by Fortinbras of Norway,
Thereto pricked° on by a most emulate° pride,
Dared to the combat, in which our valiant Ham-
   let ——
For so this side of our known world esteemed
   him ——   85
Did slay this Fortinbras. Who° by a sealed com-
   pact,°
Well ratified by law and heraldry,°
Did forfeit, with his life, all those his lands
Which he stood seized of° to the conqueror.
Against the which, a moiety competent°   90
Was gagèd° by our King, which had returnèd
To the inheritance of Fortinbras
Had he been vanquished, as by the same covenant
And carriage of the article designed°
His fell to Hamlet. Now, sir, young Fortinbras,   95
Of unimprovèd mettle° hot and full,
Hath in the skirts° of Norway here and there
Sharked° up a list of lawless resolutes,°
For food and diet,° to some enterprise   99
That hath a stomach° in 't. Which is no other ——
As it doth well appear unto our state ——
But to recover of us, by strong hand
And terms compulsatory,° those foresaid lands
So by his father lost. And this, I take it,
Is the main motive of our preparations,   105
The source of this our watch and the chief head°

---

42. scholar: As Latin was the proper language in which to address and exorcise evil spirits, a scholar was necessary. 44. harrows: distresses; lit., plows up. 47. Together with: i.e., appearing in. 48. majesty . . . Denmark: the dead King. 57–58. Without . . . eyes: unless my own eyes had vouched for it. sensible: perceived by my senses. 62. parle: parley. 63. sledded Polacks: There has been much controversy about this phrase. Q1 and Q2 read "sleaded Pollax," F1 reads "sledded Pollax." Either the late King smote his heavy (leaded) poleax on the ice, or else he attacked the Poles in their sledges. There is no further reference to this incident. 65. jump . . . hour: just at deep midnight. 68. gross . . . scope: general conclusion. 69. eruption: violent disturbance.

72. toils: wearies. subject: subjects. 74. foreign mart: purchase abroad. 75–78. Why . . . day: i.e., workers in shipyards and munition factories are working night shifts and Sundays. impress: conscription. toward: in preparation. 83. pricked: spurred. emulate: jealous. 86–95. Who . . . Hamlet: i.e., before the combat it was agreed that the victor should win the lands of the vanquished. 86. sealed compact: formal agreement. 87. heraldry: The heralds were responsible for arranging formal combats. See App. 9. 89. seized of: possessed of, a legal term. 90. moiety competent: adequate portion. 91. gaged: pledged. 94. carriage . . . designed: fulfillment of the clause in the agreement. 96. unimproved mettle: untutored, wild material, nature. 97. skirts: outlying parts. 98. Sharked: collected indiscriminately, as a shark bolts its prey. lawless resolutes: gangsters. 99. diet: maintenance. 100. stomach: resolution. 103. terms compulsatory: force. 106. chief head: main purpose.

[Margin annotations, handwritten:]
LATIN WAS PROPER LANGUAGE TO EXORCISE A SPIRIT - SO HORATIO ALONG
GHOST SPEAKS ONLY TO HAMLET - NOT TO HORATIO
EMPHASIS ON ARMOR
THIS SHOWS BAD POLITICAL STATE IN PLAY
FORT, LOST LAND TO KING HAMLET

Of this posthaste and romage° in the land.
BER. I think it be no other but e'en so.
Well may it sort° that this portentous figure   109
Comes armèd through our watch, so like the King
That was and is the question of these wars.
HOR. A mote° it is to trouble the mind's eye.
In the most high and palmy° state of Rome,
A little ere the mightiest Julius fell,   114
The graves stood tenantless, and the sheeted° dead
Did squeak and gibber° in the Roman streets.
As stars° with trains of fire and dews of blood,
Disasters° in the sun, and the moist star°
Upon whose influence Neptune's empire stands
Was sick almost to doomsday with eclipse.   120
And even the like precurse° of fierce events,
As harbingers° preceding still the fates
And prologue to the omen° coming on,
Have Heaven and earth together demonstrated
Unto our climatures° and countrymen.   125
[*Re-enter* GHOST.] But soft, behold! Lo where it
        comes again!
I'll cross it,° though it blast me. Stay, illusion!
If thou hast any sound, or use of voice,
Speak to me.
If° there be any good thing to be done   130
That may to thee do ease and grace to me,°
Speak to me.
If thou art privy to° thy country's fate,
Which, happily,° foreknowing may avoid,
Oh, speak!   135
Or if thou hast uphoarded in thy life
Extorted° treasure in the womb of earth,
For which, they say, you spirits oft walk in death,
Speak of it. Stay, and speak! [*The cock crows.*°]
        Stop it, Marcellus.
MAR. Shall I strike at it with my partisan?°   140
HOR. Do, if it will not stand.
BER.   'Tis here!
HOR.   'Tis here!
MAR. 'Tis gone!   [*Exit* GHOST.]

107. posthaste . . . romage: urgency and bustle.   109. Well . . .
sort: it would be a natural reason.   112. mote: speck of dust.
113. palmy: flourishing.   115. sheeted: in their shrouds. See
App. 16.   116. gibber: utter strange sounds.   117. As stars:
The sense of the passage is here broken; possibly a line has been
omitted after l. 116.   118. Disasters: unlucky signs. moist star:
the moon, which influences the tides.   121. precurse: forewarning.   122. harbingers: forerunners. The harbinger was an officer of the Court who was sent ahead to make the arrangements
when the Court went on progress.   123. omen: disaster.
125. climatures: regions.   127. cross it: stand in its way.
130–39. If . . . speak: In popular belief there were four reasons
why the spirit of a dead man should *walk*: (a) to reveal a secret,
(b) to utter a warning, (c) to reveal concealed treasure, (d) to
reveal the manner of its death. Horatio thus adjures the ghost
by three potent reasons, but before he can utter the fourth the
cock crows.   131. grace to me: bring me into a state of spiritual
grace.   133. privy to: have secret knowledge of.   134. happily:
by good luck.   137. Extorted: evilly acquired.   139. s.d., cock
crows: i.e., a sign that dawn is at hand. See ll. 147–64.   140. partisan: See Pl. 21a.

We do it wrong, being so majestical,
To offer it the show of violence,
For it is as the air invulnerable,   145
And our vain blows malicious mockery.
BER. It was about to speak when the cock crew.
HOR. And then it started like a guilty thing
Upon a fearful° summons. I have heard
The cock, that is the trumpet to the morn,   150
Doth with his lofty and shrill-sounding throat
Awake the god of day, and at his warning,
Whether in sea or fire, in earth or air,
The extravagant and erring° spirit hies
To his confine.° And of the truth herein   155
This present object made probation.°
MAR. It faded on the crowing of the cock.
Some say that ever 'gainst° that season comes
Wherein Our Saviour's birth is celebrated,
The bird of dawning singeth all night long.   160
And then, they say, no spirit dare stir abroad,
The nights are wholesome, then no planets° strike,
No fairy takes° nor witch hath power to charm,
So hallowed and so gracious is the time.   164
HOR. So have I heard and do in part believe it.
But look, the morn, in russet mantle clad,
Walks o'er the dew of yon high eastward hill.
Break we our watch up, and by my advice
Let us impart what we have seen tonight
Unto young Hamlet, for upon my life,   170
This spirit, dumb to us, will speak to him.
Do you consent we shall acquaint him with it,
As needful in our loves, fitting our duty?
MAR. Let's do 't, I pray. And I this morning know
Where we shall find him most conveniently.   175
                                            [*Exeunt.*]

[Handwritten margin note: RELIGIOUS IDEAS OF SHAKES.]

SCENE II. *A room of state in the castle.*

[*Flourish.*° *Enter the* KING, QUEEN, HAMLET,
    POLONIUS, LAERTES, VOLTIMAND, CORNELIUS,
            LORDS, *and* ATTENDANTS.]
KING. Though yet of Hamlet our dear brother's
        death
The memory be green,° and that it us befitted
To bear our hearts in grief and our whole kingdom
To be contracted in one brow of woe,°
Yet so far hath discretion° fought with nature°   5
That we with wisest sorrow think on him,

[Handwritten margin note: KING DEALS WELL WITH AFFAIRS OF STATE—ESPECIALLY FORTINBRAS—BUT GETS MIXED UP WITH HAMLET AROUND.]

149. fearful: causing fear.   154. extravagant . . . erring: both
words mean "wandering."   155. confine: place of confinement.   156. probation: proof.   158. 'gainst: in anticipation of.
162. planets: Planets were supposed to bring disaster. See
App. 1.   163. takes: bewitches.
    Sc. ii: s.d., Flourish: fanfare of trumpets.   2. green: fresh.
4. contracted . . . woe: i.e., every subject's forehead should be
puckered with grief.   5. discretion: common sense. nature:
natural sorrow.

Together with remembrance of ourselves.
Therefore our sometime sister,° now our Queen,
The imperial jointress° to this warlike state,
Have we, as 'twere with a defeated joy — 10
With an auspicious and a dropping eye,°
With mirth in funeral and with dirge in marriage,
In equal scale weighing delight and dole° —
Taken to wife. Nor have we herein barred
Your better wisdoms,° which have freely gone 15
With this affair along. For all, our thanks.
Now follows that you know. Young Fortinbras,
Holding a weak supposal° of our worth,
Or thinking by our late dear brother's death
Our state to be disjoint and out of frame, 20
Colleagued with the dream of his advantage,°
He hath not failed to pester us with message
Importing the surrender of those lands
Lost by his father, with all bonds of law,°
To our most valiant brother. So much for him. 25
Now for ourself, and for this time of meeting.
Thus much the business is: We have here writ
To Norway, uncle of young Fortinbras —
Who, impotent and bedrid, scarcely hears
Of this his nephew's purpose — to suppress 30
His further gait° herein, in that the levies,
The lists° and full proportions,° are all made
Out of his subject.° And we here dispatch
You, good Cornelius, and you, Voltimand,
For bearers of this greeting to old Norway, 35
Giving to you no further personal power
To business with the King more than the scope°
Of these delated articles° allow.
Farewell, and let your haste commend° your duty.
COR. & VOLT. In that and all things will we show
  our duty. 40
  KING. We doubt it nothing. Heartily farewell.
    [*Exeunt* VOLTIMAND *and* CORNELIUS.]
And now, Laertes, what's the news with you?
You told us of some suit° — what is 't, Laertes?
You cannot speak of reason to the Dane
And lose your voice. What wouldst thou beg,
  Laertes, 45
That shall not be my offer, not thy asking?

The head is not more native° to the heart,
The hand more instrumental° to the mouth,
Than is the throne of Denmark to thy father.
What wouldst thou have, Laertes?
  LAER. My dread° lord, 50
Your leave and favor to return to France,
From whence though willingly I came to Denmark
To show my duty in your coronation,
Yet now, I must confess, that duty done, 54
My thoughts and wishes bend again toward France
And bow them to your gracious leave and pardon.
  KING. Have you your father's leave? What says
    Polonius?
  POL. He hath, my lord, wrung from me my slow
    leave
By laborsome petition, and at last
Upon his will° I sealed my hard consent.° 60
I do beseech you give him leave to go.
  KING. Take thy fair hour, Laertes, time be thine,
And thy best graces spend° it at thy will!
But now, my cousin° Hamlet, and my son ——
  HAML. [*Aside*] A little more than kin and less
    than kind.° 65
  KING. How is it that the clouds still hang on you?
  HAML. Not so, my lord. I am too much i' the
    sun.
  QUEEN. Good Hamlet, cast thy nighted color° off,
And let thine eye look like a friend on Denmark.
Do not forever with thy vailèd lids° 70
Seek for thy noble father in the dust.
Thou know'st 'tis common — all that lives must die,
Passing through nature to eternity.
  HAML. Aye, madam, it is common.
  QUEEN. If it be,
Why seems it so particular with thee? 75
  HAML. Seems, madam! Nay, it is. I know not
    " seems."
'Tis not alone my inky cloak, good Mother,
Nor customary suits of solemn black,
Nor windy suspiration of forced breath —
No, nor the fruitful river° in the eye, 80
Nor the dejected havior of the visage,°
Together with all forms, moods, shapes of grief —
That can denote me truly. These indeed seem,
For they are actions that a man might play.°
But I have that within which passeth show, 85
These but the trappings° and the suits of woe.

8. sister: sister-in-law. See *Haml* Intro. p. 883a. 9. jointress: partner by marriage. 11. auspicious . . . eye: an eye at the same time full of joy and of tears. 13. dole: grief. 14–15. barred . . . wisdoms: i.e., in taking this step we have not shut out your advice. As is obvious throughout the play, the Danes chose their King by election and not by right of birth. See V.ii.65, 366. 18. weak supposal: poor opinion. 21. Colleagued . . . advantage: uniting himself with this dream that here was a good opportunity. 24. with . . . law: legally binding, as already explained in ll. 80–95, p. 886b, above. 31. gait: progress. 32. lists: rosters. proportions: military establishments. 33. subject: subjects. 37. scope: limit. 38. delated articles: detailed instructions. Claudius is following usual diplomatic procedure. Ambassadors sent on a special mission carried with them a letter of introduction and greeting to the King of the foreign Court and detailed instructions to guide them in the negotiations. 39. commend: display; lit., recommend. 43. suit: petition.

47. native: closely related. 48. instrumental: serviceable. 50. dread: dreaded, much respected. 60. will: desire. sealed . . . consent: agreed to, but with great reluctance. 63. best . . . spend: i.e., use your time well. 64. cousin: kinsman. The word was used for any near relation. 65. A . . . kind: too near a relation (uncle-father) and too little natural affection. kind: affectionate. 68. nighted color: black. Hamlet alone is in deep mourning; the rest of the Court wear gay clothes. 70. vailed lids: lowered eyelids. 80. fruitful river: stream of tears. 81. dejected . . . visage: downcast countenance. 84. play: act, as in a play. 86. trappings: ornaments.

KING. 'Tis sweet and commendable in your
    nature, Hamlet,
To give these mourning duties to your father.
But you must know your father lost a father,
That father lost, lost his, and the survivor bound 90
In filial obligation for some term
To do obsequious sorrow.° But to perséver
In obstinate condolement° is a course
Of impious stubbornness, 'tis unmanly grief.
It shows a will most incorrect to Heaven, 95
A heart unfortified,° a mind impatient,
An understanding simple and unschooled.
For what we know must be and is as common
As any the most vulgar° thing to sense,
Why should we in our peevish opposition 100
Take it to heart? Fie! 'Tis a fault to Heaven,
A fault against the dead, a fault to nature,
To reason most absurd, whose common theme
Is death of fathers, and who still hath cried,
From the first corse° till he that died today, 105
"This must be so." We pray you throw to earth
This unprevailing° woe, and think of us
As of a father. For let the world take note,
You are the most immediate° to our throne,
And with no less nobility of love 110
Than that which dearest father bears his son
Do I impart toward you. For your intent
In going back to school° in Wittenberg,
It is most retrograde° to our desire.
And we beseech you bend you° to remain 115
Here in the cheer and comfort of our eye,
Our chiefest courtier, cousin, and our son.
    QUEEN. Let not thy mother lose her prayers,
    Hamlet.
I pray thee, stay with us, go not to Wittenberg. 119
    HAML. I shall in all my best obey you, madam.
    KING. Why, 'tis a loving and a fair reply.
Be as ourself in Denmark. Madam, come,
This gentle and unforced accord of Hamlet
Sits smiling to my heart. In grace whereof,
No jocund health that Denmark drinks today 125
But the great cannon° to the clouds shall tell,
And the King's rouse° the Heaven shall bruit°
    again,
Respeaking earthly thunder. Come away.
        [*Flourish. Exeunt all but* HAML.]
    HAML. Oh, that this too too solid flesh would melt,
Thaw, and resolve itself into a dew! 130

Or that the Everlasting had not fixed
His canon° 'gainst self-slaughter! Oh, God! God!
How weary, stale, flat, and unprofitable
Seem to me all the uses° of this world!
Fie on 't, ah, fie! 'Tis an unweeded garden, 135
That grows to seed, things rank° and gross in
    nature
Possess it merely.° That it should come to this!
But two months dead! Nay, not so much, not two.
So excellent a King, that was, to this,
Hyperion° to a satyr.° So loving to my mother 140
That he might not beteem° the winds of heaven
Visit her face too roughly. Heaven and earth!
Must I remember? Why, she would hang on him
As if increase of appetite had grown 144
By what it fed on. And yet within a month ——
Let me not think on 't. — Frailty, thy name is
    woman! —
A little month, or ere those shoes were old
With which she followed my poor father's body,
Like Niobe° all tears. — Why she, even she — 149
Oh, God! A beast that wants discourse of reason°
Would have mourned longer — married with my
    uncle,
My father's brother, but no more like my father
Than I to Hercules. Within a month,
Ere yet the salt of most unrighteous tears
Had left the flushing in her gallèd° eyes, 155
She married. Oh, most wicked speed, to post°
With such dexterity° to incestuous sheets!
It is not, nor it cannot, come to good.
But break, my heart, for I must hold my tongue!
    [*Enter* HORATIO, MARCELLUS, *and* BERNARDO.]
    HOR. Hail to your lordship!
    HAML.   I am glad to see you well. 160
Horatio — or I do forget myself.
    HOR. The same, my lord, and your poor servant
    ever.
    HAML. Sir, my good friend — I'll change that
    name° with you.
And what make you from Wittenberg, Horatio?
Marcellus? 165
    MAR. My good lord?
    HAML. I am very glad to see you. [*To* BERNARDO]
    Good even, sir.
But what, in faith, make you from Wittenberg?
    HOR. A truant disposition, good my lord.
    HAML. I would not hear your enemy say so, 170
Nor shall you do my ear that violence

---

92. obsequious sorrow: the sorrow usual at funerals. **93. obstinate condolement:** lamentation disregarding the will of God. **96. unfortified:** not strengthened with the consolation of religion. **99. vulgar:** common. **105. corse:** corpse. There is unconscious irony in this remark, for the first corpse was that of Abel, also slain by his brother. **107. unprevailing:** futile. **109. most immediate:** next heir. **113. school:** university. **114. retrograde:** contrary. **115. bend you:** incline. **126. great cannon:** This Danish custom of discharging cannon when the King proposed a toast was much noted by Englishmen. **127. rouse:** deep drink. **bruit:** sound loudly, echo.

132. canon: rule, law. **134. uses:** ways. **136. rank:** coarse. **137. merely:** entirely. **140. Hyperion:** the sun god. **satyr:** a creature half man, half goat — ugly and lecherous. **141. beteem:** allow. **149. Niobe:** She boasted of her children, to the annoyance of the goddess Artemis, who slew them all. Thereafter Niobe became so sorrowful that she changed into a rock everlastingly dripping water. **150. wants . . . reason:** is without ability to reason. **155. galled:** sore. **156. post:** hasten. **157. dexterity:** nimbleness. **164. that name:** i.e., friend.

To make it truster of your own report
Against yourself. I know you are no truant.
But what is your affair in Elsinore?
We'll teach you to drink deep° ere you depart.   175
  HOR. My lord, I came to see your father's funeral.
  HAML. I pray thee do not mock me, fellow student.
I think it was to see my mother's wedding.
  HOR. Indeed, my lord, it followed hard upon.
  HAML. Thrift, thrift, Horatio! The funeral baked
    meats   180
Did coldly furnish forth the marriage tables.°
Would I had met my dearest° foe in Heaven
Or ever I had seen that day, Horatio!
My father! — Methinks I see my father.
  HOR. Oh, where, my lord?
  HAML.   In my mind's eye, Horatio.   185
  HOR. I saw him once. He was a goodly King.
  HAML. He was a man, take him for all in all.
I shall not look upon his like again.
  HOR. My lord, I think I saw him yesternight.
  HAML. Saw? Who?   190
  HOR. My lord, the King your father.
  HAML.   The King my father!
  HOR. Season your admiration° for a while
With an attent° ear till I may deliver,
Upon the witness of these gentlemen,
This marvel to you.
  HAML.   For God's love, let me hear.   195
  HOR. Two nights together had these gentlemen,
Marcellus and Bernardo, on their watch
In the dead vast and middle of the night,°
Been thus encountered. A figure like your father,
Armed at point exactly, cap-a-pie,°   200
Appears before them and with solemn march
Goes slow and stately by them. Thrice he walked
By their oppressed and fear-surprisèd eyes
Within his truncheon's° length, whilst they, dis-
    tilled°
Almost to jelly with the act of fear,   205
Stand dumb, and speak not to him. This to me
In dreadful secrecy impart they did,
And I with them the third night kept the watch.
Where, as they had delivered, both in time,   209
Form of the thing, each word made true and good,
The apparition comes. I knew your father.
These hands are not more like.
  HAML.   But where was this?
  MAR. My lord, upon the platform where we
    watched.
  HAML. Did you not speak to it?

  HOR.   My lord, I did,
But answer made it none. Yet once methought   215
It lifted up it° head and did address
Itself to motion, like as it would speak.
But even then the morning cock crew loud,
And at the sound it shrunk in haste away
And vanished from our sight.
  HAML.   'Tis very strange.   220
  HOR. As I do live, my honored lord, 'tis true,
And we did think it writ down in our duty
To let you know of it.
  HAML. Indeed, indeed, sirs, but this troubles me.
Hold you the watch tonight?
  MAR. & BER.   We do, my lord.   225
  HAML. Armed, say you?
  MAR. & BER.   Armed, my lord.
  HAML.   From top to toe?
  MAR. & BER. My lord, from head to foot.
  HAML. Then saw you not his face?
  HOR. Oh yes, my lord, he wore his beaver° up.
  HAML. What, looked he frowningly?   230
  HOR. A countenance more in sorrow than in an-
    ger.
  HAML. Pale, or red?
  HOR. Nay, very pale.
  HAML.   And fixed his eyes upon you?
  HOR. Most constantly.
  HAML.   I would I had been there.   235
  HOR. It would have much amazed you.
  HAML. Very like, very like. Stayed it long?
  HOR. While one with moderate haste might tell°
    a hundred.
  MAR. & BER. Longer, longer.
  HOR. Not when I saw 't.
  HAML.   His beard was grizzled?° No?   240
  HOR. It was as I have seen it in his life,
A sable silvered.°
  HAML.   I will watch tonight.
Perchance 'twill walk again.
  HOR.   I warrant it will.
  HAML. If it assume my noble father's person,
I'll speak to it though Hell itself should gape   245
And bid me hold my peace. I pray you all,
If you have hitherto concealed this sight,
Let it be tenable° in your silence still,
And whatsoever else shall hap tonight,
Give it an understanding, but no tongue.   250
I will requite° your loves. So fare you well.
Upon the platform, 'twixt eleven and twelve,
I'll visit you.
  ALL.   Our duty to your Honor.
  HAML. Your loves, as mine to you. Farewell.
                [Exeunt all but HAMLET.]
My father's spirit in arms! All is not well.   255

---

175. drink deep: For more on the drunken habits of the Danes, see I.iv.8–38.   **180–81. Thrift . . . tables:** they hurried on the wedding for economy's sake, so that the remains of food served at the funeral might be used cold for the wedding. **baked meats:** feast.   **182. dearest:** best-hated.   **192. Season . . . admiration:** moderate your wonder.   **193. attent:** attentive.   **198. dead . . . night:** deep, silent midnight.   **200. at . . . cap-a-pie:** complete in every detail, head to foot. See Pl. 8a.   **204. truncheon:** a general's staff. **distilled:** melted.

216. it: its.   **229. beaver:** front part of the helmet, which could be raised.   **238. tell:** count.   **240. grizzled:** gray.   **242. sable silvered:** black mingled with white.   **248. tenable:** held fast. **251. requite:** repay.

I doubt° some foul play. Would the night were
    come!
Till then sit still, my soul. Foul deeds will rise,
Though all the earth o'erwhelm them, to men's
    eyes.   *[Exit.]*

SCENE III. *A room in* POLONIUS'S *house.*

[Enter LAERTES *and* OPHELIA.*]*

LAER. My necessaries° are embarked. Farewell.
And, Sister, as the winds give benefit
And convoy is assistant,° do not sleep,
But let me hear from you.

OPH.   Do you doubt that?

LAER. For Hamlet, and the trifling of his favor,°
Hold it a fashion and a toy in blood,°
A violet in the youth of primy° nature,
Forward, not permanent, sweet, not lasting,
The perfume and suppliance of a minute° —
No more.

OPH. No more but so?

LAER.   Think it no more.   10
For Nature crescent does not grow alone
In thews and bulk,° but as this temple° waxes
The inward service of the mind and soul
Grows wide withal. Perhaps he loves you now,
And now no soil nor cautel° doth besmirch   15
The virtue of his will.° But you must fear,
His greatness weighed,° his will is not his own,
For he himself is subject to his birth.
He may not, as unvalued persons do,
Carve° for himself, for on his choice depends   20
The safety and health of this whole state,
And therefore must his choice be circumscribed°
Unto the voice and yielding of that body
Whereof he is the head. Then if he says he loves you,
It fits your wisdom so far to believe it   25
As he in his particular act and place
May give his saying deed, which is no further
Than the main voice of Denmark goes withal.
Then weigh what loss your honor may sustain
If with too credent° ear you list his songs,   30
Or lose your heart, or your chaste treasure° open
To his unmastered importunity.
Fear it, Ophelia, fear it, my dear sister,
And keep you in the rear° of your affection,
Out of the shot and danger of desire.   35

The chariest maid is prodigal enough
If she unmask her beauty to the moon.
Virtue itself 'scapes not calumnious strokes.
The canker galls the infants° of the spring
Too oft before their buttons° be disclosed,   40
And in the morn and liquid dew of youth
Contagious blastments° are most imminent.
Be wary, then, best safety lies in fear.
Youth to itself rebels, though none else near.°

OPH. I shall the effect of this good lesson keep   45
As watchman to my heart. But, good my brother,
Do not, as some ungracious pastors do,
Show me the steep and thorny way to Heaven
Whilst, like a puffed° and reckless libertine,
Himself the primrose path of dalliance° treads   50
And recks not his own rede.°

LAER.   Oh, fear me not.
I stay too long. But here my father comes.
[Enter POLONIUS.*]* A double blessing is a double
    grace,
Occasion smiles° upon a second leave.

POL. Yet here, Laertes! Aboard, aboard, for
    shame!   55
The wind sits in the shoulder of your sail
And you are stayed° for. There, my blessing with
    thee!
And these few precepts in thy memory
Look thou charácter.° Give thy thoughts no tongue,
Nor any unproportioned° thought his act.   60
Be thou familiar, but by no means vulgar.
Those friends thou hast, and their adoption tried,°
Grapple them to thy soul with hoops of steel,
But do not dull thy palm with entertainment°   64
Of each new-hatched unfledged° comrade. Beware
Of entrance to a quarrel, but being in,
Bear 't that the opposèd may beware of thee.
Give every man thy ear, but few thy voice.°
Take each man's censure,° but reserve thy judg-
    ment.
Costly thy habit° as thy purse can buy,   70
But not expressed in fancy° — rich, not gaudy.
For the apparel oft proclaims the man,
And they in France of the best rank and station
Are of a most select and generous chief in that.°

---

256. doubt: suspect.

Sc. iii: 1. necessaries: baggage.   3. convoy ... assistant: means of conveyance is available.   5. favor: i.e., toward you. 6. toy in blood: trifling impulse.   7. primy: springtime; i.e., youthful.   8. perfume ... minute: perfume which lasts only for a minute.   11-12. For ... bulk: for natural growth is not only in bodily bulk.   12. temple: i.e., the body.   15. cautel: deceit.   16. will: desire.   17. His ... weighed: when you consider his high position.   20. Carve: choose.   22. circumscribed: restricted.   30. credent: credulous.   31. chaste treasure: the treasure of your chastity.   34. in ... rear: i.e., farthest from danger.

39. canker ... infants: maggot harms the unopened buds. 40. buttons: buds.   42. Contagious blastments: infectious blasts. 44. though ... near: without anyone else to encourage it. 49. puffed: panting.   50. primrose ... dalliance: i.e., the pleasant way of love-making.   51. recks ... rede: takes no heed of his own advice.   54. Occasion smiles: i.e., here is a happy chance.   57. stayed: waited.   59. character: inscribe.   60. unproportioned: unsuitable.   62. adoption tried: friendship tested by experience.   64. dull ... entertainment: let your hand grow callous with welcome.   65. unfledged: lit., newly out of the egg, immature.   68. Give ... voice: listen to everyone but commit yourself to few.   69. censure: opinion.   70. habit: dress. 71. expressed in fancy: fantastic.   74. Are ... that: A disputed line; this is the F1 reading. Q2 reads "Or of the most select and generous, chief in that"; i.e., the best noble and gentle families are very particular in their dress. generous: of gentle birth.

[handwritten margin note:] LAERTES GIVES OUT ADVICE BUT DOESN'T USE IT HIMSELF

Neither a borrower nor a lender be,   75
For loan oft loses both itself and friend
And borrowing dulls the edge of husbandry.°
This above all: To thine own self be true,
And it must follow, as the night the day,
Thou canst not then be false to any man.   80
Farewell. My blessing season° this in thee!
   LAER. Most humbly do I take my leave, my lord.
   POL. The time invites you. Go, your servants
     tend.°
   LAER. Farewell, Ophelia, and remember well
What I have said to you.
   OPH.   'Tis in my memory locked, 85
And you yourself shall keep the key of it.
   LAER. Farewell.   [*Exit.*]
   POL. What is 't, Ophelia, he hath said to you?
   OPH. So please you, something touching the Lord
     Hamlet.
   POL. Marry,° well bethought.°   90
'Tis told me he hath very oft of late
Given private time to you, and you yourself
Have of your audience been most free and bounte-
     ous.
If it be so — as so 'tis put on me,
And that in way of caution — I must tell you   95
You do not understand yourself so clearly
As it behooves° my daughter and your honor.
What is between you? Give me up the truth.
   OPH. He hath, my lord, of late made many ten-
     ders°
Of his affection to me.   100
   POL. Affection! Pooh! You speak like a green girl,
Unsifted° in such perilous circumstance.
Do you believe his tenders, as you call them?   103
   OPH. I do not know, my lord, what I should think.
   POL. Marry, I'll teach you. Think yourself a baby
That you have ta'en these tenders° for true pay,
Which are not sterling.° Tender yourself more
     dearly,
Or — not to crack the wind of° the poor phrase,
Running it thus — you'll tender me a fool.   109
   OPH. My lord, he hath importuned me with love
In honorable fashion.
   POL. Aye, fashion° you may call it. Go to, go to.
   OPH. And hath given countenance to his speech,°
     my lord,
With almost all the holy vows of Heaven.
   POL. Aye, springes° to catch woodcocks.° I do
     know,   115
When the blood burns, how prodigal° the soul

Lends the tongue vows. These blazes,° daughter,
Giving more light than heat, extinct in both,
Even in their promise as it is a-making,
You must not take for fire. From this time   120
Be something scanter of your maiden presence,
Set your entreatments at a higher rate
Than a command to parley.° For Lord Hamlet,
Believe so much in him, that he is young,
And with a larger tether° may he walk   125
Than may be given you. In few,° Ophelia,
Do not believe his vows, for they are brokers,°
Not of that dye which their investments° show,
But mere implorators° of unholy suits,
Breathing like sanctified and pious bawds°   130
The better to beguile. This is for all.
I would not, in plain terms, from this time forth
Have you so slander any moment leisure°
As to give words or talk with the Lord Hamlet.
Look to 't, I charge you. Come your ways.   135
   OPH. I shall obey, my lord.   [*Exeunt.*]

SCENE IV. *The platform*

[*Enter* HAMLET, HORATIO, *and* MARCELLUS.]
   HAML. The air bites shrewdly.° It is very cold.
   HOR. It is a nipping and an eager° air.
   HAML. What hour now?
   HOR.   I think it lacks of twelve.
   MAR. No, it is struck.
   HOR. Indeed? I heard it not. It then draws near
     the season   5
Wherein the spirit held his wont to walk.
      [*A flourish of trumpets, and ordnance
               shot off within.°*]
What doth this mean, my lord?
   HAML. The King doth wake° tonight and takes
     his rouse,°
Keeps wassail,° and the swaggering upspring reels.°
And as he drains his draughts of Rhenish° down,
The kettledrum and trumpet thus bray out   11
The triumph of his pledge.
   HOR.   Is it a custom?
   HAML. Aye, marry, is 't.

---

77. **husbandry:** economy. 81. **season:** bring to fruit. 83. **tend:** attend. 90. **Marry:** Mary, by the Virgin Mary. **well bethought:** well remembered. 97. **behooves:** is the duty of. 99. **tenders:** offers. 102. **Unsifted:** untried. 106-09. **tenders . . . tender:** Polonius puns on "tenders," counters (used for money in games); "tender," value; "tender," show. 107. **sterling:** true currency. 108. **crack . . . of:** i.e., ride to death. 112. **fashion:** mere show. 113. **given . . . speech:** confirmed his words. 115. **springes:** snares. **woodcocks:** foolish birds. 116. **prodigal:** extravagantly.

117. **blazes:** flashes, quickly extinguished (*extinct*). 122-23. **Set . . . parley:** when you are asked to see him do not regard it as a command to negotiate. **parley:** meeting to discuss terms. 125. **tether:** rope by which a grazing animal is fastened to its peg. 126. **In few:** in short. 127. **brokers:** traveling salesmen. 128. **investments:** garments. 129. **implorators:** men who solicit. 130. **bawds:** keepers of brothels. F1 and Q2 read "bond," an easy misprint for "baud" — the Elizabethan spelling of "bawd." 133. **slander . . . leisure:** misuse any moment of leisure.
Sc. iv: 1. **shrewdly:** bitterly. 2. **eager:** sharp. 6. **s.d., within:** off stage. 8. **wake:** "makes a night of it." **rouse:** See I.ii.127,n. 9. **wassail:** revelry. **swaggering . . . reels:** reel in a riotous dance. 10. **Rhenish:** Rhine wine.

But to my mind, though I am native here
And to the manner born, it is a custom   15
More honored in the breach than the observance.
This heavy-headed revel° east and west
Makes us traduced and taxed of° other nations.
They clepe° us drunkards, and with swinish phrase
Soil our addition,° and indeed it takes   20
From our achievements, though performed at
        height,
The pith and marrow of our attribute.°
So oft it chances in particular men,
That for some vicious mole° of nature in them,
As in their birth — wherein they are not guilty,   25
Since nature cannot choose his origin —
By the o'ergrowth of some complexion,°
Oft breaking down the pales° and forts of reason,
Or by some habit that too much o'erleavens°   29
The form of plausive° manners, that these men —
Carrying, I say, the stamp of one defect,
Being Nature's livery,° or Fortune's star° —
Their virtues else — be they as pure as grace,
As infinite as man may undergo —
Shall in the general censure take corruption   35
From that particular fault. The dram of eale
Doth all the noble substance of a doubt
To his own scandal.°

        [*Enter* GHOST.]

HOR.   Look, my lord, it comes!
HAML. Angels and ministers of grace defend us!
Be thou a spirit of health or goblin damned,°   40
Bring with thee airs from Heaven or blasts from
        Hell,
Be thy intents wicked or charitable,
Thou comest in such a questionable° shape

That I will speak to thee. I'll call thee Hamlet,
King, Father, royal Dane. Oh, answer me!   45
Let me not burst in ignorance, but tell
Why thy canónized° bones, hearsèd° in death,
Have burst their cerements,° why the sepulcher
Wherein we saw thee quietly inurned°
Hath oped his ponderous and marble jaws   50
To cast thee up again. What may this mean,
That thou, dead corse, again, in complete steel,°
Revisit'st thus the glimpses of the moon,
Making night hideous, and we fools° of nature
So horridly to shake our disposition°   55
With thoughts beyond the reaches of our souls?
Say, why is this? Wherefore? What should we do?

        [GHOST *beckons* HAMLET.]

HOR. It beckons you to go away with it,
As if it some impartment° did desire
To you alone.
MAR.   Look with what courteous action   60
It waves you to a more removèd ground.
But do not go with it.
HOR.   No, by no means.
HAML. It will not speak. Then I will follow it.
HOR. Do not, my lord.
HAML.   Why, what should be the fear?
I do not set my life at a pin's fee,°   65
And for my soul, what can it do to that,
Being a thing immortal as itself?
It waves me forth again. I'll follow it.
HOR. What if it tempt you toward the flood, my
        lord,
Or to the dreadful summit of the cliff   70
That beetles o'er° his base into the sea,
And there assume some other horrible form
Which might deprive your sovereignty of reason°
And draw you into madness? Think of it.
The very place puts toys of desperation,°   75
Without more motive, into every brain
That looks so many fathoms to the sea
And hears it roar beneath.
HAML.   It waves me still.
Go on. I'll follow thee.
MAR. You shall not go, my lord.
HAML.   Hold off your hands.   80
HOR. Be ruled. You shall not go.
HAML.   My fate cries out,
And makes each petty artery in this body
As hardy as the Nemean lion's nerve.°
Still am I called. Unhand me, gentlemen.   84

17. heavy-headed revel: drinking which produces a thick head.
18. traduced . . . of: disgraced and censured by.   **19. clepe:**
call.   **20. soil . . . addition:** smirch our honor. **addition:** lit.,
title of honor added to a man's name.   **21. though . . . height:**
though of the highest merit.   **22. pith . . . attribute:** essential
part of our honor; i.e., we lose the honor due to our achievements
because of our reputation for drunkenness.   **24. mole:** blemish.
27. o'ergrowth . . . complexion: some quality allowed to overbalance the rest. See App. 3.   **28. pales:** defenses.   **29. o'er-
leavens:** mixes with.   **30. plausive:** agreeable.   **32. Nature's
livery:** i.e., inborn. **Fortune's star:** the result of ill luck. See
App. 18.   **36–38. The . . . scandal:** This is the most famous of
all disputed passages in Shakespeare's plays. The general meaning is clear: "a small portion of evil brings scandal on the whole
substance, however noble." "Eale" is an Elizabethan spelling
and pronunciation of "evil," as later in Q2 (II.ii.628); "deale"
is the spelling and pronunciation of "Devil." The difficulty lies
in "of a doubt," which is obviously a misprint for some such
word as "corrupt"; but to be satisfactory it must fit the meter
and be a plausible misprint. So far, although many guesses have
been made, none is wholly convincing. The best is perhaps "often
dout" — often put out.   **40. spirit . . . damned:** a holy spirit
or damned fiend. Hamlet, until convinced at the end of the play
scene (III.ii.298), is perpetually in doubt whether the ghost
which he sees is a good spirit sent to warn him, a devil sent to
tempt him into some damnable action, or a hallucination created
by his own diseased imagination. See II.ii.627–32.   **43. ques-
tionable:** inviting question.

47. canonized: buried with full rites according to the canon of
the Church. **hearsed:** buried.   **48. cerements:** waxen shroud,
used to wrap the bodies of the illustrious dead.   **49. inurned:**
buried.   **52. complete steel:** full armor.   **54. fools:** dupes.
55. disposition: nature.   **59. impartment:** communication.
65. fee: value.   **71. beetles o'er:** juts out over.   **73. sovereignty of reason:** control of your reason over your actions.
75. toys of desperation: desperate fancies.   **83. Nemean . . .
nerve:** sinew of a fierce beast slain by Hercules.

By Heaven, I'll make a ghost of him that lets° me!
I say, away! Go on. I'll follow thee.
                [*Exeunt* GHOST *and* HAMLET.]
HOR. He waxes desperate with imagination.
MAR. Let's follow. 'Tis not fit thus to obey him.
HOR. Have after. To what issue will this come?
MAR. Something is rotten in the state of Denmark.   90
HOR. Heaven will direct it.
MAR.   Nay, let's follow him.   [*Exeunt.*]

SCENE V. *Another part of the platform.*

[*Enter* GHOST *and* HAMLET.]
HAML. Whither wilt thou lead me? Speak. I'll go
no further.
GHOST. Mark me.
HAML.   I will.
GHOST.   My hour is almost come
When I to sulphurous and tormenting flames
Must render up myself.
HAML.   Alas, poor ghost!   4
GHOST. Pity me not, but lend thy serious hearing
To what I shall unfold.
HAML.   Speak. I am bound to hear.
GHOST. So art thou to revenge, when thou shalt
hear.
HAML. What?
GHOST.   I am thy father's spirit,
Doomed for a certain term to walk the night   10
And for the day confined to fast in fires
Till the foul crimes done in my days of nature
Are burnt and purged away. But that I am forbid
To tell the secrets of my prison house,
I could a tale unfold whose lightest word   15
Would harrow up thy soul, freeze thy young blood,
Make thy two eyes, like stars, start from their
    spheres,°
Thy knotted and combinèd° locks to part
And each particular° hair to stand an° end
Like quills upon the fretful porpentine.°   20
But this eternal blazon° must not be
To ears of flesh and blood. List, list, oh, list!
If thou didst ever thy dear father love ——
HAML. Oh, God!
GHOST. Revenge his foul and most unnatural murder.   25
HAML. Murder!
GHOST. Murder most foul, as in the best° it is,
But this most foul, strange, and unnatural.

HAML. Haste me to know 't, that I, with wings **as**
swift
As meditation or the thoughts of love,   30
May sweep to my revenge.
GHOST.   I find thee apt,
And duller shouldst thou be than the fat° weed
That roots itself in ease° on Lethe wharf°
Wouldst thou not stir in this. Now, Hamlet, hear.
'Tis given out that, sleeping in my orchard,   35
A serpent stung me — so the whole ear of Denmark
Is by a forgèd process° of my death
Rankly abused. But know, thou noble youth,
The serpent that did sting thy father's life
Now wears his crown.
HAML.   Oh, my prophetic soul!   40
My uncle!
GHOST. Aye, that incestuous, that adulterate beast,
With witchcraft of his wit, with traitorous gifts —
O wicked wit and gifts, that have the power
So to seduce! — won to his shameful lust   45
The will of my most seeming-virtuous Queen.
O Hamlet, what a falling-off was there!
From me, whose love was of that dignity
That it went hand in hand even with the vow
I made to her in marriage, and to decline   50
Upon a wretch whose natural gifts were poor
To those of mine!
But virtue, as it never will be moved
Though lewdness court it in a shape of Heaven,°
So Lust, though to a radiant angel linked,   55
Will sate itself° in a celestial bed
And prey on garbage.
But soft! Methinks I scent the morning air.
Brief let me be. Sleeping within my orchard,
My custom always of the afternoon,   60
Upon my secure hour° thy uncle stole
With juice of cursèd hebenon° in a vial,
And in the porches° of my ears did pour
The leperous distillment,° whose effect
Holds such an enmity with blood of man   65
That swift as quicksilver it courses through
The natural gates and alleys of the body,
And with a sudden vigor it doth posset°
And curd, like eager° droppings into milk,
The thin and wholesome blood. So did it mine,   70
And a most instant tetter barked° about,
Most lazarlike,° with vile and loathsome crust,
All my smooth body.
Thus was I, sleeping, by a brother's hand

---

85. lets: hinders.
    Sc. v: 17. spheres: See App. 1.   18. knotted . . . combined:
the hair that lies together in a mass.   19. particular: individual.
an: on.   20. porpentine: porcupine.   21. eternal blazon: description of eternity.   27. in . . . best: i.e., murder is foul even
when there is a good excuse.

32. fat: thick, slimy, motionless.   33. in ease: undisturbed.
Lethe wharf: the bank of Lethe, the river of forgetfulness in the
underworld.   37. forged process: false account.   54. lewdness
. . . Heaven: though wooed by Lust disguised as an angel.
56. sate itself: gorge.   61. secure hour: time of relaxation.
62. hebenon: probably henbane, a poisonous plant.   63. porches:
entrances.   64. leperous distillment: distillation causing leprosy.
68. posset: curdle.   69. eager: acid.   71. tetter barked: eruption formed a bark.   72. lazarlike: like leprosy.

Of life, of crown, of Queen, at once dispatched —
Cut off even in the blossoms of my sin,°   76
Unhouseled, disappointed, unaneled,°
No reckoning made, but sent to my account
With all my imperfections on my head.
Oh, horrible! Oh, horrible, most horrible!   80
If thou hast nature° in thee, bear it not.
Let not the royal bed of Denmark be
A couch for luxury° and damnèd incest.
But, howsoever thou pursuest this act,
Taint not thy mind, nor let thy soul contrive   85
Against thy mother aught. Leave her to Heaven
And to those thorns that in her bosom lodge
To prick and sting her. Fare thee well at once!
The glowworm shows the matin° to be near,
And 'gins to pale his uneffectual° fire.   90
Adieu, adieu, adieu! Remember me.   [*Exit.*]
  HAML. O all you host of Heaven! O earth! What
  else?
And shall I couple Hell? Oh, fie! Hold, hold, my
  heart,
And you, my sinews, grow not instant old
But bear me stiffly up. Remember thee!   95
Aye, thou poor ghost, while memory holds a seat
In this distracted globe.° Remember thee!
Yea, from the table° of my memory
I'll wipe away all trivial fond° recórds,
All saws° of books, all forms,° all pressures° past,
That youth and observation copied there,   101
And thy commandment all alone shall live
Within the book and volume of my brain,
Unmixed with baser matter. Yes, by Heaven!
O most pernicious woman!   105
O villain, villain, smiling, damnèd villain!
My tables — meet it is I set it down
[*Writing*] That one may smile, and smile, and be a
  villain.
At least I'm sure it may be so in Denmark.
So, Uncle, there you are. Now to my word.°   110
It is " Adieu, adieu! Remember me."
I have sworn 't.
  HOR. & MAR. [*Within*] My lord, my lord!
      [*Enter* HORATIO *and* MARCELLUS.]
  MAR.   Lord Hamlet!
  HOR.   Heaven secure him!
  HAML. So be it!
  MAR. Illo, ho, ho,° my lord!   115
  HAML. Hillo, ho, ho, boy! Come, bird, come.

  MAR. How is 't, my noble lord?
  HOR.   What news, my lord?
  HAML. Oh, wonderful!
  HOR. Good my lord, tell it.
  HAML.   No, you will reveal it.
  HOR. Not I, my lord, by Heaven.
  MAR.   Nor I, my lord.   120
  HAML. How say you, then, would heart of man
  once think it?
But you'll be secret?
  HOR. & MAR.   Aye, by Heaven, my lord.
  HAML. There's ne'er a villain dwelling in all Den-
  mark
But he's an arrant° knave.
  HOR. There needs no ghost, my lord, come from
  the grave   125
To tell us this.
  HAML.   Why, right, you are i' the right.
And so, without more circumstance° at all,
I hold it fit that we shake hands and part —
You as your business and desire shall point you,
For every man hath business and desire,   130
Such as it is. And for my own poor part,
Look you, I'll go pray.
  HOR. These are but wild and whirling° words, my
  lord.
  HAML. I'm sorry they offend you, heartily,
Yes, faith, heartily.
  HOR.   There's no offense, my lord.   135
  HAML. Yes, by Saint Patrick, but there is, Horatio,
And much offense too. Touching this vision here,
It is an honest° ghost, that let me tell you.
For your desire to know what is between us,
O'ermaster 't as you may. And now, good friends,
As you are friends, scholars, and soldiers,   141
Give me one poor request.
  HOR. What is 't, my lord? We will.
  HAML. Never make known what you have seen
  tonight.
  HOR. & MAR. My lord, we will not.
  HAML.   Nay, but swear 't.
  HOR.   In faith,   145
My lord, not I.
  MAR.   Nor I, my lord, in faith.
  HAML. Upon my sword.
  MAR.   We have sworn, my lord, already.
  HAML. Indeed, upon my sword,° indeed.
  GHOST. [*Beneath*] Swear.
  HAML. Ah, ha, boy! Say'st thou so? Art thou
  there, truepenny?°   150
Come on. You hear this fellow in the cellarage.
Consent to swear.

---

76. Cut . . . sin: cut off in a state of sin and so in danger of damnation. See III.iii.80–86.   **77. Unhouseled . . . unaneled:** without receiving the sacrament, not properly prepared, unanointed — without extreme unction.   **81. nature:** natural feelings. **83. luxury:** lust.   **89. matin:** morning.   **90. uneffectual:** made ineffectual by daylight.   **97. globe:** i.e., head.   **98. table:** notebook. Intellectual young men carried notebooks in which they recorded good sayings and notable observations. See III.ii.42,n. **99. fond:** trifling.   **100. saws:** wise sayings. **forms:** images in the mind. **pressures:** impressions.   **110. word:** cue.   **115. Illo . . . ho:** the falconer's cry to recall the hawk.

124. arrant: out-and-out.   **127. circumstance:** ceremony **133. whirling:** violent.   **138. honest:** true. See I.iv.40,n **148. upon . . . sword:** on the cross made by the hilt of the sword; but for soldiers the sword itself was a sacred object. **150. truepenny:** old boy.

HOR. Propose the oath, my lord.

HAML. Never to speak of this that you have seen,
Swear by my sword.

GHOST. [*Beneath*] Swear.　　　　　　　　　155

HAML. *Hic et ubique?*° Then we'll shift our
ground.
Come hither, gentlemen,
And lay your hands again upon my sword.
Never to speak of this that you have heard,
Swear by my sword.　　　　　　　　　160

GHOST. [*Beneath*] Swear.

HAML. Well said, old mole! Canst work i' the
earth so fast?
A worthy pioner!° Once more remove,° good
friends.

HOR. Oh, day and night, but this is wondrous
strange!

HAML. And therefore as a stranger give it wel-
come.　　　　　　　　　165
There are more things in Heaven and earth, Hora-
tio,
Than are dreamt of in your philosophy.
But come,
Here, as before, never, so help you mercy,
How strange or odd soe'er I bear myself,　　170
As I perchance hereafter shall think meet
To put an antic disposition° on,
That you, at such times seeing me, never shall,
With arms encumbered° thus, or this headshake,
Or by pronouncing of some doubtful phrase,　175
As "Well, well, we know," or "We could an if we
would,"
Or "If we list to speak," or "There be, an if they
might,"
Or such ambiguous giving out, to note
That you know aught of me. This not to do,
So grace and mercy at your most need help you,　180
Swear.

GHOST. [*Beneath*] Swear.

HAML. Rest, rest, perturbèd spirit! [*They swear.*]
So, gentlemen,
With all my love I do commend me to you.
And what so poor a man as Hamlet is　　　185
May do to express his love and friending° to you,
God willing, shall not lack. Let us go in together.
And still your fingers on your lips, I pray.
The time is out of joint. Oh, cursèd spite
That ever I was born to set it right!　　　190
Nay, come, let's go together.　　　　　[*Exeunt.*]

---

156. Hic et ubique: here and everywhere.　163. pioner: miner.
remove: move.　172. antic disposition: mad behavior.　174. en-
cumbered: folded.　186. friending: friendship.

Act II

SCENE I. *A room in* POLONIUS'S *house.*

[*Enter* POLONIUS *and* REYNALDO.]

POL. Give him this money and these notes, Reynaldo.

REY. I will, my lord.

POL. You shall do marvelous wisely, good Rey-
naldo,
Before you visit him, to make inquire
Of his behavior.

REY. 　　　My lord, I did intend it.　　　5

POL. Marry, well said, very well said. Look you,
sir,
Inquire me first what Danskers° are in Paris,
And how, and who, what means,° and where they
keep,°
What company, at what expense, and finding
By this encompassment and drift of question°　10
That they do know my son, come you more nearer
Than your particular demands will touch it.°
Take you, as 'twere, some distant knowledge of him,
As thus, "I know his father and his friends,
And in part him." Do you mark this, Reynaldo?　15

REY. Aye, very well, my lord.

POL. "And in part him, but," you may say, "not
well.
But if 't be he I mean, he's very wild,
Addicted so and so" — and there put on him
What forgeries° you please. Marry, none so rank°
As may dishonor him, take heed of that,　　21
But, sir, such wanton, wild, and usual slips
As are companions noted and most known
To youth and liberty.

REY. 　　　As gaming, my lord.

POL. Aye, or drinking, fencing,° swearing, quarreling,　　　　　　　　　25
Drabbing.° You may go so far.

REY. My lord, that would dishonor him.

POL. Faith, no, as you may season° it in the charge.
You must not put another scandal on him,
That he is open to incontinency.°　　　30
That's not my meaning. But breathe his faults so
quaintly°
That they may seem the taints of liberty,
The flash and outbreak of a fiery mind,
A savageness in unreclaimèd° blood,

Act II, Sc. i: 7. Danskers: Danes.　8. what means: what their
income is.　keep: live.　10. encompassment . . . question:
roundabout method of questioning.　12. your . . . it: i.e., you
won't get at the truth by straight questions.　20. forgeries:
inventions.　rank: gross.　25. fencing: A young man who
haunted fencing schools would be regarded as quarrelsome and
likely to belong to the sporting set.　26. Drabbing: whoring.
28. season: qualify.　30. open . . . incontinency: So long as
Laertes does his drabbing inconspicuously Polonius would not
be disturbed.　31. quaintly: skillfully.　34. unreclaimed:
naturally wild.

Of general assault.°

REY.   But, my good lord ——   35
POL. Wherefore should you do this?
REY.   Aye, my lord,
I would know that.
POL.   Marry, sir, here's my drift,°
And I believe it is a fetch of warrant.°
You laying these slight sullies° on my son,
As 'twere a thing a little soiled i' the working,   40
Mark you,
Your party in converse, him you would sound,
Having ever seen° in the prenominate° crimes
The youth you breathe of guilty, be assured
He closes with you in this consequence° —   45
" Good sir," or so, or " friend," or " gentleman,"
According to the phrase or the addition°
Of man and country.

REY.   Very good, my lord.   49
POL. And then, sir, does he this — he does ——
What was I about to say? By the mass, I was about
to say something. Where did I leave?
REY. At " closes in the consequence," at " friend or
so," and " gentleman."
POL. At " closes in the consequence," aye, marry,
He closes with you thus: " I know the gentleman.
I saw him yesterday, or t'other day,   56
Or then, or then, with such, or such, and, as you
     say,
There was a' gaming, there o'ertook in 's rouse,
There falling out at tennis."° Or perchance,
" I saw him enter such a house of sale,"   60
Videlicet,° a brothel, or so forth.
See you now,
Your bait of falsehood takes this carp of truth.
And thus do we of wisdom and of reach,°
With windlasses° and with assays of bias,°   65
By indirections find directions out.°
So, by my former lecture and advice,
Shall you my son. You have me, have you not?
REY. My lord, I have.
POL.   God be wi' ye, fare ye well.
REY. Good my lord!   70
POL. Observe his inclination in° yourself.
REY. I shall, my lord.
POL. And let him ply his music.
REY.   Well, my lord.
POL. Farewell!   [*Exit* REYNALDO.]

[*Enter* OPHELIA.] How now, Ophelia! What's the
     matter?
OPH. Oh, my lord, my lord, I have been so af-
     frighted!   75
POL. With what, i' the name of God?
OPH. My lord, as I was sewing in my closet,°
Lord Hamlet, with his doublet° all unbraced,
No hat upon his head, his stockings fouled,
Ungartered and down-gyved° to his ankle,   80
Pale as his shirt, his knees knocking each other,
And with a look so piteous in purport
As if he had been loosèd out of Hell
To speak of horrors, he comes before me.
POL. Mad for thy love?
OPH.   My lord, I do not know,
But truly I do fear it.   86
POL.   What said he?
OPH. He took me by the wrist and held me hard.
Then goes he to the length of all his arm,
And with his other hand thus o'er his brow,
He falls to such perusal of my face   90
As he would draw it. Long stayed he so.
At last, a little shaking of mine arm,
And thrice his head thus waving up and down,
He raised a sigh so piteous and profound
As it did seem to shatter all his bulk   95
And end his being. That done, he lets me go.
And with his head over his shoulder turned,
He seemed to find his way without his eyes;
For out o' doors he went without their helps,
And to the last bended their light on me.   100
POL. Come, go with me. I will go seek the King.
This is the very ecstasy° of love,
Whose violent property fordoes° itself
And leads the will to desperate undertakings
As oft as any passion under heaven   105
That does afflict our natures. I am sorry.
What, have you given him any hard words of late?
OPH. No, my good lord, but, as you did command,
I did repel his letters and denied
His access to me.
POL.   That hath made him mad.   110
I am sorry that with better heed and judgment
I had not quoted° him. I feared he did but trifle
And meant to wreck thee, but beshrew° my jeal-
     ousy!
By Heaven, it is as proper° to our age
To cast beyond ourselves° in our opinions   115
As it is common for the younger sort
To lack discretion. Come, go we to the King.

---

35. Of . . . assault: common to all men.   37. drift: intention.
38. fetch . . . warrant: trick warranted to work.   39. sullies:
blemishes.   43. Having . . . seen: if ever he has seen. prenominate: aforementioned.   45. closes . . . consequence: follows
up with this reply.   47. addition: title. See I.iv.20.   59. tennis: Visitors to France were much impressed by the enthusiasm of all classes of Frenchmen for tennis, which in England
was mainly a courtier's game.   61. Videlicet: namely, "viz."
64. wisdom . . . reach: of far-reaching wisdom.   65. windlasses:
roundabout methods. assays of bias: making our bowl take a
curved course. See App. 13.   66. indirections . . . out: by indirect means come at the direct truth.   71. in: for.

77. closet: private room.   78. doublet: the short close-fitting
coat which was braced to the hose by laces. When a man was re-
laxing or careless of appearance, he *unbraced*, as a modern man
takes off his coat or unbuttons his waistcoat. See Pl. 8b and notes
on p. 93a.   80. down-gyved: hanging around his ankles like fetters.   102. ecstasy: frenzy.   103. property fordoes: natural quality destroys.   112. quoted: observed carefully.   113. beshrew: a
plague on.   114. proper: natural.   115. cast . . . ourselves: be
too clever.

This must be known, which, being kept close, might
   move
More grief to hide than hate to utter love.°   119
Come.   [*Exeunt.*]

SCENE II. *A room in the castle.*

[*Flourish. Enter* KING, QUEEN, ROSENCRANTZ,
    GUILDENSTERN, *and* ATTENDANTS.]
  KING. Welcome, dear Rosencrantz and Guilden-
    stern!
Moreover° that we much did long to see you,
The need we have to use you did provoke
Our hasty sending. Something have you heard
Of Hamlet's transformation — so call it,   5
Sith° nor the exterior nor the inward man
Resembles that it was. What it should be,
More than his father's death, that thus hath put him
So much from the understanding of himself
I cannot dream of. I entreat you both   10
That, being of so young days brought up with him
And sith so neighbored to his youth and havior°
That you vouchsafe your rest° here in our Court
Some little time, so by your companies
To draw him on to pleasures, and to gather   15
So much as from occasion you may glean,
Whether aught to us unknown afflicts him thus
That opened lies within our remedy.°
  QUEEN. Good gentlemen, he hath much talked of
    you,
And sure I am two men there art not living   20
To whom he more adheres.° If it will please you
To show us so much gentry° and goodwill
As to expend your time with us a while
For the supply and profit of our hope,°
Your visitation shall receive such thanks   25
As fits a king's remembrance.
  ROS.   Both your Majesties
Might, by the sovereign power you have of us,
Put your dread pleasures more into command
Than to entreaty.
  GUIL.   But we both obey,
And here give up ourselves, in the full bent°   30
To lay our service freely at your feet,
To be commanded.
  KING. Thanks, Rosencrantz and gentle Guilden-
    stern.

  QUEEN. Thanks, Guildenstern and gentle Rosen-
    crantz.
And I beseech you instantly to visit   35
My too-much-changèd son. Go, some of you,
And bring these gentlemen where Hamlet is.
  GUIL. Heavens make our presence and our prac-
    tices
Pleasant and helpful to him!
  QUEEN.   Aye, amen! [*Exeunt* ROSENCRANTZ,
    GUILDENSTERN, *and some* ATTENDANTS.]
             [*Enter* POLONIUS.]
  POL. The ambassadors from Norway, my good
    lord,   40
Are joyfully returned.
  KING. Thou still° hast been the father of good
    news.
  POL. Have I, my lord? I assure my good liege
I hold my duty as I hold my soul,
Both to my God and to my gracious King.   45
And I do think, or else this brain of mine
Hunts not the trail of policy so sure
As it hath used to do,° that I have found
The very cause of Hamlet's lunacy.   49
  KING. Oh, speak of that. That do I long to hear.
  POL. Give first admittance to the ambassadors.
My news shall be the fruit° to that great feast.
  KING. Thyself do grace° to them and bring them
    in.   [*Exit* POLONIUS.]
He tells me, my dear Gertrude, he hath found   54
The head and source of all your son's distemper.°
  QUEEN. I doubt it is no other but the main,°
His father's death and our o'erhasty marriage.
  KING. Well, we shall sift him.
      [*Re-enter* POLONIUS, *with* VOLTIMAND
           and CORNELIUS.]
               Welcome, my good friends!
Say, Voltimand, what from our brother Norway?
  VOLT. Most fair return of greetings and desires.
Upon our first,° he sent out to suppress   61
His nephew's levies, which to him appeared
To be a preparation 'gainst the Polack,
But better looked into, he truly found
It was against your Highness, whereat, grieved   65
That so his sickness, age, and impotence
Was falsely borne in hand,° sends out arrests
On Fortinbras; which he, in brief, obeys,
Receives rebuke from Norway, and in fine°
Makes vow before his uncle never more   70
To give the assay of arms° against your Majesty.
Whereon old Norway, overcome with joy,
Gives him three thousand crowns in annual fee

118–19. which ... love: by being kept secret it may cause more
sorrow than it will cause anger by being revealed; i.e., the King
and Queen may be angry at the thought of the Prince's marrying
beneath his proper rank.
    Sc. ii: 2. Moreover: in addition to the fact that.   6. Sith:
since.   12. neighbored ... havior: so near to his youthful
manner of living.   13. vouchsafe ... rest: consent to stay.
18. opened ... remedy: if revealed, might be put right by us.
21. To ... adheres: whom he regards more highly.   22. gentry: courtesy.   24. supply ... hope: to bring a profitable conclusion to our hope.   30. in ... bent: stretched to our uttermost.

42. still: always.   47–48. Hunts ... do: is not so good at following the scent of political events as it used to be.   52. fruit:
the dessert, which comes at the end of the feast.   53. do grace:
honor; i.e., by escorting them into the royal presence.   55. distemper: mental disturbance.   56. main: principal cause.
61. first: i.e., audience.   67. borne in hand: imposed upon.
69. in fine: in the end.   71. give ... arms: make an attack.

And his commission to employ those soldiers,
So levied as before, against the Polack.   75
With an entreaty, herein further shown,

                             [*Giving a paper*]

That it might please you to give quiet pass°
Through your dominions for this enterprise,
On such regards of safety and allowance°
As therein are set down.

KING.   It likes° us well,   80
And at our more considered time we'll read,
Answer, and think upon this business.
Meantime we thank you for your well-took labor.
Go to your rest. At night we'll feast together.
Most welcome home!

            [*Exeunt* VOLTIMAND *and* CORNELIUS.]

POL.   This business is well ended.   85
My liege, and madam, to expostulate°
What majesty should be, what duty is,
Why day is day, night night, and time is time,
Were nothing but to waste night, day, and time.
Therefore, since brevity is the soul of wit   90
And tediousness the limbs and outward flourishes,°
I will be brief. Your noble son is mad.
Mad call I it, for to define true madness,
What is 't but to be nothing else but mad?
But let that go.

QUEEN.   <u>More matter, with less art.°</u>
POL. Madam, I swear I use no art at all.
That he is mad, 'tis true. 'Tis true 'tis pity,
And pity 'tis 'tis true — a foolish figure,°
But farewell it, for I will use no art.
Mad let us grant him, then. And now remains   100
That we find out the cause of this effect,
Or rather say the cause of this defect,
For this effect defective comes by cause.
Thus it remains and the remainder thus.
Perpend.°   105
I have a daughter — have while she is mine —
Who in her duty and obedience, mark,
Hath given me this. Now gather and surmise.°
[*Reads.*]
"To the celestial, and my soul's idol, the most beau-
    tified° Ophelia — "
That's an ill phrase, a vile phrase, "beautified" is a
vile phrase. But you shall hear. Thus: [*Reads.*]
"In her excellent white bosom, these," and so forth.
   QUEEN. Came this from Hamlet to her?   114
   POL. Good madam, stay awhile, I will be faithful.
[*Reads.*] "Doubt thou the stars are fire,
        Doubt that the sun doth move,
        Doubt truth to be a liar,
        But never doubt I love.   119

"O dear Ophelia, I am ill at these numbers,° I
have not art to reckon my groans, but that I love thee
best, O most best, believe it. Adieu.
   "Thine evermore, most dear lady, whilst this
               machine° is to him, HAMLET."
This in obedience hath my daughter shown me,
And more above, hath his solicitings,   126
As they fell out by time, by means and place,
All given to mine ear.

KING.   But how hath she
Received his love?

POL.   What do you think of me?
   KING. As of a man faithful and honorable.   130
   POL. I would fain prove so. But what might you
     think,
When I had seen this hot love on the wing —
As I perceived it, I must tell you that,
Before my daughter told me — what might you
Or my dear Majesty your Queen here think   135
If I had played the desk or table book,°
Or given my heart awinking, mute and dumb,
Or looked upon this love with idle sight —
What might you think? No, I went round° to work,
And my young mistress thus I did bespeak:°   140
"Lord Hamlet is a Prince, out of thy star.°
This must not be." And then I prescripts° gave her
That she should lock herself from his resort,
Admit no messengers, receive no tokens.
Which done, she took the fruits of my advice.   145
And he, repulsèd, a short tale to make,
Fell into a sadness, then into a fast,
Thence to a watch, thence into a weakness,
Thence to a lightness,° and by this declension°
Into the madness wherein now he raves   150
And all we mourn for.
   KING. Do you think this?
   QUEEN.   It may be, very like.
   POL. Hath there been such a time, I'd fain know
     that,
That I have positively said "'Tis so"
When it proved otherwise?
   KING.   Not that I know.   155
   POL. [*Pointing to his head and shoulder.*] Take
     this from this, if this be otherwise.
If circumstances lead me, I will find
Where truth is hid, though it were hid indeed
Within the center.°

---

120. numbers: verses.   124. machine: i.e., body, an affected
phrase.   136. desk ... book: i.e., acted as silent go-between
(desks and books being natural post offices for a love
letter), or been a recipient of secrets but took no action (as
desks and notebooks are the natural but inanimate places for
keeping secrets).   139. round: straight.   140. bespeak:
address.   141. out ... star: above your destiny.   142. pre-
scripts: instructions.   147-49. Fell ... lightness: Hamlet's
case history, according to Polonius, develops by stages —
melancholy, loss of appetite, sleeplessness, physical weakness,
mental instability, and finally madness.   149. declension: decline.   159. center: the very center of the earth. See App. I.

---

77. quiet pass: unmolested passage.   79. regards ... allowance: safeguard and conditions.   80. likes: pleases.   86. expostulate: indulge in an academic discussion.   91. flourishes:
ornaments.   95. art: ornament.   98. figure: i.e., a figure of
speech.   105. Perpend: note carefully.   108. surmise: guess
the meaning.   110. beautified: beautiful.

KING.   How may we try it further?

POL. You know sometimes he walks four hours together   160
Here in the lobby.

QUEEN.   So he does indeed.

POL. At such a time I'll loose° my daughter to him.
Be you and I behind an arras° then.
Mark the encounter. If he love her not,
And be not from his reason fall'n thereon,   165
Let me be no assistant for a state,
But keep a farm and carters.°

KING.   We will try it.

QUEEN. But look where sadly the poor wretch comes reading.

POL. Away, I do beseech you, both away.   169
I'll board° him presently.   [Exeunt KING, QUEEN, and ATTENDANTS.]

[Enter HAMLET, reading.] Oh, give me leave. How does my good Lord Hamlet?

HAML. Well, God-a-mercy.   *[handwritten: HE IS SEC. OF STATE BUT CALLED THIS.]*

POL. Do you know me, my lord?

HAML. Excellent well. You are a fishmonger.

POL. Not I, my lord.   175

HAML. Then I would you were so honest a man.

POL. Honest, my lord!

HAML. Aye, sir, to be honest, as this world goes, is to be one man picked out of ten thousand.

POL. That's very true, my lord.   180

HAML. For if the sun breed maggots° in a dead dog, being a god° kissing carrion° — Have you a daughter?   *[handwritten: HIS STATE OF MIND]*

POL. I have, my lord.   184

HAML. Let her not walk i' the sun. Conception is a blessing, but not as your daughter may conceive — friend, look to 't.   *[handwritten: HIS ATTIT. TO WOMEN — PRACTICALLY SAYING]*

POL. [Aside] How say you by that? Still harping on my daughter. Yet he knew me not at first, he said I was a fishmonger. He is far gone, far gone. And truly in my youth I suffered much extremity for love, very near this. I'll speak to him again. — What do you read, my lord?   193

HAML. Words, words, words.   *[handwritten: ATT. TO WRITERS]*

POL. What is the matter, my lord?

HAML. Between who?   196

POL. I mean the matter that you read, my lord.

HAML. Slanders, sir. For the satirical rogue says here that old men have gray beards, that their faces are wrinkled, their eyes purging thick amber and plum-tree gum, and that they have a plentiful lack of wit, together with most weak hams.° All which,   *[handwritten: ATTIT. TO OLD AGE]*

[left margin handwritten: THIS ALSO INDICATES OPHELIA A BAD GIRL]

[left margin handwritten: POLONIUS ACCOSTS HAM — SHOWS HAM'S STATE OF MIND THAT WORLD IS EVIL IN GENERAL]

sir, though I most powerfully and potently believe, yet I hold it not honesty to have it thus set down; for yourself, sir, should be old as I am if like a crab you could go backward.   206

POL. [Aside] Though this be madness, yet there is method° in 't. — Will you walk out of the air, my lord?   *[handwritten: POLONIUS DETECTS HAM'S m]*   210

HAML. Into my grave.

POL. Indeed, that's out of the air. [Aside] How pregnant° sometimes his replies are! A happiness° that often madness hits on, which reason and sanity could not so prosperously be delivered of. I will leave him, and suddenly contrive the means of meeting between him and my daughter. — My honorable lord, I will most humbly take my leave of you.   218

HAML. You cannot, sir, take from me anything that I will more willingly part withal — except my life, except my life, except my life.   *[handwritten: HE HAS H IMPULSES TO SUICIDE BUT WON]*

POL. Fare you well, my lord.

HAML. These tedious old fools!

[Enter ROSENCRANTZ and GUILDENSTERN.]

POL. You go to seek the Lord Hamlet. There he is.

ROS. [To POLONIUS] God save you, sir!   225
[Exit POLONIUS.]   *[handwritten: REVEN]*

GUIL. My honored lord!

ROS. My most dear lord!

HAML. My excellent good friends!° How dost thou, Guildenstern? Ah, Rosencrantz! Good lads, how do you both?   230

ROS. As the indifferent° children of the earth.

GUIL. Happy in that we are not overhappy.
On Fortune's cap we are not the very button.°

HAML. Nor the soles of her shoe?

ROS. Neither, my lord.   235

HAML. Then you live about her waist, or in the middle of her favors?   *[handwritten: HE MIGHT ATTACK HER SEX ITSELF]*

GUIL. Faith, her privates° we.

HAML. In the secret parts of Fortune? Oh, most true, she is a strumpet. What's the news?   240

ROS. None, my lord, but that the world's grown honest.   *[handwritten: BECOMES A CORRUPTION (HE IS PURITANICAL)]*

HAML. Then is Doomsday near. But your news is not true. Let me question more in particular. What have you, my good friends, deserved at the hands of Fortune, that she sends you to prison hither?   247

GUIL. Prison, my lord!

HAML. Denmark's a prison.

ROS. Then is the world one.

HAML. A goodly one, in which there are many

---

162. loose: turn loose. 163. arras: tapestry hanging. 167. keep ... carters: i.e., turn country squire — like Justice Shallow. See II Hen IV. 170. board: accost. 174. fishmonger: Hamlet is now in his "antic disposition," enjoying himself fooling Polonius. 181. sun ... maggots: a general belief. Cf. Ant & Cleo, II.vii.29–31. 182. god: Q2 and F1 read "good." carrion: flesh. 202. hams: knee joints.

208. method: order, sense. 212. pregnant: apt, meaningful. 212. happiness: good turn of phrase. 218. My ... friends: As soon as Polonius has gone, Hamlet drops his assumed madness and greets Rosencrantz and Guildenstern naturally. 231. indifferent: neither too great nor too little. 233. button: i.e., at the top. 238. privates: with a pun on "private parts" and "private," not concerned with politics.

[bottom handwritten: ONLY DOESN'T MENTION HIS MOM + CLAUDIUS — BUT THEY ARE BEHIND IT — HE WON'T DEAL WF. POLONIUS ON ANY LEVEL OF DECENC]

confines,° wards,° and dungeons, Denmark being one o' the worst.

ROS. We think not so, my lord.   254

HAML. Why, then 'tis none to you, for there is nothing either good or bad but thinking makes it so. To me it is a prison.

ROS. Why, then your ambition° makes it one. 'Tis too narrow for your mind.   259

HAML. Oh, God, I could be bounded in a nutshell and count myself a king of infinite space were it not that I have bad dreams.

GUIL. Which dreams indeed are ambition, for the very substance of the ambitious° is merely the shadow of a dream.   265

HAML. A dream itself is but a shadow.

ROS. Truly, and I hold ambition of so airy and light a quality that it is but a shadow's shadow.

HAML. Then are our beggars bodies, and our monarchs and outstretched heroes the beggars' shadows.° Shall we to the Court? For, by my fay,° I cannot reason.°   272

ROS. & GUIL. We'll wait upon you.°

HAML. No such matter. I will not sort° you with the rest of my servants, for, to speak to you like an honest man, I am most dreadfully attended.° But in the beaten way of friendship, what make you at Elsinore?   278

ROS. To visit you, my lord, no other occasion.

HAML. Beggar that I am, I am even poor in thanks, but I thank you. And sure, dear friends, my thanks are too dear a halfpenny.° Were you not sent for? Is it your own inclining? Is it a free visitation?° Come, deal justly with me. Come, come. Nay, speak.   285

GUIL. What should we say, my lord?

HAML. Why, anything, but to the purpose.° You were sent for, and there is a kind of confession in your looks which your modesties have not craft enough to color.° I know the good King and Queen have sent for you.

ROS. To what end, my lord?   292

HAML. That you must teach me. But let me conjure° you, by the rights of our fellowship,° by the consonancy° of our youth, by the obligation of our ever preserved love, and by what more dear a better

proposer could charge you withal, be even° and direct with me, whether you were sent for, or no.   299

ROS. [*Aside to* GUILDENSTERN] What say you?

HAML. [*Aside*] Nay, then, I have an eye of you. — If you love me, hold not off.

GUIL. My lord, we were sent for.   303

HAML. I will tell you why. So shall my anticipation prevent your discovery, and your secrecy to the King and Queen molt no feather.° I have of late — but wherefore I know not — lost all my mirth, forgone all custom of exercises, and indeed it goes so heavily with my disposition that this goodly frame the earth seems to me a sterile promontory.   310 This most excellent canopy,° the air, look you, this brave o'erhanging firmament,° this majestical roof fretted° with golden fire — why, it appears no other thing to me than a foul and pestilent congregation of vapors. What a piece of work is a man!   315 How noble in reason! How infinite in faculty!° In form and moving° how express° and admirable! In action how like an angel! In apprehension how like a god! The beauty of the world! The paragon of animals! And yet, to me, what is this quintessence° of dust? Man delights not me — no, nor   320 woman neither, though by your smiling you seem to say so.

ROS. My lord, there was no such stuff in my thoughts.

HAML. Why did you laugh, then, when I said "Man delights not me"?

ROS. To think, my lord, if you delight not in man, what lenten entertainment° the players shall receive from you. We coted° them on the way, and hither are they coming to offer you service.   331

HAML. He that plays the King shall be welcome, His Majesty shall have tribute of me. The adventurous knight shall use his foil and target,° the lover shall not sigh gratis, the humorous man° shall end his part in peace, the clown shall make those laugh whose lungs are tickle o' the sere,° and the lady shall say her mind freely or the blank verse shall halt° for 't. What players are they?   340

ROS. Even those you were wont to take such delight in, the tragedians of the city.

HAML. How chances it they travel? Their resi-

[Handwritten margin note: WHAT WESTERN MAN THINKS OF HIMSELF — HAML. THINKS POORLY OF MEN]

---

252. confines: places of confinement. wards: cells.   258. your ambition: Rosencrantz is feeling after one possible cause of Hamlet's melancholy — thwarted ambition.   264. substance ... ambitious: that on which an ambitious man feeds his fancies.   269–71. Then ... shadows: i.e., by your reasoning beggars are the only men of substance, for kings and heroes are by nature ambitious and therefore "the shadows of a dream." outstretched: of exaggerated reputation.   271. fay: faith. 272. reason: argue.   273. wait ... you: be your servants. 274. sort: class.   276. dreadfully attended: my attendants are a poor crowd.   282. too ... halfpenny: not worth a halfpenny. 283. free visitation: voluntary visit.   287. anything ... purpose: anything so long as it is not true.   290. color: conceal. 294. conjure: make solemn appeal to. fellowship: comradeship. 295. consonancy: concord.

298. even: straight.   304–06. So ... feather: i.e., so by my telling you first you will not be obliged to betray the secrets of the King. prevent: forestall. molt no feather: be undisturbed.   311. canopy: covering.   312. firmament: sky. 313. fretted: ornamented.   317. moving: movement. express: exact.   319. quintessence: perfection; the fifth essence, which would be left if the four elements were taken away.   329. lenten entertainment: meager welcome.   330. coted: overtook.   334. foil ... target: rapier and small shield. See Pl. 22, l, i.   335. humorous man: the man who specializes in character parts; e.g., Jaques in *AYLI*. See App. 3.   338. are ... sere: explode at a touch. The *sere* is part of the trigger mechanism of a gun which if "ticklish" will go off at a touch.   340. halt: limp.

dence, both in reputation and profit, was better both
ways.°   345

ROS. I° think their inhibition° comes by the
means of the late innovation.°

HAML. Do they hold the same estimation they did
when I was in the city? Are they so followed?

ROS. No, indeed are they not.   350

HAML. How comes it? Do they grow rusty?

ROS. Nay, their endeavor keeps in the wonted
pace.° But there is, sir, an eyrie° of children, little
eyases,° that cry out on the top of question° and
are most tyrannically° clapped for 't. These are   355
now the fashion, and so berattle° the common
stages° — so they call them — that many wearing
rapiers are afraid of goose quills° and dare scarce
come thither.   360

HAML. What, are they children? Who maintains
'em? How are they escoted?° Will they pursue the
quality° no longer than they can sing? Will they not
say afterward, if they should grow themselves to
common players — as it is most like if their means
are no better — their writers do them wrong to make
them exclaim against their own succession?°   368

ROS. Faith, there has been much to-do on both
sides, and the nation holds it no sin to tarre° them
to controversy. There was for a while no money bid
for argument° unless the poet and the player went
to cuffs° in the question.   373

HAML. Is 't possible?

GUIL. Oh, there has been much throwing-about of
brains.

HAML. Do the boys carry it away?

ROS. Aye, that they do, my lord, Hercules and his
load° too.   379

HAML. It is not very strange, for my uncle is King
of Denmark, and those that would make mows° at
him while my father lived give twenty, forty, fifty,
a hundred ducats apiece for his picture in little.
'Sblood,° there is something in this more than natural, if philosophy could find it out.   385

[Flourish of trumpets within.]

Left margin handwritten notes: THEY'LL GO UP + BE COMMON ACTORS WITHOUT A JOB — Hmm. EXCLAIMS AGAINST USE OF KIDS IN PLAY — HAMLET WONDERS WHY HE DOESN'T JUST STAB KING AT MOST CONVENIENT TIME IN A WORLD LIKE THIS, BUT DOESN'T

GUIL. There are the players.

HAML. Gentlemen, you are welcome to Elsinore.
Your hands. Come then. The appurtenance of welcome is fashion and ceremony.° Let me comply°
with you in this garb,° lest my extent° to the   390
players — which, I tell you, must show fairly outward — should more appear like entertainment°
than yours. You are welcome. But my uncle-father
and aunt-mother are deceived.

GUIL. In what, my dear lord?   395

HAML. I am but mad north-northwest.° When
the wind is southerly,° I know a hawk from a handsaw.°

[Re-enter POLONIUS.]

POL. Well be with you, gentlemen!

HAML. Hark you, Guildenstern, and you too — at
each ear a hearer. That great baby you see there is
not yet out of his swaddling clouts.°   401

ROS. Happily he's the second time come to them,
for they say an old man is twice a child.

HAML. I will prophesy he comes to tell me of the
players, mark it. You say right, sir. O' Monday
morning, 'twas so indeed.   407

POL. My lord, I have news to tell you.

HAML. My lord, I have news to tell you. When
Roscius° was an actor in Rome ——

POL. The actors are come hither, my lord.

HAML. Buzz, buzz!°

POL. Upon my honor ——   413

HAML. Then came each actor on his ass ——

POL. The° best actors in the world, either for tragedy, comedy, history, pastoral, pastoral-comical,
historical-pastoral, tragical-historical, tragical-comi-
cal-historical-pastoral, scene individable° or poem
unlimited.° Seneca cannot be too heavy, nor Plau-
tus° too light. For the law of writ° and the liberty,°
these are the only men.   421

HAML. O Jephthah,° judge of Israel, what a treasure hadst thou!

343-45. Their . . . ways: i.e., if they stayed in the city, it would
bring them more profit and fame.   346-79. I . . . too: This
is one of the several topical references in *Hamlet*. For details of the stage war between the Children's Companies,
see Gen. Intro. pp. 45a–46a.   346. inhibition: formal
prohibition.   347. innovation: riot.   352-53. endeavor . . .
pace: they try as hard as ever.   353. eyrie: nest.   354. eyases:
young hawks.   354. cry . . . question: either "cry in a shrill
voice" or perhaps "cry out the latest detail of the dispute."   355. tyrannically: outrageously.   356. berattle: abuse.
357. common stages: the professional players. The boys acted
in "private" playhouses.   359. goose quills: pens; i.e., of such
as Ben Jonson.   362. escoted: paid.   363. quality: acting profession.   368. exclaim . . . succession: abuse the profession to
which they will afterward belong.   370. tarre: urge on to fight;
generally used of encouraging a dog.   372. argument: plot
of a play. See III.ii.242.   372-73. went to cuffs: boxed each
other's ears.   378-79. Hercules . . . load: Hercules carrying the
globe on his shoulders was the sign of the Globe Playhouse.
381. mows: grimaces.   384. 'Sblood: by God's blood.

388-89. appurtenance . . . ceremony: that which pertains to welcome is formal ceremony.   389. comply: use the formality of
welcome; i.e., shake hands with you.   390. garb: fashion. extent: outward behavior.   392. entertainment: welcome.
396. north-northwest: i.e., 327° (out of 360°) of the compass.
397. wind is southerly: The south wind was considered unhealthy.
396-97. hawk . . . handsaw: Either "handsaw" is a corruption
of "heronshaw," heron, or a hawk is a tool like a pickax. The
phrase means "I'm not so mad as you think."   401. clouts:
clothes.   410. Roscius: the most famous of Roman actors.
412. Buzz, buzz: slang for "stale news."   415-21. The . . .
men: Polonius reads out the accomplishments of the actors from
the license which they have presented him. For the wording of
the actual license granted to Shakespeare's company by King
James, see Gen. Intro. p. 13a.   418. scene individable: i.e., a
play preserving the unities. See Gen. Intro. p. 42a.   418-
19. poem unlimited: i.e., a play which disregards the rules.   419-
20. Seneca . . . Plautus: the Roman writers of tragedy and comedy with whose plays every educated man was familiar.   420. law
of writ: the critical rules; i.e., classical plays. liberty: plays
freely written; i.e., "modern" drama.   422. Jephthah: The story
of Jephthah is told in Judges, Chapter II. He vowed that if suc-

POL. What a treasure had he, my lord?

HAML. Why, 425
      "One° fair daughter, and no more,
      The which he lovèd passing well."

POL. [*Aside*] Still° on my daughter.

HAML. Am I not i' the right, old Jephthah?

POL. If you call me Jephthah, my lord, I have a daughter that I love passing well. 431

HAML. Nay, that follows not.

POL. What follows, then, my lord?

HAML. Why,
      "As by lot, God wot,"° 435
and then you know,
      "It came to pass, as most like it was — "
the first row° of the pious chanson° will show you more, for look where my abridgement° comes. 439 [*Enter four or five* PLAYERS.] You are welcome, masters, welcome all. I am glad to see thee well. Welcome, good friends. Oh, my old friend!° Why, thy face is valanced° since I saw thee last. Comest thou to beard° me in Denmark? What, my young lady° and mistress! By 'r Lady, your ladyship is nearer to Heaven than when I saw you last, by the alti- 445 tude of a chopine.° Pray God your voice, like a piece of uncurrent gold, be not cracked within the ring.° Masters, you are all welcome. We'll e'en to 't like French falconers,° fly at anything we see. We'll have a speech straight. Come, give us a taste of your quality° — come, a passionate speech. 452

I. PLAY. What speech, my good lord?

HAML. I heard thee speak me a speech once, but it was never acted, or if it was, not above once; for the play, I remember, pleased not the million, 'twas caviar° to the general.° But it was — as I received it, and others, whose judgments in such matters cried in the top of mine° — an excellent play, well digested° in the scenes, set down with as much 460 modesty° as cunning. I remember one said there were no sallets° in the lines to make the matter savory, nor no matter in the phrase that might indict the author of affection,° but called it an honest

method, as wholesome as sweet, and by very 465 much more handsome than fine.° One speech in it I chiefly loved. 'Twas Aeneas' tale to Dido,° and thereabout of it especially where he speaks of Priam's° slaughter. If it live in your memory, begin at this line — let me see, let me see — 471
      "The rugged Pyrrhus,° like th' Hyrcanian
         beast,° — "
It is not so. It begins with "Pyrrhus."
      "The° rugged Pyrrhus, he whose sable° arms,
      Black as his purpose, did the night resemble 475
      When he lay couchèd in the ominous° horse,°
      Hath now this dread and black complexion
        smeared
      With heraldry° more dismal. Head to foot
      Now is he total gules, horridly tricked 479
      With blood of fathers, mothers, daughters, sons,
      Baked and impasted° with the parching streets
      That lend a tyrannous and a damnèd light
      To their lord's murder. Roasted in wrath and
        fire,
      And thus o'ersized with coagulate gore,° 484
      With eyes like carbuncles, the hellish Pyrrhus
      Old grandsire Priam seeks."
So, proceed you.

POL. 'Fore God, my lord, well spoken, with good accent and good discretion.

I. PLAY.   "Anon he finds him 490
      Striking too short at Greeks. His antique sword,
      Rebellious to his arm, lies where it falls,
      Repugnant to command.° Unequal matched,
      Pyrrhus at Priam drives, in rage strikes wide,
      But with the whiff and wind of his fell sword 495
      The unnerved father falls. Then senseless Ilium,°
      Seeming to feel this blow, with flaming top
      Stoops to his base,° and with a hideous crash
      Takes prisoner Pyrrhus' ear. For, lo! his sword,
      Which was declining° on the milky° head 500
      Of reverend Priam, seemed i' the air to stick.

---

cessful against the Ammonites he would sacrifice the first creature to meet him on his return, which was his daughter. **426-37. One . . . was:** Quotations from a ballad of Jephthah. **428. Still:** always. **435. wot:** knows. **438. row:** line. **pious chanson:** godly poem. **439. abridgement:** entertainment. Cf. *MND*, V.i.39. **441. old friend:** i.e., the leading player. **442. valanced:** bearded. A valance is a fringe hung round the sides and bottom of a bed. See Pl. 17b. **443. beard:** dare, with a pun on "valanced." **young lady:** i.e., the boy who takes the woman's parts. **446. chopine:** lady's shoe with thick cork sole. **447. cracked . . . ring:** Before coins were milled on the rim they were liable to crack. When the crack reached the ring surrounding the device, the coin was no longer valid. See Pl. 10. **450. French falconers:** They were famous for their skill in hawking. **452. quality:** skill as an actor. **457. caviar:** sturgeon's roe, a Russian delicacy not then appreciated (or known) by any but gourmets. **general:** common herd. **459. cried . . . mine:** surpassed mine. **460. digested:** composed. **461. modesty:** moderation. **462. sallets:** tasty bits. **463-64. phrase . . . affection:**

nothing in the language which could charge the author with affectation. **466. fine:** subtle. **467. Aeneas' . . . Dido:** the story of the sack of Troy as told by Aeneas to Dido, Queen of Carthage. The original is in Virgil's *Aeneid*. A similar speech occurs in Marlowe's play *Dido, Queen of Carthage*. **469. Priam:** the old King of Troy. **472. Pyrrhus:** the son of Achilles, one of the Greeks concealed in the Wooden Horse. **472. Hyrcanian beast:** the tiger. **474-541. The . . . gods:** The speech may be from some lost play of *Dido and Aeneas*, but more likely it is Shakespeare's own invention. It is written in the heavy elaborate style still popular in the dramas of the Admiral's Men. The first player delivers it with excessive gesture and emotion. **474. sable:** black. **476. ominous. horse:** the Wooden Horse by which a small Greek force was enabled to make a secret entry into Troy. **478. heraldry:** painting. The image of heraldic painting is kept up in *gules* (the heraldic term for red) and *tricked* (painted). See App. 9. **481. impasted:** turned into a crust by the heat of the burning city. **484. o'ersized . . . gore:** covered over with congealed blood. **493. Repugnant to command:** refusing to be used. **496. Ilium:** the citadel of Troy. **498. stoops . . . base:** collapses. **500. declining:** bending toward. **milky:** milk-white.

So as a painted tyrant° Pyrrhus stood,
And like a neutral to his will and matter,°
Did nothing.
But as we often see, against° some storm　　　505
A silence in the heavens, the rack° stand still,
The bold winds speechless and the orb° below
As hush as death, anon the dreadful thunder
Doth rend the region° — so after Pyrrhus' pause
Arousèd vengeance sets him new awork.　　　510
And never did the Cyclops'° hammers fall
On Mars's armor, forged for proof eterne,°
With less remorse° than Pyrrhus' bleeding sword
Now falls on Priam.　　　　　　　　　514
Out, out, thou strumpet, Fortune! All you gods,
In general synod° take away her power,
Break all the spokes and fellies° from her wheel,
And bowl the round nave° down the hill of Heaven
As low as to the fiends! "
　　POL. This is too long.　　　　　　520
　　HAML. It shall to the barber's, with your beard.
Prithee, say on. He's for a jig° or a tale of bawdry,
or he sleeps. Say on. Come to Hecuba.
　　I. PLAY. " But who, oh, who had seen the mobled°
　　　Queen — "
　　HAML. " The mobled Queen "?
　　POL. That's good, " mobled Queen " is good.
　　I. PLAY. " Run barefoot up and down, threatening
　　　the flames
With bisson rheum,° a clout° upon that head
Where late the diadem stood, and for a robe,　530
About her lank and all o'erteemèd° loins
A blanket, in the alarm of fear caught up.
Who this had seen, with tongue in venom steeped
'Gainst Fortune's state would treason have pro-
　　nounced.°
But if the gods themselves did see her then,　535
When she saw Pyrrhus make malicious sport
In mincing with his sword her husband's limbs,
The instant burst of clamor that she made,
Unless things mortal move them not at all,
Would have made milch° the burning eyes of
　　Heaven
And passion in the gods."　　　　　540

　　POL. Look whether he has not turned his **color**
and has tears in 's eyes. Prithee, no more.
　　HAML. 'Tis well; I'll have thee speak out the rest
of this soon. Good my lord, will you see the players
well bestowed?° Do you hear, let them be well used,
for they are the abstract and brief chronicles of the
time.° After your death you were better have a bad
epitaph than their ill report while you live.　　551
　　POL. My lord, I will use them according to their
desert.°
　　HAML. God's bodykins,° man, much better. Use
every man after his desert and who shall 'scape
whipping? Use them after your own honor and dignity. The less they deserve, the more merit is in your
bounty. Take them in.
　　POL. Come, sirs.　　　　　　　　559
　　HAML. Follow him, friends. We'll hear a play tomorrow. [*Exit* POLONIUS *with all the* PLAYERS *but the*
FIRST.] Dost thou hear me, old friend? Can you play
The Murder of Gonzago?
　　I. PLAY. Aye, my lord.　　　　　　564
　　HAML. We'll ha 't tomorrow night. You could, for
a need, study a speech of some dozen or sixteen lines
which I would set down and insert in 't, could you
not?
　　I. PLAY. Aye, my lord.　　　　　　569
　　HAML. Very well. Follow that lord, and look you
mock him not. [*Exit* FIRST PLAYER.] My good
friends, I'll leave you till night. You are welcome to
Elsinore.
　　ROS. Good my lord!　　　　　　　574
　　HAML. Aye, so, God be wi' ye! [*Exeunt* ROSEN-
CRANTZ *and* GUILDENSTERN.] Now I am alone.
Oh, what a rogue and peasant slave am I!
Is it not monstrous that this player here,
But in a fiction, in a dream of passion,°
Could force his soul so to his own conceit°　579
That from her working° all his visage wanned,°
Tears in his eyes, distraction° in 's aspect,°
A broken voice, and his whole function° suiting
With forms to his conceit? And all for nothing!
For Hecuba!
What's Hecuba to him or he to Hecuba,　　585
That he should weep for her? What would he do
Had he the motive and the cue for passion
That I have? He would drown the stage with tears
And cleave the general ear° with horrid speech,
Make mad the guilty and appal the free,°　　590

502. **painted tyrant:** as in the painting of a tyrant.　503. **neu-tral ... matter:** one midway (*neutral*) between his desire (*will*) and action (*matter*).　505. **against:** just before.　506. **rack:** the clouds in the upper air. Cf. *Ant & Cleo*, IV.xiv.10.　507. **orb:** world.　509. **region:** the country round.　511. **Cyclops':** of Titans, giants who aided Vulcan, the blacksmith god, to make armor for Mars, the war god.　512. **proof eterne:** everlasting protection.　513. **remorse:** pity.　516. **synod:** council.　517. **fellies:** the pieces forming the circumference of a wooden wheel.　518. **nave:** center of the wheel.　522. **jig:** bawdy dance. See App. 24.　525. **mobled:** muffled.　529. **bisson rheum:** blinding moisture. **clout:** rag.　531. **o'erteemed:** exhausted by bearing children; she had borne fifty-two.　533-34. **Who ... pronounced:** anyone who had seen this sight would with bitter words have uttered treason against the tyranny of Fortune.　540. **milch:** milky, i.e., dripping moisture.

548. **bestowed:** housed.　549-50. **abstract ... time:** they summarize and record the events of our time. Elizabethan players were often in trouble for too saucily commenting on their betters in plays dealing with history or contemporary events and persons. See Gen. Intro. pp. 41a, 45a, 48a-b, 49a-b.　552. **desert:** rank.　553. **God's bodykins:** by God's little body.　578. **dream of passion:** imaginary emotion.　579. **conceit:** imagination.　580. **her working:** i.e., the effect of imagination. **wanned:** went pale.　581. **distraction:** frenzy. **aspect:** countenance.　582. **function:** behavior.　589. **general ear:** ears of the audience.　590. **free:** innocent.

Confound the ignorant, and amaze indeed
The very faculties of eyes and ears.
Yet I,
A dull and muddy-mettled° rascal, peak,°   594
Like John-a-dreams,° unpregnant of my cause,°
And can say nothing — no, not for a King
Upon whose property° and most dear life
A damned defeat° was made. Am I a coward?
Who° calls me villain? Breaks my pate across?
Plucks off my beard and blows it in my face?   600
Tweaks me by the nose? Gives me the lie i' the
     throat
As deep as to the lungs? Who does me this?
Ha!
'Swounds,° I should take it. For it cannot be
But I am pigeon-livered° and lack gall°   605
To make oppression bitter, or ere this
I should have fatted all the region kites
With this slave's offal.° Bloody, bawdy villain!
Remorseless, treacherous, lecherous, kindless° vil-
     lain!
Oh, vengeance!   610
Why, what an ass am I! This is most brave,
That I, the son of a dear father murdered,
Prompted to my revenge by Heaven and Hell,
Must, like a whore, unpack my heart with words
And fall a-cursing like a very drab,°   615
A scullion!°
Fie upon 't! Foh! About, my brain! Hum, I have
     heard
That guilty creatures sitting at a play
Have by the very cunning of the scene
Been struck so to the soul that presently°   620
They have proclaimed their malefactions;°
For murder, though it have no tongue, will speak
With most miraculous organ. I'll have these players
Play something like the murder of my father
Before mine uncle. I'll observe his looks,   625
I'll tent° him to the quick. If he but blench,°
I know my course. The° spirit that I have seen
May be the Devil, and the Devil hath power
To assume a pleasing shape. Yea, and perhaps
Out of my weakness and my melancholy,   630
As he is very potent with such spirits,
Abuses me to damn me.° I'll have grounds°

---

594. **muddy-mettled:** made of mud, not iron. **peak:** mope.
595. **John-a-dreams:** "Sleepy Sam." **unpregnant . . . cause:**
barren of plans for vengeance.   597. **property:** personality, life.
598. **defeat:** ruin.   599–602. **Who . . . this:** Hamlet runs through
all the insults which provoked a resolute man to mortal
combat. **pate:** head. **lie . . . throat:** the bitterest of insults.
604. **'Swounds:** by God's wounds.   605. **pigeon-livered:** "as
gentle as a dove." **gall:** spirit.   606–08. **I . . . offal:** before this
I would have fed this slave's (i.e., the King's) guts to the kites.
fatted: made fat.   609. **kindless:** unnatural.   615. **drab:**
"moll."   616. **scullion:** the lowest of the kitchen servants.
620. **presently:** immediately.   621. **proclaimed . . . malefactions:** shouted out their crimes.   626. **tent:** probe. See *Cor*,
I.ix.31. **blench:** flinch.   627–32. **The . . . me:** See *Haml*
Intro. p. 883a–b.   632. **Abuses . . . me:** i.e., deceives me so that I

More relative than this.° The play's the thing
Wherein I'll catch the conscience of the King.

                                        [*Exit.*]

Act III

SCENE I. *A room in the castle.*

[*Enter* KING, QUEEN, POLONIUS, OPHELIA,
     ROSENCRANTZ, *and* GUILDENSTERN.]
KING. And can you, by no drift of circumstance,°
Get from him why he puts on this confusion,
Grating° so harshly all his days of quiet
With turbulent and dangerous lunacy?   4
ROS. He does confess he feels himself distracted,
But from what cause he will by no means speak.
GUIL. Nor do we find him forward to be
     sounded,°
But, with a crafty madness, keeps aloof
When we would bring him on to some confession
Of his true state.
QUEEN.   Did he receive you well?   10
ROS. Most like a gentleman.
GUIL. But with much forcing of his disposition.°
ROS. Niggard of question,° but of our demands
Most free in his reply.
QUEEN.   Did you assay him
To any pastime?°   15
ROS. Madam, it so fell out that certain players
We o'erraught° on the way. Of these we told him,
And there did seem in him a kind of joy
To hear of it. They are about the Court,
And, as I think, they have already order   20
This night to play before him.
POL.   'Tis most true.
And he beseeched me to entreat your Majesties
To hear and see the matter.
KING. With all my heart, and it doth much con-
     tent me
To hear him so inclined.   25
Good gentlemen, give him a further edge,°
And drive his purpose on to these delights.
ROS. We shall, my lord.
          [*Exeunt* ROSENCRANTZ *and* GUILDENSTERN.]
KING.   Sweet Gertrude, leave us too,
For we have closely° sent for Hamlet hither,
That he, as 'twere by accident, may here   30

---

may commit the sin of murder which will bring me to damnation.
grounds: reasons for action.   633. **relative . . . this:** i.e., more
convincing than the appearance of a ghost.

Act III, Sc. i: 1. **drift of circumstance:** circumstantial evidence, hint.   3. **grating:** disturbing.   7. **forward . . . sounded:**
eager to be questioned.   12. **much . . . disposition:** making a
great effort to be civil to us.   13. **Niggard of question:** not asking
many questions.   14–15. **Did . . . pastime:** did you try to interest him in any amusement.   17. **o'erraught:** overtook.
26. **edge:** encouragement.   29. **closely:** secretly.

Affront° Ophelia.
Her father and myself, lawful espials,°
Will so bestow ourselves that, seeing unseen,
We may of their encounter frankly judge
And gather by him, as he is behaved,°   35
If 't be the affliction of his love or no
That thus he suffers for.
     QUEEN.   I shall obey you.
And for your part, Ophelia, I do wish
That your good beauties be the happy cause   39
Of Hamlet's wildness. So shall I hope your virtues
Will bring him to his wonted way° again,
To both your honors.
     OPH.·   Madam, I wish it may. [*Exit* QUEEN.]
     POL. Ophelia, walk you here. Gracious,° so please
     you,
We will bestow ourselves. [*To* OPHELIA] Read on
     this book,°
That show of such an exercise may color   45
Your loneliness. We are oft to blame in this —
'Tis too much proved — that with devotion's
     visage°
And pious action we do sugar o'er
The Devil himself.
     KING. [*Aside*] Oh, 'tis too true!
How smart a lash that speech doth give my con-
     science!   50
The harlot's cheek, beautied with plastering art,
Is not more ugly to the thing that helps it°
Than is my deed to my most painted° word.
Oh, heavy burden!   54
     POL. I hear him coming. Let's withdraw, my lord.
             [*Exeunt* KING *and* POLONIUS.
             [*Enter* HAMLET.°]
     HAML. To be, or not to be — that is the question.
Whether 'tis nobler in the mind to suffer
The slings and arrows of outrageous° fortune,
Or to take arms against a sea° of troubles
And by opposing end them. To die, to sleep —   60
No more, and by a sleep to say we end
The heartache and the thousand natural shocks
That flesh is heir to. 'Tis a consummation°
Devoutly to be wished. To die, to sleep,
To sleep — perchance to dream. Aye, there's the
     rub,°   65
For in that sleep of death what dreams may come
When we have shuffled off this mortal coil°

Must give us pause. There's the respect°
That makes calamity of so long life.°   69
For who would bear the whips and scorns of time,
The oppressor's wrong, the proud man's contumely°
The pangs of déspised love, the law's delay,
The insolence of office° and the spurns
That patient merit of the unworthy takes,°
When he himself might his quietus° make   75
With a bare bodkin?° Who would fardels° bear,
To grunt and sweat under a weary life,
But that the dread of something after death,
The undiscovered country from whose bourn°
No traveler returns, puzzles the will,°   80
And makes us rather bear those ills we have
Than fly to others that we know not of?
Thus° conscience does make cowards of us all,
And thus the native hue° of resolution
Is sicklied o'er with the pale cast° of thought,   85
And enterprises of great pitch° and moment
With this regard their currents turn awry
And lose the name of action.° — Soft you now!
The fair Ophelia! Nymph, in thy orisons°
Be all my sins remembered.
     OPH.   Good my lord,   90
How does your Honor for this many a day?
     HAML. I humbly thank you — well, well, well.
     OPH. My lord, I have remembrances of yours
That I have longed long to redeliver.
I pray you now receive them.
     HAML.   No, not I.   95
I never gave you aught.
     OPH. My honored lord, you know right well you
     did,
And with them words of so sweet breath composed
As made the things more rich. Their perfume lost,
Take these again, for to the noble mind   100
Rich gifts wax poor when givers prove unkind.
There, my lord.
     HAML. Ha, ha! Are you honest?°
     OPH. My lord?
     HAML. Are you fair?   105
     OPH. What means your lordship?
     HAML. That if you be honest and fair, your hon-
esty should admit no discourse to your beauty.°

---

31. **Affront:** encounter.   32. **lawful espials:** who are justified in spying on him.   35. **by . . . behaved:** from him, from his behavior.   41. **wonted way:** normal state.   43. **Gracious:** your Majesty — addressed to the King.   44. **book:** i.e., of devotions.   47. **devotion's visage:** an outward appearance of religion.   52. **ugly . . . it:** i.e., lust, which is the cause of its artificial beauty.   53. **painted:** i.e., false.   55 s.d., **Enter Hamlet:** In Q1 the King draws attention to Hamlet's approach with the words "See where he comes poring upon a book." Hamlet is again reading, and is too much absorbed to notice Ophelia.   58. **outrageous:** cruel.   59. **sea:** i.e., an endless turmoil.   63. **consummation:** completion.   65. **rub:** impediment. See App. 13.   67. **shuffled . . . coil:** cast off this fuss of life.

68. **respect:** reason.   69. **makes . . . life:** makes it a calamity to have to live so long.   71. **contumely:** insulting behavior. 73. **insolence of office:** insolent behavior of government officials. 73–74. **spurns . . . takes:** insults which men of merit have patiently to endure from the unworthy.   75. **quietus:** discharge. See Sonnet 126.   76. **bodkin:** dagger. **fardels:** burdens, the coolie's pack.   79. **bourn:** boundary.   80. **will:** resolution, ability to act. 83–88. **Thus . . . action:** the religious fear that death may not be the end makes men shrink from heroic actions.   84. **native hue:** natural color.   85. **cast:** color.   86. **pitch:** height; used of the soaring flight of a hawk. See App. 26.   87–88. **With . . . action:** by brooding on this thought great enterprises are diverted from their course and fade away.   89. **orisons:** prayers.   103. **honest:** chaste. 107–08. **That . . . beauty:** if you are chaste and beautiful your chastity should have nothing to do with your beauty — because

OPH. Could beauty, my lord, have better commerce than with honesty?   110

HAML. Aye, truly, for the power of beauty will sooner transform honesty from what it is to a bawd° than the force of honesty can translate beauty into his likeness. This was sometime a paradox,° but now the time gives it proof. I did love you once.   116

OPH. Indeed, my lord, you made me believe so.

HAML. You should not have believed me, for virtue cannot so inoculate our old stock but we shall relish° of it. I loved you not.   120

OPH. I was the more deceived.

HAML. Get thee to a nunnery. Why wouldst thou be a breeder of sinners? I am myself indifferent honest,° but yet I could accuse me of such things that it were better my mother had not borne me. I am   125 very proud, revengeful, ambitious, with more offenses at my beck° than I have thoughts to put them in, imagination to give them shape, or time to act them in. What should such fellows as I do crawling between heaven and earth? We are arrant   130 knaves all. Believe none of us. Go thy ways to a nunnery.° Where's your father?

OPH. At home, my lord.

HAML. Let the doors be shut upon him, that he may play the fool nowhere but in 's own house. Farewell.   137

OPH. Oh, help him, you sweet Heavens!

HAML. If thou dost marry, I'll give thee this plague for thy dowry: Be thou as chaste as ice, as pure as snow — thou shalt not escape calumny.° Get thee to a nunnery, go. Farewell. Or if thou wilt needs marry, marry a fool, for wise men know well enough what monsters° you make of them. To a nunnery, go, and quickly too. Farewell.

OPH. O heavenly powers, restore him!   147

HAML. I have heard of your paintings° too, well enough. God hath given you one face and you make yourselves another. You jig,° you amble,° and you lisp,° and nickname God's creatures, and make your wantonness your ignorance.° Go to, I'll no more on 't — it hath made me mad. I say we will have no more marriages. Those that are married already, all but one, shall live; the rest shall keep as they   156 are. To a nunnery, go.   [*Exit.*]

OPH. Oh, what a noble mind is here o'erthrown! The courtier's, soldier's, scholar's, eye, tongue, sword —

The expectancy and rose° of the fair state,   160
The glass° of fashion and the mold of form,°
The observed of all observers — quite, quite down!
And I, of ladies most deject and wretched,
That sucked the honey of his music vows,
Now see that noble and most sovereign reason,   165
Like sweet bells jangled, out of tune and harsh,
That unmatched° form and feature of blown° youth
Blasted with ecstasy.° Oh, woe is me,
To have seen what I have seen, see what I see!   169
      [*Re-enter* KING *and* POLONIUS.]

KING. Love! His affections° do not that way tend,
Nor what he spake, though it lacked form a little,
Was not like madness. There's something in his soul
O'er which his melancholy sits on brood,°
And I do doubt the hatch and the disclose°
Will be some danger. Which for to prevent,   175
I have in quick determination
Thus set it down: He shall with speed to England,
For the demand of our neglected tribute.
Haply° the seas and countries different
With variable objects° shall expel   180
This something-settled° matter in his heart
Whereon his brains still beating puts him thus
From fashion of himself.° What think you on 't?

POL. It shall do well. But yet do I believe
The origin and commencement of his grief   185
Sprung from neglected love. How now, Ophelia!
You need not tell us what Lord Hamlet said,
We heard it all. My lord, do as you please,
But, if you hold it fit, after the play
Let his Queen mother all alone entreat him   190
To show his grief. Let her be round° with him,
And I'll be placed, so please you, in the ear
Of all their conference. If she find him not,
To England send him, or confine him where
Your wisdom best shall think.

KING.   It shall be so.   195
Madness in great ones must not unwatched go.
      [*Exeunt.*]

SCENE II. *A hall in the castle.*

[*Enter* HAMLET *and* PLAYERS.]

HAML. Speak the speech,° I pray you, as I pro-

---

160. **expectancy . . . rose:** bright hope. The rose is used as a symbol for beauty and perfection. Cf. *I Hen IV*, I.iii.175. 161. **glass:** mirror. **mold of form:** perfect pattern of manly beauty. 167. **unmatched:** unmatchable. **blown:** perfect, like an open flower at its best. 168. **Blasted . . . ecstasy:** ruined by madness. 170. **affections:** state of mind. 173. **sits . . . brood:** sits hatching. 174. **doubt . . . disclose:** suspect the brood which will result. 179. **Haply:** perhaps. 180. **variable objects:** novel sights. 181. **something-settled:** somewhat settled; i.e., not yet incurable. 182–83. **puts . . . himself:** i.e., separates him from his normal self. 191. **round:** direct.

Sc. ii: 1. **the speech:** which he has written. See ll. 266–67. The whole passage which follows is Shakespeare's own comment

---

(so Hamlet thinks in his bitterness) beautiful women are seldom chaste. 112. **bawd:** brothel-keeper. 115. **paradox:** statement contrary to accepted opinion. 120. **relish:** have some trace. 123–24. **indifferent honest:** moderately honorable. 127. **at . . . beck:** waiting to come when I beckon. 132. **nunnery:** i.e., a place where she will be removed from temptation. 141. **calumny:** slander. 145. **monsters:** horned beasts, cuckolds. See App. 11. 148. **paintings:** using make-up. 150. **jig:** dance lecherously. **amble:** walk artificially. 151. **lisp:** talk affectedly. 152–53. **nickname . . . ignorance:** give things indecent names and pretend to be too simple to understand their meanings.

nounced it to you, trippingly° on the tongue. But if
you mouth° it, as many of your players do, I had as
lief° the town crier spoke my lines. Nor do not saw
the air too much with your hand, thus, but use   5
all gently. For in the very torrent, tempest, and, as I
may say, whirlwind of passion, you must acquire and
beget a temperance that may give it smoothness. Oh,
it offends me to the soul to hear a robustious° peri-
wig-pated° fellow tear a passion to tatters, to   10
very rags, to split the ears of the groundlings,° who
for the most part are capable of nothing but inexplicable dumb shows° and noise. I would have such
a fellow whipped for o'erdoing Termagant° — it
out-Herods Herod. Pray you, avoid it.   16

I. PLAY. I warrant your Honor.

HAML. Be not too tame neither, but let your own
discretion be your tutor. Suit the action to the word,
the word to the action, with this special observ-   20
ance, that you o'erstep not the modesty of nature.
For anything so overdone is from° the purpose of
playing, whose end, both at the first and now, was
and is to hold as 'twere the mirror up to Nature —
to show Virtue her own feature, scorn her own   25
image, and the very age and body of the time his
form and pressure.° Now this overdone or come
tardy off, though it make the unskillful laugh, cannot but make the judicious grieve, the censure of the
which one° must in your allowance o'erweigh a   30
whole theater of others. Oh, there be players° that I
have seen play, and heard others praise — and that
highly, not to speak it profanely — that neither having the accent of Christians nor the gait of Christian,
pagan, nor man, have so strutted and bellowed   35
that I have thought some of Nature's journeymen°
had made men, and not made them well, they imitated humanity so abominably.

I. PLAY. I hope we have reformed that indiffer-
ently° with us, sir.   41

HAML. Oh, reform it altogether. And let those that
play your clowns° speak no more than is set down

Marginal handwritten notes: ON STAGE YOU MUST MAINTAIN SMOOTH SPEECH, ALTHOUGH IN A PASSION, YOU STUTTER — SO MUST BE UNREAL

for them. For there be of them that will themselves
laugh, to set on some quantity of barren spec-   45
tators to laugh too, though in the meantime some
necessary question of the play be then to be considered. That's villainous, and shows a most pitiful°
ambition in the fool that uses it. Go, make you   50
ready. [*Exeunt* PLAYERS. *Enter* POLONIUS, ROSEN-
CRANTZ, *and* GUILDENSTERN.] How now, my lord!
Will the King hear this piece of work?

POL. And the Queen too, and that presently.

HAML. Bid the players make haste. [*Exit* POLO-
NIUS.] Will you two help to hasten them?   55

ROS. & GUIL. We will, my lord.

[*Exeunt* ROSENCRANTZ *and* GUILDENSTERN.]

HAML. What ho! Horatio!

[*Enter* HORATIO.]

HOR. Here, sweet lord, at your service.

HAML. Horatio, thou art e'en as just a man
As e'er my conversation coped° withal.   60

HOR. Oh, my dear lord ——

HAML.   Nay, do not think I flatter,
For what advancement° may I hope from thee,
That no revénue hast but thy good spirits
To feed and clothe thee? Why should the poor be
    flattered?
No, let the candied° tongue lick absurd pomp   65
And crook the pregnant hinges of the knee
Where thrift may follow fawning.° Dost thou
    hear?
Since my dear soul was mistress of her choice
And could of men distinguish, her election
Hath sealed° thee for herself. For thou hast been   70
As one in suffering all that suffers nothing,
A man that fortune's buffets and rewards
Hast ta'en with equal thanks. And blest are those
Whose blood and judgment are so well commingled
That they are not a pipe° for fortune's finger   75
To sound what stop she please. Give me that man
That is not passion's slave, and I will wear him
In my heart's core — aye, in my heart of heart,
As I do thee. Something too much of this.
There is a play tonight before the King.   80
One scene of it comes near the circumstance
Which I have told thee of my father's death.
I prithee when thou seest that act afoot,
Even with the very comment° of thy soul
Observe my uncle. If his occulted° guilt   85

Marginal handwritten notes: HORATIO IS COOL ENOUGH EXCEPT AT END SHUTS HOW... REJECT ALMOST EVERYONE AS AGAINST HIM

on the actor's art and states the creed and practice of his
company as contrasted with the more violent methods of
Edward Alleyn and his fellows. See Gen. Intro. p. 41b.
2. trippingly: smoothly, easily.   **3. mouth:** "ham" it.   **4. lief:**
soon.   **9. robustious:** ranting.   **10. periwig-pated:** wearing
a wig.   **11. groundlings:** the poorer spectators, who stood in
the yard of the playhouse. See Gen. Intro. p. 53a.   **14. dumb
shows:** an old-fashioned dramatic device, still being used by the
Admiral's Men: before a tragedy, and sometimes before each act,
the characters mimed the action which was to follow. See later,
l. 145.   **15. Termagant:** God of the Saracens, who, like Herod,
was presented in early stage plays as a roaring tyrant.   **22. from:**
contrary to.   **26–27. very . . . pressure:** an exact reproduction of
the age. **form:** shape. **pressure:** imprint (of a seal).   **30. the
. . . one:** i.e., the judicious spectator.   **31. there . . . players:** An
obvious attack on Alleyn.   **41. indifferently:** moderately.   **42–43. those
. . . clowns:** A hit at Will Kempe, the former clown of Shakespeare's company. See Gen. Intro. p. 60a. Q1 adds the passage
"And then you have some again that keep one suit of jests, as a
man is known by one suit of apparel, and gentlemen quote his jests

down in their tables before they come to the play, as thus: 'Cannot you stay till I eat my porridge?' and 'You owe me a quarter's
wages,' and 'My coat wants a cullison,' and 'Your beer is sour,'
and blabbering with his lips, and thus keeping in his cinquepace
of jests, when God knows the warm clown cannot make a jest unless by chance, as the blind man catcheth a hare. Masters tell
him of it."   **49. pitiful:** contemptible.   **60. coped:** met.   **62. advancement:** promotion.   **65. candied:** sugared over with hypocrisy.   **66–67. crook . . . fawning:** bend the ready knees whenever
gain will follow flattery.   **70. sealed:** set a mark on.   **75. pipe:** an
instrument that varies its notes.   **84. comment:** close observation.   **85. occulted:** concealed.

Do not itself unkennel° in one speech
It is a damnèd ghost° that we have seen
And my imaginations are as foul
As Vulcan's° stithy.° Give him heedful note,°
For I mine eyes will rivet to his face,   90
And after we will both our judgments join
In censure of his seeming.°
HOR.   Well, my lord.
If he steal aught the whilst this play is playing,
And 'scape detecting, I will pay the theft.
    HAML. They are coming to the play. I must be
    idle.°   95
Get you a place.
    [Danish march. A flourish. Enter KING, QUEEN,
POLONIUS, OPHELIA, ROSENCRANTZ, GUILDENSTERN,
    and other LORDS attendant, with the GUARD
                carrying torches.]
KING. How fares our cousin Hamlet?
    HAML. Excellent, i' faith, of the chameleon's dish.
I eat the air, promise-crammed. You cannot feed ca-
pons so.°
    KING. I have nothing with this answer,° Hamlet.
These words are not mine.
    HAML. No, nor mine now.° [To POLONIUS] My
lord, you played once i' the university, you say?
    POL. That did I, my lord, and was accounted a
good actor.   106
    HAML. What did you enact?
    POL. I did enact Julius Caesar. I was killed i' the
Capitol. Brutus killed me.
    HAML. It was a brute part of him to kill so capital
a calf there. Be the players ready?   111
    ROS. Aye, my lord, they stay upon your patience.°
    QUEEN. Come hither, my dear Hamlet, sit by me.
    HAML. No, good Mother, here's metal more attrac-
tive.   117
    POL. [To the KING] Oh ho! Do you mark that?
    HAML. Lady, shall I lie in your lap?
                [Lying down at OPHELIA's feet]
    OPH. No, my lord.   120
    HAML. I mean, my head upon your lap?
    OPH. Aye, my lord.
    HAML. Do you think I meant country matters?°
    OPH. I think nothing, my lord.
    HAML. That's a fair thought to lie between maids'
    legs.   126
    OPH. What is, my lord?

HAML. Nothing.
    OPH. You are merry, my lord.
    HAML. Who, I?   130
    OPH. Aye, my lord.
    HAML. Oh God, your only jig-maker.° What
should a man do but be merry? For look you how
cheerfully my mother looks, and my father died
within 's two hours.   135
    OPH. Nay, 'tis twice two months, my lord.
    HAML. So long? Nay, then, let the Devil wear
black, for I'll have a suit of sables.° Oh heavens! Die
two months ago, and not forgotten yet? Then there's
hope a great man's memory may outlive his   140
life half a year. But, by 'r Lady, he must build
churches then, or else shall he suffer not thinking on,
with the hobbyhorse,° whose epitaph is "For, oh,
for oh, the hobbyhorse is forgot."   145
[Hautboys° play. The dumb show enters.° Enter a
KING and a QUEEN very lovingly, the QUEEN embracing him and he her. She kneels, and makes show of
protestation unto him. He takes her up, and declines
his head upon her neck, lays him down upon a bank
of flowers. She, seeing him asleep, leaves him. Anon
comes in a fellow, takes off his crown, kisses it, and
pours poison in the KING's ears, and exit. The QUEEN
returns, finds the KING dead, and makes passionate
action. The Poisoner, with some two or three Mutes,
comes in again, seeming to lament with her. The
dead body is carried away. The Poisoner woos the
QUEEN with gifts. She seems loath and unwilling
awhile, but in the end accepts his love.   Exeunt.]
    OPH. What means this, my lord?
    HAML. Marry, this is miching mallecho.° It means
mischief.
    OPH. Belike this show imports the argument° of
the play.   150
                [Enter PROLOGUE.]
    HAML. We shall know by this fellow. The players
cannot keep counsel, they'll tell all.
    OPH. Will he tell us what this show meant?
    HAML. Aye, or any show that you'll show him. Be
not you ashamed to show, he'll not shame to tell you
what it means.   156
    OPH. You are naught,° you are naught. I'll mark
the play.

Margin handwritten note: WHOLE PLAY SEEMS TO BE HAMLET'S CREATION ALTHOUGH IT DOESN'T STICK OUT

86. unkennel: come to light; lit., force a fox from his hole.
87. damned ghost: See II.ii.627.   89. Vulcan: the blacksmith god. stithy: smithy. heedful note: careful observation.
92. censure . . . seeming: judgment on his looks.   95. be idle:
seem crazy.   98-100. Excellent . . . so: Hamlet takes "fare"
literally as "what food are you eating." The chameleon was supposed to feed on air. promise-crammed: stuffed, like a fattened
chicken (capon) — but with empty promises.   101. I . . . answer: I cannot make any sense of your answer.   103. nor . . .
now: i.e., once words have left the lips they cease to belong to
the speaker.   112. stay . . . patience: wait for you to be ready.
123. country matters: something indecent.

132. jig-maker: composer of jigs. See App. 24.   138. suit of
sables: a quibble on "sable," black, and "sable," gown
trimmed with sable fur, worn by wealthy old gentlemen.
See Pl. 9l.   144. hobbyhorse: imitation horse worn by performers in a morris dance, an amusement much disapproved of by the
godly. See App. 24.   145 s.d., Hautboys: oboes. The dumb
show enters: Critics have been disturbed because this dumb show
cannot be exactly paralleled in any other Elizabethan play, and
because the King is apparently not disturbed by it. Shakespeare's
intention, however, in presenting a play within a play is to produce something stagy and artificial compared with the play
proper. Moreover, as Hamlet has already complained, dumb
shows were often inexplicable.   147. miching mallecho: slinking
mischief.   149. argument: plot. She too is puzzled by the dumb
show.   157. naught: i.e., disgusting.

PRO. For us, and for our tragedy,
Here stooping to your clemency, 160
We beg your hearing patiently.
HAML. Is this a prologue, or the posy of a ring?°
OPH. 'Tis brief, my lord.
HAML. As woman's love.

[*Enter two* PLAYERS, KING *and* QUEEN.]

P. KING. Full° thirty times hath Phoebus' cart°
gone round 165
Neptune's° salt wash and Tellus'° orbèd ground,
And thirty dozen moons with borrowed sheen°
About the world have times twelve thirties been,
Since love our hearts and Hymen° did our hands
Unite commutual° in most sacred bands. 170
P. QUEEN. So many journeys may the sun and
moon
Make us again count o'er ere love be done!
But, woe is me, you are so sick of late,
So far from cheer and from your former state,
That I distrust° you. Yet, though I distrust, 175
Discomfort you, my lord, it nothing must.
For women's fear and love holds quantity°
In neither aught or in extremity.°
Now what my love is, proof hath made you know,
And as my love is sized, my fear is so. 180
Where love is great, the littlest doubts are fear,
Where little fears grow great, great love grows there.
P. KING. Faith, I must leave thee,° love, and
shortly too,
My operant powers° their functions leave to do.
And thou shalt live in this fair world behind, 185
Honored, beloved, and haply one as kind
For husband shalt thou ——
P. QUEEN. Oh, confound the rest!
Such love must needs be treason in my breast.
In second husband let me be accurst!
None wed the second but who killed the first. 190
HAML. [*Aside*] Wormwood,° wormwood.
P. QUEEN. The instances° that second marriage
move
Are base respects of thrift,° but none of love.
A second time I kill my husband dead
When second husband kisses me in bed. 195
P. KING. I do believe you think what now you
speak,
But what we do determine oft we break.
Purpose is but the slave to memory,

Of violent birth but poor validity,
Which now, like fruit unripe, sticks on the tree 200
But fall unshaken when they mellow be.
Most necessary 'tis that we forget
To pay ourselves what to ourselves is debt.
What to ourselves in passion we propose,
The passion ending, doth the purpose lose. 205
The violence of either grief or joy
Their own enactures° with themselves destroy.
Where joy most revels, grief doth most lament,
Grief joys, joy grieves, on slender accident. 209
This world is not for aye,° nor 'tis not strange
That even our loves should with our fortunes
change,
For 'tis a question left us yet to prove
Whether love lead fortune or else fortune love.
The great man down, you mark his favorite flies,
The poor advanced makes friends of enemies. 215
And hitherto doth love on fortune tend,
For who not needs shall never lack a friend,
And who in want a hollow friend doth try
Directly seasons° him his enemy.
But, orderly to end where I begun, 220
Our wills and fates do so contráry run
That our devices still are overthrown,
Our thoughts are ours, their ends none of our own.
So think thou wilt no second husband wed, 224
But die thy thoughts when thy first lord is dead.
P. QUEEN. Nor earth to me give food nor Heaven
light!
Sport and repose lock from me day and night!
To desperation turn my trust and hope!
An anchor's° cheer in prison be my scope!
Each opposite that blanks° the face of joy 230
Meet what I would have well and it destroy!
Both here and hence pursue me lasting strife
If, once a widow, ever I be wife!
HAML. If she should break it now!
P. KING. 'Tis deeply sworn. Sweet, leave me here
a while. 235
My spirits grow dull, and fain I would beguile
The tedious day with sleep. [*Sleeps.*]
P. QUEEN. Sleep rock thy brain,
And never come mischance between us twain!
[*Exit.*]
HAML. Madam, how like you this play?
QUEEN. The lady doth protest too much, methinks.
HAML. Oh, but she'll keep her word. 241
KING. Have you heard the argument?° Is there no
offense in 't?
HAML. No, no, they do but jest, poison in jest ——
no offense i' the world. 245
KING. What do you call the play?

---

162. posy . . . ring: It was a pretty custom to inscribe rings with little mottoes or messages, which were necessarily brief. **165–238. Full . . . twain:** The play is deliberately written in crude rhyming verse, full of ridiculous and bombastic phrases. **165. Phoebus' cart:** the chariot of the sun. **166. Neptune:** the sea god. **Tellus:** the earth goddess. **167. borrowed sheen:** light borrowed from the sun. **170. commutual:** mutually. **175. distrust:** am anxious about. **177. quantity:** proportion. **178. In . . . extremity:** either nothing or too much. **183. leave thee:** i.e., die. **184. operant powers:** bodily strength. **191. Wormwood:** bitterness. **192. instances:** arguments. **193. respects of thrift:** considerations of gain.

207. enactures: performances. **210. aye:** ever. **219. seasons:** ripens into. **229. anchor:** anchorite, hermit. **230. blanks:** makes pale. **242. argument:** plot. When performances were given at Court it was sometimes customary to provide a written or printed synopsis of the story for the distinguished spectators.

HAML. *The Mousetrap.*° Marry, how? Tropically.° This play is the image of a murder done in
Vienna. Gonzago is the Duke's name, his wife, Baptista. You shall see anon. 'Tis a knavish piece of   250
work, but what o' that? Your Majesty, and we that
have free° souls, it touches us not. Let the galled
jade wince, our withers are unwrung.°
[*Enter* LUCIANUS.] This is one Lucianus, nephew to
the King.

OPH. You are as good as a chorus,° my lord.   255

HAML. I could interpret between you and your
love, if I could see the puppets dallying.°

OPH. You are keen, my lord, you are keen.

HAML. It would cost you a groaning to take off
my edge.   260

OPH. Still better, and worse.

HAML. So you must take your husbands.° Begin,
murderer. Pox, leave thy damnable faces and begin.
Come, the croaking raven doth bellow for revenge.

LUC. Thoughts black, hands apt, drugs fit, and
   time agreeing,   266
Confederate season, else no creature° seeing,
Thou mixture rank of midnight weeds collected,
With Hecate's ban° thrice blasted, thrice infected,
Thy natural magic and dire property°   270
On wholesome life usurp immediately.

   [*Pours the poison into the sleeper's ear.*]

HAML. He poisons him i' the garden for his estate.° His name's Gonzago. The story is extant, and
written in very choice Italian. You shall see anon
how the murderer gets the love of Gonzago's wife.

OPH. The King rises.   276

HAML. What, frighted with false fire!°

QUEEN. How fares my lord?

POL. Give o'er the play.

KING. Give me some light. Away!   280

POL. Lights, lights, lights!

   [*Exeunt all but* HAMLET *and* HORATIO.]

HAML. "Why, let the stricken deer go weep,
   The hart ungallèd play,
For some must watch while some must sleep.
   Thus runs the world away."   285
Would not this, sir, and a forest of feathers° — if the

rest of my fortunes turn Turk° with me — with two
Provincial roses° on my razed° shoes, get me a fel-
lowship° in a cry° of players, sir?

HOR. Half a share.   290

HAML. A whole one, I.
   "For thou dost know, O Damon° dear,
      This realm dismantled° was
   Of Jove himself, and now reigns here
      A very, very — pajock."°   295

HOR. You might have rhymed.

HAML. O good Horatio, I'll take the ghost's word
for a thousand pound. Didst perceive?

HOR. Very well, my lord.

HAML. Upon the talk of the poisoning?   300

HOR. I did very well note him.

HAML. Ah, ha! Come, some music! Come, the re-
corders!°
   "For if the King like not the comedy,
   Why then, belike, he likes it not, perdy."°   305
Come, some music!

   [*Re-enter* ROSENCRANTZ *and* GUILDENSTERN.]

GUIL. Good my lord, vouchsafe me a word with
you.

HAML. Sir, a whole history.

GUIL. The King, sir ——   310

HAML. Aye, sir, what of him?

GUIL. Is in his retirement marvelous distempered.°

HAML. With drink, sir?

GUIL. No, my lord, rather with choler.°   315

HAML. Your wisdom should show itself more
richer to signify this to the doctor, for for me to put
him to his purgation° would perhaps plunge him
into far more choler.   319

GUIL. Good my lord, put your discourse into some
frame,° and start not so wildly from my affair.

HAML. I am tame, sir. Pronounce.

GUIL. The Queen your mother, in most great
affliction of spirit, hath sent me to you.

HAML. You are welcome.   325

GUIL. Nay, good my lord, this courtesy is not of
the right breed. If it shall please you to make me a
wholesome answer, I will do your mother's commandment. If not, your pardon and my return shall
be the end of my business.   330

HAML. Sir, I cannot.

GUIL. What, my lord?

HAML. Make you a wholesome answer, my wit's

---

247. **Mousetrap:** The phrase was used of a device to entice a person to his own destruction (OED).   248. **Tropically:** figuratively,
with a pun on "trap."   252. **free:** innocent.   252–53. **galled . . .
unwrung:** let a nag with a sore back flinch when the saddle is put
on; our shoulders (being ungalled) feel no pain.   255. **chorus:** the
chorus sometimes introduced the characters and commented on
what was to follow. See, for instance, the Chorus in *Hen V.*
257. **puppets dallying:** Elizabethan puppets were crude marion-
ettes, popular at fairs. While the figures were put through their
motions, the puppet master explained what was happening.
262. **So . . . husbands:** i.e., as the marriage service expresses it,
"for better, for worse."   267. **confederate . . . creature:** the opportunity conspiring with me, no other creature.   269. **Hecate's
ban:** the curse of Hecate, goddess of witchcraft.   270. **property:**
nature.   273. **estate:** kingdom.   277. **false fire:** a mere show.
286. **forest of feathers:** set of plumes, much worn by players.

287. **turn Turk:** turn heathen, and treat me cruelly.   288. **Provincial roses:** rosettes, worn on the shoes. **razed:** slashed, ornamented with cuts. See Pl. 8c.   289. **fellowship:** partnership. **cry:** pack.
292. **Damon:** Damon and Pythias were types of perfect friends.
293. **dismantled:** robbed.   295. **pajock:** peacock, a strutting,
lecherous bird. These verses, and the lines above, may have come
from some ballad, otherwise lost.   303. **recorders:** wooden pipes.
See Pl. 19b.   305. **perdy:** by God.   312. **distempered:** disturbed; but Hamlet takes the word in its other sense of "drunk."
315. **choler:** anger, which Hamlet again pretends to understand
as meaning "biliousness."   317–18. **put . . . purgation:** "give
him a dose of salts."   321. **frame:** shape; i.e., "please talk sense."

diseased. But, sir, such answer as I can make you shall command, or rather, as you say, my mother. Therefore no more, but to the matter. My mother, you say —— 337

ROS. Then thus she says. Your behavior hath struck her into amazement and admiration.°

HAML. Oh, wonderful son that can so astonish a mother! But is there no sequel at the heels of this mother's admiration? Impart. 342

ROS. She desires to speak with you in her closet ere you go to bed.

HAML. We shall obey, were she ten times our mother. Have you any further trade with us?

ROS. My lord, you once did love me. 348

HAML. So I do still, by these pickers and stealers.°

ROS. Good my lord, what is your cause of distemper? You do surely bar the door upon your own liberty if you deny your griefs° to your friend.

HAML. Sir, I lack advancement.° 354

ROS. How can that be when you have the voice of the King himself for your succession in Denmark?

HAML. Aye, sir, but " While the grass grows "° — the proverb is something musty. [*Re-enter* 359 PLAYERS *with recorders.*] Oh, the recorders!° Let me see one. To withdraw° with you —— why do you go about to recover the wind° of me, as if you would drive me into a toil?°

GUIL. O my lord, if my duty be too bold, my love is too unmannerly.° 365

HAML. I do not well understand that. Will you play upon this pipe?

GUIL. My lord, I cannot.

HAML. I pray you.

GUIL. Believe me, I cannot.

HAML. I do beseech you. 371

GUIL. I know no touch of it, my lord.

HAML. It is as easy as lying. Govern these ventages° with your fingers and thumb, give it breath with your mouth, and it will discourse most eloquent music. Look you, these are the stops. 376

GUIL. But these cannot I command to any utterance of harmony, I have not the skill.

HAML. Why, look you now, how unworthy a thing you make of me! You would play upon me, 380 you would seem to know my stops, you would pluck out the heart of my mystery, you would sound me

339. admiration: wonder. 349. pickers . . . stealers: i.e., hands — an echo from the Christian's duty in the catechism to keep his hands "from picking and stealing." 353. deny . . . griefs: refuse to tell your troubles. 354. advancement: promotion. Hamlet harks back to his previous interview with Rosencrantz and Guildenstern. See II.ii.258. 358. While . . . grows: the proverb ends "the steed starves." 360. recorders: See Pl. 19b. 361. withdraw: go aside. Hamlet leads Guildenstern to one side of the stage. 362. recover . . . wind: a hunting metaphor; approach me with the wind against you. 363. toil: net. 364-65. if . . . unmannerly: if I exceed my duty by asking these questions, then my affection for you shows lack of manners; i.e., forgive me if I have been impertinent. 374. ventages: holes, stops.

from my lowest note to the top of my compass — and there is much music, excellent voice, in this little organ — yet cannot you make it speak. 'Sblood, do you think I am easier to be played on than a pipe? Call me what instrument you will, though you can fret° me, you cannot play upon me. [*Re-enter* PO-LONIUS.] God bless you, sir! 390

POL. My lord, the Queen would speak with you, and presently.

HAML. Do you see yonder cloud that's almost in shape of a camel?

POL. By the mass, and 'tis like a camel indeed.

HAML. Methinks it is like a weasel. 396

POL. It is backed like a weasel.

HAML. Or like a whale?

POL. Very like a whale.

HAML. Then I will come to my mother by 400 and by. They fool me to the top of my bent.° I will come by and by.

POL. I will say so. [*Exit* POLONIUS.]

HAML. " By and by " is easily said. Leave me, friends. [*Exeunt all but* HAMLET.] 'Tis now the very witching time° of night, 406 When churchyards yawn and Hell itself breathes out Contagion° to this world. Now could I drink hot blood, And do such bitter business as the day 409 Would quake to look on. Soft! Now to my mother. O heart, lose not thy nature, let not ever The soul of Nero° enter this firm bosom. Let me be cruel, not unnatural. I will speak daggers to her, but use none. My tongue and soul in this be hypocrites, 415 How in my words soever she be shent,° To give them seals° never, my soul, consent! [*Exit.*]

SCENE III. *A room in the castle.*

[*Enter* KING, ROSENCRANTZ, *and* GUILDENSTERN.]

KING. I like him not, nor stands it safe with us To let his madness range.° Therefore prepare you. I your commission will forthwith dispatch, And he to England shall along with you. The terms of our estate° may not endure 5 Hazard so near us as doth hourly grow Out of his lunacies.

GUIL. We will ourselves provide.°

389. fret: annoy, with a pun on the frets or bars on stringed instruments by which the fingering is regulated. See Pl. 18b. 401. top . . . bent: See II.ii.30,n. 406. witching time: when witches perform their foul rites. 408. Contagion: infection. 412. Nero: Nero killed his own mother. Hamlet is afraid that in the interview to come he will lose all self-control. 416. shent: rebuked. 417. give . . . seals: ratify words by actions. See App. 6.

Sc. iii: 2. range: roam freely. 5. terms . . . estate: i.e., one in my position. 7. ourselves provide: make our preparations

Most holy and religious fear° it is
To keep those many many bodies safe
That live and feed upon your Majesty. 10
 ROS. The single and peculiar° life is bound
With all the strength and armor of the mind
To keep itself from noyance,° but much more
That spirit upon whose weal° depends and rests
The lives of many. The cease of majesty° 15
Dies not alone, but like a gulf° doth draw
What's near it with it. It is a massy° wheel
Fixed on the summit of the highest mount,
To whose huge spokes ten thousand lesser things
Are mortised° and adjoined; which, when it falls,
Each small annexment, petty consequence,° 21
Attends° the boisterous ruin. Never alone
Did the King sigh but with a general groan.
 KING. Arm you, I pray you, to this speedy voyage,
For we will fetters put upon this fear, 25
Which now goes too free-footed.
 ROS. & GUIL. We will haste us.
  [*Exeunt* ROSENCRANTZ *and* GUILDENSTERN.]
   [*Enter* POLONIUS.]
 POL. My lord, he's going to his mother's closet.
Behind the arras I'll convey myself
To hear the process.° I'll warrant she'll tax° him
  home.
And, as you said,° and wisely was it said, 30
'Tis meet that some more audience than a mother,
Since nature makes them partial, should o'erhear
The speech, of vantage.° Fare you well, my liege.
I'll call upon you ere you go to bed
And tell you what I know.
 KING. Thanks, dear my lord. [*Exit* POLONIUS.]
Oh, my offense is rank,° it smells to Heaven. 36
It hath the primal eldest curse° upon 't,
A brother's murder. Pray can I not,
Though inclination be as sharp as will.°
My stronger guilt defeats my strong intent, 40
And like a man to double business bound,
I stand in pause where I shall first begin,
And both neglect. What if this cursèd hand
Were thicker than itself with brother's blood,
Is there not rain enough in the sweet heavens 45
To wash it white as snow? Whereto serves mercy
But to confront the visage of offense?°
And what's in prayer but this twofold force,
To be forestalled° ere we come to fall

Or pardoned being down? Then I'll look up, 50
My fault is past. But oh, what form of prayer
Can serve my turn? "Forgive me my foul mur-
  der"?
That cannot be, since I am still possessed
Of those effects° for which I did the murder —
My crown, mine own ambition, and my Queen. 55
May one be pardoned and retain the offense?°
In the corrupted currents° of this world
Offense's gilded hand may shove by justice,
And oft 'tis seen the wicked prize° itself
Buys out the law. But 'tis not so above. 60
There is no shuffling, there the action lies
In his true nature,° and we ourselves compelled
Even to the teeth and forehead° of our faults
To give in evidence. What then? What rests?
Try what repentance can. What can it not? 65
Yet what can it when one cannot repent?
Oh, wretched state! Oh, bosom black as death!
Oh, limèd° soul, that struggling to be free
Art more engaged!° Help, angels! Make assay!°
Bow, stubborn knees, and heart with strings of steel,
Be soft as sinews of the newborn babe! 71
All may be well. [*Retires and kneels.*]
   [*Enter* HAMLET.]
 HAML. Now might I do it pat, now he is praying,
And now I'll do 't. And so he goes to Heaven,°
And so am I revenged. That would be scanned: 75
A villain kills my father, and for that
I, his sole son, do this same villain send
To Heaven.
Oh, this is hire and salary,° not revenge.
He took my father grossly,° full of bread, 80
With all his crimes broad blown, as flush° as May,
And how his audit° stands who knows save
  Heaven?
But in our circumstance and course of thought,°
'Tis heavy with him. And am I then revenged,
To take him in the purging of his soul, 85
When he is fit and seasoned,° for his passage?
No.
Up, sword, and know thou a more horrid hent.°
When he is drunk asleep, or in his rage,
Or in the incestuous pleasure of his bed — 90
At gaming, swearing, or about some act
That has no relish of salvation in 't —
Then trip him, that his heels may kick at Heaven
And that his soul may be as damned and black

---

8. **fear:** anxiety. 11. **peculiar:** individual. 13. **noyance:** injury. 14. **weal:** welfare. 15. **cease of majesty:** death of a king. 16. **gulf:** whirlpool. 17. **massy:** massive. 20. **mortised:** firmly fastened. 21. **annexment . . . consequence:** attachment, smallest thing connected with it. 22. **Attends:** waits on, is involved in. 29. **process:** proceeding. **tax:** censure. 30. **as . . . said:** Actually Polonius himself had said it (III.i.189–93). 33. **of vantage:** from a place of vantage; i.e., concealment. 36. **rank:** foul. 37. **primal . . . curse:** the curse laid upon Cain, the first murderer, who also slew his brother. 39. **will:** desire. 47. **confront . . . offense:** look crime in the face. 49. **forestalled:** prevented.

54. **effects:** advantages. 56. **offense:** i.e., that for which he has offended. 57. **currents:** courses, ways. 59. **wicked prize:** the proceeds of the crime. 61–62. **there . . . nature:** in Heaven the case is tried on its own merits. 63. **teeth . . . forehead:** i.e., face to face. 68. **limed:** caught as in birdlime. 69. **engaged:** stuck fast. **assay:** attempt. 74. **And . . . Heaven:** See *Haml* Intro. p. 884a. 79 **hire . . . salary:** i.e., a kind action deserving pay. 80. **grossly:** i.e., when he was in a state of sin. See I.v.74–80. 81. **broad . . . flush:** in full blossom, as luxuriant. 82. **audit:** account. 83. **circumstance . . . thought:** as it appears to my mind. 86. **seasoned:** ripe. 88. **hent:** opportunity.

As Hell, whereto it goes. My mother stays.   95
This physic but prolongs thy sickly days.   [*Exit.*]
KING. [*Rising*] My words fly up, my thoughts re-
main below.
Words without thoughts never to Heaven go.
[*Exit.*]

SCENE IV. *The* QUEEN's *closet.*

[*Enter* QUEEN *and* POLONIUS.]
POL. He will come straight. Look you lay home
to° him.
Tell him his pranks have been too broad° to bear
with,
And that your grace hath screened and stood be-
tween
Much heat and him. I'll sconce me° even here.
Pray you, be round with him.   5
HAML. [*Within*] Mother, Mother, Mother!
QUEEN.   I'll warrant you,
Fear me not. Withdraw, I hear him coming.
[POLONIUS *hides behind the arras.*]
[*Enter* HAMLET.]
HAML. Now, Mother, what's the matter?
QUEEN. Hamlet, thou hast thy father much of-
fended.
HAML. Mother, you have my father much of-
fended.   10
QUEEN. Come, come, you answer with an idle°
tongue.
HAML. Go, go, you question with a wicked
tongue.
QUEEN. Why, how now, Hamlet!
HAML.   What's the matter now?
QUEEN. Have you forgot me?
HAML.   No, by the rood,° not so.   14
You are the Queen, your husband's brother's wife,
And — would it were not so! — you are my mother.
QUEEN. Nay, then, I'll set those to you that can
speak.
HAML. Come, come, and sit you down. You shall
not budge,
You go not till I set you up a glass°
Where you may see the inmost part of you.   20
QUEEN. What wilt thou do? Thou wilt not mur-
der me?
Help, help, ho!
POL. [*Behind*] What ho! Help, help, help!
HAML. [*Drawing*] How now! A rat? Dead, for a
ducat, dead! [*Makes a pass through the arras.*]
POL. [*Behind*] Oh, I am slain! [*Falls and dies.*]
QUEEN.   Oh me, what hast thou done?
HAML. Nay, I know not. Is it the King?   26
QUEEN. Oh, what a rash and bloody deed is this!

Sc. iv: 1. lay . . . to: be strict with.   2. broad: unrestrained.
Polonius is thinking of the obvious insolence of the remarks about
second marriage in the play scene.   4. sconce me: hide myself.
11. idle: foolish.   14. rood: crucifix.   19. glass: looking-glass.

HAML. A bloody deed! Almost as bad, good
Mother,
As kill a king and marry with his brother.
QUEEN. As kill a king!
HAML.   Aye, lady, 'twas my word.   30
[*Lifts up the arras and discovers* POLONIUS.]
Thou wretched, rash, intruding fool, farewell!
I took thee for thy better. Take thy fortune.
Thou find'st to be too busy is some danger.
Leave wringing of your hands. Peace! Sit you down,
And let me wring your heart. For so I shall   35
If it be made of penetrable stuff,
If damnèd custom have not brassed° it so
That it be proof and bulwark against sense.
QUEEN. What have I done that thou darest wag
thy tongue
In noise so rude against me?
HAML.   Such an act   40
That blurs the grace and blush of modesty,
Calls virtue hypocrite, takes off the rose
From the fair forehead of an innocent love,
And sets a blister° there — makes marriage vows
As false as dicers' oaths — Oh, such a deed   45
As from the body of contraction° plucks
The very soul, and sweet religion makes
A rhapsody of words.° Heaven's face doth glow,
Yea, this solidity and compound mass,°
With tristful visage, as against the doom,°   50
Is thought-sick at the act.
QUEEN.   Aye me, what act
That roars so loud and thunders in the index?°
HAML. Look here upon this picture,° and on this,
The counterfeit presentment° of two brothers.
See what a grace was seated on this brow —   55
Hyperion's curls, the front° of Jove himself,
An eye like Mars, to threaten and command,
A station° like the herald Mercury°
New-lighted° on a heaven-kissing hill,
A combination° and a form indeed   60
Where every god did seem to set his seal°
To give the world assurance of a man.
This was your husband. Look you now what fol-
lows.
Here is your husband, like a mildewed ear,
Blasting his wholesome brother. Have you eyes?   65
Could you on this fair mountain leave to feed

37. brassed: made brazen; i.e., impenetrable.   44. sets a blister: brands as a harlot.   46. contraction: the marriage contract.
48. rhapsody of words: string of meaningless words.   49. solidity . . . mass: i.e., solid earth.   50. tristful . . . doom: sorrowful
face, as in anticipation of Doomsday.   52. in . . . index: i.e., if
the beginning (*index*, i.e., table of contents) is so noisy, what
will follow?   53. picture: Modern producers usually interpret
the pictures as miniatures, Hamlet wearing one of his father,
Gertrude one of Claudius. In the eighteenth century, wall portraits were used.   54. counterfeit presentment: portrait.
56. front: forehead.   58. station: figure; lit., standing. Mercury:
messenger of the gods, and one of the most beautiful.   59. New-
lighted: newly alighted.   60. combination: i.e., of physical
qualities.   61. set . . . seal: guarantee as a perfect man.

And batten° on this moor? Ha! Have you eyes?
You cannot call it love, for at your age
The heyday° in the blood is tame, it's humble, 69
And waits upon the judgment. And what judgment
Would step from this to this? Sense° sure you have,
Else could you not have motion.° But sure that sense
Is apoplexed;° for madness would not err,
Nor sense to ecstasy° was ne'er so thralled°
But it reserved some quantity of choice 75
To serve in such a difference.° What devil was 't
That thus hath cozened° you at hoodman-blind?°
Eyes without feeling, feeling without sight,
Ears without hands or eyes, smelling sans° all,
Or but a sickly part of one true sense 80
Could not so mope.°
Oh, shame! Where is thy blush? Rebellious° Hell,
If thou canst mutine° in a matron's bones,
To flaming youth let virtue be as wax
And melt in her own fire. Proclaim no shame 85
When the compulsive ardor° gives the charge,
Since frost itself as actively doth burn,
And reason panders° will.
QUEEN.   O Hamlet, speak no more.
Thou turn'st mine eyes into my very soul,
And there I see such black and grainèd° spots 90
As will not leave their tinct.°
HAML.   Nay, but to live
In the rank sweat of an enseamèd° bed,
Stewed in corruption, honeying and making love
Over the nasty sty ——
QUEEN.   Oh, speak to me no more,
These words like daggers enter in my ears. 95
No more, sweet Hamlet!
HAML.   A murderer and a villain,
A slave that is not twentieth part the tithe°
Of your precedent° lord, a vice of kings,°
A cutpurse° of the empire and the rule,
That from a shelf the precious diadem stole 100
And put it in his pocket!
QUEEN.   No more!
HAML. A king of shreds and patches ——
[*Enter* GHOST] Save me, and hover o'er me with
 your wings,
You heavenly guards! What would your gracious
 figure?

QUEEN. Alas, he's mad! 105
HAML. Do you not come your tardy son to chide
That, lapsed in time and passion, lets go by
The important acting of your dread command?°
Oh, say!
GHOST. Do not forget. This visitation 110
Is but to whet thy almost blunted purpose.
But look, amazement on thy mother sits.
Oh, step between her and her fighting soul.
Conceit° in weakest bodies strongest works.
Speak to her, Hamlet.
HAML.   How is it with you, lady? 115
QUEEN. Alas, how is 't with you
That you do bend your eye on vacancy°
And with the incorporal° air do hold discourse?
Forth at your eyes your spirits wildly peep,
And as the sleeping soldiers in the alarm, 120
Your bedded° hairs, like life in excrements,°
Start up and stand an° end. O gentle son,
Upon the heat and flame of thy distemper°
Sprinkle cool patience. Whereon do you look?
HAML. On him, on him! Look you how pale he
 glares! 125
His form and cause conjoined,° preaching to stones,
Would make them capable.° Do not look upon
 me,
Lest with this piteous action you convert
My stern effects.° Then what I have to do 129
Will want true color — tears perchance for blood.
QUEEN. To whom do you speak this?
HAML.   Do you see nothing there?
QUEEN. Nothing at all, yet all that is I see.
HAML. Nor did you nothing hear?
QUEEN.   No, nothing but ourselves.
HAML. Why, look you there! Look how it steals
 away!
My father, in his habit as he lived! 135
Look where he goes, even now, out at the portal!
       [*Exit* GHOST.]
QUEEN. This is the very coinage of your brain.
This bodiless creation ecstasy°
Is very cunning in.
HAML.   Ecstasy! 139
My pulse, as yours, doth temperately keep time,
And makes as healthful music. It is not madness
That I have uttered. Bring me to the test
And I the matter will reword, which madness
Would gambol° from. Mother, for love of grace,

---

57. batten: glut yourself. 69. heyday: excitement. 71. Sense: feeling. 72. motion: desire. 73. apoplexed: paralyzed. 74. ecstasy: excitement, passion. See II.i.102. thralled: enslaved. 76. serve . . . difference: to enable you to see the difference between your former and your present husband. 77. cozened: cheated. hoodman-blind: blind-man's-buff. 79. sans: without. 81. mope: be dull. 82–88. Rebellious . . . will: i.e., if the passion (*Hell*) of a woman of your age is uncontrollable (*rebellious*), youth can have no restraints; there is no shame in a young man's lust when the elderly are just as eager and their reason (which should control desire) encourages them. 83. mutine: mutiny. 86. compulsive ardor: compelling lust. 88. panders: acts as go-between. 90. grained: dyed in the grain. 91. tinct: color. 92. enseamed: greasy. 97. tithe: tenth part. 98. precedent: former. vice of kings: caricature of a king. 99. cutpurse: thief.

107–08. That . . . command: who has allowed time to pass and passion to cool, and neglects the urgent duty of obeying your dread command. 114. Conceit: imagination. 117. vacancy: empty space. 118. incorporal: bodiless. 121. bedded: evenly laid. excrements: anything that grows out of the body, such as hair or fingernails; here hair. 122. an: on. 123. distemper: mental disturbance. 126. form . . . conjoined: his appearance and the reason for his appearance joined. 127. capable: i.e., of feeling. 128–29. convert . . . effects: change the stern action which should follow. 138. ecstasy: madness. 144. gambol: start away.

Lay not that flattering unction° to your soul,   145
That not your trespass but my madness speaks.
It will but skin and film the ulcerous place,
Whiles rank corruption, mining° all within,
Infects unseen. Confess yourself to Heaven,
Repent what's past, avoid what is to come,   150
And do not spread the compost° on the weeds
To make them ranker. Forgive me this my virtue,
For in the fatness° of these pursy° times
Virtue itself of vice must pardon beg —
Yea, curb° and woo for leave to do him good.   155
    QUEEN. O Hamlet, thou hast cleft my heart in
      twain.
    HAML. Oh, throw away the worser part of it,
And live the purer with the other half.
Good night. But go not to my uncle's bed.
Assume a virtue if you have it not.   160
That° monster, custom, who all sense doth eat,
Of habits devil,° is angel yet in this,
That to the use° of actions fair and good
He likewise gives a frock or livery
That aptly° is put on. Refrain tonight,   165
And that shall lend a kind of easiness
To the next abstinence, the next more easy.
For use almost can change the stamp° of nature,
And either the Devil,° or throw him out   169
With wondrous potency. Once more, good night.
And when you are desirous to be blest,
I'll blessing beg of you. For this same lord,
                 [*Pointing to* POLONIUS]
I do repent; but Heaven hath pleased it so,
To punish me with this, and this with me,
That I must be their scourge and minister.   175
I will bestow° him, and will answer well
The death I gave him. So again good night.
I must be cruel only to be kind.
Thus bad begins, and worse remains behind.
One word more, good lady.
    QUEEN.   What shall I do?   180
    HAML. Not this, by no means, that I bid you do.
Let the bloat° king tempt you again to bed,
Pinch wanton° on your cheek, call you his mouse,
And let him, for a pair of reechy° kisses   184
Or paddling in your neck with his damned fingers,
Make you to ravel° all this matter out,
That I essentially am not in madness,

But mad in craft. 'Twere good you let him know.
For who that's but a Queen, fair, sober, wise,
Would from a paddock,° from a bat, a gib,°   190
Such dear concernings° hide? Who would do so?
No, in despite° of sense and secrecy,
Unpeg the basket on the house's top,
Let the birds fly, and like the famous ape,°
To try conclusions,° in the basket creep   195
And break your own neck down.
    QUEEN. Be thou assured if words be made of
      breath
And breath of life, I have no life to breathe
What thou hast said to me.
    HAML. I must to England. You know that?
    QUEEN.   Alack,   200
I had forgot. 'Tis so concluded on.
    HAML. There's letters sealed, and my two school-
      fellows,
Whom I will trust as I will adders fanged,
They bear the mandate.° They must sweep my way,
And marshal me to knavery. Let it work,   205
For 'tis the sport to have the enginer°
Hoist with his own petar.° And 't shall go hard
But I will delve one yard below their mines
And blow them at the moon: Oh, 'tis most sweet
When in one line two crafts° directly meet.   210
This man shall set me packing.
I'll lug the guts into the neighbor room.
Mother, good night. Indeed this counselor
Is now most still, most secret, and most grave
Who was in life a foolish prating knave.   215
Come, sir, to draw toward an end with you.
Good night, Mother.   [*Exeunt severally,*°
        HAMLET *dragging in* POLONIUS.]

Act IV

SCENE I. *A room in the castle.*

[*Enter* KING, QUEEN, ROSENCRANTZ, *and*
       GUILDENSTERN.]
    KING. There's matter° in these sighs, these pro-
      found heaves,
You must translate. 'Tis fit we understand them.
Where is your son?

---

145. unction: healing ointment.   **148. mining:** undermining.
151. compost: manure.   **153. fatness:** grossness. **pursy:** bloated.
155. curb: bow low.   **161–65. That . . . on:** i.e., custom (bad
habits) like an evil monster destroys all sense of good and evil, but
yet can become an angel (good habits) when it makes us perform
good actions as mechanically as we put on our clothes. **162. devil:**
This is the Q2 reading; the passage is omitted in F1. Probably the
word should be "evil." **163. use:** practice. **165. aptly:** readily.
168. stamp: impression.   **169. either the Devil:** some verb such
as "shame" or "curb" has been omitted. **176. bestow:** get rid of.
182. bloat: bloated.   **183. wanton:** lewdly. **184. reechy:** foul.
186. ravel: unravel, reveal.

190. paddock: toad. **gib:** tomcat.   **191. dear concernings:**
important matters.   **192. despite:** spite.   **194. famous ape:**
The story is not known, but evidently told of an ape that
let the birds out of their cage and, seeing them fly, crept
into the cage himself and jumped out, breaking his own neck.
195. try conclusions: repeat the experiment.   **204. mandate:**
command.   **206. enginer:** engineer.   **207. petar:** petard, land
mine.   **210. crafts:** devices.   **217 s.d., Exeunt severally:** i.e.,
by separate exits. In F1 there is no break here. The King enters as soon as Hamlet has dragged the body away. Q2 marks the
break. The act division was first inserted in a quarto of 1676.
    Act IV. Sc. i: 1. matter: something serious.

QUEEN. Bestow this place° on us a little while.
   [*Exeunt* ROSENCRANTZ *and* GUILDENSTERN.]
Ah, mine own lord, what have I seen tonight!   5
KING. What, Gertrude? How does Hamlet?
QUEEN. Mad as the sea and wind when both contend
Which is the mightier. In his lawless fit,
Behind the arras hearing something stir,
Whips out his rapier, cries " A rat, a rat! "   10
And in this brainish apprehension° kills
The unseen good old man.
   KING.   Oh, heavy deed!
It had been so with us had we been there.
His liberty is full of threats to all,
To you yourself, to us, to everyone.   15
Alas, how shall this bloody deed be answered?
It will be laid to us, whose providence°
Should have kept short,° restrained and out of
   haunt,°
This mad young man. But so much was our love
We would not understand what was most fit,   20
But, like the owner of a foul disease,
To keep it from divulging° let it feed
Even on the pith° of life. Where is he gone?
   QUEEN. To draw apart the body he hath killed,
O'er whom his very madness, like some ore   25
Among a mineral of metals base,
Shows itself pure. He weeps for what is done.
   KING. O Gertrude, come away!
The sun no sooner shall the mountains touch
But we will ship him hence. And this vile deed   30
We must, with all our majesty and skill,
Both countenance° and excuse. Ho, Guildenstern!
   [*Re-enter* ROSENCRANTZ *and* GUILDENSTERN.]
Friends both, go join you with some further aid.
Hamlet in madness hath Polonius slain,   34
And from his mother's closet hath he dragged him.
Go seek him out, speak fair, and bring the body
Into the chapel. I pray you, haste in this.
   [*Exeunt* ROSENCRANTZ *and* GUILDENSTERN.]
Come, Gertrude, we'll call up our wisest friends,
And let them know both what we mean to do
And what's untimely done,°   40
Whose whisper o'er the world's diameter
As level as the cannon to his blank°
Transports his poisoned shot, may miss our name
And hit the woundless air. Oh, come away!
My soul is full of discord and dismay.   [*Exeunt.*]

4. Bestow . . . place: give place, leave us. 11. brainish apprehension: mad imagination. 17. providence: foresight. 18. short: confined. out of haunt: away from others. 22. divulging: becoming known. 23. pith: marrow. 32. countenance: take responsibility for. 40. done: A half-line has been omitted. Some editors fill the gap with "So, haply slander." 42. blank: target.

SCENE II. *Another room in the castle.*

   [*Enter* HAMLET.]
HAML. Safely stowed.
ROS. & GUIL. [*Within*] Hamlet! Lord Hamlet!
HAML. But soft, what noise? Who calls on Hamlet?
Oh, here they come.
   [*Enter* ROSENCRANTZ *and* GUILDENSTERN.]
ROS. What have you done, my lord, with the dead
   body?   5
HAML. Compounded it with dust, whereto 'tis kin.
ROS. Tell us where 'tis, that we may take it thence
And bear it to the chapel.
HAML. Do not believe it.
ROS. Believe what?   10
HAML. That I can keep your counsel and not mine
own. Besides, to be demanded of a sponge! What
replication° should be made by the son of a king?
ROS. Take you me for a sponge, my lord?   15
HAML. Aye, sir, that soaks up the King's countenance,° his rewards, his authorities. But such officers
do the King best service in the end. He keeps them,
like an ape, in the corner of his jaw, first mouthed,
to be last swallowed. When he needs what you have
gleaned, it is but squeezing you and, sponge, you
shall be dry again.   23
ROS. I understand you not, my lord.
HAML. I am glad of it. A knavish speech sleeps in
a foolish ear.°
ROS. My lord, you must tell us where the body is,
and go with us to the King.   28
HAML. The body is with the King, but the King
is not with the body.° The King is a thing ——
GUIL. A thing, my lord?
HAML. Of nothing. Bring me to him. Hide   32
fox, and all after.°   [*Exeunt.*]

SCENE III. *Another room in the castle.*

   [*Enter* KING, *attended.*]
KING. I have sent to seek him, and to find the
   body.
How dangerous is it that this man goes loose!
Yet must not we put the strong law on him.
He's loved of the distracted° multitude,
Who like not in their judgment but their eyes;°   5
And where 'tis so, the offender's scourge° is
   weighed,

Sc. ii: 14. replication: answer. 17. countenance: favor. 25–26. A . . . ear: a fool never understands the point of a sinister speech. 29–30. The . . . body: Hamlet deliberately bewilders his companions. 32–33. Hide . . . after: a form of the game of hide-and-seek. With these words Hamlet runs away from them.
  Sc. iii: 4. distracted: bewildered. 5. like . . . eyes: whose likings are swayed not by judgment but by looks. 6. scourge: punishment.

But never the offense. To bear° all smooth and
    even,
This sudden sending him away must seem
Deliberate pause.° Diseases desperate grown
By desperate appliance are relieved,   10
Or not at all.
[*Enter* ROSENCRANTZ.] How now! What hath be-
    fall'n?
ROS. Where the dead body is bestowed, my lord,
We cannot get from him.
    KING.   But where is he?
ROS. Without, my lord, guarded, to know your
    pleasure.
KING. Bring him before us.   15
ROS. Ho, Guildenstern! Bring in my lord.
    [*Enter* HAMLET *and* GUILDENSTERN.]
KING. Now, Hamlet, where's Polonius?
HAML. At supper.
KING. At supper! Where?   19
HAML. Not where he eats, but where he is eaten.
A certain convocation of politic worms° are e'en at
him. Your worm is your only emperor for diet. We
fat all creatures else to fat us, and we fat ourselves
for maggots. Your fat king and your lean beggar is
but variable service,° two dishes, but to one table.
That's the end.   26
KING. Alas, alas!
HAML. A man may fish with the worm that hath
eat of a king, and eat of the fish that hath fed of that
worm.
KING. What dost thou mean by this?
HAML. Nothing but to show you how a king may
go a progress° through the guts of a beggar.
KING. Where is Polonius?   34
HAML. In Heaven — send thither to see. If your
messenger find him not there, seek him i' the other
place yourself. But indeed if you find him not with-
in this month, you shall nose him as you go up the
stairs into the lobby.   39
KING. [*To some* ATTENDANTS] Go seek him there.
HAML. He will stay till you come.
             [*Exeunt* ATTENDANTS.]
KING. Hamlet, this deed, for thine especial safety,
Which we do tender,° as we dearly grieve
For that which thou hast done, must send thee
    hence
With fiery quickness. Therefore prepare thyself.   45
The bark is ready and the wind at help,°
The associates tend,° and every thing is bent°
For England.
HAML.   For England?
KING.   Aye, Hamlet.

HAML.   Good.
KING. So is it if thou knew'st our purposes.
HAML. I see a cherub that sees them. But, come,
for England! Farewell, dear Mother.   51
KING. Thy loving father, Hamlet.
HAML. My mother. Father and mother is man and
wife, man and wife is one flesh, and so, my mother.
Come, for England!   [*Exit.*]
KING. Follow him at foot,° tempt° him with
    speed aboard.   56
Delay it not, I'll have him hence tonight.
Away! For everything is sealed and done
That else leans on the affair. Pray you make haste.
    [*Exeunt* ROSENCRANTZ *and* GUILDENSTERN.]
And, England, if my love thou hold'st at aught —
As my great power thereof may give thee sense,   61
Since yet thy cicatrice° looks raw and red
After the Danish sword, and thy free awe°
Pays homage to us — thou mayst not coldly set
Our sovereign process,° which imports at full,   65
By letters congruing° to that effect,
The present° death of Hamlet. Do it, England,
For like the hectic° in my blood he rages,
And thou must cure me. Till I know 'tis done,
Howe'er my haps,° my joys were ne'er begun.   70
                  [*Exit.*]

SCENE IV. *A plain in Denmark.*

[*Enter* FORTINBRAS, *a* CAPTAIN *and* SOLDIERS,
             marching.]
FOR. Go, Captain, from me greet the Danish
    King.
Tell him that by his license Fortinbras
Craves the conveyance of a promised march°
Over his kingdom. You know the rendezvous.
If that His Majesty would aught with us,   5
We shall express our duty in his eye,°
And let him know so.
CAP.   I will do 't, my lord.
FOR. Go softly on.
            [*Exeunt* FORTINBRAS *and* SOLDIERS.]
[*Enter* HAMLET, ROSENCRANTZ, GUILDENSTERN, *and*
            others.]
HAML. Good sir, whose powers° are these?
CAP. They are of Norway, sir.   10
HAML. How purposed, sir, I pray you?
CAP. Against some part of Poland.

---

7. **bear**: make.   9. **Deliberate pause**: the result of careful
planning.   21. **convocation . . . worms**: an assembly of political-
minded worms.   25. **variable service**: choice of alternatives.
33. **go a progress**: make a state journey.   43. **tender**: regard
highly.   46. **at help**: favorable.   47. **associates tend**: your
companions are waiting. **bent**: ready.

56. **at foot**: at his heels. **tempt**: entice.   62. **cicatrice**: scar
There is nothing in the play to explain this incident.   63. **free
awe**: voluntary submission.   64–65. **coldly . . . process**: hesitate to carry out our royal command.   66. **congruing**: agreeing
67. **present**: immediate.   68. **hectic**: fever.   70. **Howe'er my
haps**: whatever may happen to me.
    Sc. iv: 3. **Craves . . . march**: asks for permission to transport
his army, as had already been promised. See II.ii.76–82.   6. **in
. . . eye**: before his eyes; i.e., in person.   9. **powers**: forces

HAML. Who commands them, sir?
CAP. The nephew to old Norway, Fortinbras.   14
HAML. Goes it against the main° of Poland, sir,
Or for some frontier?
CAP. Truly to speak, and with no addition,°
We go to gain a little patch of ground
That hath in it no profit but the name.
To pay five ducats, five, I would not farm it,   20
Nor will it yield to Norway or the Pole
A ranker° rate should it be sold in fee.°
HAML. Why, then the Polack never will defend it.
CAP. Yes, it is already garrisoned.
HAML. Two thousand souls and twenty thousand
     ducats   25
Will not debate the question of this straw.
This is the imposthume of° much wealth and peace,
That inward breaks, and shows no cause without
Why the man dies. I humbly thank you, sir.
CAP. God be wi' you, sir.   [Exit.]
ROS.   Will 't please you go, my lord?   30
HAML. I'll be with you straight. Go a little before.
                          [Exeunt all but HAMLET.]
How° all occasions do inform against° me
And spur my dull revenge! What is a man
If his chief good and market° of his time
Be but to sleep and feed? A beast, no more.   35
Sure, He that made us with such large discourse,
Looking before and after,° gave us not
That capability and godlike reason
To fust° in us unused. Now whether it be
Bestial oblivion, or some craven scruple   40
Of thinking too precisely on the event —
A thought which, quartered, hath but one part wis-
     dom
And ever three parts coward — I do not know
Why yet I live to say " This thing's to do,"   44
Sith I have cause, and will, and strength, and means
To do 't. Examples gross° as earth exhort me.
Witness this army, of such mass and charge,°
Led by a delicate and tender Prince
Whose spirit with divine ambition puffed
Makes mouths at the invisible event,°   50
Exposing what is mortal and unsure
To all that fortune, death, and danger dare,
Even for an eggshell.° Rightly to be great
Is not to stir without great argument,
But greatly to find quarrel in a straw   55
When honor's at the stake.° How stand I then,

That have a father killed, a mother stained,
Excitements of my reason and my blood,
And let all sleep while to my shame I see
The imminent death of twenty thousand men   60
That for a fantasy and trick° of fame
Go to their graves like beds, fight for a plot
Whereon the numbers cannot try the cause,°
Which is not tomb enough and continent°
To hide the slain? Oh, from this time forth,   65
My thoughts be bloody or be nothing worth!
                                          [Exit.]

SCENE V. *Elsinore. A room in the castle.*

[*Enter* QUEEN, HORATIO, *and a* GENTLEMAN.]
QUEEN. I will not speak with her.
GEN. She is importunate, indeed distract.°
Her mood will needs be pitied.
QUEEN   What would she have?
GEN. She speaks much of her father, says she hears
There's tricks° i' the world, and hems° and beats
     her heart,   5
Spurns enviously° at straws, speaks things in doubt
That carry but half-sense. Her speech is nothing,
Yet the unshaped use° of it doth move
The hearers to collection.° They aim° at it,   9
And botch° the words up fit to their own thoughts,
Which, as her winks and nods and gestures yield
     them,
Indeed would make one think there might be
     thought,
Though nothing sure, yet much unhappily.
HOR. 'Twere good she were spoken with, for she
     may strew
Dangerous conjectures in ill-breeding minds.   15
QUEEN. Let her come in.   [Exit GENTLEMAN.]
[Aside] To my sick soul, as sin's true nature is,
Each toy° seems prologue to some great amiss.°
So full of artless jealousy° is guilt,
It spills itself in fearing to be spilt.°   20
     [Re-enter GENTLEMAN, with OPHELIA.°]
OPH. Where is the beauteous Majesty of Den-
     mark?
QUEEN. How now, Ophelia!
OPH. [Sings.]
     " How should I your truelove know
          From another one?

---

15. main: mainland.   17. addition: exaggeration.   22. ranker:
richer. in fee: with possession as freehold.   27. imposthume
of: inward swelling caused by.   32–66. How . . . worth: The
soliloquy and all the dialogue after the exit of Fortinbras
are omitted in F1.   32. inform against: accuse.   34. market:
profit. 36–37. such . . . after: intelligence that enables us to consider the future and the past.   39. fust: grow musty.   46. gross:
large.   47. charge: expense.   50. Makes . . . event: mocks at the
unseen risk.   53. eggshell: i.e., worthless trifle.   53–56. Rightly
. . . stake: true greatness is a matter of fighting not for a mighty
cause but for the merest trifle when honor is concerned.

61. fantasy . . . trick: illusion and whim.   63. Whereon . . .
cause: a piece of ground so small that it would not hold the
combatants.   64. continent: large enough to contain.
   Sc. v: 2. distract: out of her mind.   5. tricks: trickery. hems:
makes significant noises.   6. Spurns enviously: kicks spitefully.
8. unshaped use: disorder.   9. collection: i.e., attempts to
find a sinister meaning. aim: guess.   10. botch: patch.   18. toy:
trifle. amiss: calamity.   19. artless jealousy: clumsy suspicion.
20. It . . . spilt: guilt reveals itself by its efforts at concealment.
20 s.d., Re-enter . . . Ophelia: Q1 notes "Enter Ophelia playing on a lute, and her hair down, singing."

By his cockle hat° and staff   25
    And his sandal shoon."°
QUEEN. Alas, sweet lady, what imports this song?
OPH. Say you? nay, pray you, mark. [*Sings.*]
    "He is dead and gone, lady,
      He is dead and gone,   30
    At his head a grass-green turf,
      At his heels a stone."

Oh, oh!
QUEEN. Nay, but, Ophelia ——
OPH.   Pray you, mark. [*Sings.*]
"White his shroud as the mountain snow ——"   35
    [*Enter* KING.]
QUEEN. Alas, look here, my lord.
OPH. [*Sings.*]
    "Larded° with sweet flowers,
    Which bewept to the grave did go
    With truelove showers."°
KING. How do you, pretty lady?   40
OPH. Well, God 'ild° you! They say the owl was
a baker's daughter.° Lord, we know what we are
but know not what we may be. God be at your table!
KING. Conceit upon her father.   45
OPH. Pray you let's have no words of this, but
when they ask you what it means, say you this
[*Sings*]:
    "Tomorrow is Saint Valentine's day,°
      All in the morning betime,
    And I a maid at your window,
      To be your Valentine.   50

    "Then up he rose, and donned his clothes,
      And dupped° the chamber door,
    Let in the maid, that out a maid
      Never departed more."   55
KING. Pretty Ophelia!
OPH. Indeed, la, without an oath, I'll make an end
on 't. [*Sings.*]
    "By Gis° and by Saint Charity,
      Alack, and fie for shame!   60
    Young men will do 't, if they come to 't,
      By cock, they are to blame.
    Quoth she, before you tumbled me,
      You promised me to wed."
He answers:

    "So would I ha' done, by yonder sun,   65
      An thou hadst not come to my bed."
KING. How long hath she been thus?
OPH. I hope all will be well. We must be patient.
But I cannot choose but weep to think they should
lay him i' the cold ground. My brother shall   70
know of it. And so I thank you for your good coun-
sel. Come, my coach! Good night, ladies, good night,
sweet ladies, good night, good night.   [*Exit.*]
KING. Follow her close,° give her good watch, I
pray you.   [*Exit* HORATIO.]
Oh, this is the poison of deep grief. It springs   76
All from her father's death. O Gertrude, Gertrude,
When sorrows come, they come not single spies,°
But in battalions! First, her father slain.
Next, your son gone, and he most violent author°
Of his own just remove. The people muddied,   81
Thick and unwholesome in their thoughts and
    whispers,
For good Polonius' death. And we have done but
    greenly°
In huggermugger° to inter him. Poor Ophelia
Divided from herself and her fair judgment,°   85
Without the which we are pictures,° or mere beasts.
Last, and as much containing as all these,
Her brother is in secret come from France,
Feeds on his wonder, keeps himself in clouds,
And wants not buzzers° to infect his ear   90
With pestilent speeches of his father's death,
Wherein necessity, of matter beggared,
Will nothing stick our person to arraign°
In ear and ear. O my dear Gertrude, this,
Like to a murdering piece,° in many places   95
Gives me superfluous death.   [*A noise within*]
QUEEN.   Alack, what noise is this?
KING. Where are my Switzers?° Let them guard
    the door.
[*Enter another* GENTLEMAN.] What is the matter?
GEN.   Save yourself, my lord.
The ocean, overpeering of his list,°
Eats not the flats° with more impetuous haste   100
Than young Laertes, in a riotous head,°
O'erbears your officers. The rabble call him lord,
And as the world were now but to begin,
Antiquity forgot, custom not known,
The ratifiers and props of every word,°   105

---

25. **cockle hat:** a hat adorned with a cockleshell worn by pilgrims.   26. **sandal shoon:** sandals, the proper footwear of pilgrims.   37. **Larded:** garnished.   39. **truelove showers:** the tears
of his faithful love.   41. **'ild** (yield): reward.   41–42. **owl . . .
daughter:** An allusion to a legend that Christ once went into a
baker's shop and asked for bread. The baker's wife gave him a
piece but was rebuked by her daughter for giving him too much.
Thereupon the daughter was turned into an owl.   48. **Saint . . .
day:** February 14, the day when birds are supposed to mate.
According to the old belief the first single man then seen by a
maid is destined to be her husband.   53. **dupped:** opened.
59–62. **Gis . . . cock:** for "Jesus" and "God," both words being
used instead of the sacred names, like the modern "Jeez" and
"Gee."

74. **close:** closely.   78. **spies:** scouts.   80. **author:** cause.
83. **done . . . greenly:** shown immature judgment.   84. **hugger-
mugger:** secret haste, "any which way."   85. **Divided . . . judgment:** no longer able to use her judgment.   86. **pictures:** lifeless
imitations.   90. **buzzers:** scandalmongers.   92–93. **Wherein . . .
arraign:** in which, knowing nothing of the true facts, he must
necessarily accuse us.   95. **murdering piece:** cannon loaded with
grapeshot.   97. **Switzers:** Swiss bodyguard.   99. **overpeering
. . . list:** looking over its boundary; i.e., flooding the mainland.
100. **Eats . . . flats:** floods not the flat country.   101. **in . . .
head:** with a force of rioters.   104–05. **Antiquity . . . word:** forgetting ancient rule and ignoring old custom, by which all promises must be maintained.

They cry " Choose we — Laertes shall be King! "
Caps, hands, and tongues applaud it to the clouds —
" Laertes shall be King, Laertes King! "
    QUEEN. How cheerfully on the false trail they cry!
Oh, this is counter,° you false Danish dogs!   110
                               [*Noise within*]
    KING. The doors are broke.
    [*Enter* LAERTES, *armed,* DANES *following.*]
    LAER. Where is this King? Sirs, stand you all
    without.
    DANES. No, let's come in.
    LAER.   I pray you, give me leave.
    DANES. We will, we will.
                [*They retire without the door.*]
    LAER. I thank you. Keep the door. O thou vile
    King,   115
Give me my father!
    QUEEN.   Calmly, good Laertes.
    LAER. That drop of blood that's calm proclaims
    me bastard,
Cries cuckold° to my father, brands the harlot°
Even here, between the chaste unsmirchèd brows
Of my true mother.
    KING.   What is the cause, Laertes,   120
That thy rebellion looks so giantlike?
Let him go, Gertrude. Do not fear° our person.
There's such divinity doth hedge a king°
That treason can but peep° to what it would,
Acts little of his will. Tell me, Laertes,   125
Why thou art thus incensed. Let him go, Gertrude.
Speak, man.
    LAER. Where is my father?
    KING.   Dead.
    QUEEN.   But not by him.
    KING. Let him demand his fill.
    LAER. How came he dead? I'll not be juggled
    with.   130
To Hell, allegiance! Vows, to the blackest devil!
Conscience and grace, to the profoundest pit!
I dare damnation. To this point I stand,
That both the worlds I give to negligence.°
Let come what comes, only I'll be revenged   135
Most throughly° for my father.
    KING.   Who shall stay you?
    LAER. My will, not all the world.
And for my means, I'll husband° them so well
They shall go far with little.
    KING.   Good Laertes,
If you desire to know the certainty   140
Of your dear father's death, is 't writ in your revenge

That, swoopstake,° you will draw both friend and
    foe,
Winner and loser?
    LAER. None but his enemies.
    KING.   Will you know them, then?
    LAER. To his good friends thus wide I'll ope my
    arms,   145
And like the kind life-rendering pelican,°
Repast° them with my blood.
    KING.   Why, now you speak
Like a good child and a true gentleman.
That I am guiltless of your father's death,
And am most sensibly° in grief for it,   150
It shall as level° to your judgment pierce
As day does to your eye.
    DANES.   [*Within*] Let her come in.
    LAER. How now! What noise is that?
    [*Re-enter* OPHELIA.] O heat, dry up my brains! Tears
    seven times salt
Burn out the sense and virtue of mine eye!   155
By Heaven, thy madness shall be paid with weight
Till our scale turn the beam.° O rose of May!°
Dear maid, kind sister, sweet Ophelia!
Oh heavens! Is 't possible a young maid's wits
Should be as mortal as an old man's life?   160
Nature is fine in love, and where 'tis fine
It sends some precious instance of itself
After the thing it loves.°
    OPH. [*Sings.*]
        " They bore him barefaced on the bier,
            Hey non nonny, nonny, hey nonny,   165
            And in his grave rained many a tear ——— "
Fare you well, my dove!
    LAER. Hadst thou thy wits and didst persuade re-
    venge,
It could not move thus.
    OPH. [*Sings.*]
        " You must sing down a-down   170
            An you call him a-down-a."
Oh, how the wheel° becomes it! It is the false stew-
ard, that stole his master's daughter.
    LAER. This nothing's more than matter.°   174
    OPH. There's° rosemary, that's for remembrance

---

110. **counter:** in the wrong direction of the scent. 118. **cuck-**
old: a husband deceived by his wife. **brands . . . harlot:** Convicted harlots were branded with a hot iron. Cf. III.iv.44.
122. **fear:** fear for. 123. **divinity . . . king:** divine protection
surrounds a king as with a hedge. 124. **peep:** look over, not
break through. 134. **That . . . negligence:** I do not care what
happens to me in this world or the next. 136. **throughly:** thoroughly. 138. **husband:** use economically.

142. **swoopstake:** "sweeping the board." 146. **life-rendering**
pelican: The mother pelican was supposed to feed her young
with blood from her own breast. 147. **Repast:** feed. 150. **sensi-**
bly: feelingly. 151. **level:** clearly. 157. **turn . . . beam:** weigh
down the beam of the scale. **rose of May:** perfection of young
beauty. See III.i.160. 161–63. **Nature . . . loves:** i.e., her love
for her father was so exquisite that she has sent her sanity
after him. Laertes, especially in moments of emotion, is
prone to use highly exaggerated speech. 172. **wheel:** explained
variously as the spinning wheel, Fortune's wheel, or the refrain.
The likeliest explanation is that she breaks into a little dance
at the words "You must sing," and that the *wheel* is the turn
as she circles round. 174. **This . . . matter:** this nonsense means
more than sense. 175–85. **There's . . . died:** In the language of
flowers, each has its peculiar meaning, and Ophelia distributes
them appropriately: for her brother rosemary (remembrance)
and pansies (thoughts); for the King fennel (flattery) and columbine

— pray you, love, remember. And there is pansies,
that's for thoughts.

LAER. A document° in madness, thoughts and remembrance fitted.　　　　　　　　　　　　　　179

OPH. There's fennel for you, and columbines.
There's rue for you, and here's some for me — we
may call it herb of grace o' Sundays. Oh, you must
wear your rue with a difference. There's a daisy. I
would give you some violets, but they withered all
when my father died. They say a' made a good
end. [*Sings.*]　　　　　　　　　　　　　　　186

　　"For bonny sweet Robin is all my joy."

LAER. Thought and affliction, passion, Hell itself,
She turns to favor° and to prettiness.

OPH. [*Sings.*]

　　"And will a' not come again?　　　　　190
　　And will a' not come again?
　　　No, no, he is dead,
　　　Go to thy deathbed,
　　He never will come again.

　　"His beard was as white as snow,　　195
　　All flaxen was his poll.°
　　　He is gone, he is gone,
　　　And we cast away moan.
　　God ha' mercy on his soul!"

And of all Christian souls, I pray God. God be wi'
you.　　　　　　　　　　　　　　　　　[*Exit.*]

LAER. Do you see this, O God?　　　　　201

KING. Laertes, I must commune with your grief,
Or you deny me right. Go but apart,
Make choice of whom your wisest friends you will,
And they shall hear and judge 'twixt you and me.
If by direct or by collateral° hand　　　　206
They find us touched,° we will our kingdom give,
Our crown, our life, and all that we call ours,
To you in satisfaction. But if not,
Be you content to lend your patience to us　　210
And we shall jointly labor with your soul
To give it due content.

LAER.　　　　　　　　Let this be so.
His means of death, his obscure funeral,°
No trophy, sword, nor hatchment° o'er his bones,
No noble rite nor formal ostentation,°　　215
Cry to be heard, as 'twere from Heaven to earth,
That I must call 't in question.

KING.　　　　　　　　　So you shall,
And where the offense is let the great ax fall.
I pray you, go with me.　　　　　[*Exeunt.*]

(thanklessness); for the Queen rue, called also herb o' grace
(sorrow), and daisy (light of love). Neither is worthy of violets
(faithfulness).　　**178. document:** instruction.　　**189. favŏr:**
charm.　　**196. flaxen . . . poll:** white as flax was his head.
206. collateral: i.e., as an accessory.　　**207. touched:** implicated.
213. obscure funeral: Men of rank were buried with much
ostentation. To bury Polonius "huggermugger" was thus an
insult to his memory and to his family. See App. 9.　　**214. hatch-
ment:** device of the coat of arms carried in a funeral and hung
up over the tomb.　　**215. formal ostentation:** ceremony properly
ordered.

SCENE VI. *Another room in the castle.*

　　　　　[*Enter* HORATIO *and a* SERVANT.]

HOR. What are they that would speak with me?

SER. Seafaring men, sir. They say they have letters
for you.

HOR. Let them come in.　　　　[*Exit* SERVANT.]
I do not know from what part of the world
I should be greeted, if not from Lord Hamlet.　　5

　　　　　[*Enter* SAILORS.]

1. SAIL. God bless you, sir.

HOR. Let Him bless thee too.

1. SAIL. He shall, sir, an 't please Him. There's a
letter for you, sir. It comes from the ambassador that
was bound for England — if your name be Horatio,
as I am let to know it is.　　　　　　　　11

HOR. [*Reads.*] "Horatio, when thou shalt have
overlooked° this, give these fellows some means° to
the King. They have letters for him. Ere we were
two days old at sea, a pirate of very warlike ap-　15
pointment° gave us chase. Finding ourselves too
slow of sail, we put on a compelled valor, and in the
grapple I boarded them. On the instant they got
clear of our ship, so I alone became their prisoner.
They have dealt with me like thieves of mercy;　20
but they knew what they did — I am to do a good
turn for them. Let the King have the letters I have
sent, and repair thou to me with as much speed as
thou wouldest fly death. I have words to speak in
thine ear will make thee dumb, yet are they　25
much too light for the bore of the matter.° These
good fellows will bring thee where I am. Rosencrantz and Guildenstern hold their course for England. Of them I have much to tell thee. Farewell.　30

　　　　　"He that thou knowest thine,
　　　　　　　　　　"HAMLET"

Come, I will make you way for these your letters,
And do 't the speedier that you may direct me
To him from whom you brought them. [*Exeunt.*]

SCENE VII. *Another room in the castle.*

　　　　　[*Enter* KING *and* LAERTES.]

KING. Now must your conscience my acquittance
seal,°
And you must put me in your heart for friend,
Sith you have heard, and with a knowing ear,
That he which hath your noble father slain
Pursued my life.

LAER.　　　　　It well appears. But tell me　5
Why you proceeded not against these feats,°
So crimeful and so capital° in nature,

Sc. vi: 13. overlooked: read.　**means:** access.　**16. appointment:** equipment.　**26. too . . . matter:** i.e., words fall short,
like a small shot fired from a cannon with too wide a bore.

Sc. vii: 1. my . . . seal: acquit me.　**6. feats:** acts.　**7. capital:** deserving death.

As by your safety, wisdom, all things else,
You mainly were stirred up.
    KING.   Oh, for two special reasons,
Which may to you perhaps seem much unsinewed,°
But yet to me they're strong. The Queen his mother
Lives almost by his looks, and for myself —   12
My virtue or my plague, be it either which —
She's so conjunctive° to my life and soul
That as the star moves not but° in his sphere,   15
I could not but by her. The other motive
Why to a public count° I might not go
Is the great love the general gender° bear him,
Who, dipping all his faults in their affection,°
Would, like the spring that turneth wood to stone,°
Convert his gyves to graces.° So that my arrows,   21
Too slightly timbered° for so loud a wind,
Would have reverted to my bow again
And not where I had aimed them.
    LAER.   And so have I a noble father lost,   25
A sister driven into desperate terms,°
Whose worth, if praises may go back again,°
Stood challenger on mount of all the age
For her perfections.° But my revenge will come.
    KING. Break not your sleeps for that. You must
        not think
That we are made of stuff so flat and dull   31
That we can let our beard be shook with danger
And think it pastime. You shortly shall hear more.°
I loved your father, and we love ourself,
And that, I hope, will teach you to imagine ——   35
[*Enter a* MESSENGER, *with letters.*] How now! What
    news?
    MESS. Letters, my lord, from Hamlet.
This to your Majesty, this to the Queen.
    KING. From Hamlet! Who brought them?
    MESS. Sailors, my lord, they say — I saw them
    not.
They were given me by Claudio, he received them
Of him that brought them.   41
    KING. Laertes, you shall hear them.
Leave us.   [*Exit* MESSENGER.]
[*Reads*] "High and Mighty, you shall know I am
set naked° on your kingdom. Tomorrow shall I beg
leave to see your kingly eyes, when I shall, first ask-
ing your pardon thereunto, recount the occasion of

my sudden and more strange return.
                                " HAMLET "
What should this mean? Are all the rest come
    back?
Or is it some abuse,° and no such thing?   50
    LAER. Know you the hand?
    KING. 'Tis Hamlet's character.° " Naked! "
And in a postscript here, he says " alone."
Can you advise me?
    LAER. I'm lost in it, my lord. But let him come.
It warms the very sickness in my heart   56
That I shall live and tell him to his teeth
" Thus didest thou."
    KING.   If it be so, Laertes —
As how should it be so, how otherwise? —
Will you be ruled by me?
    LAER.   Aye, my lord,   60
So you will not o'errule° me to a peace.
    KING. To thine own peace. If he be now returned,
As checking at° his voyage, and that he means
No more to undertake it, I will work him
To an exploit now ripe in my device,   65
Under the which he shall not choose but fall.
And for his death no wind of blame shall breathe,
But even his mother shall uncharge the practice°
And call it accident.
    LAER.   My lord, I will be ruled,
The rather if you could devise it so   70
That I might be the organ.°
    KING.   It falls right.
You have been talked of since your travel much,
And that in Hamlet's hearing, for a quality
Wherein they say you shine. Your sum of parts°
Did not together pluck such envy from him   75
As did that one, and that in my regard
Of the unworthiest siege.°
    LAER.   What part is that, my lord?
    KING. A very ribbon in the cap of youth,
Yet needful too; for youth no less becomes
The light and careless livery that it wears   80
Than settled age his sables and his weeds,°
Importing health and graveness. Two months since,
Here was a gentleman of Normandy.
I've seen myself, and served against, the French,
And they can well° on horseback; but this gallant
Had witchcraft in 't, he grew unto his seat,   86
And to such wondrous doing brought his horse
As had he been incorpsed and deminatured°
With the brave beast. So far he topped my thought°

That I, in forgery of shapes and tricks,°   90
Come short of what he did.
    LAER.   A Norman was 't?
    KING. A Norman.
    LAER. Upon my life, Lamond.
    KING.   The very same.
    LAER. I know him well. He is the brooch° indeed
And gem of all the nation.   95
    KING. He made confession° of you,
And gave you such a masterly report
For art and exercise in your defense,
And for your rapier most especial,
That he cried out 'twould be a sight indeed   100
If one could match you. The scrimers° of their na-
    tion,
He swore, had neither motion, guard, nor eye
If you opposed them. Sir, this report of his
Did Hamlet so envenom° with his envy
That he could nothing do but wish and beg   105
Your sudden coming o'er, to play with him.
Now, out of this ——
    LAER.   What out of this, my lord?
    KING. Laertes, was your father dear to you?
Or are you like the painting° of a sorrow,
A face without a heart?
    LAER.   Why ask you this?   110
    KING. Not that I think you did not love your
    father,
But that I know love is begun by time,
And that I see, in passages of proof,°
Time qualifies° the spark and fire of it.
There lives within the very flame of love   115
A kind of wick or snuff° that will abate it.
And nothing is at a like goodness still,°
For goodness, growing to a pleurisy,°
Dies in his own too much. That we would do
We should do when we would; for this " would "
    changes   120
And hath abatements and delays as many
As there are tongues, are hands, are accidents,
And then this " should " is like a spendthrift° sigh
That hurts by easing. But to the quick o' the ulcer.°
Hamlet comes back. What would you undertake
To show yourself your father's son in deed   126
More than in words?
    LAER.   To cut his throat i' the church.°

    KING. No place indeed should murder sanctuar-
    ize,°
Revenge should have no bounds. But, good Laertes,
Will you do this, keep close within your chamber.
Hamlet returned shall know you are come home.
We'll put on those° shall praise your excellence   132
And set a double varnish on the fame
The Frenchman gave you, bring you in fine° to-
    gether
And wager on your heads. He, being remiss,°   135
Most generous° and free from all contriving,°
Will not peruse the foils, so that with ease,
Or with a little shuffling, you may choose
A sword unbated,° and in a pass of practice°
Requite him for your father.
    LAER.   I will do 't,   140
And for that purpose I'll anoint my sword.
I bought an unction° of a mountebank°
So mortal that but dip a knife in it,
Where it draws blood no cataplasm° so rare,
Collected from all simples° that have virtue   145
Under the moon,° can save the thing from death
That is but scratched withal. I'll touch my point
With this contagion, that if I gall° him slightly,
It may be death.
    KING.   Let's further think of this,
Weigh what convenience both of time and means
May fit us to our shape.° If this should fail,   151
And that our drift look through our bad perform-
    ance,°
'Twere better not assayed. Therefore this project
Should have a back or second, that might hold
If this did blast in proof.° Soft! Let me see —   155
We'll make a solemn wager on your cunnings.
I ha 't.
When in your motion you are hot and dry —
As make your bouts° more violent to that end —
And that he calls for drink, I'll have prepared him
A chalice° for the nonce,° whereon but sipping,
If he by chance escape your venomed stuck,°   162
Our purpose may hold there. But stay, what noise?
[*Enter* QUEEN.] How now, sweet Queen!
    QUEEN. One woe doth tread upon another's heel,
So fast they follow. Your sister's drowned, Laertes.
    LAER. Drowned! Oh, where?   166

90. forgery . . . tricks: imagination of all kinds of fancy tricks.
shapes: fancies.   94. brooch: ornament.   96. confession:
report.   101. scrimers: fencers.   104. envenom: poison.
109. painting: i.e., imitation.   113. passages of proof: experiences which prove.   114. qualifies: diminishes.   116. snuff:
Before the invention of self-consuming wicks for candles, the
wick smoldered and formed a ball of soot which dimmed the
light and gave out a foul smoke.   117. still: always.
118. pleurisy: fullness.   123. spendthrift: wasteful, because
sighing was supposed to be bad for the blood.   124. quick
. . . ulcer: i.e., to come to the real issue. quick: flesh, sensitive
part.   127. cut . . . church: i.e., to commit murder in a holy
place, which would bring Laertes in danger of everlasting damnation; no crime could be worse.

128. sanctuarize: give sanctuary to.   132. put . . . those: set
on some.   134. fine: short.   135. remiss: careless.   136. generous: noble. contriving: plotting.   139. unbated: not blunted, with a sharp point. pass of practice: treacherous thrust.
142. unction: poison. mountebank: quack doctor.   144. cata-
plasm: poultice.   145. simples: herbs.   146. Under . . .
moon: herbs collected by moonlight were regarded as particularly potent.   148. gall: break the skin.   150–51. Weigh . . .
shape: consider the best time and method of carrying out our
plan.   152. drift . . . performance: intention be revealed through
bungling.   155. blast in proof: break in trial, like a cannon which
bursts when being tested.   159. bouts: attacks, in the fencing
match.   161. chalice: cup. nonce: occasion.   162. stuck:
thrust.

QUEEN. There is a willow grows aslant a brook
That shows his hoar° leaves in the glassy stream.
There with fantastic garlands did she come
Of crowflowers, nettles, daisies, and long purples
That liberal° shepherds give a grosser name,   171
But our cold maids do dead-men's-fingers call them.
There on the pendent° boughs her coronet weeds°
Clambering to hang, an envious sliver° broke,
When down her weedy trophies and herself   175
Fell in the weeping brook. Her clothes spread wide,
And mermaidlike awhile they bore her up —
Which time she chanted snatches of old tunes,
As one incapable° of her own distress,
Or like a creature native and indued°   180
Unto that element. But long it could not be
Till that her garments, heavy with their drink,
Pulled the poor wretch from her melodious lay°
To muddy death.
　　LAER.　　　　　Alas, then, she is drowned!
　　QUEEN. Drowned, drowned.   185
　　LAER. Too much of water hast thou, poor Ophelia,
And therefore I forbid my tears. But yet
It is our trick° — Nature her custom holds,
Let shame say what it will. When these° are gone,
The woman will be out.° Adieu, my lord.   190
I have a speech of fire that fain° would blaze
But that this folly douts° it.   [Exit.]
　　KING.　　　　　Let's follow, Gertrude.
How much I had to do to calm his rage!
Now fear I this will give it start again,
Therefore let's follow.   [Exeunt.]

Act V

SCENE I. *A churchyard.*

[Enter two CLOWNS,° *with spades, etc.]*
　1. CLO. Is she to be buried in Christian burial°
that willfully seeks her own salvation?

---

168. hoar: gray. The underside of the leaves of the willow
are silver-gray.　171. liberal: coarse-mouthed.　173. pendent:
hanging over the water. coronet weeds: wild flowers woven
into a crown.　174. envious sliver: malicious branch.
179. incapable: not realizing.　180. indued: endowed; i.e.,
a creature whose natural home is the water (*element*).
183. lay: song.　187–88. But . . . trick: it is our habit; i.e., to
break into tears at great sorrow.　189. these: i.e., my tears.
190. woman . . . out: I shall be a man again.　191. fain:
willingly.　192. douts: puts out.

　Act V, Sc. i: s.d., Clowns: countrymen. See Gen. Intro. p.
60a.　1. Christian burial: Suicides were not allowed burial in
consecrated ground, but were buried at crossroads. The gravediggers and the priest are professionally scandalized that Ophelia
should be allowed Christian burial solely because she is a
lady of the Court.

---

　2. CLO. I tell thee she is, and therefore make her
grave straight.° The crowner° hath sat on her, and
finds it Christian burial.   5
　1. CLO. How can that be, unless she drowned herself in her own defense?
　2. CLO. Why, 'tis found so.
　1. CLO. It must be " se offendendo,"° it cannot be
else. For here lies the point. If I drown myself   10
wittingly,° it argues an act, and an act hath three
branches — it is to act, to do, and to perform. Argal,°
she drowned herself wittingly.
　2. CLO. Nay, but hear you, goodman delver.°   15
　1. CLO. Give me leave. Here lies the water, good.
Here stands the man, good. If the man go to this
water and drown himself, it is will he, nill he° he
goes, mark you that; but if the water come to him
and drown him, he drowns not himself. Argal, he
that is not guilty of his own death shortens not his
own life.   22
　2. CLO. But is this law?
　1. CLO. Aye, marry, is 't, crowner's quest° law.
　2. CLO. Will you ha' the truth on 't? If this had
not been a gentlewoman, she should have been
buried out o' Christian burial.   28
　1. CLO. Why, there thou say'st. And the more pity
that great folks should have countenance° in this
world to drown or hang themselves more than their
even° Christian. Come, my spade. There is no ancient gentlemen but gardeners, ditchers, and   34
gravemakers. They hold up° Adam's profession.
　2. CLO. Was he a gentleman?
　1. CLO. A' was the first that ever bore arms.°
　2. CLO. Why, he had none.   39
　1. CLO. What, art a heathen? How dost thou understand the Scripture? The Scripture says Adam
digged. Could he dig without arms? I'll put another
question to thee. If thou answerest me not to the
purpose, confess thyself ——
　2. CLO. Go to.   45
　1. CLO. What is he that builds stronger than either
the mason, the shipwright, or the carpenter?
　2. CLO. The gallows-maker, for that frame outlives
a thousand tenants.   50
　1. CLO. I like thy wit well, in good faith. The gallows does well, but how does it well? It does well to
those that do ill. Now thou dost ill to say the gallows
is built stronger than the church; argal, the gallows
may do well to thee. To 't again, come.   56
　2. CLO. Who builds stronger than a mason, a shipwright, or a carpenter?

---

4. straight: straightway. crowner: coroner. See *T. Night*,
I.v.142n.　9. se offendendo: for *defendendo*, in self-defense.
11. wittingly: with full knowledge.　12. Argal: for the Latin
ergo, therefore.　15. delver: digger.　18. will he, nill he:
willy-nilly, whether he wishes or not.　24. quest: inquest.
30. countenance: favor.　33. even: fellow.　35. hold up: support.　38. bore arms: had a coat of arms — the outward sign of a
gentleman. See App. 9.

1. CLO. Aye, tell me that, and unyoke.°

2. CLO. Marry, now I can tell.   60

1. CLO. To 't.

2. CLO. Mass,° I cannot tell.

[*Enter* HAMLET *and* HORATIO, *afar off.*]

1. CLO. Cudgel thy brains no more about it, for your dull ass will not mend his pace with beating, and when you are asked this question next, say " A gravemaker." The houses that he makes last till Doomsday. Go, get thee to Yaughan,° fetch me   67 a stoup° of liquor.   [*Exit* SECOND CLOWN.]

[FIRST CLOWN *digs, and sings.*]

" In youth,° when I did love, did love,
    Methought it was very sweet,
To contract; oh, the time, for-a my behoove,°   71
    Oh, methought, there-a was nothing-a meet."

HAML. Has this fellow no feeling of his business, that he sings at grave-making?

HOR. Custom hath made it in him a property of easiness.°

HAML. 'Tis e'en so. The hand of little employment hath the daintier sense.°   78

1. CLO. [*Sings.*] " But age, with his stealing steps,
    Hath clawed me in his clutch,
And hath shipped me intil the land°
    As if I had never been such."   82

[*Throws up a skull.*]

HAML. That skull had a tongue in it, and could sing once. How the knave jowls° it to the ground, as if it were Cain's jawbone, that did the first murder! It might be the pate of a politician which this ass now o'erreaches° — one that would circumvent° God, might it not?

HOR. It might, my lord.   89

HAML. Or of a courtier, which could say " Good morrow, sweet lord! How dost thou, good lord? " This might be my lord Such-a-one that praised my lord Such-a-one's horse when he meant to beg it, might it not?

HOR. Aye, my lord.   95

HAML. Why, e'en so. And now my Lady Worm's chapless,° and knocked about the mazzard° with a sexton's spade. Here's fine revolution, an we had the trick to see 't. Did these bones cost no more the breeding but to play at loggats° with 'em? Mine ache to think on 't.   101

1. CLO. [*Sings.*] " A pickax and a spade, a spade,
    For and a shrouding sheet —
Oh, a pit of clay for to be made
    For such a guest is meet."   105

[*Throws up another skull.*]

HAML. There's another. Why may not that be the skull of a lawyer?° Where be his quiddities now, his quillets, his cases, his tenures, and his tricks? Why does he suffer this rude knave now to knock him about the sconce° with a dirty shovel, and will   110 not tell him of his action of battery? Hum! This fellow might be in 's time a great buyer of land, with his statutes, his recognizances, his fines, his double vouchers, his recoveries. Is this the fine° of his fines and the recovery of his recoveries, to have his   115 fine pate full of fine dirt? Will his vouchers vouch him no more of his purchases, and double ones too, than the length and breadth of a pair of indentures? The very conveyances of his lands will hardly lie in this box,° and must the inheritor himself have no   more, ha?   121

HOR. Not a jot more, my lord.

HAML. Is not parchment made of sheepskins?

HOR. Aye, my lord, and of calfskins too.

HAML. They are sheep and calves which seek out assurance in that. I will speak to this fellow. Whose grave's this, sirrah?

1. CLO. Mine, sir. [*Sings.*]
    " Oh, a pit of clay for to be made
      For such a guest is meet."   129

HAML. I think it be thine indeed, for thou liest in 't.

1. CLO. You lie out on 't, sir, and therefore 'tis not yours. For my part, I do not lie in 't, and yet it is mine.   135

HAML. Thou dost lie in 't, to be in 't and say it is thine. 'Tis for the dead, not for the quick, therefore thou liest.

1. CLO. 'Tis a quick lie, sir, 'twill away again, from me to you.   140

HAML. What man dost thou dig it for?

1. CLO. For no man, sir.

HAML. What woman, then?

1. CLO. For none, neither.

HAML. Who is to be buried in 't?   145

1. CLO. One that was a woman, sir, but, rest her soul, she's dead.

HAML. How absolute° the knave is! We must speak by the card,° or equivocation° will undo us.

TEDIOUSNESS OF LIFE

---

59. **unyoke:** finish the job, unyoking the plow oxen being the end of the day's work.   62. **Mass:** by the mass. 67. **Yaughan:** apparently an innkeeper near the Globe Theatre. 68. **stoup:** large pot. See Pl. 20e.   69–105. **In youth . . . meet:** The song which the gravedigger sings without much care for accuracy or sense was first printed in *Tottel's Miscellany*, 1558. 71. **behoove:** benefit.   75–76. **property of easiness:** careless habit.   77–78. **hand . . . sense:** those who have little to do are the most sensitive.   81. **shipped . . . land:** shoved me into the ground.   84. **jowls:** dashes.   87. **o'erreaches:** gets the better of. **circumvent:** get around. 97. **chapless:** without jaws. **mazzard:** head, a slang word; lit., drinking-bowl.   100. **loggats:** a game in which billets of wood or bones were stuck in the ground and knocked over by throwing at them.

107–18. **lawyer . . . indentures:** Hamlet strings out a number of the legal phrases loved by lawyers: *quiddities:* subtle arguments; *quillets:* quibbles; *tenures:* titles to property; *tricks:* knavery; *statutes:* bonds; *recognizances:* obligations; *fines:* conveyances; *vouchers:* guarantors; *recoveries:* transfers; *indentures:* agreements. See App. 6 and Pl. 11a. 110. **sconce:** head; lit., blockhouse.   114. **fine:** ending. 120. **box:** coffin.   148. **absolute:** exact.   149. **by . . . card:** exactly. The card is the mariner's compass. **equivocation:** speak-

By the Lord, Horatio, this three years I have taken note of it — the age is grown so picked° that the toe of the peasant comes so near the heel of the courtier, he galls his kibe.° How long hast thou been a grave-maker?   154

1. CLO. Of all the days i' the year, I came to 't that day that our last King Hamlet o'ercame Fortinbras.

HAML. How long is that since?

1. CLO. Cannot you tell that? Every fool can tell that. It was that very day that young Hamlet was born, he that is mad, and sent into England.   164

HAML. Aye, marry, why was he sent into England?

1. CLO. Why, because a' was mad. A' shall recover his wits there, or, if a' do not, 'tis no great matter there.

HAML. Why?

1. CLO. 'Twill not be seen in him there — there the men are as mad as he.   170

HAML. How came he mad?

1. CLO. Very strangely, they say.

HAML. How "strangely"?

1. CLO. Faith, e'en with losing his wits.

HAML. Upon what ground?

1. CLO. Why, here in Denmark. I have been sexton here, man and boy, thirty years.°

HAML. How long will a man lie i' the earth ere he rot?   179

1. CLO. I' faith, if a' be not rotten before a' die — as we have many pocky° corses nowadays that will scarce hold the laying in — a' will last you some eight year or nine year. A tanner will last you nine year.

HAML. Why he more than another?   185

1. CLO. Why, sir, his hide is so tanned with his trade that a' will keep out water a great while, and your water is a sore decayer of your whoreson° dead body. Here's a skull now. This skull has lain in the earth three and twenty years.   191

HAML. Whose was it?

1. CLO. A whoreson mad fellow's it was. Whose do you think it was?

HAML. Nay, I know not.   195

1. CLO. A pestilence on him for a mad rogue! A' poured a flagon of Rhenish on my head once. This same skull, sir, was Yorick's skull, the King's jester.

HAML. This?

1. CLO. E'en that.

HAML. Let me see. [*Takes the skull.*] Alas, poor Yorick! I knew him, Horatio — a fellow of infinite jest, of most excellent fancy. He hath borne me on his back a thousand times, and now how ab- 205 horred in my imagination it is! My gorge rises° at it. Here hung those lips that I have kissed I know not how oft. Where be your gibes now? Your gam-bols? Your songs? Your flashes of merriment that were wont to set the table on a roar? Not one 210 now, to mock your own grinning? Quite chop-fallen?° Now get you to my lady's chamber and tell her, let her paint an inch thick, to this favor° she must come — make her laugh at that. Prithee, Hora-tio, tell me one thing.

HOR. What's that, my lord?   217

HAML. Dost thou think Alexander looked o' this fashion i' the earth?

HOR. E'en so.

HAML. And smelt so? Pah!

[*Puts down the skull.*]

HOR. E'en so, my lord.

HAML. To what base uses we may return, Horatio! Why may not imagination trace the noble dust of Alexander till he find it stopping a bunghole?°

HOR. 'Twere to consider too curiously° to consider so.   228

HAML. No, faith, not a jot, but to follow him thither with modesty° enough and likelihood to lead it. As thus: Alexander died, Alexander was buried, Alexander returneth into dust; the dust is earth; of earth we make loam;° and why of that loam, whereto he was converted, might they not stop a beer barrel?   235

"Imperious Caesar, dead and turned to clay,
    Might stop a hole to keep the wind away.
  Oh, that that earth which kept the world in awe
    Should patch a wall to expel the winter's flaw!"°
But soft! But soft! Aside — here comes the King.

[*Enter* PRIESTS,° *etc., in procession; the corpse of*
Ophelia, LAERTES *and* MOURNERS *following;*
    KING, QUEEN, *their trains, etc.*]

The Queen, the courtiers — who is this they follow?
And with such maimèd° rites? This doth betoken°
The corse they follow did with desperate hand 243
Fordo° its own life. 'Twas of some estate.°

Couch° we awhile, and mark.

        [*Retiring with* HORATIO.]

LAER. What ceremony else?

HAML. That is Laertes, a very noble youth. Mark.

LAER. What ceremony else?   248

1. PRIEST. Her obsequies have been as far enlarged
As we have warranty.° Her death was doubtful,
And but that great command o'ersways the order,°
She should in ground unsanctified have lodged
Till the last trumpet; for° charitable prayers,
Shards,° flints, and pebbles should be thrown on her.
Yet here she is allowed her virgin crants,°   255
Her maiden strewments° and the bringing home
Of bell and burial.

  LAER. Must there no more be done?

  1. PRIEST.   No more be done.
We should profane the service of the dead
To sing a requiem and such rest to her   260
As to peace-parted souls.°

  LAER.   Lay her i' the earth.
And from her fair and unpolluted flesh
May violets spring! I tell thee, churlish priest,
A ministering angel shall my sister be
When thou liest howling.

  HAML.   What, the fair Ophelia! 265

  QUEEN. [*Scattering flowers*] Sweets to the sweet.
  Farewell!
I hoped thou shouldst have been my Hamlet's wife,
I thought thy bride bed to have decked, sweet maid,
And not have strewed thy grave.

  LAER.   Oh, treble woe
Fall ten times treble on that cursèd head   270
Whose wicked deed thy most ingenious sense°
Deprived thee of! Hold off the earth a while
Till I have caught her once more in mine arms.

           [*Leaps into the grave.*]
Now pile your dust upon the quick° and dead
Till of this flat a mountain you have made   275
To o'ertop old Pelion° or the skyish° head
Of blue Olympus.

  HAML. [*Advancing*] What is he whose grief
Bears such an emphasis? Whose phrase of sorrow
Conjures the wandering stars and makes them
  stand°
Like wonder-wounded hearers? This is I,   280
Hamlet the Dane.   [*Leaps into the grave.*]

LAER. The Devil take thy soul!

          [*Grappling with him*]

HAML.   Thou pray'st not well.
I prithee, take thy fingers from my throat,
For though I am not splenitive° and rash,
Yet have I in me something dangerous,   285
Which let thy wisdom fear. Hold off thy hand.

  KING. Pluck them asunder.

  QUEEN.   Hamlet, Hamlet!

  ALL.   Gentlemen——

  HOR. Good my lord, be quiet.

        [*The* ATTENDANTS *part them,
and they come out of the grave.*]

  HAML. Why, I will fight with him upon this
  theme
Until my eyelids will no longer wag.   290

  QUEEN. O my son, what theme?

  HAML. I loved Ophelia. Forty thousand brothers
Could not, with all their quantity of love,
Make up my sum. What wilt thou do for her?

  KING. Oh, he is mad, Laertes.   295

  QUEEN. For love of God, forbear him.°

  HAML. 'Swounds,° show me what thou'lt do.
Woo 't weep? Woo 't fight? Woo 't fast? Woo 't tear
  thyself?
Woo 't drink up eisel?° Eat a crocodile?
I'll do 't. Dost thou come here to whine?   300
To outface° me with leaping in her grave?
Be buried quick with her, and so will I.
And if thou prate of mountains, let them throw
Millions of acres on us, till our ground,
Singeing his pate against the burning zone, 305
Make Ossa° like a wart! Nay, an thou 'lt mouth,
I'll rant as well as thou.

  QUEEN.   This is mere madness.
And thus awhile the fit will work on him.
Anon, as patient as the female dove
When that her golden couplets° are disclosed,° 310
His silence will sit drooping.

  HAML.   Hear you, sir.
What is the reason that you use me thus?
I loved you ever. But it is no matter,
Let Hercules himself do what he may,
The cat will mew and dog will have his day.° [*Exit.*] 314

  KING. I pray thee, good Horatio, wait upon him.

           [*Exit* HORATIO.]
[*To* LAERTES] Strengthen your patience in our last
  night's speech.
We'll put the matter to the present push.°

---

245. Couch: lie down. 249–50. Her . . . warranty: the funeral rites have been as complete as may be allowed. 251. but . . . order: if the King's command had not overruled the proper procedure. 253. for: instead of. 254. Shards: pieces of broken crockery. 255. crants: wreaths of flowers — a sign that she had died unwed. 256. maiden strewments: the flowers strewn on the corpse of a maiden. 261. peace-parted souls: souls which departed in peace, fortified with the rites of the Church. 271. most . . . sense: lively intelligence. 274. quick: living. 276. Pelion: When the giants fought against the gods in order to reach Heaven, they tried to pile Mount Pelion and Mount Ossa on Mount Olympus, the highest mountain in Greece. skyish: reaching the sky. 279. stand: stand still.

284. splenitive: hot-tempered. 296. forbear him: leave him alone. 297–307. 'Swounds . . . thou: Hamlet in his excitement cries out that if Laertes wishes to make extravagant boasts of what he will do to show his sorrow, he will be even more extravagant. 299. eisel: vinegar. 301. outface: browbeat. 306. Ossa: See l. 276, n. 310. couplets: eggs, of which the dove lays two only. disclosed: hatched. 314-15. Let . . . day: i.e., let this ranting hero have his turn; mine will come sometime. 318. push: test; lit., thrust of a pike.

Good Gertrude, set some watch over your son.
This grave shall have a living monument.°   320
An hour of quiet shortly shall we see,
Till then, in patience our proceeding be.   [*Exeunt.*]

SCENE II. *A hall in the castle.*

[*Enter* HAMLET *and* HORATIO.]

HAML. So much for this, sir. Now shall you see
    the other.
You do remember all the circumstance?
    HOR. Remember it, my lord!
    HAML. Sir, in my heart there was a kind of fight-
    ing
That would not let me sleep. Methought I lay   5
Worse than the mutines in the bilboes.° Rashly,
And praised be rashness for it, let us know,
Our indiscretion sometime serves us well
When our deep plots do pall.° And that should
    learn° us
There's a divinity that shapes our ends,   10
Roughhew them how we will.°
    HOR.   That is most certain.
    HAML. Up from my cabin,
My sea gown° scarfed° about me, in the dark
Groped I to find out them,° had my desire,
Fingered their packet, and in fine withdrew   15
To mine own room again, making so bold,
My fears forgetting manners, to unseal
Their grand commission where I found, Horatio —
Oh royal knavery! — an exact command,
Larded° with many several sorts of reasons,   20
Importing Denmark's health and England's too,
With, ho! such bugs° and goblins in my life°
That, on the supervise,° no leisure bated,°
No, not to stay the grinding of the ax,
My head should be struck off.
    HOR.   Is 't possible?   25
    HAML. Here's the commission. Read it at more
    leisure
But wilt thou hear me how I did proceed?
    HOR. I beseech you.
    HAML. Being thus benetted round with vil-
    lainies —
Ere I could make a prologue to my brains,   30
They had begun the play — I sat me down,
Devised a new commission, wrote it fair.
I once did hold it, as our statists° do,

A baseness to write fair, and labored much
How to forget that learning, but, sir, now   35
It did me yeoman's service.° Wilt thou know
The effect of what I wrote?
    HOR.   Aye, good my lord.
    HAML. An earnest conjuration from the King,
As England was his faithful tributary,
As love between them like the palm might flourish,
As peace should still her wheaten garland wear   41
And stand a comma 'tween their amities,°
And many suchlike " Ases "° of great charge,°
That, on the view and knowing of these contents,
Without debatement° further, more or less,   45
He should the bearers put to sudden death,
Not shriving time allowed.°
    HOR.   How was this sealed?
    HAML. Why, even in that was Heaven ordinant.°
I had my father's signet in my purse,
Which was the model° of that Danish seal —   50
Folded the writ° up in the form of the other,
Subscribed° it, gave 't the impression,° placed it
    safely,
The changeling° never known. Now the next day
Was our sea fight, and what to this was sequent°
Thou know'st already.   55
    HOR. So Guildenstern and Rosencrantz go to 't.
    HAML. Why, man, they did make love to this em-
    ployment.
They are not near my conscience, their defeat°
Does by their own insinuation° grow.
'Tis dangerous when the baser nature comes   60
Between the pass and fell incensèd points
Of mighty opposites.°
    HOR.   Why, what a King is this!
    HAML. Does it not, think'st thee, stand me now
    upon —
He that hath killed my King and whored my
    mother,
Popped in between the election and my hopes,°   65

Thrown out his angle° for my proper° life,
And with such cozenage° — is 't not perfect con-
science,
To quit° him with this arm? And is 't not to be
damned,
To let this canker° of our nature come
In further evil?   70
  HOR. It must be shortly known to him from Eng-
land
What is the issue of the business there.
  HAML. It will be short. The interim° is mine,
And a man's life's no more than to say " One."
But I am very sorry, good Horatio,   75
That to Laertes I forgot myself,
For by the image of my cause I see
The portraiture of his. I'll court his favors.
But, sure, the bravery° of his grief did put me
Into a towering passion.
  HOR.   Peace! Who comes here?   80

    [*Enter* OSRIC.°]

  OSR. Your lordship is right welcome back to Denmark.
  HAML. I humbly thank you, sir. Dost know this
water fly?°
  HOR. No, my good lord.   84
  HAML. Thy state is the more gracious,° for 'tis a
vice to know him. He hath much land, and fertile.
Let a beast be lord of beasts and his crib shall stand
at the King's mess.° 'Tis a chough,° but, as I say,
spacious° in the possession of dirt.   90
  OSR. Sweet lord, if your lordship were at leisure, I should impart a thing to you from His Majesty.
  HAML. I will receive it, sir, with all diligence of
spirit. Put your bonnet to his right use,° 'tis for the
head.
  OSR. I thank your lordship, it is very hot.   97
  HAML. No, believe me, 'tis very cold. The wind is
northerly.
  OSR. It is indifferent° cold, my lord, indeed.   100
  HAML. But yet methinks it is very sultry and hot,
for my complexion ——
  OSR. Exceedingly, my lord. It is very sultry, as
'twere — I cannot tell how. But, my lord, His Majes-

ty bade me signify to you that he has laid a great
wager on your head. Sir, this is the matter ——
  HAML. I beseech you, remember ——   108
    [HAMLET *moves him to put on his hat.*]
  OSR. Nay, good my lord, for mine ease, in good
faith. Sir, here is newly come to Court Laertes — believe me, an absolute° gentleman, full of most excellent differences,° of very soft society° and great
showing.° Indeed, to speak feelingly° of him, he is
the card or calendar of gentry,° for you shall find in
him the continent of what part a gentleman would
see.°   116
  HAML. Sir,° his definement suffers no perdition in
you, though I know to divide him inventorially
would dizzy the arithmetic of memory, and yet but   120
yaw neither, in respect of his quick sail. But in
the verity of extolment, I take him to be a soul of
great article, and his infusion of such dearth and
rareness as, to make true diction of him, his semblable is his mirror, and who else would trace him,
his umbrage — nothing more.   125
  OSR. Your lordship speaks most infallibly of
him.
  HAML. The concernancy,° sir? Why do we wrap
the gentleman in our more rawer breath?°
  OSR. Sir?°   129
  HOR. Is 't not possible to understand in another
tongue? You will do 't, sir, really.
  HAML. What imports the nomination° of this
gentleman?
  OSR. Of Laertes?   135
  HOR. His purse is empty already, all's golden
words are spent.
  HAML. Of him, sir.
  OSR. I know you are not ignorant ——   139
  HAML. I would you did, sir. Yet, in faith, if you
did, it would not much approve° me. Well, sir?

---

66. angle: fishing rod and line. **proper:** own. **67. cozenage:** cheating. **68. quit:** pay back. **69. canker:** maggot. See I.iii.39. **73. interim:** interval; between now and the news from England.
79. bravery: excessive show. **80 s.d.,** Osric: Osric is a specimen
of the fashionable, effeminate courtier. He dresses prettily and
talks the jargon of his class, which at this time affected elaborate
and allusive metaphors and at all costs avoided saying plain things
plainly.   **83. water fly:** a useless little creature that flits about.
85. Thy . . . gracious: you are in the better state. **88–89. Let . . .
mess:** i.e., any man, however low, who has wealth enough will
find a good place at Court. **crib:** manger. **mess:** table.
89. chough: jackdaw.   **90. spacious:** wealthy.   **95. Put . . .
use:** i.e., put your hat on your head. Osric is so nice-mannered
that he cannot bring himself to wear his hat in the presence of
the Prince. See App. 7.   **100. indifferent:** moderately.

111. absolute: perfect.   **112. differences:** qualities peculiar to himself. **soft society:** gentle breeding.   **112–13. great showing:** distinguished appearance.   **113. feelingly:** with proper appreciation.
114. card . . . gentry: the very fashion plate of what a gentleman
should be.   **115–16. continent . . . see:** all the parts that should be
in a perfect gentleman.   **117–25. Sir . . . more:** Hamlet retorts in
similar but even more extravagant language. This is too much for
Osric (and for most modern readers). Hamlet's words may be paraphrased: "Sir, the description of this perfect gentleman loses
nothing in your account of him; though I realize that if one
were to try to enumerate his excellences, it would exhaust our
arithmetic, and yet" — here he changes the image to one of sailing — "we should still lag behind him as he outsails us. But in
the true vocabulary of praise, I take him to be a soul of the
greatest worth, and his perfume" — i.e., his personal essence —
"so scarce and rare that to speak truly of him, the only thing
like him is his own reflection in his mirror, and everyone else
who tries to follow him merely his shadow." **yaw:** fall off from
the course laid. **verity . . . extolment:** in true praise. **infusion:**
essence. **semblable:** resemblance. **trace:** follow. **umbrage:** shadow.
127. concernancy: i.e., what is all this talk about?   **127–28. Why
. . . breath:** why do we discuss the gentleman with our inadequate voices?   **129. Sir:** Osric is completely baffled.   **133. nomination:** naming.   **141. approve:** commend.

OSR. You are not ignorant of what excellence
Laertes is —   144

HAML. I dare not confess that, lest I should compare with him in excellence, but to know a man well
were to know himself.

OSR. I mean, sir, for his weapon,° but in the im-
putation° laid on him by them, in his meed° he's
unfellowed.°   150

HAML. What's his weapon?

OSR. Rapier and dagger.

HAML. That's two of his weapons, but, well.

OSR. The King, sir, hath wagered with him six
Barbary horses, against the which he has im-   155
poned,° as I take it, six French rapiers and poniards,
with their assigns,° as girdle, hanger,° and so —
three of the carriages, in faith, are very dear to
fancy,° very responsive to° the hilts, most delicate
carriages, and of very liberal conceit.°   160

HAML. What call you the carriages?

HOR. I knew you must be edified by the margent°
ere you had done.

OSR. The carriages, sir, are the hangers.   164

HAML. The phrase would be more germane° to
the matter if we could carry a cannon by our sides.
I would it might be hangers till then. But, on — six
Barbary horses against six French swords, their assigns, and three liberal-conceited carriages. That's
the French bet against the Danish. Why is this "imponed," as you call it?   171

OSR. The King, sir, hath laid, sir, that in a dozen
passes between yourself and him, he shall not exceed you three hits. He hath laid on twelve for
nine,° and it would come to immediate trial if your
lordship would vouchsafe the answer.

HAML. How if I answer no?   177

OSR. I mean, my lord, the opposition of your person in trial.

HAML. Sir, I will walk here in the hall. If it please
His Majesty, it is the breathing-time of day with
me.° Let the foils be brought, the gentleman willing,
and the King hold his purpose, I will win for him
an I can. If not, I will gain nothing but my shame
and the odd hits.   185

OSR. Shall I redeliver you e'en so?

HAML. To this effect, sir, after what flourish°
your nature will.

OSR. I commend my duty to your lordship.   189

HAML. Yours, yours. [*Exit* OSRIC.] He does well to
commend it himself, there are no tongues else for 's
turn.

HOR. This lapwing° runs away with the shell on
his head.

HAML. He did comply with his dug° before he
sucked it. Thus has he — and many more of the
same breed that I know the drossy° age dotes on —
only got the tune of the time and outward habit of
encounter,° a kind of yesty collection° which carries
them through and through the most fond° and   200
winnowed° opinions — and do but blow them to
their trial, the bubbles are out.°

[*Enter a* LORD.]

LORD. My lord, His Majesty commended him to
you by young Osric, who brings back to him that you
attend him in the hall. He sends to know if your
pleasure hold to play with Laertes, or that you will
take longer time.   207

HAML. I am constant to my purposes, they follow
the King's pleasure. If his fitness speaks, mine is
ready, now or whensoever, provided I be so able as
now.   211

LORD. The King and Queen and all are coming
down.

HAML. In happy time.°

LORD. The Queen desires you to use some gentle
entertainment° to Laertes before you fall to play.

HAML. She well instructs me.   [*Exit* LORD.]

HOR. You will lose this wager, my lord.   219

HAML. I do not think so. Since he went into
France I have been in continual practice, I shall win
at the odds. But thou wouldst not think how ill all's
here about my heart — but it is no matter.

HOR. Nay, good my lord —   224

HAML. It is but foolery, but it is such a kind of
gaingiving° as would perhaps trouble a woman.

HOR. If your mind dislike anything, obey it. I will
forestall their repair hither and say you are not fit.

HAML. Not a whit, we defy augury.° There's   230
special providence in the fall of a sparrow.° If it be
now, 'tis not to come; if it be not to come, it will be
now; if it be not now, yet it will come. The read-

193. **lapwing:** a pretty, lively little bird. It is so lively that it can
run about the moment it is hatched.   195. **did . . . dug:** was
ceremonious with the nipple; i.e., behaved in this fantastic way
from his infancy. See II.ii.389.   197. **drossy:** scummy, frivolous.
198–99. **tune . . . encounter:** i.e., they sing the same tune as
everyone else and have the same society manners.   199. **yesty
collection:** frothy catchwords.   200. **fond:** foolish.   201. **winnowed:** light as chaff. Winnowing is the process of fanning
the chaff from the grain.   201–02. **do . . . out:** force them to
make sense of their words and they are deflated, as Hamlet
has just deflated Osric.   214. **In . . . time:** at a good moment.   215–16. **gentle entertainment:** kindly treatment; i.e., be
reconciled after the brawl in the churchyard.   226. **gaingiv-
ing:** misgiving.   230. **augury:** omens.   231. **special . . . sparrow:** The idea comes from Matthew 10:29. "Are not two
sparrows sold for a farthing? and one of them shall not fall to
the ground without your Father."

148. **his weapon:** i.e., skill with his weapon.   149. **imputation:**
reputation. **meed:** merit.   150. **unfellowed:** without an equal.
156. **imponed:** laid down as a stake.   157. **assigns:** that which
goes with them. **hanger:** straps by which the scabbard was hung
from the belt; for specimens, see Pl. 3c.   158–59. **dear to fancy:**
of beautiful design.   159. **responsive to:** matching.   160. **liberal
conceit:** elaborately artistic.   162. **edified . . . margent:** informed by the notes. In Shakespeare's time the notes were often
printed in the margin.   165. **germane:** related.   174–75. **twelve
. . . nine:** See App. 25.   181–82. **breathing-time . . . me:** time
when I take exercise.   187. **flourish:** fanfare, elaborate phrasing.

iness is all. Since no man has aught of what he leaves,
what is 't to leave betimes? Let be.   235
[*Enter* KING, QUEEN, LAERTES, *and* LORDS, OSRIC *and*
other ATTENDANTS *with foils; a table and flagons of*
wine on it.]
   KING. Come, Hamlet, come, and take this hand
      from me.
            [*The* KING *puts* LAERTES' *hand into* HAMLET'*s.*]
   HAML. Give me your pardon, sir. I've done you
      wrong,
But pardon 't, as you are a gentleman.
This presence° knows,
And you must needs have heard, how I am pun-
      ished   240
With sore distraction. What I have done
That might your nature, honor, and exception°
Roughly awake, I here proclaim was madness.
Was 't Hamlet wronged Laertes? Never Hamlet.
If Hamlet from himself be ta'en away,°   245
And when he's not himself does wrong Laertes,
Then Hamlet does it not, Hamlet denies it.
Who does it, then? His madness. If 't be so,
Hamlet is of the faction that is wronged,
His madness is poor Hamlet's enemy.   250
Sir, in this audience
Let my disclaiming from a purposed evil°
Free me so far in your most generous thoughts
That I have shot mine arrow o'er the house,
And hurt my brother.
      LAER.   I am satisfied in nature,   255
Whose motive, in this case, should stir me most
To my revenge. But in my terms of honor
I stand aloof, and will no reconcilement
Till by some elder masters of known honor
I have a voice and precedent of peace   260
To keep my name ungored.° But till that time
I do receive your offered love like love
And will not wrong it.
      HAML.   I embrace it freely,
And will this brother's wager frankly play.
Give us the foils. Come on.
      LAER.   Come, one for me.   265
   HAML. I'll be your foil,° Laertes. In mine ignor-
      ance
Your skill shall, like a star i' the darkest night,
Stick° fiery off indeed.
      LAER.   You mock me, sir.
   HAML. No, by this hand.

239. presence: the whole Court.   242. exception: resentment.
245. If . . . away: i.e., Hamlet mad is not Hamlet.   252. Let . . .
evil: let my declaration that I did not intend any harm.
255-61. I . . . ungored: I bear you no grudge so far as concerns
my personal feelings, which would most readily move me to vengeance; but as this matter touches my honor, I cannot accept
your apology until I have been assured by those expert in matters
of honor that I may so do without loss of reputation.   266. foil:
Hamlet puns on the other meaning of foil — tin foil set behind
a gem to give it luster.   268. Stick . . . off: Shine out.

KING. Give them the foils, young Osric. Cousin
      Hamlet,   270
You know the wager?
   HAML.   Very well, my lord.
Your Grace has laid the odds o' the weaker side.
   KING. I do not fear it, I have seen you both.
But since he is bettered,° we have therefore odds.
   LAER. This is too heavy, let me see another.   275
   HAML. This likes° me well. These foils have all a
length?°   [*They prepare to play.*]
   OSR. Aye, my good lord.
   KING. Set me the stoups° of wine upon that table.
If Hamlet give the first or second hit,
Or quit° in answer of the third exchange,   280
Let all the battlements their ordnance fire.
The King shall drink to Hamlet's better breath,
And in the cup a union° shall he throw
Richer than that which four successive kings   284
In Denmark's crown have worn. Give me the cups,
And let the kettle° to the trumpet speak,
The trumpet to the cannoneer without,
The cannon to the Heavens, the Heaven to earth,
"Now the King drinks to Hamlet." Come, begin,
And you, the judges, bear a wary eye.   290
   HAML. Come on, sir.
   LAER.   Come, my lord.   [*They play.*]
   HAML.   One.
   LAER.   No.
   HAML.   Judgment.
   OSR. A hit, a very palpable° hit.
   LAER.   Well, again.
   KING. Stay, give me drink. Hamlet, this pearl is
      thine° —
Here's to thy health.
      [*Trumpets sound, and cannon shot off within.*]
                        Give him the cup.   294
   HAML. I'll play this bout first. Set it by a while.
Come. [*They play.*] Another hit, what say you?
   LAER. A touch, a touch, I do confess.
   KING. Our son shall win.
   QUEEN.   He's fat° and scant of breath.
Here, Hamlet, take my napkin, rub thy brows.
The Queen carouses to thy fortune, Hamlet.   300
   HAML. Good madam!
   KING.   Gertrude, do not drink.
   QUEEN. I will, my lord, I pray you pardon me.
                                          [*She drinks.*]
   KING. [*Aside*] It is the poisoned cup, it is too late.
   HAML. I dare not drink yet, madam — by and by.
   QUEEN. Come, let me wipe thy face.   305
   LAER. My lord, I'll hit him now.

274. bettered: considered your superior.   276. likes: pleases.
have . . . length: are all of equal length.   278. stoups: drinking-
vessels.   280. quit: strike back.   283. union: a large pearl.
286. kettle: kettledrum.   292. palpable: clear.   293. this . . .
thine: With these words the King drops the poisoned pearl
into the cup intended for Hamlet.   298. fat: out of condition.

KING.   I do not think 't.

LAER. [*Aside*] And yet 'tis almost against my
    conscience.

HAML. Come, for the third, Laertes. You but
    dally.°

I pray you pass with your best violence,

I am afeard you make a wanton of me.°   310

    LAER. Say you so? Come on.   [*They play.*]

OSR. Nothing, neither way.

LAER. Have at you now!

[LAERTES *wounds* HAMLET; *then, in scuffling, they*
    change rapiers,° and HAMLET *wounds* LAERTES.]

KING.   Part them, they are incensed.

HAML. Nay, come, again.   [*The* QUEEN *falls.*]

OSR.   Look to the Queen there, ho!

HOR. They bleed on both sides. How is it, my
    lord?   315

OSR. How is 't, Laertes?

LAER. Why, as a woodcock to mine own springe,°
    Osric,

I am justly killed with mine own treachery.

HAML. How does the Queen?

KING.   She swounds to see them bleed.

QUEEN. No, no, the drink, the drink! — O my dear
    Hamlet —   320

The drink, the drink! I am poisoned.   [*Dies.*]

HAML. Oh, villainy! Ho! Let the door be locked.

Treachery! Seek it out.   [LAERTES *falls.*]

LAER. It is here, Hamlet. Hamlet, thou art slain.

No medicine in the world can do thee good,   325

In thee there is not half an hour of life.

The treacherous instrument is in thy hand,

Unbated and envenomed. The foul practice

Hath turned itself on me. Lo, here I lie

Never to rise again. Thy mother's poisoned.   330

I can no more. The King, the King's to blame.

HAML. The point envenomed too!

Then, venom, to thy work.   [*Stabs the* KING.]

ALL. Treason! Treason!   334

KING. Oh, yet defend me, friends, I am but hurt.

HAML. Here, thou incestuous, murderous,
    damnèd Dane,

Drink off this potion. Is thy union° here?

Follow my mother.   [KING *dies.*]

LAER.   He is justly served.

It is a poison tempered° by himself.

Exchange forgiveness with me, noble Hamlet.   340

Mine and my father's death come not upon thee,°

Nor thine on me!   [*Dies.*]

HAML. Heaven make thee free of it!° I follow
    thee.

I am dead, Horatio. Wretched Queen, adieu!

You that look pale and tremble at this chance,   345

That are but mutes or audience to this act,

Had I but time — as this fell° sergeant,° Death,

Is strict in his arrest — oh, I could tell you ——

But let it be. Horatio, I am dead,

Thou livest. Report me and my cause aright   350

To the unsatisfied.°

HOR.   Never believe it.

I am more an antique Roman° than a Dane.

Here's yet some liquor left.

HAML.   As thou 'rt a man,

Give me the cup. Let go — by Heaven, I'll have 't.

O good Horatio, what a wounded name,   355

Things standing thus unknown, shall live behind
    me!

If thou didst ever hold me in thy heart,

Absent thee from felicity a while,

And in this harsh world draw thy breath in pain

To tell my story. [*March afar off, and shot within*]
          What warlike noise is this?   360

OSR. Young Fortinbras, with conquest come from
    Poland,

To the ambassadors of England gives

This warlike volley.

HAML.   Oh, I die, Horatio,

The potent poison quite o'ercrows° my spirit.

I cannot live to hear the news from England,   365

But I do prophesy the election° lights

On Fortinbras. He has my dying voice.°

So tell him, with the occurrents, more and less,

Which have solicited.° The rest is silence.   [*Dies.*]

HOR. Now cracks a noble heart. Good night,
    sweet Prince,   370

And flights of angels sing thee to thy rest!
          [*March within.*]

Why does the drum come hither?

[*Enter* FORTINBRAS, *and the* ENGLISH AMBASSADORS,
    with drum, colors, and ATTENDANTS.]

FOR. Where is this sight?

HOR.   What is it you would see?

If aught of woe or wonder, cease your search.   374

FOR. This quarry cries on havoc.° O proud Death,

What feast is toward° in thine eternal cell

That thou so many princes at a shot

So bloodily hast struck?

I. AMB.   The sight is dismal,

And our affairs from England come too late.   379

The ears are senseless that should give us hearing,

---

347. fell: dread. **sergeant:** the officer of the Court who made
arrests. **351. unsatisfied:** who do not know the truth.
352. antique Roman: like Cato and Brutus, who killed themselves
rather than survive in a world which was unpleasing to them.
364. o'ercrows: overpowers. **366. election:** as King of Denmark. See l. 65 above. **367. voice:** support. **368–69. occurrents . . . solicited:** events great and small which have caused
me to act. **375. quarry . . . havoc:** heap of slain denotes a
pitiless slaughter. See *Caesar*, III.i.273. **376. toward:** being
prepared.

---

308. dally: play. **310. make . . . me:** treat me like a child by
letting me win. **313. s.d., they . . . rapiers:** See App. 25 and
Pl. 22l. **317. springe:** snare. **337. union:** pearl, as in l. 283.
339. tempered: mixed. **341. come . . . thee:** are not on your
head. **343. Heaven . . . it:** God forgive you.

To tell him his commandment is fulfilled,
That Rosencrantz and Guildenstern are dead.
Where should we have our thanks?

HOR.   Not from his mouth
Had it the ability of life to thank you.
He never gave commandment for their death. 385
But since, so jump° upon this bloody question,°
You from the Polack wars, and you from England,
Are here arrived, give order that these bodies
High on a stage be placèd to the view,
And let me speak to the yet unknowing world 390
How these things came about. So shall you hear
Of carnal, bloody, and unnatural acts,
Of accidental judgments, casual slaughters,
Of deaths put on by cunning and forced cause,
And, in this upshot, purposes mistook 395
Fall'n on the inventors' heads.° All this can I
Truly deliver.

FOR.   Let us haste to hear it,
And call the noblest to the audience.
For me, with sorrow I embrace my fortune. 399

I have some rights of memory° in this kingdom,
Which now to claim my vantage° doth invite me.

HOR. Of that I shall have also cause to speak,
And from his mouth whose voice will draw on
    more.°
But let this same be presently performed,
Even while men's minds are wild, lest more mis-
    chance 405
On plots and errors happen.

FOR.   Let four captains
Bear Hamlet, like a soldier, to the stage.
For he was likely, had he been put on,°
To have proved most royally. And for his passage
The soldiers' music and the rites of war 410
Speak loudly for him.
Take up the bodies. Such a sight as this
Becomes the field, but here shows much amiss.
Go, bid the soldiers shoot.

    [*A dead march. Exeunt, bearing off the bodies;
       after which a peal of ordnance is shot off.*]

---

386. **jump:** exactly. See I.i.65. **question:** matter. **392–96. carnal
. . . heads:** These lines sum up the whole tragedy: Claudius'
adultery with Gertrude, his murder of his brother, the death
of Ophelia due to an accident, that of Polonius by casual
chance, Hamlet's device which caused the deaths of Rosencrantz
and Guildenstern, the plan which went awry and caused the
deaths of Claudius and Laertes.

400. **rights of memory:** rights which will be remembered; i.e.,
with the disappearance of all the family of the original
King Hamlet the situation reverts to what it was before the
death of Fortinbras' father. See I.i.80–95.   401. **vantage:**
i.e., my advantage, there being none to dispute my claim.
403. **voice . . . more:** i.e., Hamlet's dying voice will strengthen
your claim.   408. **had . . . on:** had he become King.

THE MERRY WIVES OF WINDSOR

Introduction

None of Shakespeare's plays, with the exception of *Hamlet,* is more beset with problems than *The Merry Wives of Windsor.* Text, traditions, source, topicalities, and date have all provoked endless speculation, argument, and ingenious explanation among scholars. Critics, also, have found much to discuss because the principal character in the play is Sir John Falstaff, but a Falstaff very different from the overwhelming mountain of flesh of *Henry IV.* The facts and their varying interpretations may first be considered.

1. THE TEXT: On January 18, 1602, John Busby, a printer of somewhat shady reputation, entered in the Stationers' Register a book called "An excellent and pleasant conceited Commedie of Sir John Faulstof and the merry wyves of Windesor." Busby immediately transferred the play to another printer named Arthur Johnson. Following this entry a quarto (Q1) was published with the title page: *A Most pleasaunt and excellent conceited Comedie, of Syr John Falstaffe, and the merrie Wiues of Windsor Entermixed with sundrie variable and pleasing humors, of Syr Hugh the Welch Knight, Iustice Shallow, and his wise Cousin M. Slender. With the swaggering vaine of Aunciont Pistoll, and Corporall Nym. By William Shakespeare. As it hath bene diuers times Acted by the right Honorable my Lord Chamberlaines seruants. Both before her Maiestie, and else-where.* This quarto is a piracy, and a wretched production. It leaves out many scenes and passages, and the text is bad and garbled throughout except when the Host appears. It therefore seems likely either that the printer's copy was written by someone who had come by the part of the Host, or else that the actor who played the Host himself reproduced a version of the play from what he could remember. This quarto was reprinted in 1619.

The *Merry Wives* was included with the rest of Shakespeare's plays in the first folio (F1) in 1623.

The printer's copy for F1 was presumably the work of a professional scribe. It is divided into acts and scenes, and the names of the characters who appear are grouped at the head of each scene; but the stage directions for the action are omitted, and there are various irregularities in the text. At times sentences in the F1 text are imperfect or make no sense; some, in fact, can be put right from Q1.

The difference between Q1 and F1 can best be illustrated from some specimen passages from Q1.

1. SIR HUGH EVANS WAITS FOR HIS OPPONENT (cf. III.i)

Enter Syr Hugh and Simple.

Sir Hu. I pray you do so much as see if you can espie Doctor
Cayus comming, and give me intelligence,
Or bring me vrde if you please now.

Sim. I will Sir.

Sir Hu. Ieshu ples mee, how my hart trobes, and trobes,
And then she made him bedes of Roses,
And a thousand fragrant poses,
To shallow riueres. Now so kad vdge me, my hart
Swelles more and more. Mee thinkes I can cry
Verie well. There dwelt a man in *Babylon,*
To shallow riuers and to falles,
Melodious birds sing Madrigalles.

Sim. Sir here is M. *Page,* and M. *Shallow,*
Comming hither as fast as they can.

Sir Hu. Then it is verie necessary I put vp my sword,
Pray giue me my cowne too, marke you.

Enter Page, Shallow, and Slender.

Pa. God saue you Sir *Hugh.*

Shal. God saue you M. parson.

Sir Hu. God plesse you all from his mercies sake now.

Pa. What the word and the sword, doth that agree well?

Sir Hu. There is reasons and causes in all things,
I warrant you now.

Pa. Well Sir *Hugh,* we are come to craue
Your helpe and furtherance in a matter.

Sir Hu. What is I pray you?

Pa. Ifaith tis this sir *Hugh.* There is an auncient friend of ours, a man of verie good sort, so at odds

with one patience, that I am sure you would hartily
grieue to see him. Now Sir *Hugh,* you are a schol-
ler well red, and verie perswasiue, we would in-
treate you to see if you could intreat him to patience.

   Sir Hu. I pray you who is it? Let vs know that.

   Pa. I am shure you know him, tis Doctor *Cayus.*

   Sir Hu. I had as leeue you should tel me of a
    messe of poredge,

He is an arant lowsie beggerly knaue:

And he is a coward beside.

   Pa. Why Ile laie my life tis the man

That he should fight withall.

   Enter Doctor and the Host, they offer to fight.

   Shal. Keep them asunder, take away their
    weapons.

   Host. Disarme, let them question.

   Shal. Let them keep their limbs hole, and hack
    our English.

   Doc. Hark van vrd in your eare. You be vn daga
And de Iack, coward preest.

   Sir Hu. Harke you, let vs not be laughing stockes
to other mens humors. By Ieshu I will knock your
vrinalls about your knaues cockcomes, for missing
your meetings and appointments.

   Doc. O Ieshu mine host of de garter, *Iohn
    Rogoby,*

Haue I not met him at de place he make apoint,

Haue I not?

   Sir Hu. So kad vdge me, this is the pointment
    place,

Witnes by my Host of the garter.

   Host. Peace I say gawle and gawlia, French and
    Wealch,

Soule curer, and bodie curer.

   Doc. This is verie braue, excellent.

   Host. Peace I say, heare mine host of the garter,

Am I wise? am I polliticke? am I Matchauil?

Shall I lose my doctor? No, he giues me the mo-
    tions

And the potions. Shall I lose my parson, my sir
    Hu?

No, he giues me the prouerbes, and the nouerbes:

Giue me thy hand terestiall,

So give me thy hand celestiall:

So boyes of art I haue deceiued you both,

I haue directed you to wrong places,

Your hearts are mightie, you skins are whole,

Bardolfe laie their swords to pawne, Follow me
    lads

Of peace, follow me. Ha, ra, la. Follow. *Exit Host.*

   2. FALSTAFF AND THE FAIRIES (cf. V.v.1)

   Enter sir Iohn with a Bucks head vpon him.

   Fal. This is the third time, well Ile venter,

They say there is good luck in old numbers,

Ioue transformed himselfe into a bull,

And I am here a Stag, and I thinke the fattest

In all *Windsor* forrest: well I stand here

For *Horne* the hunter, waiting my Does comming.

   Enter mistris Page, and mistris Ford.

   Mis. Pa. Sir *Iohn,* where are you?

   Fal. Art thou come my doe? what and thou too?

Welcome Ladies.

   Mi. For. I I sir Iohn, I see you will not faile,

Therefore you deserue far better than our loues,

But it grieues me for your late crosses.

   Fal. This makes amends for all.

Come diuide me betweene you, each a hanch,

For my horns Ile bequeath them to your husbands,

Do I speake like *Horne* the hunter, ha?

   Mis. Pa. God forgiue me, what noise is this?

*There is a noise of hornes, the two women run
away.*

*Enter sir Hugh like a Satyre, and boyes drest like
Fayries, mistresse Quickly, like the Queene of
Fayries: they sing a song about him, and after-
ward speake.*

   Quic: You Fayries that do haunt these shady
    groues,

Looke round about the wood if you can espie

A mortall that doth haunt our sacred round:

If such a one you can espie, giue him his due,

And leaue not till you pinch him blacke and blew:

Giue them their charge *Puck* ere they part away.

   Sir Hu. Come hither *Peane,* go to the countrie
    houses,

And when you finde a slut that lies a sleepe,

And all her dishes foule, and roome unswept,

With your long nailes pinch her till she crie,

And sweare to mend her sluttish huswiferie.

   Fai. I warrant you I will performe your will.

   Hu. Where is *Pead?* go you & see where Brokers
    sleep,

And Foxe-eyed Seriants with their mase,

Goe laie the Proctors in the street,

And pinch the lowsie Seriants face:

Spare none of these when they are a bed,

But such whose nose lookes plew and red.

   Quic. Away begon, his mind fulfill,

And looke that none of you stand still.

Some do that thing, some do this,

All do something, none amis.

   Hir Hu. I smell a man of middle earth.

   Fal. God blesse me from that wealch Fairie.

   Quic. Looke euery one about this round,

And if that any here be found,

For his presumption in this place,

Spare neither legge, arme, head, nor face.

   Sir Hu. See I haue spied one by good luck,

His bodie man, his head a buck.

   Fal. God send me good fortune now, and I care
    not.

Quic. Go strait, and do as I commaund,
And take a Taper in your hand,
And set it to his fingers endes,
And if you see it him offends,
And that he starteth at the flame,
Then is he mortall, know his name:
If with an F. it doth begin,
Why then be shure he is full of sin.
About it then, and know the truth,
Of this same metamorphised youth.
   Sir Hu. Giue me the Tapers, I will try
And if that he loue venery.
   They put the Tapers to his fingers, and he starts.
   Sir Hu. It is right indeed, he is full of lecheries
    and iniquitie.
   Quic. A little distant from him stand,
And euery one take hand in hand,
And compasse him within a ring,
First pinch him well, and after sing.
*Here they pinch him, and sing about him, & the
Doctor comes one way & steales away a boy in
red. And Slender another way he takes a boy in
greene: And Fenton steales misteris Anne, being
in white. And a noyse of hunting is made within:
and all the Fairies runne away. Falstaffe pulles
of his bucks head, and rises up. And enters* M.
Page, M. Ford, *and their wiues,* M. Shallow, Sir
Hugh.
   Fal. Horne the hunter quoth you: am I a ghost?
Sblood the Fairies hath made a ghost of me:
What hunting at this time at night?
Ile lay my life the mad Prince of *Wales*
Is stealing his fathers Deare. How now who haue
we here, what is all *Windsor* stirring? Are you
   there?
   Shal. God saue you sir *Iohn Falstaffe.*

2. THE TRADITIONS: *Queen Elizabeth's command.* There is a tradition, often repeated by
eighteenth-century editors, that Shakespeare
wrote *The Merry Wives of Windsor* by direct
command of Queen Elizabeth. This story is first
found in 1702 in a dedicatory epistle to a play
by John Dennis called *The Comical Gallant.*
Dennis's play is a rewriting of *The Merry
Wives* and he justifies himself by saying that
the original play " had pleased one of the greatest queens that ever was in the world." " This
comedy," he declares, " was written at her command, and by her direction, and she was so
eager to see it acted that she commanded it to
be finished in fourteen days; and was afterward,
as tradition tells us, very well pleased at the
representation." Dennis's words imply that the
tradition was then well known.

The three luces. There is another tradition
that, in the opening passages (I.i.1–23) of *The
Merry Wives of Windsor,* Shakespeare was
mocking Sir Thomas Lucy, who was a great
man in the neighborhood of Stratford-on-Avon
during Shakespeare's early youth and manhood.
Justice Shallow, boasting of his own importance, is supported by Master Slender:

   SLEN. All his successors gone before him hath
done't, and all his ancestors that come after him
may. They may give the dozen white luces in
their coat.
   SHAL. It is an old coat.
   EVANS. The dozen white louses do become an
old coat well. It agrees well, passant. It is a familiar beast to man, and signifies love.
   SHAL. The luce is the fresh fish. The salt fish is
an old coat.

A " luce " is a pike (fish), and " luces " were
emblazoned on the coat of arms of the Lucy
family as a kind of pun on their name. According to tradition, Shakespeare in his youth had
fallen foul of Sir Thomas Lucy. Nicholas Rowe,
in the life of Shakespeare which he added to
his edition of Shakespeare's works in 1709,
noted: " He [Shakespeare] had, by a misfortune
common enough to young fellows, fallen into
ill company; and amongst them, some that
made a frequent practice of deer-stealing, engaged him with them more than once in robbing a Park that belonged to Sir Thomas Lucy
of Cherlecot, near Stratford. For this he was
prosecuted by that gentleman, as he thought,
somewhat too severely; and in order to revenge
that ill usage, he made a ballad upon him. And
though this, probably the first essay of his poetry, be lost; yet it is said to have been so very
bitter, that it redoubled the prosecution against
him to that degree, that he was obliged to leave
his business and family in Warwickshire for
some time and shelter himself in London."
Rowe also observes: " Falstaff is allowed by
everybody to be a masterpiece. . . . Amongst
other extravagances, in *The Merry Wives of
Windsor,* he has made him a deer-stealer, that
he might at the same time remember his Warwickshire prosecutor, under the name of Justice Shallow; he has given him very near the
same coat of arms which Dugdale, in his Antiquities of that county, describes for a family
there, and makes the Welsh Parson descant very
pleasantly upon 'em. . . ."

Sir Thomas Lucy, however, was not the only Elizabethan to bear luces in his coat of arms. Dr. Leslie Hotson published an account (*Shakespeare vs. Shallow*, 1931) of his discovery that in 1596 Shakespeare fell foul of a gentleman called William Wayte. Wayte was the son of a London magistrate named William Gardiner, who had a coat of arms that also included three luces. Dr. Hotson claimed that the luce-louse joke referred to Gardiner rather than to Sir Thomas Lucy.

3. THE SOURCE: The direct source of the play is not known, but it is suspected on reasonable grounds that *The Merry Wives of Windsor* is a rewriting of an old play. If the Queen Elizabeth tradition is correct, it would be logical to assume that Shakespeare, so hardly pressed for time, would have taken up the most suitable old play in the company's stock of out-of-date play-books and transformed it by writing in parts for Falstaff and his old companions. There seem to be several traces of this old play in *The Merry Wives of Windsor* as it now stands, particularly in the passages of somewhat stiff verse, such as the conversation of Fenton and Anne Page (III.iv), the conversation of the two wives and their husbands (IV.iv), the passage between Fenton and the Host when he explains the plot to abduct Anne Page (IV.vi), the fairy scene (V.v.41–106) — wherein Pistol and Mrs. Quickly not only appear most inappropriately but also speak in verse quite different from their usual curious and individual prose — and the passage at the end of the play (V.v.233–59). If, as has been suggested, these passages are all relics of the older play, it follows that it, too, was a story of how a Windsor lady-killer was gulled at Herne's Oak.

4. LOCAL REFERENCES AND TOPICALITIES: *Windsor Castle and the Order of the Garter* (V.v.60–80). In the fairy scene, the fairies are bidden to visit Windsor Castle and anoint the chairs of the Knights of the Order of the Garter. It would seem likely that these lines were inserted for a special performance at the Garter Feast at Windsor (see App. 29). There is no corresponding speech in Q1. The passage resembles the similar instructions given to the fairies at the end of *A Midsummer Night's Dream* (V.i.408–29).

Herne the Hunter. Herne the Hunter was an ancient, legendary figure. He was said to haunt one of the great oaks in Windsor Forest, near the Castle, and to appear at midnight rattling a chain. Herne's Oak was once a well-known landmark; it stood until 1863 when it was blown down in a storm; it was then more than six hundred years old.

The Germans (IV.iii and v). In the play as it stands in F1, there is a very brief scene (IV.iii) between the Host and Bardolph concerning some Germans and a Duke who require horses from the Host. A little later (IV.v.64), Bardolph runs in:

> BARD. Out, alas, sir! Cozenage, mere cozenage!
> HOST. Where be my horses? Speak well of them, varletto.
> BARD. Run away with the cozeners. For so soon as I came beyond Eton, they threw me off from behind one of them in a slough of mire, and set spurs and away, like three German devils, three Doctor Faustuses. 71
> HOST. They are gone but to meet the Duke, villain. Do not say they be fled. Germans are honest men.
> [*Enter* SIR HUGH EVANS.]
> EVANS. Where is mine host? 75
> HOST. What is the matter, sir?
> EVANS. Have a care of your entertainments. There is a friend of mine come to town, tells me there is three cozen-germans that has cozened all the hosts of Readins, of Maidenhead, of 80 Colebrook, of horses and money. I tell you for good will, look you. You are wise, and full of gibes and vlouting-stocks, and 'tis not convenient you should be cozened. Fare you well. [*Exit.*]

In the passage in Q1 corresponding to ll. 74–81 above, Sir Hugh Evans says:

> Where is mine Host of the gartyr?
> Now my Host, I would desire you to looke now,
> To haue a care of your entertainments,
> For there is three sorts of cosen garmombles,
> Is cosen all the Host of Maidenhead and Readings.

These Germans have nothing to do with the story of the play and the episode is probably a topical allusion to a German Count Mompelgard who came to England in 1592. The Count was corpulent and found much difficulty in fitting his person to the English type of saddle. He visited Queen Elizabeth at Reading, and went on to Windsor where he was entertained for two days. On his departure, special arrangements were made for him to have the privilege of free post horses (see App. 17). The Count greatly desired to be made a Knight of the Garter and periodically wrote to the Queen. Finally, in 1597 — the Count having by this time become Duke of Wirtenburg — he was elected to the Order, but he was not invested with the insignia until 1603. A journal of the Count's visit in 1592 was kept by one of his retainers, and from the tart comments on the unfriendliness and scorn of the English toward foreigners it seems likely that the Germans had made themselves conspicuous and unpopular. However, allusions to the German visitors would only have been topical in 1592, and these passages may be survivals of an earlier source-play of *The Merry Wives.*

Pistol and Nym. As has been shown (see Gen. Intro. pp. 41b–42a), Pistol was created to be a walking parody of the great actor, Edward Alleyn, chief of the rival company, the Lord Admiral's Men. Alleyn was the leading exponent of the older style of heavy, robustious rant. Nym, on the other hand, mocks the newest development in drama; he is a living " humor "; he cannot open his mouth without a humor dropping out. The vogue for the " humors " was at its height in the two or three years after the success of Jonson's *Every Man in His Humor* (see p. 42a–b).

5. THE DATE: Various dates have been proposed for the writing of *The Merry Wives.* The date of the entry of Q1 (January 1602) shows that the play must have been written before the end of 1601, and internal evidence suggests that it was written after *II Henry IV,* which is usually assigned to the spring of 1598. Certain facts are relevant. In *The Merry Wives* Sir John Falstaff is associated with Bardolph, Pistol, Nym, and Mistress Quickly. Bardolph, Pistol, and Mistress Quickly were all prominent characters in *II Henry IV.* Nym, however, does not appear in the History Plays until *Henry V.* Now the writing of *Henry V* can be placed with some certainty in the spring of 1599 (see p. 732a). It is thus an open question whether Nym's first appearance was in *Henry V* or *The Merry Wives.* On the whole, it is a likelier guess that Nym was first created as a newcomer to *Henry V.*

There are, moreover, certain links between *The Merry Wives of Windsor* and Ben Jonson's *Every Man in His Humor,* first played in September 1598. Two of Shakespeare's characters — Ford, the jealous husband, and Slender, the silly young gentleman — have much in common with Jonson's Thorello and Stephano (renamed Kitely and Master Stephen in the 1616 version of *Every Man in His Humor*). The silly-gentleman type was new in Shakespeare's plays, and he reappears as Sir Andrew Aguecheek in *Twelfth Night,* Osric in *Hamlet,* and Roderigo in *Othello.* It is likely that the same actor played all four parts.

Taking all the facts, inferences, and traditions into account, the best guess is that Falstaff was revived to be the victim of the merry wives by royal command after he had been killed off in *Henry V* (spring 1599), and that *The Merry Wives of Windsor* was written to be acted at the Garter Feast, April 23, 1599. Dr. Hotson has proposed the date 1597 for the writing of *The Merry Wives,* but this date creates more problems than it solves.

The play itself would have caused less excitement among critics if the wooer of Mistress Ford and Mistress Page had borne any other name than Falstaff. There are certainly a number of inconsistencies in the plot. Justice Shallow at his first entry is full of threats against Falstaff, and the audience is led to believe that this situation will be developed, but it is not. Instead, Justice Shallow mellows into a kindly old gentleman who does very little. Pistol and Bardolph keep some of their old characteristics and their strange manner of speech, but they are unimportant in the story. Indeed, Shakespeare appears to have been somewhat embarrassed by having to reintroduce these survivors from the disreputable Eastcheap days of *II Henry IV.* The episode of the fairies at the conclusion of the play is unnecessary; they are introduced simply to give an opportunity for the small boys to sing and dance before the original courtly audience. But, once the inconsistencies have been forgotten, the *Merry Wives* is an excellent farce, full of amusing episodes, and it acts well on the stage. It is not, and was never intended to be, serious comedy.

The Merry Wives of Windsor

DRAMATIS PERSONAE

SIR JOHN FALSTAFF
FENTON, *a gentleman*
SHALLOW, *a country justice*
SLENDER, *cousin to Shallow*
FORD }
PAGE } *two gentlemen dwelling at Windsor*
WILLIAM PAGE, *a boy, son to Page*
SIR HUGH EVANS, *a Welsh parson*
DOCTOR CAIUS, *a French physician*
HOST *of the Garter Inn*
BARDOLPH }
PISTOL } *sharpers attending on Falstaff*
NYM }

ROBIN, *page to Falstaff*
SIMPLE, *servant to Slender*
RUGBY, *servant to Doctor Caius*

MISTRESS FORD
MISTRESS PAGE
ANNE PAGE, *her daughter*
MISTRESS QUICKLY, *servant to Doctor Caius*

SERVANTS *to Page, Ford, &c.*

SCENE — *Windsor, and the neighborhood.*

Act I

SCENE I. *Windsor. Before* PAGE's *house.*

[*Enter* JUSTICE SHALLOW, SLENDER, *and* SIR HUGH EVANS.]

SHAL. Sir° Hugh, persuade me not. I will make a Star Chamber° matter of it. If he were twenty Sir John Falstaffs, he shall not abuse Robert Shallow, Esquire.°

SLEN. In the County of Gloucester, Justice of Peace and " Coram."° 6

SHAL. Aye, Cousin Slender, and " Custalorum."°

SLEN. Aye, and " Ratolorum "° too; and a gentleman born, Master Parson, who writes himself " Armigero,"° in any bill, warrant, quittance,° or obligation, " Armigero." 11

SHAL. Aye, that I do, and have done any time these three hundred years.°

SLEN. All his successors gone before him hath done't, and all his ancestors that come after 15 him may. They may give° the dozen white luces° in their coat.

SHAL. It is an old coat.

EVANS. The dozen white louses° do become an old coat well. It agrees well, passant.° It is a familiar beast to man, and signifies love. 21

SHAL. The luce is the fresh fish. The salt fish is an old coat.°

SLEN. I may quarter,° Coz.°

SHAL. You may, by marrying. 25

EVANS. It is marring indeed, if he quarter it.

SHAL. Not a whit.

EVANS. Yes, py'r° lady. If he has a quarter of your coat, there is but three skirts° for yourself, in my simple conjectures. But that is all one. If Sir 30 John Falstaff have committed disparagements unto you, I am of the Church, and will be glad to do my benevolence to make atonements and comprimises between you.

SHAL. The Council shall hear it. It is a riot.° 35

EVANS. It is not meet the Council hear a riot. There is no fear of Got in a riot. The Council, look you, shall desire to hear the fear of Got, and not to hear a riot. Take your vizaments° in that.

SHAL. Ha! O' my life, if I were young again, the sword should end it. 41

EVANS. It is petter that friends is the sword, and end it. And there is also another device in my prain, which peradventure prings goot discretions with it — there is Anne Page, which is daughter to Master Thomas Page, which is pretty virginity. 46

Act I, Sc. i: 1. Sir: See *T Night*, III.iv.298,n. 2. Star Chamber: See Gen. Intro. p. 25a–b. 4. Esquire: gentleman owning landed property. 6. Coram: a corruption of *quorum*, the first word in one of the clauses in the commission of appointment of a magistrate. 7. Custalorum: for *custos rotulorum* (keeper of the rolls), the most important of the magistrates in a county. 8. Ratolorum: Slender's ignorant mistake for *rotulorum*. 10. Armigero: lit., bearer of arms, the official designation of a gentleman. See App. 9. quittance: discharge from debt; but Slender merely means official documents. 13. these . . . years: i.e., my family have borne arms for the last three centuries. 16. give: display as coat of arms. luces: pike. See *M Wives* Intro. pp. 937b–38a.

19. louses: Sir Hugh is never very happy with his pronunciation of English words, but the similarity between *luce* and "louse" was a common joke. 20. passant: a heraldic term for walking. 22–23. salt . . . coat: The joke has not been satisfactorily explained. 24. quarter: i.e., marry a lady of gentle family and quarter her coat of arms with my own. Coz: kinsman. 28. py'r: by our. 29. skirts: the fullness at the bottom of a doublet. See Pl. 9j,n,o. 35. Council . . . riot: See Gen. Intro. p. 25a–b. 39. vizaments: for advisement; i.e., take careful consideration.

SLEN. Mistress Anne Page? She has brown hair and speaks small° like a woman.

EVANS. It is that fery person for all the orld, 50 as just as you will desire; and seven hundred pounds of moneys, and gold, and silver is her grandsire upon his death's bed (Got deliver to a joyful resurrections!) give when she is able to overtake seventeen years old. It were a goot motion if we 55 leave our pribbles and prabbles° and desire a marriage between Master Abraham and Mistress Anne Page.

SLEN. Did her grandsire leave her seven hundred pound? 60

EVANS. Aye, and her father is make° her a petter penny.

SLEN. I know the young gentlewoman. She has good gifts.

EVANS. Seven hundred pounds and possibilities is goot gifts. 66

SHAL. Well, let us see honest Master Page. Is Falstaff there?

EVANS. Shall I tell you a lie? I do despise a liar as I do despise one that is false, or as I despise one 70 that is not true. The knight Sir John, is there, and, I beseech you, be ruled by your well-willers. I will peat the door for Master Page. [*Knocks.*] What ho! Got pless your house here!

PAGE. [*Within*] Who's there? 75

[*Enter* PAGE.]

EVANS. Here is Got's plessing, and your friend, and Justice Shallow, and here young Master Slender, that peradventures shall tell you another tale, if matters grow to your likings.

PAGE. I am glad to see your Worships well. I thank you for my venison, Master Shallow. 81

SHAL. Master Page, I am glad to see you. Much good do it your good heart! I wished your venison better. It was ill killed. How doth good Mistress Page? And I thank you always with my heart, la, with my heart. 86

PAGE. Sir, I thank you.

SHAL. Sir, I thank you, by yea and no, I do. 89

PAGE. I am glad to see you, good Master Slender.

SLEN. How does your fallow° greyhound, sir? I heard say he was outrun on Cotsall.°

PAGE. It could not be judged,° sir.

SLEN. You'll not confess, you'll not confess.

SHAL. That he will not. 'Tis your fault,° 'tis your fault. 'Tis a good dog. 96

PAGE. A cur, sir.

SHAL. Sir, he's a good dog, and a fair dog. Can there be more said? He is good and fair. Is Sir John Falstaff here? 100

PAGE. Sir, he is within, and I would I could do a good office between you.

EVANS. It is spoke as a Christians ought to speak.

SHAL. He hath wronged me, Master Page. 105

PAGE. Sir, he doth in some sort confess it.

SHAL. If it be confessed, it is not redressed. Is not that so, Master Page? He hath wronged me. Indeed he hath, at a word, he hath, believe me. Robert Shallow, Esquire, saith he is wronged. 110

PAGE. Here comes Sir John.

[*Enter* SIR JOHN FALSTAFF, BARDOLPH, NYM, *and* PISTOL.]

FAL. Now, Master Shallow, you'll complain of me to the King?

SHAL. Knight, you have beaten my men, killed my deer, and broke open my lodge. 115

FAL. But not kissed your keeper's daughter?

SHAL. Tut, a pin!° This shall be answered.

FAL. I will answer it straight. I have done all this. That is now answered.

SHAL. The Council shall know this. 120

FAL. 'Twere better for you if it were known in counsel.° You'll be laughed at.

EVANS. *Pauca verba,*° Sir John. Goot worts.

FAL. Good worts! Good cabbage. Slender, I broke your head. What matter have you against me? 126

SLEN. Marry, sir, I have matter in my head against you, and against your cony-catching° rascals, Bardolph, Nym, and Pistol.

BARD. You Banbury cheese!° 130

SLEN. Aye, it is no matter.

PIST. How now, Mephostophilus!°

SLEN. Aye, it is no matter.

NYM. Slice,° I say! *Pauca, pauca.* Slice! That's my humor.° 135

SLEN. Where's Simple, my man? Can you tell, Cousin?

EVANS. Peace, I pray you. Now let us understand. There is three umpires in this matter, as I understand; that is, Master Page, *fidelicet*° Master 140 Page, and there is myself, *fidelicet* myself, and the three party is, lastly and finally, mine host of the Garter.

PAGE. We three to hear it and end it between them. 145

EVANS. Fery goot. I will make a prief° of it in my notebook, and we will afterwards ork° upon the

---

49. small: shrill.   56. pribbles . . . prabbles: brawling and babbling. The Welshman finds a difficulty with his "b's" and his "d's."   61. is make: will provide.   91. fallow: pale brown. 92. Cotsall: Cotswold. The smooth grassy Cotswold Hills in Gloucestershire, near Shakespeare's home country, ideal ground for the sport of coursing the hare.   93. judged: fairly decided. 95. fault: misfortune.

117. pin: trifle.   122. counsel: secret.   123. *Pauca verba:* few words.   128. cony-catching: thieving. See Gen. Intro. p. 28a. 130. Banbury cheese: a very thin cream cheese, made at Banbury, about 15 miles from Stratford.   132. Mephostophilus: the name of the devil in Marlowe's *Dr. Faustus.*   134. Slice: Nym lays his hand on his sword and threatens to slice the "Banbury cheese."   135. my humor: See App. 3.   140. *fidelicet:* for *videlicet* ("viz."), namely.   146. prief: brief; summary of the case.   147. ork: work.

cause with as great discreetly as we can.

FAL. Pistol!

PIST. He hears with ears.   150

EVANS. The tevil and his tam!° What phrase is this? "He hears with ear"? Why, it is affectations.

FAL. Pistol, did you pick Master Slender's purse?

SLEN. Aye, by these gloves,° did he, or I would I might never come in mine own great chamber 157 again else, of seven groats° in mill-sixpences,° and two Edward shovelboards° that cost me two shilling and two pence apiece of Yead° Miller, by these gloves.   161

FAL. Is this true, Pistol?

EVANS. No. It is false, if it is a pickpurse.

PIST. Ha, thou mountain foreigner!° Sir John and master mine,
I combat challenge° of this latten bilbo.°   165
Word of denial in thy labras° here!
Word of denial. Froth and scum, thou liest!

SLEN. By these gloves, then, 'twas he.

NYM. Be avised,° sir, and pass good humors.° I will say "marry trap"° with you if you run the nut-hook's° humor° on me. That is the very note of it.   172

SLEN. By this hat, then, he in the red face had it, for though I cannot remember what I did when you made me drunk, yet I am not altogether an ass.   176

FAL. What say you, Scarlet and John?°

BARD. Why, sir, for my part, I say the gentleman had drunk himself out of his five sentences ——

EVANS. It is his five senses. Fie, what the ignorance is!   182

BARD. And being fap,° sir, was, as they say, cashiered, and so conclusions passed the careires.°

SLEN. Aye, you spake in Latin then too; but 186

'tis no matter. I'll ne'er be drunk whilst I live again, but in honest, civil, godly company, for this trick. If I be drunk, I'll be drunk with those that have the fear of God, and not with drunken knaves.   190

EVANS. So Got udge me, that is a virtuous mind.

FAL. You hear all these matters denied, gentlemen. You hear it.

[*Enter* ANNE PAGE, *with wine;* MISTRESS FORD *and* MISTRESS PAGE, *following.*]

PAGE. Nay, Daughter, carry the wine in. We'll drink within.   [*Exit* ANNE PAGE.]   196

SLEN. Oh, Heaven! This is Mistress Anne Page.

PAGE. How now, Mistress Ford!

FAL. Mistress Ford, by my troth,° you are very well met. By your leave, good mistress.   200

[*Kisses her.*]

PAGE. Wife, bid these gentlemen welcome. Come, we have a hot venison pasty to dinner. Come, gentlemen, I hope we shall drink down all unkindness.

[*Exeunt all except* SHALLOW, SLENDER, *and* EVANS.]

SLEN. I had rather than forty shillings I 205 had my Book of Songs and Sonnets° here. [*Enter* SIMPLE.] How now, Simple! Where have you been? I must wait on myself, must I? You have not the Book of Riddles° about you, have you?   209

SIM. Book of Riddles! Why, did you not lend it to Alice Shortcake upon Allhallowmass° last, a fortnight afore Michaelmas?°

SHAL. Come, Coz, come, Coz, we stay for you. A word with you, Coz. Marry, this, Coz. There is, as 'twere, a tender,° a kind of tender, made afar off° by Sir Hugh here. Do you understand me?   216

SLEN. Aye, sir, you shall find me reasonable. If it be so, I shall do that that is reason.

SHAL. Nay, but understand me.

SLEN. So I do, sir.   220

EVANS. Give ear to his motions, Master Slender. I will description the matter to you, if you be capacity of it.

SLEN. Nay, I will do as my cousin Shallow says. I pray you pardon me. He's a Justice of Peace in his country, simple though I stand here.   226

EVANS. But that is not the question. The question is concerning your marriage.

SHAL. Aye, there's the point, sir.

EVANS. Marry, is it, the very point of it, to Mistress Anne Page.   231

SLEN. Why, if it be so, I will marry her upon any reasonable demands.

---

151. tevil . . . tam: the Devil and his mother — a common oath. See *Oth,* IV.i.153.   **154. by . . . gloves:** a very mild oath.   **158. groats:** coins worth 4*d.* **mill-sixpences:** Elizabethan coins were usually struck out by hand, so that the edge was thin and uneven; as a result it was not difficult to "clip" the coin by paring off a thin slice. The first "milled" coins, with a thick, even rim, were made about this time. See Pl. 10a–d.   **159. shovelboards:** old shillings worn smooth, and used for the game of "shovegroat." See *II Hen IV,* II.iv.207,n.   **160. Yead:** Ned.   **164. mountain foreigner:** stranger from the (Welsh) mountains.   **165. combat challenge:** dare to mortal fight. **latten bilbo:** *Latten* is soft brass; *bilbo* is a sword from Bilboa in Spain. Pistol calls Slender a *latten bilbo* because he is long, thin, and soft.   **166. labras:** lips.   **169. avised:** cautious. **pass . . . humors:** i.e., no dirty charges here.   **170. marry trap:** i.e., you'll get yourself into trouble.   **170–71. nuthook:** lit., one who grabs, like the modern "cop" (one who cops), officer of the law. **nuthook's humor:** Nym misuses the word *humor* so grossly that it is not always possible to give the exact meaning of his words — "if you try any cop-stuff on me."   **177. Scarlet . . . John:** two of Robin Hood's Merry Men. Scarlet is appropriately applied to Bardolph because of his face. See *I Hen IV,* III.iii.27–55.   **183. fap:** "tight."   **184. conclusions . . . careires:** ran their course; i.e., anyone who gets drunk in our company will naturally conclude by getting robbed.   **185. careire** (usually spelled career): a gallop at full speed.

199. troth: truth.   **206. Book . . . Sonnets:** better known to literary students as Tottel's *Miscellany,* a very famous collection first published in 1557.   **209. Book of Riddles:** i.e., in order that Slender may shine in company.   **211. Allhallowmass:** All Saints' Day, November 1.   **212. Michaelmas:** St. Michael's day, September 29. Simple is weak on Church festivals.   **215. tender:** offer. **made . . . off:** a distant offer.

EVANS. But can you affection the 'oman? Let us command to know that of your mouth or of 235 your lips; for divers philosophers hold that the lips is parcel° of the mouth. Therefore, precisely, can you carry your good will to the maid?

SHAL. Cousin Abraham Slender, can you love her?   240

SLEN. I hope, sir, I will do as it shall become one that would do reason.

EVANS. Nay, Got's lords and his ladies! You must speak possitable,° if you can carry her your desires toward her.   245

SHAL. That you must. Will you, upon good dowry, marry her?

SLEN. I will do a greater thing than that, upon your request, Cousin, in any reason.

SHAL. Nay, conceive° me, conceive me, sweet 250 Coz. What I do is to pleasure you, Coz. Can you love the maid?

SLEN. I will marry her, sir, at your request. But if there be no great love in the beginning, yet 254 Heaven may decrease it upon better acquaintance when we are married and have more occasion to know one another. I hope upon familiarity will grow more contempt.° But if you say " Marry her," I will marry her. That I am freely dissolved, and dissolutely.°   260

EVANS. It is a fery discretion answer, save the fall° is in the ort " dissolutely." The ort is, according to our meaning, " resolutely." His meaning is good.

SHAL. Aye, I think my cousin meant well.   265

SLEN. Aye, or else I would I might be hanged, la!

SHAL. Here comes fair Mistress Anne. [Re-enter ANNE PAGE.] Would I were young for your sake, Mistress Anne!

ANNE. The dinner is on the table. My father desires your Worships' company.   271

SHAL. I will wait on him, fair Mistress Anne.

EVANS. Od's plessed will! I will not be absence at the grace.   [Exeunt SHALLOW and EVANS.]

ANNE. Will 't please your Worship to come in, sir?   276

SLEN. No, I thank you, forsooth, heartily. I am very well.

ANNE. The dinner attends° you, sir.   279

SLEN. I am not ahungry, I thank you, forsooth. Go, sirrah,° for all° you are my man, go wait upon my cousin Shallow. [Exit SIMPLE.] A justice of peace sometime may be beholding to his friend for

a man. I keep but three men and a boy yet, till 285 my mother be dead. But what though? Yet I live like a poor gentleman born.

ANNE. I may not go in without your Worship. They will not sit till you come.

SLEN. I' faith, I'll eat nothing. I thank you as much as though I did.   291

ANNE. I pray you, sir, walk in.

SLEN. I had rather walk here, I thank you. I bruised my shin th' other day with playing at sword and dagger with a master of fence;° three 295 veneys° for a dish of stewed prunes, and, by my troth, I cannot abide the smell of hot meat since. Why do your dogs bark so? Be there bears i' the town?

ANNE. I think there are, sir. I heard them talked of.   301

SLEN. I love the sport well, but I shall as soon quarrel at it as any man in England. You are afraid if you see the bear loose, are you not?

ANNE. Aye, indeed, sir.   305

SLEN. That's meat and drink to me, now. I have seen Sackerson° loose twenty times and have taken him by the chain; but, I warrant you, the women have so cried and shrieked at it that it passed. 310 But women, indeed, cannot abide 'em. They are very ill-favored rough things.

[Re-enter PAGE.]

PAGE. Come, gentle Master Slender, come. We stay for you.

SLEN. I'll eat nothing, I thank you, sir.   315

PAGE. By cock and pie,° you shall not choose, sir! Come, come.

SLEN. Nay, pray you, lead the way.

PAGE. Come on, sir.

SLEN. Mistress Anne, yourself shall go first.

ANNE. Not I, sir. Pray you keep on.   321

SLEN. Truly, I will not go first, truly, la! I will not do you that wrong.

ANNE. I pray you, sir.   324

SLEN. I'll rather be unmannerly than troublesome. You do yourself wrong, indeed, la!   [Exeunt.]

SCENE II. *The same.*

[Enter SIR HUGH EVANS and SIMPLE.]

EVANS. Go your ways, and ask of Doctor Caius' house which is the way. And there dwells one Mistress Quickly, which is in the manner of his nurse, or his dry nurse, or his cook, or his laundry, his washer, and his wringer.   5

SIM. Well, sir.

237. parcel: part.   244. possitable: positively.   250. conceive: understand.   258. contempt: emendation for the F1 "content," made by Theobald and adapted by most editors since (to match *decrease*, l. 255).   259–60. dissolved . . . dissolutely: for "resolved, and resolutely." Slender's vocabulary is slight.   262. fall: for fauit.   279. attends: awaits.   281. sirrah: a word of address used to an inferior. for all: although.

295. master of fence: professional fencer.   296. veneys: bouts — the prize being a *dish of stewed prunes*.   307. Sackerson: a famous bear used for baiting. See App. 5.   316. cock . . . pie: See *II Hen IV*, V.i.1,n.

EVANS. Nay, it is petter yet. Give her this letter, for it is a 'oman that altogether's acquaintance with Mistress Anne Page. And the letter is to desire and require her to solicit your master's desires to 10 Mistress Anne Page. I pray you be gone. I will make an end of my dinner. There's pippins and cheese to come.   [*Exeunt.*]

SCENE III. *A room in the Garter Inn.*

[*Enter* SIR JOHN FALSTAFF, HOST, BARDOLPH, NYM, PISTOL, *and* ROBIN.]

FAL. Mine host of the Garter!

HOST. What says my bully rook?° Speak scholarly and wisely.

FAL. Truly, mine host, I must turn away some of my followers.   5

HOST. Discard, bully Hercules! Cashier! Let them wag!° Trot, trot!

FAL. I sit at° ten pounds a week.

HOST. Thou'rt an emperor, Caesar, Keisar,° and Pheezar.° I will entertain° Bardolph. He shall draw,° he shall tap. Said I well, bully Hector?°   12

FAL. Do so, good mine host.

HOST. I have spoke. Let him follow. [*To* BARDOLPH] Let me see thee froth° and lime.° I am at a word.° Follow.   [*Exit.*]   16

FAL. Bardolph, follow him. A tapster is a good trade. An old cloak makes a new jerkin, a withered servingman a fresh tapster. Go. Adieu.   20

BARD. It is a life that I have desired. I will thrive.

PIST. O base Hungarian wight!° Wilt thou the spigot° wield?   [*Exit* BARDOLPH.]

NYM. He was gotten in drink. Is not the humor conceited?°   26

FAL. I am glad I am so acquit of this tinder box.° His thefts were too open. His filching was like an unskillful singer; he kept not time.

NYM. The good humor is to steal at a minute's rest.°   31

PIST. "Convey,"° the wise it call. "Steal!" Foh!

A fico° for the phrase!

FAL. Well, sirs, I am almost out at heels.

PIST. Why, then, let kibes° ensue.   35

FAL. There is no remedy. I must cony-catch.° I must shift.°

PIST. Young ravens must have food.

FAL. Which of you know Ford of this town?

PIST. I ken the wight. He is of substance good.

FAL. My honest lads, I will tell you what I am about.   42

PIST. Two yards, and more.

FAL. No quips now, Pistol! Indeed, I am in   45 the waist two yards about, but I am now about no waste. I am about thrift. Briefly, I do mean to make love to Ford's wife. I spy entertainment in her. She discourses, she carves,° she gives the leer of invitation. I can construe° the action of her familiar   50 style, and the hardest voice° of her behavior, to be Englished rightly, is "I am Sir John Falstaff's."

PIST. He hath studied her will and translated her will — out of honesty into English.   55

NYM. The anchor is deep.° Will that humor pass?

FAL. Now, the report goes she has all the rule of her husband's purse. He hath a legion of angels.°

PIST. As many devils entertain, and "To her, boy," say I.   62

NYM. The humor rises. It is good. Humor me the angels.

FAL. I have writ me here a letter to her; and   65 here another to Page's wife, who even now gave me good eyes too, examined my parts with most judicious oeillades.° Sometimes the beam of her view gilded° my foot, sometimes my portly belly.

PIST. Then did the sun on dunghill shine.   70

NYM. I thank thee for that humor.

FAL. Oh, she did so course° o'er my exteriors with such a greedy intention that the appetite of her eye did seem to scorch me up like a burning glass!° Here's another letter to her. She bears the purse   75 too. She is a region in Guiana,° all gold and bounty. I will be cheaters° to them both, and they shall be exchequers to me. They shall be my East and

---

Sc. iii: **2. bully rook:** fine fellow.   **7. wag:** go off.   **8. I . . . at:** it costs me.   **9. Keisar:** emperor.   **10. Pheezar:** probably for vizier.   **11. entertain:** employ.   **12. draw:** become a drawer — barman in a tavern who brings the drinks. **Hector:** a type of valiant hero.   **15. froth:** cheat by filling the pot of ale with an excess of froth. **lime:** adulterate with lime to take away the sourness. See *I Hen IV*, II.iv.137,n.   **15–16. at a word:** one who speaks few words.   **22. Hungarian wight:** man from the Hungary wars. The wars between Hungary and the Turks had attracted many professional soldiers, who returned to England in very poor condition.   **24. spigot:** the bung in a beer barrel. **26. conceited:** clever.   **27. tinder box:** fire maker. See *Oth*, I.i.141,n.   **30–31. minute's rest:** for minim's rest, the minim being the shortest note in music. Nym, who has expert knowledge of the matter, can pick a pocket in a flash.   **32. Convey:** the slang word for "steal." Pistol dislikes the coarser term, as being unrefined.

33. fico: the fig — an insulting gesture, made by thrusting the thumb between the first and second fingers.   **35. kibes:** blisters, chilblains. See *Lear*, I.v.9.   **36. cony-catch:** steal. See I.i.128. **37. shift:** live by my wits.   **49. carves:** behaves delicately. **50. construe:** translate.   **51. hardest voice:** the most difficult phrase.   **56. anchor is deep:** Nym's dark sayings are difficult to interpret. Probably he means "This is a deep scheme." **60. angels:** with the common pun on *angels*, coins worth 10s. See Pl. 10c.   **68. oeillades:** looks of love.   **68–69. beam . . . gilded:** It was believed that the eye shot out a beam which caused the object to be illuminated, and so visible. See *Tr & Cr*, III.iii.109 (n. on *speculation*).   **72. course:** run.   **74. burning glass:** convex lens, used for starting a fire by concentrating the sun's rays on inflammable material.   **76. Guiana:** Sir Walter Raleigh had voyaged to Guiana in 1595 and brought back tales of its vast wealth.   **77. cheaters:** for escheaters, officers of the King's Exchequer.

West Indies, and I will trade to them both.   80
[*To* PISTOL] Go bear thou this letter to Mistress
Page; [*To* NYM] and thou this to Mistress Ford. We
will thrive, lads, we will thrive.

PIST. Shall I Sir Pandarus° of Troy become,
And by my side wear steel?° Then, Lucifer take
    all!

NYM. I will run no base humor. Here, take   85
the humor-letter. I will keep the havior of reputation.°

FAL. [*To* ROBIN] Hold, sirrah, bear you these let-
    ters tightly.
Sail like my pinnace° to these golden shores.   89
Rogues, hence, avaunt! Vanish like hailstones, go!
Trudge, plod away o' the hoof! Seek shelter, pack!
Falstaff will learn the humor of the age,
French thrift,° you rogues — myself and skirted°
    page. [*Exeunt* SIR JOHN FALSTAFF *and* ROBIN.]

PIST. Let vultures gripe thy guts! For gourd and
    fullam° holds,°
And high and low beguiles the rich and poor.   95
Tester° I'll have in pouch when thou shalt lack,
Base Phrygian Turk!°

NYM. I have operations which be humors of revenge.

PIST. Wilt thou revenge?   100

NYM. By welkin° and her star!

PIST. With wit or steel?

NYM. With both the humors, I.
I will discuss the humor of this love to Page.

PIST. And I to Ford shall eke° unfold   105
    How Falstaff, varlet vile,
    His dove will prove,° his gold will hold,
    And his soft couch defile.

NYM. My humor shall not cool. I will incense
Page to deal with poison. I will possess him   110
with yellowness,° for the revolt of mine° is dangerous. That is my true humor.

PIST. Thou art the Mars of malcontents.° I second
thee. Troop on!   [*Exeunt.*]

SCENE IV. *A room in* DOCTOR CAIUS's *house.*

[*Enter* MISTRESS QUICKLY, SIMPLE, *and* RUGBY.]

QUICK. What, John Rugby! I pray thee go to the
casement, and see if you can see my master, Master

Doctor Caius, coming. If he do, i' faith, and find
anybody in the house, here will be an old° abusing
of God's patience and the king's English.   6

RUG. I'll go watch.

QUICK. Go, and we'll have a posset° for 't soon
at night, in faith, at the latter end of a sea-coal° fire.
[*Exit* RUGBY.] An honest, willing, kind fellow,   10
as ever servant shall come in house withal; and, I
warrant you, no telltale nor no breedbate.° His
worst fault is that he is given to prayer. He is something peevish that way. But nobody but has his
fault; but let that pass. Peter Simple, you say your
name is?   16

SIM. Aye, for fault of a better.

QUICK. And Master Slender's your master?

SIM. Aye, forsooth.

QUICK. Does he not wear a great round beard,
like a glover's paring knife?°   21

SIM. No, forsooth. He hath but a little wee face,°
with a little yellow beard — a Cain-colored° beard.

QUICK. A softly-sprighted° man, is he not?   25

SIM. Aye, forsooth. But he is as tall° a man of his
hands as any is between this and his head.° He hath
fought with a warrener.°

QUICK. How say you? Oh, I should remember
him. Does he not hold up his head, as it were, and
strut in his gait?   31

SIM. Yes, indeed, does he.

QUICK. Well, Heaven send Anne Page no worse
fortune! Tell Master Parson Evans I will do what
I can for your master. Anne is a good girl, and I
wish ——   36

[*Re-enter* RUGBY.]

RUG. Out, alas! Here comes my master.

QUICK. We shall all be shent.° Run in here, good
young man. Go into this closet.° He will not stay
long. [*Shuts* SIMPLE *in the closet.*] What, John   40
Rugby! John! What, John, I say! Go, John, go inquire for my master. I doubt he be not well that he
comes not home.   [*Singing.*]
    And down, down, adown-a,° &c.

[*Enter* DOCTOR CAIUS.]

CAIUS. Vat is you sing? I do not like des   45
toys.° Pray you go and vetch me in my closet *un*

Sc. iv: 4. **old:** any amount of.   8. **posset:** hot drink, usually
made with milk.   9. **sea-coal:** mined coal, brought by sea from
the north. The usual coal was charcoal.   12. **breedbate:** stirrer
up of strife.   21. **glover's . . . knife:** i.e., broad and round.
Elizabethan gentlemen were as particular about the cut of the
beard as modern women about the style of their hairdressing.
22. **wee face:** a disputed reading, given by F1. Q1 reads "a whay
coloured beard." *Wee,* meaning "little," does not occur else
where in Shakespeare.   24. **Cain-colored:** The F1 reading
Q1 spells "kane," and some editors emend to "cane-colored'
(i.e., light yellow), which is probably correct.   25. **softly-
sprighted:** gentle-spirited.   26. **tall:** valiant.   27. **between . . .
head:** a proverbial phrase for "in these parts."   28. **warrener:**
gamekeeper.   38. **shent:** rebuked.   39. **closet:** small room,
study.   44. **And . . . adown-a:** the meaningless refrain of a
popular song.   46. **toys:** trifles, rubbish.

---

83. **Pandarus:** i.e., your pander. For Pandarus, see *Tr & Cr.*
84. **And . . . steel:** and still keep my honor as a soldier.   86. **havior of reputation:** outward respectability.   89. **pinnace:** swift,
light sailing vessel, used for carrying dispatches.   93. **French
thrift:** It was a fashion to employ French pages at low wages.
skirted: wearing a full-skirted coat.   94. **gourd . . . fullam:** kinds
of false dice. **holds:** still work — Pistol will not aid Falstaff in
his base schemes so long as he can make a more honest living by
cheating at dice.   96. **Tester:** sixpence.   97. **Phrygian Turk:**
Turk was a term of abuse. Phrygia is in Asia Minor.   101. **welkin:** sky.   105. **eke:** also.   107. **prove:** test the loyalty of.
111. **yellowness:** the color of jealousy. **revolt of mine:** my desertion of Falstaff.   113. **malcontents:** See App. 4.

boitier vert° — a box, a green-a box. Do intend vat I speak? A green-a box.

QUICK. Aye, forsooth, I'll fetch it you. [*Aside*] I am glad he went not in himself. If he had 50 found the young man, he would have been horn-mad.°

CAIUS. Fe, fe, fe, fe! *Ma foi, il fait fort chaud. Je m'en vais à la cour — la grande affaire.*

QUICK. Is it this, sir?   55

CAIUS. *Oui. Mette le au mon pocket. Dépêche,* quickly. Vere is dat knave Rugby?

QUICK. What, John Rugby! John!

RUG. Here, sir!

CAIUS. You are John Rugby, and you are 60 Jack° Rugby. Come, take-a your rapier,° and come after my heel to the Court.

RUG. 'Tis ready, sir, here in the porch.

CAIUS. By my trot, I tarry too long. Od's me! *Qu'ai-j'oublié!* Dere is some simples° in my closet dat I vill not for the varld I shall leave behind. 66

QUICK. Aye me, he'll find the young man there, and be mad!   69

CAIUS. *O diable, diable!* Vat is in my closet? Villain! Larron!° [*Pulling* SIMPLE *out*] Rugby, my rapier!

QUICK. Good master, be content.

CAIUS. Wherefore shall I be content-a?

QUICK. The young man is an honest man.   75

CAIUS. What shall de honest man do in my closet? Dere is no honest man dat shall come in my closet.

QUICK. I beseech you be not so phlegmatic.° Hear the truth of it. He came of an errand to me from Parson Hugh.   81

CAIUS. Vell.

SIM. Aye, forsooth; to desire her to ——

QUICK. Peace, I pray you.   84

CAIUS. Peace-a your tongue. — Speak-a your tale.

SIM. To desire this honest gentlewoman, your maid, to speak a good word to Mistress Anne Page for my master in the way of marriage.

QUICK. This is all, indeed, la! But I'll ne'er put my finger in the fire, and need not.   91

CAIUS. Sir Hugh send-a you? Rugby, *baille*° me some paper. Tarry you a little-a while. [*Writes.*]

QUICK. [*Aside to* SIMPLE] I am glad he is so quiet. If he had been throughly moved, you 95 should have heard him so loud and so melancholy.° But notwithstanding, man, I'll do you your master what good I can. And the very yea and the no is, the French doctor, my master — I may 100

call him my master, look you, for I keep his house, and I wash, wring, brew, bake, scour, dress meat and drink, make the beds, and do all myself ——

SIM. [*Aside to* MISTRESS QUICKLY] 'Tis a great charge° to come under one body's hand.   105

QUICK. [*Aside to* SIMPLE] Are you advised o' that? You shall find it a great charge; and to be up early and down late — but notwithstanding (to tell you in your ear, I would have no words of it) my master himself is in love with Mistress Anne 110 Page. But notwithstanding that, I know Anne's mind — that's neither here nor there.

CAIUS. You jack'nape,° give-a this letter to Sir Hugh. By gar,° it is a shallenge. I will cut his troat in de park, and I will teach a scurvy jackanape priest to meddle or make.° You may be gone. 116 It is not good you tarry here. — By gar, I will cut all his two stones. By gar, he shall not have a stone to throw at his dog.   [*Exit* SIMPLE.]

QUICK. Alas, he speaks but for his friend.   120

CAIUS. It is no matter-a ver dat. Do not you tell-a me dat I shall have Anne Page for myself? By gar, I vill kill de Jack priest, and I have appointed mine host of de Jarteer to measure our weapon. By gar, I will myself have Anne Page.   126

QUICK. Sir, the maid loves you, and all shall be well. We must give folks leave to prate. What, the goodyear!°

CAIUS. Rugby, come to the Court with me.   130 By gar, if I have not Anne Page, I shall turn your head out of my door. Follow my heels, Rugby.

[*Exeunt* DOCTOR CAIUS *and* RUGBY.]

QUICK. You shall have An fool's head of 134 your own. No, I know Anne's mind for that. Never a woman in Windsor knows more of Anne's mind than I do, nor can do more than I do with her, I thank Heaven.

FEN. [*Within*] Who's within there? Ho!

QUICK. Who's there, I trow?° Come near the house, I pray you.   141

[*Enter* FENTON.]

FEN. How now, good woman! How dost thou?

QUICK. The better that it pleases your good Worship to ask.

FEN. What news? How does pretty Mistress Anne?   146

QUICK. In truth, sir, and she is pretty, and honest, and gentle, and one that is your friend. I can tell you that by the way, I praise Heaven for it. 151

FEN. Shall I do any good, think'st thou? Shall I not lose my suit?

QUICK. Troth, sir, all is in His hands above. But notwithstanding, Master Fenton, I'll be sworn 155 on a book, she loves you. Have not your Worship a

---

47. *boitier vert:* F1 and Q1 are usually wide of the mark when they attempt to reproduce Caius's French. The editors have emended.   51–52. horn-mad: mad as a stag in the spring. 61. Jack: i.e., a knave. take-a . . . rapier: i.e., to protect his master.   65. simples: drugs.   71. Larron: thief.   79. phlegmatic: She should have said "choleric." See App. 3.   92. *baille* bring.   96–97. melancholy: she means "choleric."

105. charge: responsibility.   113. jack'nape: whippersnapper. 114. gar: God.   116. make: interfere.   129. goodyear: a meaningless phrase meaning "what the deuce."   140. trow: wonder.

wart above your eye?

FEN. Yes, marry, have I. What of that?

QUICK. Well, thereby hangs a tale. Good faith, it is such another Nan.° But, I detest, an honest 160 maid as ever broke bread. We had an hour's talk of that wart. I shall never laugh but in that maid's company! But, indeed, she is given too much to allicholy° and musing. But for you — well, go to. 165

FEN. Well, I shall see her today. Hold, there's money for thee. Let me have thy voice in my behalf. If thou seest her before me, commend me.

QUICK. Will I? I' faith, that we will; and I 170 will tell your Worship more of the wart the next time we have confidence, and of other wooers.

FEN. Well, farewell. I am in great haste now.

QUICK. Farewell to your Worship. [*Exit* FENTON.] Truly, an honest gentleman. But Anne 177 loves him not, for I know Anne's mind as well as another does. Out upon 't! What have I forgot?

[*Exit.*]

Act II

SCENE I. *Before* PAGE'S *house.*

[*Enter* MISTRESS PAGE, *with a letter.*]

MRS. PAGE. What, have I scaped love letters in the holiday time° of my beauty, and am I now a subject for them? Let me see. [*Reads.*]

"Ask me no reason why I love you, for though Love use Reason for his physician,° he admits 5 him not for his counselor. You are not young, no more am I. Go to,° then, there's sympathy. You are merry, so am I. Ha, ha! Then there's more sympathy. You love sack,° and so do I. Would you desire better sympathy? Let it suffice thee, Mistress 11 Page — at the least, if the love of soldier can suffice — that I love thee. I will not say pity me — 'tis not a soldierlike phrase; but I say love me. By me,

Thine own true knight, 15
By day or night,
Or any kind of light,
With all his might
For thee to fight, JOHN FALSTAFF."

What a Herod of Jewry° is this! Oh, wicked, 20 wicked world! One that is well-nigh worn to pieces with age to show himself a young gallant! What an unweighed° behavior hath this Flemish° drunkard picked — with the Devil's name! — 25 out of my conversation, that he dares in this manner assay° me? Why, he hath not been thrice in my company! What should I say to him? I was then frugal of my mirth. Heaven forgive me! Why, I'll exhibit° a bill in the Parliament for the putting down of men. How shall I be revenged on 31 him? For revenged I will be, as sure as his guts are made of puddings.°

[*Enter* MISTRESS FORD.]

MRS. FORD. Mistress Page! Trust me, I was going to your house.

MRS. PAGE. And, trust me, I was coming to you. You look very ill. 36

MRS. FORD. Nay, I'll ne'er believe that. I have to show to the contrary.

MRS. PAGE. Faith, but you do, in my mind.

MRS. FORD. Well, I do, then. Yet, I say, I 40 could show you to the contrary. O Mistress Page, give me some counsel!

MRS. PAGE. What's the matter, woman?

MRS. FORD. Oh, woman, if it were not for one trifling respect,° I could come to such honor! 45

MRS. PAGE. Hang the trifle, woman! Take the honor. What is it? Dispense with trifles. What is it?

MRS. FORD. If I would but go to Hell for an eternal moment° or so, I could be knighted. 50

MRS. PAGE. What? Thou liest! Sir Alice Ford! These knights will hack,° and so thou shouldst not alter the article of thy gentry.°

MRS. FORD. We burn daylight.° Here, read, read. Perceive how I might be knighted. I shall think 55 the worse of fat men as long as I have an eye to make difference° of men's liking.° And yet he would not swear, praised women's modesty, and gave such orderly and well-behaved reproof 60 to all uncomeliness that I would have sworn his disposition would have gone to the truth of his words; but they do no more adhere and keep place together than the Hundredth Psalm° to the tune of "Green Sleeves."° What tempest, I trow, threw 65 this whale, with so many tuns of oil in his belly, ashore at Windsor? How shall I be revenged on

---

159-60. it . . . Nan: Mrs. Quickly is never too precise in her use of English. Her mind has presumably gone back to her praise of Anne as "pretty and honest and gentle." 164-65. allicholy: for "melancholy."

Act II, Sc. i: 2. holiday time: gay period. 5. physician: F1 reads "precisian" (which usually means Puritan preacher), which ɪ / be correct. The emendation was made by Johnson. 7. Go to: well then. 9. sack: Spanish wine, to which Falstaff was very partial. See *II Hen IV*, IV iii.102-35.

20. Herod of Jewry: regarded as a type of wicked tyrant. 23. unweighed: light. 24. Flemish: the Flemings were notable for their deep drinking. See *Oth*, II.iii.77-87. 27. assay: attempt. 30. exhibit: introduce. 32. puddings: sausages; i.e., entrails filled with meat. 45. respect: consideration. 50. moment: period. 52. hack: ride off without keeping promise. 53. article . . . gentry: your rank. 54. burn daylight: waste time. 57. make difference: distinguish. liking: physique. 64. Hundredth Psalm: "All people that on earth do dwell, /Sing to the Lord with cheerful voice." 65. "Green Sleeves": a very popular song-tune, to which (as with certain modern songs, like "John Brown's Body") various words had been fitted.

him? I think the best way were to entertain him
with hope till the wicked fire of lust have melted
him in his own grease. Did you ever hear the like?

MRS. PAGE. Letter for letter, but that the 71
name of Page and Ford differs! To thy great comfort in this mystery of ill opinions,° here's the twin
brother of thy letter. But let thine inherit° first, 75
for, I protest, mine never shall. I warrant he hath a
thousand of these letters, writ with blank space for
different names — sure, more! — and these are of
the second edition. He will print them, out of
doubt,° for he cares not what he puts into the 80
press, when he would put us two. I had rather be
a giantess and lie under Mount Pelion.° Well, I will
find you twenty lascivious turtles° ere one chaste
man.

MRS. FORD. Why, this is the very same, the very
hand, the very words. What doth he think of us?

MRS. PAGE. Nay, I know not. It makes me 86
almost ready to wrangle with mine own honesty.°
I'll entertain° myself like one that I am not acquainted withal.° For, sure, unless he know 90
some strain° in me that I know not myself, he
would never have boarded° me in this fury.

MRS. FORD. "Boarding," call you it? I'll be sure to
keep him above deck.

MRS. PAGE. So will I. If he come under my 95
hatches, I'll never to sea again. Let's be revenged
on him. Let's appoint him a meeting, give him a
show of comfort in his suit, and lead him on with
a fine-baited° delay till he hath pawned his horses
to mine host of the Garter. 100

MRS. FORD. Nay, I will consent to act any villainy
against him that may not sully the chariness° of
our honesty. Oh, that my husband saw this letter!
It would give eternal food to his jealousy. 105

MRS. PAGE. Why, look where he comes, and my
good man too. He's as far from jealousy as I am
from giving him cause, and that, I hope, is an unmeasurable distance.

MRS. FORD. You are the happier woman. 110

MRS. PAGE. Let's consult together against this
greasy knight. Come hither.   [*They retire.*]

[*Enter* FORD, *with* PISTOL, *and* PAGE, *with* NYM.]

FORD. Well, I hope it be not so.

PIST. Hope is a curtal° dog in some affairs.
Sir John affects° thy wife. 115

FORD. Why, sir, my wife is not young.

PIST. He woos both high and low, both rich and
poor,

Both young and old, one with another, Ford.
He loves the gallimaufry.° Ford, perpend.°

FORD. Love my wife! 120

PIST. With liver burning hot. Prevent,° or go
thou,
Like Sir Actaeon° he, with Ringwood° at thy
heels.
Oh, odious is the name!

FORD. What name, sir?

PIST. The horn,° I say. Farewell. 125
Take heed! Have open eye, for thieves do foot by
night.
Take heed ere summer comes, or cuckoo birds do
sing.
Away, Sir Corporal Nym! —
Believe it, Page, he speaks sense.   [*Exit.*]

FORD. [*Aside*] I will be patient. I will find out
this. 131

NYM. [*To* PAGE] And this is true. I like not the
humor of lying. He hath wronged me in some humors. I should have borne the humored letter to
her; but I have a sword, and it shall bite upon 135
my necessity. He loves your wife. There's the short
and the long. My name is Corporal Nym. I speak,
and I avouch. 'Tis true. My name is Nym, and Falstaff loves your wife. Adieu. I love not the humor
of bread and cheese,° and there's the humor of it.
Adieu.   [*Exit.*] 141

PAGE. "The humor of it," quoth 'a! Here's a fellow frights English out of his wits.

FORD. I will seek out Falstaff.

PAGE. I never heard such a drawling, affecting°
rogue. 146

FORD. If I do find it — well.

PAGE. I will not believe such a Cataian,° though
the priest o' the town commended him for a true
man. 150

FORD. 'Twas a good sensible fellow — well.

PAGE. How now, Meg!

[MISTRESS PAGE *and* MISTRESS FORD *come forward.*]

MRS. PAGE. Whither go you, George? Hark you.

MRS. FORD. How now, sweet Frank! Why art thou
melancholy? 156

FORD. I melancholy! I am not melancholy. Get
you home, go.

MRS. FORD. Faith, thou hast some crotchets° in
thy head. Now, will you go, Mistress Page? 160

MRS. PAGE. Have with you.° You'll come to dinner, George? [*Aside to* MISTRESS FORD] Look who
comes yonder. She shall be our messenger to this
paltry knight.

---

73. **mystery . . . opinions:** strange story of our alleged bad repu-
tations.   75. **inherit:** come into its own; i.e., be heard first.
79–80. **out of doubt:** for sure.   82. **Mount Pelion:** See *Haml*,
V.i.276,n.   83. **turtles:** turtle doves — the pattern of chaste loyalty.   87. **honesty:** chastity.   89. **entertain:** treat.   90. **withal:**
with.   91. **strain:** tendency.   92. **boarded:** sailed up alongside.
99. **fine-baited:** tempting and alluring.   102. **chariness:** careful
preservation.   114. **curtal:** bobtailed.   115. **affects:** loves.

119. **gallimaufry:** hotch-potch, mix up; i.e., all comers. **perpend:**
consider.   121. **Prevent:** forestall.   122. **Sir Actaeon:** See
T Andr, II.iii.63,n. **Ringwood:** a popular name for a hound.
125. **horn:** See App. 11.   140. **bread . . . cheese:** plain living,
which is all that he can now afford, since his discharge.   145. **affecting:** affected.   148. **Cataian:** Chinese, subtle rogue.
159. **crotchets:** whimsies.   161. **Have . . . you:** agreed.

MRS. FORD. [*Aside to* MISTRESS PAGE] Trust me, I
thought on her. She'll fit it.   166

[*Enter* MISTRESS QUICKLY.]

MRS. PAGE. You are come to see my daughter
Anne?

QUICK. Aye, forsooth, and, I pray, how does good
Mistress Anne?   170

MRS. PAGE. Go in with us and see. We have° an
hour's talk with you.   [*Exeunt* MISTRESS PAGE,
MISTRESS FORD, *and* MISTRESS QUICKLY.]

PAGE. How now, Master Ford!

FORD. You heard what this knave told me, did
you not?   175

PAGE. Yes, and you heard what the other told me?

FORD. Do you think there is truth in them?

PAGE. Hang 'em, slaves! I do not think the knight
would offer it. But these that accuse him in his   180
intent toward our wives are a yoke° of his discarded men, very rogues, now they be out of service.

FORD. Were they his men?

PAGE. Marry,° were they.   185

FORD. I like it never the better for that. Does he
lie° at the Garter?

PAGE. Aye, marry, does he. If he should intend
this voyage toward my wife, I would turn her
loose to him, and what he gets more of her than
sharp words, let it lie on my head.   191

FORD. I do not misdoubt my wife, but I would be
loath to turn them together. A man may be too confident. I would have nothing lie on my head. I cannot be thus satisfied.   195

PAGE. Look where my ranting host of the Garter
comes. There is either liquor in his pate or money
in his purse when he looks so merrily. [*Enter* HOST.]
How now, mine host!

HOST. How now, bully rook!° Thou'rt a gentleman. Cavaleiro° Justice, I say!   201

[*Enter* SHALLOW.]

SHAL. I follow, mine host, I follow. Good even
and twenty,° good Master Page! Master Page, will
you go with us? We have sport in hand.   205

HOST. Tell him, Cavaleiro Justice. Tell him, bully
rook.

SHAL. Sir, there is a fray to be fought between Sir
Hugh the Welsh priest and Caius the French
doctor.   210

FORD. Good mine host o' the Garter, a word with
you.   [*Drawing him aside.*]

HOST. What say'st thou, my bully rook?

SHAL. [*To* PAGE] Will you go with us to behold
it? My merry host hath had the measuring of   215

their weapons,° and, I think, hath appointed them
contrary places. For, believe me, I hear the parson
is no jester. Hark, I will tell you what our sport
shall be.   [*They converse apart.*]

HOST. Hast thou no suit against my knight, my
guest-Cavaleire?   221

FORD. None, I protest. But I'll give you a pottle°
of burnt° sack to give me recourse° to him, and
tell him my name is Brook — only for a jest.

HOST. My hand, bully. Thou shalt have   225
egress and regress — said I well? — and thy name
shall be Brook. It is a merry knight. Will you go,
Anhaires?°

SHAL. Have with you, mine host.

PAGE. I have heard the Frenchman hath good
skill in his rapier.   231

SHAL. Tut, sir, I could have told you more. In
these times you stand on distance, your passes, stoccadoes,° and I know not what. 'Tis the heart, Master Page, 'tis here, 'tis here. I have seen the   235
time with my long sword° I would have made you
four tall fellows skip like rats.

HOST. Here, boys, here, here! Shall we wag?°

PAGE. Have with you. I had rather hear them
scold than fight. [*Exeunt* HOST, SHALLOW, *and* PAGE.]

FORD. Though Page be a secure° fool and   241
stands so firmly on his wife's frailty, yet I cannot
put off my opinion so easily. She was in his company at Page's house, and what they made° there
I know not. Well, I will look further into't,   245
and I have a disguise to sound Falstaff. If I find her
honest, I lose not my labor. If she be otherwise, 'tis
labor well bestowed.   [*Exit.*]

SCENE II. *A room in the Garter Inn.*

[*Enter* SIR JOHN FALSTAFF *and* PISTOL.]

FAL. I will not lend thee a penny.

PIST. Why, then the world's mine oyster,
Which I with sword will open.°

FAL. Not a penny. I have been content, sir, you
should lay my countenance to pawn.° I have   5
grated upon° my good friends for three reprieves
for you and your coach-fellow° Nym, or else you

215–16. measuring . . . weapons: i.e., acting as umpire. For the
fight to be fair, the weapons must be of equal length. 222. pottle:
two quarts. 223. burnt: heated. recourse: access. 228. Anhaires: not satisfactorily explained. Many guesses, none of them
convincing, have been made at the meaning of this word, which
in F1 is spelled An-heires. 233–34. distance . . . stoccadoes:
fencing terms affected by the younger men. See *R & J*, II.iv.23–
27,n, and Pl. 22l. 236. long sword: See Pl. 22j and p. 99b.
See *Lear*, V.iii.275–76. 238. wag: get going. 241. secure:
self-confident, careless. 244. made: did.

Sc. ii: 2–3. world's . . . open: I will force the world to provide
me with pearls. Pistol is seldom clear. He means that he will live
by violence. 5. lay . . . pawn: make use of my reputation.
6. grated upon: made myself a nuisance to. 7. coach-fellow:
one who rides in the same cart to execution.

171. We have: we must have. 181. yoke: pair. 185. Marry:
Mary, by the Virgin. 187. lie: stay. 200. bully rook: See
I.iii.2,n. 201. Cavaleiro: Sir Knight. 202–03. Good . . .
twenty: a good evening and twenty more — a proverbial way
of greeting (much the same as "and then some." nowadays).

had looked through the grate,° like a geminy° of baboons. I am damned in Hell for swearing to 10 gentlemen my friends you were good soldiers and tall° fellows, and when Mistress Bridget lost the handle of her fan, I took't upon mine honor thou hadst it not.

PIST. Didst not thou share? Hadst thou not fifteen pence?

FAL. Reason, you rogue, reason. Think'st 15 thou I'll endanger my soul gratis? At a word, hang no more about me, I am no gibbet° for you. Go! A short knife and a throng!° To your manor of Pickthatch!° Go. You'll not bear a letter for me, you rogue! You stand upon your honor! Why, thou 20 unconfinable baseness, it is as much as I can do to keep the terms of my honor precise.° I, I, I myself sometimes, leaving the fear of God on the left hand, and hiding mine honor in my necessity, am 25 fain to shuffle, to hedge, and to lurch;° and yet you, rogue, will ensconce your rags, your cat-a-mountain° looks, your red-lattice° phrases, and your bold-beating° oaths under the shelter of your honor! You will not do it, you! 30

PIST. I do relent. What would thou more of man?
[*Enter* ROBIN.]

ROB. Sir, here's a woman would speak with you.
FAL. Let her approach.
[*Enter* MISTRESS QUICKLY.]

QUICK. Give your Worship good morrow.
FAL. Good morrow, good wife. 35
QUICK. Not so, an't° please your Worship.
FAL. Good maid, then.
QUICK. I'll be sworn;° as my mother was, the first hour I was born.
FAL. I do believe the swearer. What with me? 40
QUICK. Shall I vouchsafe your Worship a word or two?
FAL. Two thousand, fair woman, and I'll vouchsafe thee the hearing.
QUICK. There is one Mistress Ford, sir. I 45 pray, come a little nearer this ways. I myself dwell with Master Doctor Caius ——
FAL. Well, on. Mistress Ford, you say ——
QUICK. Your Worship says very true. I pray your Worship, come a little nearer this ways. 50
FAL. I warrant thee, nobody hears. Mine own people, mine own people.
QUICK. Are they so? God bless them, and make them His servants!

FAL. Well, Mistress Ford — what of her? 55
QUICK. Why, sir, she's a good creature. Lord, Lord! Your Worship's a wanton! Well, Heaven forgive you and all of us, I pray!
FAL. Mistress Ford, come, Mistress Ford ——
QUICK. Marry, this is the short and the long 60 of it. You have brought her into such a canaries° as 'tis wonderful. The best courtier of them all, when the Court lay at Windsor, could never have brought her to such a canary. Yet there has been knights, and lords, and gentlemen, with their coaches; 65 I warrant you, coach after coach, letter after letter, gift after gift, smelling so sweetly — all musk — and so rushling,° I warrant you, in silk and gold, and in such alligant° terms, and in such wine and 70 sugar of the best and the fairest that would have won any woman's heart; and, I warrant you, they could never get an eye-wink of her. I had myself twenty angels given me this morning, but I defy all angels — in any such sort, as they say — but in 75 the way of honesty. And, I warrant you, they could never get her so much as sip on a cup with the proudest of them all; and yet there has been earls — nay, which is more, pensioners.° But, I warrant you, all is one with her. 80
FAL. But what says she to me? Be brief, my good she-Mercury.°
QUICK. Marry, she hath received your letter, for the which she thanks you a thousand times, and she gives you to notify that her husband will be 85 absence from his house between ten and eleven.
FAL. Ten and eleven.
QUICK. Aye, forsooth, and then you may come and see the picture, she says, that you wot° of. 90 Master Ford, her husband, will be from home. Alas, the sweet woman leads an ill life with him! He's a very jealousy man. She leads a very frampold° life with him, good heart.
FAL. Ten and eleven. Woman, commend me to her. I will not fail her. 96
QUICK. Why, you say well. But I have another messenger to your Worship. Mistress Page hath her hearty commendations to you, too. And let me tell you in your ear, she's as fartuous° a civil 100 modest wife, and one, I tell you, that will not miss you morning nor evening prayer, as any is in Windsor, whoe'er be the other. And she bade me tell your Worship that her husband is seldom from 105 home, but she hopes there will come a time. I never knew a woman so dote upon a man. Surely, I think you have charms,° la! Yes, in truth.

---

9. grate: iron bars of the jail. geminy: pair. 12. tall: brave. 17. gibbet: gallows. 18. short . . . throng: i.e., turn cutpurse and rob in crowds. See Gen. Intro. p. 28a. 18–19. Pickt-hatch: a disreputable district in London, the haunt of prostitutes and thieves. 22. keep . . . precise: preserve my reputation. 26. shuffle . . . lurch: to make excuses, to dodge, to hide. 27. cat-a-mountain: ferocious wild cat. 28. red-lattice: tavern — because the lattice windows of taverns were painted red. See *II Hen IV*, II.ii.85–86,n. 28–29. bold-beating: bullying. 36. an't: if. 38. I'll be sworn: I swear that I am.

61. canaries: lively dance, but Mrs. Quickly uses it to mean "quandary." 68. rushling: the rustling of their silks. 70. alligant: for elegant. 79. pensioners: gentlemen of the Queen's bodyguard. See *MND*, II.i.10,n. 82. Mercury: Mercury was the messenger of the gods. 90. wot: know. 93. frampold: disagreeable. 100. fartuous: for "virtuous." 108. charms: love magic.

FAL. Not I, I assure thee. Setting the attraction of my good parts aside, I have no other charms.   111

QUICK. Blessing on your heart for't!

FAL. But, I pray thee tell me this: Has Ford's wife and Page's wife acquainted each other how they love me?   115

QUICK. That were a jest indeed! They have not so little grace, I hope. That were a trick indeed! But Mistress Page would desire you to send her your little page, of all loves.° Her husband has a marvelous infection° to the little page; and, truly,   120 Master Page is an honest man. Never a wife in Windsor leads a better life than she does. Do what she will, say what she will, take all, pay all, go to bed when she list, rise when she list, all is as she will; and, truly, she deserves it, for if there be   125 a kind woman in Windsor, she is one. You must send her your page. No remedy.

FAL. Why, I will.

QUICK. Nay, but do so, then. And, look you, he may come and go between you both; and, in   130 any case, have a nay-word,° that you may know one another's mind, and the boy never need to understand anything. For 'tis not good that children should know any wickedness. Old folks, you know, have discretion, as they say, and know the world.

FAL. Fare thee well. Commend me to them   137 both. There's my purse. I am yet thy debtor. Boy, go along with this woman. [*Exeunt* MISTRESS QUICKLY *and* ROBIN.] This news distracts me!   140

PIST. This punk° is one of Cupid's carriers.° Clap on more sails! Pursue! Up with your fights!° Give fire! She is my prize, or ocean whelm° them all!   [*Exit.*]

FAL. Say'st thou so, old Jack? Go thy ways. I'll make more of thy old body than I have done.   145 Will they yet look after thee? Wilt thou, after the expense of so much money, be now a gainer? Good body, I thank thee. Let them say 'tis grossly done. So it be fairly done, no matter.

[*Enter* BARDOLPH.]

BARD. Sir John, there's one Master Brook   150 below would fain speak with you and be acquainted with you, and hath sent your Worship a morning's draught of sack.

FAL. Brook is his name?

BARD. Aye, sir.   155

FAL. Call him in. [*Exit* BARDOLPH.] Such Brooks are welcome to me, that o'erflow such liquor. Ah ha! Mistress Ford and Mistress Page, have I encompassed° you? Go to, via!°

[*Re-enter* BARDOLPH, *with* FORD *disguised*.]

FORD. Bless you, sir!   160

FAL. And you, sir! Would you speak with me?

FORD. I make bold to press with so little preparation upon you.

FAL. You're welcome. What's your will? — Give us leave, drawer.   [*Exit* BARDOLPH.]   165

FORD. Sir, I am a gentleman that have spent much. My name is Brook.

FAL. Good Master Brook, I desire more acquaintance of you.   169

FORD. Good Sir John, I sue for yours; not to charge you, for I must let you understand I think myself in better plight for a lender than you are, the which hath something emboldened me to this unseasoned intrusion. For they say if money go before, all ways do lie open.   175

FAL. Money is a good soldier, sir, and will on.

FORD. Troth, and I have a bag of money here troubles me. If you will help to bear it, Sir John, take all, or half, for easing me of the carriage.

FAL. Sir, I know not how I may deserve to be your porter.   181

FORD. I will tell you, sir, if you will give me the hearing.

FAL. Speak, good Master Brook. I shall be glad to be your servant.   185

FORD. Sir, I hear you are a scholar — I will be brief with you — and you have been a man long known to me, though I had never so good means as desire to make myself acquainted with you. I shall discover a thing to you wherein I must very   190 much lay open mine own imperfection. But, good Sir John, as you have one eye upon my follies, as you hear them unfolded, turn another into the register° of your own, that I may pass with a reproof the easier, sith° you yourself know how easy it is to be such an offender.   196

FAL. Very well, sir. Proceed.

FORD. There is a gentlewoman in this town. Her husband's name is Ford.

FAL. Well, sir.   200

FORD. I have long loved her and, I protest to you, bestowed much on her, followed her with a doting observance,° engrossed° opportunities to meet her, fee'd° every slight occasion that could but niggardly° give me sight of her, not only bought   205 many presents to give her, but have given largely to many to know what she would have given. Briefly, I have pursued her as love hath pursued me, which hath been on the wing of all occasions.° But   210 whatsoever I have merited, either in my mind or in my means, meed,° I am sure, I have received none, unless experience be a jewel that I have purchased

119. of . . . loves: above everything else.   120. infection: for affection.   131. nay-word: password.   141. punk: bawd. carriers: messengers.   142. fights: canvas screens used on sailing ships to conceal the fighting men on deck.   143. whelm: overwhelm, drown.   158–59. encompassed: got round.   159. via: come on.

193–94. register: record.   195. sith: since.   203. observance: reverence. engrossed: bought wholesale.   204. fee'd: paid for. 204–05. niggardly: slightly.   210. wing . . . occasions: at every possible opportunity.   212. meed: reward.

at an infinite rate, and that hath taught me to say
this:

"Love like a shadow flies when substance love
　　pursues,　　　　　　　　　　　　　　　　215
Pursuing that that flies, and flying what pursues."

FAL. Have you received no promise of satisfaction at her hands?

FORD. Never.

FAL. Have you importuned her to such a purpose?　　　　　　　　　　　　　　　　　221

FORD. Never.

FAL. Of what quality was your love, then?

FORD. Like a fair house built on another man's
ground, so that I have lost my edifice by mistaking
the place where I erected it.　　　　　　　226

FAL. To what purpose have you unfolded this
to me?

FORD. When I have told you that, I have told you
all. Some say that though she appear honest to　230
me, yet in other places she enlargeth her mirth so
far that there is shrewd construction° made of her.
Now, Sir John, here is the heart of my purpose.
You are a gentleman of excellent breeding, admirable
discourse, of great admittance,° authentic° in　235
your place and person, generally allowed° for your
many warlike, courtlike, and learned preparations.°

FAL. Oh, sir!　　　　　　　　　　　　　239

FORD. Believe it, for you know it. There is money.
Spend it, spend it. Spend more. Spend all I have.
Only give me so much of your time in exchange of
it as to lay an amiable siege to the honesty of this
Ford's wife. Use your art of wooing. Win her to
consent to you. If any man may, you may as soon as
any.　　　　　　　　　　　　　　　　　246

FAL. Would it apply well to the vehemency of
your affection that I should win what you would
enjoy? Methinks you prescribe to yourself very preposterously.　　　　　　　　　　　　　250

FORD. Oh, understand my drift. She dwells so securely on the excellency of her honor that the folly
of my soul dares not present itself. She is too bright
to be looked against. Now, could I come to her with
any detection in my hand,° my desires had　255
instance and argument to commend themselves. I
could drive her then from the ward° of her purity,
her reputation, her marriage vow, and a thousand
other her defenses, which now are too too strongly
embattled against me. What say you to't, Sir
John?　　　　　　　　　　　　　　　　261

FAL. Master Brook, I will first make bold with
your money; next, give me your hand; and last, as
I am a gentleman, you shall, if you will, enjoy
Ford's wife.　　　　　　　　　　　　　265

FORD. Oh, good sir!

FAL. I say you shall.

FORD. Want no money, Sir John. You shall want
none.　　　　　　　　　　　　　　　　269

FAL. Want no Mistress Ford, Master Brook. You
shall want none. I shall be with her, I may tell you,
by her own appointment. Even as you came in to
me, her assistant, or go-between, parted from me. I
say I shall be with her between ten and eleven,　275
for at that time the jealous rascally knave her husband will be forth. Come you to me at night. You
shall know how I speed.

FORD. I am blest in your acquaintance. Do you
know Ford, sir?　　　　　　　　　　　280

FAL. Hang him, poor cuckoldly° knave! I know
him not. Yet I wrong him to call him poor. They
say the jealous, wittolly° knave hath masses of
money, for the which his wife seems to me well-favored.° I will use her as the key of the cuckoldly
rogue's coffer, and there's my harvest home.　286

FORD. I would you knew Ford, sir, that you
might avoid him if you saw him.

FAL. Hang him, mechanical° salt-butter° rogue!
I will stare him out of his wits. I will awe him　291
with my cudgel. It shall hang like a meteor° o'er
the cuckold's horns. Master Brook, thou shalt know
I will predominate over the peasant, and thou　295
shalt lie with his wife. Come to me soon at night.
Ford's a knave, and I will aggravate his style.°
Thou, Master Brook, shalt know him for knave and
cuckold. Come to me soon at night.　[*Exit.*]　299

FORD. What a damned Epicurean° rascal is this!
My heart is ready to crack with impatience. Who
says this is improvident jealousy? My wife hath
sent to him. The hour is fixed. The match is made.
Would any man have thought this? See the　305
hell of having a false woman! My bed shall be
abused, my coffers ransacked, my reputation gnawn
at, and I shall not only receive this villainous wrong
but stand under the adoption of abominable terms,°
and by him that does me this wrong. Terms!　310
Names! Amaimon sounds well, Lucifer, well, Barbason,° well, yet they are devils' additions,° the
names of fiends. But Cuckold! Wittol! Cuckold!
The Devil himself hath not such a name. Page is
an ass, a secure ass. He will trust his wife.　315
He will not be jealous. I will rather trust a Fleming° with my butter, Parson Hugh the Welshman
with my cheese, an Irishman with my aqua-vitae°

---

232. shrewd construction: evil interpretation.　235. great admittance: admitted everywhere. authentic: a man of authority.
236. allowed: recognized.　237. preparations: accomplishments.
254-55. could . . . hand: if I could tell her that I know she is
known to have had other lovers.　257. ward: defense.

281. cuckoldly: See App. 11.　283. wittolly: A wittol is a willing
cuckold.　284-85. well-favored: in good condition.　290. mechanical: base. salt-butter: one who eats cheap butter.　292. meteor: comet — a sign of disaster.　297. aggravate . . . style:
make his title (cuckold) the greater.　300. Epicurean: lustful.
309. stand . . . terms: be insulted by being called vile names.
311-12. Amaimon . . . Barbason: names of fiends.　312. additions: titles.　316-20. Fleming . . . bottle: The love of the
Flemings for butter, the Welsh for cheese, and the Irish for
whiskey was proverbial.　318. aqua-vitae: spirits

bottle, or a thief to walk my ambling gelding,° than my wife with herself. Then she plots, then she   321 ruminates, then she devises, and what they think in their hearts they may effect, they will break their hearts but they will effect. God be praised for my jealousy! Eleven o'clock the hour! I will prevent this, detect my wife, be revenged on Falstaff,   326 and laugh at Page. I will about it. Better three hours too soon than a minute too late. Fie, fie, fie! Cuckold! Cuckold! Cuckold!   [*Exit.*]   329

SCENE III. *A field near Windsor.*

[*Enter* DOCTOR CAIUS *and* RUGBY.]

CAIUS. Jack Rugby!

RUG. Sir?

CAIUS. Vat is de clock, Jack?

RUG. 'Tis past the hour, sir, that Sir Hugh promised to meet.   5

CAIUS. By gar, he has save his soul dat he is no come. He has pray his Pible well dat he is no come. By gar, Jack Rugby, he is dead already if he be come.

RUG. He is wise, sir. He knew your Worship would kill him if he came.   11

CAIUS. By gar, de herring is no dead so as I vill kill him. Take your rapier, Jack. I vill tell you how I vill kill him.

RUG. Alas, sir, I cannot fence.   15

CAIUS. Villainy,° take your rapier.

RUG. Forbear. Here's company.

[*Enter* HOST, SHALLOW, SLENDER, *and* PAGE.]

HOST. Bless thee, bully doctor!

SHAL. Save you, Master Doctor Caius!

PAGE. Now, good Master Doctor!   20

SLEN. Give you good morrow, sir.

CAIUS. Vat be all you, one, two, tree, four, come for?

HOST. To see thee fight, to see thee foin,° to see thee traverse, to see thee here, to see thee there,   25 to see thee pass thy punto, thy stock, thy reverse, thy distance, thy montant. Is he dead, my Ethiopian? Is he dead, my Francisco?° Ha, bully! What says my Aesculapius? My Galen?° My heart of elder?°

Ha! Is he dead, bully stale?° Is he dead?   31

CAIUS. By gar, he is de coward Jack priest of de vorld.° He is not show his face.

HOST. Thou art a Castalion-King-Urinal.° Hector of Greece, my boy!   35

CAIUS. I pray you bear vitness that me have stay six or seven, two, tree hours for him, and he is no come.

SHAL. He is the wiser man, Master Doctor. He is a curer of souls, and you a curer of bodies. If   40 you should fight, you go against the hair° of your professions. Is it not true, Master Page?

PAGE. Master Shallow, you have yourself been a great fighter, though now a man of peace.   45

SHAL. Bodykins,° Master Page, though I now be old and of the peace, if I see a sword out, my finger itches to make one.° Though we are justices, and doctors, and churchmen, Master Page, we have some salt of our youth in us. We are the sons of women, Master Page.   51

PAGE. 'Tis true, Master Shallow.

SHAL. It will be found so, Master Page. Master Doctor Caius, I am come to fetch you home.   54 I am sworn of the peace.° You have shewed yourself a wise physician, and Sir Hugh hath shewn himself a wise and patient churchman. You must go with me, Master Doctor.

HOST. Pardon, Guest Justice. — A word, Mounseur Mockwater.°   60

CAIUS. Mockvater! Vat is dat?

HOST. Mockwater, in our English tongue, is valor, bully.

CAIUS. By gar, den I have as much mockvater as de Englishman. Scurvy jack-dog priest! By gar, me vill cut his ears.   66

HOST. He will clapper-claw° thee tightly, bully.

CAIUS. Clapper-de-claw! Vat is dat?

HOST. That is, he will make thee amends.   70

CAIUS. By gar, me do look he shall clapper-de-claw me, for, by gar, me vill have it.

HOST. And I will provoke him to't, or let him wag.

CAIUS. Me tank you for dat.   75

HOST. And, moreover, bully — But first, Master Guest, and Master Page, and eke Cavaleiro Slender, go you through the town to Frogmore.°

---

320. ambling gelding: riding horse.
Sc. iii: 16. Villainy: villain. **24–27. foin . . . montant:** all terms of the fencing school: *foin,* fence; *traverse,* advance; *punto,* thrust; *stock* (or *stoccado*), thrust; *reverse,* a back-handed stroke; *montant,* an upright blow. This mocking of the professional jargon of the fencing masters who taught the use of the new rapier was common on the stage at this time. Jonson also mocks it in an effective scene in *Every Man in His Humor* where the gull Matthew comes to Captain Bobadil for some instruction in the art of fence. **28. Francisco:** Frenchman. **29. Aesculapius . . . Galen:** the two most famous physicians of antiquity. **30. elder:** The host is insulting Caius throughout, though the Frenchman does not know enough English to realize it. Elder is a soft and useless wood, with a center of pith — very far from a heart of oak.

31. bully stale: another insult. *Bully* is a term of endearment; *stale* means "excretion" — a matter of interest to doctors. **32–33. coward . . . vorld:** the greatest coward in the world. **34. Castalion-King-Urinal:** a king-size in chamberpots. Physicians made a special study of urine, so that this vessel was naturally associated with the profession. **Castalion-King:** Spanish King, who at this time was the most powerful monarch in Europe. **41. against . . . hair:** against the natural order. The image is from stroking an animal against the natural lie of the fur. **46. Bodykins:** by God's little body. **48. make one:** join in. **55. sworn . . . peace:** a justice of the peace, magistrate. **60. Mockwater:** one who misinterprets the signs in urine. See above l. 34, and *II Hen IV*, I.ii.1–6,n. **67. clapper-claw:** scratch and claw. **78. Frogmore:** near Windsor.

[*Aside to them.*]

PAGE. Sir Hugh is there, is he?   79

HOST. He is there. See what humor he is in, and
I will bring the doctor about° by the fields. Will it
do well?

SHAL. We will do it.   84

PAGE, SHAL., SLEN. Adieu, good Master Doctor.

[*Exeunt* PAGE, SHALLOW, *and* SLENDER.]

CAIUS. By gar, me vill kill de priest, for he speak
for a jackanape° to Anne Page.

HOST. Let him die. Sheathe thy impatience; throw
cold water on thy choler. Go about the fields with
me through Frogmore. I will bring thee where   90
Mistress Anne Page is, at a farmhouse afeasting,
and thou shalt woo her. Cried I aim?° Said I well?

CAIUS. By gar, me dank you vor dat. By gar, I
love you, and I shall procure-a you de good   95
guest, de earl, de knight, de lords, de gentlemen, my
patients.

HOST. For the which I will be thy adversary toward Anne Page. Said I well?

CAIUS. By gar, 'tis good. Vell said!   100

HOST. Let us wag, then.

CAIUS. Come at my heels, Jack Rugby.   [*Exeunt.*]

Act III

SCENE I. *A field near Frogmore.*

[*Enter* SIR HUGH EVANS *and* SIMPLE.]

EVANS. I pray you now, good Master Slender's
servingman, and friend Simple by your name,
which way have you looked for Master Caius, that
calls himself Doctor of Physic?   4

SIM. Marry, sir, the pittie-ward,° the Park-ward,°
every way; old Windsor way, and every way but
the town way.

EVANS. I most fehemently desire you you will
also look that way.

SIM. I will, sir.   [*Exit.*]   10

EVANS. Pless my soul, how full of chollors° I am,
and trempling of mind! I shall be glad if he have
deceived me. How melancholies I am! I will knog
his urinals about his knave's costard° when I have
goot opportunities for the ork. Pless my soul!   16

[*Sings.*°]

To shallow rivers, to whose falls
Melodious birds sings madrigals.°
There will we make our peds of roses,
And a thousand fragrant posies.   20
To shallow ——

Mercy on me! I have a great dispositions to cry.

[*Sings.*]

Melodious birds sing madrigals —
Whenas I sat in Pabylon° —
And a thousand vagram posies.   25
To shallow &c.

[*Re-enter* SIMPLE.]

SIM. Yonder he is coming, this way, Sir Hugh.

EVANS. He's welcome.   [*Sings.*]

To shallow rivers, to whose falls ——   29
Heaven prosper the right! What weapons is he?

SIM. No weapons, sir. There comes my master,
Master Shallow, and another gentleman, from Frogmore, over the stile, this way.

EVANS. Pray you, give me my gown, or else keep
it in your arms.   35

[*Enter* PAGE, SHALLOW, *and* SLENDER.]

SHAL. How now, Master Parson! Good morrow,
good Sir Hugh. Keep a gamester from the dice,
and a good student from his book, and it is wonderful.

SLEN. [*Aside*] Ah, sweet Anne Page!   40

PAGE. Save you, good Sir Hugh!

EVANS. Pless you from his mercy sake, all of you!

SHAL. What, the sword and the Word! Do you
study them both, Master Parson?   45

PAGE. And youthful still! In your doublet and
hose° this raw rheumatic day!

EVANS. There is reasons and causes for it.

PAGE. We are come to you to do a good office,
Master Parson.   50

EVANS. Fery well. What is it?

PAGE. Yonder is a most reverend gentleman, who,
belike having received wrong by some person, is at
most odds° with his own gravity and patience that
ever you saw.   55

SHAL. I have lived fourscore years and upward.
I never heard a man of his place, gravity, and learning, so wide of his own respect.°

EVANS. What is he?

PAGE. I think you know him. Master Doctor
Caius, the renowned French physician.   61

EVANS. Got's will, and his passion of my heart! I

---

81. **about:** a roundabout way.   87. **jackanape:** monkey on
horseback. See I.iv.113 and App. 5.   92. **Cried I aim:** A much
discussed phrase. The original reading is "cried game" in Q1,
and "cride-game" in F1. As emended it means "to encourage."
See *John*, II.i.196,n. "Cry game" was the cry of the bear keeper
in bearbaiting, meaning "Make your bets on the game." See
App. 5.
Act III, Sc. i: 5. **pittie-ward:** This has not been identified.
Park-ward: the way to Windsor Park.   11. **chollors:** angry
passions.   15. **costard:** head — a slang word, lit., apple.

16. **s.d., Sings:** Evans nervously begins to sing fragments of
Marlowe's famous poem "Come live with me, and be my love."
18. **madrigals:** part songs.   24. **Whenas . . . Pabylon:** Here in
his agitation he substitutes a line from the metrical version of
Psalm 137.   46–47. **doublet . . . hose:** i.e., without your
gown; for Sir Hugh is ready for battle. See Note on Costume,
p. 93a–b.   53–54. **at . . . odds:** is quarreling with; i.e., a man
of religion should not be waiting to fight a duel.   58. **wide . . .
respect:** acting so contrary to his profession.

had as lief you would tell me of a mess of porridge.

PAGE. Why?   65

EVANS. He has no more knowledge in Hibo-crates° and Galen,—and he is a knave besides, a cowardly knave as you would desires to be acquainted withal.

PAGE. I warrant you, he's the man should fight with him.   71

SLEN. [*Aside*] O sweet Anne Page!

SHAL. It appears so, by his weapons. Keep them asunder. Here comes Doctor Caius.

[*Enter* HOST, DOCTOR CAIUS, *and* RUGBY.]

PAGE. Nay, good Master Parson, keep in your weapon.   76

SHAL. So do you, good Master Doctor.

HOST. Disarm them, and let them question. Let them keep their limbs whole and hack our English.   80

CAIUS. I pray you, let-a me speak a word with your ear. Verefore vill you not meet-a me?

EVANS. [*Aside to* DOCTOR CAIUS] Pray you, use your patience. In good time.

CAIUS. By gar, you are de coward, de Jack dog, John ape.   86

EVANS. [*Aside to* DOCTOR CAIUS] Pray you let us not be laughingstocks to other men's humors. I desire you in friendship, and I will one way or other make you amends. [*Aloud*] I will knog   90 your urinals about your knave's cogscomb for missing your meetings and appointments.

CAIUS. Diable! Jack Rugby, mine host de Jarteer, have I not stay for him to kill him? Have I not, at de place I did appoint?   95

EVANS. As I am a Christians soul, now, look you, this is the place appointed. I'll be judgment by mine host of the Garter.

HOST. Peace, I say, Gallia° and Gaul, French and Welsh, soul-curer and body-curer!   100

CAIUS. Aye, dat is very good; excellent.

HOST. Peace, I say! Hear mine host of the Garter. Am I politic? Am I subtle? Am I a Machiavel?° Shall I lose my doctor? No, he gives me the potions and the motions. Shall I lose my parson, my   105 priest, my Sir Hugh? No, he gives me the proverbs and the noverbs. Give me thy hand, terrestrial; so. Give me thy hand, celestial; so. Boys of art,° I have deceived you both. I have directed you to   110 wrong places. Your hearts are mighty, your skins are whole, and let burnt° sack be the issue. Come, lay their swords to pawn.° Follow me, lads of peace, follow, follow, follow.

SHAL. Trust me, a mad host. Follow, gentlemen, follow.   116

SLEN. [*Aside*] O sweet Anne Page!

[*Exeunt* SHALLOW, SLENDER, PAGE, *and* HOST.]

CAIUS. Ha, do I perceive dat? Have you make-a de sot° of us, ha, ha?   119

EVANS. This is well. He has made us his vlouting-stog.° I desire you that we may be friends, and let us knog our prains together to be revenge on this same scall,° scurvy, cogging° companion, the host of the Garter.   124

CAIUS. By gar, with all my heart. He promise to bring me where is Anne Page. By gar, he deceive me too.

EVANS. Well, I will smite his noddles. Pray you, follow.   [*Exeunt.*]

SCENE II. *The street, in Windsor.*

[*Enter* MISTRESS PAGE *and* ROBIN.]

MRS. PAGE. Nay, keep your way, little gallant. You were wont to be a follower, but now you are a leader. Whether had° you rather lead mine eyes, or eye your master's heels?

ROB. I had rather, forsooth, go before you like a man than follow him like a dwarf.   6

MRS. PAGE. Oh, you are a flattering boy. Now I see you'll be a courtier.

[*Enter* FORD.]

FORD. Well met, Mistress Page. Whither go you?

MRS. PAGE. Truly, sir, to see your wife. Is she at home?   11

FORD. Aye, and as idle as she may hang together,° for want of company. I think, if your husbands were dead, you two would marry.   15

MRS. PAGE. Be sure of that—two other husbands.

FORD. Where had you this pretty weathercock?

MRS. PAGE. I cannot tell what the dickens° his name is my husband had him of.—What do you call your knight's name, sirrah?   21

ROB. Sir John Falstaff.

FORD. Sir John Falstaff!

MRS. PAGE. He, he, I can never hit on's name. There is such a league between my good man and he! Is your wife at home indeed?   26

FORD. Indeed she is.

MRS. PAGE. By your leave, sir. I am sick till I see her.   [*Exeunt* MISTRESS PAGE *and* ROBIN.]

FORD. Has Page any brains? Hath he any   30 eyes? Hath he any thinking? Sure, they sleep. He hath no use of them. Why, this boy will carry a

---

66–67. **Hibocrates:** Hippocrates — another famous physician of classical times.   99. **Gallia:** for "Wallia"—Wales.   103. **Machiavel:** subtle schemer. See *I Hen VI*, V.iv.74,n.   109. **Boys of art:** i.e., university men, graduates.   112. **burnt:** hot. 113. **lay . . . pawn:** take away their swords as pledges that they will be peaceable.

119. **sot:** fool.   120–21. **vlouting-stog:** laughingstock.   123. **scall:** scald, scabby. **cogging:** cheating.

Sc. ii: 3. **Whether had:** would.   12. **hang together:** i.e., two women as idle as you two will naturally be close friends. 18. **dickens:** polite phrase for the Devil.

letter twenty mile as easy as a cannon will shoot point-blank twelve score.° He pieces out° his 35 wife's inclination, he gives her folly motion and advantage, and now she's going to my wife, and Falstaff's boy with her. A man may hear this shower sing in the wind. And Falstaff's boy with her! Good plots, they are laid, and our revolted wives share damnation together. Well, I will 41 take him, then torture my wife, pluck the borrowed veil of modesty from the so seeming Mistress Page, divulge Page himself for a secure and willful Actaeon,° and to these violent proceedings all 45 my neighbors shall cry aim.° [*Clock heard.*] The clock gives me my cue, and my assurance bids me search. There I shall find Falstaff. I shall be rather praised for this than mocked, for it is as positive as the earth is firm that Falstaff is there. I will go. 50

[*Enter* PAGE, SHALLOW, SLENDER, HOST, SIR HUGH EVANS, *and* DOCTOR CAIUS, *and* RUGBY.]

SHAL., PAGE, &c. Well met, Master Ford.

FORD. Trust me, a good knot.° I have good cheer at home, and I pray you all go with me.

SHAL. I must excuse myself, Master Ford.

SLEN. And so must I, sir. We have appointed to dine with Mistress Anne, and I would not break with her for more money than I'll speak of. 57

SHAL. We have lingered about a match between Anne Page and my cousin Slender, and this day we shall have our answer. 60

SLEN. I hope I have your good will, Father Page.

PAGE. You have, Master Slender. I stand wholly for you. — But my wife, Master Doctor, is for you altogether.

CAIUS. Aye, be-gar, and de maid is love-a me. My nursh-a Quickly tell me so mush. 66

HOST. What say you to young Master Fenton? He capers,° he dances, he has eyes of youth, he writes verses, he speaks holiday,° he smells April and May.° He will carry't, he will carry't. 'Tis in his buttons.° He will carry't. 71

PAGE. Not by my consent, I promise you. The gentleman is of no having.° He kept company with the wild Prince and Poins.° He is of too high a region. He knows too much. No, he shall not 75 knit a knot in° his fortunes with the finger of my substance. If he take her, let him take her simply.° The wealth I have waits on my consent, and my consent goes not that way.

FORD. I beseech you heartily some of you go 80

home with me to dinner. Besides your cheer, you shall have sport. I will show you a monster. Master Doctor, you shall go. So shall you, Master Page, and you, Sir Hugh.

SHAL. Well, fare you well. We shall have 85 the freer wooing at Master Page's.

[*Exeunt* SHALLOW *and* SLENDER.]

CAIUS. Go home, John Rugby. I come anon.°

[*Exit* RUGBY.]

HOST. Farewell, my hearts. I will to my honest knight Falstaff, and drink canary° with him. 89

[*Exit.*]

FORD. [*Aside*] I think I shall drink in pipe wine° first with him. I'll make him dance. Will you go, gentles?

ALL. Have with you to see this monster.

[*Exeunt.*]

SCENE III. *A room in* FORD's *house.*

[*Enter* MISTRESS FORD *and* MISTRESS PAGE.]

MRS. FORD. What,° John! What, Robert!

MRS. PAGE. Quickly, quickly! Is the buck basket° ——

MRS. FORD. I warrant. What, Robin, I say!

[*Enter* SERVANTS *with a basket.*]

MRS. PAGE. Come, come, come. 5

MRS. FORD. Here, set it down.

MRS. PAGE. Give your men the charge.° We must be brief.

MRS. FORD. Marry, as I told you before, John and Robert, be ready here hard by in the brewhouse,° and when I suddenly call you, come forth, and 11 without any pause or staggering,° take this basket on your shoulders. That done, trudge with it in all haste, and carry it among the whitsters° in Datchet Mead,° and there empty it in the muddy ditch close by the Thames side. 16

MRS. PAGE. You will do it?

MRS. FORD. I ha' told them over and over. They lack no direction. Be gone, and come when you are called. [*Exeunt* SERVANTS.] 20

MRS. PAGE. Here comes little Robin.

[*Enter* ROBIN.]

MRS. FORD. How now, my eyas-musket!° What news with you?

---

87. anon: by and by.   **89. canary:** wine from the Canary Isles.
90. pipe wine: wine from the *pipe* (i.e., a small cask), with a pun on dancing to the music of the *pipe*.
Sc. iii: 1. What: where are you?   **2–3. buck basket:** large basket for carrying dirty linen. Dirty linen was soaked in lye beaten and washed clean in running water, and dried, sweetened, and bleached by being stretched out in the sun.   **7. charge:** instructions.   **10. brewhouse:** At this time all large houses had a brewhouse for making the beer for the household.   **12. staggering:** hesitating.   **14. whitsters:** bleachers, who bleach linen. **14–15. Datchet Mead:** a meadow by the Thames at Windsor. **22. eyas-musket:** baby sparrow hawk.

---

35. twelve score: i.e., paces. The pace was five feet; the range is thus 400 yards. **pieces out:** adds to. **44–45. Actaeon:** horned one, cuckold. See *T Andr*, II.iii.63,n. **46. cry aim:** shout encouragement. See II.iii.92,n. **52. knot:** company. **68. capers:** dances lustily. See App. 24: The Capriol. **69. holiday:** like a gay young man. **69–70. smells . . . May:** he is as fresh as spring flowers. **71. his buttons:** he has it "all sewed up." **73. having:** wealth. **74. wild . . . Poins:** See *I Hen IV* for Prince Hal and Poins. **76. knit . . . in:** mend. **77. simply:** as she is, without any dowry.

ROB. My master, Sir John, is come in at your back door, Mistress Ford, and requests your company.   26

MRS. PAGE. You little Jack-a-Lent,° have you been true to us?

ROB. Aye, I'll be sworn. My master knows not of your being here and hath threatened to put me   30 into everlasting liberty° if I tell you of it, for he swears he'll turn me away.

MRS. PAGE. Thou'rt a good boy. This secrecy of thine shall be a tailor to thee,° and shall make thee a new doublet and hose. I'll go hide me.   36

MRS. FORD. Do so. — Go tell thy master I am alone. [*Exit* ROBIN.] Mistress Page, remember you your cue.

MRS. PAGE. I warrant thee. If I do not act it, hiss° me.   [*Exit.*]   41

MRS. FORD. Go to, then. We'll use this unwholesome humidity, this gross watery pumpion.° We'll teach him to know turtles from jays.°

[*Enter* SIR JOHN FALSTAFF.]

FAL. "Have I caught" thee, "my heavenly   45 jewel?"° Why, now let me die, for I have lived long enough. This is the period° of my ambition. Oh, this blessed hour!

MRS. FORD. Oh, sweet Sir John!   49

FAL. Mistress Ford, I cannot cog,° I cannot prate, Mistress Ford. Now shall I sin in my wish. I would thy husband were dead. I'll speak it before the best lord. I would make thee my lady.

MRS. FORD. I your lady, Sir John! Alas, I should be a pitiful lady!   56

FAL. Let the Court of France show me such another. I see how thine eye would emulate the diamond. Thou hast the right arched beauty of the brow that becomes the ship tire, the tire-valiant, or any tire of Venetian admittance.°   61

MRS. FORD. A plain kerchief,° Sir John. My brows become nothing else, nor that well neither.

FAL. By the Lord, thou art a traitor to say so. Thou wouldst make an absolute° courtier, and   65 the firm fixture of thy foot would give an excellent motion to thy gait in a semicircled farthingale.° I

see what thou wert, if Fortune thy foe were not, Nature thy friend.° Come, thou canst not hide it.

MRS. FORD. Believe me, there's no such thing in me.   72

FAL. What made me love thee? Let that persuade thee there's something extraordinary in   75 thee. Come, I cannot cog and say thou art this and that, like a many of these lisping hawthorn buds° that come like women in men's apparel and smell like Bucklersbury in simple time.° I cannot. But I love thee, none but thee, and thou deservest it.   81

MRS. FORD. Do not betray me, sir. I fear you love Mistress Page.

FAL. Thou mightst as well say I love to walk by the Counter Gate,° which is as hateful to me as the reek of a limekiln.   86

MRS. FORD. Well, Heaven knows how I love you, and you shall one day find it.

FAL. Keep in that mind. I'll deserve it.

MRS. FORD. Nay, I must tell you so you do, or else I could not be in that mind.   91

ROB. [*Within*] Mistress Ford, Mistress Ford! Here's Mistress Page at the door, sweating, and blowing, and looking wildly, and would needs speak with you presently.°   95

FAL. She shall not see me. I will ensconce me behind the arras.°

MRS. FORD. Pray you, do so. She's a very tattling woman. [FALSTAFF *hides himself.*] — [*Re-enter* MISTRESS PAGE *and* ROBIN.] What's the matter? How now!   100

MRS. PAGE. O Mistress Ford, what have you done? You're shamed, you're overthrown, you're undone forever!

MRS. FORD. What's the matter, good Mistress Page?   105

MRS. PAGE. Oh, well-a-day, Mistress Ford! Having an honest man to your husband, to give him such cause of suspicion!

MRS. FORD. What cause of suspicion?

MRS. PAGE. What cause of suspicion! Out upon you! How am I mistook in you!   111

MRS. FORD. Why, alas, what's the matter?

MRS. PAGE. Your husband's coming hither, woman, with all the officers in Windsor, to search for a gentleman that he says is here now in the   115 house by your consent to take an ill advantage of his

---

27. **Jack-a-Lent:** a straw puppet, dressed in gay rags, set up in the streets, at which boys threw stones. Falstaff's page is gaily dressed.   30–31. **put . . . liberty:** i.e., "fire" me permanently.   35. **be . . . thee:** win you a new suit.   39–40. **cue . . . hiss:** An actor who forgot his part was hissed. See *Cor,* V.iii.40–42.   43. **pumpion:** watermelon.   44. **know . . . jays:** distinguish between faithful wives and birds of prey. The turtle dove represented faithful love, the jay, a loose woman.   45–46. **Have . . . jewel:** a quotation from the "second sonnet" appended to Sidney's *Astrophel and Stella* — "Have I caught my heavenly Jewel/Teaching Sleep most fair to be."   47. **period:** end.   50. **cog:** cheat.   60–61. **ship . . . admittance:** various styles of headdressing approved by Venice, which was renowned for the smartness of its women.   62. **kerchief:** head covering.   65. **absolute:** perfect.   67. **semicircled farthingale:** See Note on Costume, p. 94b.

68–69. **what . . . friend:** what sort of a woman you would be, if only you had the good fortune that your nature deserves. See App. 18. *Fortune my foe* was the name of a popular tune to which many ballads were set.   77. **hawthorn buds:** The hawthorn is a symbol for a gay young man. It flowers in early spring.   80. **Bucklersbury . . . time:** Bucklersbury was a district in London where the shops of grocers (who sold herbs and perfumes) were concentrated. **simple time:** when the fresh herbs are dried, and so perfume the air.   85. **Counter Gate:** The Counters were the prisons of the City of London. They stank vilely.   95. **presently:** immediately.   97. **arras:** hangings of tapestry.

absence. You are undone.

MRS. FORD. 'Tis not so, I hope.

MRS. PAGE. Pray Heaven it be not so that you have such a man here! But 'tis most certain 120 your husband's coming with half Windsor at his heels to search for such a one. I come before to tell you. If you know yourself clear, why, I am glad of it, but if you have a friend° here, convey, 125 convey him out. Be not amazed. Call all your senses to you. Defend your reputation, or bid farewell to your good life forever.

MRS. FORD. What shall I do? There is a gentleman my dear friend, and I fear not mine own shame so much as his peril. I had rather than a thousand pound he were out of the house. 132

MRS. PAGE. For shame! Never stand° "you had rather" and "you had rather." Your husband's here at hand. Bethink you of some conveyance. In the house you cannot hide him. Oh, how have 136 you deceived me! Look here, here is a basket. If he be of any reasonable stature, he may creep in here; and throw foul linen upon him as if it were going to bucking.° Or — it is whiting time.° Send him by your two men to Datchet Mead. 141

MRS. FORD. He's too big to go in there. What shall I do?

FAL. [*Coming forward*] Let me see't, let me see't, oh, let me see't! I'll in, I'll in. Follow your friend's counsel. I'll in. 146

MRS. PAGE. What, Sir John Falstaff! Are these your letters, knight?

FAL. I love thee. Help me away. Let me creep in here. I'll never —— 150

[*Gets into the basket. They cover him with foul linen.*]

MRS. PAGE. Help to cover your master, boy. — Call your men, Mistress Ford. — You dissembling knight!

MRS. FORD. What, John! Robert! John [*Exit* ROBIN.] — [*Re-enter* SERVANTS.] Go take up 155 these clothes here quickly. Where's the cowlstaff?° Look how you drumble!° Carry them to the laundress in Datchet Mead. Quickly, come.

[*Enter* FORD, PAGE, DOCTOR CAIUS, *and* SIR HUGH EVANS.]

FORD. Pray you, come near. If I suspect without cause, why then make sport at me. Then let 160 me be your jest. I deserve it. — How now! Whither bear you this?

SERV. To the laundress, forsooth.

MRS. FORD. Why, what have you to do whither they bear it? You were best meddle with buckwashing. 166

FORD. Buck!° I would I could wash myself of the buck! Buck, buck, buck! Aye, buck. I warrant you, buck; and of the season too, it shall appear. [*Exeunt* SERVANTS *with the basket.*] Gentlemen, I have 170 dreamed tonight. I'll tell you my dream. Here, here, here be my keys. Ascend my chambers. Search, seek, find out. I'll warrant we'll unkennel° the fox. Let me stop this way first. [*Locking the door.*] So, now uncape.° 176

PAGE. Good Master Ford, be contented. You wrong yourself too much.

FORD. True, Master Page. Up, gentlemen. You shall see sport anon. Follow me, gentlemen. [*Exit.*]

EVANS. This is fery fantastical humors and jealousies. 182

CAIUS. By gar, 'tis no the fashion of France. It is not jealous in France.

PAGE. Nay, follow him, gentlemen. See the issue of his search. 186

[*Exeunt* PAGE, DOCTOR CAIUS, *and* EVANS.]

MRS. PAGE. Is there not a double excellency in this?

MRS. FORD. I know not which pleases me better, that my husband is deceived, or Sir John. 190

MRS. PAGE. What a taking° was he in when your husband asked who was in the basket!

MRS. FORD. I am half afraid he will have need of washing, so throwing him into the water will do him a benefit. 195

MRS. PAGE. Hang him, dishonest rascal! I would all of the same strain were in the same distress.

MRS. FORD. I think my husband hath some special suspicion of Falstaff's being here, for I never saw him so gross° in his jealousy till now. 201

MRS. PAGE. I will lay a plot to try that, and we will yet have more tricks with Falstaff. His dissolute disease will scarce obey this medicine. 204

MRS. FORD. Shall we send that foolish carrion° Mistress Quickly to him and excuse his throwing into the water; and give him another hope, to betray him to another punishment?

MRS. PAGE. We will do it. Let him be sent for tomorrow, eight o'clock, to have amends. 210

[*Re-enter* FORD, PAGE, DOCTOR CAIUS, *and* SIR HUGH EVANS.]

FORD. I cannot find him. Maybe the knave bragged of that he could not compass.°

MRS. PAGE. [*Aside to* MISTRESS FORD] Heard you that?

MRS. FORD. You use me well, Master Ford, do you? 216

FORD. Aye, I do so.

---

125. **friend**: lover.   133. **Never stand**: don't keep on repeating. 140. **bucking**: washing. **whiting time**: bleaching time. See l l. 2–3, n. 156. **cowlstaff**: large pole on which the clothes basket was slung and carried on the shoulders.   157. **drumble**: hesitate.

167. **Buck**: Ford plays with the meaning "buck" (male deer), a horned beast, and so typical of a cuckold. See App. 11.   173. **unkennel**: lit., drive a fox from its earth.   176. **uncape**: reveal the hidden fox.   191. **taking**: to-do, agitation.   201. **gross**: excessive.   205. **carrion**: piece of flesh — a contemptuous word. 212. **compass**: achieve.

MRS. FORD. Heaven make you better than your thoughts!°

FORD. Amen!   220

MRS. PAGE. You do yourself mighty wrong, Master Ford.

FORD. Aye, aye, I must bear it.

EVANS. If there be anypody in the house, and in the chambers, and in the coffers, and in the presses,° Heaven forgive my sins at the day of judgment!

CAIUS. By gar, nor I too. There is nobodies.   228

PAGE. Fie, fie, Master Ford! Are you not ashamed? What spirit, what devil suggests   230 this imagination? I would not ha' your distemper° in this kind for the wealth of Windsor Castle.

FORD. 'Tis my fault, Master Page. I suffer for it.

EVANS. You suffer for a pad conscience. Your   235 wife is as honest a 'omans as I will desires among five thousand, and five hundred too.

CAIUS. By gar, I see 'tis an honest woman.

FORD. Well, I promised you a dinner. Come, come, walk in the Park. I pray you pardon me.   240 I will hereafter make known to you why I have done this. — Come, Wife. Come, Mistress Page. — I pray you pardon me. Pray heartily pardon me.

PAGE. Let's go in, gentlemen, but, trust me, we'll mock him. I do invite you tomorrow morning   245 to my house to breakfast. After, we'll abirding° together. I have a fine hawk for the bush. Shall it be so?

FORD. Anything.

EVANS. If there is one, I shall make two in the company.   251

CAIUS. If there be one or two, I shall make-a the turd.

FORD. Pray you go, Master Page.

EVANS. I pray you, now, remembrance tomorrow on the lousy knave, mine host.   256

CAIUS. Dat is good. By gar, with all my heart!

EVANS. A lousy knave, to have his gibes and his mockeries!   [Exeunt.]   260

SCENE IV. *A room in* PAGE'S *house.*

[*Enter* FENTON *and* ANNE PAGE.]

FEN. I see I cannot get thy father's love.
Therefore no more turn me to him, sweet Nan.

ANNE. Alas, how then?

FEN.   Why, thou must be thyself.
He doth object I am too great of birth,
And that, my state being galled with my expense,°
I seek to heal it only by his wealth.   6

Besides these, other bars he lays before me, —
My riots past, my wild societies —
And tells me 'tis a thing impossible
I should love thee but as a property.   10

ANNE. Maybe he tells you true.

FEN. No, Heaven so speed° me in my time to come!
Albeit I will confess thy father's wealth
Was the first motive that I wooed thee, Anne,
Yet, wooing thee, I found thee of more value   15
Than stamps in gold° or sums in sealèd bags,
And 'tis the very riches of thyself
That now I aim at.

ANNE.   Gentle Master Fenton,
Yet seek my father's love. Still seek it, sir.
If opportunity and humblest suit   20
Cannot attain it, why, then — hark you hither!
                            [*They converse apart.*]

[*Enter* SHALLOW, SLENDER, *and* MISTRESS QUICKLY.]

SHAL. Break their talk, Mistress Quickly. My kinsman shall speak for himself.

SLEN. I'll make a shaft or a bolt° on't. 'Slid,° 'tis but venturing.   25

SHAL. Be not dismayed.

SLEN. No, she shall not dismay me. I care not for that, but that I am afeard.

QUICK. Hark ye, Master Slender would speak a word with you.   30

ANNE. I come to him. [*Aside*] This is my father's choice.
Oh, what a world of vile ill-favored° faults
Looks handsome in three hundred pounds a year!

QUICK. And how does good Master Fenton? Pray you, a word with you.   35

SHAL. She's coming. To her, Coz. O boy, thou hadst a father!°

SLEN. I had a father, Mistress Anne. My uncle can tell you good jests of him. Pray you, Uncle, tell Mistress Anne the jest how my father stole two geese out of a pen, good Uncle.   41

SHAL. Mistress Anne, my cousin loves you.

SLEN. Aye, that I do, as well as I love any woman in Gloucestershire.   44

SHAL. He will maintain you like a gentlewoman.

SLEN. Aye, that I will, come cut and long-tail,° under the degree of a squire.°

SHAL. He will make you a hundred and fifty pounds jointure.°   50

---

12. speed: aid.   16. stamps in gold: gold coins.   24. shaft . . . bolt: a proverb. A *shaft* is an arrow, a *bolt* a short arrow used in the crossbow; hence the proverb means the wood will do either for an arrow or a bolt — "I'll do one thing or the other." 'Slid: by God's eyelid.   32. ill-favored: ugly.   36–37. thou . . . father: i.e., behave like a man — and not a timid woman.   46. cut . . . long-tail: a proverb meaning "whatever happens," lit., whatever kind of dog comes.   47. under . . . squire: according to the style of living of a country gentleman.   50. jointure: marriage allowance.

218–19. better . . . thoughts: a better man than your foul thoughts.   225. presses: wardrobes for clothes.   231. distemper: disease.   246. abirding: hawking or shooting small birds put up from the bushes.

Sc. iv: 5. galled . . . expense: my wealth being ruined by my extravagances. See III.ii.72–79.

ANNE. Good Master Shallow, let him woo for himself.

SHAL. Marry, I thank you for it. I thank you for that good comfort. She calls you, Coz. I'll leave you.

ANNE. Now, Master Slender —   56

SLEN. Now, good Mistress Anne —

ANNE. What is your will?

SLEN. My will! Od's heartlings,° that's a pretty jest indeed! I ne'er made my will yet, I thank Heaven. I am not such a sickly creature, I give Heaven praise.   62

ANNE. I mean, Master Slender, what would you with me?

SLEN. Truly, for mine own part, I would   65 little or nothing with you. Your father and my uncle hath made motions. If it be my luck, so; if not, happy man be his dole!° They can tell you how things go better than I can. You may ask your father. Here he comes.   70

[*Enter* PAGE *and* MISTRESS PAGE.]

PAGE. Now, Master Slender. Love him, daughter Anne. —
Why, how now! What does Master Fenton here?
You wrong me, sir, thus still to haunt my house.
I told you, sir, my daughter is disposed of.

FEN. Nay, Master Page, be not impatient.   75

MRS. PAGE. Good Master Fenton, come not to my child.

PAGE. She is no match for you.

FEN. Sir, will you hear me?

PAGE.   No, good Master Fenton.
Come, Master Shallow. Come, Son Slender, in.
Knowing my mind, you wrong me, Master Fenton.   [*Exeunt* PAGE, SHALLOW, *and* SLENDER.]

QUICK. Speak to Mistress Page.   81

FEN. Good Mistress Page, for that I love your daughter
In such a righteous fashion as I do,
Perforce, against all checks, rebukes, and manners
I must advance the colors° of my love   85
And not retire. Let me have your good will.

ANNE. Good Mother, do not marry me to yond fool.

MRS. PAGE. I mean it not. I seek you a better husband.

QUICK. That's my master, Master Doctor.

ANNE. Alas, I had rather be set quick° i' the earth   90
And bowled to death with turnips!

MRS. PAGE. Come, trouble not yourself. Good Master Fenton,
I will not be your friend nor enemy.
My daughter will I question how she loves you,

And as I find her, so am I affected.   95
Till then farewell, sir. She must needs go in.
Her father will be angry.

FEN. Farewell, gentle mistress. Farewell, Nan.

[*Exeunt* MISTRESS PAGE *and* ANNE PAGE.]

QUICK. This is my doing now. "Nay," said I, "will you cast away your child on a fool, and   100 a physician? Look on Master Fenton." This is my doing.

FEN. I thank thee, and I pray thee, once tonight Give my sweet Nan this ring. There's for thy pains.   104

QUICK. Now Heaven send thee good fortune! [*Exit* FENTON.] A kind heart he hath. A woman would run through fire and water for such a kind heart. But yet I would my master had Mistress Anne, or I would Master Slender had her, or, in sooth, I would Master Fenton had her. I will   110 do what I can for them all three, for so I have promised, and I'll be as good as my word; but speciously° for Master Fenton. Well, I must of another errand to Sir John Falstaff from my two mistresses. What a beast am I to slack it!   [*Exit.*]   115

SCENE V. *A room in the Garter Inn.*

[*Enter* SIR JOHN FALSTAFF *and* BARDOLPH.]

FAL. Bardolph, I say —

BARD. Here, sir.

FAL. Go fetch me a quart of sack. Put a toast° in't. [*Exit* BARDOLPH.] Have I lived to be carried in a basket, like a barrow of butcher's offal, and to   5 be thrown in the Thames? Well, if I be served such another trick, I'll have my brains ta'en out, and buttered, and give them to a dog for a new-year's gift. The rogues slighted° me into the river   10 with as little remorse as they would have drowned a blind bitch's puppies, fifteen i' the litter. And you may know by my size that I have a kind of alacrity in sinking. If the bottom were as deep as Hell, I should down. I had been drowned but that the   15 shore was shelvy and shallow — a death that I abhor; for the water swells a man, and what a thing should I have been when I had been swelled! I should have been a mountain of mummy.°

[*Re-enter* BARDOLPH *with sack.*]

BARD. Here's Mistress Quickly, sir, to speak with you.   21

FAL. Come, let me pour in some sack to the Thames water, for my belly's as cold as if I had swallowed snowballs for pills to cool the reins.° Call her in.   25

59. Od's heartlings: by God's little heart.   68. happy . . . dole: good luck to the man who wins. See *W Tale,* I.ii.163.   85. advance . . . colors: carry my flag forward; i.e., take the initiative in.   90. quick: alive.

112–13. speciously: for specially.
Sc. v: 3. toast: pieces of toast were floated on hot drinks.   10. slighted: slid.   19. mummy: corpse.   24. reins: kidneys.

BARD. Come in, woman!

[*Enter* MISTRESS QUICKLY.]

QUICK. By your leave. I cry you mercy.° Give your Worship good morrow.

FAL. Take away these chalices.° Go brew me a pottle of sack finely.°   30

BARD. With eggs, sir?

FAL. Simple of itself. I'll no pullet sperm in my brewage. [*Exit* BARDOLPH.] How now!

QUICK. Marry, sir, I come to your Worship from Mistress Ford.   35

FAL. Mistress Ford! I have had ford enough. I was thrown into the ford. I have my belly full of ford.

QUICK. Alas the day! Good heart, that was not her fault. She does so take on with her men. They mistook their erection.°   41

FAL. So did I mine, to build upon a foolish woman's promise.

QUICK. Well, she laments, sir, for it, that it would yearn° your heart to see it. Her husband goes   45 this morning abirding. She desires you once more to come to her, between eight and nine. I must carry her word quickly. She'll make you amends, I warrant you.

FAL. Well, I will visit her. Tell her so, and   50 bid her think what a man is. Let her consider his frailty, and then judge of my merit.

QUICK. I will tell her.

FAL. Do so. Between nine and ten, sayest thou?

QUICK. Eight and nine, sir.   55

FAL. Well, be gone. I will not miss her.

QUICK. Peace be with you, sir.   [*Exit.*]

FAL. I marvel I hear not of Master Brook. He sent me word to stay within. I like his money well. Oh, here he comes.   60

[*Enter* FORD.]

FORD. Bless you, sir!

FAL. Now, Master Brook, you come to know what hath passed between me and Ford's wife?

FORD. That, indeed, Sir John, is my business.   64

FAL. Master Brook, I will not lie to you. I was at her house the hour she appointed me.

FORD. And sped you,° sir?

FAL. Very ill-favoredly, Master Brook.

FORD. How so, sir? Did she change her determination?   70

FAL. No, Master Brook, but the peaking Cornuto° her husband, Master Brook, dwelling in a continual 'larum of jealousy, comes me in the instant of our encounter, after we had embraced, kissed, protested, and, as it were, spoke the   75 prologue of our comedy; and at his heels a rabble

of his companions, thither provoked and instigated by his distemper, and, forsooth, to search his house for his wife's love.

FORD. What, while you were there?   80

FAL. While I was there.

FORD. And did he search for you, and could not find you?

FAL. You shall hear. As good luck would have it, comes in one Mistress Page, gives intelligence   85 of Ford's approach, and, in her invention and Ford's wife's distraction, they conveyed me into a buck basket.

FORD. A buck basket!   89

FAL. By the Lord, a buck basket! Rammed me in with foul shirts and smocks, socks, foul stockings, greasy napkins, that, Master Brook, there was the rankest compound of villainous smell that ever offended nostril.

FORD. And how long lay you there?   95

FAL. Nay, you shall hear, Master Brook, what I have suffered to bring this woman to evil for your good. Being thus crammed in the basket, a couple of Ford's knaves, his hinds,° were called forth by their mistress to carry me in the name of foul   100 clothes to Datchet Lane. They took me on their shoulders, met the jealous knave their master in the door, who asked them once or twice what they had in their basket. I quaked for fear, lest the lunatic knave would have searched it, but Fate,   105 ordaining he should be a cuckold, held his hand. Well. On went he for a search, and away went I for foul clothes. But mark the sequel, Master Brook. I suffered the pangs of three several deaths: 110 first, an intolerable fright to be detected with° a jealous rotten bellwether;° next, to be compassed, like a good bilbo, in the circumference of a peck, hilt to point, heel to head;° and then, to be stopped in, like a strong distillation,° with stinking   115 clothes that fretted° in their own grease. Think of that—a man of my kidney!—think of that!— that am as subject to heat as butter, a man of continual dissolution and thaw. It was a miracle to 'scape suffocation. And in the height of this bath, when I was more than half stewed in grease, like a Dutch dish, to be thrown into the Thames, and cooled, glowing hot, in that surge, like a horseshoe! Think of that—hissing hot—think of that, Master Brook!   124

FORD. In good sadness, sir, I am sorry that for my sake you have suffered all this. My suit, then, is des-

---

27. **cry . . . mercy:** beg your pardon.   29. **chalices:** cups. 30. **finely:** carefully.   41. **erection:** for direction.   45. **yearn:** grieve.   67. **sped you:** did you make good progress?   71– 72. **Cornuto:** horned one.

99. **hinds:** servants.   111. **with:** by.   112. **bellwether:** the leader of a flock of sheep; it wore a bell round its neck.   112– 14. **compassed . . . head:** be bent round (*compassed*) until my head and my heels touched — like a rapier (*bilbo*) forced into a peck measure till point touches the hilt. It is the mark of a fine sword that it will return to the straight when the blade has been bent double.   114–15. **stopped . . . distillation:** corked in like a fermenting drink.   116. **fretted:** wore out.

perate. You'll undertake her no more?

FAL. Master Brook, I will be thrown into Etna, as I have been into Thames, ere I will leave her thus. Her husband is this morning gone abirding. I have received from her another embassy of meeting. 'Twixt eight and nine is the hour, Master Brook.   133

FORD. 'Tis past eight already, sir.

FAL. Is it? I will then address me to my appointment. Come to me at your convenient leisure, and you shall know how I speed, and the conclusion shall be crowned with your enjoying her. Adieu. You shall have her, Master Brook. Master Brook, you shall cuckold Ford.   [Exit.] 140

FORD. Hum! Ha! Is this a vision? Is this a dream? Do I sleep? Master Ford, awake! Awake, Master Ford! There's a hole made in your best coat, Master Ford. This 'tis to be married! This 'tis to have linen and buck baskets! Well, I will proclaim myself what I am. I will now take the lecher. He is at my house. He cannot 'scape me. 'Tis impossible he should. He cannot creep into a halfpenny purse, nor into a pepperbox; but, lest the Devil that guides him should aid him, I will search impossible places. Though what I am I cannot avoid, yet to be what I would not shall not make me tame. If I have horns to make one mad, let the proverb go with me — I'll be horn-mad.   [Exit.] 155

Act IV

SCENE I. *A street.*

[*Enter* MISTRESS PAGE, MISTRESS QUICKLY, *and* WILLIAM PAGE.]

MRS. PAGE. Is he at Master Ford's already, think'st thou?

QUICK. Sure he is by this, or will be presently. But, truly, he is very courageous mad about his throwing into the water. Mistress Ford desires you to come suddenly.°   5

MRS. PAGE. I'll be with her by and by.° I'll but bring my young man here to school. Look where his master comes. 'Tis a playing day,° I see. [*Enter* SIR HUGH EVANS.] How now, Sir Hugh! No school today?   10

EVANS. No, Master Slender is let the boys leave to play.°

QUICK. Blessing of his heart!

MRS. PAGE. Sir Hugh, my husband says my son profits nothing in the world at his book. I pray you

ask him some questions in his accidence.°   16

EVANS. Come hither, William. Hold up your head. Come.

MRS. PAGE. Come on, sirrah. Hold up your head. Answer your master, be not afraid.   20

EVANS. William, how many numbers is in nouns?

WILL. Two.

QUICK. Truly, I thought there had been one number more, because they say, "Od's nouns."°   25

EVANS. Peace your tattlings! What is "fair," William?

WILL. *Pulcher.*

QUICK. Polecats! There are fairer things than polecats, sure.   30

EVANS. You are a very simplicity 'oman. I pray you peace. — What is *lapis,* William?

WILL. A stone.

EVANS. And what is "a stone," William?

WILL. A pebble.   35

EVANS. No, it is *lapis.* I pray you remember in your prain.

WILL. *Lapis.*

EVANS. That is a good William. What is he, William, that does lend articles?   40

WILL. Articles are borrowed of the pronoun, and be thus declined: *Singulariter, nominativo, hic, haec, hoc.*

EVANS. *Nominativo, hig, hag, hog.* Pray you, mark. *Genitivo, hujus.* Well, what is your accusative case?   46

WILL. *Accusativo, hinc.*

EVANS. I pray you have your remembrance, child. *Accusativo, hung, hang, hog.*

QUICK. "Hang-hog" is Latin for bacon, I warrant you.   51

EVANS. Leave your prabbles, 'oman. — What is the focative case, William?

WILL. Oh, *vocativo, O.*

EVANS. Remember, William. Focative is *caret.*°

QUICK. And that's a good root.   56

EVAN. 'Oman, forbear.

MRS. PAGE. Peace!

EVANS. What is your genitive case plural, William?   60

WILL. Genitive case!

EVANS. Aye.

WILL. Genitive — *horum, harum, horum.*

QUICK. Vengeance of Jenny's case! Fie on her! Never name her, child, if she be a whore.   65

EVANS. For shame, 'oman.

QUICK. You do ill to teach the child such words. He teaches him to hick and to hack,° which they'll do fast enough of themselves, and to call "horum."

Act. IV, Sc. i: 5. suddenly: quickly.   6. by ... by: soon. 8. playing day: holiday.   11-12. is ... play: has granted a holiday.

16. accidence: Latin grammar.   25. Od's nouns: Mrs. Quickly apparently does not realize that the true meaning of this oath is "By God's wounds."   55. is caret: is missing.   68. hick ... hack: drink and whore.

Fie upon you!   70

EVANS. 'Oman, art thou lunatics? Hast thou no understandings for thy cases, and the numbers of the genders? Thou art as foolish Christian creatures as I would desires.

MRS. PAGE. Prithee hold thy peace.   75

EVANS. Show me now, William, some declensions of your pronouns.

WILL. Forsooth, I have forgot.

EVANS. It is *qui, quae, quod.* If you forget your *quie's,* your *quae's,* and your *quod's,* you must be preeches.° Go your ways, and play. Go.   81

MRS. PAGE. He is a better scholar than I thought he was.

EVANS. He is a good sprag° memory. Farewell, Mistress Page.   85

MRS. PAGE. Adieu, good Sir Hugh. [*Exit* SIR HUGH.] Get you home, boy. Come, we stay too long.
      [*Exeunt.*]

SCENE II. *A room in* FORD'S *house.*

[*Enter* SIR JOHN FALSTAFF *and* MISTRESS FORD.]

FAL. Mistress Ford, your sorrow hath eaten up my sufferance.° I see you are obsequious° in your love, and I profess requital to a hair's breadth, not only, Mistress Ford, in the simple office of love, but in all the accouterment, complement, and ceremony° of it. But are you sure of your husband now?   6

MRS. FORD. He's abirding, sweet Sir John.

MRS. PAGE. [*Within*] What ho, gossip Ford! What ho!   10

MRS. FORD. Step into the chamber, Sir John.
      [*Exit* SIR JOHN FALSTAFF.]
      [*Enter* MISTRESS PAGE.]

MRS. PAGE. How now, sweetheart! Who's at home besides yourself?

MRS. FORD. Why, none but mine own people.

MRS. PAGE. Indeed!   15

MRS. FORD. No, certainly. [*Aside to her*] Speak louder.

MRS. PAGE. Truly, I am so glad you have nobody here.

MRS. FORD. Why?   20

MRS. PAGE. Why, woman, your husband is in his old lunes° again. He so takes on yonder with my husband, so rails against all married mankind, so curses all Eve's daughters, of what complexion soever, and so buffets himself on the forehead,   25 crying, " Peer out,° peer out! " that any madness I ever yet beheld seemed but tameness, civility, and patience to this his distemper he is in now. I am

glad the fat knight is not here.

MRS. FORD. Why, does he talk of him?   30

MRS. PAGE. Of none but him, and swears he was carried out, the last time he searched for him, in a basket, protests to my husband he is now here, and hath drawn him and the rest of their company from their sport to make another experiment of his   35 suspicion. But I am glad the knight is not here. Now he shall see his own foolery.

MRS. FORD. How near is he, Mistress Page?

MRS. PAGE. Hard by, at street end. He will be here anon.   41

MRS. FORD. I am undone! The knight is here.

MRS. PAGE. Why, then you are utterly shamed, and he's but a dead man. What a woman are you! Away with him, away with him! Better shame than murder.   46

MRS. FORD. Which way should he go? How should I bestow him? Shall I put him into the basket again?
      [*Re-enter* SIR JOHN FALSTAFF.]

FAL. No, I'll come no more i' the basket. May I not go out ere he come?   51

MRS. PAGE. Alas, three of Master Ford's brothers watch the door with pistols, that none shall issue out. Otherwise you might slip away ere he came. But what make you here?   55

FAL. What shall I do? I'll creep up into the chimney.°

MRS. FORD. There they always use to discharge their birding pieces.° Creep into the kiln hole.°

FAL. Where is it?   60

MRS. FORD. He will seek there, on my word. Neither press, coffer, chest, trunk, well, vault, but he hath an abstract° for the remembrance of such places, and goes to them by his note. There is no hiding you in the house.   65

FAL. I'll go out, then.

MRS. PAGE. If you go out in your own semblance, you die, Sir John. Unless you go out disguised——

MRS. FORD. How might we disguise him?   70

MRS. PAGE. Alas the day, I know not! There is no woman's gown big enough for him. Otherwise he might put on a hat, a muffler, and a kerchief, and so escape.

FAL. Good hearts, devise something. Any extremity rather than a mischief.°   76

MRS. FORD. My maid's aunt, the fat woman of Brentford, has a gown above.

MRS. PAGE. On my word, it will serve him. She's

---

81. preeches: breeched, whipped.   84. sprag: for "sprack," quick.
   Sc. ii: 2. sufferance: suffering.   obsequious: zealous.   5. accouterment . . . ceremony: i.e., I will be the complete lover in every particular.   22. lunes: mad fits.   26. Peer out: addressed to his budding horns. See App. 11.

56–57. chimney: the great chimney in an Elizabethan house was large enough to hold a man.   58–59. discharge . . . pieces: As it was dangerous to try to extract the powder, the loaded firearm was discharged up the great chimney as a safety precaution. See Note on Arquebus (p. 99a) for loading firearms.   59. birding piece: sporting gun, fowling piece.   kiln hole: the fireplace — a narrow brick chamber — where malt is made.   63. abstract: list.   76. mischief: bodily injury.

as big as he is, and there's her thrummed hat,° and her muffler too. Run up, Sir John.   81

MRS. FORD. Go, go, sweet Sir John. Mistress Page and I will look some linen for your head.

MRS. PAGE. Quick, quick! We'll come dress you straight. Put on the gown the while.   85

[*Exit* SIR JOHN FALSTAFF.]

MRS. FORD. I would my husband would meet him in this shape. He cannot abide the old woman of Brentford. He swears she's a witch, forbade her my house, and hath threatened to beat her.   89

MRS. PAGE. Heaven guide him to thy husband's cudgel, and the Devil guide his cudgel afterwards!

MRS. FORD. But is my husband coming?

MRS. PAGE. Aye, in good sadness,° is he, and talks of the basket too, howsoever° he hath had intelligence.°   95

MRS. FORD. We'll try that; for I'll appoint my men to carry the basket again, to meet him at the door with it, as they did last time.

MRS. PAGE. Nay, but he'll be here presently.° Let's go dress him like the witch of Brentford.   100

MRS. FORD. I'll first direct my men what they shall do with the basket. Go up. I'll bring linen for him straight.   [*Exit.*]

MRS. PAGE. Hang him, dishonest varlet! We cannot misuse him enough.   105

We'll leave a proof by that which we will do,
Wives may be merry, and yet honest too.
We do not act that often jest and laugh.
'Tis old, but true: Still swine eats all the draff.°

[*Exit.*]

[*Re-enter* MISTRESS FORD *with two* SERVANTS.]

MRS. FORD. Go, sirs, take the basket again   110 on your shoulders. Your master is hard at door. If he bid you set it down, obey him. Quickly, dispatch.

[*Exit.*]

1. SERV. Come, come, take it up.

2. SERV. Pray Heaven it be not full of knight again.   116

1. SERV. I hope not. I had as lief° bear so much lead.

[*Enter* FORD, PAGE, SHALLOW, DOCTOR CAIUS, *and* SIR HUGH EVANS.]

FORD. Aye, but if it prove true, Master Page, have you any way then to unfool me again? Set   120 down the basket, villain! Somebody call my wife. Youth in a basket! Oh, you panderly° rascals! There's a knot, a ging, a pack,° a conspiracy against me. Now shall the Devil be shamed. — What, Wife, I say! Come, come forth! Behold what honest clothes you send forth to bleaching!   126

PAGE. Why, this passes,° Master Ford. You are not to go loose any longer. You must be pinioned

EVANS. Why, this is lunatics! This is mad as a mad dog!   131

SHAL. Indeed, Master Ford, this is not well, indeed.

FORD. So say I too, sir. [*Re-enter* MISTRESS FORD.] Come hither, Mistress Ford. Mistress Ford,   135 the honest woman, the modest wife, the virtuous creature, that hath the jealous fool to her husband I suspect without cause, mistress, do I?

MRS. FORD. Heaven be my witness you do, if you suspect me in any dishonesty.   140

FORD. Well said, brazen-face! Hold it out. Come forth, sirrah! [*Pulling clothes out of the basket.*]

PAGE. This passes!

MRS. FORD. Are you not ashamed? Let the clothes alone.   145

FORD. I shall find you anon.

EVANS. 'Tis unreasonable! Will you take up your wife's clothes? Come away.

FORD. Empty the basket, I say!

MRS. FORD. Why, man, why?   150

FORD. Master Page, as I am a man, there was one conveyed out of my house yesterday in this basket. Why may not he be there again? In my house I am sure he is. My intelligence is true. My jealousy is reasonable. Pluck me out all the linen.   156

MRS. FORD. If you find a man there, he shall die a flea's death.

PAGE. Here's no man.

SHAL. By my fidelity, this is not well, Master Ford, this wrongs you.   161

EVANS. Master Ford, you must pray, and not follow the imaginations of your own heart. This is jealousies.

FORD. Well, he's not here I seek for.   165

PAGE. No, nor nowhere else but in your brain.

FORD. Help to search my house this one time. If I find not what I seek, show no color for my extremity.° Let me for ever be your table sport. Let them say of me, " As jealous as Ford, that searched a hollow walnut for his wife's leman.° " Satisfy me once more. Once more search with me.   173

MRS. FORD. What ho, Mistress Page! Come you and the old woman down. My husband will come into the chamber.

FORD. Old woman! What old woman's that?

MRS. FORD. Why, it is my maid's aunt of Brentford.   179

FORD. A witch, a quean,° an old cozening quean! Have I not forbid her my house? She comes of errands, does she? We are simple men. We do not know what's brought to pass under the profession of fortunetelling. She works by charms, by spells,

---

80. thrummed hat: hat made of the waste ends from a piece of woven material. See Pl. 8c (right figure).   93. sadness: seriousness.   94. howsoever: by whatever means.   94-95. intelligence: information.   99. presently: immediately.   109. Still . . . draff: it's the quiet sow that eats all the hogwash.   117. lief: soon.   122. panderly: go-between.   123. knot . . . ging . . . pack: All three words mean gang.

127. passes: is too much.   168-69. color . . . extremity: reason for my agitation.   172. leman: lover.   180. quean: hussy.

by the figure,° and such daubery° as this is,   185
beyond our element. We know nothing. Come
down, you witch, you hag, you. Come down, I say!

MRS. FORD. Nay, good, sweet Husband! — Good
gentlemen, let him not strike the old woman.   190
[*Re-enter* SIR JOHN FALSTAFF *in woman's clothes,
and* MISTRESS PAGE.]

MRS. PAGE. Come, Mother Prat. Come, give me
your hand.

FORD. I'll prat her. [*Beating him.*] Out of my
door, you witch, you hag, you baggage, you polecat, you ronyon!° Out, out! I'll conjure you, I'll for-
tunetell you.   [*Exit* SIR JOHN FALSTAFF.]   196

MRS. PAGE. Are you not ashamed? I think you
have killed the poor woman.

MRS. FORD. Nay, he will do it. 'Tis a goodly credit
for you.   200

FORD. Hang her, witch!

EVANS. By yea and no, I think the 'oman is a
witch indeed. I like not when a 'oman has a great
peard.° I spy a great peard under his muffler.   205

FORD. Will you follow, gentlemen? I beseech you,
follow. See but the issue° of my jealousy. If I cry
out thus upon no trail, never trust me when I open
again.   209

PAGE. Let's obey his humor a little further. Come,
gentlemen.   [*Exeunt* FORD, PAGE, SHALLOW,
                          DOCTOR CAIUS, *and* SIR HUGH EVANS.]

MRS. PAGE. Trust me, he beat him most pitifully.

MRS. FORD. Nay, by the Mass, that he did not. He
beat him most unpitifully methought.   215

MRS. PAGE. I'll have the cudgel hallowed° and
hung o'er the altar. It hath done meritorious service.

MRS. FORD. What think you? May we, with the
warrant of womanhood and the witness of a   221
good conscience, pursue him with any further revenge?

MRS. PAGE. The spirit of wantonness is, sure,
scared out of him. If the Devil have him not in fee
simple° with fine and recovery,° he will never, I
think, in the way of waste,° attempt us again.°

MRS. FORD. Shall we tell our husbands how we
have served him?   229

MRS. PAGE. Yes, by all means, if it be but to scrape
the figures° out of your husband's brains. If they
can find in their hearts the poor unvirtuous fat
knight shall be any further afflicted, we two will
still be the ministers.   234

MRS. PAGE. I'll warrant they'll have him publicly
shamed; and methinks there would be no period to
the jest, should he not be publicly shamed.

MRS. PAGE. Come, to the forge with it, then. Shape
it. I would not have things cool.°   [*Exeunt.*]   240

SCENE III. *A room in the Garter Inn.*

[*Enter* HOST *and* BARDOLPH.]

BARD. Sir, the Germans° desire to have three of
your horses. The Duke himself will be tomorrow at
Court, and they are going to meet him.   4

HOST. What duke should that be comes so secretly? I hear not of him in the Court. Let me
speak with the gentlemen. They speak English?

BARD. Aye, sir. I'll call them to you.   9

HOST. They shall have my horses, but I'll make
them pay. I'll sauce° them. They have had my
house a week at command. I have turned away my
other guests. They must come off.° I'll sauce them.
Come.   [*Exeunt.*]

SCENE IV. *A room in* FORD'S *house.*

[*Enter* PAGE, FORD, MISTRESS PAGE, MISTRESS FORD,
and SIR HUGH EVANS.]

EVANS. 'Tis one of the best discretions of a 'oman
as ever I did look upon.

PAGE. And did he send you both these letters at
an instant?°

MRS. PAGE. Within a quarter of an hour.   5

FORD. Pardon me, Wife. Henceforth do what
     thou wilt.
I rather will suspect the sun with cold
Than thee with wantonness. Now doth thy honor
     stand
In him that was of late an heretic
As firm as faith.

PAGE.   'Tis well, 'tis well. No more.   10
Be not as extreme in submission
As in offense.
But let our plot go forward. Let our wives
Yet once again, to make us public sport,
Appoint a meeting with this old fat fellow,   15
Where we may take him and disgrace him for it.

FORD. There is no better way than that they
     spoke of.

PAGE. How? To send him word they'll meet him
in the Park at midnight? Fie, fie! He'll never come.

EVANS. You say he has been thrown in the   20
rivers and has been grievously peaten as an old
'oman. Methinks there should be terrors in him
that he should not come. Methinks his flesh is punished, he shall have no desires.

---

185. figure: horoscopes. daubery: dirty foolery.   195. ronyon:
scabby creature.   205. great peard: Women with hair on the
chin were suspected of being witches. See App. 23.   207. issue:
result.   216. hallowed: blessed as a holy relic.   225–26. fee
simple: as an absolute possession.   226. fine . . . recovery:
with full legal assurance.   227. way . . . again: will not attempt to rob us of our honesty again. waste: robbery, ruin.
231. figures: fancies.

239–40. to . . . cool: let us make the plan while the idea is still
hot.
     Sc. iii: 1. Germans: This conversation about the Germans,
which has nothing to do with the play, is obviously a topical
allusion. See *M Wives* Intro. p. 938b.   11. sauce: treat saucily.
13. come off: pay up.
     Sc. iv: 4. at an instant: simultaneously.

PAGE. So think I too.   25

MRS. FORD. Devise but how you'll use him when
he comes,

And let us two devise to bring him thither.

MRS. PAGE. There is an old tale goes that Herne
the Hunter,°

Sometime a keeper here in Windsor Forest,

Doth all the winter time, at still midnight,   30

Walk round about an oak, with great ragged
horns;

And there he blasts° the tree, and takes° the cattle,

And makes milch kine° yield blood, and shakes a
chain

In a most hideous and dreadful manner.   34

You have heard of such a spirit, and well you know

The superstitious idle-headed eld°

Received and did deliver to our age

This tale of Herne the Hunter for a truth.

PAGE. Why, yet there want not many that do fear

In deep of night to walk by this Herne's oak.   40

But what of this?

MRS. FORD.   Marry, this is our device:

That Falstaff at that oak shall meet with us.

PAGE. Well, let it not be doubted but he'll come.

And in this shape, when you have brought him
thither,

What shall be done with him? What is your plot?

MRS. PAGE. That likewise have we thought upon,
and thus: 46

Nan Page my daughter, and my little son,

And three or four more of their growth° we'll
dress

Like urchins,° ouphes° and fairies, green and
white,

With rounds of waxen tapers° on their heads   50

And rattles in their hands. Upon a sudden,

As Falstaff, she, and I are newly met,

Let them from forth a sawpit° rush at once

With some diffusèd° song. Upon their sight,

We two in great amazèdness will fly.   55

Then let them all encircle him about,

And, fairylike, to pinch° the unclean knight,

And ask him why that hour of fairy revel

In their so sacred paths he dares to tread

In shape profane.

MRS. FORD.   And till he tell the truth,   60

Let the supposèd fairies pinch him sound,

And burn him with their tapers.

MRS. PAGE.   The truth being known,

We'll all present ourselves, dis-horn° the spirit,

And mock him home to Windsor.

FORD.   The children must

Be practiced well to this, or they'll ne'er do't.   65

EVANS. I will teach the children their behaviors,
and I will be like a jackanapes also, to burn the
knight with my taber.°

FORD. That will be excellent. I'll go buy them
vizards.°   70

MRS. PAGE. My Nan shall be the Queen of all the
fairies,

Finely attirèd in a robe of white.°

PAGE. That silk will I go buy. [*Aside*] And in
that time

Shall Master Slender steal my Nan away   74

And marry her at Eton. Go send to Falstaff straight.

FORD. Nay, I'll to him again in name of Brook.

He'll tell me all his purpose. Sure, he'll come.

MRS. PAGE. Fear not you that. Go get us properties

And tricking° for our fairies.

EVANS. Let us about it. It is admirable pleasures
and fery honest knaveries.   81

[*Exeunt* PAGE, FORD, *and* SIR HUGH EVANS.]

MRS. PAGE. Go, Mistress Ford,

Send quickly to Sir John, to know his mind.

[*Exit* MISTRESS FORD.]

I'll to the doctor. He hath my good will,

And none but he, to marry with Nan Page.   85

That Slender, though well landed, is an idiot,

And he my husband best of all affects.°

The doctor is well moneyed and his friends

Potent at Court. He, none but he, shall have her,

Though twenty thousand worthier come to crave
her.   [*Exit.*] 90

SCENE V. *A room in the Garter Inn.*

[*Enter* HOST *and* SIMPLE.]

HOST. What wouldst thou have, boor?° What,
thick-skin? Speak, breathe, discuss! Brief, short,
quick, snap!

SIM. Marry, sir, I come to speak with Sir John
Falstaff from Master Slender.   5

HOST. There's his chamber, his house, his castle,
his standing bed, and truckle bed.° 'Tis painted
about with the story of the Prodigal,° fresh and

---

28. Herne ... Hunter: See *M Wives* Intro. p. 938b.   32. blasts:
blights. takes: bewitches.   33. milch kine: milking cows.
36. eld: old folk.   48. growth: size.   49. urchins: lit., hedgehogs, little goblins. ouphes: elves.   50. rounds ... tapers:
crowns of candles.   53. sawpit: Before the invention of the
circular saw, timber was sawn into planks by means of a long
saw worked by two men. To get the necessary length of stroke,
one man stood beneath the timber in a pit.   54. diffused: wild.
57. pinch: Fairies pinched their victims. See *Temp*, I.ii.326–30.

63. dis-horn: Falstaff, disguised as Herne the Hunter, will be
wearing horns.   68. taber: for taper.   70. vizards: masks.
72. robe of white: This is what she tells her husband. Actually
she plans to dress Nan in green. See later IV.vi.41 and V.iii.1–2.
79. tricking: costumes.   87. affects: likes.
    Sc. v: 1. boor: lout.   7. standing ... bed: The *standing bed*
was the great bed (see Pl. 17b); the *truckle bed* was a small bed,
used by a servant and pushed under the great bed by day.
7–8. painted ... Prodigal: The walls of rooms in inns were often
painted with scenes from the Bible or the classics. See Pl. 6a.
For the Prodigal Son, see Luke 15:11–32.

new. Go knock and call. He'll speak like an An-
thropophaginian° unto thee. Knock, I say.   10

SIM. There's an old woman, a fat woman, gone
up into his chamber. I'll be so bold as stay, sir, till
she come down. I come to speak with her, indeed.   15

HOST. Ha! A fat woman! The knight may be
robbed. I'll call. — Bully knight! Bully Sir John!
Speak from thy lungs military. Art thou there? It is
thine host, thine Ephesian,° calls.

FAL. [Above] How now, mine host!   20

HOST. Here's a Bohemian Tartar° tarries the
coming down of thy fat woman. Let her descend,
bully, let her descend. My chambers are honorable.
Fie! Privacy? Fie!

[Enter SIR JOHN FALSTAFF.]

FAL. There was, mine host, an old fat woman
even now with me, but she's gone.   26

SIM. Pray you, sir, was't not the wise woman° of
Brentford?

FAL. Aye, marry, was it, mussel shell.° What
would you with her?   30

SIM. My master, sir, Master Slender, sent to her,
seeing her go thorough° the streets, to know, sir,
whether one Nym, sir, that beguiled him of a
chain, had the chain or no.

FAL. I spake with the old woman about it.   35

SIM. And what says she, I pray, sir?

FAL. Marry, she says that the very same man that
beguiled Master Slender of his chain cozened him
of it.

SIM. I would I could have spoken with the
woman herself. I had other things to have spoken
with her too from him.

FAL. What are they? Let us know.

HOST. Aye, come. Quick!

SIM. I may not conceal° them, sir.   45

HOST. Conceal them, or thou diest.

SIM. Why, sir, they were nothing but about Mistress Anne Page; to know if it were my master's
fortune to have her or no.

FAL. 'Tis, 'tis his fortune.   50

SIM. What, sir?

FAL. To have her, or no. Go. Say the woman told
me so.

SIM. May I be bold to say so, sir?

FAL. Aye, sir. Like who more bold.°   55

SIM. I thank your Worship. I shall make my master glad with these tidings.   [Exit.]

HOST. Thou art clerkly,° thou art clerkly, Sir
John. Was there a wise woman with thee?   59

FAL. Aye, that there was, mine host, one that hath
taught me more wit than ever I learned before in
my life, and I paid nothing for it neither, but was
paid for my learning.   63

[Enter BARDOLPH.]

BARD. Out, alas, sir! Cozenage, mere cozenage!

HOST. Where be my horses? Speak well of them,
varletto.°

BARD. Run away with the cozeners.° For so soon
as I came beyond Eton, they threw me off from behind one of them in a slough of mire,° and set spurs
and away, like three German devils, three Doctor
Faustuses.°   71

HOST. They are gone but to meet the Duke, villain. Do not say they be fled. Germans are honest
men.

[Enter SIR HUGH EVANS.]

EVANS. Where is mine host?   75

HOST. What is the matter, sir?

EVANS. Have a care of your entertainments. There
is a friend of mine come to town, tells me there is
three cozen-germans° that has cozened all the hosts
of Readins, of Maidenhead, of Colebrook, of   80
horses and money. I tell you for good will, look you.
You are wise, and full of gibes and vlouting-stocks,°
and 'tis not convenient you should be cozened. Fare
you well.   [Exit.]

[Enter DOCTOR CAIUS.]

CAIUS. Vere is mine host de Jarteer?   85

HOST. Here, Master Doctor, in perplexity and
doubtful dilemma.

CAIUS. I cannot tell vat is dat. But it is tell-a me
dat you make grand preparation for a duke de
Jamany. By my trot, dere is no duke dat the Court
is know to come. I tell you for good vill. Adieu.   91
          [Exit.]

HOST. Hue and cry,° villain, go! — Assist me,
Knight. — I am undone! — Fly, run, hue and cry,
villain! — I am undone!

[Exeunt HOST and BARDOLPH.]

FAL. I would all the world might be cozened,   95
for I have been cozened and beaten too. If it should
come to the ear of the Court how I have been transformed, and how my transformation hath been
washed and cudgeled, they would melt me out of
my fat drop by drop, and liquor° fishermen's   100
boots with me. I warrant they would whip me with
their fine wits till I were as crestfallen° as a dried
pear. I never prospered since I forswore myself at
primero.° Well, if my wind were but long enough

9–10. Anthropophaginian: cannibal.   19. Ephesian: gay lad.
See II Hen IV, II.ii.164,n.   21. Bohemian Tartar: a picturesque word for barbarian. Tartary is South Russia.   27. wise
woman: witch. The village witch was known as the "wise
woman." She was often consulted by the superstitious in love
affairs and when things were lost or stolen.   29. mussel shell:
an empty useless thing.   32. thorough: through.   45. conceal:
for "reveal."   55. Like . . . bold: a proverbial phrase — "You
certainly can."   58. clerkly: quite a scholar.

66. varletto: knave.   67. cozeners: cheats. See M Wives Intro.
p. 939a–b.   69. slough of mire: patch of deep mud.   70–71. devils
. . . Faustuses: a reference to Marlowe's famous tragedy of
Dr. Faustus, the German magician who sold his soul to the
Devil.   79. cozen-germans: a pun on "near relations," and
"cheating (cozening) Germans."   82. vlouting-stocks: laughingstocks.   92. Hue . . . cry: See Gen. Intro. p. 28a.   100. liquor:
grease.   102. crestfallen: limp.   103–04. forswore . . . primero:
cheated at cards.

to say my prayers, I would repent. [*Enter* MISTRESS QUICKLY.] Now, whence come you?   105

QUICK. From the two parties, forsooth.

FAL. The Devil take one party, and his dam° the other! And so they shall be both bestowed. I have suffered more for their sakes more than the   110 villainous inconstancy of man's disposition is able to bear.

QUICK. And have not they suffered? Yes, I warrant, speciously° one of them. Mistress Ford, good heart, is beaten black and blue, that you cannot see a white spot about her.   116

FAL. What tell'st thou me of black and blue? I was beaten myself into all the colors of the rainbow, and I was like to be apprehended for the witch of Brentford. But that my admirable dexterity   120 of wit, my counterfeiting the action of an old woman, delivered me, the knave constable had set me i' the stocks, i' the common stocks, for a witch.

QUICK. Sir, let me speak with you in your   125 chamber. You shall hear how things go, and, I warrant, to your content. Here is a letter will say somewhat. Good hearts, what ado here is to bring you together! Sure, one of you does not serve Heaven well, that you are so crossed.°   130

FAL. Come up into my chamber.   [*Exeunt.*]

SCENE VI. *The same. Another room in the Garter Inn.*

[*Enter* FENTON *and* HOST.]

HOST. Master Fenton, talk not to me. My mind is heavy. I will give over all.°

FEN. Yet hear me speak. Assist me in my purpose,
And, as I am a gentleman, I'll give thee
A hundred pound in gold more than your loss.   5

HOST. I will hear you, Master Fenton, and I will at the least keep your counsel.

FEN. From time to time I have acquainted you
With the dear love I bear to fair Anne Page,
Who mutually hath answered my affection,   10
So far forth as herself might be her chooser,
Even to my wish. I have a letter from her
Of such contents as you will wonder at,
The mirth whereof so larded° with my matter
That neither singly can be manifested   15
Without the show of both.° Fat Falstaff
Hath a great scene. The image° of the jest
I'll show you here at large. Hark, good mine host.
Tonight at Herne's Oak, just 'twixt twelve and one,

Must my sweet Nan present° the Fairy Queen.   20
The purpose why is here; in which disguise,
While other jests are something rank on foot,°
Her father hath commanded her to slip
Away with Slender and with him at Eton
Immediately to marry. She hath consented.   25
Now, sir,
Her mother, ever strong against that match
And firm for Doctor Caius, hath appointed
That he shall likewise shuffle her away
While other sports are tasking of° their minds,   30
And at the deanery, where a priest attends,
Straight marry her. To this her mother's plot
She, seemingly obedient, likewise hath
Made promise to the doctor. Now, thus it rests:
Her father means she shall be all in white,   35
And in that habit, when Slender sees his time
To take her by the hand and bid her go,
She shall go with him. Her mother hath intended,
The better to denote her to the doctor —
For they must all be masked and vizarded —   40
That quaint° in green she shall be loose enrobed,
With ribands pendent, flaring° 'bout her head;
And when the doctor spies his vantage ripe,°
To pinch her by the hand, and, on that token,
The maid hath given consent to go with him.   45

HOST. Which means she to deceive, father or mother?

FEN. Both, my good host, to go along with me;
And here it rests — that you'll procure the vicar
To stay for me at church 'twixt twelve and one,
And, in the lawful name of marrying,   50
To give our hearts united ceremony.°

HOST. Well, husband° your device. I'll to the vicar.
Bring you the maid, you shall not lack a priest.

FEN. So shall I evermore be bound to thee.   54
Besides, I'll make a present recompense.° [*Exeunt.*]

Act V

SCENE I. *A room in the Garter Inn.*

[*Enter* SIR JOHN FALSTAFF *and* MISTRESS QUICKLY.]

FAL. Prithee no more prattling. Go. I'll hold.°
This is the third time. I hope good luck lies in odd numbers. Away! Go! They say there is divinity in odd numbers, either in nativity, chance, or death. Away!   5

---

107. **dam:** mother.   114. **speciously:** for especially.   130. **crossed:** thwarted.

    Sc. vi: 2. **give . . . all:** have nothing more to do with it. 14. **larded:** enriched.   15–16. **neither . . . both:** i.e., Nan's letter concerns both matters — our marriage and the joke against Falstaff.   17. **image:** description.

20. **present:** represent, take the part of.   22. **rank on foot:** in great abundance.   30. **tasking of:** occupying.   41. **quaint:** pretty.   42. **pendent, flaring:** hanging and fluttering.   43. **vantage ripe:** ripe opportunity.   51. **To . . . ceremony:** unite us in marriage.   52. **husband:** manage.   55. **present recompense:** immediate reward.

    Act V, Sc. i: 1. **hold:** keep my word to come.

QUICK. I'll provide you a chain,° and I'll do what I can to get you a pair of horns.

FAL. Away, I say. Time wears. Hold up your head, and mince.° [*Exit* MISTRESS QUICKLY.] — [*Enter* FORD.] How now, Master Brook! Master   10 Brook, the matter will be known tonight or never. Be you in the Park about midnight, at Herne's Oak, and you shall see wonders.

FORD. Went you not to her yesterday, sir, as you told me you had appointed?   15

FAL. I went to her, Master Brook, as you see, like a poor old man. But I came from her, Master Brook, like a poor old woman. That same knave Ford, her husband, hath the finest mad devil of jealousy in him, Master Brook, that ever governed frenzy.°   20 I will tell you: He beat me grievously, in the shape of a woman, for in the shape of man, Master Brook, I fear not Goliath with a weaver's beam;° because I know also life is a shuttle.° I am in haste. Go   25 along with me. I'll tell you all, Master Brook. Since I plucked geese, played truant, and whipped top, I knew not what 'twas to be beaten till lately. Follow me. I'll tell you strange things of this knave Ford, on whom tonight I will be revenged, and I will   30 deliver his wife into your hand. Follow. Strange things in hand, Master Brook! Follow.   [*Exeunt.*]

SCENE II. *Windsor Park.*°

[*Enter* PAGE, SHALLOW, *and* SLENDER.]

PAGE. Come, come. We'll couch° i' the Castle ditch° till we see the light of our fairies. Remember, Son Slender, my daughter.

SLEN. Aye, forsooth. I have spoke with her, and we have a nay-word° how to know one another.   5 I come to her in white,° and cry, " mum," she cries " budget,"° and by that we know one another.

SHAL. That's good too. But what needs either your " mum " or her " budget "?° The white will decipher° her well enough. It hath struck ten o'clock.   12

PAGE. The night is dark. Light and spirits will become it well. Heaven prosper our sport! No man means evil but the Devil, and we shall know him by his horns. Let's away. Follow me.   [*Exeunt.*]

SCENE III. *A street leading to the Park.*

[*Enter* MISTRESS PAGE, MISTRESS FORD, *and* DOCTOR CAIUS.]

MRS. PAGE. Master Doctor, my daughter is in green. When you see your time, take her by the hand, away with her to the deanery, and dispatch it quickly. Go before° into the Park. We two must go together.   5

CAIUS. I know vat I have to do. Adieu.

MRS. PAGE. Fare you well, sir. [*Exit* DOCTOR CAIUS.] My husband will not rejoice so much at the abuse of Falstaff as he will chafe° at the doctor's marrying my daughter. But 'tis no matter. Better a little chiding than a great deal of heartbreak.   11

MRS. FORD. Where is Nan now and her troop of fairies, and the Welsh devil Hugh?

MRS. PAGE. They are all couched in a pit hard by Herne's Oak, with obscured lights, which, at   15 the very instant of Falstaff's and our meeting, they will at once display to the night.

MRS. FORD. That cannot choose but amaze° him.

MRS. PAGE. If he be not amazed, he will be mocked. If he be amazed, he will every way be mocked.   21

MRS. FORD. We'll betray him finely.

MRS. PAGE. Against such lewdsters° and their lechery
Those that betray them do no treachery.

MRS. FORD. The hour draws on. To the Oak, to the Oak!   [*Exeunt.*]   26

SCENE IV. *Windsor Park.*

[*Enter* SIR HUGH EVANS *disguised, with others as Fairies.*]

EVANS. Trib,° trib, fairies. Come, and remember your parts. Be pold, I pray you. Follow me into the pit, and when I give the watch-'ords, do as I pid you. Come, come. Trib, trib.   [*Exeunt.*]

SCENE V. *Another part of the Park.*

[*Enter* SIR JOHN FALSTAFF *disguised as Herne.*]

FAL. The Windsor bell hath struck twelve. The minute draws on. Now, the hot-blooded gods assist

---

6. **chain:** i.e., to shake in his disguise as Herne the Hunter. 9. **mince:** walk off. 20. **governed frenzy:** caused madness. 23. **Goliath . . . beam:** Goliath, the Philistine giant slain by the boy David, was so strong that "the staff of his spear was like a weaver's beam." See I Samuel 17:7. The beam is the bar on which the threads of the warp are wound in weaving. It was formerly made of a solid tree trunk. 25. **shuttle:** the instrument used in weaving which is thrown to and fro in crossing the threads.   **Sc. ii: Windsor Park.** Editors have given a place heading to each of these brief scenes (ii,iii,iv), but on the stage they are not localized and are nothing more than the quick comings and goings of the various sets of characters. 1. **couch:** lie. 1–2. **Castle ditch:** moat. 5. **nay-word:** password. 6. **her in white:** girl wearing a white costume. 6–7. **mum . . . budget:** lit., silence. 8–9. **what . . . budget:** i.e., why these passwords? 11. **decipher:** identify.

Sc. iii: 4. **before:** ahead. 9. **chafe:** fret. 18. **amaze:** astound — a much stronger word than today. 23. **lewdsters:** lechers.

Sc. iv: 1. **Trib:** for trip, dance on your toes.

me! Remember, Jove,° thou wast a bull for thy Europa. Love set on thy horns. O powerful Love, that in some respects makes a beast a man, in some   5 other, a man a beast. You were also, Jupiter, a swan for the love of Leda. O omnipotent Love! How near the god drew to the complexion of a goose! A fault done first in the form of a beast. Oh, Jove,   10 a beastly fault! And then another fault in the semblance of a fowl. Think on't, Jove, a foul fault! When gods have hot backs, what shall poor men do? For me, I am here a Windsor stag, and the fattest, I think, i' the forest. Send me a cool rut   15 time,° Jove, or who can blame me to piss my tallow? Who comes here? My doe?

[*Enter* MISTRESS FORD *and* MISTRESS PAGE.]

MRS. FORD. Sir John! Art thou there, my deer? My male deer?   19

FAL. My doe with the black scut!° Let the sky rain potatoes.° Let it thunder to the tune of " Green Sleeves,"° hail kissing comfits,° and snow eringoes.° Let there come a tempest of provocation, I will shelter me here.

MRS. FORD. Mistress Page is come with me, Sweetheart.   26

FAL. Divide me like a bribe° buck, each a haunch. I will keep my sides to myself, my shoulders for the fellow of this walk, and my horns I bequeath your husbands. Am I a woodman,   30 ha? Speak I like Herne the Hunter? Why, now is Cupid a child of Conscience. He makes restitution.° As I am a true spirit, welcome!   [*Noise within.*]

MRS. PAGE. Alas, what noise?

MRS. FORD. Heaven forgive our sins!   35

FAL. What should this be?

MRS. FORD, MRS. PAGE. Away, away!

[*They run off.*]

FAL. I think the Devil will not have me damned, lest the oil that's in me should set Hell on fire. He would never else cross me thus.   40

[*Enter* SIR HUGH EVANS, *disguised as before;* PISTOL, *as Hobgoblin;* MISTRESS QUICKLY, ANNE PAGE, *and others, as Fairies, with tapers.*°]

QUICK. Fairies, black, grey, green, and white, You moonshine revelers and shades of night, You orphan heirs of fixèd destiny, Attend your office and your quality.° Crier Hobgoblin, make the fairy oyes.°   45

PIST. Elves, list your names. Silence, you airy toys.°

Cricket,° to Windsor chimneys shalt thou leap. Where° fires thou find'st unraked° and hearths unswept, There pinch the maids as blue as bilberry. Our radiant Queen hates sluts and sluttery.   50

FAL. They are fairies. He that speaks to them shall die. I'll wink° and couch. No man their works must eye.   [*Lies down upon his face.*]

EVANS. Where's Bede? Go you, and where you find a maid That, ere she sleep, has thrice her prayers said, Raise up the organs of her fantasy.°   55 Sleep she as sound as careless infancy. But those as° sleep and think not on their sins, Pinch them, arms, legs, backs, shoulders, sides, and shins.

QUICK. About, about! Search Windsor Castle,° elves, within and out.   60 Strew good luck, ouphes,° on every sacred room, That it may stand till the perpetual doom In state as wholesome as in state 'tis fit, Worthy the owner,° and the owner it. The several° chairs of order look you scour   65 With juice of balm and every precious flower. Each fair installment,° coat, and several crest, With loyal blazon,° evermore be blest! And nightly, meadow fairies, look you sing, Like to the Garter's compass, in a ring.°   70 Th' expressure° that it bears, green let it be, More fertile-fresh than all the field to see; And *Honi soit qui mal y pense* write In emerald tufts, flowers purple, blue, and white, Like sapphire, pearl, and rich embroidery,   75 Buckled below fair knighthood's bending knee. Fairies use flowers for their charactery.° Away! Disperse! But till 'tis one o'clock, Our dance of custom round about the oak Of Herne the Hunter let us not forget.   80

EVANS. Pray you lock hand in hand. Yourselves in order set, And twenty glowworms shall our lanterns be To guide our measure° round about the tree. But, stay. I smell a man of middle earth.°

---

46. toys: trifles. **47. Cricket**: the name of a fairy. **48–80. Where . . . forget**: The tasks and behavior of these fairies should be compared with *MND*, II.i.32–57 and V.i.378–429. **48. unraked**; not properly raked together for the night. **52. wink**: shut my eyes. **55. fantasy**: imagination — give her good dreams. **57. as**: that. **60. Windsor Castle**: See *M Wives* Intro. p. 938b. **61. ouphes**: elves. **64. owner**: i.e., Queen Elizabeth. **65. several**: individual; i.e., the chairs of the Knights of the Garter. **67. installment**: stalls. See App. 29. **67–68. coat . . . crest . . . blazon**: See App. 9. **70. Like . . . ring**: making a circle like the Garter itself. **71. expressure**: inscription. **77. charactery**: handwriting. **83. measure**: dance. See App. 24. **84. middle earth**: The earth is so called as being in the middle between Heaven and Hell.

Sc. v: 3–7. Jove . . . Leda: The god Jupiter was notorious for his love affairs with humans whom he wooed under various disguises. **15–16. rut time**: mating time. **20. scut**: little tail. **21. potatoes**: sweet potatoes, believed to cause potency in love. **21–22. "Green Sleeves"**: See II.i.65,n. **22. kissing comfits**: candies used to make the breath sweet. **eringoes**: a candied root, believed to have the same effect as potatoes, l. 21,n. **27. bribe**: F1 reads "brib'd" (stolen), which makes better sense than *bribe* (brought as a bribe). **32. restitution**: repayment for all my trouble. **40. s.d.**: See *M Wives* Intro. p. 936b for the Q1 version of this stage direction. **44. quality**: profession. **45. oyes**: the warning cry of the town crier — *oyez* (hear ye).

FAL. Heavens defend me from that Welsh fairy,
lest he transform me to a piece of cheese!   86

PIST. Vile worm, thou wast o'erlooked° even in
thy birth.

QUICK. With trial-fire° touch me his finger end.
If he be chaste, the flame will back descend
And turn him to no pain, but if he start,   90
It is the flesh of a corrupted heart.

PIST. A trial, come.

EVANS.   Come, will this wood take fire?
    [They burn him with their tapers.]

FAL. Oh, Oh, Oh!

QUICK. Corrupt, corrupt, and tainted in desire!
About him, fairies. Sing a scornful rhyme,   95
And, as you trip, still pinch him to your time.

SONG

Fie on sinful fantasy!
Fie on lust and luxury!°
Lust is but a bloody fire,
Kindled with unchaste desire,   100
Fed in heart, whose flames aspire,
As thoughts do blow them, higher and higher.
Pinch him, fairies, mutually.
Pinch him for his villainy.
Pinch him, and burn him, and turn him about,   105
Till candles and starlight and moonshine be out.

[During this song they pinch SIR JOHN FALSTAFF.
DOCTOR CAIUS *comes one way, and steals away a boy
in green,* SLENDER *another way, and takes off a boy
in white, and* FENTON *comes, and steals away* MIS-
TRESS ANNE PAGE. *A noise of hunting is heard within.
All the Fairies run away.* SIR JOHN FALSTAFF *pulls
off his buck's head, and rises.]*

[Enter PAGE, FORD, MISTRESS PAGE *and*
MISTRESS FORD.]

PAGE. Nay, do not fly. I think we have watched°
you now.
Will none but Herne the Hunter serve your turn?

MRS. PAGE. I pray you, come, hold up the jest no
higher.°   109
Now, good Sir John, how like you Windsor wives?
See you these, Husband? Do not these fair yokes°
Become the forest better than the town?

FORD. Now, sir, who's a cuckold now? Master
Brook, Falstaff's a knave, a cuckoldly knave. Here
are his horns, Master Brook. And, Master   115
Brook, he hath enjoyed nothing of Ford's but his
buck basket, his cudgel, and twenty pounds of
money, which must be paid to Master Brook. His
horses are arrested for it, Master Brook.   119

MRS. FORD. Sir John, we have had ill luck. We
could never meet. I will never take you for my love
again, but I will always count you my deer.

FAL. I do begin to perceive that I am made an
ass.   125

FORD. Aye, and an ox° too. Both the proofs are
extant.

FAL. And these are not fairies? I was three or
four times in the thought they were not fairies;
and yet the guiltiness of my mind, the sudden   130
surprise of my powers, drove the grossness of the
foppery° into a received belief, in despite of the
teeth° of all rhyme and reason, that they were
fairies. See now how wit may be made a Jack-a-
Lent,° when 'tis upon ill employment!   135

EVANS. Sir John Falstaff, serve Got, and leave
your desires, and fairies will not pinse you.

FORD. Well said, Fairy Hugh.

EVANS. And leave you your jealousies too, I pray
you.   140

FORD. I will never mistrust my wife again till
thou art able to woo her in good English.

FAL. Have I laid my brain in the sun and dried
it, that it wants matter to prevent so gross o'erreach-
ing° as this? Am I ridden with a Welsh goat°   145
too? Shall I have a coxcomb of frieze?° 'Tis time I
were choked with a piece of toasted cheese.

EVANS. Seese is not good to give putter. Your
pelly is all putter.   149

FAL. "Seese" and "putter"? Have I lived to
stand at the taunt of one that makes fritters° of
English? This is enough to be the decay of lust and
late-walking through the realm.

MRS. PAGE. Why, Sir John, do you think,   154
though we would have thrust virtue out of our
hearts by the head and shoulders, and have given
ourselves without scruple to Hell, that ever the
Devil could have made you our delight?

FORD. What, a hodge pudding?° A bag of flax?

MRS. PAGE. A puffed man?   160

PAGE. Old, cold, withered, and of intolerable entrails?

FORD. And one that is as slanderous as Satan?

PAGE. And as poor as Job?

FORD. And as wicked as his wife?   165

EVANS. And given to fornications, and to taverns,
and sack, and wine, and metheglins,° and to drink-
ings, and swearings, and starings, pribbles and
prabbles?°   169

FAL. Well, I am your theme. You have the start

---

87. o'erlooked: bewitched.   88. trial-fire: the fire which tests,
explained in ll. 89–91.   98. luxury: lechery.   107. watched:
caught.   109. hold . . . higher: do not continue the joke any
further.   111. yokes: i.e., the horns which Falstaff has been
wearing.

126. ox: i.e., a horned beast.   132. foppery: deceit.   132–33. in
. . . teeth: in the teeth of.   134–35. Jack-a-Lent: See III.iii.27,n.
144–45. o'erreaching: deception.   145. Welsh goat: because
Evans in his disguise as a satyr looks like a goat.   146. coxcomb of frieze: fool's cap made of coarse cloth. See Pl. 13c.
151. fritters: fried meat-cakes.   159. hodge pudding: pudding
made of meat stuffed into a sheep's stomach — like the Scotch
haggis.   167. metheglins: a strong drink made of fermented
honey, and especially enjoyed by Welshmen.   168–69. pribbles
. . . prabbles: See I.i.56,n.

of me. I am dejected. I am not able to answer the Welsh flannel.° Ignorance itself is a plummet° o'er me. Use me as you will.

FORD. Marry, sir, we'll bring you to Windsor, to one Master Brook, that° you have cozened of 175 money, to whom you should have been a pander. Over and above that you have suffered, I think to repay that money will be a biting affliction.

PAGE. Yet be cheerful, Knight. Thou shalt eat a posset° tonight at my house, where I will desire thee to laugh at my wife, that now laughs at 181 thee. Tell her Master Slender hath married her daughter.

MRS. PAGE. [*Aside*] Doctors doubt that.° If Anne Page be my daughter, she is, by this, Doctor Caius' wife. 186

[*Enter* SLENDER.]

SLEN. Whoa, ho! Ho, Father Page!

PAGE. Son, how now! How now, Son! Have you dispatched? 189

SLEN. Dispatched! I'll make the best in Gloucestershire know on't. Would I were hanged, la, else!

PAGE. Of what, Son?

SLEN. I came yonder at Eton to marry Mistress Anne Page, and she's a great lubberly boy. If it had not been i' the church, I would have swinged° 195 him, or he should have swinged me. If I did not think it had been Anne Page, would I might never stir! And 'tis a postmaster's boy.

PAGE. Upon my life, then, you took the wrong.

SLEN. What need you tell me that? I think 202 so, when I took a boy for a girl. If I had been married to him, for all he was in woman's apparel, I would not have had him. 205

PAGE. Why, this is your own folly. Did not I tell you how you should know my daughter by her garments?

SLEN. I went to her in white, and cried " mum," and she cried " budget," as Anne and I had 210 appointed; and yet it was not Anne, but a postmaster's boy.

MRS. PAGE. Good George, be not angry. I knew of your purpose, turned my daughter into green, and, indeed, she is now with the doctor at the deanery, and there married. 216

[*Enter* DOCTOR CAIUS.]

CAIUS. Vere is Mistress Page? By gar, I am cozened. I ha' married *un garçon,* a boy; *un paysan,*°

by gar, a boy. It is not Anne Page. By gar, I am cozened. 220

MRS. PAGE. Why, did you take her in green?

CAIUS. Aye, by gar, and 'tis a boy. By gar, I'll raise all Windsor. [*Exit.*]

FORD. This is strange. Who hath got the right Anne? 225

PAGE. My heart misgives me. Here comes Master Fenton.

[*Enter* FENTON *and* ANNE PAGE.]

How now, Master Fenton!

ANNE. Pardon, good Father! Good my Mother, pardon!

PAGE. Now, mistress, how chance you went not with Master Slender? 231

MRS. PAGE. Why went you not with Master Doctor, maid?

FEN. You do amaze° her. Hear the truth of it.
You would have married her most shamefully
Where there was no proportion held in love. 235
The truth is, she and I, long since contracted,
Are now so sure that nothing can dissolve us.
The offense is holy that she hath committed,
And this deceit loses the name of craft,
Of disobedience, or unduteous title,° 240
Since therein she doth evitate° and shun
A thousand irreligious cursèd hours
Which forcèd marriage would have brought upon her.

FORD. Stand not amazed. Here is no remedy.
In love the Heavens themselves do guide the state.
Money buys lands, and wives are sold by fate. 246

FAL. I am glad, though you have ta'en a special stand° to strike at me, that your arrow hath glanced.°

PAGE. Well, what remedy? Fenton, Heaven give thee joy! 250
What cannot be eschewed° must be embraced.

FAL. When night-dogs run, all sorts of deer are chased.

MRS. PAGE. Well, I will muse no further. Master Fenton,
Heaven give you many, many merry days!
Good Husband, let us every one go home 255
And laugh this sport o'er by a country fire,
Sir John and all.

FORD.   Let it be so. Sir John,
To Master Brook you yet shall hold your word,
For he tonight shall lie with Mistress Ford.

[*Exeunt.*]

---

172. flannel: a contemptuous name for a Welshman. Ignorance . . . plummet: there is no end to the depth of my ignorance. 175. that: whom. 180. posset: hot bedtime drink. 184. Doctors . . . that: learned men have another opinion. 195. swinged: thrashed. 218. *paysan:* peasant.

233. amaze: astonish, frighten. 240. unduteous title: title of lack of filial duty. 241. evitate: avoid. 247–48. special stand: as in a deer shoot. See *LLL*, IV.i.7–8,n. 249. glanced: missed. 251. eschewed: avoided, escaped.

The Tragedy of
TROILUS AND CRESSIDA

Introduction

The earliest record of Shakespeare's *Troilus and Cressida* is an entry in the Stationers' Register dated February 7, 1603, when it was assigned to James Roberts the printer with the note: "Entred for his copie in full Court holden this day to print when he hath gotten sufficient aucthority for yt, The booke of Troilus and Cresseda as yt is acted by my Lord Chamberlens Men." No copy of an edition of 1603 is known, and it is probable that this was a blocking entry (see Gen. Intro. p. 56a) made by Roberts at the request of the players to prevent any other printer from publishing the play. Roberts had similarly entered *As You Like It, Much Ado about Nothing,* and *Henry V* in 1600. On January 28, 1609, Richard Bonian and Henry Walley entered " a booke called the history of Troylus and Cressida," and during the year issued a quarto edition with the title *The Historie of Troylus and Cresseida. As it was acted by the Kings Maiesties seruants at the Globe. Written by William Shakespeare.* This quarto was reissued during the year with a new title page: *The Famous Historie of Troylus and Cresseid. Excellently expressing the beginning of their loues, with the conceited wooing of Pandarus Prince of Licia. Written by William Shakespeare.* To this second issue was also added a remarkable Epistle to the Reader:

A NEVER WRITER TO AN EVER READER. NEWS.

Eternal reader, you have here a new play, never staled with the stage, never clapper-clawed with the palms of the vulgar, and yet passing full of the palm comical; for it is a birth of your brain, that never undertook anything comical vainly: and were but the vain names of comedies changed for the titles of commodities, or of plays for pleas, you should see all those grand censors that now style them such vanities flock to them for the main grace of their gravities: especially this author's comedies, that are so framed to the life that they serve for the most common commentaries of all the actions of our lives showing such a dexterity, and power of wit that the most displeased with plays are pleased with his comedies. And all such dull and heavy-witted worldlings as were never capable of the wit of a comedy coming by report of them to his representations, have found that wit there that they never found in themselves, and have parted better-witted than they came, feeling an edge of wit set upon them more than ever they dreamed they had brain to grind it on. So much and such savored salt of wit is in his comedies that they seem (for their height of pleasure) to be born in that sea that brought forth Venus. Amongst all there is none more witty than this, and had I time I would comment upon it, though I know it needs not (for so much as will think your testern [sixpence] well bestowed) but for so much worth as even poor I know to be stuffed in it. It deserves such a labor as well as the best comedy in Terence or Plautus. And believe this, that when he is gone, and his comedies out of sale, you will scramble for them, and set up a new English Inquisition. Take this for a warning, and at the peril of your pleasure's loss, and judgments, refuse not, nor like this the less for not being sullied with the smoky breath of the multitude, but thank fortune for the 'scape it hath made amongst you. Since by the grand possessors' wills I believe you should have prayed for them rather than been prayed. And so I leave all such to be prayed for (for the states of their wit's healths) that will not praise it.

VALE

Troilus and Cressida was reprinted in the first folio of 1623, but there seem to have been difficulties. In two surviving copies of the folio, the first page only occurs immediately after *Romeo and Juliet;* in all other copies it was printed without pagination between *Henry VIII* (the last of the histories) and *Coriolanus* (the first of the tragedies). The likeliest explanation is that some dispute over the ownership of the play arose during the printing of the folio which was not settled until after the rest of the tragedies had been set up.

The plot of the play is twofold. The first story tells how Troilus obtained the love of Cressida with the aid of Pandarus, her uncle, and how she was taken to the Greek camp and there played the strumpet. The second story tells how the

Greeks, distressed by Achilles' withdrawal from the combat, arranged for Ajax to fight a friendly bout with Hector, and how thereafter Hector killed Achilles' young friend Patroclus, and was in turn treacherously slain by Achilles.

The tale of Troilus and Cressida was a later invention and not part of the original Greek cycle of the legends of Troy. It was so popular that " Cressida " and " Pandar " became the types of a wanton and a pimp. The best version in English was Chaucer's *Troylus and Cressyde*. The story of Achilles, Ajax, and Hector came originally from Homer's *Iliad*. In 1598 the first two of George Chapman's translations of the *Iliad* had appeared — *Seven Books of the Iliades* and *Achilles' Shield*. The books translated were I, II, VII, VIII, IX, X, XII and XVIII. From these books came Achilles' quarrel with Agamemnon and his withdrawal from the war, the character of Thersites, the combat of Ajax and Hector, the proposal to send Helen back, the embassy of Nestor and Odysseus (Ulysses) to Achilles, and the grief of Achilles for Patroclus. Shakespeare however owed little to his sources, medieval or Homeric, for anything more than the outline of the story and a few of the episodes. The plot of the play, most of the characterization, the speeches, and the situations were his own invention.

But Chapman gave an unexpected lead. He had dedicated his translation of the *Seven Books of the Iliades of Homer, Prince of Poets,* to " the most honored instance of the Achilleian virtues eternized by Divine Homer, the Earl of Essex, Earl Marshal, etc." Chapman further insisted on the parallel by addressing Essex as

Most true Achilles (whom by sacred prophecy Homer did but prefigure in his admirable object) and in whose unmatched virtues shine the dignities of the soul, and the whole excellence of royal humanity; let not the peasant-common politics of the world, that count all things servile and simple that pamper not their sensualities, burying quick in their filthy sepulchers the earth, the whole bodies and souls of honor, virtue and piety, stir your temper from perseverance in godlike pursuit of Eternity.

With this dedication before him, Shakespeare could hardly have failed to see certain remarkable likenesses between Essex and Achilles. Moreover events in the three years following the publication of Chapman's translation made the identifi-

cation more exact and significant (see Gen. Intro p. 24a).

The parallel between the situation at Essex House in the winter of 1600–01, with Essex Southampton, and Cuff snarling at the Queen and her Ministers, is so close to the situation in the play where Achilles, Patroclus, and Thersites sneer at Agamemnon, Nestor, Menelaus, Ajax and the rest that no contemporary could have missed it. It is in fact far closer to the actual events of the time than to the original situation in the *Iliad*. Nevertheless *Troilus and Cressida* is not an allegory of the fortunes of the Earl of Essex. As elsewhere, Shakespeare saw a remarkable similarity and made the most of it.

The exact date of the writing of *Troilus and Cressida* cannot be fixed, but the probable conclusion is that it was written between the autumn of 1600 and the winter of 1602. It is not likely that the play was ever publicly acted. Indeed Bonian and Walley, after stating in their first edition that it was acted at the Globe, withdrew the statement and declared in the Epistle that it " was never staled with the stage, never clapper-clawed with the palms of the vulgar." It does however bear all the signs of a play prepared for a private and select audience. There are signs also that the Troilus section of the story is in part a rewriting of an old play. In the latter part of the play, in such scenes as III.v, there are patches of rhyme and rhythm very much in the early style of *Love's Labor's Lost*.

The quarto text issued in 1609 is fairly well printed, but differs in many small points from the text printed in the folio. Each version contains short passages omitted by the other. From certain similarities in the setting of the two texts, it seems either that the folio text was printed from a copy of the quarto carefully but not uniformly corrected from a playhouse copy, or that both texts derive from a common original.

Troilus and Cressida is one of the most puzzling of Shakespeare's plays, although at times one of the most powerful. It is distinctly an unpleasant play, and has therefore been ignored by those critics who prefer to avoid the dark corners in Shakespeare's mind. Here love is smirched and mocked with a filthy bitterness, and heroism is made ridiculous. Hector the brave, the one man of heroic stature in the play, is murdered in cold blood by Achilles, another classical " hero," who is shown as insubordinate, sulky, and lovesick.

There is no romance, no beauty, no heroism, and no nobility. *Troilus and Cressida* is the work of a man in the bitterest mood of disillusionment to whom the world has become " a foul and pestilent congregation of vapors."

The play opens with a sight of Troilus and Pandarus. Troilus is almost lust-mad with desire for Cressida. In the next scene Cressida is shown as Pandarus, her uncle, tries to win her sympathy for Troilus. Cressida answers him with cynical and equivocal jests; but when she is alone she utters her true thoughts (I.ii.308); she is as hot as Troilus, but more expert. She will take him when his passion has reached white heat, but not before.

The scene then passes to the Greek camp with the generals in council (I.iii). Everything is going wrong. Agamemnon as commander opens the debate. He is followed by old Nestor, the type of reminiscent ancient who complacently observes that ill fortune is the test of valor. Then Shakespeare puts into the mouth of Ulysses one of his greatest speeches (I.iii.75); all these troubles, says Ulysses, come because men refuse to conform to the pattern of the universe, and especially Achilles, who sulks and mocks them all. The argument is interrupted by the arrival of Aeneas from Troy to bring Hector's challenge to any Greek who will meet him in single combat.

The third set of characters — Ajax, Thersites, the bitter foul-mouthed commentator, Achilles, and his minion Patroclus — is now introduced (II.i) in a short patch of quick dialogue to contrast with the oratory of the previous scene. The debate of the Greek commanders is next paralleled by another debate in Priam's palace. The theme of the Greek debate was order and chaos; the theme of the Trojans is honor and reason. Reason and moral right demand that Helen shall be sent back to her lawful husband, " honor " that she shall remain. In the next scene the contrast and the comment on what has just been said is given by Thersites — " All the argument is a cuckold and a whore." The Greek generals come to Achilles, but he treats them insultingly and they agree to exalt Ajax, who is already almost bursting with his own pride.

The story then returns to Troilus. Pandarus fetches Cressida to him and in the presence of this greasy old man the lovers declare their passion. There is a cynical contrast here to the other great declarations of love which Shakespeare had created: Bassanio and Portia (*M of Ven*, III.ii), Benedict and Beatrice (*M Ado*, IV.i.257), Romeo and Juliet (II.ii). These lovers exchange not lyric passion but bawdy jests, though at the end they reach a height of emotion when — the most bitter touch of all — they swear constancy to each other, and Pandarus ushers them into a bedchamber.

The scene next passes to the Greek camp, where the Greeks promise to fetch Cressida from Troy and to restore her to her father Calchas, the Trojan traitor, in return for the Trojan Antenor whom they have captured. The Greek generals now turn the tables on Achilles. As he sits in the door of his tent they deliberately ignore him, and when he asks Ulysses for an explanation of this unexpected behavior, Shakespeare puts into the mouth of Ulysses the magnificent speech on Time's mutability (III.iii.145).

Early next morning Troilus must leave Cressida, but before he has time to bid her farewell Aeneas is at hand with the command that she must go to her father in the Greek camp with Diomedes as her escort. Cressida for the moment is wild with grief, but she goes calmly, somewhat resentful at Troilus' insistence that she be true to him. When she arrives in the Greek camp, she greets the warriors with easy familiarity. The indecisive combat between Hector and Ajax follows, and then the Greeks, like warriors of chivalrous romance, entertain their enemies for the night. After supper Diomedes slips away. Troilus and Ulysses follow and watch. Cressida comes out to Diomedes and dallies with her new love; she easily parts with the sleeve that was Troilus' gift, and invites Diomedes to come to her. Troilus is transfixed with horror and incredulity.

Next morning the war is renewed. There is confused and general fighting. Patroclus is slain and his body is carried to Achilles, who is at last roused to action. Meanwhile Hector, wearied with the fighting, lays aside his sword and helmet, and while he is still resting unarmed is attacked by Achilles and his Myrmidons and slain in cold blood. Troilus in horror goes back to tell the news in Troy.

Although the play itself is loosely constructed and the last scenes seem to have been hastily huddled together, Shakespeare took considerable care in creating his characters. Three in particular stand out: Thersites, Ulysses, and Cressida.

Thersites is a specimen of a type not uncommon in Shakespeare's times — the political malcontent (see App. 4), a man frustrated and thwarted in his ambitions who takes his revenge on the world by posing as a fearless, blistering critic of humanity too honest and clear-sighted to be deceived by humbug and romantic notions, and who always imputes the worst of motives to every action.

Ulysses is a very different kind of commentator. He is the farsighted realist, with a vast knowledge of human motives. His analysis of the causes of the Greek disasters (I.iii.75–210) is acute wisdom. He recognizes at once that the best means of bringing Achilles to his senses is to encourage the foolish Ajax (I.iii.367–86), and when the time comes he gives the best possible advice to Achilles, reminding him of the universal truth — the touch of nature that makes the whole world kin — that men always follow the newest fashion and soon forget the old (III.iii.95–215). He also at a glance recognizes Cressida for what she is (IV.v. 54–63).

Cressida is drawn with fascinated loathing. She is the born wanton, a creature wholly sensual, passing easily from one lover to the next. Troilus is her slave, but soon she finds his devoted passion tedious, especially when he demands loyalty. She meets her match in Diomedes, who quickly discovers how to reduce her from encouragement to pleading. It is not an attractive picture; but there is no romance in *Troilus and Cressida*.

In any other play Shakespeare would have ended on a note of tragedy, a quiet close, a eulogy dignified and noble for the dead Hector. But *Troilus and Cressida* is not the story of the death of a hero; its theme is lechery and incontinent varlets, and Shakespeare gave the last word to Pandarus, a rueful comment on his own disgusting trade: " O traitors and bawds, how earnestly are you set a-work, and how ill requited! "

Troilus and Cressida

DRAMATIS PERSONAE

PRIAM, *King of Troy*

HECTOR
TROILUS
PARIS } *his sons*
DEIPHOBUS
HELENUS

MARGARELON, *a bastard son of Priam*

AENEAS } *Trojan commanders*
ANTENOR

CALCHAS, *a Trojan priest, taking part with the Greeks*

PANDARUS, *uncle to Cressida*

AGAMEMNON, *the Grecian general*

MENELAUS, *his brother*

ACHILLES
AJAX } *Grecian commanders*
ULYSSES

NESTOR
DIOMEDES } *Grecian commanders*
PATROCLUS

THERSITES, *a deformed and scurrilous Grecian*

ALEXANDER, *servant to Cressida*

SERVANT *to Troilus*

SERVANT *to Paris*

SERVANT *to Diomedes*

HELEN, *wife to Menelaus*

ANDROMACHE, *wife to Hector*

CASSANDRA, *daughter to Priam; a prophetess*

CRESSIDA, *daughter to Calchas*

TROJAN *and* GREEK SOLDIERS, *and* ATTENDANTS

SCENE — *Troy, and the Grecian camp.*

PROLOGUE°

In Troy there lies the scene. From isles of Greece
The princes orgulous,° their high blood chafed,°
Have to the port of Athens sent their ships,
Fraught° with the ministers and instruments
Of cruel war. Sixty and nine that wore   5
Their crownets° regal from the Athenian bay
Put forth toward Phrygia,° and their vow is made
To ransack Troy, within whose strong immures°
The ravishèd Helen, Menelaus' Queen,   9
With wanton Paris sleeps, and that's the quarrel.
To Tenedos° they come,
And the deep-drawing barks do there disgorge
Their warlike fraughtage. Now on Dardan° plains
The fresh and yet unbruisèd Greeks do pitch
Their brave pavilions. Priam's six-gated city,   15
Dardan, and Timbria, Helias, Chetas, Troien,
And Antenorides,° with massy° staples,
And corresponsive and fulfilling bolts,
Sperr° up the sons of Troy.
Now expectation, tickling skittish spirits,   20
On one and other side, Trojan and Greek,
Sets all on hazard. And hither am I come
A Prologue armed, but not in confidence
Of author's pen or actor's voice, but suited
In like conditions as our argument,°   25
To tell you, fair beholders, that our play
Leaps o'er the vaunt and firstlings° of those broils,
Beginning in the middle, starting thence away
To what may be digested in a play.
Like, or find fault, do as your pleasures are.   30
Now good or bad, 'tis but the chance of war.

Prologue: Shakespeare, unlike other contemporary dramatists, seldom used a prologue to introduce a play. This **Prologue** is armed, in imitation of the armed Prologues used during the stage war by Marston in *Antonio and Mellida* and Jonson in *Poetaster* (see Gen. Intro. pp. 44a, 45a). **2. orgulous:** proud. **chafed:** enraged. **4. Fraught:** laden. **6. crownets:** coronets, worn by petty kings. **7. Phrygia:** Asia Minor. **8. immures:** walls. **11. Tenedos:** a Greek island in the Aegean Sea. **13. Dardan:** Trojan. **16–17. Dardan . . . Antenorides:** the names of the gates of Troy. **17. massy:** massive. **19. Sperr:** shut.

Act I

SCENE I. *Troy. Before* PRIAM's *palace.*

[*Enter* PANDARUS *and* TROILUS.]

TRO. Call here my varlet,° I'll unarm again.
Why should I war without° the walls of Troy,
That find such cruel battle here within?
Each Trojan that is master of his heart,
Let him to field. Troilus, alas, hath none!   5
PAN. Will this gear° ne'er be mended?
TRO. The Greeks are strong and skillful to their strength,

25. argument: plot, theme.   27. vaunt . . . firstlings: van and beginning.
Act I, Sc. i: 1. varlet: servant, valet.   2. without: outside.
6. gear: business.

Fierce to their skill and to their fierceness valiant.
But I am weaker than a woman's tear,
Tamer than sleep, fonder° than ignorance, 10
Less valiant than the virgin in the night,
And skill-less as unpracticed infancy.

PAN. Well, I have told you enough of this. For my
part, I'll not meddle nor make no farther. He that
will have a cake out of the wheat must needs tarry
the grinding. 16

TRO. Have I not tarried?

PAN. Aye, the grinding. But you must tarry the
bolting.°

TRO. Have I not tarried?

PAN. Aye, the bolting. But you must tarry the
leavening. 20

TRO. Still have I tarried.

PAN. Aye, to the leavening. But here's yet in the
word "hereafter" the kneading, the making of the
cake, the heating of the oven, and the baking. Nay,
you must stay the cooling too, or you may chance to
burn your lips. 26

TRO. Patience herself, what goddess e'er she be,
Doth lesser blench° at sufferance° than I do.
At Priam's royal table do I sit,
And when fair Cressid comes into my thoughts —
So, traitor! — "When she comes!" — When is she
 thence?

PAN. Well, she looked yesternight fairer than ever
I saw her look, or any woman else.

TRO. I was about to tell thee — when my heart,
As wedgèd with a sigh, would rive° in twain 35
Lest Hector or my father should perceive me,
I have, as when the sun doth light a storm,
Buried this sigh in wrinkle of a smile.
But sorrow that is couched in seeming gladness
Is like that mirth fate turns to sudden sadness. 40

PAN. An° her hair were not somewhat darker
than Helen's — well, go to — there were no more
comparison between the women. But for my part,
she is my kinswoman. I would not, as they term it,
praise her. But I would somebody had heard her talk
yesterday, as I did. I will not dispraise your sister
Cassandra's wit, but ——

TRO. O Pandarus! I tell thee, Pandarus —
When I do tell thee, there my hopes lie drowned,
Reply not in how many fathoms deep 50
They lie indrenched.° I tell thee I am mad
In Cressid's love. Thou answer'st "she is fair,"
Pour'st in the open ulcer of my heart
Her eyes, her hair, her cheek, her gait, her voice,
Handlest in thy discourse, oh, that her hand, 55
In whose comparison all whites are ink
Writing their own reproach, to whose soft seizure
The cygnet's down is harsh, and spirit of sense

Hard as the palm of plowman.° This thou tell'st me,
As true thou tell'st me, when I say I love her. 60
But, saying thus, instead of oil and balm,
Thou lay'st in every gash that love hath given me
The knife that made it.

PAN. I speak no more than truth.

TRO. Thou dost not speak so much. 65

PAN. Faith, I'll not meddle in 't. Let her be as she
is. If she be fair, 'tis the better for her. An she be not,
she has the mends in her own hands.°

TRO. Good Pandarus, how now, Pandarus!

PAN. I have had my labor for my travail, ill-
thought-on of her and ill-thought-on of you — gone
between and between, but small thanks for my labor.

TRO. What, art thou angry, Pandarus? What,
 with me? 75

PAN. Because she's kin to me, therefore she's not
so fair as Helen. An she were not kin to me, she
would be as fair on Friday as Helen is on Sunday.°
But what care I? I care not an she were a blackamoor, 'tis all one to me. 80

TRO. Say I she is not fair?

PAN. I do not care whether you do or no. She's a
fool to stay behind her father.° Let her to the
Greeks, and so I'll tell her the next time I see her.
For my part, I'll meddle nor make no more i' the
matter.

TRO. Pandarus ——

PAN. Not I.

TRO. Sweet Pandarus ——

PAN. Pray you, speak no more to me. I will leave
all as I found it, and there an end. 91

        [*Exit. An alarum.*]

TRO. Peace, you ungracious clamors! Peace, rude
 sounds!
Fools on both sides! Helen must needs be fair
When with your blood you daily paint her thus.
I cannot fight upon this argument, 95
It is too starved a subject for my sword.
But Pandarus —— O gods, how do you plague me!
I cannot come to Cressid but by Pandar,
And he's as tetchy° to be wooed to woo
As she is stubborn-chaste against all suit. 100
Tell me, Apollo, for thy Daphne's° love,
What Cressid is, what Pandar, and what we.
Her bed is India,° there she lies, a pearl.
Between our Ilium and where she resides,
Let it be called the wild and wandering flood, 105
Ourself the merchant, and this sailing Pandar

57–59. to . . . plowman: compared with Cressida's gentle grasp,
swan's-down is hard, and the most sensitive of feeling as rough
as a plowman's hand. 68. has . . . hands: i.e., can make
herself up. 78. on Sunday: i.e., in her Sunday best.
82–83. She's . . . father: Cressida's father, Calchas, deserted to
the Greeks. 99. tetchy: touchy. 101. Daphne: one of Apollo's
unsuccessful loves. To avoid his approaches she was changed
into a laurel. 103. India: the symbol of distant, wealthy, and
romantic lands.

10. fonder: more foolish. 18. bolting: sifting of the flour.
28. blench: shy (like a horse). sufferance: pain. 35. rive:
split. 41. An: if. 51. indrenched: soaked.

Our doubtful hope, our convoy and our bark.°

    [Alarum. Enter AENEAS.]

  AENE. How now, Prince Troilus! Wherefore not
afield?

  TRO. Because not there. This woman's answer
sorts,°

For womanish it is to be from thence.   110

What news, Aeneas, from the field today?

  AENE. That Paris is returned home, and hurt.

  TRO. By whom, Aeneas?

  AENE.   Troilus, by Menelaus.

  TRO. Let Paris bleed. 'Tis but a scar to scorn. 114

Paris is gored with Menelaus' horn.°   *[Alarum.]*

  AENE. Hark, what good sport is out of town today!

  TRO. Better at home if " would I might " were
" may."

But to the sport abroad. Are you bound thither?

  AENE. In all swift haste.

  TRO.   Come, go we then together. *[Exeunt.]*

SCENE II. *The same. A street.*

[Enter CRESSIDA *and* ALEXANDER *her man.]*

  CRES. Who were those went by?

  ALEX.   Queen Hecuba and Helen.

  CRES. And whither go they?

  ALEX.   Up to the eastern tower,

Whose height commands as subject all the vale,

To see the battle. Hector, whose patience

Is as a virtue fixed, today was moved.   5

He chid Andromache and struck his armorer,

And, like as there were husbandry° in war,

Before the sun rose he was harnessed° light,

And to the field goes he, where every flower

Did, as a prophet, weep what it foresaw   10

In Hector's wrath.

  CRES.   What was his cause of anger?

  ALEX. The noise goes, this: There is among the
Greeks

A lord of Trojan blood, nephew to Hector.

They call him Ajax.°

  CRES.   Good, and what of him?

  ALEX. They say he is a very man per se,°   15

And stands alone.

  CRES. So do all men, unless they are drunk, sick,
or have no legs.

  ALEX. This man, lady, hath robbed many beasts of
their particular additions.° He is as valiant as 20
the lion, churlish as the bear, slow as the elephant —

a man into whom Nature hath so crowded humors°
that his valor is crushed into folly, his folly sauced
with discretion. There is no man hath a virtue that
he hath not a glimpse of, nor any man an at- 25
taint° but he carries some stain of it. He is melancholy without cause and merry against the hair.° He
hath the joints of everything, but everything so out
of joint that he is a gouty Briareus,° many hands
and no use, or purblind Argus,° all eyes and no
sight.   31

  CRES. But how should this man, that makes me
smile, make Hector angry?

  ALEX. They say he yesterday coped° Hector in the
battle and struck him down, the disdain and shame
whereof hath ever since kept Hector fasting and
waking.   37

        [Enter PANDARUS.]

  CRES. Who comes here?

  ALEX. Madam, your uncle Pandarus.

  CRES. Hector's a gallant man.

  ALEX. As may be in the world, lady.

  PAN. What's that? What's that?

  CRES. Good morrow, Uncle Pandarus.   43

  PAN. Good morrow, Cousin° Cressid. What do
you talk of? Good morrow, Alexander. How do you,
Cousin? When were you at Ilium?°

  CRES. This morning, Uncle.

  PAN. What were you talking of when I came?
Was Hector armed and gone ere you came to Ilium?
Helen was not up, was she?   50

  CRES. Hector was gone, but Helen was not up.

  PAN. E'en so. Hector was stirring early.

  CRES. That were we talking of, and of his anger.

  PAN. Was he angry?

  CRES. So he says here.

  PAN. True, he was so. I know the cause too. He'll
lay about him today, I can tell them that. And there's
Troilus will not come far behind him. Let them take
heed of Troilus, I can tell them that too.   61

  CRES. What, is he angry too?

  PAN. Who, Troilus? Troilus is the better man of
the two.

  CRES. Oh Jupiter! There's no comparison.   65

  PAN. What, not between Troilus and Hector? Do
you know a man if you see him?

  CRES. Aye, if I ever saw him before and knew him.

  PAN. Well, I say Troilus is Troilus.   70

  CRES. Then you say as I say, for I am sure he is not
Hector.

  PAN. No, nor Hector is not Troilus in some degrees.°

---

107. **bark:** ship.   109. **sorts:** fits.   115. **horn:** i.e., because
Menelaus is a cuckold. See App. 11.

Sc. ii: 7. **husbandry:** economy; i.e., he got up early to make
the most of daylight.   8. **harnessed:** armored.   14. **Ajax:**
See App. 4.   15. **per se:** by himself, unique.   20. **additions:**
distinctive attributes.

22. **humors:** whims. See App. 3.   26. **attaint:** disgrace.
27. **against . . . hair:** i.e., the natural lie of the hair; "against the
grain."   29. **Briareus:** a monster with a hundred hands.
30. **Argus:** a monster with a hundred eyes.   34. **coped:** encountered.   44. **Cousin:** used for any near relation.   46. **Ilium:** the
citadel of Troy, the royal palace.   73-74. **in . . . degrees:** by
some distance.

CRES. 'Tis just to each of them, he is himself.

PAN. Himself! Alas, poor Troilus! I would he were.

CRES. So he is. 79

PAN. Condition, I had gone° barefoot to India.

CRES. He is not Hector.

PAN. Himself! No, he's not himself. Would a'° were himself! Well, the gods are above, time must friend or end. Well, Troilus, well, I would my heart were in her body! No, Hector is not a better man than Troilus. 86

CRES. Excuse me.

PAN. He is elder.

CRES. Pardon me, pardon me.

PAN. Th' other's not come to 't. You shall tell me another tale when th' other's come to 't. Hector shall not have his wit this year.

CRES. He shall not need it if he have his own.

PAN. Nor his qualities.

CRES. No matter. 95

PAN. Nor his beauty.

CRES. 'Twould not become him, his own's better.

PAN. You have no judgment, Niece. Helen herself swore th' other day that Troilus, for a brown favor° — for so 'tis, I must confess — not brown neither ——

CRES. No, but brown. 104

PAN. Faith, to say truth, brown and not brown.

CRES. To say the truth, true and not true.

PAN. She praised his complexion above Paris.

CRES. Why, Paris hath color enough.

PAN. So he has.

CRES. Then Troilus should have too much. If she praised him above, his complexion is higher than his. He having color enough, and the other higher, is too flaming a praise for a good complexion. I had as lief Helen's golden tongue had commended Troilus for a copper° nose. 115

PAN. I swear to you I think Helen loves him better than Paris.

CRES. Then she's a merry Greek° indeed.

PAN. Nay, I am sure she does. She came to him th' other day into the compassed° window — and you know he has not past three or four hairs on his chin —— 122

CRES. Indeed, a tapster's arithmetic° may soon bring his particulars therein to a total.

PAN. Why, he is very young. And yet will he, within three pound, lift as much as his brother Hector. 127

CRES. Is he so young a man and so old a lifter?°

PAN. But to prove to you that Helen loves him — she came and puts me her white hand to his cloven chin ——

CRES. Juno have mercy! How came it cloven?

PAN. Why you know 'tis dimpled. I think his smiling becomes him better than any man in all Phrygia. 136

CRES. Oh, he smiles valiantly.

PAN. Does he not?

CRES. Oh yes, an 'twere a cloud in autumn.

PAN. Why, go to, then. But to prove to you that Helen loves Troilus ——

CRES. Troilus will stand to the proof, if you'll prove it so.

PAN. Troilus! Why, he esteems her no more than I esteem an addle° egg. 145

CRES. If you love an addle egg as well as you love an idle head, you would eat chickens i' the shell.

PAN. I cannot choose but laugh to think how she tickled his chin. Indeed she has a marvelous white hand, I must needs confess —— 150

CRES. Without the rack.°

PAN. And she takes upon her to spy a white hair on his chin.

CRES. Alas, poor chin! Many a wart is richer. 155

PAN. But there was such laughing! Queen Hecuba laughed, that her eyes ran o'er.

CRES. With millstones.°

PAN. And Cassandra laughed. 159

CRES. But there was more temperate fire under the pot° of her eyes. Did her eyes run o'er too?

PAN. And Hector laughed.

CRES. At what was all this laughing?

PAN. Marry,° at the white hair that Helen spied on Troilus' chin. 165

CRES. An 't had been a green hair, I should have laughed too.

PAN. They laughed not so much at the hair as at his pretty answer.

CRES. What was his answer?

PAN. Quoth she, "Here's but two and fifty hairs on your chin, and one of them is white."

CRES. This is her question. 173

PAN. That's true, make no question of that. "Two and fifty hairs," quoth he, "and one white. That white hair is my father, and all the rest are his sons."° "Jupiter!" quoth she. "Which of these hairs is Paris my husband?" "The forked one,"° quoth he. "Pluck 't out, and give it him." But there was such laughing! And Helen so blushed, and Paris so chafed, and all the rest so laughed, that it passed.

---

80. Condition . . . gone: i.e., I wish Troilus was himself even if I had to go.　**82. a':** he.　**100–01. brown favor:** dark complexion.　**115. copper:** red.　**118. merry Greek:** The Greeks were considered gay folk, so *merry Greek* came to be a proverbial phrase for a lighthearted, frivolous person.　**120. compassed:** round.　**123. tapster's arithmetic:** such slight ability to add as a bartender (*tapster*) needs.　**128. lifter:** thief.

145. addle: addled, bad.　**151. Without . . . rack:** i.e., without being put to torture. See App. 10.　**158. With millstones:** "by the pailful."　**161. pot:** socket.　**164. Marry:** Mary, by the Virgin.　**176–77. his sons:** Priam had fifty sons.　**178. forked one**: i.e., the cuckold. See App. 11.

CRES. So let it° now, for it has been a great while going by. 184

PAN. Well, Cousin, I told you a thing yesterday. Think on 't.

CRES. So I do.

PAN. I'll be sworn 'tis true. He will weep you an 'twere° a man born in April.° 189

CRES. And I'll spring up in his tears an 'twere a nettle against May. [*A retreat sounded.*]

PAN. Hark! They are coming from the field. Shall we stand up here and see them as they pass toward Ilium? Good Niece, do, sweet Niece Cressida. 195

CRES. At your pleasure.

PAN. Here, here, here's an excellent place, here we may see most bravely. I'll tell you them all by their names as they pass by, but mark Troilus above the rest. 200

[*AENEAS passes.*]

CRES. Speak not so loud.

PAN. That's Aeneas. Is not that a brave man? He's one of the flowers of Troy, I can tell you. But mark Troilus, you shall see anon.

CRES. Who's that? 205

[*ANTENOR passes.*]

PAN. That's Antenor. He has a shrewd wit, I can tell you, and he's a man good enough. He's one o' the soundest judgments in Troy, whosoever, and a proper man of person.° When comes Troilus? I'll show you Troilus anon. If he see me, you shall see him nod at me. 211

CRES. Will he give you the nod?°

PAN. You shall see.

CRES. If he do, the rich shall have more.°

[*HECTOR passes.*]

PAN. That's Hector, that, that, look you, that. There's a fellow! Go thy way, Hector! There's a brave man, Niece. Oh, brave Hector! Look how he looks! There's a countenance! Is 't not a brave man?

CRES. Oh, a brave man! 220

PAN. Is a' not? It does a man's heart good. Look you what hacks are on his helmet! Look you yonder, do you see? Look you there — there's no jesting, there's laying on, take 't off who will, as they say. There be hacks! 225

CRES. Be those with swords?

PAN. Swords! Anything, he cares not. An the Devil come to him, it's all one. By God's lid,° it does one's heart good. Yonder comes Paris, yonder comes Paris. [*PARIS passes.*] Look ye yonder, Niece. Is 't not a gallant man too, is 't not? Why, this is brave now. Who said he came hurt home today? He's not hurt. Why, this will do Helen's heart good now, ha!

Would I could see Troilus now! You shall see Troilus anon. 236

CRES. Who's that?

[*HELENUS passes.*]

PAN. That's Helenus. I marvel where Troilus is. That's Helenus. I think he went not forth today. That's Helenus. 240

CRES. Can Helenus fight, Uncle?

PAN. Helenus! No, yes, he'll fight indifferent° well. I marvel where Troilus is. Hark! Do you not hear the people cry " Troilus "? Helenus is a priest. 245

CRES. What sneaking fellow comes yonder?

[*TROILUS passes.*]

PAN. Where? Yonder? That's Deiphobus. 'Tis Troilus! There's a man, Niece! Hem! Brave Troilus! The prince of chivalry!

CRES. Peace, for shame, peace! 250

PAN. Mark him, note him. Oh, brave Troilus! Look well upon him, Niece. Look you how his sword is bloodied, and his helm more hacked than Hector's, and how he looks, and how he goes! Oh, admirable youth! He never saw° three-and-twenty. Go thy way, Troilus, go thy way! Had I a sister were a grace, or a daughter a goddess, he should take his choice. Oh, admirable man! Paris? Paris is dirt to him, and I warrant Helen, to change, would give an eye to boot.°

[*COMMON SOLDIERS pass.*]

CRES. Here come more. 261

PAN. Asses, fools, dolts! Chaff and bran, chaff and bran! Porridge after meat! I could live and die i' the eyes of° Troilus. Ne'er look, ne'er look, the eagles are gone — crows and daws,° crows and daws! I had rather be such a man as Troilus than Agamemnon and all Grece. 267

CRES. There is among the Greeks Achilles, a better man than Troilus.

PAN. Achilles! A drayman,° a porter, a very camel.

CRES. Well, well.

PAN. Well, well! Why, have you any discretion? Have you any eyes? Do you know what a man is? Is not birth, beauty, good shape, discourse, manhood, learning, gentleness, virtue, youth, liberality, and suchlike the spice and salt that season a man? 278

CRES. Aye, a minced° man. And then to be baked with no date in the pie, for then the man's date is out.°

PAN. You are such a woman! One knows not at what ward° you lie. 283

183. it: i.e., this interminable tale. 189. an 'twere: as if he was. born in April: the rainy month of Aquarius. See App. 2. 209. proper . . . person: a fine handsome man. 212. give . . . nod: i.e., recognize you. 214. rich . . . more: i.e., if he nods to you, you will be a greater noddy (simpleton) than ever. 228. lid: eyelid. 242. indifferent: fairly. 255. never saw: i.e., is not yet. 260. to boot: in addition; i.e., to get Troilus, Helen would give Paris and one of her eyes. 263–64. i' . . . of: gazing at. 265. daws: jackdaws. 270. drayman: man who drives a heavy cart. 279. minced: with a pun on mincing, affected. 280–81. date is out: time is up. 283. ward: position of defense.

CRES. Upon my back, to defend my belly; upon my wit, to defend my wiles; upon my secrecy, to defend mine honesty;° my mask,° to defend my beauty; and you, to defend all these. And at all these wards I lie, at a thousand watches.

PAN. Say one of your watches.   290

CRES. Nay, I'll watch you for that, and that's one of the chiefest of them too. If I cannot ward what I would not have hit, I can watch you for telling how I took the blow — unless it swell past hiding, and then it's past watching.°   295

PAN. You are such another!

[*Enter* TROILUS'S BOY.]

BOY. Sir, my lord would instantly speak with you.

PAN. Where?   299

BOY. At your own house. There he unarms him.

PAN. Good boy, tell him I come. [*Exit* BOY.] I doubt° he be hurt. Fare ye well, good Niece.

CRES. Adieu, Uncle.

PAN. I will be with you, Niece, by and by.

CRES. To bring, Uncle?   305

PAN. Aye, a token from Troilus.

CRES. By the same token, you are a bawd.°

[*Exit* PANDARUS.]

Words, vows, gifts, tears, and love's full sacrifice,
He offers in another's enterprise.
But more in Troilus thousandfold I see   310
Than in the glass° of Pandar's praise may be.
Yet hold I off. Women are angels, wooing.°
Things won are done, joy's soul lies in the doing.
That she beloved° knows naught that knows not this —
Men prize the thing ungained more than it is.   315
That she was never yet that ever knew°
Love got so sweet as when desire did sue.
Therefore this maxim out of love I teach:
Achievement is command; ungained, beseech.°
Then though my heart's content firm love doth bear,
Nothing of that shall from mine eyes appear.   321

[*Exeunt.*]

SCENE III. *The Grecian camp. Before*
AGAMEMNON'S *tent.*

[*Sennet.° Enter* AGAMEMNON, NESTOR, ULYSSES,
MENELAUS, *with others.*]

AGAM. Princes,
What grief hath set the jaundice on your cheeks?

The ample proposition that hope makes
In all designs begun on earth below
Fails in the promised largeness.° Checks and disasters   5
Grow in the veins of actions highest reared,°
As knots, by the conflux of meeting sap,
Infect the sound pine and divert his grain
Tortive° and errant from his course of growth.
Nor, Princes, is it matter new to us   10
That we come short of our suppose° so far
That after seven years' siege yet Troy walls stand;
Sith° every action that hath gone before,
Whereof we have recórd, trial did draw
Bias° and thwart,° not answering the aim   15
And that unbodied° figure of the thought
That gave 't surmised shape. Why then, you Princes,
Do you with cheeks abashed behold our works,
And call them shames? Which are indeed naught else
But the protractive° trials of great Jove   20
To find persistive constancy° in men.
The fineness of which metal is not found
In Fortune's love,° for then the bold and coward,
The wise and fool, the artist° and unread,
The hard and soft, seem all affined° and kin.   25
But in the wind and tempest of her frown,
Distinction with a broad and powerful fan,
Puffing at all, winnows the light away,
And what hath mass or matter, by itself
Lies rich in virtue and unmingled.°   30

NEST. With due observance of thy godlike seat,°
Great Agamemnon, Nestor shall apply
Thy latest words. In the reproof of chance°
Lies the true proof of men. The sea being smooth,
How many shallow bauble° boats dare sail   35
Upon her patient breast, making their way
With those of nobler bulk!
But let the ruffian Boreas° once enrage
The gentle Thetis,° and anon behold
The stronged-ribbed bark through liquid mountains cut,   40
Bounding between the two moist elements°
Like Perseus' horse.° Where's then the saucy boat,
Whose weak untimbered sides but even now
Corivaled° greatness? Either to harbor fled,

---

286. honesty: chastity. mask: Ladies wore masks to prevent sun tan.   295. watching: caring for.   302. doubt: am afraid. 307. bawd: one who introduces the customer to a prostitute. 311. glass: reflection.   312. wooing: while still being wooed. 314. That . . . beloved: i.e., any woman who has a lover. 316. That . . . knew: there was never a woman who did not know.   319. Achievement . . . beseech: when a woman is won, she is at her man's command; but before he has won her, he will beg.
Sc. iii: s.d., Sennet: trumpet call.

5. promised largeness: expected good results.   6. highest reared: undertaken on a large scale.   9. Tortive: twisting. 11. suppose: estimate.   13. Sith: since.   15. Bias: out of the direct course. See App. 13. thwart: awry.   16. unbodied: i.e., existing in the mind.   20. protractive: long-drawn-out. 21. persistive constancy: firmness to persist.   23. Fortune's love: i.e., when all goes well.   24. artist: scholar.   25. affined: related.   30. unmingled: i.e., with baser qualities.   31. seat: authority.   33. reproof of chance: defiance of fortune. 35. bauble: trifling.   38. Boreas: the north wind.   39. Thetis: a sea nymph, so the sea.   41. moist elements: i.e., air and water.   42. Perseus' horse: the Greek hero Perseus killed the sorceress Medea, and from her head came Pegasus, a winged horse, which Perseus rode.   44. Corivaled: competed with.

Or made a toast for Neptune. Even so   45
Doth valor's show° and valor's worth divide
In storms of Fortune. For in her ray and bright-
    ness
The herd hath more annoyance by the breese°
Than by the tiger. But when the splitting wind
Makes flexible the knees of knotted oaks,   50
And flies fled under shade, why then the thing of
    courage
As roused with rage with rage doth sympathize,
And with an accent tuned in selfsame key
Retorts to chiding Fortune.
    ULYSS.   Agamemnon,
Thou great commander, nerve° and bone of Greece,
Heart of our numbers, soul and only spirit   56
In whom the tempers and the minds of all
Should be shut up,° hear what Ulysses speaks.
Besides the applause and approbation
The which, [*To* AGAMEMNON] most mighty for thy
    place and sway,   60
[*To* NESTOR] And thou most reverend for thy
    stretched-out life,
I give to both your speeches, which were such
As Agamemnon and the hand of Greece
Should hold up high in brass,° and such again
As venerable Nestor, hatched in silver,°   65
Should with a bond of air, strong as the axletree
On which heaven rides, knit all the Greekish ears
To his experienced tongue, yet let it please both,
Thou great, and wise, to hear Ulysses speak.
    AGAM. Speak, Prince of Ithaca, and be 't of less
    expect   70
That matter needless, of importless burden,
Divide thy lips than we are confident
When rank Thersites opes his mastic jaws
We shall hear music, wit, and oracle.°   74
    ULYSS. Troy, yet upon his basis, had been down,
And the great Hector's sword had lacked a master,
But for these instances.°
The specialty of rule° hath been neglected.
And look how many Grecian tents do stand   79
Hollow upon this plain, so many hollow factions.
When that the general is not like the hive
To whom the foragers shall all repair,
What honey is expected? Degree° being vizarded,°

The unworthiest shows as fairly in the mask.°   84
The heavens themselves, the planets and this center,°
Observe degree, priority, and place,
Insisture,° course, proportion, season, form,
Office, and custom, in all line of order.
And therefore is the glorious planet Sol
In noble eminence enthroned and sphered   90
Amidst the other,° whose medicinable eye
Corrects the ill aspects of planets evil,
And posts° like the commandment of a king,
Sans° check to good and bad. But when the planets
In evil mixture to disorder wander,   95
What plagues and what portents, what mutiny,
What raging of the sea, shaking of earth,
Commotion in the winds, frights, changes, horrors,
Divert and crack, rend and deracinate,°
The unity and married calm of states   100
Quite from their fixure!° Oh, when degree is
    shaked,
Which is the ladder to all high designs,
The enterprise is sick! How could communities,
Degrees in schools° and brotherhoods in cities,
Peaceful commerce from dividable° shores,   105
The primogenitive° and due of birth,
Prerogative° of age, crowns, scepters, laurels,
But by degree, stand in authentic place?
Take but degree away, untune that string,   109
And hark, what discord follows! Each thing meets
In mere oppugnancy.° The bounded° waters
Should lift their bosoms higher than the shores,
And make a sop of all this solid globe.
Strength should be lord of imbecility,°
And the rude son should strike his father dead.   115
Force should be right, or rather, right and wrong,
Between whose endless jar° justice resides,
Should lose their names, and so should justice too.
Then everything includes itself in power,
Power into will, will into appetite,   120
And appetite, a universal wolf,
So doubly seconded with° will and power,
Must make perforce a universal prey,
And last eat up himself. Great Agamemnon,
This chaos, when degree is suffocate,   125
Follows the choking.
And this neglection of degree it is
That by a pace goes backward, with a purpose
It hath to climb.° The general's disdained

---

46. **show:** i.e., outward show.   48. **breese:** gadfly.   55. **nerve:** sinew.   58. **shut up:** confined.   64. **hold . . . brass:** set up aloft inscribed in brass for all to read.   65. **hatched in silver:** lit., inlaid with silver, streaked with white.   70–74. **Speak . . . oracle:** This obscure speech may be paraphrased: "Speak, Prince of Ithaca, for we know that we shall hear nothing worthless from you, as we know that when Thersites opens his bitter mouth we shall hear neither harmony nor sense." **mastic:** lit., scourging, satirical; a word coined by Shakespeare from *mastix* (a scourge). The word had been much in use after Dekker's play *Satiromastix; or, The Whipping of the Satirist*, 1601. See Gen. Intro. pp. 45a–46a.   77. **instances:** reasons.   78. **specialty of rule:** special authority of the commander; i.e., discipline.   83. **Degree:** rank. **being vizarded:** wearing a mask, obscured.

84. **mask:** entertainment at which all the partakers are masked.   85. **center:** earth. See App. 1.   87. **Insisture:** regularity.   91. **other:** others.   93. **posts:** rides fast. See App. 17.   94. **Sans:** without.   99. **deracinate:** root out.   101. **fixure:** fixed place.   104. **Degrees in schools:** i.e., the three degrees in universities: Bachelor, Master, Doctor.   105. **dividable:** divided.   106. **primogenitive:** right of the firstborn.   107. **Prerogative:** privilege.   111. **mere oppugnancy:** utter conflict. **bounded:** confined.   114. **Strength . . . imbecility:** i.e., the strong young man should control his feeble father.   117. **jar:** conflict.   122. **seconded with:** supported by.   127–29. **And . . . climb:** this neglect of degree makes us go back when we seek to climb.

By him one step below, he by the next, 130
That next by him beneath. So every step,
Exampled by the first pace that is sick
Of his superior, grows to an envious fever
Of pale and bloodless emulation.°
And 'tis this fever that keeps Troy on foot, 135
Not her own sinews. To end a tale of length,
Troy in our weakness stands, not in her strength.

NEST. Most wisely hath Ulysses here discovered°
The fever whereof all our power is sick. 139

AGAM. The nature of the sickness found, Ulysses,
What is the remedy?

ULYSS. The great Achilles, whom opinion crowns
The sinew and the forehand of our host,
Having his ear full of his airy fame,
Grows dainty of his worth, and in his tent 145
Lies mocking our designs. With him, Patroclus,
Upon a lazy bed, the livelong day
Breaks scurril° jests,
And with ridiculous and awkward action,
Which, slanderer, he imitation calls, 150
He pageants° us. Sometime, great Agamemnon,
Thy topless deputation° he puts on,
And like a strutting player whose conceit°
Lies in his hamstring,° and doth think it rich
To hear the wooden dialogue and sound 155
'Twixt his stretched footing° and the scaffoldage,°
Such to-be-pitied and o'erwrested° seeming
He acts thy greatness in. And when he speaks,
'Tis like a chime a-mending,° with terms un-
  squared,°
Which, from the tongue of roaring Typhon°
  dropped, 160
Would seem hyperboles. At this fusty stuff,
The large Achilles, on his pressed bed lolling,
From his deep chest laughs out a loud applause,
Cries "Excellent! 'Tis Agamemnon just.° 164
Now play me Nestor, hem, and stroke thy beard,
As he being dressed° to some oration."
That's done, as near as the extremest ends
Of parallels, as like as Vulcan and his wife.°
Yet god Achilles still cries "Excellent!
'Tis Nestor right. Now play him me, Patroclus, 170
Arming to answer in a night alarm."
And then, forsooth, the faint defects of age
Must be the scene of mirth, to cough and spit

And, with a palsy fumbling on his gorget,°
Shake in and out the rivet. And at this sport 175
Sir Valor dies, cries "Oh, enough, Patroclus,
Or give me ribs of steel! I shall split all
In pleasure of my spleen."° And in this fashion
All our abilities, gifts, natures, shapes,
Severals° and generals of grace exact, 180
Achievements, plots, orders, preventions,
Excitements to the field or speech for truce,
Success or loss, what is or is not, serves
As stuff for these two to make paradoxes.°

NEST. And in the imitation of these twain, 185
Who, as Ulysses says, opinion crowns
With an imperial voice,° many are infect.
Ajax is grown self-willed, and bears his head
In such a rein, in full as proud a place
As broad Achilles; keeps his tent like him; 190
Makes factious feasts; rails on our state of war
Bold as an oracle; and sets Thersites,
A slave whose gall coins slanders like a mint,
To match us in comparisons with dirt,
To weaken and discredit our exposure, 195
How rank soever rounded in with danger.°

ULYSS. They tax° our policy and call it cowardice,
Count wisdom as no member of the war,
Forestall prescience,° and esteem no act
But that of hand. The still and mental parts 200
That do contrive how many hands shall strike
When fitness calls them on, and know by measure
Of their observant toil the enemies' weight —
Why, this hath not a finger's dignity. 204
They call this bed work,° mappery,° closet war.
So that the ram° that batters down the wall,
For the great swing and rudeness of his poise,
They place before his hand that made the engine,
Or those that with the fineness of their souls
By reason guide his execution. 210

NEST. Let this be granted, and Achilles' horse
Makes many Thetis' sons.° [*Tucket.*°]

AGAM. What trumpet? Look, Menelaus.

MEN. From Troy.

[*Enter* AENEAS.]

AGAM. What would you 'fore our tent? 215

AENE. Is this great Agamemnon's tent, I pray you?

AGAM. Even this.

AENE. May one that is a herald and a prince
Do a fair message to his kingly ears? 219

AGAM. With surety stronger than Achilles' arm

133–34. grows . . . emulation: becomes a feverish jealousy which makes our bravery (*emulation*) pale and bloodless. 138. dis-covered: revealed. 148. scurril: scurrilous. 151. pageants: mimics. 152. topless deputation: supreme authority. 153. con-ceit: intelligence. 154. hamstring: ridiculous posing; lit., the tendon behind the knee. 156. stretched footing: exaggerated stalking. scaffoldage: stage. 157. o'erwrested: overstrained. See III.iii.23,n. 159. chime a-mending: peal of bells out of tune. unsquared: inappropriate. 160. Typhon: a roaring monster buried beneath Mount Etna. 164. just: exactly. 166. dressed: about to begin. 168. Vulcan . . . wife: Vulcan was the black-smith of the gods, unsuitably married to Venus.

174. gorget: armor for the throat. See Pl. 8a. 178. spleen: exces-sive laughter. 180. Severals: particular qualities. 184. para-doxes: absurdities. 186–87. opinion . . . voice: general opinion would wish to have commander. 195–96. exposure . . . danger: our exposure to danger however excessive. 197. tax: criticize. 199. Forestall prescience: condemn forethought. 205. bed work: armchair strategy. mappery: mere making of maps. 206. ram: battering-ram. 211–12. Achilles' . . . sons: Achilles' horse is worth many an Achilles (who was the son of Thetis). 212 s.d., Tucket: trumpet call.

'Fore all the Greekish heads, which with one voice
Call Agamemnon head and general.
   AENE. Fair leave and large security. How may
A stranger to those most imperial looks
Know them from eyes of other mortals?   225
   AGAM.   How!
   AENE. Aye.
I ask that I might waken reverence,
And bid the cheek be ready with a blush
Modest as morning when she coldly eyes
The youthful Phoebus.°   230
Which is that god in office, guiding men?
Which is the high and mighty Agamemnon?
   AGAM. This Trojan scorns us, or the men of Troy
Are ceremonious courtiers.   234
   AENE. Courtiers as free, as debonair, unarmed,
As bending° angels, that's their fame in peace.
But when they would seem soldiers, they have
     galls,°
Good arms, strong joints, true swords, and, Jove's
     accord,°
Nothing so full of heart. But peace, Aeneas,
Peace, Trojan, lay thy finger on thy lips!   240
The worthiness of praise distains° his worth
If that the praised himself bring the praise forth.
But what the repining enemy commends,
That breath fame blows, that praise, sole pure,
     transcends.   244
   AGAM. Sir, you of Troy, call you yourself Aeneas?
   AENE. Aye, Greek, that is my name.
   AGAM. What's your affair, I pray you?
   AENE. Sir, pardon, 'tis for Agamemnon's ears.
   AGAM. He hears naught privately that comes from
     Troy.   249
   AENE. Nor I from Troy come not to whisper him.
I bring a trumpet to awake his ear,
To set his sense on the attentive bent,°
And then to speak.
   AGAM.   Speak frankly as the wind.
It is not Agamemnon's sleeping hour.
That thou shalt know, Trojan, he is awake,   255
He tells thee so himself.
   AENE.   Trumpet, blow loud,
Send thy brass voice through all these lazy tents,
And every Greek of mettle, let him know
What Troy means fairly shall be spoke aloud.
                       [*Trumpet sounds.*]
We have, great Agamemnon, here in Troy   260
A prince called Hector — Priam is his father —
Who in this dull and long-continued truce
Is rusty grown. He bade me take a trumpet,
And to this purpose speak: Kings, Princes, lords!
If there be one among the fair'st of Greece   265
That holds his honor higher than his ease,

That seeks his praise more than he fears his peril,
That knows his valor and knows not his fear,
That loves his mistress more than in confession
With truant° vows to her own lips he loves,   270
And dare avow° her beauty and her worth
In other arms than hers — to him this challenge.
Hector, in view of Trojans and of Greeks,
Shall make it good, or do his best to do it,
He hath a lady, wiser, fairer, truer,   275
Than ever Greek did compass in his arms,
And will tomorrow with his trumpet call
Midway between your tents and walls of Troy,
To rouse a Grecian that is true in love.
If any come, Hector shall honor him.   280
If none, he'll say in Troy, when he retires,
The Grecian dames are sunburnt° and not worth
The splinter of a lance. Even so much.
   AGAM. This shall be told our lovers, Lord Aeneas.
If none of them have soul in such a kind,   285
We left them all at home. But we are soldiers,
And may that soldier a mere recreant° prove
That means not, hath not, or is not in love!
If then one is, or hath, or means to be,
That one meets Hector. If none else, I am he.   290
   NEST. Tell him of Nestor, one that was a man
When Hector's grandsire sucked. He is old now,
But if there be not in our Grecian host
One noble man that hath one spark of fire,
To answer for his love, tell him from me   295
I'll hide my silver beard in a gold beaver,°
And in my vantbrace° put this withered brawn,
And meeting him will tell him that my lady
Was fairer than his grandam, and as chaste
As may be in the world. His youth in flood,°   300
I'll prove this truth with my three drops of blood.
   AENE. Now Heavens forbid such scarcity of youth!
   ULYSS. Amen.
   AGAM. Fair Lord Aeneas, let me touch your hand.
To our pavilion shall I lead you, sir.   305
Achilles shall have word of this intent,
So shall each lord of Greece, from tent to tent.
Yourself shall feast with us before you go,
And find the welcome of a noble foe.
            [*Exeunt all but* ULYSSES *and* NESTOR.]
   ULYSS. Nestor!   310
   NEST. What says Ulysses?
   ULYSS. I have a young conception° in my brain.
Be you my time to bring it to some shape.
   NEST. What is 't?
   ULYSS. This 'tis: 315
Blunt wedges rive hard knots. The seeded pride
That hath to this maturity blown up

---

230. **Phoebus:** the sun.   236. **bending:** adoring.   237. **galls:**
bitterness.   238. **Jove's accord:** Jove is with them.   241. **distains:** sullies.   252. **attentive bent:** lit., stretched taut to hear.

270. **truant:** runaway.   271. **avow:** declare.   282. **sunburnt:**
i.e., mere country wenches.   287. **recreant:** traitor.   296. **beaver:**
face piece of the helmet. See Pl. 8a.   297. **vantbrace:** armor
for the forearm.   300. **His . . . flood:** though his manhood be
in its prime.   312. **young conception:** fresh idea.

In rank° Achilles must or° now be cropped,
Or, shedding,° breed a nursery of like evil,
To overbulk° us all.
    NEST.   Well, and how?   320
    ULYSS. This challenge that the gallant Hector
sends,
However it is spread in general name,
Relates in purpose only to Achilles.
    NEST. The purpose is perspicuous even as sub-
stance,
Whose grossness little characters sum up.°   325
And, in the publication, make no strain,
But that Achilles, were his brain as barren
As banks of Libya° — though Apollo knows,
'Tis dry enough — will, with great speed of judg-
ment —
Aye, with celerity — find Hector's purpose   330
Pointing on him.
    ULYSS. And wake him to the answer, think you?
    NEST. Yes, 'tis most meet. Who may you else
oppose
That can from Hector bring his honor off,°
If not Achilles? Though 't be a sportful combat,
Yet in this trial much opinion° dwells,   336
For here the Trojans taste our dear'st repute
With their finest palate. And trust to me, Ulysses,
Our imputation° shall be oddly poised°
In this wild action. For the success,   340
Although particular, shall give a scantling°
Of good or bad unto the general,°
And in such indexes, although small pricks°
To their subséquent volumes, there is seen
The baby figure of the giant mass   345
Of things to come at large. It is supposed
He that meets Hector issues from our choice.
And choice, being mutual act of all our souls,
Makes merit her election,° and doth boil
As 'twere from forth us all, a man distilled   350
Out of our virtues. Who miscarrying,
What heart from hence receives the conquering part,
To steel a strong opinion to themselves?°
Which entertained, limbs are his instruments,
In no less working than are swords and bows   355
Directive by the limbs.
    ULYSS. Give pardon to my speech.
Therefore 'tis meet Achilles meet not Hector.
Let us, like merchants, show our foulest wares,
And think perchance they'll sell. If not,   360

The luster of the better yet to show
Shall show the better. Do not consent
That ever Hector and Achilles meet,
For both our honor and our shame in this
Are dogged with two strange followers.   365
    NEST. I see them not with my old eyes. What are
they?
    ULYSS. What glory our Achilles shares from Hec-
tor,
Were he not proud, we all should share with him.
But he already is too insolent,
And we were better parch in Afric sun   370
Than in the pride and salt° scorn of his eyes,
Should he 'scape Hector fair. If he were foiled,°
Why then we did our main opinion crush
In taint of our best man.° No, make a lottery,
And by device° let blockish° Ajax draw   375
The sort° to fight with Hector. Among ourselves
Give him allowance for the better man;
For that will physic° the great Myrmidon°
Who broils in loud applause, and make him fall°
His crest that prouder than blue Iris° bends.   380
If the dull brainless Ajax comes safe off,
We'll dress him up in voices.° If he fail,
Yet go we under our opinion still
That we have better men. But, hit or miss,
Our project's life this shape of sense assumes,   385
Ajax employed plucks down Achilles' plumes.
    NEST. Ulysses,
Now I begin to relish thy advice,
And I will give a taste of it forthwith
To Agamemnon. Go we to him straight.   390
Two curs shall tame each other. Pride alone
Must tarre° the mastiffs on, as 'twere their bone.
                           [Exeunt.]

Act II

SCENE I. *The Grecian camp.*

[Enter AJAX *and* THERSITES.]
    AJAX. Thersites!
    THER. Agamemnon — how if he had boils — full,
all over, generally?
    AJAX. Thersites!
    THER. And those boils did run? — Say so — did
not the General run then? Were not that a botchy
core?°   7

---

318. **rank:** lit., overfull of blood, proud. **or:** either. 319. **shedding:**
i.e., its seeds. 320. **overbulk:** overwhelm. 325. **grossness
. . . up:** size is made up of little figures. 328. **Libya:** the
African desert. 334. **bring . . . off:** win honor. 336. **opinion:**
reputation. 339. **imputation:** good fame. **oddly poised:** unevenly
balanced. 341. **scantling:** sample. 342. **general:** army as a
whole. 343. **small pricks:** mere dots. 349. **Makes . . . election:** chooses the best man. 351–53. **Who . . . themselves:** if he
fails, what an encouragement the winning side will gain to
strengthen (*steel*) their self-confidence (*opinion*).

371. **salt:** bitter. 372. **foiled:** defeated. 373–74. **did . . . man:**
lost our reputation (*opinion*) in the failure of our best man.
375. **device:** a trick. **blockish:** blockheaded. 376. **sort:** lot.
378. **physic:** give a dose to. **Myrmidon:** i.e., Achilles, who
was commander of the Myrmidons. 379. **fall:** lower. 380. **Iris:**
the rainbow. 382. **dress . . . voices:** congratulate him loudly.
392. **tarre:** urge on to fight.
    Act II, Sc. i: 6–7. **botchy core:** boil full of matter.

AJAX. Dog!

THER. Then would come some matter from him. I see none now.

AJAX. Thou bitch wolf's son, canst thou not hear? Feel, then.   [*Strikes him.*]

THER. The plague of Greece upon thee, thou mongrel beef-witted° lord!   14

AJAX. Speak then, thou vinewed'st° leaven, speak. I will beat thee into handsomeness.

THER. I shall sooner rail thee into wit and holiness. But I think thy horse will sooner con° an oration than thou learn a prayer without book. Thou canst strike, canst thou? A red murrain° o' thy jade's° tricks!   21

AJAX. Toadstool, learn° me the proclamation.

THER. Dost thou think I have no sense,° thou strikest me thus?

AJAX. The proclamation!   25

THER. Thou art proclaimed a fool, I think.

AJAX. Do not, porpentine,° do not. My fingers itch.

THER. I would thou didst itch from head to foot, and I had the scratching of thee. I would make thee the loathsomest scab in Greece. When thou art forth in the incursions,° thou strikest as slow as another.

AJAX. I say, the proclamation!   34

THER. Thou grumblest and railest every hour on Achilles, and thou art as full of envy at his greatness as Cerberus° is at Proserpina's° beauty — aye, that thou barkest at him.

AJAX. Mistress Thersites!

THER. Thou shouldst strike him.   40

AJAX. Cobloaf!°

THER. He would pun° thee into shivers with his fist, as a sailor breaks a biscuit.

AJAX. [*Beating him*] You whoreson° cur!

THER. Do, do.   45

AJAX. Thou stool° for a witch!

THER. Aye, do, do, thou sodden-witted lord! Thou hast no more brain than I have in mine elbows, an assinego° may tutor thee. Thou scurvy-valiant ass! Thou art here but to thrash Trojans, and thou art bought and sold among those of any wit, like a barbarian slave. If thou use to beat me, I will begin at thy heel and tell what thou art by inches, thou thing of no bowels° thou!

AJAX. You dog!   55

THER. You scurvy lord!

AJAX. [*Beating him*] You cur!

THER. Mars his idiot!° Do, rudeness, do, camel, do, do.

[*Enter* ACHILLES *and* PATROCLUS.]

ACHIL. Why, how now, Ajax! Wherefore do ye thus? How now, Thersites! What's the matter, man?

THER. You see him there, do you?

ACHIL. Aye. What's the matter?

THER. Nay, look upon him.   65

ACHIL. So I do. What's the matter?

THER. Nay, but regard him well.

ACHIL. Well! Why, so I do.

THER. But yet you look not well upon him, for whosoever you take him to be, he is Ajax.

ACHIL. I know that, fool.

THER. Aye, but that fool knows not himself.

AJAX. Therefore I beat thee.   73

THER. Lo, lo, lo, lo, what modicums of wit he utters! His evasions have ears thus long.° I have bobbed° his brain more than he has beat my bones. I will buy nine sparrows for a penny, and his pia mater° is not worth the ninth part of a sparrow. This lord, Achilles — Ajax, who wears his wit in his belly and his guts in his head — I'll tell you what I say of him.   81

ACHIL. What?

THER. I say, this Ajax ——

[AJAX *offers to strike him.*]

ACHIL. Nay, good Ajax.

THER. Has not so much wit ——   85

ACHIL. Nay, I must hold you.

THER. As will stop the eye of Helen's needle, for whom he comes to fight.

ACHIL. Peace, fool!

THER. I would have peace and quietness, but the fool will not. He there, that he. Look you there!

AJAX. O thou damned cur! I shall ——

ACHIL. Will you set your wit to a fool's?   94

THER. No, I warrant you, for a fool's will shame it.

PATR. Good words, Thersites.

ACHIL. What's the quarrel?

AJAX. I bade the vile owl go learn me the tenor of the proclamation, and he rails upon me.

THER. I serve thee not.

AJAX. Well, go to, go to.

THER. I serve here voluntary.°   104

ACHIL. Your last service was sufferance, 'twas not voluntary, no man is beaten voluntary. Ajax was here the voluntary, and you as under an impress.°

THER. E'en so, a great deal of your wit too 108
lies in your sinews, or else there be liars. Hector shall have a great catch if he knock out either of your

---

14. **beef-witted:** too much meat was believed to be bad for the wits. See *T Night,* I.iii.88.   15. **vinewed'st:** moldy, emendation for Q1 "unsalted" and F1 "whinid'st."   18. **con:** learn by heart.   20. **murrain:** plague. **jade:** bad-tempered horse.   22. **learn:** tell.   23. **sense:** feeling.   27. **porpentine:** porcupine.   33. **incursions:** raids.   37. **Cerberus:** the three-headed dog guarding the mouth of Hades. **Proserpina.** Queen of the underworld.   41. **Cobloaf:** little loaf with a round head.   42. **pun:** pound.   44. **whoreson:** bastard.   46. **stool:** closestool, privy.   49. **assinego:** little ass.   54. **bowels:** mercy.

58. **Mars . . . idiot:** the fool of the god of war.   75. **evasions . . . long:** i.e., his utterances are as long as an ass's ears.   76. **bobbed:** struck.   77–78. **pia mater:** brain.   104. **voluntary:** as a volunteer.   107. **as . . . impress:** forced to serve.

brains. A' were as good crack a fusty nut with no
kernel.   112

ACHIL. What, with me too, Thersites?

THER. There's Ulysses and old Nestor, whose wit
was moldy ere your grandsires had nails on their
toes, yoke you° like draught oxen, and make you
plow up the wars.   117

ACHIL. What? What?

THER. Yes, good sooth. To, Achilles! To, Ajax!
To!

AJAX. I shall cut out your tongue.   121

THER. 'Tis no matter, I shall speak as much as
thou afterward.

PATR. No more words, Thersites, peace!   125

THER. I will hold my peace when Achilles'
brooch° bids me, shall I?

ACHIL. There's for you, Patroclus.

THER. I will see you hanged, like clotpoles,° ere I
come any more to your tents. I will keep where there
is wit stirring, and leave the faction of fools.   131
[Exit.]

PATR. A good riddance.

ACHIL. Marry, this, sir, is proclaimed through all
our host:
That Hector, by the fifth hour of the sun,
Will with a trumpet 'twixt our tents and Troy   135
Tomorrow morning call some knight to arms
That hath a stomach,° and such a one that dare
Maintain — I know not what. 'Tis trash. Farewell.
AJAX. Farewell. Who shall answer him?
ACHIL. I know not. 'Tis put to lottery, otherwise
He knew his man.   141
AJAX. Oh, meaning you. I will go learn more of
it.   [Exeunt.]

SCENE II. Troy. A room in PRIAM's palace.

[Enter PRIAM, HECTOR, TROILUS, PARIS,
and HELENUS.]

PRI. After so many hours, lives, speeches spent,
Thus once again says Nestor from the Greeks:
"Deliver Helen, and all damage else,
As honor, loss of time, travail, expense,
Wounds, friends, and what else dear that is con-
sumed   5
In hot digestion of this cormorant° war,
Shall be struck off." Hector, what say you to 't?
HECT. Though no man lesser fears the Greeks
than I
As far as toucheth my particular,

Yet, dread Priam,   10
There is no lady of more softer bowels,
More spongy to suck in the sense of fear,
More ready to cry out "Who knows what follows?"
Than Hector is. The wound° of peace is surety,
Surety secure. But modest doubt is called   15
The beacon of the wise, the tent that searches
To the bottom of the worst. Let Helen go.
Since the first sword was drawn about this question
Every tithe soul, 'mongst many thousand dismes,°
Hath been as dear as Helen — I mean, of ours.   20
If we have lost so many tenths of ours
To guard a thing not ours, nor worth to us,
Had it our name, the value of one ten,
What merit's in that reason which denies
The yielding of her up?
TRO.   Fie, fie, my brother!   25
Weigh you the worth and honor of a king
So great as our dread father in a scale
Of common ounces? Will you with counters° sum°
The past proportion of his infinite?
And buckle in a waist most fathomless   30
With spans° and inches so diminutive
As fears and reasons? Fie, for godly shame!
HEL. No marvel, though you bite so sharp at rea-
sons,
You are so empty of them. Should not our father
Bear the great sway of his affairs with reasons,   35
Because your speech hath none that tells him so?
TRO. You are for dreams and slumbers, brother
priest.
You fur your gloves with reason.° Here are your
reasons:
You know an enemy intends you harm,
You know a sword employed is perilous,   40
And reason flies the object of all harm.
Who marvels, then, when Helenus beholds
A Grecian and his sword, if he do set
The very wings of reason to his heels,
And fly like chidden Mercury from Jove,   45
Or like a star disorbed?° Nay, if we talk of reason,
Let's shut our gates, and sleep. Manhood and honor
Should have hare hearts, would they but fat their
thoughts
With this crammed reason. Reason and respect°
Make livers° pale and lustihood deject.   50

---

116. yoke you: i.e., treat you two like beasts of burden.
127. brooch: an ornament that he hangs about him; i.e., Patroclus.   129. clotpoles: blockheads.   137. stomach: i.e., for
a fight.

Sc. ii: 6. cormorant: devouring. The cormorant is a rapacious
sea bird.

14–17. wound . . . worst: peace is wounded by self-confidence
(surety), careless (secure) self-confidence; but a modest doubt of
success is like a guiding light (beacon) to the wise, or a probe (tent)
which cleans the wound to the bottom. tent: lit., a piece of lint
used to probe and clean out a wound.   19. tithe . . . dismes:
both mean tenth; i.e., since Helen came one man in ten of many
ten thousands.   28. counters: used in calculating large sums.
sum: reckon.   31. spans: little calculations; lit., the distance between thumb and little finger in the outstretched hand; i.e., 9
inches.   38. fur . . . reason: line your gloves with reasons; i.e.,
cowardly arguments.   46. disorbed: shot out of its course.
See App. 1.   49. respect: counting the consequences.   50. livers:
The liver was regarded as the seat of courage.

HECT. Brother, she is not worth what she doth
    cost
The holding.
    TRO.   What's aught but as 'tis valued?
    HECT. But value dwells not in particular will.°
It holds his estimate and dignity
As well wherein 'tis precious of itself   55
As in the prizer. 'Tis mad idolatry
To make the service greater than the god.
And the will dotes that is attributive
To what infectiously itself affects,
Without some image of the affected merit.°   60
    TRO. I take° today a wife, and my election°
Is led on in the conduct of my will,°
My will enkindled by mine eyes and ears,
Two traded° pilots 'twixt the dangerous shores
Of will and judgment. How may I avoid,   65
Although my will distaste what it elected,
The wife I chose? There can be no evasion
To blench° from this, and to stand firm by honor.
We turn not back the silks upon the merchant
When we have soiled them, nor the remainder
    viands   70
We do not throw in unrespective sieve°
Because we now are full. It was thought meet
Paris should do some vengeance on the Greeks.
Your breath of full consent bellied° his sails.
The seas and winds, old wranglers, took a truce, 75
And did him service. He touched the ports de-
    sired,
And for an old aunt whom the Greeks held captive
He brought a Grecian Queen, whose youth and
    freshness
Wrinkles Apollo's° and makes stale the morning.
Why keep we her? The Grecians keep our aunt. 80
Is she worth keeping? Why, she is a pearl,
Whose price hath launched above a thousand ships,°
And turned crowned kings to merchants.
If you'll avouch 'twas wisdom Paris went —   84
As you must needs, for you all cried " Go, go " —
If you'll confess he brought home noble prize —
As you must needs, for you all clapped your hands
And cried " Inestimable! " — why do you now
The issue° of your proper° wisdoms rate,°
And do a deed that Fortune never did,°   90
Beggar the estimation° which you prized

Richer than sea and land? Oh, theft most base,
That we have stol'n what we do fear to keep!
But thieves unworthy of a thing so stol'n,
That in their country did them that disgrace,   95
We fear to warrant in our native place!°
    CAS. [*Within*] Cry, Trojans, cry!
    PRI.   What noise? What shriek is this?
    TRO. 'Tis our mad sister, I do know her voice.
    CAS. [*Within*] Cry, Trojans!   100
    HECT. It is Cassandra.
[*Enter* CASSANDRA, *raving, with her hair about her
    ears.*]
    CAS. Cry, Trojans, cry! Lend me ten thousand
    eyes,
And I will fill them with prophetic tears.
    HECT. Peace, sister, peace!
    CAS. Virgins and boys, mid-age and wrinkled
    eld,°
Soft infancy, that nothing canst but cry,   105
Add to my clamors! Let us pay betimes
A moiety° of that mass of moan to come.
Cry, Trojans, cry! Practice your eyes with tears!
Troy must not be, nor goodly Ilion° stand,
Our firebrand brother, Paris, burns us all.   110
Cry, Trojans, cry! A Helen and a woe.
Cry, cry! Troy burns, or else let Helen go. [*Exit.*]
    HECT. Now, youthful Troilus, do not these high
    strains
Of divination in our sister work
Some touches of remorse?° Or is your blood   115
So madly hot that no discourse of reason,
Nor fear of bad success in a bad cause,
Can qualify° the same?
    TRO.   Why, Brother Hector,
We may not think the justness of each act
Such and no other than event° doth form it,   120
Nor once deject the courage of our minds,
Because Cassandra's mad. Her brainsick raptures
Cannot distaste° the goodness of a quarrel
Which hath our several honors all engaged   125
To make it gracious. For my private part,
I am no more touched than all Priam's sons.
And Jove forbid there should be done amongst us
Such things as might offend the weakest spleen°
To fight for and maintain!
    PAR. Else might the world convince° of levity
As well my undertakings as your counsels.   131
But I attest° the gods your full consent

---

53. particular will: individual desire.   58–60. And . . . merit: desire is mad when it inclines to what will cause it harm without even the show of any advantage.   61. I take: suppose that I choose. election: choice.   62. will: desire, lust.   64. traded: experienced.   68. blench: start aside, refuse.   71. unrespective sieve: senseless garbage can.   74. bellied: blew out.   79. Wrinkles Apollo's: i.e., makes the god Apollo look wrinkled.   82. Whose . . . ships: a deliberate echo of Faustus' famous address to Helen in Marlowe's *Dr. Faustus:* "Was this the face that launched a thousand ships?"   89. issue: result. proper: own. rate: estimate the value of.   90. And . . . did: i.e., show yourselves more fickle even than Fortune.   91. Beggar . . . estimation: make worthless the thing of value.

92–96. Oh . . . place: we are like thieves who have stolen something too good for us, which disgraces us in our own country; we are afraid to admit the worth of (*fear to warrant*) Helen in Troy; i.e., you were all enthusiastic when Paris brought Helen back to Troy, but now you basely pretend that she is not worth keeping.   104. eld: old age.   107. moiety: part. 109. Ilion: Ilium, the citadel of Troy.   115. remorse: pity. 118. qualify: moderate.   120. event: consequences.   124. distaste: give a bad taste to.   129. spleen: temper.   130. convince: convict.   132. attest: call to witness.

Gave wings to my propension,° and cut off
All fears attending on so dire a project.
For what, alas, can these my single arms?   135
What propugnation° is in one man's valor,
To stand the push and enmity of those
This quarrel would excite? Yet I protest
Were I alone to pass the difficulties,
And had as ample power as I have will,   140
Paris should ne'er retract what he hath done,
Nor faint in the pursuit.
    PRI.   Paris, you speak
Like one besotted on your sweet delights.
You have the honey still, but these the gall,
So to be valiant is no praise at all.   145
    PAR. Sir, I propose not merely to myself
The pleasures such a beauty brings with it,
But I would have the soil of her fair rape
Wiped off in honorable keeping her.
What treason were it to the ransacked Queen,   150
Disgrace to your great worths, and shame to me,
Now to deliver her possession up
On terms of base compulsion! Can it be
That so degenerate a strain as this
Should once set footing in your generous° bosoms?
There's not the meanest spirit on our party   156
Without a heart to dare, or sword to draw,
When Helen is defended, nor none so noble
Whose life were ill bestowed, or death unfamed,
Where Helen is the subject. Then, I say,   160
Well may we fight for her, whom, we know well,
The world's large spaces cannot parallel.
    HECT. Paris and Troilus, you have both said well,
And on the cause and question now in hand
Have glozed,° but superficially, not much   165
Unlike young men, whom Aristotle° thought
Unfit to hear moral philosophy.
The reasons you allege do more conduce
To the hot passion of distempered° blood
Than to make up a free determination   170
'Twixt right and wrong; for pleasure and revenge
Have ears more deaf than adders to the voice
Of any true decision. Nature craves
All dues be rendered to their owners. Now,
What nearer debt in all humanity   175
Than wife is to the husband? If this law
Of nature be corrupted through affection,°
And that great minds, of partial indulgence
To their benumbèd wills, resist the same,
There is a law in each well-ordered nation   180
To curb those raging appetites that are
Most disobedient and refractory.
If Helen then be wife to Sparta's King,

As it is known she is, these moral laws
Of nature and of nations speak aloud   185
To have her back returned. Thus to persist
In doing wrong extenuates not wrong,
But makes it much more heavy. Hector's opinion
Is this in way of truth. Yet ne'ertheless,
My spritely brethren, I propend° to you   190
In resolution to keep Helen still,
For 'tis a cause that hath no mean dependence
Upon° our joint and several dignities.
    TRO. Why, there you touched the life of our de-
     sign.
Were it not glory that we more affected   195
Than the performance of our heaving spleens,
I would not wish a drop of Trojan blood
Spent more in her defense. But, worthy Hector,
She is a theme of honor and renown,
A spur to valiant and magnanimous deeds   200
Whose present courage may beat down our foes,
And fame in time to come canónize° us.
For I presume brave Hector would not lose
So rich advantage of a promised glory
As smiles upon the forehead of this action   205
For the wide world's revenue.
    HECT.   I am yours,
You valiant offspring of great Priamus.
I have a roisting° challenge sent amongst
The dull and factious nobles of the Greeks
Will strike amazement to their drowsy spirits.   210
I was advértised° their great General slept
Whilst emulation° in the army crept.
This, I presume, will wake him.   [*Exeunt.*]

SCENE III. *The Grecian camp. Before the tent
    of* ACHILLES.

[*Enter* THERSITES, *solus.*]
    THER. How now, Thersites! What, lost in the
labyrinth of thy fury! Shall the elephant Ajax carry
it thus? He beats me, and I rail at him, oh, worthy
satisfaction! Would it were otherwise — that I could
beat him whilst he railed at me. 'Sfoot,° I'll learn   5
to conjure and raise devils, but I'll see some issue
of my spiteful execrations. Then there's Achilles, a
rare enginer.° If Troy be not taken till these two
undermine it, the walls will stand till they fall   10
of themselves. O thou great thunder-darter of Olympus, forget that thou art Jove, the King of gods, and,
Mercury, lose all the serpentine craft of thy cadu-
ceus° if ye take not that little little less than little wit

---

133. propension: inclination.   136. propugnation: defense.
155. generous: noble.   165. glozed: commented.   166. Aristotle:
the Greek philosopher who died 322 B.C., — about ten centuries after the siege of Troy.   169. distempered: drunken.
177. affection: lust.

190. propend: incline.   192–93. hath . . . Upon: does not lightly
concern.   202. canonize: set us in the calendar of the heroes.
208. roisting: blustering.   211. advertised: informed.   212. emulation: jealous rivalry.
    Sc. iii: 5. 'Sfoot: by God's foot.   9. enginer: engineer.
14. caduceus: Mercury's snake-entwined wand.

from them that they have! Which short-armed 15
ignorance itself knows is so abundant scarce it will
not in circumvention° deliver a fly from a spider
without drawing their massy irons and cutting the
web. After this, the vengeance on the whole 20
camp! Or rather the Neapolitan boneache,° for that
methinks is the curse dependent on those that war
for a placket.° I have said my prayers, and devil
Envy say amen. What ho! My Lord Achilles!

[*Enter* PATROCLUS.]

PATR. Who's there? Thersites! Good Thersites,
come in and rail.   26

THER. If I could ha' remembered a gilt counterfeit,° thou wouldst not have slipped out of my contemplation. But it is no matter, thyself upon thyself! The common curse of mankind, folly and 30
ignorance, be thine in great revenue! Heaven bless
thee° from a tutor, and discipline come not near
thee! Let thy blood be thy direction° till thy death!
Then if she that lays thee out says thou art a fair
corse, I'll be sworn and sworn upon 't she never 35
shrouded any but lazars.° Amen. Where's Achilles?

PATR. What, art thou devout? Wast thou in
prayer?

THER. Aye, the Heavens hear me!

PATR. Amen.

[*Enter* ACHILLES.]

ACHIL. Who's there?

PATR. Thersites, my lord.

ACHIL. Where, where? Art thou come? Why, my
cheese, my digestion, why hast thou not served thyself in to my table so many meals? Come, what's
Agamemnon?   46

THER. Thy commander, Achilles. Then tell me,
Patroclus, what's Achilles?

PATR. Thy lord, Thersites. Then tell me, I pray
thee, what's thyself?   50

THER. Thy knower, Patroclus. Then tell me, Patroclus, what art thou?

PATR. Thou mayst tell that knowest.

ACHIL. Oh, tell, tell.

THER. I'll decline° the whole question. Aga- 55
memnon commands Achilles, Achilles is my lord, I
am Patroclus' knower, and Patroclus is a fool.

PATR. You rascal!

THER. Peace, fool! I have not done.   60

ACHIL. He is a privileged man. Proceed, Thersites.

THER. Agamemnon is a fool, Achilles is a fool,
Thersites is a fool, and, as aforesaid, Patroclus is a
fool.   65

ACHIL. Derive this, come.

THER. Agamemnon is a fool to offer to command

Achilles, Achilles is a fool to be commanded of Agamemnon, Thersites is a fool to serve such a fool, and
Patroclus is a fool positive.   70

PATR. Why am I a fool?

THER. Make that demand of the prover. It suffices
me thou art. Look you, who comes here?

ACHIL. Patroclus, I'll speak with nobody. 74
Come in with me, Thersites.   [*Exit.*]

THER. Here is such patchery,° such juggling, and
such knavery! All the argument is a cuckold and a
whore, a good quarrel to draw emulous° factions
and bleed to death upon. Now, the dry serpigo° on
the subject!° And war and lechery confound all! 82
                                              [*Exit.*]

[*Enter* AGAMEMNON, ULYSSES, NESTOR, DIOMEDES, *and*
AJAX.]

AGAM. Where is Achilles?

PATR. Within his tent, but ill-disposed, my lord.

AGAM. Let it be known to him that we are here.
He shent° our messengers, and we lay by
Our appertainments,° visiting of him.   87
Let him be told so, lest perchance he think
We dare not move° the question of our place,°
Or know not what we are.

PATR.   I shall say so to him. [*Exit.*]

ULYSS. We saw him at the opening of his tent.
He is not sick.

AJAX. Yes, lion-sick, sick of proud heart. You may
call it melancholy, if you will favor the man, 95
but, by my head, 'tis pride. But why, why? Let him
show us the cause. A word, my lord.

                         [*Takes* AGAMEMNON *aside*]

NEST. What moves Ajax thus to bay° at him?

ULYSS. Achilles hath inveigled his fool from him.

NEST. Who, Thersites?   100

ULYSS. He.

NEST. Then will Ajax lack matter, if he have lost
his argument.°

ULYSS. No, you see he is his argument that 104
has his argument, Achilles.

NEST. All the better. Their fraction° is more our
wish than their faction. But it was a strong compo-
sure° a fool could disunite.

ULYSS. The amity that wisdom knits not, folly may
easily untie. [*Re-enter* PATROCLUS.] Here comes
Patroclus.   111

NEST. No Achilles with him.

ULYSS. The elephant hath joints, but none for
courtesy. His legs are legs for necessity, not for flexure.°   115

---

17. circumvention: cunning.   21. Neapolitan boneache: venereal disease.   23. placket: opening in a petticoat; i.e., wench.
27–28. gilt counterfeit: false money, counter; called also a slip.
31–32. bless thee: preserve you.   33. blood . . . direction: desires lead you.   36. lazars: lepers.   55. decline: go through.

76. patchery: pretense.   80. emulous: jealous.   81. dry serpigo: eruptions on the skin.   82. the subject: everyone.
86. shent: rebuked.   87. appertainments: privileges of rank.
89. We . . . move: we are afraid of asserting. place: i.e., as commander.   98. bay: bark.   103. argument: topic of conversation; i.e., Thersites.   106. fraction: division, quarrel.   108. composure: unity.   115. flexure: bending. It was once believed that
the elephant had no leg joints.

PATR. Achilles bids me say he is much sorry
If anything more than your sport and pleasure
Did move your greatness and this noble state
To call upon him. He hopes it is no other
But for your health and your digestion sake,   120
An after-dinner's breath.°
    AGAM.   Hear you, Patroclus.
We are too well acquainted with these answers.
But his evasion, winged thus swift with scorn,
Cannot outfly our apprehensions.°
Much attribute° he hath, and much the reason   125
Why we ascribe it to him. Yet all his virtues,
Not virtuously on his own part beheld,
Do in our eyes begin to lose their gloss —
Yea, like fair fruit in an unwholesome dish,
Are like to rot untasted. Go and tell him   130
We come to speak with him, and you shall not sin
If you do say we think him overproud
And underhonest; in self-assumption greater
Than in the note of judgment; and worthier than
    himself
Here tend° the savage strangeness he puts on,   135
Disguise the holy strength of their command,
And underwrite in an observing kind
His humorous predominance° — yea, watch
His pettish lunes,° his ebbs, his flows, as if
The passage and whole carriage of this action   140
Rode on his tide. Go tell him this, and add
That if he overhold his price so much,
We'll none of him, but let him, like an engine°
Not portable,° lie under this report:
"Bring action hither, this cannot go to war.   145
A stirring dwarf we do allowance give
Before a sleeping giant." Tell him so.
    PATR. I shall, and bring his answer presently.°
                                [*Exit.*]
    AGAM. In second voice we'll not be satisfied,   149
We come to speak with him. Ulysses, enter you.
                         [*Exit* ULYSSES.]
    AJAX. What is he more than another?
    AGAM. No more than what he thinks he is.
    AJAX. Is he so much? Do you not think he thinks
himself a better man than I am?
    AGAM. No question.   155
    AJAX. Will you subscribe° his thought and say he
is?
    AGAM. No, noble Ajax. You are as strong, as val-
iant, as wise, no less noble, much more gentle, and
altogether more tractable.   160
    AJAX. Why should a man be proud? How doth
pride grow? I know not what pride is.

AGAM. Your mind is the clearer, Ajax, and your
virtues the fairer. He that is proud eats up himself.
Pride is his own glass, his own trumpet, his own
chronicle, and whatever praises itself but in the deed
devours the deed in the praise.
    AJAX. I do hate a proud man as I hate the engen-
dering of toads.   170
    NEST. [*Aside*] Yet he loves himself. Is 't not
strange?
              [*Re-enter* ULYSSES.]
    ULYSS. Achilles will not to the field tomorrow.
    AGAM. What's his excuse?
    ULYSS.   He doth rely on none,
But carries on the stream of his dispose
Without observance or respect of any,   175
In will peculiar and in self-admission.°
    AGAM. Why will he not, upon our fair request,
Untent his person, and share the air with us?
    ULYSS. Things small as nothing, for request's sake
    only°
He makes important. Possessed he is with greatness,
And speaks not to himself but with a pride   181
That quarrels at self-breath. Imagined worth
Holds in his blood such swoln and hot discourse
That 'twixt his mental and his active parts
Kingdomed° Achilles in commotion rages   185
And batters down himself. What should I say?
He is so plaguy proud that the death tokens° of it
Cry "No recovery."
    AGAM.   Let Ajax go to him.
Dear lord, go you and greet him in his tent.
'Tis said he holds you well, and will be led   190
At your request a little from himself.
    ULYSS. O Agamemnon, let it not be so!
We'll consecrate the steps that Ajax makes
When they go from Achilles. Shall the proud lord
That bastes his arrogance with his own seam,°   195
And never suffers matter of the world
Enter his thoughts, save such as do revolve
And ruminate himself, shall he be worshiped
Of that we hold an idol more than he?°
No, this thrice worthy and right valiant lord   200
Must not so stale his palm,° nobly acquired,
Nor, by my will, assubjugate° his merit,
As amply titled as Achilles is,
By going to Achilles.
That were to enlard his fat-already pride,   205
And add more coals to Cancer when he burns
With entertaining great Hyperion.°
This lord go to him! Jupiter forbid,

---

121. breath: exercise.   124. outfly . . . apprehensions: outdis-
tance our understanding.   125. attribute: honor.   135. tend:
wait upon.   137–38. underwrite . . . predominance: submit to
but observe his moody superiority.   139. lunes: freaks.   143. engine: military machine, battering-ram.   144. Not portable: too
heavy to be moved.   148. presently: immediately.   156. subscribe: agree with.

176. self-admission: admitting only his own judgment.   179. for
. . . only: only because they are asked for.   185. Kingdomed:
like a kingdom.   187. death tokens: plague spots indicating that
the disease has taken a fatal turn.   195. seam: grease.   199. Of
. . . he: a man whom we regard as more worshipful than he.
201. stale . . . palm: make his glory cheap.   202. assubju-
gate: lower.   206–07. add . . . Hyperion: make summer hotter:
The sun (*Hyperion*) enters the sign of Cancer in June. See App. 2.

And say in thunder "Achilles go to him."

NEST. [*Aside*] Oh, this is well. He rubs the vein
   of him.°   210

DIO. [*Aside*] And how his silence drinks up this
   applause!

AJAX. If I go to him, with my armèd fist
I'll pash° him o'er the face.

AGAM. Oh, no, you shall not go.

AJAX. An a' be proud with me, I'll pheeze° his
   pride.   215
Let me go to him.

ULYSS. Not for the worth that hangs upon our
   quarrel.

AJAX. A paltry, insolent fellow!

NEST. [*Aside*] How he describes himself!

AJAX. Can he not be sociable?   220

ULYSS. [*Aside*] The raven chides blackness.

AJAX. I'll let his humors blood.°

AGAM. [*Aside*] He will be the physician that
should be the patient.

AJAX. An all men were o' my mind ——   225

ULYSS. [*Aside*] Wit would be out of fashion.

AJAX. A'° should not bear it so, a' should eat
swords first. Shall pride carry it?

NEST. [*Aside*] An 'twould, you 'd carry half.

ULYSS. [*Aside*] A' would have ten shares.   230

AJAX. I will knead him, I'll make him supple.

NEST. [*Aside*] He's not yet through° warm.
Force° him with praises. Pour in, pour in, his ambition is dry.

ULYSS. [*To* AGAMEMNON] My lord, you feed too
   much on this dislike.

NEST. Our noble General, do not do so.

DIO. You must prepare to fight without Achilles.

ULYSS. Why, 'tis this naming of him does him
   harm.
Here is a man — but 'tis before his face,   240
I will be silent.

NEST.   Wherefore should you so?
He is not emulous,° as Achilles is.

ULYSS. Know the whole world, he is as valiant.

AJAX. A whoreson dog, that shall palter thus with
us!
Would he were a Trojan!   245

NEST. What a vice were it in Ajax now ——

ULYSS. If he were proud ——

DIO. Or covetous of praise ——

ULYSS. Aye, or surly borne ——

DIO. Or strange,° or self-affected!°   250

ULYSS. Thank the Heavens, lord, thou art of sweet
   composure.
Praise him that got° thee, she that gave thee suck.

Famed be thy tutor, and thy parts of nature
Thrice-famed beyond, beyond all erudition.°
But he that disciplined thine arms to fight,   255
Let Mars divide eternity in twain
And give him half. And for thy vigor,
Bull-bearing Milo° his addition yield°
To sinewy Ajax. I will not praise thy wisdom,
Which, like a bourn,° a pale,° a shore, confines
Thy spacious and dilated° parts. Here's Nestor,
Instructed by the antiquary times,   262
He must, he is, he cannot but be wise.
But pardon, Father Nestor, were your days
As green° as Ajax', and your brain so tempered,
You should not have the eminence of him,   266
But be as Ajax.

AJAX.   Shall I call you father?

NEST. Aye, my good son.

DIO.   Be ruled by him, Lord Ajax.

ULYSS. There is no tarrying here. The hart
   Achilles
Keeps thicket. Please it our great General   270
To call together all his state of war.°
Fresh kings are come to Troy. Tomorrow
We must with all our main of° power stand fast.
And here's a lord, come knights from east to west,
And cull their flower,° Ajax shall cope the best.   275

AGAM. Go we to council. Let Achilles sleep.
Light boats sail swift, though greater hulks draw
   deep.   [*Exeunt.*]

Act III

SCENE I. *Troy. A room in* PRIAM's *palace.*

[*Enter* PANDARUS *and a* SERVANT.]

PAN. Friend you, pray you, a word. Do you not
follow° the young Lord Paris?

SERV. Aye, sir, when he goes before me.

PAN. You depend upon him, I mean?

SERV. Sir, I do depend upon the Lord.   5

PAN. You depend upon a noble gentleman. I must
needs praise him.

SERV. The Lord be praised!

PAN. You know me, do you not?

SERV. Faith, sir, superficially.   10

PAN. Friend, know me better. I am the Lord
Pandarus.

---

210. rubs . . . him: flatters his disposition.   **213. pash:** smash.
215. pheeze: do for.   **222. I'll . . . blood:** I'll bleed his moodiness. Bleeding was a recognized remedy for many complaints.
227. A': he.   **232. through:** thoroughly.   **233. Force:** stuff.
242. emulous: envious.   **250. strange:** standoffish, haughty. **self-
affected:** conceited.   **252. got:** begot.

254. erudition: learning.   **258. Milo:** a prodigiously strong
Greek athlete. **addition yield:** give up his claims to fame.
260. bourn: boundary. **pale:** fence.   **261. dilated:** spread far
and wide.   **265. green:** young.   **271. state of war:** chief commanders.   **273. main of:** full.   **275. cull . . . flower:** i.e., take
the pick of them.
Act III, Sc. i: **2. follow:** serve.

SERV. I hope I shall know your Honor better.

PAN. I do desire it.

SERV. You are in the state of grace.°   15

PAN. Grace! Not so, friend. Honor and lordship are my titles.° [*Music within*] What music is this?

SERV. I do but partly know, sir. It is music in parts.°   20

PAN. Know you the musicians?

SERV. Wholly, sir.

PAN. Who play they to?

SERV. To the hearers, sir.

PAN. At whose pleasure, friend?   25

SERV. At mine, sir, and theirs that love music.

PAN. Command, I mean, friend.

SERV. Who shall I command, sir?

PAN. Friend, we understand not one another. I am too courtly, and thou art too cunning.° At   30 whose request do these men play?

SERV. That's to 't, indeed, sir. Marry, sir, at the request of Paris my lord, who is there in person; with him, the mortal Venus, the heartblood of beauty, love's invisible soul.   35

PAN. Who, my cousin Cressida?

SERV. No, sir, Helen. Could not you find out that by her attributes?

PAN. It should seem, fellow, that thou hast not seen the Lady Cressida. I come to speak with   40 Paris from the Prince Troilus. I will make a complimental assault° upon him, for my business seethes.°

SERV. Sodden business! There's a stewed phrase indeed!

[*Enter* PARIS *and* HELEN, *attended.*]

PAN. Fair be to you, my lord, and to all this fair company! Fair desires, in all fair measure, fairly guide them! Especially to you, fair Queen! Fair thoughts be your fair pillow!   49

HELEN. Dear lord, you are full of fair words.

PAN. You speak your fair pleasure, sweet Queen. Fair Prince, here is good broken music.°

PAR. You have broke it, Cousin. And, by my life, you shall make it whole again, you shall piece it out° with a piece of your performance. Nell, he is full of harmony.   56

PAN. Truly, lady, no.

HELEN. O sir ——   59

PAN. Rude,° in sooth, in good sooth,° very rude.

PAR. Well said, my lord! Well, you say so in fits.°

PAN. I have business to my lord, dear Queen. My lord, will you vouchsafe me a word?

HELEN. Nay, this shall not hedge us out.   65 We'll hear you sing, certainly.

PAN. Well, sweet Queen, you are pleasant with me. But, marry, thus, my lord. My dear lord, and most esteemed friend, your brother Troilus ——   70

HELEN. My Lord Pandarus, honey-sweet lord ——

PAN. Go to, sweet Queen, go to — commends himself most affectionately to you ——

HELEN. You shall not bob° us out of our melody. If you do, our melancholy upon your head!   75

PAN. Sweet Queen, sweet Queen, that's a sweet Queen, i' faith.

HELEN. And to make a sweet lady sad is a sour offense.   80

PAN. Nay, that shall not serve your turn, that shall it not, in truth, la. Nay, I care not for such words, no, no. And my lord, he desires you that if the King call for him at supper, you will make his excuse.   85

HELEN. My Lord Pandarus ——

PAN. What says my sweet Queen, my very very sweet Queen?

PAR. What exploit 's in hand? Where sups he tonight?   90

HELEN. Nay, but, my lord ——

PAN. What says my sweet Queen? My cousin will fall out with you. You must not know where he sups.

PAR. I'll lay my life, with my disposer° Cressida.

PAN. No, no, no such matter, you are wide. Come, your disposer is sick.

PAR. Well, I'll make excuse.

PAN. Aye, good my lord. Why should you say Cressida? No, your poor disposer's sick.   101

PAR. I spy.

PAN. You spy! What do you spy? Come, give me an instrument. Now, sweet Queen.

HELEN. Why, this is kindly done.   105

PAN. My niece is horribly in love with a thing you have, sweet Queen.

HELEN. She shall have it, my lord, if it be not my lord Paris.

PAN. He! No, she'll none of him, they two are twain.°   111

HELEN. Falling in, after falling out, may make them three.

PAN. Come, come, I'll hear no more of this. I'll sing you a song now.   115

HELEN. Aye, aye, prithee now. By my troth, sweet lord, thou hast a fine forehead.

PAN. Aye, you may,° you may.

HELEN. Let thy song be love. This love will undo us all. O Cupid, Cupid, Cupid!   120

PAN. Love! Aye, that it shall, i' faith.

PAR. Aye, good now, love, love, nothing but love.

PAN. In good troth, it begins so. [*Sings.*]
  "Love, love, nothing but love, still more!   125
        For, oh, love's bow
        Shoots buck and doe.
        The shaft confounds,
        Not that it wounds,
  But tickles still the sore.°   130
  These lovers cry ' Oh! oh! ' they die.
    Yet that which seems the wound to kill,
  Doth turn oh! oh! to ha! ha! he!
      So dying love lives still.
  Oh! oh! a while, but ha! ha! ha!   135
  Oh! oh! groans out for ha! ha! ha! "
Heigh-ho!

HELEN. In love, i' faith, to the very tip of the nose.

PAR. He eats nothing but doves, love, and that breeds hot blood, and hot blood begets hot thoughts, and hot thoughts beget hot deeds, and hot deeds is love.   143

PAN. Is this the generation° of love? Hot blood, hot thoughts, and hot deeds? Why, they are vipers. Is love a generation of vipers? Sweet lord, who's afield today?

PAR. Hector, Deiphobus, Helenus, Antenor, and all the gallantry of Troy. I would fain have armed today, but my Nell would not have it so. How chance my brother Troilus went not?   151

HELEN. He hangs the lip at° something. You know all, Lord Pandarus.

PAN. Not I, honey-sweet Queen. I long to hear how they sped today. You'll remember your brother's excuse?

PAR. To a hair.

PAN. Farewell, sweet Queen.

HELEN. Commend me to your niece.   159

PAN. I will, sweet Queen.   [*Exit.*]
    [*A retreat sounded*]

PAR. They're come from field. Let us to Priam's hall
To greet the warriors. Sweet Helen, I must woo you
To help unarm our Hector. His stubborn buckles,
With these your white enchanting fingers touched,
Shall more obey than to the edge of steel   165
Or force of Greekish sinews. You shall do more
Than all the island kings° — disarm great Hector.

HELEN. 'Twill make us proud to be his servant, Paris.
Yea, what he shall receive of us in duty
Gives us more palm° in beauty than we have —
Yea, overshines ourself.   171

PAR. Sweet, above thought I love thee. [*Exeunt.*]

SCENE II. *An orchard to* PANDARUS' *house.*

[*Enter* PANDARUS *and* TROILUS' BOY, *meeting.*]

PAN. How now! Where's thy master? At my cousin Cressida's?

BOY. No, sir, he stays for you to conduct him thither.

PAN. Oh, here he comes. [*Enter* TROILUS.] How now, how now!   5

TRO. Sirrah,° walk off.   [*Exit* BOY.]

PAN. Have you seen my cousin?

TRO. No, Pandarus. I stalk about her door
Like a strange soul upon the Stygian° banks   10
Staying for waftage.° Oh, be thou my Charon,
And give me swift transportance to those fields
Where I may wallow in the lily beds
Proposed for the deserver! O gentle Pandarus,
From Cupid's shoulder pluck his painted wings,   15
And fly with me to Cressid!

PAN. Walk here i' the orchard, I'll bring her straight.   [*Exit.*]

TRO. I am giddy, expectation whirls me round.
The imaginary relish is so sweet   20
That it enchants my sense. What will it be
When that the watery palates taste indeed
Love's thrice repurèd° nectar? Death, I fear me,
Swounding° destruction, or some joy too fine,
Too subtle-potent, tuned too sharp in sweetness,   25
For the capacity of my ruder powers.
I fear it much, and I do fear besides
That I shall lose distinction in my joys,
As doth a battle when they charge on heaps
The enemy flying.   30
    [*Re-enter* PANDARUS.]

PAN. She's making her ready, she'll come straight.
You must be witty now. She does so blush, and
fetches her wind so short, as if she were frayed with
a sprite:° I'll fetch her. It is the prettiest villain. She
fetches her breath as short as a new-ta'en sparrow.
    [*Exit.*]

TRO. Even such a passion doth embrace my bosom.
My heart beats thicker than a feverous pulse,
And all my powers do their bestowing lose,
Like vassalage° at unawares encountering   40
The eye of majesty.
    [*Re-enter* PANDARUS *with* CRESSIDA.]

PAN. Come, come, what need you blush? Shame's a baby. Here she is now. Swear the oaths now to her that you have sworn to me. What, are you gone again? You must be watched ere you be made tame, must you? Come your ways, come your ways. An

---

130. **sore:** lit., a buck in its fourth year, with a pun on *sore*, meaning hurt. 144. **generation:** descent, breeding. 152. **hangs . . . at:** is troubled by. 167. **island kings:** kings of the Greek isles. 170. **palm:** reward.

Sc. ii: 6. **Sirrah:** term of address used to an inferior. 10. **Stygian:** the river Styx, which surrounded the underworld and across which souls were transported by Charon the ferryman. 11. **waftage:** passage. 23. **repured:** refined. 24. **Swounding:** swooning. 33–34. **frayed . . . sprite:** frightened by a ghost. 40. **vassalage:** a servant.

you draw backward, we'll put you i' the fills.° Why do you not speak to her? Come, draw this curtain° and let's see your picture. Alas the day, how   49 loath you are to offend daylight! An 'twere dark, you'd close sooner. So, so, rub on, and kiss the mistress.° How now! A kiss in fee farm!° Build there, carpenter, the air is sweet. Nay, you shall fight your hearts out ere I part you. The falcon as the tercel,° for all the ducks i' the river. Go to, go to.   56

TRO. You have bereft me of all words, lady.

PAN. Words pay no debts, give her deeds. But she'll bereave you o' the deeds too if she call your activity in question. What, billing again? Here's " In witness whereof the parties interchangeably "°   62 —— Come in, come in. I'll go get a fire.

[*Exit.*]

CRES. Will you walk in, my lord?

TRO. O Cressida, how often have I wished me thus!

CRES. Wished, my lord? — The gods grant —— O my lord!

TRO. What should they grant? What makes this pretty abruption?° What too curious dreg espies my sweet lady in the fountain of our love?   71

CRES. More dregs than water, if my fears have eyes.

TRO. Fears make devils of cherubins, they never see truly.   75

CRES. Blind fear that seeing reason leads finds safer footing than blind reason stumbling without fear. To fear the worst oft cures the worse.   79

TRO. Oh, let my lady apprehend no fear. In all Cupid's pageant there is presented no monster.

CRES. Nor nothing monstrous neither?

TRO. Nothing but our undertakings — when we vow to weep seas, live in fire, eat rocks, tame tigers, thinking it harder for our mistress to devise imposition enough than for us to undergo any difficulty imposed. This is the monstruosity in love, lady, that the will is infinite and the execution confined, that the desire is boundless and the act a slave to limit.°

CRES. They say all lovers swear more per-   91 formance than they are able, and yet reserve an ability that they never perform, vowing more than the perfection of ten, and discharging less than the tenth part of one. They that have the voice of lions and the act of hares, are they not monsters?   96

TRO. Are there such? Such are not we. Praise us as we are tasted, allow us as we prove, our head shall go bare till merit crown it. No perfection in

reversion° shall have a praise in present. We will not name desert° before his birth, and being born, his addition° shall be humble. Few words to fair faith. Troilus shall be such to Cressid as what envy can say worst shall be a mock for his truth, and what truth can speak truest, not truer than Troilus.°   106

CRES. Will you walk in, my lord?

[*Re-enter* PANDARUS.]

PAN. What, blushing still? Have you not done talking yet?

CRES. Well, Uncle, what folly I commit, I dedicate to you.

PAN. I thank you for that. If my lord get a boy of you, you'll give him me. Be true to my lord. If he flinch, chide me for it.

TRO. You know now your hostages — your uncle's word and my firm faith.   116

PAN. Nay, I'll give my word for her too. Our kindred, though they be long ere they are wooed, they are constant being won. They are burrs, I can tell you, they'll stick where they are thrown.   120

CRES. Boldness comes to me now, and brings me heart.
Prince Troilus, I have loved you night and day
For many weary months.

TRO. Why was my Cressid then so hard to win?

CRES. Hard to seem won. But I was won, my lord,
With the first glance that ever — pardon me,   126
If I confess much, you will play the tyrant.
I love you now, but not, till now, so much
But I might master it. In faith, I lie.
My thoughts were like unbridled° children, grown
Too headstrong for their mother. See, we fools!   131
Why have I blabbed? Who shall be true to us
When we are so unsecret to ourselves?
But though I loved you well, I wooed you not.
And yet, good faith, I wished myself a man,   135
Or that we women had men's privilege
Of speaking first. Sweet, bid me hold my tongue,
For in this rapture° I shall surely speak
The thing I shall repent. See, see, your silence,
Cunning in dumbness, from my weakness draws
My very soul of counsel!° Stop my mouth.   141

TRO. And shall, albeit sweet music issues thence.

PAN. Pretty, i' faith.

CRES. My lord, I do beseech you pardon me,
'Twas not my purpose thus to beg a kiss.   145
I am ashamed. Oh heavens, what have I done?
For this time will I take my leave, my lord.

TRO. Your leave, sweet Cressid?

47. fills: shafts (of a cart).   48. curtain: veil.   51–52. rub ... mistress: a metaphor from bowls. *rub on:* roll on. *mistress:* the "jack." See App. 13.   52. fee farm: perpetual possession. 56. tercel: male of a small species of hawk.   61–62. In ... interchangeably: a legal phrase in agreements, which continues "set to their hands and seals."   70. abruption: breaking off. 90. slave to limit: only able to be performed to a limited degree.

99–100. in reversion: a legal phrase meaning property which will pass on the death of some other person; so "in the future." 101. desert: merit.   102. addition: title.   102–06. Few ... Troilus: good faith needs few words. Troilus will be so true to Cressida that the worst that Envy can utter will be a mockery of the truth, and when Truth is speaking its truest, it will not be truer than Troilus.   130. unbridled: uncontrolled.   138. rapture: ecstasy.   141. soul of counsel: secret of my heart.

PAN. Leave! An you take leave till tomorrow
morning —— 150
  CRES. Pray you content you.
  TRO. What offends you, lady?
  CRES. Sir, mine own company.
  TRO. You cannot shun yourself.
  CRES. Let me go and try.
I have a kind of self resides with you, 155
But an unkind self that itself will leave
To be another's fool. I would be gone.
Where is my wit? I know not what I speak.
  TRO. Well know they what they speak that speak
    so wisely.
  CRES. Perchance, my lord, I show more craft than
    love, 160
And fell so roundly° to a large° confession
To angle for your thoughts. But you are wise,
Or else you love not, for to be wise and love
Exceeds man's might, that dwells with gods above.
  TRO. Oh, that I thought it could be in a woman —
As, if it can, I will presume in you — 166
To feed for aye her lamp and flames of love,
To keep her constancy in plight° and youth,
Outliving beauty's outward, with a mind
That doth renew swifter than blood decays! 170
Or that persuasion could but thus convince me
That my integrity and truth to you
Might be affronted with the match and weight°
Of such a winnowed purity in love.
How were I then uplifted! But alas! 175
I am as true as truth's simplicity,
And simpler than the infancy of truth.
  CRES. In that I'll war with you.
  TRO.   Oh, virtuous fight
When right with right wars who shall be most right!
True swains° in love shall in the world to come 180
Approve° their truths by Troilus. When their
  rhymes,
Full of protest, of oath and big compare,
Want similes, truth tired with iteration° —
" As true as steel, as plantage to the moon,°
As sun to day, as turtle° to her mate, 185
As iron to adamant,° as earth to the center " —
Yet, after all comparisons of truth,
As truth's authentic author to be cited,
" As true as Troilus " shall crown up the verse
And sanctify the numbers.°
  CRES.   Prophet may you be! 190
If I be false, or swerve a hair from truth,
When time is old and hath forgot itself,
When waterdrops have worn the stones of Troy,

161. roundly: directly. large: full. 168. plight: promise.
173. affronted . . . weight: met by equal truth. 180. swains:
lovers. 181. Approve: confirm. 183. iteration: simile.
184. plantage . . . moon: as plants are true to the moon. It is
still a very general belief that the growth of plants is controlled
by the moon. 185. turtle: dove. 186. adamant: the hardest
steel. 190. numbers: verses.

And blind oblivion swallowed cities up,
And mighty states characterless are grated° 195
To dusty nothing, yet let memory,
From false to false, among false maids in love,
Upbraid my falsehood! When they've said " as false
As air, as water, wind, or sandy earth,
As fox to lamb, or wolf to heifer's calf, 200
Pard° to the hind, or stepdame to her son,
" Yea," let them say, to stick the heart of falsehood,
" As false as Cressid."
  PAN. Go to, a bargain made. Seal it, seal it, I'll be
the witness. Here I hold your hand, here my cousin's.
If ever you prove false one to another, since I have
taken such pains to bring you together, let all pitiful
goers-between be called to the world's end after my
name — call them all Pandars, let all constant men
be Troiluses, all false women Cressids, and all brok-
ers-between Pandars! Say " Amen."
  TRO. Amen.
  CRES. Amen. 214
  PAN. Amen. Whereupon I will show you a chamber with a bed, which bed, because it shall not speak
of your pretty encounters, press it to death.° Away!
              [*Exeunt* TROILUS *and* CRESSIDA.]
And Cupid grant all tongue-tied maidens here
Bed, chamber, Pandar to provide this gear!   [*Exit.*]

SCENE III. *The Grecian camp.*

[*Flourish. Enter* AGAMEMNON, ULYSSES, DIOMEDES,
    NESTOR, AJAX, MENELAUS, *and* CALCHAS.]
  CAL. Now, Princes, for the service I have done
    you,
The advantage of the time prompts me aloud
To call for recompense. Appear it to your mind
That, through the sight I bear in things to love,
I have abandoned Troy, left my possession, 5
Incurred a traitor's name, exposed myself,
From certain and possessed conveniences,
To doubtful fortunes, sequestering° from me all
That time, acquaintance, custom, and condition
Made tame and most familiar to my nature, 10
And here, to do you service, am become
As new into the world, strange, unacquainted.
I do beseech you, as in way of taste,°
To give me now a little benefit
Out of those many registered in promise, 15
Which you say live to come in my behalf.
  AGAM. What wouldst thou of us, Trojan? Make
    demand.
  CAL. You have a Trojan prisoner called Antenor,
Yesterday took. Troy holds him very dear.
Oft have you — often have you thanks therefore —

195. characterless . . . grated: are ground so small that not a
letter remains. 201. Pard: panther. 217. press . . . death: see
Gen. Intro. p. 27b.
  Sc. iii: 8. sequestering: separating. 13. taste: foretaste.

Desired my Cressid in right great exchange,   21
Whom Troy hath still° denied. But this Antenor
I know is such a wrest° in their affairs
That their negotiations all must slack
Wanting his manage, and they will almost   25
Give us a prince of blood, a son of Priam,
In change of him. Let him be sent, great Princes,
And he shall buy my daughter, and her presence
Shall quite strike off° all service I have done
In most accepted pain.°
    AGAM.   Let Diomedes bear him,   30
And bring us Cressid hither. Calchas shall have
What he requests of us. Good Diomed,
Furnish you° fairly for this interchange.
Withal, bring word if Hector will tomorrow
Be answered in his challenge. Ajax is ready.   35
    DIO. This shall I undertake, and 'tis a burden
Which I am proud to bear.
                    [*Exeunt* DIOMEDES *and* CALCHAS.]
[*Enter* ACHILLES *and* PATROCLUS, *before their tent.*]
    ULYSS. Achilles stands i' the entrance of his tent.
Please it° our General pass strangely by him,
As if he were forgot, and, Princes all,   40
Lay negligent and loose regard° upon him.
I will come last. 'Tis like he'll question me
Why such unplausive° eyes are bent on him.
If so, I have derision medicinable
To use between your strangeness and his pride,   45
Which his own will shall have desire to drink.
It may do good. Pride hath no other glass
To show itself but pride, for supple knees
Feed arrogance and are the proud man's fees.
    AGAM. We'll execute your purpose and put on   50
A form of strangeness as we pass along.
So do each lord, and either greet him not
Or else disdainfully, which shall shake him more
Than if not looked on. I will lead the way.
    ACHIL. What, comes the General to speak with
me?   55
You know my mind, I'll fight no more 'gainst Troy.
    AGAM. What says Achilles? Would he aught with
us?
    NEST. Would you, my lord, aught with the General?
    ACHIL. No.
    NEST. Nothing, my lord.   60
    AGAM. The better.
               [*Exeunt* AGAMEMNON *and* NESTOR.]
    ACHIL. Good day, good day.
    MEN. How do you? How do you?   [*Exit.*]
    ACHIL. What, does the cuckold scorn me?
    AJAX. How now, Patroclus!   65

    ACHIL. Good morrow, Ajax.
    AJAX. Ha?
    ACHIL. Good morrow.
    AJAX. Aye, and good next day too.   [*Exit.*]
    ACHIL. What mean these fellows? Know they not
Achilles?   70
    PATR. They pass by strangely. They were used to
bend,
To send their smiles before them to Achilles,
To come as humbly as they used to creep
To holy altars.
    ACHIL.   What, am I poor of late?   74
'Tis certain greatness, once fall'n out with fortune,
Must fall out with men too. What the declined is,
He shall as soon read in the eyes of others
As feel in his own fall. For men, like butterflies,
Show not their mealy° wings but to the summer,
And not a man, for being simply man,   80
Hath any honor but honor for those honors
That are without him, as place, riches, and favor,
Prizes of accident as oft as merit.
Which when they fall, as being slippery standers,
The love that leaned on them as slippery too,   85
Do one pluck down another and together
Die in the fall. But 'tis not so with me.
Fortune and I are friends. I do enjoy
At ample point° all that I did possess,
Save these men's looks, who do methinks find out
Something not worth in me such rich beholding   91
As they have often given. Here is Ulysses.
I'll interrupt his reading.
How now, Ulysses!
    ULYSS.   Now, great Thetis' son!
    ACHIL. What are you reading?
    ULYSS.   A strange fellow here   95
Writes me: " That man, how dearly ever parted,°
How much in having, or without or in,
Cannot make boast to have that which he hath,
Nor feels not what he owes,° but by reflection,
As when his virtues shining upon others   100
Heat them, and they retort that heat again
To the first giver."
    ACHIL.   This is not strange, Ulysses.
The beauty that is borne here in the face
The bearer knows not, but commends itself
To others' eyes. Nor doth the eye itself,   105
That most pure spirit of sense, behold itself,
Not going from itself, but eye to eye opposed
Salutes each other with each other's form.
For speculation° turns not to itself
Till it hath traveled and is mirrored there   110

---

22. still: always.   23. wrest: controlling instrument; lit., the key which tightens the pegs in a musical instrument. 29. strike off: pay for.   30. accepted pain: agreeable labor. 33. Furnish you: equip yourself.   39. Please it: let it please . . . to.   41. regard: look.   43. unplausive: disapproving.

79. mealy: powdery.   89. At . . . point: fully.   96. how . . . parted: however richly endowed. 99. owes: owns. 109. speculation: power of sight. It was thought that the eye shot out a beam (like a searchlight) which caused the object to be visible to the beholder. So in this image *speculation* cannot see itself until the beam has passed out and been reflected back.

Where it may see itself. This is not strange at all.
　ULYSS. I do not strain at the position —°
It is familiar — but at the author's drift,
Who in his circumstance expressly proves
That no man is the lord of anything,   115
Though in and of him there be much consisting,
Till he communicate his parts to others.
Nor doth he of himself know them for aught
Till he behold them formed in the applause
Where they're extended,° who, like an arch, rever-
　　berates   120
The voice again, or like a gate of steel
Fronting the sun, receives and renders back
His figure and his heat. I was much rapt in° this,
And apprehended here immediately
The unknown Ajax.   125
Heavens, what a man is there! A very horse,
That has he knows not what. Nature, what things
　　there are,
Most abject in regard and dear in use!°
What things again most dear in the esteem   129
And poor in worth! Now shall we see tomorrow —
An act that very chance doth throw upon him —
Ajax renowned. O heavens, what some men do
While some men leave to do!
How some men creep in skittish fortune's hall
Whiles others play the idiots in her eyes!   135
How one man eats into another's pride
While pride is fasting in his wantonness!
To see these Grecian lords! Why, even already
They clap the lubber° Ajax on the shoulder
As if his foot were on brave Hector's breast   140
And great Troy shrieking.
　ACHIL. I do believe it, for they passed by me
As misers do by beggars, neither gave to me
Good word nor look. What, are my deeds forgot?
　ULYSS. Time hath, my lord, a wallet at his back
Wherein he puts alms for oblivion,   146
A great-sized monster of ingratitudes.
Those scraps are good deeds past, which are de-
　　voured
As fast as they are made, forgot as soon
As done. Perseverance, dear my lord,   150
Keeps honor bright. To have done is to hang
Quite out of fashion, like a rusty mail
In monumental mockery.° Take the instant way,
For honor travels in a strait° so narrow,
Where one but goes abreast. Keep then the path,
For emulation° hath a thousand sons   156
That one by one pursue. If you give way,
Or hedge aside from the direct forthright,°

Like to an entered tide they all rush by
And leave you hindmost.   160
Or like a gallant horse fall'n in first rank,
Lie there for pavement to the abject rear,
O'errun and trampled on. Then what they do in
　　present,
Though less than yours in past, must o'ertop yours.
For time is like a fashionable host   165
That slightly shakes his parting guest by the hand,
And with his arms outstretched, as he would fly,
Grasps in the comer. Welcome ever smiles,
And farewell goes out sighing. Oh, let not virtue seek
Remuneration for the thing it was;   170
For beauty, wit,
High birth, vigor of bone, desert in service,
Love, friendship, charity, are subjects all
To envious and calumniating time.   174
One touch of nature makes the whole world kin,°
That all with one consent praise newborn gawds,°
Though they are made and molded of things past,
And give to dust that is a little gilt
More laud than gilt o'erdusted.
The present eye praises the present object.   180
Then marvel not, thou great and complete man,
That all the Greeks begin to worship Ajax,
Since things in motion sooner catch the eye
Than what not stirs. The cry went once on thee,
And still it might, and yet it may again,   185
If thou wouldst not entomb thyself alive
And case thy reputation in thy tent,
Whose glorious deeds, but in these fields of late,
Made emulous missions 'mongst the gods them-
　　selves,
And drave great Mars to faction.°
　ACHIL.   Of this my privacy   190
I have strong reasons.
　ULYSS.   But 'gainst your privacy
The reasons are more potent and heroical.
'Tis known, Achilles, that you are in love
With one of Priam's daughters.°
　ACHIL.   Ha! Known?
　ULYSS. Is that a wonder?   195
The providence that's in a watchful state
Knows almost every grain of Plutus'° gold,
Finds bottom in the uncomprehensive° deeps,
Keeps place with thought, and almost like the gods
Does thoughts unveil in their dumb cradles.   200
There is a mystery, with whom relation
Durst never meddle,° in the soul of state,
Which hath an operation more divine

---

112. **position:** assertion.　120. **extended:** bestowed.　123. **rapt in:** taken by.　128. **abject . . . use:** despised but invaluable.　139. **lubber:** lout.　152–53. **rusty . . . mockery:** neglected suit of armor, which is a mocking memorial of the knight who once wore it.　154. **strait:** path.　156. **emulation:** jealousy.　158. **forthright:** straightforward path.

175. **One . . . kin:** one natural inclination (*touch*) unites everyone.　176. **gawds:** trifles.　189–90. **Made . . . faction:** caused the gods to grow jealous and take sides (*to faction*). In the *Iliad* each of the heroes was the favorite of one of the gods or goddesses, who were constantly squabbling.　194. **one . . . daughters:** i.e., Polyxena.　197. **Plutus:** god of wealth.　198. **uncomprehensive:** unplumbed.　201–02. **relation . . . meddle:** that which must never be pried into.

Than breath or pen can give expressure to.
All the commerce that you have had with Troy   205
As perfectly is ours as yours, my lord,
And better would it fit Achilles much
To throw down Hector than Polyxena.
But it must grieve young Pyrrhus° now at home
When fame shall in our islands sound her trump,
And all the Greekish girls shall tripping sing   211
"Great Hector's sister did Achilles win,
But our great Ajax bravely beat down him."
Farewell, my lord. I as your lover speak.
The fool slides o'er the ice that you should break.
                                        [*Exit.*]
PATR. To this effect, Achilles, have I moved you.
A woman impudent and mannish grown
Is not more loathed than an effeminate man
In time of action. I stand condemned for this,
They think my little stomach° to the war   220
And your great love to me restrains you thus.
Sweet, rouse yourself, and the weak wanton Cupid
Shall from your neck unloose his amorous fold
And, like a dewdrop from the lion's mane,
Be shook to air.
ACHIL.   Shall Ajax fight with Hector?   225
PATR. Aye, and perhaps receive much honor by
   him.
ACHIL. I see my reputation is at stake,°
My fame is shrewdly gored.°
PATR.   Oh, then beware.
Those wounds heal ill that men do give themselves.
Omission to do what is necessary   230
Seals a commission to a blank of danger,°
And danger, like an ague, subtly taints
Even then when we sit idly in the sun.
ACHIL. Go call Thersites hither, sweet Patroclus.
I'll send the fool to Ajax, and desire him   235
To invite the Trojan lords after the combat
To see us here unarmed. I have a woman's longing,°
An appetite that I am sick withal,
To see great Hector in his weeds° of peace,
To talk with him, and to behold his visage,   240
Even to my full of view.
                    [*Enter* THERSITES.]
                        —A labor saved!
THER. A wonder!
ACHIL. What?
THER. Ajax goes up and down the field asking for
himself.   245
ACHIL. How so?
THER. He must fight singly tomorrow with Hec-
tor, and is so prophetically proud of a heroical cudg-
eling that he raves in saying nothing.

ACHIL. How can that be?   250
THER. Why, a' stalks up and down like a peacock
—a stride and a stand. Ruminates like a hostess°
that hath no arithmetic but her brain to set down her
reckoning. Bites his lip with a politic regard,° as
who should say "There were wit in this head, an
'twould out." And so there is, but it lies as coldly in
him as fire in a flint, which will not show without
knocking. The man's undone forever, for if Hector
break not his neck i' the combat, he'll break 't himself in vainglory. He knows not me. I said, "Good
morrow, Ajax," and he replies "Thanks, Agamemnon." What think you of this man, that takes me for
the General? He's grown a very land fish,° lan-
guageless, a monster. A plague of opinion!° A man
may wear it on both sides, like a leather jerkin.   266
ACHIL. Thou must be my ambassador to him,
Thersites.
THER. Who, I? Why, he'll answer nobody, he professes not answering. Speaking is for beggars, he
wears his tongue in 's arms. I will put on his presence.° Let Patroclus make demands to me, you shall
see the pageant° of Ajax.   273
ACHIL. To him, Patroclus. Tell him I humbly de-
sire the valiant Ajax to invite the most valorous Hec-
tor to come unarmed to my tent, and to procure safe-
conduct for his person of the magnanimous and
most illustrious six-or-seven-times-honored Captain
General of the Grecian army, Agamemnon, et cetera.
Do this.   280
PATR. Jove bless great Ajax!
THER. Hum!
PATR. I come from the worthy Achilles——
THER. Ha!
PATR. Who most humbly desires you to invite
Hector to his tent——
THER. Hum!
PATR. And to procure safe-conduct from Aga-
memnon.
THER. Agamemnon?   290
PATR. Aye, my lord.
THER. Ha!
PATR. What say you to 't?
THER. God be wi' you, with all my heart.
PATR. Your answer, sir.
THER. If tomorrow be a fair day, by eleven of the
clock it will go one way or other. Howsoever, he
shall pay for me ere he has me.
PATR. Your answer, sir.
THER. Fare you well, with all my heart.   300
ACHIL. Why, but he is not in this tune, is he?
THER. No, but he's out o' tune thus. What music
will be in him when Hector has knocked out his

---

209. **Pyrrhus:** Achilles' son.   220. **stomach:** appetite.   227. **at
stake:** See App. 5.   228. **shrewdly gored:** grievously wounded.
231. **Seals . . . danger:** gives danger a blank check.   237. **woman's longing:** the insatiable longing of a pregnant woman.
239. **weeds:** garments.

252. **hostess:** tavernkeeper.   254. **politic regard:** the look of
a politician.   264. **land fish:** freak of nature.   265. **opinion:**
conceit.   271–72. **put . . . presence:** imitate his manner.
273. **pageant:** play.

brains I know not, but I am sure none unless the
fiddler Apollo get his sinews to make catlings° on.

ACHIL. Come, thou shalt bear a letter to him
straight.   308

THER. Let me bear another to his horse, for that's
the more capable° creature.

ACHIL. My mind is troubled like a fountain
     stirred,
And I myself see not the bottom of it.
         [*Exeunt* ACHILLES *and* PATROCLUS.]

THER. Would the fountain of your mind were
clear again, that I might water an ass at it! I had
rather be a tick in a sheep than such a valiant   315
ignorance.   [*Exit*]

Act IV

SCENE I. *Troy. A street.*

[*Enter, at one side,* AENEAS, *and* SERVANT *with a
torch; at the other,* PARIS, DEIPHOBUS, ANTENOR,
DIOMEDES, *and others, with torches.*]

PAR. See, ho! Who is that there?

DEI. It is the Lord Aeneas.

AENE. Is the Prince there in person?
Had I so good occasion to lie long
As you, Prince Paris, nothing but heavenly business
Should rob my bedmate of my company.   5

DIO. That's my mind too. Good morrow, Lord
     Aeneas.

PAR. A valiant Greek, Aeneas — take his hand —
Witness the process° of your speech, wherein
You told how Diomed a whole week by days
Did haunt you in the field.

AENE. Health to you, valiant sir,   10
During all question° of the gentle truce.
But when I meet you armed, as black defiance
As heart can think or courage execute.

DIO. The one and other Diomed embraces.
Our bloods are now in calm, and, so long, health.
But when contention and occasion° meet,   16
By Jove, I'll play the hunter for thy life
With all my force, pursuit, and policy.°

AENE. And thou shalt hunt a lion that will fly
With his face backward. In humane gentleness,   20
Welcome to Troy! Now, by Anchises'° life,
Welcome indeed! By Venus' hand I swear
No man alive can love in such a sort
The thing he means to kill more excellently.

DIO. We sympathize.° Jove, let Aeneas live,   25

If to my sword his fate be not the glory,
A thousand complete courses of the sun!
But in mine emulous honor, let him die,
With every joint a wound, and that tomorrow.

AENE. We know each other well.   30

DIO. We do, and long to know each other worse.

PAR. This is the most despiteful° gentle greeting,
The noblest hateful love, that e'er I heard of.
What business, lord, so early?

AENE. I was sent for to the King, but why I know
     not.   35

PAR. His purpose meets you. 'Twas to bring this
     Greek
To Calchas' house, and there to render° him,
For the enfreed Antenor, the fair Cressid.
Let's have your company, or, if you please,
Haste there before us. I constantly do think,   40
Or rather, call my thought a certain knowledge,
My brother Troilus lodges there tonight.
Rouse him and give him note of our approach,
With the whole quality° wherefore. I fear
We shall be much unwelcome.

AENE.   That I assure you.   45
Troilus had rather Troy were borne to Greece
Than Cressid borne from Troy.

PAR.   There is no help,
The bitter disposition of the time
Will have it so. On, lord, we'll follow you.   49

AENE. Good morrow, all. [*Exit with* SERVANT.]

PAR. And tell me, noble Diomed, faith, tell me
     true,
Even in the soul of sound good-fellowship,
Who, in your thoughts, deserves fair Helen best,
Myself or Menelaus?

DIO.   Both alike.
He merits well to have her that doth seek her   55
Not making any scruple of her soilure,°
With such a Hell of pain and world of charge.°
And you as well to keep her that defend her
Not palating° the taste of her dishonor
With such a costly loss of wealth and friends.   60
He, like a puling cuckold, would drink up
The lees and dregs of a flat tamed piece.°
You, like a lecher, out of whorish loins
Are pleased to breed out your inheritors.°
Both merits poised, each weighs nor less nor more,
But he as he, the heavier for a whore.°   66

PAR. You are too bitter to your countrywoman.

DIO. She's bitter to her country. Hear me, Paris.
For every false drop in her bawdy veins
A Grecian's life hath sunk; for every scruple°   70

---

306. catlings: catgut fiddle strings.   310. capable: intelligent.
     Act IV, Sc. i: 8. process: gist.   11. question: converse.
16. occasion: opportunity.   18. policy: cunning.   21. Anchises:
father of Aeneas, whose mother was Venus.   25. sympathize:
have the same feeling.

32. despiteful: hateful.   37. render: restore.   44. quality:
nature of the business.   56. Not . . . soilure: regardless of her
dishonor.   57. charge: expense.   59. palating: relishing.
62. flat . . . piece: woman whose best has been enjoyed by others.   64. inheritors: children.   65–66. each . . . whore: both
weigh alike, but you who have her are heavier for having a whore
as wife.   70. scruple: smallest part.

Of her contaminated carrion weight
A Trojan hath been slain. Since she could speak,
She hath not given so many good words breath
As for her Greeks and Trojans suffered death.

PAR. Fair Diomed, you do as chapmen° do,   75
Dispraise the thing that you desire to buy.
But we in silence hold this virtue well,
We'll not commend what we intend to sell.
Here lies our way.   [*Exeunt.*]

SCENE II. *Court of* PANDARUS' *house.*

[*Enter* TROILUS *and* CRESSIDA.]
TRO. Dear, trouble not yourself. The morn is cold.
CRES. Then, sweet my lord, I'll call mine uncle
    down.
He shall unbolt the gates.
TRO.   Trouble him not.
To bed, to bed. Sleep kill° those pretty eyes,
And give as soft attachment° to thy senses   5
As infants' empty of all thought!
CRES.   Good morrow, then.
TRO. I prithee now, to bed.
CRES.   Are you aweary of me?
TRO. O Cressida! But that the busy day,
Waked by the lark, hath roused the ribald crows,
And dreaming night will hide our joys no longer,
I would not from thee.
CRES.   Night hath been too brief.
TRO. Beshrew° the witch! With venomous
    wights° she stays   12
As tediously as Hell, but flies the grasps of love
With wings more momentary-swift than thought.
You will catch cold, and curse me.
CRES.   Prithee tarry.   15
You men will never tarry.
O foolish Cressid! I might have still held off,
And then you would have tarried. Hark! There's
    one up.
PAN. [*Within*] What, 's all the doors open here?
TRO. It is your uncle.   20
CRES. A pestilence on him! Now will he be mock-
    ing.
I shall have such a life!
[*Enter* PANDARUS.]
PAN. How now, how now! How go° maiden-
heads? Here, you maid! Where's my cousin Cressid?
CRES. Go hang yourself, you naughty mocking
    uncle!   26
You bring me to do — and then you flout me too.
PAN. To do what? To do what? Let her say what.
What have I brought you to do?

CRES. Come, come, beshrew your heart! You'll
    ne'er be good,   30
Nor suffer others.
PAN. Ha, ha! Alas, poor wretch! A poor capoc-
chia!° Hast not slept tonight? Would he not, a
naughty man, let it sleep? A bugbear take him!
CRES. Did not I tell you? Would he were knocked
    i' the head!   [*One knocks.*]   35
Who's that at door? Good Uncle, go and see.
My lord, come you again into my chamber.
You smile and mock me, as if I meant naughtily.
TRO. Ha, ha!
CRES. Come, you are deceived, I think of no such
    thing.   [*Knocking.*]   40
How earnestly they knock! Pray you come in.
I would not for half Troy have you seen here.
       [*Exeunt* TROILUS *and* CRESSIDA.]
PAN. Who's there? What's the matter? Will you
beat down the door? How now! What's the matter?
[*Enter* AENEAS.]
AENE. Good morrow, lord, good morrow.   46
PAN. Who's there? My Lord Aeneas! By my troth,
I knew you not. What news with you so early?
AENE. Is not Prince Troilus here?
PAN. Here! What should he do here?   50
AENE. Come, he is here, my lord, do not deny
    him.
It doth import him much° to speak with me.
PAN. Is he here, say you? 'Tis more than I know,
I'll be sworn. For my own part, I came in late. What
should he do here?   55
AENE. Who! Nay then, come, come, you'll do him
wrong ere you are ware. You'll be so true to him to
be false to him. Do not you know of him, but yet go
fetch him hither, go.
[*Re-enter* TROILUS.]
TRO. How now! What's the matter?   60
AENE. My lord, I scarce have leisure to salute you,
My matter is so rash.° There is at hand
Paris your brother and Deiphobus,
The Grecian Diomed, and our Antenor
Delivered to us, and for him forthwith,   65
Ere the first sacrifice, within this hour,
We must give up to Diomedes' hand
The Lady Cressida.
TRO.   Is it so concluded?
AENE. By Priam and the general state° of Troy.
They are at hand and ready to effect it.   70
TRO. How my achievements° mock me!
I will go meet them. And, my Lord Aeneas,
We met by chance, you did not find me here.
AENE. Good, good, my lord. The secrets of nature
Have not more gift in taciturnity.   75
       [*Exeunt* TROILUS *and* AENEAS.]

---

75. chapmen: haggling traders.
    Sc. ii: 4. kill: overcome.   5. attachment: seizure.   12. Be-
shrew: curse. wights: men.   23. How go: what's the price of.

33. capocchia: lit., knob of stick (used obscenely).   52. It . .
much: it is of great importance for him.   62. rash: urgent.
69. state: assembly.   71. achievements: winnings, luck.

PAN. Is 't possible? No sooner got but lost? The devil take Antenor! The young Prince will go mad. A plague upon Antenor! I would they had broke 's neck!

[*Re-enter* CRESSIDA.]

CRES. How now! What's the matter? Who was here?   81

PAN. Ah, ah!

CRES. Why sigh you so profoundly? Where's my lord? Gone! Tell me, sweet Uncle, what's the matter?   85

PAN. Would I were as deep under the earth as I am above!

CRES. Oh, the gods! What's the matter?

PAN. Prithee get thee in. Would thou hadst ne'er been born! I knew thou wouldst be his death. Oh, poor gentleman! A plague upon Antenor!

CRES. Good Uncle, I beseech you, on my knees I beseech you, what's the matter?   94

PAN. Thou must be gone, wench, thou must be gone, thou art changed° for Antenor. Thou must to thy father, and be gone from Troilus. 'Twill be his death, 'twill be his bane,° he cannot bear it.   99

CRES. O you immortal gods! I will not go.

PAN. Thou must.

CRES. I will not, Uncle. I have forgot my father, I know no touch of consanguinity,°
No kin, no love, no blood, no soul, so near me
As the sweet Troilus. O you gods divine!   105
Make Cressid's name the very crown of falsehood
If ever she leave Troilus! Time, force, and death
Do to this body what extremes you can,
But the strong base and building of my love
Is as the very center of the earth,   110
Drawing all things to it. I'll go in and weep——

PAN. Do, do.

CRES. Tear my bright hair and scratch my praisèd cheeks,
Crack my clear voice with sobs, and break my heart   114
With sounding Troilus. I will not go from Troy.

[*Exeunt.*]

SCENE III. *Before* PANDARUS' *house.*

[*Enter* PARIS, TROILUS, AENEAS, DEIPHOBUS, ANTENOR, *and* DIOMEDES.]

PAR. It is great morning,° and the hour prefixed
For her delivery to this valiant Greek
Comes fast upon. Good my brother Troilus,
Tell you the lady what she is to do,
And haste her to the purpose.

TRO.   Walk into her house, 5

96. **changed**: exchanged.   99. **bane**: destruction.   103. **consanguinity**: blood relationship.
Sc. iii: 1. **great morning**: broad daylight.

I'll bring her to the Grecian presently.
And to his hand when I deliver her,
Think it an altar, and thy brother Troilus
A priest, there offering to it his own heart.   [*Exit.*]

PAR. I know what 'tis to love,   10
And would, as I shall pity, I could help!
Please you walk in, my lords.   [*Exeunt.*]

SCENE IV. *A room in* PANDARUS' *house.*

[*Enter* PANDARUS *and* CRESSIDA.]

PAN. Be moderate, be moderate.

CRES. Why tell you me of moderation?
The grief is fine, full, perfect, that I taste,
And violenteth° in a sense as strong
As that which causeth it. How can I moderate it?   5
If I could temporize° with my affection,
Or brew it to a weak and colder palate,
The like allayment could I give my grief.
My love admits no qualifying dross,°
No more my grief, in such a precious loss.   10

PAN. Here, here, here he comes. [*Enter* TROILUS.]
Ah, sweet ducks!

CRES. O Troilus! Troilus!   [*Embracing him.*]

PAN. What a pair of spectacles is here! Let me embrace too. "O heart," as the goodly saying is,
     " O heart, heavy heart,
       Why sigh'st thou without breaking? "
where he answers again,
     " Because thou canst not ease thy smart   20
       By friendship nor by speaking."
There was never a truer rhyme. Let us cast away nothing, for we may live to have need of such a verse. We see it, we see it. How now, lambs!   25

TRO. Cressid, I love thee in so strained° a purity
That the blest gods, as angry with my fancy,°
More bright in zeal than the devotion which
Cold lips blow to their deities, take thee from me.

CRES. Have the gods envy?   30

PAN. Aye, aye, aye, aye, 'tis too plain a case.

CRES. And is it true that I must go from Troy?

TRO. A hateful truth.

CRES.   What, and from Troilus too?

TRO. From Troy and Troilus.

CRES.   Is it possible?

TRO. And suddenly, where injury of chance°   35
Puts back leave-taking, justles roughly by
All time of pause, rudely beguiles our lips
Of all rejoindure,° forcibly prevents
Our locked embrasures,° strangles our dear vows
Even in the birth of our own laboring breath.   40

Sc. iv: 4. **violenteth**: is violent.   6. **temporize**: compromise. 9. **qualifying dross**: alloy to make it less than pure gold. 26. **strained**: i.e., of all impurities.   27. **fancy**: love.   35. **injury of chance**: the ill done us by Fortune.   38. **rejoindure**: reunion.   39. **embrasures**: embraces.

We two, that with so many thousand sighs
Did buy each other, must poorly sell ourselves
With the rude brevity and discharge of one.
Injurious time now with a robber's haste
Crams his rich thievery° up, he knows not how.　45
As many farewells as be stars in heaven,
With distinct breath and consigned kisses to them,°
He fumbles up into a loose adieu,
And scants us with a single famished kiss
Distasted° with the salt of broken tears.　50
　　AENE. [*Within*] My Lord, is the lady ready?
　　TRO. Hark! You are called. Some say the Genius°
so
Cries "Come!" to him that instantly must die.
Bid them have patience, she shall come anon.　54
　　PAN. Where are my tears? Rain, to lay this wind,
or my heart will be blown up by the root.　[*Exit.*]
　　CRES. I must then to the Grecians?
　　TRO.　　　　　　　　　　No remedy.
　　CRES. A woeful Cressid 'mongst the merry
　　　Greeks!°
When shall we see again?
　　TRO. Hear me, my love. Be thou but true of heart.
　　CRES. I true! How now! What wicked deem° is
　　　this?　61
　　TRO. Nay, we must use expostulation° kindly,
For it is parting from us.°
I speak not "Be thou true" as fearing thee,
For I will throw my glove to° Death himself　65
That there's no maculation° in thy heart.
But "Be thou true" say I to fashion in
My sequent protestation.° Be thou true,
And I will see thee.
　　CRES. Oh, you shall be exposed, my lord, to dan-
　　　gers　70
As infinite as imminent. But I'll be true.
　　TRO. And I'll grow friend with danger. Wear this
　　　sleeve.°
　　CRES. And you this glove. When shall I see you?
　　TRO. I will corrupt the Grecian sentinels,
To give thee nightly visitation.　75
But yet, be true.
　　CRES.　　　　Oh heavens! "Be true" again!
　　TRO. Hear why I speak it, love.
The Grecian youths are full of quality,°
They're loving, well composed with gifts of nature,
And flowing o'er with arts and exercise.°　80
How novelties may move and parts with person,°

Alas, a kind of godly jealousy —
Which, I beseech you, call a virtuous sin —
Makes me afeard.
　　CRES.　　　　Oh heavens! You love me not.
　　TRO. Die I a villain, then!　85
In this I do not call your faith in question,
So mainly as my merit. I cannot sing,
Nor heel the high lavolt,° nor sweeten talk,
Nor play at subtle games — fair virtues all,
To which the Grecians are most prompt and preg-
　　　nant.°　90
But I can tell that in each grace of these
There lurks a still and dumb-discoursive° devil
That tempts most cunningly. But be not tempted.
　　CRES. Do you think I will?
　　TRO. No.　95
But something may be done that we will not.
And sometimes we are devils to ourselves,
When we will tempt the frailty of our powers,
Presuming on their changeful potency.°
　　AENE. [*Within*] Nay, good my lord!
　　TRO.　　　　Come, kiss, and let us part.　100
　　PAR. [*Within*] Brother Troilus!
　　TRO.　　　　Good Brother, come you hither,
And bring Aeneas and the Grecian with you.
　　CRES. My lord, will you be true?
　　TRO. Who, I? Alas, it is my vice, my fault.
Whiles others fish with craft for great opinion,°
I with great truth catch mere simplicity.　106
Whilst some with cunning gild their copper
　　　crowns,°
With truth and plainness I do wear mine bare.
Fear not my truth. The moral of my wit
Is "plain and true," there's all the reach of it.　110
[*Enter* AENEAS, PARIS, ANTENOR, DEIPHOBUS, *and*
　　　DIOMEDES.]
Welcome, Sir Diomed! Here is the lady
Which for Antenor we deliver you.
At the port,° lord, I'll give her to thy hand,
And by the way possess° thee what she is.
Entreat her fair, and by my soul, fair Greek,　115
If e'er thou stand at mercy of my sword,
Name Cressid and thy life shall be as safe
As Priam is in Ilion.
　　DIO.　　　　Fair Lady Cressid,
So please you, save the thanks this Prince expects.
The luster in your eye, heaven in your cheek,　120
Pleads your fair usage, and to Diomed
You shall be mistress, and command him wholly.
　　TRO. Grecian, thou dost not use me courteously,
To shame the zeal of my petition to thee
In praising her. I tell thee, lord of Greece,　125

---

45. thievery: plunder.　47. With . . . them: each farewell with its own sigh and added kiss.　50. Distasted: distasteful. 52. Genius: guardian angel.　58. merry Greeks: See I.ii.118,n. 61. deem: thought.　62. expostulation: talk.　63. For . . . us: for it is our last chance of talking.　65. throw . . . to: challenge to combat.　66. maculation: stain.　67–68. to . . . protestation: to prepare for my vow which follows.　72. sleeve: often richly embroidered and worn separately from the main garment. See note on p. 95a.　78. quality: natural gifts.　80. exercise: skill.　81. parts . . . person: accomplishments added to personal charm.

88. lavolt: lavolta, a high stepping dance. See App. 24.　90. pregnant: apt.　92. dumb-discoursive: silently eloquent.　99. changeful potency: fickle power.　105. opinion: reputation.　107. gild . . . crowns: Copper gilt was the poorest kind of imitation gold. 113. port: gate.　114. possess: tell.

She is as far high-soaring o'er thy praises
As thou unworthy to be called her servant.
I charge thee use her well, even for my charge,
For, by the dreadful Pluto,° if thou dost not,
Though the great bulk Achilles be thy guard,   130
I'll cut thy throat.

DIO.   Oh, be not moved, Prince Troilus.
Let me be privileged by my place and message
To be a speaker free. When I am hence,
I'll answer to my lust.° And know you, lord,
I'll nothing do on charge.° To her own worth   135
She shall be prized, but that° you say " Be 't so,"
I'll speak it in my spirit and honor " No! "

TRO. Come, to the port. I'll tell thee, Diomed,
This brave° shall oft make thee to hide thy head.
Lady, give me your hand, and as we walk   140
To our own selves bend we our needful talk.

[Exeunt TROILUS, CRESSIDA, *and* DIOMEDES.]
[A trumpet sounds.]

PAR. Hark! Hector's trumpet.

AENE.   How have we spent this morning!
The Prince must think me tardy and remiss,
That swore to ride before him to the field.

PAR. 'Tis Troilus' fault. Come, come, to field with
him.   145

DEI. Let us make ready straight.

AENE. Yea, with a bridegroom's fresh alacrity,
Let us address° to tend on Hector's heels.
The glory of our Troy doth this day lie   149
On his fair worth and single chivalry.° *[Exeunt.]*

SCENE V. *The Grecian camp. Lists set out.*°

[Enter AJAX, *armed;* AGAMEMNON, ACHILLES,
PATROCLUS, MENELAUS, ULYSSES, NESTOR, *and others.]*

AGAM. Here art thou in appointment° fresh and
fair,
Anticipating time with starting courage.
Give with thy trumpet a loud note to Troy,
Thou dreadful Ajax, that the appallèd air
May pierce the head of the great combatant   5
And hale° him hither.

AJAX.   Thou, trumpet,° there's my purse.
Now crack thy lungs, and split thy brazen pipe.
Blow, villain, till thy spherèd bias cheek°
Outswell the colic of puffed Aquilon.°   9
Come, stretch thy chest, and let thy eyes spout blood.

129. Pluto: king of the underworld.   134. to my lust: as I
please.   135. on charge: because I am bidden.   136. that: if.
139. brave: boast.   148. address: make ready.   150. chivalry:
knightly combat.

    Sc. v: s.d., Lists . . . out: place of combat prepared. Shake-
speare and his contemporaries, as well as earlier writers, imagined
the worthies of the Trojan war as medieval knights, fighting in
full armor, according to the rules of chivalry.   1. appointment: equipment.   6. hale: draw, haul. trumpet: trumpeter.
8. sphered . . . cheek: cheek blown out like a bowl.   9. Aquilon:
northwest wind.

Thow blow'st for Hector.   *[Trumpet sounds.]*

ULYSS. No trumpet answers.

ACHIL.   'Tis but early days.

AGAM. Is not yond Diomed, with Calchas' daughter?

ULYSS. 'Tis he, I ken° the manner of his gait,
He rises on the toe. That spirit of his   15
In aspiration lifts him from the earth.

[Enter DIOMEDES, *with* CRESSIDA.]

AGAM. Is this the Lady Cressid?

DIO.   Even she.

AGAM. Most dearly welcome to the Greeks, sweet
lady.

NEST. Our General doth salute you with a kiss.

ULYSS. Yet is the kindness but particular,   20
'Twere better she were kissed in general.

NEST. And very courtly counsel. I'll begin.
So much for Nestor.

ACHIL. I'll take that winter° from your lips, fair
lady.
Achilles bids you welcome.   25

MEN. I had good argument for kissing once.

PATR. But that's no argument for kissing now,
For thus popped Paris in his hardiment,°
And parted thus you and your argument.   29

ULYSS. O deadly gall, and theme of all our scorns!
For which we lose our heads to gild his horns.°

PATR. The first was Menelaus' kiss, this, mine.
Patroclus kisses you.

MEN.   Oh, this is trim!

PATR. Paris and I kiss evermore for him.

MEN. I'll° have my kiss, sir. Lady, by your leave.

CRES. In kissing, do you render or receive?   36

PATR. Both take and give.

CRES.   I'll make my match to live,
The kiss you take is better than you give,
Therefore no kiss.

MEN. I'll give you boot,° I'll give you three for
one.   40

CRES. You're an odd man. Give even, or give
none.

MEN. An odd man, lady! Every man is odd.

CRES. No, Paris is not, for you know 'tis true
That you are odd, and he is even with you.

MEN. You fillip° me o' the head.

CRES.   No, I'll be sworn.   45

ULYSS. It were no match, your nail against his
horn.
May I, sweet lady, beg a kiss of you?

CRES. You may.

ULYSS.   I do desire it.

14. ken: know.   24. winter: i.e., old Nestor's cold kiss.
28. hardiment: boldness.   31. gild . . . horns: i.e., to do honor
to our cuckold Menelaus.   35–52. I'll . . . you: This rhymed
passage is very similar to *LLL*, V.ii. 200–61 and 336–483.
If *Tr & Cr* is in part an old play, this passage is likely to be a
relic of the original stratum.   40. boot: advantage, extra payment.   45. fillip: flip.

CRES.   Why, beg, then.
ULYSS. Why then, for Venus' sake, give me a kiss
When Helen is a maid again, and his.°   50
CRES. I am your debtor, claim it when 'tis due.
ULYSS. Never's my day, and then a kiss of you.
DIO. Lady, a word. I'll bring you to your father.
                [*Exit with* CRESSIDA.]
NEST. A woman of quick sense.°
ULYSS.   Fie, fie upon her!   54
There's language in her eye, her cheek, her lip —
Nay, her foot speaks, her wanton spirits look out
At every joint and motive° of her body.
Oh, these encounterers, so glib of tongue,
That give accosting° welcome ere it comes,
And wide unclasp° the tables° of their thoughts   60
To every ticklish° reader! Set them down
For sluttish spoils of opportunity,°
And daughters of the game.   [*Trumpet within.*]
ALL. The Trojans' trumpet.
AGAM.   Yonder comes the troop.
[*Flourish. Enter* HECTOR, *armed;* AENEAS, TROILUS,
    and other TROJANS, *with* ATTENDANTS.]
AENE. Hail, all the state of Greece! What shall be
    done   65
To him that victory commands? Or do you purpose
A victor shall be known?° Will you the knights
Shall to the edge of all extremity°
Pursue each other, or shall they be divided
By any voice or order of the field?   70
Hector bade ask.
AGAM.   Which way would Hector have it?
AENE. He cares not. He'll obey conditions.
ACHIL. 'Tis done like Hector, but securely° done,
A little proudly, and great deal misprizing°
The knight opposed.
AENE.   If not Achilles, sir,   75
What is your name?
ACHIL.   If not Achilles, nothing.
AENE. Therefore Achilles. But whate'er, know
    this.
In the extremity of great and little,
Valor and pride excel themselves in Hector,
The one almost as infinite as all,   80
The other blank as nothing. Weigh him well,
And that which looks like pride is courtesy.
This Ajax is half made of Hector's blood.°
In love whereof, half Hector stays at home;
Half heart, half hand, half Hector comes to seek   85
This blended knight, half Trojan and half Greek.

ACHIL. A maiden° battle, then? Oh, I perceive
    you.
                [*Re-enter* DIOMEDES.]
AGAM. Here is Sir Diomed. Go, gentle knight,
Stand by our Ajax. As you and Lord Aeneas
Consent upon the order of their fight,   90
So be it, either to the uttermost
Or else a breath. The combatants being kin
Half stints their strife before their strokes begin.
          [AJAX *and* HECTOR *enter the lists.*]
ULYSS. They are opposed already.
AGAM. What Trojan is that same that looks so
    heavy?   95
ULYSS. The youngest son of Priam, a true knight,
Not yet mature, yet matchless, firm of word,
Speaking in deeds and deedless in his tongue,
Not soon provoked nor being provoked soon
    calmed;
His heart and hand both open and both free;   100
For what he has he gives, what thinks he shows,
Yet gives he not till judgment guide his bounty,
Nor dignifies an impair° thought with breath;
Manly as Hector, but more dangerous,
For Hector in his blaze of wrath subscribes   105
To tender objects,° but he in heat of action
Is more vindicative° than jealous love.
They call him Troilus, and on him erect
A second hope, as fairly built as Hector.
Thus says Aeneas, one that knows the youth   110
Even to his inches, and with private soul°
Did in great Ilion thus translate° him to me.
        [*Alarum.* HECTOR *and* AJAX *fight.*]
AGAM. They are in action.
NEST. Now, Ajax, hold thine own!
TRO.   Hector, thou sleep'st.
Awake thee!   115
AGAM. His blows are well disposed. There, Ajax!
DIO. You must no more.   [*Trumpets cease.*]
AENE.   Princes, enough, so please you.
AJAX. I am not warm yet, let us fight again.
DIO. As Hector pleases.
HECT.   Why, then will I no more.
Thou art, great lord, my father's sister son,   120
A cousin-german° to great Priam's seed.
The obligation of our blood forbids
A gory emulation 'twixt us twain.
Were thy commixtion° Greek and Trojan so
That thou couldst say, "This hand is Grecian all,
And this is Trojan, the sinews of this leg   126
All Greek and this all Troy, my mother's blood
Runs on the dexter° cheek and this sinister°
Bounds in my father's," by Jove multipotent,

---

50. **his:** i.e., restored to Menelaus.   54. **sense:** feeling.   57. **motive:** limb.   59. **accosting:** Theobald's emendation for "coasting"; i.e., one who takes the initiative. Cf. *T Night,* I.iii. 52–64.   60. **unclasp:** open. **tables:** notebook.   61. **ticklish:** lecherous.   62. **sluttish . . . opportunity:** sluts to be picked up as desired.   67. **A . . . known:** i.e., a combat to a decisive end.   68. **edge . . . extremity:** to the death.   73. **securely:** foolhardily.   74. **misprizing:** disdaining.   83. **half . . . blood:** explained later at ll. 120–35.

Thou shouldst not bear from me a Greekish mem-
　ber°　　　　　　　　　　　　　　　　130
Wherein my sword had not impressure made
Of our rank feud. But the just gods gainsay°
That any drop thou borrow'dst from thy mother,
My sacred aunt, should by my mortal sword
Be drained! Let me embrace thee, Ajax.　　135
By him that thunders, thou hast lusty arms.
Hector would have them fall upon him thus.
Cousin, all honor to thee!
　　AJAX.　　　　　　　　I thank thee, Hector.
Thou art too gentle and too free° a man.
I came to kill thee, Cousin, and bear hence　140
A great addition° earnèd in thy death.
　　HECT. Not Neoptolemus° so mirable,°
On whose bright crest Fame with her loud'st
　　Oyes°
Cries, "This is he," could promise to himself
A thought of added honor torn from Hector.　145
　　AENE. There is expectance here from both the
　　sides,
What further you will do.
　　HECT.　　　　　　　We'll answer it,
The issue° is embracement. Ajax, farewell.
　　AJAX. If I might in entreaties find success —
As seld I have the chance — I would desire　150
My famous cousin to our Grecian tents.
　　DIO. 'Tis Agamemnon's wish, and great Achilles
Doth long to see unarmed the valiant Hector.
　　HECT. Aeneas, call my brother Troilus to me.
And signify this loving interview　　　　155
To the expecters° of our Trojan part,
Desire them home. Give me thy hand, my cousin.
I will go eat with thee, and see your knights.
　　AJAX. Great Agamemnon comes to meet us here.
　　HECT. The worthiest of them tell me name by
　　name,　　　　　　　　　　　　　　160
But for Achilles, my own searching eyes
Shall find him by his large and portly size.
　　AGAM. Worthy of arms! As welcome as to one
That would be rid of such an enemy,
But that's no welcome. Understand more clear　165
What's past and what's to come is strewed with
　　husks
And formless ruin of oblivion.°
But in this extant° moment, faith and troth,
Strained purely from all hollow bias-drawing,°
Bids thee, with most divine integrity,　　170
From heart of very heart, great Hector, welcome.
　　HECT. I thank thee, most imperious Agamemnon.

　　AGAM. [*To* TROILUS] My well-famed lord of Troy,
　　no less to you.
　　MEN. Let me confirm my princely brother's greet-
　　ing.
You brace of warlike brothers, welcome hither.　175
　　HECT. Who must we answer?
　　AENE.　　　　　　　　The noble Menelaus.
　　HECT. Oh, you, my lord! By Mars his gauntlet,
　　thanks!
Mock not that I affect the untraded° oath,
Your quondam° wife swears still by Venus' glove.
She's well, but bade me not commend her to you.
　　MEN. Name her not now, sir, she's a deadly theme.
　　HECT. Oh, pardon, I offend.　　　　　182
　　NEST. I have, thou gallant Trojan, seen thee oft,
Laboring for destiny,° make cruel way
Through ranks of Greekish youth. And I have seen
　　thee,　　　　　　　　　　　　　185
As hot as Perseus,° spur thy Phrygian steed,
Despising many forfeits and subduements,°
When thou hast hung° thy advancèd sword i' the
　　air,
Not letting it decline on the declined,
That I have said to some my standers-by　　190
"Lo, Jupiter is yonder, dealing life!"
And I have seen thee pause and take thy breath
When that a ring of Greeks have hemmed thee in,
Like an Olympian° wrestling. This have I seen.
But this thy countenance, still locked in steel,°　195
I never saw till now. I knew thy grandsire,
And once fought with him. He was a soldier good,
But, by great Mars the captain of us all,
Never like thee. Let an old man embrace thee,
And, worthy warrior, welcome to our tents.　200
　　AENE. 'Tis the old Nestor.
　　HECT. Let me embrace thee, good old chronicle,°
That hast so long walked hand in hand with time.
Most reverend Nestor, I am glad to clasp thee.
　　NEST. I would my arms could match thee in con-
　　tention,　　　　　　　　　　　　205
As they contend with thee in courtesy.
　　HECT. I would they could.
　　NEST. Ha!　　　　　　　　　　　　208
By his white beard, I'd fight with thee tomorrow.
Well, welcome, welcome! — I have seen the time.
　　ULYSS. I wonder now how yonder city stands,
When we have here her base and pillar by us.
　　HECT. I know your favor, Lord Ulysses, well.
Ah, sir, there's many a Greek and Trojan dead
Since first I saw yourself and Diomed　　215
In Ilion, on your Greekish embassy.

---

130. member: limb.　132. gainsay: forbid.　139. free: generous.　141. addition: honor.　142. Neoptolemus: son of Achilles,
but presumably Achilles is meant.　mirable: marvelous.
143. Oyes: Oyez (hear ye), the herald's warning to his hearers.　148. issue: end.　156. expecters: supporters; lit., those
who wait for news.　166–67. husks . . . oblivion: in time to
come nothing will be left but shapeless ruins.　168. extant: present.　169. bias-drawing: crooked dealing.

178. untraded: unusual.　179. quondam: former.　184. Laboring . . . destiny: working for Fate.　186. Perseus: See I.iii.
42,n.　187. forfeits . . . subduements: men vanquished who
have forfeited their lives.　188. hung: i.e., refrained from striking.　194. Olympian: god.　195. still . . . steel: always enclosed
in armor. See IV.v.s.d.,n (p. 1005a), and Pl. 8a.　202. chronicle:
i.e., record of the past.

ULYSS. Sir, I foretold you then what would ensue.
My prophecy is but half his journey yet,
For yonder walls that pertly front° your town,   219
Yond towers whose wanton tops do buss° the clouds,
Must kiss their own feet.
     HECT.   I must not believe you.
There they stand yet, and modestly I think
The fall of every Phrygian stone will cost
A drop of Grecian blood. The end crowns all,
And that old common arbitrator, Time,   225
Will one day end it.
     ULYSS.   So to him we leave it.
Most gentle and most valiant Hector, welcome.
After the General, I beseech you next
To feast with me and see me at my tent.
     ACHIL. I shall forestall thee, Lord Ulysses, thou!
Now, Hector, I have fed mine eyes on thee,   231
I have with exact view perused thee, Hector,
And quoted° joint by joint.
     HECT.   Is this Achilles?
     ACHIL. I am Achilles.   234
     HECT. Stand fair, I pray thee. Let me look on thee.
     ACHIL. Behold thy fill.
     HECT.   Nay, I have done already.
     ACHIL. Thou art too brief. I will the second time,
As I would buy thee, view thee limb by limb.
     HECT. Oh, like a book of sport thou'lt read me
       o'er,
But there's more in me than thou under-
       stand'st.   240
Why dost thou so oppress me with thine eye?
     ACHIL. Tell me, you Heavens, in which part of his
       body
Shall I destroy him? Whether there, or there, or
       there?
That I may give the local wound a name,
And make distinct the very breach whereout   245
Hector's great spirit flew. Answer me, Heavens!
     HECT. It would discredit the blest gods, proud
       man,
To answer such a question. Stand again.
Think'st thou to catch my life so pleasantly
As to prenominate° in nice conjecture   250
Where thou wilt hit me dead?
     ACHIL.   I tell thee yea.
     HECT. Wert thou an oracle to tell me so,
I'd not believe thee. Henceforth guard thee well,
For I'll not kill thee there, nor there, nor there,
But, by the forge that stithied° Mars his helm,   255
I'll kill thee everywhere — yea, o'er and o'er.
You wisest Grecians, pardon me this brag.
His insolence draws folly from my lips,
But I'll endeavor deeds to match these words,
Or may I never ——
     AJAX.   Do not chafe thee, Cousin.   260

And you, Achilles, let these threats alone
Till accident or purpose bring you to 't.
You may have every day enough of Hector,
If you have stomach. The general state, I fear,
Can scarce entreat you to be odd with him.°   265
     HECT. I pray you let us see you in the field.
We have had pelting° wars since you refused
The Grecians' cause.
     ACHIL.   Dost thou entreat me, Hector?
Tomorrow do I meet thee, fell° as death,
Tonight all friends.
     HECT.   Thy hand upon that match.   270
     AGAM. First, all you peers of Greece, go to my tent,
There in the full convive we.° Afterward,
As Hector's leisure and your bounties shall
Concur together, severally° entreat him.   274
Beat loud the tabourines,° let the trumpets blow,
That this great soldier may his welcome know.
           [*Exeunt all but* TROILUS *and* ULYSSES.]
     TRO. My Lord Ulysses, tell me, I beseech you,
In what place of the field doth Calchas keep?°
     ULYSS. At Menelaus' tent, most princely Troilus.
There Diomed doth feast with him tonight,   280
Who neither looks upon the heaven nor earth,
But gives all gaze and bent of amorous view
On the fair Cressid.
     TRO. Shall I, sweet lord, be bound to you so much,
After we part from Agamemnon's tent,   285
To bring me thither?
     ULYSS.   You shall command me, sir.
As gentle tell me, of what honor was
This Cressida in Troy? Had she no lover there
That wails her absence?
     TRO. Oh, sir, to such as boasting show their scars.
A mock is due. Will you walk on, my lord?   291
She was beloved, she loved; she is, and doth.
But still sweet love is food for fortune's tooth.
                               [*Exeunt.*]

Act V

SCENE I. *The Grecian camp. Before* ACHILLES'
tent.

[*Enter* ACHILLES *and* PATROCLUS.]
     ACHIL. I'll heat his blood with Greekish wine to-
       night,
Which with my scimitar I'll cool tomorrow.
Patroclus, let us feast him to the height.
     PATR. Here comes Thersites.

263–65. You . . . him: i.e., you can fight Hector any day you choose, but our army (*general state*) can hardly persuade you to come out.   267. pelting: paltry.   269. fell: fearful.   272. convive we: let us feast.   274. severally: individually.   275. tabourines: drums.   278. keep: lodge.

219. front: stand in front of.   220. buss: kiss.   233. quoted: noted.   250. prenominate: foretell.   255. stithied: forged.

[*Enter* THERSITES.]

ACHIL. How now, thou core° of envy!
Thou crusty batch° of nature, what's the news? 5

THER. Why, thou picture of what thou seemest,
and idol of idiot-worshipers, here's a letter for thee.

ACHIL. From whence, fragment?

THER. Why, thou full dish of fool, from Troy. 10

PATR. Who keeps the tent now?°

THER. The surgeon's box, or the patient's wound.°

PATR. Well said, adversity! And what needs these
tricks?

THER. Prithee be silent, boy, I profit not by thy
talk. Thou art thought to be Achilles' male varlet.

PATR. Male varlet, you rogue! What's that? 19

THER. Why, his masculine whore. Now the rotten
diseases of the south,° the guts-griping, ruptures,
catarrhs, loads o' gravel i' the back, lethargies, cold
palsies, raw eyes, dirt-rotten livers, wheezing lungs,
bladders full of imposthume,° sciaticas, limekilns i'
the palm,° incurable boneache, and the riveled fee
simple of the tetter,° take and take again such preposterous discoveries!° 28

PATR. Why, thou damnable box of envy thou,
what mean'st thou to curse thus?

THER. Do I curse thee?

PATR. Why, no, you ruinous butt,° you whoreson
indistinguishable° cur, no. 33

THER. No! Why art thou then exasperate, thou
idle immaterial skein of sleave silk, thou green sarcenet flap for a sore eye, thou tassel of a prodigal's
purse thou?° Ah, how the poor world is pestered
with such water flies,° diminutives of nature!

PATR. Out, gall! 40

THER. Finch-egg!°

ACHIL. My sweet Patroclus, I am thwarted quite
From my great purpose in tomorrow's battle.
Here is a letter from Queen Hecuba,
A token from her daughter, my fair love, 45
Both taxing° me and gaging° me to keep
An oath that I have sworn. I will not break it.
Fall Greeks, fail fame, honor or go or stay,
My major vow lies here, this I'll obey.
Come, come, Thersites, help to trim my tent. 50

This night in banqueting must all be spent.
Away, Patroclus!

[*Exeunt* ACHILLES *and* PATROCLUS.]

THER. With too much blood and too little brain,
these two may run mad, but if with too much brain
and too little blood they do, I'll be a curer 55
of madmen. Here's Agamemnon, an honest fellow
enough and one that loves quails,° but he has not so
much brain as earwax. And the goodly transformation of Jupiter there, his brother, the bull, the primitive statue and oblique° memorial of cuckolds, 60
a thrifty shoeing horn in a chain hanging at his
brother's leg — to what form but that he is should
wit larded° with malice and malice forced° with
wit turn him to? To an ass were nothing, he is both
ass and ox. To an ox were nothing, he is both 65
ox and ass. To be a dog, a mule, a cat, a fitchew,° a
toad, a lizard, an owl, a puttock,° or a herring without a rope, I would not care. But to be Menelaus! I
would conspire against destiny. Ask me not what I
would be if I were not Thersites, for I care not 70
to be the louse of a lazar,° so I were not Menelaus.
Hoy-day!° Spirits and fires!

[*Enter* HECTOR, TROILUS, AJAX, AGAMEMNON, ULYSSES,
NESTOR, MENELAUS, *and* DIOMEDES, *with lights.*]

AGAM. We go wrong, we go wrong.

AJAX. No, yonder 'tis,
There, where we see the lights.

HECT. I trouble you. 75

AJAX. No, not a whit.

[*Re-enter* ACHILLES.]

ULYSS. Here comes himself to guide you.

ACHIL. Welcome, brave Hector, welcome, Princes
all.

AGAM. So now, fair Prince of Troy, I bid good
night.
Ajax commands the guard to tend on you.

HECT. Thanks and good night to the Greeks' General. 80

MEN. Good night, my lord.

HECT. Good night, sweet Lord Menelaus.

THER. Sweet draught.° Sweet, quoth a'! Sweet
sink, sweet sewer.

ACHIL. Good night and welcome, both at once, to
those
That go or tarry. 85

AGAM. Good night.

[*Exeunt* AGAMEMNON *and* MENELAUS.]

ACHIL. Old Nestor tarries, and you too, Diomed,
Keep Hector company an hour or two.

DIO. I cannot, lord, I have important business
The tide° whereof is now. Good night, great Hector.

Act V, Sc. i: **4. core**: center of a boil. **5. crusty batch**:
overbaked loaf; i.e., black, hard, and bitter. **11. Who . . . now**:
i.e., the news that Thersites has a letter from Troy quickly
brings Achilles out of his tent. **12. The . . . wound**: Thersites
deliberately misunderstands tent as lint. See II.ii.16,n. **21. south**:
regarded as an unhealthy quarter. **24. imposthume**: abscess.
24–25. limekilns . . . palm: arthritis. **26–27. riveled . . . tetter**: permanent ownership (*fee simple*) of eruptions (*tetter*)
that pucker (*rivel*) the skin. **28. discoveries**: revelations.
32. ruinous butt: broken-down barrel. **33. indistinguishable**:
shapeless. **34–38. thou . . . thou**: Thersites now turns to curse
Patroclus's appearance. Patroclus is played as a dapper effeminate youth, prettily dressed in green silk. **sleave silk**: skein
of raw silk. **sarcenet**: fine soft silk. **39. water flies**: useless little
creatures that flit about. Cf. *Haml.*, V.ii.83. **41. Finch-egg**:
i.e., little smooth thing. **46. taxing**: blaming. **gaging**: pledging.

57. quails: courtesans. **60. oblique**: indirect, symbolic.
63. larded: basted. **forced**: stuffed. **66. fitchew**: polecat. **67. puttock**: kite. **71. lazar**: leper. **72. Hoy-day**: an exclamation
of surprise, as he sees lights approaching. **82. draught**: privy.
90. tide: decisive moment.

HECT. Give me your hand.   91

ULYSS. [*Aside to* TROILUS] Follow his torch, he goes to Calchas' tent.

I'll keep you company.

TRO.   Sweet sir, you honor me.

HECT. And so good night.

[*Exit* DIOMEDES; ULYSSES *and* TROILUS *following.*]

ACHIL. Come, come, enter my tent.   94

[*Exeunt* ACHILLES, HECTOR, AJAX, *and* NESTOR.]

THER. That same Diomed's a false-hearted rogue, a most unjust knave. I will no more trust him when he leers than I will a serpent when he hisses. He will spend his mouth° and promise, like Brabbler the hound, but when he performs, astronomers 100 foretell it.° It is prodigious,° there will come some change,° the sun borrows of the moon when Diomed keeps his word. I will rather leave to see° Hector than not to dog him. They say he keeps a Trojan drab and uses the traitor Calchas' tent. I'll after. Nothing but lechery! All incontinent varlets! 106

[*Exit.*]

SCENE II. *The same. Before* CALCHAS' *tent.*

[*Enter* DIOMEDES.]

DIO. What, are you up here, ho? Speak.

CAL. [*Within*] Who calls?

DIO. Diomed. Calchas, I think. Where's your daughter?

CAL. [*Within*] She comes to you.

[*Enter* TROILUS *and* ULYSSES, *at a distance; after them,* THERSITES.]

ULYSS. Stand where the torch may not discover us.

[*Enter* CRESSIDA.]

TRO. Cressid comes forth to him.   6

DIO.   How now, my charge!

CRES. Now, my sweet guardian! Hark, a word with you.   [*Whispers.*]

TRO. Yea, so familiar!

ULYSS. She will sing any man at first sight.

THER. And any man may sing her, if he can take her cliff.° She's noted.°   11

DIO. Will you remember?

CRES. Remember! Yes.

DIO. Nay, but do, then, And let your mind be coupled with your words. 15

TRO. What should she remember?

ULYSS. List.

CRES. Sweet honey Greek, tempt me no more to folly.

THER. Roguery!

DIO. Nay, then ——

CRES. I'll tell you what ——

DIO. Foh, foh! Come, tell a pin.° You are forsworn.

CRES. In faith, I cannot. What would you have me do?

THER. A juggling trick — to be secretly open.

DIO. What did you swear you would bestow on me?   25

CRES. I prithee do not hold me to mine oath. Bid me do anything but that, sweet Greek.

DIO. Good night.

TRO. Hold, patience!

ULYSS. How now, Trojan!   30

CRES. Diomed ——

DIO. No, no, good night. I'll be your fool no more.

TRO. Thy better° must.

CRES. Hark, one word in your ear.

TRO. Oh, plague and madness!   35

ULYSS. You are moved, Prince. Let us depart, I pray you, Lest your displeasure should enlarge itself To wrathful terms. This place is dangerous, The time right deadly. I beseech you, go.

TRO. Behold, I pray you!

ULYSS.   Nay, good my lord, go off. 40 You flow to great distraction.° Come, my lord.

TRO. I pray thee stay.

ULYSS.   You have not patience, come.

TRO. I pray you stay. By Hell and all Hell's torments, I will not speak a word.

DIO.   And so good night.

CRES. Nay, but you part in anger.

TRO.   Doth that grieve thee? 45 Oh, withered truth!

ULYSS.   Why, how now, lord!

TRO.   By Jove, I will be patient.

CRES.   Guardian! — Why, Greek!

DIO. Foh, foh! Adieu, you palter.

CRES. In faith, I do not. Come hither once again.

ULYSS. You shake, my lord, at something. Will you go?   50 You will break out.

TRO.   She strokes his cheek!

ULYSS.   Come, come.

TRO. Nay, stay, by Jove. I will not speak a word. There is between my will and all offenses A guard of patience. Stay a little while.   54

THER. How the devil luxury,° with his fat rump and potato finger,° tickles these together! Fry, lechery, fry!

DIO. But will you, then?

---

99. spend . . . mouth: bark.   100–01. astronomers . . . it: astrologers prophesy it. See App. 2.   101. prodigious: an omen. 102. change: revolution.   103. leave to see: lose seeing. Sc. ii: 11. cliff: clef, a key in music. noted: observed, with a pun on musical notes.

22. pin: trifle.   33. better: i.e., Troilus.   41. distraction: agitation.   55. luxury: lechery.   56. potato finger: The sweet potato was supposed to provoke lust.

CRES. In faith, I will, la. Never trust me else.
DIO. Give me some token for the surety of it.   60
CRES. I'll fetch you one.   [*Exit.*]
ULYSS. You have sworn patience.
TRO.   Fear me not, sweet lord.
I will not be myself, nor have cognition
Of what I feel. I am all patience.
[*Re-enter* CRESSIDA.] Now the pledge, now, now,
    now!   65
    CRES. Here, Diomed, keep this sleeve.
TRO. O beauty! Where is thy faith?
ULYSS.   My lord——
TRO. I will be patient, outwardly I will.
CRES. You look upon that sleeve, behold it well.
He loved me. — O false wench! — Give 't me
    again.   70
    DIO. Whose was 't?
CRES. It is no matter, now I have 't again.
I will not meet with you tomorrow night.
I prithee, Diomed, visit me no more.   74
    THER. Now she sharpens. Well said, whetstone!
DIO. I shall have it.
CRES.   What, this?
DIO.   Aye, that.
CRES. Oh, all you gods! O pretty, pretty pledge!
Thy master now lies thinking in his bed
Of thee and me, and sighs, and takes my glove,
And gives memorial dainty kisses to it,   80
As I kiss thee. Nay, do not snatch it from me.
He that takes that doth take my heart withal.
    DIO. I had your heart before, this follows it.
TRO. I did swear patience.
CRES. You shall not have it, Diomed, faith, you
    shall not.   85
I'll give you something else.
    DIO. I will have this. Whose was it?
CRES.   It is no matter.
DIO. Come, tell me whose it was.
CRES. 'Twas one's that loved me better than you
    will.
But now you have it, take it.
    DIO.   Whose was it?   90
CRES. By all Diana's waiting women° yond,
And by herself, I will not tell you whose.
    DIO. Tomorrow will I wear it on my helm,
And grieve his spirit that dares not challenge it.
    TRO. Wert thou the Devil, and worest it on thy
    horn,   95
It should be challenged.
    CRES. Well, well, 'tis done, 'tis past. And yet it is
    not.
I will not keep my word.
    DIO.   Why then, farewell.
Thou never shalt mock Diomed again.   99
    CRES. You shall not go. One cannot speak a word
But it straight starts you.

91. **waiting women:** i.e., the stars. Diana being the moon.

DIO.   I do not like this fooling.
THER. Nor I, by Pluto. But that that likes° not
you pleases me best.
    DIO.   What, shall I come? The hour?
CRES. Aye, come. O Jove! Do come. I shall be
    plagued.   105
    DIO. Farewell till then.
CRES.   Good night. I prithee come.
                              [*Exit* DIOMEDES.]
Troilus, farewell! One eye yet looks on thee,
But with my heart the other eye doth see.
Ah, poor our sex! This fault in us I find,
The error of our eye directs our mind.   110
What error leads must err. Oh, then conclude
Minds swayed by eyes are full of turpitude.   [*Exit.*]
    THER. A proof of strength she could not publish
    more
Unless she said " My mind is now turned whore."
    ULYSS. All's done, my lord.
TRO.   It is.
ULYSS.   Why stay we, then?
TRO. To make a recordation to° my soul   116
Of every syllable that here was spoke.
But if I tell how these two did coact,
Shall I not lie in publishing a truth?
Sith° yet there is a credence in my heart,   120
An esperance° so obstinately strong
That doth invert the attest° of eyes and ears,
As if those organs had deceptious functions,
Created only to calumniate.
Was Cressid here?
    ULYSS.   I cannot conjure,° Trojan.   125
TRO. She was not, sure.
ULYSS.   Most sure she was.
TRO. Why, my negation hath no taste of madness.°
ULYSS. Nor mine, my lord. Cressid was here but
    now.
    TRO. Let it not be believed for womanhood!
Think, we had mothers. Do not give advantage   130
To stubborn critics, apt without a theme
For depravation, to square° the general sex
By Cressid's rule.° Rather think this not Cressid.
    ULYSS. What hath she done, Prince, that can soil
    our mothers?
    TRO. Nothing at all, unless that this were she.   135
    THER. Will a' swagger himself out on 's own eyes?
TRO. This she? No, this is Diomed's Cressida.
If beauty have a soul, this is not she.
If souls guide vows, if vows be sanctimonies,
If sanctimony be the gods' delight,   140
If there be rule in unity itself,
This is not she. Oh, madness of discourse

102. **likes:** pleases.   116. **recordation to:** remembrance in-
120. **Sith:** since.   121. **esperance:** hope.   122. **invert ... attest:** refuse to believe the evidence.   125. **I ... conjure:** i.e.,
these were not spirits.   127. **negation ... madness:** my
denial has no taint of madness; i.e., I am not mad **to deny it**
132. **square:** measure.   133. **rule:** carpenter's rule.

That cause sets up with and against itself!
Bifold authority! Where reason can revolt
Without perdition, and loss assume all reason   145
Without revolt.° This is, and is not, Cressid!
Within my soul there doth conduce a fight
Of this strange nature, that a thing inseparate°
Divides more wider than the sky and earth,
And yet the spacious breadth of this division   150
Admits no orifex° for a point as subtle
As Ariachne's broken woof° to enter.
Instance,° oh instance, strong as Pluto's gates,
Cressid is mine, tied with the bonds of Heaven.
Instance, oh instance, strong as Heaven itself,   155
The bonds of Heaven are slipped, dissolved, and
    loosed,
And with another knot, five-finger-tied,
The fractions of her faith, orts° of her love,
The fragments, scraps, the bits and greasy relics
Of her o'ereaten° faith, are bound to Diomed.   160
  ULYSS. May worthy Troilus be half attached
With° that which here his passion doth express?
  TRO. Aye, Greek, and that shall be divulgèd well
In characters as red as Mars his heart
Inflamed with Venus. Never did young man fancy
With so eternal and so fixed a soul.   166
Hark, Greek. As much as I do Cressid love,
So much by weight hate I her Diomed.
That sleeve is mine that he'll bear on his helm.
Were it a casque° composed by Vulcan's skill,   170
My sword should bite it. Not the dreadful spout°
Which shipmen do the hurricano call,
Constringed in mass° by the almighty sun,
Shall dizzy with more clamor Neptune's ear
In his descent than shall my prompted sword   175
Falling on Diomed.
  THER. He'll tickle it for his concupy.°
  TRO. O Cressid! O false Cressid! False, false, false!
Let all untruths stand by thy stainèd name,
And they'll seem glorious.
  ULYSS.   Oh, contain yourself.   180
Your passion draws ears hither.
            [*Enter* AENEAS.]
  AENE. I have been seeking you this hour, my lord.
Hector by this is arming him in Troy,
Ajax your guard stays to conduct you home.
  TRO. Have with you, Prince. My courteous lord,
    adieu.   185

142–46. Oh . . . revolt: a mad argument that is at the same time
for and against itself. Divided authority where reason can
turn against itself without becoming madness, and destruction
(*loss*) become reasonable; i.e., it is both reasonable and insane to believe or to disbelieve what I have seen. 148. insepa-
rate: inseparable. 151. orifex: point of entry. 152. Ariachne's
. . . woof: the thread of a spider's web. Ariachne for Arachne,
who was turned into a spider. 153. Instance: proof. 158. orts:
scraps. 160. o'ereaten: overeaten, gorged. 161–62. attached
With: affected by. 170. casque: helmet. 171. spout: water-
spout. 173. Constringed in mass: drawn together. 177. He'll
. . . concupy: he'll be tickled for his lust.

Farewell, revolted fair! And, Diomed,
Stand fast, and wear a castle on thy head!°
  ULYSS. I'll bring you to the gates.
  TRO. Accept distracted thanks.   189
    [*Exeunt* TROILUS, AENEAS, *and* ULYSSES.]
  THER. Would I could meet that rogue Diomed! I
would croak like a raven, I would bode,° I would
bode. Patroclus will give me anything for the intelligence of this whore. The parrot will not do more
for an almond° than he for a commodious° drab.
Lechery, lechery! Still wars and lechery! Nothing
else holds fashion. A burning devil take them! 197
                                     [*Exit.*]

SCENE III. *Troy. Before* PRIAM'S *palace.*

    [*Enter* HECTOR *and* ANDROMACHE.]
  AND. When was my lord so much ungently tem-
    pered
To stop his ears against admonishment?
Unarm, unarm, and do not fight today.
  HECT. You train° me to offend you, get you in.
By all the everlasting gods, I'll go!   5
  AND. My dreams will sure prove ominous to the
    day.
  HECT. No more, I say.
           [*Enter* CASSANDRA.]
  CAS.   Where is my brother Hector?
  AND. Here, Sister, armed, and bloody in intent.
Consort with me in loud and dear petition,
Pursue we him on knees, for I have dreamed   10
Of bloody turbulence, and this whole night
Hath nothing been but shapes and forms of slaugh-
    ter.
  CAS. Oh, 'tis true.
  HECT.   Ho! Bid my trumpet sound!
  CAS. No notes of sally, for the Heavens, sweet
    Brother.
  HECT. Be gone, I say. The gods have heard me
    swear.   15
  CAS. The gods are deaf to hot and peevish° vows.
They are polluted offerings, more abhorred
Than spotted livers in the sacrifice.
  AND. Oh, be persuaded! Do not count it holy
To hurt by being just. It is as lawful,   20
For we would give much, to use violent **thefts**
And rob in the behalf of charity.
  CAS. It is the purpose that makes strong the vow.
But vows to every purpose must not hold.
Unarm, sweet Hector.
  HECT.   Hold you still, I say.   25

187. wear . . . head: i.e., nothing less than a castle will protect
you. 191. bode: prophesy disaster. 194–95. parrot . . . almond: The love of parrots for almonds is proverbial. 195. com-
modious: accommodating.
    Sc. iii: 4. train: encourage. 16. peevish: obstinate.

Mine honor keeps the weather of° my fate.
Life every man holds dear, but the dear man
Holds honor far more precious-dear than life.
[*Enter* TROILUS.] How now, young man! Mean'st
    thou to fight today?
    AND. Cassandra, call my father to persuade.   30
                        [*Exit* CASSANDRA.]
    HECT. No, faith, young Troilus. Doff thy harness,
    youth.
I am today i' the vein of chivalry.°
Let grow thy sinews till their knots be strong,
And tempt not yet the brushes of the war.
Unarm thee, go, and doubt thou not, brave boy,   35
I'll stand today for thee and me and Troy.
    TRO. Brother, you have a vice of mercy in you
Which better fits a lion than a man.
    HECT. What vice is that, good Troilus? Chide me
    for it.
    TRO. When many times the captive Grecian falls,
Even in the fan and wind of your fair sword,   41
You bid them rise and live.
    HECT. Oh, 'tis fair play.
    TRO.   Fool's play, by Heaven, Hector.
    HECT. How now! How now!
    TRO.   For the love of all the gods,
Let's leave the hermit pity with our mother,   45
And when we have our armors buckled on,
The venomed vengeance ride upon our swords,
Spur them to ruthful work,° rein them from ruth!
    HECT. Fie, savage, fie!
    TRO.   Hector, then 'tis wars.
    HECT. Troilus, I would not have you fight today.
    TRO. Who should withhold me?   51
Not fate, obedience, nor the hand of Mars
Beckoning with fiery truncheon my retire —
Not Priamus and Hecuba on knees,
Their eyes o'ergallèd° with recourse° of tears;   55
Nor you, my brother, with your true sword
    drawn —
Opposed to hinder me should stop my way
But by my ruin.
    [*Re-enter* CASSANDRA, *with* PRIAM.]
    CAS. Lay hold upon him, Priam, hold him fast.
He is thy crutch. Now if thou lose thy stay,   60
Thou on him leaning and all Troy on thee,
Fall all together.
    PRI.   Come, Hector, come, go back.
Thy wife hath dreamed, thy mother hath had vi-
    sions,
Cassandra doth foresee, and I myself
Am like a prophet suddenly enrapt,°   65
To tell thee that this day is ominous.
Therefore, come back.

    HECT.   Aeneas is afield,
And I do stand engaged° to many Greeks,
Even in the faith of valor, to appear
This morning to them.
    PRI.   Aye, but thou shalt not go.   70
    HECT. I must not break my faith.
You know me dutiful, therefore, dear sir,
Let me not shame respect, but give me leave
To take that course by your consent and voice
Which you do here forbid me, royal Priam.   75
    CAS. O Priam, yield not to him!
    AND.   Do not, dear Father.
    HECT. Andromache, I am offended with you.
Upon the love you bear me, get you in.
                    [*Exit* ANDROMACHE.]
    TRO. This foolish, dreaming, superstitious girl
Makes all these bodements.°
    CAS.   Oh, farewell, dear Hector!   80
Look how thou diest! Look how thy eye turns pale!
Look how thy wounds do bleed at many vents!°
Hark how Troy roars, how Hecuba cries out!
How poor Andromache shrills her dolors forth!
Behold, distraction, frenzy, and amazement,   85
Like witless antics,° one another meet,
And all cry "Hector! Hector's dead! Oh, Hector!"
    TRO. Away! Away!
    CAS. Farewell. Yet, soft! Hector, I take my leave.
Thou dost thyself and all our Troy deceive.   [*Exit.*]
    HECT. You are amazed, my liege, at her exclaim.
Go in and cheer the town. We'll forth and fight,
Do deeds worth praise and tell you them at night.
    PRI. Farewell. The gods with safety stand about
    thee!
    [*Exeunt severally*° PRIAM *and* HECTOR.
                             Alarum.]
    TRO. They are at it, hark! Proud Diomed, believe,
I come to lose my arm or win my sleeve.   96
            [*Enter* PANDARUS.]
    PAN. Do you hear, my lord? Do you hear?
    TRO. What now?
    PAN. Here's a letter come from yond poor girl.
    TRO. Let me read.   100
    PAN. A whoreson tisick,° a whoreson rascally
tisick so troubles me, and the foolish fortune of this
girl; and what one thing, what another, that I shall
leave you one o' these days. And I have a rheum in
mine eyes too, and such an ache in my bones that,
unless a man were cursed, I cannot tell what to think
on 't. What says she there?   107
    TRO. Words, words, mere words, no matter from
    the heart.
The effect doth operate another way.
                  [*Tearing the letter*]
Go, wind, to wind, there turn and change together.

---

26. keeps . . . of: has the advantage of.   32. i' . . . chivalry:
i.e., fighting for honor.   48. ruthful work: work that will rouse
pity; i.e., be ruthless.   55. o'ergalled: inflamed. recourse:
flowing.   65. enrapt: inspired.

68. engaged: pledged.   80. bodements: gloomy prophecies.
82. vents: openings.   86. antics: buffoons.   94 s.d. severally:
by different exits.   101. tisick: cough.

My love with words and errors still she feeds,   **111**
But edifies another with her deeds.

                   [*Exeunt severally.*]

SCENE IV. *The field between Troy and the Grecian camp.*

[*Alarums. Excursions. Enter* THERSITES.]

THER. Now they are clapper-clawing° one another. I'll go look on. That dissembling abominable varlet Diomed has got that same scurvy doting foolish young knave's sleeve of Troy there in his helm. I would fain see them meet, that that same young **5** Trojan ass, that loves the whore there, might send that Greekish whoremasterly villain with the sleeve back to the dissembling luxurious drab, of a sleeveless° errand. O' the t'other side, the policy of those crafty swearing rascals, that stale old mouse- **10** eaten dry cheese Nestor, and that same dog fox Ulysses, is not proved worth a blackberry. They set me up in policy° that mongrel cur Ajax against that dog of as bad a kind, Achilles. And now is the cur Ajax prouder than the cur Achilles, and will **15** not arm today, whereupon the Grecians begin to proclaim barbarism,° and policy grows into an ill opinion.° Soft! Here comes sleeve, and t'other.

[*Enter* DIOMEDES *and* TROILUS.]

TRO. Fly not, for shouldst thou take the river Styx, I would swim after.

DIO.   Thou dost miscall retire.   **21**
I do not fly, but advantageous care
Withdrew me from the odds of multitude.
Have at thee!   **24**

THER. Hold thy whore, Grecian! Now for thy whore, Trojan! Now the sleeve, now the sleeve!

     [*Exeunt* TROILUS *and* DIOMEDES, *fighting.*]
          [*Enter* HECTOR.]

HECT. What art thou, Greek? Art thou for Hector's match?
Art thou of blood and honor?   **29**

THER. No, no, I am a rascal,° a scurvy railing knave, a very filthy rogue.

HECT. I do believe thee. Live.   [*Exit.*]

THER. God-a-mercy° that thou wilt believe me, but a plague break thy neck for frighting me! What's become of the wenching rogues? I think they have swallowed one another. I would laugh at that miracle — yet in a sort lechery eats itself. I'll seek **37** them.   [*Exit.*]

SCENE V. *Another part of the field.*

[*Enter* DIOMEDES *and* SERVANT.]

DIO. Go, go, my servant, take thou Troilus' horse,
Present the fair steed to my Lady Cressid.
Fellow, commend my service to her beauty.
Tell her I have chastised the amorous Trojan,
And am her knight by proof.

SERV.   I go, my lord. [*Exit.*]   **5**
            [*Enter* AGAMEMNON.]

AGAM. Renew, renew! The fierce Polydamas
Hath beat down Menon. Bastard Margarelon
Hath Doreus prisoner,
And stands colossus-wise,° waving his beam,°
Upon the pashed corses° of the kings   **10**
Epistrophus and Cedius. Polyxenes is slain,
Amphimachus and Thoas deadly hurt,
Patroclus ta'en or slain, and Palamedes
Sore hurt and bruised. The dreadful sagittary°
Appals our numbers. Haste we, Diomed,   **15**
To reinforcement, or we perish all.
            [*Enter* NESTOR.]

NEST. Go, bear Patroclus' body to Achilles,
And bid the snail-paced Ajax arm for shame.
There is a thousand Hectors in the field.
Now here he fights on Galathe his horse,   **20**
And there lacks work. Anon he's there afoot,
And there they fly or die, like scalèd sculls°
Before the belching whale. Then is he yonder,
And there the strawy° Greeks, ripe for his edge,
Fall down before him like the mower's swath. **25**
Here, there, and everywhere he leaves and takes,
Dexterity so obeying appetite
That what he will he does, and does so much
That proof is called impossibility.
           [*Enter* ULYSSES.]

ULYSS. Oh, courage, courage, Princes! Great Achilles   **30**
Is arming, weeping, cursing, vowing vengeance.
Patroclus' wounds have roused his drowsy blood,
Together with his mangled Myrmidons,°
That noseless, handless, hacked and chipped, come to him,
Crying on Hector. Ajax hath lost a friend,   **35**
And foams at mouth, and he is armed, and at it,
Roaring for Troilus, who hath done today
Mad and fantastic execution,
Engaging and redeeming of himself
With such a careless force and forceless care **40**
As if that luck, in very spite of cunning,
Bade him win all.

Sc. iv: **1. clapper-clawing:** scratching and clawing. **9. sleeveless:** futile. **12–13. set . . . policy:** thought it a clever plan to support. **17. proclaim barbarism:** declare that ignorance is preferable. **17–18. policy . . . opinion:** cleverness gets a bad name. **30. rascal:** lit., a deer in poor condition. **33. God-a-mercy:** thank God.

Sc. v: **9. colossus-wise:** See *Caesar*, I.ii.135–38. **beam:** huge spear. **10. pashed corses:** mangled corpses. **14. sagittary:** a centaur, half man, half horse, who helped the Trojans. **22. scalèd sculls:** shoals of scaly fish. **24. strawy:** weak as straw. **33. Myrmidons:** Achilles' followers.

[*Enter* AJAX.]

AJAX. Troilus! Thou coward Troilus!   [*Exit.*]

DIO.   Aye, there, there.

NEST. So, so, we draw together.

       [*Enter* ACHILLES.]

ACHIL.   Where is this Hector?

Come, come, thou boy-queller,° show thy face,   45

Know what it is to meet Achilles angry.

Hector! Where's Hector? I will none but Hector.

                    [*Exeunt.*]

SCENE VI. *Another part of the field.*

[*Enter* AJAX.]

AJAX. Troilus, thou coward Troilus, show thy
head!

       [*Enter* DIOMEDES.]

DIO. Troilus, I say! Where's Troilus?

AJAX.   What wouldst thou?

DIO. I would correct him.

AJAX. Were I the General, thou shouldst have my
office

Ere that correction.° Troilus, I say! What, Troilus! 5

       [*Enter* TROILUS.]

TRO. O traitor Diomed! Turn thy false face, thou
traitor,

And pay thy life thou owest me for my horse.

DIO. Ha, art thou there?

AJAX. I'll fight with him alone. Stand, Diomed.

DIO. He is my prize, I will not look upon.   10

TRO. Come both, you cogging° Greeks, have at
you both!   [*Exeunt, fighting.*]

       [*Enter* HECTOR.]

HECT. Yea, Troilus? Oh, well fought, my youngest brother!

       [*Enter* ACHILLES.]

ACHIL. Now do I see thee, ha! Have at thee, Hector!

HECT. Pause, if thou wilt.

ACHIL. I do disdain thy courtesy, proud Trojan.

Be happy that my arms are out of use.   16

My rest and negligence befriends thee now,

But thou anon shalt hear of me again.

Till when, go seek thy fortune.   [*Exit.*]

HECT.   Fare thee well.

I would have been much more a fresher man   20

Had I expected thee.

[*Re-enter* TROILUS.] How now, my brother!

TRO. Ajax hath ta'en Aeneas. Shall it be?

No, by the flame of yonder glorious heaven,

He shall not carry him. I'll be ta'en too,

Or bring him off.° Fate, hear me what I say!   25

I reck not though I end my life today.   [*Exit.*]

   [*Enter one in sumptuous armor.*]

HECT. Stand, stand, thou Greek, thou art a goodly
mark.

No? Wilt thou not? I like thy armor well.

I'll frush° it, and unlock the rivets all,   29

But I'll be master of it. Wilt thou not, beast, abide?

Why then, fly on, I'll hunt thee for thy hide.

                   [*Exeunt.*]

SCENE VII. *Another part of the field.*

[*Enter* ACHILLES, *with* MYRMIDONS.]

ACHIL. Come here about me, you my Myrmidons,

Mark what I say. Attend me where I wheel.

Strike not a stroke, but keep yourselves in breath.

And when I have the bloody Hector found,

Empale° him with your weapons round about,   5

In fellest manner execute your aims.

Follow me, sirs, and my proceedings eye.

It is decreed Hector the great must die.   [*Exeunt.*]

   [*Enter* MENELAUS *and* PARIS, *fighting: then*
THERSITES.]

THER. The cuckold and the cuckold-maker are at
it. Now, bull! Now, dog! 'Loo,° Paris, 'loo! Now,
my double-henned sparrow! 'Loo, Paris, 'loo! The
bull has the game. Ware horns, ho!   12

   [*Exeunt* PARIS *and* MENELAUS.]

     [*Enter* MARGARELON.]

MAR. Turn, slave, and fight.

THER. What art thou?

MAR. A bastard son of Priam's.   15

THER. I am a bastard too, I love bastards. I am a
bastard begot, bastard instructed, bastard in mind,
bastard in valor, in everything illegitimate. One bear
will not bite another, and wherefore should one bastard? Take heed, the quarrel's most ominous to us.
If the son of a whore fight for a whore, he tempts
judgment. Farewell, bastard.   [*Exit.*]

MAR. The Devil take thee, coward!   [*Exit.*]

SCENE VIII. *Another part of the field.*

[*Enter* HECTOR.]

HECT. Most putrefied core, so fair without,

Thy goodly armor thus hath cost thy life.

Now is my day's work done. I'll take good breath.

Rest, sword, thou hast thy fill of blood and death.

       [*Puts off his helmet and hangs
his shield behind him.*]

---

45. boy-queller: boy-killer, because he has killed Patroclus.
   Sc. vi: 5. Ere . . . correction: before you should take from
me the privilege of correcting him.   **11. cogging:** cheating.
25. bring . . . off: rescue him.

29. frush: bruise.
   Sc. vii: 5. Empale: hedge in.   **10. Now . . . 'Loo:** Thersites
shouts encouragement as if a spectator in the bullring. See
App. 5.

[*Enter* ACHILLES *and* MYRMIDONS.]

ACHIL. Look, Hector, how the sun begins to set,
How ugly night comes breathing at his heels.   6
Even with the vail° and darking of the sun
To close the day up, Hector's life is done.
   HECT. I am unarmed, forgo this vantage, Greek.
   ACHIL. Strike, fellows, strike, this is the man I
     seek.   [HECTOR *falls.*]
So, Ilion, fall thou next! Now, Troy, sink down!
Here lies thy heart, thy sinews, and thy bone.   12
On, Myrmidons, and cry you all amain,
"Achilles hath the mighty Hector slain."
                [*A retire sounded*]
Hark! A retire upon our Grecian part.   15
   MYR. The Trojan trumpets sound the like, my
     lord.
   ACHIL. The dragon wing of night o'erspreads the
     earth,
And stickler-like° the armies separates.
My half-supped sword that frankly would have fed,
Pleased with this dainty bait, thus goes to bed.   20
              [*Sheathes his sword.*]
Come, tie his body to my horse's tail.
Along the field I will the Trojan trail.
         [*Exeunt. A retreat sounded.*]

SCENE IX. *Another part of the field.*

[*Enter* AGAMEMNON, AJAX, MENELAUS, NESTOR,
DIOMEDES, *and the rest, marching. Shouts within.*]

   AGAM. Hark! Hark! What shout is that?
   NEST. Peace, drums!
[*Within*] "Achilles! Achilles! Hector's slain!
     Achilles!"
   DIO. The bruit° is Hector's slain, and by Achilles.
   AJAX. If it be so, yet bragless let it be,   5
Great Hector was a man as good as he.
   AGAM. March patiently along. Let one be sent
To pray Achilles see us at our tent.
If in his death the gods have us befriended,   9
Great Troy is ours, and our sharp wars are ended.
            [*Exeunt, marching.*]

SCENE X. *Another part of the field.*

[*Enter* AENEAS, PARIS, ANTENOR, *and* DEIPHOBUS.]

   AENE. Stand, ho! Yet are we masters of the field.
Never go home, here starve we out the night.

Sc. viii: 7. **vail:** lowering.   18. **stickler-like:** The *stickler*
was the umpire who intervened in a friendly combat.
Sc. ix: 4. **bruit:** rumor.

[*Enter* TROILUS.]

   TRO. Hector is slain.
   ALL.   Hector! The gods forbid!
   TRO. He's dead, and at the murderer's horse's tail
In beastly sort dragged through the shameful field.
Frown on, you Heavens, effect your rage with speed!
Sit, gods, upon your thrones, and smile at Troy!   7
I say, at once let your brief plagues be mercy,
And linger not our sure destructions on!
   AENE. My lord, you do discomfort all the host.   10
   TRO. You understand me not that tell me so.
I do not speak of flight, of fear, of death,
But dare all imminence° that gods and men
Address° their dangers in. Hector is gone.
Who shall tell Priam so, or Hecuba?   15
Let him that will a screech owl aye° be called
Go in to Troy, and say there "Hector's dead."
There is a word will Priam turn to stone,
Make wells and Niobes° of the maids and wives,
Cold statues of the youth, and, in a word,   20
Scare Troy out of itself. But march away.
Hector is dead, there is no more to say.
Stay yet. You vile abominable tents,
Thus proudly pight° upon our Phrygian plains,
Let Titan° rise as early as he dare,   25
I'll through and through you! And, thou great-sized
     coward,
No space of earth shall sunder our two hates.
I'll haunt thee like a wicked conscience still,°
That moldeth goblins swift as frenzy's thoughts.
Strike a free march to Troy! With comfort go.   30
Hope of revenge shall hide our inward woe.
        [*Exeunt* AENEAS *and* TROJANS.]
[*As* TROILUS *is going out, enter, from the other side,*
     PANDARUS.]

   PAN. But hear you, hear you!
   TRO. Hence, broker lackey! Ignomy and shame
Pursue thy life, and live aye with thy name!   [*Exit.*]
   PAN. A goodly medicine for my aching bones! O
world, world, world! Thus is the poor agent de-
spised! O traitors and bawds, how earnestly are you
set a-work, and how ill requited! Why should our
endeavor be so loved and the performance so
loathed? What verse for it? What instance for it?
Let me see: 41
   "Full merrily the humblebee doth sing
     Till he hath lost his honey and his sting,
     And being once subdued in armèd tail,
     Sweet honey and sweet notes together fail."   45
Good traders in the flesh, set this in your painted
cloths:°
   "As many as be here of Pandar's hall,

Sc. x: 13. **imminence:** impending evil.   14. **Address:** make
ready.   16. **aye:** always.   19. **Niobe:** She wept so grievously
for her dead children that she was turned into a stone fountain.
24. **pight:** pitched.   25. **Titan:** the sun.   28. **still:** always.
46-47. **painted cloths:** imitation tapestry, painted with Scriptural or allegorical scenes. See Pl. 6a.

Your eyes, half out, weep out at Pandar's fall.
Or if you cannot weep, yet give some groans,   50
Though not for me, yet for your aching bones.
Brethren and sisters of the hold-door trade,
Some two months hence my will shall here be
   made.
It should be now, but that my fear is this —

Some gallèd° goose of Winchester° would hiss.
Till then I'll sweat and seek about for eases,   56
And at that time bequeath you my diseases."

                       [*Exit.*]

55. **galled:** sore. **goose of Winchester:** prostitute. Prostitutes were called "Winchester geese" because they inhabited property in Southwark owned by the Bishop of Winchester.

ALL'S WELL THAT ENDS WELL

Introduction

All's Well That Ends Well was originally printed in the first folio (F1) in 1623. There are some difficulties in the text; a few essential stage directions have been omitted, and there is inconsistency in the names given to persons in the speech headings. It may be that the printer had for copy an original manuscript which — unlike the best texts in F1 — was not adequately edited or prepared for the press.

The play seems never to have been popular; scholars have found no contemporary mention or quotation. There is, therefore, no external fact by which the date of writing can be determined, nor is there any topical allusion or other clue within the play itself. The style is uneven, but in the best passages, both verse and prose, there is a maturity which shows that the play was written in the latter half of Shakespeare's career. It is usual to set *All's Well* alongside *Measure for Measure* (partly, it must be admitted, because both plays include the "bed trick" whereby a reluctant husband is cheated into giving his wife her due rights) and to assign as a date "somewhere between 1601 and 1604."

The source of *All's Well* is a story in Boccaccio's *Decameron,* reproduced and translated in an English version in William Painter's *Palace of Pleasure,* 1566. The story runs as follows:

A French nobleman, called Isnardo, Count of Rossiglione, was sickly and maintained in his household a physician named Gerado of Narbona. The Count had an only son called Beltramo, who was brought up with other children of his own age, among whom was the physician's daughter, Giletta, "who fervently fell in love with Beltramo, more than was meet for a maiden of her age."

When Count Isnardo died, Beltramo was left in the custody of the King and was sent to Paris, whither Giletta was unable to follow him. But at length she heard that the King was suffering from a most painful fistula on his breast which no physician could cure. Giletta therefore determined to try to heal the King by using some of the knowledge that she had learned from her father. She journeyed to Paris and with great difficulty at last persuaded the King to allow her to try the cure. As a reward for her success she asked for Beltramo as her husband. The King agreed; Beltramo was very angry, but he dared not refuse.

As soon as the marriage had been celebrated, Beltramo, pretending that he was going home, made off to Tuscany where he took service with the Florentines in their war with the "Senois." Meanwhile Giletta returned to Rossiglione and was received as Countess. From the first she managed her husband's estate with such wisdom that all his subjects rejoiced exceedingly; but when she sent two knights to Beltramo asking him to come back, he churlishly replied to her messengers, "'Let her do what she list; for I do purpose to dwell with her when she shall have this ring'" — meaning a ring which he wore — "'upon her finger, and a son in her arms begotten by me.'"

When Giletta heard these hard conditions, she was very sorrowful. She summoned the chief men of her country and told them that since she was loath that the Count for her sake should live in perpetual exile, she would spend the rest of her life in pilgrimages. So she went away, dressed as a pilgrim, accompanied only by a maid and a servant. Then she set out for Florence, where she soon learned that Beltramo was making love to a poor but virtuous gentlewoman who lived with her mother. Giletta visited these two, told her story, and promised to give the poor girl a handsome dowry with which she could obtain a suitable husband.

Then she made a proposal:

"'I think it requisite, that by someone whom you trust, that you give knowledge to the Count my husband, that your daughter is, and shall be at his commandment; and to the intent she may be well assured that he loveth her indeed above any other, that she prayeth him to send her a ring that he weareth upon his finger, which ring she heard tell he loved very dearly: and when he sendeth the ring, you shall give it unto me, and afterward send him word, that your daughter is ready to accomplish his pleasure, and then you shall cause him secretly to come hither, and place me by him (instead of your daughter) peradventure God will give me the grace, that I may be with child, and so having this ring on my finger, and the child in mine arms begotten by him, I shall recover him, and by your means continue with him, as a wife ought to do with her husband.' "

The mother at first was reluctant, " but in few days with great subtlety, following the order wherein she was instructed, she had gotten the ring, although it was with the Count's ill will, and took order that the Countess instead of her daughter did lie with him. And at the first meeting, so affectuously desired by the Count, God so disposed the matter that the Countess was begotten with child, of two goodly sons, and her delivery chanced at the due time. Whereupon the gentlewoman, not only contented the Countess at that time with the company of her husband, but at many other times so secretly that it was never known, the Count not thinking that he had lain with his wife, but with her whom he loved."

Count Beltramo, having by this time heard that his wife had departed from Rossiglione, went back to his home. Meanwhile Giletta waited in Florence until she had been delivered of twins, and then, still in her pilgrim's garb, she returned to her husband's palace at a time when he was holding a great feast. She came into the hall, went up to her husband, and then, falling down at his feet, showed how she had fulfilled all his conditions. " 'It is now time,' said she, ' if thou keep promise, that I should be received as thy wife.' "

Thereupon she told the whole tale, which greatly amazed the Count and all those standing by; and he himself was so much moved that he abated his rigor, and — the tale ends — " from that time forth he loved and honored her as his dear spouse and wife."

Shakespeare followed the main story quite closely, especially in the interview between Giletta and the King; but he added the characters of the old Countess — the most likable of all his elderly mothers — Lafeu, the clown, and the whole subplot which concerns Parolles.

All's Well That Ends Well is rarely acted, and it has seldom received much praise from critics, who usually agree with Samuel Johnson's judgment:

This play has many delightful scenes, though not sufficiently probable, and some happy characters, though not new, nor produced by any deep knowledge of human nature. Parolles is a boaster and a coward, such as has always been the sport of the stage, but perhaps never raised more laughter or contempt than in the hands of Shakespeare.

I cannot reconcile my heart to Bertram, a man noble without generosity, and young without truth, who marries Helen as a coward. and leaves her as a profligate; when she is dead by his unkindness, sneaks home to a second marriage, is accused by a woman whom he has wronged, defends himself by falsehood, and is dismissed to happiness.

There is, however, more to be said in favor of the play than Johnson allows. The characterization is clever and the persons are alive even if unattractive. Moreover the subplot — the trick played on Parolles — is excellent theater, and indeed may well be based on some incident that actually occurred during the wars in France. Twentieth-century readers and playgoers are disturbed by some of the moral implications in the play, which are far removed from modern conventions. They resent the device by which Helena wins Bertram as her husband, for they feel that the young man has been unfairly trapped; they resent the conditions on which he will accept Helena as his wife; and finally they feel outraged when Helena fulfills those conditions. Shakespeare's audiences would have felt little of this embarrassment, for stories of this kind, which tell of the cleverness of a woman in love, were quite common in medieval romances. Moreover, once Bertram has become Helena's lawful husband, no matter by what means, she has every right to obtain her dues as his wife, and if she is forced into trickery, that is the fault of her husband. Modern readers may find such plots and motives distasteful; Elizabethan readers and playgoers did not.

Nevertheless, Shakespeare seems not to have taken his story too seriously. *All's Well That Ends Well* is just an "interlude," a means of passing away a couple of hours with a play that never demands too much emotion or thought. But, as so often, Shakespeare makes his characters come to life. He has asked himself the question: if this story had really happened, what sort of people would these characters have been? And the answer is that the young woman was too eager, and the young man too spiteful. The real improbability which shakes our credulity is that such a series of adventures could end in general reconciliation and affection. The same doubt occurs in other comedies. But Shakespeare's comedies end as the wedding bells ring out. We need not disturb ourselves unduly by speculating about Bertram and Helena after ten years of married life.

All's Well That Ends Well

DRAMATIS PERSONAE

KING OF FRANCE
DUKE OF FLORENCE
BERTRAM, *Count of Rousillon*
LAFEU, *an old lord*
PAROLLES, *a follower of Bertram*
STEWARD ⎱ *servants to the Countess of*
LAVACHE, *a Clown* ⎰ *Rousillon*
A PAGE

COUNTESS OF ROUSILLON, *mother to Bertram*

HELENA, *a gentlewoman protected by the Countess*
AN OLD WIDOW *of Florence*
DIANA, *daughter to the Widow*
VIOLENTA ⎱ *neighbors and friends to the Widow*
MARIANA ⎰

LORDS, OFFICERS, SOLDIERS, *&c., French and Florentine*

SCENE — *Rousillon; Paris; Florence; Marseilles.*

Act I

SCENE I. *Rousillon. The* COUNT'S *palace.*

[*Enter* BERTRAM, *the* COUNTESS OF ROUSILLON, HELENA, *and* LAFEU, *all in black.*]
COUNTESS. In delivering° my son from me, I bury a second husband.
BER. And I in going, madam, weep o'er my father's death anew; but I must attend His Majesty's command, to whom I am now in ward,° evermore in subjection. 6
LAF. You shall find of the King a husband, madam; you, sir, a father. He that so generally° is at all times good, must of necessity hold his virtue to you,° whose worthiness would stir it up where 10 it wanted, rather than lack it where there is such abundance.°
COUNTESS. What hope is there of His Majesty's amendment?°
LAF. He hath abandoned his physicians, 15 madam, under whose practices he hath persecuted Time with hope° and finds no other advantage in the process but only the losing of hope by time.
COUNTESS. This young gentlewoman had a father — oh, that "had"! How sad a passage° 'tis! — 20 whose skill was almost as great as his honesty; had it stretched so far, would have made nature im-

mortal, and death should have play° for lack of work. Would, for the King's sake, he were living! I think it would be the death of the King's disease. 26
LAF. How called you the man you speak of, madam?
COUNTESS. He was famous, sir, in his profession, and it was his great right to be so — Gerard de Narbon. 31
LAF. He was excellent indeed, madam. The King very lately spoke of him admiringly and mourningly. He was skillful enough to have lived still,° if knowledge could be set up against mortality.° 36
BER. What is it, my good lord, the King languishes of?
LAF. A fistula,° my lord.
BER. I heard not of it before. 40
LAF. I would it were not notorious. Was this gentlewoman the daughter of Gerard de Narbon?
COUNTESS. His sole child, my lord, and be- 44 queathed to my overlooking. I have those hopes of her good that her education promises. Her dispositions° she inherits, which makes fair gifts fairer, for where an unclean mind carries virtuous qualities,° there commendations go with pity.° They are virtues and traitors too. In her they are the better 50 for their simpleness. She derives° her honesty and achieves° her goodness.
LAF. Your commendations, madam, get from her tears.
COUNTESS. 'Tis the best brine a maiden can 55 season° her praise in. The remembrance of her father never approaches her heart, but the tyranny

---

Act I, Sc. i: 1. **delivering**: sending away. 5. **in ward**: An heir who succeeded to his estate while still legally under age was placed "in ward," i.e., under the protection of a guardian who acted as trustee for the estate and arranged a suitable marriage for his ward. Young noblemen were usually wards of the sovereign. 8. **generally**: usually. 9-10. **hold . . . you**: continue to behave virtuously to you. 10-12. **whose . . . abundance**: your worthiness would stir him to treat you honorably even if he lacked virtue; as it is, you are not likely to be without good treatment from one who has such abundance of virtues. 14. **amendment**: recovery. 16-17. **persecuted . . . hope**: kept on pestering Time with the vain hope of cure. 20. **passage**: passing away.

23. **play**: i.e., nothing to do. 35. **still**: for ever. 36. **mortality**: i.e., the fact that all men must die. 39. **fistula**: abscess. 46-47. **dispositions**: natural qualities. 48. **virtuous qualities**: accomplishments. 49. **commendations . . . pity**: i.e., her praises are qualified with regret. 51. **derives**: inherits. 52. **achieves**: acquires. See App. 18. 56. **season**: lit., to add salt as a preservative. See *T Night,* I.i.28-32.

of her sorrows takes all livelihood from her cheek.
No more of this, Helena, go to, no more, lest 60
it be rather thought you affect° a sorrow than to
have ——

HEL. I do affect a sorrow, indeed, but I have it
too.

LAF. Moderate lamentation is the right of the
dead, excessive grief the enemy to the living. 65

COUNTESS. If the living be enemy to the grief, the
excess makes it soon mortal.°

BER. Madam, I desire your holy wishes.

LAF. How understand we that?

COUNTESS. Be thou blest, Bertram, and succeed
    thy father 70
In manners, as in shape! Thy blood and virtue
Contend for empire in thee, and thy goodness
Share with thy birthright!° Love all, trust a few,
Do wrong to none. Be able for thine enemy
Rather in power than use,° and keep thy friend 75
Under thy own life's key. Be checked° for silence,
But never taxed° for speech. What Heaven more
    will,
That thee may furnish, and my prayers pluck down,
Fall on thy head! — Farewell, my lord.
'Tis an unseasoned° courtier. Good my lord, 80
Advise him.

LAF.   He cannot want the best
That shall attend his love.

COUNTESS. Heaven bless him! Farewell, Bertram.
                                 [*Exit.*]

BER. [*To* HELENA] The best wishes that can be
forged in your thoughts be servants to you! Be 85
comfortable to my mother, your mistress, and make
much of her.

LAF. Farewell, pretty lady. You must hold the
credit of your father. [*Exeunt* BERTRAM *and* LAFEU.]

HEL. Oh, were that all! I think not on my father,
And these great tears grace his remembrance more
Than those I shed for him. What was he like? 92
I have forgot him. My imagination
Carries no favor° in 't but Bertram's.
I am undone. There is no living, none, 95
If Bertram be away. 'Twere all one
That I should love a bright particular star
And think to wed it, he is so above me.
In his bright radiance and collateral light
Must I be comforted, not in his sphere.° 100
The ambition in my love thus plagues itself.
The hind that would be mated by the lion

Must die for love. 'Twas pretty, though a plague,
To see him every hour, to sit and draw
His archéd brows, his hawking° eye, his curls, 105
In our heart's table° — heart too capable
Of every line and trick of his sweet favor.
But now he's gone, and my idolatrous fancy°
Must sanctify his relics.° Who comes here?
           [*Enter* PAROLLES.]

[*Aside*] One that goes with him. I love him for his
    sake, 110
And yet I know him a notorious liar,
Think him a great way fool, solely° a coward.
Yet these fixed evils sit so fit in him
That they take place° when virtue's steely° bones
Look bleak i' the cold wind. Withal, full oft we see
Cold wisdom waiting on superfluous folly.° 116

PAR. Save° you, fair queen!

HEL. And you, monarch!

PAR. No.

HEL. And no. 120

PAR. Are you meditating on virginity?

HEL. Aye. You have some stain° of soldier in you.
Let me ask you a question. Man is enemy to virginity. How may we barricado° it against him?

PAR. Keep him out. 126

HEL. But he assails, and our virginity, though
valiant, in the defense, yet is weak. Unfold to us
some warlike resistance.

PAR. There is none. Man, sitting down before°
you, will undermine you and blow you up. 131

HEL. Bless° our poor virginity from underminers
and blowers up! Is there no military policy how
virgins might blow up men?

PAR. Virginity being blown down, man will 135
quicklier be blown up. Marry,° in blowing him
down again, with the breach yourselves made you
lose your city. It is not politic in the commonwealth
of nature to preserve virginity. Loss of virginity is
rational° increase, and there was never virgin 140
got° till virginity was first lost. That° you were
made of is metal° to make virgins. Virginity by being once lost may be ten times found. By being ever
kept, it is ever lost. 'Tis too cold a companion.
Away with 't! 145

HEL. I will stand for 't a little, though therefore
I die a virgin.

---

61. **affect:** pretend, with a pun on the meaning "are in love
with."   67. **excess . . . mortal:** i.e., excessive grief soon kills
itself.   71–73. **Thy . . . birthright:** may the qualities (*blood and
virtue*) which you inherit from your father contend with your
own natural goodness; and may your goodness be as great as
your high rank.   74–75. **Be . . . use:** let your strength be as
great as that of your enemy, but don't use it.   76. **checked:**
rebuked.   77. **taxed:** censured.   80. **unseasoned:** inexperienced.
94. **favor:** face.   99–100. **In . . . sphere:** I can only get reflected
light from him; I cannot move in his orbit.

105. **hawking:** keen as a hawk's.   106. **table:** notebook.
108. **fancy:** love.   109. **sanctify . . . relics:** venerate the tokens
of himself which he leaves behind.   112. **solely:** entirely.
113–14. **Yet . . . place:** yet these evil qualities are so much part
of him (*sit so fit*) that they seem natural (*take place*) — i.e.,
Helena prefers Parolles as he is, for all his faults; an air of virtue
in him would be hypocritical.   114. **steely:** unyielding, rigid.
116. **Cold . . . folly:** a famished wise manservant to (*waiting on*)
a rich fool.   117. **Save:** God save.   122. **stain:** quality.
125. **barricado:** erect a barricade.   130. **sitting . . . before:**
laying siege to.   132. **Bless:** God preserve.   136. **Marry:** Mary,
by the Virgin.   140. **rational:** reasonable.   141. **got:** begotten.
That: that which.   142. **metal:** material.

PAR. There's little can be said in 't. 'Tis against the rule of nature. To speak on the part of virginity is to accuse your mothers, which is most infalli- 150 ble° disobedience. He that hangs himself is a virgin. Virginity murders itself and should be buried in highways° out of all sanctified limit,° as a desper- ate offendress against nature. Virginity breeds mites, much like a cheese; consumes itself to the very 155 paring, and so dies with feeding his own stomach. Besides, virginity is peevish, proud, idle, made of self-love, which is the most inhibited° sin in the canon.° Keep it not. You cannot choose but lose by 't. Out with 't! Within ten year it will make 160 itself ten, which is a goodly increase, and the princi- pal itself not much the worse. Away with 't!

HEL. How might one do, sir, to lose it to her own liking? 164

PAR. Let me see. Marry, ill, to like him that ne'er it likes. 'Tis a commodity will lose the gloss with lying.° The longer kept, the less worth. Off with 't while 'tis vendible.° Answer the time of request. Virginity, like an old courtier, wears her cap 170 out of fashion, richly suited, but unsuitable,° just like the brooch and the toothpick, which wear not now.° Your date is better in your pie and your porridge than in your cheek,° and your virginity, your old virginity, is like one of our French 175 withered pears: It looks ill, it eats drily. Marry, 'tis a withered pear. It was formerly better. Marry, yet 'tis a withered pear. Will you any thing with it?°

HEL. Not my virginity yet.° ——
There shall your master have a thousand loves,
A mother, and a mistress, and a friend, 181
A phoenix,° captain, and an enemy,
A guide, a goddess, and a sovereign,
A counselor, a traitress, and a dear;
His humble ambition, proud humility, 185
His jarring concord, and his discord dulcet,
His faith, his sweet disaster; with a world
Of pretty, fond, adoptious christendoms
That blinking Cupid gossips.° Now shall he ——

I know not what he shall. God send him well! 190
The Court's a learning place, and he is one ——
PAR. What one, i'faith?
HEL. That I wish well. 'Tis pity ——
PAR. What's pity?
HEL. That wishing well had not a body in 't 195
Which might be felt; that we, the poorer born,
Whose baser stars° do shut us up in wishes,°
Might with effects of them follow our friends
And show what we alone must think, which never
Returns us thanks. 200

[Enter PAGE.]

PAGE. Monsieur Parolles, my lord calls for you.

[Exit.]

PAR. Little Helen, farewell. If I can remember thee, I will think of thee at Court.

HEL. Monsieur Parolles, you were born under a charitable star.° 205

PAR. Under Mars, I.

HEL. I especially think under Mars.

PAR. Why under Mars?

HEL. The wars have so kept you under that you must needs be born under Mars. 210

PAR. When he was predominant.

HEL. When he was retrograde, I think, rather.

PAR. Why think you so?

HEL. You go so much backward when you fight.

PAR. That's for advantage. 215

HEL. So is running away when fear proposes the safety, but the composition that your valor and fear makes in you is a virtue of a good wing; and I like the wear well.° 219

PAR. I am so full of businesses I cannot answer thee acutely. I will return perfect courtier, in the which my instruction shall serve to naturalize° thee so thou wilt be capable of a courtier's counsel and understand what advice shall thrust upon thee; else thou diest in thine unthankfulness, and thine 225 ignorance makes thee away.° Farewell. When thou hast leisure, say thy prayers. When thou hast none, remember thy friends. Get thee a good husband, and use him as he uses thee. So, farewell. [Exit.]

HEL. Our remedies oft in ourselves do lie, 231
Which we ascribe to Heaven. The fated sky
Gives us free scope.° Only doth backward pull
Our slow designs when we ourselves are dull.
What power is it which mounts my love so high,
That makes me see, and cannot feed mine eye? 236
The mightiest space in fortune nature brings

150-51. infallible: certain. 152-53. buried in highways: i.e., as a suicide. See *Haml*, V.i.1,n and ll.250-54. 153. out . . . limit: away from all consecrated ground. 158. inhibited: forbidden. 159. canon: ecclesiastical law. 167. lying: lack of use. 169. vend- ible; salable. 171. richly . . . unsuitable: of rich material but un- fashionable. 172-73. brooch . . . now: i.e., brooches and tooth- picks are no longer in the fashion. Toothpicks were the sign of a traveler and were in fashion when *John* was written. See *John*, I.i.190. 173-74. date . . . cheek: it is better to use a date for pies and porridge than to let your withered cheek "date" you as an old maid. 178. Will . . . it: what's the good of it? 179. Not . . . yet: The text here is disturbed. Some lines have been lost in which Helena comments on the departure of Bertram for the Court where he will find new loves. 182. phoenix: rarity. See *Temp*, III.iii.23,n. 187-89. with . . . gossips: i.e., he will give his new love all the pretty, foolish (*fond*) adopted names (*adoptious christendoms*) which the blind (*winking*) god of love bestows like a godfather (*gossip*).

197. baser stars: poorer fortunes. shut . . . wishes: confine us to wishing. 204-05. born . . . star: See App. 1. 217-19. but . . . well: but your courage and your timidity have made an agreement (*composition*), and that makes you fly well; and (she adds consolingly) I like your new suit — for Parolles is very vain about his fashionable clothes. 222. naturalize: familiarize. 226. makes . . . away: destroys you. 232-33. fated . . . scope: in spite of the influence of the stars (*sky*) we have plenty of free will.

To join like likes and kiss like native things.°
Impossible be strange attempts to those
That weigh their pains in sense and do suppose
What hath been cannot be.° Who ever strove   241
To show her merit that did miss her love?
The King's disease — my project may deceive me,
But my intents are fixed, and will not leave me.
                                        [*Exit.*]

SCENE II. *Paris. The* KING's *palace.*

[*Flourish° of cornets. Enter the* KING OF FRANCE
        with letters, and divers ATTENDANTS.]
    KING. The Florentines and Senoys° are by the
        ears,
Have fought with equal fortune, and continue
A braving war.°
    LORD.   So 'tis reported, sir.
    KING. Nay, 'tis most credible. We here receive it
A certainty, vouched from our cousin° Austria,   5
With caution, that the Florentine will move° us
For speedy aid; wherein our dearest friend
Prejudicates° the business and would seem
To have us make denial.
    1. LORD.   His love and wisdom,
Approved so to your Majesty, may plead   10
For amplest credence.
    KING.   He hath armed° our answer,
And Florence is denied before he comes.
Yet, for our gentlemen that mean to see
The Tuscan service,° freely have they leave
To stand on either part.°
    2. LORD.   It well may serve   15
A nursery° to our gentry, who are sick°
For breathing° and exploit.
    KING.   What's he comes here?
    [*Enter* BERTRAM, LAFEU, *and* PAROLLES.]
    1. LORD. It is the Count Rousillon, my good lord,
Young Bertram.
    KING.   Youth, thou bear'st thy father's face.
Frank nature, rather curious° than in haste,   20
Hath well composed thee. Thy father's moral parts
Mayst thou inherit too! Welcome to Paris.
    BER. My thanks and duty are your Majesty's.

    KING. I would I had that corporal° soundness
        now
As when thy father and myself in friendship   25
First tried our soldiership! He did look far
Into the service of the time and was
Discipled of° the bravest. He lasted long,
But on us both did haggish° age steal on
And wore us out of act.° It much repairs me   30
To talk of your good father. In his youth
He had the wit which I can well observe
Today in our young lords; but they may jest
Till their own scorn return to them unnoted
Ere they can hide their levity in honor.°   35
So like a courtier, contempt nor bitterness
Were in his pride or sharpness. If they were,
His equal had awaked them, and his honor,
Clock to itself, knew the true minute when
Exception° bid him speak, and at this time   40
His tongue obeyed his hand. Who° were below him
He used as creatures of another place,°
And bowed his eminent top to their low ranks,
Making them proud of his humility,
In their poor praise he humbled. Such a man   45
Might be a copy to these younger times,
Which, followed well, would demonstrate them
        now
But goers backward.°
    BERT.   His good remembrance, sir,
Lies richer in your thoughts than on his tomb.
So in approof lives not his epitaph   50
As in your royal speech.°
    KING. Would I were with him! He would always
        say —
Methinks I hear him now; his plausive° words
He scattered not in ears, but grafted them   54
To grow there and to bear — "Let me not live," —
This his good melancholy oft began,
On the catastrophe° and heel of pastime,°
When it was out — "Let me not live," quoth he,
"After my flame lacks oil, to be the snuff°
Of younger spirits, whose apprehensive° senses   60
All but new things disdain, whose judgments are
Mere fathers of their garments,° whose constancies
Expire before their fashions." This he wished.
I, after him, do after him wish too,

237–38. The . . . things: in spite of the greatest difference in
fortunes, nature will join like with like and bring them together
as if they were naturally equal.   **239–41. Impossible . . . be:**
The passage may be freely paraphrased: "Those who calculate
the difficulties and suppose that nothing can be changed will
never achieve a daring plan."
    Sc. ii: s.d., Flourish: notes of music announcing the entry of
an important person.   **1. Senoys:** people of Sienna.   **3. braving:**
defiant.   **5. cousin:** kinsman.   **6. move:** petition.   **8. Pre-
judicates:** passes judgment on beforehand.   **11. armed:** fortified.
14. Tuscan service: the campaign in northern Italy.   **15. stand
. . . part:** to serve in either army.   **16. nursery:** training ground.
sick: eager, longing.   **17. breathing:** exercise.   **20. curious:**
careful.

24. corporal: bodily.   **28. Discipled of:** taught by.   **29. haggish:**
that makes haggard.   **30. act:** strength.   **33–35. but . . . honor:**
i.e., our modern young courtiers, unlike the late Count, cannot
combine wit with honor; they just go on jesting until one is tired
of their cynicism.   **40. Exception:** that which moved his anger.
41. Who: those who.   **42. He . . . place:** treated as if they were
his equals.   **47–48. would . . . backward:** would show that they
followed the good old days.   **50–51. So . . . speech:** your commendation is a better proof of his good qualities than the words
inscribed on his tomb.   **53. plausive:** agreeable.   **57. On . . .
pastime:** after he had enjoyed some pleasure. **catastrophe:** end.
59. snuff: like the offensive smoke of an extinguished oil lamp.
60. apprehensive: witty.   **61–62. whose . . . garments:** who
are only capable of inventing a new fashion.

Since I nor wax nor honey can bring home,° 65
I quickly were dissolvèd° from my hive
To give some laborers room.
   2. LORD.   You are loved, sir.
They that least lend it you shall lack you first.°
   KING. I fill a place, I know't. How long is 't,
     Count,
Since the physician at your father's died? 70
He was much famed.
   BER.   Some six months since, my lord.
   KING. If he were living, I would try him yet.
Lend me an arm. The rest have worn me out
With several applications.° Nature and sickness
Debate it at their leisure. Welcome, Count. 75
My son's no dearer.
   BER. Thank your Majesty. [*Exeunt. Flourish.*]

SCENE III. *Rousillon. The* COUNT's *palace.*

[*Enter* COUNTESS, STEWARD, *and* CLOWN.]
   COUNTESS. I will now hear. What say you of this
gentlewoman?
   STEW. Madam, the care I have had to even° your
content° I wish might be found in the calendar° of
my past endeavors, for then we wound our 5
modesty and make foul the clearness of our deservings when of ourselves we publish them.°
   COUNTESS. What does this knave here? Get you
gone, sirrah.° The complaints I have heard of 10
you I do not all believe. 'Tis my slowness that I do
not, for I know you lack not folly to commit them,
and have ability enough to make such knaveries
yours.
   CLO. 'Tis not unknown to you, madam, I am a
poor fellow. 16
   COUNTESS. Well, sir.
   CLO. No, madam, 'tis not so well that I am poor,
though many of the rich are damned. But, if I may
have your ladyship's good will to go to the 20
world,° Isbel the woman and I will do as we may.
   COUNTESS. Wilt thou needs be a beggar?
   CLO. I do beg your good will in this case.
   COUNTESS. In what case?
   CLO. In Isbel's case and mine own. Service is 25
no heritage,° and I think I shall never have the

blessing of God till I have issue o' my body; for they
say barnes° are blessings.
   COUNTESS. Tell me thy reason why thou wilt
marry. 29
   CLO. My poor body, madam, requires it. I am
driven on by the flesh, and he must needs go that
the Devil drives.
   COUNTESS. Is this all your Worship's reason?
   CLO. Faith, madam, I have other holy reasons,
such as they are. 35
   COUNTESS. May the world know them?
   CLO. I have been, madam, a wicked creature, as
you and all flesh and blood are; and, indeed, I do
marry that I may repent.
   COUNTESS. Thy marriage, sooner than thy wickedness. 41
   CLO. I am out o' friends, madam, and I hope to
have friends for my wife's sake.
   COUNTESS. Such friends are thine enemies, knave.
   CLO. You're shallow, madam, in great friends,
for the knaves come to do that for me which I 45
am aweary of. He that ears° my land spares my
team and gives me leave to in the crop. If I be his
cuckold,° he's my drudge. He that comforts my
wife is the cherisher of my flesh and blood. He that
cherishes my flesh and blood loves my flesh and 50
blood. He that loves my flesh and blood is my
friend. Ergo,° he that kisses my wife is my friend.
If men could be contented to be what they are,
there were no fear in marriage. For young 55
Charbon the puritan and old Poysam° the papist,
howsome'er their hearts are severed in religion,
their heads are both one. They may jowl° horns together like any deer i' the herd.
   COUNTESS. Wilt thou ever be a foul-mouthed and
calumnious knave? 61
   CLO. A prophet I, madam, and I speak the truth
the next° way. [*Sings.*]
     "For I the ballad will repeat,
       Which men full true shall find; 65
     Your marriage comes by destiny,
       Your cuckoo sings by kind."°
   COUNTESS. Get you gone, sir. I'll talk with you
more anon.
   STEW. May it please you, madam, that he bid
Helen come to you. Of her I am to speak. 71
   COUNTESS. Sirrah, tell my gentlewoman I would
speak with her; Helen, I mean.
   CLO. [*Sings.*]

---

65. **wax . . . home:** i.e., since I have become a mere drone.
66. **dissolved:** removed. 68. **They . . . first:** those that love you
least will miss you first. 74. **several applications:** i.e., each
physician trying out his own cure.
   Sc. iii: 3–4. **even . . . content:** satisfy your wishes. **even:** lit.,
to balance. 4. **calendar:** register. 5–7. **for . . . them:** we
offend against modesty and befoul our record when we boast
of our good deeds. 10. **sirrah:** term of address used to an
inferior. 20–21. **go . . . world:** get married. See *M Ado*,
II.i.330–32. 25–26. **Service . . . heritage:** a proverb meaning
"Servingmen amass no wealth." It was a common complaint
that gentlemen were no longer generous to their servants; hence

a servingman was not regarded as a suitable wooer by the
thrifty father of a marriageable girl. The whole problem was set
out at length in a pamphlet called *A Health to the Gentlemanly
Profession of Serving Men*, 1598. 28. **barnes:** bairns, children.
46. **ears:** plows. 48. **cuckold:** See App. 11. 52. **Ergo:** therefore. 56. **Charbon . . . Poysam:** possibly "Flesheater" and
"Fisheater." 58. **jowl:** clash. 63. **next:** nearest. 67. **kind:**
according to his nature. See App. 11.

"'Was this fair face the cause,'° quoth she,
  'Why the Grecians sackèd Troy?   75
Fond° done, done fond,
  Was this King Priam's joy?'
With that she sighèd as she stood,
With that she sighèd as she stood,
  And gave this sentence then: 80
'Among nine bad if one be good,
Among nine bad if one be good,
  There's yet one good in ten.'"

COUNTESS. What, one good in ten? You corrupt
the song, sirrah.   85

CLO. One good woman in ten, madam, which is
a purifying o' the song. Would God would serve
the world so all the year! We'd find no fault with
the tithewoman° if I were the parson. One in ten,
quoth a'!° An° we might have a good woman   90
born but one every blazing star,° or at an earthquake, 'twould mend the lottery well.° A man may
draw his heart out ere a' pluck one.

COUNTESS. You'll be gone, sir knave, and do as I
command you.   95

CLO. That man should be at woman's command,
and yet no hurt done! Though honesty be no puritan, yet it will do no hurt. It will wear the surplice
of humility over the black gown° of a big heart. I
am going, forsooth. The business is for Helen to
come hither.   [*Exit.*] 101

COUNTESS. Well, now.

STEW. I know, madam, you love your gentlewoman entirely.

COUNTESS. Faith, I do. Her father bequeathed her
to me, and she herself, without other advantage,
may lawfully make title to as much love as she
finds. There is more owing her than is paid, and
more shall be paid her than she'll demand.   109

STEW. Madam, I was very late° more near her
than I think she wished me. Alone she was, and
did communicate to herself her own words to her
own ears. She thought, I dare vow for her, they
touched not any stranger sense.° Her matter was
she loved your son. Fortune, she said, was no   115
goddess, that had put such difference betwixt their
two estates, Love no god, that would not extend his
might only where qualities were level, Dian no°
queen of virgins that would suffer her poor   120
knight° surprised without rescue in the first assault
or ransom afterward. This she delivered in the most
bitter touch of sorrow that e'er I heard virgin exclaim in; which I held my duty speedily to acquaint
you withal, sithence,° in the loss° that may happen,
it concerns you something to know it.   126

COUNTESS. You have discharged this honestly.
Keep it to yourself. Many likelihoods informed me
of this before, which hung so tottering in the balance that I could neither believe nor misdoubt.   130
Pray you leave me. Stall° this in your bosom, and I
thank you for your honest care. I will speak with
you further anon.   [*Exit* STEWARD.]

         [*Enter* HELENA.]

Even so it was with me when I was young.
  If ever we are nature's, these° are ours. This
     thorn   135
Doth to our rose° of youth rightly belong.
  Our blood to us, this to our blood is born.°
It is the show and seal of nature's truth
Where love's strong passion is impressed in youth.
By our remembrances of days foregone,   140
Such were our faults, or then we thought them
     none.
Her eye is sick on 't. I observe her now.

HEL. What is your pleasure, madam?

COUNTESS.   You know, Helen,
I am a mother to you.

HEL. Mine honorable mistress.

COUNTESS.   Nay, a mother 145
Why not a mother? When I said "a mother,"
Methought you saw a serpent. What's in "mother"
That you start at it? I say I am your mother,
And put you in the catalogue of those
That were enwombèd mine.° 'Tis often seen   150
Adoption strives with nature,° and choice breeds
A native slip° to us from foreign seeds.
You ne'er oppressed me with a mother's groan,
Yet I express to you a mother's care.
God's mercy, maiden! Does it curd thy blood   155
To say I am thy mother? What's the matter,
That this distempered° messenger of wet,
The many-colored Iris,° rounds thine eye?
Why? That you are my daughter?

HEL.   That I am not.

---

74. Was . . . cause: i.e., the face of Helen of Troy, of whom Marlowe wrote the famous line, "Was this the face that launched a thousand ships?" The original ballad from which the Clown quotes (or misquotes) is lost.   **76. Fond:** foolishly.   **89. tithe-woman:** the tenth woman, sent along as part of the tithe. See Gen. Intro. p. 19a.   **90. quoth a':** says he. **An:** if.   **91. one . . . star:** every comet appears. The appearance of a comet was supposed to foretell some strange event, such as the birth or death of a superman. See *Caesar,* II.ii.30–31, and *I Hen IV,* III.i.13–43.   **92. mend . . . well:** improve the chances in the lottery, which in Elizabethan lotteries were about one in forty.   **98–99. surplice . . . gown:** Ministers of the Church of England were by law obliged to wear the surplice. The puritanically inclined preferred the black Geneva gown, but many of them, to avoid being ejected from their church livings, reluctantly wore the hated garment.   **110. late:** lately   **114. touched . . . sense:** i.e., were not overheard.

118. Dian no: "Dian no" has been added by editors. F1 reads here "were level, Queen of virgins."   **120–21. poor knight:** i.e., a follower of Diana, vowed to perpetual chastity.   **125. sithence:** since. **loss:** harm.   **131. Stall:** keep shut.   **135. these:** i.e., passions.   **136. rose:** The rose is often used as the symbol of youth. See *Haml,* IV.v.157.   **137. Our . . . born:** passion (*blood*) is born in our blood.   **150. enwombed mine:** my natural children.   **151. Adoption . . . nature:** i.e., we love our adopted children as well as our own.   **152. slip:** a grafting.   **157. dis-tempered:** ill-humored.   **158. many-colored Iris:** sparkling tear. Iris was the rainbow goddess.

COUNTESS. I say I am your mother.
HEL.   Pardon, madam.   160
The Count Rousillon cannot be my brother.
I am from humble, he from honored name;
No note upon° my parents, his all noble.
My master, my dear lord he is, and I
His servant live, and will his vassal° die.   165
He must not be my brother.
    COUNTESS.   Nor I your mother?
    HEL. You are my mother, madam. Would you
      were —
So that my lord your son were not my brother —
Indeed my mother! Or were you both our mothers,
I care no more for than I do for Heaven   170
So I were not his sister. Can't no other,°
But I your daughter, he must be my brother?
    COUNTESS. Yes, Helen, you might be my daugh-
      ter-in-law.
God shield° you mean it not, daughter and mother
So strive upon your pulse. What, pale again?   175
My fear hath catched your fondness.° Now I see
The mystery of your loneliness and find
Your salt tears' head.° Now to all sense 'tis gross°
You love my son. Invention is ashamed,°
Against the proclamation of thy passion,   180
To say thou dost not. Therefore tell me true;
But tell me then, 'tis so; for look, thy cheeks
Confess it, th' one to th' other, and thine eyes
See it so grossly shown in thy behaviors
That in their kind° they speak it. Only sin   185
And hellish obstinacy tie thy tongue,
That truth should be suspected. Speak, is't so?
If it be so, you have wound a goodly clew.°
If it be not, forswear 't. Howe'er, I charge thee,
As Heaven shall work in me for thine avail,   190
To tell me truly.
    HEL.   Good madam, pardon me!
    COUNTESS. Do you love my son?
    HEL.   Your pardon, noble mistress!
    COUNTESS. Love you my son?
    HEL.   Do not you love him, madam?
    COUNTESS. Go not about. My love hath in 't a
      bond°
Whereof the world takes note. Come, come, disclose
The state of your affection, for your passions   196
Have to the full appeached.°
    HEL.   Then, I confess,
Here on my knee before high Heaven and you,
That before you, and next unto high Heaven,
I love your son.   200
My friends were poor but honest. So's my love.

Be not offended, for it hurts not him
That he is loved of me. I follow him not
By any token of presumptuous suit,
Nor would I have him till I do deserve him,   205
Yet never know how that desert should be.
I know I love in vain, strive against hope.
Yet in this captious and intenible sieve°
I still pour in the waters of my love,
And lack not to lose still. Thus, Indian-like,°   210
Religious in mine error, I adore
The sun, that looks upon his worshiper
But knows of him no more. My dearest madam,
Let not your hate encounter with my love
For loving where you do. But if yourself,   215
Whose agèd honor cites° a virtuous youth,
Did ever in so true a flame of liking
Wish chastely and love dearly that your Dian
Was both herself and Love, oh, then give pity
To her whose state is such that cannot choose   220
But lend and give where she is sure to lose,
That seeks not to find that her search implies,
But riddlelike lives sweetly where she dies!
    COUNTESS. Had you not lately an intent — speak
      truly —
To go to Paris?
    HEL.   Madam, I had.
    COUNTESS.   Wherefore? Tell true.   225
    HEL. I will tell truth. By grace itself I swear.
You know my father left me some prescriptions
Of rare and proved effects, such as his reading
And manifest experience had collected
For general sovereignty,° and that he willed me
In heedful'st reservation to bestow them,   231
As notes whose faculties inclusive were
More than they were in note.° Amongst the rest
There is a remedy approved, set down,
To cure the desperate languishings whereof   235
The King is rendered° lost.
    COUNTESS.   This was your motive
For Paris, was it? Speak.
    HEL. My lord your son made me to think of this,
Else Paris, and the medicine, and the King
Had from the conversation of my thoughts   240
Haply been absent then.
    COUNTESS.   But think you, Helen,
If you should tender your supposèd aid,
He would receive it? He and his physicians
Are of a mind; he, that they cannot help him,
They, that they cannot help. How shall they credit
A poor unlearnèd virgin when the schools,   246

---

163. No . . . upon: nothing remarkable about. 165. vassal: slave. 171. Can't . . . other: can it not be otherwise? 174. shield: forbid. 176. fondness: folly. 178. head: origin. gross: clear. 179. Invention is ashamed: i.e., you cannot pretend. 185. kind: nature; i.e., tears. 188. clew: ball of thread. 194. My . . . bond: i.e., I am bound by nature to love my son. 197. appeached: given you away.

208. captious . . . sieve: this sieve which receives all that I pour in but retains none. The reading is an emendation of the F1 "this captious and imtenible Sive." 210. Indian-like: like a worshiper of idols. 216. cites: evidences. 230. general sovereignty: remedy for every complaint. 232–33. whose . . . note: whose power to cure was greater in fact than in the notebook; i.e., unlike many famous remedies, they had been proved efficacious. 236. rendered: given up for.

Emboweled of their doctrine, have left off
The danger to itself?°
    HEL.   There's something in 't
More than my father's skill, which was the great'st
Of his profession, that his good receipt   250
Shall for my legacy be sanctified
By the luckiest stars in Heaven; and would your
    Honor
But give me leave to try success, I'd venture
The well-lost life of mine on His Grace's cure
By such a day and hour.
    COUNTESS.   Dost thou believe 't?   255
    HEL. Aye, madam, knowingly.
    COUNTESS. Why, Helen, thou shalt have my leave
    and love,
Means and attendants, and my loving greetings
To those of mine in Court. I'll stay at home
And pray God's blessing into thy attempt.   260
Be gone tomorrow, and be sure of this:
What I can help thee to, thou shalt not miss.
                                [Exeunt.]

Act II

SCENE I. *Paris. The* KING's *palace.*

[Flourish of cornets. Enter the KING, *attended with
divers° young* LORDS *taking leave for the Florentine
war,* BERTRAM, *and* PAROLLES.]
    KING. Farewell, young lords. These warlike prin-
    ciples
Do not throw from you;° and you, my lords, fare-
    well.
Share the advice betwixt you. If both gain, all
The gift doth stretch itself as 'tis received,
And is enough for both.
    1. LORD.   'Tis our hope, sir,   5
After well-entered soldiers,° to return
And find your Grace in health.
    KING. No, no, it cannot be; and yet my heart
Will not confess he owes° the malady
That doth my life besiege. Farewell, young lords.
Whether I live or die, be you the sons   11
Of worthy Frenchmen. Let higher° Italy —
Those bated° that inherit but the fall
Of the last monarchy° — see that you come,
Not to woo honor, but to wed it. When   15

The bravest questant° shrinks, find what you seek,
That fame may cry you loud. I say farewell.
    2. LORD. Health at your bidding serve your Maj-
    esty!
    KING. Those girls of Italy, take heed of them.
They say our French lack of language to deny   20
If they demand. Beware of being captives
Before you serve.
    BOTH.   Our hearts receive your warnings.
    KING. Farewell. Come hither to me.   *[Exit.]*
    1. LORD. *[To* BERTRAM] O my sweet lord, that you
    will stay behind us!
    PAR. 'Tis not his fault, the spark.°
    2. LORD.   Oh, 'tis brave wars!   25
    PAR. Most admirable. I have seen those wars.
    BER. I am commanded° here, and kept a coil°
    with
"Too young," and "the next year," and "'tis too
    early."
    PAR. An° thy mind stand to 't, boy, steal away
    bravely.   29
    BER. I shall stay here the forehorse to a smock,°
Creaking my shoes on the plain masonry,
Till honor be bought up° and no sword worn
But one to dance with! By heaven, I'll steal away.
    1. LORD. There's honor in the theft.
    PAR.   Commit it, Count.   34
    2. LORD. I am your accessary; and so, farewell.
    BER. I grow to you, and our parting is a tortured
body.   36
    1. LORD. Farewell, Captain.
    2. LORD. Sweet Monsieur Parolles!
    PAR. Noble heroes, my sword and yours are   40
kin. Good sparks and lustrous, a word, good metals.
You shall find in the regiment of the Spinii one
Captain Spurio, with his cicatrix,° an emblem of
war, here on his sinister° cheek. It was this very
sword entrenched it. Say to him I live, and observe
his reports for me.   46
    1. LORD. We shall, noble Captain.
                              [Exeunt LORDS.]
    PAR. Mars dote on you for his novices!° What
    will ye do?
    BER. Stay. The King.   50
                    [Re-enter KING.]
    PAR. *[Aside to* BERTRAM] Use a more spacious
ceremony to the noble lords. You have restrained
yourself within the list° of too cold an adieu. Be

247–48. Emboweled . . . itself: emptied of their knowledge, have
left the disease to cure itself.
    Act II, Sc. i: s.d., **divers:** various.   **1–2. These . . . you:**
don't forget the advice about soldiering which I have just given
you.   **6. After . . . soldiers:** when we are experienced soldiers.
9. owes: owns; i.e., I will not regard my sickness as hopeless.
12. higher: i.e., the Adriatic side.   **13. bated:** excepted.   **13–
14. Those . . . monarchy:** an obscure passage, perhaps meaning
"with the exception of those who profit by the fall of the late
King."

16. questant: seeker.   **25. spark:** i.e., Bertram, who (as we
learn at l. 27) is not allowed to go with the rest to the wars.
27. commanded: ordered to stay. **kept a coil:** fussed over.
29. An: if.   **30. forehorse . . . smock:** forced to be the drudge
of dames. The forehorse was the leader of a wagon team. Bertram's complaint is that he must stay with the Court ladies while
the other young men are making their names in the war.
smock: female, lit., woman's nightgown. See *R & J*, II.iv.109.
32. bought up: sold out.   **43. cicatrix:** scar.   **44. sinister:** left.
48. Mars . . . novices: may the god of war regard you as his
special pupils.   **53. list:** boundary.

more expressive to them; for they wear themselves
in the cap of the time,° there do muster true   55
gait,° eat, speak, and move under the influence of
the most received star.° And though the Devil lead
the measure,° such are to be followed. After them,
and take a more dilated° farewell.

BER. And I will do so.   60

PAR. Worthy fellows, and like to prove most sin-
ewy° swordmen. [*Exeunt* BERTRAM *and* PAROLLES.]
                    [*Enter* LAFEU.]

LAF. [*Kneeling.*] Pardon, my lord, for me and for
my tidings.

KING. I'll fee° thee to stand up.°

LAF. Then here's a man stands that has brought
his pardon.   65
I would you had kneeled, my lord, to ask me mercy,
And that at my bidding you could so stand up.

KING. I would I had, so I had broke thy pate°
And asked thee mercy for 't.

LAF. Good faith, across.° But, my good lord, 'tis
thus: 70
Will you be cured of your infirmity?

KING. No.

LAF. Oh, will you eat no grapes, my royal fox?°
Yes, but you will my noble grapes an if
My royal fox could reach them. I have seen a med-
icine   75
That's able to breathe life into a stone,
Quicken a rock, and make you dance canary°
With spritely fire and motion; whose simple touch
Is powerful to araise King Pepin,° nay,
To give great Charlemain a pen in 's hand   80
And write to her a love-line.

KING.   What " her " is this?

LAF. Why, Doctor She. My lord, there's one ar-
rived,
If you will see her. Now, by my faith and honor,
If seriously I may convey my thoughts
In this my light deliverance,° I have spoke   85
With one that, in her sex, her years, profession,
Wisdom, and constancy, hath amazed me more

54–55. wear . . . time: i.e., like a brooch worn on the cap, they
are in favor. See *Haml*, II.ii.233 and Pl. 8d.   55–56. muster . . .
gait: a difficult phrase, perhaps meaning "gather together."
56–57. influence . . . star: i.e., take care to be friendly with
these young lords, for they are in favor just now. See App. 1.
58. measure: dance. See App. 24.   59. dilated: extended.
62. sinewy: muscular.   64. I'll . . . up: Lafeu, as a good courtier,
kneels to make his request of the King, who, like Henri IV, the
then King of France, is very affable and familiar with his courtiers. He bids Lafeu rise and forget ceremony. fee: reward.
68. so . . . pate: so long as I had cracked your head first.
70. across: i.e., clumsily, and not full tilt like a brave tilter.
See *AYLI*, III.iv.45,n.   73. Oh . . . fox: i.e., you don't believe
you can be cured, so you'll not listen to talk of remedies. In the
fable, when the fox could not reach the grapes, he muttered
that he did not want them, because they were sour anyway.
77. canary: a quick, lively dance.   79. araise . . . Pepin: fetch
King Pepin out of his grave. Pepin was the son of Charlemagne
and had been dead since A.D. 810.   85. light deliverance: gay
way of talking.

Than I dare blame my weakness. Will you see
her —
For that is her demand — and know her business?
That done, laugh well at me.

KING.   Now, good Lafeu,   90
Bring in the admiration,° that we with thee
May spend our wonder too or take off° thine
By wondering how thou took'st it.

LAF.   Nay, I'll fit° you,
And not be all day neither.   [*Exit.*]

KING. Thus he his special nothing ever prologues.°   95
          [*Re-enter* LAFEU, *with* HELENA.]

LAF. Nay, come your ways.

KING.   This haste hath wings indeed.

LAF. Nay, come your ways.
This is His Majesty, say your mind to him.
A traitor you do look like, but such traitors   99
His Majesty seldom fears. I am Cressid's uncle,°
That dare leave two together. Fare you well. [*Exit.*]

KING. Now, fair one, does your business follow
us?

HEL. Aye, my good lord.
Gerard de Narbon was my father;
In what he did profess, well found.°

KING.   I knew him.   105

HEL. The rather will I spare my praises toward
him.
Knowing him is enough. On's bed of death
Many receipts he gave me; chiefly one,
Which, as the dearest° issue of his practice
And of his old experience the only darling,   110
He bade me store up as a triple° eye,
Safer than mine own two, more dear. I have so.
And hearing your high Majesty is touched
With that malignant cause° wherein the honor
Of my dear father's gift stands chief in power,°
I come to tender° it and my appliance,°   116
With all bound humbleness.

KING.   We thank you, maiden,
But may not be so credulous of cure,
When our most learnèd doctors leave us and
The congregated College° have concluded   120
That laboring art can never ransom nature
From her inaidible estate.° I say we must not
So stain our judgment or corrupt our hope
To prostitute our past-cure malady
To empirics,° or to dissever so   125

91. admiration: wonder.   92. take off: cause you to lose.
93. fit: satisfy.   95. prologues: introduces.   100. Cressid's
uncle: Pandarus was the go-between in the love affair of Troilus
and Cressida. See *Tr & Cr*.   105. well found: of sound learning.
109. dearest: most valuable.   111. triple: third; i.e., to value it
as dearly as one of my eyes.   114. cause: case, disease.   114–
15. wherein . . . power: which my father's prescription is most
able to cure.   116. tender: offer. appliance: application of the
remedy.   120. congregated College: the whole College of Physicians.   122. inaidible estate: incurable condition.   125. empirics: quacks.

Our great self and our credit to esteem
A senseless help, when help past sense we deem.
HEL. My duty, then, shall pay me for my pains.
I will no more enforce mine office on you,
Humbly entreating from your royal thoughts 130
A modest one, to bear me back again.
KING. I cannot give thee less, to be called grateful.
Thou thought'st to help me, and such thanks I give
As one near death to those that wish him live.
But what at full I know, thou know'st no part,
I knowing all my peril, thou no art. 136
HEL. What I can do can do no hurt to try,
Since you set up your rest° 'gainst remedy.
He that of greatest works is finisher
Oft does them by the weakest minister. 140
So Holy Writ in babes hath judgment shown
When judges have been babes. Great floods have
flown
From simple sources, and great seas have dried
When miracles have by the greatest been denied.
Oft expectation fails, and most oft there 145
Where most it promises; and oft it hits
Where hope is coldest and despair most fits.
KING. I must not hear thee. Fare thee well, kind
maid.
Thy pains not used must by thyself be paid.
Proffers not took reap thanks for their reward.°
HEL. Inspirèd merit so by breath° is barred. 151
It is not so with Him that all things knows
As 'tis with us that square our guess by shows;°
But most it is presumption in us when
The help of Heaven we count the act of men. 155
Dear sir, to my endeavors give consent.
Of Heaven, not me, make an experiment.
I am not an impostor that proclaim
Myself against the level of mine aim;°
But know I think, and think I know most sure,
My art is not past power, nor you past cure. 161
KING. Art thou so confident? Within what space
Hopest thou my cure?
HEL. The great'st Grace lending grace,
Ere twice the horses of the sun shall bring
Their fiery torcher° his diurnal ring,° 165
Ere twice in murk° and occidental damp°
Moist Hesperus° hath quenched his sleepy lamp,
Or four and twenty times the pilot's glass°
Hath told the thievish minutes how they pass,
What is infirm from your sound parts shall fly, 170
Health shall live free, and sickness freely die.°

KING. Upon thy certainty and confidence
What darest thou venture?
HEL. Tax of° impudence,
A strumpet's boldness, a divulgèd shame 174
Traduced by odious ballads,° my maiden's name
Seared° otherwise; ne° worse of worst extended,°
With vilest torture let my life be ended.
KING. Methinks in thee some blessed spirit doth
speak
His powerful sound within an organ weak;
And what impossibility would slay 180
In common sense, sense saves another way.°
Thy life is dear; for all that life can rate
Worth name of life in thee hath estimate,° —
Youth, beauty, wisdom, courage, all
That happiness and prime° can happy call. 185
Thou this to hazard needs must intimate
Skill infinite or monstrous desperate.
Sweet practicer,° thy physic I will try,
That ministers° thine own death if I die.
HEL. If I break time, or flinch in property° 190
Of what I spoke, unpitied let me die,
And well deserved. Not helping, death's my fee,
But if I help, what do you promise me?
KING. Make thy demand.
HEL. But will you make it even?°
KING. Aye, by my scepter and my hopes of
Heaven. 195
HEL. Then shalt thou give me with thy kingly
hand
What husband in thy power I will command.
Exempted be from me the arrogance
To choose from forth the royal blood of France,
My low and humble name to propagate 200
With any branch or image of thy state;
But such a one, thy vassal, whom I know
Is free for me to ask, thee to bestow.
KING. Here is my hand. The premises° observed,
Thy will by my performance shall be served. 205
So make the choice of thy own time, for I,
Thy resolved patient, on thee still rely.
More should I question thee, and more I must,
Though more to know could not be more to trust —
From whence thou camest, how tended on — but
rest 210
Unquestioned welcome, and undoubted blest.
Give me some help here, ho! If thou proceed
As high as word, my deed shall match thy deed.
[Flourish. Exeunt.]

138. set ... rest: See *R & J*, IV.v.6,n. 150. Proffers ...
reward: although I do not take your offer, yet it deserves a reward
of gratitude. 151. by breath: by your words. 153. square
... shows: reckon by outward appearances. 158–59. proclaim
... aim: i.e., that boast more than I can perform. 165. torcher:
torchbearer, light-bringer; i.e., the sun. diurnal ring: daily
circuit. 166. murk: darkness. occidental damp: his descent
into the western ocean. 167. Hesperus: the evening star.
168. glass: hourglass. 171. Health ... die: or, in simpler
words: "In two days you will be a fit man."

173. Tax of: to be blamed for. 175. odious ballads: See App. 8.
176. Seared: branded. ne: nor. extended: prolonged. 180–
81. And ... way: i.e., though my common sense tells me that
you cannot be as skillful as you say, yet I have a feeling that you
may be. 183. estimate: value. 185. prime: youthfulness.
188. practicer: practitioner, physician. 189. ministers: causes.
190. property: exact fulfillment. 194. make it even: fulfill my
demand. 204. premises: conditions.

SCENE II. *Rousillon. The* COUNT'S *palace.*

[*Enter* COUNTESS *and* CLOWN.]

COUNTESS. Come on, sir. I shall now put you to
the height of your breeding.°

CLO. I will show myself highly fed and lowly
taught. I know my business is but° to the Court.

COUNTESS. To the Court! Why, what place 5
make you special, when you put off that with such
contempt? But to the Court!

CLO. Truly, madam, if God have lent a man any
manners, he may easily put it off at Court. He that
cannot make a leg,° put off's cap, kiss his hand, 10
and say nothing, has neither leg, hands, lip, nor
cap; and, indeed, such a fellow, to say precisely,
were not for the Court. But for me, I have an answer will serve all men.

COUNTESS. Marry, that's a bountiful answer that
fits all questions. 16

CLO. It is like a barber's chair that fits all buttocks, the pin° buttock, the quatch° buttock, the
brawn° buttock, or any buttock.

COUNTESS. Will your answer serve fit to° all
questions? 21

CLO. As fit as ten groats° is for the hand of an
attorney, as your French crown° for your taffeta
punk,° as Tib's rush° for Tom's forefinger, as a
pancake for Shrove Tuesday,° a morris° for 25
May Day, as the nail to his hole, the cuckold to his
horn, as a scolding quean° to a wrangling knave, as
the nun's lip to the friar's mouth, nay, as the pud-
ding° to his skin.

COUNTESS. Have you, I say, an answer of such fitness for all questions? 31

CLO. From below your duke to beneath your constable, it will fit any question.

COUNTESS. It must be an answer of most monstrous size that must fit all demands. 35

CLO. But a trifle neither, in good faith, if the
learned should speak truth of it. Here it is, and all
that belongs to 't. Ask me if I am a courtier. It
shall do you no harm to learn. 39

COUNTESS. To be young again, if we could! I will
be a fool in question, hoping to be the wiser by
your answer. I pray you, sir, are you a courtier?

CLO. Oh, Lord, sir!° There's a simple putting
off. More, more, a hundred of them. 44

COUNTESS. Sir, I am a poor friend of yours that
loves you.

CLO. Oh, Lord, sir! Thick,° thick, spare not me.

COUNTESS. I think, sir, you can eat none of this
homely meat.

CLO. Oh, Lord, sir! Nay, put me to 't, I warrant
you. 51

COUNTESS. You were lately whipped, sir, as I
think.

CLO. Oh, Lord, sir! Spare not me.

COUNTESS. Do you cry, " Oh, Lord, sir! " at your
whipping, and " Spare not me "? Indeed your 55
" Oh, Lord, sir! " is very sequent° to your whipping. You would answer very well to a whipping
if you were but bound to 't.°

CLO. I ne'er had worse luck in my life in my
" Oh, Lord, sir! " I see things may serve long, but
not serve ever. 61

COUNTESS. I play the noble housewife with the
time
To entertain 't so merrily with a fool.

CLO. Oh, Lord, sir! Why, there 't serves well
again. 65

COUNTESS. An end, sir. To your business. Give
Helen this,
And urge her to a present° answer back.
Commend me to my kinsmen and my son.
This is not much.

CLO. Not much commendation to them. 70

COUNTESS. Not much employment for you. You
understand me?

CLO. Most fruitfully. I am there before my legs.

COUNTESS. Haste you again.   [*Exeunt severally.*]

SCENE III. *Paris. The* KING'S *palace.*

[*Enter* BERTRAM, LAFEU, *and* PAROLLES.]

LAF. They say miracles are past, and we have our
philosophical persons, to make modern° and familiar things supernatural and causeless. Hence is
it that we make trifles of terrors, ensconcing° ourselves into seeming knowledge when we should submit ourselves to an unknown fear.° 7

PAR. Why, 'tis the rarest argument of° wonder
that hath shot out in our latter times.

BER. And so 'tis.

LAF. To be relinquished of the artists° —— 10

Sc. ii: 1–2. **put . . . breeding**: give you a task which will show
whether you are fit for high society. 4. **but**: merely. 10. **make
a leg**: bow to his betters. See App. 7. 18. **pin**: i.e., small and
narrow. **quatch**: fat. 19. **brawn**: muscular. 20. **serve . . .
to**: suit. 22. **ten groats**: 3s. 4d. — the groat being worth 4d.
23. **French crown**: worth about 6s. 23–24. **taffeta punk**: prostitute wearing taffeta. 24. **rush**: a ring made of a rush, used in a
mock wedding. 25. **pancake . . . Tuesday**: Shrove Tuesday
is the day before Ash Wednesday. It was (and still is) the English
custom to eat pancakes on that day — a final feast before the
Lenten fast begins. **morris**: See App. 24: Country Dances.
27. **quean**: slut. 28–29. **pudding**: sausage.

43. **Oh . . . sir**: The phrase was at this time in the mouth of
every boneheaded young courtier as an answer to any question.
47. **Thick**: quicker. 56. **sequent**: a good answer to. 58. **bound
to 't**: forced to endure it. 67. **present**: immediate.
    Sc. iii: 2. **modern**: ordinary. 4. **ensconcing**: protecting.
6–7. **we . . . fear**: i.e., we should admit that we have seen a real
miracle. 8. **argument of**: matter for. 10. **relinquished . . .
artists**: given up by the experts.

PAR. So I say.

LAF. Both of Galen and Paracelsus° ——

PAR. So I say.

LAF. Of all the learned and authentic° fellows ——

PAR. Right. So I say.   15

LAF. That gave him out incurable ——

PAR. Why, there 'tis. So say I too.

LAF. Not to be helped° ——

PAR. Right. As 'twere, a man assured of a ——

LAF. Uncertain life, and sure death.   20

PAR. Just, you say well; so would I have said.

LAF. I may truly say it is a novelty to the world.

PAR. It is, indeed. If you will have it in showing,°
you shall read it in — what do ye call there?

LAF. A showing of a heavenly effect in an earthly
actor.

PAR. That's it. I would have said the very same.

LAF. Why, your dolphin is not lustier.° 'Fore me,
I speak in respect ——   31

PAR. Nay, 'tis strange, 'tis very strange, that is the
brief and the tedious of it; and he's of a most faci-
nerious° spirit that will not acknowledge it to be
the ——

LAF. Very hand of Heaven.   37

PAR. Aye, so I say.

LAF. In a most weak ——

PAR. And debile° minister, great power, great
transcendence,° which should, indeed, give us a
further use to be made than alone the recovery of
the King, as to be ——   43

LAF. Generally thankful.

PAR. I would have said it. You say well. Here
comes the King.   46

[*Enter* KING, HELENA, *and* ATTENDANTS.]

LAF. Lustig,° as the Dutchman° says. I'll like a
maid the better, whilst I have a tooth in my head.
Why, he's able to lead her a coranto.°

PAR. *Mort du vinaigre!*° Is not this Helen?   50

LAF. 'Fore God, I think so.

KING. Go, call before me all the lords in Court.
Sit, my preserver, by thy patient's side,
And with this healthful hand, whose banished
     sense
Thou hast repealed,° a second time receive   55
The confirmation of my promised gift,°
Which but attends thy naming.

[*Enter three or four* LORDS.]

Fair maid, send forth thine eyes. This youthful par-
cel
Of noble bachelors stand at my bestowing,
O'er whom both sovereign power and father's
     voice   60
I have to use. Thy frank election° make.
Thou hast power to choose, and they none to for-
sake.

HEL. To each of you one fair and virtuous mistress
Fall, when Love please! Marry, to each, but one!

LAF. I'd give bay Curtal° and his furniture°   65
My mouth no more were broken than° these boys'
And writ° as little beard.

KING.   Peruse them well.
Not one of those but had a noble father.

HEL. Gentlemen,
Heaven hath through me restored the King to
     health.   70

ALL. We understand it, and thank Heaven for
you.

HEL. I am a simple maid, and therein wealthiest
That I protest I simply am a maid.
Please it your Majesty, I have done already.
The blushes in my cheeks thus whisper me: 75
"We blush that thou shouldst choose; but, be re-
fused,
Let the white death sit° on thy cheek for ever.
We'll ne'er come there again."

KING.   Make choice, and see —
Who shuns thy love shuns all his love in me.

HEL. Now, Dian, from thy altar do I fly,°   80
And to imperial Love, that God most high,
Do my sighs stream. Sir, will you hear my suit?

1. LORD. And grant it.

HEL.   Thanks, sir. All the rest is mute.

LAF. I had rather be in this choice than throw
ames-ace° for my life.   85

HEL. The honor, sir, that flames in your fair eyes
Before I speak, too threateningly replies.
Love make your fortunes twenty times above
Her that so wishes and her humble love!

2. LORD. No better, if you please.

HEL.   My wish receive,   90
Which great Love grant! And so, I take my leave.

LAF. Do all they deny her? An they were sons of
mine, I'd have them whipped, or I would send
them to the Turk to make eunuchs of.

---

12. Galen . . . Paracelsus: famous physicians of antiquity.
14. authentic: certified.   18. helped: cured.   24. showing:
writing.   30. lustier: merrier.   34–35. facinerious: wicked.
40. debile: feeble.   41. transcendence: beyond all experience.
47. Lustig: lustily. Dutchman: German.   49. lead . . . coranto:
be her partner in a lively dance. See App. 24.   50. *Mort du
vinaigre:* lit., death of vinegar — a meaningless oath which
Parolles tries to pass off as evidence of his travels.   55. repealed:
called back from banishment.   56. promised gift: See II.i.196–
97.

61. frank election: free choice.   65. bay Curtal: the name of a
bay horse with a docked tail. furniture: saddlery.   66. My . . .
than: I had lost as few teeth as.   67. writ: i.e., produced,
showed.   76–77. be . . . sit: if your chosen one refuses you, then
may death make white.   80. Dian . . . fly: i.e., I will now desert
the goddess of single life. With these words Helena rises and goes
round to each of the four young men in turn, coming to Bertram
last. Lafeu and Parolles stand apart and comment.   85. ames-
ace: a throw of double-one in dice; i.e., I would rather be her
choice than to throw dice for my own life — and lose.

HEL. Be not afraid that I your hand should take.
I'll never do you wrong for your own sake.   96
Blessing upon your vows! And in your bed
Find fairer fortune, if you ever wed!

LAF. These boys are boys of ice, they'll none have
her. Sure, they are bastards to the English. The
French ne'er got° 'em.   101

HEL. You are too young, too happy, and too good
To make yourself a son out of my blood.

4. LORD. Fair one, I think not so.

LAF. There's one grape yet. I am sure thy   105
father drunk wine.° But if thou be'st not an ass, I
am a youth of fourteen. I have known thee already.

HEL. [*To* BERTRAM] I dare not say I take you, but
I give
Me and my service, ever whilst I live,   110
Into your guiding power. This is the man.

KING. Why, then, young Bertram, take her. She's
thy wife.

BER. My wife, my liege!° I shall beseech your
Highness,
In such a business give me leave to use
The help of mine own eyes.

KING.   Know'st thou not, Bertram,   115
What she has done for me?

BER.   Yes, my good lord,
But never hope to know why I should marry her.

KING. Thou know'st she has raised me from my
sickly bed.

BER. But follows it, my lord, to bring me down°
Must answer for your raising? I know her well.
She had her breeding° at my father's charge.   121
A poor physician's daughter my wife! Disdain
Rather corrupt me ever!°

KING. 'Tis only title thou disdain'st in her, the
which
I can build up. Strange is it that our bloods,°   .125
Of color, weight, and heat, poured all together,
Would quite confound distinction, yet stand off
In differences so mighty. If she be
All that is virtuous, save what thou dislikest,
A poor physician's daughter, thou dislikest   130
Of virtue for the name. But do not so.
From lowest place when virtuous things proceed,
The place is dignified by the doer's deed.
Where great additions swell's,° and virtue none,
It is a dropsied° honor. Good alone   135
Is good without a name. Vileness is so.

The property° by what it is should go,
Not by the title. She is young, wise, fair.
In these to nature she's immediate heir,
And these breed honor. That is honor's scorn   140
Which challenges itself as honor's born,
And is not like the sire.° Honors thrive
When rather from our acts we them derive
Than our foregoers.° The mere word's° a slave
Deboshed° on every tomb, on every grave   145
A lying trophy, and as oft is dumb
Where dust and damned oblivion is the tomb
Of honored bones indeed. What should be said?
If thou canst like this creature as a maid,
I can create the rest.° Virtue and she   150
Is her own dower, honor and wealth from me.

BER. I cannot love her, nor will strive to do 't.

KING. Thou wrong'st thyself if thou shouldst
strive to choose.°

HEL. That you are well restored, my lord, I'm
glad.
Let the rest go.°   155

KING. My honor's at the stake; which to defeat,
I must produce my power. Here, take her hand,
Proud scornful boy, unworthy this good gift;
That dost in vile misprision° shackle up
My love and her desert; that canst not dream,   160
We, poising us in her defective scale,°
Shall weigh thee to the beam; that wilt not know
It is in us to plant thine honor where
We please to have it grow. Check thy contempt.
Obey our will, which travails in° thy good.   165
Believe not thy disdain, but presently°
Do thine own fortunes that obedient right
Which both thy duty owes and our power claims,
Or I will throw thee from my care for ever
Into the staggers° and the careless lapse   170
Of youth and ignorance, both my revenge and hate
Loosing upon thee, in the name of justice,
Without all terms of pity. Speak! Thine answer!

BER. Pardon, my gracious lord, for I submit
My fancy° to your eyes. When I consider   175
What great creation and what dole° of honor
Flies where you bid it, I find that she, which late
Was in my nobler thoughts most base, is now

137. **property**: natural quality.   140–42. **That . . . sire**: it is a disgrace to honor whenever a man declares (*challenges*) that he is honorable merely because of the title he has inherited, and not because of the honorable qualities which won that title for his ancestor.   144. **foregoers**: ancestors. **mere word**: i.e., honor.   145. **Deboshed**: debauched, disgraced.   150. **create . . . rest**: give her a title which will make her "honorable."   153. **if . . . choose**: if you presume to choose contrary to my command. As ward Bertram has no choice in the matter, See I.i.5,n.   155. **Let . . . go**: if he will not have me, so be it. Helena is prepared to let Bertram go, but the King now regards his refusal as contemptuous.   159. **misprision**: contempt.   161. **poising . . . scale**: when I add my weight to hers, you will be light indeed.   165. **travails in**: labors for.   166. **presently**: immediately.   170. **staggers**: giddiness.   175. **fancy**: love.   176. **dole**: portion

101. **got**: begot.   106. **father . . . wine**: was no water drinker; i.e., milksop.   113. **liege**: lord.   119. **bring me down**: disgrace me.   121. **breeding**: education.   122–23. **Disdain . . . ever**: may I be shamed forever. Bertram's objection to marrying Helena is that she is not his social equal — a matter of supreme importance in Shakespeare's time.   125–28. **bloods . . . mighty**: i.e., there is no real difference between her blood and yours or mine, except for inequality in rank which you regard so highly.   134. **Where . . . swell's**: where we are puffed up merely by titles (*additions*).   135. **dropsied**: swollen by disease.

The praisèd of the King; who, so ennobled,
Is as't were born so.

KING.   Take her by the hand,   180
And tell her she is thine; to whom I promise
A counterpoise,° if not to thy estate
A balance more replete.°

BER.   I take her hand.

KING. Good fortune and the favor of the King
Smile upon this cóntract, whose ceremony   185
Shall seem expedient on the now-born brief°
And be performed tonight. The solemn feast
Shall more attend upon the coming space,
Expecting° absent friends.° As thou lovest her,
Thy love's to me religious, else, does err.   190

[*Exeunt all but* LAFEU *and* PAROLLES.]

LAF. Do you hear, monsieur? A word with you.

PAR. Your pleasure, sir?

LAF. Your lord and master did well to make his
recantation.   195

PAR. Recantation! My lord! My master!

LAF. Aye. Is it not a language I speak?

PAR. A most harsh one, and not to be understood
without bloody succeeding. My master!   200

LAF. Are you companion to the Count Rousillon?

PAR. To any count, to all counts, to what is man.

LAF. To what is count's man. Count's master is
of another style.

PAR. You are too old, sir. Let it satisfy you, you
are too old.

LAF. I must tell thee, sirrah, I write man,° to
which title age cannot bring thee.   209

PAR. What I dare too well do, I dare not do.

LAF. I did think thee, for two ordinaries,° to be a
pretty wise fellow. Thou didst make tolerable vent°
of thy travel. It might pass. Yet the scarfs and the
bannerets about thee did manifoldly dissuade me
from believing thee a vessel of too great a   215
burden.° I have now found° thee. When I lose thee
again, I care not. Yet art thou good for nothing but
taking up,° and that thou'rt scarce worth.

PAR. Hadst thou not the privilege of antiquity
upon thee ——   221

LAF. Do not plunge thyself too far in anger, lest
thou hasten thy trial, which if —— Lord have mercy
on thee for a hen!° So, my good window of lattice,
fare thee well. Thy casement I need not open, for I
look through thee. Give me thy hand.   226

PAR. My lord, you give me most egregious° indignity.

LAF. Aye, with all my heart, and thou art worthy
of it.   231

PAR. I have not, my lord, deserved it.

LAF. Yes, good faith, every dram° of it; and I
will not bate° thee a scruple.°

PAR. Well, I shall be wiser.   235

LAF. Ev'n as soon as thou canst, for thou hast to
pull at a smack° o' the contrary.° If ever thou be'st
bound in thy scarf and beaten, thou shalt find what
it is to be proud of thy bondage. I have a desire to
hold my acquaintance with thee, or rather my   240
knowledge, that I may say in the default,° "He is
a man I know."

PAR. My lord, you do me most insupportable vexation.

LAF. I would it were Hell pains for thy sake,   245
and my poor doing eternal. For doing I am past, as
I will by thee, in what motion age will give me
leave.°   [*Exit.*]

PAR. Well, thou hast a son shall take this disgrace
off me, scurvy, old, filthy, scurvy lord! Well, I   250
must be patient. There is no fettering of authority.
I'll beat him, by my life, if I can meet him with any
convenience, an he were double and double a lord.
I'll have no more pity of his age than I would have
of —— I'll beat him, an if I could but meet him
again.   256

[*Re-enter* LAFEU.]

LAF. Sirrah, your lord and master's married.
There's news for you! You have a new mistress.

PAR. I most unfeignedly beseech your lordship to
make some reservation of your wrongs. He is my
good lord. Whom I serve above is my Master.   261

LAF. Who? God?

PAR. Aye, sir.

LAF. The Devil it is that's thy master. Why dost
thou garter° up thy arms o' this fashion? Dost
make hose° of thy sleeves? Do other servants so?
Thou wert best set thy lower part where thy nose
stands. By mine honor, if I were but two hours
younger, I'd beat thee. Methinks thou art a general offense, and every man should beat thee. I   270

---

182. counterpoise: a reward which shall make her equal to you.
182–83. if . . . replete: if not a gift of lands, something more
valuable — e.g., a title.   185–86. whose . . . brief: the ceremony of marriage shall follow quickly (*expedient*) on my present
(*now-born*) command. brief: a royal command.   187–89. solemn
. . . friends: the formal wedding feast shall wait (*attend*) until
the time when (*coming space*) absent friends have arrived.
189. Expecting: awaiting.   208. write man: declare myself to
be a man.   211. two ordinaries: for the space of two meals.
212. tolerable vent: sufficient account.   213–16. Yet . . . burden:
yet you did not carry the outward signs of being a vessel of any
great size or importance. Lafeu means that Parolles at first gave
out that he was a great traveler, but he has since shown himself
to be insignificant. Large vessels were elaborately decorated with
flags and streamers. See Pl. 7b.   216. found: "found" and
"found out."   218. taking up: picking up, as a thing found
in the streets.

224. hen: silly, cackling creature.   227. egregious: flagrant.
233. dram: small part, lit., one sixteenth of an ounce.   234. bate:
diminish. scruple: lit., one third of a dram.   236–37. for . . .
contrary: for you'll have to taste the opposite; i.e., you'll soon
show yourself a fool. smack: taste.   241. in . . . default: if need
shall arise.   246–48. For . . . leave: I'm too old to do much to
you; but I will now leave you ([go] *by thee*) as fast as my old
age will let me.   265. garter: tie. Parolles is wearing exagger-
atedly full sleeves which need a band to control them.   266. hose:
See Notes on Costume, p. 93a–b.

think thou wast created for men to breathe° themselves upon thee.

PAR. This is hard and undeserved measure, my lord.

LAF. Go to, sir. You were beaten in Italy for   275 picking a kernel out of a pomegranate.° You are a vagabond, and no true traveler. You are more saucy with lords and honorabl̄ personages than the commission of your birth and virtue gives you heraldry.° You are not worth another word, else I'd call you knave. I leave you.   [*Exit.*]   281

PAR. Good, very good. It is so, then. Good, very good. Let it be concealed awhile.

[*Re-enter* BERTRAM.]

BER. Undone and forfeited to cares forever!

PAR. What's the matter, sweetheart?   285

BER. Although before the solemn priest I have sworn,

I will not bed her.

PAR. What, what, sweetheart?

BER. Oh, my Parolles, they have married me!

I'll to the Tuscan wars, and never bed her.   290

PAR. France is a dog-hole, and it no more merits The tread of a man's foot. To the wars!

BER. There's letters from my mother. What the import is,

I know not yet.

PAR. Aye, that would be known. To the wars, my boy, to the wars!   295

He wears his honor in a box unseen

That hugs his kicky-wicky° here at home,

Spending his manly marrow in her arms,

Which should sustain the bound and high curvet°

Of Mars's fiery steed. To° other regions   300

France is a stable; we that dwell in 't jades.°

Therefore, to the war!

BER. It shall be so. I'll send her to my house,

Acquaint my mother with my hate to her

And wherefore I am fled, write to the King   305

That which I durst not speak. His present gift

Shall furnish me to those Italian fields

Where noble fellows strike. War is no strife

To the dark house and the detested wife.   309

PAR. Will this *capriccio*° hold in thee, art sure?

BER. Go with me to my chamber, and advise me.

I'll send her straight away. Tomorrow

I'll to the wars, she to her single sorrow.

PAR. Why, these balls° bound. There's noise in it. 'Tis hard.

A young man married is a man that's marred.   315

Therefore away, and leave her bravely. Go!

The King has done you wrong, but, hush, 'tis so.

[*Exeunt.*]

SCENE IV. *Paris. The* KING'S *palace.*

[*Enter* HELENA *and* CLOWN.]

HEL. My mother greets me kindly. Is she well?

CLO. She is not well, but yet she has her health. She's very merry, but yet she is not well. But thanks be given, she's very well and wants nothing i' the world; but yet she is not well.   5

HEL. If she be very well, what does she ail, that she's not very well?

CLO. Truly, she's very well indeed, but for two things.

HEL. What two things?   10

CLO. One, that she's not in Heaven, whither God send her quickly! The other, that she's in earth, from whence God send her quickly!

[*Enter* PAROLLES.]

PAR. Bless you, sir, my fortunate lady!

HEL. I hope, sir, I have your good will to have mine own good fortunes.   16

PAR. You had my prayers to lead them on, and to keep them on, have them still. Oh, my knave, how does my old lady?

CLO. So that you had her wrinkles and I her money, I would she did as you say.   21

PAR. Why, I say nothing.

CLO. Marry, you are the wiser man, for many a man's tongue shakes out° his master's undoing. To say nothing, to do nothing, to know nothing,   25 and to have nothing is to be a great part of your title,° which is within a very little of nothing.

PAR. Away! Thou'rt a knave.

CLO. You should have said, sir, before° a knave thou'rt a knave; that's, before me thou'rt a knave. This had been truth, sir.   31

PAR. Go to, thou art a witty fool. I have found thee.°

CLO. Did you find me in yourself, sir? Or were you taught to find me? The search, sir, was   35 profitable, and much fool may you find in you, even to the world's pleasure and the increase of laughter.

PAR. A good knave, i' faith, and well fed. Madam, my lord will go away tonight.   40

A very serious business calls on him.

The great prerogative and rite of love,

Which, as your due, time claims, he does acknowledge,

But puts it off to a compelled restraint,°

---

271. breathe: exercise.   275–76. You . . . pomegranate: i.e., you were so despised that men beat you on the slightest excuse. 278–80. commission . . . heraldry: i.e., you have no legitimate claim through either your good family or your personality. See App. 9.   297. kicky-wicky: little wife.   299. curvet: prancing of a high-spirited horse.   300. To: compared with.   301. jades: horses of poor quality.   310. *capriccio*: caprice.   314. balls: tennis balls — made of leather stuffed with hair. A well-made **tennis ball** rebounded from the hard court with a good smack.

Sc. iv: 24. shakes out: causes. The metaphor is from shaking out rubbish from the lap.   27. title: what you own.   29. before: in the presence of.   32–33. found thee: found you out.   44. puts . . . restraint: circumstances compel him to postpone it.

Whose want, and whose delay, is strewed with
    sweets,   45
Which they distil now in the curbèd time,°
To make the coming hour o'erflow with joy
And pleasure drown the brim.

HEL.   What's his will else?

PAR. That you will take your instant leave o' the
    King
And make this haste as your own good proceeding,°
Strengthened with what apology you think   51
May make it probable need.°

HEL.   What more commands he?

PAR. That, having this obtained, you presently
Attend his further pleasure.

HEL. In every thing I wait upon his will.   55

PAR. I shall report it so.

HEL. I pray you. [*Exit* PAROLLES.] Come, sirrah.
                            [*Exeunt.*]

SCENE V. *Paris. The* KING's *palace.*

[*Enter* LAFEU *and* BERTRAM.]

LAF. But I hope your lordship thinks not him a
soldier.

BER. Yes, my lord, and of very valiant approof.°

LAF. You have it from his own deliverance.°

BER. And by other warranted testimony.   5

LAF. Then my dial° goes not true. I took this lark
for a bunting.°

BER. I do assure you, my lord, he is very great in
knowledge, and accordingly valiant.

LAF. I have then sinned against his experience
and transgressed against his valor, and my state   11
that way is dangerous,° since I cannot yet find in
my heart to repent. Here he comes. I pray you make
us friends. I will pursue the amity.°   15

[*Enter* PAROLLES.]

PAR. [*To* BERTRAM] These things shall be done,
sir.

LAF. Pray you, sir, who's his tailor?

PAR. Sir?

LAF. Oh, I know him well, I, sir. He, sir, 's a
good workman, a very good tailor.   21

BER. [*Aside to* PAROLLES] Is she gone to the
King?

PAR. She is.

BER. Will she away tonight?

PAR. As you'll have her.   25

BER. I have writ my letters, casketed my treasure,

Given order for our horses, and tonight,
When I should take possession of the bride,
End ere I do begin.

LAF. A good traveler is something° at the   30
latter end of a dinner, but one that lies three thirds
and uses a known truth to pass a thousand nothings
with should be once heard and thrice beaten. God
save you, Captain.   34

BER. Is there any unkindness between my lord
and you, Monsieur?

PAR. I know not how I have deserved to run into
my lord's displeasure.

LAF. You have made shift° to run into 't, boots
and spurs and all, like him that leaped into the   40
custard; and out of it you'll run again, rather than
suffer question for your residence.°

BER. It may be you have mistaken him, my lord.

LAF. And shall do so ever, though I took him   45
at 's prayers. Fare you well, my lord; and believe
this of me: There can be no kernel in this light
nut. The soul of this man is his clothes. Trust him
not in matter of heavy consequence. I have kept of
them tame° and know their natures. Farewell,   50
Monsieur. I have spoken better of you than you have
or will to deserve at my hand, but we must do good
against evil.   [*Exit.*]

PAR. An idle lord, I swear.

BER. I think so.   55

PAR. Why, do you not know him?

BER. Yes, I do know him well, and common
speech
Gives him a worthy pass.° Here comes my clog.°

[*Enter* HELENA.]

HEL. I have, sir, as I was commanded from you,
Spoke with the King, and have procured his leave
For present parting. Only he desires   61
Some private speech with you.

BER.   I shall obey his will.
You must not marvel, Helen, at my course,
Which holds not color with the time,° nor does
The ministration and requirèd office   65
On my particular.° Prepared I was not
For such a business. Therefore am I found
So much unsettled. This drives me to entreat you
That presently you take your way for home,
And rather muse° than ask why I entreat you;   70
For my respects° are better than they seem,
And my appointments° have in them a need

---

46. **Which . . . time:** i.e., the joy of that time will be concentrated (*distilled*) because of the present forced delay (*curbed time*).   50. **your . . . proceeding:** as if it was your own proposal. 52. **probable need:** plausible excuse.

     Sc. v: 3. **approof:** proved valor.   4. **deliverance:** speech. 6. **dial:** watch.   7. **bunting:** a bird resembling a lark — but no songster.   11–12. **my . . . dangerous:** I am therefore in a state of sin.   15. **amity:** friendship.

30. **something:** a person to be highly regarded.   39. **made shift:** contrived.   42. **suffer . . . residence:** than stay to justify your remaining there — in Lafeu's displeasure.   49–50. **kept . . . tame:** have kept such specimens as pets.   58. **worthy pass:** good reputation. **clog:** a weight fastened round the leg of a beast to prevent it from straying.   64. **Which . . . time:** which seems so unsuitable (for a newly married man).   64–66. **nor . . . particular:** nor does that which you expect of me — i.e., my giving you the due of marriage.   70. **muse:** wonder.   71. **respects:** reasons. 72. **appointments:** purposes.

Greater than shows itself at the first view
To you that know them not. This to my mother.
                        [*Giving a letter.*]
'Twill be two days ere I shall see you. So   75
I leave you to your wisdom.
     HEL.   Sir, I can nothing say
But that I am your most obedient servant.
     BER. Come, come, no more of that.
     HEL.   And ever shall
With true observance seek to eke out that
Wherein toward me my homely stars have failed
To equal my great fortune.
     BER.   Let that go.   81
My haste is very great. Farewell. Hie home.
     HEL. Pray, sir, your pardon.
     BER.   Well, what would you say?
     HEL. I am not worthy of the wealth I owe;
Nor dare I say 'tis mine, and yet it is —   85
But, like a timorous thief, most fain would steal
What law does vouch mine own.
     BER.   What would you have?
     HEL. Something, and scarce so much. Nothing,
     indeed.
I would not tell you what I would, my lord. Faith,
     yes.   90
Strangers and foes do sunder,° and not kiss.
     BER. I pray you, stay not, but in haste to horse.
     HEL. I shall not break your bidding, good my
     lord.
     BER. Where are my other men, Monsieur? —
     Farewell!   [*Exit* HELENA.]
Go thou toward home, where I will never come   95
Whilst I can shake my sword or hear the drum.
Away, and for our flight.
     PAR.   Bravely, *coragio!*°   [*Exeunt.*]

Act III

SCENE I. *Florence. The* DUKE'S *palace.*

[*Flourish. Enter the* DUKE *of Florence, attended;
the two Frenchmen with a troop of soldiers.*]
     DUKE. So that from point to point now have you
     heard
The fundamental reasons of this war,
Whose great decision hath much blood let forth
And more thirsts after.
     1. LORD.   Holy seems the quarrel
Upon your Grace's part, black and fearful   5
On the opposer.
     DUKE. Therefore we marvel much our cousin
     France

Would in so just a business shut his bosom
Against our borrowing prayers.°
     2. LORD.   Good my lord,
The° reasons of our state I cannot yield   10
But like a common and an outward man
That the great figure of a council frames
By self-unable motion; therefore dare not
Say what I think of it, since I have found
Myself in my incertain grounds to fail   15
As often as I guessed.
     DUKE.   Be it his pleasure.
     1. LORD. But I am sure the younger of our nature,
That surfeit° on their ease, will day by day
Come here for physic.
     DUKE.   Welcome shall they be,
And all the honors that can fly from us   20
Shall on them settle. You know your places well.
When better fall, for your avails they fell.°
Tomorrow to the field.   [*Flourish. Exeunt.*]

SCENE II. *Rousillon. The* COUNT'S *palace.*

[*Enter* COUNTESS *and* CLOWN.]
     COUNTESS. It hath happened all as I would have
had it, save that he comes not along with her.
     CLO. By my troth,° I take my young lord to be a
very melancholy man.
     COUNTESS. By what observance, I pray you?   5
     CLO. Why, he will look upon his boot and sing,
mend the ruff° and sing, ask questions and sing,
pick his teeth and sing. I know a man that had this
trick of melancholy sold a goodly manor for a
song.   10
     COUNTESS. Let me see what he writes, and when
he means to come.   [*Opening a letter.*]
     CLO. I have no mind to Isbel since I was at Court.
Our old ling° and our Isbels o' the country are
nothing like your old ling and your Isbels o'   15
the Court. The brains of my Cupid's knocked out,
and I begin to love as an old man loves money, with
no stomach.
     COUNTESS. What have we here?
     CLO. E'en that you have there.   [*Exit.*]   20
     COUNTESS. [*Reads.*] "I have sent you a daughter-
in-law. She hath recovered° the King and undone
me. I have wedded her, not bedded her, and sworn
to make the 'not' eternal. You shall hear I am run
away. Know it before the report come. If there   25

Act III, Sc. i: **9. borrowing prayers:** petitions for help. **10–
13. The . . . motion:** i.e., I do not know the reason for our policy,
though, like any other man in the street, I can guess what is
decided by our Council. **13. self-unable motion:** impotent
guess. **18. surfeit:** grow sick. **22. When . . . fell:** i.e., when
better places become vacant, you will get them.
Sc. ii: **3. troth:** truth. **7. ruff:** See Note on Men's Costume,
p. 94a. **14. ling:** salt cod. **22. recovered:** cured.

---

91. sunder: part.   **97.** *coragio:* courage.

be breadth enough in the world, I will hold a long
distance. My duty to you.
                    Your unfortunate son,
                        BERTRAM."
This is not well, rash and unbridled boy,   30
To fly the favors of so good a King,
To pluck his indignation on thy head
By the misprising° of a maid too virtuous
For the contempt of empire.°
             [Re-enter CLOWN.*]*
CLO. Oh, madam, yonder is heavy news 35
within between two soldiers and my young lady!
   COUNTESS. What is the matter?
   CLO. Nay, there is some comfort in the news,
some comfort. Your son will not be killed so soon as
I thought he would.   40
   COUNTESS. Why should he be killed?
   CLO. So say I, madam, if he run away, as I hear
he does. The danger is in standing to 't.° That's the
loss of men, though it be the getting of children.
Here they come will tell you more. For my part, I
only hear your son was run away.   *[Exit.]* 46
   [Enter HELENA *and two* GENTLEMEN.*]*
   1. GENT. Save you, good madam.
   HEL. Madam, my lord is gone, forever gone.
   2. GENT. Do not say so.
   COUNTESS. Think upon patience. Pray you, gentle-
men,   50
I have felt so many quirks° of joy and grief
That the first face of neither, on the start,
Can woman me° unto 't. Where is my son, I pray
   you?
   2. GENT. Madam, he's gone to serve the Duke of
   Florence.   54
We met him thitherward,° for thence we came,
And after some dispatch° in hand at Court,
Thither we bend again.
   HEL. Look on his letter, madam. Here's my pass-
   port.
[Reads.] "When thou canst get the ring upon my
finger which never shall come off, and show 60
me a child begotten of thy body that I am father to,
then call me husband. But in such a ' then ' I write
a ' never.' "
This is a dreadful sentence.
   COUNTESS. Brought you this letter, gentlemen?
   1. GENT.   Aye, madam, 65
And for the contents' sake are sorry for our pains.
   COUNTESS. I prithee, lady, have a better cheer.
If thou engrossest° all the griefs are thine,
Thou robb'st me of a moiety.° He was my son,
But I do wash his name out of my blood,   70

And thou art all my child. Towards Florence is he?
   2. GENT. Aye, madam.
   COUNTESS.   And to be a soldier?
   2. GENT. Such is his noble purpose, and, believe 't,
The Duke will lay upon him all the honor
That good convenience° claims.
   COUNTESS.   Return you thither? 75
   1. GENT. Aye, madam, with the swiftest wing of
   speed.
   HEL. *[Reads.]* " Till I have no wife, I have noth-
   ing in France."
'Tis bitter.
   COUNTESS. Find you that there?
   HEL.   Aye, madam.
   1. GENT. 'Tis but the boldness of his hand, haply,°
which his heart was not consenting to.   80
   COUNTESS. Nothing in France until he have no
   wife!
There's nothing here that is too good for him
But only she, and she deserves a lord
That twenty such rude boys might tend upon
And call her hourly, mistress. Who was with him?
   1. GENT. A servant only, and a gentleman   86
Which I have sometime known.
   COUNTESS.   Parolles, was it not?
   1. GENT. Aye, my good lady, he.
   COUNTESS. A very tainted fellow, and full of
   wickedness.
My son corrupts a well-derivèd nature   90
With his inducement.°
   1. GENT.   Indeed, good lady,
The fellow has a deal of that too-much
Which holds him much to have.°
   COUNTESS. Y'are welcome, gentlemen.
I will entreat you, when you see my son,   95
To tell him that his sword can never win
The honor that he loses. More I'll entreat you
Written to bear along.
   2. GENT.   We serve you, madam,
In that and all your worthiest affairs.
   COUNTESS. Not so, but as we change our courte-
   sies.°   100
Will you draw near?
                 [Exeunt COUNTESS *and* GENTLEMEN.*]*
   HEL. " Till I have no wife, I have nothing in
   France."
Nothing in France until he has no wife!
Thou shalt have none, Rousillon, none in France;
Then hast thou all again. Poor lord! Is 't I   105
That chase thee from thy country and expose
Those tender limbs of thine to the event
Of the none-sparing war? And is it I

---

33. misprising: undervaluing.   **34. For . . . empire:** i.e., so
worthy that one would lose an empire to win her.   **43. standing to 't:** i.e., not running away.   **51. quirks:** sudden turns.
53. woman me: i.e., make me weep.   **55. thitherward:** on his
way thither.   **56. dispatch:** necessary business.   **68. engrossest:**
corner the market in.   **69. moiety:** share.   **75. convenience:** fitness.   **79. haply:** perhaps.   **90–91. My
. . . inducement:** i.e., my son's natural good is corrupted by his
influence.   **92–93. The . . . have:** i.e., he has too much evil influence over Bertram, who regards him too highly.   **100. as . . .
courtesies:** a polite phrase (like "You're welcome") — I will
allow you to serve me as I am allowed to serve you.

That drive thee from the sportive Court, where
   thou
Wast shot at with fair eyes, to be the mark   110
Of smoky muskets? O you leaden messengers
That ride upon the violent speed of fire,
Fly with false aim! Move the still-peering° air,
That sings with piercing. Do not touch my lord.
Whoever shoots at him, I set him there.   115
Whoever charges on his forward breast,
I am the caitiff° that do hold him to 't,
And, though I kill him not, I am the cause
His death was so effected. Better 'twere
I met the ravin° lion when he roared   120
With sharp constraint of hunger. Better 'twere
That all the miseries which nature owes
Were mine at once. No, come thou home, Rousillon,
Whence honor but of danger wins a scar,
As oft it loses all.° I will be gone.   125
My being here it is that holds thee hence.
Shall I stay here to do 't? No, no, although
The air of paradise did fan the house
And angels officed° all. I will be gone,
That pitiful rumor may report my flight   130
To consolate thine ear. Come, night; end, day!
For with the dark, poor thief, I'll steal away. [*Exit.*]

SCENE III. *Florence. Before the* DUKE's *palace.*

[*Flourish. Enter the* DUKE *of Florence,* BERTRAM,
   PAROLLES, SOLDIERS, *Drum, and Trumpets.*]
  DUKE. The General of our Horse° thou art, and
   we,
Great in our hope, lay our best love and credence
Upon thy promising fortune.
  BER.   Sir, it is
A charge too heavy for my strength; but yet
We'll strive to bear it for your worthy sake   5
To the extreme edge of hazard.
  DUKE.   Then go thou forth,
And Fortune play upon thy prosperous helm°
As thy auspicious mistress!
  BER.   This very day,
Great Mars, I put myself into thy file.°   9
Make me but like my thoughts, and I shall prove
A lover of thy drum, hater of love.   [*Exeunt.*]

SCENE IV. *Rousillon. The* COUNT's *palace.*

[*Enter* COUNTESS *and* STEWARD.]
  COUNTESS. Alas! And would you take the letter
   of her?
Might you not know she would do as she has done
By sending me a letter? Read it again.
  STEW. [*Reads.*]
" I am Saint Jaques' pilgrim,° thither gone.
   Ambitious love hath so in me offended   5
That barefoot plod I the cold ground upon,
   With sainted vow my faults to have amended.
Write, write, that from the bloody course of war
   My dearest master, your dear son, may hie.°
Bless him at home in peace, whilst I from far   10
   His name with zealous fervor sanctify.°
His taken° labors bid him me forgive.
   I, his despiteful Juno,° sent him forth
From courtly friends with camping foes to live,
   Where death and danger dogs the heels of
    worth.   15
He is too good and fair for Death and me;
   Whom° I myself embrace to set him free."
  COUNTESS. Ah, what sharp stings are in her
   mildest words!
Rinaldo, you did never lack advice° so much
As letting her pass so. Had I spoke with her,   20
I could have well diverted her intents,
Which thus she hath prevented.
  STEW.   Pardon me, madam.
If I had given you this at overnight,
She might have been o'erta'en; and yet she writes
Pursuit would be but vain.
  COUNTESS.   What angel shall   25
Bless this unworthy husband? He cannot thrive
Unless her prayers, whom Heaven delights to hear
And loves to grant, reprieve him from the wrath
Of greatest justice. Write, write, Rinaldo,
To this unworthy husband of his wife.   30
Let every word weigh heavy of her worth
That he does weigh too light. My greatest grief,
Though little he do feel it, set down sharply.
Dispatch the most convenient messenger.
When haply he shall hear that she is gone,   35
He will return, and hope I may that she,
Hearing so much, will speed her foot again,
Led hither by pure love. Which of them both
Is dearest to me, I have no skill in sense
To make distinction. Provide this messenger.   40
My heart is heavy and mine age is weak.
Grief would have tears, and sorrow bids me speak.
                         [*Exeunt.*]

---

113. still-peering: This is the F1 reading; there have been many
guesses at the right reading, none satisfactory. **117. caitiff:**
wretch. **120. ravin:** ravenous. **124–25. Whence . . . all:** from
the place where a man at best wins only an honorable scar but
often loses his life. **129. officed:** were the household servants.

  Sc. iii: 1. General . . . Horse: It seems at first sight improbable that a man so young should be given this important
command even in a play, but actually royal favorites (such as
the Earl of Essex) were given similar positions of responsibility
at a tender age. It was, however, usual to provide them with an
experienced officer as adviser. **7. helm:** helmet. **9. file:** troop.

  Sc. iv: 4. Saint . . . pilgrim: I am making a pilgrimage to the
shrine of St. James (a very famous shrine at Compostela in
Spain). **9. hie:** hasten. **11. sanctify:** make holy by my
prayers. **12. taken:** which he has undertaken. **13. despiteful
Juno:** spiteful Juno, the jealous wife of Jupiter, king of the gods.
17. Whom: i.e., Death. **19. advice:** good sense.

SCENE V. *Florence. Without the walls.*
A tucket° afar off.

[*Enter an old* WIDOW *of Florence,* DIANA, VIOLENTA,
and MARIANA, *with other* CITIZENS.]

WID. Nay, come, for if they do approach the city,
we shall lose all the sight.

DIA. They say the French Count has done most
honorable service.

WID. It is reported that he has taken their 5
greatest commander, and that with his own hand
he slew the Duke's brother. [*Tucket.*] We have lost
our labor. They are gone a contrary way. Hark!
You may know by their trumpets.

MAR. Come, let's return again and suffice 10
ourselves with the report of it. Well, Diana, take
heed of this French Earl.° The honor of a maid is
her name, and no legacy is so rich as honesty.

WID. I have told my neighbor how you have been
solicited by a gentleman his companion. 16

MAR. I know that knave. Hang him! One Parolles. A filthy officer he is in those suggestions for the
young Earl. Beware of them, Diana. Their promises, enticements, oaths, tokens, and all these 20
engines° of lust are not the things they go under.
Many a maid hath been seduced by them, and the
misery is, example,° that so terrible shows in the
wreck of maidenhood, cannot for all that 25
dissuade succession,° but that they are limed with
the twigs° that threaten them. I hope I need not to
advise you further, but I hope your own grace will
keep you where you are, though there were no further danger known but the modesty which is so
lost. 30

DIA. You shall not need to fear me.

WID. I hope so. [*Enter* HELENA, *disguised like a*
PILGRIM.] Look, here comes a pilgrim. I know she
will lie° at my house. Thither they send one another. I'll question her. God save you, pilgrim!
Whither are you bound? 36

HEL. To Saint Jaques le Grand.
Where do the palmers° lodge, I do beseech you?

WID. At the Saint Francis here beside the port.°

HEL. Is this the way? 40

WID. Aye, marry, is't. [*A march afar.*] Hark you!
They come this way.
If you will tarry, holy pilgrim,
But till the troops come by,
I will conduct you where you shall be lodged,
The rather, for I think I know your hostess 45

As ample° as myself.

HEL.   Is it yourself?

WID. If you shall please so, pilgrim.

HEL. I thank you and will stay upon your leisure.

WID. You came, I think, from France?

HEL.   I did so.

WID. Here you shall see a countryman of yours
That has done worthy service.

HEL.   His name, I pray you? 51

DIA. The Count Rousillon. Know you such a
one?

HEL. But by the ear, that hears most nobly of
him.
His face I know not.

DIA.   Whatsome'er he is,
He's bravely taken here. He stole from France, 55
As 'tis reported, for the King had married him
Against his liking. Think you it is so?

HEL. Aye, surely, mere° the truth. I know his
lady.

DIA. There is a gentleman that serves the Count
Reports but coarsely of her.

HEL.   What's his name? 60

DIA. Monsieur Parolles.

HEL.   Oh, I believe with him,
In argument of praise, or to the worth
Of the great Count himself, she is too mean
To have her name repeated. All her deserving
Is a reservèd honesty,° and that 65
I have not heard examined.°

DIA.   Alas, poor lady!
'Tis a hard bondage to become the wife
Of a detesting lord.

WID. I warrant good creature, wheresoe'er she is,
Her heart weighs sadly. This young maid might do
her 70
A shrewd° turn if she pleased.

HEL.   How do you mean?
May be the amorous Count solicits her
In the unlawful purpose.

WID.   He does indeed,
And brokes° with all that can in such a suit
Corrupt the tender honor of a maid; 75
But she is armed for him and keeps her guard
In honestest defense.

MAR.   The gods forbid else!

WID. So, now they come.
[*Drum and Colors. Enter* BERTRAM, PAROLLES, *and*
the whole army.]
That is Antonio, the Duke's eldest son.
That, Escalus.

HEL.   Which is the Frenchman?

DIA.   He; 80
That with the plume. 'Tis a most gallant fellow.

Sc. v: s.d., **tucket:** trumpet call denoting the approach of an
important person. **12. Earl:** Count. **21. engines:** devices.
24. example: i.e., the precedent of others' ruin. **26. dissuade
succession:** prevent others from being deceived in turn. **26–
27. limed . . . twigs:** caught in the same trap. Birdlime is a
sticky substance spread on twigs on which the bird is caught
and held fast. **34. lie:** lodge. **38. palmers:** pilgrims. See
R & J, I.v.102,n. **39. port:** city gate.

46. ample: well. **58. mere:** absolutely. **65. reserved honesty:**
well-guarded chastity. **66. examined:** questioned. **71. shrewd:**
nasty, bitter. **74. brokes:** makes offers.

I would he loved his wife. If he were honester,
He were much goodlier. Is 't not a handsome gen-
   tleman?
  HEL. I like him well.
  DIA. 'Tis pity he is not honest. Yond's that same
   knave   85
That leads him to these places.° Were I his lady,
I would poison that vile rascal.
  HEL.   Which is he?
  DIA. That jackanapes with scarves.° Why is he
melancholy?
  HEL. Perchance he's hurt i' the battle.   90
  PAR. Lose our drum!° Well.
  MAR. He's shrewdly vexed° at something. Look,
he has spied us.
  WID. Marry, hang you!
  MAR. And your courtesy, for a ring carrier!° 95
     [*Exeunt* BERTRAM, PAROLLES, *and army.*]
  WID. The troop is past. Come, pilgrim, I will
   bring you
Where you shall host.° Of enjoined° penitents
There's four or five, to great Saint Jaques bound,
Already at my house.
  HEL.   I humbly thank you.
Please it this matron and this gentle maid   100
To eat with us tonight, the charge and thanking
Shall be for me; and, to requite you further,
I will bestow some precepts of° this virgin
Worthy the note.
  BOTH. We'll take your offer kindly. [*Exeunt.*]

SCENE VI. *Camp before Florence.*

[*Enter* BERTRAM *and the two French* LORDS.]
  2. LORD. Nay, good my lord, put him to 't.° Let
him have his way.
  1. LORD. If your lordship find him not a hilding,°
hold me no more in your respect.
  2. LORD. On my life, my lord, a bubble.   5
  BER. Do you think I am so far deceived in him?
  2. LORD. Believe it, my lord, in mine own direct
knowledge, without any malice, but to speak of him
as my kinsman, he's a most notable coward, an infinite and endless liar, an hourly promise-   10
breaker, the owner of no one good quality worthy
your lordship's entertainment.
  1. LORD. It were fit you knew him, lest, reposing

too far in his virtue, which he hath not, he   15
might at some great and trusty business in a main
danger fail you.
  BER. I would I knew in what particular action to
try him.
  1. LORD. None better than to let him fetch   20
off° his drum, which you hear him so confidently
undertake to do.
  2. LORD. I with a troop of Florentines will suddenly surprise him. Such I will have whom I am
sure he knows not from the enemy. We will   25
bind and hoodwink° him so that he shall suppose
no other but that he is carried into the leaguer° of
the adversaries when we bring him to our own
tents. Be but your lordship present at his examination. If he do not, for the promise of his life   30
and in the highest compulsion of base fear, offer to
betray you and deliver all the intelligence° in his
power against you, and that with the divine forfeit
of his soul upon oath, never trust my judgment in
any thing.   35
  1. LORD. Oh, for the love of laughter, let him
fetch his drum. He says he has a stratagem for 't.
When your lordship sees the bottom of his success
in 't, and to what metal this counterfeit lump of
ore will be melted, if you give him not John   40
Drum's entertainment,° your inclining cannot be
removed. Here he comes.
         [*Enter* PAROLLES.]
  2. LORD. [*Aside to* BERTRAM] Oh, for the love of
laughter, hinder not the honor of his design. Let
him fetch off his drum in any hand.°   45
  BER. How now, monsieur! This drum sticks
sorely in your disposition.°
  1. LORD. A pox° on 't, let it go. 'Tis but a drum.
  PAR. "But a drum"! Is 't "but a drum"? A 50
drum so lost! There was excellent command — to
charge in with our horse upon our own wings, and
to rend our own soldiers!
  1. LORD. That was not to be blamed in the command of the service. It was a disaster of war   55
that Caesar himself could not have prevented if he
had been there to command.
  BER. Well, we cannot greatly condemn our success. Some dishonor we had in the loss of that drum,
but it is not to be recovered.   60
  PAR. It might have been recovered.
  BER. It might, but it is not now.
  PAR. It is to be recovered. But that the merit of
service is seldom attributed to the true and exact

---

86. to . . . places: to our house.   88. jackanapes . . . scarves:
overdressed monkey.   91. Lose . . . drum: See later III.vi.20,n.
92. shrewdly vexed: bitterly annoyed.   95. ring carrier: a
bawd, one who brings a token for an improper assignation.
97. host: lodge. enjoined: bound by an oath.   103. precepts of:
advice on.
  Sc. vi: 1. put . . . to 't: compel him to do it.   3. hilding:
worthless creature.

20–21. fetch off: rescue. In each company of soldiers there was
a flag and a drum; to lose either in fight was a great disgrace.
Hence Parolles' apparent eagerness to recover his company's
drum.   26. hoodwink: blindfold.   27. leaguer: camp.   32. intelligence: information.   40–41. John . . . entertainment: a
proverbial phrase meaning "a good beating."   45. in . . . hand:
whatever happens.   46–47. sticks . . . disposition: is causing
you a lot of worry.   49. pox: plague, lit., venereal disease.

performer, I would have that drum or another,° or "*Hic Jacet.*"°   66

BER. Why, if you have a stomach, to 't, monsieur, if you think your mystery° in stratagem can bring this instrument of honor again into his native quarter, be magnanimous° in the enterprise, 70 and go on. I will grace the attempt for a worthy exploit. If you speed well in it, the Duke shall both speak of it and extend to you what further becomes his greatness, even to the utmost syllable of your worthiness.   75

PAR. By the hand of a soldier, I will undertake it.

BER. But you must not now slumber in it.

PAR. I'll about it this evening, and I will presently pen down my dilemmas,° encourage myself in 80 my certainty, put myself into my mortal preparation,° and by midnight look to hear further from me.

BER. May I be bold to acquaint His Grace you are gone about it?   85

PAR. I know not what the success will be, my lord, but the attempt I vow.

BER. I know thou'rt valiant, and, to the possibility° of thy soldiership, will subscribe for thee. Farewell.

PAR. I love not many words.   [*Exit.*] 91

2. LORD. No more than a fish loves water. Is not this a strange fellow, my lord, that so confidently seems to undertake this business, which he knows is not to be done; damns himself to do, and dares better be damned than to do 't?   96

1. LORD. You do not know him, my lord, as we do. Certain it is that he will steal himself into a man's favor and for a week escape a great deal of discoveries; but when you find him out, you have him ever after.   101

BER. Why, do you think he will make no deed at all of this that so seriously he does address himself unto?

2. LORD. None in the world, but return with 105 an invention and clap upon you two or three probable lies. But we have almost embossed° him. You shall see his fall tonight; for indeed he is not for your lordship's respect.

1. LORD. We'll make you some sport with 110 the fox ere we case° him. He was first smoked° by the old Lord Lafeu. When his disguise and he is parted, tell me what a sprat° you shall find him;

which you shall see this very night.

2. LORD. I must go look my twigs.° He shall be caught.   115

BER. Your brother he shall go along with me.

2. LORD. As 't please your lordship. I'll leave you.   [*Exit.*]

BER. Now will I lead you to the house and show you
The lass I spoke of.

1. LORD.   But you say she's honest.

BER. That's all the fault. I spoke with her but once   120
And found her wondrous cold, but I sent to her,
By this same coxcomb that we have i' the wind,°
Tokens and letters which she did resend;
And this is all I have done. She's a fair creature.
Will you go see her?

1. LORD.   With all my heart, my lord. 125
    [*Exeunt.*]

SCENE VII. *Florence. The* WIDOW'S *house.*

[*Enter* HELENA *and* WIDOW.]

HEL. If you misdoubt me that I am not she,
I know not how I shall assure you further,
But I shall lose the grounds I work upon.°

WID. Though my estate be fallen, I was well born,
Nothing acquainted with these businesses,   5
And would not put my reputation now
In any staining act.

HEL.   Nor would I wish you.
First, give me trust, the Count he is my husband,
And what to your sworn counsel° I have spoken
Is so from word to word; and then you cannot, 10
By the good aid that I of you shall borrow,
Err in bestowing it.

WID.   I should believe you,
For you have showed me that which well approves
You're great in fortune.

HEL.   Take this purse of gold,
And let me buy your friendly help thus far,   15
Which I will overpay and pay again
When I have found it. The Count he woos your daughter,
Lays down his wanton siege before her beauty,
Resolved to carry her. Let her in fine° consent
As we'll direct her how 'tis best to bear it.   20
Now his important° blood will naught deny
That she'll demand. A ring the County° wears
That downward hath succeeded in his house
From son to son, some four or five descents

65. another: i.e., one belonging to the enemy.   66. *Hic Jacet:* "Here Lies" — the words set on a tombstone; i.e., "I'll die in the attempt."   68. mystery: expert knowledge.   70. magnanimous: courageous.   80. dilemmas: a list of arguments for and against a certain course of action.   81–82. put . . . preparation: prepare myself for death.   88–89. possibility: extreme limits of. 107. embossed: driven him, like an animal, to extreme exhaustion.   111. case: strip him of his skin. smoked: found out. 113. sprat: worthless thing, lit., a small fish caught in shoals and sold very cheap.

115. twigs: See III.v.26–27,n.   122. have . . . wind: are hunting.
    Sc. vii: 3. But . . . upon: i.e., unless (*but*) I reveal my secret.
9. sworn counsel: promised secrecy.   19. in fine: in short.
21. important: eager.   22. County: Count.

Since the first father wore it. This ring he holds   25
In most rich choice,° yet in his idle fire,
To buy his will, it would not seem too dear,
Howe'er repented after.

WID.   Now I see
The bottom of your purpose.

HEL. You see it lawful, then. It is no more,   30
But that your daughter, ere she seems as won,
Desires this ring, appoints him an encounter,
In fine, delivers me to fill the time,
Herself most chastely absent. After this,
To marry° her, I'll add three thousand crowns   35
To what is past° already.

WID.   I have yielded.
Instruct my daughter how she shall perséver,°
That time and place with this deceit so lawful
May prove coherent.° Every night he comes
With musics of all sorts and songs composed   40
To her unworthiness. It nothing steads° us
To chide him from our eaves, for he persists
As if his life lay on 't.

HEL.   Why then tonight
Let us assay our plot; which,° if it speed,°
Is wicked meaning in a lawful deed,   45
And lawful meaning in a lawful act,
Where both not sin, and yet a sinful fact.
But let's about it.   [*Exeunt.*]

Act IV

SCENE I. *Without the Florentine camp.*

[*Enter* SECOND FRENCH LORD, *with five or six other* SOLDIERS *in ambush.*]

2. LORD. He can come no other way but by this hedgecorner. When you sally upon him, speak what terrible language you will. Though you understand it not yourselves, no matter, for we must not seem to understand him, unless some one among us whom we must produce for an interpreter.   7

1. SOLD. Good Captain, let me be the interpreter.

2. LORD. Art not acquainted with him? Knows he not thy voice?   11

1 SOLD. No, sir, I warrant you.

2. LORD. But what linsey-woolsey° hast thou to speak to us again?

1. SOLD. E'en such as you speak to me.   15

2. LORD. He must think us some band of strangers° i' the adversary's entertainment. Now he hath a smack° of all neighboring languages. Therefore° we must everyone be a man of his own fancy, not to know what we speak one to another. So we   20 seem to know, is to know straight our purpose. Choughs' language,° gabble enough, and good enough. As for you, interpreter, you must seem very politic. But couch,° ho! Here he comes to beguile two hours in a sleep, and then to return and swear the lies he forges.   26

[*Enter* PAROLLES.]

PAR. Ten o'clock. Within these three hours 'twill be time enough to go home. What shall I say I have done? It must be a very plausive° invention that carries it. They begin to smoke° me, and   30 disgraces have of late knocked too often at my door. I find my tongue is too foolhardy, but my heart hath the fear of Mars before it and of his creatures, not daring the reports of my tongue.   35

2. LORD. [*Aside*] This is the first truth that e'er thine own tongue was guilty of.

PAR. What the Devil should move° me to undertake the recovery of this drum, being not ignorant of the impossibility, and knowing I had no   40 such purpose? I must give myself some hurts and say I got them in exploit. Yet slight ones will not carry it. They will say, " Came you off with so little? " And great ones I dare not give. Wherefore, what's the instance? Tongue, I must put you   45 into a butter-woman's° mouth, and buy myself another of Bajazet's mule° if you prattle me into these perils.

2. LORD. [*Aside*] Is it possible he should know what he is, and be that he is?   49

PAR. I would the cutting of my garments would serve the turn, or the breaking of my Spanish sword.

2. LORD. [*Aside*] We cannot afford you so.°

PAR. Or the baring° of my beard, and to say it was in stratagem.   55

2. LORD. [*Aside*] 'Twould not do.

PAR. Or to drown my clothes, and say I was stripped.

2. LORD. [*Aside*] Hardly serve.

PAR. Though I swore I leaped from the window of the citadel ——   61

---

25. In . . . choice: in high regard.   35. To marry: i.e., toward her dowry.   36. past: given.   37. persever: carry on.   39. coherent: consistent.   41. steads: helps.   44. speed: succeed.   44–47. which . . . fact: Helena means that Bertram has wicked designs in that he is hoping to seduce Diana, but his action in fact will be lawful, since he will be having intercourse with his own wife, even though his act in intention is sinful.

Act IV, Sc. i: 13. linsey-woolsey: lit., a cloth made of linen and wool, so "hodgepodge."

16–17. strangers: foreigners.   18. smack: smattering.   18-21. Therefore . . . purpose: i.e., we must all speak some imaginary language (*fancy*), and though we don't know each other's meaning, so long as we seem to know, we shall achieve our purpose.   22. Choughs' language: jackdaws' chatter.   24. couch: lie down.   29. plausive: plausible.   30. smoke: suspect.   38. move: persuade.   46. butter-woman: women who sold butter in the markets, notorious for their shrill tongues.   47. Bajazet's mule: not satisfactorily explained. Bajazet is a character in Marlowe's *Tamburlane* who is monstrously maltreated and laments accordingly.   53. afford . . . so: let you off so easily.   54. baring: shaving.

2. LORD. [*Aside*] How deep?

PAR. Thirty fathom.

2. LORD. [*Aside*] Three great oaths would scarce make that be believed. 65

PAR. I would I had any drum of the enemy's. I would swear I recovered it.

2. LORD. [*Aside*] You shall hear one anon.°

PAR. A drum now of the enemy's ——
                       [*Alarum° within.*]

2. LORD. *Throca movousus, cargo, cargo, cargo.*

ALL. *Cargo, cargo, cargo, villianda par corbo, cargo.* 72

PAR. Oh, ransom, ransom! Do not hide mine eyes.   [*They seize and blindfold him.*]

1. SOLD. *Boskos thromuldo boskos.* 75

PAR. I know you are the Muskos' regiment, And I shall lose my life for want of language. If there be here German, or Dane, low Dutch, Italian, or French, let him speak to me. I'll 79 Discover° that which shall undo the Florentine.

1. SOLD. *Boskos vauvado.* I understand thee and can speak thy tongue. *Kerelybonto,* sir, betake thee to thy faith,° for seventeen poniards° are at thy bosom.

PAR. Oh! 85

1. SOLD. Oh, pray, pray, pray! *Manka revania dulche.*

2. LORD. *Oscorbidulchos volivorco.*

1. SOLD. The General is content to spare thee yet, And, hoodwinked as thou art, will lead thee on To gather from thee. Haply thou mayst inform 91 Something to save thy life.

PAR.   Oh, let me live! And all the secrets of our camp I'll show, Their force, their purposes — nay, I'll speak that Which you will wonder at.

1. SOLD.   But wilt thou faithfully? 95

PAR. If I do not, damn me.

1. SOLD. *Acordo linta.*
Come on. Thou art granted space.°
           [*Exit, with* PAROLLES *guarded.*
            A short alarum within.]

2. LORD. Go tell the Count Rousillon and my brother,
We have caught the woodcock° and will keep him muffled° 100
Till we do hear from them.

2. SOLD.   Captain, I will.

2. LORD. A'° will betray us all unto ourselves. Inform on that.

2. SOLD. So I will, sir.

2. LORD. Till then I'll keep him dark and safely locked.   [*Exeunt.*] 105

SCENE II. *Florence. The* WIDOW'S *house.*

[*Enter* BERTRAM *and* DIANA.]

BER. They told me that your name was Fontibell.

DIA. No, my good lord, Diana.

BER.   Titled goddess!
And worth it with addition!° But, fair soul,
In your fine frame hath love no quality?
If the quick fire of youth light not your mind, 5
You are no maiden, but a monument.°
When you are dead, you should be such a one
As you are now; for you are cold and stern,
And now you should be as your mother was
When your sweet self was got. 10

DIA. She then was honest.

BER.   So should you be.

DIA.   No.
My mother did but duty; such, my lord,
As you owe to your wife.

BER.   No more o' that!
I prithee do not strive against my vows.
I was compelled to her, but I love thee 15
By love's own sweet constraint, and will for ever
Do thee all rights of service.

DIA.   Aye, so you serve us
Till we serve you; but when you have our roses,
You barely leave our thorns to prick ourselves,
And mock us with our bareness.

BER.   How have I sworn! 20

DIA. 'Tis not the many oaths that makes the truth,
But the plain single vow that is vowed true.
What is not holy, that we swear not by,
But take the High'st to witness. Then, pray you tell me,
If I should swear by Jove's° great attributes 25
I loved you dearly, would you believe my oaths
When I did love you ill?° This has no holding,°
To swear by Him whom I protest to love,
That I will work against Him.° Therefore your oaths
Are words and poor conditions,° but unsealed —°
At least in my opinion.

BER.   Change it, change it. 31
Be not so holy-cruel.° Love is holy,

Sc. ii: **3. addition:** title added to the original name.   **6. monument:** i.e., cold as stone.   **25. Jove:** used instead of "God" to avoid the penalties laid down in the statute against profanity in plays. See p. 653b.   **27. When . . . ill:** when in fact I did not love you at all. **holding:** validity.   **28–29. Him . . . Him:** Jove; i.e., God.   **30. poor conditions:** worthless. **unsealed:** unconfirmed. Diana's argument (ll. 21–31) is that Bertram's oaths, though made by all that is holy, are themselves invalid, for he is in fact preparing to commit an unholy act.   **32. holy-cruel:** so cruel by being chaste.

68. anon: by and by.   **69. s.d., Alarum:** battle noises off stage. **80. Discover:** reveal.   **82–83. betake . . . faith:** say your prayers.   **83. poniards:** daggers.   **98. space:** temporary reprieve.   **100. woodcock:** a very foolish bird. See *T Night,* II.v.92. **muffled:** wrapped up.   **102. A':** he.

And my integrity ne'er knew the crafts
That you do charge men with. Stand no more off,
But give thyself unto my sick desires,   35
Who then recover. Say thou art mine, and ever
My love, as it begins, shall so perséver.

DIA. I see that men make rope's in such a scarre
That we'll forsake ourselves.° Give me that ring.

BER. I'll lend it thee, my dear, but have no power
To give it from me.°

DIA.   Will you not, my lord?   41

BER. It is an honor 'longing to our house,
Bequeathèd down from many ancestors,
Which were the greatest obloquy i' the world
In me to lose.

DIA.   Mine honor's such a ring.   45
My chastity's the jewel of our house,
Bequeathèd down from many ancestors,
Which were the greatest obloquy i' the world
In me to lose. Thus your own proper° wisdom
Brings in the champion Honor on my part   50
Against your vain assault.

BER.   Here, take my ring.
My house, mine honor, yea, my life, be thine,
And I'll be bid by thee.

DIA. When midnight comes, knock at my cham-
ber window.
I'll order take my mother shall not hear.   55
Now will I charge you in the band° of truth,
When you have conquered my yet maiden bed,
Remain there but an hour, nor speak to me.
My reasons are most strong, and you shall know
them
When back again this ring shall be delivered.   60
And on your finger in the night I'll put
Another ring, that what in time proceeds
May token to the future our past deeds.
Adieu, till then. Then fail not. You have won
A wife of me, though there my hope be done.   65

BER. A heaven on earth I have won by wooing
thee.   [Exit.]

DIA. For which live long to thank both Heaven
and me!
You may so in the end.
My mother told me just how he would woo,
As if she sat in 's heart. She says all men   70
Have the like oaths. He had sworn to marry me
When his wife's dead; therefore I'll lie with him

When I am buried. Since Frenchmen are so braid,
Marry that will, I live and die a maid.
Only in this disguise I think 't no sin   75
To cozen° him that would unjustly win.   [Exit.]

SCENE III. *The Florentine camp.*

[*Enter the two French* LORDS *and some two or three*
SOLDIERS.]

1. LORD. You have not given him his mother's letter?

2. LORD. I have delivered it an hour since. There
is something in 't that stings his nature, for on the
reading it he changed almost into another man.   6

1. LORD. He has much worthy blame laid upon
him for shaking off so good a wife and so sweet a
lady.

2. LORD. Especially he hath incurred the   10
everlasting displeasure of the King, who had even
tuned his bounty to sing happiness to him. I will
tell you a thing, but you shall let it dwell darkly
with you.

1. LORD. When you have spoken it, 'tis dead, and
I am the grave of it.   16

2. LORD. He hath perverted a young gentlewoman here in Florence, of a most chaste renown; and
this night he fleshes° his will in the spoil of her
honor. He hath given her his monumental° ring
and thinks himself made in the unchaste composition.°   22

1. LORD. Now, God delay° our rebellion! As we
are ourselves, what things are we!

2. LORD. Merely our own traitors. And as in the
common course of all treasons we still° see them
reveal themselves till° they attain to their abhorred
ends, so he that in this action contrives against his
own nobility, in his proper stream o'erflows himself.°   30

1. LORD. Is it not meant damnable in us to be
trumpeters of our unlawful intents? We shall not
then have his company tonight?

2. LORD. Not till after midnight, for he is dieted°
to his hour.

1. LORD. That approaches apace. I would gladly
have him see his company° anatomized,° that we
might take a measure of his own judgments,

38–39. I . . . ourselves: This passage has not yet been explained,
though many attempts have been made; nor is the meaning of
the word *scarre* known. Presumably the reading of F1 is corrupt.
The difficulty lies in *make rope's*, which should perhaps be some
such word as "entrap's" or even "may rap's." If so, the line
would read: "I see that men may rap (*enrapture*) us in such a
scare (*panic*) that we forget ourselves." Whatever the right
reading, it is clear that the vehemence of Bertram's speech makes
Diana pretend to be overcome by his urgency. **41. from me:**
away. **49. proper:** own. **56. band:** bond.

73. braid: The word is not known elsewhere. Presumably it
means deceitful. **76. cozen:** cheat.

Sc. iii: 19. fleshes: gratifies. **20. monumental:** memorial,
ancestral. **21–22. composition:** bargain. **23. delay:** prevent.
26. still: always. **27. till:** when. **28–30. he . . . himself:** so
he who in this act plots against his own noble reputation drowns
himself in the current of his own lusts by revealing his own disgrace. **34. dieted:** restricted. **37. company:** companion (i.e.,
Parolles). **anatomized:** minutely dissected, shown up.

wherein so curiously he had set this counterfeit.°

2. LORD. We will not meddle with him till he
come, for his presence must be the whip of   42
the other.

1. LORD. In the meantime, what hear you of these
wars?   46

2. LORD. I hear there is an overture° of peace.

1. LORD. Nay, I assure you, a peace concluded.

2. LORD. What will Count Rousillon do then?
Will he travel higher,° or return again into France?

1. LORD. I perceive by this demand you are   52
not altogether of his council.

2. LORD. Let it be forbid, sir. So should I be a
great deal of° his act.   55

1. LORD. Sir, his wife some two months since fled
from his house. Her pretense° is a pilgrimage to
Saint Jaques le Grand, which holy undertaking
with most austere sanctimony° she accomplished;
and, there residing, the tenderness of her   60
nature became as a prey to her grief, in fine, made
a groan of her last breath, and now she sings in
Heaven.

2. LORD. How is this justified?°

1. LORD. The stronger part of it by her own   65
letters, which makes her story true, even to the
point of her death. Her death itself, which could
not be her office to say is come, was faithfully confirmed by the rector of the place.

2. LORD. Hath the Count all this intelligence?   70

1. LORD. Aye, and the particular confirmations,
point from point, to the full arming of the verity.°

2. LORD. I am heartily sorry that he'll be glad of
this.   75

1. LORD. How mightily sometimes we make us
comforts of our losses!

2. LORD. And how mightily some other times we
drown our gain in tears! The great dignity that his
valor hath here acquired for him shall at home be
encountered with a shame as ample.   82

1. LORD. The web of our life is of a mingled yarn,
good and ill together. Our virtues would be proud
if our faults whipped them not, and our crimes
would despair if they were not cherished by our
virtues. [*Enter a* MESSENGER.] How now!   87
Where's your master!

SERV. He met the Duke in the street, sir, of whom
he hath taken a solemn leave. His lordship will   90
next morning for France. The Duke hath offered
him letters of commendations to the King.

2. LORD. They shall be no more than needful

there, if they were more than they can commend.°

1. LORD. They cannot be too sweet for the   95
King's tartness. Here's his lordship now. [*Enter*
BERTRAM.] How now, my lord! Is 't not after mid-
night?

BER. I have tonight dispatched sixteen businesses,
a month's length apiece, by an abstract of success.°
I have congied with° the Duke, done my adieu   100
with his nearest, buried a wife, mourned for her,
writ to my lady mother I am returning, entertained
my convoy,° and between these main parcels of dispatch effected many nicer° needs. The last was the
greatest, but that I have not ended yet.   106

2. LORD. If the business be of any difficulty, and
this morning your departure hence, it requires haste
of your lordship.

BER. I mean the business is not ended, as   110
fearing to hear of it hereafter. But shall we have
this dialogue between the fool and the soldier?
Come, bring forth this counterfeit module,° has deceived me, like a double-meaning prophesier.°   115

2. LORD. Bring him forth. Has sat i' the stocks all
night, poor gallant knave.

BER. No matter. His heels have deserved it in
usurping his spurs° so long. How does he carry
himself?   120

2. LORD. I have told your lordship already the
stocks carry him. But to answer you as you would
be understood, he weeps like a wench that had shed
her milk. He hath confessed himself to Morgan,
whom he supposes to be a friar, from the time   125
of his remembrance to this very instant disaster of
his setting i' the stocks. And what think you he
hath confessed?

BER. Nothing of me, has a'?

2. LORD. His confession is taken, and it shall   130
be read to his face. If your lordship be in 't, as I
believe you are, you must have the patience to hear
it.

[*Enter* PAROLLES *guarded, and* FIRST SOLDIER.]

BER. A plague upon him! Muffled! He can say
nothing of me. Hush, hush!   135

1. LORD. Hoodman° comes! *Portotartarossa.*

1. SOLD. He calls for the tortures. What will you
say without 'em?

PAR. I will confess what I know without con-

93–94. They . . . commend: i.e., he will need all the commendation he can get.   **99. abstract of success:** to give you a summary
of my success.   **100. congied with:** made my ceremonial bow
to; i.e., taken formal leave.   **103–04. entertained my convoy:**
hired my transport to take me home.   **105. nicer:** used with
double meaning — "less important" and "wanton" (i.e., his
affair with Diana).   **114. module:** image.   **115. double-meaning prophesier:** like a riddling prophet — whose prophesies can
be interpreted in two ways.   **119. usurping . . . spurs:** Since
spurs were a mark of knighthood, Parolles had no right to wear
them.   **136. Hoodman:** blind man.

37–39. that . . . counterfeit: so that he may have a truer estimate
of the worth of his own judgment, which has so elaborately
overvalued this pretender.   **47. overture:** offer.   **51. higher:**
into the more northern parts.   **54–55. be . . . of:** be deeply involved in.   **57. pretense:** intention.   **59. sanctimony:** holiness.
64. justified: proved.   **72. arming . . . verity:** confirmation of
the truth.

straint.° If ye pinch me like a pasty,° I can say no
more.   141

1. SOLD. *Bosko chimurcho.*

1. LORD. *Boblibindo chicurmurco.*

1. SOLD. You are a merciful General. — Our General bids you answer to what I shall ask you out of
a note.   146

PAR. And truly, as I hope to live.

1. SOLD. [*Reads.*] "First demand of him how
many horse the Duke is strong." — What say you
to that?   150

PAR. Five or six thousand, but very weak and
unserviceable. The troops are all scattered, and the
commanders very poor rogues, upon my reputation
and credit, and as I hope to live.

1. SOLD. Shall I set down your answer so?   155

PAR. Do. I'll take the sacrament on 't, how and
which way you will.

BER. [*To two* LORDS] All's one to him. What a
past-saving slave is this!   159

1. LORD. You're deceived, my lord. This is Monsieur Parolles, the gallant militarist° — that was his
own phrase — that had the whole theoric° of war
in the knot of his scarf, and the practice in the
chape° of his dagger.

2. LORD. I will never trust a man again for   165
keeping his sword clean, nor believe he can have
everything in him by wearing his apparel neatly.

1. SOLD. Well, that's set down.   169

PAR. Five or six thousand horse, I said — I will
say true — or thereabouts, set down, for I'll speak
truth.

1. LORD. He's very near the truth in this.

BER. But I con° him no thanks for 't, in the nature he delivers it.   175

PAR. Poor rogues, I pray you say.

1. SOLD. Well, that's set down.

PAR. I humbly thank you, sir. A truth's a truth,
the rogues are marvelous poor.   179

1. SOLD. [*Reads.*] "Demand of him of what
strength they are afoot." — What say you to that?

PAR. By my troth, sir, if I were to live this present hour,° I will tell true. Let me see. Spurio, a hundred and fifty; Sebastian, so many; Corambus,   185
so many; Jacques, so many; Guiltian, Cosmo, Lodowick, and Gratii, two hundred and fifty each; mine
own company, Chitopher, Vaumond, Bentii, two
hundred and fifty each; so that the muster file, rotten and sound, upon my life, amounts not to   190
fifteen thousand poll,° half of the which dare not
shake the snow from off their cassocks,° lest they

shake themselves to pieces.

BER. What shall be done to him?

1. LORD. Nothing, but let him have thanks.   19[5]
Demand of him my condition, and what credit I
have with the Duke.

1. SOLD. Well, that's set down. [*Reads.*] "You
shall demand of him whether one Captain Dumain°
be i' the camp, a Frenchman; what his reputation is
with the Duke; what his valor, honesty, and   200
expertness in wars; or whether he thinks it were not
possible, with well-weighing° sums of gold, to corrupt him to a revolt." — What say you to this?
What do you know of it?   205

PAR. I beseech you, let me answer to the particular of the inter'gatories.° Demand them singly.

1. SOLD. Do you know this Captain Dumain?

PAR. I know him. A' was a botcher's°   21[0]
'prentice in Paris, from whence he was whipped for
getting the shrieve's fool° with child — a dumb innocent that could not say him nay.

BER. Nay, by your leave, hold your hands,°   21[5]
though I know his brains are forfeit to the next tile
that falls.°

1. SOLD. Well, is this Captain in the Duke of
Florence's camp?

PAR. Upon my knowledge, he is, and lousy.   220

1. LORD. Nay, look not so upon me. We shall
hear of your lordship anon.

1. SOLD. What is his reputation with the Duke?

PAR. The Duke knows him for no other but   225
a poor officer of mine, and writ to me this other day
to turn him out o' the band. I think I have his letter in my pocket.

1. SOLD. Marry, we'll search.

PAR. In good sadness,° I do not know.   230
Either it is there, or it is upon a file with the Duke's
other letters in my tent.

1. SOLD. Here 'tis. Here's a paper. Shall I read it
to you?

PAR. I do not know if it be it or no.   235

BER. Our interpreter does it well.

1. LORD. Excellently.

1. SOLD. [*Reads.*]

"Dian, the Count's a fool, and full of gold" ——

PAR. That is not the Duke's letter, sir. That is an
advertisement° to a proper maid in Florence,   240
one Diana, to take heed of the allurement of one
Count Rousillon, a foolish idle boy, but for all that

139–40. constraint: force.   **140. pinch . . . pasty:** The crust of a
pie was pinched into fancy shapes.   **161. militarist:** military
expert.   **162. theoric:** theory.   **164. chape:** the metal protection at the bottom of the sheath of a dagger.   **174. con:** give,
lit., learn.   **183–84. if . . . hour:** if I survive this present time;
i.e., if you spare me.   **191. poll:** head.   **192. cassocks:** soldiers'
coats.

199. Dumain: As is clear from the dialogue which follows, this
First Lord is named Dumain. See *LLL* Intro. p. 395b.   **203. well-
weighing:** weighty.   **207. inter'gatories:** questions delivered on
oath. See *M of Ven*, V.i.298,n.   **211. botcher:** odd-job tailor.
213. shrieve's fool: idiot woman, put under the charge of the
sheriff, who was responsible for the care of the insane poor.
215. hold . . . hands: said to Dumain, who is about to strike
the unwitting Parolles.   **216–17. forfeit . . . falls:** i.e., some unheroic accident will destroy him.   **230. sadness:** seriousness.
240. advertisement: warning.

very ruttish. I pray you, sir, put it up again.

1. SOLD. Nay, I'll read it first, by your favor. 245

PAR. My meaning in 't, I protest, was very honest in the behalf of the maid; for I knew the young Count to be a dangerous and lascivious boy, who is a whale to virginity and devours up all the fry° it finds. 250

BER. Damnable both-sides° rogue!

1. SOLD. [Reads.]
"When he swears oaths, bid him drop gold, and take it;
After he scores, he never pays the score.
Half won is match well made; match, and well make it.°
He ne'er pays after-debts, take it before. 255
And say a soldier, Dian, told thee this:
Men are to mell° with, boys are not to kiss.
For count of this, the Count's a fool, I know it,
Who pays before, but not when he does owe it.
Thine, as he vowed to thee in thine ear, 260
                PAROLLES."

BER. He shall be whipped through the army with this rhyme in 's forehead.

2. LORD. This is your devoted friend, sir, the manifold linguist and the armipotent° soldier. 265

BER. I could endure anything before but a cat,° and now he's a cat to me.

1. SOLD. I perceive, sir, by the General's looks, we shall be fain° to hang you.

PAR. My life, sir, in any case. Not that I am 270 afraid to die, but that, my offenses being many, I would repent out the remainder of nature. Let me live, sir, in a dungeon, i' the stocks, or any where, so I may live.

1. SOLD. We'll see what may be done, so you 275 confess freely. Therefore, once more to this Captain Dumain. You have answered to his reputation with the Duke and to his valor. What is his honesty?

PAR. He will steal, sir, an egg out of a 280 cloister. For rapes and ravishments he parallels Nessus.° He professes not keeping of oaths; in breaking 'em he is stronger than Hercules. He will lie, sir, with such volubility that you would think truth were a fool. Drunkenness is his best 285 virtue, for he will be swine-drunk, and in his sleep he does little harm, save to his bedclothes about him; but they know his conditions° and lay him in

straw. I have but little more to say, sir, of his 290 honesty. He has everything that an honest man should not have. What an honest man should have, he has nothing.

1. LORD. I begin to love him for this.

BER. For this description of thine honesty? A pox upon him for me, he's more and more a cat. 295

1. SOLD. What say you to his expertness in war?

PAR. Faith, sir, has led the drum before the English tragedians.° To belie him I will not, and more of his soldiership I know not, except, in that 300 country he had the honor to be the officer at a place there called Mile End,° to instruct for the doubling of files.° I would do the man what honor I can, but of this I am not certain.

1. LORD. He hath out-villained villainy so far 305 that the rarity redeems him.

BER. A pox on him, he's a cat still.

1. SOLD. His qualities being at this poor price, I need not to ask you if gold will corrupt him to revolt. 310

PAR. Sir, for a *quart d'écu*° he will sell the fee simple° of his salvation, the inheritance of it, and cut the entail° from all remainders,° and a perpetual succession for it perpetually. 314

1. SOLD. What's his brother, the other Captain Dumain?

2. LORD. Why does he ask him of me?

1. SOLD. What's he?

PAR. E'en a crow o' the same nest; not altogether so great as the first in goodness, but greater a 320 great deal in evil. He excels his brother for a coward, yet his brother is reputed one of the best that is. In a retreat he outruns any lackey.° Marry, in coming on he has the cramp. 324

1. SOLD. If your life be saved, will you undertake to betray the Florentine?

PAR. Aye, and the Captain of his Horse, Count Rousillon.

1. SOLD. I'll whisper with the General, and know his pleasure. 330

PAR. [Aside] I'll no more drumming. A plague of all drums! Only to seem to deserve well, and to beguile the supposition of that lascivious young boy the Count, have I run into this danger. Yet who

---

249. fry: small fish.   **251. both-sides**: every way.   **254. match . . . it**: i.e., before you let him have what he wants, see that you first get your reward.   **257. mell**: mingle.   **265. armipotent**: most valiant — a pompous word. See *LLL*, V.ii.651.   **266. endure . . . cat**: Bertram is one of those men who has a horror of cats. See *M of Ven*, IV.i.47–50.   **269. fain**: obliged.   **282. Nessus**: a centaur (a creature half man and half horse) who attempted to rape Deianira, the wife of Hercules, by whom he was promptly transfixed with an arrow. See *Ant & Cleo*, IV.xii.43,n. **289. conditions**: habits.

297–98. led . . . tragedians: When a company of players proposed to play in a country town, they marched through the streets, with a drum leading. Such a drummer was a very poor kind of soldier.   **302. Mile End**: Able-bodied Londoners were expected in emergency to serve as soldiers in the trainbands (an elementary form of National Guard). They received one day's training each year in the fields at Mile End Green outside the city on Midsummer Day. This performance was regarded as a joke.   **302–03. doubling of files**: infantry drill.   **311. quart d'écu**: spelt *cardecu* in F1; a French coin worth about 25¢.   **311–12. fee simple**: absolute possession.   **313. entail**: right of succession. **remainders**: those who come into possession on the death of a legatee.   **323. lackey**: civilian servant to a captain.

would have suspected an ambush where I was taken?   336

1. SOLD. There is no remedy, sir, but you must die. The General says you that have so traitorously discovered the secrets of your army and made such pestiferous reports of men very nobly held can 340 serve the world for no honest use. Therefore you must die. Come, headsman, off with his head.

PAR. Oh, Lord, sir, let me live, or let me see my death!°   345

1. SOLD. That shall you, and take your leave of all your friends. [*Unblinding him.*] So, look about you. Know you any here?

BER. Good morrow, noble Captain.

2. LORD. God bless you, Captain Parolles.   350

1. LORD. God save you, noble Captain.

2. LORD. Captain, what greeting will you to my Lord Lafeu? I am for France.

1. LORD. Good Captain, will you give me a copy of the sonnet you writ to Diana in behalf of 355 the Count Rousillon? An I were not a very coward, I'd compel it of you. But fare you well.

[*Exeunt* BERTRAM *and* LORDS.]

1. SOLD. You are undone, Captain, all but your scarf. That has a knot on 't yet.   359

PAR. Who cannot be crushed with a plot?

1. SOLD. If you could find out a country where but women were that had received so much shame, you might begin an impudent nation. Fare ye well, sir. I am for France too. We shall speak of you there.   [*Exit, with* SOLDIERS.]   365

PAR. Yet am I thankful. If my heart were great, 'Twould burst at this. Captain I'll be no more, But I will eat, and drink, and sleep as soft As captain shall. Simply the thing I am Shall make me live. Who knows himself a braggart, Let him fear this, for it will come to pass   371 That every braggart shall be found an ass. Rust, sword! Cool, blushes! And, Parolles, live Safest in shame! Being fooled, by foolery thrive! There's place and means for every man alive.   375 I'll after them.   [*Exit.*]

SCENE IV. *Florence. The* WIDOW'S *house.*

[*Enter* HELENA, WIDOW, *and* DIANA.]

HEL. That you may well perceive I have not wronged you,
One of the greatest in the Christian world
Shall be my surety, 'fore° whose throne 'tis needful,
Ere I can perfect mine intents, to kneel.
Time was I did him a desirèd office,   5
Dear almost as his life; which gratitude

Through flinty Tartar's° bosom would peep forth
And answer thanks. I duly am informed
His Grace is at Marseilles, to which place
We have convenient convoy.° You must know   10
I am supposèd dead. The army breaking,°
My husband hies him home, where, Heaven aiding,
And by the leave of my good lord the King,
We'll be before our welcome.

WID.   Gentle madam,
You never had a servant to whose trust   15
Your business was more welcome.

HEL.   Nor you, mistress,
Ever a friend whose thoughts more truly labor
To recompense your love. Doubt not but Heaven
Hath brought me up to be° your daughter's dower,
As it hath fated her to be my motive°   20
And helper to a husband. But, O strange men!
That° can such sweet use make of what they hate,
When saucy trusting of the cozened° thoughts
Defiles the pitchy night: so lust doth play
With what it loathes for that which is away.   25
But more of this hereafter. You, Diana,
Under my poor instructions yet must suffer
Something in my behalf.

DIA.   Let death and honesty
Go with your impositions,° I am yours
Upon your will to suffer.°

HEL.   Yet, I pray you!   30
But with the word° the time will bring on summer,
When briers shall have leaves as well as thorns
And be as sweet as sharp. We must away.
Our wagon is prepared, and time revives° us.
ALL'S WELL THAT ENDS WELL. Still the fine's the crown.°   35
Whate'er the course, the end is the renown.

[*Exeunt.*]

SCENE V. *Rousillon. The* COUNT'S *palace.*

[*Enter* COUNTESS, LAFEU, *and* CLOWN.]

LAF. No, no, no, your son was misled with a snipt-taffeta° fellow there, whose villainous saffron° would have made all the unbaked and doughy

---

7. **Tartar:** The Tartars lived in South Russia and were proverbial for cruelty.   10. **convoy:** transport.   11. **breaking:** disbanding, demobilizing.   19. **to be:** i.e., the means of providing.   20. **motive:** means.   23. **cozened:** cheated.   22–25. **That . . . away:** i.e., that, when they are cheated in the darkness, can find such pleasure in what they really hate. So Bertram found pleasure in my hated company because he thought that I was Diana. 29. **impositions:** tasks laid on me.   29–30. **I . . . suffer:** I will endure whatever you ask me.   31. **with . . . word:** in a word, soon.   34. **revives:** restores.   35. **fine's . . . crown:** a translation of the Latin proverb *Finis coronat opus*, the end crowns the work.

     Sc. v: 2. **snipt-taffeta:** a man wearing a suit of taffeta cut out in places to show the lining. **saffron:** yellow, the color of cowards and jealous men.

344–45. **see my death:** i.e., have the bandage taken off my eyes. Sc. iv: 3. **'fore:** before.

youth of a nation in his color. Your daughter-in-law had been alive at this hour, and your son here 5 at home, more advanced by the King than by that red-tailed humblebee I speak of.

COUNTESS. I would I had not known him. It was the death of the most virtuous gentlewoman that ever nature had praise for creating. If she had partaken of my flesh and cost me the dearest groans of a mother, I could not have owed her a more rooted love.

LAF. 'Twas a good lady, 'twas a good lady. We may pick a thousand salads ere we light on such another herb. 16

CLO. Indeed, sir, she was the sweet marjoram° of the salad, or rather, the herb of grace.°

LAF. They are not herbs, you knave. They are nose herbs.° 20

CLO. I am no great Nebuchadnezzar, sir. I have not much skill in grass.°

LAF. Whether° dost thou profess thyself, a knave or a fool?

CLO. A fool, sir, at a woman's service, and a knave at a man's. 26

LAF. Your distinction?

CLO. I would cozen° the man of his wife and do his service.

LAF. So you were a knave at his service, indeed. 31

CLO. And I would give his wife my bauble,° sir, to do her service.

LAF. I will subscribe for thee thou art both knave and fool. 35

CLO. At your service.

LAF. No, no, no.

CLO. Why, sir, if I cannot serve you, I can serve as great a prince as you are.

LAF. Who's that? A Frenchman? 40

CLO. Faith, sir, a' has an English name, but his fisnomy° is more hotter in France than there.

LAF. What prince is that?

CLO. The Black Prince,° sir, alias, the Prince of Darkness, alias, the Devil. 45

LAF. Hold thee, there's my purse. I give thee not this to suggest thee from thy master° thou talkest of. Serve him still.

CLO. I am a woodland fellow, sir, that always loved a great fire, and the master I speak of 50 ever keeps a good fire. But, sure, he is the Prince of the world. Let his nobility remain in 's Court. I am for the house with the narrow gate,° which I take to be too little for pomp to enter. Some that humble themselves may, but the many will be 55 too chill and tender,° and they'll be for the flowery way that leads to the broad gate and the great fire.°

LAF. Go thy ways, I begin to be aweary of thee, and I tell thee so before because I would not 60 fall out with thee. Go thy ways. Let my horses be well looked to, without any tricks.

CLO. If I put any tricks upon 'em, sir, they shall be jades' tricks,° which are their own right by the law of nature. [Exit.] 65

LAF. A shrewd° knave and an unhappy.°

COUNTESS. So he is. My lord that's gone made himself much sport out of him. By his authority he remains here, which he thinks is a patent° for his sauciness; and indeed he has no pace,° but runs where he will. 71

LAF. I like him well. 'Tis not amiss. And I was about to tell you, since I heard of the good lady's death and that my lord your son was upon his return home, I moved the King my master to 75 speak in the behalf of my daughter; which, in the minority of them both, His Majesty, out of a self-gracious remembrance, did first propose. His Highness hath promised me to do it, and to stop up 80 the displeasure he hath conceived against your son there is no fitter matter. How does your ladyship like it?

COUNTESS. With very much content, my lord, and I wish it happily effected.

LAF. His Highness comes post° from Marseilles, of as able body as when he numbered thirty. 86 He will be here tomorrow, or I am deceived by him that in such intelligence hath seldom failed.

COUNTESS. It rejoices me that I hope I shall see him ere I die. I have letters that my son will be 90 here tonight. I shall beseech your lordship to remain with me till they meet together.

LAF. Madam, I was thinking with what manners I might safely be admitted.°

COUNTESS. You need but plead your honorable privilege.° 96

LAF. Lady, of that I have made a bold charter,° but I thank my God it holds yet.

---

17. sweet marjoram: a herb used in salads. **18. herb of grace:** rue. **20. nose herbs:** used for the scent, not the taste. **21–22. Nebuchadnezzar . . . grass:** Nebuchadnezzar was smitten with madness "and he did eat grass as oxen, and his body was wet with the dew of heaven." See Daniel 4: 28–37. **23. Whether:** which of two. **28. cozen:** cheat. **32. bauble:** lit., the stick surmounted with a fool's head carried by clowns. A specimen is shown at the bottom of Pl. 12f. **42. fisnomy:** physiognomy, face. **44. Black Prince:** the famous son of Edward III who was the terror of the French. See App. 28. The clown, however, refers also to the Devil as the Black Prince because he was the Prince of Darkness and in religious art was represented as black. **47. suggest . . . master:** to suggest that you should leave your master — the Devil.

53. house . . . gate: Heaven. **56. chill . . . tender:** i.e., will prefer the hotter place. **56–57. flowery . . . fire:** or, as the porter in *Macb* (II.iii.20–21) puts it, "the primrose way to the everlasting bonfire"; i.e., Hell. **64. jades' tricks:** vicious habits of bad-tempered horses. **66. shrewd:** bitter. **unhappy:** unlucky. **69. patent:** license. **70. pace:** restraint. **85. post:** See App. 17. **93–94. I . . . admitted:** I was wondering how I could with politeness be present. **95–96. honorable privilege:** the right of a councilor to be admitted to the king's presence. **97. charter:** claim.

[*Re-enter* CLOWN.]

CLO. Oh, madam, yonder's my lord your son with a patch of velvet° on 's face. Whether 100 there be a scar under 't or no, the velvet knows, but 'tis a goodly patch of velvet. His left cheek is a cheek of two pile and a half,° but his right cheek is worn bare.

LAF. A scar nobly got, or a noble scar, is a good livery° of honor; so belike is that. 106

CLO. But it is your carbonadoed° face.

LAF. Let us go see your son, I pray you. I long to talk with the young noble soldier.

CLO. Faith, there's a dozen of 'em, with 110 delicate fine hats and most courteous feathers, which bow the head and nod at every man. [*Exeunt.*]

Act V

SCENE I. *Marseilles. A street.*

[*Enter* HELENA, WIDOW, *and* DIANA, *with two* ATTENDANTS.]

HEL. But this exceeding posting° day and night Must wear your spirits low. We cannot help it. But since you have made the days and nights as one To wear your gentle limbs in my affairs, Be bold you do so grow in my requital 5 As nothing can unroot you.° In happy time,°

[*Enter a* GENTLEMAN.°]

This man may help me to His Majesty's ear, If he would spend his power.° God save you, sir.

GENT. And you.

HEL. Sir, I have seen you in the Court of France.

GENT. I have been sometimes there. 11

HEL. I do presume, sir, that you are not fallen From the report that goes upon your goodness, And therefore, goaded with most sharp occasions, Which lay nice manners by, I put you to 15 The use of your own virtues, for the which I shall continue thankful.

GENT. What's your will?

HEL. That it will please you To give this poor petition to the King

And aid me with that store of power you have 20 To come into his presence.

GENT. The King's not here.

HEL. Not here, sir!

GENT. Not, indeed. He hence removed last night and with more haste Than is his use.

WID. Lord, how we lose our pains!

HEL. ALL'S WELL THAT ENDS WELL yet, 25 Though time seem so adverse and means unfit. I do beseech you, whither is he gone?

GENT. Marry, as I take it, to Rousillon, Whither I am going.

HEL. I do beseech you, sir, Since you are like to see the King before me, 30 Commend the paper to his gracious hand, Which I presume shall render you no blame But rather make you thank your pains for it. I will come after you with what good speed Our means will make us means.

GENT. This I'll do for you. 35

HEL. And you shall find yourself to be well thanked, Whate'er falls more.° We must to horse again. Go, go, provide. [*Exeunt.*]

SCENE II. *Rousillon. Before the* COUNT's *palace.*

[*Enter* CLOWN, *and* PAROLLES, *following.*]

PAR. Good Monsieur Lavache,° give my Lord Lafeu this letter. I have ere now, sir, been better known to you, when I have held familiarity with fresher clothes; but I am now, sir, muddled in Fortune's mood° and smell somewhat strong of her strong displeasure. 6

CLO. Truly, Fortune's displeasure is but sluttish if it smell so strongly as thou speakest of. I will henceforth eat no fish of Fortune's buttering. Prithee allow the wind.° 10

PAR. Nay, you need not to stop your nose, sir. I spake but by a metaphor.

CLO. Indeed, sir, if your metaphor stink, I will stop my nose, or against any man's metaphor. Prithee get thee further. 15

PAR. Pray you, sir, deliver me this paper.

CLO. Foh! Prithee stand away. A paper from Fortune's closestool° to give to a nobleman! Look, here he comes himself. [*Enter* LAFEU.] Here is a 20 purr of Fortune's, sir, or of Fortune's cat — but not

---

100. patch of velvet: downy beard.   103. two ... half: Three-pile velvet was the thickest quality, and two-pile second-rate. Bertram's youthful beard is thus only moderately thick.   106. livery: badge, sign that the wearer is the servant of honor.   107. carbonadoed: sliced — like a steak for the broiling.

Act V, Sc. i: 1. exceeding posting: excessive haste.   5–6. Be ... you: be assured that you are so much in my debt (*requital*) that nothing can remove you from my friendship.   6. In ... time: at a lucky moment — a phrase to denote the fortunate arrival of someone just when wanted. s.d., Enter a gentleman: F1 reads *Enter a gentle Astringer* — a gentleman falconer. 8. spend ... power: use his influence.

37. Whate'er ... more: whatever else may happen.
Sc. ii: 1. Monsieur Lavache: F1 reads "Lavatch." This name has greatly puzzled editors; it means "cow." This is the only occasion when the Clown is named; and it is a sign of Parolles' degradation that he addresses the Clown so respectfully. The once fashionable Parolles is now filthy and bedraggled. 5. mood: whim, with a pun on "mud."   10. allow ... wind: stand to windward.   19. closestool: the toilet.

a musk cat° — that has fallen into the unclean fish-
pond of her displeasure, and, as he says, is muddied
withal. Pray you, sir, use the carp as you may, for
he looks like a poor, decayed, ingenious, foolish,   25
rascally knave. I do pity his distress in my similes of
comfort and leave him to your lordship.   [*Exit.*]

PAR. My lord, I am a man whom Fortune hath
cruelly scratched.

LAF. And what would you have me to do?   30
'Tis too late to pare her nails now. Wherein have
you played the knave with Fortune, that she should
scratch you, who of herself is a good lady and
would not have knaves thrive long under her?
There's a *quart d'écu*° for you. Let the justices
make you and Fortune friends.° I am for other
business.   36

PAR. I beseech your Honor to hear me one single
word.

LAF. You beg a single penny more. Come, you
shall ha 't. Save your word.   40

PAR. My name, my good lord, is Parolles.

LAF. You beg more than "word," then. Cox my
passion!° Give me your hand. How does your
drum?

PAR. Oh, my good lord, you were the first that
found me!°   46

LAF. Was I, in sooth? And I was the first that
lost thee.

PAR. It lies in you, my lord, to bring me in some
grace, for you did bring me out.   50

LAF. Out upon thee, knave! Dost thou put upon
me at once both the office of God and the Devil?
One brings thee in grace and the other brings thee
out. [*Trumpets sound.*] The King's coming. I
know by his trumpets. Sirrah, inquire further after
me. I had talk of you last night. Though you are a
fool and a knave, you shall eat. Go to,° follow.

PAR. I praise God for you.   [*Exeunt.*]

SCENE III. *Rousillon. The* COUNT'S *palace.*

[*Flourish. Enter* KING, COUNTESS, LAFEU, *the two*
FRENCH LORDS, *with* ATTENDANTS.]

KING. We lost a jewel of her, and our esteem°
Was made much poorer by it; but your son,
As mad in folly, lacked the sense to know
Her estimation home.°

COUNTESS.   'Tis past, my liege,
And I beseech your Majesty to make it   5
Natural rebellion, done i' the blaze of youth,

When oil and fire, too strong for reason's force,
O'erbears it and burns on.

KING.   My honored lady,
I have forgiven and forgotten all,
Though my revenges were high bent° upon him
And watched the time to shoot.

LAF.   This I must say   11
But first I beg my pardon — the young lord
Did to His Majesty, his mother, and his lady
Offense of mighty note, but to himself
The greatest wrong of all. He lost a wife   15
Whose beauty did astonish the survey
Of richest eyes, whose words all ears took captive,
Whose dear perfection hearts that scorned to serve
Humbly called mistress.

KING.   Praising what is lost   19
Makes the remembrance dear. Well, call him hither.
We are reconciled, and the first view shall kill
All repetition. Let him not ask our pardon.
The nature of his great offense is dead,
And deeper than oblivion we do bury
The incensing relics° of it. Let him approach,   25
A stranger, no offender, and inform him
So 'tis our will he should.

GENT.   I shall, my liege.   [*Exit.*]

KING. What says he to your daughter? Have you
spoke?

LAF. All that he is hath reference to your Highness.°

KING. Then shall we have a match. I have letters
sent me   30
That set him high in fame.

[*Enter* BERTRAM.]

LAF.   He looks well on 't.

KING. I am not a day of season,°
For thou mayst see a sunshine and a hail
In me at once. But to the brightest beams
Distracted clouds give way. So stand thou forth.   35
The time is fair again.

BER.   My high-repented blames,
Dear sovereign, pardon to me.

KING.   All is whole.
Not one word more of the consumèd time.
Let's take the instant by the forward top,°
For we are old, and on our quick'st decrees   40
The inaudible and noiseless foot of Time
Steals ere we can effect them. You remember
The daughter of this lord?

BER. Admiringly,° my liege, at first
I stuck my choice upon her, ere my heart   45

10. high bent: stretched like a bow ready to shoot.   25. incensing relics: reminders that would kindle my rage.   29. All
. . . Highness: he submits everything to your Highness's decision.   32. day of season: seasonable, fine day.   39. take . . .
top: take Time by the forelock; i.e., make the most of the present.
44. Admiringly: with wonder.   44–55. Admiringly . . . it: i.e.,
my first choice was Lafeu's daughter, but I did not dare to declare
my love. As a result, Contempt lent me a *perspective* which made

22. musk cat: the animal from which the perfume is taken; also
a foppish courtier, which Parolles has ceased to be.   34. *quart
d'écu:* See IV.iii.311,n.   34–35. justices . . . friends: i.e., appeal
to the justices for charity from public funds.   42–43. Cox my
passion: by God's suffering.   46. found me: showed me up.
57. Go to: an exclamation of impatience.

Sc. iii: 1. esteem: reputation.   4. home: thoroughly.

Durst make too bold a herald of my tongue;
Where the impression of mine eye infixing,
Contempt his scornful perspective° did lend me,
Which warped the line of every other favor,
Scorned a fair color, or expressed it stolen,   50
Extended or contracted all proportions
To a most hideous object. Thence it came
That she whom all men praised and whom myself,
Since I have lost, have loved, was in mine eye
The dust that did offend it.
     KING.   Well excused.   55
That thou didst love her strikes some scores away
From the great compt;° but love that comes too late,
Like a remorseful° pardon slowly carried,
To the great sender turns a sour offense,
Crying, " That's good that's gone." Our rash faults
Make trivial price of serious things we have,   61
Not knowing them until we know their grave.
Oft our displeasures, to ourselves unjust,
Destroy our friends and after weep their dust.
Our own love waking cries to see what's done,   65
While shameful hate sleeps out the afternoon.
Be this sweet Helen's knell, and now forget her.
Send forth your amorous token for fair Magdalen.°
The main consents are had,° and here we'll stay
To see our widower's second marriage day.   70
     COUNTESS. Which better than the first, O dear
     Heaven, bless!
Or, ere they meet, in me, O nature, cesse!°
     LAF. Come on, my son,° in whom my house's
     name
Must be digested,° give a favor° from you
To sparkle in the spirits of my daughter,   75
That she may quickly come. [BERTRAM *gives a*
     ring.] By my old beard
And every hair that's on 't, Helen, that's dead,
Was a sweet creature. Such a ring as this,
The last° that e'er I took her leave at Court,
I saw upon her finger.
     BER.   Hers it was not.   80
     KING. Now, pray you let me see it, for mine eye,
While I was speaking, oft was fastened to 't.
                        [*Takes the ring.*]
This ring was mine, and when I gave it Helen,
I bade her, if her fortunes ever stood
Necessitied to help, that by this token   85
I would relieve her. Had you that craft to reave°
     her

Of what should stead° her most?
     BER.   My gracious sovereign,
Howe'er it pleases you to take it so,
The ring was never hers.
     COUNTESS.   Son, on my life,
I have seen her wear it, and she reckoned it   90
At her life's rate.
     LAF.   I am sure I saw her wear it.
     BER. You are deceived, my lord. She never saw it.
In Florence was it from a casement thrown me,
Wrapped in a paper which contained the name
Of her that threw it. Noble she was and thought
I stood engaged.° But when I had subscribed   96
To mine own fortune° and informed her fully
I could not answer in that course of honor
As she had made the overture, she ceased
In heavy satisfaction,° and would never   100
Receive the ring again.
     KING.   Plutus° himself,
That knows the tinct and multiplying medicine,°
Hath not in nature's mystery more science°
Than I have in this ring. 'Twas mine, 'twas Helen's,
Whoever gave it you. Then, if you know   105
That you are well acquainted with yourself,
Confess 'twas hers, and by what rough enforcement
You got it from her. She called the saints to surety
That she would never put it from her finger
Unless she gave it to yourself in bed,   110
Where you have never come, or sent it us
Upon her great disaster.
     BER.   She never saw it.
     KING. Thou speak'st it falsely, as I love mine
     honor,   113
And makest conjectural fears to come into me
Which I would fain shut out. If it should prove
That thou art so inhuman — 'twill not prove so —
And yet I know not. Thou didst hate her deadly,
And she is dead, which nothing but to close
Her eyes myself could win me to believe
More than to see this ring. Take him away.   120
                [GUARDS *seize* BERTRAM.]
My fore-past proofs, howe'er the matter fall,
Shall tax my fears of little vanity,
Having vainly feared too little.° Away with him!
We'll sift this matter further.
     BER.   If you shall prove

---

every other face (*favor*) look unattractive. Thus Helena, whom everyone praised, and whom now I find I loved, offended me like dust in my eye.   **48. perspective:** a glass that produces a distorted image.   **57. compt:** account.   **58. remorseful:** merciful; i.e., like a pardon which comes after the man has been executed. **68. Magdalen:** spelt "Maudlin" in F1 and so pronounced. **69. main . . . had:** those most concerned (Lafeu the father, the Countess, and the King himself) have agreed.   **72. cesse:** cease. **73. son:** son-in-law to be.   **74. digested:** combined. **favor:** token. **79. last:** last time.   **86. reave:** deprive.

87. stead: help.   **96. engaged:** pledged, but some editors read "ungaged."   **96–97. subscribed . . . fortune:** admitted my condition; i.e., that I was married to Helena.   **100. heavy satisfaction:** sad recognition of the hopelessness of her love.   **101. Plutus:** the god of riches — an expert in the value of precious metals. **102. tinct . . . medicine:** the nature and medicinal value of gold. See App. 21.   **103. science:** expert knowledge.   **121–23. My . . . little:** the previous experiences I have had of Bertram, whatever the result of the present inquiry, shall blame (*tax*) me for having had too little anxiety, because, foolishly, I have not been fearful enough; i.e., I have not been sufficiently suspicious of this young man.

This ring was ever hers, you shall as easy   125
Prove that I husbanded her bed in Florence,
Where yet she never was.   [*Exit, guarded.*]
    KING. I am wrapped in dismal thinkings.
            [*Enter a* GENTLEMAN.]
    GENT.   Gracious sovereign,
Whether I have been to blame or no, I know not.
Here's a petition from a Florentine,   130
Who hath for four or five removes° come short
To tender it herself. I undertook it,
Vanquished thereto by the fair grace and speech
Of the poor suppliant, who by this I know
Is here attending. Her business looks in her   135
With an importing visage,° and she told me,
In a sweet verbal brief,° it did concern
Your Highness with herself.
    KING. [*Reads.*] "Upon his many protestations to
marry me when his wife was dead — I blush   140
to say it — he won me. Now is the Count Rousillon
a widower. His vows are forfeited to me, and my
honor's paid to him. He stole from Florence, taking
no leave, and I follow him to his country for justice.
Grant it me, O King! In you it best lies. Otherwise a seducer flourishes, and a poor maid is
undone.   147
              DIANA CAPILET."
    LAF. I will buy me a son-in-law in a fair, and toll°
for this. I'll none of him.
    KING. The Heavens have thought well on thee,
    Lafeu,   150
To bring forth this discovery. Seek these suitors.
Go speedily and bring again the Count.
I am afeard the life of Helen, lady,
Was foully snatched.
    COUNTESS.   Now, justice on the doers!
           [*Re-enter* BERTRAM, *guarded.*]
    KING. I wonder, sir, sith° wives are monsters to
    you   155
And that you fly them as you swear them lordship,
Yet you desire to marry.
          [*Enter* WIDOW *and* DIANA.]
              What woman's that?
    DIA. I am, my lord, a wretched Florentine,
Derivèd° from the ancient Capilet.
My suit, as I do understand, you know,   160
And therefore know how far I may be pitied.
    WID. I am her mother, sir, whose age and honor
Both suffer under this complaint we bring,
And both shall cease,° without your remedy.°
    KING. Come hither, Count. Do you know these
    women?   165
    BER. My lord, I neither can nor will deny

But that I know them. Do they charge me further?
    DIA. Why do you look so strange upon your wife?
    BER. She's none of mine, my lord.
    DIA.   If you shall marry,
You give away this hand, and that is mine;   170
You give away Heaven's vows, and those are mine;
You give away myself, which is known mine;
For I by vow am so embodied yours
That she which marries you must marry me,
Either both or none.   175
    LAF. Your reputation comes too short for my
daughter. You are no husband for her.
    BER. My lord, this is a fond° and desperate crea-
ture
Whom sometime I have laughed with. Let your
    Highness
Lay a more noble thought upon mine honor   180
Than for to think that I would sink it here.
    KING. Sir, for my thoughts, you have them ill to
    friend
Till your deeds gain them. Fairer prove your honor
Than in my thought it lies.
    DIA.   Good my lord,
Ask him upon his oath if he does think   185
He had not my virginity.
    KING. What say'st thou to her?
    BER.   She's impudent, my lord,
And was a common gamester to the camp.
    DIA. He does me wrong, my lord; if I were so,
He might have bought me at a common price.   190
Do not believe him. Oh, behold this ring,
Whose high respect and rich validity
Did lack a parallel. Yet for all that
He gave it to a commoner o' the camp,
If I be one.
    COUNTESS. He blushes, and 'tis it.   195
Of six preceding ancestors, that gem,
Conferred by testament to the sequent issue,°
Hath it been owed° and worn. This is his wife.
That ring's a thousand proofs.
    KING.   Methought you said
You saw one here in Court could witness it.   200
    DIA. I did, my lord, but loath am to produce
So bad an instrument. His name's Parolles.
    LAF. I saw the man today, if man he be.
    KING. Find him, and bring him hither.
             [*Exit an* ATTENDANT.]
    BER.   What of him?
He's quoted° for a most perfidious slave,   205
With all the spots o' the world taxed° and de-
boshed,°
Whose nature sickens but to speak a truth.
Am I or that or this for what he'll utter,
That will speak any thing?

---

131. removes: the movements of the Court from place to place.
135–36. looks . . . visage: looks important.   137. verbal brief:
instruction by word of mouth.   148. toll: pay market fees;
i.e., I'll sell Bertram and buy another son-in-law.   155. sith:
since.   159. Derived: descended.   164. cease: die. without . . .
remedy: unless you give me relief.

178. fond: foolish.   197. sequent issue: succeeding heir.
198. owed: owned.   205. quoted: notorious.   206. taxed: accused. deboshed: disgraced.

KING.   She hath that ring of yours.
BER. I think she has. Certain it is I liked her 210
And boarded° her i' the wanton way of youth.
She knew her distance° and did angle for me,
Madding my eagerness with her restraint,
As all impediments in fancy's° course
Are motives of more fancy; and, in fine, 215
Her infinite cunning, with her modern° grace,
Subdued me to her rate. She got the ring,
And I had that which any inferior might
At market price have bought.
  DIA.   I must be patient.
You, that have turned off a first so noble wife, 220
May justly diet me.° I pray you yet —
Since you lack virtue, I will lose a husband —
Send for your ring, I will return it home,
And give me mine again.
  BER.   I have it not.
  KING. What ring was yours, I pray you?
  DIA.   Sir, much like 225
The same upon your finger.
  KING. Know you this ring? This ring was his of
  late.
  DIA. And this was it I gave him, being abed.
  KING. The story then goes false you threw it him
Out of a casement.
  DIA.   I have spoke the truth. 230
       [Enter PAROLLES.]
  BER. My lord, I do confess the ring was hers.
  KING. You boggle shrewdly,° every feather starts
  you.
Is this the man you speak of?
  DIA.   Aye, my lord.
  KING. Tell me, sirrah — but tell me true, I charge
  you,
Not fearing the displeasure of your master, 235
Which on your just proceeding I'll keep off —
By him and by this woman here what know you?
  PAR. So please your Majesty, my master hath
been an honorable gentleman. Tricks he hath had
in him, which gentlemen have. 240
  KING. Come, come, to the purpose. Did he love
this woman?
  PAR. Faith, sir, he did love her, but how?
  KING. How, I pray you?
  PAR. He did love her, sir, as a gentleman loves a
woman. 246
  KING. How is that?
  PAR. He loved her, sir, and loved her not.
  KING. As thou art a knave, and no knave. What
an equivocal companion° is this! 250

  PAR. I am a poor man, and at your Majesty's
command.
  LAF. He's a good drum, my lord, but a naughty°
orator.
  DIA. Do you know he promised me marriage?
  PAR. Faith, I know more than I'll speak. 256
  KING. But wilt thou not speak all thou knowest?
  PAR. Yes, so please your Majesty. I did go between them, as I said, but more than that, he loved
her. For indeed he was mad for her, and 260
talked of Satan, and of Limbo,° and of Furies, and
I know not what. Yet I was in that credit with
them at that time that I knew of their going to bed,
and of other motions, as promising her marriage,
and things which would derive me ill will to 265
speak of. Therefore I will not speak what I know.
  KING. Thou hast spoken all already unless thou
canst say they are married. But thou art too fine° in
thy evidence. Therefore stand aside. 270
This ring, you say, was yours?
  DIA.   Aye, my good lord.
  KING. Where did you buy it? Or who gave it
  you?
  DIA. It was not given me, nor I did not buy it.
  KING. Who lent it you?
  DIA.   It was not lent me neither.
  KING. Where did you find it, then?
  DIA.   I found it not. 275
  KING. If it were yours by none of all these ways,
How could you give it him?
  DIA.   I never gave it him.
  LAF. This woman's an easy glove, my lord. She
goes off and on at pleasure. 279
  KING. This ring was mine. I gave it his first wife.
  DIA. It might be yours or hers, for aught I know.
  KING. Take her away. I do not like her now.
To prison with her, and away with him.
Unless thou tell'st me where thou hadst this ring,
Thou diest within this hour.
  DIA.   I'll never tell you. 285
  KING. Take her away.
  DIA.   I'll put in bail,° my liege.
  KING. I think thee now some common customer.
  DIA. By Jove, if ever I knew man, 'twas you.
  KING. Wherefore hast thou accused him all this
  while? 289
  DIA. Because he's guilty, and he is not guilty.
He knows I am no maid, and he'll swear to 't.
I'll swear I am a maid, and he knows not.
Great King, I am no strumpet, by my life.
I am either maid, or else this old man's wife. 294
  KING. She does abuse our ears. To prison with
  her. 295

---

211. **boarded:** had intercourse with. 212. **distance:** difference
in rank. 214. **fancy:** love. 216. **modern:** worthless, commonplace. 221. **diet me:** give me my medicine. 232. **boggle
shrewdly:** shy excessively, like a frightened horse. 250. **equivocal companion:** quibbling rascal.

253. **naughty:** worthless. 261. **Limbo:** the place where good but
unbaptized souls linger; but here Parolles means Hell. 269. **fine:**
clever, subtle. 286. **bail:** a surety.

DIA. Good mother, fetch my bail. Stay, royal sir.
[*Exit* WIDOW.]
The jeweler that owes the ring is sent for,
And he shall surety me.° But for this lord
Who hath abused me, as he knows himself,   299
Though yet he never harmed me, here I quit° him.
He knows himself my bed he hath defiled,
And at that time he got his wife with child.
Dead though she be, she feels her young one kick.
So there's my riddle — one that's dead is quick.°
And now behold the meaning.
[*Re-enter* WIDOW, *with* HELENA.]
    KING.   Is there no exorcist°   305
Beguiles the truer office of mine eyes?
Is 't real that I see?
    HEL.   No, my good lord.
'Tis but the shadow of a wife you see,
The name and not the thing.
    BER.   Both, both. Oh, pardon!   309
HEL. O my good lord, when I was like this maid,
I found you wondrous kind.° There is your ring;
And, look you, here's your letter. This it says:
"When from my finger you can get this ring
And are by me with child," &c.° This is done.
Will you be mine, now you are doubly won?   315
    BER. If she, my liege, can make me know this
clearly,
I'll love her dearly, ever, ever dearly.
    HEL. If it appear not plain and prove untrue,
Deadly divorce step between me and you!

298. surety me: be my bail.   **300. quit:** release from debt
304. quick: means both "living" and "pregnant."   **305. exorcist:** one who calls up the spirits of the dead.   **310–11. when
. . . kind:** when you thought that I was Diana I found you were
very affectionate.   **314. &c:** As the player was provided with
the property letter, there was no need to write it into the part;
see *Caesar*, II.i.47,n.

O my dear mother, do I see you living?   320
    LAF. Mine eyes smell onions. I shall weep anon.
[*To* PAROLLES] Good Tom Drum, lend me a hand-
kercher. So;
I thank thee. Wait on me home. I'll make sport
with thee.
Let thy courtesies alone;° they are scurvy ones.
    KING. Let us from point to point this story know,
To make the even° truth in pleasure flow.   326
[*To* DIANA] If thou be'st yet a fresh uncroppèd
flower,
Choose thou thy husband, and I'll pay thy dower;
For I can guess that by thy honest aid
Thou kept'st a wife herself, thyself a maid.   330
Of that and all the progress, more and less,
Resolvedly° more leisure shall express.
All yet seems well, and if it end so meet,
The bitter past, more welcome is the sweet.
[*Flourish.*]

EPILOGUE°

    KING. The King's a beggar, now the play is
done.
All is well ended, if this suit be won,   336
That you express content; which we will pay,
With strife° to please you, day exceeding day.
Ours be your patience then, and yours our parts.
Your gentle hands lend us, and take our hearts.
[*Exeunt.*]

324. Let . . . alone: stop making courtesies to me.   **326. even:**
exact.   **332. Resolvedly:** until the truth is all told.   **Epilogue:**
see note on the Epilogue to *II Hen IV*.   **338. With strife·**
striving.

The Tragedy of
OTHELLO, THE MOOR OF VENICE

Introduction

Othello was probably written in 1602. The earliest definite record of a performance occurs in the Court Accounts of King James I, which shows that it was played before the King on November 1, 1604. There are few certain indications of the date of writing, but some phrases were picked out of the play and embodied in the pirated version of *Hamlet* known as the first quarto (Q1), published in 1603. *Othello* probably followed either *Hamlet* or *Twelfth Night*.

The direct source of the play is not known. It is obviously derived from a story in the *Hecato-mithi* (*Hundred Tales*) of Giraldi Cinthio, published in Venice in 1566, of which the outline runs as follows:

In Venice, there lived a Moor, valiant, handsome and highly regarded for his skill in war. A young lady named Disdemona fell in love with him, and he with her. In spite of objections from her parents, they married and lived happily in Venice. After a while the Moor was sent to command the garrison in Cyprus. Disdemona went with him and they safely reached the island. In their company were a captain, who was a favorite with the Moor, and an ensign; both were accompanied by their wives. The ensign fell desperately in love with Disdemona, but as she showed no interest in him, he supposed that she must be in love with the captain. So the ensign grew to hate them both. Soon afterward the captain was deprived of his rank for having attacked a soldier of the guard. Disdemona was greatly grieved, and endeavored to reconcile her husband to him. When the Moor told the ensign how his wife was asking him to restore the captain to favor, the ensign saw his chance and began to hint that the lady was in love with the captain. The Moor indignantly demanded proof, which the ensign found difficult to obtain; but at last he managed to steal the handkerchief embroidered in the Moorish fashion which her husband had given her. This handkerchief the ensign left on the captain's bed. The captain's wife was expert at embroidery, and she began to copy the work, and the ensign took care that the Moor should come on her while she was so engaged.

The Moor was now firmly convinced of his wife's guilt, and he bribed the ensign to kill the captain. One night as the captain was on his way to visit a courtesan, the ensign struck him such a blow in the right thigh that he cut off his leg. When the news reached Disdemona, she showed great grief, which confirmed the Moor's suspicions. So he plotted with the ensign to kill her. The ensign suggested that he should beat her with a stocking filled with sand, and when she was dead pull down part of the ceiling to make it appear an accident. This plan was carried out, and Disdemona was killed, to the great grief of everyone who knew her. But in a short while the Moor's feelings changed; he began to feel such sorrow at the death of his wife that he became almost mad, and realizing that the ensign was the cause of his loss, he hated him so bitterly that he would have slain him had he been able, but instead he turned him out of his company.

The ensign now began to plot against the Moor. He went to the captain, who had recovered from his wound, and told him that it was the Moor who had cut off his leg because of his jealous suspicions, and that Disdemona had in fact been murdered by her husband. Thereupon the captain accused the Moor, and the rulers of Venice commanded that the Moor should be brought back to the city. He was put to torture to persuade him to reveal the truth, but he denied everything. After some days in prison he was condemned to perpetual banishment. He was ultimately slain by the kinsfolk of Disdemona.

No English version of this tale is known, and it differs in many details from Shakespeare's play.

The text of *Othello* is difficult. There are three early versions: a quarto of 1622, the text of the first folio of 1623, and a later quarto of 1630. All three texts have many minor differences. That of F1 is the best, and has obviously been carefully prepared for the printer; it gives about 160 lines not found in the first quarto. On the other hand, the folio text has been most delicately refined, presumably to conform with an Act of Parliament of 1606 which forbade the use of the name of God in stage plays. It omits all the oaths which are found in the quarto; even such harmless remarks as " faith " and " pray " have been cut out or changed. On the whole the quarto is inferior to the folio; it adds a few lines of its own, but its readings are usually weaker. The quarto was probably printed from an earlier version of the playhouse manuscript, and the folio from a later copy revised and refined. The text used in modern editions is a compound of quarto and folio.

Othello is perhaps Shakespeare's greatest triumph as a stage play; it lacks the magnificent irrelevancies of *Hamlet* or the vastness of *Lear,* but it gains over both in concentration and design. There are, however, certain problems in *Othello* about which critics have argued endlessly. The first is the "time" problem, which is discussed in Appendix 22. The second is the problem of Iago's motives. Many different answers have been given by critics and actors.

Othello himself is a good example of the "tragic hero" as defined by Aristotle; he is a good man of great and simple virtues but with the fatal flaw of believing that men are what they seem. He is also a Moor, and so to Shakespeare and his audience a "black man." There was little color prejudice in Shakespeare's time, and on the stage the Moor was sometimes a heroic character. Indeed, the Moors in the sixteenth century were so powerful that they were greatly dreaded by all who had traffic in the Mediterranean.

Othello is a man of royal blood, proud of his descent. He has some characteristics of the savage, a hyperbolical utterance when roused and an unreasoning passion, but he is not portrayed as in any way an alien. He is "the noble Moor," a man "all-in-all sufficient."

He is also a professional soldier, a type common in literature and in life. In English literature there is a long line of distinguished military gentlemen with pleasant simple virtues and failings, beginning with Chaucer's Knight and coming down through Uncle Toby to Henry Esmond. Professional soldiers are inevitably molded by their profession. They are more exposed to physical danger than the civilian, but often sheltered from mental problems. They are faced with the duty of carrying out their orders in the most efficient way, but it is for the civilian to decide why the orders should first be given. Hence doubt and uncertainty are alien to the soldierly mind. "To be once in doubt," says Othello, "is once to be resolved." As soon as he has cleared up a situation, he acts quickly without further question. These qualities are admirable in the field, but by his marriage with a society lady of Venice, Othello finds himself involved in new problems in which his training and experience count for nothing. His love for Desdemona is not youthful passion, but a mature and mutual understanding, and this makes Iago's suggestion the more abhorrent to him. Othello is not a soldier of society who haunts Courts and capitals. He has lived all his life in camp and campaigns, and knows nothing of women.

Desdemona is the first woman who has ever come into Othello's life. She is a complete contrast, a lady moving in the best society of Venice, which was the most sophisticated and luxurious of all European cities, and particularly renowned for its ladies of pleasure. By convention Desdemona is often played as a perfect specimen of the Victorian young lady; but she is not so simple. Desdemona knew what she wanted and she won it in her own way, as is clear from Othello's account of their courtship. In public she has plenty of self-possession. Before the Duke she knows her own mind and states her case boldly. She takes the first opportunity of trying to prove that she can have her own way with her husband when she wishes; she easily persuades Othello to grant that Cassio may be allowed to plead his own cause. It is an unfortunate triumph, and brings about her destruction. When next she returns to Othello she is still in the same happy frame of mind, confident that he will do anything for her; but he has changed, for Iago has been working on him unceasingly. She cannot understand the alteration and she tries to win Othello back again by the same technique as before, which in the circumstances is disastrous. Desdemona has her weaknesses. She is soon thrown into panic by Othello's unexpected fury. In crises, she prefers to evade rather than face unpleasantness. She is, in short, a lively, vivacious, young woman moving in the best Venetian society. She wanted her man and she won him, but she knows very little of him and she realizes only too soon that he is utterly different from "the wealthy curlèd darlings of our nation." Her bewildered and pathetic simplicity at the end reveals that she was after all an inexperienced girl to whom the thought of disloyalty was so impossible that she could not even imagine jealousy in her husband.

Iago is one of Shakespeare's most subtle villains. He is an Italian, and therefore in Elizabethan eyes malignant by nature. There were many such in other plays, and indeed stories of real life in sixteenth-century Italy produce characters as ruthless and devilish. Iago loves mischief for its own sake and finds cruelty amusing. He believes that all women are false, and if Desdemona is true to Othello, it is because so far she has had no chance to be otherwise. Yet even so, given this character, why did he act as he did? Coleridge spoke of Iago's "motiveless malignity"; Hazlitt replied that Iago's motive was a perverted love of power. The fact is, however, that Iago's motives for the whole tragedy are laid bare in the first bitter outburst to Roderigo (I.i. 8–33). Shakespeare's audiences were well trained. No modern dramatist would dare to give such essential information in the first thirty-five lines.

Iago is a professional soldier. He has climbed up from the lowest rank until he is now within reach of the top. He naturally expects that Othello will select him as second in command, and his vanity is in part justified, for he is in many ways a greater man than Cassio. When he is rejected, he suffers the bitter blow which will come to everyone at some time or other when he sees himself passed over in favor of someone whom he despises. Injured vanity is a wrong to the essential self. This is the main cause of Iago's anger. It is not a dignified cause. Hence he refuses to face it out with his own conscience. He shies away from the sour truth that Othello considers Cassio to be a better soldier than himself. He begins to invent causes for Othello's choice — any excuse to get even with Othello. At any cost he will ease the writhing anguish of his hurt vanity by destroying those who have wronged him and all that they value most. These things are revealed in his soliloquies. Iago therefore begins with a lust to hurt both Othello and Cassio through Desdemona, but he soon becomes fascinated by his own cleverness and inextricably and fatally entangled in his own plot.

So Desdemona and Othello are brought to destruction. When Iago makes his foul suggestion, Othello feels, and how naturally, that he has been fooled. Who was he to know anything about the ways of a Venetian lady? "Honest" Iago, of course, knows everything:

> This honest creature doubtless
> Sees and knows more, much more, than he unfolds.

Not the least of Iago's subtlety is that he seems always to be keeping something back, to know more than he reveals. The incident which finally convinces Othello is the sight of the precious handkerchief in Cassio's hand. Had Desdemona been calmer, she would have remembered when she lost it; had Othello been less simple-minded, he would have asked Cassio how he came by it. But it is now too late. When he has seen Cassio giving Bianca the handkerchief, the situation is cleared up. There remains no doubt in Othello's mind; he must now do his duty, as he understands it.

The end is most moving. Othello is purged of all personal animosity. He sees Desdemona's death as a duty laid on him, and he does not consult his own heart when duty is concerned. In the last scene he approaches the bed not stealthily as a murderer, but as embodied vengeance, vindicating manhood wronged by the faithlessness of woman. Then, too late, he learns the truth, and his universe falls about him.

On the stage, *Othello* is the most often successfully acted of all Shakespeare's tragedies. The drama is perfectly constructed, and the theme is universal; jealousy in love is one of the commonest of human failings. Nevertheless there are certain changes in emphasis in the story of *Othello* as it affects modern spectators and readers, who are often inclined to regard Brabantio as a specimen of the heavy, slightly comic father. Like other fathers in Shakespeare's plays, such as old Capulet, Polonius, or Lear, he misunderstands his daughter and, to us at least, his anger that she should have chosen to wed Othello without first asking his leave is unseemly, unsympathetic, and crude. This was not the view in Shakespeare's day. Desdemona, as a lady of great family, was expected to make a suitable marriage with one of her own rank. The notion that anyone was free to marry at fancy was not generally held. It was utterly inconceivable that a girl of Desdemona's rank should run off in the night with a stranger, however distinguished. Brabantio is so dumfounded that he brings wild charges of witchcraft against Othello, for witchcraft is the only rational explanation of such an incredible breach of normal decent behavior. Brabantio was, therefore, a much-wronged man, and Desdemona was punished, albeit too brutally, for committing a sin against what at that time was regarded as fundamental decency.

Othello

DRAMATIS PERSONAE

DUKE OF VENICE
BRABANTIO, *a Senator*
OTHER SENATORS
GRATIANO, *brother to Brabantio*
LODOVICO, *kinsman to Brabantio*
OTHELLO, *a noble Moor in the service of the Venetian state*
CASSIO, *his lieutenant*
IAGO, *his ancient*
MONTANO, *Othello's predecessor in the government of Cyprus*

RODERIGO, *a Venetian gentleman*
CLOWN, *servant to Othello*

DESDEMONA, *daughter to Brabantio and wife to Othello*
EMILIA, *wife to Iago*
BIANCA, *mistress to Cassio*

SAILOR, MESSENGER, HERALD, OFFICERS, GENTLEMEN, MUSICIANS, *and* ATTENDANTS

SCENE — *Venice: a seaport in Cyprus.*

Act I

SCENE I. *Venice. A street.*

[*Enter* RODERIGO *and* IAGO.]

ROD. Tush, never tell me. I take it much unkindly
That thou, Iago, who hast had° my purse
As if the strings were thine, shouldst know of this.

IAGO. 'Sblood,° but you will not hear me.
If ever I did dream of such a matter,   5
Abhor me.

ROD. Thou told'st me thou didst hold him in thy hate.

IAGO. Despise me if I do not. Three great ones of the city,
In personal suit° to make me his Lieutenant,
Off-capped° to him. And, by the faith of man,   10
I know my price, I am worth no worse a place.
But he, as loving his own pride and purposes,
Evades them, with a bombast circumstance°
Horribly stuffed with epithets of war.°
And, in conclusion,   15
Nonsuits° my mediators, for, "Certes,"° says he,
"I have already chose my officer."
And what was he?
Forsooth, a great arithmetician,°
One Michael Cassio, a Florentine,   20
A fellow almost damned in a fair wife,°

That never set a squadron in the field,
Nor the division of a battle° knows
More than a spinster, unless the bookish theoric,°
Wherein the toged° Consuls° can propose   25
As masterly as he — mere prattle without practice
Is all his soldiership. But he, sir, had the election.
And I, of whom his eyes had seen the proof
At Rhodes, at Cyprus, and on other grounds   29
Christian and heathen, must be beleed° and calmed
By debitor and creditor. This countercaster,°
He, in good time,° must his Lieutenant be,
And I — God bless the mark!° — his Moorship's Ancient.°

ROD. By Heaven, I rather would have been his hangman.

IAGO. Why, there's no remedy. 'Tis the curse of service,   35
Preferment goes by letter and affection,
And not by old gradation,° where each second
Stood heir to the first. Now, sir, be judge yourself
Whether I in any just term am affined°
To love the Moor.

ROD.   I would not follow him, then.   40

IAGO. Oh, sir, content you,
I follow him to serve my turn upon him.
We cannot all be masters, nor all masters
Cannot be truly followed. You shall mark
Many a duteous and knee-crooking knave   45

Act I, Sc. i: 2. had: i.e., used.   4. 'Sblood: by God's blood.
9. In ... suit: making this request in person.   10. Off-capped: stood cap in hand.   13. bombast circumstance: bombastic phrases. Bombast is cotton padding used to stuff out a garment.   14. stuffed ... war: padded out with military terms.
16. Nonsuits: rejects the petition of. Certes: assuredly.
19. arithmetician: Contemporary books on military tactics are full of elaborate diagrams and numerals to explain military formations. Cassio is a student of such books.   21. almost ... wife: A much-disputed phrase. There is an Italian proverb, "You have married a fair wife? You are damned." If Iago has this in mind, he means by *almost* that Cassio is about to marry.

23. division ... battle: organization of an army.   24. bookish theoric: student of war; not a practical soldier.   25. toged: wearing a toga. Consuls: councilors. Cf. I.ii.43.   30. beleed: placed on the lee (or unfavorable) side.   31. countercaster: calculator (repeating the idea of arithmetician). Counters were used in making calculations.   32. in ... time: A phrase expressing indignation.   33. God ... mark: An exclamation of impatience. Ancient: ensign, the third officer in the company of which Othello is Captain and Cassio Lieutenant.   36–37. Preferment ... gradation: promotion comes through private recommendation and favoritism and not by order of seniority.   39. affined: tied by affection.

That doting on his own obsequious bondage
Wears out his time, much like his master's ass,
For naught but provender, and when he's old,
    cashiered.°
Whip me such honest knaves. Others there are
Who, trimmed in forms and visages of duty,°   50
Keep yet their hearts attending on themselves,
And throwing but shows of service° on their lords
Do well thrive by them, and when they have lined
    their coats
Do themselves homage.° These fellows have some
    soul,
And such a one do I profess myself. For, sir,   55
It is as sure as you are Roderigo,
Were I the Moor, I would not be Iago.
In following him, I follow but myself.
Heaven is my judge, not I for love and duty,
But seeming so, for my peculiar° end.   60
For when my outward action doth demónstrate
The native act and figure of my heart°
In compliment extern,° 'tis not long after
But I will wear my heart upon my sleeve
For daws° to peck at. I am not what I am.°   65
ROD. What a full fortune° does the thick-lips owe°
If he can carry 't thus!°
IAGO.   Call up her father,
Rouse him. Make after him, poison his delight,
Proclaim him in the streets. Incense her kinsmen,
And though he in a fertile climate dwell,   70
Plague him with flies. Though that his joy be joy,
Yet throw such changes of vexation on 't
As it may lose some color.°
ROD. Here is her father's house, I'll call aloud.
IAGO. Do, with like timorous° accent and dire yell
As when, by night and negligence, the fire   76
Is spied in populous cities.
ROD. What ho, Brabantio! Signior Brabantio, ho!
IAGO. Awake! What ho, Brabantio! Thieves!
    Thieves! Thieves!
Look to your house, your daughter and your bags!°
Thieves! Thieves!   81

[BRABANTIO *appears above, at a window.*]

BRA. What is the reason of this terrible summons?
What is the matter there?
ROD. Signior, is all your family within?
IAGO. Are your doors locked?
BRA.   Why, wherefore ask you this?   85

IAGO. 'Zounds,° sir, you're robbed. For shame,
    put on your gown,°
Your heart is burst, you have lost half your soul.
Even now, now, very now, an old black ram
Is tupping° your white ewe. Arise, arise,
Awake the snorting° citizens with the bell,   90
Or else the Devil° will make a grandsire of you.
Arise, I say.
BRA.   What, have you lost your wits?
ROD. Most reverend signior, do you know my
    voice?
BRA. Not I. What are you?
ROD. My name is Roderigo.   94
BRA.   The worser welcome.
I have charged thee not to haunt about my doors.
In honest plainness thou hast heard me say
My daughter is not for thee, and now, in madness,
Being full of supper and distempering draughts,°
Upon malicious bravery° dost thou come   100
To start° my quiet.
ROD. Sir, sir, sir ——
BRA.   But thou must needs be sure
My spirit and my place have in them power
To make this bitter to thee.
ROD.   Patience, good sir.
BRA. What tell'st thou me of robbing? This is
    Venice,   105
My house is not a grange.°
ROD.   Most grave Brabantio,
In simple and pure soul I come to you.
IAGO. 'Zounds, sir, you are one of those that will
not serve God if the Devil bid you. Because we come
to do you service and you think we are ruffians,   110
you'll have your daughter covered with a Barbary°
horse, you'll have your nephews° neigh to you, you'll
have coursers for cousins,° and jennets° for ger-
mans.°
BRA. What profane wretch art thou?   115
IAGO. I am one, sir, that comes to tell you your
daughter and the Moor are now making the beast
with two backs.
BRA. Thou art a villain.
IAGO.   You are — a Senator.
BRA. This thou shalt answer. I know thee, Roder-
igo.   120
ROD. Sir, I will answer anything. But I beseech you
If 't be your pleasure and most wise consent,
As partly I find it is, that your fair daughter,
At this odd-even° and dull° watch o' the night,
Transported with no worse nor better guard   125

---

48. **cashiered:** dismissed. The word at this time did not imply
dishonorable discharge.   50. **trimmed . . . duty:** decking themselves out with the outward forms of loyal service.   52. **throwing . . . service:** serving merely in outward show.   54. **Do . . .
homage:** serve themselves. **homage:** an outward act signifying
obedience.   60. **peculiar:** particular, personal.   62. **native . . .
heart:** natural actions and shape of my secret designs. 63. **extern:**
outward.   65. **daws:** jackdaws; i.e., fools. **I . . . am:** i.e., I am in
secret a devil.   66. **full fortune:** overflowing good luck. **owe:**
own. 67. **carry 't thus:** i.e., bring off this marriage.   72–73. **throw
. . . color:** cause him some annoyance by way of variety to
tarnish his joy.   75. **timorous:** terrifying.   80. **bags:** moneybags.

86. **'Zounds:** by God's wounds. **gown:** dressing gown.   89. **tup-
ping:** covering.   90. **snorting:** snoring.   91. **Devil:** The Devil in
old pictures and woodcuts was represented as black.   99. **distempering draughts:** liquor that makes senseless.   100. **bravery:**
defiance.   101. **start:** startle.   106. **grange:** lonely farm.
111. **Barbary:** Moorish.   112. **nephews:** grandsons.   113. **cousins:**
near relations. **jennets:** Moorish ponies.   114. **germans:** kinsmen.   124. **odd-even:** about midnight. **dull:** heavy, sleepy.

But with a knave of common hire, a gondolier,
To the gross clasps of a lascivious Moor —
If this be known to you, and your allowance,°
We then have done you bold and saucy wrongs.
But if you know not this, my manners tell me   130
We have your wrong rebuke. Do not believe
That from the sense of all civility°
I thus would play and trifle with your reverence.
Your daughter, if you have not given her leave,
I say again, hath made a gross revolt,°   135
Tying her duty, beauty, wit, and fortunes
In an extravagant° and wheeling° stranger
Of here and everywhere. Straight satisfy yourself.
If she be in her chamber or your house,
Let loose on me the justice of the state   140
For thus deluding you.
   BRA.   Strike on the tinder,° ho!
Give me a taper!° Call up all my people!
This accident is not unlike my dream.   *SUPERSTITIOUS*
Belief of it oppresses me already.
Light, I say! Light!   [*Exit above.*]
   IAGO.   Farewell, for I must leave you.   145
It seems not meet, nor wholesome to my place,°
To be produced — as if I stay I shall —
Against the Moor. For I do know the state,
However this may gall° him with some check,°
Cannot with safety cast° him. For he's embarked
With such loud reason to the Cyprus wars,   151
Which even now stand in act,° that, for their souls,
Another of his fathom° they have none
To lead their business. In which regard,
Though I do hate him as I do Hell pains,   155
Yet for necessity of present life   *← HIS DECEIT*
I must show out a flag° and sign of love,
Which is indeed but sign. That you shall surely find
   him,
Lead to the Sagittary° the raisèd search,   159
And there will I be with him. So farewell.   [*Exit.*]
[*Enter, below,* BRABANTIO, *in his nightgown, and* SERVANTS *with torches.*]
   BRA. It is too true an evil. Gone she is,
And what's to come of my despisèd time°
Is naught but bitterness. Now, Roderigo,
Where didst thou see her? Oh, unhappy girl!
With the Moor, say'st thou? Who would be a
   father!   165

How didst thou know 'twas she? Oh, she deceives   *DISTRACTED*
   me
Past thought! What said she to you? Get more ta-
   pers.
Raise all my kindred. Are they married, think you?
   ROD. Truly, I think they are.
   BRA. Oh Heaven! How got she out? Oh, treason
     of the blood!°   170
Fathers, from hence trust not your daughters' minds
By what you see them act. Are there not charms°   *SUPERSTITIOUS*
By which the property° of youth and maidhood
May be abused?° Have you not read, Roderigo,
Of some such thing?
   ROD.   Yes, sir, I have indeed.   175
   BRA. Call up my brother. Oh, would you had had
     her!
Some one way, some another. Do you know
Where we may apprehend her and the Moor?
   ROD. I think I can discover him, if you please
To get good guard and go along with me.   180
   BRA. Pray you, lead on. At every house I'll call,   *HIS*
I may command° at most. Get weapons, ho!   *POWER +*
And raise some special officers of night.   *DES.'S*
On, good Roderigo, I'll deserve your pains.°
               [*Exeunt.*]   *STRENGTH*
                       OF LOVE

SCENE II. *Another street.*

[*Enter* OTHELLO, IAGO, *and* ATTENDANTS
with torches.]

   IAGO. Though in the trade of war I have slain
     men,
Yet do I hold it very stuff° o' the conscience
To do no contrivèd° murder. I lack iniquity
Sometimes to do me service. Nine or ten times
I had thought to have yerked° him here under the
     ribs.   *HIS*   5
   OTH. 'Tis better as it is.   *WISE ATTITUDE*
   IAGO.   Nay, but he prated
And spoke such scurvy and provoking terms
Against your honor
That, with the little godliness I have,   *← "HONEST*
I did full hard forbear him.° But I pray you, sir,   *IAGO"*   10
Are you fast° married? Be assured of this,
That the Magnifico° is much beloved,
And hath in his effect° a voice potential
As double as° the Duke's. He will divorce you,
Or put upon you what restraint and grievance   15

128. your allowance: by your permission.   132. from ... civility: disregarding all sense of decent behavior.   135. gross revolt: indecent rebellion.   137. extravagant: vagabond. wheeling: wandering.   141. tinder: the primitive method of making fire, used before the invention of matches. A spark, made by striking flint on steel, fell on the tinder, some inflammable substance such as charred linen, which was blown into flame.   142. taper: candle.   146. place: i.e., as Othello's officer.   149. gall: make sore. check: rebuke.   150. cast: dismiss from service.   152. stand in act: are on the point of beginning.   153. fathom: depth.   157. flag: a sign of welcome.   159. Sagittary: presumably some building in Venice, not identified, used as a meeting place for the Council.   162. what's ... time: the rest of my wretched life.

170. treason ... blood: treachery of my own child.   172. charms: magic spells.   173. property: nature.   174. abused: deceived. 182. command: find supporters.   184. deserve ... pains: reward your labor.
   Sc. ii: 2. stuff: material, nature.   3. contrived: deliberately planned.   5. yerked: jabbed.   10. full ... him: had a hard job to keep my hands off him.   11. fast: securely.   12. Magnifico: the title of the chief men of Venice.   13. in ... effect: what he can do.   13–14. potential ... as: twice as powerful as.

The law, with all his might to enforce it on,
Will give him cable.°
OTH.   Let him do his spite.
My services which I have done the signiory°
Shall outtongue his complaints. 'Tis yet to know° —
Which, when I know that boasting is an honor,   20
I shall promulgate° — I fetch my life and being°
From men of royal siege,° and my demerits°
May speak unbonneted° to as proud a fortune
As this that I have reached. For know, Iago,
But that I love the gentle Desdemona,   25
I would not my unhoused° free condition
Put into circumscription and confine°
For the sea's worth. But look! What lights come
    yond?
IAGO. Those are the raisèd father and his friends.
You were best go in.
OTH.   Not I, I must be found.   30
My parts,° my title, and my perfect° soul
Shall manifest me rightly. Is it they?
IAGO. By Janus,° I think no.
[*Enter* CASSIO, *and certain* OFFICERS *with torches.*]
OTH. The servants of the Duke, and my Lieuten-
ant.
The goodness of the night upon you, friends!   35
What is the news?
CAS.   The Duke does greet you, General,
And he requires your haste-posthaste° appearance,
Even on the instant.
OTH.   What is the matter, think you?
CAS. Something from Cyprus, as I may divine.
It is a business of some heat. The galleys°   40
Have sent a dozen sequent° messengers
This very night at one another's heels,
And many of the consuls, raised and met,
Are at the Duke's already. You have been hotly
    called for
When, being not at your lodging to be found,   45
The Senate hath sent about three several° quests
To search you out.
OTH. 'Tis well I am found by you.
I will but spend a word here in the house
And go with you.   [*Exit.*]

CAS.   Ancient, what makes he here?
IAGO. Faith, he tonight hath boarded a land car-
rack.°   50
If it prove lawful prize, he's made forever.
CAS. I do not understand.
IAGO.   He's married.
CAS.   To who?
[*Re-enter* OTHELLO.]
IAGO. Marry,° to —— Come, Captain, will you
go?
OTH.   Have with you.
CAS. Here comes another troop to seek for you.
IAGO. It is Brabantio. General, be advised,°   55
He comes to bad intent.
[*Enter* BRABANTIO, RODERIGO, *and* OFFICERS *with
torches and weapons.*]
OTH.   Holloa! Stand there!
ROD. Signior, it is the Moor.
BRA.   Down with him, thief!
[*They draw on both sides.*]
IAGO. You, Roderigo! Come, sir, I am for you.
OTH. Keep up° your bright swords, for the dew
will rust them.
Good signior, you shall more command with years
Than with your weapons.   61
BRA. O thou foul thief, where hast thou stowed
my daughter?
Damned as thou art, thou hast enchanted her.
For I'll refer me to all things of sense°
If she in chains of magic were not bound,   65
Whether a maid so tender, fair, and happy,
So opposite to marriage that she shunned
The wealthy curlèd darlings of our nation,
Would ever have, to incur a general mock,
Run from her guardage° to the sooty bosom   70
Of such a thing as thou, to fear, not to delight.
Judge me the world if 'tis not gross in sense°
That thou hast practiced on her with foul charms,
Abused her delicate youth with drugs or minerals
That weaken motion.° I'll have 't disputed on,°   75
'Tis probable, and palpable° to thinking.
I therefore apprehend and do attach° thee
For an abuser of the world, a practicer
Of arts inhibited and out of warrant.°
Lay hold upon him. If he do resist,   80
Subdue him at his peril.
OTH.   Hold your hands,
Both you of my inclining and the rest.
Were it my cue to fight, I should have known it
Without a prompter. Where will you that I go

17. cable: rope.   18. signiory: the state of Venice.   19. 'Tis . . .
know: it has still to be made known.   21. promulgate: proclaim.
fetch . . . being: am descended.   22. royal siege: throne. demerits: deserts.   23. unbonneted: A disputed phrase. Usually it
means "without a cap"; i.e., in sign that the wearer is standing
before a superior. But Othello means that his merits are such that
he need show deference to no man.   26. unhoused: unmarried.
27. confine: confinement.   31. parts: abilities. perfect: ready.
33. Janus: the two-faced God of the Romans, an appropriate
deity for Iago.   37. haste-posthaste: with the quickest possible
speed. When it was necessary to urge the postboy to greater
speed than usual, the letter or dispatch was inscribed "haste,
posthaste." The Earl of Essex once inscribed a letter "haste,
haste, haste posthaste, haste for life." See App. 17.   40. galleys:
Venetian ships manned and rowed by slaves; the fastest of
craft.   41. sequent: following one after another.   46. several:
separate.

50. carrack: the largest type of Spanish merchant ship.
53. Marry: Mary, by the Virgin — with a pun.   55. advised:
careful.   59. Keep up: sheathe.   64. refer . . . sense: i.e., by
every rational consideration.   70. guardage: guardianship.
72. gross in sense: i.e., plain to the perception.   75. motion:
sense. disputed on: argued in the courts of law.   76. palpable:
clear.   77. attach: arrest.   79. arts . . . warrant: forbidden and
illegal acts; i.e., magic and witchcraft.

To answer this your charge?

BRA.   To prison, till fit time   85
Of law and course of direct session°
Call thee to answer.

OTH.   What if I do obey?
How may the Duke be therewith satisfied,
Whose messengers are here about my side
Upon some present° business of the state   90
To bring me to him?

1. OFF.   'Tis true, most worthy signior.
The Duke's in Council, and your noble self
I am sure is sent for.

BRA.   How! The Duke in Council!
In this time of the night! Bring him away.
Mine's not an idle° cause. The Duke himself,   95
Or any of my brothers of the state,
Cannot but feel this wrong as 'twere their own.
For if such actions may have passage free,°
Bondslaves and pagans shall our statesmen be.

             [*Exeunt.*]

SCENE III. *A council chamber.*

[*The* DUKE *and* SENATORS *sitting at a table,* OFFICERS *attending.*]

DUKE. There is no composition° in these news°
That gives them credit.

1. SEN.   Indeed they are disproportioned.
My letters say a hundred and seven galleys.

DUKE. And mine, a hundred and forty.

2. SEN.   And mine, two hundred.
But though they jump not on a just account° —   5
As in these cases, where the aim reports,°
'Tis oft with difference — yet do they all confirm
A Turkish fleet, and bearing up° to Cyprus.

DUKE. Nay, it is possible enough to judgment.
I do not so secure me in the error,°   10
But the main article° I do approve
In fearful° sense.

SAILOR. [*Within*] What ho! What ho! What ho!

1. OFF. A messenger from the galleys.

       [*Enter* SAILOR.]

DUKE.   Now, what's the business?

SAIL. The Turkish preparation makes for Rhodes.
So was I bid report here to the state   15
By Signior Angelo.

DUKE. How say you by this change?

1. SEN.   This cannot be,
By no assay of reason.° 'Tis a pageant°
To keep us in false gaze.° When we consider
The importancy of Cyprus to the Turk,   20
And let ourselves again but understand
That as it more concerns the Turk than Rhodes,
So may he with more facile question bear° it,
For that it stands not in such warlike brace°
But altogether lacks the abilities   25
That Rhodes is dressed° in — if we make thought
   of this,
We must not think the Turk is so unskillful
To leave that latest which concerns him first,
Neglecting an attempt of ease and gain
To wake and wage° a danger profitless.   30

DUKE. Nay, in all confidence, he's not for Rhodes.

1. OFF. Here is more news.

       [*Enter a* MESSENGER.]

MESS. The Ottomites,° Reverend and Gracious,
Steering with due course toward the isle of Rhodes,
Have there injointed° them with an after-fleet.°   35

1. SEN. Aye, so I thought. How many, as you
   guess?

MESS. Of thirty sail. And now they do restem°
Their backward course, bearing with frank appearance°
Their purposes toward Cyprus. Signior Montano,
Your trusty and most valiant servitor,   40
With his free duty recommends you thus,°
And prays you to believe him.

DUKE. 'Tis certain then for Cyprus.
Marcus Luccicos, is not he in town?

1. SEN. He's now in Florence.   45

DUKE. Write from us to him, post-posthaste dispatch.

1. SEN. Here comes Brabantio and the valiant
   Moor.

     [*Enter* BRABANTIO, OTHELLO, IAGO, RODERIGO,
           and OFFICERS.]

DUKE. Valiant Othello, we must straight employ
   you
Against the general enemy Ottoman.
[*To* BRABANTIO] I did not see you. Welcome, gentle
   signior,   50
We lacked your counsel and your help tonight.

BRA. So did I yours. Good your Grace, pardon
   me,
Neither my place nor aught I heard of business
Hath raised me from my bed, nor doth the general
   care
Take hold on me. For my particular° grief   55

[handwritten margin note: PRIVATE & SORROWS IN PUBLIC WORLD]

---

86. course . . . session: trial in the ordinary courts, where witches and other criminals are tried — and not by special commission as a great man.   90. present: immediate.   95. idle: trivial. 98. have . . . free: be freely allowed.

     Sc. iii: 1. composition: agreement. news: reports.   5. jump . . . account: do not agree with an exact estimate.   6. aim reports: i.e., intelligence reports of an enemy's intention often differ in the details.   8. bearing up: making course for.   10. I . . . error: I do not consider myself free from danger, because the reports may not all be accurate.   11. main article: general purport.   12. fearful: to be feared.

18. assay of reason: reasonable test. pageant: show.   19. false gaze: looking the wrong way.   23. with . . . bear: take it more easily.   24. brace: state of defense.   26. dressed: prepared. 30. wage: risk.   33. Ottomites: Turks.   35. injointed: joined. after-fleet: following, second fleet.   37. restem: steer again. 38. frank appearance: no attempt at concealment.   41. With . . . thus: with all due respect thus advises.   55. particular: personal.

Is of so floodgate° and o'erbearing nature
That it engluts° and swallows other sorrows,
And it is still itself.
    DUKE.   Why, what's the matter?
    BRA. My daughter! Oh, my daughter!
    ALL.   Dead?
    BRA.   Aye, to me.
She is abused, stol'n from me and corrupted   60
By spells and medicines bought of mountebanks.°
For nature so preposterously to err,
Being not deficient, blind, or lame of sense,
Sans° witchcraft could not.
    DUKE. Whoe'er he be that in this foul proceeding
Hath thus beguiled your daughter of herself°   66
And you of her, the bloody book of law
You shall yourself read in the bitter letter
After your own sense — yea, though our proper° son
Stood in your action.
    BRA.   Humbly I thank your Grace.   70
Here is the man, this Moor, whom now, it seems,
Your special mandate for the state affairs
Hath hither brought.
    ALL.   We are very sorry for 't.
    DUKE. [*To* OTHELLO] What in your own part can
      you say to this?
    BRA. Nothing but this is so.   75
    OTH. Most potent, grave, and reverend signiors,
My very noble and approved° good masters,
That I have ta'en away this old man's daughter,
It is most true — true, I have married her.
The very head and front° of my offending   80
Hath this extent, no more. Rude° am I in my speech,
And little blest with the soft phrase of peace.
For since these arms of mine had seven years' pith°
Till now some nine moons wasted, they have used
Their dearest° action in the tented field.   85
And little of this great world can I speak,
More than pertains to feats of broil and battle,
And therefore little shall I grace my cause
In speaking for myself. Yet, by your gracious pa-
    tience,
I will a round unvarnished tale° deliver   90
Of my whole course of love — what drugs, what
    charms,
What conjuration and what mighty magic —
For such proceeding I am charged withal —
I won his daughter.
    BRA.   A maiden never bold,
Of spirit so still and quiet that her motion   95

Blushed at herself,° and she — in spite of nature,
Of years, of country, credit,° everything —
To fall in love with what she feared to look on!
It is a judgment maimed and most imperfect
That will confess° perfection so could err   100
Against all rules of nature, and must be driven
To find out practices° of cunning Hell
Why this should be. I therefore vouch° again
That with some mixtures° powerful o'er the blood,°
Or with some dram conjured° to this effect,   105
He wrought upon her.
    DUKE.   To vouch this is no proof
Without more certain and more overt° test
Than these thin habits° and poor likelihoods°
Of modern seeming° do prefer° against him.
    I. SEN. But, Othello, speak.   110
Did you by indirect and forcèd° courses
Subdue and poison this young maid's affections?
Or came it by request, and such fair question
As soul to soul affordeth?
    OTH.   I do beseech you
Send for the lady to the Sagittary,   115
And let her speak of me before her father.
If you do find me foul in her report,
The trust, the office I do hold of you,
Not only take away, but let your sentence
Even fall upon my life.
    DUKE.   Fetch Desdemona hither.   120
    OTH. Ancient, conduct them, you best know the
      place.   [*Exeunt* IAGO *and* ATTENDANTS.]
And till she come, as truly as to Heaven
I do confess the vices of my blood,
So justly to your grave ears I'll present
How I did thrive in this fair lady's love   125
And she in mine.
    DUKE.   Say it, Othello.
    OTH. Her father loved me, oft invited me,
Still° questioned me the story of my life
From year to year, the battles, sieges, fortunes,   130
That I have passed.
I ran it through, even from my boyish days
To the very moment that he bade me tell it.
Wherein I spake of most disastrous chances,°
Of moving accidents° by flood and field,   135
Of hairbreadth 'scapes i' the imminent deadly
    breach,°
Of being taken by the insolent foe
And sold to slavery, of my redemption thence,

---

56. floodgate: i.e., like water rushing through an opened sluice.
57. engluts: swallows. 61. mountebanks: quack doctors, who
dealt in poisons and love potions. Cf. *Haml,* IV.vii.142.
64. Sans: without. 66. beguiled . . . herself: cheated your
daughter of herself; i.e., caused her to be "beside herself."
69. proper: own. 77. approved: tested; i.e., found good masters
by experience. 80. front: forehead. 81. Rude: rough, uncul-
tured. 83. pith: marrow. 85. dearest: most important.
90. round . . . tale: direct, unadorned account.

95–96. Of . . . herself: she was so shy that she blushed at the
slightest cause. motion: outward behavior. 97. credit: reputation. 100. will confess: would believe. 102. practices: plots.
103. vouch: declare. 104. mixtures: drugs. blood: passions.
105. conjured: mixed with spells. 107. overt: open. 108. thin
habits: slight evidence; lit., thin clothes. poor likelihoods: unconvincing charges. 109. modern seeming: slight suspicion. prefer: make a charge against. 111. forced: unnatural. 129. Still:
always, continually. 134. chances: accidents. 135. accidents:
occurrences. 136. breach: assault on a city. See Pl. 12a.

And portance° in my travels' history.
Wherein of antres° vast and deserts idle,°   140
Rough quarries, rocks, and hills whose heads touch
     heaven,
It was my hint° to speak — such was the process.°
And of the cannibals that each other eat,
The anthropophagi,° and men whose heads
Do grow beneath their shoulders.° This to hear
Would Desdemona seriously incline.   146
But still the house affairs would draw her thence,
Which ever as she could with haste dispatch,
She'd come again, and with a greedy ear
Devour up my discourse. Which I observing,   150
Took once a pliant° hour and found good means
To draw from her a prayer of earnest heart
That I would all my pilgrimage dilate,°
Whereof by parcels° she had something heard,
But not intentively.° I did consent,   155
And often did beguile her of° her tears
When I did speak of some distressful stroke
That my youth suffered. My story being done,
She gave me for my pains a world of sighs.
She swore, in faith, 'twas strange, 'twas passing
     strange,   160
'Twas pitiful, 'twas wondrous pitiful.
She wished she had not heard it, yet she wished
That Heaven had made her° such a man. She
     thanked me,
And bade me, if I had a friend that loved her,
I should but teach him how to tell my story   165
And that would woo her. Upon this hint I spake.
She loved me for the dangers I had passed,
And I loved her that she did pity them.
This only is the witchcraft I have used.
Here comes the lady, let her witness it.   170

     [*Enter* DESDEMONA, IAGO, *and* ATTENDANTS.]
DUKE. I think this tale would win my daughter
     too.
Good Brabantio,
Take up this mangled matter at the best.°
Men do their broken weapons rather use
Than their bare hands.
   BRA.   I pray you hear her speak.   175
If she confess that she was half the wooer,
Destruction on my head if my bad blame
Light on the man! Come hither, gentle mistress.
Do you perceive in all this noble company
Where most you owe obedience?
   DES.   My noble Father,   180
I do perceive here a divided duty.

To you I am bound for life and education,
My life and education both do learn° me
How to respect you, you are the lord of duty,°
I am hitherto your daughter. But here's my hus-
     band,   185
And so much duty as my mother showed
To you, preferring you before her father
So much I challenge that I may profess
Due to the Moor my lord.
   BRA.   God be with you! I have done.
Please it your Grace, on to the state affairs.   190
I had rather to adopt a child than get° it.
Come hither, Moor.
I here do give thee that with all my heart
Which, but thou hast already, with all my heart
I would keep from thee. For your sake, jewel,   195
I am glad at soul I have no other child,
For thy escape would teach me tyranny,
To hang clogs on them. I have done, my lord.
   DUKE. Let me speak like yourself, and lay a sen-
     tence°
Which, as a grise° or step, may help these lovers
Into your favor.   201
When remedies are past, the griefs are ended
By seeing the worst, which late on hopes depended.°
To mourn a mischief that is past and gone
Is the next way to draw new mischief on.   205
What cannot be preserved when fortune takes,
Patience her injury a mockery makes.°
The robbed that smiles steals something from the
     thief.
He robs himself that spends a bootless° grief.
   BRA. So° let the Turk of Cyprus us beguile,   210
We lose it not so long as we can smile.
He bears the sentence well that nothing bears
But the free comfort which from thence he hears.
But he bears both the sentence and the sorrow
That, to pay grief, must of poor patience borrow.
These sentences, to sugar or to gall,   216
Being strong on both sides, are equivocal.
But words are words. I never yet did hear
That the bruisèd heart was piercèd through the ear.
I humbly beseech you, proceed to the affairs of
     state.   220
   DUKE. The Turk with a most mighty preparation
makes for Cyprus. Othello, the fortitude of the place

---

183. learn: teach.   **184. lord of duty:** the man to whom I owe
duty.   **191. get:** beget.   **199. sentence:** proverbial saying.
200. grise: degree, step.   **202–03. When . . . depended:** our
anxieties end when the feared event happens.   **207. Patience . . .
makes:** i.e., when we are not unduly disturbed by our misfortunes, we mock Fortune.   **209. bootless:** vain.   **210–19. So . . .
ear:** Brabantio retaliates sarcastically with a few "sentences"
of his own: Let the Turk take Cyprus; it is no loss if we smile at it.
It is easy enough to produce sententious consolation, it costs
nothing; but the man who has to endure both consolation and the
sorrow itself must needs be patient. These sentences work both
ways; mere words hurt no one. Cf. Leonato's similar outburst,
M Ado, V.i.3–38.

139. portance: bearing.   **140. antres:** caves. **idle:** worthless.
142. hint: occasion. **process:** proceeding, order.   **144. anthropophagi:** cannibals.   **144–45. men . . . shoulders:** See *Temp*,
III.iii.46–47,n.   **151. pliant:** suitable.   **153. dilate:** relate at
length.   **154. parcels:** portions.   **155. intentively:** intently.
156. beguile . . . of: draw from her.   **163. her:** for her.   **173. Take
. . . best:** make the best settlement you can of this confused business.

is best known to you, and though we have there a
substitute° of most allowed° sufficiency,° yet opinion, a sovereign mistress of effects, throws a more
safer voice on you.° You must therefore be content
to slubber° the gloss of your new fortunes with this
more stubborn and boisterous expedition.   229

OTH. The tyrant custom, most grave Senators,
Hath made the flinty and steel couch of war
My thrice-driven° bed of down. I do agnize°
A natural and prompt alacrity
I find in hardness,° and do undertake
These present wars against the Ottomites.   235
Most humbly therefore bending to your state,
I crave fit disposition for my wife,
Due reference of place° and exhibition,°
With such accommodation and besort°
As levels with her breeding.°

DUKE.   If you please,   240
Be 't at her father's.

BRA.   I'll not have it so.

OTH. Nor I.

DES.   Nor I. I would not there reside,
To put my father in impatient thoughts
By being in his eye. Most gracious Duke,
To my unfolding° lend your prosperous° ear,   245
And let me find a charter° in your voice
To assist my simpleness.

DUKE. What would you, Desdemona?

DES. That I did love the Moor to live with him,
My downright violence and storm of fortunes   250
May trumpet to the world. My heart's subdued
Even to the very quality of my lord.°
I saw Othello's visage in his mind,
And to his honors and his valiant parts
Did I my soul and fortunes consecrate.   255
So that, dear lords, if I be left behind,
A moth of peace,° and he go to the war,
The rites for which I love him are bereft me,
And I a heavy interim° shall support
By his dear absence. Let me go with him.   260

OTH. Let her have your voices.
Vouch° with me, Heaven, I therefore beg it not
To please the palate of my appetite,
Nor to comply with heat — the young affects
In me defunct° — and proper satisfaction,   265

But to be free and bounteous° to her mind.°
And Heaven defend° your good souls, that you think
I will your serious and great business scant
For she is with me. No, when light-winged toys°
Of feathered Cupid seel° with wanton dullness   270
My speculative and officed instruments,°
That my disports° corrupt and taint my business,
Let housewives make a skillet° of my helm,
And all indign° and base adversities
Make head against° my estimation!°   275

DUKE. Be it as you shall privately determine,
Either for her stay or going. The affair cries haste,
And speed must answer 't. You must hence tonight.

DES. Tonight, my lord?

DUKE.   This night.

OTH.   With all my heart.

DUKE. At nine i' the morning here we'll meet
again.   280
Othello, leave some officer behind,
And he shall our commission° bring to you,
With such things else of quality and respect
As doth import you.°

OTH.   So please your Grace, my Ancient,
A man he is of honesty and trust.   285
To his conveyance I assign my wife,
With what else needful your good grace shall think
To be sent after me.

DUKE.   Let it be so.
Good night to everyone. [*To* BRABANTIO] And, noble
signior,
If virtue no delighted beauty lack,   290
Your son-in-law is far more fair than black.°

I. SEN. Adieu, brave Moor. Use Desdemona well.

BRA. Look to her, Moor, if thou hast eyes to see.
She has deceived her father, and may thee.°

         [*Exeunt* DUKE, SENATORS, OFFICERS, *etc.*]

OTH. My life upon her faith! Honest Iago,   295
My Desdemona must I leave to thee.
I prithee, let thy wife attend on her,
And bring them after in the best advantage.°
Come, Desdemona, I have but an hour
Of love, of worldly matters and direction,   300
To spend with thee. We must obey the time.

         [*Exeunt* OTHELLO *and* DESDEMONA.]

---

224. substitute: deputy commander. **allowed:** admitted. **sufficiency:** efficiency. **224–27. yet . . . you:** yet public opinion,
which controls our actions, is such that we regard you as a safer
choice. **228. slubber:** tarnish. **232. thrice-driven:** three times
refined. **agnize:** confess. **234. hardness:** hardship. **238. Due
. . . place:** i.e., that she shall be treated as becomes my wife.
exhibition: allowance. **239. besort:** attendants. **240. levels
. . . breeding:** as suits her birth. **245. unfolding:** plan; lit., revealing. **prosperous:** favorable. **246. charter:** privilege.
249–52. That . . . lord: my love for the Moor is publicly shown by
the way in which I have violently taken my fortunes in my hands;
my heart has become a soldier like my husband. **quality:** profession. **257. moth of peace:** a useless creature living in luxury.
259. interim: interval. **262. Vouch:** certify. **264–65. young
. . . defunct:** in me the passion of youth is dead.

266. bounteous: generous. **to . . . mind:** Othello repeats Desdemona's claim that this is a marriage of minds. **267. defend:** forbid. **269. toys:** trifles. **270. seel:** close up; a technical term
from falconry. See App. 26. **271. speculative . . . instruments:**
powers of sight and action; i.e., my efficiency as your general.
272. disports: amusements. **273. skillet:** saucepan. **274. in-
dign:** unworthy. **275. Make . . . against:** overcome. **estimation:** reputation. **282. commission:** formal document of appointment. **283–84. With . . . you:** with other matters that concern
your position and honor. **290–91. If . . . black:** if worthiness is a
beautiful thing in itself, your son-in-law, though black, has
beauty. **293–94. Look . . . thee:** Iago in the background takes
note of these words, and later reminds Othello of them with
deadly effect. See III.iii.206. **298. in . . . advantage:** at the best
opportunity.

ROD. Iago!

IAGO. What say'st thou, noble heart?

ROD. What will I do, thinkest thou?

IAGO. Why, go to bed and sleep.   305

ROD. I will incontinently° drown myself.

IAGO. If thou dost, I shall never love thee after. Why, thou silly gentleman!

ROD. It is silliness to live when to live is torment, and then have we a prescription to die when death is our physician.   311

IAGO. Oh, villainous! I have looked upon the world for four times seven years, and since I could distinguish betwixt a benefit and an injury I never found man that knew how to love himself. Ere I would say I would drown myself for the love of a guinea hen, I would change my humanity with a baboon.   318

ROD. What should I do? I confess it is my shame to be so fond,° but it is not in my virtue° to amend it.

IAGO. Virtue! A fig! 'Tis in ourselves that we are thus or thus. Our bodies are gardens, to the which our wills° are gardeners. So that if we will plant nettles or sow lettuce, set hyssop and weed up   325 thyme, supply it with one gender° of herbs or distract it with many, either to have it sterile with idleness or manured with industry — why, the power and corrigible° authority of this lies in our wills. If the balance of our lives had not one scale of   330 reason to poise° another of sensuality, the blood and baseness of our natures would conduct us to most preposterous conclusions. But we have reason to cool our raging motions, our carnal stings,° our unbitted° lusts, whereof I take this that you call love to be a sect or scion.°   337

ROD. It cannot be.

IAGO. It is merely a lust of the blood and a permission of the will. Come, be a man. Drown thyself! Drown cats and blind puppies. I have professed me thy friend, and I confess me knit to thy deserving with cables of perdurable° toughness. I could never better stead° thee than now. Put money in thy purse, follow thou the wars, defeat thy favor with an   345 usurped beard° — I say put money in thy purse. It cannot be that Desdemona should long continue her love to the Moor — put money in thy purse — nor he his to her. It was a violent commencement,   350 and thou shalt see an answerable sequestration° — put but money in thy purse. These Moors are changeable in their wills. — Fill thy purse with money. The

food that to him now is as luscious as locusts° shall be to him shortly as bitter as coloquintida.°   355 She must change for youth. When she is sated with his body, she will find the error of her choice. She must have change, she must — therefore put money in thy purse. If thou wilt needs damn thyself, do it a more delicate way than drowning. Make all   360 the money thou canst.° If sanctimony and a frail vow betwixt an erring° barbarian and a supersubtle Venetian be not too hard for my wits and all the tribe of Hell, thou shalt enjoy her — therefore make money. A pox of drowning thyself! It is clean out of the way. Seek thou rather to be hanged in   366 compassing° thy joy than to be drowned and go without her.

ROD. Wilt thou be fast to my hopes if I depend on the issue?   370

IAGO. Thou art sure of me. Go, make money. I have told thee often, and I retell thee again and again, I hate the Moor. My cause is hearted,° thine hath no less reason. Let us be conjunctive° in our revenge against him. If thou canst cuckold° him,   375 thou dost thyself a pleasure, me a sport. There are many events in the womb of time, which will be delivered. Traverse,° go, provide thy money. We will have more of this tomorrow. Adieu.   380

ROD. Where shall we meet i' the morning?

IAGO. At my lodging.

ROD. I'll be with thee betimes.°

IAGO. Go to, farewell. Do you hear, Roderigo?

ROD. What say you?   386

IAGO. No more of drowning, do you hear?

ROD. I am changed. I'll go sell all my land. [*Exit.*]

IAGO. Thus do I ever make my fool my purse, For I mine own gained knowledge should profane If I would time expend with such a snipe   391 But for my sport and profit. I hate the Moor, And it is thought abroad that 'twixt my sheets He has done my office. I know not if 't be true, But I for mere suspicion in that kind   395 Will do as if for surety. He holds me well, The better shall my purpose work on him. Cassio's a proper° man. Let me see now, To get his place, and to plume up° my will In double knavery —— How, how? — Let's see. — After some time, to abuse Othello's ear   401 That he is too familiar with his wife. He hath a person and a smooth dispose To be suspected,° framed to make women false.

---

306. **incontinently:** immediately.   320. **fond:** foolishly in love. **virtue:** manhood.   324. **wills:** desires.   326. **gender:** kind. 329. **corrigible;** correcting, directing.   331. **poise:** weigh. 335. **carnal stings:** fleshly desires.   336. **unbitted:** uncontrolled. 337. **sect or scion:** Both words mean a slip taken from a tree and planted to produce a new growth.   343. **perdurable:** very hard.   344. **stead:** help.   345–46. **defeat . . . beard:** disguise your face by growing a beard.   351. **answerable sequestration:** corresponding separation; i.e., reaction.

354. **locusts:** It is not known what fruit was called a locust. 355. **coloquintida:** known as "bitter apple," a form of gherkin from which a purge was made.   360–61. **Make . . . canst:** turn all you can into ready cash.   362. **erring:** vagabond.   367. **compassing:** achieving.   373. **hearted:** heartfelt.   374. **conjunctive:** united.   375. **cuckold:** make him a cuckold. See App. 11. 379. **Traverse:** quickstep.   384. **betimes:** in good time, early. 398. **proper:** handsome.   399. **plume up:** glorify.   403–04. **He . . . suspected:** an easy way with him that is naturally suspected.

The Moor is of a free and open nature   405
That thinks men honest that but seem to be so,
And will as tenderly be led by the nose
As asses are.
I have 't. It is engendered.° Hell and night   409
Must bring this monstrous birth to the world's light.
                             [*Exit.*]

Act II

SCENE I. *A seaport in Cyprus. An open place near the wharf.*

[*Enter* MONTANO *and two* GENTLEMEN.]

MON. What from the cape can you discern at sea?
1. GENT. Nothing at all. It is a high-wrought
     flood.°
I cannot 'twixt the heaven and the main°
Descry a sail.
   MON. Methinks the wind hath spoke aloud at
     land,   5
A fuller blast ne'er shook our battlements.
If it hath ruffianed° so upon the sea,
What ribs of oak, when mountains melt on them,
Can hold the mortise?° What shall we hear of this?
   2. GENT. A segregation° of the Turkish fleet.   10
For do but stand upon the foaming shore,
The chidden billow seems to pelt the clouds,
The wind-shaked surge, with high and monstrous
     mane,
Seems to cast water on the burning Bear,°
And quench the guards of the ever-fixèd Pole.°   15
I never did like molestation° view
On the enchafèd° flood.
   MON.   If that the Turkish fleet
Be not ensheltered and embayed,° they are
     drowned.
It is impossible to bear it out.

[*Enter a* THIRD GENTLEMAN.]

   3. GENT. News, lads! Our wars are done.   20
The desperate tempest hath so banged the Turks
That their designment halts.° A noble ship of Venice
Hath seen a grievous wreck and sufferance°
On most part of their fleet.

MON. How! Is this true?
   3. GENT.   The ship is here put in,   25
A Veronesa. Michael Cassio,
Lieutenant to the warlike Moor Othello,
Is come on shore, the Moor himself at sea,
And is in full commission° here for Cyprus.
   MON. I am glad on 't. 'Tis a worthy governor.   30
   3. GENT. But this same Cassio, though he speak of
     comfort
Touching the Turkish loss, yet he looks sadly
And prays the Moor be safe, for they were parted
With foul and violent tempest.
   MON.   Pray Heavens he be,
For I have served him, and the man commands   35
Like a full° soldier. Let's to the seaside, ho!
As well to see the vessel that's come in
As to throw out our eyes for brave Othello,
Even till we make the main and the aerial blue
An indistinct regard.°
   3. GENT.   Come, let's do so.   40
For every minute is expectancy
Of more arrivance.°

[*Enter* CASSIO.]

   CAS. Thanks, you the valiant of this warlike isle
That so approve the Moor! Oh, let the heavens
Give him defense against the elements,   45
For I have lost him on a dangerous sea.
   MON. Is he well shipped?°
   CAS. His bark is stoutly timbered, and his pilot
Of very expert and approved allowance.°
Therefore my hopes, not surfeited° to death,   50
Stand in bold cure.°   [*A cry within:*
                     "A sail, a sail, a sail!"]

[*Enter a* FOURTH GENTLEMAN.]

   CAS. What noise?
   4. GENT. The town is empty. On the brow o' the
     sea
Stand ranks of people, and they cry "A sail!"   54
   CAS. My hopes do shape° him for the governor.
                          [*Guns heard*]
   2. GENT. They do discharge their shot of courtesy.
Our friends, at least.
   CAS.   I pray you, sir, go forth,
And give us truth who 'tis that is arrived.
   2. GENT. I shall.   [*Exit.*]
   MON. But, good Lieutenant, is your General
     wived?   60
   CAS. Most fortunately. He hath achieved° a maid
That paragons° description and wild fame,
One that excels the quirks of blazoning pens
And in the essential vesture of creation

---

409. **engendered**: conceived.
     Act II, Sc. i: 2. **high-wrought flood**: heavy sea.   **3. main**:
sea.   7. **ruffianed**: played the ruffian.   9. **hold . . . mortise**:
remain fast joined.   10. **segregation**: separation.   14. **Bear**:
the Great Bear.   15. **guards . . . Pole**: stars in the "tail" of the
Little Bear constellation.   16. **molestation**: disturbance.
17. **enchafed**: angry.   18. **embayed**: anchored in some bay.
22. **designment halts**: plan is made lame.   23. **sufferance**:
damage.

29. **in . . . commission**: with full powers. See I.iii.281–82.
36. **full**: perfect.   39–40. **Even . . . regard**: until we can no longer
distinguish between sea and sky.   41–42. **For . . . arrivance**:
every minute more arrivals are expected.   47. **well shipped**: in a
good ship.   49. **approved allowance**: proved skill.   50. **surfeited**: sickened.   51. **Stand . . . cure**: have every hope of cure.
55. **shape**: imagine.   61. **achieved**: won.   62. **paragons**: surpasses.

Does tire the ingener.°

[*Re-enter* SECOND GENTLEMAN.] How now! Who has
    put in?   65

  2. GENT. 'Tis one Iago, Ancient to the General.

  CAS. He has had most favorable and happy speed.
Tempests themselves, high seas, and howling
    winds,
The guttered° rocks, and congregated sands,
Traitors ensteeped° to clog the guiltless keel,   70
As having sense of beauty, do omit
Their mortal natures,° letting go safely by
The divine Desdemona.

  MON.   What is she?

  CAS. She that I spake of, our great Captain's cap-
    tain,
Left in the conduct° of the bold Iago,   75
Whose footing° here anticipates our thoughts
A sennight's° speed. Great Jove, Othello guard,
And swell his sail with thine own powerful breath,
That he may bless this bay with his tall ship,
Make love's quick pants in Desdemona's arms,   80
Give renewed fire to our extincted° spirits,
And bring all Cyprus comfort.

  [*Enter* DESDEMONA, EMILIA, IAGO, RODERIGO,
        and ATTENDANTS.]
            Oh, behold,
The riches of the ship is come on shore!
Ye men of Cyprus, let her have your knees.
Hail to thee, lady! And the grace of Heaven,   85
Before, behind thee, and on every hand,
Enwheel° thee round!

  DES.   I thank you, valiant Cassio.
What tidings can you tell me of my lord?

  CAS. He is not yet arrived, nor know I aught
But that he's well and will be shortly here.   90

  DES. Oh, but I fear—— How lost you company?

  CAS. The great contention of the sea and skies
Parted our fellowship.° — But, hark! A sail.

    [*A cry within:* "A sail, a sail!" *Guns heard.*]

  2. GENT. They give their greeting to the citadel.
This likewise is a friend.

  CAS.   See for the news. [*Exit* GENTLEMAN.]
Good Ancient, you are welcome. [*To* EMILIA] Wel-
    come, mistress.
Let it not gall your patience, good Iago,
That I extend my manners.° 'Tis my breeding°
That gives me this bold show of courtesy.°   100
                    [*Kissing her.*]

  IAGO. Sir, would she give you so much of her lips
As of her tongue she oft bestows on me,
You'd have enough.

  DES.   Alas, she has no speech.

  IAGO. In faith, too much,
I find it still° when I have list° to sleep.   105
Marry, before your ladyship, I grant,
She puts her tongue a little in her heart
And chides with thinking.

  EMIL. You have little cause to say so.

  IAGO. Come on, come on. You are pictures° out of
    doors,   110
Bells° in your parlors, wildcats in your kitchens,
Saints in your injuries,° devils being offended,
Players in your housewifery, and housewives in your
    beds.

  DES. Oh, fie upon thee, slanderer!

  IAGO. Nay, it is true, or else I am a Turk.°   115
You rise to play, and go to bed to work.

  EMIL. You shall not write my praise.

  IAGO.   No, let me not.

  DES. What wouldst thou write of me if thou
    shouldst praise me?

  IAGO. O gentle lady, do not put me to 't,
For I am nothing if not critical.°   120

  DES. Come on, assay.° — There's one gone to the
    harbor?

  IAGO. Aye, madam.

  DES. I am not merry, but I do beguile
The thing I am by seeming otherwise.
Come, how wouldst thou praise me?   125

  IAGO. I am about it, but indeed my invention
Comes from my pate as birdlime does from
    frieze° —
It plucks out brains and all. But my Muse labors,
And thus she is delivered.
If she be fair and wise, fairness and wit,   130
The one's for use, the other useth it.

  DES. Well praised! How if she be black and witty?

  IAGO. If she be black, and thereto have a wit,
She'll find a white° that shall her blackness fit.

  DES. Worse and worse.   135

  EMIL. How if fair and foolish?

  IAGO. She never yet was foolish that was fair,
For even her folly helped her to an heir.

  DES. These are old fond paradoxes° to make fools
laugh i' the alehouse. What miserable praise hast
thou for her that's foul and foolish?   141

63–65. One . . . ingener: one that is too good for the fancy
phrases (*quirks*) of painting pens (i.e., poets) and in her absolute
perfection wearies the artist (i.e., the painter). (Cassio is full of
gallant phrases and behavior, in contrast to Iago's bluntness.) **ingener:** inventor. **69. guttered:** worn into channels. **70. en-
steeped:** submerged. **71–72. omit . . . natures:** forbear their
deadly nature. **75. conduct:** escort. **76. footing:** arrival.
77. sennight: week. **81. extincted:** extinguished. **87. En-
wheel:** encompass. **93. fellowship:** company. **99. extend my
manners:** i.e., salute your wife. **breeding:** bringing-up. **100. bold
. . . courtesy:** i.e., of saluting your wife with a kiss — a piece of
presumptuous behavior which indicates that Cassio regards himself as Iago's social superior. **105. still:** continuously. **list:** desire.
110. pictures: i.e., painted and dumb. **111. Bells:** i.e., ever
clacking. **112. Saints . . . injuries:** saints when you hurt anyone
else. **115. Turk:** heathen. **120. critical:** bitter. **121. assay:**
try. **126–27. my . . . frieze:** my literary effort (*invention*) is as
hard to pull out of my head as frieze (cloth with a nap) stuck to
birdlime. **134. white:** with a pun on *wight* (l. 159), man, person.
139. fond paradoxes: foolish remarks, contrary to general
opinion.

IAGO. There's none so foul, and foolish thereunto,
But does foul pranks which fair and wise ones do.

DES. Oh, heavy ignorance! Thou praisest the worst
best. But what praise couldst thou bestow on a deserving woman indeed, one that in the authority of
her merit did justly put on the vouch of very malice
itself?°   148

IAGO. She that was ever fair and never proud,
Had tongue at will° and yet was never loud,
Never lacked gold and yet went never gay,
Fled from her wish and yet said " Now I may."
She that, being angered, her revenge being nigh,
Bade her wrong stay and her displeasure fly.
She that in wisdom never was so frail   155
To change the cod's head for the salmon's tail.°
She that could think and ne'er disclose her mind,
See suitors following and not look behind.
She was a wight, if ever such wight were ——

DES. To do what?   160

IAGO. To suckle fools and chronicle small beer.°

DES. Oh, most lame and impotent conclusion! Do
not learn of him, Emilia, though he be thy husband.
How say you, Cassio? Is he not a most profane and
liberal° counselor?   165

CAS. He speaks home,° madam. You may relish°
him more in the soldier than in the scholar.

IAGO. [*Aside*] He° takes her by the palm. Aye,
well said, whisper. With as little a web as this will I
ensnare as great a fly as Cassio. Aye, smile upon   170
her, do, I will gyve° thee in thine own courtship.
You say true, 'tis so indeed. If such tricks as these
strip you out of your Lieutenantry, it had been better
you had not kissed your three fingers° so oft, which
now again you are most apt to play the sir° in.   175
Very good, well kissed! An excellent courtesy! 'Tis
so indeed. Yet again your fingers to your lips? Would
they were clyster pipes° for your sake! [*Trumpet
within.*] The Moor! I know his trumpet.   180

CAS. 'Tis truly so.

DES. Let's meet him and receive him.

CAS. Lo where he comes!

[*Enter* OTHELLO *and* ATTENDANTS.]

OTH. O my fair warrior!°

DES.   My dear Othello!

OTH. It gives me wonder great as my content   185
To see you here before me. O my soul's joy!
If after every tempest come such calms,

May the winds blow till they have wakened death!
And let the laboring bark climb hills of seas
Olympus-high,° and duck again as low   190
As Hell's from Heaven! If it were now to die,
'Twere now to be most happy, for I fear
My soul hath her content so absolute
That not another comfort like to this
Succeeds in unknown fate.   194

DES.   The Heavens forbid
But that our loves and comforts should increase,
Even as our days do grow!

OTH.   Amen to that, sweet powers!
I cannot speak enough of this content.
It stops me here,° it is too much of joy.
And this, and this, the greatest discords be   200
That e'er our hearts shall make!

[*Kissing her*]

IAGO. [*Aside*]   Oh, you are well tuned now,
But I'll set down the pegs° that make this music,
As honest as I am.

OTH.   Come, let us to the castle.
News, friends. Our wars are done, the Turks are
drowned.
How does my old acquaintance of this isle?   205
Honey, you shall be well desired in Cyprus,
I have found great love amongst them. O my sweet,
I prattle out of fashion,° and I dote
In mine own comforts. I prithee, good Iago,
Go to the bay and disembark my coffers.°   210
Bring thou the master° to the citadel.
He is a good one, and his worthiness
Does challenge° much respect. Come, Desdemona,
Once more well met at Cyprus.   214

[*Exeunt all but* IAGO *and* RODERIGO.]

IAGO. Do thou meet me presently° at the harbor.
Come hither. If thou beest valiant — as they say base
men being in love have then a nobility in their natures more than is native to them — list me. The
Lieutenant tonight watches on the court of guard.°
First, I must tell thee this. Desdemona is directly in
love with him.   221

ROD. With him! Why, 'tis not possible.

IAGO. Lay thy finger thus,° and let thy soul be instructed. Mark me with what violence she first loved
the Moor, but for° bragging and telling her   225
fantastical lies. And will she love him still for prating? Let not thy discreet heart think it. Her eye must
be fed, and what delight shall she have to look on the
Devil?° When the blood is made dull with the act

146–48. one . . . itself: one so deserving that even malice would
declare her good.   150. tongue . . . will: a ready flow of words.
156. To . . . tail: to prefer the tail end of a good thing to the
head of a poor thing.   161. chronicle . . . beer: write a whole
history about trifles (*small beer:* thin drink).   165. liberal:
gross.   166. home: to the point. relish: appreciate.   168–79. He
. . . sake: As so often, Shakespeare without using elaborate stage
directions exactly indicates the action in the dialogue. Cf. *W Tale,*
I.ii.111–18.   171. gyve: fetter.   174. kissed . . . fingers: a
gesture of gallantry.   175. play . . . sir: act the fine gentleman.   179 clyster pipes: an enema syringe.   184. warrior:
because she 's a soldier's wife. See I.iii.249.

190. Olympus-high: high as Olympus, the highest mountain in
Greece.   199. here: i.e., in the heart.   202. set . . . pegs: i.e.,
make you sing in a different key. A stringed instrument was
tuned by the pegs.   208. prattle . . . fashion: talk idly.
210. coffers: trunks.   211. master: captain of the ship.   213. challenge: claim.   215. presently: immediately.   219. watches . . .
guard: is on duty with the guard. The court of guard meant
both the guard itself and the guardroom.   223. finger thus: i.e.,
on the lips.   225. but for: only for.   229. Devil: See I.i.91,n.

of sport, there should be, again to inflame it   230
and to give satiety a fresh appetite, loveliness in favor,° sympathy in years, manners, and beauties, all
which the Moor is defective in. Now, for want of
these required conveniences, her delicate tenderness
will find itself abused, begin to heave the   235
gorge,° disrelish and abhor the Moor. Very nature
will instruct her in it and compel her to some second
choice. Now, sir, this granted — as it is a most pregnant and unforced position° — who stands so emi-
nently in the degree of this fortune as Cassio   240
does? A knave very voluble, no further conscion-
able° than in putting on the mere form of civil and
humane seeming° for the better compassing of his
salt° and most hidden loose affection? Why, none,
why, none. A slipper° and subtle knave, a finder-
out of occasions, that has an eye can stamp   246
and counterfeit advantages,° though true advantage
never present itself. A devilish knave! Besides, the
knave is handsome, young, and hath all those requi-
sites in him that folly and green° minds look   250
after. A pestilent complete knave, and the woman
hath found him already.

ROD. I cannot believe that in her. She's full of
most blest condition.°   255

IAGO. Blest fig's-end!° The wine she drinks is
made of grapes. If she had been blest, she would
never have loved the Moor. Blest pudding! Didst
thou not see her paddle° with the palm of his hand?
Didst not mark that?   260

ROD. Yes, that I did, but that was but courtesy.

IAGO. Lechery, by this hand, an index° and obscure prologue to the history of lust and foul
thoughts. They met so near with their lips that
their breaths embraced together. Villainous   265
thoughts, Roderigo! When these mutualities° so
marshal the way, hard at hand comes the master and
main exercise, the incorporate° conclusion. Pish!
But, sir, be you ruled by me. I have brought you
from Venice. Watch you tonight. For the com-   270
mand, I'll lay 't upon you. Cassio knows you not.
I'll not be far from you. Do you find some occasion
to anger Cassio, either by speaking too loud, or taint-
ing° his discipline, or from what other course you
please which the time shall more favorably   275
minister.°

ROD. Well.

IAGO. Sir, he is rash and very sudden in choler,°
and haply° may strike at you. Provoke him, that he
may, for even out of that will I cause these of   280
Cyprus to mutiny, whose qualification° shall come
into no true taste again but by the displanting° of
Cassio. So shall you have a shorter journey to your
desires by the means I shall then have to pre-   285
fer° them, and the impediment most profitably removed without the which there were no expectation
of our prosperity.

ROD. I will do this, if I can bring it to any opportunity.   290

IAGO. I warrant thee. Meet me by and by at the
citadel. I must fetch his necessaries ashore. Farewell.

ROD. Adieu.   [*Exit.*]

IAGO. That Cassio loves her, I do well believe it.
That she loves him, 'tis apt and of great credit.°   296
The Moor, howbeit that I endure him not,
Is of a constant, loving, noble nature,
And I dare think he'll prove to Desdemona
A most dear husband. Now, I do love her too,   300
Not out of absolute lust, though peradventure
I stand accountant for as great a sin,
But partly led to diet° my revenge
For that I do suspect the lusty Moor   304
Hath leaped into my seat. The thought whereof
Doth like a poisonous mineral° gnaw my inwards.
And nothing can or shall content my soul
Till I am evened with him, wife for wife.
Or failing so, yet that I put the Moor
At least into a jealousy so strong   310
That judgment° cannot cure. Which thing to do,
If this poor trash of Venice, whom I trash°
For his quick hunting,° stand the putting-on,°
I'll have our Michael Cassio on the hip,
Abuse him to the Moor in the rank garb° —   315
For I fear Cassio with my nightcap too —
Make the Moor thank me, love me, and reward me
For making him egregiously° an ass
And practicing upon° his peace and quiet
Even to madness. 'Tis here, but yet confused.   320
Knavery's plain face is never seen till used.   [*Exit.*]

---

278. choler: anger.   279. haply: perhaps.   281. qualification:
appeasement.   282. displanting: removal.   286. prefer: promote.   296. apt ... credit: likely and very credible.   303. diet:
feed.   306. poisonous mineral: corrosive poison. See I.ii.74.
311. judgment: reason.   312. trash ... trash: rubbish ... discard.   312–13. trash ... hunting: F1 reads "trace" and Q1
"crush." If the emendation "trash" is correct, it means "hold
back from outrunning the pack." Cf. *Temp.*, I.ii.81,n.   313. putting-on: encouraging.   315. rank garb: gross manner; i.e., by
accusing him of being Desdemona's lover.   318. egregiously:
notably.   319. practicing upon: plotting against.

---

232. favor: face.   235–36. heave ... gorge: retch. gorge: throat.
238–39. pregnant ... position: very significant and probable argument.   241–42. no ... conscionable: who has no more conscience.   243. humane seeming: courteous appearance.   244. salt:
lecherous.   245. slipper: slippery.   246–47. stamp ... advantages: forge false opportunities.   250. green: inexperienced,
foolish.   255. condition: disposition.   256. Blest fig's-end:
blest nonsense, a phrase used as a substitute in contempt for a
phrase just used, as is also *blest pudding* (l.258).   259. paddle:
play.   262. index: table of contents.   266. mutualities: mutual
exchanges.   268. incorporate: bodily.   274. tainting: disparag-
ing.   276. minister: provide.

SCENE II. *A street.*

[*Enter a* HERALD *with a proclamation,* PEOPLE *following.*]

HER. It is Othello's pleasure, our noble and valiant General, that upon certain tidings now arrived, importing the mere perdition° of the Turkish fleet, every man put himself into triumph° — some to dance, some to make bonfires, each man to what 5 sport and revels his addiction° leads him. For, besides these beneficial news, it is the celebration of his nuptial. So much was his pleasure should be proclaimed. All offices° are open, and there is full liberty of feasting from this present hour of five till 10 the bell have told eleven. Heaven bless the isle of Cyprus and our noble General Othello! [*Exeunt.*]

SCENE III. *A hall in the castle.*

[*Enter* OTHELLO, DESDEMONA, CASSIO, *and* ATTENDANTS.]

OTH. Good Michael, look you to the guard tonight. Let's teach ourselves that honorable stop, Not to outsport discretion.°

CAS. Iago hath direction what to do, But notwithstanding with my personal eye 5 Will I look to 't.

OTH. 　　　　　Iago is most honest. Michael, good night. Tomorrow with your earliest° Let me have speech with you. Come, my dear love, The purchase made, the fruits are to ensue — That profit's yet to come 'tween me and you. 10 Good night.

[*Exeunt* OTHELLO, DESDEMONA, *and* ATTENDANTS.]

[*Enter* IAGO.]

CAS. Welcome, Iago. We must to the watch.

IAGO. Not this hour, Lieutenant, 'tis not yet ten o' the clock. Our General cast° us thus early for the love of his Desdemona, who let us not therefore blame. He hath not yet made wanton the night with her, and she is sport for Jove. 17

CAS. She's a most exquisite lady.

IAGO. And, I'll warrant her, full of game.

CAS. Indeed she's a most fresh and delicate creature. 21

IAGO. What an eye she has! Methinks it sounds a parley to provocation.°

CAS. An inviting eye, and yet methinks right modest.

IAGO. And when she speaks, is it not an alarum° to love? 27

CAS. She is indeed perfection.

IAGO. Well, happiness to their sheets! Come, Lieutenant, I have a stoup° of wine, and here without are a brace of Cyprus gallants that would fain° have a measure to the health of black Othello. 33

CAS. Not tonight, good Iago. I have very poor and unhappy brains for drinking. I could well wish courtesy would invent some other custom of entertainment.

IAGO. Oh, they are our friends. But one cup — I'll drink for you. 39

CAS. I have drunk but one cup tonight, and that was craftily qualified° too, and behold what innovation° it makes here. I am unfortunate in the infirmity, and dare not task° my weakness with any more. 44

IAGO. What, man! 'Tis a night of revels. The gallants desire it.

CAS. Where are they?

IAGO. Here at the door. I pray you call them in.

CAS. I'll do 't, but it dislikes° me. [*Exit.*]

IAGO. If I can fasten but one cup upon him, 50 With that which he hath drunk tonight already He'll be as full of quarrel and offense As my young mistress' dog. Now my sick fool Roderigo, Whom love hath turned almost the wrong side out, To Desdemona hath tonight caroused° 55 Potations pottle-deep,° and he's to watch. Three lads of Cyprus, noble swelling° spirits That hold their honors in a wary distance,° The very elements° of this warlike isle, Have I tonight flustered with flowing cups, 60 And they watch too. Now, 'mongst this flock of drunkards, Am I to put our Cassio in some action That may offend the isle. But here they come. If consequence do but approve my dream,° My boat sails freely, both with wind and stream. 65

[*Re-enter* CASSIO, *with him* MONTANO *and* GENTLEMEN, SERVANTS *following with wine.*]

CAS. 'Fore God, they have given me a rouse° already.

MON. Good faith, a little one — not past a pint, as I am a soldier.

IAGO. Some wine, ho! [*Sings.*] 70

26. alarum: call to arms. 31. stoup: large drinking vessel. See Pl. 20e. 32. fain: gladly. 41. craftily qualified: cunningly mixed. 42. innovation: revolution, disturbance. 43. task: burden. 49. dislikes: displeases. 55. caroused: drunk healths. 56. pottle-deep: "bottoms up"; a pottle held two quarts. 57. swelling: bursting with pride. 58. hold . . . distance: "have a chip on their shoulders." 59. very elements: typical specimens. 64. If . . . dream: if what follows proves my dream true. 66. rouse: a deep drink.

Sc. ii: 3. mere perdition: absolute destruction. 4. put . . . triumph: celebrate. 6. addiction: inclination. 9. offices: the kitchen and buttery — i.e., free food and drink for all.

Sc. iii: 3. outsport discretion: let the fun go too far. 7. with . . . earliest: very early. 14. cast: dismissed. 22–23. sounds . . . provocation: invites to a love talk.

He shows his drunken state

" And let me the cannikin° clink, clink,
    And let me the cannikin clink.
        A soldier's a man,
        A life's but a span.°
    Why, then let a soldier drink."   75
Some wine, boys!

CAS. 'Fore God, an excellent song.

IAGO. I learned it in England, where indeed they are most potent in potting.° Your Dane, your German, and your swag-bellied° Hollander — Drink, ho! — are nothing to your English.   81

CAS. Is your Englishman so expert in his drinking?

IAGO. Why, he drinks you with facility your Dane dead drunk, he sweats not° to overthrow your Almain,° he gives your Hollander a vomit° ere the next pottle can be filled.   87

CAS. To the health of our General!

MON. I am for it, Lieutenant, and I'll do you justice.   90

IAGO. O sweet England! [*Sings.*]
" King Stephen was a worthy peer,
    His breeches cost him but a crown.
He held them sixpence all too dear,°
    With that he called the tailor lown.°   95

"He was a wight of high renown,
    And thou art but of low degree.
'Tis pride that pulls the country down.
    Then take thine auld cloak about thee."
Some wine, ho!   100

CAS. Why, this is a more exquisite song than the other.

IAGO. Will you hear 't again?

CAS. No, for I hold him to be unworthy of his place that does those things. Well, God's above all, and there be souls must be saved and there be souls must not be saved.   107

IAGO. It's true, good Lieutenant.

CAS. For mine own part — no offense to the General, nor any man of quality° — I hope to be saved.

IAGO. And so do I too, Lieutenant.   112

CAS. Aye, but, by your leave, not before me. The Lieutenant is to be saved before the Ancient. Let's have no more of this, let's to our affairs. God   115 forgive us our sins! Gentlemen, let's look to our business. Do not think, gentlemen, I am drunk. This is my Ancient, this is my right hand and this is my left. I am not drunk now, I can stand well enough and speak well enough.   120

ALL. Excellent well.

CAS. Why, very well, then, you must not think then that I am drunk.   [*Exit.*]

MON. To the platform,° masters. Come, let's set the watch.°   125

IAGO. You see this fellow that is gone before.
He is a soldier fit to stand by Caesar
And give direction. And do but see his vice.
'Tis to his virtue a just equinox,°
The one as long as the other. 'Tis pity of him.   130
I fear the trust Othello puts him in
On some odd time° of his infirmity
Will shake this island.

MON.   But is he often thus?

IAGO. 'Tis evermore the prologue to his sleep.
He'll watch the horologe a double set,°   135
If drink rock not his cradle.

MON.   It were well
The General were put in mind of it.
Perhaps he sees it not, or his good nature
Prizes the virtue that appears in Cassio
And looks not on his evils. Is not this true?   140

                    [*Enter* RODERIGO.]

IAGO. [*Aside to him*] How now, Roderigo! I pray you, after the Lieutenant. Go.   [*Exit* RODERIGO.]

MON. And 'tis great pity that the noble Moor
Should hazard such a place as his own second
With one of an ingraft° infirmity.   145
It were an honest action to say
So to the Moor.

IAGO.   Not I, for this fair island.
I do love Cassio well, and would do much
To cure him of this evil — But, hark! What noise?

                    [*A cry within:* " Help! help! "]

            [*Re-enter* CASSIO, *driving in* RODERIGO.]

CAS. 'Zounds! You rogue! You rascal!

MON.   What's the matter, Lieutenant?   150

CAS. A knave teach me my duty!
But I'll beat the knave into a wicker bottle.°

ROD. Beat me!

CAS. Dost thou prate, rogue? [*Striking* RODERIGO.]

MON.   Nay, good Lieutenant, [*Staying him.*]
I pray you, sir, hold your hand.

CAS.   Let me go, sir,
Or I'll knock you o'er the mazzard.°

MON.   Come, come, you're drunk.   155

CAS. Drunk!   [*They fight.*]

---

71. cannikin: drinking pot. See Pl. 20e.   74. span: lit., the measure between the thumb and little finger of the outstretched hand; about 9 inches.   79. potent in potting: desperate drinkers. For the Danes' potency in potting see *Haml*, I.iv.8–38.   80. swag-bellied: with loose bellies. Germans and Dutchmen were almost as famous for drinking as the Danes.   85. sweats not: has no need to labor excessively.   86. Almain: German. 86. gives . . . vomit: drinks as much as will make a Dutchman throw up.   94. sixpence . . . dear: too dear by sixpence. 95. lown: lout.   111. quality: rank.

124. platform: the level place on the ramparts where the cannon were mounted.   124–25. set . . . watch: mount guard.   129. just equinox: exact equal.   132. some . . . time: some time or other. 135. watch . . . set: stay awake the clock twice round.   145. ingraft: engrafted, firmly fixed.   152. But . . . bottle: One of those bad-tempered threatening phrases which have no very exact meaning, like "I'll knock him into a cocked hat." wicker bottle: large bottle covered with wicker, demijohn.   154. mazzard: head, a slang word.

IAGO. [*Aside to* RODERIGO] Away, I say. Go out
   and cry a mutiny.°   [*Exit* RODERIGO.]
Nay, good Lieutenant! God's will, gentlemen!
Help, ho!—Lieutenant—sir—Montano—sir—
Help, masters!—Here's a goodly watch indeed!
                    [*A bell rings.*]
Who's that that rings the bell?—Diablo,° ho!   160
The town will rise. God's will, Lieutenant, hold—
You will be shamed forever.
     [*Re-enter* OTHELLO *and* ATTENDANTS.]
OTH.   What is the matter here?
MON. 'Zounds, I bleed still, I am hurt to the death.
                          [*Faints.*]
OTH. Hold, for your lives!   165
IAGO. Hold, ho! Lieutenant—sir—Montano—
   gentlemen—
Have you forgot all sense of place and duty?
Hold! The General speaks to you. Hold, hold, for
   shame!
OTH. Why, how now, ho! From whence ariseth
   this?
Are we turned Turks, and to ourselves do that   170
Which Heaven hath forbid the Ottomites?
For Christian shame, put by this barbarous brawl.
He that stirs next to carve for his own rage°
Holds his soul light, he dies upon his motion.°
Silence that dreadful bell. It frights the isle   175
From her propriety.° What is the matter, masters?
Honest Iago, that look'st dead with grieving,
Speak, who began this? On thy love, I charge
   thee.
IAGO. I do not know. Friends all but now, even
   now,
In quarter and in terms like bride and groom   180
Devesting° them for bed. And then, but now,
As if some planet had unwitted men,°
Swords out, and tilting° one at other's breast
In opposition bloody. I cannot speak
Any beginning to this peevish odds,°   185
And would in action glorious I had lost
Those legs that brought me to a part of it!
OTH. How comes it, Michael, you are thus for-
   got?°
CAS. I pray you, pardon me, I cannot speak.
OTH. Worthy Montano, you were wont be civil.°
The gravity and stillness° of your youth   191
The world hath noted, and your name is great
In mouths of wisest censure.° What's the matter
That you unlace° your reputation thus,

And spend your rich opinion° for the name   195
Of a night brawler? Give me answer to it.
   MON. Worthy Othello, I am hurt to danger.
Your officer, Iago, can inform you—
While I spare speech, which something now offends
   me—
Of all that I do know. Nor know I aught   200
By me that's said or done amiss this night,
Unless self-charity° be sometimes a vice,
And to defend ourselves it be a sin
When violence assails us.
OTH.   Now, by Heaven,
My blood begins my safer guides to rule,   205
And passion, having my best judgment collied,°
Assays to lead the way. If I once stir,
Or do but lift this arm, the best of you
Shall sink in my rebuke. Give me to know
How this foul rout° began, who set it on,   210
And he that is approved° in this offense,
Though he had twinned with me, both at a birth,
Shall lose me. What! In a town of war,
Yet wild, the people's hearts brimful of fear,
To manage° private and domestic quarrel,   215
In night, and on the court and guard of safety!
'Tis monstrous. Iago, who began 't?
   MON. If partially affined, or leagued in office,
Thou dost deliver° more or less than truth,
Thou art no soldier.
IAGO.   Touch me not so near.   220
I had rather have this tongue cut from my mouth
Than it should do offense to Michael Cassio.
Yet I persuade myself to speak the truth
Shall nothing wrong him. Thus it is, General.
Montano and myself being in speech,   225
There comes a fellow crying out for help,
And Cassio following him with determined sword
To execute upon him. Sir, this gentleman
Steps in to Cassio and entreats his pause.°
Myself the crying fellow did pursue,   230
Lest by his clamor—as it so fell out—
The town might fall in fright. He, swift of foot,
Outran my purpose, and I returned the rather
For that I heard the clink and fall of swords,
And Cassio high in oath, which till tonight   235
I ne'er might say before. When I came back—
For this was brief—I found them close together,
At blow and thrust, even as again they were
When you yourself did part them.
More of this matter cannot I report.   240
But men are men, the best sometimes forget.
Though Cassio did some little wrong to him,
As men in rage strike those that wish them best,

---

157. **cry . . . mutiny:** cry that a mutiny has broken out; i.e., raise
a riot.   160. **Diablo:** the Devil.   173. **carve . . . rage:** to satisfy
his hunger for rage.   174. **upon . . . motion:** at his first movement.   176. **propriety:** natural behavior.   181. **Devesting:** taking off their clothes.   182. **planet . . . men:** as if some evil star
had made men mad. See App. 1.   183. **tilting:** thrusting.
185. **peevish odds:** silly disagreement.   188. **are . . . forgot:**
have so forgotten yourself.   190. **civil:** well behaved.   191. **stillness:** staid behavior.   193. **censure:** judgment.   194. **unlace:**
undo.

195. **spend . . . opinion:** lose your good reputation.   202. **self-
charity:** love for oneself.   206. **collied:** darkened.   210. **rout:**
riot, uproar.   211. **approved:** proved guilty.   215. **manage:** be
concerned with.   218–19. **If . . . deliver:** if, because you are influenced by partiality or because he is your fellow officer, you report. **affined:** bound.   229. **entreats . . . pause:** begs him to stop.

Yet surely Cassio, I believe, received
From him that fled some strange indignity,   245
Which patience could not pass.

OTH.   I know, Iago,
Thy honesty and love doth mince this matter,
Making it light to Cassio. Cassio, I love thee,
But never more be officer of mine.
[*Re-enter* DESDEMONA, *attended.*] Look, if my gentle
       love be not raised up!   250
I'll make thee an example.

DES.   What's the matter?

OTH. All's well now, sweeting.° Come away to
       bed. [*To* MONTANO, *who is led off*]
Sir, for your hurts, myself will be your surgeon.
Lead him off.
Iago, look with care about the town,   255
And silence those whom this vile brawl distracted.
Come, Desdemona. 'Tis the soldiers' life
To have their balmy slumbers waked with strife.

              [*Exeunt all but* IAGO *and* CASSIO.]

IAGO. What, are you hurt, Lieutenant?

CAS. Aye, past all surgery.   260

IAGO. Marry, Heaven forbid!

CAS. Reputation, reputation, reputation! Oh, I
have lost my reputation! I have lost the immortal
part of myself, and what remains is bestial. My reputation, Iago, my reputation!   265

IAGO. As I am an honest man, I thought you had
received some bodily wound. There is more sense
in that than in reputation. Reputation is an idle and
most false imposition,° oft got without merit and
lost without deserving. You have lost no repu-   270
tation at all unless you repute yourself such a loser.
What, man! There are ways to recover the General
again. You are but now cast in his mood,° a punishment more in policy° than in malice — even so as
one would beat his offenseless dog to affright an imperious lion.° Sue to him again and he's yours.   277

CAS. I will rather sue to be despised than to deceive so good a commander with so slight, so
drunken, and so indiscreet an officer. Drunk? And
speak parrot?° And squabble? Swagger? Swear?
And discourse fustian° with one's own shadow? O
thou invisible spirit of wine, if thou hast no name to
be known by, let us call thee devil!   284

IAGO. What was he that you followed with your
sword? What had he done to you?

CAS. I know not.   TO PROTECT HIMSELF

IAGO. Is 't possible?   288

CAS. I remember a mass of things, but nothing
distinctly — a quarrel, but nothing wherefore. Oh

God, that men should put an enemy in their mouths
to steal away their brains! That we should, with joy,
pleasance,° revel, and applause, transform ourselves
into beasts!   294

IAGO. Why, but you are now well enough. How
came you thus recovered?

CAS. It hath pleased the devil drunkenness to give
place to the devil wrath. One unperfectness shows
me another, to make me frankly despise myself.   300

IAGO. Come, you are too severe a moraler.° As the
time, the place, and the condition of this country
stands, I could heartily wish this had not befall-
en. But since it is as it is, mend it for your own
good.   305

CAS. I will ask him for my place again, he shall
tell me I am a drunkard! Had I as many mouths as
Hydra,° such an answer would stop them all. To be
now a sensible man, by and by a fool, and presently a beast! Oh, strange! Every inordinate° cup is
unblest, and the ingredient is a devil.   312

IAGO. Come, come, good wine is a good familiar
creature, if it be well used. Exclaim no more against
it. And, good Lieutenant, I think you think I love
you.

CAS. I have well approved it, sir. I drunk!   317

IAGO. You or any man living may be drunk at
some time, man. I'll tell you what you shall do. Our
General's wife is now the General. I may say so in
this respect, for that he hath devoted and given up
himself to the contemplation, mark, and denote-
ment° of her parts and graces. Confess yourself
freely to her, importune her help to put you in your
place again. She is of so free, so kind, so apt,° so
blessed a disposition, she holds it a vice in her   325
goodness not to do more than she is requested. This
broken joint between you and her husband entreat
her to splinter° and, my fortunes against any lay°
worth naming, this crack of your love shall grow
stronger than it was before.   331

CAS. You advise me well.

IAGO. I protest, in the sincerity of love and honest
kindness.

CAS. I think it freely, and betimes in the morning
I will beseech the virtuous Desdemona to undertake
for me. I am desperate of my fortunes if they check
me here.°

IAGO. You are in the right. Good night, Lieutenant, I must to the watch.   340

CAS. Good night, honest Iago.   [*Exit.*]

IAGO. And what's he then that says I play the vil-
       lain?

---

252. **sweeting**: sweetheart.   269. **imposition**: a quality laid on
a man by others.   273. **cast . . . mood**: dismissed because he is in
a bad mood.   275. **in policy**: i.e., because he must appear to be
angry before the Cypriots.   275–77. **even . . . lion**: a proverb
meaning that when the lion sees the dog beaten, he will know
what is coming to him.   281. **speak parrot**: babble.   282. **fustian**:
nonsense; lit., cheap cloth.

293. **pleasance**: a gay time.   301. **moraler**: moralizer.   307. **Hydra**: a hundred-headed beast slain by Hercules.   311. **inordinate**:
excessive.   322. **denotement**: careful observation.   324. **apt**:
ready.   329. **splinter**: put in splints.   329. **lay**: bet.   337–38. I
. . . **here**: I despair of my future if my career is stopped short
here.

When this advice is free I give and honest,
Probal° to thinking, and indeed the course
To win the Moor again? For 'tis most easy   345
The inclining Desdemona to subdue
In any honest suit. She's framed° as fruitful
As the free elements.° And then for her
To win the Moor, were 't to renounce his baptism,
All seals and symbols of redeemèd sin,   350
His soul is so enfettered to her love
That she may make, unmake, do what she list,
Even as her appetite shall play the god
With his weak function.° How am I then a villain
To counsel Cassio to this parallel course,   355
Directly to his good? Divinity of Hell!
When devils will the blackest sins put on,
They do suggest° at first with heavenly shows,
As I do now. For whiles this honest fool
Plies° Desdemona to repair his fortunes,   360
And she for him pleads strongly to the Moor,
I'll pour this pestilence into his ear,
That she repeals° him for her body's lust.
And by how much she strives to do him good,
She shall undo her credit with the Moor.   365
So will I turn her virtue into pitch,
And out of her own goodness make the net
That shall enmesh them all.

[*Enter* RODERIGO.] How now, Roderigo!
  ROD. I do follow here in the chase, not like a hound
that hunts but one that fills up the cry.° My   370
money is almost spent, I have been tonight exceed-
ingly well cudgeled, and I think the issue will be I
shall have so much experience for my pains and so,
with no money at all and a little more wit, return
again to Venice.   375
  IAGO. How poor are they that have not patience!
What wound did ever heal but by degrees?
Thou know'st we work by wit and not by witch-
  craft,
And wit depends on dilatory Time.°
Does 't not go well? Cassio hath beaten thee,   380
And thou by that small hurt hast cashiered Cassio.
Though other things grow fair against the sun,
Yet fruits that blossom first will first be ripe.°
Content thyself awhile. By the mass, 'tis morning.
Pleasure and action make the hours seem short.   385
Retire thee, go where thou art billeted.
Away, I say. Thou shalt know more hereafter.
Nay, get thee gone. [*Exit* RODERIGO.] Two things are
  to be done:

My wife must move for° Cassio to her mistress,
I'll set her on,   390
Myself the while to draw the Moor apart
And bring him jump° when he may Cassio find
Soliciting his wife. Aye, that's the way.
Dull not device° by coldness and delay.   [*Exit.*]

Act III

SCENE I. *Before the castle.*

[*Enter* CASSIO *and some* MUSICIANS.]
  CAS. Masters, play here, I will content your
    pains°—
Something that's brief, and bid "Good morrow,
    General."°   [*Music.*]
              [*Enter* CLOWN.]
  CLO. Why, masters, have your instruments been
in Naples,° that they speak i' the nose thus?
  1. MUS. How, sir, how?   5
  CLO. Are these, I pray you, wind instruments?
  1. MUS. Aye, marry are they, sir.
  CLO. Oh, thereby hangs a tail.
  1. MUS. Whereby hangs a tale, sir?   9
  CLO. Marry, sir, by many a wind instrument that
I know. But, masters, here's money for you. And the
General so likes your music that he desires you, for
love's sake, to make no more noise with it.
  1. MUS. Well, sir, we will not.   15
  CLO. If you have any music that may not be heard,
to 't again. But, as they say, to hear music the General does not greatly care.
  1. MUS. We have none such, sir.
  CLO. Then put up your pipes in your bag, for I'll
away. Go, vanish into air, away!   21
              [*Exeunt* MUSICIANS.]
  CAS. Dost thou hear, my honest friend?
  CLO. No, I hear not your honest friend, I hear you.
  CAS. Prithee keep up thy quillets.° There's a poor
piece of gold for thee. If the gentlewoman that attends the General's wife be stirring, tell her there's
one Cassio entreats her a little favor of speech. Wilt
thou do this?   28
  CLO. She is stirring, sir. If she will stir hither, I
shall seem to notify unto her.
  CAS. Do, good my friend.   [*Exit* CLOWN.]

---

344. **Probal:** probable.   347. **framed:** made.   348. **free ele-**
ments: i.e., the air.   354. **function:** intelligence.   358. **suggest:**
seduce.   360. **Plies:** vigorously urges.   363. **repeals:** calls
back.   370. **one . . . cry:** See *MND*, IV.i.127–28,n.   379. **And
. . . Time:** and cleverness must wait for Time, who is in no hurry.
382–83. **Though . . . ripe:** though the fruit ripens in the sun, yet
the first fruit to ripen will come from the earliest blossoms;
i.e., our first plan — to get Cassio cashiered — has succeeded,
the rest will soon follow.

389. **move for:** petition for.   392. **jump:** at the moment, just.
394. **Dull . . . device:** do not spoil the plan.
  Act III, Sc. i: 1. content . . . pains: reward your labor.   **2. bid
. . . General:** It was a common custom to play or sing a song beneath the bedroom window of a distinguished guest or of a newly
wedded couple on the morning after their wedding night.   **4. in
Naples:** a reference to the Neapolitan (i.e., venereal) disease.
24. keep . . . quillets: put away your wisecracks.

[*Enter* IAGO.] In happy time,° Iago.
  IAGO. You have not been abed, then?
  CAS. Why, no, the day had broke
Before we parted. I have made bold, Iago,   35
To send in to your wife. My suit to her
Is that she will to virtuous Desdemona
Procure me some access.
  IAGO.   I'll send her to you presently,
And I'll devise a mean to draw the Moor
Out of the way, that your convérse and business 40
May be more free.
  CAS. I humbly thank you for 't. [*Exit* IAGO.] I
    never knew
A Florentine more kind° and honest.
            [*Enter* EMILIA.]
  EMIL. Good morrow, good Lieutenant. I am sorry
For your displeasure,° but all will sure be well. 45
The General and his wife are talking of it,
And she speaks for you stoutly. The Moor replies
That he you hurt is of great fame in Cyprus
And great affinity,° and that in wholesome wisdom
He might not but° refuse you. But he protests he
    loves you,   50
And needs no other suitor but his likings°
To take the safest occasion by the front
To bring you in° again.
  CAS.   Yet I beseech you,
If you think fit, or that it may be done,
Give me advantage of some brief discourse 55
With Desdemona alone.
  EMIL.   Pray you, come in.
I will bestow you where you shall have time
To speak your bosom freely.°
  CAS.   I am much bound to you. [*Exeunt.*]

(margin notes: IRONY— CASSIO SHOULD HAVE WAITED ON GOING TO DES. WILL RESULT IN TROUBLE)

        SCENE II. *A room in the castle.*

[*Enter* OTHELLO, IAGO, *and* GENTLEMEN.]
  OTH. These letters give, Iago, to the pilot,
And by him do my duties° to the Senate.
That done, I will be walking on the works.°
Repair there to me.
  IAGO.   Well, my good lord, I'll do 't.
  OTH. This fortification, gentlemen, shall we
    see 't?   5
  GENT. We'll wait upon your lordship. [*Exeunt.*]

(margin notes: IAGO IS CLOSER TO OTH. NOW + CAN WORK ON HIM — They will meet later p. 30 C.N.)

SCENE III. *The garden of the castle.*

    [*Enter* DESDEMONA, CASSIO, *and* EMILIA.]
  DES. Be thou assured, good Cassio, I will do
All my abilities in thy behalf.
  EMIL. Good madam, do. I warrant it grieves my
    husband
As if the case were his.
  DES. Oh, that's an honest fellow. Do not doubt,
    Cassio,   5
But I will have my lord and you again
As friendly as you were.
  CAS.   Bounteous madam,
Whatever shall become of Michael Cassio,
He's never anything but your true servant. 9
  DES. I know 't. I thank you. You do love my lord.
You have known him long, and be you well as-
    sured
He shall in strangeness stand no farther off
Than in a politic distance.°
  CAS.   Aye, but, lady,
That policy may either last so long,
Or feed upon such nice and waterish diet,° 15
Or breed itself so out of circumstance,°
That, I being absent and my place supplied,°
My General will forget my love and service.
  DES. Do not doubt° that. Before Emilia here
I give thee warrant of thy place.° Assure thee, 20
If I do vow a friendship, I'll perform it
To the last article. My lord shall never rest.
I'll watch him tame° and talk him out of patience,
His bed shall seem a school, his board a shrift.°
I'll intermingle every thing he does 25
With Cassio's suit. Therefore be merry, Cassio,
For thy solicitor shall rather die
Than give thy cause away.
    [*Enter* OTHELLO *and* IAGO, *at a distance.*]
  EMIL. Madam, here comes my lord.
  CAS. Madam, I'll take my leave.   30
  DES. Nay, stay and hear me speak.
  CAS. Madam, not now. I am very ill at ease,
Unfit for mine own purposes.°
  DES. Well, do your discretion.   [*Exit* CASSIO.]
  IAGO. Ha! I like not that.
  OTH. What dost thou say?   35
  IAGO. Nothing, my lord. Or if — I know not
    what.
  OTH. Was not that Cassio parted from my wife?

(margin notes: TURNING PT. 1st proof of guilt)

32. In . . . time: i.e., I am glad to see you.   43. Florentine . . . kind: Iago is a Venetian. Cassio means: even one of my own people could not have been kinder.   45. your displeasure: i.e., that Othello is displeased with you.   49. affinity: kindred. 50. might . . . but: i.e., he must.   51. likings: affections. 52–53. safest . . . in: to take the first opportunity to restore you to your position. front: forehead; i.e., to take Time by the forelock.   58. speak . . . freely: declare what is on your mind.   Sc. ii: 2. do . . . duties: express my loyalty.   3. works: fortifications.

Sc. iii: 12–13. He . . . distance: i.e., his apparent coldness to you shall only be so much as his official position demands for reasons of policy.   15. nice . . . diet: have such weak encouragement.   16. breed . . . circumstance: become so used to the situation.   17. supplied: filled by another.   19. doubt: fear. 20. give . . . place: guarantee that you will be restored to your position.   23. watch . . . tame: as wild hawks are made tame by keeping them from sleep. See App. 26.   24. shrift: place of confession and absolution.   33. Unfit . . . purposes: in no condition to plead my own cause.

IAGO. Cassio, my lord! No, sure, I cannot think it,
That he would steal away so guilty-like,
Seeing you coming.

OTH.   I do believe 'twas he.   40

DES. How now, my lord!
I have been talking with a suitor here,
A man that languishes in your displeasure.

OTH. Who is 't you mean?

DES. Why, your Lieutenant, Cassio. Good my
lord,   45
If I have any grace or power to move you,
His present reconciliation take.°
For if he be not one that truly loves you,
That errs in ignorance and not in cunning,°
I have no judgment in an honest face.   50
I prithee call him back.

OTH.   Went he hence now?

DES. Aye, sooth, so humbled
That he hath left part of his grief with me,
To suffer with him. Good love, call him back.

OTH. Not now, sweet Desdemona, some other
time.   55

DES. But shall 't be shortly?

OTH.   The sooner, sweet, for you.

DES. Shall 't be tonight at supper?

OTH.   No, not tonight.

DES. Tomorrow dinner then?

OTH.   I shall not dine at home.
I meet the captains at the citadel.

DES. Why, then tomorrow night or Tuesday
morn,   60
On Tuesday noon, or night, on Wednesday morn.
I prithee name the time, but let it not
Exceed three days. In faith, he's penitent,
And yet his trespass, in our common reason° —   64
Save that, they say, the wars must make examples
Out of their best — is not almost° a fault
To incur a private check.° When shall he come?
Tell me, Othello. I wonder in my soul
What you would ask me that I should deny,   69
Or stand so mammering° on. What! Michael Cassio,
That came a-wooing with you, and so many a
time
When I have spoke of you dispraisingly
Hath ta'en your part — to have so much to do
To bring him in! Trust me, I could do much ——

OTH. Prithee, no more. Let him come when he
will.   75
I will deny thee nothing.

DES.   Why, this is not a boon.°
'Tis as I should entreat you wear your gloves,
Or feed on nourishing dishes, or keep you warm,
Or sue to you to do a peculiar° profit

To your own person. Nay, when I have a suit   80
Wherein I mean to touch your love indeed,
It shall be full of poise° and difficult weight,°
And fearful to be granted.°

OTH.   I will deny thee nothing.
Whereon I do beseech thee grant me this,
To leave me but a little to myself.   85

DES. Shall I deny you? No. Farewell, my lord.

OTH. Farewell, my Desdemona. I'll come to thee
straight.

DES. Emilia, come. Be as your fancies teach you.°
Whate'er you be, I am obedient.

         [*Exeunt* DESDEMONA *and* EMILIA.]

OTH. Excellent wretch! Perdition catch my soul
But I do love thee! And when I love thee not,   91
Chaos° is come again.

IAGO. My noble lord ——

OTH.   What dost thou say, Iago?

IAGO. Did Michael Cassio,° when you wooed my
lady,
Know of your love?   95

OTH. He did, from first to last. Why dost thou
ask?

IAGO. But for a satisfaction of my thought,
No further harm.

OTH.   Why of thy thought, Iago?

IAGO. I did not think he had been acquainted with
her.

OTH. Oh yes, and went between us very oft.   100

IAGO. Indeed!

OTH. Indeed! Aye, indeed. Discern'st thou aught
in that?
Is he not honest?

IAGO. Honest, my lord!

OTH. Honest! Aye, honest.

IAGO. My lord, for aught I know.

OTH. What dost thou think?

IAGO. Think, my lord!   105

OTH. Think, my lord! By Heaven, he echoes me
As if there were some monster in his thought
Too hideous to be shown. Thou dost mean some-
thing.
I heard thee say even now thou likedst not that
When Cassio left my wife. What didst not like?
And when I told thee he was of my counsel   111
In my whole course of wooing, thou criedst "In-
deed!"
And didst contract and purse thy brow together
As if thou then hadst shut up in thy brain
Some horrible conceit.° If thou dost love me,   115
Show me thy thought.

---

47. His . . . take: accept his immediate apology and forgive him.
49. in cunning: knowingly.   64. common reason: common sense.
66. not almost: hardly.   67. check: rebuke.   70. mammering:
hesitating.   76. boon: great favor.   79. peculiar: particular.

82. poise: weight in the scales. difficult weight: hard to estimate.   83. fearful . . . granted: only granted with a sense of
fear.   88. Be . . . you: please yourself.   92. Chaos: the utter
confusion that existed before order was established in the universe. The idea of order and chaos is worked out elaborately in
Tr & Cr, I.iii.83–124.   94. Did . . . Cassio: See App. 22.
115. conceit: conception, notion.

IAGO. My lord, you know I love you.

OTH.   I think thou dost,
And for° I know thou'rt full of love and honesty
And weigh'st thy words before thou givest them
          breath,
Therefore these stops of thine fright me the more.
For such things in a false disloyal knave   121
Are tricks of custom, but in a man that's just
They're close delations,° working from the heart,
That passion cannot rule.

IAGO.   For Michael Cassio,
I dare be sworn I think that he is honest.   125

OTH. I think so too.

IAGO.   Men should be what they seem,
Or those that be not, would they might seem none!°

OTH. Certain, men should be what they seem.

IAGO. Why, then I think Cassio's an honest man.

OTH. Nay, yet there's more in this.   130
I prithee speak to me as to thy thinkings,
As thou dost ruminate, and give thy worst of
          thoughts
The worst of words.

IAGO.   Good my lord, pardon me.
Though I am bound to every act of duty,
I am not bound to that all slaves are free to.   135
Utter my thoughts? Why, say they are vile and false,
As where's that palace whereinto foul things
Sometimes intrude not? Who has a breast so pure
But some uncleanly apprehensions
Keep leets and law days, and in session sit   140
With meditations lawful?°

OTH. Thou dost conspire against thy friend, Iago,
If thou but think'st him wronged and makest his
          ear
A stranger to thy thoughts.

IAGO.   I do beseech you —
Though I perchance am vicious in my guess,   145
As, I confess, it is my nature's plague
To spy into abuses, and oft my jealousy°
Shapes faults that are not — that your wisdom yet,
From one that so imperfectly conceits,°
Would take no notice, nor build yourself a trouble
Out of his scattering° and unsure observance.°   151
It were not for your quiet nor your good,
Nor for my manhood, honesty, or wisdom,
To let you know my thoughts.

OTH.   What dost thou mean?

IAGO. Good name in man and woman, dear my
          lord,   155

Is the immediate° jewel of their souls.
Who steals my purse steals trash — 'tis something,
          nothing,
'Twas mine, 'tis his, and has been slave to thou-
          sands —
But he that filches from me my good name
Robs me of that which not enriches him   160
And makes me poor indeed.

OTH. By Heaven, I'll know thy thoughts.

IAGO. You cannot if my heart were in your hand,
Nor shall not whilst 'tis in my custody.

OTH. Ha!

IAGO.   Oh, beware, my lord, of jealousy.   165
It is the green-eyed monster which doth mock°
The meat° it feeds on. That cuckold lives in bliss
Who, certain of his fate, loves not his wronger.°
But, oh, what damnèd minutes tells he o'er   169
Who dotes, yet doubts, suspects, yet strongly loves!

OTH. Oh, misery!

IAGO. Poor and content is rich, and rich enough,
But riches fineless° is as poor as winter
To him that ever fears he shall be poor.
Good Heaven, the souls of all my tribe defend   175
From jealousy!

OTH.   Why, why is this?
Think'st thou I'd make a life of jealousy,
To follow still the changes of the moon
With fresh suspicions? No, to be once in doubt
Is once to be resolved.° Exchange me for a goat   180
When I shall turn the business of my soul
To such exsufflicate and blown surmises,
Matching thy inference.° 'Tis not to make me jeal-
          ous
To say my wife is fair, feeds well, loves company,
Is free of speech, sings, plays, and dances well.   185
Where virtue is, these are more virtuous.
Nor from mine own weak merits will I draw
The smallest fear or doubt of her revolt,°
For she had eyes, and chose me. No, Iago,
I'll see before I doubt, when I doubt, prove,   190
And on the proof, there is no more but this —
Away at once with love or jealousy!

IAGO. I am glad of it, for now I shall have reason
To show the love and duty that I bear you
With franker spirit. Therefore, as I am bound,   195
Receive it from me. I speak not yet of proof.
Look to your wife. Observe her well with Cassio.
Wear your eye thus, not jealous nor secure.°

---

118. **for:** since.   123. **close delations:** concealed accusations.
127. **seem none:** i.e., not seem to be honest men.   138–41. **Who
. . . lawful:** whose heart is so pure but that some foul suggestion
will sit on the bench alongside lawful thoughts; i.e., foul thoughts
will rise even on the most respectable occasions. **leet:** court
held by the lord of the manor. **law days:** days when courts sit.
session: sitting of the court.   147. **jealousy:** suspicion.   149. **conceits:** conceives, imagines.   151. **scattering:** scattered, casual.
observance: observation.

156. **immediate:** most valuable.   166. **doth mock:** makes a
mockery of.   167. **meat:** i.e., victim.   167–68. **That . . .
wronger:** i.e., the cuckold who hates his wife and knows her falseness is not tormented by suspicious jealousy. See App. 11.
173. **fineless:** limitless.   179–80. **to . . . resolved:** whenever I
find myself in doubt I at once seek out the truth.   181–83. **When
. . . inference:** when I shall allow that which concerns me most
dearly to be influenced by such trifling suggestions as yours.
exsufflicate: blown up, like a bubble.   188. **revolt:** faithlessness.
198. **secure:** overconfident.

I would not have your free and noble nature
Out of self-bounty° be abused, look to 't.   200
I know our country disposition well.
In Venice° they do let Heaven see the pranks
They dare not show their husbands. Their best con-
    science
Is not to leave 't undone, but keep 't unknown.
OTH. Dost thou say so?   205
IAGO. She did deceive her father,° marrying you,
And when she seemed to shake and fear your looks,
She loved them most.
OTH.   And so she did.
IAGO.   Why, go to, then.
She that so young could give out such a seeming
To seel° her father's eyes up close as oak ——   210
He thought 'twas witchcraft — but I am much to
    blame.
I humbly do beseech you of your pardon
For too much loving you.
OTH.   I am bound to thee forever.
IAGO. I see this hath a little dashed your spirits.
OTH. Not a jot, not a jot.
IAGO.   I' faith, I fear it has.   215
I hope you will consider what is spoke
Comes from my love, but I do see you're moved.
I am to pray you not to strain my speech
To grosser issues° nor to larger reach°
Than to suspicion.   220
OTH. I will not.
IAGO.   Should you do so, my lord,
My speech should fall into such vile success°
As my thoughts aim not at. Cassio's my worthy
    friend. —
My lord, I see you're moved.
OTH.   No, not much moved.
I do not think but Desdemona's honest.°   225
IAGO. Long live she so! And long live you to think
    so!
OTH. And yet, how nature erring from itself ——
IAGO. Aye, there's the point. As — to be bold with
    you —
Not to affect° many proposed matches°
Of her own clime, complexion, and degree,   230
Whereto we see in all things nature tends° ——
Foh! One may smell in such a will most rank,°
Foul disproportion, thoughts unnatural.

But pardon me. I do not in position
Distinctly speak of her, though I may fear   235
Her will, recoiling to her better judgment,
May fall to match° you with her country forms,°
And happily° repent.
OTH.   Farewell, farewell.
If more thou dost perceive, let me know more.
Set on thy wife to observe. Leave me, Iago.   240
IAGO. [*Going*] My lord, I take my leave.
OTH. Why did I marry? This honest creature
    doubtless
Sees and knows more, much more, than he unfolds.
IAGO. [*Returning*] My lord, I would I might en-
    treat your honor
To scan this thing no further. Leave it to time.   245
Though it be fit that Cassio have his place,
For sure he fills it up with great ability,
Yet if you please to hold him off awhile,
You shall by that perceive him and his means.
Note if your lady strain his entertainment°   250
With any strong or vehement importunity —
Much will be seen in that. In the meantime,
Let me be thought too busy in my fears —
As worthy cause I have to fear I am —
And hold her free, I do beseech your Honor.   255
OTH. Fear not my government.°
IAGO. I once more take my leave.   [*Exit.*]
OTH. This fellow's of exceeding honesty,
And knows all qualities,° with a learned spirit,   259
Of human dealings.° If I do prove her haggard,
Though that her jesses were my dear heartstrings,
I'd whistle her off and let her down the wind
To prey at fortune.° Haply, for I am black
And have not those soft parts of conversation
That chamberers° have, or for I am declined   265
Into the vale of years — yet that's not much —
She's gone, I am abused, and my relief
Must be to loathe her. Oh, curse of marriage,
That we can call these delicate creatures ours,
And not their appetites! I had rather be a toad   270
And live upon the vapor of a dungeon
Than keep a corner in the thing I love
For others' uses. Yet, 'tis the plague of great ones,
Prerogatived° are they less than the base.
'Tis destiny unshunnable, like death.   275
Even then this forkèd plague° is fated to us
When we do quicken.° Desdemona comes.

---

200. **self-bounty:** natural goodness.   202. **In Venice:** Venice was notorious for its loose women; the Venetian courtesans were among the sights of Europe and were much commented upon by travelers.   206. **She . . . father:** Iago deliberately echoes Brabantio's parting words. See I.iii.293–94.   210. **seel:** blind. See I.iii.270,n.   219. **grosser issues:** worse conclusions. **larger reach:** i.e., more widely.   222. **success:** result.   225. **honest:** When applied to Desdemona, "honest" means "chaste," but applied to Iago it has the modern meaning of "open and sincere."   229. **affect:** be inclined to. **proposed matches:** offers of marriage.   231. **in . . . tends:** i.e., a woman naturally marries a man of her own country, color, and rank.   232. **will . . . rank:** desire most lustful.

237. **match:** compare. **country forms:** the appearance of her countrymen; i.e., white men.   238. **happily:** haply, by chance.   250. **strain . . . entertainment:** urge you to receive him.   256. **government:** self-control.   259. **qualities:** different kinds.   259–60. **with . . . dealings:** with wide experience of human nature.   260–63. **If . . . fortune:** Othello keeps up the imagery of falconry throughout. He means: If I find that she is wild, I'll whistle her off the game and let her go where she will, for she's not worth keeping. See App. 26. **haggard:** a wild hawk. **jesses:** the straps attached to a hawk's legs.   265. **chamberers:** playboys.   274. **Prerogatived:** privileged.   276. **forked plague:** i.e., to be a cuckold.   277. **quicken:** stir in our mother's womb.

[*Re-enter* DESDEMONA *and* EMILIA.] If she be false, oh,
 then Heaven mocks itself!
I'll not believe 't.
 DES.   How now, my dear Othello!
Your dinner, and the generous° islanders 280
By you invited, do attend your presence.
 OTH. I am to blame.
 DES.   Why do you speak so faintly?
Are you not well?
 OTH. I have a pain upon my forehead here.
 DES. Faith, that's with watching,° 'twill away
 again. 285
Let me but bind it hard, within this hour
It will be well.
 OTH.   Your napkin° is too little,
   [*He puts the handkerchief from him,*
         and she drops it.]
Let it alone. Come, I'll go in with you.
 DES. I am very sorry that you are not well.
   [*Exeunt* OTHELLO *and* DESDEMONA.]
 EMIL. I am glad I have found this napkin. 290
This was her first remembrance from the Moor.
My wayward° husband hath a hundred times
Wooed me to steal it, but she so loves the token,
For he conjured° her she should ever keep it,
That she reserves it evermore about her 295
To kiss and talk to. I'll have the work ta'en out,°
And give 't Iago. What he will do with it
Heaven knows, not I.
I nothing but to please his fantasy.°
   [*Re-enter* IAGO.]
 IAGO. How now! What do you here alone? 300
 EMIL. Do not you chide, I have a thing for you.
 IAGO. A thing for me? It is a common thing——
 EMIL. Ha!
 IAGO. To have a foolish wife. 304
 EMIL. Oh, is that all? What will you give me now
For that same handkerchief?
 IAGO.   What handkerchief?
 EMIL. What handkerchief!
Why, that the Moor first gave to Desdemona,
That which so often you did bid me steal.
 IAGO. Hast stol'n it from her? 310
 EMIL. No, faith, she let it drop by negligence,
And, to the advantage,° I being here took 't up.
Look, here it is.
 IAGO. A good wench. Give it me.
 EMIL. What will you do with 't, that you have
  been so earnest
To have me filch it? 314
 IAGO. [*Snatching it*] Why, what's that to you?
 EMIL. If 't be not for some purpose of import,

Give 't me again. Poor lady, she'll run mad
When she shall lack it.
 IAGO. Be not acknown on 't,° I have use for it.
Go, leave me.   [*Exit* EMILIA.]
I will in Cassio's lodging lose this napkin, 321
And let him find it. Trifles light as air
Are to the jealous confirmations strong
As proofs of Holy Writ. This may do something.
The Moor already changes with my poison. 325
Dangerous conceits are in their natures poisons,
Which at the first are scarce found to distaste,°
But with a little° act upon the blood
Burn like the mines of sulphur. I did say so.°
Look where he comes!
[*Re-enter* OTHELLO.] Not poppy,° nor mandragora,°
Nor all the drowsy syrups of the world, 331
Shall ever medicine thee to that sweet sleep
Which thou owedst° yesterday.
 OTH.   Ha! Ha! False to me?
 IAGO. Why, how now, General! No more of that.
 OTH. Avaunt!° Be gone! Thou hast set me on the
 rack.° 335
I swear 'tis better to be much abused
Than but to know 't a little.
 IAGO.   How now, my lord!
 OTH. What sense had I of her stol'n hours of lust?
I saw 't not, thought it not, it harmed not me.
I slept the next night well, was free and merry. 340
I found not Cassio's kisses on her lips.
He that is robbed, not wanting° what is stol'n,
Let him not know 't and he's not robbed at all.
 IAGO. I am sorry to hear this.
 OTH. I had been happy if the general camp, 345
Pioners° and all, had tasted her sweet body,
So I had nothing known. Oh, now forever
Farewell the tranquil mind! Farewell content!
Farewell the plumèd° troop and the big wars
That make ambition virtue! Oh, farewell, 350
Farewell the neighing steed and the shrill trump,
The spirit-stirring drum, the ear-piercing fife,
The royal banner and all quality,°
Pride, pomp, and circumstance of glorious war!
And, O you mortal engines,° whose rude throats
The immortal Jove's dread clamors counterfeit,°
Farewell! Othello's occupation's gone! 357
 IAGO. Is 't possible, my lord?
 OTH. Villain, be sure thou prove my love a whore,
Be sure of it, give me the ocular proof. 360

319. **Be . . . on't:** know nothing about it. 327. **distaste:** taste
unpleasantly. 328. **with a little:** in a little while. 329. **I . . .**
so: As Iago says this, Othello is seen approaching, with all the
signs of his agitation outwardly visible. 330. **poppy:** opium.
mandragora: called also mandrake, a root used as a drug to bring
sleep. See Pl. 12e. 333. **owedst:** owned, possessed. 335. **Avaunt:**
be off! **on . . . rack:** i.e., in torment. See App. 10. 342. **wanting:**
missing. 346. **Pioners:** pioneers, the lowest type of soldier.
349. **plumed:** wearing plumes in the helmet. 353. **quality:** military rank. 355. **mortal engines:** deadly cannon. 356. **counter-**
feit: imitate.

280. **generous:** noble, of gentle blood. 285. **watching:** lack of
sleep. 287. **napkin:** handkerchief. 292. **wayward:** unaccount-
able. 294. **conjured:** begged with an oath. 296. **work . . . out:**
pattern copied. 299. **fantasy:** whim. 312. **to . . . advantage:**
thereby giving me the opportunity.

Or by the worth of man's eternal soul,
Thou hadst been better have been born a dog
Than answer my waked wrath!
    IAGO.   Is 't come to this?
    OTH. Make me to see 't, or at the least so prove it
That the probation° bear no hinge nor loop   365
To hang a doubt on, or woe upon thy life!
    IAGO. My noble lord——
    OTH. If thou dost slander her and torture me,
Never pray more, abandon all remorse.°
On horror's head horrors accumulate,   370
Do deeds to make Heaven weep, all earth amazed,
For nothing canst thou to damnation add
Greater than that.
    IAGO.   Oh, grace! Oh, Heaven defend me!
Are you a man? Have you a soul or sense?   374
God be wi' you, take mine office. O wretched fool,
That livest to make thine honesty a vice!
O monstrous world! Take note, take note, O world,
To be direct and honest is not safe.
I thank you for this profit,° and from hence   379
I'll love no friend, sith° love breeds such offense.
    OTH. Nay, stay. Thou shouldst be honest.
    IAGO. I should be wise, for honesty's a fool,
And loses that it works for.
    OTH.   By the world,
I think my wife be honest, and think she is not.
I think that thou art just, and think thou art not.
I'll have some proof. Her name, that was as fresh
As Dian's° visage, is now begrimed and black   387
As mine own face. If there be cords, or knives,
Poison, or fire, or suffocating streams,
I'll not endure it. Would I were satisfied!   390
    IAGO. I see, sir, you are eaten up with passion.
I do repent me that I put it to you.
You would be satisfied?
    OTH.   Would! Nay, I will.
    IAGO. And may, but, how? How satisfied, my
    lord?
Would you, the supervisor,° grossly gape on?   395
Behold her topped?
    OTH.   Death and damnation! Oh!
    IAGO. It were a tedious difficulty, I think,
To bring them to that prospect.° Damn them then,
If ever mortal eyes do see them bolster°
More than their own! What then? How then?   400
What shall I say? Where's satisfaction?
It is impossible you should see this,
Were they as prime° as goats, as hot as monkeys,
As salt° as wolves in pride,° and fools as gross
As ignorance made drunk. But yet I say   405
If imputation° and strong circumstances,

Which lead directly to the door of truth,
Will give you satisfaction, you may have 't.
    OTH. Give me a living° reason she's disloyal.
    IAGO. I do not like the office.   410
But sith I am entered in this cause so far,
Pricked° to 't by foolish honesty and love,
I will go on. I lay with Cassio lately,
And being troubled with a raging tooth,
I could not sleep.   415
There are a kind of men so loose of soul
That in their sleeps will mutter their affairs.
One of this kind is Cassio.
In sleep I heard him say "Sweet Desdemona,
Let us be wary, let us hide our loves."   420
And then, sir, would he gripe° and wring my
    hand,
Cry "O sweet creature!" and then kiss me hard,
As if he plucked up kisses by the roots
That grew upon my lips. Then laid his leg   424
Over my thigh, and sighed and kissed, and then
Cried "Cursed fate that gave thee to the Moor!"
    OTH. Oh, monstrous! Monstrous!
    IAGO.   Nay, this was but his dream.
    OTH. But this denoted a foregone conclusion.
'Tis a shrewd doubt,° though it be but a dream.
    IAGO. And this may help to thicken other proofs
That do demónstrate thinly.
    OTH.   I'll tear her all to pieces.   431
    IAGO. Nay, but be wise. Yet we see nothing done,
She may be honest yet. Tell me but this:
Have you not sometimes seen a handkerchief   434
Spotted with strawberries° in your wife's hand?
    OTH. I gave her such a one, 'twas my first gift.
    IAGO. I know not that. But such a handkerchief—
I am sure it was your wife's—did I today
See Cassio wipe his beard with.
    OTH.   If it be that——
    IAGO. If it be that, or any that was hers,   440
It speaks against her with the other proofs.
    OTH. Oh, that the slave had forty thousand lives!
One is too poor, too weak, for my revenge.
Now do I see 'tis true. Look here, Iago,
All my fond love thus do I blow to Heaven—   445
'Tis gone.
Arise, black Vengeance, from thy hollow cell!
Yield up, O Love, thy crown and hearted° throne
To tyrannous hate! Swell, bosom, with thy fraught,°
For 'tis of aspics'° tongues!
    IAGO.   Yet be content.   450
    OTH. Oh, blood, blood, blood!
    IAGO. Patience, I say. Your mind perhaps may
    change.

---

365. **probation:** proof.   369. **remorse:** pity.   379. **profit:** profitable lesson.   380. **sith:** since.   387. **Dian:** Diana, goddess of chastity.   395. **supervisor:** looker-on.   398. **prospect:** sight.   399. **bolster:** sleep together.   403. **prime:** lustful.   404. **salt:** eager. **in pride:** in heat.   406. **imputation:** probability.

409. **living:** tangible.   412. **Pricked:** spurred on.   421. **gripe:** grip.   429. **shrewd doubt:** bitter suspicion.   435. **with strawberries:** with a pattern of strawberries.   448. **hearted:** in my heart.   449. **fraught:** freight, load.   450. **aspic:** asp, a small poisonous snake. See *Ant & Cleo*, V.ii.351–56.

[handwritten: TRAGIC THAT HE WONT CHANGE NOW ONCE HATE IS AROUSED]

OTH. Never, Iago. Like to the Pontic Sea,
Whose icy current and compulsive course
Ne'er feels retiring ebb but keeps due on   455
To the Propontic and the Hellespont;°
Even so my bloody thoughts, with violent pace,
Shall ne'er look back, ne'er ebb to humble love,
Till that capable° and wide revenge   459
Swallow them up. Now, by yond marble Heaven,
In the due reverence of a sacred vow   [*Kneels.*]
I here engage° my words.

IAGO.   Do not rise yet.   [*Kneels.*]
Witness, you ever burning lights above,
You elements that clip° us round about,
Witness that here Iago doth give up   465
The execution of his wit, hands, heart,
To wronged Othello's service! Let him command,
And to obey shall be in me remorse,°
What bloody business ever.   [*They rise.*]

OTH.   I greet thy love,
Not with vain thanks, but with acceptance bounteous,   470
And will upon the instant put thee to 't.°
Within these three days let me hear thee say
That Cassio's not alive.

IAGO. My friend is dead. 'Tis done at your request.
But let her live.

OTH. Damn her, lewd minx! Oh, damn her!   475
Come, go with me apart. I will withdraw,
To furnish me with some swift means of death
For the fair devil. Now art thou my Lieutenant.

IAGO. I am your own forever.   [*Exeunt.*]

SCENE IV. *Before the castle.*

[*Enter* DESDEMONA, EMILIA, *and* CLOWN.]

DES. Do you know, sirrah, where Lieutenant Cassio lies?

CLO. I dare not say he lies anywhere.

DES. Why, man?

CLO. He's a soldier, and for one to say a soldier lies is stabbing.   6

DES. Go to. Where lodges he?

CLO. To tell you where he lodges is to tell you where I lie.

DES. Can anything be made of this?   10

CLO. I know not where he lodges, and for me to devise a lodging, and say he lies here or he lies there, were to lie in mine own throat.

DES. Can you inquire him out and be edified by report?°   15

CLO. I will catechize the world for him; that is, make questions and by them answer.

DES. Seek him, bid him come hither. Tell him I *[handwritten: IRONY — SHE THINKS OTH. WILL FORGIVE CASS.]* have moved my lord on his behalf and hope all will be well.   20

CLO. To do this is within the compass of man's wit, and therefore I will attempt the doing it.   [*Exit.*]

DES. Where should I lose that handkerchief, Emilia?

EMIL. I know not, madam. *[handwritten: IRONY — SHE THINKS HE IS FREE FROM JEALOUSY]*

DES. Believe me, I had rather have lost my purse
Full of crusados.° And, but my noble Moor   26
Is true of mind and made of no such baseness
As jealous creatures are, it were enough
To put him to ill thinking.

EMIL.   Is he not jealous?   29

DES. Who, he? I think the sun where he was born
Drew all such humors° from him.

EMIL.   Look where he comes.

DES. I will not leave him now till Cassio
Be called to him.
[*Enter* OTHELLO.] How is 't with you, my lord?

OTH. Well, my good lady. [*Aside*] Oh, hardness to dissemble!
How do you, Desdemona?

DES.   Well, my good lord.   35

OTH. Give me your hand. This hand is moist,° my lady.

DES. It yet has felt no age nor known no sorrow.

OTH. This argues fruitfulness and liberal heart.
Hot, hot, and moist — this hand of yours requires
A sequester° from liberty, fasting and prayer,   40
Much castigation, exercise devout.
For here's a young and sweating devil here,
That commonly rebels. 'Tis a good hand,
A frank one.

DES.   You may indeed say so,
For 'twas that hand that gave away my heart.   45

OTH. A liberal° hand. The hearts of old gave hands,
But our new heraldry is hands, not hearts.°

DES. I cannot speak of this. Come now, your promise.

453–56. Like . . . Hellespont: In Pliny's *Natural History*, translated by Philemon Holland in 1601, it was noted that "the sea Pontus (Black Sea) evermore floweth and runneth out into Propontis (Sea of Marmora) but the sea never returneth back again within Pontus." Hellespont: the Dardanelles. 459. capable: comprehensive, complete. 462. engage: pledge. 464. elements . . . clip: skies that embrace, surround. 468. remorse: solemn obligation. 471. put . . . to't: put you to the proof.

Sc. iv: 14–15. edified by report: enlightened by the information. Desdemona speaks with mock pomposity. 26. crusados: small gold Portuguese coins. 31. humors: moods; lit., dampnesses. 36. moist: a hot moist palm was believed to show desire. 40. sequester: separation. 46. liberal: overgenerous. 46–47. The . . . hearts: once love and deeds went together, but now it is all deeds (i.e., faithlessness) and no love. This phrase has been taken as a reference to the order of baronets created by James I in 1611, who bore on their heraldic coats of arms the device of the "bloody hand of Ulster." If so, the lines are a later addition; but the reference is very doubtful. The contrast between hearts (true love and faith) and hands (actions) is natural (see *Lear* I.ii. 72–73). As Othello's passions rise, he ceases to be entirely coherent.

OTH. What promise, chuck?°
DES. I have sent to bid Cassio come speak with
    you.   50
OTH. I have a salt and sorry rheum° offends me.
Lend me thy handkerchief.
DES.   Here, my lord.
OTH. That which I gave you.
DES. I have it not about me.
OTH. Not?
DES. No indeed, my lord.
OTH. That's a fault. That handkerchief   55
Did an Egyptian° to my mother give.
She was a charmer, and could almost read
The thoughts of people. She told her while she kept
    it
'Twould make her amiable and subdue my father
Entirely to her love, but if she lost it   60
Or made a gift of it, my father's eye
Should hold her loathed and his spirits should hunt
After new fancies. She dying gave it me,
And bid me, when my fate would have me wive,
To give it her. I did so. And take heed on 't,   65
Make it a darling like your precious eye.
To lose 't or give 't away were such perdition
As nothing else could match.
DES.   Is 't possible?
OTH. 'Tis true. There's magic in the web of it.
A sibyl° that had numbered in the world   70
The sun to course two hundred compasses
In her prophetic fury° sewed the work.
The worms were hallowed that did breed the silk,
And it was dyed in mummy° which the skillful
Conserved° of maidens' hearts.
DES.   Indeed! Is 't true? 75
OTH. Most veritable, therefore look to 't well.
DES. Then would to God that I had never seen 't.
OTH. Ha! Wherefore?
DES. Why do you speak so startlingly and rash?
OTH. Is 't lost? Is 't gone? Speak, is it out o' the
    way?   80
DES. Heaven bless us!
OTH. Say you?
DES. It is not lost, but what an if it were?
OTH. How!
DES. I say it is not lost.
OTH. Fetch 't, let me see it.   85
DES. Why, so I can, sir, but I will not now.
This is a trick to put me from my suit.
Pray you let Cassio be received again.
OTH. Fetch me the handkerchief. My mind mis-
    gives.

DES. Come, come,   90
You'll never meet a more sufficient man.
OTH. The handkerchief!
DES.   I pray talk me of Cassio.
OTH. The handkerchief!
DES.   A man that all his time
Hath founded his good fortunes on your love,
Shared dangers with you ——   95
OTH. The handkerchief!
DES. In sooth, you are to blame.
OTH. Away!   [*Exit.*]
EMIL. Is not this man jealous?
DES. I ne'er saw this before.   100
Sure there's some wonder in this handkerchief.
I am most unhappy in the loss of it.
EMIL. 'Tis not a year or two shows us a man.°
They are all but stomachs and we all but food.
They eat us hungerly, and when they are full 105
They belch us. Look you, Cassio and my husband.
        [*Enter* CASSIO *and* IAGO.]
IAGO. There is no other way, 'tis she must do 't.
And, lo, the happiness!° Go and impórtune her.
DES. How now, good Cassio! What's the news
    with you?
CAS. Madam, my former suit. I do beseech you
That by your virtuous means I may again   111
Exist, and be a member of his love
Whom I with all the office of my heart
Entirely honor. I would not be delayed.
If my offense be of such mortal kind   115
That nor my service past nor present sorrows
Nor purposed merit in futurity°
Can ransom me into his love again,
But to know so must be my benefit.
So shall I clothe me in a forced content   120
And shut myself up in some other course
To Fortune's alms.°
DES.   Alas, thrice-gentle Cassio!
My advocation° is not now in tune.
My lord is not my lord, nor should I know him
Were he in favor as in humor altered.°   125
So help me every spirit sanctified,
As I have spoken for you all my best
And stood within the blank° of his displeasure
For my free speech! You must awhile be patient.
What I can do I will, and more I will   130
Than for myself I dare. Let that suffice you.
IAGO. Is my lord angry?

---

49. **chuck:** a term of affection, but not the kind of word with
which a person of Othello's dignity would normally address his
wife. He is beginning to treat her with contemptuous familiarity.
See IV.ii.24.   51. **rheum:** common cold.   56. **Egyptian:** gypsy.
70. **sibyl:** prophetess.   72. **fury:** inspiration.   74. **mummy:** a
concoction made from Egyptian mummies.   75. **Conserved:**
prepared.

103. **'Tis . . . man:** it does not take a couple of years for us to
discover the nature of a man; i.e., he soon shows his real nature.   108. **And . . . happiness:** what good luck, here she is.
117. **Nor . . . futurity:** nor my good resolutions for the future.
119–22. **But . . . alms:** if I know that Othello will not restore me
to my position, it will have this benefit: I shall force myself
to be contented and try my luck elsewhere. **Fortune's alms:** what
Fortune may give me.   123. **advocation:** advocacy, pleading.
125. **favor . . . altered:** as changed in face as in mood.
128. **blank:** aim. The blank is the bull's-eye of a target.

EMIL.   He went hence but now,
And certainly in strange unquietness.

IAGO. Can he be angry? I have seen the cannon
When it hath blown his ranks into the air,   135
And, like the Devil, from his very arm
Puffed his own brother, and can he be angry?
Something of moment then. I will go meet him.
There's matter in 't indeed if he be angry.

DES. I prithee do so. [*Exit* IAGO.] Something sure
of state,   140
Either from Venice, or some unhatched practice
Made demonstrable° here in Cyprus to him,
Hath puddled° his clear spirit. And in such cases
Men's natures wrangle with inferior things,
Though great ones are their object.° 'Tis even so,
For let our finger ache and it indues°   146
Our other healthful members even to that sense
Of pain. Nay, we must think men are not gods,
Nor of them look for such observancy
As fits the bridal.° Beshrew me° much, Emilia,   150
I was, unhandsome warrior° as I am,
Arraigning his unkindness with my soul,
But now I find I had suborned the witness,°
And he's indicted falsely.

EMIL. Pray Heaven it be state matters, as you
think,   155
And no conception nor no jealous toy°
Concerning you.

DES. Alas the day, I never gave him cause!

EMIL. But jealous souls will not be answered so.
They are not ever jealous for the cause,   160
But jealous for they are jealous. 'Tis a monster
Begot upon itself, born on itself.

DES. Heaven keep that monster from Othello's
mind!

EMIL. Lady, amen.

DES. I will go seek him. Cassio, walk hereabout.
If I do find him fit, I'll move your suit,   166
And seek to effect it to my uttermost.

CAS. I humbly thank your ladyship.

[*Exeunt* DESDEMONA *and* EMILIA.]
[*Enter* BIANCA.]

BIAN. Save you, friend Cassio!

CAS.   What make you from° home?
How is it with you, my most fair Bianca?   170
I' faith, sweet love, I was coming to your house.

BIAN. And I was going to your lodging, Cassio.
What, keep a week away? Seven days and nights?

Eightscore eight hours? And lovers' absent hours,
More tedious than the dial eightscore times?°   175
Oh, weary reckoning!

CAS.   Pardon me, Bianca.
I have this while with leaden thoughts been pressed,
But I shall in a more continuate time°
Strike off this score of absence. Sweet Bianca,
[*Giving her* DESDEMONA's *handkerchief*]
Take me this work out.°

BIAN.   O Cassio, whence came this?   180
This is some token from a newer friend.
To the felt absence now I feel a cause.
Is 't come to this? Well, well.

CAS.   Go to, woman!
Throw your vile guesses in the Devil's teeth,   184
From whence you have them. You are jealous now
That this is from some mistress, some remembrance.
No, by my faith, Bianca.

BIAN.   Why, whose is it?

CAS. I know not, sweet. I found it in my chamber.
I like the work well. Ere it be demanded —
As like enough it will — I'd have it copied.   190
Take it, and do 't, and leave me for this time.

BIAN. Leave you! Wherefore?

CAS. I do attend here on the General,
And think it no addition,° nor my wish,
To have him see me womaned.°

BIAN.   Why, I pray you?   195

CAS. Not that I love you not.

BIAN.   But that you do not love me.
I pray you bring me on the way a little,
And say if I shall see you soon at night.

CAS. 'Tis but a little way that I can bring you,
For I attend here. But I'll see you soon.   200

BIAN. 'Tis very good, I must be circumstanced.°

[*Exeunt.*]

Act IV

SCENE I. *Cyprus. Before the castle.*

[*Enter* OTHELLO *and* IAGO.]

IAGO. Will you think so?

OTH.   Think so, Iago!

IAGO.   What,
To kiss in private?

OTH.   An unauthorized kiss.

IAGO. Or to be naked with her friend in bed

141–42. unhatched ... demonstrable: some plot, not yet matured, which has been revealed.   143. puddled: muddied, stirred up.   143–45. in ... object: when men are disturbed by great matters, they show their temper in small things.   146. indues: endows, pervades.   150. bridal: honeymoon. Beshrew me: plague on me.   151. unhandsome warrior: clumsy soldier. Desdemona continually thinks of herself as Othello's companion in arms. Cf. I.iii.249ff.   153. suborned ... witness: corrupted the evidence; i.e., it is my fault, not his.   156. jealous toy: silly suspicion.   169. make ... from: are you doing away from.

174–75. And ... times: when one's lover is absent for a week does it not seem far longer than a hundred and sixty clock hours?   178. continuate time: i.e., when my time is not continually being interrupted.   180. Take ... out: copy this pattern.   194. addition: honor.   195. womaned: with a girl.   201. circumstanced: put off.

An hour or more, not meaning any harm?

OTH. Naked in bed, Iago, and not mean harm!   5
It is hypocrisy against the Devil.°
They that mean virtuously and yet do so,
The Devil their virtue tempts and they tempt
     Heaven.°

IAGO. So° they do nothing, 'tis a venial° slip.
But if I give my wife a handkerchief ——   10

OTH. What then?

IAGO. Why, then, 'tis hers, my lord, and being
     hers,
She may, I think, bestow 't on any man.

OTH. She is protectress of her honor too.
May she give that?   15

IAGO. Her honor is an essence that's not seen.
They have it very oft that have it not.°
But for the handkerchief ——

OTH. By Heaven, I would most gladly have forgot
     it.
Thou said'st — oh, it comes o'er my memory,   20
As doth the raven o'er the infected house,°
Boding° to all — he had my handkerchief.

IAGO. Aye, what of that?

OTH.   That's not so good now.

IAGO.   What,
If I had said I had seen him do you wrong?
Or heard him say — as knaves be such abroad,   25
Who having, by their own importunate suit,
Or voluntary dotage° of some mistress,
Convincèd or supplied° them, cannot choose
But they must blab ——

OTH.   Hath he said anything?

IAGO. He hath, my lord, but be you well assured,
No more than he'll unswear.

OTH.   What hath he said?   31

IAGO. Faith, that he did —— I know not what he
     did.

OTH. What? What?

IAGO. Lie ——

OTH.   With her?

IAGO.   With her, on her, what you will.   34

OTH. Lie° with her! Lie on her! — We say lie
on her when they belie her. — Lie with her!
'Zounds, that's fulsome!° Handkerchief — confessions — handkerchief! — To confess, and be hanged
for his labor. First to be hanged, and then to confess.
I tremble at it. Nature would not invest herself in
such shadowing passion without some instruc-   41

tion.° It is not words that shake me thus. Pish!
Noses, ears, and lips. Is 't possible? — Confess? —
Handkerchief? — Oh, devil!   [*Falls in a trance.*]

IAGO. Work on,   45
My medicine, work! Thus credulous fools are
     caught,
And many worthy and chaste dames even thus,
All guiltless, meet reproach. What ho! My lord!
My lord, I say! Othello! [*Enter* CASSIO.] How now,
     Cassio!

CAS. What's the matter?   50

IAGO. My lord is fall'n into an epilepsy.
This is his second fit, he had one yesterday.

CAS. Rub him about the temples.

IAGO.   No, forbear,
The lethargy° must have his quiet course.
If not, he foams at mouth and by and by   55
Breaks out to savage madness. Look, he stirs.
Do you withdraw yourself a little while,
He will recover straight. When he is gone,
I would on great occasion speak with you.
                       [*Exit* CASSIO.]
How is it, General? Have you not hurt your head?°

OTH. Dost thou mock me?   61

IAGO.   I mock you! No, by Heaven.
Would you would bear your fortune like a man!

OTH. A hornèd man's a monster and a beast.

IAGO. There's many a beast, then, in a populous
     city,
And many a civil° monster.   65

OTH. Did he confess it?

IAGO.   Good sir, be a man.
Think every bearded fellow that's but yoked°
May draw with you.° There's millions now alive
That nightly lie in those unproper beds
Which they dare swear peculiar.° Your case is bet-
     ter.   70
Oh, 'tis the spite of Hell, the Fiend's archmock,
To lip° a wanton in a secure couch°
And to suppose her chaste! No, let me know,
And knowing what I am, I know what she shall be.

OTH. Oh, thou art wise, 'tis certain.

IAGO.   Stand you awhile apart,   75
Confine yourself but in a patient list.°
Whilst you were here o'erwhelmèd with your
     grief —
A passion most unsuiting such a man —
Cassio came hither. I shifted him away,

Act IV, Sc. i: 6. hypocrisy ... Devil: "double-crossing the Devil"; i.e., they are behaving in a most suspicious way. 7–8. They ... Heaven: i.e., those who go to bed together and mean no harm are asking the Devil to tempt them, and they make God suspect their innocence. 9. So: so long as. venial: pardonable. 17. They ... not: i.e., many are honored who have no honor. 21. As ... house: i.e., as a bird of prey waits for its victim to die. 22. Boding: foretelling evil. 27. dotage: infatuation. 28. Convinced or supplied: overcome or satisfied their desires. 35–44. Lie ... devil: Othello breaks into incoherent muttering before he falls down in a fit. 37. fulsome: disgusting.

40–42. Nature ... instruction: nature would not fill me with such overwhelming emotion unless there was some cause. 54. lethargy: epileptic fit. Cf. *II Hen IV*, I.ii.127–29. 60. Have ... head: With brutal cynicism Iago asks whether Othello is suffering from cuckold's headache. 65. civil: sober, well-behaved citizen. 67. yolked: married. 68. draw ... you: lit., be your yoke fellow, share your fate. 69–70. That ... peculiar: that lie nightly in beds which they believe are their own but which others have shared. 72. lip: kiss. secure couch: lit., a carefree bed; i.e., a bed which has been used by the wife's lover, but secretly. 76. patient list: confines of patience.

And laid good 'scuse upon your ecstasy,°   80
Bade him anon return and here speak with me,
The which he promised. Do but encave° yourself,
And mark the fleers,° the gibes, and notable scorns,
That dwell in every region of his face.
For I will make him tell the tale anew,   85
Where, how, how oft, how long ago, and when
He hath and is again to cope° your wife.
I say but mark his gesture. Marry, patience,
Or I shall say you are all in all in spleen,°
And nothing of a man.

OTH.   Dost thou hear, Iago?   90
I will be found most cunning in my patience,
But — dost thou hear? — most bloody.

IAGO.   That's not amiss,
But yet keep time in all. Will you withdraw?
                                    [OTHELLO *retires*.]
Now will I question Cassio of Bianca,
A housewife° that by selling her desires   95
Buys herself bread and clothes. It is a creature
That dotes on Cassio, as 'tis the strumpet's plague
To beguile many and be beguiled by one.
He, when he hears of her, cannot refrain
From the excess of laughter. Here he comes.   100
[*Re-enter* CASSIO.] As he shall smile, Othello shall go
                                    mad,
And his unbookish° jealousy must construe°
Poor Cassio's smiles, gestures, and light behavior
Quite in the wrong. How do you now, Lieutenant?

CAS. The worser that you give me the addition°
Whose want even kills me.   106

IAGO. Ply° Desdemona well, and you are sure
                                    on 't.
Now, if this suit lay in Bianca's power,
How quickly should you speed!

CAS.   Alas, poor caitiff!°

OTH. Look how he laughs already!   110

IAGO. I never knew a woman love man so.

CAS. Alas, poor rogue! I think, i' faith, she loves
                                    me.

OTH. Now he denies it faintly and laughs it out.

IAGO. Do you hear, Cassio?

OTH.   Now he impórtunes him   115
To tell it o'er. Go to. Well said, well said.

IAGO. She gives it out that you shall marry her.
Do you intend it?

CAS. Ha, ha, ha!   120

OTH. Do you triumph, Roman?° Do you triumph?

CAS. I marry her! What, a customer!° I prithee

bear some charity to my wit. Do not think it so unwholesome. Ha, ha, ha!   125

OTH. So, so, so, so. They laugh that win.°

IAGO. Faith, the cry goes that you shall marry her.

CAS. Prithee say true.

IAGO. I am a very villain else.

OTH. Have you scored° me? Well.   130

CAS. This is the monkey's own giving out. She is
persuaded I will marry her out of her own love and
flattery, not out of my promise.

OTH. Iago beckons me, now he begins the story.

CAS. She was here even now. She haunts me in
every place. I was the other day talking on the sea
bank with certain Venetians, and thither comes the
bauble,° and, by this hand, she falls me thus about
my neck ——   140

OTH. Crying " O dear Cassio! " as it were. His gesture imports it.

CAS. So hangs and lolls and weeps upon me, so
hales° and pulls me. Ha, ha, ha!   144

OTH. Now he tells how she plucked him to my
chamber. Oh, I see that nose of yours, but not that
dog I shall throw it to.

CAS. Well, I must leave her company.

IAGO. Before me!° Look where she comes.   149

CAS. 'Tis such another fitchew!° Marry, a perfumed one. [*Enter* BIANCA.] What do you mean by
this haunting of me?

BIAN. Let the Devil and his dam° haunt you!
What did you mean by that same handkerchief you
gave me even now? I was a fine fool to take it.   155
I must take out the work? A likely piece of work,
that you should find it in your chamber and not
know who left it there! This is some minx's token,
and I must take out the work? There, give it your
hobbyhorse.° Wheresoever you had it, I'll take out
no work on 't.   161

CAS. How now, my sweet Bianca! How now! How
now!

OTH. By Heaven, that should be my handkerchief!   165

BIAN. An° you'll come to supper tonight, you
may. An you will not, come when you are next prepared for.   [*Exit*.]

IAGO. After her, after her.

CAS. Faith, I must, she'll rail i' the street else.   171

IAGO. Will you sup there?

CAS. Faith, I intend so.

IAGO. Well, I may chance to see you, for I would
very fain° speak with you.   175

CAS. Prithee, come, will you?

IAGO. Go to. Say no more.   [*Exit* CASSIO.]

80. ecstasy: fit.   82. encave: hide.   83. fleers: scornful grins.
87. cope: encounter.   89. spleen: hot temper. Cf. *I Hen IV,*
V.ii.19.   95. housewife: hussy.   102. unbookish: unlearned,
simple.   construe: interpret.   105. addition: title (Lieutenant)
which he has lost.   107. Ply: urge.   109. caitiff: wretch.
121. triumph, Roman: The word "triumph" suggests "Roman"
because the Romans celebrated their victories with triumphs,
elaborate shows, and processions. Cf. *Caesar,* I.i.56.   123. customer: harlot.

126. They . . . win: a proverbial saying. See *Temp,* II.i.33.
130. scored: marked, as with a blow from a whip.   139. bauble:
toy, plaything.   144. hales: hauls, drags.   149. Before me:
by my soul, a mild oath.   150. fitchew: polecat, a creature most
demonstrative in the mating season.   153. dam: mother.
160. hobbyhorse: harlot.   166. An: if   175. fain: gladly.

OTH. [*Advancing*] How shall I murder him, Iago?

IAGO. Did you perceive how he laughed at his vice? 181

OTH. Oh, Iago!

IAGO. And did you see the handkerchief?

OTH. Was that mine?

IAGO. Yours, by this hand. And to see how he prizes the foolish woman your wife! She gave it him, and he hath given it his whore. 187

OTH. I would have him nine years a-killing. A fine woman! A fair woman! A sweet woman!

IAGO. Nay, you must forget that.

OTH. Aye, let her rot, and perish, and be damned tonight, for she shall not live. No, my heart is turned to stone, I strike it and it hurts my hand. Oh, the world hath not a sweeter creature. She might lie by an emperor's side, and command him tasks. 196

IAGO. Nay, that's not your way.°

OTH. Hang her! I do but say what she is, so delicate with her needle, an admirable musician — oh, she will sing the savageness out of a bear — of so high and plenteous wit and invention —— 201

IAGO. She's the worse for all this.

OTH. Oh, a thousand thousand times. And then, of so gentle a condition!°

IAGO. Aye, too gentle. 205

OTH. Nay, that's certain. But yet the pity of it, Iago! O Iago, the pity of it, Iago!

IAGO. If you are so fond° over her iniquity, give her patent° to offend, for if it touch not you, it comes near nobody. 210

OTH. I will chop her into messes.° Cuckold me!

IAGO. Oh, 'tis foul in her.

OTH. With mine officer!

IAGO. That's fouler. 215

OTH. Get me some poison, Iago, this night. I'll not expostulate° with her, lest her body and beauty unprovide° my mind again. This night, Iago. 218

IAGO. Do it not with poison, strangle her in her bed, even the bed she hath contaminated.

OTH. Good, good. The justice of it pleases. Very good.

IAGO. And for Cassio, let me be his undertaker.° You shall hear more by midnight. 225

OTH. Excellent good. [*A trumpet within.*] What trumpet is that same?

IAGO. Something from Venice, sure. 'Tis Lodovico

Come from the Duke. And see, your wife is with him.

[*Enter* LODOVICO, DESDEMONA, *and* ATTENDANTS.]

LOD. God save the worthy General!

OTH. With all my heart, sir. 229

LOD. The Duke and Senators of Venice greet you. [*Gives him a letter.*]

OTH. I kiss the instrument° of their pleasures. [*Opens the letter, and reads.*]

DES. And what's the news, good Cousin Lodovico?

IAGO. I am very glad to see you, signior. Welcome to Cyprus.

LOD. I thank you. How does Lieutenant Cassio?

IAGO. Lives, sir. 236

DES. Cousin, there's fall'n between him and my lord

An unkind breach, but you shall make all well.

OTH. Are you sure of that?

DES. My lord?

OTH. [*Reads.*] "This fail you not to do, as you will——" 240

LOD. He did not call, he's busy in the paper. Is there division 'twixt my lord and Cassio?

DES. A most unhappy one. I would do much To atone° them, for the love I bear to Cassio.

OTH. Fire and brimstone!

DES. My lord?

OTH. Are you wise?° 245

DES. What, is he angry?

LOD. Maybe the letter moved him, For, as I think, they do command him home, Deputing Cassio in his government.°

DES. By my troth,° I am glad on 't.

OTH. Indeed!

DES. My lord?

OTH. I am glad to see you mad.

DES. Why, sweet Othello? 250

OTH. Devil! [*Striking her.*]

DES. I have not deserved this.

LOD. My lord, this would not be believed in Venice

Though I should swear I saw 't. 'Tis very much.° Make her amends, she weeps.

OTH. O devil, devil! 255 If that the earth could teem with a woman's tears, Each drop she falls would prove a crocodile.° Out of my sight!

DES. I will not stay to offend you. [*Going.*]

LOD. Truly, an obedient lady. I do beseech your lordship, call her back. 260

OTH. Mistress!

DES. My lord?

---

197. Nay . . . way: i.e., don't get soft thoughts about her. 204. condition: nature. 208. fond: foolish. 209. patent: a grant by the King of some special privilege. 211. messes: little pieces. 217. expostulate: argue. 218. unprovide: weaken. 224. be . . . undertaker: undertake to manage his business. In Shakespeare's plays the word does *not* mean "mortician."

231. instrument: i.e., the official letter which he has just received. 244. atone: reconcile. 245. Are . . . wise: i.e., in saying you bear love to Cassio. 248. in . . . government: in his place as governor. 249. troth: truth. 254. 'Tis . . . much: this is too much. 256–57. If . . . crocodile: if the earth could breed from woman's tears, each tear that she lets fall would become a crocodile. It was believed that the crocodile would cry and sob to attract the sympathetic passer-by, who was then snapped up.

OTH. What would you with her, sir?
LOD.   Who, I, my lord?
OTH. Aye, you did wish that I would make her
    turn.
Sir, she can turn and turn, and yet go on
And turn again. And she can weep, sir, weep.   265
And she's obedient, as you say, obedient,
Very obedient. Proceed you in your tears.
Concerning this, sir — oh, well-painted passion!° —
I am commanded home. Get you away.
I'll send for you anon. Sir, I obey the mandate,   270
And will return to Venice. Hence, avaunt!
                    [*Exit* DESDEMONA.]
Cassio shall have my place. And, sir, tonight,
I do entreat that we may sup together.
You are welcome, sir, to Cyprus. Goats and mon-
    keys!   [*Exit.*]
LOD. Is this the noble Moor whom our full Senate
Call all-in-all sufficient? This the nature   276
Whom passion could not shake? Whose solid vir-
    tue
The shot of accident nor dart of chance
Could neither graze nor pierce?
IAGO.   He is much changed.
LOD. Are his wits safe? Is he not light of brain?
IAGO. He's that he is. I may not breathe my cen-
    sure°   281
What he might be. If what he might he is not,
I would to Heaven he were!°
LOD.   What, strike his wife!
IAGO. Faith, that was not so well, yet would I knew
That stroke would prove the worst!
LOD.   Is it his use?°   285
Or did the letters work upon his blood,
And new-create this fault?
IAGO.   Alas, alas!
It is not honesty in me to speak
What I have seen and known. You shall observe
    him,
And his own courses° will denote him so   290
That I may save my speech. Do but go after,
And mark how he continues.
LOD. I am sorry that I am deceived in him.
                    [*Exeunt.*]

SCENE II. *A room in the castle.*

[*Enter* OTHELLO *and* EMILIA.]
OTH. You have seen nothing, then?
EMIL. Nor ever heard, nor ever did suspect.

OTH. Yes, you have seen Cassio and she together.
EMIL. But then I saw no harm, and then I heard
Each syllable that breath made up between them.   5
OTH. What, did they never whisper?
EMIL.   Never, my lord.
OTH. Nor send you out o' the way?
EMIL. Never.
OTH. To fetch her fan, her gloves, her mask, nor
    nothing?
EMIL. Never, my lord.   10
OTH. That's strange.
EMIL. I durst, my lord, to wager she is honest,
Lay down my soul at stake.° If you think other,
Remove your thought, it doth abuse your bosom.
If any wretch have put this in your head,   15
Let Heaven requite it with the serpent's curse!°
For if she be not honest, chaste, and true,
There's no man happy, the purest of their wives
Is foul as slander.
OTH. Bid her come hither. Go.   [*Exit* EMILIA.]
She says enough. Yet she's a simple bawd°   20
That cannot say as much. This is a subtle whore,
A closet° lock and key of villainous secrets.
And yet she'll kneel and pray, I have seen her do 't.
        [*Enter* DESDEMONA *with* EMILIA.]
DES. My lord, what is your will?
OTH.   Pray, chuck,° come hither.
DES. What is your pleasure?
OTH.   Let me see your eyes.   25
Look in my face.
DES.   What horrible fancy's this?
OTH. [*To* EMILIA] Some of your function,° mis-
    tress.
Leave procreants alone and shut the door,
Cough, or cry hem, if anybody come.
Your mystery,° your mystery. Nay, dispatch.°   30
                    [*Exit* EMILIA.]
DES. Upon my knees, what doth your speech im-
    port?
I understand a fury in your words,
But not the words.
OTH. Why, what art thou?
DES. Your wife, my lord, your true and loyal wife.
OTH. Come, swear it, damn thyself,   35
Lest, being like one of Heaven,° the devils them-
    selves
Should fear to seize thee. Therefore be double-
    damned.
Swear thou art honest.
DES.   Heaven doth truly know it.

Sc. ii: **13. at stake:** as the stake, the bet.   **16. serpent's
curse:** i.e., the curse laid on the serpent in the Garden of Eden.
20. bawd: keeper of a brothel.   **22. closet:** box in which secret
papers are kept.   **24. chuck:** See III.iv.49,n.   **27. Some . . .
function:** get about your business; i.e., prostitution. Othello pretends that Emilia is keeper of a brothel and Desdemona one of
the women.   **30. mystery:** profession. **dispatch:** be quick.
36. being . . . Heaven: because you look like an angel.

268. **well-painted passion:** cleverly imitated emotion; *passion* is
any violent emotion.   281. **censure:** opinion, judgment.   283. I
. . . were: I wish he were the man he ought to be. Once more
Iago hints that he is holding back some unpleasant fact.   285. Is
. . . use: does he always behave like this?   290. **courses:** ways,
behavior.

OTH. Heaven truly knows that thou art false as
     Hell.
DES. To whom, my lord? With whom? How am
     I false?   40
OTH. O Desdemona! Away! Away! Away!
DES. Alas the heavy day! Why do you weep?
Am I the motive of these tears, my lord?
If haply you my father do suspect
An instrument of this your calling-back,   45
Lay not your blame on me. If you have lost him,
Why, I have lost him too.
     OTH.   Had it pleased Heaven
To try me with affliction, had they rained
All kinds of sores and shames on my bare head,
Steeped me in poverty to the very lips,   50
Given to captivity me and my utmost hopes,
I should have found in some place of my soul
A drop of patience. But, alas, to make me
A fixèd figure for the time of scorn
To point his slow unmoving finger at!°   55
Yet could I bear that too, well, very well.
But there where I have garnered up my heart,°
Where either I must live or bear no life,
The fountain from the which my current runs
Or else dries up — to be discarded thence!   60
Or keep it as a cistern for foul toads
To knot and gender° in! Turn thy complexion there,
Patience, thou young and rose-lipped cherubin —
Aye, there, look grim as Hell!
     DES. I hope my noble lord esteems me honest.   65
OTH. Oh, aye, as summer flies are in the sham-
     bles,°
That quicken even with blowing.° O thou weed,
Who art so lovely fair and smell'st so sweet
That the sense aches at thee, would thou hadst ne'er
     been born!   69
DES. Alas, what ignorant sin have I committed?
OTH. Was this fair paper,° this most goodly book,
Made to write " whore " upon? What committed!
Committed! O thou public commoner!°
I should make very forges of my cheeks°
That would to cinders burn up modesty   75
Did I but speak thy deeds. What committed!
Heaven stops the nose at it, and the moon winks.
The bawdy wind, that kisses all it meets,
Is hushed within the hollow mine° of earth
And will not hear it. What committed!   80
Impudent strumpet!

54–55. A . . . at: A difficult image, much discussed. F1 reads
"slow and moving finger"; Q1 reads "slow unmoving." Probably
it means "a perpetual mark for scorn to point at with motionless finger." time of scorn: (perhaps) scorn for all time. 57. garnered . . . heart: stored the harvest of my love. 62. gender:
mate. 66. shambles: slaughterhouse. 67. quicken . . . blowing: come to life as soon as the eggs are laid. 71. fair paper: i.e.,
her white body. 73. public commoner: one who offers herself to
all comers. 74. I . . . cheeks: i.e., my cheeks would be as hot as
a forge if I told the truth. 79. hollow mine: i.e., the cave where
the winds were supposed to be kept.

DES.   By Heaven, you do me wrong.
OTH. Are not you a strumpet?
DES.   No, as I am a Christian.
If to preserve this vessel for my lord
From any other foul unlawful touch
Be not to be a strumpet, I am none.   85
OTH. What, not a whore?
DES.   No, as I shall be saved.
OTH. Is 't possible?
DES. Oh, Heaven forgive us!
OTH.   I cry you mercy, then.
I took you for that cunning whore of Venice
That married with Othello. [*Raising his voice.*]
     You, mistress,   90
That have the office opposite to Saint Peter,°
And keep the gate of Hell!
[*Re-enter* EMILIA.] You, you, aye, you!
We have done our course, there's money for your
     pains.   93
I pray you turn the key, and keep our counsel.°
                                        [*Exit.*]
EMIL. Alas, what does this gentleman conceive?°
How do you, madam? How do you, my good lady?
DES. Faith, half-asleep.
EMIL. Good madam, what's the matter with my
     lord?
DES. With who?
EMIL. Why, with my lord, madam.   100
DES. Who is thy lord?
EMIL.   He that is yours, sweet lady.
DES. I have none. Do not talk to me, Emilia.
I cannot weep, nor answer have I none
But what should go by water.° Prithee tonight
Lay on my bed my wedding sheets. Remember,   105
And call thy husband hither.
EMIL.   Here's a change indeed! [*Exit.*]
DES. 'Tis meet I should be used so, very meet.
How have I been behaved that he might stick
The small'st opinion on my least misuse?°
              [*Re-enter* EMILIA *with* IAGO.]
IAGO. What is your pleasure, madam? How is 't
     with you?   110
DES. I cannot tell. Those that do teach young babes
Do it with gentle means and easy tasks.
He might have chid me so, for, in good faith,
I am a child to chiding.
IAGO.   What's the matter, lady? 114
EMIL. Alas, Iago, my lord hath so bewhored her,
Thrown such despite and heavy terms upon her,
As true hearts cannot bear.
DES. Am I that name, Iago?
IAGO.   What name, fair lady?

91. office . . . Peter: St. Peter kept the keys to Heaven.
94. counsel: i.e., secret. 95. conceive: imagine. 104. should
. . . water: be expressed in tears. 108–09. How . . . misuse:
what have I done that he could find the smallest reason to find
fault with my least mistake?

DES. Such as she says my lord did say I was.   119

EMIL. He called her whore. A beggar in his drink
Could not have laid such terms upon his callet.°

IAGO. Why did he so?

DES. I do not know. I am sure I am none such.

IAGO. Do not weep, do not weep. Alas the day!

EMIL. Hath she forsook so many noble matches,
Her father and her country and her friends,   126
To be called whore? Would it not make one weep?

DES. It is my wretched fortune.

IAGO.   Beshrew him for 't!
How comes this trick upon him?

DES.   Nay, Heaven doth know.

EMIL. I will be hanged if some eternal villain,
Some busy and insinuating rogue,   131
Some cogging, cozening° slave, to get some office,
Have not devised this slander. I'll be hanged else.

IAGO. Fie, there is no such man, it is impossible.

DES. If any such there be, Heaven pardon him!

EMIL. A halter pardon him! And Hell gnaw his
bones!   136
Why should he call her whore? Who keeps her company?
What place? What time? What form? What likelihood?
The Moor's abused by some most villainous knave,
Some base notorious knave, some scurvy fellow.
O Heaven, that such companions° Thou'dst unfold,°
And put in every honest hand a whip   142
To lash the rascals naked through the world
Even from the east to the west!

IAGO.   Speak withindoor.°

EMIL. Oh, fie upon them! Some such squire° he
was   145
That turned your wit the seamy side without,
And made you to suspect me with the Moor.

IAGO. You are a fool. Go to.°

DES.   O good Iago,
What shall I do to win my lord again?   149
Good friend, go to him, for, by this light of Heaven,
I know not how I lost him. Here I kneel.
If e'er my will did trespass 'gainst his love
Either in discourse of thought or actual deed,
Or that mine eyes, mine ears, or any sense
Delighted them in any other form,   155
Or that I do not yet, and ever did,
And ever will, though he do shake me off
To beggarly divorcement, love him dearly,
Comfort forswear° me! Unkindness may do much,
And his unkindness may defeat° my life,   160
But never taint my love. I cannot say " whore,"
It doth abhor me now I speak the word.

To do the act that might the addition° earn
Not the world's mass of vanity° could make me.

IAGO. I pray you be content, 'tis but his humor.
The business of the state does him offense,   166
And he does chide with you.

DES. If 'twere no other ——

IAGO. 'Tis but so, I warrant. [*Trumpets within.*]
Hark how these instruments summon to supper!
The messengers of Venice stay the meat.°   170
Go in, and weep not, all things shall be well.

[*Exeunt* DESDEMONA *and* EMILIA.]
[*Enter* RODERIGO.] How now, Roderigo!

ROD. I do not find that thou dealest justly with me.

IAGO. What in the contrary?   175

ROD. Every day thou daffest° me with some device, Iago, and rather, as it seems to me now, keepest from me all conveniency° than suppliest me with the least advantage of hope. I will indeed no longer endure it, nor am I yet persuaded to put up in peace what already I have foolishly suffered.   182

IAGO. Will you hear me, Roderigo?

ROD. Faith, I have heard too much, for your words and performances are no kin together.

IAGO. You charge me most unjustly.   186

ROD. With naught but truth. I have wasted myself out of my means. The jewels you have had from me to deliver to Desdemona would half have corrupted a votarist.° You have told me she hath received them, and returned me expectations and comforts of sudden respect and acquaintance, but I find none.

IAGO. Well, go to, very well.   194

ROD. Very well! Go to! I cannot go to, man, nor 'tis not very well. By this hand, I say 'tis very scurvy, and begin to find myself fopped° in it.

IAGO. Very well.   198

ROD. I tell you 'tis not very well. I will make myself known to Desdemona. If she will return me my jewels, I will give over my suit and repent my unlawful solicitation. If not, assure yourself I will seek satisfaction of you.

IAGO. You have said now.°

ROD. Aye, and said nothing but what I protest intendment of doing.   206

IAGO. Why, now I see there's mettle° in thee, and even from this instant do build on thee a better opinion than ever before. Give me thy hand, Roderigo. Thou hast taken against me a most just exception,° but yet I protest I have dealt most directly in thy affair.   211

ROD. It hath not appeared.

IAGO. I grant indeed it hath not appeared, and

121. laid . . . callet: used such words about his moll.   132. cogging, cozening: deceiving, cheating.   141. companions: low creatures. unfold: bring to light.   144. Speak withindoor: don't shout so loud that all the street will hear you.   145. squire: fine fellow.   148. Go to: An expression of derision.   159. forswear: repudiate.   160. defeat: destroy.

163. addition: title. Cf. IV.i.105.   164. vanity: i.e., riches.
170. meat: serving of supper.   176. thou daffest: you put me aside. Cf. *I Hen IV*, IV.i.96.   178. conveniency: opportunity.
190. votarist: one who has taken a vow, here a nun.   197. fopped: fooled.   204. You . . . now: or in modern slang, "Oh yeah."
207. mettle: metal, good stuff.   209. just exception: reasonable grievance.

your suspicion is not without wit° and judgment.
But, Roderigo, if thou hast that in thee indeed 216
which I have greater reason to believe now than ever
— I mean purpose, courage, and valor — this night
show it. If thou the next night following enjoy not
Desdemona, take me from this world with treachery
and devise engines° for my life. 222

ROD. Well, what is it? Is it within reason and compass?

IAGO. Sir, there is especial commission come from
Venice to depute Cassio in Othello's place.

ROD. Is that true? Why, then Othello and Desdemona return again to Venice. 228

IAGO. Oh, no. He goes into Mauritania, and takes
away with him the fair Desdemona, unless his abode
be lingered here by some accident. Wherein none can
be so determinate° as the removing of Cassio. 233

ROD. How do you mean, " removing of " him?

IAGO. Why, by making him uncapable° of Othello's place, knocking out his brains.

ROD. And that you would have me to do? 237

IAGO. Aye, if you dare do yourself a profit and a
right. He sups tonight with a harlotry,° and thither
will I go to him. He knows not yet of his honorable
fortune. If you will watch his going thence, which I
will fashion to fall out between twelve and one, you
may take him at your pleasure. I will be near to
second your attempt, and he shall fall between us.
Come, stand not amazed at it, but go along 245
with me. I will show you such a necessity in his
death that you shall think yourself bound to put it
on him. It is now high suppertime, and the night
grows to waste. About it. 250

ROD. I will hear further reason for this.

IAGO. And you shall be satisfied. [Exeunt.]

SCENE III. *Another room in the castle.*

[*Enter* OTHELLO, LODOVICO, DESDEMONA, EMILIA, *and*
ATTENDANTS.]

LOD. I do beseech you, sir, trouble yourself no
further.

OTH. Oh, pardon me, 'twill do me good to walk.

LOD. Madam, good night. I humbly thank your
ladyship.

DES. Your Honor is most welcome.

OTH.   Will you walk, sir?
Oh — Desdemona —— 5

DES. My lord?

OTH. Get you to bed on the instant, I will be returned forthwith. Dismiss your attendant there.
Look it be done.

DES. I will, my lord. 10
[*Exeunt* OTHELLO, LODOVICO, *and* ATTENDANTS.]

EMIL. How goes it now? He looks gentler than
he did.

DES. He says he will return incontinent.°
He hath commanded me to go to bed,
And bade me to dismiss you.

EMIL.   Dismiss me! 14

DES. It was his bidding, therefore, good Emilia,
Give me my nightly wearing,° and adieu.
We must not now displease him.

EMIL. I would you had never seen him!

DES. So would not I. My love doth so approve°
him 19
That even his stubbornness, his checks, his frowns —
Prithee, unpin me — have grace and favor in them.

EMIL. I have laid those sheets you bade me on the
bed.

DES. All's one. Good faith, how foolish are our
minds!
If I do die before thee, prithee shroud me
In one of those same sheets.

EMIL.   Come, come, you talk. 25

DES. My mother had a maid called Barbara.
She was in love, and he she loved proved mad
And did forsake her. She had a song of " willow "° —
An old thing 'twas, but it expressed her fortune,
And she died singing it. That song tonight 30
Will not go from my mind. I have much to do
But to go hang my head all at one side
And sing it like poor Barbara. Prithee, dispatch.

EMIL. Shall I go fetch your nightgown?

DES.   No, unpin me here.
This Lodovico is a proper man. 35

EMIL. A very handsome man.

DES. He speaks well.

EMIL. I know a lady in Venice would have walked
barefoot to Palestine for a touch of his nether°
lip. 40

DES. [*Singing*]
" The poor soul sat sighing by a sycamore tree,
Sing all a green willow.
Her hand on her bosom, her head on her knee,
Sing willow, willow, willow.
The fresh streams ran by her, and murmured her
moans, 45
Sing willow, willow, willow.
Her salt tears fell from her, and softened the
stones — "
Lay by these — [*Singing*]
" Sing willow, willow, willow."
Prithee, hie thee, he'll come anon.° — [*Singing*] 50
" Sing all a green willow must be my garland.

---

215. **wit**: wisdom.   222. **engines**: instruments of torture.
233. **determinate**: decisive.   235. **uncapable**: unable to take.
239. **harlotry**: harlot.

Sc. iii: 12. **incontinent**: immediately.   16. **nightly wearing**:
nightgown.   19. **approve**: commend.   28. **willow**: the emblem
of the forlorn lover.   39. **nether**: lower.   50. **anon**: soon.

Let nobody blame him, his scorn I approve —— "
Nay, that's not next. Hark! Who is 't that knocks?
  EMIL. It's the wind.
  DES. [*Singing*]
" I called my love false love, but what said he then?
    Sing willow, willow, willow.   56
  If I court moe° women, you'll couch with moe
    men."
So get thee gone, good night. Mine eyes do itch.
Doth that bode weeping?
  EMIL.   'Tis neither here nor there.
  DES. I have heard it said so. Oh, these men, these
    men!   60
Dost thou in conscience think — tell me, Emilia —
That there be women do abuse their husbands
In such gross kind? *[handwritten: SHOWS HER INNOCENCE]*
  EMIL.   There be some such, no question.
  DES. Wouldst thou do such a deed for all the
    world?
  EMIL. Why, would not you?
  DES.   No, by this heavenly light!   65
  EMIL. Nor I neither by this heavenly light. I might
do 't as well i' the dark.
  DES. Wouldst thou do such a deed for all the
    world?
  EMIL. The world's a huge thing. It is a great price
For a small vice.
  DES.   In troth, I think thou wouldst not.   70
  EMIL. In troth, I think I should, and undo 't when
I had done. Marry, I would not do such a thing for
a joint ring,° nor for measures of lawn,° nor for
gowns, petticoats, nor caps, nor any petty exhibi-
tion;° but for the whole world — why, who would
not make her husband a cuckold to make him a
monarch? I should venture Purgatory for 't.   77
  DES. Beshrew me if I would do such a wrong
For the whole world.
  EMIL. Why, the wrong is but a wrong i' the
world, and having the world for your labor, 'tis a
wrong in your own world and you might quickly
make it right.
  DES. I do not think there is any such woman.   84
  EMIL. Yes, a dozen, and as many to the vantage°
as would store° the world they played for.
But I do think it is their husbands' faults
If wives do fall. Say that they slack their duties
And pour our treasures into foreign laps,
Or else break out in peevish jealousies,   90
Throwing restraint° upon us, or say they strike us,
Or scant our former having in despite,°

Why, we have galls,° and though we have some
  grace,
Yet have we some revenge. Let husbands know
Their wives have sense like them. They see and smell
And have their palates both for sweet and sour,   96
As husbands have. What is it that they do
When they change us for others? Is it sport?
I think it is. And doth affection breed it?
I think it doth. Is 't frailty that thus errs?   100
It is so too. And have not we affections,
Desires for sport, and frailty, as men have?
Then let them use us well. Else let them know
The ills we do, their ills instruct us so.
  DES. Good night, good night. Heaven me such
  uses° send,   105
Not to pick bad from bad, but by bad mend!
[handwritten: HER CHRISTIAN MORALS]
                            [*Exeunt.*]

Act V

SCENE I. *Cyprus. A street.*

[*Enter* IAGO *and* RODERIGO.]

  IAGO. Here, stand behind this bulk,° straight° will
  he come.
Wear thy good rapier bare, and put it home.
Quick, quick, fear nothing, I'll be at thy elbow.
It makes us, or it mars us. Think on that,
And fix most firm thy resolution.   5
  ROD. Be near at hand, I may miscarry in 't.
  IAGO. Here, at thy hand. Be bold, and take thy
  stand.   [*Retires.*]
  ROD. I have no great devotion to the deed,
And yet he hath given me satisfying reasons.
'Tis but a man gone. Forth, my sword. He dies.   10
  IAGO. I have rubbed this young quat° almost to the
  sense,°
And he grows angry. Now, whether he kill Cassio,
Or Cassio him, or each do kill the other,
Every way makes my gain. Live Roderigo,
He calls me to a restitution large°   15
Of gold and jewels that I bobbed° from him
As gifts to Desdemona.
It must not be. If Cassio do remain,
He hath a daily beauty in his life
That makes me ugly,° and besides, the Moor   20
May unfold° me to him. There stand I in much
  peril.

[handwritten right margin: WHY BOTH CASSIO & RODE. MUST DIE]

57. moe: more.   73. joint ring: ring made in two pieces, a lover's
gift. measures of lawn: lengths of finest lawn, or as a modern
woman would say, "sheer nylon."   74–75. petty exhibition:
small allowance of money.   85. as . . . vantage: and more too;
vantage is that added to the exact weight to give generous measure.   86. store: stock, fill up.   91. Throwing restraint: putting
restraints.   92. scant . . . despite: for spite cut down our allowance.

93. galls: bile, the cause of bitterness.   105. uses: practices.
Act V, Sc. i: 1. bulk: stall outside a shop. straight: straightway.   11. quat: pimple. to . . . sense: to the quick, to the raw.
15. large: full.   16. bobbed: cheated.   19–20. He . . . ugly:
by comparison with him I am a poor thing. Iago is conscious of
his lack of social graces.   21. unfold: expose.

No, he must die. Be 't so. I hear him coming.
                     [*Enter* CASSIO.]
ROD. I know his gait, 'tis he. Villain, thou diest!
                   [*Makes a pass at* CASSIO.]
CAS. That thrust had been mine enemy indeed
But that my coat is better than thou know'st.° 25
I will make proof of thine.
              [*Draws, and wounds* RODERIGO.]
ROD.   Oh, I am slain!
       [IAGO *from behind wounds* CASSIO
                 in the leg, and exit.]
CAS. I am maimed for ever. Help, ho! Murder!
   Murder!   [*Falls.*]
           [*Enter* OTHELLO.]
OTH. The voice of Cassio. Iago keeps his word.
ROD. Oh, villain that I am!
OTH.   It is even so.
CAS. Oh, help, ho! Light! A surgeon!   30
OTH. 'Tis he. O brave Iago, honest and just,
That hast such noble sense of thy friend's wrong!
Thou teachest me. Minion,° your dear lies dead,
And your unblest fate hies.° Strumpet, I come!
Forth of my heart those charms, thine eyes, are
   blotted.   35
Thy bed lust-stained shall with lust's blood be
   spotted.   [*Exit.*]
       [*Enter* LODOVICO *and* GRATIANO.]
CAS. What ho! No watch?° No passage?° Mur-
   der! Murder!
GRA. 'Tis some mischance, the cry is very dire-
   ful.
CAS. Oh, help!
LOD. Hark!   40
ROD. Oh, wretched villain!
LOD. Two or three groan. It is a heavy° night.
These may be counterfeits.° Let's think 't unsafe
To come in to the cry without more help.
ROD. Nobody come? Then shall I bleed to death.
LOD. Hark!
      [*Re-enter* IAGO, *with a light.*]
GRA. Here's one comes in his shirt, with light and
   weapons.   46
IAGO. Who's there? Whose noise is this that cries
   on° murder?
LOD. We do not know.
IAGO.   Did not you hear a cry?
CAS. Here, here! For Heaven's sake, help me!
IAGO.   What's the matter? 50
GRA. This is Othello's Ancient, as I take it.
LOD. The same indeed, a very valiant fellow.
IAGO. What are you here that cry so grievously?
CAS. Iago? Oh, I am spoiled, undone by villains!
Give me some help.   55

IAGO. Oh me, Lieutenant! What villains have done
   this?
CAS. I think that one of them is hereabout,
And cannot make away.
IAGO.   Oh, treacherous villains!
[*To* LODOVICO *and* GRATIANO.] What are you there?
   Come in and give some help.
ROD. Oh, help me here!   60
CAS. That's one of them.
IAGO. Oh, murderous slave! Oh, villain!
               [*Stabs* RODERIGO.]
ROD. Oh, damned Iago! Oh, inhuman dog!
IAGO. Kill men i' the dark! Where be these bloody
   thieves?
How silent is this town! Ho! Murder! Murder!
What may you be? Are you of good or evil?   65
LOD. As you shall prove us, praise us.
IAGO. Signior Lodovico?
LOD. He, sir.
IAGO. I cry you mercy. Here's Cassio hurt by vil-
   lains.
GRA. Cassio!   70
IAGO. How is 't, brother?
CAS. My leg is cut in two.
IAGO.   Marry, Heaven forbid!
Light, gentlemen. I'll bind it with my shirt.
          [*Enter* BIANCA.]
BIAN. What is the matter, ho? Who is 't that
   cried?
IAGO. Who is 't that cried!   75
BIAN. Oh, my dear Cassio! My sweet Cassio! Oh,
Cassio, Cassio, Cassio!
IAGO. Oh, notable strumpet! Cassio, may you sus-
   pect
Who they should be that have thus mangled you?
CAS. No.   80
GRA. I am sorry to find you thus. I have been to
   seek you.
IAGO. Lend me a garter. So. Oh, for a chair,
To bear him easily hence!
BIAN. Alas, he faints! Oh, Cassio, Cassio, Cassio!
IAGO. Gentlemen all, I do suspect this trash   85
To be a party in this injury.
Patience awhile, good Cassio. Come, come,
Lend me a light. Know we this face or no?
Alas, my friend and my dear countryman
Roderigo? No — yes, sure. Oh Heaven! Roderigo.
GRA. What, of Venice?   91
IAGO. Even he, sir. Did you know him?
GRA.   Know him! Aye.
IAGO. Signior Gratiano? I cry you gentle pardon.°
These bloody accidents must excuse my manners,
That so neglected you.
GRA.   I am glad to see you. 95
IAGO. How do you, Cassio? Oh, a chair, a chair!
GRA. Roderigo!

---

25. **coat . . . know'st:** i.e., I wear mail under my coat. 33. **Min-ion:** darling, in a bad sense. 34. **hies:** comes on quickly. 37. **watch:** police. See Gen. Intro. p. 18a. **No passage:** nobody passing. 42. **heavy:** thick. 43. **counterfeits:** fakes. 47. **cries on:** cries out.

93. **I . . . pardon:** I beg you kindly pardon me.

IAGO. He, he, 'tis he. [*A chair brought in*] Oh,
    that's well said, the chair.
Some good man bear him carefully from hence.
I'll fetch the General's surgeon. [*To* BIANCA] For
    you, mistress,   100
Save you your labor. He that lies slain here, Cassio,
Was my dear friend. What malice was between you?
    CAS. None in the world, nor do I know the man.
    IAGO. [*To* BIANCA] What, look you pale? Oh, bear
        him out o' the air.
        [CASSIO *and* RODERIGO *are borne off.*]
Stay you, good gentlemen. Look you pale, mistress?
Do you perceive the gastness° of her eye?   106
Nay, if you stare, we shall hear more anon.
Behold her well, I pray you look upon her.
Do you see, gentlemen? Nay, guiltiness will speak,
Though tongues were out of use.   110
        [*Enter* EMILIA.]
    EMIL. 'Las, what's the matter? What's the matter,
        husband?
    IAGO. Cassio hath here been set on in the dark
By Roderigo, and fellows that are 'scaped.
He's almost slain, and Roderigo dead.   114
    EMIL. Alas, good gentlemen! Alas, good Cassio!
    IAGO. This is the fruit of whoring. Prithee, Emilia,
Go know of Cassio where he supped tonight.
What, do you shake at that?
    BIAN. He supped at my house, but I therefore
        shake not.
    IAGO. Oh, did he so? I charge you, go with me.
    EMIL. Fie, fie upon thee, strumpet!   121
    BIAN. I am no strumpet, but of life as honest
As you that thus abuse me.
    EMIL.   As I! Foh! Fie upon thee!
    IAGO. Kind gentlemen, let's go see poor Cassio
        dressed.°
Come, mistress, you must tell 's another tale.   125
Emilia, run you to the citadel,
And tell my lord and lady what hath happed!
Will you go on? I pray. [*Aside*] This is the night
That either makes me or fordoes° me quite.
        [*Exeunt.*]

SCENE II. *A bedchamber in the castle.* DESDE-
MONA *in bed asleep, a light burning.*

        [*Enter* OTHELLO.]
    OTH. It is the cause,° it is the cause, my soul.
Let me not name it to you, you chaste stars!
It is the cause. Yet I'll not shed her blood,

Nor scar that whiter skin of hers than snow
And smooth as monumental alabaster.°   5
Yet she must die, else she'll betray more men.
Put out the light, and then put out the light.
If I quench thee, thou flaming minister,°
I can again thy former light restore,
Should I repent me. But once put out thy light,   10
Thou cunning'st° pattern of excelling nature,
I know not where is that Promethean heat°
That can thy light relume.° When I have plucked
    the rose,
I cannot give it vital growth again,
It needs must wither. I'll smell it on the tree.   15
        [*Kissing her*]
Ah, balmy breath, that dost almost persuade
Justice to break her sword! One more, one more.
Be thus when thou art dead, and I will kill thee,
And love thee after. One more, and this the last.
So sweet was ne'er so fatal. I must weep,   20
But they are cruel tears. This sorrow's heavenly,
It strikes where it doth love. She wakes.
    DES. Who's there? Othello?
    OTH.   Aye, Desdemona.
    DES. Will you come to bed, my lord?
    OTH. Have you prayed tonight, Desdemona?   25
    DES. Aye, my lord.
    OTH. If you bethink yourself of any crime
Unreconciled as yet to Heaven and grace,
Solicit for it straight.
    DES. Alas, my lord, what may you mean by that?
    OTH. Well, do it, and be brief. I will walk by.   30
I would not kill thy unpreparèd spirit.
No, Heaven forfend! I would not kill thy soul.°
    DES. Talk you of killing?
    OTH. Aye, I do.
    DES. Then Heaven have mercy on me!
    OTH. Amen, with all my heart!
    DES. If you say so, I hope you will not kill me.   35
    OTH. Hum!
    DES. And yet I fear you, for you are fatal° then
When your eyes roll so. Why I should fear I know
    not,
Since guiltiness I know not, but yet I feel I fear.
    OTH. Think on thy sins.
    DES.   They are loves I bear to you. 40
    OTH. Aye, and for that thou diest.
    DES. That death's unnatural that kills for loving.
Alas, why gnaw you so your nether lip?
Some bloody passion shakes your very frame.
These are portents,° but yet I hope, I hope,   45

106. **gastness:** ghastly look.   124. **dressed:** i.e., his wound
dressed.   129. **fordoes:** ruins.
    Sc. ii: 1. **It . . . cause:** The meaning of the opening lines of
this speech has been much discussed. The *cause* is Desdemona's
supposed faithlessness; Othello, at this moment, sees himself as
embodied vengeance, the venger of man betrayed by woman.

5. **monumental alabaster:** Alabaster is white translucent stone,
much used for memorial effigies on Elizabethan tombs.   8. **minister:** servant.   11. **cunning'st:** most skillfully made.   12. **Promethean heat:** fire from Heaven. Prometheus stole fire from
Heaven and first gave it to man.   13. **relume:** relight.   27–32. **If
. . . soul:** Othello will be a merciful murderer. Cf. *Haml,* I.v.76–
80. **forfend:** forbid.   37. **fatal:** deadly.   45. **portents:** signs
foretelling disaster.

They do not point on me.

OTH.   Peace, and be still!

DES. I will so. What's the matter?

OTH. That handkerchief which I so loved and gave thee
Thou gavest to Cassio.

DES.   No, by my life and soul!
Send for the man, and ask him.

OTH.   Sweet soul, take heed,   50
Take heed of perjury, thou art on thy deathbed.

DES. Aye, but not yet to die.

OTH.   Yes, presently.°
Therefore confess thee freely of thy sin,
For to deny each article with oath
Cannot remove nor choke the strong conception°
That I do groan withal. Thou art to die.   56

DES. Then Lord have mercy on me!

OTH.   I say amen.

DES. And have you mercy too! I never did
Offend you in my life, never loved Cassio
But with such general warranty° of Heaven   60
As I might love. I never gave him token.

OTH. By Heaven, I saw my handkerchief in 's hand.
O perjured woman! Thou dost stone° my heart,
And makest me call what I intend to do
A murder, which I thought a sacrifice.   65
I saw the handkerchief.

DES.   He found it, then,
I never gave it him. Send for him hither.
Let him confess a truth.

OTH.   He hath confessed.

DES. What, my lord?

OTH. That he hath used thee.

DES.   How? Unlawfully?   70

OTH. Aye.

DES. He will not say so.

OTH.   No, his mouth is stopped.
Honest Iago hath ta'en order for 't.

DES. Oh, my fear interprets! What, is he dead?

OTH. Had all his hairs been lives, my great revenge
Had stomach for them all.   75

DES. Alas, he is betrayed, and I undone!

OTH. Out, strumpet! Weep'st thou for him to my face?

DES. Oh, banish me, my lord, but kill me not!

OTH. Down, strumpet!

DES. Kill me tomorrow, let me live tonight!   80

OTH. Nay, if you strive——

DES. But half an hour!

OTH.   Being done, there is no pause.

DES. But while I say one prayer!

OTH.   It is too late.
[*He stifles her.*]

EMIL. [*Within*] My lord, my lord! What ho! My lord, my lord!

OTH. What noise is this? Not dead? Not yet quite dead?   85
I that am cruel am yet merciful,
I would not have thee linger in thy pain.
So, so.

EMIL. [*Within*] What ho! My lord, my lord!

OTH.   Who's there?

EMIL. [*Within*] Oh, good my lord, I would speak a word with you!   90

OTH. Yes, 'tis Emilia. By and by. She's dead.
'Tis like she comes to speak of Cassio's death.
The noise was here. Ha! No more moving?
Still as the grave. Shall she come in? Were 't good?
I think she stirs again. No. What's best to do?   95
If she come in, she'll sure speak to my wife.
My wife! My wife! What wife? I have no wife.
Oh, insupportable! Oh, heavy hour!
Methinks it should be now a huge eclipse
Of sun and moon, and that the affrighted globe   100
Should yawn at alteration.°

EMIL.   [*Within*] I do beseech you
That I may speak with you, O good my lord!

OTH. I had forgot thee. Oh, come in, Emilia.
Soft, by and by. Let me the curtains° draw.   104
Where art thou?   [*Unlocks the door.*]
[*Enter* EMILIA.] What's the matter with thee now?

EMIL. Oh, my good lord, yonder 's foul murders done!

OTH. What, now?

EMIL. But now, my lord.

OTH. It is the very error° of the moon.
She comes more nearer earth than she was wont
And makes men mad.   111

EMIL. Cassio, my lord, hath killed a young Venetian
Called Roderigo.

OTH.   Roderigo killed!
And Cassio killed!

EMIL.   No, Cassio is not killed.

OTH. Not Cassio killed! Then murder's out of tune,   115
And sweet revenge grows harsh.

DES. Oh, falsely, falsely murdered!

EMIL.   Alas, what cry is that?

OTH. That! What?

EMIL. Out and alas! That was my lady's voice.
Help! Help, ho! Help! O lady, speak again!   120
Sweet Desdemona! O sweet mistress, speak!

DES. A guiltless death I die.

EMIL. Oh, who hath done this deed?

DES. Nobody, I myself. Farewell.

---

52. presently: at once.   55. conception: thought.   60. warranty: permission.   63. stone: turn to stone.

101. yawn at alteration: gape with wonder at some monstrous change.   104. curtains: i.e., of the bed. See Pl. 17b.   109. error: wandering out of her proper course.

Commend me to my kind lord. Oh, farewell!   125
                                        [*Dies.*]
OTH. Why, how should she be murdered?
EMIL. Alas, who knows?
OTH. You heard her say herself it was not I.
EMIL. She said so. I must needs report the truth.
OTH. She's like a liar gone to burning Hell.
'Twas I that killed her.
EMIL.   Oh, the more angel she,   130
And you the blacker devil!
OTH. She turned to folly,° and she was a whore.
EMIL. Thou dost belie her, and thou art a devil.
OTH. She was false as water.
EMIL.   Thou art rash as fire to say
That she was false. Oh, she was heavenly true!   135
OTH. Cassio did top her, ask thy husband else.
Oh, I were damned beneath all depth in Hell
But that I did proceed upon just grounds
To this extremity. Thy husband knew it all.
EMIL. My husband!   140
OTH. Thy husband.
EMIL. That she was false to wedlock?
OTH. Aye, with Cassio. Nay, had she been true,
If Heaven would make me such another world
Of one entire and perfect chrysolite,°   145
I'd not have sold her for it.
EMIL. My husband!
OTH.   Aye, 'twas he that told me first.
An honest man he is, and hates the slime
That sticks on filthy deeds.
EMIL.   My husband!
OTH. What needs this iteration,° woman? I say
  thy husband.   150
EMIL. Oh, mistress, villainy hath made mocks with
  love!
My husband say that she was false!
OTH.   He, woman.
I say thy husband. Dost understand the word?
My friend, thy husband, honest, honest Iago.
EMIL. If he say so, may his pernicious soul   155
Rot half a grain a day! He lies to the heart.
She was too fond of her most filthy bargain.
OTH. Ha!
EMIL. Do thy worst.
This deed of thine is no more worthy Heaven   160
Than thou wast worthy her.
OTH.   Peace, you were best.
EMIL. Thou hast not half that power to do me
  harm
As I have to be hurt. O gull!° O dolt!°
As ignorant as dirt! Thou hast done a deed ——
I care not for thy sword, I'll make thee known,   165
Though I lost twenty lives. Help! Help, ho! Help!
The Moor hath killed my mistress! Murder! Murder!

[*Enter* MONTANO, GRATIANO, IAGO, *and others.*]
MON. What is the matter? How now, General!
EMIL. Oh, are you come, Iago? You have done
  well,
That men must lay their murders on your neck.   170
GRA. What is the matter?
EMIL. Disprove this villain, if thou be'st a man.
He says thou told'st him that his wife was false.
I know thou didst not, thou'rt not such a villain.
Speak, for my heart is full.   175
IAGO. I told him what I thought, and told no more
Than what he found himself was apt° and true.
EMIL. But did you ever tell him she was false?
IAGO. I did.
EMIL. You told a lie, an odious, damnèd lie,   180
Upon my soul, a lie, a wicked lie!
She false with Cassio! Did you say with Cassio?
IAGO. With Cassio, mistress. Go to, charm your
  tongue.°
EMIL. I will not charm my tongue, I am bound to
  speak.
My mistress here lies murdered in her bed.   185
ALL. Oh, Heavens forfend!
EMIL. And your reports have set the murder on.
OTH. Nay, stare not, masters. It is true indeed.
GRA. 'Tis a strange truth.
MON. Oh, monstrous act!
EMIL.   Villainy, villainy, villainy!   190
I think upon 't. I think I smell 't. Oh, villainy!
I thought so then.° I'll kill myself for grief.
Oh, villainy, villainy!
IAGO. What, are you mad? I charge you, get you
  home.
EMIL. Good gentlemen, let me have leave to
  speak.   195
'Tis proper I obey him, but not now.
Perchance, Iago, I will ne'er go home.
OTH. Oh! Oh! Oh!   [*Falling on the bed.*]
EMIL.   Nay, lay thee down and roar,
For thou hast killed the sweetest innocent
That e'er did lift up eye.
OTH.   [*Rising*] Oh, she was foul!   200
I scarce did know you, Uncle. There lies your niece,
Whose breath indeed these hands have newly
  stopped.
I know this act shows horrible and grim.
GRA. Poor Desdemona! I am glad thy father's
  dead.
Thy match was mortal° to him, and pure grief   205
Shore his old thread in twain.° Did he live now,
This sight would make him do a desperate turn ——
Yea, curse his better angel from his side,

177. apt: likely.   183. charm . . . tongue: be silent.   192. I . . .
then: i.e., I suspected this earlier — as for example when Iago
took the handkerchief. See III.iii.313.   205. match . . . mortal:
i.e., grief at this marriage killed him.   206. Shore . . . twain:
cut his thread of life in two.

132. folly: lewdness.   145. chrysolite: a semiprecious stone,
usually green in color.   150. iteration: repetition.   163. gull:
dupe. dolt: dull-witted ass.

And fall to reprobation.°

OTH. 'Tis pitiful, but yet Iago knows   210
That she with Cassio hath the act of shame
A thousand times committed. Cassio confessed it.
And she did gratify his amorous works
With that recognizance° and pledge of love
Which I first gave her, I saw it in his hand.   215
It was a handkerchief, an antique token
My father gave my mother.

EMIL. Oh, Heaven! Oh, heavenly powers!

IAGO. 'Zounds! Hold your peace.

EMIL.   'Twill out, 'twill out. I peace!
No, I will speak as liberal as the north.°   220
Let Heaven and men and devils, let them all,
All, all, cry shame against me, yet I'll speak.

IAGO. Be wise, and get you home.

EMIL.   I will not. [IAGO *offers to stab* EMILIA.]

GRA.   Fie!
Your sword upon a woman!

EMIL. O thou dull Moor! That handkerchief thou
speak'st of   225
I found by fortune and did give my husband,
For often with a solemn earnestness,
More than indeed belonged to such a trifle,
He begged of me to steal it.

IAGO.   Villainous whore!

EMIL. She give it Cassio! No, alas, I found it,   230
And I did give 't my husband.

IAGO.   Filth, thou liest!

EMIL. By Heaven, I do not, I do not, gentlemen.
Oh, murderous coxcomb!° What should such a fool
Do with so good a wife?

OTH.   Are there no stones° in Heaven
But what serve for the thunder? Precious villain!
           [*He runs at* IAGO. IAGO, *from behind,*
                 stabs EMILIA, *and exit.*]

GRA. The woman falls. Sure, he hath killed his
wife.   236

EMIL. Aye, aye. Oh, lay me by my mistress' side.

GRA. He's gone, but his wife's killed.

MON. 'Tis a notorious villain. Take you this
weapon,
Which I have here recovered from the Moor.   240
Come, guard the door without, let him not pass,
But kill him rather. I'll after that same villain,
For 'tis a damnèd slave.
           [*Exeunt all but* OTHELLO *and* EMILIA.]

OTH.   I am not valiant neither.
But every puny whipster° gets my sword.
But why should honor outlive honesty?   245
Let it go all.

EMIL.   What did thy song bode, lady?
Hark, canst thou hear me? I will play the swan,

And die in music.° [*Singing*]
     " Willow, willow, willow."
Moor, she was chaste. She loved thee, cruel Moor,
So come my soul to bliss as I speak true.   250
So speaking as I think, I die, I die.   [*Dies.*]

OTH. I have another weapon in this chamber.
It is a sword of Spain,° the ice brook's temper.° —
Oh, here it is. Uncle, I must come forth.

GRA. [*Within*] If thou attempt it, it will cost thee
dear.   255
Thou hast no weapon, and perforce must suffer.

OTH. Look in upon me then, and speak with me,
Or, naked° as I am, I will assault thee.
           [*Re-enter* GRATIANO.]

GRA. What is the matter?

OTH.   Behold, I have a weapon,
A better never did itself sustain   260
Upon a soldier's thigh. I have seen the day
That with this little arm and this good sword
I have made my way through more impediments
Than twenty times your stop. But, oh, vain boast!
Who can control his fate? 'Tis not so now.   265
Be not afraid, though you do see me weaponed.
Here is my journey's end, here is my butt°
And very sea mark of my utmost sail.°
Do you go back dismayed? 'Tis a lost fear.
Man but a rush° against Othello's breast,   270
And he retires. Where should Othello go?
Now, how dost thou look now? O ill-starred wench!
Pale as thy smock! When we shall meet at compt,°
This look of thine will hurl my soul from Heaven
And fiends will snatch at it. Cold, cold, my girl!
Even like thy chastity. Oh, cursèd slave!   276
Whip me, ye devils,
From the possession of this heavenly sight!
Blow me about in winds! Roast me in sulphur!
Wash me in steep-down gulfs° of liquid fire!   280
O Desdemona! Desdemona! Dead!
Oh! Oh! Oh!
     [*Enter* LODOVICO, MONTANO, CASSIO *carried in a chair,*
         and OFFICERS *with* IAGO, *prisoner.*]

LOD. Where is this rash and most unfortunate
man?

OTH. That's he that was Othello. Here I am.

LOD. Where is that viper? Bring the villain forth.

OTH. I look down toward his feet,° but that's a
fable.   286

247–48. play . . . music: i.e., I will sing at my death. It was believed that swans sang once only, just before they died. **253. sword of Spain:** Spanish swords and rapiers, from Toledo or Bilbao, were famous. **ice . . . temper:** hardened in ice-cold water. **258. naked:** unarmed. **267. butt:** aim. **268. And . . . sail:** the mark that I have reached the end of my voyage. **sea mark:** a conspicuous object by which the mariner checks his course. **270. Man . . . rush:** attack with only a reed. **273. compt:** account; i.e., the Day of Judgment. **280. steep-down gulfs:** sheer whirlpools. **286. toward . . . feet:** i.e., to see if he has the cloven hoof of a devil.

---

209. reprobation: damnation; i.e., by self-murder.   214. recognizance: badge, token.   220. liberal . . . north: as freely as the north wind, which is loud and bitter.   233. coxcomb: conceited fool.   234. stones: thunderbolts.   244. whipster: whippersnapper.

If that thou be'st a devil,° I cannot kill thee.

                                   [*Wounds* IAGO.]

LOD. Wrench his sword from him.

IAGO.   I bleed, sir, but not killed.

OTH. I am not sorry neither. I'd have thee live,

For, in my sense, 'tis happiness to die.   290

LOD. O thou Othello, that wert once so good,

Fall'n in the practice° of a damnèd slave,

What shall be said to thee?

OTH.   Why, anything.

An honorable murderer, if you will,

For naught did I in hate, but all in honor.   295

LOD. This wretch hath part confessed his villainy.

Did you and he consent in Cassio's death?

OTH. Aye.

CAS. Dear General, I never gave you cause.

OTH. I do believe it, and I ask your pardon.   300

Will you, I pray, demand that demidevil

Why he hath thus ensnared my soul and body?

IAGO. Demand me nothing. What you know, you

     know.

From this time forth I never will speak word.

LOD. What, not to pray?

GRA.   Torments will ope your lips.   305

OTH. Well, thou dost best.

LOD. Sir, you shall understand what hath befall'n,

Which, as I think, you know not. Here is a letter

Found in the pocket of the slain Roderigo,

And here another. The one of them imports   310

The death of Cassio to be undertook

By Roderigo.

OTH. Oh, villain!

CAS.   Most heathenish and most gross!

LOD. Now here's another discontented paper,

Found in his pocket too. And this, it seems,   315

Roderigo meant to have sent this damnèd villain

But that, belike, Iago in the interim

Came in and satisfied him.

OTH.   Oh, the pernicious caitiff!

How came you, Cassio, by that handkerchief

That was my wife's?

CAS.   I found it in my chamber.   320

And he himself confessed but even now

That there he dropped it for a special purpose

Which wrought to his desire.

OTH.   O fool! Fool! Fool!

CAS. There is besides in Roderigo's letter

How he upbraids Iago, that he made him   325

Brave° me upon the watch, whereon it came

That I was cast.° And even but now he spake

After long seeming dead, Iago hurt him,

Iago set him on.

LOD. You must forsake this room, and go with us.

Your power and your command is taken off,   331

And Cassio rules in Cyprus. For this slave,

If there be any cunning cruelty

That can torment him much and hold him long,°

It shall be his. You shall close prisoner rest   335

Till that the nature of your fault be known

To the Venetian state. Come, bring away.

OTH. Soft you,° a word or two before you go.

I have done the state some service, and they know 't.

No more of that. I pray you, in your letters,   340

When you shall these unlucky deeds relate,

Speak of me as I am, nothing extenuate,

Nor set down aught in malice. Then must you speak

Of one that loved not wisely but too well,

Of one not easily jealous, but, being wrought,   345

Perplexed in the extreme, of one whose hand,

Like the base Indian, threw a pearl away

Richer than all his tribe° — of one whose subdued

     eyes,

Albeit unusèd to the melting mood,

Drop tears as fast as the Arabian trees   350

Their medicinal gum. Set you down this,

And say besides that in Aleppo once,

Where a malignant and a turbaned Turk

Beat a Venetian and traduced° the state,

I took by the throat the circumcisèd dog   355

And smote him, thus.   [*Stabs himself.*]

LOD. Oh, bloody period!

GRA.   All that's spoke is marred.°

OTH. I kissed thee ere I killed thee. No way but

     this,

Killing myself, to die upon a kiss.

                  [*Falls on the bed, and dies.*]

CAS. This did I fear, but thought he had no

     weapon.   360

For he was great of heart.

LOD.   [*To* IAGO] O Spartan° dog,

More fell° than anguish, hunger, or the sea!

Look on the tragic loading° of this bed,

This is thy work. The object poisons sight,

Let it be hid.° Gratiano, keep the house,   365

And seize upon the fortunes of the Moor,

For they succeed on you. To you, Lord Governor,

Remains the censure of this hellish villain,

The time, the place, the torture.

Oh, enforce it!

Myself will straight aboard, and to the state   370

This heavy act with heavy heart relate.   [*Exeunt.*]

---

287. It . . . devil: if you are an evil spirit and no man.   292. Fall'n
. . . practice: destroyed by the plotting.   326. Brave: dare, insult.   327. cast: dismissed.

334. hold . . . long: i.e., in dying.   338. Soft you: pause awhile.
347–48. base . . . tribe: A much discussed passage. F1 reads
"Iudean" (Judean), and if correct it would refer to Judas Iscariot, who betrayed Jesus. Shakespeare does not elsewhere use
the word "Judean," and he does associate India with pearls, as
in *Tr & Cr*, I.i.105: "Her bed is India, There she lies a pearl."
354. traduced: insulted.   357. marred: spoiled.   361. Spartan:
i.e., hardhearted.   362. fell: cruel.   363. loading: burden — the
bodies of Desdemona and Othello.   365. Let . . . hid: At these
words the curtains are closed across the inner stage (or chamber, if
this scene was acted aloft), concealing all three bodies. See Pl. 5b.

MEASURE FOR MEASURE

Introduction

Measure for Measure was played before the Court of King James I on December 26, 1604. Apart from this one fact recorded in the Revels Accounts [1] nothing is known of the play, but the style suggests that it was then fairly new. It was first printed in the first folio (F1) in 1623, where the text omits some essential stage direction and contains many corrupt lines and wrong line divisions. There are also a number of passages of indifferent writing which may be the work of a second hand.

The nearest parallel to the story of the play in Elizabethan times occurs in a dramatic piece called *Promos and Cassandra* written by George Whetstone and published in 1578. Four years later Whetstone published a prose version of the story in a collection called *The Heptameron of Civil Discourses*. The outline of the story is as follows:

In Julio in Hungary, Lord Promos revived an old law by which incontinence was punished by the death of the man and the perpetual shame of the woman. As a result a young gentleman called Andrugio was condemned to death. His sister, Cassandra, thereupon petitioned Lord Promos to pardon her brother. Promos was so much delighted with her beauty and conversation that he reprieved Andrugio, but after a while his liking changed to lust and he demanded that she should ransom her brother by sacrificing her honor. Cassandra, won over by her brother's pleading, reluctantly agreed on the condition that Promos should then pardon her brother and marry her. Promos promised to abide by these conditions, but as soon as he had satisfied his will he commanded the jailer to present Cassandra with her brother's head. The jailer, however, befriended Andrugio and instead brought to Cassandra the head of a newly executed felon, and then set Andrugio free. Cassandra thereupon complained to the King, who hastened to do justice on Promos. He commanded that Promos should marry Cassandra and forthwith be beheaded, but no sooner had the marriage been solemnized than Cassandra begged the King to spare her new husband. When the King refused, Andrugio, perceiving the grief of his sister, came forward and at the risk of his own life begged the King to be merciful. The King was so greatly moved that he pardoned Andrugio and Promos.

Although the story in its general details resembles the story of the play, it is likely that some other version, possibly one of the many Elizabethan plays now lost, was the actual source of *Measure for Measure*. But even if Shakespeare took his outline from Whetstone, he added Lucio and the affairs of Pompey from his own imagination, and very considerably altered the details and the motivation of the plot.

Measure for Measure is one of Shakespeare's unpleasant plays, and has, on the whole, been roughly treated by the earlier critics, though some modern writers have praised it as a highly moral play on the theme of "judge not that ye be not judged." It is not surprising that critics should disagree, for the play presents a stark problem in human conduct: When a woman is offered the choice of saving a condemned man — her brother, as it happens — at the cost of her own chastity, what should she do? As Shakespeare states the problem there is no simple answer.

The play opens quickly. Vincentio, Duke of Vienna, declares that he is about to travel incognito to Poland. He appoints Angelo to be his Deputy with full powers of life and death, and he disappears. It is not necessarily ironical that the Deputy should be named Angelo, for he is by most recognized standards a good man; he is austere, conscientious, and efficient, and he alone can be trusted to cleanse the morals of Vienna without fear of unpopularity. Angelo immediately begins a long overdue reformation. Brothels are pulled down, and an old fierce law whereby incontinence is punished by death is put into force. One of the offenders against this law is a young gentleman named Claudio who finds himself in prison awaiting execution. Claudio's friends are horrified, especially Lucio. Claudio sees that his only possible chance of reprieve lies in an appeal for mercy. So he sends Lucio to fetch his sister Isabella to plead with Deputy Angelo.

Isabella is a proper match for Angelo. She too is austere and cold-blooded. Indeed, when Lucio

---

[1] I.e., the sums expended on entertainment for the Court.

calls upon her she is about to take her vows as a nun and is complaining that the rules of the order are not strict enough. Nevertheless, she consents to plead for her brother and with Lucio she goes to the Deputy. Her appeal is so eloquent and moving that it has the most unexpected and devastating result. Suddenly the old restraint snaps, and Angelo in a moment is mad to commit that very offense which he has spent his life in suppressing. He becomes raging with desire for Isabella. So he tells her to come again. When she returns he makes her the monstrous proposal that he will pardon Claudio at the price of her yielding to his will. Naturally Isabella is shocked, but she is not frightened, for, as she reflects, her brother, being an honorable young man, will naturally prefer to die to save her honor.

All this, with the comic business of the disreputable but ever cheerful Pompey, takes up the first two acts. Meanwhile the Duke, instead of going to Poland, has disguised himself as a friar and is watching events. In this guise he is allowed to enter the jail to minister to the prisoners. The third act opens in the prison with the supposed friar exhorting Claudio not to be afraid of death, with the result that Claudio is in the right frame of mind to die cheerfully when Isabella enters to tell him of her conversation with the Deputy. At first she says that there is no hope of reprieve, but when she goes on to repeat Angelo's offer and to say complacently that she would gladly give her life for her brother, there comes over the wretched Claudio an appalling horror of death, and he pleads with his sister to save his life at Angelo's price. Thus twice disillusioned by the faithlessness of man, Isabella turns from him with fury and loathing. Here is the problem fairly and freely stated — since Angelo will grant mercy on no other terms, which is to be sacrificed, Claudio's life or Isabella's honor?

Much of the irritation which critics feel with *Measure for Measure* is caused by Shakespeare's refusal either to give an answer to the question or to present the case sentimentally. There is no clear line between black and white. Angelo is neither ruffian nor seducer, but a man caught by the wildest, fiercest, most irrational, and most irresistible passion. In his sane moments he is the man of the highest principles. Nor is Isabella a warmhearted, generous, self-sacrificing heroine; she is hard, cold, and self-righteous, for it requires no exalted nobility to preserve her own honor at the cost of her brother's life. Nor is Claudio, from what we see of him, particularly worth saving. The trouble is that Shakespeare has made his characters human beings and not idealized types.

At this point in the play Angelo, Isabella, and Claudio are in such a tangle that for each of them disaster seems inevitable; but thereafter instead of making his story a tragedy of human frailties, Shakespeare changes the whole direction of the play and converts it into a thriller of the conventional type. The problem ceases to be one of ethics and becomes one of plot: how to save Claudio, reward Isabella, cheat Angelo, and bring a happy ending to all.

The disguised Duke now takes charge. As it happened, there was another lady in the case. Five years earlier Angelo had been betrothed to Mariana of the moated grange, but her dowry was lost in a shipwreck, and he in a most ungentlemanly manner repudiated the bargain. Yet in spite of all she still loves him. So the Duke proposes that Isabella shall pretend to agree to Angelo's condition, but that they shall meet in some dark spot where Mariana shall take her place. And this is done. To most moderns the solution is distasteful and hardly creditable to the two women or the supposed friar. It would not, however, have shocked Shakespeare's audience. According to accepted notions, Mariana had a moral if not a legal claim on Angelo as her husband (see Gen. Intro. p. 20a). Moreover, marriage included certain obligations on each party which Shakespeare elsewhere calls "bedright." If Angelo refused Mariana her rights as a wife, she was justified in obtaining them by trickery.

Once Angelo has, as he thinks, seduced Isabella, he suffers the natural and inevitable reaction, which is itself as fierce as the original passion. He now loathes himself and loathes Isabella so bitterly that instead of pardoning Claudio as he had promised, he sends an order that Claudio shall instantly be beheaded, and further, that there may be no doubt in his own mind, he commands the head to be sent to him. All this the disguised Duke learns during his visit to the prison.

Here is an unexpected turn. The Duke first suggests that the head of Barnardine, who is awaiting execution, shall be shaved and otherwise disguised and substituted for Claudio's. But Barnardine thwarts this plan by refusing to be beheaded. However, by good luck another prisoner has just died, and by further good luck his head is not unlike Claudio's. So the head is dispatched to Angelo and passes the inspection. The play must now be wound up.

The Duke sends a message announcing his return to Vienna and commands that all petitioners with a grievance shall attend him. He appears without his disguise and is greeted by Angelo and the rest. The two women come forward and accuse Angelo, who replies that either they are mad or else are the tools of some plotter. Thereupon the Duke leaves Angelo to try the case and withdraws to return a few moments later in his friar's disguise. The " friar " is closely questioned and ordered to be sent to prison, but in the scuffle his cowl is pulled off and he is revealed as Angelo's Prince. Angelo thus stands convicted and can only confess his guilt. There remains the passing of judgments. The Duke declares that Angelo must legally marry Mariana forthwith and after due penitence be forgiven. Lucio, who has made some very slanderous observations on the Duke, is condemned to whipping and to marrying a prostitute. Claudio is forgiven and told to marry his mistress. And as for Isabella, the Duke decides to make her his own wife. The ending, to say the least, is more symmetrical than convincing.

It is not, however, necessarily a blemish in a play, especially an Elizabethan play, that the story should be improbable. Few of Shakespeare's comedies could possibly have happened in real life, but usually no one takes the stories too seriously, because they never touch the deeper levels of emotion. This play in its earlier and middle scenes has been too powerful. Emotions have been so painfully stirred by the central problem that the critical instincts demand an answer. A profound moral issue has been stated, and we are not to be satisfied by a series of plots and stratagems, no matter how ingenious.

Measure for Measure indeed is marred by a certain confusion of purpose. Shakespeare the working playwright wished to provide his company with a new play on an old theme. It was a familiar story, with the commonest tricks of the theater: disguises, surprises, distressed virgins, thwarted seducers, and a happy ending. But Shakespeare the expert in humanity took charge. He treated his puppets seriously, and he made them human, with the result that the soul of the play became too great for its body.

Measure for Measure

DRAMATIS PERSONAE

VINCENTIO, *the Duke*
ANGELO, *Deputy*
ESCALUS, *an ancient lord*
CLAUDIO, *a young gentleman*
LUCIO, *a fantastic*
TWO OTHER GENTLEMEN
PROVOST
THOMAS }
PETER } *two friars*
A JUSTICE
VARRIUS
ELBOW, *a simple constable*
FROTH, *a foolish gentleman*

POMPEY, *servant to Mistress Overdone*
ABHORSON, *an executioner*
BARNARDINE, *a dissolute prisoner*

ISABELLA, *sister to Claudio*
MARIANA, *betrothed to Angelo*
JULIET, *beloved of Claudio*
FRANCISCA, *a nun*
MISTRESS OVERDONE, *a bawd*

LORDS, OFFICERS, CITIZENS, BOY, *and* ATTENDANTS

SCENE — *Vienna.*

Act I

SCENE I. *An apartment in the* DUKE'S *palace.*

[*Enter* DUKE, ESCALUS, LORDS *and* ATTENDANTS.]
DUKE. Escalus.
ESCAL. My lord.
DUKE. Of government the properties to unfold
Would seem in me to affect speech and discourse,°
Since I am put° to know that your own science° 5
Exceeds, in that, the lists° of all advice
My strength can give you. Then no more remains,
But that to your sufficiency, as your worth is able,°
And let them work. The nature of our people, 10
Our city's institutions, and the terms°
For common justice, you're as pregnant° in
As art and practice hath enriched any
That we remember. There is our commission,°
From which we would not have you warp.° Call
     hither, 15
I say, bid come before us Angelo.
                         [*Exit an* ATTENDANT.]
What figure° of us think you he will bear?
For you must know, we have with special soul
Elected him our absence to supply,°
Lent him our terror, dressed him with our love, 20
And given his deputation° all the organs°
Of our own power. What think you of it?

Act I, Sc. i: 3-4. Of . . . discourse: i.e., for me to tell you
about the principles (*properties*) of governing would seem to be
mere desire to make a speech. 5. put: made. science: expert
knowledge. 6. lists: limits. 9. But . . . able: A sentence
seems to have been omitted between "sufficiency" and "able."
11. terms: periods when the courts sit. 12. pregnant: expert.
14. commission: formal document setting out in detail the duties
of his appointment. 15. warp: deviate. 17. figure: likeness.
19. our . . . supply: to fill up our place when absent. 21. deputation: appointment to act as my deputy. organs: instruments.

ESCAL. If any in Vienna be of worth
To undergo such ample grace and honor,
It is Lord Angelo.
     DUKE.   Look where he comes. 25
                         [*Enter* ANGELO.]
     ANG. Always obedient to your Grace's will,
I come to know your pleasure.
     DUKE.   Angelo,
There is a kind of character° in thy life,
That to th' observer doth thy history
Fully unfold. Thyself and thy belongings 30
Are not thine own so proper as to waste
Thyself upon thy virtues, they on thee.°
Heaven doth with us as we with torches do,
Not light them for themselves; for if our virtues
Did not go forth of us, 'twere all alike 35
As if we had them not. Spirits are not finely
     touched°
But to fine issues, nor Nature never lends
The smallest scruple° of her excellence
But, like a thrifty goddess, she determines
Herself the glory of a creditor, 40
Both thanks and use. But I do bend my speech
To one that can my part in him advértise.°
Hold° therefore, Angelo. —
In our remove° be thou at full ourself.
Mortality° and mercy in Vienna 45
Live in thy tongue and heart. Old Escalus,
Though first in question, is thy secondary.°
Take thy commission.
     ANG.   Now, good my lord,

28. character: stamp, impression. 30-32. Thyself . . . thee:
i.e., your good qualities are not your own private property to be
wasted on yourself. 36. touched: tested. 38. scruple: minute
part. 42. my . . . advertise: teach me how to govern. 43. Hold:
observe, remember. 44. remove: absence. 45. Mortality:
power to condemn to death. 47. Though . . . secondary: though
first summoned, is your subordinate.

Let there be some more test made of my metal°
Before so noble and so great a figure   50
Be stamped upon it.
   DUKE.   No more evasion.
We have with a leavened° and preparèd choice
Proceeded to you, therefore take your honors.
Our haste from hence is of so quick condition
That it prefers itself,° and leaves unquestioned°   55
Matters of needful value. We shall write to you,
As time and our concernings shall impórtune,
How it goes with us, and do look to know
What doth befall you here. So fare you well.
To the hopeful execution do I leave you   60
Of your commissions.
   ANG.   Yet give leave, my lord,
That we may bring you something on the way.
   DUKE. My haste may not admit it,
Nor need you, on mine honor, have to do
With any scruple.° Your scope is as mine own,   65
So to enforce or qualify the laws
As to your soul seems good. Give me your hand.
I'll privily away. I love the people,
But do not like to stage me to their eyes.
Though it do well, I do not relish well   70
Their loud applause and Aves vehement,°
Nor do I think the man of safe discretion
That does affect° it. Once more, fare you well.
   ANG. The Heavens give safety to your purposes!
   ESCAL. Lead forth and bring you back in happi-
    ness!   75
   DUKE. I thank you. Fare you well.   [*Exit.*]
   ESCAL. I shall desire you, sir, to give me leave
To have free speech with you, and it concerns me
To look into the bottom of° my place.
A power I have, but of what strength and nature   80
I am not yet instructed.
   ANG. 'Tis so with me. Let us withdraw together,
And we may soon our satisfaction have
Touching that point.
   ESCAL.   I'll wait upon your Honor.
                 [*Exeunt.*]

SCENE II. *A street.*

[*Enter* LUCIO *and two* GENTLEMEN.]
   LUCIO. If the Duke, with the other dukes, come
not to composition° with the King of Hungary, why
then all the dukes fall upon the King.

   1. GENT. Heaven grant us its peace, but not the
King of Hungary's!   5
   2. GENT. Amen.
   LUCIO. Thou concludest like the sanctimonious pirate that went to sea with the Ten Commandments,
but scraped one out of the table.
   2. GENT. " Thou shalt not steal? "   10
   LUCIO. Aye, that he razed.
   1. GENT. Why, 'twas a commandment to command
the captain and all the rest from their functions.°
They put forth to steal. There's not a soldier of us
all that in the thanksgiving before meat do relish
the petition well that prays for peace.
   2. GENT. I never heard any soldier dislike it.
   LUCIO. I believe thee, for I think thou never wast
where grace was said.   20
   2. GENT. No? A dozen times at least.
   1. GENT. What, in meter?
   LUCIO. In any proportion° or in any language.
   1. GENT. I think or in any religion.
   LUCIO. Aye, why not? Grace is grace,° despite   25
of all controversy. As, for example, thou thyself art
a wicked villain, despite of all grace.
   1. GENT. Well, there went but a pair of shears between us.°
   LUCIO. I grant, as there may between the lists°
and the velvet. Thou art the list.   31
   1. GENT. And thou the velvet. Thou art good velvet, thou'rt a three-piled° piece, I warrant thee. I had
as lief be a list of an English kersey° as be piled as
thou art piled, for a French velvet. Do I speak feel-
ingly° now?   36
   LUCIO. I think thou dost, and indeed with most
painful feeling of thy speech I will, out of thine
own confession, learn to begin thy health, but whilst
I live forget to drink after thee.   40
   1. GENT. I think I have done myself wrong, have
I not?
   2. GENT. Yes, that thou hast, whether thou art
tainted or free.
           [*Enter* MISTRESS OVERDONE.]
   LUCIO. Behold, behold, where Madam Mitigation
comes! I have purchased as many diseases under   46
her roof as come to ——
   2. GENT. To what, I pray?
   LUCIO. Judge.
   2. GENT. To three thousand dolors° a year.   50
   1. GENT. Aye, and more.
   LUCIO. A French crown° more.

49. **metal:** mettle; i.e., material, worth. "Mettle" and "metal" were the same word in Shakespeare's time. 52. **leavened:** allowed to work like leaven; i.e., mature consideration. 55. **prefers itself:** takes precedence. **unquestioned:** undiscussed. 64–65. **have . . . scruple:** i.e., hesitate to use your power to the full. 68–71. **I . . . vehement:** a tactful compliment to King James I, who (unlike Queen Elizabeth) disliked cheering crowds. **Aves:** salutations. 73. **affect:** desire. 79. **look . . . of:** examine carefully.
   Sc. ii: 2. **composition:** agreement.

13. **from . . . functions:** to forbid them to fulfill their tasks. 23. **proportion:** meter. 25. **Grace is grace:** with a pun on grace, meaning holy life. 28–29. **there . . . us:** i.e., we were cut from the same piece. 30. **lists:** the outer edge or selvage, which is made of plain material. 33. **three-piled:** i.e., thick velvet of the best quality, with a pun on piled, meaning made bald as a result of the French (venereal) disease. 34. **kersey:** thick woolen cloth. 36. **feelingly:** i.e., to make you feel pain. 50. **dolors:** with a pun on dollars. 52. **French crown:** the same joke as in ll. 32–34 above.

1. GENT. Thou art always figuring° diseases in me, but thou art full of error. I am sound.

LUCIO. Nay, not as one would say healthy, 55 but so sound as things that are hollow. Thy bones are hollow, impiety has made a feast of thee.

1. GENT. How now! Which of your hips has the most profound sciatica? 60

MRS. OV. Well, well, there's one yonder arrested and carried to prison was worth five thousand of you all.

2. GENT. Who's that, I pray thee?

MRS. OV. Marry,° sir, that's Claudio, Signior Claudio. 66

1. GENT. Claudio to prison? 'Tis not so.

MRS. OV. Nay, but I know 'tis so. I saw him arrested, saw him carried away, and, which is more, within these three days his head to be chopped off.

LUCIO. But after all this fooling, I would not have it so. Art thou sure of this? 72

MRS. OV. I am too sure of it. And it is for getting Madam Julietta with child.

LUCIO. Believe me, this may be. He promised 75 to meet me two hours since, and he was ever precise in promise-keeping.

2. GENT. Besides, you know, it draws something near to the speech we had to such a purpose. 79

1. GENT. But most of all, agreeing with the proclamation.

LUCIO. Away! Let's go learn the truth of it.

[*Exeunt* LUCIO *and* GENTLEMEN.]

MRS. OV. Thus, what with the war, what with the sweat,° what with the gallows, and what with poverty, I am custom-shrunk.° [*Enter* POMPEY.] 85 How now! What's the news with you?

POM. Yonder man is carried to prison.

MRS. OV. Well, what has he done?

POM. A woman.

MRS. OV. But what's his offense? 90

POM. Groping for trouts in a peculiar° river.

MRS. OV. What, is there a maid with child by him?

POM. No, but there's a woman with maid by him. You have not heard of the proclamation, have you?

MRS. OV. What proclamation, man? 95

POM. All houses° in the suburbs° of Vienna must be plucked down.

MRS. OV. And what shall become of those in the city?

POM. They shall stand for seed. They had 100 gone down too but that a wise burgher put in for them.°

MRS. OV. But shall all our houses of resort in the suburbs be pulled down? 105

POM. To the ground, mistress.

MRS. OV. Why, here's a change indeed in the commonwealth! What shall become of me?

POM. Come, fear not you. Good counselors 110 lack no clients. Though you change your place, you need not change your trade, I'll be your tapster° still. Courage! There will be pity taken on you. You that have worn your eyes almost out in the service, you will be considered. 115

MRS. OV. What's to do here, Thomas Tapster? *POMPEY* Let's withdraw.

POM. Here comes Signior Claudio, led by the Provost° to prison, and there's Madam Juliet.

[*Exeunt.*]

[*Enter* PROVOST, CLAUDIO, JULIET, *and* OFFICERS.°]

CLAUD. Fellow, why dost thou show me thus to the world?
Bear me to prison, where I am committed.

PROV. I do it not in evil disposition,
But from Lord Angelo by special charge.

CLAUD. Thus can the demigod Authority
Make us pay down for our offense by weight° 125
The words of Heaven° — on whom it will, it will;
On whom it will not, so; yet still 'tis just.

[*Re-enter* LUCIO *and two* GENTLEMEN.]

LUCIO. Why, how now, Claudio! Whence comes this restraint?°

CLAUD. From too much liberty, my Lucio, liberty.
As surfeit° is the father of much fast, 130
So every scope° by the immoderate use
Turns to restraint. Our natures do pursue,
Like rats that ravin° down their proper bane,°
A thirsty evil, and when we drink we die.

LUCIO. If I could speak so wisely under an 135 arrest, I would send for certain of my creditors. And yet, to say the truth, I had as lief have the foppery° of freedom as the morality of imprisonment. What's thy offense, Claudio?

CLAUD. What but to speak of would offend again.

LUCIO. What, is 't murder? 141

CLAUD. No.

LUCIO. Lechery?

CLAUD. Call it so.

PROV. Away, sir! You must go. 143

CLAUD. One word, good friend. Lucio, a word with you.

LUCIO. A hundred, if they'll do you any good. Is lechery so looked after?°

---

53. **figuring**: calculating, imagining. 65. **Marry**: Mary, by the Virgin. 84. **sweat**: sweating sickness, a form of the plague. 85. **I . . . custom-shrunk**: my trade is failing. 91. **peculiar**: private. 96. **houses**: brothels. **suburbs**: The most notorious London brothels were located in the suburbs. 101–102. **put . . . them**: made a bid for them.

112. **tapster**: bartender, the waiter who brings the drinks; i.e. pimp. 119. **Provost**: officer of the law. 120 s.d.: At this point the folio marks a new scene. 125. **pay . . . weight**: pay heavily for. 126. **words of Heaven**: possibly a reference to Romans 9: 15–18. "I will have mercy on whom I will have mercy . . . therefore hath He mercy on whom He will have mercy, and whom He will He hardeneth." Here also there seems to be some omission in the text. 128. **restraint**: arrest. 130. **surfeit**: excess. 131. **scope**: liberty. 133. **ravin**: devour greedily. **bane**: poison. 137. **foppery**: folly. 148. **looked after**: seriously regarded.

CLAUD. Thus stands it with me. Upon a true con-
tráct°
I got possession of Julietta's bed.   150
You know the lady. She is fast my wife,
Save that we do the denunciation lack
Of outward order.° This we came not to,
Only for propagation° of a dower
Remaining in the coffer° of her friends,   155
From whom we thought it meet° to hide our love
Till time had made them° for us. But it chances
The stealth of our most mutual entertainment
With character° too gross is writ on Juliet.
   LUCIO. With child, perhaps?
     CLAUD.   Unhappily, even so.   160
And the new Deputy now for the Duke —
Whether it be the fault and glimpse° of newness,
Or whether that the body public be
A horse whereon the governor doth ride,
Who, newly in the seat, that it may know   165
He can command, lets it straight feel the spur —
Whether the tyranny be in his place,
Or in his eminence that fills it up,
I stagger in.° But this new governor
Awakes me all the enrollèd penalties   170
Which have, like unscoured° armor, hung by the
    wall
So long that nineteen zodiacs° have gone round
And none of them been worn; and, for a name,°
Now puts° the drowsy and neglected act
Freshly on me. 'Tis surely for a name.   175
   LUCIO. I warrant it is. And thy head stands so
tickle° on thy shoulders that a milkmaid, if she be
in love, may sigh it off. Send after the Duke, and ap-
peal to him.
   CLAUD. I have done so, but he's not to be found. I
    prithee,   180
Lucio, do me this kind service.
This day my sister should the cloister enter
And there receive her approbation.°
Acquaint her with the danger of my state,
Implore her, in my voice, that she make friends   185
To the strict Deputy, bid herself assay° him.
I have great hope in that, for in her youth
There is a prone° and speechless dialect
Such as move men. Beside, she hath prosperous art
When she will play with reason and discourse,   190
And well she can persuade.
   LUCIO. I pray she may, as well for the encourage-

ment of the like, which else would stand under griev-
ous imposition, as for the enjoying of thy life, who
I would be sorry should be thus foolishly lost at a
game of ticktack.° I'll to her.   196
   CLAUD. I thank you, good friend Lucio.
   LUCIO. Within two hours.
   CLAUD.   Come, officer, away! [*Exeunt.*]

SCENE III. *A monastery.*

[*Enter* DUKE *and* FRIAR THOMAS.]
   DUKE. No, holy Father, throw away that thought,
Believe not that the dribbling dart° of love
Can pierce a complete° bosom. Why I desire thee
To give me secret harbor hath a purpose
More grave and wrinkled° than the aims and ends
Of burning youth.
   FRI. T.   May your Grace speak of it?   6
   DUKE. My holy sir, none better knows than you
How I have ever loved the life removed,°
And held in idle price° to haunt assemblies
Where youth, and cost° and witless bravery° keeps.
I have delivered to Lord Angelo,   11
A man of stricture° and firm abstinence,
My absolute power and place here in Vienna,
And he supposes me traveled to Poland,
For so I have strewed it in the common ear,   15
And so it is received. Now, pious sir,
You will demand of me why I do this.
   FRI. T. Gladly, my lord.
   DUKE. We have strict statutes and most biting
    laws,
The needful bits and curbs to headstrong weeds,°
Which for this fourteen years we have let slip,   21
Even like an o'ergrown lion in a cave,
That goes not out to prey. Now, as fond° fathers,
Having bound up the threatening twigs of birch
Only to stick it in their children's sight   25
For terror, not to use, in time the rod
Becomes more mocked than feared, so our decrees,
Dead to infliction,° to themselves are dead,
And liberty° plucks justice by the nose,
The baby beats the nurse, and quite athwart°   30
Goes all decorum.
   FRI. T.   It rested in° your Grace
To unloose this tied-up justice when you pleased.

149. true contract: betrothal. See Gen. Intro. p. 20a.   152–53. denunciation . . . order: lack formal pronouncement of the marriage ceremony.   154. propagation: increase.   155. coffer: safekeeping; lit., strongbox.   156. meet: fit.   157. made them: i.e.,
our friends, and so approving our marriage.   159. character:
handwriting.   162. fault . . . glimpse: mistaken glamor.
169. stagger in: am uncertain.   171. unscoured: rusty.   172. zo-
diacs: years. See App. 1.   173. name: notable example.
174. puts: applies.   177. tickle: unsteadily.   183. approbation:
novitiate, period of trial.   186. assay: attempt, i.e., to persuade
him.   188. prone: effective.

196. ticktack: lit., a game played on a board with pegs fitted
into holes.   Sc. iii: 2. dribbling dart: arrow feebly shot.   3. complete:
fully protected.   5. wrinkled: i.e., suitable for an experienced man.   8. removed: private.   9. in . . . price: as worthless.   10. cost: extravagance. bravery: ostentation.   12. stric-
ture: strict life.   20. weeds: Theobald's emendation of "steeds"
is preferable.   23. fond: foolish.   28. Dead to infliction: i.e.,
never carried into effect.   29. liberty: license.   30. athwart:
awry, in the wrong direction.   31. rested in: was in the power
of.

And it in you more dreadful would have seemed
Than in Lord Angelo.
  DUKE.   I do fear too dreadful.
Sith° 'twas my fault to give the people scope,   35
'Twould be my tyranny to strike and gall them
For what I bid them do. For we bid this be done
When evil deeds have their permissive pass,°
And not the punishment. Therefore indeed, my
    father,
I have on Angelo imposed the office,   40
Who may, in the ambush° of my name, strike
    home,
And yet my nature never in the fight
To do in slander.° And to behold his sway,
I will, as 'twere a brother of your order,
Visit both prince and people, therefore I prithee 45
Supply me with the habit,° and instruct me
How I may formally in person bear me
Like a true friar.° Moe° reasons for this action
At our more leisure shall I render you,
Only, this one: <u>Lord Angelo is precise,</u>   50
<u>Stands at a guard with envy,° scarce confesses</u>
<u>That his blood flows or that his appetite</u>
<u>Is more to bread than stone. Hence shall we see,</u>
<u>If power change purpose, what our seemers be.°</u>
                              [*Exeunt.*]

SCENE IV. *A nunnery.*

[*Enter* ISABELLA *and* FRANCISCA.]
  ISAB. And have you nuns no farther privileges?
  FRAN. Are not these large enough?
  ISAB. Yes, truly. I speak not as desiring more,
But rather wishing a more strict restraint   4
Upon the sisterhood, the votarists° of Saint Clare.°
  LUCIO. [*Within*] Ho! Peace be in this place!
  ISAB.   Who's that which calls?
  FRAN. It is a man's voice. Gentle Isabella,
Turn you the key,° and know his business of him.
You may, I may not, you are yet unsworn.
When you have vowed, you must not speak with
    men   10
But in the presence of the prioress.
Then, if you speak, you must not show your face,
Of if you show your face, you must not speak.
He calls again. I pray you answer him.   [*Exit.*]

35. Sith: since.   **38. permissive pass:** permission to pass.
41. in ... ambush: under the cover.   **42–43. And ... slander:**
and yet never in the fray bring slander on my name.   **46. habit:**
garment.   **47–48. formally ... friar:** accurately impersonate a
real friar.   **48. Moe:** more.   **51. Stands ... envy:** is on his
guard against malice.   **54. If ... be:** i.e., if power changes his
nature from what it seems to be.
    Sc. iv: 5. votarists: nuns. **Saint Clare:** The order of St. Clare
of Assisi was founded in 1212. The nuns followed strict rules,
and gave themselves to meditation and educating the young.
8. Turn ... key: unlock the door.

ISAB. Peace and prosperity! Who is 't that calls?
                  [*Enter* LUCIO.]
  LUCIO. Hail, virgin, if you be, as those cheek roses
Proclaim you are no less! Can you so stead° me 17
As bring me to the sight of Isabella,
A novice of this place, and the fair sister
To her unhappy brother Claudio?   20
  ISAB. Why " her unhappy brother "? Let me ask
The rather, for I now must make you know
I am that Isabella and his sister.
  LUCIO. Gentle and fair, your brother kindly greets
    you.
Not to be weary° with you, he's in prison.   25
  ISAB. Woe me! For what?
  LUCIO. For that which, if myself might be his
    judge,
He should receive his punishment in thanks.
He hath got his friend° with child.
  ISAB. Sir, make me not your story.°
  LUCIO.   It is true. 30
I would not — though 'tis my familiar sin
With maids to seem the lapwing,° and to jest,
Tongue far from heart — play with all virgins so.
I hold you as a thing enskied° and sainted,
By your renouncement, an immortal spirit,   35
And to be talked with in sincerity,
As with a saint.
  ISAB. You do blaspheme the good in mocking
    me.
  LUCIO. Do not believe it. Fewness° and truth, 'tis
    thus:
Your brother and his lover have embraced.   40
As those that feed grow full — as blossoming time,
That from the seedness° the bare fallow brings
To teeming foison° — even so her plenteous womb
Expresseth his full tilth and husbandry.
  ISAB. Someone with child by him? — My cousin
    Juliet?   45
  LUCIO. Is she your cousin?
  ISAB. Adoptedly, as school maids change their
    names
By vain, though apt, affection.
  LUCIO.   She it is.
  ISAB. Oh, let him marry her.
  LUCIO.   This is the point.
The Duke is very strangely gone from hence,   50
Bore many gentlemen, myself being one,
In hand, and hope of action.° But we do learn
By those that know the very nerves° of state,
His givings-out were of an infinite distance

17. stead: help.   **25. weary:** wearisome.   **29. friend:** mistress.
30. story: theme for jest.   **32. lapwing:** a bird which leads
intruders away from its nest by pretending to be injured; so
deceiver.   **34. enskied:** heavenly.   **39. Fewness:** briefly.
42. seedness: sowing.   **43. foison:** plenty.   **51–52. Bore ...
action:** deluded (*bore in hand*) many, including me, that we were
going to war (*action*); i.e., in which Lucio would have served as
an officer.   **53. nerves:** sinews.

From his true-meant design.° Upon his place,   55
And with full line of his authority,
Governs Lord Angelo, a man whose blood
Is very snow broth, one who never feels
The wanton stings and motions of the sense,
But doth rebate° and blunt his natural edge   60
With profits of the mind, study and fast.
He — to give fear to use and liberty,°
Which have for long run by° the hideous law,
As mice by lions — hath picked out an act
Under whose heavy sense° your brother's life   65
Falls into forfeit. He arrests him on it,
And follows close the rigor of the statute,
To make him an example. All hope is gone
Unless you have the grace by your fair prayer
To soften Angelo. And that's my pith of° business
'Twixt you and your poor brother.   71
     ISAB. Doth he so seek his life?
     LUCIO.   Has censured° him
Already, and, as I hear, the Provost hath
A warrant for his execution.
     ISAB. Alas! What poor ability's in me   75
To do him good?
     LUCIO.   Assay the power you have.
     ISAB. My power? Alas, I doubt——
     LUCIO.   Our doubts are traitors,
And make us lose the good we oft might win
By fearing to attempt. Go to Lord Angelo,
And let him learn to know when maidens sue,   80
Men give like gods, but when they weep and kneel,
All their petitions are as freely theirs
As they themselves would owe them.°
     ISAB. I'll see what I can do.
     LUCIO.   But speedily.
     ISAB. I will about it straight,   85
No longer staying but to give the Mother
Notice of my affair. I humbly thank you.
Commend me to my brother. Soon at night
I'll send him certain word of my success.
     LUCIO. I take my leave of you.   89
     ISAB.   Good sir, adieu. [*Exeunt.*]

Act II

SCENE I. *A hall in* ANGELO's *house.*

[*Enter* ANGELO, ESCALUS, *and a* JUSTICE, PROVOST,
OFFICERS, *and other* ATTENDANTS, *behind.*]
     ANG. We must not make a scarecrow of the law,
Setting it up to fear° the birds of prey,

And let it keep one shape till custom make it
Their perch, and not their terror.
     ESCAL.   Aye, but yet
Let us be keen, and rather cut a little   5
Than fall,° and bruise to death. Alas, this gentle-
     man,
Whom I would save, had a most noble father!
Let but your Honor know,
Whom I believe to be most strait in virtue,
That in the working of your own affections,   10
Had time cohered° with place or place with wish-
     ing,
Or that the resolute acting of your blood
Could have attained the effect of your own purpose,
Whether you had not sometime in your life
Erred in this point which now you censure him,   15
And pulled the law upon you.
     ANG. 'Tis one thing to be tempted, Escalus,
Another thing to fall. I not deny,
The jury, passing on the prisoner's life,
May in the sworn twelve have a thief or two   20
Guiltier than him they try. What's open made to
     justice,
That justice seizes. What know the laws
That thieves do pass on° thieves? 'Tis very preg-
     nant,°
The jewel that we find, we stoop and take't,
Because we see it, but what we do not see   25
We tread upon, and never think of it.
You may not so extenuate his offense
For° I have had such faults, but rather tell me
When I that censure him do so offend,
Let mine own judgment pattern out my death,   30
And nothing come in partial.° Sir, he must die.
     ESCAL. Be it as your wisdom will.
     ANG.   Where is the Provost?
     PROV. Here, if it like° your Honor.
     ANG.   See that Claudio
Be executed by nine tomorrow morning.
Bring him his confessor, let him be prepared,   35
For that's the utmost of his pilgrimage.°
                            [*Exit* PROVOST.]
     ESCAL. [*Aside*] Well, Heaven forgive him, and
     forgive us all!
Some rise by sin, and some by virtue fall.
Some run from brakes of ice,° and answer none,°
And some condemnèd for a fault alone.°   40
     [*Enter* ELBOW, *and* OFFICERS *with* FROTH
           and POMPEY.]
     ELB. Come, bring them away. If these be good
people in a commonweal that do nothing but use

54–55. His . . . design: his declared intentions were very different from his true plan.   60. rebate: abate, dull.   62. use . . .
liberty: customary licentiousness.   63. run by: ignored.
65. sense: meaning, intention.   70. my . . . of: the main purpose of my.   72. censured: passed sentence on.   83. As . . .
them: as if they themselves possessed them; i.e., had the granting.
     Act II, Sc. i: 2. fear: frighten.

6. fall: let fall, strike.   11. cohered: agreed.   23. pass on:
i.e., pass judgment on. pregnant: obvious.   28. For: because.
31. nothing . . . partial: no partiality be shown to me.   33. like:
please.   36. utmost . . . pilgrimage: limit of his life on earth.
39. brakes of ice: a curious phrase, probably corrupt; *brakes:*
lit., thickets. answer none: are never called to account.   40. fault
alone: i.e., a single lapse which is no crime.

their abuses° in common houses, I know no law. Bring them away.

ANG. How now, sir! What's your name? And 45 what's the matter?

ELB. If it please your Honor, I am the poor Duke's constable, and my name is Elbow. I do lean upon justice, sir, and do bring in here before your good Honor two notorious benefactors. 50

ANG. Benefactors? Well, what benefactors are they? Are they not malefactors?

ELB. If it please your Honor, I know not well what they are. But precise° villains they are, that I am 55 sure of, and void of° all profanation in the world that good Christians ought to have.

ESCAL. This comes off well. Here's a wise officer.

ANG. Go to.° What quality are they of? Elbow is your name? Why dost thou not speak, Elbow? 60

POM. He cannot, sir, he's out at elbow.

ANG. What are you, sir?

ELB. He, sir! A tapster, sir, parcel-bawd,° one that serves a bad woman, whose house, sir, was, as 65 they say, plucked down in the suburbs. And now she professes a hothouse,° which I think is a very ill house too.

ESCAL. How know you that?

ELB. My wife, sir, whom I detest° before Heaven and your Honor —— 70

ESCAL. How? Thy wife?

ELB. Aye, sir — whom, I thank Heaven, is an honest woman ——

ESCAL. Dost thou detest her therefore?

ELB. I say, sir, I will detest myself also, as 75 well as she, that this house, if it be not a bawd's house, it is pity of her life, for it is a naughty house.

ESCAL. How dost thou know that, constable?

ELB. Marry, sir, by my wife, who if she had 80 been a woman cardinally° given, might have been accused in fornication, adultery, and all uncleanliness there.

ESCAL. By the woman's means?

ELB. Aye, sir, by Mistress Overdone's means. 85 But as she spit in his face, so she defied him.

POM. Sir, if it please your Honor, this is not so.

ELB. Prove it before these varlets° here, thou honorable man, prove it.

ESCAL. Do you hear how he misplaces?° 90

POM. Sir, she came in great with child, and longing, saving your Honor's reverence,° for stewed prunes. Sir, we had but two in the house, which at

that very distant time stood, as it were, in a fruit dish, a dish of some threepence — your Honors 95 have seen such dishes, they are not China dishes, but very good dishes ——

ESCAL. Go to, go to. No matter for the dish, sir.

POM. No indeed, sir, not of a pin, you are therein in the right. But to the point. As I say, this 100 Mistress Elbow, being, as I say, with child, and being great-bellied, and longing, as I said, for prunes, and having but two in the dish, as I said, Master Froth here, this very man, having eaten the rest, as I said, and, as I say, paying for them very honestly — for, as you know, Master Froth, I could not give you threepence again. 107

FROTH. No indeed.

POM. Very well — you being then, if you be remembered, cracking the stones of the foresaid prunes ——

FROTH. Aye, so I did indeed.

POM. Why, very well. I telling you then, if 110 you be remembered, that such a one and such a one were past cure of the thing you wot° of, unless they kept very good diet, as I told you —— 116

FROTH. All this is true.

POM. Why, very well, then ——

ESCAL. Come, you are a tedious fool. To the purpose. What was done to Elbow's wife that he 120 hath cause to complain of? Come me to what was done to her.

POM. Sir, your Honor cannot come to that yet.

ESCAL. No, sir, nor I mean it not.

POM. Sir, but you shall come to it, by your 125 Honor's leave. And I beseech you, look into Master Froth here, sir, a man of fourscore pound a year, whose father died at Hallowmas° — was't not at Hallowmas, Master Froth?

FROTH. Allhallond Eve.° 130

POM. Why, very well, I hope here be truths. He, sir, sitting, as I say, in a lower chair, sir — 'twas in the Bunch of Grapes,° where, indeed, you have a delight to sit, have you not? 135

FROTH. I have so, because it is an open room, and good for winter.

POM. Why, very well, then, I hope here be truths.

ANG. This will last out a night in Russia When nights are longest there. I'll take my leave, And leave you to the hearing of the cause, 141 Hoping you'll find good cause to whip them all.

ESCAL. I think no less. Good morrow to your lordship. [*Exit* ANGELO.]

Now, sir, come on. What was done to Elbow's wife, once more? 145

POM. Once, sir? There was nothing done to her once.

---

43. abuses: improper behavior. 55. precise: puritanical. 56. void of: free from. 59. Go to: get on. 64. parcel-bawd: partly bawd (i.e., pimp), — and partly tapster. 67. professes a hothouse: her business is a brothel. 69. detest: for "protest." 81. cardinally: for "carnally." 88. varlets: knaves. 90. misplaces: mistakes the meanings of his words. 92. saving . . . reverence: begging your Honor's pardon — a phrase used to apologize for an improper remark.

115. wot: know. 128. Hallowmas: All Saints' Day, November 1. 130. Allhallond Eve: Halloween, October 31. 134. Bunch of Grapes: the name of a room.

ELB. I beseech you, sir, ask him what this man did to my wife.

POM. I beseech your Honor, ask me.　　150

ESCAL. Well, sir, what did this gentleman to her?

POM. I beseech you, sir, look in this gentleman's face. Good Master Froth, look upon his Honor, 'tis for a good purpose. Doth your Honor mark his face?

ESCAL. Aye, sir, very well.　　156

POM. Nay, I beseech you mark it well.

ESCAL. Well, I do so.

POM. Doth your Honor see any harm in his face?

ESCAL. Why, no.

POM. I'll be supposed° upon a book, his face is the worst thing about him. Good, then. If his face be the worst thing about him, how could Mas-　165 ter Froth do the constable's wife any harm? I would know that of your Honor.

ESCAL. He's in the right. Constable, what say you to it?

ELB. First, an it like you,° the house is a re-　170 spected house. Next, this is a respected fellow, and his mistress is a respected woman.

POM. By this hand, sir, his wife is a more re-spected person than any of us all.

ELB. Varlet, thou liest, thou liest, wicked varlet! The time is yet to come that she was ever respected° with man, woman, or child.　　177

POM. Sir, she was respected with him before he married with her.

ESCAL. Which is the wiser here? Justice or Iniquity? Is this true?

ELB. O thou caitiff!° O thou varlet! O thou wicked Hannibal!° I respected with her before I was mar-ried to her! If ever I was respected with her, or　185 she with me, let not your Worship think me the poor Duke's officer. Prove this, thou wicked Hanni-bal, or I'll have mine action of battery° on thee.

ESCAL. If he took you a box o' th' ear, you might have your action of slander too.　　190

ELB. Marry, I thank your good Worship for it. What is't your Worship's pleasure I shall do with this wicked caitiff?

ESCAL. Truly, officer, because he hath some of-fenses in him that thou wouldst discover if thou　195 couldst, let him continue in his courses till thou knowest what they are.

ELB. Marry, I thank your Worship for it. Thou seest, thou wicked varlet, now, what's come　200 upon thee. Thou art to continue now, thou varlet, thou art to continue.

ESCAL. Where were you born, friend?

FROTH. Here in Vienna, sir.

ESCAL. Are you of fourscore pounds a year?

FROTH. Yes, an 't please you, sir.　　205

ESCAL. So. What trade are you of, sir?

POM. A tapster, a poor widow's tapster.

ESCAL. Your mistress' name?

POM. Mistress Overdone.

ESCAL. Hath she had any more than one husband?

POM. Nine, sir, Overdone by the last.

ESCAL. Nine! Come hither to me, Master Froth. Master Froth, I would not have you acquainted with tapsters. They will draw you,° Master Froth,　215 and you will hang them. Get you gone, and let me hear no more of you.

FROTH. I thank your Worship. For mine own part, I never come into any room in a taphouse but I am drawn in.　　220

ESCAL. Well, no more of it, Master Froth. Fare-well. [Exit FROTH.] Come you hither to me, Master Tapster. What's your name, Master Tapster?

POM. Pompey.　　225

ESCAL. What else?

POM. Bum, sir.

ESCAL. Troth,° and your bum is the greatest thing about you, so that, in the beastliest sense, you　229 are Pompey the Great. Pompey, you are partly a bawd, Pompey, howsoever you color° it in being a tapster, are you not? Come, tell me true. It shall be the better for you.

POM. Truly, sir, I am a poor fellow that would live.　　235

ESCAL. How would you live, Pompey? By being a bawd? What do you think of the trade, Pompey? Is it a lawful trade?

POM. If the law would allow it, sir.

ESCAL. But the law will not allow it, Pompey, nor it shall not be allowed in Vienna.　　240

POM. Does your Worship mean to geld and splay° all the youth of the city?

ESCAL. No, Pompey.

POM. Truly, sir, in my poor opinion, they will to't, then. If your Worship will take order for the　245 drabs° and the knaves, you need not to fear the bawds.

ESCAL. There are pretty orders beginning. I can tell you. It is but heading° and hanging.　　250

POM. If you head and hang all that offend that way but° for ten year together, you'll be glad to give out a commission for more heads. If this law hold in Vienna ten year, I'll rent the fairest house in it after° threepence a bay.° If you live to see this come　255 to pass, say Pompey told you so.

ESCAL. Thank you, good Pompey, and in requital

---

163. supposed: for "deposed"; i.e., sworn as a witness.　170. an ... you: if it please you.　176. respected: Elbow thinks it means "suspected."　183. caitiff: rogue.　184. Hannibal: for "Cannibal."　188. battery: Elbow, as Escalus points out, is mixed in his legal terms.

215. draw you: draw drink for you, with a pun on hang, draw, and quarter.　228. Troth: in truth.　231. color: conceal.　241. splay: castrate.　246. drabs: whores.　250. heading: beheading.　252. but: only.　254. after: at the rate of.　255. bay: bay window.

of your prophecy, hark you. I advise you, let me not
find you before me again upon any complaint whatsoever — no, not for dwelling where you do.°   260
If I do, Pompey, I shall beat you to your tent, and
prove a shrewd Caesar° to you. In plain dealing,
Pompey, I shall have you whipped. So for this time,
Pompey, fare you well.   265

POM. I thank your Worship for your good counsel.
[*Aside*] But I shall follow it as the flesh and fortune
shall better determine.
Whip me? No, no, let carman whip his jade.°   269
The valiant heart's not whipped out of his trade.
[*Exit.*]

ESCAL. Come hither to me, Master Elbow, come
hither, Master Constable. How long have you been
in this place of constable?

ELB. Seven year and a half, sir.

ESCAL. I thought by your readiness in the of-   275
fice you had continued in it sometime. You say seven
years together?

ELB. And a half, sir.

ESCAL. Alas, it hath been great pains to you. They
do you wrong to put you so oft upon 't.° Are   280
there not men in your ward sufficient to serve it?

ELB. Faith, sir, few of any wit in such matters. As
they are chosen, they are glad to choose me for
them. I do it for some piece of money, and go
through with all.   285

ESCAL. Look you bring me in the names of some
six or seven, the most sufficient of your parish.

ELB. To your Worship's house, sir?

ESCAL. To my house. Fare you well. [*Exit* ELBOW.]
What's o'clock, think you?   290

JUST. Eleven, sir.

ESCAL. I pray you home to dinner with me.

JUST. I humbly thank you.

ESCAL. It grieves me for the death of Claudio,
But there's no remedy.   295

JUST. Lord Angelo is severe.

ESCAL.   It is but needful.
Mercy is not itself that oft looks so,
Pardon is still° the nurse of second woe.
But yet — poor Claudio! There is no remedy.   299
Come, sir.   [*Exeunt.*]

SCENE II. *Another room in the same.*

[*Enter* PROVOST *and a* SERVANT.]

SERV. He's hearing of a cause. He will come
straight.
I'll tell him of you.

PROV.   Pray you, do. [*Exit* SERVANT.] I'll know
His pleasure, maybe he will relent. Alas,
He hath but as offended in a dream!°
All sects, all ages smack of this vice, and he   5
To die for 't!

[*Enter* ANGELO.]

ANG.   Now what's the matter, Provost?

PROV. Is it your will Claudio shall die tomorrow?

ANG. Did not I tell thee yea? Hadst thou not
order?
Why dost thou ask again?

PROV.   Lest I might be too rash.
Under your good correction,° I have seen   10
When, after execution, Judgment hath
Repented o'er his doom.

ANG.   Go to. Let that be mine.
Do you your office, or give up your place,
And you shall well be spared.

PROV.   I crave your Honor's pardon.
What shall be done, sir, with the groaning Juliet?
She's very near her hour.   16

ANG.   Dispose of her
To some more fitter place, and that with speed.

[*Re-enter* SERVANT.]

SERV. Here is the sister of the man condemned
Desires access to you.

ANG.   Hath he a sister?

PROV. Aye, my good lord, a very virtuous maid
And to be shortly of a sisterhood,   21
If not already.

ANG. Well, let her be admitted.   [*Exit* SERVANT.]
See you the fornicatress be removed.
Let her have needful, but not lavish, means,
There shall be order for 't.

[*Enter* ISABELLA *and* LUCIO.]

PROV.   God save your Honor!   25

ANG. Stay a little while. [*To* ISABELLA] You're
welcome.
What's your will?

ISAB. I am a woeful suitor to your Honor,
Please but your Honor hear me.

ANG.   Well, what's your suit?

ISAB. There is a vice that most I do abhor,
And most desire should meet the blow of justice,   30
For which I would not plead but that I must,
For which I must not plead but that I am
At war 'twixt will and will not.

ANG.   Well, the matter?

ISAB. I have a brother is condemned to die.
I do beseech you, let it be his fault,°   35
And not my brother.

PROV. [*Aside*] Heaven give thee moving graces!

ANG. Condemn the fault, and not the actor of it?
Why, every fault's condemned ere it be done.

Mine were the very cipher of a function,°
To fine the faults whose fine stands in recórd°   40
And let go by the actor.
    ISAB.   Oh, just but severe law!
I had a brother,° then. — Heaven keep your Honor!
    LUCIO. [*Aside to* ISABELLA] Give 't not o'er so. To
    him again, entreat him,
Kneel down before him, hang upon his gown.
You are too cold. If you should need a pin,°   45
You could not with more tame a tongue desire it.
To him, I say!
    ISAB. Must he needs die?
    ANG.   Maiden, no remedy.
    ISAB. Yes, I do think that you might pardon him,
And neither Heaven nor man grieve at the mercy.
    ANG. I will not do 't.
    ISAB.   But can you, if you would?
    ANG. Look, what I will not, that I cannot do.   52
    ISAB. But might you do 't, and do the world no
    wrong,
If so your heart were touched with that remorse°
As mine is to him?
    ANG.   He's sentenced, 'tis too late.   55
    LUCIO. [*Aside to* ISABELLA] You are too cold.
    ISAB. Too late? Why, no. I, that do speak a word,
May call it back again. Well, believe this,
No ceremony° that to great ones 'longs° —
Not the king's crown, nor the deputed sword,°   60
The marshal's truncheon,° nor the judge's robe —
Become them with one half so good a grace
As mercy does.
If he had been as you, and you as he,
You would have slipped like him, but he, like you,
Would not have been so stern.
    ANG.   Pray you be gone.   66
    ISAB. I would to Heaven I had your potency°
And you were Isabel! Should it then be thus?
No, I would tell what 'twere to be a judge,
And what a prisoner.
    LUCIO. [*Aside to* ISABELLA] Aye, touch him,
    there's the vein.
    ANG. Your brother is a forfeit of the law,
And you but waste your words.
    ISAB.   Alas, alas!
Why, all the souls that were were forfeit once,
And He that might the vantage° best have took
Found out the remedy. How would you be   75
If He, which is the top of judgment,° should
But judge you as you are? Oh, think on that,

And mercy then will breathe within your lips,
Like man new-made.
    ANG.   Be you content, fair maid.
It is the law, not I, condemn your brother.   80
Were he my kinsman, brother, or my son,
It should be thus with him. He must die tomor-
row.
    ISAB. Tomorrow! Oh, that's sudden! Spare him,
    spare him!
He's not prepared for death. Even for our kitchens
We kill the fowl of season.° Shall we serve Heaven
With less respect than we do minister   86
To our gross selves? Good, good my lord, bethink
    you,
Who is it that hath died for this offense?
There's many have committed it.
    LUCIO. [*Aside to* ISABELLA] Aye, well said.
    ANG. The law hath not been dead, though it hath
    slept.   90
Those many had not dared to do that evil
If the first that did the edíct infringe
Had answered° for his deed. Now 'tis awake,
Takes note of what is done, and, like a prophet,
Looks in a glass° that shows what future evils,   95
Either now, or by remissness new-conceived,
And so in progress to be hatched and born,
Are now to have no súccessive degrees,°
But, ere they live, to end.
    ISAB.   Yet show some pity.
    ANG. I show it most of all when I show justice,
For then I pity those I do not know,   101
Which a dismissed offense would after gall,
And do him right that, answering one foul wrong,
Lives not to act another. Be satisfied,
Your brother dies tomorrow, be content.   105
    ISAB. So you must be the first that gives his sen-
    tence,
And he, that suffers. Oh, it is excellent
To have a giant's strength, but it is tyrannous
To use it like a giant.
    LUCIO. [*Aside to* ISABELLA] That's well said.
    ISAB. Could great men thunder   110
As Jove himself does, Jove would ne'er be quiet,
For every pelting,° petty officer
Would use his Heaven for thunder.
Nothing but thunder! Merciful Heaven,
Thou rather with thy sharp and sulphurous bolt
Split'st the unwedgeable and gnarlèd oak   116
Than the soft myrtle. But man, proud man,
Dressed in a little brief authority,
Most ignorant of what he's most assured,
His glassy essence,° like an angry ape,   120
Plays such fantastic tricks before high Heaven

---

39. cipher . . . function: an office worth nothing.   40. fine . . .
record: punish faults that are already condemned.   42. had a
brother: i.e., he is as good as dead.   45. pin: worthless trifle.
54. remorse: pity.   59. ceremony: symbol of greatness. Cf. *Hen
V*, IV.i.253–301. 'longs: belongs.   6o. deputed sword: the sword
of Justice, carried before the Deputy, and symbolizing his power.
61. truncheon: staff of office.   67. potency: power.   74. vantage: advantage; i.e., to punish mankind.   76. top of judgment:
Supreme Judge.

85. of season: at the proper time of year.   93. answered: been
condemned.   95. glass: i.e., a magic glass which shows the future.   98. successive degrees: successors.   112. pelting: paltry.   120. glassy essence: fragile nature.

As make the angels weep — who, with our spleens,°
Would all themselves laugh mortal.°
   LUCIO. [*Aside to* ISABELLA] Oh, to him, to him,
     wench! He will relent,
He's coming, I perceive 't.
   PROV. [*Aside*] Pray Heaven she win him!   125
   ISAB. We cannot weigh our brother with ourself.
Great men may jest with saints, 'tis wit in them,
But in the less foul profanation.
   LUCIO. Thou'rt i' the right, girl, more o' that.
   ISAB. That in the captain's but a choleric° word
Which in the soldier is flat blasphemy.   131
   LUCIO. [*Aside to* ISABELLA] Art avised° o' that?
     More on't.
   ANG. Why do you put these sayings upon me?
   ISAB. Because authority, though it err like others,
Hath yet a kind of medicine in itself   135
That skins the vice o' the top.° Go to your bosom,
Knock there, and ask your heart what it doth know
That's like my brother's fault. If it confess
A natural guiltiness such as is his,
Let it not sound a thought upon your tongue   140
Against my brother's life.
   ANG.   [*Aside*] She speaks, and 'tis
Such sense that my sense breeds° with it. Fare you
well.
   ISAB. Gentle my lord, turn back.
   ANG. I will bethink me. Come again tomorrow.
   ISAB. Hark how I'll bribe you. Good my lord, turn
     back.   145
   ANG. How? Bribe me?
   ISAB. Aye, with such gifts that Heaven shall share
     with you.
   LUCIO. [*Aside to* ISABELLA] You had marred all
     else.
   ISAB. Not with fond sicles° of the tested gold,
Or stones whose rates are either rich or poor   150
As fancy values them, but with true prayers
That shall be up at Heaven and enter there
Ere sunrise, prayers from preservèd souls,
From fasting maids whose minds are dedicate
To nothing temporal.
   ANG.   Well, come to me tomorrow.   155
   LUCIO. [*Aside to* ISABELLA] Go to, 'tis well. Away!
   ISAB. Heaven keep your Honor safe!
   ANG. [*Aside*] Amen.
For I am that way going to temptation,
Where prayers cross.°
   ISAB.   At what hour tomorrow
Shall I attend your lordship?
   ANG.   At any time 'fore noon.   160

   ISAB. 'Save° your Honor!
      [*Exeunt* ISABELLA, LUCIO, *and* PROVOST.]
   ANG.   From thee — even from thy virtue!
What's this, what's this? Is this her fault or mine?
The tempter or the tempted, who sins most?
Ha!
Not she, nor doth she tempt. But it is I   165
That, lying by the violet in the sun,
Do as the carrion does, not as the flower,
Corrupt with virtuous season.° Can it be
That modesty may more betray our sense
Than woman's lightness? Having waste ground
   enough,   170
Shall we desire to raze the sanctuary,
And pitch our evils there? Oh, fie, fie, fie!
What dost thou, or what art thou, Angelo?
Dost thou desire her foully for those things
That make her good? Oh, let her brother live.   175
Thieves for their robbery have authority
When judges steal themselves. What, do I love her,
That I desire to hear her speak again
And feast upon her eyes? What is't I dream on?
O cunning enemy, that to catch a saint   180
With saints dost bait thy hook! Most dangerous
Is that temptation that doth goad us on
To sin in loving virtue. Never could the strumpet,
With all her double vigor, art and nature,°
Once stir my temper, but this virtuous maid   185
Subdues me quite. Ever till now,
When men were fond,° I smiled, and wondered
   how.   [*Exit.*]

SCENE III. *A room in a prison.*

[*Enter, severally,*° DUKE *disguised as a friar,
and* PROVOST.]

   DUKE. Hail to you, Provost! So I think you are.
   PROV. I am the Provost. What's your will, good
     Friar?
   DUKE. Bound by my charity and my blest order,
I come to visit the afflicted spirits
Here in the prison. Do me the common right   5
To let me see them, and to make me know
The nature of their crimes, that I may minister
To them accordingly.
   PROV. I would do more than that, if more were
     needful.
[*Enter* JULIET.] Look, here comes one — a gentle-
   woman of mine   10

---

122. with . . . spleens: if they had our spleens. The spleen was
regarded as the seat of laughter.   123. laugh mortal: laugh
themselves to death.   130. choleric: hot-tempered.   132. avised:
advised, aware.   136. skins . . . top: covers the sore, but does
not heal it.   142. breeds: quickens, stirs.   149. sicles: shekels.
159. cross: are at cross-purposes.

161. 'Save: God save.   165–68. But . . . season: i.e., the same
sun brings the violet to its full sweetness and causes the carrion
to stink. Corrupt: decay. virtuous: giving strength. season:
summer sun.   184. art . . . nature: See App. 18.   187. fond:
doting, foolish.
   Sc. iii: 8.d. severally: by separate entrances.

Who, falling in the flaws° of her own youth,
Hath blistered° her report.° She is with child,
And he that got it, sentenced, a young man
More fit to do another such offense
Than die for this.   15
    DUKE. When must he die?
    PROV.   As I do think, tomorrow.
[*To* JULIET] I have provided for you. Stay awhile,
And you shall be conducted.
    DUKE. Repent you, fair one, of the sin you carry?
    JUL. I do, and bear the shame most patiently.   20
    DUKE. I'll teach you how you shall arraign your
        conscience,
And try your penitence, if it be sound
Or hollowly put on.
    JUL.   I'll gladly learn.
    DUKE. Love you the man that wronged you?   24
    JUL. Yes, as I love the woman that wronged him.
    DUKE. So, then, it seems your most offenseful act
Was mutually committed?
    JUL.   Mutually.
    DUKE. Then was your sin of heavier kind than his.
    JUL. I do confess it, and repent it, Father.
    DUKE. 'Tis meet so, Daughter. But lest you do re-
        pent   30
As that° the sin hath brought you to this shame,
Which sorrow is always toward ourselves, not
        Heaven,
Showing we would not spare Heaven° as we love it,
But as we stand in fear——
    JUL. I do repent me as it is an evil,   35
And take the shame with joy.
    DUKE.   There rest.
Your partner, as I hear, must die tomorrow,
And I am going with instruction° to him.
Grace go with you. *Benedicite!*   [*Exit.*]
    JUL. Must die tomorrow! Oh, injurious love,   40
That respites me a life whose very comfort
Is still a dying horror!°
    PROV.   'Tis pity of him. [*Exeunt.*]

SCENE IV. *A room in* ANGELO'S *house.*

[*Enter* ANGELO.]
    ANG. When I would pray and think, I think and
        pray
To several subjects.° Heaven hath my empty words,
Whilst my invention,° hearing not my tongue,
Anchors on Isabel. Heaven in my mouth,

As if I did but only chew His name,   5
And in my heart the strong and swelling evil
Of my conception.° The state, whereon I studied,
Is like a good thing, being often read,
Grown feared° and tedious. Yea, my gravity,
Wherein — let no man hear me — I take pride,   10
Could I with boot° change for an idle plume°
Which the air beats for vain.° O place, O form,
How often dost thou with thy case,° thy habit,°
Wrench awe from fools, and tie the wiser souls
To thy false seeming! Blood, thou art blood.   15
Let's write good angel on the Devil's horn;
'Tis not the Devil's crest.°
[*Enter a* SERVANT.] How now! Who's there?
    SERV. One Isabel, a sister, desires access to you.
    ANG. Teach her the way. Oh heavens!
Why does my blood thus muster to my heart,   20
Making both it unable for itself,
And dispossessing all my other parts
Of necessary fitness?
So play the foolish throngs with one that swoons,
Come all to help him, and so stop the air   25
By which he should revive. And even so
The general subject° to a well-wished king
Quit their own part, and in obsequious fondness
Crowd to his presence, where their untaught love
Must needs appear offense.°
[*Enter* ISABELLA.] How now, fair maid?   30
    ISAB. I am come to know your pleasure.
    ANG. That you might know° it would much better
        please me
Than to demand what 'tis. Your brother cannot live.
    ISAB. Even so. — Heaven keep your Honor!
    ANG. Yet may he live awhile, and, it may be,   35
As long as you or I. Yet he must die.
    ISAB. Under your sentence?
    ANG. Yea.
    ISAB. When, I beseech you? That in his reprieve,
Longer or shorter, he may be so fitted°   40
That his soul sicken not.
    ANG. Ha! Fie, these filthy vices! It were as good
To pardon him that hath from nature stolen
A man already made, as to remit°
Their saucy sweetness that do coin Heaven's image
In stamps° that are forbid. 'Tis all as easy   46

11. **flaws:** gusts of passion.   12. **blistered:** blemished. **report:**
reputation.   31. **As that:** because.   33. **spare Heaven:** i.e.,
avoid grieving God.   38. **instruction:** religious counsel.   40-42. **Oh
. . . horror:** oh, destroying love that spares my life everlastingly (*still*) deprived by horrible death of my true love.
    Sc. iv: 2. **several subjects:** i.e., contrary purposes.   3. **in-
vention:** imagination, power of expression.

7. **conception:** thought.   9. **feared:** the F1 reading. Some editors emend to "seared": withered.   11. **boot:** advantage. **plume:**
feather, the mark of the brainless gallant.   12. **the . . . vain:**
vainly fans the air.   13. **case:** outside. **habit:** garment.
16-17. **Let's . . . crest:** If the reading is correct, the passage
probably means "since desire (*blood*) is natural, let us call the
Devil a good angel, and then his horn is the badge of an angel
and not a devil"; i.e., Angelo is saying, "To hell with my respectability. Evil, be thou my good."   27. **general subject:**
common crowd.   27-30. **The . . . offense:** See I.i.68,n.   32. **know:**
Angelo cynically sees a double meaning in "pleasure" and
"know" — i.e., have carnal knowledge.   40. **fitted:** prepared
for death.   44. **remit:** forgive.   46. **stamps:** lit., the dies by
which coins were stamped.

Falsely to take away a life true made
As to put metal in restrainèd means
To make a false one.°

ISAB. 'Tis set down so in Heaven, but not in
    earth.   50

ANG. Say you so? Then I shall pose you° quickly.
Which had you rather — that the most just law
Now took your brother's life, or, to redeem him,
Give up your body to such sweet uncleanness
As she that he hath stained?

ISAB.   Sir, believe this,   55
I had rather give my body than my soul.

ANG. I talk not of your soul. Our compelled sins
Stand more for number than for accompt.°

ISAB.   How say you?°

ANG. Nay, I'll not warrant that, for I can speak
Against the thing I say. Answer to this: 60
I, now the voice of the recorded law,
Pronounce a sentence on your brother's life.
Might there not be a charity in sin
To save this brother's life?

ISAB.   Please you to do't,
I'll take it as a peril to my soul,   65
It is no sin at all, but charity.

ANG. Pleased you° to do't at peril of your soul,
Were equal poise° of sin and charity.

ISAB. That I do beg his life, if it be sin,
Heaven let me bear it! You granting of my suit,   70
If that be sin, I'll make it my morn prayer
To have it added to the faults of mine,
And nothing of your answer.

ANG.   Nay, but hear me.
Your sense pursues not mine.° Either you are ig-
    norant,   74
Or seem so, craftily, and that's not good.

ISAB. Let me be ignorant, and in nothing good,
But graciously to know I am no better.

ANG. Thus wisdom wishes to appear most bright
When it doth tax° itself, as these black masks
Proclaim an enshield° beauty ten times louder   80
Than beauty could, displayed. But mark me,
To be receivèd plain, I'll speak more gross:
Your brother is to die.

ISAB. So.

ANG. And his offense is so, as it appears,   85
Accountant° to the law upon that pain.°

ISAB. True.

ANG. Admit no other way to save his life —
As I subscribe not that, nor any other,

But in the loss of question° — that you, his sister,
Finding yourself desired of such a person   91
Whose credit with the judge, or own great place,
Could fetch your brother from the manacles
Of the all-building° law; and that there were
No earthly mean to save him, but that either   95
You must lay down the treasures of your body
To this supposed, or else to let him suffer —
What would you do?

ISAB. As much for my poor brother as myself.
That is, were I under the terms of death,   100
The impression of keen whips I'd wear as rubies,
And strip myself to death, as to a bed
That longing have been sick for, ere I'd yield
My body up to shame.

ANG.   Then must your brother die.

ISAB. And 'twere the cheaper way.   105
Better it were a brother died at once
Than that a sister, by redeeming him,
Should die forever.

ANG. Were not you, then, as cruel as the sentence
That you have slandered so?   110

ISAB. Ignomy in ransom° and free pardon
Are of two houses.° Lawful mercy
Is nothing kin to foul redemption.

ANG. You seemed of late to make the law a tyrant,
And rather proved the sliding of your brother   115
A merriment than a vice.

ISAB. Oh, pardon me, my lord. It oft falls out,
To have what we would have, we speak not what
    we mean.
I something do excuse the thing I hate
For his advantage that I dearly love.   120

ANG. We are all frail.

ISAB.   Else° let my brother die,
If not a feodary,° but only he
Owe° and succeed thy weakness.

ANG. Nay, women are frail too.

ISAB. Aye, as the glasses where they view them-
    selves,   125
Which are as easy broke as they make forms.°
Women! — Help Heaven! Men their creation mar
In profiting by° them. Nay, call us ten times frail,
For we are soft as our complexions are,
And credulous to° false prints.°

ANG.   I think it well.   130
And from this testimony of your own sex —
Since, I suppose, we are made to be no stronger
Than faults may shake our frames — let me be
    bold —

46–49. 'tis . . . one: i.e., it is much the same to take away the life of a man lawfully begotten as to create an illegitimate child (lit., to make a false coin by using metal in a forbidden way). 51. pose you: put a difficult question to you. 58. Stand . . . accompt: are counted but not charged up against us. How . . . you: i.e., do you really mean it? 67. Pleased you: if you agreed. 68. poise: weight. 74. Your . . . mine: You do not mean the same as I. 79. tax: censure. 80. enshield: concealed. 86. Accountant: forfeit. pain: penalty.

89–90. As . . . question: as I do not admit this, or anything else, but for the sake of argument; "loss" is probably a corrupt reading. 94. all-building: this is the F1 reading; Theobald's emendation "all-binding" is preferable. 111. Ignomy in ransom: an ignominious payment for release. 112. two houses: i.e., different families. 121–23. Else . . . weakness: Another corrupt passage. 122. feodary: confederate. 123. Owe: own. 126. forms: appearances, reflections. 128. profiting by: taking advantage of. 130. credulous to: deceived by. prints: impressions.

I do arrest your words.° Be that you are,
That is, a woman. If you be more, you're none. 135
If you be one — as you are well expressed
By all external warrants — show it now,
By putting on the destined livery.°
    ISAB. I have no tongue but one. Gentle my lord,
Let me entreat you speak the former language.°
    ANG. Plainly conceive, I love you.   141
    ISAB. My brother did love Juliet,
And you tell me that he shall die for it.
    ANG. He shall not, Isabel, if you give me love.
    ISAB. I know your virtue hath a license in 't,   145
Which seems a little fouler than it is,
To pluck on others.
    ANG.   Believe me, on mine honor,
My words express my purpose.
    ISAB. Ha! Little honor to be much believed,
And most pernicious purpose! — Seeming, seem-
    ing! —   150
I will proclaim thee, Angelo, look for 't.
Sign me a present° pardon for my brother,
Or with an outstretched throat I'll tell the world
    aloud
What man thou art.
    ANG.   Who will believe thee, Isabel?
My unsoiled name, the austereness of my life,   155
My vouch° against you, and my place i' the state,
Will so your accusation overweigh
That you shall stifle in your own report,
And smell of calumny. I have begun,
And now I give my sensual race the rein.   160
Fit thy consent to my sharp appetite,
Lay by all nicety and prolixious° blushes
That banish what they sue for. Redeem thy brother
By yielding up thy body to my will,
Or else he must not only die the death,   165
But thy unkindness shall his death draw out
To lingering sufferance.° Answer me tomorrow,
Or, by the affection° that now guides me most,
I'll prove a tyrant to him. As for you,   169
Say what you can, my false o'erweighs your
    true.   [*Exit.*]
    ISAB. To whom should I complain? Did I tell this,
Who would believe me? Oh, perilous mouths,
That bear in them one and the selfsame tongue,
Either of condemnation or approof,°
Bidding the law make curtsy to their will,   175
Hooking both right and wrong to the appetite,
To follow as it draws! I'll to my brother.
Though he hath fall'n by prompture° of the blood,
Yet hath he in him such a mind of honor

That had he twenty heads to tender° down   180
On twenty bloody blocks, he'd yield them up
Before his sister should her body stoop
To such abhorred pollution.
Then, Isabel, live chaste, and, Brother, die.
More than our brother is our chastity.   185
I'll tell him yet of Angelo's request,
And fit his mind to death, for his soul's rest.   [*Exit.*]

Act III

SCENE I. *A room in the prison.*

[*Enter* DUKE *disguised as before,* CLAUDIO, *and*
             PROVOST.]
    DUKE. So then, you hope of pardon from Lord
    Angelo?
    CLAUD. The miserable have no other medicine
But only hope.
I've hope to live, and am prepared to die.   4
    DUKE. Be absolute for° death. Either death or life
Shall thereby be the sweeter. Reason thus with life:
If I do lose thee, I do lose a thing
That none but fools would keep. A breath thou art,
Servile to all the skyey° influences
That dost this habitation where thou keep'st   10
Hourly afflict. Merely,° thou art death's fool,
For him thou labor'st by thy flight to shun,
And yet runn'st toward him still. Thou art not noble,
For all the accommodations° that thou bear'st
Are nursed by baseness.° Thou'rt by no means val-
    iant,   15
For thou dost fear the soft and tender fork°
Of a poor worm.° Thy best of rest is sleep,
And that thou oft provokest, yet grossly fear'st
Thy death, which is no more. Thou art not thyself,
For thou exist'st on many a thousand grains   20
That issue out of dust. Happy thou art not,
For what thou hast not, still thou strivest to get,
And what thou hast, forget'st. Thou art not certain,
For thy complexion shifts to strange effects,°
After° the moon. If thou art rich, thou'rt poor,   25
For, like an ass whose back with ingots bows,
Thou bear'st thy heavy riches but a journey,
And death unloads thee. Friend hast thou none,
For thine own bowels,° which do call thee sire,

134. arrest ... words: take you at your word.   138. destined
livery: i.e., the frailty of your sex.   140. former language: i.e.,
before you began to make these proposals.   152. present: immediate.   156. vouch: declaration.   162. prolixious: superfluous.
167. sufferance: suffering.   168. affection: lust.   174. approof:
approval.   178. prompture: inciting.

    Act III, Sc. i: 5. absolute for: certain of.   9. skyey: i.e.,
of the stars. See App. 1.   11. Merely: entirely.   14. accommo-
dations: comforts.   15. nursed by baseness: supplied by
base means.   16. fork: forked tongue, which was believed to contain the sting.   17. worm: snake.   24. complexion: constitution
(varying as the balance of the humors changes). See App. 3.
shifts ... effects: constantly changes.   25. After: like.   29. bowels: offspring.

The mere effusion of thy proper° loins,   30
Do curse the gout, serpigo,° and the rheum°
For ending thee no sooner. Thou hast nor youth nor
    age,
But, as it were, an after-dinner's sleep,
Dreaming on both; for all thy blessed youth
Becomes as agèd, and doth beg the alms   35
Of palsied eld.° And when thou art old and rich,
Thou hast neither heat, affection, limb, nor beauty,
To make thy riches pleasant. What's yet in this
That bears the name of life? Yet in this life   39
Lie hid moe thousand deaths. Yet death we fear,
That makes these odds all even.

CLAUD.   I humbly thank you.
To sue to live, I find I seek to die,
And, seeking death, find life. Let it come on.

ISAB. [*Within*] What ho! Peace here, grace and
    good company!

PROV. Who's there? Come in. The wish deserves a
    welcome.   45

DUKE. Dear sir, ere long I'll visit you again.

CLAUD. Most holy sir, I thank you.

                        [*Enter* ISABELLA.]

ISAB. My business is a word or two with Claudio.

PROV. And very welcome. Look, signior, here's
    your sister.

DUKE. Provost, a word with you.   50

PROV. As many as you please.

DUKE. Bring me to hear them speak where I may
be concealed.

                        [*Exeunt* DUKE *and* PROVOST.]

CLAUD. Now, Sister, what's the comfort?

ISAB. Why,   55
As all comforts are, most good, most good indeed.
Lord Angelo, having affairs to Heaven,
Intends you for his swift ambassador,
Where you shall be an everlasting leiger.°
Therefore your best appointment° make with speed,
Tomorrow you set on.

CLAUD.   Is there no remedy?   61

ISAB. None but such remedy as, to save a head,
To cleave a heart in twain.

CLAUD.   But is there any?

ISAB. Yes, Brother, you may live.
There is a devilish mercy in the judge,   65
If you'll implore it, that will free your life,
But fetter you till death.

CLAUD.   Perpetual durance?°

ISAB. Aye, just, perpetual durance, a restraint,
Though all the world's vastidity° you had,
To a determined scope.°

CLAUD.   But in what nature?   70

ISAB. In such a one as, you consenting to't,
Would bark your honor from that trunk you bear,
And leave you naked.

CLAUD.   Let me know the point.°

ISAB. Oh, I do fear thee, Claudio, and I quake
Lest thou a feverous life shouldst entertain,   75
And six or seven winters more respect
Than a perpetual honor. Darest thou die?
The sense of death is most in apprehension,°
And the poor beetle that we tread upon
In corporal sufferance° finds a pang as great   80
As when a giant dies.

CLAUD.   Why give you me this shame?
Think you I can a resolution fetch
From° flowery tenderness? If I must die,
I will encounter darkness° as a bride,
And hug it in mine arms.   85

ISAB. There spake my brother, there my father's
    grave
Did utter forth a voice. Yes, thou must die.
Thou art too noble to conserve a life
In base appliances.° This outward-sainted Deputy,
Whose settled° visage and deliberate° word   90
Nips youth i' the head, and follies doth emmew°
As falcon doth the fowl,° is yet a devil.
His filth within being cast,° he would appear
A pond as deep as Hell.

CLAUD.   The prenzie° Angelo!

ISAB. Oh, 'tis the cunning livery° of Hell,   95
The damned'st body to invest° and cover
In prenzie guards!° Dost thou think,° Claudio? —
If I would yield him my virginity,
Thou mightst be freed.

CLAUD.   Oh, Heavens, it cannot be!

ISAB. Yes, he would give 't thee, from this rank of-
    fense,   100
So to offend him still. This night's the time
That I should do what I abhor to name,
Or else thou diest tomorrow.

CLAUD.   Thou shalt not do't.

ISAB. Oh, were it but my life,
I'd throw it down for your deliverance   105
As frankly° as a pin.

CLAUD.   Thanks, dear Isabel.

ISAB. Be ready, Claudio, for your death tomorrow.

CLAUD. Yes. Has he affections° in him

---

30. **proper:** own.   31. **serpigo:** a skin disease. **rheum:** excessive moisture, supposed to cause catarrh and rheumatism.   35–36. **alms . . . eld:** charity for a paralyzed old man.   59. **leiger:** a resident ambassador, as distinguished from an ambassador extraordinary sent on a special mission.   60. **appointment:** preparation.   67. **durance:** imprisonment.   69. **vastidity:** immensity.   70. **determined scope:** fixed limit.

73. **point:** i.e., truth.   78. **The . . . apprehension:** the physical feeling of death is mostly imagination.   80. **corporal sufferance:** bodily suffering.   82–83. **resolution . . . From:** find courage in.   84. **darkness:** death.   89. **In . . . appliances:** by low means.   90. **settled:** firm, solemn. **deliberate:** severe.   91. **emmew:** keep in the coop.   92. **As . . . fowl:** because the hen fears to come out when the hawk is overhead.   93. **cast:** vomited.   94. **prenzie:** a doubtful word which does not appear elsewhere and is probably a misprint; by the context it should mean "prim," "respectable."   95. **livery:** uniform.   96. **invest:** clothe.   97. **guards:** braid sewn on as ornament to a livery. **Dost . . . think:** would you believe it.   106. **frankly:** freely.   108. **affections:** feelings.

That thus can make him bite the law by the nose,
When he would force° it? Sure, it is no sin,   110
Or of the deadly seven it is the least.
   ISAB. Which is the least?
   CLAUD. If it were damnable, he being so wise,
Why would he for the momentary trick
Be perdurably fined?° — O Isabel!   115
   ISAB. What says my brother?
   CLAUD.   Death is a fearful thing.
   ISAB. And shamèd life a hateful.
   CLAUD. Aye, but to die, and go we know not
     where,
To lie in cold obstruction° and to rot,
This sensible° warm motion° to become   120
A kneaded clod° and the delighted spirit
To bathe in fiery floods, or to reside
In thrilling° region of thick-ribbèd ice —
To be imprisoned in the viewless° winds,
And blown with restless violence round about   125
The pendent world, or to be worse than worst
Of those that lawless and incertain thought
Imagine howling — 'tis too horrible!
The weariest and most loathèd worldly life
That age, ache, penury, and imprisonment   130
Can lay on nature is a paradise
To what we fear of death.
   ISAB. Alas, alas!
   CLAUD.   Sweet sister, let me live.
What sin you do to save a brother's life,
Nature dispenses with° the deed so far   135
That it becomes a virtue.
   ISAB.   O you beast!
O faithless coward! O dishonest wretch!
Wilt thou be made a man out of my vice?
Is't not a kind of incest, to take life
From thine own sister's shame? What should I
     think?   140
Heaven shield my mother played my father fair!
For such a warpèd slip of wilderness°
Ne'er issued from his blood. Take my defiance!
Die, perish! Might but my bending down
Reprieve thee from thy fate, it should proceed.   145
I'll pray a thousand prayers for thy death,
No word to save thee.
   CLAUD. Nay, hear me, Isabel.
   ISAB.   Oh, fie, fie, fie!
Thy sin's not accidental, but a trade.
Mercy to thee would prove itself a bawd.   150
'Tis best that thou diest quickly.
   CLAUD.   Oh, hear me, Isabella!

[*Re-enter* DUKE.]

   DUKE. Vouchsafe a word, young sister, but **one**
     word.
   ISAB. What is your will?
   DUKE. Might you dispense with your leisure, I
would by and by° have some speech with you.   155
The satisfaction I would require is likewise your
own benefit.
   ISAB. I have no superfluous leisure. My stay must
be stolen out of other affairs, but I will attend you
awhile.   [*Walks apart.*]
   DUKE. Son, I have overheard what hath passed between you and your sister. Angelo had never the
purpose to corrupt her, only he hath made an assay
of her virtue to practice his judgment° with   165
the disposition of natures. She, having the truth of
honor in her, hath made him that gracious denial
which he is most glad to receive. I am confessor to
Angelo, and I know this to be true. Therefore prepare yourself to death. Do not satisfy your   170
resolution° with hopes that are fallible.° Tomorrow
you must die, go to your knees, and make ready.
   CLAUD. Let me ask my sister pardon. I am so out
of love with life that I will sue to be rid of it.
   DUKE. Hold you there. Farewell.   [*Exit* CLAUDIO.]
Provost, a word with you!   176

[*Re-enter* PROVOST.]

   PROV. What's your will, Father?
   DUKE. That now you are come, you will be gone.
Leave me awhile with the maid. My mind   180
promises with my habit no loss° shall touch her by
my company.
   PROV. In good time.

[*Exit* PROVOST. ISABELLA *comes forward.*]

   DUKE. The hand that hath made you fair hath
made you good. The goodness that is cheap in beauty
makes beauty brief in goodness, but grace, be-   185
ing the soul of your complexion, shall keep the body
of it ever fair. The assault that Angelo hath made to
you fortune hath conveyed to my understanding, and
but that frailty hath examples for his falling, I   190
should wonder at Angelo. How will you do to content this substitute,° and to save your brother?
   ISAB. I am now going to resolve him.° I had rather
my brother die by the law than my son should   195
be unlawfully born. But oh, how much is the good
Duke deceived in Angelo! If ever he return and I
can speak to him, I will open my lips in vain, or discover his government.°
   DUKE. That shall not be much amiss.° Yet,   200
as the matter now stands, he will avoid your accu-

---

110. force: enforce.   115. perdurably fined: everlastingly punished.   119. in . . . obstruction: i.e., stiff and cold.   120. sensible: feeling. motion: living body.   121. kneaded clod: i.e.,
turned into earth.   123. thrilling: freezing.   124. view-
less: invisible.   135. dispenses with: grants absolution for.
142. warped . . . wilderness: degenerate throwback. The metaphor is of a cultivated fruit tree which reverts to the original
wild stock.

155. by . . . by: at once.   165. practice . . . judgment: experiment.   170–71. satisfy . . . resolution: feed your certainty;
i.e., do not deceive yourself.   171. fallible: false.   181. loss:
harm.   192. content . . . substitute: satisfy this deputy.
194. resolve him: give him my answer.   199. discover . . .
government: i.e., reveal his misgovernment.   200. That . . .
amiss: there is not much wrong with that.

sation, he made trial of you only. Therefore fasten your ear on my advisings. To the love I have in doing good a remedy presents itself. I do make myself believe that you may most uprighteously 205 do a poor wronged lady a merited benefit, redeem your brother from the angry law, do no stain to your own gracious person, and much please the absent Duke, if peradventure he shall ever return to 210 have hearing of this business.

ISAB. Let me hear you speak farther. I have spirit to do anything that appears not foul in the truth of my spirit.

DUKE. Virtue is bold, and goodness never 215 fearful. Have you not heard speak of Mariana, the sister of Frederick the great soldier who miscarried at sea?

ISAB. I have heard of the lady, and good words went with her name. 220

DUKE. She should this Angelo have married, was affianced° to her by oath, and the nuptial appointed. Between which time of the contract and limit° of the solemnity, her brother Frederick was 225 wrecked at sea, having in that perished vessel the dowry of his sister. But mark how heavily this befell to the poor gentlewoman. There she lost a noble and renowned brother, in his love toward her ever most kind and natural, with him the portion and 230 sinew of her fortune, her marriage dowry, with both her combinate° husband, this well-seeming° Angelo.

ISAB. Can this be so? Did Angelo so leave her?

DUKE. Left her in her tears, and dried not one of them with his comfort, swallowed his vows 235 whole, pretending in her discoveries of dishonor. In few,° bestowed her on° her own lamentation, which she yet wears for his sake, and he, a marble° to her tears, is washed with them, but relents not.

ISAB. What a merit were it in death to take 240 this poor maid from the world! What corruption in this life, that it will let this man live! But how out of this can she avail?

DUKE. It is a rupture that you may easily heal. And the cure of it not only saves your brother, but keeps you from dishonor in doing it. 245

ISAB. Show me how, good Father.

DUKE. This forenamed maid hath yet in her the continuance of her first affection. His unjust unkindness, that in all reason should have quenched 250 her love, hath, like an impediment in the current, made it more violent and unruly. Go you to Angelo, answer his requiring with a plausible obedience, agree with his demands to the point. Only refer yourself to this advantage:° first, that your stay 255

with him may not be long, that the time may have all shadow and silence in it, and the place answer to convenience. This being granted in course — and now follows all — we shall advise this wronged maid to stead up your appointment,° go in your 260 place. If the encounter acknowledge itself hereafter, it may compel him to her recompense. And here, by this, is your brother saved, your honor untainted, the poor Mariana advantaged, and the corrupt 265 Deputy scaled.° The maid will I frame° and make fit for his attempt. If you think well to carry this as you may, the doubleness of the benefit defends the deceit from reproof. What think you of it?

ISAB. The image° of it gives me content al- 270 ready, and I trust it will grow to a most prosperous perfection.

DUKE. It lies much in your holding up.° Haste you speedily to Angelo. If for this night he entreat you to his bed, give him promise of satisfaction. 275 I will presently to Saint Luke's. There, at the moated grange,° resides this dejected Mariana. At that place call upon me, and dispatch with Angelo, that it may be quickly.

ISAB. I thank you for this comfort. Fare you 280 well, good Father.   [*Exeunt severally.*]

SCENE II. *The street before the prison.*

[*Enter, on one side,* DUKE *disguised as before; on the other,* ELBOW, *and* OFFICERS *with* POMPEY.]

ELB. Nay, if there be no remedy for it but that you will needs buy and sell men and women like beasts, we shall have all the world drink brown and white bastard.°

DUKE. Oh heavens! what stuff is here? 5

POM. 'Twas never merry world since, of two usuries,° the merriest was put down, and the worser allowed by order of law a furred gown° to keep him warm, and furred with fox and lambskins too, to signify that craft, being richer than innocency, 10 stands for the facing.°

ELB. Come your way, sir. 'Bless you, good Father Friar.

DUKE. And you, good Brother Father. What offense hath this man made you, sir? 15

ELB. Marry, sir, he hath offended the law. And, sir, we take him to be a thief too, sir, for we have found upon him, sir, a strange picklock,° which we have sent to the Deputy.

260. stead . . . appointment: keep the appointment in your stead. 266. scaled: weighed. frame: prepare.   270. image: thought. 273. It . . . up: i.e., the success of the plan depends on your support. 276–77. moated grange: a large farm surrounded by a moat.
Sc. ii: 4. bastard: lit., a sweet Spanish wine. 6–7. two usuries: i.e., prostitution and moneylending. 8. furred gown: gown trimmed with fox fur, the outward sign of wealth. See Pl. 9l. 10–11. craft . . . facing: cunning is represented by the trimming (*facing*). 18. picklock: skeleton key. See Pl. 13c.

222. affianced: betrothed: See Gen. Intro. p. 20a. 224. limit: appointed date. 231. combinate: affianced. well-seeming: hypocritical.   237. In few: briefly. bestowed . . . on: i.e., left her to. 238. marble: i.e., coldhearted. 254–55. Only . . . advantage: only demand for yourself this condition.

DUKE. Fie, sirrah! A bawd, a wicked bawd!　20
The evil that thou causest to be done,
That is thy means to live. Do thou but think
What 'tis to cram a maw° or clothe a back
From such a filthy vice. Say to thyself,
" From their abominable and beastly touches　25
I drink, I eat, array myself, and live."
Canst thou believe thy living is a life,
So stinkingly depending?° Go mend, go mend.

POM. Indeed, it does stink in some sort, sir, but
yet, sir, I would prove ——　30

DUKE. Nay, if the Devil have given thee proofs
for sin,
Thou wilt prove his. Take him to prison, officer.
Correction and instruction must both work
Ere this rude beast will profit.

ELB. He must before the Deputy, sir, he has　35
given him warning. The Deputy cannot abide a
whoremaster. If he be a whoremonger, and comes
before him, he were as good go a mile on his errand.°

DUKE. That we were all, as some would seem to
be,　40
From our faults, as faults from seeming, free!

ELB. His neck will come to your waist — a cord,°
sir.

POM. I spy comfort, I cry bail. Here's a gentleman
and a friend of mine.

[*Enter* LUCIO.]

LUCIO. How now, noble Pompey! What, at　45
the wheels° of Caesar? Art thou led in triumph?
What, is there none of Pygmalion's images,° newly
made woman, to be had now, for putting the hand
in the pocket and extracting it clutched?° What　49
reply, ha? What sayest thou to this tune, matter and
method? Is't not drowned i' the last rain, ha? What
sayest thou, Trot?° Is the world as it was, man?
Which is the way? Is it sad, and few words? Or
how? The trick of it?

DUKE. Still thus, and thus, still worse!　55

LUCIO. How doth my dear morsel, thy mistress?
Procures she still, ha?

POM. Troth, sir, she hath eaten up all her beef,
and she is herself in the tub.°

LUCIO. Why, 'tis good, it is the right of it, it　60
must be so. Ever your fresh whore and your pow-

dered° bawd — an unshunned° consequence, it must
be so. Art going to prison, Pompey?

POM. Yes, faith, sir.

LUCIO. Why, 'tis not amiss, Pompey. Fare-　65
well. Go say I sent thee thither. For debt, Pompey?
Or how?

ELB. For being a bawd, for being a bawd.

LUCIO. Well then, imprison him. If imprisonment
be the due of a bawd, why, 'tis his right. Bawd　70
is he doubtless, and of antiquity too, bawd-born.
Farewell, good Pompey. Commend me to the prison,
Pompey. You will turn good husband° now, Pompey, you will keep the house.　74

POM. I hope, sir, your good Worship will be my
bail.

LUCIO. No, indeed will I not, Pompey. It is not the
wear.° I will pray, Pompey, to increase your bondage. If you take it not patiently, why, your mettle°
is the more. Adieu, trusty Pompey. 'Bless you,
Friar.　81

DUKE. And you.

LUCIO. Does Bridget paint° still, Pompey, ha?

ELB. Come your ways, sir, come.

POM. You will not bail me, then, sir?　85

LUCIO. Then, Pompey, nor now. What news
abroad, Friar? What news?

ELB. Come your ways, sir, come.

LUCIO. Go to kennel, Pompey, go. [*Exeunt* ELBOW,
POMPEY, *and* OFFICERS.] What news, Friar, of the
Duke?

DUKE. I know none. Can you tell me of any?

LUCIO. Some say he is with the Emperor of Russia, other some,° he is in Rome. But where is he,
think you?　95

DUKE. I know not where, but wheresoever, I wish
him well.

LUCIO. It was a mad fantastical trick of him to
steal from the state, and usurp° the beggary he was
never born to. Lord Angelo dukes it well in his absence, he puts transgression to't.　101

DUKE. He does well in't.

LUCIO. A little more lenity to lechery would do no
harm in him. Something too crabbed that way,
Friar.　105

DUKE. It is too general a vice, and severity must
cure it.

LUCIO. Yes, in good sooth, the vice is of a great
kindred, it is well allied. But it is impossible to ex-
tirp° it quite, Friar, till eating and drinking be put
down. They say this Angelo was not made by　111
man and woman after this downright way of creation. Is it true, think you?

DUKE. How should he be made, then?

23. maw: stomach.　28. stinkingly depending: depending on
such stinking support.　38. go . . . errand: make a fruitless
journey.　42. His . . . cord: The Friar, as part of the garb of his
order, wears a cord round his waist. Such a cord, says Elbow, will
be used for hanging Pompey.　46. wheels: i.e., chariot wheels.
See II.i.263.　47. Pygmalion's images: Pygmalion created a
statue of a woman so beautiful that he fell in love with it, whereupon Aphrodite gave it life. This story had been retold in luscious
verse by Marston in *Pygmalion's Image* in 1598. Lucio asks
whether there is no pretty woman to help the bawd in his distress.　49. clutched: i.e., with a handful of money.　52. Trot:
a comtemptuous phrase, usually used of an old woman.　59. tub:
the pickle tub, used for the cure of venereal disease by
means of sweating. Cf. *Hen V*, II.i.78–81.

62. powdered: pickled, steeped in brine. unshunned: inevitable.
73. husband: housekeeper.　78. wear: fashion.　79. mettle:
with a pun on metal; i.e., irons.　83. paint: make herself up.
94. other some: some others.　99. usurp: falsely assume.
110. extirp: root out.

LUCIO. Some report a sea maid° spawned him; some, that he was begot between two stockfishes.° But it is certain that when he makes water, his 117 urine is congealed ice. That I know to be true, and he is a motion generative,° that's infallible.

DUKE. You are pleasant, sir, and speak apace.°

LUCIO. Why, what a ruthless thing is this in 121 him, for the rebellion of a codpiece° to take away the life of a man! Would the Duke that is absent have done this? Ere he would have hanged a man for the getting a hundred bastards, he would 125 have paid for the nursing a thousand. He had some feeling of the sport, he knew the service, and that instructed him to mercy.

DUKE. I never heard the absent Duke much detected for° women. He was not inclined that way.

LUCIO. Oh, sir, you are deceived. 131

DUKE. 'Tis not possible.

LUCIO. Who, not the Duke? Yes, your beggar of fifty,° and his use was to put a ducat in her 134 clackdish.° The Duke had crotchets° in him. He would be drunk too, that let me inform you.

DUKE. You do him wrong, surely.

LUCIO. Sir, I was an inward of his. A shy fellow was the Duke. And I believe I know the cause of his withdrawing. 140

DUKE. What, I prithee, might be the cause?

LUCIO. No, pardon, 'tis a secret must be locked within the teeth and the lips. But this I can let you understand, the greater file° of the subject° held the Duke to be wise. 145

DUKE. Wise! Why, no question but he was.

LUCIO. A very superficial, ignorant, unweighing fellow.

DUKE. Either this is envy in you, folly, or mistaking. The very stream of his life and the busi- 150 ness he hath helmed° must, upon a warranted need,° give him a better proclamation.° Let him be but testimonied in his own bringings-forth,° and he shall appear to the envious a scholar, a statesman, and a soldier. Therefore you speak unskillfully, or if 155 your knowledge be more, it is much darkened in your malice.

LUCIO. Sir, I know him, and I love him.

DUKE. Love talks with better knowledge, and knowledge with dearer love. 160

LUCIO. Come, sir, I know what I know.

DUKE. I can hardly believe that, since you know not what you speak. But if ever the Duke return, as our prayers are he may, let me desire you to make your answer before him. If it be honest you 165 have spoke, you have courage to maintain it. I am bound to call upon you, and, I pray you, your name?

LUCIO. Sir, my name is Lucio, well known to the Duke. 170

DUKE. He shall know you better, sir, if I may live to report you.

LUCIO. I fear you not.

DUKE. Oh, you hope the Duke will return no more, or you imagine me too unhurtful an op- 175 posite. But indeed I can do you little harm. You'll forswear this again.

LUCIO. I'll be hanged first. Thou art deceived in me, Friar. But no more of this. Canst thou tell if Claudio die tomorrow or no? 180

DUKE. Why should he die, sir?

LUCIO. Why? For filling a bottle with a tundish.° I would the Duke we talk of were returned again. This ungenitured° agent will unpeople the province with continency; sparrows must not build in 185 his house eaves, because they are lecherous. The Duke yet would have dark deeds darkly answered, he would never bring them to light. Would he were returned! Marry, this Claudio is condemned 189 for untrussing.° Farewell, good Friar. I prithee pray for me. The Duke, I say to thee again, would eat mutton on Fridays.° He's not past it yet, and I say to thee he would mouth° with a beggar though she smelt brown bread and garlic. Say that I said 194 so. Farewell.   [*Exit.*]

DUKE. No might nor greatness in mortality°
Can censure 'scape; back-wounding calumny
The whitest virtue strikes. What king so strong
Can tie the gall up in the slanderous tongue?
But who comes here? 200

[*Enter* ESCALUS, PROVOST, *and* OFFICERS *with*
MISTRESS OVERDONE.]

ESCAL. Go, away with her to prison!

MRS. OV. Good my lord, be good to me. Your Honor is accounted a merciful man, good my lord.

ESCAL. Double and treble admonition, and still forfeit° in the same kind! This would make 205 mercy swear and play the tyrant.

PROV. A bawd of eleven years' continuance, may it please your Honor.

MRS. OV. My lord, this is one Lucio's infor- 210 mation against me. Mistress Kate Keepdown was with child by him in the Duke's time, he promised her marriage. His child is a year and a quarter old, come Philip and Jacob.° I have kept it myself, and see how he goes about to abuse me! 215

---

115. **sea maid:** mermaid.   116. **stockfishes:** dried codfish. 119. **motion generative:** a masculine puppet.   120. **apace:** excessively.   122. **rebellion . . . codpiece:** i.e., because his lust got the better of him. **codpiece:** See Pl. 8c and comment on p. 93b. 130. **detected for:** suspected of.   133–34. **your . . . fifty:** he had an affair with an old beggarwoman.   135. **clackdish:** wooden bowl carried by beggars. **crotchets:** odd ways.   144. **file:** lit., list, quantity. **subject:** people.   151. **helmed:** steered. **upon . . . need:** if assurance is needed.   152. **proclamation:** report. 153. **bringings-forth:** actions.

182. **tundish:** funnel.   184. **ungenitured:** impotent.   190. **untrussing:** taking down his breeches.   191–92. **eat . . . Fridays:** lit., be no fasting man; *mutton* also means a prostitute. 193. **mouth:** kiss.   196. **mortality:** human life.   205. **forfeit:** offending.   214. **Philip . . . Jacob:** St. Philip and St. James Day (May 1).

ESCAL. That fellow is a fellow of much license. Let him be called before us. Away with her to prison! Go to, no more words. [*Exeunt* OFFICERS *with* MISTRESS OVERDONE.] Provost, my brother Angelo will not be altered, Claudio must die tomorrow. Let him be furnished with divines, and have all chari- 221 table preparation. If my brother wrought by my pity,° it should not be so with him.

PROV. So please you, this friar hath been 224 with him, and advised him for the entertainment of death.

ESCAL. Good even, good Father.

DUKE. Bliss and goodness on you!

ESCAL. Of whence are you?

DUKE. Not of this country, though my chance is now   230
To use it for my time. I am a brother
Of gracious order, late come from the See°
In special business from His Holiness.

ESCAL. What news abroad i' the world?

DUKE. None but that there is so great a fever 235 on goodness that the dissolution° of it must cure it. Novelty is only in request, and it is as dangerous to be aged in any kind of course as it is virtuous to be constant in any undertaking. There is scarce truth enough alive to make societies secure, but se- 240 curity enough to make fellowships accurst° — much upon this riddle runs the wisdom of the world. This news is old enough, yet it is every day's news. I pray you, sir, of what disposition was the Duke? 244

ESCAL. One that, above all other strifes, contended especially to know himself.

DUKE. What pleasure was he given to?

ESCAL. Rather rejoicing to see another merry than merry at anything which professed to make 249 him rejoice — a gentleman of all temperance. But leave we him to his events,° with a prayer they may prove prosperous, and let me desire to know how you find Claudio prepared. I am made to understand that you have lent him visitation.   254

DUKE. He professes to have received no sinister measure° from his judge, but most willingly humbles himself to the determination of justice. Yet had he framed to himself, by the instruction° of his 258 frailty, many deceiving promises of life, which I, by my good leisure, have discredited to him, and now is he resolved to die.

ESCAL. You have paid the Heavens your function,° and the prisoner the very debt of your calling.° 263 I have labored for the poor gentleman to the extrem-

est shore° of my modesty. But my brother 265 Justice have I found so severe that he hath forced me to tell him he is indeed Justice.°

DUKE. If his own life answer the straitness of his proceeding, it shall become him well, wherein if he chance to fail, he hath sentenced himself.   270

ESCAL. I am going to visit the prisoner. Fare you well.

DUKE. Peace be with you!
          [*Exeunt* ESCALUS *and* PROVOST.]

He° who the sword of Heaven will bear   275
Should be as holy as severe,
Pattern in himself to know,
Grace to stand and virtue go,
More nor less to others paying
Than by self-offenses weighing.   280
Shame to him whose cruel striking
Kills for faults of his own liking!
Twice treble shame on Angelo,
To weed my vice and let his grow!
Oh, what may man within him hide,   285
Though angel on the outward side!
How may likeness made in crimes,
Making practice on the times,
To draw with idle spiders' strings
Most ponderous and substantial things!°   290
Craft against vice I must apply.
With Angelo tonight shall lie
His old betrothèd but despisèd,
So disguise shall, by the disguisèd,
Pay with falsehood false exacting,   295
And perform an old contracting.   [*Exit.*]

Act IV

SCENE I. *The moated grange at* ST. LUKE'S.

[*Enter* MARIANA *and a* BOY.]
BOY. [*Sings.*]
Take, O, take those lips away
     That so sweetly were forsworn,
And those eyes, the break of day,°
     Lights that do mislead the morn.
But my kisses bring again, bring again,   5
Seals of love, but sealed in vain, sealed in vain.
MARI. Break off thy song, and haste thee quick away.
Here comes a man of comfort, whose advice

222–23. wrought ... pity: acted as mercifully as I would. 232. See: i.e., Rome.   236. dissolution: death.   240–41. security ... accurst: since everyone nowadays demands security there is no true friendship.   251. events: own affairs. 255–56. sinister measure: unjust sentence.   258. instruction: prompting.   262. You ... function: you have done your duty toward God.   263. debt ... calling: what your holy office demands.

265. shore: limit.   267. indeed Justice: i.e., Justice without mercy.   275–96. He ... contracting: Most critics believe this passage in rhymed octosyllabic verse was not written by Shakespeare.   287–90. How ... things: an obscure passage which has not been satisfactorily explained.
Act IV, Sc. i: 3. break of day: i.e., like the dawn.

Hath often stilled my brawling° discontent.

                [Exit BOY.*]*

[Enter DUKE *disguised as before.]* I cry you mercy,°
   sir, and well could wish   10
You had not found me here so musical.
Let me excuse me, and believe me so,
My mirth it much displeased, but pleased my woe.
  DUKE. 'Tis good, though music oft hath such a
   charm
To make bad good, and good provoke to harm. 15
I pray you tell me, hath anybody inquired for me
here today? Much upon this time have I promised
here to meet.
  MARI. You have not been inquired after. I have
sat here all day.   20

            [Enter ISABELLA.*]*

  DUKE. I do constantly believe you. The time is
come even now. I shall crave your forbearance a
little. Maybe I will call upon you anon, for some ad-
vantage to yourself.
  MARI. I am always bound to you.   *[Exit.]*
  DUKE. Very well met, and well come.   26
What is the news from this good Deputy?
  ISAB. He hath a garden circummured° with brick,
Whose western side is with a vineyard backed,
And to that vineyard is a planchèd° gate   30
That makes his opening with this bigger key.
This other doth command a little door
Which from the vineyard to the garden leads.
There have I made my promise
Upon the heavy middle of the night   35
To call upon him.
  DUKE. But shall you on your knowledge find this
   way?
  ISAB. I have ta'en a due and wary° note upon 't.
With whispering and most guilty diligence,
In action all of precept,° he did show me   40
The way twice o'er.
  DUKE.   Are there no other tokens
Between you 'greed concerning her observance?°
  ISAB. No, none, but only a repair i' the dark,
And that I have possessed him my most stay
Can be but brief. For I have made him know   45
I have a servant comes with me along
That stays upon° me, whose persuasion is°
I come about my brother.
  DUKE.   'Tis well borne up.°
I have not yet made known to Mariana
A word of this. What ho! Within! Come forth! 50

[Re-enter MARIANA.*]* I pray you be acquainted with
  this maid,
She comes to do you good.

  ISAB.   I do desire the like.
  DUKE. Do you persuade yourself that I respect
  you?°
  MARI. Good Friar, I know you do, and have found
  it.
  DUKE. Take, then, this your companion by the
  hand,   55
Who hath a story ready for your ear.
I shall attend your leisure. But make haste,
The vaporous night approaches.
  MARI. Will't please you walk aside?

          [Exeunt MARIANA *and* ISABELLA.*]*

  DUKE. O place and greatness, millions of false eyes
Are stuck upon thee! Volumes of report   61
Run with these false and most contrarious quests°
Upon thy doings! Thousand escapes of wit
Make thee the father of their idle dreams,
And rack° thee in their fancies!

[Re-enter MARIANA *and* ISABELLA.*]* Welcome, how
  agreed?   65
  ISAB. She'll take the enterprise upon her, Father,
If you advise it.
  DUKE.   It is not my consent
But my entreaty too.
  ISAB.   Little have you to say
When you depart from him, but, soft and low,
"Remember now my brother."
  MARI.   Fear me not.   70
  DUKE. Nor, gentle Daughter, fear you not at all.
He is your husband on a precontráct.
To bring you thus together, 'tis no sin,
Sith° that the justice of your title to him
Doth flourish° the deceit. Come, let us go.   75
Our corn's to reap, for yet our tithe's° to sow.

                         [Exeunt.]

SCENE II. *A room in the prison.*

        [Enter PROVOST *and* POMPEY.*]*

  PROV. Come hither, sirrah. Can you cut off a man's
head?
  POM. If the man be a bachelor, sir, I can. But if he
be a married man, he's his wife's head, and I can
never cut off a woman's head.   5
  PROV. Come, sir, leave me your snatches° and
yield me a direct answer. Tomorrow morning are
to die Claudio and Barnardine. Here is in our prison
a common executioner, who in his office lacks 10
a helper. If you will take it on you to assist him, it
shall redeem you from your gyves.° If not, you shall

9. brawling: noisy.   10. cry . . . mercy: beg your pardon.
28. circummured: walled round. See Pl. 16a.   30. planched:
planked. 38. wary: careful.   40. In . . . precept: instructing
me by his gestures. 42. her observance: what she must observe.
47. stays upon: waits for. whose . . . is: who has been told.
48. borne up: planned.

53. respect you: esteem.   62. quests: following of the scent.
65. rack: stretch, pull to pieces.   74. Sith: since.   75. flourish: embellish.   76. tithe's: the F1 reading. Some editions
emend to "tilth," plowing.
    Sc. ii: 6. snatches: wisecracks.   12. gyves: fetters.

have your full time of imprisonment, and your deliverance with an unpitied whipping, for you have
been a notorious bawd.   15

POM. Sir, I have been an unlawful bawd time out
of mind, but yet I will be content to be a lawful hangman. I would be glad to receive some instruction
from my fellow partner.

PROV. What ho! Abhorson! Where's Abhorson,
there?   20

[*Enter* ABHORSON.]

ABHOR. Do you call, sir?

PROV. Sirrah, here's a fellow will help you tomorrow in your execution. If you think it meet, com-
pound° with him by the year, and let him abide   25
here with you. If not, use him for the present, and
dismiss him. He cannot plead his estimation° with
you, he hath been a bawd.

ABHOR. A bawd, sir? Fie upon him! He will discredit our mystery.°   30

PROV. Go to, sir, you weigh equally.° A feather
will turn the scale.   [*Exit.*]

POM. Pray, sir, by your good favor — for surely,
sir, a good favor° you have, but that you have a
hanging look — do you call, sir, your occupation°
a mystery?   36

ABHOR. Aye, sir, a mystery.

POM. Painting, sir, I have heard say, is a mystery,
and your whores, sir, being members of my occupation, using painting, do prove my occupation   40
a mystery. But what mystery there should be in
hanging, if I should be hanged, I cannot imagine.

ABHOR. Sir, it is a mystery.

POM. Proof?   45

ABHOR. Every true man's apparel fits your thief.
If it be too little for your thief, your true man thinks
it big enough; if it be too big for your thief, your
thief thinks it little enough. So every true man's apparel fits your thief.°   50

[*Re-enter* PROVOST.]

PROV. Are you agreed?

POM. Sir, I will serve him, for I do find your hangman is a more penitent trade than your bawd. He
doth oftener ask forgiveness.°   55

PROV. You, sirrah, provide your block and your
ax tomorrow four o'clock.

ABHOR. Come on, bawd, I will instruct thee in my
trade. Follow.

POM. I do desire to learn, sir. And I hope, if you
have occasion to use me for your own turn, you   60

shall find me yare;° for truly, sir, for your kindness
I owe you a good turn.

PROV. Call hither Barnardine and Claudio.

[*Exeunt* POMPEY *and* ABHORSON.]

The one has my pity, not a jot the other,
Being a murderer, though he were my brother.   65

[*Enter* CLAUDIO.] Look, here's the warrant, Claudio,
for thy death.
'Tis now dead midnight, and by eight tomorrow
Thou must be made immortal. Where's Barnardine?

CLAUD. As fast locked up in sleep as guiltless labor
When it lies starkly in the traveler's bones.°   70
He will not wake.

PROV.   Who can do good on him?
Well, go, prepare yourself. [*Knocking within.*] But
hark, what noise? —
Heaven give your spirits comfort!   [*Exit* CLAUDIO.]
By and by.° —
I hope it is some pardon or reprieve
For the most gentle Claudio.

[*Enter* DUKE *disguised as before.*] Welcome, Father.

DUKE. The best and wholesomest spirits of the
night   76
Envelop you, good Provost! Who called here of late?

PROV. None, since the curfew rung.

DUKE. Not Isabel?

PROV.   No.

DUKE.   They will, then, ere't be long.

PROV. What comfort is for Claudio?   80

DUKE. There's some in hope.

PROV.   It is a bitter Deputy.

DUKE. Not so, not so, his life is paralleled
Even with the stroke and line of his great justice.°
He doth with holy abstinence subdue
That in himself which he spurs on his power   85
To qualify° in others. Were he mealed° with that
Which he corrects, then were he tyrannous,
But this being so, he's just.   [*Knocking within.*]
Now are they come.   [*Exit* PROVOST.]
This is a gentle Provost. Seldom when°
The steelèd° jailer is the friend of men.   90

[*Knocking within.*]

How now! What noise? That spirit's possessed with
haste
That wounds the unsisting° postern with these
strokes.

[*Re-enter* PROVOST.]

PROV. There he must stay until the officer
Arise to let him in. He is called up.

DUKE. Have you no countermand for Claudio yet,

---

25. **compound**: contract.   27. **estimation**: worth.   30. **mystery**:
trade practiced by skilled craftsmen.   31. **weigh equally**: i.e.,
you both follow a despised occupation.   34. **favor**: with double
meaning of "kindness" and "face."   35. **occupation**: trade, work
performed with the hands. Cf. *Caesar,* I.ii.269.   46–50. **Every
. . . thief**: i.e., an honest man's clothes suit the thief who steals
them.   55. **ask forgiveness**: It was part of the etiquette of
an execution for the hangman to ask for the forgiveness of his
victim.

61. **yare**: handy.   69–70. **As . . . bones**: i.e., like the innocent
sleep that comes to the weary traveler. **starkly**: stiffly.   73. **By . . .
by**: in a moment — in answer to the knocking.   82–83. **his . . .
justice**: i.e., his good life and his sense of justice seem parallel like
the lines in a diagram.   86. **qualify**: moderate. **mealed**: spotted.
89. **Seldom when**: it is seldom that.   90. **steeled**: hardhearted.
92. **unsisting**: The word is not otherwise known, and is variously
emended; e.g., unresisting, unassisting.

But he must die tomorrow?

PROV.   None, sir, none.   96

DUKE. As near the dawning, Provost, as it is,
You shall hear more ere morning.

PROV.   Happily°
You something know, yet I believe there comes
No countermand — no such example have we.   100
Besides, upon the very siege° of justice
Lord Angelo hath to the public ear
Professed the contrary.
[*Enter a* MESSENGER.] This is his lordship's man.

DUKE. And here comes Claudio's pardon.

MESS. [*Giving a paper*] My lord hath sent   105
you this note, and by me this further charge, that
you swerve not from the smallest article of it, neither
in time, matter, or other circumstance. Good morrow, for, as I take it, it is almost day.

PROV. I shall obey him.   [*Exit* MESSENGER.]

DUKE. [*Aside*] This is his pardon, purchased by
such sin   111
For which the pardoner himself is in.
Hence hath offense his quick celerity
When it is borne in high authority.
When vice makes mercy, mercy's so extended   115
That for the fault's love is the offender friended.
Now, sir, what news?

PROV. I told you. Lord Angelo, belike thinking
me remiss in mine office, awakens me with this unwonted putting-on° — methinks strangely, for   120
he hath not used it before.

DUKE. Pray you, let's hear.

PROV. [*Reads.*] "Whatsoever you may hear to the
contrary, let Claudio be executed by four of the
clock, and in the afternoon Barnardine. For   125
my better satisfaction, let me have Claudio's head
sent me by five. Let this be duly performed, with a
thought that more depends on it than we must yet
deliver. Thus fail not to do your office, as you will
answer it at your peril." What say you to this,   130
sir?

DUKE. What is that Barnardine who is to be executed in the afternoon?

PROV. A Bohemian born, but here nursed up and
bred, one that is a prisoner nine years old.   135

DUKE. How came it that the absent Duke had not
either delivered him to his liberty or executed him?
I have heard it was ever his manner to do so.

PROV. His friends still wrought reprieves for him.
And indeed his fact,° till now in the govern-   140
ment of Lord Angelo, came not to an undoubtful°
proof.

DUKE. It is now apparent?   144

PROV. Most manifest, and not denied by himself.

DUKE. Hath he borne himself penitently in prison?
How seems he to be touched?

PROV. A man that apprehends death no more
dreadfully but as a drunken sleep — careless,   149
reckless, and fearless of what's past, present, or to
come, insensible of mortality and desperately mortal.°

DUKE. He wants advice.°

PROV. He will hear none. He hath evermore had
the liberty of the prison. Give him leave to es-   155
cape hence, he would not. Drunk many times a day,
if not many days entirely drunk. We have very oft
awaked him as if to carry him to execution, and
showed him a seeming warrant for it. It hath   160
not moved him at all.

DUKE. More of him anon. There is written in your
brow, Provost, honesty and constancy. If I read it
not truly, my ancient skill beguiles me, but in the
boldness of my cunning° I will lay myself in   165
hazard. Claudio, whom here you have warrant to
execute, is no greater forfeit to the law than Angelo
who hath sentenced him. To make you understand
this in a manifested effect, I crave but four   170
days' respite, for the which you are to do me both a
present and a dangerous courtesy.

PROV. Pray, sir, in what?

DUKE. In the delaying death.

PROV. Alack, how may I do it, having the   175
hour limited,° and an express command, under penalty, to deliver his head in the view of Angelo? I
may make my case as Claudio's, to cross° this in the
smallest.

DUKE. By the vow of mine Order I warrant   180
you, if my instructions may be your guide. Let this
Barnardine be this morning executed, and his head
borne to Angelo.

PROV. Angelo hath seen them both, and will discover the favor.°   185

DUKE. Oh, death's a great disguiser, and you may
add to it. Shave the head, and tie° the beard, and
say it was the desire of the penitent to be so bared
before his death. You know the course is com-   190
mon. If anything fall to you upon this more than
thanks and good fortune, by the saint whom I profess, I will plead against it with my life.

PROV. Pardon me, good Father, it is against my
oath.

DUKE. Were you sworn to the Duke, or to the
Deputy?   195

PROV. To him, and to his substitutes.

DUKE. You will think you have made no offense
if the Duke avouch the justice of your dealing?   200

PROV. But what likelihood is in that?

DUKE. Not a resemblance, but a certainty. Yet
since I see you fearful, that neither my coat, integ-

151–52. **insensible . . . mortal:** having no thought of death and in
a desperate state of deadly sin.   153. **advice:** spiritual counsel.   165. **cunning:** skill.   176. **limited:** appointed.   178. **cross:**
thwart.   185. **favor:** face.   188. **tie:** trim short.

98. **Happily:** perhaps.   101. **siege:** seat.   120. **putting-on:** urging.   140. **fact:** deed, crime.   141. **undoubtful:** certain.

rity, nor persuasion can with ease attempt you, I will go further than I meant, to pluck all fears 205 out of you. [*Producing a letter*] Look you, sir, here is the hand and seal of the Duke. You know the character,° I doubt not, and the signet is not strange to you.

PROV. I know them both.   210

DUKE. The contents of this is the return of the Duke. You shall anon overread it at your pleasure, where you shall find within these two days he will be here. This is a thing that Angelo knows not, for he this very day receives letters of strange tenor 215 — perchance of the Duke's death, perchance entering into some monastery — but, by chance, nothing of what is writ. Look, the unfolding star° calls up the shepherd. Put not yourself into amazement 220 how these things should be. All difficulties are but easy when they are known. Call your executioner, and off with Barnardine's head. I will give him a present shrift° and advise him for a better place. Yet you are amazed, but this shall absolutely re- 225 solve you. Come away, it is almost clear dawn.

[*Exeunt.*]

SCENE III. *Another room in the same.*

[*Enter* POMPEY.]

POM. I am as well acquainted° here as I was in our house of profession. One would think it were Mistress Overdone's own house, for here be many of her old customers. First, here's young Master 5 Rash. He's in for a commodity of brown paper and old ginger, ninescore and seventeen pounds, of which he made five marks, ready money. Marry, then ginger was not much in request, for the old women were all dead.° Then is there here one Master 10 Caper, at the suit of Master Threepile the mercer, for some four suits of peach-colored satin, which now peaches° him a beggar. Then have we here young Dizy, and young Master Deep-vow, and Master 15 Copper-spur, and Master Starve-lackey the rapier and dagger man,° and young Drop-heir that killed lusty Pudding, and Master Forthlight the tilter,° and brave Master Shooty° the great traveler, and wild Half-can that stabbed Pots, and I think forty 20

more — all great doers in our trade, and are now " for the Lord's sake."°

[*Enter* ABHORSON.]

ABHOR. Sirrah, bring Barnardine hither.

POM. Master Barnardine! You must rise and be hanged, Master Barnardine!

ABHOR. What ho, Barnardine!   25

BARNAR. [*Within*] A pox o' your throats! Who makes that noise there? What are you?

POM. Your friends, sir, the hangman. You must be so good, sir, to rise and be put to death.

BARNAR. [*Within*] Away, you rogue, away! I am sleepy.   30

ABHOR. Tell him he must awake, and that quickly too.

POM. Pray, Master Barnardine, awake till you are executed, and sleep afterward.   35

ABHOR. Go in to him and fetch him out.

POM. He is coming, sir, he is coming, I hear his straw rustle.

ABHOR. Is the ax upon the block, sirrah?

POM. Very ready, sir.   40

[*Enter* BARNARDINE.]

BARNAR. How now, Abhorson? What's the news with you?

ABHOR. Truly, sir, I would desire you to clap into° your prayers, for look you, the warrant's come.   45

BARNAR. You rogue, I have been drinking all night, I am not fitted for 't.

POM. Oh, the better, sir, for he that drinks all night and is hanged betimes in the morning may sleep the sounder all the next day.   50

ABHOR. Look you, sir, here comes your ghostly° Father. Do we jest now, think you?

[*Enter* DUKE *disguised as before.*]

DUKE. Sir, induced by my charity, and hearing how hastily you are to depart, I am come to advise you, comfort you, and pray with you.   55

BARNAR. Friar, not I. I have been drinking hard all night, I will have more time to prepare me, or they shall beat out my brains with billets.° I will not consent to die this day, that's certain.

DUKE. O sir, you must, and therefore I beseech you   60
Look forward on the journey you shall go.

BARNAR. I swear I will not die today for any man's persuasion.

DUKE. But hear you.

BARNAR. Not a word. If you have anything to 65 say to me, come to my ward,° for thence will not I today.   [*Exit.*]

DUKE. Unfit to live or die. O gravel° heart!

---

208. **character:** handwriting.   219. **unfolding star:** the morning star which summons the shepherd to lead his sheep from the fold.   224. **present shrift:** immediate absolution.
    Sc. iii: 1. **well acquainted:** have as many acquaintances. 6–10. **commodity . . . dead:** Interest on loans had been fixed by Act of Parliament at 10%, but moneylenders evaded the statute by the legal device of "commodities." In return for a loan of cash the borrower also purchased a parcel (*commodity*) of worthless goods, such as lutestrings, for which he promised to pay back a much higher sum. Master Rash's "commodity" consisted of brown paper and ginger. **marks:** 13*s.*4*d.*   14. **peaches:** denounces.   16–17. **rapier . . . man:** bully.   18. **tilter:** fencer. 19. **Shooty:** i.e., shoe tie.

22. **for . . . sake:** Prisoners were obliged to pay for their own food in prisons. Those who had no money were allowed to appeal to the charity of passers by to give them alms "for the Lord's sake."   44. **clap into:** get going with.   51. **ghostly:** spiritual.   58. **billet:** a thick stick.   66. **ward:** cell.   68. **gravel:** hard as stone.

After him, fellows, bring him to the block.
[Exeunt ABHORSON and POMPEY.]
[Enter PROVOST.]

PROV. Now, sir, how do you find the prisoner?   70
DUKE. A creature unprepared, unmeet for death,
And to transport him in the mind he is
Were damnable.
PROV.   Here in the prison, Father,
There died this morning of a cruel fever
One Ragozine, a most notorious pirate,   75
A man of Claudio's years, his beard and head
Just of his color. What if we do omit
This reprobate till he were well inclined,
And satisfy the Deputy with the visage
Of Ragozine, more like to Claudio?   80
DUKE. Oh, 'tis an accident that Heaven provides!
Dispatch it presently,° the hour draws on
Prefixed by Angelo. See this be done,
And sent according to command, whiles I
Persuade this rude wretch willingly to die.   85
PROV. This shall be done, good Father, presently.
But Barnardine must die this afternoon.
And how shall we continue Claudio,
To save me from the danger that might come
If he were known alive?
DUKE.   Let this be done.   90
Put them in secret holds, both Barnardine and
Claudio.
Ere twice the sun hath made his journal° greeting
To the under generation,° you shall find
Your safety manifested.
PROV. I am your free dependant.°   95
DUKE. Quick, dispatch, and send the head to
Angelo.   [*Exit* PROVOST.]
Now will I write letters to Angelo —
The Provost, he shall bear them — whose contents
Shall witness to him I am near at home,
And that, by great injunctions, I am bound   100
To enter publicly. Him I'll desire
To meet me at the consecrated fount,
A league below the city, and from thence,
By cold gradation° and well-balanced form,
We shall proceed with Angelo.   105
[Re-enter PROVOST.]

PROV. Here is the head, I'll carry it myself.
DUKE. Convenient is it. Make a swift return,
For I would commune with you of such things
That want no ear but yours.
PROV.   I'll make all speed. [*Exit.*]
ISAB. [*Within*] Peace ho, be here!   110
DUKE. The tongue of Isabel. She's come to know
If yet her brother's pardon be come hither.
But I will keep her ignorant of her good,
To make her heavenly comforts of despair

When it is least expected.
[Enter ISABELLA.]

ISAB.   Ho, by your leave!   115
DUKE. Good morning to you, fair and gracious
daughter.
ISAB. The better, given me by so holy a man.
Hath yet the Deputy sent my brother's pardon?
DUKE. He hath released him, Isabel, from the
world.
His head is off, and sent to Angelo.   120
ISAB. Nay, but it is not so.
DUKE. It is no other. Show your wisdom, Daughter,
In your close° patience.
ISAB. Oh, I will to him and pluck out his eyes!
DUKE. You shall not be admitted to his sight.   125
ISAB. Unhappy Claudio! Wretched Isabel!
Injurious world! Most damnèd Angelo!
DUKE. This nor hurts him nor profits you a jot.
Forbear it therefore, give your cause to Heaven.
Mark what I say, which you shall find   130
By every syllable a faithful verity.
The Duke comes home tomorrow — nay, dry your
eyes,
One of our covent,° and his confessor,
Gives me this instance.° Already he hath carried
Notice to Escalus and Angelo,   135
Who do prepare to meet him at the gates,
There to give up their power. If you can, pace° your
wisdom
In that good path that I would wish it go,
And you shall have your bosom° on this wretch,
Grace of the Duke, revenges to your heart,   140
And general honor.
ISAB.   I am directed by you.
DUKE. This letter, then, to Friar Peter give.
'Tis that he sent me of the Duke's return.
Say, by this token, I desire his company
At Mariana's house tonight. Her cause and yours
I'll perfect° him withal, and he shall bring you   146
Before the Duke, and to the head° of Angelo
Accuse him home and home. For my poor self,
I am combinèd° by a sacred vow,
And shall be absent. Wend you with this letter.   150
Command these fretting waters from your eyes
With a light heart. Trust not my holy Order
If I pervert your course. — Who's here?
[Enter LUCIO.]

LUCIO. Good even. Friar, where's the Provost?
DUKE. Not within, sir.   155
LUCIO. O pretty Isabella, I am pale at mine heart
to see thine eyes so red. Thou must be patient. I am
fain to dine and sup with water and bran, I dare not

---

82. **presently:** immediately.   92. **journal:** daily.   93. **under generation:** i.e., the Antipodes.   95. **your . . . dependant:** entirely your servant.   104. **cold gradation:** deliberate steps.

123. **close:** secret.   133. **covent:** convent, monastery.   134. **instance:** news.   137. **pace:** direct.   139. **your bosom:** what your heart desires.   146. **perfect:** fully inform.   147. **head:** face.   149. **combined:** bound.

for my head fill my belly, one fruitful meal   160
would set me to't. But they say the Duke will be
here tomorrow. By my troth, Isabel, I loved thy
brother. If the old fantastical Duke of dark corners°
had been at home, he had lived.   [*Exit* ISABELLA.]

DUKE. Sir, the Duke is marvelous little be-   166
holding to your reports, but the best is, he lives not
in them.°

LUCIO. Friar, thou knowest not the Duke so well
as I do. He's a better woodman° than thou takest
him for.   170

DUKE. Well, you'll answer this one day. Fare ye
well.

LUCIO. Nay, tarry, I'll go along with thee. I can
tell thee pretty tales of the Duke.   175

DUKE. You have told me too many of him already,
sir, if they be true. If not true, none were enough.

LUCIO. I was once before him for getting a wench
with child.   180

DUKE. Did you such a thing?

LUCIO. Yes, marry did I. But I was fain to forswear it, they would else have married me to the
rotten medlar.°

DUKE. Sir, your company is fairer than hon-   185
est. Rest you well.°

LUCIO. By my troth, I'll go with thee to the lane's
end. If bawdy talk offend you, we'll have very little
of it. Nay, Friar, I am a kind of burr, I shall   189
stick.   [*Exeunt.*]

SCENE IV. *A room in* ANGELO's *house.*

[*Enter* ANGELO *and* ESCALUS.]

ESCAL. Every letter he hath writ hath disvouched°
other.

ANG. In most uneven and distracted manner. His
actions show much like to madness. Pray Heaven his
wisdom be not tainted! And why meet him at   5
the gates, and redeliver our authorities there?

ESCAL. I guess not.

ANG. And why should we proclaim it in an   8
hour before his entering that if any crave redress of
injustice, they should exhibit their petitions in the
street?

ESCAL. He shows his reason for that. To have a
dispatch of complaints, and to deliver us from   13
devices° hereafter, which shall then have no power
to stand against us.

ANG. Well, I beseech you let it be proclaimed betimes i' the morn. I'll call you at your house. Give

notice to such men of sort° and suit° as are to meet
him.   20

ESCAL. I shall, sir. Fare you well.

ANG. Good night.   [*Exit* ESCALUS.]
This deed unshapes° me quite, makes me unpreg-
nant,°
And dull to all proceedings. A deflowered maid!
And by an eminent body that enforced   25
The law against it! But that her tender shame
Will not proclaim against her maiden loss,°
How might she tongue me! Yet reason dares her
no.°
For my authority bears of a credent bulk°
That no particular scandal once can touch   30
But it confounds the breather. He should have lived,
Save that his riotous youth, with dangerous sense,°
Might in the times to come have ta'en revenge
By so receiving a dishonored life
With ransom of such shame. Would yet he had
lived!   35
Alack, when once our grace we have forgot,
Nothing goes right. We would, and we would not.
  [*Exit.*]

SCENE V. *Fields without the town.*

[*Enter* DUKE *in his own habit, and* FRIAR PETER.]

DUKE. These letters at fit time deliver me.°
  [*Giving letters*]
The Provost knows our purpose and our plot.
The matter being afoot, keep your instruction,
And hold you ever to our special drift,°
Though sometimes you do blench° from this to
that,   5
As cause doth minister. Go call at Flavius' house,
And tell him where I stay. Give the like notice
To Valentius, Rowland, and to Crassus,
And bid them bring the trumpets to the gate.   9
But send me Flavius first.

FRI. P.   It shall be speeded well.   [*Exit.*]
[*Enter* VARRIUS.]

DUKE. I thank thee, Varrius, thou hast made good
haste.
Come, we will walk. There's other of our friends
Will greet us here anon, my gentle Varrius.
  [*Exeunt.*]

19. sort: high rank. suit: with petitions.   23. unshapes: upsets.
unpregnant: unapt.   27. maiden loss: loss of virginity.   28. dares
... no: tells her not to.   29. credent bulk: my authority is so
great that I will be believed.   32. sense: feeling.
    Sc. v: 1. me: for me.   4. drift: purpose.   5. blench: start
aside.

164. dark corners: always meeting women in the dark.
167–68. lives ... them: i.e., they are lies.   169. woodman: hunter; i.e., of women.   184. medlar: fruit of the apple kind, eaten
only when it has gone soft.   186. Rest ... well: I bid you farewell.
    Sc. iv: 1. disvouched: contradicted.   14. devices: plots.

SCENE VI. *Street near the city gate.*

[*Enter* ISABELLA *and* MARIANA.]

ISAB. To speak so indirectly I am loath.
I would say the truth, but to accuse him so,
That is your part. Yet I am advised to do it —
He says, to veil full purpose.°
　MARI.　　　　　　　　Be ruled by him.
ISAB. Besides, he tells me that if peradventure　5
He speak against me on the adverse side,
I should not think it strange, for 'tis a physic
That's bitter to sweet end.
　MARI. I would Friar Peter ——
　ISAB.　　　　　Oh, peace! The Friar is come.
[*Enter* FRIAR PETER.]
FRI. P. Come, I have found you out a stand° most
　fit,　　　　　　　　　　　　　　　　　　　10
Where you may have such vantage° on the Duke,
He shall not pass you. Twice have the trumpets
　sounded,
The generous° and gravest citizens
Have hent° the gates, and very near upon
The Duke is entering.Therefore hence, away!　15
　　　　　　　　　　　　　　　　　[*Exeunt.*]

Act V

SCENE I. *The city gate.*

[MARIANA *veiled,* ISABELLA, *and* FRIAR PETER, *at their*
stand. Enter DUKE, VARRIUS, LORDS, ANGELO, ESCALUS,
　LUCIO, PROVOST, OFFICERS, *and* CITIZENS,
　　　　　at several doors.]
DUKE. My very worthy cousin,° fairly met!
Our old and faithful friend, we are glad to see you.
　ANG. & ESCAL. Happy return be to your royal
　　Grace!
　DUKE. Many and hearty thankings to you both.
We have made inquiry of you, and we hear　5
Such goodness of your justice that our soul
Cannot but yield you forth to public thanks,
Forerunning more requital.°
　ANG.　　　　You make my bonds° still greater.
DUKE. Oh, your desert speaks loud, and I should
　wrong it
To lock it in the wards of covert bosom°　10
When it deserves, with characters° of brass,

Sc. vi: 4. **veil . . . purpose:** not to reveal our full plan.
10. **stand:** place.　11. **vantage:** advantageous position.　13. **gen-**
erous: well-born.　14. **hent:** occupied.
　Act V, Sc. i: 1. **cousin:** kinsman.　8. **Forerunning . . . re-**
quital: preceding other forms of reward. **bonds:** debts.　10. **cov-**
ert bosom: i.e., the secrecy of my heart.　11. **characters:** letters.

A forted° residence 'gainst the tooth of time
And razure of oblivion. Give me your hand,
And let the subject° see, to make them know
That outward courtesies would fain proclaim　15
Favors that keep within. Come, Escalus,
You must walk by us on our other hand.
And good supporters are you.
[FRIAR PETER *and* ISABELLA *come forward.*]
　FRI. P. Now is your time. Speak loud, and kneel
　before him.　　　　　　　　　　　　　　　19
　ISAB. Justice, O royal Duke! Vail your regard°
Upon a wronged, I would fain have said, a maid!
O worthy prince, dishonor not your eye
By throwing it on any other object
Till you have heard me in my true complaint,
And given me justice, justice, justice, justice!　25
　DUKE. Relate your wrongs. In what? By whom?
　Be brief.
Here is Lord Angelo shall give you justice.
Reveal yourself to him.
　ISAB.　　　　　　O worthy Duke,
You bid me seek redemption of the Devil.
Hear me yourself, for that which I must speak　30
Must either punish me, not being believed,
Or wring redress from you. Hear me, O hear me,
　here!
　ANG. My lord, her wits, I fear me, are not firm.
She hath been a suitor to me for her brother
Cut off by course of justice ——
　ISAB.　　　　　　By course of justice!　35
　ANG. And she will speak most bitterly and strange.
　ISAB. Most strange, but yet most truly, will I speak.
That Angelo's forsworn, is it not strange?
That Angelo's a murderer, is't not strange?
That Angelo is an adulterous thief,　　　　40
A hypocrite, a virgin-violator,
Is it not strange and strange?
　DUKE.　　　　Nay, it is ten times strange.
　ISAB. It is not truer he is Angelo
Than this is all as true as it is strange.
Nay, it is ten times true, for truth is truth　45
To the end of reckoning.
　DUKE.　　　　　　Away with her! — Poor soul,
She speaks this in the infirmity of sense.
　ISAB. O Prince, I conjure thee, as thou believest
There is another comfort than this world,
That thou neglect me not, with that opinion　50
That I am touched with madness! Make not impos-
　sible
That which but seems unlike. 'Tis not impossible
But one, the wicked'st caitiff° on the ground,
May seem as shy, as grave, as just, as absolute°
As Angelo. Even so may Angelo,　　　　55
In all his dressings,° characts,° titles, forms,

---

12. **forted:** fortified.　14. **the subject:** my subjects.　20. **Vail**
. . . regard: lower your glance.　53. **caitiff:** wretch.　54. **abso-**
lute: perfect.　56. **dressings:** outward shows. **characts:** marks
of distinction.

Be an archvillain — believe it, royal Prince.
If he be less, he's nothing, but he's more
Had I more name for badness.
    DUKE.   By mine honesty,
If she be mad — as I believe no other —   60
Her madness hath the oddest frame of sense,
Such a dependency of thing on thing,
As e'er I heard in madness.
    ISAB.   O gracious Duke,
Harp not on that, nor do not banish reason
For inequality,° but let your reason serve   65
To make the truth appear where it seems hid,
And hide the false seems true.
    DUKE.   Many that are not mad
Have, sure, more lack of reason. What would you
    say?
    ISAB. I am the sister of one Claudio,
Condemned upon the act of fornication   70
To lose his head, condemned by Angelo.
I, in probation° of a sisterhood,
Was sent to by my brother, one Lucio
As then the messenger ——
    LUCIO.   That's I, an't like° your Grace.
I came to her from Claudio, and desired her   75
To try her gracious fortune with Lord Angelo
For her poor brother's pardon.
    ISAB.   That's he indeed.
    DUKE. You were not bid to speak.
    LUCIO.   No, my good lord,
Nor wished to hold my peace.
    DUKE.   I wish you now, then.
Pray you take note of it. And when you have   80
A business for yourself, pray Heaven you then
Be perfect.
    LUCIO.   I warrant your Honor.
    DUKE. The warrant's for yourself, take heed to't.
    ISAB. This gentleman told somewhat of my
    tale ——
    LUCIO. Right.   85
    DUKE. It may be right, but you are i' the wrong
To speak before your time. Proceed.
    ISAB.   I went
To this pernicious caitiff Deputy ——
    DUKE. That's somewhat madly spoken.
    ISAB.   Pardon it.
The phrase is to the matter.°   90
    DUKE. Mended again. The matter — proceed.
    ISAB. In brief — to set the needless process by,
How I persuaded, how I prayed, and kneeled,
How he refelled° me, and how I replied —
For this was of much length — the vile conclu-
    sion
I now begin with grief and shame to utter.   96
He would not, but by gift of my chaste body

To his concupiscible° intemperate lust,
Release my brother, and, after much debatement,
My sisterly remorse° confutes mine honor,   100
And I did yield to him. But the next morn betimes,
His purpose surfeiting,° he sends a warrant
For my poor brother's head.
    DUKE.   This is most likely!
    ISAB. Oh, that it were as like° as it is true!
    DUKE. By Heaven, fond° wretch, thou know'st
    not what thou speak'st,   105
Or else thou art suborned° against his honor
In hateful practice.° First, his integrity
Stands without blemish. Next, it imports no reason
That with such vehemency he should pursue   109
Faults proper° to himself. If he had so offended,
He would have weighed thy brother by himself,
And not have cut him off. Someone hath set you on.
Confess the truth, and say by whose advice
Thou camest here to complain.
    ISAB.   And is this all?
Then, O you blessed ministers above,   115
Keep me in patience, and with ripened time
Unfold the evil which is here wrapped up
In countenance!° — Heaven shield your Grace from
    woe,
As I, thus wronged, hence unbelievèd go!   119
    DUKE. I know you'd fain be gone. — An officer!
To prison with her! — Shall we thus permit
A blasting and a scandalous breath to fall
On him so near us? This needs must be a practice.
Who knew of your intent and coming hither?   124
    ISAB. One that I would were here, Friar Lodo-
    wick.
    DUKE. A ghostly Father, belike. Who knows that
    Lodowick?
    LUCIO. My lord, I know him, 'tis a meddling friar,
I do not like the man. Had he been lay,° my lord,
For certain words he spake against your Grace   129
In your retirement, I had swinged° him soundly.
    DUKE. Words against me! This's a good friar, be-
    like!
And to set on this wretched woman here
Against our substitute! Let this friar be found.
    LUCIO. But yesternight, my lord, she and that
    friar,
I saw them at the prison. A saucy friar,   135
A very scurvy fellow.
    FRI. P. Blessed be your royal Grace!
I have stood by, my lord, and I have heard
Your royal ear abused. First, hath this woman
Most wrongfully accused your substitute,   140
Who is as free from touch or soil with her

---

65. inequality: injustice.   72. probation: novitiate.   74. an't
like: if it please.   90. to ... matter: fitting.   94. refelled:
refused.   98. concupiscible: lecherous.   100. remorse: pity.   102. surfeiting: sickening after excess.   104. like: likely.   105. fond:
foolish.   106. suborned: bribed to make a false accusation.
107. practice: plot.   110. proper: belonging.   118. countenance:
favoritism.   128. lay: a layman.   130. swinged: thrashed.

As she from one ungot.°
DUKE.   We did believe no less.
Know you that Friar Lodowick that she speaks
of?
FRI. P. I know him for a man divine and holy,
Not scurvy, nor a temporary° meddler   145
As he's reported by this gentleman,
And, on my trust, a man that never yet
Did, as he vouches, misreport your Grace.
LUCIO. My lord, most villainously, believe it.
FRI. P. Well, he in time may come to clear him-
self,   150
But at this instant he is sick, my lord,
Of a strange fever. Upon his mere request —
Being come to knowledge that there was complaint
Intended 'gainst Lord Angelo — came I hither,
To speak, as from his mouth, what he doth know
Is true and false, and what he with his oath   156
And all probation° will make up full clear,
Whensoever he's convented.° First, for this woman,
To justify this worthy nobleman,
So vulgarly and personally accused,   160
Her shall you hear disprovèd to her eyes
Till she herself confess it.
DUKE.   Good Friar, let's hear it.
[ISABELLA *is carried off guarded;*
and MARIANA *comes forward.*]
Do you not smile at this, Lord Angelo? —
O Heaven, the vanity of wretched fools! —
Give us some seats. Come, Cousin Angelo,   165
In this I'll be impartial,° be you judge
Of your own cause. Is this the witness, Friar?
First, let her show her face, and after speak.
MARI. Pardon, my lord, I will not show my face
Until my husband bid me.   170
DUKE. What, are you married?
MARI. No, my lord.
DUKE. Are you a maid?
MARI. No, my lord.
DUKE. A widow, then?   175
MARI. Neither, my lord.
DUKE. Why, you are nothing, then — neither
maid, widow, nor wife?
LUCIO. My lord, she may be a punk,° for many of
them are neither maid, widow, nor wife.   180
DUKE. Silence that fellow. I would he had some
cause
To prattle for himself.
LUCIO. Well, my lord.
MARI. My lord, I do confess I ne'er was married,
And I confess, besides, I am no maid.   185
I have known° my husband, yet my husband
Knows not that ever he knew me.

LUCIO. He was drunk, then, my lord. It can be no
better.   190
DUKE. For the benefit of silence, would thou wert
so too!
LUCIO. Well, my lord.
DUKE. This is no witness for Lord Angelo.
MARI. Now I come to't, my lord.
She that accuses him of fornication   195
In selfsame manner doth accuse my husband,
And charges him, my lord, with such a time
When I'll depose° I had him in mine arms
With all the effect of love.
ANG. Charges she moe° than me?
MARI.   Not that I know.   200
DUKE. No? You say your husband.
MARI. Why, just, my lord, and that is Angelo,
Who thinks he knows that he ne'er knew my body,
But knows he thinks that he knows Isabel's.   204
ANG. This is a strange abuse. Let's see thy face.
MARI. My husband bids me, now I will unmask.
[*Unveiling.*]
This is that face, thou cruel Angelo,
Which once thou sworest was worth the looking on.
This is the hand which, with a vowed contráct,
Was fast belocked in thine. This is the body   210
That took away the match° from Isabel,
And did supply thee at thy garden house
In her imagined person.
DUKE.   Know you this woman?
LUCIO. Carnally, she says.
DUKE.   Sirrah, no more!
LUCIO. Enough, my lord.   215
ANG. My lord, I must confess I know this woman.
And five years since there was some speech of mar-
riage
Betwixt myself and her, which was broke off,
Partly for that her promisèd proportions°
Came short of composition,° but in chief   220
For that her reputation was disvalued
In levity.° Since which time of five years
I never spake her with, saw her, nor heard from her,
Upon my faith and honor.
MARI.   Noble Prince,
As there comes light from Heaven and words from
breath,   225
As there is sense in truth and truth in virtue,
I am affianced° this man's wife as strongly
As words could make up vows. And, my good lord,
But Tuesday night last gone in's garden house
He knew me as a wife. As this is true,   230
Let me in safety raise me from my knees,
Or else for ever be confixèd° here,
A marble monument!

142. ungot: unbegotten.   145. temporary: in temporal matters.
157. probation: proof.   158. convented: summoned.   166. be
impartial: take no part.   179. punk: whore.   186. known: had
intercourse with.

198. depose: give evidence.   200. moe: more.   211. match:
meeting.   219. proportions: possessions, dowry.   220. composition: agreement.   221–22. was . . . levity: made worthless
by loose behavior.   227. affianced: betrothed.   232. confixed:
firmly fixed.

ANG.   I did but smile till now.
Now, good my lord, give me the scope of justice,
My patience here is touched. I do perceive   235
These poor informal° women are no more
But instruments of some more mightier member
That sets them on. Let me have way, my lord,
To find this practice out.
DUKE.   Aye, with my heart,
And punish them to your height of pleasure.   240
Thou foolish friar, and thou pernicious woman,
Compact° with her that's gone, think'st thou thy
        oaths,
Though they would swear down each particular
        saint,
Were testimonies against his worth and credit   244
That's sealed in approbation?° You, Lord Escalus,
Sit with my cousin, lend him your kind pains°
To find out this abuse, whence 'tis derived.
There is another friar that set them on.
Let him be sent for.
FRI. P. Would he were here, my lord! For he in-
        deed   250
Hath set the women on to this complaint.
Your Provost knows the place where he abides,
And he may fetch him.
DUKE.   Go, do it instantly.   [*Exit* PROVOST.]
And you, my noble and well-warranted cousin,
Whom it concerns to hear this matter forth,   255
Do with your injuries as seems you best,
In any chastisement. I for a while will leave you,
But stir not you till you have well determined°
Upon these slanderers.   259
ESCAL. My lord, we'll do it throughly.° [*Exit*
DUKE.] Signior Lucio, did not you say you knew
that Friar Lodowick to be a dishonest person?
LUCIO. "*Cucullus non facit monachum.*"° Hon-
est in nothing but in his clothes, and one that hath
spoke most villainous speeches of the Duke.   265
ESCAL. We shall entreat you to abide here till he
come, and enforce° them against him. We shall find
this friar a notable fellow.
LUCIO. As any in Vienna, on my word.   269
ESCAL. Call that same Isabel here once again. I
would speak with her. [*Exit an* ATTENDANT.] Pray
you, my lord, give me leave to question, you shall
see how I'll handle her.
LUCIO. Not better than he, by her own report.
ESCAL. Say you?   275
LUCIO. Marry, sir, I think if you handled her privately, she would sooner confess. Perchance publicly
she'll be ashamed.
ESCAL. I will go darkly° to work with her.

LUCIO. That's the way, for women are light at
midnight.   281
[*Re-enter* OFFICERS *with* ISABELLA; *and* PROVOST *with
the* DUKE *in his friar's habit.*]
ESCAL. Come on, mistress. Here's a gentlewoman
denies all that you have said.
LUCIO. My lord, here comes the rascal I spoke of,
here with the Provost.   285
ESCAL. In very good time. Speak not you to him
till we call upon you.
LUCIO. Mum.
ESCAL. Come, sir, did you set these women on
to slander Lord Angelo? They have confessed you
did.
DUKE. 'Tis false.   291
ESCAL. How! Know you where you are?
DUKE. Respect to your great place! And let the
        Devil
Be sometime honored for his burning throne!   295
Where is the Duke? 'Tis he should hear me speak.
ESCAL. The Duke's in us,° and we will hear you
        speak.
Look you speak justly.
DUKE. Boldly, at least. But, oh, poor souls,
Come you to seek the lamb here of the fox?   300
Good night to your redress! Is the Duke gone?
Then is your cause gone too. The Duke's unjust,
Thus to retort° your manifest appeal,
And put your trial in the villain's mouth
Which here you come to accuse.   305
LUCIO. This is the rascal, this is he I spoke of.
ESCAL. Why, thou unreverend and unhallowed
        friar,
Is't not enough thou hast suborned these women
To accuse this worthy man, but, in foul mouth,
And in the witness of his proper° ear,   310
To call him villain? And then to glance from him
To the Duke himself, to tax° him with injustice?
Take him hence, to the rack with him! We'll touse°
        you
Joint by joint, but we will know his purpose.
What, "unjust"!
DUKE.   Be not so hot. The Duke   315
Dare no more stretch this finger of mine than he
Dare rack his own. His subject am I not,
Nor here provincial.° My business in this state
Made me a looker-on here in Vienna,
Where I have seen corruption boil and bubble   320
Till it o'errun the stew° — laws for all faults,
But faults so countenanced that the strong statutes
Stand like the forfeits° in a barber's shop,
As much in mock as mark.°

236. informal: crazy.   242. Compact: confederate.   245. sealed
in approbation: warranted as true.   246. pains: trouble.   258. determined: decided.   260. throughly: thoroughly.   263. Cucullus
... monachum: a cowl does not make a monk.   267. enforce:
bring home, declare.   279. darkly: subtly.

297. in us: represented by us.   303. retort: reject.   310. proper:
own.   312. tax: charge.   313. touse: tear.   318. provincial:
a member of this ecclesiastical province.   321. stew: caldron.
323. forfeits: teeth extracted by barbers (who were also surgeons and dentists) strung up as trophies of their trade.   324. As
... mark: to be mocked at as much as observed.

ESCAL. Slander to the state! Away with him to
    prison!   325
ANG. What can you vouch against him, Signior
    Lucio?
Is this the man that you did tell us of?
LUCIO. 'Tis he, my lord. Come hither, goodman
baldpate. Do you know me?   330
DUKE. I remember you, sir, by the sound of your
voice. I met you at the prison, in the absence of the
Duke.
LUCIO. Oh, did you so? And do you remember
what you said of the Duke?   335
DUKE. Most notedly, sir.
LUCIO. Do you so, sir? And was the Duke a flesh-
monger, a fool, and a coward, as you then reported
him to be?
DUKE. You must, sir, change persons with me ere
you make that my report. You indeed spoke so of
him, and much more, much worse.   340
LUCIO. O thou damnable fellow! Did not I pluck
thee by the nose for thy speeches?
DUKE. I protest I love the Duke as I love myself.
ANG. Hark how the villain would close° now,
after his treasonable abuses!   345
ESCAL. Such a fellow is not to be talked withal.
Away with him to prison! Where is the Provost?
Away with him to prison! Lay bolts enough upon
him. Let him speak no more. Away with those gig-
lets° too, and with the other confederate companion!
DUKE. [*To the* PROVOST] Stay, sir, stay awhile.
ANG. What, resists he? Help him, Lucio.
LUCIO. Come, sir, come, sir, come, sir. Foh,   355
sir! Why, you bald-pated, lying rascal, you must be
hooded, must you? Show your knave's visage, with
a pox to you! Show your sheepbiting° face, and be
hanged an hour! Will't not off?   360
[*Pulls off the friar's hood, and discovers the Duke.*]
    DUKE. Thou art the first knave that e'er madest a
    Duke.
First, Provost, let me bail these gentle three.
[*To* LUCIO] Sneak not away, sir, for the Friar and
    you
Must have a word anon. Lay hold on him.
LUCIO. This may prove worse than hanging.   365
DUKE. [*To* ESCALUS] What you have spoke I par-
don. Sit you down.
We'll borrow place of him. [*To* ANGELO] Sir, by
your leave.
Hast thou or word, or wit, or impudence,
That yet can do thee office? If thou hast,
Rely upon it till my tale be heard,   370
And hold no longer out.
    ANG.   O my dread lord,
I should be guiltier than my guiltiness
To think I can be undiscernible°

When I perceive your Grace, like power divine,
Hath looked upon my passes.° Then, good Prince,
No longer session° hold upon my shame,   376
But let my trial be mine own confession.
Immediate sentence then, and sequent° death,
Is all the grace I beg.
    DUKE.   Come hither, Mariana.
Say, wast thou e'er contracted to this woman?   380
ANG. I was, my lord.
    DUKE. Go take her hence, and marry her in-
    stantly.
Do you the office, Friar, which consummate,
Return him here again. Go with him, Provost.
    [*Exeunt* ANGELO, MARIANA, FRIAR PETER,
            and PROVOST.]
ESCAL. My lord, I am more amazed at his dis-
honor   385
Than at the strangeness of it.
    DUKE.   Come hither, Isabel.
Your friar is now your Prince. As I was then
Advértising° and holy to your business,
Not changing heart with habit, I am still
Attorneyed° at your service.
    ISAB.   Oh, give me pardon   390
That I, your vassal,° have employed and pained
Your unknown sovereignty!
    DUKE.   You are pardoned, Isabel.
And now, dear maid, be you as free to us.
Your brother's death, I know, sits at your heart,
And you may marvel why I obscured myself,   395
Laboring to save his life, and would not rather
Make rash remonstrance° of my hidden power
Than let him so be lost. O most kind maid,
It was the swift celerity of his death,
Which I did think with slower foot came on,   400
That brained my purpose. But peace be with him!
That life is better life, past fearing death,
Than that which lives to fear. Make it your comfort,
So happy is your brother.
    ISAB.   I do, my lord.
    [*Re-enter* ANGELO, MARIANA, FRIAR PETER,
            and PROVOST.]
DUKE. For this new-married man approaching
here,   405
Whose salt° imagination yet hath wronged
Your well-defended honor, you must pardon
For Mariana's sake. But as he adjudged your
    brother —
Being criminal, in double violation
Of sacred chastity, and of promise breach   410
Thereon dependent, for your brother's life —
The very mercy of the law cries out
Most audible, even from his proper tongue,

---

344. close: "climb down."   349. giglets: wantons.   359. sheep-
biting: sheepstealing.   373. undiscernible: not revealed.

375. passes: acts, trespasses.   376. session: trial.   378. sequent: following.   388. Advertising: attentive.   390. Attorneyed: employed as your pleader.   391. vassal: slave.   397. rash
remonstrance: hasty demonstration.   406. salt: lustful.

"An Angelo for Claudio, death for death!"   414
Haste still pays haste, and leisure answers leisure,
Like doth quit° like, and measure still for measure.
Then, Angelo, thy fault's thus manifested,
Which, though thou wouldst deny, denies thee vantage.
We do condemn thee to the very block   419
Where Claudio stooped to death, and with like haste.
Away with him!

MARI.   O my most gracious lord,
I hope you will not mock me with a husband.

DUKE. It is your husband mocked you with a husband.
Consenting to the safeguard of your honor,
I thought your marriage fit, else imputation,°   425
For that he knew you, might reproach your life
And choke your good to come. For his possessions,
Although by confiscation they are ours,
We do instate and widow you withal,°
To buy you a better husband.

MARI.   O my dear lord,   430
I crave no other, nor no better man.

DUKE. Never crave him, we are definitive.°

MARI. Gentle my liege ——   [*Kneeling.*]

DUKE.   You do but lose your labor.
Away with him to death! [*To* LUCIO] Now, sir, to you.

MARI. O my good lord! Sweet Isabel, take my part,   435
Lend me your knees, and all my life to come
I'll lend you all my life to do you service.

DUKE. Against all sense you do impórtune her.
Should she kneel down in mercy of this fact,
Her brother's ghost his pavèd° bed would break,
And take her hence in horror.   441

MARI.   Isabel,
Sweet Isabel, do yet but kneel by me,
Hold up your hands, say nothing, I'll speak all.
They say best men are molded out of faults,
And, for the most, become much more the better
For being a little bad. So may my husband.   446
O Isabel, will you not lend a knee?

DUKE. He dies for Claudio's death.

ISAB.   Most bounteous sir,   [*Kneeling.*]
Look, if it please you, on this man condemned
As if my brother lived. I partly think   450
A due sincerity governed his deeds,
Till he did look on me. Since it is so,
Let him not die. My brother had but justice,
In that he did the thing for which he died.
For Angelo,   455
His act did not o'ertake his bad intent,°
And must be buried but as an intent

That perished by the way. Thoughts are no subjects,°
Intents but merely thoughts.

MARI.   Merely, my lord.

DUKE. Your suit's unprofitable. Stand up, I say.
I have bethought me of another fault.   461
Provost, how came it Claudio was beheaded
At an unusual hour?

PROV.   It was commanded so.

DUKE. Had you a special warrant for the deed?

PROV. No, my good lord, it was by private message.   465

DUKE. For which I do discharge you of your office.
Give up your keys.

PROV.   Pardon me, noble lord.
I thought it was a fault, but knew it not,
Yet did repent me, after more advice.°
For testimony whereof, one in the prison   470
That should by private order else have died
I have reserved alive.

DUKE.   What's he?

PROV.   His name is Barnardine.

DUKE. I would thou hadst done so by Claudio.
Go fetch him hither, let me look upon him.
         [*Exit* PROVOST.]

ESCAL. I am sorry one so learned and so wise   475
As you, Lord Angelo, have still° appeared
Should slip so grossly, both in the heat of blood
And lack of tempered judgment afterward.

ANG. I am sorry that such sorrow I procure.
And so deep sticks it in my penitent heart   480
That I crave death more willingly than mercy.
'Tis my deserving, and I do entreat it.
     [*Re-enter* PROVOST, *with* BARNARDINE, CLAUDIO
            muffled,° and JULIET.]

DUKE. Which is that Barnardine?

PROV.   This, my lord.

DUKE. There was a friar told me of this man.
Sirrah, thou art said to have a stubborn soul   485
That apprehends no further than this world,
And squarest° thy life according. Thou'rt condemned.
But, for those earthly faults, I quit° them all,
And pray thee take this mercy to provide
For better times to come. Friar, advise him,   490
I leave him to your hand. What muffled fellow's that?

PROV. This is another prisoner that I saved,
Who should have died when Claudio lost his head,
As like almost to Claudio as himself.
         [*Unmuffles* CLAUDIO.]

DUKE. [*To* ISABELLA] If he be like your brother, for his sake   495
Is he pardoned, and, for your lovely sake,

---

416. quit: pay for.   425. imputation: slander.   429. instate . . . withal: bestow on you as his widow.   432. definitive: resolute. 440. paved: Persons of rank were buried inside the church beneath the pavement.   456. His . . . intent: he did not commit the act which he intended.

458. no subjects: not subject to punishment.   469. advice: consideration.   476. still: always.   482 s.d., muffled: i.e., his face concealed in a muffler.   487. squarest: measurest. 488. quit: forgive.

Give me your hand and say you will be mine,
He is my brother too. But fitter time for that.
By this Lord Angelo perceives he's safe,
Methinks I see a quickening in his eye.   500
Well, Angelo, your evil quits° you well.
Look that you love your wife, her worth worth
    yours.
I find an apt remission° in myself,
And yet here's one in place I cannot pardon.
[*To* LUCIO] You, sirrah, that knew me for a fool, a
    coward,   505
One all of luxury,° an ass, a madman,
Wherein have I so deserved of you
That you extol me thus?
    LUCIO. 'Faith, my lord, I spoke it but according to
the trick. If you will hang me for it, you may, but I
had rather it would please you I might be whipped.
    DUKE. Whipped first, sir, and hanged after. LUCIO
Proclaim it, Provost, round about the city,
If any woman wronged by this lewd fellow —   515
As I have heard him swear himself there's one
Whom he begot with child — let her appear
And he shall marry her. The nuptial finished,
Let him be whipped and hanged.
    LUCIO. I beseech your Highness, do not marry me
to a whore. Your Highness said even now I made
you a Duke. Good my lord, do not recompense me
in making me a cuckold.

501. quits: pays back.   503. remission: readiness to forgive.
506. luxury: lust.

    DUKE. Upon mine honor, thou shalt marry her.
Thy slanders I forgive, and therewithal   525
Remit thy other forfeits.° — Take him to prison,
And see our pleasure herein executed.
    LUCIO. Marrying a punk, my lord, is pressing to
death° whipping, and hanging.
    DUKE. Slandering a prince deserves it.   530
                    [*Exeunt* OFFICERS *with* LUCIO.]
She, Claudio, that you wronged, look you restore.
Joy to you, Mariana! Love her, Angelo.
I have confessed her,° and I know her virtue.
Thanks, good friend Escalus, for thy much goodness,
There's more behind° that is more gratulate.°   535
Thanks, Provost, for thy care and secrecy.
We shall employ thee in a worthier place.
Forgive him, Angelo, that brought you home
The head of Ragozine for Claudio's.
The offense pardons itself. Dear Isabel,   540
I have a motion° much imports your good,
Whereto if you'll a willing ear incline,
What's mine is yours, and what is yours is mine.
So bring us to our palace, where we'll show
What's yet behind, that's meet you all should know.
                    [*Exeunt.*]

526. forfeits: punishments.   528–29. pressing to death: See
Gen. Intro. p. 27b.   533. confessed her: heard her confession;
i.e., when he was posing as a friar.   535. behind: to come.
gratulate: gratifying.   541. motion: proposal.

THE TRAGEDY OF KING LEAR

Introduction

The Tragedy of King Lear is usually regarded by critics as Shakespeare's greatest play, but it is not his most popular, for there is something terrifying in the grandeur of the tragedy and its immense pessimism. Nor is the play often acted on the stage, for the part of Lear requires an actor of exceptional range of emotional expression. Indifferently produced, Lear is tedious, but when greatly acted it is almost too intolerably moving.

King Lear can be more precisely dated than most of Shakespeare's plays. On November 26, 1607, Nathaniel Butter and John Busby entered in the Register of the Stationers' Company and so claimed their right to print " A booke called Master William Shakespeare his historye of King Lear, as yt was played before the Kinges maiestie at Whitehall vppon Sainct Stephens night (December 26) at Christmas Last, by his maiesties servantes playinge vsually at the Globe on the Banksyde."

Lear was thus acted before King James and his Court in the Christmas holidays of 1606. The earliest quarto of the play (Q1) is dated 1608. There are also some evidences in the play itself which show that Shakespeare wrote it between February and December 1606. Gloucester's observations on " these late eclipses in the sun and moon " probably refer to notable eclipses that occurred on September 27 and October 2, 1605. To the superstitious, an eclipse was always an alarming event. Shakespeare, however, took these speeches from a pamphlet called Strange, fearful and true news which happened at Carlstadt in the Kingdom of Croatia. It was translated from the High Dutch and told of fearful signs and portents, which according to the editor, one Edward Gresham, an almanac-writer, were divine warnings of threatening disasters:

The Earth's and Moon's late and horrible obscurations, the frequent eclipsations of the fixed bodies; by the wandering, the fixed stars, I mean the planets, within these few years more than ordinary, shall without doubt (salved divine inhibition) have their effects no less admirable than the positions unusual. Which PEUCER with many more too long to rehearse out of continual observation and the consent of all

authors noted to be new leagues, traitorous designments, catching at kingdoms, translation of empire, downfall of men in authority, emulations, ambition, innovations, factious sects, schisms and much disturbance and troubles in religion and matters of the Church, with many other things infallible in sequent such orbical positions and phenomenes.

The preface to this astonishing work was dated February 11, 1606. The similarity of phrase, rhythm, and sentiment is too close to have been accidental. Shakespeare also took a few details from A declaration of egregious popish impostures to withdraw the hearts of her Majesty's subjects from their allegiance, and from the truth of the Christian religion, professed in England, under the pretense of casting out devils. This book was written in 1602–03 by the Reverend Samuel Harsnett, chaplain to the Bishop of London. Harsnett had taken considerable part in the controversies which raged around John Darrell the exorcist (see T. Night Intro. p. 847a–b), and was the author of the official exposure of Darrell's claims. After the Darrell controversy had died down, Harsnett turned to attack the Jesuit exorcists in A Declaration. From this book Shakespeare took also the names of Edgar's fiends — Fraretto, Flibbertigibbet, Hopdidance, Modo and Mahu.

The text of King Lear is difficult. Q1 is very badly printed and full of errors. Many verse lines are printed as prose, the punctuation is chaotic, and misprints and meaningless phrases are common. There has been considerable controversy among scholars about the origin of this text but so far no wholly convincing explanation has been put forward to account for all its peculiarities. The version of the play printed in the first folio in 1623 was based on a copy of Q1 which had been very carefully corrected and much revised; it omits about three hundred lines and adds a few new passages. Editors in preparing a modern text usually make an amalgamation of Q1 and F1, adapting those readings which seem best.

The story of King Lear and his three daughters was well known. It was one of the many fables which old chroniclers had inserted into the history of England to bridge the gap between Biblical history and the time when records of fact begin. In Holinshed's *Chronicles,* for instance, it is stated that:

Leir the son of Baldud was admitted ruler over the Britons, in the year of the world 3105, at what time Joash reigned in Judah. This Leir was a prince of right noble demeanor, governing his land and subjects in great wealth. He made the town of Caerleir now called Leicester, which standeth upon the river of Sore. It is written that he had by his wife three daughters without other issue, whose names were Gonorilla, Regan, and Cordeilla, which daughters he greatly loved, but especially Cordeilla, the youngest, far above the two elder. When this Leir therefore was come to great years, and began to wax unwieldy through age, he thought to understand the affections of his daughters toward him, and prefer her whom he best loved to the succession over the kingdom. Whereupon he first asked Gonorilla, the eldest, how well she loved him: who calling her gods to record, protested that she loved him more than her own life, which by right and reason should be most dear unto her. With which answer the father being well pleased, turned to the second, and demanded of her how well she loved him: who answered (confirming her sayings with great oaths) that she loved him more than tongue could express, and far above all other creatures of the world.

Then called he his youngest daughter Cordeilla before him, and asked of her what account she made of him, unto whom she made this answer as followeth: " Knowing the great love and fatherly zeal that you have always born toward me (for the which I may not answer you otherwise than I think, and as my conscience leadeth me) I protest unto you that I have loved you ever, and will continually (while I live) love you as my natural father. And if you would more understand of the love that I bear you, ascertain yourself that so much as you have, so much you are worth, and so much I love you, and no more." The father, being nothing content with this answer, married his two eldest daughters, the one unto Henninus the Duke of Cornwall, and the other unto Maglanus the Duke of Albania, betwixt whom he willed and ordained that his land should be divided after his death, and the one half thereof immediately should be assigned to them in hand: but for the third daughter Cordeilla he reserved nothing.

There are various versions of the rest of the story, but all agree in the general outline: that after Lear had foolishly disinherited his youngest daughter, he was driven out by his two elder daughters and at last made his way to France.

Here his youngest daughter received him kindly and raised an army to restore him to his kingdom. In the war which followed, the two wicked sisters and their husbands were destroyed. The story is related in Spenser's *Fairie Queene,* Book 2, Canto X, Stanza 32, and concludes thus:

So to his crown she him restored again,
  In which he died, made ripe for death by eld,
  And after willed it should to her remain.
  Who peaceably the same long time did weld,
  And all men's hearts in due obedience held,
  Till that her sisters' children, woxen strong,
  Through proud ambition, against her rebelled,
  And overcommen kept in prison long,
Till weary of that wretched life, herself she hong.

Spenser was the first to call the youngest daughter Cordelia. In the other versions she is Cordeil, Cordeilla, or Cordella. Shakespeare took the name from Spenser, but he was the first to give the plot an unhappy ending. He thus transmuted an old tale in which evil is punished and good restored into a tremendous and pessimistic drama, of which Gloucester's words form the most fitting motto:

As flies to wanton boys are we to the gods.
  They kill us for their sport.

The whole conception of the play is Shakespeare's own; he owed nothing to his sources for the madness of Lear, Kent's devotion, the storm, the fool, Oswald, and above all the ending with Cordelia hanged and Lear dying of old age and a broken heart.

Shakespeare's play has a double plot. Parallel with the sufferings of Lear at the hands of his daughters runs the story of Gloucester, who is destroyed by his own base son. This story was apparently suggested by a brief tale in Sir Philip Sidney's romance *Arcadia* of an old Prince of Paphlagonia who was similarly served by a bastard son.

Shakespeare, however, was not the first to write a play on the theme. In Henslowe's *Diary* there are two mentions of performances of a " King Lear " at the Rose theater in 1594. This play, or yet another on the theme was published in 1605 as *The True Chronicle History of King Leir and his three daughters, Gonorill, Ragan and Cordella.* The play of *King Leir* is very crude. It begins with Leir proclaiming that, since he has lost his wife, his daughters lack a mother's care and must marry. The first scenes follow the familiar story. Ragan and Gonorill are bestowed on Cornwall and Cambria, and Cordella is cast out, but she finds a protector in the Gallian King, who follows her in disguise, falls in love, and takes her back with him to France. Gonorill soon tires of Leir and ill-treats him. Leir is deserted by all except Perillus, who remains as his faithful but rather ineffective councilor. Perillus advises him to go to Ragan, but she likewise ill-treats him. The two old men then wander away. A murderer is sent in pursuit to kill them, but he relents because whenever he is about to commit the deed a clap of thunder warns him to desist. At last Leir and Perillus reach the coast of Britain and pass over to France, where they land. There, as it happens, the Gallian King and Cordella, having disguised themselves as countryfolk, are spending a day by the seashore. They come on the two old men, half-starving. Leir at first does not recognize his wronged daughter. When Cordella reveals herself, he kneels to her for forgiveness, but she insists that it is her duty to kneel, and the two indulge in a competition of kneeling for about sixty lines. Thereafter, the Gallian King invades Britain. There is a short battle in which the wicked daughters are defeated and Leir and his party are victorious. In this play, as in all other versions except Shakespeare's, Leir is restored to his kingdom.

In writing *King Lear,* Shakespeare thus had the advantage that the story was quite familiar to his audience. He could therefore begin where he wished without elaborate explanation. Shakespeare's *Lear* opens at the moment when the old King has already decided in council that he will divide his kingdom and is about to ratify the decision in a public ceremony at which his daughters are expected to play their parts. It is the last time when the old King is ever to appear in his full majesty, and he expects his vanity to be humored to the full. Goneril and Regan easily fall in with this mood, but Cordelia, bitterly resentful of the order to "heave her heart into her mouth," suffers from a kind of paralysis of the will. Whatever she might have wished to say on any other occasion, all that she can utter is "Nothing." To Lear it is the worst public affront that he has ever suffered and, coming so unexpectedly from his best-loved daughter, it arouses in him the spirit of wrath. His plans are upset, Kent, his one faithful follower, is cast out, and Lear is alone. The play thus reaches its decisive moment in the very first scene. Thereafter we are shown how this tyrannical old man is goaded beyond endurance until his spirit breaks and he is purged of his wrath.

Lear dominates the first scene. He is still King, but as soon as he has resigned his crown, he ceases to be the master and becomes the subject of his daughters. He refuses to realize the change, and in Goneril's house he behaves in complete disregard of her wishes or convenience. When she protests at the ill behavior of his followers, her words are sneering and unkind, but not unreasonable. Lear's terrible curse is not justified (I.iv.297–312). Sending Kent before him, he rushes away to find Regan, his second daughter. When he reaches Gloucester's castle, whither Regan and Cornwall, her husband, have removed, the first person to greet him is Kent, his messenger, locked in the stocks as if he were no better than a common vagabond. When Regan treats him more coldly even than Goneril, and later, when Goneril herself arrives, Lear is left no choice but abject submission. This is too much for the proud old man and in his ungovernable rage he dashes out into the storm, followed by Kent and the Fool.

Lear's madness can be traced step by step. As events develop it becomes inevitable. A man of such violent temper must never be checked, or disaster will follow; he has no reserve of emotion or restraint. Cordelia angers him and she is cursed. Goneril offends him and she is cursed to the limits of malediction. Regan and Goneril both offend him and Lear's language fails, for he has exhausted the power of relieving emotion by words, and he cannot and will not allow anger the relief of tears. The only other relief possible is madness. The tragedy of Lear is that he brings his suffering on his own head by a grievous stupidity.

Linked to the story of Lear and his three daughters is the story of Gloucester and his two sons. Edmund, the bastard, is the most interesting and unscrupulous villain created by Shakespeare. He has every quality which makes for material success. He has a clear head; he is an opportunist; he has no scruples or conscience and is therefore unhampered by those restraints which check normal men; he is indeed the perfect egoist. In the play Edmund is shown climbing step by step to the highest rung. First he ousts his brother from his father's favor. Next he betrays his father to Cornwall and so becomes Earl of Gloucester. Then complications arise as both sisters fall in love with him. He plays with them both, waiting to see which of them will give him the greater advantage. After the battle, when Lear and Cordelia are his prisoners, he orders them to be murdered, for he now sees the final step. With the old King dead and both daughters in his power, there is nothing to prevent him from winning the crown.

Lear is a difficult play for modern readers. Shakespeare was always experimenting; in this play he experimented with the possibilities of a concentrated poetic imagery that is most elaborate and at times exceedingly difficult to comprehend.

The use of a particular kind of symbolic imagery is especially remarkable and well worth detailed study. The play abounds in animal images. In *Hamlet* man was "the paragon of animals." In *Lear* he is "hog in sloth, fox in stealth, wolf in greediness, dog in madness, lion in prey." It is as if Shakespeare wished to portray a world in which most men and women are beasts, and only the exceptional few redeem "Nature from the general curse." Apart from this use of images which constantly recur, Shakespeare effected a grim irony by the use of two words which sound throughout the play like the tolling of a knell: "nature" and "nothing."

Lear, Gloucester, and Edmund each in turn call on Nature. To the old fathers Nature is the goddess of natural affection by whose law children are naturally loyal to their parents. To Edmund — the "natural" son — Nature is the goddess of the wild; he is "natural" man because he is by nature a beast. "Nature," "natural," and "unnatural" recur again and again with every shade of meaning and misunderstanding.

There is also a devastating irony in the word "nothing." Cordelia at the critical moment can only utter "Nothing," and Lear replies "Nothing will come of nothing." He is wrong — from this one word "nothing" begins the whole devastating tragedy.

King Lear

DRAMATIS PERSONAE

[Handwritten annotation: THE GOOD MEN & WOMEN ARE STUPID. THE BAD MEN & WOMEN ARE CLEVER & SHARP.]

LEAR, *King of Britain* — *[80 YRS. OLD]*
KING OF FRANCE *[CORDELIA'S SUITORS]*
DUKE OF BURGUNDY
DUKE OF CORNWALL — *[REGAN'S HUSBAND]*
DUKE OF ALBANY — *[GONERIL'S HUSBAND]*
EARL OF KENT — *[FAITHFUL, HONEST COURTIER (AGE 48)]*
EARL OF GLOUCESTER
EDGAR, *son to Gloucester* *[GODSON OF KING, "Poor Tom"]*
EDMUND, *bastard son to Gloucester*
CURAN, *a courtier*
OLD MAN, *tenant to Gloucester*
DOCTOR
FOOL — *[SUPPOSED TO REMIND KING THAT HE WAS JUST MORTAL]*

OSWALD, *steward to Goneril*
A CAPTAIN *employed by Edmund*
GENTLEMAN *attendant on Cordelia*
HERALD
SERVANTS *to Cornwall*
GONERIL *[OLDEST]*
REGAN *daughters to Lear*
CORDELIA *[YOUNGEST]*
[100] KNIGHTS *of Lear's train,* CAPTAINS, MESSENGERS, SOLDIERS, *and* ATTENDANTS
[MONSIEUR LA FAR — MARSHAL OF Fr...]
SCENE — *Britain.*

[Handwritten annotation: DIVIDING KINGDOM IS A FOOLISH THING TO DO — SHOWN LATER.]

Act I

[Handwritten annotation: KENT & GLOUCESTER — HIS ADVISORS THAT DO NOT REALLY ADVISE HIM.]

SCENE I.° KING LEAR's *palace.*

[*Enter* KENT, GLOUCESTER, *and* EDMUND.]

KENT. I thought the King had more affected° the Duke of Albany than Cornwall.

GLO. It did always seem so to us. But now, in the division of the kingdom, it appears not which of the Dukes he values most, for equalities are so weighed that curiosity in neither can make choice of either's moiety.° 7

[Handwritten annotation: PAYS TO THE TWO MEN ARE ALREADY EQUALLY ASSIGNED — BEFORE HE HAS DAUGHTERS EXPRESS THEIR LOVE]

KENT. Is not this your son, my lord?

GLO. His breeding, sir, hath been at my charge. I have so often blushed to acknowledge him that now I am brazed° to it. 11

KENT. I cannot conceive° you.

GLO. Sir, this young fellow's mother could. Whereupon she grew round-wombed, and had indeed, sir, a son for her cradle ere she had a husband for her bed. Do you smell a fault?

KENT. I cannot wish the fault undone, the issue° of it being so proper.° 18

GLO. But I have, sir, a son by order of law, some year elder than this, who yet is no dearer in my account. Though this knave came something saucily into the world before he was sent for, yet was his mother fair, there was good sport at his making,

and the whoreson° must be acknowledged. Do you know this noble gentleman, Edmund? 25

EDM. No, my lord.

GLO. My Lord of Kent. Remember him hereafter as my honorable friend.

EDM. My services to your lordship.

KENT. I must love you, and sue to know you better. 31

EDM. Sir, I shall study deserving.°

GLO. He hath been out nine years, and away he shall again. The King is coming.

[*Sennet.° Enter one bearing a coronet,*° KING LEAR, CORNWALL, ALBANY, GONERIL, REGAN, CORDELIA, *and* ATTENDANTS.]

LEAR. Attend° the lords of France and Burgundy, Gloucester. 35

GLO. I shall, my liege.

[*Exeunt* GLOUCESTER *and* EDMUND.]

LEAR. Meantime we shall express our darker purpose.°
Give me the map there. Know that we have divided
In three our kingdom. And 'tis our fast intent
To shake all cares and business from our age, 40
Conferring them on younger strengths while we
Unburdened crawl toward death. Our son° of Cornwall,
And you, our no less loving son of Albany,
We have this hour a constant will° to publish 44
Our daughters' several° dowers, that future strife

[Handwritten top margin: CORDELIA DRIVES LEAR TO "A TERRIBLE RAGE — BUT SHE REACTS TO SISTERS BY DECIDING SHE HAS NOTHING TO SAY — STUBBORNLY STICKS TO DECISION (LIKE HER DAD)]

May be prevented° now. The Princes, France and
    Burgundy,
Great rivals in our youngest daughter's love,
Long in our Court have made their amorous so-
    journ,
And here are to be answered. Tell me, my daugh-
    ters,
Since now we will divest us both of rule,   50
Interest of territory, cares of state,
Which of you shall we say doth love us most?
That we our largest bounty may extend
Where nature doth with merit challenge.° Goneril,
Our eldest-born, speak first.   55

  GON. Sir, I love you more than words can wield°
the matter,
Dearer than eyesight, space, and liberty,
Beyond what can be valued, rich or rare,
No less than life, with grace, health, beauty, honor,
As much as child e'er loved or father found —   60
A love that makes breath poor and speech unable —
Beyond all manner of so much° I love you.

  COR. [*Aside*] What shall Cordelia do? Love, and
be silent.

LEAR. Of all these bounds, even from this line to
    this,   64
With shadowy forests and with champains riched,°
With plenteous rivers and wide-skirted meads,°
We make thee lady. To thine and Albany's issue
Be this perpetual. What says our second daughter,
Our dearest Regan, wife to Cornwall? Speak.   70

  REG. I am made of that self metal° as my sister,
And prize me at her worth.° In my true heart
I find she names my very deed of love,
Only she comes too short. That I profess
Myself an enemy to all other joys   75
Which the most precious square of sense possesses,°
And find I am alone felicitate°
In your dear Highness' love.

  COR.   [*Aside*] Then poor Cordelia!
And yet not so, since I am sure my love's
More ponderous than my tongue.   80

  LEAR. To thee and thine hereditary ever
Remain this ample third of our fair kingdom,
No less in space, validity° and pleasure
Than that conferred on Goneril. Now, our joy,
Although the last, not least, to whose young love   85
The vines of France and milk of Burgundy
Strive to be interested,° what can you say to draw

[Handwritten left-margin notes: BY DOING THIS HE MAKES DIVISION OF HIS PRIVATE ESTATE / KINGDOM; CRUCIAL MOMENT — TRAGEDY; HER RESPONSE IS TO GONERIL; HAS TRUE LOVE BUT STUBBORN; ENOUGH NOT TO COMPETE W. SISTERS SINCE I KNOWS HER LOVE IS TRUER THAN THEIRS; HER REST-PONSE IS TO REGAN]

A third more opulent than your sisters? Speak.

  COR. Nothing, my lord.°

  LEAR. Nothing!   90

  COR. Nothing.

  LEAR. Nothing will come of nothing.° Speak
again.

  COR. Unhappy that I am, I cannot heave
My heart into my mouth. I love your Majesty
According to my bond,° nor more nor less.   95

  LEAR. How, how, Cordelia! Mend your speech a
    little,
Lest it may mar your fortunes.

  COR.   Good my lord,
You have begot me, bred me, loved me. I
Return those duties back as are right fit,
Obey you, love you, and most honor you.
Why have my sisters husbands if they say   100
They love you all? Haply,° when I shall wed,
That lord whose hand must take my plight° shall
    carry
Half my love with him, half my care and duty.
Sure, I shall never marry like my sisters,
To love my father all.   105

  LEAR. But goes thy heart with this?

  COR.   Aye, good my lord.

  LEAR. So young, and so untender?

  COR. So young, my lord, and true.

  LEAR. Let it be so. Thy truth then be thy dower.
For, by the sacred radiance of the sun,   111
The mysteries of Hecate,° and the night,
By all the operation of the orbs°
From whom we do exist and cease to be,
Here I disclaim° all my paternal care,   115
Propinquity,° and property of blood,°
And as a stranger to my heart and me
Hold thee from this forever. The barbarous Scyth-
    ian,°
Or he that makes his generation messes
To gorge his appetite° shall to my bosom   120
Be as well neighbored, pitied, and relieved°
As thou my sometime daughter.

  KENT.   Good my liege ——

  LEAR. Peace, Kent!
Come not between the dragon° and his wrath.
I loved her most, and thought to set my rest°   125

[Handwritten right-column notes: SHOWS STUBBORN AS DAD + NOTHING PRECIPITATES LEAR'S FALL; NOT TRUE — LOVE IS NOT DIVISIBLE IN THIS WAY]

---

89. **Nothing, my lord:** See Intro. *Lear*, p. 1138a.   92. **Nothing
. . . nothing:** the old maxim *Ex nihilo nihil fit.*   95. **bond:** i.e.,
the tie of natural affection and duty which binds daughter to
father.   102. **Haply:** it may happen.   103. **plight:** promise made
at betrothal.   112. **Hecate:** goddess of witchcraft. Cf. *Macb*,
II.i.52; III.ii.41–43.   113. **orbs:** stars.   115. **disclaim:** renounce.
116. **Propinquity:** relationship. **property of blood:** claim which
you have as being of my blood.   118. **Scythian:** inhabitant of
South Russia, regarded as the worst kind of savage.   119–20. **Or
. . . appetite:** or he that feeds gluttonously on his own children.
121. **relieved:** helped in distress.   124. **dragon:** the Dragon of
Britain was Lear's heraldic device and also a symbol of his ferocity.   125. **set . . . my rest:** lit., to risk all — a term in the card
game called primero. Lear uses it with the double meaning of
"find rest."

46. **prevented:** forestalled.   54. **Where . . . challenge:** where
natural affection and desert have an equal claim on my bounty.
56. **wield:** declare.   62. **Beyond . . . much:** i.e., beyond all these
things.   65. **champains riched:** enriched with fertile fields.
66. **wide-skirted meads:** extensive pasture lands.   71. **self metal:**
same material.   72. **prize . . . worth:** value me at the same price.
76. **most . . . possesses:** feeling in the highest degree possesses. **square:** the carpenter's rule; i.e., measurement.   77. **fe-
licitate:** made happy.   79–80. **love's . . . tongue:** love is heavier
than my words.   83. **validity:** value.   87. **interested:** have a
share in.

On her kind nursery.° Hence, and avoid° my sight!
So be my grave my peace, as here I give
Her father's heart from her! Call France. Who stirs?
Call Burgundy. Cornwall and Albany,   129
With my two daughters' dowers digest° this third.
Let pride, which she calls plainness,° marry her.
I do invest you jointly with my power,
Pre-eminence,° and all the large effects
That troop with majesty.° Ourself, by monthly
    course,°
With reservation of a hundred knights   135
By you to be sustained, shall our abode
Make with you by due turns. Only we still retain
The name and all the additions° to a king.
The sway, revenue, execution of the rest,
Belovèd Sons, be yours, which to confirm,   140
This coronet° part betwixt you.

KENT.   Royal Lear,
Whom I have ever honored as my King,
Loved as my father, as my master followed,
As my great patron thought on in my prayers——

LEAR. The bow is bent and drawn, make from the
    shaft.°   145

KENT. Let it fall rather, though the fork° invade
The region of my heart. Be Kent unmannerly
When Lear is mad. What wouldst thou do, old
    man?°
Think'st thou that duty shall have dread to speak
When power to flattery bows? To plainness honor's
    bound   150
When majesty stoops to folly.° Reverse thy doom,°
And in thy best consideration check
This hideous rashness. Answer my life my judgment,
Thy youngest daughter does not love thee least,
Nor are those empty-hearted whose low sound   155
Reverbs° no hollowness.

LEAR.   Kent, on thy life, no more.

KENT. My life I never held but as a pawn°
To wage against thy enemies, nor fear to lose it,
Thy safety being the motive.

LEAR.   Out of my sight!

KENT. See better, Lear, and let me still remain
The true blank° of thine eye.   161

LEAR. Now, by Apollo——

KENT.   Now, by Apollo, King.
Thou swear'st thy gods in vain.

LEAR.   O vassal!° Miscreant!°
        [*Laying his hand on his sword.*]

ALB. & CORN. Dear sir, forbear.

KENT. Do.
Kill thy physician, and the fee bestow   166
Upon the foul disease. Revoke thy doom,
Or whilst I can vent clamor° from my throat
I'll tell thee thou dost evil.

LEAR.   Hear me, recreant!°
On thy allegiance,° hear me!   170
Since thou hast sought to make us break our vow,
Which we durst never yet, and with strained° pride
To come between our sentence and our power° —
Which nor our nature nor our place can bear,
Our potency made good° — take thy reward.   175
Five days we do allot thee, for provision°
To shield thee from diseases of the world,
And on the sixth to turn thy hated back
Upon our kingdom. If on the tenth day following
Thy banished trunk° be found in our dominions,
The moment is thy death. Away! By Jupiter,   181
This shall not be revoked.

KENT. Fare° thee well, King. Sith° thus thou wilt
    appear,
Freedom lives hence, and banishment is here.
[*To* CORDELIA] The gods to their dear shelter take
    thee, maid,   185
That justly think'st and hast most rightly said!
[*To* REGAN *and* GONERIL] And your large° speeches
    may your deeds approve,°
That good effects° may spring from words of love.
Thus Kent, O Princes, bids you all adieu.   189
He'll shape his old course in a country new.   [*Exit.*]
[*Flourish.° Re-enter* GLOUCESTER, *with* FRANCE,
       BURGUNDY, *and* ATTENDANTS.]

GLO. Here's France and Burgundy, my noble lord.

LEAR. My lord of Burgundy,
We first address toward you, who with this King
Hath rivaled for our daughter. What, in the least,
Will you require° in present° dower with her,   195
Or cease your quest of love?

BUR.   Most royal Majesty,

---

126. nursery: care. avoid: depart from.   130. digest: absorb.
131. plainness: honest plain speech.   133. Pre-eminence: authority.   133–34. large . . . majesty: the outward show of power
that goes with rule.   134. course: turn.   138. additions: titles
of honor.   141. coronet: i.e., the coronet which was to have been
the symbol of Cordelia's kingdom.   145. shaft: arrow.   146. fork:
point of a forked arrow. See Pl. 22a.   148. old man: Kent, who
is as quick-tempered as Lear, has lost control of his tongue. The
phrase to a still ruling king is grossly insulting.   149–51. Think'st
. . . folly: This is one of many passages in *Lear* where the abstract
is strikingly and effectively used for the person. It means: "Do
you think that a man who keeps his sense of duty will be afraid
to speak when he sees a king yielding to his flatterers? An
honorable man is forced to speak plainly when a king becomes
a fool."   151. doom: sentence.   156. Reverbs: re-echoes.
157. pawn: a pledge to be sacrificed.   161. blank: aim; i.e.,
something which you look at. The blank is the center of the target.

163. vassal: wretch. Miscreant: lit., misbeliever.   168. vent
clamor: utter a cry.   169. recreant: traitor.   170. On . . .
allegiance: The most solemn form of command that can be laid
upon a subject, for to disobey it is to commit high treason.
172. strained: excessive.   173. To . . . power: to interpose yourself between my decree and my royal will; i.e., to make me revoke an order.   175. Our . . . good: my power being now asserted.   176. for provision: for making your preparations.
180. trunk: body.   183–90. Fare . . . new: The rhyme in this
passage and elsewhere in the play is used for the particular purpose of stiffening the speech and giving it a special prophetic or
moral significance; cf. III.vi.109–20.   183. Sith: since.
187. large: fine-sounding. approve: i.e., be shown in deeds.
188. effects: results.   190 s.d., Flourish: trumpet fanfare.
195. require: request. present: immediate.

I crave no more than what your Highness offered,
Nor will you tender° less.
  LEAR.   Right noble Burgundy,
When she was dear° to us, we did hold her so,
But now her price is fall'n. Sir, there she stands. 200
If aught within that little seeming substance,°
Or all of it, with our displeasure pieced°
And nothing more, may fitly like° your Grace,
She's there, and she is yours.
  BUR.   I know no answer.
  LEAR. Will you, with those infirmities she owes,°
Unfriended, new-adopted to our hate, 206
Dowered with our curse and strangered with our
    oath,°
Take her, or leave her?
  BUR.   Pardon me, royal sir,
Election makes not up on such conditions.°
  LEAR. Then leave her, sir. For, by the power that
    made me, 210
I tell you all her wealth. [*To* FRANCE] For you, great
    King,
I would not from your love make such a stray,°
To match you where I hate. Therefore beseech you
To avert your liking° a more worthier way
Than on a wretch whom Nature° is ashamed 215
Almost to acknowledge hers.
  FRANCE.   This is most strange,
That she that even but now was your best object,
The argument° of your praise, balm of your age,
Most best, most dearest, should in this trice of time
Commit a thing so monstrous, to dismantle° 220
So many folds of favor. Sure, her offense
Must be of such unnatural degree
That monsters it,° or your forevouched° affection
Fall'n into taint.° Which to believe of her
Must be a faith that reason without miracle 225
Could never plant in me.°
  COR.   I yet beseech your Majesty —
If for I want that glib and oily art,
To speak and purpose not,° since what I well intend
I'll do 't before I speak — that you make known
It is no vicious blot,° murder, or foulness, 230
No unchaste action or dishonored step,
That hath deprived me of your grace and favor,

198. **tender:** offer.   199. **dear:** in the double sense of "beloved" and "valuable."   201. **little ... substance:** creature that seems so small. Part of Lear's anger with Cordelia is that so small a body seems to hold so proud a heart.   202. **pieced:** added to it.   203. **fitly like:** suitably please.   205. **owes:** possesses. 207. **strangered ... oath:** made a stranger to me by my oath. 209. **Election ... conditions:** i.e., one does not choose one's wife on such conditions.   212. **from ... stray:** remove myself so far from showing love to you.   214. **avert ... liking:** turn your affection.   215. **Nature:** See *Lear* Intro. p. 1139b.   218. **argument:** topic.   220. **dismantle:** lit., take off (as a cloak).   223. **monsters it:** makes it a monster. **forevouched:** previously declared. 224. **Fall'n ... taint:** become bad.   224–26. **Which ... me:** that is so contrary to reason that only a miracle could make me believe it.   228. **and ... not:** and not mean it.   230. **vicious blot:** vicious act which blots my honor.

But even for want of that for which I am richer,
A still-soliciting° eye, and such a tongue
As I am glad I have not, though not to have it 235
Hath lost me in° your liking.
  LEAR.   Better thou
Hadst not been born than not to have pleased me
    better.
  FRANCE. Is it but this? A tardiness in nature°
Which often leaves the history unspoke
That it intends to do? My Lord of Burgundy, 240
What say you to the lady? Love's not love
When it is mingled with regards that stand
Aloof from the entire point.° Will you have her?
She is herself a dowry.
  BUR.   Royal Lear,
Give but that portion which yourself proposed, 245
And here I take Cordelia by the hand,
Duchess of Burgundy.
  LEAR. Nothing. I have sworn, I am firm.
  BUR. I am sorry then you have so lost a father
That you must lose a husband.
  COR.   Peace be with Burgundy! 250
Since that respects of fortune° are his love,
I shall not be his wife.
  FRANCE. Fairest Cordelia, that art most rich being
    poor,
Most choice forsaken, and most loved despised,
Thee and thy virtues here I seize upon, 255
Be it lawful I take up what's cast away.
Gods, gods! 'Tis strange that from their cold'st
    neglect
My love should kindle to inflamed respect.°
Thy dowerless daughter, King, thrown to my
    chance,
Is Queen of us, of ours, and our fair France. 260
Not all the dukes of waterish° Burgundy
Can buy this unprized precious maid of me.
Bid them farewell, Cordelia, though unkind.
Thou losest here, a better where to find.
  LEAR. Thou hast her, France. Let her be thine,
    for we 265
Have no such daughter, nor shall ever see
That face of hers again. Therefore be gone
Without our grace, our love, our benison.°
Come, noble Burgundy. [*Flourish. Exeunt all but*
    FRANCE, GONERIL, REGAN, *and* CORDELIA.]
  FRANCE. Bid farewell to your sisters. 270
  COR. The jewels of our father,° with washed° eyes
Cordelia leaves you. I know you what you are,

234. **still-soliciting:** always begging favors.   236. **lost me in:** deprived me of.   238. **tardiness in nature:** natural slowness. 242–43. **When ... point:** when it is mixed with other motives (the amount of the dowry) which have nothing to do with the thing itself (love).   251. **respects of fortune:** considerations of my dowry.   258. **inflamed respect:** warmer affection. 261. **waterish:** with the double meaning of "with many rivers" and "feeble."   268. **benison:** blessing.   271. **The ... father:** i.e., creatures whom my father values so highly. **washed:** weeping, but also made clearsighted by tears.

[Handwritten left margin: CORDELIA KNOWS THAT 2 SISTERS WILL MISTREAT HIM, BUT SHE IS TOO STUBBORN TO REPENT TO LEAR]

And, like a sister, am most loath to call
Your faults as they are named. Use well our father.
To your professèd° bosoms I commit him.   275
But yet, alas, stood I within his grace,°
I would prefer° him to a better place.
So farewell to you both.

REG. Prescribe not us our duties.

GON.   Let your study
Be to content your lord, who hath received you   280
At Fortune's alms.° You have obedience scanted,°
And well are worth the want that you have wanted.°

COR. Time shall unfold what plaited° cunning
    hides.
Who cover faults, at last shame them derides.
Well may you prosper!

FRANCE.   Come, my fair Cordelia. 285
         [*Exeunt* FRANCE *and* CORDELIA.]

GON. Sister,° it is not a little I have to say of what
most nearly appertains to us both. I think our father
will hence tonight.

REG. That's most certain, and with you, next
month with us.   290

GON. You see how full of changes his age is; the
observation we have made of it hath not been little.
He always loved our sister most, and with what poor
judgment he hath now cast her off appears too
grossly.

REG. 'Tis the infirmity of his age. Yet he hath ever
but slenderly known himself.   297

GON. The best and soundest of his time hath been
but rash. Then must we look to receive from his age
not alone the imperfections of long-ingrafted condition,° but therewithal the unruly waywardness
that infirm and choleric years bring with them.   303

REG. Such unconstant starts° are we like to have
from him as this of Kent's banishment.

GON. There is further compliment° of leave-taking between France and him. Pray you, let's hit° together. If our father carry authority with such dis-
positions° as he bears, this last surrender of his will
but offend us.   310

[Handwritten left margin: PROBLEM]

REG. We shall further think on 't.

GON. We must do something, and i' the heat.°
                 [*Exeunt.*]

SCENE II. *The* EARL OF GLOUCESTER'S *castle.*

[*Enter* EDMUND, *with a letter.*]

EDM. Thou, Nature, art my goddess; to thy law
My services are bound. Wherefore should I
Stand in the plague of custom, and permit
The curiosity of nations to deprive me,   4
For that I am some twelve or fourteen moonshines
Lag of a brother?° Why bastard? Wherefore
     base?
When my dimensions are as well compact,°
My mind as generous° and my shape as true,
As honest madam's issue? Why brand they us
With base? With baseness? Bastardy? Base, base?
Who in the lusty stealth of nature take   11
More composition and fierce quality°
Than doth, within a dull, stale, tired bed,
Go to the creating a whole tribe of fops°
Got° 'tween asleep and wake? Well then,   15
Legitimate Edgar, I must have your land. *[Handwritten: HE CONTIN]*
Our father's love is to the bastard Edmund *[Handwritten: CONTIN]*
As to the legitimate — fine word, "legitimate"! *[Handwritten: STEP]*
Well, my legitimate, if this letter speed° *[Handwritten: UPd]*
And my invention° thrive, Edmund the base   20
Shall top the legitimate. I grow, I prosper. *[Handwritten: ALMOST]*
Now, gods, stand up for bastards! *[Handwritten: MAKES KING]*
       [*Enter* GLOUCESTER.] *[Handwritten: EXCEPT TH EDGAR W]*

GLO. Kent banished thus! And France in choler
     parted!
And the King gone tonight! Subscribed° his power!
Confined to exhibition!° All this done   25
Upon the gad!° Edmund, how now! What news? *[Handwritten: TO]*

EDM. So please your lordship, none.
         [*Putting up the letter.*]

GLO. Why so earnestly seek you to put up that letter?

EDM. I know no news, my lord.

GLO. What paper were you reading?   30

EDM. Nothing, my lord.°

GLO. No? What needed then that terrible dis-
patch° of it into your pocket? The quality of nothing hath not such need to hide itself. Let's see. Come,
if it be nothing, I shall not need spectacles.   36

EDM. I beseech you, sir, pardon me. It is a letter
from my brother that I have not all o'erread, and for

---

275. **professed**: which profess such love.   276. **within . . . grace**: in his favor.   277. **prefer**: promote.   281. **At . . . alms**: as an act of charity from Fortune. **scanted**: neglected.   282. **And . . . wanted**: and well deserve the same lack of love which you have shown.   283. **plaited**: pleated, enfolded. Cf. ll. 220–21. 286–312. **Sister . . . heat**: The abrupt change from rhyme to prose marks the change from the emotion of the previous episodes to the cynical frankness of the two sisters.   301–02. **long-ingrafted condition**: temper which has long been part of his nature. 304. **unconstant starts**: sudden outbursts.   306. **compliment**: formality.   307. **hit**: agree.   309. **dispositions**: frame of mind. 312. **i' the heat**: while the iron is hot.

[Handwritten bottom: EDMUND MOVES FROM BEGINNING — (FATHER HAD USED COARSE LANGUAGE BEFORE KENT — BUT COARSENESS)]

Sc. ii: 1. **Thou, Nature**: Edmund, the "natural" son of his father, appeals to Nature, whose doctrine is every man ruthlessly for himself.   2–6. **Wherefore . . . brother**: Why should I allow myself to be plagued by custom and nice distinctions (*curiosity*) which deprive me of my natural rights, because I am a year younger (*lag*: lagging behind) than my legitimate brother? 7. **compact**: put together, framed. 8. **generous**: noble. 12. **More . . . quality**: more fiber and ferocity.   14. **fops**: fools.   15. **Got**: begotten.   19. **speed**: prosper. 20. **invention**: plan. 24. **Subscribed**: signed away.   25. **Confined to exhibition**: reduced to a pension. 26. **gad**: prick of a goad; i.e., the spur of the moment.   31. **Nothing, my lord**: Gloucester's tragedy also begins with the word "nothing." See I i.89.   32–33. **terrible dispatch**: i.e., hasty thrusting.

so much as I have perused, I find it not fit for your o'erlooking.° 40

GLO. Give me the letter, sir.

EDM. I shall offend, either to detain or give it. The contents, as in part I understand them, are to blame.

GLO. Let's see, let's see. 44

EDM. I hope, for my brother's justification, he wrote this but as an essay° or taste of my virtue.

GLO. [*Reads.*] " This policy and reverence of age° makes the world bitter to the best of our times,° keeps our fortunes from us till our oldness cannot relish them. I begin to find an idle and fond° 50 bondage in the oppression of aged tyranny, who sways not as it hath power, but as it is suffered.° Come to me, that of this I may speak more. If our father would sleep till I waked him, you should enjoy half his revenue forever, and live the beloved 55 of your brother, EDGAR."

Hum! Conspiracy! — " Sleep till I waked him, you should enjoy half his revenue! " — My son Edgar! Had he a hand to write this? A heart and brain to breed it in? When came this to you? Who brought it?

EDM. It was not brought me, my lord, there's the cunning of it. I found it thrown in at the casement° of my closet.° WINDOW OF HIS ROOM 65

GLO. You know the character° to be your brother's?

EDM. If the matter were good, my lord, I durst swear it were his, but in respect of that, I would fain think it were not.

GLO. It is his.

EDM. It is his hand, my lord, but I hope his heart is not in the contents. 73

GLO. Hath he never heretofore sounded you in this business?

EDM. Never, my lord. But I have heard him oft maintain it to be fit that, sons at perfect age and fathers declining, the father should be as ward to the son, and the son manage his revenue. 79

GLO. Oh, villain, villain! His very opinion in the letter! Abhorred villain! Unnatural, detested, brutish villain! Worse than brutish! Go, sirrah, seek him — aye, apprehend him. Abominable villain! Where is he? 84

EDM. I do not well know, my lord. If it shall please you to suspend your indignation against my brother till you can derive from him better testimony of his intent, you should run a certain course.° Where, if you violently proceed against him, mistaking his purpose, it would make a great gap° in your own 90

honor and shake in pieces the heart of his obedience.° I dare pawn down my life for him that he hath wrote this to feel° my affection to your honor and to no further pretense of danger. 95

GLO. Think you so?

EDM. If your honor judge it meet, I will place you where you shall hear us confer of this, and by an auricular assurance° have your satisfaction, and that without any further delay than this very evening.

GLO. He cannot be such a monster — 102

EDM. Nor is not, sure.

GLO. — to his father, that so tenderly and entirely loves him. Heaven and earth! Edmund, seek 105 him out, wind me into him,° I pray you. Frame the business after your own wisdom. I would unstate myself, to be in a due resolution.°

EDM. I will seek him, sir, presently,° convey° the business as I shall find means, and acquaint you withal. 111

GLO. These late eclipses° in the sun and moon portend no good to us. Though the wisdom of nature° can reason° it thus and thus, yet nature finds itself scourged by the sequent° effects. Love cools, 115 friendship falls off, brothers divide. In cities, mutinies; in countries, discord; in palaces, treason; and the bond cracked 'twixt son and father. This villain of mine comes under the prediction, there's son against father. The King falls from bias of na- 120 ture,° there's father against child. We have seen the best of our time. Machinations, hollowness, treachery, and all ruinous disorders follow us disquietly to our graves. Find out this villain, Edmund, it shall lose thee nothing. Do it carefully. And the noble and true-hearted Kent banished! His offense, honesty! 'Tis strange. [*Exit.*] 127

EDM. This is the excellent foppery° of the world, that when we are sick in fortune — often the surfeit° of our own behavior — we make guilty of our 130 disasters the sun, the moon, and the stars, as if we were villains by necessity, fools by heavenly compulsion; knaves, thieves, and treachers by spherical predominance;° drunkards, liars, and adulterers by an enforced obedience of planetary influence;° 135 and all that we are evil in, by a divine thrusting on

---

91. shake . . . obedience: cause him no longer to obey you loyally. 94. feel: test. 100. auricular assurance: proof heard with your own ears. 106. wind . . . him: worm your way into his confidence for me. 107–08. I . . . resolution: I would lose my earldom to learn the truth. This is one of many touches of bitter irony in this tragedy, for it is not until he has "unstated himself" that Gloucester does indeed learn the truth about his two sons. 109. presently: at once. convey: manage. 112. These . . . eclipses: See Intro. *Lear*, p. 1136a and App. 2. 113. wisdom of nature: i.e., a rational explanation. 114. reason: explain. 115. sequent: subsequent. 120–21. bias of nature: natural inclination. See App. 13. 128. foppery: folly. 129. surfeit: lit., eating to excess and its results. 133–34. treachers . . . predominance: traitors because the stars so decreed when we were born. 135. enforced . . . influence: because we were forced to be so in obeying the influence of the stars.

40. o'erlooking: reading. 46. essay: trial. 47. policy . . . age: this custom of respecting old men. 48. best . . . times: i.e., when we are still young. 50. fond: foolish. 52. suffered: allowed. 64. casement: window. 65. closet: room. 66. character: handwriting. 88. certain course: i.e., know where you are going. 90. gap: hole.

— an admirable evasion of whoremaster° man, to lay his goatish disposition to the charge of a star!° My father compounded with my mother under the dragon's tail, and my nativity° was under Ursa   140 Major,° so that it follows I am rough and lecherous. Tut, I should have been that I am had the maiden-liest star in the firmament twinkled on my bas-   144 tardizing. Edgar—— [*Enter* EDGAR.] And pat he comes like the catastrophe° of the old comedy. My cue is villainous melancholy, with a sigh like Tom o' Bedlam.° Oh, these eclipses do portend these divisions! Fa, sol, la, mi.°

EDG. How now, Brother Edmund! What serious contemplation are you in?   151

EDM. I am thinking, Brother, of a prediction I read this other day, what should follow these eclipses.

EDG. Do you busy yourself about that?   155

EDM. I promise you the effects he writes of succeed° unhappily, as of unnaturalness between the child and the parent; death, dearth, dissolutions of ancient amities;° divisions in state, menaces and maledictions against King and nobles; needless diffidences,° banishment of friends, dissipation of cohorts,° nuptial breaches, and I know not what.   163

EDG. How long have you been a sectary astronomical?°

EDM. Come, come, when saw you my father last?

EDG. Why, the night gone by.   168

EDM. Spake you with him?

EDG. Aye, two hours together.

EDM. Parted you in good terms? Found you no displeasure in him by word or countenance?

EDG. None at all.   173

EDM. Bethink yourself wherein you may have offended him. And at my entreaty forbear his presence till some little time hath qualified° the heat of his displeasure, which at this instant so rageth in him that with the mischief of your person it would scarcely allay.°

EDG. Some villain hath done me wrong.   180

EDM. That's my fear. I pray you have a continent forbearance° till the speed of his rage goes slower, and, as I say, retire with me to my lodging, from whence I will fitly bring you to hear my lord speak.

Pray ye, go, there s my key. If you do stir abroad, go armed.   186

EDG. Armed, Brother!

EDM. Brother, I advise you to the best — go armed. I am no honest man if there be any good meaning toward you. I have told you what I have seen and heard, but faintly, nothing like the image and horror of it. Pray you, away.   192

EDG. Shall I hear from you anon?

EDM. I do serve you in this business.

[*Exit* EDGAR.]

A credulous father, and a brother noble,   195
Whose nature is so far from doing harms
That he suspects none, on whose foolish honesty
My practices° ride easy. I see the business.
Let me, if not by birth, have lands by wit.   199
All with me's meet° that I can fashion fit.° [*Exit*.]

SCENE III. *The* DUKE OF ALBANY'S *palace*.

[*Enter* GONERIL *and* OSWALD, *her steward*.]

GON. Did my father strike my gentleman for chiding of his fool?°

OSW. Yes, madam.

GON. By day and night he wrongs me. Every hour He flashes into one gross crime or other That sets us all at odds. I'll not endure it.   5 His knights grow riotous, and himself upbraids us On every trifle. When he returns from hunting, I will not speak with him. Say I am sick. If you come slack of former services,° You shall do well, the fault of it I'll answer.   10

OSW. He's coming, madam, I hear him. [*Horns within*.]

GON. Put on what weary negligence you please, You and your fellows, I'd have it come to question.° If he distaste it, let him to our sister, Whose mind and mine, I know, in that are one,   15 Not to be overruled. Idle old man, That still would manage those authorities That he hath given away! Now, by my life, Old fools are babes again, and must be used With checks as flatteries when they are seen abused. Remember what I tell you.

OSW.   Very well, madam.   21

GON. And let his knights have colder looks among you.
What grows of it, no matter, advise your fellows so. I would breed from hence occasions,° and I shall,

---

137. whoremaster: lecherous.   137–38. to ... star: to say that some star caused him to have the morals of a goat.   140. nativity: moment of birth.   140–41. Ursa Major: the Great Bear. 146. catastrophe: the final episode.   146–48. my ... Bedlam: I must now pretend to be a melancholic and sigh like a lunatic beggar. Tom o' Bedlam was a lunatic discharged from Bedlam (Bethlehem Hospital for lunatics). See II.iii.14.   149. Fa ... mi: Edmund hums to himself.   156. succeed: follow.   159. amities: friendships.   162. diffidences: distrusts.   162–63. dissipation of cohorts: breaking-up of established friendships (lit., of troops of soldiers).   164. sectary astronomical: a follower of the sect of astrologers.   176. qualified: lessened.   178–79. with ... allay: it would scarcely be lessened even if he did you some bodily injury.   181–82. continent forbearance: self-control which will keep you from any rash action.

198. practices: plots.   200. meet: suitable. fashion fit: make fit my purposes.
Sc. iii: 1. fool: professional jester. See Pl. 12j, 13c.   9. come ... services: do not wait on him as efficiently as you used to.   13. to question: or in modern slang, to a showdown.   19–20. Old ... abused: old men must be treated like babies, and scolded, not flattered, when they are naughty.   24. breed ... occasions: find excuses for taking action.

That I may speak. I'll write straight to my sister   25
To hold my very course. Prepare for dinner.
                                    [*Exeunt.*]

SCENE IV. *A hall in the same.*

[*Enter* KENT, *disguised.*]

KENT. If but as well I other accents borrow
That can my speech defuse,° my good intent
May carry through itself to that full issue
For which I razed° my likeness. Now, banished
    Kent,
If thou canst serve where thou dost stand con-
    demned,   5
So may it come, thy master whom thou lovest
Shall find thee full of labors.

[*Horns within.*° *Enter* LEAR, KNIGHTS, *and*
                    ATTENDANTS.]

LEAR. Let me not stay a jot for dinner. Go get it
ready. [*Exit an* ATTENDANT.] How now! What art
thou?   10
KENT. A man, sir.
LEAR. What dost thou profess?° What wouldst
thou with us?   13
KENT. I do profess to be no less than I seem — to
serve him truly that will put me in trust, to love him
that is honest, to converse with him that is wise and
says little, to fear judgment,° to fight when I cannot
choose, and to eat no fish.°   18
LEAR. What art thou?
KENT. A very honest-hearted fellow, and as poor
as the King.
LEAR. If thou be as poor for a subject as he is for
a king, thou art poor enough. What wouldst thou?
KENT. Service.   25
LEAR. Who wouldst thou serve?
KENT. You.
LEAR. Dost thou know me, fellow?
KENT. No, sir, but you have that in your counte-
nance° which I would fain call master.   30
LEAR. What's that?
KENT. Authority.
LEAR. What services canst thou do?   33
KENT. I can keep honest counsel, ride, run, mar a
curious tale in telling it,° and deliver a plain message
bluntly. That which ordinary men are fit for, I am
qualified in, and the best of me is diligence.
LEAR. How old art thou?
KENT. Not so young, sir, to love a woman for

singing, nor so old to dote on her for anything. I
have years on my back forty-eight.   42
LEAR. Follow me, thou shalt serve me. If I like
thee no worse after dinner, I will not part from thee
yet. Dinner, ho, dinner! Where's my knave? My
fool? Go you, and call my fool hither. [*Exit an* AT-
TENDANT. *Enter* OSWALD.] You, you, sirrah, where's
my daughter?
OSW. So please you —   [*Exit.*]
LEAR. What says the fellow there? Call the clot-
poll° back. [*Exit a* KNIGHT.] Where's my fool, ho? I
think the world's asleep. [*Re-enter* KNIGHT.]   52
How now! Where's that mongrel?
KNIGHT. He says, my lord, your daughter is not
well.   55
LEAR. Why came not the slave back to me when I
called him?
KNIGHT. Sir, he answered me, in the roundest°
manner, he would not.
LEAR. He would not!   60
KNIGHT. My lord, I know not what the matter is,
but, to my judgment, your Highness is not enter-
tained° with that ceremonious affection° as you
were wont. There's a great abatement of kindness
appears as well in the general dependents° as in the
Duke himself also and your daughter.   67
LEAR. Ha! Sayest thou so?
KNIGHT. I beseech you pardon me, my lord, if I be
mistaken, for my duty cannot be silent when I think
your Highness wronged.   71
LEAR. Thou but rememberest° me of mine own
conception. I have perceived a most faint neglect°
of late, which I have rather blamed as mine own
jealous curiosity° than as a very pretense° and purpose of unkindness. I will look further into 't. But
where's my fool? I have not seen him this two
days.   78
KNIGHT. Since my young lady's going into France,
sir, the fool hath much pined away.
LEAR. No more of that, I have noted it well. Go
you, and tell my daughter I would speak with her.
[*Exit an* ATTENDANT.] Go you, call hither my   84
fool. [*Exit an* ATTENDANT. *Re-enter* OSWALD.] Oh, you
sir, you, come you hither, sir. Who am I, sir?
OSW. My lady's father.
LEAR. My lady's father! My lord's knave. You
whoreson dog! You slave! You cur!   89
OSW. I am none of these, my lord, I beseech your
pardon.

Sc. iv: 2. defuse: make indistinct, disguise.   4. razed: lit.,
shaved off, disguised.   7 s.d., within: off stage.   12. What . . .
profess: what is your profession?   17. judgment: The Day of
Judgment; i.e., I have a conscience.   18. eat no fish: I don't
observe fast days, and am therefore no Catholic.   30. countenance: bearing.   34–35. mar . . . it: I'm not one to delight in
overelaborate (*curious*) phrases when telling my tale; i.e., he
will have none of the fantastic talk of the typical courtier — such
as Shakespeare mocks in the character of Osric (see *Haml,*
V.ii.81–201). Kent himself mimics this fashion later (II.ii.111–14).

51. clotpoll: clodpole, blockhead.   58. roundest: plainest.
63. entertained: treated.   ceremonious affection: affection
which shows itself in ceremony. Manners even between children
and parents were very formal. Neglect of courtesies to the ex-
King shows deliberate disrespect.   66. dependents: servants of
the house.   72. rememberest: remind.   73. faint neglect: i.e.,
the "weary negligence" commanded by Goneril (I.iii.12).
75. jealous curiosity: excessive suspicion.   pretense: deliberate
intention.

[handwritten margin note: OSWALD TALKS BACK TO KING SO KING TRIPS HIM]

LEAR. Do you bandy° looks with me, you rascal?
                           [*Striking him.*]
OSW. I'll not be struck, my lord.   94
KENT. Nor tripped neither, you base football
player.   [*Tripping up his heels.*]
LEAR. I thank thee, fellow. Thou servest me, and
I'll love thee.   98
KENT. Come, sir, arise, away! I'll teach you differ-
ences.° Away, away! If you will measure your lub-
ber's length again, tarry. But away! Go to, have you
wisdom? So.   [*Pushes* OSWALD *out.*]
LEAR. Now, my friendly knave, I thank thee.
There's earnest° of thy service.   104
                     [*Giving* KENT *money.*]
[*Enter* FOOL.]
FOOL. Let me hire him too. Here's my coxcomb.°
            [*Offering* KENT *his cap.*]
LEAR. How now, my pretty knave! How dost
thou?
FOOL. Sirrah, you were best take my coxcomb.
KENT. Why, fool?   110
FOOL. Why, for taking one's part that's out of
favor. Nay, an thou canst not smile as the wind sits,°
thou'lt catch cold shortly. There, take my coxcomb.
Why, this fellow hath banished two on 's daughters,
and done the third a blessing against his will. If thou
follow him, thou must needs wear my coxcomb.
How now, Nuncle! Would I had two coxcombs and
two daughters!   118
LEAR. Why, my boy?
FOOL. If I gave them all my living, I'd keep my
coxcombs myself. There's mine, beg another of thy
daughters.
LEAR. Take heed, sirrah, the whip.°   123
FOOL. Truth's a dog must to kennel. He must be
whipped out, when Lady the brach° may stand by
the fire and stink.
LEAR. A pestilent gall to me!°
FOOL. Sirrah, I'll teach thee a speech.
LEAR. Do.
FOOL. Mark it, Nuncle: 130
   "Have more than thou showest,
   Speak less than thou knowest,
   Lend less than thou owest,°
   Ride more than thou goest,°

Learn more than thou trowest,°   135
Set less than thou throwest.°
Leave thy drink and thy whore,
And keep in-a-door,
And thou shalt have more
Than two tens to a score."°   140
KENT. This is nothing, fool.
FOOL. Then 'tis like the breath of an unfeed law-
yer. You gave me nothing for 't. Can you make no
use of nothing, Nuncle?
LEAR. Why, no, boy, nothing can be made out of
nothing.°   146
FOOL. [*To* KENT] Prithee tell him so much the
rent of his land comes to. He will not believe a fool.
LEAR. A bitter fool!   150
FOOL. Dost thou know the difference, my boy, be-
tween a bitter fool and a sweet fool?
LEAR. No, lad, teach me.
FOOL.   "That lord that counseled thee
       To give away thy land,   155
   Come place him here by me,
       Do thou for him stand.
   The sweet and bitter fool
       Will presently appear —
   The one in motley° here,   160
       The other found out there."
LEAR. Dost thou call me fool, boy?
FOOL. All thy other titles thou hast given away.
That thou wast born with.
KENT. This is not altogether fool, my lord.   165
FOOL. No, faith, lords and great men will not let
me.° If I had a monopoly° out, they would have part
on 't. And ladies too, they will not let me have all the
fool to myself, they'll be snatching. Give me an egg,
Nuncle, and I'll give thee two crowns.
LEAR. What two crowns shall they be?   172
FOOL. Why, after I have cut the egg in the middle
and eat up the meat, the two crowns of the egg.
When thou clovest thy crown i' the middle and gavest away both parts, thou borest thine ass on thy
back o'er the dirt.° Thou hadst little wit in thy bald
crown when thou gavest thy golden one away. If I
speak like myself° in this, let him be whipped that
first finds it so. [*Singing*]   180
   "Fools had ne'er less wit in a year,
   For wise men are grown foppish,
   And know not how their wits to wear,
       Their manners are so apish."°

---

92. bandy: lit., hit the ball to and fro as in tennis. **100. dif-**
ferences: of rank. **104. earnest:** money given on account of
services to be rendered. Lear thus formally engages Kent as his
servant. **105. coxcomb:** the cap shaped like a cock's comb
(crest) worn by the professional fool. **112. an . . . sits:** i.e.,
if you can't curry favor with those in power. **117. Nuncle:**
Uncle. **123. the whip:** The fool's profession was precarious,
and in real life too smart a joke brought its painful reward.
In March 1605 Stone, a professional fool, was whipped for commenting on the diplomatic mission about to sail for Spain that
"there went sixty fools into Spain, besides my Lord Admiral
and his two sons." **125. Lady . . . brach:** Lady the pet bitch.
127. A . . . me: this pestilent fool rubs me on a sore spot.
133. owest: possess. **134. goest:** walk.

135. trowest: know. **136. Set . . . throwest:** don't bet a larger
stake than you can afford to lose. **139–40. And . . . score:**
and then your money will increase. **145–46. nothing . . . noth-**
ing: Lear unconsciously repeats himself. See I.i.92. **160. motley:**
the particolored uniform worn by a fool. **166–67. will . . . me:**
i.e., keep all my folly to myself. **167. monopoly:** a royal patent
giving the holders the sole right to deal in some commodity. The
granting of such monopolies to courtiers was one of the crying
scandals of the time. **176–77. thine . . . dirt:** an old tale of the
typical simple-minded countryman. **179. like myself:** i.e., like
a fool. **181–84. Fools . . . apish:** there's no job left for fools

LEAR. When were you wont to be so full of songs, sirrah?   186

FOOL. I have used it, Nuncle, ever since thou madest thy daughters thy mother. For when thou gavest them the rod and puttest down thine own breeches, [*Singing*]   190

   " Then they for sudden joy did weep,
      And I for sorrow sung,
     That such a king should play bopeep,
      And go the fools among."   194

Prithee, Nuncle, keep a schoolmaster that can teach thy fool to lie. I would fain learn to lie.

LEAR. An° you lie, sirrah, we'll have you whipped.

FOOL. I marvel what kin thou and thy daughters are. They'll have me whipped for speaking true, thou'lt have me whipped for lying, and sometimes I am whipped for holding my peace. I had rather be any kind o' thing than a fool. And yet I would not be thee, Nuncle. Thou hast pared thy wit o' both sides and left nothing i' the middle. Here comes one o' the pairings.   206

[*Enter* GONERIL.]

LEAR. How now, Daughter! What makes that frontlet° on? Methinks you are too much of late i' the frown.   209

FOOL. Thou wast a pretty fellow when thou hadst no need to care for her frowning. Now thou art an O without a figure.° I am better than thou art now. I am a fool, thou art nothing. [*To* GONERIL] Yes, forsooth, I will hold my tongue, so your face bids me, though you say nothing.   215

   " Mum, mum.
   He that keeps nor crust nor crumb,°
   Weary of all, shall want some."

[*Pointing to* LEAR] That's a shealed peascod.°

GON. Not only, sir, this your all-licensed° fool, But other of your insolent retinue   221
Do hourly carp° and quarrel, breaking forth
In rank and not to be endurèd riots. Sir,
I had thought, by making this well known unto you,
To have found a safe redress, but now grow fearful
By what yourself too late have spoke and done   226
That you protect this course and put it on°
By your allowance.° Which if you should, the fault
Would not 'scape censure, nor the redresses sleep,
Which, in the tender of a wholesome weal,   230
Might in their working do you that offense
Which else were shame, that then necessity
Will call discreet proceeding.°

FOOL. For, you know, Nuncle,
   " The hedge sparrow fed the cuckoo° so long   235
     That it had it head bit off by it young."
So out went the candle, and we were left darkling.°

LEAR. Are you our daughter?

GON. Come, sir,   239
I would you would make use of that good wisdom
Whereof I know you are fraught,° and put away
These dispositions° that of late transform you
From what you rightly are.

FOOL. May not an ass know when the cart draws the horse? Whoop, Jug! I love thee.°   245

LEAR. Doth any here know me? This is not Lear. Doth Lear walk thus? Speak thus? Where are his eyes?
Either his notion° weakens, his discernings
Are lethargied° —— Ha! Waking? 'Tis not so.
Who is it that can tell me who I am?   250

FOOL. Lear's shadow.

LEAR. I would learn that, for, by the marks of sovereignty,° knowledge, and reason, I should be false persuaded I had daughters.   255

FOOL. Which they will make an obedient father.

LEAR. Your name, fair gentlewoman?

GON. This admiration,° sir, is much o' the savor
Of° other your new pranks. I do beseech you
To understand my purposes aright.   260
As you are old and reverend, you should be wise.
Here do you keep a hundred knights and squires,
Men so disordered,° so deboshed° and bold,
That this our Court, infected with their manners,
Shows like a riotous inn. Epicurism° and lust   265
Make it more like a tavern or a brothel
Than a graced° palace. The shame itself doth speak
For instant remedy. Be then desired
By her that else will take the thing she begs
A little to disquantity your train,°   270
And the remainder that shall still depend,°
To be such men as may besort° your age,
Which know themselves and you.

LEAR.   Darkness and devils!
Saddle my horses, call my train together.
Degenerate bastard! I'll not trouble thee.   275
Yet have I left a daughter.

GON. You strike my people, and your disordered rabble

nowadays, because the wise men are so like them. **apish:** like apes, who always imitate.   **198. An:** if.   **208. frontlet:** frown; lit., a band worn on the forehead.   **211–12. an . . . figure:** a cipher.   **217. crumb:** inside of the loaf.   **219. shealed peascod:** a shelled peapod.   **220. all-licensed:** allowed to take all liberties.   **222. carp:** find fault.   **227. put it on:** encourage it.   **228. allowance:** approval.   **230–33. Which . . . proceeding:** if you continue to be a nuisance I shall be forced to keep my state peaceful by taking measures which will annoy you and would at other times be shameful toward a father, but would be justified as mere discretion.   **235. cuckoo:** for the habits of the cuckoo see App. II.   **237. darkling:** in the dark.   **241. fraught:** stored, endowed.   **242. dispositions:** moods.   **245. Whoop . . . thee:** one of the meaningless cries made by the fool to distract attention.   **248. notion:** understanding.   **249. lethargied:** paralyzed.   **253–54. marks of sovereignty:** the outward signs which show that I am King.   **258. admiration:** pretended astonishment.   **258–59. much . . . Of:** tastes much the same as.   **263. disordered:** disorderly. **deboshed:** debauched.   **265. Epicurism:** self-indulgence, riotous living.   **267. graced:** gracious.   **270. disquantity . . . train:** diminish the number of your followers.   **271. depend:** be your dependents.   **272. besort:** be suitable for.

Make servants of their betters.
[*Enter* ALBANY.]
LEAR. Woe, that too late repents. — [*To* ALBANY]
   Oh, sir, are you come?
Is it your will? Speak, sir. Prepare my horses. 280
Ingratitude, thou marble-hearted fiend,
More hideous when thou show'st thee in a child
Than the sea monster!
ALB.   Pray, sir, be patient.
LEAR. [*To* GONERIL] Detested kite!° Thou liest.
My train are men of choice and rarest parts,° 285
That all particulars of duty know,
And in the most exact regard support
The worships of their name.° O most small fault,
How ugly didst thou in Cordelia show! 289
That, like an engine, wrenched my frame of nature
From the fixed place,° drew from my heart all love
And added to the gall.° O Lear, Lear, Lear!
Beat at this gate, that let thy folly in
                   [*Striking his head*]
And thy dear judgment out!° Go, go, my people.
ALB. My lord, I am guiltless, as I am ignorant
Of what hath moved you.
LEAR.   It may be so, my lord. 296
Hear, Nature, hear,° dear goddess, hear!
Suspend thy purpose if thou didst intend
To make this creature fruitful.
Into her womb convey sterility.   300
Dry up in her the organs of increase,°
And from her derogate° body never spring
A babe to honor her! If she must teem,°
Create her child of spleen,° that it may live
And be a thwart disnatured° torment to her. 305
Let it stamp wrinkles in her brow of youth,
With cadent° tears fret° channels in her cheeks,
Turn all her mother's pains and benefits
To laughter and contempt, that she may feel
How sharper than a serpent's tooth it is   310
To have a thankless child! Away, away!   [*Exit.*]
ALB. Now, gods that we adore, whereof comes this?
GON. Never afflict yourself to know the cause,
But let his disposition have that scope
That dotage gives it.   315
          [*Re-enter* LEAR.]
LEAR. What, fifty of my followers at a clap!°
Within a fortnight!°
ALB.   What's the matter, sir?

LEAR. I'll tell thee. [*To* GONERIL] Life and death!
   I am ashamed
That thou hast power to shake my manhood° thus,
That these hot tears, which break from me perforce,
Should make thee worth them. Blasts and fogs upon
   thee!   321
The untented woundings° of a father's curse
Pierce every sense about thee! Old fond° eyes,
Beweep this cause again, I'll pluck ye out
And cast you with the waters that you lose   325
To temper° clay. Yea, is it come to this?
Let it be so. Yet have I left a daughter
Who I am sure is kind and comfortable.°
When she shall hear this of thee, with her nails
She'll flay thy wolvish visage. Thou shalt find   330
That I'll resume the shape which thou dost think
I have cast off forever. Thou shalt, I warrant thee.
     [*Exeunt* LEAR, KENT, *and* ATTENDANTS.]
GON. Do you mark that, my lord?
ALB. I° cannot be so partial, Goneril,
To the great love I bear you ——   335
GON. Pray you, content. What, Oswald, ho!
[*To the* FOOL] You, sir, more knave than fool, after
   your master.
FOOL. Nuncle Lear, Nuncle Lear, tarry, take the
fool with thee.°
   "A fox, when one has caught her,   340
     And such a daughter,
     Should sure to the slaughter,
     If my cap would buy a halter.
     So the fool follows after."   [*Exit.*]
GON. This man hath had good counsel. A hundred
   knights!   345
'Tis politic° and safe to let him keep
At point° a hundred knights. Yes, that on every
   dream,
Each buzz,° each fancy, each complaint, dislike,
He may enguard his dotage with their powers
And hold our lives in mercy. Oswald, I say!   350
ALB. Well, you may fear too far.
GON.   Safer than trust too far.
Let me still take away the harms I fear,
Not fear still to be taken.° I know his heart.
What he hath uttered I have writ my sister.
If she sustain him and his hundred knights   355
When I have showed the unfitness ——

---

284. **kite:** the lowest of the birds of prey, an eater of offal.
285. **parts:** accomplishments.   287–88. **in . . . name:** and in
every minute detail uphold their honorable names.   290–91. **like
. . . place:** like a little instrument (e.g., a lever) dislodged my
firm nature.   292. **gall:** bitterness.   293–94. **Beat . . . out:** the
first signs of madness in Lear.   297. **Hear . . . hear:** In making
this terrible curse, Lear also calls on Nature, but as goddess
of natural affection. Cf. I.ii.1–22.   301. **increase:** childbearing.
302. **derogate:** debased.   303. **teem:** conceive.   304. **spleen:**
malice.   305. **thwart disnatured:** perverse and unnatural.
307. **cadent:** falling. **fret:** wear away.   316. **at a clap:** at one
blow.   316–17. **What . . . fortnight:** As Lear goes out he learns

that Goneril has herself already begun to take steps "a little to
disquantity his train" by ordering that fifty of them shall depart
within a fortnight. To a man who regards his own dignity so
highly, this fresh blow is devastating.   319. **shake my manhood:** i.e., with sobs.   322. **untented woundings:** raw wounds.
A tent was a small roll of lint used to clean out a wound
before it was bound up.   323. **fond:** foolish.   326. **temper:** mix.
328. **comfortable:** full of comfort.   334–35. **I . . . you:** i.e., although my love makes me partial to you, yet I must protest.
338–39. **take . . . thee:** i.e., take your fool and your own folly.
346. **politic:** good policy.   347. **At point:** fully armed.   348. **buzz:**
rumor.   352–53. **Let . . . taken:** let me always remove what I
fear will harm me rather than live in perpetual fear.

[*Re-enter* OSWALD.] How now, Oswald!
What, have you writ that letter to my sister?

OSW. Yes, madam.

GON. Take you some company, and away to horse.
Inform her full of my particular fear,   360
And thereto add such reasons of your own
As may compact it more.° Get you gone,
And hasten your return. [*Exit* OSWALD.] No, no, my
     lord,
This milky gentleness and course° of yours
Though I condemn not, yet, under pardon,   365
You are much more attasked° for want of wisdom
Than praised for harmful mildness.°

ALB. How far your eyes may pierce I cannot tell.
Striving to better, oft we mar what's well.

GON. Nay, then ——   370

ALB. Well, well, the event.°   [*Exeunt.*]

SCENE V. *Court before the same.*

[*Enter* LEAR, KENT, *and* FOOL.]

LEAR. Go you before to Gloucester with these letters. Acquaint my daughter no further with anything you know than comes from her demand out
of the letter. If your diligence be not speedy, I shall
be there afore you.   5

KENT. I will not sleep, my lord, till I have delivered
your letter.   [*Exit.*]

FOOL. If a man's brains were in 's heels, were 't
not in danger of kibes?°

LEAR. Aye, boy.   10

FOOL. Then I prithee be merry. Thy wit shall ne'er
go slipshod.°

LEAR. Ha, ha, ha!

FOOL. Shalt see thy other daughter will use thee
kindly,° for though she's as like this as a crab's° like
an apple, yet I can tell what I can tell.   16

LEAR. Why, what canst thou tell, my boy?

FOOL. She will taste as like this as a crab does to
a crab. Thou canst tell why one's nose stands i' the
middle on 's face?   20

LEAR. No.

FOOL. Why, to keep one's eyes of either side 's
nose, that what a man cannot smell out he may spy
into.

LEAR. I did her wrong ——   25

FOOL. Canst tell how an oyster makes his shell?

LEAR. No.

FOOL. Nor I neither, but I can tell why a snail has
a house.   30

LEAR. Why?

FOOL. Why, to put 's head in, not to give it away
to his daughters and leave his horns without a case.

LEAR. I will forget my nature. — So kind a father!
— Be my horses ready?   36

FOOL. Thy asses are gone about 'em. The reason
why the seven stars are no more than seven is a
pretty reason.

LEAR. Because they are not eight?   40

FOOL. Yes, indeed. Thou wouldst make a good
fool.

LEAR. To take 't again perforce!° Monster ingratitude!

FOOL. If thou wert my fool, Nuncle, I'd have thee
beaten for being old before thy time.   46

LEAR. How's that?

FOOL. Thou shouldst not have been old till thou
hadst been wise.

LEAR. Oh, let me not be mad, not mad, sweet
     Heaven!   50
Keep me in temper.° I would not be mad!
[*Enter* GENTLEMAN.] How now! Are the horses
     ready?

GENT. Ready, my lord.

LEAR. Come, boy.

FOOL. She that's a maid now and laughs at my departure   55
Shall not be a maid long, unless things be cut shorter.
     [*Exeunt.*]

Act II

SCENE I. *The* EARL OF GLOUCESTER's *castle.*

[*Enter* EDMUND *and* CURAN, *meeting.*]

EDM. Save thee,° Curan.

CUR. And you, sir. I have been with your father,
and given him notice that the Duke of Cornwall and
Regan his Duchess will be here with him this night.

EDM. How comes that?   6

CUR. Nay, I know not. You have heard of the
news abroad — I mean the whispered ones, for they
are yet but ear-kissing° arguments?

EDM. Not I. Pray you what are they?   10

CUR. Have you heard of no likely wars toward
'twixt the Dukes of Cornwall and Albany?

EDM. Not a word.   14

CUR. You may do, then, in time. Fare you well,
sir.   [*Exit.*]

---

362. compact it more: make my argument more convincing.
364. milky . . . course: this milksop behavior.   **366. attasked:**
blamed.   **367. harmful mildness:** a mildness which may prove
harmful.   **371. the event:** i.e., we must see what will happen.

     Sc. v: 9. kibes: chilblains.   **11–12. Thy . . . slipshod:** i.e.,
you don't need slippers, for you have no brains to be protected
from chilblains.   **15. kindly:** after her kind; i.e., nature.
crab: crab apple.

43. To . . . perforce: I will take back my kingdom by force.
51. temper: sanity.

     Act II, Sc. i: 1. Save thee: God save thee.   **9. ear-kissing:**
whispered close in the ear.

EDM. **The Duke be here tonight?** The better! Best!
This weaves itself perforce into my business.
My father hath set guard to take my brother,
And I have one thing, of a queasy question,°
Which I must act. Briefness and fortune, work!   20
Brother, a word, descend.° Brother, I say!
[*Enter* EDGAR.] My father watches. O sir, fly this
    place.
Intelligence° is given where you are hid.
You have now the good advantage of the night.   24
Have you not spoken 'gainst the Duke of Cornwall?
He's coming hither, now, i' the night, i' the haste,
And Regan with him. Have you nothing said
Upon his party 'gainst the Duke of Albany?
Advise yourself.
    EDG.   I am sure on 't, not a word.
    EDM. I hear my father coming. Pardon me,   30
In cunning° I must draw my sword upon you.
Draw. Seem to defend yourself. Now quit you well.°
Yield. Come before my father. Light, ho, here!
Fly, Brother. Torches, torches! So farewell.
                         [*Exit* EDGAR.]
Some blood drawn on me would beget opinion°   35
                        [*Wounds his arm.*]
Of my more fierce endeavor. I have seen drunkards
Do more than this in sport. Father, Father!
Stop, stop! No help?
    [*Enter* GLOUCESTER *and* SERVANTS *with torches.*]
    GLO. Now, Edmund, where's the villain?
    EDM. Here stood he in the dark, his sharp sword
    out,   40
Mumbling° of wicked charms, conjuring the moon°
To stand 's auspicious° mistress.
    GLO.   But where is he?
    EDM. Look, sir, I bleed.
    GLO.   Where is the villain, Edmund?
    EDM. Fled this way, sir. When by no means he
    could ——
    GLO. Pursue him, ho! — Go after.
              [*Exeunt some* SERVANTS.]
       "By no means" what?   45
    EDM. Persuade me to the murder of your lordship,
But that I told him the revenging gods
'Gainst parricides did all their thunders bend,
Spoke with how manifold and strong a bond
The child was bound to the father. Sir, in fine,°   50
Seeing how loathly opposite I stood°
To his unnatural purpose, in fell° motion

With his prepared° sword he charges home
My unprovided° body, lanced mine arm.
But when he saw my best alarumed spirits°   55
Bold in the quarrel's right, roused to the encounter,
Or whether gasted° by the noise I made,
Full suddenly he fled.
    GLO.   Let him fly far.
Not in this land shall he remain uncaught,
And found — dispatch.° The noble Duke my mas-
    ter,   60
My worthy arch and patron,° comes tonight.
By his authority I will proclaim it,
That he which finds him shall deserve our thanks,
Bringing the murderous caitiff° to the stake.°
He that conceals him, death.   65
    EDM. When I dissuaded him from his intent
And found him pight° to do it, with curst° speech
I threatened to discover him. He replied,
"Thou unpossessing bastard! Dost thou think,
If I would stand against thee, could the reposal   70
Of any trust, virtue, or worth in thee
Make thy words faithed?° No. What I should
    deny —
As this I would, aye, though thou didst produce
My very character° — I'd turn it all°
To thy suggestion,° plot, and damnèd practice.°   75
And thou must make° a dullard of the world
If they not thought the profits of my death
Were very pregnant and potential spurs°
To make thee seek it."
    GLO.   Strong and fastened° villain!
Would he deny his letter? I never got° him.   80
                  [*Tucket° within*]
Hark, the Duke's trumpets! I know not why he
    comes.
All ports I'll bar,° the villain shall not 'scape,
The Duke must grant me that. Besides, his pic-
    ture
I will send far and near, that all the kingdom
May have due note of him, and of my land,   85
Loyal and natural° boy, I'll work the means
To make thee capable.°   *HE WILL GIVE*
EARLDOM OF GLOUCESTER TO EDMUND

19. **queasy question:** which needs delicate handling; *queasy* means on the point of vomiting.   21. **descend:** i.e., from the chamber where he has been hiding.   23. **Intelligence:** information.   31. **In cunning:** as a pretense.   32. **quit . . . well:** defend yourself well. Here they clash their swords together.   35. **beget opinion:** give the impression.   41–42. **Mumbling . . . mistress:** This is the kind of story which would especially appeal to Gloucester. Cf. I.ii.112.   41. **conjuring . . . moon:** calling on Hecate, goddess of witchcraft.   42. **auspicious:** favorable.   50. **in fine:** in short.   51. **how . . . stood:** with what loathing I opposed.   52. **fell:** fearful.

53. **prepared:** drawn.   54. **unprovided:** unguarded.   55. **my . . . spirits:** my stoutest spirits called out by the alarm.   57. **gasted:** terrified.   60. **And . . . dispatch:** and when he's found, kill him.   61. **arch . . . patron:** chief support and protector.   64. **caitiff:** wretch; lit., captive. **to . . . stake:** i.e., place of execution.   67. **pight:** determined. **curst:** bitter.   72. **faithed:** believed.   74. **character:** handwriting. Cf. I.ii.66. **turn it all:** make it appear to be.   75. **suggestion:** idea. **practice:** plot.   76–79. **make . . . it:** you would have to make people dull indeed before they would disbelieve that your chief motive was to benefit by my death.   78. **pregnant . . . spurs:** obvious and powerful encouragements.   79. **fastened:** confirmed.   80. **got:** begot. s.d., **Tucket:** trumpet call.   82. **ports . . . bar:** I'll have the seaports watched to prevent his escape.   86. **natural:** i.e., one who has the proper feelings of son to father. Gloucester does not as yet realize what "nature" means to Edmund. See I.ii.1.   87. **capable:** i.e., legitimate; lit., capable of succeeding **as my** heir.

[*Enter* CORNWALL, REGAN, *and* ATTENDANTS.]

CORN. How now, my noble friend! Since I came
    hither,
Which I can call but now, I have heard strange
    news.

REG. If it be true, all vengeance comes too short
Which can pursue the offender. How dost, my lord?

GLO. Oh, madam, my old heart is cracked, is
    cracked!   92

REG. What, did my father's godson seek your life?
He whom my father named? Your Edgar?

GLO. Oh, lady, lady, shame would have it hid!   95

REG. Was he not companion with the riotous
    knights
That tend upon my father?

GLO. I know not, madam. 'Tis too bad, too bad.

EDM. Yes, madam, he was of that consort.°   99

REG. No marvel then, though he were ill affected.°
'Tis they have put him on° the old man's death,
To have the waste and spoil of his revènues.
I have this present evening from my sister
Been well informed of them, and with such cautions
That if they come to sojourn at my house,   105
I'll not be there.

CORN.   Nor I, assure thee, Regan.
Edmund, I hear that you have shown your father
A childlike office.°

EDM.   'Twas my duty, sir.

GLO. He did bewray° his practice, and received
This hurt you see, striving to apprehend him.   110

CORN. Is he pursued?

GLO.   Aye, my good lord.

CORN. If he be taken, he shall never more
Be feared of doing° harm. Make your own purpose,
How in my strength you please.° For you, Edmund,
Whose virtue and obedience doth this instant   115
So much commend itself, you shall be ours.
Natures of such deep trust we shall much need.
You we first seize on.

EDM.   I shall serve you, sir,
Truly, however else.

GLO.   For him I thank your Grace.

CORN. You know not why we came to visit
    you ——   120

REG. Thus out of season, threading dark-eyed
    night.°
Occasions, noble Gloucester, of some poise,°
Wherein we must have use of your advice.
Our father he hath writ, so hath our sister,
Of differences, which I least thought it fit   125
To answer from° our home. The several messengers

From hence attend dispatch.° Our good old friend,
Lay comforts to your bosom, and bestow
Your needful counsel to our business,
Which craves the instant use.°

GLO.   I serve you, madam.   130
Your Graces are right welcome. [*Flourish. Exeunt.*]

SCENE II. *Before* GLOUCESTER's *castle.*

[*Enter* KENT *and* OSWALD, *severally.*°]

OSW. Good dawning to thee, friend. Art of this
house?

KENT. Aye.

OSW. Where may we set our horses?

KENT. I' the mire.

OSW. Prithee, if thou lovest me, tell me.

KENT. I love thee not.

OSW. Why, then I care not for thee.

KENT. If I had thee in Lipsbury pinfold,° I would
make thee care for me.   10

OSW. Why dost thou use me thus? I know thee
not.

KENT. Fellow, I know thee.

OSW. What dost thou know me for?   14

KENT. A° knave, a rascal, an eater of broken
meats; a base, proud, shallow, beggarly, three-suited,
hundred-pound, filthy, worsted-stocking knave; a
lily-livered, action-taking knave; a whoreson, glass-
gazing, superserviceable, finical rogue; one-trunk-
inheriting slave; one that wouldst be a bawd in   20
way of good service, and art nothing but the composition of a knave, beggar, coward, pander, and the
son and heir of a mongrel bitch — one whom I will
beat into clamorous whining if thou deniest the least
syllable of thy addition.   26

OSW. Why, what a monstrous fellow art thou,
thus to rail on one that is neither known of thee nor
knows thee!   29

KENT. What a brazen-faced varlet art thou, to

127. **attend dispatch:** are waiting to be sent back.   130. **craves
. . . use:** requires immediate action.
  Sc. ii: s.d., severally: by different entrances.   9. **Lipsbury
pinfold:** This phrase has not been convincingly explained.
A pinfold is a village pound, a small enclosure in which strayed
beasts are kept until reclaimed by their owners; a pinfold was a
good place for a fight whence neither side could escape.   15–26. **A
. . . addition:** Kent here sums up the characteristics of the more
unpleasant kind of gentleman servingman of whom Oswald is a
fair specimen (see App. 14). **broken meats:** remains of food
sent down from the high table. **three-suited:** allowed three suits
a year. **hundred-pound:** i.e., the extent of his wealth. **worsted-
stocking:** no gentleman, or he would have worn silk. **lily-livered:**
cowardly. **action-taking knave:** one who goes to law instead of
risking a fight. **glass-gazing:** always looking at himself in a
mirror. **superserviceable:** too eager to do what his master
wishes. **finical:** finicky. **one-trunk-inheriting:** whose whole
inheritance from his father will go into one trunk. **bawd . . .
service:** ready to serve his master's lusts if it will please him.
composition: mixture. **pander:** pimp. **addition:** lit., title of
honor added to a man's name.

99. **consort:** party.   100. **though . . . affected:** if he had traitorous thoughts.   101. **put . . . on:** persuaded him to cause.
108. **childlike office:** filial service.   109. **bewray:** reveal.
113. **of doing:** because he might do.   113–14. **Make . . . please:**
use my authority for any action you care to take.   121. **threading . . . night:** making our way through the darkness.   122. **poise:**
weight.   126. **from:** away from.

deny thou knowest me! Is it two days ago since I
tripped up thy heels and beat thee before the King?
Draw, you rogue. For though it be night, yet the
moon shines. I'll make a sop o' the moonshine of
you.° Draw, you whoreson cullionly° barber- 35
monger,° draw.   [*Drawing his sword.*]

osw. Away! I have nothing to do with thee.

KENT. Draw, you rascal. You come with letters
against the King, and take vanity the puppet's part°
against the royalty of her father. Draw, you rogue, or
I'll so carbonado° your shanks. Draw, you rascal,
come your ways.   42

osw. Help, ho! Murder! Help!

KENT. Strike, you slave. Stand, rogue, stand, you
neat slave, strike.   [*Beating him.*]

osw. Help, ho! Murder! Murder!   46

[*Enter* EDMUND, *with his rapier drawn,* CORNWALL,
     REGAN, GLOUCESTER, *and* SERVANTS.]

EDM. How now! What's the matter?

         [*Parting them.*]

KENT. With you, goodman boy,° an you please.
Come, I'll flesh you,° come on, young master.

GLO. Weapons! Arms! What's the matter here?

CORN. Keep peace, upon your lives.   52
He dies that strikes again. What is the matter?

REG. The messengers from our sister and the
King.   55

CORN. What is your difference?° Speak.

osw. I am scarce in breath, my lord.

KENT. No marvel, you have so bestirred your
valor. You cowardly rascal, Nature disclaims in thee.
A tailor made thee.°   60

CORN. Thou art a strange fellow — a tailor make
a man?

KENT. Aye, a tailor, sir. A stonecutter or a painter
could not have made him so ill, though he had been
but two hours at the trade.   65

CORN. Speak yet, how grew your quarrel?

osw. This ancient ruffian, sir, whose life I have
spared at suit of his gray beard ——   68

KENT. Thou whoreson zed! Thou unnecessary
letter!° My lord, if you will give me leave, I will

tread this unbolted° villain into mortar, and daub
the walls of a jakes° with him. Spare my gray beard,
you wagtail?°

CORN. Peace, sirrah!

You beastly knave, know you no reverence?°   75

KENT. Yes, sir, but anger hath a privilege.°

CORN. Why art thou angry?

KENT. That such a slave as this should wear a
sword,
Who wears no honesty. Such smiling rogues as these,
Like rats, oft bite the holy cords a-twain   80
Which are too intrinse to unloose;° smooth° every
passion
That in the natures of their lords rebel;
Bring oil to fire, snow to their colder moods;
Renege, affirm,° and turn their halcyon° beaks
With every gale and vary of their masters,   85
Knowing naught, like dogs, but following.
A plague upon your epileptic visage!
Smile you my speeches, as I were a fool?
Goose,° if I had you upon Sarum° plain,
I'd drive ye cackling home to Camelot.°   9'

CORN. What, art thou mad, old fellow?

GLO. How fell you out? Say that.

KENT. No contraries hold more antipathy
Than I and such a knave.

CORN. Why dost thou call him knave? What is his
fault?   95

KENT. His countenance likes me not.°

CORN. No more perchance does mine, nor his, nor
hers.

KENT. Sir, 'tis my occupation to be plain.
I have seen better faces in my time
Than stands on any shoulder that I see   100
Before me at this instant.

CORN.   This° is some fellow
Who, having been praised for bluntness, doth affect
A saucy roughness,° and constrains the garb
Quite from his nature.° He cannot flatter, he —
An honest mind and plain — he must speak truth!
An they will take it, so. If not, he's plain.   106
These kind of knaves I know, which in this plain-
ness

34–35. sop . . . you: Not satisfactorily explained, but obviously
something unpleasant; probably Kent means no more than "I'll
make a wet mess of you."   35. cullionly: base.   36. barber-
monger: a man always in the barber's shop. Elizabethan gentlemen frequented the beauty parlor as much as our modern ladies
do.   39. vanity . . . part: Vanity appeared as an evil character in
the old Morality plays of the early sixteenth century, which still
survived in a degenerate form in puppet shows exhibited at fairs.
41. carbonado: lit., a steak slashed for cooking, so "slice."
49. goodman boy: my young man. Edmund is still a young man,
but it was an insult to call him boy. Cf. *R & J*, I.v.79–80;
Cor, V.vi.101–13.   50. flesh you: give you your first fight.
Cf. *I Hen IV*, V.iv.133–34.   56. difference: disagreement.
59–60. Nature . . . thee: Nature refuses to own you, you are
nothing but clothes — from the English proverb "The tailor
makes the man."   69–70. zed . . . letter: because z does not
exist in Latin and is not necessary in the English alphabet, since
s can usually take its place.

71. unbolted: unsifted, coarse.   72. jakes: privy.   73. wagtail:
a small bird which wags its tail up and down as it struts.
75. know . . . reverence: i.e., do you have the impertinence to
raise your voice in the presence of your betters?   76. anger . . .
privilege: something must be allowed to a man who has lost temper.   80–81. bite . . . unloose: i.e., cause the bonds of holy
matrimony to be broken by serving the lusts of their employers.
81. smooth: help to gratify.   84. Renege, affirm: deny or agree;
i.e., a perfect "yes man." halcyon: kingfisher. A kingfisher
hung up by the neck was supposed to turn its bill into the prevailing wind.   89–90. Goose . . . Camelot: These lines cannot be
explained. Sarum: Salisbury Plain, in the south of England.
Camelot: the home of King Arthur and the knights of his Round
Table.   96. His . . . not: I don't like his face.   101–10. This . . .
nicely: See App. 4.   103. saucy roughness: impudent rudeness.
103–04. constrains . . . nature: affects a manner which is quite
unnatural.

KING LEAR

Harbor more craft and more corrupter ends
Than twenty silly ducking observants
That stretch their duties nicely.°   110
  KENT. Sir,° in good faith, in sincere verity,
Under the allowance of your great aspèct,
Whose influence, like the wreath of radiant fire
On flickering Phoebus'° front ——
  CORN.   What mean'st by this? 114
  KENT. To go out of my dialect, which you discommend so much. I know, sir, I am no flatterer. He that beguiled you in a plain accent was a plain knave, which, for my part, I will not be, though I should win your displeasure to entreat me to 't.°   120
  CORN. What was the offense you gave him?
  OSW. I never gave him any.
It pleased the King his master very late
To strike at me, upon his misconstruction,°   124
When he, conjunct,° and flattering his displeasure,
Tripped me behind; being down, insulted, railed,
And put upon him such a deal of man
That worthied him,° got praises of the King
For him attempting° who was self-subdued,°
And in the fleshment° of this dread exploit   130
Drew on me here again.
  KENT.   None of these rogues and cowards
But Ajax is their fool.°
  CORN.   Fetch forth the stocks!
You stubborn° ancient knave, you reverend° braggart,
We'll teach you ——
  KENT.   Sir, I am too old to learn.
Call not your stocks for me. I serve the King, 135
On whose employment I was sent to you.
You shall do small respect, show too bold malice
Against the grace and person of my master,
Stocking his messenger.°
  CORN. Fetch forth the stocks! As I have life and honor,   140

109–10. silly . . . nicely: silly servants who are always bowing to their masters as they strain to carry out their orders. *111–14. Sir . . . front:* Kent now changes his tone from the honest blunt man to the affected courtier. See I.iv.34. *Phoebus:* the sun god. *116–20. He . . . to't:* the man who posed as blunt and honest and deceived you was simply a knave. I shall never be a knave, even if you ask me and are angry because I refuse. *124. upon . . . misconstruction:* because he deliberately misinterpreted my words. *125. conjunct:* i.e., joining with the King. *128. worthied him:* got him favor. *129. attempting:* attacking. *self-subdued:* made no resistance. *130. fleshment:* excitement. *131–32. None . . . fool:* This cryptic but devastating remark rouses Cornwall to fury, for he realizes from Kent's insolent tone, manner, and gesture that by "Ajax" he is himself intended. Ajax was the ridiculous braggart of the Greek army whom Shakespeare had already dramatized in *Tr & Cr.* The name Ajax had further unsavory significances for the original audience, for "Ajax" was a common synonym for a jakes — a very evil-smelling place. Kent thus implies "All these knaves and cowards are fooling this stinking braggart." See App. 4. *133. stubborn:* rude. *reverend:* old. *137–39. You . . . messenger:* As the King's representative, Kent is entitled to respectful treatment; to put him in the stocks is to offer an intolerable insult to the King. See ll. 147–54 below and II.iv.22–24.

There shall he sit till noon.
  REG. Till noon! Till night, my lord, and all night too.
  KENT. Why, madam, if I were your father's dog, You should not use me so.
  REG.   Sir, being his knave, I will.
  CORN. This is a fellow of the selfsame color   145
Our sister speaks of. Come, bring away° the stocks!
                              [*Stocks brought out*]
  GLO. Let me beseech your Grace not to do so.
His fault is much, and the good King his master
Will check° him for 't. Your purposed low correction°
Is such as basest and contemned'st° wretches   150
For pilferings and most common trespasses
Are punished with. The King must take it ill
That he, so slightly valued in his messenger,
Should have him thus restrained.
  CORN.   I'll answer that.
  REG. My sister may receive it much more worse
To have her gentleman abused, assaulted,   156
For following her affairs. Put in his legs.
                    [KENT *is put in the stocks.*]
Come, my good lord, away.
          [*Exeunt all but* GLOUCESTER *and* KENT.]
  GLO. I am sorry for thee, friend. 'Tis the Duke's pleasure,
Whose disposition all the world well knows   160
Will not be rubbed° nor stopped. I'll entreat for thee.
  KENT. Pray do not, sir. I have watched and traveled hard,
Some time I shall sleep out, the rest I'll whistle.
A good man's fortune may grow out at heels.°
Give you good morrow!°   165
  GLO. The Duke's to blame in this, 'twill be ill-taken.
                                         [*Exit.*]
  KENT. Good King, that must approve the common saw,°
Thou out of Heaven's benediction comest
To the warm sun!°
Approach, thou beacon to this underglobe,°   170
That by thy comfortable beams I may
Peruse this letter! Nothing almost sees miracles
But misery.° I know 'tis from Cordelia,
Who hath most fortunately been informed
Of my obscurèd course,° and shall find time   175
From this enormous state,° seeking to give

146. bring away: fetch out. *149. check:* rebuke, punish. *purposed . . . correction:* the degrading punishment which you propose. *150. contemned'st:* most despised. *161. rubbed:* turned aside, a metaphor from the game of bowls. *164. A . . . heels:* even a good man may suffer a shabby fate. *165. Give . . . morrow:* a good morning to you. *167. approve . . . saw:* stress the truth of the common proverb. *168–69. Thou . . . sun:* you are coming out of the shade into the heat. *170. beacon . . . underglobe:* the rising sun. *172–73. Nothing . . . misery:* only those who are wretched appreciate miracles. *175. obscured course:* i.e., my actions in disguise. *176. this . . . state:* these wicked times.

Losses their remedies. All weary and o'erwatched,
Take vantage, heavy eyes, not to behold
This shameful lodging.   179
Fortune, good night. Smile once more, turn thy
     wheel!   [*Sleeps.*]

SCENE III. *A wood.*

[*Enter* EDGAR.]

EDG. I heard myself proclaimed,°
And by the happy° hollow of a tree
Escaped the hunt. No port is free, no place,
That guard and most unusual vigilance
Does not attend my taking.° Whiles I may 'scape   5
I will preserve myself, and am bethought°
To take the basest and most poorest shape
That ever penury in contempt of man
Brought near to beast.° My face I'll grime with filth,
Blanket° my loins, elf° all my hair in knots,   10
And with presented nakedness° outface
The winds and persecutions of the sky.
The country gives me proof and precedent°
Of Bedlam beggars,° who with roaring voices
Strike in their numbed and mortified° bare
     arms   15
Pins, wooden pricks, nails, sprigs of rosemary,
And with this horrible object, from low° farms,
Poor pelting° villages, sheepcotes and mills,
Sometime with lunatic bans,° sometime with pray-
     ers,   19
Enforce their charity. Poor Turlygod! Poor Tom!°
That's something yet. Edgar I nothing am.°   [*Exit.*]

SCENE IV. *Before* GLOUCESTER'S *castle.* KENT *in the stocks.*

[*Enter* LEAR, FOOL, *and* GENTLEMAN.]

LEAR. 'Tis strange that they should so depart from
     home
And not send back my messenger.
   GENT.   As I learned,

Sc. iii: 1. **proclaimed**: See II.i.82–85.   2. **happy**: lucky.
5. **attend my taking**: watch to take me.   6. **am bethought**: have
decided.   8–9. **penury . . . beast**: poverty, to show that man
is a contemptible creature, reduced to the level of a beast.
10. **Blanket**: cover with only a blanket. **elf**: mat. Matted hair
was believed to be caused by elves. Cf. *R & J*, I.iv.88–91.
11. **with . . . nakedness**: bold in my nakedness.   13. **proof . . .
precedent**: examples.   14. **Bedlam beggars**: lunatics discharged
from Bedlam (or Bethlehem) Hospital, the London madhouse.
These sturdy beggars were the terror of the countryside. See
I.ii.148.   15. **mortified**: numbed.   17. **low**: humble.   18. **pelting**: paltry.   19. **bans**: curses.   20. **Poor . . . Tom**: Edgar rehearses the names which a bedlam calls himself.   21. **That's . . .
am**: there's still a chance for me; as Edgar I am a dead man.

The night before there was no purpose° in them
Of this remove.
   KENT.   Hail to thee, noble master!
   LEAR. Ha!   5
Makest thou this shame thy pastime?°
   KENT.   No, my lord.
   FOOL. Ha, ha! He wears cruel° garters. Horses are
tied by the heads, dogs and bears by the neck, mon-
keys by the loins, and men by the legs. When a man's
overlusty at legs,° then he wears wooden nether-
stocks.°   11
   LEAR. What's he that hath so much thy place mis-
     took
To set thee here?
   KENT.   It is both he and she,
Your son and daughter.
   LEAR. No.   15
   KENT. Yes.
   LEAR. No, I say.
   KENT. I say yea.
   LEAR. No, no, they would not.
   KENT. Yes, they have.   20
   LEAR. By Jupiter, I swear no.
   KENT. By Juno, I swear aye.
   LEAR.   They durst not do 't,
They could not, would not do 't. 'Tis worse than
     murder
To do upon respect° such violent outrage.
Resolve° me with all modest haste which way   25
Thou mightest deserve, or they impose, this usage,
Coming from us.°
   KENT.   My lord, when at their home
I did commend your Highness' letters to them,
Ere I was risen from the place that showed
My duty kneeling, came there a reeking post,°   30
Stewed in his haste, half-breathless, panting forth
From Goneril his mistress salutations,
Delivered letters, spite of intermission,°
Which presently° they read. On whose contents
They summoned up their meiny,° straight took
     horse,   35
Commanded me to follow and attend
The leisure of their answer, gave me cold looks.
And meeting here the other messenger,
Whose welcome, I perceived, had poisoned mine —
Being the very fellow that of late   40
Displayed so saucily° against your Highness —
Having more man than wit about me, drew.
He raised the house with loud and coward cries.

Sc. iv: 3. **purpose**: intention.   6. **Makest . . . pastime**: are
you sitting there for amusement?   7. **cruel**: with a pun on
"crewel" — worsted.   10. **overlusty at legs**: i.e., a vagabond.
11. **netherstocks**: stockings.   24. **upon respect**: the respect due
to me, their King and father.   25. **Resolve**: inform.   27. **Coming . . . us**: Lear uses the royal "we" — "from us, the King."
30. **reeking post**: sweating messenger.   33. **spite of intermission**:
in spite of the delay in reading my letter (which should have come
first).   34. **presently**: immediately.   35. **meiny**: followers.
41. **Displayed so saucily**: behaved so insolently.

Your son and daughter found this trespass worth°
The shame which here it suffers.   45

FOOL. Winter's not gone yet° if the wild geese fly
that way.
      " Fathers that wear rags
          Do make their children blind,
      But fathers that bear bags°   50
          Shall see their children kind.
      Fortune, that arrant whore,
      Ne'er turns the key° to the poor."
But for all this, thou shalt have as many dolors° for
thy daughters as thou canst tell° in a year.   55

LEAR. Oh,° how this mother swells up toward my
    heart!
Hysterica passio, down, thou climbing sorrow,
Thy element's° below! Where is this daughter?

KENT. With the Earl, sir, here within.   59

LEAR. Follow me not, stay here.   [*Exit.*]

GENT. Made you no more offense but what you
speak of?

KENT. None.
How chance the King comes with so small a train?

FOOL. An thou hadst been set i' the stocks for that
question, thou hadst well deserved it.   66

KENT. Why, fool?

FOOL. We'll° set thee to school to an ant, to teach
thee there's no laboring i' the winter. All that follow
their noses° are led by their eyes but blind men,   70
and there's not a nose among twenty but can smell
him that's stinking. Let go thy hold when a great
wheel runs down a hill, lest it break thy neck with
following it, but the great one that goes up the hill,
let him draw thee after. When a wise man gives   75
thee better counsel, give me mine again. I would
have none but knaves follow it, since a fool gives it.

    " That sir which serves and seeks for gain,
      And follows but for form,°
    Will pack° when it begins to rain,   80
      And leave thee in the storm.

    " But I will tarry, the fool will stay,
      And let the wise man fly.
    The knave turns fool that runs away,   85
      The fool no knave, perdy."°

KENT. Where learned you this, fool?

FOOL. Not i' the stocks, fool.
    [*Re-enter* LEAR, *with* GLOUCESTER.]

LEAR. Deny to speak with me? They are sick?
    They are weary?
They have traveled all the night? Mere fetches,°   90
The images° of revolt and flying off.
Fetch me a better answer.

GLO.   My dear lord,
You know the fiery quality° of the Duke,
How unremovable and fixed he is
In his own course.   95

LEAR. Vengeance! Plague! Death! Confusion!
Fiery? What quality? Why, Gloucester, Gloucester,
I'd speak with the Duke of Cornwall and his wife.

GLO. Well, my good lord, I have informed them
so.

LEAR. Informed them! Dost thou understand me,
man?   100

GLO. Aye, my good lord.

LEAR. The King would speak with Cornwall, the
dear father
Would with his daughter speak, commands her
service.
Are they informed of this? My breath and blood!
"Fiery"? "The fiery Duke"? Tell the hot Duke
that——   105
No, but not yet. Maybe he is not well.
Infirmity doth still neglect all office
Whereto our health is bound.° We are not our-
selves
When nature being oppressed commands the mind
To suffer with the body. I'll forbear,   110
And am fall'n out with my more headier will,°
To take the indisposed and sickly fit
For the sound man. [*Looking on* KENT] Death on
my state! Wherefore
Should he sit here? This act persuades me
That this remotion° of the Duke and her   115
Is practice° only. Give me my servant forth.°
Go tell the Duke and 's wife I'd speak with them,
Now, presently. Bid them come forth and hear me,
Or at their chamber door I'll beat the drum
Till it cry sleep to death.°   120

GLO. I would have all well betwixt you.   [*Exit.*]

LEAR. Oh, me, my heart, my rising heart! But
down!°   122

FOOL. Cry to it, Nuncle, as the cockney° did to
the eels when she put 'em i' the paste alive. She
knapped° 'em o' the coxcombs with a stick, and
cried " Down, wantons, down! " 'Twas her brother
that, in pure kindness to his horse, buttered his hay.

---

44. worth: deserving.   46. Winter's ... yet: there's more
trouble to come.   50. bear bags: have money.   53. turns ...
key: opens the door.   54. dolors: with a pun on "dollars."
55. tell: count.   56–58. Oh ... below: The *mother*, called also
hysterica passio, was an overwhelming feeling of physical distress
and suffocation. Lear's mental suffering is now beginning to cause
a physical breakdown. This sensation, and the violent throbbing
of his heart until finally it ceases, can be traced in Lear's speeches.
See ll. 122, 138, 200–01; III.iv.14.   58. element: natural place.
68–77. We'll ... it: The fool is so much amused at Kent's
discomfiture that he strings off a series of wise sayings to
show his own clearer understanding of Lear's state.   69–70. follow ... noses: go straight ahead.   80. but ... form: merely
for show.   81. pack: clear out.   86. perdy: by God.

90. fetches: excuses.   91. images: exact likenesses.   93. quality: nature.   107–08. Infirmity ... bound: when a man is sick,
he neglects his proper duty.   111. am ... will: regret my hasti-
ness.   115. remotion: removal.   116. practice: pretense. Give
... forth: release my servant at once.   120. cry ... death: kill
sleep by its noise.   122. Oh ... down: See ll. 56–58.   123. cockney: Londoner.   125. knapped: cracked.

HE DOESN'T KNOW OWN DAUGHTERS

[*Re-enter* GLOUCESTER, *with* CORNWALL, REGAN, *and*
SERVANTS.]
LEAR. Good morrow to you both.
CORN.   Hail to your Grace! [KENT *is set at liberty.*]
REG. I am glad to see your Highness.   130
LEAR. Regan, I think you are, I know what reason
I have to think so. If thou shouldst not be glad,
I would divorce me from thy mother's tomb,
Sepúlchring an adultress.° [*To* KENT] Oh, are you
    free?
Some other time for that. Belovèd Regan,   135
Thy sister's naught.° O Regan, she hath tied
Sharp-toothed unkindness, like a vulture, here.
                      [*Points to his heart.*]
I can scarce speak to thee, thou'lt not believe
With how depraved a quality —— O Regan!   139
   REG. I pray you, sir, take patience. I have hope
You less know how to value her desert
Than she to scant her duty.
     LEAR.   Say, how is that?
   REG. I cannot think my sister in the least
Would fail her obligation. If, sir, perchance
She have restrained the riots of your followers,   145
'Tis on such ground and to such wholesome end
As clears her from all blame.
     LEAR. My curses on her!
   REG.   Oh, sir, you are old,
Nature in you stands on the very verge
Of her confine.° You should be ruled and led   150
By some discretion that discerns your state
Better than you yourself. Therefore I pray you
That to our sister you do make return.
Say you have wronged her, sir.
     LEAR.   Ask her forgiveness?   154
Do you but mark how this becomes the house.° —
[*Kneeling*] "Dear daughter, I confess that I am old,
Age is unnecessary. On my knees I beg
That you'll vouchsafe me raiment, bed, and food."
   REG. Good sir, no more, these are unsightly tricks.
Return you to my sister.
     LEAR.   [*Rising*] Never, Regan.   160
She hath abated me of half my train,
Looked black upon me, struck me with her tongue,
Most serpentlike, upon the very heart.
All the stored vengeances of Heaven fall
On her ingrateful top!° Strike her young bones,
You taking airs, with lameness.
   CORN.   Fie, sir, fie!   166
     LEAR. You nimble lightnings, dart your blinding
    flames
Into her scornful eyes. Infect her beauty,
You fen-sucked fogs,° drawn by the powerful sun
To fall° and blast her pride.   170

REG. Oh, the blest gods! So will you wish on me
When the rash mood is on.
   LEAR. No, Regan, thou shalt never have my curse.
Thy tender-hefted° nature shall not give
Thee o'er to harshness. Her eyes are fierce, but thine
Do comfort and not burn. 'Tis not in thee   176
To grudge my pleasures, to cut off my train,
To bandy hasty words, to scant my sizes,°
And in conclusion to oppose the bolt°
Against my coming in. Thou better know'st   180
The offices of nature, bond of childhood,
Effects of courtesy, dues of gratitude.
Thy half o' the kingdom hast thou not forgot,
Wherein I thee endowed.
   REG.   Good sir, to the purpose.°
   LEAR. Who put my man i' the stocks?
                       [*Tucket within.*]
   CORN.   What trumpet's that?   185
   REG. I know 't, my sister's. This approves° her
    letter,
That she would soon be here.
           [*Enter* OSWALD.]   Is your lady come?
   LEAR. This is a slave whose easy-borrowed pride
Dwells in the fickle grace of her he follows.°
Out, varlet,° from my sight!
   CORN.   What means your Grace?   190
   LEAR. Who stocked my servant? Regan, I have
    good hope
Thou didst not know on 't. Who comes here?
[*Enter* GONERIL.]   O Heavens,
If you do love old men, if your sweet sway
Allow° obedience, if yourselves are old,
Make it your cause. Send down, and take my part!
[*To* GONERIL] Art not ashamed to look upon this
    beard?   196
O Regan, wilt thou take her by the hand?
   GON. Why not by the hand, sir? How have I of-
    fended?
All's not offense that indiscretion finds
And dotage terms so.°
   LEAR.   O sides, you are too tough,   200
Will you yet hold?° How came my man i' the
    stocks?
   CORN. I set him there, sir. But his own disorders
Deserved much less advancement.°
   LEAR.   You! Did you?
   REG. I pray you, Father, being weak, seem so.°
If till the expiration of your month   205
You will return and sojourn with my sister,

133–34. divorce . . . adultress: i.e., I would suspect that your
dead mother had been false to me.   136. naught: wicked.
150. confine: boundary, edge.   155. becomes . . . house: i.e.,
suits my dignity.   165. top: head.   169. fen-sucked fogs: Cf.
I.iv.321.   170. fall: fall upon.

174. tender-hefted: gently framed.   178. scant my sizes: reduce
my allowances.   179. oppose . . . bolt: bar the door.   184. Good
. . . purpose: and in good time to; or, please talk sense.
186. approves: confirms.   188–89. whose . . . follows: who soon
puts on airs because his fickle mistress favors him.   190. varlet:
knave.   194. Allow: approve of.   199–200. that . . . so: because a silly old man says so. See L.i.149–51,n.   200–01. O
. . . hold: See II.iv.56–58,n, above.   203. advancement: promotion.   204. seem so: i.e., behave suitably.

Dismissing half your train, come then to me.
I am now from home and out of that provision
Which shall be needful for your entertainment.°
  LEAR. Return to her, and fifty men dismissed?
No, rather I abjure° all roofs, and choose   211
To wage against the enmity o' the air,
To be a comrade with the wolf and owl —
Necessity's sharp pinch! Return with her?   214
Why, the hot-blooded France, that dowerless took
Our youngest-born — I could as well be brought
To knee his throne and, squirelike,° pension beg
To keep base life afoot. Return with her?
Persuade me rather to be slave and sumpter°
To this detested groom.   [*Pointing at* OSWALD.]
  GON.   At your choice, sir.   220
  LEAR. I prithee, Daughter, do not make me mad.
I will not trouble thee, my child. Farewell.
We'll no more meet, no more see one another.
But yet thou art my flesh, my blood, my daughter,
Or rather a disease that's in my flesh   225
Which I must needs call mine. Thou art a boil,
A plague sore, an embossed carbuncle,°
In my corrupted blood. But I'll not chide thee.
Let shame come when it will, I do not call it.
I do not bid the thunderbearer° shoot,   230
Nor tell tales of thee to high-judging Jove.
Mend when thou canst, be better at thy leisure.
I can be patient, I can stay with Regan,
I and my hundred knights.
  REG.   Not altogether so.
I looked not for you yet, nor am provided   235
For your fit welcome. Give ear, sir, to my sister,
For those that mingle reason with your passion
Must be content to think you old,° and so ——
But she knows what she does.
  LEAR.   Is this well spoken?
  REG. I dare avouch° it, sir. What, fifty followers?
Is it not well? What should you need of more?   241
Yea, or so many, sith° that both charge and danger°
Speak 'gainst so great a number? How in one house
Should many people under two commands
Hold amity? 'Tis hard, almost impossible.   245
  GON. Why might not you, my lord, receive attendance
From those that she calls servants or from mine?
  REG. Why not, my lord? If then they chanced to slack° you,
We could control them. If you will come to me,
For now I spy a danger, I entreat you   250
To bring but five and twenty. To no more

Will I give place or notice.
  LEAR. I gave you all ——
  REG.   And in good time you gave it.
  LEAR. Made you my guardians, my depositaries,°
But kept a reservation° to be followed   255
With such a number. What, must I come to you
With five and twenty, Regan? Said you so?
  REG. And speak 't again, my lord, no more with me.
  LEAR. Those wicked creatures yet do look well-favored,°
When others are more wicked. Not being the worst
Stands in some rank of praise.° [*To* GONERIL] I'll go with thee.   261
Thy fifty yet doth double five and twenty,
And thou art twice her love.
  GON.   Hear me, my lord.
What need you five and twenty, ten, or five,
To follow in a house where twice so many   265
Have a command to tend you?
  REG.   What need one?
  LEAR. Oh,° reason not the need. Our basest beggars
Are in the poorest thing superfluous.°
Allow not nature more than nature needs,
Man's life's as cheap as beast's. Thou art a lady.   270
If only to go warm were gorgeous,
Why, nature needs not what thou gorgeous wear'st,
Which scarcely keeps thee warm. But for true need ——
You Heavens, give me that patience, patience I need!
You see me here, you gods, a poor old man,   275
As full of grief as age, wretched in both.
If it be you that stirs these daughters' hearts
Against their father, fool me not so much
To bear it tamely.° Touch me with noble anger,
And let not women's weapons, water drops,   280
Stain my man's cheeks! No, you unnatural hags,
I will have such revenges on you both
That all the world shall —— I will do such things ——
What they are, yet I know not, but they shall be
The terrors of the earth. You think I'll weep.   285
No, I'll not weep.°
I have full cause of° weeping, but this heart
Shall break into a hundred thousand flaws°
Or ere I'll weep. O fool, I shall go mad!
    [*Exeunt* LEAR, GLOUCESTER, KENT, *and* FOOL.]

209. entertainment: maintenance.   211. abjure: refuse with an oath.   217. squirelike: like a servant.   219. sumpter: pack horse, beast of burden.   227. embossed carbuncle: swollen boil. 230. thunderbearer: Jupiter.   237–38. those . . . old: those who consider your passion with reason realize that you are old — and should be wise.   240. avouch: guarantee.   242. sith: since. charge . . . danger: expense and risk of maintaining.   248. slack: neglect.

254. depositaries: trustees.   255. reservation: condition. See I.i.134–41.   259. well-favored: handsome.   260–61. Not . . . praise: i.e., since Goneril is not so bad as Regan, that is one thing in her favor.   267–74. Oh . . . need: the needs of a beggar are very different from the needs of a king — but above all Lear needs not dignity but patience.   267–68. Our . . . superfluous: even the few possessions of a beggar are not absolutely necessary. 278–79. fool . . . tamely: do not degrade me so much that I just tamely endure it.   286. No . . . weep: See *Lear* Intro. p. 1138b. 287. of: for.   288. flaws: broken pieces.

CORN. Let us withdraw, 'twill be a storm.   290
[Storm and tempest.]
REG. This house is little. The old man and his people
Cannot be well bestowed.
GON. 'Tis his own blame. Hath put himself from rest,
And must needs taste his folly.
REG. For his particular,° I'll receive him gladly,
But not one follower.
GON.   So am I purposed.   296
Where is my Lord of Gloucester?
CORN. Followed the old man forth. He is returned.
[Re-enter GLOUCESTER.]
GLO. The King is in high rage.
CORN.   Whither is he going?   299
GLO. He calls to horse, but will I know not whither.
CORN. 'Tis best to give him way, he leads himself.
GON. My lord, entreat him by no means to stay.
GLO. Alack, the night comes on, and the bleak winds
Do sorely ruffle. For many miles about
There's scarce a bush.
REG.   Oh, sir, to willful men   305
The injuries that they themselves procure
Must be their schoolmasters. Shut up your doors.
He is attended with a desperate train,
And what they may incense° him to, being apt°
To have his ear abused,° wisdom bids fear.   310
CORN. Shut up your doors, my lord, 'tis a wild night.
My Regan counsels well. Come out o' the storm.
[Exeunt.]

[handwritten: LEAR HAS STORM IN HEAD]
[handwritten: REAL STORM MAY BE TO COMPLEMENT ONE IN HEAD.]

Act III

[handwritten: HE HAS SOMETHING W/ SECRECY EVEN HIS OWN SECRECY]

SCENE I. *A heath.*

[Storm still.° Enter KENT and a GENTLEMAN, meeting.]

KENT. Who's there, besides foul weather?
GENT. One minded like the weather, most unquietly.
KENT. I know you. Where's the King?
GENT. Contending with the fretful elements.
Bids the wind blow the earth into the sea,   5
Or swell the curlèd waters 'bove the main,°
That things might change or cease; tears his white hair,

Which the impetuous blasts, with eyeless° rage,
Catch in their fury, and make nothing of;
Strives in his little world of man° to outscorn   10
The to-and-fro-conflicting wind and rain.
This night, wherein the cub-drawn bear° would couch,°
The lion and the belly-pinchèd° wolf
Keep their fur dry, unbonneted° he runs,
And bids what will take all.
KENT.   But who is with him?   15
GENT. None but the fool, who labors to outjest
His heart-struck injuries.
KENT.   Sir, I do know you,
And dare, upon the warrant of my note,°
Commend a dear° thing to you. There is division,
Although as yet the face of it be covered   20
With mutual cunning, 'twixt Albany and Cornwall,
Who have — as who have not that their great stars
Throned and set high?° — servants, who seem no less,
Which are to France the spies and speculations°
Intelligent of our state° — what hath been seen,
Either in snuffs and packings° of the Dukes,   26
Or the hard rein which both of them have borne
Against the old kind King, or something deeper,
Whereof perchance these are but furnishings° ——
But true it is, from France there comes a power°   30
Into this scattered kingdom, who already,
Wise in our negligence, have secret feet
In some of our best ports and are at point°
To show their open banner. Now to you.
If on my credit° you dare build so far   35
To make your speed to Dover, you shall find
Some that will thank you, making just report
Of how unnatural and bemadding sorrow
The King hath cause to plain.°
I am a gentleman of blood° and breeding,   40
And from some knowledge and assurance° offer
This office° to you.
GENT. I will talk further with you.
KENT.   No, do not.
For confirmation that I am much more
Than my outwall,° open this purse and take   45
What it contains. If you shall see Cordelia ——

[handwritten alongside: KENT KNOWS A LOT / ABOUT WHAT'S GOING ON]

8. **eyeless:** blind.   10. **little . . . man:** It was a common Elizabethan idea, sometimes elaborately worked out, that individual man was a little world (microcosm) and reproduced in himself the universe (macrocosm).   12. **cub-drawn bear:** she-bear sucked dry, and therefore hungry. **couch:** take shelter.   13. **belly-pinched:** ravenous.   14. **unbonneted:** without a hat.   18. **upon . . . note:** guaranteed by my observation of you.   19. **dear:** precious.   22–23. **that . . . high:** whom Fate has set in a great position.   24. **speculations:** informers.   25. **Intelligent . . . state:** report on the state of our affairs.   26. **snuffs . . . packings:** resentment and plotting against each other.   29. **furnishings:** excuses. The sentence is not finished.   30. **power:** army.   33. **at point:** on the point of, about to.   35. **credit:** trustworthiness.   39. **plain:** complain.   40. **blood:** noble family.   41. **knowledge . . . assurance:** sure knowledge.   42. **office:** undertaking.   45. **outwall:** outside.

295. **his particular:** himself personally.   309. **incense:** incite. **apt:** ready.   310. **abused:** deceived.
Act III, Sc. i: s.d., **still:** continuing.   6. **main:** mainland.

[handwritten: THEY HAD SCIENTIFIC BASIS FOR ASTROLOGY — NATURE & MAN THOUGHT OF AS ONE THING]

[Handwritten top margin: EDGAR & KENT BOTH WON'T REVEAL]

[Handwritten: RATHER STUPID]

As fear not but you shall — show her this ring,
And she will tell you who your fellow° is
That yet you do not know. Fie on this storm!
I will go seek the King.
GENT.   Give me your hand.   50
Have you no more to say?
KENT. Few words, but, to effect, more than all
      yet —
That when we have found the King — in which your
      pain°
That way, I'll this — he that first lights on him   54
Holloa the other.   [*Exeunt severally.*]

SCENE II. *Another part of the heath.*
      Storm still.

[*Enter* LEAR *and* FOOL.]
LEAR. Blow, winds, and crack your cheeks! Rage!
      Blow!
You cataracts and hurricanoes,° spout
Till you have drenched our steeples, drowned the
      cocks!° *[Handwritten: ANACHRONISM — They were A]*
You sulphurous and thought-executing° fires, *[Handwritten: Reminder]*
Vaunt-couriers° to oak-cleaving thunderbolts,   5 *[Handwritten: OF]*
Singe my white head! And thou, all-shaking thun- *[Handwritten: POSSIBILITY]*
      der,
Smite flat the thick rotundity o' the world! *[Handwritten: OF BETRAYING]*
Crack nature's molds,° all germens° spill at once *[Handwritten: CHRIST]*
That make ingrateful man!   9
FOOL. O Nuncle, Court holy water° in a dry
house is better than this rain water out o' door. Good
Nuncle, in, and ask thy daughters' blessing. Here's
a night pities neither wise man nor fool.
LEAR. Rumble thy bellyful! Spit, fire! Spout, rain!
Nor rain, wind, thunder, fire, are my daughters.   15
I tax° not you, you elements, with unkindness.
I never gave you kingdom, called you children,
You owe me no subscription.° Then let fall
Your horrible pleasure. Here I stand, your slave,
A poor, infirm, weak, and despised old man.   20
But yet I call you servile ministers°
That have with two pernicious daughters joined
Your high-engendered battles° 'gainst a head
So old and white as this. Oh, oh! 'Tis foul!
FOOL. He that has a house to put 's head in has a
good headpiece.   26

[Handwritten right margin: FOOL MAKES SEX REMARKS]

"The° codpiece° that will house
      Before the head has any,
The head and he shall louse
      So beggars marry many.   30
The man that makes his toe
      What he his heart should make
Shall of a corn cry woe,
      And turn his sleep to wake."
For there was never yet fair woman but she made
mouths in a glass.°   36
LEAR. No, I will be the pattern of all patience,
I will say nothing.
[*Enter* KENT.]
KENT. Who's there?
FOOL. Marry,° here's grace and a codpiece — that's
a wise man and a fool.   41
KENT. Alas, sir, are you here? Things that love
night
Love not such nights as these. The wrathful skies
Gallow° the very wanderers of the dark   44
And make them keep their caves. Since I was man,
Such sheets of fire, such bursts of horrid thunder,
Such groans of roaring wind and rain, I never
Remember to have heard. Man's nature cannot
carry°
The affliction nor the fear.
LEAR.   Let the great gods,
That keep this dreadful pother° o'er our heads,   50
Find out their enemies now. Tremble, thou wretch,
That hast within thee undivulgèd crimes
Unwhipped of justice. Hide thee, thou bloody hand,
Thou perjured, and thou simular man of virtue°
That art incestuous. Caitiff, to pieces shake,   55
That under covert and convenient seeming°
Hast practiced on man's life. Close pent-up guilts,
Rive your concealing continents° and cry
These dreadful summoners grace.° I am a man
More sinned against than sinning.
KENT.   Alack, bareheaded!   60
Gracious my lord, hard by here is a hovel.
Some friendship will it lend you 'gainst the tempest.
Repose you there while I to this hard house —
More harder than the stones whereof 'tis raised,

27–34. The . . . wake: the man who goes wenching before he has
a roof over his head will become a lousy beggar. The man who is
kinder to his toe than to his heart will be kept awake by his
corns — i.e., Lear has been kinder to his feet (his daughters)
than to his heart (himself). The Fool's remarks, especially
when cryptic and indecent, are not easy to paraphrase.
27. codpiece: lit., the opening in the hose. See Pl. 8c and comment
on p. 93b.   **35–36. made . . . glass:** made faces in a mirror.
40. Marry: Mary, by the Virgin.   **44. Gallow:** terrify.
48. carry: endure.   **50. pother:** turmoil.   **54. simular . . . virtue:** a man who pretends to be virtuous.   **56. under . . . seeming:** under a false appearance of propriety.   **57. Rive . . . continents:** split open that which covers and conceals you.
58–59. cry . . . grace: ask for mercy from these dreadful summoners. The summoner was the officer of the ecclesiastical court
who summoned a man to appear to answer a charge of im-
morality. See Gen. Intro. p. 26a.

---

48. fellow: companion.   **53. pain:** labor.
   Sc. ii: **2. hurricanoes:** waterspouts.   **3. cocks:** weathercocks
on top of the steeples.   **4. thought-executing:** killing as quick
as thought.   **5. Vaunt-couriers:** forerunners.   **8. nature's molds:**
the molds in which men are made. **germens:** seeds of life.
10. Court . . . water: flattery of great ones.   **16. tax:** accuse.
18. subscription: submission.   **21. servile ministers:** servants
who slavishly obey your masters.   **23. high-engendered battles:**
armies begotten on high.

Which even but now, demanding after you,   65
Denied me to come in — return, and force
Their scanted courtesy.

LEAR.   My wits begin to turn.
Come on, my boy. How dost, my boy? Art cold?
I am cold myself. Where is this straw, my fellow?
The art of our necessities is strange,   70
That can make vile things precious.° Come, your
     hovel.
Poor fool and knave, I have one part in my heart
That's sorry yet for thee.

FOOL. [*Singing*]
    " He° that has and a little tiny wit —
      With hey, ho, the wind and the rain —   75
      Must make content with his fortunes fit,°
      For the rain it raineth every day."

LEAR. True, my good boy. Come, bring us to this
    hovel.   [*Exeunt* LEAR *and* KENT.]

FOOL. This is a brave night to cool a courtesan.
I'll speak a prophecy° ere I go: 80
" When priests are more in word than matter,
When brewers mar their malt with water,
When nobles are their tailors' tutors,°
No heretics burned, but wenches' suitors,
When every case in law is right,   85
No squire in debt, nor no poor knight,
When slanders do not live in tongues,
Nor cutpurses come not to throngs,
When usurers tell their gold i' the field,
And bawds and whores do churches build —   90
Then shall the realm of Albion°
Come to great confusion.
Then comes the time, who lives to see 't,
That going shall be used with feet."°   94
This prophecy Merlin shall make, for I live before
    his time.°   [*Exit.*]

SCENE III. GLOUCESTER's *castle.*

[*Enter* GLOUCESTER *and* EDMUND.]

GLO. Alack, alack, Edmund, I like not this unnatural dealing. When I desired their leave that I might
pity him,° they took from me the use of mine own

house, charged me, on pain of their perpetual displeasure, neither to speak of him, entreat for him,
nor any way sustain° him.   6

EDM. Most savage and unnatural!

GLO. Go to, say you nothing. There's a division betwixt the Dukes, and a worse matter than that. I
have received a letter this night, 'tis dangerous   10
to be spoken. — I have locked the letter in my closet.
These injuries the King now bears will be revenged
home.° There is part of a power already footed.° We
must incline to the King. I will seek him and privily°
relieve him. Go you, and maintain talk with   15
the Duke, that my charity be not of him perceived.
If he ask for me, I am ill and gone to bed. Though I
die for it, as no less is threatened me, the King my
old master must be relieved. There is some   20
strange thing toward, Edmund. Pray you be careful.
                       [*Exit.*]

EDM. This courtesy, forbid thee,° shall the Duke
Instantly know, and of that letter too.
This seems a fair deserving,° and must draw me
That which my father loses, no less than all.   25
The younger rises when the old doth fall.   [*Exit.*]

*THERE ARE SMALL TOUCHES OF
EDMUND REPENTING.*

SCENE IV. *The heath. Before a hovel.*

[*Enter* LEAR, KENT, *and* FOOL.]

KENT. Here is the place, my lord. Good my lord,
    enter.
The tyranny° of the open night's too rough
For nature to endure.   [*Storm still.*]

LEAR.   Let me alone.

KENT. Good my lord, enter here.

LEAR.   Wilt break my heart?

KENT. I had rather break mine own. Good my
    lord, enter.   5

LEAR. Thou think'st 'tis much that this conten-
    tious° storm
Invades us to the skin. So 'tis to thee,
But where the greater malady is fixed°
The lesser is scarce felt. Thou'dst shun a bear,
But if thy flight lay toward the raging sea   10
Thou'dst meet the bear i' the mouth. When the
    mind's free°
The body's delicate. The tempest in my mind
Doth from my senses take all feeling else
Save what beats there.° Filial ingratitude!
Is it not as this mouth should tear this hand   15

70–71. art . . . precious: our needs are like the art of the alchemist (who was forever experimenting to try to transmute base
metal into gold). See App. 21.   74–77. He . . . day: another
stanza of the song which the Fool in *Twelfth Night* sings at the
end of the play.   76. Must . . . fit: i.e., must be content with a
fortune as slim as his wit.   80–94. prophecy . . . feet: The fool
gives a list of common events, pretending that they are never
likely to happen. The prophecy is a parody of riddling prophecies popular at this time which were attributed to Merlin, the old
magician of King Arthur's Court.   83. nobles . . . tutors: Young
noblemen and gallants were very particular about the fashion and
cut of their clothes.   91. Albion: England.   94. going . . . feet:
feet will be used for walking.   95. This . . . time: A piece of
mock pedantry, for — according to Holinshed's *Chronicles* —
King Lear died some generations before King Arthur.
    Sc. iii: 3. him: Lear.

6. sustain: relieve.   13. home: to the utmost. footed: landed.
14. privily: secretly.   22. forbid thee: forbidden to thee.   24. This
. . . deserving: i.e., by betraying my father, I shall deserve
much of (be rewarded by) the Duke.
    Sc. iv: 2. tyranny: cruelty.   6. contentious: striving against
us.   8. the . . . fixed: i.e., in the mind.   11. free: i.e., from
cares.   14. what . . . there: i.e., the mental anguish which
is increased by the thumping of Lear's overtaxed heart.

For lifting food to 't? But I will punish home.
No, I will weep no more. In such a night
To shut me out! Pour on, I will endure.
In such a night as this! O Regan, Goneril!
Your old kind father, whose frank heart gave
     all ——   20
Oh, that way madness lies, let me shun that,
No more of that.

KENT.   Good my lord, enter here.

LEAR. Prithee, go in thyself, seek thine own ease.
This tempest will not give me leave to ponder
On things would hurt me more. But I'll go in.   25
[*To the* FOOL] In, boy, go first. You houseless pov-
     erty° ——
Nay, get thee in. I'll pray, and then I'll sleep.

                    [FOOL *goes in.*]

Poor naked wretches, wheresoe'er you are,
That bide° the pelting of this pitiless storm,
How shall your houseless heads and unfed sides,   30
Your looped and windowed° raggedness, defend you
From seasons such as these? Oh, I have ta'en
Too little care of this! Take physic, pomp.°
Expose thyself to feel what wretches feel,
That thou mayst shake the superflux° to them   35
And show the Heavens more just.

EDG. [*Within*] Fathom and half, fathom and half!
Poor Tom!

        [*The* FOOL *runs out from the hovel.*]

FOOL. Come not in here, Nuncle, here's a spirit.
Help me, help me!   40

KENT. Give me thy hand. Who's there?

FOOL. A spirit, a spirit. He says his name's Poor
Tom.

KENT. What art thou that dost grumble there i'
     the straw?
Come forth.   45

      [*Enter* EDGAR *disguised as a madman.*]

EDG. Away! The foul fiend follows me!
" Through the sharp hawthorn blows the cold
     wind."
Hum! Go to thy cold bed and warm thee.

LEAR. Hast thou given all to thy two daughters?
And art thou come to this?°   50

EDG. Who gives anything to Poor Tom? Whom
the foul fiend hath led through fire and through
flame, through ford and whirlpool, o'er bog and
quagmire, that hath laid knives under his pillow
and halters in his pew,° set ratsbane° by his   55
porridge, made him proud of heart to ride on a bay
trotting horse over four-inched° bridges, to course°

his own shadow for a traitor. Bless thy five wits!°
Tom's a-cold. Oh, do de, do de, do de. Bless thee from
whirlwinds, star-blasting,° and taking!° Do Poor
Tom some charity, whom the foul fiend vexes. There
could I have him now, and there, and there   62
again, and there.°   [*Storm still.*]

LEAR. What, have his daughters brought him to
     this pass?
Couldst thou save nothing? Didst thou give them
     all?

FOOL. Nay, he reserved a blanket,° else we had
been all shamed.   67

LEAR. Now, all the plagues that in the pendulous°
     air
Hang fated o'er men's faults light on thy daugh-
     ters!

KENT. He hath no daughters, sir.   71

LEAR. Death, traitor! Nothing could have subdued
     nature
To such a lowness but his unkind daughters.
Is it the fashion that discarded fathers
Should have thus little mercy on their flesh?   75
Judicious punishment! 'Twas this flesh begot
Those pelican° daughters.

EDG.   " Pillicock sat on Pillicock Hill.
          Halloo, halloo, loo, loo! "°

FOOL. This cold night will turn us all to fools and
madmen.   81

EDG. Take heed o' the foul fiend. Obey thy parents, keep thy word justly, swear not, commit not
with man's sworn spouse, set not thy sweet heart on
proud array. Tom's a-cold.

LEAR. What hast thou been?   86

EDG. A servingman,° proud in heart and mind,
that curled my hair, wore gloves in my cap, served
the lust of my mistress's heart and did the act of darkness with her, swore as many oaths as I spake   90
words and broke them in the sweet face of Heaven.
One that slept in the contriving of lust and waked
to do it. Wine loved I deeply, dice dearly, and in
woman outparamoured° the Turk.° False of heart,
light of ear, bloody of hand, hog in sloth,° fox in   95
stealth, wolf in greediness, dog in madness, lion in
prey. Let not the creaking of shoes nor the rustling
of silks betray thy poor heart to woman. Keep thy
foot out of brothels, thy hand out of plackets,°

---

26. **houseless poverty:** poor homeless people.   29. **bide:** endure.
31. **looped ... windowed:** full of holes and gaps.   33. **Take ...
pomp:** i.e., cure yourselves, you great men.   35. **superflux:**
superfluity, what you do not need.   49–50. **Hast ... this:** At
the sight of the supposed lunatic Lear goes quite mad. Such utter
destitution, he says, can only have been caused by daughters as
unkind as his own.   55. **pew:** seat. **ratsbane:** rat poison.
57. **four-inched:** i.e., narrow. **course:** hunt after.

58. **five wits:** i.e., common wit, imagination, fantasy, estimation, and memory.   60. **star-blasting:** evil caused by a
planet. **taking:** malignant influence of fairies. Cf. *Haml.*, I.i.163.
61–63. **There ... there:** Poor Tom is chasing his own vermin.
66. **blanket:** i.e., his only covering. See II.iii.10.   68. **pendulous:**
overhanging.   77. **pelican:** The pelican was the pattern of
devoted motherhood because it fed its young on its own blood;
but when the young grew strong, they turned on their parents.
78–79. **Pillicock ... loo:** an old rhyme.   87–97. **A servingman
... prey:** This is another description of the gentleman servingman. See II.ii.15–26.   94. **outparamoured:** had more mistresses
than. **the Turk:** the Turkish Emperor.   95. **hog in sloth:** See
Lear Intro. p. 1139a.   99. **plackets:** openings in a petticoat.

thy pen from lenders' books,° and defy the foul fiend.   101

" Still through the hawthorn blows the cold wind.
 Says suum, mun, ha, no, nonny.
 Dolphin my boy, my boy, sessa! Let him trot by."
                                                    [*Storm still.*]

LEAR. Why, thou wert better in thy grave   104
than to answer with thy uncovered body this extremity of the skies. Is man no more than this? Consider him well. Thou° owest the worm no silk, the
beast no hide, the sheep no wool, the cat no perfume.° Ha! Here's three on 's are sophisticated.
Thou art the thing itself. Unaccommodated   110
man is no more but such a poor, bare, forked animal
as thou art. Off, off, you lendings!° Come, unbutton
here.   [*Tearing off his clothes.*]   113

FOOL. Prithee, Nuncle, be contented, 'tis a naughty
night to swim in. Now a little fire in a wild field
were like an old lecher's heart, a small spark, all the
rest on 's body cold. Look, here comes a walking
fire.   119

[*Enter* GLOUCESTER, *with a torch.*]

EDG. This is the foul fiend Flibbertigibbet. He be-
gins at curfew° and walks till the first cock, he gives
the web and the pin,° squints the eye and makes the
harelip, mildews the white wheat and hurts the poor
creature of earth.
 " Saint° Withold footed thrice the 'old,°   125
 He met the nightmare° and her ninefold.°
   Bid her alight,
   And her troth plight,
 And aroint thee, witch, aroint° thee! "

KENT. How fares your Grace?   130
LEAR. What's he?
KENT. Who's there? What is 't you seek?
GLO. What are you there? Your names?
EDG. Poor Tom, that eats the swimming frog, the
toad, the tadpole, the wall newt, and the water;   135
that in the fury of his heart, when the foul fiend
rages, eats cow dung for sallets;° swallows the old
rat and the ditch dog;° drinks the green mantle of

100. pen . . . books: The debtor often acknowledged the debt by
signing in the lender's account book. There are many such
acknowledgments in Henslowe's *Diary* (see Gen. Intro. p. 65a).
107–13. Thou . . . here: There is usually an underlying sense in
Lear's ravings. The bedlam, he says, has not borrowed silk from
the silkworm, or furs from the beast, or wool from the sheep to
cover himself. Kent, the Fool, and he himself are therefore
sophisticated — adulterated, wearing coverings not their own.
Natural man, *unaccommodated* (i.e., not provided with such
conveniences), is just a naked animal. Lear will therefore
strip himself naked and cease to be artificial.   108–09. cat . . .
perfume: a perfume taken from the civet cat, which has glands
that function in the same manner as the skunk's.   112. lendings:
things borrowed.   121. curfew: sounded at 9 P.M.   122. web . . .
pin: eye diseases, cataract.   125–29. Saint . . . thee: a charm to
keep horses from suffering from nightmare.   125. 'old: wold,
uncultivated downland.   126. nightmare: nightmare was believed to be caused by a fiend. ninefold: nine young.   129. a-
roint: be gone.   137. sallets: salads.   138. ditch dog: dog
drowned in a ditch.

the standing pool; who is whipped from tithing to
tithing,° and stock-punished, and imprisoned;   140
who hath had three suits° to his back, six shirts to
his body, horse to ride, and weapon to wear.
 " But mice and rats and such small deer
 Have been Tom's food for seven long year."
Beware my follower. Peace, Smulkin,° peace, thou
   fiend!   146
GLO. What, hath your Grace no better company?
EDG. The Prince of Darkness is a gentleman.
Modo he's called, and Mahu.
GLO. Our flesh and blood is grown so vile, my
   lord,   150
That it doth hate what gets° it.
EDG. Poor Tom's a-cold.
GLO. Go in with me. My duty cannot suffer
To obey in all your daughters' hard commands.
Though their injunction be to bar my doors   155
And let this tyrannous night take hold upon you,
Yet have I ventured to come seek you out
And bring you where both fire and food is ready.
LEAR. First let me talk with this philosopher.
What is the cause of thunder?°   160
KENT. Good my lord, take his offer, go into the
   house.
LEAR. I'll talk a word with this same learnèd
   Theban.°
What is your study?°
EDG. How to prevent the fiend and to kill vermin.
LEAR. Let me ask you one word in private.   165
KENT. Impórtune him once more to go, my lord.
His wits begin to unsettle.
GLO. Canst thou blame him?   [*Storm still.*]
His daughters seek his death. Ah, that good Kent!
He said it would be thus, poor banished man!
Thou say'st the King grows mad. I'll tell thee,
   friend,   170
I am almost mad myself. I had a son,
Now outlawed from my blood. He sought my life
But lately, very late. I loved him, friend,
No father his son dearer. Truth to tell thee,   174
The grief hath crazed my wits. What a night's this!
I do beseech your Grace ——
LEAR.   Oh, cry you mercy, sir.
Noble philosopher, your company.
EDG. Tom's a-cold.
GLO. In, fellow, there, into the hovel. Keep thee
   warm.
LEAR. Come, let's in all.
KENT.   This way, my lord.
LEAR.   With him,   180
I will keep still with my philosopher.

140. tithing: district, parish.   141. three suits: See II.ii.16.
145–49. Smulkin . . . Mahu: familiar spirits. See *Lear* Intro.
p. 1136b.   151. gets: begets.   160. cause of thunder: This was
much disputed by philosophers of the time.   162. Theban: i.e.,
Greek philosopher.   163. study: particular interest, or in
modern academic jargon, "special field."

KENT. Good my lord, soothe him, let him take the
  fellow.
GLO. Take him you on.
KENT. Sirrah, come on, go along with us.
LEAR. Come, good Athenian.°   185
GLO. No words, no words. Hush.
EDG. " Child° Rowland to the dark tower came.
    His word was still ' Fie, foh, and fum,
      I smell the blood of a British man.' "
                                        [*Exeunt.*]

SCENE V. GLOUCESTER's *castle*.

[*Enter* CORNWALL *and* EDMUND.]

CORN. I will have my revenge ere I depart his
house.
EDM. How, my lord, I may be censured,° that na-
ture° thus gives way to loyalty, something fears me
to think of.   5
CORN. I now perceive it was not altogether your
brother's evil disposition made him seek his death,
but a provoking merit, set a-work by a reprovable
badness in himself.°   9
EDM. How malicious is my fortune, that I must
repent to be just!° This is the letter he spoke of,
which approves° him an intelligent party° to the
advantages of France. Oh heavens, that this treason
were not, or not I the detector!   14
CORN. Go with me to the Duchess.
EDM. If the matter of this paper be certain, you
have mighty business in hand.
CORN. True or false, it hath made thee Earl of
Gloucester. Seek out where thy father is, that he
may be ready for our apprehension.°   20
EDM. [*Aside*] If I find him comforting the King,
it will stuff his suspicion more fully. — I will per-
sever° in my course of loyalty, though the conflict be
sore between that and my blood.   24
CORN. I will lay trust upon thee, and thou shalt
find a dearer father in my love.   [*Exeunt.*]

---

185. Athenian: like "Theban," l. 162.   187–89. Child . . . man:
jumbled snatches of old ballads. *Child* in old ballads is used
of young warriors who have not yet been knighted.
    Sc. v: 3. censured: judged.   4. nature: i.e., natural affection
toward my father yielding to loyalty to my Duke. For Edmund's
real sentiments on nature see I.ii.1–2.   8–9. but . . . himself: i.e.,
but a good quality in Edgar that provoked him to commit murder
because of the reprehensible badness in Gloucester.   11. repent . . . just: be sorry because I have acted rightly (in betraying my father).   12. approves: proves. intelligent party: spy,
one with secret information.   20. apprehension: arrest.   23. persever: persevere.

SCENE VI.° *A chamber in a farmhouse adjoining the castle.*

[*Enter* GLOUCESTER, LEAR, KENT, FOOL, *and* EDGAR.]

GLO. Here is better than the open air, take it
thankfully. I will piece out the comfort with what
addition I can. I will not be long from you.
KENT. All the power of his wits has given way to
his impatience.° The gods reward your kindness!   6
                                    [*Exit* GLOUCESTER.]
EDG. Fraretto° calls me, and tells me Nero° is
an angler in the lake of darkness. Pray, innocent,°
and beware the foul fiend.
FOOL. Prithee, Nuncle, tell me whether a madman
be a gentleman or a yeoman.°   11
LEAR. A king, a king!
FOOL. No, he's a yeoman that has a gentleman to
his son, for he's a mad yeoman that sees his son a
gentleman before him.°   15
LEAR. To have a thousand with red burning spits°
Come hissing in upon 'em ——
EDG. The foul fiend bites my back.
FOOL. He's mad that trusts in the tameness of a
wolf, a horse's health, a boy's love, or a whore's
oath.
LEAR. It shall be done, I will arraign them
  straight.°   22
[*To* EDGAR] Come, sit thou here, most learned jus-
  ticer.°
[*To the* FOOL] Thou, sapient° sir, sit here. Now, you
  she-foxes!
EDG. Look where he stands and glares! Wantest
thou eyes at trial,° madam?   26
  " Come o'er the bourn, Bessy, to me."
FOOL. " Her boat hath a leak,
      And she must not speak
    Why she dares not come over to thee."   30
EDG. The foul fiend haunts poor Tom in the voice
of a nightingale. Hopdance° cries in Tom's belly for

    Sc. vi: In this scene Lear is completely mad, the Fool is
half-witted, and Edgar is pretending to be a lunatic.   6. impatience: suffering.   7. Fraretto: another fiend's name from
Harsnett's book. See *Lear* Intro. p. 1136a.   Nero: the debauched
Roman Emperor who fiddled while Rome burned.   8. innocent:
fool.   10–11. whether . . . yeoman: The fool is much interested
in the social status of a madman and proceeds to discuss the
problem.   yeoman: farmer, a notoriously wealthy class at this
time.   13–15. No . . . him: Many yeomen farmers who had become wealthy by profiteering from the wars and dearths sent
their sons to London to learn to become gentlemen, as fifty years
ago Chicago meat packers sent their sons to Harvard and their
daughters to England, to be presented at Court. This social
change was much commented on, and is illustrated in Jonson's
comedy *Every Man out of His Humour.*   16. spits: thin iron rods
thrust through meat on which the meat was turned before the fire
in roasting; very useful weapons in emergency.   22. straight:
straightway.   23. justicer: judge.   24. sapient: wise.
25–26. Wantest . . . trial: can you not see who is at your trial
(i.e., this fiend)? But Edgar is deliberately talking madly.
32. Hopdance: another name from Harsnett.

two white herring. Croak not,° black angel, I have
no food for thee.

KENT. How do you, sir? Stand you not so
    amazed.°   35
Will you lie down and rest upon the cushions?

LEAR. I'll see their trial first. Bring in the evidence.
[*To* EDGAR] Thou robèd man of justice,° take thy
    place.
[*To the* FOOL] And thou, his yokefellow of equity,°
Bench° by his side. [*To* KENT] You are o' the com-
    mission,°   40
Sit you too.

EDG. Let us deal justly.
    "Sleepest or wakest thou, jolly shepherd?
        Thy sheep be in the corn,
    And for one blast of thy minikin° mouth, 45
        Thy sheep shall take no harm."
Purr! The cat is gray.

LEAR. Arraign her first. 'Tis Goneril. I here take
my oath before this honorable assembly, she kicked
the poor King her father.   50

FOOL. Come hither, mistress. Is your name Goneril?

LEAR. She cannot deny it.

FOOL. Cry you mercy,° I took you for a joint
stool.°   55

LEAR. And here's another, whose warped° looks
    proclaim
What store° her heart is made on. Stop her there!
Arms, arms, sword, fire! Corruption° in the place!
False justicer, why hast thou let her 'scape?

EDG. Bless thy five wits!   60

KENT. Oh, pity! Sir, where is the patience now,
That you so oft have boasted to retain?

EDG. [*Aside*] My tears begin to take his part so
    much
They'll mar my counterfeiting.°

LEAR. The little dogs and all,   65
Tray, Blanch, and Sweetheart, see, they bark at me.

EDG. Tom will throw his head at them. Avaunt,
you curs!
    Be thy mouth or black or white,
    Tooth that poisons if it bite,   70
    Mastiff, greyhound, mongrel grim,
    Hound or spaniel, brach° or lym,°
    Or bobtail tike or trundletail,°

Tom will make them weep and wail.
For, with throwing thus my head,   75
Dogs leap the hatch, and all are fled.
Do de, de, de. Sessa! Come, march to wakes° and
fairs and market towns. Poor Tom, thy horn° is
dry.   79

LEAR. Then let them anatomize° Regan, see what
breeds about her heart. Is there any cause in nature
that makes these hard hearts? [*To* EDGAR] You, sir, I
entertain° for one of my hundred, only I do not like
the fashion of your garments. You will say they are
Persian attire,° but let them be changed.   86

KENT. Now, good my lord, lie here and rest
awhile.

LEAR. Make no noise, make no noise. Draw the
curtains. So, so, so.° We'll go to supper i' the morning. So, so, so.   91

FOOL. And I'll go to bed at noon.°
    [*Re-enter* GLOUCESTER.]

GLO. Come hither, friend. Where is the King my
master?

KENT. Here, sir, but trouble him not. His wits are
gone.

GLO. Good friend, I prithee take him in thy arms.
I have o'erheard a plot of death upon him.   96
There is a litter° ready, lay him in 't,
And drive toward Dover, friend, where thou shalt
    meet
Both welcome and protection. Take up thy master.
If thou shouldst dally° half an hour, his life,   100
With thine and all that offer to defend him,
Stand in assured loss. Take up, take up,
And follow me, that will to some provision
Give thee quick conduct.

KENT.   Oppressèd nature sleeps.
This rest might yet have balmed° thy broken sin-
    ews,   105
Which, if convenience will not allow,
Stand in hard cure.° [*To the* FOOL] Come, help to
    bear thy master.
Thou must not stay behind.

GLO.   Come, come, away.
    [*Exeunt all but* EDGAR.]

EDG. When we our betters see bearing our woes,
We scarcely think our miseries our foes.   110

---

33. Croak not: don't rumble in my empty belly. The correct
Elizabethan word for this embarrassing manifestation is "wam-
ble."   **35. amazed:** astonished — a strong word.   **38. robed
. . . justice:** another glance at Edgar's blanket.   **39. yokefellow
of equity:** partner in the law.   **40. Bench:** sit on the judge's
bench. **commission:** Persons of high rank or those accused of
extraordinary crimes were not tried before the ordinary courts,
but by a commission specially appointed.   **45. minikin:** dainty.
55. Cry . . . mercy: I beg your pardon. **joint stool:** wooden
stool of joiner's work. See Pl. 17a.   **56. warped:** malignant.
57. store: material. **58. Corruption:** bribery.   **63–64. My . . .
counterfeiting:** i.e., I am so sorry for the King that I can hardly
keep up this pretense.   **72. brach:** bitch. **lym:** bloodhound.
73. trundletail: curly tail.

77. wakes: merrymakings.   **78. horn:** a horn bottle carried by
beggars in which they stored the drink given by the charitable.
80. anatomize: dissect.   **84. entertain:** engage.   **86. Persian
attire:** i.e., of a magnificent and foreign fashion. There had
been considerable interest in Persia for some years, especially
after the return of some of the followers of Sir Anthony Shirley
from his famous expedition. See *T. Night* Intro. p. 845a.   **90. So
. . . so:** In dialogue "so, so" usually indicates action. Here
Lear imagines the bed curtains are being drawn.   **92. And . . .
noon:** i.e., if it's suppertime in the morning, it will be bedtime at
noon. The fool disappears after this scene.   **97. litter:** a form
of bed or stretcher enclosed by curtains used for carrying the
sick or the wealthy.   **100. dally:** hesitate.   **105. balmed:**
soothed.   **107. Stand . . . cure:** will hardly be cured.

Who alone suffers suffers most i' the mind,
Leaving free things and happy shows behind.
But then the mind much sufferance doth o'erskip
When grief hath mates, and bearing fellowship.°
How light and portable my pain seems now   115
When that which makes me bend makes the King
     bow,
He childed as I fathered! Tom, away!
Mark the high noises,° and thyself° bewray
When false opinion, whose wrong thought defiles
     thee,
In thy just proof repeals° and reconciles thee.   120
What will hap more tonight, safe 'scape the King!
Lurk,° lurk.   [*Exit.*]

SCENE VII. GLOUCESTER's *castle.*

[*Enter* CORNWALL, REGAN, GONERIL, EDMUND, *and*
SERVANTS.]

   CORN. Post speedily to my lord your husband.°
Show him this letter. The army of France is landed.
Seek out the traitor Gloucester.
           [*Exeunt some of the* SERVANTS.]
   REG. Hang him instantly.
   GON. Pluck out his eyes.   5
   CORN. Leave him to my displeasure. Edmund,
keep you our sister company. The revenges we are
bound to take upon your traitorous father are not fit
for your beholding. Advise the Duke, where you are
going, to a most festinate° preparation. We are
bound to the like. Our posts° shall be swift and in-
telligent° betwixt us. Farewell, dear Sister. Fare-
well, my Lord of Gloucester.°   13
[*Enter* OSWALD.] How now! Where's the King?
   OSW. My Lord of Gloucester° hath conveyed him
hence.   15
Some five or six and thirty of his knights,
Hot questrists° after him, met him at gate,
Who, with some other of the lords dependents,°
Are gone with him toward Dover, where they boast
To have well-armèd friends.

109–14. **When ... fellowship:** when we see better men than ourselves suffering as we do, our sufferings seem slight. The man
who suffers endures most in his mind because he contrasts his
present misery with his happy past; but when he has companions
in misery (*bearing fellowship*), his mind suffers less.   118. **high
noises:** i.e., the "hue and cry" of the pursuers. See Gen. Intro.
p. 28a.   118–20. **thyself ... thee:** do not reveal yourself until
the belief in your guilt is proved wrong and you are called back.
120. **repeals:** calls back from banishment.   122. **Lurk:** lie hid.
     Sc. vii: 1. **Post ... husband:** These words are addressed to
Goneril. **Post:** ride fast.   10. **festinate:** hasty.   11. **posts:**
messengers. See App. 17.   12. **intelligent:** full of information.
13. **Lord of Gloucester:** i.e., Edmund, who has been promoted for
his treachery.   15. **Lord of Gloucester:** i.e., the old Earl.
17. **questrists:** seekers.   18. **lords dependents:** lords of his
party.

   CORN.   Get horses for your mistress.   20
   GON. Farewell, sweet lord, and Sister.
   CORN. Edmund, farewell.
     [*Exeunt* GONERIL, EDMUND, *and* OSWALD.]
           Go seek the traitor Gloucester.
Pinion him like a thief, bring him before us.
               [*Exeunt other* SERVANTS.]
Though well we may not pass° upon his life
Without the form of justice, yet our power   25
Shall do a courtesy to our wrath,° which men
May blame but not control. Who's there? The
     traitor?
[*Enter* GLOUCESTER, *brought in by two or three.*]
   REG. Ungrateful fox! 'Tis he.
   CORN. Bind fast his corky° arms.
   GLO. What mean your Graces? Good my friends,
     consider   30
You are my guests. Do me no foul play, friends.
   CORN. Bind him, I say.   [SERVANTS *bind him.*]
   REG.   Hard, hard. O filthy traitor!
   GLO. Unmerciful lady as you are, I'm none.
   CORN. To this chair bind him. Villain, thou shalt
     find ——   [REGAN *plucks his beard.*]
   GLO. By the kind gods, 'tis most ignobly done
To pluck me by the beard.°   36
   REG. So white, and such a traitor!
   GLO.   Naughty lady,
These hairs which thou dost ravish° from my
     chin
Will quicken° and accuse thee. I am your host.
With robbers' hands my hospitable favors°   40
You should not ruffle thus. What will you do?
   CORN. Come, sir, what letters had you late from
     France?
   REG. Be simple answerer, for we know the truth.
   CORN. And what confederacy° have you with the
     traitors
Late footed in the kingdom?   45
   REG. To whose hands have you sent the lunatic
     King?
Speak.
   GLO. I have a letter guessingly set down,
Which came from one that's of a neutral heart,
And not from one opposed.
   CORN.   Cunning.
   REG.   And false
   CORN. Where hast thou sent the King?
   GLO.   To Dover.   50
   REG. Wherefore to Dover? Wast thou not charged
     at peril° ——
   CORN. Wherefore to Dover? Let him first answer
     that.

---

24. **pass:** pass judgment on.   25–26. **yet ... wrath:** yet because
we are all-powerful we will give way to our wrath.   29. **corky:**
dry and withered.   36. **pluck ... beard:** the greatest indignity
that could be offered.   38. **ravish:** seize.   39. **quicken:** come
to life.   40. **hospitable favors:** the face of your host.   44. **confederacy:** alliance, understanding.   51. **at peril:** under penalty.

GLO. I am tied to the stake, and I must stand the
course.°

REG. Wherefore to Dover, sir?   55

GLO. Because I would not see thy cruel nails
Pluck out his poor old eyes, nor thy fierce sister
In his anointed° flesh stick boarish fangs.
The sea, with such a storm as his bare head
In hell-black night endured, would have buoyed up,°
And quenched the stellèd fires.°   61
Yet, poor old heart, he holp° the heavens to rain.
If wolves had at thy gate howled that stern time,
Thou shouldst have said, " Good porter, turn the
key,"°
All cruels else subscribed.° But I shall see   65
The wingèd vengeance overtake such children.

CORN. See 't shalt thou never. Fellows, hold the
chair.
Upon these eyes of thine I'll set my foot.

GLO. He that will think to live till he be old,
Give me some help! Oh, cruel! Oh, you gods!   70
          [GLOUCESTER's *eye is put out.*]

REG. One side will mock another, the other too.

CORN. If you see vengeance ——

1. SERV.   Hold your hand, my lord.
I have served you ever since I was a child,
But better service have I never done you
Than now to bid you hold.

REG.   How now, you dog!   75

1. SERV. If you did wear a beard upon your chin,
I'd shake it on this quarrel. What do you mean?

CORN. My villain!
   [*They draw and fight.* CORNWALL *is wounded.*]

1. SERV. Nay, then, come on, and take the chance
of anger.

REG. Give me thy sword. A peasant stand up thus!
     [*Takes a sword and runs at him behind.*]

1. SERV. Oh, I am slain! My lord, you have one eye
left
To see some mischief on him. Oh!   [*Dies.*]

CORN. Lest it see more, prevent it. Out, vile jelly!
Where is thy luster now?
         [*Puts out* GLOUCESTER's *other eye.*]

GLO. All dark and comfortless. Where's my son
Edmund?   85
Edmund, enkindle all the sparks° of nature,
To quit° this horrid act.

REG.   Out, treacherous villain!
Thou call'st on him that hates thee. It was he
That made the overture° of thy treasons to us,
Who is too good to pity thee.   90

GLO. Oh, my follies! Then Edgar was abused.
Kind gods, forgive me that, and prosper him!

REG. Go thrust him out at gates, and let him
smell
His way to Dover.   [*Exit one with* GLOUCESTER.]
         How is 't, my lord? How look you?

CORN. I have received a hurt. Follow me, lady.
Turn out that eyeless villain. Throw this slave   96
Upon the dunghill. Regan, I bleed apace.°
Untimely comes this hurt. Give me your arm.
         [*Exit* CORNWALL, *led by* REGAN.]

2. SERV. I'll never care what wickedness I do
If this man come to good.

3. SERV.   If she live long,   100
And in the end meet the old course of death,°
Women will all turn monsters.

2. SERV. Let's follow the old Earl, and get the bed-
lam°
To lead him where he would. His roguish madness
Allows itself to anything.   105

3. SERV. Go thou. I'll fetch some flax and whites of
eggs
To apply to his bleeding face. Now, Heaven help
him!   [*Exeunt severally.*]

Act IV

SCENE I. *The heath.*

        [*Enter* EDGAR.]

EDG. Yet better thus, and known to be con-
temned,°
Than still° contemned and flattered. To° be worst,
The lowest and most dejected thing of fortune,
Stands still in esperance, lives not in fear.
The lamentable change is from the best,   5
The worst returns to laughter. Welcome then,
Thou unsubstantial air that I embrace!
The wretch that thou hast blown unto the worst
Owes nothing to thy blasts. — But who comes here?
   [*Enter* GLOUCESTER, *led by an* OLD MAN.]
My father, poorly led?° World, world, O world!
But that thy strange mutations make us hate thee,

54. I . . . course: like a bear in the bear pit I must endure the
onslaught. See App. 5.   58. anointed: i.e., anointed as a king,
and therefore holy.   60. buoyed up: swelled up.   61. stelled
fires: the light of the stars.   62. holp: helped.   64. turn . . .
key: open the gate.   65. All . . . subscribed: all other cruel
things were on his side.   86. enkindle . . . sparks: i.e., blow into
flame your natural love.   87. quit: requite.   89. overture:
revelation.

97. apace: quickly, profusely.   101. old . . . death: natural
death in old age.   103. bedlam: i.e., Poor Tom. See I.ii.148;
II.iii.14.
     Act IV, Sc. i: 1. contemned: despised; i.e., as a beggar.
2. still: always.   2–12. To . . . age: when a man has reached the
lowest state of misfortune, he has hope (*esperance*) for the
better, and no fear for the worse. The change to be lamented
is when the best turn to bad; the worst can only change
to joy. After this poor consolation that nothing worse can happen to him, Edgar sees his blinded father and continues (l. 10):
One would not trouble to live to old age except to spite the
world.   10. poorly led: led by one poor old man — and not accompanied by the usual party of servants.

Life would not yield to age.   12

OLD MAN. Oh, my good lord, I have been your tenant, and your father's tenant, these fourscore years.

GLO. Away, get thee away. Good friend, be gone.
Thy comforts can do me no good at all,   17
Thee they may hurt.

OLD MAN. Alack, sir, you cannot see your way.

GLO. I have no way and therefore want no eyes.
I stumbled when I saw. Full oft 'tis seen,   21
Our means secure us, and our mere defects
Prove our commodities.° Ah, dear Son Edgar,
The food° of thy abusèd father's wrath,
Might I but live to see thee in my touch,   25
I'd say I had eyes again!

OLD MAN.   How now! Who's there?

EDG. [*Aside*] Oh gods! Who is 't can say " I am
at the worst "?
I am worse than e'er I was.

OLD MAN.   'Tis poor mad Tom.

EDG. [*Aside*] And worse I may be yet. The worst
is not
So long as we can say " This is the worst."°   30

OLD MAN. Fellow, where goest?

GLO.   Is it a beggarman?

OLD MAN. Madman and beggar too.

GLO. He has some reason, else he could not beg.
I' the last night's storm I such a fellow saw,
Which made me think a man a worm. My son   35
Came then into my mind, and yet my mind
Was then scarce friends with him. I have heard more
     since.
As flies to wanton boys are we to the gods,
They kill us for their sport. A THEME OF PLAY

EDG.   [*Aside*] How should this be?
Bad is the trade that must play fool to sorrow,   40
Angering itself and others.° Bless thee, master!

GLO. Is that the naked fellow?

OLD MAN.   Aye, my lord.

GLO. Then, prithee get thee gone. If for my sake
Thou wilt o'ertake us hence a mile or twain
I' the way toward Dover, do it for ancient love,   45
And bring some covering for this naked soul,
Who I'll entreat to lead me.

OLD MAN.   Alack, sir, he is mad.

GLO. 'Tis the times' plague° when madmen lead
     the blind.
Do as I bid thee, or rather do thy pleasure.
Above the rest, be gone.   50

OLD MAN. I'll bring him the best 'parel° that I
have,
Come on 't what will.   [*Exit*.]

GLO. Sirrah, naked fellow ——

EDG. Poor Tom's a-cold. [*Aside*] I cannot daub°
it further.

GLO. Come hither, fellow.   55

EDG. [*Aside*] And yet I must. — Bless thy sweet
eyes, they bleed.

GLO. Know'st thou the way to Dover?

EDG. Both stile and gate, horseway and footpath.
Poor Tom hath been scared out of his good wits.
Bless thee, good man's son, from the foul fiend!   60
Five fiends have been in Poor Tom at once — of lust,
as Obidicut; Hobbididence, prince of dumbness;
Mahu, of stealing; Modo, of murder; Flibbertigibbet,° of mopping and mowing,° who since possesses
chambermaids and waiting-women. So, bless thee,
master!   66

GLO. Here, take this purse, thou whom the Heav-
ens' plagues
Have humbled to all strokes.° That I am wretched
Makes thee the happier. Heavens, deal so still!
Let the superfluous and lust-dieted man,   70
That slaves your ordinance, that will not see
Because he doth not feel, feel your power quickly.°
So distribution should undo excess°
And each man have enough. Dost thou know
     Dover?

EDG. Aye, master.   75

GLO. There is a cliff whose high and bending°
head
Looks fearfully in the confinèd deep.
Bring me but to the very brim of it,
And I'll repair the misery thou dost bear
With something rich about me. From that place   80
I shall no leading need.

EDG.   Give me thy arm.
Poor Tom shall lead thee.   [*Exeunt*.]

SCENE II. *Before the* DUKE OF ALBANY'S *palace*.

[*Enter* GONERIL *and* EDMUND.]

GON. Welcome, my lord. I marvel our mild husband
Not met us on the way.

[*Enter* OSWALD.] Now, where's your master?

OSW. Madam, within, but never man so changed.
I told him of the army that was landed.

---

54. daub: plaster it over, pretend.   **62–64. Obidicut . . .
Flibbertigibbet:** these names also come from Harsnett. See *Lear*
Intro. p. 1136b.   **64. mopping . . . mowing:** making faces and
grimaces. Cf. *Temp*, IV.i.47.   **68. humbled . . . strokes:** made
so humble that you can endure anything.   **69–72. Heavens . . .
quickly:** you gods, deal with others as you have dealt with me; let
the man who has too much and pampers his own lusts, who regards your commands as contemptuously as he regards his
slaves, that will not understand until he is hurt, feel your power
quickly. This passage echoes Lear's words (III.iv.33–36).
73. So . . . excess: then the man with too much would distribute
his excessive wealth.   **76. bending:** overhanging.

22–23. Our . . . commodities: when we are well off we grow careless, and then our misfortunes prove blessings. **24. food:** object.
29–30. The . . . worst: so long as a man is alive, he may yet
reach a lower depth of misery. **40–41. Bad . . . others:** this
business of pretending to be mad and fooling a man in such distress as Gloucester is now hateful. **48. times' plague:** a sign of
these diseased times. **51. 'parel:** apparel.

He smiled at it. I told him you were coming.   5
His answer was " The worse." Of Gloucester's
      treachery
And of the loyal service of his son
When I informed him, then he called me sot
And told me I had turned the wrong side out.   9
What most he should dislike seems pleasant to him,
What like, offensive.
      GON. [*To* EDMUND] Then shall you go no further.
It is the cowish° terror of his spirit,
That dares not undertake.° He'll not feel wrongs
Which tie° him to an answer. Our wishes on the way
May prove effects.° Back, Edmund, to my brother.
Hasten his musters° and conduct his powers.°   16
I° must change arms at home and give the distaff°
Into my husband's hands. This trusty servant
Shall pass between us. Ere long you are like to hear,
If you dare venture in your own behalf,   20
A mistress's° command. Wear this. Spare speech.
                              [*Giving a favor.*]
Decline your head. This kiss, if it durst speak,
Would stretch thy spirits up into the air.
Conceive,° and fare thee well.
      EDM. Yours in the ranks of death.
      GON. My most dear Gloucester!   [*Exit* EDMUND.]
Oh, the difference of man and man!   26
To thee a woman's services are due,
My fool° usurps my body.
      OSW.   Madam, here comes my lord.   [*Exit.*]
                              [*Enter* ALBANY.]
      GON. I have been worth the whistle.°
      ALB.   O Goneril!
You are not worth the dust which the rude wind   30
Blows in your face. I fear your disposition.
That° nature which contemns it origin
Cannot be bordered certain in itself.
She that herself will sliver° and disbranch
From her material sap,° perforce must wither   35
And come to deadly use.
      GON. No more, the text is foolish.°
      ALB. Wisdom and goodness to the vile seem vile.

Filths savor but themselves.° What have you done?
Tigers, not daughters, what have you performed?
A father, and a gracious agèd man   41
Whose reverence even the head-lugged bear° would
      lick,
Most barbarous, most degenerate, have you madded!
Could my good brother° suffer you to do it?
A man, a prince, by him so benefited!   45
If that the Heavens do not their visible spirits°
Send quickly down to tame these vile offenses,
It will come.
Humanity must perforce prey on itself,
Like monsters of the deep.°
      GON.   Milk-livered° man!   50
That bear'st a cheek for blows, a head for wrongs,
Who hast not in thy brows an eye discerning
Thine honor from thy suffering;° that not know'st
Fools do those villains pity who are punished
Ere they have done their mischief.° Where's thy
      drum?   55
France spreads his banners in our noiseless land,
With plumèd helm thy state begins to threat,
Whiles thou, a moral° fool, sit'st still and criest
" Alack, why does he so? "
      ALB.   See thyself, devil!
Proper deformity° seems not in the fiend   60
So horrid as in woman.
      GON.   O vain fool!
      ALB. Thou changèd and self-covered° thing, for
      shame,
Bemonster not thy feature.° Were 't my fitness
To let these hands obey my blood,°
They are apt enough to dislocate and tear   65
Thy flesh and bones. Howe'er° thou art a fiend,
A woman's shape doth shield thee.
      GON. Marry, your manhood!° Mew!°
                              [*Enter a* MESSENGER.]
      ALB. What news?
      MESS. O my good lord, the Duke of Cornwall's
      dead,   70
Slain by his servant, going to put out
The other eye of Gloucester.

Sc. ii: **12. cowish:** cowardly.   **13. undertake:** show initiative, venture.   **14. tie:** force.   **14–15. Our . . . effects:** our hopes (of love) as we rode together may be fulfilled.   **16. musters:** troops which have been collected. **powers:** forces.   **17–18. I . . . hands:** I must become the soldier and leave my husband to do the spinning.   **17. distaff:** stick used in spinning, essentially the work of the housewife.   **21. mistress's:** in the double sense of lady and lover. Edmund, having disposed of his brother and father, now looks higher; he will through Goneril become possessed of her half of the kingdom of Lear.   **24. Conceive:** use your imagination.   **28. My fool:** i.e., my husband is no more than a fool to me.   **29. worth . . . whistle:** There is a proverb "'Tis a poor dog that is not worth the whistle." Goneril means: I was once worth being regarded as your dog.   **32–36. That . . . use:** that creature which despises its father (*origin*) cannot be kept within bounds; she that cuts herself off from her family tree will perish and like a dead branch come to the burning.   **34. sliver:** slice off.   **35. material sap:** that sap which is part of herself.   **37. text is foolish:** i.e., this is a silly sermon.

39. Filths . . . themselves: the filthy like the taste only of filth.   **42. head-lugged bear:** a bear with its head torn by the hounds. See App. 5.   **44. good brother:** Cornwall.   **46. visible spirits:** avenging spirits in visible form.   **49–50. Humanity . . . deep:** A thought more than once expressed by Shakespeare — that when natural law is broken, men will degenerate into beasts and prey on each other. Cf. *Tr & Cr*, I.iii.101–24; Gen. Intro. p. 7b–8a.   **50. Milk-livered:** cowardly; the liver was regarded as the seat of courage.   **52–53. Who . . . suffering:** who cannot see when the insults which you endure are dishonorable to you.   **54–55. Fools . . . mischief:** only a fool pities a villain when he is punished to prevent his committing a crime.   **58. moral:** moralizing.   **60. Proper deformity:** deformity natural to a fiend.   **62. self-covered:** hiding your true self (i.e., devil) under the guise of a woman.   **63. Bemonster . . . feature:** do not change your shape into a fiend.   **64. blood:** anger.   **66. Howe'er:** although.   **68. Marry . . . manhood:** you're a fine specimen of a man! Mew: a catcall.

[handwritten margin note:] ALBANY WAKES UP + SEES GONERIL IS NO GOOD

ALB.   Gloucester's eyes!
MESS. A servant that he bred, thrilled with re-morse,°
Opposed against the act, bending his sword
To his great master, who thereat enraged   75
Flew on him and amongst them felled him dead,
But not without that harmful stroke which since
Hath plucked him after.
ALB.   This shows you are above,
You justicers, that these our nether crimes°
So speedily can venge. But, oh, poor Gloucester!   80
Lost he his other eye?
MESS.   Both, both, my lord.
This letter, madam, craves a speedy answer.
'Tis from your sister.
GON.   [Aside] One way I like this well,
But being widow, and my Gloucester° with her,   85
May all the building in my fancy pluck°
Upon my hateful life. Another way,
The news is not so tart. — I'll read, and answer.
    [Exit.]
ALB. Where was his son when they did take his eyes?
MESS. Come with my lady hither.
ALB.   He is not here.   90
MESS. No, my good lord, I met him back again.°
ALB. Knows he the wickedness?
MESS. Aye, my good lord, 'twas he informed against him,
And quit the house on purpose, that their punishment
Might have the freer course.
ALB.   Gloucester, I live   95
To thank thee for the love thou show'dst the King,
And to revenge thine eyes. Come hither, friend.
Tell me what more thou know'st.   [Exeunt.]

SCENE III. *The French camp near Dover.*

[*Enter* KENT *and a* GENTLEMAN.]
KENT. Why the King of France is so suddenly gone back know you the reason?
GENT. Something he left imperfect in the state which since his coming-forth is thought of, which imports to the kingdom so much fear and danger that his personal return was most required and necessary.   7
KENT. Who hath he left behind him general?
GENT. The Marshal of France, Monsieur La Far.
KENT. Did your letters pierce the Queen to any demonstration of grief?   *YES*   12

73. thrilled ... remorse: trembling with pity.   79. nether crimes: crimes committed on earth below.   85. my Gloucester: i.e., Edmund.   86. May ... pluck: may pull down my castle in the air (i.e., her desire to marry Edmund).   91. met ... again: met him as he was on his way back.

GENT. Aye, sir. She took them, read them in my presence,
And now and then an ample tear trilled down
Her delicate cheek. It seemed she was a queen   15
Over her passion,° who most rebel-like
Sought to be king o'er her.
KENT.   Oh, then it moved her.
GENT. Not to a rage. Patience and Sorrow strove
Who should express her goodliest.° You have seen
Sunshine and rain at once. Her smiles and tears   20
Were like a better way.° Those happy smilets°
That played on her ripe lip seemed not to know
What guests were in her eyes, which parted thence
As pearls from diamonds dropped. In brief,
Sorrow would be a rarity most beloved   25
If all could so become it.°
KENT.   Made she no verbal question?
GENT. Faith, once or twice she heaved the name of "Father"
Pantingly forth, as if it pressed her heart,
Cried "Sisters! Sisters! Shame of ladies! Sisters!
Kent! Father! Sisters! What, i' the storm? i' the night?
Let pity not be believed!" There she shook   30
The holy water from her heavenly eyes,
And clamor-moistened.° Then away she started
To deal with grief alone.
KENT.   It is the stars,
The stars above us, govern our conditions,   35
Else one self° mate and mate could not beget
Such different issues.° You spoke not with her since?
GENT. No.
KENT. Was this before the King returned?
GENT.   No, since.
KENT. Well, sir, the poor distressèd Lear's i' the town,   40
Who sometime in his better tune remembers
What we are come about, and by no means
Will yield to see his daughter.
GENT.   Why, good sir?
KENT. A sovereign° shame so elbows° him. His own unkindness
That stripped her from his benediction, turned her
To foreign casualties,° gave her dear rights   46
To his doghearted daughters. These things sting
His mind so venomously that burning shame
Detains him from Cordelia.
GENT.   Alack, poor gentleman!

Sc. iii: 16. passion: emotion.   19. express ... goodliest: make her seem more beautiful.   21. like ... way: even more lovely. smilets: little smiles.   25–26. Sorrow ... it: if everyone looked so beautiful in sorrow, it would be a quality much sought after.   33. clamor-moistened: wet her cries of grief with tears.   36. self: same.   37. issues: children.   44. sovereign: overpowering. elbows: plucks him by the elbow, reminding him of the past.   46. casualties: chances, accidents.

[Handwritten margin note:] AFTER TIME, CORDELIA SEES WHAT HAPPENED WHEN SHE LEFT HER FATHER TO 2 SISTERS + IT MOVES HER; HER LOVE FOR HIM OVERCOMES HER OBSTINANT SELF

KENT. Of Albany's and Cornwall's powers you
  heard not?   50
GENT. 'Tis so, they are afoot.
  KENT. Well, sir, I'll bring you to our master Lear,
And leave you to attend him. Some dear cause°
Will in concealment wrap me up awhile.
When I am known aright, you shall not grieve   55
Lending° me this acquaintance. I pray you, go
Along with me.   [*Exeunt.*]

SCENE IV. *The same. A tent.*

[*Enter, with drum and colors,*° CORDELIA, DOCTOR,
and SOLDIERS.]

  COR. Alack, 'tis he. Why, he was met even now
As mad as the vexed sea, singing aloud,
Crowned with rank fumiter and furrow weeds,
With burdocks, hemlock, nettles, cuckoo flowers,
Darnel,° and all the idle weeds that grow   5
In our sustaining° corn. A century° send forth.
Search every acre in the high-grown° field,
And bring him to our eye. [*Exit an* OFFICER.] What
  can man's wisdom
In the restoring his bereavèd sense?
He that helps him take all my outward worth.°   10
  DOCT. There is means, madam.
Our foster nurse° of nature is repose,
The which he lacks. That to provoke in him
Are many simples operative,° whose power
Will close the eye of anguish.
  COR.   All blest secrets,   15
All you unpublished virtues° of the earth,
Spring with my tears! Be aidant and remediate°
In the good man's distress! Seek, seek for him,
Lest his ungoverned rage dissolve the life
That wants the means to lead it.°

[*Enter a* MESSENGER.]

  MESS.   News, madam.   20
The British powers are marching hitherward.
  COR. 'Tis known before, our preparation stands
In expectation of them.° O dear Father,
It is thy business that I go about,
Therefore great France   25
My mourning and important° tears hath pitied.
No blown° ambition doth our arms incite,

53. dear cause: important reason.   56. Lending: bestowing on.
    Sc. iv: s.d., drum . . . colors: a drummer and a soldier carry-
ing a flag.   3–5. fumiter . . . Darnel: These are all English wild
flowers and weeds.   6. sustaining: which maintains life.   century: company of a hundred soldiers.   7. high-grown: The
season is therefore late summer.   10. outward worth: visible
wealth.   12. foster nurse: the nurse who feeds.   14. simples
operative: efficacious herbs.   16. unpublished virtues: secret
remedies.   17. aidant . . . remediate: helpful and remedial.
20. wants . . . it: that has no sense to guide it.   22–23. our . . .
them: our army is ready to meet them.   26. important: importunate, pleading   27. blown: puffed up.

But love, dear love, and our agèd father's right.
Soon may I hear and see him!   [*Exeunt.*]

SCENE V. GLOUCESTER'S *castle.*

[*Enter* REGAN *and* OSWALD.]

  REG. But are my brother's powers set forth?
  OSW.   Aye, madam.
  REG. Himself in person there?
  OSW.   Madam, with much ado.
Your sister is the better soldier.
  REG. Lord Edmund spake not with your lord at
    home?
  OSW. No, madam.   5
  REG. What might import my sister's letter to him?
  OSW. I know not, lady.
  REG. Faith, he is posted° hence on serious matter.
It was great ignorance, Gloucester's eyes being out,
To let him live. Where he arrives he moves   10
All hearts against us. Edmund, I think, is gone,
In pity of his misery, to dispatch
His nighted° life, moreover to descry
The strength o' the enemy.   14
  OSW. I must needs after him, madam, with my
    letter.
  REG. Our troops set forth tomorrow. Stay with us,
The ways are dangerous.
  OSW.   I may not, madam.
My lady charged my duty° in this business.
  REG. Why should she write to Edmund? Might
    not you
Transport her purposes by word? Belike,   20
Something — I know not what — I'll love thee
    much,
Let me unseal the letter.
  OSW.   Madam, I had rather —
  REG. I know your lady does not love her husband,
I am sure of that. And at her late being here   24
She gave strange œillades° and most speaking looks
To noble Edmund. I know you are of her bosom.°
  OSW. I, madam?
  REG. I speak in understanding. You are, I know 't.
Therefore I do advise you, take this note.°
My lord is dead, Edmund and I have talked,   30
And more convenient is he for my hand
Than for your lady's. You may gather more.
If you do find him, pray you give him this,
And when your mistress hears thus much from you,
I pray desire her call her wisdom to her.   35
So, fare you well.
If you do chance to hear of that blind traitor,

Sc. v: 8. is posted: has ridden fast.   13. nighted: blinded.
18. charged my duty: entrusted it to me as a solemn duty.
25. œillades: loving looks.   26. of . . . bosom: in her confidence.
29. take . . . note: observe this.

Preferment° falls on him that cuts him off.

osw. Would I could meet him, madam! I should
show   39
What party I do follow.

reg.   Fare thee well.   [*Exeunt.*]

SCENE VI. *Fields near Dover.*

[*Enter* gloucester, *and* edgar *dressed like a
peasant.*]

glo. When shall we come to the top of that same
hill?

edg. You do climb up it now. Look how we labor.

glo. Methinks the ground is even.

edg.   Horrible steep.
Hark, do you hear the sea?

glo.   No, truly.

edg. Why then your other senses grow imperfect
By your eyes' anguish.

glo.   So may it be, indeed.   6
Methinks thy voice is altered, and thou speak'st
In better phrase and matter than thou didst.

edg. You're much deceived. In nothing am I
changed
But in my garments.

glo.   Methinks you're better-spoken.   10

edg. Come on, sir, here's the place. Stand still.
How° fearful
And dizzy 'tis to cast one's eyes so low!
The crows and choughs° that wing the midway air
Show scarce so gross as beetles. Halfway down
Hangs one that gathers samphire,° dreadful trade!
Methinks he seems no bigger than his head.   16
The fishermen that walk upon the beach
Appear like mice, and yond tall anchoring bark°
Diminished to her cock° — her cock, a buoy
Almost too small for sight. The murmuring surge
That on the unnumbered idle pebbles chafes   21
Cannot be heard so high. I'll look no more,
Lest my brain turn and the deficient sight
Topple down headlong.°

glo.   Set me where you stand.

edg. Give me your hand. You are now within a
foot   25
Of the extreme verge. For all beneath the moon
Would I not leap upright.

glo.   Let go my hand.
Here, friend, 's another purse, in it a jewel

Well worth a poor man's taking. Fairies and gods°
Prosper it with thee! Go thou further off.   30
Bid me farewell, and let me hear thee going.

edg. Now fare you well, good sir.

glo.   With all my heart.

edg. Why I do trifle thus with his despair
Is done to cure it.°

glo. [*Kneeling*] O you mighty gods!
This world I do renounce, and in your sights   35
Shake patiently my great affliction off.
If° I could bear it longer and not fall
To quarrel with your great opposeless wills,
My snuff° and loathèd part of nature should
Burn itself out. If Edgar live, oh, bless him!   40
Now, fellow, fare thee well.   [*He falls forward.°*]

edg.   Gone, sir. Farewell.
And yet I know not how conceit° may rob
The treasury of life when life itself
Yields to the theft.° Had he been where he thought,
By this had thought been past. Alive or dead?   45
Ho, you sir! Friend! Hear you, sir! Speak!
Thus might he pass° indeed. Yet he revives.
What are you, sir?

glo.   Away, and let me die.

edg. Hadst thou been aught but gossamer,° feath-
ers, air,
So many fathom down precipitating,   50
Thou'dst shivered like an egg. But thou dost breathe,
Hast heavy substance, bleed'st not, speak'st, art
sound.
Ten masts at each° make not the altitude
Which thou hast perpendicularly fell.
Thy life's a miracle. Speak yet again.   55

glo. But have I fall'n, or no?

edg. From the dread summit of this chalky
bourn.°
Look up a-height, the shrill-gorged° lark so far
Cannot be seen or heard. Do but look up.

glo. Alack, I have no eyes.   60

29. **Fairies . . . gods:** As this tale is pre-Christian, it is natural
for the characters to call on the gods of the "elder world."
33–34. **Why . . . it:** Edgar's purpose is to persuade his blinded
father to go on living by the thought that he has been miraculously preserved after falling from a great height. When Gloucester begins to recover from the shock, Edgar has dropped his
pretense of being a bedlam and speaks in a natural (but still
disguised) voice.   37–40. **If . . . out:** if I could endure my misery
longer without quarreling with the wish of Heaven, I would wait
for the rest of my hateful life to burn itself out.   39. **snuff:** lit.,
smoking end of a burnt out candle.   41 s.d., **falls forward.** To
be effective this episode needs an actor who is not afraid of
hurting himself, for unless Gloucester's fall is heavy it is
quite unconvincing. After his fall, he lies stunned for a few
moments.   42. **conceit:** imagination.   44. **Yields . . . theft:** i.e.,
is willing to die.   47. **pass:** pass away, die.   49. **gossamer:** the
parachute-like web made by a species of small spider by which it
floats through the air.   53. **Ten . . . each:** ten masts, one on top
of the other.   57. **bourn:** boundary.   58. **shrill-gorged:** shrill-
throated. The lark is a small brown bird which flies to a great
height and there remains fluttering and singing a shrill but
beautiful song.

38. **Preferment:** promotion.
Sc. vi: **11–24. How . . . headlong:** This vivid description of
the cliffs at Dover seems to have been written from direct observation. The King's Players visited Dover in September 1606.
13. **choughs:** jackdaws.   15. **samphire:** a strongly perfumed
plant which grows on the chalk cliffs of Dover.   18. **bark:** ship.
19. **cock:** cockboat, the small ship's boat, usually towed behind.
23–24. **deficient . . . headlong:** my sight failing, cause me to
topple headlong.

Is wretchedness deprived that benefit,
To end itself by death? 'Twas yet some comfort
When misery could beguile° the tyrant's rage
And frustrate his proud will.

EDG.   Give me your arm.
Up, so. How is 't? Feel you your legs? You stand.
GLO. Too well, too well.
EDG.   This is above all strangeness. 66
Upon the crown o' the cliff, what thing was that
Which parted from you?
GLO.   A poor unfortunate beggar.
EDG. As I stood here below, methought his eyes
Were two full moons, he had a thousand noses, 70
Horns whelked° and waved like the enridgèd° sea.
It was some fiend, therefore, thou happy father,
Think that the clearest° gods, who make them honors
Of men's impossibilities,° have preserved thee.
GLO. I do remember now. Henceforth I'll bear 75
Affliction till it do cry out itself
"Enough, enough," and die. That thing you speak of,
I took it for a man. Often 'twould say
"The fiend, the fiend." He led me to that place.
EDG. Bear free° and patient thoughts. But who
     comes here?   80

[*Enter* LEAR, *fantastically dressed with wild flowers.*]

The safer sense will n'er accommodate
His master thus.°
LEAR. No,° they cannot touch me for coining, I
am the King himself.
EDG. O thou side-piercing sight!   85
LEAR. Nature's above art° in that respect. There's
your press money. That fellow handles his bow like
a crowkeeper,° draw me a clothier's yard.° Look,
look, a mouse! Peace, peace, this piece of toasted
cheese will do 't. There's my gauntlet,° I'll prove it
on a° giant. Bring up the brown bills.° Oh, well-

flown, bird! I' the clout,° i' the clout. Hewgh!° Give
the word.°   93
EDG. Sweet marjoram.°
LEAR. Pass.
GLO. I know that voice.   96
LEAR. Ha! Goneril, with a white beard! They
flattered me like a dog, and told me I had white
hairs in my beard ere the black ones were there. To
say "aye" and "no" to everything that I said!
"Aye" and "no" too was no good divinity.° 101
When the rain came to wet me once and the wind to
make me chatter, when the thunder would not peace
at my bidding, there I found 'em, there I smelt 'em
out. Go to, they are not men o' their words. They
told me I was everything. 'Tis a lie, I am not ague-
proof.   107
GLO. The trick° of that voice I do well remember.
Is 't not the King?
LEAR.   Aye, every inch a king.
When I do stare, see how the subject quakes.   110
I pardon that man's life. What was thy cause?
Adultery?
Thou shalt not die. Die for adultery! No.
The wren goes to 't, and the small gilded fly
Does lecher in my sight.   115
Let copulation thrive, for Gloucester's bastard son
Was kinder to his father than my daughters
Got 'tween the lawful sheets.
To 't, luxury,° pell-mell! For I lack soldiers.
Behold yond simpering dame,   120
Whose face between her forks° presages snow,
That minces virtue° and does shake the head
To hear of pleasure's name.
The fitchew,° nor the soilèd° horse, goes to 't
With a more riotous appetite.   125
Down from the waist they are Centaurs,°
Though women all above.
But to° the girdle do the gods inherit,
Beneath is all the fiends'.
There's Hell, there's darkness, there's the sulphur-
     ous pit,   130
Burning, scalding, stench, consumption, fie, fie, fie,
Pah, pah! Give me an ounce of civet,° good apothe-
cary, to sweeten my imagination. There's money for
thee.
GLO. Oh, let me kiss that hand!   135
LEAR. Let me wipe it first, it smells of mortality.
GLO. O ruined piece of nature! This great world
Shall so wear out to naught.° Dost thou know me?

---

63. beguile: cheat (by death). 71. whelked: with spiral twists.
enridged: wavy. 73. clearest: most glorious. 73–74. who . . .
impossibilities: who cause themselves to be honored by performing miracles impossible to men. 80. free: innocent.
81–82. The . . . thus: a man in his right senses would never adorn
himself thus. Edgar with unconscious irony repeats Lear's "accommodated." See III.iv.110. 83–93. No . . . word: Lear's
madness has a sort of logical coherence. He begins by saying that
he cannot be charged with coining, because it was his right as
king to issue the coin, a natural right. From coin his mind goes to
the use of coin as *press money* for soldiers (money given to a
conscripted recruit as token that he has been engaged), thence
to the recruits at archery practice. Then his mind is distracted
by a mouse, but comes back to his quarrel with his sons-in-law.
He will throw down his gauntlet as a challenge to single combat
against any odds. He comes back to the archery range, and a
good shot right in the bull's-eye. 86. Nature's . . . art: See
App. 18. 88. crowkeeper: a man hired to scare away crows from
the crop. clothier's yard: The expert archer drew his arrow back
a full yard to the ear. 90. gauntlet: glove, token of challenge.
90–91. prove . . . a: i.e., fight even a. 91. brown bills: i.e., the
infantry. See Pl. 21c. brown: varnished to keep from rusting.
92. clout: the canvas target. Hewgh: imitation of the whiz
of the arrow. 93. word: password. 94. marjoram: a savory
herb. 101. no . . . divinity: i.e., false doctrine. 108. trick: peculiar note. 119. luxury: lust. 121. forks: legs. 122. minces
virtue: walks with a great air of virtue. 124. fitchew: polecat,
a creature demonstratively oversexed. soiled: fed on spring
grass. 126. Centaurs: creatures half man and half stallion.
128. But to: only down to. 132. civet: perfume. See III.iv
108–09,n. 137–38. O . . . naught: O ruined masterpiece of nature, the universe likewise will come to nothing.

LEAR. I remember thine eyes well enough. Dost thou squiny° at me? No, do thy worst, blind Cupid,° I'll not love. Read thou this challenge, mark but the penning on 't.   142

GLO. Were all the letters suns, I could not see one.

EDG. I would not take this from report. It is, And my heart breaks at it.

LEAR. Read.   146

GLO. What, with the case of eyes?

LEAR. Oh ho, are you there with me?° No eyes in your head, nor no money in your purse? Your eyes are in a heavy case, your purse in a light. Yet you see how this world goes.   151

GLO. I see it feelingly.

LEAR. What, art mad? A man may see how this world goes with no eyes. Look with thine ears. See how yond Justice rails upon yond simple thief. Hark, in thine ear. Change places and, handy-dandy,° which is the Justice, which is the thief? Thou hast seen a farmer's dog bark at a beggar?   159

GLO. Aye, sir.

LEAR. And the creature run from the cur? There thou mightst behold the great image of authority.° A dog's obeyed in office. Thou rascal beadle,° hold thy bloody hand! Why dost thou lash that whore? Strip thine own back.   165 Thou hotly lust'st to use her in that kind° For which thou whip'st her. The usurer hangs the cozener.° Through tattered clothes small vices do appear, Robes and furred gowns hide all. Plate sin with gold And the strong lance of justice hurtless breaks.   170 Arm it in rags, a pigmy's straw does pierce it. None does offend, none, I say, none, I'll able° 'em. Take that of me, my friend, who have the power To seal the accuser's lips. Get thee glass eyes° And, like a scurvy° politician, seem   175 To see the things thou dost not. Now, now, now, now. Pull off my boots. Harder, harder. So.

EDG. Oh, matter and impertinency° mixed! Reason in madness!   179

LEAR. If thou wilt weep my fortunes, take my eyes. I know thee well enough. Thy name is Gloucester. Thou must be patient, we came crying hither. Thou know'st the first time that we smell the air, We wawl and cry. I will preach to thee. Mark.

GLO. Alack, alack the day!   185

LEAR. When we are born, we cry that we are come To this great stage of fools. This 's a good block.° It were a delicate stratagem to shoe A troop of horse with felt. I'll put 't in proof,° And when I have stol'n upon these sons-in-law, Then, kill, kill, kill, kill, kill, kill!   191

[Enter a GENTLEMAN, with ATTENDANTS.]

GENT. Oh, here he is. Lay hand upon him. Sir, Your most dear daughter ——

LEAR. No rescue? What, a prisoner? I am even The natural fool of Fortune.° Use me well,   195 You shall have ransom.° Let me have a surgeon, I am cut to the brains.

GENT.   You shall have anything.

LEAR. No seconds?° All myself? Why, this would make a man a man of salt,° To use his eyes for garden waterpots,   200 Aye, and laying autumn's dust.

GENT. Good sir ——

LEAR. I will die bravely, like a smug bridegroom.° What! I will be jovial. Come, come, I am a king, My masters, know you that.

GENT. You are a royal one, and we obey you.   205

LEAR. Then there's life in 't. Nay, an you get it, you shall get it by running. Sa, sa, sa, sa.°

[Exit running. ATTENDANTS follow.]

GENT. A sight most pitiful in the meanest wretch, Past speaking of in a king! Thou hast one daughter Who redeems nature from the general curse   210 Which twain have brought her to.°

EDG. Hail, gentle sir.

GENT.   Sir, speed you. What's your will?

EDG. Do you hear aught, sir, of a battle toward?°

GENT. Most sure and vulgar.° Everyone hears that Which can distinguish sound.

EDG.   But, by your favor,   215 How near's the other army?

GENT. Near and on speedy foot, the main descry Stands on the hourly thought.°

EDG.   I thank you, sir. That's all.

GENT. Though that the Queen on special cause is here, Her army is moved on.

---

187. block: hat; lit., the block on which a felt hat is molded. From hat Lear's mind turns to felt.   189. put ... proof: try it out.   195. natural ... Fortune: born to be fooled by Fortune. 196. ransom: Prisoners of good family could buy their freedom from their captors. Cf. Hen V, IV.iii.79–125.   198. No seconds: no one to help me.   199. man of salt: because tears are salt.   202. like ... bridegroom: It was said of Lord Grey of Wilton, who was led out as if to be executed on December 9, 1603, that he "had such gaiety and cheer in his countenance that he seemed a dapper young bridegroom."   207. Sa ... sa: a cry used sometimes in sudden action.   210–11. Who ... to: See Lear Intro. p. 1139b.   213. toward: at hand.   214. vulgar: common, in everyone's mouth.   217–18. the ... thought: the main body is expected to come into sight at any time now.

---

140. squiny: look sideways, like a prostitute.   140–41. blind Cupid: the usual sign hung over a brothel.   148. are ... me: do you agree with me?   157. handy-dandy: the nursery game of "Handy-pandy, sugar candy, which hand will you have?" 162. image of authority: figure showing the true meaning of authority.   164. beadle: parish officer.   166. kind: manner. 167. usurer ... cozener: the swindler hangs the crook. 172. able: give power to.   174. glass eyes: spectacles. 175. scurvy: lit., with skin disease, "lousy."   178. matter ... impertinency: sense and nonsense.

EDG.   I thank you, sir.   [*Exit* GENTLEMAN.]
GLO.   You ever-gentle gods, take my breath from
me.   221
Let not my worser spirit tempt me again
To die before you please!
EDG.   Well pray you, Father.
GLO.   Now, good sir, what are you?
EDG.   A most poor man, made tame to fortune's
blows,   225
Who, by the art° of known and feeling sorrows,
Am pregnant to° good pity. Give me your hand.
I'll lead you to some biding.°
GLO.   Hearty thanks.
The bounty and the benison° of Heaven
To boot, and boot!°

[*Enter* OSWALD.]

OSW.   A proclaimed° prize! Most happy!   230
That eyeless head of thine was first framed flesh
To raise my fortunes. Thou old unhappy traitor,
Briefly thyself remember.° The sword is out
That must destroy thee.
GLO.   Now let thy friendly hand
Put strength enough to 't.   [EDGAR *interposes*.]
OSW.   Wherefore, bold peasant,   235
Darest thou support a published° traitor? Hence,
Lest that the infection of his fortune take
Like hold on thee! Let go his arm.
EDG.   Chill° not let go, zir, without vurther 'ca-
sion.°
OSW.   Let go, slave, or thou diest!   241
EDG.   Good gentleman, go your gait,° and let poor
volk pass. An chud° ha' been zwaggered out of my
life, 'twould not ha' been zo long as 'tis by a vort-
night. Nay, come not near th' old man, keep out,
che vor ye,° or I'se try whether your costard° or my
ballow° be the harder. Chill be plain with you.   247
OSW.   Out, dunghill!   [*They fight*.]
EDG.   Chill pick your teeth, zir. Come, no matter
vor your foins.°   [OSWALD *falls*.]
OSW.   Slave, thou hast slain me. Villain, take my
purse.
If ever thou wilt thrive, bury my body,
And give the letters which thou find'st about me
To Edmund Earl of Gloucester. Seek him out   254
Upon the British party. Oh, untimely death!
Death!   [*Dies*.]
EDG.   I know thee well — a serviceable° villain,
As duteous to the vices of thy mistress

As badness would desire.
GLO.   What, is he dead?
EDG.   Sit you down, Father, rest you.   260
Let's see these pockets. The letters that he speaks of
May be my friends. He's dead. I am only sorry
He had no other deathsman. Let us see.
Leave, gentle wax,° and, manners, blame us not.
To know our enemies' minds, we'd rip their hearts,
Their papers is more lawful. [*Reads*.]   266
"Let our reciprocal vows be remembered. You
have many opportunities to cut him off. If your will
want not,° time and place will be fruitfully offered.
There is nothing done if he return the conqueror.
Then am I the prisoner, and his bed my jail, from
the loathed warmth whereof deliver me, and supply
the place for your labor.   274
"Your — wife, so I would say — affectionate
servant,   GONERIL."
Oh, undistinguished space° of woman's will!
A plot upon her virtuous husband's life,
And the exchange my brother! Here, in the sands,
Thee I'll rake up,° the post unsanctified°   281
Of murderous lechers, and in the mature time
With this ungracious paper strike the sight
Of the death-practiced° Duke. For him 'tis well
That of thy death and business I can tell.   285
GLO.   The King is mad. How° stiff° is my vile
sense,°
That I stand up, and have ingenious° feeling
Of my huge sorrows! Better I were distract.°
So should my thoughts be severed from my griefs,
And woes by wrong imaginations lose   290
The knowledge of themselves.   [*Drum afar off*]
EDG.   Give me your hand.
Far off methinks I hear the beaten drum.
Come, Father, I'll bestow you with a friend.
[*Exeunt*.]

SCENE VII. *A tent in the French camp*. LEAR
on a bed asleep, soft music playing,
GENTLEMAN, *and others attending*.

[*Enter* CORDELIA, KENT, *and* DOCTOR.]
COR.   O thou good Kent, how shall I live and
work,
To match thy goodness? My life will be too short,
And every measure fail me.
KENT.   To be acknowledged, madam, is o'erpaid.
All my reports go with the modest truth,   5

---

226. art: long experience.   227. pregnant to: able to conceive.
228. biding: resting-place.   229. benison: blessing.   230. To
... boot: in the highest degree. proclaimed: Cf. IV.v.37–8.
233. thyself remember: prepare for death — by confessing your
sins.   236. published: publicly proclaimed.   239–48. Chill ...
you: Edgar speaks stage rustic dialect.   240. Chill: I'll. vurther 'casion: further occasion, reason.   242. go ... gait: go
your own way.   243. chud: should.   246. che ... ye: I warn
yer. costard: head; lit., apple.   247. ballow: cudgel.   250. foins:
thrusts.   257. serviceable: diligent.

264. Leave ... wax: Here he breaks the seal. See App. 6.
268–69. will ... not: desire is not lacking. *Will* means both
willingness and lust.   278. undistinguished space: limitless,
extending beyond the range of sight.   281. rake up: hide in the
dust. post unsanctified: unholy messenger.   284. death-prac-
ticed: whose death is plotted.   286–88. How .. sorrows: i.e.,
if only I could go mad and forget my sorrows. stiff: strong
sense: sanity. ingenious: sensitive. distract: mad.

Nor more nor clipped, but so.°
    COR.   Be better suited.°
These weeds° are memories of those worser hours.
I prithee put them off.
    KENT.   Pardon me, dear madam,
Yet to be known shortens my made intent.°
My boon° I make it that you know me not   10
Till time and I think meet.
    COR. Then be 't so, my good lord. [*To the* DOCTOR]
    How does the King?
    DOCT. Madam, sleeps still.
    COR. O you kind gods,
Cure this great breach in his abusèd nature!   15
The untuned and jarring senses, oh, wind up°
Of this child-changèd° father!
    DOCT.   So please your Majesty
That we may wake the King. He hath slept long.
    COR. Be governed by your knowledge, and pro-
      ceed
I' the sway° of your own will. Is he arrayed?   20
    GENT. Aye, madam. In the heaviness of his sleep
We put fresh garments on him.
    DOCT. Be by, good madam, when we do awake
    him.
I doubt not of his temperance.°
    COR.   Very well.
    DOCT. Please you, draw near. Louder the music
    there!   25
    COR. O my dear Father! Restoration hang
Thy medicine on my lips, and let this kiss
Repair those violent harms that my two sisters
Have in thy reverence made!
    KENT.   Kind and dear Princess!
    COR. Had you not been their father, these white
    flakes   30
Had challenged pity of them. Was this a face
To be opposed against the warring winds?
To stand against the deep dread-bolted thunder?
In the most terrible and nimble stroke
Of quick, cross lightning?° To watch — poor
    perdu!° —   35
With this thin helm? Mine enemy's dog,
Though he had bit me, should have stood that night
Against my fire, and wast thou fain, poor Father,
To hovel thee with swine and rogues forlorn
In short and musty straw? Alack, alack!   40
'Tis wonder that thy life and wits at once
Had not concluded all. He wakes. Speak to him.
    DOCT. Madam, do you, 'tis fittest.

    COR. How does my royal lord? How fares your
    Majesty?
    LEAR. You do me wrong to take me out o' the
    grave.   45
Thou art a soul in bliss,° but I am bound
Upon a wheel of fire that mine own tears
Do scald like molten lead.
    COR.   Sir, do you know me?
    LEAR. You are a spirit, I know. When did you
    die?
    COR. Still, still far wide!   50
    DOCT. He's scarce awake. Let him alone awhile.
    LEAR. Where have I been? Where am I? Fair day-
    light?
I am mightily abused. I should e'en die with pity
To see another thus. I know not what to say.
I will not swear these are my hands. Let's see,   55
I feel this pin prick. Would I were assured
Of my condition!
    COR.   Oh, look upon me, sir,
And hold your hands in benediction o'er me.
No, sir, you must not kneel.
    LEAR.   Pray do not mock me.
I am a very foolish fond old man,   60
Fourscore and upward, not an hour more nor less,
And, to deal plainly,
I fear I am not in my perfect mind.
Methinks I should know you and know this man,
Yet I am doubtful, for I am mainly ignorant   65
What place this is, and all the skill I have
Remembers not these garments, nor I know not
Where I did lodge last night. Do not laugh at me,
For, as I am a man, I think this lady
To be my child Cordelia.
    COR.   And so I am, I am.   70
    LEAR. Be your tears wet? Yes, faith. I pray weep
    not.
If you have poison for me, I will drink it.
I know you do not love me, for your sisters
Have, as I do remember, done me wrong.
You have some cause, they have not.
    COR.   No cause, no cause.   75
    LEAR. Am I in France?
    KENT.   In your own kingdom, sir.
    LEAR. Do not abuse me.
    DOCT. Be comforted, good madam. The great
    rage,
You see, is killed in him. And yet it is danger
To make him even o'er° the time he has lost.   80
Desire him to go in, trouble him no more
Till further settling.
    COR. Will 't please your Highness walk?
    LEAR.   You must bear with me.
Pray you now, forget and forgive. I am old and
    foolish.
    [*Exeunt all but* KENT *and* GENTLEMAN.]

Sc. vii: **6. Nor . . . so:** neither exaggerated nor curtailed, but
exact. **suited:** garbed. **7. weeds:** garments; i.e., his livery
as Lear's servant. **9. Yet . . . intent:** my plan will be frustrated
if I am revealed now. **10. boon:** request for a favor. **16. wind
up:** i.e., as the loose string of a musical instrument is tightened.
17. child-changed: transformed by the treatment of his
children. **20. sway:** direction. **24. temperance:** sanity.
35. cross lightning: forked lightning. **perdu:** sentry in an exposed position.

46. bliss: Heaven. **80. even o'er:** go over.

[handwritten: REGAN IS MORE VIGOROUS + DIREC WITH EDMUND]

GENT. Holds it true, sir, that the Duke of Corn-
wall was so slain?   86
KENT. Most certain, sir.
GENT. Who is conductor of his people?
KENT. As 'tis said, the bastard son of Gloucester.
GENT. They say Edgar, his banished son, is with
the Earl of Kent in Germany.   91
KENT. Report is changeable.° 'Tis time to look
about. The powers of the kingdom approach apace.
GENT. The arbiterment° is like to be bloody. Fare
you well, sir.   [*Exit.*]
KENT. My point and period° will be throughly°
wrought,   97
Or well or ill, as this day's battle's fought. [*Exit.*]

Act V

[handwritten: BATTLE IS KIND OF A FINAL POLITICAL ACT — HE HAS CAUSED THIS BATTLE]

SCENE I. *The British camp near Dover.*

[*Enter, with drum and colors,* EDMUND, REGAN,
GENTLEMEN, *and* SOLDIERS.]
EDM. Know° of the Duke if his last purpose hold,
Or whether since he is advised by aught
To change the course. He's full of alteration
And self-reproving. Bring his constant° pleasure.
                          [*To a* GENTLEMAN, *who goes out.*]
REG. Our sister's man is certainly miscarried.   5
EDM. 'Tis to be doubted,° madam.
REG.   Now, sweet lord,
You know the goodness I intend upon you.
Tell me, but truly, but then speak the truth,
Do you not love my sister?
EDM.   In honored love.   9
REG. But have you never found my brother's way
To the forfended° place?
EDM.   That thought abuses° you.
REG. I am doubtful that you have been conjunct
And bosomed with her, as far as we call hers.°
EDM. No, by mine honor, madam.
REG. I never shall endure her. Dear my lord,   15
Be not familiar with her.
EDM.   Fear me not. —
She and the Duke her husband!
[*Enter, with drum and colors,* ALBANY, GONERIL, *and*
SOLDIERS.]
GON. [*Aside*] I had rather lose the battle than that
sister
Should loosen him and me.

ALB. Our very loving sister, well bemet.   20
Sir, this I hear: The King is come to his daughter,
With others whom the rigor of our state°
Forced to cry out.° Where I could not be honest,
I never yet was valiant. For this business,
It toucheth us, as France invades our land,   25
Not bolds the King, with others, whom I fear
Most just and heavy causes make oppose.°
EDM. Sir, you speak nobly.
REG.   Why is this reasoned?°
GON. Combine together 'gainst the enemy,
For these domestic and particular broils   30
Are not the question here.
ALB.   Let's then determine
With the ancient of war° on our proceedings.
EDM. I shall attend you presently at your tent.
REG. Sister, you'll go with us?
GON. No.   35
REG. 'Tis most convenient. Pray you go with us.
GON. [*Aside*] Oh ho, I know the riddle.° — I
will go.
[*As they are going out, enter* EDGAR *disguised.*]
EDG. If e'er your Grace had speech with man so
poor,
Hear me one word.
ALB.   I'll overtake you. Speak.
                  [*Exeunt all but* ALBANY *and* EDGAR.]
EDG. Before you fight the battle, ope this letter.
If you have victory, let the trumpet sound   41
For him that brought it. Wretched though I seem,
I can produce a champion that will prove
What is avouchèd° there. If you miscarry,
Your business of the world hath so an end,   45
And machination ceases. Fortune love you!
ALB. Stay till I have read the letter.
EDG.   I was forbid it.
When time shall serve, let but the herald cry
And I'll appear again.   49
ALB. Why, fare thee well. I will o'erlook° thy
paper.   [*Exit* EDGAR.]
                  [*Re-enter* EDMUND.]
EDM. The enemy's in view. Draw up your powers.
Here is the guess° of their true strength and forces
By diligent discovery, but your haste
Is now urged on you.
ALB.   We will greet the time.° [*Exit.*]
EDM. To° both these sisters have I sworn my love,

92. Report . . . changeable: rumors are not reliable.   94. arbiterment: decision.   97. point . . . period: lit., full stop; the end
of my chapter. throughly: thoroughly.
Act V, Sc. i: 1. Know: learn.   4. constant: firm; i.e., final
decision.   6. doubted: feared.   11. forfended: forbidden.
abuses: wrongs; i.e., you should not have such a thought.
12–13. I . . . hers: I am afraid that you have been united in intimacy with her in every way.

22. rigor . . . state: our harsh government.   23. cry out: protest.
24–27. For . . . oppose: this business concerns us particularly,
not because France is encouraging Lear and others who rightly
oppose us, but because he is invading our country.   28. reasoned:
argued.   32. ancient of war: experienced commanders.   37. Oh
. . . riddle: i.e., you are afraid to leave me alone with Edmund.
44. avouched: declared.   50. o'erlook: read.   52. guess:
estimate.   54. greet . . . time: i.e., go to meet our enemy.
55–69. To . . . debate: Edmund has now reached the crisis in his
fortunes. Both sisters are in love with him, he can have either.
Or he can aim higher and, with Lear and Cordelia out of the way,
achieve the whole kingdom for himself.

[handwritten: ALBANY WANTS TO MAKE A BIG ISSUE OF FIGHTING EDMUND SO TELLS EDMUND TO OPEN LETTER JUST BEFORE BATTLE]

Each jealous of the other, as the stung   56
Are of the adder. Which of them shall I take?
Both? One? Or neither? Neither can be enjoyed
If both remain alive. To take the widow
Exasperates, makes mad her sister Goneril,   60
And hardly shall I carry out my side,°
Her husband being alive. Now then we'll use
His countenance° for the battle, which being done,
Let her who would be rid of him devise
His speedy taking-off. As for the mercy   65
Which he intends to Lear and to Cordelia,
The battle done, and they within our power,
Shall never see his pardon, for my state
Stands on me to defend, not to debate.°   [_Exit._]

SCENE II. _A field between the two camps._

[_Alarum within. Enter, with drum and colors,_ LEAR,
CORDELIA, _and_ SOLDIERS, _over the stage; and exeunt._
            Enter EDGAR _and_ GLOUCESTER.]

    EDG. Here, Father, take the shadow of this tree
For your good host. Pray that the right may thrive.
If ever I return to you again,
I'll bring you comfort.
    GLO.   Grace go with you, sir! [_Exit_ EDGAR.]
      [_Alarum and retreat within. Re-enter_ EDGAR.]
    EDG. Away, old man. Give me thy hand, away!
King Lear hath lost, he and his daughter ta'en.°
Give me thy hand, come on.   7
    GLO. No farther, sir. A man may rot even here.
    EDG. What, in ill thoughts again? Men° must
      endure
Their going hence, even as their coming hither.   10
Ripeness° is all. Come on.
    GLO.   And that's true too. [_Exeunt._]

SCENE III. _The British camp near Dover._

[_Enter, in conquest, with drum and colors,_ EDMUND,
LEAR _and_ CORDELIA, _as prisoners,_ CAPTAIN, SOLDIERS,
                    etc.]

    EDM. Some officers take them away. Good guard,
Until their greater pleasures° first be known
That are to censure them.
    COR.   We are not the first
Who with best meaning have incurred the worst.
For thee, oppressèd King, am I cast down.   5
Myself could else outfrown false fortune's frown.°

Shall we not see these daughters and these sisters?
    LEAR. No, no, no, no! Come, let's away to prison.
We two alone will sing like birds i' the cage.
When thou dost ask me blessing, I'll kneel down   10
And ask of thee forgiveness. So we'll live,
And pray, and sing, and tell old tales, and laugh
At gilded butterflies,° and hear poor rogues
Talk of Court news. And we'll talk with them too,
Who loses and who wins, who's in, who's out,   15
And take upon 's the mystery of things°
As if we were God's spies. And we'll wear out,
In a walled prison, packs and sects of great ones
That ebb and flow by the moon.°
    EDM.   Take them away.
    LEAR. Upon such sacrifices, my Cordelia,   20
The gods themselves throw incense. Have I caught
      thee?
He that parts us shall bring a brand° from Heaven,
And fire us° hence like foxes. Wipe thine eyes.
The goodyears° shall devour them, flesh and fell,°
Ere they shall make us weep. We'll see 'em starve
      first.   25
Come.   [_Exeunt_ LEAR _and_ CORDELIA, _guarded._]
    EDM. Come hither, Captain, hark.
Take thou this note. Go follow them to prison.
One step I have advanced thee. If thou dost
As this instructs thee, thou dost make thy way
To noble fortunes. Know thou this, that men   30
Are as the time is.° To be tender-minded
Does not become a sword.° Thy great employment
Will not bear question.° Either say thou'lt do 't,
Or thrive by other means.
    CAPT.   I'll do 't, my lord.
    EDM. About it, and write happy° when thou hast
      done.   35
Mark, I say, instantly, and carry it so
As I have set it down.
    CAPT. I cannot draw a cart, nor eat dried oats.
If it be man's work, I'll do 't.   [_Exit._]
[_Flourish. Enter_ ALBANY, GONERIL, REGAN, _another_
            CAPTAIN, _and_ SOLDIERS.]
    ALB. Sir, you have shown today your valiant
      strain,°   40
And fortune led you well. You have the captives
That were the opposites° of this day's strife.
We do require them of you, so to use them
As we shall find their merits and our safety
May equally determine.

13. gilded butterflies: i.e., Court folk.   16. take . . . things:
pretend to understand deep secrets.   18–19. packs . . . moon:
parties at Court whose fortunes change monthly.   22. a brand:
fire.   23. fire us: drive us out by fire.   24. goodyears: The
phrase "what the goodyear" meant "what the deuce"; hence
"goodyear" means something vaguely evil. Lear is talking
baby talk — "The bogeymen shall have them." fell: skin.
30–31. men . . . is: i.e., in brutal times men must be brutes.
32. sword: soldier.   32–33. Thy . . . question: the duty now laid on
you is too important and brutal to be argued about.   35. happy:
fortunate.   40. strain: blood, courage.   42. opposites: opponents.

61. my side: i.e., of the bargain.   63. countenance: authority.
68–69. for . . . debate: my fortune is now in such a state that I
must act, not argue.
    Sc. ii: 6. ta'en: taken.   9–11. Men . . . all: Shakespeare had
already expressed this stoical view of life in _Haml,_ V.ii.231.
11. Ripeness: perfect readiness.
    Sc. iii: 2. their . . . pleasures: the will of my superiors.
3–6. We . . . frown: See I.i.183–90,n.

EDM.   Sir, I thought it fit   45
To send the old and miserable King
To some retention and appointed guard,°
Whose age has charms in it, whose title more,
To pluck the common bosom° on his side
And turn our impressed lances° in our eyes   50
Which do command them. With him I sent the
      Queen,
My reason all the same, and they are ready
Tomorrow or at further space to appear
Where you shall hold your session.° At this time
We sweat and bleed. The friend hath lost his friend,
And the best quarrels, in the heat, are cursed   56
By those that feel their sharpness.°
The question of Cordelia and her father
Requires a fitter place.
     ALB.   Sir, by your patience,
I hold you but a subject° of this war,   60
Not as a brother.
     REG.   That's as we list to grace him.
Methinks our pleasure might have been demanded
Ere you had spoke so far. He led our powers,
Bore the commission of my place and person,°
The which immediacy may well stand up   65
And call itself your brother.°
     GON.   Not so hot.
In his own grace he doth exalt himself
More than in your addition.°
     REG.   In my rights,
By me invested, he compeers° the best.
     GON. That were the most, if he should husband
      you.   70
     REG. Jesters do oft prove prophets.
     GON.   Holloa, holloa!
That eye that told you so looked but a-squint.
     REG. Lady, I am not well, else I should answer
From a full-flowing stomach.° General,
Take thou my soldiers, prisoners, patrimony,   75
Dispose of them, of me, the walls are thine.°
Witness the world that I create thee here
My lord and master.
     GON.   Mean you to enjoy him?
     ALB. The let-alone° lies not in your goodwill.
     EDM. Nor in thine, lord.
     ALB.   Half-blooded fellow, yes.   80
     REG. [To EDMUND] Let the drum strike, and prove
      my title thine.

     ALB. Stay yet, hear reason. Edmund, I arrest thee
On capital treason,° and in thine attaint°
This gilded serpent. [Pointing to GONERIL] For
      your claim, fair Sister,
I bar it in the interest of my wife.   85
'Tis she is subcontracted° to this lord,
And I, her husband, contradict your bans.°
If you will marry, make your loves to me.
My lady is bespoke.°
     GON.   An interlude!°
     ALB. Thou art armed, Gloucester. Let the trumpet
      sound.   90
If none appear to prove upon thy person
Thy heinous,° manifest, and many treasons,
There is my pledge. [Throwing down a glove] I'll
      prove it on thy heart
Ere I taste bread, thou art in nothing less
Than I have here proclaimed thee.
     REG.   Sick, oh, sick!   95
     GON. [Aside] If not, I'll ne'er trust medicine.°
     EDM. [Throwing down a glove] There's my ex-
      change. What in the world he is
That names me traitor, villainlike he lies.°
Call by thy trumpet. He that dares approach,
On him, on you — who not? — I will maintain
My truth and honor firmly.   101
     ALB. A herald, ho!
     EDM.   A herald, ho, a herald!
     ALB. Trust to thy single° virtue, for thy soldiers,
All levied in my name, have in my name
Took their discharge.
     REG.   My sickness grows upon me.   105
     ALB. She is not well. Convey her to my tent.
      [Exit REGAN, led.]
[Enter a HERALD.] Come hither, herald. — Let the
      trumpet sound. —
And read out this.   108
     CAPT. Sound, trumpet!   [A trumpet sounds.]
     HER. [Reads.] "If any man of quality or degree°
within the lists° of the army will maintain upon Ed-
mund, supposed Earl of Gloucester, that he is a
manifold traitor, let him appear by the third sound
of the trumpet. He is bold in his defense."   114
     EDM. Sound!   [First trumpet.]
     HER. Again!   [Second trumpet.]
Again!   [Third trumpet.]
      [Trumpet answers within.]
[Enter EDGAR at the third sound, armed, with a
      trumpet before him.]

---

47. **retention . . . guard:** where he can be kept and properly guarded.   49. **common bosom:** the sympathies of our soldiers. 50. **impressed lances:** the soldiers we have conscripted.   54. **session:** trial.   56–57. **And . . . sharpness:** i.e., with the battle hardly over we are in no condition to judge this matter calmly. 60. **subject:** i.e., not one who gives orders.   64. **commission . . . person:** commission appointing him commander as my deputy. 65–66. **The . . . brother:** since he is my general, he is fit to be considered your equal.   68. **your addition:** the title which you have given him. See I.i.138.   69. **compeers:** equals.   74. **full-flowing stomach:** in full wrath.   76. **walls . . . thine:** i.e., you have won the outer defenses.   79. **let-alone:** power to prevent.

83. **capital treason:** treason deserving death. **and . . . attaint:** and accused with you (attaint: impeachment).   86. **subcontracted:** already betrothed.   87. **bans:** notice of intention to marry, read out in church for three Sundays previous to the marriage. 89. **bespoke:** already reserved. **An interlude:** i.e., this is mere play-acting.   92. **heinous:** odious.   96. **medicine:** poison. 98. **villainlike . . . lies:** he lies like a villain. This is the lie direct, which was a direct challenge to mortal combat. Cf. AYLI, V.iv.69–108.   103. **single:** solitary, unaided.   110. **quality or degree:** rank or high position.   111. **lists:** roll call, roster.

ALB. Ask him his purposes, why he appears
Upon this call o' the trumpet.°

HER.   What are you?   119
Your name, your quality? And why you answer
This present summons?

EDG.   Know my name is lost,
By treason's tooth bare-gnawn and canker-bit.°
Yet am I noble as the adversary
I come to cope.°

ALB.   Which is that adversary?

EDG. What's he that speaks for Edmund, Earl of
    Gloucester?   125

EDM. Himself. What say'st thou to him?

EDG.   Draw thy sword,
That if my speech offend a noble heart,
Thy arm may do thee justice. Here is mine.
Behold, it is the privilege of mine honors,
My oath, and my profession.° I protest,   130
Mauger° thy strength, youth, place, and eminence,
Despite thy victor sword and fire-new° fortune,
Thy valor and thy heart, thou art a traitor,
False to thy gods, thy brother, and thy father,
Conspirant° 'gainst this high illustrious Prince,   135
And from the extremest upward of thy head
To the descent and dust below thy foot
A most toad-spotted° traitor. Say thou " No,"
This sword, this arm, and my best spirits are bent
To prove upon thy heart, whereto I speak,   140
Thou liest.

EDM. In wisdom I should ask thy name,
But since thy outside looks so fair and warlike
And that thy tongue some say of breeding° breathes,
What safe and nicely° I might well delay
By rule of knighthood I disdain and spurn.   145
Back do I toss these treasons to thy head,
With the hell-hated lie o'erwhelm thy heart,
Which for they yet glance by and scarcely bruise,
This sword of mine shall give them instant way   149
Where they shall rest forever. Trumpets, speak!

        [*Alarums. They fight.* EDMUND *falls.*]

ALB. Save him, save him!

GON.   This is practice,° Gloucester.
By the law of arms thou wast not bound to answer
An unknown opposite. Thou art not vanquished,
But cozened° and beguiled.

ALB.   Shut your mouth, dame,
Or with this paper° shall I stop it. Hold, sir,   155

Thou worse than any name, read thine own evil.
No tearing, lady. I perceive you know it.

GON. Say if I do, the laws are mine, not thine.
Who can arraign me for 't?

ALB.   Most monstrous!   159
Know'st thou this paper?

GON.   Ask me not what I know. [*Exit.*]

ALB. Go after her. She's desperate, govern° her.

EDG. What you have charged me with, that have
    I done,
And more, much more. The time will bring it out.
'Tis past, and so am I. But what art thou
That hast this fortune on me? If thou 'rt noble,
I do forgive thee.

EDG.   Let's exchange charity.   166
I am no less in blood than thou art, Edmund.
If more, the more thou hast wronged me.
My name is Edgar, and thy father's son.
The gods are just, and of our pleasant vices   170
Make instruments to plague us.°
The dark and vicious place where thee he got°
Cost him his eyes.

EDM.   Thou hast spoken right, 'tis true.
The wheel is come full circle,° I am here.

ALB. Methought thy very gait did prophesy   175
A royal nobleness. I must embrace thee.
Let sorrow split my heart if ever I
Did hate thee or thy father!

EDG.   Worthy Prince, I know 't.

ALB. Where have you hid yourself?   179
How have you known the miseries of your father?

EDG. By nursing them, my lord. List a brief tale,
And when 'tis told, oh, that my heart would
    burst!
The bloody proclamation to escape°
That followed me so near — Oh, our lives' sweet-
    ness!
That we the pain of death would hourly die   185
Rather than die at once!° — taught me to shift
Into a madman's rags, to assume a semblance
That very dogs disdained. And in this habit
Met I my father with his bleeding rings,   189
Their precious stones new-lost, became his guide,
Led him, begged for him, saved him from despair,
Never — oh, fault! — revealed myself unto him
Until some half-hour past, when I was armed.
Not sure, though hoping, of this good success,
I asked his blessing, and from first to last   195
Told him my pilgrimage. But his flawed heart —
Alack, too weak the conflict to support! —
'Twixt two extremes of passion, joy and grief,

118–19. Ask . . . trumpet: The combat follows the normal procedure of chivalry. Cf. *Rich II*, I.iii. Edgar is wearing full
armor, his face concealed by his closed helmet. See Pl. 8a.
122. canker-bit: corrupted by maggots.   124. cope: meet, encounter.   130. profession: i.e., as a knight.   131. Mauger:
in spite of.   132. fire-new: brand-new — like a new coin.
135. Conspirant: conspiring.   138. toad-spotted: i.e., venomous
as a toad. Cf. *AYLI*, II.i.13.   143. say of breeding: accent
of a gentleman.   144. nicely: i.e., if I stood on niceties of
procedure.   151. practice: treachery.   154. cozened: cheated.
155. this paper: her love letter to Edmund, which Edgar had
taken from Oswald's corpse. See IV.vi.267–76.

161. govern: control.   170–71. of . . . us: This is the answer to
Gloucester's lighthearted words at the opening of the play — " Do
you smell a fault?" (I.i.16)   172. got: begot.   174. The . . .
circle: i.e., I end as I began — an outcast of fortune.   183. The
. . . escape: in order to escape after the proclamation for my arrest. See II.iii.1.   184–86. Oh . . . once: life is so sweet to us that
we will endure the pains of death hourly if only we can live.

Burst smilingly.°

EDM.   This speech of yours hath moved me,
And shall perchance do good. But speak you on.
You look as you had something more to say.   201

ALB. If there be more, more woeful, hold it in,
For I am almost ready to dissolve,
Hearing of this.

EDG.   This would have seemed a period°
To such as love not sorrow, but another,   205
To amplify too much, would make much more,
And top extremity.°
Whilst I was big in clamor,° came there in a man
Who, having seen me in my worst estate,   209
Shunned my abhorred society. But then, finding
Who 'twas that so endured, with his strong arms
He fastened on my neck, and bellowed out
As he'd burst heaven, threw him on my father,
Told the most piteous tale of Lear and him
That ever ear received. Which in recounting   215
His grief grew puissant,° and the strings of life°
Began to crack. Twice then the trumpets sounded,
And there I left him tranced.°

ALB.   But who was this?

EDG. Kent, sir, the banished Kent, who in disguise
Followed his enemy King,° and did him service
Improper for a slave.   221

[*Enter a* GENTLEMAN, *with a bloody knife.*]

GENT. Help, help, oh, help!

EDG.   What kind of help?

ALB.   Speak, man.

EDG. What means this bloody knife?

GENT.   'Tis hot, it smokes.
It came even from the heart of — oh, she's dead!

ALB. Who dead? Speak, man.   225

GENT. Your lady, sir, your lady. And her sister
By her is poisoned. She hath confessed it.

EDM. I was contracted° to them both. All three
Now marry in an instant.

EDG.   Here comes Kent.   229

ALB. Produce the bodies, be they alive or dead.
       [*Exit* GENTLEMAN.]
This judgment of the Heavens, that makes us tremble,
Touches us not with pity.
       [*Enter* KENT.] Oh, is this he?
The time will not allow the compliment
Which very manners urges.

KENT.   I am come
To bid my King and master aye good night.   235
Is he not here?

ALB.   Great thing of us forgot!

Speak, Edmund, where's the King? And where's
Cordelia?
See's thou this object, Kent?

[*The bodies of* GONERIL *and* REGAN *are brought in.*]

KENT. Alack, why thus?

EDM.   Yet Edmund was beloved.°
The one the other poisoned for my sake,   240
And after slew herself.

ALB. Even so. Cover their faces.

EDM. I pant for life. Some good I mean to do,
Despite of mine own nature. Quickly send —
Be brief in it — to the castle, for my writ   245
Is on the life of Lear and on Cordelia.
Nay, send in time.

ALB.   Run, run, oh, run!

EDG. To who, my lord? Who hath the office? Send
Thy token of reprieve.°

EDM. Well thought on. Take my sword.   250
Give it the Captain.

ALB.   Haste thee, for thy life.   [*Exit* EDGAR.]

EDM. He hath commission from thy wife and me
To hang Cordelia in the prison and
To lay the blame upon her own despair,
That she fordid° herself.   255

ALB. The gods defend her! Bear him hence
awhile.   [EDMUND *is borne off.*]

[*Re-enter* LEAR, *with* CORDELIA *dead in his arms,*
EDGAR, CAPTAIN, *and others following.*]

LEAR. Howl, howl, howl, howl! Oh, you are men
of stones.
Had I your tongues and eyes, I'd use them so
That heaven's vault should crack. She's gone forever!
I know when one is dead and when one lives.   260
She's dead as earth. Lend me a looking-glass.
If that her breath will mist or stain the stone,°
Why, then she lives.

KENT.   Is this the promised end?°

EDG. Or image of that horror?

ALB.   Fall and cease.°

LEAR. This feather stirs, she lives. If it be so,   265
It is a chance which does redeem all sorrows
That ever I have felt.

KENT. [*Kneeling*] Oh, my good master!

LEAR. Prithee, away.

EDG.   'Tis noble Kent, your friend.

LEAR. A plague upon you, murderers, traitors all!
I might have saved her. Now she's gone forever!
Cordelia, Cordelia! Stay a little. Ha!   270
What is 't thou say'st? Her voice was ever soft,
Gentle and low, an excellent thing in woman.
I killed the slave that was a-hanging thee.

CAPT. 'Tis true, my lords, he did.

196–99. But . . . smilingly: In the performance the significance of Edgar's speech can easily be missed. Gloucester has died from excessive emotion (*passion*), and Kent is near his end. 204. period: end. 207. top extremity: exceed the extreme limit of what could be endured. 208. clamor: grief. 216. puissant: powerful, overwhelming. strings of life: heartstrings. 218. tranced: in a faint. 220. enemy King: the King who had declared him an enemy. 228. contracted: betrothed.

239. Yet . . . beloved: The bastard's last grim triumph — two women died for his love. 249. token of reprieve: sign that the are reprieved. 255. fordid: destroyed. 262. stone: glas 263. the . . . end: i.e., Doomsday. 264. Fall . . . cease: i.e let Doomsday come and the world end.

LEAR.   Did I not, fellow?   275
I have seen the day with my good biting falchion°
I would have made them skip. I am old now,
And these same crosses° spoil me. Who are you?⌉
Mine eyes are not o' the best, I'll tell you straight⌋

KENT. If fortune brag of two she loved and hated,
One of them we behold.   281

LEAR. This is a dull sight. Are you not Kent?

KENT.   The same,
Your servant Kent. Where is your servant Caius?

LEAR. He's a good fellow, I can tell you that.   284
He'll strike, and quickly too. He's dead and rotten.

KENT. No, my good lord, I am the very man°——

LEAR. I'll see that straight.

KENT. That from your first of difference° and decay
Have followed your sad steps.

LEAR.   You are welcome hither.

KENT. Nor no man else. All's cheerless, dark, and
deadly.   290
Your eldest daughters have fordone themselves,
And desperately are dead.

LEAR.   Aye, so I think.

ALB. He knows not what he says, and vain is it
That we present us to him.

EDG.   Very bootless.°

[Enter a CAPTAIN.]

CAPT. Edmund is dead, my lord.

ALB.   That's but a trifle here.   295
You lords and noble friends, know our intent.
What comfort to this great decay° may come
Shall be applied. For us, we will resign,
During the life of this old Majesty,
To him our absolute power.

[To EDGAR and KENT] You, to your rights,   300
With boot,° and such addition as your honors
Have more than merited. All friends shall taste
The wages of their virtue, and all foes
The cup of their deservings. Oh, see, see!°

LEAR. And my poor fool° is hanged! No, no, no⌉
life!   305
Why should a dog, a horse, a rat, have life
And thou no breath at all? Thou'lt come no more,
Never, never, never, never, never!
Pray you, undo this button.° Thank you, sir.
Do you see this? Look on her, look, her lips,⌉   310
Look there, look there!   ⌐Dies.⌉

EDG.   He faints. My lord, my lord!

KENT. Break, heart, I prithee break!

EDG.   Look up, my lord.

KENT. Vex not his ghost. Oh, let him pass! He
hates him
That would upon the rack° of this tough world
Stretch him out longer.

EDG.   He is gone indeed.   315

KENT. The wonder is he hath endured so long.
He but usurped his life.

ALB. Bear them from hence. Our present business
Is general woe. [To KENT and EDGAR] Friends of my
soul, you twain
Rule in this realm and the gored state sustain.   320

KENT. I have a journey, sir, shortly to go.
My master calls me,° I must not say no.

ALB. The weight of this sad time we must obey,
Speak what we feel, not what we ought to say.   324
The oldest hath borne most. We that are young
Shall never see so much, nor live so long.

[Exeunt, with a dead march.]

---

276. **falchion:** curved sword. 278. **crosses:** troubles. 283–86. **Your . . . man:** This is the first and only mention of a Caius, which was apparently the name assumed by Kent in his disguise. 288. **difference:** changed state. 294. **bootless:** useless. 297. **decay:** i.e., Lear.

301. **boot:** advantage. 304. **Oh . . . see:** There is a sudden change in Lear. 305. **fool:** Cordelia; *fool* is often used as a term of affection. 309. **Pray . . . button:** For the last time Lear is oppressed by the violent beating of his heart before it is stilled forever. 314. **rack:** See App. 10. 322. **calls me:** i.e., to follow him into the darkness.

THE TRAGEDY OF MACBETH

Introduction

In some ways *The Tragedy of Macbeth* is the least satisfactory of the four great tragedies, though the great scenes — the murder of Duncan, the banquet scene, the sleepwalking scene — are as powerful as anything Shakespeare ever wrote. Apart from Macbeth and his wife, the characterization — especially of the minor persons — is far less detailed than in *Lear* or *Hamlet*. Indeed there is a general agreement amongst scholars that *Macbeth* has not been finished with the same care as the others and that other hands than Shakespeare's have contributed to the play. The speech of the bleeding captain, if not the whole of I.ii, and the operatic episode between Hecate and the witches (III.v and IV.i) are not in Shakespeare's manner. Thomas Middleton, who wrote a play called *The Witch* about 1612, is often considered the author of these passages, especially as the songs to which reference is made in the stage directions of IV.i are given in full in *The Witch*.

There are other indications in the text itself, either that Shakespeare was himself revising or rewriting an old play, or that he had a collaborator. These are most noticeable in the last Act, where the rhymes and diction are often feeble or forced, and the rhythm unlike Shakespeare's. The differences can best be seen by comparing two small link scenes. These are II.iv and III.vi. The conversation in the first scene between Ross and the old man is not in Shakespeare's usual style, while the speech of Lennox is by contrast full of the subtlest tones and hints of meaning.

Macbeth was probably written in 1606. The remarks of the Porter about equivocation — "Faith here's an equivocator, that could swear in both the scales against either scale, who committed treason enough for God's sake, yet could not equivocate to Heaven" — are a likely reference to the notorious trial and execution of Father Garnet for being an accessory to the Gunpowder Plot. Garnet admitted that he had deliberately deceived his accusers, and justified himself by the doctrine of equivocation (see Gen. Intro. p. 17a and App. 20).

If, as is likely, the inconsistencies of style are due to hasty writing, then it is possible that the play was written by command as one of the plays to be given before King James I and the King of Denmark during the latter's notable visit to England in the summer of 1606. Shakespeare's company were the King's Players, and it would be natural for them to be commanded to produce a story of Scottish history touching on the ancestry of their patron. In the previous summer, when King James made a visit in state to the University of Oxford, three little boys, dressed as nymphs, greeted him with a short Latin speech, reminding him of the ancient legend of the Three Sisters who had prophesied future glory to Banquo's descendants.

Macbeth was being played in London in 1611, and was one of several plays visited by Dr. Simon Forman, a well-known astrologer of the time, who wrote as follows:[1]

In *Macbeth* at the Globe, 1610 (1611), the 20 of April (Saturday), there was to be observed, first, how Macbeth and Banquo, two noblemen of Scotland, riding through a wood; there stood before them three women fairies or nymphs, and saluted Macbeth, saying three times unto him, " Hail Macbeth, King of Codon [Cawdor]; for thou shalt be a king, but shalt beget no kings, etc." Then said Banquo, " What, all to Macbeth and nothing to me? " " Yes," said the nymphs, " hail to thee Banquo, thou shalt beget kings, yet be no king." And so they departed and came to the court of Scotland, to Duncan, King of Scots, and it was in the days of Edward the Confessor. And Duncan bade them both kindly welcome, and made Macbeth forthwith Prince of Northumberland, and sent him home to his own castle; and appointed Macbeth to provide for him, for he would sup with him the next day at night; and did so. And Macbeth contrived to kill Duncan and through the persuasion of his wife did that night murder the king in his own castle, being his guest. And there were many prodigies seen that night and the day before. And when Macbeth had murdered the king, the blood on his hands could not be washed off by any means, nor from his wife's hands, which handled the bloody daggers in hiding them; by which

[1] E. K. Chambers, *William Shakespeare*, II, 337. The original manuscript is in the Bodleian Library at Oxford; its genuineness was at one time suspected but has now been established.

means they became both much amazed and affronted. The murder being known, Duncan's two sons fled, the one to England, the [other to] Wales, to save themselves. They being fled, they were supposed guilty of the murder of their father, which was nothing so. Then was Macbeth crowned king; and then he for fear of Banquo, his old companion, that he should beget kings but be no king himself, he contrived the death of Banquo, and caused him to be murdered on the way as he rode. The next night, being at supper with his noblemen whom he had bid to a feast, to the which also Banquo should have come, he began to speak of noble Banquo, and to wish that he were there. And as he thus did, standing up to drink a carouse to him, the ghost of Banquo came and sat down in his chair behind him. And he, turning about to sit down again, saw the ghost of Banquo, which fronted him so, that he fell into a great passion of fear and fury, uttering many words about his murder; by which, when they heard that Banquo was murdered they suspected Macbeth.

Then Macduff fled to England to the king's son; and so they raised an army, and came into Scotland. And at Dunston Anyse [Dunsinane] overthrew Macbeth. In the meantime while Macduff was in England, Macbeth slew Macduff's wife and children, and after in the battle Macduff slew Macbeth.

Observe also how Macbeth's queen did rise in the night in her sleep and walk, and talked and confessed all, and the doctor noted her words.

Macbeth was first printed in F1 in 1623, where the text is not very satisfactory and shows some signs of cutting and alteration. The main story of the play was derived from two episodes in Holinshed's *Chronicles*. The first is the history of Macbeth, from which the main outline of the plot was taken. The second, which provided the details of the murder of Duncan, is the story of the murder of King Duff by Donwald, who also was encouraged by an ambitious wife. The story of Macbeth was followed fairly closely. In Holinshed, the incident of the three witches is thus told:

Shortly after happened a strange and uncouth wonder, which afterward was the cause of much trouble in the realm of Scotland, as ye shall after hear. It fortuned as Macbeth and Banquo journeyed toward Forres, where the King then lay, they went sporting by the way together without other company, save only themselves, passing through the woods and fields, when suddenly in the midst of a laund [lawn, open place] there met them three women in strange and wild apparel, resembling creatures of elder world, whom when they atten-

tively beheld, wondering much at the sight, the first of them spake and said: " All hail, Macbeth, Thane of Glammis! " (for he had lately entered into that dignity and office by the death of his father Sinell). The second of them said: " Hail, Macbeth, Thane of Cawder! " But the third said: " All hail, Macbeth, that hereafter shalt be King of Scotland! "

Then Banquo: " What manner of women " (saith he) " are you, that seem so little favorable unto me, whereas to my fellow here, besides high offices, ye assign also the kingdom, appointing forth nothing for me at all? " " Yes," (saith the first of them) " we promise greater benefits unto thee than unto him, for he shall reign indeed, but with an unlucky end; neither shall he leave any issue behind him to succeed in his place, where contrarily thou indeed shalt not reign at all, but of thee those shall be born which shall govern the Scottish kingdom by long order of continual descent." Herewith the foresaid women vanished immediately out of their sight. This was reputed at the first but some vain fantastical illusion by Macbeth and Banquo, insomuch that Banquo would call Macbeth, in jest, King of Scotland, and Macbeth again would call him in sport likewise the father of many kings. But afterward the common opinion was that these women were either the weird sisters, that is (as ye would say) the goddesses of destiny, or else some nymphs or fairies, imbued with knowledge of prophecy by their necromantical science, because everything came to pass as they had spoken. For shortly after, the Thane of Cawder being condemned at Forres of treason against the King committed, his lands, livings, and offices were given of the King's liberality to Macbeth.

The same night after, at supper, Banquo jested with him and said: " Now, Macbeth, thou hast obtained those things which the two former sisters prophesied, there remaineth only for thee to purchase that which the third said should come to pass." Whereupon Macbeth revolving the thing in his mind, began even then to devise how he might attain to the kingdom; but yet he thought with himself that he must tarry a time, which should advance him thereto (by the divine Providence) as it had come to pass in his former preferment. But shortly after it chanced that King Duncan, having two sons by his wife which was the daughter of Siward, Earl of Northumberland, he made the elder of them, called Malcolm, Prince of Cumberland, as it were thereby to appoint him his successor in the kingdom, immediately after his decease. Macbeth, sore troubled herewith, for that he saw by this means his hope sore hindered (where, by the old laws of the realm, the ordinance was that if he that should succeed were not of able age to take the charge upon himself, he that was next of blood unto him should be admitted), he began to take counsel how he might usurp the kingdom by force, having a just quarrel so to do (as he took the matter) for that Duncan did what in him lay to defraud him of all manner of title and claim which he might in time to come pretend unto the crown.

The words of the three weird sisters also (of whom before you have heard) greatly encouraged him hereunto, but specially his wife lay sore upon him to attempt the thing, as she that was very ambitious, burning in unquenchable desire to bear the name of a Queen. At length therefore, communicating his purposed intent with his trusty friends, amongst whom Banquo was the chiefest, upon confidence of their promised aid, he slew the King at Enverns [Inverness], or (as some say) at Botgosvane, in the sixth year of his reign. Then having a company about him of such as he had made privy to his enterprise, he caused himself to be proclaimed King, and forthwith went unto Scone, where (by common consent) he received the investure of the kingdom according to the accustomed manner. The body of Duncan was first conveyed unto Elgin, and there buried in kingly wise; but afterward it was removed and conveyed unto Colmekill, and there laid in a sepulcher amongst his predecessors, in the year after the birth of our Saviour, 1046.

The murder of King Duff by Donwald was thus described:

Donwald thus being the more kindled in wrath by the words of his wife, determined to follow her advice in the execution of so heinous an act. Whereupon devising with himself for a while, which way he might best accomplish his cursed intent, at length gat opportunity, and sped his purpose as followeth. It chanced that the King, upon the day before he purposed to depart forth of the castle, was long in his oratory at his prayers, and there continued till it was late in the night. At the last, coming forth, he called such afore him as had faithfully served him in pursuit and apprehension of the rebels, and giving them hearty thanks, he bestowed sundry honorable gifts amongst them, of the which number Donwald was one, as he that had been ever accounted a most faithful servant to the King.

At length, having talked with them a long time, he got him into his privy chamber, only with two of his chamberlains, who having brought him to bed, came forth again, and then fell to banqueting with Donwald and his wife, who had prepared divers delicate dishes, and sundry sorts of drinks for their rear supper or collation, whereat they sat up so long till they had charged their stomachs with such full gorges that their heads were no sooner got to the pillow but asleep they were so fast that a man might have removed the chamber over them sooner than to have awakened them out of their drunken sleep.

Then Donwald, though he abhorred the act greatly in heart, yet through instigation of his wife he called four of his servants unto him (whom he had made privy to his wicked intent before, and framed to his purpose with large gifts) and now declaring unto them after what sort they should work the feat, they gladly obeyed his instructions, and speedily going about the murder they enter the chamber (in which the King lay) a little before cock's crow, where they secretly cut his throat as he lay sleeping, without any buskling [bustling, noise] at all; and immediately by a postern gate they carried forth the dead body into the fields, and throwing it upon an horse there provided ready for that purpose, they convey it unto a place about two miles distant from the castle, where they stayed, and gat certain laborers to help them to turn the course of a little river running through the fields there, and digging a deep hole in the channel, they bury the body in the same, ramming it up with stones and gravel so closely that setting the water in the right course again, no man could perceive that anything had been newly digged there. This they did by order appointed them by Donwald as is reported, for that the body should not be found and by bleeding (when Donwald should be present) declare him to be guilty of the murder. For such an opinion men have, that the dead corpse of any man being slain will bleed abundantly if the murderer be present. But for what consideration soever they buried him there, they had no sooner finished the work but that they slew them whose help they used herein, and straightwise thereupon fled into Orkney.

Donwald, about the time that the murder was in doing, got him amongst them that kept the watch, and so continued in company with them all the residue of the night. But in the morning when the noise was raised in the King's chamber how the King was slain, his body conveyed away, and the bed all berayed with blood, he with the watch ran thither, as though he had known nothing of the matter, and breaking into the chamber and finding cakes of blood in the bed and on the floor about the sides of it, he forthwith slew the chamberlains, as guilty of that heinous murder, and then like a mad man running to and fro, he ransacked every corner within the castle as though it had been to have seen if he might have found either the body or any of the murderers hid in any privy place. But at length coming to the postern gate and finding it open, he burdened [accused] the chamberlains, whom he had slain, with all the fault, they having the keys of the gates committed to their keeping all the night, and therefore it could not be otherwise (said he) but that they were of counsel in committing of that most detestable murder.

Finally, such was his own earnest diligence in the

severe inquisition and trial of the offenders herein, that some of the lords began to mislike the matter, and to smell forth shrewd tokens that he should not be altogether clear himself. But for so much as they were in that country, where he had the whole rule, what by reason of his friends and authority together, they doubted to utter what they thought, till time and place should better serve thereunto, and hereupon they got them away every man to his home.

According to the *Chronicles,* Macbeth reigned well for some years, until he began to brood on the words of the three weird sisters that the kingdom should come to Banquo's posterity. He therefore planned to have Banquo slain, but Fleance, Banquo's son, escaped. Hereafter Macbeth's character degenerated until " he found such sweetness by putting his nobles thus to death that his earnest thirst for blood in his own behalf might in no wise be satisfied." He was warned by a prophecy against Macduff:

And surely hereupon had he put Macduff to death, but that a certain witch, whom he had in great trust, had told that he should never be slain with man born of any woman, nor vanquished till the wood of Bernane came to the castle of Dunsinane. By this prophecy Macbeth put all fear out of his heart, supposing he might do what he would, without any fear to be punished for the same, for by the one prophecy he believed it was impossible for any man to vanquish him, and by the other impossible to slay him. This vain hope caused him to do many outrageous things, to the grievous oppression of his subjects. At length Macduff, to avoid peril of life, purposed with himself to pass into England, to procure Malcolm Cammore to claim the crown of Scotland. But this was not so secretly devised by Macduff but that Macbeth had knowledge given him thereof; for kings (as is said) have sharp sight like unto lynx, and long ears like unto Midas. For Macbeth had, in every nobleman's house, one sly fellow or other in fee with him, to reveal all that was said or done within the same, by which sight he oppressed the most part of the nobles of his realm."

The long passage between Malcolm and Macduff (IV.iii) follows the *Chronicles* closely, for Holinshed recorded the conversation at some length; but the final battle in which Macbeth was killed took place not in Dunsinane castle but on the open field; Macduff pursued Macbeth on horseback and overtook him. Then:

Macbeth, perceiving that Macduff was hard at his back, leapt beside his horse, saying: " Thou traitor, what meaneth it that thou shouldest thus in vain follow me that am not appointed to be slain by any creature that is born of a woman? Come on therefore, and receive thy reward which thou has deserved for thy pains! " and therewithal he lifted up his sword, thinking to have slain him.

But Macduff, quickly avoiding from his horse, ere he came at him, answered (with his naked sword in his hand) saying: " It is true, Macbeth, and now shall thine insatiable cruelty have an end, for I am even he that thy wizards have told thee of, who was never born of my mother, but ripped out of her womb." Therewithal he stepped unto him, and slew him in the place. Then cutting his head from his shoulders, he set it upon a pole, and brought it unto Malcolm. This was the end of Macbeth, after he had reigned seventeen years over the Scottishmen.

To a greater extent than the other great tragedies *Macbeth* is a tragedy of fate. All the tragedies illustrate the idea that there's a divinity that shapes our ends. It may simply be a comet which foretells the death of princes, or the darker feeling that

As flies to wanton boys are we to the gods.
They kill us for their sport.

Yet, until the end, some way of escape seems possible. But Macbeth from the beginning is the plaything of that evil power which uses the witches as his ministers. When Macbeth first appears with Banquo, he has been brooding on treason, and the prophecy that he shall be " Thane of Cawdor " and " King hereafter " comes pat on his thoughts. The first prophecy is fulfilled at once. Thereafter Macbeth is caught by fate.

Macbeth's character is a mixture of good and evil qualities. He has bravery and nobility counterbalanced by ambition. Above all he is controlled by an overpowering imagination which makes him see not only what the results of an action will be, but also its essential meaning. The third scene ends with the tragic foreboding that the prophecy will be fulfilled; Macbeth has already foreseen the manner of its fulfilling and he is horrified by the sight. Nevertheless his loyalty and his ambition are evenly balanced until he comes into the presence of his wife. Lady Macbeth is at the same time greater and lesser than her husband. She has a hardness which he lacks, but she has none of his subtlety and perception. She knows her husband well and despises him a little, but to satisfy her ambition, which is the crude desire to have her man King, she will devote herself soul and body to evil.

So the murder is accomplished, although Macbeth realizes that this deed is not only evil in itself, but will bring inevitable retribution. When Duncan is dead, the contrast between man and wife becomes more vivid. Macbeth is overwhelmed with the significance of his filthy deed. His wife is concerned only with the details of what must be done next — with facts. She has no imagination. This passage between Macbeth and Lady Macbeth after the murder is one of the finest examples of " atmosphere " ever created in drama.

The imagery used in this scene, and indeed throughout the whole play, is notable. Three ideas are predominant; blood, water, and darkness. From this point onward, the tragedy is splashed with blood. Once the murder has been committed, the blood of Duncan drips down the stairs after Macbeth until it pervades his whole universe, and he stands alone in a universal sea of blood. Lady Macbeth still thinks that a little water will clear them of this deed; Macbeth knows that all great Neptune's ocean will never make them clean.

Upon this intensity of horror breaks in the knocking. Coleridge objected to this vulgar porter, but he is dramatically essential. After the intensity of what has just gone before, some change or explosion is necessary to release the emotional tension, and crude laughter is the most effective. It brings us back to earth. The murder is discovered, Malcolm and Donalbain escape, and Fate begins to turn her wheel.

This ends the first part of the play. The second part begins with Act III. Macbeth is King, and the third prophecy has been fulfilled; but there were other prophecies made to Banquo. Macbeth is beginning to realize that it has all been in vain. One murder begets another. Macbeth's degeneration is swift and terrible. Banquo is murdered,

and inevitably Fleance escapes. The second part of the play ends with the murder of Banquo.

Macbeth again seeks the witches; having no earthly friends, he will put his trust in them. As before, he is given three prophecies.

The last act brings the tragedy to its close. It begins with the sleepwalking scene, which sums up and concentrates the full horror of the whole business. The resistance of this hard, practical woman has broken down. She was the real cause and the agent of the tragedy. In the words which she utters in her sleep, she gives her own answer to the casual remark that " a little water clears us of this deed." This is the true dramatic irony, tragic and terrible, where the easiest remarks have the most ghastly significance and are echoed by a kind of devilish chuckle.

Macbeth now has only the prophecies left to defend and comfort him as the avengers gather round. Lady Macbeth is dying, and when he learns that she has gone the full realization of his own tragedy comes to him:

> Life's but a walking shadow, a poor player
> That struts and frets his hour upon the stage
> And then is heard no more. It is a tale
> Told by an idiot, full of sound and fury,
> Signifying nothing.

So everything was futile, the murder of Duncan and all the blood, for life itself has no meaning.

Two things are particularly worth noting about this play. The first is that *Macbeth* is a chronicle play and, as with Shakespeare's other plays of British history, Holinshed was its source. Yet Shakespeare has moved a long way from his last chronicle play of *Henry V*. The second is that Macbeth is a play with a villain as hero. It was twelve years since Shakespeare last wrote a chronicle with the villain as hero — *Richard III*. These two plays have much in common — ghosts, prophecies, spirits, ambitious villains, soliloquies, and the idea of a brooding fate; but a comparison of the two will show how Shakespeare had grown.

Macbeth

DRAMATIS PERSONAE

DUNCAN, *King of Scotland*
MALCOLM } *his sons*
DONALBAIN
MACBETH } *generals of the King's army*
BANQUO
MACDUFF
LENNOX
ROSS
MENTEITH } *noblemen of Scotland*
ANGUS
CAITHNESS
FLEANCE, *son to Banquo*
SIWARD, *Earl of Northumberland, general of the English forces*
YOUNG SIWARD, *his son*
SEYTON, *an officer attending on Macbeth*
BOY, *son to Macduff*

AN ENGLISH DOCTOR
A SCOTCH DOCTOR
A SERGEANT
A PORTER
AN OLD MAN

LADY MACBETH
LADY MACDUFF
GENTLEWOMAN *attending on Lady Macbeth*

HECATE
THREE WITCHES
APPARITIONS
LORDS, GENTLEMEN, OFFICERS, SOLDIERS, MURDERERS, ATTENDANTS, AND MESSENGERS

SCENE — *Scotland; England.*

Act I

SCENE I. *A desert place.*

[*Thunder and lightning. Enter* THREE WITCHES.°]
1. WITCH. When shall we three meet again
In thunder, lightning, or in rain?
2. WITCH. When the hurly-burly's° done,
When the battle's lost and won.
3. WITCH. That will be ere the set of sun.   5
1. WITCH. Where the place?
2. WITCH.   Upon the heath.
3. WITCH. There to meet with Macbeth.
1. WITCH. I come, Graymalkin.°
ALL. Paddock° calls. — Anon!°   10
Fair is foul, and foul is fair.
Hover through the fog and filthy air.   [*Exeunt.*]

SCENE II. *A camp near Forres.*

[*Alarum within.*° *Enter* DUNCAN, MALCOLM,
DONALBAIN, LENNOX, *with* ATTENDANTS,
meeting a bleeding SERGEANT.]
DUN. What bloody man is that? He can report,
As seemeth by his plight, of the revolt
The newest state.
MAL.   This is the sergeant

Act I, Sc. i: s.d., Enter . . . witches: See App. 23.   3. hurly-burly: commotion.   9. Graymalkin: a common name for a gray cat; it is the First Witch's familiar spirit.   10. Paddock: toad. Anon: at once, "I am coming."
Sc. ii: s.d., Alarum within: trumpet call to arms, off stage.

Who like a good and hardy soldier fought
'Gainst my captivity. Hail, brave friend!   5
Say to the King the knowledge of the broil
As thou didst leave it.
SERG.   Doubtful it stood,
As two spent swimmers that do cling together
And choke their art.° The merciless Macdonwald —
Worthy to be a rebel, for to that   10
The multiplying villainies of nature
Do swarm upon him — from the western isles
Of kerns and gallowglasses° is supplied.°
And fortune, on his damnèd quarrel smiling,
Showed° like a rebel's whore. But all's too weak.   15
For brave Macbeth — well he deserves that name —
Disdaining fortune, with his brandished steel,
Which smoked with bloody execution,
Like valor's minion° carvèd out his passage
Till he faced the slave,   20
Which ne'er shook hands, nor bade farewell to him,
Till he unseamed him° from the nave to the chaps,°
And fixed his head upon our battlements.
DUN. Oh, valiant Cousin! Worthy gentleman!
SERG. As whence the sun 'gins his reflection°   25
Shipwrecking storms and direful thunders break,
So from that spring whence comfort seemed to come

9. choke . . . art: i.e., prevent each other from swimming. art: skill.   13. kerns . . . gallowglasses: types of wild Irish soldiers. The kern fought on foot, the gallowglass was armed with an ax and fought on horseback. supplied: aided.   15. Showed: appeared.   19. minion: darling.   22. unseamed him: ripped Macdonwald open. nave . . . chaps: from navel to cheeks.   25. whence . . . reflection: from that quarter where the sun first appears; i.e., the east.

Discomfort swells. Mark, King of Scotland, mark.
No sooner justice had, with valor armed,
Compelled these skipping kerns to trust their heels,
But the Norweyan° lord, surveying vantage,°   31
With furbished° arms and new supplies of men,
Began a fresh assault.
    DUN.   Dismayed not this
Our captains, Macbeth and Banquo?
    SERG.   Yes,
As sparrows eagles, or the hare the lion.   35
If I say sooth,° I must report they were
As cannons overcharged with double cracks,°
So they
Doubly redoubled strokes upon the foe.
Except they meant to bathe in reeking° wounds,
Or memorize another Golgotha,°   40
I cannot tell ——
But I am faint, my gashes cry for help.
    DUN. So well thy words become thee as thy
      wounds.
They smack of honor both. Go get him surgeons.
                   [Exit SERGEANT, *attended.]*
Who comes here?
               [Enter ROSS.]
    MAL.   The worthy Thane° of Ross.   45
    LEN. What a haste looks through his eyes! So
      should he look
That seems to speak things strange.
    ROSS.   God save the King!
    DUN. Whence camest thou, worthy Thane?
    ROSS.   From Fife, great King,
Where the Norweyan banners flout° the sky
And fan our people cold.   50
Norway himself, with terrible numbers,
Assisted by that most disloyal traitor
The Thane of Cawdor, began a dismal conflict,
Till that Bellona's bridegroom,° lapped in proof,°
Confronted him with self-comparisons,°   55
Point against point rebellious, arm 'gainst arm,
Curbing his lavish° spirit. And, to conclude,
The victory fell on us.
    DUN.   Great happiness!
    ROSS. That now
Sweno, the Norways' king, craves composition.°
Nor would we deign him burial of his men   60
Till he disbursèd, at Saint Colme's inch,°

Ten thousand dollars to our general use.
    DUN. No more that Thane of Cawdor shall de-
      ceive
Our bosom interest.° Go pronounce his present°
    death,
And with his former title greet Macbeth.   65
    ROSS. I'll see it done.
    DUN. What he hath lost noble Macbeth hath won.
                          [Exeunt.]

SCENE III. *A heath.*

    [Thunder. Enter the THREE WITCHES.]
    1. WITCH. Where hast thou been, Sister?
    2. WITCH. Killing swine.°
    3. WITCH. Sister, where thou?
    1. WITCH. A sailor's wife had chestnuts in her lap,
And mounched, and mounched, and mounched.
    "Give me," quoth I.   5
"Aroint thee,° witch!" the rump-fed° ronyon°
    cries.
Her husband's to Aleppo gone, master o' the *Tiger.*
But in a sieve I'll thither sail
And, like a rat without a tail,
I'll do, I'll do, and I'll do.   10
    2. WITCH. I'll give thee a wind.
    1. WITCH. Thou'rt kind.
    3. WITCH. And I another.
    1. WITCH. I myself have all the other,
And the very ports they blow,°   15
All the quarters that they know
I' the shipman's card.°
I will drain him dry as hay.
Sleep shall neither night nor day
Hang upon his penthouse lid.°   20
He shall live a man forbid.°
Weary sennights° nine times nine
Shall he dwindle, peak,° and pine.
Though his bark° cannot be lost,
Yet it shall be tempest-tost.   25
Look what I have.
    2. WITCH. Show me, show me.
    1. WITCH. Here I have a pilot's thumb,
Wrecked as homeward he did come.
                     [Drum within.]
    3. WITCH. A drum, a drum!   30
Macbeth doth come.

ALL. The weird° sisters, hand in hand,
Posters° of the sea and land,
Thus do go about, about.
Thrice to thine, and thrice to mine,   35
And thrice again, to make up nine.
Peace! The charm's wound up.°

[*Enter* MACBETH *and* BANQUO.]

MACB. So foul and fair a day I have not seen.

BAN. How far is 't called to Forres?° What are these
So withered, and so wild in their attire,   40
That look not like the inhabitants o' the earth
And yet are on 't? Live you? Or are you aught
That man may question? You seem to understand me,
By each at once her choppy° finger laying
Upon her skinny lips. You should be women,   45
And yet your beards° forbid me to interpret
That you are so.

MACB.   Speak, if you can. What are you?

1. WITCH. All hail, Macbeth! Hail to thee, Thane of Glamis!

2. WITCH. All hail, Macbeth! Hail to thee, Thane of Cawdor!

3. WITCH. All hail, Macbeth, that shalt be King hereafter!   50

BAN. Good sir, why do you start, and seem to fear
Things that do sound so fair? I' the name of truth,
Are ye fantastical,° or that indeed
Which outwardly ye show? My noble partner
You greet with present grace and great prediction
Of noble having° and of royal hope,   56
That he seems rapt° withal. To me you speak not.
If you can look into the seeds of time
And say which grain will grow and which will not,
Speak then to me, who neither beg nor fear   60
Your favors nor your hate.

1. WITCH. Hail!

2. WITCH. Hail!

3. WITCH. Hail!

1. WITCH. Lesser than Macbeth, and greater.   65

2. WITCH. Not so happy,° yet much happier.

3. WITCH. Thou shalt get° kings, though thou be none.

So all hail, Macbeth and Banquo!

1. WITCH. Banquo and Macbeth, all hail!   69

MACB. Stay, you imperfect speakers, tell me more.
By Sinel's° death I know I am Thane of Glamis,
But how of Cawdor? The Thane of Cawdor lives,

A prosperous gentleman, and to be King
Stands not within the prospect of belief,
No more than to be Cawdor. Say from whence   75
You owe° this strange intelligence?° Or why
Upon this blasted heath you stop our way
With such prophetic greeting? Speak, I charge you.

[WITCHES *vanish*.]

BAN. The earth hath bubbles as the water has,   79
And these are of them. Whither are they vanished?

MACB. Into the air, and what seemed corporal° melted
As breath into the wind. Would they had stayed!

BAN. Were such things here as we do speak about?
Or have we eaten on the insane root°
That takes the reason prisoner?   85

MACB. Your children shall be kings.

BAN.   You shall be King.

MACB. And Thane of Cawdor too. Went it not so?

BAN. To the selfsame tune and words. Who's here?

[*Enter* ROSS *and* ANGUS.]

ROSS. The King hath happily received, Macbeth,
The news of thy success. And when he reads   90
Thy personal venture in the rebels' fight,
His wonders and his praises do contend
Which should be thine or his.° Silenced° with that,
In viewing o'er the rest o' the selfsame day,
He finds thee in the stout Norweyan ranks,   95
Nothing afeard of what thyself didst make,
Strange images of death.° As thick as hail
Came post with post,° and every one did bear
Thy praises in his kingdom's great defense,
And poured them down before him.

ANG.   We are sent   100
To give thee, from our royal master, thanks,
Only to herald thee° into his sight,
Not pay thee.

ROSS. And for an earnest° of a greater honor,
He bade me, from him, call thee Thane of Cawdor.
In which addition,° hail, most worthy Thane!   106
For it is thine.

BAN.   What, can the Devil speak true?

MACB. The Thane of Cawdor lives. Why do you dress me
In borrowed robes?

ANG.   Who was the Thane lives yet,
But under heavy judgment bears that life   110
Which he deserves to lose. Whether he was combined

---

32. weird: having to do with destiny, spelt "weyard" and "weyward" in F₁.   **33. Posters:** quick riders.   **37. wound up:** i.e., completed.   **39. Forres:** a town about 25 miles from Inverness.   **44. choppy:** chapped.   **46. your beards:** For a woman to have a beard was sinister. When Falstaff escapes disguised as a witch, Parson Evans remarks, "By yea and no, I think the 'oman is a witch indeed. I like not when a 'oman has a great peard." (*Merry Wives*, I.v.202)   **53. fantastical:** creatures of the imagination.   **56. having:** possessions.   **57. rapt:** in a trance.   **66. happy:** lucky.   **67. get:** beget.   **71. Sinel:** Macbeth's father.

76. owe: own, possess. **intelligence:** knowledge.   **81. corporal:** corporeal, of bodily substance.   **84. insane root:** henbane or hemlock, supposed to cause madness.   **93. thine or his:** whether he should wonder or praise you. **Silenced:** speechless with admiration.   **97. Strange . . . death:** i.e., Macbeth was threatened with death, and caused death.   **98. post . . . post:** See App. 17.   **102. herald thee:** act as the herald bringing you into the King's presence.   **104. earnest:** lit., money given on account of the main payment.   **106. addition:** title of honor.

With those of Norway, or did line° the rebel
With hidden help and vantage,° or that with both
He labored in his country's wreck, I know not.
But treasons capital,° confessed and proved,   115
Have overthrown him.
    MACB. [*Aside*] Glamis, and Thane of Cawdor.
The greatest is behind.° — Thanks for your
       pains. —
Do you not hope your children shall be kings,
When those that gave the Thane of Cawdor to me
Promised no less to them?
    BAN.   That, trusted home,°   120
Might yet enkindle° you unto the crown,
Besides the Thane of Cawdor. But 'tis strange.
And oftentimes, to win us to our harm,
The instruments of darkness tell us truths,
Win us with honest trifles, to betray 's   125
In deepest consequence.°
Cousins, a word, I pray you.
    MACB.   [*Aside*] Two truths are told
As happy prologues to the swelling act
Of the imperial theme.° — I thank you, gentle-
       men. —
[*Aside*] This supernatural soliciting°   130
Cannot be ill, cannot be good. If ill,
Why hath it given me earnest of success,
Commencing in a truth? I am Thane of Cawdor.
If good, why do I yield to that suggestion
Whose horrid image doth unfix my hair   135
And make my seated° heart knock at my ribs,
Against the use of nature?° Present fears
Are less than horrible imaginings.
My thought, whose murder yet is but fantastical,°
Shakes so my single state of man° that function
Is smothered in surmise,° and nothing is   141
But what is not.
    BAN.   Look how our partner's rapt.
    MACB. [*Aside*] If chance will have me King, why,
       chance may crown me,
Without my stir.
    BAN.   New honors come upon him,
Like our strange garments,° cleave not to their mold
But with the aid of use.
    MACB.   [*Aside*] Come what come may,   146
Time and the hour runs through° the roughest day.
    BAN. Worthy Macbeth, we stay upon your leisure.

MAC. Give me your favor. My dull brain was
       wrought
With things forgotten. Kind gentlemen, your pains°
Are registered° where every day I turn   151
The leaf to read them. Let us toward the King.
Think upon what hath chanced, and at more time,
The interim having weighed it,° let us speak
Our free hearts each to other.
    BAN.   Very gladly.   155
    MACB. Till then, enough. Come, friends.
                               [*Exeunt.*]

SCENE IV. *Forres. The palace.*

[*Flourish.*° *Enter* DUNCAN, MALCOLM, DONALBAIN,
       LENNOX, *and* ATTENDANTS.]
    DUN. Is execution done on Cawdor? Are not
Those in commission° yet returned?
    MAL.   My liege,
They are not yet come back. But I have spoke
With one that saw him die, who did report
That very frankly he confessed his treasons,   5
Implored your Highness' pardon, and set forth
A deep repentance. Nothing in his life
Became him like the leaving it. He died
As one that had been studied in his death
To throw away the dearest thing he owed   10
As 'twere a careless trifle.°
    DUN.   There's no art
To find the mind's construction in the face.°
He was a gentleman on whom I built
An absolute trust.
    [*Enter* MACBETH, BANQUO, ROSS, *and* ANGUS.]
           O worthiest Cousin!
The sin of my ingratitude even now   15
Was heavy on me. Thou art so far before
That swiftest wing of recompense is slow
To overtake thee. Would thou hadst less deserved,
That the proportion both of thanks and payment
Might have been mine! Only I have left to say,   20
More is thy due than more than all can pay.
    MACB. The service and the loyalty I owe,
In doing it, pays itself. Your Highness' part
Is to receive our duties. And our duties
Are to your throne and state children and servants,°
Which do but what they should, by doing every-
       thing   26

112. **line:** support.   113. **vantage:** assistance.   115. **capital:** deserving death.   117. **behind:** yet to come.   120. **home:** fully. 121. **enkindle:** set you on fire to get.   126. **In . . . consequence:** in matters of the greatest importance.   128–29. **prologues . . . theme:** the first two truths are like the prologue to a powerful scene which will lead me to the crown.   130. **soliciting:** incitement.   136. **seated:** embedded.   137. **Against . . . nature:** in an unnatural way, as if it had broken loose.   139. **whose . . . fantastical:** in which murder is as yet only imagined.   140. **single . . . man:** Man was often regarded as a "microcosm," or universe in miniature, with all the functions of a kingdom existing in himself. **state:** kingdom.   140–41. **function . . . surmise:** action is choked by imagination.   145. **Like . . . garments:** like a new suit of clothes.   147. **runs through:** comes to the end of.

150. **pains:** troubles.   151. **registered:** recorded; i.e., in my heart.   154. **The . . . it:** having considered it meanwhile.
    Sc. iv: s.d., **Flourish:** trumpet fanfare.   2. **in commission:** For important state trials the accused was tried not by the ordinary courts but by a body of great persons summoned by a special commission.   9–11. **studied . . . trifle:** made it his study to throw away his life as a mere trifle.   11–12. **There's . . . face:** i.e., there is no method of discovering a man's character from his face.   24–25. **our . . . servants:** i.e., we owe duty to you as our King as if we were your children or servants.

Safe toward° your love and honor.
DUN.   Welcome hither.
I have begun to plant thee, and will labor
To make thee full of growing. Noble Banquo,
That hast no less deserved, nor must be known   30
No less to have done so, let me infold thee
And hold thee to my heart.
BAN.   There if I grow,
The harvest is your own.
DUN.   My plenteous joys,
Wanton° in fullness, seek to hide themselves
In drops of sorrow. Sons, kinsmen, thanes,   35
And you whose places are the nearest, know,
We will establish our estate° upon
Our eldest, Malcolm, whom we name hereafter
The Prince of Cumberland. Which honor must
Not unaccompanied invest him only,   40
But signs of nobleness, like stars, shall shine
On all deservers. From hence to Inverness,
And bind us further to you.
MACB. The rest is labor, which is not used for
    you.°
I'll be myself the harbinger,° and make joyful   45
The hearing of my wife with your approach,
So humbly take my leave.
DUN.   My worthy Cawdor!
MACB. [*Aside*] The Prince of Cumberland! That
    is a step
On which I must fall down or else o'erleap,
For in my way it lies. Stars, hide your fires,   50
Let not light see my black and deep desires.
The eye wink° at the hand, yet let that be
Which the eye fears, when it is done, to see. [*Exit.*]
DUN. True, worthy Banquo, he is full so° valiant,
And in his commendations I am fed,   55
It is a banquet to me. Let's after him,
Whose care is gone before to bid us welcome.
It is a peerless kinsman.   [*Flourish. Exeunt.*]

SCENE V. *Inverness.* MACBETH's *castle.*

[*Enter* LADY MACBETH, *reading a letter.*]
LADY M. " They met me in the day of success, and
I have learned by the perfectest report they have more
in them than mortal knowledge. When I burned in
desire to question them further, they made themselves air, into which they vanished. Whiles° I stood
rapt in the wonder of it, came missives° from the   6
King, who all-hailed me ' Thane of Cawdor,' by
which title, before, these weird sisters saluted me,
and referred me to the coming-on of time, with
' Hail, King that shalt be! ' This have I thought   10
good to deliver thee, my dearest partner of greatness,
that thou mightst not lose the dues of rejoicing° by
being ignorant of what greatness is promised thee.
Lay it to thy heart, and farewell."
Glamis thou art, and Cawdor, and shalt be
What thou art promised. Yet do I fear thy nature.
It is too full o' the milk of human kindness
To catch the nearest way. Thou wouldst be great,
Art not without ambition, but without   20
The illness° should attend it. What thou wouldst
    highly,
That wouldst thou holily — wouldst not play false,
And yet wouldst wrongly win. Thou'dst have, great
    Glamis,
That which cries " Thus thou must do, if thou have
    it,
And that which rather thou dost fear to do   25
Than wishest should be undone." Hie° thee hither,
That I may pour my spirits in thine ear,
And chastise with the valor of my tongue
All that impedes thee from the golden round°
Which fate and metaphysical° aid doth seem   30
To have thee crowned withal.
    [*Enter a* MESSENGER.] What is your tidings?
MESS. The King comes here tonight.
LADY M.   Thou'rt mad to say it.
Is not thy master with him? Who, were 't so,
Would have informed for preparation.°
MESS. So please you, it is true. Our Thane is com-
    ing.   35
One of my fellows had the speed of° him,
Who, almost dead for breath, had scarcely more
Than would make up his message.
LADY M.   Give him tending,°
He brings great news.   [*Exit* MESSENGER.]
             The raven himself is hoarse
That croaks the fatal entrance of Duncan   40
Under my battlements. Come, you spirits
That tend on mortal thoughts, unsex me here,
And fill me, from the crown to the toe, topfull
Of direst cruelty! Make thick my blood,
Stop up the accéss and passage to remorse,°   45
That no compunctious visitings of nature°
Shake my fell purpose, nor keep peace between
The effect and it!° Come to my woman's breasts,
And take my milk for gall,° you murdering minis-
    ters,°

27. Safe toward: with sure regard for.   **34. Wanton:** grow wild.
37. establish . . . estate: settle our kingdom on; i.e., by declaring him to be our heir.   **44. The . . . you:** i.e., anything done
for you is pleasure, everything else is tedious.   **45. harbinger:** an
official of the Court who made preparations for lodging when the
King went on progress.   **52. wink:** shut; i.e., be blind to what
I do.   **54. full so:** as fully — as you say.
Sc. v: **5. Whiles:** while.   **6. missives:** messengers.

12. dues of rejoicing: what is due to rejoicing, joy.   **21. illness:** wickedness.   **26. Hie:** hasten.   **29. golden round:** the
crown.   **30. metaphysical:** supernatural.   **34. informed . . .
preparation:** informed me so that I might be prepared.   **36. had
. . . of:** overtook.   **38. tending:** attention.   **45. remorse:** pity.
46. compunctious . . . nature: natural feelings of pity. **compunctious:** remorseful   **48. The . . . it:** i.e., pity and the effecting
of my dreadful (*fell*) purpose.   **49. take . . . gall:** turn my milk
to gall (i.e., bitterness). **murdering ministers:** spirits of murder.

Wherever in your sightless° substances   50
You wait on nature's mischief! Come, thick night,
And pall° thee in the dunnest° smoke of Hell,
That my keen knife see not the wound it makes,
Nor Heaven peep through the blanket of the dark°
To cry " Hold, hold! "
[*Enter* MACBETH.] Great Glamis! Worthy Cawdor!
Greater than both, by the all-hail hereafter!   56
Thy letters have transported me beyond
This ignorant present, and I feel now
The future in the instant.
     MACB.   My dearest love,
Duncan comes here tonight.
     LADY M.   And when goes hence?   60
     MACB. Tomorrow, as he purposes.
     LADY M.   Oh, never
Shall sun that morrow see!
Your face, my Thane, is as a book where men
May read strange matters. To beguile° the time,
Look like the time, bear welcome in your eye,   65
Your hand, your tongue. Look like the innocent
     flower
But be the serpent under 't. He that's coming
Must be provided for. And you shall put
This night's great business into my dispatch,
Which shall to all our nights and days to come   70
Give solely sovereign sway° and masterdom.
     MACB. We will speak further.
     LADY M.   Only look up clear.°
To alter favor° ever is to fear.
Leave all the rest to me.   [*Exeunt.*]

SCENE VI. *Before* MACBETH's *castle.*

[*Hautboys*° *and torches. Enter* DUNCAN, MALCOLM,
DONALBAIN, BANQUO, LENNOX, MACDUFF, ROSS,
ANGUS, *and* ATTENDANTS.]
     DUN. This castle hath a pleasant seat,° the air
Nimbly° and sweetly recommends itself
Unto our gentle senses.
     BAN.   This guest of summer,
The temple-haunting martlet,° does approve°
By his loved mansionry° that the heaven's breath   5
Smells wooingly here. No jutty,° frieze,°
Buttress, nor coign of vantage° but this bird

Hath made his pendent bed and procreant cradle.°
Where they most breed and haunt, I have observed
The air is delicate.
           [*Enter* LADY MACBETH.]
     DUN.   See, see, our honored hostess!   10
The love that follows us sometime is our trouble,
Which still we thank as love. Herein I teach you
How you shall bid God 'ild° us for your pains,
And thank us for your trouble.
     LADY M.   All our service
In every point twice done, and then done double,   15
Were poor and single business to contend°
Against those honors deep and broad wherewith
Your Majesty loads our house. For those of old,
And the late dignities heaped up to them,
We rest your hermits.°
     DUN.   Where's the Thane of Cawdor?   20
We coursed° him at the heels, and had a purpose
To be his purveyor.° But he rides well,
And his great love, sharp as his spur, hath holp° him
To his home before us. Fair and noble hostess,
We are your guest tonight.
     LADY M.   Your servants ever   25
Have theirs, themselves, and what is theirs, in
     compt,°
To make their audit at your Highness' pleasure,
Still to return your own.°
     DUN.   Give me your hand,
Conduct me to mine host. We love him highly,
And shall continue our graces toward him.   30
By your leave, hostess.   [*Exeunt.*]

SCENE VII. MACBETH's *castle.*

[*Hautboys and torches. Enter a* SEWER,° *and divers*
SERVANTS *with dishes and service, and pass over*
     the stage. Then enter MACBETH.]
     MACB. If it were done when 'tis done, then 'twere
     well
It were done quickly. If the assassination
Could trammel up the consequence, and catch,
With his surcease, success,° that but this blow
Might be the be-all and the end-all here,   5
But° here, upon this bank and shoal of time,

---

50. sightless: unseen.   **52. pall:** cover as with a pall. **dunnest:** darkest.   **54. Nor . . . dark:** nor Heaven (i.e., some good spirit) peer through the darkness which covers as with a blanket. **64. beguile:** deceive.   **71. sovereign sway:** royal, absolute power.   **72. clear:** i.e., with a look of innocence.   **73. alter favor:** change countenance; i.e., to look as if you were afraid. **Sc. vi: s.d.,** Hautboys: oboes.   **1. seat:** situation.   **2. Nimbly:** briskly.   **4. martlet:** a species of swallow which builds for her nest a little round mud cell under the eaves of the roof. **approve:** demonstrate.   **5. mansionry:** building.   **6. jutty:** part of a building which juts out. **frieze:** horizontal band of masonry. **7. coign of vantage:** convenient corner.

8. procreant cradle: cradle where the young are hatched. **13. God 'ild:** God reward.   **16. poor . . . contend:** poor and weak in comparison.   **20. rest . . . hermits:** remain bound to pray for you. **hermit:** beadsman, one who prays for the soul of a benefactor. Cf. *Rich II*, III.ii.116.   **21. coursed:** chased. **22. purveyor:** an officer who went ahead to make preparation for the provisions when the Court went on progress. See *harbinger* (I.iv.45,n).   **23. holp:** helped.   **26. compt:** account.   **28. Still . . . own:** always to give you back your own; i.e., all that we have is yours, and we must make an account of it when you demand it.
     Sc. vii: s.d., sewer: server.   **2–4. If . . . success:** i.e., if only the murder could have no aftereffects but be final and successful at Duncan's death (*surcease*). **trammel:** to entangle in a net.   **6. But:** even.

We'd jump° the life to come. But in these cases
We still have judgment here, that we but teach
Bloody instructions, which being taught return   9
To plague the inventor. This even-handed justice
Commends the ingredients of our poisoned chalice°
To our own lips. He's here in double trust.
First, as I am his kinsman and his subject,
Strong both against the deed. Then, as his host,
Who should against his murderer shut the door,   15
Not bear the knife myself. Besides, this Duncan
Hath borne his faculties° so meek, hath been
So clear° in his great office, that his virtues
Will plead like angels trumpet-tongued against
The deep damnation of his taking-off.   20
And pity, like a naked newborn babe,°
Striding the blast, or Heaven's cherubin horsed
Upon the sightless couriers° of the air,
Shall blow the horrid deed in every eye,
That tears shall drown the wind. I have no spur   25
To prick the sides of my intent, but only
Vaulting ambition, which o'erleaps itself
And falls on the other.°
[*Enter* LADY MACBETH.] How now! What news?
   LADY M. He has almost supped. Why have you
      left the chamber?
   MACB. Hath he asked for me?
   LADY M.   Know you not he has?   30
   MACB. We will proceed no further in this business.
He hath honored me of late, and I have bought
Golden opinions from all sorts of people,
Which would be worn now in their newest gloss,
Not cast aside so soon.
   LADY M.   Was the hope drunk   35
Wherein you dressed yourself? Hath it slept since?
And wakes it now, to look so green and pale
At what it did so freely?° From this time
Such I account thy love. Art thou afeard°
To be the same in thine own act and valor   40
As thou art in desire? Wouldst thou have that
Which thou esteem'st the ornament of life°
And live a coward in thine own esteem,
Letting " I dare not " wait upon " I would,"
Like the poor cat i' the adage?°
   MACB.   Prithee, peace.   45
I dare do all that may become a man.

Who dares do more is none.
   LADY M.   What beast was 't then
That made you break° this enterprise to me?
When you durst do it, then you were a man,
And to be more than what you were, you would   50
Be so much more the man. Nor time nor place
Did then adhere,° and yet you would make both.
They have made themselves, and that their fitness
      now
Does unmake you. I have given suck, and know
How tender 'tis to love the babe that milks me.   55
I would, while it was smiling in my face,
Have plucked my nipple from his boneless gums
And dashed the brains out, had I so sworn as you
Have done to this.
   MACB.   If we should fail?
   LADY M.   We fail!
But screw your courage to the sticking-place   60
And we'll not fail. When Duncan is asleep —
Whereto the rather shall his day's hard journey
Soundly invite him — his two chamberlains
Will I with wine and wassail° so convince°
That memory, the warder of the brain,   65
Shall be a fume, and the receipt of reason
A limbec only.° When in swinish sleep
Their drenchèd natures lie as in a death,
What cannot you and I perform upon
The unguarded Duncan? What not put upon   70
His spongy° officers, who shall bear the guilt
Of our great quell?°
   MACB.   Bring forth men-children only,
For thy undaunted mettle° should compose
Nothing but males. Will it not be received,   74
When we have marked with blood those sleepy two
Of his own chamber, and used their very daggers,
That they have done 't?
   LADY M.   Who dares receive it other,
As we shall make our griefs and clamor roar
Upon his death?
   MACB.   I am settled, and bend up°
Each corporal agent to this terrible feat.   80
Away, and mock the time with fairest show.
False face must hide what the false heart doth know.
                                        [*Exeunt.*]

7. jump: risk.   11. chalice: cup.   17. faculties: powers.   18. clear:
innocent.   21. naked . . . babe: i.e., an object which moves the
hardest-hearted to pity.   23. sightless couriers: unseen messengers.   28. other: i.e., side.   38. freely: without compulsion.
39. afeard: afraid, scared.   42. ornament of life: i.e., the crown.
45. adage: proverb. The proverb is common and runs "The cat
would eat fish but would not wet her feet."

48. break: reveal.   51-52. Nor . . . adhere: there was then no
suitable time or place for the murder.   64. wassail: carousing.
convince: overcome.   65-67. memory . . . only: memory, which
keeps watch in the brain, will be confused by the fumes of drink
and the reason become like a still (*limbec*) distilling only confused thoughts. Cf. *Temp,* V.i.64-68. receipt: receptacle; i.e.,
that part of the brain which contains the reason.   71. spongy:
that soak up drink like a sponge.   72. quell: murder.   73. mettle: material.   79. bend up: stretch tight (as a strung bow).

Act II

SCENE I.° *Inverness. Court of* MACBETH's
castle.

[*Enter* BANQUO, *and* FLEANCE *bearing a torch before
him.*]

BAN. How goes the night, boy?

FLE. The moon is down, I have not heard the
clock.

BAN. And she goes down at twelve.

FLE.　　　　　　　　　　　I take 't 'tis later, sir.

BAN. Hold, take my sword. There's husbandry°
in Heaven,

Their candles are all out. Take thee that too.°　5

A heavy summons° lies like lead upon me,

And yet I would not sleep. Merciful powers,

Restrain in me the cursèd thoughts that nature

Gives way to in repose!

[*Enter* MACBETH, *and a* SERVANT *with a torch.*]
　　　　　　Give me my sword.

Who's there?　　　　　　　　　　　　　　10

MACB. A friend.

BAN. What, sir, not yet at rest? The King's abed.

He hath been in unusual pleasure, and

Sent forth great largess° to your offices.°

This diamond he greets your wife withal,　　15

By the name of most kind hostess, and shut up

In measureless content.°

MACB.　　　　　　　　Being unprepared,

Our will became the servant to defect,

Which else should free have wrought.°

BAN.　　　　　　　　　　　All's well.

I dreamed last night of the three weird sisters.　20

To you they have showed some truth.

MACB.　　　　　　　　I think not of them.

Yet when we can entreat an hour to serve,

We would spend it in some words upon that business,

If you would grant the time.

BAN.　　　　　　　　At your kind'st leisure.

MACB. If you shall cleave to my consent, when
'tis,°　　　　　　　　　　　　　　　　25

It shall make honor for you.

BAN.　　　　　　　So° I lose none

In seeking to augment it, but still keep

My bosom franchised and allegiance clear,

I shall be counseled.

MACB.　　　　　　　Good repose the while!

BAN. Thanks, sir. The like to you!　　　　30

[*Exeunt* BANQUO *and* FLEANCE.]

MACB. Go bid thy mistress, when my drink is
ready,

She strike upon the bell. Get thee to bed.

[*Exit* SERVANT.]

Is this a dagger which I see before me,

The handle toward my hand? Come, let me clutch
thee.

I have thee not, and yet I see thee still.　　35

Art thou not, fatal vision, sensible°

To feeling as to sight? Or art thou but

A dagger of the mind, a false creation,

Proceeding from the heat-oppressèd brain?

I see thee yet, in form as palpable°　　　40

As this which now I draw.

Thou marshal'st° me the way that I was going,

And such an instrument I was to use.

Mine eyes are made the fools o' the other senses,

Or else worth all the rest. I see thee still,　45

And on thy blade and dudgeon° gouts° of blood,

Which was not so before. There's no such thing.

It is the bloody business which informs°

Thus to mine eyes. Now o'er the one half-world

Nature seems dead, and wicked dreams abuse　50

The curtained° sleep. Witchcraft celebrates

Pale Hecate's° offerings, and withered murder,

Alarumed by his sentinel, the wolf,

Whose howl 's his watch,° thus with his stealthy
pace,

With Tarquin's ravishing strides,° toward his design　　　　　　　　　　　　　　　　55

Moves like a ghost. Thou sure and firm-set earth,

Hear not my steps, which way they walk, for fear

Thy very stones prate of my whereabout,

And take the present horror° from the time,　59

Which now suits° with it. Whiles I threat, he lives.

Words to the heat of deeds too cold breath gives.

[*A bell rings.*]

I go, and it is done. The bell invites me.

Hear it not, Duncan, for it is a knell

That summons thee to Heaven, or to Hell. [*Exit.*]

Act II, Sc. i: The divisions into acts and scenes, though
made in F1, are not always apt. There is no pause in the action from I.vii to the end of II.iii.　**4. husbandry:** economy.
5. that too: i.e., his buckler.　**6. heavy summons:** i.e., I am
very weary. Cf. *Caesar*, IV.iii.267–69.　**14. largess:** gifts of
money. **offices:** servants' quarters.　**16–17. shut . . . content:**
he has ended the day in the greatest content.　**17–19. Being . . .
wrought:** i.e., as we were not properly prepared, our entertainment was not so good as we would have wished; it would otherwise have been more lavish.　**25. If . . . 'tis:** if you will be one
of my party, when it is formed.　**26–29. So . . . counseled:** so
long as I do not lose my honor in seeking to increase it, but keep
my faith free (*franchised*) and my loyalty unstained, I will be
on your side. In the *Chronicle* Banquo was said to have been a
fellow conspirator against Duncan. Since, however, Banquo was
the ancestor of King James I, Shakespeare was careful to acquit
him of such treachery.　**42. marshal'st:** conductest.　**46. dudgeon:**
handle. **gouts:** drops.　**48. informs:** creates forms.　**51. curtained:**
with the bed curtains drawn.　**52. Hecate:** goddess of witchcraft.
See later III.v.　**54. howl's . . . watch:** who tells the time by
howling.　**55. Tarquin's . . . strides:** Tarquin, the last King of
Rome, was so overcome by his lust for Lucrece that he ravished
her. The story is told in Shakespeare's *Rape of Lucrece*.　**59. present
horror:** i.e., the silence of midnight.　**60. suits:** matches.

SCENE II. *The same.*

[*Enter* LADY MACBETH.]

LADY M. That which hath made them drunk hath
    made me bold,
What hath quenched them hath given me fire.
    Hark! Peace!
It was the owl that shrieked, the fatal bellman,
Which gives the stern'st good night.° He is about it.
The doors are open, and the surfeited° grooms°   5
Do mock their charge° with snores. I have drugged
    their possets,°
That death and nature do contend about them,
Whether they live or die.

MACB.   [*Within*] Who's there? What ho!

LADY M. Alack, I am afraid they have awaked   10
And 'tis not done. The attempt and not the deed
Confounds us. Hark! I laid their daggers ready,
He could not miss 'em. Had he not resembled
My father as he slept, I had done 't.

[*Enter* MACBETH.]   My husband!

MACB. I have done the deed. Didst thou not hear
    a noise?   15

LADY M. I heard the owl scream and the crickets
    cry.
Did not you speak?

MACB.   When?

LADY M.   Now.

MACB.   As I descended?

LADY M. Aye.

MACB. Hark!
Who lies i' the second chamber?

LADY M.   Donalbain.   20

MACB. This is a sorry sight.
                    [*Looking on his hands.*]

LADY M. A foolish thought, to say a sorry sight.

MACB. There's one did laugh in 's sleep, and one
    cried " Murder! "
That they did wake each other. I stood and heard
    them.   24
But they did say their prayers, and addressed them
Again to sleep.

LADY M.   There are two lodged together.

MACB. One cried " God bless us! " and " Amen "
    the other,
As they had seen me with these hangman's hands.°

Listening their fear, I could not say " Amen "
When they did say " God bless us! "

LADY M.   Consider it not so deeply.   30

MACB. But wherefore could not I pronounce
    " Amen "?
I had most need of blessing, and " Amen "
Stuck in my throat.

LADY M.   These deeds must not be thought
After these ways. So, it will make us mad.

MACB. Methought I heard a voice cry " Sleep no
    more!   35
Macbeth does murder sleep " — the innocent sleep,
Sleep that knits up the raveled sleave° of care,
The death of each day's life, sore labor's bath,
Balm of hurt minds, great nature's second course,°
Chief nourisher in life's feast ——

LADY M.   What do you mean?   40

MACB. Still° it cried " Sleep no more! " to all the
    house.
" Glamis hath murdered sleep, and therefore Caw-
    dor
Shall sleep no more. Macbeth shall sleep no
    more."

LADY M. Who was it that thus cried? Why, worthy
    Thane,
You do unbend° your noble strength to think   45
So brainsickly of things. Go get some water
And wash this filthy witness from your hand.
Why did you bring these daggers from the place?
They must lie there. Go carry them, and smear
The sleepy grooms with blood.

MACB.   I'll go no more.   50
I am afraid to think what I have done,
Look on 't again I dare not.

LADY M.   Infirm of purpose!
Give me the daggers. The sleeping and the dead
Are but as pictures. 'Tis the eye of childhood
That fears a painted devil. If he do bleed,   55
I'll gild° the faces of the grooms withal,
For it must seem their guilt.   [*Exit.*]
                    [*Knocking within.*]

MACB.   Whence is that knocking?
How is 't with me when every noise appals me?
What hands are here? Ha! They pluck out mine
    eyes!
Will all great Neptune's ocean wash this blood   60
Clean from my hand? No, this my hand will
    rather
The multitudinous seas incarnadine,°
Making the green one red.

                    [*Re-enter* LADY MACBETH.]

LADY M. My hands are of your color, but I shame

Sc. ii: 3–4. **fatal . . . night:** On the night before an execution in London the bell of St. Sepulcher's Church (near Newgate
prison) was tolled, and at midnight the bellman rang a hand-bell
outside the cell of the condemned, bidding him think on his
sins. This custom had been established by Robert Dow, merchant
tailor, in 1604.   **5. surfeited:** overfed. **groom:** servant of the
chamber, who slept at the foot of the King's bed.   **6. charge:**
him whom they are responsible for watching. **possets:** warm drink
of milk and ale, taken as a nightcap.   **28. hangman's hands:**
To Shakespeare's audience, fresh from the excitements of the
execution of the plotters in the Gunpowder Treason, this image
would be full of ghastly significance. It was the hangman's business to tear the vitals out of his victim before hacking him into
pieces. See Gen. Intro. 17a, 27b.

37. raveled sleave: tangled skein.   **39. second course:** i.e.,
the main part of a feast.   **41. Still:** continuously.   **45. unbend:**
relax.   **56. gild:** a grim pun. Shakespeare's contemporaries
were however not very exact in their names for colors, and they
often confused "red" and "gold." Cf. II.iii.118 and *Temp.*
V.i. 279–80.   **62. incarnadine:** make red.

To wear a heart so white. [*Knocking within.*] I hear
　a knocking　　　　　　　　　　　　　　　　　65
At the south entry. Retire we to our chamber.
A little water clears us of this deed.°
How easy is it then! Your constancy
Hath left you unattended. [*Knocking within.*]
　Hark! More knocking.
Get on your nightgown,° lest occasion call us　70
And show us to be watchers.° Be not lost
So poorly in your thoughts.
　MACB. To know my deed, 'twere best not know
　myself.　　　　　　　　　　　[*Knocking within.*]
Wake Duncan with thy knocking! I would thou
　couldst!　　　　　　　　　　　　　[*Exeunt.*]

SCENE III. *The same.*

[*Enter a* PORTER.° *Knocking within.*]

　PORT. Here's a knocking indeed! If a man were
porter of Hell gate, he should have old° turning the
key.° [*Knocking within.*] Knock, knock, knock!
Who's there, i' the name of Beelzebub? Here's a
farmer that hanged himself on th' expectation of　5
plenty.° Come in time, have napkins° enow° about
you, here you'll sweat for 't. [*Knocking within.*]
Knock, knock! Who's there, in th' other devil's
name? Faith, here's an equivocator,° that could
swear in both the scales against either scale, who　10
committed treason enough for God's sake, yet could
not equivocate to Heaven. Oh, come in, equivocator.
[*Knocking within.*] Knock, knock, knock! Who's
there? Faith, here's an English tailor come hither,
for stealing out of a French hose.° Come in, tailor,
here you may roast your goose.° [*Knocking　16
within.*] Knock, knock, never at quiet! What are
you? But this place is too cold for Hell. I'll devil-
porter it no further. I had thought to have let in
some of all professions that go the primrose　20

way° to the everlasting bonfire. [*Knocking within.*]
Anon, anon! I pray you remember the porter.
　　　　　　　　　　　　　　[*Opens the gate.*]

[*Enter* MACDUFF *and* LENNOX.]

　MACD. Was it so late, friend, ere you went to bed
That you do lie so late?　　　　　　　　　　25
　PORT. Faith, sir, we were carousing till the second
cock.° And drink, sir, is a great provoker of three
things.
　MACD. What three things does drink especially
provoke?　　　　　　　　　　　　　　　30
　PORT. Marry, sir, nose-painting, sleep, and urine.
Lechery, sir, it provokes and unprovokes. It provokes the desire, but it takes away the performance.
Therefore much drink may be said to be an equivocator with lechery. It makes him and it mars　35
him, it sets him on and it takes him off, it persuades
him and disheartens him, makes him stand to and
not stand to; in conclusion, equivocates him in a
sleep and giving him the lie, leaves him.　　40
　MACD. I believe drink gave thee the lie last night.
　PORT. That it did, sir, i' the very throat on me.
But I requited° him for his lie, and I think being
too strong for him, though he took up my legs some-
time, yet I made a shift° to cast° him.　　　46
　MACD. Is thy master stirring?
[*Enter* MACBETH]. Our knocking has awaked him.
　Here he comes.
　LEN. Good morrow, noble sir.
　MACB.　　　　　　　　Good morrow, both.
　MACD. Is the King stirring, worthy Thane?
　MACB.　　　　　　　　　　　　Not yet.　50
　MACD. He did command me to call timely on him.
I have almost slipped the hour.
　MACB.　　　　　　　　I'll bring you to him.
　MACD. I know this is a joyful trouble to you,
But yet 'tis one.
　MACB. The labor we delight in physics° pain.　55
This is the door.
　MACD.　　　I'll make so bold to call,
For 'tis my limited service.°　　　　　　[*Exit.*]
　LEN. Goes the King hence today?
　MACB.　　　　　　　He does. He did appoint so.
　LEN. The night has been unruly. Where we lay,
Our chimneys were blown down, and, as they say,
Lamentings heard i' the air, strange screams of
　death,　　　　　　　　　　　　　　61
And prophesying with accents terrible
Of dire combustion° and confused events
New-hatched to the woeful time. The obscure bird°
Clamored the livelong night. Some say the earth　65

---

67. A . . . deed: See V.i.48 and *Macb* Intro. p. 1188a.　70. nightgown: dressing gown.　70–71. lest . . . watchers: lest something
should cause us to be summoned, and we should be found still
out of bed.
　Sc. iii: s.d., Enter a porter: See *Macb* Intro. p. 1188a.
2. old: slang for "any amount of."　2–3. turning . . . key:
opening the door.　5–6. farmer . . . plenty: Farmers who hoarded
corn in the hope of high prices in a time of dearth were often the
subject for jest and satire. In Jonson's *Every Man out of His
Humor* Sordido the farmer believes from the weather forecast in
his almanac that the harvest will fail. When his hopes of profiteering are disappointed he hangs himself, but is cut down by his
neighbors.　When he revives, he abuses them for cutting and not
untying the rope.　6. napkins: towels. enow: enough.　9. equivocator: See *Macb* Intro. p. 1184a and App. 20.　14–15. English . . . hose: It was double theft; he not only stole the fashion
but helped himself to some of the cloth, for French hose at
this time were very full and baggy. See Pl. 8b and comment
on p. 93b.　16. goose: with a pun on goose, the tailor's pressing
iron.

20–21. primrose way: the broad and pleasant path that leads to
Hell.　26–27. second cock: 3 A.M. First cock was midnight and
third cock an hour before dawn. Cf. *R & J*, IV.iv.3–4.　44. requited: paid him back.　46. made a shift: managed. cast: throw
up.　55. physics: cures.　57. limited service: duty assigned me.
63. dire combustion: some terrific event about to blaze out.
64. obscure bird: owl.

Was feverous and did shake.

MACB.   'Twas a rough night.

LEN. My young remembrance cannot parallel
A fellow to it.

     [*Re-enter* MACDUFF.]

MACD. O horror, horror, horror! Tongue nor heart
Cannot conceive nor name thee.

MACB. & LEN.   What's the matter?   70

MACD. Confusion now hath made his masterpiece.
Most sacrilegious murder hath broke ope
The Lord's anointed temple, and stole thence
'The life o' the building.

MACB.   What is 't you say? The life?

LEN. Mean you His Majesty?   75

MACD. Approach the chamber, and destroy your
    sight
With a new Gorgon.° Do not bid me speak.
See, and then speak yourselves.

     [*Exeunt* MACBETH *and* LENNOX.]
            Awake, awake!
Ring the alarum bell. Murder and treason!
Banquo and Donalbain! Malcolm! Awake!   80
Shake off this downy sleep, death's counterfeit,
And look on death itself! Up, up, and see
The great doom's image!° Malcolm! Banquo!
As from your graves rise up, and walk like sprites,
To countenance° this horror. Ring the bell.   85

           [*Bell rings.*]

     [*Enter* LADY MACBETH.]

LADY M. What's the business,
That such a hideous trumpet calls to parley°
The sleepers of the house? Speak, speak!

MACD.   O gentle lady,
'Tis not for you to hear what I can speak.
The repetition, in a woman's ear,   90
Would murder as it fell.

     [*Enter* BANQUO.] O Banquo, Banquo!
Our royal master's murdered.

LADY M.   Woe, alas!
What, in our house?

BAN.   Too cruel anywhere.
Dear Duff, I prithee, contradict thyself,
And say it is not so.   95

     [*Re-enter* MACBETH *and* LENNOX, *with* ROSS.]

MACB. Had I but died an hour before this chance,
I had lived a blessèd time, for from this instant
There's nothing serious in mortality.°
All is but toys.° Renown and grace is dead,
The wine of life is drawn, and the mere lees   100
Is left this vault° to brag of.

     [*Enter* MALCOLM *and* DONALBAIN.]

DON. What is amiss?

MACB.   You are, and do not know 't.

The spring, the head, the fountain of your blood
Is stopped, the very source of it is stopped.

MACD. Your royal father's murdered.

MAL.   Oh, by whom?   105

LEN. Those of his chamber, as it seemed, had
    done 't.
Their hands and faces were all badged° with blood,
So were their daggers, which unwiped we found
Upon their pillows.
They stared, and were distracted, no man's life   110
Was to be trusted with them.

MACB. Oh, yet I do repent me of my fury,
That I did kill them.

MACD.   Wherefore did you so?

MACB. Who can be wise, amazed, temperate and
    furious,
Loyal and neutral, in a moment? No man.   115
The expedition° of my violent love
Outrun the pauser reason.° Here lay Duncan,
His silver skin laced with his golden blood,°
And his gashed stabs looked like a breach in nature
For ruin's wasteful entrance. There, the murderers,
Steeped in the colors of their trade, their daggers
Unmannerly breeched° with gore. Who could re-
    frain   122
That had a heart to love, and in that heart
Courage to make 's love known?

LADY M.   Help me hence, ho!

MACD. Look to the lady.

MAL. [*Aside to* DONALBAIN] Why do we hold our
    tongues,   125
That most may claim this argument for ours?°

DON. [*Aside to* MALCOLM] What should be spoken
    here, where our fate,
Hid in an auger hole,° may rush and seize us?
Let's away,   129
Our tears are not yet brewed.°

MAL. [*Aside to* DONALBAIN] Nor our strong sorrow
Upon the foot of motion.°

BAN. Look to the lady.

     [LADY MACBETH *is carried out.*]
And when we have our naked frailties hid,
That suffer in exposure,° let us meet,
And question this most bloody piece of work,
To know it further. Fears and scruples shake us.
In the great hand of God I stand, and thence   136

---

77. **Gorgon:** the snake-headed monster Medusa, so terrible to look upon that it turned those who saw it to stone.   83. **great . . . image:** the picture of the Day of Doom.   85. **countenance:** to be in keeping with.   87. **parley:** conference of war.   98. **mortality:** human life.   99. **toys:** trifles.   101. **vault:** universe.

107. **badged:** marked; lit., wearing a badge as a servant of murder.   116. **expedition:** hasty action.   117. **pauser reason:** reason which causes a man to pause before acting.   118. **laced . . . blood:** overlaid with blood as a garment is ornamented with gold. Macbeth in his attempt to conceal his guilt uses highflown and exaggerated language. **golden:** red. See II.ii.56.   122. **Unmannerly breeched:** covered as with breeches in an unbecoming way.   126. **That . . . ours:** i.e., who are most concerned with this business.   128. **auger hole:** a small hole made by an auger; i.e., destruction may come on us from the smallest circumstance.   130. **Our . . . brewed:** we have not yet had time for weeping.   131. **Upon . . . motion:** is not yet moving.   132–33. **our . . . exposure:** i.e., when we have put on our clothes. All but Macduff have come straight from their beds.

Against the undivulged pretense° I fight
Of treasonous malice.
   MACD.   And so do I.
   ALL.   So all.
   MACB. Let's briefly put on manly readiness,
And meet i' the hall together.
   ALL.   Well contented.   140
       [Exeunt all but MALCOLM *and* DONALBAIN.]
   MAL. What will you do? Let's not consort° with
them.
To show an unfelt sorrow is an office
Which the false man does easy. I'll to England.
   DON. To Ireland, I. Our separated fortune
Shall keep us both the safer. Where we are   145
There's daggers in men's smiles. The near in blood,
The nearer bloody.°
   MAL.   This murderous shaft° that's shot
Hath not yet lighted,° and our safest way
Is to avoid the aim. Therefore to horse,
And let us not be dainty° of leave-taking,   150
But shift away. There's warrant in that theft
Which steals itself when there's no mercy left.°
                          [Exeunt.]

SCENE IV. *Outside* MACBETH's *castle.*

       [Enter ROSS *with an* OLD MAN.]
   OLD MAN. Threescore and ten I can remember
well.
Within the volume of which time I have seen
Hours dreadful and things strange, but this sore
   night
Hath trifled former knowings.°
   ROSS.   Ah, good Father,
Thou seest the heavens, as troubled with man's act,
Threaten his bloody stage. By the clock 'tis day,   6
And yet dark night strangles the traveling lamp.°
Is 't night's predominance,° or the day's shame,°
That darkness does the face of earth entomb
When living light should kiss it?
   OLD MAN.   'Tis unnatural,   10
Even like the deed that's done. On Tuesday last
A falcon towering in her pride of place°
Was by a mousing owl hawked at and killed.

ROSS. And Duncan's horses — a thing most
   strange and certain —
Beauteous and swift, the minions of their race,   15
Turned wild in nature, broke their stalls, flung out,
Contending 'gainst obedience, as they would make
War with mankind.
   OLD MAN.   'Tis said they eat each other.
   ROSS. They did so, to the amazement of mine eyes,
That looked upon 't.
       [Enter MACDUFF.] Here comes the good Macduff.
How goes the world, sir, now?
   MACD.   Why, see you not?   21
   ROSS. Is 't known who did this more than bloody
   deed?
   MACD. Those that Macbeth hath slain.
   ROSS.   Alas the day!
What good could they pretend?°
   MACD.   They were suborned.°
Malcolm and Donalbain, the King's two sons,   25
Are stol'n away and fled, which puts upon them
Suspicion of the deed.
   ROSS.   'Gainst nature still.
Thriftless ambition, that wilt ravin up°
Thine own life's means!° Then 'tis most like
The sovereignty will fall upon Macbeth.   30
   MACD. He is already named,° and gone to Scone
To be invested.
   ROSS.   Where is Duncan's body?
   MACD. Carried to Colmekill,°
The sacred storehouse of his predecessors
And guardian of their bones.
   ROSS.   Will you to Scone?   35
   MACD. No, Cousin, I'll to Fife.
   ROSS.   Well, I will thither.
   MACD. Well, may you see things well done there.
   Adieu!
Lest our old robes sit easier than our new!
   ROSS. Farewell, Father.
   OLD MAN. God's benison° go with you, and with
   those   40
That would make good of bad and friends of foes!
                          [Exeunt.]

137. **undivulged pretense:** the intention of the crime which has not yet been revealed. Cf. *W Tale*, III.ii.17–18.   141. **consort:** associate with.   146–47. **The . . . bloody:** the nearer we are by blood relationship to the King, the more likely to be murdered. 147. **shaft:** arrow. 148. **lighted:** come to earth. 150. **dainty:** particular. 151–52. **There's . . . left:** i.e., we are justified in stealing away in these merciless times.

    Sc. iv: 4. trifled . . . knowings: everything I have known before is a trifle compared with this. 7. **strangles . . . lamp:** blots out the sun. **traveling:** either moving in its course or struggling. In Shakespeare's time "travel" and "travail" (strive) were the same word. F1 spells "travailing." 8. **predominance:** supremacy. **day's shame:** i.e., is the day ashamed of this dreadful deed and so unwilling to show its face. 12. **towering . . . place:** towering proudly aloft.

Act III

SCENE I. *Forres. The palace.*

       [Enter BANQUO.]
   BAN. Thou hast it now. King, Cawdor, Glamis,
   all,
As the weird women promised, and I fear

24. **pretend:** allege. **suborned:** bribed.   28. **ravin up:** devour greedily. 29. **own . . . means:** i.e., parent. 31. **named:** elected. 33. **Colmekill:** Iona, the ancient burying place of the Kings of Scotland. 40. **benison:** blessing.

Thou play'dst most foully for 't. Yet it was said
It should not stand in thy posterity,
But that myself should be the root and father   5
Of many kings. If there come truth from them —
As upon thee, Macbeth, their speeches shine —
Why, by the verities on thee made good,
May they not be my oracles as well
And set me up in hope? But hush, no more.   10

[*Sennet*° *sounded. Enter* MACBETH, *as King;* LADY
MACBETH, *as Queen;* LENNOX, ROSS, LORDS, LADIES,
and ATTENDANTS.]

MACB. Here's our chief guest.
LADY M.   If he had been forgotten,
It had been as a gap in our great feast,
And all-thing° unbecoming.
MACB. Tonight we hold a solemn° supper, sir,
And I'll request your presence.
BAN.   Let your Highness   15
Command upon me, to the which my duties
Are with a most indissoluble tie
Forever knit.
MACB. Ride you this afternoon?
BAN.   Aye, my good lord.   20
MACB. We should have else desired your good ad-
  vice,
Which still° hath been both grave and prosperous,
In this day's council, but we'll take tomorrow.
Is 't far you ride?
BAN. As far, my lord, as will fill up the time   25
'Twixt this and supper. Go not my horse the better,
I must become a borrower of the night
For a dark hour or twain.
MACB.   Fail not our feast.
BAN. My lord, I will not.
MACB. We hear our bloody cousins are bestowed
In England and in Ireland, not confessing   31
Their cruel parricide, filling their hearers
With strange invention. But of that tomorrow,
When therewithal we shall have cause of state
Craving us jointly.° Hie° you to horse. Adieu,   35
Till you return at night. Goes Fleance with you?
BAN. Aye, my good lord. Our time does call
  upon 's.°
MACB. I wish your horses swift and sure of foot,
And so I do commend you to their backs.   39
Farewell.   [*Exit* BANQUO.]
Let every man be master of his time
Till seven at night. To make society
The sweeter welcome, we will keep ourself
Till suppertime alone. While° then, God be with
  you!
                    [*Exeunt all but* MACBETH
                        and an ATTENDANT.]

Sirrah, a word with you. Attend° those men   45
Our pleasure?
ATT. They are, my lord, without° the palace gate.
MACB. Bring them before us.   [*Exit* ATTENDANT.]
                          To be thus is nothing,
But to be safely thus. Our fears in Banquo
Stick deep, and in his royalty of nature°   50
Reigns that which would be feared. 'Tis much he
  dares,
And to° that dauntless temper of his mind,
He hath a wisdom that doth guide his valor
To act in safety. There is none but he
Whose being I do fear. And under him   55
My Genius is rebuked, as it is said
Mark Antony's was by Caesar.° He chid the sisters
When first they put the name of King upon me,
And bade them speak to him. Then prophetlike
They hailed him father to a line of kings.   60
Upon my head they placed a fruitless crown
And put a barren scepter in my gripe,°
Thence to be wrenched with an unlineal° hand,
No son of mine succeeding. If 't be so,
For Banquo's issue have I filed° my mind,   65
For them the gracious Duncan have I murdered,
Put rancors° in the vessel of my peace
Only for them, and mine eternal jewel°
Given to the common enemy of man°
To make them kings — the seed of Banquo kings!
Rather than so, come, Fate, into the list,°   71
And champion° me to the utterance!° Who's there?
[*Re-enter* ATTENDANT, *with* TWO MURDERERS.]
Now go to the door, and stay there till we call.
                          [*Exit* ATTENDANT.]
Was it not yesterday we spoke together?
1. MUR. It was, so please your Highness.
MACB.   Well then, now   75
Have you considered of my speeches? Know
That it was he in the times past which held you
So under fortune,° which you thought had been
Our innocent self. This I made good° to you
In our last conference, passed in probation° with
  you,   80
How you were borne in hand,° how crossed, the in-
  struments,
Who wrought with them, and all things else that
  might
To half a soul and to a notion crazed°

---

45. Attend: wait.   47. without: outside.   50. royalty of nature: kingly nature.   52. to: added to.   56–57. My . . . Caesar:
See *Ant & Cleo,* II.iii.18–29, and *Caesar,* II.i.66.   62. gripe:
grip.   63. unlineal: not descended from me.   65. filed: defiled.
67. rancors: bitterness.   68. eternal jewel: i.e., immortal
soul.   69. common . . . man: the Devil.   71. list: place of combat.   72. champion: fight against in single combat. to . . .
utterance: *à l'outrance,* to the uttermost, a term in chivalry for a
combat to the death.   77–78. held . . . fortune: was the cause
of your bad fortune.   79. made good: demonstrated.
80. passed in probation: proved.   81. borne in hand: deceived.
83. notion crazed: even to a half-wit.

Act III, Sc. i: 10 s.d., Sennet: a trumpet call.   13. all-
thing: every way.   14. solemn: ceremonious. See III.iv.1.
22. still: always.   35. Craving us jointly: demanding the attention of both of us. Hie: hasten.   37. Our . . . upon 's: our
business is urgent.   44. While: till.

Say "Thus did Banquo."

1. MUR.　　　　　　　　You made it known to us.

MACB. I did so, and went further, which is now
Our point of second meeting. Do you find　　86
Your patience so predominant in your nature
That you can let this go? Are you so gospeled,°
To pray for this good man and for his issue,
Whose heavy hand hath bowed° you to the grave
And beggared yours forever?

1. MUR.　　　　　　We are men, my liege.　91

MACB. Aye, in the catalogue ye go for men,
As hounds and greyhounds, mongrels, spaniels, curs,
Shoughs,° water rugs° and demiwolves,° are clept°
All by the name of dogs. The valued file°　　95
Distinguishes the swift, the slow, the subtle,
The housekeeper, the hunter, every one
According to the gift which bounteous Nature
Hath in him closed,° whereby he does receive
Particular addition from the bill　　　　100
That writes them all alike.° And so of men.
Now if you have a station in the file,°
Not i' the worst rank of manhood, say it,
And I will put that business in your bosoms
Whose execution takes your enemy off,　　105
Grapples you to the heart and love of us,
Who wear our health but sickly in his life°
Which in his death were perfect.

2. MUR.　　　　　　　I am one, my liege,
Whom the vile blows and buffets of the world
Have so incensed that I am reckless what　　110
I do to spite the world.

1. MUR.　　　　　And I another
So weary with disasters, tugged with° fortune,
That I would set my life on any chance
To mend it or be rid on 't.

MACB.　　　　　　　Both of you
Know Banquo was your enemy.

BOTH MURS.　　　　　True, my lord.　115

MACB. So is he mine, and in such bloody distance°
That every minute of his being thrusts
Against my near'st of life.° And though I could
With barefaced power sweep him from my sight
And bid my will avouch° it, yet I must not,　120
For certain friends that are both his and mine,
Whose loves I may not drop, but wail his fall°
Who I myself struck down. And thence it is
That I to your assistance do make love,

Masking° the business from the common eye　125
For sundry weighty reasons.

2. MUR.　　　　　　We shall, my lord,
Perform what you command us.

1. MUR.　　　　　　Though our lives ——

MACB. Your spirits shine through you. Within this
　　hour at most
I will advise you where to plant yourselves,
Acquaint you with the perfect spy o' the time,°　130
The moment on 't. For 't must be done tonight,
And something° from the palace, always thought
That I require a clearness.° And with him —
To leave no rubs° nor botches in the work —
Fleance his son, that keeps him company,　135
Whose absence is no less material to me
Than is his father's, must embrace the fate
Of that dark hour. Resolve yourselves apart.°
I'll come to you anon.

BOTH MURS.　　　We are resolved, my lord.

MACB. I'll call upon you straight. Abide within.
　　　　　　　　　　　　[*Exeunt* MURDERERS.]
It is concluded. Banquo, thy soul's flight,　141
If it find Heaven, must find it out tonight. [*Exit.*]

SCENE II. *The palace.*

[*Enter* LADY MACBETH *and a* SERVANT.]

LADY M. Is Banquo gone from Court?

SERV. Aye, madam, but returns again tonight.

LADY M. Say to the King I would attend his leisure
For a few words.

SERV.　　　Madam, I will.　　[*Exit.*]

LADY M.　　　　Naught's had, all's spent,
Where our desire is got without content.　　5
'Tis safer to be that which we destroy
Than by destruction dwell in doubtful joy.
[*Enter* MACBETH.] How now, my lord! Why do you
　　keep alone,
Of sorriest fancies your companions making,
Using those thoughts which should indeed have
　　died　　10
With them they think on? Things without all
　　remedy
Should be without regard. What's done is done.

MACB. We have scotched° the snake, not killed it.
She'll close° and be herself, whilst our poor malice
Remains in danger of her former tooth.°　　15

---

88. so gospeled: such a good Christian.　90. bowed: bent down
double.　94. Shoughs: shaggy-haired dogs. water rugs: dogs
used to the water. demiwolves: dogs which are half wolf. clept:
called.　95. valued file: list of those considered first class.
99. in . . . closed: enclosed in him.　99–101. whereby . . . alike:
i.e., from his special quality, each kind of dog has his particular
distinction (*addition*) which makes him more than a mere
"dog."　102. station . . . file: place.　107. in . . . life: so long
as he is alive.　112. tugged with: pulled about by.　116. distance: disagreement, quarrel.　118. near'st of life: inmost being,
myself.　120. avouch: justify.　122. wail . . . fall: pretend to
lament his death.

125. Masking: hiding.　130. Acquaint . . . time: send someone
to tell you the exact moment.　132. something: some distance.
133. clearness: i.e., that no suspicion falls on me.　134. rubs:
impediments. See App. 13.　138. Resolve . . . apart: make up
your minds by yourselves.

Sc. ii: 13. scotched: wounded slightly. F1 reads "scorched."
14. close: heal.　14–15. whilst . . . tooth: while we for all our
hatred are in as great danger from her as before.

But let the frame of things disjoint, both the worlds
    suffer,°
Ere we will eat our meal in fear and sleep
In the affliction of these terrible dreams
That shake us nightly. Better be with the dead,
Whom we, to gain our peace, have sent to peace,   20
Than on the torture of the mind to lie
In restless ecstasy.° Duncan is in his grave,
After life's fitful fever he sleeps well.
Treason has done his worst. Nor steel, nor poison,
Malice domestic, foreign levy, nothing,   25
Can touch him further.
    LADY M.   Come on,
Gentle my lord, sleek o'er your rugged looks,°
Be bright and jovial among your guests tonight.
    MACB. So shall I, love, and so, I pray, be you.
Let your remembrance apply to Banquo,   30
Present him eminence,° both with eye and tongue,
Unsafe the while,° that we
Must lave° our honors in these flattering streams
And make our faces vizards° to our hearts,
Disguising what they are.
    LADY M.   You must leave this.   35
    MACB. Oh, full of scorpions is my mind, dear wife!
Thou know'st that Banquo, and his Fleance, lives.
    LADY M. But in them Nature's copy's not eterne.°
    MACB. There's comfort yet, they are assailable.
Then be thou jocund. Ere the bat hath flown   40
His cloistered flight,° ere to black Hecate's summons
The shard-borne° beetle with his drowsy hums
Hath rung night's yawning peal, there shall be done
A deed of dreadful note.
    LADY M.   What's to be done?
    MACB. Be innocent of the knowledge, dearest
    chuck,°   45
Till thou applaud the deed. Come, seeling night,°
Scarf° up the tender eye of pitiful day,
And with thy bloody and invisible hand
Cancel and tear to pieces that great bond°
Which keeps me pale! Light thickens, and the crow
Makes wing to the rooky° wood.   51
Good things of day begin to droop and drowse
Whiles night's black agents to their preys do rouse.
Thou marvel'st at my words. But hold thee still,
Things bad begun make strong themselves by ill.
So prithee go with me.   [*Exeunt.*]

---

16. let . . . suffer: let the universe fall to pieces, let heaven and
earth perish.   22. ecstasy: madness.   27. sleek . . . looks: make
smooth your wild looks.   31. Present . . . eminence: make much
of him.   32. Unsafe . . . while: we are unsafe so long as.   33. lave:
bathe.   34. vizards: masks.   38. Nature's . . . eterne: i.e., man
holds his life only on a temporary lease (*copy*) — not perpetual
freehold — from Nature.   41. cloistered flight: flight in cloisters.
42. shard-borne: borne aloft by its horny wings.   45. chuck:
chick.   46. seeling night: an image from the taming of hawks.
See App. 26.   47. Scarf: blindfold.   49. great bond: lit., that
which binds me; i.e., Banquo's life.   51. rooky: murky.

SCENE III. *A park near the palace.*

[*Enter three* MURDERERS.°]
    1. MUR. But who did bid thee join with us?
    3. MUR.   Macbeth.
    2. MUR. He needs not our mistrust, since he de-
    livers
Our offices,° and what we have to do,
To the direction just.°
    1. MUR.   Then stand with us.
The west yet glimmers with some streaks of day.   5
Now spurs the lated° traveler apace
To gain the timely inn, and near approaches
The subject of our watch.
    3. MUR.   Hark! I hear horses.
    BAN. [*Within*] Give us a light there, ho!
    2. MUR.   Then 'tis he. The rest
That are within the note of expectation°   10
Already are i' the Court.
    1. MUR.   His horses go about.
    3. MUR. Almost a mile. But he does usually —
So all men do — from hence to the palace gate
Make it their walk.
    2. MUR.   A light, a light!
    [*Enter* BANQUO, *and* FLEANCE *with a torch.*]
    3. MUR.   'Tis he.
    1. MUR. Stand to 't.   15
    BAN. It will be rain tonight.
    1. MUR.   Let it come down.
        [*They set upon* BANQUO.]
    BAN. Oh, treachery! Fly, good Fleance, fly, fly, fly!
Thou mayst revenge. O slave!
        [*Dies.* FLEANCE *escapes.*]
    3. MUR. Who did strike out the light?
    1. MUR.   Was 't not the way?
    3. MUR. There's but one down, the son is fled.
    2. MUR.   We have lost   20
Best half of our affair.
    1. MUR. Well, let's away and say how much is
    done.   [*Exeunt.*]

SCENE IV. *Hall in the palace.*

[*A banquet prepared. Enter* MACBETH, LADY
MACBETH, ROSS, LENNOX, LORDS, *and* ATTENDANTS.]
    MACB. You know your own degrees,° sit down.
    At first
And last the hearty welcome.
    LORDS.   Thanks to your Majesty.

Sc. iii: s.d., three Murderers: The presence of the third
murderer is not explained, but he is presumably the "perfect
spy o' the time." See III.i.130.   3. offices: duty.   4. To . . .
just: in exact detail.   6. lated: belated.   10. within . . . expectation: noted as expected at the feast.
    Sc. iv: 1. degrees: ranks. This is a state banquet at which
each guest sits according to his rank.

MACB. Ourself will mingle with society
And play the humble host.
Our hostess keeps her state,° but in best time   5
We will require her welcome.
     LADY M. Pronounce it for me, sir, to all our friends,
For my heart speaks they are welcome.
         [*Enter* FIRST MURDERER, *to the door.*]
     MACB. See, they encounter thee with their hearts'
thanks.
Both sides are even.° Here I'll sit i' the midst.   10
Be large in mirth,° anon we'll drink a measure°
The table round. [*Approaching the door.*] There's
     blood upon thy face.
     MUR. 'Tis Banquo's then.
     MACB. 'Tis better thee without than he within.
Is he dispatched?   15
     MUR. My lord, his throat is cut. That I did for
     him.
     MACB. Thou art the best o' the cutthroats. Yet he's
good
That did the like for Fleance. If thou didst it,
Thou art the nonpareil.°
     MUR.   Most royal sir.
Fleance is 'scaped.   20
     MACB. [*Aside*] Then comes my fit again. I had
     else been perfect,
Whole as the marble, founded as the rock,
As broad and general as the casing° air.   23
But now I am cabined, cribbed,° confined, bound in
To saucy° doubts and fears. — But Banquo's safe?
     MUR. Aye, my good lord. Safe in a ditch he bides,
With twenty trenchèd gashes on his head,
The least a death to nature.°
     MACB.   Thanks for that.   28
[*Aside*] There the grown serpent lies. The worm°
     that's fled
Hath nature that in time will venom breed,
No teeth for the present. Get thee gone. Tomorrow
We'll hear ourselves again.   [*Exit* MURDERER.]
     LADY M.   My royal lord,
You do not give the cheer. The feast° is sold
That is not often vouched, while 'tis a-making,
'Tis given with welcome. To feed were best at home,
From thence the sauce to meat is ceremony,   36
Meeting were bare without it.
     MACB.   Sweet remembrancer!
Now good digestion wait on appetite,
And health on both!
     LEN.   May 't please your Highness sit.

[*The* GHOST OF BANQUO *enters, and sits in* MACBETH's
place.]
     MACB. Here had we now our country's honor
     roofed°   40
Were the graced° person of our Banquo present,
Who may I rather challenge for unkindness
Than pity for mischance!
     ROSS.   His absence, sir,
Lays blame upon his promise. Please 't your High-
ness
To grace us with your royal company.   45
     MACB. The table's full.
     LEN.   Here is a place reserved, sir.
     MACB. Where?
     LEN. Here, my good lord. What is 't that moves
     your Highness?
     MACB. Which of you have done this?
     LORDS.   What, my good lord?
     MACB. Thou canst not say I did it. Never shake
Thy gory locks at me.   51
     ROSS. Gentlemen, rise. His Highness is not well.
     LADY M. Sit, worthy friends. My lord is often thus,
And hath been from his youth. Pray you keep seat,
The fit is momentary, upon a thought°   55
He will again be well. If much you note him,
You shall offend him and extend his passion.°
Feed, and regard him not. Are you a man?
     MACB. Aye, and a bold one, that dare look on that
Which might appall the Devil.
     LADY M.   Oh, proper stuff!   60
This is the very painting of your fear.
This is the air-drawn dagger which you said
Led you to Duncan. Oh, these flaws° and starts,
Impostors to true fear, would well become
A woman's story at a winter's fire,   65
Authorized by her grandam.° Shame itself!
Why do you make such faces? When all's done,
You look but on a stool.°
     MACB. Prithee see there! Behold! Look! Lo! How
     say you?
Why, what care I? If thou canst nod, speak too.   70
If charnel houses° and our graves must send
Those that we bury back, our monuments
Shall be the maws of kites.°   [*Exit* GHOST.]
     LADY M.   What, quite unmanned in folly?
     MACB. If I stand here, I saw him.
     LADY M.   Fie, for shame!

---

5. keeps . . . state: i.e., sits on her throne apart.   10. even: equal.   11. large in mirth: unrestrained in your enjoyment. measure: toast; lit., a quantity of drink.   19. nonpareil: without an equal.   23. casing: enclosing.   24. cribbed: hampered. 25. saucy: insolent.   28. nature: natural life.   29. worm: a little snake. Cf. *Ant & Cleo*, V.ii.243.   33–36. feast . . . ceremony: i.e., there is no hospitality at a feast where the guests are not made welcome; without welcome, it is a mere bought dinner — one can feed better at home; when one is away from home, ceremony should accompany the feast.

40. our . . . roofed: all the most honorable men in the country under our roof.   41. graced: honored.   55. upon a thought: as quick as thought.   57. extend . . . passion: increase his fit. 63. flaws: lit., gusts of wind.   66. Authorized . . . grandam: vouched for by her grandmother.   68. You . . . stool: Unlike the ghost which appeared on the battlements to Hamlet and his friends, Banquo's ghost is a hallucination, visible only to Macbeth. It has, however, almost always been the custom on the stage to have it visible. See s.d. at l. 39. stool: joined stool. See Pl. 17a. Only those of highest rank sat on chairs.   71. charnel houses: See App. 16.   72–73. our . . . kites: our graves shall be in the bellies of birds of prey.

MACB. Blood hath been shed ere now, i' the olden
    time,   75
Ere humane statute purged the gentle weal° —
Aye, and since too, murders have been performed
Too terrible for the ear. The time has been
That when the brains were out, the man would die,
And there an end. But now they rise again,   80
With twenty mortal murders on their crowns,°
And push us from our stools. This is more strange
Than such a murder is.

LADY M.   My worthy lord,
Your noble friends do lack you.

MACB.   I do forget.
Do not muse at me, my most worthy friends.   85
I have a strange infirmity, which is nothing
To those that know me. Come, love and health to
    all,
Then I'll sit down. Give me some wine, fill full.
I drink to the general joy o' the whole table,
And to our dear friend Banquo, whom we miss.   90
Would he were here! To all and him we thirst,
And all to all.

LORDS.   Our duties, and the pledge.
             [Re-enter GHOST.]

MACB. Avaunt!° And quit my sight! Let the earth
    hide thee!
Thy bones are marrowless, thy blood is cold,
Thou hast no speculation° in those eyes   95
Which thou dost glare with.

LADY M.   Think of this, good peers,
But as a thing of custom.° 'Tis no other,
Only it spoils the pleasure of the time.

MACB. What man dare, I dare.
Approach thou like the rugged Russian bear,   100
The armed rhinoceros, or the Hyrcan° tiger.
Take any shape but that° and my firm nerves
Shall never tremble. Or be alive again,
And dare me to the desert° with thy sword.
If trembling I inhabit then, protest me   105
The baby of a girl.° Hence, horrible shadow!
Unreal mockery, hence!   *[Exit* GHOST.]
          Why, so. Being gone,
I am a man again. Pray you sit still.

LADY M. You have displaced° the mirth, broke the
    good meeting,
With most admired° disorder.

MACB.   Can such things be,   110
And overcome° us like a summer's cloud,

Without our special wonder? You make me strange
Even to the disposition that I owe°
When now I think you can behold such sights
And keep the natural ruby of your cheeks   115
When mine is blanched with fear.

ROSS.   What sights, my lord?

LADY M. I pray you speak not, he grows worse and
    worse.
Question enrages him. At once, good night.
Stand not upon the order of your going,°
But go at once.

LEN.   Good night, and better health   120
Attend His Majesty!

LADY M.   A kind good night to all!
             [Exeunt all but MACBETH
             and LADY MACBETH.]

MACB. It will have blood. They say blood will have
    blood.
Stones have been known to move and trees to speak.
Augurs° and understood relations° have
By maggot pies and choughs° and rooks brought
    forth   125
The secret'st man of blood. What is the night?

LADY M. Almost at odds° with morning, which is
    which.

MACB. How say'st thou that Macduff denies his
    person
At our great bidding?

LADY M.   Did you send to him, sir?

MACB. I hear it by the way, but I will send.   130
There's not a one of them but in his house
I keep a servant feed.° I will tomorrow,
And betimes° I will, to the weird sisters.
More shall they speak, for now I am bent° to know,
By the worst means, the worst. For mine own good
All causes shall give way. I am in blood   136
Stepped in so far that should I wade no more,
Returning were as tedious as go o'er.
Strange things I have in head that will to hand,
Which must be acted ere they may be scanned.°

LADY M. You lack the season of all natures, sleep.°

MACB. Come, we'll to sleep. My strange and self-
    abuse°   142
Is the initiate fear° that wants hard use.
We are yet but young in deed.   *[Exeunt.]*

112. special wonder: universal astonishment. Macbeth cannot
understand why the others are seemingly so calm.   113. owe:
own, possess.   119. Stand . . . going: do not wait to take leave
in order of rank. The disorderly end to the banquet contrasts
with its formal beginning (l. 1).   124. Augurs: auguries, omens.
understood relations: the relation between the omen and what
it signifies.   125. maggot pies . . . choughs: magpies and jackdaws, birds which were regarded as having mystic qualities.
127. at odds: striving.   132. feed: in my pay as a spy.   133. betimes: in good time.   134. bent: eager — like a taut bowstring.
140. scanned: examined.   141. the . . . sleep: sleep, which (like
salt) gives seasoning to keep nature fresh.   142. self-abuse:
self-deception.   143. initiate fear: a novice's fear; i e., when I
have more experience in murder I shall not be troubled with
apparitions.

76. Ere . . . weal: before humane laws made the state civilized.
81. twenty . . . crowns: with twenty deadly wounds on their
heads.   93. Avaunt: be gone.   95. speculation: power of sight.
97. custom: common occurrence.   101. Hyrcan: from Hyrcania,
south of the Caspian Sea, where according to Pliny's *Natural
History* tigers roamed.   102. that: i.e., the specter of Banquo.
104. desert: i.e., a place where neither of us could escape.
105-06. If . . . girl: i.e., if then I live trembling (show myself a
coward), proclaim that I am the baby of a young girl.   109. displaced: upset.   110. admired: to be wondered at.   111. overcome: come over, overshadow.

SCENE V. *A heath.*

[Thunder. Enter the THREE WITCHES, *meeting* HECATE.°*]*

1. WITCH. Why, how now, Hecate! You look
    angerly.°

HEC. Have I not reason, beldams° as you are,
Saucy and overbold? How did you dare
To trade and traffic with Macbeth
In riddles and affairs of death,   5
And I, the mistress of your charms,
The close contriver° of all harms,
Was never called to bear my part,
Or show the glory of our art?
And, which is worse, all you have done   10
Hath been but for a wayward° son,
Spiteful and wrathful, who, as others do,
Loves for his own ends, not for you.
But make amends now. Get you gone,
And at the pit of Acheron°   15
Meet me i' the morning. Thither he
Will come to know his destiny.
Your vessels and your spells provide,
Your charms and everything beside.
I am for the air, this night I'll spend   20
Unto a dismal and a fatal end.
Great business must be wrought ere noon.
Upon the corner of the moon
There hangs a vaporous drop profound.
I'll catch it ere it come to ground,   25
And that distilled by magic sleights°
Shall raise such artificial sprites°
As by the strength of their illusion
Shall draw him on to his confusion.°
He shall spurn fate, scorn death, and bear   30
His hopes 'bove wisdom, grace, and fear.
And you all know security°
Is mortals' chiefest enemy.
    [Music and a song within: " Come away,°
                  come away *" etc.]*
Hark! I am called. My little spirit, see,   34
Sits in a foggy cloud and stays for me.   *[Exit.]*

1. WITCH. Come, let's make haste, she'll soon be
    back again.   *[Exeunt.]*

SCENE VI. *Forres. The palace.*

[Enter LENNOX *and another* LORD.*]*

LEN. My former speeches have but hit your
    thoughts,

Which can interpret farther.° Only I say
Things have been strangely borne.° The gracious
    Duncan
Was pitied of° Macbeth. Marry,° he was dead.
And the right-valiant Banquo walked too late,   5
Whom, you may say, if 't please you, Fleance killed,
For Fleance fled. Men must not walk too late.
Who cannot want° the thought how monstrous
It was for Malcolm and for Donalbain
To kill their gracious father? Damnèd fact!   10
How it did grieve Macbeth! Did he not straight,
In pious rage, the two delinquents tear
That were the slaves of drink and thralls° of sleep?
Was not that nobly done? Aye, and wisely too,
For 'twould have angered any heart alive   15
To hear the men deny 't. So that I say
He has borne all things well. And I do think
That had he Duncan's sons under his key —
As, an 't° please Heaven, he shall not — they should
    find
What 'twere to kill a father. So should Fleance.   20
But, peace! For from broad° words, and 'cause he
    failed
His presence° at the tyrant's feast, I hear
Macduff lives in disgrace. Sir, can you tell
Where he bestows himself?

LORD.   The son of Duncan,
From whom this tyrant holds the due of birth,   25
Lives in the English Court, and is received
Of the most pious Edward° with such grace
That the malevolence of fortune nothing
Takes from his high respect.° Thither Macduff
Is gone to pray the holy King, upon his aid   30
To wake Northumberland and warlike Siward,
That by the help of these, with Him above
To ratify the work, we may again
Give to our tables meat, sleep to our nights,
Free from our feasts and banquets bloody knives,
Do faithful homage and receive free honors° —   36
All which we pine for now. And this report
Hath so exasperate the King that he
Prepares for some attempt of war.

LEN.   Sent he to Macduff?

LORD. He did. And with an absolute " Sir, not I,"
The cloudy° messenger turns me his back,   41
And hums, as who should say " You'll rue the time
That clogs° me with this answer."

LEN.   And that well might
Advise him to a caution, to hold what distance

Sc. v: s.d., Hecate: goddess of witchcraft. See *Macb* Intro.
p. 1184a.   1. angerly: angrily.   2. beldams: hags.   7. close contriver: secret inventor.   11. wayward: perverse.   15. Acheron:
Hell.   26. sleights: devices.   27. artificial sprites: spirits
created by magic art.   29. confusion: destruction.   32. security: false sense of safety.   33. s.d., Come away: The words
of this song and of "Black Spirits" (IV.i.43) occur in a play
called *The Witch* by Thomas Middleton.

Sc. vi: 1–2. hit . . . farther: given you matter from which to
draw conclusions.   3. borne: managed.   4. of: by. Marry:
Mary, by the Virgin.   8. want: be without.   13. thralls: slaves.
19. an't: if it.   21. broad: too free.   21–22. failed . . . presence:
failed to appear.   27. most . . . Edward: King Edward the
Confessor (died 1066), regarded as a most saintly person.
28–29. malevolence . . . respect: in spite of his misfortunes he is
regarded with the highest respect.   36. free honors: honors bestowed on free men, and not as a reward for crimes.   41. cloudy:
surly.   43. clogs: obstructs.

His wisdom can provide. Some holy angel   45
Fly to the Court of England and unfold
His message ere he come, that a swift blessing
May soon return to this our suffering country
Under a hand accursed!

   LORD.   I'll send my prayers with him.   [*Exeunt.*]

Act IV

SCENE I.° *A cavern. In the middle, a boiling
caldron.*

[*Thunder. Enter the* THREE WITCHES.]

1. WITCH. Thrice the brinded° cat hath mewed.
2. WITCH. Thrice and once the hedgepig° whined.
3. WITCH. Harpier° cries " 'Tis time, 'tis time."
1. WITCH. Round about the caldron go.
In the poisoned entrails throw.   5
Toad, that under cold stone
Days and nights has thirty-one
Sweltered° venom sleeping got,
Boil thou first i' the charmèd pot.
   ALL.   Double, double toil and trouble,   10
Fire burn and caldron bubble.
2. WITCH. Fillet of a fenny° snake,
In the caldron boil and bake.
Eye of newt and toe of frog,
Wool of bat and tongue of dog,   15
Adder's fork° and blindworm's sting,°
Lizard's leg and howlet's° wing,
For a charm of powerful trouble,
Like a Hell broth boil and bubble.
   ALL.   Double, double toil and trouble,   20
Fire burn and caldron bubble.
3. WITCH. Scale of dragon, tooth of wolf,
Witches' mummy,° maw and gulf°
Of the ravined° salt-sea shark,
Root of hemlock digged i' the dark,   25
Liver of blaspheming Jew,
Gall of goat and slips of yew
Slivered° in the moon's eclipse,
Nose of Turk and Tartar's lips,
Finger of birth-strangled babe   30
Ditch-delivered° by a drab,

Make the gruel thick and slab.°
Add thereto a tiger's chaudron,°
For the ingredients of our caldron.
   ALL.   Double, double toil and trouble,   35
Fire burn and caldron bubble.
2. WITCH. Cool it with a baboon's blood,
Then the charm is firm and good.
      [*Enter* HECATE *to the other* THREE WITCHES.]
   HEC.   Oh, well done! I commend your pains,
And everyone shall share i' the gains.   40
And now about the caldron sing
Like elves and fairies in a ring,
Enchanting all that you put in.
      [*Music and a song:* " Black Spirits,"° etc.
                 HECATE *retires.*]
2. WITCH. By the pricking of my thumbs,
Something wicked this way comes.   45
  Open, locks,
  Whoever knocks!
         [*Enter* MACBETH.]
   MACB.   How now, you secret, black, and midnight
     hags!
What is 't you do?
   ALL.   A deed without a name.
   MACB.   I conjure you, by that which you profess,°
Howe'er you come to know it, answer me.   51
Though you untie the winds° and let them fight
Against the churches; though the yesty° waves
Confound and swallow navigation up;
Though bladed° corn be lodged° and trees blown
    down;   55
Though castles topple on their warders' heads;
Though palaces and pyramids do slope
Their heads to their foundations; though the treas-
    ure
Of nature's germens° tumble all together,
Even till destruction sicken — answer me   60
To what I ask you.
   1. WITCH.   Speak.
   2. WITCH.   Demand.
   3. WITCH.   We'll answer.
   1. WITCH. Say, if thou'dst rather hear it from our
    mouths,
Or from our masters?
   MACB.   Call 'em, let me see 'em.
   1. WITCH. Pour in sow's blood that hath eaten
Her nine farrow,° grease that's sweaten   65
From the murderer's gibbet° throw
Into the flame.
   ALL.   Come, high or low,

Act IV, Sc. i: See *Macb* Intro. p. 1184a.   **1. brinded:** brin-
dled, striped.   **2. hedgepig:** hedgehog.   **3. Harpier:** the name
of a familiar spirit.   **8. Sweltered:** sweated out.   **12. fenny:**
from a fen.   **16. fork:** tongue. **blindworm's sting:** the blindworm
is a small snakelike legless lizard; it does not, in fact, have
a sting.   **17. howlet:** small owl.   **23. mummy:** dried corpse.
Mummy from Egypt was formerly considered a potent drug, and
regularly stocked by old-time druggists. **maw . . . gulf:** belly
and gullet.   **24. ravined:** ravenous.   **28. Slivered:** sliced.
31. Ditch-delivered: born in a ditch.

32. slab: like thick mud.   **33. chaudron:** entrails.   **43. s.d.,**
Black Spirits: See III.v.33,n.   **50. profess:** i.e., the art of witchcraft.   **52. untie . . . winds:** Witches were reputed to be
able to control the winds.   **53. yesty:** foaming.   **55. bladed:** in
the ear. **lodged:** laid flat.   **59. nature's germens:** the seeds
of matter, all living things.   **65. farrow:** young.   **66. gibbet:**
gallows on which the bodies of executed criminals were hung as a
warning.

Thyself and office deftly show!

[*Thunder.* FIRST APPARITION: *an armed Head.*]

MACB. Tell me, thou unknown power ——

1. WITCH.　　　　　　　He knows thy thought.

Hear his speech, but say thou naught.　　　　70

1. APP. Macbeth! Macbeth! Macbeth! Beware Macduff,

Beware the Thane of Fife. Dismiss me. Enough.

[*Descends.*]

MACB. Whate'er thou art, for thy good caution thanks.

Thou hast harped° my fear aright. But one word more ——

1. WITCH. He will not be commanded. Here's another,　　　　75

More potent than the first.

[*Thunder.* SECOND APPARITION: *a bloody Child.*]

2. APP. Macbeth! Macbeth! Macbeth!

MACB. Had I three ears, I'd hear thee.

2. APP. Be bloody, bold, and resolute, laugh to scorn

The power of man, for none of woman born　　80

Shall harm Macbeth.　　　　　　[*Descends.*]

MACB. Then live, Macduff. What need I fear of thee?

But yet I'll make assurance double sure,

And take a bond of fate.° Thou shalt not live,

That I may tell pale-hearted fear it lies,　　　85

And sleep in spite of thunder.

[*Thunder.* THIRD APPARITION: *a Child crowned, with a tree in his hand.*]

　　　　　　　　　　　What is this

That rises like the issue of a king,

And wears upon his baby brow the round

And top of sovereignty?°

ALL.　　　　　　Listen, but speak not to 't.

3. APP. Be lion-mettled, proud, and take no care

Who chafes, who frets, or where conspirers are.　91

Macbeth shall never vanquished be until

Great Birnam Wood to high Dunsinane Hill

Shall come against him.　　　　[*Descends.*]

MACB.　　　　　　That will never be.

Who can impress° the forest, bid the tree　　95

Unfix his earthbound root? Sweet bodements!°

Good!

Rebellion's head, rise never till the wood

Of Birnam rise, and our high-placed Macbeth

Shall live the lease of nature,° pay his breath

To time and mortal custom. Yet my heart　　100

Throbs to know one thing. Tell me, if your art

Can tell so much. Shall Banquo's issue ever

Reign in this kingdom?

ALL.　　　　　　Seek to know no more.

---

74. harped: hit upon.　84. bond of fate: i.e., to force fate to keep the agreement, he will kill Macduff.　88–89. round . . . sovereignty: a crown.　95. impress: conscript.　96. bodements: prophecies.　99. lease of nature: the natural length of life. Cf. III.ii.38.

MACB. I will be satisfied. Deny me this,

And an eternal curse fall on you! Let me know.　105

Why sinks that caldron? And what noise is this?

[*Hautboys.*]

1. WITCH. Show!

2. WITCH. Show!

3. WITCH. Show!

ALL. Show his eyes, and grieve his heart.　　110

Come like shadows, so depart!

[*A show of eight* KINGS,° *the last with a glass° in his hand,* BANQUO'S GHOST *following.*]

MACB. Thou art too like the spirit of Banquo. Down!

Thy crown does sear mine eyeballs. And thy hair,

Thou other gold-bound brow, is like the first.

A third is like the former. Filthy hags!　　115

Why do you show me this? A fourth! Start, eyes!

What, will the line stretch out to the crack of doom?

Another yet! A seventh! I'll see no more.

And yet the eighth appears, who bears a glass

Which shows me many more, and some I see　120

That twofold balls and treble scepters° carry.

Horrible sight! Now I see 'tis true,

For the blood-boltered° Banquo smiles upon me,

And points at them for his. What, is this so?

1. WITCH. Aye, sir, all this is so. But why　125

Stands Macbeth thus amazedly?

Come, Sisters, cheer we up his sprites,°

And show the best of our delights.

I'll charm the air to give a sound

While you perform your antic round,°　　130

That this great King may kindly say

Our duties did his welcome pay.

[*Music. The* WITCHES *dance, and then vanish, with* HECATE.]

MACB. Where are they? Gone? Let this pernicious hour

Stand aye accursèd in the calendar!

Come in, without there!

[*Enter* LENNOX.]

LEN.　　　　　What's your Grace's will?　135

MACB. Saw you the weird sisters?

LEN.　　　　　　　No, my lord.

MACB. Came they not by you?

LEN.　　　　　　No indeed, my lord.

MACB. Infected be the air whereon they ride,

And damned all those that trust them! I did hear

The galloping of horse. Who was 't came by?　140

LEN. 'Tis two or three, my lord, that bring you word

Macduff is fled to England.

---

111. s.d., A . . . kings: a dumb show, figures passing across the back of the stage in silent action. glass: mirror.　121. twofold . . . scepters: i.e., the insignia of the Kingdoms of England, Scotland, and Ireland united in 1603 when King James VI of Scotland (Banquo's descendant) became also James I of England.　123. blood-boltered: with his hair matted with blood.　127. sprites: spirits.　130. antic round: fantastic dance.

MACB.   Fled to England!

LEN. Aye, my good lord.

MACB. [*Aside*] Time, thou anticipatest my dread
exploits.

The flighty purpose never is o'ertook   145
Unless the deed go with it.° From this moment
The very firstlings° of my heart shall be
The firstlings of my hand. And even now,
To crown my thoughts with acts, be it thought and
done.

The castle of Macduff I will surprise,   150
Seize upon Fife, give to the edge o' the sword
His wife, his babes, and all unfortunate souls
That trace him in his line.° No boasting like a fool,
This deed I'll do before this purpose cool.   154
But no more sights! — Where are these gentlemen?
Come, bring me where they are.   [*Exeunt.*]

SCENE II. *Fife.* MACDUFF'S *castle.*

[*Enter* LADY MACDUFF, *her* SON, *and* ROSS.]

L. MACD. What had he done, to make him fly the
land?

ROSS. You must have patience, madam.

L. MACD.   He had none.
His flight was madness. When our actions do not,
Our fears do make us traitors.

ROSS.   You know not
Whether it was his wisdom or his fear.   5

L. MACD. Wisdom! To leave his wife, to leave his
babes,
His mansion and his titles,° in a place
From whence himself does fly? He loves us not,
He wants the natural touch. For the poor wren,
The most diminutive of birds, will fight,   10
Her young ones in her nest, against the owl.
All is the fear and nothing is the love,
As little is the wisdom, where the flight
So runs against all reason.

ROSS.   My dearest coz,°
I pray you school° yourself. But, for your husband,
He is noble, wise, judicious, and best knows   16
The fits o' the season.° I dare not speak much fur-
ther.
But cruel are the times, when we are traitors
And do not know ourselves, when we hold rumor
From what we fear, yet know not what we fear,   20
But float upon a wild and violent sea
Each way and move.° I take my leave of you.

145–46. The . . . it: the plan is never fulfilled unless carried
out at once.   147. firstlings: lit., first fruits.   153. trace . . .
line: i.e., are related to him.
     Sc. ii: 7. titles: possessions; lit., that to which he has a
title.   14. coz: cousin.   15. school: discipline.   17. fits . . .
season: sudden changes of the times.   21–22. But . . . move:
like a ship, powerless in a tempest, carried hither and thither.

Shall not be long but I'll be here again.
Things at the worst will cease, or else climb upward
To what they were before. My pretty cousin,   25
Blessing upon you!

L. MACD. Fathered he is, and yet he's fatherless.

ROSS. I am so much a fool, should I stay longer,
It would be my disgrace and your discomfort.
I take my leave at once.   [*Exit.*]

L. MACD.   Sirrah, your father's dead.   30
And what will you do now? How will you live?

SON. As birds do, Mother.

L. MACD.   What, with worms and flies?

SON. With what I get, I mean, and so do they.

L. MACD. Poor bird! Thou'dst never fear the net
nor lime,°
The pitfall nor the gin.°   35

SON. Why should I, Mother? Poor birds they are
not set for.°
My father is not dead, for all your saying.

L. MACD. Yes, he is dead. How wilt thou do for a
father?

SON. Nay, how will you do for a husband?

L. MACD. Why, I can buy me twenty at any
market.   40

SON. Then you'll buy 'em to sell again.

L. MACD. Thou speak'st with all thy wit, and yet,
i' faith,
With wit enough for thee.

SON. Was my father a traitor, Mother?

L. MACD. Aye, that he was.   45

SON. What is a traitor?

L. MACD. Why, one that swears and lies.

SON. And be all traitors that do so?

L. MACD. Every one that does so is a traitor, and
must be hanged.   50

SON. And must they all be hanged that swear and
lie?

L. MACD. Every one.

SON. Who must hang them?

L. MACD. Why, the honest men.   55

SON. Then the liars and swearers are fools, for
there are liars and swearers enow to beat the honest
men and hang up them.

L. MACD. Now, God help thee, poor monkey! But
how wilt thou do for a father?   60

SON. If he were dead, you'd weep for him. If you
would not, it were a good sign that I should quickly
have a new father.

L. MACD. Poor prattler, how thou talk'st!

[*Enter a* MESSENGER.]

MESS. Bless you, fair dame! I am not to you
known,   65
Though in your state of honor I am perfect.°
I doubt° some danger does approach you nearly.

34. lime: birdlime.   35. gin: snare.   36. Poor . . . for: no one
sets a trap for a poor bird.   66. state . . . perfect: I well know
you to be an honorable person.   67. doubt: suspect.

If you will take a homely° man's advice,
Be not found here. Hence, with your little ones.
To fright you thus, methinks I am too savage,　70
To do worse to you were fell° cruelty,
Which is too nigh your person. Heaven preserve
　you!
I dare abide no longer.　　　　　　　[*Exit.*]
　L. MACD.　　　　　Whither should I fly?
I have done no harm. But I remember now
I am in this earthly world, where to do harm　75
Is often laudable, to do good sometime
Accounted dangerous folly. Why, then, alas,
Do I put up that womanly defense,
To say I have done no harm? — What are these
　faces?
　　　　　[*Enter* MURDERERS.]
　I. MUR. Where is your husband?　　　　80
　L. MACD. I hope, in no place so unsanctified
Where such as thou mayst find him.
　I. MUR.　　　　　　He's a traitor.
　SON. Thou liest, thou shag-eared° villain!
　I. MUR.　　　　What, you egg!° [*Stabbing him.*]
Young fry° of treachery!
　SON.　　　　He has killed me, Mother.　84
Run away, I pray you!　　　　　　[*Dies.*]
　　　[*Exit* LADY MACDUFF, *crying* "Murder!"
　　　Exeunt MURDERERS, *following her.*]

SCENE III.° *England. Before the* KING'S
　　　　　palace.

　　　[*Enter* MALCOLM *and* MACDUFF.]
　MAL. Let us seek out some desolate shade, and
　there
Weep our sad bosoms empty.
　MACD.　　　　　　Let us rather
Hold fast the mortal° sword, and like good men
Bestride our downfall'n birthdom.° Each new morn
New widows howl, new orphans cry, new sorrows
Strike Heaven on the face, that it resounds　6
As if it felt with Scotland and yelled out
Like syllable of dolor.°
　MAL.　　　　　What I believe, I'll wail,
What know, believe. And what I can redress,
As I shall find the time to friend,° I will.　10
What you have spoke, it may be so perchance.
This tyrant, whose sole name° blisters our tongues,
Was once thought honest. You have loved him well,

He hath not touched you yet. I am young, but
　something
You may deserve of him through me, and wisdom
To offer up a weak, poor, innocent lamb　16
To appease an angry god.
　MACD. I am not treacherous.
　MAL.　　　　　　But Macbeth is.
A good and virtuous nature may recoil
In an imperial charge.° But I shall crave your par-
　don.　　　　　　　　　　　　　20
That which you are, my thoughts cannot transpose.°
Angels are bright still, though the brightest fell.
Though all things foul would wear the brows of
　grace,
Yet grace must still look so.°
　MACD.　　　　I have lost my hopes.
　MAL. Perchance even there where I did find my
　doubts.　　　　　　　　　　　　25
Why in that rawness° left you wife and child,
Those precious motives, those strong knots of love,
Without leave-taking? I pray you
Let not my jealousies be your dishonors,　29
But mine own safeties.° You may be rightly just,
Whatever I shall think.
　MACD.　　　　Bleed, bleed, poor country.
Great tyranny, lay thou thy basis sure,
For goodness dare not check thee. Wear thou thy
　wrongs,
The title is affeered.° Fare thee well, lord.
I would not be the villain that thou think'st　35
For the whole space that's in the tyrant's grasp
And the rich East to boot.
　MAL.　　　　　Be not offended.
I speak not as in absolute fear of you.
I think our country sinks beneath the yoke.
It weeps, it bleeds, and each new day a gash　40
Is added to her wounds. I think withal
There would be hands uplifted in my right,
And here from gracious England have I offer
Of goodly thousands. But for all this,
When I shall tread upon the tyrant's head,　45
Or wear it on my sword, yet my poor country
Shall have more vices than it had before,
More suffer and more sundry ways than ever,
By him that shall succeed.
　MACD.　　　　What should he be?
　MAL. It is myself I mean, in whom I know　50
All the particulars of vice so grafted°
That when they shall be opened, black Macbeth
Will seem as pure as snow, and the poor state
Esteem him as a lamb, being compared

---

68. homely: simple, plain.　71. fell: fierce.　83. shag-eared:
hairy-eared. egg: i.e., unhatched traitor.　84. fry: spawn.
　Sc. iii: The conversation between Malcolm and Macduff
comes from the *Chronicle*.　3. mortal: deadly.　4. birthdom:
native land.　6–8. that . . . dolor: that even the heavens resound as if they echoed the lamentations of Scotland.　10. time
to friend: the time to be friendly.　12. sole name: very name
by itself.

19–20. A . . . charge: even a good man may degenerate and do a
wicked deed if ordered by a king.　21. transpose: alter.　24. look
so: i.e., like itself, gracious.　26. rawness: unprotected state.
29–30. Let . . . safeties: i.e., I am suspicious not because I
would dishonor you but would look after my own safety.　34. title
is affeered: legal right is confirmed.　51. grafted: engrafted, in-
grown.

With my confineless harms.

MACD.   Not in the legions 55
Of horrid Hell can come a devil more damned
In evils to top Macbeth.

MAL.   I grant him bloody,
Luxurious,° avaricious, false, deceitful,
Sudden, malicious, smacking of every sin
That has a name. But there's no bottom, none, 60
In my voluptuousness.° Your wives, your daughters,
Your matrons and your maids, could not fill up
The cistern of my lust, and my desire
All continent impediments would o'erbear°
That did oppose my will. Better Macbeth 65
Than such a one to reign.

MACD.   Boundless intemperance
In nature is a tyranny. It hath been
The untimely emptying of the happy throne,
And fall of many kings. But fear not yet
To take upon you what is yours. You may 70
Convey your pleasures in a spacious plenty,°
And yet seem cold,° the time° you may so hood-
    wink.
We have willing dames enough. There cannot be
That vulture in you to devour so many
As will to greatness dedicate themselves, 75
Finding it so inclined.°

MAL.   With this there grows
In my most ill-composed affection such
A stanchless° avarice that, were I King,
I should cut off the nobles for their lands,
Desire his jewels and this other's house. 80
And my more-having would be as a sauce
To make me hunger more, that I should forge
Quarrels unjust against the good and loyal,
Destroying them for wealth.

MACD.   This avarice
Sticks deeper, grows with more pernicious root 85
Than summer-seeming° lust, and it hath been
The sword of° our slain kings. Yet do not fear.
Scotland hath foisons° to fill up your will
Of your mere own.° All these are portable,°
With other graces weighed.° 90

MAL. But I have none. The king-becoming
    graces —
As justice, verity, temperance, stableness,°
Bounty, perseverance, mercy, lowliness,

Devotion, patience, courage, fortitude —
I have no relish of° them, but abound 95
In the division of each several crime,°
Acting it many ways. Nay, had I power, I should
Pour the sweet milk of concord into Hell,
Uproar the universal peace, confound
All unity on earth.

MACD.   Oh, Scotland, Scotland! 100

MAL. If such a one be fit to govern, speak.
I am as I have spoken.

MACD.   Fit to govern!
No, not to live. O nation miserable!
With an untitled° tyrant bloody-sceptered,
When shalt thou see thy wholesome days again,
Since that the truest issue of thy throne° 106
By his own interdiction° stands accursed,
And does blaspheme his breed? Thy royal father
Was a most sainted King. The Queen that bore thee,
Oftener upon her knees than on her feet, 110
Died every day she lived.° Fare thee well!
These evils thou repeat'st upon thyself
Have banished me from Scotland. O my breast,
Thy hope ends here!

MAL.   Macduff, this noble passion,°
Child of integrity, hath from my soul 115
Wiped the black scruples, reconciled my thoughts
To thy good truth and honor. Devilish Macbeth
By many of these trains° hath sought to win me
Into his power, and modest wisdom plucks me
From overcredulous haste. But God above 120
Deal between thee and me! For even now
I put myself to thy direction, and
Unspeak mine own detraction, here abjure
The taints and blames I laid upon myself,
For strangers to my nature. I am yet 125
Unknown to woman, never was forsworn,°
Scarcely have coveted what was mine own,
At no time broke my faith, would not betray
The Devil to his fellow, and delight
No less in truth than life. My first false speaking
Was this upon myself. What I am truly 131
Is thine and my poor country's to command,
Whither indeed, before thy here-approach,
Old Siward, with ten thousand warlike men,
Already at a point,° was setting forth. 135
Now we'll together, and the chance of goodness
Be like our warranted quarrel! Why are you silent?

MACD. Such welcome and unwelcome things at
    once

---

55. confineless harms: the uncontrollable evil which I shall commit.   58. Luxurious: lustful.   61. voluptuousness: lust.
64. All . . . o'erbear: would overcome all restraining barriers.
71. Convey . . . plenty: find plenty of room in which to indulge your pleasures secretly.   72. cold: chaste. time: i.e., the world.
73–76. There . . . inclined: however greedy you are, there will be as many women eager to satisfy one in your great position.   78. stanchless: insatiable.   86. summer-seeming: which lasts like summer; i.e., only for a season.   87. sword of: which has killed.   88. foisons: plenty.   89. mere own: absolute property. portable: endurable.   90. With . . . weighed: so long as there are good qualities to counterbalance them.   92. stableness: constancy.

95. relish of: taste for.   96. division . . . crime: in every part of each particular kind of crime.   104. untitled: having no legal right to be King.   106. issue . . . throne: child of your King.   107. interdiction: exclusion.   111. Died . . . lived: i.e., lived continually in a state of grace. The phrase comes from I Corinthians 15:31: "I protest by your rejoicing which I have in Christ Jesus our Lord, I die daily."   114. Passion: emotion.
118. trains: enticements.   126. was forsworn: broke my oath.
135. at a point: ready for action.

'Tis hard to reconcile.

[*Enter a* DOCTOR.]

MAL. Well, more anon. Comes the King forth, I
pray you?   140

DOCT. Aye, sir, there are a crew of wretched souls
That stay his cure.° Their malady convinces
The great assay of art,° but at his touch,
Such sanctity hath Heaven given his hand,   144
They presently° amend.

MAL.   I thank you, Doctor. [*Exit* DOCTOR.]

MACD. What's the disease he means?

MAL.   'Tis called the Evil.°
A most miraculous work in this good King,
Which often, since my here-remain in England,
I have seen him do. How he solicits Heaven,
Himself best knows. But strangely visited people,
All swoln° and ulcerous, pitiful to the eye,   151
The mere° despair of surgery, he cures,
Hanging a golden stamp° about their necks,
Put on with holy prayers. And 'tis spoken,
To the succeeding royalty he leaves   155
The healing benediction. With this strange virtue
He hath a heavenly gift of prophecy,
And sundry blessings hang about his throne
That speak him full of grace.

[*Enter* ROSS.]

MACD.   See, who comes here?   159

MAL. My countryman, but yet I know him not.

MACD. My ever gentle° cousin, welcome hither.

MAL. I know him now. Good God, betimes° remove
The means that makes us strangers!

ROSS.   Sir, amen.

MACD. Stands Scotland where it did?

ROSS.   Alas, poor country!
Almost afraid to know itself! It cannot   165
Be called our mother, but our grave. Where nothing
But who knows nothing is once seen to smile;
Where sighs and groans and shrieks that rend the
air
Are made, not marked; where violent sorrow seems
A modern ecstasy.° The dead man's knell   170
Is there scarce asked for who, and good men's lives
Expire before the flowers in their caps,
Dying or ere they sicken.

MACD.   Oh, relation
Too nice,° and yet too true!

MAL.   What's the newest grief?

ROSS. That of an hour's age doth hiss the speaker.°
Each minute teems° a new one.

MACD.   How does my wife?   176

ROSS. Why, well.

MACD.   And all my children?

ROSS.   Well too.

MACD. The tyrant has not battered at their peace?

ROSS. No, they were well at peace when I did
leave 'em.

MACD. Be not a niggard° of your speech. How
goes 't?   180

ROSS. When I came hither to transport the tidings,
Which I have heavily borne, there ran a rumor
Of many worthy fellows that were out,°
Which was to my belief witnessed° the rather,
For that I saw the tyrant's power° afoot.   185
Now is the time of help, your eye in Scotland
Would create soldiers, make our women fight,
To doff° their dire distresses.

MAL.   Be 't their comfort
We are coming thither. Gracious England hath
Lent us good Siward and ten thousand men —   190
An older and a better soldier none
That Christendom gives out.

ROSS.   Would I could answer
This comfort with the like! But I have words
That would be howled out in the desert air,
Where hearing should not latch° them.

MACD.   What concern they?   195
The general cause? Or is it a fee grief
Due to some single breast?°

ROSS.   No mind that's honest
But in it shares some woe, though the main part
Pertains to you alone.

MACD.   If it be mine,
Keep it not from me, quickly let me have it.   200

ROSS. Let not your ears despise my tongue forever,
Which shall possess them with the heaviest sound
That ever yet they heard.

MACD.   Hum! I guess at it.

ROSS. Your castle is surprised, your wife and babes
Savagely slaughtered. To relate the manner   205
Were, on the quarry° of these murdered deer,
To add the death of you.

MAL.   Merciful Heaven!
What, man! Ne'er pull your hat upon your brows.°
Give sorrow words. The grief that does not speak
Whispers the o'erfraught° heart and bids it break.

---

142. stay . . . cure: wait for him to heal them.   142–43. convinces . . . art: defeats the attempts of the medical art.
145. presently: immediately.   146. the Evil: scrofula, a skin
disease. Holinshed notes that King Edward the Confessor "used
to help those that were vexed with the disease commonly called
the King's Evil and left that virtue as it was a portion of inheritance unto his successors." The reference here is dragged in as
a compliment to King James I who was at first unwilling to continue the practice of touching sufferers until urged by his English Ministers.   151. swoln: swollen.   152. mere: utter, sheer.
153. stamp: medal.   161. gentle: noble.   162. betimes: soon.
170. modern ecstasy: slight mental disturbance.   174. nice: exact.

175. That . . . speaker: i.e., there are so many sorrows that a
report only one hour old is hissed as stale news.   176. teems:
gives birth to.   180. niggard: sparing.   183. out: i.e., in rebellion.   184. witnessed: confirmed.   185. power: army.
188. doff: put off.   195. latch: catch.   196–97. fee . . . breast:
a grief which belongs to a single owner.   206. quarry: heap of
slain deer after a hunt. Cf. *Haml*, V.ii.375.   208. What . . .
brows: one of many instances when the action is described in the
dialogue.   210. o'erfraught: overladen.

MACD. My children too?

ROSS.　　　　　Wife, children, servants, all　211
That could be found.

MACD.　　　　　　And I must be from thence!
My wife killed too?

ROSS.　　　　I have said.

MAL.　　　　　　　　Be comforted.
Let's make us medicines of our great revenge,
To cure this deadly grief.　　　　　　　215

MACD. He has no children.° All my pretty ones?
Did you say all? O Hellkite! All?
What, all my pretty chickens and their dam
At one fell swoop?

MAL. Dispute° it like a man.

MACD.　　　　　　　I shall do so,　220
But I must also feel it as a man.
I cannot but remember such things were,
That were most precious to me. Did Heaven look on
And would not take their part? Sinful Macduff,
They were all struck for thee! Naught° that I am,
Not for their own demerits, but for mine,　226
Fell slaughter on their souls. Heaven rest them now!

MAL. Be this the whetstone of your sword. Let
　　grief
Convert to anger, blunt not the heart, enrage it.

MACD. Oh, I could play the woman with mine
　　eyes,　　　　　　　　　　　　　230
And braggart with my tongue! But, gentle Heavens,
Cut short all intermission.° Front to front°
Bring thou this fiend of Scotland and myself,
Within my sword's length set him. If he 'scape,
Heaven forgive him too!

MAL.　　　　　This tune goes manly.　235
Come, go we to the King. Our power is ready,
Our lack is nothing but our leave.° Macbeth
Is ripe for shaking, and the powers above
Put on their instruments. Receive what cheer you
　　may.
The night is long that never finds the day.　240
　　　　　　　　　　　　　　　　　　[*Exeunt.*]

Act V

SCENE I. *Dunsinane. Anteroom in the castle.*

[*Enter a* DOCTOR OF PHYSIC *and a*
WAITING GENTLEWOMAN.]

DOCT. I have two nights watched with you, but
can perceive no truth in your report. When was it
she last walked?　　　　　　　　　　　　3

GEN. Since His Majesty went into the field,° I
have seen her rise from her bed, throw her nightgown upon her, unlock her closet,° take forth paper,
fold it, write upon 't, read it, afterward seal it, and
again return to bed, yet all this while in a most fast
sleep.　　　　　　　　　　　　　　　9

DOCT. A great perturbation in nature, to receive at
once the benefit of sleep and do the effects of watching! In this slumbery agitation, besides her walking
and other actual performances, what, at any time,
have you heard her say?　　　　　　　　15

GEN. That, sir, which I will not report after her.

DOCT. You may to me, and 'tis most meet you
should.

GEN. Neither to you nor anyone, having no witness to confirm my speech. [*Enter* LADY MAC-　21
BETH, *with a taper.*°] Lo you, here she comes! This
is her very guise,° and, upon my life, fast asleep.
Observe her. Stand close.°

DOCT. How came she by that light?　　　25

GEN. Why, it stood by her. She has light by her
continually, 'tis her command.

DOCT. You see, her eyes are open.

GEN. Aye, but their sense is shut.

DOCT. What is it she does now? Look how she
rubs her hands.　　　　　　　　　　　31

GEN. It is an accustomed action with her to seem
thus washing her hands. I have known her continue
in this a quarter of an hour.

LADY M. Yet here's a spot.　　　　　　35

DOCT. Hark! She speaks. I will set down what
comes from her, to satisfy my remembrance the more
strongly.

LADY M. Out, damned spot! Out, I say! One, two
— why, then 'tis time to do 't. Hell is murky.　40
Fie, my lord, fie! A soldier, and afeard? What need
we fear who knows it, when none can call our power
to account? Yet who would have thought the old
man to have had so much blood in him?　　45

DOCT. Do you mark that?

LADY M. The Thane of Fife had a wife. Where is
she now? What, will these hands ne'er be clean?°
No more o' that, my lord, no more o' that. You mar
all with this starting.　　　　　　　　50

DOCT. Go to, go to. You have known what you
should not.

GEN. She has spoke what she should not, I am
sure of that. Heaven knows what she has known.

LADY M. Here's the smell of the blood still. All the
perfumes of Arabia will not sweeten this little hand.
Oh, oh, oh!

DOCT. What a sigh is there! The heart is sorely
charged.°　　　　　　　　　　　　60

216. He . . . children: either Malcolm has no children and so cannot truly sympathize; or — more probably — Macbeth has no
children and so Macduff can never exact a full vengeance.
220. Dispute: strive against.　225. Naught: worthless.　232. intermission: interval between actions. Front to front: face to face.
237. leave: permission to go.

Act V, Sc. i: 4. went . . . field: set out with his army.
6. closet: chest containing private papers.　22. s.d., taper:
candle.　23. guise: custom — as described in ll. 4–9.　24. close:
hidden.　48. these . . . clean: Cf. II.ii.67.　60. charged:
burdened.

GEN. I would not have such a heart in my bosom
for the dignity of the whole body.

DOCT. Well, well, well——

GEN. Pray God it be, sir.　　　　　　　　　64

DOCT. This disease is beyond my practice. Yet I
have known those which have walked in their sleep
who have died holily in their beds.

LADY M. Wash your hands, put on your nightgown, look not so pale. I tell you yet again, Banquo's
buried, he cannot come out on 's grave.　　　71

DOCT. Even so?

LADY M. To bed, to bed, there's knocking at the
gate. Come, come, come, come, give me your hand.
What's done cannot be undone. To bed, to bed, 75
to bed.　　　　　　　　　　　　　　　[Exit.]

DOCT. Will she go now to bed?

GEN. Directly.

DOCT. Foul whisperings are abroad. Unnatural
deeds
Do breed unnatural troubles. Infected minds 80
To their deaf pillows will discharge their secrets.
More needs she the divine than the physician.
God, God forgive us all! Look after her,
Remove from her the means of all annoyance,°
And still° keep eyes upon her. So good night. 85
My mind she has mated° and amazed my sight.
I think, but dare not speak.

GEN.　　　　　Good night, good Doctor. [Exeunt.]

SCENE II. *The country near Dunsinane.*

[*Drum and colors.*° *Enter* MENTEITH, CAITHNESS,
ANGUS, LENNOX, *and* SOLDIERS.]

MENT. The English power is near, led on by Mal-
colm,
His uncle Siward, and the good Macduff.
Revenges burn in them, for their dear° causes
Would to the bleeding and the grim alarm°
Excite the mortified° man.

ANG.　　　　　　　Near Birnam Wood 5
Shall we well meet them. That way are they coming.

CAITH. Who knows if Donalbain be with his
brother?

LEN. For certain, sir, he is not. I have a file°
Of all the gentry. There is Siward's son,
And many unrough° youths that even now 10
Protest their first of manhood.°

MENT.　　　　　　What does the tyrant?

CAITH. Great Dunsinane he strongly fortifies.
Some say he's mad. Others, that lesser hate him,

Do call it valiant fury. But for certain
He cannot buckle his distempered cause 15
Within the belt of rule.°

ANG.　　　　　　　Now does he feel
His secret murders sticking on his hands,
Now minutely revolts upbraid his faith breach.°
Those he commands move only in command,
Nothing in love. Now does he feel his title 20
Hang loose about him, like a giant's robe
Upon a dwarfish thief.

MENT.　　　　　　Who then shall blame
His pestered° senses to recoil and start,
When all that is within him does condemn
Itself for being there?

CAITH.　　　　　Well, march we on, 25
To give obedience where 'tis truly owed.
Meet we the medicine of the sickly weal,°
And with him pour we, in our country's purge,
Each drop of us.

LEN.　　　　　Or so much as it needs
To dew° the sovereign flower° and drown the
weeds.　　　　　　　　　　　　　30
Make we our march toward Birnam.

[*Exeunt, marching.*]

SCENE III. *Dunsinane. A room in the castle.*

[*Enter* MACBETH, DOCTOR, *and* ATTENDANTS.]

MACB. Bring me no more reports, let them fly all.
Till Birnam Wood remove to Dunsinane 2
I cannot taint° with fear. What's the boy Malcolm?
Was he not born of woman? The spirits that know
All mortal consequences° have pronounced me thus·
"Fear not, Macbeth, no man that's born of woman
Shall e'er have power upon thee." Then fly, false
thanes,　　　　　　　　　　　　　　7
And mingle with the English epicures.°
The mind I sway by and the heart I bear
Shall never sag with doubt nor shake with fear. 10
[*Enter a* SERVANT.] The Devil damn thee black,°
thou cream-faced loon!°
Where got'st thou that goose look?

SERV. There is ten thousand——

MACB.　　　　　　　Geese, villain?

SERV.　　　　　　　Soldiers, sir.

MACB. Go prick thy face and overred° thy fear,

84. annoyance: harm.　　85. still: continuously.　　86. mated:
confounded.
　　Sc. ii: s.d., Drum and colors: a drummer and a soldier carrying a flag.　3. dear: heartfelt.　4. alarm: call to arms.
5. mortified: half-dead.　8. file: list. Cf. III.i.95.　10. un-
rough: smooth-chinned.　11. Protest . . . manhood: show that
they have hardly reached manhood.

15–16. buckle . . . rule: keep his evil cause under control.
18. Now . . . breach: his disloyalty is blamed every minute by
those who rebel against him.　23. pestered: troubled.
27. medicine . . . weal: that which will heal the commonwealth;
i.e., Malcolm and his party.　30. dew: water. sovereign flower:
in the double meaning of "all-powerful healing herb" and "true
King."
　　Sc. iii: 3. taint: be infected.　5. mortal consequences:
human fate.　8. epicures: gluttons; i.e., no soldiers.　11. Devil
. . . black: Black was the Devil's own color, and it was believed
that, when the Devil had claimed a soul as his own, the body
turned black. Cf. *Haml* Intro. p. 883a. loon: fool.　14. overred:
make red.

Thou lily-livered° boy. What soldiers, patch?°   15
Death of thy soul! Those linen° cheeks of thine
Are counselors to fear. What soldiers, wheyface?
   SERV. The English force, so please you.
   MACB. Take thy face hence.   [*Exit* SERVANT.]
               Seyton! — I am sick at heart,
When I behold —— Seyton, I say! — This push°
Will cheer me ever or disseat° me now.   21
I have lived long enough. My way° of life
Is fall'n into the sear,° the yellow leaf,
And that which should accompany old age,
As honor, love, obedience, troops of friends,   25
I must not look to have, but in their stead
Curses, not loud but deep, mouth-honor, breath,
Which the poor heart would fain deny, and dare not.
Seyton!

         [*Enter* SEYTON.]

   SEY. What's your gracious pleasure?
   MACB.   What news more?   30
   SEY. All is confirmed, my lord, which was re-
ported.
   MACB. I'll fight till from my bones my flesh be
hacked.
Give me my armor.
   SEY.   'Tis not needed yet.
   MACB. I'll put it on.
Send out moe° horses, skirr° the country round,   35
Hang those that talk of fear. Give me mine armor.
How does your patient, Doctor?
   DOCT.   Not so sick, my lord,
As she is troubled with thick-coming fancies
That keep her from her rest.
   MACB.   Cure her of that.
Canst thou not minister to a mind diseased,   40
Pluck from the memory a rooted sorrow,
Raze out the written troubles of the brain,
And with some sweet oblivious antidote
Cleanse the stuffed° bosom of that perilous stuff
Which weighs upon the heart?
   DOCT.   Therein the patient   45
Must minister to himself.
   MACB. Throw physic to the dogs, I'll none of it.
Come, put mine armor on, give me my staff.
Seyton, send out. Doctor, the thanes fly from me.
Come, sir, dispatch.° If thou couldst, Doctor, cast
The water° of my land, find her disease   51
And purge it to a sound and pristine° health,

I would applaud thee to the very echo,
That should applaud again. Pull 't off, I say.
What rhubarb, senna,° or what purgative drug   55
Would scour these English hence? Hear'st thou of
them?
   DOCT. Aye, my good lord, your royal preparation
Makes us hear something.
   MACB.   Bring it after me.
I will not be afraid of death and bane
Till Birnam Forest come to Dunsinane.   60
   DOCT. [*Aside*] Were I from Dunsinane away and
clear,
Profit again should hardly draw me here.
                   [*Exeunt.*]

SCENE IV. *Country near Birnam Wood.*

[*Drum and colors. Enter* MALCOLM, *old* SIWARD *and
his* SON, MACDUFF, MENTEITH, CAITHNESS, ANGUS,
LENNOX, ROSS, *and* SOLDIERS, *marching.*]
   MAL. Cousins, I hope the days are near at hand
That chambers will be safe.°
   MENT.   We doubt it nothing.
   SIW. What wood is this before us?
   MENT.   The wood of Birnam.
   MAL. Let every soldier hew him down a bough,
And bear 't before him. Thereby shall we shadow°
The numbers of our host, and make discovery   6
Err in report of us.
   SOLDS.   It shall be done.
   SIW. We learn no other but the confident tyrant
Keeps still in Dunsinane, and will endure
Our setting down before 't.°
   MAL.   'Tis his main hope.   10
For where there is advantage to be given,
Both more and less° have given him the revolt,
And none serve with him but constrainèd° things
Whose hearts are absent too.
   MACD.   Let our just censures
Attend the true event,° and put we on   15
Industrious soldiership.
   SIW.   The time approaches
That will with due decision make us know
What we shall say we have and what we owe.°
Thoughts speculative their unsure hopes relate,
But certain issue strokes must arbitrate.°   20
Toward which advance the war.
                [*Exeunt, marching.*]

---

15. **lily-livered:** white-livered, cowardly. **patch:** fool.   16. **linen:** i.e., pale as linen.   20. **push:** attack; lit., push of pike, decisive assault.   21. **disseat:** unseat.   22. **way:** Dr. Johnson conjectured that the correct reading was "May" (i.e., springtime). This is very likely, as the image of May for youth at its prime is common. Cf. Sonnet 73.1.   23. **sear:** dry and withered.   35. **moe:** more. **skirr:** scour.   44. **stuffed:** overfull.   50. **dispatch:** be quick — addressed to the servant who is buckling on the armor.   50–51. **cast . . . water:** Inspection or "casting" of the urine (called uroscopy) as an aid to diagnosis was the common practice of contemporary physicians. Cf. *II Hen IV,* I.ii.1–6.   52. **pristine:** former.

55. **senna:** purgative herb.
Sc. iv: 2. **chambers . . . safe:** i.e., a man will have nothing to fear in his own home.   5. **shadow:** conceal.   10. **setting . . . before 't:** siege.   12. **more . . . less:** i.e., men of all ranks.   13. **constrained:** forced.   14–15. **Let . . . event:** let us wait until after the battle before passing judgment on that.   18. **owe:** own.   19–20. **Thoughts . . . arbitrate:** these guesses are mere hopes; we shall only find out for certain by strokes. **arbitrate:** decide.

SCENE V. *Dunsinane. Within the castle.*

[*Enter* MACBETH, SEYTON, *and* SOLDIERS, *with drum and colors.*]

MACB. Hang out our banners on the outward
    walls.
The cry is still " They come." Our castle's strength
Will laugh a siege to scorn. Here let them lie
Till famine and the ague° eat them up.
Were they not forced° with those that should be
    ours,   5
We might have met them dareful, beard to beard,
And beat them backward home.
      [*A cry of women within.*] What is that noise?
SEY. It is the cry of women, my good lord. [*Exit.*]
MACB. I have almost forgot the taste of fears.
The time has been my senses would have cooled 10
To hear a night shriek, and my fell of hair°
Would at a dismal treatise° rouse and stir
As life were in 't. I have supped full with horrors.
Direness, familiar to my slaughterous thoughts,
Cannot once start me.°
      [*Re-enter* SEYTON.] Wherefore was that cry? 15
SEY. The Queen, my lord, is dead.
MACB. She should have died hereafter,°
There would have been a time for such a word.
Tomorrow, and tomorrow, and tomorrow
Creeps in this petty pace from day to day,   20
To the last syllable of recorded time,
And all our yesterdays have lighted fools
The way to dusty death. Out, out, brief candle!
Life's but a walking shadow, a poor player
That struts and frets his hour upon the stage   25
And then is heard no more. It is a tale
Told by an idiot, full of sound and fury,
Signifying nothing.
[*Enter a* MESSENGER.] Thou comest to use thy tongue,
    thy story quickly.
MESS. Gracious my lord,   30
I should report that which I say I saw,
But know not how to do it.
    MACB.   Well, say, sir.
MESS. As I did stand my watch upon the hill,
I looked toward Birnam, and anon methought
The wood began to move.
    MACB.   Liar and slave!   35
MESS. Let me endure your wrath if 't be not so.
Within this three mile may you see it coming,
I say, a moving grove.
    MACB.   If thou speak'st false,
Upon the next tree shalt thou hang alive
Till famine cling° thee. If thy speech be sooth,° 40
I care not if thou dost for me as much.

Sc. v: 4. ague: fever.   5. forced: reinforced.   11. fell of
hair: the hair on my scalp.   12. treatise: discourse.   15. start
me: make me start.   17. She . . . hereafter: she would have
died at some time or other.   40. cling: wither. sooth: truth.

I pull in° resolution,° and begin
To doubt the equivocation° of the fiend
That lies like truth. " Fear not, till Birnam Wood
Do come to Dunsinane." And now a wood   45
Comes toward Dunsinane. Arm, arm, and out!
If this which he avouches does appear,
There is nor flying hence nor tarrying here.
I 'gin to be aweary of the sun,   49
And wish the estate o' the world were now undone.
Ring the alarum bell! Blow, wind! Come, wrack!°
At least we'll die with harness° on our back.
                              [*Exeunt.*]

SCENE VI. *Dunsinane. Before the castle.*

[*Drum and colors. Enter* MALCOLM, *old* SIWARD,
   MACDUFF, *and their* ARMY, *with boughs.*]

MAL. Now near enough. Your leavy° screens
    throw down,
And show like those you are. You, worthy Uncle,
Shall, with my cousin, your right noble son,
Lead our first battle.° Worthy Macduff and we
Shall take upon 's what else remains to do,   5
According to our order.
    SIW.   Fare you well.
Do we but find the tyrant's power tonight,
Let us be beaten if we cannot fight.
    MACD. Make all our trumpets speak, give them all
    breath,   9
Those clamorous harbingers° of blood and death.
                                [*Exeunt.*]

SCENE VII. *Another part of the field.*

[*Alarums. Enter* MACBETH.]

MACB. They have tied me to a stake, I cannot fly,
But bearlike I must fight the course.° What's he
That was not born of woman? Such a one
Am I to fear, or none.
      [*Enter* YOUNG SIWARD.]
YOUNG SIW. What is thy name?
    MACB.   Thou'lt be afraid to hear it.   5
YOUNG SIW. No, though thou call'st thyself a hot-
    ter name
Than any is in Hell.
    MACB.   My name's Macbeth.
YOUNG SIW. The Devil himself could not pro-
    nounce a title
More hateful to mine ear.

42. pull in: rein in, check. resolution: courage.   43. equivo-
cation: quibbling. See II.iii.9, and App. 20.   51. wrack: wreck.
52. harness: armor.
   Sc. vi: 1. leavy: leafy.   4. battle: division.   10. harbinger:
See I.iv.45,n.
   Sc. vii: 1–2. They . . . course: See App. 5.

MACB.   No, nor more fearful.
YOUNG SIW. Thou liest, abhorrèd tyrant. With my
  sword   10
I'll prove the lie thou speak'st.
        [*They fight, and* YOUNG SIWARD *is slain.*]
MACB.   Thou wast born of woman.
But swords I smile at, weapons laugh to scorn,
Brandished by man that's of a woman born. [*Exit.*]
        [*Alarums. Enter* MACDUFF.]
MACD. That way the noise is. Tyrant, show thy
  face!
If thou be'st slain and with no stroke of mine,   15
My wife and children's ghosts will haunt me still.
I cannot strike at wretched kerns° whose arms
Are hired to bear their staves.° Either thou, Mac-
  beth,
Or else my sword, with an unbattered edge,
I sheathe again undeeded. There thou shouldst be,
By this great clatter, one of greatest note   21
Seems bruited.° Let me find him, Fortune!
And more I beg not.   [*Exit. Alarums.*]
        [*Enter* MALCOLM *and old* SIWARD.]
SIW. This way, my lord, the castle's gently ren-
  dered.°
The tyrant's people on both sides do fight,   25
The noble thanes do bravely in the war,
The day almost itself professes yours,
And little is to do.
MAL.   We have met with foes
That strike beside us.°
SIW.   Enter, sir, the castle. [*Exeunt. Alarum.*]

SCENE VIII. *Another part of the field.*

        [*Enter* MACBETH.]
MACB. Why should I play the Roman fool and die
On mine own sword?° Whiles I see lives, the gashes
Do better upon them.
        [*Enter* MACDUFF.]
MACD.   Turn, hellhound, turn!
MACB. Of all men else I have avoided thee.
But get thee back, my soul is too much charged   5
With blood of thine already.
MACD.   I have no words.
My voice is in my sword, thou bloodier villain
Than terms can give thee out!   [*They fight.*]
MACB.   Thou losest labor.
As easy mayst thou the intrenchant° air
With thy keen sword impress° as make me bleed.

Let fall thy blade on vulnerable crests.°   11
I bear a charmèd life, which must not yield
To one of woman born.
MACD.   Despair thy charm,
And let the angel whom thou still° hast served
Tell thee Macduff was from his mother's womb   15
Untimely ripped.
MACB. Accursèd be that tongue that tells me so,
For it hath cowed my better part of man!
And be these juggling fiends no more believed
That palter° with us in a double sense,   20
That keep the word of promise to our ear
And break it to our hope. I'll not fight with thee.
MACD. Then yield thee, coward,
And live to be the show and gaze o' the time.
We'll have thee, as our rarer monsters are,   25
Painted upon a pole,° and underwrit,
" Here may you see the tyrant."
MACB.   I will not yield,
To kiss the ground before young Malcolm's feet,
And to be baited° with the rabble's curse.
Though Birnam Wood be come to Dunsinane,   30
And thou opposed, being of no woman born,
Yet I will try the last. Before my body
I throw my warlike shield. Lay on, Macduff,
And damned be him that first cries " Hold,
  enough! "   [*Exeunt, fighting. Alarums.*]
[*Retreat. Flourish. Enter, with drum and colors,*
  MALCOLM, *old* SIWARD, ROSS, *the other* THANES,
        and SOLDIERS.]
MAL. I would the friends we miss were safe ar-
  rived.   35
SIW. Some must go off.° And yet, by these I see,
So great a day as this is cheaply bought.
MAL. Macduff is missing, and your noble son.
ROSS. Your son, my lord, has paid a soldier's debt.
He only lived but till he was a man,   40
The which no sooner had his prowess confirmed
In the unshrinking station° where he fought
But like a man he died.
SIW.   Then he is dead?
ROSS. Aye, and brought off the field. Your cause
  of sorrow
Must not be measured by his worth, for then   45
It hath no end.
SIW.   Had he his hurts before?
ROSS. Aye, on the front.
SIW.   Why then, God's soldier be he!
Had I as many sons as I have hairs,
I would not wish them to a fairer death.
And so his knell is knolled.
MAL.   He's worth more sorrow,   50
And that I'll spend for him.

---

17. kerns: See I.ii.13.   18. staves: i.e., spears.   22. bruited:
revealed by the noise.   24. gently rendered: easily surrendered.
29. beside us: on our side.

    Sc. viii: 1–2. play . . . sword: For instances of *Roman fools*,
who killed themselves in the moment of defeat, see *Caesar*,
V.iii.23–46; V.v.44–51.   9. intrenchant: that cannot be cut.
10. impress: make an impression on.

11. vulnerable crests: heads that can be wounded.   14. still:
always.   20. palter: juggle.   26. Painted . . . pole: i.e., on a
placard stuck on a pole.   29. baited: worried, as a bear by
hounds.   36. go off: die.   42. unshrinking station: i.e., by
standing firm and undismayed when he fought with Macbeth.

SIW.   He's worth no more.
They say he parted well and paid his score.°
And so God be with him! Here comes newer com-
    fort.
    [*Re-enter* MACDUFF, *with* MACBETH'*s head.*]
    MACD. Hail, King! For so thou art. Behold where
        stands
The usurper's cursèd head. The time is free.°   55
I see thee compassed with thy kingdom's pearl,°
That speak my salutation in their minds,
Whose voices I desire aloud with mine:
Hail, King of Scotland!
    ALL.   Hail, King of Scotland!   [*Flourish.*]
    MAL. We shall not spend a large expense of time
Before we reckon with your several° loves,   61

And make us even with you.° My thanes and kins-
    men,
Henceforth be Earls, the first that ever Scotland
In such an honor named. What's more to do,
Which would be planted newly with the time,   65
As calling home our exiled friends abroad
That fled the snares of watchful tyranny,
Producing forth the cruel ministers
Of this dead butcher and his fiendlike Queen,
Who, as 'tis thought, by self and violent hands   70
Took off her life — this, and what needful else
That calls upon us, by the grace of Grace
We will perform in measure,° time, and place.
So thanks to all at once and to each one,
Whom we invite to see us crowned at Scone.   75
                                        [*Flourish. Exeunt.*]

52. score: debt.   55. time is free: i.e., liberty is restored.
56. compassed . . . pearl: surrounded by the pearl (or as we now
say, flower) of the kingdom.   61. several: separate, individual.

62. even . . . you: i.e., by paying what we owe.   73. measure
i.e., full measure.

The Tragedy of
ANTONY AND CLEOPATRA

Introduction

The Tragedy of Antony and Cleopatra was probably written in 1607 or 1608. On May 20, 1608, Edward Blount, the stationer, entered in the Stationers' Register two books, the first being "A book called The book of Pericles Prince of Tyre," and the second "A book called Antony and Cleopatra." *Pericles* was printed separately in a quarto in 1609. No quarto of *Antony and Cleopatra* is known, and the play first appeared in the folio (F1) in 1623. The play may have been written a year or two before the entry, for in 1607 Samuel Daniel, who in 1594 had already written a tragedy called *Cleopatra* in the manner of Seneca, produced a new edition with alterations that have some resemblance to passages in Shakespeare's play. Shakespeare may, of course, have followed Daniel. From the evidence of style, it seems likely that *Antony and Cleopatra* came after *Macbeth* and *Lear*. The style is easier, and the imagery less concentrated.

Antony and Cleopatra is the sequel to *Julius Caesar*. As before, Shakespeare took his story from North's Plutarch (see *Caesar* Intro. p. 809b) but he had fewer difficulties. North's translation of the "Life of Marcus Antonius" gave him all the facts and the matter for many of the finest speeches. The drama begins four years after the murder of Julius Caesar. The Triumvirs — the "Big Three" — have overcome the party of Brutus and Cassius and now the Roman world has been divided between them, Antony's share being the rich East. When the play begins Antony is at the height of his passion for Cleopatra, before his fortunes have begun to decline. The story as given in Plutarch's "Life of Marcus Antonius" is full, and Shakespeare, as usual, selected and rearranged those incidents which he needed to make a good play. At times, indeed, he followed Plutarch so closely that he did little more than turn North's fine prose into finer blank verse. Thus the gorgeous description of Antony's first meeting with Cleopatra (II.ii. 190–245) appeared in North's prose as follows:

Antonius being thus inclined, the last and extremest mischiefs of all other (to wit, the love of Cleopatra) lighted on him, who did waken and stir up many vices yet hidden in him, and were never seen to any. And if any spark of goodness or hope of rising were left him, Cleopatra quenched it straight, and made it worse than before. The manner how he fell in love with her was this. Antonius, going to make war with the Parthians, sent to command Cleopatra to appear personally before him when he came into Cilicia, to answer unto such accusations as were laid against her, being this: that she had aided Cassius and Brutus in their war against him. The messenger sent unto Cleopatra to make his summons unto her was called Dellius, who when he had thoroughly considered her beauty, the excellent grace and sweetness of her tongue, he nothing mistrusted that Antonius would do any hurt to so noble a lady, but rather assured himself that within a few days she should be in great favor with him. Thereupon he did her great honor, and persuaded her to come into Cilicia as honorably furnished as she could possible; and bade her not to be afraid at all of Antonius, for he was a more courteous lord than any that she had ever seen. Cleopatra, on the other side, believing Dellius' words, and guessing by the former access and credit she had with Julius Caesar and Cnaeus Pompey (the son of Pompey the Great) only for her beauty, she began to have good hope that she might more easily win Antonius. For Caesar and Pompey knew her when she was but a young thing, and knew not then what the world meant; but now she went to Antonius at the age when a woman's beauty is at the prime, and she also of best judgment.

So she furnished herself with a world of gifts, store of gold and silver and of riches and other sumptuous ornaments, as is credible enough she might bring from so great a house and from so wealthy and rich a realm as Egypt was. But yet she carried nothing with her wherein she trusted more than in herself, and in the charms and enchantment of her passing beauty and grace. Therefore when she was sent unto by divers letters, both from Antonius himself and also from his friends, she made so light of it and mocked Antonius so much that she disdained to set forward otherwise but to take her

barge in the river of Cydnus, the poop whereof was
of gold, the sails of purple, and the oars of silver,
which kept stroke in rowing after the sound of the
music of flutes, hautboys, cithers, viols, and such
other instruments as they played upon in the barge.
And now for the person of herself: She was laid
under a pavilion of cloth-of-gold of tissue, appareled
and attired like the goddess Venus commonly
drawn in picture; and hard by her, on either hand
of her, pretty fair boys, appareled as painters do set
forth god Cupid, with little fans in their hands
with the which they fanned wind upon her. Her
ladies and gentlewomen also, the fairest of them,
were appareled like the nymphs Nereides (which
are the mermaids of the waters) and like the
Graces, some steering the helm, others tending
the tackle and ropes of the barge, out of the which
there came a wonderful passing sweet savor of perfumes that perfumed the wharf's side, pestered with
innumerable multitudes of people. Some of them
followed the barge all along the river's side, others
also ran out of the city to see her coming in, so that
in the end there ran such multitudes of people one
after another to see her that Antonius was left post-
alone in the market place in his imperial seat to
give audience. And there went a rumor in the people's mouths that the goddess Venus was come to
play with the god Bacchus for the general good of
all Asia.

Another passage which Shakespeare took over
and adapted was the conversation between the
soothsayer and Antonius (II.iii.10–30):

But in all other manner of sports and exercises,
wherein they passed the time away the one with the
other, Antonius was ever inferior unto Caesar, and
always lost, which grieved him much. With Antonius there was a soothsayer or astronomer of
Egypt that could cast a figure and judge of men's
nativities to tell them what should happen to them.
He, either to please Cleopatra or else for that he
found it so by his art, told Antonius plainly that his
fortune (which of itself was excellent good, and
very great) was altogether blemished and obscured
by Caesar's fortune; and therefore he counseled him
utterly to leave his company and to get him as far
from him as he could. " For thy demon," said he,
"(that is to say, the good angel and spirit that
keepeth thee) is afraid of his, and being courageous
and high when he is alone becometh fearful and
timorous when he cometh near unto the other."
Howsoever it was, the events ensuing proved the
Egyptian's words true.

The final scene of Cleopatra's death (V.ii) was
also described in some detail by Plutarch:

There was a young gentleman, Cornelius Dolabella, that was one of Caesar's very great familiars
and besides did bear no ill will unto Cleopatra. He
sent her word secretly, as she had requested him,
that Caesar determined to take his journey through
Syria and that within three days he would send
her away before with her children. When this was
told Cleopatra, she requested Caesar that it would
please him to suffer her to offer the last oblations
of the dead unto the soul of Antonius. . . .

Then having ended these doleful plaints, [she]
crowned the tomb with garlands and sundry nosegays and marvelous lovingly embraced the same,
she commanded they should prepare her bath, and
when she had bathed and washed herself she fell
to her meat and was sumptuously served. Now
whilst she was at dinner there came a countryman
and brought her a basket. The soldiers that warded
at the gates asked him straight what he had in his
basket. He opened his basket and took out the leaves
that covered the figs and showed them that they
were figs he brought. They all of them marveled to
see so goodly figs. The countryman laughed to hear
them, and bade them take some if they would. They
believed he told them truly, and so bade him carry
them in. After Cleopatra had dined, she sent a certain table [tablet] written and sealed unto Caesar
and commanded them all to go out of the tomb
where she was, except for the two women; then she
shut the doors to her. Caesar when he had received
this table, and began to read her lamentation and
petition requesting him that he would let her be
buried with Antonius, found straight what she
meant and thought to have gone thither himself.
Howbeit, he sent one before in all haste that might
be to see what it was.

Her death was very sudden. For those whom
Caesar sent unto her ran thither in all haste possible, and found the soldiers standing at the gate,
mistrusting nothing, nor understanding of her
death. But when they had opened the doors, they
found Cleopatra stark-dead, laid upon a bed of
gold attired and arrayed in her royal robes, and one
of her two women, which was called Iras, dead at
her feet, and her other woman called Charmian
half-dead and trembling, trimming the diadem
which Cleopatra wore upon her head. One of the
soldiers, seeing her, angrily said unto her: " Is that
well done, Charmian? " " Very well," said she
again, " and meet for a Princess descended from the
race of so many noble Kings." She said no more,
but fell down dead hard by the bed.

Some report that this aspic was brought unto her
in the basket with figs and that she had commanded them to hide it under the fig leaves, so that
when she should think to take out the figs the aspic
should bite her before she should see her; howbeit,

that when she would have taken away the leaves for the figs she perceived it and said: " Art thou here then? " And so, her arm being naked, she put it to the aspic to be bitten. Others say again that she kept it in a box and that she did prick and thrust it with a spindle of gold, so that the aspic being angered withal, leaped out with great fury, and bit her in the arm. Howbeit, few can tell the truth. For they report also that she had hidden poison in a hollow razor which she carried in the hair of her head. And yet was there no mark seen on her body or any sign discerned that she was poisoned, neither also did they find this serpent in her tomb. But it was reported only that there were seen certain fresh steps or tracks where it had gone, on the tomb side toward the sea, and specially by the door side. Some say also that they found two little pretty bitings in her arm, scant to be discerned, the which it seemed Caesar himself gave credit unto, because in his triumph he carried Cleopatra's image with an asp biting her arm. And thus goeth the report of her death.

Here Shakespeare took his incidents from Plutarch, but the dialogue is almost all his own.

The reputation of *Antony and Cleopatra* as a play has suffered unjustly because of changes in the convention of the stage. As printed in a modern edition, the play has an impossible multiplicity of scenes. In Act IV alone fifteen are marked, each with its appropriate locality. But Shakespeare did not think of these little episodes in terms of place; neither in F1 nor in the original production was there division into acts and scenes. Shakespeare indeed was stretching to the utmost the possibilities of the Globe stage. Episode succeeds episode in different parts of the stage,[1] giving an illusion of the rush of events as each of the chief persons nears the climax of his fortune. The direction of this play must have needed careful and elaborate timing. Only when *Antony and Cleopatra* is acted with speed on a bare stage in the Elizabethan convention are its magnificent planning and superb poetry fully revealed. Such an effect is quite impossible on any stage where scenery must be changed or where there is any attempt to give a realistic background.

Nevertheless, *Antony and Cleopatra* does demand of spectator and reader a closer attention than is usual. By 1608 Shakespeare had so

[1] The student will find it interesting to work out the Elizabethan staging of *Antony and Cleopatra*; but he should use the original stage directions of the folio and not those of a modern text. See Gen. Intro. pp. 56a–58b.

trained his audience that from the first flourish of the trumpets they were intent to follow every word.

The play is remarkable for its characterization and for the peculiar quality of its poetry. As before, in *Julius Caesar,* Shakespeare reduces the complex events of history to the simple clash of personality. The protagonists are Octavius Caesar (nephew and heir of Julius Caesar), Antony, and Cleopatra. Antony has already appeared in *Julius Caesar.* He is a full character, a man who enjoys pleasures of every kind, but who can also endure the extremes of hardship. He has subtlety of intellect, which does not, however, prevent him from deceiving himself, and great personal charm. In the earlier play, he outwitted Brutus and Cassius by his greater knowledge of man and by sheer personality; and it was his generalship and leading which ultimately gave the victory to Caesar's party. In *Antony and Cleopatra* he is shown in his decadence. Though the others still recognize his good qualities, he becomes besotted with passion and degenerates into a fool; and before his death he is little better than an " old ruffian."

Character can be developed in a drama in many ways, by the actions and words of the character himself and by what others say of him. The great dramatist combines every method, subtly and imperceptibly building up the impression in the mind of the spectator. Antony is spoken of by everyone. Caesar brings out his worst, Lepidus with his tactful apologies reveals his greatest weaknesses. In this play, Shakespeare invented a character to be the commentator on the action. Enobarbus stands for sanity, common sense, and cynicism. Enobarbus himself is a " character." A blunt, cynical soldier, he is the absolutely honest man, the kind of person that Iago pretended to be. He is thus a natural commentator and, significantly, he is Shakespeare's own invention, for the name alone occurs in Plutarch. The contrast between Enobarbus and his master is brought out in the very beginning. Whenever Antony becomes at all sentimental, Enobarbus brings him back to his senses. Enobarbus follows Antony's fortunes until nearly the end, and then he deserts him not because Antony is beaten but because Antony has degenerated into a fool; and then when Antony sends his treasure after him, Enobarbus realizes that after all he was wrong and that Antony for all his faults was a divine master, and this treachery breaks his heart. It is through Enobarbus that the divine streak in Antony is finally displayed.

Octavius, Antony's opponent, is shown as a very young man, and the contrast between their ages becomes more marked toward the end of the play. In fact Antony was thirty-nine at the time of Julius Caesar's death, Octavius twenty years younger. Octavius is a cold-blooded young man who moves unemotionally to gain his own ends. He sacrifices his sister in his game with Antony; he remains sober during the drunken party on Pompey's galley; he alone can look Cleopatra straight in the face without any quickening of the pulse. He is in fact Fortune's prudent darling.

Nevertheless the whole story and success of the play must turn on Cleopatra. Many have told the story of this woman who fascinated two Emperors, and their estimates differ widely. Shakespeare, however, followed Plutarch; to him Cleopatra is a magnificent courtesan, a creature of gaiety, instinct, and passion with few, if any, higher feelings than the enjoyment of the moment; but yet she is unique among women and can therefore defy all normal rules of propriety and morality. The part, incidentally, was played by a boy, but this was not necessarily a disadvantage. A good boy actor, well trained, is capable of a great range of emotion, and had his boy not been up to the part, Shakespeare would never have written it.

It needs vast skill to create such a character so convincingly that we can sympathize with Antony's passion for her. She is shown in her infinite variety as a woman of amazing charm and personality, quite apart from her physical beauty. She gives a lesson to Charmian on how to keep her man (I.iii) and at all times, except at the very end, she can control and fascinate Antony. She is, nevertheless, a quick-tempered beauty, as the unfortunate messenger discovers (II.v), but her anger is soon allayed, and the contrast is seen in her self-satisfied analysis of Antony's new wife. Cleopatra knows that she has nothing to fear from a widow of thirty with a round face, brown hair, a low forehead, and no majesty in her movement.

Shakespeare must also show how she appeals to others. This is more difficult. He achieves it in the gorgeous description of her first meeting with Antony (II.ii.190–231), which is pronounced not by Antony or by one of her adorers but by the cynic Enobarbus. If Cleopatra can produce this effect on Enobarbus, she must indeed have been a charmer. The other side of her nature is brought out as clearly. Toward the end, when Antony's fortunes are hopeless, Thyreus comes from Octavius. Cleopatra, who is thinking of changing sides, sets about fascinating Caesar's messenger. Antony overhears her. He has heard that tone before, and he rounds on her with a flow of abuse as vile as Enobarbus' speech was lyrical.

Her death is magnificent. She must live in brightness or she will wither, and when she knows that there remains only for her to be carried to Rome to be displayed as Caesar's most interesting captive, she realizes that the time has come for the dark. She dies as spectacularly as she lives, and Charmian pronounces her epitaph:

> Now boast thee, Death, in thy possession lies
> A lass unparalleled. Downy windows, close,
> And golden Phoebus, never be beheld
> Of eyes again so royal!

Antony and Cleopatra

DRAMATIS PERSONAE

ANTONY ⎫
OCTAVIUS CAESAR ⎬ *triumvirs*
LEPIDUS ⎭

SEXTUS POMPEIUS

DOMITIUS ENOBARBUS ⎫
VENTIDIUS ⎪
EROS ⎪
SCARUS ⎬ *friends to Antony*
DERCETAS ⎪
DEMETRIUS ⎪
PHILO ⎭

MECAENAS ⎫
AGRIPPA ⎪
DOLABELLA ⎪
PROCULEIUS ⎬ *friends to Caesar*
THYREUS ⎪
GALLUS ⎭

MENAS ⎫
MENECRATES ⎬ *friends to Sextus Pompeius*
VARRIUS ⎭

TAURUS, *lieutenant general to Caesar*
CANIDIUS, *lieutenant general to Antony*
SILIUS, *an officer in Ventidius's army*
EUPHRONIUS, *an ambassador from Antony to Caesar*
ALEXAS *HER CONFIDENCIAL SECRETARY*
MARDIAN, *a eunuch* ⎫
SELEUCUS *TREASURER* ⎬ *attendants on Cleopatra*
DIOMEDES *HER MESSENGER TO ANTONY* ⎭
A SOOTHSAYER
A CLOWN

CLEOPATRA, *Queen of Egypt*
OCTAVIA, *sister to Caesar, and wife to Antony*
CHARMIAN ⎫ *attendants on Cleopatra*
IRAS ⎭

OFFICERS, SOLDIERS, MESSENGERS, *and other*
ATTENDANTS

SCENE — *In several parts of the Roman Empire.*

Act I

[handwritten: IT SHOWS SOCIETY IS BEING AFFECTED BY THIS —]

SCENE I. *Alexandria. A room in* CLEOPATRA'S *palace.*

[handwritten: ACTIONS OF CENTRAL CHAR. (PRIVATE) WORKS ON PUBLIC ORDER]

[*Enter* DEMETRIUS *and* PHILO.]

PHI. Nay, but this dotage of our General's
O'erflows the measure.° Those his goodly eyes,
That o'er the files° and musters of the war
Have glowed like plated° Mars, now bend, now turn
The office and devotion of their view°   5
Upon a tawny° front.° His captain's heart,
Which in the scuffles of great fights hath burst
The buckles on his breast, reneges all temper,°
And is become the bellows and the fan°
To cool a gypsy's° lust. *[handwritten: PLAY MIGHT AS WELL HAVE BEGUN HERE]*
[*Flourish.*° *Enter* ANTONY, CLEOPATRA, *her* LADIES,
the train, with EUNUCHS *fanning her.*]
                    Look where they come.   10
Take but good note, and you shall see in him

The triple pillar° of the world transformed
Into a strumpet's fool. Behold and see.
  CLEO. If it be love indeed, tell me how much.
  ANT. There's beggary in the love that can be reck-
    oned.   15
  CLEO. I'll set a bourn° how far to be beloved.
  ANT. Then must thou needs find out new Heaven,
    new earth.
              [*Enter an* ATTENDANT.]
  ATT. News, my good lord, from Rome ——
  ANT.   Grates° me. The sum.°
  CLEO. Nay, hear them,° Antony.
Fulvia° perchance is angry, or who knows   20
If the scarce-bearded Caesar have not sent
His powerful mandate° to you, "Do this, or this.
Take in that kingdom, and enfranchise° that.
Perform 't, or else we damn° thee."
  ANT.   How, my love!
  CLEO. Perchance! Nay, and most like.   25
You must not stay here longer, your dismission°
Is come from Caesar, therefore hear it, Antony.
Where's Fulvia's process?° Caesar's, I would say?
    Both? *[handwritten: TAUNTS HIM TO REINFORCE HIS DEVOTION TO HER]*

[handwritten right margin: SHE LIKENS LOVE TO A TERRITORIAL POSSESSION SINCE EMP. TILL END]

Act I, Sc. i: 2. O'erflows . . . measure: exceeds all calculation.   3. files: ranks.   4. plated: in armor.   4–5. now . . .
view: gaze with devoted service.   6. tawny: dusky; lit., yellow-
ish-brown. front: forehead.   8. reneges . . . temper: refuses all
self-restraint.   9. bellows . . . fan: i.e., alternately rousing and
allaying.   10. gypsy: Gypsies were supposed to have come from
Egypt, hence their name. Shakespeare thought of Cleopatra as a
dusky Queen; actually she was descended from one of the Mace-
donian generals of Alexander the Great. s.d., Flourish: fanfare
of trumpets.

12. triple pillar: one of the three pillars; i.e., the Triumvirate
(Big Three). See *Ant & Cleo* Intro. p. 1219a.   16. bourn:
boundary.   18. Grates: bores; lit., jars. The sum: give me a
summary.   19. them: i.e., the news.   20. Fulvia: Antony's
legal wife, a managing and shrewish lady.   22. mandate: command.   23. enfranchise: set free.   24. damn: condemn.   26. dismission: dismissal.   28. process: summons to appear before
a court of law.

Call in the messengers. As I am Egypt's Queen,
Thou blushest, Antony, and that blood of thine   30
Is Caesar's homager.° Else so° thy cheek pays shame
When shrill-tongued Fulvia scolds. The messengers!

ANT. Let Rome in Tiber melt, and the wide arch
Of the ranged empire° fall! Here is my space.
Kingdoms are clay. Our dungy° earth alike   35
Feeds beast as man. The nobleness of life
Is to do thus, when such a mutual pair

                 [*Embracing.*]

And such a twain can do 't, in which I bind,
On pain of punishment, the world to weet
We stand up peerless.°

CLEO.   Excellent falsehood!   40
Why did he marry Fulvia and not love her?
I'll seem the fool I am not, Antony
Will be himself.°

ANT.   But stirred by Cleopatra.
Now, for the love of Love and her soft hours,
Let's not confound° the time with conference
     harsh.°   45
There's not a minute of our lives should stretch
Without some pleasure now. What sport tonight?

CLEO. Hear the ambassadors.

ANT.   Fie, wrangling Queen!
Whom everything becomes, to chide, to laugh,
To weep, whose every passion fully strives   50
To make itself, in thee, fair and admired!
No messenger but thine, and all alone
Tonight we'll wander through the streets and note
The qualities° of people. Come, my Queen.
Last night you did desire it. Speak not to us.   55

    [*Exeunt* ANTONY *and* CLEOPATRA *with their train.*]

DEM. Is Caesar with Antonius prized so slight?

PHI. Sir, sometimes, when he is not Antony,
He comes too short of that great property°
Which still° should go with Antony.

DEM.   I am full sorry
That he approves the common liar,° who   60
Thus speaks of him at Rome. But I will hope
Of better deeds tomorrow. Rest you happy!

                     [*Exeunt.*]

SCENE II. *The same. Another room.*

[*Enter* CHARMIAN, IRAS, ALEXAS, *and a* SOOTHSAYER.]

CHAR. Lord Alexas, sweet Alexas, most anything Alexas, almost most absolute° Alexas, where's the soothsayer that you praised so to the Queen? Oh, that I knew this husband which you say must charge his horns with garlands!°   5

ALEX. Soothsayer!

SOOTH. Your will?

CHAR. Is this the man? Is 't you, sir, that know things?

SOOTH. In nature's infinite book of secrecy
A little I can read.

ALEX.   Show him your hand.   10

           [*Enter* ENOBARBUS.]

ENO. Bring in the banquet° quickly, wine enough Cleopatra's health to drink.

CHAR. Good sir, give me good fortune.

SOOTH. I make not, but foresee.

CHAR. Pray then, foresee me one.   15

SOOTH. You shall be yet far fairer than you are.

CHAR. He means in flesh.

IRAS. No, you shall paint when you are old.

CHAR. Wrinkles forbid!

ALEX. Vex not his prescience.° Be attentive.   20

CHAR. Hush!

SOOTH. You shall be more beloving than beloved.

CHAR. I had rather heat my liver with drinking.

ALEX. Nay, hear him.   24

CHAR. Good now,° some excellent fortune! Let me be married to three Kings in a forenoon, and widow them all. Let me have a child at fifty, to whom Herod of Jewry may do homage.° Find me to marry me with Octavius Caesar, and companion me with my mistress.   30

SOOTH. You shall outlive the lady whom you serve.

CHAR. Oh, excellent! I love long life better than figs.

SOOTH. You have seen and proved° a fairer former fortune
Than that which is to approach.   34

CHAR. Then belike my children shall have no names.° Prithee, how many boys and wenches° must I have?

SOOTH. If every of your wishes had a womb,
And fertile every wish, a million.

CHAR. Out, fool! I forgive thee for a witch.°   40

---

31. **Caesar's homager:** one who pays homage to Caesar; i.e., recognizes him as a superior. **Else so:** or else. 33–34. **wide . . . empire:** This is one of the many concentrated phrases in *Ant & Cleo* which convey their meaning emotionally and are so difficult to paraphrase. The image is of the sweep of a great arch, stone supporting stone. **ranged:** set in order. 35. **dungy:** manured. 36–40. **The . . . peerless:** i.e., love is the noblest thing in life; when such a pair as we are in each other's arms, I force the world to know that our love is without a rival. **weet:** know. 42–43. **I'll . . . himself:** i.e., even if I fool myself that Antony loves me, Antony won't pretend. 45. **confound:** waste. **conference harsh:** rough talk. 54. **qualities:** characteristics. 58. **property:** personal quality. 59. **still:** always. 60. **approves . . . liar:** proves that the lies commonly told about him are true.

Sc. ii: 2. **absolute:** perfect. 4–5. **charge . . . garlands:** wear a wreath on his horns like an ox going to be sacrificed; i.e., when I shall make him a cuckold. See App. 11. 11. **banquet:** wine and light refreshments, not the main feast. 20. **prescience:** power of foresight. 25. **Good now:** now, my good man. 27–28. **Herod . . . homage:** Herod was always represented as a ferocious tyrant. A child to whom he would do homage would thus have considerable character. 33. **proved:** experienced. 35–36. **have . . . names:** i.e., be bastards. 36. **wenches:** girls. 40. **I . . . witch:** you are a wizard, so I forgive you your plain speaking.

ALEX. You think none but your sheets are privy to° your wishes.

CHAR. Nay, come, tell Iras hers.

ALEX. We'll know all our fortunes.

ENO. Mine and most of our fortunes tonight shall be — drunk to bed.   46

IRAS. There's a palm presages° chastity, if nothing else.

CHAR. E'en as the o'erflowing Nilus presageth famine!   50

IRAS. Go, you wild bedfellow, you cannot sooth-say.

CHAR. Nay, if an oily palm be not a fruitful prognostication,° I cannot scratch mine ear. Prithee, tell her but a workaday fortune.   55

SOOTH. Your fortunes are alike.

IRAS. But how, but how? Give me particulars.

SOOTH. I have said.   59

IRAS. Am I not an inch of fortune better than she?

CHAR. Well, if you were but an inch of fortune better than I, where would you choose it?

IRAS. Not in my husband's nose.

CHAR. Our worser thoughts Heavens mend! Alexas — come, his fortune, his fortune! Oh, let   65 him marry a woman that cannot go,° sweet Isis,° I beseech thee! And let her die too, and give him a worse! And let worse follow worse, till the worst of all follow him laughing to his grave, fiftyfold a cuckold! Good Isis, hear me this prayer, though thou deny me a matter of more weight. Good Isis, I beseech thee!   72

IRAS. Amen. Dear goddess, hear that prayer of the people! For as it is a heartbreaking to see a handsome man loose-wived, so it is a deadly sorrow to behold a foul knave uncuckolded. Therefore, dear Isis, keep decorum,° and fortune him accordingly!   78

CHAR. Amen.

ALEX. Lo, now, if it lay in their hands to make me a cuckold, they would make themselves whores but they'd do 't!

ENO. Hush! Here comes Antony.

CHAR.   Not he, the Queen.

[*Enter* CLEOPATRA.]

CLEO. Saw you my lord?

ENO. No, lady.

CLEO. Was he not here?

CHAR. No, madam.   85

CLEO. He was disposed to mirth, but on the sudden

A Roman° thought hath struck him. Enobarbus!

ENO. Madam?

CLEO. Seek him, and bring him hither. Where's Alexas?   89

ALEX. Here, at your service. My lord approaches.

CLEO. We will not look upon him. Go with us.

[*Exeunt.*]

[*Enter* ANTONY *with a* MESSENGER *and* ATTENDANTS.]

MESS. Fulvia thy wife first came into the field.

ANT. Against my brother Lucius?

MESS. Aye.

But soon that war had end, and the time's state°   95 Made friends of them, jointing their force 'gainst Caesar,

Whose better issue° in the war from Italy

Upon the first encounter drave them.

ANT.   Well, what worst?

MESS. The nature of bad news infects° the teller.

ANT. When it concerns the fool or coward. On.

Things that are past are done with me. 'Tis thus —

Who tells me true, though in his tale lie death,   102

I hear him as he flattered.°

MESS.   Labienus —

This is stiff news — hath with his Parthian force

Extended° Asia from Euphrates,   105

His conquering banner shook from Syria

To Lydia and to Ionia,

Whilst ——

ANT. Antony, thou wouldst say ——

MESS.   Oh, my lord!

ANT. Speak to me home,° mince not the general tongue.°

Name Cleopatra as she is called in Rome.   110

Rail thou in Fulvia's phrase, and taunt my faults

With such full license as both truth and malice

Have power to utter. Oh, then we bring forth weeds

When our quick minds lie still, and our ills told us

Is as our earing.° Fare thee well awhile.   115

MESS. At your noble pleasure.   [*Exit.*]

ANT. From Sicyon,° ho, the news! Speak there!

1. ATT. The man from Sicyon, is there such a one?

2. ATT. He stays upon your will.

ANT.   Let him appear.

These strong Egyptian fetters I must break,   120

Or lose myself in dotage.

[*Enter another* MESSENGER.] What are you?

2. MESS. Fulvia thy wife is dead.

ANT.   Where died she?

2. MESS. In Sicyon.   123

Her length of sickness, with what else more serious

95. time's state: state of the times.   97. better issue: greater success.   99. infects: brings disaster on.   103. as . . . flattered: as if he brought me good news.   105. Extended: seized on.   109. home: plainly. general tongue: what everyone is saying.   113-15. Oh . . . earing: i.e., when we do not use our minds to consider what should be done, we suffer from the evils which follow idleness, but to have our misfortunes told us produces good results. still: fallow, unused. earing: plowing.   117. Sicyon: a town in Greece where Antony had parted from Fulvia.

41-42. privy to: know the secrets of.   47. presages: foretells.   53-54. oily . . . prognostication: A moist palm was believed to be a sign of an amorous disposition. fruitful prognostication: indication of wantonness.   66. cannot go: is no use. Isis: Egyptian goddess of the moon.   78. decorum: a sense of what is appropriate.   87. Roman: i.e., solemn.

Importeth thee to know, this bears. [*Gives a letter.*]
　　ANT. Forbear° me. [*Exit* SECOND MESSENGER.]
There's a great spirit gone! Thus did I desire it.
What our contempts do often hurl from us,
We wish it ours again. The present pleasure,
By revolution lowering,° does become
The opposite of itself. She's good, being gone,　130
The hand could° pluck her back that shoved her on.
I must from this enchanting Queen break off.
Ten thousand harms, more than the ills I know,
My idleness doth hatch. How now! Enobarbus!
　　　　　　[*Re-enter* ENOBARBUS.]
　　ENO. What's your pleasure, sir?　　　　　135
　　ANT. I must with haste from hence.
　　ENO. Why, then we kill all our women. We see
how mortal an unkindness is to them. If they suffer
our departure, death's the word.°
　　ANT. I must be gone.　　　　　　　　　140
　　ENO. Under a compelling occasion° let women die.
It were pity to cast them away for nothing, though
between them and a great cause they should be esteemed nothing. Cleopatra, catching but the least
noise of this, dies instantly. I have seen her die twenty
times upon far poorer moment.° I do think there is
mettle° in death which commits some loving act
upon her, she hath such a celerity in dying.°
　　ANT. She is cunning past man's thought.　　150
　　ENO. Alack, sir, no, her passions° are made of
nothing but the finest part of pure love. We cannot
call her winds and waters sighs and tears, they are
greater storms and tempests than almanacs° can report. This cannot be cunning in her. If it be, she
makes a shower of rain as well as Jove.　　157
　　ANT. Would I had never seen her!
　　ENO. Oh, sir, you had then left unseen a wonderful piece of work, which not to have been blest
withal would have discredited your travel.°
　　ANT. Fulvia is dead.　　　　　　　　162
　　ENO. Sir?
　　ANT. Fulvia is dead.
　　ENO. Fulvia!
　　ANT. Dead.　　　　　　　　　　　166
　　ENO. Why, sir, give the gods a thankful sacrifice.
When it pleaseth their deities to take the wife of a
man from him, it shows to man the tailors of the
earth, comforting therein, that when old robes are
worn out there are members to make new.° If　171

there were no more women but Fulvia, then had you
indeed a cut,° and the case to be lamented. This grief
is crowned with consolation. Your old smock brings
forth a new petticoat. And indeed the tears live in an
onion° that should water this sorrow.　　　177
　　ANT. The business she hath broachèd° in the state
Cannot endure my absence.
　　ENO. And the business you have broached here
cannot be without you, especially that of Cleopatra's,
which wholly depends on your abode.　　　182
　　ANT. No more light answers. Let our° officers
Have notice what we purpose. I shall break
The cause of our expedience° to the Queen　185
And get her leave to part. For not alone
The death of Fulvia, with more urgent touches,°
Do strongly speak to us, but the letters too
Of many our contriving friends° in Rome
Petition us at home. Sextus Pompeius　　190
Hath given the dare to Caesar, and commands
The empire of the sea. Our slippery people,
Whose love is never linked to the deserver
Till his deserts are past, begin to throw
Pompey the Great and all his dignities　　195
Upon his son,° who, high in name and power,
Higher than both in blood and life, stands up
For the main soldier.° Whose quality,° going on,
The sides o' the world may danger. Much is breed-
　　ing
Which, like the courser's hair, hath yet but life　200
And not a serpent's poison.° Say our pleasure,
To such whose place is under us, requires
Our quick remove from hence.
　　ENO. I shall do 't.　　　　　　[*Exeunt.*]

SCENE III. *The same. Another room.*

[*Enter* CLEOPATRA, CHARMIAN, IRAS, *and* ALEXAS.]
　　CLEO. Where is he?
　　CHAR.　　　　　I did not see him since.
　　CLEO. See where he is, who's with him, what he
　　does.
I did not send you. If you find him sad,
Say I am dancing; if in mirth, report
That I am sudden sick. Quick, and return.　　5
　　　　　　　　　[*Exit* ALEXAS.]
　　CHAR. Madam, methinks if you did love him
　　dearly,

125. Forbear: leave.　129. By . . . lowering: changed to the
opposite by a turn of the wheel.　131. could: would if it could.
138-39. If . . . word: if they have to endure our departing, they
swear they'll die.　141. Under . . . occasion: if it's really
necessary.　147. moment: occasion.　148. mettle: material,
good stuff.　149. celerity in dying: speed at dying; i.e., death
is like one of her lovers, to whom she yields very willingly.
151. passions: emotions.　155. almanacs: See App. 2.　161. discredited . . . travel: i.e., you would have missed one of the most
interesting sights in the world.　168-71. When . . . new: i.e.,
the gods are like tailors; when one suit is worn out they can
make a new one. members: people.　173. cut: loss.　176-77. tears . . . onion: i.e., you'll have to use
an onion if you want to shed tears for Fulvia.　178. broached:
caused. To broach is to open a cask.　183. our: Antony assumes
the tone of a commander asserting himself.　185. expedience:
hasty departure.　187. touches: matters which touch us.
189. contriving friends: friends who plot for us.　194-96. begin . . . son: begin to think young Pompey as worthy a man as
his father.　197-98. stands . . . soldier: intends to become the
supreme soldier.　198. quality: position, success.　200-01. courser's . . . poison: It was commonly believed that a horse's hair
left in water would turn into a living creature.

You do not hold the method to enforce
The like from him.
  CLEO.   What should I do I do not?
  CHAR. In each thing give him way, cross him in
    nothing.
  CLEO. Thou teachest like a fool the way to lose
    him.   10
  CHAR. Tempt him not so too far, I wish, forbear.°
In time we hate that which we often fear.°
But here comes Antony.
                [*Enter* ANTONY.]
  CLEO.   I am sick and sullen.
  ANT. I am sorry to give breathing° to my pur-
    pose ——   14
  CLEO. Help me away, dear Charmian, I shall fall.
It cannot be thus long, the sides of nature
Will not sustain it.
  ANT.   Now, my dearest Queen ——
  CLEO. Pray you stand farther from me.
  ANT.   What's the matter?
  CLEO. I know, by that same eye, there's some good
news.
What says the married woman? You may go.   20
Would she had never given you leave to come!
Let her not say 'tis I that keep you here.
I have no power upon you, hers you are.
  ANT. The gods best know ——
  CLEO.   Oh, never was there queen
So mightily betrayed! Yet at the first   25
I saw the treasons planted.
  ANT.   Cleopatra ——
  CLEO. Why should I think you can be mine and
    true,
Though you in swearing shake the thronèd gods,
Who have been false to Fulvia? Riotous madness,
To be entangled with those mouth-made vows 30
Which break themselves in swearing!
  ANT.   Most sweet Queen ——
  CLEO. Nay, pray you seek no color° for your
    going,
But bid farewell and go. When you sued staying,°
Then was the time for words. No going then.
Eternity was in our lips and eyes,   35
Bliss in our brows' bent, none our parts so poor
But was a race of Heaven.° They are so still,
Or thou, the greatest soldier of the world,
Art turned the greatest liar.
  ANT.   How now, lady!
  CLEO. I would I had thy inches, thou shouldst
    know   40
There were a heart in Egypt.
  ANT.   Hear me, Queen.

The strong necessity of time commands
Our services awhile, but my full heart
Remains in use with you. Our Italy
Shines o'er with civil swords.° Sextus Pompeius 45
Makes his approaches to the port of Rome.
Equality of two domestic powers
Breed scrupulous faction.° The hated, grown to
    strength,
Are newly grown to love. The condemned Pompey,
Rich in his father's honor, creeps apace 50
Into the hearts of such as have not thrived
Upon the present state, whose numbers threaten,
And quietness grown sick of rest would purge
By any desperate change. My more particular,
And that which most with you should safe° my go-
    ing,   55
Is Fulvia's death.
  CLEO. Though age from folly could not give me
    freedom,
It does from childishness. Can Fulvia die?°
  ANT. She's dead, my Queen.
Look here, and at thy sovereign leisure read 60
The garboils° she awaked. At the last, best.
See when and where she died.
  CLEO.   Oh, most false love!
Where be the sacred vials° thou shouldst fill
With sorrowful water? Now I see, I see,
In Fulvia's death, how mine received shall be. 65
  ANT. Quarrel no more, but be prepared to know
The purposes I bear, which are, or cease,°
As you shall give the advice. By the fire
That quickens Nilus' slime,° I go from hence
Thy soldier, servant, making peace or war 70
As thou affect'st.°
  CLEO.   Cut my lace,° Charmian, come,
But let it be. I am quickly ill and well,
So° Antony loves.
  ANT.   My precious Queen, forbear,
And give true evidence to his love, which stands
An honorable trial.
  CLEO.   So Fulvia told me. 75
I prithee, turn aside and weep for her,
Then bid adieu to me, and say the tears
Belong to Egypt. Good now, play one scene
Of excellent dissembling,° and let it look
Like perfect honor.
  ANT.   You'll heat my blood. No more. 80
  CLEO. You can do better yet, but this is meetly.°

Sc. iii: **11. I . . . forbear:** please forbear to torment him.
12. fear: frighten.   **14. breathing:** breath, words.   **32. color:**
excuse.   **33. sued staying:** begged to be allowed to stay.
37. race of Heaven: belonged to some heavenly creatures. She is
reminding Antony of his own words (I.i.36–40).

45. civil swords: swords drawn in civil war.   **47–48. Equality . . .
faction:** when parties are equally balanced, each side is cautious
in taking action.   **55. safe:** make safe; i.e., you need not
fear that I am returning to my wife.   **58. Can . . . die:** the
mistress's bitter sneer that the legal wife lives forever.   **61. garboils:** commotions.   **63. vials:** tear bottles.   **67. which . . .
cease:** which shall be carried out or canceled.   **68–69. By . . .
slime:** by the sun which makes fertile the mud of the Nile.
71. affect'st: desire. **Cut . . . lace:** See *Rich III*, IV.i.34,n.
73. So: so long as.   **79. dissembling:** hypocrisy.   **81. meetly:**
good.

ANT. Now, by my sword —

CLEO.   And target.° Still he mends,
But this is not the best. Look, prithee, Charmian,
How this Herculean° Roman does become
The carriage of his chafe.°   85

ANT. I'll leave you, lady.

CLEO.   Courteous lord, one word.
Sir, you and I must part, but that's not it.
Sir, you and I have loved, but there's not it —
That you know well. Something it is I would ——
Oh, my oblivion is a very Antony,   90
And I am all forgotten.°

ANT.   But that your royalty
Holds idleness your subject, I should take you
For idleness itself.°

CLEO.   'Tis sweating labor
To bear such idleness so near the heart
As Cleopatra this. But, sir, forgive me,   95
Since my becomings° kill me when they do not
Eye well° to you. Your honor calls you hence,
Therefore be deaf to my unpitied folly,
And all the gods go with you! Upon your sword
Sit laurel victory! And smooth success   100
Be strewed before your feet!

ANT.   Let us go. Come,
Our separation so abides and flies
That thou residing here go'st yet with me,
And I hence fleeting here remain with thee.°   104
Away!   [Exeunt.]

SCENE IV. *Rome.* CAESAR's *house.*

[Enter OCTAVIUS CAESAR, *reading a letter,* LEPIDUS,
and their train.]

CAES. You may see, Lepidus, and henceforth
   know,
It is not Caesar's natural vice to hate
Our great competitor.° From Alexandria
This is the news. He fishes, drinks, and wastes
The lamps of night in revel, is not more manlike   5
Than Cleopatra, nor the Queen of Ptolemy
More womanly than he. Hardly gave audience, or
Vouchsafed° to think he had partners. You shall find
   there
A man who is the abstract of all faults
That all men follow.°

LEP.   I must not think there are   10
Evils enow° to darken all his goodness.
His faults in him seem as the spots of Heaven,
More fiery by night's blackness,° hereditary
Rather than purchased,° what he cannot change
Than what he chooses.   15

CAES. You are too indulgent. Let us grant it is not
Amiss to tumble on the bed of Ptolemy,
To give a kingdom for a mirth,° to sit
And keep the turn of tippling with a slave,
To reel the streets at noon and stand the buffet°   20
With knaves that smell of sweat. Say this becomes
   him —
As his composure° must be rare indeed
Whom these things cannot blemish — yet must
   Antony
No way excuse his soils° when we do bear
So great weight in his lightness.° If he filled   25
His vacancy° with his voluptuousness,
Full surfeits° and the dryness of his bones°
Call on him for 't.° But to confound such time
That drums him from his sport and speaks as loud
As his own state and ours,° 'tis to be chid   30
As we rate boys who, being mature in knowledge,
Pawn their experience to their present pleasure,
And so rebel to judgment.°

                    [Enter a MESSENGER.]

LEP.   Here's more news.

MESS. Thy biddings have been done, and every
   hour,
Most noble Caesar, shalt thou have report   35
How 'tis abroad. Pompey is strong at sea,
And it appears he is beloved of those
That only have feared Caesar. To the ports
The discontents° repair, and men's reports
Give him° much wronged.

CAES.   I should have known no less.   40
It hath been taught us from the primal state°
That he which is was wished until he were,°
And the ebbed man, ne'er loved till ne'er worth love,
Comes deared by being lacked.° This common body,

11. enow: enough.   12–13. His . . . blackness: i.e., as the black
night shows up the stars, so Antony's good qualities make the
bad more conspicuous.   Lepidus is always anxious to avoid
trouble and tries to prevent the differences between Caesar and
Antony from coming to a head.   13–14. hereditary . . . purchased: born in him rather than acquired.   18. mirth: jest.
20. stand . . . buffet: exchange blows.   22. composure: nature.
24. soils: blemishes.   25. weight . . . lightness: trouble because
of his frivolity.   26. vacancy: leisure hours.   27. surfeits:
excesses of eating and drinking. dryness . . . bones: the results
of loose living.   28. Call . . . for't: call him to a reckoning.
28–30. confound . . . ours: but to waste that time which summons him from sport to his duty and demands that he attend to
his business and ours.   30–33. 'tis . . . judgment: is to be
worthy of blame, as we rebuke boys who indulge in pleasures
which by experience and judgment they know to be harmful.
39. discontents: discontented.   40. Give him: give him out to
be.   41. primal state: the very beginning.   42. That . . . were:
i.e., the "coming man" is desired until he has "arrived" — and
then everyone hates him.   43–44. And . . . lacked: the man

82. target: shield. See Pl. 9d.   84. Herculean: Antony claimed
to be descended from Hercules.   84–85. does . . . chafe: how
fine he looks when he is angry. chafe: annoyance.   90–91. Oh
. . . forgotten: A cry of pathos, another of Shakespeare's un-
translatable phrases; "even when I forget everything I remember
only Antony, though he utterly forgets me."   91–93. But . . .
itself: I would regard you as idleness personified were it not
that idleness is one of your subjects.   96. becomings: graces.
97. Eye well: seem good.   102–04. Our . . . thee: or, as Sidney
put it, "My true love hath my heart, and I have his." fleeting:
sailing.

Sc. iv: 3. competitor: partner.   8. Vouchsafed: condescended.
9–10. abstract . . . follow: is a summary of all human faults.

Pompey is up but same forces that brought him up will bring him down (handwritten)

Like to a vagabond flag upon the stream,   45
Goes to and back, lackeying the varying tide,
To rot itself with motion.°
   MESS.   Caesar, I bring thee word,
Menecrates and Menas, famous pirates,
Make the sea serve them, which they ear and wound
With keels of every kind. Many hot inroads   50
They make in Italy. The borders maritime
Lack blood° to think on 't, and flush° youth revolt.
No vessel can peep forth but 'tis as soon
Taken as seen, for Pompey's name strikes more
Than could his war resisted.
   CAES.   Antony,   55
Leave thy lascivious wassails.° When thou once
Wast beaten from Modena, where thou slew'st
Hirtius and Pansa, consuls, at thy heel
Did famine follow, whom thou fought'st against,
Though daintily brought up, with patience more
Than savages could suffer. Thou didst drink   61
The stale° of horses and the gilded° puddle
Which beasts would cough at. Thy palate then did
    deign
The roughest berry on the rudest hedge —
Yea, like the stag when snow the pasture sheets,   65
The barks of trees thou browsedst. On the Alps
It is reported thou didst eat strange flesh
Which some did die to look on. And all this —
It wounds thine honor that I speak it now —
Was borne so like a soldier that thy cheek   70
So much as lanked not.°
   LEP.   'Tis pity of him.
   CAES. Let his shames quickly
Drive him to Rome. 'Tis time we twain
Did show ourselves i' the field, and to that end
Assemble we immediate council. Pompey   75
Thrives in our idleness.
   LEP.   Tomorrow, Caesar,
I shall be furnished to inform you rightly
Both what by sea and land I can be able
To front° this present time.
   CAES.   Till which encounter,
It is my business too. Farewell.   80
   LEP. Farewell, my lord. What you shall know
    meantime
Of stirs abroad, I shall beseech you, sir,

whose power has slipped away is never loved till he is not worth
loving and becomes precious because of his absence. **44–47. This
. . . motion:** the common herd are like a flag floating this way
and that on the water, as the tide ebbs and flows, till it
rots by the constant movement. "Flag" is usually interpreted
as water iris; if so, this is the only time that Shakespeare uses
the word in this sense. More probably he had noticed some actual flag trailing in the waters of the Thames and carried up
and down by the tide till it rotted away. **lackeying:** following
like a servant; Theobald's emendation for F1 "lacking." Shakespeare does not elsewhere use "lackey" as a verb. **52. Lack
blood:** go pale. **flush:** in full vigor. **56. wassails:** revels.
stale: urine. **gilded:** covered with a yellow film. **71. lanked not:**
did not grow thin. **79. front:** confront.

To let me be partaker.
   CAES.   Doubt not, sir.
I knew it for my bond.°   [*Exeunt.*

SCENE V. *Alexandria.* CLEOPATRA's *palace.*

[*Enter* CLEOPATRA, CHARMIAN, IRAS, *and* MARDIAN.]
   CLEO. Charmian!
   CHAR. Madam?
   CLEO. Ha, ha!
Give me to drink mandragora.°
   CHAR.   Why, madam?
   CLEO. That I might sleep out this great gap of
    time   5
My Antony is away.
   CHAR.   You think of him too much.
   CLEO. Oh, 'tis treason!
   CHAR.   Madam, I trust not so.
   CLEO. Thou, eunuch Mardian!
   MAR.   What's your Highness' pleasure?
   CLEO. Not now to hear thee sing, I take no
    pleasure
In aught a eunuch has. 'Tis well for thee   10
That, being unseminared,° thy freer thoughts
May not fly forth of Egypt. Hast thou affections?
   MAR. Yes, gracious madam.
   CLEO. Indeed!
   MAR. Not in deed, madam, for I can do nothing
But what indeed is honest to be done.   16
Yet have I fierce affections, and think
What Venus did with Mars.
   CLEO.   O Charmian,
Where think'st thou he is now? Stands he, or sits
    he?
Or does he walk? Or is he on his horse?   20
O happy horse, to bear the weight of Antony!
Do bravely, horse! For wot'st thou° whom thou
    movest?
The demi-Atlas° of this earth, the arm
And burgonet° of men. He's speaking now,
Or murmuring, " Where's my serpent of old Nile? "
For so he calls me. Now I feed myself   26
With most delicious poison. Think on me,
That am with Phoebus'° amorous pinches black
And wrinkled deep in time?° Broad-fronted°
    Caesar,
When thou wast here above the ground, I was   30
A morsel for a monarch. And great Pompey
Would stand and make his eyes grow in my brow.
There would he anchor his aspéct° and die

83. I . . . bond: it is part of my agreement with you.
   Sc. v: 4. mandragora: mandrake, a sleep-inducing drug. Cf.
Oth, III.iii.330. **11. unseminared:** gelded. **22. wot'st thou:**
do you know. **23. demi-Atlas:** i.e., upholding half the world.
Atlas bore the Earth upon his shoulders. **24. burgonet:** helmet.
See Pl. 22d. **28. Phoebus:** the sun god. **29. in time:** by time.
Broad-fronted: with wide forehead. **33. aspect:** look.

THE FACT THAT CAESAR GETS INFORMATION FROM ALL OVER SUGGESTS HE IS ON TOP OF THINGS (GOOD LEADER)

With looking on his life.
                    [Enter ALEXAS.]
  ALEX.   Sovereign of Egypt, hail!
  CLEO. How much unlike art thou Mark Antony!
Yet, coming from him, that great medicine hath   36
With his tinct gilded thee.°
How goes it with my brave Mark Antony?
  ALEX. Last thing he did, dear Queen,
He kissed — the last of many doubled kisses —   40
This Orient pearl. His speech sticks in my heart.
  CLEO. Mine ear must pluck it thence.
  ALEX.   " Good friend," quoth he,
" Say the firm Roman to great Egypt sends
This treasure of an oyster. At whose foot,
To mend the petty present, I will piece°   45
Her opulent throne with kingdoms. All the East,
Say thou, shall call her mistress." So he nodded,
And soberly did mount an arm-gaunt° steed,
Who neighed so high that what I would have spoke
Was beastly dumbed by him.
  CLEO.   What, was he sad or merry?   50
  ALEX. Like to the time o' the year between the ex-
tremes
Of hot and cold, he was nor sad nor merry.
  CLEO. Oh, well-divided disposition! Note him,
Note him, good Charmian, 'tis the man, but note
    him.
He was not sad, for he would shine on those   55
That make their looks by his; he was not merry,
Which seemed to tell them his remembrance lay
In Egypt with his joy; but between both.
Oh, heavenly mingle! Be'st thou sad or merry,
The violence of either thee becomes   60
So does it no man else. Met'st thou my posts?°
  ALEX. Aye, madam, twenty several messengers.
Why do you send so thick?
  CLEO.   Who's born that day
When I forget to send to Antony
Shall die a beggar. Ink and paper, Charmian.   65
Welcome, my good Alexas. Did I, Charmian,
Ever love Caesar so?
  CHAR.   Oh, that brave Caesar!
  CLEO. Be choked with such another emphasis!
Say the brave Antony.
  CHAR.   The valiant Caesar!
  CLEO. By Isis, I will give thee bloody teeth   70
If thou with Caesar paragon° again
My man of men.
  CHAR.   By your most gracious pardon,
I sing but after you.
  CLEO.   My salad days,°

SUGGESTS IT TAKES TIME TO LEARN TO LOVE

When I was green in judgment, cold in blood,
To say as I said then! But come, away,   75
Get me ink and paper.
He shall have every day a several° greeting,
Or I'll unpeople Egypt.   [Exeunt.]

Act II

SCENE I. *Messina.* POMPEY'S *house.*

[Enter POMPEY, MENECRATES, and MENAS, in warlike
                        manner.]
  POM. If the great gods be just, they shall assist
The deeds of justest men.
  MENE.   Know, worthy Pompey,
That what they do delay, they not deny.
  POM. Whiles we are suitors to their throne,
    decays
The thing we sue for.
  MENE.   We, ignorant of ourselves,   5
Beg often our own harms, which the wise powers
Deny us for our good. So find we profit
By losing of our prayers.
  POM.   I shall do well.
The people love me, and the sea is mine.
My powers are crescent,° and my auguring° hope
Says it will come to the full. Mark Antony   11
In Egypt sits at dinner, and will make
No wars withoutdoors. Caesar gets money where
He loses hearts. Lepidus flatters both,
Of both is flattered, but he neither loves   15
Nor either cares for him.
  MEN.   Caesar and Lepidus
Are in the field. A mighty strength they carry.
  POM. Where have you this? 'Tis false.
  MEN.   From Silvius, sir.
  POM. He dreams. I know they are in Rome to-
        gether,
Looking for Antony. But all the charms of love,   20
Salt° Cleopatra, soften thy waned° lip!
Let witchcraft join with beauty, lust with both!
Tie up the libertine in a field of feasts,
Keep his brain fuming. Epicurean cooks
Sharpen with cloyless° sauce his appetite,   25
That sleep and feeding may prorogue° his honor
Even till a Lethed dullness!°
[Enter VARRIUS.]   How now, Varrius!
  VAR. This is most certain that I shall deliver.
Mark Antony is every hour in Rome

36–37. medicine . . . thee: i.e., the very sight of Antony has been
like a dose of tincture of gold. See App. 21.   45. piece: enlarge.   48. arm-gaunt: a much-disputed word not satisfactorily
explained, unless, perhaps, lean and hard from bearing armor.
61. posts: messengers. See App. 17.   71. paragon: make equal.
73. salad days: i.e., when I was green and inexperienced.

78. several: separate.
  Act II, Sc. i: 10. crescent: growing. auguring: prophesying
good.   21. Salt: lustful. waned: withered.   25. cloyless: of
which he never has too much. 26. prorogue: suspend. 27. Lethed
dullness: dull forgetfulness. Lethe was the river of forgetfulness in the underworld.

Expected. Since he went from Egypt 'tis   30
A space° for farther travel.
  POM.   I could have given less matter
A better ear. Menas, I did not think
This amorous surfeiter would have donned his helm
For such a petty war. His soldiership
Is twice the other twain. But let us rear   35
The higher our opinion,° that our stirring
Can from the lap of Egypt's widow pluck
The ne'er-lust-wearied Antony.
  MEN.   I cannot hope
Caesar and Antony shall well greet together.
His wife that's dead did trespasses to Caesar,   40
His brother warred upon him — although I think
Not moved by Antony.
  POM.   I know not, Menas,
How lesser enmities may give way to greater.
Were 't not that we stand up against them all,
'Twere pregnant° they should square° between
  themselves,   45
For they have entertainèd° cause enough
To draw their swords. But how the fear of us
May cément their divisions and bind up
The petty difference, we yet not know.
Be 't as our gods will have 't! It only stands   50
Our lives upon to use our strongest hands.°
Come, Menas.   [*Exeunt.*]

1st time you put 2 from opposite sides together

SCENE II. *Rome. The house of* LEPIDUS.

[*Enter* ENOBARBUS *and* LEPIDUS.]

 LEP. Good Enobarbus, 'tis a worthy deed
And shall become you well, to entreat your Captain
To soft and gentle speech.
  ENO.   I shall entreat him
To answer like himself. If Caesar move him,
Let Antony look over Caesar's head   5
And speak as loud as Mars. By Jupiter,
Were I the wearer of Antonius' beard,
I would not shave 't today.°
  LEP.   'Tis not a time
For private stomaching.°
  ENO.   Every time
Serves for the matter that is then born in 't.   10
 LEP. But small to greater matters must give way.
 ENO. Not if the small come first.
 LEP.   Your speech is passion.
But pray you stir no embers up. Here comes
The noble Antony.

His assumes Antony wants to trump Caesar — sign of disrespect

Lepidus — soft argument
Enobarbus — directness

[*Enter* ANTONY *and* VENTIDIUS.]

 ENO.   And yonder, Caesar.
[*Enter* CAESAR, MECAENAS, *and* AGRIPPA.]
 ANT. If we compose° well here, to Parthia.   15
Hark, Ventidius.

Shows he is mature & planned

 CAES.   I do not know,
Mecaenas. Ask Agrippa.

Doesn't know

 LEP.   Noble friends,
That which combined us was most great, and let not
A leaner action rend us. What's amiss,
May it be gently heard. When we debate   20
Our trivial difference loud, we do commit
Murder in healing wounds. Then, noble partners,
The rather for I earnestly beseech,
Touch you the sourest points with sweetest terms,
Nor curstness° grow to the matter.
  ANT.   'Tis spoken well.   25
Were we before our armies and to fight,
I should do thus.   [*Flourish.*]
 CAES. Welcome to Rome.
 ANT. Thank you.
 CAES. Sit.

Whoever sits down shows submissiveness to other

 ANT. Sit, sir.
 CAES. Nay, then.

Antony gets right to sit

 ANT. I learn you take things ill which are not so,
Or being, concern you not.

Antony has had much more exp. in speeches & so Caesar gives in

 CAES.   I must be laughed at   30
If, or for° nothing or a little, I
Should say myself offended, and with you
Chiefly i' the world — more laughed at that I should
Once name you derogately° when to sound your
  name
It not concerned me.
  ANT.   My being in Egypt, Caesar,   35
What was 't to you?
 CAES. No more than my residing here at Rome
Might be to you in Egypt. Yet if you there
Did practice on° my state, your being in Egypt
Might be my question.°
  ANT.   How intend° you "practiced"?   40
 CAES. You may be pleased to catch at mine intent
By what did here befall me. Your wife and brother
Made wars upon me, and their contestation
Was theme for you,° you were the word° of war.
 ANT. You do mistake your business. My brother
  never   45
Did urge me in his act. I did inquire it,
And have my learning° from some true reports°
That drew their swords with you. Did he not rather
Discredit my authority with yours,

---

31. A space: i.e., time. **35–36. rear . . . opinion:** have a better opinion of ourselves. **45. pregnant:** likely. **square:** quarrel. **46. entertained:** received. **50–51. It . . . hands:** our lives depend on our using our hands strongly.
  Sc. ii: 7–8. Were . . . today: i.e., I would dare Caesar to insult me. To pluck at a man's beard was a deadly insult. Cf. *Lear*, III.vii.35–36, 76–77. **9. private stomaching:** squabbling over personal grievances.

15. compose: come to terms. **25. curstness:** bitterness. **31. or for:** either for. **34. derogately:** disparagingly. **39. practice on:** plot against. **40. question:** affair. **intend:** mean. **43–44. contestation . . . you:** fighting with me a subject which concerned you. **44. word:** watchword; i.e., they claimed that they were fighting for you. **47. learning:** information. **reports:** reporters. As often, Shakespeare uses the abstract for the concrete word.

[handwritten top margin: SOME OF ANTONY'S POSITION ERODED BY VOLUME OF COMPLAINTS — HE THUS HAS TO APOLOGIZE + ADMIT HE IS WRONG]

And make the wars alike against my stomach,°   50
Having alike your cause?° Of this my letters
Before did satisfy you. If you'll patch a quarrel,°
As matter whole you have not to make it with,
It must not be with this.

CAES.   You praise yourself
By laying defects of judgment to me, but   55
You patched up your excuses.

ANT.   Not so, not so.
I know you could not lack, I am certain on 't,
Very necessity of this thought, that I,
Your partner in the cause 'gainst which he fought,
Could not with graceful eyes attend° those wars   60
Which fronted° mine own peace. As for my wife,
I would you had her spirit in such another.
The third o' the world is yours, which with a snaffle°
You may pace° easy, but not such a wife.

[handwritten: BOTH SM ABOUT]

ENO. Would we had all such wives, that the   65
men might go to wars with the women!

[handwritten left margin: ENO. IS SPEAKING OUT RUDELY + FLIPLY — BUT ANT.]

[handwritten: SAME THING — BUT]

ANT. So much uncurbable, her garboils, Caesar,
Made out of her impatience, which not wanted
Shrewdness of policy too, I grieving grant
Did you too much disquiet.° For that you must   70
But say I could not help it.

[handwritten: ENO. HAS TO BITE TO IT]

CAES.   I wrote to you
When rioting in Alexandria. You
Did pocket up my letters, and with taunts
Did gibe my missive° out of audience.

[handwritten left margin: TRUE — 2nd CHARGE]

ANT.   Sir,
He fell upon me ere admitted.° Then   75
Three Kings I had newly feasted and did want
Of what I was i' the morning. But next day
I told him of myself, which was as much
As to have asked him pardon. Let this fellow
Be nothing of our strife. If we contend,   80
Out of our question wipe him.

CAES.   You have broken
The article of your oath, which you shall never
Have tongue to charge me with.

[handwritten left margin: TRUE — 3rd CHARGE]

LEP.   Soft, Caesar!
ANT. No, Lepidus, let him speak.
The honor is sacred which he talks on now,   85
Supposing that I lacked it. But on, Caesar,
The article of my oath.

CAES. To lend me arms and aid when I required
    them,

The which you both denied.

ANT.   Neglected rather,
And then when poisoned hours had bound me up
From mine own knowledge. As nearly as I may,   91
I'll play the penitent to you, but mine honesty
Shall not make poor my greatness, nor my power
Work without it.° Truth is that Fulvia,
To have me out of Egypt, made wars here,   95
For which myself, the ignorant motive, do
So far ask pardon as befits mine honor
To stoop in such a case.

LEP.   'Tis noble-spoken.
MEC. If it might please you to enforce no further
The griefs between ye, to forget them quite   100
Were to remember that the present need
Speaks to atone° you.

LEP.   Worthily spoken, Mecaenas.
ENO. Or if you borrow one another's love for the
instant, you may, when you hear no more words of
Pompey, return it again. You shall have time to
wrangle in when you have nothing else to do.   107
ANT. Thou art a soldier only. Speak no more.
ENO. That truth should be silent I had almost
    forgot.   110
ANT. You wrong this presence,° therefore speak
    no more.
ENO. Go to, then, your considerate stone.°
CAES. I do not much dislike the matter, but
The manner, of his speech. For 't cannot be
We shall remain in friendship, our conditions°   115
So differing in their acts. Yet if I knew
What hoop° should hold us stanch,° from edge to
    edge
O' the world I would pursue it.

AGR.   Give me leave, Caesar.
CAES. Speak, Agrippa.
AGR. Thou hast a sister by the mother's side,
Admired Octavia. Great Mark Antony   121
Is now a widower.

CAES.   Say not so, Agrippa.
If Cleopatra heard you, your reproof
Were well deserved of rashness.

ANT. I am not married, Caesar. Let me hear   125
Agrippa further speak.
AGR. To hold you in perpetual amity,
To make you brothers and to knit your hearts
With an unslipping knot, take Antony°
Octavia to his wife, whose beauty claims   130
No worse a husband than the best of men,
Whose virtue and whose general graces speak

50. **stomach:** inclination.   51. **Having . . . cause:** i.e., those who fought against you were fighting against me.   52. **patch a quarrel:** make a quarrel out of patches.   60. **with . . . attend:** could not pay favorable attention to.   61. **fronted:** opposed. 63. **snaffle:** a bit without a curb, used only with a horse easy to manage.   64. **pace:** ride.   67–70. **So . . . disquiet:** I regretfully admit that her brawls (*garboils*), caused by an impatience which was not indeed without deliberate shrewdness, caused you too much anxiety (*disquiet*). Antony is finding it difficult to keep his end up against Caesar's direct accusations, and the logical sequence of his thought suffers.   74. **gibe my missive:** mock my messenger.   75. **ere admitted:** before he was given permission **to come in.**

92–94. **but . . . it:** i.e., but even if I am honest, I am not going to be too humble, nor will I use my power dishonestly.   102. **atone:** make one, reconcile.   111. **presence:** noble company; lit., presence chamber, the room in Court where Caesar gave formal audiences.   112. **your . . . stone:** i.e., I'll say nothing but think quite a bit.   115. **conditions:** natures.   117. **hoop:** i.e., like that of a barrel. **stanch:** free from leaks.   129. **take Antony:** let Antony take.

That which none else can utter. By this marriage
All little jealousies which now seem great,
And all great fears which now import° their dan-
    gers,   135
Would then be nothing. Truths would be tales°
Where now half-tales be truths. Her love to both
Would each to other and all loves to both
Draw after her. Pardon what I have spoke,
For 'tis a studied,° not a present, thought,°   140
By duty ruminated.

    ANT.   Will Caesar speak?
    CAES. Not till he hears how Antony is touched
With what is spoke already.

    ANT.   What power is in Agrippa
If I would say, " Agrippa, be it so,"
To make this good?

    CAES.   The power of Caesar, and 145
His power unto Octavia.

    ANT.   May I never
To this good purpose, that so fairly shows,
Dream of impediment! Let me have thy hand.
Further this act of grace, and from this hour
The heart of brothers govern in our loves   150
And sway our great designs!

    CAES.   There is my hand.
A sister I bequeath you whom no brother
Did ever love so dearly. Let her live
To join our kingdoms and our hearts, and never
Fly off our loves again!

    LEP.   Happily, amen!   155
    ANT. I did not think to draw my sword 'gainst
    Pompey,
For he hath laid strange courtesies and great
Of late upon me. I must thank him only,
Lest my remembrance suffer ill report,
At heel of that, defy him.

    LEP.   Time calls upon 's.   160
Of us must Pompey presently° be sought,
Or else he seeks out us.

    ANT.   Where lies he?
    CAES. About the Mount Misenum.
    ANT.   What's his strength
By land?
    CAES. Great and increasing. But by sea 165
He is an absolute master.

    ANT.   So is the fame.°
Would we had spoke together! Haste we for it.
Yet ere we put ourselves in arms, dispatch we
The business we have talked of.

    CAES.   With most gladness,
And do invite you to my sister's view,°   170
Whither straight I'll lead you.

    ANT.   Let us, Lepidus,

Not lack your company.

    LEP.   Noble Antony,
Not sickness should detain me.

    [*Flourish. Exeunt* CAESAR, ANTONY, *and* LEPIDUS.]
    MEC. Welcome from Egypt, sir.   174
    ENO. Half the heart of Caesar, worthy Mecaenas!
My honorable friend Agrippa!

    AGR. Good Enobarbus!

    MEC. We have cause to be glad that matters are so
well digested. You stayed well by 't° in Egypt. 180

    ENO. Aye, sir, we did sleep day out of counte-
nance, and made the night light with drinking.

    MEC. Eight wild boars roasted whole at a break-
fast and but twelve persons there. Is this true? 185

    ENO. This was but as a fly by an eagle. We had
much more monstrous matter of feast which worthily deserved noting.

    MEC. She's a most triumphant lady, if report be
square to° her.   190

    ENO. When she first met Mark Antony, she pursed
up° his heart, upon the river of Cydnus.°

    AGR. There she appeared indeed,° or my reporter
devised well for her.°

    ENO. I° will tell you.   195
The barge she sat in, like a burnished throne,
Burned on the water. The poop° was beaten gold,
Purple the sails, and so perfumèd that
The winds were lovesick with them. The oars were
    silver,
Which to the tune of flutes kept stroke and made
The water which they beat to follow faster,   201
As amorous of their strokes. For her own person,
It beggared all description. She did lie
In her pavilion, cloth of gold of tissue,°
O'er picturing that Venus where we see   205
The fancy outwork nature.° On each side her
Stood pretty dimpled boys, like smiling Cupids,
With divers-colored° fans, whose wind did seem
To glow° the delicate cheeks which they did cool,
And what they undid did.

    AGR.   Oh, rare for Antony! 210
    ENO. Her gentlewomen, like the Nereides,°
So many mermaids, tended her i' the eyes,
And made their bends adornings.° At the helm
A seeming mermaid steers. The silken tackle°

---

135. **import**: bring with them. 136. **tales**: i.e., not regarded seriously. 140. **studied**: carefully considered. **present thought**: a thought that has just occurred to me. 161. **presently**: immediately. 166. **fame**: report. 170. **sister's view**: to visit my sister.

180. **stayed . . . by't**: had a good time. 190. **square to**: accurate about. 191–92. **pursed up**: put in the bag. 192. **Cydnus**: a river in Asia Minor. 193. **appeared indeed**: made a good show. 194. **devised . . . her**: wrote her up well. 195–245. **I . . . riggish**: For the original of this famous description see *Ant & Cleo* Intro. pp. 1219b–1220a. It is superb artistry to give this rapturous and lyrical account of Cleopatra to the cynical Enobarbus. 197. **poop**: stern. 204. **cloth . . . tissue**: "sheer" cloth of gold. 206. **fancy . . . nature**: the imagination of the artist surpasses nature. See Pl. 7a. 208. **divers-colored**: different-colored. 209. **glow**: make blush. 211. **Nereides**: sea nymphs. 212–13. **tended . . . adornings**: a much-discussed phrase; probably meaning "they watched her slightest glance as they prettily bent to fulfill her pleasure." 214. **tackle**: rigging.

Swell with the touches of those flower-soft hands
That yarely frame the office.° From the barge   216
A strange invisible perfume hits the sense
Of the adjacent wharfs. The city cast
Her people out upon her. And Antony,
Enthronèd i' the market place, did sit alone,   220
Whistling to the air, which, but for vacancy,°
Had gone to gaze on Cleopatra too,
And made a gap in nature.

AGR.   Rare Egyptian!

ENO. Upon her landing, Antony sent to her,
Invited her to supper. She replied   225
It should be better he became her guest,
Which she entreated. Our courteous Antony,
Whom ne'er the word of " No " woman heard
    speak,
Being barbered ten times o'er, goes to the feast,
And, for his ordinary,° pays his heart   230
For what his eyes eat only.

AGR.   Royal wench!

She made great Caesar lay his sword to bed.
He plowed her, and she cropped.

ENO.   I saw her once
Hop forty paces through the public street.
And having lost her breath, she spoke, and panted,
That she did make defect perfection,   236
And breathless, power breathe forth.

MEC. Now Antony must leave her utterly.

ENO. Never. He will not.
Age cannot wither her, nor custom stale   240
Her infinite variety. Other women cloy
The appetites they feed, but she makes hungry
Where most she satisfies. For vilest things
Become themselves in her, that the holy priests
Bless her when she is riggish.°   245

MEC. If beauty, wisdom, modesty, can settle
The heart of Antony, Octavia is
A blessèd lottery° to him.

AGR.   Let us go.
Good Enobarbus, make yourself my guest   249
Whilst you abide here.

ENO.   Humbly, sir, I thank you.   [*Exeunt.*]

SCENE III. *The same.* CAESAR'S *house.*

[*Enter* ANTONY, CAESAR, OCTAVIA *between them, and*
ATTENDANTS.]

ANT. The world and my great office will some-
    times
Divide me from your bosom.

OCT.   All which time
Before the gods my knee shall bow my prayers
To them for you.

ANT.   Good night, sir. My Octavia,
Read not my blemishes in the world's report.   5
I have not kept my square,° but that to come
Shall all be done by the rule. Good night, dear lady.
Good night, sir.

CAES. Good night.   [*Exeunt all but* ANTONY.]
            [*Enter* SOOTHSAYER.]

ANT. Now, sirrah,° you do wish yourself in
    Egypt?   10

SOOTH. Would I had never come from thence, nor
    you
Thither!

ANT. If you can, your reason?

SOOTH.   I see it in
My motion,° have it not in my tongue. But yet
Hie you° to Egypt again.

ANT.   Say to me   15
Whose fortunes shall rise higher, Caesar's or mine?

SOOTH. Caesar's.
Therefore, O Antony, stay not by his side.
Thy demon,° that thy spirit which keeps thee, is
Noble, courageous, high, unmatchable,   20
Where Caesar's is not. But near him thy angel
Becomes a fear,° as being o'erpowered. Therefore
Make space enough between you.

ANT.   Speak this no more.

SOOTH. To none but thee, no more but when to
    thee.
If thou dost play with him at any game,   25
Thou art sure to lose, and, of that natural luck,
He beats thee 'gainst the odds. Thy luster thickens°
When he shines by. I say again, thy spirit
Is all afraid to govern thee near him,
But he away, 'tis noble.

ANT.   Get thee gone.   30
Say to Ventidius I would speak with him.
                 [*Exit* SOOTHSAYER.]
He shall to Parthia. Be it art or hap,
He hath spoken true. The very dice obey him,
And in our sports my better cunning faints°
Under his chance.° If we draw lots, he speeds.°   35
His cocks do win the battle still° of mine
When it is all to naught, and his quails° ever
Beat mine, inhooped, at odds. I will to Egypt.
And though I make this marriage for my peace,
I' the East my pleasure lies.
      [*Enter* VENTIDIUS.] Oh, come, Ventidius,   40
You must to Parthia. Your commission's° ready.
Follow me, and receive 't.   [*Exeunt.*]

216. yarely . . . office: carry out their task like good sailors.
Cf. *Temp,* I.i.4–7.   **221. but . . . vacancy:** but that it would
have caused a vacuum.   **230. ordinary:** dinner.   **245. riggish:**
wanton.   **248. lottery:** prize in a lottery.

Sc. iii: 6. kept my square: kept straight; lit., within the
boundary.   **10. sirrah:** my man, a term used to an inferior.
12–13. in My motion: by intuition.   **14. Hie you:** hasten.
19. demon: the spirit which watches over you; guardian angel.
21–22. angel . . . fear: your guardian angel is afraid.   **27. luster
thickens:** brightness grows dim.   **34. cunning faints:** knowledge fails.   **35. chance:** luck. **speeds:** wins.   **36. still:** always.
37. quails: Quail-fighting was a popular sport in Egypt. The
two birds were set down within a hoop and fought till one was
driven out.   **41. commission:** document of appointment.

SCENE IV. *The same. A street.*

[*Enter* LEPIDUS, MECAENAS, *and* AGRIPPA.]

LEP. Trouble yourselves no further. Pray you
    hasten
Your generals after.

AGR.   Sir, Mark Antony *Following Antony's own*
Will e'en but kiss Octavia, and we'll follow.

LEP. Till I shall see you in your soldier's dress,
Which will become you both, farewell.

MEC.   We shall, 5
As I conceive° the journey, be at the Mount
Before you, Lepidus.

LEP.   Your way is shorter.
My purposes do draw me much about.°
You'll win two days upon me.

MEC. & AGR.   Sir, good success! 9

LEP. Farewell.   [*Exeunt.*]

SCENE V. *Alexandria.* CLEOPATRA's *palace.*

[*Enter* CLEOPATRA, CHARMIAN, IRAS, *and* ALEXAS.]

CLEO. Give me some music — music, moody food
Of us that trade in love.

ALL.   The music, ho!

[*Enter* MARDIAN *the eunuch.*]

CLEO. Let it alone, let's to billiards. Come, Charmian.

CHAR. My arm is sore. Best play with Mardian.

CLEO. As well a woman with a eunuch played 5
As with a woman. Come, you'll play with me, sir?

MAR. As well as I can, madam.

CLEO. And when goodwill is showed, though 't
    come too short,
The actor may plead pardon. I'll none now.
Give me mine angle,° we'll to the river. There, 10
My music playing far off, I will betray
Tawny-finned fishes. My bended hook shall pierce
Their slimy jaws, and as I draw them up,
I'll think them every one an Antony,
And say "Ah, ha! You're caught."

CHAR.   'Twas merry when 15
You wagered on your angling, when your diver
Did hang a salt fish on his hook, which he
With fervency drew up.

CLEO.   That time — oh, times! —
I laughed him out of patience, and that night
I laughed him into patience. And next morn, 20
Ere the ninth hour, I drunk him to his bed,
Then put my tires° and mantles on him whilst
I wore his sword Philippan.°

[*Enter a* MESSENGER.]   Oh, from Italy!

Ram thou thy fruitful tidings in mine ears,
That long time have been barren.

MESS.   Madam, madam —— 25

CLEO. Antonius dead! If thou say so, villain,
Thou kill'st thy mistress. But well and free,
If thou so yield him, there is gold, and here
My bluest veins to kiss — a hand that Kings
Have lipped, and trembled kissing. 30

MESS. First, madam, he is well.

CLEO.   Why, there's more gold.
But, sirrah, mark, we use
To say the dead are well. Bring it to that,
The gold I give thee will I melt and pour
Down thy ill-uttering throat. 35

MESS. Good madam, hear me.

CLEO.   Well, go to,° I will.
But there's no goodness in thy face. If Antony
Be free and healthful — so tart a favor°
To trumpet such good tidings! If not well,
Thou shouldst come like a Fury° crowned with
    snakes, 40
Not like a formal man.°

MESS.   Will 't please you hear me?

CLEO. I have a mind to strike thee ere thou
    speak'st.
Yet if thou say Antony lives, is well,
Or friends with Caesar or not captive to him,
I'll set thee in a shower of gold and hail° 45
Rich pearls upon thee.

MESS.   Madam, he's well.

CLEO.   Well said.

MESS. And friends with Caesar.

CLEO.   Thou'rt an honest man.

MESS. Caesar and he are greater friends than ever.

CLEO. Make thee a fortune from me.

MESS.   But yet, madam ——

CLEO. I do not like "But yet." It does allay 50
The good precédence.° Fie upon "But yet"!
"But yet" is as a jailer to bring forth
Some monstrous malefactor. Prithee, friend,
Pour out the pack of matter° to mine ear,
The good and bad together. He's friends with
    Caesar, 55
In state of health, thou say'st, and thou say'st free.

MESS. Free, madam! No, I made no such report.
He's bound unto Octavia.

CLEO.   For what good turn?

MESS. For the best turn i' the bed.

CLEO.   I am pale, Charmian.

MESS. Madam, he's married to Octavia. 60

CLEO. The most infectious pestilence upon thee!

[*Strikes him down.*]

Sc. iv: 6. conceive: understand.   8. draw . . . about: make
me take a much longer way.

Sc. v: 10. angle: fishing rod.   22. tires: headdresses.
23. sword Philippan: the sword he wore at the Battle of Philippi.

36. go to: get on.   38. so . . . favor: such a sour expression.
40. Fury: fiend.   41. formal man: man of normal shape.
45. hail: rain down like hail.   50-51. allay . . . precedence: mix
something base with the goodness that has gone before.   54. pack
of matter: all the contents of the bag at once.

MESS. Good madam, patience.

CLEO. What say you? Hence, [*Strikes him again.*]
Horrible villain! Or I'll spurn thine eyes
Like balls before me, I'll unhair thy head.
        [*She hales him up and down.*]
Thou shalt be whipped with wire, and stewed in
    brine,   65
Smarting in lingering pickle.

MESS.   Gracious madam,
I that do bring the news made not the match.

CLEO. Say 'tis not so, a province I will give thee
And make thy fortunes proud. The blow thou hadst
Shall make thy peace for moving me to rage,   70
And I will boot° thee with what gift beside
Thy modesty can beg.

MESS.   He's married, madam.

CLEO. Rogue, thou hast lived too long.
                       [*Draws a knife.*]

MESS.   Nay, then I'll run.
What mean you, madam? I have made no fault.
                          [*Exit.*]

CHAR. Good madam, keep yourself within your-
    self.   75
The man is innocent.

CLEO. Some innocents 'scape not the thunderbolt.
Melt Egypt into Nile! And kindly creatures
Turn all to serpents! Call the slave again.
Though I am mad, I will not bite him. Call.   80

CHAR. He is afeard to come.

CLEO.   I will not hurt him. [*Exit* CHARMIAN.]
These hands do lack nobility, that they strike
A meaner than myself, since I myself
Have given myself the cause.
[*Re-enter* CHARMIAN *and* MESSENGER.] Come hither,
    sir.
Though it be honest, it is never good   85
To bring bad news. Give to a gracious message
A host of tongues, but let ill tidings tell
Themselves when they be felt.

MESS.   I have done my duty.

CLEO. Is he married?
I cannot hate thee worser than I do   90
If thou again say " Yes."

MESS.   He's married, madam.

CLEO. The gods confound thee! Dost thou hold
    there still?

MESS. Should I lie, madam?

CLEO.   Oh, I would thou didst,
So half my Egypt were submerged and made
A cistern for scaléd snakes! Go get thee hence.   95
Hadst thou Narcissus° in thy face, to me
Thou wouldst appear most ugly. He is married?

MESS. I crave your Highness' pardon.

CLEO.   He is married?

MESS. Take no offense that I would not offend you.
To punish me for what you make me do   100
Seems much unequal.° He's married to Octavia.

CLEO. Oh, that his fault should make a knave of
    thee,
That art not what thou'rt sure of! Get thee hence.
The merchandise which thou hast brought from
    Rome   104
Are all too dear for me. Lie they upon thy hand,
And be undone by 'em!   [*Exit* MESSENGER.]

CHAR.   Good your Highness, patience.

CLEO. In praising Antony, I have dispraised
    Caesar.

CHAR. Many times, madam.

CLEO.   I am paid for 't now.
Lead me from hence,
I faint. O Iras, Charmian! 'Tis no matter.   110
Go to the fellow, good Alexas. Bid him
Report the feature of Octavia, her years,
Her inclination,° let him not leave out
The color of her hair. Bring me word quickly.
                     [*Exit* ALEXAS.]
Let him forever go, let him not —— Charmian,   115
Though he be painted one way like a Gorgon,°
The other way's a Mars. [*To* MARDIAN] Bid you
    Alexas
Bring me word how tall she is. Pity me, Charmian,
But do not speak to me. Lead me to my chamber.
                         [*Exeunt.*]

SCENE VI. *Near Misenum.*

[*Flourish. Enter* POMPEY *and* MENAS *from one side,
with drum and trumpet; at another,* CAESAR, ANTONY,
LEPIDUS, ENOBARBUS, MECAENAS, *with* SOLDIERS
marching.]

POM. Your hostages I have, so have you mine,
And we shall talk before we fight.

CAES.   Most meet
That first we come to words, and therefore have we
Our written purposes before us sent.
Which if thou hast considered, let us know   5
If 'twill tie up thy discontented sword
And carry back to Sicily much tall° youth
That else must perish here.

POM.   To you all three,
The Senators° alone of this great world,
Chief factors° for the gods, I do not know   10
Wherefore my father should revengers want,
Having a son and friends, since Julius Caesar,
Who at Philippi the good Brutus ghosted,°

---

71. boot: benefit.   96. Narcissus: a youth so beautiful that
he fell in love with his own reflection in the water and perished
seeking it.

101. unequal: unfair.   113. inclination: what she likes and dislikes.   116. Gorgon: a creature so terrible to look on that all
who saw her turned to stone.
    Sc. vi: 7. tall: brave.   9. Senators: councilors, governors.
10. factors: agents.   13. ghosted: haunted. See *Caesar*, IV.iii
275–87.

There saw you laboring for him. What was 't
That moved pale Cassius to conspire, and what 15
Made the all-honored honest Roman, Brutus,
With the armed rest, courtiers of beauteous freedom,
To drench° the Capitol, but that they would
Have one man but a man? And that is it
Hath made me rig my navy, at whose burden 20
The angered ocean foams, with which I meant
To scourge the ingratitude that despiteful° Rome
Cast on my noble father.

CAES.   Take your time

ANT. Thou canst not fear° us, Pompey, with thy
    sails, 24
We'll speak with thee at sea. At land, thou know'st
How much we do o'ercount thee.

POM.   At land indeed
Thou dost o'ercount° me of my father's house.
But since the cuckoo° builds not for himself,
Remain in 't as thou mayst.

LEP.   Be pleased to tell us —
For this is from the present° — how you take 30
The offers we have sent you.

CAES.   There's the point.

ANT. Which do not be entreated to, but weigh
What it is worth embraced.

CAES.   And what may follow,
To try a larger fortune.

POM.   You have made me offer
Of Sicily, Sardinia, and I must 35
Rid all the sea of pirates. Then, to send
Measures of wheat to Rome. This 'greed upon,
To part with unhacked edges° and bear back
Our targes undinted.°

CAES., ANT., & LEP. That's our offer.

POM.   Know, then,
I came before you here a man prepared 41
To take this offer. But Mark Antony
Put me to some impatience. Though I lose
The praise of it by telling, you must know
When Caesar and your brother were at blows, 45
Your mother came to Sicily and did find
Her welcome friendly.

ANT.   I have heard it, Pompey,
And am well studied° for a liberal thanks
Which I do owe you.

POM.   Let me have your hand.
I did not think, sir, to have met you here. 50

ANT. The beds i' the East are soft, and thanks to
    you,
That called me timelier than my purpose hither,
For I have gained by 't.

CAES.   Since I saw you last
There is a change upon you.

POM.   Well, I know not
What counts° harsh Fortune casts upon my face, 55
But in my bosom shall she never come
To make my heart her vassal.°

LEP.   Well met here.

POM. I hope so, Lepidus. Thus we are agreed.
I crave our composition° may be written
And sealed between us.

CAES.   That's the next to do. 60

POM. We'll feast each other ere we part, and let's
Draw lots who shall begin.

ANT.   That will I, Pompey.

POM. No, Antony, take the lot.
But, first or last, your fine Egyptian cookery 64
Shall have the fame. I have heard that Julius Caesar
Grew fat with feasting there.

ANT.   You have heard much.

POM. I have fair meanings, sir.

ANT.   And fair words to them.

POM. Then so much have I heard.
And I have heard, Apollodorus carried ——

ENO. No more of that. He did so.

POM.   What, I pray you? 70

ENO. A certain Queen to Caesar in a mattress.

POM. I know thee now. How farest thou, soldier?

ENO.   Well,
And well am like to do, for I perceive
Four feasts are toward.

POM.   Let me shake thy hand.
I never hated thee. I have seen thee fight 75
When I have envied thy behavior.

ENO.   Sir,
I never loved you much, but I ha' praised ye
When you have well deserved ten times as much
As I have said you did.

POM.   Enjoy thy plainness,
It nothing ill becomes thee. 80
Aboard my galley I invite you all.
Will you lead, lords?

CAES., ANT., & LEP. Show us the way, sir.

POM.   Come.
    [*Exeunt all but* MENAS *and* ENOBARBUS.]

MEN. [*Aside*] Thy father, Pompey, would ne'er
have made this treaty. — You and I have known,°
sir. 86

ENO. At sea, I think.

MEN. We have, sir.

ENO. You have done well by water.

MEN. And you by land. 90

ENO. I will praise any man that will praise me,
though it cannot be denied what I have done by land.

MEN. Nor what I have done by water. 94

---

18. drench: i.e., with blood. 22. despiteful: hateful, cruel.
24. fear: frighten. 27. o'ercount: outbid. Antony had bought
the house of the elder Pompey and refused to pay for it.
28. cuckoo: See App. 11. 30. For . . . present: i.e., this wrangling is off the point. 38. unhacked edges: i.e., without fighting.
39. targes undinted: shields undented. 48. am . . . studied:
have long thought. Cf. II.ii.156–60.

55. counts: accounts; i.e., whether my debts to Fortune are
recorded in my face. 57. vassal: slave. 59. composition:
agreement. 85. known: met before.

ENO. Yes, something you can deny for your own safety. You have been a great thief by sea.

MEN. And you by land.

ENO. There I deny my land service. But give me your hand, Menas. If our eyes had authority, here they might take two thieves kissing.   101

MEN. All men's faces are true, whatsome'er their hands are.

ENO. But there is never a fair woman has a true face.   105

MEN. No slander, they steal hearts.

ENO. We came hither to fight with you.

MEN. For my part, I am sorry it is turned to a drinking. Pompey doth this day laugh away his fortune.   110

ENO. If he do, sure he cannot weep 't back again.

MEN. You've said, sir. We looked not for Mark Antony here. Pray you, is he married to Cleopatra?

ENO. Caesar's sister is called Octavia.   116

MEN. True, sir, she was the wife of Caius Marcellus.

ENO. But she is now the wife of Marcus Antonius.

MEN. Pray ye, sir?   120

ENO. 'Tis true.

MEN. Then is Caesar and he forever knit together.

ENO. If I were bound to divine° of this unity, I would not prophesy so.   125

MEN. I think the policy of that purpose made more° in the marriage than the love of the parties.

ENO. I think so too. But you shall find the band that seems to tie their friendship together will be the very strangler of their amity. Octavia is of a holy, cold, and still conversation.°   131

MEN. Who would not have his wife so?

ENO. Not he that himself is not so, which is Mark Antony. He will to his Egyptian dish again. Then shall the sighs of Octavia blow the fire up in Caesar, and, as I said before, that which is the strength of their amity shall prove the immediate author° of their variance. Antony will use his affection where it is. He married but his occasion here.°   140

MEN. And thus it may be. Come, sir, will you aboard? I have a health for you.

ENO. I shall take it, sir. We have used our throats in Egypt.   144

MEN. Come, let's away.   [*Exeunt.*]

---

124. divine: prophesy.   126–27. policy . . . more: political advantage of that arrangement had more to do with.   131. still conversation: "dumb" behavior.   138. author: cause.   140. married . . . here: married to suit his immediate need.

SCENE VII. *On board* POMPEY'S *galley, off Misenum.*

[*Music plays. Enter two or three* SERVANTS, *with a banquet.*°]

1. SERV. Here they'll be, man. Some o' their plants° are ill-rooted already, the least wind i' the world will blow them down.

2. SERV. Lepidus is high-colored.   5

1. SERV. They have made him drink alms drink.°

2. SERV. As they pinch° one another by the disposition,° he cries out "No more," reconciles them to his entreaty and himself to the drink.

1. SERV. But it raises the greater war between him and his discretion.   11

2. SERV. Why, this it is to have a name in great men's fellowship. I had as lief have a reed that will do me no service as a partisan° I could not heave.

1. SERV. To be called into a huge sphere, and   16 not to be seen to move in 't, are the holes where eyes should be, which pitifully disaster the cheeks.°

[*A sennet*° *sounded. Enter* CAESAR, ANTONY, LEPIDUS, POMPEY, AGRIPPA, MECAENAS, ENOBARBUS, MENAS, *with other* CAPTAINS.]

ANT. [*To* CAESAR] Thus do they, sir. They take the flow o' the Nile   20
By certain scales i' the pyramid. They know
By the height, the lowness, or the mean if dearth
Or foison° follow. The higher Nilus swells,
The more it promises. As it ebbs, the seedsman
Upon the slime and ooze scatters his grain,   25
And shortly comes to harvest.

LEP. You've strange serpents there.

ANT. Aye, Lepidus.

LEP. Your serpent of Egypt is bred now of your mud by the operation of your sun. So is your crocodile.°   31

ANT. They are so.

POM. Sit — and some wine! A health to Lepidus!

LEP. I am not so well as I should be, but I'll ne'er out.°   36

ENO. Not till you have slept. I fear me you'll be in till then.

LEP. Nay, certainly I have heard the Ptolemies' pyramises° are very goodly things — without contradiction, I have heard that.   41

Sc. vii: s.d., banquet: dessert and wine.   2. plants: soles of the feet, with a pun on growing plants.   6. alms drink: dregs given to the beggars.   7. pinch: irritate.   7–8. by . . . disposition: according to each man's nature.   15. partisan: a heavy weapon. See Pl. 21a.   16–18. To . . . cheeks: a complex image; it may be paraphrased "to be summoned to occupy a great and conspicuous place, like a planet in the sky, and then to be a failure, is to be like eyeless sockets which pitifully scar the face."   19 s.d., sennet: trumpet call.   23. foison: plenty.   29–31. Your . . . crocodile: This was very generally believed.   35–36. I'll . . . out: I'll never refuse a drink. Lepidus is by this time very fuddled.   40. pyramises: the nearest Lepidus can get to "pyramides," the Elizabethan form of pyramids. See V.ii.61.

MEN. [*Aside to* POMPEY] Pompey, a word.

POM. [*Aside to* MENAS] Say in mine ear. What is 't?

MEN. [*Aside to* POMPEY] Forsake thy seat, I do beseech thee, Captain,
And hear me speak a word.

POM. [*Aside to* MENAS] Forbear me till anon.° —
This wine for Lepidus! 45

LEP. What manner o' thing is your crocodile?

ANT. It is shaped, sir, like itself, and it is as broad as it hath breadth. It is just so high as it is, and moves with it own organs. It lives by that which nourisheth it, and the elements° once out of it, it transmigrates.

LEP. What color is it of? 52

ANT. Of it° own color too.

LEP. 'Tis a strange serpent.

ANT. 'Tis so. And the tears of it are wet.

CAES. Will this description satisfy him?

ANT. With the health that Pompey gives him, else he is a very epicure.° 58

POM. [*Aside to* MENAS] Go hang, sir, hang! Tell me of that? Away!
Do as I bid you. — Where's this cup I called for?

MEN. [*Aside to* POMPEY] If for the sake of merit thou wilt hear me, 61
Rise from thy stool.

POM. [*Aside to* MENAS] I think thou'rt mad. The matter? [*Rises, and walks aside.*]

MEN. I have ever held my cap off to thy fortunes.°

POM. Thou hast served me with much faith. What's else to say?
Be jolly, lords.

ANT. These quicksands, Lepidus — 65
Keep off them, for you sink.°

MEN. Wilt thou be lord of all the world?

POM. What say'st thou?

MEN. Wilt thou be lord of the whole world? That's twice.

POM. How should that be?

MEN. But entertain it,
And though thou think me poor, I am the man 70
Will give thee all the world.

POM. Hast thou drunk well?

MEN. No, Pompey, I have kept me from the cup.
Thou art, if thou darest be, the earthly Jove.
Whate'er the ocean pales° or sky inclips°
Is thine if thou wilt ha 't.

POM. Show me which way. 75

MEN. These three world-sharers, these competitors,
Are in thy vessel. Let me cut the cable,

And when we are put off, fall to their throats.
All there is thine.

POM. Ah, this thou shouldst have done,
And not have spoke on 't! In me 'tis villainy, 80
In thee 't had been good service. Thou must know
'Tis not my profit that does lead mine honor,
Mine honor, it. Repent that e'er thy tongue
Hath so betrayed thine act. Being done unknown,
I should have found it afterward well done, 85
But must condemn it now. Desist, and drink.

MEN. [*Aside*] For this
I'll never follow thy palled° fortunes more.
Who seeks and will not take when once 'tis offered
Shall never find it more.

POM. This health to Lepidus! 90

ANT. Bear him ashore. I'll pledge it for him, Pompey.

ENO. Here's to thee, Menas!

MEN. Enobarbus, welcome!

POM. Fill till the cup be hid.

ENO. There's a strong fellow, Menas.
[*Pointing to the* ATTENDANT *who carries off* LEPIDUS.]

MEN. Why? 95

ENO. A' bears the third part of the world, man, see'st not?

MEN. The third part then is drunk. Would it were all,
That it might go on wheels!°

ENO. Drink thou, increase the reels.° 100

MEN. Come.

POM. This is not yet an Alexandrian feast.°

ANT. It ripens toward it. Strike the vessels,° ho!
Here's to Caesar!

CAES. I could well forbear 't.
It's monstrous labor when I wash my brain 105
And it grows fouler.

ANT. Be a child o' the time.

CAES. Possess it,° I'll make answer.
But I had rather fast from all four days
Than drink so much in one.

ENO. [*To* ANTONY] Ha, my brave Emperor! 110
Shall we dance now the Egyptian Bacchanals,°
And celebrate our drink?

POM. Let's ha 't, good soldier.

ANT. Come, let's all take hands
Till that the conquering wine hath steeped our sense
In soft and delicate Lethe.

ENO. All take hands. 115
Make battery to our ears with the loud music,
The while I'll place you. Then the boy shall sing,
The holding° every man shall bear as loud
As his strong sides can volley.

---

44. anon: by and by. **50. elements:** The word is used with a large range of meanings. Antony here means "life." **53. it:** its. **58. epicure:** i.e., expert drinker. **63. held . . . fortunes:** i.e., have been your faithful servant. **65-66. These . . . sink:** Lepidus here lapses into a coma. **74. pales:** fences in. **inclips:** embraces.

88. palled: decayed. **99. on wheels:** fast; from the proverb "The world goes on wheels." **100. reels:** revelry. **102. Alexandrian feast:** i.e., as rowdy as those given by Cleopatra. **103. Strike . . . vessels:** either "tap fresh casks" or "bang the cups on the tables." **107. Possess it:** have it your own way. **111. Bacchanals:** dances to Bacchus, the god of wine. **118. holding:** refrain.

[*Music plays.* ENOBARBUS *places them hand in hand.*]
THE SONG

Come, thou monarch of the vine,   120
Plumpy Bacchus with pink eyne!°
In thy fats° our cares be drowned,
With thy grapes our hairs be crowned.
Cup us, till the world go round,
Cup us, till the world go round!   125

CAES. What would you more? Pompey, good
    night. Good brother,
Let me request you off.° Our graver business
Frowns at this levity. Gentle lords, let's part,
You see we have burnt our cheeks. Strong Enobarb
Is weaker than the wine, and mine own tongue   130
Splits what it speaks. The wild disguise hath almost
Anticked us all.° What needs more words? Good
    night.
Good Antony, your hand.
    POM.   I'll try you on the shore.
    ANT. And shall, sir. Give 's your hand.
    POM.   O Antony,
You have my father's house. — But what? We are
    friends.   135
Come, down into the boat.
    ENO.   Take heed you fall not.
        [*Exeunt all but* ENOBARBUS *and* MENAS.]
Menas, I'll not on shore.
    MEN.   No, to my cabin.
These drums! These trumpets, flutes! What!
Let Neptune° hear we bid a loud farewell   139
To these great fellows. Sound and be hanged, sound
    out!   [*Sound a flourish, with drums.*]
    ENO. Hoo! says a'. There's my cap.
    MEN. Hoo! Noble Captain, come.   [*Exeunt.*]

Act III

SCENE I. *A plain in Syria.*

[*Enter* VENTIDIUS *as it were in triumph,° with* SILIUS,
and other ROMANS, OFFICERS, *and* SOLDIERS, *the dead
body of* PACORUS *borne before him.*]
    VEN. Now, darting Parthia,° art thou struck, and
    now
Pleased fortune does of Marcus Crassus' death

121. eyne: eyes.   122. fats: vats, casks.   127. request . . . off:
beg you to come away.   132. Anticked us all: turned us all into
clowns.   139. Neptune: the god of the sea.
    Act III, Sc. i: s.d., Ventidius . . . triumph: Ventidius had
been sent to Parthia by Antony (II.iii.40–45) to avenge the
death of the Roman leader Crassus, defeated and killed by the
Parthians under King Orodes in Mesopotamia in 53 B.C.
1. darting Parthia: The Parthians had defeated the heavy-armed
and slow-moving Roman legions by their method of fighting.
They rode light-armed on horses from which they shot arrows into
the close ranks, and were away before the Romans could catch
them.

Make me revenger. Bear the King's son's body
Before our army. Thy Pacorus, Orodes,
Pays this for Marcus Crassus.
    SIL.   Noble Ventidius,   5
Whilst yet with Parthian blood thy sword is warm,
The fugitive Parthians follow. Spur through Media,
Mesopotamia, and the shelters whither
The routed fly. So thy grand° Captain Antony
Shall set thee on triumphant chariots and   10
Put garlands on thy head.
    VEN.   O Silius, Silius,
I have done enough. A lower place, note well,
May make too great an act.° For learn this, Silius —
Better to leave undone than by our deed
Acquire too high a fame when him we serve's away.
Caesar and Antony have ever won   16
More in their officer than person. Sossius,
One of my place in Syria, his lieutenant,
For quick accumulation of renown,
Which he achieved by the minute, lost his favor.   20
Who does i' the wars more than his Captain can
Becomes his Captain's Captain. And ambition,
The soldier's virtue, rather makes choice of loss
Than gain which darkens him.
I could do more to do Antonius good,   25
But 'twould offend him, and in his offense
Should my performance perish.
    SIL.   Thou hast, Ventidius, that
Without the which a soldier and his sword
Grants scarce distinction. Thou wilt write to
    Antony?
    VEN. I'll humbly signify what in his name,   30
That magical word of war, we have effected,
How with his banners and his well-paid ranks
The ne'er-yet-beaten horse of Parthia
We have jaded° out o' the field.
    SIL.   Where is he now?
    VEN. He purposeth to Athens. Whither, with what
    haste   35
The weight° we must convey with 's will permit,
We shall appear before him. On, there, pass along!
                    [*Exeunt.*]

SCENE II. *Rome. An antechamber in* CAESAR'S
house.

[*Enter* AGRIPPA *at one door and* ENOBARBUS *at
another.*]
    AGR. What, are the brothers parted?
    ENO. They have dispatched° with Pompey. He is
    gone,

9. grand: great.   12–13. A . . . act: i.e., a subordinate commander can do too well.   34. jaded: reduced to jades; i.e., poor-
spirited nags.   36. The weight: i.e., the body of Pacorus and
the loot.
    Sc. ii: 2. dispatched: finished their business.

The other three are sealing.° Octavia weeps
To part from Rome, Caesar is sad, and Lepidus
Since Pompey's feast, as Menas says, is troubled   5
With the greensickness.°

AGR.   'Tis° a noble Lepidus.

ENO. A very fine one. Oh, how he loves Caesar!

AGR. Nay, but how dearly he adores Mark
    Antony!

ENO. Caesar? Why, he's the Jupiter of men.

AGR. What's Antony? The god of Jupiter.   10

ENO. Spake you of Caesar? How! The nonpareil!°

AGR. O Antony! O thou Arabian bird!°

ENO. Would you praise Caesar, say " Caesar." Go
    no further.

AGR. Indeed he plied them both with excellent
    praises.

ENO. But he loves Caesar best, yet he loves
    Antony.   *PARALLELISM*   15
Ho! Hearts, tongues, figures, scribes, bards, poets,
    cannot
Think, speak, cast,° write, sing, number° — ho! —
His love to Antony. But as for Caesar,
Kneel down, kneel down, and wonder.

AGR.   Both he loves.

ENO. They are his shards,° and he their beetle.
    [*Trumpet within.*] So,   20
This is to horse. Adieu, noble Agrippa.

AGR. Good fortune, worthy soldier, and farewell.
    [*Enter* CAESAR, ANTONY, LEPIDUS, *and* OCTAVIA.]

ANT. No further, sir.

CAES. You take from me a great part of myself.
Use me well in 't. Sister, prove such a wife   25
As my thoughts make thee, and as my farthest band
Shall pass on thy approof.° Most noble Antony,
Let not the piece of virtue which is set
Betwixt us as the cément of our love,
To keep it builded, be the ram° to batter   30
The fortress of it. For better might we
Have loved without this mean° if on both parts
This be not cherished.

ANT.   Make me not offended
In your distrust.

CAES.   I have said.

ANT.   You shall not find,
Though you be therein curious,° the least cause   35
For what you seem to fear. So the gods keep you,
And make the hearts of Romans serve your ends!
We will here part.

CAES. Farewell, my dearest Sister, fare thee well.
The elements° be kind to thee, and make   40
Thy spirits all of comfort! Fare thee well.

OCT. My noble brother!

ANT. The April's in her eyes. It is love's spring,
And these the showers to bring it on. Be cheerful.

OCT. Sir, look well to my husband's house,
    and ——

CAES.   What,   45
Octavia?

OCT.   I'll tell you in your ear.

ANT. Her tongue will not obey her heart, nor can
Her heart inform her tongue,° the swan's-down
    feather,
That stands upon the swell at full of tide
And neither way inclines.   50

ENO. [*Aside to* AGRIPPA] Will Caesar weep?

AGR. [*Aside to* ENOBARBUS] He has a cloud in 's
    face.°

ENO. [*Aside to* AGRIPPA] He were the worse for
    that were he a horse.°
So is he, being a man.

AGR. [*Aside to* ENOBARBUS] Why, Enobarbus,
When Antony found Julius Caesar dead,
He cried almost to roaring, and he wept   55
When at Philippi he found Brutus slain.

ENO. [*Aside to* AGRIPPA] That year indeed he was
    troubled with a rheum.°
What willingly he did confound° he wailed,°
Believe 't, till I wept too.

CAES.   No, sweet Octavia,
You shall hear from me still. The time shall not   60
Outgo my thinking on you.

ANT.   Come, sir; come,
I'll wrestle° with you in my strength of love.
Look, here I have you, thus I let you go,
And give you to the gods.

CAES.   Adieu. Be happy!   64

LEP. Let all the number of the stars give light
To thy fair way!

CAES.   Farewell, farewell! [*Kisses* OCTAVIA.]

ANT.   Farewell!
    [*Trumpets sound. Exeunt.*]

SCENE III. *Alexandria.* CLEOPATRA's *palace.*

[*Enter* CLEOPATRA, CHARMIAN, IRAS, *and* ALEXAS.]

CLEO. Where is the fellow?

ALEX.   Half afeard to come.

CLEO. Go to, go to.

---

3. sealing: See App. 6.   **6. greensickness:** a form of anemia common to teen-age girls.   **6–20. 'Tis . . . beetle:** Agrippa and Enobarbus mimic Lepidus's tactful efforts to keep his partners from quarreling.   **11. nonpareil:** unparalleled.   **12. Arabian bird:** phoenix; i.e., unique creature. See *Temp*, III.iii.21–23,n.   **17. cast:** reckon. **number:** make verses.   **20. shards:** the horny wings of the beetle.   **26–27. as . . . approof:** as my most extravagant bond (*band*) shall guarantee. **approof:** proof of your behavior.   **30. ram:** battering ram.   **32. mean:** means. **35. be . . . curious:** make most careful inquiry.

40. elements: i.e., sea and sky.   **47–48. Her . . . tongue:** she is so full of emotion that she can neither speak nor be silent. **51. cloud . . . face:** i.e., looks as if he would weep.   **52. were . . . horse:** a "cloud in the face" is also a dark patch between a horse's eyes, believed to denote bad temper.   **57. rheum:** cold. **58. confound:** overthrow. **wailed:** wept over.   **62. wrestle:** i.e., they embrace at parting.

[handwritten: SHE HAS CORRUPTED THIS INFORMATION]

[*Enter* MESSENGER.]   Come hither, sir.

ALEX.   Good Majesty,
Herod of Jewry dare not look upon you
But when° you are well pleased.

CLEO.   That Herod's head
I'll have. But how, when Antony is gone   5
Through whom I might command it? Come thou
    near.

MESS. Most gracious Majesty ——

CLEO. Didst thou behold Octavia?

MESS. Aye, dread Queen.

CLEO. Where?   10

MESS. Madam, in Rome
I looked her in the face, and saw her led
Between her brother and Mark Antony.

CLEO. Is she as tall as me?

MESS.   She is not, madam.

CLEO. Didst hear her speak? Is she shrill-tongued
    or low?   15

MESS. Madam, I heard her speak. She is low-
    voiced.

CLEO. That's not so good. He cannot like her long.

CHAR. Like her! Oh, Isis! 'Tis impossible.

CLEO. I think so, Charmian. Dull of tongue and
    dwarfish.
What majesty is in her gait? Remember,   20
If e'er thou look'dst on majesty.

MESS.   She creeps.
Her motion and her station are as one.
She shows a body rather than a life,
A statue than a breather.°

CLEO.   Is this certain?

MESS. Or I have no observance.

CHAR.   Three in Egypt   25
Cannot make better note.

CLEO.   He's very knowing,
I do perceive 't. There's nothing in her yet.
The fellow has good judgment.

CHAR.   Excellent.

CLEO. Guess at her years, I prithee.

MESS.   Madam,
She was a widow ——

CLEO.   Widow! Charmian, hark.   30

MESS. And I do think she's thirty.

CLEO. Bear'st thou her face in mind? Is 't long or
    round?

MESS. Round even to faultiness.

CLEO. For the most part, too, they are foolish that
    are so.
Her hair, what color?   35

MESS. Brown, madam, and her forehead
As low° as she would wish it.

CLEO.   There's gold for thee.

[handwritten in margin: Getting standards of beauty]

Thou must not take my former sharpness ill.
I will employ thee back again, I find thee
Most fit for business. Go make thee ready,   40
Our letters are prepared.   [*Exit* MESSENGER.]

CHAR.   A proper° man.

CLEO. Indeed he is so. I repent me much
That so I harried him. Why, methinks, by him,
This creature's no such thing.°

CHAR.   Nothing, madam.

CLEO. The man hath seen some majesty, and
    should know.   45

CHAR. Hath he seen majesty? Isis else defend,°
And serving you so long!

CLEO. I have one thing more to ask him yet, good
    Charmian.
But 'tis no matter, thou shalt bring him to me
Where I will write. All may be well enough.   50

CHAR. I warrant you, madam.

                            [*Exeunt.*]

SCENE IV. *Athens. A room in* ANTONY'S *house.*

[*Enter* ANTONY *and* OCTAVIA.]

ANT. Nay, nay, Octavia, not only that —
That were excusable, that and thousands more
Of semblable° import — but he hath waged
New wars 'gainst Pompey, made his will, and read
    it
To public ear,   5
Spoke scantly° of me. When perforce he could not
But pay me terms of honor,° cold and sickly
He vented° them, most narrow measure lent me.
When the best hint° was given him, he not took 't,
Or did it from his teeth.°

OCT.   O my good lord,   10
Believe not all. Or if you must believe,
Stomach° not all. A more unhappy lady,
If this division chance, ne'er stood between,
Praying for both parts.
The good gods will mock me presently   15
When I shall pray, " Oh, bless my lord and hus-
    band! "
Undo that prayer, by crying out as loud,
" Oh, bless my brother! " Husband win, win brother,
Prays, and destroys the prayer — no midway
'Twixt these extremes at all.

ANT.   Gentle Octavia,   20
Let your best love draw to that point° which seeks
Best to preserve it. If I lose mine honor,
I lose myself. Better I were not yours

---

41. **proper**: fine.   44. **This . . . thing**: i.e., nothing to worry about.
46. **defend**: forbid.
     Sc. iv: 3. **semblable**: like.   6. **scantly**: disrespectfully.
6-7. **could . . . honor**: was obliged to say honorable things about
me.   8. **vented**: uttered.   9. **hint**: opportunity.   10. **from . . .
teeth**: i.e., gave me lip service only.   12. **Stomach**: be angry
at.   21. **draw . . . point**: i.e., be bestowed on me.

Sc. iii: 4. **But when**: except when.   21-24. **She . . . breather**:
i.e., Octavia is insignificant and demure; moving or standing,
she is a dummy.   36. **low**: A low forehead showed lack of intelligence.

Than yours so branchless.° But, as you requested,
Yourself shall go between 's. The meantime, lady,
I'll raise the preparation of a war   26
Shall stain° your brother. Make your soonest haste,
So your desires are yours.

OCT.   Thanks to my lord.
The Jove of power make me most weak, most weak,
Your reconciler! Wars 'twixt you twain would be
As if the world should cleave, and that slain men
Should solder up the rift.   32

ANT. When it appears to you where this begins,
Turn your displeasure that way, for our faults
Can never be so equal that your love   35
Can equally move with them. Provide your going,
Choose your own company, and command what
     cost
Your heart has mind to.   [*Exeunt.*]

SCENE V. *The same. Another room.*

[*Enter* ENOBARBUS *and* EROS, *meeting.*]

ENO. How now, friend Eros!

EROS. There's strange news come, sir.

ENO. What, man?

EROS. Caesar and Lepidus have made wars upon
Pompey.

ENO. This is old. What is the success?°   6

EROS. Caesar, having made use of him in the wars
'gainst Pompey, presently denied him rivality,°
would not let him partake in the glory of the action.
And not resting here, accuses him of letters he had
formerly wrote to Pompey, upon his own appeal,°
seizes him. So the poor third is up,° till death enlarge his confine.°   13

ENO. Then, world, thou hast a pair of chaps,° no
     more,
And throw between them all the food thou hast,
They'll grind the one the other. Where's Antony?

EROS. He's walking in the garden — thus, and
     spurns°   17
The rush° that lies before him, cries " Fool
     Lepidus! "
And threats the throat of that his officer
That murdered Pompey.

ENO.   Our great navy's rigged.   20

EROS. For Italy and Caesar. More, Domitius.
My lord desires you presently. My news
I might have told hereafter.

ENO.   'Twill be naught.

But let it be. Bring me to Antony.   24

EROS. Come, sir.   [*Exeunt.*]

SCENE VI. *Rome.* CAESAR'S *house.*

[*Enter* CAESAR, AGRIPPA, *and* MECAENAS.]

CAES. Contemning° Rome, he has done all this,
     and more,
In Alexandria. Here's the manner of 't.
I' the market place, on a tribunal° silvered
Cleopatra and himself in chairs of gold
Were publicly enthroned. At the feet sat   5
Caesarion,° whom they call my father's° son,
And all the unlawful issue° that their lust
Since then hath made between them. Unto her
He gave the stablishment° of Egypt, made her
Of lower Syria, Cyprus, Lydia,   10
Absolute Queen.

MEC.   This in the public eye?

CAES. I' the common show place, where they
     exercise.
His sons he there proclaimed the Kings of Kings.
Great Media, Parthia, and Armenia
He gave to Alexander. To Ptolemy he assigned   15
Syria, Cilicia, and Phoenicia. She
In the habiliments° of the goddess Isis
That day appeared, and oft before gave audience,
As 'tis reported, so.

MEC.   Let Rome be thus
Informed.

AGR.   Who, queasy with his insolence   20
Already, will their good thoughts call from him.

CAES. The people know it, and have now received
His accusations.

AGR.   Who does he accuse?

CAES. Caesar. And that, having in Sicily
Sextus Pompeius spoiled, we had not rated him°   25
His part o' the isle. Then does he say he lent me
Some shipping unrestored. Lastly, he frets
That Lepidus of the Triumvirate
Should be deposed, and, being, that we detain
All his revenue.

AGR.   Sir, this should be answered.   30

CAES. 'Tis done already, and the messenger gone.
I have told him Lepidus was grown too cruel,
That he his high authority abused
And did deserve his change.° For what I have con-
     quered,
I grant him part, but then in his Armenia   35
And other of his conquered kingdoms I
Demand the like.

---

24. **branchless:** without branches; i.e., lopped of honors.
27. **stain:** discredit.

     Sc. v: 6. **success:** result.   8. **rivality:** partnership.   11. **ap-
peal:** accusation.   12. **poor . . . up:** i.e., so No. 3 of the Big
Three is in jail.   13. **enlarge . . . confine:** make wider his
place of confinement.   14. **pair of chaps:** an upper and a lower
jaw; i.e., Antony and Octavius.   17. **spurns:** kicks at.   18. **rush:**
i.e., one of the rushes with which the floor was strewn.

     Sc. vi: 1. **Contemning:** despising.   3. **tribunal:** high throne.
6. **Caesarion:** the son of Cleopatra by Julius Caesar. **father's:**
Octavius was the adopted son of Julius Caesar.   7. **unlawful
issue:** bastard children.   9. **stablishment:** rule.   17. **habiliments:** robes.   25. **rated him:** given as his share.   34. **change:**
i.e., of fortune.

MEC. He'll never yield to that.

CAES. Nor must not then be yielded to in this.

[*Enter* OCTAVIA, *with her train.*]

OCT. Hail, Caesar, and my lord! Hail, most dear
Caesar!

CAES. That ever I should call thee castaway! 40

OCT. You have not called me so, nor have you
cause.

CAES. Why have you stol'n upon us thus? You
come not
Like Caesar's sister. The wife of Antony
Should have an army for an usher,° and
The neighs of horse to tell of her approach 45
Long ere she did appear. The trees by the way
Should have borne men, and expectation fainted,°
Longing for what it had not. Nay, the dust
Should have ascended to the roof of Heaven,
Raised by your populous troops. But you are come
A market maid to Rome, and have prevented° 51
The ostentation° of our love, which left unshown
Is often left unloved. We should have met you
By sea and land, supplying every stage
With an augmented greeting.

OCT.   Good my lord, 55
To come thus was I not constrained,° but did it
On my free will. My lord, Mark Antony,
Hearing that you prepared for war, acquainted
My grieved ear withal, whereon I begged
His pardon for return.

CAES.   Which soon he granted, 60
Being an obstruct° 'tween his lust and him.

OCT. Do not say so, my lord.

CAES.   I have eyes upon him,
And his affairs come to me on the wind.
Where is he now?

OCT.   My lord, in Athens.

CAES. No, my most wronged sister, Cleopatra 65
Hath nodded him to her. He hath given his empire
Up to a whore, who now are levying
The Kings o' the earth for war. He hath assembled
Bocchus, the King of Libya; Archelaus,
Of Cappadocia; Philadelphos, King 70
Of Paphlagonia; the Thracian King, Adallas;
King Malchus of Arabia; King of Pont;
Herod of Jewry; Mithridates, King
Of Comagene; Polemon and Amyntas,
The Kings of Mede and Lycaonia, 75
With a more larger list of scepters.

OCT.   Aye, me, most wretched,
That have my heart parted betwixt two friends
That do afflict each other!

CAES.   Welcome hither.
Your letters did withhold° our breaking-forth

Till we perceived both how you were wrong led 80
And we in negligent danger.° Cheer your heart.
Be you not troubled with the time,° which drives
O'er your content these strong necessities,
But let determined things to destiny
Hold unbewailed their way.° Welcome to Rome,
Nothing more dear to me. You are abused 86
Beyond the mark° of thought. And the high gods,
To do you justice, make them ministers
Of us and those that love you. Best of comfort,
And ever welcome to us.

AGR.   Welcome, lady. 90

MEC. Welcome, dear madam.
Each heart in Rome does love and pity you.
Only the adulterous Antony, most large
In his abominations, turns you off,
And gives his potent regiment° to a trull° 95
That noises it° against us.

OCT.   Is it so, sir?

CAES. Most certain. Sister, welcome. Pray you,
Be ever known to patience. My dear'st sister!

[*Exeunt.*]

SCENE VII. *Near Actium.* ANTONY's *camp.*

[*Enter* CLEOPATRA *and* ENOBARBUS.]

CLEO. I will be even with thee, doubt it not.

ENO. But why, why, why?°

CLEO. Thou hast forspoke° my being in these
wars,
And say'st it is not fit.

ENO.   Well, is it, is it?

CLEO. If not denounced against us, why should
not we 5
Be there in person?°

ENO.   [*Aside*] Well, I could reply.
If we should serve with horse and mares together,
The horse were merely° lost, the mares would bear
A soldier and his horse.

CLEO.   What is 't you say? 10

ENO. Your presence needs must puzzle Antony,
Take from his heart, take from his brain, from 's
time,
What should not then be spared. He is already
Traduced° for levity, and 'tis said in Rome
That Photinus, a eunuch, and your maids 15
Manage this war.

---

81. **negligent danger:** danger through our own neglect. 82. **time:** these difficult days. 84–85. **But . . . way:** Caesar, as the soothsayer had warned Antony (II.iii.15–30), was a man of destiny. **determined . . . destiny:** that which is decided by Fate. 87. **mark:** limit. 95. **potent regiment:** great authority. **trull:** whore. 96. **noises it:** is clamorous.

Sc. vii: 2. **But . . . why:** Enobarbus has no respect for Cleopatra, whom he treats not as a queen but as Antony's mistress and plaything. 3. **forspoke:** spoken against. 5–6. **If . . . person:** even if war has not been declared against me, why should I not be there? 8. **merely:** utterly. 14. **Traduced:** criticized.

---

44. **usher:** gentleman in attendance. 47. **expectation fainted:** people in the crowd should have fainted in their eagerness to see you. 51. **prevented:** forestalled. 52. **ostentation:** ceremonious show. 56. **constrained:** forced. 61. **obstruct:** obstruction. 79. **withhold:** keep back.

CLEO.   Sink Rome, and their tongues rot
That speak against us! A charge we bear i' the war,
And as the president of my kingdom will
Appear there for a man. Speak not against it,
I will not stay behind.

ENO.   Nay, I have done.   20
Here comes the Emperor.

    [*Enter* ANTONY *and* CANIDIUS.]

ANT.   Is it not strange, Canidius,
That from Tarentum and Brundusium
He could so quickly cut° the Ionian sea,
And take in° Toryne? You have heard on 't, sweet?

CLEO. Celerity is never more admired   25
Than by the negligent.

ANT.   A good rebuke,
Which might have well becomed the best of men,
To taunt at slackness. Canidius, we
Will fight with him by sea.

CLEO.   By sea. What else?

CAN. Why will my lord do so?

ANT.   For that he dares us to 't.   30

ENO. So hath my lord dared him to single fight.

CAN. Aye, and to wage this battle at Pharsalia,
Where Caesar fought with Pompey. But these offers,
Which serve not for his vantage, he shakes off,
And so should you.

ENO.   Your ships are not well manned,   35
Your mariners are muleters,° reapers, people
Ingrossed by swift impress.° In Caesar's fleet
Are those that often have 'gainst Pompey fought.
Their ships are yare,° yours heavy. No disgrace
Shall fall you for refusing him at sea,   40
Being prepared for land.

ANT.   By sea, by sea.

ENO. Most worthy sir, you therein throw away
The absolute soldiership° you have by land,
Distract° your army, which doth most consist
Of war-marked° footmen, leave unexecuted   45
Your own renownèd knowledge,° quite forgo
The way which promises assurance, and
Give up yourself merely° to chance and hazard
From firm security.

ANT.   I'll fight at sea.

CLEO. I have sixty sails, Caesar none better.   50

ANT. Our overplus of shipping will we burn,
And with the rest full-manned, from the head of
    Actium
Beat the approaching Caesar. But if we fail,
We then can do 't at land.

[*Enter a* MESSENGER.]   Thy business?   54

MESS. The news is true, my lord, he is descried.°

Caesar has taken Toryne.

ANT. Can he be there in person? 'Tis impossible.
Strange that his power° should be. Canidius,
Our nineteen legions thou shalt hold by land,   59
And our twelve thousand horse. We'll to our ship.
Away, my Thetis!°

[*Enter a* SOLDIER.]   How now, worthy soldier?

SOLD. O noble Emperor, do not fight by sea,
Trust not to rotten planks. Do you misdoubt
This sword and these my wounds? Let the Egyptians
And the Phoenicians go a-ducking.° We   65
Have used to conquer standing on the earth
And fighting foot to foot.

ANT.   Well, well. Away!

[*Exeunt* ANTONY, CLEOPATRA, *and* ENOBARBUS.]

SOLD. By Hercules, I think I am i' the right.

CAN. Soldier, thou art. But his whole action grows
Not in the power on 't.° So our leader's led,   70
And we are women's men.

SOLD.   You keep by land
The legions and the horse whole, do you not?

CAN. Marcus Octavius, Marcus Justeius,
Publicola, and Caelius, are for sea.   74
But we keep whole by land. This speed of Caesar's
Carries beyond belief.

SOLD.   While he was yet in Rome,
His power went out in such distractions° as
Beguiled all spies.

CAN.   Who's his lieutenant, hear you?

SOLD. They say one Taurus.

CAN.   Well I know the man.

    [*Enter a* MESSENGER.]

MESS. The Emperor calls Canidius.   80

CAN. With news the time's with labor,° and
    throes° forth
Each minute some.   [*Exeunt.*]

SCENE VIII.° *A plain near Actium.*

[*Enter* CAESAR, *and* TAURUS, *with his army,
marching.*]

CAES. Taurus!

TAUR. My lord?

CAES. Strike not by land, keep whole. Provoke not
    battle
Till we have done at sea. Do not exceed
The prescript of this scroll.° Our fortune lies
Upon this jump.°   [*Exeunt.*]

---

58. power: army.   61. Thetis: sea nymph.   65. go a-ducking: take to the water.   69–70. his . . . on 't: he is not wholly guided by military reasons.   77. distractions: small parties.   81. with labor: in childbirth. throes: i.e., produces news.

Sc. viii: There are no scene divisions in F1. This division into little scenes, each with its different locality, was made by editors in the eighteenth century. See *Ant & Cleo* Intro., p. 1221a.   5. prescript . . . scroll: what is laid down in these written orders.   6. jump: hazard.

23. cut: cut across.   24. take in: occupy.   36. muleters: muleteers, mule-drivers.   37. Ingrossed . . . impress: hurriedly conscripted.   39. yare: easily handled.   43. absolute soldiership: overwhelming superiority.   44. Distract: confuse.   45. warmarked: veteran.   45–46. leave . . . knowledge: i.e., make no use of your superior generalship.   48. merely: utterly.   55. descried: observed.

SCENE IX. *Another part of the plain.*

[*Enter* ANTONY *and* ENOBARBUS.]
ANT. Set we our squadrons on yond side o' the hill,
In eye of Caesar's battle, from which place
We may the number of the ships behold,
And so proceed accordingly.   [*Exeunt.*]

SCENE X. *Another part of the plain.*

[*Enter* CANIDIUS, *marching with his land army one
way; and* TAURUS, *the lieutenant of* CAESAR, *with his
army, the other way. After their going-in is heard
the noise of a sea fight.*]
[*Alarum. Enter* ENOBARBUS.]
ENO. Naught, naught, all naught! I can behold no
longer!
The *Antoniad,* the Egyptian Admiral,°
With all their sixty, fly and turn the rudder.
To see 't mine eyes are blasted.
[*Enter* SCARUS.]
SCAR.   Gods and goddesses,
All the whole synod° of them!
ENO.   What's thy passion?   5
SCAR. The greater cantle° of the world is lost
With very ignorance. We have kissed away
Kingdoms and provinces.
ENO.   How appears the fight?
SCAR. On our side like the tokened pestilence,°
Where death is sure. Yon ribaudrèd nag° of
Egypt —   10
Whom leprosy o'ertake! — i' the midst o' the fight,
When vantage like a pair of twins appeared,
Both as the same or rather ours the elder° —
The breese upon her, like a cow in June!° —
Hoists sails and flies.   15
ENO. That I beheld.
Mine eyes did sicken at the sight, and could not
Endure a further view.
SCAR.   She once being loofed,°
The noble ruin of her magic, Antony,
Claps on his sea wing, and like a doting mallard,°
Leaving the fight in height,° flies after her.   21
I never saw an action of such shame.
Experience, manhood, honor, ne'er before
Did violate so itself.
ENO.   Alack, alack!
[*Enter* CANIDIUS.]
CAN. Our fortune on the sea is out of breath,   25

Sc. x: **2. Admiral:** the Egyptian flagship.   **5. synod:** assembly.   **6. cantle:** slice.   **9. tokened pestilence:** plague when the red spots appear which denote death.   **10. ribaudred nag:** foul mare.   **12–13. vantage . . . elder:** victory seemed to favor both sides, and ours rather than theirs.   **14. breese . . . June:** like a cow stung by a gadfly in the summer.   **18. loofed:** luffed, her ship turned into the wind.   **20. doting mallard:** lovesick wild drake.   **21. in height:** at its fiercest.

And sinks most lamentably. Had our General
Been what he knew himself, it had gone well.
Oh, he has given example for our flight
Most grossly by his own!
ENO.   Aye, are you thereabouts?
Why then, good night indeed.   30
CAN. Toward Peloponnesus are they fled.
SCAR. 'Tis easy to 't, and there I will attend°
What further comes.
CAN.   To Caesar will I render
My legions and my horse. Six Kings already
Show me the way of yielding.
ENO.   I'll yet follow   35
The wounded chance° of Antony, though my reason
Sits in the wind against me.°   [*Exeunt.*]

SCENE XI. *Alexandria.* CLEOPATRA'S *palace.*

[*Enter* ANTONY *with* ATTENDANTS.]
ANT. Hark! The land bids me tread no more
upon 't,
It is ashamed to bear me. Friends, come hither.
I am so lated° in the world that I
Have lost my way forever. I have a ship
Laden with gold. Take that, divide it. Fly,   5
And make your peace with Caesar.
ALL.   Fly! Not we.
ANT. I have fled myself, and have instructed
cowards
To run and show their shoulders.° Friends, be gone.
I have myself resolved upon a course
Which has no need of you. Be gone.   10
My treasure's in the harbor, take it. Oh,
I followed that I blush to look upon.
My very hairs do mutiny, for the white
Reprove the brown for rashness, and they them
For fear and doting. Friends, be gone. You shall   15
Have letters from me to some friends that will
Sweep your way for you. Pray you, look not sad,
Nor make replies of loathness. Take the hint
Which my despair proclaims, let that be left
Which leaves itself. To the seaside straightway.   20
I will possess you of that ship and treasure.
Leave me, I pray, a little. Pray you now.
Nay, do so, for indeed I have lost command,
Therefore I pray you. I'll see you by and by.
[*Sits down.*]
[*Enter* CLEOPATRA *led by* CHARMIAN *and* IRAS, EROS
following.]
EROS. Nay, gentle madam, to him, comfort him.
IRAS. Do, most dear Queen.   26
CHAR. Do! Why, what else?

32. attend: await.   **36. wounded chance:** damaged fortune. **36–37 reason . . . me:** good sense is against me.
    Sc. xi: **3. lated:** belated; i.e., lost in the dark.   **8. show . . . shoulders:** i.e., their backs in flight.

CLEO. Let me sit down. Oh, Juno!

ANT. No, no, no, no, no.

EROS. See you here, sir?   30

ANT. Oh, fie, fie, fie!

CHAR. Madam!

IRAS. Madam, O good Empress!

EROS. Sir, sir!

ANT. Yes, my lord, yes. He° at Philippi kept   35
His sword e'en like a dancer,° while I struck
The lean and wrinkled Cassius. And 'twas I
That the mad Brutus ended.° He alone
Dealt on lieutenantry° and no practice° had
In the brave squares° of war. Yet now —— No
     matter.   40

CLEO. Ah! Stand by.

EROS. The Queen, my lord, the Queen.

IRAS. Go to him, madam, speak to him.
He is unqualitied° with very shame.

CLEO. Well then, sustain me.° Oh!   45

EROS. Most noble sir, arise, the Queen approaches.
Her head's declined, and death will seize her but°
Your comfort makes the rescue.

ANT. I have offended reputation,°
A most unnoble swerving.

EROS.   Sir, the Queen.   50

ANT. Oh, whither hast thou led me, Egypt? See
How I convey my shame out of thine eyes
By looking back what I have left behind
Stroyed° in dishonor.

CLEO.   O my lord, my lord,
Forgive my fearful sails! I little thought   55
You would have followed.

ANT.   Egypt, thou knew'st too well
My heart was to thy rudder tied by the strings,
And thou shouldst tow me after. O'er my spirit
Thy full supremacy thou knew'st, and that
Thy beck might from the bidding of the gods   60
Command me.

CLEO.   Oh, my pardon!

ANT.   Now I must
To the young man send humble treaties,° dodge
And palter in the shifts of lowness,° who
With half the bulk o' the world played as I pleased,
Making and marring fortunes. You did know   65
How much you were my conqueror, and that
My sword, made weak by my affection, would
Obey it on all cause.

CLEO.   Pardon, pardon!

35. He: Octavius Caesar.   **36. Sword . . . dancer:** i.e., for show
not use.   **36–38. while . . . ended:** Antony is lying. For the
deaths of Cassius and Brutus see *Caesar*, V.iii.45–46; V.v.50–51.
39. Dealt on lieutenantry: let his subordinates do the fighting.
practice: experience. **40. squares:** squadrons. **44. unqualitied:**
unmanned, having lost his natural quality. **45. sustain
me:** As before, Cleopatra faints to attract his sympathy. See
I.iii.71. **47. but:** unless. **49. reputation:** honor. **54. Stroyed:**
destroyed. **62. treaties:** proposals for an armistice.
62–63. dodge . . . lowness: make shifty excuses in my reduced
state.

ANT. Fall° not a tear, I say. One of them rates°
All that is won and lost. Give me a kiss,   70
Even this repays me. We sent our schoolmaster. *SHOWS CAESAR*
Is he come back? Love, I am full of lead. *IS INSULTED*
Some wine, within there, and our viands! Fortune *BY*
     knows *ANTONY—*
We scorn her most when most she offers blows. *ANTONY SUGGESTS CAESAR HAS*
     [*Exeunt.*] *SOMETHING TO LEARN*

SCENE XII. *Egypt.* CAESAR'S *camp.*

[*Enter* CAESAR, DOLABELLA, THYREUS, *with others.*]

CAES. Let him appear that's come from Antony.
Know you him?

DOL.   Caesar, 'tis his schoolmaster. *DOLA. PUTS*
An argument that he is plucked when hither *BEST POSSIBLE*
He sends so poor a pinion° of his wing, *LIGHT ON MATTER*
Which had superfluous Kings for messengers   5 *BY SAYING TO CAESAR*
Not many moons gone by. *THAT*

[*Enter* EUPHRONIUS, *ambassador from* ANTONY.] *ANTONY HAS*

CAES.   Approach, and speak. *NO FOLLOWERS*

EUPH. Such as I am, I come from Antony. *LEFT*
I was of late as petty to his ends°
As is the morn dew on the myrtle leaf
To his grand sea.

CAES.   Be 't so. Declare thine office.   10

EUPH. Lord of his fortunes he salutes thee, and
Requires° to live in Egypt. Which not granted,
He lessens his requests, and to thee sues
To let him breathe between the heavens and earth,
A private man in Athens. This for him.   15
Next, Cleopatra does confess thy greatness,
Submits her to thy might, and of thee craves
The circle° of the Ptolemies for her heirs,
Now hazarded to thy grace.°

CAES.   For Antony,
I have no ears to his request. The Queen   20
Of audience nor desire shall fail, so° she
From Egypt drive her all-disgracèd friend,
Or take his life there. This if she perform,
She shall not sue unheard. So to them both.

EUPH. Fortune pursue thee!

CAES.   Bring him through the bands.°   25
     [*Exit* EUPHRONIUS.]
[*To* THYREUS] To try thy eloquence, now 'tis time.
     Dispatch.
From Antony win Cleopatra. Promise,
And in our name, what she requires. Add more,
From thine invention,° offers. Women are not
In their best fortunes strong, but want will per-
     jure   30

69. Fall: let fall. **rates:** is worth.
   Sc. xii: 4. pinion: feather. **8. petty . . . ends:** insignificant
to his intentions. **12. Requires:** requests. **18. circle:** crown.
19. hazarded . . . grace: yours to dispose of as you will. **21. so:**
so long as. **25. bands:** companies, army. **29. From . . . invention:** as it occurs to you.

The ne'er-touched vestal. Try thy cunning, Thyreus.
Make thine own edict for thy pains,° which we
Will answer as a law.
    THYR.   Caesar, I go.
    CAES. Observe how Antony becomes his flaw,°
And what thou think'st his very action speaks   35
In every power that moves.°
    THYR.   Caesar, I shall. [*Exeunt.*]

SCENE XIII. *Alexandria.* CLEOPATRA's *palace.*

[*Enter* CLEOPATRA, ENOBARBUS, CHARMIAN, *and* IRAS.]
    CLEO. What shall we do, Enobarbus?
    ENO.   Think, and die.
    CLEO. Is Antony or we in fault for this?
    ENO. Antony only, that would make his will°
Lord of his reason. What though you fled
From that great face of war, whose several ranges°
Frighted each other, why should he follow?   6
The itch of his affection should not then
Have nicked° his captainship, at such a point,
When half to half the world opposed, he being
The mered question.° 'Twas a shame no less   10
Than was his loss to course° your flying flags
And leave his navy gazing.
    CLEO.   Prithee, peace.
[*Enter* ANTONY, *with* EUPHRONIUS *the Ambassador.*]
    ANT. Is that his answer?
    EUPH. Aye, my lord.
    ANT. The Queen shall then have courtesy so she
Will yield us up.
    EUPH.   He says so.
    ANT.   Let her know 't.   16
To the boy Caesar send this grizzled head,
And he will fill thy wishes to the brim
With principalities.°
    CLEO.   That head, my lord?
    ANT. To him again. Tell him he wears the rose
Of youth upon him, from which the world should
    note   21
Something particular. His coin, ships, legions,
May be a coward's, whose ministers would prevail
Under the service of a child as soon
As i' the command of Caesar. I dare him therefore
To lay his gay comparisons° apart   26
And answer me declined,° sword against sword,
Ourselves alone. I'll write it. Follow me.
             [*Exeunt* ANTONY *and* EUPHRONIUS.]

    ENO. [*Aside*] Yes, like enough, high-battled°
    Caesar will
Unstate his happiness° and be staged to the show
Against a sworder!° I see men's judgments are   31
A parcel of their fortunes,° and things outward
Do draw the inward quality after them,
To suffer all alike. That he should dream,
Knowing all measures,° the full Caesar will   35
Answer his emptiness! Caesar, thou hast subdued
His judgment too.
             [*Enter an* ATTENDANT.]
    ATT.   A messenger from Caesar.
    CLEO. What, no more ceremony? See, my women,
Against the blown rose° may they stop their nose
That kneeled unto the buds. Admit him, sir.   40
             [*Exit* ATTENDANT.]
    ENO. [*Aside*] Mine honesty and I begin to
    square.°
The loyalty well held to fools does make
Our faith mere folly. Yet he that can endure
To follow with allegiance a fall'n lord
Does conquer him that did his master conquer,   45
And earns a place i' the story.
             [*Enter* THYREUS.]
    CLEO.   Caesar's will?
    THYR. Hear it apart.
    CLEO.   None but friends. Say boldly.
    THYR. So, haply,° are they friends to Antony.
    ENO. He needs as many, sir, as Caesar has,
Or needs not us. If Caesar please, our master
Will leap to be his friend. For us, you know
Whose he is we are, and that is Caesar's.
    THYR.
Thus then, thou most renowned. Caesar entreats
Not to consider in what case thou stand'st
Further than he is Caesar.°
    CLEO.   Go on. Right royal.   55
    THYR. He knows that you embrace not Antony
As you did love but as you feared him.
    CLEO.   Oh!
    THYR. The scars upon your honor therefore he
Does pity as constrainèd° blemishes
Not as deserved.
    CLEO.   He is a god and knows   60
What is most right. Mine honor was not yielded,
But conquered merely.
    ENO.   [*Aside*] To be sure of that,

---

32. **Make . . . pains:** make your own terms for your labors. 34. **how . . . flaw:** how Antony behaves now he is a broken man. 35–36. **And . . . moves:** and how his actions reveal his state of mind.
    Sc. xiii: 3. **will:** lust.   5. **ranges:** ranks.   8. **nicked:** snipped, cut short.   10. **mered question:** sole matter in dispute. 11. **course:** chase after.   19. **principalities:** kingdoms.   26. **gay comparisons:** the gay signs that he is a young man.   27. **declined:** in my decline.

29. **high-battled:** with his great army.   30. **Unstate . . . happiness:** lay aside his superiority.   30–31. **staged . . . sworder:** make a public exhibition of himself by fighting a professional swordsman.   31–32. **men's . . . fortunes:** men's judgments are part (*parcel*) of their fortunes; i.e., a defeated man becomes a fool. 35. **Knowing . . . measures:** having had experience of all kinds of fortune.   39. **blown rose:** rose that has shed its petals. 41. **square:** quarrel.   48. **haply:** perhaps.   53–55. **Caesar . . . Caesar:** Caesar begs you to forget that you have been defeated by him and to remember only that he is Caesar; i.e., a generous victor.   59. **constrained:** forced.

I will ask Antony. Sir, sir, thou art so leaky
That we must leave thee to thy sinking, for
Thy dearest quit thee.   [*Exit.*]

THYR.   Shall I say to Caesar   65
What you require of him? For he partly begs
To be desired to give. It much would please him
That of his fortunes you should make a staff
To lean upon. But it would warm his spirits
To hear from me you had left Antony,   70
And put yourself under his shroud,°
The universal landlord.

CLEO.   What's your name?

THYR. My name is Thyreus.

CLEO.   Most kind messenger,
Say to great Caesar this: In deputation°
I kiss his conquering hand. Tell him I am prompt
To lay my crown at 's feet, and there to kneel. 76
Tell him from his all-obeying° breath I hear
The doom of Egypt.

THYR.   'Tis your noblest course.
Wisdom and fortune combating together,
If that the former dare but what it can,   80
No chance may shake it. Give me grace° to lay
My duty on your hand.°

CLEO.   Your Caesar's father oft,
When he hath mused of taking kingdoms in,
Bestowed his lips on that unworthy place
As it rained kisses.
                    [*Re-enter* ANTONY *and* ENOBARBUS.]

ANT.   Favors, by Jove that thunders! 85
What art thou, fellow?

THYR.   One that but performs
The bidding of the fullest man and worthiest
To have command obeyed.

ENO.   [*Aside*] You will be whipped.

ANT. Approach, there! Ah, you kite!° Now, gods
    and devils!
Authority melts from me. Of late, when I cried
    " Ho! "   90
Like boys unto a muss,° Kings would start forth
And cry " Your will? " Have you no ears?
I am Antony yet.
[*Enter* ATTENDANTS.] Take hence this Jack,° and
    whip him.

ENO. [*Aside*] 'Tis better playing with a lion's
    whelp
Than with an old one dying.

ANT.   Moon and stars!   95
Whip him. Were 't twenty of the greatest tributaries
That do acknowledge Caesar, should I find them
So saucy with the hand of she here — what's her
    name

Since she was Cleopatra?° Whip him, fellows,
Till, like a boy, you see him cringe his face   100
And whine aloud for mercy. Take him hence.

THYR. Mark Antony ——

ANT.   Tug him away. Being whipped,
Bring him again. This Jack of Caesar's shall
Bear us an errand to him.
                    [*Exeunt* ATTENDANTS, *with* THYREUS.]
You were half-blasted ere I knew you. Ha!   105
Have I my pillow left unpressed in Rome,
Forborne the getting° of a lawful race,
And by a gem of women, to be abused°
By one that looks on feeders?°

CLEO.   Good my lord ——

ANT. You have been a boggler° ever.   110
But when we in our viciousness grow hard —
Oh, misery on 't! — the wise gods seel° our eyes,
In our own filth drop our clear judgments, make us
Adore our errors, laugh at 's while we strut
To our confusion.°

CLEO.   Oh, is 't come to this?   115

ANT. I found you as a morsel cold upon
Dead Caesar's trencher. Nay, you were a fragment
Of Cneius Pompey's, besides what hotter hours,
Unregistered in vulgar fame, you have
Luxuriously° picked out. For I am sure,   120
Though you can guess what temperance should be,
You know not what it is.

CLEO.   Wherefore is this?

ANT. To let a fellow that will take rewards
And say " God quit you! "° be familiar with
My playfellow, your hand, this kingly seal   125
And plighter of high hearts! Oh, that I were
Upon the hill of Basan,° to outroar
The hornèd herd! For I have savage cause,
And to proclaim it civilly were like
A haltered neck which does the hangman thank
For being yare about him.
                    [*Re-enter* ATTENDANTS, *with* THYREUS.]
                         Is he whipped?   131

I. ATT. Soundly, my lord.

ANT.   Cried he? And begged he pardon?

I. ATT. He did ask favor.

ANT. If that thy father live, let him repent
Thou wast not made his daughter. And be thou
    sorry   135
To follow Caesar in his triumph, since
Thou hast been whipped for following him. Hence-
forth

---

71. shroud: covering, protection.   74. In deputation: by means
of you his deputy.   77. all-obeying: which all obey.   81. grace:
favor.   81–82. to . . . hand: to kiss your hand.   89. kite: the
lowest of the birds of prey, an offal-eater.   91. muss: a game
in which something is scrambled for.   93. Jack: knave.

99. Since . . . Cleopatra: now that she is no longer Cleopatra.
107. getting: begetting.   108. abused: shamed.   109. feeders:
beggars who whine for food.   110. boggler: shifty thing.
112. seel: close up. See App. 26.   115. confusion: destruction.
120. Luxuriously: lustfully.   124. God . . . you: God reward
you, — the beggar's thanks.   127. hill of Basan: a reminiscence
of Psalm 68 (in the Prayer Book version): "as the hill of Basan,
so is God's hill; even a high hill as the hill of Basan . . . fat bulls
of Basan close me in on every side."

The white hand of a lady fever thee,°
Shake thou to look on 't. Get thee back to Caesar,
Tell him thy entertainment. Look thou say   140
He makes me angry with him, for he seems
Proud and disdainful, harping on what I am,
Not what he knew I was. He makes me angry,
And at this time most easy 'tis to do 't,
When my good stars that were my former guides
Have empty left their orbs° and shot their fires   146
Into the abysm of Hell. If he mislike
My speech and what is done, tell him he has
Hipparchus, my enfranchèd° bondman, whom
He may at pleasure whip, or hang, or torture,   150
As he shall like, to quit me.° Urge it thou.
Hence with thy stripes, begone!   [*Exit* THYREUS.]
    CLEO. Have you done yet?
    ANT.   Alack, our terrene° moon
Is now eclipsed, and it portends alone
The fall of Antony.
    CLEO.   I must stay his time.°   155
    ANT. To flatter Caesar, would you mingle eyes
With one that ties his points?°
    CLEO.   Not know me yet?
    ANT. Coldhearted toward me?
    CLEO.   Ah, dear, if I be so,
From my cold heart let Heaven engender hail
And poison it in the source, and the first stone   160
Drop in my neck. As it determines,° so
Dissolve my life! The next Caesarion smite!
Till by degrees the memory of my womb,
Together with my brave Egyptians all,
By the discandying° of this pelleted° storm   165
Lie graveless, till the flies and gnats of Nile
Have buried them for prey!
    ANT.   I am satisfied.
Caesar sits down in Alexandria, where
I will oppose his fate. Our force by land
Hath nobly held. Our severed navy too   170
Have knit again, and fleet,° threatening most sealike.
Where hast thou been, my heart? Dost thou hear,
    lady?
If from the field I shall return once more
To kiss these lips, I will appear in blood.
I and my sword will earn our chronicle.°   175
There's hope in 't yet.
    CLEO. That's my brave lord!
    ANT. I will be treble-sinewed, hearted, breathed,°
And fight maliciously.° For when mine hours
Were nice° and lucky, men did ransom lives   180

Of me for jests, but now I'll set my teeth
And send to darkness all that stop me. Come,
Let's have one other gaudy° night. Call to me
All my sad captains, fill our bowls once more.
Let's mock the midnight bell.
    CLEO.   It is my birthday.   185
I had thought to have held it poor, but since my lord
Is Antony again, I will be Cleopatra.
    ANT. We will yet do well.
    CLEO. Call all his noble captains to my lord.
    ANT. Do so, we'll speak to them. And tonight I'll
    force   190
The wine peep through their scars. Come on, my
    Queen,
There's sap in 't yet. The next time I do fight
I'll make death love me, for I will contend
Even with his pestilent scythe.
                [*Exeunt all but* ENOBARBUS.]
    ENO. Now he'll outstare the lightning. To be
    furious   195
Is to be frighted out of fear, and in that mood
The dove will peck the estridge.° And I see still,
A diminution in our Captain's brain
Restores his heart. When valor preys on reason,
It eats the sword it fights with. I will seek   200
Some way to leave him.   [*Exit.*]

Act IV

SCENE I. *Before Alexandria.* CAESAR'S *camp.*

[*Enter* CAESAR, AGRIPPA, *and* MECAENAS, *with his
    army;* CAESAR *reading a letter.*]
    CAES. He calls me boy,° and chides as° he had
    power
To beat me out of Egypt. My messenger
He hath whipped with rods, dares me to personal
    combat,
Caesar to Antony. Let the old ruffian know
I have many other ways to die, meantime   5
Laugh at his challenge.
    MEC.   Caesar must think,
When one so great begins to rage, he's hunted
Even to falling. Give him no breath, but now
Make boot° of his distraction. Never anger
Made good guard for itself.
    CAES.   Let our best heads   10
Know that tomorrow the last of many battles
We mean to fight. Within our files there are
Of those that served Mark Antony but late

---

138. fever thee: give you fever.   **146. orbs:** spheres. See App. I.
149. enfranched: freed.   **151. quit me:** get even with me.
153. terrene: earthly.   **155. stay . . . time:** i.e., wait till his
rage has blown itself out.   **157. ties . . . points:** i.e., acts as
his valet. See *I Hen IV*, II.iv.238–39. **161. determines:** comes to
an end, melts.   **165. discandying:** dissolving. **pelleted:** i.e., hail.
171. fleet: float.   **175. our chronicle:** our place in history.
178. breathed: have my breath again.   **179. maliciously:**
furiously.   **180. nice:** delicate, particular.

183. gaudy: rowdy.   **197. estridge:** hawk.
    Act IV, Sc. i: 1. boy: a bitter insult. See *Cor*, V.vi.101–13.
as: as if.   **9. Make boot:** take advantage.

Enough to fetch him in. See it done.
And feast the army, we have store to do 't,   15
And they have earned the waste. Poor Antony!
                                      [*Exeunt.*]

SCENE II. *Alexandria.* CLEOPATRA's *palace.*

[*Enter* ANTONY, CLEOPATRA, ENOBARBUS, CHARMIAN,
      IRAS, ALEXAS, *with others.*]

ANT. He will not fight with me, Domitius?
ENO.   No.
ANT. Why should he not?
ENO. He thinks, being twenty times of better for-
    tune,
He is twenty men to one.
ANT.   Tomorrow, soldier,
By sea and land I'll fight. Or I will live   5
Or bathe my dying honor in the blood
Shall° make it live again. Woo 't° thou fight well?
ENO. I'll strike, and cry " Take all."°
ANT.   Well said. Come on.
Call forth my household servants. Let's tonight
Be bounteous at our meal.
[*Enter three or four* SERVITORS.] Give me thy hand,
Thou hast been rightly honest — so hast thou — 11
Thou — and thou — and thou. You have served me
    well,
And Kings have been your fellows.
CLEO. [*Aside to* ENOBARBUS] What means this?
ENO. [*Aside to* CLEOPATRA] 'Tis one of those odd
    tricks which sorrow shoots
Out of the mind.
ANT.   And thou art honest too.   15
I wish I could be made so many men,
And all of you clapped up° together in
An Antony, that I might do you service
So good as you have done.
SERV.   The gods forbid!
ANT. Well, my good fellows, wait on me tonight.
Scant not my cups, and make as much of me 21
As when mine empire was your fellow too
And suffered my command.
CLEO. [*Aside to* ENOBARBUS] What does he mean?
ENO. [*Aside to* CLEOPATRA] To make his followers
    weep.
ANT.   Tend me tonight.
Maybe it is the period° of your duty.   25
Haply you shall not see me more, or if,
A mangled shadow, perchance tomorrow
You'll serve another master. I look on you
As one that takes his leave. Mine honest friends,
I turn you not away, but like a master 30
Married to your good service, stay till death.

Tend me tonight two hours, I ask no more,
And the gods yield° you for 't!
ENO.   What mean you, sir,
To give them this discomfort? Look, they weep,
And I, an ass, am onion-eyed.° For shame, 35
Transform us not to women.
ANT.   Ho, ho, ho!
Now the witch take me° if I meant it thus!
Grace grow where those drops fall! My hearty
    friends,
You take me in too dolorous a sense. 39
For I spake to you for your comfort, did desire you
To burn this night with torches. Know, my hearts,
I hope well of tomorrow, and will lead you
Where rather I'll expect victorious life
Than death and honor. Let's to supper, come, 44
And drown consideration.°   [*Exeunt.*]

SCENE III. *The same. Before the palace.*

[*Enter two* SOLDIERS *to their guard.*]

1. SOLD. Brother, good night. Tomorrow is the
    day.
2. SOLD. It will determine one way. Fare you well.
Heard you of nothing strange about the streets?
1. SOLD. Nothing. What news?
2. SOLD. Belike 'tis but a rumor. Good night to
    you.   5
1. SOLD. Well, sir, good night.
             [*Enter two other* SOLDIERS.]
2. SOLD. Soldiers, have careful watch.
3. SOLD. And you. Good night, good night.
[*They place themselves in every corner of the stage.*]
4. SOLD. Here we. And if tomorrow
Our navy thrive, I have an absolute hope 10
Our landmen will stand up.
3. SOLD.   'Tis a brave army,
And full of purpose.
      [*Music of hautboys° as under the stage.*]
4. SOL.   Peace! What noise?
1. SOLD.   List, list!
2. SOLD. Hark!
1. SOLD.   Music i' the air.
3. SOLD.   Under the earth.
4. SOLD. It signs well,° does it not?
3. SOLD.   No.
1. SOLD.   Peace, I say!
What should this mean?   15
2. SOLD. 'Tis the god Hercules, whom Antony
    loved,
Now leaves him.

---

33. yield: reward. 35. am onion-eyed: can't help weeping.
37. witch . . . me: may I be bewitched. 45. consideration:
worry.
    Sc. iii: 12 s.d., hautboys: oboes 14. It . . . well: it is a good
sign.

Sc. ii: 7. Shall: which shall. Woo 't: wilt. 8. Take all:
i.e., no mercy, the winner takes all. 17. clapped up: fastened.
25. period: end.

1. SOLD. Walk. Let's see if other watchmen
Do hear what we do.

2. SOLD.   How now, masters!

ALL. [*Speaking together*] How now! How now!
Do you hear this?

1. SOLD. Aye, is 't not strange?   20

3. SOLD. Do you hear, masters? Do you hear?

1. SOLD. Follow the noise so far as we have
quarter.°

Let's see how it will give off.°

ALL. Content. 'Tis strange.   [*Exeunt.*]

SCENE IV. *The same. A room in the palace.*

[*Enter* ANTONY *and* CLEOPATRA, CHARMIAN *and others
attending.*]

ANT. Eros! Mine armor, Eros!

CLEO.   Sleep a little.

ANT. No, my chuck.° Eros, come. Mine armor,
Eros!

[*Enter* EROS *with armor.*]

Come, good fellow, put mine iron on.
If fortune be not ours today, it is
Because we brave her. Come.

CLEO.   Nay, I'll help too.   5
What's this for?

ANT.   Ah, let be, let be! Thou art
The armorer of my heart. False, false. This, this.

CLEO. Sooth, la, I'll help. Thus it must be.

ANT.   Well, well,
We shall thrive now. Seest thou, my good fellow?
Go put on thy defenses.

EROS.   Briefly, sir.   10

CLEO. Is not this buckled well?

ANT.   Rarely, rarely.
He that unbuckles this till we do please
To daff 't° for our repose shall hear a storm.
Thou fumblest, Eros, and my Queen's a squire°
More tight° at this than thou. Dispatch. O love,   15
That thou couldst see my wars today, and knew'st
The royal occupation!° Thou shouldst see
A workman in 't.

[*Enter an armed* SOLDIER.] Good morrow to thee,
welcome.

Thou look'st like him that knows a warlike charge.
To business that we love we rise betime,   20
And go to 't with delight.

SOLD.   A thousand, sir,
Early though 't be, have on their riveted trim,°
And at the port° expect you.

[*Shout. Trumpets flourish.*]

[*Enter* CAPTAINS *and* SOLDIERS.]

CAPT. The morn is fair. Good morrow, General.

ALL. Good morrow, General.

ANT.   'Tis well blown,° lads.   25
This morning, like the spirit of a youth
That means to be of note, begins betimes.
So, so, come, give me that. This way, well said.
Fare thee well, dame, whate'er becomes of me.
This is a soldier's kiss.° Rebukable   30
And worthy shameful check it were to stand
On more mechanic compliment.° I'll leave thee
Now like a man of steel. You that will fight,
Follow me close, I'll bring you to 't. Adieu.

[*Exeunt* ANTONY, EROS, CAPTAINS, *and* SOLDIERS.]

CHAR. Please you, retire to your chamber.

CLEO.   Lead me.   35
He goes forth gallantly. That he and Caesar might
Determine this great war in single fight!
Then Antony —— But now —— Well, on.

[*Exeunt.*]

SCENE V. *Alexandria.* ANTONY's *camp.*

[*Trumpets sound. Enter* ANTONY *and* EROS, *a* SOLDIER
meeting them.]

SOLD. The gods make this a happy day to Antony!

ANT. Would thou and those thy scars had once
prevailed
To make me fight at land!

SOLD.   Hadst thou done so,
The Kings that have revolted and the soldier
That has this morning left thee would have still   5
Followed thy heels.

ANT.   Who's gone this morning?

SOLD.   Who!
One ever near thee. Call for Enobarbus,
He shall not hear thee, or from Caesar's camp
Say "I am none of thine."

ANT.   What say'st thou?

SOLD.   Sir,
He is with Caesar.

EROS.   Sir, his chests and treasure   10
He has not with him.

ANT.   Is he gone?

SOLD.   Most certain.

ANT. Go, Eros, send his treasure after. Do it,
Detain no jot, I charge thee. Write to him —
I will subscribe° — gentle adieus and greetings.
Say that I wish he never find more cause   15
To change a master. Oh, my fortunes have
Corrupted honest men! Dispatch. Enobarbus!

[*Exeunt.*]

---

22. **quarter:** the limit of the sentry's beat.   23. **give off:** end.
   Sc. iv: 2. **chuck:** chick.   13. **daff 't:** doff it, put it off.
14. **squire:** the duty of the squire was to arm his knight.
15. **tight:** handy.   17. **royal occupation:** i.e., war, the work
for kings.   22. **riveted trim:** riveted finery; i.e., armor.
23. **port:** gate.

25. **blown:** i.e., the "flourish."   30. **soldier's kiss:** i.e., a
quick one.   32. **mechanic compliment:** the long leave-taking of a
civilian.
   Sc. v: 14. **subscribe:** sign.

SCENE VI. *Alexandria.* CAESAR's *camp.*

[*Flourish. Enter* CAESAR *with* AGRIPPA, ENOBARBUS,
and others.]

CAES. Go forth, Agrippa, and begin the fight.
Our will is Antony be took alive.
Make it so known.

AGR.   Caesar, I shall.   [*Exit.*]

CAES. The time of universal peace is near.   5
Prove this a prosperous day, the three-nooked°
world
Shall bear the olive freely.

            [*Enter a* MESSENGER.]

MESS.   Antony
Is come into the field.

CAES.   Go charge Agrippa
Plant those that have revolted in the van,
That Antony may seem to spend his fury   10
Upon himself.   [*Exeunt all but* ENOBARBUS.]

ENO. Alexas did revolt, and went to Jewry
On affairs of Antony, there did persuade
Great Herod to incline himself to Caesar
And leave his master Antony. For this pains   15
Caesar hath hanged him. Canidius and the rest
That fell away have entertainment,° but
No honorable trust. I have done ill,
Of which I do accuse myself so sorely
That I will joy no more.

            [*Enter a* SOLDIER *of* CAESAR's.]

SOLD.   Enobarbus, Antony   20
Hath after thee sent all thy treasure, with
His bounty overplus.° The messenger
Came on my guard, and at thy tent is now
Unloading of his mules.

ENO.   I give it you.

SOLD. Mock not, Enobarbus.   25
I tell you true. Best you safed° the bringer
Out of the host. I must attend mine office,
Or would have done 't myself. Your Emperor
Continues still a Jove.   [*Exit.*]

ENO. I am alone the villain of the earth,   30
And feel I am so most. O Antony,
Thou mine of bounty, how wouldst thou have paid
My better service when my turpitude
Thou dost so crown with gold! This blows° my
heart.
If swift thought break it not, a swifter mean   35
Shall outstrike thought. But thought will do 't, I feel.
I fight against thee! No. I will go seek
Some ditch wherein to die, the foul'st best fits
My latter part of life.   [*Exit.*]

Sc. vi: 6. **three-nooked:** three-cornered. **17. entertainment:**
employment. **22. overplus:** in addition. **26. safed:** conducted
safely. **34. blows:** swells to bursting.

SCENE VII. *Field of battle between the camps.*

[*Alarum. Drums and trumpets. Enter* AGRIPPA *and
others.*]

AGR. Retire, we have engaged ourselves too far.
Caesar himself has work, and our oppression°
Exceeds what we expected.   [*Exeunt.*]

[*Alarums. Enter* ANTONY, *and* SCARUS *wounded.*]

SCAR. O my brave Emperor, this is fought indeed!
Had we done so at first, we had droven them home
With clouts° about their heads.

ANT.   Thou bleed'st apace.   6

SCAR. I had a wound here that was like a T,
But now 'tis made an H.°   [*Retreat afar off.*]

ANT.   They do retire.

SCAR. We'll beat 'em into bench holes.° I have yet
Room for six scotches° more.   10

            [*Enter* EROS.]

EROS. They are beaten, sir, and our advantage
serves
For a fair victory.

SCAR.   Let us score their backs
And snatch 'em up, as we take hares, behind.
'Tis sport to maul a runner.

ANT.   I will reward thee
Once for thy spritely comfort, and tenfold   15
For thy good valor. Come thee on.

SCAR.   I'll halt° after.   [*Exeunt.*]

SCENE VIII. *Under the walls of Alexandria.*

[*Alarum. Enter* ANTONY, *in a march;* SCARUS, *with
others.*]

ANT. We have beat him to his camp. Run one
before
And let the Queen know of our gests.° Tomorrow,
Before the sun shall see 's, we'll spill the blood
That has today escaped. I thank you all,
For doughty-handed° are you, and have fought   5
Not as you served the cause, but as 't had been
Each man's like mine. You have shown all Hectors.°
Enter the city, clip° your wives, your friends,
Tell them your feats whilst they with joyful tears
Wash the congealment from your wounds and kiss
The honored gashes whole. [*To* SCARUS] Give me
thy hand.   11

Sc. vii: 2. **oppression:** opposition. **6. clouts:** rags; i.e.,
bandages. **7–8. like . . . H:** The "T" has not been satisfactorily
explained. "H" and "ache" were pronounced alike, and the pun
is common. **9. bench holes:** the seats of privies. **10. scotches:**
gashes; i.e., I have room for a few more wounds on my body.
16. halt: limp.
Sc. viii: 2. **gests:** deeds. **5. doughty-handed:** stalwart.
7. Hectors: Hector was the heroic champion of the Trojans in
the war against the Greeks. See *Tr & Cr.* **8. clip:** embrace.

[*Enter* CLEOPATRA, *attended.*] To this great fairy° I'll
  commend thy acts,
Make her thanks bless thee. O thou day o' the world,°
Chain mine armed neck. Leap thou, attire and all,
Through proof of harness° to my heart, and there
Ride on the pants triumphing!
    CLEO.   Lord of lords!   16
O infinite virtue,° comest thou smiling from
The world's great snare° uncaught?
    ANT.   My nightingale,
We have beat them to their beds. What, girl! though
  gray
Do something mingle with our younger brown, yet
  ha' we
A brain that nourishes our nerves° and can   20
Get goal for goal of youth. Behold this man.
Commend unto his lips thy favoring hand.
Kiss it, my warrior. He hath fought today
As if a god in hate of mankind had
Destroyed in such a shape.   25
    CLEO.   I'll give thee, friend,
An armor all of gold. It was a King's.
    ANT. He has deserved it, were it carbuncled°
Like holy Phoebus' car.° Give me thy hand.
Through Alexandria make a jolly march,   30
Bear our hacked targets like the men that owe°
  them.
Had our great palace the capacity
To camp this host, we all would sup together
And drink carouses° to the next day's fate,
Which promises royal peril. Trumpeters,   35
With brazen din blast you the city's ear.
Make mingle with our rattling tabourines,°
That Heaven and earth may strike their sounds to-
  gether,
Applauding our approach.   [*Exeunt.*]

    2. SOLD.   Stand close, and list him.
    ENO. Be witness to me, O thou blessèd moon,
When men revolted shall upon recòrd
Bear hateful memory, poor Enobarbus did
Before thy face repent!
    1. SOLD.   Enobarbus!
    3. SOLD.   Peace!   10
Hark further.
    ENO. O sovereign mistress of true melancholy,°
The poisonous damp of night disponge° upon me,
That life, a very rebel to my will,
Mày hang no longer on me. Throw my heart   15
Against the flint and hardness of my fault,
Which, being dried with grief, will break to powder
And finish all foul thoughts. O Antony,
Nobler than my revolt is infamous,
Forgive me in thine own particular,°   20
But let the world rank me in register
A master leaver and a fugitive.
O Antony! O Antony!   [*Dies.*]
    2. SOLD.   Let's speak to him.
    1. SOLD. Let's hear him, for the things he speaks
May concern Caesar.
    3. SOLD.   Let's do so. But he sleeps.   25
    1. SOLD. Swoons rather, for so bad a prayer as his
Was never yet for sleep.
    2. SOLD.   Go we to him.
    3. SOLD. Awake, sir, awake. Speak to us.
    2. SOLD.   Hear you, sir?
    1. SOLD. The hand of death hath raught° him.
        [*Drums afar off.*] Hark! The drums   30
Demurely wake the sleepers. Let us bear him
To the court of guard, he is of note. Our hour
Is fully out.
    3. SOLD. Come on, then, he may recover yet.
                    [*Exeunt with the body.*]

SCENE IX. CAESAR'S *camp.*

[SENTINELS *at their post.*]
    1. SOLD. If we be not relieved within this hour,
We must return to the court of guard.° The night
Is shiny, and they say we shall embattle
By the second hour i' the morn.
    2. SOLD.   This last day was
A shrewd° one to 's.
    [*Enter* ENOBARBUS.]
    ENO.   Oh, bear me witness, night ——   5
    3. SOLD. What man is this?

SCENE X. *Between the two camps.*

[*Enter* ANTONY *and* SCARUS, *with their army.*]
    ANT. Their preparation is today by sea.
We please them not by land.
    SCAR.   For both, my lord.
    ANT. I would they'd fight i' the fire or i' the air.°
We'd fight there too. But this it is. Our foot
Upon the hills adjoining to the city   5
Shall stay with us. Order for sea is given,
They have put forth the haven,
Where their appointment° we may best discover
And look on their endeavor.   [*Exeunt.*]

12. fairy: charmer.   13. day . . . world: brightest creature in the
world.   15. proof of harness: armor of proof.   17. virtue: valor.
18. world's . . . snare: i.e., the uncertain risk of war.   21. nerves:
sinews.   28. carbuncled: set with gems.   29. car: chariot.
31. owe: own.   34. carouses: healths drunk to the bottom of the
cup.   37. tabourines: drums.
    Sc. ix: 2. court of guard: guardroom.   5. shrewd: bitter.

12. O . . . melancholy: the moon.   13. disponge: squeeze out as
from a sponge.   20. in . . . particular: as far as it concerns
you.   30. raught: laid hold on.
    Sc. x: 3. i' . . . air: i.e., in the other two elements. See App. 3.
8. appointment: purpose.

SCENE XI. *Another part of the same.*

[*Enter* CAESAR, *and his army.*]

CAES. But being charged,° we will be still by land,
Which, as I take 't, we shall, for his best force
Is forth° to man his galleys.° To the vales,
And hold our best advantage.   [*Exeunt.*]

SCENE XII. *Hills adjoining to Alexandria.*

[*Enter* ANTONY *and* SCARUS.]

ANT. Yet they are not joined. Where yond pine
     does stand
I shall discover all. I'll bring thee word
Straight how 'tis like to go.   [*Exit.*]
SCAR.   Swallows have built
In Cleopatra's sails their nests. The augurers°
Say they know not, they cannot tell, look grimly,   5
And dare not speak their knowledge. Antony
Is valiant, and dejected, and by starts
His fretted° fortunes give him hope, and fear,
Of what he has, and has not.

[*Alarum afar off, as at a seafight.*]
[*Re-enter* ANTONY.]

ANT.   All is lost.
This foul Egyptian hath betrayed me.   10
My fleet hath yielded to the foe, and yonder
They cast their caps up and carouse together
Like friends long lost. Triple-turned whore!° 'Tis
     thou
Hast sold me to this novice, and my heart
Makes only wars on thee. Bid them all fly,   15
For when I am revenged upon my charm,
I have done all. Bid them all fly. Begone.

[*Exit* SCARUS.]

O sun, thy uprise shall I see no more.
Fortune and Antony part here, even here
Do we shake hands. All come to this? The hearts
That spanieled° me at heels, to whom I gave   21
Their wishes, do discandy, melt their sweets
On blossoming Caesar, and this pine is barked,°
That overtopped them all. Betrayed I am.
O this false soul of Egypt! This grave charm,°
Whose eye becked° forth my wars and called them
     home,   26
Whose bosom was my crownet,° my chief end,
Like a right gypsy° hath at fast and loose°

Beguiled me to the very heart of loss.°
What, Eros, Eros!

[*Enter* CLEOPATRA.] Ah, thou spell! Avaunt!   30
CLEO. Why is my lord enraged against his love?
ANT. Vanish, or I shall give thee thy deserving,
And blemish° Caesar's triumph. Let him take thee,
And hoist thee up to the shouting plebeians.
Follow his chariot, like the greatest spot   35
Of all thy sex. Most monsterlike, be shown
For poor'st diminutives, for doits.° And let
Patient Octavia plow thy visage up
With her preparèd nails.   [*Exit* CLEOPATRA.]
     'Tis well thou'rt gone,
If it be well to live. But better 'twere   40
Thou fell'st into my fury, for one death
Might have prevented many. Eros, ho!
The shirt of Nessus° is upon me. Teach me,
Alcides,° thou mine ancestor, thy rage.
Let me lodge Lichas on the horns o' the moon,   45
And with those hands that grasped the heaviest club
Subdue my worthiest self. The witch shall die.
To the young Roman boy she hath sold me, and I
     fall
Under this plot. She dies for 't. Eros, ho!   [*Exit.*]

SCENE XIII. *Alexandria.* CLEOPATRA's *palace.*

[*Enter* CLEOPATRA, CHARMIAN, IRAS, *and* MARDIAN.]

CLEO. Help me, my women! Oh, he is more mad
Than Telamon° for his shield. The boar of Thes-
     saly°
Was never so embossed.°
CHAR.   To the monument!
There lock yourself, and send him word you are
     dead.
The soul and body rive° not more in parting   5
Than greatness going off.
CLEO.   To the monument!
Mardian, go tell him I have slain myself.
Say that the last I spoke was " Antony,"
And word it, prithee, piteously. Hence, Mardian,   9
And bring me how he takes my death. To the monu-
     ment!   [*Exeunt.*]

29. **very . . . loss:** center of loss, utter loss.   33. **blemish:** spoil, because it would lack Cleopatra.   36–37. **monsterlike . . . doits:** like a rare freak to be shown to the commonest of the people for pennies.   43. **shirt of Nessus:** The centaur Nessus, when fatally wounded by Hercules, told Deianira (Hercules' bride) to dip a shirt in the blood. The shirt was brought to Hercules by Lichas, his page, but when he put it on, it stuck to his flesh and began to consume him. In his agony Hercules threw Lichas into the sea and killed himself.   44. **Alcides:** Hercules.

Sc. xiii: 2. **Telamon:** Ajax, who went mad when the shield of the dead hero Achilles was awarded to Ulysses instead of himself. **boar of Thessaly:** a boar sent by the goddess Diana into the kingdom of Calydon and slain by Meleager.   3. **embossed:** foaming at the mouth, hard-driven.   5. **rive:** split.

Sc. xi: 1. **But . . . charged:** unless we are charged.   3. **forth:** gone forth. **galleys:** ships propelled by oars.
Sc. xii: 4. **augurers:** officials who foretold the future by observing omens of various kinds.   8. **fretted:** frayed. 13. **Triple-turned whore:** whore who has double-crossed three men, i.e., Pompey, Julius Caesar, and himself.   21. **spanieled:** fawned on like spaniels.   23. **pine is barked:** i.e., I am like a pine stripped of its bark.   25. **grave charm:** great sorceress. 26. **becked:** beckoned.   27. **crownet:** coronet.   28. **gypsy:** See I.i.10. **fast . . . loose:** a trickster's game.

[handwritten marginalia: CLEO DOESN'T DEFEND HERSELF — DOESN'T UNDERSTAND HIS ANGER]

SCENE XIV. *The same. Another room.*

[*Enter* ANTONY *and* EROS.]

ANT. Eros, thou yet behold'st me?

EROS.   Aye, noble lord.

ANT. Sometime we see a cloud that's dragonish,°
A vapor sometime like a bear or lion,
A towered citadel, a pendent° rock,
A forkèd mountain, or blue promontory   5
With trees upon 't that nod unto the world
And mock our eyes with air. Thou hast seen these
         signs,
They are black vesper's pageants.°

EROS.   Aye, my lord.

ANT. That which is now a horse, even with a
         thought
The rack dislimns° and makes it indistinct   10
As water is in water.

EROS.   It does, my lord.

ANT. My good knave Eros, now thy Captain is
Even such a body. Here I am Antony,
Yet cannot hold this visible shape, my knave.
I made these wars for Egypt, and the Queen —   15
Whose heart I thought I had, for she had mine,
Which, whilst it was mine, had annexed unto 't
A million moe,° now lost — she, Eros, has
Packed cards° with Caesar, and false-played my
         glory
Unto an enemy's triumph.   20
Nay, weep not, gentle Eros, there is left us
Ourselves to end ourselves.

[*Enter* MARDIAN.]   Oh, thy vile lady!
She has robbed me of my sword.

MAR.   No, Antony.
My mistress loved thee, and her fortunes mingled
With thine entirely.

ANT.   Hence, saucy eunuch, peace! 25
She hath betrayed me, and shall die the death.

MAR. Death of one person can be paid but once,
And that she has discharged. What thou wouldst do
Is done unto thy hand. The last she spake
Was "Antony! Most noble Antony!"   30
Then in the midst a tearing groan did break
The name of Antony. It was divided
Between her heart and lips. She rendered° life,
Thy name so buried in her.

ANT.   Dead, then?

MAR.   Dead.

ANT. Unarm, Eros. The long day's task is done,
And we must sleep. [*To* MARDIAN] That thou de-
         part'st hence safe   36
Does pay thy labor richly. Go.   [*Exit* MARDIAN.]

Off, pluck off.
The sevenfold shield of Ajax cannot keep
The battery from my heart.° Oh, cleave, my sides!
Heart, once be stronger than thy continent,°   40
Crack thy frail case! Apace, Eros, apace!
No more a soldier. Bruisèd pieces,° go,
You have been nobly borne. From me° awhile.

[*Exit* EROS.]

I will o'ertake thee, Cleopatra, and
Weep for my pardon. So it must be, for now   45
All length° is torture. Since the torch is out,
Lie down and stray no farther. Now all labor
Mars what it does. Yea, very force entangles
Itself with strength. Seal° then, and all is done.
Eros! — I come, my Queen. Eros! — Stay for me.
Where souls do couch on flowers, we'll hand in
         hand,   51
And with our sprightly port° make the ghosts gaze.
Dido and her Aeneas° shall want troops,°
And all the haunt be ours. Come, Eros, Eros!

[*Re-enter* EROS.]

EROS. What would my lord?

ANT.   Since Cleopatra died   55
I have lived in such dishonor that the gods
Detest my baseness. I, that with my sword
Quartered the world, and o'er green Neptune's back
With ships made cities, condemn myself to lack
The courage of a woman — less noble mind   60
Than she which by her death our Caesar tells
"I am conqueror of myself." Thou art sworn, Eros,
That when the exigent° should come — which now
Is come indeed — when I should see behind me
The inevitable prosecution° of   65
Disgrace and horror, that, on my command,
Thou then wouldst kill me. Do 't, the time is come.
Thou strikest not me, 'tis Caesar thou defeat'st.
Put color in thy cheek.

EROS.   The gods withhold me!
Shall I do that which all the Parthian darts,   70
Though enemy, lost aim and could not?

ANT.   Eros,
Wouldst thou be windowed° in great Rome and
         see
Thy master thus with pleached° arms, bending
         down
His corrigible° neck, his face subdued
To penetrative° shame, whilst the wheeled seat   75
Of fortunate Caesar, drawn before him, branded

38–39. sevenfold . . . heart: even the seven thicknesses of hide
of Ajax's shield cannot keep off the troubles which assault my
heart.   40. continent: that which contains it.   42. pieces:
i.e., of armor.   43. From me: leave me.   46. length: prolonging
of life.   49. Seal: complete the business. See App. 6.
52. sprightly port: lively bearing.   53. Dido . . . Aeneas: typical
lovers-till-death in classical story. See *Temp*, II.i.76. troops:
admiring followers.   63. exigent: emergency.   65. prosecution:
pursuit.   72. windowed: standing at a window.   73. pleached:
folded.   74. corrigible: submissive.   75. penetrative: penetrating.

Sc. xiv: 2. dragonish: shaped like a serpent.   4. pendent:
hanging in the air.   8. black . . . pageants: sights seen in the
evening.   10. rack dislimns: drifting cloud paints out.   18. moe:
more.   19. Packed cards: i.e., cheated in the deal.   33. rendered: gave up.

His baseness that ensued?°

EROS.   I would not see 't.

ANT. Come, then, for with a wound I must be
     cured.

Draw that thy honest sword, which thou hast worn
Most useful for thy country.

EROS.   O sir, pardon me!   80

ANT. When I did make thee free, sworest thou not
     then

To do this when I bade thee? Do it at once,
Or thy precédent services are all
But accidents unpurposed. Draw, and come.

EROS. Turn from me then that noble countenance,
Wherein the worship of the whole world lies.   86

ANT. Lo thee!   [*Turning from him.*]

EROS. My sword is drawn.

ANT.   Then let it do at once
The thing why thou hast drawn it.

EROS.   My dear master,
My Captain, and my Emperor, let me say,   90
Before I strike this bloody stroke, farewell.

ANT. 'Tis said, man, and farewell.

EROS. Farewell, great chief. Shall I strike now?

ANT.   Now, Eros.

EROS. Why, there then. Thus I do escape the
     sorrow

Of Antony's death.   [*Kills himself.*]

ANT.   Thrice nobler than myself!   95
Thou teachest me, O valiant Eros, what
I should and thou couldst not. My Queen and Eros
Have by their brave instruction got upon° me
A nobleness in record. But I will be
A bridegroom in my death,° and run into 't   100
As to a lover's bed. Come then, and, Eros,
Thy master dies thy scholar. To do thus
         [*Falling on his sword.*]
I learned of thee. How! Not dead? Not dead?
The guard, ho! Oh, dispatch me!
       [*Enter* DERCETAS *and* GUARD.]

I. GUARD.   What's the noise?

ANT. I have done my work ill, friends. Oh, make
     an end   105
Of what I have begun.

2. GUARD.   The star is fallen.

I. GUARD. And time is at his period.°

ALL.   Alas, and woe!

ANT. Let him that loves me strike me dead.

I. GUARD.   Not I.

2. GUARD. Nor I.   109

3. GUARD. Nor anyone.   [*Exeunt* GUARD.]

DER. Thy death and fortunes bid thy followers fly.
This sword but shown to Caesar, with this tidings,
Shall enter me with him.°

[*Enter* DIOMEDES.]

DIO. Where's Antony?

DER.   There, Diomed, there.

DIO.   Lives he?   114

Wilt thou not answer, man?   [*Exit* DERCETAS.]

ANT. Art thou there, Diomed? Draw thy sword,
     and give me

Sufficing strokes for death.

DIO.   Most absolute **lord,**
My mistress Cleopatra sent me to thee.

ANT. When did she send thee?

DIO.   Now, my lord.

ANT.   Where is she?

DIO. Locked in her monument. She had a prophe-
     sying fear   120
Of what hath come to pass. For when she saw —
Which never shall be found — you did suspect
She had disposed° with Caesar, and that your rage
Would not be purged, she sent you word she was
     dead;
But fearing since how it might work, hath sent   125
Me to proclaim the truth, and I am come,
I dread too late.

ANT. Too late, good Diomed. Call my guard, I
 · ·   prithee.

DIO. What ho, the Emperor's guard! The guard,
     what ho!

Come, your lord calls.   130
    [*Enter four or five of the* GUARD *of* ANTONY.]

ANT. Bear me, good friends, where Cleopatra
     bides.
'Tis the last service that I shall command you.

I. GUARD. Woe, woe are we, sir, you may not live
     to wear

All your true followers out.

ALL.   Most heavy day!

ANT. Nay, good my fellows, do not please sharp
     Fate   135
To grace it with your sorrows.° Bid that welcome
Which comes to punish us, and we punish it
Seeming to bear it lightly. Take me up.
I have led you oft. Carry me now, good friends,
And have my thanks for all.   140
         [*Exeunt, bearing* ANTONY.]

SCENE XV. *The same. A monument.*

[*Enter* CLEOPATRA, *and her maids aloft, with*
CHARMIAN, *and* IRAS.]

CLEO. O Charmian, I will never go from hence.

CHAR. Be comforted, dear madam.

CLEO.   No, I will not.
All strange and terrible events are welcome,
But comforts we despise. Our size of sorrow,

76–77. branded . . . ensued: marked as with a brand the baseness
of the man who followed.   98. instruction . . . upon: example
won over.   100. bridegroom . . . death: Cf. *Lear,* IV.vi.202.
107. period: end.   113. enter . . . him: get me into his favor.

123. disposed: come to terms.   135–36. please . . . sorrows: i.e.,
do not let cruel Fate rejoice because it has made you sad.

Proportioned to our cause, must be as great   5
As that which makes it.
[*Enter, below,* DIOMEDES.] How now! Is he dead?
   DIO. His death's upon him, but not dead.
Look out o' the other side your monument.
His guard have brought him thither.
    [*Enter, below,* ANTONY, *borne by the* GUARD.]
   CLEO.   O sun,
Burn the great sphere° thou movest in! Darkling°
   stand   10
The varying shore o' the world. O Antony,
Antony, Antony! Help, Charmian, help. Iras, help.
Help, friends below. Let's draw him hither.
   ANT.   Peace!
Not Caesar's valor hath o'erthrown Antony,
But Antony's hath triumphed on itself.   15
   CLEO. So it should be, that none but Antony
Should conquer Antony, but woe 'tis so!
   ANT. I am dying, Egypt, dying, only
I here importune death awhile° until
Of many thousand kisses the poor last   20
I lay upon thy lips.
   CLEO.   I dare not, dear,
Dear my lord, pardon, I dare not,
Lest I be taken. Not the imperious show
Of the full-fortuned Caesar ever shall
Be brooched with me.° If knife, drugs, serpents, have
   Edge, sting, or operation, I am safe.   25
Your wife Octavia, with her modest eyes
And still conclusion,° shall acquire no honor
Demuring° upon me. But come, come, Antony—
Help me, my women — we must draw thee up.   30
Assist, good friends.
   ANT.   Oh, quick, or I am gone.
   CLEO. Here's sport indeed! How heavy weighs my
   lord!
Our strength is all gone into heaviness.°
That makes the weight. Had I great Juno's power,
The strong-winged Mercury° should fetch thee up
And set thee by Jove's side. Yet come a little —   36
Wishers were ever fools — oh, come, come, come,
    [*They heave* ANTONY *aloft to* CLEOPATRA.]
And welcome, welcome! Die where thou hast lived.
Quicken° with kissing. Had my lips that power,
Thus would I wear them out.
   ALL.   A heavy sight!   40
   ANT. I am dying, Egypt, dying.
Give me some wine, and let me speak a little.
   CLEO. No, let me speak, and let me rail so high

That the false housewife° Fortune break her wheel,
Provoked by my offense.
   ANT.   One word, sweet Queen.   45
Of Caesar seek your honor, with your safety. Oh!
   CLEO. They do not go together.
   ANT.   Gentle, hear me.
None about Caesar trust but Proculeius.
   CLEO. My resolution and my hands I'll trust,
None about Caesar.   50
   ANT. The miserable change now at my end
Lament nor sorrow at, but please your thoughts
In feeding them with those my former fortunes
Wherein I lived the greatest Prince o' the world,
The noblest, and do now not basely die,   55
Not cowardly put off my helmet to
My countryman, a Roman by a Roman
Valiantly vanquished. Now my spirit is going,
I can no more.
   CLEO.   Noblest of men, woo 't die?
Hast thou no care of me? Shall I abide   60
In this dull world, which in thy absence is
No better than a sty? Oh, see, my women,
                     [ANTONY *dies.*]
The crown o' the earth doth melt. My lord!
Oh, withered is the garland° of the war,
The soldier's pole° is fall'n. Young boys and girls
Are level now with men. The odds° is gone,   66
And there is nothing left remarkable
Beneath the visiting moon.   [*Faints.*]
   CHAR.   Oh, quietness, lady!
   IRAS. She's dead too, our sovereign.
   CHAR.   Lady!
   IRAS.   Madam!
   CHAR. O madam, madam, madam!
   IRAS.   Royal Egypt,   70
Empress!
   CHAR. Peace, peace, Iras!
   CLEO. No more, but e'en a woman, and com-
   manded
By such poor passion as the maid that milks
And does the meanest chares.° It were for me   75
To throw my scepter at the injurious° gods,
To tell them that this world did equal theirs
Till they had stol'n our jewel. All's but naught.
Patience is sottish,° and impatience does
Become a dog that's mad. Then is it sin   80
To rush into the secret house of death
Ere death dare come to us? How do you, women?
What, what! Good cheer! Why, how now, Char-
   mian!
My noble girls! Ah, women, women, look,
Our lamp is spent, it's out! Good sirs, take heart. 85
We'll bury him, and then, what's brave,° what's
   noble,

   Sc. xv: 10. sphere: course. See App. 1. Darkling: in the
dark.   19. importune ... awhile: beg death to forbear for a
while.   23–25. Not ... me: the triumphal procession of the all-
fortunate Caesar shall never be ornamented with me. brooched:
worn like a brooch.   28. still conclusion: quiet disapproval.
29. Demuring: looking primly.   33. heaviness: grief.   35. Mercury: the messenger of the gods, who wore winged sandals.
39. Quicken: make live.

44. housewife: hussy.   64. garland: ornament, glory.   65. pole:
the guiding star.   66. odds: superiority.   75. chares: chores.
76. injurious: who injure us.   79. sottish: stupid.   86. brave: fine.

Let's do it after the high Roman fashion,
And make death proud to take us. Come, away.
This case° of that huge spirit now is cold.
Ah, women, women! Come, we have no friend   90
But resolution° and the briefest end.

[*Exeunt, those above bearing off* ANTONY's *body.*]

Act V

SCENE I. *Alexandria.* CAESAR's *camp.*

[*Enter* CAESAR, AGRIPPA, DOLABELLA, MECAENAS,
GALLUS, PROCULEIUS, *and others, his council of war.*]

CAES. Go to him, Dolabella, bid him yield.
Being so frustrate,° tell him he mocks
The pauses that he makes.°

DOL.   Caesar, I shall. [*Exit.*]

[*Enter* DERCETAS, *with the sword of* ANTONY.]

CAES. Wherefore is that? And what art thou that
   darest
Appear thus to us?

DER.   I am called Dercetas.   5
Mark Antony I served, who best was worthy
Best to be served. Whilst he stood up and spoke,
He was my master, and I wore my life
To spend upon his haters. If thou please
To take me to thee, as I was to him   10
I'll be to Caesar. If thou pleasest not,
I yield thee up my life.

CAES.   What is 't thou say'st?

DER. I say, O Caesar, Antony is dead.

CAES. The breaking of so great a thing should
   make
A greater crack. The round world   15
Should have shook lions into civil streets,
And citizens to their dens.° The death of Antony
Is not a single doom.° In the name lay
A moiety° of the world.

DER.   He is dead, Caesar.
Not by a public minister of justice,   20
Nor by a hired knife, but that self hand
Which writ his honor in the acts it did
Hath, with the courage which the heart did lend it,
Splitted the heart. This is his sword.
I robbed his wound of it. Behold it stained   25
With his most noble blood.

CAES.   Look you sad, friends?
The gods rebuke me, but it is tidings

To wash the eyes of Kings.

AGR.   And strange it is
That nature must compel us to lament
Our most persisted deeds.

MEC.   His taints and honors   30
Waged equal° with him.

AGR.   A rarer spirit never
Did steer humanity. But you, gods, will give us
Some faults to make us men. Caesar is touched.

MEC. When such a spacious mirror's set before
   him,°
He needs must see himself.

CAES.   O Antony!   35
I have followed thee to this. But we do lance
Diseases in our bodies. I must perforce
Have shown to thee such a declining day,
Or look on thine. We could not stall° together
In the whole world. But yet let me lament,   40
With tears as sovereign° as the blood of hearts,
That thou, my brother, my competitor
In top of all design,° my mate in empire,
Friend and companion in the front of war,
The arm of mine own body and the heart   45
Where mine his thoughts did kindle, that our stars
Unreconciliable° should divide
Our equalness to this. Hear me, good friends ——
But I will tell you at some meeter° season.

[*Enter an* EGYPTIAN.] The business of this man looks
   out of him,   50
We'll hear him what he says. Whence are you?

EGYP. A poor Egyptian yet.° The Queen my mis-
   tress,
Confined in all she has, her monument,
Of thy intents desires instruction,
That she preparedly may frame herself   55
To the way she's forced to.

CAES.   Bid her have good heart.
She soon shall know of us, by some of ours,
How honorable and how kindly we
Determine for her, for Caesar cannot live   59
To be ungentle.°

EGYP.   So the gods preserve thee! [*Exit.*]

CAES. Come hither, Proculeius. Go and say
We purpose her no shame. Give her what comforts
The quality of her passion° shall require,
Lest in her greatness by some mortal° stroke
She do defeat us, for her life in Rome   65
Would be eternal in our triumph.° Go,

---

89. case: i.e., body.   91. resolution: courage.

    Act V, Sc. i: 2. frustrate: thwarted.   2–3. mocks . . . makes: delays are a mockery.   15–17. The . . . dens: i.e., at Antony's death there should have been omens such as accompanied the end of Julius Caesar. See *Caesar,* I.iii–II.ii.   18. single doom: the death of one man.   19. moiety: half, large part.

31. Waged equal: were an equal match.   34. a . . . him: i.e., in Antony's fortune he saw a reflection of his own.   39. stall: lit., share the same stall.   41. sovereign: powerful.   42–43. competitor . . . design: partner in the greatest achievements. 46–47. stars Unreconciliable: fate which would not allow us to agree.   49. meeter: fitter.   52. yet: still; i.e., until you tell us our fate.   60. ungentle: ungenerous.   63. quality . . . passion: nature of her emotion.   64. mortal: fatal. 65–66. for . . . triumph: the fame of our triumphant return to Rome would be everlasting if we could carry her alive in the procession.

And with your speediest bring us what she says
And how you find of her.
　　PRO.　　　　　　　Caesar, I shall.　　[*Exit.*]
　　CAES. Gallus, go you along.　　[*Exit* GALLUS.]
　　　Where's Dolabella,
To second Proculeius?
　　ALL.　　　　　　Dolabella!　　　　　70
　　CAES. Let him alone, for I remember now
How he's employed. He shall in time be ready.
Go with me to my tent, where you shall see
How hardly I was drawn into this war,
How calm and gentle I proceeded still　　　75
In all my writings. Go with me, and see
What I can show in this.　　　　[*Exeunt.*]

CAESAR FEELS WEAK FOR CRYING— + MUST JUSTIFY HIMSELF BY SHOWING THEM HIS LETTERS

SCENE II. *Alexandria. The monument.*

　　[*Enter* CLEOPATRA, CHARMIAN, *and* IRAS.]
　　CLEO. My desolation does begin to make
A better life. 'Tis paltry to be Caesar.
Not being Fortune, he's but Fortune's knave,°
A minister° of her will. And it is great
To do that thing that ends all other deeds,　　5
Which shackles accidents and bolts up change,°
Which sleeps, and never palates more the dug,
The beggar's nurse and Caesar's.°
　　[*Enter, to the gates of the monument,* PROCULEIUS,
　　　　　GALLUS, *and* SOLDIERS.]
　　PRO. Caesar sends greeting to the Queen of Egypt,
And bids thee study on what fair demands　　10
Thou mean'st to have him grant thee.
　　CLEO.　　　　　　　What's thy name?
　　PRO. My name is Proculeius.
　　CLEO.　　　　　　　　Antony
Did tell me of you, bade me trust you, but
I do not greatly care to be deceived,
That have no use for trusting. If your master　15
Would have a Queen his beggar, you must tell him
That majesty, to keep decorum,° must
No less beg than a kingdom. If he please
To give me conquered Egypt for my son,
He gives me so much of mine own as I　　20
Will kneel to him with thanks.
　　PRO.　　　　　　　Be of good cheer.
You're fall'n into a princely hand, fear nothing.
Make your full reference° freely to my lord,

Who is so full of grace that it flows over
On all that need. Let me report to him　　　25
Your sweet dependency,° and you shall find
A conqueror that will pray in aid for kindness°
Where he for grace is kneeled to.
　　CLEO.　　　　　　　Pray you tell him
I am his fortune's vassal° and I send him
The greatness he has got.° I hourly learn　　30
A doctrine of obedience, and would gladly
Look him i' the face.
　　PRO.　　　　　This I'll report, dear lady.
Have comfort, for I know your plight is pitied
Of him that caused it.
　　GAL. You see how easily she may be surprised.　35
[*Here* PROCULEIUS *and two of the* GUARD *ascend the
monument by a ladder placed against a window, and,
having descended, come behind* CLEOPATRA. *Some of
the* GUARD *unbar and open the gates.*°]
Guard her till Caesar come.　　　　[*Exit.*]
　　IRAS. Royal Queen!
　　CHAR. O Cleopatra! Thou art taken, Queen!
　　CLEO. Quick, quick, good hands.
　　　　　　　　　　　[*Drawing a dagger.*]
　　PRO.　　　　Hold, worthy lady, hold.
　　　　　　　　　　[*Seizes and disarms her.*]
Do not yourself such wrong, who are in this　40
Relieved,° but not betrayed.
　　CLEO.　　　　　　What, of death too,
That rids our dogs of languish?°
　　PRO.　　　　　　　Cleopatra,
Do not abuse my master's bounty by
The undoing of yourself. Let the world see
His nobleness well acted, which your death　45
Will never let come forth.
　　CLEO.　　　　　　Where art thou, Death?
Come hither, come! Come, come, and take a Queen
Worth many babes and beggars!
　　PRO.　　　　　　　Oh, temperance, lady!
　　CLEO. Sir, I will eat no meat, I'll not drink, sir.
If idle talk will once be necessary,　　　50
I'll not sleep neither. This mortal house° I'll ruin,
Do Caesar what he can. Know, sir, that I
Will not wait pinioned° at your master's Court,
Nor once be chastised with the sober eye
Of dull Octavia. Shall they hoist me up　　55
And show me to the shouting varletry°
Of censuring Rome? Rather a ditch in Egypt

Sc. ii: **3. knave:** attendant.　**4. minister:** servant.　**6. Which
. . . change:** lit., which fetters chance and locks up misfortune;
i.e., which puts an end to the uncertainties of life.　**7–8. Which
. . . Caesar's:** F1 reads "dung." There is no need to alter it.
The passage then means, "death makes us sleep and never more
eat the dung (i.e., food grown out of manure), which nourishes
alike a beggar and Caesar." It is an echo of Antony's "our dungy
earth alike feeds beast and man" (I.i.35–36). These morbid
broodings on the various transmutations of matter are common in
the early seventeenth century.　**17. keep decorum:** i.e., the only
request which a Queen can rightly ask is a kingdom.　**23. reference:** request.

26. sweet dependency: willing dependence.　**27. pray . . . kindness:** petition to be allowed to do you kindness.　**29. vassal:**
slave.　**29–30. I . . . got:** i.e., I admit that he is in every way
superior.　**35. s.d., Here . . . gates:** There is no stage direction
in F1, which however prints *Pro* before l. 33, "This, I'll report,"
and again before l. 35, "You see how easily . . ." The stage direction in the text was devised by Malone from the passage in Plutarch, but editors do not explain how the action could have been
carried out on the stage of the Globe.　**41. Relieved:** aided.
42. languish: wasting-away.　**51. mortal house:** i.e., body.
53. pinioned: bound like a criminal.　**56. shouting varletry:**
mob of yelling slaves.

Be gentle grave unto me! Rather on Nilus' mud
Lay me stark-naked, and let the water flies
Blow me into abhorring!° Rather make   60
My country's high pyramides my gibbet,
And hang me up in chains!
    PRO.   You do extend
These thoughts of horror further than you shall
Find cause in Caesar.

                 [*Enter* DOLABELLA.]
    DOL.   Proculeius,
What thou hast done thy master Caesar knows,   65
And he hath sent for thee. For the Queen,
I'll take her to my guard.
    PRO.   So, Dolabella,
It shall content me best. Be gentle to her.
[*To* CLEOPATRA] To Caesar I will speak what you
    shall please,
If you'll employ me to him.
    CLEO.   Say I would die.   70
          [*Exeunt* PROCULEIUS *and* SOLDIERS.]
    DOL. Most noble Empress, you have heard of me?
    CLEO. I cannot tell.
    DOL.   Assuredly you know me.
    CLEO. No matter, sir, what I have heard or known.
You laugh when boys or women tell their dreams —
Is 't not your trick?
    DOL.   I understand not, madam.   75
    CLEO. I dreamed there was an Emperor Antony.
Oh, such another sleep, that I might see
But such another man!
    DOL.   If it might please ye ——
    CLEO. His face was as the heavens, and therein
    stuck
A sun and moon, which kept their course and
    lighted   80
The little O, the earth.
    DOL.   Most sovereign creature ——
    CLEO. His legs bestrid the ocean. His reared arm
Crested° the world. His voice was propertied
As all the tunèd spheres,° and that to friends.
But when he meant to quail° and shake the orb,   85
He was as rattling thunder. For his bounty,
There was no winter in 't, an autumn 'twas
That grew the more by reaping. His delights
Were dolphinlike, they showed his back above
The element they lived in.° In his livery   90
Walked crowns and crownets,° realms and islands
    were
As plates° dropped from his pocket.
    DOL.   Cleopatra ——

    CLEO. Think you there was, or might be, such a
    man
As this I dreamed of?
    DOL.   Gentle madam, no.
    CLEO. You lie, up to the hearing of the gods.   95
But if there be, or ever were, one such,
It's past the size of dreaming. Nature wants stuff
To vie strange forms with fancy, yet to imagine
An Antony were nature's piece 'gainst fancy,
Condemning shadows quite.°
    DOL.   Hear me, good madam.   100
Your loss is as yourself, great, and you bear it
As answering to the weight. Would I might never
O'ertake pursued success but I do feel,
By the rebound of yours, a grief that smites
My very heart at root.
    CLEO.   I thank you, sir.   105
Know you what Caesar means to do with me?
    DOL. I am loath to tell you what I would you
    knew.
    CLEO. Nay, pray you, sir ——
    DOL.   Though he be honorable ——
    CLEO. He'll lead me then in triumph?
    DOL. Madam, he will, I know 't.   110
     [*Flourish and shout within:* " Make way there.
                            Caesar! "]

     [*Enter* CAESAR, GALLUS, PROCULEIUS, MECAENAS,
        SELEUCUS, *and others of his train.*]
    CAES. Which is the Queen of Egypt?
    DOL. It is the Emperor, madam.
                        [CLEOPATRA *kneels.*]
    CAES. Arise, you shall not kneel.
I pray you, rise, rise, Egypt.
    CLEO.   Sir, the gods   115
Will have it thus. My master and my lord
I must obey.
    CAES.   Take to you no hard thoughts.
The record of what injuries you did us,
Though written in our flesh, we shall remember
As things but done by chance.
    CLEO.   Sole sir o' the world,   120
I cannot project° mine own cause so well
To make it clear, but do confess I have
Been laden with like frailties which before
Have often shamed our sex.
    CAES.   Cleopatra, know
We will extenuate° rather than enforce.°   125
If you apply yourself to our intents,°
Which toward you are most gentle, you shall find
A benefit in this change. But if you seek
To lay on me a cruelty by taking

---

60. **Blow . . . abhorring:** lay their eggs in me until I become
loathsome.   83. **Crested:** surmounted, as a crest does a coat of
arms.   83–84. **propertied . . . spheres:** had the quality of music
like the perfect harmony of the spheres. See App. 1.   85. **quail:**
make quail.   88–90. **His . . . in:** as a dolphin shows his back
above the water, so Antony in his pleasures showed himself
above ordinary men.   90–91. **In . . . crownets:** Kings and Princes
wore his livery (i.e., were his servants).   92. **plates:** silver coins.

97–100. **Nature . . . quite:** Nature cannot invent such strange
creatures as we can imagine, but to create the form of Antony was
Nature's masterpiece, better than any unreal thing created by
imagination; i.e., the real Antony was finer than anything that
could be imagined.   121. **project:** set forth.   125. **extenuate:**
excuse. **enforce:** emphasize.   126. **If . . . intents:** if you carry
out our wishes.

Antony's course, you shall bereave yourself 130
Of my good purposes and put your children
To that destruction which I'll guard them from
If thereon you rely. I'll take my leave.
   CLEO. And may, through all the world. 'Tis
      yours, and we, 134
Your scutcheons° and your signs of conquest, shall
Hang in what place you please. Here, my good
   lord.
   CAES. You shall advise me in all for Cleopatra.
   CLEO. This is the brief° of money, plate, and
   jewels
I am possessed of. 'Tis exactly valued,
Not petty things admitted.° Where's Seleucus? 140
   SEL. Here, madam.
   CLEO. This is my treasurer. Let him speak, my
   lord,
Upon his peril, that I have reserved
To myself nothing. Speak the truth, Seleucus.
   SEL. Madam, 145
I had rather seal my lips than to my peril
Speak that which is not.
   CLEO.   What have I kept back?
   SEL. Enough to purchase what you have made
   known.
   CAES. Nay, blush not, Cleopatra. I approve
Your wisdom in the deed.
   CLEO.   See, Caesar! Oh, behold 150
How pomp° is followed! Mine will now be yours,
And should we shift estates,° yours would be mine.
The ingratitude of this Seleucus does
Even make me wild. O slave, of no more trust
Than love that's hired! What, goest thou back?
   Thou shalt 155
Go back, I warrant thee, but I'll catch thine eyes,
Though they had wings. Slave, soulless villain, dog!
O rarely base!
   CAES.   Good Queen, let us entreat you.
   CLEO. O Caesar, what a wounding shame is this,
That thou vouchsafing here to visit me, 160
Doing the honor of thy lordliness
To one so meek, that mine own servant should
Parcel° the sum of my disgraces by
Addition of his envy!° Say, good Caesar,
That I some lady° trifles have reserved, 165
Immoment toys,° things of such dignity
As we greet modern° friends withal. And say
Some nobler token I have kept apart
For Livia and Octavia, to induce
Their mediation. Must I be unfolded 170
With° one that I have bred? The gods! It smites me

---

135. scutcheons: painted coats of arms displayed at funerals and other ceremonial occasions. 138. brief: inventory. 140. Not . . . admitted: not even the trifles omitted. 151. pomp: greatness. 152. shift estates: change places. 163. Parcel: add to. 164. envy: malice. 165. lady: feminine. 166. Immoment toys: valueless trifles. 167. modern: slight. 170–71. unfolded With: exposed by.

Beneath the fall I have. [*To* SELEUCUS] Prithee go
   hence,
Or I shall show the cinders° of my spirits
Through the ashes of my chance.° Wert thou a man,
Thou wouldst have mercy on me.
   CAES.   Forbear, Seleucus. [*Exit* SELEUCUS.]
   CLEO. Be it known that we, the greatest, are mis-
   thought° 176
For things that others do, and when we fall,
We answer others' merits in our name,°
Are therefore to be pitied.
   CAES.   Cleopatra,
Not what you have reserved, nor what acknowl-
   edged, 180
Put we i' the roll of conquest.° Still be 't yours.
Bestow it at your pleasure, and believe
Caesar's no merchant, to make prize° with you
Of things that merchants sold. Therefore be cheered.
Make not your thoughts your prisons. No, dear
   Queen, 185
For we intend so to dispose you as
Yourself shall give us counsel. Feed, and sleep.
Our care and pity is so much upon you
That we remain your friend. And so adieu.
   CLEO. My master, and my lord!
   CAES.   Not so. Adieu. 190
   [*Flourish. Exeunt* CAESAR *and his train.*]
   CLEO. He words me, girls, he words me, that I
   should not
Be noble to myself. But, hark thee, Charmian.
               [*Whispers to* CHARMIAN.]
   IRAS. Finish, good lady. The bright day is done,
And we are for the dark.
   CLEO.   Hie° thee again.
I have spoke already, and it is provided. 195
Go put it to the haste.
   CHAR.   Madam, I will.
           [*Re-enter* DOLABELLA.]
   DOL. Where is the Queen?
   CHAR.   Behold, sir. [*Exit.*]
   CLEO.   Dolabella!
   DOL. Madam, as thereto sworn by your command,
Which my love makes religion to obey,
I tell you this. Caesar through Syria 200
Intends his journey, and within three days
You with your children will he send before.
Make your best use of this. I have performed
Your pleasure and my promise.
   CLEO.   Dolabella,
I shall remain your debtor.
   DOL.   I your servant. 205
Adieu, good Queen, I must attend on Caesar.
   CLEO. Farewell, and thanks. [*Exit* DOLABELLA.]

---

173. cinders: hot coals. 174. chance: misfortune. 176. misthought: misjudged. 178. We . . . name: we are responsible for the deeds of others done in our name. 181. Put . . . conquest: we shall record in the inventory of the victory. 183. make prize: estimate the value. 194. Hie: hasten.

Now, Iras, what think'st thou?
Thou, an Egyptian puppet,° shalt be shown
In Rome, as well as I. Mechanic° slaves   210
With greasy aprons, rules and hammers, shall
Uplift us to the view. In their thick breaths,
Rank of gross diet, shall we be enclouded
And forced to drink their vapor.

IRAS.   The gods forbid!

CLEO. Nay, 'tis most certain, Iras. Saucy lictors°
Will catch at us like strumpets, and scald rhymers°
Ballad us out o' tune. The quick comedians°   216
Extemporally° will stage us and present
Our Alexandrian revels. Antony
Shall be brought drunken forth, and I shall see
Some squeaking Cleopatra boy° my greatness   220
I' the posture of a whore.

IRAS.   Oh, the good gods!

CLEO. Nay, that's certain.

IRAS. I'll never see 't, for I am sure my nails
Are stronger than mine eyes.

CLEO.   Why, that's the way
To fool their preparation, and to conquer   225
Their most absurd intents.

[*Re-enter* CHARMIAN.]   Now, Charmian!
Show me, my women, like a Queen. Go fetch
My best attires. I am again for Cydnus,°
To meet Mark Antony. Sirrah° Iras, go.
Now, noble Charmian, we'll dispatch indeed,   230
And when thou hast done this chare I'll give thee
     leave
To play till Doomsday. Bring our crown and all.
               [*Exit* IRAS. *A noise within.*]
Wherefore's this noise?
           [*Enter a* GUARDSMAN.]

GUARD.   Here is a rural fellow
That will not be denied your Highness' presence.
He brings you figs.   235

CLEO. Let him come in.   [*Exit* GUARDSMAN.]
           What poor an instrument
May do a noble deed! He brings me liberty.
My resolution's placed, and I have nothing
Of woman in me. Now from head to foot
I am marble-constant,° now the fleeting moon   240
No planet is of mine.
[*Re-enter* GUARDSMAN, *with* CLOWN° *bringing
in a basket.*]

GUARD.   This is the man.

CLEO. Avoid, and leave him.   [*Exit* GUARDSMAN.]
Hast thou the pretty worm° of Nilus there

That kills and pains not?   244

CLO. Truly, I have him. But I would not be the
party that should desire you to touch him, for his
biting is immortal.° Those that do die of it do seldom or never recover.   248

CLEO. Rememberest thou any that have died on 't?

CLO. Very many, men and women too. I heard of
one of them no longer than yesterday — a very honest woman, but something given to lie, as a woman
should not do but in the way of honesty — how she
died of the biting of it, what pain she felt. Truly,
she makes a very good report o' the worm. But he that
will believe all that they say shall never be saved
by half that they do. But this is most fallible,° the
worm's an odd worm.

CLEO. Get thee hence. Farewell.   260

CLO. I wish you all joy of the worm.
           [*Setting down his basket.*]

CLEO. Farewell.

CLO. You must think this, look you, that the worm
will do his kind.°

CLEO. Aye, aye. Farewell.   265

CLO. Look you, the worm is not to be trusted but
in the keeping of wise people, for indeed there is no
goodness in the worm.

CLEO. Take thou no care, it shall be heeded.

CLO. Very good. Give it nothing, I pray you, for it
is not worth the feeding.   271

CLEO. Will it eat me?

CLO. You must not think I am so simple but I
know the Devil himself will not eat a woman. I
know that a woman is a dish for the gods, if the
Devil dress° her not. But truly these same whoreson°
devils do the gods great harm in their women, for in
every ten that they make, the devils mar five.

CLEO. Well, get thee gone. Farewell.   280

CLO. Yes, forsooth. I wish you joy o' the worm.
           [*Exit.*]

[*Re-enter* IRAS *with a robe, crown, etc.*]

CLEO. Give me my robe, put on my crown. I have
Immortal longings° in me. Now no more
The juice of Egypt's grape shall moist this lip.   285
Yare,° yare, good Iras, quick. Methinks I hear
Antony call. I see him rouse himself
To praise my noble act, I hear him mock
The luck of Caesar, which the gods give men
To excuse their afterwrath.° Husband, I come.   290
Now to that name my courage prove my title!
I am fire and air. My other elements
I give to baser life. So, have you done?

---

208. **puppet:** i.e., we shall become characters in puppet shows.
209. **Mechanic:** slave laborers.   214. **lictors:** officers of the
law.   215. **scald rhymers:** scabby poets. See App. 8.   216. **quick
comedians:** quick-witted players.   217. **Extemporally:** impromptu.   220. **squeaking . . . boy:** some boy player with a
squeaky voice act Cleopatra.   228. **Cyndus:** Cleopatra's thoughts
turn back to her first meeting with Antony. See II.ii.191–231.
229. **Sirrah:** The word was sometimes addressed to women.
240. **marble-constant:** as firm and coldhearted as marble in my
resolve.   241. **s.d., Clown:** countryman.   243. **worm:** snake.

247. **immortal:** for "mortal." As is usual with Shakespeare's
humbler characters, this clown loves long words without being
too sure of their meanings.   258. **fallible:** for "infallible."
264. **will . . . kind:** will act according to his nature.   276. **dress:**
make ready. **whoreson:** bastard, son of a bitch.   284. **Immortal
longings:** longings for immortality.   286. **Yare:** quick.
289–90. **which . . . afterwrath:** the gods give men excessive good
luck which afterward brings down on them Divine wrath.

Come, then, and take the last warmth of my lips.
Farewell, kind Charmian. Iras, long farewell.   295
    [*Kisses them.* IRAS *falls and dies.*]
Have I the aspic° in my lips? Dost fall?
If thou and nature can so gently part,
The stroke of death is as a lover's pinch,
Which hurts, and is desired. Dost thou lie still?
If thus thou vanishest, thou tell'st the world   300
It is not worth leave-taking.
  CHAR. Dissolve, thick cloud, and rain, that I may
  say
The gods themselves do weep!
  CLEO.   This proves me base.
If she first meet the curlèd Antony,
He'll make demand of her, and spend that kiss   305
Which is my Heaven to have. Come, thou mortal°
 wretch,
  [*To an asp, which she applies to her breast*]
With thy sharp teeth this knot intrinsicate°
Of life at once untie. Poor venomous fool,
Be angry, and dispatch. Oh, couldst thou speak,
That I might hear thee call great Caesar ass   310
Unpolicied!°
  CHAR. Oh, Eastern star!
  CLEO.   Peace, peace!
Dost thou not see my baby at my breast,
That sucks the nurse asleep?
  CHAR.   Oh, break! Oh, break!
  CLEO. As sweet as balm, as soft as air, as gentle —
O Antony! — Nay, I will take thee too.   315
    [*Applying another asp to her arm.*]
What should I stay ——   [*Dies.*]
  CHAR. In this vile world? So, fare thee well.
Now boast thee, Death, in thy possession lies
A lass unparalleled. Downy windows,° close,
And golden Phoebus, never be beheld   320
Of eyes again so royal! Your crown's awry.
I'll mend it,° and then play.
    [*Enter the* GUARD, *rushing in.*]
  I. GUARD. Where is the Queen?
  CHAR.   Speak softly, wake her not.
  I. GUARD. Caesar hath sent ——
  CHAR. Too slow a messenger.   [*Applies an asp.*]
Oh, come apace,° dispatch. I partly feel thee.   325
  I. GUARD. Approach, ho! All's not well. Caesar's
  beguiled.
  2. GUARD. There's Dolabella sent from Caesar. Call
  him.
  I. GUARD. What work is here! Charmian, is this
  well done?
  CHAR. It is well done, and fitting for a Princess
Descended of so many royal Kings.   330

Ah, soldier.   [*Dies.*]
    [*Re-enter* DOLABELLA.]
  DOL. How goes it here?
  2. GUARD.   All dead.
  DOL.   Caesar, thy thoughts
Touch their effects° in this. Thyself art coming
To see performed the dreaded act which thou
So sought'st to hinder.   335
  [*Within.* " A way there, a way for Caesar!"]
    [*Re-enter* CAESAR *and his train.*]
  DOL. O sir, you are too sure an augurer.
That you did fear is done.
  CAES.   Bravest° at the last,
She leveled at° our purposes, and being royal,
Took her own way. The manner of their deaths?
I do not see them bleed.
  DOL.   Who was last with them?   341
  I. GUARD. A simple countryman that brought her
  figs.
This was his basket.
  CAES.   Poisoned, then.
  I. GUARD.   O Caesar,
This Charmian lived but now, she stood and spake.
I found her trimming up the diadem   345
On her dead mistress. Tremblingly she stood,
And on the sudden dropped.
  CAES.   O noble weakness!
If they had swallowed poison, 'twould appear
By external swelling. But she looks like sleep,
As she would catch another Antony   350
In her strong toil of grace.°
  DOL.   Here, on her breast,
There is a vent° of blood, and something blown.°
The like is on her arm.
  I. GUARD. This is an aspic's trail. And these fig
  leaves
Have slime upon them, such as the aspic leaves   355
Upon the caves of Nile.
  CAES.   Most probable
That so she died, for her physician tells me
She hath pursued conclusions° infinite
Of easy ways to die. Take up her bed,
And bear her women from the monument.   360
She shall be buried by her Antony.
No grave upon the earth shall clip° in it
A pair so famous. High events as these
Strike those that make them, and their story is
No less in pity than his glory which   365
Brought them to be lamented. Our army shall
In solemn show attend this funeral,
And then to Rome. Come, Dolabella, see
High order in this great solemnity.   [*Exeunt.*]

---

296. **aspic:** asp, a small poisonous snake. 306. **mortal:** deadly.
307. **intrinsicate:** intricate. 310–11. **ass Unpolicied:** cheated
in his politic tricks. 319. **Downy windows:** eyelids soft as down.
322. **mend it:** put it straight. 325. **apace:** quickly.

333. **Touch . . . effects:** are fulfilled. 337. **Bravest:** finest.
338. **leveled at:** aimed at, guessed. 351. **toil of grace:** snare
of her beauty. 352. **vent:** discharge. **blown:** swollen. 358. **conclusions:** experiments. 362. **clip:** embrace.

THE TRAGEDY OF CORIOLANUS

Introduction

Very little is known of the date or the circumstances of the writing or the production of *The Tragedy of Coriolanus*. There are no contemporary references to the play, which was first published in the first folio (F1) in 1623. On the evidence of style alone, *Coriolanus* is usually dated 1607–09. There are a few passages in the play itself which would have been topically significant during these years, but they are not sufficiently definite to be indisputable evidence of date.

1. From mid-May to the end of July 1607 there was very serious rioting in England, particularly in the counties of Northamptonshire, Warwick, and Leicester. Considerable grievance was felt when rich men began to enclose the common lands and to convert tillage into pasture. The rioters tore down the hedges and filled up the ditches. In the country district there was very general sympathy for them. These disturbances were hotly discussed and were attributed to various causes. According to Howe's *Annals,* the rioters themselves declared that they wished

the prevention of further depopulation, the increase and continuance of tillage to relieve their wives and children, and chiefly because it had been credibly reported unto them by many that of very late years there were three hundred and forty towns decayed and depopulated, and that they supposed by this insurrection and casting down of enclosures to cause reformation.

As the rioters did not yield to persuasion and did not obey proclamations, some of the leaders were arrested and executed for high treason. This was the most serious civil disturbance in England for forty years. A play in which the chief motive is the clash of interests between the " rich " and the " poor " would therefore have had some special significance at this time.

2.   You are no surer, no,
Than is the coal of fire upon the ice. (I.i.176–77)

In the winter of 1607–08 occurred the worst frost for fifty-three years, to which there are many references. The following is from Howe's *Annals:*

The eighth of December began the hard frost which continued seven days and then thawed gently five days' space. And the two and twentieth the same month the frost began again very violently so as within four days many persons did walk halfway over the Thames upon the ice, and by the thirtieth of December the multitude at every ebb and half-flood passed over the Thames in divers places. And although the violence of the frost abated now and then, yet it held from the third of January until the fifteenth of the same, so as many set up booths and stands of sundry things to sell upon the ice, and some shot at pricks and played at bowls and other exercises of pleasure upon the ice.

On January 8, John Chamberlain wrote:

Above Westminster the Thames is quite frosted over and the Archbishop came from Lambeth on Twelfth Day over the ice to the Court. Many fantastical experiments are daily put in practice, as certain youths burned a gallon of wine upon the ice and made all the passengers partakers.[1]

3.
            And in the brunt of seventeen battles since,
            He lurched all swords of the garland.

This rare phrase (II.ii.104–05) is echoed in Ben Jonson's *Epicoene; or, The Silent Woman.*

You have lurched your friends of the better half of the garland, by concealing this part of the plot.

Epicoene was produced in 1609 or 1610.

4.   wants not spirit
  To say he'll turn your current in a ditch
            And make your channel his? (III.i.95–97)

This poetic image is an echo of the gossip caused by a sensational and much-discussed project when Hugh Middleton, goldsmith, obtained permission to bring clean water into London by channels from streams in Hertfordshire. His project was begun on February 20, 1609, and finished on Michaelmas Day 1613, during which time, according to Howe's *Annals,* Master Middleton " spent much money, endured despite and derisions of the vulgar and envious, answered many

---

1 *Letters Written by John Chamberlain*, ed. by N. E. McClure, 2 vols., American Philosophical Society, 1936, Vol. I, p. 253.

causeless hindrances and complaints of sundry persons through whose ground he was to cut his water passage."

The source of *Coriolanus* is the life of Caius Martius Coriolanus in North's translation of Plutarch's *Lives* (see *Caesar* Intro. p. 809a). Shakespeare followed his source closely, although for his own purposes he compressed the story and somewhat altered the incidents. In Plutarch there were two insurrections, both occurring after the capture of Corioli, when the plebeians withdrew in a body from Rome. The enemies of Rome, hearing of this trouble, began to invade Roman territory, which caused the Senate to appeal to the people, but they would not yield. Accordingly:

The Senate, being afraid of their departure, did send unto them certain of the pleasantest old men, and the most acceptable to the people among them. Of those Menenius Agrippa was he who was sent for chief man of the message from the Senate. He, after many good persuasions and gentle requests made to the people on the behalf of the Senate, knit up his oration in the end with a notable tale, in this manner: That on a time all the members of man's body did rebel against the belly, complaining of it that it only remained in the midst of the body without doing anything, neither did bear any labor to the maintenance of the rest; whereas all other parts and members did labor painfully, and were very careful to satisfy the appetites and desires of the body. And so the belly, all this notwithstanding, laughed at their folly, and said: "It is true I first receive all meats that nourish man's body; but afterward I send it again to the nourishment of other parts of the same. Even so (quoth he) O you, my masters, and citizens of Rome, the reason is alike between the Senate and you. For matters being well digested, and their counsels thoroughly examined, touching the benefit of the commonwealth, the Senators are cause of the common commodity that cometh unto every one of you."

The people were persuaded by this appeal and by the promise that tribunes should be appointed:

So Junius Brutus and Sicinius Vellutus were the first tribunes of the people that were chosen, who had only been the causers and procurers of this sedition. Hereupon, the city being grown again to good quiet and unity, the people immediately went to the wars, showing that they had a good will to do better than ever they did, and to be very willing to obey the magistrates in that they would command concerning the wars.

North's Plutarch served Shakespeare well, for the narrative is clear and full of vivid description of events and persons. Martius himself is thus described:

This man also is a good proof to confirm some men's opinions, that a rare and excellent wit untaught doth bring forth many good and evil things together, as a fat soil that lieth unmanured bringeth forth both herbs and weeds. For this Martius' natural wit and great heart did marvelously stir up his courage, to do and attempt notable acts. But on the other side, for lack of education he was so choleric and impatient that he would yield to no living creature, which made him churlish, uncivil, and altogether unfit for any man's conversation. Yet men marveling much at his constancy, that he was never overcome with pleasure, nor money, and how he would endure easily all manner of pains and travails, thereupon they well liked and commended his stoutness and temperancy. But for all that, they could not be acquainted with him, as one citizen useth to be with another in the city.

Many of the incidents and speeches in the play were followed very closely. Thus the episode in Act IV, scene iv, where Coriolanus enters the house of Aufidius, was based on the following passage by Plutarch:

It was even twilight when he entered the city of Antium, and many people met him in the streets, but no man knew him. So he went directly to Tullus Aufidius' house, and when he came thither, he got him up straight to the chimney hearth and sat him down, and spake not a word to any man, his face all muffled over. They of the house, spying him, wondered what he should be, and yet they durst not bid him rise. For ill-favoredly muffled and disguised as he was, yet there appeared a certain majesty in his countenance and in his silence. Whereupon they went to Tullus, who was at supper, to tell him of the strange disguising of this man. Tullus rose presently from the board, and coming toward him, asked him what he was, and wherefore he came. Then Martius unmuffled himself, and after he had paused awhile, making no answer, he said unto him:

"If thou knowest me not yet, Tullus, and seeing me, dost not perhaps believe me to be the man I am indeed, I must of necessity bewray myself to be that I am. I am Caius Martius, who hath done to thyself particularly, and to all the Volsces generally, great hurt and mischief, which I cannot deny for my surname of Coriolanus that I bear. For I never had other benefit nor recompense of the true and painful service I have done, and the extreme dangers I have been in, but this only surname — a good memory and witness of the malice and displeasure thou shouldest bear me. Indeed the name only remaineth with me. For the rest the envy and cruelty of the people of Rome have taken from me, by the sufferance of the dastardly nobility and magistrates, who have forsaken me, and let me be banished by the people. This extremity hath now driven me to come as a poor suitor, to take thy chimney hearth, not of any hope I have to save my life thereby; for if I had feared death, I would not have come hither to have put myself in hazard, but pricked forward with desire to be revenged of them that thus have banished me; which now I do begin, in putting my person into the hands of their enemies.

"Wherefore, if thou hast any heart to be wreaked [revenged] of the injuries thy enemies have done thee, speed thee now, and let my misery serve thy turn, and so use it as my service may be a benefit to the Volsces, promising thee that I will fight with better goodwill for all you than I did when I was against you, knowing that they fight more valiantly who know the force of the enemy than such as have never proved it. And if it be so that thou dare not, and that thou art weary to prove fortune any more, then am I also weary to live any longer. And it were no wisdom in thee to save the life of him who hath been heretofore thy mortal enemy, and whose service now can nothing help nor pleasure thee."

Tullus, hearing what he said, was a marvelous glad man, and taking him by the hand, he said unto him: "Stand up, O Martius, and be of good cheer, for in proffering thyself unto us thou doest us great honor, and by this means thou mayest hope also of greater things at all the Volsces' hands." So he feasted him for that time, and entertained him in the honorablest manner he could, talking with him of no other matter at that present. But within few days after they fell to consultation together, in what sort they should begin their wars.

The scene (V.iii) where the ladies of Rome make their final and successful plea to Coriolanus also follows the original very closely:

Now was Martius set then in his chair of state, with all the honors of a general, and when he had spied the women coming afar off, he marveled what the matter meant. But afterward, knowing his wife which came foremost, he determined at the first to persist in his obstinate and inflexible rancor. But overcome in the end with natural affection, and being altogether altered to see them, his heart would not serve him to tarry their coming to his chair, but, coming down in haste, he went to meet them, and first he kissed his mother, and embraced her a pretty while, then his wife and little children. And Nature so wrought with him that the tears fell from his eyes, and he could not keep himself from making much of them, but yielded to the affection of his blood, as if he had been violently carried with the fury of a most swift-running stream. After he had thus lovingly received them, and perceiving that his mother Volumnia would begin to speak to him, he called the chiefest of the council of the Volsces to hear what she would say. Then she spake in this sort:

"If we held our peace, my son, and determined not to speak, the state of our poor bodies, and present sight of our raiment, would easily bewray to thee what life we have led at home since thy exile and abode abroad. But think now with thyself how much more unfortunate than all the women living we are come hither, considering that the sight which should be most pleasant to all other to behold, spiteful Fortune had made most fearful to us — making myself to see my son, and my daughter here her husband, besieging the walls of his native country; so as that which is the only comfort to all other in their adversity and misery, to pray unto the gods and to call to them for aid, is the only thing which plungeth us into most deep perplexity. For we cannot, alas! together pray both for victory to our country and for safety of thy life also; but a world of grievous curses — yea, more than any mortal enemy can heap upon us — are forcibly wrapped up in our prayers. For the bitter sop of most hard choice is offered thy wife and children, to forgo one of the two: either to lose the person of thyself or the nurse of their native country.

"For myself, my son, I am determined not to tarry till Fortune, in my lifetime, do make an end of this war. For if I cannot persuade thee rather to do good unto both parties than to overthrow and destroy the one, preferring love and nature before the malice and calamity of wars, thou shalt see, my son, and trust unto it, thou shalt no sooner march forward to assault thy country but thy foot shall tread upon thy mother's womb that brought thee first into this world. And I may not defer to see the day, either that my son be led prisoner in triumph by his natural countrymen or that he himself do triumph of them, and of his natural country. For if it were so that my request tended to save thy country in destroying the Volsces, I must confess thou wouldest hardly and doubtfully resolve on that. For as to destroy thy natural country, it is altogether unmeet and unlawful, so were it not just, and less honorable, to betray those that put their trust in thee.

"But my only demand consisteth to make a jail delivery of all evils, which delivereth equal benefit and safety both to the one and the other, but most honorable for the Volsces. For it shall appear that, having victory in their hands, they have of special favor granted us singular graces, peace and amity, albeit themselves have no less part of both than we. Of which good, if so it came to pass, thyself is the only author, and so hast thou the only honor. But if it fail and fall out contrary, thyself alone deservedly shalt carry the shameful reproach and burden of either party. So, though the end of war be uncertain, yet this notwithstanding is most certain, that if it be thy chance to conquer, this benefit shalt thou reap of thy goodly conquest, to be chronicled the plague and destroyer of thy country. And if Fortune overthrow thee, then the world will say that through desire to revenge thy private injuries thou hast forever undone thy good friends, who did most lovingly and courteously receive thee."

Martius gave good ear unto his mother's words, without interrupting her speech at all, and after she had said what she would, he held his peace a pretty while, and answered not a word. Hereupon she began again to speak unto him, and said: "My son, why dost thou not answer me? Dost thou think it good altogether to give place unto thy choler and desire of revenge, and thinkest thou it not honesty for thee to grant thy mother's request in so weighty a cause? Dost thou take it honorable for a noble man to remember the wrongs and injuries done him, and dost not in like case think it an honest noble man's part to be thankful for the goodness that parents do show to their children, acknowledging the duty and reverence they ought to bear unto them? No man living is more bound to show himself thankful in all parts and respects than thyself, who so unnaturally showest all ingratitude. Moreover (my son) thou hast sorely taken of thy country, exacting grievous payments upon them in revenge of the injuries offered thee. Besides, thou hast not hitherto showed thy poor mother any courtesy. And therefore it is not only honest, but due unto me, that without compulsion I should obtain my so just and reasonable request of thee. But since by reason I cannot persuade thee to it, to what purpose do I defer my last hope?" And with these words, herself, his wife and children, fell down upon their knees before him.

Martius, seeing that, could refrain no longer, but went straight and lift her up, crying out, "Oh, Mother, what have you done to me?" And holding her hard by the right hand, "Oh, Mother," said he, "you have won a happy victory for your country, but mortal and unhappy for your son; for I see myself vanquished by you alone." These words being spoken openly, he spake a little apart with his mother and wife, and then let them return again to Rome, for so they did request him. And so remaining in camp that night, the next morning he dislodged and marched homeward into the Volsces' country again, who were not all of one mind, nor all alike contented. For some misliked him and that he had done. Other, being well pleased that peace should be made, said that neither the one nor the other deserved blame nor reproach. Other, though they misliked that was done, did not think him an ill man for that he did, but said he was not to be blamed, though he yielded to such a forcible extremity. Howbeit no man contraried his departure, but all obeyed his commandment, more for respect of his worthiness and valiancy than for fear of his authority.

Coriolanus has never been a general favorite. In 1934 it was played in Paris at a time of political tension and caused riots between extremists of both right and left. The play, nevertheless, is admirably written and Shakespeare preserves a unity of tone throughout. There is no digression, secondary plot, or clowning. Indeed the strength of *Coriolanus* is also its undoing; Shakespeare has shown up the weaknesses of all shades of political parties so clearly that few readers feel themselves untouched.

Shakespeare indeed seems to have had no great affection for any of his characters except Virgilia. This is unusual, for even Edmund and Iago, his greatest studies of evil, have qualities which appeal, if not to our affection, at least to our admiration. The character of Caius Marcius Coriolanus is a full-length and remorseless study of a man of limited mentality. Coriolanus is a professional soldier. He judges everyone by his military value; if the Roman citizens cannot fight, let them starve. He has all the assurance of the ignorant man who can get his own way by force because no one dares resist him. In war he is invaluable, in peace an impossible member of the state. His good qualities are simple. He has immense physical courage and a surprising tenderness for his wife; for Virgilia has all the womanly weaknesses so conspicuously wanting in Volumnia.

Virgilia cares nothing for decorations or military honors so long as her man comes back to her; she brings out his tenderest qualities. His ferocity he owes to his mother Volumnia, who is a portrait of the old-fashioned Roman matron, a type which Shakespeare seems not to have admired. In some ways the play is as much a tragedy of Volumnia as of Coriolanus. He is his mother's creation, and in the end she has the bitterness of destroying him. When he returns as leader of the Volscians, it is her appeal which saves Rome. She overcomes him and molds him to her will, as she has always done; but she saves the city at the cost of her son's life.

Coriolanus is one of Shakespeare's few political plays, and much critical comment has been expended on the supposed antidemocratic feeling exhibited in the crowd scenes. Two charges are made against the crowds in *Coriolanus* and in *Julius Caesar:* they are fickle, and their breath stinks. The second fact was indeed obvious to any Londoner who attended the Globe Theater. The first accusation is more serious.

At the beginning of the play, the crowd is shown as hungry and starving. They suspect the patricians, and from what is seen of Coriolanus and his friends, their suspicions are not unreasonable. All crowds, and even quite intelligent persons, at times of economic disturbance lay the blame for scarcities or the black market on the obviously prosperous. The plebeians of Rome have no reason to love Caius Marcius at any time, yet after his achievements at Corioli they are willing in a moment of generosity to forgive him the past and to elect him Consul. But when the Tribunes work on their feelings, a natural reaction follows and the citizens agree that they have made a mistake: Coriolanus has not deserved their love.

In the eyes of the patricians the Tribunes are villainous demagogues, yet they have a case. They are in the difficult position of all labor leaders who have to decide whether they should secure the immediate advantage of their own people or continue to endure intolerable conditions for the sake of the larger unit, the state. At all times Caius Marcius is the enemy of the people, and when he is driven out, the state for a while benefits; but the Tribunes in solving one problem have created a greater, for Coriolanus was the only man who could keep Aufidius in check. Now both Coriolanus and Aufidius are at the gates of Rome. So the Tribunes are made to learn the first political lesson, which is that a crowd will follow a successful leader but will desert him as soon as he seems to be failing. There is however no need to regard the Roman crowds as exceptionally fickle. Humanity in the mass respects only success. Even in modern democracies an educated electorate has been known to desert its leader.

[Handwritten top margin: MARCIUS HAS NO POLITICAL SENSE — HE IS A PRIVATE PERSON (LIKE RICH. II.) (SO NO DEVOTION TO COUNTRY & BAD AS A "GENERAL" FIGURE)]

Coriolanus

DRAMATIS PERSONAE

[Handwritten: MOST FEROCIOUS WARRIOR IN HISTORY]

CAIUS MARCIUS, *afterward* CAIUS MARCIUS CORIOLANUS
TITUS LARTIUS } *generals against the Volscians*
COMINIUS
MENENIUS AGRIPPA, *friend to Coriolanus*
SICINIUS VELUTUS } *tribunes of the people*
JUNIUS BRUTUS
YOUNG MARCIUS, *son of Coriolanus*
A ROMAN HERALD
TULLUS AUFIDIUS, *general of the Volscians*
LIEUTENANT *to Aufidius*
CONSPIRATORS *with Aufidius*
A CITIZEN *of Antium*

TWO VOLSCIAN GUARDS
VOLUMNIA, *mother to Coriolanus*
VIRGILIA, *wife to Coriolanus*
VALERIA, *friend to Virgilia*
GENTLEWOMAN *attending on Virgilia*

ROMAN *and* VOLSCIAN SENATORS, PATRICIANS, AEDILES,
LICTORS, SOLDIERS, CITIZENS, MESSENGERS, SERVANTS
to Aufidius, and other ATTENDANTS

SCENE — *Rome and the neighborhood; Corioli and
the neighborhood; Antium.*

Act I

[Handwritten: CRITICALLY A REFLECTIVE GROUP OF PEOPLE]

SCENE I. *Rome. A street.*

[Handwritten across columns: MOB IS ANALYTICAL, CONSIDERATE, + MORAL]

[*Enter a company of mutinous* CITIZENS, *with staves,
clubs, and other weapons.*]

1. CIT. Before we proceed any further, hear me
speak.
ALL. Speak, speak.
1. CIT. You are all resolved rather to die than to
famish?   5
ALL. Resolved, resolved.
1. CIT. First, you know Caius Marcius is chief
enemy to the people.
ALL. We know 't, we know 't.   9
1. CIT. Let us kill him, and we'll have corn° at
our own price. Is 't a verdict?
ALL. No more talking on 't. Let it be done—
away, away!
2. CIT. One word, good citizens.   14
1. CIT. We are accounted poor citizens, the patricians, good. What authority surfeits° on would relieve us. If they would yield us but the superfluity°
while it were wholesome, we might guess they relieved us humanely, but they think we are too   19
dear.° The leanness that afflicts us, the object of our
misery, is as an inventory to particularize their abundance,° our sufferance is a gain to them. Let us revenge this with our pikes,° ere we become rakes.°

[Handwritten left margin: THEY WANT TO GET FOOD BY KILLING MARCIUS — UNLIKE MOST MOBS THAT TAKE ACTION & DON'T SPEAK]

[Handwritten lower left: MOBS DON'T SPEAK LIKE THIS — DON'T WORRY ABOUT DIFF. BETWEEN REVENGE + HUNGER]

Act I, Sc. i: 10. corn: wheat, barley, oats, rye, but *not* our
"corn," which was not known in Shakespeare's time and in
England today is called maize or Indian corn.   16. surfeits:
feeds to excess.   17. superfluity: what they do not need.
20. dear: expensive.   20–21. The ... abundance: our leanness,
which is the reason why we are miserable, is an indication of their
prosperity; i.e., the poorer we are, the richer they become.
23. pikes: pitchforks. rakes: i.e., as lean as rakes.

For the gods know I speak this in hunger for bread,
not in thirst for revenge.   25
2. CIT. Would you proceed especially against
Caius Marcius?
ALL. Against him first. He's a very dog to the
commonalty.   29
2. CIT. Consider you what services he has done
for his country?
1. CIT. Very well, and could be content to give
him good report for 't but that he pays himself with
being proud.
2. CIT. Nay, but speak not maliciously.   35
1. CIT. I say unto you, what he hath done famously, he did it to that end. Though soft-con-
scienced men can be content to say it was for his
country, he did it to please his mother and to be
partly proud,° which he is, even to the altitude of his
virtue.°   41
2. CIT. What he cannot help in his nature you ac-
count a vice in him. You must in no way say he is
covetous.
1. CIT. If I must not, I need not be barren of accusations. He hath faults, with surplus, to tire in
repetition. [*Shouts within.*] What shouts are these?
The other side o' the city is risen. Why stay we
prating here? To the Capitol!
ALL. Come, come.   50
1. CIT. Soft! Who comes here?
[*Enter* MENENIUS AGRIPPA.]
2. CIT. Worthy Menenius Agrippa, one that hath
always loved the people.
1. CIT. He's honest enough. Would all the rest
were so!   55
MEN. What work's, my countrymen, in hand?
Where go you

39–40. to ... proud: partly to be proud.   40–41. altitude ...
virtue: i.e., his pride is as high as his courage.

[Handwritten bottom: PLEBEIANS + PATRICIANS]
[Handwritten: COMMONERS & MOB]
[Handwritten: GOV. IN HANDS OF THESE FATHERS]

With bats° and clubs? The matter? Speak, I pray
  you.
   1. CIT. Our business is not unknown to the Sen-
ate. They have had inkling, this fortnight, what we
intend to do, which now we'll show 'em in deeds.
They say poor suitors have strong breaths. They
shall know we have strong arms too.   62
   MEN. Why, masters, my good friends, mine hon-
    est neighbors,
Will you undo yourselves?
   1. CIT. We cannot, sir, we are undone already.
   MEN. I tell you, friends, most charitable care
Have the patricians of you. For your wants,
Your suffering in this dearth, you may as well
Strike at the Heaven with your staves as lift them
Against the Roman state, whose course will on   71
The way it takes, cracking ten thousand curbs
Of more strong link asunder than can ever
Appear in your impediment.° For the dearth,
The gods, not the patricians, make it, and   75
Your knees to them, not arms, must help. Alack,
You are transported by calamity°
Thither where more attends you, and you slander
The helms° o' the state, who care for you like
    fathers,
When you curse them as enemies.   80
   1. CIT. Care for us! True, indeed! They ne'er
cared for us yet. Suffer us to famish, and their store-
houses crammed with grain; make edicts for usury,
to support usurers; repeal daily any wholesome act
established against the rich, and provide more
piercing° statutes daily to chain up and restrain the
poor. If the wars eat us not up, they will, and there's
all the love they bear us.   89
   MEN. Either you must
Confess yourselves wondrous malicious
Or be accused of folly. I shall tell you
A pretty tale. It may be you have heard it,
But since it serves my purpose, I will venture
To stale 't° a little more.   95
   1. CIT. Well, I'll hear it, sir. Yet you must not
think to fob off° our disgrace with a tale. But, an 't
please you, deliver.°
   MEN. There° was a time when all the body's mem-
    bers
Rebelled against the belly, thus accused it: 100
That only like a gulf° it did remain
I' the midst o' the body, idle and unactive,
Still cupboarding the viand,° never bearing

Like labor with the rest, where the other instru-
    ments   104
Did see and hear, devise, instruct, walk, feel,
And, mutually participate,° did minister
Unto the appetite and affection° common
Of the whole body. The belly answered ——   109
   1. CIT. Well, sir, what answer made the belly?
   MEN. Sir, I shall tell you. With a kind of smile,
Which ne'er came from the lungs, but even thus —
For, look you, I may make the belly smile
As well as speak — it tauntingly replied
To the discontented members, the mutinous parts
That envied his receipt° — even so most fitly   116
As you malign our Senators for that
They are not such as you.
   1. CIT.   Your belly's answer? What!
The kingly crowned head, the vigilant eye,
The counselor heart, the arm our soldier,   120
Our steed the leg, the tongue our trumpeter,
With other muniments and petty helps°
In this our fabric, if that they ——
   MEN.   What then?
'Fore me,° this fellow speaks! What then? What
    then?
   1. CIT. Should by the cormorant° belly be re-
    strained,   125
Who is the sink o' the body ——
   MEN.   Well, what then?
   1. CIT. The former agents, if they did complain,
What could the belly answer?
   MEN.   I will tell you.
If you'll bestow a small — of what you have little —
Patience awhile, you'st hear the belly's answer.
   1. CIT. You're long about it.
   MEN.   Note me this, good friend. 131
Your most grave belly was deliberate,
Not rash like his accusers, and thus answered:
" True is it, my incorporate° friends," quoth he,
" That I receive the general food at first,   135
Which you do live upon, and fit it is,
Because I am the storehouse and the shop
Of the whole body. But, if you do remember,
I send it through the rivers of your blood,
Even to the Court, the heart, to the seat o' the brain.
And through the cranks° and offices° of man, 141
The strongest nerves° and small inferior veins
From me receive that natural competency
Whereby they live. And though that all at once,
You, my good friends " — this says the belly, mark
   me ——   145

---

57. bats: cudgels.   71–74. whose . . . impediment: i.e., which
will continue on its course, overcoming far stronger impediments
than you can offer. curbs: restraints; lit., the chain of the bit
which passes round the lower jaw of the horse. in . . . impediment: in anything you can do to hinder.   77. transported by
calamity: carried away by the storm of ill fortune.   79. helms:
steersmen.   87. piercing: oppressive.   95. stale 't: make staler by
repeating. F1 reads "scale't."   97. fob off: put off with a trick.
98. deliver: hand it out, tell your tale.   99–150. There . . . to 't:
See *Cor* Intro. p. 1266a.   101. gulf: whirlpool.   103. viand: food.

106. mutually participate: in mutual partnership.   108. affection: desire.   116. his receipt: what he received.   122. muniments . . . helps: fortifications and minor defenses.   124. 'Fore
me: a mild oath, substituted for "before God."   125. cormorant:
a sea bird noted for its greed.   134. incorporate: united in one
body.   141. cranks: winding passages. offices: parts of the house
where the work is done; e.g., kitchen and pantry.   142. nerves:
sinews.

[handwritten marginalia at top: MARCIUS' DEF. OF GOOD GENERAL { 1.) RAPID MOVEMENT OF TROOPS 2.) KNOWING LOCAT. OF ENEMY]

1. CIT. Aye, sir, well, well.

MEN.   " Though all at once cannot
See what I do deliver out to each,
Yet I can make my audit up, that all
From me do back receive the flour of all,   149
And leave me but the bran." What say you to 't?

1. CIT. It was an answer. How apply you this?

MEN. The Senators of Rome are this good belly,
And you the mutinous members. For examine
Their counsels and their cares, digest things rightly
Touching the weal o' the common,° you shall find
No public benefit which you receive   156
But it proceeds or comes from them to you
And no way from yourselves. What do you think,
You, the great toe of this assembly?

1. CIT. I the great toe! Why the great toe?   160

MEN. For that being one o' the lowest, basest,
poorest,
Of this most wise rebellion, thou go'st foremost.
Thou rascal,° that art worst in blood to run,°
Lead'st first to win some vantage.
But make you ready your stiff bats and clubs.   165
Rome and her rats are at the point of battle,
The one side must have bale.°

     [*Enter* CAIUS MARCIUS.] Hail, noble Marcius!

MAR. Thanks. What's the matter, you dissentious°
rogues,
That, rubbing the poor itch of your opinion,°
Make yourselves scabs?

1. CIT.   We have ever your good word.   170

MAR. He that will give good words to thee will
flatter
Beneath abhorring.° What would you have, you
curs,
That like nor peace nor war? The one affrights you,
The other makes you proud. He that trusts to you,
Where he should find you lions, finds you hares,
Where foxes, geese. You are no surer, no,   176
Than is the coal of fire upon the ice,
Or hailstone in the sun. Your virtue° is
To make him worthy whose offense subdues him°
And curse that justice did it. Who deserves greatness
Deserves your hate. And your affections are   181
A sick man's appetite, who desires most that
Which would increase his evil. He that depends
Upon your favors swims with fins of lead
And hews down oaks with rushes.° Hang ye! Trust
ye?   185
With every minute you do change a mind,
And call him noble that was now your hate,

Him vile that was your garland. What's the matter,
That in these several places of the city
You cry against the noble Senate, who,   190
Under the gods, keep you in awe,° which else
Would feed on one another? What's their seeking?

MEN. For corn at their own rates, whereof, they
say,
The city is well stored.

MAR.   Hang 'em! They say!
They'll sit by the fire and presume to know   195
What's done i' the Capitol; who's like to rise,
Who thrives and who declines; side factions° and
give out
Conjectural marriages; making parties strong
And feebling such as stand not in their liking
Below their cobbled shoes. They say there's grain
enough!   200
Would the nobility lay aside their ruth°
And let me use my sword, I'd make a quarry°
With thousands of these quartered° slaves, as high
As I could pick° my lance.

MEN. Nay, these are almost thoroughly persuaded,
For though abundantly they lack discretion,   206
Yet are they passing° cowardly. But I beseech you,
What says the other troop?

MAR.   They are dissolved. Hang 'em!
They said they were a-hungry; sighed forth prov-
erbs,
That hunger broke stone walls, that dogs must eat,
That meat was made for mouths, that the gods sent
not   211
Corn for the rich men only. With these shreds
They vented their complainings, which being an-
swered,
And a petition granted them, a strange one—
To break the heart of generosity°   215
And make bold power look pale—they threw their
caps
As they would hang them on the horns o' the moon,
Shouting their emulation.°

MEN.   What is granted them?

MAR. Five Tribunes to defend their vulgar wis-
doms,
Of their own choice. One's Junius Brutus,   220
Sicinius Velutus, and I know not—— 'Sdeath!°
The rabble should have first unroofed the city
Ere so prevailed with me. It will in time
Win upon power° and throw forth greater themes
For insurrection's arguing.

MEN.   This is strange.   225

---

155. weal . . . common: welfare of the common people.   163. rascal: lean deer, not worth hunting. worst . . . run: in the poorest
condition for running.   167. bale: injury.   168. dissentious:
seditious.   169. opinion: self-esteem.   172. Beneath abhorring:
i.e., "disgusting" would be too weak a word for flattery given to
this crowd.   178. virtue: i.e., your idea of manhood.   179. whose
. . . him: who is brought low by his own wrongdoing.
185. rushes: The rush is often used as a symbol for weakness, as
in the phrase "a broken reed."

191. awe: obedience.   197. side factions: take sides with parties.
201. ruth: pity.   202. quarry: heap of slaughtered deer after the
hunt. Cf. *Haml*, V.ii.375; *Macb*, IV.iii.206.   203. quartered:
cut in quarters.   204. pick: throw.   207. passing: exceedingly.
215. heart of generosity: the heart of the gentry.   218. emulation: rivalry; i.e., vying with each other in shouting.
221. 'Sdeath: by God's death.   224. Win . . . power: overcome
authority.

[handwritten at bottom: TRIBUNES HAVE FULL STATUS AS MAGISTRATES OF STATE]

[Handwritten across top: MARCIUS CAN BE CALLED PROUD SINCE LEAVES AT OFFICIAL PRAISE & WON'T SHOW SCARS — (SINCE WON'T ACCEPT PUBLIC PRAISE — FEARS HE IS ABOVE IT)]

MAR. Go get you home, you fragments!
    [*Enter a* MESSENGER, *hastily.*]
MESS. Where's Caius Marcius?
MAR.   Here. What's the matter?
MESS. The news is, sir, the Volsces are in arms.
MAR. I am glad on 't. Then we shall ha' means to
  vent
Our musty superfluity.° See, our best elders.   230
[*Enter* COMINIUS, TITUS LARTIUS, *and other* SENATORS;
    JUNIUS BRUTUS *and* SICINIUS VELUTUS.]
I. SEN. Marcius, 'tis true that you have lately told
  us —
The Volsces are in arms.
MAR.   They have a leader,
Tullus Aufidius, that will put you to 't.°
I sin in envying his nobility,
And were I anything but what I am,   235
I would wish me only he.
COM.   You have fought together?
MAR. Were half to half the world by the ears,°
  and he
Upon my party, I'd revolt, to make
Only my wars with him. He is a lion
That I am proud to hunt.
I. SEN.   Then, worthy Marcius,   240
Attend upon Cominius to these wars.
COM. It is your former promise. *[Handwritten: SHOWS MAR. JUST LOVES FIGHTING (NOT HIS COUNTRY) + WANTS]*
MAR.   Sir, it is,
And I am constant.° Titus Lartius, thou
Shalt see me once more strike at Tullus' face.
What, art thou stiff?° Stand'st out?°
LART.   No, Caius Marcius.   245
I'll lean upon one crutch and fight with t'other,
Ere stay behind this business.
         Oh, true-bred!
I. SEN. Your company to the Capitol, where, I
  know, *[Handwritten: TO MEET AUFIDIUS]*
Our greatest friends attend us.
LART.   [*To* COMINIUS] Lead you on.
[*To* MARCIUS] Follow Cominius. We must follow
  you,   250
Right worthy you priority.°
COM.   Noble Marcius!
I. SEN. [*To the* CITIZENS] Hence to your homes,
  be gone!
MAR.   Nay, let them follow.
The Volsces have much corn. Take these rats thither
To gnaw their garners.° Worshipful mutiners,°
Your valor puts well forth.° Pray follow.   255
      [CITIZENS *steal away. Exeunt all
      but* SICINIUS *and* BRUTUS.]

SIC. Was ever man so proud as is this Marcius?
BRU. He has no equal.
SIC. When we were chosen Tribunes for the peo-
  ple ——
BRU. Marked you his lip and eyes?
SIC.   Nay, but his taunts.
BRU. Being moved, he will not spare to gird° the
  gods.   260
SIC. Bemock the modest moon.
BRU. The present wars devour him! He is grown
Too proud to be so° valiant.
SIC.   Such a nature,
Tickled with good success, disdains the shadow
Which he treads on at noon. But I do wonder   265
His insolence can brook to be commanded
Under Cominius.
BRU.   Fame, at the which he aims,
In whom already he's well graced, cannot
Better be held, nor more attained, than by
A place below the first. For what miscarries   270
Shall be the general's fault, though he perform
To the utmost of a man, and giddy censure°
Will then cry out of Marcius "Oh, if he
Had borne° the business!"
SIC.   Besides, if things go well,
Opinion, that so sticks on Marcius, shall   275
Of his demerits° rob Cominius.
BRU.   Come.
Half all Cominius' honors are to Marcius,
Though Marcius earned them not. And all his faults
To Marcius shall be honors, though indeed
In aught he merit not.
SIC.   Let's hence, and hear   280
How the dispatch is made,° and in what fashion,
More than his singu!arity,° he goes
Upon this present action.
BRU.   Let's along.   [*Exeunt.*]

[Handwritten right margin: THEN SAY HE PREFERED TO BE 2nd IN COMMAND SO CAN'T BE BLAMED. WHY IS HE 2 nd IN COMMAND — BECAUSE HE's NOT AMBITIOUS OR GREEDY (HE JUST WANTS TO FIGHT)]

SCENE II. *Corioli. The Senate House.*

[*Enter* TULLUS AUFIDIUS, *with* SENATORS *of Corioli.*]
I. SEN. So your opinion is, Aufidius,
That they of Rome are entered in° our counsels,
And know how we proceed.
AUF.   Is it not yours?
What ever have been thought on in this state
That could be brought to bodily act ere Rome   5
Had circumvention?° 'Tis not four days gone
Since I heard thence. These are the words — I think
I have the letter here — yes, here it is.

229–30. vent . . . superfluity: dispose of our stale excess; i.e.,
some of these unnecessary rogues will be killed.   233. put . . .
to 't: keep you busy.   237. by . . . ears: i.e., quarreling.   243. constant: firm to my promise.   245. stiff: obstinate. Stand'st out:
i.e., will you oppose?   251. Right . . . priority: it is right that
you should go first.   254. garners: granaries. mutiners: mutineers.   255. puts . . . forth: makes a good show.

260. gird: taunt.   263. to be so: i.e., because he is so.
272. giddy censure: fickle opinion.   274. borne: been in charge
of.   276. demerits: deserts.   281. dispatch is made: business
is settled.   282. singularity: own peculiar behavior.
    Sc. ii: 2. are . . . in: have access to.   6. circumvention:
means of circumventing it.

[*Reads.*] " They have pressed a power,° but it is not known

Whether for east or west. The dearth is great,　10
The people mutinous. And it is rumored,
Cominius, Marcius your old enemy,
Who is of Rome worse hated than of° you,
And Titus Lartius, a most valiant Roman,
These three lead on this preparation　15
Whither 'tis bent.° Most likely 'tis for you.
Consider of it."

　　1. SEN.　　　Our army's in the field.
We never yet made doubt but Rome was ready
To answer us.

　　AUF.　　　Nor did you think it folly
To keep your great pretenses veiled till when　20
They needs must show themselves, which in the hatching,°
It seemed, appeared to Rome. By the discovery
We shall be shortened in our aim,° which was
To take in many towns ere almost Rome
Should know we were afoot.

　　2. SEN.　　　Noble Aufidius,　25
Take your commission,° hie° you to your bands.°
Let us alone to guard Corioli.
If they set down before 's,° for the remove°
Bring up your army, but I think you'll find
They've not prepared for us.

　　AUF.　　　Oh, doubt not that,　30
I speak from certainties. Nay, more,
Some parcels° of their power are forth already,
And only hitherward. I leave your Honors.
If we and Caius Marcius chance to meet,
'Tis sworn between us, we shall ever strike　35
Till one can do no more.

　　ALL.　　　The gods assist you!
　　AUF. And keep your Honors safe!
　　1. SEN.　　　Farewell.
　　2. SEN.　　　Farewell.
　　ALL. Farewell.　　　[*Exeunt.*]

VOLUMNIA — FERIOUS WOMAN —
PROUD OF CORIO's 27 WOUNDS

SCENE III. *Rome. A room in* MARCIUS' *house.*

[*Enter* VOLUMNIA *and* VIRGILIA. *They set them down on two low stools, and sew.*]

　　VOL. I pray you, Daughter, sing, or express yourself in a more comfortable sort. If my son were my husband, I should freelier rejoice in that absence wherein he won honor than in the embracements of his bed where he would show most love. When　5
yet he was but tender-bodied, and the only son of my womb; when youth with comeliness plucked all

gaze his way;° when, for a day of kings' entreaties, a mother should not sell him an hour from her beholding — I, considering how honor would become such a person, that it was no better than picturelike to hang by the wall° if renown made it not stir, was pleased to let him seek danger where he was like to find fame. To a cruel war I sent him, from whence he returned, his brows bound with　15
oak.° I tell thee, Daughter, I sprang not more in joy at first hearing he was a man-child than now in first seeing he had proved himself a man.

　　VIR. But had he died in the business, madam, how then?

　　VOL. Then his good report° should have been　20
my son, I therein would have found issue.° Hear me profess sincerely. Had I a dozen sons, each in my love alike and none less dear than thine and　25
my good Marcius, I had rather had eleven die nobly for their country than one voluptuously° surfeit out of action.

[*Enter a* GENTLEWOMAN.]

　　GEN. Madam, the Lady Valeria is come to visit you.

　　VIR. Beseech you, give me leave to retire myself.

　　VOL. Indeed you shall not.　31
Methinks I hear hither your husband's drum,
See him pluck Aufidius down by the hair,
As children from a bear, the Volsces shunning him.
Methinks I see him stamp thus, and call thus:　35
" Come on, you cowards! You were got° in fear,
Though you were born in Rome." His bloody brow
With his mailed hand then wiping, forth he goes,
Like to a harvestman that's tasked to° mow
Or all, or° lose his hire.　40

　　VIR. His bloody brow! Oh, Jupiter, no blood!

　　VOL. Away, you fool! It more becomes a man
Than gilt his trophy.° The breasts of Hecuba,
When she did suckle Hector, looked not lovelier
Than Hector's forehead when it spit forth blood　45
At Grecian sword, contemning.° Tell Valeria
We are fit to bid her welcome.

[*Exit* GENTLEWOMAN.]

　　VIR. Heavens bless° my lord from fell° Aufidius!

　　VOL. He'll beat Aufidius' head below his knee,
And tread upon his neck.　50

[*Enter* VALERIA, *with an* USHER° *and* GENTLEWOMAN.]

　　VAL. My ladies both, good day to you.

---

9. **pressed a power:** drafted an army.　13. **of:** by.　16. **bent:** intended.　21. **hatching:** disclosing.　23. **be . . . aim:** fall short of our aim.　26. **commission:** document formally appointing him as commander. **hie:** hasten. **bands:** companies.　27. **set . . . before 's:** besiege us. **remove:** relief.　32. **parcels:** detachments.

Sc. iii: **7–8. when . . . way:** when he was so attractive a youth that everyone stared at him.　**12. hang . . . wall:** i.e., in idleness.　**15–16. bound . . . oak:** wearing a garland of oak leaves, the Roman equivalent of the Congressional Medal.　**20. good report:** fame.　**21. issue:** children.　**27. voluptuously:** luxuriously.　**36. got:** begotten.　**39. tasked to:** given the task of.　**40. Or . . . or:** either . . . or.　**43. Than . . . trophy:** than gilt is appropriate on his memorial. In Shakespeare's time much gilt was used on the memorials and monuments in English churches.　**46. contemning:** disdaining.　**48. bless:** protect. **fell:** fierce.　**50 s.d., usher:** gentleman acting as escort.

VOL. Sweet madam.

VIR. I am glad to see your ladyship.

VAL. How do you both? You are manifest house-keepers.° What are you sewing here? A fine spot,° in good faith. How does your little son?   57

VIR. I thank your ladyship, well, good madam.

VOL. He had rather see the swords and hear a drum than look upon his schoolmaster.   61

VAL. O' my word, the father's son. I'll swear 'tis a very pretty boy. O' my troth,° I looked upon him o' Wednesday half an hour together, has such a con-firmed° countenance. I saw him run after a gilded butterfly, and when he caught it, he let it go   66 again; and after it again, and over and over he comes, and up again; catched it again. Or whether his fall enraged him, or how 'twas, he did so set his teeth and tear it — oh, I warrant, how he mammocked° it!

VOL. One on 's father's moods.   72

VAL. Indeed, la, 'tis a noble child.

VIR. A crack,° madam.

VAL. Come, lay aside your stitchery. I must have you play the idle huswife with me this afternoon.

VIR. No, good madam, I will not out of doors.

VAL. Not out of doors!

VOL. She shall, she shall.   80

VIR. Indeed, no, by your patience. I'll not over the threshold till my lord return from the wars.

VAL. Fie, you confine yourself most unreasonably. Come, you must go visit the good lady that lies in.°

VIR. I will wish her speedy strength, and visit   87 her with my prayers, but I cannot go thither.

VOL. Why, I pray you?   90

VIR. 'Tis not to save labor, nor that I want love.

VAL. You would be another Penelope.° Yet they say all the yarn she spun in Ulysses' absence did but fill Ithaca full of moths. Come, I would your cam-bric° were sensible° as your finger, that you might leave pricking it for pity. Come, you shall go with us.   97

VIR. No, good madam, pardon me. Indeed I will not forth.

VAL. In truth, la, go with me, and I'll tell you ex-cellent news of your husband.

VIR. Oh, good madam, there can be none yet.

VAL. Verily, I do not jest with you. There came news from him last night.

VIR. Indeed, madam?   105

VAL. In earnest, it's true, I heard a Senator speak it. Thus it is. The Volsces have an army forth, against

whom Cominius the general is gone, with one part of our Roman power. Your lord and Titus Lartius are set down before their city Corioli. They nothing doubt prevailing,° and to make it brief wars. This is true, on mine honor. And so I pray go with us.

VIR. Give me excuse, good madam, I will obey you in everything hereafter.   115

VOL. Let her alone, lady. As she is now, she will but disease our better mirth.

VAL. In troth, I think she would. Fare you well, then. Come, good sweet lady. Prithee, Virgilia, turn thy solemnness out o' door and go along with us.

VIR. No, at° a word, madam. Indeed, I must   122 not. I wish you much mirth.

VAL. Well then, farewell.   [Exeunt.]

SCENE IV. Before Corioli.

[Enter, with drum and colors, MARCIUS, TITUS LARTIUS, CAPTAINS and SOLDIERS. To them a MESSENGER.]

MAR. Yonder comes news. A wager they have met.

LART. My horse to yours, no.

MAR.   'Tis done.

LART.   Agreed.

MAR. Say, has our general met the enemy?

MESS. They lie in view, but have not spoke as yet.

LART. So, the good horse is mine.

MAR.   I'll buy him of you.   5

LART. No, I'll nor sell nor give him. Lend you him
I will
For half a hundred years. Summon the town.

MAR. How far off lie these armies?

MESS.   Within this mile and half.

MAR. Then shall we hear their larum,° and they
ours.
Now, Mars, I prithee, make us quick in work,   10
That we with smoking swords may march from
hence
To help our fielded° friends! Come, blow thy blast.
[They sound a parley.° Enter two SENATORS with
others, on the walls.]
Tullus Aufidius, is he within your walls?

1. SEN. No, nor a man that fears you less than
he —
That's lesser than a little. Hark, our drums   15
[Drum afar off.]
Are bringing forth our youth! We'll break our walls
Rather than they shall pound° us up. Our gates,

55–56. manifest housekeepers: obviously being good housewives. 56. spot: pattern.   63. O' my troth: by my truth.   65. con-firmed: determined.   71. mammocked: tore it to pieces. 74. crack: imp.   86. lies in: has had a baby.   92. Penelope: the wife of Ulysses. After the siege of Troy she waited for ten years for her husband to return to their home in Ithaca. To put off the persistent wooers who wished to marry her, she said that she must first complete a piece of weaving, which she unraveled each night.   95. cambric: fine linen. sensible: sensitive.

111–12. They . . . prevailing: they have every confidence that they will win.   122. at: in.
    Sc. iv: 9. larum: alarum, call to arms.   12. fielded: in the field. s.d., sound a parley: i.e., trumpet call summoning to a conference.   17. pound: shut up as in a pound.

Handwritten annotation at top: MARCIUS IS A GREAT FIGHTER, BUT A BAD GENERAL (PRIVATE) (PUBLIC)

Which yet seem shut, we have but pinned with
    rushes,°
They'll open of themselves. Hark you, far off!
                   [*Alarum° far off.*]
There is Aufidius. List what work he makes   20
Amongst your cloven° army.
MAR.   Oh, they are at it!
  LART. Their noise be our instruction. Ladders, ho!
       [*Enter the army of the Volsces.*]
  MAR. They fear us not, but issue forth their city.
Now put your shields before your hearts and fight
With hearts more proof° than shields. Advance,
    brave Titus.   25
They do disdain us much beyond our thoughts,°
Which makes me sweat with wrath. Come on, my
    fellows.
He that retires, I'll take him for a Volsce,
And he shall feel mine edge.
     [*Alarum. The* ROMANS *are beaten back to their*
          trenches. Re-enter MARCIUS, *cursing.*]
  MAR. All the contagion of the south° light on you,
You shames of Rome! You herd of —— Boils and
    plagues   31
Plaster you o'er, that you may be abhorred
Farther than seen, and one infect another
Against the wind a mile!° You souls of geese,
That bear the shapes of men, how have you run   35
From slaves that apes would beat! Pluto° and Hell!
All hurt behind, backs red, and faces pale
With flight and agued° fear! Mend,° and charge
    home,
Or, by the fires of Heaven,° I'll leave the foe   39
And make my wars on you. Look to 't. Come on.
If you'll stand fast, we'll beat them to their wives,
As they us to our trenches followed.
     [*Another alarum. The Volsces fly, and*
         MARCIUS *follows them to the gates.*]
So, now the gates are ope. Now prove good seconds.°
'Tis for the followers Fortune widens them,
Not for the flyers. Mark me, and do the like.   45
                  [*Enters the gates.*]
  1. SOL. Foolhardiness — not I.
  2. SOL.   Nor I. [MARCUS *is shut in.*]
  1. SOL. See, they have shut him in.
  ALL.   To the pot,° I warrant him.
                 [*Alarum continues.*]
         [*Re-enter* TITUS LARTIUS.]
  LART. What is become of Marcius?

Handwritten annotations: THEM FOLLOW LARTIUS — SINCE GOOD SENSE — BUT WON'T FOLLOW MARCIUS; SOLDIERS WON'T FOLLOW MARCIUS WITHIN GATES

  ALL.   Slain, sir, doubtless.
  1. SOL. Following the flyers at the very heels,
With them he enters, who, upon the sudden,   50
Clapped to their gates. He is himself alone,
To answer° all the city.
  LART.   O noble fellow!
Who sensibly° outdares his senseless sword,
And, when it bows, stands up! Thou art left,
    Marcius.
A carbuncle° entire, as big as thou art,   55
Were not so rich a jewel. Thou wast a soldier
Even to Cato's° wish, not fierce and terrible
Only in strokes; but, with thy grim looks and
The thunderlike percussion of thy sounds,
Thou madest thine enemies shake as if the world   60
Were feverous and did tremble.
     [*Re-enter* MARCIUS, *bleeding, assaulted by the*
       enemy.]
  1. SOL.   Look, sir.
  LART.   Oh, 'tis Marcius!
Let's fetch him off,° or make remain alike.°
       [*They fight, and all enter the city.*]

    SCENE V. *Within Corioli. A street.*

     [*Enter certain* ROMANS, *with spoils.*]
  1. ROM. This will I carry to Rome.
  2. ROM. And I this.
  3. ROM. A murrain° on 't! I took this for silver.
         [*Alarum contines still afar off.*]
   [*Enter* MARCIUS *and* TITUS LARTIUS *with a trumpet.*]
  MAR. See here these movers° that do prize their
    hours   5
At a cracked° drachma!° Cushions, leaden spoons,
Irons of a doit,° doublets that hangmen would
Bury with those that wore them,° these base slaves,
Ere yet the fight be done, pack up. Down with them!
And hark what noise the General makes! To him!
There is the man of my soul's hate, Aufidius,   11
Piercing our Romans. Then, valiant Titus, take
Convenient numbers to make good the city,
Whilst I, with those that have the spirit, will haste
To help Cominius.
  LART.   Worthy sir, thou bleed'st.   15
Thy exercise hath been too violent
For a second course° of fight.
  MAR.   Sir, praise me not,

---

18. **pinned ... rushes:** fastened only with rushes.   19 s.d.,
alarum: see l. 9.   21. **cloven:** cleft, cut-up.   25. **proof:** tough,
tested like the best armor.   26. **They ... thoughts:** they despise
us more than we can think.   30. **south:** A wind from the south
was believed to bring fog, sickness, and bad luck.   34. **Against
... mile:** even when you are a mile off and the wind is blowing
against you.   36. **Pluto:** god and ruler of the underworld.
38. **agued:** shivering. **Mend:** pull yourselves together.   39. **fires
of Heaven:** stars.   43. **seconds:** supports.   47. **To ... pot:** lit.,
melting-pot; i.e., it's all up with him.

52. **answer:** oppose.   53. **sensibly:** endowed with feeling.
55. **carbuncle:** The term was used for any precious stone of a
transparent red.   57. **Cato's:** Cato the Censor was famous for
his austere views on life and conduct.   62. **fetch ... off:**
rescue him. **alike:** i.e., bloody.
Sc. v: 3. **murrain:** plague.   5. **movers:** creatures, human only
because they move.   6. **cracked:** worthless. **drachma:** a Greek
coin.   7. **Irons ... doit:** ironmongery not worth half a cent.
7–8. **doublets ... them:** The clothes of the executed were the
hangman's perquisite. For doublets, see Pl. 8b and comment on
p. 93a.   17. **course:** round. See App. 5.

My work hath yet not warmed me.° Fare you well.
The blood I drop is rather physical°
Than dangerous to me. To Aufidius thus   20
I will appear, and fight.

LART.   Now the fair goddess Fortune
Fall deep in love with thee, and her great charms
Misguide thy opposers' swords! Bold gentleman,
Prosperity be thy page!°

MAR.   Thy friend no less
Than those she placeth highest! So farewell.   25

LART. Thou worthiest Marcius! [*Exit* MARCIUS.]
Go sound thy trumpet in the market place,
Call thither all the officers o' the town,
Where they shall know our mind. Away!

                         [*Exeunt.*]

WHILE MARCIUS CURSES HIS MEN,   IN VICTORY

SCENE VI. *Near the camp of* COMINIUS.

COMINIUS PRAISES HIS MEN IN DEFEAT

[*Enter* COMINIUS, *as it were in retire, with* SOLDIERS.]

COM. Breathe you,° my friends. Well fought. We
   are come off°
Like Romans, neither foolish in our stands
Nor cowardly in retire. Believe me, sirs,
We shall be charged again. Whiles we have struck,
By interims and conveying gusts° we have heard   5
The charges of our friends. Ye Roman gods,
Lead their successes as we wish our own,
That both our powers, with smiling fronts encoun-
   tering,
May give you thankful sacrifice!

[*Enter a* MESSENGER.]   Thy news?

MESS. The citizens of Corioli have issued,   10
And given to Lartius and to Marcius battle.
I saw our party to their trenches driven,
And then I came away.

COM.   Though thou speak'st truth,
Methinks thou speak'st not well. How long is 't
   since?

MESS. Above an hour, my lord.   15

COM. 'Tis not a mile, briefly° we heard their
   drums.
How couldst thou in a mile confound° an hour
And bring thy news so late?

MESS.   Spies of the Volsces
Held me in chase, that I was forced to wheel°
Three or four miles about. Else had I, sir,   20
Half an hour since brought my report.

                    [*Enter* MARCIUS.]

COM.   Who's yonder,

That does appear as he were flayed? Oh, gods!
He has the stamp° of Marcius, and I have
Beforetime seen him thus.

   MAR.   Come I too late?

COM. The shepherd knows not thunder from a
   tabor°   25
More than I know the sound of Marcius' tongue
From every meaner man.

   MAR.   Come I too late?

COM. Aye, if you come not in the blood of others,
But mantled in your own.

   MAR.   Oh, let me clip° ye
In arms as sound as when I wooed, in heart   30
As merry as when our nuptial day was done,
And tapers° burned to bedward!°

   COM.   Flower of warriors,
How is 't with Titus Lartius?

MAR. As with a man busied about decrees —
Condemning some to death, and some to exile;   35
Ransoming him or pitying, threatening the other;
Holding Corioli in the name of Rome,
Even like a fawning greyhound in the leash,
To let him slip at will.

   COM.   Where is that slave
Which told me they had beat you to your trenches?
Where is he? Call him hither.

   MAR.   Let him alone,   41
He did inform the truth. But for our gentlemen,
The common file° — a plague! Tribunes for
   them! —
The mouse ne'er shunned the cat as they did budge°
From rascals worse than they.

   COM.   But how prevailed you?   45

MAR. Will the time serve to tell? I do not think.
Where is the enemy? Are you lords o' the field?
If not, why cease you till you are so?

   COM.   Marcius,
We have at disadvantage fought, and did
Retire to win our purpose.   50

   MAR. How lies their battle?° Know you on which
   side
They have placed their men of trust?

   COM.   As I guess, Marcius,
Their bands i' the vaward° are the Antiates,
Of their best trust, o'er them Aufidius,
Their very heart of hope.°

   MAR.   I do beseech you,   55
By all the battles wherein we have fought,
By the blood we have shed together, by the vows

18. My . . . me: I have not yet warmed up to any work worth
praising.   19. physical: salutary, healthful. Bloodletting was a
cure in many complaints.   24. Prosperity . . . page: may good
fortune be your page (i.e., servant) to attend on you.

Sc. vi: 1. Breathe you: take breath, pause. are . . . off: have
left the fight.   5. By . . . gusts: at intervals borne to us by the
wind.   16. briefly: a short while since.   17. confound: waste.
19. wheel: make a detour.

23. stamp: impression, appearance.   25. tabor: small drum, an
instrument of peace. See Pl. 13d.   29. clip: embrace.   32. tapers:
candles. bedward: toward bed.   42–43. gentlemen . . . file: the
gentlemen who served as volunteers, usually in the commander's
own company, were the pick of the army. The *common file* — the
ordinary soldiers — were usually unwilling conscripts. See Gen.
Intro. p. 31a. file: list, roster. Cf. *Macb*, III.i.95.   44. budge:
shrink.   51. battle: army.   53. vaward: vanguard.   55. heart
of hope: greatest hope.

We have made to endure friends, that you directly
Set me against Aufidius and his Antiates.
And that you not delay the present but,   60
Filling the air with swords advanced° and darts,
We prove° this very hour.
    COM.   Though I could wish
You were conducted to a gentle bath,
And balms applied to you, yet dare I never
Deny your asking. Take your choice of those   65
That best can aid your action.
    MAR.   Those are they
That most are willing. If any such be here —
As it were sin to doubt — that love this painting°
Wherein you see me smeared, if any fear
Lesser his person than an ill report,   70
If any think brave death outweighs bad life
And that his country's dearer than himself,
Let him alone, or so many so minded,
Wave thus, to express his disposition,
And follow Marcius.   75
    [*They all shout, and wave their swords, take him
       up in their arms, and cast up their caps.*]
Oh, me alone! Make you a sword of me?°
If these shows be not outward, which of you
But is four Volsces? None of you but is
Able to bear against the great Aufidius
A shield as hard as his. A certain number,   80
Though thanks to all, must I select from all. The rest
Shall bear the business in some other fight,
As cause will be obeyed.° Please you to march,
And four shall quickly draw out my command,°
Which men are best inclined.
    COM.   March on, my fellows.   85
Make good this ostentation° and you shall
Divide° in all with us.   [*Exeunt.*]

SCENE VII. *The gates of Corioli.*

[*TITUS LARTIUS, having set a guard upon Corioli,
going with drum and trumpet toward* COMINIUS
and CAIUS MARCIUS, *enters with a* LIEUTENANT,
other SOLDIERS, *and a* SCOUT.]
    LART. So, let the ports° be guarded. Keep your
       duties

As I have set them down. If I do send, dispatch
Those centuries° to our aid. The rest will serve
For a short holding. If we lose the field,
We cannot keep the town.
    LIEU.   Fear not our care, sir.   5
    LART. Hence, and shut your gates upon 's.
Our guider, come, to the Roman camp conduct us.
                              [*Exeunt.*]

SCENE VIII. *A field of battle between the Roman and the Volscian camps.*

[*Alarum as in battle. Enter, from opposite sides,
MARCIUS and AUFIDIUS.*]
    MAR. I'll fight with none but thee, for I do hate
       thee
Worse than a promise-breaker.
    AUF.   We hate alike.
Not Afric owns a serpent I abhor
More than thy fame and envy. Fix thy foot.
    MAR. Let the first budger° die the other's slave,   5
And the gods doom him after!
    AUF.   If I fly, Marcius,
Holloa° me like a hare.
    MAR.   Within these three hours, Tullus,
Alone I fought in your Corioli walls
And made what work I pleased. 'Tis not my blood
Wherein thou seest me masked. For thy revenge   10
Wrench up° thy power to the highest.
    AUF.   Wert thou the Hector
That was the whip of your bragged progeny,°
Thou shouldst not 'scape me here.
[*They fight, and certain Volsces come in the aid of
AUFIDIUS. MARCIUS fights till they be driven in
breathless.*]
Officious, and not valiant, you have shamed me   14
In your condemnèd seconds.°   [*Exeunt.*]

SCENE IX. *The Roman camp.*

[*Flourish.° Alarum. A retreat is sounded. Enter
from one side,* COMINIUS *with the* ROMANS; *from the
other side,* MARCIUS, *with his arm in a scarf.*]
    COM. If I should tell thee o'er° this thy day's work,
Thou'lt not believe thy deeds. But I'll report it
Where Senators shall mingle tears with smiles;
Where great patricians shall attend,° and shrug,°

---

61. advanced: raised.   **62. prove:** try our luck.   **68. painting:**
i.e., blood.   **76. Oh . . . me:** do you wave me aloft as if I were a
sword? There has been much dispute about this line. It is to
be noted that the main difficulties in this play occur in the
speeches of Marcius when he is under emotional stress. It was
presumably Shakespeare's intention to show him as a man who
became incoherent at moments of excitement; the difficulties,
therefore, are not due to any corruption of the text but to
Marcius' emotion. See later III.i.102; III.iii.68.   **83. As . . .
obeyed:** as occasion demands.   **84. And . . . command:** and four
officers shall quickly select the volunteers who are to go with me.
86. Make . . . ostentation: let this show of eagerness be made
good in battle.   **87. Divide:** i.e., the loot.
    Sc. vii: 1. ports: gates.

3. centuries: companies of a hundred men each.
    Sc. viii: 5. budger: one who gives way.   **7. Holloa:** shout at,
to make me run faster.   **11. Wrench up:** as with a lever or a jack.
11–12. Hector . . . progeny: that Hector who scourged your
ancestors, about whom you boasted so much. (Either Shakespeare or Aufidius is in error, for Hector was the champion of the
Trojans from whom the Romans claimed to be descended.)
15. condemned seconds: "damned help."
    Sc. ix: s.d., Flourish: trumpet fanfare.   **1. tell . . . o'er:** re-
peat to you.   **4. attend:** listen. **shrug:** i.e., doubt.

I' the end admire;° where ladies shall be frighted   5
And, gladly quaked,° hear more; where the dull
    Tribunes
That, with the fusty plebeians, hate thine honors
Shall say against their hearts° "We thank the gods
Our Rome hath such a soldier."
Yet camest thou to a morsel of this feast,   10
Having fully dined before.

    [*Enter* TITUS LARTIUS, *with his power, from the
        pursuit.*]
    LART.   O General,
Here is the steed, we the caparison.°
Hadst thou beheld——
    MAR.   Pray now, no more. My mother,
Who has a charter to extol her blood,°
When she does praise me grieves me. I have done
As you have done, that's what I can — induced   16
As you have been, that's for my country.
He that has but effected his goodwill°
Hath overta'en mine act.
    COM.   You shall not be
The grave of your deserving,° Rome must know   20
The value of her own. 'Twere a concealment
Worse than a theft, no less than a traducement,°
To hide your doings and to silence that
Which, to the spire and top of praises vouched,°
Would seem but modest. Therefore I beseech you —
In sign of what you are, not to reward   26
What you have done — before our army hear me.
    MAR. I have some wounds upon me, and they
        smart
To hear themselves remembered.
    COM.   Should they not,
Well might they fester 'gainst ingratitude,   30
And tent° themselves with death. Of all the horses,
Whereof we have ta'en good and good store, of all
The treasure in this field achieved and city,
We render you the tenth, to be ta'en forth
Before the common distribution, at   35
Your only° choice.
    MAR.   I thank you, General,
But cannot make my heart consent to take
A bribe to pay my sword. I do refuse it,
And stand upon my common part with those
That have beheld the doing.°   40

    [*A long flourish. They all cry* "Marcius! Marcius!"
cast up their caps and lances. COMINIUS *and* LARTIUS
                       stand bare.°]
    MAR. May° these same instruments, which you
        profane,
Never sound more! When drums and trumpets shall
I' the field prove flatterers, let Courts and cities be
Made all of false-faced soothing!°
When steel grows soft as the parasite's silk,   45
Let him be made a coverture for the wars!
No more, I say! For that I have not washed
My nose that bled, or foiled° some debile° wretch,
Which without note here's many else have done,
You shout me forth   50
In acclamations hyperbolical,
As if I loved my little should be dieted
In praises sauced with lies.°
    COM.   Too modest are you,
More cruel to your good report than grateful
To us that give you truly. By your patience,   55
If 'gainst yourself you be incensed, we'll put you,
Like one that means his proper° harm, in manacles,
Then reason safely with you. Therefore be it known,
As to us, to all the world, that Caius Marcius   59
Wears this war's garland.° In token of the which,
My noble steed, known to the camp, I give him,
With all his trim belonging.° And from this time,
For what he did before Corioli, call him,
With all the applause and clamor of the host,
CAIUS MARCIUS CORIOLANUS. Bear   65
The addition° nobly ever!
    [*Flourish. Trumpets sound, and drums.*]

5. admire: be overwhelmed with astonishment. 6. quaked: made to tremble. 8. against ... hearts: although they dislike you. 12. Here ... caparison: Coriolanus is the horse himself, the rest of us merely its coverings. caparison: a long saddlecloth used on ceremonial occasions. 14. charter ... blood: special privilege to praise her own child. 18. effected ... will: done his best. 20. grave ... deserving: your deserts shall not be buried with you for lack of recognition. 22. traducement: slander. 24. spire ... vouched: publicly declared as high as the tops of church spires. 31. tent: A tent was a roll of linen inserted into a wound to cleanse it; "to tent" is thus to cleanse. So, Cominius says, Marcius' wounds might be expected to fester and bring death if his fellow soldiers should neglect to give him the praises due to him. 36. only: sole. 39–40. stand ... doing: I will take my share with everyone else who was in the action. 40 s.d., bare: bareheaded, as a mark of honor. See App. 7. 41–46. May ... wars: a difficult and much disputed passage, much emended by editors. F1 reads: "May these same Instruments, which you prophane,/Never sound more: when Drums and Trumpets shall/I' th' field prove flatterers, let Courts and Cities be/Made all of false-fac'd soothing:/When Steele grows soft, as the Parasites Silke,/Let him be made an Overture for th' Warres." The main difficulty is in the word "overture," which elsewhere in Shakespeare means discovery, exposure, or proposal (see *Lear*, III.vii.89; *W Tale*, II.i.172; *T Night*, I.v.224). Editors have therefore substituted "coverture," which means "covering" (Cf. *M Ado*, III.i.30), but it does not greatly help the sense. The F1 reading can however be interpreted as it stands, for the word "overture" in Elizabethan speech sometimes means "overthrower." Coriolanus is weak from his wounds and, as often when in a state of high emotion, he becomes incoherent (see I.vi.76; III.iii.68). He means "when drums and trumpets are debased by being used for flattery (and not to sound charges), then Courts and cities (where peaceful parasites live) will naturally be full of smooth falsehood. When steel (the soldiers' covering) grows as soft as the courtier's silk, then the courtier overthrows the honor of war." More briefly, his meaning is: "When soldiers turn flatterers, they behave like civilians and bring dishonor on war." 44. false-faced soothing: deceitful flattery. 48. foiled: overthrown. debile: feeble. 52–53. my ... lies: my small accomplishment should be given a fancy diet of lies. 57. proper: own. 60. Wears ... garland: i.e., carries the chief honor of this war. 62. trim belonging: equipment and harness in fine condition. 66. addition: title of honor added to a man's name, and so honor.

ALL. Caius Marcius Coriolanus!
COR.   I will go wash,
And when my face is fair,° you shall perceive
Whether I blush or no. Howbeit, I thank you.   70
I mean to stride your steed, and at all times
To undercrest your good addition
To the fairness of my power.°
COR.   So, to our tent,
Where ere we do repose us we will write
To Rome of our success. You, Titus Lartius,   75
Must to Corioli back. Send us to Rome
The best,° with whom we may articulate°
For their own good and ours.
LART.   I shall, my lord.
COR. The gods begin to mock me. I, that now
Refused most princely gifts, am bound to beg   80
Of my lord General.
COM.   Take 't, 'tis yours. What is 't?
COR. I sometime lay° here in Corioli
At a poor man's house, he used me kindly.
He cried to me, I saw him prisoner,
But then Aufidius was within my view   85
And wrath o'erwhelmed my pity. I request you
To give my poor host freedom.
COM.   Oh, well begged!
Were he the butcher of my son, he should
Be free as is the wind. Deliver him, Titus.
LART. Marcius, his name?
COR.   By Jupiter, forgot.   90
I am weary, yea, my memory is tired.
Have we no wine here?
COM.   Go we to our tent.
The blood upon your visage dries, 'tis time
It should be looked to. Come.   [*Exeunt.*]

SCENE X. *The camp of the Volsces.*

[*A flourish. Cornets. Enter* TULLUS AUFIDIUS, *bloody,
with two or three* SOLDIERS.]
AUF. The town is ta'en!
I. SOL. 'Twill be delivered back on good condition.°
AUF. Condition!
I would I were a Roman, for I cannot,
Being a Volsce, be that I am. Condition!   5
What good condition can a treaty find
I' the part that is at mercy?° Five times, Marcius,
I have fought with thee, so often hast thou beat me,
And wouldst do so, I think, should we encounter
As often as we eat. By the elements,°   10

If e'er again I meet him beard to beard,
He's mine, or I am his. Mine emulation°
Hath not that honor in 't it had, for where
I thought to crush him in an equal force,
True sword to sword, I'll potch° at him some way,
Or wrath or craft may get him.
I. SOL.   He's the Devil.   16
AUF. Bolder, though not so subtle. My valor's
poisoned
With only suffering stain by him, for him
Shall fly out of itself. Nor sleep nor sanctuary,
Being naked, sick, nor fane° nor Capitol,   20
The prayers of priests nor times of sacrifice,
Embarquements° all of fury, shall lift up
Their rotten privilege and custom 'gainst
My hate to Marcius. Where I find him, were it
At home, upon my brother's guard,° even there,   25
Against the hospitable canon,° would I
Wash my fierce hand in 's heart. Go you to the city.
Learn how 'tis held, and what they are that must
Be hostages for Rome.
I. SOL.   Will not you go?
AUF. I am attended° at the cypress grove. I pray
you —   30
'Tis south the city mills — bring me word thither
How the world goes, that to the pace of it
I may spur on my journey.
I. SOL.   I shall, sir.   [*Exeunt.*]

Act II

SCENE I. *Rome. A public place.*

[*Enter* MENENIUS, *with the two* TRIBUNES *of the
people,* SICINIUS *and* BRUTUS.]
MEN. The augurer° tells me we shall have news
tonight.
BRU. Good or bad?
MEN. Not according to the prayer of the people,
for they love not Marcius.   5
SIC. Nature teaches beasts to know their friends.
MEN. Pray you, who does the wolf love?
SIC. The lamb.
MEN. Aye, to devour him, as the hungry plebeians would the noble Marcius.   11
BRU. He's a lamb indeed, that baas like a bear.
MEN. He's a bear indeed, that lives like a lamb.

---

69. fair: clean. 72–73. undercrest . . . power: I will wear this
good honor as a crest as far as I possibly can. 77. best: i.e.,
chief men of Corioli. articulate: draw up articles of peace.
82. lay: lodged.
    Sc. x: 2. condition: terms. 7. I' . . . mercy: on the beaten
side. 10. elements: sky and sea.

12. emulation: jealousy. 15. potch: poke at. 20. fane:
temple. 22. Embarquements: things that hinder. 25. upon
. . . guard: with my brother guarding him. 26. hospitable
canon: law of hospitality. 30. attended: waited for.
    Act II, Sc. i: 1. augurer: official who foretold future events
from various omens. Cf. *Caesar,* II.ii.37–40.

You two are old men. Tell me one thing that I shall ask you.

BOTH. Well, sir.   17

MEN. In what enormity is Marcius poor in, that you two have not in abundance?

BRU. He's poor in no one fault, but stored with all.

SIC. Especially in pride.   22

BRU. And topping all others in boasting.

MEN. This is strange now. Do you two know how you are censured° here in the city, I mean of us o' the right-hand file?° Do you?   26

BOTH. Why, how are we censured?

MEN. Because you talk of pride now — will you not be angry?

BOTH. Well, well, sir, well.   30

MEN. Why, 'tis no great matter, for a very little thief of occasion° will rob you of a great deal of patience. Give your dispositions the reins,° and be angry at your pleasures — at the least, if you take it as a pleasure to you in being so. You blame Marcius for being proud?

BRU. We do it not alone, sir.   37

MEN. I know you can do very little alone, for your helps are many,° or else your actions would grow wondrous single.° Your abilities are too infantlike for doing much alone. You talk of pride. Oh, that you could turn your eyes toward the napes of your necks and make but an interior survey of your good selves! Oh, that you could!   44

BOTH. What then, sir?

MEN. Why, then you should discover a brace of unmeriting,° proud, violent, testy magistrates, alias fools, as any in Rome.   49

SIC. Menenius, you are known well enough too.

MEN. I am known to be a humorous° patrician, and one that loves a cup of hot wine with not a drop of allaying Tiber° in 't; said to be something imperfect in favoring the first complaint,° hasty and tinderlike° upon too trivial motion;° one that   55
converses more with the buttock of the night than with the forehead of the morning. What I think I utter, and spend my malice in my breath. Meeting two such wealsmen° as you are — I cannot call you Lycurguses° — if the drink you give me touch my   60
palate adversely, I make a crooked face at it. I can't say your Worships have delivered the matter well when I find the ass in compound with the major part

of your syllables.° And though I must be content to bear with those that say you are reverend grave   66
men, yet they lie deadly that tell you you have good faces. If you see this in the map of my microcosm,° follows it that I am known well enough too? What harm can your bisson conspectuities° glean out of this character, if I be known well enough too?   72

BRU. Come, sir, come, we know you well enough.

MEN. You know neither me, yourselves, nor anything. You are ambitious for poor knaves' caps and legs.° You wear out a good wholesome forenoon in hearing a cause between an orange wife and a fosset-seller,° and then rejourn° the controversy of three-pence to a second day of audience. When you   80
are hearing a matter between party and party, if you chance to be pinched with the colic, you make faces like mummers;° set up the bloody flag against° all patience; and in roaring for a chamber pot, dismiss the controversy bleeding,° the more entangled by your hearing. All the peace you make in their cause is calling both the parties knaves. You are a pair of strange ones.   89

BRU. Come, come, you are well understood to be a perfecter giber° for the table than a necessary bencher° in the Capitol.

MEN. Our very priests must become mockers if they shall encounter such ridiculous subjects as   94
you are. When you speak best unto the purpose, it is not worth the wagging of your beards, and your beards deserve not so honorable a grave as to stuff a botcher's° cushion or to be entombed in an ass's packsaddle. Yet you must be saying Marcius is proud, who, in a cheap estimation,° is worth all   101
your predecessors since Deucalion,° though peradventure some of the best of 'em were hereditary hangmen. Godden° to your Worships. More of your conversation would infect my brain, being the herdsmen of the beastly plebeians. I will be bold to take my leave of you.   [BRUTUS and SICINIUS go aside.]
[Enter VOLUMNIA, VIRGILIA, and VALERIA.] How now, my as fair as noble ladies — and the moon, were she

64–65. ass . . . syllables: there is "ass" (stupidity) in everything you say.   68. map . . . microcosm: i.e., face. Man was often regarded as a little universe (*microcosm*) which reproduces all the qualities of the great universe (macrocosm). The idea has already been elaborately worked out by Menenius in the fable of the belly. See I.i.99. Cf. *II Hen IV*, IV.iii.116.   71. bisson conspectuities: blear-eyed visions.   75–76. poor . . . legs: i.e., outward marks of respect. See App. 7.   78–79. orange . . . seller: a woman who sells oranges and a seller of wooden faucets for barrels, whose disputes are not of great importance.   79. rejourn: adjourn.   83. mummers: dancers in mumming dances, where the dancers disguised themselves and performed various rowdy antics.   set . . . against: declared war on — a red flag being a sign of defiance.   86. bleeding: unhealed.   91. perfecter giber: better at making jokes.   92. bencher: Senator.   99. botcher: a mender of torn clothes.   101. cheap estimation: at a low valuation.   102. Deucalion: in classical legend Deucalion (like Noah in Genesis) survived the great flood that wiped out mankind.   104. Godden: good evening.

25. censured: judged, estimated.   26. right-hand file: i.e., by those of the Right, the patricians.   31–32. very . . . occasion: a very slight cause, like a thief.   33. Give . . . reins: let your feelings take control.   39. helps . . . many: i.e., you have your crowd to back you up.   40. single: feeble.   48. unmeriting: undeserving.   51. humorous: whimsical.   53. allaying Tiber: Tiber water to dilute it.   53–54. something . . . complaint: rather too prone not to listen to both sides of the case.   55. tinderlike: i.e., catching fire easily.   motion: impulse.   59. wealsmen: statesmen.   60. Lycurguses: Lycurgus, who drew up the constitution and laws of Sparta, was regarded as a man of godlike wisdom.

...bler — whither do you follow your   109

...le Menenius, my boy Marcius ap-
...t love of Juno, let's go.
...cius coming home!

...aye, worthy Menenius, and with most prosperous approbation.°

MEN. Take my cap, Jupiter,° and I thank thee.
Hoo! Marcius coming home?   116

VIR. & VAL. Nay, 'tis true.

VOL. Look, here's a letter from him. The state°
hath another, his wife another, and I think there's
one at home for you.   120

MEN. I will make my very house reel tonight. A
letter for me?

VIR. Yes, certain — there's a letter for you, I
saw 't.   124

MEN. A letter for me! It gives me an estate of
seven years' health, in which time I will make a lip°
at the physician. The most sovereign prescription in
Galen° is but empiricutic,° and, to this preservative,° of no better report than a horse drench.°
Is he not wounded? He was wont to come home
wounded.   131

VIR. Oh, no, no, no.

VOL. Oh, he is wounded, I thank the gods for 't.

MEN. So do I too, if it be not too much. Brings a'°
victory in his pocket? The wounds become him.

VOL. On 's brows. Menenius, he comes the   137
third time home with the oaken garland.

MEN. Has he disciplined° Aufidius soundly?

VOL. Titus Lartius writes they fought together,
but Aufidius got off.   141

MEN. And 'twas time for him too, I'll warrant him
that. An° he had stayed by him, I would not have
been so fidiused° for all the chests in Corioli and the
gold that's in them. Is the Senate possessed° of
this?   146

VOL. Good ladies, let's go. Yes, yes, yes, the Senate
has letters from the General, wherein he gives my
son the whole name° of the war. He hath in this
action outdone his former deeds doubly.   151

VAL. In troth, there's wondrous things spoke of
him.

MEN. Wondrous! Aye, I warrant you, and not
without his true purchasing.°   155

VIR. The gods grant them true!

VOL. True! Pow, wow.°

MEN. True! I'll be sworn they are true. Where is
he wounded? [*To the* TRIBUNES] God save your
good Worships! Marcius is coming home. He has
more cause to be proud. Where is he wounded?   162

VOL. I' the shoulder and i' the left arm. There will
be large cicatrices° to show the people when he shall
stand for his place.° He received in the repulse of
Tarquin seven hurts i' the body.   166

MEN. One i' the neck, and two i' the thigh —
there's nine that I know.

VOL. He had, before this last expedition, twenty-
five wounds upon him.

MEN. Now it's twenty-seven. Every gash was an
enemy's grave. [*A shout and flourish.*] Hark! The
trumpets.   173

VOL. These are the ushers° of Marcius. Before
him he carries noise, and behind him he leaves tears.
Death, that dark spirit, in 's nervy° arm doth lie,
Which, being advanced,° declines,° and then men
die.   178

[*A sennet.° Trumpets sound. Enter* COMINIUS *and*
TITUS LARTIUS; *between them,* CORIOLANUS, *crowned
with an oaken garland; with* CAPTAINS *and* SOLDIERS,
and a HERALD.]

HER. Know, Rome, that all alone Marcius did fight
Within Corioli gates, where he hath won,   180
With fame, a name to Caius Marcius — these
In honor follows Coriolanus.°
Welcome to Rome, renowned Coriolanus!
                                        [*Flourish.*]

ALL. Welcome to Rome, renownèd Coriolanus!

COR. No more of this, it does offend my heart.
Pray now, no more.

COM.   Look, sir, your mother!

COR.   Oh,
You have, I know, petitioned all the gods   187
For my prosperity!   [*Kneels.*]

VOL.   Nay, my good soldier, up.
My gentle Marcius, worthy Caius, and
By deed-achieving honor° newly named —   190
What is it? — Coriolanus must I call thee? ——
But, oh, thy wife!

COR.   My gracious silence, hail!
Wouldst thou have laughed had I come coffined
home,
That weep'st to see me triumph? Ah, my dear,°
Such eyes the widows in Corioli wear,   195
And mothers that lack sons.

---

114. **prosperous approbation:** highest fame.   115. **Take . . .
Jupiter:** i.e., he throws his cap into the air. Jupiter is the god of
the sky. The characters in Shakespeare's *Coriolanus* were dressed
in Elizabethan and not Roman costumes.   118. **state:** the
Government; i.e., the Senate.   126. **lip:** face.   128. **Galen:** a
Roman writer on medical matters who in Shakespeare's time was
regarded as the supreme authority. He lived in the second century A.D., several centuries after Coriolanus' time. **empiricutic:**
empirical, mere quackery.   128–29. **to . . . preservative:** compared with this cordial.   129. **horse drench:** purge given to a
horse, a crude form of medicine.   135. **a':** he.   139. **disciplined:**
beaten.   143. **An:** if.   144. **fidiused:** i.e., given the treatment
which Aufidius received.   145. **possessed:** informed.   150. **name:**
glory.   155. **true purchasing:** honest acquisition.

157. **Pow, wow:** a phrase of strong contempt.   164. **cicatrices:**
scars.   165. **stand . . . place:** be a candidate for election.
174. **ushers:** escorts.   177. **nervy:** sinewy.   178. **advanced:**
raised. **declines:** falls. **s.d., sennet:** a few notes on the trumpet.
181–82. **these . . . Coriolanus:** *Coriolanus* is added as an honorable addition to *Caius Marcius*.   190. **deed-achieving honor:**
honor which comes from heroic achievement.   194. **my dear:**
In Shakespeare's time this was a very strong term of affection.

MEN.   Now the gods crown thee!

COR. And live you yet? [*To* VALERIA] O my sweet
  lady, pardon.

VOL. I know not where to turn. Oh, welcome
  home.
And welcome, General. And ye're welcome all.

   MEN. A hundred thousand welcomes. I could
    weep,   200
And I could laugh, I am light and heavy. Welcome.
A curse begin at very root on 's heart
That is not glad to see thee! You are three
That Rome should dote on. Yet, by the faith of men,
We have some old crab trees° here at home that will
  not   205
Be grafted to your relish.° Yet welcome, warriors.
We call a nettle but a nettle, and
The faults of fools but folly.

   COM.   Ever right.

   COR. Menenius, ever, ever.

   HER. Give way there, and go on.

   COR. [*To* VOLUMNIA *and* VIRGILIA] Your hand, and
  yours.   210
Ere in our own house I do shade my head,
The good patricians must be visited,
From whom I have received not only greetings,
But with them change° of honors.

   VOL.   I have lived
To see inherited my very wishes   215
And the buildings of my fancy.° Only
There's one thing wanting, which I doubt not but
Our Rome will cast upon thee.

   COR.   Know, good Mother,
I had rather be their servant in my way
Than sway° with them in theirs.

   COM.   On, to the Capitol! 220
  [*Flourish. Cornets. Exeunt in state, as before.*]
    [BRUTUS *and* SICINIUS *come forward.*]

   BRU. All tongues speak of him, and the bleared
  sights
Are spectacled° to see him. Your prattling nurse
Into a rapture° lets her baby cry
While she chats° him. The kitchen malkin° pins
Her richest lockram° 'bout her reechy° neck, 225
Clambering the walls to eye him. Stalls, bulks,° win-
  dows,
Are smothered up, leads° filled and ridges horsed
With variable complexions,° all agreeing
In earnestness to see him. Seld-shown flamens°

Do press among the popular throngs, and puff 230
To win a vulgar station.° Our veiled dames
Commit the war of white and damask in
Their nicely gawded cheeks to the wanton spoil
Of Phoebus' burning kisses.° Such a pother,
As if that whatsoever god who leads him   235
Were slyly crept into his human powers,
And gave him graceful posture.

   SIC.   On the sudden
I warrant him Consul.

   BRU.   Then our office may,
During his power, go sleep.

   SIC. He cannot temperately transport his honors
From where he should begin and end, but will 241
Lose those he hath won.

   BRU.   In that there's comfort.

   SIC.   Doubt not
The commoners, for whom we stand, but they
Upon their ancient malice will forget°
With the least cause these his new honors, which
That he will give them make I as little question 246
As he is proud to do 't.

   BRU.   I heard him swear,
Were he to stand for Consul, never would he
Appear i' the market place, nor on him put
The napless vesture of humility,°   250
Nor showing, as the manner is, his wounds
To the people, beg their stinking breaths.

   SIC.   'Tis right.

   BRU. It was his word. Oh, he would miss it rather
Than carry it but by the suit of the gentry° to him,
And the desire of the nobles.

   SIC.   I wish no better 255
Than have him hold that purpose and to put it
In execution.

   BRU.   'Tis most like he will.

   SIC. It shall be to him then, as our good wills.°
A sure destruction.

   BRU.   So it must fall out
To him or our authorities. For an end,°   260
We must suggest° the people in what hatred

---

205. **crab trees:** crab-apple trees. 206. **to ... relish:** to suit your taste. 214. **change:** addition, variety. 216. **buildings ... fancy:** my castles in the air. 220. **sway:** rule. 221–22. **bleared ... spectacled:** the shortsighted put on spectacles. 223. **rapture:** fit. 224. **chats:** chatters about. **malkin:** slut. 225. **lockram:** linen collar. **reechy:** dirty. 226. **bulks:** wooden projections in front of a shop. 227. **leads:** i.e., rooftops covered with lead. 227–28. **ridges ... complexions:** the ridges of the roofs thronged with crowds of all sorts sitting astride. Cf. the account of the crowd at Queen Elizabeth's funeral in App. 16. 229. **Seld-shown flamens:** priests seldom seen in public.

231. **vulgar station:** place in the crowd. 231–34. **Our ... kisses:** our veiled ladies of fashion risk their dainty pink and white cheeks in the hot sunshine. Cf. *AYLI*, I.iii.114,n. **nicely gawded:** carefully colored. **Phoebus:** the sun god. 242–44. **Doubt ... forget:** without doubt the common people, whom we represent, because of their ancient hatred for him will forget. 250. **napless ... humility:** the threadbare toga which shows humility. According to North's *Plutarch* "the custom of Rome was at that time that such as did sue for any office should for certain days before be in the market place only with a poor gown on their backs, and without any coat underneath, to pray the citizens to remember them at the day of election; which was thus devised either to move the people the more by requesting them in such humble apparel, or else because they might show them their wounds they had gotten in the wars in the service of the commonwealth, as manifest marks and testimonies of their valiantness." 254. **but ... gentry:** otherwise than at the request of the gentlemen. 258. **good wills:** best efforts. 260. **For an end:** to bring matters to a head. 261. **suggest:** prompt.

He still° hath held them; that to 's power he would
Have made them mules,° silenced their pleaders and
Dispropertied° their freedoms, holding them,
In human action and capacity,   265
Of no more soul nor fitness for the world
Than camels in the war, who have their provand°
Only for bearing burdens, and sore blows
For sinking under them.

SIC.   This, as you say, suggested
At some time when his soaring insolence   270
Shall touch the people — which time shall not want,
If he be put upon 't,° and that's as easy
As to set dogs on sheep — will be his fire
To kindle their dry stubble, and their blaze
Shall darken him forever.

           [*Enter a* MESSENGER.]

BRU.   What's the matter?   275
MESS. You are sent for to the Capitol. 'Tis thought
That Marcius shall be Consul.
I have seen the dumb men throng to see him and
The blind to hear him speak. Matrons flung gloves,
Ladies and maids their scarfs and handkerchers,
Upon him as he passed. The nobles bended,   281
As to Jove's statue, and the commons made
A shower and thunder with their caps and shouts.
I never saw the like.

BRU.   Let's to the Capitol,
And carry with us ears and eyes for the time,°   285
But hearts for the event.°

SIC.   Have with you.°   [*Exeunt.*]

SCENE II. *The same. The Capitol.*

[*Enter two* OFFICERS, *to lay cushions.*]

1. OFF. Come, come, they are almost here. How
many stand for consulships?

2. OFF. Three, they say. But 'tis thought of everyone Coriolanus will carry it.   4

1. OFF. That's a brave fellow, but he's vengeance°
proud, and loves not the common people.

2. OFF. Faith, there have been many great men
that have flattered the people who ne'er loved them,
and there be many that they have loved they   10
know not wherefore. So that if they love they know
not why, they hate upon no better a ground. Therefore for Coriolanus neither to care whether they love
or hate him manifests the true knowledge he has in
their disposition, and out of his noble carelessness
lets them plainly see 't.   17

1. OFF. If he did not care whether he had their
love or no, he waved indifferently° 'twixt doing

them neither good nor harm. But he seeks their hate
with greater devotion than they can render it him,
and leaves nothing undone that may fully discover
him their opposite.° Now, to seem to affect° the
malice and displeasure of the people is as bad as that
which he dislikes, to flatter them for their love.   26

2. OFF. He hath deserved worthily of his country.
And his ascent is not by such easy degrees as those
who, having been supple° and courteous to the people, bonneted,° without any further deed to have
them° at all into their estimation and report.   31
But he hath so planted his honors in their eyes and
his actions in their hearts that for their tongues to be
silent and not confess so much were a kind of ungrateful injury. To report otherwise were a malice
that, giving itself the lie, would pluck reproof and
rebuke from every ear that heard it.   38

1. OFF. No more of him, he's a worthy man. Make
way, they are coming.

[*A sennet. Enter, with* LICTORS *before them,* COMIN-
IUS *the Consul,* MENENIUS, CORIOLANUS, SENATORS,
SICINIUS *and* BRUTUS. *The* SENATORS *take
their places; the* TRIBUNES *take their
places by themselves.* CORIOLANUS
stands.]

MEN. Having determined of° the Volsces and
To send for Titus Lartius, it remains,
As the main point of this our after-meeting,
To gratify° his noble service that
Hath thus stood for his country. Therefore please
     you,   45
Most reverend and grave elders, to desire
The present Consul, and last General
In our well-found° successes, to report
A little of that worthy work performed
By Caius Marcius Coriolanus, whom   50
We met here both to thank and to remember
With honors like himself.

1. SEN.   Speak, good Cominius.
Leave nothing out for length, and make us think
Rather our state's defective for requital
Than we to stretch it out.° [*To the* TRIBUNES] Mas-
     ters o' the people,   55
We do request your kindest ears, and after,
Your loving motion toward the common body,
To yield what passes here.°

SIC.   We are convented
Upon a pleasing treaty,° and have hearts

---

262. still: always.   263. mules: beasts of burden.   264. Dis-
propertied: dispossessed them of.   267. provand: fodder.
272. put upon 't: moved to do it.   285. for ... time: for the
present.   286. for ... event: for the future. Have ... you:
agreed.
     Sc. ii: 5. vengeance: with a vengeance.   19. waved indiffer-
ently: wavered impartially.

23–24. discover ... opposite: reveal him as their enemy.   24. affect: desire.   29. supple: obsequious.   30. bonneted: with their
hats in their hands. See App. 7.   30–31. have them: got themselves.   41. determined of: made our decisions concerning.
44. gratify: give a token of gratitude to, reward.   48. well-
found: fortunate.   53–55. make ... out: rather make us think
that Rome lacks the means to reward him properly than that we
should be unwilling to be generous.   57–58. Your ... here: your
friendly influence with the common body to agree to what is
passed here.   58–59. We ... treaty: we have met to discuss a
pleasant motion.

Inclinable to honor and advance   60
The theme of our assembly.

    BRU.   Which the rather
We shall be blessed° to do if he remember
A kinder value of the people than
He hath hereto prized them at.

    MEN.   That's off,° that's off,
I would you rather had been silent. Please you   65
To hear Cominius speak?

    BRU.   Most willingly.
But yet my caution was more pertinent
Than the rebuke you give it.

    MEN.   He loves your people,
But tie him not to be their bedfellow.
Worthy Cominius, speak. [CORIOLANUS *offers to go
    away.*] Nay, keep your place.   70

    1. SEN. Sit, Coriolanus, never shame to hear
What you have nobly done.

    COR.   Your Honors' pardon.
I had rather have my wounds to heal again
Than hear say how I got them.

    BRU.   Sir, I hope
My words disbenched° you not.

    COR.   No, sir. Yet oft   75
When blows have made me stay, I fled from words.
You soothed not,° therefore hurt not. But your
    people,
I love them as they weigh.°

    MEN.   Pray now, sit down.

    COR. I had rather have one scratch my head i' the
    sun
When the alarum were struck than idly sit   80
To hear my nothings monstered.°   [*Exit.*]

    MEN.   Masters of the people,
Your multiplying spawn how can he flatter —
That's thousand to one good one° — when you now
    see
He had rather venture all his limbs for honor   84
Than one on 's° ears to hear it? Proceed, Cominius.

    COM. I shall lack voice. The deeds of Coriolanus
Should not be uttered feebly. It is held
That valor is the chiefest virtue and
Most dignifies the haver. If it be,
The man I speak of cannot in the world   90
Be singly counterpoised.° At sixteen years,
When Tarquin made a head for° Rome, he fought
Beyond the mark of others.° Our then dictator,
Whom with all praise I point at, saw him fight
When with his Amazonian chin° he drove   95

62. blessed: happy.   64. That's off: leave that out.   75. dis-
benched: caused you to leave your seat.   77. soothed not: did
not flatter.   78. as . . . weigh: i.e., very lightly.   81. monstered: exaggerated.   83. That's . . . one: in which only one in a
thousand is any good.   85. one on 's: one of his.   91. singly
counterpoised: counterbalanced by any single man.   92. made
. . . for: raised an army against.   93. Beyond . . . others: beyond anything that others effected.   95. Amazonian chin:
beardless like an Amazon. The Amazons were the women soldiers
of Scythia (South Russia).

The bristled lips before him. He bestrid
An o'erpress'd Roman, and i' the Consul's view
Slew three opposers. Tarquin's self he met,
And struck him on his knee. In that day's feats,
When he might act the woman in the scene,°   100
He proved the best man i' the field, and for his meed°
Was brow-bound with the oak. His pupil age
Man-entered thus,° he waxed like a sea,
And in the brunt of seventeen battles since,   104
He lurched all swords of the garland.° For this last,
Before and in Corioli, let me say,
I cannot speak him home.° He stopped the flyers,
And by his rare example made the coward
Turn terror into sport. As weeds before
A vessel under sail, so men obeyed,   110
And fell below his stem.° His sword, death's stamp,°
Where it did mark, it took. From face to foot
He was a thing of blood, whose every motion
Was timed with dying cries. Alone he entered
The mortal° gate of the city, which he painted   115
With shunless destiny;° aidless came off,°
And with a sudden reinforcement struck
Corioli like a planet.° Now all's his.
When, by and by, the din of war gan° pierce
His ready sense, then straight his doubled spirit 120
Requickened what in flesh was fatigate,°
And to the battle came he, where he did
Run reeking° o'er the lives of men as if
'Twere a perpetual spoil.° And till we called
Both field and city ours, he never stood   125
To ease his breast with panting.

    MEN.   Worthy man!

    1. SEN. He cannot but with measure fit° the
    honors
Which we devise him.

    COM.   Our spoils he kicked at,
And looked upon things precious as they were
The common muck of the world. He covets less   130
Than misery itself would give,° rewards
His deeds with doing them, and is content
To spend the time to end it.°

100. act . . . scene: Coriolanus was more fitted to take the part
of a woman than that of a hero. At this time women's parts in
plays were taken by boys. See Gen. Intro. p. 59b. The number of
images taken from the stage in this play is notable. See II.ii.149;
III.i.105–06; V.iii.40–42.   101. meed: reward.   102–03. His
. . . thus: his boyhood being thus turned into manhood.
105. lurched . . . garland: he won all the honors himself. lurched:
lit., won a love set (won all the points in the game).   107. speak
. . . home: speak of him adequately.   111. stem: prow. stamp:
lit., that which makes an impression, particularly the mold used for
stamping coins.   115. mortal: deadly.   115–16. painted . . . destiny: made red with death that could not be avoided.   116. came
off: withdrew as victor.   118. planet: thunderbolt.   119. gan: began.   121. fatigate: wearied.   123. Run reeking: i.e., wherever he
went, there was a reek (hot steam) of blood.   124. spoil: slaughter.
Cf. *Caesar*, III.i.206.   127. He . . . fit: he will be a very fit
man for.   130–31. He . . . give: his desires are less than what belongs to the most wretched creature.   132–33. is . . . it: i.e., the
action is its own reward.

MEN.   He's right noble.
Let him be called for.
     I. SEN.   Call Coriolanus.
     OFF. He doth appear.   135
         [*Re-enter* CORIOLANUS.]
     MEN. The Senate, Coriolanus, are well pleased
To make thee Consul.
     COR.   I do owe them still°
My life and services.
     MEN.   It then remains
That you do speak to the people.
     COR.   I do beseech you
Let me o'erleap° that custom, for I cannot   140
Put on the gown,° stand naked, and entreat them,
For my wounds' sake, to give their suffrage.° Please
    you
That I may pass this doing.
     SIC.   Sir, the people
Must have their voices, neither will they bate°
One jot of ceremony.
     MEN.   Put° them not to 't.   145
Pray you, go fit you to the custom, and
Take to you, as your predecessors have,
Your honor with your form.°
     COR.   It is a part
That I shall blush in acting, and might well
Be taken from the people.
     BRU.   Mark you that?   150
     COR. To brag unto them thus I did, and thus,
Show them the unaching scars which I should hide,
As if I had received them for the hire
Of their breath only!
     MEN.   Do not stand upon 't.°
We recommend to you, Tribunes of the people,   155
Our purpose to them. And to our noble Consul
Wish we all joy and honor.
     SENS. To Coriolanus come all joy and honor!
     [*Flourish of cornets. Exeunt all but* SICINIUS *and*
                BRUTUS.]
     BRU. You see how he intends to use the people.
     SIC. May they perceive 's intent! He will require
    them°   160
As if he did contemn° what he requested
Should be in them to give.
     BRU.   Come, we'll inform them
Of our proceedings here. On the market place,
I know, they do attend us.   [*Exeunt.*]

---

137. still: always.   140. o'erleap: omit.   141. Put . . . gown: See
II.i.250; II.iii.44.   142. suffrage: vote.   144. bate: omit.
145. Put: force.   147–48. Take . . . form: before you assume
your honorable office you must, as have all who have gone before
you, observe the formalities of election.   154. Do . . . upon 't: do
not insist upon it.   160. require them: ask their votes.   161. contemn: despise.

SCENE III. *The same. The Forum.*

[*Enter seven or eight* CITIZENS.]
     I. CIT. Once,° if he do require our voices, we
ought not to deny him.
     2. CIT. We may, sir, if we will.
     3. CIT. We have power in ourselves to do it, but it
is a power that we have no power to do. For if he   5
show us his wounds and tell us his deeds, we are to
put our tongues into those wounds and speak for
them. So, if he tell us his noble deeds, we must also
tell him our noble acceptance of them. Ingratitude
is monstrous. And for the multitude to be ingrateful
were to make a monster of the multitude, of the
which we being members, should bring ourselves to
be monstrous members.   14
     I. CIT. And to make us no better thought of, a
little help will serve, for once we stood up about
the corn, he himself stuck not° to call us the many-
headed multitude.   18
     3. CIT. We have been called so of many, not that
our heads are some brown, some black, some auburn,
some bald, but that our wits are so diversely colored.
And truly I think if all our wits were to issue out of
one skull, they would fly east, west, north, south,
and their consent of one direct way° should be at
once to all the points o' the compass.   26
     2. CIT. Think you so? Which way do you judge
my wit would fly?
     3. CIT. Nay, your wit will not so soon out as an-
other man's will, 'tis strongly wedged up in a blockhead. But if it were at liberty, 'twould, sure, southward.°   32
     2. CIT. Why that way?
     3. CIT. To lose itself in a fog, where being three
parts melted away with rotten dews, the fourth
would return for conscience' sake, to help to get thee
a wife.   37
     2. CIT. You are never without your tricks.° You
may, you may.
     3. CIT. Are you all resolved to give your voices?
But that's no matter, the greater part carries it. I
say, if he would incline to the people, there was never
a worthier man.   43
     [*Enter* CORIOLANUS *in a gown of humility,*°
                with MENENIUS.]
Here he comes, and in the gown of humility. Mark
his behavior. We are not to stay all together, but to
come by him where he stands, by ones, by twos, and
by threes. He's to make his requests by particu-   47
lars,° wherein every one of us has a single honor, in
giving him our own voices with our own tongues.

Sc. iii: 1. Once: in a word.   17. stuck not: did not hesitate.
25. consent . . . way: the nearest they would get to agreeing to.
32. southward: See I.iv.30,n.   38. tricks: jokes.   43. s.d.,
gown . . . humility: See II.i.250.   48. by particulars: one by one.

Therefore follow me, and I'll direct you how you
shall go by him.   52
  ALL. Content, content.   [*Exeunt* CITIZENS.]
  MEN. O sir, you are not right. Have you not
    known
The worthiest men have done 't?
  COR.   What must I say? —   55
"I pray, sir " —— Plague upon 't! I cannot bring
My tongue to such a pace. "Look, sir, my wounds!
I got them in my country's service when
Some certain of your brethren roared, and ran
From the noise of our own drums."
  MEN.   Oh me, the gods!   60
You must not speak of that. You must desire them
To think upon you.
  COR.   Think upon me! Hang 'em!
I would they would forget me, like the virtues
Which our divines lose by 'em.°
  MEN.   You'll mar all.
I'll leave you. Pray you, speak to 'em, I pray you,   65
In wholesome° manner.   [*Exit.*]
  COR.   Bid them wash their faces,
And keep their teeth clean. [*Re-enter two of the* CITI-
ZENS.] So, here comes a brace.
[*Re-enter a third* CITIZEN.] You know the cause, sir,
of my standing here.
  3. CIT. We do, sir. Tell us what hath brought you
to 't.   70
  COR. Mine own desert.
  2. CIT. Your own desert!
  COR. Aye, but not mine own desire.
  3. CIT. How! Not your own desire!
  COR. No, sir, 'twas never my desire yet to trouble
the poor with begging.   76
  3. CIT. You must think if we give you anything,
we hope to gain by you.
  COR. Well then, I pray your price o' the consulship?   80
  1. CIT. The price is to ask it kindly.
  COR. Kindly! Sir, I pray, let me ha 't. I have
wounds to show you, which shall be yours in private.
— Your good voice, sir, what say you?
  2. CIT. You shall ha 't, worthy sir.   85
  COR. A match,° sir. There's in all two worthy
voices begged. I have your alms. Adieu.
  3. CIT. But this is something odd.
  2. CIT. An 'twere to give again — but 'tis no
matter.   [*Exeunt the three* CITIZENS.]
      [*Re-enter two other* CITIZENS.]
  COR. Pray you now, if it may stand with the tune
of your voices that I may be Consul, I have here the
customary gown.
  4. CIT. You have deserved nobly of your country,
and you have not deserved nobly.   95

  COR. Your enigma?
  4. CIT. You have been a scourge to ner enemies,
you have been a rod to her friends.° You have not
indeed loved the common people.   99
  COR. You should account me the more virtuous
that I have not been common in my love. I will, sir,
flatter my sworn brother,° the people, to earn a
dearer° estimation of them. 'Tis a condition° they
account gentle.° And since the wisdom of their
choice is rather to have my hat than my heart,   105
I will practice the insinuating° nod, and be off to
them most counterfeitly;° that is, sir, I will counterfeit the bewitchment° of some popular man, and
give it bountiful to the desirers. Therefore, beseech
you, I may be Consul.   110
  5. CIT. We hope to find you our friend, and therefore give you our voices heartily.
  4. CIT. You have received many wounds for your
country.
  COR. I will not seal° your knowledge with   114
showing them. I will make much of your voices, and
so trouble you no farther.
  BOTH CITS. The gods give you joy, sir heartily!
                     [*Exeunt.*]
  COR. Most sweet voices!
Better° it is to die, better to starve,   120
Than crave the hire which first we do deserve.°
Why in this woolvish toge° should I stand here,
To beg of Hob and Dick° that do appear
Their needless vouches?° Custom calls me to 't.
What custom wills, in all things should we do 't,
The dust on ántique time would lie unswept,   126
And mountainous error be too highly heaped
For truth to o'erpeer.° Rather than fool it so,
Let the high office and the honor go
To one that would do thus. I am half-through.   130
The one part suffered, the other will I do.
[*Re-enter three* CITIZENS *more.*] Here come moe°
    voices.
Your voices. For your voices I have fought,
Watched° for your voices, for your voices bear
Of wounds two dozen odd. Battles thrice six   135
I have seen, and heard of, for your voices have

97–98. You . . . friends: though you have scourged our enemies
with a cat-o'-nine-tails, you have also beaten our friends with a
rod.   **102. sworn brother:** brother in arms. Two knights sometime swore to each other to share all dangers and prosperity alike.
103. dearer: more valuable. **condition:** manner of behavior.
104. gentle: the mark of a gentleman. **106. insinuating:**
flattering.   **106–07. be . . . counterfeitly:** take off my hat in a
most deceptive way. **108. bewitchment:** winning behavior. For
an example, see *Rich II*, I.iv.23–36. **114. seal:** complete. See
App. 6. **120–31. Better . . . do:** for a similar use of rhyme see
Lear, I.i.183,n. **121. crave . . . deserve:** beg for pay which we
have already earned. **122. woolvish toge:** i.e., like a wolf in
sheep's clothing. The toga (*toge*) was the gown worn by upper
class Romans. **123. Hob . . . Dick:** "Tom, Dick, and Harry."
124. vouches: guarantees. **128. o'erpeer:** look over the top.
132. moe: more. **134. Watched:** kept guard.

Done many things, some less, some more. Your voices.
Indeed, I would be Consul.

6. CIT. He has done nobly, and cannot go without
any honest man's voice.   140

7. CIT. Therefore let him be Consul. The gods give
him joy, and make him good friend to the people!

ALL. Amen, amen. God save thee, noble Consul!
                         [*Exeunt.*]

COR. Worthy voices!   145
[*Re-enter* MENENIUS, *with* BRUTUS *and* SICINIUS.]

MEN. You have stood your limitation,° and the
    Tribunes
Endue you with the people's voice.° Remains
That in the official marks° invested you
Anon do meet the Senate.

COR.   Is this done?

SIC. The custom of request° you have discharged.
The people do admit you, and are summoned   151
To meet anon upon your approbation.°

COR. Where? At the Senate House?

SIC.   There, Coriolanus.

COR. May I change these garments?

SIC.   You may, sir.

COR. That I'll straight do and, knowing myself
    again,   155
Repair to the Senate House.

MEN. I'll keep you company. Will you along?

BRU. We stay here for the people.

SIC.   Fare you well.
          [*Exeunt* CORIOLANUS *and* MENENIUS.]
He has it now, and, by his looks, methinks
'Tis warm at 's heart.   160

BRU. With a proud heart he wore his humble
    weeds.°
Will you dismiss the people?
            [*Re-enter* CITIZENS.]

SIC. How now, my masters! Have you chose this
    man?

1. CIT. He has our voices, sir.   164

BRU. We pray the gods he may deserve your loves.

2. CIT. Amen, sir. To my poor unworthy notice,
He mocked us when he begged our voices.

3. CIT.   Certainly
He flouted° us downright.

1. CIT. No, 'tis his kind of speech, he did not mock
    us.   169

2. CIT. Not one amongst us save yourself but says
He used us scornfully. He should have showed us
His marks of merit, wounds received for 's country.

SIC. Why, so he did, I am sure.

CITIZENS. No, no, no man saw 'em.

3. CIT. He said he had wounds which he could
    show in private,

And with his hat, thus waving it in scorn,   175
" I would be Consul," says he. " Aged custom,
But by your voices,° will not so permit me.
Your voices therefore." When we granted that,
Here was " I thank you for your voices. Thank you.
Your most sweet voices. Now you have left your
    voices,   180
I have no further° with you." Was not this mockery?

SIC. Why, either were you ignorant to see 't,°
Or, seeing it, of such childish friendliness
To yield your voices?

BRU.   Could you not have told him,
As you were lessoned,° when he had no power,   185
But was a petty servant to the state,
He was your enemy, ever spake against
Your liberties and the charters° that you bear
I' the body of the weal?° And now, arriving
A place of potency and sway o' the state,°   190
If he should still malignantly remain
Fast foe to the plebeii,° your voices might
Be curses to yourselves? You should have said
That as his worthy deeds did claim no less
Than what he stood for, so his gracious nature   195
Would think upon you for your voices, and
Translate° his malice toward you into love,
Standing your friendly lord.

SIC.   Thus to have said,
As you were foreadvised, had touched° his spirit
And tried his inclination, from him plucked   200
Either his gracious promise, which you might,
As cause had called you up, have held him to;°
Or else it would have galled° his surly nature,
Which easily endures not article°
Tying him to aught. So, putting him to rage,   205
You should have ta'en the advantage of his choler,°
And passed him unelected.

BRU.   Did you perceive
He did solicit you in free° contempt
When he did need your loves, and do you think
That his contempt shall not be bruising to you   210
When he hath power to crush? Why, had your
    bodies
No heart among you? Or had you tongues to cry
Against the rectorship of judgment?°

SIC.   Have you
Ere now denied the asker? And now again,
Of him that did not ask but mock, bestow   215

---

146. limitation: appointed time.   147. Endue . . . voice: confirm (lit., clothe) you as duly chosen by the people.   148. official marks: insignia of office.   150. custom of request: the customary request for the people's approval.   152. approbation: formal confirmation.   161. weeds: garments.   168. flouted: mocked.

177. But . . . voices: unless you give me your approval.   181. no further: no more business.   182. were . . . see 't: were you too ignorant to notice it?   185. lessoned: taught.   188. charters: privileges.   189. weal: state.   190. A . . . state: a position of power where he can direct the affairs of state.   192. plebeii: plebeians, common people.   197. Translate: transform.   199. touched: tested.   200–02. from . . . to: extracted from him some kindly promise which on some later occasion you might have made him keep.   203. galled: rubbed sore.   204. article: condition.   206. choler: anger.   208. free: openly expressed.   213. Against . . . judgment: contrary to the rule of reason; i.e., why did you agree to a decision so contrary to common sense?

Your sued-for tongues?°

3. CIT. He's not confirmed, we may deny him yet.

2. CIT. And will deny him.

I'll have five hundred voices of that sound.

1. CIT. I twice five hundred, and their friends to
    piece 'em.°   220

BRU. Get you hence instantly, and tell those
    friends
They have chose a Consul that will from them take
Their liberties, make them of no more voice
Than dogs that are as often beat for barking
As therefore kept to do so.

SIC.   Let them assemble,   225
And, on a safer judgment, all revoke
Your ignorant election. Enforce° his pride
And his old hate unto you. Besides, forget not
With what contempt he wore the humble weed,
How in his suit° he scorned you. But your loves,
Thinking upon his services, took from you   231
The apprehension of his present portance,°
Which most gibingly, ungravely,° he did fashion°
After° the inveterate hate he bears you.

BRU.   Lay
A fault on us, your Tribunes, that we labored,   235
No impediment between, but that° you must
Cast your election on him.

SIC.   Say you chose him
More after our commandment than as guided
By your own true affections, and that your minds,
Preoccupied with what you rather must do   240
Than what you should, made you against the grain°
To voice him Consul. Lay the fault on us.

BRU. Aye, spare us not. Say we read lectures to
    you,
How youngly he began to serve his country,   244
How long continued. And what stock he springs of,
The noble house o' the Marcians, from whence came
That Ancus Marcius, Numa's daughter's son,
Who, after great Hostilius, here was King.
Of the same house Publius and Quintus were,
That our best water brought by conduits hither,
And Censorinus, nobly named so,   251
Twice being by the people chosen censor,
Was his great ancestor.°

213–16. Have . . . tongues: have you not, in the past, refused
your votes to the man who asked for them? Do you now give your
votes to one who mocks and did not even ask?   220. piece 'em:
add to them.   227. Enforce: lay stress on.   230. suit: petition
for votes.   232. apprehension . . . portance: proper understanding of his present attitude toward you.   233. ungravely: without dignity. fashion: frame, contrive.   234. After: according
to.   236. No . . . that: that there should be nothing to prevent.   241. against . . . grain: against the natural inclination.
249–53. Of . . . ancestor: F1 reads: "of the same House,
Publius and *Quintus* were/That our best Water, brought by Conduits hither,/And Nobly nam'd, so twice being Censor,/Was his
great Ancestor." The passage from Plutarch reads: "of the
same house were Publius and Quintus, who brought to Rome their
best water they had by conduits. Censorinus also came of that
family, that was so surnamed because the people had chosen

SIC.   One thus descended,
That hath beside well in his person wrought°
To be set high in place, we did commend   255
To your remembrances. But you have found,
Scaling° his present bearing with his past,
That he's your fixed enemy, and revoke
Your sudden approbation.

BRU.   Say you ne'er had done 't —
Harp on that still — but by our putting on.   260
And presently, when you have drawn your number,
Repair to the Capitol.

CITS.   We will so. Almost all
Repent in their election.   [*Exeunt* CITIZENS.]

BRU.   Let them go on.
This mutiny were better put in hazard
Than stay, past doubt, for greater.°   265
If, as his nature is, he fall in rage
With their refusal, both observe and answer
The vantage of his anger.°

SIC.   To the Capitol, come.
We will be there before the stream o' the people,
And this shall seem, as partly 'tis, their own 270
Which we have goaded onward.   [*Exeunt.*]

Act III

SCENE I. *Rome. A street.*

[*Cornets. Enter* CORIOLANUS, MENENIUS, *all the*
GENTRY, COMINIUS, TITUS LARTIUS, *and other*
SENATORS.]

COR. Tullus Aufidius then had made new head?°

LART. He had, my lord, and that it was which
    caused
Our swifter composition.°

COR. So then the Volsces stand but as at first,
Ready, when time shall prompt them, to make road
Upon 's° again.

COM.   They are worn, Lord Consul, so   6
That we shall hardly in our ages see
Their banners wave again.

COR.   Saw you Aufidius?

LART. On safeguard° he came to me, and did curse
Against the Volsces, for they had so vilely   10
Yielded the town. He is retired to Antium.

him censor twice." Some words or a line have obviously been
omitted from F1, which editors have variously restored.
253–54. One . . . wrought: not only because of his noble descent, but also because of his own distinction.   257. Scaling:
weighing, comparing.   264–65. This . . . greater: it is better
to risk a riot now than to wait for a greater which is bound to
come in the future.   268. vantage . . . anger: advantage which
his anger will give us.

    Act III, Sc. i: 1. made . . . head: collected new forces. Cf.
II.ii.92.   3. composition: coming to terms.   5–6. make . . .
Upon 's: invade.   9. safeguard: safe conduct.

COR. Spoke he of me?

LART.   He did, my lord.

COR.   How? What?

LART. How often he had met you, sword to sword;
That of all things upon the earth he hated
Your person most; that he would pawn his fortunes
To hopeless restitution° so he might   16
Be called your vanquisher.

COR.   At Antium lives he?

LART. At Antium.

COR. I wish I had a cause to seek him there,
To oppose his hatred fully. Welcome home.   20
[*Enter* SICINIUS *and* BRUTUS.] Behold, these are the
     Tribunes of the people,
The tongues o' the common mouth. I do despise
     them,
For they do prank them° in authority
Against all noble sufferance.°

SIC.   Pass no further.

COR. Ha! What is that?   25

BRU. It will be dangerous to go on. No further.

COR. What makes this change?

MEN. The matter?

COM. Hath he not passed the noble and the com-
     mon?

BRU. Cominius, no.

COR.   Have I had children's voices?   30

1. SEN. Tribunes, give way, he shall to the market
     place.

BRU. The people are incensed against him.

SIC.   Stop,
Or all will fall in broil.

COR.   Are these your herd?
Must these have voices, that can yield them now
And straight disclaim their tongues? What are your
     offices?°   35
You being their mouths, why rule you not their
     teeth?
Have you not set them on?

MEN.   Be calm, be calm.

COR. It is a purposed thing,° and grows by plot,
To curb the will of the nobility.
Suffer 't, and live with° such as cannot rule,   40
Nor ever will be ruled.

BRU.   Call 't not a plot.
The people cry you mocked them, and of late,
When corn was given them gratis, you repined,°
Scandaled° the suppliants for the people, called
     them
Time-pleasers, flatterers, foes to nobleness.   45

COR. Why, this was known before.

BRU.   Not to them all.

COR. Have you informed them sithence?°

BRU.   How! I inform them!

COM. You are like to do such business.

BRU.   Not unlike,
Each way, to better yours.°

COR. Why then should I be Consul? By yond
     clouds,   50
Let me deserve so ill as you, and make me
Your fellow Tribune.

SIC.   You show too much of that
For which the people stir. If you will pass
To where you are bound,° you must inquire your
     way,
Which you are out of, with a gentler spirit,   55
Or never be so noble as a Consul,
Nor yoke with° him for Tribune.

MEN.   Let's be calm.

COM. The people are abused,° set on. This
     paltering°
Becomes not Rome, nor has Coriolanus
Deserved this so dishonored rub,° laid falsely   60
I' the plain way of his merit.

COR.   Tell me of corn!
This was my speech, and I will speak 't again ——

MEN. Not now, not now.

1. SEN.   Not in this heat, sir, now.

COR. Now, as I live, I will. My nobler friends,
I crave their pardons.   65
For the mutable, rank-scented many,° let them
Regard me as I do not flatter, and
Therein behold themselves. I say again,
In soothing them, we nourish 'gainst our Senate
The cockle° of rebellion, insolence, sedition,   70
Which we ourselves have plowed for, sowed and
     scattered,
By mingling them with us, the honored number,
Who lack not virtue, no, nor power, but that
Which they have given to beggars.°

MEN.   Well, no more.

1. SEN. No more words, we beseech you.

COR.   How! No more!   75
As for my country I have shed my blood,
Not fearing outward force, so shall my lungs
Coin words till their decay against those measles°
Which we disdain should tetter° us, yet sought
The very way to catch them.

BRU.   You speak o' the people   80
As if you were a god to punish, not
A man of their infirmity.

---

47. sithence: since then.   **48–49. Not . . . yours:** I certainly am likely to do what I can to get the better of you.   **53–54. pass . . . bound:** reach the consulship which you aim at.   **57. yoke with:** serve with.   **58. abused:** deceived. **paltering:** trickery. **60. rub:** obstacle. See App. 13.   **66. rank-scented many:** stinking multitude.   **70. cockle:** a weed that grows in the wheat. **73–74. Who . . . beggars:** who still have plenty of valor and power, except for what we have given away to beggars. **78. measles:** plague spots.   **79. tetter:** break out on our skins. Cf. *Haml,* I.v.71.

---

16. hopeless restitution: beyond all hope of recovery. **23. prank them:** make themselves fine fellows. **24. Against . . . sufferance:** beyond the endurance of the nobles. **35. offices:** duties. **38. purposed thing:** "frame-up."   **40. live with:** you will have to live with.   **43. repined:** were dissatisfied.   **44. Scandaled:** spoke harshly about.

SIC.   'Twere well
We let the people know 't.
     MEN.   What, what? His choler?
     COR. Choler!
Were I as patient as the midnight sleep,   85
By Jove, 'twould be my mind!
     SIC.   It is a mind
That shall remain a poison where it is,
Not poison any further.
     COR.   Shall remain!
Hear you this Triton° of the minnows? Mark you
His absolute " shall "?
     COM.   'Twas from the canon.°
     COR.   " Shall "!   90
O good but most unwise patricians! Why,
You grave but reckless Senators, have you thus
Given Hydra° here to choose an officer
That with his peremptory " shall," being but
The horn and noise o' the monster's, wants not
    spirit   95
To say he'll turn your current in a ditch
And make your channel his?° If he have power,
Then vail your ignorance;° if none, awake
Your dangerous lenity. If you are learned,
Be not as common fools; if you are not,   100
Let them have cushions by you.° You are plebeians
If they be Senators. And they are no less
When, both your voices blended, the great'st taste
Most palates theirs.° They choose their magistrate,
And such a one as he, who puts his " shall,"   105
His popular " shall," against a graver bench
Than ever frowned in Greece. By Jove himself,
It makes the Consuls base! And my soul aches
To know, when two authorities are up,
Neither supreme, how soon confusion°   110
May enter 'twixt the gap of both and take
The one by the other.
     COM.   Well, on to the market place.
     COR. Whoever gave that counsel, to give forth
The corn o' the storehouse gratis, as 'twas used
Sometime in Greece ——
     MEN.   Well, well, no more of that.   115
     COR. Though there the people had more absolute
    power,
I say they nourished disobedience, fed
The ruin of the state.
     BRU.   Why, shall the people give
One that speaks thus their voice?

     COR.   I'll give my reasons,
More worthier than their voices. They know the
    corn   120
Was not our recompense,° resting well assured
They ne'er did service for 't. Being pressed to the
    war,
Even when the navel° of the state was touched,
They would not thread the gates.° This kind of
    service
Did not deserve corn gratis. Being i' the war,   125
Their mutinies and revolts, wherein they showed
Most valor, spoke not for them. The accusation
Which they have often made against the Senate,
All cause unborn,° could never be the native
Of our so frank donation.° Well, what then?   130
How shall this bosom multiplied° digest
The Senate's courtesy? Let deeds express
What's like to be their words: " We did request it,
We are the greater poll,° and in true fear
They gave us our demands." Thus we debase   135
The nature of our seats, and make the rabble
Call our cares fears, which will in time
Break ope the locks o' the Senate and bring in
The crows to peck the eagles.
     MEN.   Come, enough.
     BRU. Enough, with overmeasure.
     COR.   No, take more.   140
What may be sworn by, both divine and human,
Seal what I end withal! This double worship,
Where one part does disdain with cause, the other
Insult without all reason; where gentry, title, wis-
    dom,°
Cannot conclude° but by the yea and no   145
Of general ignorance — it must omit
Real necessities, and give way the while
To unstable slightness. Purpose so barred, it follows
Nothing is done to purpose. Therefore, beseech
    you —
You that will be less fearful than discreet,°   150
That love the fundamental part of state
More than you doubt the change on 't,° that prefer
A noble life before a long, and wish
To jump° a body with a dangerous physic
That's sure of death without it — at once pluck out
The multitudinous tongue. Let them not lick   156
The sweet which is their poison. Your dishonor°

89. **Triton**: the trumpeter of Neptune, the sea god.   90. **from . . . canon**: contrary to law.   93. **Hydra**: a many-headed beast slain by Hercules.   96–97. **turn . . . his**: he will direct your stream into a ditch and use your watercourse for his own. See *Cor* Intro. p. 1265b.   98. **vail . . . ignorance**: lower your ignorance; i.e., have more sense.   101. **have . . . you**: i.e., share equally in the government with you.   102–04. **And . . . theirs**: Once more Coriolanus, in his excitement, grows incoherent. He means that they are no less than Senators if when you vote together you must submit to eating what the more numerous plebeians like best. Cf. I.vi.76; III.iii.68.   110. **confusion**: utter ruin.

121. **our recompense**: given by us as a reward for service.   123. **navel**: very center.   124. **thread . . . gates**: pass through the gates in single file — on the way to war.   129. **All . . . unborn**: without any cause.   129–30. **native . . . donation**: true reason for our generous gift.   131. **bosom multiplied**: i.e., bosom of the "rank-scented many," the mob.   134. **We . . . poll**: we have more votes.   144. **gentry . . . wisdom**: the gentlemen, the nobles, and the wise men; another instance of Shakespeare's frequent use of abstract words for the concrete.   145. **conclude**: reach a decision.   150. **less . . . discreet**: i.e., wise men rather than cowards.   152. **doubt . . . on't**: fear a revolution.   154. **jump**: risk   157. **Your dishonor**: i.e., the dishonorable condition to which you have now sunk.

Mangles true judgment and bereaves the state
Of that integrity which should become 't,
Not having the power to do the good it would   160
For the ill which doth control 't.

BRU.   Has said enough.

SIC. Has spoken like a traitor, and shall answer
As traitors do.

COR.   Thou wretch, despite° o'erwhelm thee!
What should the people do with these bald Trib-
     unes?   165
On whom depending, their obedience fails
To the greater bench.° In a rebellion,
When what's not meet, but what must be, was law,
Then were they chosen. In a better hour,
Let what is meet be said it must be meet,   170
And throw their power i' the dust.

BRU. Manifest treason!

SIC.   This a Consul? No.

BRU. The Aediles,° ho!

     [*Enter an* AEDILE.] Let him be apprehended.

SIC. Go, call the people [*Exit* AEDILE.], in whose
     name myself
Attach° thee as a traitorous innovator,°   175
A foe to the public weal. Obey, I charge thee,
And follow to thine answer.°

COR.   Hence, old goat!

SENS., ETC. We'll surety° him.

COM.   Aged sir, hands off.

COR. Hence, rotten thing! Or I shall shake thy
     bones
Out of thy garments.

SIC.   Help, ye citizens!   180

[*Enter a rabble of* CITIZENS, *with the* AEDILES.]

MEN. On both sides, more respect.

SIC. Here's he that would take from you all your
     power.

BRU. Seize him, Aediles!

CITS. Down with him! Down with him!

SENS., ETC. Weapons, weapons, weapons!   185

         [*They all bustle about* CORIOLANUS.]

ALL THE PEOPLE. Tribunes! — Patricians! — Citi-
     zens! — What ho!

Sicinius! — Brutus! — Coriolanus! — Citizens! —
Peace, peace, peace! — Stay! Hold! Peace!

MEN. What is about to be? I am out of breath.
Confusion's° near. I cannot speak. You, Tribunes
To the people! Coriolanus, patience!   191
Speak, good Sicinius.

SIC.   Hear me, people. Peace!

CITS. Let's hear our Tribune. Peace! — Speak,
speak, speak.

SIC. You are at point to lose your liberties.

Marcius would have all from you, Marcius,   195
Whom late you have named for Consul.

MEN.   Fie, fie, fie!
This is the way to kindle, not to quench.

1. SEN. To unbuild the city, and to lay all flat.

SIC. What is the city but the people?

CITS.   True,
The people are the city.   200

BRU. By the consent of all, we were established
The people's magistrates.

CITS.   You so remain.

MEN. And so are like to do.

COM. That is the way to lay the city flat,
To bring the roof to the foundation,   205
And bury all which yet distinctly ranges°
In heaps and piles of ruin.

SIC.   This deserves death.

BRU. Or let us stand to our authority,
Or let us lose it. We do here pronounce,
Upon the part o'° the people, in whose power   210
We were elected theirs, Marcius is worthy
Of present death.

SIC.   Therefore lay hold of him,
Bear him to the rock Tarpeian,° and from thence
Into destruction cast him.

BRU.   Aediles, seize him!

CITS. Yield, Marcius, yield!

MEN.   Hear me one word.
Beseech you, Tribunes, hear me but a word.   216

AEDI. Peace, peace!

MEN. [*To* BRUTUS] Be that you seem, truly your
     country's friend,
And temperately proceed to what you would
Thus violently redress.

BRU.   Sir, those cold ways,   220
That seem like prudent helps, are very poisonous
Where the disease is violent. Lay hands upon him,
And bear him to the rock.

COR.   No, I'll die here. [*Drawing his sword.*]
There's some among you have beheld me fighting.
Come, try upon yourselves what you have seen me.

MEN. Down with that sword! Tribunes, with-
     draw awhile.   226

BRU. Lay hands upon him.

MEN.   Help Marcius, help,
You that be noble, help him, young and old!

CITS. Down with him, down with him!

     [*In this mutiny, the* TRIBUNES, *the* AEDILES,
                       and the PEOPLE, *are beat in.*]

MEN. Go, get you to your house, be gone, away!
All will be naught° else.

2. SEN.   Get you gone.

COM.   Stand fast.   231

---

164. despite: contempt.   167. greater bench: the more honorable assembly; i.e., the Senate.   173. Aediles: officers of the law.
175. Attach: arrest. innovator: revolutionary.   177. to . . . answer: to answer the charge against you.   178. surety: go bail for.
190. Confusion: See l. 110.

206. ranges: stands orderly.   210. Upon . . . o': on behalf of.
213. rock Tarpeian: a precipitous rock on the Capitoline Hill in
Rome. Traitors were executed by being thrown from this rock.
231. naught: ruined.

We have as many friends as enemies.
  MEN. Shall it be put to that?
    I. SEN.   The gods forbid!
I prithee, noble friend, home to thy house.
Leave us to cure this cause.
  MEN.   For 'tis a sore upon us   235
You cannot tent° yourself. Be gone, beseech you.
  COM. Come, sir, along with us.
    COR. I would they were barbarians — as they are,
Though in Rome littered — not Romans — as they
    are not,
Though calved i' the porch o' the Capitol ——
  MEN.   Be gone.   240
Put not your worthy rage into your tongue.
One time will owe another.°
  COR.   On fair ground
I could beat forty of them.
  MEN.   I could myself
Take up a brace o' the best of them — yea, the two
    Tribunes.
  COM. But now 'tis odds beyond arithmetic,   245
And manhood is called foolery when it stands
Against a falling fabric.° Will you hence
Before the tag° return? Whose rage doth rend
Like interrupted waters,° and o'erbear
What they are used to bear.
  MEN.   Pray you be gone.   250
I'll try whether my old wit be in request
With those that have but little. This must be
    patched
With cloth of any color.
  COM.   Nay, come away.
        [*Exeunt* CORIOLANUS, COMINIUS, *and others.*]
  I. PAT. This man has marred his fortune.
  MEN. His nature is too noble for the world.   255
He would not flatter Neptune for his trident,
Or Jove for 's power to thunder. His heart's his
    mouth —
What his breast forges, that his tongue must vent,
And, being angry, does forget that ever
He heard the name of death.   [*A noise within.*]
Here's goodly work!
  2. PAT.   I would they were abed!   261
  MEN. I would they were in Tiber! What the
    vengeance!
Could he not speak 'em fair?
        [*Re-enter* BRUTUS *and* SICINIUS, *with the rabble.*]
  SIC.   Where is this viper
That would depopulate the city and
Be every man himself?
  MEN.   You worthy Tribunes ——   265
  SIC. He shall be thrown down the Tarpeian rock
With rigorous hands. He hath resisted law,

And therefore law shall scorn him further trial
Than the severity of the public power,
Which he so sets at naught.
    I. CIT.   He shall well know   270
The noble Tribunes are the people's mouths,
And we their hands.
    CITS. He shall, sure on 't.
  MEN.   Sir, sir ——
  SIC. Peace!
  MEN. Do not cry havoc° where you should but
    hunt   275
With modest warrant.
  SIC.   Sir, how comes 't that you
Have holp° to make this rescue?
  MEN.   Hear me speak.
As I do know the Consul's worthiness,
So can I name his faults ——
  SIC.   Consul! What Consul?
  MEN. The Consul Coriolanus.
  BRU.   He Consul!   280
  CITS. No, no, no, no, no.
  MEN. If, by the Tribunes' leave, and yours, good
    people,
I may be heard, I would crave a word or two,
The which shall turn° you to no further harm
Than so much loss of time.
  SIC.   Speak briefly then,   285
For we are peremptory° to dispatch
This viperous traitor. To eject him hence
Were but one danger, and to keep him here
Our certain death. Therefore it is decreed
He dies tonight.
  MEN.   Now the good gods forbid   290
That our renownèd Rome, whose gratitude
Toward her deservèd children is enrolled
In Jove's own book, like an unnatural dam
Should now eat up her own!
  SIC. He's a disease that must be cut away.   295
  MEN. Oh, he's a limb that has but a disease —
Mortal to cut it off, to cure it easy.
What has he done to Rome that's worthy death?
Killing our enemies, the blood he hath lost —
Which, I dare vouch, is more than that he hath   300
By many an ounce — he dropped it for his country.
And what is left, to lose it by his country
Were to us all that do 't and suffer it
A brand° to the end o' the world
  SIC.   This is clean kam.°
  BRU. Merely° awry. When he did love his coun-
    try,   305
It honored him.
  MEN.   The service of the foot

236. tent: cleanse. Cf. I.ix.31.   242. One . . . another: i.e., our
turn will come.   247. falling fabric: falling house.   248. tag:
rabble.   249. interrupted waters: waters that have burst their
banks.

275. havoc: the cry of "no quarter." See *Caesar*, III.i.270–75.
277. holp: helped.   284. turn: put.   286. peremptory: firmly
determined.   304. brand: dishonorable mark. For certain
offenses, the guilty were branded with red-hot irons. clean kam:
quite wrong.   305. Merely: entirely.

Being once gangrened, is not then respected
For what before it was.

BRU.   We'll hear no more.
Pursue him to his house and pluck him thence,
Lest his infection, being of catching nature,   310
Spread further.

MEN.   One word more, one word.
This tiger-footed rage, when it shall find
The harm of unscanned swiftness,° will, too late,
Tie leaden pounds° to 's heels. Proceed by process,°
Lest parties,° as he is beloved, break out,   315
And sack great Rome with Romans.

BRU.   If it were so——
SIC. What do ye talk?
Have we not had a taste of his obedience?
Our Aediles smote? Ourselves resisted? Come.

MEN. Consider this. He has been bred i' the wars
Since he could draw a sword, and is ill schooled   321
In bolted° language — meal and bran together
He throws without distinction. Give me leave,
I'll go to him and undertake to bring him
Where he shall answer, by a lawful form,   325
In peace, to his utmost peril.°

I. SEN.   Noble Tribunes,
It is the humane way. The other course
Will prove too bloody, and the end of it
Unknown to the beginning.

SIC.   Noble Menenius,
Be you then as the people's officer.   330
Masters, lay down your weapons.

BRU.   Go not home.
SIC. Meet on the market place. We'll attend you
   there,
Where, if you bring not Marcius, we'll proceed
In our first way.

MEN.   I'll bring him to you.
[*To the* SENATORS] Let me desire your company. He
   must come,   335
Or what is worst will follow.

I. SEN.   Pray you, let's to him. [*Exeunt.*]

SCENE II. *A room in* CORIOLANUS'S *house.*

[*Enter* CORIOLANUS, *with* PATRICIANS.]
COR. Let them pull all about mine ears, present me
Death on the wheel,° or at wild horses' heels,°
Or pile ten hills on the Tarpeian rock,
That the precipitation might downstretch
Below the beam° of sight, yet will I still   5
Be thus to them.

I. PAT.   You do the nobler.
COR. I muse° my mother
Does not approve me further,° who was wont
To call them woolen vassals,° things created
To buy and sell with groats,° to show bare heads   10
In congregations, to yawn, be still, and wonder
When one but of my ordinance° stood up
To speak of peace or war.
[*Enter* VOLUMNIA.]   I talk of you.
Why did you wish me milder? Would you have me
False to my nature? Rather say I play   15
The man I am.

VOL.   O sir, sir, sir,
I would have had you put your power well on
Before you had worn it out.

COR.   Let go.
VOL. You might have been enough the man you
   are
With striving less to be so. Lesser had been   20
The thwartings of your dispositions if
You had not showed them how ye were disposed
Ere they lacked power to cross you.

COR.   Let them hang.
VOL. Aye, and burn too.
[*Enter* MENENIUS *with the* SENATORS.]
MEN. Come, come, you have been too rough,
   something too rough.   25
You must return and mend it.

I. SEN.   There's no remedy,
Unless, by not so doing, our good city
Cleave in the midst, and perish.

VOL.   Pray be counseled.
I have a heart as little apt° as yours,
But yet a brain that leads my use of anger   30
To better vantage.

MEN.   Well said, noble woman!
Before he should thus stoop to the herd, but that
The violent fit o' the time° craves it as physic
For the whole state, I would put mine armor on,
Which I can scarcely bear.

COR.   What must I do?   35
MEN. Return to the Tribunes.
COR.   Well, what then? What then?
MEN. Repent what you have spoke.
COR. For them! I cannot do it to the gods.
Must I then do 't to them?

VOL.   You are too absolute,°
Though therein you can never be too noble   40
But when extremities speak.° I have heard you say
Honor and policy,° like unsevered° friends,

313. unscanned swiftness: ill-considered haste.   314. pounds:
weights. process: legal proceeding.   315. parties: rival parties.
322. bolted: lit., sifted, carefully chosen.   326. to . . . peril: i.e.,
under penalty of death.
     Sc. ii: 2. Death . . . wheel: i.e., break me on the wheel—a
lingering death. wild . . . heels: torn to pieces by wild horses.
5. beam: range.

7. muse: wonder.   8. approve . . . further: show more approval
of my actions.   9. woolen vassals: slaves that wear wool; i.e.,
cheap clothes.   10. To . . . groats: whose business is only with
"dimes." groat: fourpence.   12. ordinance: rank.   29. apt:
ready; i.e., to yield to the plebeians.   33. violent . . . time: i.e.,
the present riots.   39. absolute: unbending.   41. But . . .
speak: except when extreme dangers demand.   42. policy:
craftiness. unsevered: inseparable.

I' the war do grow together. Grant that, and tell me,
In peace what each of them by the other lose,
That they combine not there.

COR.   Tush, tush!

MEN.   A good demand.   45

VOL. If it be honor in your wars to seem
The same you are not, which, for your best ends,
You adopt your policy, how is it less or worse
That it shall hold companionship in peace
With honor, as in war, since that to both   50
It stands in like request?°

COR.   Why force you this?°

VOL. Because that now it lies you on° to speak
To the people — not by your own instruction,
Nor by the matter which your heart prompts you,
But with such words that are but roted in°   55
Your tongue, though but bastards and syllables
Of no allowance° to your bosom's truth.
Now this no more dishonors you at all
Than to take in a town with gentle words,
Which else would put you to your fortune° and   60
The hazard of much blood.
I would dissemble° with my nature where
My fortunes and my friends at stake required
I should do so in honor. I am in this,°
Your wife, your son, these Senators, the nobles,   65
And you will rather show our general louts°
How you can frown than spend a fawn upon 'em
For the inheritance° of their loves and safeguard
Of what that want might ruin.

MEN.   Noble lady!
Come, go with us, speak fair. You may salve° so   70
Not what is dangerous present, but the loss
Of what is past.

VOL.   I prithee now, my son,
Go° to them, with this bonnet in thy hand,
And thus far having stretched it, here be with them,
Thy knee bussing° the stones — for in such business
Action is eloquence, and the eyes of the ignorant   76
More learnèd than the ears — waving thy head,
Which often thus, correcting thy stout heart,
Now humble as the ripest mulberry
That will not hold° the handling. Or say to them
Thou art their soldier, and being bred in broils°   81
Hast not the soft way which, thou dost confess,
Were fit for thee to use, as they to claim,
in asking their good loves. But thou wilt frame°

51. in . . . request: is equally required; i.e., "policy" is as necessary in peace as in war. force . . . this: urge this argument. 52. lies . . . on: is your duty to. 55. roted in: learned by heart. 57. Of . . . allowance: not acknowledged. 60. put . . . fortune: cause you to risk all. 62. dissemble: play the hypocrite. 64. in this: in this matter. 66. general louts: those louts that make up the populace. 68. inheritance: possession. 70. salve: heal. 73–86. Go . . . person: Here, as often, Shakespeare uses the dialogue for stage direction. Volumnia plucks the hat off his head and shows him by her own actions how he should act his part. 75. bussing: kissing. 80. hold: endure. 81. broils: fights. 84. frame: make.

Thyself, forsooth, hereafter theirs, so far   85
As thou hast power and person.

MEN.   This but done,
Even as she speaks, why, their hearts were yours.
For they have pardons, being asked, as free
As words to little purpose.

VOL.   Prithee now,
Go, and be ruled.° Although I know thou hadst
rather   90
Follow thine enemy in a fiery gulf°
Than flatter him in a bower.°

[*Enter* COMINIUS.]   Here is Cominius.

COM. I have been i' the market place, and, sir, 'tis fit
You make strong party,° or defend yourself
By calmness or by absence. All's in anger.   95

MEN. Only fair speech.

COM.   I think 'twill serve, if he
Can thereto frame his spirit.

VOL.   He must, and will.
Prithee now, say you will, and go about it.

COR. Must I go show them my unbarbed sconce?°
Must I,
With my base tongue, give to my noble heart   100
A lie that it must bear? Well, I will do 't.
Yet, were there but this single plot° to lose,
This mold of Marcius, they to dust should grind it,
And throw 't against the wind. To the market
place!
You have put me now to such a part° which never
I shall discharge to the life.°

COM.   Come, come, we'll prompt you.   106

VOL. I prithee now, sweet son, as thou hast said
My praises made thee first a soldier, so,
To have my praise for this, perform a part
Thou hast not done before.

COR.   Well, I must do 't.   110
Away, my disposition, and possess me
Some harlot's spirit! My throat of war be turned,
Which quired with° my drum, into a pipe
Small as an eunuch, or the virgin voice
That babies lulls asleep! The smiles of knaves   115
Tent° in my cheeks, and schoolboys' tears take up
The glasses of my sight!° A beggar's tongue
Make motion through my lips, and my armed knees,
Who bowed but in my stirrup, bend like his
That hath received an alms! I will not do 't,   120
Lest I surcease° to honor mine own truth,
And by my body's action teach my mind
A most inherent baseness.

VOL.   At thy choice, then.

90. ruled: obedient. 91. gulf: whirlpool. 92. bower: i.e., a place for love-making. 94. You . . . party: have a large party with you. 99. unbarbed sconce: unarmed head. sconce: lit., blockhouse. 102. plot: plot of earth; i.e., his own body, a common poetic image. 105. part: actor's part. 106. discharge . . . life: act realistically. See II.ii.100,n. 113. quired with: sang to the tune of. 116. Tent: encamp. 117. glasses . . . sight: eyeballs. 121. surcease: cease.

To beg of thee, it is my more dishonor
Than thou of them. Come all to ruin, let   125
Thy mother rather feel thy pride than fear
Thy dangerous stoutness, for I mock at death
With as big heart as thou. Do as thou list.°
Thy valiantness was mine, thou suck'dst it from me,
But owe° thy pride thyself.

COR.   Pray be content.   130
Mother, I am going to the market place,
Chide me no more. I'll mountebank° their loves,
Cog° their hearts from them, and come home be-
    loved
Of all the trades in Rome. Look, I am going.
Commend me to my wife. I'll return Consul,   135
Or never trust to what my tongue can do
I' the way of flattery further.

VOL.   Do your will.   [*Exit.*]
COM. Away! The tribunes do attend you. Arm
    yourself°
To answer mildly, for they are prepared
With accusations, as I hear, more strong   140
Than are upon you yet.

COR. The word° is "mildly." Pray you let us go.
Let them accuse me by invention,° I
Will answer in mine honor.

MEN.   Aye, but mildly.   144
COR. Well, mildly be it then. Mildly!   [*Exeunt.*]

SCENE III. *The same. The Forum.*

[*Enter* SICINIUS *and* BRUTUS.]

BRU. In this point charge him home,° that he
    affects°
Tyrannical power. If he evade us there,
Enforce him with° his envy to° the people,
And that the spoil got on° the Antiates
Was ne'er distributed.

[*Enter an* AEDILE.]   What, will he come?   5
AED. He's coming.
BRU.   How accompanied?
AED. With old Menenius and those Senators
That always favored him.
SIC.   Have you a catalogue
Of all the voices that we have procured,
Set down by the poll?°
AED.   I have, 'tis ready.   10
SIC. Have you collected them by tribes?
AED.   I have.
SIC. Assemble presently° the people hither.

And when they hear me say "It shall be so
I' the right and strength o' the commons," be it
    either
For death, for fine, or banishment, then let them,
If I say fine, cry "Fine," if death, cry "Death,"   16
Insisting on the old prerogative°
And power i' the truth° o' the cause.

AED.   I shall inform them.
BRU. And when such time they have begun to cry,
Let them not cease, but with a din confused   20
Enforce the present execution
Of what we chance to sentence.

AED.   Very well.
SIC. Make them be strong, and ready for this hint°
When we shall hap to give 't them.

BRU.   Go about it.   [*Exit* AEDILE.]
Put him to choler straight.° He hath been used   25
Ever to conquer and to have his worth
Of contradiction.° Being once chafed,° he cannot
Be reined again to temperance. Then he speaks
What's in his heart, and that is there which looks
With us to break his neck.

SIC.   Well, here he comes.   30

[*Enter* CORIOLANUS, MENENIUS, *and* COMINIUS, *with*
SENATORS *and* PATRICIANS.]

MEN. Calmly, I do beseech you.
COR. Aye, as an ostler,° that for the poorest piece
Will bear the knave by the volume.° The honored
    gods
Keep Rome in safety, and the chairs of justice
Supplied with worthy men! Plant love among 's!   35
Throng our large temples with the shows° of
    peace,
And not our streets with war!

I. SEN.   Amen, amen.
MEN. A noble wish.

[*Re-enter* AEDILE, *with* CITIZENS.]

SIC. Draw near, ye people.
AED. List to your Tribunes, audience. Peace, I say!
COR. First, hear me speak.
BOTH TRIBUNES.   Well, say. Peace, ho!   41
COR. Shall I be charged no further than this pres-
    ent?
Must all determine here?°
SIC.   I do demand,
If you submit you° to the people's voices,
Allow their officers, and are content   45
To suffer lawful censure° for such faults
As shall be proved upon you.
COR.   I am content.

---

128. **as . . . list:** as you please.   130. **owe:** own.   132. **mounte-**
bank: win them over like a cheap trickster at a fair.   133. **Cog:**
cheat.   138. **Arm yourself:** be prepared.   142. **word:** password.
143. **Let . . . invention:** let them invent accusations.
    Sc. iii: 1. **charge . . . home:** press your accusation. **affects:**
seeks.   3. **Enforce . . . with:** stress. **envy to:** hatred of.   4. **got**
on: won from.   10. **by . . . poll:** man by man.   12. **presently:**
immediately.

17. **prerogative:** sovereign right.   18. **truth:** justice.   23. **hint:**
occasion.   25. **Put . . . straight:** make him lose his temper at
once.   26–27. **his . . . contradiction:** full allowance to contradict.   27. **chafed:** rubbed, made angry.   32. **ostler:** man who
tends horses.   32–33. **for . . . volume:** i.e., for a penny will
submit to be called knave by the bookful.   36. **shows:** pageants.
43. **determine here:** be concluded here.   44. **you:** yourself.
46. **censure:** judgment.

MEN. Lo, citizens, he says he is content.
The warlike service he has done, consider. Think
Upon the wounds his body bears, which show   50
Like graves i' the holy churchyard.
    COR.   Scratches with briers,
Scars to move laughter only.
    MEN.   Consider further
That when he speaks not like a citizen,
You find him like a soldier. Do not take
His rougher accents for malicious sounds,   55
But, as I say, such as become a soldier
Rather than envy you.°
    COM.   Well, well, no more.
    COR. What is the matter
That being passed for Consul with full voice,
I am so dishonored that the very hour   60
You take it off again?
    SIC.   Answer to us.
    COR. Say, then. 'Tis true, I ought so.
    SIC. We charge you that you have contrived° to
        take
From Rome all seasoned office,° and to wind°
Yourself into a power tyrannical,   65
For which you are a traitor to the people.
    COR. How! Traitor!
    MEN.   Nay, temperately — your promise.
    COR. The° fires i' the lowest Hell fold in° the
        people!
Call me their traitor! Thou injurious° Tribune!
Within thine eyes sat twenty thousand deaths,°   70
In thy hands clutched as many millions, in
Thy lying tongue both numbers, I would say
" Thou liest " unto thee with a voice as free
As I do pray the gods.
    SIC.   Mark you this, people?
    CITS. To the rock, to the rock with him!
    SIC.   Peace!   75
We need not put new matter to his charge.
What you have seen him do and heard him speak,
Beating your officers, cursing yourselves,
Opposing laws with strokes, and here defying
Those whose great power must try him. Even this,
So criminal and in such capital kind,°   81
Deserves the extremest death.
    BRU.   But since he hath
Served well for Rome —
    COR.   What do you prate of service?
    BRU. I talk of that that know it.
    COR. You?   85
    MEN. Is this the promise that you made your
        mother?

COM. Know, I pray you ——
    COR.   I'll know no further.
Let them pronounce the steep Tarpeian death,
Vagabond exile, flaying, pent° to linger
But with a grain a day, I would not buy   90
Their mercy at the price of one fair word,
Nor check my courage for what they can give,
To have 't with saying " Good morrow."
    SIC.   For that he has,
As much as in him lies, from time to time
Envied against° the people, seeking means   95
To pluck away their power, as now at last
Given hostile strokes, and that not in the presence
Of dreaded justice but on the ministers
That do distribute it — in the name o' the people,
And in the power of us the Tribunes, we,   100
Even from this instant, banish him our city,
In peril of precipitation
From off the rock Tarpeian, never more
To enter our Rome gates. I' the people's name
I say it shall be so.   105
    CITS. It shall be so, it shall be so, let him away.
He's banished, and it shall be so.
    COM. Hear me, my masters, and my common
        friends ——
    SIC. He's sentenced, no more hearing.
    COM.   Let me speak.
I have been Consul, and can show for Rome   110
Her enemies' marks upon me. I do love
My country's good with a respect more tender,
More holy and profound, than mine own life,
My dear wife's estimate,° her womb's increase
And treasure of my loins. Then if I would   115
Speak that ——
    SIC.   We know your drift. — Speak what?
    BRU. There's no more to be said but he is banished,
As enemy to the people and his country.
It shall be so.
    CITS.   It shall be so, it shall be so.
    COR. You common cry° of curs! Whose breath I
        hate   120
As reek o' the rotten fens, whose loves I prize
As the dead carcasses of unburied men
That do corrupt my air, I banish you,
And here remain with your uncertainty!°
Let every feeble rumor shake your hearts,   125
Your enemies, with nodding of their plumes,°
Fan you into despair! Have the power still
To banish your defenders, till at length
Your ignorance, which finds not till it feels,
Making not reservation of yourselves,   130
Still your own foes, deliver you as most
Abated captives to some nation

---

57. **envy you:** express hatred for you. 63. **contrived:** plotted.
64. **seasoned office:** long-established offices. **wind:** insinuate.
68–74. **The . . . gods:** Once again Coriolanus becomes incoherent
with rage. Cf. I.vi.76; III.i.102. 68. **fold in:** enclose. 69. **injurious:** insulting. 70. **Within . . . deaths:** even if you had
twenty thousand deaths in your glance. 81. **capital kind:**
deserving death.

89. **pent:** shut in.   95. **Envied against:** shown hatred for.
114. **estimate:** honor.   120. **cry:** pack.   124. **And . . . uncertainty:** may you remain here in a state of confusion. 126. **plumes:**
i.e., on their helmets.

That won you without blows!° Despising,
For you, the city, thus I turn my back.
There is a world elsewhere.　　　　　　　　135

　　　　　　　[*Exeunt* CORIOLANUS, COMINIUS,
　　　MENENIUS, SENATORS *and* PATRICIANS.]

AED. The people's enemy is gone, is gone!
CITS. Our enemy is banished! He is gone! Hoo!
　　Hoo!

　　　　[*They all shout, and throw up their caps.*]

SIC. Go, see him out at gates, and follow him,
As he hath followed you, with all despite.°
Give him deserved vexation.° Let a guard　　140
Attend us through the city.
　　CITS. Come, come, let's see him out at gates, come.
The gods preserve our noble Tribunes! Come.

　　　　　　　　　　　　　　　[*Exeunt.*]

Act IV

SCENE I. *Rome. Before a gate of the city.*

[*Enter* CORIOLANUS, VOLUMNIA, VIRGILIA, MENENIUS,
COMINIUS, *with the young nobility of Rome.*]

COR. Come, leave your tears, a brief farewell. The
　　beast
With many heads butts me away. Nay, Mother,
Where is your ancient courage? You were used
To say extremity° was the trier of spirits,
That common chances common men could bear,　5
That when the sea was calm all boats alike
Showed mastership in floating. Fortune's blows,
When most struck home, being gentle wounded,
　　craves
A noble cunning.° You were used to load me
With precepts that would make invincible　　10
The heart that conned° them.
　　VIR. Oh, heavens! Oh, heavens!
　　COR.　　　　　Nay, I prithee, woman ——
VOL. Now the red pestilence° strike all trades in
　　Rome,
And occupations° perish!
　　COR.　　　　　What, what, what!　14
I shall be loved when I am lacked.° Nay, Mother,
Resume that spirit when you were wont to say

If you had been the wife of Hercules,
Six of his labors you'd have done, and saved
Your husband so much sweat. Cominius,
Droop not, adieu. Farewell, my wife, my mother.
I'll do well yet. Thou old and true Menenius,　21
Thy tears are salter than a younger man's,
And venomous to thine eyes. My sometime General,
I have seen thee stern, and thou hast oft beheld
Heart-hardening spectacles. Tell these sad women
'Tis fond° to wail inevitable strokes,　　26
As 'tis to laugh at 'em. My mother, you wot° well
My hazards still° have been your solace. And
Believe 't not lightly — though I go alone,
Like to a lonely dragon that his fen　　30
Makes feared and talked of more than seen — your
　　son
Will or exceed the common, or be caught
With cautelous° baits and practice.°
　　VOL.　　　　My first son,
Whither wilt thou go? Take good Cominius
With thee awhile. Determine on some course　35
More than a wild exposture° to each chance
That starts i' the way before thee.
　　COR.　　　　Oh, the gods!
COM. I'll follow thee a month, devise with thee
Where thou shalt rest, that thou mayst hear of us
And we of thee. So, if the time thrust forth　40
A cause for thy repeal,° we shall not send
O'er the vast world to seek a single man
And lose advantage,° which doth ever cool
I' the absence of the needer.
　　COR.　　　　Fare ye well.
Thou hast years upon thee, and thou art too full　45
Of the wars' surfeits° to go rove with one
That's yet unbruised. Bring me but out at gate.
Come, my sweet wife, my dearest mother, and
My friends of noble touch,° when I am forth,
Bid me farewell, and smile. I pray you come.　50
While I remain above the ground you shall
Hear from me still, and never of me aught
But what is like me formerly.
　　MEN.　　　　That's worthily
As any ear can hear. Come, let's not weep.
If I could shake off but one seven years　　55
From these old arms and legs, by the good gods,
I'd with thee every foot.
　　COR.　　　　Give me thy hand.
Come.　　　　　　　　　　　[*Exeunt.*]

128–33. till . . . blows: till at last your ignorance (which will not
be revealed till you suffer for it and which makes you always your
own worst enemies) shall deliver you as most humiliated (*abated*)
captives to some nation that wins you without blows.　**139. de-**
spite: spite.　**140. vexation:** torment.
　Act IV, Sc. i: 4. extremity: misfortune.　**7–9. Fortune's . . .**
cunning: when Fortune's blows strike home, to remain true to
one's birth (*gentle*) under the wound demands a noble knowledge;
i.e., only the noble heart can endure the blows of Fortune bravely.
Cf. *Tr & Cr,* I.iii.33–37.　**9. cunning:** skill.　**11. conned:**
learned by heart.　**13. red pestilence:** one of the forms of the
dreaded plague.　**14. occupations:** tradesmen.　**15. lacked:**
missed.

26. fond: foolish.　**27. wot:** know.　**28. still:** always.　**33. cau-**
telous: crafty. **practice:** plotting.　**36. exposture:** exposure.
41. repeal: recall from banishment.　**43. advantage:** the opportunity.　**45–46. thou . . . surfeits:** you are sick of too much war.
surfeits: state of overfullness.　**49. noble touch:** proved nobility.
touch: tested by the touchstone. See *Rich III*, IV.ii.8,n.

SCENE II. *The same. A street near the gate.*

[*Enter the two* TRIBUNES, SICINIUS *and* BRUTUS, *with the* AEDILE.]

SIC. Bid them all home, he's gone, and we'll no
  further.
The nobility are vexed, whom we see have sided°
In his behalf.
  BRU.   Now we have shown our power,
Let us seem humbler after it is done
Than when it was a-doing.
  SIC.   Bid them home.   5
Say their great enemy is gone, and they
Stand in their ancient strength.
  BRU.   Dismiss them home.   [*Exit* AEDILE.]
Here comes his mother.
  [*Enter* VOLUMNIA, VIRGILIA, *and* MENENIUS.]
  SIC.   Let's not meet her.
  BRU.   Why?
  SIC. They say she's mad.
  BRU. They have ta'en note of° us. Keep on your
  way.   10
  VOL. Oh, ye're well met. The hoarded plague°
  o' the gods
Requite your love!
  MEN.   Peace, peace, be not so loud.
  VOL. If that I could for weeping, you should
  hear ——
Nay, and you shall hear some. [*To* BRUTUS] Will you
  be gone?
  VIR. [*To* SICINIUS] You shall stay too. I would I
  had the power   15
To say so to my husband.
  SIC.   Are you mankind?°
  VOL. Aye, fool, is that a shame? Note but this fool.
Was not a man my father? Hadst thou foxship°
To banish him that struck more blows for Rome
Than thou hast spoken words?
  SIC.   Oh, blessed Heavens!   20
  VOL. Moe noble blows than ever thou wise words,
And for Rome's good. I'll tell thee what, yet go.
Nay, but thou shalt stay too. I would my son
Were in Arabia,° and thy tribe before him,
His good sword in his hand.
  SIC.   What then?
  VIR.   What then!   25
He'd make an end of thy posterity.°
  VOL. Bastards and all.
Good man, the wounds that he does bear for Rome!
  MEN. Come, come, peace.
  SIC. I would he had continued to his country   30
As he began, and not unknit himself

The noble knot° he made.
  BRU.   I would he had.
  VOL. "I would he had!" 'Twas you incensed the
  rabble,
Cats, that can judge as fitly of his worth
As I can of those mysteries which Heaven   35
Will not have earth to know.
  BRU.   Pray let us go.
  VOL. Now pray, sir, get you gone.
You have done a brave deed. Ere you go, hear this:
As far as doth the Capitol exceed
The meanest house in Rome, so far my son —   40
This lady's husband here, this, do you see? —
Whom you have banished, does exceed you all.
  BRU. Well, well, we'll leave you.
  SIC.   Why stay we to be baited°
With one that wants her wits?
  VOL.   Take my prayers with you.
                           [*Exeunt* TRIBUNES.]
I would the gods had nothing else to do   45
But to confirm my curses! Could I meet 'em
But once a day, it would unclog° my heart
Of what lies heavy to 't.
  MEN.   You have told them home,
And, by my troth, you have cause. You'll sup with
  me?
  VOL. Anger's my meat. I sup upon myself,   50
And so shall starve with feeding. Come, let's go.
Leave this faint puling,° and lament as I do,
In anger, Juno-like.° Come, come, come.
            [*Exeunt* VOLUMNIA *and* VIRGINIA.]
  MEN. Fie, fie, fie!   [*Exit.*]

SCENE III. *A highway between Rome and
        Antium.*

[*Enter a* ROMAN *and a* VOLSCE, *meeting.*]

  ROM. I know you well, sir, and you know me.
Your name, I think, is Adrian.
  VOLS. It is so, sir. Truly, I have forgot you.
  ROM. I am a Roman, and my services are, as you
are, against 'em. Know you me yet?   5
  VOLS. Nicanor? No.
  ROM. The same, sir.
  VOLS. You had more beard when I last saw you,
but your favor is well appeared by your tongue.°
What's the news in Rome? I have a note from the
Volscian state, to find you out there. You have well
saved me a day's journey.   12
  ROM. There hath been in Rome strange insurrec-

Sc. ii: 2. sided: taken sides.   10. ta'en . . . of: noticed.
11. hoarded plague: plague kept in store for a special punishment.   16. mankind: a mannish woman.   18. foxship: low
cunning.   24. Arabia: i.e., the desert, where there is no escaping.
26. posterity: descendants, tribe.

32. noble knot: i.e., that which bound Rome to him.   43. baited:
worried, like a bear by the hounds.   47. unclog: take the weight
from.   52. puling: whining.   53. Juno-like: Juno was Queen
of Heaven; her anger therefore was thunderous.
Sc. iii: 9. favor . . . tongue: face is seen in your speech; i.e.,
your Latin accent shows that you are a Roman.

tions, the people against the Senators, patricians, and nobles.

vols. Hath been! Is it ended, then? Our state think not so. They are in a most warlike preparation, and hope to come upon them in the heat of their division. 19

rom. The main blaze of it is past, but a small thing would make it flame again. For the nobles receive so to heart the banishment of that worthy Coriolanus that they are in a ripe aptness° to take all power from the people, and to pluck from them their Tribunes forever. This lies glowing, I can tell you, and is almost mature for the violent breaking-out. 27

vols. Coriolanus banished!

rom. Banished, sir.

vols. You will be welcome with this intelligence,° Nicanor. 31

rom. The day serves well for them now. I have heard it said the fittest time to corrupt a man's wife is when she's fallen out with her husband. Your noble Tullus Aufidius will appear well in these wars, his great opposer, Coriolanus, being now in no request of° his country. 38

vols. He cannot choose. I am most fortunate thus accidentally to encounter you. You have ended my business, and I will merrily accompany you home.

rom. I shall, between this and supper, tell you most strange things from Rome, all tending to the good of their adversaries. Have you an army ready, say you? 46

vols. A most royal one, the centurions and their charges,° distinctly° billeted, already in the entertainment,° and to be on foot at an hour's warning. 50

rom. I am joyful to hear of their readiness, and am the man, I think, that shall set them in present° action. So, sir, heartily well met, and most glad of your company. 54

vols. You take my part from me, sir. I have the most cause to be glad of yours.

rom. Well, let us go together. [*Exeunt.*]

SCENE IV. *Antium. Before* AUFIDIUS'S *house.*

[*Enter* CORIOLANUS *in mean apparel, disguised and muffled.*]

cor. A goodly city is this Antium. City,
'Tis I that made thy widows. Many an heir
Of these fair edifices 'fore° my wars
Have I heard groan and drop. Then know me not,

Lest that thy wives with spits,° and boys with stones,
In puny battle slay me.
[*Enter a* CITIZEN.]   Save you,° sir. 6
cit. And you.
cor.   Direct me, if it be your will,
Where great Aufidius lies. Is he in Antium?
cit. He is, and feasts the nobles of the state
At his house this night.
cor.   Which is his house, beseech you? 10
cit. This, here before you.
cor.   Thank you, sir. Farewell. [*Exit* CITIZEN.]
O world, thy slippery turns! Friends now fast sworn,
Whose double bosoms seem to wear one heart,
Whose hours, whose bed, whose meal and exercise
Are still together, who twin, as 'twere, in love 15
Unseparable, shall within this hour,
On a dissension of a doit,° break out
To bitterest enmity. So fellest° foes,
Whose passions and whose plots have broke their sleep
To take the one the other, by some chance, 20
Some trick not worth an egg, shall grow dear friends
And interjoin their issues.° So with me.
My birthplace hate I, and my love's upon
This enemy town. I'll enter. If he slay me,
He does fair justice. If he give me way, 25
I'll do his country service. [*Exit.*]

SCENE V. *The same. A hall in* AUFIDIUS'S *house.*

[*Music within. Enter a* SERVINGMAN.]
1. serv. Wine, wine, wine!—What service is here! I think our fellows are asleep. [*Exit.*]
[*Enter another* SERVINGMAN.]
2. serv. Where's Cotus? My master calls for him. Cotus! [*Exit.*]
[*Enter* CORIOLANUS.]
cor. A goodly house. The feast smells well, but I Appear not like a guest. 6
[*Re-enter the* FIRST SERVINGMAN.]
1. serv. What would you have, friend? Whence are you? Here's no place for you. Pray go to the door. [*Exit.*]
cor. I have deserved no better entertainment,°
In being Coriolanus. 11
[*Re-enter* SECOND SERVINGMAN.]
2. serv. Whence are you, sir? Has the porter° his

---

5. **spits:** iron rods on which meat was roasted, useful domestic weapons.   6. **Save you:** God bless you.   17. **dissension . . . doit:** quarrel not worth half a cent. **doit:** half a farthing.   18. **fellest:** fiercest.   22. **interjoin . . . issues:** arrange for their children to intermarry.

Sc. v: 10. **entertainment:** reception.   12. **porter:** keeper of the outer gate.

23. **ripe aptness:** ready and eager.   31. **intelligence:** news. 37–38. **in . . . of:** not required by.   48. **charges:** men in their command. **distinctly:** individually.   48–49. **in . . . entertainment:** hired.   52. **present:** immediate.

Sc. iv: 3. **'fore:** before.

Handwritten margin notes: AUFIDIUS IS IMPATIENT — USE OF SAME TERMS INDICATES A PT. BY SKAKES.

eyes in his head that he gives entrance to such companions?° Pray get you out.

COR. Away!   15

2. SERV. Away! Get you away.

COR. Now thou'rt troublesome.

2. SERV. Are you so brave?° I'll have you talked with anon.°

[*Enter a* THIRD SERVINGMAN. *The first meets him.*]

3. SERV. What fellow's this?   20

1. SERV. A strange one as ever I looked on. I cannot get him out o' the house. Prithee call my master to him.   [*Retires.*]

3. SERV. What have you to do here, fellow? Pray you avoid° the house.   25

COR. Let me but stand, I will not hurt your hearth.

3. SERV. What are you?

COR. A gentleman.

3. SERV. A marvelous poor one.   30

COR. True, so I am.

3. SERV. Pray you, poor gentleman, take up some other station,° here's no place for you. Pray you avoid. Come.   34

COR. Follow your function,° go and batten on cold bits.°   [*Pushes him away from him.*]

3. SERV. What, you will not? Prithee tell my master what a strange guest he has here.

2. SERV. And I shall.   [*Exit.*]

3. SERV. Where dwell'st thou?   40

COR. Under the canopy.°

3. SERV. Under the canopy!

COR. Aye.

3. SERV. Where's that?

COR. I' the city of kites and crows.   45

3. SERV. I' the city of kites and crows! What an ass it is! Then thou dwell'st with daws° too?

COR. No, I serve not thy master.

3. SERV. How, sir! Do you meddle with my master?   51

COR. Aye, 'tis an honester service than to meddle with thy mistress. Thou pratest, and pratest. Serve with thy trencher,° hence!   [*Beats him away.*
                                 Exit THIRD SERVINGMAN.]

[*Enter* AUFIDIUS *with the* SECOND SERVINGMAN.]

AUF. Where is this fellow?   55

2. SERV. Here, sir. I'd have beaten him like a dog but for disturbing the lords within.   [*Retires.*]

AUF. Whence comest thou? What wouldst thou? Thy name?

Why speak'st not? Speak, man. What's thy name?

COR. [*Unmuffling.*]   If, Tullus,   60
Not yet thou knowest me and, seeing me, dost not
Think me for the man I am, necessity

Commands me name myself.

AUF.   What is thy name?

COR. A name unmusical to the Volscians' ears,
And harsh in sound to thine.

AUF.   Say, what's thy name?   65
Thou hast a grim appearance, and thy face
Bears a command in 't. Though thy tackle's° torn,
Thou show'st a noble vessel. What's thy name?

COR. Prepare thy brow to frown. — Know'st thou
        me yet?

AUF. I know thee not. — Thy name?   70

COR. My name is Caius Marcius, who hath done
To thee particularly, and to all the Volsces,
Great hurt and mischief — thereto witness may
My surname, Coriolanus. The painful° service,
The extreme dangers, and the drops of blood   75
Shed for my thankless country are requited
But with that surname, a good memory,°
And witness of the malice and displeasure
Which thou shouldst bear me. Only that name remains.

The cruelty and envy of the people,   80
Permitted by our dastard° nobles, who
Have all forsook me, hath devoured the rest,
And suffered me by the voice of slaves to be
Whooped° out of Rome. Now this extremity
Hath brought me to thy hearth. Not out of hope —
Mistake me not — to save my life, for if   86
I had feared death, of all the men i' the world
I would have 'voided thee, but in mere spite,
To be full quit of° those my banishers,
Stand I before thee here. Then if thou hast   90
A heart of wreak° in thee that wilt revenge
Thine own particular wrongs, and stop those
        maims
Of shame° seen through thy country, speed thee
        straight,
And make my misery serve thy turn. So use it
That my revengeful services may prove   95
As benefits to thee, for I will fight
Against my cankered° country with the spleen°
Of all the underfiends.° But if so be
Thou darest not this and that to prove more fortunes°
Thou'rt tired, then, in a word, I also am   100
Longer to live most weary, and present
My throat to thee and to thy ancient malice,
Which not to cut would show thee but a fool,
Since I have ever followed thee with hate,
Drawn tuns° of blood out of thy country's breast,

---

14. companions: low fellows. 18. brave: insolent. 19. anon: at once. 25. avoid: get out of. 33. station: standing place. 35. Follow . . . function: do your job. 35–36. batten . . . bits: feed on the scraps. 41. canopy: the heavens. 47. daws: jackdaws. 54. trencher: wooden plate.

67. tackle: rigging. 74. painful: laborious. 77. memory: memorial. 81. dastard: cowardly. 84. Whooped: pursued with shouts of derision. 89. full . . . of: fully revenged on. 91. wreak: vengeance. 92–93. maims . . . shame: shameful injuries. 97. cankered: eaten up by the maggots of ingratitude. spleen: anger. 98. underfiends: the fiends below. 99. prove . . . fortunes: risk the fortune of war again. 105. tuns: barrels. A *tun* is a large cask, used especially for wine.

And cannot live but to thy shame° unless　　106
It be to do thee service.
　　　AUF.　　　　　　　O Marcius, Marcius!
Each word thou hast spoke hath weeded from my
　　　heart
A root of ancient envy.° If Jupiter
Should from yond cloud speak divine things,　110
And say " 'Tis true," I'd not believe them more
Than thee, all-noble Marcius. Let me twine
Mine arms about that body where-against
My grainèd ash° a hundred times hath broke,
And scarred the moon with splinters. Here I clip°
The anvil of my sword, and do contest　　116
As hotly and as nobly with thy love
As ever in ambitious strength I did
Contend against thy valor. Know thou first,
I loved the maid I married, never man　　120
Sighed truer breath, but that I see thee here,
Thou noble thing! more dances my rapt° heart
Than when I first my wedded mistress saw
Bestride my threshold. Why, thou Mars! I tell thee
We have a power on foot, and I had purpose　125
Once more to hew thy target° from thy brawn,°
Or lose mine arm for 't. Thou hast beat me out
Twelve several times, and I have nightly since
Dreamed of encounters 'twixt thyself and me.
We have been down together in my sleep,　　130
Unbuckling helms,° fisting each other's throat,
And waked half-dead with nothing. Worthy Mar-
　　　cius,
Had we no quarrel else to Rome but that
Thou art thence banished, we would muster all
From twelve to seventy, and pouring war　　135
Into the bowels of ungrateful Rome,
Like a bold flood o'erbear. Oh, come, go in,
And take our friendly Senators by the hands,
Who now are here taking their leaves of me,
Who am prepared against your territories,　　140
Though not for Rome itself.
　　　COR.　　　　　　　You bless me, gods!
　　　AUF. Therefore, most absolute° sir, if thou wilt
　　　have
The leading of thine own revenges, take
The one half of my commission, and set down —
As best thou art experienced, since thou know'st
Thy country's strength and weakness — thine own
　　　ways,　　146
Whether to knock against the gates of Rome,
Or rudely visit them in parts remote,
To fright them, ere destroy. But come in.
Let me commend° thee first to those that shall　150
Say yea to thy desires. A thousand welcomes!

---

106. cannot . . . shame: i.e., while I live I am a record of your
shame.　109. envy: hatred.　114. grainèd ash: the stout ash
shaft of my spear.　115. clip: embrace.　122. rapt: enraptured.
126. target: small shield. See Pl. 9d. brawn: the muscles of the
arm.　131. helms: helmets.　142. absolute: perfect.　150. commend: introduce.

And more a friend than e'er an enemy;
Yet, Marcius, that was much. Your hand. Most welcome!　[*Exeunt* CORIOLANUS *and* AUFIDIUS. *The
two* SERVINGMEN *come forward.*]
　　　1. SERV. Here's a strange alteration!　　154
　　　2. SERV. By my hand, I had thought to have
strucken° him with a cudgel, and yet my mind gave
me° his clothes made a false report of him.
　　　1. SERV. What an arm he has! He turned me about
with his finger and his thumb as one would set up
a top.　　161
　　　2. SERV. Nay, I knew by his face that there was
something in him. He had, sir, a kind of face, methought —— I cannot tell how to term it.
　　　1. SERV. He had so, looking as it were —— Would
I were hanged, but I thought there was more in him
than I could think.　　167
　　　2. SERV. So did I, I'll be sworn. He is simply° the
rarest man i' the world.
　　　1. SERV. I think he is. But a greater soldier than
he, you wot one.　　171
　　　2. SERV. Who? My master?
　　　1. SERV. Nay, it's no matter for that.
　　　2. SERV. Worth six on him.
　　　1. SERV. Nay, not so neither. But I take him to be
the greater soldier.　　176
　　　2. SERV. Faith, look you, one cannot tell how to say
that. For the defense of a town, our General is excellent.
　　　1. SERV. Aye, and for an assault too.　　180
　　　　　[*Re-enter* THIRD SERVINGMAN.]
　　　3. SERV. O slaves, I can tell you news, news, you
rascals!
　　　1. & 2. SERV. What, what, what? Let's partake.
　　　3. SERV. I would not be a Roman, of all nations. I
had as lieve° be a condemned man.　　186
　　　1. & 2. SERV. Wherefore? Wherefore?
　　　3. SERV. Why, here's he that was wont to thwack°
our General — Caius Marcius.
　　　1. SERV. Why do you say thwack our General?
　　　3. SERV. I do not say thwack our General,　192
but he was always good enough for him.
　　　2. SERV. Come, we are fellows and friends. He was
ever too hard for him, I have heard him say so himself.　　196
　　　1. SERV. He was too hard for him directly, to say
the troth on 't. Before Corioli he scotched° him and
notched him like a carbonado.°
　　　2. SERV. An he had been cannibally given, he
might have broiled and eaten him too.　　201
　　　1. SERV. But more of thy news?
　　　3. SERV. Why, he is so made on here within as if
he were son and heir to Mars — set at upper end o'

---

156. strucken: hit.　156–57. gave me: told me, misgave me.
168. simply: without other description.　186. lieve: soon.
189. thwack: wallop.　198. scotched: slashed.　199. carbonado: steak scored for grilling.

the table, no question asked him by any of the Senators, but they stand bald° before him. Our General himself makes a mistress of him, sanctifies himself with 's hand,° and turns up the white o' the eye to his discourse. But the bottom of the news is, our General is cut i' the middle, and but one half of 210 what he was yesterday, for the other has half, by the entreaty and grant of the whole table. He'll go, he says, and sowl° the porter of Rome gates by the ears. He will mow all down before him, and leave his passage polled.° 215

2. SERV. And he's as like to do 't as any man I can imagine.

3. SERV. Do 't! He will do 't, for look you, sir, he has as many friends as enemies, which friends, sir, as it were, durst not, look you, sir, show themselves, as we term it, his friends whilst he's in directitude.°

1. SERV. Directitude! What's that? 222

3. SERV. But when they shall see, sir, his crest up again and the man in blood, they will out of their burrows, like conies° after rain, and revel all with him. 227

1. SERV. But when goes this forward?

3. SERV. Tomorrow, today, presently. You shall have the drum struck up this afternoon. 'Tis, as it were, a parcel° of their feast, and to be executed ere they wipe their lips. 232

2. SERV. Why, then we shall have a stirring world again. This peace is nothing° but to rust iron, increase tailors, and breed ballad-makers.°

1. SERV. Let me have war, say I. It exceeds peace as far as day does night, it's spritely,° waking, audible,° and full of vent.° Peace is a very apoplexy,° lethargy, mulled,° deaf, sleepy, insensible, a getter of more bastard children than war's a destroyer of men. 241

2. SERV. 'Tis so. And as war, in some sort, may be said to be a ravisher, so it cannot be denied but peace is a great maker of cuckolds.°

1. SERV. Aye, and it makes men hate one another.

3. SERV. Reason,° because they then less need 247 one another. The wars for my money. I hope to see Romans as cheap° as Volscians. They are rising,° they are rising. 250

1. & 2. SERV. In, in, in, in!   [*Exeunt.*]

---

206. bald: bareheaded, as a sign of respect.   207-08. sanctifies . . . hand: touches him with his hand as if he were something holy. 213. sowl: pull out.   215. polled: shorn.   221. directitude: Servants in Shakespeare's plays often use big words without knowing their meanings; possibly he intended "discredit." 226. conies: rabbits.   231. parcel: part.   234. This . . . nothing: When *Coriolanus* was written many of Shakespeare's contemporaries, especially unemployed ex-captains, openly lamented the end of the Spanish wars.   235. ballad-makers: See App. 8. 237. spritely: full of spirit.   238. audible: quick to hear. full of vent: full of excited talk. apoplexy: lethargy. See *II Hen IV,* I.ii.122–28.   239. mulled: warm and drowsy.   245. cuckolds: deceived husbands.   247. Reason: with good reason.   249. cheap: poor things. are rising: i.e., have finished dinner.

SCENE VI. *Rome. A public place.*

[*Enter the two* TRIBUNES, SICINIUS *and* BRUTUS.]

SIC. We hear not of him, neither need we fear him.
His remedies are tame° i' the present peace
And quietness of the people, which before
Were in wild hurry. Here do we make his friends
Blush that the world goes well, who rather had,   5
Though they themselves did suffer by 't, behold
Dissentious numbers pestering° streets than see
Our tradesmen singing in their shops and going
About their functions friendly.

BRU.   We stood to 't in good time.

[*Enter* MENENIUS.] Is this Menenius?   10

SIC. 'Tis he, 'tis he. Oh, he is grown most kind
Of late. Hail, sir!

MEN.   Hail to you both!

SIC. Your Coriolanus is not much missed
But with° his friends. The commonwealth doth stand,
And so would do were he more angry at it.   15

MEN. All's well, and might have been much better if
He could have temporized.°

SIC.   Where is he, hear you?

MEN. Nay, I hear nothing. His mother and his wife
Hear nothing from him.

[*Enter three or four* CITIZENS.]

CITS. The gods preserve you both!

SIC.   Godden, our neighbors.   20

BRU. Godden to you all, godden to you all.

1. CIT. Ourselves, our wives, and children, on our knees,
Are bound to pray for you° both.

SIC.   Live, and thrive!

BRU. Farewell, kind neighbors. We wished Coriolanus
Had loved you as we did.

CITS.   Now the gods keep you!   25

BOTH TRIBS. Farewell, farewell.

[*Exeunt* CITIZENS.]

SIC. This is a happier and more comely time
Than when these fellows ran about the streets
Crying confusion.

BRU.   Caius Marcius was
A worthy officer i' the war, but insolent,   30
O'ercome with pride, ambitious past all thinking,
Self-loving——

SIC.   And affecting one sole throne,
Without assistance.°

MEN.   I think not so.

Sc. vi: 2. remedies . . . tame: the actions he would have taken (had he been Consul) are no longer dangerous.   7. pestering: crowding.   14. But with: except by.   17. temporized: compromised.   23. Are . . . you: i.e., as our benefactors and patrons. 32-33. affecting . . . assistance: aiming to be King by himself.

SIC. We should by this, to all our lamentation,°
If he had gone forth° Consul, found it so.   35
BRU. The gods have well prevented it, and Rome
Sits safe and still without him.
                    [*Enter an* AEDILE.]
AED.   Worthy Tribunes,
There is a slave, whom we have put in prison,
Reports the Volsces with two several powers°
Are entered in the Roman territories,   40
And with the deepest malice of the war
Destroy what lies before 'em.
MEN.   'Tis Aufidius,
Who, hearing of our Marcius' banishment,
Thrusts forth his horns° again into the world,
Which were inshelled when Marcius stood for
          Rome,   45
And durst not once peep out.
SIC.   Come, what talk you
Of Marcius?
BRU. Go see this rumorer whipped. It cannot be
The Volsces dare break with us.
MEN.   Cannot be!
We have record that very well it can,
And three examples of the like have been   50
Within my age.° But reason with the fellow
Before you punish him, where he heard this,
Lest you shall chance to whip your information°
And beat the messenger who bids beware
Of what is to be dreaded.
SIC.   Tell not me.   55
I know this cannot be.
BRU.   Not possible.
                    [*Enter a* MESSENGER.]
MESS. The nobles in great earnestness are going
All to the Senate House. Some news is come
That turns their countenances.°
SIC.   'Tis this slave.
Go whip him 'fore the people's eyes. His raising, 60
Nothing but his report.
MESS.   Yes, worthy sir,
The slave's report is seconded,° and more,
More fearful, is delivered.°
SIC.   What more fearful?
MESS. It is spoke freely out of many mouths —
How probable I do not know — that Marcius,   65
Joined with Aufidius, leads a power 'gainst Rome,
And vows revenge as spacious as between
The young'st and oldest thing.°
SIC.   This is most likely!
BRU. Raised only that the weaker sort may wish
Good Marcius home again.

SIC.   The very trick° on 't.   70
MEN. This is unlikely.
He and Aufidius can no more atone°
Than violentest contrariety.
                    [*Enter a* SECOND MESSENGER.]
2. MESS. You are sent for to the Senate.
A fearful army, led by Caius Marcius   75
Associated with Aufidius, rages
Upon our territories, and have already
O'erborne° their way, consumed with fire, and took
What lay before them.
                    [*Enter* COMINIUS.]
COM. Oh, you have made good work!
MEN.   What news? What news?   80
COM. You have holp to ravish your own daugh-
          ters, and
To melt the city leads° upon your pates,
To see your wives dishonored to your noses ——
MEN. What's the news? What's the news?
COM. Your temples burned in their cement, and
Your franchises,° whereon you stood,° confined   86
Into an auger's bore.°
MEN.   Pray now, your news? —
You have made fair work, I fear me. — Pray, your
          news? —
If Marcius should be joined with Volscians ——
COM.   If!
He is their god. He leads them like a thing   90
Made by some other deity than nature,
That shapes man better. And they follow him,
Against us brats, with no less confidence
Than boys pursuing summer butterflies,
Or butchers killing flies.
MEN.   You have made good work, 95
You and your apron men,° you that stood so much
Upon the voice of occupation° and
The breath of garlic-eaters!
COM. He'll shake your Rome about your ears.
MEN.   As Hercules
Did shake down mellow fruit. You have made fair
          work!   100
BRU. But is this true, sir?
COM.   Aye, and you'll look pale
Before you find it other. All the regions
Do smilingly revolt, and who resist
Are mocked for valiant ignorance°
And perish constant° fools. Who is 't can blame
          him?   105

---

34. to . . . lamentation: to the sorrow of us all.   35. gone forth:
been elected.   39. several powers: separate armies.   44. Thrusts
. . . horns: i.e., like a snail.   51. age: lifetime.   53. information: teacher.   59. turns . . . countenances: makes them look
pale.   62. seconded: supported.   63. delivered: related, told.
67–68. as . . . thing: i.e., that he will spare neither young nor
old.

70. trick: device.   72. atone: be friends.   78. O'erborne: i.e.,
like a river in flood.   82. melt . . . leads: the roofs of buildings were often covered with lead. When a building caught fire
the molten lead was a considerable danger to the fire-fighters.
86. franchises: privileges; e.g., of being able to refuse to confirm the election of a Consul. stood: insisted.   87. auger's
bore: a tiny hole such as is made by an auger.   96. apron men:
artisans. Cf. *Caesar*, I.i.7.   97. voice of occupation: vote of
the workingman.   104. valiant ignorance: being brave fools.
105. constant: loyal.

Your enemies and his find something in him.
  MEN. We are all undone unless
The noble man have mercy.
  COM.   Who shall ask it?
The Tribunes cannot do 't for shame, the people
Deserve such pity of him as the wolf   110
Does of the shepherds. For his best friends, if they
Should say " Be good to Rome," they charged° him
   even
As those should do that had deserved his hate,
And therein showed like enemies.
  MEN.   'Tis true.
If he were putting to my house the brand°   115
That should consume it, I have not the face
To say " Beseech you, cease." You have made fair
   hands,°
You and your crafts!° You have crafted fair!
  COM.   You have brought
A trembling upon Rome such as was never
So incapable of help.
  BOTH TRIBS.   Say not we brought it.   120
  MEN. How! Was it we? We loved him, but, like
   beasts
And cowardly nobles, gave way unto your clusters,°
Who did hoot him out o' the city.
  COM.   But I fear
They'll roar him in again. Tullus Aufidius,
The second name of men,° obeys his points°   125
As if he were his officer.° Desperation
Is all the policy, strength, and defense
That Rome can make against them.
            [Enter a troop of CITIZENS.]
  MEN.   Here come the clusters.
And is Aufidius with him? You are they
That made the air unwholesome when you cast 130
Your stinking greasy caps in hooting at
Coriolanus' exile. Now he's coming,
And not a hair upon a soldier's head
Which will not prove a whip. As many coxcombs°
As you threw caps up will he tumble down,   135
And pay you for your voices. 'Tis no matter,
If he could burn us all into one coal,
We have deserved it.
  CITS. Faith, we hear fearful news.
  1. CIT.   For mine own part,
When I said banish him, I said 'twas pity.   140
  2. CIT. And so did I.
  3. CIT. And so did I, and, to say the truth, so did
very many of us. That we did, we did for the best,
and though we willingly consented to his banishment, yet it was against our will.   146

  COM. Ye're goodly things, you voices!
  MEN.   You have made
Good work, you and your cry!° Shall 's to the Capi-
   tol?
  COM. Oh, aye, what else?
             [Exeunt COMINIUS *and* MENENIUS.]
  SIC. Go, masters, get you home, be not dismayed.
These are a side that would be glad to have   151
This true which they so seem to fear. Go home,
And show no sign of fear.
  1. CIT. The gods be good to us! Come, masters,
let's home. I ever said we were i' the wrong when
we banished him.   156
  2. CIT. So did we all. But come, let's home.
                   [Exeunt CITIZENS.]
  BRU. I do not like this news.
  SIC. Nor I.   159
  BRU. Let's to the Capitol. Would half my wealth
Would buy this for a lie!
  SIC.   Pray let us go.   *[Exeunt.]*

SCENE VII. *A camp, at a small distance*
from Rome.

     [Enter AUFIDIUS, *with his* LIEUTENANT.]
  AUF. Do they still fly to the Roman?
  LIEU. I do not know what witchcraft's in him, but
Your soldiers use him as the grace 'fore meat,
Their talk at table, and their thanks at end,
And you are darkened in this action, sir,   5
Even by your own.°
  AUF.   I cannot help it now,
Unless, by using means, I lame the foot
Of our design. He bears himself more proudlier,
Even to my person, than I thought he would
When first I did embrace him. Yet his nature   10
In that's no changeling,° and I must excuse
What cannot be amended.
  LIEU.   Yet I wish, sir —
I mean for your particular° — you had not
Joined in commission with him, but either
Had borne the action of yourself or else   15
To him had left it solely.
  AUF. I understand thee well, and be thou sure,
When he shall come to his account, he knows not
What I can urge against him. Although it seems,
And so he thinks, and is no less apparent   20
To the vulgar eye, that he bears all things fairly,
And shows good husbandry° for the Volscian state,
Fights dragonlike, and does achieve° as soon
As draw his sword, yet he hath left undone

---

112. **charged:** accused.   115. **brand:** firebrand.   117. **have . . .
hands:** have done a fine job.   118. **crafts:** trade-unions.
122. **clusters:** mobs.   125. **second . . . men:** the most famous
after Coriolanus. **points:** trumpet calls, by which a commander
issued his orders.   126. **officer:** lieutenant.   134. **coxcombs:**
heads, lit., the fool's cap. See Pl. 13c.

148. **cry:** See III.iii.120,n.
  Sc. vii: 6. **own:** i.e., soldiers.   11. **no changeling:** i.e., is
true to his nature. A changeling was a child substituted by
the fairies for one they had stolen.   13. **your particular:** as
far as concerns yourself.   22. **husbandry:** management.
23. **achieve:** win.

That which shall break his neck or hazard mine 25
Whene'er we come to our account.
    LIEU. Sir, I beseech you, think you he'll carry
      Rome?
    AUF. All places yield to him ere he sits down,°
And the nobility of Rome are his.
The Senators and patricians love him too. 30
The Tribunes are no soldiers, and their people
Will be as rash in the repeal° as hasty
To expel him thence. I think he'll be to Rome
As is the osprey to the fish,° who takes it
By sovereignty of nature.° First he was 35
A noble servant to them, but he could not
Carry his honors even.° Whether 'twas pride,
Which out of° daily fortune ever taints°
The happy° man, whether defect of judgment,
To fail in the disposing of those chances 40
Which he was lord of, or whether nature,
Not to be other than one thing, not moving
From the casque to the cushion,° but commanding
    peace
Even with the same austerity and garb°
As he controlled the war, but one of these — 45
As he hath spices° of them all, not all,
For I dare so far free him — made him feared,
So hated, and so banished. But he has a merit,
To choke it in the utterance.° So our virtues
Lie in the interpretation of the time, 50
And power, unto itself most commendable,
Hath not a tomb so evident as a chair
To extol what it hath done.°
One fire drives out one fire — one nail, one nail.
Rights by rights fouler, strengths by strengths do
    fail. 55
Come, let's away. When, Caius, Rome is thine,
Thou art poor'st of all, then shortly art thou mine.
                  [Exeunt.]

---

28. sits down: lays siege.   **32. rash . . . repeal:** hasty to call him
back.   **34. osprey . . . fish:** The osprey is a species of fish-eating
hawk. It was believed that it so fascinated fishes that they
turned up their bellies to be more easily caught.   **35. sovereignty of nature:** natural superiority.   **37. even:** well balanced.
38. out of: in the course of. **taints:** infects.   **39. happy:** lucky.
42–43. not . . . cushion: not able to adjust himself from war to
peace. **casque:** helmet.   **44. austerity . . . garb:** severe behavior.
46. spices: flavors.   **48–49. But . . . utterance:** his merit should
have caused the sentence of banishment to be suppressed.
49–53. So . . . done: a difficult sentence. If the reading is correct,
the meaning appears to be: "Our good qualities depend on the
value which our contemporaries give them; and a man of power,
however worthy he may consider himself, is brought to destruction when he praises himself from his own chair of office"; i.e.,
a proud man brings ruin on himself by his pride.

Act V

SCENE I. *Rome. A public place.*

[*Enter* MENENIUS, COMINIUS, SICINIUS *and* BRUTUS,
the two TRIBUNES, *with others.*]

    MEN. No, I'll not go. You hear what he hath said
Which was sometime° his General, who loved him
In a most dear particular.° He called me father,
But what o' that? Go, you that banished him,
A mile before his tent fall down, and knee 5
The way into his mercy. Nay, if he coyed°
To hear Cominius speak, I'll keep at home.
    COM. He would not seem to know me.
    MEN.   Do you hear?
    COM. Yet one time he did call me by my name.
I urged our old acquaintance, and the drops 10
That we have bled together. Coriolanus
He would not answer to, forbade all names.
He was a kind of nothing, titleless,
Till he had forged himself a name o' the fire
Of burning Rome.
    MEN.   Why, so. You have made good work! 15
A pair of Tribunes that have racked° for Rome,
To make coals cheap. A noble memory!
    COM. I minded him how royal 'twas to pardon
When it was less expected. He replied
It was a bare petition° of a state 20
To one whom they had punished.
    MEN.   Very well.
Could he say less?
    COM. I offered° to awaken his regard
For 's private friends. His answer to me was
He could not stay to pick them in a pile 25
Of noisome musty chaff. He said 'twas folly,
For one poor grain or two, to leave unburned,
And still to nose° the offense.
    MEN.   For one poor grain or two!
I am one of those. His mother, wife, his child,
And this brave fellow too, we are the grains. 30
You are the musty chaff, and you are smelt
Above the moon. We must be burned for you.
    SIC. Nay, pray be patient. If you refuse your aid
In this so never-needed° help, yet do not
Upbraid 's with our distress. But sure, if you 35
Would be your country's pleader, your good tongue,
More than the instant army we can make,°
Might stop our countryman.
    MEN.   No, I'll not meddle.
    SIC. Pray you, go to him.
    MEN.   What should I do?

    Act V, Sc. i: 2. sometime: at one time.   **3. In . . . particular:**
in a most personal manner.   **6. coyed:** disdained.   **16. racked:**
strained, made great efforts.   **20. bare petition:** paltry request.
23. offered: attempted.   **28. nose:** smell.   **34. so never-needed:**
never so much needed as now.   **37. the . . . make:** the army we
can raise at short notice.

BRU. Only make trial what your love can do   40
For Rome, toward Marcius.
MEN.   Well, and say that Marcius
Return me, as Cominius is returned,
Unheard — what then?
But as a discontented friend, grief-shot°
With his unkindness? Say 't be so?
SIC.   Yet your goodwill   45
Must have that thanks from Rome after the
    measure
As you intended well.°
MEN.   I'll undertake 't.
I think he'll hear me. Yet, to bite his lip
And hum at good Cominius much unhearts° me.
He was not taken well,° he had not dined.   50
The veins unfilled, our blood is cold, and then
We pout upon the morning, are unapt
To give or to forgive. But when we have stuffed
These pipes and these conveyances of our blood
With wine and feeding, we have suppler souls   55
Than in our priestlike fasts. Therefore I'll watch
    him
Till he be dieted to my request,°
And then I'll set upon him.
BRU. You know the very road into his kindness,
And cannot lose your way.
MEN.   Good faith, I'll prove him,   60
Speed how it will.° I shall ere long have knowledge
Of my success.   [*Exit.*]
COM.   He'll never hear him.
SIC.   Not?
COM. I tell you, he does sit in gold,° his eye
Red as 'twould burn Rome, and his injury
The jailer to his pity.° I kneeled before him.   65
'Twas very faintly he said " Rise," dismissed me
Thus, with his speechless hand. What he would do,
He sent in writing after me, what he would not,
Bound with an oath to yield to his conditions.°
So that all hope is vain   70
Unless his noble mother, and his wife,
Who, as I hear, mean to solicit him
For mercy to his country. Therefore let's hence,
And with our fair entreaties haste them on.
                                        [*Exeunt.*]

44. grief-shot: struck by grief.   46–47. after . . . well: in proportion to your efforts.   49. unhearts: disheartens.   50. not . . .
well: not approached at a good moment.   57. dieted . . . request: till his stomach be in a fit state for me to ask.   61. Speed
. . . will: whatever the result may be.   63. sit in gold: i.e., on a
gold throne like a conqueror.   64–65. his . . . pity: his sense of
anger locking up his sense of pity.   69. Bound . . . conditions: he
is bound by an oath to observe the conditions of his appointment
as General.

SCENE II. *Entrance to the Volscian camp before Rome. Two* SENTINELS *on guard.*

[*Enter to them* MENENIUS.]
1. SEN. Stay. Whence are you?
2. SEN.   Stand, and go back.
MEN. You guard like men, 'tis well. But, by your
    leave,
I am an officer of state, and come
To speak with Coriolanus.
1. SEN.   From whence?
MEN.   From Rome.
1. SEN. You may not pass, you must return. Our
    General   5
Will no more hear from thence.
2. SEN. You'll see your Rome embraced with fire
    before
You'll speak with Coriolanus.
MEN.   Good my friends,
If you have heard your General talk of Rome,
And of his friends there, it is lots to blanks°   10
My name hath touched your ears. It is Menenius.
1. SEN. Be it so, go back. The virtue° of your
    name
Is not here passable.°
MEN.   I tell thee, fellow,
Thy General is my lover. I have been
The book° of his good acts, whence men have
    read   15
His fame unparalleled haply amplified.°
For I have ever verified° my friends,
Of whom he's chief, with all the size that verity
Would without lapsing suffer. Nay, sometimes,
Like to a bowl upon a subtle° ground,   20
I have tumbled past° the throw, and in his praise
Have almost stamped the leasing.° Therefore,
    fellow,
I must have leave to pass.
1. SEN. Faith, sir, if you had told as many lies in
his behalf as you have uttered words in your own,
you should not pass here — no, though it were as
virtuous to lie as to live chastely. Therefore go
back.   28
MEN. Prithee, fellow, remember my name is
Menenius, always factionary on° the party of your
General.
2. SEN. Howsoever° you have been his liar, as you
say you have, I am one that, telling true under him,
must say you cannot pass. Therefore go back.   35

Sc. ii: 10. lots to blanks: i.e., winning tickets in a lottery
to blank tickets. In an Elizabethan lottery the chances of a
prize were about one in forty.   12. virtue: power.   13. passable:
valid to let you pass.   15. book: the record.   16. haply amplified: perchance exaggerated.   17. verified: borne witness to.
20. subtle: tricky. See App. 13.   21. tumbled past: overshot.
22. stamped . . . leasing: given the lie (*leasing*) the impression
(*stamp*) of truth.   30. factionary on: a keen supporter of.
33. Howsoever: even if you have.

MEN. Has he dined, canst thou tell? For I would not speak with him till after dinner.

1. SEN. You are a Roman, are you?

MEN. I am, as thy General is.   39

1. SEN. Then you should hate Rome, as he does. Can you, when you have pushed out your gates the very defender of them and, in a violent popular ignorance, given your enemy your shield, think to front° his revenges with the easy groans of old women, the virginal palms of your daughters,   45 or with the palsied° intercession of such a decayed dotant° as you seem to be? Can you think to blow out the intended fire your city is ready to flame in with such weak breath as this? No, you are deceived. Therefore back to Rome, and prepare for your execution. You are condemned. Our General has sworn you out° of reprieve and pardon.   54

MEN. Sirrah, if thy captain knew I were here, he would use me with estimation.°

1. SEN. Come, my captain knows you not.

MEN. I mean, thy General.   58

1. SEN. My General cares not for you. Back, I say, go, lest I let forth your half-pint of blood. — Back — that's the utmost of your having — back.

MEN. Nay, but, fellow, fellow ——

[*Enter* CORIOLANUS *and* AUFIDIUS.]

COR. What's the matter?   64

MEN. Now, you companion, I'll say an errand for° you. You shall know now that I am in estimation, you shall perceive that a Jack guardant cannot office° me from my son Coriolanus. Guess but by my entertainment with him if thou standest not i' the state of° hanging, or of some death more long in   70 spectatorship° and crueler in suffering. Behold now presently, and swoon for what's to come upon thee. The glorious gods sit in hourly synod° about thy particular° prosperity, and love thee no worse than thy old father Menenius does! O my son, my   75 son! Thou art preparing fire for us. Look thee, here's water to quench it. I was hardly° moved to come to thee, but being assured none but myself could move thee, I have been blown out of your gates with   80 sighs, and conjure thee to pardon Rome and thy petitionary° countrymen. The good gods assuage thy wrath, and turn the dregs of it upon this varlet here — this, who, like a block,° hath denied my access to thee.   85

COR. Away!

MEN. How! Away!

COR. Wife, mother, child, I know not. My affairs

Are servanted to° others. Though I owe° My revenge properly,° my remission° lies   90 In Volscian breasts. That we have been familiar, Ingrate° forgetfulness shall poison rather Than pity note how much. Therefore be gone. Mine ears against your suits are stronger than Your gates against my force. Yet, for I loved thee, Take this along — I writ it for thy sake,   96 And would have sent it. [*Gives him a letter.*] Another word, Menenius, I will not hear thee speak. This man, Aufidius, Was my beloved in Rome. Yet thou behold'st.

AUF. You keep a constant temper.   100

[*Exeunt* CORIOLANUS *and* AUFIDIUS.]

1. SEN. Now, sir, is your name Menenius?

2. SEN. 'Tis a spell, you see, of much power. You know the way home again.

1. SEN. Do you hear how we are shent° for keeping your greatness back?   105

2. SEN. What cause do you think I have to swoon?

MEN. I neither care for the world nor your General. For such things as you, I can scarce think there's any, ye're so slight.° He that hath a will to die   110 by himself fears it not from another. Let your General do his worst. For you, be that you are, long, and your misery increase with your age! I say to you, as I was said to, Away!   [*Exit.*]

1. SEN. A noble fellow, I warrant him.   115

2. SEN. The worthy fellow is our General. He's the rock, the oak not to be wind-shaken.   [*Exeunt.*]

SCENE III. *The tent of* CORIOLANUS.

[*Enter* CORIOLANUS, AUFIDIUS, *and others.*]

COR. We will before the walls of Rome tomorrow Set down our host.° My partner in this action, You must report to the Volscian lords how plainly° I have borne this business.

AUF.   Only their ends You have respected, stopped your ears against   5 The general suit° of Rome, never admitted A private whisper — no, not with such friends That thought them sure of you.

COR.   This last old man, Whom with a cracked heart I have sent to Rome, Loved me above the measure of a father —   10 Nay, godded° me indeed. Their latest refuge° Was to send him, for whose old love I have, Though I showed sourly to him, once more offered The first conditions, which they did refuse

<hr>

44. front: confront.   46. palsied: paralyzed.   47. dotant: dodderer.   53–54. sworn . . . out: sworn not to.   56. estimation: respect.   65. say . . . for: tell a tale of.   67. Jack . . . office: Jack-in-office cannot keep.   69–70. i' . . . of: in danger of.   70–71. more . . . spectatorship: which gives the spectators a longer show.   73. synod: council.   74. particular: very own.   77. hardly: with difficulty.   82. petitionary: pleading.   84. block: block of wood, blockhead.

89. servanted to: under the orders of. owe: own.   90. properly: as my own. remission: power to forgive.   92. Ingrate: ungrateful.   104. shent: rebuked.   110. slight: hardly noticeable.   Sc. iii: 2. Set . . . host: i.e., begin the siege. Cf. I.ii.28.   3. plainly: honestly.   6. suit: petition.   11. godded: treated as a god. latest refuge: last resort.

And cannot now accept. To grace him only   15
That thought he could do more, a very little
I have yielded to. Fresh embassies and suits,
Nor from the state nor private friends, hereafter
Will I lend ear to. [*Shout within.*] Ha! What shout
     is this?
Shall I be tempted to infringe my vow   20
In the same time 'tis made? I will not.
[*Enter, in mourning habits,* VIRGILIA, VOLUMNIA,
leading young MARCIUS, VALERIA, *and* ATTENDANTS.]
My wife comes foremost, then the honored mold
Wherein this trunk° was framed, and in her hand
The grandchild to her blood. But out, affection!
All bond and privilege of nature, break!°   25
Let it be virtuous to be obstinate.
What is that curtsy worth? Or those doves' eyes,
Which can make gods forsworn? I melt, and am not
Of stronger earth than others. My mother bows,
As if Olympus to a molehill should   30
In supplication nod. And my young boy
Hath an aspéct of intercession° which
Great Nature cries " Deny not." Let the Volsces
Plow Rome and harrow Italy. I'll never
Be such a gosling to obey instinct, but stand   35
As if a man were author° of himself
And knew no other kin.
     VIR.   My lord and husband!
     COR. These eyes are not the same I wore in Rome.
     VIR. The sorrow that delivers us thus changed
Makes you think so.
     COR.   Like a dull actor° now   40
I have forgot my part and I am out,
Even to a full disgrace. Best of my flesh,
Forgive my tyranny, but do not say,
For that " Forgive our Romans." Oh, a kiss
Long as my exile, sweet as my revenge!   45
Now, by the jealous Queen of Heaven,° that kiss
I carried from thee, dear, and my true lip
Hath virgined it° e'er since. You gods! I prate,
And the most noble mother of the world
Leave unsaluted. Sink, my knee, i' the earth,   50
                      [*Kneels.*]
Of thy deep duty more impression show
Than that of common sons.
     VOL.   Oh, stand up blest
Whilst, with no softer cushion than the flint,
I kneel before thee and unproperly
Show duty, as mistaken all this while   55
Between the child and parent.   [*Kneels.*]
     COR.   What is this?
Your knees to me? To your corrected son?
Then let the pebbles on the hungry beach

Fillip° the stars, then let the mutinous winds
Strike the proud cedars 'gainst the fiery sun,   60
Murdering impossibility,° to make
What cannot be, slight work.
     VOL.   Thou art my warrior,
I holp to frame thee. Do you know this lady?
     COR. The noble sister of Publicola,
The moon of Rome,° chaste as the icicle   65
That's curdied° by the frost from purest snow
And hangs on Dian's temple — dear Valeria!
     VOL. This is a poor epitome° of yours,
Which by the interpretation of full time°
May show like all yourself.
     COR.   The god° of soldiers,   70
With the consent of supreme Jove, inform°
Thy thoughts with nobleness, that thou mayst prove
To shame unvulnerable, and stick i' the wars
Like a great sea mark,° standing every flaw°
And saving those that eye thee!
     VOL.   Your knee, sirrah.   75
     COR. That's my brave boy!
     VOL. Even he, your wife, this lady, and myself
Are suitors to you.
     COR.   I beseech you, peace.
Or if you'd ask, remember this before.
The thing I have forsworn to° grant may never   80
Be held by you denials. Do not bid me
Dismiss my soldiers, or capitulate°
Again with Rome's mechanics. Tell me not
Wherein I seem unnatural. Desire not
To allay my rages and revenges with   85
Your colder reasons.
     VOL.   Oh, no more, no more!
You have said you will not grant us anything,
For we have nothing else to ask but that
Which you deny already. Yet we will ask,
That, if you fail in our request, the blame   90
May hang upon your hardness. Therefore hear us.
     COR. Aufidius, and you Volsces, mark, for we'll
Hear naught from Rome in private. Your request?
     VOL. Should° we be silent and not speak, our
     raiment
And state of bodies would bewray° what life   95
We have led since thy exile. Think with thyself
How more unfortunate than all living women

59. **Fillip:** flip, dash against.   61. **Murdering impossibility:** i.e., make impossible events happen; no disaster can seem impossible when his mother, whom he had worshiped, kneels to him. 65. **moon of Rome:** i.e., the very goddess of chastity, for Diana was worshiped as the moon. 66. **curdied:** curdled. 68. **epitome:** shorter edition. Here Volumnia takes Coriolanus' son by the hand. 69. **interpretation . . . time:** when time shall have fully interpreted him, keeping up the image of "epitome." 70. **The god:** i.e., may the god. 71. **inform:** form, make. 74. **sea mark:** a conspicuous landmark seen from the sea which enables a navigator to check his position. **flaw:** gust of wind. 80. **forsworn to:** sworn not to. 82. **capitulate:** agree to conditions of surrender. 94–191. **Should . . . peace:** See *Cor* Intro. p. 1267b for the original of this speech. 95. **bewray:** betray, reveal.

23. **trunk:** body. 25. **All . . . break:** break every tie and claim of my natural love for mother, wife, and son. 32. **aspect of intercession:** pleading look. 36. **author:** maker. 40. **dull actor:** another image taken from the playhouse. Cf. II.ii.100, and Sonnet 23, 1–2. 46. **Queen of Heaven:** Juno. 48. **virgined it:** kept it chaste.

Are we come hither. Since that thy sight, which
　　should
Make our eyes flow with joy, hearts dance with
　　comforts,
Constrains them weep and shake with fear and sor-
　　row, 100
Making the mother, wife, and child to see
The son, the husband, and the father tearing
His country's bowels out. And to poor we
Thine enmity's most capital.° Thou barr'st us
Our prayers to the gods, which is a comfort 105
That all but we enjoy. For how can we,
Alas! how can we for our country pray,
Whereto we are bound, together with thy victory,
Whereto we are bound? Alack, or we must lose
The country, our dear nurse, or else thy person, 110
Our comfort in the country. We must find
An evident° calamity, though we had
Our wish, which side should win. For either thou
Must, as a foreign recreant,° be led
With manacles thorough our streets, or else 115
Triumphantly tread on thy country's ruin,
And bear the palm° for having bravely shed
Thy wife and children's blood. For myself, son,
I purpose not to wait on fortune till
These wars determine.° If I cannot persuade thee
Rather to show a noble grace to both parts° 121
Than seek the end of one, thou shalt no sooner
March to assault thy country than to tread —
Trust to 't, thou shalt not — on thy mother's womb
That brought thee to this world.
　　VIR.　　　　　　　　　Aye, and mine, 125
That brought you forth this boy, to keep your name
Living to time.
　　BOY.　　　　　A' shall not tread on me.
I'll run away till I am bigger, but then I'll fight.
　　COR.　Not of a woman's tenderness to be
Requires nor child nor woman's face to see.° 130
I have sat too long. 　　　　　　　　[*Rising.*]
　　VOL.　　　　　　Nay, go not from us thus.
If it were so that our request did tend
To save the Romans, thereby to destroy
The Volsces whom you serve, you might condemn
　　us
As poisonous of your honor. No, our suit 135
Is that you reconcile them. While the Volsces
May say " This mercy we have showed," the Ro-
　　mans,
" This we received," and each in either side
Give the all-hail° to thee, and cry " Be blest
For making up this peace! " Thou know'st, great
　　son, 140

The end of war's uncertain, but this certain,
That if thou conquer Rome, the benefit
Which thou shalt thereby reap is such a name
Whose repetition will be dogged with curses,
Whose chronicle thus writ: " The man was noble,
But with his last attempt he wiped it out, 146
Destroyed his country, and his name remains
To the ensuing age abhorred." Speak to me, son,
Thou hast affected° the fine strains° of honor,
To imitate the graces of the gods, 150
To tear with thunder the wide cheeks o' the air,
And yet to charge thy sulphur with a bolt
That should but rive an oak.° Why dost not speak?
Think'st thou it honorable for a noble man 154
Still to remember wrongs? Daughter, speak you.
He cares not for your weeping. Speak thou, boy.
Perhaps thy childishness will move him more
Than can our reasons. There's no man in the world
More bound to 's mother, yet here he lets me prate
Like one i' the stocks.° Thou hast never in thy life
Showed thy dear mother any courtesy, 161
When she, poor hen, fond of no second brood,
Has clucked thee to the wars and safely home,
Loaden° with honor. Say my request's unjust,
And spurn me back. But if it be not so, 165
Thou art not honest, and the gods will plague thee,
That thou restrain'st from me the duty which
To a mother's part belongs. He turns away.
Down, ladies, let us shame him with our knees.
To his surname Coriolanus 'longs° more pride 170
Than pity to our prayers. Down — an end,
This is the last. So we will home to Rome,
And die among our neighbors. Nay, behold 's.
This boy, that cannot tell what he would have,
But kneels and holds up hands for fellowship,° 175
Does reason° our petition with more strength
Than thou hast to deny 't. Come, let us go.
This fellow had a Volscian to his mother,
His wife is in Corioli, and his child
Like him by chance. Yet give us our dispatch.° 180
I am hushed until our city be afire,
And then I'll speak a little.
　　COR.　[*After holding her by the hand, silent*] O
　　　Mother, Mother!
What have you done? Behold, the Heavens do ope,
The gods look down, and this unnatural scene
They laugh at. O my mother, Mother! Oh! 185
You have won a happy victory to Rome,
But, for your son, believe it, oh, believe it,
Most dangerously you have with him prevailed,
If not most mortal° to him. But let it come.

104. capital: deadly.　112. evident: manifest.　114. recreant:
traitor.　117. bear . . . palm: receive the palm of victory.
120. determine: end.　121. parts: sides.　129–30. Not . . . see:
unless a man is to become as tender as a woman, he must not look
at his child or his wife.　139. all-hail: the salutation given to
kings. Cf. *Rich II*, IV.i.167–69; *Macb*, I.v.56.

149. affected: loved. strains: instincts.　151–53. To . . . oak: to
make a noise that would split the air and yet to load your gunpowder with a cannon ball which would only split an oak.
160. one . . . stocks: i.e., a railing vagabond. See App. 10.
164. Loaden: laden.　170. 'longs: belongs.　175. fellowship:
partnership, friendship.　176. reason: argue.　180. dispatch:
dismissal.　189. mortal: mortally.

Aufidius, though I cannot make true wars,　　190
I'll frame convenient° peace. Now, good Aufidius,
Were you in my stead, would you have heard
A mother less? Or granted less, Aufidius?

AUF.　I was moved withal.

COR.　　　　　　　　I dare be sworn you were.
And, sir, it is no little thing to make　　195
Mine eyes to sweat compassion. But, good sir,
What peace you'll make, advise me. For my part,
I'll not to Rome, I'll back with you, and pray you,
Stand to me° in this cause. O Mother! Wife!

AUF.　[*Aside*] I am glad thou hast set thy mercy
　　and thy honor　　200
At difference in thee. Out of that I'll work
Myself a former fortune.°

　　　　　[*The* LADIES *make signs to* CORIOLANUS.]

COR.　[*To* VOLUMNIA, VIRGILIA, *etc.*] Aye, by and
by —
But we will drink together, and you shall bear
A better witness back than words, which we
On like conditions will have countersealed.°　　205
Come, enter with us. Ladies, you deserve
To have a temple built you. All the swords
In Italy, and her confederate arms,
Could not have made this peace.　　　[*Exeunt.*]

SCENE IV.　*Rome. A public place.*

[*Enter* MENENIUS *and* SICINIUS.]

MEN.　See you yond coign° o' the Capitol, yond
cornerstone?

SIC.　Why, what of that?

MEN.　If it be possible for you to displace it with
your little finger, there is some hope the ladies of　　5
Rome, especially his mother, may prevail with him.
But I say there is no hope in 't. Our throats are sentenced, and stay upon° execution.

SIC.　Is 't possible that so short a time can alter the
condition of a man?　　10

MEN.　There is differency between a grub and a
butterfly, yet your butterfly was a grub. This Marcius
is grown from man to dragon. He has wings, he's
more than a creeping thing.

SIC.　He loved his mother dearly.　　15

MEN.　So did he me. And he no more remembers
his mother now than an eight-year-old horse. The
tartness of his face sours ripe grapes. When he
walks, he moves like an engine,° and the ground
shrinks before his treading. He is able to pierce a

corslet° with his eye, talks like a knell, and his hum°
is a battery. He sits in his state° as a thing made for
Alexander.° What he bids be done is finished with
his bidding.° He wants nothing of a god but eternity
and a Heaven to throne in.　　26

SIC.　Yes, mercy, if you report him truly.

MEN.　I paint him in the character.° Mark what
mercy his mother shall bring from him. There is no
more mercy in him than there is milk in a male tiger
— that shall our poor city find. And all this is long
of° you.　　32

SIC.　The gods be good unto us!

MEN.　No, in such a case the gods will not be good
unto us. When we banished him, we respected not
them, and he returning to break our necks, they respect not us.　　37

[*Enter a* MESSENGER.]

MESS.　Sir, if you'd save your life, fly to your house.
The plebeians have got your fellow Tribune
And hale° him up and down, all swearing if　　40
The Roman ladies bring not comfort home,
They'll give him death by inches.

[*Enter another* MESSENGER.]

SIC.　　　　　　　　What's the news?

2. MESS.　Good news, good news. The ladies have
prevailed,
The Volscians are dislodged,° and Marcius gone.
A merrier day did never yet greet Rome —　　45
No, not the expulsion of the Tarquins.

SIC.　　　　　　　　Friend,
Art thou certain this is true? Is it most certain?

2. MESS.　As certain as I know the sun is fire.
Where have you lurked° that you make doubt of it?
Ne'er through an arch so hurried the blown tide°
As the recomforted through the gates. Why, hark
you!　　51

[*Trumpets, hautboys, drums beat, all together.*]

The trumpets, sackbuts,° psalteries,° and fifes,
Tabors° and cymbals and the shouting Romans,
Make the sun dance. Hark you!　[*A shout within.*]

MEN.　　　　　　　　This is good news.
I will go meet the ladies. This Volumnia　　55
Is worth of Consuls, Senators, patricians,
A cityful, of Tribunes, such as you,
A sea and land full. You have prayed well today.
This morning for ten thousand of your throats
I'd not have given a doit. Hark how they joy!　　60

[*Music still, with shouts.*]

---

191. **convenient:** suitable.　199. **Stand to me:** support me.
201-02. **I'll . . . fortune:** I will restore my own fortunes to what
they were.　203-05. **you . . . countersealed:** you shall take back
not only an oral promise but a written and sealed agreement.
　Sc. iv: 1. coign: corner.　8. **stay upon:** wait for.　19. **engine:**
battering-ram, a heavy, lumbering machine.

21. **corslet:** breastplate. **hum:** grunt.　22. **state:** chair of state.
22-23. **thing . . . Alexander:** like a statue of Alexander the Great.
24-25. **What . . . bidding:** his orders are carried out by the time
he has finished giving them.　28. **in . . . character:** in his true
character.　31-32. **long of:** because of.　40. **hale:** haul.　44. **are
dislodged:** have abandoned the siege.　49. **lurked:** been hiding.
50. **Ne'er . . . tide:** This image is taken from the rush of waters
between the arches of London Bridge. See Gen. Intro. p. 16b.
52. **sackbut:** a form of trombone. **psalteries:** stringed instruments played with both hands.　53. **Tabors:** drums.

SIC. First, the gods bless you for your tidings.
Next,
Accept my thankfulness.

2. MESS.   Sir, we have all
Great cause to give great thanks.

SIC.   They are near the city?

2. MESS. Almost at point to enter.

SIC.   We will meet them,   64
And help the joy.   [*Exeunt.*]

SCENE V. *The same. A street near the gate.*

[*Enter two* SENATORS *with* VOLUMNIA, VIRGILIA,
VALERIA, *etc., passing over the stage, followed
by* PATRICIANS *and others.*]

1. SEN. Behold our patroness, the life of Rome!
Call all your tribes together, praise the gods,
And make triumphant fires,° strew flowers before
them.
Unshout the noise° that banished Marcius,
Repeal him with the welcome of his mother,   5
Cry " Welcome, ladies, welcome! "

ALL.   Welcome, ladies,
Welcome!

[*A flourish with drums and trumpets. Exeunt.*]

SCENE VI. *Corioli. A public place.*

[*Enter* TULLUS AUFIDIUS, *with* ATTENDANTS.]

AUF. Go tell the lords o' the city I am here.
Deliver them this paper. Having read it,
Bid them repair to the market place, where I,
Even in theirs and in the commons' ears,
Will vouch the truth of it. Him I accuse   5
The city ports° by this hath entered, and
Intends to appear before the people, hoping
To purge° himself with words. Dispatch.

[*Exeunt* ATTENDANTS.]

[*Enter three or four* CONSPIRATORS *of* AUFIDIUS'
faction.]

Most welcome!

1. CON.   How is it with our General?

AUF.   Even so   10
As with a man by his own alms empoisoned,
And with his charity slain.

2. CON.   Most noble sir,
If you do hold the same intent wherein
You wished us parties, we'll deliver you
Of your great danger.

AUF.   Sir, I cannot tell.   15
We must proceed as we do find the people.

3. CON. The people will remain uncertain whilst
'Twixt you there's difference, but the fall of either
Makes the survivor heir of all.

AUF.   I know it,
And my pretext to strike at him admits   20
A good construction. I raised him, and I pawned
Mine honor for his truth. Who being so heightened,
He watered his new plants with dews of flattery,
Seducing so my friends. And, to this end,
He bowed° his nature, never known before   25
But to be rough, unswayable, and free.

3. CON.   Sir, his stoutness
When he did stand for Consul, which he lost
By lacking of stooping ——

AUF.   That I would have spoke of.
Being banished for 't, he came unto my hearth,   30
Presented to my knife his throat. I took him,
Made him joint servant with me, gave him way
In all his own desires — nay, let him choose
Out of my files,° his projects to accomplish,
My best and freshest men, served his designments°
In mine own person, holp to reap the fame   36
Which he did end all his,° and took some pride
To do myself this wrong. Till at the last
I seemed his follower, not partner, and
He waged me with his countenance, as if   40
I had been mercenary.°

1. CON.   So he did, my lord.
The army marveled at it, and in the last,
When he had carried Rome and that we looked
For no less spoil than glory ——

AUF.   There was it
For which my sinews° shall be stretched upon him.
At a few drops of women's rheum,° which are   46
As cheap as lies, he sold the blood and labor
Of our great action. Therefore shall he die,
And I'll renew me in his fall. But hark!

[*Drums and trumpets sound, with great shouts of
the people.*]

1. CON. Your native town you entered like a post,°
And had no welcomes home, but he returns,   51
Splitting the air with noise.

2. CON.   And patient fools,
Whose children he hath slain, their base throats tear
With giving him glory.

3. CON.   Therefore, at your vantage,°
Ere he express himself, or move the people   55
With what he would say, let him feel your sword,
Which we will second. When he lies along,°
After your way his tale pronounced shall bury
His reasons with his body.

25. **bowed:** forced.   **34. files:** ranks.   **35. designments:** designs.   **36–37. holp . . . his:** helped to reap the crop of his fame, which he gathered up as all his own.   **40–41. waged . . . mercenary:** gave me patronizing looks, as if I had been his hired man.   **45. sinews:** strength.   **46. rheum:** moisture, tears.   **50. post:** a postboy, whom no one notices.   **54. at . . . vantage:** take your opportunity.   **57. along:** stretched out.

Sc. v: 3. **triumphant fires:** bonfires of joy.   4. **Unshout . . .
noise:** i.e., reverse your decision.

Sc. vi: 6. **ports:** gates.   8. **purge:** clear.

AUF.   Say no more.
Here come the lords.   60
        [*Enter the* LORDS *of the city.*]
LORDS. You are most welcome home.
        AUF.   I have not deserved it.
But, worthy lords, have you with heed perused
What I have written to you?
        LORDS.   We have.
        I. LORD.   And grieve to hear 't.
What faults he made before the last, I think
Might have found easy fines.° But there to end   65
Where he was to begin, and give away
The benefit of our levies, answering us
With our own charge,° making a treaty where
There was a yielding — this admits no excuse.
        AUF. He approaches. You shall hear him.   70
[*Enter* CORIOLANUS, *marching with drum and colors,
        the commoners being with him.*]
        COR. Hail, lords! I am returned your soldier,
No more infected with my country's love
Than when I parted hence, but still subsisting°
Under your great command. You are to know
That prosperously I have attempted, and   75
With bloody passage led your wars even to
The gates of Rome. Our spoils we have brought
        home
Do more than counterpoise° a full third part
The charges of the action. We have made peace,
With no less honor to the Antiates   80
Than shame to the Romans. And we here deliver,
Subscribed° by the Consuls and patricians,
Together with the seal o' the Senate, what
We have compounded° on.
        AUF.   Read it not, noble lords,
But tell the traitor,° in the highest degree   85
He hath abused your powers.
        COR. Traitor! How now!
        AUF.   Aye, traitor, Marcius!
        COR.   Marcius!
        AUF. Aye, Marcius, Caius Marcius. Dost thou
        think
I'll grace thee with that robbery, thy stol'n name
Coriolanus, in Corioli?   90
You lords and heads o' the state, perfidiously
He has betrayed your business, and given up,
For certain drops of salt, your city Rome —
I say "your city" — to his wife and mother,

Breaking his oath and resolution like   95
A twist° of rotten silk, never admitting
Council o' the war,° but at his nurse's tears
He whined and roared away your victory,
That pages blushed at him, and men of heart
Looked wondering each at other.
        COR.   Hear'st thou, Mars?   100
        AUF. Name not the god, thou boy of tears!°
        COR.   Ha!
        AUF. No more.
        COR. Measureless liar, thou hast made my heart
Too great for what contains it. " Boy! " O slave!
Pardon me, lords, 'tis the first time that ever   105
I was forced to scold. Your judgments, my grave
        lords,
Must give this cur the lie. And his own notion° —
Who wears my stripes impressed upon him, that
Must bear my beating to his grave — shall join
To thrust the lie unto him.   110
        I. LORD. Peace, both, and hear me speak.
        COR. Cut me to pieces, Volsces, men and lads,
Stain all your edges° on me. " Boy! " False hound!
If you have writ your annals true,° 'tis there
That, like an eagle in a dovecote, I   115
Fluttered your Volscians in Corioli.
Alone I did it. " Boy! "
        AUF.   Why, noble lords,
Will you be put in mind of his blind fortune,°
Which was your shame, by this unholy braggart
'Fore your own eyes and ears?
        ALL CONS.   Let him die for 't.   120
        ALL THE PEOPLE. Tear him to pieces. — Do it pres-
ently. — He killed my son. — My daughter. — He
killed my cousin Marcus. — He killed my father.
        2. LORD. Peace, ho! No outrage. Peace!   125
The man is noble, and his fame folds in
This orb o' the earth.° His last offenses to us
Shall have judicious° hearing. Stand, Aufidius,
And trouble not the peace.
        COR.   Oh, that I had him,
With six Aufidiuses, or more, his tribe,   130
To use my lawful sword!
        AUF.   Insolent villain!
        ALL CONS. Kill, kill, kill, kill, kill him!
        [*The* CONSPIRATORS *draw, and kill* CORIOLANUS.
                        AUFIDIUS *stands on his body.*]
        LORDS.   Hold, hold, hold, hold!
        AUF. My noble masters, hear me speak.

---

65. fines: penalties.   **66–68. give . . . charge:** give away the
profitable spoils which should have been taken, and leave us to
pay for the wars ourselves. In Shakespeare's time, when the doctrine of total war had not yet been established, the winning side
expected to make a profit out of the plunder brought home.
Coriolanus admits (ll. 76–78) that the spoils have only paid for
about a third of the expenses.   **73. subsisting:** continuing.
78. counterpoise: counterbalance.   **82. Subscribed:** signed.
84. compounded: agreed.   **85. traitor:** As before, the accusation
that he is a traitor moves Coriolanus to ungovernable fury. Cf.
III.iii.66.

96. twist: skein.   **96–97. never . . . war:** never asking the advice of his council of war. (It was normal for a commander's
commission to include a clause that in all major decisions he
should consult his council of war, composed of senior commanders.)
101. boy of tears: crybaby. To call a man a "boy" was a gross
and deliberate insult. Cf. *R & J*, III.i.69; *M Ado*, V.i.83–85.
107. notion: sense.   **113. edges:** i.e., swords.   **114. If . . . true:**
if your history books tell the truth.   **118. blind fortune:** lucky
success.   **126–27. folds . . . earth:** is universal.   **128. judicious:** judicial; i.e., in a court of law.

1. LORD.   O Tullus ——

2. LORD. Thou hast done a deed whereat valor will
   weep.

3. LORD. Tread not upon him. Masters all, be
   quiet.   135
Put up your swords.

   AUF. My lords, when you shall know — as in this
      rage
Provoked by him, you cannot — the great danger
Which this man's life did owe you,° you'll rejoice
That he is thus cut off. Please it your Honors   140
To call me to your Senate, I'll deliver°
Myself your loyal servant, or endure
Your heaviest censure.°

   1. LORD.   Bear from hence his body,
And mourn you for him. Let him be regarded

As the most noble corse° that ever herald°   145
Did follow to his urn.°

   2. LORD.   His own impatience
Takes from Aufidius a great part of blame.
Let's make the best of it.

   AUF.   My rage is gone,
And I am struck with sorrow. Take him up.
Help, three o' the chiefest soldiers, I'll be one. 150
Beat thou the drum, that it speak mournfully.
Trail your steel pikes.° Though in this city he
Hath widowed and unchilded many a one
Which to this hour bewail the injury,
Yet he shall have a noble memory.   155
Assist.   [*Exeunt, bearing the body of* CORIOLANUS.
                          A dead march sounded.]

138–39. **the . . . you:** the great danger you were in so long as this man was alive. 141. **deliver:** submit. 143. **censure:** condemnation.

145. **corse:** corpse. **herald:** See App. 9. 146. **urn:** tomb. 152. **Trail . . . pikes:** At military funerals the pikemen marched in the procession with pikes trailed and reversed. See Pl. 9a.

TIMON OF ATHENS

Introduction

Timon of Athens was first printed in the first folio in 1623, where it is included — apparently as an afterthought — among the tragedies, between *Romeo and Juliet* and *Julius Caesar*. It was at first intended that *Troilus and Cressida* should follow *Romeo and Juliet* (see *Tr & Cr* Intro. p. 973b) but for some reason it was removed, leaving a gap of thirty pages between the last page of *Romeo and Juliet,* numbered 79, and the first page of *Julius Caesar,* numbered 109. *Timon,* however, is eight pages shorter than *Troilus and Cressida,* and so the pagination of the folio is considerably disturbed; the pages of *Timon* are numbered 80, 81, 82, 81, 82, 83 and thence continuously to 98. There seems, therefore, to have been some understandable hesitation on the part of the editors of the first folio whether to include or to omit *Timon of Athens.*

The text of *Timon* is difficult. At times the play runs smoothly, with all the speeches well written and the action consistent and even; but at other times the diction in the folio breaks down into a confused medley of blank verse, rhymed verse, free verse, and mere doodling. This unevenness is not so obvious in an edited text, as editors have to some extent smoothed away the difficulties. Thus the F1 version of I.ii.197–223 runs:

> *Fla.* What will this come to?
> He commands vs to prouide, and giue great
>   guifts, and all out of an empty Coffer:
> Nor will he know his Purse, or yeeld me this,
> To shew him what a Begger his heart is,
> Being of no power to make his wishes good.
> His promises flye so beyond his state,
> That what he speaks is all in debt, he ows for
>   eu'ry word:
> He is so kinde, that he now payes interest for't;
> His Land's put to their Bookes. Well, would I
>   were
> Gently put out of Office, before I were forc'd out:
> Happier is he that has no friend to feede,
> Then such that do e'ne Enemies exceede.
> I bleed inwardly for my Lord.   *Exit*
> *Tim.* You do your selues much wrong,
> You bate too much of your owne merits,

Heere my Lord, a trifle of our Loue.
> *2 Lord.* With more then common thankes
> I will receyue it.
> *3 Lord.* O he's the very soule of Bounty.
> *Tim.* And now I remember my Lord, you gaue good words the other day of a Bay Courser I rod on. Tis yours because you lik'd it.
> *1 L.* Oh, I beseech you pardon mee, my Lord, in that.
> *Tim.* You may take my word my Lord: I know no man can iustly praise, but what he does affect. I weighe my Friends affection with mine owne: Ile tell you true, Ile call to you.

Various explanations have been offered for the difficulties of the text, such as revision of Shakespeare's work, or revision of another man's work by Shakespeare, or inept cutting of the play for performance. The likeliest guess is that of E. K. Chambers,[1] that *Timon* is the first version of a play which Shakespeare never finished. The passage quoted above is just the kind of rough draft that comes from an author whose inspiration is flagging or who is tired or bored with what he is writing.

There is no external fact — such as contemporary mention or quotation — by which the date of *Timon* can be checked, but the style is unmistakably that of Shakespeare's later period, when he wrote *Lear* and *Coriolanus* (1606–1609). Some of the speeches in *Timon* are echoes of passages and sentiments in the maturer tragedies, as if Shakespeare were imitating or borrowing from his own work. Thus Timon's curses on Athens and on mankind (IV.i.1–40, IV.iii.1–43) are an echo of Coriolanus's curse on Rome when he too was banished (III.iii.120–35), or a kind of rewriting of the mad speeches of Lear.

Some critics, impressed by the power of these speeches, have interpreted the play as a serious expression of Shakespeare's own sentiments at a period of some vast and intimate emotional crisis in his life. This kind of criticism, first made fashionable by the Victorian scholar Ed-

[1] *William Shakespeare: A Study of Facts and Problems,* i. 482.

ward Dowden (see pp. 82b–83a), has from time to time been repeated even by the younger critics of the 1930's and 1940's. An examination of the plays written between 1600 and 1610 would, however, have revealed to these critics the fact that the Timon type of character was quite common on the stage. In play after play there appeared a misanthrope who railed on the world with bitter vituperation.

The direct source of *Timon* is a casual anecdote in North's Plutarch (see *Caesar* Intro. pp. 809b–10a); it occurs in the "Life of Marcus Antonius," which Shakespeare had already used in the writing of both *Julius Caesar* and *Antony and Cleopatra*. The story is this:

Antonius, he forsook the city and company of his friends, and built him a house in the sea by the isle of Pharos, upon certain forced mounts which he caused to be cast into the sea, and dwelt there as a man that banished himself from all men's company, saying that he would lead Timon's life, because he had the like wrong offered him, that was before offered unto Timon; and that for the unthankfulness of those he had done good unto, and whom he took to be his friends, he was angry with all men and would trust to no man. This Timon was a citizen of Athens, that lived about the war of Peloponnesus, as appeareth by Plato and Aristophanes' comedies; in the which they mocked him, calling him a viper and malicious man unto mankind, to shun all other men's companies but the company of young Alcibiades, a bold and insolent youth, whom he would greatly feast and make much of, and kissed him very gladly. Apemantus wondering at it, asked him the cause what he meant to make so much of that young man alone, and to hate all others. Timon answered him: "I do it," said he, "because I know that one day he shall do great mischief unto the Athenians." This Timon sometimes would have Apemantus in his company, because he was much like of his nature and conditions, and also followed him in manner of life. On a time when they solemnly celebrated the feast called *Chœ* at Athens (to wit, the feasts of the dead where they make sprinklings and sacrifices for the dead) and that they two then feasted together by themselves, Apemantus said unto the other: "Oh, here is a trim banquet, Timon!" Timon answered again: "Yea," said he, "so thou wert not here." It is reported of him also, that this Timon on a time (the people having assembled in the market place about dispatch of some affairs) got up into the pulpit for orations, where the orators commonly use to speak unto the

people; and silence being made, every man listening to hear what he would say, because it was a wonder to see him in that place, at length he began to speak in this manner: "My lords of Athens, I have a little yard at my house where there groweth a fig tree, on the which many citizens have hanged themselves; and because I mean to make some building on the place, I thought good to let you all understand it, that, before the fig tree be cut down, if any of you be desperate, you may there in time go hang yourselves." He died in the city of Hales, and was buried upon the seaside. Now it chanced so, that the sea getting in, it compassed his tomb round about, that no man could come to it; and upon the same was written this epitaph:

Here lies a wretched corse, of wretched soul bereft:
Seek not my name: a plague consume you wicked wretches left!

It is reported that Timon himself, when he lived, made this epitaph; for that which is commonly rehearsed was not his, but made by the poet Callimachus:

Here lie I, Timon, who alive all living men did hate:
Pass by and curse thy fill: but pass, and stay not here thy gait.

Many other things could we tell you of this Timon, but this little shall suffice at this present.

From Plutarch's "Life of Alcibiades" Shakespeare might also have gathered some interesting details; but he seems to have taken little except the general impression that Alcibiades was a young gentleman who turned against his native city of Athens.

The story of Timon appears also in one of the *Dialogues* of the second-century Greek writer Lucian. In this version Timon appeals to the god Zeus to drop his thunderbolts on those ingrates who have taken his wealth and turn on him now that he is no more than a poor farm laborer. Zeus is at last aroused by Timon's prayers and orders Hermes, the messenger of the gods, to take Riches to Timon, but Riches demurs because Timon had treated him so badly in the past, and a long argument follows on the proper use of wealth. At last Riches agrees to go with Hermes. They find Timon digging; his companions nowadays are Poverty, Toil, Endurance, Wisdom, and Manliness. Timon greets Hermes and Riches rudely, but when persuaded that Riches is a gift from Zeus he reluctantly relents with the remark that they are bringing him ill luck because he is most nappy in his poverty, and with renewed wealth he will again be full of cares. Timon discovers a treasure and thereupon resolves to buy the farm where he is working, but to keep his wealth to himself. Almost at once his former parasites begin to gather — Gnathonides the toady, Philiades the flatterer, Demas the orator, and Thrasycles the philosopher, who preaches temperance best when drunk. Timon drives them all away.

There is little in this version — except for the discovery of the treasure — to suggest that Shakespeare used it, and the tone and moral implications are quite different from those in the play.

Timon is generally regarded as an unsatisfactory play. The characterization is poor and the plot as uneven as the poetry. The play begins with one of Shakespeare's favorite openings in his later dramas. Certain characters of minor importance — artists whom Timon is patronizing — enter and discuss him. Then, as they are talking, the curtains at the back of the stage open, and Timon himself appears, surrounded by his parasites. The first act thus displays the prosperity and the magnificent extravagance of Timon.

In the second act the situation begins to change. As Timon's creditors sense that he has reached the end of his inheritance, they hasten to retrieve what they have lent the spendthrift. Timon for a while is too stupid to face realities and rebukes his old steward for trying to force him to understand the facts. Even when ruined, Timon still believes that those who have sponged on him in his affluence will show themselves good friends in his ruin. When at last he is forced to realize that others are less open-handed than himself, he goes mad and departs to live with the beasts of the woods.

Meanwhile Alcibiades, his young soldier friend, has also suffered from the ingratitude of man. When he begs the Senate for the life of a friend who has killed his enemy in private quarrel, he is refused; and when he continues to plead, he is banished from Athens. Alcibiades' reply to this treatment is not solitary brooding like Timon's but a mad desire for vengeance.

So far, however, the plot has been fairly coherent; thereafter it rapidly disintegrates. In the fourth act Timon has reached the woods and turned beast. Accidentally, he finds gold, and a series of episodes follows in which he disposes of his gold where he thinks it will do the most harm, giving generously to Alcibiades and his two harlots, and then to a gang of bandits because they can always be relied on to injure their fellows. The news of his wealth soon spreads and the procession of his old flatterers begins; but Timon is no longer deceived, refuses to listen to any of them, and leaves the stage to die, presumably from moral indignation, for no other cause of his end is suggested.

Three brief episodes end the play. The senators of Athens express their fear of Alcibiades. A soldier finds Timon's tomb and takes an impression of the inscription. Alcibiades and his army come up to Athens; the senators submit; the soldier gives Alcibiades the copy of the inscription; and Alcibiades makes a final speech in which he promises to spare Athens.

Timon is not one of Shakespeare's great characters. He is hardly at any time much more than a personification, first of Reckless Prodigality and then of Mad Misanthropy, for he is shown only on the outside and his personality has therefore neither depth, variety, nor humanity. In Shakespeare's other mature plays, the major characters are seen from all sides. Coriolanus, for instance, in spite of his overwhelming pride, which is as much an obsession as the prodigality of Timon, is set off against his friend Menenius, his mother, his wife, his fellow soldiers, his Volscian enemy Aufidius, and his Roman enemies, the two tribunes. We thus see him as warrior, son, husband, father, friend, and politician. He is also given speeches and soliloquies in which to explain if not to justify the motives for his arrogance. But Timon has neither friends, wife, rivals, nor even enemies by whose aid we may see into his heart; nor, in the earlier scenes of the play, is he given any speech or soliloquy to justify his inept squanderings, which are indeed the sign not of generosity but of a crude form of vanity and a desire for applause.

It is impossible to say why the play was left in its present state, and there have been many guesses. But even the greatest writers sometimes flag and lose their inspiration. Moreover by 1609 the misanthropic type was ceasing to attract playgoers, who were turning to newer and less exacting kinds of dramatic entertainment.

Timon of Athens

DRAMATIS PERSONAE

TIMON, *a noble Athenian*
LUCIUS ⎫
LUCULLUS ⎬ *flattering lords*
SEMPRONIUS ⎭
VENTIDIUS, *one of Timon's false friends*
ALCIBIADES, *an Athenian captain*
APEMANTUS, *a churlish philosopher*
FLAVIUS, *steward to Timon*
POET ⎫
PAINTER ⎬
JEWELER ⎬
MERCHANT ⎭
AN OLD ATHENIAN
FLAMINIUS ⎫
LUCILIUS ⎬ *servants to Timon*
SERVILIUS ⎭

CAPHIS ⎫
PHILOTUS ⎬ *servants to Timon's creditors and to*
TITUS ⎬ *the Lords*
HORTENSIUS ⎬
And others ⎭
A PAGE
A FOOL
THREE STRANGERS

PHRYNIA ⎫ *mistresses to Alcibiades*
TIMANDRA ⎭

CUPID *and* AMAZONS *in the mask*

Other LORDS, SENATORS, OFFICERS, BANDITTI, *and*
ATTENDANTS

SCENE — *Athens, and the neighboring woods.*

Act I

SCENE I. *Athens. A hall in* TIMON's *house.*

[*Enter* POET, PAINTER, JEWELER, MERCHANT, *and others, at several*° *doors.*]

POET. Good day, sir.
PAIN.   I am glad you're well.
POET. I have not seen you long. How goes the world?
PAIN. It wears,° sir, as it grows.
POET.   Aye, that's well known.
But what particular rarity? What strange,
Which manifold record not matches?° See,   5
Magic of bounty!° All these spirits thy power
Hath conjured to attend. I know the merchant.
     PAIN. I know them both. Th' other's a jeweler.
     MER. [*To the* JEWELER] Oh, 'tis a worthy lord!
     JEW.   Nay, that's most fixed.°
     MER. A most incomparable man, breathed,° as
          it were,   10
To an untirable and continuate goodness.
He passes.°

Act I, Sc. i: s.d., several: separate. 3. wears: wastes away.
4–5. But . . . matches: what is strange in that? What is there
that cannot be paralleled in history? 6. Magic of bounty: i.e.,
Timon, whose generosity is magical. 9. fixed: certain.
10. breathed: exercised by constant practice. 12. passes:
surpasses.

JEW.   I have a jewel here ——
MER. Oh, pray, let's see 't. For the Lord Timon, sir?
JEW. If he will touch the estimate.° But, for that ——
POET. [*Reciting to himself.*] "When we for recompense have praised the vile,   15
It stains the glory in that happy verse
Which aptly sings the good."
     MER. [*Looking on the jewel.*] 'Tis a good form.°
     JEW. And rich. Here is a water,° look ye.
     PAIN. [*To the* POET] You are rapt,° sir, in some work, some dedication
To the great lord.
POET.   A thing slipped idly from me.   20
Our poesy is as a gum which oozes
From whence 'tis nourished. The fire i' the flint
Shows not till it be struck. Our gentle flame
Provokes itself, and like the current, flies
Each bound it chafes.° What have you there?   25
     PAIN. A picture, sir. When comes your book forth?
     POET. Upon the heels of my presentment,° sir.
Let's see your piece.

---

14. touch . . . estimate: pay the price. 17. form: design.
18. water: luster of a diamond. 19. rapt: poetically inspired,
absorbed. 24–25. flies . . . chafes: swirls back each time it
meets an obstacle. 27. heels . . . presentment: directly I have
presented the first copy. A book which was dedicated to a distinguished patron was not offered for sale to the public until the patron had accepted his copy.

PAIN. 'Tis a good piece.

POET. So 'tis. This comes off well and excellent.

PAIN. Indifferent.°

POET.   Admirable! How this grace   30
Speaks his own standing.° What a mental power
This eye shoots forth! How big imagination
Moves in this lip! To the dumbness of the gesture
One might interpret.°

PAIN. It is a pretty mocking° of the life.   35
Here is a touch. Is 't good?

POET.   I will say of it
It tutors° nature. Artificial strife
Lives in these touches, livelier than life.

     [*Enter certain* SENATORS, *and pass over.*]

PAIN. How this lord is followed!

POET. The senators of Athens. Happy man!   40

PAIN. Look, moe!°

POET. You see this confluence,° this great flood
of visitors.
I have in this rough work shaped out a man
Whom this beneath° world doth embrace and hug
With amplest entertainment. My° free drift   45
Halts not particularly, but moves itself
In a wide sea of wax. No leveled° malice
Infects one comma° in the course I hold,
But flies an eagle flight, bold and forth on,
Leaving no tract behind.   50

PAIN. How shall I understand you?

POET.   I will unbolt° to you.
You see how all conditions, how all minds,
As well of glib and slippery creatures as
Of grave and austere quality, tender down°
Their services to Lord Timon. His° large fortune,
Upon his good and gracious nature hanging,   56
Subdues and properties to his love and tendance
All sorts of hearts — yea, from the glass-faced° flat-
terer
To Apemantus, that few things loves better
Than to abhor himself. Even he drops down   60
The knee before him, and returns in peace,
Most rich in Timon's nod.

PAIN.   I saw them speak together.

POET. Sir, I have upon a high and pleasant hill
Feigned° Fortune to be throned. The base o' the
mount
Is ranked with all deserts,° all kind of natures   65
That labor on the bosom of this sphere°
To propagate their states.° Amongst them all
Whose eyes are on this sovereign lady° fixed,
One do I personate of Lord Timon's frame,°   69
Whom Fortune with her ivory hand wafts° to her,
Whose present grace to present slaves and servants
Translates his rivals.°

PAIN.   'Tis conceived to scope.°
This throne, this Fortune, and this hill, methinks,
With one man beckoned from the rest below,
Bowing his head against the steepy mount   75
To climb his happiness, would be well expressed
In our condition.°

POET.   Nay, sir, but hear me on.
All those which were his fellows but of late,
Some better than his value,° on the moment
Follow his strides, his lobbies fill with tendance,   80
Rain sacrificial° whisperings in his ear,
Make sacred even his stirrup,° and through him
Drink the free air.°

PAIN.   Aye, marry,° what of these?

POET. When Fortune in her shift and change of
mood   84
Spurns down her late beloved, all his dependants
Which labored after him to the mountain's top
Even on their knees and hands let him slip down,
Not one accompanying his declining foot.

PAIN. 'Tis common.
A thousand moral° paintings I can show   90
That shall demónstrate these quick blows of For-
tune's
More pregnantly° than words. Yet you do well
To show Lord Timon that mean eyes° have seen
The foot above the head.°

     [*Trumpets sound. Enter* LORD TIMON, *addressing
himself courteously to every suitor, a* MESSENGER
from VENTIDIUS *talking with him,* LUCILIUS *and
other servants following.*]

---

30. Indifferent: so-so.   **30–31. Admirable . . . standing:** this is
excellent; you have represented the gracious appearance of
Timon.   **34. interpret:** give life to.   **35. mocking:** imitation.
37. tutors: teaches, is better than the real thing.   **41. moe:**
more.   **42. confluence:** crowd.   **44. beneath:** i.e., the earth
which is underneath Heaven.   **45–50. My . . . behind:** This
poet (as becomes a poet in this age of "metaphysical" poetry)
is above making a plain statement but must use a variety of
images. His general meaning is that there is no malice or satire
in his work; it is all plain and smooth — like the surface of wax
which has been melted and has gone hard and smooth. In ll. 47–50
he varies the image to the straight course of a bullet and the
direct flight of an eagle which leaves no trace (*tract*) behind.
47. leveled: aimed like a gun.   **48. comma:** smallest point.
51. unbolt: open up.   **54. tender down:** lay on the ground as
offerings.   **55–58. His . . . hearts:** his great wealth, joined to
his good nature, subdues and wins over (*properties*) all kinds of
men, so that they love him and crowd his house (*tendance*).
58. glass-faced: reflecting the whim of the flattered.

64. Feigned: pretended, imagined.   **65. ranked . . . deserts:**
shows all sorts of men in rows (ranks).   **66. sphere:** world.
67. propagate . . . states: increase their own fortunes.   **68. sovereign lady:** i.e., Fortune.   **69. frame:** appearance.   **70. wafts:**
beckons.   **71–72. Whose . . . rivals:** whose present good fortune
turns all his rivals into his slaves.   **72. 'Tis . . . scope:** you have
succeeded in your aim.   **77. condition:** art; i.e., we artists are
well able to express the climbing fortunes of Timon.   **79. Some
. . . value:** some wealthier than he once was.   **81. sacrificial:**
adoring.   **82. Make . . . stirrup:** It was a sign of respect to hold
the stirrup of a great man as he mounted his horse. Timon's followers even regard this action as something holy.   **82–83. through
. . . air:** pretend that they breathe by his permission.   **83. marry:**
Mary, by the Virgin.   **90. moral:** symbolical.   **92. pregnantly:**
aptly.   **93. mean eyes:** humble observers.   **94. The . . . head:**
i.e., that men can change places.

TIM. *Ventidius is* Imprisoned is he, say you?
MESS. Aye, my good lord, five talents° is his
   debt,   95
His means most short, his creditors most strait.°
Your honorable letter he desires
To those have shut him up, which failing,
Periods° his comfort.
   TIM.   Noble Ventidius! Well,
I am not of that feather° to shake off   100
My friend when he must need me. I do know him
A gentleman that well deserves a help,
Which he shall have. I'll pay the debt and free him.
   MESS. Your lordship ever binds° him.
   TIM. Commend me to him. I will send his ran-
      som,   105
And, being enfranchised, bid him come to me.
'Tis not enough to help the feeble up,
But to support him after. Fare you well.
   MESS. All happiness to your Honor!   [*Exit.*]
         [*Enter an* OLD ATHENIAN.]
   OLD ATH. Lord Timon, hear me speak.
   TIM.   Freely, good father. 110
   OLD ATH. Thou hast a servant named Lucilius.
   TIM. I have so. What of him?
   OLD ATH. Most noble Timon, call the man before
      thee.
   TIM. Attends he here, or no? Lucilius!
   LUC. Here, at your lordship's service.   115
   OLD ATH. This fellow here, Lord Timon, this thy
      creature,
By night frequents my house. I am a man
That from my first have been inclined to thrift,
And my estate deserves an heir more raised
Than one which holds a trencher.°
   TIM.   Well, what further? 120
   OLD ATH. One only daughter have I, no kin else
On whom I may confer what I have got.
The maid is fair, o' the youngest° for a bride,
And I have bred her at my dearest cost
In qualities of the best. This man of thine   125
Attempts her love. I prithee, noble lord,
Join with me to forbid him her resort.
Myself have spoke in vain.
   TIM.   The man is honest.
   OLD ATH. Therefore he will be, Timon.
His honesty rewards him in itself.   130
It must not bear° my daughter.
   TIM.   Does she love him?
   OLD ATH. She is young and apt.
Our own precedent° passions do instruct us

What levity's in youth.
   TIM. [*To* LUCILIUS] Love you the maid?   134
   LUC. Aye, my good lord, and she accepts of it.
   OLD ATH. If in her marriage my consent be miss-
      ing,
I call the gods to witness I will choose
Mine heir from forth the beggars of the world
And dispossess her all.
   TIM.   How shall she be endowed
If she be mated with an equal husband?   140
   OLD ATH. Three talents on the present; in future,
      all.
   TIM. This gentleman of mine hath served me
      long.
To build his fortune I will strain a little,
For 'tis a bond in men.° Give him thy daughter.
What you bestow, in him I'll counterpoise,°   145
And make him weigh with her.
   OLD ATH.   Most noble lord,
Pawn° me to this your honor, she is his.
   TIM. My hand to thee. Mine honor on my
      promise.
   LUC. Humbly I thank your lordship. Never may
That state or fortune fall into my keeping   150
Which is not owed to you!°
         [*Exeunt* LUCILIUS *and* OLD ATHENIAN.]
   POET. Vouchsafe° my labor, and long live your
      lordship!
   TIM. I thank you. You shall hear from me anon.°
Go not away. What have you there, my friend?
   PAIN. A piece of painting, which I do beseech
Your lordship to accept.
   TIM.   Painting is welcome. 156
The painting is almost the natural man;
For since dishonor traffics with man's nature,
He is but outside.° These penciled° figures are
Even such as they give out. I like your work, 160
And you shall find I like it. Wait attendance
Till you hear further from me.
   PAIN.   The gods preserve ye!
   TIM. Well fare you, gentleman. Give me your
      hand.
We must needs dine together. Sir, your jewel
Hath suffered under praise.°
   JEW.   What, my lord! Dispraise? 165
   TIM. A mere satiety of commendations.
If I should pay you for 't as 'tis extolled,
It would unclew° me quite.
   JEW.   My lord, 'tis rated°
As those which sell would give. But you well know

---

95. talents: A talent (so far as it is possible to give a modern
equivalent) was worth about $1,250; but the word is used poeti-
cally for a great sum.   96. strait: strict.   99. Periods: puts an
end to.   100. of . . . feather: that kind of bird.   104. ever
binds: i.e., makes him your debtor forever.   120. holds a
trencher: is a servant. A trencher is a wooden plate.   123. o' . . .
youngest: almost too young to be.   131. bear: carry off.
133. precedent: i.e., felt in youth.

144. bond in men: i.e., one is bound to help a faithful servant.
145. counterpoise: give equal weight.   147. Pawn: pledge.
149–51. Never . . . you: I shall owe all my fortunes to you forever.   152. Vouchsafe: accept.   153. anon: presently.
158–59. For . . . outside: when a man is dishonorable, he is true
only in appearance.   159. penciled: painted.   165. under
praise: through excessive praise.   168. unclew: unwind (like
a ball of wool); i.e., ruin. rated: valued.

Things of like value, differing in the owners, 170
Are prizèd by their masters. Believe 't, dear lord,
You mend° the jewel by the wearing it.

TIM. Well mocked.

MER. No, my good lord. He speaks the common
tongue,
Which all men speak with him.   175

TIM. Look who comes here. Will you be chid?°

[*Enter* APEMANTUS.]

JEW. We'll bear, with your lordship.

MER.   He'll spare none.

TIM. Good morrow to thee, gentle Apemantus!

APE. Till I be gentle, stay thou for thy good morrow;
When thou art Timon's dog, and these knaves honest.°   180

TIM. Why dost thou call them knaves? Thou
know'st them not.

APE. Are they not Athenians?

TIM. Yes.

APE. Then I repent not.

JEW. You know me, Apemantus?   185

APE. Thou know'st I do. I called thee by thy
name.

TIM. Thou art proud, Apemantus.

APE. Of nothing so much as that I am not like
Timon.   190

TIM. Whither art going?

APE. To knock out an honest Athenian's brains.

TIM. That's a deed thou'lt die for.

APE. Right, if doing nothing be death by the
law.°   196

TIM. How likest thou this picture, Apemantus?

APE. The best for the innocence.°

TIM. Wrought he not well that painted it?   200

APE. He wrought better that made the painter;
and yet he's but a filthy piece of work.

PAIN. You're a dog.

APE. Thy mother's of my generation.° What's
she, if I be a dog?   205

TIM. Wilt dine with me, Apemantus?

APE. No, I eat not lords.

TIM. An° thou shouldst, thou'dst anger ladies.

APE. Oh, they eat lords. So they come by great
bellies.   210

TIM. That's a lascivious apprehension.°

APE. So thou apprehend'st it. Take it for thy labor.

TIM. How dost thou like this jewel, Apemantus?

APE. Not so well as plain-dealing, which will not
cost a man a doit.°   217

TIM. What dost thou think 'tis worth?

APE. Not worth my thinking. How now, poet!

POET. How now, philosopher!   221

APE. Thou liest.

POET. Art not one?

APE. Yes.

POET. Then I lie not.   225

APE. Art not a poet?

POET. Yes.

APE. Then thou liest. Look in thy last work,
where thou hast feigned him a worthy fellow.

POET. That's not feigned. He is so.   230

APE. Yes, he is worthy of thee, and to pay thee for
thy labor. He that loves to be flattered is worthy o'
the flatterer. Heavens, that I were a lord!

TIM. What wouldst do then, Apemantus?   235

APE. E'en as Apemantus does now — hate a lord
with my heart.

TIM. What, thyself?

APE. Aye.

TIM. Wherefore?   240

APE. That I had no angry wit to be a lord.° Art
not thou a merchant?

MER. Aye, Apemantus.

APE. Traffic confound thee,° if the gods will not!

MER. If traffic do it, the gods do it.   246

APE. Traffic's thy god, and thy god confound thee!

[*Trumpet sounds. Enter a* MESSENGER.]

TIM. What trumpet's that?

MESS. 'Tis Alcibiades, and some twenty horse,
All of companionship.°   251

TIM. Pray, entertain them. Give them guide to us.

[*Exeunt some* ATTENDANTS.]

[*To the* PAINTER] You must needs dine with me. Go
not you hence
Till I have thanked you. When dinner's done,
Show me this piece. I am joyful of your sights.°

[*Enter* ALCIBIADES, *with the rest.*]

Most welcome, sir!

APE.   So, so, there!   256

Aches° contract and starve your supple joints!
That there should be small love 'mongst these
sweet knaves,
And all this courtesy! The strain of man's bred out
Into baboon and monkey.   260

ALC. Sir, you have saved my longing, and I feed
Most hungerly on your sight.

TIM.   Right, welcome, sir!

---

172. **mend:** increase the value of.   176. **Will . . . chid:** now look out for abuse.   179–80. **Till . . . honest:** you won't get a "good morrow" from me till you have become a dog and these men are turned honest.   195–96. **if . . . law:** if it's a capital offense to do nothing — for, since no honest Athenian has any brains, they cannot be knocked out.   199. **innocence:** simplicity; i.e., it's a childish piece of work.   204. **generation:** breed.   208. **An:** if.   211. **apprehension:** thought.

217. **doit:** small Dutch coin, "cent."   241. **That . . . lord:** This is the reading of F1 and is usually emended by editors to "so hungry a," "angry wish," "empty wit," etc. If the reading is correct, then Apemantus is cursing himself because he lacks the usual hot temper of a great man.   245. **Traffic . . . thee:** may you be ruined by your trade.   251. **All of companionship:** all close friends.   255. **sights:** i.e., what you have to show.   257. **Aches:** pronounced as a dissyllable like "H's."

Ere we depart, we'll share a bounteous time
In different pleasures. Pray you, let us in.

                 [*Exeunt all but* APEMANTUS.]
              [*Enter two* LORDS.]

1. LORD. What time o' day is 't, Apemantus?   265
APE. Time to be honest.
1. LORD. That times serves still.°
APE. The most accursèd thou, that still omitt'st it.
2. LORD. Thou art going to Lord Timon's feast?
APE. Aye, to see meat fill knaves and wine heat
    fools.   271
2. LORD. Fare thee well, fare thee well.
APE. Thou art a fool to bid me farewell twice.
2. LORD. Why, Apemantus?   274
APE. Shouldst have kept one to thyself, for I
mean to give thee none.
1. LORD. Hang thyself!
APE. No, I will do nothing at thy bidding. Make
thy requests to thy friend.
2. LORD. Away, unpeaceable dog, or I'll spurn
thee hence!   281
APE. I will fly, like a dog, the heels o' the ass.

                              [*Exit.*]
1. LORD. He's opposite to° humanity. Come, shall
    we in
And taste Lord Timon's bounty? He outgoes   285
The very heart of kindness.
2. LORD. He pours it out. Plutus, the God of Gold,
Is but his steward. No meed° but he repays
Sevenfold above itself, no gift to him
But breeds the giver a return exceeding   290
All use of quittance.°
1. LORD.   The noblest mind he carries
That ever governed man.
2. LORD. Long may he live in fortunes! Shall we
    in?
1. LORD. I'll keep you company.   [*Exeunt.*]

SCENE II. *A banqueting room in* TIMON's
house.

[*Hautboys° playing loud music. A great banquet
served in,* FLAVIUS *and others attending; and then
enter* LORD TIMON, ALCIBIADES, LORDS, SENATORS, *and*
    VENTIDIUS. *Then comes, dropping° after all,*
    APEMANTUS, *discontentedly, like himself.*]

VEN. Most honored Timon,
It hath pleased the gods to remember my father's
    age
And call him to long peace.
He is gone happy, and has left me rich.
Then, as in grateful virtue I am bound   5

To your free° heart, I do return those talents,°
Doubled with thanks and service, from whose help
I derived liberty.
TIM.   Oh, by no means,
Honest Ventidius. You mistake my love.
I gave it freely ever, and there's none   10
Can truly say he gives if he receives.
If our betters play at that game, we must not dare
To imitate them. Faults that are rich are fair.°
VEN. A noble spirit!
TIM. Nay, my lords, ceremony° was but devised
    at first   15
To set a gloss on faint deeds, hollow welcomes,
Recanting goodness, sorry ere 'tis shown;°
But where there is true friendship, there needs none.
Pray, sit. More welcome are ye to my fortunes
Than my fortunes to me.   [*They sit.*] 20
1. LORD. My lord, we always have confessed it.
APE. Ho, ho, confessed it! Hanged° it, have you
not?
TIM. Oh, Apemantus, you are welcome.
APE.   No,
You shall not make me welcome.
I come to have thee thrust me out of doors.   25
TIM. Fie, thou'rt a churl.° Ye've got a humor°
    there
Does not become a man. 'Tis much to blame.
They say, my lords, "*Ira furor brevis est;*"° but
yond man is ever angry. Go, let him have a table by
himself, for he does neither affect° company, nor is
he fit for 't indeed.   31
APE. Let me stay at thine apperil,° Timon.
I come to observe. I give thee warning on 't.
TIM. I take no heed of thee. Thou'rt an Athenian,
therefore welcome. I myself would have no power.
Prithee let my meat make thee silent.°   37
APE. I scorn thy meat. 'Twould choke me, for I
should ne'er flatter thee. O you gods, what a number of men eat Timon, and he sees 'em not! It
grieves me to see so many dip their meat in one
man's blood; and all the madness is° he cheers
them up, too.
I wonder men dare trust themselves with men.   44
Methinks they should invite them without knives;°
Good for their meat, and safer for their lives.
There's much example for 't. The fellow that sits

6. free: generous. return . . . talents: See I.i.94–108.   13. Faults
. . . fair: the faults of the rich are regarded as good deeds.
15. ceremony: Some editions add before this line the stage direction "They stand ceremoniously looking on Timon." Formal
banquets were marked by elaborate ceremony between host and
guests. See *Macb*, III.iv.33–37.   17. sorry . . . shown: i.e., a
sign of friendship given reluctantly.   22. confessed . . . Hanged:
an allusion to the proverb "Confess and be hanged." See *Oth*,
IV.i.38.   26. churl: boor.   humor: temperament.   28. Ira . . .
est: anger is a short fit of madness.   30. affect: like.   32. apperil: peril.   36–37. I . . . silent: I cannot make you quiet, but
perhaps my food will.   42. all . . . is: what makes it all so mad
is.   45. without knives: It was usual for guests to bring their
own knives with them.

267. That . . . still: there's always time for that.   284. opposite
to: the enemy of.   288. meed: reward, gift.   291. use of quittance: normal rate of exchange.
    Sc. ii: s.d., Hautboys: oboes. dropping: slouching.

next him now parts bread with him, pledges the
breath of him in a divided draught,° is the readiest
man to kill him. 'T has been proved. If I were a
huge man, I should fear to drink at meals,   51
Lest they should spy my windpipe's dangerous
    notes.°
Great men should drink with harness° on their
    throats.
TIM. My lord, in heart;° and let the health go
    round.   54
2. LORD. Let it flow this way, my good lord.
APE. Flow this way! A brave fellow. He keeps his
tides well. Those healths will make thee and thy
state look ill, Timon. Here's that which is too weak
to be a sinner, honest water, which ne'er left man i'
the mire.   60
This and my food are equals. There's no odds.
Feasts are too proud to give thanks to the gods.

APEMANTUS's *Grace*

Immortal gods, I crave no pelf.°
I pray for no man but myself.
Grant I may never prove so fond°   65
To trust man on his oath or bond,
Or a harlot for her weeping,
Or a dog that seems asleeping,
Or a keeper with my freedom,
Or my friends, if I should need 'em.   70
Amen. So fall to 't.
Rich men sin, and I eat root.

[Eats and drinks.]

Much good dich° thy good heart, Apemantus!
TIM. Captain Alcibiades, your heart's in the field°
now.   75
ALC. My heart is ever at your service, my lord.
TIM. You had rather be at a breakfast of enemies
than a dinner of friends.   79
ALC. So they were bleeding new, my lord, there's
no meat like 'em. I could wish my best friend at
such a feast.
APE. Would all those flatterers were thine enemies, then, that then thou mightst kill 'em and bid
me to 'em!   85
1. LORD. Might we but have that happiness, my
lord, that you would once use our hearts,° whereby
we might express some part of our zeals, we should
think ourselves for ever perfect.   90
TIM. Oh, no doubt, my good friends, but the gods
themselves have provided that I shall have much
help from you. How had you been my friends else?
Why have you that charitable title from thousands,
did not you chiefly belong to my heart? I have 95

told more of you° to myself than you can with modesty speak in your own behalf, and thus far I confirm you. O you gods, think I, what need we have
any friends if we should ne'er have need of   100
'em? They were the most needless creatures living
should we ne'er have use for 'em, and would most
resemble sweet instruments hung up in cases that
keep their sounds to themselves. Why, I have often wished myself poorer that I might come   105
nearer to you. We are born to do benefits; and what
better or properer° can we call our own than the
riches of our friends? Oh, what a precious comfort
'tis to have so many, like brothers, command- 110
ing one another's fortunes! O joy, e'en made away
ere 't can be born!° Mine eyes cannot hold out water,° methinks. To forget their faults, I drink to
you.
APE. Thou weep'st to make them° drink, Timon.
2. LORD. Joy had the like conception in our eyes,
And at that instant, like a babe° sprung up.   116
APE. Ho, ho! I laugh to think that babe a bastard.
3. LORD. I promise you, my lord, you moved me
    much.
APE. Much!   [*Tucket,° within.*]
TIM. What means that trump?
                        [*Enter a* SERVANT.]
                                How now!   120
SERV. Please you, my lord, there are certain ladies
most desirous of admittance.
TIM. Ladies! What are their wills?
SERV. There comes with them a forerunner, my
lord, which bears that office to signify their pleas-
ures.   126
TIM. I pray, let them be admitted.
                        [*Enter* CUPID.°]
CUP. Hail to thee, worthy Timon! And to all
That of his bounties taste! The five best Senses
Acknowledge thee their patron, and come freely
To gratulate° thy plenteous bosom. Th' Ear,   131
Taste, Touch, and Smell, pleased from thy table
    rise.
They only now come but to feast thine eyes.
TIM. They're welcome all. Let 'em have kind ad-
    mittance.
Music, make their welcome!   [*Exit* CUPID.] 135
1. LORD. You see, my lord, how ample you're be-
    loved.
[*Music. Re-enter* CUPID, *with a mask of* LADIES° *as*

49. divided draught: a drink shared by two.   52. Lest . . . notes:
i.e., lest when they noticed that my throat was occupied in drinking, they should cut it.   53. harness: armor.   54. in heart:
from the bottom of my heart.   63. pelf: cash.   65. fond:
foolish.   73. dich: do it.   74. in . . . field: i.e., thinking of
battles.   87. use . . . hearts: test our true feelings.

96. told . . . you: promised you more.   107. properer: more
one's own.   111–12. e'en . . . born: i.e., which dissolves into
tears as soon as one thinks of it.   112–13. hold . . . water:
refrain from tears.   114. make them: encourage.   116. babe:
a tear was sometimes called a "baby in the eye."   119. s.d.,
Tucket: trumpet call to announce a new arrival.   127. s.d.,
Enter Cupid: See *R & J*, I.iv.1–3,n.   131. gratulate: pay honor
to.   136. s.d., mask . . . ladies: These elaborate entertainments
were called masques because originally those taking part, being
amateurs of good or noble family, disguised themselves in masks.
See Gen. Intro. p. 47b, and *Hen VIII*, I.iv.50–108.

Amazons, with lutes° in their hands, dancing and playing.]

APE. Hoyday,° what a sweep of vanity° comes
   this way!
They dance! They are mad women.
Like° madness is the glory of this life,
As this pomp shows to a little oil and root.   140
We make ourselves fools to disport ourselves,
And spend our flatteries to drink those men
Upon whose age we void it up again
With poisonous spite and envy.
Who lives that's not depravèd or depraves?   145
Who dies that bears not one spurn° to their graves
Of their friends' gift?
I should fear those that dance before me now
Would one day stamp upon me. 'T has been done.
Men shut their doors against a setting sun.   150
[*The* LORDS *rise from table, with much adoring of*
   TIMON; *and to show their loves, each singles out an*
   AMAZON, *and all dance, men with women, a lofty*
   strain or two to the hautboys, and cease.]
   TIM. You have done our pleasures much grace,
   fair ladies,
Set a fair fashion on our entertainment,
Which was not half so beautiful and kind.
You have added worth unto 't and luster,
And entertained me with mine own device.°   155
I am to thank you for 't.
   1. LADY. My lord, you take us even at the best.°
   APE. Faith, for the worst is filthy, and would not
hold° taking, I doubt me.
   TIM. Ladies, there is an idle banquet° attends
   you.   160
Please you to dispose yourselves.
   ALL LADIES. Most thankfully, my lord.
         [*Exeunt* CUPID *and* LADIES.]
   TIM. Flavius!
   FLAV. My lord?
   TIM. The little casket bring me hither.   164
   FLAV. Yes, my lord. [*Aside*] More jewels yet!
There is no crossing him in 's humor.°
Else I should tell him — well, i' faith, I should —
When all's spent, he'd be crossed° then, an he
   could.
'Tis pity bounty had not eyes behind,   169

That man might ne'er be wretched for his mind.°
                      [*Exit.*]
   1. LORD. Where be our men?
   SERV. Here, my lord, in readiness.
   2. LORD. Our horses!
     [*Re-enter* FLAVIUS, *with the casket.*]
   TIM.   O my friends,
I have one word to say to you. Look you, my good
   lord,
I must entreat you honor me so much   175
As to advance° this jewel. Accept it, and wear it,
Kind my lord.
   1. LORD.   I am so far already in your gifts —
   ALL. So are we all.
           [*Enter a* SERVANT.]
   SERV. My lord, there are certain nobles of the
   Senate   180
Newly alighted and come to visit you.
   TIM. They are fairly° welcome.
   FLAV.   I beseech your Honor
Vouchsafe me a word. It does concern you near.
   TIM. Near! Why, then another time I'll hear thee.
I prithee let's be provided to show them entertain-
   ment.   185
   FLAV. [*Aside*] I scarce know how.
        [*Enter another* SERVANT.]
   2. SERV. May it please your Honor, Lord Lucius
Out of his free love hath presented to you
Four milk-white horses, trapped° in silver.   189
   TIM. I shall accept them fairly. Let the presents
Be worthily entertained.°
       [*Enter a* THIRD SERVANT.]
              How now! What news?
   3. SERV. Please you, my lord, that honorable gen-
tleman, Lord Lucullus, entreats your company to-
morrow to hunt with him, and has sent your Hon-
or two brace of greyhounds.   195
   TIM. I'll hunt with him; and let them be re-
   ceived,
Not without fair reward.
   FLAV. [*Aside*]   What will this come to?
He commands us to provide and give great gifts,
And all out of an empty coffer.°
Nor will he know his purse, or yield me this: 200
To show him what a beggar his heart is,
Being of no power to make his wishes good.
His promises fly so beyond his state
That what he speaks is all in debt, he owes
For every word. He is so kind that he now   205
Pays interest for 't. His land's put to their books.°
Well, would I were gently put out of office
Before I were forced out!

136. s.d., lutes: See Pl. 18d.   137. Hoyday: heyday — a
meaningless exclamation of disapproval. sweep of vanity:
crowd of overdressed women.   139–44. Like . . . envy: this wild
display (*glory*) is as mad as an extravagant feast (*pomp*) compared
with a philosopher's frugal fare (*oil and roots*). We make fools of
ourselves in our amusements and waste flattery when we praise
excessively (*drink up*) those men whom later we shall vomit up
through sheer spite and envy.   146. spurn: contemptuous gibe.
155. own device: i.e., masque which I composed.   157. take
. . . best: treat us most honorably.   159. hold: be worth.
160. idle banquet: trifling refreshment (such as jellies, etc.)
after a large feast or entertainment.   166. humor: mood.
168. crossed: thwarted.

169–70. 'Tis . . . mind: it is a pity that a man cannot see that
his generosity will soon cause him wretchedness.   176. advance:
promote, honor by wearing.   182. fairly: very.   189. trapped:
with harnesses adorned with silver.   191. entertained: looked
after.   199. coffer: treasure chest.   206. put . . . books:
pawned.

Happier is he that has no friend to feed
Than such that do e'en enemies exceed.°   210
I bleed inwardly for my lord.   [*Exit.*]
TIM.   You do yourselves
Much wrong; you bate° too much of your own
    merits.
Here, my lord, a trifle of our love.
2. LORD. With more than common thanks I will
    receive it.
3. LORD. Oh, he's the very soul of bounty!   215
TIM. And now I remember, my lord, you gave
Good words the other day of a bay courser° RIDING
I rode on. 'Tis yours, because you liked it. HORSE
3. LORD. Oh, I beseech you, pardon me, my lord,
    in that.
TIM. You may take my word, my lord. I know
    no man   220
Can justly praise but what he does affect.°
I weigh my friend's affection with mine own.
I'll tell you true. I'll call to° you.
ALL LORDS.   Oh, none so welcome.
TIM. I take all and your several° visitations
So kind to heart 'tis not enough to give.   225
Methinks, I could deal kingdoms to my friends,
And ne'er be weary. Alcibiades,
Thou art a soldier, therefore seldom rich.
It comes in charity to thee;° for all thy living
Is 'mongst the dead, and all the lands thou hast
Lie in a pitched field.°
ALC.   Aye, defiled land, my lord.   231
1. LORD. We are so virtuously bound ——
TIM.   And so
Am I to you.
2. LORD.   So infinitely endeared ——
TIM. All to you. Lights, more lights!
1. LORD.   The best of happiness,   234
Honor, and fortunes keep with you, Lord Timon!
TIM. Ready for his friends.
    [*Exeunt all but* APEMANTUS *and* TIMON.]
APE.   What a coil's° here!
Serving of becks° and jutting out of bums!°
I doubt whether their legs be worth the sums   238
That are given for 'em.° Friendship's full of dregs.
Methinks false hearts should never have sound legs.
Thus honest fools lay out their wealth on court'sies.
TIM. Now, Apemantus, if thou wert not sullen,
I would be good to thee.
APE. No, I'll nothing; for if I should be bribed

too, there would be none left to rail upon thee,   245
and then thou wouldst sin the faster. Thou givest so
long, Timon, I fear me thou wilt give away thyself
in paper° shortly. What needs these feasts, pomps,
and vainglories?   249
TIM. Nay, an you begin to rail on society once,°
I am sworn not to give regard to you. Farewell, and
come with better music.°   [*Exit.*]
APE. So.
Thou wilt not hear me now. Thou shalt not then.
I'll lock thy heaven° from thee.   255
Oh, that men's ears should be
To counsel deaf, but not to flattery!   [*Exit.*]

Act II

SCENE I. *A* SENATOR'S *house.*

[*Enter a* SENATOR, *with papers in his hands.*]
SEN. And late° five thousand. To Varro and to
    Isidore
He owes nine thousand, besides my former sum, 25,000 —
Which makes it five and twenty. Still in motion TIMON
Of raging waste?° It cannot hold; it will not. OWES
If I want gold, steal but a beggar's dog   5
And give it Timon — why, the dog coins gold.
If I would sell my horse and buy twenty moe
Better than he — why, give my horse to Timon.
Ask nothing, give it him — it foals me straight
And able horses.° No porter° at his gate,   10
But rather one that smiles and still° invites
All that pass by. It cannot hold. No reason
Can found his state in safety.° Caphis, ho!
Caphis, I say!
    [*Enter* CAPHIS.]
CAPH.   Here, sir. What is your pleasure?
SEN. Get on your cloak, and haste you to Lord
    Timon.   15
Importune him for my moneys. Be not ceased°
With slight denial, nor then silenced, when
" Commend me to your master," and the cap
Plays in the right hand,° thus. But tell him,

247–48. give . . . paper: you'll find yourself in the pillory with
your folly set out on a placard. See App. 10.   250. an . . . once:
as soon as you.   252. with . . . music: in a better mood.
255. heaven: benefit.

Act II, Sc. i: 1. late: recently.   3–4. Still . . . waste: still
keeping up this everlasting waste.   9–10. it . . . horses: it at
once brings me back horses in return, and good horses too; i.e.,
Timon always repays a present with something better.   10. porter: i.e., to keep out the rogues.   11. still: perpetually.   12–13. No
. . . safety: no reasonable man can believe that he is solvent.
16. ceased: silenced.   18–19. cap . . . hand: i.e., when Timon
takes off his cap as a tribute to me. See App. 7.

209–10. Happier . . . exceed: it is better to have no dependent
friends than to support a crowd who will do more harm than one's
enemies.   212. bate: abate, make too little of.   217. courser:
riding horse.   221. affect: like.   223. call to: i.e., on you when
I am in need.   224. several: individual.   229. It . . . thee: it is
true charity to be generous to you.   231. pitched field: battlefield.   236. coil: fuss.   237. Serving of becks: humble bows.
bums: backsides.   238–39. their . . . 'em: all this humble bowing is worth what it costs. See App. 7.

My uses   cry to me, I must serve my turn   20
Out of mine own.° His days and times are past,
And my reliances on his fracted dates°
Have smit my credit. I love and honor him,
But must not break my back to heal his finger.
Immediate are my needs, and my relief°   25
Must not be tossed and turned to me in words,
But find supply immediate. Get you gone.
Put on a most importunate aspéct,°
A visage of demand; for I do fear,
When° every feather sticks in his own wing,   30
Lord Timon will be left a naked gull,
Which flashes now a phoenix. Get you gone.
     CAPH. I go, sir.
     SEN. "I go, sir!" Take the bonds along with you,
And have the dates in compt.°
     CAPH.   I will, sir.
     SEN.   Go. [*Exeunt.*]   35

SCENE II. *A hall in* TIMON's *house.*

     [*Enter* FLAVIUS, *with many bills in his hand.*]
     FLA. No care, no stop! So senseless of expense
That he will neither know° how to maintain it,
Nor cease his flow of riot,° takes no account
How things go from him, nor resumes° no care
Of what is to continue.° Never mind   5
Was to be so unwise, to be so kind.°
What shall be done? He will not hear till feel.°
I must be round° with him, now he comes from
    hunting.
Fie, fie, fie, fie!
     [*Enter* CAPHIS, *with the* SERVANTS *of* ISIDORE
               and of VARRO.]
     CAPH.   Good even, Varro.
What, you come for money?
     VAR. SERV.   Is 't not your business too?   10
     CAPH. It is; and yours too, Isidore?
     ISI. SERV.   It is so.
     CAPH. Would we were all discharged!°
     VAR. SERV.   I fear it.
     CAPH. Here comes the lord.

     [*Enter* TIMON, ALCIBIADES, LORDS, *and others.*]
     TIM. So soon as dinner's done, we'll forth again,
My Alcibiades. [*To* CAPHIS] With me? What is
    your will?   15
     CAPH. My lord, here is a note of certain dues.
     TIM. Dues! Whence are you?
     CAPH.   Of Athens here, my lord.
     TIM. Go to my steward.
     CAPH. Please it your lordship, he hath put me off
To the succession of new days° this month.   20
My master is awaked by great occasion
To call upon his own, and humbly prays you
That with your other noble parts you'll suit
In giving him his right.°
     TIM.   Mine honest friend,
I prithee but repair to me next morning.   25
     CAPH. Nay, good my lord ——
     TIM.   Contain thyself, good friend.
     VAR. SERV. One Varro's servant, my good lord ——
     ISI. SERV.   From Isidore.
He humbly prays your speedy payment.
     CAPH. If you did know, my lord, my master's
    wants ——
     VAR. SERV. 'Twas due on forfeiture,° my lord, six
    weeks   30
And past.
     ISI. SERV. Your steward puts me off, my lord,
And I am sent expressly to your lordship.
     TIM. Give me breath.
I do beseech you, good my lords, keep on.   35
I'll wait upon you instantly.
               [*Exeunt* ALCIBIADES, LORDS, &c.]
[*To* FLAVIUS]   Come hither. Pray you,
How goes the world, that I am thus encountered
With clamorous demands of date-broke bonds
And the detention of long-since-due debts
Against my honor?
     FLAV.   Please you, gentlemen,   40
The time is unagreeable to this business.
Your importunacy cease till after dinner,
That I may make his lordship understand
Wherefore you are not paid.
     TIM. Do so, my friends. See them well enter-
    tained.   [*Exit.*]   45
     FLAV. Pray draw near.   [*Exit.*]
          [*Enter* APEMANTUS *and* FOOL.]
     CAPH. Stay, stay, here comes the fool with Ape-
mantus.
Let's ha' some sport with 'em.
     VAR. SERV. Hang him, he'll abuse us.
     ISI. SERV. A plague upon him, dog!   50
     VAR. SERV. How dost, fool?
     APE. Dost dialogue° with thy shadow?

---

20. **uses:** needs.   **20–21: serve . . . own:** use my own money
to serve my own needs.   **22. fracted dates:** broken promises
of repayment.   **25. relief:** repayment.   **28. aspect:** look.
30–32. When . . . phoenix: when every borrowed feather which
now makes Timon as bright as the phoenix has been repaid, he
will be as naked as a newly hatched gull. The gull is used as the
type of silly bird. For the magnificence and rarity of the phoenix,
see *Temp,* III.iii.23,n.   **35. have . . . compt:** note the dates
when each is due. **compt:** reckoning.
     Sc. ii: 2. know: understand.   **3. flow of riot:** extravagance.
4. resumes: takes.   **5. Of . . . continue:** how we can carry on.
5–6. Never . . . kind: never was anyone so foolishly kind. This
is one of a number of lines which have been jotted down in draft,
but not completed. See *Timon* Intro. p. 1315b.   **7. till feel:** till
he is made to feel.   **8. round:** straight.   **12. discharged:** sent
away with what we have come for.

20. To . . . days: from one day to the next.   **23–24. That . . .
right:** that you will show your usual noble nature in paying what
is due to him.   **30. on forfeiture:** i.e., the debt was due on penalty of forfeiture.   **52. dialogue:** converse.

VAR. SERV. I speak not to thee.

APE. No, 'tis to thyself. [*To the* FOOL] Come away.　　　55

ISI. SERV. There's the fool hangs on your back already.

APE. No, thou stand'st single, thou'rt not on him yet.

CAPH. Where's the fool now?　　　59

APE. He last asked the question. Poor rogues, and usurers' men! Bawds° between gold and want!

ALL SERV. What are we, Apemantus?

APE. Asses.

ALL SERV. Why?　　　65

APE. That you ask me what you are, and do not know yourselves. Speak to 'em, fool.

FOOL. How do you, gentlemen?

ALL SERV. Gramercies,° good fool. How does your mistress?　　　70

FOOL. She's e'en setting on water to scald such chickens as you are. Would we could see you at Corinth!°

APE. Good! Gramercy.

[*Enter* PAGE.] WITH 2 LETTERS

FOOL. Look you, here comes my mistress'　　　75
page.

PAGE. [*To the* FOOL] Why, how now, captain! What do you in this wise company? How dost thou, Apemantus?

APE. Would I had a rod in my mouth, that I might answer thee profitably.　　　80

PAGE. Prithee, Apemantus, read me the superscription° of these letters. I know not which is which.

APE. Canst not read?

PAGE. No.　　　85

APE. There will little learning die, then, that day thou art hanged. This is to Lord Timon, this to Alcibiades. Go. Thou wast born a bastard, and thou'lt die a bawd.　　　89

PAGE. Thou wast whelped a dog, and thou shalt famish a dog's death. Answer not, I am gone.

[*Exit.*]

APE. E'en so thou outrun'st grace.° Fool, I will go with you to Lord Timon's.

FOOL. Will you leave me there?　　　95

APE. If Timon stay at home. You three serve three usurers?

ALL SERV. Aye. Would they served us!

APE. So would I — as good a trick as ever hangman served thief.　　　100

FOOL. Are you three usurers' men?

ALL SERV. Aye, fool.

FOOL. I think no usurer but has a fool to his serv-

OWNS A BROTHEL

ant. My mistress° is one, and I am her fool. When men come to borrow of your masters, they　105 approach sadly and go away merry, but they enter my mistress' house merrily and go away sadly. The reason of this?

VAR. SERV. I could render one.　　　109

APE. Do it then, that we may account thee a whoremaster° and a knave; which notwithstanding, thou shalt be no less esteemed.

VAR. SERV. What is a whoremaster, fool?　　　113

FOOL. A fool in good clothes, and something like thee. 'Tis a spirit. Sometime 't appears like a lord, sometime like a lawyer, sometime like a philosopher, with two stones moe than 's artificial one.° He is very often like a knight, and, generally, in all shapes that man goes up and down in from fourscore to thirteen, this spirit walks in.　　　121

VAR. SERV. Thou art not altogether a fool.

FOOL. Nor thou altogether a wise man. As much foolery as I have, so much wit thou lack'st.

APE. That answer might have become Apemantus.　　　126

ALL SERV. Aside, aside! Here comes Lord Timon.

[*Re-enter* TIMON *and* FLAVIUS.]

APE. Come with me, fool, come.

FOOL. I do not always follow lover, elder brother, and woman; sometime the philosopher.°　　　131

[*Exeunt* APEMANTUS *and* FOOL.]

FLAV. [*To* SERVANTS] Pray you, walk near. I'll speak with you anon.　　　[*Exeunt* SERVANTS.]

TIM. You make me marvel. Wherefore, ere this time,

Had you not fully laid my state before me,

That I might so have rated my expense　　　135

As I had leave of means?°

FLAV.　　　　　　　　You would not hear me

At many leisures I proposed.

TIM.　　　　　　　　Go to.

Perchance° some single vantages you took

When my indisposition put you back,

And that unaptness made your minister　　　140

Thus to excuse yourself.

FLAV.　　　　　　　Oh, my good lord,

At many times I brought in my accounts,

Laid them before you. You would throw them off

And say you found them in mine honesty.　　　144

When for some trifling present you have bid me

Return so much, I have shook my head and wept —

---

104. **My mistress:** She keeps a brothel, like Mistress Overdone in *M for Meas.*　111. **whoremaster:** one who frequents brothels. 118. **stones . . . one:** learned men still practiced alchemy and endeavored to discover the philosopher's stone. See App. 21. 130–31. **I . . . philosopher:** I do not always follow lovers (who are mad), elder brothers (who are extravagant), or women (who are fickle); I sometimes follow a wise man.　135–36. **rated . . . means:** have reckoned my spending according to my means. 138–41. **Perchance . . . yourself:** You may occasionally have raised the matter when I was unwilling to hear you, and you have used that reluctance as an excuse.

---

61. **Bawds:** go-betweens.　69. **Gramercies:** thanks a lot. 73. **Corinth:** slang for a brothel.　81–82. **superscription:** name of the addressee.　93. **outrun'st grace:** i.e., a knave goes faster than a good man.

Yea, 'gainst the authority of manners prayed you
To hold your hand more close. I did endure
Not seldom nor no slight checks when I have
Prompted° you in the ebb of your estate   150
And your great flow of debts. My lovèd lord,
Though you hear now, too late, yet now's a time:
The greatest of your having lacks a half°
To pay your present debts.
    TIM.   Let all my land be sold.
    FLAV. 'Tis all engaged,° some forfeited and gone,
And what remains will hardly stop the mouth   156
Of present dues. The future comes apace.°
What shall defend the interim? And at length
How goes our reckoning?°
    TIM. To Lacedaemon° did my land extend.   160
    FLAV. Oh, my good lord, the world is but a word.
Were it all yours to give it in a breath,
How quickly were it gone!
    TIM.   You tell me true.
    FLAV. If you suspect my husbandry° or falsehood,
Call me before the exactest auditors,   165
And set me on the proof. So the gods bless me,
When all our offices have been oppressed
With riotous feeders, when our vaults have wept
With drunken spilth° of wine, when every room
Hath blazed with lights and brayed with minstrelsy,
I have retired me to a wasteful cock°   171
And set mine eyes at flow.
    TIM.   Prithee no more.
    FLAV. Heavens, have I said, the bounty of this
        lord!
How many prodigal bits have slaves and peasants
This night englutted! Who is not Timon's?   175
What heart, head, sword, force, means, but is Lord
        Timon's?
Great Timon, noble, worthy, royal Timon!
Ah, when the means are gone that buy this praise,
The breath is gone whereof this praise is made.
Feast won, fast lost;° one cloud of winter showers,
These flies are couched.°
    TIM.   Come, sermon me no further.   181
No villainous bounty yet hath passed my heart.
Unwisely, not ignobly, have I given.
Why dost thou weep? Canst thou the conscience
        lack°
To think I shall lack friends? Secure thy heart.°

If I would broach° the vessels of my love   186
And try the argument of hearts° by borrowing,
Men and men's fortunes could I frankly use
As I can bid thee speak.
    FLAV.   Assurance bless your thoughts!°
    TIM. And in some sort these wants of mine are
        crowned,   190
That I account them blessings;° for by these
Shall I try friends. You shall perceive how you
Mistake my fortunes. I am wealthy in my friends.
Within there! Flaminius! Servilius!
[*Enter* FLAMINIUS, SERVILIUS, *and other* SERVANTS.]
    SERVANTS. My lord? My lord?   195
    TIM. I will dispatch you severally:° you to Lord
Lucius; to Lord Lucullus you. I hunted with His
Honor today. You to Sempronius. Commend me to
their loves, and I am proud, say, that my occasions
have found time to use 'em toward a supply of
money. Let the request be fifty talents.   202
    FLAM. As you have said, my Lord.
    FLAV. [*Aside*] Lord Lucius and Lucullus? Hum!
    TIM. Go you, sir, to the Senators—   205
Of whom, even to the state's best health,° I have
Deserved this hearing — bid 'em send o' the instant
A thousand talents to me.
    FLAV.   I have been bold,
For that I knew it the most general way,
To them to use your signet and your name,°   210
But they do shake their heads, and I am here
No richer in return.
    TIM.   Is 't true? Can 't be?
    FLAV. They answer, in a joint and corporate voice,
That now they are at fall,° want treasure, cannot
Do what they would; are sorry — you are honor-
        able —   215
But yet they could have wished — they know not —
Something hath been amiss — a noble nature
May catch a wrench° — would all were well — 'tis
        pity —
And so, intending other serious matters,
After distasteful looks and these hard fractions,°
With certain half-caps° and cold-moving nods   221
They froze me into silence.
    TIM.   You gods, reward them!
Prithee, man, look cheerly. These old fellows
Have their ingratitude in them hereditary.

---

150. **Prompted:** reminded.   153. **The . . . half:** the full extent
of your present wealth is less than enough to pay half of your
debts.   155. **engaged:** pawned as security.   157. **apace:**
quickly.   158–59. **What . . . reckoning:** how shall we meet the
debts of the near future, and the final reckoning?   160. **Lacedaemon:** Sparta.   164. **husbandry:** management.   169. **spilth:**
spilling.   171. **wasteful cock:** This phrase has been much debated. As it stands it means: "I have sat beside the running tap
of a cask and there wept" — which seems hardly in keeping
with the nature of Flavius. Editors emend *cock* in various ways,
such as "couch," "cot," "compt" (account).   180. **Feast . . .
lost:** friends won by feasting are soon lost.   181. **are couched:**
hide.   184. **conscience lack:** be so without conscience as to believe.   185. **Secure . . . heart:** don't worry.

186. **broach:** set flowing, lit., insert the spigot in a cask.   187. **argument of hearts:** appeal to their generosity.   189. **Assurance
. . . thoughts:** may your thoughts turn out true.   190–91. **And
. . . blessings:** and in a way these needs of mine are lucky
(*crowned*), so that they are blessings to me.   196. **severally:**
separately.   206. **even . . . health:** i.e., I have deserved the
greatest help from the state.   208–10. **I . . . name:** I have even
sent them letters, in your name and sealed with your seal (*signet*),
for I knew that was the likeliest (*most general*) way of getting a
favorable answer.   214. **at fall:** at low tide.   218. **catch a
wrench:** strain itself, slip up.   220. **fractions:** broken sentences.
221. **half-caps:** perfunctory acknowledgments.

Their blood is caked, 'tis cold, it seldom flows. 225
'Tis lack of kindly° warmth they are not kind,
And nature, as it grows again toward earth,
Is fashioned for the journey, dull and heavy.°
[*To a* SERVANT] Go to Ventidius. [*To* FLAVIUS]
    Prithee be not sad. 229
Thou art true and honest. Ingeniously° I speak,
No blame belongs to thee. [*To* SERVANT] Ventidius
    lately
Buried his father, by whose death he's stepped
Into a great estate. When he was poor,
Imprisoned, and in scarcity of friends,
I cleared him with five talents. Greet him from me.
Bid him suppose some good necessity 236
Touches his friend, which craves to be remembered
With those five talents. [*Exit* SERVANT.]
[*To* FLAVIUS] That had, give 't these fellows
To whom 'tis instant due. Ne'er speak or think
That Timon's fortunes 'mong his friends can sink.
    FLAV. I would I could not think it. That thought
      is bounty's foe;° 241
Being free° itself, it thinks all others so. [*Exeunt.*]

Act III

SCENE I. *A room in* LUCULLUS's *house.*

[FLAMINIUS *waiting. Enter a* SERVANT *to him.*]
    SERV. I have told my lord of you. He is coming
down to you.
    FLAM. I thank you, sir.
        [*Enter* LUCULLUS.]
    SERV. Here's my lord.
    LUCUL. [*Aside*] One of Lord Timon's men? 5
A gift, I warrant. Why, this hits right.° I dreamt
of a silver basin and ewer tonight.—Flaminius,
honest Flaminius, you are very respectively° welcome, sir. Fill me some wine. [*Exit* SERVANT.] And
how does that honorable, complete, free-hearted
gentleman of Athens, thy very bountiful good lord
and master? 11
    FLAM. His health is well, sir.
    LUCUL. I am right glad that his health is well, sir.
And what hast thou there under thy cloak, pretty
Flaminius? 15
    FLAM. Faith, nothing but an empty box, sir,
which, in my lord's behalf, I come to entreat your

Honor to supply; who, having great and instant
occasion to use fifty talents, hath sent to your lordship to furnish him, nothing doubting your present
assistance therein. 21
    LUCUL. La, la, la, la! "Nothing doubting," says
he? Alas, good lord! A noble gentleman 'tis, if he
would not keep so good a house.° Many a time 25
and often I ha' dined with him, and told him on 't,
and come again to supper to him, of purpose to have
him spend less; and yet he would embrace no counsel, take no warning by my coming. Every man has
his fault, and honesty° is his. I ha' told him on 't,
but I could ne'er get him from 't. 31
    [*Re-enter* SERVANT, *with wine.*]
    SERV. Please your lordship, here is the wine.
    LUCUL. Flaminius, I have noted thee always wise.
Here's to thee.
    FLAM. Your lordship speaks your pleasure.° 35
    LUCUL. I have observed thee always for a to-
wardly° prompt spirit — give thee thy due — and
one that knows what belongs to reason, and canst
use the time well if the time use thee well. Good
parts° in thee. [*To* SERVANT] Get you gone, 40
sirrah.° [*Exit* SERVANT.] Draw nearer, honest Flaminius. Thy lord's a bountiful gentleman. But thou
art wise, and thou knowest well enough, although
thou comest to me, that this is no time to lend 45
money, especially upon bare friendship, without
security. Here's three solidares° for thee. Good boy,
wink at me, and say thou saw'st me not.° Fare thee
well.
    FLAM. Is 't possible the world should so much
      differ, 49
And we alive that lived?° Fly, damnèd baseness,
To him that worships thee! [*Throwing back the
      money.*]
    LUCUL. Ha! Now I see thou art a fool, and fit for
thy master. [*Exit.*]
    FLAM. May these add to the number that may
      scald thee!
Let molten coin be thy damnation,° 55
Thou disease of a friend, and not himself!
Has friendship such a faint and milky heart,
It turns° in less than two nights? Oh, you gods,
I feel my master's passion!° This slave,
Unto his honor, has my lord's meat in him.° 60
Why should it thrive and turn to nutriment,
When he is turned to poison?

---

226. **kindly:** natural. 227–28. **And . . . heavy:** i.e., as men
grow older they become meaner. 230. **Ingeniously:** frankly.
241. **That . . . foe:** i.e., the thought that men are grateful causes
a lack of generosity, for it proves false in experience. 242. **free:**
generous.

Act III, Sc. i: 6. **hits right:** comes true. 8. **respectively:**
particularly.

25. **keep . . . house:** live so extravagantly. 30. **honesty:** open-
handedness. 35. **speaks . . . pleasure:** you are pleased to say
so. 36–37. **towardly:** willing. 40. **parts:** qualities. 41. **sirrah:**
term of address used to an inferior. 47. **solidares:** small coins,
"dimes." 48. **wink . . . not:** shut your eyes and say that you
never saw me. 49–50. **Is 't . . . lived:** is it possible that we
should live to see men change so quickly? 54–55. **May . . .
damnation:** i.e., may you go to Hell and have boiling metal
poured over you. 58. **turns:** curdles, goes sour. 59. **passion:**
indignation. 59–60. **This . . . him:** this slave has been made
honorable by the dinners which my lord has given him.

Oh, may diseases only work upon 't!
And when he's sick to death, let not that part of
   nature
Which my lord paid for be of any power   65
To expel sickness, but prolong his hour!°   [*Exit.*]

SCENE II. *A public place.*

[*Enter* LUCIUS, *with three* STRANGERS.]

LUC. Who, the Lord Timon? He is my very good
friend, and an honorable gentleman.
  1. STRA. We know him for no less, though we are
but strangers to him. But I can tell you one thing,
my lord, and which I hear from common   5
rumors: Now Lord Timon's happy hours are done
and past, and his estate shrinks from him.
  LUC. Fie, no, do not believe it. He cannot want
for money.   10
  2. STRA. But believe you this, my lord, that not
long ago one of his men was with the Lord Lucullus
to borrow so many talents; nay, urged extremely
for 't, and showed what necessity belonged to 't, and
yet was denied.   15
  LUC. How!
  2. STRA. I tell you, denied, my lord.
  LUC. What a strange case was that! Now, before
the gods, I am ashamed on 't. Denied that honorable
man! There was very little honor showed in 't.   20
For my own part, I must needs confess I have received some small kindnesses from him, as money,
plate, jewels, and suchlike trifles, nothing comparing to his. Yet, had he mistook° him and sent to
me, I should ne'er have denied his occasion° so
many talents.   26

[*Enter* SERVILIUS.]

SER. See, by good hap, yonder's my lord. I have
sweat° to see His Honor. My honored lord!
  LUC. Servilius! You are kindly met, sir. Fare   30
thee well. Commend me to thy honorable virtuous
lord, my very exquisite friend.
  SER. May it please your Honor, my lord hath
sent ——
  LUC. Ha! What has he sent? I am so much   35
endeared to that lord. He's ever sending. How shall
I thank him, think'st thou? And what has he sent
now?
  SER. Has only sent his present occasion now, my
lord, requesting your lordship to supply his instant
use with so many talents.   41
  LUC. I know his lordship is but merry with me.
He cannot want fifty-five hundred talents.
  SER. But in the meantime he wants° less, my
   lord.

If his occasion were not virtuous,   45
I should not urge it half so faithfully.
  LUC. Dost thou speak seriously, Servilius?
  SER. Upon my soul, 'tis true, sir.
  LUC. What a wicked beast was I to disfurnish
myself against° such a good time° when I   50
might ha' shown myself honorable! How unluckily
it happened that I should purchase the day before
for a little part, and undo a great deal of honor!°
Servilius, now, before the gods, I am not able to do
— the more beast, I say! I was sending to use°   55
Lord Timon myself, these gentlemen can witness,
but I would not, for the wealth of Athens, I had
done 't now. Commend me bountifully to his good
lordship, and I hope His honor will conceive   60
the fairest° of me, because° I have no power to be
kind; and tell him this from me: I count it one of
my greatest afflictions, say, that I cannot pleasure
such an honorable gentleman. Good Servilius, will
you befriend me so far as to use mine own words to
him?   65
  SER. Yes, sir, I shall.
  LUC. I'll look you out a good turn,° Servilius.

[*Exit* SERVILIUS.]

True, as you said, Timon is shrunk indeed,
And he that's once denied° will hardly speed.°

[*Exit.*]

  1. STRA. Do you observe this, Hostilius?
  2. STRA.   Aye, too well.   70
  1. STRA. Why, this is the world's soul, and just of
   the same piece
Is every flatterer's spirit. Who can call him
His friend that dips in the same dish?° For, in
My knowing, Timon has been this lord's father,°
And kept his credit with his purse,°   75
Supported his estate — nay, Timon's money
Has paid his men their wages. He ne'er drinks,
But Timon's silver treads upon his lip;
And yet — oh, see the monstrousness of man
When he looks out in an ungrateful shape! —   80
He does deny him, in respect of his,°
What charitable men afford to beggars.
  3. STRA. Religion groans at it.
  1. STRA.   For mine own part,
I never tasted Timon in my life,
Nor came any of his bounties over me   85

---

66. prolong . . . hour: i.e., may he die slowly.
Sc. ii: 24. mistook: doubted. 25. occasion: need. 28. sweat:
made great efforts. 44. wants: requires.

49–50. disfurnish . . . time: leave myself unprovided to do such
a good turn. against: in anticipation of. 52–53. purchase . . .
honor: have made a purchase yesterday for a small sum which
leaves me unable to win honor by helping Timon. 55. sending
to use: asking for a loan. 60–61. conceive . . . fairest: think
most kindly. because: even though. 67. look . . . turn: think
of some way of befriending you. 69. once denied: refused a
loan. speed: prosper. 73. dips . . . dish: It was customary for
friends to sit together, four at a table (or mess), and to help
themselves from one common dish. 74. father: i.e., a father to
him. 75. kept . . . purse: stood security for his debts. 81. in
. . . his: when it comes to giving some of his own money.

To mark me for his friend; yet, I protest,
For his right noble mind, illustrious virtue,
And honorable carriage,
Had his necessity made use of° me,
I would have put my wealth into donation,°   90
And the best half should have returned to him,
So much I love his heart. But I perceive
Men must learn now with pity to dispense,
For policy° sits above conscience.   [*Exeunt.*]

SCENE III. *A room in* SEMPRONIUS' *house.*

[*Enter* SEMPRONIUS, *and a* SERVANT OF TIMON's.]
SEM. Must he needs trouble me in 't — hum! —
  'bove all others?
He might have tried Lord Lucius or Lucullus;
And now Ventidius is wealthy too,
Whom he redeemed from prison. All these
Owe their estates unto him.
SERV.   My lord,   5
They have all been touched° and found base metal,
  for
They have all denied him.
  SEM.   How! Have they denied him?
Has Ventidius and Lucullus denied him?
And does he send to me? Three? Hum!
It shows but little love or judgment in him.   10
Must I be his last refuge? His friends, like physi-
  cians,
Thrive, give him over.° Must I take the cure upon
  me?
Has° much disgraced me in 't. I'm angry at him,
That might have known my place. I see no sense
  for 't,
But his occasions might have wooed me first,   15
For, in my conscience, I was the first man
That e'er received gift from him.
And does he think so backwardly of me now
That I'll requite it last? No.
So it may prove an argument of laughter   20
To the rest, and 'mongst lords I be thought a fool.
I'd rather than the worth of thrice the sum
Had sent to me first, but for my mind's sake;°
I'd such a courage° to do him good. But now
  return.
And with their faint reply this answer join;   25
Who bates° mine honor shall not know my coin.
                        [*Exit.*]
SERV. Excellent! Your lordship's a goodly villain.

The° Devil knew not what he did when he made
man politic. He crossed himself by 't, and I cannot
think but in the end the villainies of man will set
him clear. How fairly this lord strives to appear
foul! Takes virtuous copies to be wicked, like
those that under hot ardent zeal would set whole
realms on fire.
Of such a nature is his politic love.   35
This was my lord's best hope. Now all are fled
Save only the gods. Now his friends are dead.
Doors° that were ne'er acquainted with their
  wards°
Many a bounteous year must be employed
Now to guard sure their master.   40
And this is all a liberal course allows.°
Who cannot keep his wealth must keep° his house.
                        [*Exit.*]

SCENE IV. *A hall in* TIMON's *house.*

[*Enter two* SERVANTS OF VARRO, *and the* SERVANT OF
  LUCIUS, *meeting* TITUS, HORTENSIUS, *and other*
  SERVANTS *of* TIMON's *creditors, waiting his*
                  coming out.]
1. VAR. SERV. Well met. Good morrow, Titus and
  Hortensius.
TIT. The like to you, kind Varro.
HOR.   Lucius!
What, do we meet together?
  LUC. SERV.   Aye, and I think
One business does command us all, for mine
Is money.
  TIT. So is theirs and ours.
                [*Enter* PHILOTUS.]
LUC. SERV.   And Sir Philotus too!
PHI. Good day at once.
  LUC. SERV.   Welcome, good brother.
What do you think the hour?
  PHI.   Laboring° for nine.
LUC. SERV. So much?
  PHI.   Is not my lord seen yet?
LUC. SERV.   Not yet.
PHI. I wonder on 't. He was wont to shine at
  seven.   10

28–32. The . . . wicked: The servant is disgusted at the hypocrisy of Sempronius in excusing his meanness by pleading that
his honor is injured. The speech may be paraphrased: "The
Devil made a mistake when he made man crafty. He thwarted
(*crossed*) himself; but yet men in the end will see to it that the
Devil is justified. This lord tries to make out that he is acting
honorably when he does a foul deed, and imitates honorable
men as a justification for his wickedness." 38–40. Doors . . .
master: The doors in Timon's house, which once were kept
open to welcome his guests, must now be locked to protect their
master. 38. wards: locks, lit., the bars inside a lock which fit
the key. 41. And . . . allows: this is the end of too liberal a
way of life. 42. keep: guard.
  Sc. iv: 8. Laboring: about to bring forth.

89. made . . . of: ask for help from. 90. put . . . donation:
have made a gift of my own wealth. *Donation* is a legal term
meaning "formal transfer of property as a gift." 94. policy:
craftiness.
  Sc. iii: 6. touched: tested. See *Rich III*, IV.ii.8,n. 12. give
. . . over: abandon hope of his recovery. 13. Has: he has.
23. mind's sake: for my good intentions toward him. 24. courage: determination. 26. bates: lessens.

LUC. SERV. Aye, but the days are waxed shorter
    with him.
You must consider that a prodigal course
Is like the sun's, but not, like his, recoverable.°
I fear
'Tis deepest winter in Lord Timon's purse;
That is, one may reach deep enough and yet   15
Find little.
    PHI.   I am of your fear for that.
    TIT. I'll show you how to observe a strange event.
Your lord sends now for money.
    HOR.   Most true, he does.
    TIT. And he wears jewels now of Timon's gift,
For which I wait for money.   20
    HOR. It is against my heart.
    LUC. SERV.   Mark how strange it shows
Timon in this should pay more than he owes.
And e'en as if your lord should wear rich jewels,
And send for money for 'em.
    HOR. I'm weary of this charge,° the gods can
    witness.   25
I know my lord hath spent of Timon's wealth,
And now ingratitude makes it worse than stealth.
    1. VAR. SERV. Yes, mine's three thousand crowns.
    What's yours?
    LUC. SERV. Five thousand mine.
    1. VAR. SERV. 'Tis much deep; and it should seem
    by the sum   30
Your master's confidence was above mine,°
Else, surely, his had equaled.
                [*Enter* FLAMINIUS.]
    TIT. One of Lord Timon's men.
    LUC. SERV. Flaminius! Sir, a word. Pray, is my
lord ready to come forth?   35
    FLAM. No, indeed he is not.
    TIT. We attend° his lordship. Pray signify so
much.
    FLAM. I need not tell him that. He knows you
are too diligent.   [*Exit.*]   40
        [*Enter* FLAVIUS *in a cloak, muffled.*°]
    LUC. SERV. Ha! Is not that his steward muffled so?
He goes away in a cloud.° Call him, call him!
    TIT. Do you hear, sir?
    2. VAR. SERV. By your leave, sir ——
    FLAV. What do ye ask of me, my friend?   45
    TIT. We wait for certain money here, sir.
    FLAV.   Aye,
If money were as certain as your waiting,
'Twere sure enough,

Why then preferred° you not your sums and bills
When your false masters eat of my lord's meat?   50
Then they could smile and fawn upon his debts,
And take down the interest into their gluttonous
    maws.
You do yourselves but wrong to stir me up.
Let me pass quietly.
Believe 't, my lord and I have made an end.   55
I have no more to reckon, he to spend.
    LUC. SERV. Aye, but this answer will not serve.
    FLAV. If 'twill not serve, 'tis not so base as you,
For you serve knaves.   [*Exit.*]
    1. VAR. SERV. How! What does his cashiered°
Worship mutter?   61
    2. VAR. SERV. No matter what. He's poor, and
that's revenge enough. Who can speak broader than
he that has no house to put his head in? Such may
rail against great buildings.   65
             [*Enter* SERVILIUS.]
    TIT. Oh, here's Servilius. Now we shall know
some answer.
    SER. If I might beseech you, gentlemen, to repair
some other hour, I should derive much from 't;°
for, take 't of my soul, my lord leans wondrously to
discontent. His comfortable temper has forsook   71
him. He's much out of health and keeps his chamber.
    LUC. SERV. Many do° keep their chambers are not
    sick.
And if it be so far beyond his health,°   75
Methinks he should the sooner pay his debts,
And make a clear way to the gods.°
    SERV.   Good gods!
    TIT. We cannot take this for answer, sir.
    FLAM. [*Within*] Servilius, help! My lord! My
    lord!
     [*Enter* TIMON, *in a rage,* FLAMINIUS *following.*]
    TIM. What, are my doors opposed against my
    passage?   80
Have I been ever free, and must my house
Be my retentive enemy, my jail?
The place which I have feasted, does it now,
Like all mankind, show me an iron heart?
    LUC. SERV. Put in now,° Titus.   85
    TIT. My lord, here is my bill.
    LUC. SERV. Here's mine.
    HOR. And mine, my lord.
    BOTH VAR. SERV. And ours, my lord.
    PHI. All our bills.   90
    TIM. Knock me down with 'em. Cleave me to the
    girdle.°
    LUC. SERV. Alas, my lord ——

12–13. prodigal . . . recoverable: i.e., the course of an extravagant man is like that of the sun: He has plenty of sunshine in
the summer, but little in the winter; but the prodigal's winter
is not like that of the sun, for it has no return of summer.
25. charge: instruction to collect the money.   31. Your . . .
mine: your master trusted Timon more than mine did, for he
lent him more money.   37. attend: wait for.   40. s.d., muffled:
with his head covered   42. cloud: huff.

49. preferred: put in.   60. cashiered: dismissed.   69. derive
. . . from 't: be much obliged.   74. Many do: many who do.
75. if . . . health: if he is as sick as you say.   77. make . . .
gods: go to Heaven with a clear conscience.   85. Put in now:
now's your chance to present your bill.   91. girdle: waist.

TIM. Cut my heart in sums.

TIT. Mine, fifty talents.

TIM. Tell° out my blood.   95

LUC. SERV. Five thousand crowns, my lord.

TIM. Five thousand drops pays that. What yours?
And yours?

1. VAR. SERV. My lord——

2. VAR. SERV. My lord——

TIM. Tear me, take me, and the gods fall upon°
you!   [*Exit.*] 100

HOR. Faith, I perceive our masters may throw
their caps at their money. These debts may well be
called desperate ones, for a madman owes 'em.
                                              [*Exeunt.*]

[*Re-enter* TIMON *and* FLAVIUS.]

TIM. They have e'en put my breath from me, the
slaves.

Creditors? Devils!   105

FLAV. My dear lord——

TIM. What if it should be so.

FLAV. My lord——

TIM. I'll have it so. My steward!

FLAV. Here, my lord.   110

TIM. So fitly?° Go bid all my friends again,
Lucius, Lucullus, and Sempronius — all.
I'll once more feast the rascals.

FLAV.   Oh, my lord,
You only speak from your distracted soul.
There is not so much left to furnish out   115
A moderate table.

TIM.   Be it not in thy care.
Go,
I charge thee, invite them all. Let in the tide
Of knaves once more. My cook and I'll provide.
                                              [*Exeunt.*]

SCENE V. *The Senate House.*

[*The* SENATE *sitting.*]

1. SEN. My lord, you have my voice° to it. The
fault's
Bloody. 'Tis necessary he should die.
Nothing emboldens sin so much as mercy.

2. SEN. Most true. The law shall bruise him.

[*Enter* ALCIBIADES, *attended.*]

ALC. Honor, health, and compassion° to the
Senate!   5

1. SEN. Now, Captain?

ALC. I am an humble suitor to your virtues;
For pity is the virtue of the law,
And none but tyrants use it cruelly.
It pleases time and fortune to lie heavy   10
Upon a friend of mine, who in hot blood
Hath stepped into the law, which is past depth

To those that without heed do plunge into 't.
He is a man, setting his fate aside,
Of comely virtues.   15
Nor did he soil the fact° with cowardice —
An honor in him which buys out his fault —
But with a noble fury and fair spirit,
Seeing his reputation touched to death,
He did oppose his foe;   20
And with such sober and unnoted° passion
He did behave° his anger, ere 'twas spent,
As if he had but proved an argument.

1. SEN. You undergo too strict a paradox,°
Striving to make an ugly deed look fair.   25
Your words have took such pains as if they labored
To bring manslaughter into form and set quarrel-
ing
Upon the head of valor;° which indeed
Is valor misbegot and came into the world
When sects and factions were newly born.   30
He's truly valiant that can wisely suffer
The worst that man can breathe,° and make his
wrongs
His outsides, to wear them like his raiment, care-
lessly,
And ne'er prefer° his injuries to his heart
To bring it into danger.   35
If wrongs be evils and enforce us kill,
What folly 'tis to hazard life for ill!

ALC. My lord——

1. SEN. You cannot make gross sins look clear.°
To revenge is no valor, but to bear.°

ALC. My lords, then, under favor, pardon me
If I speak like a captain.   41
Why do fond° men expose themselves to battle,
And not endure all threats? Sleep upon 't,
And let the foes quietly cut their throats
Without repugnancy?° If there be   45
Such valor in the bearing, what make we
Abroad?° Why then women are more valiant
That stay at home, if bearing carry it;°
And the ass more captain than the lion, the felon
Loaden with irons wiser than the judge,   50
If wisdom be in suffering. O my lords,
As you are great, be pitifully° good.
Who cannot condemn rashness in cold blood?

16. **fact**: deed.   21. **unnoted**: calm, without fury.   22. **behave**:
emendation for "behoove"; i.e., his anger was as cool as if he
was conducting a debate.   24. **undergo . . . paradox**: you try
to maintain an argument that is self-contradictory.   27–28. **To
. . . valor**: to make manslaughter something admirable and
quarreling a necessary part of valor.   32. **breathe**: utter.
34. **prefer**: offer; i.e., the valiant man should endure his injuries;
he should not take them too seriously, to his own disaster.
38. **clear**: innocent.   39. **To . . . bear**: it is valor to endure an
injury, not to revenge it.   42. **fond**: foolish.   45. **repugnancy**:
fighting back.   45–47. **If . . . Abroad**: if it is so brave to endure
injuries, why should we soldiers fight in foreign lands?   48. **bearing . . . it**: i.e., mere endurance is preferable.   52. **pitifully**:
mercifully.

95. **Tell**: count.   100. **fall upon**: destroy.   111. **fitly**: conveniently.

Sc. v: 1. **voice**: vote.   5. **compassion**: a spirit of mercy.

To kill, I grant, is sin's extremest gust,°
But in defense, by mercy 'tis most just.°   55
To be in anger is impiety,
But who is man that is not angry?
Weigh but the crime with this.
   2. SEN. You breathe in vain.
   ALC.   In vain! His service done
At Lacedaemon and Byzantium°   60
Were a sufficient briber for his life.
   1. SEN. What's that?
   ALC. I say, my lords, he has done fair service,
And slain in fight many of your enemies.
How full of valor did he bear himself   65
In the last conflict, and made plenteous wounds!
   2. SEN. He has made too much plenty with 'em.
He's a sworn rioter. He has a sin°
That often drowns him and takes his valor prisoner.
If there were no foes, that were enough   70
To overcome him. In that beastly fury
He has been known to commit outrages
And cherish factions. 'Tis inferred° to us
His days are foul and his drink dangerous.
   1. SEN. He dies.
   ALC. Hard fate! He might have died in war.   75
My lords, if not for any parts° in him —
Though his right arm might purchase his own time
And be in debt to none° — yet, more to move you,
Take my deserts to his and join 'em both.
And, for I know your reverend ages love   80
Security,° I'll pawn my victories, all
My honors to you upon his good returns.°
If by this crime he owes the law his life,
Why, let the war receive 't in valiant gore;
For law is strict, and war is nothing more.   85
   1. SEN. We are for law. He dies. Urge it no more,
On height of our displeasure. Friend or brother,
He forfeits his own blood that spills another.
   ALC. Must it be so? It must not be. My lords,
I do beseech you, know me.   90
   2. SEN. How!
   ALC. Call me to your remembrances.
   3. SEN. What!
   ALC. I cannot think but your age has forgot me.
It could not else be I should prove so base
To sue and be denied such common grace.   95
My wounds ache at you.
   1. SEN.   Do you dare our anger?
'Tis in few words, but spacious in effect.
We banish thee for ever.
   ALC.   Banish me!

Banish your dotage. Banish usury,
That makes the Senate ugly.   100
   1. SEN. If after two days' shine Athens contain thee,
Attend our weightier judgment. And, not to swell our spirit,°
He shall be executed presently.° [Exeunt SENATORS.]
   ALC. Now the gods keep you old enough that you may live
Only in bone, that none may look on you!°   105
I'm worse than mad. I have kept back their foes
While they have told° their money and let out
Their coin upon large interest — I myself
Rich only in large hurts. All those for this?
Is this the balsam° that the usuring Senate   110
Pours into captains' wounds? Banishment!
It comes not ill. I hate not to be banished.
It is a cause worthy my spleen and fury,
That I may strike at Athens. I'll cheer up
My discontented troops and lay for hearts.°   115
'Tis honor with most lands to be at odds.
Soldiers should brook as little wrongs as gods.°
                            [Exit.]

SCENE VI. *A banqueting room in* TIMON's *house.*

[*Music. Tables set out.* SERVANTS *attending. Enter divers* LORDS, SENATORS, *and others, at several doors.*]
   1. LORD. The good time of day to you, sir.
   2. LORD. I also wish it to you. I think this honorable lord did but try° us this other day.
   1. LORD. Upon that were my thoughts tiring° when we encountered. I hope it is not so low   5 with him as he made it seem in the trial of his several friends.
   2. LORD. It should not be, by the persuasion of his new feasting.   9
   1. LORD. I should think so. He hath sent me an earnest inviting, which many my near occasions° did urge me to put off; but he hath conjured me beyond them, and I must needs appear.   14
   2. LORD. In like manner was I in debt to my importunate business, but he would not hear my excuse. I am sorry, when he sent to borrow of me, that my provision was out.

102. **swell . . . spirit:** make us even more angry. 103. **presently:** immediately. 104–05. **Now . . . you:** a much-discussed passage. It means: "May you go on living till you have become mere skeletons whom none care to regard." Alcibiades in his mad anger prays that these comfortable old men may endure all the penalties of extreme old age — dotage, ugliness, neglect. 107. **told:** counted. 110. **balsam:** balm, healing ointment. 115. **lay . . . hearts:** strike to the heart; i.e., wage deadly war. 117. **Soldiers . . . gods:** soldiers should put up with (*brook*) wrongs as little as the gods do; i.e., should revenge them as quickly. **Sc. vi: 3. try:** put to the test. 4. **tiring:** busying themselves. 12. **many . . . occasions:** my own urgent affairs.

54. **gust:** blast of wind. 55. **But . . . just:** but to kill in self-defense is regarded as justifiable by merciful men. 60. **Lacedaemon . . . Byzantium:** Sparta and Constantinople. 68. **sin:** i.e., drunkenness. 73. **inferred:** reported. 76. **parts:** good qualities. 77–78. **Though . . . none:** though his bravery might be considered to have paid in full for his pardon. 81. **Security:** peaceful ease. 82. **upon . . . returns:** that he will make good.

1. LORD. I am sick of that grief too, as I understand how all things go.   20

2. LORD. Every man here's so. What would he have borrowed of you?

1. LORD. A thousand pieces.

2. LORD. A thousand pieces!

1. LORD. What of you?   25

2. LORD. He sent to me, sir —— Here he comes.

[*Enter* TIMON *and* ATTENDANTS.]

TIM. With all my heart, gentlemen both. And how fare you?

1. LORD. Ever at the best, hearing well of your lordship.   30

2. LORD. The swallow follows not summer more willing than we your lordship.

TIM. [*Aside*] No more willingly leaves winter. Such summer birds are men. — Gentlemen, our dinner will not recompense this long stay.° Feast   35
your ears with the music awhile, if they will fare so harshly o' the trumpet's sound.° We shall to 't presently.°

1. LORD. I hope it remains not unkindly with your lordship that I returned you an empty messenger.

TIM. Oh, sir, let it not trouble you.

2. LORD. My noble lord ——

TIM. Ah, my good friend, what cheer?   44

2. LORD. My most honorable lord, I am e'en sick of shame that, when your lordship this other day sent to me, I was so unfortunate a beggar.°

TIM. Think not on 't, sir.   49

2. LORD. If you had sent but two hours before ——

TIM. Let it not cumber your better remembrance.
[*The banquet brought in.*] Come, bring in all together.

2. LORD. All covered dishes!°   55

1. LORD. Royal cheer, I warrant you.

3. LORD. Doubt not that, if money and the season can yield it.

1. LORD. How do you? What's the news?   60

3. LORD. Alcibiades is banished. Hear you of it?

1, 2. LORD. Alcibiades banished!

3. LORD. 'Tis so, be sure of it.

1. LORD. How? How?

2. LORD. I pray you, upon what?   65

TIM. My worthy friends, will you draw near?

3. LORD. I'll tell you more anon. Here's a noble feast toward.°

2. LORD. This is the old° man still.

3. LORD. Will 't hold? Will 't hold?   70

2. LORD. It does. But time will° — and so ——

3. LORD. I do conceive.

TIM. Each man to his stool with that spur as he

would to the lip of his mistress. Your diet shall be in all places alike. Make not a city feast° of it,   75
to let the meat cool ere we can agree upon the first place. Sit, sit. The gods require our thanks.

You great benefactors, sprinkle our society with thankfulness. For your own gifts, make   80
yourselves praised; but reserve still to give,° lest your deities be despised. Lend to each man enough, that one need not lend to another; for were your godheads to borrow of men, men would forsake   85
the gods. Make the meat be beloved more than the man that gives it. Let no assembly of twenty be without a score of villains. If there sit twelve women at the table, let a dozen of them be — as they are. The rest of your fees,° O gods — the Senators   90
of Athens, together with the common lag° of people — what is amiss in them, you gods, make suitable for destruction. For these my present friends, as they are to me nothing, so in nothing bless them, and to nothing are they welcome.   95
Uncover, dogs, and lap.   [*The dishes are uncovered and seen to be full of warm water.*]

SOME SPEAK. What does his lordship mean?

SOME OTHER. I know not.

TIM. May you a better feast never behold,
You knot° of mouth friends! Smoke and lukewarm water
Is your perfection. This is Timon's last.   100
Who stuck and spangled° you with flatteries
Washes it off, and sprinkles in your faces
Your reeking villainy.

[*Throwing the water in their faces.*]
                                        Live loathed and long,
Most smiling, smooth, detested parasites,   104
Courteous destroyers, affable wolves, meek bears,
You fools of Fortune,° trencher friends,° Time's flies,
Cap-and-knee slaves,° vapors, and minute-jacks!°
Of man and beast the infinite malady
Crust you quite o'er!° What, dost thou go?   109
Soft! Take thy physic first — thou too — and thou!
Stay. I will lend thee money, borrow none.
[*Throws the dishes at them, and drives them out.*]
What, all in motion? Henceforth be no feast
Whereat a villain's not a welcome guest.
Burn, house! Sink, Athens! Henceforth hated be

75. **city feast:** ceremonial banquet, at which every guest is on his dignity.   81. **still to give:** do not give everything you have.   90. **fees:** the meaning is doubtful.   91. **lag:** rabble, for the Fɪ reading "leg."   99. **knot:** gang.   101. **stuck . . . spangled:** make you sparkle with the jewels he stuck on you.   106. **fools of Fortune:** fools who follow Fortune (and desert when things go wrong).   **trencher friends:** friends only for the food you can guzzle.   107. **Cap-and-knee slaves:** fawning obsequious beggars. See App. 7. **minute-jacks:** the figure on a clock which strikes the hours, used as a type of senseless flattering beggar. See *Rich III,* IV.ii.117, and *Rich II,* V.v.60.   108-09. **Of . . . o'er:** may every disease suffered by man or beast cover you all over with blotches. For *crust,* see *Haml,* I.v.71-73.

35. **stay:** wait.   36-37. **fare . . . sound:** care to listen to the harsh notes of the trumpet.   37-38. **to 't presently:** dine at once.   47. **beggar:** i.e., without any money myself.   55. **covered dishes:** i.e., implying an elaborate formal dinner, not just refreshments.   68. **toward:** about to happen.   69. **old:** i.e., as he used to be.   71. **time will:** i.e., show.

Of Timon, man, and all humanity!   [*Exit.*]   115
[*Re-enter the* LORDS, SENATORS, *&c.*]
1. LORD. How now, my lords!
2. LORD. Know you the quality of Lord Timon's
fury?
3. LORD. Push! Did you see my cap?
4. LORD. I have lost my gown.   120
1. LORD. He's but a mad lord, and naught but hu-
mor° sways him. He gave me a jewel th' other day,
and now he has beat it out of my hat. Did you see
my jewel?
3. LORD. Did you see my cap?   125
2. LORD. Here 'tis.
4. LORD. Here lies my gown.
1. LORD. Let's make no stay.
2. LORD. Lord Timon's mad.
3. LORD.   I feel 't upon my bones.   130
4. LORD. One day he gives us diamonds, next day
stones.   [*Exeunt.*]

Act IV

SCENE I. *Without the walls of Athens.*

[*Enter* TIMON.]

TIM. Let me look back upon thee. O thou wall,
That girdlest in those wolves, dive in the earth,
And fence not Athens! Matrons, turn incontinent!
Obedience fail in children! Slaves and fools,   4
Pluck the grave wrinkled Senate from the bench,
And minister° in their steads! To general filths°
Convert o' the instant, green virginity!
Do 't in your parents' eyes! Bankrupts, hold fast.°
Rather than render back, out with your knives,
And cut your trusters' throats! Bound servants,°
     steal!   10
Large-handed robbers your grave masters are,
And pill° by law. Maid, to thy master's bed!
Thy mistress is o' the brothel. Son of sixteen,
Pluck the lined° crutch from thy old limping sire,
With it beat out his brains! Piety and fear,   15
Religion to the gods, peace, justice, truth,
Domestic awe,° night rest and neighborhood,°
Instruction, manners, mysteries° and trades,

121–22. **humor:** whim, madness. See App. 3.
     Act IV, Sc. i: 6. **minister:** rule. **general filths:** common harlots.
8. **hold fast:** don't pay your debts. 10. **Bound servants:**
apprentices, bound by agreement to serve faithfully. 12. **pill:**
rob. 14. **lined:** padded. 17. **Domestic awe:** obedience due
to parents. With this curse, compare Ulysses' speech on the confusion that follows neglect of "degree" (*Tr & Cr,* I.iii.101–24).
neighborhood: neighborliness. 18. **mysteries:** skilled trades —
in which the spirit of brotherhood was strong.

Degrees, observances, customs and laws,
Decline° to your confounding contraries,°   20
And let confusion live! Plagues incident to men,
Your potent and infectious fevers heap
On Athens, ripe for stroke! Thou cold sciatica,
Cripple our Senators, that their limbs may halt°
As lamely as their manners! Lust and liberty°   25
Creep in the minds and marrows of our youth,
That 'gainst the stream of virtue they may strive,
And drown themselves in riot! Itches, blains,°
Sow all the Athenian bosoms, and their crop
Be general leprosy! Breath infect breath,   30
That their society, as their friendship, may
Be merely° poison! Nothing I'll bear from thee
But nakedness, thou détestable town!
Take thou that too, with multiplying bans!°
Timon will to the woods, where he shall find   35
The unkindest beast more kinder than mankind.
The gods confound — hear me, you good gods
     all! —
The Athenians both within and out that wall!
And grant, as Timon grows, his hate may grow
To the whole race of mankind, high and low!   40
Amen.   [*Exit.*]

SCENE II. *Athens.* TIMON'S *house.*

[*Enter* FLAVIUS, *with two or three* SERVANTS.]
1. SERV. Hear you, Master Steward, where's our
     master?
Are we undone? Cast off? Nothing remaining?
FLAV. Alack, my fellows, what should I say to
     you?
Let me be recorded by the righteous gods,
I am as poor as you.
1. SERV.   Such a house broke!   5
So noble a master fall'n! All gone! And not
One friend to take his fortune by the arm°
And go along with him!
2. SERV.   As we do turn our backs
From our companion thrown into his grave,
So his familiars to his buried fortunes°   10
Slink all away, leave their false vows with him,
Like empty purses picked, and his poor self,
A dedicated beggar to the air,
With his disease of all-shunned poverty,
Walks, like Contempt, alone. More of our fellows.
[*Enter other* SERVANTS.]
FLAV. All broken implements of a ruined house.
3. SERV. Yet do our hearts wear Timon's livery.
That see I by our faces. We are fellows° still,

---

20. **Decline:** fall away. **confounding contraries:** destructive opposites. 24. **halt:** limp. 25. **liberty:** licentiousness. 28. **blains:**
sores. 32. **merely:** entirely. 34. **bans:** curses.
     Sc. ii: 7. **take . . . arm:** support him in his troubles. 10. **fa-
miliars . . . fortunes:** who were his close friends before he lost
his money. 18. **fellows:** friends and equals.

Serving alike in sorrow. Leaked is our bark,
And we, poor mates, stand on the dying deck,   20
Hearing the surges threat. We must all part
Into this sea of air.
FLAV.   Good fellows all,
The latest° of my wealth I'll share amongst you.
Wherever we shall meet, for Timon's sake
Let's yet be fellows. Let's shake our heads and say,
As 'twere a knell° unto our master's fortunes,   26
"We have seen better days." Let each take some.
Nay, put out all your hands. Not one word more.
Thus part we rich in sorrow, parting poor.
[SERVANTS embrace, and part several ways.]
Oh, the fierce wretchedness that glory° brings us!
Who would not wish to be from wealth exempt,   31
Since riches point to misery and contempt?
Who would be so mocked with glory? Or to live
But in a dream of friendship?
To have his pomp and all what state compounds°
But only painted,° like his varnished friends?   36
Poor honest lord, brought low by his own heart,
Undone by goodness! Strange, unusual blood,
When man's worst sin is he does too much good!
Who then dares to be half so kind again?   40
For bounty, that makes gods, does still mar men.
My dearest lord, blest to be most accursed,
Rich only to be wretched, thy great fortunes
Are made thy chief afflictions. Alas, kind lord!
He's flung° in rage from this ingrateful seat   45
Of monstrous friends, nor has he with him to
Supply his life, or that which can command it.°
I'll follow, and inquire him out.
I'll ever serve his mind with my best will.   49
Whilst I have gold, I'll be his steward still.   [Exit.]

SCENE III. *Woods and cave, near the seashore.*

[Enter TIMON, from the cave.]
TIM. O blessed breeding sun, draw from the
    earth
Rotten humidity. Below thy sister's orb°
Infect the air! Twinned° brothers of one womb,
Whose procreation, residence, and birth
Scarce is dividant,° touch them with several° for-
    tunes,   5
The greater scorns the lesser. Not nature,
To whom all sores lay siege, can bear great fortune
But by contempt of nature.°

Raise me° this beggar and deny 't that lord;
The senator shall bear contempt hereditary,°   10
The beggar native honor.
It is the pasture lards° the rother's° sides,
The want that makes him lean. Who dares, who
    dares,
In purity of manhood stand upright
And say "This man's a flatterer"? If one be,   15
So are they all, for every grise° of fortune
Is smoothed by that below. The learnèd pate
Ducks to the golden fool.° All is oblique;
There's nothing level in our cursèd natures
But direct villainy. Therefore be abhorred   20
All feasts, societies and throngs of men!
His semblable,° yea, himself, Timon disdains.
Destruction fang° mankind! Earth, yield me roots!
[Digging.]
Who seeks for better of thee, sauce his palate
With thy most operant° poison! What is here?   25
Gold? Yellow, glittering, precious gold? No, gods,
I am no idle votarist.° Roots, you clear Heavens!
Thus much of this will make black white, foul fair,
Wrong right, base noble, old young, coward valiant.
Ha, you gods! Why this? What this, you gods?
    Why, this   30
Will lug° your priests and servants from your sides,
Pluck stout men's pillows from below their heads.°
This yellow slave
Will knit and break religions, bless the accursed,
Make the hoar° leprosy adored, place° thieves,   35
And give them title, knee,° and approbation
With senators on the bench. This is it
That makes the wappened° widow wed again —
She, whom the spital house° and ulcerous sores
Would cast the gorge° at — this embalms and
    spices   40
To the April day° again. Come, damnèd earth,
Thou common whore of mankind, that put'st odds
Among the rout of nations,° I will make thee
Do thy right nature. [March afar off.] Ha! A
    drum? Thou'rt quick,°
But yet I'll bury thee. Thou'lt go, strong thief,   45
When gouty keepers of thee cannot stand.

9. me: for me.   10. bear . . . hereditary: inherit contempt as
natural to his rank.   12. lards: makes fat. rother: horned beast.
An ingenious emendation for the F1 reading "brothers." The
word "rother" is not however used elsewhere by Shakespeare.
16. grise: step.   17–18. learned . . . fool: i.e., "The college
president flatters the millionaire."   22. semblable: likeness.
23. fang: tear with its fangs.   25. operant: powerful.   27. idle
votarist: one who offers a meaningless prayer.   31. lug: tug.
32. Pluck . . . heads: i.e., cause strong men to be smothered in
their beds.   35. hoar: white. place: give office to.   36. knee:
marks of respect.   38. wappened: tired.   39. spital house:
hospital for venereal diseases.   40. cast . . . gorge: vomit.
40–41. embalms . . . day: makes as sweet smelling as April
flowers.   42–43. put'st . . . nations: makes quarrels between
the rabble (rout) of nations.   44. quick: living — because gold
can accomplish so much.

23. latest: last.   26. knell: parting bell. See App. 19.   30. glory:
ostentation.   35. state compounds: magnificence collects.
36. painted: outward show.   45. flung: rushed away.   47. can
. . . it: money to buy the means of life.
    Sc. iii: 2. sister's orb: the moon.   3–6. Twinned . . . lesser:
give to twin brothers, who have lived in the same womb, such
different fortunes that the greater may scorn the less.   5. dividant: divided. several: different.   6–8. Not . . . nature: even
human nature, liable to every kind of disease, can only endure
great wealth by despising itself.

Nay, stay thou out for earnest.°

[Keeping some gold.]
[Enter ALCIBIADES, *with drum and fife, in warlike manner;* PHRYNIA *and* TIMANDRA.]

ALC.   What art thou there? Speak.

TIM. A beast, as thou art. The canker° gnaw thy heart
For showing me again the eyes of man!

ALC. What is thy name? Is man so hateful to thee,
That art thyself a man?   50

TIM. I am Misanthropos° and hate mankind.
For thy part, I do wish thou wert a dog,
That I might love thee something.

ALC.   I know thee well,   55
But in thy fortunes am unlearned and strange.°

TIM. I know thee too, and more than that I know thee
I not desire to know. Follow thy drum.
With man's blood paint the ground, gules, gules.°
Religious canons,° civil laws are cruel.   60
Then what should war be? This fell° whore of thine
Hath in her more destruction than thy sword,
For all her cherubin look.

PHR.   Thy lips rot off!

TIM. I will not kiss thee. Then the rot returns
To thine own lips again.   65

ALC. How came the noble Timon to this change?

TIM. As the moon does, by wanting light to give;
But then renew I could not, like the moon.
There were no suns to borrow of.

ALC. Noble Timon, what friendship may I do thee?

TIM. None, but to maintain my opinion.   70

ALC. What is it, Timon?

TIM. Promise me friendship, but perform none.
If thou wilt not promise, the gods plague thee, for
thou art a man. If thou dost perform, confound
thee, for thou art a man!   75

ALC. I have heard in some sort of thy miseries.

TIM. Thou saw'st them when I had prosperity.

ALC. I see them now. Then was a blessèd time.

TIM. As thine is now, held with a brace of harlots.

TIMA. Is this the Athenian minion° whom the world   80
Voiced so regardfully?°

TIM.   Art thou Timandra?

TIMA. Yes.

TIM. Be a whore still. They love thee not that use thee.
Give them diseases, leaving with thee their lust.
Make use of thy salt° hours. Season° the slaves   85
For tubs and baths.° Bring down rose-cheeked youth
To the tub-fast° and the diet.

TIMA.   Hang thee, monster!

ALC. Pardon him, sweet Timandra, for his wits
Are drowned and lost in his calamities.
I have but little gold of late, brave Timon,   90
The want whereof doth daily make revolt
In my penurious band. I have heard and grieved
How cursèd Athens, mindless of thy worth,   93
Forgetting thy great deeds when neighbor states,
But for thy sword and fortune, trod upon them ——

TIM. I prithee beat thy drum, and get thee gone.

ALC. I am thy friend and pity thee, dear Timon.

TIM. How dost thou pity him whom thou dost trouble?
I had rather be alone.

ALC.   Why, fare thee well.
Here is some gold for thee.

TIM.   Keep it, I cannot eat it.

ALC. When I have laid proud Athens on a heap ——   101

TIM. Warr'st thou 'gainst Athens?

ALC.   Aye, Timon, and have cause.

TIM. The gods confound them all in thy conquest,
And thee after, when thou hast conquered!

ALC. Why me, Timon?

TIM.   That by killing of villains
Thou wast born to conquer my country.   106
Put up thy gold. Go on — here's gold — go on.
Be as a planetary plague,° when Jove
Will o'er some high-viced° city hang his poison
In the sick air. Let not thy sword skip one.   110
Pity not honored age for his white beard.
He is an usurer. Strike me the counterfeit matron.
It is her habit° only that is honest,
Herself's a bawd. Let not the virgin's cheek
Make soft thy trenchant° sword; for those milk paps,   115
That through the window bars bore° at men's eyes
Are not within the leaf° of pity writ,
But set them down horrible traitors. Spare not the babe

---

85. salt: bawdy. **Season:** make ready, lit., salt. **86. tubs . . . baths:** The treatment for venereal disease was a course of hot baths. **87. tub-fast:** the sweating treatment. **108. planetary plague:** a plague sent by an evil planet. See App. 1. **109. high-viced:** vicious. **113. habit:** dress. **115. trenchant:** carving. **116. window . . . bore:** F1 reads "through the window Barne bore at"; Dr. Johnson emended to "windowbars." The passage then means "fascinate men's eyes as they are exposed through the openings in the bosom of the dress." In Shakespeare's time it was fashionable for unmarried women to bare the breasts. **117. within . . . leaf:** on the page.

---

47. earnest: money given on account of the main sum to come. **48. canker:** canker worm, maggot. **51. Misanthropos:** man hater. **56. fortunes . . . strange:** am ignorant of what misfortunes have come to you. **59. gules:** heraldic word for red. See *Haml*, II.ii.478–79, and App. 9. **60. canons:** laws. **61. fell:** fearful. **80. Athenian minion:** darling of Athens. **81. Voiced so regardfully:** praised so honorably.

Whose dimpled smiles from fools exhaust their
   mercy.
Think it a bastard whom the oracle   120
Hath doubtfully pronounced thy throat shall cut,°
And mince it sans° remorse. Swear against objects.°
Put armor on thine ears and on thine eyes,
Whose proof° nor yells of mothers, maids, nor
   babes,
Nor sight of priests in holy vestments bleeding   125
Shall pierce a jot. There's gold to pay thy soldiers.
Make large confusion; and, thy fury spent,
Confounded be thyself! Speak not, be gone.

ALC. Hast thou gold yet? I'll take the gold thou
   givest me,
Not all thy counsel.   130
   TIM. Dost thou or dost thou not, Heaven's curse
   upon thee!
   PHR., TIMA. Give us some gold, good Timon.
   Hast thou more?
   TIM. Enough to make a whore forswear her
   trade,
And to make whores, a bawd. Hold up, you sluts,
Your aprons mountant.° You are not oathable.°
Although, I know you'll swear, terribly swear,
Into strong shudders and to heavenly agues   137
The immortal gods that hear you, spare your oaths;
I'll trust to your conditions. Be whores still,
And he whose pious breath seeks to convert you
Be strong in whore, allure him, burn him up.   141
Let your close fire predominate his smoke,°
And be no turncoats. Yet may your pains six
   months
Be quite contrary;° and thatch your poor thin roots
With burdens of the dead° — some that were
   hanged.   145
No matter — wear them, betray with them. Whore
   still.
Paint till a horse may mire upon your face.
A pox of wrinkles!°
   PHR., TIMA. Well, more gold. What then?
Believe 't that we'll do any thing for gold.   150
   TIM. Consumptions sow

In hollow bones of man. Strike their sharp shins,
And mar men's spurring.° Crack the lawyer's voice,
That he may never more false title plead,
Nor sound his quillets° shrilly. Hoar° the flamen,°
That scolds against the quality° of flesh,   156
And not believes himself. Down with the nose,
Down with it flat. Take the bridge quite away
Of him that, his particular to foresee,
Smells from the general weal.° Make curled-pate
   ruffians bald,   160
And let the unscarred braggarts° of the war
Derive some pain from you. Plague all,
That your activity may defeat and quell
The source of all erection. There's more gold.
Do you damn others, and let this damn you,   165
And ditches grave you all!°
   PHR., TIMA. More counsel with more money,
   bounteous Timon.
   TIM. More whore, more mischief first. I have
   given you earnest.
   ALC. Strike up the drum towards Athens! Fare-
   well, Timon.
If I thrive well, I'll visit thee again.   170
   TIM. If I hope well, I'll never see thee more.
   ALC. I never did thee harm.
   TIM. Yes, thou spokest well of me.
   ALC.   Call'st thou that harm?
   TIM. Men daily find it. Get thee away, and take
Thy beagles° with thee.   175
   ALC. We but offend him. Strike!° [*Drum beats.
   Exeunt* ALCIBIADES, PHRYNIA, *and* TIMANDRA.]
   TIM. That nature, being sick of man's unkind-
   ness,
Should yet be hungry! Common mother, thou,
                            [*Digging.*]
Whose womb unmeasurable and infinite breast
Teems, and feeds all; whose self-same mettle,°
Whereof thy proud child, arrogant man, is puffed,
Engenders the black toad and adder blue,   181
The gilded newt and eyeless venomed worm,°
With all the abhorrèd births below crisp° heaven
Whereon Hyperion's° quickening fire doth shine;
Yield him, who all thy human sons doth hate,   185
From forth thy plenteous bosom one poor root!
Ensear° thy fertile and conceptious° womb;
Let it no more bring out ingrateful man!

120–21. **bastard . . . cut:** In the Greek myth of Oedipus the oracle had prophesied that the babe would kill his father. As a result he was exposed to death but was rescued by a kindhearted shepherd, and so lived to fulfill the prophecy.   122. **sans:** without.   **Swear . . . objects:** a difficult phrase; in this context it means: "Swear not to spare that which moves pity."   124. **proof:** strength, impenetrability.   135. **mountant:** uplifted.   **oathable:** to be believed on oath.   142. **Let . . . smoke:** let the heat of your lust overcome the smoke of his eloquence.   143–44. **Yet . . . contrary:** A much disputed sentiment. Probably Timon means: "May you in your turn suffer from venereal disease for six months." Among the more devastating results of the disease were loss of hair, ulcers, rotting of the flesh, loss of the nose, softening of the bones, over which Timon gloats in ll. 151–66.   144–45. **thatch . . . dead:** See *M of Ven*, III.ii.92–96,n.   148. **pox of wrinkles:** to Hell with wrinkles — because paint will conceal them.

153. **mar . . . spurring:** because of sore heels.   155. **quillets:** subtleties.   **Hoar:** cover with white blotches.   **flamen:** priest.   156. **quality:** nature.   159–60. **his . . . weal:** another difficult phrase. The general meaning is: "He that in following his own desires separates himself from the general good."   161. **unscarred braggarts:** unwounded boasters.   166. **ditches . . . all:** may you be buried in ditches.   175. **beagles:** women, lit., small hounds.   **Strike:** beat the drum.   179. **mettle:** material.   182. **eyeless . . . worm:** the "blind-worm" a legless lizard resembling a snake, common in England.   183. **crisp:** covered with curly clouds.   184. **Hyperion:** the sun god.   187. **Ensear:** dry up.   **conceptious:** able to conceive.

Go great with° tigers, dragons, wolves and bears.
Teem with new monsters, whom thy upward face
Hath to the marbled mansion° all above   191
Never presented! — Oh, a root! Dear thanks! —
Dry up thy marrows, vines, and plow-torn leas,°
Whereof ingrateful man, with liquorish° draughts
And morsels unctuous, greases his pure mind,   195
That from it all consideration° slips!

         [*Enter* APEMANTUS.]

More man? Plague, plague!
   APE. I was directed hither. Men report
Thou dost affect° my manners and dost use them.
     TIM. 'Tis then because thou dost not keep a dog,
Whom I would imitate. Consumption catch thee!
     APE. This is in thee a nature but infected,°   202
A poor unmanly melancholy sprung
From change of fortune. Why this spade? This
     place?
This slave-like habit? And these looks of care?   205
Thy flatterers yet wear silk, drink wine, lie soft,
Hug their diseased perfumes,° and have forgot
That ever Timon was. Shame not these woods
By putting on the cunning of a carper.°
Be thou a flatterer now, and seek to thrive   210
By that which has undone thee. Hinge thy knee,
And let his very breath whom thou'lt observe
Blow off thy cap. Praise his most vicious strain,
And call it excellent. Thou wast told thus.
Thou gavest thine ears like tapsters° that bade wel-
     come   215
To knaves and all approachers. 'Tis most just
That thou turn rascal. Hadst thou wealth again,
Rascals should have 't. Do not assume my likeness.
     TIM. Were I like thee, I'd throw away myself.
     APE. Thou hast cast away thyself, being like thy-
     self,   220
A madman so long, now a fool. What, think'st
That the bleak air, thy boisterous chamberlain,°
Will put thy shirt on warm? Will these mossed
     trees,
That have outlived the eagle, page° thy heels
And skip when thou point'st out? Will the cold
     brook,   225
Candied with ice, caudle thy morning taste°
To cure thy o'ernight's surfeit? Call the creatures
Whose naked natures live in all the spite
Of wreakful° heaven, whose bare unhousèd
     trunks,°

To the conflicting elements exposed,   230
Answer mere nature. Bid them flatter thee.
Oh, thou shalt find ——
     TIM.   A fool of thee. Depart.
     APE. I love thee better now than e'er I did.
     TIM. I hate thee worse.
     APE.   Why?
     TIM.   Thou flatter'st misery.
     APE. I flatter not, but say thou art a caitiff.°   235
     TIM. Why dost thou seek me out?
     APE.   To vex thee.
     TIM. Always a villain's office or a fool's.
Dost please thyself in 't?
     APE.   Aye.
     TIM.   What! A knave too?
     APE. If thou didst put this sour-cold habit on
To castigate thy pride, 'twere well. But thou   240
Dost it enforcedly. Thou'dst courtier be again,
Wert thou not beggar. Willing° misery
Outlives incertain pomp, is crowned before.
The one is filling still, never complete,
The other at high wish. Best state, contentless,   245
Hath a distracted and most wretched being,
Worse than the worst, content.
Thou shouldst desire to die, being miserable.
     TIM. Not by his breath that is more miserable.
Thou art a slave whom Fortune's tender arm   250
With favor never clasped, but bred a dog.
Hadst thou, like us from our first swath,° proceeded
The sweet degrees° that this brief world affords
To such as may the passive drugs° of it
Freely command, thou wouldst have plunged thy-
     self   255
In general riot, melted down thy youth
In different beds of lust, and never learned
The icy precepts of respect,° but followed
The sugared game before thee. But myself,
Who had the world as my confectionary,°   260
The mouths, the tongues, the eyes and hearts of
     men
At duty,° more than I could frame employment,
That numberless upon me stuck, as leaves
Do on the oak, have with one winter's brush
Fell from their boughs, and left me open, bare   265
For every storm that blows. I, to bear this,

---

189. Go . . . with: be pregnant with, conceive.   191. marbled mansion: the sky mottled with gray clouds.   193. leas: plow lands.   194. liquorish: delightful.   196. consideration: thought for anything but sensual pleasure.   199. affect: imitate.   202. infected: i.e., you are not a genuine born melancholic; you have merely caught the complaint. See App. 4.   207. diseased perfumes: their diseased scented mistresses.   209. cunning . . . carper: expert knowledge of a cynic.   215. tapsters: bartenders.   222. chamberlain: valet.   224. page: follow like a page.   226. caudle . . . taste: provide a warm morning drink.   229. wreakful: vengeful. trunks: bodies.

235. caitiff: wretch.   242–47. Willing . . . content: the man who is willingly melancholic lives longer than the wealthy man with his uncertainties and gets his reward (*is crowned*) sooner. The wealthy man is never satisfied, never full; the melancholy man always has what he desires (*at high wish*). The rich man has no content because he is a distracted and most wretched being; but the man who is in the lowest condition is content. For similar sentiments, see Edgar's attempted consolation in *Lear* (IV.i.1–9).   252. swath: swaddling clothes, "diaper."   252–53. proceeded . . . degrees: graduated through the stages.   254. drugs: drudges, lower servants.   258. respect: decency.   260. confectionary: the place in a great house where the sweetmeats and preserves were made and kept.   262. At duty: at my service.

That never knew but better,° is some burden.
Thy nature did commence in sufferance,° time
Hath made thee hard in 't. Why shouldst thou hate
   men?
They never flattered thee. What hast thou given?
If thou wilt curse, thy father, that poor rag,   271
Must be thy subject, who in spite put stuff
To some she-beggar and compounded thee
Poor rogue hereditary.° Hence, be gone!
If thou hadst not been born the worst of men,   275
Thou hadst been a knave and flatterer.

APE.   Art thou proud yet?
TIM. Aye, that I am not thee.
APE.   I, that I was
No prodigal.
TIM.   I, that I am one now.
Were all the wealth I have shut up in thee,
I'd give thee leave to hang it. Get thee gone.   280
That the whole life of Athens were in this!
Thus would I eat it.   [*Eating a root.*]
APE.   Here, I will mend thy feast.
              [*Offering him a root.*]
TIM. First mend my company. Take away thyself.
APE. So I shall mend mine own, by the lack of
   thine.
TIM. 'Tis not well mended so, it is but botched;°
If not, I would it were.   286
APE. What wouldst thou have to° Athens?
TIM. Thee thither in a whirlwind. If thou wilt,
Tell them there I have gold. Look, so I have.
APE. Here is no use for gold.
TIM.   The best and truest,
For here it sleeps, and does no hired harm.   291
APE. Where liest o' nights, Timon?
TIM.   Under that's above me.
Where feed'st thou o' days, Apemantus?
APE. Where my stomach finds meat, or, rather,
where I eat it.   295
TIM. Would poison were obedient and knew my
mind!
APE. Where wouldst thou send it?
TIM. To sauce thy dishes.   299
APE. The middle of humanity thou never knew-
est, but the extremity of both ends. When thou wast
in thy gilt and thy perfume, they mocked thee for
too much curiosity.° In thy rags thou know'st none,
but art despised for the contrary. There's a medlar°
for thee. Eat it.   305
TIM. On what I hate I feed not.
APE. Dost hate a medlar?
TIM. Aye, though it look like thee.
APE. An thou hadst hated meddlers sooner, thou

shouldst have loved thyself better now. What   310
man didst thou ever know unthrift that was beloved after his means?°
TIM. Who, without those means thou talk'st of,
didst thou ever know beloved?
APE. Myself.   315
TIM. I understand thee. Thou hadst some means
to keep a dog.
APE. What things in the world canst thou nearest
compare to thy flatterers?   319
TIM. Women nearest; but men, men are the
things themselves. What wouldst thou do with the
world, Apemantus, if it lay in thy power?
APE. Give it the beasts, to be rid of the men.
TIM. Wouldst thou have thyself fall in the confu-
sion° of men, and remain a beast with the beasts?
APE. Aye, Timon.   326
TIM. A beastly ambition, which the gods grant
thee t' attain to! If thou wert the lion, the fox would
beguile thee. If thou wert the lamb, the fox would
eat thee. If thou wert the fox, the lion would   330
suspect thee, when peradventure thou wert accused
by the ass. If thou wert the ass, thy dullness would
torment thee, and still thou livedst but as a breakfast to the wolf. If thou wert the wolf, thy   335
greediness would afflict thee, and oft thou shouldst
hazard thy life for thy dinner. Wert thou the unicorn,° pride and wrath would confound thee and
make thine own self the conquest of thy fury. Wert
thou a bear, thou wouldst be killed by the   340
horse. Wert thou a horse, thou wouldst be seized by
the leopard. Wert thou a leopard, thou wert ger-
man° to the lion, and the spots° of thy kindred
were jurors on thy life.° All thy safety were   345
remotion,° and thy defense absence. What beast
couldst thou be that were not subject to a beast?
And what a beast art thou already that seest not
thy loss in transformation!   349
APE. If thou couldst please me with speaking to
me, thou mightst have hit upon it here. The commonwealth of Athens is become a forest of beasts.
TIM. How has the ass broke the wall, that thou
art out of the city?   355
APE. Yonder comes a poet and a painter. The
plague of company light upon thee! I will fear to
catch it, and give way. When I know not what else
to do, I'll see thee again.   359
TIM. When there is nothing living but thee, thou
shalt be welcome. I had rather be a beggar's dog
than Apemantus.

---

267. **never . . . better:** always enjoyed the best.   268. **sufferance:** hardship.   274. **Poor . . . hereditary:** born a poor rogue.
285. **botched:** clumsily patched.   287. **have to:** wish might
happen to.   303. **curiosity:** fastidiousness.   304. **medlar:** a
fruit somewhat like a small brown apple, eaten when it has begun to go soft.

311–12. **unthrift . . . means:** an extravagant man who was loved
after his money had gone.   324–25. **confusion:** destruction.
337–38. **unicorn:** See *Caesar*, II.i.204,n.   343–44. **german:**
related to. It was believed that leopards were born as the result
of the mating of a "pard" and a lioness.   344. **spots:** crimes,
with a pun on the leopard's spots.   345. **jurors . . . life:** i.e.,
would condemn you to death.   346. **remotion:** in moving away.

APE. Thou art the cap° of all the fools alive. 363

TIM. Would thou wert clean enough to spit upon!

APE. A plague on thee! Thou art too bad to curse.

TIM. All villains that do stand by thee are pure.

APE. There is no leprosy but what thou speakst.

TIM. If I name thee.

I'll beat thee, but I should infect my hands.

APE. I would my tongue could rot them off! 370

TIM. Away, thou issue of a mangy dog!

Choler does kill me that thou art alive.

I swoon to see thee.

APE. Would thou wouldst burst!

TIM. Away, thou tedious rogue! I am sorry I shall lose

A stone by thee.   [*Throws a stone at him.*]

APE. Beast!

TIM.   Slave!

APE.   Toad!

TIM.   Rogue, rogue, rogue! 375

I am sick of this false world, and will love naught

But even the mere necessities upon 't.

Then, Timon, presently° prepare thy grave.

Lie where the light foam of the sea may beat

Thy gravestone daily. Make thine epitaph, 380

That death in me at others' lives may laugh.

[*To the gold*] O thou sweet king-killer, and dear divorce

'Twixt natural son and sire! Thou bright defiler

Of Hymen's° purest bed! Thou valiant Mars! 384

Thou ever young, fresh, loved, and delicate wooer,

Whose blush doth thaw the consecrated snow°

That lies on Dian's° lap! Thou visible god,

That solder'st close impossibilities

And makest them kiss! That speak'st with every tongue

To every purpose! O thou touch° of hearts! 390

Think thy slave man rebels, and by thy virtue

Set them into confounding odds, that beasts

May have the world in empire!

APE.   Would 'twere so!

But not till I am dead. I'll say thou hast gold.

Thou wilt be thronged to shortly.

TIM.   Thronged to!

APE.   Aye. 395

TIM. Thy back, I prithee.

APE.   Live, and love thy misery!

TIM. Long live so, and so die! [*Exit* APEMANTUS.]

I am quit.

Moe° things like men? Eat, Timon, and abhor them.

[*Enter* BANDITTI.]

1. BAN. Where should he have this gold? It is

some poor fragment, some slender ort° of his 400

remainder. The mere want of gold and the falling-

from of his friends drove him into this melancholy.

2. BAN. It is noised he hath a mass of treasure. 405

3. BAN. Let us make the assay° upon him. If he

care not for 't, he will supply us easily. If he cov-

etously reserve it, how shall 's get it?

2. BAN. True; for he bears it not about him. 'Tis hid.

1. BAN. Is not this he? 410

BANDITTI. Where?

2. BAN. 'Tis his description.

3. BAN. He. I know him.

BANDITTI. Save thee, Timon.

TIM. Now, thieves? 415

BANDITTI. Soldiers, not thieves.

TIM. Both too; and women's sons.

BANDITTI. We are not thieves, but men that much do want.

TIM. Your greatest want is you want much of meat.

Why should you want? Behold, the earth hath roots. 420

Within this mile break forth a hundred springs.

The oaks bear mast,° the briers scarlet hips.°

The bounteous housewife, Nature, on each bush

Lays her full mess before you. Want! Why want?

1. BAN. We cannot live on grass, on berries, water,

As beasts and birds and fishes. 426

TIM. Nor on the beasts themselves, the birds and fishes.

You must eat men. Yet thanks I must you con°

That you are thieves professed, that you work not

In holier shapes. For there is boundless theft 430

In limited° professions. Rascal thieves,

Here's gold. Go suck the subtle blood o' the grape

Till the high fever seethe your blood to froth,

And so 'scape hanging. Trust not the physician;

His antidotes are poison, and he slays 435

Moe than you rob. Take wealth and lives together.

Do villainy, do, since you protest to do 't,

Like workmen. I'll example you with thievery:

The sun's a thief, and with his great attraction

Robs the vast sea. The moon's an arrant° thief,

And her pale fire she snatches from the sun. 441

The sea's a thief, whose liquid surge resolves

The moon into salt tears. The earth's a thief

That feeds and breeds by a composture° stol'n

From general excrement. Each thing's a thief. 445

The laws, your curb and whip, in their rough power

Have unchecked theft. Love not yourselves. Away,

---

363. **cap**: top, lit., the fool's cockscomb. 378. **presently**: at once. 384. **Hymen**: god of marriage. 386. **consecrated snow**: i.e., the symbol of holy chastity. 387. **Dian**: Diana, goddess of chastity. 390. **touch**: test, touchstone. See *Rich III*, IV.ii.8,n. 398. **Moe**: more.

400. **ort**: scrap. 406. **assay**: attempt. 422. **mast**: acorns. **hips**: the ripe fruits of the wild rose. 428. **thanks . . . con**: I must learn to be thankful to you. 431. **limited**: restricted, governed by rules of admission. 440. **arrant**: out and out. 444. **composture**: compost, manure.

Rob one another. There's more gold. Cut throats.
All that you meet are thieves. To Athens go,
Break open shops. Nothing can you steal,   450
But thieves do lose it. Steal not less for this
I give you, and gold confound you howsoe'er!
Amen.

3. BAN. Has almost charmed me from my profession by persuading me to it.   455

1. BAN. 'Tis in the malice of mankind that he thus advises us, not to have us thrive in our mystery.°

2. BAN. I'll believe him as an enemy and give over my trade.   460

1. BAN. Let us first see peace in Athens. There is no time so miserable but a man may be true.

[*Exeunt* BANDITTI.]

[*Enter* FLAVIUS.]

FLAV. Oh, you gods!
Is yond despised and ruinous man my lord?   465
Full of decay and failing? Oh, monument
And wonder of good deeds evilly bestowed!
What an alteration of honor
Has desperate want made!
What viler thing upon the earth than friends   470
Who can bring noblest minds to basest ends!
How rarely does it meet with this time's guise,
When man was wished to love his enemies!°
Grant I may ever love, and rather woo
Those that would mischief me° than those that do!
Has caught me in his eye. I will present   476
My honest grief unto him and, as my lord,
Still serve him with my life. — My dearest master!

TIM. Away! What art thou?

FLAV.   Have you forgot me, sir?

TIM. Why dost ask that? I have forgot all men.
Then, if thou grant'st thou'rt a man, I have forgot
thee.   481

FLAV. An honest poor servant of yours.

TIM. Then I know thee not.
I never had honest man about me, I. All
I kept were knaves, to serve in meat to villains.

FLAV. The gods are witness,   486
Ne'er did poor steward wear a truer grief
For his undone lord than mine eyes for you.

TIM. What, dost thou weep? Come nearer. Then
I love thee
Because thou art a woman, and disclaim'st   490
Flinty mankind, whose eyes do never give°
But thorough° lust and laughter. Pity's sleeping.
Strange times, that weep with laughing, not with
weeping!

FLAV. I beg of you to know me, good my lord,

To accept my grief, and whilst this poor wealth
lasts,   495
To entertain° me as your steward still.

TIM. Had I a steward
So true, so just, and now so comfortable?°
It almost turns my dangerous nature mild.
Let me behold thy face. Surely this man   500
Was born of woman.°
Forgive my general and exceptless° rashness,
You perpetual-sober gods! I do proclaim
One honest man. Mistake me not — but one!
No more, I pray — and he's a steward.   505
How fain would I have hated all mankind!
And thou redeem'st thyself. But all save thee
I fell° with curses.
Methinks thou art more honest now than wise;
For by oppressing and betraying me,   510
Thou mightst have sooner got another service.
For many so arrive at second masters,
Upon their first lord's neck. But tell me true —
For I must ever doubt, though ne'er so sure —
Is not thy kindness subtle, covetous,   515
If not a usuring kindness and as rich men deal
gifts,
Expecting in return twenty for one?

FLAV. No, my most worthy master, in whose
breast
Doubt and suspect, alas, are placed too late.
You should have feared false times when you did
feast.   520
Suspect still comes where an estate is least.°
That which I show, Heaven knows, is merely love,
Duty, and zeal to your unmatchèd mind,
Care of your food and living; and — believe it,
My most honored lord —   525
For any benefit that points to me,
Either in hope or present, I'd exchange
For this one wish; that you had power and wealth
To requite me by making rich yourself.

TIM. Look thee, 'tis so! Thou singly° honest man,
Here, take. The gods, out of my misery,   531
Have sent thee treasure. Go live rich and happy,
But thus conditioned: Thou shalt build from men,°
Hate all, curse all, show charity to none,
But let the famished flesh slide from the bone   535
Ere thou relieve the beggar. Give to dogs
What thou deniest to men. Let prisons swallow 'em,
Debts wither 'em to nothing. Be men like blasted
woods,
And may diseases lick up their false bloods!
And so farewell, and thrive.

FLAV.   Oh, let me stay   540

457–58. mystery: trade.   472–73. How . . . enemies: how seldom is it fashionable in these times for a man to obey the command to love his enemies.   475. would . . . me: openly wish me harm.   491. give: i.e., weep.   492. thorough: through.   496. entertain: employ.   498. comfortable: full of comfort. 500–01. Surely . . . woman: See *Tr & Cr*, V.ii.129–33.   502. exceptless: that makes no exceptions.   508. fell: knock down. 521. Suspect . . . least: suspicion only comes when a man is poor. 530. singly: sole.   533. from men: far away from men.

And comfort you, my master.

TIM.   If thou hatest curses
Stay not. Fly whilst thou art blest and free.
Ne'er see thou man, and let me ne'er see thee.
                     [*Exeunt severally.*]

Act V

SCENE I. *The woods. Before* TIMON'S *cave.*

[*Enter* POET *and* PAINTER, TIMON *watching them from his cave.*]

PAIN. As I took note of the place, it cannot be far
where he abides.

POET. What's to be thought of him? Does the rumor hold for true that he's so full of gold?   4

PAIN. Certain. Alcibiades reports it. Phrynia and
Timandra had gold of him. He likewise enriched
poor straggling soldiers with great quantity. 'Tis
said he gave unto his steward a mighty sum.

POET. Then this breaking° of his has been but a
try for° his friends.   11

PAIN. Nothing else. You shall see him a palm° in
Athens again, and flourish with the highest. Therefore 'tis not amiss we tender our loves to him in
this supposed distress of his. It will show   15
honestly in us, and is very likely to load our purposes with what they travail for,° if it be a just and
true report that goes of his having.

POET. What have you now to present unto him?

PAIN. Nothing at this time but my visitation.
Only I will promise him an excellent piece.   21

POET. I must serve him so too, tell him of an intent that's coming toward him.

PAIN. Good as the best. Promising° is the very
air o' the time. It opens the eyes of expectation.   25
Performance is even the duller for his act, and, but
in the plainer and simpler kind of people, the deed
of saying is quite out of use. To promise is most
courtly and fashionable. Performance is a kind of
will or testament which argues a great sickness in
his judgment that makes it.   31
       [TIMON *comes from his cave, behind.*]

TIM. [*Aside*] Excellent workman! Thou canst
not paint a man so bad as is thyself.

POET. I am thinking what I shall say I have   35
provided for him. It must be a personating° of himself, a satire against the softness of prosperity, with
a discovery° of the infinite flatteries that follow
youth and opulency.   39

TIM. [*Aside*] Must thou needs stand for a vil-
lain° in thine own work? Wilt thou whip thine
own faults in other men? Do so, I have gold for
thee.

POET. Nay, let's seek him.
Then do we sin against our own estate,
When we may profit meet, and come too late.   45

PAIN. True.
When the day serves, before black-cornered° night,
Find what thou want'st by free and offered light.
Come.

TIM. [*Aside*] I'll meet you at the turn.° What a
     god's gold,   50
That he is worshiped in a baser temple
Than where swine feed!
'Tis thou that rigg'st the bark° and plough'st the
     foam,
Settlest admired reverence in a slave.°
To thee be worship! And thy saints for aye   55
Be crowned with plagues, that thee alone obey!
Fit I meet them.   [*Coming forward.*]

POET. Hail, worthy Timon!

PAIN.   Our late noble master!

TIM. Have I once lived to see two honest men?

POET. Sir,   60
Having often of your open bounty tasted,
Hearing you were retired, your friends fall'n off,
Whose thankless natures — O abhorrèd spirits! —
Not all the whips of heaven are large enough —
What! To you,   65
Whose starlike nobleness gave life and influence
To their whole being! I am rapt,° and cannot cover
The monstrous bulk of this ingratitude
With any size of words.

TIM. Let it go naked, men may see 't the better.
You that are honest, by being what you are   71
Make them best seen and known.

PAIN.   He and myself
Have travailed° in the great shower of your gifts,
And sweetly felt it.

TIM.   Aye, you are honest men.

PAIN. We are hither come to offer you our service.   75

Act V, Sc. i: 10. breaking: bankruptcy. 11. try for: experiment to test. 12. palm: palm tree, the type of flourishing prosperity, as in Psalm 92:12 — "The righteous shall flourish like
the palm tree: he shall grow like a cedar in Lebanon." 16–17. load
... for: bring us the reward we are laboring for. 24–31. Promising ... it: everyone promises nowadays. It makes people
hopeful. Fulfillment of the promises is almost a disappointment
and, except among simple folk, no one does what he says he will.
Fashionable people make promises, but to carry them out is like
the bequests in a foolish will made by a sick man who is not in
his right mind.

36. personating: representation. 38. discovery: revelation.
40–41. stand ... villain: reveal yourself a villain. 47. black-
cornered: that makes corners dark. 50. at ... turn: when you
turn round. These two have been walking up and down at the
front of the main stage while Timon lurks at the rear. 53. bark:
ship. 54. Settlest ... slave: causes a slave to have excessive
wonder. 67. rapt: filled with rapture, poetic inspiration.
73. travailed: labored.

TIM. Most honest men! Why, how shall I requite
   you?
Can you eat roots and drink cold water? No.
   BOTH. What we can do, we'll do, to do you serv-
      ice.
   TIM. Ye're honest men. Ye've heard that I have
      gold.   79
I am sure you have. Speak truth. Ye're honest men.
   PAIN. So it is said, my noble lord; but therefore
Came not my friend nor I.
   TIM. Good honest men! Thou draw'st a counter-
      feit°
Best in all Athens. Thou'rt indeed the best.
Thou counterfeit'st most lively.°
   PAIN.   So, so, my lord.   85
   TIM. E'en so, sir, as I say. And, for thy fiction,
Why, thy verse swells with stuff so fine and smooth
That thou art even natural° in thine art.
But for all this, my honest-natured friends,
I must needs say you have a little fault.   90
Marry, 'tis not monstrous in you. Neither wish I
You take much pains to mend.
   BOTH.   Beseech your Honor
To make it known to us.
   TIM.   You'll take it ill.
   BOTH. Most thankfully, my lord.
   TIM.   Will you, indeed?
   BOTH. Doubt it not, worthy lord.   95
   TIM. There's never a one of you but trusts a
      knave
That mightily deceives you.
   BOTH.   Do we, my lord?
   TIM. Aye, and you hear him cog,° see him dis-
      semble,°
Know his gross patchery,° love him, feed him,
Keep in your bosom, yet remain assured   100
That he's a made-up° villain.
   PAIN. I know none such, my lord.
   POET.   Nor I.
   TIM. Look you, I love you well. I'll give you gold.
Rid me these villains from your companies.
Hang them or stab them, drown them in a
   draught,°   105
Confound them by some course, and come to me.
I'll give you gold enough.
   BOTH. Name them, my lord, let's know them.
   TIM. You° that way, and you this, but two in
      company;
Each man apart, all single and alone,   110
Yet an archvillain keeps him company.
If, where thou art, two villains shall not be,

Come not near him. If thou wouldst not reside
But where one villain is, then him abandon.
Hence, pack!° There's gold. You came for gold, ye
   slaves.   115
[To PAINTER] You have work for me, there's pay-
   ment. Hence!
[To POET] You are an alchemist,° make gold of
   that.
Out, rascal dogs!   [Beats them out,
            and then retires into his cave.]
      [Enter FLAVIUS and two SENATORS.]
   FLAV. It is in vain that you would speak with
      Timon,
For he is set so only to himself   120
That nothing but himself which looks like man
Is friendly with him
   1. SEN.   Bring us to his cave.
It is our part and promise to the Athenians
To speak with Timon.
   2. SEN.   At all times alike   124
Men are not still the same. 'Twas time and griefs
That framed him thus. Time, with his fairer hand,
Offering the fortunes of his former days,
The former man may make him. Bring us to him,
And chance it as it may.
   FLAV.   Here is his cave.   129
Peace and content be here! Lord Timon! Timon!
Look out, and speak to friends. The Athenians
By two of their most reverend Senate greet thee.
Speak to them, noble Timon.
      [TIMON comes from his cave.]
   TIM. Thou sun, that comfort'st, burn! Speak, and
      be hanged.
For each true word, a blister! And each false   135
Be as a cauterizing to the root o' the tongue,
Consuming it with speaking!
   1. SEN.   Worthy Timon——
   TIM. Of none but such as you, and you of Timon.
   1. SEN. The Senators of Athens greet thee, Timon.
   TIM. I thank them and would send them back the
      plague,   140
Could I but catch it for them.
   1. SEN.   Oh, forget
What we are sorry for ourselves in thee.°
The Senators with one consent of love
Entreat thee back to Athens; who have thought
On special dignities, which vacant lie   145
For thy best use and wearing.
   2. SEN.   They confess
Toward thee forgetfulness too general, gross;
Which now the public body, which doth seldom
Play the recanter,° feeling in itself
A lack of Timon's aid, hath sense withal   150

Of it own fail, restraining aid to Timon,°
And send forth us to make their sorrowed render,°
Together with a recompense more fruitful
Than their offense can weigh down by the
    dram° —   154
Aye, even such heaps and sums of love and wealth
As shall to thee blot out what wrongs were theirs
And write in thee the figures° of their love,
Ever to read them thine.

    TIM.   You witch° me in it,
Surprise me to the very brink of tears.
Lend me a fool's heart and a woman's eyes,   160
And I'll beweep these comforts, worthy Senators.
    1. SEN. Therefore, so please thee to return with
      us,
And of our Athens, thine and ours, to take
The captainship, thou shalt be met with thanks,
Allowed° with absolute power, and thy good name
Live with authority. So soon we shall drive back
Of Alcibiades the approaches wild,   167
Who, like a boar too savage, doth root up
His country's peace.
    2. SEN.   And shakes his threatening sword
Against the walls of Athens.
    1. SEN.   Therefore, Timon ——   170
    TIM. Well, sir, I will. Therefore, I will, sir, thus:
If Alcibiades kill my countrymen,
Let Alcibiades know this of Timon,
That Timon cares not. But if he sack fair Athens
And take our goodly aged men by the beards,   175
Giving our holy virgins to the stain
Of contumelious,° beastly, mad-brained war,
Then let him know — and tell him Timon speaks
    it —
In pity of our aged and our youth,
I cannot choose but tell him that I care not,   180
And let him take 't at worst; for their knives care
    not
While you have throats to answer. For myself,
There's not a whittle° in the unruly camp,
But I do prize it at my love before°
The reverend'st throat in Athens. So I leave you
To the protection of the prosperous gods,   186
As thieves to keepers.
    FLAV.   Stay not. All's in vain.
    TIM. Why, I was writing of my epitaph.
It will be seen tomorrow. My long sickness
Of health and living now begins to mend,   190
And nothing brings me all things. Go, live still;

Be Alcibiades your plague, you his,
And last so long enough!
    1. SEN.   We speak in vain.
    TIM. But yet I love my country, and am not
One that rejoices in the common wreck,   195
As common bruit° doth put it.
    1. SEN.   That's well spoke.
    TIM. Commend me to my loving country-
    men ——
    1. SEN. These words become your lips as they pass
    through them.
    2. SEN. And enter in our ears like great triumph-
    ers
In their applauding gates.
    TIM.   Commend me to them,   200
And tell them that, to ease them of their griefs,
Their fears of hostile strokes, their aches, losses,
Their pangs of love, with other incident° throes
That nature's fragile vessel doth sustain
In life's uncertain voyage, I will some kindness do
    them: 205
I'll teach them to prevent° wild Alcibiades' wrath.
    1. SEN. I like this well. He will return again.
    TIM. I have a tree° which grows here in my
    close°
That mine own use° invites me to cut down,
And shortly must I fell it. Tell my friends,   210
Tell Athens, in the sequence of degree°
From high to low throughout, that whoso please
To stop affliction, let him take his haste,
Come hither ere my tree hath felt the ax,
And hang himself. I pray you do my greeting.   215
    FLAV. Trouble him no further. Thus you still°
    shall find him.
    TIM. Come not to me again, but say to Athens
Timon hath made his everlasting mansion
Upon the beachèd verge° of the salt flood,
Who° once a day with his embossèd° froth   220
The turbulent surge shall cover. Thither come,
And let my gravestone be your oracle.
Lips, let sour words go by and language end.
What is amiss, plague and infection mend!   224
Graves only be men's works, and death their gain!
Sun, hide thy beams! Timon hath done his reign.
                        [Retires to his cave.]
    1. SEN. His discontents are unremovably
Coupled to nature.°
    2. SEN. Our hope in him is dead. Let us return
And strain what other means is left unto us   230
In our dear° peril.
    1. SEN.   It requires swift foot.   [Exeunt.]

---

151. Of . . . Timon: of its (it) own failure in refusing to help Timon in his distress.   152. sorrowed render: sorrowful confession.   154. dram: lit., the sixteenth of an ounce, a very small weight; i.e., the recompense shall by far outweigh the injury. 157. figures: i.e., value.   158. witch: charm.   165. Allowed: invested.   177. contumelious: insolent.   183. whittle: small clasp knife.   184. prize . . . before: value it more highly.

196. bruit: rumor.   203. incident: accompanying.   206. prevent: forestall.   208. I . . . tree: See Timon Intro. p. 1316b. close: private garden.   209. use: convenience.   211. sequence of degree: order of rank.   216. still: always.   219. verge: shore. 220. Who: i.e., the flood. embossed: foamy.   228. Coupled to nature: part of his nature.   231. dear: excessive.

SCENE II. *Before the walls of Athens.*

[*Enter two* SENATORS *and a* MESSENGER.]

1. SEN. Thou hast painfully discovered.° Are his files°
As full as thy report?

MESS.   I have spoke the least.
Besides, his expedition° promises
Present° approach.

2. SEN. We stand much hazard if they bring not
    Timon.   5

MESS. I met a courier, one mine ancient friend,
Whom, though in general part we were opposed,
Yet our old love made a particular force°
And made us speak like friends. This man was rid-
    ing
From Alcibiades to Timon's cave   10
With letters of entreaty which imported
His fellowship i' the cause against your city,
In part for his sake moved.°

1. SEN.   Here come our brothers.

[*Enter* SENATORS *from* TIMON.]

3. SEN. No talk of Timon, nothing of him expect.
The enemies' drum is heard, and fearful scouring°
Doth choke the air with dust. In, and prepare. 16
Ours is the fall, I fear, our foes the snare. [*Exeunt.*]

SCENE III. *The woods.* TIMON'S *cave, and a rude tomb seen.*

[*Enter a* SOLDIER, *seeking* TIMON.]

SOLD. By all description this should be the place.
Who's here? Speak, ho! No answer! What is this?
Timon is dead, who hath outstretched his span.°
Some beast read this. There does not live a man.°
Dead, sure, and this his grave. What's on this
    tomb   5
I cannot read. The character I'll take with wax.°
Our captain hath in every figure° skill,
An aged interpreter,° though young in days.
Before proud Athens he's set down° by this,
Whose fall the mark of his ambition is. [*Exit.*] 10

SCENE IV. *Before the walls of Athens.*

[*Trumpets sound. Enter* ALCIBIADES
with his powers.]

ALC. Sound to this coward and lascivious town
Our terrible approach.   [*A parley sounded.*]

[*Enter* SENATORS *upon the walls.*]

Till now you have gone on and filled the time
With all licentious measure, making your wills
The scope of justice.° Till now myself and such 5
As slept within° the shadow of your power
Have wandered with our traversed arms° and
    breathed
Our sufferance vainly.° Now the time is flush,°
When crouching marrow° in the bearer strong
Cries of itself "No more." Now° breathless wrong
Shall sit and pant in your great chairs of ease, 11
And pursy insolence shall break his wind
With fear and horrid flight.

1. SEN.   Noble and young,
When thy first griefs were but a mere conceit,°
Ere thou hadst power or we had cause of fear, 15
We sent to thee to give thy rages balm,°
To wipe out our ingratitude with loves
Above their quantity.

2. SEN.   So did we woo
Transformèd Timon to our city's love
By humble message and by promised means. 20
We were not all unkind, nor all deserve
The common stroke of war.

1. SEN.   These walls of ours
Were not erected by their hands from whom
You have received your griefs,° nor are they such
That these great towers, trophies, and schools
    should fall   25
For private faults in them.

2. SEN.   Nor are they living
Who were the motives that you first went out.
Shame, that they wanted cunning, in excess
Hath broke their hearts.° March, noble lord,
Into our city with thy banners spread.   30
By decimation and a tithèd death° —
If thy revenges hunger for that food
Which nature loathes — take thou the destined
    tenth,

Sc. ii: 1. Thou ... discovered: your information is painful.
files: ranks, numbers. 3. expedition: haste. 4. Present:
immediate. 7–8. though ... force: although we were on opposing sides, yet our ancient friendship had a personal appeal.
13. In ... moved: which had been partly undertaken for Timon's
sake. 15. scouring: scurrying, haste.

Sc. iii: 3. outstretched ... span: stretched out his span of
life. 4. Some ... man: the beasts will have to read this, for
there are no men living hereabouts. 6. character ... wax: I
will make an impression of the writing (*character*) in wax.
7. figure: writing — the soldier is illiterate. 8. aged interpreter:
has great experience in interpretation. 9. set down: has started
the siege.

Sc. iv: 4–5. making ... justice: making justice depend on
your desires. 6. slept within: were oppressed by. 7. traversed
arms: with arms reversed in sign of mourning. 7–8. breathed
... vainly: uttered our grievances without redress. 8. flush:
in full bloom. 9. crouching marrow: strength (*marrow*) ready
for the spring. 10–13. Now ... flight: now we who have been
wronged shall pant after our exertions and sit in your comfortable
chairs while overfat (*pursy*) insolent men shall break their wind
with fear as they run away. 14. conceit: imagination. 16. balm:
healing ointment. 24. griefs: grievances. 28–29. Shame ...
hearts: they have died of broken hearts because they were not
clever enough. 31. decimation .. death: the selection of one
man in ten to be put to death.

And **by** the hazard of the spotted die°
Let die the spotted.°

    1. SEN.   All have not offended.   35
For those that were, it is not square° to take
On those that are, revenges. Crimes, like lands,
Are not inherited. Then, dear countryman,
Bring in thy ranks, but leave without° thy rage.
Spare thy Athenian cradle and those kin   40
Which, in the bluster of thy wrath, must fall
With those that have offended. Like a shepherd
Approach the fold and cull° the infected forth,
But kill not all together.

    2. SEN.   What thou wilt,
Thou rather shalt enforce it with thy smile   45
Than hew to 't with thy sword.

    1. SEN.   Set but thy foot
Against our rampired° gates, and they shall ope;
So° thou wilt send thy gentle heart before
To say thou'lt enter friendly.

    2. SEN.   Throw thy glove,°
Or any token of thine honor else,   50
That thou wilt use the wars as thy redress,
And not as our confusion. All thy powers
Shall make their harbor in our town till we
Have sealed° thy full desire.

    ALC.   Then there's my glove.
Descend, and open your uncharged ports.°   55
Those enemies of Timon's and mine own,
Whom you yourselves shall set out for reproof,°
Fall, and no more; and to atone° your fears
With my more noble meaning, not a man
Shall pass his quarter° or offend the stream   60

---

34. hazard . . . die: by the luck of a throw of the dice.
35. spotted: guilty.   **36. square:** just.   **39. without:** outside.
43. cull: pick out.   **47. rampired:** protected with ramparts.
48. So: so long as.   **49. Throw . . . glove:** i.e., as a token.
54. sealed: formally made agreement with.   **55. uncharged ports:** unassaulted gates.   **57. reproof:** punishment.   **58. atone:** reconcile.   **60. pass . . . quarter:** leave his quarters, go out of bounds.

Of regular justice in your city's bounds,
But shall be rendered° to your public laws
At heaviest answer.°

    BOTH.   'Tis most nobly spoken.
    ALC. Descend, and keep your words.
        [*The* SENATORS *descend, and open the gates.*]
                [*Enter* SOLDIER.]
    SOLD. My noble General, Timon is dead,   65
Entombed upon the very hem° o' the sea,
And on his gravestone this insculpture,° which
With wax I brought away, whose soft impression
Interprets for my poor ignorance.

    ALC. [*Reads.*]
"Here lies° a wretched corse, of wretched soul be-
    reft.   70
Seek not my name. A plague consume you wicked
    caitiffs left!
Here lie I, Timon, who, alive, all living men did
    hate.
Pass by and curse thy fill, but pass and stay not
    here thy gait."
These well express in thee thy latter spirits.   74
Though thou abhorr'dst in us our human griefs,
Scorn'dst our brain's flow and those our droplets
    which
From niggard nature fall, yet rich conceit°
Taught thee to make vast Neptune weep for aye
On thy low grave, on faults forgiven. Dead
Is noble Timon, of whose memory   80
Hereafter more. Bring me into your city,
And I will use the olive° with my sword,
Make war breed peace, make peace stint° war,
    make each
Prescribe to other as each other's leech.°
Let our drums strike.   [*Exeunt.*]   85

---

62. rendered: handed over.   **63. answer:** penalty.   **66. hem:** edge.   **67. insculpture:** inscription.   **70. Here lies:** See *Timon* Intro. p. 1316b.   **77. conceit:** imagination.   **82. use . . . olive:** bring peace.   **83. stint:** stop.   **84. leech:** physician.

PERICLES

Introduction

Pericles was one of three plays which, though printed in quarto during Shakespeare's lifetime with his name on the title page, were *not* included in the first folio of 1623, either because the editors knew that Shakespeare had written only a part of each play or because there was some difficulty over the copyright. The other two were entitled *The London Prodigal. As it was plaide by the Kings Maiesties seruants. By William Shakespeare . . . 1605* and *A Yorkshire Tragedy. Not so New as Lamentable and true. Acted by his Maiesties Players at the Globe. Written by W. Shakespeare . . . 1608.* All three plays (together with four others, now known not to have been written by Shakespeare) were subsequently included in the third folio of 1664; but only *Pericles* is still retained in the canon of Shakespeare's work, though there is little trace of his hand in any passage before Act III. With the third act the style changes and much of the remainder of the play may well be Shakespeare's writing, but if so it is Shakespeare far below his best. Most critics are agreed, however, that the prose scenes of the brothel (IV.ii and vi) are undoubtedly his. The earlier scenes of the play, especially I.iv and II.vi and v, are puerile melodrama and so badly written that they might almost be parodies of Elizabethan drama at its worst. The poor quality of these scenes may be partly due to the fact that the text of the play was a piracy.

Pericles was entered in the Stationers' Register on May 20, 1608: " Edward Blount. Entred for his copie vnder thandes of Sir George Buck knight and Master Warden Seton A booke called. the booke of Pericles prynce of Tyre." The name of Sir George Buc indicates that the entry refers to a play, because Buc was Master of the Revels and so responsible for the censorship and supervision of plays. No quarto was printed by Blount, and the entry, like that of *Much Ado about Nothing* (see p. 697a), may have been made to block the printing of the play (see Gen. Intro. p. 66a). If this was the intention, it was unsuccessful, for in 1609 another printer produced an edition with the title page: *The Late, And much Admired Play, Called Pericles, Prince of Tyre. With the true Relation of the whole Historie, aduentures, and fortunes of the said Prince: As also, The no lesse strange, and worthy accidents, in the Birth and Life, of his Daughter Mariana. As it hath been diuers and sundry times acted by his Maiesties Seruants at the Globe on the Banck-side. By William Shakespeare. Imprinted at London for Henry Gosson, and are to be solde at the signe of the Sunne in Pater-noster row, &c. 1609.* This play was popular and was reprinted in 1611 and 1619.

The story of Pericles was well known in English and European literature. It first appeared as a Roman tale in the fifth or sixth century A.D. It was retold in an English version in Gower's *Confessio Amantis.* John Gower, a contemporary of Chaucer, died in 1408, and his tomb, with a recumbent effigy, is still to be seen in St. Saviour's Church Southwark — near the site of the Globe playhouse — where Shakespeare's brother Edmund was buried on December 31, 1607. That Gower's tale is the ultimate source of the play is shown by the appearance of " Ancient Gower " as Prologue. The tale was again told in English in Laurence Twine's *Pattern of Painful Adventures,* 1576. In both Gower's and Twine's versions the hero of the story is called Appolinus. In 1608 a novel by George Wilkins was printed, entitled *The Painfull Aduentures of Pericles Prince of Tyre. Being the true History of the Play of Pericles, as it was lately presented by the worthy and ancient Poet Iohn Gower. 1608.*

Gower's story is as follows:

King Antiochus lived in sin with his daughter. To prevent her marriage, he made a statute that any suitor who sought her hand must first answer a question; if he could not answer, he lost his head; and many heads decorated Antiochus' gate.

At length Appolinus of Tyre, " a young, a fresh, a lusty knight." came as suitor. The King put to him the question, which was:

With felony I am upbore
I eat and have it naught forbore
My mother's flesh, whose housébond
My father for to seek I fond,
Which is the son eke of my wife.
Hereof I am inquisitive;
And who that can my talé save,
All quiet he shall my daughter have;
Of his answer and if he fail
He shall be dead withouté fail.

Appolinus divined the meaning of the riddle, but Antiochus, fearing his own shame if the answer were published, put off the reply for thirty days, and Appolinus, fearing the vengeance of Antiochus, fled away to his own city of Tyre, whence he entered a ship laden with wheat and departed, to the great sorrow of his people. Meanwhile Antiochus had sent his servant Taliart to Tyre to murder Appolinus.

So Appolinus came to Tharsis and took lodging with a rich burgher and his wife, named Strangulio and Dionise. At that time the city of Tharsis was suffering from a great famine, which Appolinus relieved with the wheat from his ship, and the citizens in gratitude erected a statue in his honor. But soon a man named Hellicane came from Tyre to warn Appolinus that Antiochus was still seeking to kill him.

Once more, therefore, Appolinus fled away by sea, but his ship was wrecked, and he was cast ashore naked. In this unhappy and hopeless state a poor fisherman befriended him and set him on his way to the city of Pentapolis where he found the people crowding to the games. Appolinus entered as a competitor and overcame all others, which caused the King to invite him to supper. The stranger showed such signs of sadness that the King sent his daughter to console him, and at length she persuaded him to tell her his story. The King was full of pity at the sad tale and commanded his daughter to sing and play to the stranger. At length she handed Appolinus the harp, and he in his turn played and sang " like an angel," an accomplishment which indicated that he was of gentle birth. The girl asked that Appolinus should be her teacher. She fell hotly in love with him, but for very shame she dared not declare her love, and in this unhappy state she began to pine away. Soon there came three princes to ask for her hand in marriage. The daughter then wrote a letter to her father revealing how matters

stood with her, whereupon the King tactfully dismissed the suitors and showed the letter to Appolinus, who was delighted; and the marriage was joyously celebrated. Soon afterward men came from Tyre to seek Appolinus —

for they him told
That for vengeance, as God it would,
Antiochus as men may wit [know]
With thunder and lightning is forsmit.
His daughter hath the samé chance;
So they be both in o' balance.

Appolinus therefore sailed for Tyre, with his wife, now in the later stages of pregnancy, and a nurse called Lichorida. At sea a great storm arose, and the Queen was delivered of a girl, but so distressing was her labor that she lay to all appearances dead. Appolinus swooned for very sorrow; when he recovered, the master of the ship demanded that the corpse of the Queen be thrown overboard, because the sea will not hold in itself any creature which is dead. The body was therefore laid in a coffer, with gold and jewels and a letter —

I, King of Tyre, Appolinus
Do all manner of men to wit
That hear and see this letter writ,
That helpless without reed [succor]
Here lieth a King's daughter dead.
And who that happeth her to find
For charity take in his mind
And so that she shall be begrave [buried]
With this treasure, which he shall have.

The coffer was cast up at Ephesim and there found by Cerimon, a great physician. He restored the body to life, and the lady, supposing her husband and child to be dead, thereafter entered the religious state in the temple of Diana.

Meanwhile Appolinus had reached Tharsis where he entrusted the infant, who had been called Thaise, to Strangulio and Dionise.

Time passed and Thaise was now fourteen years old, having been brought up as companion to Dionise's daughter; but she so far surpassed her companion that Dionise grew jealous and ordered her bondman, Theophilus by name, to take Thaise down to the seashore and there slay her. The bondman prepared to carry out his orders, but Thaise's pitiful cries roused some pirates who were hiding by the seashore; they emerged, seized the girl, and carried her off to

Mitilene, where they sold her to Leonin, master of a brothel. A number of young men sought her favors, but her sorrow moved them to pity and they left her untouched. This enraged Leonin, who sent his own servant to overcome her; but he, too, was so touched by her innocence that he spared her. At length Leonin yielded to her plea that she be allowed to make her keep by teaching gentlewomen, and her skill as a teacher of the citole and harp and the use of proverbs attracted so many pupils that she became famous.

Theophilus escaped when the pirates seized Thaise; he went back to Dionise and declared that the girl was dead and buried. Dionise made a great show of sorrow and gave out that Thaise had died suddenly. A fine tomb was erected with the epitaph:

> O ye that this behold,
> Lo, here lieth she, the which was hold
> The fairest and the flower of all;
> The name Thaïsis men call.
> The King of Tyre, Appolinus,
> Her father was: now lieth she thus.
> Fourteen year she was of age
> When Death her took to his voyage.

When the news of Thaise's death was brought to Appolinus, he again boarded ship, and in great sorrow came to Mitilene. Here Athenagoras, lord of the place, sent Thaise to comfort him. At first Appolinus treated her roughly, and even smote her; but she answered so gently that he was finally won over and asked her name. She told him her tale, and Appolinus, with great joy, recognized his own daughter. Athenagoras asked for her hand in marriage, and they were wedded.

Appolinus then decided to go on to Tharsis to avenge himself on Dionise; but he was told in a dream to go instead to Ephesim, where he found his wife, long supposed dead. He then continued his journey to Tharsis, where Strangulio and Dionise were duly punished for their wickedness; they were hanged, drawn, burned, and their ashes scattered to the winds. Meanwhile a letter came from Pentapolis saying that the King was dead and inviting Appolinus to take over the kingdom. Thus at length, after many trials and difficulties, everything ended happily for Appolinus and his family.

Such, in outline, is Gower's tale. Twine's version is a prose rendering of the story, using the same names. In his version Wilkins used Twine to some extent. Although he changed the name of Appolinus to Pericles and Thaise to Marina, he took over from Twine the song that Marina sang to her father. The parallels between Wilkins' novel and the play *Pericles* are very close. The riddle is the same, and in the same words; the devices used in the tournament are the same, as is the letter placed in the coffer with the body of Pericles' supposedly dead wife. Wilkins was a minor dramatist; but the only play he wrote by himself, and not in collaboration, is *The Miseries of Enforced Marriage,* presented by the King's Men and printed in 1607. There seems little reason to doubt Wilkins' statement on the title page that the novel is a prose version of Shakespeare's play. If so, *Pericles* was written by 1608. Some scholars have suggested that Wilkins may even have had a hand in writing it.

Pericles has some critical interest. The attempt, not entirely successful, to reproduce Gower's four-stress line and vocabulary is interesting, for such deliberate imitations of fourteenth-century verse were rare in Shakespeare's time. As a play, *Pericles* is an early specimen of the new mode so successfully exploited by Beaumont and Fletcher (see Gen. Intro. pp. 49b–50a). The fashion for gloomy and misanthropic tragedies was passing, and the interest of playgoers was all for the new tragicomedy, exciting, romantic, and melodramatic, but seldom touching the deeper emotions. If indeed *Pericles* can be considered Shakespeare's, it is his first attempt to write a play dealing with two generations, of which *The Winter's Tale* and *The Tempest* are the best examples. It is not too farfetched to suggest that these plays owed their existence partly to the fact that the King's Men had a boy actor who was a considerable success in such parts as Marina, Perdita, Imogen, and Miranda.

Pericles

DRAMATIS PERSONAE

ANTIOCHUS, *King of Antioch*
PERICLES, *Prince of Tyre*
HELICANUS ⎱ *two lords of Tyre*
ESCANES ⎰
SIMONIDES, *King of Pentapolis*
CLEON, *Governor of Tarsus*
LYSIMACHUS, *Governor of Mytilene*
CERIMON, *a lord of Ephesus*
THALIARD, *a lord of Antioch*
PHILEMON, *servant to Cerimon*
LEONINE, *servant to Dionyza*
MARSHAL
A PANDER
BOULT, *his servant*

THE DAUGHTER *of Antiochus*
DIONYZA, *wife to Cleon*
THAISA, *daughter to Simonides*
MARINA, *daughter to Pericles and Thaisa*
LYCHORIDA, *nurse to Marina*

A BAWD
LORDS, KNIGHTS, GENTLEMEN, SAILORS, PIRATES,
    FISHERMEN, *and* MESSENGERS

DIANA
GOWER, *as Chorus*

SCENE — *Dispersedly in various countries.*

Act I

CHORUS

Before the palace of Antioch.

[*Enter* GOWER° *as Chorus.*]
GOW. To sing a song that old was sung,
From ashes° ancient Gower is come,
Assuming man's infirmities°
To glad your ear and please your eyes.
It hath been sung at festivals   5
On ember eves° and holy-ales,°
And lords and ladies in their lives
Have read it for restoratives.°
The purchase° is to make men glorious;
Et bonum quo antiquius, eo melius.°   10
If you, born in these latter times
When wit's more ripe, accept my rhymes,
And that to hear an old man sing
May to your wishes pleasure bring,
I life would wish, and that I might   15
Waste it for you like taper light.°

This Antioch then Antiochus the Great
Built up, this city, for his chiefest seat,
The fairest in all Syria.
I tell you what mine authors say: 20
This king unto him took a fere,°
Who died and left a female heir,
So buxom,° blithe and full of face
As° Heaven had lent her all His grace;
With whom the father liking took,   25
And her to incest did provoke.
Bad child, worse father! To entice his own
To evil should be done by none.
But custom what they did begin
Was with long use account° no sin.   30
The beauty of this sinful dame
Made many princes thither frame°
To seek her as a bedfellów,
In marriage-pleasures playfellów;
Which to prevent he made a law,   35
To keep her still° and men in awe,
That whoso asked her for his wife,
His riddle told not,° lost his life.
So for her many a wight° did die,
As yon grim looks° do testify.   40
What now ensues, to the judgment of your eye
I give, my cause who best can justify.°   [*Exit.*]

Act I, Chorus: s.d., Gower: See *Per* Intro. p. 1349b.   **2. From ashes:** from the dead.   **3. Assuming . . . infirmities:** resuming a human shape.   **6. ember eves:** the evening before ember days — periods of three days' fast, observed in the Catholic Church four times each year. **holy-ales:** In earlier times, instead of whist drives, bazaars, or bingo, it was customary to raise money for church or charitable purposes by ale-drinking parties. **8. restoratives:** recreations.   **9. purchase:** gain, profit.   **10. *Et . . . melius:*** and a good thing, the more ancient the better it is.   **16. Waste . . . light:** spend my life for you as the candles are spent by which you read.

21. fere: mate.   **23. buxom:** lively.   **24. As:** as if.   **30. account:** accounted.   **32. frame:** direct their journey.   **36. still:** always.   **38. His . . . not:** if he could not tell the answer to the riddle.   **39. wight:** man.   **40. yon . . . looks:** i.e., the heads of the unsuccessful suitors.   **41–42. What . . . justify:** what follows (i.e., this play) I leave to you spectators who are the best judges of my case.

SCENE I. *Antioch. A room in the palace.*

[*Enter* ANTIOCHUS, PRINCE PERICLES,
and FOLLOWERS.]

ANT. Young Prince of Tyre, you have at large re-
  ceived°
The danger of the task you undertake.
  PER. I have, Antiochus, and with a soul
Emboldened with the glory of her praise,
Think death no hazard in this enterprise.   5
  ANT. Bring in our daughter, clothéd like a bride
For° the embracements even of Jove himself,
At whose conception, till Lucina reigned,°
Nature this dowry gave to glad her presence,°
The senate house of planets° all did sit   10
To knit in her their best perfections.

[*Music. Enter* ANTIOCHUS' DAUGHTER.]

  PER. See where she comes, appareled like the
  spring,
Graces her subjects,° and her thoughts the king
Of every virtue gives° renown to men!
Her face the book of praises, where is read   15
Nothing but curious° pleasures, as from thence
Sorrow were ever razed° and testy wrath
Could never be her mild companion.°
You gods that made me man and sway in love,
That have inflamed desire in my breast   20
To taste the fruit of yon celestial tree
Or die in the adventure, be my helps,
As I am son and servant to your will,
To compass such a boundless happiness!
  ANT. Prince Pericles ——   25
  PER. That would be son to great Antiochus.
  ANT. Before thee stands this fair Hesperides,°
With golden fruit, but dangerous to be touched;
For deathlike dragons here affright thee hard.
Her face, like Heaven, enticeth thee to view   30
Her countless glory, which desert must gain,
And which, without desert,° because thine eye
Presumes to reach, all thy whole heap must die.
Yon sometimes famous princes, like thyself,
Drawn by report, adventurous by desire,   35
Tell thee, with speechless tongues and semblance
  pale,
That without covering,° save yon field of stars,
Here they stand martyrs, slain in Cupid's wars;

And with dead cheeks advise thee to desist
For going on death's net,° whom none resist.   40
  PER. Antiochus, I thank thee, who hath taught
My frail mortality to know itself
And by those fearful objects to prepare
This body, like to them, to what I must;°
For death remembered should be like a mirror   45
Who tells us life's but breath, to trust it error.
I'll make my will then, and, as sick men do,
Who know the world, see Heaven, but, feeling woe,
Gripe° not at earthly joys as erst° they did,
So I bequeath a happy peace to you   50
And all good men, as every prince should do;
My riches to the earth from whence they came;
But my unspotted fire of love to you.
[*To the* PRINCESS.] Thus ready for the way of life or
  death,
I wait the sharpest blow.   55
  ANT. Scorning advice, read the conclusion then,
Which read and not expounded, 'tis decreed,
As these before thee thou thyself shalt bleed.
  DAU. Of all 'sayed yet,° mayst thou prove pros-
  perous!
Of all 'sayed yet, I wish thee happiness!   60
  PER. Like a bold champion I assume the lists,°
Nor ask advice of any other thought
But faithfulness and courage. [*He reads the riddle.*]
    "I am no viper, yet I feed
    On mother's flesh which did me breed.   65
    I sought a husband, in which labor
    I found that kindness in a father.
    He's father, son, and husband mild;
    I mother, wife, and yet his child.
    How they may be, and yet in two,   70
    As you will live, resolve it you."
[*Aside*] Sharp physic is the last. But O you powers
That give Heaven countless eyes to view men's acts,
Why cloud they not their sights perpetually
If this be true which makes me pale to read it?   75
Fair glass of light, I loved you, and could still,
Were not this glorious casket° stored with ill.
But I must tell you, now my thoughts revolt;
For he's no man on whom perfections wait°
That, knowing sin within, will touch the gate.   80
You are a fair viol° and your sense the strings,
Who, fingered to make man his lawful music,
Would draw Heaven down and all the gods to
  hearken,
But being played upon before your time,
Hell only danceth at so harsh a chime.   85
Good sooth,° I care not for you.

Sc. i: **1. at . . . received:** been fully informed about.   **7. For:**
i.e., fit for.   **8. At . . . reigned:** from the time of her conception
till her birth. Lucina was the goddess of childbirth.   **9. glad . . .
presence:** make her delightful to all who see her.   **10. senate
. . . planets:** i.e., all the lucky stars. See App. 1.   **13. Graces
. . . subjects:** i.e., she is endowed with every grace.   **14. gives:**
i.e., which gives.   **16. curious:** exquisite.   **17. razed:** rooted
out.   **18. mild companion:** the companion of one so amiable.
27. Hesperides: the garden where grew trees bearing golden
fruit, guarded by dragons. It was one of Hercules' labors to
gather the fruit.   **32. without desert:** because you do not deserve
her.   **37. without covering:** unburied.

40. going . . . net: running into the net of destruction.   **44. I
must:** i.e., die.   **49. Gripe:** grip. **erst:** once.   **59. Of . . . yet:**
of all who have as yet assayed (attempted).   **61. assume . . .
lists:** enter as a combatant. **lists:** See *Rich II*, I.iii.s.d.   **77. casket:** small box used for holding jewels.   **79. on . . . wait:** who
is at all perfect.   **81. viol:** See Pl. 18c.   **86. sooth:** truth.

ANT. Prince Pericles, touch not,° upon thy life,
For that's an article within our law
As dangerous as the rest. Your time's expired.
Either expound now or receive your sentence.   90
PER. Great King,
Few love to hear the sins they love to act.
'Twould braid° yourself too near for me to tell it.
Who has a book of all that monarchs do,
He's more secure to keep it shut than shown.   95
For vice repeated° is like the wandering wind,
Blows° dust in others' eyes to spread itself;
And yet the end of all is bought thus dear,
The breath is gone, and the sore eyes see clear
To stop the air would hurt them.° The blind mole casts   100
Copped° hills towards Heaven to tell the earth is°
    thronged
By man's oppression, and the poor worm doth die
    for 't.
Kings are earth's gods; in vice their law's their will;
And if Jove stray, who dares say Jove doth ill?
It is enough you know; and it is fit,   105
What being more known grows worse, to smother
    it.
All love the womb that their first being bred,
Then give my tongue like leave to love my head.
ANT. [*Aside*] Heaven, that I had thy head! He
    has found the meaning.
But I will gloze° with him. — Young Prince of
    Tyre,   110
Though by the tenor of our strict edict,
Your exposition misinterpreting,
We might proceed to cancel of your days,
Yet hope, succeeding° from so fair a tree
As your fair self, doth tune us otherwise.   115
Forty days longer we do respite you.
If by which time our secret be undone,
This mercy shows we'll joy in such a son.
And until then your entertain shall be
As doth befit our honor and your worth.   120
        [*Exeunt all but* PERICLES.]
PER. How courtesy would seem to cover sin,
When what is done is like an hypocrite,
The which is good in nothing but in sight!
If it be true that I interpret false,
Then were it certain you were not so bad   125
As with foul incest to abuse your soul;
Where now you're both a father and a son
By your untimely claspings with your child —
Which pleasure fits a husband, not a father —

And she an eater of her mother's flesh   130
By the defiling of her parent's bed;
And both like serpents are, who though they feed
On sweetest flowers, yet they poison breed.
Antioch, farewell! For wisdom sees, those men
Blush° not in actions blacker than the night   135
Will shun no course to keep them from the light.
One sin, I know, another doth provoke.
Murder's as near to lust as flame to smoke.
Poison and treason are the hands of sin,
Aye, and the targets° to put off the shame.   140
Then, lest my life be cropped to keep you clear,
By flight I'll shun the danger which I fear.   [*Exit.*]
        [*Re-enter* ANTIOCHUS.]
ANT. He hath found the meaning, for the which
    we mean
To have his head.
He must not live to trumpet forth my infamy,   145
Nor tell the world Antiochus doth sin
In such a loathéd manner;
And therefore instantly this prince must die,
For by his fall my honor must keep high.
Who attends us there?
        [*Enter* THALIARD.]
THAL. Doth your Highness call?   150
ANT. Thaliard,
You are of our chamber,° and our mind partakes°
Her private actions to your secrecy;
And for your faithfulness we will advance you.   154
Thaliard, behold, here's poison, and here's gold.
We hate the Prince of Tyre, and thou must kill him.
It fits thee not to ask the reason why,
Because we bid it. Say, is it done?
THAL.   My lord,
'Tis done.
ANT.   Enough.   160
        [*Enter a* MESSENGER.]
Let your breath cool yourself, telling° your haste.
MESS. My lord, Prince Pericles is fled.   [*Exit.*]
ANT.   As thou
Wilt live, fly after, and like an arrow shot
From a well experienced archer hits the mark
His eye doth level° at, so thou ne'er return   165
Unless thou say " Prince Pericles is dead."
THAL. My lord,
If I can get him within my pistol's length,
I'll make him sure enough. So, farewell to your
    Highness.
ANT. Thaliard, adieu! [*Exit* THALIARD.] Till
    Pericles be dead,   170
My heart can lend no succor to my head.°   [*Exit.*]

---

87. **touch not:** i.e., her hand.   93. **braid:** unbraid, bring shame to.   96. **repeated:** talked about.   97. **Blows:** which blows.   98–100. **And . . . them:** the final result, so dearly achieved, is that, when the dust dies down, the sore eyes see clearly how to stop the breeze which would hurt them; i.e., it is safer to say nothing than to raise a dust.   101. **Copped:** vaulted. **to . . . is:** to tell the earth that it is.   110. **gloze:** speak soothingly.   114. **succeeding:** issuing.

135. **Blush:** i.e., who blush.   140. **targets:** shields.   152. **of . . . chamber:** i.e., a personal servant, specially trusted. **partakes:** shares.   161. **telling:** which tells.   165. **level:** aim.   171. **My . . . head:** my thoughts can give me no pleasure.

SCENE II. *Tyre. A room in the palace.*

[*Enter* PERICLES.]

PER. [*To* LORDS *without*°] Let none disturb us. —
Why should this change of thoughts,
The sad companion, dull-eyed melancholy,
Be my so used° a guest as not an hour
In the day's glorious walk or peaceful night,
The tomb where grief should sleep, can breed me
    quiet?   5
Here pleasures court mine eyes, and mine eyes shun
    them,
And danger, which I feared, is at Antioch,
Whose arm seems far too short to hit me here.
Yet neither pleasure's art can joy my spirits,
Nor yet the other's distance comfort me.   10
Then it is thus: The° passions of the mind,
That have their first conception by mis-dread,
Have after-nourishment and life by care;
And what was first but fear what might be done
Grows elder now and cares it be not done.   15
And so with me: The great Antiochus,
'Gainst whom I am too little to contend,
Since he's so great can make his will his act,
Will think me speaking, though I swear to silence.
Nor boots it° me to say I honor him   20
If he suspect I may dishonor him;
And what may make him blush in being known,
He'll stop the course by which it might be known.
With hostile forces he'll o'erspread the land,
And with the ostent° of war will look so huge,   25
Amazement shall drive courage from the state,
Our men be vanquished ere they do resist,
And subjects punished that ne'er thought offense;
Which care of them, not pity of myself,
Who am no more but as the tops of trees   30
Which fence° the roots they grow by and defend
    them,
Makes both my body pine and soul to languish,
And punish that before that he would punish.°

[*Enter* HELICANUS, *with other* LORDS.]

1. LORD. Joy and all comfort in your sacred breast!
2. LORD. And keep your mind, till you return to
    us,   35
Peaceful and comfortable!
HEL. Peace, peace, and give experience tongue.°
They do abuse the King that flatter him.
For flattery is the bellows blows up sin,

The thing the which is flattered, but a spark   40
To which that blast gives heat and stronger glow-
    ing;
Whereas reproof, obedient and in order,
Fits kings, as they are men, for° they may err.
When Signior Sooth° here does proclaim a peace,
He flatters you, makes war upon your life.   45
Prince, pardon me, or strike me, if you please.
I cannot be much lower than my knees.
PER. All leave us else, but let your cares o'erlook°
What shipping and what lading's° in our haven,
And then return to us. [*Exeunt* LORDS.] Helicanus,
    thou   50
Hast moved us. What seest thou in our looks?
HEL. An angry brow, dread lord.
PER. If there be such a dart° in princes' frowns,
How durst thy tongue move anger to our face?
HEL. How dare the plants look up to heaven,
    from whence   55
They have their nourishment?
PER.   Thou know'st I have power
To take thy life from thee.
HEL. [*Kneeling*] I have ground the ax myself.
Do you but strike the blow.
PER. Rise, prithee, rise. Sit down. Thou art no
    flatterer.   60
I thank thee for it; and Heaven forbid
That kings should let their ears hear their faults
    hid!
Fit counselor and servant for a prince,
Who by thy wisdom makest a prince thy servant,
What wouldst thou have me do?
HEL.   To bear with patience   65
Such griefs as you yourself do lay upon yourself.
PER. Thou speak'st like a physician, Helicanus,
That minister'st a potion unto me
That thou wouldst tremble to receive thyself.
Attend° me then. I went to Antioch,   70
Where, as thou know'st, against the face of death
I sought the purchase of a glorious beauty
From whence an issue° I might propagate
Are arms° to princes and bring joys to subjects.
Her face was to mine eye beyond all wonder,   75
The rest — hark in thine ear — as black as incest;
Which by my knowledge found, the sinful father
Seemed not to strike, but smooth. But thou know'st
    this:
'Tis time to fear when tyrants seem to kiss.
Which fear so grew in me, I hither fled   80
Under the covering of a careful° night,
Who seemed my good protector, and, being here,
Bethought me what was past, what might succeed.°

Sc. ii: 1. s.d., **without:** standing outside.   **3. used:** familiar.
11–15. The . . . done: excessive fears (*passions of the mind*) that
are first conceived through dread are increased by anxiety, and
what was first a fear that something evil might happen (*mis-
dread*) turns into precaution that it shall not; i.e., I was at first
afraid Antiochus would injure me, but now I shall take precaution that he cannot.   **20. boots it:** is it advantageous.
25. ostent: display.   **31. fence:** protect.   **33. And . . . punish:**
i.e., by my excessive fear I punish myself before Antiochus
punishes me.   **37. give . . . tongue:** give me leave to speak out
of my experience.

43. for: because.   **44. Signior Sooth:** "Mr. Smoothtongue."
48. o'erlook: see.   **49. lading:** cargo.   **53. dart:** i.e., danger.
70. Attend: listen to.   **73. an issue:** children.   **74. Are arms:**
that are arms.   **81. careful:** taking care of me.   **83. succeed:**
come next.

I knew him tyrannous, and tyrants' fears
Decrease not, but grow faster than the years.   85
And should he doubt° it, as no doubt he doth,
That I should open to the listening air
How many worthy princes' bloods were shed
To keep his bed of blackness unlaid ope,°
To lop that doubt he'll fill this land with arms,   90
And make pretense of wrong that I have done him;
When all for mine (if I may call) offense°
Must feel war's blow, who spares not innocence.
Which love to all, of which thyself art one,
Who now reprovest me for it ——

HEL.   Alas, sir!   95
PER. Drew sleep out of mine eyes, blood from my
   cheeks,
Musings into my mind, with thousand doubts
How I might stop this tempest ere it came;
And finding little comfort to relieve them,
I thought it princely charity to grieve them.   100
   HEL. Well, my lord, since you have given me
     leave to speak,
Freely will I speak. Antiochus you fear;
And justly, too, I think, you fear the tyrant,
Who either by public war or private treason
Will take away your life.   105
Therefore, my lord, go travel for a while,
Till that his rage and anger be forgot,
Or till the Destinies do cut his thread of life.°
Your rule direct to any° — if to me,
Day serves not light more faithful than I'll be.   110
   PER. I do not doubt thy faith;
But should he wrong my liberties in my absence?
   HEL. We'll mingle our bloods together in the
     earth
From whence we had our being and our birth.
   PER. Tyre, I now look from thee then, and to
     Tarsus   115
Intend° my travel, where I'll hear from thee,
And by whose letters I'll dispose myself.
The care I had and have of subjects' good
On thee I lay, whose wisdom's strength can bear it.
I'll take thy word for faith, not ask thine oath;   120
Who shuns not to break one will sure crack both.
But in our orbs° we'll live so round and safe
That time of both this truth shall ne'er convince,°
Thou show'st a subject's shine, I a true prince.
                          [*Exeunt.*]

---

86. doubt: suspect.   89. unlaid ope: concealed.   92. if . . .
offense: if what I have done may be called offense.   108. Destinies . . . life: See *M N D*, V.i.343–48.   109. direct to any:
entrust to someone.   116. Intend: direct.   122. orbs: courses
of life, spheres. See App. 1.   123. That . . . convince: i.e., that
time will prove that both of us are true to our faiths. convince:
convict of falsehood.

[*Enter* THALIARD.]
THAL. So, this is Tyre, and this the Court. Here
must I kill King Pericles, and if I do it not, I am
sure to be hanged at home. 'Tis dangerous. Well, I
perceive he was a wise fellow° and had good discre-
tion that, being bid to ask what he would of the   5
King, desired he might know none of his secrets.
Now do I see he had some reason for 't, for if a king
bid a man be a villain, he's bound by the indenture°
of his oath to be one. Hush! Here come the lords of
Tyre.   10
[*Enter* HELICANUS *and* ESCANES, *with other* LORDS.]
HEL. You shall not need, my fellow peers of Tyre,
Further to question me of your King's departure.
His sealed commission° left in trust with me
Doth speak sufficiently he's gone to travel.
   THAL. [*Aside*] How! The King gone!   15
   HEL. If further yet you will be satisfied,
Why, as it were unlicensed° of your loves,
He would depart, I'll give some light unto you.
Being at Antioch ——
   THAL. [*Aside*] What from Antioch?
   HEL. Royal Antiochus — on what cause I know
     not ——   20
Took some displeasure at him; at least he judged so.
And doubting lest that he had erred or sinned,
To show his sorrow, he'd correct himself;°
So puts himself unto the shipman's toil,°   24
With whom each minute threatens life or death.
   THAL. [*Aside*] Well, I perceive I shall not be
hanged now, although I would; but since he's gone,
the King's seas must please. He 'scaped the land to
perish at the sea. I'll present myself. — Peace to the
lords of Tyre!   30
   HEL. Lord Thaliard from Antiochus is welcome.
   THAL. From him I come
With message unto princely Pericles,
But since my landing I have understood   34
Your lord has betook himself to unknown travels.
My message must return from whence it came.
   HEL. We have no reason to desire it,
Commended to our master, not to us.°
Yet, ere you shall depart, this we desire,
As friends to Antioch, we may feast in Tyre.   40
                          [*Exeunt.*]

Sc. iii: 4. wise fellow: The story is told of King Lysimachus
and a poet called Philides.   8. indenture: agreement. See App. 6.
13. sealed commission: official appointment as deputy in
Pericles' absence. See *M for Meas*, I.i.14,n.   17. unlicensed:
without first obtaining leave.   22–23. And . . . himself: and,
not being sure whether he had committed some error or fault,
punishes himself to show his sorrow.   24. puts . . toil: submits
himself to the perils of a sea voyage.   37–38. We . . . us: we
do not desire to read a message intended only for our master.

SCENE IV. *Tarsus. A room in the Governor's house.*

[*Enter* CLEON *the Governor of Tarsus, with* DIONYZA *and others.*]

CLE. My Dionyza, shall we rest us here,
And by relating tales of others' griefs,
See if 'twill teach us to forget our own?
  DIO. That were to blow at fire in hope to quench it,
For who digs° hills because they do aspire°   5
Throws down one mountain to cast up a higher.
O my distressed lord, even such our griefs are.
Here they're but felt, and seen with Mischief's eyes,
But like to groves, being topped,° they higher rise.
  CLE. O Dionyza,   10
Who wanteth° food, and will not say he wants it,
Or can conceal his hunger till he famish?
Our tongues and sorrows do sound deep
Our woes into the air. Our eyes do weep
Till tongues fetch breath that may proclaim them
     louder,   15
That, if Heaven° slumber while their creatures
     want,
They° may awake their helps to comfort them.
I'll then discourse our woes, felt several years,
And, wanting breath to speak, help me with tears.
  DIO. I'll do my best, sir.   20
  CLE. This Tarsus, o'er which I have the govern-
     ment,
A city on whom Plenty held full hand —
For Riches° strewed herself even in the streets, —
Whose towers bore heads so high they kissed the
     clouds,
And strangers ne'er beheld but wondered at,   25
Whose men and dames so jetted° and adorned,
Like one another's glass to trim° them by.
Their tables were stored full to glad the sight,
And not so much to feed on as delight.
All poverty was scorned, and pride so great,   30
The name of help grew odious to repeat.°
  DIO. Oh, 'tis too true.
  CLE. But see what Heaven can do! By this our
     change,
These mouths, who but of late earth, sea and air
Were all too little to content and please,   35
Although they gave their creatures in abundance,
As houses are defiled° for want of use,
They° are now starved for want of exercise.
Those palates who, not yet two summers younger,

Must have inventions° to delight the taste   40
Would now be glad of bread, and beg for it.
Those mothers who, to nousle° up their babes,
Thought naught too curious° are ready now
To eat those little darlings whom they loved.
So sharp are hunger's teeth that man and wife   45
Draw lots who first shall die to lengthen life.
Here stands a lord, and there a lady weeping.
Here many sink, yet those which see them fall
Have scarce strength left to give them burial.
Is not this true?   50
  DIO. Our cheeks and hollow eyes do witness it.
  CLE. Oh, let those cities that of Plenty's cup
And her prosperities so largely taste,
With their superfluous riots,° hear these tears!
The misery of Tarsus may be theirs.   55
     [*Enter a* LORD.]
  LORD. Where's the Lord Governor?
  CLE. Here.
Speak out thy sorrows which thou bring'st in haste,
For comfort is too far for us to expect.
  LORD. We have descried upon our neighboring
     shore,   60
A portly° sail of ships make hitherward.
  CLE. I thought as much.
One sorrow never comes but brings an heir
That may succeed as his inheritor.
And so in ours: Some neighboring nation,   65
Taking advantage of our misery,
Hath stuffed these hollow vessels with their power°
To beat us down, the which are down already,
And make a conquest of unhappy me,
Whereas° no glory's got to overcome.   70
  LORD. That's the least fear,° for, by the sem-
     blance°
Of their white flags displayed, they bring us peace,
And come to us as favorers, not as foes.
  CLE. Thou speak'st like him 's untutored to re-
     peat.°
Who makes the fairest show means most deceit.   75
But bring they what they will and what they can,
What need we fear?
The ground's the lowest, and we are half way there.
Go tell their General we attend° him here,   79
To know for what he comes, and whence he comes,
And what he craves.
  LORD. I go, my lord.   [*Exit.*]
  CLE. Welcome is peace, if he on peace consist;°
If wars, we are unable to resist.
     [*Enter* PERICLES *with* ATTENDANTS.]

Sc. iv: 5. digs: digs up. aspire: are high.   9. topped: cut,
lopped.   11. wanteth: needs.   16. Heaven: the gods.   17. They:
i.e., the gods.   23. Riches: a singular word.   26. jetted: be-
jeweled.   27. trim: adorn.   31. The . . . repeat: everyone was
so proud and rich that none ever thought of asking for help —
a line forced for the sake of the rhyme at the end.   37. are
defiled: grow filthy.   38. They: i.e., the mouths.

40. inventions: novelties — plain food was not good enough.
42. nousle: cuddle, "spoil."   43. curious: elaborate, "fancy."
54. riots: extravagances.   61. portly: imposing.   67. power:
soldiers.   70. Whereas: where.   71. That's . . . fear: there
is small need to fear that. semblance: appearance.   74. untutored to repeat: one untaught to give an accurate report; i.e., an
inexperienced fool.   79. attend: await.   83. consist: stand upon

PER. Lord Governor, for so we hear you are,   85
Let not our ships and number of our men
Be like a beacon fired° to amaze° your eyes.
We have heard your miseries as far as Tyre,
And seen the desolation of your streets.
Nor come we to add sorrow to your tears,   90
But to relieve them of their heavy load;
And these our ships, you happily° may think
Are like the Trojan Horse° was stuffed within
With bloody veins expecting overthrow,°   94
Are stored with corn° to make your needy bread,
And give them life whom hunger starved half dead.
    ALL. The gods of Greece protect you!
And we'll pray for you.
    PER.   Arise, I pray you, rise.
We do not look for reverence, but for love
And harborage for ourself, our ships and men.   100
    CLE. The which when any shall not gratify,
Or pay you with unthankfulness in thought,
Be it our wives, our children, or ourselves,
The curse of Heaven and men succeed° their evils!°
Till when — the which I hope shall ne'er be seen —
Your Grace is welcome to our town and us.   106
    PER. Which welcome we'll accept, feast here
    awhile,
Until our stars that frown lend us a smile.
                          [*Exeunt.*]

Act II

CHORUS

[*Enter* GOWER.]
   GOW. Here have you seen a mighty king
His child, I wis,° to incest bring;
A better prince and benign lord,
That will prove awful both in deed and word
Be quiet then, as men should be,   5
Till he hath passed necessity.°
I'll show you those in troubles reign,°
Losing a mite,° a mountain gain.
The good in conversation,°

To whom I give my benison,°   10
Is still at Tarsus, where each man
Thinks all is Writ° he spoken can;°
And, to remember° what he does,
Build his statue to make him glorious.
But tidings to the contrary   15
Are brought your eyes. What need speak I?
[DUMB SHOW:° *Enter, at one door,* PERICLES, *talking with* CLEON; *all the train° with them. Enter, at another door, a* GENTLEMAN, *with a letter to* PERICLES. PERICLES *shows the letter to* CLEON, *gives the* MESSENGER *a reward, and knights° him. Exit* PERICLES *at one door, and* CLEON *at another.*]
Good Helicane, that stayed at home,
Not to eat honey like a drone
From others' labors, for though° he strive
To killen° bad, keep good alive;   20
And to fulfill his Prince's desire,
Sends word of all that haps in Tyre:
How Thaliard came full bent with sin
And had intent to murder him,
And that in Tarsus was not best   25
Longer for him to make his rest.
He, doing so, put forth to seas,
Where when men been,° there's seldom ease.
For now the wind begins to blow.
Thunder above and deeps below   30
Make such unquiet that the ship
Should° house him safe is wrecked and split,
And he, good Prince, having all lost,
By waves from coast to coast is tossed.
All perishen of man, of pelf,°   35
Ne° aught escapen but himself;
Till fortune, tired with doing bad,
Threw him ashore to give° him glad.
And here he comes. What shall be next,   39
Pardon old Gower — this longs the text.°   [*Exit.*]

SCENE I. *Pentapolis. An open place by the seaside.*

[*Enter* PERICLES, *wet.*]
   PER. Yet cease your ire, you angry stars of
   Heaven!
Wind, rain, and thunder, remember earthly man
Is but a substance that must yield to you,
And I, as fits my nature, do obey you.
Alas, the sea hath cast me on the rocks,   5

---

87. beacon fired: warning of an approaching enemy. See *II Hen IV*, IV.iii.116,n. amaze: terrify.   92. happily: perhaps. 93. Trojan Horse: After ten years' siege the Greeks ultimately captured Troy by trickery. They pretended to sail away, but left behind as a memorial a great Wooden Horse which the Trojans were persuaded to bring into their city. The Horse, however, was filled with soldiers. 94. With . . . overthrow: with bloody soldiers waiting (*expecting*) to overthrow Troy. 95. corn: grain. 104. succeed: follow, fall upon. evils: i.e., ungrateful thoughts.
    Act II. Chorus: 2. I wis: certainly — one of several archaic forms used to give an antique flavor to Gower's speeches. 6. passed necessity: i.e., until he has fulfilled his destiny. 7. in . . . reign: whose reigns are full of troubles. 8. mite: minute portion. 9. conversation: duty, life.

10. benison: blessing.   12. Thinks . . . can: thinks that everything that Pericles utters (*speken*) is holy — another example of pseudoantique diction. Writ: holy scriptures.   13. remember: commemorate.   16. s.d., Dumb show: See *Haml*, III.ii.14,n and l. 145, s.d.,n. train: attendants. knights: See *II Hen VI*, IV.ii.127–28,n.   19. for though: although.   20. killen: kill. 28. been: are.   32. Should: which should.   35. All . . . pelf: all the men and the goods perished.   36. Ne: nor.   38. give: make.   40. this . . . text: this belongs to the story of the play.

Washed me from shore to shore, and left me breath
Nothing to think on but ensuing death.
Let it suffice the greatness of your powers
To have bereft a prince of all his fortunes,
And, having thrown him from your watery grave,
Here to have death in peace is all he'll crave.   11

[*Enter* THREE FISHERMEN.]

1. FISH. What ho, Pilch!°

2. FISH. Ha, come and bring away the nets!

1. FISH. What, Patchbreech, I say!

3. FISH. What say you, master?   15

1. FISH. Look how thou stirrest now! Come away,
or I'll fetch thee with a wanion.°

3. FISH. Faith, master, I am thinking of the poor
men that were cast away before us even now.   20

1. FISH. Alas, poor souls, it grieved my heart to
hear what pitiful cries they made to us to help them,
when, well-a-day,° we could scarce help ourselves.

3. FISH. Nay, master, said not I as much when I
saw the porpus,° how he bounced and tumbled?
They say they're half fish, half flesh. A plague on
them, they ne'er come but I look to be washed.°
Master, I marvel how the fishes live in the sea.   30

1. FISH. Why, as men do a-land; the great ones
eat up the little ones. I can compare our rich misers
to nothing so fitly as to a whale: A' plays and tum-
bles, driving the poor fry before him, and at last
devours them all at a mouthful. Such whales   35
have I heard on o' the land, who never leave gaping
till they've swallowed the whole parish, church,
steeple, bells, and all.°

PER. [*Aside*] A pretty moral.

3. FISH. But, master, if I had been the sexton,   40
I would have been that day in the belfry.

2. FISH. Why, man?

3. FISH. Because he should have swallowed me,
too, and when I had been in his belly, I would have
kept such a jangling of the bells that he should   45
never have left till he cast° bells, steeple, church, and
parish, up again. But if the good King Simonides
were of my mind —

PER. [*Aside*] Simonides!

3. FISH. We would purge the land of these   50
drones that rob the bee of her honey.

PER. [*Aside*] How from the finny subject° of the
sea
These fishers tell the infirmities of men,
And from their watery empire recollect
All that may men approve° or men detect! —   55
Peace be at your labor, honest fishermen.

2. FISH. Honest! Good fellow, what's that? If it
be a day fits you, search out of the calendar, and nobody look after it.°   59

PER. May° see the sea hath cast upon your coast.

2. FISH. What a drunken knave was the sea to
cast thee in our way!

PER. A man whom both the waters and the wind
In that vast tennis court have made the ball
For them to play upon entreats you pity him.   65
He asks of you, that never used to beg.

1. FISH. No, friend, cannot you beg? Here's them
in our country of Greece gets more with begging
than we can do with working.

2. FISH. Canst thou catch any fishes then?   70

PER. I never practiced it.

2. FISH. Nay, then thou wilt starve, sure, for here's
nothing to be got nowadays, unless thou canst fish
for 't.

PER. What I have been I have forgot to know,   75
But what I am want teaches me to think on:
A man thronged up° with cold. My veins are chill,
And have no more of life than may suffice
To give my tongue that heat to ask your help;
Which if you shall refuse, when I am dead,   80
For that I am a man, pray see me buriéd.

1. FISH. Die quoth-a?° Now gods forbid 't! And
I have a gown here. Come, put it on. Keep thee
warm. Now, afore me, a handsome fellow! Come,
thou shalt go home, and we'll have flesh for   85
holidays, fish for fasting days, and moreo'er pud-
dings° and flapjacks, and thou shalt be welcome.

PER. I thank you, sir.

2. FISH. Hark° you, my friend. You said you
could not beg.   90

PER. I did but crave.

2. FISH. But crave! Then I'll turn craver too, and
so I shall 'scape whipping.

PER. Why, are all your beggars whipped then?

2. FISH. Oh, not all, my friend, not all; for if   95
all your beggars were whipped, I would wish no
better office than to be beadle. But, master, I'll go
draw up the net.   [*Exit with* THIRD FISHERMAN.]

PER. [*Aside*] How well this honest mirth becomes their labor!   99

1. FISH. Hark you, sir, do you know where ye are?

PER. Not well.

1. FISH. Why, I'll tell you. This is called Pentapolis, and our King the good Simonides.

Sc. i: 12. Pilch: leather coat.   17. wanion: vengeance.
23. well-a-day: alas.   26. porpus: porpoise.   29. washed: wet
through.   36–38. leave . . . all: a reference to the common
grievance — which had led to severe rioting in 1607 — that rich
men, by enclosing common lands and substituting sheep raising
for agriculture, had depopulated (*swallowed up*) many villages.
46. cast: threw up.   52. subject: subjects, inhabitants.
55. approve: commend.

57–59. Honest . . . it: Pericles steps forward and surprises the
fisherman, who exclaims: "Who are you, calling us honest?
If this day suits you, look into the almanac and see what
luck it will bring you; you can keep it!"   60. May: you may.
77. thronged up: overwhelmed.   82. quoth-a: says he.   86–
87. puddings: sausages.   89–97. Hark . . . beadle: The laws
against beggars were very severe. A man charged with begging
was put in the stocks, whipped, and sent to his own parish to be
put to work. To "crave," however, is a more gentlemanly word
than to "beg," and so not liable to the penalties. See *Lear*,
III.iv.134–42.

PER. The good Simonides, do you call him?   105

1. FISH. Aye, sir, and he deserves so to be called for his peaceable reign and good government.

PER. He is a happy king, since he gains from his subjects the name of good by his government. How far is his court distant from this shore?   111

1. FISH. Marry,° sir, half a day's journey. And I'll tell you, he hath a fair daughter, and tomorrow is her birthday; and there are princes and knights come from all parts of the world to just° and tourney° for her love.   116

PER. Were my fortunes equal to my desires, I could wish to make one there.°

1. FISH. Oh, sir, things must be as they may, and what a man cannot get, he may lawfully deal for. His wife's soul —   121

[*Re-enter* SECOND *and* THIRD FISHERMEN, *drawing up a net.*]

2. FISH. Help, master, help! Here's a fish hangs in the net, like a poor man's right in the law;° 'twill hardly come out. Ha! Bots° on 't, 'tis come at last, and 'tis turned to a rusty armor.°   125

PER. An armor, friends! I pray you let me see it. Thanks, Fortune, yet, that after all thy crosses° Thou givest me somewhat to repair myself, And though it was mine own, part of my heritage, Which my dead father did bequeath to me   130 With this strict charge, even as he left his life, " Keep it, my Pericles; it hath been a shield 'Twixt me and death " — and pointed to this brace° — " For that it saved me, keep it. In like necessity — The which the gods protect thee from! —may defend thee."   135 It kept where I kept,° I so dearly loved it, Till the rough seas, that spare not any man, Took it in rage, though calmed have given 't again. I thank thee for 't. My shipwreck now's no ill, Since I have here my father's gift in 's will.   140

1. FISH. What mean you, sir?

PER. To beg of you, kind friends, this coat of worth,° For it was sometime target° to a King. I know it by this mark. He loved me dearly, And for his sake I wish the having of it;   145 And that you'd guide me to your sovereign's Court, Where with it I may appear a gentleman; And if that ever my low fortune's better,

I'll pay your bounties, till then rest your debtor.

1. FISH. Why, wilt thou tourney for the lady?   150

PER. I'll show the virtue I have borne in arms.

1. FISH. Why, do 'e take it, and the gods give thee good on 't!

2. FISH. Aye, but hark you, my friend, 'twas we that made up this garment through the rough   155 seams of the waters. There are certain condolements, certain vails.° I hope, sir, if you thrive, you'll remember from whence you had them.

PER. Believe 't, I will. By your furtherance° I am clothed in steel,   160 And spite of all the rapture° of the sea This jewel holds his building on my arm.° Unto thy value I will mount myself Upon a courser,° whose delightful steps Shall make the gazer joy to see him tread.   165 Only, my friend, I yet am unprovided Of a pair of bases.°

2. FISH. We'll sure provide. Thou shalt have my best gown to make thee a pair, and I'll bring thee to the Court myself.   170

PER. Then honor be but a goal to my will.° This day I'll rise, or else add ill to ill.   [*Exeunt.*]

SCENE II. *The same. A public way or platform leading to the lists.° A pavilion by the side of it for the reception of the* KING, PRINCESS, LORDS, &c.

[*Enter* SIMONIDES, THAISA,° LORDS, *and* ATTENDANTS.]

SIM. Are the knights ready to begin the triumph?°

1. LORD. They are, my liege, And stay° your coming to present themselves.

SIM. Return° them. We are ready, and our daughter, In honor of whose birth these triumphs are,   5 Sits here, like beauty's child, whom nature gat° For men to see, and seeing, wonder at.   [*Exit a* LORD.]

THAI. It pleaseth you, my royal Father, to express My commendations great, whose merit's less.

SIM. It's fit it should be so, for princes are   10 A model which Heaven makes like to itself. As jewels lose their glory if neglected,

---

112. **Marry:** Mary, by the Virgin.   115. **just:** joust, tilt. In tilting, knights in full armor charged each other on horseback with long wooden lances.   115–16. **tourney:** take part in a tournament.   118. **make . . . there:** take part.   123. **poor . . . law:** like a poor man caught in the net of the law. Note in these plays (*Per* and *Cym*) the constant jibes at the abuses of the times.   124. **Bots:** lit., worms in the guts. See Pl. 8a and Note on p. 95a–b.   127. **crosses:** trials, burdens.   133. **brace:** protection for the arm.   136. **kept:** stayed.   142. **coat of worth:** suit of armor.   143. **target:** protection.

156–57. **condolements . . . vails:** marks of sympathy . . . perquisites. Both words are polite synonyms for "tip."   160. **furtherance:** aid.   161. **rapture:** fury.   162. **This . . arm:** i.e., I still retain this jewel (which I can sell).   164. **courser:** charger.   167. **bases:** skirt of the doublet. See Pl. 13b.   171. **goal . . . will:** incentive to my desires.

Sc. ii: s.d., **lists:** barriers erected round the place of combat. **Thaisa:** a three-syllable word.   1. **triumph:** festivities.   3. **stay:** wait for.   4. **Return:** answer.   6. **gat:** begat.

So princes their renowns it not respected.
'Tis now your honor, daughter, to entertain°
The labor of each knight in his device.°   15
    THAI. Which, to preserve mine honor, I'll per-
    form.
    [*Enter a* KNIGHT; *he passes over, and his* SQUIRE
       presents his shield to the PRINCESS.]
    SIM. Who is the first that doth prefer° himself?
    THAI. A knight of Sparta, my renowned Father,
And the device he bears upon his shield
Is a black Ethiope reaching at the sun;   20
The word, " *Lux tua vita mihi.*"°
    SIM. He loves you well that holds his life of you.
                 [*The* SECOND KNIGHT *passes.*]
Who is the second that presents himself?
    THAI. A prince of Macedon, my royal Father,
And the device he bears upon his shield   25
Is an armed knight that's conquered by a lady;
The motto thus, in Spanish, " *Piu por dulzura que*
    por fuerza."°   [*The* THIRD KNIGHT *passes.*]
    SIM. And what's the third?
    THAI.   The third of Antioch,
And his device, a wreath of chivalry;
The word, " *Me pompae provexit apex.*"°   30
              [*The* FOURTH KNIGHT *passes.*]
    SIM. What is the fourth?
    THAI. A burning torch that's turned upside
    down;
The word, " *Quod me alit, me extinguit.*"°
    SIM. Which shows that beauty hath his power and
    will,
Which can as well inflame as it can kill.   35
             [*The* FIFTH KNIGHT *passes.*]
    THAI. The fifth, an hand environed° with clouds,
Holding out gold that's by the touchstone° tried;
The motto thus, " *Sic spectanda fides.*"°
      [*The* SIXTH KNIGHT, PERICLES, *passes.*]
    SIM. And what's
The sixth and last, the which the knight himself°
With such a graceful courtesy delivered?   41
    THAI. He seems to be a stranger, but his present
    is
A withered branch, that's only green at top;
The motto, " *In hac spe vivo.*"°
    SIM. A pretty moral —   45
From the dejected state wherein he is,
He hopes by you his fortunes yet may flourish.

    1. LORD. He had need mean° better than his out-
    ward show
Can any way speak in his just commend,
For by his rusty outside he appears   50
To have practiced more the whipstock° than the
    lance.
    2. LORD. He well may be a stranger, for he comes
To an honored triumph strangely furnished.
    3. LORD. And on set purpose let his armor rust
Until this day, to scour it in the dust.   55
    SIM. Opinion's° but a fool that makes us scan
The outward habit by the inward man.°
But stay, the knights are coming. We will withdraw
Into the gallery.   [*Exeunt.*]
    [*Great shouts within, and all cry* " The mean°
        knight! "]

SCENE III. *The same. A hall of state. A banquet*
prepared.

    [*Enter* SIMONIDES, THAISA, LORDS, KNIGHTS,
        and ATTENDANTS.]
    SIM. Knights,
To say you're welcome were superfluous.
To place upon the volume of your deeds,
As in a title page,° your worth in arms,
Were more than you expect, or more than's fit,   5
Since every worth in show commends itself.
Prepare for mirth, for mirth becomes a feast.
You are princes and my guests.
    THAI. But you, my knight and guest,
To whom this wreath of victory I give,   10
And crown you king of this day's happiness.
    PER. 'Tis more by fortune, lady, than my merit.
    SIM. Call it by what you will, the day is yours,
And here, I hope, is none that envies it.
In framing an artist, art hath thus decreed,   15
To make some good, but others to exceed;
And you are her labored° scholar. Come, queen o'
    the feast —
For, Daughter, so you are — here take your place.
Marshal the rest as they deserve their grace.
    KNIGHTS. We are honored much by good Simon-
    ides.   20
    SIM. Your presence glads our days. Honor we
    love;
For who hates honor hates the gods above.
    MARSHAL. Sir, yonder is your place.
    PER.   Some other is more fit.

---

14. entertain: welcome.   15. device: In a tilt each knight carried
a shield on which was painted a "device" (called also an impresa),
a symbol with an appropriate motto. See Gen. Intro. p. 15a
(under March 31, 1612).   17. prefer: present.   21. *Lux . . .
mihi:* your light is life to me.   27. *Piu . . . fuerza:* rather by
gentleness than by force.   30. *Me . . . apex:* the crown of glory
has carried me forward.   33. *Quod . . . extinguit:* what nurtures
me kills me.   36. environed: surrounded.   37. touchstone:
See *Rich III*, IV.ii.8,n.   38. *Sic . . . fides:* thus must faith be
tried.   40. himself: i.e., without a squire.   44. *In . . . vivo:*
in this hope I live.

48. mean: means.   51. whipstock: i.e., he looks more like a
carter than a knight.   56. Opinion: popular judgment.   56–
57. scan . . . man: judge a man's character by his outward
appearance.   59. s.d., mean: shabby. These cries indicate that
Pericles has won the contest.
    Sc. iii: 4. As . . . page: i.e., elaborately set out. For a specimen,
see Pl. 14a.   17. labored: on whom she has spent most labor.

1. KNIGHT. Contend not, sir, for we are gentle-
men
That neither in our hearts nor outward eyes   25
Envy the great nor do the low despise.
PER. You are right courteous knights.
SIM.   Sit, sir, sit.
[*Aside*] By Jove, I wonder, that is king of thoughts,
These cates resist me, he not thought upon.°   29
THAI. [*Aside*] By Juno, that is queen of marriage,
All viands that I eat do seem unsavory,
Wishing him my meat. — Sure he's a gallant gentle-
man.
SIM. He's but a country° gentleman,
Has done no more than other knights have done,
Has broken a staff or so; so let it pass.   35
THAI. [*Aside*] To me he seems like diamond to
glass.
PER. [*Aside*] Yon King's to me like to my father's
picture,
Which tells me in that glory once he was,
Had princes sit, like stars, about his throne,
And he the sun, for them to reverence.   40
None that beheld him but, like lesser lights,
Did vail° their crowns to his supremacy,
Where now his son's like a glowworm in the night,
The which hath fire in darkness, none in light.
Whereby I see that Time's the King of men: 45
He's both their parent, and he is their grave,
And gives them what he will, not what they crave.
SIM. What, are you merry, knights?
KNIGHTS. Who can be other in this royal pres-
ence?
SIM. Here, with a cup that's stored unto the
brim —   50
As you do love, fill to your mistress' lips —
We drink this health to you.
KNIGHTS.   We thank your Grace.
SIM. Yet pause awhile.
Yon knight doth sit too melancholy,
As if the entertainment in our Court   55
Had not a show might countervail° his worth.
Note it not you, Thaisa?
THAI. What is 't to me, my Father?
SIM.   Oh, attend, my Daughter.
Princes in this should live like gods above,
Who freely give to every one that comes   60
To honor them;
And princes not doing so are like to gnats,
Which make a sound, but killed are wondered at.°
Therefore to make his entrance more sweet,

Here, say we drink this standing-bowl° of wine to
him.   65
THAI. Alas, my father, it befits not me
Unto a stranger knight to be so bold.
He may my proffer take for an offense,
Since men take women's gifts for impudence.
SIM. How!   70
Do as I bid you, or you'll move° me else.
THAI. [*Aside*] Now, by the gods, he could not
please me better.
SIM. And furthermore tell him we desire to know
of him
Of whence he is, his name and parentage.   74
THAI. The King my father, sir, has drunk to you.
PER. I thank him.
THAI. Wishing it so much blood unto your life.
PER. I thank both him and you, and pledge° him
freely.
THAI. And further he desires to know of you
Of whence you are, your name and parentage.   80
PER. A gentleman of Tyre, my name, Pericles.
My education been in arts and arms;
Who, looking for adventures in the world,
Was by the rough seas reft of ships and men,
And after shipwreck driven upon this shore.   85
THAI. He thanks your Grace, names himself
Pericles,
A gentleman of Tyre,
Who only by misfortune of the seas
Bereft of ships and men, cast on this shore.
SIM. Now, by the gods, I pity his misfortune,   90
And will awake him from his melancholy.
Come, gentlemen, we sit too long on trifles,
And waste the time, which looks for other revels.
Even in your armors, as you are addressed,°
Will very well become a soldier's dance.   95
I will not have excuse, with saying this
Loud music is too harsh for ladies' heads,
Since they love men in arms as well as beds.
[*The* KNIGHTS *dance.*]
So, this was well asked, 'twas so well performed.
Come, sir,
Here's a lady that wants breathing° too,   101
And I have heard, you knights of Tyre
Are excellent in making ladies trip,°
And that their measures° are as excellent.
PER. In those that practice them they are, my
lord.   105
SIM. Oh, that's as much as you would be denied
Of your fair courtesy.°
[*The* KNIGHTS *and* LADIES *dance.*]
Unclasp, unclasp.

28–29. By . . . upon: by Jove, who is ruler of our thoughts, I am
astonished. These delicacies (*cates*) do not please me, for this
stranger was not one that I had expected as a suitor for my
daughter.   **33. country:** i.e., simple, of no great rank.   **42. vail:**
lower.   **56. countervail:** counterbalance, is not good enough for.
63. wondered at: i.e., that so much noise could come from so
small a creature.

65. standing-bowl: a bowl with a stem. See Pl. 20h.   **71. move:**
anger.   **78. pledge:** drink a health to.   **94. addressed:** dressed.
101. breathing: exercise.   **103. trip:** dance, with a quibble on
"go astray."   **104. measures:** courtly dances. See App. 24.
106–07. that's . . . courtesy: you are denying that you have such
courtly accomplishments.

Thanks, gentlemen, to all. All have done well,
[*To* PERICLES] But you the best. Pages and lights,
  to conduct
These knights unto their several° lodgings! Yours,
  sir,   110
We have given order to be next our own.
  PER. I am at your Grace's pleasure.
  SIM. Princes, it is too late to talk of love,
And that's the mark I know you level at.
Therefore each one betake him to his rest.   115
Tomorrow all for speeding° do their best.
                                [*Exeunt.*]

SCENE IV. *Tyre. A room in the Governor's house.*

[*Enter* HELICANUS *and* ESCANES.°]

  HEL. No, Escanes, know this of me,
Antiochus from incest lived not free;
For which, the most high gods not minding°
  longer
To withhold the vengeance that they had in store,
Due to this heinous capital offense,   5
Even in the height and pride of all his glory,
When he was seated in a chariot
Of an inestimable value, and his daughter with him,
A fire from Heaven came and shrivelled up   9
Their bodies even to loathing; for they so stunk
That all those eyes adored° them ere their fall
Scorn now their hand should give them burial.
  ESC. 'Twas very strange.
  HEL.   And yet but justice, for though
This king were great, his greatness was no guard
To bar Heaven's shaft,° but sin had his reward. 15
  ESC. 'Tis very true.
        [*Enter two or three* LORDS.]
  1. LORD. See, not a man in private conference
Or council has respect with him° but he.
  2. LORD. It shall no longer grieve without re-
  proof.°
  3. LORD. And cursed be he that will not second
  it.   20
  1. LORD. Follow me then. Lord Helicane, a word.
  HEL. With me? And welcome. Happy day, my
  lords.
  1. LORD. Know that our griefs are risen to the top,
And now at length they overflow their banks.
  HEL. Your griefs! For what? Wrong not your
  Prince you love.   25
  1. LORD. Wrong not yourself, then, noble Helicane,

But if the Prince do live, let us salute him,
Or know what ground's made happy by his breath.
If in the world he live, we'll seek him out;
If in his grave he rest, we'll find him there;   30
And be resolved he lives to govern us,
Or dead, give 's cause to mourn his funeral
And leave us to our free election.°
  2. LORD. Whose death's indeed the strongest in
  our censure;°
And knowing this kingdom is without a head — 35
Like goodly buildings left without a roof
Soon fall to ruin — your noble self,
That best know how to rule and how to reign,
We thus submit unto, our sovereign.
  ALL. Live, noble Helicane!   40
  HEL. For honor's cause, forbear your suffrages.°
If that you love Prince Pericles, forbear.
Take I your wish, I leap into the seas,
Where's hourly trouble for a minute's ease.°
A twelvemonth longer, let me entreat you   45
To forbear the absence of your King;
If in which time expired he not return,
I shall with agéd patience bear your yoke.
But if I cannot win you to this love,
Go search like nobles, like noble subjects,   50
And in your search spend your adventurous worth;
Whom if you find and win unto return,
You shall like diamonds sit about his crown.
  1. LORD. To wisdom he's a fool that will not yield,
And, since Lord Helicane enjoineth us,   55
We with our travels will endeavor it.
  HEL. Then you love us, we you, and we'll clasp
  hands.
When peers thus knit, a kingdom ever stands.
                           [*Exeunt.*]

SCENE V. *Pentapolis. A room in the palace.*

[*Enter* SIMONIDES, *reading a letter, at one door. The* KNIGHTS *meet him.*]

  1. KNIGHT. Good morrow to the good Simonides.
  SIM. Knights, from my daughter this I let you
  know,
That for this twelvemonth she'll not undertake
A married life.
Her reason to herself is only known,   5
Which from her by no means can I get.
  2. KNIGHT. May we not get access to her, my
  lord?
  SIM. Faith, by no means. She hath so strictly
Tied her to her chamber that 'tis impossible.   9

110. **several:** separate, individual.   116. **speeding:** success.
  Sc. iv: s.d., **Escanes:** pronounced Éscanés.   3. **minding:** caring, willing.   11. **adored:** that adored.   15. **shaft:** punishment, lit., arrow.   18. **has . . . him:** is highly regarded.   19. **It . . . reproof:** i.e., such favoritism shall not be longer endured without protest (*reproof*).

33. **to . . . election:** to make free choice of a successor.   34. **Whose . . . censure:** in our judgment (*censure*) it is most likely that he is dead.   41. **forbear . . . suffrages:** do not give your votes to me.   43–44. **Take . . . ease:** if I agree to what you wish, I shall leap into a sea of troubles which will give one hour of disquiet for every minute of ease.

One twelve moons° more she'll wear Diana's livery.°
This by the eye of Cynthia° hath she vowed,
And on her virgin honor will not break it.

　　3. KNIGHT. Loath to bid farewell, we take our
　　leaves.　　　　　　　　　[*Exeunt* KNIGHTS.]
　　SIM. So,
They are well dispatched; now to my daughter's
　　letter.　　　　　　　　　　　　　　15
She tells me here, she'll wed the stranger knight,
Or never more to view nor day nor light.
'Tis well, mistress. Your choice agrees with mine.
I like that well. Nay, how absolute° she's in 't,
Not minding whether I dislike or no!　　　20
Well, I do commend her choice,
And will no longer have it be delayed.
Soft! Here he comes. I must dissemble it.°
　　　　　　　[*Enter* PERICLES.]
　　PER. All fortune to the good Simonides!
　　SIM. To you as much, sir! I am beholding to you
For your sweet music this last night. I do　　26
Protest my ears were never better fed
With such delightful pleasing harmony.
　　PER. It is your Grace's pleasure to commend,
Not my desert.
　　SIM.　　　　Sir, you are Music's master.　　30
　　PER. The worst of all her scholars, my good lord.
　　SIM. Let me ask you one thing:
What do you think of my daughter, sir?
　　PER. A most virtuous Princess.
　　SIM. And she is fair too, is she not?　　35
　　PER. As a fair day in summer, wondrous fair.
　　SIM. Sir, my daughter thinks very well of you —
Aye, so well, that you must be her master,
And she will be your scholar. Therefore look to it.
　　PER. I am unworthy for her schoolmaster.　　40
　　SIM. She thinks not so. Peruse this writing else.
　　PER. [*Aside*] What's here?
A letter, that she loves the knight of Tyre!
'Tis the King's subtlety to have my life. —
Oh, seek not to entrap me, gracious lord,　　45
A stranger and distresséd gentleman
That never aimed so high to love your daughter,
But bent all offices° to honor her.
　　SIM. Thou hast bewitched my daughter, and thou
　　art
A villain.　　　　　　　　　　　50
　　PER. By the gods, I have not.
Never did thought of mine levy offense,
Nor never did my actions yet commence

A deed might gain her love or your displeasure.
　　SIM. Traitor, thou liest.
　　PER.　　　　　　Traitor!
　　SIM.　　　　　　　　　Aye, traitor.　　55
　　PER. Even in his throat — unless it be the
　　King° —
That calls me traitor, I return the lie.°
　　SIM. [*Aside*] Now, by the gods, I do applaud his
　　courage.
　　PER. My actions are as noble as my thoughts,
That never relished of a base descent.　　60
I came unto your Court for Honor's cause,
And not to be a rebel to her state;
And he that otherwise accounts of me,
This sword shall prove he's Honor's enemy.
　　SIM. No?　　　　　　　　　　65
Here comes my daughter, she can witness it.
　　　　　　　[*Enter* THAISA.]
　　PER. Then, as you are as virtuous as fair,
Resolve° your angry father if my tongue
Did e'er solicit, or my hand subscribe,
To any syllable that made love to you.　　70
　　THAI. Why, sir, say if you had,
Who takes offense at that would make me glad?
　　SIM. Yea, mistress, are you so peremptory?°
[*Aside*] I am glad on 't with all my heart. —
I'll tame you. I'll bring you in subjection.　　75
Will you, not having my consent,
Bestow your love and your affections
Upon a stranger? [*Aside*] Who, for aught I know,
May be, nor can I think the contrary,
As great in blood as I myself. —　　80
Therefore hear you, mistress. Either frame
Your will to mine — and you, sir, hear you,
Either be ruled by me, or I'll make you —
Man and wife.　　　　　　　　84
Nay, come, your hands and lips must seal it too,
And being joined, I'll thus your hopes destroy;
And for a further grief — God give you joy!
What, are you both pleased?
　　THAI.　　　　　　Yes, if you love me, sir.
　　PER. Even as my life my blood that fosters it.
　　SIM. What, are you both agreed?　　90
　　BOTH. Yes, if 't please your Majesty.
　　SIM. It pleaseth me so well that I will see you
　　wed,
And then, with what haste you can, get you to bed.
　　　　　　　　　　　　[*Exeunt.*]

56–57. Even . . . lie: A "lie in the throat" was the bitterest
insult that could be offered; by "returning" the lie the injured
party challenges his opponent to mortal combat. See *Haml*,
II.ii.599–604.　56. unless . . . King: because a king is exempt
from any challenge by a subject.　68. Resolve: inform.　73. peremptory: determined.

Sc. v: 10. One . . . moons: a year. wear . . . livery: serve the
goddess of single life.　11. Cynthia: Diana.　19. absolute:
resolute.　23. dissemble it: pretend otherwise.　48. all offices:
every effort.

Act III

CHORUS

[*Enter* GOWER.]
GOW. Now sleep y-slakèd hath the rout.°
No din but snores the house about,
Made louder by the o'erfed breast
Of this most pompous marriage feast.
The cat, with eyne° of burning coal,   5
Now couches 'fore the mouse's hole,
And crickets sing at the oven's mouth,
E'er the blither° for their drouth.°
Hymen° hath brought the bride to bed,
Where, by the loss of maidenhead,   10
A babe is molded.° Be attent,
And time that is so briefly spent
With your fine fancies quaintly eche.°
What's dumb in show I'll plain with speech.
[DUMB SHOW: *Enter* PERICLES *and* SIMONIDES *at one
door, with* ATTENDANTS. *A* MESSENGER *meets them,
kneels, and gives* PERICLES *a letter.* PERICLES *shows it*
SIMONIDES. *The* LORDS *kneel to the former. Then en-
ter* THAISA *with child,° with* LYCHORIDA, *a nurse.
The* KING *shows her the letter; she rejoices. She and*
PERICLES *take leave of her father, and depart with*
LYCHORIDA *and their* ATTENDANTS. *Then exeunt*
SIMONIDES *and the rest.*]
By many a dern° and painful perch°   15
Of Pericles the careful search,
By the four opposing coigns°
Which the world together joins,
Is made with all due diligence
That horse and sail and high expense   20
Can stead° the quest. At last from Tyre,
Fame° answering the most strange inquire,
To the Court of King Simonides
Are letters brought, the tenor these:
Antiochus and his daughter dead,   25
The men of Tyrus on the head
Of Helicanus would set on
The crown of Tyre, but he will none.
The mutiny he there hastes t' oppress;°
Says to 'em, if King Pericles   30
Come not home in twice six moons,
He, obedient to their dooms,°
Will take the crown. The sum of this,
Brought hither to Pentapolis,

Y-ravishéd° the regions round,   35
And every one with claps can sound,
" Our heir apparent is a king!
Who dreamed, who thought of such a thing? "
Brief, he must hence depart to Tyre.
His Queen with child makes her desire —   40
Which who shall cross? — along to go.
Omit we all their dole° and woe.
Lychorida, her nurse, she takes,
And so to sea. Their vessel shakes
On Neptune's billow. Half the flood   45
Hath their keel cut;° but Fortune's mood
Varies again. The grisled° North
Disgorges such a tempest forth
That, as a duck for life that dives,
So up and down the poor ship drives.
The lady shrieks and well-a-near°
Does fall in travail° with her fear,
And what ensues in this fell° storm
Shall for itself itself perform.
I nill° relate, action may   55
Conveniently the rest convey;
Which might not what by me is told.°
In your imagination hold
This stage the ship, upon whose deck
The sea-tossed Pericles appears to speak. [*Exit.*]   60

SCENE I.

[*Enter* PERICLES, *on shipboard.*]
PER. Thou God of this great vast,° rebuke these
     surges
Which wash both Heaven and Hell; and thou, that
     hast
Upon the winds command, bind them in brass,
Having called them from the deep! Oh, still
Thy deafening dreadful thunders! Gently quench
Thy nimble sulfurous flashes! Oh, how, Lychor-
     ida,   6
How does my Queen? — Thou stormest venom-
     ously.
Wilt thou spit all thyself? The seaman's whistle
Is as a whisper in the ears of death,
Unheard. — Lychorida! — Lucina,° O   10
Divinest patroness and midwife gentle
To those that cry° by night, convey thy deity
Aboard our dancing boat; make swift the pangs
Of my Queen's travails! — Now, Lychorida!
[*Enter* LYCHORIDA, *with an Infant.*]

Act III, Chorus: 1. y-slaked . . . rout: has quieted the crowd.
The prefix "y-," used here (and at l. 35) to give an antique flavor
to the speech, was by 1609 archaic. See II. Chorus. 2,n.   5. eyne:
eyes.   8. blither: more merrily. drouth: thirst.   9. Hymen:
god of marriage.   11. molded: conceived.   13. quaintly eche:
ingeniously eke out, prolong.   14. s.d., with child: pregnant.
15. dern: dreary. perch: journeying, lit., a measurement of land
(5½ yards).   17. coigns: corners.   21. stead: assist.   22. Fame:
report — of the search for Pericles.   29. oppress: subdue.
32. dooms: decisions.

35. Y-ravished: greatly excited.   42. dole: lamentation.
45–46. Half . . . cut: their ship had made half the distance.
47. grisled: gray.   51. well-a-near: well-a-day, alas.   52. travail: labor of childbirth.   53. fell: dreadful.   55. nill: will not.
57. Which . . . told: i.e., the action could not conveniently have
shown what I have told you.
Sc. i: 1. vast: wide ocean.   10. Lucina: goddess of child
birth. See I.i.8.   12. cry: are in pain.

LYC. Here is a thing too young for such a place,
Who, if it had conceit,° would die, as I 16
Am like to do. Take in your arms this piece
Of your dead Queen.
    PER.   How, how, Lychorida!
    LYC. Patience, good sir. Do not assist° the storm.
Here's all that is left living of your Queen — 20
A little daughter. For the sake of it
Be manly, and take comfort.
    PER.   O you gods!
Why do you make us love your goodly gifts,
And snatch them straight away? We here below
Recall not what we give, and therein may 25
Use honor with you.°
    LYC.   Patience, good sir,
Even for this charge.°
    PER.   Now, mild may be thy life!
For a more blustrous birth had never babe.
Quiet and gentle thy conditions! For
Thou art the rudeliest° welcome to this world 30
That ever was prince's child. Happy what follows!
Thou hast as chiding a nativity°
As fire, air, water, earth and heaven can make
To herald thee from the womb. Even at the first
Thy loss is more than can thy portage° quit. 35
With all thou canst find here.° Now, the good gods
Throw their best eyes upon 't!
                [Enter two SAILORS.]
    1. SAIL. What courage, sir? God save you!
    PER. Courage enough. I do not fear the flaw.°
It hath done to me the worst. Yet, for the love 40
Of this poor infant, this fresh new seafarer,
I would it would be quiet.
    1. SAIL. Slack the bolins° there! Thou wilt not,
wilt thou?° Blow, and split thyself.
    2. SAIL. But sea room,° an the brine and 45
cloudy billow kiss the moon, I care not.
    1. SAIL. Sir, your Queen must overboard. The sea
works high, the wind is loud, and will not lie till
the ship be cleared of the dead.
    PER. That's your superstition. 50
    1. SAIL. Pardon us, sir. With us at sea it hath been
still° observed, and we are strong in custom. There-

fore briefly yield her, for she must overboard
straight.
    PER. As you think meet. Most wretched Queen!
    LYC. Here she lies, sir. 56
    PER. A terrible childbed hast thou had, my dear.
No light, no fire, the unfriendly elements
Forgot thee utterly. Nor have I time
To give thee hallowed to thy grave, but straight
Must cast thee, scarcely coffined, in the ooze,° 61
Where, for a monument upon thy bones,
And aye-remaining° lamps, the belching whale
And humming water must o'erwhelm thy corpse,
Lying with simple shells. O Lychorida, 65
Bid Nestor bring me spices, ink and paper,
My casket and my jewels, and bid Nicander
Bring me the satin coffer.° Lay the babe
Upon the pillow. Hie° thee, whiles I say
A priestly farewell to her. Suddenly,° woman. 70
                  [Exit LYCHORIDA.]
    2. SAIL. Sir, we have a chest beneath the hatches,
caulked and bitumed° ready.
    PER. I thank thee. Mariner, say what coast is this?
    2. SAIL. We are near Tarsus.
    PER. Thither, gentle mariner, 75
Alter thy course for Tyre. When canst thou reach
    it?
    2. SAIL. By break of day, if the wind cease.
    PER. Oh, make for Tarsus!
There will I visit Cleon, for the babe
Cannot hold out to Tyrus. There I'll leave it 80
At careful nursing.° Go thy ways, good mariner.
I'll bring the body presently.°   *[Exeunt.]*

SCENE II. *Ephesus. A room in* CERIMON'S *house.*

[Enter CERIMON, *a* SERVANT, *and some persons who
have been shipwrecked.]*
    CER. Philemon, ho!
                [Enter PHILEMON.]
    PHIL. Doth my lord call?
    CER. Get fire and meat for these poor men.
'T has been a turbulent and stormy night.
    SERV. I have been in many, but such a night as
    this, 5
Till now, I ne'er endured.
    CER. Your master will be dead ere you return.
There's nothing can be ministered to nature
That can recover him. [*To* PHILEMON] Give this to
    the 'pothecary,
And tell me how it works.

---

16. conceit: intelligence.   19. assist: i.e., by your lamentations.
24–26. We . . . you: i.e., we men do not take back the gifts which
we have given you gods, and so treat you honorably — not like
you who have taken away my wife almost as soon as you have
given her to me.   27. charge: i.e., the babe which has been
entrusted to you.   30. rudeliest: given the roughest.   32. chiding a nativity: threatening horoscope. See App. 1.   34–36. Even
. . . here: This difficult sentence presumably means: "Even at
the moment of your birth you have lost more than all the good
that may come to you in life hereafter."   35. portage: lit.,
bearing; i.e., fortune. See *Oth*, I.iii.139, "portance in my travel's
history."   39. flaw: gust of wind.   43. bolins: bowlines, ropes
used for steadying a sail in a high wind.   43–44. Thou . . . thou:
He threatens a hesitating sailor.   45. But . . . room: if only we
can gain sea room. See *Temp*, I.i.1, s.d.,n., where the situation is
similar.   52. still: always.

61. ooze: bottom of the sea.   63. aye-remaining: lamps always
burning. It was a Roman custom to keep lamps burning in
tombs.   68. satin coffer: box where the silks are kept.   69. Hie:
hasten.   70. Suddenly: quickly.   72. bitumed: made water-
tight with bitumen (pitch).   81. nursing: i.e., with a wet nurse.
82. presently: immediately.

[*Exeunt all but* CERIMON.]
[*Enter two* GENTLEMEN.]

1. GENT.   Good morrow.   10
2. GENT. Good morrow to your lordship.
CER.   Gentlemen,
Why do you stir so early?
1. GENT. Sir.
Our lodgings, standing bleak upon the sea,
Shook as the earth did quake.   15
The very principals° did seem to rend
And all-to° topple. Pure surprise and fear
Made me to quit the house.
2. GENT. That is the cause we trouble you so early.
'Tis not our husbandry.°
CER.   Oh, you say well.   20
1. GENT. But I much marvel that your lordship,
    having
Rich tire about you,° should at these early hours
Shake off the golden slumber of repose.
'Tis most strange,
Nature should be so conversant with pain,°   25
Being thereto not compelled.
CER.   I hold it ever
Virtue and cunning° were endowments greater
Than nobleness and riches. Careless heirs
May the two latter darken and expend,
But immortality attends the former,   30
Making a man a god. 'Tis known I ever
Have studied physic, through which secret art,
By turning o'er° authorities, I have,
Together with my practice, made familiar
To me and to my aid the blest infusions°   35
That dwell in vegetives,° in metals, stones;
And I can speak of the disturbances
That nature works, and of her cures, which doth
    give me
A more content in course of true delight
Than to be thirsty after tottering honor,   40
Or tie my treasure up in silken bags
To please the fool and death.
2. GENT. Your Honor has through Ephesus
    poured forth
Your charity, and hundreds call themselves
Your creatures, who by you have been restored;
And not your knowledge, your personal pain, but
    even   46
Your purse, still open, hath built Lord Cerimon
Such strong renown as time shall never ——
[*Enter two or three* SERVANTS *with a chest.*]
1. SERV. So, lift there.
1. SERV.   What is that?

1. SERV.   Sir, even now
Did the sea toss upon our shore this chest.   50
'Tis of some wreck.
CER.   Set 't down. Let's look upon 't.
2. GENT. 'Tis like a coffin, sir.
CER.   Whate'er it be,
'Tis wondrous heavy. Wrench it open straight.
If the sea's stomach be o'ercharged with gold,
'Tis a good constraint of fortune it belches upon
    us.°   55
2. GENT. 'Tis so, my lord.
CER.   How close 'tis caulked and bitumed!
Did the sea cast it up?
1. SERV. I never saw so huge a billow, sir,
As tossed it upon shore.
CER.   Wrench it open.
Soft! It smells most sweetly in my sense.   60
2. GENT. A delicate odor.
CER. As ever hit my nostril. So, up with it.
Oh, you most potent gods! What's here? A corse!°
1. GENT. Most strange!
CER. Shrouded in cloth of state,° balmed° and
    entreasured   65
With full bags of spices! A passport, too!
Apollo perfect me in the characters!°
[*Reads from a scroll.*]
    " Here I give to understand,
        If e'er this coffin drive a-land,
    I, King Pericles, have lost   70
        This Queen, worth all our mundane cost.
    Who finds her, give her burying.
        She was the daughter of a King.
    Besides this treasure for a fee,
        The gods requite his charity! "   75
If thou livest, Pericles, thou hast a heart
That even cracks for woe! This chanced tonight.
2. GENT. Most likely, sir.
CER.   Nay, certainly tonight,
For look how fresh she looks! They were too rough
That threw her in the sea. Make a fire within.   80
Fetch hither all my boxes in my closet.°
[*Exit a* SERVANT.]
Death may usurp on nature many hours,
And yet the fire of life kindle again
The o'erpressed° spirits. I heard of an Egyptian
That had nine hours lien° dead,   85
Who was by good appliance recovered.
[*Re-enter a* SERVANT, *with boxes, napkins, and fire.*]
Well said, well said; the fire and cloths.
The rough and woeful music that we have,
Cause it to sound, beseech you.   89

Sc. ii: **16. principals:** main supports.   **17. all-to:** all together.
20. husbandry: early rising — showing a careful nature.   **21-
22. having . . . you:** lit., richly clothed — being a man of such
wealth.   **25. Nature . . . pain:** that you should be so concerned
with pain, i.e., with the study of medicine.   **27. cunning:**
skill.   **33. turning o'er:** studying.   **35. infusions:** distillations.
36. vegetives: plants.

55. 'Tis . . . us: i.e., it is good that fortune has forced the
sea to vomit up this chest on our coast.   **63. corse:** corpse.
65. cloth of state: costly wrappings.   **balmed:** anointed with
perfumes.   **67. perfect . . . characters:** enable me to decipher
the writing (*characters*).   **81. closet:** small room, study.
84. o'erpressed: overcome.   **85. lien:** lain.

The viol° once more. How thou stirr'st, thou block!
The music there! I pray you, give her air.
Gentlemen,
This Queen will live. Nature awakes; a warmth
Breathes out of her. She hath not been entranced
Above five hours. See how she 'gins to blow°   95
Into life's flower again!
    1. GEN.   The Heavens
Through you increase our wonder, and set up
Your fame for ever.
    CER.   She is alive! Behold,
Her eyelids, cases to those heavenly jewels
Which Pericles hath lost, begin to part   100
Their fringes of bright gold. The diamonds
Of a most praised water° do appear
To make the world twice rich. Live,
And make us weep to hear your fate, fair creature,
Rare as you seem to be.   [*She moves.*]
    THAI.   O dear Diana,   105
Where am I? Where's my lord? What world is
    this?
    2. GENT. Is not this strange?
    1. GENT.   Most rare.
    CER.   Hush, my gentle neighbors!
Lend me your hands. To the next chamber bear
    her.
Get linen. Now this matter must be looked to,
For her relapse is mortal.° Come, come,   110
And Aesculapius° guide us!
        [*Exeunt, carrying her away.*]

SCENE III. *Tarsus. A room in the Governor's
house.*

[*Enter* PERICLES, CLEON, DIONYZA, *and* LYCHORIDA
with MARINA *in her arms.*]
    PER. Most honored Cleon, I must needs be gone.
My twelve months are expired, and Tyrus stands
In a litigious peace.° You, and your lady,
Take from my heart all thankfulness! The gods
Make up the rest upon you!   5
    CLE. Your shafts° of fortune, though they hurt
    you mortally,
Yet glance full wanderingly° on us.°
    DIO.   O your sweet Queen!
That the strict fates had pleased you had brought
    her hither,
To have blessed mine eyes with her!
    PER.   We cannot but obey
The powers above us. Could I rage and roar   10

As doth the sea she lies in, yet the end
Must be as 'tis. My gentle babe Marina, whom,
For she was born at sea I have named so, here
I charge your charity withal, leaving her
The infant of your care, beseeching you   15
To give her princely training, that she may be
Mannered as she is born.
    CLE.   Fear not, my lord, but think
Your Grace, that fed my country with your corn,
For which the people's prayers still fall upon you,
Must in your child be thought on. If neglection°
Should therein make me vile, the common body,   21
By you relieved, would force me to my duty;
But if to that my nature need a spur,
The gods revenge it upon me and mine
To the end of generation!°
    PER.   I believe you.   25
Your honor and your goodness teach me to 't
Without your vows. Till she be married, madam,
By bright Diana, whom we honor, all
Unscissored shall this hair of mine remain,
Though I show ill° in 't. So I take my leave.   30
Good madam, make me blessèd in your care
In bringing up my child.
    DIO.   I have one myself,
Who shall not be more dear to my respect°
Than yours, my lord.
    PER.   Madam, my thanks and prayers.
    CLE. We'll bring your Grace e'en to the edge o'
    the shore,   35
Then give you up to the masked° Neptune° and
The gentlest winds of heaven.
    PER.   I will embrace
Your offer. Come, dearest madam. Oh, no tears,
Lychorida, no tears.
Look to your little mistress, on whose grace   40
You may depend hereafter. Come, my lord.
        [*Exeunt.*]

SCENE IV. *Ephesus. A room in* CERIMON'S
house.

[*Enter* CERIMON *and* THAISA.]
    CER. Madam, this letter and some certain jewels
Lay with you in your coffer, which are
At your command. Know you the character?
    THAI. It is my lord's.
That I was shipped at sea, I well remember,   5
Even on my eaning time;° but whether there
Delivered, by the holy gods,
I cannot rightly say. But since King Pericles,
My wedded lord, I ne'er shall see again,

---

90. viol: See Pl. 18c. 95. blow: open out like a bud. 102. water:
luster. 110. relapse is mortal: if she has a relapse, it will be
fatal. 111. Aesculapius: god of medicine.
    Sc. iii: 3. litigious peace: a peace disturbed by constant law-
suits. 6. shafts: arrows. 7. glance . . . us: pass by us —
without hitting. wanderingly: emendation for the quarto
"wondringly."

---

20. neglection: neglect. 25. end of generation: until the last
generation. 30. show ill: appear ill-kempt, untidy. 33. to my
respect: in my love. 36. masked: i.e., hiding his face beneath
a calm sea. Neptune: the sea god.
    Sc. iv: 6. eaning time: time of delivery.

A vestal livery° will I take me to,   10
And never more have joy.
    CER. Madam, if this you purpose as ye speak,
Diana's temple is not distant far,
Where you may abide till your date° expire.
Moreover, if you please, a niece of mine   15
Shall there attend you.
    THAI. My recompense is thanks, that's all;
Yet my good will is great, though the gift small.
                            [Exeunt.]

Act IV

CHORUS

[Enter GOWER.*]*
    GOW. Imagine Pericles arrived at Tyre,
Welcomed and settled to his own desire.
His woeful Queen we leave at Ephesus,
Unto Diana there's a votaress.
Now to Marina bend your mind,   5
Whom our fast-growing scene must find°
At Tarsus, and by Cleon trained
In music, letters; who hath gained
Of education all the grace
Which makes her both the heart and place   10
Of general wonder. But, alack,
That monster Envy, oft the wrack°
Of earnéd praise, Marina's life
Seeks to take off by treason's° knife.
And in this kind° hath our Cleon   15
One daughter, and a wench full grown,
Even ripe for marriage rite. This maid
Hight° Philoten; and it is said
For certain in our story, she
Would ever with Marina be.   20
Be 't when she weaved the sleided° silk
With fingers long, small, white as milk;
Or when she would with sharp needle wound
The cambric, which she made more sound
By hurting it;° or when to the lute   25
She sung, and made the night bird mute,
That still records with moan;° or when
She would with rich and constant pen°
Vail° to her mistress Dian; still
This Philoten contends in skill   30

With absolute Marina: So
With the dove of Paphos° might the **crow**
Vie° feathers white. Marina gets
All praises, which are paid as debts,
And not as given. This so darks   35
In Philoten all graceful marks
That Cleon's wife, with envy rare,
A present° murderer does prepare
For good Marina, that her daughter
Might stand peerless° by this slaughter.   40
The sooner her vile thoughts to stead,°
Lychorida, our nurse, is dead,
And curséd Dionyza hath
The pregnant instrument of wrath
Prest° for this blow. The unborn event   45
I do commend to your content.
Only I carry wingéd time
Post° on the lame feet of my rhyme,
Which never could I so convey
Unless your thoughts went on my **way**.   50
Dionyza does appear
With Leonine, a murderer.   *[Exit.]*

SCENE I. *Tarsus. An open place near the seashore.*

[Enter DIONYZA *with* LEONINE.*]*
    DIO. Thy oath remember. Thou hast sworn to do 't.
'Tis but a blow which never shall be known.
Thou canst not do a thing in the world so soon°
To yield thee so much profit. Let not conscience,
Which is but cold, inflaming love i' thy bosom,   5
Inflame too nicely,° nor let pity, which
Even women have cast off, melt thee, but be
A soldier° to thy purpose.
    LEO. I will do 't. But yet she is a goodly creature.
    DIO. The fitter then the gods should have her.   10
Here she comes weeping for her only mistress'°
death. Thou art resolved?
    LEO. I am resolved.
    [Enter MARINA, *with a basket of flowers.]*
    MAR. No, I will rob Tellus° of her weed,°
To strew thy green° with flowers. The yellows, blues,   15
The purple violets, and marigolds,
Shall as a carpet hang upon thy grave
While summer days do last. Aye me! Poor maid,
Born in a tempest when my mother died,

---

10. **vestal livery:** i.e., a life devoted to celibacy.   14. **date:** span of life.
    Act IV, Chorus: 6. our . . . find: i.e., imagine an interval (of fourteen years) till Marina is grown up.   **12. wrack:** wreck.   14. **treason:** treachery.   15. **in . . . kind:** i.e., like Marina.   18. **Hight:** called.   21. **sleided:** unwrought, in the skein.   24–25. **sound . . . it:** i.e., although she injures the material by pricking it, yet she improves it with her embroidery.   26–27. **night . . . moan:** the nightingale, which sings a sad song.   28. **pen:** i.e., poetry.   29. **Vail:** do homage.

32. **Paphos:** an island sacred to the goddess Venus.   33. **Vie:** compete against.   38. **present:** immediate.   40. **peerless:** unrivaled.   41. **stead:** aid.   45. **Prest:** ready.   48. **Post:** hastily.
    Sc. i: 3. soon: quickly.   6. **nicely:** scrupulously.   8. **soldier:** i.e., pitiless and bold.   11. **only mistress:** i.e., her dearly loved nurse. See Chorus ll. 41–42.   14. **Tellus:** the earth. **weed:** garment — the flowers.   15. **green:** the green turf on thy grave.

This world to me is like a lasting storm,   20
Whirring° me from my friends.
   DIO. How now, Marina! Why do you keep alone?
How chance my daughter is not with you?
Do not consume your blood with sorrowing.°   24
You have a nurse of me. Lord, how your favor's°
Changed with this unprofitable woe!
Come, give me your flowers ere the sea° mar it.°
Walk with Leonine. The air is quick° there,
And it pierces and sharpens the stomach.   29
Come, Leonine, take her by the arm, walk with her.
   MAR. No, I pray you, I'll not bereave° you of your
     servant.
   DIO. Come, come.
I love the King your father and yourself
With more than foreign heart.° We every day
Expect him here. When he shall come, and find   35
Our paragon° to all reports thus blasted,
He will repent the breadth of his great voyage,
Blame both my lord and me, that we have taken
No care to your best courses. Go, I pray you,
Walk, and be cheerful once again. Reserve   40
That excellent complexion, which did steal
The eyes of young and old. Care not for me.
I can go home alone.
   MAR.   Well, I will go,
But yet I have no desire to it.
   DIO. Come, come, I know 'tis good for you.   45
Walk half an hour, Leonine, at the least.
Remember what I have said.
   LEO.   I warrant you, madam.
   DIO. I'll leave you, my sweet lady, for a while.
Pray, walk softly,° do not heat your blood.
What! I must have care of you.
   MAR.   My thanks, sweet madam.   50
               [Exit DIONYZA.]
Is this wind westerly that blows?
   LEO.   Southwest.
   MAR. When I was born, the wind was north.
   LEO.   Was 't so?
   MAR. My father, as nurse said, did never fear,
But cried "Good seamen!" to the sailors, galling
His kingly hands, haling° ropes,   55
And, clasping to the mast, endured a sea
That almost burst the deck.
   LEO. When was this?
   MAR. When I was born.
Never was waves nor wind more violent,   60
And from the ladder tackle° washes off

A canvas-climber.° "Ha!" says one, "Wilt out?"°
And with a dropping° industry they skip
From stem to stern. The boatswain whistles, and
The master° calls and trebles their confusion.   65
   LEO. Come, say your prayers.
   MAR. What mean you?
   LEO. If you require a little space for prayer,
I grant it. Pray, but be not tedious,
For the gods are quick of ear, and I am sworn   70
To do my work with haste.
   MAR.   Why will you kill me?
   LEO. To satisfy my lady.
   MAR. Why would she have me killed?
Now, as I can remember, by my troth,°
I never did her hurt in all my life.   75
I never spake bad word, nor did ill turn
To any living creature. Believe me, la,
I never killed a mouse, nor hurt a fly.
I trod upon a worm against my will,
But I wept for it. How have I offended,   80
Wherein my death might yield her any profit,
Or my life imply her any danger?
   LEO. My commission°
Is not to reason of the deed, but do 't.   84
   MAR. You will not do 't for all the world, I hope.
You are well-favored,° and your looks foreshow
You have a gentle heart. I saw you lately
When you caught hurt in parting two that fought.
Good sooth, it showed well in you. Do so now.
Your lady seeks my life. Come you between,   90
And save poor me, the weaker.
   LEO.   I am sworn,   [He seizes her.]
And will dispatch.
             [Enter PIRATES.]
   1. PIR. Hold, villain!   [LEONINE runs away.]
   2. PIR. A prize! A prize!
   3. PIR. Half-part,° mates, half-part. Come   95
let's have her aboard suddenly.
        [Exeunt PIRATES with MARINA.]
           [Re-enter LEONINE.]
   LEO. These roguing° thieves serve the great pi-
rate Valdes,
And they have seized Marina. Let her go.
There's no hope she will return. I'll swear she's
dead,
And thrown into the sea. But I'll see further.   100
Perhaps they will but please themselves upon her,
Not carry her aboard. If she remain,
Whom they have ravished must by me be slain.
                [Exit.]

---

21. **Whirring:** whirling.   24. **consume . . . sorrowing:** It was
believed that sighs consumed the blood and so shortened life.
25. **favor:** face.   27. **sea:** i.e., your tears. **it:** i.e., the bunch
of flowers.   28. **quick:** lively.   31. **bereave:** deprive.   34. **more
. . . heart:** i.e., as if he were one of our own nation.   36. **paragon:**
incomparable beauty.   49. **softly:** gently.   55. **haling:** hauling.
61. **ladder tackle:** rope ladder.

62. **canvas-climber:** a sailor climbing up to the sails. **Wilt out:**
i.e., "Are you leaving?" — a grim jest as the sailor is washed
overboard.   63. **dropping:** dripping wet.   65. **master:** captain.
74. **troth:** truth.   83. **commission:** instructions.   86. **well-
favored:** handsome.   95. **Half-part:** equal shares.   97. **roguing:**
vagabond.

SCENE II. *Mytilene. A room in a brothel.*

[*Enter* PANDER, BAWD,° *and* BOULT.]

PAN. Boult!

BOULT. Sir?

PAN. Search the market narrowly. Mytilene is full of gallants. We lost too much money this mart° by being too wenchless.   5

BAWD. We were never so much out of creatures. We have but poor three, and they can do no more than they can do; and they with continual action are even as good as rotten.   9

PAN. Therefore let's have fresh ones, whate'er we pay for them. If there be not a conscience to be used in every trade,° we shall never prosper.   13

BAWD. Thou sayest true. 'Tis not our bringing up of poor bastards — as, I think, I have brought up some eleven —   16

BOULT. Aye, to eleven,° and brought them down again. But shall I search the market?

BAWD. What else, man? The stuff we have, a strong wind will blow it to pieces, they are so pitifully sodden.°   21

PAN. Thou sayest true. They're too unwholesome, o' conscience. The poor Transylvanian is dead that lay with the little baggage.

BOULT. Aye, she quickly pooped° him. She   25
made him roast meat for worms. But I'll go search the market.   [*Exit.*]

PAN. Three or four thousand chequins° were as pretty a proportion to live quietly, and so give over.°   30

BAWD. Why to give over, I pray you? Is it a shame to get° when we are old?

PAN. Oh, our credit comes not in like the commodity, nor the commodity wages not with the   35
danger.° Therefore, if in our youths we could pick up some pretty estate, 'twere not amiss to keep our door hatched.° Besides, the sore terms we stand upon with the gods° will be strong° with us for giving o'er.

BAWD. Come, other sorts offend as well as we.   40

PAN. As well as we! Aye, and better too. We offend worse. Neither is our profession any trade. It's no calling. But here comes Boult.

[*Re-enter* BOULT, *with the* PIRATES *and* MARINA.]

BOULT. [*To* MARINA] Come your ways. My masters, you say she's a virgin?   45

I. PIR. Oh, sir, we doubt it not.

BOULT. Master, I have gone through° for this piece, you see. If you like her, so; if not, I have lost my earnest.°

BAWD. Boult, has she any qualities?   50

BOULT. She has a good face, speaks well, and has excellent good clothes. There's no farther necessity of qualities can make her be refused.°

BAWD. What's her price, Boult?   54

BOULT. I cannot be bated° one doit° of a thousand pieces.°

PAN. Well, follow me, my masters. You shall have your money presently. Wife, take her in. Instruct her what she has to do, that she may not be raw in her entertainment.°   60

[*Exeunt* PANDER *and* PIRATES.]

BAWD. Boult, take you the marks of her, the color of her hair, complexion, height, her age, with warrant of her virginity, and cry, "He that will give most shall have her first." Such a maidenhead were no cheap thing, if men were as they have been. Get this done as I command you.   66

BOULT. Performance shall follow.   [*Exit.*]

MAR. Alack that Leonine was so slack, so slow! He should have struck, not spoke; or that these pirates,
Not enough barbarous, had not o'erboard thrown me   70
For to seek my mother!

BAWD. Why lament you, pretty one?

MAR. That I am pretty.   74

BAWD. Come, the gods have done their part in you.°

MAR. I accuse them not.

BAWD. You are light° into my hands, where you are like to live.°

MAR. The more my fault,
To 'scape his hands where I was like to die.   80

BAWD. Aye, and you shall live in pleasure.

MAR. No.

BAWD. Yes, indeed shall you, and taste gentlemen of all fashions. You shall fare well. You shall have the difference of all complexions.° What! Do you stop your ears?   86

MAR. Are you a woman?

BAWD. What would you have me be, an° I be not a woman?

Sc. ii: s.d., **pander, bawd:** The pander's business was to bring in the clients; the bawd (a woman) managed the establishment.   **4. mart:** convention of businessmen.   **12–13. If . . . trade:** if tradesmen do not give honest value.   **17. to eleven:** till they were eleven years old.   **21. sodden:** rotten.   **25. pooped:** sunk.   **28–30. Three . . . over:** if we could make three or four thousand chequins, that would be enough to retire and live on. **chequins:** small gold coins, worth about $2.00 each.   **32. get:** earn.   **34–36. our . . . danger:** our reputation does not increase with the growth of business (*commodity*); nor is the business worth the danger.   **38. hatched:** shut.   **38–39. sore . . . gods:** the anger of the gods at our way of life.   **39. strong:** i.e., a strong argument.

47. gone through: made an offer.   **49. earnest:** payment on account, deposit.   **52–53. There's . . . refused:** there are no other reasons why you should reject my buy.   **55. bated:** let off. **doit:** small Dutch coin, "cent."   **56. pieces:** presumably chequins (see above, l. 30).   **60. raw . . . entertainment:** show lack of experience in entertaining her customers.   **75–76. done . . . you:** have done well for you.   **77. light:** alighted, have come into.   **78. live:** have a good time.   **85. difference . . . complexions:** men of every kind.   **88. an:** if.

MAR. An honest woman, or not a woman.   90

BAWD. Marry, whip thee, gosling. I think I shall
have something to do with you. Come, you're a
young foolish sapling, and must be bowed° as I
would have you.

MAR. The gods defend me!   95

BAWD. If it please the gods to defend you by men,
then men must comfort you, men must feed you,
men must stir you up. Boult's returned.

[*Re-enter* BOULT.]

Now, sir, hast thou cried her through the market?   99

BOULT. I have cried her almost to the number of
her hairs. I have drawn her picture with my voice.

BAWD. And I prithee tell me, how dost thou find
the inclination of the people, especially of the
younger sort?   105

BOULT. Faith, they listened to me as they would
have hearkened to their father's testament. There
was a Spaniard's mouth so watered that he went to
bed to her very description.   109

BAWD. We shall have him here tomorrow with
his best ruff° on.

BOULT. Tonight, tonight. But, mistress, do you
know the French knight that cowers i' the hams?°

BAWD. Who, Monsieur Veroles?   115

BOULT. Aye, he. He offered to cut a caper° at the
proclamation; but he made a groan at it, and swore
he would see her tomorrow.

BAWD. Well, well, as for him, he brought his disease hither. Here he does but repair it. I know   120
he will come in our shadow to scatter his crowns in
the sun.°

BOULT. Well, if we had of every nation a traveler, we should lodge them with this sign.°   124

BAWD. Pray you, come hither awhile. You have
fortunes coming upon you. Mark me: you must
seem to do that fearfully which you commit willingly, despise profit where you have most gain. To
weep that you live as ye do makes pity in your   130
lovers; seldom but that pity begets you a good opinion, and that opinion a mere° profit.

MAR. I understand you not.

BOULT. Oh, take her home, mistress, take her
home. These blushes of hers must be quenched with
some present practice.   136

BAWD. Thou sayest true, i' faith, so they must; for
your bride goes to that with shame which is her
way to go with warrant.°

BOULT. Faith, some do, and some do not. But,
mistress, if I have bargained for the joint ——   141

BAWD. Thou mayst cut a morsel off the spit.°

BOULT. I may so.

BAWD. Who should deny it? Come, young one, I
like the manner of your garments well.   145

BOULT. Aye, by my faith, they shall not be
changed yet.

BAWD. Boult, spend thou that in the town. Report what a sojourner we have. You'll lose nothing
by custom.° When nature framed this piece,   150
she meant thee a good turn. Therefore say what a
paragon she is, and thou hast the harvest out of
thine own report.

BOULT. I warrant you, mistress, thunder shall not
so awake the beds of eels° as my giving out   155
her beauty stir up the lewdly inclined. I'll bring
home some tonight.

BAWD. Come your ways. Follow me.

MAR. If fires be hot, knives sharp, or waters deep,
Untied I still my virgin knot will keep.   160
Diana, aid my purpose!

BAWD. What have we to do with Diana? Pray
you, will you go with us?   [*Exeunt.*]

SCENE III. *Tarsus. A room in the Governor's
house.*

[*Enter* CLEON *and* DIONYZA.]

DIO. Why, are you foolish? Can it be undone?

CLE. O Dionyza, such a piece of slaughter
The sun and moon ne'er looked upon!

DIO.   I think
You'll turn a child again.

CLE. Were I chief lord of all this spacious world,
I'd give it to undo the deed. O lady,   6
Much less in blood than virtue,° yet a princess
To equal any single crown o' the earth
I' the justice of compare!° O villain Leonine,
Whom thou hast poisoned too!   10
If thou hadst drunk to him,° 't had been a kindness
Becoming well thy fact.° What canst thou say
When noble Pericles shall demand his child?

DIO. That she is dead. Nurses are not the fates
To foster it, nor ever to preserve.   15
She died at night.° I'll say so. Who can cross° it?
Unless you play the pious innocent,
And for an honest attribute cry out,
"She died by foul play."

CLE.   Oh, go to. Well, well,

142. **spit:** i.e., while the roast is still cooking. A joint of meat was
roasted by being skewered on a thin iron rod (*spit*) which was
revolved slowly before a hot fire.   149–50. **lose . . . custom:**
find plenty of customers.   155. **beds of eels:** Eels are believed
to be excited by thunder and then to bite more readily.

Sc. iii: 7. **Much . . . virtue:** your (i.e., Marina's) virtue was
even greater than your nobility of birth.   9. **I' . . . compare:**
if the comparison was fair.   11. **drunk to him:** i.e., poisoned yourself at the same time   12. **fact:** deed.   16. **at night:** in her sleep.
cross: deny.

93. **bowed:** bent.   111. **ruff:** See Notes on Costume, p. 94a.
114. **cowers . . . hams:** has bent knees.   116. **cut a caper:** See
App. 24: The Capriol.   121–22. **he . . . sun:** he will come inside
our house to throw his money about.   124. **sign:** See App. 12.
132. **mere:** sheer, great.   139. **with warrant:** lawfully.

Of all the faults beneath the heavens, the gods   20
Do like this worst.
DIO.   Be one of those that think
The petty wrens of Tarsus will fly hence
And open° this to Pericles. I do shame
To think of what a noble strain you are,
And of how coward a spirit.
CLE.   To° such proceeding   25
Who ever but his approbation added,
Though not his prime consent, he did not flow
From honorable sources.
DIO.   Be it so, then.
Yet none does know but you, how she came dead,
Nor none can know, Leonine being gone.   30
She did distain° my child, and stood between
Her and her fortunes. None would look on her,
But cast their gazes on Marina's face,
Whilst ours was blurted° at, and held a malkin,°
Not worth the time of day. It pierced me thorough;°
And though you call my course unnatural,   36
You not your child well loving, yet I find
It greets me° as an enterprise of kindness
Performed to your sole daughter.
CLE.   Heavens forgive it!
DIO. And as for Pericles,   40
What should he say? We wept after her hearse,
And yet we mourn. Her monument
Is almost finished, and her epitaphs
In glittering golden characters express
A general praise to her, and care in us   45
At whose expense 'tis done.
CLE.   Thou art like the harpy,°
Which, to betray, dost with thine angel's face,
Seize with thine eagle's talons.
DIO. You are like one that superstitiously
Doth swear to the gods that winter kills the flies;°
But yet I know you'll do as I advise. [*Exeunt.*] 51

SCENE IV.

[*Enter* GOWER, *before the monument of* MARINA *at
Tarsus.*]

GOW. Thus time we waste,° and longest leagues
    make short;
Sail seas in cockles,° have and wish but for 't;
Making, to take your imagination,
From bourn° to bourn, region to region.
By you being pardoned, we commit no crime   5

To use one language in each several clime
Where our scenes seem to live. I do beseech you
To learn of me, who stand i' the gaps° to teach you
The stages of our story. Pericles
Is now again thwarting° the wayward seas,   10
Attended on by many a lord and knight,
To see his daughter, all his life's delight.
Old Helicanus goes along. Behind
Is left to govern it, you bear in mind
Old Escanes, whom Helicanus late   15
Advanced in time to great and high estate.
Well-sailing ships and bounteous winds have
    brought
This king to Tarsus — think his pilot thought;°
So with his steerage shall your thoughts grow on —
To fetch his daughter home, who first is gone.   20
Like motes° and shadows see them move awhile.
Your ears unto your eyes I'll reconcile.
[DUMB SHOW: *Enter* PERICLES *at one door, with all
his train;* CLEON *and* DIONYZA *at the other.* CLEON
shows PERICLES *the tomb; whereat* PERICLES *makes
lamentation, puts on sackcloth, and in a mighty pas-
sion° departs. Then exeunt* CLEON, DIONYZA, *and
                                            the rest.*]

See how belief may suffer by foul show!
This borrowed° passion stands for true old woe;
And Pericles, in sorrow all devoured,   25
With sighs shot through and biggest tears o'er-
    showered,
Leaves Tarsus and again embarks. He swears
Never to wash his face, nor cut his hairs.
He puts on sackcloth, and to sea. He bears
A tempest, which his mortal vessel° tears,   30
And yet he rides it out. Now please you wit°
The epitaph is for Marina writ
By wicked Dionyza.
    [*Reads the incription on* MARINA's *monument.*]
" The fairest, sweet'st and best, lies here,
Who withered in her spring of year.   35
She was of Tyrus the King's daughter,
On whom foul death hath made this slaughter.
Marina was she called; and at her birth,
Thetis,° being proud, swallowed some part o' the
    earth.
Therefore the earth, fearing to be o'erflowed,   40
Hath Thetis' birth-child on the Heavens bestowed;
Wherefore she does, and swears she'll never stint,°
Make raging battery° upon shores of flint."
No visor° does become black villainy
So well as soft and tender flattery.   45

---

23. open: tell. 25–28. To . . . sources: no man who even sanc-
tioned such a deed, let alone instigated it, could be honorable.
31. distain: cast a stain on. 34. blurted: sneered. malkin:
slut. 35. thorough: through. 38. It . . . me: I rejoice at it.
46. harpy: See *Temp,* III.iii.52,s.d.,n. 49–50. You . . . flies:
you are so scared of the gods that you will apologize for the
death of a fly which the winter killed.
    Sc. iv: 1. waste: pass over quickly. 2. cockles: small
boats. 4. bourn: boundary.

8. gaps: intervals. 10. thwarting: crossing. 18. think . . .
thought: think that he has been transported as quick as thought.
21. motes: specks in the sunbeam. 22. s.d., passion: emotion.
24. borrowed: unreal. 30. mortal vessel: i.e., his body.
31. wit: know. 39. Thetis: daughter of Neptune, the sea god.
42. stint: stop. 43. battery: battering. 44. visor: mask.

Let Pericles believe his daughter's dead,
And bear his courses° to be orderèd
By Lady Fortune, while our scene must play
His daughter's woe and heavy well-a-day
In her unholy service. Patience, then,   50
And think you now are all in Mytilene.   [*Exit.*]

SCENE V. *Mytilene. A street before the brothel.*

[*Enter, from the brothel, two* GENTLEMEN.]

1. GENT. Did you ever hear the like?

2. GENT. No, nor never shall do in such a place as
this, she being once gone.

1. GENT. But to have divinity preached there! Did
you ever dream of such a thing?   5

2. GENT. No, no. Come, I am for no more bawdy
houses. Shall 's go hear the vestals° sing?

1. GENT. I'll do anything now that is virtuous, but
I am out of the road of rutting for ever.   [*Exeunt.*]

SCENE VI. *The same. A room in the brothel.*

[*Enter* PANDER, BAWD, *and* BOULT.]

PAN. Well, I had rather than twice the worth of
her she had ne'er come here.

BAWD. Fie, fie upon her! She's able to freeze the
god Priapus,° and undo a whole generation. We
must either get her ravished or be rid of her.   5
When she should do for clients her fitment° and do
me the kindness of our profession, she has me her
quirks,° her reasons, her master reasons, her prayers, her knees; that she would make a puritan of the
Devil, if he should cheapen° a kiss of her.   10

BOULT. Faith, I must ravish her, or she'll disfurnish us of all our cavaliers and make our swearers
priests.

PAN. Now, the pox° upon her green-sickness°
for me!   15

BAWD. Faith, there's no way to be rid on 't but by
the way to the pox. Here comes the Lord Lysimachus disguised.

BOULT. We should have both lord and lown° if
the peevish baggage would but give way to customers.   21

[*Enter* LYSIMACHUS.]

LYS. How now! How a° dozen of virginities?

BAWD. Now, the gods to-bless° your Honor!

BOULT. I am glad to see your Honor in good
health.   25

LYS. You may so. 'Tis the better for you that your
resorters stand upon sound legs. How now, wholesome iniquity, have you that a man may deal withal,
and defy the surgeon?

BAWD. We have here one, sir, if she would — but
there never came her like in Mytilene.   31

LYS. If she'd do the deed of darkness, thou
wouldst say.

BAWD. Your Honor knows what 'tis to say well
enough.   35

LYS. Well, call forth, call forth.

BOULT. For flesh and blood, sir, white and red,
you shall see a rose; and she were a rose indeed, if
she had but ——

LYS. What, prithee?   40

BOULT. Oh, sir, I can be modest.

LYS. That dignifies the renown of a bawd no less
than it gives a good report to a number to be
chaste.°   [*Exit* BOULT.]

BAWD. Here comes that which grows to the stalk;
never plucked yet, I can assure you. [*Re-enter*   46
BOULT *with* MARINA.] Is she not a fair creature?

LYS. Faith, she would serve after a long voyage at
sea. Well, there's for you. Leave us.

BAWD. I beseech your Honor, give me leave. A
word, and I'll have done presently.   51

LYS. I beseech you, do.

BAWD. [*To* MARINA] First, I would have you note,
this is an honorable man.

MAR. I desire to find him so, that I may worthily
note him.   56

BAWD. Next, he's the Governor of this country,
and a man whom I am bound to.

MAR. If he govern the country, you are bound to
him indeed; but how honorable he is in that, I know
not.   61

BAWD. Pray you, without any more virginal fencing,° will you use him kindly? He will line your
apron with gold.

MAR. What he will do graciously, I will thankfully receive.   66

LYS. Ha' you done?

BAWD. My lord, she's not paced° yet. You must
take some pains to work her to your manage.°
Come, we will leave His Honor and her together.
Go thy ways.   70

[*Exeunt* BAWD, PANDER, *and* BOULT.]

LYS. Now, pretty one, how long have you been
at this trade?

MAR. What trade, sir?

---

47. courses: direction of his life.
   Sc. v: 7. vestals: virgin priestesses of Diana.
   Sc. vi: 4. Priapus: god of copulation.   6. fitment: job.
8. quirks: quibbles.   10. cheapen: bargain for.   14. pox:
plague: lit., venereal disease. green-sickness: a form of anemia common in teen-age girls.   19. lown: men of low birth.
22. How a: what's the price of.   23. to-bless: bless exceedingly.

42–44. That . . . chaste: i.e., it is as remarkable (in a brothel)
to find a bawd modest as it is to find women chaste.   62–
63. virginal fencing: pretended modesty.   68. paced: ready for
the saddle, exercised — like a fresh horse — to be ready for
mounting.   69. manage: horsemanship.

LYS. Why, I cannot name 't but I shall offend.   75
MAR. I cannot be offended with my trade. Please
you to name it.
LYS. How long have you been of this profession?
MAR. E'er since I can remember.   79
LYS. Did you go to 't so young? Were you a
gamester at five or at seven?
MAR. Earlier too, sir, if now I be one.
LYS. Why, the house you dwell in proclaims you
to be a creature of sale.   84
MAR. Do you know this house to be a place of
such resort, and will come into 't? I hear say you are
of honorable parts and are the Governor of this
place.
LYS. Why, hath your principal made known unto
you who I am?   90
MAR. Who is my principal?
LYS. Why, your herb woman° — she that sets
seeds and roots of shame and iniquity. Oh, you have
heard something of my power, and so stand aloof
for more serious wooing. But I protest to thee, 95
pretty one, my authority shall not see thee,° or else
look friendly upon thee. Come, bring me to some
private place. Come, come.
MAR. If you were born to honor, show it now;
If put upon you, make the judgment good   100
That thought you worthy of it.
LYS. How's this? How's this? Some more; be
  sage.
MAR.   For me
That am a maid, though most ungentle fortune
Have placed me in this sty, where, since I came,
Diseases have been sold dearer than physic, 105
Oh, that the gods
Would set me free from this unhallowed place,
Though they did change me to the meanest bird
That flies i' the purer air!
LYS.   I did not think
Thou couldst have spoke so well — ne'er dreamed
  thou couldst.   110
Had I brought hither a corrupted mind,
Thy speech had altered it. Hold, here's gold for
  thee.
Persèver in that clear way thou goest,
And the gods strengthen thee!
MAR.   The good gods preserve you!
LYS. For me, be you thoughten°   115
That I came with no ill intent, for to me
The very doors and windows savor vilely.
Fare thee well. Thou art a piece of virtue, and
I doubt not but thy training hath been noble.
Hold, here's more gold for thee.   120
A curse upon him, die he like a thief,
That robs thee of thy goodness! If thou dost

Hear from me, it shall be for thy good.
          [*Re-enter* BOULT.]
BOULT. I beseech your Honor, one piece for me.
LYS. Avaunt, thou damnèd doorkeeper!   126
Your house, but for this virgin that doth prop it,
Would sink and overwhelm you. Away!   [*Exit.*]
BOULT. How's this? We must take another course
with you. If your peevish chastity, which is not
worth a breakfast in the cheapest country under the
cope,° shall undo a whole household, let me be
gelded like a spaniel. Come your ways.
MAR. Whither would you have me?   135
BOULT. I must have your maidenhead taken off,
or the common hangman shall execute it. Come
your ways. We'll have no more gentlemen driven
away. Come your ways, I say.
          [*Re-enter* BAWD.]
BAWD. How now! What's the matter?   140
BOULT. Worse and worse, mistress. She has here
spoken holy words to the Lord Lysimachus.
BAWD. Oh, abominable!
BOULT. She makes our profession as it were to
stink afore the face of the gods.   145
BAWD. Marry, hang her up for ever!
BOULT. The nobleman would have dealt with her
like a nobleman, and she sent him away as cold as a
snowball, saying his prayers too.   149
BAWD. Boult, take her away. Use her at thy pleas-
ure. Crack the glass of her virginity, and make the
rest malleable.
BOULT. An if she were a thornier piece of ground
than she is, she shall be ploughed.
MAR. Hark, hark, you gods!   155
BAWD. She conjures.° Away with her! Would she
had never come within my doors! Marry, hang you!
She's born to undo us. Will you not go the way of
womenkind? Marry, come up, my dish of chastity
with rosemary and bays!°   [*Exit.*] 160
BOULT. Come, mistress, come your ways with me.
MAR. Whither wilt thou have me?
BOULT. To take from you the jewel you hold so
dear.   165
MAR. Prithee tell me one thing first.
BOULT. Come now, your one thing.
MAR. What canst thou wish thine enemy to be?
BOULT. Why, I could wish him to be my master,
or rather, my mistress.°   170
MAR. Neither of these are so bad as thou art,
Since they do better thee in their command.
Thou hold'st a place for which the pained'st° fiend
Of Hell would not in reputation change.
Thou art the damned doorkeeper to every   175
Coistrel° that comes inquiring for his Tib,°

---

92. **herb woman:** lit., one who grows herbs.   96. **my . . . thee:**
I shall overlook your offenses.   115. **be . . . thoughten:** be
assured.

132. **cope:** heaven.   156. **conjures:** is calling upon spirits.
160. **with . . . bays:** garnished with herbs.   169–70. **to . . . mistress:** i.e., as vile as the pander and the bawd.   173. **pained'st:**
most tormented.   176. **Coistrel:** groom. **Tib:** "Moll."

To the choleric fisting° of every rogue
Thy ear is liable. Thy food is such
As hath been belched on by infected lungs.

BOULT. What would you have me do? Go to   180
the wars, would you? Where a man may serve
seven years for the loss of a leg, and have not money
enough in the end to buy him a wooden one?

MAR. Do any thing but this thou doest. Empty
Old receptacles, or common shores, of filth;   186
Serve by indenture° to the common hangman.
Any of these ways are yet better than this.
For what thou professest, a baboon, could he speak,
Would own a name too dear.° Oh, that the gods
Would safely deliver me from this place!   191
Here, here's gold for thee.
If that thy master would gain by me,
Proclaim that I can sing, weave, sew, and dance,
With other virtues which I'll keep from boast,   195
And I will undertake all these to teach.
I doubt not but this populous city will
Yield many scholars.

BOULT. But can you teach all this you speak of?
MAR. Prove that I cannot, take me home again,
And prostitute me to the basest groom   201
That doth frequent your house.

BOULT. Well, I will see what I can do for thee. If
I can place thee, I will.

MAR. But amongst honest women.   205
BOULT. Faith, my acquaintance lies little amongst
them. But since my master and mistress have bought
you, there's no going but by their consent. Therefore I will make them acquainted with your purpose, and I doubt not but I shall find them   210
tractable enough. Come, I'll do for thee what I can.
Come your ways.   [Exeunt.]

Act V

CHORUS

[Enter GOWER.]
GOW. Marina thus the brothel 'scapes, and
    chances
Into an honest house, our story says.
She sings like one immortal, and she dances
As goddesslike to her admirèd lays.°
Deep clerks she dumbs,° and with her needle°
    composes   5
Nature's own shape of bud, bird, branch, or berry,

That even her art sisters° the natural roses,
Her inkle,° silk, twin with the rubied cherry,
That pupils lacks she none of noble race,
Who pour their bounty on her, and her gain   10
She gives the cursèd bawd. Here we her place,
And to her father turn our thoughts again,
Where we left him, on the sea. We there him lost;
Whence, driven before the winds, he is arrived
Here where his daughter dwells, and on this coast
Suppose him now at anchor. The city strived   16
God Neptune's annual feast to keep; from whence
Lysimachus our Tyrian ship espies —
His banners sable,° trimmed with rich expense —
And to him in his barge with fervor hies.   20
In your supposing once more put your sight
Of heavy Pericles. Think this his bark,
Where what is done in action, more, if might,°
Shall be discovered. Please you, sit, and hark.
                                        [Exit.]

SCENE I. *On board* PERICLES' *ship, off Mytilene.
A close pavilion° on deck, with a curtain be-
fore it;* PERICLES *within it, reclined on a couch.
A barge lying beside the Tyrian vessel.*

[*Enter two* SAILORS, *one belonging to the Tyrian
vessel, the other to the barge; to them* HELICANUS.]
TYR. SAIL. [*To the* SAILOR *of Mytilene*] Where is
    Lord Helicanus? He can resolve° you.
Oh, here he is.
Sir, there is a barge put off from Mytilene,
And in it is Lysimachus the Governor,
Who craves to come aboard. What is your will?   5
HEL. That he have his. Call up some gentlemen.
TYR. SAIL. Ho, gentlemen! My lord calls.
            [*Enter two or three* GENTLEMEN.]
I. GENT. Doth your lordship call?
HEL. Gentlemen, there is some of worth would
come aboard. I pray, greet him fairly.   10
            [*The* GENTLEMEN *and the two* SAILORS
                descend, and go on board the barge.]
[*Enter from thence,* LYSIMACHUS, *and* LORDS, *with
    the* GENTLEMEN *and the two* SAILORS.]
TYR. SAIL. Sir,
This is the man that can, in aught you would,
Resolve you.
LYS. Hail, reverend sir! The gods preserve you!
HEL. And you, sir, to outlive the age I am,   15
And die as I would do.
LYS.   You wish me well.
Being on shore, honoring of Neptune's triumphs,

---

177. **choleric fisting:** hot-tempered cuffing.   187. **indenture:**
agreement. See App. 6.   190. **Would . . . dear:** i.e., would
disown the name of pander.

Act V, Chorus: 4. **lays:** songs.   5. **Deep . . . dumbs:** puts
learned scholars to silence. **needle:** pronounced as one syllable.

7. **sisters:** matches.   8. **inkle:** embroidered tape.   19. **sable:**
black. For a *trimmed* ship, see Pl. 7b.   23. **if might:** if it were
possible.

Sc. i: s.d., close pavilion: private tent. All these details were
added by eighteenth-century editors. Q1 simply notes: "*Enter
Helicanus, to him 2. Saylers.*"   1. **resolve:** inform you.

Seeing this goodly vessel ride before us,
I made to it, to know of whence you are.
   HEL. First, what is your place?
   LYS.   I am the Governor   20
Of this place you lie before.
   HEL. Sir,
Our vessel is of Tyre, in it the King,
A man who for this three months hath not spoken
To any one, nor taken sustenance   25
But to prorogue° his grief.
   LYS. Upon what ground is his distemperature?°
   HEL. 'Twould be too tedious to repeat,
But the main grief springs from the loss
Of a belovéd daughter and a wife.   30
   LYS. May we not see him?
   HEL. You may,
But bootless° is your sight. He will not speak
To any.
   LYS. Yet let me obtain my wish.   35
   HEL. Behold him. [PERICLES discovered.°] This
      was a goodly person
Till the disaster that, one mortal night,
Drove him to this.
   LYS. Sir King, all hail! The gods preserve you!
Hail, royal sir!   40
   HEL. It is in vain. He will not speak to you.
   I. LORD. Sir,
We have a maid in Mytilene, I durst wager
Would win some words of him.
   LYS.   'Tis well bethought.
She, questionless,° with her sweet harmony   45
And other chosen attractions, would allure,
And make a battery° through his deafened parts,
Which now are midway stopped.
She is all happy as the fairest of all,
And with her fellow maids is now upon   50
The leafy shelter that abuts against
The island's side. [Whispers to a LORD, who goes
      off in the barge of LYSIMACHUS.]
   HEL. Sure, all's effectless; yet nothing we'll omit
That bears recovery's name. But, since your kindness
We have stretched thus far, let us beseech you   55
That for our gold we may provision have,
Wherein we are not destitute for want,
But weary for the staleness.°
   LYS.   Oh, sir, a courtesy
Which if we should deny, the most just gods
For every graff° would send a caterpillar,   60
And so inflict our province. Yet once more
Let me entreat to know at large the cause

Of your King's sorrow.
   HEL.   Sit, sir, I will recount it to you.
But see, I am prevented.
   [Re-enter, from the barge, LORD, with MARINA,
       and a young LADY.]
   LYS.   Oh, here is
The lady that I sent for. Welcome, fair one! —   65
Is 't not a goodly presence?
   HEL.   She's a gallant lady.
   LYS. She's such a one that, were I well assured
Came of a gentle kind and noble stock,
I'd wish no better choice, and think me rarely wed.
Fair ne, all° goodness that consists in bounty.   70
Expect even here, where is a kingly patient.
If that thy prosperous and artificial feat°
Can draw him but to answer thee in aught,
Thy sacred physic shall receive such pay
As thy desires can wish.
   MAR.   Sir, I will use   75
My utmost skill in his recovery, provided
That none but I and my companion maid
Be suffered to come near him.
   LYS.   Come, let us leave her,
And the gods make her prosperous!   80
           [MARINA sings.]
   LYS. Marked he your music?
   MAR.   No, nor looked on us.
   LYS. See, she will speak to him.
   MAR. Hail, sir! My lord, lend ear.
   PER. Hum, ha!
   MAR. I am a maid,   85
My lord, that ne'er before invited eyes,
But have been gazed on like a comet.° She speaks,
My lord, that may be hath endured a grief
Might equal yours, if both were justly weighed.
Though wayward fortune did malign° my state,
My derivation was from ancestors   91
Who stood equivalent with mighty kings.
But time hath rooted out my parentage,
And to the world and awkward casualties°
Bound me in servitude. [Aside] I will desist;   95
But there is something glows upon my cheek,
And whispers in mine ear, " Go not till he speak."
   PER. My fortunes — parentage — good parent-
      age —
To equal mine! — was it not thus? What say you?
   MAR. I said, my lord, if you did know my parent-
      age,   100
You would not do me violence.
   PER. I do think so. Pray you, turn your eyes upon
      me.
You are like something that — What country-
   woman?

---

26. prorogue: keep in being.   27. Upon . . . distemperature:
what is the cause of his sickness.   33. bootless: vain.   36. s.d.,
discovered: i.e., the curtain at the back of the stage is drawn
aside, revealing Pericles.   45. questionless: without doubt.
47. battery: assault.   58. staleness: lack of variety of food on
board ship.   60. graff: branch grafted in a fruit tree.

70–75. all . . . wish: i.e., if you are successful, your reward will
be great.   72. artificial feat: artistic skill.   87. comet: i.e., a
prodigious and fearful wonder. See Caesar, II.ii.30–31.   90. malign: treat maliciously.   94. awkward casualties: perverse
happenings.

Here of these shores?

MAR. No, nor of any shores.
Yet I was mortally brought forth, and am 105
No other than I appear.

PER. I am great with woe,° and shall deliver
weeping.
My dearest wife was like this maid, and such a one
My daughter might have been: my Queen's square
brows,
Her stature to an inch, as wandlike straight, 110
As silver-voiced, her eyes as jewel-like
And cased as richly, in pace another Juno,
Who starves the ears she feeds, and makes them
hungry,
The more she gives them speech. Where do you
live? 114

MAR. Where I am but a stranger. From the deck
You may discern the place.

PER. Where were you bred?
And how achieved you these endowments which
You make more rich to owe?°

MAR. If I should tell my history, it would seem
Like lies disdained in the reporting.

PER. Prithee speak. 120
Falseness cannot come from thee, for thou look'st
Modest as Justice, and thou seem'st a palace
For the crowned Truth to dwell in. I will believe
thee,
And make my senses credit thy relation° 124
To points that seem impossible; for thou look'st
Like one I loved indeed. What were thy friends?
Didst thou not say, when I did push thee back —
Which was when I perceived thee — that thou
camest
From good descending?

MAR. So indeed I did.

PER. Report thy parentage. I think thou said'st
Thou hadst been tossed from wrong to injury, 131
And that thou thought'st thy griefs might equal
mine
If both were opened.

MAR. Some such thing
I said, and said no more but what my thoughts
Did warrant me was likely.

PER. Tell thy story. 135
If thine considered prove the thousandth part
Of my endurance, thou art a man, and I
Have suffered like a girl. Yet thou dost look
Like Patience gazing on kings' graves and smiling
Extremity out of act.° What were thy friends? 140
How lost thou them? Thy name, my most kind
virgin?
Recount. I do beseech thee. Come, sit by me.

MAR. My name is Marina.

107. great . . . woe: in the throes of woe — like a woman in
childbirth. 118. owe: own. 124. relation: story. 139-
40. smiling . . . act: disarming Calamity (*Extremity*) by a smile.

PER. Oh, I am mocked,
And thou by some incensèd god sent hither
To make the world to laugh at me.

MAR. Patience, good sir, 145
Or here I'll cease.

PER. Nay, I'll be patient.
Thou little know'st how thou dost startle me,
To call thyself Marina.

MAR. The name
Was given me by one that had some power — 150
My father, and a king.

PER. How! A king's daughter
And called Marina?

MAR. You said you would believe me;
But, not to be a troubler of your peace,
I will end here.

PER. But are you flesh and blood?
Have you a working pulse? And are no fairy? 155
Motion! Well, speak on. Where were you born?
And wherefore called Marina?

MAR. Called Marina
For I was born at sea.

PER. At sea! What mother?

MAR. My mother was the daughter of a King,
Who died the minute I was born, 160
As my good nurse Lychorida hath oft
Delivered° weeping.

PER. Oh, stop there a little!
[*Aside*] This is the rarest dream that e'er dull
sleep
Did mock sad fools withal. This cannot be.
My daughter's buried. — Well, where were you
bred? 165
I'll hear you more, to the bottom of your story,
And never interrupt you.

MAR. You scorn. Believe me, 'twere best I did
give o'er.

PER. I will believe you by the syllable
Of what you shall deliver. Yet, give me leave. 170
How came you in these parts? Where were you
bred?

MAR. The King my father did in Tarsus leave
me,
Till cruel Cleon, with his wicked wife,
Did seek to murder me; and having wooed 174
A villain to attempt it, who having drawn° to do 't,
A crew of pirates came and rescued me,
Brought me to Mytilene. But, good sir,
Whither will you have me? Why do you weep? It
may be,
You think me an impostor. No, good faith.
I am the daughter to King Pericles, 180
If good King Pericles be.

PER. Ho, Helicanus!

HEL. Calls my lord?

PER. Thou art a grave and noble Councillor,

162. Delivered: related. 175. drawn: i.e., his sword.

Most wise in general. Tell me, if thou canst,   185
What this maid is, or what is like to be,
That thus hath made me weep.
    HEL.   I know not, but
Here is the Regent, sir, of Mytilene
Speaks nobly of her.
    LYS.   She never would tell
Her parentage. Being demanded that,   190
She would sit still and weep.
    PER. O Helicanus, strike me, honored sir.
Give me a gash, put me to present pain,
Lest this great sea of joys rushing upon me
O'erbear the shores of my mortality,°   195
And drown me with their sweetness. — Oh, come
    hither,
Thou that beget'st him that did thee beget;°
Thou that wast born at sea, buried at Tarsus,
And found at sea again! Oh Helicanus,
Down on thy knees! Thank the holy gods as loud
As thunder threatens us. This is Marina. —   201
What was thy mother's name? Tell me but that,
For truth can never be confirmed enough,
Though doubts did ever sleep.
    MAR. First, sir, I pray, what is your title?   205
    PER.   I
Am Pericles of Tyre. But tell me now
My drowned Queen's name, as in the rest you said
Thou hast been godlike perfect,
The heir of kingdoms and another like
To Pericles thy father.   210
    MAR. Is it no more to be your daughter than
To say my mother's name was Thaisa?
Thaisa was my mother, who did end
The minute I began.
    PER. Now, blessing on thee! Rise, thou art my
    child.   215
Give me fresh garments. Mine own, Helicanus.
She is not dead at Tarsus, as she should have been,
By savage Cleon. She shall tell thee all,
When thou shalt kneel, and justify° in knowledge
She is thy very Princess. Who is this?   220
    HEL. Sir, 'tis the Governor of Mytilene,
Who, hearing of your melancholy state,
Did come to see you.
    PER.   I embrace you.
Give me my robes. I am wild in my beholding.°
O Heavens bless my girl! But, hark, what music?
Tell Helicanus, my Marina, tell him   226
O'er, point by point, for yet he seems to doubt
How sure you are my daughter. But what music?
    HEL. My lord, I hear none.
    PER. None!   230
The music of the spheres!° List, my Marina.

LYS. It is not good to cross him. Give him way.°
PER. Rarest sounds! Do ye not hear?
LYS.   My lord, I hear.   [Music.]
PER. Most heavenly music!
It nips me unto listening, and thick slumber   235
Hangs upon mine eyes. Let me rest.   [Sleeps.]
    LYS. A pillow for his head —
So, leave him all. Well, my companion friends,
If this but answer to my just belief,
I'll well remember you.   240
        [Exeunt all but PERICLES.]
    [DIANA appears to PERICLES in a vision.]
    DIANA. My temple stands in Ephesus. Hie thee
    thither,
And do upon mine altar sacrifice.
There, when my maiden priests are met together,
Before the people all,
Reveal how thou at sea didst lose thy wife.   245
To mourn thy crosses, with thy daughter's, call
And give them repetition to the life.°
Or perform my bidding, or° thou livest in woe,
Do it, and happy, by my silver bow!°
Awake, and tell thy dream.   [Disappears.]   250
    PER. Celestial Dian, goddess argentine,°
I will obey thee. Helicanus!
    [Re-enter HELICANUS, LYSIMACHUS, and MARINA.]
    HEL.   Sir?
    PER. My purpose was for Tarsus, there to strike
The inhospitable Cleon, but I am
For other service first. Toward Ephesus   255
Turn our blown sails. Eftsoons° I'll tell thee why.
    [To LYSIMACHUS] Shall we refresh us, sir, upon
    your shore,
And give you gold for such provision
As our intents will need?
    LYS. Sir,   260
With all my heart; and, when you come ashore,
I have another suit.
    PER.   You shall prevail,
Were it to woo my daughter, for it seems
You have been noble towards her.
    LYS.   Sir, lend me your arm.
    PER. Come, my Marina.   [Exeunt.]   265

SCENE II.

[Enter GOWER, before the temple of DIANA
at Ephesus.]
    GOW. Now our sands are almost run;
More a little, and then dumb.

195. mortality: life.   197. Thou . . . beget: i.e., who gives
second birth to your father.   219. justify: be assured.   224. beholding: to look upon — because he has kept his vow. See
III.iii.27–30.   231. music . . . spheres: See App. I. spheres:
planets.   232. It . . . way: Since the music of the spheres was inaudible
to mortal ears, Lysimachus supposes that Pericles is raving.
246–47. To . . . life: lament your sorrows (crosses) and your
daughter's, and loudly tell the story again as it happened (to the
life).   248. Or . . . or: either . . . or.   249. silver bow: the new
moon. Diana was also goddess of the moon.   251. argentine:
silver shining.   256. Eftsoons: soon.

This, my last boon, give me —
For such kindness must relieve me —
That you aptly will suppose 5
What pageantry, what feats, what shows,
What minstrelsy and pretty din,
The regent made in Mytilene
To greet the King. So he thrived
That he is promised to be wived 10
To fair Marina, but in no wise
Till he had done his sacrifice,
As Dian bade. Whereto being bound,
The interim, pray you, all confound.
In feathered briefness° sails are filled, 15
And wishes fall out as they're willed.
At Ephesus, the temple see,
Our King and all his company.
That he can hither come so soon,
Is by your fancies' thankful doom.° [*Exit.*] 20

SCENE III. *The temple of* DIANA *at Ephesus;* THAISA *standing near the altar, as high priestess; a number of* VIRGINS *on each side;* CERIMON *and other inhabitants of Ephesus attending.*°

[*Enter* PERICLES, *with his train;*° LYSIMACHUS, HELICANUS, MARINA, *and a* LADY.]

PER. Hail, Dian! To perform thy just command,
I here confess myself the King of Tyre,
Who, frighted from my country, did wed
At Pentapolis the fair Thaisa.
At sea in childbed died she, but brought forth 5
A maid-child called Marina, who, O Goddess,
Wears yet thy silver livery.° She at Tarsus
Was nursed with Cleon, who at fourteen years
He sought to murder; but her better stars
Brought her to Mytilene, 'gainst whose shore 10
Riding,° her fortunes brought the maid aboard us,
Where, by her own most clear remembrance, she
Made known herself my daughter.
THAI. Voice and favor!
You are, you are — O royal Pericles! —— [*Faints.*]
PER. What means the nun? She dies! Help, gentlemen! 15
CER. Noble sir,
If you have told Diana's altar true,
This is your wife.
PER. Reverend appearer,° no.
I threw her overboard with these very arms.
CER. Upon this coast, I warrant you.

PER. 'Tis most certain. 20
CER. Look to the lady. Oh, she's but overjoyed.
Early in blustering morn this lady was
Thrown upon this shore. I oped° the coffin,
Found there rich jewels, recovered° her, and placed her
Here in Diana's temple.
PER. May we see them? 25
CER. Great sir, they shall be brought you to my house,
Whither I invite you. Look, Thaisa is
Recovered.
THAI. Oh, let me look!
If he be none of mine, my sanctity
Will to my sense bend no licentious ear, 30
But curb it, spite of seeing.° Oh, my lord,
Are you not Pericles? Like him you spake,
Like him you are. Did you not name a tempest,
A birth, and death?
PER. The voice of dead Thaisa!
THAI. That Thaisa am I, supposèd dead 35
And drowned.
PER. Immortal Dian!
THAI. Now I know you better.
When we with tears parted° Pentapolis,
The King my father gave you such a ring.
[*Shows a ring.*]
PER. This, this. No more, you gods! Your present kindness 40
Makes my past miseries sports. You shall do well
That on the touching of her lips I may
Melt, and no more be seen. Oh, come, be buried
A second time within these arms.
MAR. My heart
Leaps to be gone into my mother's bosom. 45
[*Kneels to* THAISA.]
PER. Look, who kneels here! Flesh of thy flesh, Thaisa;
Thy burden at the sea, and called Marina
For she was yielded° there.
THAI. Blest, and mine own!
HEL. Hail, madam, and my Queen!
THAI. I know you not.
PER. You have heard me say, when I did fly from Tyre, 50
I left behind an ancient substitute.
Can you remember what I called the man?
I have named him oft.
THAI. 'Twas Helicanus then.
PER. Still confirmation.°
Embrace him, dear Thaisa; this is he. 55
Now do I long to hear how you were found,

Sc. ii: **15. feathered briefness:** swift as wings. **20. Is ... doom:** is caused by the kindly (*thankful*) judgment of your imaginations.
Sc. iii: **s.d.:** These directions also were added by the editors. **train:** attendants. **7. silver livery:** the white garments of a virgin. **11. Riding:** as we lay at anchor. **18. appearer:** stranger, lit., one who appears.

23. oped: opened. **24. recovered:** restored to life. **29–31. If ... seeing:** if he is not indeed my husband, my vow of celibacy will not yield to any lustful desire, but restrain it in spite of the joy of seeing one like Pericles. **38. parted:** left. **48. yielded:** brought to birth. **54. Still confirmation:** more proof.

How possibly preserved, and who to thank,
Besides the gods, for this great miracle.
   THAI. Lord Cerimon, my lord. This man,
Through whom the gods have shown their power,
     that can   60
From first to last resolve you.
   PER.   Reverend sir,
The gods can have no mortal° officer
More like a god than you. Will you deliver
How this dead Queen relives?
   CER.   I will, my lord.
Beseech you, first go with me to my house,   65
Where shall be shown you all was found with her,
How she came placed here in the temple,
No needful thing omitted.
   PER. Pure Dian, bless thee for thy vision! I
Will offer night oblations° to thee. Thaisa,   70
This Prince, the fair-betrothéd of your daughter,
Shall marry her at Pentapolis. And now,
This ornament°
Makes° me look dismal will I clip to form,°
And what this fourteen years no razor touched, 75
To grace thy marriage day, I'll beautify.
   THAI. Lord Cerimon hath letters of good credit,
     sir,
My father's dead.
   PER. Heavens make a star of him! Yet there, my
     Queen,

We'll celebrate their nuptials, and ourselves   80
Will in that kingdom spend our following° days.
Our son and daughter shall in Tyrus reign.
Lord Cerimon, we do our longing stay
To hear the rest untold. Sir, lead 's the way.
                              [Exeunt.]

               [Enter GOWER.*]*
   GOW. In Antiochus and his daughter you have
     heard   85
Of monstrous lust the due and just reward.
In Pericles, his Queen and daughter, seen,
Although assailed with fortune fierce and keen,
Virtue preserved from fell destruction's blast,
Led on by Heaven and crowned with joy at last. 90
In Helicanus may you well descry
A figure of truth, of faith, of loyalty.
In reverend Cerimon there well appears
The worth that learnèd charity aye wears.
For wicked Cleon and his wife, when fame   95
Had spread their cursèd deed and honored name
Of Pericles, to rage the city turn,
That him and his they in his palace burn.
The gods for murder seemèd so content
To punish, although not done, but meant.°   100
So, on your patience evermore attending,
New joy wait on you! Here our play has ending.
                               [Exit.]

---

62. mortal: human.   **70. oblations:** offerings.   **73. ornament:** i.e., his shaggy hair and beard.   **74. Makes:** which makes. **form:** neatness.

81. following: which follow.   **99–100. The . . . meant:** the gods were pleased to punish a murder which, although not effected, was planned.

CYMBELINE

Introduction

Cymbeline was first printed in the first folio (F1) of 1623, where it stands at the end of the volume as the last of the tragedies. The F1 text is on the whole good and has been divided into acts and scenes. Cymbeline is one of the group of three plays on the theme of reconciliation which Shakespeare wrote at the end of his career as a dramatist, the others being *The Winter's Tale* and *The Tempest*.

Cymbeline was probably written in 1610. It was among those plays being acted in London in the early months of 1611 that were seen and summarized by Dr. Simon Forman (see *Macb,* Intro. p. 1184b). In Forman's notebook the date of the performance is not recorded, but *Cymbeline* comes between a notice of *Macbeth,* seen on April 20, 1611, and a play on Richard II, seen on April 30. Forman's account reads: [1]

Remember also the story of Cymbeline, King of England, in Lucius' time; how Lucius came from Octavius Caesar for tribute, and being denied, after sent Lucius with a great army of soldiers who landed at Milford Haven, and after were vanquished by Cymbeline, and Lucius taken prisoner; and all by means of three outlaws, of the which two of them were the sons of Cymbeline, stolen from him when they were but two years old by an old man whom Cymbeline banished; and he kept them as his own sons twenty years with him in a cave. And how one of them slew Cloten, that was the Queen's son, going to Milford Haven to seek the love of Imogen, the King's daughter, whom he had banished also for loving his daughter; and how the Italian that came from her love conveyed himself into a chest, and said it was a chest of plate sent from her love and others, to be presented to the King. And in the deepest of the night, she being asleep, he opened the chest, and came forth of it, and viewed her in her bed, and the marks of her body, and took away her bracelet, and after accused her of adultery to her love, etc. And in the end how he came with the Romans into England and was taken prisoner, and after revealed to Imogen, who had turned herself into man's apparel and fled to meet her love at Milford Haven, and

[1] E. K. Chambers, *William Shakespeare*, Vol. II, pp. 338–39.

chanced to fall on the cave in the woods where her two brothers were; and how by eating a sleeping dram they thought she had been dead, and laid her in the woods, and the body of Cloten by her, in her love's apparel that he left behind him; and how she was found by Lucius, etc.

Apart from this account, there is no other direct evidence for the date of writing, though the style shows that *Cymbeline* was written in Shakespeare's latest period.

The story of *Cymbeline* is elaborate, complicated, and farfetched even for an Elizabethan play; and it includes nearly every ingredient known to melodrama. The central theme concerns a young and innocent girl, married for true love, who is harassed by a wicked stepmother, ill-treated by her father, pursued by a hated and boorish brute, falsely accused of unchastity, forced to flee in disguise as a boy, befriended by savage mountaineers (who are natural gentlemen and turn out to be her longlost brothers), and finally triumphantly restored to her repentant husband. In addition, we are given such stock items as a faithful servant, a good doctor, a penitent villain, heroic Britons, chivalric Romans, battle scenes, a prison scene, ghosts, music, abundant moralizing, drugs which produce the appearance of death, a severed head, and even the convenient birthmark — a " sanguine star " — by which the lost heir is at last recognized and restored.

The historical scenes, which tell how Cymbeline, King of Britain — for the story is supposed to take place in the first century B.C. — had trouble with the Romans, came in part from Holinshed's *Chronicles,* so often used by Shakespeare. But Shakespeare's use of the *Chronicles* in writing *Cymbeline* was very different from his debt in the *Henry IV* and *Henry VI* plays, where he followed the narrative closely. In Holinshed's account of Cymbeline there was less material for drama, for in the early pages of the *Chronicles* Holinshed was usually brief (and wholly unreliable) in his picturesque fables of the kings of Britain in pre-Saxon days.

According to Holinshed —

Kymbeline or Cimbeline, the son of Theomantius, was of the Britons made king after the decease of his father, in the year of the world 3944, after the building of Rome 728, and before the birth of our Saviour 33. This man (as some write) was brought up at Rome, and there made knight by Augustus Caesar, under whom he served in the wars, and was in such favor with him, that he was at liberty to pay his tribute or not.

The episode of the fight in the narrow lane (V.iii.1–58) was also taken from Holinshed— but from an incident in Scottish history which occurred when, nearly a thousand years after the reign of Cymbeline, the Scots king was fighting Danish invaders:

[The Danes] rushed forth with such violence upon their adversaries, that first the right, and then after the left wing of the Scots, was constrained to retire and flee back, the middle ward stoutly yet keeping their ground: but the same stood in such danger, being now left naked on the sides, that the victory must needs have remained with the Danes, had not a renewer of the battle come in time, by the appointment (as is to be thought) of Almighty God.

For as it chanced, there was in the next field at the same time an husbandman, with two of his sons busy about his work, named Hay, a man strong and stiff in making and shape of body, but endued with a valiant courage. This Hay beholding the king with the most part of the nobles, fighting with great valiancy in the middle ward, now destitute of the wings, and in great danger to be oppressed by the great violence of his enemies, caught a plow beam in his hand, and with the same exhorting his sons to do the like, hasted toward the battle, there to die rather amongst others in defense of his country, than to remain alive after the discomfiture in miserable thralldom and bondage of the cruel and most unmerciful enemies. There was near to the place of the battle, a long lane fenced on the sides with ditches and walls made of turf, through the which the Scots which fled were beaten down by the enemies on heaps.

Here Hay with his sons, supposing they might best stay the flight, placed themselves overthwart the lane, beat them back whom they met fleeing, and spared neither friend nor foe: but down they went all such as came within their reach, wherewith divers hardy personages cried unto their fellows to return back unto the battle, for there was a new power of Scottishmen come to their succors, by whose aid the victory might be easily obtained of their most cruel adversaries the Danes: therefore might they choose whether they would be slain of their own fellows coming to their aid, or to return again to fight with the enemies. The Danes being here stayed in the lane by the great valiancy of the father and the sons, thought verily there had been some great succors of Scots come to the aid of their king, and thereupon ceasing from further pursuit, fled back in great disorder unto the other of their fellows fighting with the middle ward of the Scots.

The story of Imogen, Posthumus, and Iachimo was derived from a tale in Boccaccio's *Decameron* (Second Day, Ninth Tale), which may be paraphrased as follows:

Certain Italian merchants, gathered in Paris, after a jolly evening began to tell stories about their wives of whose loyalty they had a low opinion. But one of them, a Genoese called Bernarbo Lomellin, declared that he had a perfect wife and that it would be impossible to find a woman more chaste. Among the merchants was a young man called Ambrogiuolo da Piacenza, who began to mock Bernarbo, and to declare that if he had access to the lady, he would soon have the same success with her as with every other woman that he had encountered. At this, Bernarbo grew so angry that he was willing to wager his own head against one thousand crowns that Ambrogiuolo would not succeed in his attempt. However, the wager ultimately fixed was that Bernarbo would pay five thousand florins if Ambrogiuolo succeeded, and win one thousand if he failed.

Ambrogiuolo set out for Genoa, where he made careful inquiries and soon learned that the lady was indeed as good as her husband had boasted. Realizing that his design was hopeless and being unwilling to lose his money, Ambrogiuolo bribed a poor woman who worked in the house to convey him in a chest into the lady's bedroom. Late that night, Ambrogiuolo opened the chest and stepped out; and since there was a light in the room he was able to note the pictures and other details. Then he approached the bed and uncovered the lady, perceiving under her left breast a mole surrounded with golden hairs. He also took from the lady's boxes, a purse, a gown, a ring, and a girdle, and so returned into the chest.

Ambrogiuolo hastened back to Paris with his trophies and claimed that he had won the wager. When he described the room and produced the articles he had stolen, Bernarbo acknowledged the accuracy of his tale but declared that he might have come by the tokens through one of the servants, and that better evidence was needed to win the bet. To this Ambrogiuolo retorted, "This should be enough; but since you require something further, I will satisfy you. I say that the Lady Zinevra, your wife, has a mole under her left breast, around which are about six golden hairs."

When Bernarbo heard these words he was struck to the heart and admitted that Ambrogiuolo had indeed won the wager. On the next day, having paid his bet, Bernarbo set out for Genoa. He did not go home but stayed at one of his estates about twenty miles outside the city. From here he sent one of his servants with a letter to his wife telling her to come out and meet him; but he ordered the servant to slay her on the way. The lady was very glad to receive the letter, and next day rode forth with the servant to meet her husband. When they came to a deep and lonely gorge, the servant drew a knife and was about to slay his mistress; but she pleaded with him so hard that he consented to give her some of his clothes and to take hers to Bernarbo with the tale that she was dead. Bernarbo thereafter returned to Genoa, where he was much blamed for this supposed cruelty.

Meanwhile the poor lady, disguised as a man, made her way to the seacoast where she was taken into service by a Catalan gentleman called Signor Encararch. She now took the name of Sicurano da Finale. Sometime later the Catalan gentleman sailed to Alexandria, where the Soldan [Sultan] was so much attracted by the good service of Sicurano that he begged the Catalan for him. Sicurano quickly rose in the favor of the Soldan and was sent to Acre as governor and captain of the guard for the protection of the merchants there. Now, it so happened that Sicurano, as "he" was looking into a shop belonging to a Venetian, saw the very purse and girdle that had been stolen by Ambrogiuolo. He asked the shopkeeper, who was Ambrogiuolo himself, how he had come by these articles. Ambrogiuolo replied that they had been given to him by a lady named Zinevra, wife to Bernarbo Lomellin, with whom he had spent the night; she had prayed him to keep them as a token of her love. In consequence, he had won a bet from Bernarbo, and Bernarbo had had Zinevra put to death.

Sicurano thus realized why her husband had treated her so cruelly. On returning to Alexandria, she caused the Soldan to be interested in Ambrogiuolo, and by a device she also caused Bernarbo to come to Alexandria. In the presence of the Soldan, Ambrogiuolo confessed the truth.

Then Sicurano, turning to the Soldan, said that she would produce the lady if the Soldan would punish the evildoers. The Soldan agreed. At this Sicurano, bursting into tears, cried out that she was the unfortunate Lady Zinevra, and rending her robes made it clear to the Sultan that she was in fact a woman. Bernardo was forgiven for his cruelty and restored to his lady who was highly favored by the Sultan; but Ambrogiuolo was bound to a stake and left with his bare flesh anointed with honey to be eaten away by the flies and wasps of that country.

As a whole *Cymbeline* has many resemblances to Beaumont and Fletcher's *Philaster* (see Gen. Intro. p. 50a), which also concerns the misfortunes of a faithful lady, who owing to hasty misunderstanding is scorned, maligned, and ill-treated by her truelove. If, as is likely, *Philaster* was the earlier play, Shakespeare was following rather than creating a new vogue for tragicomedy. Certainly *Cymbeline* with its endlessly involved complexity and its long last scene of explanations, revelations, and reconciliations, is a very different play from any that Shakespeare had hitherto written. Some critics, however, believe that Shakespeare did not write the whole of this play. The speeches of the apparitions in V.iv.30–122 are dreary doggerel and do little better than repeat information already given in I.i.1–62. There is no generally accepted explanation for this episode. Perhaps in the original production the oracular paper was first introduced at V.v.429, and the actors, feeling that the scene of its giving should have been shown, caused this passage to be written in. Perhaps the first appearance of the ghosts of the aged parents was confined to wordless dumb show, which proved unintelligible, and so had to be fitted with words. Whatever the origin, the verses can hardly have been written by Shakespeare.

On the whole, therefore, *Cymbeline* has not won the approval of critics. Indeed, Dr. Johnson poured over it the vial of his indignation:

This play has many just sentiments, some natural dialogues, and some pleasing scenes, but they are obtained at the expense of much incongruity. To remark the folly of the fiction, the absurdity of the conduct, the confusion of the names and manners of different times, and the impossibility of the events in any system of life, were to waste criticism upon unresisting imbecility, upon faults too evident for detection, and too gross for aggravation.

Yet Dr. Johnson is too brutal; in spite of the stale stage tricks, *Cymbeline* has many incidents and speeches composed in Shakespeare's finest manner.

Cymbeline

DRAMATIS PERSONAE

CYMBELINE, *King of Britain*
CLOTEN, *son to the Queen by a former husband*
POSTHUMUS° LEONATUS, *a gentleman, husband to Imogen*
BELARIUS, *a banished lord, disguised under the name of Morgan*
GUIDERIUS } *sons to Cymbeline, disguised under the names of Polydore and Cadwal, supposed sons to Morgan*
ARVIRAGUS }
PHILARIO, *friend to Posthumus* } *Italians*
IACHIMO, *friend to Philario* }
CAIUS LUCIUS, *General of the Roman forces*
PISANIO, *servant to Posthumus*
CORNELIUS, *a physician*
A ROMAN CAPTAIN
TWO BRITISH CAPTAINS

A FRENCHMAN, *friend to Philario*
TWO LORDS *of Cymbeline's Court*
TWO GENTLEMEN *of the same*
TWO JAILERS

QUEEN, *wife to Cymbeline*
IMOGEN, *daughter to Cymbeline by a former Queen*
HELEN, *a lady attending on Imogen*

LORDS, LADIES, ROMAN SENATORS, TRIBUNES, *a* SOOTH-SAYER, *a* DUTCHMAN, *a* SPANIARD, MUSICIANS, OFFICERS, CAPTAINS, SOLDIERS, MESSENGERS, *and other* ATTENDANTS
APPARITIONS

SCENE — *Britain, Rome.*

Act I

SCENE I. *Britain. The garden of* CYMBELINE's *palace.*

[*Enter two* GENTLEMEN.]

1. GENT. You do not meet a man but frowns. Our bloods
No more obey the Heavens than our courtiers
Still seem as does the King.°
2. GENT.   But what's the matter?
1. GENT. His daughter, and the heir of 's kingdom, whom
He purposed to his wife's sole son — a widow   5
That late he married — hath referred° herself
Unto a poor but worthy gentleman. She's wedded,
Her husband banished, she imprisoned. All
Is outward sorrow, though I think the King
Be touched at very heart.
2. GENT.   None but the King?   10
1. GENT. He that hath lost her too. So is the Queen,
That most desired the match; but not a courtier,
Although they wear their faces to the bent°
Of the King's looks, hath a heart that is not
Glad at the thing they scowl at.
2. GENT.   And why so?   15

1. GENT. He that hath missed the Princess is a thing
Too bad for bad report, and he that hath her —
I mean, that married her, alack, good man! —
And therefore banished is a creature such
As, to seek through the regions of the earth   20
For one his like, there would be something failing
In him that should compare.° I do not think
So fair an outward and such stuff within
Endows a man but he.°
2. GENT.   You speak him far.
1. GENT. I do extend him, sir, within himself,°
Crush him together rather than unfold   26
His measure duly.
2. GENT.   What's his name and birth?
1. GENT. I cannot delve him to the root.° His father
Was called Sicilius, who did join his honor
Against the Romans with Cassibelan,   30
But had his titles by° Tenantius, whom
He served with glory and admired success,
So gained the sur-addition° Leonatus;
And had, besides this gentleman in question,
Two other sons, who in the wars o' the time   35
Died with their swords in hand. For which their father,

Dramatis Personae: **Posthumus:** accented Posthúmus.
Act I, Sc. i: **1–3. Our . . . King:** just as our passions (*bloods*) obey the stars (*Heavens*), so our courtiers always (*still*) appear to follow the moods of the King.   **6. referred:** transferred; i.e., married.   **13. bent:** inclination.

22. In . . . compare: should be chosen as comparison.   **23-**
24. So . . . he: no man is so fair outwardly and inwardly.
25. extend . . . himself: exhibit (*extend*) him as he is.   **28. delve . . . root:** trace him back to his first ancestor.   **31. by:** i.e., won his titles from.   **33. sur-addition:** title of honor added to a man's name.

Then old and fond of issue,° took such sorrow
That he quit being,° and his gentle lady,
Big of° this gentleman our theme, deceased
As he was born. The King he takes the babe   40
To his protection, calls him Posthumus Leonatus,
Breeds him and makes him of his bedchamber;°
Puts to him all the learnings that his time
Could make him the receiver of, which he took,
As we do air, fast as 'twas ministered,   45
And in 's spring became a harvest, lived in Court —
Which rare it is to do — most praised, most loved,
A sample to the youngest, to the more mature
A glass that feated° them, and to the graver
A child that guided dotards.° To his mistress,   50
For whom he now is banished, her own price
Proclaims how she esteemed him and his virtue.
By her election° may be truly read
What kind of man he is.

    2. GENT.   I honor him
Even out of your report. But, pray you tell me,   55
Is she sole child to the King?

    1. GENT.   His only child.
He had two sons — if this be worth your hearing,
Mark it — the eldest of them at three years old,
I' the swathing° clothes the other,° from their
    nursery
Were stolen, and to this hour no guess in knowl-
    edge   60
Which way they went.

    2. GENT.   How long is this ago?

    1. GENT. Some twenty years.

    2. GENT. That a King's children should be so
    conveyed!°
So slackly guarded, and the search so slow
That could not trace them!

    1. GENT.   Howsoe'er 'tis strange,   65
Or that the negligence may well be laughed at,
Yet is it true, sir.

    2. GENT.   I do well believe you.

    1. GENT. We must forbear.° Here comes the gen-
    tleman,
The Queen, and Princess.   [*Exeunt.*]

    [*Enter the* QUEEN, POSTHUMUS *and* IMOGEN.]

    QUEEN. No, be assured you shall not find me,
    Daughter,   70
After the slander of most stepmothers,°
Evil-eyed unto you. You're my prisoner, but
Your jailer shall deliver you the keys
That lock up your restraint.° For you, Posthumus,

So soon as I can win the offended King,   75
I will be known your advocate. Marry,° yet
The fire of rage is in him, and 'twere good
You leaned unto° his sentence with what patience
Your wisdom may inform° you.

    POST.   Please your Highness,
I will from hence today.

    QUEEN.   You know the peril.°   80
I'll fetch a turn about the garden, pitying
The pangs of barred° affections, though the King
Hath charged you should not speak together.
                         [*Exit.*]

    IMO.   Oh,
Dissembling° courtesy! How fine° this tyrant   84
Can tickle where she wounds! My dearest Husband,
I something fear my father's wrath, but nothing —
Always reserved my holy duty — what
His rage can do on me. You must be gone,
And I shall here abide the hourly shot
Of angry eyes, not comforted to live,   90
But that there is this jewel in the world
That I may see again.

    POST.   My Queen! My mistress!
O lady, weep no more, lest I give cause
To be suspected of more tenderness
Than doth become a man! I will remain   95
The loyal'st husband that did e'er plight troth.
My residence in Rome at one Philario's,
Who to my father was a friend, to me
Known but by letter. Thither write, my Queen,
And with mine eyes I'll drink the words you send,
Though ink be made of gall.°   101

    [*Re-enter* QUEEN.]

    QUEEN.   Be brief, I pray you.
If the King come, I shall incur I know not
How much of his displeasure. [*Aside*] Yet I'll move
    him
To walk this way. I never do him wrong
But he does buy my injuries to be friends;   105
Pays dear for my offenses.°   [*Exit.*]

    POST.   Should we be taking leave
As long a term as yet we have to live,
The loathness to depart would grow. Adieu!

    IMO. Nay, stay a little.
Were you but riding forth to air yourself,   110
Such parting were too petty. Look here, love.
This diamond was my mother's. Take it, heart,
But keep it till you woo another wife,
When Imogen is dead.

POST.   How, how! Another?
You gentle gods, give me but this I have,   115
And sear up° my embracements from a next
With bonds of death! [*Putting on the ring.*] Re-
main, remain thou here
While sense° can keep it on! And, sweetest, fairest,
As I my poor self did exchange for you
To your so infinite loss, so in our trifles   120
I still win of you. For my sake wear this.
It is a manacle of love. I'll place it
Upon this fairest prisoner.
              [*Putting a bracelet on her arm.*]
IMO.   Oh, the gods!
When shall we see again?
          [*Enter CYMBELINE and LORDS.*]
POST.   Alack, the King!
CYM. Thou basest thing, avoid! Hence, from my
sight!   125
If after this command thou fraught° the Court
With thy unworthiness, thou diest. Away!
Thou'rt poison to my blood.
POST.   The gods protect you
And bless the good remainders of the Court!
I am gone.   [*Exit.*]
IMO.   There cannot be a pinch in death   130
More sharp than this is.
CYM.   O disloyal thing,
That shouldst repair my youth,° thou heap'st
A year's age on me!
IMO.   I beseech you, sir,
Harm not yourself with your vexation.
I am senseless of° your wrath. A touch° more rare°
Subdues all pangs, all fears.
CYM.   Past grace? Obedience?   136
IMO. Past hope, and in despair; that way, past
grace.
CYM. That mightst have had the sole son of my
Queen!
IMO. Oh, blessèd, that I might not! I chose an
eagle,
And did avoid a puttock.°   140
CYM. Thou took'st a beggar, wouldst have made
my throne
A seat for baseness.°
IMO.   No, I rather added
A luster to it.
CYM.   O thou vile one!
IMO.   Sir,
It is your fault that I have loved Posthumus.
You bred him as my playfellow, and he is   145

A man worth any woman, overbuys me
Almost the sum he pays.°
CYM.   What, art thou mad!
IMO. Almost, sir. Heaven restore me! Would I
were
A neat-herd's° daughter, and my Leonatus
Our neighbor shepherd's son!
CYM.   Thou foolish thing!   150
          [*Re-enter QUEEN.*]
They were again together. You have done
Not after our command. Away with her,
And pen her up.
QUEEN.   Beseech your patience. Peace,
Dear Lady Daughter, peace! Sweet sovereign,
Leave us to ourselves, and make yourself some com-
fort   155
Out of your best advice.
CYM.   Nay, let her languish
A drop of blood a day, and, being aged,
Die of this folly! [*Exeunt CYMBELINE and LORDS.*]
QUEEN.   Fie! You must give way.
          [*Enter PISANIO.*]
Here is your servant. — How now, sir! What news?
PIS. My lord your son drew on my master.
QUEEN.   Ha!   160
No harm, I trust, is done?
PIS.   There might have been,
But that my master rather played than fought,
And had no help of anger. They were parted
By gentlemen at hand.
QUEEN.   I am very glad on 't.
IMO. Your son's my father's friend. He takes his
part.   165
To draw upon an exile! Oh, brave sir!
I would they were in Afric both together,°
Myself by with a needle, that I might prick
The goer-back.° Why came you from your master?
PIS. On his command. He would not suffer me
To bring him to the haven;° left these notes   171
Of what commands I should be subject to
When 't pleased you to employ me.
QUEEN.   This hath been
Your faithful servant. I dare lay° mine honor
He will remain so.
PIS.   I humbly thank your Highness.   175
QUEEN. Pray walk awhile.
IMO.   About some half-hour hence,
I pray you speak with me. You shall at least
Go see my lord aboard. For this time leave me.
                                        [*Exeunt.*]

---

116. **sear up**: shrivel.   118. **sense**: life.   126. **fraught**: burden.
132. **repair my youth**: make me feel young again.   135. **senseless of**: incapable of feeling. **touch**: sensation (i.e., the loss of
Posthumus). **rare**: intense, unique.   140. **puttock**: kite — a
carrion-eating hawk.   142. **seat . . . baseness**: i.e., your children
who would have succeeded to the throne would not have been
of pure royal blood.

146–47. **overbuys . . . pays**: whatever he pays for me is almost
too much; i.e., he is worth far more than I am.   149. **neat-
herd's**: cowherd's.   167. **Afric . . . together**: i.e., that Cloten
and Posthumus were alone in the desert with no one to interfere.
See *Cor*, IV.ii.23–25.   169. **goer-back**: the one who ran away.
171. **haven**: harbor.   174. **lay**: pawn, bet.

SCENE II. *The same. A public place.*

[*Enter* CLOTEN *and two* LORDS.]

1. LORD. Sir, I would advise you to shift a shirt.° The violence of action hath made you reek° as a sacrifice. Where air comes out, air comes in. There's none abroad so wholesome as that you vent.°   5

CLO. If my shirt were bloody, then to shift it. Have I hurt him?

2. LORD. [*Aside*] No, faith, not so much as his patience.   9

1. LORD. Hurt him! His body's a passable° carcass if he be not hurt. It is a throughfare for steel if it be not hurt.

2. LORD. [*Aside*] His steel was in debt.° It went o' the backside the town.°

CLO. The villain would not stand me.   15

2. LORD. [*Aside*] No; but he fled forward still, toward your face.

1. LORD. Stand you! You have land enough of your own, but he added to your having, gave you some ground.   20

2. LORD. [*Aside*] As many inches as you have oceans. Puppies!

CLO. I would they had not come between us.

2. LORD. [*Aside*] So would I, till you had   25 measured how long a fool you were upon the ground.

CLO. And that she should love this fellow and refuse me!

2. LORD. [*Aside*] If it be a sin to make a true election, she is damned.   30

1. LORD. Sir, as I told you always, her beauty and her brain go not together. She's a good sign,° but I have seen small reflection of her wit.

2. LORD. [*Aside*] She shines not upon fools, lest the reflection should hurt her.   35

CLO. Come, I'll to my chamber. Would there had been some hurt done!

2. LORD. [*Aside*] I wish not so, unless it had been the fall of an ass, which is no great hurt.

CLO. You'll go with us?   40

1. LORD. I'll attend your lordship.

CLO. Nay, come, let's go together.

2. LORD. Well, my lord.   [*Exeunt.*]

SCENE III. *A room in* CYMBELINE's *palace.*

[*Enter* IMOGEN *and* PISANIO.]

IMO. I would thou grew'st unto the shores o' the haven

And question'dst every sail. If he should write And I not have it, 'twere a paper lost As offered mercy is.° What was the last That he spake to thee?

PIS.   It was his Queen, his Queen! 5

IMO. Then waved his handkerchief?

PIS.   And kissed it, madam.

IMO. Senseless linen! Happier therein than I! And that was all?

PIS.   No, madam. For so long As he could make me° with this eye or ear Distinguish him from others, he did keep   10 The deck, with glove, or hat, or handkerchief, Still waving, as the fits and stirs of 's mind Could best express how slow his soul sailed on, How swift his ship.

IMO.   Thou shouldst have made him As little as a crow, or less, ere left   15 To aftereye him.°

PIS.   Madam, so I did.

IMO. I would have broke mine eyestrings,° cracked them, but To look upon him till the diminution Of space had pointed him sharp as my needle — Nay, followed him till he had melted from   20 The smallness of a gnat to air, and then Have turned mine eye and wept. But, good Pisanio, When shall we hear from him?

PIS.   Be assured, madam, With his next vantage.°

IMO. I did not take my leave of him, but had   25 Most pretty things to say. Ere I could tell him How I would think on him at certain hours, Such thoughts and such, or I could make him swear The she's of Italy should not betray   29 Mine interest and his honor, or have charged him, At the sixth hour of morn, at noon, at midnight, To encounter me with orisons — for then I am in Heaven for him° — or ere I could Give him that parting kiss which I had set   34 Betwixt two charming° words, comes in my father, And, like the tyrannous breathing of the North,° Shakes all our buds from growing.

[*Enter a* LADY.]

LADY.   The Queen, madam, Desires your Highness' company.

IMO. Those things I bid you do, get them dispatched.

Sc. ii: **1. shift a shirt:** change your shirt — because it is wet with the perspiration of your efforts. **2. reek:** steam. **5. vent:** give off. **10. passable:** has a way through, i.e., is full of holes. **13. steel . . . debt:** his sword did not fulfill its promises; i.e., he played the coward. **13–14. went . . . town:** skulked away like a debtor fearing arrest. **32. sign:** outward appearance only. See App. 12.

Sc. iii: **3–4. 'twere . . . is:** it were as if the pardon for a condemned man went astray. **9. As . . . me:** as I could make him out. **15–16. ere . . . him:** before you ceased (*left*) following him with your gaze. **17. eyestrings:** the muscles or tendons of the eye, supposed to break when a man went blind. **24. vantage:** opportunity. **32–33. encounter . . . him:** meet me in his prayers (*orisons*). The idea is that when she is at her prayers Imogen's soul is out of her body; if Posthumus prays at the same time their souls may meet. **35. charming:** enchanting. **36. breathing . . . North:** like the bitter north wind, which brings frosts in the spring.

I will attend the Queen.

PIS.   Madam, I shall. [*Exeunt.*] 40

SCENE IV.° *Rome.* PHILARIO'S *house.*

[*Enter* PHILARIO, IACHIMO, *a* FRENCHMAN, *a* DUTCH-MAN, *and a* SPANIARD.]

IACH. Believe it, sir, I have seen him in Britain. He was then of a crescent note,° expected to prove so worthy as since he hath been allowed the name of.° But I could then have looked on him without the help of admiration,° though the catalogue of his endowments had been tabled° by his side and I to peruse him by items.   7

PHI. You speak of him when he was less furnished than now he is with that which makes him both without and within.°

FRENCH. I have seen him in France. We had very many there could behold the sun with as firm eyes as he.°   13

IACH. This matter of marrying his King's daughter, wherein he must be weighed rather by her value than his own, words him, I doubt not, a great deal from the matter.°

FRENCH. And then his banishment.   18

IACH. Aye, and the approbation° of those that weep this lamentable divorce under her colors are wonderfully to extend him; be it but to fortify her judgment, which else an easy battery might lay flat for taking a beggar without less quality. But how comes it he is to sojourn with you? How creeps acquaintance?°   25

PHI. His father and I were soldiers together, to whom I have been often bound for no less than my life. Here comes the Briton. Let him be so entertained amongst you as suits° with gentlemen of your knowing to a stranger of his quality. 30 [*Enter* POSTHUMUS] I beseech you all, be better known to this gentleman, whom I commend to you as a noble friend of mine. How worthy he is I will leave to appear hereafter, rather than story him in his own hearing.   35

FRENCH. Sir, we have known° together in Orleans.

POST. Since when I have been debtor to you for courtesies which I will be ever to pay and yet pay still.°   40

FRENCH. Sir, you o'errate my poor kindness. I was glad I did atone° my countryman and you. It had been pity you should have been put together with so mortal° a purpose as then each bore, upon importance° of so slight and trivial a nature. 45

POST. By your pardon, sir, I° was then a young traveler, rather shunned to go even with° what I heard than in my every action to be guided by others' experiences; but upon my mended judgment — if I offend not to say it is mended — my quarrel was not altogether slight.   51

FRENCH. Faith, yes, to be put to the arbitrement° of swords, and by such two that would, by all likelihood, have confounded° one the other, or have fallen both.   55

IACH. Can we with manners ask what was the difference?

FRENCH. Safely, I think. 'Twas a contention in public, which may without contradiction suffer the report. It was much like an argument that fell 60 out last night, where each of us fell in praise of our country mistresses. This gentleman at that time vouching — and upon warrant of bloody affirmation — his to be more fair, virtuous, wise, chaste, constant-qualified,° and less attemptable than any the rarest of our ladies in France.   66

IACH. That lady is not now living, or this gentleman's opinion, by this,° worn out.

POST. She holds her virtue still, and I my mind.

IACH. You must not so far prefer her 'fore ours of Italy.   71

POST. Being so far provoked as I was in France, I would abate her nothing,° though I profess myself her adorer, not her friend.°

IACH. As fair and as good — a kind of hand- 75 in-hand comparison — had been something too fair and too good for any lady in Britany.° If she went before others I have seen, as that diamond of yours outlusters many I have beheld, I could not but believe she excelled many; but I have not seen 80

Sc. iv: The conversation throughout this scene is in the affected "pregnant" style used by young gallants of the period. **2. crescent note**: growing reputation. **3–4. allowed ... of**: acknowledged. **5. admiration**: gaping wonder. **6. tabled**: tabulated. **10. without ... within**: perfect in body and mind. **12–13. behold ... he**: It was believed that only the eagle — the king of birds — could look straight into the sun. The Frenchman means that there are plenty of others who could compare with Posthumus for excellence. **16–17. words ... matter**: causes him to be slanderously reported. **19–23. approbation ... quality**: the approval of those who sympathize with him for his forced separation from his lady greatly extols (*extends*) his reputation, even if it be only to support her choice; for had she married a lesser man her good name would have been disgraced for choosing a beggar of poor reputation. **24–25. creeps acquaintance**: how does he succeed in creeping into your friendship? **29. suits**: befits.

36. known: been acquainted. **39–40. which ... still**: i.e., however much I repay, I shall always be in your debt. **42. atone**: reconcile. **44. mortal**: deadly. **44–45. importance**: affair. **46–51. I ... slight**: i.e., I was an inexperienced traveler in those days, and I tended to disagree with (*shunned to go even with*) the advice of others rather than be guided by their experiences. Nevertheless, upon further consideration I still hold that it was not an unimportant matter. **52. arbitrement**: decision by mortal combat. **54. confounded**: destroyed. **65. constant-qualified**: endowed with the quality of constancy. **68. by this**: by this time. **73. abate ... nothing**: not allow anything to be taken from her reputation. **74. friend**: lover. **77. Britany**: Britain.

the most precious diamond that is, nor you the lady.°

POST. I praised her as I rated° her: so do I my stone.

IACH. What do you esteem it at?   85

POST. More than the world enjoys.

IACH. Either your unparagoned° mistress is dead, or she's outprized by a trifle.

POST. You are mistaken. The one may be sold or given if there were wealth enough for the   90 purchase or merit for the gift. The other is not a thing for sale, and only the gift of the gods.°

IACH. Which the gods have given you?

POST. Which, by their graces, I will keep.   95

IACH. You may wear her in title° yours. But you know strange fowl light upon neighboring ponds. Your ring may be stolen too. So your brace of unprizable estimations, the one is but frail and the other casual.° A cunning thief or a that way   100 accomplished courtier would hazard the winning both of first and last.

POST. Your Italy contains none so accomplished a courtier to convince° the honor of my   105 mistress, if, in the holding or loss of that, you term her frail. I do nothing doubt you have store of thieves. Notwithstanding, I fear not my ring.

PHI. Let us leave here, gentlemen.   109

POST. Sir, with all my heart. This worthy signior, I thank him, makes no stranger of me. We are familiar at first.

IACH. With five times so much conversation, I should get ground of your fair mistress, make her go back even to the yielding, had I admittance and opportunity to friend.°   116

POST. No, no.

IACH. I dare thereupon pawn the moiety° of my estate to your ring, which in my opinion o'ervalues it something. But I make my wager rather   120 against your confidence than her reputation, and, to bar your offense herein too, I durst attempt it against any lady in the world.

POST. You are a great deal abused° in too bold a persuasion, and I doubt not you sustain what you're worthy of by your attempt.   126

IACH. What's that?

POST. A repulse — though your attempt, as you call it, deserve more, a punishment too.

PHI. Gentlemen, enough of this. It came in too suddenly. Let it die as it was born, and I pray you be better acquainted.   132

IACH. Would I had put my estate and my neighbor's on the approbation° of what I have spoke!

POST. What lady would you choose to assail?   136

IACH. Yours, whom in constancy you think stands so safe. I will lay you ten thousand ducats to your ring that, commend me to the Court where your lady is, with no more advantage than the   140 opportunity of a second conference, and I will bring from thence that honor of hers which you imagine so reserved.

POST. I will wage against your gold, gold to it. My ring I hold dear as my finger. 'Tis part of it.   145

IACH. You are afraid, and therein the wiser. If you buy ladies' flesh at a million a dram, you cannot preserve it from tainting; but I see you have some religion° in you, that you fear.

POST. This is but a custom in your tongue. You bear a graver purpose, I hope.   151

IACH. I am the master of my speeches and would undergo° what's spoken, I swear.

POST. Will you? I shall but lend my diamond till your return. Let there be covenants drawn   155 between 's. My mistress exceeds in goodness the hugeness of your unworthy thinking. I dare you to this match. Here's my ring.

PHI. I will have it no lay.°

IACH. By the gods, it is one. If I bring you   160 no sufficient testimony that I have enjoyed the dearest bodily part of your mistress, my ten thousand ducats are yours; so is your diamond too. If I come off and leave her in such honor as you have trust in, she your jewel, this your jewel, and my gold   165 are yours, provided I have your commendation for my more free entertainment.°

POST. I embrace these conditions. Let us have articles betwixt us. Only, thus far you shall answer: if you make your voyage upon her and give me   170 directly to understand you have prevailed, I am no further your enemy; she is not worth our debate. If she remain unseduced, you not making it appear otherwise, for your ill opinion and the assault you have made to her chastity, you shall answer me with your sword.   176

IACH. Your hand. A covenant. We will have these things set down by lawful counsel,° and straight away for Britain, lest the bargain should catch cold and starve. I will fetch my gold and have our two wagers recorded.   181

POST. Agreed. [*Exeunt* POSTHUMUS *and* IACHIMO.]

FRENCH. Will this hold, think you?

PHI. Signior Iachimo will not from it. Pray let us follow 'em.   [*Exeunt.*]

80–82. but . . . lady: but I have not seen the most precious diamond in the world, nor you the fairest lady.   83. rated: valued.   87. unparagoned: without an equal.   92. only . . . gods: given by the gods alone — and therefore not to be sold or given away.   96. in title: as nominal owner.   100. casual: a matter of chance.   105. convince: overcome.   116. to friend: to help me.   118. moiety: half.   124. abused: deceived.

135. approbation: proof.   149. religion: scruple.   153. undergo: undertake.   159. lay: bet.   166–67. commendation . . . entertainment: your letter that I am to be welcomed.   178. lawful counsel: lawyers.

SCENE V. *Britain. A room in* CYMBELINE'S *palace.*

[*Enter* QUEEN, LADIES, *and* CORNELIUS.]

QUEEN. Whiles° yet the dew's on ground, gather
  those flowers.
Make haste. Who has the note° of them?
  1. LADY.   I, madam.
QUEEN. Dispatch.°   [*Exeunt* LADIES.]
Now, Master Doctor, have you brought those
  drugs?
  COR. Pleaseth your Highness, aye. Here they are,
  madam;   [*Presenting a small box*] 5
But I beseech your grace, without offense —
My conscience bids me ask — wherefore you have
Commanded of me these most poisonous com-
  pounds,
Which are the movers° of a languishing death,
But, though slow, deadly.
  QUEEN.   I wonder, Doctor,   10
Thou ask'st me such a question. Have I not been
Thy pupil long? Hast thou not learned° me how
To make perfumes? Distil? Preserve? Yea, so
That our great King himself doth woo me oft
For my confections?° Having thus far proceeded —
Unless thou think'st me devilish — is 't not meet
That I did amplify my judgment in   17
Other conclusions?° I will try the forces
Of these thy compounds on such creatures as
We count not worth the hanging, but none human,
To try the vigor of them and apply   21
Allayments to their act,° and by them gather
Their several virtues and effects.
  COR.   Your Highness
Shall from this practice but make hard your heart.
Besides, the seeing these effects will be   25
Both noisome and infectious.
  QUEEN.   Oh, content thee.

[*Enter* PISANIO.]

[*Aside*] Here comes a flattering rascal. Upon him
Will I first work. He's for his master,
And enemy to my son. — How now, Pisanio! —
Doctor, your service for this time is ended. 30
Take your own way.
  COR. [*Aside*]   I do suspect you, madam,
But you shall do no harm.
  QUEEN. [*To* PISANIO] Hark thee, a word.
  COR. [*Aside*] I do not like her. She doth think
  she has
Strange lingering poisons. I do know her spirit,
And will not trust one of her malice with   35
A drug of such damned nature. Those she has

Will stupefy and dull the sense awhile,
Which first, perchance, she'll prove on cats and
  dogs,
Then afterward up higher; but there is
No danger in what show of death it makes,   40
More than the locking up the spirits a time,
To be more fresh, reviving. She is fooled
With a most false effect, and I the truer,
So to be false with her.
  QUEEN.   No further service, Doctor,
Until I send for thee.
  COR.   I humbly take my leave. [*Exit.*] 45
  QUEEN. Weeps she still, say'st thou? Dost thou
  think in time
She will not quench° and let instructions enter
Where folly now possesses? Do thou work.
When thou shalt bring me word she loves my son,
I'll tell thee on the instant thou art then   50
As great as is thy master — greater, for
His fortunes all lie speechless, and his name
Is at last gasp. Return he cannot, nor
Continue where he is. To shift his being°
Is to exchange one misery with another,   55
And every day that comes comes to decay
A day's work in him.° What shalt thou expect,
To be depender on a thing that leans,°
Who cannot be new built, nor has no friends,
So much as but to prop him? [*The* QUEEN *drops the
  box.* PISANIO *takes it up.*] Thou takest up   60
Thou know'st not what, but take it for thy labor.
It is a thing I made which hath the King
Five times redeemed from death. I do not know
What is more cordial.° Nay, I prithee take it.
It is an earnest° of a further good   65
That I mean to thee. Tell thy mistress how
The case stands with her. Do 't as from thyself.
Think what a chance thou changest on,° but think
Thou hast thy mistress still, to boot,° my son,
Who shall take notice of thee. I'll move the King
To any shape of thy preferment such   71
As thou'lt desire; and then myself, I chiefly,
That set thee on to this desert, am bound
To load thy merit richly. Call my women.
Think on my words.   [*Exit* PISANIO.]
                    A sly and constant knave, 75
Not to be shaked; the agent for his master,
And the remembrancer° of her to hold
The hand-fast° to her lord. I have given him that
Which, if he take, shall quite unpeople her

Sc. v: 1. Whiles: while. 2. note: list. 3. Dispatch: make
haste. 9. movers: causes. 12. learned: taught. 15. confections: preparations. 17–18. amplify . . . conclusions: increase my knowledge by other experiments. 22. Allayments
. . . act: antidotes.

47. quench: put out, let her love die down. 54. being: place of
living. 56–57. And . . . him: i.e., each day makes his condition
worse. 58. leans: is collapsing. 64. cordial: remedial.
65. earnest: a small payment made on account of the main sum
to come. 68. Think . . . on: think of the good fortune which
will come when you change your loyalty. 69. to boot: in
addition. 77. remembrancer: reminder. 78. hand-fast: trothplight.

Of liegers° for her sweet,° and which she after,   80
Except she bend her humor, shall be assured
To taste of too.
            [*Re-enter* PISANIO *with* LADIES.]
            So, so. Well done, well done.
The violets, cowslips, and the primroses,
Bear to my closet. — Fare thee well, Pisanio.
Think on my words.   [*Exeunt* QUEEN *and* LADIES.]
PIS.   And shall do;   85
But when to my good lord I prove untrue,
I'll choke myself. There's all I'll do for you. [*Exit.*]

SCENE VI. *The same. Another room in the palace.*

            [*Enter* IMOGEN *alone.*]
IMO. A father cruel, and a stepdame false,
A foolish suitor to a wedded lady,
That hath her husband banished. Oh, that husband!
My supreme crown of grief! And those repeated
Vexations of it! Had I been thief-stol'n,   5
As my two brothers, happy! But most miserable
Is the desire that's glorious.° Blest be those,
How mean soe'er, that have their honest wills,
Which seasons comfort.° Who may this be? Fie!
            [*Enter* PISANIO *and* IACHIMO.]
PIS. Madam, a noble gentleman of Rome   10
Comes from my lord with letters.
IACH.   Change you, madam?
The worthy Leonatus is in safety,
And greets your Highness dearly.
            [*Presents a letter.*]
IMO.   Thanks, good sir.
You're kindly welcome.   14
    IACH. [*Aside*] All of her that is out of door° most rich!
If she be furnished with a mind so rare,
She is alone the Arabian bird,° and I
Have lost the wager. Boldness be my friend!
Arm me, Audacity, from head to foot!
Or, like the Parthian, I shall flying fight;°   20
Rather, directly fly.
    IMO. [*Reads.*] "He is one of the noblest note, to
whose kindnesses I am most infinitely tied. Reflect
upon him accordingly, as you value your trust ——
            LEONATUS."   25
So far I read aloud.
But even the very middle of my heart

Is warmed by the rest, and takes it thankfully.
You are as welcome, worthy sir, as I
Have words to bid you, and shall find it so   30
In all that I can do.
IACH.   Thanks, fairest lady.
What, are men mad? Hath nature given them eyes
To see this vaulted arch° and the rich crop
Of sea and land, which can distinguish 'twixt
The fiery orbs above and the twinned stones°   35
Upon the numbered beach,° and can we not
Partition° make with spectacles so precious
'Twixt fair and foul?
IMO.   What makes your admiration?°
IACH. It cannot be i' the eye, for apes and monkeys,   39
'Twixt two such she's, would chatter this way and
Contemn with mows° the other; nor i' the judgment,
For idiots, in this case of favor,° would
Be wisely definite; nor i' the appetite:
Sluttery,° to such neat excellence opposed,
Should make desire vomit emptiness,   45
Not so allured to feed.
IMO. What is the matter, trow?°
IACH.   The° cloyed will° —
That satiate yet unsatisfied desire, that tub
Both filled and running — ravening first the lamb,
Longs after for the garbage.
IMO.   What, dear sir,   50
Thus raps° you? Are you well?
IACH.   Thanks, madam, well.
[*To* PISANIO] Beseech you, sir,
Desire my man's abode° where I did leave him.
He's strange and peevish.°
PIS.   I was going, sir,
To give him welcome.   [*Exit.*]   55
    IMO. Continues well my lord? His health, beseech you?
IACH. Well, madam.
IMO. Is he disposed to mirth? I hope he is.
IACH. Exceeding pleasant; none a stranger there
So merry and so gamesome. He is called   60

---

80. liegers: resident ambassadors — Pisanio being Posthumus's representative in the Court. **sweet:** i.e., husband.
    Sc. vi: 6–7. But . . . glorious: i.e., princesses are most unhappy compared with the lowly. **9. Which . . . comfort:** i.e., honest country folk who find their joys in the produce of the seasons. **15. out of door:** visible, i.e., her physical attributes. **17. Arabian bird:** the phoenix, the symbol of rarity. See *Temp,* III.iii.23,n. **20. Parthian . . . fight:** See *Ant & Cleo,* III.i.1,n.

33. vaulted arch: the sky. **35. twinned stones:** worthless pebbles lying side by side and indistinguishable. **36. numbered beach:** the beach with its innumerable stones. **37. Partition:** distinction. **38. admiration:** excessive wonder. **41. Contemn . . . mows:** show their contempt by grimacing. The gist of Iachimo's feigned "admiration" is that the beauty of Imogen, compared with that of all other women, would move even apes and idiots to excessive wonder. **42. case of favor:** in this matter of beauty. **44–46. Sluttery . . . feed:** i.e., even a slut who hates neatness would be disturbed. Iachimo in his feigned ecstasy raves so much that his words lack grammar and logic. **47. trow:** can you tell me? **47–50. The . . . garbage:** i.e., a lustful man, always unsatisfied, after devouring the innocent victim, goes after filth. See *Haml,* I.v.53–57. This remark is by way of prelude to his vile accusation of Posthumus at ll. 118–35. **47. will:** lust. **51. raps:** makes you so enraptured. **53. abode:** abiding. **54. strange . . . peevish:** a stranger and upset.

The Briton reveler.

IMO.   When he was here
He did incline to sadness, and ofttimes
Not knowing why.

IACH.   I never saw him sad.
There is a Frenchman his companion, one
An eminent monsieur, that, it seems, much loves
A Gallian girl at home. He furnaces   66
The thick sighs° from him, whiles the jolly
          Briton —
Your lord, I mean — laughs from 's free lungs,
          cries, " Oh,
Can my sides hold, to think that man, who knows
By history, report, or his own proof,   70
What woman is — yea, what she cannot choose
But must be — with his free hours languish for
Assurèd° bondage? "°

IMO.   Will my lord say so?
IACH. Aye, madam, with his eyes in flood with
          laughter.
It is a recreation to be by   75
And hear him mock the Frenchman. But, Heavens
          know
Some men are much to blame.

IMO.   Not he, I hope.
IACH. Not he; but yet Heaven's bounty towards
          him might
Be used more thankfully. In himself 'tis much.
In you, which I account his beyond all talents,°
Whilst I am bound to wonder, I am bound   81
To pity too.

IMO.   What do you pity, sir?
IACH. Two creatures heartily.

IMO.   Am I one, sir?
You look on me. What wreck discern you in me
Deserves your pity?

IACH.   Lamentable! What,   85
To hide me from the radiant sun, and solace
I' the dungeon by a snuff?°

IMO.   I pray you, sir,
Deliver with more openness your answers
To my demands. Why do you pity me?

IACH. That others do,   90
I was about to say, enjoy your —— But
It is an office of the gods to venge it,
Not mine to speak on 't.

IMO.   You do seem to know
Something of me, or what concerns me. Pray you —
Since doubting things go ill° often hurts more   95
Than to be sure they do; for certainties
Either are past remedies, or, timely knowing,
The remedy then born — discover° to me

What both you spur and stop.°

IACH.   Had I this cheek   99
To bathe my lips upon; this hand, whose touch,
Whose every touch, would force the feeler's soul
To the oath of loyalty; this object, which
Takes prisoner the wild motion of mine eye,
Fixing it only here; should I, damned then,
Slaver with lips as common° as the stairs   105
That mount the Capitol, join gripes with hands
Made hard with hourly falsehood — falsehood, as
With labor; then by-peeping in an eye
Base and unlustrous as the smoky light
That's fed with stinking tallow? It were fit   110
That all the plagues of Hell should at one time
Encounter such revolt.°

IMO.   My lord, I fear,
Has forgot Britain.

IACH.   And himself. Not I,
Inclined to this intelligence, pronounce   114
The beggary of his change, but 'tis your graces
That from my mutest conscience to my tongue
Charms° this report out.

IMO.   Let me hear no more.
IACH. O dearest soul, your cause doth strike my
          heart
With pity that doth make me sick! A lady
So fair, and fastened to an empery,°   120
Would make the great'st king double to be part-
          nered
With tomboys° hired with that self exhibition
Which your own coffers yield!° With diseased ven-
          tures
That play with all infirmities for gold
Which rottenness can lend nature! Such boiled
          stuff°   125
As well might poison poison! Be revenged,
Or she that bore you was no Queen and you
Recoil from your great stock.

IMO.   Revenged!
How should I be revenged? If this be true —
As I have such a heart that both mine ears   130
Must not in haste abuse — if it be true,
How should I be revenged?

IACH.   Should he make me
Live like Diana's priest,° betwixt cold sheets,
Whiles he is vaulting variable ramps,°
In your despite, upon your purse?° Revenge it.
I dedicate myself to your sweet pleasure,   136

---

99. **spur . . . stop:** keep half revealing and half concealing.
105. **Slaver . . . common:** i.e., foul myself by kissing harlots.
112. **revolt:** disloyalty.   117. **Charms:** bewitches.   120. **empery:** empire.   122. **tomboys:** wantons.   122–23. **hired . . .
yield:** bought with that same (*self*) money (*exhibition*) which you
yourself gave him.   125. **boiled stuff:** creatures from the
venereal hospital, where the disease was treated by hot sweating
baths.   133. **Diana's priest:** Diana was the goddess of chastity.
134. **variable ramps:** a succession of whores.   135. **upon . . .
purse:** at your expense.

66–67. **furnaces . . . sighs:** sighs like a furnace.   73. **Assured
bondage:** the bonds of married life. **Assured:** betrothed.   80. **talents:** riches.   87. **snuff:** smoky candle.   95. **doubting . . . ill:**
suspecting that things are going wrong.   98. **discover:** reveal.

More noble than that runagate° to your bed,
And will continue fast to your affection,
Still close as sure.°

IMO.   What ho, Pisanio!   139
IACH. Let me my service tender on your lips.
IMO. Away! I do condemn mine ears that have
So long attended thee. If thou wert honorable,
Thou wouldst have told this tale for virtue, not
For such an end thou seek'st, as base as strange.
Thou wrong'st a gentleman who is as far   145
From thy report as thou from honor, and
Solicit'st here a lady that disdains
Thee and the Devil alike. What ho, Pisanio!
The King my father shall be made acquainted
Of thy assault. If he shall think it fit   150
A saucy stranger in his Court to mart°
As in a Romish stew,° and to expound
His beastly mind to us, he hath a Court
He little cares for, and a daughter who
He not respects at all. What ho, Pisanio!   155
IACH. O happy Leonatus! I may say
The credit that thy lady hath of thee
Deserves thy trust, and thy most perfect goodness
Her assured credit. Blessed live you long!
A lady to the worthiest stir that ever   160
Country called his, and you his mistress, only
For the most worthiest fit! Give me your pardon.
I have spoke this to know if your affiance°
Were deeply rooted, and shall make your lord
That which he is new o'er;° and he is one   165
The truest mannered, such a holy witch°
That he enchants societies into him.
Half all men's hearts are his.

IMO.   You make amends.
IACH. He sits 'mongst men like a descended god.
He hath a kind of honor sets him off   170
More than a mortal seeming. Be not angry,
Most mighty Princess, that I have adventured
To try your taking of a false report, which hath
Honored with confirmation your great judgment
In the election of a sir so rare,   175
Which you know cannot err. The love I bear him
Made me to fan you thus, but the gods made you,
Unlike all others, chaffless.° Pray your pardon.
IMO. All's well, sir. Take my power i 'the Court
for yours.
IACH. My humble thanks. I had almost forgot
To entreat your Grace but in a small request,   181
And yet of moment too, for it concerns
Your lord. Myself and other noble friends
Are partners in the business.

IMO.   Pray, what is 't?
IACH. Some dozen Romans of us, and your
lord —   185
The best feather of our wing — have mingled sums
To buy a present for the Emperor,
Which I, the factor° for the rest, have done
In France. 'Tis plate of rare device and jewels
Of rich and exquisite form, their values great;   190
And I am something curious,° being strange,°
To have them in safe stowage. May it please you
To take them in protection?

IMO.   Willingly,
And pawn mine honor for their safety. Since
My lord hath interest in them, I will keep them
In my bedchamber.

IACH.   They are in a trunk   196
Attended by my men. I will make bold
To send them to you only for this night.
I must aboard tomorrow.

IMO.   Oh, no, no.   199
IACH. Yes, I beseech, or I shall short my word°
By lengthening my return. From Gallia
I crossed the seas on purpose and on promise
To see your Grace.

IMO.   I thank you for your pains;
But not away tomorrow!

IACH.   Oh, I must, madam.
Therefore I shall beseech you, if you please   205
To greet your lord with writing, do 't tonight.
I have outstood my time, which is material
To the tender of our present.°

IMO.   I will write.
Send your trunk to me. It shall safe be kept
And truly yielded° you. You're very welcome.   210
                                        [*Exeunt.*]

Act II

SCENE I. *Britain. Before* CYMBELINE'S *palace.*

[*Enter* CLOTEN *and two* LORDS.]

CLO. Was there ever man had such luck! When I
kissed the jack, upon an upcast° to be hit away! I
had a hundred pound on 't; and then a whoreson
jackanapes must take me up° for swearing, as if I
borrowed mine oaths of him, and might not spend

---

137. runagate: deserter.   **139. close as sure:** as secret as faithful.   **151. mart:** bargain.   **152. stew:** brothel.   **163. affiance:** confidence.   **165. new o'er:** i.e., even worthier than before.   **166. witch:** The word was used for men as well as women.   **177–78. fan . . . chaffless:** The worthless chaff was separated from the grain by fanning it with a winnowing fan. **chaffless:** without fault.

188. factor: agent.   **191. curious:** anxious, careful. **strange:** a stranger.   **200. short my word:** come short of my promise.   **207–08. material . . . present:** a matter of importance in offering our present to the Emperor.   **210. yielded:** returned.

Act II, Sc. i: **2. jack . . . upcast:** See App. 13. An *upcast* is a throw which drives away the opponent's bowl from the jack. **4. take me up:** rebuke.

them at my pleasure.   6

1. LORD. What got he by that? You have broke his pate° with your bowl.

2. LORD. [*Aside*] If his wit had been like him that broke it, it would have run all out.   10

CLO. When a gentleman is disposed to swear, it is not for any standers-by to curtail his oaths, ha?

2. LORD. No, my lord; [*Aside*] nor crop the ears° of them.   15

CLO. Whoreson dog! I give him satisfaction?° Would he had been one of my rank!

2. LORD. [*Aside*] To have smelt° like a fool.

CLO. I am not vexed more at any thing in the earth. A pox° on 't! I had rather not be so noble as I am. They dare not fight with me because of the Queen my mother. Every Jack-slave hath his bellyful of fighting, and I must go up and down like a cock that nobody can match.   24

2. LORD. [*Aside*] You are cock and capon too, and you crow, cock, with your comb on.°

CLO. Sayest thou?

2. LORD. It is not fit your lordship should undertake every companion° that you give offense to.   30

CLO. No, I know that; but it is fit I should commit offense to my inferiors.

2. LORD. Aye, it is fit for your lordship only.

CLO. Why, so I say.

1. LORD. Did you hear of a stranger that's come to Court tonight?   36

CLO. A stranger, and I not know on 't!

2. LORD. [*Aside*] He's a strange fellow himself, and knows it not.

1. LORD. There's an Italian come, and 'tis thought, one of Leonatus' friends.   41

CLO. Leonatus! a banished rascal; and he's another, whatsoever he be. Who told you of this stranger?

1. LORD. One of your lordship's pages.   45

CLO. Is it fit I went to look upon him? Is there no derogation° in 't?

2. LORD. You cannot derogate, my lord.

CLO. Not easily, I think.   49

2. LORD. [*Aside*] You are a fool granted. Therefore your issues,° being foolish, do not derogate.

CLO. Come, I'll go see this Italian. What I have

lost today at bowls I'll win tonight of him. Come, go.   55

2. LORD. I'll attend your lordship.

              [*Exeunt* CLOTEN *and* FIRST LORD.]

That such a crafty devil as is his mother
Should yield the world this ass! A woman that
Bears all down° with her brain, and this her son
Cannot take two from twenty, for his heart,°   60
And leave eighteen. Alas, poor Princess,
Thou divine Imogen, what thou endurest
Betwixt a father by thy stepdame governed,
A mother hourly coining plots, a wooer
More hateful than the foul expulsion is   65
Of thy dear husband, than that horrid act
Of the divorce he'd make! The Heavens hold firm
The walls of thy dear honor, keep unshaked
That temple, thy fair mind, that thou mayst stand
To enjoy thy banished lord and this great land!

                          [*Exit.*]

SCENE II. IMOGEN's *bedchamber in* CYMBELINE's *palace. A trunk in one corner of it.*

[IMOGEN *in bed, reading, a* LADY *attending.*]

IMO. Who's there? My woman Helen?

LADY.   Please you, madam.

IMO. What hour is it?

LADY.   Almost midnight, madam.

IMO. I have read three hours then. Mine eyes are weak.
Fold down the leaf where I have left. To bed.
Take not away the taper, leave it burning,   5
And if thou canst awake by four o' the clock,
I prithee call me. Sleep hath seized me wholly.

                      [*Exit* LADY.]

To your protection I commend me, gods!
From fairies and the tempters of the night
Guard me, beseech ye!   10

              [*Sleeps.* IACHIMO *comes from the trunk.*]

IACH. The crickets sing, and man's o'erlabored sense
Repairs itself by rest. Our Tarquin° thus
Did softly press the rushes° ere he wakened
The chastity he wounded. Cytherea,°
How bravely thou becomest thy bed! Fresh lily!   15
And whiter than the sheets! That I might touch
But kiss; one kiss! Rubies° unparagoned,°
How dearly they do 't! 'Tis her breathing that
Perfumes the chamber thus. The flame o' the taper
Bows toward her and would underpeep her lids

---

8. **pate**: head.   12–13. **curtail . . . ears**: Cloten uses *curtail* in the sense of "cut short," lit., to cut short the tail of a dog or horse. The 2nd Lord puns on this sense with *crop the ears* — with a suggestion of the punishment given to those who stood in the pillory for perjury and similar offenses.   16. **I . . . satisfaction**: i.e., did he expect me to fight with him?   18. **smelt**: with a pun on Cloten's *rank*, which also means "the coarse scent of a fox."   20. **pox**: lit., venereal disease.   26. **comb on**: i.e., wearing the cockscomb cap of the professional fool. See Pl. 13c.   29–30. **undertake . . . companion**: fight with every low fellow.   47. **51. derogation . . . derogate**: act unbecoming to my rank . . . behave in a degenerate manner.   51. **issues**: actions with secondary meaning of "your children."

59. **Bears . . . down**: subdues all.   60. **for . . . heart**: to save his life.

Sc. ii: 12. **Tarquin**: The story of how Tarquin ravished the chaste Lucrece is told in Shakespeare's *Lucrece*.   13. **rushes**: used as floor covering.   14. **Cytherea**: a title of the goddess Venus.   17. **Rubies**: i.e., Imogen's lips. **unparagoned**: unequaled.

To see the encloséd lights, now canopied   21
Under these windows,° white and azure, laced°
With blue of heaven's own tinct.° But my design —
To note the chamber. I will write all down.
Such and such pictures; there the window; such   25
The adornment of her bed; the arras,° figures,
Why, such and such; and the contents o' the story.
Ah, but some natural notes about her body
Above ten thousand meaner movables°
Would testify to enrich mine inventory.   30
O sleep, thou ape° of death, lie dull upon her,
And be her sense but as a monument,
Thus in a chapel lying! Come off, come off.
                    [*Taking off her bracelet.*]
As slippery as the Gordian knot° was hard!
'Tis mine, and this will witness outwardly,   35
As strongly as the conscience does within,
To the madding of her lord. On her left breast
A mole cinque-spotted,° like the crimson drops°
I' the bottom of a cowslip. Here's a voucher°
Stronger than ever law could make. This secret   40
Will force him think I have picked the lock and
    ta'en
The treasure of her honor. No more. To what end?
Why should I write this down, that's riveted,
Screwed to my memory? She hath been reading
    late
The tale of Tereus. Here the leaf's turned down   45
Where Philomel° gave up. I have enough.
To the trunk again, and shut the spring of it.
Swift, swift, you dragons of the night, that dawning
May bare the raven's eye!° I lodge in fear.
Though this a heavenly angel, Hell is here.   50
                        [*Clock strikes.*]
One, two, three. Time, time!
        [*Goes into the trunk. The scene closes.*]

SCENE III. *An antechamber adjoining*
IMOGEN's *apartments.*

[*Enter* CLOTEN *and* LORDS.]

1. LORD. Your lordship is the most patient man in
loss, the most coldest that ever turned up ace.°
    CLO. It would make any man cold to lose.   4
    1. LORD. But not every man patient after the no-
ble temper of your lordship. You are most hot and
furious when you win.
    CLO. Winning will put any man into courage. If I
could get this foolish Imogen, I should have gold

enough. It's almost morning, is 't not?   10
    1. LORD. Day, my lord.
    CLO. I would this music would come. I am ad-
vised to give her music o' mornings. They say it will
penetrate. [*Enter* MUSICIANS.] Come on. Tune.   14
If you can penetrate her with your fingering, so.
We'll try with tongue too. If none will do, let her
remain, but I'll never give o'er. First, a very excellent good-conceited° thing; after, a wonderful sweet
air, with admirable rich words to it; and then let
her consider.   20

                    SONG

    Hark, hark, the lark at Heaven's gate sings,
        And Phoebus° 'gins arise,
    His steeds to water at those springs
        On chaliced flowers that lies;
    And winking Mary-buds° begin   25
        To ope their golden eyes.
    With every thing that pretty is,
        My lady sweet, arise.
            Arise, arise!   30

    CLO. So, get you gone. If this penetrate, I will
consider your music the better. If it do not, it is a
vice in her ears which horsehairs, and calves' guts,°
nor the voice of unpaved° eunuch to boot, can never
amend.   [*Exeunt* MUSICIANS.]   35
    2. LORD. Here comes the King.
    CLO. I am glad I was up so late, for that's the rea-
son I was up so early. He cannot choose but take
this service I have done fatherly. [*Enter* CYMBELINE
and QUEEN.] Good morrow to your Majesty and to
my gracious Mother.   41
    CYM. Attend you here the door of our stern
        daughter?
Will she not forth?
    CLO. I have assailed her with music, but she
vouchsafes no notice.   45
    CYM. The exile of her minion° is too new.
She hath not yet forgot him. Some more time
Must wear the print of his remembrance out,
And then she's yours.
    QUEEN.   You are most bound to the King,
Who lets go by no vantages that may   50
Prefer° you to his daughter. Frame yourself
To orderly soliciting, and be friended
With aptness of the season.° Make denials
Increase your services. So seem as if
You were inspired to do those duties which   55
You tender to her; that you in all obey her,
Save when command to your dismission tends,°

22. windows: i.e., eyelids. laced: patterned.   23. tinct: color.
26. arras: tapestry hangings. 29. movables: furniture. 31. ape:
imitator. 34. Gordian knot: See *Hen V*, I.i.46,n. 38. cinque-
spotted: with five spots. drops: spots. 39. voucher: guarantee.
45–46. Tereus . . . Philomel: See *T Andr* Intro. p. 295b–96a.
49. bare . . . eye: make the raven open his eye.
    Sc. iii: 3. ace: one — the lowest throw in dice.

18. good-conceited: full of fine fancy. 22. Phoebus: the sun
god. 25. winking Mary-buds: marigolds with shut eyes.
33. horsehairs . . . guts: i.e., fiddle bows and strings. 34. un-
paved: castrated. 46. minion: darling. 51. Prefer: recommend. 52–53. friended . . . season: make the best use of your
chances. 57. Save . . . tends: except when she orders you to
go away.

And therein you are senseless.°
CLO.   Senseless! Not so.
       [*Enter a* MESSENGER.]
MESS. So like° you, sir, ambassadors from Rome.
The one is Caius Lucius.
CYM.   A worthy fellow,   60
Albeit he comes on angry purpose now;
But that's no fault of his. We must receive him
According to the honor of his sender,
And toward himself, his goodness forespent on us,
We must extend our notice.° Our dear Son,   65
When you have given good morning to your mistress,
Attend the Queen and us. We shall have need
To employ you toward this Roman. Come, our
    Queen.   [*Exeunt all but* CLOTEN.]
CLO. If she be up, I'll speak with her. If not,
Let her lie still and dream. By your leave, ho!   70
             [*Knocks.*]
I know her women are about her. What
If I do line one of their hands? 'Tis gold
Which buys admittance. Oft it doth, yea, and makes
Diana's rangers° false° themselves, yield up
Their deer to the stand° o' the stealer; and 'tis gold
Which makes the true man killed and saves the
    thief —   76
Nay, sometime hangs both thief and true man.
    What
Can it not do and undo? I will make
One of her women lawyer to me, for
I yet not understand the case myself.   80
By your leave.   [*Knocks.*]
      [*Enter a* LADY.]
LADY. Who's there that knocks?
CLO.   A gentleman.
LADY.   No more?
CLO. Yes, and a gentlewoman's son.
LADY.   That's more
Than some whose tailors are as dear as yours
Can justly boast of. What's your lordship's pleasure?   85
CLO. Your lady's person. Is she ready?
LADY.   Aye,
To keep her chamber.
CLO.   There is gold for you.
Sell me your good report.
LADY. How! My good name? Or to report of you
What I shall think is good? The Princess!   90
         [*Exit* LADY.]
     [*Enter* IMOGEN.]
CLO. Good morrow, fairest. Sister, your sweet
    hand.

IMO. Good morrow, sir. You lay out too much
    pains
For purchasing but trouble. The thanks I give
Is telling you that I am poor of thanks
And scarce can spare them.
CLO.   Still I swear I love you.   95
IMO. If you but said so, 'twere as deep° with me.
If you swear still, your recompense is still
That I regard it not.
CLO.   This is no answer.
IMO. But that you shall not say I yield being
    silent,   100
I would not speak.° I pray you spare me. Faith,
I shall unfold equal discourtesy
To your best kindness. One of your great knowing°
Should learn, being taught, forbearance.
CLO. To leave you in your madness, 'twere my sin.
I will not.   105
IMO. Fools are not mad folks.
CLO.   Do you call me fool?
IMO. As I am mad, I do.
If you'll be patient, I'll no more be mad.
That cures us both. I am much sorry, sir,
You put me to forget a lady's manners   110
By being so verbal;° and learn now for all
That I, which know my heart, do here pronounce
By the very truth of it I care not for you,
And am so near the lack of charity —
To accuse myself — I hate you, which I had rather
You felt than make 't my boast.
CLO.   You sin against   116
Obedience, which you owe your father. For
The contract you pretend with that base wretch,
One bred of alms and fostered with cold dishes,°
With scraps o' the Court, it is no contract, none;
And° though it be allowed in meaner parties —
Yet who than he more mean? — to knit their souls,
On whom there is no more dependency
But brats and beggary, in self-figured knot,   124
Yet you are curbed from that enlargement° by
The consequence o' the crown, and must not soil
The precious note of it with a base slave,
A hilding for a livery, a squire's cloth,
A pantler, not so eminent.°
IMO.   Profane fellow!
Wert thou the son of Jupiter, and no more   130

---

58. senseless: without perception.   59. like: please.   64–65. And . . . notice: since he was formerly good to us, we must treat him courteously.   74. rangers: foresters, attendants. Diana, the goddess of the chase and chastity, was attended by nymphs. false: betray.   75. stand: standing place. See *LLL,* IV.i.7–8,n.

96. deep: weighty.   100–01. But . . . speak: I only speak because otherwise you would say that my silence gives assent.   103. knowing: intelligence.   111. verbal: full of words.   119. fostered . . . dishes: fed on the leftovers sent down from the high table. 121–24. And . . . knot: common people — and who could be more common than Posthumus — may unite their souls (i.e., marry), but the result will be nothing more than brats and poverty in a union as poor as themselves (*self-figured knot*).   125. enlargement: freedom.   128–29. hilding . . . eminent: a worthless creature, fit only to be a servant and wear the livery of a squire, not even fit to be a pantryman (*pantler*) — one of the lower offices in the household.

But what thou art besides, thou wert too base
To be his groom. Thou wert dignified enough,
Even to the point of envy, if 'twere made
Comparative for° your virtues to be styled
The underhangman of his kingdom and hated   135
For being preferred so well.°

CLO.   The south fog° rot him!
IMO. He never can meet more mischance than
    come
To be but named of thee. His meanest garment,
That ever hath but clipped° his body, is dearer
In my respect° than all the hairs above thee,   140
Were they all made such men. How now, Pisanio!

         [*Enter* PISANIO.]

CLO. "His garment!" Now, the Devil ——
IMO. To Dorothy my woman hie thee pres-
    ently° ——
CLO. "His garment!"
IMO.   I am spirited with° a fool,
Frighted and angered worse. Go bid my woman
Search for a jewel that too casually   146
Hath left mine arm. It was thy master's. 'Shrew
    me°
If I would lose it for a revenue
Of any king's in Europe! I do think
I saw 't this morning. Confident I am   150
Last night 'twas on mine arm. I kissed it.
I hope it be not gone to tell my lord
That I kiss aught but he.
PIS.   'Twill not be lost.
IMO. I hope so. Go and search.   [*Exit* PISANIO.]
CLO.   You have abused me.
" His meanest garment!"
IMO.   Aye, I said so, sir.   155
If you will make 't an action,° call witness to 't.
CLO. I will inform your father.
IMO.   Your mother too.
She's my good lady, and will conceive,° I hope,
But the worst of me. So, I leave you, sir,
To the worst of discontent.   [*Exit.*]
CLO.   I'll be revenged.   160
" His meanest garment!" Well.   [*Exit.*]

SCENE IV. *Rome.* PHILARIO'S *house.*

     [*Enter* POSTHUMUS *and* PHILARIO.]

POST. Fear it not, sir. I would I were so sure
To win the King as I am bold her honor
Will remain hers.
PHI.   What means do you make to him?

POST. Not any, but abide the change of time,
Quake° in the present winter's state, and wish   5
That warmer days would come. In these feared
    hopes,
I barely gratify your love.° They failing,
I must die much your debtor.
PHI. Your very goodness and your company
O'erpays all I can do. By this,° your King   10
Hath heard of great Augustus. Caius Lucius
Will do 's commission throughly.° And I think
He'll grant the tribute, send the arrearages,
Or look upon our Romans, whose remembrance
Is yet fresh in their grief.°
POST.   I do believe,   15
Statist° though I am none, nor like to be,
That this will prove a war, and you shall hear
The legions now in Gallia sooner landed
In our not-fearing Britain than have tidings
Of any penny tribute paid. Our countrymen   20
Are men more ordered° than when Julius Caesar
Smiled at their lack of skill but found their courage
Worthy his frowning° at. Their discipline,
Now mingled with their courages, will make known
To their approvers° they are people such   25
That mend upon the world.

         [*Enter* IACHIMO.]

PHI.   See! Iachimo!
POST. The swiftest harts have posted° you by
    land,
And winds of all the corners kissed your sails,
To make your vessel nimble.
PHI.   Welcome, sir.
POST. I hope the briefness of your answer made
The speediness of your return.
IACH.   Your lady   31
Is one of the fairest that I have looked upon.
POST. And therewithal the best, or let her beauty
Look through a casement° to allure false hearts
And be false with them.
IACH.   Here are letters for you.   35
POST. Their tenor good, I trust.
IACH.   'Tis very like.
PHI. Was Caius Lucius in the Britain Court
When you were there?
IACH.   He was expected then,
But not approached.
POST.   All is well yet.
Sparkles this stone° as it was wont? Or is 't not   40

---

134. Comparative for: corresponding to.   136. preferred so
well: getting such undeserved promotion. south fog: regarded as
bringing fever and misfortune. See *Cor,* I.iv.30,n.   139. clipped:
embraced.   140. respect: estimation.   143. presently: immediately.   144. spirited with: haunted by.   147. 'Shrew me:
beshrew, bad luck to.   156. make 't an action: go to law about
it.   158. conceive: think.

Sc. iv: 5. Quake: shiver.   7. barely . . . love: i.e., I cannot
repay you, but merely pay back love for love.   10. By this:
by this time.   12. throughly: thoroughly.   15. fresh . . . grief:
still painful to them.   16. Statist: statesman.   21. ordered:
disciplined.   23. frowning: anger.   25. approvers: those who
try their worth.   27. swiftest . . . posted: i.e., you must have
ridden on the swiftest of deer to get back so quickly.   34. Look
. . . casement: i.e., like a harlot, encouraging the passers-by.
casement: window opening on a hinge.   40. stone: i.e., the
diamond which is the wager. See I.iv.146–58.

Too dull for your good wearing?
　　IACH.　　　　　　　　If I had lost it,
I should have lost the worth of it in gold.
I'll make a journey twice as far to enjoy
A second night of such sweet shortness which
Was mine in Britain; for the ring is won.　　45
　　POST. The stone's too hard to come by.
　　IACH.　　　　　　　　Not a whit,
Your lady being so easy.
　　POST.　　　　　　Make not, sir,
Your loss your sport. I hope you know that we
Must not continue friends.
　　IACH.　　　　　　Good sir, we must,
If you keep covenant. Had I not brought　　50
The knowledge of your mistress home,° I grant
We were to question farther; but I now
Profess myself the winner of her honor,
Together with your ring, and not the wronger
Of her or you, having proceeded but　　55
By both your wills.
　　POST.　　　　　If you can make 't apparent
That you have tasted her in bed, my hand
And ring is yours. If not, the foul opinion
You had of her pure honor gains or loses
Your sword or mine, or masterless leaves both　　60
To who shall find them.
　　IACH.　　　　　Sir, my circumstances,
Being so near the truth as I will make them,
Must first induce you to believe; whose strength
I will confirm with oath, which I doubt not
You'll give me leave to spare when you shall find
You need it not.°
　　POST.　　　　Proceed
　　IACH.　　　　　First, her bedchamber —　　66
Where, I confess, I slept not, but profess
Had that was well worth watching — it was hanged
With tapestry of silk and silver; the story
Proud Cleopatra, when she met her Roman,　　70
And Cydnus swelled above the banks, or for
The press of boats or pride° — a piece of work
So bravely done, so rich, that it did strive
In workmanship and value, which I wondered
Could be so rarely and exactly wrought,　　75
Since the true life on 't was ——
　　POST.　　　　　　This is true,
And this you might have heard of here, by me,
Or by some other.
　　IACH.　　　　More particulars
Must justify my knowledge.
　　POST.　　　　　　So they must,
Or do your honor injury.
　　IACH.　　　　　　The chimney　　80
Is south the chamber, and the chimney piece,°

Chaste Dian bathing. Never saw I figures
So likely to report themselves.° The cutter
Was as another nature, dumb, outwent her,
Motion and breath left out.°
　　POST.　　　　　　This is a thing　　85
Which you might from relation likewise reap,
Being, as it is, much spoke of.
　　IACH.　　　　　　The roof o' the chamber
With golden cherubins is fretted.° Her andirons —
I had forgot them — were two winking Cupids
Of silver, each on one foot standing, nicely　　90
Depending on their brands.°
　　POST.　　　　　　This is her honor!°
Let it be granted you have seen all this — and
　　praise
Be given to your remembrance — the description
Of what is in her chamber nothing saves
The wager you have laid.
　　IACH. Then, if you can,　[*Showing the bracelet*]
Be pale. I beg but leave to air this jewel. See!　　96
And now 'tis up again. It must be married
To that your diamond. I'll keep them.
　　POST.　　　　　　　Jove!
Once more let me behold it. Is it that
Which I left with her?
　　IACH.　　　　　Sir — I thank her — that.　　100
She stripped it from her arm. I see her yet.
Her pretty action did outsell her gift,
And yet enriched it too. She gave it me
And said she prized it once.
　　POST.　　　　　May be she plucked it off
To send it me.
　　IACH.　　　She writes so to you, doth she?　　105
　　POST. Oh, no, no, no! 'Tis true. Here, take this
　　too.　　　　　　　[*Gives the ring.*]
It is a basilisk° unto mine eye,
Kills me to look on 't. Let there be no honor
Where there is beauty; truth, where semblance;
　　love,　　109
Where there's another man. The vows of women
Of no more bondage be to where° they are made
Than they are to their virtues, which is nothing.
Oh, above measure false!
　　PHI.　　　　　Have patience, sir,
And take your ring again. 'Tis not yet won.
It may be probable she lost it, or　　115
Who knows if one of her women, being corrupted,
Hath stol'n it from her?
　　POST.　　　　　　Very true,
And so, I hope, he came by 't. Back my ring.
Render to me some corporal° sign about her

50–51. Had . . . home: if I had not been intimate with your mistress.　64–66. which . . . not: i.e., my evidence will be so clear that you will not need an oath to confirm it.　70–72. Proud . . . pride: See *Ant & Cleo*, II.ii.191–231.　81. chimney piece: carving on the mantelpiece.

83. likely . . . themselves: almost able to speak.　84–85. outwent . . . out: surpassed nature, except that his figures could not move or speak.　88. fretted: carved.　91. Depending . . . brands: leaning on the logs they support. This . . . honor: so this is all you can produce against her honor.　107. basilisk: See *Rich III*, I.ii.151,n.　111. where: i.e., those to whom they swear.　119. corporal: bodily.

More evident than this; for this was stol'n.   120
  IACH. By Jupiter, I had it from her arm.
  POST. Hark you, he swears; by Jupiter he swears.
'Tis true — nay, keep the ring — 'tis true. I am
    sure
She would not lose it. Her attendants are
All sworn and honorable. They induced to steal it!
And by a stranger! No, he hath enjoyed her.   126
The cognizance° of her incontinency
Is this: She hath bought the name of whore thus
    dearly.
There, take thy hire, and all the fiends of Hell
Divide themselves between you!
  PHI.   Sir, be patient.   130
This is not strong enough to be believed
Of one persuaded well of ——
  POST.   Never talk on 't.
She hath been colted° by him.
  IACH.   If you seek
For further satisfying, under her breast —
Worthy the pressing — lies a mole, right proud   135
Of that most delicate lodging. By my life,
I kissed it, and it gave me present hunger
To feed again, though full. You do remember
This stain upon her?
  POST.   Aye, and it doth confirm
Another stain as big as Hell can hold,   140
Were there no more but it.
  IACH.   Will you hear more?
  POST. Spare your arithmetic. Never count the
    turns.
Once, and a million!
  IACH.   I'll be sworn ——
  POST.   No swearing.
If you will swear you have not done 't, you lie,
And I will kill thee if thou dost deny   145
Thou'st made me cuckold.
  IACH.   I'll deny nothing.
  POST. Oh, that I had her here to tear her limb-
    meal!°
I will go there and do 't, i' the Court, before
Her father. I'll do something ——   [*Exit.*]
  PHI.   Quite besides
The government of patience! You have won.   150
Let's follow him and pervert the present wrath
He hath against himself.
  IACH.   With all my heart. [*Exeunt.*]

SCENE V. *Another room in* PHILARIO'S *house.*

[*Enter* POSTHUMUS.]
  POST. Is there no way for men to be, but women
Must be half-workers?° We are all bastards,

127. cognizance: badge, sign.   133. colted: mounted.   147. limb-
meal: limb from limb.
  Sc. v: 2. half-workers: sharers in procreation.

And that most venerable man which I
Did call my father was I know not where
When I was stamped.° Some coiner with his tools
Made me a counterfeit. Yet my mother seemed   6
The Dian of that time: so doth my wife
The nonpareil of this. Oh, vengeance, vengeance!
Me of my lawful pleasure she restrained,
And prayed me oft forbearance; did it with   10
A pudency° so rosy, the sweet view on 't
Might well have warmed old Saturn,° that I
    thought her
As chaste as unsunned snow. Oh, all the devils!
This yellow° Iachimo in an hour — was 't not? —
Or less — at first? — perchance he spoke not, but
Like a full-acorned boar, a German one,   16
Cried "Oh!" and mounted, found no opposition
But what he looked for should oppose and she
Should from encounter guard. Could I find out
The woman's part in me! For there's no motion°
That tends to vice in man but I affirm   21
It is the woman's part. Be it lying, note it
The woman's; flattering, hers; deceiving, hers;
Lust and rank thoughts, hers, hers; revenges, hers;
Ambitions, covetings, change of prides,° disdain,
Nice° longing, slanders, mutability,   26
All faults that may be named, nay, that Hell knows,
Why, hers, in part or all, but rather all.
For even to vice
They are not constant, but are changing still°   30
One vice, but of a minute old, for one
Not half so old as that. I'll write against them,
Detest them, curse them. Yet 'tis greater skill
In a true hate to pray they have their will.   34
The very devils cannot plague them better. [*Exit.*]

Act III

SCENE I. *Britain. A hall in* CYMBELINE'S *palace.*

[*Enter in state,* CYMBELINE, QUEEN, CLOTEN, *and*
LORDS *at one door, and at another,* CAIUS
LUCIUS *and* ATTENDANTS.]
  CYM. Now say what would Augustus Caesar
    with us?
  LUC. When Julius Caesar, whose remembrance
    yet

5. stamped: coined, begotten.   11. pudency: modesty.   12. Saturn: the father of the god Jupiter, and so the type of old age.
14. yellow: Yellow symbolized various qualities. Here it indicates
"treacherous."   20. motion: inclination.   25. change of prides:
variety of vanities.   26. Nice: capricious.   30. still: continually.

Lives in men's eyes and will to ears and tongues
Be theme and hearing° ever, was in this Britain
And conquered it, Cassibelan, thine uncle° —   5
Famous in Caesar's praises no whit less
Than in his feats deserving it — for him
And his succession granted Rome a tribute,
Yearly three thousand pounds, which by thee lately
Is left untendered.
     QUEEN.   And, to kill the marvel,°   10
Shall be so ever.
     CLO.   There be many Caesars
Ere such another Julius. Britain is
A world by itself, and we will nothing pay
For wearing our own noses.
     QUEEN.   That opportunity
Which then they had to take from 's, to resume   15
We have again. Remember, sir, my liege,°
The Kings your ancestors, together with
The natural bravery of your isle, which stands
As Neptune's park,° ribbed and paled° in   20
With rocks unscalable and roaring waters,
With sands that will not bear your enemies' boats,
But suck them up to the topmast. A kind of con-
          quest
Caesar made here, but made not here his brag
Of " Came, and saw, and overcame."° With
          shame —   24
The first that ever touched him — he was carried
From off our coast, twice beaten, and his ship-
          ping —
Poor ignorant baubles!° — on our terrible seas,
Like eggshells moved upon their surges, cracked
As easily 'gainst our rocks; for joy whereof   29
The famed Cassibelan, who was once at point° —
Oh, giglot° fortune! — to master Caesar's sword,
Made Lud's Town° with rejoicing fires bright
And Britons strut with courage.
     CLO. Come, there's no more tribute to be paid.
Our kingdom is stronger than it was at that   35
time, and, as I said, there is no moe° such Caesars.
Other of them may have crooked° noses, but to
owe° such straight arms, none.
     CYM. Son, let your mother end.
     CLO. We have yet many among us can gripe°   40
as hard as Cassibelan. I do not say I am one, but I
have a hand. Why tribute? Why should we pay
tribute? If Caesar can hide the sun from us with a
blanket or put the moon in his pocket, we will pay

him tribute for light; else, sir, no more tribute,
pray you now.   46
     CYM. You must know,
Till the injurious° Romans did extort
This tribute from us, we were free. Caesar's ambi-
          tion,
Which swelled so much that it did almost stretch
The sides o' the world, against all color° here   51
Did put the yoke upon 's; which to shake off
Becomes a warlike people, whom we reckon
Ourselves to be.
     CLO., LORDS. We do.
     CYM.   Say then to Caesar,
Our ancestor was that Mulmutius° which   55
Ordained our laws, whose use the sword of Caesar
Hath too much mangled, whose repair and fran-
          chise°
Shall, by the power we hold, be our good deed,
Though Rome be therefore angry. Mulmutius made
     our laws,
Who was the first of Britain which did put   60
His brows within a golden crown and called
Himself a King.
     LUC.   I am sorry, Cymbeline,
That I am to pronounce Augustus Caesar —
Caesar, that hath moe kings his servants than
Thyself domestic officers — thine enemy.   65
Receive it from me, then. War and confusion
In Caesar's name pronounce I 'gainst thee. Look
For fury not to be resisted. Thus defied,
I thank thee for myself.
     CYM.   Thou art welcome, Caius.
Thy Caesar knighted me. My youth I spent   70
Much under him. Of him I gathered honor,
Which he to seek of me again, perforce,
Behoves me keep at utterance.° I am perfect°
That the Pannonians and Dalmatians° for
Their liberties are now in arms, a precedent   75
Which not to read° would show the Britons cold.
So Caesar shall not find them.
     LUC.   Let proof speak.
     CLO. His Majesty bids you welcome. Make pas-
time with us a day or two, or longer. If you seek us
afterwards in other terms, you shall find us in our
salt-water girdle. If you beat us out of it, it is yours.
If you fall in the adventure, our crows shall fare the
better for you; and there's an end.   83
     LUC. So, sir.

---

4. **hearing**: story.   5. **uncle**: Cassivelaunus, leader of the resistance against Julius Caesar's second invasion of Britain (54 B.C.).
10. **kill . . . marvel**: end your wonder.   16. **liege**: lord.   19. **park**: enclosure. **ribbed . . . paled**: fenced and enclosed.   24. **Came . . . overcame**: See *II Hen IV*, IV.iii.44,n.   27. **baubles**: toys, trifles.   30. **at point**: just about.   31. **giglot**: wanton.   32. **Lud's Town**: London. According to the legend recorded by Holinshed and others, London was first called Troynovant (New Troy), but afterward renamed Lud's Town as a mark of respect for King Lud.   36. **moe**: more.   37. **crooked**: hooked.   38. **owe**: own.   40. **gripe**: grip.

48. **injurious**: insolent.   51. **color**: reason, justice.   55. **Mulmutius**: according to Holinshed, the first King of Britain to be crowned with a golden crown, indicating that he was a king and not merely a tribal chief.   57. **repair . . . franchise**: i.e., by bringing restitution and freedom to the kingdom founded by Mulmutius.   73. **keep at utterance**: preserve by combat to the death. **perfect**: accurately informed.   74. **Pannonians . . . Dalmatians**: tribes, living on the east shores of the Adriatic Sea, who rebelled against the Romans A.D. 6 and were only subdued after a three years' war.   76. **Which . . . read**: which if neglected.

CYM. I know your master's pleasure, and he
　mine.
All the remain° is "Welcome."　　　　　　[*Exeunt.*]

SCENE II. *Another room in the palace.*

[*Enter* PISANIO, *with a letter.*]

PIS. How! Of adultery? Wherefore write you not
What monster's her accuser? Leonatus!
O master! What a strange infection
Is fall'n into thy ear! What false Italian,
As poisonous-tongued as handed, hath prevailed　5
On thy too ready hearing? Disloyal! No.
She's punished for her truth and undergoes,
More goddesslike than wifelike, such assaults
As would take in some virtue. O my master!
Thy mind to her is now as low as were　　10
Thy fortunes. How! That I should murder her?
Upon the love and truth and vows which I
Have made to thy command? I, her? Her blood?
If it be so to do good service, never
Let me be counted serviceable. How look I,　15
That I should seem to lack humanity
So much as this fact° comes to? [*Reading*]
　　　　　　　　　　　" Do 't. The letter
　That I have sent her, by her own command
　Shall give thee opportunity."
　　　　　　　　　　　Oh, damned paper!
Black as the ink that's on thee! Senseless bauble,　20
Art thou a feodary° for this act, and look'st
So virginlike° without? Lo, here she comes.
I am ignorant in what I am commanded.

[*Enter* IMOGEN.]

IMO. How now, Pisanio!
PIS. Madam, here is a letter from my lord.　25
IMO. Who? Thy lord? That is my Lord Leonatus!
Oh, learned indeed were that astronomer
That knew the stars as I his characters.°
He'd lay the future open. You good gods,
Let what is here contained relish of love,　30
Of my lord's health, of his content, yet not
That we two are asunder. Let that grieve him.
Some griefs are medicinable.° That is one of them,
For it doth physic love. Of his content,
All but in that! Good wax, thy leave.° Blest be　35
You bees that make these locks of counsel!° Lovers
And men in dangerous bonds pray not alike.
Though forfeiters° you cast in prison, yet

You clasp young Cupid's tables.° Good news, gods!
[*Reads.*] "Justice,° and your father's wrath, should
he take me in his dominion, could not be so　41
cruel to me, as you, O the dearest of creatures, would
even renew me with your eyes. Take notice that I
am in Cambria,° at Milford Haven. What your own
love will out of this advise you, follow. So he wishes
you all happiness, that remains loyal to his vow, and
your, increasing in love,
　　　　　　LEONATUS POSTHUMUS."　49
Oh, for a horse with wings! Hear'st thou, Pisanio?
He is at Milford Haven. Read, and tell me
How far 'tis thither. If one of mean affairs°
May plod it in a week, why may not I
Glide thither in a day? Then, true Pisanio —　54
Who long'st, like me, to see thy lord; who long'st —
Oh, let me bate° — but not like me — yet long'st,
But in a fainter kind — oh, not like me,
For mine's beyond beyond. Say, and speak
　　thick° —
Love's counselor should fill the bores of hearing
To the smothering of the sense — how far it is　60
To this same blessèd Milford; and by the way
Tell me how Wales was made so happy as
To inherit such a haven. But, first of all,
How we may steal from hence, and for the gap　64
That we shall make in time from our hence-going
And our return to excuse; but first, how get hence.
Why should excuse be born or ere begot?
We'll talk of that hereafter. Prithee speak
How many score of miles may we well ride
'Twixt hour and hour?
PIS.　　　　　One score 'twixt sun and sun,　70
Madam, 's enough for you, and too much too.
IMO. Why, one that rode to 's execution, man,
Could never go so slow. I have heard of riding
　wagers,
Where horses have been nimbler than the sands
That run i' the clock's behalf. But this is foolery.
Go bid my woman feign a sickness, say　　76
She'll home to her father, and provide me presently
A riding suit no costlier than would fit
A franklin's° housewife.
PIS.　　　　　Madam, you're best consider.
IMO. I see before me,° man, nor here, nor here,
Nor what ensues, but have a fog in them　　81
That I cannot look through. Away, I prithee.
Do as I bid thee. There's no more to say.
Accessible is none but Milford way.°　　[*Exeunt.*]

86. remain: for the rest, so far as you yourself are concerned.
　Sc. ii: 17. fact: deed.　21. feodary: confederate, accessory.
22. virginlike° white.　28. characters: handwriting.　33. medicinable: good for health.　35. Good . . . leave: See App. 6: Letters.　36. locks of counsel: safeguards of secrets; i.e., wax seals.　38. forfeiters: those who seal bonds and forfeit them.

39. tables: writing book.　40–43. Justice . . . eyes: i.e., if only I could see you again, it would recompense me for all that your father could do to me.　44. Cambria: Wales.　52. mean affairs: humble business.　56. bate: abate; i.e., your longing cannot be as strong as mine.　58. thick: fast — with the words all running together.　79. franklin: farmer.　80. I . . . me: I look straight ahead.　84. Accessible . . . way: the road to Milford is the only road for me.

SCENE III. *Wales; a mountainous country with a cave.*

[*Enter* BELARIUS, GUIDERIUS, *and* ARVIRAGUS.]

BEL. A goodly day not to keep house with such
Whose roof's as low as ours!° Stoop, boys. This gate
Instructs you how to adore the Heavens,° and bows
    you
To a morning's holy office.° The gates of monarchs
Are arched so high that giants may jet° through   5
And keep their impious turbans on without
Good morrow to the sun. Hail, thou fair Heaven!
We house i' the rock, yet use thee not so hardly
As prouder livers do.

GUI.   Hail, Heaven!

ARV.   Hail, Heaven!

BEL. Now for our mountain sport. Up to yond
    hill!   10
Your legs are young. I'll tread these flats. Consider,
When you above perceive me like a crow,
That it is place which lessens and sets off;°
And you may then revolve what tales I have told
    you
Of courts, of princes, of the tricks in war.   15
This service is not service, so being done,
But being so allowed.° To apprehend thus
Draws us a profit from all things we see,
And often, to our comfort, shall we find
The sharded° beetle in a safer hold   20
Than is the full-winged eagle. Oh, this life
Is nobler than attending for a check,°
Richer than doing nothing for a bauble,
Prouder than rustling in unpaid-for silk.
Such gain the cap° of him that makes 'em fine,   25
Yet keeps his book uncrossed° — no life to ours.

GUI. Out of your proof° you speak. We, poor un-
    fledged,
Have never winged from view o' the nest, nor
    know not
What air's from home. Haply° this life is best
If quiet life be best, sweeter to you   30
That have a sharper known, well corresponding
With your stiff age. But unto us it is

A cell of ignorance, traveling abed,°
A prison for a debtor that not dares
To stride a limit.°

ARV.   What should we speak of   35
When we are old as you? When we shall hear
The rain and wind beat dark December, how
In this our pinching cave shall we discourse
The freezing hours away? We have seen nothing.
We are beastly,° subtle as the fox for prey,   40
Like warlike as the wolf for what we eat.
Our valor is to chase what flies. Our cage
We make a choir as doth the prisoned bird,
And sing our bondage freely.

BEL.   How you speak!
Did you but know the city's usuries,   45
And felt them knowingly; the art o' the Court,
As hard to leave as keep, whose top to climb
Is certain falling, or so slippery that
The fear's as bad as falling; the toil o' the war,
A pain° that only seems to seek out danger   50
I' the name of fame and honor, which dies i' the
    search,
And hath as oft a slanderous epitaph
As record of fair act, nay, many times,
Doth ill deserve by doing well; what's worse,   54
Must curtsy at the censure.° Oh, boys, this story
The world may read in me. My body's marked
With Roman swords, and my report was once
First with the best of note. Cymbeline loved me,
And when a soldier was the theme, my name
Was not far off. Then was I as a tree   60
Whose boughs did bend with fruit, but in one night,
A storm, or robbery, call it what you will,
Shook down my mellow hangings, nay, my leaves,
And left me bare to weather.

GUI.   Uncertain favor!

BEL. My fault being nothing, as I have told you
    oft,   65
But that two villains, whose false oaths prevailed
Before my perfect honor, swore to Cymbeline
I was confederate with the Romans. So
Followed my banishment, and this twenty years
This rock and these demesnes° have been my
    world,   70
Where I have lived at honest freedom, paid
More pious debts to Heaven than in all
The fore-end° of my time. But up to the moun-
    tains!
This is not hunters' language. He that strikes
The venison first shall be the lord o' the feast.   75
To him the other two shall minister,
And we will fear no poison, which attends
In place of greater state. I'll meet you in the valleys.

Sc. iii: 1–2. A . . . ours: i.e., it's too fine a day for us to stay in our humble cave.   2–3. gate . . . Heavens: i.e., by having to stoop low to enter the cave you learn to bow to the gods.   4. office: service, worship.   5. jet: strut.   11–13. Consider . . . off: reflect, when from high above I seem as small as a crow, that the difference between one man and another is just a matter of where each is standing.   17. allowed: admitted; i.e., service is only accounted as good as it is acknowledged; its true worth is of no value.   20. sharded: having hard shiny wings.   22. attending . . . check: waiting in attendance merely to be snubbed.   25. gain . . . cap: win the obsequious flattery. See App. 7.   26. book uncrossed: with the debt still not canceled. Debts were recorded in the lender's book and signed by the debtor. When the debt was paid, the entry was crossed off.   27. proof: experience.   29. Haply: perhaps.

33. traveling abed: mere dreaming.   35. stride a limit: venture boldly.   40. beastly: as ignorant as beasts.   50. pain: labor.   55. curtsy . . . censure: receive rebukes with a bow.   70. demesnes: domains, territory.   73. fore-end: first part.

[*Exeunt* GUIDERIUS *and* ARVIRAGUS.]
How hard it is to hide the sparks of nature!
These boys know little they are sons to the King,
Nor Cymbeline dreams that they are alive.   81
They think they are mine, and though trained up
 thus meanly
I' the cave wherein they bow, their thoughts do hit
The roofs of palaces, and nature prompts them
In simple and low things to prince it much   85
Beyond the trick of others. This Polydore,
The heir of Cymbeline and Britain, who
The King his father called Guiderius — Jove!
When on my three-foot° stool I sit and tell
The warlike feats I have done, his spirits fly out 90
Into my story. Say " Thus mine enemy fell,
And thus I set my foot on 's neck "; even then
The princely blood flows in his cheek, he sweats,
Strains his young nerves, and puts himself in pos-
 ture   94
That acts my words. The younger brother, Cadwal,
Once Arviragus, in as like a figure
Strikes life into my speech and shows much more
His own conceiving.° Hark, the game is roused!
O Cymbeline! Heaven and my conscience knows
Thou didst unjustly banish me; whereon,   100
At three and two years old, I stole these babes,
Thinking to bar thee of succession° as
Thou reft'st me of my lands. Euriphilé,
Thou wast their nurse. They took thee for their
 mother,
And every day do honor to her grave.   105
Myself, Belarius, that am Morgan called,
They take for natural father. The game is up.
          [*Exit.*]

SCENE IV. *Country near Milford Haven.*

[*Enter* PISANIO *and* IMOGEN.]

IMO. Thou told'st me, when we came from
 horse,° the place
Was near at hand. Ne'er longed my mother so
To see me first, as I have now. Pisanio! Man!
Where is Posthumus? What is in thy mind,
That makes thee stare thus? Wherefore breaks that
 sigh   5
From the inward of thee? One but painted thus
Would be interpreted a thing perplexed
Beyond self-explication.° Put thyself
Into a havior of less fear, ere wildness°
Vanquish my staider senses. What's the matter? 10
Why tender'st° thou that paper to me with

A look untender? If 't be summer news,
Smile to 't before, if winterly, thou need'st
But keep that countenance still. My husband's
 hand!   14
That drug-damned° Italy hath outcraftied° him,
And he's at some hard point.° Speak, man. Thy
 tongue
May take off some extremity, which to read
Would be even mortal° to me.
 PIS.   Please you, read,
And you shall find me, wretched man, a thing
The most disdained of fortune.   20
 IMO. [*Reads*] " Thy mistress, Pisanio, hath played
the strumpet in my bed, the testimonies whereof lie
bleeding in me. I speak not out of weak surmises,
but from proof as strong as my grief and as 25
certain as I expect my revenge. That part thou, Pisanio, must act for me if thy faith be not tainted with
the breach of hers. Let thine own hands take away
her life. I shall give thee opportunity at Milford
Haven. She hath my letter for the purpose; 30
where, if thou fear to strike, and to make me certain it is done, thou art the pander° to her dishonor,
and equally to me disloyal."
 PIS. What shall I need to draw my sword? The
 paper
Hath cut her throat already. No, 'tis Slander, 35
Whose edge is sharper than the sword, whose
 tongue
Outvenoms all the worms° of Nile, whose breath
Rides on the posting° winds and doth belie
All corners of the world. Kings, queens, and
 states,°
Maids, matrons, nay, the secrets of the grave 40
This viperous Slander enters. — What cheer,
 madam?
 IMO. False to his bed! What is it to be false?
To lie in watch° there, and to think on him?
To weep 'twixt clock and clock? If sleep charge°
 nature,
To break it with a fearful dream of him 45
And cry myself awake? That's false to 's bed, is it?
 PIS. Alas, good lady!
 IMO. I false! Thy conscience witness. Iachimo,
Thou didst accuse him of incontinency.
Thou then look'dst like a villain; now, methinks,
Thy favor's° good enough. Some jay° of Italy 51
Whose mother was her painting° hath betrayed
 him.

---

89. three-foot: three-legged. **98. conceiving:** imagination.
102. bar . . . succession: deprive you of heirs.
 Sc. iv: **1. came . . . horse:** dismounted from our horses.
8. self-explication: explanation. **9. wildness:** madness.
11. tender'st: offerest.

15. drug-damned: damned for its poisonings. Italians were
believed to be capable of any villainy. **outcraftied:** overcome
him by some subtle trick. **16. at . . . point:** in extreme difficulty.
18. mortal: deadly. **32. pander:** one who procures customers
for a whore. See *Tr & Cr.* **37. worms:** serpents. See *Ant &
Cleo,* V.ii.241–81. **38. posting:** traveling fast. **39. states:**
statesmen. **43. watch:** wakefulness. **44. charge:** overcome.
51. favor: face. **jay:** harlot. **52. Whose . . painting:** who was
taught to beautify herself from her babyhood.

Poor I am stale,° a garment out of fashion;
And, for I am richer than to hang by the walls,
I must be ripped.° To pieces with me! Oh,   55
Men's vows are women's traitors! All good seeming,
By thy revolt, O Husband, shall be thought
Put on for villainy,° not born where 't grows,
But worn a bait for ladies.
    PIS.   Good madam, hear me.
    IMO. True honest men being heard, like false
      Aeneas,°   60
Were in his time thought false, and Sinon's°
      weeping
Did scandal many a holy tear, took pity
From most true wretchedness: so thou Posthumus,
Wilt lay the leaven° on all proper° men.
Goodly and gallant shall be false and perjured 65
From thy great fail. Come, fellow, be thou honest.
Do thou thy master's bidding. When thou see'st
    him,
A little witness my obedience. Look!
I draw the sword myself. Take it, and hit
The innocent mansion of my love, my heart.   70
Fear not. 'Tis empty of all things but grief.
Thy master is not there, who was indeed
The riches of it. Do his bidding. Strike.
Thou mayst be valiant in a better cause,
But now thou seem'st a coward.
    PIS.   Hence, vile instrument! 75
Thou shalt not damn my hand.
    IMO.   Why, I must die,
And if I do not by thy hand, thou art
No servant of thy master's. Against self-slaughter
There is a prohibition so divine
That cravens° my weak hand. Come, here's my
    heart —   80
Something's afore 't. Soft, soft! We'll no defense —
Obedient as the scabbard. What is here?
The scriptures of the loyal Leonatus,
All turned to heresy? Away, away,
Corrupters of my faith! You shall no more   85
Be stomachers° to my heart. Thus may poor fools
Believe false teachers. Though those that are be-
    trayed
Do feel the treason sharply, yet the traitor
Stands in worse case of woe.
And thou, Posthumus, thou that didst set up   90
My disobedience 'gainst the King my father,
And make me put into contempt the suits

Of princely fellows,° shalt hereafter find
It is no act of common passage,° but
A strain of rareness; and I grieve myself   95
To think, when thou shalt be disedged° by her
That now thou tirest° on, how thy memory
Will then be panged° by me. Prithee dispatch.
The lamb entreats the butcher. Where's thy knife?
Thou art too slow to do thy master's bidding, 100
When I desire it too.
    PIS.   Oh, gracious lady,
Since I received command to do this business
I have not slept one wink.
    IMO.   Do 't, and to bed then.
    PIS. I'll wake mine eyeballs blind first.
    IMO.   Wherefore then
Didst undertake it? Why hast thou abused°   105
So many miles with a pretense?° This place?
Mine action, and thine own? Our horses' labor?
The time inviting thee? The pérturbed Court,
For my being absent? Whereunto I never
Purpose return. Why hast thou gone so far   110
To be unbent when thou hast ta'en thy stand,
The elected deer° before thee?
    PIS.   But to win time
To lose so bad employment, in the which
I have considered of a course. Good lady,
Hear me with patience.
    IMO.   Talk thy tongue weary. Speak. 115
I have heard I am a strumpet, and mine ear,
Therein false struck, can take no greater wound,
Nor tent° to bottom that. But speak.
    PIS.   Then, madam.
I thought you would not back again.
    IMO.   Most like,
Bringing me here to kill me.
    PIS.   Not so, neither. 120
But if I were as wise as honest, then
My purpose would prove well. It cannot be
But that my master is abused. Some villain,
Aye, and singular° in his art, hath done you both
This cursed injury.   125
    IMO. Some Roman courtesan.
    PIS.   No, on my life.
I'll give but notice you are dead, and send him
Some bloody sign of it; for 'tis commanded
I should do so. You shall be missed at Court,
And that will well confirm it.
    IMO.   Why, good fellow, 130
What shall I do the while? Where bide? How live?
Or in my life what comfort, when I am
Dead to my husband?
    PIS.   If you'll back to the Court ——

---

53. stale: out of date.   **54–55. for . . . ripped:** I am too good
material to be left hanging on the wall; I must be cut up.
Imogen is here almost hysterical in her grief and so not wholly
coherent.   **56–58. All . . . villainy:** hereafter, when a man appears honorable, it will be thought that he is pretending for his
own evil purposes.   **60. false Aeneas:** See *Temp*, II.i.76,n.
61. Sinon's: See *III Hen VI*, III.ii.190,n.   **64. leaven:** that
which causes a substance to ferment and go rotten. **proper:**
handsome.   **80. cravens:** makes cowardly.   **86. stomachers:**
protectors. See Pl. 3b, and Note on Women's Costume, p. 94b.

93. fellows: equals — not commoners, like Posthumus.   **94. passage:** occurrence.   **96. disedged:** have taken off the edge of
your appetite.   **97. tirest:** feedest greedily on.   **98. panged;**
pained.   **105. abused:** wasted.   **106. pretense:** a plan that you
never intended to carry out.   **112. elected deer:** selected victim.
118. tent: probe. See *Cor*, I.ix.31,n.   **124. singular:** expert.

IMO. No Court, no father, nor no more ado
With that harsh, noble, simple nothing,   135
That Cloten, whose love suit hath been to me
As fearful as a siege.
   PIS.   If not at Court,
Then not in Britain must you bide.
   IMO.   Where then?
Hath Britain all the sun that shines? Day, night,
Are they not but in Britain? I' the world's volume
Our Britain seems as of it, but not in 't;   141
In a great pool a swan's nest. Prithee think
There's livers° out of Britain.
   PIS.   I am most glad
You think of other place. The ambassador,
Lucius the Roman, comes to Milford Haven   145
Tomorrow. Now, if you could wear a mind
Dark as your fortune is and but disguise
That which to appear itself must not yet be
But by self-danger, you should tread a course°
Pretty and full of view,° yea, haply, near   150
The residence of Posthumus; so nigh at least
That though his actions were not visible, yet
Report should render him hourly to your ear
As truly as he moves.
   IMO.   Oh, for such means,
Though peril to my modesty, not death on 't,   155
I would adventure!
   PIS.   Well then, here's the point:
You must forget to be a woman. Change
Command into obedience, fear and niceness —
The handmaids of all women, or, more truly,   159
Woman it pretty self — into a waggish courage,
Ready in gibes, quick-answered, saucy, and
As quarrelous as the weasel; nay, you must
Forget° that rarest treasure of your cheek,
Exposing it — but, oh, the harder heart!
Alack, no remedy! — to the greedy touch   165
Of common-kissing Titan, and forget
Your laborsome and dainty trims,° wherein
You made great Juno angry.°
   IMO.   Nay, be brief.
I see into thy end, and am almost
A man already.
   PIS.   First, make yourself but like one.   170
Fore-thinking this, I have already fit —
'Tis in my cloak-bag — doublet, hat, hose,° all
That answer to them. Would you, in their serving°
And with what imitation you can borrow
From youth of such a season,° 'fore noble Lucius

Present yourself, desire his service, tell him   176
Wherein you're happy° — which you'll make him know
If that his head have ear in music — doubtless
With joy he will embrace you; for he's honorable,
And, doubling that, most holy. Your means abroad
— You have me, rich,° and I will never fail   181
Beginning nor supplyment.°
   IMO.   Thou art all the comfort
The gods will diet me with. Prithee away.
There's more to be considered, but we'll even°
All that good time will give us. This attempt   185
I am soldier to, and will abide it with
A prince's courage. Away, I prithee.
   PIS. Well, madam, we must take a short farewell,
Lest, being missed, I be suspected of   189
Your carriage from the Court. My noble mistress,
Here is a box. I had it from the Queen.°
What's in 't is precious. If you are sick at sea
Or stomach-qualmed° at land, a dram of this
Will drive away distemper.° To some shade,
And fit you to your manhood. May the gods   195
Direct you to the best!
   IMO. Amen. I thank thee.   [*Exeunt severally.*°]

SCENE V. *A room in* CYMBELINE'S *palace.*

[*Enter* CYMBELINE, QUEEN, CLOTEN, LUCIUS, *and*
LORDS.]

   CYM. Thus far, and so farewell.
   LUC.   Thanks, royal sir.
My Emperor hath wrote I must from hence,
And am right sorry that I must report ye
My master's enemy.
   CYM.   Our subjects, sir,
Will not endure his yoke, and for ourself   5
To show less sovereignty than they, must needs
Appear unkinglike.
   LUC.   So, sir. I desire of you
A conduct° overland to Milford Haven.
Madam, all joy befall your Grace and you!
   CYM. My lords, you are appointed for that office.
The due of honor in no point omit.   11
So farewell, noble Lucius.
   LUC.   Your hand, my lord.
   CLO. Receive it friendly, but from this time forth
I wear it as your enemy.
   LUC.   Sir, the event°

---

143. **livers:** people who live.   149. **tread a course:** follow a path.   150. **Pretty . . . view:** i.e., giving you a full view of what is going on.   163–66. **Forget . . . Titan:** expose your delicate complexion to the sun (*Titan*).   167. **laborsome . . . trims:** the labor which you spend on making yourself pretty.   168. **Juno angry:** make the Queen of Heaven jealous.   172. **doublet . . . hose:** See Note on Men's Costume, p. 93a.   173. **in . . . serving:** with their help.   175 **such a season:** of the age and rank of the clothes.

177. **happy:** lucky, clever; i.e., in singing.   180–81. **Your . . . rich:** you have me to keep you richly supplied with money.   182. **supplyment:** continued supply.   184. **even:** keep up with.   191. **box . . . Queen:** See I.v.60–66.   193. **stomach-qualmed:** have a feeling of nausea.   194. **distemper:** illness.   196. **s.d., severally:** by separate exits.

Sc. v: 8. **conduct:** escort.   14. **event:** sequel, what happens next.

Is yet to name the winner. Fare you well.   15
    CYM. Leave not the worthy Lucius, good my
      lords,
Till he have crossed the Severn.° Happiness!
              [*Exeunt* LUCIUS *and* LORDS.]
    QUEEN. He goes hence frowning, but it honors us
That we have given him cause.
    CLO.   'Tis all the better.
Your valiant Britons have their wishes in it.   20
    CYM. Lucius hath wrote already to the Emperor
How it goes here. It fits us therefore ripely°
Our chariots and our horsemen be in readiness.
The powers° that he already hath in Gallia°
Will soon be drawn to head, from whence he
      moves   25
His war for Britain.
    QUEEN.   'Tis not sleepy business°
But must be looked to speedily and strongly.
    CYM. Our expectation that it would be thus
Hath made us forward.° But, my gentle Queen,
Where is our daughter? She hath not appeared   30
Before the Roman, nor to us hath tendered
The duty of the day. She looks us like°
A thing more made of malice than of duty.
We have noted it. Call her before us, for
We have been too slight in sufferance.°
              [*Exit an* ATTENDANT.]
    QUEEN.   Royal sir,   35
Since the exile of Posthumus, most retired
Hath her life been, the cure whereof, my lord,
'Tis time must do. Beseech your Majesty,
Forbear sharp speeches to her. She's a lady
So tender of rebukes that words are strokes,   40
And strokes death to her.
             [*Re-enter* ATTENDANT.]
    CYM.   Where is she, sir? How
Can her contempt be answered?
    ATTEN.   Please you, sir,
Her chambers are all locked, and there's no answer
That will be given to the loud'st of noise we make.
    QUEEN. My lord, when last I went to visit her,
She prayed me to excuse her keeping close;   46
Whereto constrained by her infirmity,
She should that duty leave unpaid to you
Which daily she was bound to proffer. This
She wished me to make known, but our great Court
Made me to blame in memory.
    CYM.   Her doors locked?   51
Not seen of late? Grant, Heavens, that which I fear
Prove false!   [*Exit.*]
    QUEEN. Son, I say, follow the King.
    CLO. That man of hers, Pisanio, her old servant,

I have not seen these two days.
    QUEEN.   Go, look after. [*Exit* CLOTEN.]   55
Pisanio, thou that stand'st so° for Posthumus!
He hath a drug of mine. I pray his absence
Proceed by swallowing that, for he believes
It is a thing most precious. But for her,
Where is she gone? Haply, despair hath seized her,
Or, winged with fervor of her love, she's flown   61
To her desired Posthumus. Gone she is
To death or to dishonor, and my end
Can make good use of either. She being down,
I have the placing of the British crown.   65
             [*Re-enter* CLOTEN.]
How now, my Son!
    CLO.   'Tis certain she is fled.
Go in and cheer the King. He rages. None
Dare come about him.
    QUEEN. [*Aside*]   All the better. May   68
This night forestall him of the coming day!° [*Exit.*]
    CLO. I love and hate her. For she's fair and royal,
And that she hath all courtly parts more exquisite
Than lady, ladies, woman. From every one
The best she hath, and she, of all compounded,
Outsells them all. I love her therefore. But
Disdaining me and throwing favors on   **75**
The low Posthumus slanders so her judgment
That what's else rare is choked; and in that point
I will conclude to hate her — nay, indeed,
To be revenged upon her. For when fools
Shall ——
             [*Enter* PISANIO.]
Who is here? What, are you packing,° sirrah?°   80
Come hither. Ah, you precious pander! Villain,
Where is thy lady? In a word, or else
Thou art straightway with the fiends.
    PIS.   Oh, good my lord!
    CLO. Where is thy lady? Or, by Jupiter —
I will not ask again. Close° villain,   85
I'll have this secret from thy heart, or rip
Thy heart to find it. Is she with Posthumus?
From whose so many weights of baseness cannot
A dram° of worth be drawn.
    PIS.   Alas, my lord,
How can she be with him? When was she missed?
He is in Rome.
    CLO.   Where is she, sir? Come nearer.   91
No farther halting. Satisfy me home°
What is become of her.
    PIS. Oh, my all-worthy lord!
    CLO.   All-worthy villain!
Discover where thy mistress is at once,   95
At the next word. No more of " worthy lord! "

---

17. **Severn:** the river dividing England from Wales.   22. **fits
. . . ripely:** is time that.   24. **powers:** forces. **Gallia:** France.
26. **sleepy business:** a time to be leisurely.   29. **forward:**
prepared.   32. **looks us like:** seems to be.   35. **too . . . sufferance:** too easy going.

56. **stand'st so:** art so firm a support.   69. **forestall . . . day:**
may he die this night.   80. **packing:** conspiring. **sirrah:** a term
used to an inferior.   85. **Close:** secretive.   89. **dram:** the smallest weight, lit., one-sixteenth of an ounce.   92. **home:** thoroughly.

Speak, or thy silence on the instant is
Thy condemnation and thy death.
     PIS.   Then, sir,
This paper° is the history of my knowledge
Touching her flight.   [*Presenting a letter.*]
     CLO.   Let's see 't. I will pursue her   100
Even to Augustus' throne.
     PIS. [*Aside*]   Or° this, or perish.
She's far enough, and what he learns by this
May prove his travel,° not her danger.
     CLO.   Hum!
     PIS. [*Aside*] I'll write to my lord she's dead. O
    Imogen,
Safe mayst thou wander, safe return again!   105
     CLO. Sirrah, is this letter true?
     PIS. Sir, as I think.
     CLO. It is Posthumus' hand. I know 't. Sirrah, if
thou wouldst not be a villain, but do me true service, undergo those employments wherein I   110
should have cause to use thee with a serious industry, that is, what villainy soe'er I bid thee do, to perform it directly and truly, I would think thee an
honest man. Thou shouldst neither want my means
for thy relief, nor my voice for thy preferment.   116
     PIS. Well, my good lord.
     CLO. Wilt thou serve me? For° since patiently and
constantly thou hast stuck to the bare fortune of
that beggar Posthumus, thou canst not, in the   120
course of gratitude, but be a diligent follower of
mine. Wilt thou serve me?
     PIS. Sir, I will.
     CLO. Give me thy hand. Here's my purse. Hast
any of thy late master's garments in thy possession?   125
     PIS. I have, my lord, at my lodging the same suit
he wore when he took leave of my lady and mistress.
     CLO. The first service thou dost me, fetch that
suit hither. Let it be thy first service. Go.   130
     PIS. I shall, my lord.   [*Exit.*]
     CLO. Meet thee at Milford Haven — I forgot to
ask him one thing; I'll remember 't anon — even
there, thou villain Posthumus, will I kill thee. I
would these garments were come. She said   135
upon a time — the bitterness of it I now belch from
my heart — that she held the very garment of Posthumus in more respect than my noble and natural
person, together with the adornment of my   140
qualities. With that suit upon my back, will I ravish her; first kill him, and in her eyes. There shall
she see my valor, which will then be a torment to
her contempt. He on the ground, my speech of in-

sultment ended on his dead body, and when   145
my lust hath dined — which, as I say, to vex her I
will execute in the clothes that she so praised — to
the Court i'll knock her back, foot her home again.
She hath despised me rejoicingly, and I'll be merry
in my revenge. [*Re-enter* PISANIO, *with the clothes.*]
Be those the garments?   151
     PIS. Aye, my noble lord.
     CLO. How long is 't since she went to Milford
Haven?
     PIS. She can scarce be there yet.   155
     CLO. Bring this apparel to my chamber. That is
the second thing that I have commanded thee. The
third is that thou wilt be a voluntary mute to my
design. Be but duteous, and true preferment shall
tender itself to thee. My revenge is now at Milford.
Would I had wings to follow it! Come, and be true.
                                 [*Exit.*]
     PIS. Thou bid'st me to my loss; for, true to thee
Were to prove false, which I will never be,
To him that is most true. To Milford go,   165
And find not her whom thou pursuest. Flow, flow,
You heavenly blessings, on her! This fool's speed
Be crossed° with slowness; labor be his meed!°
                                 [*Exit.*]

SCENE VI. *Wales, before the cave of* BELARIUS.

[*Enter* IMOGEN, *in boy's clothes.*]
     IMO. I see a man's life is a tedious one.
I have tired myself, and for two nights together
Have made the ground my bed. I should be sick,
But that my resolution helps me. Milford,
When from the mountain top Pisanio showed thee,
Thou wast within a ken.° Oh, Jove! I think   6
Foundations° fly the wretched; such, I mean,
Where they should be relieved. Two beggars told
    me
I could not miss my way. Will poor folks lie,
That have afflictions on them, knowing 'tis   10
A punishment or trial? Yes. No wonder,
When rich ones scarce tell true. To lapse in fullness°
Is sorer than to lie for need, and falsehood
Is worse in kings than beggars. My dear lord,
Thou art one o' the false ones. Now I think on thee,
My hunger's gone, but even before I was   16
At point to sink for food. But what is this?
Here is a path to 't. 'Tis some savage hold.°
I were best not call. I dare not call. Yet famine,
Ere clean it o'erthrow nature, makes it valiant.   20

Plenty and peace breeds cowards. Hardness ever
Of hardiness is mother. Ho! Who's here?
If any thing that's civil,° speak; if savage,
Take or lend. Ho! No answer? Then I'll enter.
Best draw my sword, and if mine enemy   25
But fear the sword like me, he'll scarcely look on 't.
Such a foe, good Heavens!   [*Exit, to the cave.*]
     [*Enter* BELARIUS, GUIDERIUS, *and* ARVIRAGUS.]
     BEL. You, Polydore, have proved best woodman° and
Are master of the feast. Cadwal and I
Will play the cook and servant. 'Tis our match.°
The sweat of industry would dry and die,   31
But for the end it works to. Come. Our stomachs
Will make what's homely savory. Weariness
Can snore upon the flint, when resty° sloth
Finds the down pillow hard. Now, peace be here,
Poor house, that keep'st thyself!°
     GUI.   I am throughly weary.   36
     ARV. I am weak with toil, yet strong in appetite.
     GUI. There is cold meat i' the cave. We'll browse on that
Whilst what we have killed be cooked.
     BEL. [*Looking into the cave*]   Stay, come not in.
But that it eats our victuals, I should think   41
Here were a fairy.
     GUI.   What's the matter, sir?
     BEL. By Jupiter, an angel! Or, if not,
An earthly paragon! Behold divineness
No elder than a boy!   45
          [*Re-enter* IMOGEN.]
     IMO. Good masters, harm me not.
Before I entered here, I called, and thought
To have begged or bought what I have took. Good troth,°
I have stol'n naught, nor would not, though I had found
Gold strew'd i' the floor. Here's money for my meat.
I would have left it on the board so soon   51
As I had made my meal, and parted
With prayers for the provider.
     GUI.   Money, youth?
     ARV. All gold and silver rather turn to dirt!
As 'tis no better reckoned, but of those   55
Who worship dirty gods.
     IMO.   I see you're angry.
Know, if you kill me for my fault, I should
Have died had I not made it.
     BEL.   Whither bound?
     IMO. To Milford Haven.
     BEL. What's your name?   60
     IMO. Fidele,° sir. I have a kinsman who

Is bound for Italy. He embarked at Milford,
To whom being going, almost spent with hunger,
I am fall'n in° this offense.
     BEL.   Prithee, fair youth,
Think us no churls, nor measure our goods minds
By this rude place we live in. Well encountered!°
'Tis almost night. You shall have better cheer   67
Ere you depart, and thanks to stay and eat it.
Boys, bid him welcome.
     GUI.   Were you a woman, youth,
I should woo hard but be your groom.° In honesty,
I bid for you as I'd buy.°
     ARV.   I'll make 't my comfort   71
He is a man. I'll love him as my brother;
And such a welcome as I'd give to him
After long absence, such is yours. Most welcome!
Be sprightly, for you fall 'mongst friends.
     IMO.   'Mongst friends,   75
If brothers. [*Aside*] Would it had been so, that they
Had been my father's sons! Then had my prize
Been less, and so more equal ballasting
To thee, Posthumus.°
     BEL.   He wrings° at some distress.
     GUI. Would I could free 't!
     ARV.   Or I, whate'er it be,   80
What pain it cost, what danger! Gods!
     BEL.   Hark, boys. [*Whispering.*]
     IMO. Great men,
That had a court no bigger than this cave,
That did attend themselves and had the virtue
Which their own conscience sealed them — laying by   85
That nothing-gift of differing multitudes° —
Could not outpeer° these twain. Pardon me, gods!
I'd change my sex to be companion with them,
Since Leonatus' false.
     BEL.   It shall be so.   89
Boys, we'll go dress our hunt.° Fair youth, come in.
Discourse is heavy, fasting. When we have supped,
We'll mannerly demand thee of thy story
So far as thou wilt speak it.
     GUI.   Pray draw near.
     ARV. The night to the owl and morn to the lark less welcome.
     IMO. Thanks, sir.   95
     ARV. I pray, draw near.   [*Exeunt.*]

64. am . . . in: have committed.   **66. Well encountered:** welcome.   **70.** but . . . groom: only to be your husband.   **70–71. In . . . buy:** truly, I mean business.   **77–79. Had . . . Posthumus:** i.e., if these men had indeed been my brothers then I should have been of humble birth and so equal in birth to Posthumus.   **79. wrings:** shows signs of grief.   **85–86. laying . . . multitudes:** laying aside the worthless flattery of the crowd that is of lower rank than themselves.   **87. outpeer:** be greater than.   **90. dress . . . hunt:** prepare our game for dinner.

23. civil: civilized.   **28. woodman:** hunter.   **30. match:** agreement, wager.   **34. resty:** restless, impatient.   **36. keep'st thyself:** hast no servant to look after thee.   **48. troth:** truth.   **61. Fidele:** pronounced as a three-syllable word, with the accent on the second syllable.

SCENE VII. *Rome. A public place.*

[*Enter two* SENATORS *and* TRIBUNES.]
1. SEN. This is the tenor° of the Emperor's writ:
That since the common men are now in action
'Gainst the Pannonians and Dalmatians
And that the legions now in Gallia are
Full weak to undertake our wars against   5
The fall'n off° Britons, that we do incite
The gentry to this business. He creates
Lucius Proconsul; and to you the Tribunes,
For this immediate levy he commends
His absolute commission.° Long live Caesar!   10
   1. TRI. Is Lucius General of the forces?
   2. SEN.   Aye.
   1. TRI. Remaining now in Gallia?
   1. SEN.   With those legions
Which I have spoke of, whereunto your levy
Must be supplyant.° The words of your commis-
   sion
Will tie you to° the numbers and the time   15
Of their dispatch.
   1. TRI.   We will discharge our duty. [*Exeunt.*]

Act IV

SCENE I. *Wales, near the cave of* BELARIUS.

[*Enter* CLOTEN *alone.*]
CLO. I am near to the place where they should
meet, if Pisanio have mapped it truly. How fit° his
garments serve me! Why should his mistress, who
was made by Him that made the tailor, not be fit°
too? The rather — saving reverence° of the   5
word — for 'tis said a woman's fitness comes by fits.°
Therein I must play the workman. I dare speak it
to myself — for it is not vainglory for a man and
his glass to confer in his own chamber — I   10
mean the lines of my body are as well drawn as his.
No less young, more strong, not beneath him in fortunes, beyond him in the advantage of the time,
above him in birth, alike conversant in general   15
services,° and more remarkable in single oppositions;° yet this imperceiverant° thing loves him in

my despite.° What mortality is!° Posthumus, thy
head, which now is growing upon thy shoulders,
shall within this hour be off, thy mistress   20
enforced,° thy garments cut to pieces before thy
face. And all this done, spurn her home to her father, who may haply be a little angry for my so
rough usage; but my mother, having power of   25
his testiness, shall turn all into my commendations.
My horse is tied up safe. Out, sword, and to a sore
purpose! Fortune, put them into my hand! This is
the very description of their meeting place, and the
fellow dares not deceive me.   [*Exit.*]

SCENE II. *Before the cave of* BELARIUS.

[*Enter, from the cave,* BELARIUS, GUIDERIUS,
ARVIRAGUS, *and* IMOGEN.]
BEL. [*To* IMOGEN] You are not well. Remain here
   in the cave.
We'll come to you after hunting.
   ARV. [*To* IMOGEN]   Brother, stay here.
Are we not brothers?
   IMO.   So man and man should be,
But clay and clay differs in dignity,
Whose dust is both alike.° I am very sick.   5
   GUI. Go you to hunting. I'll abide with him.
   IMO. So sick I am not, yet I am not well,
But not so citizen° a wanton as
To seem to die ere sick. So please you, leave me.
Stick to your journal course.° The breach of cus-
   tom   10
Is breach of all. I am ill, but your being by me
Cannot amend me. Society is no comfort
To one not sociable. I am not very sick,
Since I can reason of it. Pray you, trust me here.
I'll rob none but myself, and let me die,   15
Stealing so poorly.°
   GUI.   I love thee. I have spoke it.
How much the quantity, the weight as much,
As I do love my father.
   BEL.   What! How! How!
   ARV. If it be sin to say so, sir, I yoke me
In my good brother's fault. I know not why   20
I love this youth, and I have heard you say
Love's reason's without reason. The bier at door
And a demand who is 't shall die, I'd say
" My father, not this youth."
   BEL. [*Aside*]   Oh, noble strain!°
Oh, worthiness of nature! Breed of greatness!   25

Sc. vii: 1. **tenor**: general purpose.   6. **fall'n off**: revolted.
9–10. **commends . . . commission**: grants you the fullest powers.
14. **supplyant**: an addition.   15. **tie . . . to**: lay down.
   Act IV, Sc. i: 2. **fit**: suitably.   4. **fit**: used in an obscene sense.
5. **saving reverence**: an apology for an improper remark —
sometimes abbreviated to "sir reverence."   6. **fitness . . . fits**:
whims come by fits and starts.   15–16. **general services**:
service in the wars.   16–17. **oppositions**: fights.   17. **imper-
ceiverant**: unperceiving, stupid.

---

18. **my despite**: in spite of me. **What . . . is**: how frail is human
life.   21. **enforced**: raped.
   Sc. ii: 4–5. **But . . . alike**: living men (*clay and clay*) are of
different ranks but all are equal in death (*dust*).   8. **citizen**:
effeminate.   10. **journal course**: daily custom; i.e., the morning
hunt.   16. **Stealing so poorly**: being such a poor thief.   24. **strain**:
natural quality — for the boy is royal by birth.

Cowards father cowards and base things sire base.
Nature hath meal and bran,° contempt and grace.
I'm not their father, yet who this should be
Doth miracle itself, loved before me.° —
'Tis the ninth hour o' the morn.

ARV.   Brother, farewell.   30
IMO.   I wish ye sport.
ARV.   You health. So please you, sir.
IMO.   [*Aside*] These are kind creatures. Gods,
   what lies I have heard!
Our courtiers say all's savage but at Court.
Experience, oh, thou disprovest report!
The imperious seas breed monsters; for the dish
Poor tributary rivers as sweet fish.°   36
I am sick still, heartsick. Pisanio,
I'll now taste of thy drug.   [*Swallows some.*]
GUI.   I could not stir° him.
He said he was gentle,° but unfortunate;
Dishonestly afflicted, but yet honest.   40
ARV.   Thus did he answer me, yet said, hereafter
I might know more.
BEL.   To the field, to the field!
We'll leave you for this time. Go in and rest.
ARV.   We'll not be long away.
BEL.   Pray be not sick,
For you must be our housewife.°
IMO.   Well or ill,   45
I am bound to you.
BEL.   And shalt be ever.
                  [*Exit* IMOGEN, *to the cave.*]
This youth, howe'er distressed, appears he hath had
Good ancestors.
ARV.   How angel-like he sings!
GUI.   But his neat cookery! He cut our roots
In characters,°
And sauced our broths, as° Juno had been sick,
And he her dieter.°
ARV.   Nobly he yokes   51
A smiling with a sigh, as if the sigh
Was that it was for not being such a smile,
The smile mocking the sigh, that it would fly
From so divine a temple to commix   55
With winds that sailors rail at.
GUI.   I do note
That grief and patience, rooted in him both,
Mingle their spurs° together.
ARV.   Grow, patience!
And let the stinking elder,° grief, untwine

His perishing root with the increasing vine!   60
BEL.   It is great° morning. Come, away! — Who's
   there?
                [*Enter* CLOTEN.]
CLO.   I cannot find those runagates.° That villain
Hath mocked me. I am faint.
BEL.   "Those runagates!"
Means he not us? I partly know him. 'Tis
Cloten, the son o' the Queen. I fear some ambush.
I saw him not these many years, and yet   66
I know 'tis he. We are held as outlaws. Hence!
GUI.   He is but one. You and my brother search
What companies° are near. Pray you away.
Let me alone with him.
       [*Exeunt* BELARIUS *and* ARVIRAGUS.]
CLO.   Soft! What are you   70
That fly me thus? Some villain mountaineers?
I have heard of such. What slave art thou?
GUI.   A thing
More slavish did I ne'er than answering
A slave without a knock.°
CLO.   Thou art a robber,
A lawbreaker, a villain. Yield thee, thief.   75
GUI.   To who? To thee? What art thou? Have
   not I
An arm as big as thine? A heart as big?
Thy words, I grant, are bigger, for I wear not
My dagger in my mouth. Say what thou art,
Why I should yield to thee.
CLO.   Thou villain base,   80
Know'st° me not by my clothes?
GUI.   No, nor thy tailor, rascal,
Who is thy grandfather. He made those clothes,
Which, as it seems, make thee.
CLO.   Thou precious varlet,
My tailor made them not.
GUI.   Hence then, and thank
The man that gave them thee. Thou art some fool.
I am loath to beat thee.
CLO.   Thou injurious° thief,   86
Hear but my name, and tremble.
GUI.   What's thy name?
CLO.   Cloten, thou villain.
GUI.   Cloten, thou double villain, be thy name,
I cannot tremble at it. Were it Toad, or Adder, Spi-
   der,   90
'Twould move me sooner.
CLO.   To thy further fear,
Nay, to thy mere° confusion, thou shalt know
I am son to the Queen.
GUI.   I am sorry for 't, not seeming
So worthy as thy birth.
CLO.   Art not afeard?

27. meal . . . bran: good and worthless.   **28–29. yet . . . me:** yet I wonder who this "boy" can be who by some miracle is loved more than me.   **35–36. The . . . fish:** the all powerful (*imperious*) sea breeds monsters, but the little rivers produce fish as good for food.   **38. stir:** get him to tell his story.   **39. gentle:** of gentle birth.   **45. housewife:** stay-at-home.   **49. characters:** letters, shapes.   **50. as:** as if.   **51. dieter:** one who regulates the diet.   **58. spurs:** roots.   **59. stinking elder:** Judas Iscariot, according to legend, hanged himself on an elder, which is thus an ill-omened tree. Elders were sometimes used as supports for the vine.

61. great: broad, full.   **62. runagates:** runaways — Imogen and Posthumus.   **69. companies:** companions.   **72–74. A . . . knock:** i.e., I should be a slave like you if I did not greet such a slave as you with a blow.   **81. Know'st:** recognizest.   **86. injurious:** insulting.   **92. mere:** sheer, utter.

GUI. Those that I reverence, those I fear, the wise.
At fools I laugh, not fear them.
CLO.   Die the death.°   96
When I have slain thee with my proper° hand,
I'll follow those that even now fled hence,
And on the gates of Lud's Town set your heads.
Yield, rustic mountaineer. [*Exeunt, fighting.*] 100
    [*Re-enter* BELARIUS *and* ARVIRAGUS.]
  BEL. No companies abroad?
  ARV. None in the world. You did mistake him,
    sure.
  BEL. I cannot tell. Long is it since I saw him,
But time hath nothing blurred those lines of favor°
Which then he wore. The snatches in his voice 105
And burst of speaking° were as his. I am absolute°
'Twas very Cloten.
  ARV.   In this place we left them.
I wish my brother make good time with him,
You say he is so fell.°
  BEL.   Being scarce made up,
I mean, to man, he had not apprehension 110
Of roaring terrors; for defect of judgment
Is oft the cause of fear.° But see, thy brother.
    [*Re-enter* GUIDERIUS *with* CLOTEN's *head.*]
  GUI. This Cloten was a fool, an empty purse.
There was no money in 't. Not Hercules
Could have knocked out his brains, for he had
    none.   115
Yet I not doing this, the fool had borne
My head as I do his.
  BEL.   What hast thou done?
  GUI. I am perfect what;° cut off one Cloten's
    head,
Son to the Queen, after his own report,
Who called me traitor, mountaineer, and swore,
With his own single hand he'd take us in,° 121
Displace our heads where — thank the gods! —
    they grow,
And set them on Lud's Town.
  BEL.   We are all undone.
  GUI. Why, worthy Father, what have we to lose
But that he swore to take, our lives? The law 125
Protects not us. Then why should we be tender
To let an arrogant piece of flesh threat us,
Play judge and executioner, all himself,
For we do fear the law? What company
Discover you abroad?
  BEL.   No single soul 130
Can we set eye on, but in all safe reason
He must have some attendants. Though his humor
Was nothing but mutation,° aye, and that

From one bad thing to worse, not frenzy, not
Absolute madness could so far have raved 135
To bring him here alone. Although perhaps
It may be heard at Court that such as we
Cave here, hunt here, are outlaws, and in time
May make some stronger head,° the which he
    hearing —
As it is like him — might break out, and swear
He'd fetch us in. Yet is 't not probable 141
To come alone, either he so undertaking,
Or they so suffering. Then on good ground we fear,
If we do fear this body hath a tail
More perilous than the head.
  ARV.   Let ordinance° 145
Come as the gods foresay it. Howsoe'er,
My brother hath done well.
  BEL.   I had no mind
To hunt this day. The boy Fidele's sickness
Did make my way long forth.°
  GUI.   With his own sword,
Which he did wave against my throat, I have ta'en
His head from him. I'll throw 't into the creek 151
Behind our rock, and let it to the sea,
And tell the fishes he's the Queen's son, Cloten.
That's all I reck.°   [*Exit.*]
  BEL.   I fear 'twill be revenged.
Would, Polydore, thou hadst not done 't! Though
    valor   155
Becomes thee well enough.
  ARV.   Would I had done 't,
So the revenge alone pursued me! Polydore,
I love thee brotherly, but envy much
Thou hast robbed me of this deed. I would revenges,
That possible strength might meet,° would seek us
    through 160
And put us to our answer.
  BEL.   Well, 'tis done.
We'll hunt no more today, nor seek for danger
Where there's no profit. I prithee, to our rock.
You and Fidele play the cooks. I'll stay
Till hasty Polydore return, and bring him 165
To dinner presently.
  ARV.   Poor sick Fidele!
I'll willingly to him. To gain his color°
I'd let a parish° of such Clotens blood,
And praise myself for charity.   [*Exit.*]
  BEL.   O thou Goddess,
Thou divine Nature, how thyself thou blazon'st°
In these two princely boys! They are as gentle 171

---

96. Die ... death: i.e., you are doomed.   97. proper: own.
104. lines of favor: features.   105–06. snatches ... speaking:
habit of speaking in spurts.   106. absolute: certain.   109. fell:
fierce.   111–12. defect ... fear: i.e., one would have expected
such a fool to be a coward.   118. I ... what: I know quite well.
121. in: i.e., as prisoners.   132–33. humor ... mutation: he
had a most changeable and unstable nature.

139. make ... head: gather a stronger company.   145. ordinance: what is ordained.   149. long forth: seem long.   154. reck:
care.   160. That ... meet: within our powers of opposing.
167. gain ... color: bring back the color to his cheeks.   168. let
a parish: let a whole parish bleed. For bloodletting, see *Rich II*,
I.i.153–57,n.   170. blazon'st: paintest. The word is a heraldic
term, appropriately applied to the two boys as being of royal
blood. See App. 9.

As zephyrs blowing below the violet,
Not wagging his sweet head, and yet as rough,
Their royal blood enchafed,° as the rudest wind
That by the top doth take the mountain pine   175
And make him stoop to the vale.° 'Tis wonder
That an invisible instinct should frame them
To royalty unlearned, honor untaught,
Civility not seen from other, valor
That wildly grows in them but yields a crop   180
As if it had been sowed. Yet still it's strange
What Cloten's being here to us portends,
Or what his death will bring us.

          [*Re-enter* GUIDERIUS.]

GUI.   Where's my brother?
I have sent Cloten's clotpoll° down the stream
In embassy to his mother. His body's hostage   185
For his return.   [*Solemn music.*]
BEL.   My ingenious° instrument!
Hark, Polydore, it sounds! But what occasion
Hath Cadwal now to give it motion? Hark!
GUI. Is he at home?
BEL.   He went hence even now.
GUI. What does he mean? Since death of my
          dear'st mother,   190
It did not speak before. All solemn things
Should answer solemn accidents. The matter?
Triumphs for nothing and lamenting toys°
Is jollity for apes° and grief for boys.
Is Cadwal mad?

[*Re-enter* ARVIRAGUS *with* IMOGEN, *as dead, bearing
          her in his arms.*]

BEL.   Look, here he comes,   195
And brings the dire occasion in his arms
Of what we blame him for!
ARV.   The bird is dead
That we have made so much on. I had rather
Have skipped from sixteen years of age to sixty,
To have turned my leaping time into a crutch,   200
Than have seen this.
GUI.   O sweetest, fairest lily!
My brother wears thee not the one half so well
As when thou grew'st thyself.
BEL.   O melancholy!
Who ever yet could sound thy bottom? Find   204
The ooze, to show what coast thy sluggish crare
Might easiliest harbor in?° Thou blessed thing!
Jove knows what man thou mightst have made;
          but I,°

174. enchafed: irritated.   176. vale: valley.   184. clotpoll:
blockhead.   186. ingenious: cunningly made.   193. toys:
trifles; i.e., why is he playing a solemn dirge for the death of this
fool Cloten.   194. apes: idiots.   204–06. sound . . . in: It
was formerly the practice of mariners, when uncertain of their
position, to make a sounding with a lead weight covered with
grease. When raised, some of the sea bottom stuck to the weight,
and according to what was thus revealed the position and the
nature of the anchorage was estimated. A muddy bottom (*ooze*)
was best anchorage for a small merchant ship (*crare*).   207. but
I: I know.

Thou diedst, a most rare boy, of melancholy.
How found you him?
ARV.   Stark,° as you see;
Thus smiling, as some fly had tickled slumber,   210
Not as death's dart, being laughed at; his right
          cheek
Reposing on a cushion.
GUI.   Where?
ARV.   O' the floor;
His arms thus leagued.° I thought he slept, and put
My clouted brogues° from off my feet, whose rude-
          ness
Answered my steps too loud.
GUI.   Why, he but sleeps.   215
If he be gone, he'll make his grave a bed.
With female fairies will his tomb be haunted,
And worms will not come to thee.°
ARV.   With fairest flowers,
Whilst summer lasts and I live here, Fidele,
I'll sweeten thy sad grave. Thou shalt not lack   220
The flower that's like thy face, pale primrose, nor
The azured° harebell, like thy veins, no, nor
The leaf of eglantine,° whom, not to slander,
Outsweetened not thy breath. The ruddock°
          would
With charitable bill° — O bill, sore shaming   225
Those rich-left heirs that let their fathers lie
Without a monument! — bring thee all this,
Yea, and furred moss besides when flowers are none,
To winter-ground° thy corse.°
GUI.   Prithee have done,
And do not play in wenchlike words with that   230
Which is so serious. Let us bury him,
And not protract with admiration what
Is now due° debt? To the grave!
ARV.   Say where shall 's lay him?
GUI. By good Euriphilé, our mother.
ARV.   Be 't so;
And let us, Polydore, though now our voices   235
Have got the mannish crack, sing him to the
          ground,
As once our mother, use like note and words,
Save that " Euriphilé " must be " Fidele."
GUI. Cadwal,
I cannot sing. I'll weep and word it with thee;   240
For notes of sorrow out of tune are worse
Than priests and fanes° that lie.
ARV.   We'll speak it then.

209. Stark: stiff.   213. leagued: united, folded.   214. clouted
brogues: patched heavy shoes, studded with nails.   218. worms
. . . thee: i.e., the fairies will keep his body from corruption.
222. azured: pale blue.   223. eglantine: sweetbrier.   224. rud-
dock: robin. The English robin is a little bird with a red breast,
about the size of a sparrow; it is a lusty songster.   225. With
. . . bill: The robin is said to bring leaves in its bill to cover the
dead, as in the story of the babes in the wood.   229. winter-
ground: cover in winter. corse: corpse.   233. due: i.e., to the
dead.   242. fanes: temples.

BEL. Great griefs, I see, medicine° the less, for
    Cloten
Is quite forgot. He was a Queen's son, boys,
And though he came our enemy, remember   245
He was paid for that. Though mean and mighty,
    rotting
Together, have one dust, yet reverence,
That angel of the world, doth make distinction
Of place 'tween high and low. Our foe was princely,
And though you took his life as being our foe,   250
Yet bury him as a Prince.
GUI.   Pray you fetch him hither.
Thersites' body is as good as Ajax,°
When neither are alive.
ARV.   If you'll go fetch him,
We'll say our song the whilst. Brother, begin.
                     [*Exit* BELARIUS.]
GUI. Nay, Cadwal, we must lay his head to the
    east.   255
My father hath a reason for 't.
ARV.   'Tis true.
GUI. Come on then and remove him.
ARV.   So. Begin.

SONG

GUI.   Fear no more the heat o the sun,
         Nor the furious winter's rages.
     Thou thy worldly task hast done,   260
         Home art gone and ta'en thy wages.
     Golden° lads and girls all must,
     As° chimney sweepers, come to dust.
ARV.   Fear no more the frown o' the great.
         Thou art past the tyrant's stroke.   265
     Care no more to clothe and eat.
         To thee the reed is as the oak.
     The scepter, learning, physic,° must
     All follow this and come to dust.
GUI.   Fear no more the lightning flash,   270
ARV.   Nor the all-dreaded thunderstone.°
GUI.   Fear not slander, censure rash.
ARV.   Thou hast finished joy and moan.
BOTH. All lovers young, all lovers must
     Consign to° thee and come to dust.   275
GUI.   No exorciser° harm thee!
ARV.   Nor no witchcraft charm thee!
GUI.   Ghost unlaid forbear° thee!
ARV.   Nothing ill come near thee!
BOTH. Quiet consummation° have,   280
     And renownèd be thy grave!
[*Re-enter* BELARIUS *with the body of* CLOTEN.]

GUI. We have done our obsequies. Come, lay him
    down.
BEL. Here's a few flowers, but 'bout midnight
    more.
The herbs that have on them cold dew o' the night
Are strewing fitt'st for graves. Upon their faces.
You were as flowers, now withered: even so   286
These herblets shall, which we upon you strow.°
Come on, away. A part upon our knees.
The ground that gave them first has them again.
Their pleasures here are past, so is their pain.   290
     [*Exeunt* BELARIUS, GUIDERIUS, *and* ARVIRAGUS.]
IMO. [*Awaking*] Yes, sir, to Milford Haven.
     Which is the way? —
I thank you. — By yond bush? — Pray, how far
    thither?
'Ods pittikins!° Can it be six mile yet? —
I have gone all night. — Faith, I'll lie down and
    sleep.   294
But, soft! No bedfellow! Oh, gods and goddesses!
                [*Seeing the body of* CLOTEN.]
These flowers are like the pleasures of the world;
This bloody man, the care on 't. I hope I dream,
For so I thought I was a cave keeper
And cook to honest creatures; but 'tis not so.
'Twas but a bolt° of nothing, shot at nothing, 300
Which the brain makes of fumes.° Our very eyes
Are sometimes like our judgments, blind. Good
    faith,
I tremble still with fear; but if there be
Yet left in Heaven as small a drop of pity
As a wren's eye, feared gods, a part of it!   305
The dream's here still. Even when I wake, it is
Without me as within me; not imagined, felt.
A headless man! The garments of Posthumus!
I know the shape of 's leg. This is his hand,
His foot Mercurial,° his Martial° thigh,   310
The brawns° of Hercules; but his Jovial° face —
Murder in Heaven? — How! 'Tis gone. Pisanio
All curses madded Hecuba° gave the Greeks,
And mine to boot,° be darted on thee! Thou,
Conspired with that irregulous° devil Cloten,   315
Hast here cut off my lord. To write and read
Be henceforth treacherous! Damned Pisanio
Hath with his forgèd letters — damned Pisanio —
From this most bravest vessel of the world
Struck the main top! O Posthumus! Alas,   320
Where is thy head? Where's that? Aye me!

---

243. medicine: cure.   252. Thersites . . . Ajax: Thersites was the foul-mouthed jester in the Greek army besieging Troy, Ajax one of the heroes. See *Tr & Cr.*   262. Golden: wealthy. 263. As: as well as.   268. scepter . . . physic: kings, learned men, physicians.   271. thunderstone: thunderbolt.   275. Consign to: come to the same end as.   276. exorciser: one who conjures up the spirits of the dead.   278. forbear: leave alone. 280. consummation: end.

287. strow: strew.   293. 'Ods pittikins: by God's pity. 300. bolt: arrow.   301. fumes: vapors, illusions.   310. Mercurial: of Mercury, the messenger of the gods, a pattern of beauty. As she wakes to full realization, Imogen examines first the feet, and so looks upward to the missing head. Martial: of Mars, the god of war.   311. brawns: muscles of the arm. Jovial: of Jupiter.   313. madded Hecuba: Hecuba was the Queen of Troy who lost all when the Greeks sacked the city. See the Player's speech, *Haml*, II.ii.471–541, especially ll. 524–41. 314. to boot: in addition.   315. irregulous: knowing no law.

Where's that?
Pisanio might have killed thee at the heart
And left this head on. How should this be? Pisanio?
'Tis he and Cloten. Malice and lucre° in them
Have laid this woe here. Oh, 'tis pregnant,° preg-
nant!   325
The drug he gave me, which he said was precious
And cordial to me, have I not found it
Murderous to the senses? That confirms it home.°
This is Pisanio's deed, and Cloten's. Oh!
Give color to my pale cheek with thy blood,   330
That we the horrider may seem to those
Which chance to find us. Oh, my lord, my lord!
                              [*Falls on the body.*]
[*Enter* LUCIUS, *a* CAPTAIN *and other* OFFICERS, *and
a* SOOTHSAYER.]

CAP. To them the legions garrisoned in Gallia
After your will have crossed the sea, attending
You here at Milford Haven with your ships.   335
They are in readiness.
LUC.   But what from Rome?
CAP. The Senate hath stirred up the confiners°
And gentlemen of Italy, most willing spirits
That promise noble service, and they come
Under the conduct of bold Iachimo,   340
Sienna's brother.°
LUC.   When expect you them?
CAP. With the next benefit o' the wind.
LUC.   This forwardness
Makes our hopes fair. Command our present num-
bers
Be mustered. Bid the captains look to 't. Now, sir,
What have you dreamed of late of this war's pur-
pose?   345
SOOTH. Last night the very gods showed me a
vision —
I fast and prayed for their intelligence — thus:
I saw Jove's bird, the Roman eagle, winged
From the spongy° south to this part of the west,
There vanished in the sunbeams; which por-
tends —   350
Unless my sins abuse my divination —
Success to the Roman host.
LUC.   Dream often so,
And never false. Soft, ho! What trunk is here
Without his top? The ruin speaks that sometime
It was a worthy building. How! A page!   355
Or dead, or sleeping on him? But dead rather,
For nature doth abhor to make his bed
With the defunct, or sleep upon the dead.
Let's see the boy's face.
CAP.   He's alive, my lord.
LUC. He'll then instruct us of this body. Young
one,   360

Inform us of thy fortunes, for it seems
They crave to be demanded. Who is this
Thou makest thy bloody pillow? Or who was he
That, otherwise than noble nature did,
Hath altered that good picture? What's thy interest
In this sad wreck? How came it? Who is it?   366
What art thou?
IMO.   I am nothing. Or if not,
Nothing to be were better. This was my master,
A very valiant Briton and a good,
That here by mountaineers lies slain. Alas!   370
There is no more such masters. I may wander
From East to Occident, cry out for service,
Try many, all good, serve truly, never
Find such another master.
LUC.   'Lack,° good youth!   374
Thou movest no less with thy complaining than
Thy master in bleeding. Say his name, good friend.
IMO. Richard du Champ. [*Aside*] If I do lie and
do
No harm by it, though the gods hear, I hope
They'll pardon it. — Say you, sir?
LUC.   Thy name?
IMO.   Fidele, sir.   379
LUC. Thou dost approve° thyself the very same.
Thy name well fits thy faith, thy faith thy name.
Wilt take thy chance with me? I will not say
Thou shalt be so well mastered, but be sure,
No less beloved. The Roman Emperor's letter
Sent by a consul to me should not sooner   385
Than thine own worth prefer° thee. Go with me.
IMO. I'll follow, sir. But first, an 't please the
gods,
I'll hide my master from the flies, as deep
As these poor pickaxes° can dig; and when
With wild wood-leaves and weeds I ha' strewed his
grave   390
And on it said a century° of prayers,
Such as I can, twice o'er, I'll weep and sigh,
And leaving so his service, follow you,
So please you entertain me.
LUC.   Aye, good youth;
And rather father thee than master thee.   395
My friends,
The boy hath taught us manly duties. Let us
Find out the prettiest daisied plot we can
And make him with our pikes and partisans°
A grave. Come, arm° him. Boy, he is preferred   400
By thee to us, and he shall be interred
As soldiers can. Be cheerful. Wipe thine eyes.
Some falls are means the happier to arise.
                                    [*Exeunt.*]

---

324. lucre: a bribe.   325. pregnant: obvious.   328. home:
entirely.   337. confiners: inhabitants.   341. Sienna's brother:
brother to the Duke of Sienna.   349. spongy: damp, full of rain.

374. 'Lack: alack.   380. approve: prove the truth of your name,
Fidele — i.e., "faithful."   386. prefer: bring promotion.
389. pickaxes: fingers.   391. century: hundred.   399. pikes
... partisans: See Pls. 21a, 21d.   400. arm: support.

SCENE III. *A room in* CYMBELINE's *palace.*

[*Enter* CYMBELINE, LORDS, PISANIO, *and* ATTENDANTS.]
CYM. Again; and bring me word how 'tis with
     her.   [*Exit an* ATTENDANT.]
A fever with the absence of her son,
A madness, of which her life's in danger. Heavens,
How deeply you at once do touch me! Imogen,
The great part of my comfort, gone; my Queen   5
Upon a desperate° bed, and in a time
When fearful wars point at me; her son gone,
So needful for this present. It strikes me past
The hope of comfort. But for thee, fellow,
Who needs must know of her departure and   10
Dost seem so ignorant, we'll enforce it from thee
By a sharp torture.
PIS.   Sir, my life is yours,
I humbly set it at your will. But, for my mistress,
I nothing know where she remains, why gone,
Nor when she purposes return. Beseech your High-
     ness,   15
Hold me your loyal servant.
I. LORD.   Good my liege,
The day that she was missing he was here.
I dare be bound he's true and shall perform
All parts of his subjection loyally. For Cloten,
There wants no diligence in seeking him,   20
And will, no doubt, be found.
CYM.   The time is troublesome.
[*To* PISANIO] We'll slip° you for a season, but our
     jealousy°
Does yet depend.°
I. LORD.   So please your Majesty,
The Roman legions, all from Gallia drawn,
Are landed on your coast with a supply°   25
Of Roman gentlemen by the Senate sent.
   CYM. Now for° the counsel of my son and
     Queen!
I am amazed with matter.°
I. LORD.   Good my liege,
Your preparation can affront no less
Than what you hear of.° Come more, for more
     you're ready.   30
The want is but to put those powers in motion
That long to move.
CYM.   I thank you. Let's withdraw,
And meet the time as it seeks us. We fear not
What can from Italy annoy us, but
We grieve at chances° here. Away!   35
                       [*Exeunt all but* PISANIO.]
   PIS. I heard no letter from my master since

I wrote him Imogen was slain. 'Tis strange.
Nor hear I from my mistress, who did promise
To yield me often tidings. Neither know I
What is betid to Cloten, but remain   40
Perplexed in all. The Heavens still must work.°
Wherein I am false I am honest, not true, to be true.
These present wars shall find I love my country
Even to the note o' the King,° or I'll fall in them.
All other doubts, by time let them be cleared.   45
Fortune brings in some boats that are not steered.
                            [*Exit.*]

SCENE IV. *Wales. Before the cave of* BELARIUS.

[*Enter* BELARIUS, GUIDERIUS, *and* ARVIRAGUS.]
GUI. The noise is round about us.
BEL.   Let us from it.
ARV. What pleasure, sir, find we in life to lock it
From action and adventure?
GUI.   Nay, what hope
Have we in hiding us? This way the Romans
Must or for Britons slay us, or receive us   5
For barbarous and unnatural revolts
During their use and slay us after.°
BEL.   Sons,
We'll higher to the mountains, there secure° us.
To the King's party there's no going. Newness
Of Cloten's death — we being not known, not
     mustered   10
Among the bands° — may drive us to a render°
Where we have lived, and so extort from 's that
Which we have done, whose answer would be
     death
Drawn on with torture.
GUI.   This is, sir, a doubt
In such a time nothing becoming you,   15
Nor satisfying us.
ARV.   It is not likely
That when they hear the Roman horses neigh,
Behold their quartered fires,° have both their eyes
And ears so cloyed importantly° as now,
That they will waste their time upon our note,°   20
To know from whence we are.
BEL.   Oh, I am known
Of many in the army. Many years,
Though Cloten then but young, you see, not wore
     him
From my remembrance. And besides, the King
Hath not deserved my service nor your loves,   25

Sc. iii: **6. desperate:** without hope of recovery.   **22. slip:** let you go. **jealousy:** suspicion.   **23. depend:** remain.   **25. supply:** reinforcement.   **27. Now for:** if only I now had.   **28. amazed . . . matter:** utterly bewildered by these affairs.   **29–30. Your . . . of:** you have forces strong enough to resist (*affront*) all these that are reported.   **35. chances:** happenings.

41. work: act.   **44. to . . . King:** as the King shall see.   **Sc. iv: 5–7. or . . . after:** the Romans will either slay us as Britons or regard us as barbarous and unnatural traitors, and after they have used us, slay us.   **8. secure:** make safe.   **11. bands:** army. **render:** account.   **18. quartered fires:** the bivouac fires in their quarters.   **19. cloyed importantly:** filled up with urgent matters.   **20. upon . . . note:** taking any notice of us.

Who find in my exile the want of breeding,
The certainty of this hard life; aye hopeless
To have the courtesy your cradle promised,
But to be still° hot summer's tanlings° and
The shrinking slaves of winter.

GUI.   Than be so   30
Better to cease to be. Pray, sir, to the army.
I and my brother are not known. Yourself
So out of thought, and thereto so o'ergrown,°
Cannot be questioned.°

ARV.   By this sun that shines,
I'll thither. What thing is it that I never   35
Did see man die! Scarce ever looked on blood
But that of coward hares, hot goats, and venison!
Never bestrid a horse, save one that had
A rider like myself,° who ne'er wore rowel°
Nor iron on his heel! I am ashamed   40
To look upon the holy sun, to have
The benefit of his blest beams, remaining
So long a poor unknown.

GUI.   By Heavens, I'll go.
If you will bless me, sir, and give me leave,
I'll take the better care, but if you will not,   45
The hazard therefore due fall on me by
The hands of Romans!

ARV.   So say I. Amen.
BEL. No reason I, since of your lives you set
So slight a valuation, should reserve
My cracked one to more care. Have with you, boys!
If in your country° wars you chance to die,   51
That is my bed too, lads, and there I'll lie.
Lead, lead. [*Aside*] The time seems long. Their
     blood thinks scorn°
Till it fly out and show them princes born.
                                        [*Exeunt.*]

Act V

SCENE I. *Britain. The Roman camp.*

[*Enter* POSTHUMUS, *with a bloody handkerchief.*]
POST. Yea, bloody cloth, I'll keep thee, for I
     wished
Thou shouldst be colored thus. You married ones,
If each of you should take this course, how many
Must murder wives much better than themselves
For wrying° but a little! O Pisanio!   5
Every good servant does not all commands!

No bond but° to do just ones. Gods, if you
Should have ta'en vengeance on my faults, I never
Had lived to put on this. So had you saved
The noble Imogen to repent, and struck   10
Me, wretch more worth your vengeance. But, alack,
You snatch some hence for little faults; that's love,
To have them fall no more. You some permit
To second° ills with ills, each elder° worse,
And make them dread it, to the doers' thrift.°   15
But Imogen is your own. Do your best wills,
And make me blest to obey! I am brought hither
Among the Italian gentry, and to fight
Against my lady's kingdom. 'Tis enough
That, Britain, I have killed thy mistress. Peace,   20
I'll give no wound to thee. Therefore, good
     Heavens,
Hear patiently my purpose. I'll disrobe me
Of these Italian weeds° and suit myself
As does a Briton peasant. So I'll fight
Against the part° I come with; so I'll die   25
For thee, O Imogen, even for whom my life
Is every breath a death. And thus, unknown,
Pitied nor hated, to the face of peril
Myself I'll dedicate. Let me make men know
More valor in me than my habits° show.   30
Gods, put the strength o' the Leonati in me!
To shame the guise o' the world,° I will begin
The fashion, less without and more within. [*Exit.*]

SCENE II. *Field of battle between the British and Roman camps.*

[*Enter, from one side,* LUCIUS, IACHIMO, IMOGEN, *and and the* ROMAN ARMY; *from the other side, the* BRITISH ARMY, LEONATUS POSTHUMUS *following, like a poor soldier.*° *They march over and go out. Then enter again, in skirmish,* IACHIMO *and* POSTHUMUS. *He vanquisheth and disarmeth* IACHIMO, *and then leaves him.*]

IACH. The heaviness and guilt within my bosom
Takes off my manhood. I have belied a lady,
The Princess of this country, and the air on 't
Revengingly enfeebles me; or could this carl,°
A very drudge of nature's, have subdued me   5
In my profession? Knighthoods and honors, borne
As I wear mine, are titles but of scorn.
If° that thy gentry, Britain, go before

7. No . . . but: he is obliged only. 14. second: follow. elder: later. 15. thrift: profit. 23. weeds: garments. 25. part: party, side. 30. habits: clothes. 32. To . . . world: i.e., the world assumes that a peasant is not so good a man as a lord; I will show otherwise.
   Sc. ii: s.d., like . . . soldier: Posthumus's change into and out of the costume of a poor soldier is rapid. Presumably he donned a ragged cloak for this scene. In V.iii. he starts the scene as a Briton, but by l. 75 he has again resumed his Roman guise. 4. carl: churl, peasant. 8–9. If . . . lords: if your gentlemen are as superior to your peasants as this peasant is better than

This lout as he exceeds our lords, the odds   9
Is that we scarce are men and you are gods. [*Exit.*]
[*The battle continues. The* BRITONS *fly.* CYMBELINE
is taken. Then enter, to his rescue, BELARIUS, GUI-
DERIUS, *and* ARVIRAGUS.]

BEL. Stand, stand! We have the advantage of the
     ground.
The lane is guarded. Nothing routs us but
The villainy of our fears.
GUI., ARV.   Stand, stand, and fight!
[*Re-enter* POSTHUMUS, *and seconds the* BRITONS.
They rescue CYMBELINE *and exeunt. Then re-
enter* LUCIUS, IACHIMO, *and* IMOGEN.]

LUC. Away, boy, from the troops, and save thy-
     self.
For friends kill friends, and the disorder's such   15
As war were hoodwinked.°
IACH.   'Tis their fresh supplies.
LUC. It is a day turned strangely. Or betimes
Let's reinforce° or fly.   [*Exeunt.*]

SCENE III. *Another part of the field.*

[*Enter* POSTHUMUS *and a* BRITISH LORD.]

LORD. Camest thou from where they made the
     stand?
POST.   I did
Though you, it seems, come from the fliers.°
LORD.   I did.
POST. No blame be to you, sir; for all was
     lost,
But that the Heavens fought. The King himself
Of his wings destitute, the army broken,   5
And but the backs of Britons seen, all flying
Through a straight° lane — the enemy full-hearted,
Lolling the tongue with slaughtering, having
     work
More plentiful than tools to do 't, struck down
Some mortally, some slightly touched, some falling
Merely through fear, that the straight pass was
     dammed   11
With dead men hurt behind and cowards living
To die with lengthened shame.
LORD.   Where was this lane?
POST. Close by the battle, ditched, and walled
     with turf,
Which gave advantage to an ancient soldier   15
(An honest one, I warrant) who deserved
So long a breeding as his white beard came to,
In doing this for 's country. Athwart the lane,
He, with two striplings — lads more like to run
The country base° than to commit such slaughter,

With faces fit for masks, or rather fairer   21
Than those for preservation cased, or shame° —
Made good the passage, cried to those that fled,
" Our Britain's harts° die flying, not our men.
To darkness fleet souls that fly backwards. Stand,
Or we are Romans, and will give you that°   26
Like beasts which you shun beastly, and may save
But to look back in frown.° Stand, stand! " These
     three,
Three thousand confident,° in act as many —
For three performers are the file° when all   30
The rest do nothing — with this word " Stand,
     stand,"
Accommodated° by the place, more charming
With their own nobleness, which could have turned
A distaff° to a lance, gilded° pale looks,
Part shame, part spirit renewed; that some, turned
     coward   35
But by example — oh, a sin in war,
Damned in the first beginners! — 'gan to look
The way that they did, and to grin like lions
Upon the pikes o' the hunters. Then began
A stop i' the chaser, a retire;° anon   40
A rout, confusion thick. Forthwith they fly
Chickens the way which they stooped eagles;°
     slaves,
The strides they victors made.° And now our
     cowards,
Like fragments in hard voyages, became
The life o' the need.° Having found the back door
     open   45
Of the unguarded hearts, Heavens, how they
     wound!
Some slain before, some dying, some their friends
O'erborne i' the former wave.° Ten chased by one
Are now each one the slaughterman of twenty.
Those that would die or ere° resist are grown   50
The mortal bugs° o' the field.
LORD.   This was strange chance.
A narrow lane, an old man, and two boys.

21–22. With . . . shame: with faces as fair as — or fairer than — those of young ladies, who wear masks to preserve their complexions from the weather, or to hide their blushes of shame. **24. harts:** deer. **26. give . . . that:** will kill you. **27–28. and . . . frown:** i.e., you may save your lives if you merely look fierce. **29. Three . . . confident:** as confident as if they had been three thousand. **30. file:** the whole army. **32. Accommodated:** aided. **34. distaff:** the staff used in spinning, a symbol of womanly achievements. **gilded:** made red. **40. stop . . . retire:** i.e., those who had been pursuing were stopped and forced to fly. **41–42. they . . . eagles:** they fly like chickens by the same route as they had formerly swooped (*stooped*) like eagles on their prey. **42–43. slaves . . . made:** like slaves they go back over the places they had passed as victors. **44–45. fragments . . . need:** like the broken bits of biscuit which save the lives (*life o' the need*) of the sailors when the voyage is too long. **47–48. Some . . . wave:** in their ferocity they strike the dead, the dying, and even their friends who are on the ground. **50. or ere:** rather than. **51. mortal bugs:** deadly fiends.

---

our lords.   **16. hoodwinked:** blindfolded.   **18. reinforce:** renew the attack.
     Sc. iii: **2. fliers:** those who fled.   **7. straight:** narrow.
19–20. run . . . base: to play prisoners' base — a boy's game.

POST. Nay, do not wonder at it. You are made
Rather to wonder at the things you hear
Than to work any. Will you rhyme upon 't   55
And vent° it for a mockery? Here is one:
"Two boys, an old man twice a boy, a lane,
Preserved the Britons, was the Romans' bane."°
    LORD. Nay, be not angry, sir.
    POST.   'Lack, to what end?
Who dares not stand his foe, I'll be his friend;°   60
For if he'll do as he is made to do,
I know he'll quickly fly my friendship too.
You have put me into rhyme.°
    LORD.   Farewell. You're angry.   [*Exit.*]
    POST. Still going?° This is a lord!° Oh, noble
        misery!   64
To be i' the field, and ask "What news?" of me!
Today how many would have given their honors
To have saved their carcasses! Took heel to do 't,
And yet died too! I, in mine own woe charmed,°
Could not find Death where I did hear him groan,
Nor feel him where he struck. Being an ugly mon-
        ster,   70
'Tis strange he hides him in fresh cups, soft beds,
Sweet words, or hath moe° ministers than we
That draw his knives i' the war. Well, I will find
        him.
For being now a favorer to the Briton,
No more a Briton, I have resumed again   75
The part° I came in. Fight I will no more,
But yield me to the veriest hind° that shall
Once touch my shoulder.° Great the slaughter is
Here made by the Roman; great the answer be
Britons must take. For me, my ransom's death.   80
On either side I come to spend my breath,
Which neither here I'll keep nor bear again,
But end it by some means for Imogen.
    [*Enter two* BRITISH CAPTAINS *and* SOLDIERS.]
    I. CAP. Great Jupiter be praised! Lucius is taken.
'Tis thought the old man and his sons were angels.
    2. CAP. There was a fourth man, in a silly° habit,
That gave the affront with them.
    I. CAP.   So 'tis reported,   87
But none of 'em can be found. Stand! Who's there?
    POST. A Roman,
Who had not now been drooping here if seconds°
Had answered him.
    2. CAP.   Lay hands on him. A dog!   91
A leg of Rome shall not return to tell

What crows have pecked them here. He brags his
        service
As if he were of note.° Bring him to the King.
[*Enter* CYMBELINE, BELARIUS, GUIDERIUS, ARVIRAGUS,
PISANIO, *and* ROMAN CAPTIVES. *The* CAPTAINS *present*
POSTHUMUS *to* CYMBELINE, *who delivers him over to
a* JAILER. *Then exeunt omnes.*]

SCENE IV. *A British prison.*

    [*Enter* POSTHUMUS *and two* JAILERS.]
    I. JAIL. You shall not now be stol'n, you have
        locks upon you.
So graze as you find pasture.
    2. JAIL.   Aye, or a stomach. [*Exeunt* JAILERS.]
    POST. Most welcome, bondage! For thou art a
        way,
I think, to liberty. Yet am I better
Than one that's sick o' the gout, since he had
        rather   5
Groan so in perpetuity than be cured
By the sure physician, Death, who is the key
To unbar these locks. My conscience, thou art
        fettered
More than my shanks and wrists. You good gods,
        give me
The penitent instrument° to pick that bolt,   10
Then, free for ever! Is 't enough I am sorry?
So children temporal fathers do appease.
Gods are more full of mercy. Must I repent?
I cannot do it better than in gyves,°
Desired more than constrained. To satisfy,   15
If of my freedom 'tis the main part, take
No stricter render° of me than my all.
I know you are more clement than vile men,
Who of their broken debtors take a third,
A sixth, a tenth, letting them thrive again   20
On their abatement.° That's not my desire.
For Imogen's dear life take mine, and though
'Tis not so dear, yet 'tis a life. You coined it.
'Tween man and man they weigh not every stamp.°
Though light, take pieces for the figure's sake.°   25
You rather mine, being yours; and so, great powers,
If you will take this audit, take this life
And cancel these cold bonds. O Imogen!
I'll speak to thee in silence.   [*Sleeps.*]
[*Solemn music. Enter, as in an apparition,* SICILIUS
LEONATUS, *father to* POSTHUMUS, *an old man, attired
like a warrior, leading in his hand an ancient ma-
tron, his wife and mother to* POSTHUMUS, *with music
before them. Then, after other music, follow the*

---

56. **vent**: utter, publish.   58. **bane**: destruction.   60. **Who . . .
friend**: i.e., I'll be the friend of every coward.   63. **You . . .
rhyme**: you have forced me to turn poet.   64. **Still going**: still
on the run?   **This . . . lord**: The continual criticism of noblemen
who are false to their ideals is very noticeable in this play.
68. **charmed**: having a charmed life.   72. **moe**: more.   75–76. **I
. . . part**: Here presumably he doffs his British soldier's garb. See
Sc. ii,s.d.,n.   77. **hind**: peasant.   78. **touch my shoulder**: the
formal sign of arrest.   86. **silly**: simple.   90. **seconds**: helpers.

94. **of note**: some important person.
    Sc. iv: 10. **penitent instrument**: i.e., true penitence to free
my conscience.   14. **gyves**: fetters.   17. **render**: account.
21. **abatement**: reduction.   24. **stamp**: coin.   25. **Though . . .
sake**: light coins are accepted at the face value.

two young LEONATI, *brothers to* POSTHUMUS, *with wounds as they died in the wars. They circle* POSTHUMUS *round as he lies sleeping.*]

SIC.   No more, thou thunder master,° show   30
     Thy spite on mortal flies.°
   With Mars fall out, with Juno chide,
     That thy adulteries
       Rates° and revenges.
   Hath my poor boy done aught but well,   35
     Whose face I never saw?
   I died whilst in the womb he stayed
     Attending° nature's law;
   Whose father then — as men report
     Thou orphans' father art —   40
   Thou shouldst have been, and shielded him
     From this earth-vexing smart.

MOTH.   Lucina° lent not me her aid,
     But took me in my throes,°
   That from me was Posthumus ript,
     Came crying 'mongst his foes,   46
       A thing of pity!

SIC.   Great nature, like his ancestry,
     Molded the stuff so fair
   That he deserved the praise o' the world,   50
     As great Sicilius' heir.

1. BRO.   When once he was mature for man,
     In Britain where was he
   That could stand up his parallel,
     Or fruitful object be   55
   In eye of Imogen, that best
     Could deem his dignity?

MOTH.   With marriage wherefore was he mocked,
     To be exiled, and thrown
   From Leonati seat, and cast   60
     From her his dearest one,
       Sweet Imogen?

SIC.   Why did you suffer Iachimo,
     Slight thing of Italy,
   To taint his nobler heart and brain
     With needless jealousy,   66
   And to become the geck° and scorn
     O' the other's villainy?

2. BRO.   For this, from stiller seats we came,
     Our parents and us twain,   70
   That striking in our country's cause
     Fell bravely and were slain,
   Our fealty and Tenantius'° right

1. BRO.   With honor to maintain.
   Like hardiment° Posthumus hath   75
     To Cymbeline performed.
   Then, Jupiter, thou King of gods,
     Why hast thou thus adjourned
   The graces for his merits due,
     Being all to dolors° turned?   80

SIC.   Thy crystal window ope. Look out.
     No longer exercise
   Upon a valiant race thy harsh
     And potent injuries.

MOTH.   Since, Jupiter, our son is good,   85
     Take off his miseries.

SIC.   Peep through thy marble mansion, help,
     Or we poor ghosts will cry
   To the shining synod° of the rest
     Against thy deity.   90

BOTH BROS.   Help, Jupiter, or we appeal,
     And from thy justice fly.

[JUPITER *descends°* *in thunder and lightning, sitting upon an eagle. He throws a thunderbolt. The* GHOSTS *fall on their knees.*]

JUP.   No more, you petty spirits of region low,
     Offend our hearing. Hush! How dare you ghosts
   Accuse the thunderer, whose bolt, you know,   95
     Sky-planted, batters all rebelling coasts?
   Poor shadows of Elysium,° hence, and rest
     Upon your never-withering banks of flowers.
   Be not with mortal accidents opprest.   99
     No care of yours it is. You know 'tis ours.

Whom best I love I cross,° to make my gift,
   The more delayed, delighted. Be content.
Your low-laid son our godhead will uplift.
   His comforts thrive, his trials well are spent.   104
Our jovial star reigned at his birth, and in
   Our temple was he married. Rise, and fade.
He shall be lord of Lady Imogen,
   And happier much by his affliction made.
This tablet lay upon his breast, wherein
   Our pleasure his full fortune doth confine;
And so away. No farther with your din   111
   Express impatience, lest you stir up mine.

---

75. hardiment: courageous action. **80. dolors:** grief. **89. synod:** council. **92. s.d., Jupiter descends:** In the stage directions of plays in the 1580's and early 1590's, there are several notes for introducing gods and goddesses from "above" by means of a pulley. This kind of primitive ingenuity had by now gone out of fashion, and Shakespeare does not use it elsewhere. **97. Elysium:** paradise. **101. cross:** thwart.

30. thunder master: i.e., Jupiter. **31. mortal flies:** men who die like flies. **34. Rates:** rebukes, scolds. **38. Attending:** waiting for. **43. Lucina:** the goddess of childbirth. **44. throes:** labor pains. **67. geck:** fool. **73. Tenantius:** King Cymbeline's father. See I.i.31.

Mount, eagle, to my palace crystalline.
  [*Ascends.*]
SIC. He came in thunder. His celestial breath
    Was sulphurous to smell. The holy eagle
    Stooped, as to foot° us. His ascension is   116
    More sweet than our blest fields. His royal
      bird
    Prunes the immortal wing and cloys°his
      beak,
    As when his god is pleased.
ALL.   Thanks, Jupiter!   119
SIC. The marble pavement closes, he is entered
    His radiant roof. Away! And, to be blest,
    Let us with care perform his great behest.
      [*The* GHOSTS *vanish.*]
POST. [*Waking*] Sleep, thou hast been a grand-
    sire, and begot
A father to me, and thou hast created
A mother and two brothers. But, oh, scorn!   125
Gone! They went hence so soon as they were born,
And so I am awake. Poor wretches that depend
On greatness' favor dream as I have done,
Wake, and find nothing. But, alas, I swerve.
Many dream not to find, neither deserve,   130
And yet are steeped in favors; so am I,
That have this golden chance, and know not why.
What fairies haunt this ground? A book? O rare
    one!
Be not, as is our fangled° world, a garment
Nobler than that it covers.° Let thy effects   135
So follow, to be most unlike our courtiers,
As good as promise.
[*Reads.*] "When° as a lion's whelp shall, to himself
unknown, without seeking find, and be embraced
by a piece of tender air, and when from a stately
cedar shall be lopped branches, which, being dead
many years, shall after revive, be jointed to the old
stock, and freshly grow, then shall Posthumus end
his miseries, Britain be fortunate and flourish in
peace and plenty."   145
'Tis still a dream, or else such stuff as madmen
Tongue, and brain not. Either both, or nothing,
Or senseless speaking, or a speaking such
As sense cannot untie. Be what it is,
The action of my life is like it, which   150
I'll keep, if but for sympathy.°
      [*Re-enter* JAILERS.]
I. JAIL. Come, sir, are you ready for death?
POST. Overroasted rather; ready long ago.
I. JAIL. Hanging is the word, sir. If you be ready
for that, you are well cooked.   155
POST. So, if I prove a good repast to the spectators,

the dish pays the shot.°
I. JAIL. A heavy reckoning for you, sir. But the
comfort is you shall be called to no more payments,
fear no more tavern bills, which are often the   160
sadness of parting, as the procuring of mirth. You
come in faint for want of meat, depart reeling with
too much drink, sorry that you have paid too much,
and sorry that you are paid too much,° purse   165
and brain both empty, the brain the heavier for being too light, the purse too light, being drawn of
heaviness. Of this contradiction you shall now be
quit. Oh, the charity of a penny cord! It sums   170
up thousands in a trice. You have no true debitor
and creditor but it; of what's past, is, and to come,
the discharge. Your neck, sir, is pen, book, and
counters;° so the acquittance° follows.
POST. I am merrier to die than thou art to live.   176
I. JAIL. Indeed, sir, he that sleeps feels not the
toothache; but a man that were to sleep your sleep,
and a hangman to help him to bed, I think he
would change places with his officer; for, look you,
sir, you know not which way you shall go.   182
POST. Yes, indeed do I, fellow.
I. JAIL. Your Death has eyes in 's head then. I
have not seen him so pictured.° You must either be
directed by some that take upon them to know,   186
or to take upon yourself that which I am sure
you do not know, or jump the after-inquiry° on
your own peril; and how you shall speed in your
journey's end, I think you'll never return to tell
one.   191
POST. I tell thee, fellow, there are none want eyes
to direct them the way I am going but such as
wink° and will not use them.   194
I. JAIL. What an infinite mock is this, that a man
should have the best use of eyes to see the way of
blindness! I am sure hanging's the way of winking.
      [*Enter a* MESSENGER.]
MESS. Knock off his manacles. Bring your prisoner to the King.   200
POST. Thou bringest good news; I am called to be
made free.
I. JAIL. I'll be hanged then.   203
POST. Thou shalt be then freer than a jailer; no
bolts for the dead.   [*Exeunt all but* FIRST JAILER.]
I. JAIL. Unless a man would marry a gallows and
beget young gibbets,° I never saw one so prone.°
Yet, on my conscience, there are verier knaves desire to live, for all he be a Roman; and there   210
be some of them too, that die against their wills. So

---

116. **foot:** grasp with the claws.   118. **cloys:** probably for "claws" — rubs the beak on the talons.   134. **fangled:** fantastic.   134–35. **garment . . . covers:** i.e., a book which has a better cover than contents.   138–45. **When . . . plenty:** explained later at V.v.435–58.   151. **sympathy:** the resemblance.

157. **shot:** cost of the dinner.   165. **are . . . much:** i.e., with a headache.   175. **counters:** used in making calculations. **acquittance:** discharge of the debt.   184–85. **Death . . . pictured:** Death is usually pictured as a skeleton with an eyeless skull.   188. **jump . . . after-inquiry:** risk the judgment to come.   194. **wink:** close the eyes.   207. **gibbets:** gallows. **prone:** eager for execution.

should I if I were one. I would we were all of one
mind, and one mind good. Oh, there were desolation of jailers and gallowses! I speak against my
present profit, but my wish hath a preferment°
in 't.   *[Exit.]*

SCENE V. CYMBELINE'S *tent.*

[Enter CYMBELINE, BELARIUS, GUIDERIUS, ARVIRAGUS,
PISANIO, LORDS, OFFICERS, *and* ATTENDANTS.*]*

CYM. Stand by my side, you whom the gods have
    made
Preservers of my throne. Woe is my heart
That the poor soldier that so richly fought,
Whose rags shamed gilded arms, whose naked
    breast
Stepped before targes of proof,° cannot be found.
He shall be happy that can find him, if   6
Our grace can make him so.
    BEL.   I never saw
Such noble fury in so poor a thing,
Such precious deeds in one that promised naught
But beggary and poor looks.
    CYM.   No tidings of him?   10
    PIS. He hath been searched among the dead and
    living,
But no trace of him.
    CYM.   To my grief, I am
The heir of his reward;° *[To* BELARIUS, GUIDERIUS,
    and ARVIRAGUS*]* which I will add
To you, the liver, heart, and brain° of Britain,
By whom I grant she lives. 'Tis now the time   15
To ask of whence you are. Report it.
    BEL.   Sir,
In Cambria° are we born, and gentlemen.
Further to boast were neither true nor modest,
Unless I add we are honest.
    CYM.   Bow° your knees.
Arise my knights o' the battle. I create you   20
Companions to our person, and will fit you
With dignities becoming your estates.
            [Enter CORNELIUS *and* LADIES.*]*
There's business in these faces. Why so sadly
Greet you our victory? You look like Romans,
And not o' the Court of Britain.
    COR.   Hail, great King!   25
To sour your happiness, I must report
The Queen is dead.
    CYM.   Who worse than a physician
Would this report become? But I consider

By medicine life may be prolonged, yet death
Will seize the doctor too. How ended she?   30
    COR. With horror, madly dying, like her life,
Which, being cruel to the world, concluded
Most cruel to herself. What she confessed
I will report, so please you. These her women
Can trip me if I err, who with wet cheeks   35
Were present when she finished.°
    CYM.   Prithee say.
    COR. First, she confessed she never loved you,
    only
Affected greatness got by you, not you;
Married your royalty, was wife to your place,
Abhorred your person.
    CYM.   She alone knew this;   40
And, but she spoke in dying, I would not
Believe her lips in opening° it. Proceed.
    COR. Your daughter, whom she bore in hand° to
    love
With such integrity, she did confess
Was as a scorpion to her sight, whose life,   45
But that her flight prevented° it, she had
Ta'en off by poison.
    CYM.   Oh, most delicate fiend!
Who is 't can read a woman? Is there more?
    COR. More, sir, and worse. She did confess she
    had
For you a mortal mineral,° which, being took,   50
Should by the minute feed on life and lingering
By inches waste you; in which time she purposed,
By watching, weeping, tendance, kissing, to
O'ercome you with her show, and in time,
When she had fitted you with her craft, to work
Her son into the adoption of the crown.   56
But, failing of her end by his strange absence,
Grew shameless-desperate, opened (in despite
Of Heaven and men)° her purposes, repented
The evils she hatched were not effected, so   60
Despairing died.
    CYM.   Heard you all this, her women?
    LADIES. We did, so please your Highness.
    CYM.   Mine eyes
Were not in fault, for she was beautiful,
Mine ears that heard her flattery, nor my heart
That thought her like her seeming. It had been
    vicious   65
To have mistrusted her. Yet, O my daughter,
That it was folly in me, thou mayst say,
And prove it in thy feeling.° Heaven mend all!
[Enter LUCIUS, IACHIMO, *the* SOOTHSAYER, *and other*
ROMAN PRISONERS, *guarded;* POSTHUMUS *behind, and*
                IMOGEN.]*
Thou comest not, Caius, now for tribute. That   69

---

215. **wish . . . preferment:** I wish a better job for myself.
   Sc. v: 5. targes of proof: proven shields (tested for their
impenetrability).   **13. heir . . . reward:** i.e., I inherit (hold)
what he should have received.   **14. liver . . . brain:** the three
vital organs, supposed to be the seats of courage, affection, and
intelligence.   **17. Cambria:** Wales.   **19. Bow:** bend, kneel.
For the ceremony of dubbing a knight, see *II Hen VI*, IV.ii.127–
28,n.

36. finished: ended, died.   **42. opening:** revealing.   **43. bore
in hand:** pretended.   **46. prevented:** forestalled.   **50. mortal
mineral:** deadly poison.   **58–59. opened . . . men:** revealed in
spite of what gods or men might do.   **68. prove . . . feeling:** you
have been made to prove my folly by your sufferings.

The Britons have razed out,° though with the loss
Of many a bold one, whose kinsmen have made suit
That their good souls may be appeased with slaugh-
 ter
Of you their captives, which ourself have granted.
So think of your estate.
    LUC. Consider, sir, the chance of war. The day
Was yours by accident. Had it gone with us,   76
We should not, when the blood was cool, have
 threatened
Our prisoners with the sword. But since the gods
Will have it thus, that nothing but our lives
May be called ransom, let it come. Sufficeth   80
A Roman with a Roman's heart can suffer.
Augustus lives to think on 't; and so much
For my peculiar care.° This one thing only
I will entreat: My boy, a Briton born,
Let him be ransomed. Never master had   85
A page so kind, so duteous, diligent,
So tender over his occasions,° true,
So feat,° so nurselike. Let his virtue join
With my request, which I'll make bold your High-
 ness
Cannot deny. He hath done no Briton harm,   90
Though he have served a Roman. Save him, sir,
And spare no blood beside.
    CYM.   I have surely seen him.
His favor° is familiar to me. Boy,
Thou hast looked thyself into my grace,
And art mine own. I know not why nor wherefore
To say, live, boy. Ne'er thank thy master. Live;   96
And ask of Cymbeline what boon thou wilt,
Fitting my bounty and thy state, I'll give it;
Yea, though thou do demand a prisoner,
The noblest ta'en.
    IMO.   I humbly thank your Highness.   100
    LUC. I do not bid thee beg my life, good lad,
And yet I know thou wilt.
    IMO.   No, no. Alack,
There's other work in hand. I see a thing
Bitter to me as death. Your life, good master,
Must shuffle for itself.
    LUC.   The boy disdains me,   105
He leaves me, scorns me. Briefly die their joys
That place them on the truth of girls and boys.
Why stands he so perplexed?
    CYM.   What wouldst thou, boy?
I love thee more and more. Think more and more
What's best to ask. Know'st him thou look'st on?
  Speak,   110
Wilt have him live? Is he thy kin? Thy friend?
    IMO. He is a Roman, no more kin to me
Than I to your Highness, who, being born your
 vassal,°

70. razed out: erased.   83. peculiar care: personal trouble.
87. occasions: duties as a servant.   88. feat: dexterous.
93. favor: face.   113. vassal: servant.

Am something nearer.
    CYM.   Wherefore eyest him so?
    IMO. I'll tell you, sir, in private, if you please
To give him hearing.
    CYM.   Aye, with all my heart,   116
And lend my best attention. What's thy name?
    IMO. Fidele, sir.
    CYM.   Thou'rt my good youth, my page.
I'll be thy master. Walk with me. Speak freely.
    [CYMBELINE *and* IMOGEN *converse apart.*]
    BEL. Is not this boy revived from death?
    ARV.   One sand another   120
Not more resembles that sweet rosy lad
Who died, and was Fidele. What think you?
    GUI. The same dead thing alive.
    BEL. Peace, peace! See further. He eyes us not.
  Forbear.
Creatures may be alike. Were 't he, I am sure   125
He would have spoke to us.
    GUI.   But we saw him dead.
    BEL. Be silent. Let's see further.
    PIS. [*Aside*]   It is my mistress.
Since she is living, let the time run on
To good or bad.
    [CYMBELINE *and* IMOGEN *come forward.*]
    CYM.   Come, stand thou by our side.
Make thy demand aloud. [*To* IACHIMO] Sir, step
  you forth.   130
Give answer to this boy, and do it freely,
Or, by our greatness and the grace of it,
Which is our honor, bitter torture shall
Winnow the truth from falsehood. On, speak to
  him.
    IMO. My boon is that this gentleman may render°
Of whom he had this ring.
    POST. [*Aside*]   What's that to him?   136
    CYM. That diamond upon your finger, say
How came it yours?
    IACH. Thou'lt torture me to leave unspoken that
Which, to be spoke, would torture thee.
    CYM.   How! Me?   140
    IACH. I am glad to be constrained° to utter that
Which torments me to conceal. By villainy
I got this ring. 'Twas Leonatus' jewel,
Whom thou didst banish, and — which more may
  grieve thee,
As it doth me — a nobler sir ne'er lived   145
'Twixt sky and ground. Wilt thou hear more, my
  lord?
    CYM. All that belongs to this.
    IACH.   That paragon, thy daughter,
For whom my heart drops blood and my false
  spirits
Quail to remember — Give me leave. I faint.
    CYM. My daughter! What of her? Renew thy
  strength.   150

135. render: give an account.   141. constrained: forced.

I had rather thou shouldst live while nature will
Than die ere I hear more. Strive, man, and speak.
    IACH. Upon a time — unhappy was the clock
That struck the hour! — it was in Rome — accurst
The mansion where! — 'twas at a feast — oh, would
Our viands had been poisoned, or at least   156
Those which I heaved to head? — the good Post-
    humus —
What should I say? He was too good to be
Where ill men were, and was the best of all
Amongst the rarest of good ones — sitting sadly,
Hearing us praise our loves of Italy   161
For beauty that made barren the swelled boast
Of him that best could speak; for feature, laming
The shrine of Venus, or straight-pight° Minerva,
Postures beyond brief nature; for condition,   165
A shop of all the qualities that man
Loves woman for; besides that hook of wiving,°
Fairness which strikes the eye ——
    CYM.   I stand on fire.
Come to the matter.
    IACH.   All too soon I shall,
Unless thou wouldst grieve quickly. This Posthu-
    mus,   170
Most like a noble lord in love and one
That had a royal lover, took his hint,
And not dispraising whom we praised — therein
He was as calm as virtue — he began
His mistress' picture,° which° by his tongue being
    made,   175
And then a mind put in 't, either our brags
Were cracked of kitchen trulls, or his description
Proved us unspeaking sots.
    CYM.   Nay, nay, to the purpose.
    IACH. Your daughter's chastity — there it begins.
He spake of her as Dian had hot dreams°   180
And she alone were cold; whereat I, wretch,
Made scruple° of his praise, and wagered with him
Pieces of gold 'gainst this which then he wore
Upon his honored finger, to attain
In suit° the place of 's bed and win this ring   185
By hers and mine adultery. He, true knight,
No lesser of her honor confident
Than I did truly find her, stakes this ring,
And would so had it been a carbuncle
Of Phoebus' wheel;° and might so safely, had it
Been all the worth of 's car. Away to Britain   191
Post° I in this design. Well may you, sir,

Remember me at Court, where I was taught
Of your chaste daughter the wide difference
'Twixt amorous° and villainous. Being thus
    quenched   195
Of hope, not longing, mine Italian brain
'Gan in your duller Britain operate
Most vilely; for my vantage, excellent;
And, to be brief, my practice° so prevailed
That I returned with simular° proof enough   200
To make the noble Leonatus mad
By wounding his belief in her renown
With tokens thus, and thus, averring notes
Of chamber-hanging, pictures, this her bracelet
Oh, cunning, how I got it! — nay, some marks   205
Of secret on her person, that he could not
But think her bond of chastity quite cracked,
I having ta'en the forfeit.° Whereupon —
Methinks I see him now ——
    POST. [*Advancing*]   Aye, so thou dost,
Italian fiend! Aye me, most credulous fool,   210
Egregious murderer, thief, anything
That's due to all the villains past, in being,
To come! Oh, give me cord, or knife, or poison,
Some upright justicer!° Thou, King, send out
For torturers ingenious. It is I   215
That all the abhorred things o' the earth amend
By being worse than they.° I am Posthumus,
That killed thy daughter. Villainlike, I lie —
That caused a lesser villain than myself,
A sacrilegious thief, to do 't. The temple   220
Of virtue was she; yea, and she herself.
Spit, and throw stones, cast mire upon me, set
The dogs o' the street to bay me. Every villain
Be called Posthumus Leonatus, and
Be villainy less than 'twas! O Imogen!   225
My queen, my life, my wife! O Imogen,
Imogen, Imogen!
    IMO.   Peace, my lord. Hear, hear ——
    POST. Shall 's have a play of this?° Thou scornful
    page,
There lie thy part.   [*Striking her. She falls.*]
    PIS.   Oh, gentlemen, help!
Mine and your mistress! Oh, my Lord Posthumus!
You ne'er killed Imogen till now. Help, help!   231
Mine honored lady!
    CYM.   Does the world go round?
    POST. How come these staggers° on me?
    PIS.   Wake, my mistress!
    CYM. If this be so, the gods do mean to strike me

---

164. **straight-pight:** lit., pitched upright; i.e., most dignified.
167. **hook of wiving:** i.e., beauty which allures a man to marry.
175. **picture:** description. 175–78. **which . . . sots:** which was
so excellent, when one thought about it, that it showed either
that we had boasted (*cracked*) about mere sluts, or else he was
so much better in describing beauty that he appeared like fools
in our lack of skill. 180. **as . . . dreams:** as if even the goddess
of chastity had lustful dreams. 182. **scruple:** doubt. 185. **In
suit:** by asking for it. 189–90. **carbuncle . . . wheel:** a jewel
from the wheel of the sun god's chariot. 192. **Post:** hasten.

195. **amorous:** true loving. 199. **practice:** plot, treachery.
200. **simular:** pretended. 208. **forfeit:** that which was forfeited
by the breaking of the bond; i.e., her honor. 214. **justicer:**
judge. 216–17. **all . . . they:** i.e., my crime is so bad that it
makes all other vile things seem better. 227–28. **Peace . . .
this:** When hearers of a speech were moved to applause they
exclaimed "hear, hear." Posthumus is enraged when the supposed page apparently treats his protestation as a piece of good
acting. 233. **staggers:** giddiness.

To death with mortal° joy.

PIS.   How fares my mistress?   235
IMO. Oh, get thee from my sight.
Thou gavest me poison. Dangerous fellow, hence!
Breathe not where princes are.
CYM.   The tune of Imogen!
PIS. Lady,
The gods throw stones of sulphur on me if   240
That box I gave you was not thought by me
A precious thing. I had it from the Queen.
CYM. New matter still?
IMO.   It poisoned me.
COR.   Oh, gods!
I left out one thing which the Queen confessed
Which must approve thee honest. "If Pisanio   245
Have," said she, "given his mistress that confec-
   tion°
Which I gave him for cordial, she is served
As I would serve a rat."
CYM.   What's this, Cornelius?
COR. The Queen, sir, very oft importuned me
To temper° poisons for her, still° pretending   250
The satisfaction of her knowledge only
In killing creatures vile, as cats and dogs,
Of no esteem. I, dreading that her purpose
Was of more danger, did compound for her
A certain stuff, which, being ta'en, would cease°
The present power of life, but in short time   256
All offices of nature should again
Do their due functions. — Have you ta'en of it?
IMO. Most like I did, for I was dead.
BEL.   My boys,
There was our error.
GUI.   This is, sure, Fidele.   260
IMO. [To POTHUMUS] Why did you throw your
   wedded lady from you?
Think that you are upon a rock, and now
Throw me again.°   [Embracing him.]
POST.   Hang there like fruit, my soul,
Till the tree die!
CYM.   How now, my flesh, my child!
What, makest thou me a dullard° in this act? 265
Wilt thou not speak to me?
IMO. [Kneeling]   Your blessing sir.
BEL. [To GUIDERIUS and ARVIRAGUS] Though you
   did love this youth, I blame ye not.
You had a motive for 't.

CYM.   My tears that fall
Prove holy water on thee! Imogen,
Thy mother's° dead.
IMO.   I am sorry for 't, my lord.   270
CYM. Oh, she was naught,° and long° of her it
   was
That we meet here so strangely. But her son
Is gone, we know not how nor where.
PIS.   My lord,
Now fear is from me, I'll speak troth.° Lord Cloten,
Upon my lady's missing, came to me   275
With his sword drawn, foamed at the mouth, and
   swore
If I discovered not which way she was gone,
It was my instant death. By accident,
I had a feigned letter of my master's
Then in my pocket, which directed him   280
To seek her on the mountains near to Milford,
Where, in a frenzy, in my master's garments,
Which he enforced from me, away he posts
With unchaste purpose, and with oath to violate
My lady's honor. What became of him   285
I further know not.
GUI.   Let me end the story.
I slew him there.
CYM.   Marry, the gods forfend!°
I would not thy good deeds should from my lips
Pluck a hard sentence. Prithee, valiant youth,
Deny 't again.
GUI.   I have spoke it, and I did it.   290
CYM. He was a Prince.
GUI. A most incivil° one. The wrongs he did me
Were nothing princelike; for he did provoke me
With language that would make me spurn the sea
If it could so roar to me. I cut off 's head,   295
And am right glad he is not standing here
To tell this tale of mine.
CYM.   I am sorry for thee.
By thine own tongue thou art condemned and must
Endure our law. Thou'rt dead.
IMO.   That headless man
I thought had been my lord.
CYM.   Bind the offender,   300
And take him from our presence.
BEL.   Stay, sir King.
This man is better than the man he slew,
As well descended as thyself, and hath
More of thee merited than a band of Clotens
Had ever scar for.° [To the GUARD] Let his arms
   alone.   305
They were not born for bondage.
CYM.   Why, old soldier,

---

235. mortal: deadly.   246. confection: compound.   250. temper: mix. still: always.   255. cease: suspend.   262-63. Think
. . . again: a difficult and much discussed phrase. Imogen means:
"Now that you know me, embrace me again, and see whether
you still wish to cast me from you." Several explanations (all
rather farfetched) are possible. E.g., "Now, if you still think
me a traitor, throw me off the rock" — as Roman traitors were
thrown from the Tarpeian Rock (see *Cor,* III.i.213,n); or perhaps "rock" is a misprint for "lock," a wrestling term meaning
a firm hold.   265. dullard: i.e., an actor who has forgotten his
part and cannot speak.

270. mother: stepmother.   271. naught: wicked. long: because
274. troth: truth.   287. forfend: forbid.   292. incivil: barbarous.   304-05. band . . . for: than a whole army of Clotens
who were wounded in battle for you.

Wilt thou undo the worth thou art unpaid for°
By tasting of our wrath? How of descent
As good as we?

    ARV. In that he spake too far.

    CYM. And thou shalt die for 't.

    BEL. We will die all three. 310
But I will prove that two on 's° are as good
As I have given out him. My Sons, I must
For mine own part unfold a dangerous speech,
Though haply well for you.

    ARV. Your danger's ours.

    GUI. And our good his.

    BEL. Have at it then, by leave. 315
Thou hadst, great King, a subject who
Was called Belarius.

    CYM. What of him? He is
A banished traitor.

    BEL. He it is that hath
Assumed this age,° indeed a banished man.
I know not how a traitor.

    CYM. Take him hence. 320
The whole world shall not save him.

    BEL. Not too hot.
First pay me for the nursing of thy sons,
And let it be confíscate all so soon
As I have received it.

    CYM. Nursing of my sons!

    BEL. I am too blunt and saucy. Here's my knee.
Ere I arise I will prefer° my sons. 326
Then spare not the old father. Mighty sir,
These two young gentlemen, that call me father
And think they are my sons, are none of mine.
They are the issue of your loins, my liege, 330
And blood of your begetting.

    CYM. How! My issue!

    BEL. So sure as you your father's. I, old Morgan,
Am that Belarius whom you sometime banished.
Your pleasure was my mere offense,° my punish-
    ment
Itself, and all my treason. That I suffered 335
Was all the harm I did. These gentle Princes —
For such and so they are — these twenty years
Have I trained up. Those arts they have as I
Could put into them. My breeding was, sir, as 339
Your Highness knows. Their nurse, Euriphilé,
Whom for the theft I wedded, stole these children
Upon my banishment. I moved her to 't,
Having received the punishment before
For that which I did then. Beaten for loyalty
Excited me to treason. Their° dear° loss, 345

The more of you 'twas felt, the more it shaped
Unto my end of stealing them. But, gracious sir,
Here are your sons again, and I must lose
Two of the sweet'st companions in the world.
The benediction of these covering Heavens 350
Fall on their heads like dew! For they are worthy
To inlay heaven with stars.

    CYM. Thou weep'st and speak'st.
The service that you three have done is more
Unlike° than this thou tell'st. I lost my children.
If these be they, I know not how to wish 355
A pair of worthier sons.

    BEL. Be pleased awhile.
This gentleman, whom I call Polydore,
Most worthy Prince, as yours, is true Guiderius.
This gentleman, my Cadwal, Arviragus, 359
Your younger princely son. He, sir, was lapped°
In a most curious° mantle, wrought by the hand
Of his Queen mother, which for more probation°
I can with ease produce.

    CYM. Guiderius had
Upon his neck a mole, a sanguine star.°
It was a mark of wonder.

    BEL. This is he, 365
Who hath upon him still that natural stamp.
It was wise nature's end in the donation,
To be his evidence now.

    CYM. Oh, what am I?
A mother to the birth of three? Ne'er mother
Rejoiced deliverance more. Blest pray you be, 370
That, after this strange starting from your orbs,°
You may reign in them now! O Imogen,
Thou hast lost by this a kingdom.

    IMO. No, my lord.
I have got two worlds by 't. O my gentle brothers,
Have we thus met? Oh, never say hereafter 375
But I am truest speaker. You called me brother
When I was but your sister; I you brothers,
When ye were so indeed.

    CYM. Did you e'er meet?

    ARV. Aye, my good lord.

    GUI. And at first meeting loved,
Continued so until we thought he died. 380

    COR. By the Queen's dram she swallowed.

    CYM. Oh, rare instinct!
When shall I hear all through? This fierce abridg-
    ment
Hath to it circumstantial branches, which
Distinction should be rich in.° Where? How lived
    you? 384

---

307. worth . . . for: the services you have done me for which you have not yet been rewarded. **311. on 's:** of us. **319. Assumed . . . age:** acted this part of an old man. **326. prefer:** cause to be promoted. **334. Your . . . offense:** i.e., the only offense I committed was to annoy you. **345–47. Their . . . them:** because I knew that you would feel their loss greatly, the more was I moved (*shaped*) to steal them. **345. dear:** great.

354. Unlike: extraordinary. **360. lapped:** wrapped. **361. curious:** elaborately embroidered. **362. probation:** proof. **364. sanguine star:** red birthmark. **371. starting . . . orbs:** leaving your natural course. The image is that of a planet which leaves its proper motion. See App. 1. **382–84. This . . . in:** i.e., this wild summary of your adventures has many details, all of which should be told to make the tale complete.

And when came you to serve our Roman captive?
How parted with your brothers? How first met
    them?
Why fled you from the Court? And whither?
    These,
And your three motives° to the battle, with
I know not how much more, should be demanded;
And all the other by-dependances°   390
From chance to chance; but nor° the time nor place
Will serve our long inter'gatories.° See,
Posthumus anchors upon Imogen,
And she, like harmless lightning, throws her eye
On him, her brothers, me, her master, hitting   395
Each object with a joy. The counterchange°
Is severally° in all. Let's quit this ground
And smoke° the temple with our sacrifices.
[*To* BELARIUS] Thou art my brother; so we'll hold
    thee ever.
    IMO. You are my father too, and did relieve me
To see this gracious season.
    CYM.   All o'erjoyed,   401
Save these in bonds. Let them be joyful too,
For they shall taste our comfort.
    IMO.   My good master,
I will yet do you service.
    LUC.   Happy be you!   404
    CYM. The forlorn soldier that so nobly fought,
He would have well becomed° this place and graced
The thankings of a King.
    POST.   I am, sir,
The soldier that did company these three
In poor beseeming.° 'Twas a fitment° for
The purpose I then followed. That I was he,   410
Speak, Iachimo. I had you down, and might
Have made you finish.
    IACH. [*Kneeling*] I am down again.
But now my heavy conscience sinks my knee,
As then your force did. Take that life, beseech
    you,
Which I so often owe. But your ring first,   415
And here the bracelet of the truest Princess
That ever swore her faith.
    POST.   Kneel not to me.
The power that I have on you is to spare you,
The malice towards you to forgive you. Live,
And deal with others better.
    CYM.   Nobly doomed!°   420
We'll learn our freeness° of a son-in-law.

Pardon's the word to all.
    ARV.   You holp° us, sir,
As you did mean indeed to be our brothers.
Joyed are we that you are.
    POST. Your servant, Princes. Good my Lord of
    Rome,   425
Call forth your soothsayer. As I slept, methought
Great Jupiter, upon his eagle backed,
Appeared to me, with other spritely shows°
Of mine own kindred. When I waked, I found
This label° on my bosom, whose containing   430
Is so from sense in hardness that I can
Make no collection° of it. Let him show
His skill in the construction.°
    LUC.   Philarmonus!
    SOOTH. Here, my good lord.
    LUC.   Read and declare the meaning.
    SOOTH. [*Reads.*] "When as a lion's whelp   435
shall, to himself unknown, without seeking find,
and be embraced by a piece of tender air, and when
from a stately cedar shall be lopped branches, which,
being dead many years, shall after revive, be jointed
to the old stock and freshly grow, then shall Post-
humus end his miseries, Britain be fortunate and
flourish in peace and plenty."
Thou, Leonatus, art the lion's whelp.
The fit and apt construction of thy name,
Being Leo-natus,° doth import so much.   445
[*To* CYMBELINE] The piece of tender air, thy virtu-
    ous daughter,
Which we call *mollis aer;* and *mollis aer*
We term it *mulier;* which *mulier* I divine
Is this most constant wife, who even now,
Answering the letter of the oracle,   450
Unknown to you, unsought, were clipped° about
With this most tender air.
    CYM.   This hath some seeming,
    SOOTH. The lofty cedar, royal Cymbeline,
Personates thee, and thy lopped branches point
Thy two sons forth; who, by Belarius stol'n,   455
For many years thought dead, are now revived,
To the majestic cedar joined, whose issue
Promises Britain peace and plenty.
    CYM.   Well,
My peace we will begin. And, Caius Lucius,
Although the victor, we submit to Caesar   460
And to the Roman Empire, promising
To pay our wonted tribute, from the which
We were dissuaded by our wicked Queen;
Whom Heavens in justice both on her and hers
Have laid most heavy hand.   465

---

388. your . . . motives: the reasons which brought you there.
390. by-dependances: additional circumstances.   391. nor:
neither.   392. inter'gatories: questions. See *M of Ven,* V.i.298,n.
396. counterchange: the exchange (of looks).   397. severally:
separately; i.e., each is looking at the other.   398. smoke:
fill with smoke.   406. becomed: become, adorned.   409. beseeming: outward appearance. fitment: fit disguise.   420. doomed:
judged, sentenced.   421. freeness: generosity.

422. holp: helped.   428. spritely shows: supernatural visions.   430. label: piece of paper, note.   432. collection:
sense.   433. construction: interpretation.   445. Leo-natus:
Lion-born.   451. clipped: embraced.

SOOTH. The fingers of the powers above do tune
The harmony of this peace. The vision,
Which I made known to Lucius ere the stroke
Of this yet scarce-cold battle, at this instant
Is full accomplished: For the Roman eagle,   470
From south to west on wing soaring aloft,
Lessened herself and in the beams o' the sun
So vanished; which foreshowed our princely eagle,
The imperial Caesar, should again unite
His favor with the radiant Cymbeline,   475
Which shines here in the West.

CYM.   Laud we the gods,
And let our crooked smokes climb to their nostrils
From our blest altars. Publish we this peace
To all our subjects. Set we forward. Let
A Roman and a British ensign wave   480
Friendly together. So through Lud's Town march;
And in the temple of great Jupiter
Our peace we'll ratify, seal it with feasts.
Set on there! Never was° a war did cease,
Ere bloody hands were washed, with such a peace.
                      [*Exeunt.*]

484. Never was: never before did.

THE WINTER'S TALE

Introduction

The Winter's Tale is one of the last of Shakespeare's plays. It was probably written in 1610 or 1611. Dr. Simon Forman, a well-known astrologer of the time, described a performance which he had seen at the Globe on May 15, 1611.[1] Forman's note runs as follows:

In *The Winter's Tale* at the Globe, 1611, the 15 of May (Wednesday),

Observe there how Leontes, the King of Sicilia, was overcome with jealousy of his wife with the King of Bohemia, his friend, that came to see him; and how he contrived his death and would have had his cup bearer to have poisoned; who gave the King of Bohemia warning thereof and fled with him to Bohemia.

Remember also how he sent to the Oracle of Apollo and the answer of Apollo, that she was guiltless and that the king was jealous etc.; and how except the child was found again that was lost, the king should die without issue; for the child was carried into Bohemia and there laid in a forest and brought up by a shepherd; and the King of Bohemia's son married that wench; and how they fled into Sicilia to Leontes; and the shepherd having showed the letter of the nobleman by whom Leontes sent away that child and the jewels found about her, she was known to be Leontes' daughter, and was then sixteen years old.

Remember also the rogue that came in all tattered like coll pixie [a mischievous fairy], and how he feigned him sick and to have been robbed of all that he had; and how he cozened the poor man of all his money; and after came to the sheep shear with a peddler's pack and there cozened them again of all their money; and how he changed apparel with the King of Bohemia's son; and then how he turned courtier etc. Beware of trusting feigned beggars or fawning fellows.

There are records in the Revels Accounts that the play was acted at Court by the King's Players on November 5, 1611, and again in February 1613 during the festivities to celebrate the marriage of Princess Elizabeth, daughter of King James I, to the Elector Palatine.

The play was first printed in the first folio (F1) in 1623. The original text was probably set up from a copy of the play made by a professional scribe. There are few difficulties except that in the F1 text the characters who are to appear are gathered at the head of each scene, in imitation of the manner used in printing classical plays, and most of the entrances and exits have been omitted.

The source of the play is one of Robert Greene's most popular novels, *Pandosto: The Triumph of Time* (see Gen. Intro. p. 37b). It was published in 1588 and reprinted in 1592, 1595, and 1607. Shakespeare took most of his incidents from the novel, but he used his material freely. The outline of the story runs as follows:

Pandosto, King of Bohemia, is happily married to Bellaria. They have one child, a boy called Garinter. Egistus, King of Sicilia, who had been brought up with Pandosto, comes to visit them with a great train of followers. He is treated with great courtesy and hospitality, and Bellaria especially is so attentive to her husband's old friend that they frequently walk together in the garden " where they two in private and pleasant devices would pass away the time to both their contents."

After a while Pandosto begins to suffer from melancholy. He grows suspicious of his wife and at length so insanely jealous that he orders Franion, his cupbearer, to poison Egistus. Franion reveals the command to Egistus, and the two, together with Egistus' followers, sail away to Sicilia. Pandosto is so angry at being thus outwitted that he causes his wife to be imprisoned and issues a public proclamation that she has committed adultery with Egistus and has plotted to murder him. In prison Bellaria gives birth to a daughter. Pandosto's first inclination is to cause both wife and daughter to be burned, but his nobles protest and he yields so far as to grant that the babe shall be abandoned in a cockboat in the open sea.

Pandosto next assembles his courtiers and accuses Bellaria in open court. She answers his accusation boldly and demands that evidence shall be produced. This increases Pandosto's anger, but he yields to her plea to send to the Isle of Delphos to inquire of the Oracle of Apollo. When the sealed answer of the god has been brought back, the Queen is publicly indicted. Then the oracle is opened and read out:

SUSPICION IS NO PROOF: JEALOUSY IS AN UNEQUAL JUDGE: BELLARIA IS CHASTE: EGISTUS BLAMELESS:

---

[1] E. K. Chambers, *William Shakespeare*, ii, 340.

FRANION A TRUE SUBJECT: PANDOSTO JEALOUS: HIS
BABE AN INNOCENT: AND THE KING SHALL LIVE WITH-
OUT AN HEIR IF THAT WHICH IS LOST BE NOT FOUND.

The King is immediately convinced of his error,
and so overcome by remorse that he begs his nobles
to ask Bellaria to forgive him; but at that moment
news comes that the boy Garinter has died suddenly. At this shock, Bellaria falls down dead
and Pandosto can hardly be prevented from killing himself. He orders that the bodies of his wife
and son be buried in a rich sepulcher, whither
once a day he will repair to bewail his misfortune.

Meanwhile the boat carrying Pandosto's daughter has drifted ashore on the coast of Sicilia. The
babe, who is almost dead from hunger and cold, is
discovered by a poor shepherd called Porrus; she is
wrapped in a mantle of scarlet richly embroidered
with gold, with a gold chain about her neck. Porrus
takes her home to his wife, and since they are childless, they decide to bring her up as their own. The
child is named Fawnia and grows up to be a girl
of surpassing beauty and excellent intelligence.
Meanwhile Egistus' only son, Prince Dorastus, has
grown into manhood, but he refuses his father's urgent command that he should take a wife. Soon
afterward, while out hawking, he comes upon
Fawnia, and immediately they fall in love with
each other. They meet again, but Fawnia, who has
realized that her lover is the Prince, declares that
she will receive him only as a shepherd. So Dorastus disguises himself as a shepherd and comes to
woo her. They plight troth, but as Dorastus knows
that his father will never consent to the marriage,
he collects money and jewels so that they may run
away and live in Italy until the King is either dead
or reconciled.

The love of Fawnia for Dorastus is observed by
the old shepherd and his wife, who are greatly
troubled. Porrus decides to go to Court, taking the
mantle with him that he may show the King how
Fawnia was found. Meanwhile, Dorastus confides
in his old servant Capnio, and then on the appointed day he fetches Fawnia and they board a
ship bound for Italy. Meanwhile Capnio has encountered Porrus on his way to the palace. Realizing that if Porrus is allowed to tell his tale all will
be revealed, Capnio causes the old shepherd to be
taken forcibly on board.

The ship puts out to sea, but is turned out of her
course by a violent storm and enters a harbor in
Bohemia. By Capnio's advice, Dorastus changes his
name to Meleagrus, and conceals his identity. The
report of Fawnia's beauty is soon carried to the
Court, whither the lovers are summoned. King
Pandosto immediately falls in love with the beautiful girl, and that he may woo her for himself, he
sends Dorastus and Capnio to prison. Fawnia rejects his advances with scorn.

By this time Egistus has heard the story and has
guessed the identity of "Meleagrus." He sails to
Bohemia, where he and his old friend King Pandosto are reconciled. Then he asks that Prince Dorastus be released and that Capnio, Porrus, and
Fawnia be executed. When the offenders are
brought forth, old Porrus is at last able to tell his
story. Pandosto recognizes his daughter, and the
young lovers are married; but soon afterward Pandosto again falls into melancholy and is so overcome with remorse at his conduct toward his wife
and daughter that he kills himself.

In writing *The Winter's Tale* Shakespeare
took over the main details of the story, but he
invented many situations and all the dialogue,
except for an occasional phrase. He changed the
names of the characters and he added Paulina,
Antigonus, and the young shepherd. The most
important change, however, was in the ending.
He brings Hermione back to life after sixteen
years and he spares Leontes. Shakespeare also
invented Autolycus, though he adopted some of
the rascal's tricks from the *Conny-catching* pamphlets in which Greene had described the ways
of the professional rogues about London. The
incident where Autolycus picks the pocket of
the Clown (IV.iv) had already been described
in the *Second and Last Part of Conny-catching*
as "A kind conceit of a foist [pickpocket] performed in Paul's."

There walked in the middle walk a plain country
farmer, a man of good wealth, who had a well-lined
purse only barely thrust up in a round slop; which
a crew of foists having perceived, their hearts were
set on fire to have it, and everyone had a fling at
him, but all in vain, for he kept his hand close in
his pocket, and his purse fast in his fist like a subtle
churl that either had been forewarned of Paul's, or
else had aforetime smoked some of that faculty.
Well, howsoever, it was impossible to do any good
with him, he was so wary. The foists, spying this,
strained their wits to the highest string how to
compass this bung; yet could not all their politic
conceits fetch the farmer over, for jostle him, chat
with him, offer to shake him by the hand — all
would not serve to get his hand out of his pocket.

At last one of the crew that for his skill might
have been doctorate in his mystery amongst them
all chose out a good foist, one of a nimble hand and
great agility, and said to the rest thus: " Masters,
it shall not be said such a base peasant shall slip
away from such a crew of gentlemen foists as we

are and not have his purse drawn; and therefore this time I'll play the stall myself, and if I hit him not home, count me for a bungler forever." And so left them, and went to the farmer and walked directly before him and next him three or four turns. At last, standing still, he cried out, " Alas, honest man, help me, I am not well." And with that sunk down suddenly in a sown [swoon]. The poor farmer, seeing a proper young gentleman (as he thought) fall dead afore him, stepped to him, held him in his arms, rubbed him and chafed him. At this there gathered a great multitude of people about him, and the whilst the foist drew the farmer's purse and away. By that the other thought the feat was done, he began to come something to himself again, and so, half-staggering, stumbled out of Paul's and went after the crew where they had appointed to meet, and there boasted of his wit and experience.

The Winter's Tale is a better play to see on the stage than to read. It is full of good theater, though critics have from time to time found blemishes in its construction. As with *Pericles, Cymbeline,* and *The Tempest,* the theme of the play is reconciliation. Wrongs committed by one generation are reconciled in the children. Such a theme requires the passage of many years. Shakespeare therefore divided the play into two parts, the first showing how Leontes unjustly accused his wife Hermione, the second how the daughter whom he supposed to have been lost was miraculously restored, and how Hermione came back to life.

The story is frankly " a winter's tale " — and " A sad tale's best for winter " — in which no one expects any probability. Nevertheless, to make the story plausible, the original motives for Leontes' jealousy must be credible. Shakespeare is sometimes criticized because Leontes' jealousy bursts forth without any apparent cause. Nevertheless, there are some warning signs before the explosion. Leontes is an obstinate man. He will not listen to Polixenes' very reasonable desire to go home. He is piqued by Polixenes' refusal to stay, and is ready to think unreasonably of him. When Hermione succeeds almost at once in making Polixenes change his mind, the sudden thought comes to Leontes that there must be something between them, and in a moment he is on the verge of what Elizabethans called " horn madness." The jealous husband is a common butt in comedies and farces, in which exact truth to life is not to be expected. In *The Winter's Tale* Shakespeare treats jealousy tragically, and to be satisfactory it must also be convincing. To appreciate Leontes' outburst, we must look not only at Leontes, but at what Leontes sees, and with his distorted vision (I.i. 108). The success of this scene depends therefore on the acting of Hermione, whose natural and innocent friendliness must be so presented that it might conceivably give some cause for suspicion to a diseased mind.

The curse of jealousy is that it breeds from suspicion. Once started, any little incident becomes strong proof. Moreover, in drama there must always be contraction of time. In a novel, or in reality, jealousy may be fed by a succession of incidents gradually accumulating day after day. In a play, all these must be compressed within a few scenes.

Leontes' character is well brought out in the opening scene. He is an obstinate and immature person, and therefore the more opposition he meets, the stronger his obstinacy becomes. He has also an inordinate fear of ridicule and gossip. Leontes thus works himself into an unreasoning passion of jealousy, and the moment he has revealed his fantastic suspicion to Camillo, he is caught in his own foolishness. He knows that there is neither proof nor evidence, though his mind is so unbalanced that he would not listen if there were. When he cannot persuade any of his followers to believe his accusations, he gambles wildly and appeals to the oracle of the god.

The oracle of Apollo is the axle on which this play turns. Here too stage presentation is needed, for in the acting the oracle must be treated with all the marks of reverence and religious awe. When the sealed judgment of the oracle has been brought back, Hermione is indicted. It is an excellent trial scene, and full of excitement. Once Hermione is allowed to defend herself, she answers the charge with such impressive dignity that Leontes quickly becomes the defendant in his own action. She too appeals to the oracle. The judgment of the oracle is opened, and Hermione is decisively vindicated. Leontes has appealed to Divine judgment. Now he spurns the verdict, and is at once the victim of Divine wrath. The sudden contrasts of this scene, the noise of Leontes' fury, the horrified silence of his Court, broken by the hurried footsteps of the distressed messenger, are magnificently dramatic. The scene ends with Leontes contrite, and Hermione apparently dead.

When the play is dissected in the study, it becomes a little difficult to explain, or to believe in, Paulina's action. How or why did she keep Hermione concealed for sixteen years? " How " is not easily explained, but after all this is a " winter's tale." " Why " is clear. Paulina and all have seen that the god Apollo is now controlling the fate of Sicilia. He has vindicated Hermione, but he has also said that the King shall live without an heir until that which is lost is found. Leontes must therefore be kept away from Hermione at all costs. Paulina acts for the best as she sees it.

The third scene in Act III is a link scene between the two parts of the play. There Shakespeare shows us that the babe Perdita is saved. This is his normal method of telling a story; [2] he does not keep back such essential information in order that he may end his play with a surprise in the last scene. He does, however, deliberately try to persuade us that Hermione is dead.

The interval between the two parts of the play is bridged by the appearance of Time to announce the passing of sixteen years. The story then continues at the sheepshearing feast, when young Prince Florizel and Perdita, the natural

[2] See *M. Ado* Intro. p. 699b.

Queen of the shepherds, fall in love. Florizel is a young man of considerable personality, who will brave his father and sacrifice a kingdom for his love. The plot now moves very quickly. On Camillo's advice, Florizel and Perdita run away to Sicilia, where they are received by Leontes; but almost at once Polixenes arrives in hot pursuit, and at last the truth is revealed.

Shakespeare has been much criticized because he did not present in the action either the meeting between Polixenes and Leontes, or the scene where the old shepherd produces the proof of Perdita's birth, or the recognition of Perdita by her father. In this matter Shakespeare's judgment was better than that of his critics. Had these three powerful and emotional episodes been shown, the final squaring-up would inevitably have been prolonged, and the emotions of the audience would have been exhausted before the end. The ending of the play is not Leontes' discovery of his daughter, nor his reconciliation with his wife, nor the vindication of Hermione, but the reunion of mother and daughter. Hermione has been wronged. The last scene is hers. Her existence has been carefully concealed from everyone until suddenly she comes to life. This scene also needs the living actor. In the reading it is fantastic. When well acted on the stage, it is most pathetic and moving.

The Winter's Tale

DRAMATIS PERSONAE

LEONTES, *King of Sicilia*
MAMILLIUS, *young Prince of Sicilia*
CAMILLO ⎫
ANTONIGUS ⎪
CLEOMENES ⎬ *four lords of Sicilia*
DION ⎭
POLIXENES, *King of Bohemia*
FLORIZEL, *Prince of Bohemia*
ARCHIDAMUS, *a lord of Bohemia*
OLD SHEPHERD, *reputed father of Perdita*
CLOWN, *his son*
AUTOLYCUS, *a rogue*
A MARINER

A JAILER
HERMIONE, *Queen to Leontes*
PERDITA, *daughter to Leontes and Hermione*
PAULINA, *wife to Antigonus*
EMILIA, *a lady attending on Hermione*
MOPSA ⎫
DORCAS ⎬ *shepherdesses*

Other LORDS *and* GENTLEMEN, LADIES, OFFICERS *and*
SERVANTS, SHEPHERDS, *and* SHEPHERDESSES.

TIME, *as Chorus*

SCENE — *Partly in Sicilia, and partly in Bohemia.*

Act I

SCENE I. *Antechamber in* LEONTES' *palace.*

[*Enter* CAMILLO *and* ARCHIDAMUS.]

ARC. If you shall chance, Camillo, to visit Bohemia
on the like occasion whereon my services are now on
foot,° you shall see, as I have said, great difference
betwixt our Bohemia and your Sicilia.   5
   CAM. I think this coming summer the King of
Sicilia means to pay Bohemia the visitation which he
justly owes him.
   ARC. Wherein our entertainment shall shame us
we will be justified in our loves,° for indeed ——
   CAM. Beseech you ——   11
   ARC. Verily, I speak it in the freedom of my
knowledge. We cannot with such magnificence —
in so rare —— I know not what to say. We will give
you sleepy drinks, that your senses, unintelligent of
our insufficience,° may, though they cannot praise
us, as little accuse us.   17
   CAM. You pay a great deal too dear for what's
given freely.
   ARC. Believe me, I speak as my understanding instructs me, and as mine honesty puts it to utterance.
   CAM. Sicilia cannot show himself overkind to   23
Bohemia.° They were trained together in their child-
hoods, and there rooted betwixt them then such an
affection, which cannot choose but branch° now.

Since their more mature dignities and royal necessities made separation of their society,° their en-   28
counters, though not personal, have been royally
attorneyed° with interchange of gifts, letters, loving
embassies, that they have seemed to be together,
though absent; shook hands, as over a vast;° and
embraced, as it were, from the ends of opposed
winds.° The Heavens continue their loves!   35
   ARC. I think there is not in the world either malice
or matter to alter it. You have an unspeakable comfort of your young Prince Mamillius. It is a gentleman of the greatest promise that ever came into my
note.   40
   CAM. I very well agree with you in the hopes of
him. It is a gallant child, one that indeed physics the
subject,° makes old hearts fresh. They that went on
crutches ere he was born desire yet their life to see
him a man.   45
   ARC. Would they else be content to die?
   CAM. Yes, if there were no other excuse why they
should desire to live.
   ARC. If the King had no son, they would de-   49
sire to live on crutches till he had one.   [*Exeunt.*]

SCENE II. *A room of state in the same.*

[*Enter* LEONTES, HERMIONE, MAMILLIUS, POLIXENES,
CAMILLO, *and* ATTENDANTS.]

   POL. Nine changes of the watery star hath been
The shepherd's note° since we have left our throne

Act I, Sc. i: 2–3. on . . . foot: i.e., as attendant on your King.
Both lords use somewhat exaggerated speech as they pay polite
compliments to each other.   9–10. Wherein . . . loves: although
we shall not be able to entertain you so lavishly, yet our love
will be as genuine.   15–16. unintelligent . . . insufficience: not
be able to realize our shortcomings.   23–24. Sicilia . . . Bohemia:
Leontes, King of Sicilia . . . and Polixenes, King of Bohemia.
26. branch: put out branches as it grows to maturity.

28. society: companionship.   28–30. encounters . . . attorneyed:
their meetings have been made through deputies.   33. vast: great
distance.   34–35. opposed winds: the opposite ends of the earth.
42–43. physics . . . subject: is good medicine for the whole nation.
   Sc. ii: 1–2. Nine . . . note: i.e., it is now nine months. watery
star: the moon. Polixenes also in making his formal farewell
speaks in the elaborate vocabulary of compliment.

Without a burden.° Time as long again
Would be filled up, my brother, with our thanks,
And yet we should, for perpetuity,   5
Go hence in debt. And therefore, like a cipher,°
Yet standing in rich place, I multiply
With one "We thank you" many thousands moe°
That go before it.

LEON.   Stay your thanks a while,
And pay them when you part.

POL.   Sir, that's tomorrow. 10
I° am questioned by my fears of what may chance
Or breed upon our absence, that may blow
No sneaping° winds at home to make us say
"This is put forth too truly." Besides, I have
    stayed
To tire your royalty.°

LEON.   We are tougher, brother, 15
Than you can put us to 't.

POL.   No longer stay.

LEON. One sevennight° longer.

POL.   Very sooth,° tomorrow.

LEON. We'll part the time between 's,° then, and
    in that
I'll no gainsaying.°

POL.   Press me not, beseech you, so.
There is no tongue that moves — none, none i' the
    world —   20
So soon as yours could win me. So it should now
Were there necessity in your request, although
'Twere needful I denied it. My affairs
Do even drag me homeward, which to hinder
Were in your love a whip to me,° my stay 25
To you a charge and trouble. To save both,
Farewell, our brother.

LEON.   Tongue-tied our Queen? Speak you.

HER. I had thought, sir, to have held my peace
    until
You had drawn oaths from him not to stay. You, sir,
Charge° him too coldly. Tell him you are sure 30
All in Bohemia's well, this satisfaction
The bygone day proclaimed. Say this to him,
He's beat from his best ward.°

LEON.   Well said, Hermione.

HER. To tell he longs to see his son were strong.
But let him say so then, and let him go. 35
But let him swear so and he shall not stay,
We'll thwack him hence with distaffs.°

Yet of your royal presence I'll adventure
The borrow of a week. When at Bohemia
You take my lord, I'll give him my commission°
To let him there a month behind the gest 41
Prefixed° for 's parting. Yet, good deed, Leontes,
I love thee not a jar° o' the clock behind
What lady she her lord. You'll stay?

POL.   No, madam.

HER. Nay, but you will?

POL.   I may not, verily. 45

HER. Verily!
You put me off with limber vows,° but I,
Though you would seek to unsphere the stars° with
    oaths,
Should yet say "Sir, no going." Verily,
You shall not go. A lady's "verily"'s 50
As potent as a lord's. Will you go yet?
Force me to keep you as a prisoner,
Not like a guest; so you shall pay your fees°
When you depart, and save your thanks. How say
    you? 54
My prisoner? Or my guest? By your dread "verily,"
One of them you shall be.

POL.   Your guest, then, madam.
To be your prisoner should import offending,
Which is for me less easy to commit
Than you to punish.

HER.   Not your jailer, then,
But your kind hostess. Come, I'll question you 60
Of my lord's tricks and yours when you were
    boys.
You were pretty lordings° then?

POL.   We were, fair Queen,
Two lads that thought there was no more behind°
But such a day tomorrow as today,
And to be boy eternal.

HER.   Was not my lord 65
The verier wag° o' the two?

POL. We were as twinned lambs that did frisk i'
    the sun,
And bleat the one at the other. What we changed°
Was innocence for innocence, we knew not
The doctrine of ill-doing, nor dreamed 70
That any did. Had we pursued that life,
And our weak spirits ne'er been higher reared
With stronger blood,° we should have answered
    Heaven

3. burden: occupant.   6. cipher: the figure o, which means nothing in itself, but much in 10,000.   8. moe: more.   11–14. I . . . truly: i.e., my fears make me ask myself what evil may be happening in my absence, lest some ill wind at home may cause me to say they were only too true. sneaping: withering.   15. royalty: your royal behavior.   17. sevennight: week. sooth: truth. 18. part . . . between 's: split the difference between us. 19. gainsaying: refusal. 24–25. which . . . me: it would be a punishment to keep me from home, even though in your love you wish me to stay. 30. Charge: make demand of. 32–33. Say . . . ward: if you tell him that all is well in Bohemia, he is driven from his best defense. ward: position of defense in sword play. 36–37. But . . . distaffs:

i.e., if he swears that he wants to go home to see his son, we women will understand that plea and send him packing. thwack: beat. distaff: the wooden rod used in spinning, a woman's occupation.   40. commission: permission.   41–42. gest Prefixed: time allotted.   43. jar: tick.   47. limber vows: slender protestations; something stronger than "verily" is needed to prove that he is forced to go.   48. unsphere . . . stars: pull the stars out of their courses. See App. I.   53. pay . . . fees: a prisoner had to pay the fees due to his jailer before he could be released.   62. lordings: little lords.   63. behind: to come.   66. verier wag: naughtier boy.   68. changed: exchanged.   72–73. And . . . blood: if we had never grown more passionate as we grew stronger.

Boldly " Not guilty," the imposition cleared
Hereditary ours.°

HER.   By this we gather   75
You have tripped since.

POL.   O my most sacred lady!
Temptations have since then been born to 's. For
In those unfledged° days was my wife a girl,
Your precious self had then not crossed the eyes
Of my young playfellow.

HER.   Grace to boot!°   80
Of this make no conclusion,° lest you say
Your Queen and I are devils. Yet go on.
The offenses we have made you do we'll answer
If you first sinned with us, and that with us
You did continue fault, and that you slipped not   85
With any but with us.

LEON.   Is he won yet?

HER. He'll stay, my lord.

LEON.   At my request he would not.
Hermione, my dearest, thou never spokest
To better purpose.

HER.   Never?

LEON.   Never but once.

HER. What! Have I twice said well? When was 't
     before?   90
I prithee tell me, cram 's with praise, and make 's
As fat as tame things.° One good deed dying tongue-
     less
Slaughters a thousand waiting upon that.°
Our praises are our wages. You may ride 's
With one soft kiss a thousand furlongs ere   95
With spur we heat an acre. But to the goal.
My last good deed was to entreat his stay.
What was my first? It has an elder sister,
Or I mistake you. Oh, would her name were Grace!
But once before I spoke to the purpose — when?
Nay, let me have 't, I long.

LEON.   Why, that was when   101
Three crabbèd° months had soured themselves to
     death
Ere I could make thee open thy white hand
And clap° thyself my love. Then didst thou utter
" I am yours forever."

HER.   'Tis grace indeed.   105
Why, lo you now,° I have spoke to the purpose twice.
The one forever earned a royal husband,
The other for some while a friend.°

LEON.   [Aside] Too hot, too hot!
To mingle friendship far is mingling bloods.
I have tremor cordis° on me. My heart dances,   110
But not for joy, not joy. This entertainment°
May a free face° put on, derive a liberty
From heartiness, from bounty, fertile bosom,°
And well become the agent. 'T may, I grant,
But to be paddling palms° and pinching fingers,
As now they are, and making practiced smiles,   116
As in a looking-glass, and then to sigh, as 'twere
The mort° o' the deer — oh, that is entertainment
My bosom likes not, nor my brows!° Mamillius,
Art thou my boy?

MAM.   Aye, my good lord.

LEON.   I' fecks!°   120
Why, that's my bawcock.° What, hast smutched°
     thy nose?
They say it is a copy out of mine. Come, captain,
We must be neat — not neat,° but cleanly, captain.
And yet the steer, the heifer, and the calf
Are all called neat. — Still virginaling°   125
Upon his palm! — How now, you wanton calf!
Art thou my calf?

MAM.   Yes, if you will, my lord.

LEON. Thou want'st a rough pash,° and the
     shoots° that I have,
To be full like me. Yet they say we are
Almost as like as eggs. Women say so,   130
That will say anything. But were they false
As o'erdyed blacks,° as wind, as waters, false
As dice are to be wished by one that fixes
No bourn 'twixt his and mine,° yet were it true
To say this boy were like me. Come, Sir Page,   135
Look on me with your welkin° eye. Sweet villain!
Most dear'st! My collop!° Can thy dam ——? May't
     be? —
Affection,° thy intention stabs the center!
Thou dost make possible things not so held,
Communicatest with dreams — how can this be? —
With what's unreal thou coactive art,°   141

74-75. the . . . ours: i.e., we were such innocents then that even the original sin (which all men inherit from Adam) should have been forgiven.   78. unfledged: when we were still in the nest.   80. Grace to boot: Heaven help me!   81. make no conclusion: do not carry the argument to a further conclusion.   92. tame things: beasts fattened for eating.   92–93. One . . . that: if one good deed is not rewarded by praise, a thousand others which might have followed are killed off.   102. crabbed: wretched.   104. clap: clasp hands on the bargain.   106. lo . . . now: well now!   108. a friend: With these words, Hermione leads Polixenes aside, holding his hand, and chattering to him gaily. As Leontes watches them, he is suddenly overcome by the devastating thought that Polix-

enes is something more than a friend to his wife. "Friend" in Shakespeare's day sometimes meant "lover." See M for Meas, I.iv.29.   110. tremor cordis: palpitation of the heart.   111. entertainment: kindly treatment.   112. free face: innocent appearance.   113. fertile bosom: natural kindliness.   115. paddling palms: playing with each other's hands.   118. mort: the blast on the horn denoting the death of the deer and the end of the hunt.   119. brows: Leontes hereafter becomes obsessed by the thought that he is a cuckold. See App. 11.   120. I' fecks: faith.   121. bawcock: fine cock. smutched: smudged.   123. not neat: he shies away from neat (calf), as it implies another horned beast.   125. virginaling: playing as on the virginals. See Pl. 19f.   128. pash: head. shoots: growth; i.e., hair.   132. o'erdyed blacks: black material so often dyed that it has become rotten.   132–34. false . . . mine: as false as a dishonest gambler would wish the dice to be who observes no boundary (bourn) between his and mine.   136. welkin: blue as the sky.   137. collop: lit., a slice, so slice of me. dam: mother.   138. Affection: is it affection that she shows? Her intention (i.e., lust) stabs me to the heart. The whole passage is deliberately incoherent as Leontes' monstrous thoughts take shape.   141. thou . . . art: you join with.

And fellow'st° nothing. Then 'tis very credent
Thou mayst cojoin with something; and thou dost,
And that beyond commission,° and I find it,
And that to the infection of my brains   145
And hardening of my brows.

POL.   What means Sicilia?

HER. He something seems unsettled.

POL.   How, my lord!
What cheer? How is 't with you, best Brother?

HER.   You look
As if you held a brow of much distraction.°
Are you moved, my lord?

LEON.   No, in good earnest.   150
How sometimes nature° will betray its folly,
Its tenderness, and make itself a pastime
To harder bosoms!° Looking on the lines
Of my boy's face, methought I did recoil
Twenty-three years, and saw myself unbreeched,°
In my green velvet coat, my dagger muzzled°   156
Lest it should bite its master, and so prove,
As ornaments oft do, too dangerous.
How like, methought, I then was to this kernel,
This squash,° this gentleman. Mine honest friend,
Will you take eggs for money?°   161

MAM. No, my lord, I'll fight.

LEON. You will! Why, happy man be 's dole!° My
brother,
Are you so fond of your young Prince as we
Do seem to be of ours?

POL.   If at home, sir,   165
He's all my exercise, my mirth, my matter —
Now my sworn friend, and then mine enemy,
My parasite,° my soldier, statesman, all.
He makes a July's day short as December,
And with his varying childness° cures in me   170
Thoughts that would thick my blood.

LEON.   So stands this squire
Officed with me.° We two will walk, my lord,
And leave you to your graver steps. Hermione,
How thou lovest us show in our brother's wel-
come.
Let what is dear in Sicily be cheap.   175
Next to thyself and my young rover, he's
Apparent° to my heart.

HER.   If you would seek us,
We are yours i' the garden. Shall 's attend you there?

LEON. To your own bents° dispose you. You'll be
found,
Be you beneath the sky. [*Aside*] I am angling now,
Though you perceive me not how I give line.   181
Go to, go to!
How she holds up the neb,° the bill, to him!
And arms her with the boldness of a wife
To her allowing° husband!

[*Exeunt* POLIXENES, HERMIONE, *and* ATTENDANTS.]
               Gone already!   185
Inch-thick, knee-deep, o'er head and ears a forked
one!°
Go, play, boy, play. Thy mother plays, and I
Play too, but so disgraced a part whose issue
Will hiss me to my grave. Contempt and clamor
Will be my knell. Go, play, boy, play. There have
been,   190
Or I am much deceived, cuckolds ere now.
And many a man there is, even at this present,
Now, while I speak this, holds his wife by the arm,
That little thinks she has been sluiced in 's absence
And his pond fished by his next neighbor, by   195
Sir Smile, his neighbor. Nay, there's comfort in 't
Whiles other men have gates and those gates opened,
As mine, against their will. Should all despair
That have revolted wives, the tenth of mankind
Would hang themselves. Physic for 't there is none.
It is a bawdy planet, that will strike   201
Where 'tis predominant,° and 'tis powerful, think it,
From east, west, north, and south. Be it concluded,
No barricado° for a belly, know 't,
It will let in and out the enemy   205
With bag and baggage. Many thousand on 's
Have the disease and feel 't not. How now, boy!

MAM. I am like you, they say.

LEON.   Why, that's some comfort.
What, Camillo there?

CAM. Aye, my good lord.   210

LEON. Go play, Mamillius. Thou'rt an honest man.
               [*Exit* MAMILLIUS.]
Camillo, this great sir will yet stay longer.

CAM. You had much ado to make his anchor hold.
When you cast out, it still came home.

LEON.   Didst note it?

CAM. He would not stay at your petitions, made
His business more material.°

LEON.   Didst perceive it?   216
[*Aside*] They're here° with me already, whispering,
rounding°
" Sicilia is a so-forth." 'Tis far gone

---

142. fellow'st: are companion to.   **144. commission:** i.e., what is lawful.   **148-49. You . . . distraction:** from the wrinkles in your brow you appear to be much worried.   **151. nature:** natural feelings.   **152-53. pastime . . . bosoms:** a joke to coarser minds. **155. unbreeched:** as a small boy, not yet old enough to wear breeches.   **156. muzzled:** fastened in its sheath.   **160. squash:** the peapod before it is ripe. Cf. *T Night*, I.v.166.   **161. eggs . . . money:** a proverb meaning to accept worthless trifles for good money; i.e., be imposed upon.   **163. happy . . . dole:** a common proverb meaning "May it be his luck to be happy."   **168. parasite:** hanger-on.   **170. varying childness:** the varying moods of a child.   **171-72. So . . . me:** this young man stands in the same relation to me.   **177. Apparent:** heir apparent, next in succession.

179. bents: inclinations.   **183. neb:** beak.   **185. allowing:** approving.   **186. forked one:** cuckold.   **201-02. bawdy . . . predominant:** we live under the influence of a planet that makes us bawdy. See App. 1. Cf. *Lear*, I.ii.128-41.   **204. barricado:** defense to keep the enemy out.   **215-16. made . . . material:** i.e., he said his business was too important.   **217. here:** i.e., they make the V sign at me — which in Shakespeare's time meant "You are a cuckold." **rounding:** murmuring.

When I shall gust° it last. — How came 't, Camillo,
That he did stay?
    CAM.   At the good Queen's entreaty.   220
    LEON. At the Queen's be 't. "Good" should be
    pertinent,°
But, so it is, it is not. Was this taken°
By any understanding pate but thine?
For thy conceit is soaking,° will draw in
More than the common blocks.° Not noted, is 't,
But of the finer natures? By some severals   226
Of headpiece extraordinary?° Lower messes°
Perchance are to this business purblind? Say.
    CAM. Business, my lord! I think most understand
Bohemia stays here longer.
    LEON.   Ha!
    CAM.   Stays here longer.   230
    LEON. Aye, but why?
    CAM. To satisfy your Highness, and the entreaties
Of our most gracious mistress.
    LEON.   Satisfy!°
The entreaties of your mistress! Satisfy!
Let that suffice. I have trusted thee, Camillo,   235
With all the nearest things to my heart, as well
My chamber councils.° Wherein, priestlike, thou
Hast cleansed my bosom, I from thee departed
Thy penitent reformed. But we have been
Deceived in thy integrity, deceived   240
In that which seems so.
    CAM.   Be it forbid, my lord!
    LEON. To bide upon 't,° thou art not honest, or
If thou inclinest that way, thou art a coward
Which hoxes° honesty behind, restraining
From course required. Or else thou must be counted
A servant grafted° in my serious trust   246
And therein negligent; or else a fool
That seest a game played home, the rich stake
    drawn,°
And takest it all for jest.
    CAM.   My gracious lord,
I may be negligent, foolish, and fearful.   250
In every one of these no man is free
But that his negligence, his folly, fear,
Among the infinite doings of the world,
Sometime puts forth.° In your affairs, my lord,
If ever I were willful-negligent,   255
It was my folly. If industriously

I played the fool, it was my negligence,
Not weighing well the end. If° ever fearful
To do a thing where I the issue doubted,
Whereof the execution did cry out   260
Against the nonperformance, 'twas a fear
Which oft infects the wisest. These, my lord,
Are such allowed° infirmities that honesty
Is never free of. But, beseech your Grace,
Be plainer with me, let me know my trespass   265
By its own visage. If I then deny it,
'Tis none of mine.
    LEON.   Ha' not you seen, Camillo —
But that's past doubt, you have, or your eyeglass°
Is thicker than a cuckold's horn — or heard,
For to a vision so apparent rumor   270
Cannot be mute° — or thought, for cogitation°
Resides not in that man that does not think —
My wife is slippery? If thou wilt confess,
Or else be impudently negative,
To have nor eyes nor ears nor thought, then say
My wife's a hobbyhorse,° deserves a name   276
As rank° as any flax wench that puts to
Before her trothplight.° Say 't and justify 't.
    CAM. I would not be a stander-by to hear
My sovereign mistress clouded so without   280
My present° vengeance taken. 'Shrew my heart,
You never spoke what did become you less
Than this, which to reiterate were sin
As deep as that, though true.
    LEON.   Is whispering nothing?
Is leaning cheek to cheek? Is meeting noses?   285
Kissing with inside lip? Stopping the career
Of laughter with a sigh — a note infallible
Of breaking honesty?° — Horsing° foot on foot?
Skulking in corners? Wishing clocks more swift?
Hours, minutes? Noon, midnight? And all eyes
Blind with the pin and web° but theirs, theirs only,
That would unseen be wicked? Is this nothing?   292
Why, then the world and all that's in 't is nothing,
The covering sky is nothing, Bohemia nothing,
My wife is nothing, nor nothing have these nothings
If this be nothing.
    CAM.   Good my lord, be cured   296
Of this diseased opinion, and betimes,
For 'tis most dangerous.
    LEON.   Say it be, 'tis true.
    CAM. No, no, my lord.
    LEON.   It is. You lie, you lie.

---

219. gust: taste, get to hear of.   221. pertinent: i.e., *good* should be (but is not) the right word for her.   222. taken: observed. 224. conceit is soaking: understanding quickly absorbs the truth. 225. blocks: blockheads.   226–27. severals . . . extraordinary: individuals of unusual intelligence.   227. messes: those who sit at the lower tables in the hall.   233. Satisfy: Leontes, who is in the mood to see a double meaning in everything, takes *satisfy* to mean "satisfy her lust." 237. chamber councils: state secrets. 242. To . . . upon 't: to insist on it.   244. hoxes: cripples; lit., hamstrings, cuts the tendon behind the knee.   246. grafted: planted.   248. played . . . drawn: in grim earnest, great winnings made.   254. puts forth: grows leaves and flowers like a plant.

258–62. If . . . wisest: if I ever feared to do a thing which ought to have been done rather then left undone because I was doubtful of the consequences, it was a fear that often afflicts the wisest. 263. allowed: excusable.   268. eyeglass: the lens of the eye. 270–71. to . . . mute: for in a matter so clear to sight gossip cannot be silent.   271. cogitation: power of thought.   276. hobbyhorse: loose woman.   277. rank: foul.   277–78. flax wench . . . trothplight: any common creature that anticipates her marriage. flax wench: lit., a woman who spins flax, "factory hand." 281. present: immediate.   288. breaking honesty: virtue giving way. Horsing: setting.   291. pin . . . web: cataract of the eye.

I say thou liest, Camillo, and I hate thee,   300
Pronounce thee a gross lout, a mindless slave,
Or else a hovering temporizer° that
Canst with thine eyes at once see good and evil,
Inclining to them both. Were my wife's liver
Infected as her life, she would not live   305
The running of one glass.°
    CAM.   Who does infect her?
    LEON. Why, he that wears her like her medal,
      hanging
About his neck, Bohemia. Who if I
Had servants true about me, that bare eyes
To see alike mine honor as their profits,   310
Their own particular thrifts,° they would do that
Which should undo more doing. Aye, and thou,
His cupbearer — whom I from meaner form
Have benched and reared to worship,° who mayst
    see
Plainly as Heaven sees earth and earth sees Heaven,
How I am galled° — mightst bespice° a cup,   316
To give mine enemy a lasting wink,
Which draught to me were cordial.°
    CAM.   Sir, my lord,
I could do this, and that with no rash potion,
But with a lingering dram° that should not work
Maliciously like poison. But I cannot   321
Believe this crack° to be in my dread mistress,
So sovereignly being honorable.°
I have loved thee ——
    LEON.   Make that thy question,° and go rot!
Dost think I am so muddy, so unsettled,   325
To appoint myself in this vexation;° sully
The purity and whiteness of my sheets,
Which to preserve is sleep, which being spotted
Is goads, thorns, nettles, tails of wasps;
Give scandal to the blood o' the Prince my son,   330
Who I do think is mine and love as mine,
Without ripe moving° to 't? Would I do this?
Could man so blench?°
    CAM.   I must believe you, sir.
I do, and will fetch off° Bohemia for 't,
Provided that when he's removed, your Highness
Will take again your Queen as yours at first,   336
Even for your son's sake, and thereby for sealing
The injury of tongues° in Courts and kingdoms

Known and allied to yours.
    LEON.   Thou dost advise me
Even so as I mine own course have set down.   340
I'll give no blemish to her honor, none.
    CAM. My lord,
Go then, and with a countenance as clear
As friendship wears at feasts, keep with° Bohemia
And with your Queen. I am his cupbearer.   345
If from me he have wholesome beverage,
Account me not your servant.
    LEON.   This is all.
Do 't and thou hast the one half of my heart,
Do 't not, thou splitt'st thine own.
    CAM.   I'll do 't, my lord.
    LEON. I will seem friendly, as thou hast advised
    me.   [Exit.]
    CAM. O miserable lady! But for me,   351
What case stand I in? I must be the poisoner
Of good Polixenes. And my ground° to do 't
Is the obedience to a master, one
Who, in rebellion with himself, will have   355
All that are his so too. To do this deed,
Promotion follows. If I could find example
Of thousands that had struck anointed kings
And flourished after, I 'd not do 't. But since
Nor brass nor stone nor parchment° bears not one,
Let villainy itself forswear 't.° I must   361
Forsake the Court. To do 't, or no, is certain
To me a breakneck. Happy star reign now!°
Here comes Bohemia.
    [Re-enter POLIXENES.]
    POL.   This is strange. Methinks
My favor here begins to warp.° Not speak?   365
Good day, Camillo.
    CAM.   Hail, most royal sir!
    POL. What is the news i' the Court?
    CAM.   None rare, my lord.
    POL. The King hath on him such a countenance
As° he had lost some province, and a region
Loved as he loves himself. Even now I met him
With customary compliment,° when he,   371
Wafting his eyes to the contrary and falling
A lip of much contempt,° speeds from me, and
So leaves me to consider what is breeding°
That changes thus his manners.   375
    CAM. I dare not know, my lord.
    POL. How! Dare not! Do not. Do you know, and
    dare not?
Be intelligent° to me. 'Tis thereabouts,°

---

302. **hovering temporizer:** a man of no principles.   306. **running . . . glass:** one turn of the hourglass.   311. **particular thrifts:** special advantages.   313–14. **meaner . . . worship:** from sitting at the bottom end of the bench have promoted to sit amongst the nobility.   316. **galled:** rubbed sore. **bespice:** add spice to; i.e., poison.   318. **cordial:** a tonic.   320. **lingering dram:** a dose that would work slowly.   322. **crack:** flaw.   323. **sovereignly . . . honorable:** so supremely honorable.   324. **Make . . . question:** i.e., if you doubt my words.   326. **appoint . . . vexation:** to cause myself this grief deliberately. **appoint:** lit., dress myself in.   332. **ripe moving:** good reason to move me.   333. **blench:** lit., shy like a horse at imaginary fears.   334. **fetch off:** remove, make way with.   337–38. **sealing . . . tongues:** stopping malicious gossip.

344. **keep with:** keep company with.   353. **ground:** reason.   360. **Nor . . . parchment:** i.e., every kind of record.   361. **forswear 't:** swear not to do it.   363. **Happy . . . now:** may some lucky star direct us.   365. **warp:** shrink.   369. **As:** as if.   371. **customary compliment:** usual salutation.   372–73. **Wafting . . . contempt:** turning his eyes away from me and making a contemptuous movement with his lower lip. **falling:** letting fall.   374. **breeding:** hatching.   378. **Be intelligent:** tell me. **'Tis thereabouts:** i.e., you are hinting at something.

For, to yourself, what you do know, you must,
'And cannot say, you dare not. Good Camillo,   380
Your changed complexions are to me a mirror
Which shows me mine changed too, for I must be
A party in this alteration, finding
Myself thus altered with 't.

CAM.   There is a sickness
Which puts some of us in distemper,° but   385
I cannot name the disease. And it is caught
Of you that yet are well.

POL.   How! Caught of me!
Make me not sighted like the basilisk.°
I have looked on thousands who have sped° the
          better
By my regard, but killed none so. Camillo —   390
As you are certainly a gentleman, thereto
Clerklike experienced,° which no less adorns
Our gentry than our parents' noble names,
In whose success we are gentle° — I beseech you
If you know aught which does behoove my knowl-
          edge,   395
Thereof to be informed, imprison 't not
In ignorant concealment.

CAM.   I may not answer.

POL. A sickness caught of me, and yet I well!
I must be answered. Dost thou hear, Camillo?
I conjure° thee, by all the parts° of man   400
Which honor does acknowledge, whereof the least
Is not this suit of mine, that thou declare
What incidency° thou dost guess of harm
Is creeping toward me — how far off, how near,
Which way to be prevented if to be,   405
If not, how best to bear it.

CAM.   Sir, I will tell you,
Since I am charged in honor° and by him
That I think honorable. Therefore mark my coun-
          sel,
Which must be ev'n as swiftly followed as
I mean to utter it, or both yourself and me   410
Cry lost, and so good night!

POL.   On, good Camillo.

CAM. I am appointed him° to murder you.

POL. By whom, Camillo?

CAM.   By the King.

POL.   For what?

CAM. He thinks — nay, with all confidence he
          swears,
As he had seen 't, or been an instrument   415
To vice° you to 't — that you have touched his
          Queen
Forbiddenly.

POL.   Oh then, my best blood turn
To an infected jelly, and my name
Be yoked with his that did betray the Best!°
Turn then my freshest reputation to   420
A savor° that may strike the dullest nostril
Where I arrive, and my approach be shunned —
Nay, hated too, worse than the great'st infection
That e'er was heard or read!

CAM.   Swear his thought over
By each particular star in Heaven and   425
By all their influences, you may as well
Forbid the sea for to obey the moon
As or by oath° remove or counsel shake
The fabric of his folly, whose foundation
Is piled upon his faith, and will continue   430
The standing of his body.°

POL.   How should this grow?

CAM. I know not. But I am sure 'tis safer to
Avoid what's grown than question how 'tis born.
If therefore you dare trust my honesty,
That lies enclosèd in this trunk° which you   435
Shall bear along impawned,° away tonight!
Your followers I will whisper to the business,
And will by twos and threes at several posterns°
Clear them o' the city. For myself, I'll put
My fortunes to your service, which are here   440
By this discovery lost. Be not uncertain,
For, by the honor of my parents, I
Have uttered truth. Which if you seek to prove,
I dare not stand by, nor shall you be safer
Than one condemned by the King's own mouth,
          thereon   445
His execution sworn.

POL.   I do believe thee.
I saw his heart in 's face. Give me thy hand.
Be pilot to me and thy places shall
Still neighbor mine. My ships are ready, and
My people did expect my hence departure   450
Two days ago. This jealousy
Is for a precious creature. As she's rare,
Must it be great. And as his person's mighty,
Must it be violent. And as he does conceive
He is dishonored by a man which ever   455
Professed° to him, why, his revenges must
In that be made more bitter. Fear o'ershades me.
Good expedition be my friend, and comfort
The gracious Queen, part of his theme, but nothing
Of his ill-ta'en suspicion!° Come, Camillo,   460
I will respect thee as a father if

419. that . . . Best: i.e., Judas Iscariot, who betrayed Jesus.
421. savor: stink.   428. oath: i.e., even if you swear that you are
innocent he will not believe you.   431. standing . . . body: so
long as he can stand.   435. trunk: body.   436. impawned: as a
pledge of my faith.   438. several posterns: different gates.
456. Professed: i.e., that he was a true friend.   458–60. Good . . .
suspicion: may my speedy departure help me to escape and bring
comfort to the gracious Queen who is partly the cause of his
anger, but not a true cause for suspicion.

385. distemper: mental sickness.   388. basilisk: a fabulous serpent able to kill by its glance. See *Rich III*, I.ii.151,n.   389. sped:
fared.   392. Clerklike experienced: with the experience of a man
of education.   394. In . . . gentle: from whom by descent we are
called gentlemen.   400. conjure: solemnly demand. parts: qualities.   403. incidency: likelihood.   407. charged in honor: bound
by my honor.   412. him: by him.   416. vice: screw, force.

Thou bear'st my life off hence. Let us avoid.°
　CAM. It is in mine authority to command
The keys of all the posterns. Please your Highness
To take the urgent hour.° Come, sir, away.　465
　　　　　　　　　　　　　　　　[*Exeunt.*]

Act II

SCENE I. *A room in* LEONTES' *palace.*

[*Enter* HERMIONE, MAMILLIUS, *and* LADIES.]
　HER. Take the boy to you. He so troubles me
'Tis past enduring.
　1. LADY.　　　　　Come, my gracious lord,
Shall I be your playfellow?
　MAM.　　　　　　No, I'll none of you.
　1. LADY. Why, my sweet lord?
　MAM. You'll kiss me hard, and speak to me as if
I were a baby still. I love you better.　　　6
　2. LADY. And why so, my lord?
　MAM.　　　　　　Not for because
Your brows are blacker — yet black brows, they say,
Become some women best, so that there be not
Too much hair there, but in a semicircle,　10
Or a half-moon made with a pen.
　2. LADY.　　　　Who taught you this?
　MAM. I learned it out of women's faces. Pray now,
What color are your eyebrows?
　1. LADY.　　　　　Blue, my lord.
　MAM. Nay, that's a mock. I have seen a lady's nose
That has been blue, but not her eyebrows.
　1. LADY.　　　　　Hark ye,　15
The Queen your mother rounds apace. We shall
Present our services to a fine new Prince
One of these days, and then you'd wanton° with us,
If we would have you.
　2. LADY.　　　　She is spread of late
Into a goodly bulk. Good time encounter her!°　20
　HER. What wisdom stirs amongst you? Come, sir,
　　now
I am for you again. Pray you, sit by us
And tell 's a tale.
　MAM.　　　　Merry or sad shall 't be?
　HER. As merry as you will.
　MAM. A sad tale's best for winter. I have one　25
Of sprites and goblins.
　HER.　　　　Let's have that, good sir.
Come on, sit down. Come on, and do your best
To fright me with your sprites, you're powerful at it.
　MAM. There was a man ——

HER.　　　　　Nay, come, sit down, then on.
　MAM. Dwelt by a churchyard — I will tell it
　　softly.　　　　　　　　　　　　　　30
Yon crickets° shall not hear it.
　HER.　　　　　Come on, then,
And give 't me in mine ear.
　　　[*Enter* LEONTES, *with* ANTIGONUS, LORDS, *and*
　　　　　　　　OTHERS.]
　LEON. Was he met there? His train? Camillo
　　with him?
　1. LORD. Behind the tuft of pines I met them.
　　Never
Saw I men scour° so on their way. I eyed them　35
Even to their ships.
　LEON.　　　　How blest am I
In my just censure,° in my true opinion!
Alack, for lesser knowledge, how accursed
In being so blest! There may be in the cup
A spider° steeped and one may drink, depart,　40
And yet partake° no venom, for his knowledge
Is not infected. But if one present
The abhorred ingredient to his eye, make known
How he hath drunk, he cracks his gorge,° his sides,
With violent hefts.° I have drunk, and seen the
　　spider.　　　　　　　　　　　　　　45
Camillo was his help in this, his pander.°
There is a plot against my life, my crown,
All's true that is mistrusted.° That false villain
Whom I employed was pre-employed by him.
He has discovered° my design, and I　　50
Remain a pinched° thing — yea, a very trick
For them to play at will. How came the posterns
So easily open?
　1. LORD.　　　By his great authority,
Which often hath no less prevailed than so
On your command.
　LEON.　　　　I know 't too well.　55
Give me the boy. I am glad you did not nurse him.
Though he does bear some signs of me, yet you
Have too much blood in him.
　HER.　　　　　What is this? Sport?
　LEON. Bear the boy hence, he shall not come about
　　her.
Away with him! And let her sport herself　60
With that she's big with, for 'tis Polixenes
Has made thee swell thus.
　HER.　　　　　But I'd say he had not,
And I'll be sworn you would believe my saying,
Howe'er you lean to the nayward.°
　LEON.　　　　　You, my lords,
Look on her, mark her well. Be but about　65

To say " She is a goodly lady " and
The justice of your hearts will thereto add
" 'Tis pity she's not honest, honorable."
Praise her but for this her withoutdoor form,°
Which on my faith deserves high speech, and
    straight   70
The shrug, the hum or ha, these petty brands
That calumny doth use. Oh, I am out,°
That mercy does, for calumny will sear°   73
Virtue itself. These shrugs, these hums and ha's,
When you have said " She's goodly," come between
Ere you can say " She's honest." But be 't known,
From him that has most cause to grieve it should be,
She's an adulteress.
    HER.   Should a villain say so,
The most replenished° villain in the world,
He were as much more villain. You, my lord,   80
Do but mistake.
    LEON.   You have mistook, my lady,
Polixenes for Leontes. O thou thing!
Which I'll not call a creature of thy place,°
Lest barbarism,° making me the precedent,
Should a like language use to all degrees,   85
And mannerly distinguishment leave out
Betwixt the prince and beggar.° I have said
She's an adulteress, I have said with whom.
More, she's a traitor, and Camillo is
A federary° with her; and one that knows,   90
What she should shame to know herself
But with her most vile principal, that she's
A bedswerver,° even as bad as those
That vulgars° give bold'st titles — aye, and privy°
To this their late escape.
    HER.   No, by my life,   95
Privy to none of this. How will this grieve you
When you shall come to clearer knowledge, that
You thus have published° me! Gentle my lord,
You scarce can right me throughly° then to say
You did mistake.
    LEON.   No. If I mistake   100
In those foundations which I build upon,
The center° is not big enough to bear
A schoolboy's top. Away with her, to prison!
He who shall speak for her is afar-off guilty
But that he speaks.°
    HER.   There's some ill planet° reigns.   105

69. **withoutdoor form:** outward shape. 72. **out:** wrong. 73. **sear:** brand. 79. **replenished:** complete. 83. **creature . . . place:** one in your royal position. 84. **barbarism:** the ignorant multitude. 85–87. **Should . . . beggar:** should use the same low word to women of every rank, and omit the distinction which showed the difference between a queen and beggarwoman. 90. **federary:** confederate. 93. **bedswerver:** false to the marriage bed. 94. **vulgars:** the lowest creatures. **privy:** sharing the secret of. 98. **published:** publicly proclaimed. 99. **throughly:** thoroughly. 102. **center:** the center of the Earth, what was regarded as the pivot of the universe. 104–05. **afar-off . . . speaks:** is partially guilty even for speaking well of her. 105. **ill planet:** See I.ii.201,n. The notion of the evil influence of the stars runs through this part of the play.

I must be patient till the Heavens look
With an aspéct° more favorable. Good my lords,
I am not prone to weeping, as our sex
Commonly are, the want of which vain dew
Perchance shall dry your pities. But I have   110
That honorable grief lodged here which burns
Worse than tears drown. Beseech you all, my lords,
With thoughts so qualified° as your charities
Shall best instruct you, measure° me. And so
The King's will be performed!
    LEON.   Shall I be heard?   115
    HER. Who is 't that goes with me? Beseech your
    Highness,
My women may be with me, for you see
My plight requires it. Do not weep, good fools,°
There is no cause. When you shall know your mistress
Has deserved prison, then abound in tears   120
As I come out. This action I now go on
Is for my better grace. Adieu, my lord.
I never wished to see you sorry, now
I trust I shall. My women, come, you have leave.
    LEON. Go, do our bidding. Hence!   125
            [*Exit* QUEEN, *guarded, with* LADIES.]
    1. LORD. Beseech your Highness, call the Queen
    again.
    ANT. Be certain what you do, sir, lest your justice
Prove violence, in the which three great ones suffer,
Yourself, your Queen, your son.
    1. LORD.   For her, my lord,
I dare my life lay down and will do 't, sir,   130
Please you to accept it, that the Queen is spotless
I' the eyes of Heaven and to you. I mean
In this which you accuse her.
    ANT.   If it prove
She's otherwise, I'll keep my stables where
I lodge my wife, I'll go in couples° with her,   135
Than when I feel and see her no farther trust her.
For every inch of woman in the world,
Aye, every dram° of woman's flesh, is false
If she be.
    LEON. Hold your peaces.
    1. LORD.   Good my lord —— 139
    ANT. It is for you we speak, not for ourselves.
You are abused, and by some putter-on°
That will be damned for 't. Would I knew the villain,
I would land-damn° him. Be she honor-flawed,
I have three daughters — the eldest is eleven,   144
The second and the third, nine, and some five —
If this prove true, they'll pay for 't. By mine honor,

107. **aspect:** See App. 1. 113. **qualified:** mixed with kindness; to "qualify" is lit. to mix water with strong drink. 114. **measure:** judge. 118. **fools:** The word is sometimes used as a term of endearment. 135. **go in couples:** tied together like a pair of greyhounds. 138. **dram:** minute portion. 141. **putter-on:** suggesting knave. 143. **land-damn:** a much-disputed word, otherwise unknown. It obviously means something unpleasant.

I'll geld 'em all, fourteen they shall not see,
To bring false generations.° They are coheirs,
And I had rather glib° myself than they
Should not produce fair issue.

LEON.   Cease, no more.   150
You smell this business with a sense as cold
As is a dead man's nose. But I do see 't and feel 't
As you feel doing thus,° and see withal
The instruments° that feel.

ANT.   If it be so,
We need no grave to bury honesty.   155
There's not a grain of it the face to sweeten
Of the whole dungy earth.

LEON.   What! Lack I credit?°

I. LORD. I had rather you did lack than I, my lord,
Upon this ground.° And more it would content me
To have her honor true than your suspicion,   160
Be blamed for 't how you might.

LEON.   Why, what need we°
Commune with you of this, but rather follow
Our forceful instigation?° Our prerogative
Calls not your counsels,° but our natural goodness
Imparts this. Which if you, or stupefied   165
Or seeming so in skill,° cannot or will not
Relish a truth like us, inform yourselves
We need no more of your advice. The matter,
The loss, the gain, the ordering on 't, is all
Properly ours.

ANT.   And I wish, my liege,   170
You had only in your silent judgment tried it,
Without more overture.°

LEON.   How could that be?
Either thou art most ignorant by age,
Or thou wert born a fool. Camillo's flight,
Added to their familiarity —   175
Which was as gross° as ever touched conjecture,°
That lacked sight only, naught for approbation°
But only seeing, all other circumstances
Made up to the deed — doth push on this proceed-
ing.
Yet, for a greater confirmation,   180
For in an act of this importance 'twere
Most piteous to be wild,° I have dispatched in post°
To sacred Delphos,° to Apollo's temple,
Cleomenes and Dion, whom you know
Of stuffed sufficiency.° Now from the oracle   185

They will bring all, whose spiritual counsel had,
Shall stop or spur me. Have I done well?

I. LORD. Well done, my lord.

LEON. Though I am satisfied and need no more
Than what I know, yet shall the oracle   190
Give rest to the minds of others, such as he
Whose ignorant credulity will not
Come up to the truth. So have we thought it good
From our free° person she should be confined,
Lest that the treachery of the two fled hence   195
Be left her to perform. Come, follow us.
We are to speak in public, for this business
Will raise us all.

ANT.   [Aside] To laughter, as I take it,   199
If the good truth were known.   [Exeunt.]

SCENE II. A prison.

[Enter PAULINA, a GENTLEMAN, and ATTENDANTS.]

PAUL. The keeper of the prison, call to him.
Let him have knowledge who I am.
                              [Exit GENTLEMAN.]
                              Good lady,
No Court in Europe is too good for thee.
What dost thou, then, in prison?
[Re-enter GENTLEMAN, with the JAILER.] Now, good
sir,
You know me, do you not?

JAIL.   For a worthy lady,   5
And one who much I honor.

PAUL.   Pray you, then,
Conduct me to the Queen.

JAIL.   I may not, madam.
To the contrary I have express commandment.

PAUL. Here's ado,
To lock up honesty and honor from   10
The access of gentle visitors! Is 't lawful, pray you,
To see her women? Any of them? Emilia?

JAIL. So please you, madam,
To put apart these your attendants, I
Shall bring Emilia forth.

PAUL.   I pray now, call her.   15
Withdraw yourselves.
                    [Exeunt GENTLEMAN and ATTENDANTS.]

JAIL.   And, madam,
I must be present at your conference.

PAUL. Well, be 't so, prithee.   [Exit JAILER.]
Here's such ado to make no stain a stain   19
As passes coloring.°
[Re-enter JAILER, with EMILIA.] Dear gentlewoman,
How fares our gracious lady?

EMIL. As well as one so great and so forlorn
May hold together. On her frights and griefs,
Which never tender lady hath borne greater,

148. To ... generations: to produce bastards.   149. glib: geld.
153. doing thus: He makes some gesture, probably clenching his
own fists.   154. instruments: i.e., the fingers.   157. Lack I
credit: am I not believed?   159. ground: foundation.   161. Why
... we: Leontes, being unable to persuade his nobles by argument, falls back on his dignity and speaks to them with the royal
"we."   163. forceful instigation: powerful incentive.   163-64. Our
... counsels: as your King I am under no obligation to ask
your advice.   166. skill: cunning.   172. overture: disclosure.
176. gross: obvious. touched conjecture: caused suspicion.
177. approbation: proof.   182. wild: rash. in post: hastily. See
App. 17.   183. Delphos: See W Tale Intro. p. 1429b.   185. Of
... sufficiency: fully competent.

194. free: guiltless.
Sc. ii: 20. passes coloring: outdoes any painting.

She is something° before her time delivered.   25
   PAUL. A boy?
   EMIL.   A daughter, and a goodly babe,
Lusty and like to live. The Queen receives
Much comfort in 't, says " My poor prisoner,
I am innocent as you."
   PAUL.   I dare be sworn.
These dangerous unsafe lunes° i' the King, be-
   shrew° them!   30
He must be told on 't, and he shall. The office
Becomes a woman best, I'll take 't upon me.
If I prove honey-mouthed,° let my tongue blister
And never to my red-looked° anger be
The trumpet any more. Pray you, Emilia,   35
Commend my best obedience° to the Queen.
If she dares trust me with her little babe,
I'll show 't the King and undertake to be
Her advocate to the loud'st. We do not know
How he may soften at the sight o' the child.   40
The silence often of pure innocence
Persuades when speaking fails.
   EMIL.   Most worthy madam,
Your honor and your goodness is so evident
That your free° undertaking cannot miss
A thriving issue.° There is no lady living   45
So meet° for this great errand. Please your ladyship
To visit the next room, I'll presently°
Acquaint the Queen of your most noble offer,
Who but today hammered of° this design,
But durst not tempt° a minister of honor,°   50
Lest she should be denied.
   PAUL.   Tell her, Emilia,
I'll use that tongue I have. If wit flow from 't
As boldness from my bosom, let 't not be doubted
I shall do good.
   EMIL.   Now be you blest for it!   54
I'll to the Queen. Please you, come something nearer.
   JAIL. Madam, if 't please the Queen to send the
   babe,
I know not what I shall incur to pass it,°
Having no warrant.°
   PAUL.   You need not fear it, sir.
This child was prisoner to the womb, and is
By law and process of great nature thence   60
Freed and enfranchised° — not a party to
The anger of the King, nor guilty of,
If any be, the trespass of the Queen.
   JAIL. I do believe it.
   PAUL. Do not you fear. Upon mine honor, I   65
Will stand betwixt you and danger.   [Exeunt.]

SCENE III. *A room in* LEONTES' *palace.*

[*Enter* LEONTES, ANTIGONUS, LORDS, *and* SERVANTS.]
   LEON. Nor night nor day no rest. It is but weak-
   ness
To bear the matter thus, mere weakness. If
The cause were not in being° — part o' the cause,
She the adulteress, for the harlot King
Is quite beyond mine arm, out of the blank°   5
And level° of my brain, plotproof.° But she
I can hook to me. Say that she were gone,
Given to the fire, a moiety° of my rest
Might come to me again. Who's there?
   I. SERV.   My lord?
   LEON. How does the boy?
   I. SERV.   He took good rest tonight,   10
'Tis hoped his sickness is discharged.°
   LEON. To see his nobleness!
Conceiving the dishonor of his mother,
He straight declined, drooped, took it deeply,
Fastened and fixed the shame on 't in himself,   15
Threw off his spirit,° his appetite, his sleep,
And downright languished. Leave me solely.° Go,
See how he fares. [*Exit* SERVANT.] Fie, fie! No
   thought of him.°
The very thought of my revenges that way
Recoil upon me. In himself too mighty,   20
And in his parties, his alliance,° let him be
Until a time may serve. For present vengeance,
Take it on her. Camillo and Polixenes
Laugh at me, make their pastime at my sorrow.
They should not laugh if I could reach them, nor
Shall she within my power.
       [*Enter* PAULINA, *with a* CHILD.]
   I. LORD.   You must not enter.   26
   PAUL. Nay, rather, good my lords, be second° to
   me.
Fear you his tyrannous passion more, alas,
Than the Queen's life? A gracious innocent soul,
More free° than he is jealous.
   ANT.   That's enough.   30
   2. SERV. Madam, he hath not slept tonight, com-
   manded
None should come at him.
   PAUL.   Not so hot, good sir.
I come to bring him sleep. 'Tis such as you,
That creep like shadows by him and do sigh
At each his needless heavings, such as you   35
Nourish the cause of his awaking. I
Do come with words as medicinal° as true,

---

25. **something:** somewhat. 30. **lunes:** mad fits. **beshrew:** plague
on. 33. **honey-mouthed:** sweet in words. 34. **red-looked:** red-
faced. 36. **best obedience:** a formal phrase of respectful compliment. 44. **free:** voluntary. 45. **thriving issue:** successful result. 46. **meet:** fitting. 47. **presently:** immediately. 49. **hammered of:** kept on thinking about. 50. **tempt:** try, approach.
minister of honor: one of the chief ministers. 57. **what . . . it:**
what risks I run if I let it pass out of the prison. 58. **warrant:**
written order. 61. **enfranchised:** set at liberty.

Sc. iii: 3. **were . . . being:** was not real. Leontes in his agitation speaks in half-formed sentences. 5. **blank:** lit., the center
of the target. 6. **level:** aim. **plotproof:** proof against my plots.
8. **moiety:** part. 11. **discharged:** gone from him. 16. **Threw
. . . spirit:** became dispirited. 17. **solely:** alone. 18. **him:** i.e.,
Polixenes. 21. **his . . . alliance:** those who side with him, his
allies. 27. **second:** support. 30. **free:** innocent. 37. **medicinal:** healing.

Honest as either, to purge him of that humor°
'That presses° him from sleep.

LEON.　　　　　　　　　　What noise there, ho?

PAUL. No noise, my lord, but needful conference°
About some gossips° for your Highness.

LEON.　　　　　　　　　　How!　　41
Away with that audacious lady! Antigonus,
I charged thee that she should not come about me.
I knew she would.

ANT.　　　　　I told her so, my lord,
On your displeasure's peril and on mine,　　45
She should not visit you.

LEON.　　　　　What, canst not rule her?

PAUL. From all dishonesty he can. In this,
Unless he take the course that you have done,
Commit me for committing honor, trust it,
He shall not rule me.

ANT.　　　　　La you now,° you hear.　　50
When she will take the rein I let her run,
But she'll not stumble.

PAUL.　　　　　Good my liege, I come —
And I beseech you hear me, who professes
Myself your loyal servant, your physician,
Your most obedient counselor, yet that dares　　55
Less appear so in comforting° your evils
Than such as most seem yours — I say I come
From your good Queen.

LEON.　　　　　Good Queen!

PAUL.　　　　　Good Queen, my lord.
Good Queen, I say good Queen,
And would by combat make her good, so were I　　60
A man, the worst about you.

LEON.　　　　　Force her hence.

PAUL. Let him that makes but trifles of his eyes
First hand me. On mine own accord I'll off,
But first I'll do my errand. The good Queen,
For she is good, hath brought you forth a daugh-
ter —　　65
Here 'tis — commends it to your blessing.

[*Laying down the* CHILD.]

LEON.　　　　　Out!
A mankind° witch! Hence with her, out o' door!
A most intelligencing° bawd!

PAUL.　　　　　Not so.
I am as ignorant in that as you
In so entitling me, and no less honest　　70
Than you are mad — which is enough, I'll warrant,
As this world goes, to pass for honest.

LEON.　　　　　Traitors!
Will you not push her out? Give her the bastard.
Thou dotard! Thou art woman-tired,° unroosted°

By thy Dame Partlet° here. Take up the bastard,　　75
Take 't up, I say. Give 't to thy crone.°

PAUL.　　　　　Forever°
Unvenerable be thy hands if thou
Takest up the Princess by that forced baseness°
Which he has put upon 't!

LEON.　　　　　He dreads his wife.

PAUL. So I would you did. Then 'twere past all
　　doubt　　80
You'd call your children yours.

LEON.　　　　　A nest of traitors!

ANT. I am none, by this good light.

PAUL.　　　　　Nor I, nor any
But one that's here, and that's himself. For he
The sacred honor of himself, his Queen's,
His hopeful son's, his babe's, betrays to slander,　　85
Whose sting is sharper than the sword's, and will
　　not —
For as the case now stands, it is a curse
He cannot be compelled to 't — once remove
The root of his opinion, which is rotten
As ever oak or stone was sound.

LEON.　　　　　A callat°　　90
Of boundless tongue, who late hath beat her husband
And now baits° me! This brat is none of mine,
It is the issue of Polixenes.
Hence with it, and together with the dam
Commit them to the fire!

PAUL.　　　　　It is yours,　　95
And, might we lay the old proverb to your charge,
So like you 'tis the worse. Behold, my lords,
Although the print° be little, the whole matter
And copy of the father — eye, nose, lip,　　99
The trick of 's frown, his forehead, nay, the valley,°
The pretty dimples of his chin and cheek,
His smiles,
The very mold and frame of hand, nail, finger.
And thou, good goddess Nature, which hast made it
So like to him that got° it, if thou hast　　105
The ordering° of the mind too, 'mongst all colors
No yellow° in 't, lest she suspect, as he does,
Her children not her husband's!

LEON.　　　　　A gross hag!
And, lozel,° thou art worthy to be hanged
That wilt not stay her tongue.

ANT.　　　　　Hang all the husbands　　110
That cannot do that feat, you'll leave yourself
Hardly one subject.

LEON.　　　　　Once more, take her hence.

---

38. humor: mental illness. See App. 3.　39. presses: keeps.
40. needful conference: necessary consideration.　41. gossips:
godparents.　50. La ... now: there now.　56. comforting: bringing
true comfort to.　67. mankind: mannish woman.　68. intelli-
gencing: cunning and full of secrets.　74. woman-tired: henpecked. unroosted: driven off the perch.

75. Dame Partlet: the nagging hen in the story of *Reynard the
Fox.*　76. crone: withered old woman.　76–79. Forever ...
upon 't: i.e., he tells you to pick up the "bastard"; if you obey his
command and thereby admit that this child is not a true Princess,
may your hands be despised forever.　78. forced baseness: the
base birth which he forces on her.　90. callat: drab.　92. baits:
worries.　98. print: type.　100. valley: little cleft in the chin.
105. got: begot.　106. ordering: regulation.　107. yellow: the
color of jealousy.　109. lozel: low fellow.

PAUL. A most unworthy and unnatural lord
Can do no more.

LEON.   I'll ha' thee burned.

PAUL.   I care not.
It is a heretic that makes the fire,   115
Not she which burns in 't. I'll not call you tyrant,
But this most cruel usage of your Queen —
Not able to produce more accusation
Than your own weak-hinged fancy — something
     savors
Of tyranny, and will ignoble make you —   120
Yea, scandalous to the world.

LEON.   On your allegiance,°
Out of the chamber with her! Were I a tyrant,
Where were her life? She durst not call me so
If she did know me one. Away with her!   124

PAUL. I pray you, do not push me, I'll be gone.
Look to your babe, my lord, 'tis yours. Jove send her
A better guiding spirit! What needs these hands?°
You, that are thus so tender o'er his follies,
Will never do him good, not one of you.   129
So, so. Farewell, we are gone.   [*Exit.*]

LEON. Thou, traitor, hast set on thy wife to this.
My child? Away with 't! Even thou, that hast
A heart so tender o'er it, take it hence
And see it instantly consumed with fire,
Even thou and none but thou. Take it up straight.
Within this hour bring me word 'tis done,   136
And by good testimony° or I'll seize thy life,
With what thou else call'st thine. If thou refuse
And wilt encounter with my wrath, say so.
The bastard brains with these my proper° hands
Shall I dash out. Go, take it to the fire,   141
For thou set'st on thy wife.

ANT.   I did not, sir.
These lords, my noble fellows, if they please,
Can clear me in 't.

LORDS.   We can. My royal liege,
He is not guilty of her coming hither.   145

LEON. You're liars all.

I. LORD. Beseech your Highness, give us better
     credit.
We have always truly served you, and beseech you
So to esteem of us. And on our knees we beg,
As recompense of our dear services   150
Past and to come, that you do change this purpose,
Which being so horrible, so bloody, must
Lead on to some foul issue. We all kneel.

LEON. I am a feather for each wind that blows.
Shall I live on to see this bastard kneel   155
And call me father? Better burn it now
Than curse it then. But be it, let it live.
It shall not, neither. You, sir, come you hither,

You that have been so tenderly officious
With Lady Margery, your midwife there,   160
To save this bastard's life — for 'tis a bastard,
So sure as this beard's gray° — what will you adven-
     ture
To save this brat's life?

ANT.   Anything, my lord,
That my ability may undergo,
And nobleness impose. At least thus much: 165
I'll pawn° the little blood which I have left
To save the innocent — anything possible.

LEON. It shall be possible. Swear by this sword
Thou wilt perform my bidding.

ANT.   I will, my lord.

LEON. Mark and perform it. Seest thou? For the
     fail   170
Of any point in 't shall not only be
Death to thyself but to thy lewd-tongued° wife,
Whom for this time we pardon. We enjoin° thee,
As thou art liegeman° to us, that thou carry
This female bastard hence, and that thou bear it
To some remote and desert place quite out   176
Of our dominions, and that there thou leave it,
Without more mercy, to it° own protection
And favor of the climate. As by strange fortune
It came to us, I do in justice charge thee,   180
On thy soul's peril and thy body's torture,
That thou commend it strangely° to some place
Where chance may nurse or end it. Take it up.

ANT. I swear to do this, though a present death
Had been more merciful. Come on, poor babe.   185
Some powerful spirit instruct the kites and ravens
To be thy nurses! Wolves and bears, they say,
Casting their savageness aside, have done
Like offices of pity. Sir, be prosperous
In more than this deed does require!° And blessing
Against this cruelty fight on thy side,   191
Poor thing, condemned to loss!

                    [*Exit with the* CHILD.]

LEON.   No, I'll not rear
Another's issue.

                    [*Enter a* SERVANT.]

SERV.   Please your Highness, posts
From those you sent to the oracle are come
An hour since. Cleomenes and Dion,   195
Being well° arrived from Delphos, are both landed,
Hasting to the Court.

I. LORD.   So please you, sir, their speed
Hath been beyond account.

LEON.   Twenty-three days
They have been absent. 'Tis good speed, foretells
The great Apollo suddenly° will have   200

---

121. On ... allegiance: the most solemn command that can be laid by a sovereign on his subject; to disobey is to commit high treason. 127. What ... hands: i.e., you need not push me. 137. testimony: proof. 140. proper: own.

162. beard's gray: i.e., Antigonus' beard, which Leontes seizes. 166. pawn: pledge. 172. lewd-tongued: foul-mouthed. 173. enjoin: command. 174. liegeman: true subject. 178. it: its. 182. commend it strangely: commit it as a stranger. 190. require: deserve. 196. well: safely. 200. suddenly: quickly.

The truth of this appear. Prepare you, lords,
Summon a session,° that we may arraign°
Our most disloyal lady. For as she hath
Been publicly accused, so shall she have
A just and open trial. While she lives   205
My heart will be a burden to me. Leave me,
And think upon my bidding.   [*Exeunt.*]

Act III

SCENE I.° *A seaport in Sicilia.*

[*Enter* CLEOMENES *and* DION.]
CLE. The climate's delicate, the air most sweet,
Fertile the isle, the temple much surpassing
The common praise it bears.
DION.   I shall report,
For most it caught me, the celestial habits° —
Methinks I so should term them — and the reverence
Of the grave wearers. Oh, the sacrifice!   6
How ceremonious, solemn, and unearthly
It was i' the offering!
CLE.   But of all, the burst
And the ear-deafening voice o' the oracle,
Kin to Jove's thunder, so surprised my sense   10
That I was nothing.
DION.   If the event° o' the journey
Prove as successful to the Queen — oh, be 't so! —
As it hath been to us rare, pleasant, speedy,
The time is worth the use on 't.
CLE.   Great Apollo
Turn all to the best! These proclamations,   15
So forcing faults upon Hermione,
I little like.
DION.   The violent carriage° of it
Will clear or end the business. When the oracle,
Thus by Apollo's great divine sealed up,
Shall the contents discover, something rare°   20
Even then will rush to knowledge. Go. Fresh horses!
And gracious be the issue!   [*Exeunt.*]

SCENE II. *A court of justice.*

[*Enter* LEONTES, LORDS, *and* OFFICERS.]
LEON. This sessions, to our great grief we pro-
          nounce,
Even pushes° 'gainst our heart. The party tried

The daughter of a King, our wife, and one
Of us too much beloved. Let us be cleared°
Of being tyrannous, since we so openly   5
Proceed in justice, which shall have due course,
Even to the guilt or the purgation.°
Produce the prisoner.
OFF. It is His Highness' pleasure that the Queen
Appear in person here in court. Silence!   10
[*Enter* HERMIONE, *guarded,* PAULINA, *and* LADIES
attending.]
LEON. Read the indictment.
OFF. [*Reads.*] "Hermione, Queen to the worthy
Leontes, King of Sicilia, thou art here accused and
arraigned of high treason, in committing adultery
with Polixenes, King of Bohemia, and conspir-   15
ing with Camillo to take away the life of our Sover-
eign Lord the King, thy royal husband. The pre-
tense° whereof being by circumstances partly laid
open, thou, Hermione, contrary to the faith and al-
legiance of a true subject, didst counsel and aid them,
for their better safety, to fly away by night."   22
HER. Since what I am to say must be but that
Which contradicts my accusation, and
The testimony on my part no other   25
But what comes from myself, it shall scarce boot°
          me
To say " Not guilty." Mine integrity,°
Being counted falsehood, shall, as I express it,°
Be so received. But thus, if Powers Divine
Behold our human actions, as they do,   30
I doubt not then but innocence shall make
False accusation blush and tyranny
Tremble at patience. You, my lord, best know,
Who least will seem to do so, my past life
Hath been as continent, as chaste, as true,   35
As I am now unhappy — which is more
Than history can pattern, though devised
And played to take spectators.° For behold me
A fellow of the royal bed, which owe°
A moiety° of the throne, a great King's daughter,
The mother to a hopeful Prince, here standing   41
To prate and talk for life and honor 'fore
Who please to come and hear. For life, I prize it
As I weigh grief, which I would spare. For honor,
'Tis a derivative from me to mine,°   45
And only that I stand for. I appeal
To your own conscience, sir, before Polixenes
Came to your Court, how I was in your grace,
How merited to be so; since he came,
With what encounter so uncurrent I   50

---

202. session: court of law. arraign: formally accuse.
Act III, Sc. i: The purpose of this short scene is to stress the
importance of the oracle on which the plot now turns. 4. celestial habits: heavenly robes. 11. event: result. 17. violent
carriage: headstrong manner of proceeding. 20. rare: unexpected.
Sc. ii: 2. pushes: thrusts.

4. cleared: shown innocent. 7. purgation: acquittal. 18. pretense: intention. 26. boot: be of advantage to. 27. integrity:
truthfulness. 28. as . . . it: even as I say it. 37–38. history
. . . spectators: can be paralleled in history, even though turned
into a play specially written to move an audience. 39. owe:
possess. 40. moiety: share. 45. derivative . . . mine: passes
as an inheritance to my son.

Have strained, to appear thus.° If one jot beyond
The bound of honor, or in act or will
That way inclining, hardened be the hearts
Of all that hear me, and my near'st of kin
Cry fie° upon my grave!

LEON.   I ne'er heard yet   55
That any of these bolder vices wanted
Less impudence to gainsay° what they did
Than to perform it first.

HER.   That's true enough,
Though 'tis a saying, sir, not due to me.

LEON. You will not own it.

HER.   More than mistress of   60
Which comes to me in name of fault I must not
At all acknowledge.° For Polixenes,
With whom I am accused, I do confess
I loved him as in honor he required,
With such a kind of love as might become   65
A lady like me, with a love even such,
So and no other, as yourself commanded.
Which not to have done I think had been in me
Both disobedience and ingratitude
To you and toward your friend, whose love had
          spoke   70
Even since it could speak, from an infant, freely
That it was yours. Now, for conspiracy,
I know not how it tastes, though it be dished
For me to try how. All I know of it
Is that Camillo was an honest man,   75
And why he left your Court, the gods themselves,
Wotting° no more than I, are ignorant.

LEON. You knew of his departure, as you know
What you have underta'en to do in 's absence.

HER. Sir,   80
You speak a language that I understand not.
My life stands in the level° of your dreams,
Which I'll lay down.

LEON.   Your actions are my dreams.
You had a bastard by Polixenes,
And I but dreamed it. As you were past all shame —
Those of your fact° are so — so past all truth. 86
Which to deny concerns more than avails;° for as
Thy brat hath been cast out, like to itself,
No father owning it — which is, indeed,
More criminal in thee than it — so thou   90
Shalt feel our justice, in whose easiest passage
Look for no less than death.

HER.   Sir, spare your threats.
The bug° which you would fright me with I seek.

To me can life be no commodity.°
The crown and comfort of my life, your favor, 95
I do give lost, for I do feel it gone,
But know not how it went. My second joy
And first-fruits of my body, from his presence
I am barred like one infectious. My third comfort,
Starred° most unluckily, is from my breast,   100
The innocent milk in it most innocent mouth,
Haled° out to murder. Myself on every post
Proclaimed a strumpet, with immodest hatred
The childbed privilege° denied which 'longs°
To women of all fashion; lastly, hurried   105
Here to this place i' the open air before
I have got strength of limit.° Now, my liege,
Tell me what blessings I have here alive,
That I should fear to die? Therefore proceed.
But yet hear this, mistake me not, no life —   110
I prize it not a straw — but for mine honor,
Which I would free, if I shall be condemned
Upon surmises, all proofs sleeping else°
But what your jealousies awake, I tell you
'Tis rigor and not law. Your Honors all,   115
I do refer me° to the oracle.
Apollo be my judge!

1. LORD.   This your request
Is altogether just. Therefore bring forth,
And in Apollo's name, his oracle.

                    [Exeunt certain OFFICERS.]

HER. The emperor of Russia was my father.   120
Oh, that he were alive, and here beholding
His daughter's trial! That he did but see
The flatness° of my misery, yet with eyes
Of pity, not revenge!

[Re-enter OFFICERS, with CLEOMENES and DION.]

OFF. You here shall swear upon this sword of jus-
          tice   125
That you, Cleomenes and Dion, have
Been both at Delphos, and from thence have brought
This sealed-up oracle by the hand delivered
Of great Apollo's priest, and that since then
You have not dared to break the holy seal   130
Nor read the secrets in 't.

CLE. & DION.   All this we swear.

LEON. Break up the seals° and read.

OFF. [Reads.] "Hermione is chaste: Polixenes
blameless: Camillo a true subject: Leontes a jealous
tyrant: his innocent babe truly begotten: and the
King shall live without an heir if that which is lost
be not found."   137

LORDS. Now blessed be the great Apollo!

HER.   Praised!

49–51. since . . . thus: I charge you to say since Polixenes came to
Court what intercourse I have had with him that was unlawful,
which causes me to appear as a prisoner.   55. fie: a word expressing strong contempt.   57. gainsay: deny.   60–62. More . . .
acknowledge: I must not acknowledge more faults than are
naturally mine.   77. Wotting: if they know.   82. level: range,
so in danger of being hit by.   86. your fact: who act as you have
done.   87. Which . . . avails: you may choose to deny it, but
it will have no effect.   93. bug: bogey.

94. commodity: advantage.   100. Starred: fated.   102. Haled:
hauled.   104. childbed privilege: the privilege of lying-in after
confinement. 'longs: belongs.   107. strength of limit: strength to
endure it.   113. all . . . else: all other proof being neglected.
116. refer me: appeal.   123. flatness: abjectness.   132. Break
. . . seals: open. See App. 6.

LEON. Hast thou read truth?

OFF.   Aye, my lord, even so
As it is here set down.   140

LEON. There is no truth at all i' the oracle.
The sessions shall proceed. This is mere falsehood.

[*Enter* SERVANT.]

SERV. My lord the King, the King!

LEON.   What is the business?

SERV. O sir, I shall be hated to report it!
The Prince your son, with mere conceit° and fear
Of the Queen's speed,° is gone.

LEON.   How! Gone!

SERV.   Is dead.   146

LEON. Apollo's angry, and the Heavens them-
    selves
Do strike at my injustice. [HERMIONE *faints.*] How
    now there!

PAUL. This news is mortal° to the Queen. Look
    down
And see what death is doing.

LEON.   Take her hence.   150
Her heart is but o'erchargèd,° she will recover.
I have too much believed mine own suspicion.
Beseech you, tenderly apply to her
Some remedies for life.

[*Exeunt* PAULINA *and* LADIES, *with* HERMIONE.]
                         Apollo, pardon
My great profaneness 'gainst thine oracle!   155
I'll reconcile me to Polixenes,
New-woo my Queen, recall the good Camillo,
Whom I proclaim a man of truth, of mercy.
For, being transported by my jealousies
To bloody thoughts and to revenge, I chose   160
Camillo for the minister to poison
My friend Polixenes, which had been done
But that the good mind of Camillo tardied°
My swift command, though I with death and with
Reward did threaten and encourage him.   165
Not doing it and being done, he, most humane
And filled with honor, to my kingly guest
Unclasped my practice,° quit his fortunes here,
Which you knew great, and to the hazard
Of all incertainties himself commended,   170
No richer than his honor.° How he glisters°
Thorough° my rust! And how his piety°
Does my deeds make the blacker!

[*Re-enter* PAULINA.]

PAUL.   Woe the while!°
Oh, cut my lace,° lest my heart, cracking it,
Break too!

I. LORD. What fit° is this, good lady?   175

145. conceit: thought. 146. speed: misfortune, plight. 149. mortal: deadly, fatal. 151. o'erchargèd: overfull of emotion.
163. tardied: delayed in obeying. 168. Unclasped my practice:
revealed my plot. 171. No . . . honor: having nothing else but
his honor. glisters: glitters, shines bright. 172. Thorough:
through. piety: goodness. 173. Woe . . . while: woe on this
time. 174. cut my lace: See *Rich III*, IV.i.34,n. 175. fit: mad fit.

PAUL. What studied° torments, tyrant, hast for
    me?
What wheels? Racks? Fires? What flaying? Boiling
In leads or oils?° What old or newer torture
Must I receive, whose every word deserves
To taste of thy most worst? Thy tyranny,   180
Together working with thy jealousies,
Fancies too weak for boys, too green and idle
For girls of nine, oh, think what they have done,
And then run mad indeed, stark-mad! For all
Thy bygone fooleries were but spices° of it.   185
That thou betray'dst Polixenes, 'twas nothing.
That did but show thee, of a fool, inconstant
And damnable ingrateful. Nor was 't much
Thou wouldst have poisoned good Camillo's honor
To have him kill a King — poor trespasses,   190
More monstrous standing by.° Whereof I reckon
The casting-forth to crows thy baby daughter
To be or none or little, though a devil
Would have shed water out of fire ere done 't.
Nor is 't directly laid to thee, the death   195
Of the young Prince, whose honorable thoughts,
Thoughts high for one so tender, cleft the heart
That could conceive° a gross and foolish sire
Blemished° his gracious dam. This is not, no,
Laid to thy answer. But the last — O lords,   200
When I have said, cry "Woe!" — The Queen, the
    Queen,
The sweet'st, dear'st creature's dead,° and venge-
    ance for 't
Not dropped down yet.

I. LORD.   The higher powers forbid!

PAUL. I say she's dead, I'll swear 't. If word nor
    oath
Prevail not, go and see. If you can bring   205
Tincture or luster° in her lip, her eye,
Heat outwardly or breath within, I'll serve you
As I would do the gods. But, O thou tyrant!
Do not repent these things, for they are heavier
Than all thy woes can stir. Therefore betake thee
To nothing but despair. A thousand knees   211
Ten thousand years together,° naked, fasting,
Upon a barren mountain, and still winter
In storm perpetual, could not move the gods
To look that way thou wert.

176. studied: carefully thought-out. 177–78. What . . . oils:
See App. 10. 185. spices: slight tastes. 190–91. poor . . . by:
slight offenses compared with your monstrous crimes. 198. conceive: imagine. 199. Blemished: defiled. 201–02. Queen . . .
dead: The author of a "winter's tale" must not be pressed too in-
sistently for details which he has omitted. It is clear from this
speech, and from Leontes' words at the end (V.iii.139–40), that
Paulina at this moment and Leontes a little later both believed
Hermione to be dead indeed. It is never disclosed how Hermione
was later found to be alive, nor is there any hint to the audience.
This is the one important occasion in all Shakespeare's plays
where he introduces a major surprise in the last scene. 206. Tincture or luster: color or brightness. 211–12. A . . . together: if
you were to kneel on a thousand knees for ten thousand years.

LEON.   Go on, go on,   215
Thou canst not speak too much. I have deserved
All tongues to talk their bitterest.
    I. LORD.   Say no more.
Howe'er the business goes, you have made fault
I' the boldness of your speech.
    PAUL.   I am sorry for 't.
All faults I make, when I shall come to know them,
I do repent. Alas! I have showed too much   221
The rashness of a woman. He is touched
To the noble heart. What's gone and what's past
        help
Should be past grief. Do not receive affliction
At my petition. I beseech you, rather   225
Let me be punished that have minded° you
Of what you should forget. Now, good my liege,
Sir, royal sir, forgive a foolish woman.
The love I bore your Queen — lo, fool again!
I'll speak of her no more, nor of your children, 230
I'll not remember you of° my own lord,
Who is lost too. Take your patience to you,°
And I'll say nothing.
    LEON.   Thou didst speak but well
When most the truth, which I receive much better
Than to be pitied of thee. Prithee bring me   235
To the dead bodies of my Queen and son.
One grave shall be for both, upon them shall
The causes of their death appear, unto
Our shame perpetual. Once a day I'll visit
The chapel where they lie, and tears shed there   240
Shall be my recreation. So long as nature
Will bear up with this exercise,° so long
I daily vow to use it. Come and lead me
To these sorrows.   [*Exeunt.*]

SCENE III. *Bohemia. A desert country near
            the sea.*

[*Enter* ANTIGONUS, *with a* CHILD, *and a* MARINER.]
    ANT. Thou art perfect,° then, our ship hath
        touched upon
The deserts of Bohemia?°
    MAR.   Aye, my lord, and fear
We have landed in ill time. The skies look grimly
And threaten present blusters. In my conscience,
The Heavens with that we have in hand are angry
And frown upon 's.   6
    ANT. Their sacred wills be done! Go, get aboard,
Look to thy bark. I'll not be long before

I call upon thee.
    MAR. Make your best haste, and go not   10
Too far i' the land. 'Tis like to be loud weather.
Besides, this place is famous for the creatures
Of prey that keep° upon 't.
    ANT.   Go thou away.
I'll follow instantly.
    MAR.   I am glad at heart
To be so rid o' the business.   [*Exit.*]
    ANT.   Come, poor babe.   15
I have heard, but not believed, the spirits o' the dead
May walk again. If such thing be, thy mother
Appeared to me last night, for ne'er was dream
So like a waking. To me comes a creature,
Sometimes her head on one side, some another.   20
I never saw a vessel of like sorrow,
So filled and so becoming. In pure white robes,
Like very sanctity,° she did approach
My cabin where I lay, thrice bowed before me,
And, gasping to begin some speech, her eyes   25
Became two spouts. The fury spent, anon
Did this break from her: " Good Antigonus,
Since fate, against thy better disposition,
Hath made thy person for the thrower-out
Of my poor babe, according to thine oath,   30
Places remote° enough are in Bohemia.
There weep and leave it crying, and for the babe
Is counted lost forever, Perdita°
I prithee call 't. For this ungentle business,
Put on thee by my lord, thou ne'er shalt see   35
Thy wife Paulina more." And so, with shrieks,
She melted into air. Affrighted much,
I did in time collect myself, and thought
This was so, and no slumber.° Dreams are toys,°
Yet for this once — yea, superstitiously —   40
I will be squared° by this. I do believe
Hermione hath suffered death, and that
Apollo would, this being indeed the issue
Of King Polixenes, it should here be laid,
Either for life or death, upon the earth   45
Of its right father. Blossom,° speed thee well!
There lie, and there thy character.° There these,°
Which may, if fortune please, both breed° thee,
        pretty,
And still rest thine. The storm begins. Poor wretch,
That for thy mother's fault art thus exposed   50
To loss and what may follow! Weep I cannot,
But my heart bleeds, and most accursed am I
To be by oath enjoined to this. Farewell!
The day frowns more and more. Thou'rt like to have
A lullaby too rough. I never saw   55

---

226. **minded:** reminded.   231. **remember . . . of:** make you remember.   232. **Take . . . you:** be patient.   241–42. **nature . . .
exercise:** nature permits me to continue this devotion.

Sc. iii: 1. **perfect:** certain.   2. **deserts of Bohemia:** Bohemia,
as Ben Jonson and other wiseacres have pointed out, has no seacoast. Shakespeare, however, took his geography from Greene.
See *W Tale* Intro. p. 1430a.

13. **keep:** live.   23. **very sanctity:** holiness itself.   31. **remote:**
deserted.   33. **Perdita:** i.e., the lost one.   39. **This . . . slumber:**
this was real and not a dream. **toys:** trifles.   41. **squared:** ruled.
46. **Blossom:** little flower.   47. **character:** writing; i.e., the account of Perdita's birth which Antigonus has prepared and which
later reveals her origin. **these:** i.e., the box of gold and jewels.
48. **breed:** pay for your bringing up.

The heavens so dim by day. A savage clamor!°
Well may I get aboard! This is the chase.°
I am gone forever.   [*Exit, pursued by a bear.*°]
                    [*Enter a* SHEPHERD.]

SHEP. I would there were no age between ten and
three and twenty, or that youth would sleep out   60
the rest. For there is nothing in the between but getting wenches with child, wronging the ancientry,°
stealing, fighting. — Hark you now! Would any but
these boiled brains° of nineteen and two and twenty
hunt this weather? They have scared away two of
my best sheep, which I fear the wolf will sooner find
than the master. If anywhere I have them, 'tis by
the seaside, browsing of ivy. Good luck, an 't be thy
will! What have we here? Mercy on 's, a barne,° a
very pretty barne! A boy or a child,° I wonder?   70
A pretty one, a very pretty one. Sure, some scape.°
Though I am not bookish, yet I can read waiting
gentlewoman in the scape. This has been some stair-
work, some trunkwork,° some behind-door work.
They were warmer that got this than the poor thing
is here. I'll take it up for pity. Yet I'll tarry till my
son come, he hallooed but even now. Whoa, ho,
hoa!
                    [*Enter* CLOWN.°]

CLO. Hilloa, loa!   80
SHEP. What, art so near? If thou'lt see a thing to
talk on when thou art dead and rotten, come hither.
What ailest thou, man?
CLO. I have seen two such sights, by sea and by
land! But I am not to say it is a sea, for it is now the
sky. Betwixt the firmament° and it you cannot thrust
a bodkin's° point.
SHEP. Why, boy, how is it?   88
CLO. I would you did but see how it chafes, how it
rages, how it takes up° the shore! But that's not to
the point. Oh, the most piteous cry of the poor souls!
Sometimes to see 'em, and not to see 'em — now the
ship boring the moon with her mainmast, and anon
swallowed with yest° and froth, as you'd thrust a
cork into a hogshead. And then for the land   95
service,° to see how the bear tore out his shoulder
bone, how he cried to me for help and said his name

was Antigonus, a nobleman. But to make an end of
the ship, to see how the sea flapdragoned° it. But
first, how the poor souls roared, and the sea mocked
them, and how the poor gentleman roared and the
bear mocked him, both roaring louder than the sea
or weather.   104
SHEP. Name of mercy, when was this, boy?
CLO. Now, now. I have not winked since I saw
these sights. The men are not yet cold under water,
nor the bear half dined on the gentleman. He's at it
now.   109
SHEP. Would I had been by, to have helped the
old man!
CLO. I would you had been by the ship side, to
have helped her. There your charity would have
lacked footing.°   114
SHEP. Heavy matters! Heavy matters! But look
thee here, boy. Now bless thyself. Thou mettest with
things dying, I with things newborn. Here's a sight
for thee, look thee, a bearing cloth° for a squire's°
child! Look thee here, take up, take up, boy, open 't.
So, let's see. It was told me I should be rich by the
fairies.° This is some changeling.° Open 't. What's
within, boy?   123
CLO. You're a made old man. If the sins of your
youth are forgiven you, you're well to live. Gold! All
gold!
SHEP. This is fairy gold, boy, and 'twill prove so.
Up with 't, keep it close. Home, home, the next°
way. We are lucky, boy, and to be so still requires
nothing but secrecy. Let my sheep go. Come, good
boy, the next way home.   131
CLO. Go you the next way with your findings. I'll
go see if the bear be gone from the gentleman, and
how much he hath eaten. They are never curst° but
when they are hungry. If there be any of him left,
I'll bury it.   136
SHEP. That's a good deed. If thou mayest discern
by that which is left of him what he is, fetch me to
the sight of him.
CLO. Marry° will I, and you shall help to put him
i' the ground.   141
SHEP. 'Tis a lucky day, boy, and we'll do good
deeds on 't.   [*Exeunt.*]

---

56. savage clamor: i.e., the noise of the hunt.   **57. chase:** the
beast being hunted.   **58 s.d., Exit . . . bear:** this famous stage
direction comes from F1. It is often claimed that a real bear was
used. Bears appear in other plays of the time, and tame bears
were not unknown; but a bear on its hind legs is of all beasts the
most easily personated by a man.   **62. ancientry:** the elderly
and respectable.   **64. boiled brains:** lunatics.   **69. barne:** bairn,
child.   **70. child:** baby girl.   **71. scape:** fun.   **74. trunkwork:**
hiding in chests.   **79 s.d., Clown:** rustic.   **86. firmament:** vault
of heaven.   **87. bodkin:** pin.   **90. takes up:** rushes up.   **94. yest:**
yeast, foam.   **95–96. land service:** what was done on land.

99. flapdragoned: swallowed it up. Swallowing flapdragons
(lighted raisins floating on liquor) was a winter amusement.
114. footing: a chance of helping.   **118. bearing-cloth:** christening robe.   **squire:** gentleman of wealth.   **121–22. rich . . . fairies:**
made rich by the fairies. The simple-minded believed that the
fairies could bring gold to bestow on those whom they favored;
but fairy gold was liable to disappear as mysteriously as it
came.   **122. changeling:** a child taken or left by the fairies in
exchange for another.   **128. next:** nearest.   **134. curst:** savage.
140. Marry: Mary, by the Virgin.

Act IV

SCENE I.

[Enter TIME, *the Chorus.°]*

TIME. I, that please some, try all, both joy and
        terror
Of good and bad, that makes and unfolds error,
Now take upon me, in the name of Time,
To use my wings.° Impute it not a crime
To me or my swift passage that I slide   5
O'er sixteen years and leave the growth untried°
Of that wide gap, since it is in my power
To o'erthrow law and in one self-born hour
To plant and o'erwhelm custom. Let me pass
The same I am, ere ancient'st order was   10
Or what is now received. I witness to
The times that brought them in. So shall I do
To the freshest things now reigning, and make stale
The glistering of this present, as my tale
Now seems to it. Your patience this allowing,   15
I turn my glass° and give my scene such growing
As° you had slept between. Leontes leaving,°
The effects of his fond° jealousies so grieving
That he shuts up himself, imagine me,
Gentle spectators, that I now may be   20
In fair Bohemia. And remember well,
I mentioned a son o' the King's, which Florizel
I now name to you, and with speed so pace°
To speak of Perdita, now grown in grace
Equal with wondering. What of her ensues   25
I list not° prophesy, but let Time's news
Be known when 'tis brought forth. A shepherd's
        daughter,
And what to her adheres,° which follows after,
Is the argument° of Time. Of this allow
If ever you have spent time worse ere now.   30
If never, yet that Time himself doth say
He wishes earnestly you never may.   *[Exit.]*

SCENE II. *Bohemia. The palace of* POLIXENES.

[Enter POLIXENES *and* CAMILLO.]

POL. I pray thee, good Camillo, be no more importunate. 'Tis a sickness denying thee anything, a
death to grant this.   3
CAM. It is fifteen years since I saw my country.

Though I have for the most part been aired abroad,°
I desire to lay my bones there. Besides, the penitent
King, my master, hath sent for me, to whose feeling
sorrows I might be some allay° — or I o'erween° to
think so, which is another spur to my departure.   10
POL. As thou lovest me, Camillo, wipe not out the
rest of thy services by leaving me now. The need I
have of thee thine own goodness hath made. Better
not to have had thee than thus to want° thee. Thou,
having made me businesses which none without thee
can sufficiently manage, must either stay to execute
them thyself or take away with thee the very services thou hast done — which if I have not enough
considered, as too much I cannot, to be more thankful to thee shall be my study, and my profit   20
therein, the heaping friendships.° Of that fatal country Sicilia prithee speak no more, whose very naming punishes me with the remembrance of that
penitent, as thou callest him, and reconciled King,
my brother, whose loss of his most precious Queen
and children are even now to be afresh lamented.
Say to me, when sawest thou the Prince Florizel, my
son? Kings are no less unhappy, their issue not being
gracious,° than they are in losing them when they
have approved° their virtues.   32
CAM. Sir, it is three days since I saw the Prince.
What his happier affairs may be are to me unknown.
But I have missingly noted° he is of late much retired from Court and is less frequent to° his princely
exercises than formerly he hath appeared.   38
POL. I have considered so much, Camillo, and
with some care. So far that I have eyes under my
service which look upon his removedness,° from
whom I have this intelligence, that he is seldom
from° the house of a most homely shepherd, a man,
they say, that from very nothing, and beyond the
imagination of his neighbors, is grown into an unspeakable estate.   46
CAM. I have heard, sir, of such a man, who hath
a daughter of most rare note. The report of her is
extended more than can be thought to begin from
such a cottage.   50
POL. That's likewise part of my intelligence, but
I fear the angle° that plucks our son thither. Thou
shalt accompany us to the place, where we will,
not appearing what we are, have some question with
the shepherd, from whose simplicity I think it not
uneasy° to get the cause of my son's resort thither.
Prithee be my present partner in this business, and
lay aside the thoughts of Sicilia.   58

Act IV, Sc. i: s.d., Time, the Chorus: Shakespeare seldom
uses a symbolic character to introduce an act. Here *Time,* with
his hourglass, symbolizes the passage of sixteen years. In the
modern theater a note on the program is sufficient.   4. use my
wings: fly over a great space.   6. untried: unexperienced, not
shown.   16. glass: hourglass.   17. As: as if. Leontes leaving:
i.e., shifting the action away from Sicilia to Bohemia.   18. fond:
foolish.   23. pace: go on.   26. list not: do not care to.   28. adheres: belongs.   29. argument: plot of the play.

Sc. ii: 5. aired abroad: lived in the air of a foreign country.
9. allay: alleviation. o'erween: presume.   14. want: be without.
21. heaping friendships: acts of friendship which you heap on me.
31. gracious: full of grace.   32. approved: proved.   36. missingly noted: noticed because I missed him.   37. frequent to:
frequently at.   41. look . . . removedness: spy on his absence.
43. from: out of.   52. angle: fishhook.   56. uneasy: difficult.

CAM. I willingly obey your command.

POL. My best Camillo! We must disguise ourselves. [*Exeunt.*]

SCENE III. *A road near the* SHEPHERD'S *cottage.*

[*Enter* AUTOLYCUS,° *singing.*]

AUT.
" When daffodils begin to peer,°
  With heigh! the doxy° over the dale,
Why, then comes in the sweet o' the year,
  For the red blood reigns in the winter's pale.°

" The white sheet bleaching on the hedge,   5
  With heigh! the sweet birds, oh, how they sing!
Doth set my pugging° tooth on edge,
  For a quart of ale is a dish for a king.

" The lark, that tirra-lyra chants,
  With heigh! with heigh! the thrush and the jay,
Are summer songs for me and my aunts,°   11
  While we lie tumbling in the hay."

I have served Prince Florizel and in my time wore three-pile,° but now I am out of service:

" But shall I go mourn for that, my dear?   15
    The pale moon shines by night.
  And when I wander here and there,
    I then do most go right.

" If tinkers may have leave to live,
    And bear the sow-skin budget,°   20
  Then my account I well may give,
    And in the stocks avouch it."°

My traffic is sheets. When the kite builds, look to lesser linen.° My father named me Autolycus, who being, as I am, littered under Mercury,° was likewise a snapper-up of unconsidered trifles. With   26
die and drab I purchased this caparison,° and my revenue is the silly cheat.° Gallows and knock are too powerful on the highway.° Beating and hanging are terrors to me. For the life to come, I sleep out the thought of it. A prize! A prize!   32

[*Enter* CLOWN.]

CLO. Let me see, every 'leven wether tods,° every tod yields pound and odd shilling, fifteen hundred shorn, what comes the wool to?

AUT. [*Aside*] If the springe° hold, the cock's° mine.   37

CLO. I cannot do't without counters.° Let me see, what am I to buy for our sheepshearing feast? Three pound of sugar, five pound of currants, rice — what will this sister of mine do with rice? But my father hath made her mistress of the feast, and she lays it on. She hath made me four and twenty nosegays for the shearers, three-man songmen° all, and very good ones. But they are most of them means° and bases, but one puritan amongst them, and he sings   47
psalms to hornpipes. I must have saffron to color the warden pies,° mace,° dates — none, that's out of my note° — nutmegs, seven, a race° or two of ginger, but that I may beg, four pound of prunes, and as many of raisins o' the sun.°   52

AUT. Oh, that ever I was born!

[*Groveling on the ground.*]

CLO. I' the name of me ——

AUT. Oh, help me, help me! Pluck but off these rags, and then death, death!   56

CLO. Alack, poor soul! Thou hast need of more rags to lay on thee rather than have these off.

AUT. O sir, the loathsomeness of them offends me more than the stripes I have received, which are mighty ones and millions.   61

CLO. Alas, poor man! A million of beating may come to a great matter.

AUT. I am robbed, sir, and beaten, my money and apparel ta'en from me, and these detestable things put upon me.   66

CLO. What, by a horseman or a footman?

AUT. A footman, sweet sir, a footman.

CLO. Indeed, he should be a footman by the garments he has left with thee. If this be a horseman's coat, it hath seen very hot service. Lend me thy hand, I'll help thee. Come, lend me thy hand.   73

[*Helping him up.*]

AUT. O good sir, tenderly. Oh!

CLO. Alas, poor soul!

AUT. O good sir, softly, good sir! I fear, sir, my shoulder blade is out.   77

CLO. How now! Canst stand?

AUT. Softly, dear sir [*Picks his pocket.*], good sir, softly. You ha' done me a charitable office.

Sc. iii: s.d., Autolycus: See *W Tale* Intro. p. 1430b.   1. When . . . peer: i.e., in early spring.   2. doxy: tramp's moll.   4. in . . . pale: in place of winter's pale blood.   7. pugging: thieving.   11. aunts: women.   14. three-pile: the thickest and costliest kind of velvet.   20. budget: tool bag.   22. stocks . . . it: acknowledge my trade (i.e., vagabondage) in the stocks.   23–24. My . . . linen: my line is stealing the sheets that are drying and bleaching on the hedges, just as a kite snatches up small pieces when it is building its nest.   25. littered . . . Mercury: born when the planet Mercury is in the ascendant. In classical legend Autolycus was the son of the god Mercury, and a most skillful thief.   26–27. With . . . caparison: dicing and drabbing have brought me this outfit (i.e., rags).   28. cheat: in thieves' language, the "sucker."   28–29. Gallows . . . highway: I am too scared of the gallows and hard knocks to become a highwayman.

33. 'leven . . . tods: eleven sheep make a tod of wool (about 28 lbs.).   36. springe: snare. cock: woodcock; i.e., victim.   38. counters: used for calculating large sums.   45. three-man songmen: singers of three-part songs.   46. means: tenors.   49. warden pies: pies made of warden pears. mace: a spice used for flavoring.   49–50. out . . . note: not in my note of what must be bought.   50. race: root.   52. raisins . . . sun: sun-dried raisins.

CLO. Dost lack any money? I have a little money
for thee.   83

AUT. No, good sweet sir. No, I beseech you, sir. I
have a kinsman not past three-quarters of a mile
hence, unto whom I was going. I shall there have
money, or anything I want. Offer me no money, I
pray you, that kills my heart.°

CLO. What manner of fellow was he that robbed
you?   90

AUT. A fellow, sir, that I have known to go about
with troll-my-dames.° I knew him once a servant of
the Prince. I cannot tell, good sir, for which of his
virtues it was, but he was certainly whipped out of
the Court.   95

CLO. His vices, you would say, there's no virtue
whipped out of the Court. They cherish it° to make
it stay there, and yet it will no more but abide.°   99

AUT. " Vices " I would say, sir. I know this man
well. He hath been since an ape-bearer,° then a
process-server,° a bailiff. Then he compassed a motion of the Prodigal Son,° and married a tinker's
wife within a mile where my land and living lies,
and, having flown over° many knavish professions,
he settled only in rogue.° Some call him Autolycus.

CLO. Out upon him! Prig,° for my life, prig.   108
He haunts wakes, fairs, and bearbaitings.

AUT. Very true, sir — he, sir, he. That's the rogue
that put me into this apparel.   111

CLO. Not a more cowardly rogue in all Bohemia.
If you had but looked big and spit at him, he'd have
run.

AUT. I must confess to you, sir, I am no fighter. I
am false of heart that way, and that he knew, I warrant him.

CLO. How do you now?   118

AUT. Sweet sir, much better than I was. I can
stand and walk. I will even take my leave of you,
and pace softly toward my kinsman's.   121

CLO. Shall I bring thee on the way?

AUT. No, good-faced sir. No, sweet sir.

CLO. Then fare thee well. I must go buy spices for
our sheepshearing.   125

AUT. Prosper you, sweet sir! [Exit CLOWN.] Your
purse is not hot enough to purchase your spice. I'll
be with you at your sheepshearing, too. If I make
not this cheat bring out another and the shearers
prove sheep, let me be unrolled° and my name put
in the book of virtue! [Sings.]   131

" Jog on, jog on, the footpath way,
     And merrily hent° the stile-a.
A merry heart goes all the day,   134
     Your sad tires in a mile-a."   [Exit.]

SCENE IV. _The_ SHEPHERD'S _cottage._

[_Enter_ FLORIZEL _and_ PERDITA.]

FLO. These your unusual weeds° to each part of
     you
Do give a life. No shepherdess, but Flora
Peering in April's front.° This your sheepshearing
Is as a meeting of the petty gods,
And you the queen on't.

PER.   Sir, my gracious lord,   5
To chide at your extremes° it not becomes me.
Oh, pardon, that I name them! Your high self,
The gracious mark o' the land,° you have obscured
With a swain's° wearing, and me, poor lowly maid,
Most goddesslike pranked up.° But that our feasts
In every mess have folly and the feeders   11
Digest it with a custom, I should blush
To see you so attired, sworn, I think,
To show myself a glass.°

FLO.   I bless the time
When my good falcon made her flight across   15
Thy father's ground.°

PER.   Now Jove afford you cause!°
To me the difference forges dread,° your greatness
Hath not been used to fear. Even now I tremble
To think your father, by some accident,
Should pass this way as you did. Oh, the Fates!   20
How would he look, to see his work, so noble,
Vilely bound up?° What would he say? Or how
Should I, in these my borrowed flaunts,° behold
The sternness of his presence?

FLO.   Apprehend°
Nothing but jollity. The gods themselves,   25
Humbling their deities to love, have taken

---

133. hent: leap.

     Sc. iv: 1. weeds: garments. Perdita is dressed like the goddess
Flora in a costume provided by Prince Florizel (ll. 9–10). Florizel
is dressed in a matching costume as her lover (ll. 8–9).
2–3. Flora . . . front: Flora, the goddess of flowers, appearing
early in April. 6. extremes: exaggerations. 8. gracious . . . land:
the "observed of all observers." 9. swain: young countryman, a
word much used by pastoral poets. 10. pranked up: dressed up.
10–14. But . . . glass: if it were not that in our feasts someone
plays the fool in every party and the rest excuse it as part of the
fun, I should blush to see you dressed as my companion, and I
would swear you did it to make me see myself reflected in you
(i.e., too gay for a humble shepherdess). sworn: This is the F1
reading. Many editors emend to "swoon" or "swound," which
makes better sense. 15–16. When . . . ground: In _Pandosto_, the
young Prince first encountered his love while hawking. See
W Tale Intro. p. 1430a. 16. afford . . . cause: give you good
reason for "blessing the time." 17. the . . . dread: the difference in rank between us makes me afraid. 21–22. his . . . up:
to see the work of which he was the author bound in so poor a
cover. 23. flaunts: finery. 24. Apprehend: think.

---

88. kills my heart: breaks my heart.   92. troll-my-dames: a
game in which balls were rolled through hoops on a board.
98. cherish it: treat it lovingly.   99. abide: make a short stay.
Cynical remarks about Court life are common at this date.
101. ape-bearer: owner of a tame monkey.   102. process-server:
sheriff's officer — a despised occupation.   102–03. compassed . . .
Son: acquired a puppet show of the story of the Prodigal Son.
106. flown over: tried his hand at.   107. settled . . . rogue:
settled down to become a rogue.   108. Prig: thief.   130. unrolled:
struck off the roll of thieves.

The shapes of beasts upon them. Jupiter
Became a bull, and bellowed; the green Neptune
A ram, and bleated; and the fire-robed god,
Golden Apollo,° a poor humble swain,   30
As I seem now. Their transformations
Were never for a piece of beauty rarer,
Nor in a way so chaste, since my desires
Run not before mine honor, nor my lusts
Burn hotter than my faith.

PER.   Oh, but, sir,   35
Your resolution cannot hold when 'tis
Opposed, as it must be, by the power of the King.
One of these two must be necessities,
Which then will speak, that you must change this
     purpose,
Or I my life.°

FLO.   Thou dearest Perdita,   40
With these forced° thoughts I prithee darken not
The mirth o' the feast. Or° I'll be thine, my fair,
Or not my father's. For I cannot be
Mine own, nor anything to any, if
I be not thine. To this I am most constant,   45
Though destiny say no. Be merry, gentle.
Strangle such thoughts as these with anything
That you behold the while. Your guests are coming.
Lift up your countenance,° as it were the day
Of celebration of that nuptial which   50
We two have sworn shall come.

PER.   O Lady Fortune,
Stand you auspicious!

FLO.   See, your guests approach.
Address yourself to entertain them sprightly,°
And let's be red with mirth.

[*Enter* SHEPHERD, CLOWN, MOPSA, DORCAS, *and others,*
     with POLIXENES *and* CAMILLO *disguised.*]

SHEP. Fie, Daughter! When my old wife lived,
     upon   55
This day she was both pantler,° butler, cook,
Both dame and servant — welcomed all, served all;
Would sing her song and dance her turn, now here,
At upper end o' the table, now i' the middle,
On his shoulder, and his. Her face o' fire   60
With labor and the thing she took to quench it
She would to each one sip. You are retired,°
As if you were a feasted one and not
The hostess of the meeting. Pray you, bid
These unknown friends to 's welcome, for it is   65
A way to make us better friends, more known.
Come, quench your blushes and present yourself
That which you are, mistress o' the feast. Come on,
And bid us welcome to your sheepshearing,

As your° good flock shall prosper.

PER.   [*To* POLIXENES] Sir, welcome.   70
It is my father's will I should take on me
The hostessship o' the day. [*To* CAMILLO] You're
     welcome, sir.
Give me those flowers there, Dorcas. Reverend sirs,
For you there's rosemary and rue,° these keep
Seeming and savor° all the winter long.   75
Grace and remembrance be to you both,
And welcome to our shearing!

POL.   Shepherdess,
A fair one are you. Well you fit our ages
With flowers of winter.

PER.   Sir, the year growing ancient,
Not yet on summer's death nor on the birth   80
Of trembling winter, the fairest flowers o' the sea-
     son°
Are our carnations and streaked gillyvors,°
Which some call nature's bastards. Of that kind
Our rustic garden's barren, and I care not
To get slips of them.

POL.   Wherefore, gentle maiden,   85
Do you neglect them?

PER.   For I have heard it said
There is an art which in their piedness shares
With great creating Nature.°

POL.   Say there be,
Yet Nature is made better by no mean°
But Nature makes that mean. So, over that art   90
Which you say adds to Nature, is an art
That Nature makes. You see, sweet maid, we marry
A gentler scion° to the wildest stock,
And make conceive a bark of baser kind
By bud of nobler race.° This is an art   95
Which does mend Nature — change it rather, but
The art itself is Nature.

PER.   So it is.

POL. Then make your garden rich in gillyvors,
And do not call them bastards.

PER.   I'll not put
The dibble° in earth to set one slip of them,   100
No more than were I painted° I would wish
This youth should say 'twere well, and only there-
     fore
Desire to breed by me. Here's flowers for you,
Hot lavender, mints, savory, marjoram,
The marigold that goes to bed wi' the sun   105

29–30. **fire-robed . . . Apollo:** Apollo was god of the sun.
38–40. **One . . . life:** when the King opposes our marriage, either
you must leave me or I must die.   41. **forced:** far-fetched, unnatural.   42. **Or:** either.   49. **Lift . . . countenance:** look up
cheerfully.   53. **sprightly:** with gay spirits.   56. **pantler:** keeper
of the pantry.   62. **are retired:** withdraw yourself.

70. **As your:** as you hope that your.   74. **rosemary . . . rue:**
These in the language of flowers mean "remembrance" and
"grace."   75. **Seeming . . . savor:** appearance and fragrance.
81. **season:** i.e., summer.   82. **streaked gillyvors:** probably the
streaked variety of clove pink.   88. **There . . . nature:** their
streaks are caused by artificial crossing and not by natural
growth. Perdita finds something distastefully unnatural in the
process.   89. **mean:** method.   93. **scion:** slip for grafting.
94–95. **And . . . race:** make the baser stock bring forth the cultivated.   100. **dibble:** tool used for making holes in the ground for
planting.   101. **painted:** made up to look more beautiful than I am.

And with him rises weeping.° These are flowers
Of middle summer, and I think they are given
To men of middle age. You're very welcome.

CAM. I should leave grazing were I of your flock,
And only live by gazing.

PER.   Out, alas!   110
You'd be so lean that blasts of January
Would blow you through and through. Now, my
     fair'st friend,
I would I had some flowers o' the spring that might
Become your time of day, and yours, and yours,
That wear upon your virgin branches yet   115
Your maidenheads growing. O° Proserpina,
For the flowers now that frighted thou let'st fall
From Dis's wagon! — daffodils,
That come before the swallow dares, and take
The winds of March with beauty; violets dim,   120
But sweeter than the lids of Juno's eyes
Or Cytherea's° breath; pale primroses,
That die unmarried, ere they can behold
Bright Phoebus in his strength, a malady
Most incident to maids; bold oxlips° and   125
The crown imperial;° lilies of all kinds,
The flower-de-luce° being one! — oh, these I lack
To make you garlands of, and my sweet friend,
To strew him o'er and o'er!

FLO.   What, like a corse?°
PER. No, like a bank for love to lie and play on,
Not like a corse; or if, not to be buried,   131
But quick and in mine arms. Come, take your
     flowers.
Methinks I play as I have seen them do
In Whitsun pastorals.° Sure this robe of mine
Does change my disposition.

FLO.   What you do   135
Still betters what is done. When you speak, sweet,
I'd have you do it ever. When you sing,
I'd have you buy and sell so, so give alms,
Pray so, and, for the ordering your affairs,
To sing them too. When you do dance, I wish you
A wave o' the sea, that you might ever do   141
Nothing but that, move still, still so,
And own no other function. Each your doing,
So singular° in each particular,
Crowns what you are doing in the present deeds,°
That all your acts are queens.

PER.   O Doricles,°   146
Your praises are too large.° But that your youth,
And the true blood which peeps fairly through 't,
Do plainly give you out an unstained° shepherd,
With wisdom I might fear, my Doricles,   150
You wooed me the false way.

FLO.   I think you have
As little skill° to fear as I have purpose
To put you to 't. But come, our dance, I pray.
Your hand, my Perdita. So turtles° pair
That never mean to part.

PER.   I'll swear for 'em.   155
POL. This is the prettiest lowborn lass that ever
Ran on the greensward. Nothing she does or seems
But smacks° of something greater than herself,
Too noble for this place.

CAM.   He tells her something
That makes her blood look out. Good sooth, she is
The queen of curds and cream.

CLO.   Come on, strike up!°   161
DOR. Mopsa must be your mistress. Marry, garlic,
To mend her kissing with!°

MOP.   Now, in good time!°
CLO. Not a word, a word, we stand upon our
     manners.°
Come, strike up!

          [*Music. Here a dance of*
          SHEPHERDS *and* SHEPHERDESSES.]

POL. Pray, good shepherd, what fair swain is this
Which dances with your daughter?

SHEP. They call him Doricles, and boasts himself
To have a worthy feeding.° But I have it
Upon his own report and I believe it,   170
He looks like sooth.° He says he loves my daughter.
I think so too, for never gazed the moon
Upon the water as he'll stand and read
As 'twere my daughter's eyes. And, to be plain,
I think there is not half a kiss to choose   175
Who loves another best.

POL.   She dances featly.°
SHEP. So she does anything, though I report it
That should be silent. If young Doricles
Do light upon her, she shall bring him that
Which he not dreams of.   180

          [*Enter* SERVANT.]

SERV. O master, if you did but hear the peddler
at the door, you would never dance again after a
tabor° and pipe — no, the bagpipe could not move
you. He sings several tunes faster than you'll tell°

105–06. goes . . . weeping: closes at sunset and opens in the
morning wet with dew.   116–27. O . . . one: Proserpina, according to the myth, was gathering flowers in her garden when Pluto
(or *Dis*) carried her off in a chariot to his kingdom of the underworld. The flowers are all early spring flowers which bloom in
March or April.   122. Cytherea: Venus. [125. oxlips: a cross
between cowslip and primrose.   126. crown imperial: a form of
lily with a cluster of yellow pendant flowers.   127. flower-de-
luce: wild iris.   129. corse: corpse.   134. Whitsun pastorals:
country morris dances performed at Whitsuntide. Whitsun
(Pentecost) is a feast which falls seven weeks after Easter. See
App. 24.   144. singular: unique.   145. in . . . deeds: what you
are doing at present.

146. Doricles: the name which Florizel has assumed when disguised as a shepherd.   147. large: exaggerated.   149. unstained:
pure.   152. skill: cause.   154. turtles: turtledoves.   158. smacks:
tastes.   161. strike up: i.e., the music.   162–63. garlic . . . with:
you'll need to eat garlic to avoid smelling her breath.   163. in
. . . time: "I like that!"   164. we . . . manners: we are on our
best behavior.   169. feeding: pasture.   171. sooth: truth.
176. featly: neatly.   183. tabor: small drum, a shepherd's instrument. See Pl. 13d.   184. tell: count.

money, he utters them as he had eaten ballads° and all men's ears grew to° his tunes. 186

CLO. He could never come better,° he shall come in. I love a ballad but even too well, if it be doleful matter merrily set down, or a very pleasant thing indeed and sung lamentably. 190

SERV. He hath songs for man or woman, of all sizes, no milliner can so fit his customers with gloves. He has the prettiest love songs for maids, so without bawdry, which is strange, with such delicate burdens of dildos and fadings,° "jump her 195 and thump her." And where some stretch-mouthed° rascal would, as it were, mean mischief and break a foul gap° into the matter, he makes the maid to answer "Whoop, do me no harm, good man," puts him off, slights him, with "Whoop, do me no harm, good man." 201

POL. This is a brave fellow.

CLO. Believe me, thou talkest of an admirable conceited° fellow. Has he any unbraided wares?° 204

SERV. He hath ribbons of all the colors i' the rainbow, points° more than all the lawyers in Bohemia can learnedly handle, though they come to him by the gross — inkles,° caddises,° cambrics, 208 lawns.° Why, he sings 'em over as they were gods or goddesses, you would think a smock° were a she-angel, he so chants to the sleeve hand° and the work about the square° on 't. 212

CLO. Prithee bring him in, and let him approach singing.

PER. Forewarn him that he use no scurrilous 215 words in 's tunes. [Exit SERVANT.]

CLO. You have of° these peddlers that have more in them than you'd think, Sister.

PER. Aye, good brother, or go about to think.

[Enter AUTOLYCUS, singing.]

AUT.

"Lawn as white as driven snow, 220
Cypress° black as e'er was crow,
Gloves as sweet as damask roses,°
Masks° for faces and for noses,
Bugle° bracelet, necklace amber,
Perfume for a lady's chamber, 225
Golden quoifs° and stomachers°
For my lads to give their dears,

Pins and poking sticks° of steel,
What maids lack from head to heel.
Come buy of me, come, come buy, come buy,
Buy, lads, or else your lasses cry. 231
Come buy."

CLO. If I were not in love with Mopsa, thou shouldst take no money of me, but being enthralled° as I am, it will also be the bondage of° certain ribbons and gloves. 236

MOP. I was promised them against° the feast, but they come not too late now.

DOR. He hath promised you more than that, or there be liars.

MOP. He hath paid you all he promised you. Maybe he has paid you more which will shame you to give him again. 243

CLO. Is there no manners left among maids? Will they wear their plackets° where they should bear their faces? Is there not milking time, when you are going to bed, or kiln hole,° to whistle off these secrets, but you must be tittletattling before all our guests? 'Tis well they are whispering. Clamor° your tongues, and not a word more. 251

MOP. I have done. Come, you promised me a tawdry lace° and a pair of sweet gloves.

CLO. Have I not told thee how I was cozened° by the way and lost all my money? 255

AUT. And indeed, sir, there are cozeners abroad, therefore it behooves men to be wary.

CLO. Fear not thou, man, thou shalt lose nothing here.

AUT. I hope so, sir, for I have about me many parcels of charge.° 261

CLO. What hast here? Ballads?

MOP. Pray now, buy some. I love a ballad in print o' life, for then we are sure they are true.

AUT. Here's one to a very doleful tune, how a usurer's wife was brought to bed of twenty money-bags at a burden, and how she longed to eat adders' heads and toads carbonadoed.° 268

MOP. Is it true, think you?

AUT. Very true, and but a month old.

DOR. Bless me° from marrying a usurer! 271

AUT. Here's the midwife's name to 't, one Mistress Taleporter, and five or six honest wives that were present. Why should I carry lies abroad?

MOP. Pray you now, buy it.

CLO. Come on, lay it by. And let's first see moe ballads. We'll buy the other things anon. 278

AUT. Here's another ballad of a fish that appeared

185. ballads: See App. 8. 186. grew to: were stuck fast to. 187. better: more welcome. 195. burdens . . . fadings: with refrains of *dildo* and *fading* in the songs. 196. stretch-mouthed: wide-mouthed. 198. foul gap: dirty crack. 204. conceited: intelligent. unbraided wares: untarnished, not shop-soiled. 206. points: laces for fastening doublet and hose together. See Notes on Contemporary Costume, pp. 93a–95b. 208. inkles: tapes. caddises: worsted tape for garters. 209. lawns: fine linens. 210. smock: nightdress. 211. sleeve hand: cuff. 212. square: embroidered neck square. 217. You . . . of: some of. 221. Cypress: crape. 222. Gloves . . . roses: perfumed gloves. 223. Masks: Fashionable ladies wore masks to protect their faces from the sun. 224. Bugle: long bead. 226. quoif: headdress. stomachers: embroidered fronts for women's dresses.

228. poking sticks: metal rods used for ironing the pleats in a ruff. 234. enthralled: enslaved. 235. be . . . of: I shall take into servitude. 237. against: in time for. 245. plackets: petticoats. 247. kiln hole: the fireplace where malt is made, a convenient place for gossip. 250. Clamor: silence. 253. tawdry lace: silk necktie. 254. cozened: cheated. 261. parcels of charge: goods of value. 268. carbonadoed: grilled. 271. Bless me: save me.

upon the coast on Wednesday the fourscore of April,
forty thousand fathom above water, and sung this
ballad against the hard hearts of maids. It was
thought she was a woman, and was turned into a
cold fish for she would not exchange flesh with one
that loved her. The ballad is very pitiful and as
true.

DOR. Is it true too, think you?   287
AUT. Five Justices' hands at it, and witnesses more
than my pack will hold.

CLO. Lay it by too. Another.
AUT. This is a merry ballad, but a very pretty one.
MOP. Let's have some merry ones.   293
AUT. Why, this is a passing° merry one and goes
to the tune of " Two maids wooing a man." There's
scarce a maid westward° but she sings it. 'Tis in request, I can tell you.

MOP. We can both sing it. If thou'lt bear a part,
thou shalt hear. 'Tis in three parts.
DOR. We had the tune on 't a month ago.   300
AUT. I can bear my part, you must know 'tis my
occupation.° Have at it with you.

AUT., DOR., & MOP.

A. " Get you hence, for I must go
      Where it fits not you to know.
          D. Whither? M. Oh, whither? D. Whither?
M.   It becomes thy oath full well,   306
      Thou to me thy secrets tell.
          D. Me too, let me go thither.

M. " Or thou goest to the grange° or mill.
D.   If to either, thou dost ill.   310
          A. Neither. D. What, neither? A. Neither.
D.   Thou hast sworn my love to be.
M.   Thou hast sworn it more to me.
      Then whither goest? Say, whither? "   314

CLO. We'll have this song out anon by ourselves.
My father and the gentlemen are in sad° talk, and
we'll not trouble them. Come, bring away thy pack
after me. Wenches, I'll buy for you both. Peddler,
let's have the first choice. Follow me, girls.   320
                     [Exit with DORCAS and MOPSA.]
AUT. And you shall pay well for 'em.
                              [Follows singing.]
" Will you buy any tape,
      Or lace for your cape,
   My dainty duck, my dear-a?
      Any silk, any thread,   325
      Any toys° for your head,
   Of the new'st, and finest, finest wear-a?
      Come to the peddler,
      Money's a meddler   329
   That doth utter° all men's ware-a." [Exit.]

294. passing: exceedingly.   296. westward: in the west country.
302. occupation: business. The ballad-seller used to sing his ballads before selling them.   309. grange: large farmhouse.
316. sad: serious.   326. toys: trifles, ornaments.   330. utter: sell.

[Re-enter SERVANT.]

SERV. Master, there is three carters, three shepherds, three neatherds,° three swineherds, that have
made themselves all men of hair. They call themselves saltiers,° and they have a dance which   334
the wenches say is a gallimaufry° of gambols, because they are not in 't. But they themselves are o'
the mind, if it be not too rough for some that know
little but bowling,° it will please plentifully.   339

SHEP. Away! We'll none on 't. Here has been too
much homely foolery already. I know, sir, we weary
you.

POL. You weary those that refresh us. Pray let's
see these four threes of herdsmen.   344

SERV. One three of them, by their own report, sir,
hath danced before the King, and not the worst of
the three but jumps twelve foot and a half by the
squier.°

SHEP. Leave your prating. Since these good men
are pleased, let them come in, but quickly now.   351
SERV. Why, they stay at door, sir.   [Exit.]
       [Here a dance of twelve SATYRS.]

POL. O Father, you'll know more of that here-
after.
[To CAMILLO] Is it not too far gone? 'Tis time to
       part them.
He's simple and tells much. How now, fair shep-
       herd!   355
Your heart is full of something that does take
Your mind from feasting. Sooth,° when I was young
And handed° love as you do, I was wont
To load my she with knacks.° I would have ran-
       sacked
The peddler's silken treasury and have poured it
To her acceptance. You have let him go   361
And nothing marted° with him. If your lass
Interpretation should abuse° and call this
Your lack of love or bounty, you were straited°
For a reply — at least if you make a care   365
Of happy holding her.
FLO.   Old sir, I know
She prizes not such trifles as these are.
The gifts she looks from me are packed and locked
Up in my heart, which I have given already,
But not delivered. Oh, hear me breathe my life   370
Before this ancient sir, who, it should seem,
Hath sometime loved! I take thy hand, this hand,
As soft as dove's down and as white as it,
Or Ethiopian's tooth, or the fanned° snow that's
       bolted°   374
By the Northern blasts twice o'er.

332. neatherds: cowmen.   334. saltiers: satyrs.   335. gallimaufry: mix-up, medley.   339. bowling: bowls, a quiet game.
349. squier: carpenter's rule.   357. Sooth: in truth.   358. handed:
handled.   359. knacks: trifles, little gifts.   362. marted: traded.
363. Interpretation . . . abuse: should misinterpret your meanness.   364. straited: in a difficulty.   374. fanned: blown.
bolted: sifted, like fine flour.

POL.   What follows this?
How prettily the young swain seems to wash
The hand was fair before! I have put you out.
But to your protestation, let me hear
What you profess.
FLO.   Do, and be witness to 't.
POL. And this my neighbor too?
FLO.   And he, and more   380
Than he, and men, the earth, the Heavens, and all.
That were I crowned the most imperial monarch,
Thereof most worthy, were I the fairest youth
That ever made eye swerve,° had force and knowl-
    edge
More than was ever man's, I would not prize them
Without her love, for her employ them all,   386
Commend them and condemn them to her service
Or to their own perdition.
POL.   Fairly offered.
CAM. This shows a sound affection.
SHEP.   But, my daughter,
Say you the like to him?
PER.   I cannot speak   390
So well, nothing so well — no, nor mean better.
By the pattern of mine own thoughts I cut out
The purity of his.
SHEP.   Take hands, a bargain!
And, friends unknown, you shall bear witness to 't.
I give my daughter to him, and will make   395
Her portion equal his.
FLO.   Oh, that must be
I' the virtue of your daughter.° One being dead,°
I shall have more than you can dream of yet,
Enough then for your wonder. But come on,
Contract us 'fore these witnesses.°
SHEP.   Come, your hand,   400
And, Daughter, yours.
POL.   Soft, swain, awhile, beseech you.
Have you a father?
FLO.   I have, but what of him?
POL. Knows he of this?
FLO.   He neither does nor shall.
POL. Methinks a father
Is at the nuptial of his son a guest   405
That best becomes the table. Pray you once more,
Is not your father grown incapable
Of reasonable affairs?° Is he not stupid
With age and altering rheums?° Can he speak?
    Hear?   409
Know man from man? Dispute his own estate?°

Lies he not bedrid? And again does nothing
But what he did being childish?
FLO.   No, good sir,
He has his health and ampler strength indeed
Than most have of his age.
POL.   By my white beard,
You offer him, if this be so, a wrong   415
Something unfilial. Reason° my son
Should choose himself a wife, but as good reason
The father, all whose joy is nothing else
But fair posterity,° should hold some counsel°
In such a business.
FLO.   I yield all this,   420
But for some other reasons, my grave sir,
Which 'tis not fit you know, I not acquaint
My father of this business.
POL.   Let him know 't.
FLO. He shall not.
POL.   Prithee let him.
FLO.   No, he must not.
SHEP. Let him, my son. He shall not need to
    grieve   425
At knowing of thy choice.
FLO.   Come, come, he must not.
Mark our contract.
POL.   Mark your divorce, young sir,
    [Discovering° himself.]
Whom son I dare not call, thou art too base
To be acknowledged. Thou a scepter's heir,
That thus affects a sheep hook!° Thou old traitor,
I am sorry that by hanging thee I can   431
But shorten thy life one week. And thou, fresh piece
Of excellent witchcraft, who of force° must know
The royal fool thou copest° with ——
SHEP.   Oh, my heart!
POL. I'll have thy beauty scratched with briers, and
    made   435
More homely than thy state. For thee, fond° boy,
If I may ever know thou dost but sigh
That thou no more shalt see this knack° — as never
I mean thou shalt — we'll bar thee from succession,
Not hold thee of our blood — no, not our kin —
Far than Deucalion off.° Mark thou my words.   441
Follow us to the Court. Thou churl,° for this time,
Though full of our displeasure, yet we free thee
From the dead blow° of it. And you, enchantment —
Worthy enough a herdsman, yea, him too,   445

---

384. **made ... swerve:** made women look at him.   396–97. **Oh ... daughter:** only in the worth of your daughter can you equal my wealth.   397. **One ... dead:** i.e., when the King my father is dead.   400. **Contract ... witnesses:** In Shakespeare's time a contract made before witnesses was legally binding. Hence Polixenes' hasty interruption before the lovers join hands. See Gen. Intro. p. 20a.   407–08. **incapable ... affairs:** not capable of looking after his own affairs rationally.   409. **altering rheums:** diseases which change his nature.   410. **Dispute ... estate:** discuss his own business.

416. **Reason:** it is reasonable that.   418–19. **joy ... posterity:** joy lies solely in his son being father of worthy children. In this speech Polixenes explains the normal Elizabethan theory of marriage: a man must choose a wife acceptable in rank to his parents because by her he will breed children to prolong the family.   419. **hold ... counsel:** give some advice.   427 s.d., **Discovering:** revealing.   430. **sheep hook:** shepherd's crook; i.e., a shepherdess.   433. **of force:** necessarily.   434. **copest:** hast to do with.   436. **fond:** foolish.   438. **knack:** trifle.   441. **Far ... off:** as far back as Deucalion, who in classical myth was, like Noah in Genesis, the survivor of the great flood.   442. **churl:** boor.   444. **dead blow:** blow which will strike you dead.

That makes himself, but for our honor therein,
Unworthy thee° — if ever henceforth thou
These rural latches to his entrance open,
Or hoop his body more with thy embraces,
I will devise a death as cruel for thee   450
As thou art tender to 't.°   [*Exit.*]
    PER.   Even here undone!
I was not much afeard, for once or twice
I was about to speak and tell him plainly
The selfsame sun that shines upon his Court
Hides not his visage from our cottage but   455
Looks on alike. Will 't please you, sir, be gone?
I told you what would come of this. Beseech you,
Of your own state take care. This dream of mine —
Being now awake, I'll queen it no inch farther,
But milk my ewes and weep.
    CAM.   Why, how now, Father!   460
Speak ere thou diest.
    SHEP.   I cannot speak, nor think,
Nor dare to know that which I know. O sir!
You have undone a man of fourscore three,
That thought to fill his grave in quiet — yea,
To die upon the bed my father died,   465
To lie close by his honest bones. But now
Some hangman must put on my shroud and lay me
Where no priest shovels in dust. O cursèd wretch,
That knew'st this was the Prince, and wouldst ad-
    venture
To mingle faith with him! Undone! Undone!   470
If I might die within this hour, I have lived
To die when I desire.   [*Exit.*]
    FLO.   Why look you so upon me?
I am but sorry, not afeard, delayed,
But nothing altered. What I was, I am,
More straining on for plucking back, not following
My leash unwillingly.°
    CAM.   Gracious my lord,   476
You know your father's temper. At this time
He will allow no speech, which I do guess
You do not purpose to him, and as hardly
Will he endure your sight as yet, I fear.   480
Then, till the fury of His Highness settle,
Come not before him.
    FLO.   I not purpose it.
I think, Camillo?°
    CAM.   Even he, my lord.
    PER. How often have I told you 'twould be thus!
How often said, my dignity would last   485
But till 'twere known!
    FLO.   It cannot fail but by
The violation of my faith, and then

Let Nature crush the sides o' the earth together
And mar° the seeds within! Lift up thy looks.
From my succession wipe me, Father, I   490
Am heir to my affection.°
    CAM.   Be advised.
    FLO. I am, and by my fancy.° If my reason
Will thereto be obedient, I have reason.
If not, my senses, better pleased with madness,
Do bid it welcome.
    CAM.   This is desperate, sir.   495
    FLO. So call it. But it does fulfill my vow,
I needs must think it honesty. Camillo,
Not for Bohemia, nor the pomp that may
Be thereat° gleaned — for all the sun sees, or
The close earth wombs,° or the profound seas hide
In unknown fathoms — will I break my oath   501
To this my fair beloved. Therefore I pray you,
As you have ever been my father's honored friend,
When he shall miss me — as, in faith, I mean not
To see him any more — cast your good counsels
Upon his passion. Let myself and fortune   506
Tug° for the time to come. This you may know
And so deliver, I am put to sea
With her whom here I cannot hold onshore.
And most oppórtune° to our need I have   510
A vessel rides° fast by, but not prepared
For this design. What course I mean to hold
Shall nothing benefit your knowledge, nor
Concern me the reporting.°
    CAM.   O my lord!
I would your spirit were easier for advice,   515
Or stronger for your need.
    FLO.   Hark, Perdita. [*Drawing her aside.*]
I'll hear you by and by.
    CAM.   He's irremovable,
Resolved for flight. Now were I happy if
His going I could frame to serve my turn,
Save him from danger, do him love and honor,   520
Purchase the sight again of dear Sicilia
And that unhappy King, my master, whom
I so much thirst to see.
    FLO.   Now, good Camillo,
I am so fraught° with curious° business that
I leave out ceremony.
    CAM.   Sir, I think   525
You have heard of my poor services, i' the love
That I have borne your father?
    FLO.   Very nobly
Have you deserved. It is my father's music
To speak your deeds, not little of his care
To have them recompensed as thought on.

445–47. yea . . . thee: yes, and also good enough for my son, who would not be good enough for you if the honor of my family was not concerned.   451. As . . . to 't: as you are too gentle to endure it.   475–76. More . . . unwillingly: like a greyhound, held back by the leash, I strain to be let loose.   483. I . . . Camillo: Here Florizel recognizes Camillo through his disguise.

489. mar: destroy.   491. heir . . . affection: my love is my inheritance.   492. fancy: love.   499. thereat: i.e., in the Court of my father.   500. wombs: hides within itself.   507. Tug: pull against each other.   510. opportune: fortunate.   511. rides: is at anchor.   512–14. What . . . reporting: it will be better for you not to know, and I do not intend to tell you, where I mean to go.   524. fraught: burdened. curious: that requires all my attention.

CAM.   Well, my lord,   530
If you may please to think I love the King,
And through him what is nearest to him, which is
Your gracious self, embrace but my direction,°
If your more ponderous° and settled° project
May suffer alteration. On mine honor   535
I'll point you where you shall have such receiving
As shall become your highness° — where you may
Enjoy your mistress — from the whom, I see,
There's no disjunction° to be made but by
As Heavens forefend! your ruin — marry her,   540
And with my best endeavors in your absence
Your discontenting father strive to qualify°
And bring him up to liking.
    FLO.   How, Camillo,
May this, almost a miracle, be done?   544
That I may call thee something more than man
And after that trust to thee.
    CAM.   Have you thought on
A place whereto you'll go?
    FLO.   Not any yet.
But as the unthought-on accident is guilty
To what we wildly do,° so we profess
Ourselves to be the slaves of chance, and flies   550
Of every wind that blows.
    CAM.   Then list° to me.
This follows, if you will not change your purpose
But undergo this flight — make for Sicilia,
And there present yourself and your fair Princess,
For so I see she must be, 'fore Leontes.   555
She shall be habited° as it becomes
The partner of your bed. Methinks I see
Leontes opening his free arms and weeping   558
His welcomes forth; asks thee the son forgiveness,
As 'twere i' the father's person;° kisses the hands
Of your fresh Princess; o'er and o'er divides him
'Twixt his unkindness and his kindness;° the one
He chides to Hell and bids the other grow
Faster than thought or time.
    FLO.   Worthy Camillo,
What color for my visitation° shall I   565
Hold up before him?
    CAM.   Sent by the King your father
To greet him and to give him comforts. Sir,
The manner of your bearing toward him, with
What you as from your father shall deliver,   569
Things known betwixt us three, I'll write you down.
The which shall point you forth at every sitting°
What you must say, that he shall not perceive

But that you have your father's bosom° there
And speak his very heart.
    FLO.   I am bound to you.
There is some sap° in this.
    CAM.   A course more promising   575
Than a wild dedication of yourselves
To unpathed waters, undreamed shores, most
    certain
To miseries enough, no hope to help you
But as you shake off one to take another —
Nothing so certain as your anchors, who   580
Do their best office if they can but stay you
Where you'll be loath to be.° Besides, you know
Prosperity's the very bond of love,
Whose fresh complexion and whose heart together
Affliction alters.
    PER.   One of these is true.   585
I think affliction may subdue the cheek,
But not take in° the mind.
    CAM.   Yea, say you so?
There shall not at your father's house these seven
    years
Be born another such.
    FLO.   My good Camillo,
She is as forward of her breeding as   590
She is i' the rear o' her birth.°
    CAM.   I cannot say 'tis pity
She lacks instructions,° for she seems a mistress
To most that teach.
    PER.   Your pardon, sir, for this
I'll blush you thanks.
    FLO.   My prettiest Perdita!
But oh, the thorns we stand upon! Camillo,   595
Preserver of my father, now of me,
The medicine of° our house, how shall we do?
We are not furnished° like Bohemia's son,
Nor shall appear in Sicilia.
    CAM.   My lord,   599
Fear none of this. I think you know my fortunes
Do all lie there. It shall be so my care
To have you royally appointed° as if
The scene you play were mine. For instance, sir,
That you may know you shall not want, one
    word.   [*They talk aside.*]   604
       [*Re-enter* AUTOLYCUS.]
AUT. Ha, ha! What a fool Honesty is! And Trust,
his sworn brother,° a very simple gentleman! I have
sold all my trumpery, not a counterfeit stone, not a

---

533. embrace . . . direction: follow my advice.   534. ponderous: weighty. settled: fixed.   537. highness: high rank.   539. disjunction: separation.   542. qualify: mollify.   548–49. unthought-on . . . do: unexpected accident is the cause of our acting in this wild way.   551. list: listen.   556. habited: clothed.   560. As . . . person: as if you were your father.   561–62. o'er . . . kindness: he is divided between his unkind behavior to your father and his welcome to you.   565. color . . . visitation: excuse for my visit.   571. point . . . sitting: give you exact instructions for each conference.

573. bosom: heart, approval.   575. sap: life.   580–82. Nothing . . . be: i.e., the most sure thing about such a voyage is that wherever you anchor you will be miserable, but more miserable if you sail on.   587. take in: capture.   590–91. She . . . birth: she is in her nature as high above what one would expect in a shepherd's daughter as she is beneath me in her humble birth.   592. lacks instructions: has had no schooling.   597. medicine of: that which keeps healthy.   598. furnished: provided for.   602. royally appointed: equipped like a prince.   606. sworn brother: See *M Ado*, I.i.72–73,n.

ribbon, glass, pomander,° brooch, table book,° ballad, knife, tape, glove, shoe tie, bracelet, horn ring,
to keep my pack from fasting.° They throng   610
who should buy first as if my trinkets had been hal-
lowed° and brought a benediction to the buyer. By
which means I saw whose purse was best in picture,°
and what I saw to my good use I remembered. My
clown, who wants but something° to be a reasonable man, grew so in love with the wenches' song
that he would not stir his pettitoes° till he had both
tune and words, which so drew the rest of the herd
to me that all their other senses stuck in ears.   620
You might have pinched a placket, it was senseless.
'Twas nothing to geld a codpiece° of a purse. I
would have filed keys off that hung in chains. No
hearing, no feeling, but my sir's song and admiring
the nothing of it. So that in this time of lethargy°
I picked and cut most of their festival purses, and
had not the old man come in with a whoobub°
against his daughter and the King's son and scared
my choughs° from the chaff, I had not left a purse
alive in the whole army.   630

[CAMILLO, FLORIZEL, *and* PERDITA *come forward.*]

CAM. Nay, but my letters, by this means being
          there
So soon as you arrive, shall clear that doubt.

FLO. And those that you'll procure from King
          Leontes ——

CAM. Shall satisfy your father.

PER.   Happy be you!
All that you speak shows fair.

CAM.   Who have we here? [*Seeing* AUTOLYCUS]
We'll make an instrument of this, omit   636
Nothing may give us aid.

AUT. If they have overheard me now, why, hanging.

CAM. How now, good fellow! Why shakest thou
so? Fear not, man, here's no harm intended to thee.

AUT. I am a poor fellow, sir.   643

CAM. Why, be so still, here's nobody will steal
that° from thee. Yet for the outside of thy property
we must make an exchange. Therefore disease° thee
instantly, — thou must think there's a necessity in 't
— and change garments with this gentleman.
Though the pennyworth on his side be the worst,
yet hold thee, there's some boot.°   650

AUT. I am a poor fellow, sir. [*Aside*] I know ye
well enough.

CAM. Nay, prithee dispatch.° The gentleman is
half flayed° already.   654

AUT. Are you in earnest, sir? [*Aside*] I smell the
trick on 't.

FLO. Dispatch, I prithee.

AUT. Indeed, I have had earnest,° but I cannot
with conscience take it.   659

CAM. Unbuckle, unbuckle.

[FLORIZEL *and* AUTOLYCUS *exchange garments.*]
Fortunate mistress — let my prophecy
Come home to ye!° — you must retire yourself
Into some covert.° Take your sweetheart's hat
And pluck it o'er your brows, muffle your face,
Dismantle you,° and, as you can, disliken°   665
The truth of your own seeming,° that you may —
For I do fear eyes over — to shipboard
Get undescried.°

PER.   I see the play so lies
That I must bear a part.

CAM.   No remedy.
Have you done there?

FLO.   Should I now meet my father,   670
He would not call me son.

CAM. Nay, you shall have no hat.

                           [*Giving it to* PERDITA.]
Come, lady, come. Farewell, my friend.

AUT.   Adieu, sir.

FLO. O Perdita, what have we twain forgot!
Pray you, a word.

CAM. [*Aside*] What I do next shall be to tell the
          King   675
Of this escape and whither they are bound,
Wherein my hope is I shall so prevail
To force him after. In whose company
I shall review° Sicilia, for whose sight
I have a woman's longing.°

FLO.   Fortune speed° us!   680
Thus we set on, Camillo, to the seaside.

CAM. The swifter speed, the better.

                 [*Exeunt* FLORIZEL, PERDITA, *and* CAMILLO.]

AUT. I understand the business, I hear it. To° have
an open ear, a quick eye, and a nimble hand is necessary for a cutpurse. A good nose is requisite also,
to smell out work for the other senses. I see this is
the time that the unjust man doth thrive. What an
exchange had this been without boot! What a boot is
here with this exchange! Sure the gods do this year
connive° at us, and we may do anything ex-   690
tempore.° The Prince himself is about a piece of

608. pomander: ball of perfume. table book: notebook.   610. to
. . . fasting: i.e., the pack is quite empty.   612. hallowed: blessed
by the Pope.   613. best . . . picture: had most faces; i.e., coins
with the King's head.   616. wants . . . something: just lacks
something; i.e., wits.   618. pettitoes: trotters.   622. codpiece:
See Pl. 8c and comment on p. 93b.   625. lethargy: lack of feeling.
627. whoobub: hubbub.   629. choughs: jackdaws, simpletons.
645. that: i.e., your poverty.   646. disease: take off your "case";
i.e., coat.   649–50. Though . . . boot: though the value of the exchange is worse for him, yet here is something extra for you —
whereupon Camillo gives him money. boot: advantage.

653. dispatch: be quick.   654. flayed: skinned.   658. earnest:
money on account.   661–62. let . . . ye: may my prophecy — that
you shall be a "fortunate mistress" — come true.   663. covert:
thicket.   665. Dismantle you: take off your cloak. disliken: disguise.   666. The . . . seeming: your true appearance.   668. undescried: undiscovered.   679. review: see again.   680. woman's
longing: as keen a desire as pregnant women have for certain
foods. speed: be lucky to.   683–702. To . . . work: See *W Tale*
Intro. p. 1430b.   690. connive: wink.   691. extempore: without
preparation.

iniquity, stealing away from his father with his clog° at his heels. If I thought it were a piece of honesty to acquaint the King withal, I would not do 't. I hold it the more knavery to conceal it, and therein am I constant° to my profession.   698

[*Re-enter* CLOWN *and* SHEPHERD.] Aside, aside, here is more matter for a hot° brain. Every lane's end, every shop, church, session, hanging, yields a careful man work.

CLO. See, see, what a man you are now! There is no other way but to tell the King she's a changeling° and none of your flesh and blood.   705

SHEP. Nay, but hear me.

CLO. Nay, but hear me.

SHEP. Go to,° then.

CLO. She being none of your flesh and blood, your flesh and blood has not offended the King, and   710 so your flesh and blood is not to be punished by him. Show those things you found about her, those secret things, all but what she has with her. This being done, let the law go whistle, I warrant you.   715

SHEP. I will tell the King all, every word — yea, and his son's pranks too, who I may say is no honest man, neither to his father nor to me, to go about to make me the King's brother-in-law.   720

CLO. Indeed, brother-in-law was the farthest off you could have been to him, and then your blood had been the dearer° by I know how much an ounce.

AUT. [*Aside*] Very wisely, puppies!   725

SHEP. Well, let us to the King. There is that in this fardel° will make him scratch his beard.

AUT. [*Aside*] I know not what impediment this complaint may be to the flight of my master.

CLO. Pray heartily he be at palace.   731

AUT. [*Aside*] Though I am not naturally honest, I am so sometimes by chance. Let me pocket up my peddler's excrement.° [*Takes off his false beard.*] How now, rustics! Whither are you bound?   735

SHEP. To the palace, an it like° your Worship.

AUT. Your affairs there — what, with whom, the condition of that fardel, the place of your dwelling, your names, your ages, of what having,° breeding, and anything that is fitting to be known, discover.°

CLO. We are but plain fellows, sir.   742

AUT. A lie, you are rough and hairy. Let° me have no lying. It becomes none but tradesmen, and they often give us soldiers the lie. But we pay them for

it with stamped coin, not stabbing steel, therefore they do not give us the lie.   748

CLO. Your Worship had like to have given us one if you had not taken yourself with the manner.°

SHEP. Are you a courtier, an 't like° you, sir?

AUT. Whether it like me or no, I am a courtier. Seest thou not the air of the Court in these enfoldings?° Hath not my gait in it the measure of   755 the Court? Receives not thy nose Court odor from me? Reflect I not on thy baseness Court contempt? Thinkest thou, for that I insinuate,° or toaze° from thee thy business, I am therefore no courtier? I am courtier cap-à-pie,° and one that will either push on or pluck back thy business there. Whereupon I command thee to open° thy affair.   763

SHEP. My business, sir, is to the King.

AUT. What advocate hast thou to him?

SHEP. I know not, an 't like you.

CLO. Advocate's the court word for a pheasant.° Say you have none.

SHEP. None, sir, I have no pheasant, cock nor hen.   770

AUT. How blessed are we that are not simple men! Yet nature might have made me as these are, Therefore I will not disdain.°

CLO. This cannot be but° a great courtier.

SHEP. His garments are rich, but he wears them not handsomely.   776

CLO. He seems to be the more noble in being fantastical. A great man, I'll warrant. I know by the picking on 's teeth.°

AUT. The fardel there? What's i' the fardel? Wherefore that box?   781

SHEP. Sir, there lies such secrets in this fardel and box which none must know but the King, and which he shall know within this hour if I may come to the speech of him.   785

AUT. Age,° thou hast lost thy labor.

SHEP. Why, sir?

AUT. The King is not at the palace. He is gone aboard a new ship to purge melancholy° and air himself. For if thou beest capable of things serious, thou must know the King is full of grief.   791

SHEP. So 'tis said, sir, about his son, that should have married a shepherd's daughter.

AUT. If that shepherd be not in handfast,° let him fly. The curses he shall have, the tortures he shall feel, will break the back of man, the heart of monster.

---

693. clog: a weight fastened to his leg; i.e., Perdita.   **698. constant:** true.   **700. hot:** quick.   **704. changeling:** See III.iii.122,n.   **708. Go to:** go on.   **724. dearer:** more valuable.   **727. fardel:** bundle.   **734. excrement:** beard; lit., that which grows out of a man. Autolycus now assumes the superior manners and affected speech of a courtier toward a countryman.   **736. as . . . like:** if it pleases.   **740. having:** wealth.   **741. discover:** reveal to me.   **743–48. Let . . . lie:** "To give the lie" is to call a man a liar — a deadly insult to a soldier, which was answered with a stab. But when tradesmen give the lie by selling false goods, they make their customers pay for it.

750. if . . . manner: if you had not caught yourself in the act (of lying).   **751. an 't like:** if it please.   **755. enfoldings:** coverings.   **758. insinuate:** wind myself into. **toaze:** comb; lit., to card wool ready for spinning.   **761. cap-à-pie:** head to foot.   **763. open:** explain.   **768. Advocate's . . . pheasant:** *advocate* is the word they use at Court for the bribe of a pheasant.   **773. disdain:** be proud.   **774. cannot . . . but:** must be.   **779. picking . . . teeth:** Toothpicks were a foreign fashion; to possess one showed that the owner had traveled.   **786. Age:** old man.   **789. purge melancholy:** A drastic purge was one of the remedies for melancholy.   **794. in handfast:** locked up.

CLO. Think you so, sir? 798

AUT. Not he alone shall suffer what wit can make heavy and vengeance bitter; but those that are germane° to him, though removed fifty times, shall all come under the hangman. Which though it be great pity, yet it is necessary. An old sheep-whistling rogue, a ram-tender, to offer to have his daughter come into grace!° Some say he shall be stoned, but that death is too soft for him say I. Draw our throne into a sheepcote!° All deaths are too few, the sharpest too easy. 808

CLO. Has the old man e'er a son, sir, do you hear, an 't like you, sir?

AUT. He has a son, who shall be flayed alive; then, 'nointed° over with honey, set on the head of a wasp's nest; then stand till he be three-quarters and a dram° dead; then recovered again with aqua vitae° or some other hot infusion; then, raw as he is, 815 and in the hottest day prognostication° proclaims, shall he be set against a brick wall, the sun looking with a southward eye upon him, where he is to behold him with flies blown° to death. But what talk we of these traitorly rascals, whose miseries are 820 to be smiled at, their offenses being so capital?° Tell me, for you seem to be honest plain men, what you have to the King. Being something gently considered,° I'll bring you where he is aboard, tender° your persons to his presence, whisper him in your behalfs. And if it be in man besides the King to effect your suits, here is man shall do it. 827

CLO. He seems to be of great authority. Close with him, give him gold, and though authority be a stubborn bear, yet he is oft led by the nose with gold. Show the inside of your purse to the outside of his hand, and no more ado. Remember " stoned," and " flayed alive." 834

SHEP. An 't please you, sir, to undertake the business for us, here is that gold I have. I'll make it as much more and leave this young man in pawn till I bring it you.

AUT. After I have done what I promised?

SHEP. Aye, sir. 840

AUT. Well, give me the moiety.° Are you a party in this business?

CLO. In some sort, sir. But though my case° be a pitiful one, I hope I shall not be flayed out of it.

AUT. Oh, that's the case of the shepherd's son. Hang him, he'll be made an example. 846

CLO. Comfort, good comfort! We must to the King and show our strange sights. He must know 'tis none of your daughter nor my sister, we are gone else. Sir, I will give you as much as this old man does when the business is performed, and remain, as he says, your pawn till it be brought you. 853

AUT. I will trust you. Walk before toward the seaside. Go on the right hand. I will but look upon the hedge and follow you.

CLO. We are blest in this man, as I may say, even blest.

SHEP. Let's before as he bids us. He was provided° to do us good. 860

[*Exeunt* SHEPHERD *and* CLOWN.]

AUT. If I had a mind to be honest, I see Fortune would not suffer me. She drops booties in my mouth. I am courted now with a double occasion,° gold and a means to do the Prince my master good, which who knows how that may turn back to my advancement? I will bring these two moles, these blind ones, aboard him. If he think it fit to shore them° again and that the complaint they have to the King concerns him nothing, let him call me rogue for being so far officious, for I am proof against that title and what shame else belongs to 't. To him will I 872 present them. There may be matter in it.   [*Exit.*]

Act V

SCENE I. *A room in* LEONTES' *palace.*

[*Enter* LEONTES, CLEOMENES, DION, PAULINA, *and* SERVANTS.]

CLE. Sir, you have done enough, and have performed
A saintlike sorrow. No fault could you make
Which you have not redeemed, indeed paid down
More penitence than done trespass. At the last,
Do as the Heavens have done, forget your evil, 5
With them forgive yourself.

LEON.   Whilst I remember
Her and her virtues, I cannot forget
My blemishes in them,° and so still think of
The wrong I did myself. Which was so much
That heirless it hath made my kingdom, and 10
Destroyed the sweet'st companion that e'er man
Bred his hopes out of.

PAUL.   True, too true, my lord.
If, one by one, you wedded all the world,
Or from the all that are took something good
To make a perfect woman, she you killed 15
Would be unparalleled.

801. germane: related.   805. grace: favor.   806–07. Draw . . . sheepcote: make our King a relative of a shepherd. 812. 'nointed: anointed.   814. dram: a very small weight. aqua vitae: spirits. 816. prognostication: The common penny *Almanack and Prognostication*, published annually, gave confident forecasts of the weather. See App. 2.   819. blown: made to swell.   821. capital: deserving death.   823–24. gently considered: on the considerations proper to a gentleman; i.e., cash in advance.   824. tender: introduce.   841. moiety: half.   843. case: with the double meaning of "affair" and "outer covering."

859. provided: sent by Providence.   863. double occasion: twofold benefit.   868. shore them: put them ashore.

Act V, Sc. i: 8. My . . . them: my faults toward them.

LEON.　　　　　　　　I think so. Killed!
She I killed! I did so, but thou strikest me
Sorely to say I did. It is as bitter
Upon thy tongue as in my thought. Now, good
　　now,°
Say so but seldom.
　　CLE.　　　　　Not at all, good lady.　　20
You might have spoken a thousand things that
　　would
Have done the time more benefit and graced
Your kindness better.°
　　PAUL.　　　　　You are one of those
Would have him wed again.
　　DION.　　　　　If you would not so,
You pity not the state, nor the remembrance　25
Of his most sovereign name,° consider little
What dangers, by His Highness' fail of issue,°
May drop upon his kingdom and devour
Incertain lookers-on.° What were more holy
Than to rejoice the former Queen is well?°　30
What holier than, for royalty's repair,°
For present comfort and for future good,
To bless the bed of majesty again
With a sweet fellow° to 't?
　　PAUL.　　　　　There is none worthy,
Respecting° her that's gone. Besides, the gods　35
Will have fulfilled their secret purposes.
For has not the divine Apollo said,
Is 't not the tenor° of his oracle,
That King Leontes shall not have an heir
Till his lost child be found? Which that it shall　40
Is all as monstrous to our human reason°
As my Antigonus to break his grave
And come again to me, who, on my life,
Did perish with the infant. 'Tis your counsel
My lord should to the Heavens be contrary,　45
Oppose against their wills. [*To* LEONTES] Care not
　　for issue,
The crown will find an heir. Great Alexander
Left his to the worthiest, so his successor
Was like to be the best.
　　LEON.　　　　　Good Paulina,
Who hast the memory of Hermione,　　50
I know, in honor, oh, that ever I
Had squared me to° thy counsel! — Then, even now
I might have looked upon my Queen's full eyes,
Have taken treasure from her lips ——
　　PAUL.　　　　　And left them
More rich for what they yielded.

LEON.　　　　　Thou speak'st truth.　55
No more such wives, therefore, no wife. One worse,
And better used, would make her sainted spirit
Again possess her corpse, and on this stage,
Where we offenders now appear soul-vexed,
And begin, " Why to me? "°
　　PAUL.　　　　　Had she such power,　60
She had just cause.
　　LEON.　　　　　She had, and would incense me
To murder her I married.
　　PAUL.　　　　　I should so.
Were I the ghost that walked, I'd bid you mark
Her eye, and tell me for what dull part in 't
You chose her. Then I'd shriek that even your ears
Should rift° to hear me, and the words that fol-
　　lowed　　66
Should be " Remember mine."
　　LEON.　　　　　Stars, stars,
And all eyes else dead coals! Fear thou no wife.
I'll have no wife, Paulina.
　　PAUL.　　　　　Will you swear
Never to marry but by my free leave?　　70
　　LEON. Never, Paulina, so be blest my spirit!
　　PAUL. Then, good my lords, bear witness to his
　　oath.
　　CLE. You tempt him overmuch.
　　PAUL.　　　　　Unless another,
As like Hermione as is her picture,
Affront his eye.
　　CLE.　　　Good madam ——
　　PAUL.　　　　　I have done.　75
Yet, if my lord will marry — if you will, sir,
No remedy but you will — give me the office
To choose you a Queen. She shall not be so young
As was your former, but she shall be such
As, walked your first Queen's ghost,° it should take
　　joy　　80
To see her in your arms.
　　LEON.　　　　　My true Paulina,
We shall not marry till thou bid'st us.
　　PAUL.　　　　　That
Shall be when your first Queen's again in breath,
Never till then.
　　　　[*Enter a* GENTLEMAN.]
　　GEN. One that gives out himself Prince Florizel,
Son of Polixenes, with his Princess, she　　86
The fairest I have yet beheld, desires access
To your high presence.
　　LEON.　　　　　What with him? He comes not
Like to his father's greatness. His approach,
So out of circumstance° and sudden, tells us　90
'Tis not a visitation framed,° but forced
By need and accident. What train?

GEN.   But few,
And those but mean.

LEON.   His Princess, say you, with him?

GEN. Aye, the most peerless piece of earth,° I
    think,
That e'er the sun shone bright on.

PAUL.   O Hermione, 95
As every present time doth boast itself
Above a better gone, so must thy grave
Give way to what's seen now! Sir,° you yourself
Have said and writ so, but your writing now
Is colder than that theme. " She had not been, 100
Nor was not to be equaled " — thus your verse
Flowed with her beauty once. 'Tis shrewdly ebbed°
To say you have seen a better.

GEN.   Pardon, madam.
The one I have almost forgot — your pardon —
The other, when she has obtained your eye, 105
Will have your tongue too. This is a creature,
Would she begin a sect, might quench the zeal
Of all professors° else, make proselytes
Of who she but bid follow.

PAUL.   How! Not women?

GEN. Women will love her that she is a woman
More worth than any man, men that she is 111
The rarest of all women.

LEON.   Go, Cleomenes,
Yourself, assisted with your honored friends,
Bring them to our embracement.°
            [Exeunt CLEOMENES and others.]
                    Still, 'tis strange
He thus should steal upon us.

PAUL.   Had our Prince, 115
Jewel of children, seen this hour, he had paired
Well with this lord. There was not full a month
Between their births.

LEON. Prithee, no more, cease. Thou know'st
He dies to me again when talked of. Sure, 120
When I shall see this gentleman, thy speeches
Will bring me to consider that which may
Unfurnish° me of reason. They are come.
[Re-enter CLEOMENES and others, with FLORIZEL and
            PERDITA.]
Your mother was most true to wedlock, Prince,
For she did print your royal father off,° 125
Conceiving you. Were I but twenty-one,
Your father's image is so hit in you,°
His very air, that I should call you Brother,
As I did him, and speak of something wildly
By us performed before. Most dearly welcome! 130

And your fair Princess — goddess! — oh, alas!
I lost a couple that 'twixt heaven and earth
Might thus have stood begetting wonder as
You, gracious couple, do. And then I lost —
All mine own folly — the society, 135
Amity° too, of your brave father, whom,
Though bearing misery,° I desire my life
Once more to look on him.

FLO.   By his command
Have I here touched Sicilia, and from him
Give you all greetings that a king at friend° 140
Can send his brother. And but infirmity,
Which waits upon worn times,° hath something
            seized
His wished ability, he had himself
The lands and waters 'twixt your throne and his
Measured to look upon you, whom he loves — 145
He bade me say so — more than all the scepters
And those that bear them living.

LEON.   O my brother,
Good gentleman! The wrongs I have done thee stir
Afresh within me, and these thy offices,°
So rarely kind, are as interpreters 150
Of my behindhand slackness!° Welcome hither,
As is the spring to the earth. And hath he too
Exposed this paragon° to the fearful usage,
At least ungentle, of the dreadful Neptune,
To greet a man not worth her pains, much less 155
The adventure of her person?

FLO.   Good my lord,
She came from Libya.°

LEON.   Where the warlike Smalus,
That noble honored lord, is feared and loved?

FLO. Most royal sir, from thence, from him whose
            daughter 159
His tears proclaimed his, parting with her. Thence,
A prosperous south wind friendly, we have crossed,
To execute the charge° my father gave me
For visiting your Highness. My best train°
I have from your Sicilian shores dismissed,
Who for Bohemia bend, to signify 165
Not only my success in Libya, sir,
But my arrival, and my wife's, in safety
Here where we are.

LEON.   The blessèd gods
Purge all infection from our air whilst you
Do climate° here! You have a holy father, 170
A graceful gentleman, against whose person,
So sacred as it is, I have done sin.

---

94. earth: i.e., flesh.   98–103. Sir . . . better: Paulina turns on
the gentleman-poet for his insincerity in forgetting the former
extravagance of his praises of Hermione.   102. shrewdly ebbed:
has, like the tide, bitterly begun to decline.   108. professors:
those who profess a zeal for religion, particularly the Puritans.
114. to . . . embracement: that we may welcome them.   123. Un-
furnish: deprive.   125. print . . . off: strike off an exact copy
of your father.   127. hit in you: exactly reproduced in you.

136. Amity: friendship.   137. Though . . . misery: though bearing my burden of sorrow.   140. at friend: being in a state of
friendship.   141–42. but . . . times: but that weakness which
comes with old age has somewhat prevented him from being able
to do as he desired.   149. offices: acts of courtesy.   151. my . . .
slackness: my slackness in not sending to greet him before this.
153. paragon: perfect creature.   156–57. Good . . . Libya: Florizel here tells the tale prepared for him by Camillo.   162. charge:
command.   163. My . . . train: most of my followers.   170. climate: remain in our country.

For which the Heavens, taking angry note,
Have left me issueless, and your father's blest,
As he from Heaven merits it, with you   175
Worthy his goodness. What might I have been,
Might I a son and daughter now have looked on,
Such goodly things as you!

           [*Enter a* LORD.]
LORD.   Most noble sir,
That which I shall report will bear no credit
Were not the proof so nigh. Please you, great sir,
Bohemia greets you from himself by me,   181
Desires you to attach° his son, who has —
His dignity and duty both cast off —
Fled from his father, from his hopes, and with
A shepherd's daughter.
LEON.   Where's Bohemia? Speak.   185
LORD. Here in your city, I now came from him.
I speak amazedly,° and it becomes
My marvel and my message. To your Court
Whiles he was hastening, in the chase, it seems,
Of this fair couple, meets he on the way   190
The father of this seeming lady and
Her brother, having both their country quitted
With this young Prince.
FLO.   Camillo has betrayed me,
Whose honor and whose honesty till now
Endured all weathers.
LORD.   Lay 't so to his charge.   195
He's with the King your father.
LEON.   Who? Camillo?
LORD. Camillo, sir, I spake with him, who now
Has these poor men in question. Never saw I
Wretches so quake. They kneel, they kiss the earth,
Forswear° themselves as often as they speak.   200
Bohemia stops his ears, and threatens them
With divers deaths° in death.
PER.   O my poor father!
The Heaven sets spies upon us, will not have
Our contract celebrated.
LEON.   You are married?
FLO. We are not, sir, nor are we like to be,   205
The stars, I see, will kiss the valleys first.
The odds for high and low's alike.°
LEON.   My lord,
Is this the daughter of a king?
FLO.   She is
When once she is my wife.
LEON. That "once" I see by your good father's
    speed   210
Will come on very slowly. I am sorry,
Most sorry, you have broken from his liking
Where you were tied in duty, and as sorry
Your choice is not so rich in worth as beauty,
That you might well enjoy her.
FLO.   Dear, look up.   215

Though Fortune, visible an enemy,°
Should chase us with my father, power no jot
Hath she to change our loves. Beseech you, sir,
Remember since you owed no more to time
Than I do now.° With thought of such affections,
Step forth mine advocate. At your request   221
My father will grant precious things as trifles.
LEON. Would he do so, I'd beg your precious mis-
    tress,
Which he counts but a trifle.
PAUL.   Sir, my liege,
Your eye hath too much youth in 't.° Not a month
'Fore your Queen died she was more worth such
    gazes   226
Than what you look on now.
LEON.   I thought of her,
Even in these looks I made. [*To* FLORIZEL] But your
    petition
Is yet unanswered. I will to your father.
Your honor not o'erthrown by your desires,°   230
I am friend to them and you. Upon which errand
I now go toward him, therefore follow me
And mark what way I make.° Come, good my lord.
                                [*Exeunt.*]

SCENE II.° *Before* LEONTES' *palace.*

[*Enter* AUTOLYCUS *and a* GENTLEMAN.]

AUT. Beseech you, sir, were you present at this relation?
1. GEN. I was by at the opening of the fardel, heard
the old shepherd deliver the manner° how he found
it. Whereupon, after a little amazedness,° we were
all commanded out of the chamber. Only this methought I heard the shepherd say — he found the
child.   8
AUT. I would most gladly know the issue of it.
1. GEN. I make a broken delivery° of the business,
but the changes I perceived in the King and Camillo
were very notes of admiration.° They seemed almost, with staring on one another, to tear the cases°
of their eyes. There was speech in their dumbness,
language in their very gesture, they looked as   15
they had heard of a world ransomed or one destroyed. A notable passion° of wonder appeared in
them, but the wisest beholder that knew no more
but seeing could not say if the importance° were joy

---

182. attach: arrest.   187. amazedly: confusedly.   200. Forswear: deny on oath.   202. divers deaths: different kinds of death.   207. odds . . . alike: bad luck comes to high and low alike.

216. visible an enemy: who is clearly our enemy.   219–20. Remember . . . now: remember when you were as young as I am.   225. Your . . . in 't: i.e., you are too much attracted by this lady. Paulina is alarmed by Leontes' obvious interest in Perdita.   230. Your . . . desires: provided that you have not behaved dishonorably toward her.   233. mark . . . make: see what success I have.

    Sc. ii: See *W Tale* Intro. p. 1432b.   4. deliver . . . manner: relate the circumstances.   5. amazedness: confused wonder.   10. broken delivery: disjointed account.   12. admiration: great wonder.   13. cases: sockets.   17. passion: emotion.   19. importance: import.

or sorrow. But in the extremity of the one, it must
needs be.   21
[*Enter another* GENTLEMAN.] Here comes a gentleman that haply knows more. The news, Rogero?

2. GEN. Nothing but bonfires. The oracle is fulfilled, the King's daughter is found. Such a deal of
wonder is broken out within this hour that ballad-
makers° cannot be able to express it.   27
[*Enter a third* GENTLEMAN.] Here comes the Lady
Paulina's steward. He can deliver you more. How
goes it now, sir? This news which is called true is so
like an old tale that the verity of it is in strong suspicion. Has the King found his heir?   32

3. GEN. Most true, if ever truth were pregnant by
circumstance.° That which you hear you'll swear
you see, there is such unity in the proofs. The mantle
of Queen Hermione's, her jewel about the neck of it,
the letters of Antigonus found with it, which they
know to be his character,° the majesty of the crea-
ture° in resemblance of the mother, the affection
of nobleness° which Nature shows above her   40
breeding,° and many other evidences proclaim her
with all certainty to be the King's daughter. Did you
see the meeting of the two Kings?

2. GEN. No.   45

3. GEN. Then have you lost a sight which was to
be seen, cannot be spoken of. There might you have
beheld one joy crown another, so and in such manner that it seemed sorrow wept to take leave of them,
for their joy waded in tears. There was casting-   50
up of eyes, holding-up of hands, with countenance
of such distraction that they were to be known by
garment, not by favor.° Our King, being ready to
leap out of himself for joy of his found daughter, as
if that joy were now become a loss, cries " Oh,   55
thy mother, thy mother! " then asks Bohemia forgiveness, then embraces his son-in-law, then again
worries he his daughter with clipping° her. Now he
thanks the old shepherd, which stands by like a
weather-bitten conduit of many kings' reigns.°   60
I never heard of such another encounter, which
lames report to follow it and undoes description to
do it.°

2. GEN. What, pray you, became of Antigonus,
that carried hence the child?   65

3. GEN. Like an old tale still, which will have matter to rehearse, though credit be asleep and not an
ear open.° He was torn to pieces with a bear. This

avouches° the shepherd's son, who has not only his
innocence, which seems much, to justify him, but a
handkerchief and rings of his that Paulina knows.

1. GEN. What became of his bark and his followers?   73

3. GEN. Wrecked the same instant of their master's
death and in the view of the shepherd. So that all the
instruments which aided to expose the child were
even then lost when it was found. But oh, the noble
combat that 'twixt joy and sorrow was fought in
Paulina! She had one eye declined for the loss of   80
her husband, another elevated that the oracle was fulfilled. She lifted the Princess from the earth, and so
locks her in embracing as if she would pin her to her
heart that she might no more be in danger of losing.   85

1. GEN. The dignity of this act was worth the audience of kings and princes, for by such was it acted.

3. GEN. One of the prettiest touches of all, and that
which angled for mine eyes, caught the water   90
though not the fish, was when, at the relation of the
Queen's death, with the manner how she came to 't
bravely confessed and lamented by the King, how
attentiveness wounded his daughter till, from one
sign of dolor° to another, she did, with an " Alas,"
I would fain° say bleed tears, for I am sure my heart
wept blood. Who was most marble° there changed
color, some swooned, all sorrowed. If all the world
could have seen 't, the woe had been universal.   100

1. GEN. Are they returned to the Court?

3. GEN. No. The Princess, hearing of her mother's
statue, which is in the keeping of Paulina — a piece
many years in doing and now newly performed by
that rare Italian master, Julio Romano,° who,   105
had he himself eternity° and could put breath into
his work, would beguile Nature of her custom,° so
perfectly he is her ape.° He so near to Hermione hath
done Hermione that they say one would speak to her
and stand in hope of answer. — Thither with all
greediness of affection are they gone, and there they
intend to sup.   112

2. GEN. I thought she had some great matter there
in hand, for she hath privately twice or thrice a day,
ever since the death of Hermione, visited that removed house. Shall we thither, and with our company piece° the rejoicing?   117

1. GEN. Who would be thence that has the benefit
of access? Every wink of an eye, some new grace
will be born. Our absence makes us unthrifty to our
knowledge.° Let's along.   [*Exeunt* GENTLEMEN.]
AUT. Now had I not the dash of my former   122

---

27. ballad-makers: See App. 8.   33–34. pregnant . . . circumstance: probable by the evidence.   38. character: handwriting.
39. creature: child; i.e., Perdita.   39–40. affection . . . nobleness: natural nobility.   41. breeding: upbringing.   51–53. with
. . . favor: i.e., their faces were so changed by their emotions
that they could only be recognized by their garments, not by
their looks.   58. clipping: embracing.   60. weather-bitten . . .
reigns: like a weather-worn fountain that has stood for many
years.   62–63. lames . . . it: makes any tale seem lame and is beyond description.   66–68. which . . . open: which the teller insists on telling though no one will believe it or listen.

69. avouches: corroborates.   95. dolor: grief.   96. fain: gladly.
98. marble: firm.   105. Julio Romano: a famous Italian artist
who died in 1546.   106. eternity: i.e., unlimited time for his
work.   107. beguile . . . custom: cheat Nature of her power to
create living things.   108. ape: imitator.   117. piece: complete;
lit., add a piece to.   120–21. unthrifty . . . knowledge: careless in
acquiring knowledge; i.e., we shall miss the latest news.

life in me, would preferment drop on my head. I
brought the old man and his son aboard the Prince,
told him I heard them talk of a fardel and I 125
know not what. But he at that time, overfond of the
shepherd's daughter — so he then took her to be —
who began to be much seasick, and himself little
better, extremity of weather continuing, this mystery
remained undiscovered. But 'tis all one to me, for
had I been the finder-out of this secret, it would not
have relished° among my other discredits. 133
[*Enter* SHEPHERD *and* CLOWN.] Here come those I
have done good to against my will, and already appearing in the blossoms of their fortune.°

SHEP. Come, boy, I am past moe children, but thy
sons and daughters will be all gentlemen born. 138

CLO. You are well met, sir. You denied° to fight
with me this other day because I was no gentleman
born. See you these clothes? Say you see them not
and think me still no gentleman born. You were
best say these robes are not gentlemen born. Give
me the lie,° do, and try whether I am not now a
gentleman born. 145

AUT. I know you are now, sir, a gentleman born.

CLO. Aye, and have been so any time these four
hours.

SHEP. And so have I, boy. 149

CLO. So you have. But I was a gentleman born before my father, for the King's son took me by the
hand and called me Brother, and then the two
Kings called my father Brother, and then the Prince
my brother and the Princess my sister called my
father Father. And so we wept, and there was the
first gentlemanlike tears that ever we shed. 156

SHEP. We may live, son, to shed many more.

CLO. Aye, or else 'twere hard luck, being in so pre-
posterous° estate as we are. 159

AUT. I humbly beseech you, sir, to pardon me all
the faults I have committed to your Worship, and
to give me your good report to the Prince my master.

SHEP. Prithee, son, do, for we must be gentle now
we are gentlemen. 165

CLO. Thou wilt amend thy life?

AUT. Aye, an it like your good Worship.

CLO. Give me thy hand. I will swear to the Prince
thou art as honest a true fellow as any is in Bohemia.

SHEP. You may say it, but not swear it. 171

CLO. Not swear it, now I am a gentleman? Let
boors and franklins° say it, I'll swear it.

SHEP. How if it be false, son? 175

CLO. If it be ne'er so false, a true gentleman may
swear it in the behalf of his friend. And I'll swear to
the Prince thou art a tall fellow of thy hands° and

that thou wilt not be drunk; but I know thou art no
tall fellow of thy hands and that thou wilt be drunk.
But I'll swear it, and I would thou wouldst be a tall
fellow of thy hands. 182

AUT. I will prove so, sir, to my power.

CLO. Aye, by any means prove a tall fellow. If I
do not wonder how thou darest venture to be drunk,
not being a tall fellow, trust me not. Hark! The
Kings and the Princes, our kindred, are going to see
the Queen's picture. Come, follow us. We'll be thy
good masters. [*Exeunt.*]

SCENE III. *A chapel in* PAULINA's *house.*

[*Enter* LEONTES, POLIXENES, FLORIZEL, PERDITA,
CAMILLO, PAULINA, LORDS, *and* ATTENDANTS.]

LEON. O grave and good Paulina, the great comfort
That I have had of thee!

PAUL.   What, sovereign sir,
I did not well, I meant well. All my services
You have paid home.° But that you have vouch-
 safed
With your crowned brother and these your con-
 tracted   5
Heirs of your kingdoms my poor house to visit,
It is a surplus of your grace,° which never
My life may last to answer.

LEON.   O Paulina,
We honor you with trouble. But we came
To see the statue of our Queen. Your gallery 10
Have we passed through, not without much content
In many singularities,° but we saw not
That which my daughter came to look upon,
The statue of her mother.

PAUL.   As she lived peerless,
So her dead likeness, I do well believe, 15
Excels whatever yet you looked upon
Or hand of man hath done. Therefore I keep it
Lonely, apart. But here it is. Prepare
To see the life as lively mocked° as ever 19
Still sleep mocked death. Behold, and say 'tis well.
  [PAULINA *draws a curtain, and discovers*
     HERMIONE *standing like a statue.*]
I like your silence, it the more shows off
Your wonder. But yet speak. First you, my liege.
Comes it not something near?

LEON.   Her natural posture!
Chide me, dear stone, that I may say indeed
Thou art Hermione. Or rather thou art she 25
In thy not chiding, for she was as tender
As infancy and grace. But yet, Paulina,

133. relished: found favor. 136. blossoms . . . fortune: showing
in their new finery their good fortune. See ll. 141–45. 139. denied: refused. 143–44. Give . . . lie: Cf. IV.iv.743–51. 159. preposterous: for "prosperous." 174. boors . . . franklins: peasants
and farmers. 178. tall . . . hands: brave man of action.

Sc. iii: 4. paid home: fully rewarded. 7. surplus . . . grace:
addition to your favor. 12. singularities: rare works of art.
19. lively mocked: exactly mimicked.

Hermione was not so much wrinkled, nothing
So agèd as this seems.

POL.   Oh, not by much.   29
PAUL. So much the more our carver's excellence,
Which lets go by some sixteen years and makes her
As° she lived now.

LEON.   As now she might have done,
So much to my good comfort as it is
Now piercing to my soul. Oh, thus she stood,
Even with such life of° majesty, warm life,   35
As now it coldly stands, when first I wooed her!
I am ashamed. Does not the stone rebuke me
For being more stone than it? O royal piece,
There's magic in thy majesty, which has
My evils conjured to remembrance and   40
From thy admiring daughter took the spirits,
Standing like stone with thee.

PER.   And give me leave,
And do not say 'tis superstition, that
I kneel and then implore her blessing. Lady,
Dear Queen, that ended when I but began,   45
Give me that hand of yours to kiss.

PAUL.   Oh, patience!
The statue is but newly fixed,° the color's
Not dry.

CAM. My lord, your sorrow was too sore laid on,
Which sixteen winters cannot blow away,   50
So many summers dry. Scarce any joy
Did ever so long live, no sorrow
But killed itself much sooner.

POL.   Dear my brother,
Let him that was the cause of this have power
To take off so much grief from you as he   55
Will piece up° in himself.

PAUL.   Indeed, my lord,
If I had thought the sight of my poor image
Would thus have wrought° you — for the stone is
     mine —
I'd not have showed it.

LEON.   Do not draw the curtain.
PAUL. No longer shall you gaze on 't, lest your
     fancy°   60
May think anon it moves.

LEON.   Let be, let be.
Would I were dead, but that, methinks, already ——
What was he that did make it? See, my lord,
Would you not deem it breathed? And that those
     veins
Did verily bear blood?

POL.   Masterly done.   65
The very life seems warm upon her lip.

LEON. The fixture of her eye has motion in 't,°
As we are mocked with art.

32. **As:** as if.   35. **life of:** living.   47. **fixed:** painted. It was customary in England to paint statues in lifelike colors.
56. **piece up:** make up.   58. **wrought:** affected.   60. **fancy:** imagination.   67. **The ... in 't:** even the fixed look in the eye seems to have life.

PAUL.   I'll draw the curtain.
My lord's almost so far transported° that
He'll think anon it lives.

LEON.   O sweet Paulina,   70
Make me to think so twenty years together!
No settled° senses of the world can match
The pleasure of that madness. Let 't alone.

PAUL. I am sorry, sir, I have thus far stirred you,
     but
I could afflict you farther.

LEON.   Do, Paulina,   75
For this affliction has a taste as sweet
As any cordial° comfort. Still, methinks
There is an air comes from her. What fine chisel
Could ever yet cut breath? Let no man mock me,
For I will kiss her.

PAUL.   Good my lord, forbear.   80
The ruddiness upon her lip is wet,
You'll mar it if you kiss it, stain your own
With oily painting. Shall I draw the curtain?

LEON. No, not these twenty years.

PER.   So long could I
Stand by, a looker-on.

PAUL.   Either forbear,   85
Quit presently the chapel, or resolve you
For more amazement. If you can behold it,
I'll make the statue move indeed, descend
And take you by the hand. But then you'll think,
Which I protest against, I am assisted   90
By wicked powers.

LEON.   What you can make her do
I am content to look on, what to speak
I am content to hear, for 'tis as easy
To make her speak as move.

PAUL.   It is required
You do awake your faith. Then all stand still.   95
On — those that think it is unlawful business°
I am about, let them depart.

LEON.   Proceed.
No foot shall stir.

PAUL.   Music, awake her, strike! [*Music.*]
'Tis time, descend, be stone no more, approach.
Strike all that look upon with marvel. Come,   100
I'll fill your grave up. Stir — nay, come away,
Bequeath to death your numbness, for from him
Dear life redeems you. You perceive she stirs.

               [HERMIONE *comes down.*]
Start not, her actions shall be holy as
You hear my spell is lawful. Do not shun her   105
Until you see her die again, for then
You kill her double. Nay, present your hand.
When she was young you wooed her, now in age
Is she become the suitor?

LEON.   Oh, she's warm!

69. **transported:** taken out of himself, excited.   72. **settled:** sane.   77. **cordial:** heartwarming.   96. **unlawful business:** i.e., black magic.

If this be magic, let it be an art 110
Lawful as eating.
  POL.   She embraces him.
  CAM. She hangs about his neck.
If she pertain to life, let her speak too.
  POL. Aye, and make 't manifest where she has
    lived,
Or how stolen from the dead.
  PAUL.   That she is living, 115
Were it but told you, should be hooted at
Like an old tale. But it appears she lives,
Though yet she speak not. Mark a little while.
Please you to interpose, fair madam. Kneel
And pray your mother's blessing. Turn, good lady,
Our Perdita is found.
  HER.   You gods, look down, 121
And from your sacred vials pour your graces
Upon my daughter's head! Tell me, mine own,
Where hast thou been preserved? Where lived?
  How found
Thy father's Court? For thou shalt hear that I, 125
Knowing by Paulina that the oracle
Gave hope thou wast in being,° have preserved
Myself to see the issue.°
  PAUL.   There's time enough for that,
Lest they desire upon this push° to trouble
Your joys with like relation. Go together, 130
You precious winners all. Your exultation

Partake to° everyone. I, an old turtle,°
Will wing me to some withered bough and there
My mate, that's never to be found again,
Lament till I am lost.
  LEON.   Oh, peace, Paulina! 135
Thou shouldst a husband take by my consent,
As I by thine a wife. This is a match,
And made between 's by vows. Thou hast found
    mine,
But how is to be questioned. For I saw her,
As I thought, dead, and have in vain said many 140
A prayer upon her grave. I'll not seek far —
For him, I partly know his mind — to find thee
An honorable husband. Come, Camillo,
And take her by the hand, whose worth and honesty
Is richly noted and here justified° 145
By us, a pair of kings. Let's from this place.
What! Look upon my brother.° Both your par-
    dons,
That e'er I put between your holy looks
My ill suspicion. This your son-in-law, 149
And son unto the King, whom, Heavens directing,
Is trothplight to your daughter. Good Paulina,
Lead us from hence, where we may leisurely
Each one demand and answer to his part
Performed in this wide gap of time since first 154
We were dissevered.° Hastily lead away. [Exeunt.]

127. in being: still living.   **128. issue:** sequel.   **129. push:** excitement.   **132. Partake to:** share with. **turtle:** turtledove.   **145. justified:** proved true.   **147. brother:** i.e., Polixenes.   **155. dissevered:** separated.

THE TEMPEST

Introduction

So far as is known or guessed, *The Tempest* is Shakespeare's last comedy. It is natural, therefore, even if dangerous, to regard it with some sentiment and to identify Prospero, the old magician bidding farewell to his art, with Shakespeare making his final appearance as a playwright. Whether we indulge this fancy — and it is no more than a fancy — or not, *The Tempest* certainly contains some of Shakespeare's finest and maturest poetry, and reveals his supreme mastery over English blank verse.

The Tempest was written about 1611. There is a record in the Revels Accounts which shows that the play was acted by the King's Players in Whitehall before King James, on Hallowmas Night (November 1) in 1611. It was again played at Court as one of the fourteen plays acted by the same company in February 1613 during the wedding festivities of the Princess Elizabeth and the Elector Palatine.

The Tempest was first published in the first folio (F1) in 1623. The text is interesting, for it was unusually well prepared for the press. It is divided into acts and scenes, and the stage directions are full and elaborate.

No complete source for *The Tempest* has been found. A German play called the *Comedy of the Beautiful Sidea,* written by Jacob Ayrer of Nuremberg sometime before 1605, has some resemblances. There is a magician Prince with a spirit attendant and an only daughter who falls in love with the son of her father's enemy. There may be some connection between this play and *The Tempest,* for Ayrer wrote other plays which were adapted from plays taken over to Germany by English players; but stories of a magician with an only daughter who falls in love are common in all fairy tales. There are, however, pieces and fragments from other sources which Shakespeare obviously found useful. The story of the shipwreck and of the mysterious island owes a good deal to an event which was recent and sensational and of which there are several contemporary comments. It is thus described in Howe's *Annals:*

In the year 1609 the Adventurers and Company of Virginia sent from London a fleet of eight ships with people to supply and make strong the Colony in Virginia, Sir Thomas Gates being General in a ship of 300 ton. In this ship was also Sir George Somers, who was Admiral, and Captain Newport Vice-Admiral, and with them about 160 persons. This ship was Admiral, and kept company with the rest of the fleet to the height of 30 degrees, and being then assembled to consult touching divers matters, they were surprised with a most extreme violent storm which scattered the whole fleet; yet all the rest of the fleet bent their course for Virginia, where by God's special favor they arrived safely, but this great ship, though new, and far stronger than any of the rest, fell into a great leak, so as mariners and passengers were forced for three days' space to do their utmost to save themselves from sudden sinking. But notwithstanding their incessant pumping, and casting out of water by buckets, and all other means, yet the water covered all the goods within the hold, and all men were utterly tired and spent in strength, and overcome with labor, and hopeless of any succor. Most of them were gone to sleep, yielding themselves to the mercy of the sea, being all very desirous to die upon any shore wheresoever. Sir George Somers, sitting at the stern, seeing the ship desperate of relief, looking every minute when the ship would sink, he espied land, which according to his and Captain Newport's opinion they judged it should be that dreadful coast of the Bermodes, which islands were of all nations said and supposed to be enchanted and inhabited with witches and devils, which grew by reason of accustomed monstrous thunder, storm, and tempest, near unto those islands. Also for that the whole coast is so wondrous dangerous of rocks that few can approach them but with unspeakable hazard of shipwreck. Sir George Somers, Sir Thomas Gates, Captain Newport, and the rest suddenly agreed of two evils to choose the least, and so in a kind of desperate resolution directed the ship mainly for these islands, which by God's divine providence at a high water ran right between two strong rocks, where it stuck fast without breaking. Which gave leisure and good opportunity for them to hoist out their boat, and to land all their men as well sailors, as soldiers, and others in good safety, and being come ashore, they were soon refreshed and cheered, the soil and air being most sweet and delicate. The salt water did great spoil to most of the ship's lading and victual, yet some meal was well recovered, with many particular things for their common use, and they all humbly thanked

God for His great mercy in so preserving them from destruction.

Then presently they sought farther into the island for food, which being never yet inhabited by any people, was overgrown with woods, and the woods replenished with wild swine, which swine as it is very probable swam thither out of some shipwreck. They found also great multitude of fowl of sundry kinds, being then in a manner very tame. They found some fruit, as mulberries, pears, and palmytoes [palmettos], with stately cedar trees. And in the sea, and in the rocks, great plenty of most pleasant and wholesome fish.

Here of necessity they were constrained to stay almost ten months, in which space by the special mercy and Divine Providence of Almighty God to make good the discovery of the islands unto them, that they by diligence and industry saved so much of the timber, tackling, and other things out of their great ship which lay wrecked and stuck fast between two rocks as therewithal, and with such supply of stuff as they found in those islands, they builded their two vessels, the lesser whereof so soon as it was finished, it was manned, and sent to go to the Colony in Virginia, to signify unto them how all things had happened with their commanders and their company, and that they would shortly set sail for Virginia. And when the bigger vessel was finished, and victualed with swine's flesh, and with what else that place would afford them, these Commanders, with all their company, embarked themselves, and by God's great mercy arrived safely at Virginia, when all Englishmen deemed them to be utterly cast away.

News of these events reached England in the early autumn of 1610, and two pamphlets were printed — *A Discovery of the Barmudas* and *A Declaration of the Estate of the Colony in Virginia.* About a year later, William Strachey, who was one of those cast ashore on Bermuda, wrote *A True Reportory of the Wreck and Redemption of Sir Thomas Gates upon and from the Islands of the Bermudas.* This was not printed until 1625, but as a number of phrases in Strachey's report seem to have been caught up into *The Tempest,* it is possible that Shakespeare saw it in manuscript.

Prospero's island is not, however, situated in the West Indies, but in the Mediterranean, somewhere off the direct course between Tunis and Naples. Shakespeare's idea of the magic island may also have been first suggested by a passage in William Parry's *New and Large Discourse of the Travels of Sir Anthony Shirley,*

Knight, describing Shirley's astonishing journeyings in Persia and Russia. This book came out in 1601, and Shakespeare seems to have read it, for he refers more than once to Shirley's Persian adventure. Parry describes how

within two days' passage of Candia [Crete], as we came toward Ciprus (which I had almost omitted) there is also a Greekish isle (whose name — I am ashamed therefore — I have quite forgotten), whereupon we touched and watered, which is some half-mile over, having one religious house therein and alone, with about some twenty Greek friggots [friars] inhabiting the same, which is (as we thought) another Eden, and the most pleasant place that ever our eyes beheld for the exercise of a solitary and contemplative life; for it is furnished with the foison of all God's good blessings. All kind of fruits (as apples, pears, plums, oranges, lemons, pomegranates, and the like) in great abundance groweth there; with most pleasant gardens, replenished with all manner of odoriferous flowers and wholesome herbs for sallets and medicines; wherein breaketh forth many fresh and crystalclear springs of water; having therewithal cattle (as beeves and muttons there naturally bred) more than sufficient to serve that house. In our travels many times, falling into dangers and unpleasant places, this only island would be the place where we would wish ourselves to end our lives.

Another book which Shakespeare obviously read when writing *The Tempest* was John Florios' translation of Montaigne's *Essays,* published in 1603, for a passage from the Essay "Of the Cannibals" (No. XXX) is followed very closely in Gonzalo's little discourse of his ideal commonwealth (II.i). Montaigne notes how one of his servants told him of a tribe of savages which followed the rule of nature:

. . . it is a nation, would I answer Plato, that hath no kind of traffic, no knowledge of letters, no intelligence of numbers, no name of magistrate, nor of politic superiority; no use of service, of riches or of poverty; no contracts, no successions, no partitions, no occupation but idle; no respect of kindred, but common; no apparel but natural; no manuring of lands, no use of wine, corn, or metal. The very words that import lying, falsehood, treason, dissimulations, covetousness, envy, detraction, and pardon were never heard of amongst them. How dissonant would he find his imaginary commonwealth from this perfection.

The Tempest was thus a play written for the Court of King James I, a play performed at a memorable Court wedding, and a fairy tale. Any working dramatist writes his play to suit his actors and his audience. For the last seven or eight years, the English Court had taken particular delight in masques (see Gen. Intro. p. 47b). *The Tempest* is not a masque, though there is inserted a little device which is a masque in miniature in honor of the betrothal of Ferdinand and Miranda. A masque was essentially an amateur affair, and not suited to the rougher audience of the Elizabethan playhouse, nor did the professional companies have the capital to invest in such costly devices. But when acting at Court for a special occasion, they had the use of stage machinery and scenery for such episodes as the storm at sea or the banquet which vanishes " by a quaint device." The King's Players had also extras for dancing and, if necessary, singing.

The Tempest has all the familiar incidents of the fairy tale: the magician with the familiar spirit and a beautiful daughter. But even a fairy tale may be used for a serious theme. The theme of *The Tempest,* as of *The Winter's Tale,* is reconciliation. This theme had interested Shakespeare not a little. In his early tragedy *Romeo and Juliet* he treated it tragically; the eternal feud between the families of Capulet and Montague is ended only when two young lovers have died as a sacrifice to the stupidity of their parents. A story of reconciliation telling of two generations must necessarily cover a long stretch of time. In *The Winter's Tale,* Shakespeare divided his play into two parts, with an interval of sixteen years symbolically indicated by Time as a Chorus. In *The Tempest,* he evolved a plot which not only brings the two generations together, but does actually preserve the unity of time, for the whole action on the stage occurs within the time of real events and almost in the same place.

If a dramatist is to construct his play of two generations and at the same time keep the unity of time, he must either choose a story so well known to the audience that they need only be told at what point the play begins, or if the story is new, quite early some explanation of past events must be given. Such explanations can be very tedious and artificial. Shakespeare begins with a stirring, noisy scene, a ship at sea in great peril. The ship runs aground. Then, in the quiet that follows, there enter an elderly man and his daughter. Here begins the glimpse into past history which is necessary before the story can move further. Critics differ in their opinions about the interpretation of this scene. To some, Prospero is yet another specimen of Shakespeare's somewhat overbearing, tyrannical fathers, like Capulet or Polonius. To others, he is a shy, gentle, melancholy student. The impression which the character will make on an audience depends on the interpretation of this scene. The common view is that, though technically excellent, the scene is inclined to be difficult. Prospero, as he tells his story, keeps interjecting: " Thou attend'st not. — Dost thou hear? " as if he were an incompetent schoolteacher trying to keep the attention of an undisciplined class. Miranda, too, seems a little lacking in politeness when she cannot at least pretend to be listening.

There is another and likelier interpretation. Hitherto, Miranda has known nothing of her father's past; now she must learn. As a Duke Prospero has been a failure; he must now tell his daughter and be judged by her. It is a humiliating moment — a trial which at some time or other comes to all parents when for the first time their children look at them frankly and critically. When Prospero comes to tell his story, he lives again in the past and speaks musingly to himself more than to her. His ejaculations are in fact pleas to Miranda because he is so desperately anxious that she shall judge his case favorably and pass a merciful verdict. It is also necessary, as a matter of mere stage technique, that a long speech shall be broken up, or it becomes tedious. Miranda says little not because she is inattentive or unsympathetic, but because she is amazed at this strange tale, not knowing what will come next.

The play is now ready to move. Miranda is asleep when Ariel — a spirit of the air — appears. Except to Prospero and to the audience, Ariel, unless assuming a disguise, is always invisible to the other characters.

We are next introduced to Caliban, who in contrast with Ariel is a creature all earth. He is Shakespeare's portrait of the horrid savage. Caliban was greatly admired by critics of the eighteenth century as a marvelous effort of the imagination. Shakespeare seemed not to have shared the views of his contemporary Montaigne that savages are naturally gentle creatures, though it is perhaps unfair to judge by this specimen, whose mother was a witch and father a devil. With such heredity one hardly expects refinement. Yet Shakespeare is always fair to Caliban. He has his case and is allowed to state it. It is not surprising that he should be fascinated by Stephano and Trinculo, with their divine liquor.

The plot is now on the move, and hereafter Prospero makes his victims dance to his music. Ferdinand comes in, and at first glance, he and Miranda " change eyes." This to the Elizabethans was the ideal form of true love:

Who ever loved that loved not at first sight?

But Prospero, so that things may not be too easy for Ferdinand, pretends to be rough and terrifying, and from that moment Ferdinand becomes Miranda's slave.

After this idyllic scene, a very different and less ideal set of people are introduced. They are Prospero's wrongers, Alonso, the father of Ferdinand, and the wicked pair Sebastian and Antonio. Also in this party is Gonzalo, the old councilor, who is a sort of refined version of Polonius. The bold, bad men Sebastian and Antonio plot Alonso's murder so nicely and so grimly. Their conversation is admirably invented — neither of them quite likes to give plain words to a plain, dirty action. But this is a fairy tale, and no blood is to be shed; besides, Prospero and Ariel always have the situation well in hand. So Alonso is saved and the party wander away to their predestined meeting place with Prospero.

Next, to clean the palate of the unpleasant taste of this scene, follows a passage of first-class low comedy. Trinculo, the jester, encounters the cowering Caliban. There is a kind of parody here of Miranda's first sight of a human being. Then comes Stephano, the drunken butler, and finds Trinculo covered by Caliban's cloak, and all three go off inspired by liquor.

Shakespeare then repeats the pattern. Ferdinand and Miranda pass from love to courtship and a pledging of troth. To high romance the natural contrast is low comedy when Stephano, Trinculo, and Caliban re-enter, with Caliban the only man among them with a plan. He will murder Prospero. It is part of Caliban's simplicity that he mistakes the nature of Stephano, who has not the stuff in him to make a murderer.

Now Prospero has everything ready for the conversion of Alonso, and to crown Alonso's sorrow there comes the sudden, unexpected, overwhelming denunciation of Ariel. Thereafter Prospero, knowing that all is as he would have it, relents toward Ferdinand and accepts him, and in honor of the lovers presents a little wedding masque, which is suddenly broken off as he remembers the plot. It is the excuse for one of the most famous, oft-quoted, and finest of Shakespeare's speeches.

The play is now working toward an end. The three plotters, Caliban, Stephano, and Trinculo, are punished; they were poor plotters after all. A few gay cloths on a line easily turned them aside. Finally, all Prospero's enemies are brought before him and forgiven. To Alonso, his son is restored, and both old men are reconciled in the happiness of their children. *The Tempest* is a very simple story.

In *The Tempest,* Shakespeare has finally achieved complete mastery over words in the blank-verse form. This power is shown throughout the play, but particularly in some of Prospero's greatest speeches, such as " Our revels now are ended " (IV.i.148), or in his farewell to his art (V.i.33). There is in these speeches a kind of organ note not hitherto heard. Shakespeare's thought was as deep as in his tragedies, but now he was able to express each thought with perfect meaning and its own proper harmony. Of his comedies, certainly *The Tempest* is Shakespeare's greatest dramatic poem. Unlike some of his other plays, it is better in the reading than on the stage.

The Tempest

DRAMATIS PERSONAE

ALONSO, *King of Naples*
SEBASTIAN, *his brother*
PROSPERO, *the right Duke of Milan*
ANTONIO, *his brother, the usurping Duke of Milan*
FERDINAND, *son to the King of Naples*
GONZALO, *an honest old councilor*
ADRIAN }
FRANCISCO } *lords*
CALIBAN, *a savage and deformed slave*
TRINCULO, *a jester*
STEPHANO, *a drunken butler*
MASTER *of a ship*
BOATSWAIN

MARINERS

MIRANDA, *daughter to Prospero*

ARIEL, *an airy spirit*

IRIS }
CERES }
JUNO } *presented by spirits*
NYMPHS }
REAPERS }

OTHER SPIRITS, *attending on Prospero*

SCENE — *A ship at sea: an uninhabited island.*

Act I

SCENE I. *On a ship at sea. A tempestuous noise of thunder and lightning heard.°*

[*Enter a* SHIPMASTER *and a* BOATSWAIN.]
MAST. Boatswain!
BOATS. Here, master. What cheer?
MAST. Good,° speak to the mariners. Fall to't yarely,° or we run ourselves aground. Bestir, bestir.
[*Exit.*]

[*Enter* MARINERS.]
BOATS. Heigh, my hearts! Cheerly, cheerly, my 6 hearts! Yare, yare! Take in the topsail.° Tend° to the master's whistle. Blow till thou burst thy wind, if room° enough!

[*Enter* ALONSO, SEBASTIAN, ANTONIO, FERDINAND, GONZALO, *and others.*]
ALON. Good boatswain, have care. Where's the master? Play the men.° 11
BOATS. I pray now, keep below.
ANT. Where is the master, boatswain?
BOATS. Do you not hear him? You mar our labor. Keep your cabins. You do assist the storm. 15
GON. Nay, good, be patient.
BOATS. When the sea is. Hence! What cares these roarers for the name of King? To cabin. Silence! Trouble us not.
GON. Good, yet remember whom thou hast aboard. 21

BOATS. None that I more love than myself. You are a councilor. If you can command these elements to silence, and work the peace of the present,° we will not hand a rope more. Use your authority. If you cannot, give thanks you have lived so long, and make yourself ready in your cabin for the mischance of the hour, if it so hap. Cheerly, good hearts! 29 Out of our way, I say. [*Exit.*]
GON. I have great comfort from this fellow. Methinks he hath no drowning mark upon him; his complexion is perfect gallows.° Stand fast, good Fate, to his hanging. Make the rope of his destiny our cable, for our own doth little advantage. If 35 he be not born to be hanged, our case is miserable.
[*Exeunt.*]

[*Re-enter* BOATSWAIN.]
BOATS. Down with the topmast! Yare! Lower, lower! Bring her to try with main course.° [*A cry within.*] A plague upon this howling! They are louder than the weather or our office.° 40
[*Re-enter* SEBASTIAN, ANTONIO, *and* GONZALO.] Yet again! What do you here? Shall we give o'er, and drown? Have you a mind to sink?
SEB. A pox o' your throat, you bawling, blasphemous, incharitable dog!
BOATS. Work you, then. 45
ANT. Hang, cur! Hang, you whoreson,° insolent noisemaker. We are less afraid to be drowned than thou art. SHOWS HE'S TRYING TO BE BRAVE
GON. I'll warrant him for drowning,° though the

Act I, Sc. i: s.d., On . . . heard: The ship is in great danger. The wind is blowing hard from the sea; on the other side lies the rocky island, and between there is too little sea room for her to sail past without being driven ashore by the drift. For the type of ship, see Pl. 7b. 3. Good: my good man. 4. yarely: quickly, smartly. 7. Take . . . topsail: i.e., to lessen the drift. Tend: attend. 9. room: sea room. 11. Play . . . men: act like men.

24. work . . . present: bring us peace at once. 32–33. hath . . . gallows: Gonzalo remembers the proverb "He that is born to be hanged will never be drowned," and the boatswain looks like a gallows bird. 38. try . . . course: i.e., use only the mainsail to heave her to. course: sail. 40. office: business. 46. whoreson: bastard. 49. warrant . . . drowning: guarantee him against drowning.

[Handwritten margin note top right:] WHY HASN'T HE TOLD HER THE STORY BEFORE? HE WAS ASHAMED TO HAVE TO TELL HER HE MESSED UP THE GOV —

ship were no stronger than a nutshell and as leaky as
an unstanched wench.   51
   BOATS. Lay her ahold,° ahold! Set her two
courses.° Off to sea again, lay her off.

     [Enter MARINERS wet.]

   MAR. All lost! To prayers, to prayers! All lost!   55
   BOATS. What, must our mouths be cold?°
   GON. The King and Prince at prayers! Let's assist
     them,
For our case is as theirs.
   SEB.   I'm out of patience.
   ANT. We are merely cheated of our lives by
     drunkards.
This wide-chapped° rascal — would thou mightst lie
     drowning
The washing of ten tides!°
   GON.   He'll be hanged yet,   61
Though every drop of water swear against it
And gape at widest to glut° him.

     [A confused noise within: "Mercy on us!"
     — "We split, we split!" — "Farewell my
     wife and children!" — "Farewell, brother!"
     — "We split, we split, we split!"]

   ANT. Let's all sink with the King. *LOOK TO*
   SEB. Let's take leave of him. *PREVIOUS LINES* 68

     [Exeunt ANTONIO and SEBASTIAN.]

   GON. Now would I give a thousand furlongs of
sea for an acre of barren ground, long heath,° brown
furze,° anything. The wills above be done! But   72
I would fain die a dry death.   [Exeunt.]

SCENE II. *The island. Before* PROSPERO'S *cell.*

     [Enter PROSPERO and MIRANDA.]

   MIRA. If by your art, my dearest father, you have
Put the wild waters in this roar, allay° them.
The sky, it seems, would pour down stinking pitch
But that the sea, mounting to the welkin's° cheek,
Dashes the fire out. Oh, I have suffered   5
With those that I saw suffer! A brave vessel,
Who had no doubt some noble creature in her,
Dashed all to pieces. Oh, the cry did knock
Against my very heart! Poor souls, they perished!
Had I been any god of power, I would   10
Have sunk the sea within the earth or ere
It should the good ship so have swallowed and
The fraughting° souls within her.
   PRO.   Be collected.°

---

52. **ahold:** close to the wind.   52–53. **two courses:** two sails; i.e.,
set the foresail as well. The maneuver of heaving-to has failed;
the boatswain now hopes to get the ship moving into the wind
enough to pass the island.   56. **mouths be cold:** Here the boatswain abandons hope and falls to drinking.   60. **wide-chapped:**
large-cheeked, because full of liquor.   61. **washing . . . tides:**
Pirates were hanged on the seashore and left until three high
tides had passed over them.   63. **glut:** swallow.   71. **long
heath:** rough grass.   72. **furze:** a prickly bushy shrub.
    Sc. ii: 2. **allay:** abate.   4. **welkin:** sky.   13. **fraughting:** lit.,
who were her freight. **collected:** calm.

No more amazement. Tell your piteous heart
There's no harm done.
   MIRA.   Oh, woe the day!
   PRO.   No harm.   15
I have done nothing but in care of thee, *PROCRAS-*
Of thee, my dear one, thee, my daughter, who *TINATE*
Art ignorant of what thou art, naught knowing *ALWAYS*
Of whence I am, nor that I am more better
Than Prospero, master of a full° poor cell,   20
And thy no greater father.
   MIRA.   More to know
Did never meddle° with my thoughts.
   PRO.   'Tis time
I should inform thee farther. Lend thy hand,
And pluck my magic garment from me. — So.

     [Lays down his mantle.]

Lie there, my art. Wipe thou thine eyes, have com-
     fort.   25
The direful spectacle of the wreck, which touched
The very virtue of compassion in thee,
I have with such provision° in mine art
So safely ordered that there is no soul,
No, not so much perdition° as a hair,   30
Betid° to any creature in the vessel
Which thou heard'st cry, which thou saw'st sink. Sit
     down,
For thou must now know farther.
   MIRA.   You have often
Begun to tell me what I am, but stopped,
And left me to a bootless inquisition,°   35
Concluding "Stay, not yet."
   PRO.   The hour's now come,
The very minute bids thee ope thine ear.
Obey, and be attentive. Canst thou remember
A time before we came unto this cell?
I do not think thou canst, for then thou wast not   40
Out° three years old.
   MIRA.   Certainly, sir, I can.
   PRO. By what? By any other house or person?
Of anything the image tell me that
Hath kept with thy remembrance.
   MIRA.   'Tis far off,
And rather like a dream than an assurance   45
That my remembrance warrants. Had I not
Four or five women once that tended me?
   PRO. Thou hadst, and more, Miranda. But how
     is it
That this lives in thy mind? What seest thou else
In the dark backward and abysm of time?°   50
If thou remember'st aught ere thou camest here,
How thou camest here thou mayst.
   MIRA.   But that I do not.

---

20. **full:** exceedingly.   22. **meddle:** interfere; i.e., cause to be
curious.   28. **provision:** foresight.   30. **perdition:** loss.
31. **Betid:** befallen.   35. **bootless inquisition:** vain inquiry.
41. **Out:** more than.   50. **abysm of time:** i.e., the past, which is
like a dark abyss.

PRO. Twelve year since, Miranda, twelve year since,
Thy father was the Duke of Milan, and
A prince of power.

MIRA.   Sir, are not you my father?   55

PRO. Thy mother was a piece of virtue, and
She said thou wast my daughter, and thy father
Was Duke of Milan, and his only heir
A Princess, no worse issued.

MIRA.   Oh, the Heavens!
What foul play had we that we came from thence?
Or blessèd was't we did?

PRO.   Both, both, my girl.   61
By foul play, as thou say'st, were we heaved thence,
But blessedly holp° hither.

MIRA.   Oh, my heart bleeds
To think o' the teen° that I have turned you to,
Which is from my remembrance! Please you, far-
ther.   65

PRO. My brother, and thy uncle, called Antonio —
I pray thee mark me — that a brother should
Be so perfidious! — he whom, next thyself,
Of all the world I loved, and to him put
The manage° of my state — as at that time   70
Through all the signories° it was the first,
And Prospero the prime° Duke, being so reputed
In dignity, and for the liberal arts°
Without a parallel, those being all my study —
The government I cast upon my brother,   75
And to my state grew stranger, being transported
And rapt in secret studies. Thy false uncle —
Dost thou attend me?

MIRA.   Sir, most heedfully.

PRO. Being once perfected° how to grant suits,
How to deny them, who to advance, and who   80
To trash for overtopping,° new-created°
The creatures that were mine, I say, or changed 'em,
Or else new-formed 'em — having both the key°
Of officer and office, set all hearts i' the state
To what tune pleased his ear, that now he was   85
The ivy which had hid my princely trunk,
And sucked my verdure out on't. Thou attend'st
not.°

MIRA. Oh, good sir, I do.

PRO.   I pray thee, mark me.
I, thus neglecting worldly ends, all dedicated
To closeness° and the bettering of my mind   90
With that which, but by being so retired,°
O'erprized all popular rate,° in my false brother

Awaked an evil nature. And my trust,
Like a good parent, did beget of him
A falsehood in its contrary as great   95
As my trust was, which had indeed no limit,
A confidence sans° bound. He being thus lorded,
Not only with what my revenue yielded,
But what my power might else exact, like one
Who having into truth, by telling of it,   100
Made such a sinner of his memory,
To credit his own lie, he did believe
He was indeed the Duke° — out o' the substitution,
And executing the outward face of royalty,
With all prerogative.° — Hence his ambition grow-
ing ——   105
Dost thou hear?

MIRA.   Your tale, sir, would cure deafness.

PRO. To have no screen between this part he played
And him he played it for, he needs will be
Absolute Milan.° Me, poor man, my library
Was dukedom large enough. Of temporal royalties°
He thinks me now incapable; confederates,°   111
So dry° he was for sway, wi' the King of Naples
To give him annual tribute, do him homage,
Subject his coronet to his crown,° and bend
The dukedom, yet unbowed — alas, poor Milan! —
To most ignoble stooping.

MIRA.   Oh, the Heavens!   116

PRO. Mark his condition, and the event,° then tell me
If this might be a brother.

MIRA.   I should sin
To think but nobly of my grandmother.
Good wombs have borne bad sons.

PRO.   Now the condition.   120
This King of Naples, being an enemy
To me inveterate, hearkens my brother's suit.
Which was that he, in lieu o' the premises,°
Of homage, and I know not how much tribute,
Should presently° extirpate° me and mine   125
Out of the dukedom, and confer fair Milan,
With all the honors, on my brother. Whereon,
A treacherous army levied, one midnight
Fated to the purpose did Antonio open
The gates of Milan, and, i' the dead of darkness   130
The ministers for the purpose hurried thence
Me and thy crying self.

---

63. holp: helped. 64. teen: sorrow. 70. manage: management.
71. signories: lordships. 72. prime: leading. 73. liberal arts:
academic learning. 79. perfected: become perfect by practice.
81. trash . . . overtopping: check for running ahead, a metaphor
from training a pack of hounds. new-created: made them new
creatures — by altering their minds. 83. key: tool used for
tuning a stringed instrument. 87. Thou . . . not: See *Temp*
Intro. p. 1473a. 90. closeness: privacy. 91. but . . . retired:
except that it kept me away from state affairs. 92. O'erprized
. . . rate: was worth more than it is commonly regarded.

97. sans: without. 97–103. He . . . Duke: he, getting such
greatness not only from my wealth but also by abusing my power,
began to believe as he had hitherto pretended, that he was in
truth the Duke. 103–05. out . . . prerogative: from being my
substitute and acting outwardly as Duke with all the rights of a
ruler. 109. Absolute Milan: Duke of Milan in fact. 110. temporal royalties: worldly power. 111. confederates: conspires.
112. dry: thirsty. 114. Subject . . . crown: i.e., pay homage as
to his overlord. The coronet was worn as a symbol by rulers of
lower rank than that of King. 117. event: sequel. 123. in . . .
premises: in return for these conditions. 125. presently: immediately. extirpate: root out.

MIRA.   Alack, for pity!
I, not remembering how I cried out then.
Will cry it o'er again. It is a hint°
That wrings mine eyes to't.
    PRO.   Hear a little further,   135
And then I'll bring thee to the present business
Which now's upon 's, without the which this story
Were most impertinent.
    MIRA.   Wherefore did they not
That hour destroy us?
    PRO.   Well demanded, wench.   139
My tale provokes that question. Dear, they durst not,
So dear the love my people bore me, nor set
A mark so bloody on the business, but
With colors fairer painted their foul ends.
In few,° they hurried us aboard a bark,   144
Bore us some leagues to sea, where they prepared
A rotten carcass of a butt,° not rigged,
Nor tackle, sail, nor mast. The very rats
Instinctively have quit it. There they hoist us,
To cry to the sea that roared to us, to sigh
To the winds, whose pity, sighing back again,   150
Did us but loving wrong.
    MIRA.   Alack, what trouble
Was I then to you!
    PRO.   Oh, a cherubin
Thou wast that did preserve me. Thou didst smile,
Infusèd with a fortitude from Heaven,   154
When I have decked the sea with drops full salt,
Under my burden groaned, which raised in me
An undergoing stomach° to bear up
Against what should ensue.
    MIRA.   How came we ashore?
    PRO. By Providence divine.
Some food we had, and some fresh water, that   160
A noble Neapolitan, Gonzalo,
Out of his charity, who being then appointed
Master of this design, did give us, with
Rich garments, linens, stuffs, and necessaries,
Which since have steaded much.° So, of his gentle-
    ness,   165
Knowing I loved my books, he furnished me
From mine own library with volumes that
I prize above my dukedom.
    MIRA.   Would I might
But ever see that man!
    PRO.   Now I arise. [*Resumes his mantle.*]
Sit still, and hear the last of our sea sorrow.   170
Here in this island we arrived, and here
Have I, thy schoolmaster, made thee more profit
Than other princes can that have more time
For vainer hours, and tutors not so careful.
    MIRA. Heavens thank you for't! And now I pray
     you, sir,   175

For still 'tis beating° in my mind, your reason
For raising this sea storm?
    PRO.   Know thus far forth.°
By accident most strange, bountiful Fortune,
Now my dear lady,° hath mine enemies
Brought to this shore. And by my prescience°   180
I find my zenith° doth depend upon
A most auspicious star, whose influence
If now I court not,° but omit, my fortunes
Will ever after droop. Here cease more questions.
Thou art inclined to sleep, 'tis a good dullness,   185
And give it way. I know thou canst not choose. [*MIRANDA sleeps.*]
Come away, servant, come. I am ready now.
Approach, my Ariel, come.
                    [*Enter* ARIEL.]
    ARI. All hail, great master! Grave sir, hail! I come
To answer thy best pleasure, be 't to fly,   190
To swim, to dive into the fire, to ride
On the curled clouds, to thy strong bidding task°
Ariel and all his quality.°
    PRO.   Hast thou, spirit,
Performed to point° the tempest that I bade thee?
    ARI. To every article.   195
I boarded the King's ship. Now on the beak,
Now in the waist,° the deck, in every cabin,
I flamed amazement.° Sometime I'd divide,
And burn in many places; on the topmast,   199
The yards and bowsprit, would I flame distinctly,
Then meet and join. Jove's lightnings, the precur-
    sors°
O' the dreadful thunderclaps, more momentary
And sight-outrunning were not. The fire and cracks
Of sulphurous roaring the most mighty Neptune
Seem to besiege, and make his bold waves tremble —
Yea, his dread trident shake.
    PRO.   My brave spirit!   206
Who was so firm, so constant, that this coil°
Would not infect his reason?
    ARI.   Not a soul
But felt a fever of the mad° and played
Some tricks of desperation.° All but mariners   210
Plunged in the foaming brine, and quit the vessel,
Then all afire with me. The King's son, Ferdinand,
With hair upstaring — then like reeds, not hair —
Was the first man that leaped, cried, " Hell is empty,

134. hint: occasion.   144. In few: in a few words.   146. butt:
tub.   157. undergoing stomach: courage to endure, the stomach
being regarded as the seat of valor.   165. have . . . much: have
been of great benefit.

176. beating: throbbing.   177. Know . . . forth: i.e., I will now
tell you more.   179. Now . . . lady: Fortune (once my foe) is
now kind to me.   180. prescience: foreknowledge.   181. zenith:
the highest point of my fortunes.   183. court not: do not seek
to win.   192. task: impose a task on.   193. quality: ability.
194. to point: in all points, exactly.   197. waist: that part of
the ship which lies between forecastle and poop. See Pl. 7a
and 6a.   198. flamed amazement: appeared in the form of fire
which caused amazement. This phenomenon, known as Saint
Elmo's fire or a corposant, is sometimes seen on ships during a
storm.   201. precursors: forerunners.   207. coil: confusion.
209. fever . . . mad: fever of madness.   210. tricks of desperation: desperate tricks.

And all the devils are here."

PRO.   Why, that's my spirit!   215
But was not this nigh shore?

ARI.   Close by, my master.

PRO. But are they, Ariel, safe?

ARI.   Not a hair perished,
On their sustaining° garments not a blemish,
But fresher than before. And, as thou badest me,
In troops I have dispersed them 'bout the isle.   220
The King's son have I landed by himself,
Whom I left cooling of the air with sighs
In an odd angle° of the isle, and sitting
His arms in this sad knot.°

PRO.   Of the King's ship,
The mariners, say how thou hast disposed,   225
And all the rest o' the fleet,

ARI.   Safely in harbor
Is the King's ship — in the deep nook where once
Thou call'dst me up at midnight to fetch dew
From the still-vexed Bermoothes,° there she's hid.
The mariners all under hatches stowed,   230
Who, with a charm joined to their suffered labor,°
I have left asleep. And for the rest o' the fleet,
Which I dispersed, they all have met again,
And are upon the Mediterranean flote,°
Bound sadly home for Naples,   235
Supposing that they saw the King's ship wrecked
And his great person perish.

PRO.   Ariel, thy charge
Exactly is performed. But there's more work.
What is the time o' the day?

ARI.   Past the midseason.

PRO. At least two glasses.° The time 'twixt six and
now   240
Must by us both be spent most preciously.

ARI. Is there more toil? Since thou dost give me
pains,°
Let me remember° thee what thou hast promisèd,
Which is not yet performed me.

PRO.   How now? Moody?
What is't thou canst demand?

ARI.   My liberty.   245

PRO. Before the time be out? No more!

ARI.   I prithee
Remember I have done thee worthy service,
Told thee no lies, made thee no mistakings, served
Without or grudge or grumblings. Thou didst
promise
To bate° me a full year.

PRO.   Dost thou forget   250
From what a torment I did free thee?

ARI.   No.

PRO. Thou dost, and think'st it much to tread the
ooze
Of the salt deep,
To run upon the sharp wind of the North,
To do me business in the veins o' the earth   255
When it is baked with frost.

ARI.   I do not, sir.

PRO. Thou liest, malignant thing! Hast thou forgot
The foul witch Sycorax, who with age and envy
Was grown into a hoop?° Hast thou forgot her?

ARI. No, sir.

PRO.   Thou hast. Where was she born?
Speak, tell me.   260

ARI. Sir, in Argier.°

PRO.   Oh, was she so? I must
Once in a month recount what thou hast been,
Which thou forget'st. This damned witch Sycorax,
For mischiefs manifold and sorceries terrible
To enter human hearing,° from Argier,   265
Thou know'st, was banished. For one thing she did°
They would not take her life. Is not this true?

ARI. Aye, sir.

PRO. This blue-eyed° hag was hither brought
with child,
And here was left by the sailors. Thou, my slave,
As thou report'st thyself, wast then her servant.   271
And, for thou wast a spirit too delicate
To act her earthy and abhorred commands,
Refusing her grand hests,° she did confine thee,
By help of her more potent ministers   275
And in her most unmitigable° rage,
Into a cloven pine. Within which rift
Imprisoned thou didst painfully remain
A dozen years. Within which space she died,
And left thee there, where thou didst vent thy
groans   280
As fast as mill wheels strike.° Then was this is-
land —
Save for the son that she did litter here,
A freckled whelp hag-born° — not honored with
A human shape.

ARI.   Yes, Caliban her son.

PRO. Dull thing, I say so, he, that Caliban   285
Whom now I keep in service. Thou best know'st
What torment I did find thee in. Thy groans
Did make wolves howl and penetrate the breasts
Of ever-angry bears. It was a torment
To lay upon the damned, which Sycorax   290
Could not again undo. It was mine art,
When I arrived and heard thee, that made gape
The pine and let thee out.

ARI.   I thank thee, master.

---

218. sustaining: which bore them up.   223. angle: corner.
224. in . . . knot: sadly folded. Ariel imitates the posture.
229. still-vexed Bermoothes: ever stormy Bermudas.   231. joined
. . . labor: as well as the labor they had endured.   234. flote:
sea.   240. glasses: i.e., hours; turns of the hourglass.   242. pains:
toil.   243. remember: remind.   250. bate: abate, lessen.

259. grown . . . hoop: bent double.   261. Argier: Algiers.   265. To
. . . hearing: for a human being to hear.   266. one . . . did: This
good action is not recalled.   269. blue-eyed: with dark rings
under the eyes.   274. hests: commands.   276. unmitigable:
absolute.   281. mill . . . strike: i.e., the continuous clack of a
water mill.   283. hag-born: child of a hag.

PRO. If thou more murmur'st, I will rend an oak°
And peg thee in his knotty entrails till   295
Thou hast howled away twelve winters.
    ARI.   Pardon, master.
I will be correspondent° to command,
And do my spiriting° gently.
    PRO.   Do so, and after two days
I will discharge thee.
    ARI.   That's my noble master!
What shall I do? Say what. What shall I do?   300
    PRO. Go make thyself like a nymph o' the sea.
Be subject to no sight but thine and mine, invisible
To every eyeball else. Go take this shape,
And hither come in't. Go, hence with diligence!
                         [*Exit* ARIEL.]
Awake, dear heart, awake! Thou hast slept well.
Awake!
    MIRA. The strangeness of your story put   306
Heaviness in me.
    PRO.   Shake it off. Come on,
We'll visit Caliban my slave, who never
Yields us kind answer.
    MIRA.   'Tis a villain, sir,
I do not love to look on.
    PRO.   But, as 'tis,   310
We cannot miss° him. He does make our fire,
Fetch in our wood, and serves in offices
That profit us. What ho! Slave! Caliban!
Thou earth,° thou! Speak.
    CAL. [*Within*]   There's wood enough within.
    PRO. Come forth, I say! There's other business for
      thee.   315
Come, thou tortoise! When?
[*Re-enter* ARIEL *like a water nymph.*] Fine apparition! My quaint° Ariel,
Hark in thine ear.
    ARI.   My lord, it shall be done. [*Exit.*]
    PRO. Thou poisonous slave, got° by the Devil himself
Upon thy wicked dam,° come forth!   320
          [*Enter* CALIBAN.]
    CAL. As wicked dew as e'er my mother brushed
With raven's feather from unwholesome fen
Drop on you both! A southwest° blow on ye
And blister you all o'er!
    PRO. For this, be sure, tonight thou shalt have
      cramps,   325
Side stitches that shall pen thy breath up. Urchins°
Shall, for that vast° of night that they may work,
All exercise on thee. Thou shalt be pinched
As thick as honeycomb, each pinch more stinging

invisible

Than bees that made 'em.
    CAL.   I must eat my dinner.   330
This island's mine, by Sycorax my mother,
Which thou takest from me. When thou camest first,
Thou strokedst me, and madest much of me, wouldst
      give me
Water with berries in't.° And teach me how
To name the bigger light, and how the less,   335
That burn by day and night. And then I loved thee,
And showed thee all the qualities° o' th' isle,
The fresh springs, brine pits, barren place and fertile.
Cursèd be I that did so! All the charms
Of Sycorax, toads, beetles, bats, light on you!   340
For I am all the subjects that you have,
Which first was mine own king. And here you sty°
      me
In this hard rock whiles you do keep from me
The rest o' th' island.
    PRO.   Thou most lying slave,
Whom stripes° may move, not kindness! I have used
      thee,   345
Filth as thou art, with human care, and lodged thee
In mine own cell till thou didst seek to violate
The honor of my child.
    CAL. Oh ho, oh ho! Would 't had been done!
Thou didst prevent me. I had peopled else   350
This isle with Calibans.
    PRO.   Abhorrèd slave,
Which any print° of goodness wilt not take,
Being capable of all ill! I pitied thee,
Took pains to make thee speak, taught thee each
      hour   354
One thing or other. When thou didst not, savage,
Know thine own meaning, but wouldst gabble like
A thing most brutish, I endowed thy purposes
With words that made them known. But thy vile
      race,
Though thou didst learn, had that in't which good
      natures
Could not abide to be with. Therefore wast thou
Deservedly confined into this rock,   361
Who hadst deserved more than a prison.
    CAL. You taught me language, and my profit on't
Is I know how to curse. The red plague° rid° you
For learning° me your language!
    PRO.   Hagseed,° hence!   365
Fetch us in fuel, and be quick, thou'rt best,
To answer other business. Shrug'st thou, malice?
If thou neglect'st, or dost unwillingly
What I command, I'll rack thee with old° cramps,

---

294. rend an oak: i.e., a far worse torment than imprisonment in a pine.   **297. correspondent:** agreeable, submissive.   **298. spiriting:** my work as a spirit.   **311. miss:** do without.   **314. earth:** lump of dirt.   **317. quaint:** elegant.   **319. got:** begotten. **320. dam:** mother.   **323. southwest:** regarded as an unhealthy wind.   **326. Urchins:** goblins, or hedgehogs.   **327. vast:** desolate period.

334. Water . . . in't: Shakespeare apparently took this from Strachey's account, which records that the castaways made a pleasant drink from cedar berries. See *Temp* Intro. p. 1472a. **337. qualities:** good spots.   **342. sty:** pen.   **345. stripes:** blows. **352. print:** impression.   **364. red plague:** bubonic plague. **rid:** destroy.   **365. learning:** teaching. **Hagseed:** son of a hag. **369. old:** abundant.

Fill all thy bones with aches,° make thee roar   370
That beasts shall tremble at thy din.
CAL.   No, pray thee.
[*Aside*] I must obey. His art is of such power
It would control my dam's god, Setebos,   373
And make a vassal° of him.
PRO.   So, slave. Hence!
                              [*Exit* CALIBAN.]
[*Re-enter* ARIEL, *invisible, playing and singing;*
    FERDINAND *following.*]
ARI. [*Sings.*]
    " Come unto these yellow sands,
        And then take hands.
    Curtsied when you have and kissed
        The wild waves whist,°
    Foot it featly° here and there,   380
        And, sweet sprites, the burden° bear."
BURDEN. [*Dispersedly*]° " Hark, hark! "
                              " Bowwow."
ARI. " The watchdogs bark."
BURDEN. [*Dispersedly*]   " Bowwow."
ARI. " Hark, hark! I hear
        The strain of strutting chanticleer   385
        Cry Cock-a-diddle-dow."
FER. Where should this music be? I' th' air or th'
    earth?
It sounds no more, and, sure, it waits upon
Some god o' th' island. Sitting on a bank,
Weeping again the King my father's wreck,   390
This music crept by me upon the waters,
Allaying both their fury and my passion°
With its sweet air. Thence I have followed it,
Or it hath drawn me rather. But 'tis gone.   395
No, it begins again.
ARI. [*Sings.*]
    " Full fathom five thy father lies,
        Of his bones are coral made,
    Those are pearls that were his eyes.
        Nothing of him that doth fade   400
    But doth suffer a sea change
        Into something rich and strange.
    Sea nymphs hourly ring his knell."
BURDEN.   " Dingdong."
ARI. " Hark! Now I hear them. — Dingdong,
    bell."
                                    404
FER. The ditty does remember my drowned father.
This is no mortal business, nor no sound
That the earth owes.° — I hear it now above me.
PRO. The fringèd curtains of thine eye advance,°
And say what thou seest yond.
MIRA.   What is't? A spirit?
Lord, how it looks about! Believe me, sir,   410

It carries a brave form.° But 'tis a spirit.
    PRO. No, wench, it eats and sleeps and hath such
    senses
As we have, such. This gallant which thou seest
Was in the wreck, and but he's something stained
With grief, that's beauty's canker,° thou mightst
    call him   415
A goodly person. He hath lost his fellows,
And strays about to find 'em.
    MIRA.   I might call him
A thing divine, for nothing natural
I ever saw so noble.
    PRO.   [*Aside*] It goes on,° I see,   419
As my soul prompts it. Spirit, fine spirit! I'll free thee
Within two days for this.
    FER.   Most sure, the goddess
On whom these airs attend!° Vouchsafe my prayer
May know if you remain upon this island,°
And that you will some good instruction give
How I may bear me° here. My prime request,   425
Which I do last pronounce, is, O you wonder!
If you be maid or no?°
    MIRA.   No wonder, sir,
But certainly a maid.
    FER.   My language! Heavens!
I am the best of them° that speak this speech,
Were I but where 'tis spoken.
    PRO.   How? The best?   430
What wert thou if the King of Naples heard thee?
    FER. A single° thing, as I am now, that wonders
To hear thee speak of Naples. He does hear me,
And that he does I weep. Myself am Naples,
Who with mine eyes, never since at ebb,° beheld
The King my father wrecked.
    MIRA.   Alack, for mercy!   436
    FER. Yes, faith, and all his lords, the Duke of
    Milan
And his brave son being twain.°
    PRO.   [*Aside*] The Duke of Milan
And his more braver daughter could control thee,
If now 'twere fit to do't. At the first sight   440
They have changed eyes.° Delicate Ariel,
I'll set thee free for this. [*To* FERDINAND] A word,
    good sir.
I fear you have done yourself some wrong. A word.
    MIRA. Why speaks my father so ungently? This
Is the third man that e'er I saw, the first   445
That e'er I sighed for. Pity move my father
To be inclined my way!

411. brave form: fine shape.   415. canker: maggot.   419. It . . .
on: i.e., Prospero's plan that Miranda and Ferdinand shall fall in
love.   422. attend: wait on.   422-23. Vouchsafe . . . island:
grant my prayer, which is to know whether you inhabit this
island.   425. bear me: behave myself.   427. maid or no: i.e., a
mortal or a goddess.   429. best of them: i.e., I am now King of
Naples since my father's death.   438. single: lonely.   435. never
. . . ebb: i.e., have not ceased to flow.   438. twain: i.e., two of
those drowned.   441. changed eyes: fallen in love.

370. aches: a two-syllable word, pronounced like "h's."
374. vassal: slave.   379. whist: silent.   380. featly: smartly.
381. burden: refrain.   382 s.d., Dispersedly: from different
sides.   392. passion: emotion, sorrow.   407. owes: owns, possesses.   408. advance: raise.

FER.   Oh, if a virgin,
And your affection not gone forth,° I'll make you
The Queen of Naples.

PRO.   Soft, sir! One word more.
[*Aside*] They are both in either's powers. But this
   swift business   450
I must uneasy make, lest too light winning
Make the prize light. [*To* FERDINAND] One word
   more. I charge thee
That thou attend me. Thou dost here usurp
The name thou owest not, and hast put thyself
Upon this island as a spy, to win it   455
From me, the lord on 't.

FER.   No, as I am a man.

MIRA. There's nothing ill can dwell in such a
   temple.°
If the ill spirit have so fair a house,
Good things will strive to dwell with 't.

PRO.   Follow me.
Speak not you for him, he's a traitor. Come,   460
I'll manacle thy neck and feet together.
Sea water shalt thou drink, thy food shall be
The fresh-brook mussels, withered roots, and husks
Wherein the acorn cradled. Follow.

FER.   No.
I will resist such entertainment till   465
Mine enemy has more power.
      [*Draws, and is charmed from moving.*]

MIRA.   O dear Father,
Make not too rash a trial of him, for
He's gentle, and not fearful.°

PRO.   What! I say,
My foot my tutor?° Put thy sword up, traitor,
Who makest a show but darest not strike, thy con-
   science   470
Is so possessed with guilt. Come from thy ward,°
For I can here disarm thee with this stick
And make thy weapon drop.

MIRA.   Beseech you, Father.

PRO. Hence! Hang not on my garments.

MIRA.   Sir, have pity.
I'll be his surety.

PRO.   Silence! One word more   475
Shall make me chide thee, if not hate thee. What!
An advocate for an impostor! Hush!
Thou think'st there is no more such shapes as he,
Having seen but him and Caliban. Foolish wench!
To the most of men this is a Caliban,   480
And they to him are angels.

MIRA.   My affections
Are, then, most humble. I have no ambition
To see a goodlier man.

PRO.   Come on, obey.
Thy nerves° are in their infancy again,
And have no vigor in them.

FER.   So they are.   485
My spirits, as in a dream, are all bound up.
My father's loss, the weakness which I feel,
The wreck of all my friends, nor this man's threats,
To whom I am subdued, are but light to me
Might I but through my prison once a day   490
Behold this maid. All corners else o' th' earth
Let liberty make use of, space enough
Have I in such a prison.

PRO.   [*Aside*] It works.
      [*To* FERDINAND] Come on.
Thou hast done well, fine Ariel!
      [*To* FERDINAND] Follow me.   494
[*To* ARIEL] Hark what thou else shalt do me.

MIRA.   Be of comfort.
My father's of a better nature, sir,
Than he appears by speech. This is unwonted°
Which now came from him.

PRO.   Thou shalt be as free
As mountain winds. But then exactly do
All points of my command.

ARI.   To the syllable.   500

PRO. Come, follow. Speak not for him. [*Exeunt.*]

Act II

SCENE I. *Another part of the island.*

[*Enter* ALONSO, SEBASTIAN, ANTONIO, GONZALO,
   ADRIAN, FRANCISCO, *and others.*]

GON. Beseech you, sir, be merry. You have cause,
So have we all, of joy, for our escape
Is much beyond our loss. Our hint° of woe
Is common. Every day some sailor's wife,   4
The masters of some merchant,° and the merchant,°
Have just our theme of woe. But for the miracle —
I mean our preservation — few in millions
Can speak like us. Then wisely, good sir, weigh
Our sorrow with our comfort.

ALON.   Prithee, peace.

SEB. He receives comfort like cold porridge.   10

ANT. The visitor° will not give him o'er so.

SEB. Look, he's winding up the watch of his wit.
By and by it will strike.

GON. Sir ——

484. nerves: sinews.   497. unwonted: unusual.
   Act II, Sc. i: 3. hint: occasion. See I.ii.134.   5. masters . . .
merchant: captains of merchant ships. the merchant: i.e., the
owner.   11. visitor: visiting minister. See *T Night*, IV.ii.25–26.
Sebastian means that Gonzalo will insist on having his say
whether Alonso wishes to hear it or not.

448. gone forth: i.e., been bestowed on someone else.   457. temple:
i.e., beautiful body.   468. fearful: to be feared.   469. My . . .
tutor: The head is the tutor to the body, but Miranda (who is by
nature subordinate and so the foot) is trying to tell her father
what he should do.   471. ward: position of defense.

SEB. One. Tell.° 15

GON. When every grief is entertained° that's offered,

Comes to the entertainer ——

SEB. A dollar.

GON. Dolor comes to him, indeed. You have spoken truer than you purposed. 20

SEB. You have taken it wiselier than I meant you should.

GON. Therefore, my lord ——

ANT. Fie, what a spendthrift is he of his tongue!

ALON. I prithee, spare. 25

GON. Well, I have done. But yet ——

SEB. He will be talking.

ANT. Which, of he or Adrian, for a good wager, first begins to crow?

SEB. The old cock. 30

ANT. The cockerel.

SEB. Done. The wager?

ANT. A laughter.°

SEB. A match!

ADR. Though this island seem to be desert ——

SEB. Ha, ha, ha! — So, you're paid.° 36

ADR. Uninhabitable, and almost inaccessible ——

SEB. Yet ——

ADR. Yet ——

ANT. He could not miss 't.° 40

ADR. It must needs be of subtle, tender, and delicate temperance.

ANT. Temperance was a delicate wench.

SEB. Aye, and a subtle, as he most learnedly delivered.° 45

ADR. The air breathes upon us here most sweetly.

SEB. As if it had lungs, and rotten ones.

ANT. Or as 'twere perfumed by a fen.

GON. Here is everything advantageous to life.

ANT. True — save means to live. 50

SEB. Of that there's none, or little.

GON. How lush and lusty the grass looks! How green!

ANT. The ground indeed is tawny.

SEB. With an eye° of green in't. 55

ANT. He misses not much.

SEB. No, he doth but mistake the truth totally.

GON. But the rarity° of it is — which is indeed almost beyond credit° ——

SEB. As many vouched° rarities are. 60

GON. That our garments, being, as they were, drenched in the sea, hold notwithstanding their freshness and glosses, being rather new-dyed than stained with salt water.

ANT. If but one of his pockets could speak,° would it not say he lies? 66

SEB. Aye, or very falsely pocket up his report.

GON. Methinks our garments are now as fresh as when we put them on first in Afric, at the marriage of the King's fair daughter Claribel to the King of Tunis. 71

SEB. 'Twas a sweet marriage, and we prosper well in our return.

ADR. Tunis was never graced° before with such a paragon to° their Queen. 75

GON. Not since Widow Dido's° time.

ANT. Widow! A pox° o' that! How came that widow in?° Widow Dido!

SEB. What if he had said " Widower Aeneas " too? Good Lord, how you take it! 80

ADR. "Widow Dido," said you? You make me study of that. She was of Carthage, not of Tunis.

GON. This Tunis, sir, was Carthage.

ADR. Carthage?

GON. I assure you, Carthage. 85

ANT. His word is more than the miraculous harp.°

SEB. He hath raised the wall, and houses too.

ANT. What impossible matter will he make easy next?

SEB. I think he will carry this island home in his pocket, and give it his son for an apple. 91

ANT. And, sowing the kernels of it in the sea, bring forth more islands.

GON. Aye.

ANT. Why, in good time. 95

GON. Sir, we were talking that our garments seem now as fresh as when we were at Tunis at the marriage of your daughter, who is now Queen.

ANT. And the rarest that e'er came there.

SEB. Bate,° I beseech you, Widow Dido. 100

ANT. Oh, Widow Dido! Aye, Widow Dido.

GON. Is not, sir, my doublet° as fresh as the first day I wore it? I mean, in a sort.°

ANT. That sort was well fished for.°

GON. When I wore it at your daughter's marriage? 105

ALON. You cram these words into mine ears against

65. pockets ... speak: i.e., his pockets are still wet.　74. graced: honored.　75. to: for.　76. Widow Dido: Dido was the Queen of Carthage (near the modern Tunis) who entertained Aeneas on his way from Troy to Italy. She was a widow and had vowed eternal fidelity to the memory of her husand, but she fell in love with Aeneas. When he deserted her, she committed suicide.　77. pox: plague; lit., venereal disease.　77–78. How ... in: why do you call her a widow?　86. His ... harp: According to the legends told by Ovid, the walls of Thebes came together at the music of Amphion's harp. By a like miracle Gonzalo has erected a Carthage at Tunis.　100. Bate: except.　102. doublet: See Pl. 8b and comment on p. 93a.　103. in a sort: after a fashion.　104. That ... for: i.e., he had to add "after a fashion."

15. Tell: count.　16. entertained: received.　33. A laughter: the winner is to have the laugh on the loser, on the principle of the proverb "He laughs that wins." Cf. Oth, IV.i.126. (Kittredge).　36. Ha ... paid: F1 divides the speech: "Sebastian: Ha, ha, ha. Antonio: So, you're paid"; i.e., you've had your laugh as winner.　40. He ... miss 't: i.e., if he begins the first clause with "though," he is sure to follow it up with a "yet."　45. delivered: declared.　55. eye: tinge.　58. rarity: strange thing.　59. credit: belief.　60. vouched: guaranteed.

The stomach of my sense. Would I had never
Married my daughter there! For, coming thence,
My son is lost and, in my rate,° she too
Who is so far from Italy removed   110
I ne'er again shall see her. O thou mine heir
Of Naples and of Milan, what strange fish
Hath made his meal on thee?

FRAN.   Sir, he may live.
I saw him beat the surges° under him,
And ride upon their backs. He trod the water,   115
Whose enmity he flung aside, and breasted
The surge most swoln° that met him. His bold head
'Bove the contentious waves he kept, and oared
Himself with his good arms in lusty stroke
To the shore, that o'er his wave-worn basis bowed,°
As stooping to relieve him. I not doubt   121
He came alive to land.

ALON.   No, no, he's gone.

SEB. Sir, you may thank yourself for this great
    loss,
That would not bless our Europe with your
    daughter,
But rather lose her to an African,   125
Where she, at least, is banished from your eye
Who hath cause to wet° the grief on 't.

ALON.   Prithee, peace.

SEB. You were kneeled to, and importuned other-
    wise,
By all of us, and the fair soul herself
Weighed° between loathness° and obedience, at   129
Which end o' the beam° should bow. We have lost
    your son,
I fear, forever. Milan and Naples have
Mo° widows in them of this business' making
Than we bring men to comfort them.
The fault's your own.

ALON.   So is the dear'st° o' the loss.   135

GON. My lord Sebastian,
The truth you speak doth lack some gentleness,
And time to speak it in. You rub the sore
When you should bring the plaster.

SEB.   Very well.

ANT. And most chirurgeonly.°   140

GON. It is foul weather in us all, good sir,
When you are cloudy.

SEB.   Foul weather?

ANT.   Very foul.

GON. Had I plantation° of this isle, my lord ——

ANT. He'd sow 't with nettle seed.

SEB.   Or docks, or mallows.°

GON. And were the King on 't, what would I do?

SEB. 'Scape being drunk for want of wine.   146

GON. I' the commonwealth° I would by con-
    traries°
Execute all things, for no kind of traffic°
Would I admit, no name of magistrate.
Letters° should not be known; riches, poverty,   150
And use of service,° none; contract,° succession,°
Bourn,° bound° of land, tilth,° vineyard, none;
No use of metal,° corn, or wine, or oil;
No occupation° — all men idle, all;
And women too, but innocent and pure;   155
No sovereignty ——

SEB.   Yet he would be King on't.

ANT. The latter end of his commonwealth forgets
the beginning.

GON. All things in common nature should pro-
    duce
Without sweat or endeavor. Treason, felony,   160
Sword, pike, knife, gun, or need of any engine°
Would I not have. But Nature should bring
    forth,
Of it° own kind, all foison,° all abundance,
To feed my innocent people.

SEB. No marrying 'mong his subjects?   165

ANT. None, man — all idle, whores and knaves.

GON. I would with such perfection govern, sir,
To excel the Golden Age.°

SEB.   'Save° His Majesty!

ANT. Long live Gonzalo!

GON.   And — do you mark me, sir?

ALON. Prithee, no more. Thou dost talk nothing to
me.   171

GON. I do well believe your Highness, and did it
to minister occasion° to these gentlemen, who are of
such sensible° and nimble lungs that they always use
to laugh at nothing.   175

ANT. 'Twas you we laughed at.

GON. Who in this kind of merry fooling am nothing to you. So you may continue and laugh at nothing still.

ANT. What a blow was there given!   180

SEB. An° it had not fallen flat-long.°

GON. You are gentlemen of brave mettle,° you
would lift the moon out of her sphere° if she would
continue in it five weeks without changing.

---

147. I' . . . commonwealth: For the origin of this passage see
Temp Intro. p. 1472b. by contraries: contrary to the usual plan.
148. traffic: trade.   150. Letters: learning.   151. use of service:
no one should have servants. contract: legal agreements. succession: right of inheritance.   152. Bourn: boundary. bound:
limit; i.e., private property rights. tilth: tillage.   153. use of
metal: i.e., exchange of money.   154. occupation: manual labor.
161. engine: instrument of warfare.   163. it: its. foison: plenty.
168. Golden Age: the days of perfect innocence at the beginning
of the world. 'Save: God save.   173. minister occasion: provide
opportunity.   174. sensible: sensitive.   181. An: if. flat-long:
on the flat side of the sword.   182. mettle: material, stuff.
183. sphere: course.

109. rate: estimation.   114. surges: waves.   117. swoln: swollen.   120. his . . . bowed: hung over its base, which had been
worn away by the sea.   127. wet: weep for.   130. Weighed:
balanced. loathness: reluctance.   131. end . . . beam: which
scale should sink.   133. Mo: more.   135. dear'st: most grievous.   140. chirurgeonly: like a good surgeon.   143. plantation:
colonization, but Antonio pretends to take it literally as "planting."   144. docks or mallows: common English weeds.

[*Enter* ARIEL (*invisible*) *playing solemn music.*]
SEB. We would so, and then go a-batfowling.°
ANT. Nay, good my lord, be not angry.   186
GON. No, I warrant you, I will not adventure my
discretion so weakly.° Will you laugh me asleep,
for I am very heavy?
ANT. Go sleep, and hear us.   190
[*All sleep except* ALONSO, SEBASTIAN, *and* ANTONIO.]
ALON. What, all so soon asleep! I wish mine eyes
Would, with themselves, shut up my thoughts. I find
They are inclined to do so.
SEB.   Please you, sir,
Do not omit the heavy offer° of it.
It seldom visits sorrow. When it doth,   195
It is a comforter.
ANT.   We two, my lord,
Will guard your person while you take your rest,
And watch your safety.
ALON.   Thank you. — Wondrous heavy.
          [ALONSO *sleeps. Exit* ARIEL.]
SEB. What a strange drowsiness possesses them!
ANT. It is the quality° o' the climate.
SEB.   Why   200
Doth it not then our eyelids sink? I find not
Myself disposed to sleep.
ANT.   Nor I. My spirits are nimble.
They fell together all, as by consent,
They dropped as by a thunderstroke. What might,
Worthy Sebastian? — Oh, what might? — No
          more. —   205
And yet methinks I see it in thy face,
What thou shouldst be. The occasion speaks thee,°
          and
My strong imagination sees a crown
Dropping upon thy head.
SEB.   What, art thou waking?°
ANT. Do you not hear me speak?
SEB.   I do, and surely   210
It is a sleepy language, and thou speak'st
Out of thy sleep. What is it thou didst say?
This is a strange repose, to be asleep
With eyes wide-open — standing, speaking, moving,
And yet so fast asleep.
ANT.   Noble Sebastian,   215
Thou let'st thy fortune sleep — die, rather —
          wink'st
Whiles thou art waking.
SEB.   Thou dost snore distinctly.
There's meaning in thy snores.
ANT. I am more serious than my custom. You
Must be so too, if heed me,° which to do   220

Trebles thee o'er.
SEB.   Well, I am standing water.°
ANT. I'll teach you how to flow.°
SEB.   Do so. To ebb
Hereditary sloth instructs me.
ANT.   Oh,
If you but knew how you the purpose cherish
Whiles thus you mock it! How, in stripping it,   225
You more invest it! Ebbing men, indeed,
Most often do so near the bottom run
By their own fear or sloth.°
SEB.   Prithee, say on.
The setting° of thine eye and cheek proclaim
A matter° from thee, and a birth, indeed,   230
Which throes thee much to yield.°
ANT.   Thus, sir.
Although this lord of weak remembrance, this,°
Who shall be of as little memory
When he is earthed, hath here almost persuaded —
For he's a spirit of persuasion, only   235
Professes to persuade — the King his son's alive,
'Tis as impossible that he's undrowned
As he that sleeps here swims.
SEB.   I have no hope
That he's undrowned.
ANT.   Oh, out of that " no hope "
What great hope have you! No hope that way is
Another way so high a hope that even   241
Ambition cannot pierce a wink beyond,
But doubt discovery there.° Will you grant with me
That Ferdinand is drowned?
SEB.   He's gone.
ANT.   Then tell me,
Who's the next heir of Naples?
SEB.   Claribel.   245
ANT. She that is Queen of Tunis, she that dwells
Ten leagues beyond man's life,° she that from
          Naples
Can have no note, unless the sun were post° —
The man i' the moon's too slow — till newborn
          chins
Be rough and razorable.° She that from whom   250
We all were sea-swallowed, though some cast° again,

---

185. **batfowling:** hunting for birds at night with the aid of torches
and sticks or bats.   187–88. **adventure . . . weakly:** risk my reputation as a discreet man so easily, by showing anger at such as
you.   194. **omit . . . offer:** do not lose this chance of sleeping.
200. **quality:** nature.   207. **occasion . . . thee:** opportunity calls
you.   209. **waking:** awake.   220. **if . . . me:** if you will listen
to me.

221. **Trebles . . . o'er:** makes you three times the man you are.
standing water: i.e., at the turning of the tide, for which for a while
neither ebbs nor flows.   222. **flow:** advance (like the rising tide).
224–28. **If . . . sloth:** if you would only realize how much you are
moved by the prospect of becoming King, even while you mock it;
how in stripping it of its glamour you make it more attractive.
Ebbing men (i.e., the lazy and unambitious) often run aground
through fear or sloth.   229. **setting:** expression.   230. **matter:**
something serious.   231. **throes . . . yield:** is very painful to bring
forth.   232. **this . . . this:** i.e., Francisco. See ll. 113–22.
240–43. **No . . . there:** i.e., your certainty that the true heir is
drowned gives you a greater hope in another direction (i.e., of
being King yourself), where even your ambition cannot look
higher.   247. **Ten . . . life:** ten leagues farther than a man could
travel in his lifetime.   248. **post:** messenger.   249–50. **newborn
. . . razorable:** i.e., newborn children are grown men.   251. **cast:**
vomited up.

And by that destiny, to perform an act
Whereof what's past is prologue, what to come,
In yours and my discharge.°

SEB.   What stuff is this! How say you?
'Tis true, my brother's daughter's Queen of Tunis,
So is she heir of Naples, 'twixt which regions   256
There is some space.

ANT.   A space whose every cubit
Seems to cry out, "How shall that Claribel
Measure us° back to Naples? Keep° in Tunis,
And let Sebastian wake." Say this were death   260
That now hath seized them — why, they were no
     worse
Than now they are. There be that can rule Naples
As well as he that sleeps, lords that can prate
As amply and unnecessarily
As this Gonzalo. I myself could make   265
A chough of as deep chat.° Oh, that you bore
The mind that I do! What a sleep were this
For your advancement! Do you understand me?

SEB. Methinks I do.

ANT.   And how does your content
Tender your own good fortune?

SEB.   I remember   270
You did supplant your brother Prospero.

ANT.   True.
And look how well my garments sit upon me,
Much feater° than before. My brother's servants
Were then my fellows,° now they are my men.°

SEB. But — for your conscience.   275

ANT. Aye, sir, where lies that? If 'twere a kibe,
'Twould put me to my slipper.° But I feel not
This deity in my bosom. Twenty consciences,
That stand 'twixt me and Milan, candied be they,
And melt ere they molest!° Here lies your brother,
No better than the earth he lies upon   281
If he were that which now he's like, that's dead.
Whom I, with this obedient steel, three inches of it,
Can lay to bed forever whiles you, doing thus,
To the perpetual wink° for aye might put   285
This ancient morsel, this Sir Prudence who
Should not upbraid our course. For all the rest,
They'll take suggestion as a cat laps milk,
They'll tell the clock to° any business that
We say befits the hour.

SEB.   Thy case, dear friend,   290
Shall be my precedent. As thou got'st Milan,
I'll come by Naples. Draw thy sword. One stroke

Shall free thee from the tribute which thou payest,
And I the King shall love thee.

ANT.   Draw together,
And when I rear my hand, do you the like,   295
To fall° it on Gonzalo.

SEB.   Oh, but one word. [*They talk apart.*]
[*Re-enter* ARIEL, *invisible.*]

ARI. My master through his art foresees the danger
That you, his friend, are in, and sends me forth —
For else his project dies — to keep them living.
           [*Sings in* GONZALO'S *ear.*]
    "While you here do snoring lie,   300
      Open-eyed conspiracy
       His time° doth take.
    If of life you keep a care,
    Shake off slumber, and beware.
      Awake, awake!"   305

ANT. Then let us both be sudden.

GON.   Now, good angels
Preserve the King!   [*They wake.*]

ALON. Why, how now? Ho, awake! — Why are
     you drawn?
Wherefore this ghastly looking?

GON.   What's the matter?

SEB. Whiles we stood here securing° your repose,
Even now, we heard a hollow burst of bellowing
Like bulls, or rather lions. Did 't not wake you?   312
It struck mine ear most terribly.

ALON.   I heard nothing.

ANT. Oh, 'twas a din to fright a monster's ear,
To make an earthquake! Sure, it was the roar   315
Of a whole herd of lions.

ALON.   Heard you this, Gonzalo?

GON. Upon mine honor, sir, I heard a humming,
And that a strange one too, which did awake me.
I shaked you, sir, and cried. As mine eyes opened
I saw their weapons drawn. — There was a noise,
That's verily.° 'Tis best we stand upon our guard,
Or that we quit this place. Let's draw our weapons.

ALON. Lead off this ground, and let's make further
     search   323
For my poor son.

GON.   Heavens keep him from these beasts!
For he is sure i' th' island.

ALON.   Lead away.

ARI. Prospero my lord shall know what I have
     done.
So, King, go safely on to seek thy son.   [*Exeunt.*]

SCENE II. *Another part of the island.*

[*Enter* CALIBAN *with a burden of wood. A noise of
thunder heard.*]

CAL. All the infections that the sun sucks up
From bogs, fens, flats, on Prosper fall, and make him

---

254. discharge: task to be performed.   259. Measure us: retrace
her journey after us. Keep: let her remain.   266. chough . . .
chat: I could make a jackdaw (*chough*, rhyming with rough) talk
as profoundly as he does. 273. feater: more trimly. 274. fellows:
equals. men: servants. 276–77. kibe . . . slipper: a chilblain which
would make me wear a slipper. 278–80. Twenty . . . molest:
i.e., if twenty consciences had stood between me and the dukedom of Milan, I should have let them melt like candy before
they would have disturbed me. Other editors take "candied" to
mean "frozen." 285. perpetual wink: everlasting sleep. 289. tell
. . . to: say it is time for.

296. fall: let fall.   302. time: opportunity.   310. securing:
keeping safe.   321. verily: truth.

1.) CAL. MAKES SAME MISTAKE HE DID W/ PROSPERO
2.) NO LOYALTY

By inchmeal° a disease! His spirits hear me,
And yet I needs must curse. But they'll nor pinch,
Fright me with urchin shows,° pitch me i' the mire,
Nor lead me, like a firebrand,° in the dark   6
Out of my way, unless he bid 'em. But
For every trifle are they set upon me —
Sometime like apes, that mow° and chatter at me,
And after bite me; then like hedgehogs, which   10
Lie tumbling in my barefoot way and mount°
Their pricks at my footfall. Sometime am I
All wound with adders, who with cloven tongues
Do hiss me into madness.
          [*Enter* TRINCULO.] Lo, now, lo!
Here comes a spirit of his, and to torment me   15
For bringing wood in slowly. I'll fall flat.
Perchance he will not mind me.

TRIN. Here's neither bush nor shrub to bear off
any weather at all, and another storm brewing, I
hear it sing i' the wind. Yond same black cloud,   20
yond huge one, looks like a foul bombard° that
would shed his liquor. If it should thunder as it did
before, I know not where to hide my head. Yond
same cloud cannot choose but fall by pailfuls. What
have we here? A man or a fish? Dead or alive?   25
A fish — he smells like a fish, a very ancient and fish-
like smell, a kind of not of the newest Poor John.° A
strange fish! Were I in England now, as once I was,
and had but this fish painted,° not a holiday fool
there but would give a piece of silver. There would
this monster make a man° — any strange beast   31
there makes a man. When they will not give a doit°
to relieve a lame beggar, they will lay out ten to see
a dead Indian. Legged like a man! And his fins like
arms! Warm, o' my troth! I do now let loose   35
my opinion, hold it no longer — this is no fish, but
an islander that hath lately suffered by a thunderbolt.
[*Thunder.*] Alas, the storm is come again! Best
way is to creep under his gaberdine,° there is no
other shelter hereabout. Misery acquaints a man   40
with strange bedfellows. I will here shroud° till the
dregs of the storm be past.
          [*Enter* STEPHANO, *singing, a bottle in his hand*.]
STE.   " I shall no more to sea, to sea,
                    Here shall I die ashore ——"   45
This is a very scurvy° tune to sing at a man's funeral.
Well, here's my comfort.   [*Drinks. Sings.*]
" The master, the swabber, the boatswain, and I,
          The gunner, and his mate,
     Loved Mall, Meg, and Marian, and Margery,   50
          But none of us cared for Kate.

For she had a tongue with a tang,°
     Would cry to a sailor, Go hang!
She loved not the savor° of tar nor of pitch,   54
Yet a tailor might scratch her where'er she did itch.
     Then, to sea, boys, and let her go hang! "

This is a scurvy tune too, but here's my comfort.
          [*Drinks.*]
CAL. Do not torment me. — Oh!   58
STE. What's the matter? Have we devils here? Do
you put tricks upon 's with salvages° and men of
Ind,° ha? I have not 'scaped drowning to be afeard
now of your four legs, for it hath been said,   62
As proper° a man as ever went on four legs cannot
make him give ground. And it shall be said so again
while Stephano breathes at nostrils.
CAL. The spirit torments me. — Oh!   66
STE. This is some monster of the isle with four
legs, who hath got, as I take it, an ague.° Where the
devil should he learn our language? I will give him
some relief, if it be but for that. If I can recover°
him, and keep him tame, and get to Naples with
him, he's a present for any emperor that ever trod on
neat's leather.°   73
CAL. Do not torment me, prithee, I'll bring my
wood home faster.
STE. He's in his fit now, and does not talk after
the wisest. He shall taste of my bottle. If he have
never drunk wine afore, it will go near to remove his
fit. If I can recover him, and keep him tame, I will
not take too much for him.° He shall pay for him
that hath him, and that soundly.   81
CAL. Thou dost me yet but little hurt, thou wilt
anon, I know it by thy trembling.° Now Prosper
works upon thee.   84
STE. Come on your ways. Open your mouth, here
is that which will give language to you, cat. Open
your mouth, this will shake your shaking, I can tell
you, and that soundly. You cannot tell who's your
friend. Open your chaps° again.   89
TRIN. I should know that voice. It should be —
but he is drowned, and these are devils. — Oh, defend me!   92
STE. Four legs and two voices — a most delicate
monster! His forward voice, now, is to speak well of
his friend, his backward voice is to utter foul
speeches and to detract. If all the wine in my bottle
will recover him, I will help his ague. Come. —
Amen! I will pour some in thy other mouth.   99
TRIN. Stephano!
STE. Doth thy other mouth call me? Mercy, mercy!

Sc. ii: **3. inchmeal:** by inches.   **5. urchin shows:** the appearance of goblins. See I.ii.326.   **6. firebrand:** will-o'-the-wisp.
9. mow: make faces.   **11. mount:** raise.   **21. bombard:** large
black leathern jug. See Pl. 17f.   **27. Poor John:** dried salt fish.
29. had . . . painted: had a poster of this fish painted.   **31. make
a man:** i.e., his fortune.   **32. doit:** a small Dutch coin, a cent.
39. gaberdine: cloak.   **41. shroud:** cover myself.   **46. scurvy:**
"lousy."

52. tang: a sharp sound.   **54. savor:** taste.   **60. salvages:** savages.   **60–61. men of Ind:** natives of India.   **63. proper:** fine.
68. ague: fever, which makes him shiver.   **71. recover:** cure.
73. neat's leather: i.e., shoes.   **79–80. I . . . him:** I'll not take
even an excessive price.   **83. trembling:** Trinculo is the trembler,
for he believes that the voice of Stephano comes from a ghost.
Trinculo is a natural coward.   **89. chaps:** chops, jaws.

This is a devil and no monster. I will leave him, I
have no long spoon.°   103

TRIN. Stephano! If thou beest Stephano, touch me,
and speak to me, for I am Trinculo — be not afeard
— thy good friend Trinculo.

STE. If thou beest Trinculo, come forth. I'll pull
thee by the lesser legs. If any be Trinculo's legs, these
are they. Thou art very Trinculo indeed! How
camest thou to be the siege° of this mooncalf?° Can
he vent Trinculos?   111

TRIN. I look him to be killed with a thunderstroke. But art thou not drowned, Stephano? I hope,
now, thou art not drowned. Is the storm overblown?
I hid me under the dead mooncalf's gaberdine for
fear of the storm. And art thou living, Stephano? O
Stephano, two Neapolitans 'scaped!   117

STE. Prithee do not turn me about, my stomach is
not constant.°

CAL. [*Aside*] These be fine things, an if they be
not sprites.
That's a brave god, and bears celestial liquor.
I will kneel to him.   122

STE. How didst thou 'scape? How camest thou
hither? Swear, by this bottle, how thou camest
hither. I escaped upon a butt of sack,° which the
sailors heaved o'erboard, by this bottle, which I made
of the bark of a tree with mine own hands, since I
was cast ashore.   128

CAL. I'll swear upon that bottle to be thy true subject, for the liquor is not earthly.

STE. Here, swear, then, how thou escapedst.

TRIN. Swam ashore, man, like a duck. I can swim
like a duck, I'll be sworn. *OFFERS CAL A DRINK* 133

STE. Here, kiss the book. Though thou canst swim
like a duck, thou art made like a goose.

TRIN. O Stephano, hast any more of this?

STE. The whole butt, man. My cellar is in a rock
by the seaside, where my wine is hid. How now,
mooncalf! How does thine ague?   139

CAL. Hast thou not dropped from Heaven?

STE. Out o' the moon, I do assure thee. I was the
man 'i the moon when time was.°   142

CAL. I have seen thee in her, and I do adore thee.
My mistress showed me thee, and thy dog, and thy
bush.°

STE. Come, swear to that, kiss the book. I will furnish it anon with new contents. Swear.   147

Allegiance of Caliban to these two.

TRIN. By this good light, this is a very shallow
monster! I afeard of him! A very weak monster!
The man i' the moon! A most poor credulous mon-
ster! Well drawn,° monster, in good sooth!°   151

CAL. I'll show thee every fertile inch o' th' island,
And I will kiss thy foot. I prithee be my god.

TRIN. By this light, a most perfidious and drunken
monster! When's god's asleep, he'll rob his bottle.

CAL. I'll kiss thy foot, I'll swear myself thy subject
STE. Come on, then, down, and swear.

TRIN. I shall laugh myself to death at this puppy-
headed monster. A most scurvy monster! I could find
in my heart to beat him ——   160

STE. Come, kiss.

TRIN. But that the poor monster's in drink. An
abominable monster!

CAL. I'll show thee the best springs, I'll pluck thee
    berries,
I'll fish for thee, and get thee wood enough.
A plague upon the tyrant that I serve!
I'll bear him no more sticks, but follow thee,
Thou wondrous man.°   168

TRIN. A most ridiculous monster, to make a wonder of a poor drunkard!

CAL. I prithee let me bring thee where crabs°
    grow.   171
And I with my long nails will dig thee pignuts,°
Show thee a jay's nest, and instruct thee how
To snare the nimble marmoset.° I'll bring thee
To clustering filberts, and sometimes I'll get thee
Young scamels° from the rock. Wilt thou go with
    me?   176

STE. I prithee now, lead the way, without any
more talking. Trinculo, the King and all our company else being drowned, we will inherit here. Here,
bear my bottle, fellow Trinculo, we'll fill him by and
by again.   181

CAL. [*Sings drunkenly.*]
    " Farewell, master, farewell, farewell! "

TRIN. A howling monster, a drunken monster!

CAL. " No more dams I'll make for fish.
            Nor fetch in firing   185
            At requiring,
        Nor scrape trencher,° nor wash dish.
        'Ban, 'Ban, Cacaliban
        Has a new master. — Get a new man."
Freedom, heyday! Heyday, freedom! Freedom, hey-
day, freedom!   191

STE. O brave monster! Lead the way.   [*Exeunt.*]

---

103. I . . . spoon: "He that sups with the Devil needs a long
spoon" — a proverb from the time when men dipped into a common dish. A long spoon was needed, as the Devil's claws were long
and sharp, and his table manners nasty.   110. siege: excrement.
mooncalf: misshapen monster, freak.   119. constant: steady.
Trinculo is pawing him all over, and turning him round in his
excitement.   125. sack: a dry wine from Spain. For Falstaff on
the merits of sack, see *II Hen IV*, IV.iii.102–35.   142. when
. . . was: once upon a time.   144–45. thee . . . bush: the man
in the moon had his dog and bush of thorns, as Quince knew.
See *MND*, III.i.60.

151. drawn: sucked. sooth: truth. 168. Thou . . . man: See *Temp*
Intro. p. 1474a. 171. crabs: crab apples. 172. pignut: called
also earthnut, a plant producing edible tubers. 174. marmoset:
kind of small monkey. 176. scamels: a much-discussed word
which does not occur elsewhere and so has been variously interpreted or emended, the likeliest guess being seamel: sea gull.
187. trencher: wooden plate.

PERFECT LOVE

Act III

SCENE I. *Before* PROSPERO'S *cell.*

[*Enter* FERDINAND, *bearing a log.*]

FER. There be some sports are painful, and their
   labor
Delight in them sets off.° Some kinds of baseness
Are nobly undergone, and most poor matters
Point° to rich ends. This my mean task
Would be as heavy to me as odious, but   5
The mistress which I serve quickens° what's dead
And makes my labors pleasures. Oh, she is
Ten times more gentle than her father's crabbèd,
And he's composed of harshness. I must remove
Some thousands of these logs, and pile them up,   10
Upon a sore injunction.° My sweet mistress
Weeps when she sees me work, and says such base-
   ness
Had never like executor.° I forget.
But these sweet thoughts do even refresh my labors,
Most busy lest when I do it.°

[*Enter* MIRANDA, *and* PROSPERO *at a distance,*°
   unseen.]

MIRA.   Alas, now, pray you   15
Work not so hard. I would the lightning had
Burned up those logs that you are enjoined to pile!
Pray set it down and rest you. When this burns,
'Twill weep° for having wearied you. My father
Is hard at study, pray now, rest yourself.   20
He's safe for these three hours.

FER.   O most dear mistress,
The sun will set before I shall discharge
What I must strive to do.

MIRA.   If you'll sit down,
I'll bear your logs the while. Pray give me that,
I'll carry it to the pile.

FER.   No, precious creature,   25
I had rather crack my sinews, break my back,
Than you should such dishonor undergo
While I sit lazy by.

MIRA.   It would become me
As well as it does you. And I should do it
With much more ease, for my goodwill is to it,   30
And yours it is against.

PRO.   Poor worm, thou art infected!

This visitation° shows it.

MIRA.   You look wearily.

FER. No, noble mistress, 'tis fresh morning with
   me
When you are by at night. I do beseech you —
Chiefly that I might set it in my prayers —   35
What is your name?

MIRA.   Miranda. — O my father,
I have broke your hest° to say so!

FER.   Admired Miranda!°
Indeed the top° of admiration! Worth
What's dearest to the world! Full many a lady
I have eyed with best regard, and many a time   40
The harmony of their tongues hath into bondage
Brought my too diligent ear. For several° virtues
Have I liked several women, never any
With so full soul but some defect in her
Did quarrel with the noblest grace she owed,   45
And put it to the foil.° But you, oh, you,
So perfect and so peerless, are created
Of every creature's best!

MIRA.   I do not know
One of my sex, no woman's face remember
Save, from my glass, mine own. Nor have I seen   50
More that I may call men than you, good friend,
And my dear father. How features are abroad,
I am skill-less of.° But, by my modesty,
The jewel in my dower, I would not wish
Any companion in the world but you,   55
Nor can imagination form a shape
Besides yourself to like of. But I prattle
Something too wildly, and my father's precepts
I therein do forget.

FER.   I am, in my condition,
A prince, Miranda, I do think, a king —   60
I would not so! — and would no more endure
This wooden slavery° than to suffer
The flesh fly blow° my mouth. Hear my soul speak.
The very instant that I saw you did
My heart fly to your service, there resides,   65
To make me slave to it, and for your sake
Am I this patient logman.

MIRA.   Do you love me?

FER. O Heaven, O earth, bear witness to this
   sound,
And crown what I profess with kind event°
If I speak true! If hollowly, invert   70
What best is boded° me to mischief! I,
Beyond all limit of what else i' the world,

Act III, Sc. i: **1–2. their . . . off:** the delight which they bring
outweighs the fatigue.   **4. Point:** lead.   **6. quickens:** brings to
life.   **11. injunction:** a command enforced with penalties against
disobedience.   **13. executor:** performer.   **15. Most . . . it:** This
line has been much discussed and may be corrupt. It means
apparently "I am most busy when I am idle, for then I think
so many sweet thoughts." **lest:** least. **s.d., and . . . distance:** F1
simply reads "Enter Miranda and Prospero." They obviously do
not enter together, and on the Elizabethan stage probably Prospero entered on the balcony above, as later (III.iii.19). The balcony was a most convenient place for eavesdroppers. See Pl. 5b.
19. weep: i.e., drip with sap when burning.

32. visitation: visit.   **37. hest:** command. **Admired Miranda:** a
play on her name, for *miranda* in Latin means "she who ought to
be wondered at." "Admired" at this time had a stronger meaning
than today. **38. top:** summit. **42. several:** separate, individual.
46. put . . . foil: bring it to disgrace. **52–53. features . . . of:** I
have no experience of how people look elsewhere. **62. wooden
slavery:** i.e., task of having to carry wood. **63. blow:** lay its eggs
on, foul. **69. event:** result. **71. What . . . boded:** the best
fate that is prophesied.

Do love, prize, honor you.

MIRA.   I am a fool
To weep at what I am glad of.

PRO.   Fair encounter
Of two most rare affections! Heavens rain grace   75
On that which breeds between 'em!

FER.   Wherefore weep you?

MIRA. At mine unworthiness, that dare not offer
What I desire to give, and much less take
What I shall die to want.° But this is trifling,
And all the more it seeks to hide itself,   80
The bigger bulk it shows. Hence, bashful cunning!
And prompt me, plain and holy innocence!
I am your wife, if you will marry me.
If not, I'll die your maid. To be your fellow°
You may deny me, but I'll be your servant,   85
Whether you will or no.

FER.   My mistress, dearest,
And I thus humble ever.

MIRA.   My husband, then?

FER. Aye, with a heart as willing°
As bondage e'er of freedom. Here's my hand.

MIRA. And mine, with my heart in 't. And now
    farewell   90
Till half an hour hence.

FER.   A thousand thousand!°

[*Exeunt* FERDINAND *and* MIRANDA *severally.*°]

PRO. So glad of this as they I cannot be,
Who° are surprised withal,° but my rejoicing
At nothing can be more. I'll to my book,
For yet ere suppertime must I perform   95
Much business appertaining.   [*Exit.*]

SCENE II. *Another part of the island.*

[*Enter* CALIBAN, STEPHANO, *and* TRINCULO.]

STE. Tell not me. — When the butt is out, we will
drink water, not a drop before. Therefore bear up,°
and board 'em. Servant-monster, drink to me.   4

TRIN. Servant-monster! The folly of this island!°
They say there's but five upon this isle. We are three
of them. If th' other two be brained like us, the state
totters.

STE. Drink, servant-monster, when I bid thee. Thy
eyes are almost set° in thy head.   10

TRIN. Where should they be set else? He were a
brave monster indeed if they were set in his tail.

STE. My man-monster hath drowned his tongue in
sack. For my part, the sea cannot drown me. I swam,

ere I could recover the shore, five-and-thirty leagues°
off and on. By this light, thou shalt be my lieutenant,
monster, or my standard.°   17

TRIN. Your lieutenant, if you list. He's no standard.

STE. We'll not run, Monsieur Monster.

TRIN. Nor go neither, but you'll lie, like dogs, and
yet say nothing neither.

STE. Mooncalf, speak once in thy life, if thou beest
a good mooncalf.   25

CAL. How does thy Honor? Let me lick thy shoe.
I'll not serve him, he is not valiant.

TRIN. Thou liest, most ignorant monster. I am in
case° to jostle a constable. Why, thou deboshed° fish
thou, was there ever man a coward that hath drunk
so much sack as I today? Wilt thou tell a monstrous
lie, being but half a fish and half a monster?   33

CAL. Lo, how he mocks me! Wilt thou let him,
my lord?

TRIN. "Lord," quoth he! That a monster should
be such a natural!°

CAL. Lo, lo, again! Bite him to death, I prithee.

STE. Trinculo, keep a good tongue in your   40
head. If you prove a mutineer — the next tree! The
poor monster's my subject, and he shall not suffer
indignity.

CAL. I thank my noble lord. Wilt thou be pleased
to hearken once again to the suit I made to thee?   45

STE. Marry,° will I. Kneel and repeat it. I will
stand, and so shall Trinculo.

[*Enter* ARIEL, *invisible.*]

CAL. As I told thee before, I am subject to a tyrant,
a sorcerer, that by his cunning hath cheated me of
the island.   50

ARI. Thou liest.

CAL. Thou liest,° thou jesting monkey thou.
I would my valiant master would destroy thee!
I do not lie.

STE. Trinculo, if you trouble him any more in 's
tale, by this hand, I will supplant° some of your
teeth.   57

TRIN. Why, I said nothing.

STE. Mum, then, and no more. Proceed.

CAL. I say, by sorcery he got this isle.   60
From me he got it. If thy greatness will
Revenge it on him — for I know thou darest,
But this thing dare not——

STE. That's most certain.

CAL. Thou shalt be lord of it, and I'll serve thee.

STE. How now shall this be compassed?°   66
Canst thou bring me to the party?

---

79. **want:** be without. 84. **fellow:** equal. See II.i.274. 88. **willing:** eager. 91. **thousand thousand:** i.e., farewells. **s.d., severally:** by different exits. 93. **Who:** i.e., Ferdinand and Miranda.
withal: therewith.

    Sc. ii: 2. bear up: crowd on more sail. 5. **The . . . island:**
what a silly place this island is. 10. **set:** closed, dazed with
drink.

15. **league:** three miles. 17. **standard:** standard-bearer (or ensign), the junior officer in the company, the others being the
captain and the lieutenant. Caliban is now too unsteady to be a
satisfactory *standard*. 29. **in case:** in a condition. **deboshed:**
debauched. 38. **natural:** born fool. 46. **Marry:** Mary, by the
Virgin. 52. **Thou liest:** Caliban supposes the voice to be Trinculo's. 56. **supplant:** displace. 66. **compassed:** brought about.

CAL. Yea, yea, my lord. I'll yield him thee asleep,
Where thou mayst knock a nail into his head.

ARI. Thou liest, thou canst not.   70

CAL. What a pied ninny's° this! Thou scurvy
     patch!°
I do beseech thy greatness, give him blows,
And take his bottle from him. When that's gone,
He shall drink naught but brine, for I'll not show
     him
Where the quick freshes° are.   75

STE. Trinculo, run into no further danger. Interrupt the monster one word further and, by this hand, I'll turn my mercy out o' doors and make a stockfish° of thee.

TRIN. Why, what did I? I did nothing. I'll go
farther off.   81

STE. Didst thou not say he lied?

ARI. Thou liest.

STE. Do I so? Take thou that. [*Beats him.*] As
you like this, give me the lie° another time.   85

TRIN. I did not give the lie. Out o' your wits, and
hearing too? A pox o' your bottle! This can sack
and drinking do. A murrain° on your monster, and
the devil take your fingers!

CAL. Ha, ha, ha!   90

STE. Now, forward with your tale. — Prithee,
stand farther off.

CAL. Beat him enough. After a little time
I'll beat him too.

STE.   Stand farther. — Come, proceed.

CAL. Why, as I told thee, 'tis a custom with him
I' th' afternoon to sleep. There thou mayst brain
     him,   96
Having first seized his books, or with a log
Batter his skull, or paunch° him with a stake,
Or cut his weasand° with thy knife. Remember
First to possess his books, for without them   100
He's but a sot, as I am, nor hath not
One spirit to command. They all do hate him
As rootedly° as I. Burn but his books.
He has brave utensils° — for so he calls them —
Which, when he has a house, he'll deck withal.   105
And that most deeply to consider is
The beauty of his daughter. He himself
Calls her a nonpareil.° I never saw a woman
But only Sycorax my dam and she,
But she as far surpasseth Sycorax   110
As great'st does least.

STE.   Is it so brave a lass?

CAL. Aye, lord, she will become thy bed, I warrant,
And bring thee forth brave brood.

STE. Monster, I will kill this man. His daughter
and I will be King and Queen — save our Graces! —
and Trinculo and thyself shall be Viceroys. Dost
thou like the plot, Trinculo?   117

TRIN. Excellent.

STE. Give me thy hand. I am sorry I beat thee, but
while thou livest keep a good tongue in thy head.

CAL. Within this half-hour will he be asleep.
Wilt thou destroy him then?

STE.   Aye, on mine honor.

ARI. This will I tell my master.

CAL. Thou makest me merry, I am full of pleasure.
Let us be jocund. Will you troll° the catch°   126
You taught me but whilere?°

STE. At thy request, monster, I will do reason,°
any reason. — Come on, Trinculo, let us sing.
[*Sings.*]   "Flout° 'em and scout° 'em,
       And scout 'em and flout 'em.   131
       Thought is free."

CAL. That's not the tune.
     [ARIEL *plays the tune on a tabor° and pipe.*]

STE. What is this same?

TRIN. This is the tune of our catch, played by the
picture of Nobody.°   136

STE. If thou beest a man, show thyself in thy likeness. If thou beest a devil, take 't as thou list.

TRIN. Oh, forgive me my sins!

STE. He that dies pays all debts. I defy thee. Mercy
upon us!   141

CAL. Art thou afeard?

STE. No, monster, not I.

CAL. Be not afeard. The isle is full of noises,°
Sounds and sweet airs that give delight and hurt not.
Sometimes a thousand twangling instruments   146
Will hum about mine ears, and sometime voices
That, if I then had waked after long sleep,
Will make me sleep again. And then, in dreaming,
The clouds methought would open and show riches
Ready to drop upon me, that when I waked,   151
I cried to dream again.

STE. This will prove a brave kingdom to me,
where I shall have my music for nothing.

CAL. When Prospero is destroyed.   155

STE. That shall be by and by.° I remember the
story.

TRIN. The sound is going away. Let's follow it,
and after do our work.

STE. Lead, monster, we'll follow. I would I could
see this taborer, he lays it on.   161

TRIN. Wilt come? I'll follow, Stephano. [*Exeunt.*]

---

71. **pied ninny**: patched fool, because Trinculo as a jester wears motley, the "patched" or particolored dress of his profession. See Pl. 13c. **patch**: fool.   75. **quick freshes**: running springs of fresh water.   79. **stockfish**: dried cod, beaten to make it tender. 85. **give . . . lie**: call me a liar.   88. **murrain**: plague.   98. **paunch**: stab him in the belly.   99. **weasand**: windpipe.   103. **rootedly**: fixedly.   104. **utensils**: furnishings.   108. **nonpareil**: without an equal.

126. **troll**: sing. **catch**: See *T Night*, II.iii.60,n. | 127. **whilere**: just now.   128. **reason**: anything within reason.   130. **Flout**: mock. **scout**: deride.   133 **s.d., tabor**: small drum. See Pl. 13d. 136. **picture of Nobody**: i.e., by an invisible player. There is a picture of Nobody in a play called *Nobody and Some-body*, printed 1606. It is all head and no body, like Humpty Dumpty. 144. **noises**: music.   156. **by . . . by**: in the near future.

SCENE III. *Another part of the island.*

[*Enter* ALONSO, SEBASTIAN, ANTONIO, GONZALO, ADRIAN, FRANCISCO, *and others.*]

GON. By'r Lakin,° I can go no further, sir,
My old bones ache. Here's a maze trod, indeed,
Through forthrights and meanders!° By your patience,
I needs must rest me.

ALON.   Old lord, I cannot blame thee,
Who am myself attached with° weariness,   5
To the dulling of my spirits. Sit down and rest.
Even here I will put off my hope, and keep it
No longer for my flatterer. He is drowned
Whom thus we stray to find, and the sea mocks
Our frustrate° search on land. Well, let him go.   10

ANT. [*Aside to* SEBASTIAN] I am right glad that
    he's so out of hope.
Do not, for one repulse, forgo the purpose
That you resolved to effect.

SEB. [*Aside to* ANTONIO] The next advantage
Will we take throughly.°

ANT. [*Aside to* SEBASTIAN] Let it be tonight,
For now they are oppressed with travel, they   15
Will not, nor cannot, use such vigilance
As when they are fresh.

SEB. [*Aside to* ANTONIO] I say tonight. No more.
                    [*Solemn and strange music.*]

ALON. What harmony is this? — My good friends,
    hark!

GON. Marvelous sweet music!

[*Enter* PROSPERO *above, invisible. Enter several strange Shapes, bringing in a banquet.° They dance about it with gentle actions of salutation, and, inviting the King, etc., to eat, they depart.*]

ALON. Give us kind keepers, Heavens! — What
    were these?   20

SEB. A living drollery.° Now° I will believe
That there are unicorns, that in Arabia
There is one tree, the phoenix'° throne, one phoenix
At this hour reigning there.

ANT.   I'll believe both,
And what does else want credit,° come to me   25
And I'll be sworn 'tis true. Travelers ne'er did lie,
Though fools at home condemn 'em.

GON.   If in Naples
I should report this now, would they believe me?

If I should say I saw such islanders —
For, certes,° these are people of the island —   30
Who, though they are of monstrous shape, yet note
Their manners are more gentle-kind than of
Our human generation° you shall find
Many — nay, almost any.

PRO.   [*Aside*] Honest lord,   34
Thou hast said well, for some of you there present
Are worse than devils.

ALON.   I cannot too much muse°
Such shapes, such gesture, and such sound, expressing —
Although they want the use of tongue — a kind
Of excellent dumb discourse.

PRO.   [*Aside*] Praise in departing.°

FRAN. They vanished strangely.

SEB.   No matter, since   40
They have left their viands behind, for we have
    stomachs. —
Will 't please you taste of what is here?

ALON.   Not I.

GON. Faith, sir, you need not fear. When we were
    boys,
Who would believe that there were mountaineers
Dewlapped° like bulls, whose throats had hanging
    at 'em   45
Wallets of flesh? Or that there were such men
Whose heads stood in their breasts?° Which now
    we find
Each putter-out of five for one° will bring us
Good warrant of.

ALON.   I will stand to and feed,
Although my last. No matter, since I feel   50
The best is past. Brother, my lord the Duke,
Stand to, and do as we.

[*Thunder and lightning. Enter* ARIEL, *like a harpy,° claps his wings upon the table, and, with a quaint device,° the banquet vanishes.*]

ARI. You are three men of sin, whom Destiny —
That hath to instrument this lower world

---

30. **certes:** certainly.   33. **generation:** breed.   36. **muse:** wonder at.   39. **Praise in departing:** a proverb meaning "Don't give thanks for your entertainment until you see how it will end."   45. **Dewlapped:** having folds of loose skin hanging from the throat.   46–47. **men . . . breasts:** Sir Walter Raleigh in his account of Guiana (1595) noted "a nation of people whose heads appear not above their shoulders; which though it may be thought a mere fable, yet for mine own part I am resolved it is true, because every child in the provinces of Arromaia and Canuri affirms the same. They are called Ewaipanoma. They are reported to have their eyes in their shoulders, and their mouths in the middle of their breasts, and that a long train of hair groweth backward between their shoulders."   48. **putter-out . . . one:** In Shakespeare's time voyages to distant and strange ports were so risky that the traveler sometimes left a sum of money with a merchant at home on condition that he should receive five times the amount if he returned; if he did not, the premium was forfeited.   52 s.d., **harpy:** a foul creature, half bird of prey, half woman. This episode was suggested by an event in Virgil's *Aeneid* when the harpies seize and foul the food of Aeneas and his followers. **quaint device:** piece of ingenious stage machinery.

Sc. iii: 1. **By'r Lakin:** by Our Lady.   2–3. **Here's . . . meanders:** we have wandered as in a maze by straight paths (*forthrights*) and winding paths (*meanders*).   5. **attached with:** overcome by; lit., arrested.   10. **frustrate:** vain.   14. **throughly:** thoroughly.   19 s.d., **banquet:** light refreshments, such as fruit and jellies.   21. **drollery:** puppet show.   21–27. **Now . . . 'em:** i.e., after this we can believe any fantastic traveler's yarn.   23. **phoenix:** a mythical bird. According to the legend only one phoenix was alive at a time. It lived for five hundred years. Then it built itself a nest of spices, which were set alight by the rapid beating of its wings. From the ashes a new phoenix was born.   25. **want credit:** is not believed.

And what is in 't° — the never-surfeited° sea   55
Hath caused to belch up you. And on this island,
Where man doth not inhabit — you 'mongst men
Being most unfit to live. I have made you mad,
And even with suchlike valor men hang and drown
Their proper° selves.

    [ALONZO, SEBASTIAN, *etc., draw their swords.*]
         You fools! I and my fellows   60
Are ministers of Fate. The elements
Of whom your swords are tempered may as well
Wound the loud winds, or with bemocked-at stabs
Kill the still-closing° waters, as diminish
One dowle° that's in my plume.° My fellow minis-
    ters   65
Are like invulnerable. If you could hurt,
Your swords are now too massy° for your strengths,
And will not be uplifted. But remember —
For that's my business to you — that you three
From Milan did supplant good Prospero,   70
Exposed unto the sea, which hath requit° it,
Him and his innocent child. For which foul deed
The powers, delaying not forgetting, have
Incensed the seas and shores — yea, all the crea-
    tures —
Against your peace. Thee of thy son, Alonso,   75
They have bereft, and do pronounce by me
Lingering perdition° — worse than any death
Can be at once — shall step by step attend
You and your ways. Whose wraths to guard you
    from —
Which here, in this most desolate isle, else falls   80
Upon your heads — is nothing but° heart sorrow
And a clear° life ensuing.
[*He vanishes in thunder; then, to soft music, enter
the Shapes again, and dance, with mocks° and
mows,° and carrying out the table.*]
    PRO. Bravely the figure of this harpy hast thou
Performed, my Ariel, a grace it had, devouring.°
Of my instruction hast thou nothing bated°   85
In what thou hadst to say. So, with good life°
And observation° strange,° my meaner ministers°
Their several kinds° have done. My high charms
    work,
And these mine enemies are all knit up°
In their distractions.° They now are in my power,

And in these fits I leave them while I visit   91
Young Ferdinand — whom they suppose is
    drowned —
And his and mine loved darling.   [*Exit above.*]
    GON. I' the name of something holy, sir, why stand
    you
In this strange stare?
    ALON.   Oh, it is monstrous, monstrous!   95
Methought the billows spoke, and told me of it,
The winds did sing it to me, and the thunder,
That deep and dreadful organ pipe, pronounced
The name of Prosper. It did bass my trespass.°
Therefore my son i' th' ooze is bedded, and   100
I'll seek him deeper than e'er plummet° sounded,
And with him there lie mudded.   [*Exit.*]
    SEB.   But one fiend at a time,
I'll fight their legions o'er.
    ANT.   I'll be thy second.
        [*Exeunt* SEBASTIAN *and* ANTONIO.]
    GON. All three of them are desperate. Their great
    guilt,
Like poison given to work a great time after,   105
Now 'gins to bite the spirits. I do beseech you
That are of suppler joints, follow them swiftly,
And hinder them from what this ecstasy°
May now provoke them to.
    ADR.   Follow, I pray you. [*Exeunt.*]

Act IV

SCENE I. *Before* PROSPERO'S *cell.*

[*Enter* PROSPERO, FERDINAND, *and* MIRANDA.]
    PRO. If I have too austerely punished you,
Your compensation makes amends. For I
Have given you here a third° of mine own life,
Or that for which I live, who once again
I tender° to thy hand. All thy vexations   5
Were but my trials of thy love, and thou
Hast strangely° stood the test. Here, afore Heaven,
I ratify this my rich gift. O Ferdinand,
Do not smile at me that I boast her off,°
For thou shalt find she will outstrip all praise   10
And make it halt° behind her.
    FER.   I do believe it
Against an oracle.°

53–55. **Destiny . . . in 't:** Destiny (Providence), which uses this world below and its powers as its instrument.   55. **never-surfeited:** never overfull. A surfeit is an excess of food. Even the sea, which can retain most things, cannot stomach Alonso and his fellow sinners.   60. **proper:** own.   64. **still-closing:** always closing up; i.e., which cannot be wounded.   65. **dowle:** downy feather. **plume:** wing.   67. **massy:** heavy.   71. **requit:** paid back.   77. **perdition:** destruction.   81. **is . . . but:** i.e., only repentance will guard you from destruction.   82. **clear:** innocent. **s.d., mocks:** mocking gestures. **mows:** grimaces.   84. **grace . . . devouring:** the action of devouring was splendidly (*bravely*) performed.   85. **bated:** abated, left out.   86. **with . . . life:** realistically.   87. **observation:** obedience. **strange:** unusual. **meaner ministers:** lesser servants.   88. **several kinds:** particular tasks.   89. **knit up:** entangled.   90. **distractions:** fits of madness.

99. **bass my trespass:** proclaim my sin in a deep note.   101. **plummet:** the lead weight at the end of a cord used by sailors to discover the depth of the water.   108. **ecstasy:** mad fit. See *Haml,* III.iv.137–44.

    Act IV, Sc. i: 3. third: i.e., a great part of.   5. **tender:** hand over.   7. **strangely:** exceptionally.   9. **boast . . . off:** boast about her.   11. **halt:** come limping; i.e., she will excel all praise.   12. **Against an oracle:** i.e., even if a god had said the contrary.

PRO. **Then,** as my gift, and thine own acquisition
Worthily purchased, take my daughter. But
If thou dost break her virgin knot before   15
All sanctimonious° ceremonies may
With full and holy rite be ministered,
No sweet aspersion° shall the Heavens let fall
To make this contract grow;° but barren hate,
Sour-eyed disdain, and discord shall bestrew   20
The union of your bed with weeds so loathly
That you shall hate it both. Therefore take heed,
As Hymen's° lamps shall light you.

FER.   As I hope
For quiet days, fair issue,° and long life,
With such love as 'tis now, the murkiest den,   25
The most opportune place, the strong'st suggestion°
Our worser genius° can, shall never melt
Mine honor into lust, to take away
The edge of that day's celebration
When I shall think or Phoebus' steeds are foundered,
Or Night kept chained below.°

PRO.   Fairly spoke.   31
Sit, then, and talk with her, she is thine own.
What, Ariel! My industrious servant, Ariel!

[Enter ARIEL.*]*

ARI. What would my potent master? Here I am.

PRO. Thou and thy meaner fellows your last
    service   35
Did worthily perform, and I must use you
In such another trick. Go bring the rabble,
O'er whom I give thee power, here to this place.
Incite them to quick motion, for I must
Bestow upon the eyes of this young couple   40
Some vanity° of mine art. It is my promise,
And they expect it from me.

ARI.   Presently?°

PRO. Aye, with a twink.°

ARI. Before you can say, " come," and " go,"
And breathe twice and cry, " so, so,"   45
Each one, tripping on his toe,
Will be here with mop° and mow.
Do you love me, master? No?   48

PRO. Dearly, my delicate Ariel. Do not approach
Till thou dost hear me call.

ARI.   Well, I conceive.° *[Exit.]*

PRO. Look thou be true. Do not give dalliance°
Too much the rein. The strongest oaths are straw
To the fire i' the blood. Be more abstemious,
Or else, good night your vow!

FER.   I warrant you, sir,

The white cold virgin snow upon my heart   55
Abates the ardor of my liver.°

PRO.   Well.
Now come, my Ariel! Bring a corollary°
Rather than want° a spirit. Appear, and pertly!°
No tongue! All eyes! Be silent.   *[Soft music.]*

[Enter IRIS.°*]*

IRIS. Ceres,° most bounteous lady, thy rich leas°
Of wheat, rye, barley, vetches, oats, and pease;   61
Thy turfy mountains, where live nibbling sheep,
And flat meads° thatched with stover,° them to
    keep;
Thy banks with pioned and twilled brims,°
Which spongy April at thy hest° betrims°   65
To make cold nymphs chaste crowns; and thy
    broom° groves,
Whose shadow the dismissed° bachelor loves,
Being lasslorn;° thy pole-clipped° vineyard;
And thy sea marge,° sterile and rocky-hard,
Where thou thyself dost air — the Queen o' the Sky,°
Whose watery arch° and messenger am I,   71
Bids thee leave these, and with her sovereign grace,
Here on this grassplot, in this very place,
To come and sport. — Her peacocks° fly amain.°
Approach, rich Ceres, her to entertain.   75

[Enter CERES.*]*

CER. Hail, many-colored messenger, that ne'er
Dost disobey the wife of Jupiter;
Who, with thy saffron° wings, upon my flowers
Diffusest honey drops, refreshing showers,
And with each end of thy blue bow dost crown   80
My bosky° acres and my unshrubbed down,°
Rich scarf° to my proud earth. — Why hath thy
    Queen
Summoned me hither, to this short-grassed green?

IRIS. A contract of true love to celebrate,
And some donation° freely to estate°   85
On the blest lovers.

CER.   Tell me, heavenly bow,

56. **liver:** passion. The liver was regarded as the seat of passion.
57. **corollary:** excess; i.e., too many rather than too few.
58. **want:** be without. **pertly:** briskly.   59 s.d., **Enter Iris:** Prospero now produces a little wedding masque in honor not only of the lovers, Ferdinand and Miranda, but as a compliment to the Princess Elizabeth and her bridegroom. See *Temp* Intro. p. 1471a and Gen. Intro. p. 47b. **Iris:** the female messenger of the gods, also the personification of the rainbow.   60. **Ceres:** goddess of corn and plenty. **leas:** arable lands.   63. **meads:** meadows. **thatched . . . stover:** covered over with grass for fodder.
64. **pioned . . . brims:** a difficult phrase, much disputed and emended. The likeliest explanation is that *pioned* means dug, and *twilled*, heaped up; i.e., with high banks. 65. **hest:** command. **betrims:** trims with wild flowers, especially kingcups, a kind of buttercup that grows by streams. 66. **broom:** a shrub with yellow flowers. 67. **dismissed:** rejected. 68. **lasslorn:** without his girl. **pole-clipped:** poles embraced by vines. 69. **sea marge:** seashore. 70. **Queen . . . Sky:** the goddess Juno, wife of Jupiter.
71. **watery arch:** i.e., the rainbow. 74. **peacocks:** birds sacred to Juno. **amain:** swiftly. 78. **saffron:** yellow. 81. **bosky:** wooded. **unshrubbed down:** rolling open country, without shrubs.
82. **scarf:** adornment.   85. **donation:** present. **estate:** donate

16. **sanctimonious:** religious.   18. **aspersion:** blessing; lit., sprinkling.   19. **grow:** prosper.   23. **Hymen:** the god of marriage.   24. **issue:** children.   26. **suggestion:** temptation. 27. **worser genius:** evil angel.   30–31. **or . . . below:** either the horses of the Sun have fallen or Night has been imprisoned; i.e., my wedding day, when night seems never to come.   41. **vanity:** display.   42. **Presently:** at once.   43. **twink:** the twinkling of an eye.   47. **mop:** grimace.   50. **conceive:** understand. 51. **dalliance:** fondling.

If Venus or her son, as thou dost know,
Do now attend the Queen? Since they did plot
The means that dusky Dis° my daughter got,
Her and her blind boy's° scandaled° company 90
I have forsworn.

IRIS. Of her society
Be not afraid. I met Her Deity
Cutting the clouds towards Paphos,° and her son
Dove-drawn° with her. Here thought they to have
done
Some wanton charm upon this man and maid, 95
Whose vows are, that no bedright shall be paid
Till Hymen's torch° be lighted. But in vain,
Mars's hot minion° is returned again.
Her waspish-headed° son has broke his arrows,
Swears he will shoot no more, but play with spar-
rows, 100
And be a boy right out.

CER. High'st Queen of state,
Great Juno, comes. I know her by her gait.

[Enter JUNO.]

JUNO. How does my bounteous sister? Go with
me
To bless this twain, that they may prosperous be,
And honored in their issue. 105

[They sing.]

JUNO. "Honor, riches, marriage blessing,
Long continuance, and increasing,
Hourly joys be still° upon you!
Juno sings her blessings on you."

CER. "Earth's increase, foison° plenty, 110
Barns and garners never empty,
Vines with clustering bunches growing,
Plants with goodly burden bowing,
Spring come to you at the farthest
In the very end of harvest!° 115
Scarcity and want shall shun you,
Ceres' blessing so is on you."

FER. This is a most majestic vision, and
Harmonious charmingly. May I be bold
To think these spirits?

PRO. Spirits which by mine art 120
I have from their confines° called to enact
My present fancies.°

FER. Let me live here ever.

So rare a wondered° father and a wise
Makes this place Paradise.

[JUNO and CERES whisper, and send IRIS
on employment.]

PRO. Sweet, now silence!
Juno and Ceres whisper seriously, 125
There's something else to do. Hush, and be mute,
Or else our spell is marred.

IRIS. You nymphs, called Naiads,° of the win-
dring° brooks,
With your sedged° crowns and ever-harmless looks,
Leave your crisp° channels, and on this green land
Answer your summons. Juno does command. 131
Come, temperate° nymphs, and help to celebrate
A contract of true love. Be not too late.

[Enter certain NYMPHS.]

You sunburned sicklemen,° of August weary,
Come hither from the furrow, and be merry. 135
Make holiday, your rye-straw hats put on,
And these fresh nymphs encounter every one
In country footing.°

[Enter certain REAPERS, properly habited. They join
with the NYMPHS in a graceful dance, towards the
end whereof PROSPERO starts suddenly, and speaks.
After which, to a strange, hollow, and confused
noise, they heavily° vanish.]

PRO. [Aside] I had forgot that foul conspiracy
Of the beast Caliban and his confederates 140
Against my life. The minute of their plot
Is almost come. [To the SPIRITS] Well done! Avoid,°
no more!

FER. This is strange. Your father's in some passion
That works him strongly.

MIRA. Never till this day
Saw I him touched with anger so distempered.°

PRO. You do look, my son, in a movèd sort,° 146
As if you were dismayed. Be cheerful, sir.
Our revels now are ended. These our actors,
As I foretold you, were all spirits, and
Are melted into air, into thin air. 150
And, like the baseless fabric° of this vision,
The cloud-capped towers, the gorgeous palaces,
The solemn temples, the great globe itself—
Yea, all which it inherit — shall dissolve
And, like this insubstantial pageant faded, 155
Leave not a rack° behind. We are such stuff
As dreams are made on, and our little life
Is rounded° with a sleep. Sir, I am vexed.
Bear with my weakness, my old brain is troubled.

89. dusky Dis: Pluto, god of the underworld, and so dark. He
seized Ceres' daughter Persephone and carried her down to his
kingdom. 90. blind boy: Cupid. scandaled: scandalous. 93. Paphos: in Sicily, a town sacred to Venus. 94. Dove-drawn: in a
chariot drawn by doves. 97. Hymen's torch: The torches of the
wedding god were lit to escort bride and bridegroom to bed.
98. Mars's . . . minion: Mars' lusty darling; i.e., Venus.
99. waspish-headed: quick-tempered. 108. still: always.
110. foison: bounteous harvest. 114–15. Spring . . . harvest:
may spring follow autumn; i.e., may there be no bitterness of
winter in your lives. Cf. Ant & Cleo, V.ii.86–88 for a similar
image. 121. confines: places of confinement. 122. fancies:
devices of my imagination.

123. wondered: wonderful. 128. Naiads: water nymphs. win-
dring: wandering, winding. 129. sedged: covered with sedge, a
kind of water grass. 130. crisp: curled, rippling. 132. temperate:
chaste. 134. sicklemen: reapers, who cut the wheat with sickles.
138. footing: dancing. s.d., heavily: sorrowfully. 142. Avoid: be
gone. 145. distempered: disturbed. 146. moved sort: as if you
were distressed. 151. baseless fabric: unreal stuff. 156. rack:
cloud. 158. rounded: completed; i.e., life is but a moment of
consciousness in an everlasting sleep.

Be not disturbed with my infirmity. 160
If you be pleased, retire into my cell,
And there repose. A turn or two I'll walk,
To still my beating° mind.
  FER. & MIRA.   We wish your peace. [*Exeunt.*]
  PRO. Come with a thought. I thank thee, Ariel.
    Come.
        [*Enter ARIEL.*]
  ARI. Thy thoughts I cleave to. What's thy pleasure?
  PRO.   Spirit, 165
We must prepare to meet with Caliban.
  ARI. Aye, my commander. When I presented°
    Ceres,
I thought to have told thee of it, but I feared
Lest I might anger thee.
  PRO. Say again, where didst thou leave these
    varlets?° 170
  ARI. I told you, sir, they were red-hot with drinking,
So full of valor that they smote the air
For breathing in their faces, beat the ground
For kissing of their feet, yet always bending°
Toward their project. Then I beat my tabor. 175
At which, like unbacked° colts, they pricked their
    ears,
Advanced their eyelids, lifted up their noses
As° they smelt music. So I charmed their ears,
That, calflike, they my lowing followed through
Toothed briers, sharp furzes,° pricking goss,° and
    thorns 180
Which entered their frail shins. At last I left them
I' the filthy-mantled° pool beyond your cell,
There dancing up to the chins, that the foul lake
O'erstunk their feet.
  PRO.   This was well done, my bird.
Thy shape invisible retain thou still. 185
The trumpery° in my house, go bring it hither,
For stale° to catch these thieves.
  ARI.   I go, I go. [*Exit.*]
  PRO. A devil, a born devil, on whose nature
Nurture° can never stick, on whom my pains,
Humanely taken, all, all lost, quite lost. 190
And as with age his body uglier grows,
So his mind cankers.° I will plague them all,
Even to roaring.
    [*Re-enter ARIEL, loaden with glistering° apparel,
        etc.*]
    Come, hang them on this line.°

[*PROSPERO and ARIEL remain, invisible. Enter
CALIBAN, STEPHANO, and TRINCULO, all wet.*]
  CAL. Pray you, tread softly, that the blind mole
    may not
Hear a footfall. We now are near his cell. 195
  STE. Monster, your fairy, which you say is a harmless fairy, has done little better than played the jack°
with us.
  TRIN. Monster, I do smell all horse piss, at which
my nose is in great indignation. 200
  STE. So is mine. Do you hear, monster? If I should
take a displeasure against you, look you ——
  TRIN. Thou wert but a lost monster.
  CAL. Good my lord, give me thy favor still.
Be patient, for the prize I'll bring thee to 205
Shall hoodwink this mischance.° Therefore speak
    softly.
All's hushed as midnight yet.
  TRIN. Aye, but to lose our bottles in the pool ——
  STE. There is not only disgrace and dishonor in
that, monster, but an infinite loss. 210
  TRIN. That's more to me than my wetting. Yet
this is your harmless fairy, monster.
  STE. I will fetch off° my bottle, though I be o'er
ears° for my labor. 214
  CAL. Prithee, my King, be quiet. See'st thou here,
This is the mouth o' the cell. No noise, and enter.
Do that good mischief which may make this island
Thine own forever, and I, thy Caliban,
For aye thy footlicker.
  STE. Give me thy hand. I do begin to have bloody
thoughts. 221
  TRIN. O King Stephano!° O peer! O worthy
Stephano! Look what a wardrobe here is for thee!
  CAL. Let it alone, thou fool, it is but trash.
  TRIN. Oh ho, monster! We know what belongs to
a frippery.° O King Stephano! 226
  STE. Put off that gown, Trinculo. By this hand,
I'll have that gown.
  TRIN. Thy Grace shall have it.
  CAL. The dropsy drown this fool! What do you
    mean 230
To dote thus on such luggage?° Let 's alone,
And do the murder first. If he awake
From toe to crown he'll fill our skins with pinches,
Make us strange stuff. 234
  STE. Be you quiet, monster. Mistress° line, is not
this my jerkin? Now is the jerkin under the line.
Now, jerkin, you are like to lose your hair and prove
a bald jerkin.

163. beating: throbbing. Cf. I.ii.176. 167. presented: either introduced the masques or acted the part of Ceres. There is, however, very little time for a change of costume between Ariel's exit at l. 50 and Ceres' entry at l. 75. 170. varlets: knaves. 174. bending: inclining. 176. unbacked: never saddled. 178. As: as if. 180. furzes: See I.i.72,n. goss: gorse. 182. filthy-mantled: covered with scum. 186. trumpery: cheap finery. 187. stale: bait. 189. Nurture: education. 192. cankers: grows malignant. 193 s.d., glistering: glittering. line: lime tree.

197. jack: knave. 206. hoodwink . . . mischance: blindfold this misfortune; i.e., make us forget it. 213. fetch off: rescue. 214. o'er ears: up to my ears in the pond. 222. O . . . Stephano: The sight of all the clothes reminds Trinculo of the old ballad "King Stephen was a worthy peer." See *Oth*, II.iii.92-99. 226. frippery: secondhand-clothes shop. 231. luggage: baggage, which will hinder them. 235-40. Mistress . . . Grace: These lines have mystified editors, and indeed elaborate Elizabethan

TRIN. Do, do. We steal by line and level, an 't like
your Grace.   240

STE. I thank thee for that jest — here's a garment
for 't. Wit shall not go unrewarded while I am King
of this country. "Steal by line and level" is an excellent pass of pate° — there's another garment for 't.

TRIN. Monster, come, put some lime° upon   246
your fingers, and away with the rest.

CAL. I will have none on 't. We shall lose our time,
And all be turned to barnacles,° or to apes
With foreheads villainous low.   250

STE. Monster, lay to your fingers. Help to bear
this away where my hogshead of wine is, or I'll turn
you out of my kingdom. Go to, carry this.

TRIN. And this.

STE. Aye, and this.   255

[*A noise of hunters heard. Enter divers* SPIRITS, *in
shape of dogs and hounds, hunting them about,*
PROSPERO *and* ARIEL *setting them on.*]

PRO. Hey, Mountain, hey!

ARI. Silver! There it goes, Silver!

PRO. Fury, Fury! There, Tyrant,° there! Hark,
hark!

[CALIBAN, STEPHANO, *and* TRINCULO *are driven out.*]

Go charge my goblins that they grind their joints
With dry convulsions. Shorten up their sinews   260
With agèd cramps,° and more pinch-spotted make
     them
Then pard° or cat-o'-mountain.°

ARI.   Hark, they roar!

PRO. Let them be hunted soundly. At this hour
Lie at my mercy all mine enemies.
Shortly shall all my labors end, and thou   265
Shalt have the air at freedom. For a little
Follow, and do me service.   [*Exeunt.*]

jokes, especially when made by a half-drunk butler, are not always easy to follow. Stephano begins by addressing the lime tree
as "Mistress Line" as if he were talking to the dealer in an old-
clothes shop. He appeals to her to decide whether the jerkin is his
or Trinculo's. Having taken the jerkin for himself, he then puns
on "under the line" (i.e., south of the Equator), where the various skin diseases common to long voyages in the tropics caused
hair to fall out. Trinculo caps the remark by a further pun on
"line and level"; i.e., "on the square," lit., by the bricklayer's
instruments for ensuring perpendicular and horizontal exactness.
245. pass of pate: sally of wit.   **246. lime:** birdlime, to make
them sticky, because Caliban disgustedly drops the garments.
249. barnacles: tree geese. It was believed, even by serious bot-
anists, that from the barnacles, which grow on rotten wood im-
mersed in sea water, emerged creatures which grew into birds
like geese.   **256–58. Mountain . . . Silver . . . Fury . . . Tyrant:**
the names of the hounds.   **261. aged cramps:** the cramps which
come with old age.   **262. pard:** leopard. **cat-o'-mountain:** mountain cat.

Act V

SCENE I. *Before the cell of* PROSPERO.

[*Enter* PROSPERO *in his magic robes, and* ARIEL.]

PRO. Now does my project gather to a head.
My charms crack not,° my spirits obey, and Time
Goes upright with his carriage.° How's the day?

ARI. On the sixth hour, at which time, my lord,
You said our work should cease.

PRO.   I did say so   5
When first I raised the tempest. Say, my spirit,
How fares the King and 's followers?

ARI.   Confined together
In the same fashion as you gave in charge,
Just as you left them — all prisoners, sir,
In the line grove° which weather-fends° your cell.
They cannot budge till your release. The King,   11
His brother, and yours abide all three distracted,
And the remainder mourning over them,
Brimful of sorrow and dismay. But chiefly
Him that you termed, sir, "The good old lord, Gon-
     zalo."   15
His tears run down his beard like winter's drops
From eaves of reeds.° Your charm so strongly works
     'em
That if you now beheld them, your affections
Would become tender.

PRO.   Dost thou think so, spirit?

ARI. Mine would, sir, were I human.

PRO.   And mine shall.   20
Hast thou, which art but air, a touch, a feeling
Of their afflictions, and shall not myself,
One of their kind, that relish° all as sharply,
Passion° as they, be kindlier moved than thou art?
Though with their high wrongs I am struck to the
     quick,   25
Yet with my nobler reason 'gainst my fury
Do I take part. The rarer action is
In virtue than in vengeance.° They being penitent,
The sole drift° of my purpose doth extend
Not a frown further. Go release them, Ariel.   30
My charms I'll break, their senses I'll restore,
And they shall be themselves.

ARI.   I'll fetch them, sir.   [*Exit.*]

PRO. Ye elves of hills, brooks, standing lakes, and
     groves,
And ye that on the sands with printless foot°
Do chase the ebbing Neptune° and do fly him   35

Act V, Sc. i: 2. crack not: do not break down.   **2–3. Time . . .
carriage:** Time bears his burden without stooping, because
it has now grown so light.   **10. line grove:** grove of lime trees.
weather-fends: protects from the weather.   **17. eaves of reeds:** a
thatched roof.   **23. relish:** feel.   **24. Passion:** suffer emotion.
27–28. rarer . . . vengeance: it is a finer action to be self-controlled
than to take vengeance.   **29. drift:** intention.   **34. printless
foot:** without leaving a footprint.   **35. ebbing Neptune:** i.e., the
outgoing tide.

When he comes back; you demipuppets° that
By moonshine do the green sour° ringlets° make,
Whereof the ewe not bites; and you whose pastime
Is to make midnight mushrooms° that rejoice
To hear the solemn curfew,° by whose aid — 40
Weak masters though ye be — I have bedimmed
The noontide sun, called forth the mutinous winds,
And 'twixt the green sea and the azured vault°
Set roaring war. To the dread rattling thunder
Have I given fire, and rifted° Jove's stout oak 45
With his own bolt. The strong-based promontory
Have I made shake, and by the spurs° plucked up
The pine and cedar. Graves at my command
Have waked their sleepers, oped, and let 'em forth
By my so potent art. But this rough magic 50
I here abjure, and when I have required
Some heavenly music — which even now I do —
To work mine end upon their senses, that
This airy charm is for, I'll break my staff,
Bury it certain fathoms in the earth, 55
And deeper than did ever plummet° sound
I'll drown my book.° [Solemn music.]
[Re-enter ARIEL before; then ALONSO, with a frantic
gesture, attended by GONZALO; SEBASTIAN and
ANTONIO in like manner, attended by ADRIAN
and FRANCISCO. They all enter the circle which
PROSPERO had made, and there stand charmed,
which PROSPERO observing, speaks:]
A solemn air,° and the best comforter
To an unsettled fancy, cure thy brains,
Now useless, boiled° within thy skull! There stand,
For you are spell-stopped. 61
Holy Gonzalo, honorable man,
Mine eyes, even sociable° to the show of thine,
Fall° fellowly° drops. The charm dissolves apace,°
And as the morning steals upon the night, 65
Melting the darkness, so their rising senses
Begin to chase the ignorant fumes° that mantle°
Their clearer reason. O good Gonzalo,
My true preserver, and a loyal sir
To him thou follow'st! I will pay thy graces 70
Home° both in word and deed. Most cruelly
Didst thou, Alonso, use me and my daughter.
Thy brother was a furtherer in the act.

Thou art pinched for 't now, Sebastian. Flesh and
  blood,
You, brother mine, that entertained ambition, 75
Expelled remorse° and nature, who with Sebas-
  tian —
Whose inward pinches therefore are most strong —
Would here have killed your King, I do forgive thee,
Unnatural though thou art. Their understanding
Begins to swell, and the approaching tide 80
Will shortly fill the reasonable shore°
That now lies foul and muddy. Not one of them
That yet looks on me, or would know me. Ariel,
Fetch me the hat and rapier in my cell.
I will discase° me, and myself present 85
As I was sometime Milan.° Quickly, spirit.
Thou shalt ere long be free.
  ARI. [Sings and helps to attire him.]
    "Where the bee sucks, there suck I.
      In a cowslip's bell I lie,
      There I couch° when owls do cry. 90
    On the bat's back I do fly
      After summer merrily.
    Merrily, merrily shall I live now
    Under the blossom that hangs on the bough."
  PRO. Why, that's my dainty Ariel! I shall miss
    thee, 95
But yet thou shalt have freedom. So, so, so.°
To the King's ship, invisible as thou art.
There shalt thou find the mariners asleep
Under the hatches. The master and the boatswain
Being awake, enforce them to this place, 100
And presently, I prithee.
  ARI. I drink the air before me, and return
Or ere your pulse twice beat. [Exit.]
  GON. All torment, trouble, wonder, and amaze-
    ment
Inhabits here. Some heavenly power guide us 105
Out of this fearful country!
  PRO. Behold, Sir King,
The wrongèd Duke of Milan, Prospero.
For more assurance that a living prince
Does now speak to thee, I embrace thy body,
And to thee and thy company I bid 110
A hearty welcome.
  ALON. Whether thou be'st he or no,
Or some enchanted trifle° to abuse° me,
As late I have been, I not know. Thy pulse
Beats, as of° flesh and blood, and since I saw thee,
The affliction of my mind amends, with which, 115
I fear, a madness held me. This must crave —

36. demipuppets: tiny creatures, half the size of a puppet.
37. sour: i.e., unacceptable to the cattle. ringlets: fairy rings,
circles of grass of a darker green often seen in English meadows,
supposed to be caused by the fairies dancing in a ring. 39. midnight mushrooms: As mushrooms grow in a single night, they
were thought to be the work of fairies. 40. curfew: rung at
9 P.M. to warn people to go indoors. Thereafter the fairies can
work without interruption. 43. azured vault: blue sky.
45. rifted: split. 47. spurs: roots. 56. plummet: See III.iii.101,n.
57. book: i.e., of magic spells. 58. air: musical air. 60. boiled:
boiling. Cf. MND, V.i.4, "Lovers and madmen have such seething brains." 63. sociable: of fellow feeling. 64. Fall: let fall.
fellowly: in sympathy. apace: quickly. 67. ignorant fumes:
mists of ignorance. mantle: cloak. 70–71. pay . . . Home: reward your kind deeds fully.

76. remorse: pity. 81. reasonable shore: shore of reason; i.e.,
sanity is beginning to flow back like the incoming tide. 85. dis-
case: remove my outer garment. Prospero is still in his magic
robe and so not recognized by his former associates. 86. As . . .
Milan: as I was when I was Duke of Milan. 90. couch: lie.
96. So, so, so: "so," used thus, often indicates movement. Cf.
Lear, III.vi.90. 112. enchanted trifle: hallucination caused by
enchantment. abuse: deceive. 114. as of: as if composed of.

An if this be at all° — a most strange story.
Thy dukedom I resign, and do entreat
Thou pardon me my wrongs.° — But how should
    Prospero
Be living and be here?

PRO.   First, noble friend,   120
Let me embrace thine age, whose honor cannot
Be measured or confined.

GON.   Whether this be
Or be not, I'll not swear.

PRO.   You do yet taste
Some subtilties° o' the isle, that will not let you
Believe things certain. Welcome, my friends all!
[*Aside to* SEBASTIAN *and* ANTONIO] But you, my
    brace of lords, were I so minded,   126
I here could pluck His Highness' frown upon you,
And justify you traitors. At this time
I will tell no tales.

SEB.   [*Aside*] The Devil speaks in him.

PRO.   No.
For you, most wicked sir, whom to call brother   130
Would even infect my mouth, I do forgive
Thy rankest fault — all of them — and require
My dukedom of thee, which perforce I know
Thou must restore.

ALON.   If thou be'st Prospero,
Give us particulars of thy preservation —   135
How thou hast met us here, who three hours
    since
Were wrecked upon this shore, where I have lost —
How sharp the point of this remembrance is! —
My dear son Ferdinand.

PRO.   I am woe for't,° sir.

ALON. Irreparable is the loss, and Patience   140
Says it is past her cure.

PRO.   I rather think
You have not sought her help of whose soft grace
For the like loss I have her sovereign° aid,
And rest myself content.

ALON.   You the like loss!

PRO. As great to me as late, and, supportable   145
To make the dear loss, have I means much weaker
Than you may call to comfort you, for I
Have lost my daughter.

ALON.   A daughter?
O Heavens, that they were living both in Naples,
The King and Queen there! That they were, I wish
Myself were mudded in that oozy bed   151
Where my son lies. When did you lose your daugh-
    ter?

PRO. In this last tempest. I perceive these lords
At this encounter do so much admire°
That they devour their reason, and scarce think   155

Their eyes do offices of truth,° their words
Are natural breath. But howsoe'er you have
Been jostled from your senses, know for certain
That I am Prospero, and that very Duke
Which was thrust forth of Milan, who most strangely
Upon this shore where you were wrecked was
    landed,   161
To be the lord on 't. No more yet of this,
For 'tis a chronicle of day by day,
Not a relation for a breakfast, nor
Befitting this first meeting. Welcome, sir.   165
This cell's my Court. Here have I few attendants,
And subjects none abroad. Pray you look in.
My dukedom since you have given me again,
I will requite° you with as good a thing,
At least bring forth a wonder to content ye   170
As much as me my dukedom.
[*Here* PROSPERO *discovers*° FERDINAND *and* MIRANDA
    playing at chess.]

MIRA. Sweet lord, you play me false.

FER.   No, my dear'st love,
I would not for the world.

MIRA. Yes, for a score of kingdoms you should
    wrangle,
And I would call it fair play.

ALON.   If this prove   175
A vision of the island, one dear son
Shall I twice lose.

SEB.   A most high miracle!

FER. Though the seas threaten, they are merciful.
I have cursed them without cause.   [*Kneels.*]

ALON.   Now all the blessings
Of a glad father compass thee about!   180
Arise, and say how thou camest here.

MIRA.   Oh, wonder!
How many goodly creatures are there here!
How beauteous mankind is! Oh, brave new world,
That has such people in 't!

PRO.   'Tis new to thee.

ALON. What is this maid with whom thou wast at
    play?   185
Your eld'st° acquaintance cannot be three hours.
Is she the goddess that hath severed us,
And brought us thus together?

FER.   Sir, she is mortal,
But by immortal Providence she's mine.
I chose her when I could not ask my father   190
For his advice, nor thought I had one. She
Is daughter to this famous Duke of Milan,
Of whom so often I have heard renown
But never saw before, of whom I have
Received a second life, and second father   195
This lady makes him to me.

ALON.   I am hers.

---

117. **An . . . all**: if this is really true.   119. **my wrongs**: the
wrongs which I have committed.   123–24. **You . . . subtilties**:
you still have the taste of the magic nature.   139. **woe for't**: sorry
for it.   143. **sovereign**: all-powerful.   154. **admire**: wonder.

156. **offices of truth**: true service.   169. **requite**: pay back.
171 **s.d., discovers**: reveals by drawing back the curtain.
186. **eld'st**: longest.

But oh, how oddly will it sound that I
Must ask my child° forgiveness!
    PRO.   There, sir, stop.
Let us not burden our remembrances with
A heaviness that's gone.
    GON.   I have inly wept,   200
Or should have spoke ere this. Look down, you gods,
And on this couple drop a blessèd crown!
For it is you that have chalked forth° the way
Which brought us hither.
    ALON.   I say Amen, Gonzalo!
    GON. Was Milan thrust from Milan, that his issue
Should become Kings of Naples? Oh, rejoice   206
Beyond a common joy! And set it down
With gold on lasting pillars. In one voyage
Did Claribel her husband find at Tunis
And Ferdinand, her brother, found a wife   210
Where he himself was lost, Prospero his dukedom
In a poor isle, and all of us ourselves
When no man was his own.
    ALON. [*To* FERDINAND *and* MIRANDA] Give me your
      hands.
Let grief and sorrow still embrace° his heart
That doth not wish you joy!
    GON.   Be it so! Amen!   215
[*Re-enter* ARIEL, *with the* MASTER *and* BOATSWAIN
      amazedly° *following.*]
Oh, look, sir, look, sir! Here is more of us.
I prophesied if a gallows were on land,
This fellow could not drown.° Now, blasphemy,°
That swear'st grace o'erboard,° not an oath on
    shore?   219
Hast thou no mouth by land? What is the news?
    BOATS. The best news is that we have safely found
Our King and company. The next, our ship —
Which, but three glasses since, we gave out split —
Is tight and yare and bravely rigged as when
We first put out to sea.
    ARI. [*Aside to* PROSPERO] Sir, all this service   225
Have I done since I went.
    PRO. [*Aside to* ARIEL] My tricksy° spirit!
    ALON. These are not natural events, they
    strengthen
From strange to stranger. Say, how came you hither?
    BOATS. If I did think, sir, I were well awake,
I'd strive to tell you. We were dead of sleep,   230
And — how we know not — all clapped° under
    hatches,
Where, but even now, with strange and several
    noises
Of roaring, shrieking, howling, jingling chains,

And mo diversity of sounds, all horrible,
We were awaked, straightway at liberty,   235
Where we, in all her trim, freshly beheld
Our royal, good, and gallant ship, our master
Capering° to eye her. — On a trice, so please you,
Even in a dream, were we divided from them,
And were brought moping hither.
    ARI. [*Aside to* PROSPERO] Was 't well done?   240
    PRO. [*Aside to* ARIEL] Bravely, my diligence. Thou
    shalt be free.
    ALON. This is as strange a maze as e'er men trod,
And there is in this business more than nature
Was ever conduct of. Some oracle
Must rectify° our knowledge.
    PRO.   Sir, my liege,   245
Do not infest your mind with beating on
The strangeness of this business. At picked leisure
Which shall be shortly, single° I'll resolve° you,
Which to you shall seem probable, of every
These happened accidents. Till when, be cheerful,
And think of each thing well. [*Aside to* ARIEL] Come
    hither, spirit.   251
Set Caliban and his companions free,
Untie the spell. [*Exit* ARIEL.] How fares my gracious
    sir?
There are yet missing of your company
Some few odd lads that you remember not.   255
[*Re-enter* ARIEL, *driving in* CALIBAN, STEPHANO, *and*
    TRINCULO, *in their stolen apparel.*]
    STE. Every man shift for all the rest, and let no
man take care for himself, for all is but fortune. —
Coragio,° bully-monster, coragio!
    TRIN. If these be true spies° which I wear in my
head, here's a goodly sight.   260
    CAL. Oh, Setebos, these be brave spirits indeed!
How fine my master is! I am afraid
He will chastise me.
    SEB.   Ha, ha!
What things are these, my lord Antonio?
Will money buy 'em?
    ANT.   Very like. One of them   265
Is a plain fish, and no doubt marketable.
    PRO. Mark but the badges° of these men, my
    lords,
Then say if they be true. This misshapen knave,
His mother was a witch, and one so strong   269
That could control the moon, make flows and ebbs,
And deal in her command,° without her power.°
These three have robbed me, and this demidevil —
For he's a bastard one — had plotted with them
To take my life. Two of these fellows you

---

198. my child: i.e., Miranda, who is about to become his daughter-in-law.   **203. chalked forth:** marked out (as with a chalk line).   **214. still embrace:** always cling to.   **215 s.d., amazedly:** in amazement.   **217–18. gallows ... drown:** see I.i.32–33.   **218. blasphemy:** you blasphemer.   **219. That ... o'erboard:** that by your swearing drives the grace of God away.   **226. tricksy:** clever.   **231. clapped:** shut in.

238. Capering: dancing for joy.   **245. rectify:** prove true.   **248. single:** alone. **resolve:** inform.   **258. Coragio:** courage.   **259. spies:** eyes.   **267. badges:** A nobleman's servant wore a badge displaying his master's coat of arms.   **271. deal ... command:** i.e., take over the moon's power of controlling the tides. **without ... power:** without the aid of the moon.

Must know and own, this thing of darkness I   275
Acknowledge mine.
    CAL.   I shall be pinched to death.
    ALON. Is not this Stephano, my drunken butler?
    SEB. He is drunk now. Where had he wine?
    ALON. And Trinculo is reeling ripe. Where should
      they   279
Find this grand liquor that hath gilded 'em?° —
How camest thou in this pickle?
    TRIN. I have been in such a pickle since I saw you
last that I fear me will never out of my bones. I shall
not fear flyblowing.°
    SEB. Why, how now, Stephano!   285
    STE. Oh, touch me not. — I am not Stephano, but
    a cramp.
    PRO. You'd be King o' the isle, sirrah?
    STE. I should have been a sore one, then.
    ALON. This is a strange thing as e'er I looked on.
                       [*Pointing to* CALIBAN.]
    PRO. He is as disproportioned in his manners°
As in his shape. Go, sirrah, to my cell.   291
Take with you your companions. As you look
To have my pardon, trim° it handsomely.
    CAL. Aye, that I will, and I'll be wise hereafter,
And seek for grace.° What a thrice-double ass   295
Was I to take this drunkard for a god
And worship this dull fool!
    PRO.   Go to, away!
    ALON. Hence, and bestow your luggage where you
    found it.
    SEB. Or stole it, rather.   299
          [*Exeunt* CALIBAN, STEPHANO, *and* TRINCULO.]
    PRO. Sir, I invite your Highness and your train
To my poor cell, where you shall take your rest
For this one night. Which, part of it, I'll waste
With such discourse as I not doubt shall make it
Go quick away — the story of my life,
And the particular accidents° gone by   305
Since I came to this isle. And in the morn
I'll bring you to your ship, and so to Naples,
Where I have hope to see the nuptial
Of these our dear-belovèd solemnized,

And thence retire me to my Milan, where   310
Every third thought shall be my grave.
    ALON.   I long
To hear the story of your life, which must
Take the ear strangely.
    PRO.   I'll deliver all,
And promise you calm seas, auspicious° gales,
And sail so expeditious that shall catch   315
Your royal fleet far off. [*Aside to* ARIEL] My Ariel,
    chick,
That is thy charge. Then to the elements
Be free, and fare thou well! Please you, draw near.
                             [*Exeunt.*]

EPILOGUE°

SPOKEN BY PROSPERO

Now my charms are all o'erthrown,
And what strength I have's mine own,
Which is most faint. Now, 'tis true,
I must be here confined by you,
Or sent to Naples. Let me not,   5
Since I have my dukedom got,
And pardoned the deceiver, dwell
In this bare island by your spell,
But release me from my bands°
With the help of your good hands.°   10
Gentle breath° of yours my sails
Must fill, or else my project fails,
Which was to please. Now I want°
Spirits to enforce, art to enchant,
And my ending is despair   15
Unless I be relieved by prayer
Which pierces so that it assaults
Mercy itself, and frees all faults.
As you from crimes would pardoned be,
Let your indulgence set me free.   20

314. auspicious: favorable.
    Epilogue: A concluding epilogue is fairly common in Elizabethan plays, especially those performed before a Courtly audience. It is usually a conventional apology for the inadequacies of the performance, and an appeal for applause. Cf. the epilogues in *MND, AYLI,* and *II Hen IV.* **9. bands:** bonds. **10. good hands:** i.e., by clapping. **11. Gentle breath:** kindly criticism.
13. want: lack.

280. gilded 'em: made them glow. **284. fear flyblowing:** i.e., shall never go bad, for I have been so well pickled. **290. manners:** behavior. **293. trim:** make tidy. **295. grace:** favor.
305. accidents: events.

THE FAMOUS HISTORY OF THE LIFE OF KING HENRY THE EIGHTH

Introduction[1]

The Famous History of the Life of King Henry VIII was acted as a new play at the Globe playhouse on June 16, 1613. The performance was memorable, partly for its lavish and realistic production, and partly because some smoldering wadding from one of the "chambers" discharged in I.iv.49 set the thatched roof ablaze so that the playhouse was burned to the ground (see Gen. Intro. p. 50).

Henry VIII was first printed in the first folio (F1) of 1623. The text is good and contains a remarkable number of very elaborate stage directions for the various scenes of pageantry (see for instance II.iv, IV.i.35, and V.v). These were retained without change by the editors.

Henry VIII is usually regarded as the last surviving play Shakespeare wrote; but for about one hundred years, editors have questioned whether Shakespeare himself actually wrote more than a small part of it. In 1850 James Spedding, who was famous for his elaborate and scholarly edition of the works of Francis Bacon, first suggested that *Henry VIII* was mostly the work of John Fletcher. There is no external evidence that Fletcher or anyone else collaborated with Shakespeare; the case rests entirely on the internal evidence of changes of style within the play. Spedding assigned I.i, I.ii, II.i, II.ii, III.ii.1–203, and V.i to Shakespeare and all the rest to Fletcher.

Some specimens will show the differences of rhythm, accentuation, and phrase which have been claimed as marking difference in authorship. Thus, in III.ii.166–79, Wolsey answers the angry King:

> My sovereign, I confess your royal graces,
> Showered on me daily, have been more than
>   could
> My studied purposes requite, which went
> Beyond all man's endeavors. My endeavors
> Have ever come too short of my desires,
> Yet filed with my abilities. Mine own ends

[1] See also App. 28.

> Have been mine so that evermore they pointed
> To the good of your most sacred person and
> The profit of the state. For your great graces
> Heaped upon me, poor undeserver, I
> Can nothing render but allegiant thanks,
> My prayers to Heaven for you, my loyalty,
> Which ever has and ever shall be growing,
> Till death, that winter, kill it.

This passage is attributed to Shakespeare.

At line 350 Wolsey soliloquizes:

> So farewell to the little good you bear me.
> Farewell! A long farewell, to all my greatness!
> This is the state of man: Today he puts forth
> The tender leaves of hopes; tomorrow blossoms
> And bears his blushing honors thick upon him;
> The third day comes a frost, a killing frost,   355
> And, when he thinks, good easy man, full surely
> His greatness is aripening, nips his root,
> And then he falls, as I do. I have ventured,
> Like little wanton boys that swim on bladders,
> This many summers in a sea of glory,   360
> But far beyond my depth. My high-blown pride
> At length broke under me, and now has left me,
> Weary and old with service, to the mercy
> Of a rude stream that must forever hide me.   364
> Vain pomp and glory of this world, I hate ye.
> I feel my heart new opened. Oh, how wretchèd
> Is that poor man that hangs on princes' favors!
> There is, betwixt that smile we would aspire to,
> That sweet aspéct of princes, and their ruin,
> More pangs and fears than wars or women have.
> And when he falls, he falls like Lucifer,   371
> Never to hope again.

The rhythms of this second passage, with their "weak" endings "left͡ me" (l. 362), "hide͡ me" (l. 364), "hate͡ ye" (l. 365), are claimed to be more in Fletcher's style than in Shakespeare's. Mechanical tests of style, however, are not entirely conclusive, but rather attempts to justify personal intuition and taste, and in recent years several scholars have maintained that the whole play was written by Shakespeare.

As with the earlier History Plays, the source of *Henry VIII* was mainly Holinshed's *Chronicles,* but incidents in the life of Thomas Cranmer were taken from John Foxe's *Book of Martyrs,* a popular and lurid account of the sufferings of Protestants, chiefly in the reign of Queen Mary, Henry VIII's elder daughter.

Some extracts from Holinshed and Foxe will show how closely Shakespeare followed his sources.

1. THE MEETING OF THE TWO KINGS (cf. I.i.4–10)

The two Kings met in the vale of Andren, accompanied with such a number of the nobility of both realms so richly appointed in apparel and costly jewels, as chains, collars of SS, and other the like ornaments to set forth their degrees and estates, that a wonder it was to behold and view them in their order and rooms, which every man kept according to his appointment.

The two Kings meeting in the field, either saluted other in most loving wise, first on horseback, and, after alighting on foot, eftsoons embraced with courteous words, to the great rejoicing of the beholders; and, after they had thus saluted each other, they went both together into a rich tent of cloth of gold, there set up for the purpose, in the which they passed the time in pleasant talk, banqueting, and loving devices till it drew toward the evening, and then departed for that night, the one to Guisnes, the other to Ard.

2. THE INDIGNATION OF THE DUKE OF BUCKINGHAM (cf.I.i.158–93)

The Peers of the realm (receiving letters to prepare themselves to attend the King in this journey, and no apparent necessary cause expressed, why nor wherefore) seemed to grudge that such a costly journey should be taken in hand to their importunate charges and expenses without consent of the whole board of the Council. But, namely, the Duke of Buckingham (being a man of a lofty courage, but not most liberal) sore repined that he should be at so great charges for his furniture forth at this time, saying that he knew not for what cause so much money should be spent about the sight of a vain talk to be had, and communication to be ministered of things of no importance. Wherefore he sticked not to say that it was an intolerable matter to obey such a vile and importunate person. The Duke indeed could not abide the Cardinal, and specially he had of late conceived an inward malice against him for Sir William Bulmer's cause, whose trouble was only procured by the Cardinal, who first caused him to be cast in prison. Now such grievous words as the Duke thus uttered against him came to the Cardinal's ear, whereupon he cast before hand all ways possible to have him in a trip, that he might cause him to leap headless.

3. KNEVET'S REVELATIONS (cf. I.ii.129–214)

This Knevet, being had in examination before the Cardinal, disclosed all the Duke's life. And first he uttered that the Duke was accustomed by way of talk to say how he meant so to use the matter that he would attain to the crown if King Henry chanced to die without issue, and that he had talk and conference of that matter on a time with George Neville, Lord of Abergavenny, unto whom he had given his daughter in marriage, and also that he threatened to punish the Cardinal for his manifold misdoings, being without cause his mortal enemy.

The Cardinal, having gotten that which he sought for, encouraged, comforted, and procured Knevet, with many comfortable words and great promises that he should with a bold spirit and countenance object and lay these things to the Duke's charge, with more if he knew [disclosed] it when time required. Then Knevet, partly provoked with desire to be revenged, and partly moved with hope of reward, openly confessed that the Duke had once fully determined to devise means how to make the King away, being brought into a full hope that he should be King by a vain prophecy which one Nicholas Hopkins, a monk of an house of the Chartreux order beside Bristow [Bristol], called Henton, sometime his confessor, had opened unto him.

The Cardinal, having thus taken the examination of Knevet, went unto the King, and declared unto him that his person was in danger by such traitorous purpose as the Duke of Buckingham had conceived in his heart, and showed how that now there is manifest tokens of his wicked pretense, wherefore he exhorted the King to provide for his own surety with some speed. The King, hearing the accusation, enforced to the uttermost by the Cardinal, made this answer, "If the Duke have deserved to be punished, let him have according to his deserts."

4. QUEEN KATHARINE'S SPEECH (cf. II.iv.13–57)

"Sir," (quoth she) "I desire you to do me justice and right, and take some pity upon me, for I am a poor woman, and a stranger, born out of your dominion, having here no indifferent [impartial] counsel, and less assurance of friendship. Alas, sir, what have I offended you, or what occasion of displeasure have I showed you, intending thus to put me from you after this sort? I take God to my judge, I have been to you a true and humble wife, ever conformable to your will and pleasure; that never contraried or gainsaid anything thereof, and, being always contented with all things wherein you had any delight, whether little or much, without grudge or displeasure, I loved for your sake all them whom you loved, whether they were my friends or enemies.

"I have been your wife these twenty years and more, and you have had by me divers children. If there be any just cause that you can allege against me, either of dishonesty [unchastity] or matter lawful to put me from you, I am content to depart to my shame and rebuke; and if there be none, then I pray you to let me have justice at your hand. The King, your father, was in his time of excellent wit, and the King of Spain, my father, Ferdinando, was reckoned one of the wisest princes that reigned in Spain many years before. It is not to be doubted but that they had gathered as wise councillors unto them of every realm as to their wisdoms they thought meet, who deemed the marriage between you and me good and lawful, etc. Wherefore, I humbly desire you to spare me until I may know what counsel my friends in Spain will advertise [advise] me to take, and, if you will not, then your pleasure be fulfilled."

5. THE CHARACTER OF CARDINAL WOLSEY

This Cardinal (as Edmund Campion in his history of Ireland describeth him) was a man undoubtedly born to honor: I think (saith he) some Prince's bastard, no butcher's son, exceeding wise, fair spoken, high minded, full of revenge, vicious of his body, lofty to his enemies, were they never so big; to those that accepted and sought his friendship wonderful courteous, a ripe schoolman, thrall to affections [slave to his passions], brought abed with flattery, insatiable to get, and more princely in bestowing, as appeareth by his two colleges at Ipswich and Oxenford, the one overthrown with his fall, the other unfinished, and yet, as it lieth for an house of students, considering all the appurtenances, incomparable through Christendom, whereof Henry the Eighth is now called founder, because he let it stand. He held and enjoyed at once the bishoprics of York, Duresme [Durham], and Winchester, the dignities of Lord Cardinal, Legate, and Chancellor, the Abbey of Saint Albans, divers priories, sundry fat benefices *In commendam;* a great preferrer of his servants, an advancer of learning, stout in every quarrel, never happy till this his overthrow. Wherein he showed such moderation, and ended so perfectly, that the hour of his death did him more honor than all the pomp of his life passed.

6. THE ATTEMPT TO GET RID OF CRANMER (cf. V.ii AND iii)

[This story was taken from John Foxe's *Acts and Monuments* (first printed in 1563), more popularly known as *The Book of Martyrs*.]

And so, incontinently upon the receipt of the King's token, they all rose and carried to the King his ring, surrendering that matter, as the order and use was, into his own hands.

When they were all come to the King's presence, his Highness, with a severe countenance, said unto them, "Ah, my Lords, I thought I had had wiser men of my Council than now I find you. What discretion was this in you, thus to make the Primate of the Realm, and one of you in office, to wait at the Council chamber door amongst serving men! You might have considered that he was a Councillor as well as you, and you had no such commission of me so to handle him. I was content that you should try him as a Councillor, and not as a mean subject. But now I well perceive that things be done against him maliciously, and, if some of you might have had your minds, you would have tried him to the uttermost. But I do you all to wit, and protest that if a Prince may be beholding unto his subject," and so (solemnly laying his hand upon his breast) said: "By the faith I owe to God, I take this man here, my Lord of Canterbury, to be of all other a most faithful subject unto us, and one to whom we are much beholding," giving him great commendations otherwise. And with that, one or two of the chiefest of the Council, making their excuse, declared that in requesting his indurance [imprisonment], it was rather meant for his trial and his purgation against the common fame and slander of the world, than for any malice conceived against him. "Well, well, my Lords," quoth the King, "take him and well use him, as he is worthy to be, and make no more ado." And with that every man caught him by the hand and made fair weather of altogethers, which might easily be done with that man.

Henry VIII dramatizes incidents that were not far remote from Shakespeare's own times. The play opens soon after the famous meeting of Henry with the French King, Francis I, in 1520, at the Field of Cloth of Gold, so called because of the extravagance and magnificence displayed by all who took part, and ends with the baptism of the Princess Elizabeth, who was born in 1533 and who became Queen Elizabeth in 1558. It was natural, therefore, for Shakespeare to include a prophecy of the glories of her long reign, which had ended in 1603, and a flattering eulogy of her successor, King James I, then reigning (V.v.15–63). Nevertheless, there is a considerable vein of irony running throughout the play. The King suffers scruples of conscience that his first marriage with the Spanish Princess, Katharine of Aragon, was unlawful, but he does not act on these scruples until after he has fallen in love with Anne Bullen (Boleyn) at the masque at Cardinal Wolsey's palace; and the meeting is Shakespeare's addition to his source. To emphasize this secondary cause of the rejection of Queen Katharine, the scene where the King welcomes the Papal Legate who has come to England to judge the case (II.ii) is immediately followed by the cynical conversation of the old lady and Anne Bullen, who is lavishly rewarded by the King for favors not yet received (II.iii). There is again bitter irony in some of Wolsey's last speeches. When he hears that Sir Thomas More has been chosen Lord Chancellor in his place, Wolsey calls down a blessing on his successor (III.ii.397-99):

> that his bones,
> When he has run his course and sleeps in bless-
> ings,
> May have a tomb of orphans' tears wept on 'em!

More was beheaded in 1535 for refusing to assent to the King's action in declaring himself Supreme Head of the Church in England. Wolsey also blesses and warns his secretary, Thomas Cromwell. Cromwell too fell under the King's displeasure and was beheaded in 1540.

There is thus little glamour in the events or persons. King Henry, known in English history as bluff King Hal, is hot tempered, easily led by Wolsey, and tyrannical, but at least generous in word to his first wife. Wolsey is the villain of the piece; he is an upstart with infinite greed for possessions and boundless ambitions, for he hopes to be made pope, and so to become his sovereign's sovereign. By contrast, Thomas Cranmer, who becomes prominent in the last scenes of the play, is very meek, but with the suggestion either that he was entirely subservient to the King, or that his seeming humility may be a subtler way to power than the arrogance of Wolsey. Anne has little chance of showing her character, and we are left in doubt whether she was the innocent victim of a King who was said to have "spared no man in his wrath, or woman in his lust," or a sly minx who betrays her mistress in her ambition to be made Queen. Only Queen Katharine is an entirely sympathetic character, a woman who maintains her dignity even when wronged, insulted, and betrayed. For Shakespeare's contemporaries, to

whom the events in the reign of King Henry VIII were still vital issues, the play would have been more remarkable for what it omitted than for what it showed.

Henry VIII is not one of Shakespeare's best Chronicle plays, though the individual scenes are lively and well written. It is a series of colorful episodes from history rather than a serious drama of cause and event. It begins with the fall of the Duke of Buckingham, who is destroyed by the malice of Cardinal Wolsey; this episode is so presented that it brings out the overbearing and unscrupulous pride of the Cardinal and his malign influence over his King. Wolsey is next shown in all his magnificence, patronizing one of his own lavish entertainments, at which, unfortunately for him, Anne Bullen is among the guests and attracts the King's roving eye. After a pathetic scene in which Buckingham is led to execution (II.i), the business of the royal divorce is set moving and leads up to the elaborate scene of the trial of Queen Katharine (II.iv). But Wolsey has now overreached himself; he opposes the King's marriage with Anne Bullen, for he has other plans of his own, and by mischance certain of his papers fall into the King's hands. The King therefore discards his minister, and Wolsey's fall is shown in a long-drawn-out passage wherein the pathos of fallen pomp is revealed. Nevertheless, even in ruin, Wolsey still keeps his greatness of mind. The pageantry of the coronation of Anne (IV.i.36) follows; and then, as contrast and comment on her triumph, there is shown the death of the much-injured Katharine, in the course of which Shakespeare introduces, with considerable effect, the account of the death of Wolsey and the final comment on his character (IV.ii). Cranmer now takes the center of the stage, and the intrigues of his fellow Councillors are drastically thwarted by the King. The play ends abruptly with the triumph of the christening of the little Princess and Cranmer's prophecy of the golden age which will follow when she becomes Queen of England. *Henry VIII* is thus a pageant to be seen rather than a play to be read, though the high moments and the great speeches, such as Buckingham's farewell (II.i.55-136), Queen Katharine's defense (II.iv.13-57), and Wolsey's farewell speeches (III.ii.350-457), are fine specimens of mature dramatic verse.

Henry VIII

DRAMATIS PERSONAE

KING HENRY *the Eighth*
CARDINAL WOLSEY
CARDINAL CAMPEIUS
CAPUCIUS, *Ambassador from the Emperor Charles V*
CRANMER, *Archbishop of Canterbury*
DUKE OF NORFOLK
DUKE OF BUCKINGHAM
DUKE OF SUFFOLK
EARL OF SURREY
LORD CHAMBERLAIN
LORD CHANCELLOR
GARDINER, *Bishop of Winchester*
BISHOP *of Lincoln*
LORD ABERGAVENNY
LORD SANDS
SIR HENRY GUILDFORD
SIR THOMAS LOVELL
SIR ANTHONY DENNY
SIR NICHOLAS VAUX
SECRETARIES *to Wolsey*
CROMWELL, *servant to Wolsey*
GRIFFITH, *gentleman usher to Queen Katharine*
THREE GENTLEMEN

DOCTOR BUTTS, *physician to the King*
GARTER, *King-at-Arms*
SURVEYOR *to the Duke of Buckingham*
BRANDON
SERGEANT-AT-ARMS

DOORKEEPER *of the Council Chamber*
PORTER, *and his* MAN
PAGE *to Gardiner*
A CRIER

QUEEN KATHARINE, *wife to King Henry, afterward divorced*
ANNE BULLEN, *her Maid of Honor, afterward Queen*
AN OLD LADY, *friend to Anne Bullen*
PATIENCE, *woman to Queen Katharine*

Several LORDS *and* LADIES *in the Dumb Shows;* WOMEN *attending upon the* QUEEN; SCRIBES, OFFICERS, GUARDS, *and other* ATTENDANTS

SPIRITS

SCENE — *London; Westminster; Kimbolton.*

THE PROLOGUE

I come no more to make you laugh. Things now
That bear a weighty and a serious brow,
Sad, high, and working,° full of state and woe,
Such noble scenes as draw the eye to flow,
We now present. Those that can pity, here   5
May, if they think it well, let fall a tear.
The subject will deserve it. Such as give
Their money out of hope they may believe
May here find truth, too. Those that come to see
Only a show or two, and so agree   10
The play may pass, if they be still and willing,
I'll undertake may see away their shilling
Richly in two short hours.° Only they
That come to hear a merry bawdy play,
A noise of targets,° or to see a fellow   15
In a long motley coat guarded with yellow°
Will be deceived; for,° gentle hearers, know,
To rank our chosen truth with such a show
As fool and fight is, beside forfeiting
Our own brains and the opinion that we bring   20
To make that only true we now intend,
Will leave us never an understanding friend.
Therefore, for goodness' sake, and as you are known
The first and happiest hearers of the town,
Be sad,° as we would make ye. Think ye see   25
The very persons of our noble story
As they were living. Think you see them great
And followed with the general throng and sweat
Of thousand friends. Then, in a moment, see
How soon this mightiness meets misery;   30
And if you can be merry then, I'll say
A man may weep upon his wedding day.

17–22. for . . . friend: for, gentle spectators (*hearers*), you must know that to make cheap (*rank*) true history with clowning and knockabout (*fool and fight*) will not only show us to be brainless and make us lose our reputation for displaying truth but lose us every intelligent friend in the audience. **25. sad:** serious.

Prologue: 3. working: moving.   **13. two . . . hours:** See *R & J*, Prologue, l. 12, n.   **15. noise of targets:** clashing of shields.   **16. motley . . . yellow:** the dress of the professional fool, ornamented (*guarded*) with braid. yellow: the fool's color.

Act I

SCENE I. *London. An antechamber in the palace.*

[*Enter the* DUKE OF NORFOLK *at one door; at the other, the* DUKE OF BUCKINGHAM *and the* LORD ABERGAVENNY.]

BUCK. Good morrow, and well met. How have
    ye done
Since last we saw° in France?
    NOR.   I thank your Grace,
Healthful, and ever since a fresh admirer
Of what I saw there.
    BUCK.   An untimely ague°
Stayed me a prisoner in my chamber when   5
Those suns of glory, those two lights° of men,
Met in the vale of Andren.°
    NOR.   'Twixt Guynes° and Arde.°
I was then present, saw them salute on horseback,
Beheld them, when they 'lighted,° how they clung
In their embracement, as they grew together;   10
Which had they, what four throned ones could
    have weighed
Such a compounded one?°
    BUCK.   All the whole time
I was my chamber's prisoner.
    NOR.   Then you lost
The view of earthly glory. Men might say,   14
Till this time pomp was single, but now married
To one above itself.° Each following day
Became the next day's master, till the last
Made former wonders its. Today the French,
All clinquant,° all in gold, like heathen gods,
Shone down the English; and tomorrow they   20
Made Britain India.° Every man that stood
Showed like a mine.° Their dwarfish pages were
As cherubins,° all gilt. The madams too,
Not used to toil, did almost sweat to bear
The pride° upon them, that their very labor   25
Was to them as a painting.° Now this masque°
Was cried incomparable; and the ensuing night

Made it a fool and beggar. The° two Kings,
Equal in luster, were now best, now worst,
As presence° did present them; him in eye   30
Still him in praise;° and being present both,
'Twas said they saw but one, and no discerner
Durst wag his tongue in censure.° When these
    suns —
For so they phrase 'em — by their heralds chal-
    lenged
The noble spirits to arms, they did perform   35
Beyond thought's compass.° That former fabulous
    story,
Being now seen possible enough, got credit,
That Bevis was believed.°
    BUCK.   Oh, you go far.
    NOR. As I belong to worship° and affect
In honor honesty, the tract of everything   40
Would by a good discourser lose some life
Which action's self was tongue to.° All was royal.
To the disposing of it naught rebelled.
Order gave each thing view. The office did
Distinctly his full function.°
    BUCK.   Who did guide —   45
I mean, who set the body and the limbs
Of this great sport together, as you guess?
    NOR. One, certes,° that promises no element°
In such a business.
    BUCK.   I pray you, who, my lord?   49
    NOR. All this was ordered by the good discretion
Of the right reverend Cardinal of York.
    BUCK. The Devil speed him! No man's pie is
    freed
From his ambitious finger. What had he
To do in these fierce vanities? I wonder
That such a keech° can with his very bulk   55
Take up the rays o' the beneficial sun
And keep it from the earth.
    NOR.   Surely, sir,
There's in him stuff that puts him to these ends;
For, being not propped by ancestry, whose grace
Chalks° successors their way, nor called upon   60
For high feats done to the crown, neither allied
To eminent assistants, but, spiderlike,
Out of his self-drawing web he gives us note°

Act I, Sc. i: **2. saw:** met.   **4. ague:** fever.   **6. two lights:** Henry VIII and the French King.   **7. Andren . . . Guynes . . . Arde:** The two towns lie on either side of the valley of Andren, which was neutral ground, as at this time Guynes was in English hands.   **9. 'lighted:** dismounted.   **11–12. Which . . one:** if they had been actually united, that one person would have been as powerful as any other four kings.   **15–16. Till . . . itself:** hitherto courtly display was confined to one court, but now that the two Courts were united, the pomp was greatly increased.   **19. clinquant:** glittering.   **21. Made . . . India:** made Britain as rich as India. India was the symbol of riches.   **22. mine:** gold mine.   **23. cherubins:** It was usual to gild the carved cherubins in a church.   **25. pride:** splendor.   **26. Was . . . painting:** made them high-colored. **masque:** See Gen. Intro. p. 47b.

28–33. The . . . censure: The general meaning of this involved sentence is: "The two Kings were so magnificent that no one could say which exceeded the other."   **30. presence:** public appearance.   **30–31. him . . . praise:** i.e., when one alone was present, that one was most highly praised.   **33. censure:** criticism.   **36. compass:** range.   **38. Bevis . . . believed:** one could even believe the marvels in *Bevis of Southampton* (a medieval romance).   **39. As . . . worship:** as I am a nobleman.   **40–42. tract . . . to:** the description (*tract*) of everything, however good the describer, would lose something of what it was in fact (*action*).   **44–45. office . . . function:** every official fulfilled his task (*function*) perfectly.   **48. certes:** for sure. **element:** natural ability.   **55. keech:** lump of suet — an allusion to the fact that Wolsey was a butcher's son.   **60. Chalks:** marks out.   **63. gives us note:** points out to us.

The force of his own merit makes his way —
A gift that Heaven gives for him, which buys   65
A place next to the King.

ABER.   I cannot tell
What Heaven hath given him. Let some graver eye
Pierce into that. But I can see his pride
Peep through each part of him. Whence has he
     that?
If not from Hell, the Devil is a niggard,°   70
Or has given all before, and he begins
A new hell in himself.

BUCK.   Why the Devil,
Upon this French going out,° took he upon him,
Without the privity° o' the King, to appoint
Who should attend on him? He makes up the file°
Of all the gentry, for the most part such   76
To whom as great a charge as little honor
He meant to lay upon; and his own letter,
The honorable board of Council out,
Must fetch him in he° papers.°

ABER.   I do know   80
Kinsmen of mine, three at the least, that have
By this so sickened their estates that never
They shall abound as formerly.

BUCK.   Oh, many
Have broke their backs with laying manors on 'em°
For this great journey. What did this vanity   85
But minister communication of
A most poor issue?°

NOR.   Grievingly I think
The peace between the French and us not values°
The cost that did conclude it.

BUCK.   Every man
After the hideous storm that followed was   90
A thing inspired and, not consulting, broke
Into a general prophecy: That this tempest,
Dashing the garment of this peace, aboded°
The sudden breach on 't.

NOR.   Which is budded out;°
For France hath flawed the league,° and hath
     attached   95
Our merchants' goods at Bordeaux.

ABER.   Is it therefore
The Ambassador is silenced?

NOR.   Marry,° is 't.

ABER. A proper title of a peace,° and purchased
At a superfluous° rate!

BUCK.   Why, all this business
Our reverend Cardinal carried.

NOR.   Like it your Grace,°   100
The state takes notice of the private difference
Betwixt you and the Cardinal. I advise you —
And take it from a heart that wishes towards you
Honor and plenteous safety — that you read
The Cardinal's malice and his potency°   105
Together; to consider further that
What his high hatred would effect wants not°
A minister° in his power. You know his nature,
That he's revengeful, and I know his sword   109
Hath a sharp edge. It's long and 't may be said
It reaches far, and where 'twill not extend,
Thither he darts° it. Bosom up° my counsel;
You'll find it wholesome. Lo, where comes that rock
That I advise your shunning.   114
[*Enter* CARDINAL WOLSEY, *the purse° borne before
him, certain of the* GUARD, *and two* SECRETARIES *with
papers. The* CARDINAL *in his passage fixeth his eye
on* BUCKINGHAM, *and* BUCKINGHAM *on him, both full
of disdain.*]

WOL. The Duke of Buckingham's surveyor,° ha?
Where's his examination?°

I. SEC.   Here, so please you.   116

WOL. Is he in person ready?

I. SEC.   Aye, please your Grace.

WOL. Well, we shall then know more, and Buck-
     ingham
Shall lessen this big look.

        [*Exeunt* WOLSEY *and his train.*]

BUCK. This butcher's cur is venom-mouthed,
     and I   120
Have not the power to muzzle him; therefore best
Not wake him in his slumber. A beggar's book°
Outworths a noble's blood.

NOR.   What, are you chafed?°
Ask God for temperance. That's the appliance° only
Which your disease requires.

BUCK.   I read in 's looks   125
Matter against me, and his eye reviled

---

70. Devil . . . niggard: the Devil is stingy. Pride is one of the three deadly sins that come from the Devil, the others being wrath and envy. **73. going out:** expedition. **74. privity:** secret knowledge. **75. file:** list. **78–80. and . . . papers:** and the sole authority of the Cardinal (the Council being disregarded in this matter) is enough to compel the attendance of any man whose name he writes down (*papers*). **he:** whom he. **84. broke . . . 'em:** have ruined themselves by pawning their manors to pay for the journey. **85–87. What . . . issue:** what was the poor result (*issue*) of all this vain display? **88. not values:** is not worth. **93. aboded:** foretold. **94. budded out:** has come to pass. **95. flawed . . . league:** broken the treaty. **97. Marry:** Mary, by the Virgin.

8. A . . . peace: spoken ironically — "This peace is a fine purchase"; i.e., the title deed of the purchase is faulty. **99. superfluous:** extravagant, excessive. **100. Like . . . Grace:** if it may please your Grace — an apology for offering advice which has not been asked for. **105. potency:** power. **107. wants not:** is not without. **108. minister:** servant; i.e., means of satisfying his hate. **111–12. extend . . . darts:** where it will not reach by itself, he thrusts it. **112. Bosom up:** take to heart. **114. s.d., the purse:** the bag containing the Great Seal, which is always kept in the possession of the Lord Chancellor of England wherever he goes. **115. surveyor:** overseer of a great estate. **116. examination:** testimony given under oath. **122. book:** book of accounts in which are recorded the debts of his enemies. **123. chafed:** enraged. **124. appliance:** remedy.

Me as his abject object.° At this instant
He bores me with some trick. He's gone to the
      King;
I'll follow and outstare him.
NOR.   Stay, my lord,
And let your reason with your choler° question   130
What 'tis you go about. To climb steep hills
Requires slow pace at first. Anger is like
A full-hot horse, who being allowed his way,
Self-mettle° tires him. Not a man in England
Can advise me like you. Be to yourself   135
As you would to your friend.
BUCK.   I'll to the King,
And from a mouth of honor° quite cry down
This Ipswich° fellow's insolence, or proclaim
There's difference in no persons.°
NOR.   Be advised.°
Heat not a furnace for your foe so hot   140
That it do singe yourself. We may outrun
By violent swiftness that which we run at,
And lose by overrunning. Know you not
The fire that mounts° the liquor till 't run o'er
In seeming to augment it wastes it? Be advised.
I say again, there is no English soul   146
More stronger to direct you than yourself
If with the sap of reason you would quench,
Or but allay, the fire of passion.
BUCK.   Sir,
I am thankful to you, and I'll go along   150
By your prescription. But this top-proud° fellow —
Whom from the flow of gall I name not, but
From sincere motions° — by intelligence°
And proofs as clear as founts in July° when
We see each grain of gravel, I do know   155
To be corrupt and treasonous.
NOR.   Say not "treasonous"
BUCK. To the King I'll say 't, and make my
      vouch° as strong
As shore of rock. Attend.° This holy fox,
Or wolf, or both — for he is equal ravenous
As he is subtle, and as prone to mischief   160
As able to perform 't, his mind and place
Infecting one another, yea, reciprocally —
Only to show his pomp as well in France
As here at home, suggests the King our master
To this last costly treaty, the interview   165
That swallowed so much treasure and like a glass
Did break i' the rinsing.
NOR.   Faith, and so it did.

BUCK. Pray, give me favor, sir. This cunning
      Cardinal
The articles o' the combination drew
As himself pleased, and they were ratified   170
As he cried, "Thus let be," to as much end
As give a crutch to the dead. But our Count-Cardi-
      nal
Has done this, and 'tis well; for worthy Wolsey,
Who cannot err, he did it. Now this follows —
Which, as I take it, is a kind of puppy   175
To the old dam° Treason — Charles the Emperor,
Under pretense to see the Queen his aunt —
For 'twas indeed his color,° but he came
To whisper Wolsey — here makes visitation.
His fears were that the interview betwixt   180
England and France might through their amity
Breed him some prejudice, for from this league
Peeped harms that menaced him. He privily
Deals with our Cardinal, and, as I trow° —
Which I do well, for I am sure the Emperor   185
Paid ere he promised, whereby his suit was granted
Ere it was asked — but when the way was made
And paved with gold, the Emperor thus desired:
That he would please to alter the King's course
And break the foresaid peace. Let the King know,
As soon he shall by me, that thus the Cardinal 191
Does buy and sell his honor as he pleases,
And for his own advantage.
NOR.   I am sorry
To hear this of him, and could wish he were
Something mistaken° in 't.
BUCK.   No, not a syllable.   195
I do pronounce him in that very shape
He shall appear in proof.°
[Enter BRANDON, a SERGEANT-AT-ARMS before him,
      and two or three of the GUARD.]
BRAN. Your office, Sergeant. Execute it.
SERG.   Sir,
My lord the Duke of Buckingham, and Earl
Of Hereford, Stafford, and Northampton, I   200
Arrest thee of high treason, in the name
Of our most sovereign King.
BUCK.   Lo you,° my lord,
The net has fall'n upon me! I shall perish
Under device and practice.°
BRAN.   I am sorry
To see you ta'en from liberty, to look on   205
The business present.° 'Tis His Highness' pleasure
You shall to the Tower.
BUCK.   It will help me nothing
To plead mine innocence, for that dye is on me
Which makes my whitest part black. The will of
      Heaven

127. abject object: a thing beneath his contempt.   130. choler:
wrath.   134. Self-mettle: natural ardor. mettle: lit., material.
137. from . . . honor: speaking as a nobleman.   138. Ipswich:
Wolsey's birthplace.   139. difference . . . persons: i.e., that
high rank is no longer regarded. advised: cautious.   144. mounts:
causes to rise.   151. top-proud: excessively proud.   153. motions: motives. intelligence: information.   154. founts in July:
streams running clear when the spring floods no longer make them
muddy.   157. vouch: testimony.   158. Attend: listen.

176. dam: mother.   178. color: excuse.   184. trow: know.
195. mistaken: misrepresented.   197. in proof: when it comes
to the trial.   202. Lo you: now you see.   204. practice: plotting.   205–06. to . . . present: to be a witness of this present
affair.

Be done in this and all things! I obey.   210
O my Lord Abergavenny, fare you well!
   BRAN. Nay, he must bear you company. [*To*
     ABERGAVENNY] The King
Is pleased you shall to the Tower till you know
How he determines further.
   ABER.   As the Duke said,
The will of Heaven be done, and the King's pleas-
     ure
By me obeyed!
   BRAN.   Here is a warrant from   216
The King to attach Lord Montacute, and the bodies
Of the Duke's confessor, John de la Car,
One Gilbert Peck, his chancellor ——
   BUCK.   So, so.
These are the limbs o' the plot. No more, I hope.
   BRAN. A monk o' the Chartreux.°
   BUCK.   Oh, Nicholas Hopkins?
   BRAN.   He.   221
   BUCK. My surveyor is false. The o'ergreat Cardi-
     nal
Hath showed him gold. My life is spanned° al-
     ready.
I am the shadow of poor Buckingham,
Whose figure even this instant cloud puts on   225
By darkening my clear sun. My lord, farewell.
                       [*Exeunt.*]

SCENE II. *The same. The Council Chamber.*

[*Cornets. Enter* KING HENRY, *leaning on the* CARDI-
NAL'S *shoulder, the nobles, and* SIR THOMAS LOVELL.
The CARDINAL *places himself under*° *the* KING'S *feet
on his right side.*]
   KING. My life itself, and the best heart° of it,
Thanks you for this great care. I stood i' the level°
Of a full-charged confederacy,° and give thanks
To you that choked it. Let be called before us
That gentleman of Buckingham's. In person   5
I'll hear him his confessions justify,°
And point by point the treasons of his master
He shall again relate.
[*A noise within, crying,* "Room for the Queen!"
Enter QUEEN KATHARINE, *ushered by the* DUKE OF
NORFOLK, *and the* DUKE OF SUFFOLK. *She kneels. The*
KING *riseth from his state,*° *takes her up, kisses and
placeth her by him.*]
   Q. KATH. Nay, we must longer kneel. I am a
     suitor.   9
   KING. Arise, and take place by us. Half your suit
Never name to us. You have half our power.

The other moiety° ere you ask is given.
Repeat your will, and take it.
   Q. KATH.   Thank your Majesty.
That you would love yourself, and in that love
Not unconsidered leave your honor nor   15
The dignity of your office, is the point
Of my petition.
   KING.   Lady mine, proceed.
   Q. KATH. I am solicited, not by a few,
And those of true condition,° that your subjects
Are in great grievance. There have been commis-
     sions   20
Sent down among 'em which hath flawed° the heart
Of all their loyalties, wherein, although,
My good Lord Cardinal, they vent reproaches
Most bitterly on you as putter on°
Of these exactions, yet the King our master —   25
Whose honor Heaven shield from soil! — even he
     escapes not
Language unmannerly — yea, such which breaks
The sides of loyalty and almost appears
In loud rebellion.
   NOR.   Not almost appears —
It doth appear. For upon these taxations,   30
The clothiers all, not able to maintain
The many to them 'longing,° have put off°
The spinsters, carders, fullers, weavers,° who,
Unfit for other life, compelled by hunger
And lack of other means, in desperate manner   35
Daring the event to the teeth,° are all in uproar,
And Danger° serves among them.
   KING.   Taxation!
Wherein? And what taxation? My Lord Cardinal,
You that are blamed for it alike with us,
Know you of this taxation?
   WOL.   Please you, sir,   40
I know but of a single part° in aught
Pertains to the state, and front but in that file°
Where others tell steps° with me.
   Q. KATH.   No, my lord,
You know no more than others. But° you frame
Things that are known alike which are not whole-
     some   45
To those which would not know them and yet must
Perforce be their acquaintance. These exactions
Whereof my sovereign would have note they are

---

12. moiety: half.   19. condition: disposition, loyalty.   21. flawed:
broken.   24. putter on: the cause.   32. 'longing: belonging,
employed by them. put off: discharged.   33. spinsters . . .
weavers: those employed in the manufacture of cloth. Spinsters
spin the thread, carders comb the wool for impurities, fullers
cleanse the wool, and weavers weave it into cloth.   36. Daring
. . . teeth: daring even death by rebellion.   37. Danger: risk
of destruction.   41. I . . . part: I am only an individual.
42. front . . . file: am only the first in the ranks.   43. tell steps:
keep pace.   44–47. But . . . acquaintance: you originate decisions which are made known to each member of the Council,
and which they dislike and would prefer not to know, and yet
perforce they must.

---

221. Chartreux: Charterhouse.   223. spanned: ended.
   Sc. ii: s.d., places . . . under: sits at the feet of.   1. best
heart: very center.   2. i' . . . level: within the aim.   3. Of . . .
confederacy: a loaded conspiracy.   6. justify: prove.   8. s.d.,
state: throne standing beneath a canopy. See Pl. 12d.

Most pestilent to the hearing, and to bear 'em,
The back is sacrifice to° the load. They say   50
They are devised by you, or else you suffer
Too hard an exclamation.°
    KING.   Still exaction!
The nature of it? In what kind, let's know,
Is this exaction?
    Q. KATH.   I am much too venturous
In tempting of your patience but am boldened   55
Under your promised pardon. The subjects' grief°
Comes through commissions which compel from
    each
The sixth part of his substance, to be levied
Without delay; and the pretense for this
Is named your wars in France. This makes bold
    mouths.   60
Tongues spit their duties out, and cold hearts freeze
Allegiance in them. Their curses now
Live where their prayers did, and it's come to pass
This tractable obedience is a slave
To each incensèd will.° I would your Highness 65
Would give it quick consideration, for
There is no primer° business.
    KING.   By my life,
This is against our pleasure.
    WOL.   And° for me,
I have no further gone in this than by
A single voice, and that not passed me but   70
By learned approbation of the judges. If I am
Traduced by ignorant tongues — which neither
    know
My faculties nor person, yet will be
The chronicles of my doing° — let me say
'Tis but the fate of place,° and the rough brake° 75
That virtue must go through. We must not stint
Our necessary actions in the fear
To cope° malicious censurers, which ever,
As ravenous fishes, do a vessel follow
That is new-trimmed,° but benefit no further   80
Than vainly longing. What we oft do best,
By sick interpreters, once° weak ones, is
Not ours or not allowed; what worst, as oft,
Hitting a grosser quality, is cried up
For our best act.° If we shall stand still   85

In fear our notion will be mocked or carped at,
We should take root here where we sit, or sit
State-statues° only.
    KING.   Things done well,
And with a care, exempt themselves from fear;
Things done without example,° in their issue° 90
Are to be feared. Have you a precedent
Of this commission? I believe, not any.
We must not rend our subjects from our laws,
And stick them in our will.° Sixth part of each?
A trembling° contribution! Why, we take   95
From every tree lop,° bark, and part o' the timber,
And, though we leave it with a root, thus hacked,
The air will drink the sap. To every county
Where this is questioned send our letters with
Free pardon to each man that has denied   100
The force of this commission. Pray, look to 't.
I put it to your care.
    WOL. [*To the* SECRETARY] A word with you.
Let there be letters writ to every shire
Of the King's grace and pardon. The grieved com-
    mons
Hardly conceive of me.° Let it be noised   105
That through our intercession this revokement
And pardon comes. I shall anon advise you
Further in the proceeding.   [*Exit* SECRETARY.]
            [*Enter* SURVEYOR.]
    Q. KATH. I am sorry that the Duke of Bucking-
    ham
Is run in your displeasure.
    KING.   It grieves many.   110
The gentleman is learned and a most rare speaker;
To nature none more bound;° his training such
That he may furnish and instruct great teachers,
And never seek for aid out of himself.° Yet see,
When these so noble benefits shall prove   115
Not well disposed, the mind growing once corrupt,
They turn to vicious forms, ten times more ugly
Than ever they were fair. This man so complete,
Who was enrolled 'mongst wonders, and when we,
Almost with ravished° listening, could not find 120
His hour of speech a minute, he, my lady,
Hath into monstrous habits° put the graces
That once were his, and is become as black
As if besmeared in Hell. Sit by us. You shall hear —
This was his gentleman in trust — of him   125
Things to strike honor sad. Bid him recount
The fore-recited practices,° whereof
We cannot feel too little, hear too much.

---

50. sacrifice to: broken by.   **51–52. or . . . exclamation:** or you are too unjustly denounced.   **56. grief:** grievance.   **64–65. This . . . will:** obedience, which ought to hold men in loyalty, has been subdued by every man's angry passion (*will*).   **67. primer:** more urgent.   **68–71. And . . . judges:** I have taken no further part in this affair than to give my support (*voice*), and that was not given without the approval of the learned judges.   **73–74. yet . . . doing:** yet will act as historians (and critics) of my actions.   **75. place:** those in high position. **brake:** thorn bush.   **78. cope:** encounter.   **80. new-trimmed:** newly cleaned and equipped.   **81–83. What . . allowed:** our best actions are by jaundiced — that is, by weak — critics either declared not to be ours or not credited to us.   **82. once:** in a word, namely.   **83–85. what . . . act:** our worst actions, appealing to the baser nature of our critics, are praised as our best.

88. State-statues: dummies, not statesmen.   **90. example:** precedent. **issue:** result.   **93–94. rend . . . will:** deprive our people of their legal rights and treat them arbitrarily.   **95. trembling:** fearful.   **96. lop:** the small branches.   **105. Hardly . . . me:** regard me bitterly.   **112. To . . . bound:** no one has greater natural ability.   **114. out of himself:** i.e., from others.   **120. ravished:** enchanted.   **122. habits:** garments.   **127. fore-recited practices:** plots already divulged.

WOL. Stand forth, and with bold spirit relate what you,
Most like a careful subject, have collected   130
Out of the Duke of Buckingham.
    KING.   Speak freely.
    SURV. First, it was usual with him — every day
It would infect his speech — that if the King
Should without issue die, he'll carry it so
To make the scepter his. These very words   135
I've heard him utter to his son-in-law,
Lord Abergavenny, to whom by oath he menaced
Revenge upon the Cardinal.
    WOL.   Please your Highness, note
This dangerous conception in this point.
Not friended by his wish,° to your high person   140
His will is most malignant, and it stretches
Beyond you to your friends.
    Q. KATH.   My learned Lord Cardinal,
Deliver all with charity.
    KING.   Speak on.
How grounded he his title to the crown   144
Upon our fail? To this point hast thou heard him
At any time speak aught?
    SURV.   He was brought to this
By a vain prophecy of Nicholas Henton.°
    KING. What was that Henton?
    SURV.   Sir, a Chartreux° friar,
His confessor, who fed him every minute
With words of sovereignty.
    KING.   How know'st thou this?   150
    SURV. Not long before your Highness sped° to
      France,
The Duke being at the Rose,° within the parish
Saint Lawrence Poultney,° did of me demand
What was the speech among the Londoners
Concerning the French journey. I replied   155
Men feared the French would prove perfidious,
To the King's danger. Presently° the Duke
Said 'twas the fear indeed, and that he doubted°
'Twould prove the verity of certain words
Spoke by a holy monk " that oft," says he,   160
" Hath sent to me, wishing me to permit
John de la Car, my chaplain, a choice hour
To hear from him a matter of some moment;
Whom after under the confession's seal
He solemnly had sworn that what he spoke   165
My chaplain to no creature living but
To me should utter, with demure° confidence
This pausingly ensued: ' Neither the King nor 's
    heirs,
Tell you the Duke, shall prosper. Bid him strive

140. Not . . . wish: not getting his desire — that the King should
die naturally without an heir.   147. Henton: this is the F1 reading. The friar was previously called Hopkins. See I.i.221 and
Hen VIII Intro. p. 1503b.   148. Chartreux: Carthusian.
151. sped: set out for.   152. Rose: a tavern.   153. Saint . . .
Poultney: a London parish.   157. Presently: at once.
158. doubted: suspected.   167. demure: solemn.

To gain the love o' the commonalty. The Duke   170
Shall govern England.' "
    Q. KATH.   If I know you well,
You were the Duke's surveyor and lost your office
On the complaint o' the tenants. Take good heed
You charge not in your spleen° a noble person
And spoil your nobler soul. I say, take heed;   175
Yes, heartily beseech you.
    KING.   Let him on.
Go forward.
    SURV.   On my soul, I'll speak but truth.
I told my lord the Duke by the Devil's illusions
The monk might be deceived, and that 'twas dan-
    gerous for him
To ruminate on this so far, until   180
It forged° him some design, which, being believed,
It was much like to do. He answered, " Tush,
It can do me no damage," adding further
That, had the King in his last sickness failed,
The Cardinal's and Sir Thomas Lovell's heads   185
Should have gone off.
    KING.   Ha! What, so rank?° Ah ha!
There's mischief in this man. Canst thou say
    further?
    SURV. I can, my liege.
    KING.   Proceed.
    SURV.   Being at Greenwich,
After your Highness had reproved the Duke
About Sir William Bulmer ——
    KING.   I remember   190
Of such a time. Being my sworn servant,
The Duke retained him his. But on. What hence?
    SURV. " If," quoth he, " I for this had been com-
    mitted
As to the Tower I thought, I would have played
The part my father meant to act upon   195
The usurper Richard; who, being at Salisbury,
Made suit to come in 's presence; which if granted,
As he made semblance of his duty,° would
Have put his knife into him."
    KING.   A giant traitor!
    WOL. Now, madam, may His Highness live in
    freedom,   200
And this man out of prison?
    Q. KATH.   God mend all!
    KING. There's something more would out of thee.
    What say'st?
    SURV. After " the Duke his father," with the
    " knife,"
He stretched him, and with one hand on his dag-
    ger,
Another spread on 's breast, mounting his eyes,   205
He did discharge a horrible oath whose tenor

174. spleen: rancor, bad temper.   181. forged: shaped, caused
him to make.   186. rank: puffed up.   198. semblance . . .
duty: pretended to be a loyal subject. For the fate of Buckingham's father, see Rich III, especially V.i.

Was, were he evil used, he would outgo
His father by as much as a performance
Does an irresolute purpose.
KING.   There's his period,°
To sheathe his knife in us. He is attached;°   210
Call him to present° trial. If he may
Find mercy in the law, 'tis his. If none,
Let him not seek 't of us. By day and night!
He's traitor to the height.°   [*Exeunt.*]

SCENE III. *An antechamber in the palace.*

[*Enter the* LORD CHAMBERLAIN *and* LORD SANDS.]
CHAM. Is 't possible the spells of France should
      juggle
Men into such strange mysteries?°
SAN.   New customs,
Though they be never so ridiculous,
Nay, let 'em be° unmanly, yet are followed.
CHAM. As far as I see, all the good our English   5
Have got by the late voyage is but merely
A fit or two o' the face;° but they are shrewd° ones,
For when they hold 'em, you would swear directly
Their very noses had been Councilors
To Pepin or Clotharius,° they keep state° so.   10
SAN. They have all new legs,° and lame ones.
      One would take it
That never saw 'em pace before, the spavin°
Or springhalt° reigned among 'em.
CHAM.   Death! My lord,
Their clothes are after such a pagan cut, too,
That, sure, they've worn out Christendom.°
      [*Enter* SIR THOMAS LOVELL.]
                              How now!   15
What news, Sir Thomas Lovell?
LOV.   Faith, my lord,
I hear of none but the new proclamation
That's clapped° upon the Court Gate.
CHAM.   What is 't for?
LOV. The reformation of our traveled gallants
That fill the Court with quarrels, talk, and tailors.
CHAM. I'm glad 'tis there. Now I would pray our
      monsieurs   21
To think an English courtier may be wise,
And never see the Louvre.°
LOV.   They must either,
For so run the conditions, leave those remnants

Of fool and feather° that they got in France,   25
With all their honorable points of ignorance°
Pertaining thereunto, as fights and fireworks,
Abusing better men than they can be
Out of a foreign wisdom, renouncing clean   29
The faith they have in tennis° and tall stockings,
Short blistered° breeches and those types° of travel,
And understand again like honest men,
Or pack to their old playfellows.° There, I take it,
They may, *cum privilegio,*° wear away   34
The lag° end of their lewdness and be laughed at.
SAN. 'Tis time to give 'em physic, their diseases
Are grown so catching.
CHAM.   What a loss our ladies
Will have of these trim vanities!
LOV.   Aye, marry,
There will be woe indeed, lords. The sly whoresons
Have got a speeding trick° to lay down° ladies. 40
A French song and a fiddle has no fellow.°
SAN. The Devil fiddle 'em! I am glad they are
      going,
For, sure, there's no converting of 'em. Now
An honest country lord, as I am, beaten
A long time out of play, may bring his plain song°
And have an hour of hearing, and, by 'r lady,   46
Held current° music too.
CHAM.   Well said, Lord Sands.
Your colt's tooth° is not cast yet.
SAN.   No, my lord,
Nor shall not while I have a stump.
CHAM.   Sir Thomas,
Whither were you agoing?
LOV.   To the Cardinal's. 50
Your lordship is a guest too.
CHAM.   Oh, 'tis true.
This night he makes a supper, and a great one,
To many lords and ladies. There will be
The beauty of this kingdom, I'll assure you.
LOV. That churchman bears a bounteous mind in-
      deed,   55
A hand as fruitful as the land that feeds us.
His dews fall every where.
CHAM.   No doubt he's noble.
He had a black mouth that said other of him.
SAN. He may, my lord; has wherewithal. In him
Sparing° would show a worse sin than ill doctrine.
Men of his way should be most liberal.   61
They are set here for examples.

---

209. **period:** end.   210. **attached:** arrested.   211. **present:** immediate.   214. **height:** utmost.
  Sc. iii: 2. **strange mysteries:** fantastical behavior.   4. **let ... be:** so long as they are.   7. **fit ... face:** affected way of screwing up the face. **shrewd:** nasty.   10. **Pepin or Clotharius:** ancient kings of France of the 6th and 8th centuries. **state:** pomposity.   11. **new legs:** new ways of making a curtsy.   12. **spavin:** swelling in the knee joints.   13. **springhalt:** lameness.   15. **worn ... Christendom:** got tired of any fashion that a Christian might wear.   18. **clapped:** fastened.   23. **Louvre:** the palace of the French king in Paris.

25. **fool ... feather:** silly manners and fantastical dress.   26. **points of ignorance:** nice distinctions.   30. **tennis:** a very popular game in France.   31. **blistered:** puffed out like a blister. **types:** signs.   33. **pack ... playfellows:** go back quickly to France and stay there.   34. *cum privilegio:* with the King's special allowance — the formal phrase used in a special grant.   35. **lag:** tail.   40. **speeding trick:** successful device. **lay down:** overcome.   41. **fellow:** equal.   45. **plain song:** simple melody; i.e., the honest English way of singing.   47. **Held current:** regarded as up to date.   48. **colt's tooth:** i.e., you're still frisky.   60. **Sparing:** meanness.

CHAM.　　　　　　　　　　　True, they are so;
But few now give so great ones. My barge° stays.
Your lordship shall along. Come, good Sir Thomas,
We shall be late else; which I would not be,　　　65
For I was spoke to, with Sir Henry Guildford,
This night to be comptrollers.°
　　SAN.　　　　　　I am your lordship's.　　[*Exeunt*]

SCENE IV. *A hall in York Place.*

[*Hautboys.° A small table under a state for the* CAR-
DINAL, *a longer table for the guests. Then enter*
ANNE BULLEN *and divers other* LADIES *and* GENTLE-
MEN *as guests, at one door; at another door, enter*
SIR HENRY GUILDFORD.]

GUILD. Ladies, a general welcome from His
　　　Grace
Salutes ye all. This night he dedicates
To fair content and you. None here, he hopes,
In all this noble bevy,° has brought with her
One care abroad. He would have all as merry　　5
As, first, good company, good wine, good welcome
Can make good people.
　　[*Enter* LORD CHAMBERLAIN, LORD SANDS, *and*
　　　　　　　SIR THOMAS LOVELL.]
　　　　　　　　　Oh, my lord, you're tardy.
The very thought of this fair company
Clapped wings to me.
　　CHAM.　　　You are young, Sir Harry Guildford.
SAN. Sir Thomas Lovell, had the Cardinal　　10
But half my lay thoughts in him, some of these
Should find a running banquet° ere they rested
I think would better please 'em. By my life,
They are a sweet society of fair ones.
　　LOV. Oh, that your lordship were but now con-
　　　fessor　　　　　　　　　　　　　　　　　15
To one or two of these!
　　SAN.　　　　　　　I would I were.
They should find easy penance.
　　LOV.　　　　　　　　　Faith, how easy?
SAN. As easy as a down bed would afford it.
　　CHAM. Sweet ladies, will it please you sit? Sir
　　　Harry,
Place you° that side. I'll take the charge of this.　20
His Grace is entering. Nay, you must not freeze.
Two women placed together makes cold weather.
My Lord Sands, you are one will keep 'em waking.
Pray, sit between these ladies.
　　SAN.　　　　　　　　By my faith,
And thank your lordship. By your leave, sweet
　　ladies.　　　　　　　　　　　　　　　　　25

If I chance to talk a little wild, forgive me.
I had it from my father.
　　ANNE.　　　　　　Was he mad, sir?
SAN. Oh, very mad, exceeding mad, in love too.
But he would bite none; just as I do now,
He would kiss you twenty with a breath.°
　　　　　　　　　　　　　　　[*Kisses her.*]
CHAM.　　　　　　　　Well said, my lord.　　30
So, now you're fairly seated. Gentlemen,
The penance lies on you if these fair ladies
Pass away frowning.
　　SAN.　　　　　　For my little cure,°
Let me alone.
　　[*Hautboys. Enter* CARDINAL WOLSEY, *and takes
　　　　　　　his state.*]
　　WOL. You're welcome, my fair guests. That noble
　　　lady　　　　　　　　　　　　　　　　　35
Or gentleman that is not freely merry
Is not my friend. This, to confirm my welcome;
And to you all, good health.　　　　[*Drinks.*]
　　SAN.　　　　　　　Your Grace is noble.
Let me have such a bowl may° hold my thanks
And save me so much talking.
　　WOL.　　　　　　My Lord Sands,　　40
I am beholding to you. Cheer your neighbors.
Ladies, you are not merry. Gentlemen,
Whose fault is this?
　　SAN.　　　　　　The red wine first must rise
In their fair cheeks, my lord. Then we shall have
　　'em
Talk us to silence.
　　ANNE.　　　　You are a merry gamester,　　45
My Lord Sands.
　　SAN.　　　　　Yes, if I make my play.°
Here's to your ladyship; and pledge it, madam,
For 'tis to such a thing ——
　　ANNE.　　　　　　　You cannot show me.
SAN. I told your Grace they would talk anon.
　　[*Drum and trumpet. Chambers° discharged.*]
　　WOL.　　　　　　　　　What's that?
CHAM. Look out there, some of ye.
　　　　　　　　　　　　　　[*Exit* SERVANT.]
　　WOL.　　　　　　What warlike voice,　　50
And to what end, is this? Nay, ladies, fear not.
By all the laws of war you're privileged.
　　[*Re-enter* SERVANT.]
CHAM. How now! What is 't?
　　SERV.　　　　　　　A noble troop of strangers,
For so they seem. They've left their barge and
　　landed,
And hither make, as great ambassadors　　　55
From foreign princes.
　　WOL.　　　　　Good Lord Chamberlain,

---

63. **barge:** For traveling on the Thames, wealthy men had private
barges rowed by servants.　67. **comptrollers:** masters of ceremonies.
　Sc. iv: s.d., Hautboys: oboes.　4. **bevy:** collection.　12. **running banquet:** light refreshments.　20. **Place you:** arrange the
places on.

30. **kiss . . . breath:** kiss twenty without drawing breath.
33. **cure:** parish — continuing the metaphor of l. 15.　39. **may:**
which may.　46. **make my play:** win.　49. s.d., **Chambers:**
small cannon. For the sad consequences see Gen. Intro. p. 50b.

Go, give 'em welcome. You can speak the French
  tongue.
And pray receive 'em nobly and conduct 'em
Into our presence, where this Heaven of beauty   59
Shall shine at full upon them. Some attend him.
        [*Exit* CHAMBERLAIN, *attended.
        All rise, and tables removed.*]
You have now a broken° banquet, but we'll mend
  it.
A good digestion to you all. And once more
I shower a welcome on ye. Welcome all.
[*Hautboys. Enter the* KING *and others, as masqu-
  ers,° habited like shepherds, ushered by the*
  LORD CHAMBERLAIN. *They pass directly before°
  the* CARDINAL, *and gracefully salute him.*]
A noble company! What are their pleasures?
    CHAM. Because they speak no English, thus they
        prayed   65
To tell your Grace: that, having heard by fame
Of this so noble and so fair assembly
This night to meet here, they could do no less,
Out of the great respect they bear to beauty,
But leave their flocks, and under your fair con-
        duct°   70
Crave leave to view these ladies and entreat
An hour of revels with 'em.
    WOL.   Say, Lord Chamberlain,
They have done my poor house grace, for which I
        pay 'em
A thousand thanks and pray 'em take their pleas-
        ures. [*They choose. The* KING *chooses* ANNE
        BULLEN.]
    KING. The fairest hand I ever touched! O Beauty,
Till now I never knew thee! [*Music. Dance.*]   76
    WOL. My lord!
    CHAM.   Your Grace?
    WOL.   Pray tell 'em thus much from me:
There should be one amongst 'em, by his person,
More worthy this place than myself; to whom,
If I but knew him, with my love and duty   80
I would surrender it.
    CHAM.   I will, my lord.
                [*Whispers to the Masquers.*]
    WOL. What say they?
    CHAM.   Such a one, they all confess,
There is indeed; which they would have your Grace
Find out, and he will take it.
    WOL.   Let me see then   84
By all your good leaves, gentlemen, here I'll make
My royal choice.

    KING. [*Unmasking.*]   Ye have found him,
        Cardinal.
You hold a fair assembly. You do well, lord.
You are a churchman, or, I'll tell you, Cardinal,
I should judge now unhappily.°
    WOL.   I am glad
Your Grace is grown so pleasant.
    KING.   My Lord Chamberlain,   90
Prithee come hither. What fair lady's that?
    CHAM. An 't please your Grace, Sir Thomas
        Bullen's daughter,
The Viscount Rochford, one of Her Highness'
        women.
    KING. By Heaven, she is a dainty one. Sweetheart,
I were unmannerly to take you out°   95
And not to kiss you. A health, gentlemen!
Let it go round.
    WOL. Sir Thomas Lovell, is the banquet ready
I' the privy chamber?
    LOV.   Yes, my lord.
    WOL.   Your Grace,
I fear, with dancing is a little heated.   100
    KING. I fear, too much.
    WOL.   There's fresher air, my lord,
In the next chamber.
    KING. Lead in your ladies, every one. Sweet
        partner,
I must not yet forsake you. Let's be merry,
Good my Lord Cardinal. I have half a dozen
        healths   105
To drink to these fair ladies, and a measure°
To lead 'em once again; and then let's dream
Who's best in favor. Let the music knock it.°
                [*Exeunt with trumpets.*]

Act II

SCENE I. *Westminster. A street.*

[*Enter two* GENTLEMEN, *meeting.*]
    1. GENT. Whither away so fast?
    2. GENT.   Oh, God save ye!
Even to the Hall,° to hear what shall become
Of the great Duke of Buckingham.
    1. GENT.   I'll save you
That labor, sir. All's now done but the ceremony
Of bringing back the prisoner.
    2. GENT.   Were you there?   5

---

61. broken: interrupted.   63. s.d., masquers: i.e., in disguise
and masked. Masques in the time of Henry VIII were different
from the later Court entertainment. They resembled the type of
amusement offered by Navarre to the Princess in *LLL* V.ii.157–
265 rather than the elaborate entertainments of the Court of
King James I (see Gen. Intro. p. 47b). directly before: immediately in front of.   70. conduct: escort, guardianship.

89. judge . . unhappily: think suspiciously.   95. take . . . out:
choose you as my partner.   106. measure: See App. 24.
108. knock it: strike up.
    Act II, Sc. i: 2. the Hall: Westminster Hall, adjoining the
Houses of Parliament. Here the judges, each in his own court,
sat to decide civil cases. For great state trials the whole hall was
used.

1. GENT. Yes, indeed was I.

2. GENT.   Pray speak what has happened.

1. GENT. You may guess quickly what.

2. GENT.   Is he found guilty?

1. GENT. Yes, truly is he, and condemned upon 't.

2. GENT. I am sorry for 't.

1. GENT.   So are a number more.

2. GENT. But, pray, how passed it?

1. GENT. I'll tell you in a little. The great Duke
Came to the bar, where to his accusations
He pleaded still not guilty and alleged
Many sharp reasons to defeat the law.
The King's Attorney, on the contrary,   15
Urged on the examinations, proofs, confessions
Of divers witnesses, which the Duke desired
To have brought *viva voce* to his face;
At which appeared against him his surveyor;
Sir Gilbert Peck,° his chancellor; and John Car,
Confessor to him; with that devil monk,   21
Hopkins, that made this mischief.

2. GENT.   That was he
That fed him with his prophecies?

1. GENT.   The same.
All these accused him strongly, which he fain°
Would have flung from him, but indeed he could
    not;   25
And so his peers upon his° evidence
Have found him guilty of high treason. Much
He spoke, and learnedly, for life, but all
Was either pitied in him or forgotten.°

2. GENT. After all this, how did he bear himself?

1. GENT. When he was brought again to the bar
    to hear   31
His knell° rung out, his judgment, he was stirred
With such an agony he sweat extremely
And something spoke in choler, ill and hasty.
But he fell to° himself again and sweetly   35
In all the rest showed a most noble patience.

2. GENT. I do not think he fears death.

1. GENT.   Sure, he does not.
He never was so womanish. The cause
He may a little grieve at.

2. GENT.   Certainly
The Cardinal is the end° of this.

1. GENT.   'Tis likely,   40
By all conjectures. First, Kildare's attainder,°
Then Deputy of Ireland, who removed,°
Earl Surrey was sent thither, and in haste too,
Lest he should help his father.°

2. GENT.   That trick of state°

Was a deep envious one.

1. GENT.   At his return   45
No doubt he will requite it. This is noted,
And generally:° Whoever the King favors,
The Cardinal instantly will find employment,
And far enough from Court, too.

2. GENT.   All the commons
Hate him perniciously and, o' my conscience,   50
Wish him ten fathom deep. This Duke as much
They love and dote on, call him bounteous Buck-
    ingham,
The mirror of all courtesy——

1. GENT.   Stay there, sir,
And see the noble ruined man you speak of.

[*Enter* BUCKINGHAM *from his arraignment, tipstaves*° *before him, the ax with the edge toward
him,*° *halberds*° *on each side, accompanied with* SIR
THOMAS LOVELL, SIR NICHOLAS VAUX, SIR WILLIAM
SANDS, *and common people, &c.*]

2. GENT. Let's stand close and behold him.

BUCK.   All good people,   55
You that thus far have come to pity me,
Hear what I say, and then go home and lose° me.
I have this day received a traitor's judgment,
And by that name must die. Yet, Heaven bear wit-
    ness,
And if I have a conscience, let it sink° me   60
Even as the ax falls if I be not faithful!
The law I bear no malice for my death.
'T has done upon the premises° but° justice;
But those that sought it I could wish more Chris-
    tians.
Be what they will, I heartily forgive 'em.   65
Yet let 'em look they glory not in mischief,
Nor build their evils on the graves of great men,
For then my guiltless blood must cry against 'em.
For further life in this world I ne'er hope,
Nor will I sue, although the King have mercies   70
More than I dare make faults. You few that loved
    me
And dare be bold to weep for Buckingham,
His noble friends and fellows,° whom to leave
Is only bitter to him only dying,°
Go with me, like good angels, to my end,   75
And as the long divorce of steel° falls on me,
Make of your prayers one sweet sacrifice
And lift my soul to Heaven. Lead on, o' God's
    name.

LOV. I do beseech your Grace, for charity,
If ever any malice in your heart   80

---

20. Sir . . . Peck: He was a priest. For the title "Sir," see
T Night, III.iv.298,n.   24. his: willingly.   26. his: i.e., Hopkins'.
28–29. all . . . forgotten: his words caused only pity or were
passed over.   32. knell: condemnation, lit., death bell. See App.
19.   35. fell to: recovered.   40. end: ultimate cause.   41. attainder: accusation of treason.   42. removed: dismissed from
his office.   44. father: father-in-law. See later III.ii.260–64.
state: policy.

47. generally: universally.   54. s.d., tipstaves: officers of the
law. ax . . . him: a sign that he has been condemned to death.
halberds: guards carrying halberds. See Pl. 21b.   57. lose: forget.   60. sink: destroy.   63. premises: evidence offered. but:
only.   73. fellows: companions.   74. Is . . . dying: i.e., the
only bitterness in death is to leave my friends.   76. divorce of
steel: separation of soul and body caused by the ax.

Were hid against me, now to forgive me frankly.

BUCK. Sir Thomas Lovell, I as free forgive you
As I would be forgiven. I forgive all.
There cannot be those numberless offenses
'Gainst me that I cannot take peace with. No black
    envy   85
Shall mark my grave. Commend me to His Grace,
And if he speak of Buckingham, pray tell him
You met him half in Heaven. My vows and prayers
Yet are the King's and, till my soul forsake,
Shall cry for blessings on him. May he live   90
Longer than I have time to tell° his years!
Ever beloved and loving may his rule be!
And when old Time shall lead him to his end,
Goodness and he fill up one monument!

    LOV. To the water side I must conduct your
    Grace,   95
Then give my charge up to Sir Nicholas Vaux,
Who undertakes° you to your end.

    VAUX.   Prepare there.
The Duke is coming. See the barge be ready,
And fit it with such furniture as suits
The greatness of his person.

    BUCK.   Nay, Sir Nicholas,   100
Let it alone. My state° now will but mock me.
When I came hither, I was Lord High Constable
And Duke of Buckingham; now, poor Edward
    Bohun.
Yet I am richer than my base accusers,   104
That never knew what truth meant. I now seal° it,
And with that blood will make 'em one day groan
    for 't.
My noble father, Henry of Buckingham,
Who first raised head° against usurping Richard,
Flying for succor to his servant Banister,
Being distressed, was by that wretch betrayed   110
And without trial fell. God's peace be with him!
Henry the Seventh succeeding, truly pitying
My father's loss, like a most royal prince
Restored me to my honors and out of ruins
Made my name once more noble. Now his son,
Henry the Eighth, life, honor, name, and all   116
That made me happy, at one stroke has taken
For ever from the world. I had my trial,
And must needs say, a noble one, which makes
    me
A little happier than my wretched father.   120
Yet thus far we are one in fortunes. Both
Fell by our servants, by those men we loved most —
A most unnatural and faithless service!
Heaven has an end in all. Yet, you that hear me,
This from a dying man receive as certain: 125
Where you are liberal of your loves and counsels

Be sure you be not loose,° for those you make
    friends
And give your hearts to, when they once perceive
The least rub° in your fortunes, fall away
Like water from ye, never found again   130
But where they mean to sink ye. All good people,
Pray for me! I must now forsake ye. The last hour
Of my long weary life is come upon me.
Farewell!   134
And when you would say something that is sad,
Speak how I fell. I have done, and God forgive me!
          [*Exeunt* DUKE *and train.*]

    1. GENT. Oh, this is full of pity! Sir, it calls,
I fear, too many curses on their heads
That were the authors.

    2. GENT.   If the Duke be guiltless,
'Tis full of woe. Yet I can give you inkling   140
Of an ensuing evil, if it fall,
Greater than this.

    1. GENT.   Good angels keep it from us!
What may it be? You do not doubt my faith,°
    sir?

    2. GENT. This secret is so weighty, 'twill require
A strong faith to conceal it.

    1. GENT.   Let me have it.   145
I do not talk much.

    2. GENT.   I am confident.
You shall, sir. Did you not of late days hear
A buzzing° of a separation
Between the King and Katharine?

    1. GENT.   Yes, but it held not;
For when the King once heard it, out of anger   150
He sent command to the Lord Mayor straight
To stop the rumor and allay those tongues
That durst disperse it.

    2. GENT.   But that slander, sir,
Is found a truth now. For it grows again
Fresher than e'er it was, and held for certain   155
The King will venture at it. Either the Cardinal,
Or some about him near, have, out of malice
To the good Queen, possessed him with a scruple°
That will undo her. To confirm this, too,
Cardinal Campeius is arrived, and lately;   160
As all think, for this business.

    1. GENT.   'Tis the Cardinal;
And merely to revenge him on the Emperor
For not bestowing on him at his asking
The Archbishopric of Toledo, this is purposed.

    2. GENT. I think you have hit the mark; but is 't
    not cruel
That she should feel the smart of this? The Cardi-
    nal   166
Will have his will, and she must fall.

    1. GENT.   'Tis woeful.

---

91. tell: count.   97. undertakes: is in charge of.   101. state:
i.e., to treat me with the ceremony due to my rank.   105. seal:
confirm my truth by death.   108. head: an army.

127. loose: too liberal.   129. rub: impediment, check.   143. faith:
trustworthiness.   148. buzzing: rumor.   158. possessed . . .
scruple: caused him to feel a scruple of conscience.

We are too open here° to argue this.
Let's think in private more.   [*Exeunt.*]

SCENE II. *An antechamber in the palace.*

[*Enter the* LORD CHAMBERLAIN, *reading a letter.*]
CHAM. "My lord, the horses your lordship sent
for, with all the care I had, I saw well chosen, rid-
den,° and furnished.° They were young and hand-
some, and of the best breed in the North. When
they were ready to set out for London, a man of my
Lord Cardinal's, by commission° and main power,°
took 'em from me with this reason: His master
would be served before a subject, if not before the
King; which stopped our mouths, sir."   10
I fear he will indeed. Well, let him have them.
He will have all, I think.
   [*Enter to the* LORD CHAMBERLAIN, *the* DUKES OF
        NORFOLK *and* SUFFOLK.]
NOR. Well met, my Lord Chamberlain.
CHAM. Good day to both your Graces.
SUF. How is the King employed?
CHAM.   I left him private,°   15
Full of sad thoughts and troubles.
NOR.   What's the cause?
CHAM. It seems the marriage with his brother's
wife
Has crept too near his conscience.
SUF.   No, his conscience
Has crept too near another lady.
NOR.   'Tis so.   19
This is the Cardinal's doing, the King-Cardinal.
That blind priest, like the eldest son° of Fortune,
Turns what he list. The King will know° him one
day.
SUF. Pray God he do! He'll never know himself
else.
NOR. How holily he works in all his business!
And with what zeal! For, now he has cracked the
league   25
Between us and the Emperor, the Queen's great
nephew,
He dives into the King's soul, and there scatters
Dangers, doubts, wringing° of the conscience,
Fears and despairs — and all these for his marriage.
And out of all these to restore the King,   30
He counsels a divorce, a loss of her
That, like a jewel, has hung twenty years
About his neck, yet never lost her luster,
Of her that loves him with that excellence
That angels love good men with, even of her   35

That, when the greatest stroke of fortune° falls,
Will bless the King. And is not this course pious?
   CHAM. Heaven keep me from such counsel! 'Tis
most true
These news are everywhere. Every tongue speaks
'em,
And every true heart weeps for 't. All that dare   40
Look into these affairs see this main end,°
The French King's sister. Heaven will one day
open
The King's eyes, that so long have slept upon
This bold bad man.
SUF.   And free us from his slavery.
NOR. We had need pray,   45
And heartily, for our deliverance,
Or this imperious man will work° us all
From princes into pages. All men's honors
Lie like one lump before him, to be fashioned
Into what pitch° he please.
SUF.   For me, my lords,   50
I love him not, nor fear him; there's my creed.
As I am made without him,° so I'll stand,
If the King please. His curses and his blessings
Touch me alike. They're breath I not believe in.
I knew him, and I know him; so I leave him   55
To him that made him proud, the Pope.
NOR.   Let's in,
And with some other business put the King
From these sad thoughts that work too much upon
him.
My lord, you'll bear us company?
CHAM.   Excuse me.
The King has sent me otherwhere. Besides,   60
You'll find a most unfit time to disturb him.
Health to your lordships.
NOR.   Thanks, my good Lord Chamberlain.
   [*Exit* LORD CHAMBERLAIN, *and the* KING
    draws° *the curtain and sits reading pensively.*]
SUF. How sad he looks! Sure, he is much af-
flicted.
KING. Who's there, ha?
NOR.   Pray God he be not angry.
KING. Who's there, I say? How dare you thrust
yourselves   65
Into my private meditations?
Who am I? Ha?
NOR. A gracious King that pardons all offenses,
Malice ne'er meant. Our breach of duty this way
Is business of estate° in which we come   70
To know your royal pleasure.
KING.   Ye are too bold.

---

168. We . . . here: i.e., this is too public a place.
   Sc. ii: 2-3. ridden: broken in. 3. furnished: equipped with
saddlery. 6. commission: the power granted him by the
Cardinal. main power: sheer force. 15. private: by himself.
21. eldest son: spoiled child. See *M Ado*, II.i.10. 22. know: find
him out. 28. wringing: torment.

36. fortune: misfortune. 41. main end: chief objective.
47. work: reduce. 50. pitch: usually means the top of the flight
of a hawk. The image, however, is that of the lump of clay which
the potter converts into whatever kind of vessel he chooses.
52. made . . . him: owe nothing to him. 62. s.d., draws: pulls
aside the curtain of the inner stage. 70. estate: state.

Go to,° I'll make ye know your times of business.
Is this an hour for temporal affairs, ha?
[*Enter* WOLSEY *and* CAMPEIUS, *with a commission.*]
Who's there? My good Lord Cardinal? O my Wolsey,
The quiet of my wounded conscience,   75
Thou art a cure fit for a King. [*To* CAMPEIUS]
     You're welcome,
Most learnèd reverend sir, into our kingdom.
Use us and it. [*To* WOLSEY] My good lord, have
     great care
I be not found a talker.°
    WOL.   Sir, you cannot.
I would your Grace would give us but an hour   80
Of private conference.
    KING. [*To* NORFOLK *and* SUFFOLK] We are busy.
     Go.
    NOR. [*Aside to* SUFFOLK] This priest has no pride
     in him?
    SUF. [*Aside to* NORFOLK]   Not to speak of.
I would not be so sick,° though, for his place.
But this cannot continue.
    NOR. [*Aside to* SUFFOLK] If it do,
I'll venture one have-at-him.°
    SUF. [*Aside to* NORFOLK] I another.   85
         [*Exeunt* NORFOLK *and* SUFFOLK.]
    WOL. Your Grace has given a precedent of wisdom
Above all princes in committing freely
Your scruple to the voice of Christendom.
Who can be angry now? What envy reach you?
The Spaniard,° tied by blood and favor to her,   90
Must now confess, if they have any goodness,
The trial just and noble. All the clerks° —
I mean the learnèd ones — in Christian kingdoms
Have their free voices.° Rome, the nurse of judgment,
Invited by your noble self, hath sent   95
One general tongue° unto us, this good man,
This just and learnèd priest, Cardinal Campeius,
Whom once more I present unto your Highness.
    KING. And once more in mine arms I bid him
     welcome   99
And thank the Holy Conclave° for their loves.
They have sent me such a man I would have wished
     for.
    CAM. Your Grace must needs deserve all strangers' loves,
You are so noble. To your Highness' hand

I tender my commission, by whose virtue,   104
The Court of Rome commanding, you, my Lord
Cardinal of York, are joined with me their servant
In the unpartial° judging of this business.
    KING. Two equal men. The Queen shall be acquainted
Forthwith for what you come. Where's Gardiner?
    WOL. I know your Majesty has always loved her
So dear in heart not to deny her that   111
A woman of less place might ask by law —
Scholars allowed freely to argue for her.
    KING. Aye, and the best she shall have; and my
     favor
To him that does best. God forbid else. Cardinal,
Prithee call Gardiner to me, my new secretary.
I find him a fit fellow.   [*Exit* WOLSEY.]
     [*Re-enter* WOLSEY, *with* GARDINER.]
    WOL. [*Aside to* GARDINER] Give me your hand.
Much joy and favor to you.   118
You are the King's now.
    GARD. [*Aside to* WOLSEY] But to be commanded
For ever by your Grace, whose hand has raised me.
    KING. Come hither, Gardiner.
            [*Walks and whispers.*]
    CAM. My Lord of York, was not one Doctor Pace
In this man's place before him?
    WOL.   Yes, he was.   123
    CAM. Was he not held a learnèd man?
    WOL.   Yes, surely.
    CAM. Believe me, there's an ill opinion spread, then,
Even of yourself, Lord Cardinal.
    WOL.   How! Of me?   126
    CAM. They will not stick to say you envied him,
And fearing he would rise, he was so virtuous,
Kept him a foreign man still,° which so grieved
     him
That he ran mad and died.
    WOL.   Heaven's peace be with him!   130
That's Christian care enough. For living murmurers
There's places of rebuke. He was a fool,
For he would needs be virtuous. That good fellow,
If I command him, follows my appointment.
I will have none so near else. Learn this, Brother,
We live not to be gripèd° by meaner persons.   136
    KING. Deliver this with modesty to the Queen.
            [*Exit* GARDINER.]
The most convenient place that I can think of
For such receipt of learning° is Blackfriars.°
There ye shall meet about this weighty business.
My Wolsey, see it furnished.° Oh, my lord,   141
Would it not grieve an able man to leave

72. Go to: an exclamation of impatience.   79. talker: i.e., one that does not act.   83. sick: eager.   85. have-at-him: blow — from the exclamation "have at you," made as a note of warning to an opponent when delivering a decisive blow.   90. Spaniard: the Spaniards, for Queen Katherine was daughter of Ferdinand of Spain.   92. clerks: scholars.   94. Have . . . voices: are allowed to give their opinions freely.   96. One . . . tongue: one to represent the Church.   100. Holy Conclave: the College of Cardinals.

107 unpartial: impartial.   129. foreign . . . still: continuously employed on duties abroad.   136. gripèd: distressed, pained.   139. such . . . learning: to accommodate such a concourse of learnèd men. Blackfriars: a famous Dominican monastery in the heart of London.   141. furnished: made ready with furniture.

So sweet a bedfellow? But, conscience, conscience!
Oh, 'tis a tender place; and I must leave her.

                        [*Exeunt.*]

SCENE III. *An antechamber of the* QUEEN'S *apartments.*

[*Enter* ANNE BULLEN *and an* OLD LADY.]

ANNE. Not for that neither. Here's the pang that
    pinches.
His Highness having lived so long with her, and
    she
So good a lady that no tongue could ever
Prounounce dishonor of her — by my life,
She never knew harmdoing — Oh, now, after   5
So many courses of the sun enthroned,
Still growing in a majesty and pomp, the which
To leave a thousandfold more bitter than
'Tis sweet at first to acquire — after this process,°
To give her the avaunt!° It is a pity   10
Would move a monster.
    OLD L.   Hearts of most hard temper°
Melt and lament for her.
    ANNE.   Oh, God's will! Much better
She ne'er had known pomp. Though 't be temporal,
Yet if that quarrel, Fortune,° do divorce
It from the bearer, 'tis a sufferance panging°   15
As soul and body's severing.
    OLD L.   Alas, poor lady!
She's a stranger now again.
    ANNE.   So much the more
Must pity drop upon her. Verily,
I swear 'tis better to be lowly born
And range with humble livers in content   20
Than to be perked up° in a glistering° grief
And wear a golden sorrow.
    OLD L.   Our content
Is our best having.
    ANNE.   By my troth and maidenhead,
I would not be a queen.
    OLD L.   Beshrew me,° I would,
And venture maidenhead for 't; and so would you,
For all this spice of your hypocrisy.   26
You, that have so fair parts of woman on you,
Have, too, a woman's heart, which ever yet
Affected° eminence, wealth, sovereignty;
Which, to say sooth, are blessings, and which
    gifts —

Saving your mincing° — the capacity   31
Of your soft cheveril° conscience would receive
If you might please to stretch it.
    ANNE.   Nay, good troth.°
    OLD L. Yes, troth, and troth. You would not be a
    queen?
    ANNE. No, not for all the riches under Heaven.
    OLD L. 'Tis strange. A threepence bowed° would
    hire me,   36
Old as I am, to queen it. But, I pray you,
What think you of a duchess? Have you limbs
To bear that load of title?
    ANNE.   No, in truth.
    OLD L. Then you are weakly made. Pluck off° a
    little.   40
I would not be a young count in your way
For more than blushing comes to. If your back
Cannot vouchsafe this burden, 'tis too weak
Ever to get° a boy.
    ANNE.   How you do talk!
I swear again I would not be a queen   45
For all the world.
    OLD L.   In faith, for little England
You'd venture an emballing.° I myself
Would for Carnarvonshire,° although there
    'longed
No more to the crown but that. Lo, who comes
    here?
           [*Enter the* LORD CHAMBERLAIN.]
    CHAM. Good morrow, ladies. What were 't worth
    to know   50
The secret of your conference?
    ANNE.   My good lord,
Not your demand. It values not your asking.°
Our mistress' sorrows we were pitying.
    CHAM. It was a gentle business, and becoming
The action of good women. There is hope   55
All will be well.
    ANNE.   Now, I pray God, amen!
    CHAM. You bear a gentle mind, and heavenly
    blessings
Follow such creatures. That you may, fair lady,
Perceive I speak sincerely and high note's
Ta'en of your many virtues, the King's Majesty
Commends his good opinion of you and   61
Does purpose honor to you no less flowing°
Than Marchioness of Pembroke, to which title
A thousand pound a year annual support
Out of his grace he adds.
    ANNE.   I do not know   65

Sc. iii: **9. process:** what has gone before. **10. give . . .
avaunt:** tell her to be gone. **11. hard temper:** i.e., hard as
iron. **14. that . . . Fortune:** a much discussed phrase. F1 reads:
"Though't be temporal, / Yet if that quarrel. Fortune, do divorce / It from the bearer, 'tis a sufferance, panging" etc. Perhaps the simplest explanation is to take *quarrel* as meaning
"quarrelsome person." **15. sufferance panging:** a suffering as
painful. **21. perked up:** decked out. **glistering:** glittering.
24. Beshrew me: ill luck to me. **29. Affected:** longed for.

31. Saving . . . mincing: in spite of your prudish airs. **32. chev-
eril:** soft as a kid leather glove. **33. troth:** truth. **36. bowed:**
bent. **40. Pluck off:** i.e., come down a step lower; if a duke is
too high for your ambitions, what about an earl (*count*)? **44. get:**
beget. **47. emballing:** assault. **48. Carnarvonshire:** a bleak
and barren county in Wales. **52. Not . . . asking:** our talk is
not worth your asking. **62. flowing:** magnificent.

What kind of my obedience I should tender.
More than my all is nothing; nor my prayers
Are not° words duly hallowed,° nor my wishes
More worth than empty vanities; yet prayers and
    wishes
Are all I can return. Beseech your lordship,   70
Vouchsafe to speak my thanks and my obedience,
As from a blushing handmaid, to His Highness,
Whose health and royalty I pray for.
    CHAM.   Lady,
I shall not fail to approve° the fair conceit°
The King hath of you. [*Aside*] I have perused her
    well.   75
Beauty and honor in her are so mingled
That they have caught the King; and who knows
    yet
But from this lady may proceed a gem
To lighten all this isle? —I'll to the King,
And say I spoke with you.
    ANNE.   My honored lord.   80
                [*Exit* LORD CHAMBERLAIN.]
    OLD L. Why, this it is. See, see!
I have been begging sixteen years in Court,
Am yet a courtier beggarly, nor could
Come pat° betwixt too early and too late
For any suit of pounds;° and you, oh, Fate!   85
A very fresh fish here —fie, fie, fie upon
This compelled° fortune! —have your mouth filled
    up
Before you open it.
    ANNE.   This is strange to me.
    OLD L. How tastes it? Is it bitter? Forty pence,
    no.
There was a lady once —'tis an old story —   90
That would not be a queen, that would she not,
For all the mud in Egypt. Have you heard it?
    ANNE. Come, you are pleasant.
    OLD L.   With your theme, I could
O'ermount° the lark. The Marchioness of Pem-
    broke!
A thousand pounds a year for pure respect!°   95
No other obligation! By my life,
That promises moe° thousands. Honor's train
Is longer than his foreskirt. By this time
I know your back will bear a duchess. Say,
Are you not stronger than you were?
    ANNE.   Good lady,   100
Make yourself mirth with your particular fancy,
And leave me out on 't. Would I had no being
If this salute° my blood a jot. It faints me
To think what follows.

The Queen is comfortless, and we forgetful   105
In our long absence. Pray, do not deliver
What here you've heard to her.
    OLD L.   What do you think me? [*Exeunt.*]

SCENE IV. *A hall in Blackfriars.*

[*Trumpets, sennet,° and cornets. Enter two* VER-
GERS,° *with short silver wands; next them, two*
SCRIBES, *in the habit of doctors; after them, the*
ARCHBISHOP OF CANTERBURY *alone; after him, the*
BISHOPS OF LINCOLN, ELY, ROCHESTER, *and* SAINT
ASAPH. *Next them, with some small distance, follows a* GENTLEMAN *bearing the purse, with the great
seal, and a cardinal's hat; then two* PRIESTS, *bearing
each a silver cross; then a* GENTLEMAN USHER *bareheaded, accompanied with a* SERGEANT-AT-ARMS
bearing a silver mace; then two GENTLEMEN *bearing
two great silver pillars;° after them, side by side,
the two* CARDINALS; *two* NOBLEMEN *with the sword
and mace. The* KING *takes place under the cloth of
state. The two* CARDINALS *sit under him as judges.
The* QUEEN *takes place some distance from the
KING. The* BISHOPS *place themselves on each side
the court in manner of a consistory;° below them,
the* SCRIBES. *The* LORDS *sit next the* BISHOPS. *The rest
of the* ATTENDANTS *stand in convenient order about
the stage.*]
    WOL. Whilst our commission from Rome is read,
Let silence be commanded.
    KING.   What's the need?
It hath already publicly been read,
And on all sides the authority allowed.
You may then spare that time.
    WOL.   Be 't so. Proceed.   5
    SCRIBE. Say, "Henry King of England, come in-
to the court."
    CRIER. Henry King of England, &c.°
    KING. Here.
    SCRIBE. Say, "Katharine Queen of England, come
into the court."   11
    CRIER. Katharine Queen of England, &c.
    [*The* QUEEN *makes no answer, rises out of
her chair, goes about° the court, comes to the
KING, and kneels at his feet; then speaks.*]
    Q. KATH. Sir,° I desire you do me right and jus-
tice,
And to bestow your pity on me; for
I am a most poor woman, and a stranger,   15
Born out of your dominions, having here

67–68. nor . . . not: i.e., are.   68. hallowed: made holy.   74. approve: confirm. conceit: thought, opinion.   84. pat: just right.
85. suit of pounds: petition for money.   87. compelled: which
you cannot refuse.   94. O'ermount: fly higher than.   95. pure
respect: merely as a mark of honor.   97. moe: more.   103. salute: act upon; i.e., make me excited.

Sc. iv: s.d., sennet: trumpet call to announce the approach of
important persons. Vergers: ushers. pillars: insignia of office, in
the form of a pillar. consistory: ecclesiastical court.   8. &c.,: i.e.,
he repeats the full sentence as ordered.   12. s.d., about: round.
13–57. Sir . . . fulfilled: This speech should be compared with
Hermione's defense, *W Tale*, III.ii.23–117.

No judge indifferent,° nor no more assurance
Of equal° friendship and proceeding. Alas, sir,
In what have I offended you? What cause
Hath my behavior given to your displeasure   20
That thus you should proceed to put me off
And take your good grace from me? Heaven witness
I have been to you a true and humble wife,
At all times to your will conformable,
Ever in fear to kindle your dislike,   25
Yea, subject to your countenance, glad or sorry
As I saw it inclined. When was the hour
I ever contradicted your desire,
Or made it not mine too? Or which of your friends
Have I not strove to love, although I knew   30
He were mine enemy? What friend of mine
That had to him derived your anger did I
Continue in my liking? Nay, gave notice
He was from thence discharged? Sir, call to mind
That I have been your wife, in this obedience, 35
Upward of twenty years, and have been blest
With many children by you. If in the course
And process of this time you can report,
And prove it too, against mine honor aught,
My bond to wedlock, or my love and duty,   40
Against your sacred person, in God's name,
Turn me away, and let the foul'st contempt
Shut door upon me, and so give me up
To the sharp'st kind of justice. Please you, sir,
The King your father was reputed for   45
A prince most prudent, of an excellent
And unmatched wit and judgment. Ferdinand
My father, King of Spain, was reckoned one
The wisest prince that there had reigned by many
A year before. It is not to be questioned   50
That they had gathered a wise council to them
Of every realm, that did debate this business,
Who deemed our marriage lawful. Wherefore I
    humbly
Beseech you, sir, to spare me till I may
Be by my friends in Spain advised, whose counsel
I will implore. If not, i' the name of God,   56
Your pleasure be fulfilled!
    WOL.   You have here, lady,
And of your choice, these reverend fathers, men
Of singular integrity and learning,
Yea, the elect o' the land, who are assembled   60
To plead your cause. It shall be therefore bootless°
That longer you desire the court, as well
For your own quiet as to rectify
What is unsettled in the King.
    CAM.   His Grace
Hath spoken well and justly. Therefore, madam,
It's fit this royal session do proceed   66
And that without delay their arguments

Be now produced and heard.
    Q. KATH.   Lord Cardinal,
To you I speak.
    WOL.   Your pleasure, madam?
    Q. KATH.   Sir,
I am about to weep; but, thinking that   70
We are° a Queen, or long have dreamed so, cer-
    tain°
The daughter of a King, my drops of tears
I'll turn to sparks of fire.
    WOL.   Be patient yet.
    Q. KATH. I will when you are humble — nay, be-
    fore,
Or God will punish me. I do believe,   75
Induced by potent circumstances,° that
You are mine enemy, and make my challenge
You shall not be my judge. For it is you
Have blown this coal° betwixt my lord and me,
Which God's dew quench! Therefore I say again
I utterly abhor — yea, from my soul   81
Refuse — you for my judge, whom, yet once more,
I hold my most malicious foe, and think not
At all a friend to truth.
    WOL.   I do profess
You speak not like yourself, who ever yet   85
Have stood to charity and displayed the effects
Of disposition gentle and of wisdom
O'ertopping woman's power. Madam, you do me
    wrong.
I have no spleen° against you, nor injustice
For you or any. How far I have proceeded,   90
Or how far further shall, is warranted
By a commission from the Consistory° —
Yea, the whole Consistory of Rome. You charge me
That I have blown this coal. I do deny it.
The King is present. If it be known to him   95
That I gainsay° my deed, how may he wound,
And worthily, my falsehood! Yea, as much
As you have done my truth. If he know
That I am free of your report,° he knows
I am not of your wrong.° Therefore in him   100
It lies to cure me, and the cure is to
Remove these thoughts from you; the which before
His Highness shall speak in, I do beseech
You, gracious madam, to unthink your speaking,
And to say so no more.
    Q. KATH.   My lord, my lord,   105
I am a simple woman, much too weak
To oppose your cunning. You're meek and humble-
    mouthed.

71. We are: She uses the royal "we" as a sign that she is on her dignity as a Queen. **certain:** certainly.   **76. Induced . . . circumstances:** having strong reasons.   **79. blown . . . coal:** The image is that of blowing on a piece of charcoal to restore the hot glow.   **89. spleen:** anger, malice.   **92. Consistory:** Papal Court.   **96. gainsay:** deny.   **99. free . . . report:** clear of what you charge me with.   **100. not . . . wrong:** i.e., since the charge is false, you wrong me.

17. indifferent: impartial.   **18. equal:** just.   **61. bootless:** profitless.

You sign your place and calling, in full seeming,
With meekness and humility,° but your heart
Is crammed with arrogancy, spleen, and pride.   110
You have, by fortune and His Highness' favors,
Gone slightly o'er low steps° and now are mounted
Where powers° are your retainers, and your words,
Domestics to you, serve your will as 't please
Yourself pronounce their office.° I must tell you
You tender° more your person's honor° than   116
Your high profession spiritual; that again
I do refuse you for my judge, and here,
Before you all, appeal unto the Pope,
To bring my whole cause 'fore His Holiness,   120
And to be judged by him.
    [*She curtsies to the* KING, *and offers to depart.*]
    CAM.   The Queen is obstinate,
Stubborn to justice, apt to accuse it, and
Disdainful to be tried by 't. 'Tis not well.
She's going away.
    KING. Call her again.   125
    CRIER. Katharine Queen of England, come into
      the court.
    GENT. USHER. Madam, you are called back.
    Q. KATH. What need you note it? Pray you, keep
      your way.
When you are called, return. Now the Lord help!
They vex me past my patience. Pray you, pass on.
I will not tarry, no, nor ever more   131
Upon this business my appearance make
In any of their courts.
         [*Exeunt* QUEEN, *and her* ATTENDANTS.]
    KING.   Go thy ways, Kate.
That man i' the world who shall report he has
A better wife, let him in naught be trusted   135
For speaking false in that.° Thou art alone°
— If thy rare qualities, sweet gentleness,
Thy meekness saintlike, wifelike government,°
Obeying in commanding, and thy parts
Sovereign and pious else,° could speak thee out —
The Queen of earthly queens. She's noble born,
And like her true nobility she has   142
Carried herself towards me.
    WOL.   Most gracious sir,
In humblest manner I require your Highness
That it shall please you to declare in hearing   145
Of all these ears — for where I am robbed and
    bound,
There must I be unloosed, although not there
At once and fully satisfied — whether ever I

Did broach° this business to your Highness, or
Laid any scruple in your way which might   150
Induce you to the question on 't? Or ever
Have to you, but with thanks to God for such
A royal lady, spake one the least word that might
Be to the prejudice of her present state
Or touch° of her good person?
    KING.   My Lord Cardinal,   155
I do excuse you. Yea, upon mine honor,
I free you from 't. You are not to be taught°
That you have many enemies that know not
Why they are so, but, like to village curs,
Bark when their fellows do. By some of these   160
The Queen is put in anger. You're excused.
But will you be more justified? You ever
Have wished the sleeping of this business, never de-
    sired
It to be stirred, but oft have hindered, oft,
The passages° made toward it. On my honor,   165
I speak my good Lord Cardinal to this point
And thus far clear him. Now, what moved me to 't,
I will be bold with time and your attention.
Then mark the inducement.° Thus it came; give
    heed to 't.
My conscience first received a tenderness,   170
Scruple, and prick, on certain speeches uttered
By the Bishop of Bayonne, then French ambassa-
    dor,
Who had been hither sent on the debating
A marriage 'twixt the Duke of Orleans and
Our daughter Mary. I' the progress of this business,
Ere a determinate resolution,° he —   176
I mean the Bishop — did require a respite°
Wherein he might the King his lord advertise
Whether our daughter were legitimate,
Respecting this our marriage with the dowager,°
Sometimes° our brother's wife. This respite shook
The bosom of my conscience, entered me,   182
Yea, with a splitting power, and made to tremble
The region of my breast; which forced such way
That many mazed considerings° did throng   185
And pressed in with this caution. First, methought
I stood not in the smile of Heaven, who had
Commanded nature that my lady's womb,
If it conceived a male child by me, should
Do no more offices of life to 't than   190
The grave does to the dead; for her male issue
Or° died where they were made, or shortly after
This world had aired them. Hence I took a thought
This was a judgment on me that my kingdom,

108–09. You . . . humility: i.e., outwardly you seem to be full of that meekness and humility which should be the sign of a priest. 112. Gone . . . steps: been promoted quickly. 113. powers: men of high rank. 113–15. words . . . office: your words, like servants, obey you in any duty (*office*) which you command. 116. tender: regard. person's honor: personal dignity. 136. speaking . . . that: i.e., a man who says he has a better wife than I is a liar. alone: without a rival. 138. government: self-control. 140. else: in addition.

149. broach: open up. The image is from opening a new cask. 155. touch: tainting. 157. You . . . taught: there is no need for me to tell you. 165. passages: approaches. 169. inducement: what induced me to act. 176. Ere . . . resolution: before a decision was finally made. 177. respite: postponement of the discussion. 180. dowager: widow. 181. Sometimes: formerly. 185. mazed considerings: bewildered thoughts. 192. Or: either.

Well worthy the best heir o' the world, should not
Be gladded in 't by me. Then follows that   196
I weighed the danger which my realms stood in
By this my issue's fail,° and that gave to me
Many a groaning throe.° Thus hulling° in
The wild sea of my conscience I did steer   200
Toward this remedy whereupon we are
Now present here together; that's to say,
I meant to rectify my conscience, which
I then did feel full sick and yet not well,°
By° all the reverend fathers of the land   205
And doctors learned. First I began in private
With you, my Lord of Lincoln. You remember
How under my oppression° I did reek°
When I first moved° you.
    LIN.   Very well, my liege.
    KING. I have spoke long. Be pleased yourself to
      say   210
How far you satisfied me.
    LIN.   So please your Highness,
The question did at first so stagger me,
Bearing a state of mighty moment° in 't
And consequence of dread, that° I committed
The daring'st counsel which I had to doubt,   215
And did entreat your Highness to this course
Which you are running here.
    KING.   I then moved you,
My Lord of Canterbury, and got your leave
To make this present summons. Unsolicited°
I left° no reverend person in this court,   220
But by particular consent proceeded
Under your hands and seals.° Therefore, go on.
For no dislike i' the world against the person
Of the good Queen, but the sharp thorny points
Of my allegèd reasons, drive this forward.   225
Prove but our marriage lawful, by my life
And kingly dignity, we are contented
To wear our mortal state° to come with her,
Katharine our Queen, before the primest creature
That's paragoned° o' the world.
    CAM.   So please your Highness,   230
The Queen being absent, 'tis a needful fitness
That we adjourn this court till further day.
Meanwhile must be an earnest motion
Made to the Queen to call back her appeal
She intends unto His Holiness.

KING. [*Aside*]   I may perceive   235
These Cardinals trifle with me. I abhor
This dilatory sloth and tricks of Rome.
My learned and well-belovèd servant Cranmer,
Prithee return. With thy approach, I know,   239
My comfort comes along. — Break up the court.
I say set on. [*Exeunt in manner as they entered.*]

Act III

SCENE I. *London. The* QUEEN's *apartments.*

[*The* QUEEN *and her* WOMEN, *as at work*.]
    Q. KATH. Take thy lute,° wench. My soul grows
      sad with troubles.
Sing, and disperse 'em if thou canst. Leave working.
              SONG
     Orpheus° with his lute made trees,
     And the mountain tops that freeze
       Bow themselves when he did sing.   5
    To his music plants and flowers
    Ever sprung, as sun and showers
      There had made a lasting spring.

    Every thing that heard him play,
    Even the billows of the sea,   10
      Hung their heads, and then lay by.
    In sweet music is such art,
    Killing care and grief of heart
      Fall asleep, or hearing die.
           [*Enter a* GENTLEMAN.]
    Q. KATH. How now!   15
    GENT. An 't° please your Grace, the two great
      Cardinals
Wait in the presence.°
    Q. KATH.   Would they speak with me?
    GENT. They willed me say so, madam.
    Q. KATH.   Pray Their Graces
To come near. [*Exit* GENTLEMAN.] What can be
    their business   19
With me, a poor weak woman fall'n from favor?
I do not like their coming. Now I think on 't,
They should be good men, their affairs as righteous.
But all hoods make not monks.°
[*Enter the two* CARDINALS, WOLSEY *and* CAMPEIUS.]
    WOL.   Peace to your Highness!
    Q. KATH. Your Graces find me here part of° a
      housewife;   24

---

198. issue's fail: lack of an heir.   199. throe: pang. hulling:
The image is that of a ship in a high storm, with all the sails
furled, driven by the tempest.   204. yet . . . well: is still uneasy.   205. By: with the help of.   208. oppression: distress.
reek: sweat, lit., steam.   209. moved: mentioned the matter to.
213. moment: importance.   214–17. that . . . here: I was doubtful about advising the most daring course and so begged your
Highness to take the action which you are now taking.   219. Unsolicited: unasked.   220. left: omitted.   222. Under . . . seals:
with your formal written approval.   228. wear . . . state: live
the rest of our natural life.   230. paragoned: held up as unrivaled.

Act III, Sc. i: 1. lute: See Pl. 18d.   3. Orpheus: See *M of
Ven*, V.i.80,n.   16. An 't: if it.   17. presence: the room in a
palace where public audiences are given.   23. all . . . monks:
a common proverb, from the Latin *cucullus non facit monachum.*
See *T Night*, I.v.62, *M for Meas*, V.i.263.   24. part of: partly—
for she is sewing.

I would be all,° against° the worst may happen.
What are your pleasures with me, reverend lords?
　WOL. May it please you, noble madam, to with-
　　draw
Into your private chamber, we shall give you
The full cause of our coming.
　Q. KATH.　　　　　　　Speak it here.　29
There's nothing I have done yet, o' my conscience,
Deserves a corner. Would all other women
Could speak this with as free a soul as I do!
My lords, I care not, so much I am happy
Above a number,° if my actions
Were tried by every tongue, every eye saw 'em,　35
Envy° and base opinion° set against 'em,
I know my life so even.° If your business
Seek me out, and that way I am wife in,°
Out with it boldly. Truth loves open dealing.
　WOL. *Tanta est erga te mentis integritas, regina
serenissima*°　——　　　　　　　　　41
　Q. KATH. Oh, good my lord, no Latin.
I am not such a truant since my coming
As not to know the language I have lived in.
A strange tongue makes my cause more strange,
　suspicious.　　　　　　　　　　　45
Pray speak in English. Here are some will thank
　you,
If you speak truth, for their poor mistress' sake.
Believe me, she has had much wrong. Lord Cardi-
　nal,
The willing'st sin I ever yet committed
May be absolved in English.
　WOL.　　　　　　　Noble lady,　50
I am sorry my integrity should breed ——
And service to His Majesty and you ——
So deep suspicion where all faith was meant.
We come not by the way of accusation
To taint that honor every good tongue blesses,　55
Nor to betray you any way to sorrow ——
You have too much, good lady —— but to know
How you stand minded in the weighty difference
Between the King and you, and to deliver,
Like free and honest men, our just opinions　60
And comforts to your cause.
　CAM.　　　　　Most honored madam,
My Lord of York, out of his noble nature,
Zeal and obedience he still° bore your Grace,
Forgetting, like a good man, your late censure°
Both of his truth and him (which was too far),　65
Offers, as I do, in a sign of peace,

His service and his counsel.
　Q. KATH. [*Aside*]　　　　To betray me. ——
My lords, I thank you both for your good wills.
Ye speak like honest men; pray God, ye prove so!
But how to make ye suddenly an answer　70
In such a point of weight, so near mine honor,
More near my life, I fear, with my weak wit,
And to such men of gravity and learning,
In truth, I know not. I was set at° work
Among my maids, full little, God knows, looking
Either for such men or such business.　76
For her sake that I have been° —— for I feel
The last fit° of my greatness —— good your Graces,
Let me have time and counsel for my cause.
Alas, I am a woman, friendless, hopeless!　80
　WOL. Madam, you wrong the King's love with
　　these fears.
Your hopes and friends are infinite.
　Q. KATH.　　　　　　In England
But little for my profit. Can you think, lords,
That any Englishman dare give me counsel?
Or be a known friend, 'gainst His Highness' pleas-
　ure ——　　　　　　　　　　　85
Though he be grown so desperate to be honest° ——
And live a subject?° Nay, forsooth, my friends,
They that must weigh out my afflictions,
They that my trust must grow to, live not here.
They are, as all my other comforts, far hence　90
In mine own country, lords.
　CAM.　　　　　I would your Grace
Would leave your griefs and take my counsel.
　Q. KATH.　　　　　　　How, sir?
　CAM. Put your main cause into the King's pro-
　　tection.
He's loving and most gracious. 'Twill be much
Both for your honor better and your cause;　95
For if the trial of the law o'ertake ye,
You'll part away disgraced.
　WOL.　　　　　He tells you rightly.
　Q. KATH. Ye tell me what ye wish for both —— my
　　ruin.
Is this your Christian counsel? Out upon ye!
Heaven is above all yet. There sits a judge　100
That no king can corrupt.
　CAM.　　　　　Your rage mistakes us.
　Q. KATH. The more shame for ye. Holy men I
　　thought ye,
Upon my soul, two reverend cardinal virtues;°
But cardinal sins and hollow hearts I fear ye.
Mend 'em, for shame, my lords. Is this your com-
　fort?　　　　　　　　　　　105
The cordial that ye bring a wretched lady,

---

25. all: i.e., if I am divorced I shall have to be a complete house-wife and look after myself. **against:** in anticipation of. **34. Above a number:** more than many. **36. Envy:** hatred. **base opinion:** evil-minded talk. **37. even:** innocent. **38. that . . . in:** what sort of wife I am. **40–41.** *Tanta . . . serenissima:* so great is the freedom of our minds from malice, most serene Queen. The Cardinal speaks Latin so that the women may not understand. **63. still:** always. **64. censure:** bitter criticism.

74. set at: put to. **77. For . . . been:** for what I have once been. **78. fit:** period. **86. desperate . . . honest:** so reckless that he dares to be my friend. **87. live a subject:** and still live. **103. cardinal virtues:** the Seven Cardinal (or essential) Virtues, which counterbalance the Seven Deadly Sins, with a pun on the rank of the two visitors.

A woman lost among ye, laughed at, scorned?
I will not wish ye half my miseries;
I have more charity. But say I warned ye;
Take heed, for Heaven's sake, take heed, lest at
    once   110
The burden of my sorrows fall upon ye.
  wol. Madam, this is a mere distraction.°
You turn the good we offer into envy."
  q. kath. Ye turn me into nothing. Woe upon ye,
And all such false professors!° Would you have
  me —   115
If you have any justice, any pity,
If ye be any thing but churchmen's habits° —
Put my sick cause into his hands that hates me?
Alas, has banished me his bed already,
His love, too long ago! I am old, my lords,   120
And all the fellowship I hold now with him
Is only my obedience. What can happen
To me above this wretchedness? All your studies
Make me a curse like this.°
  cam.   Your fears are worse.°
  q. kath. Have I lived thus long — let me speak
  myself,   125
Since virtue finds no friends — a wife, a true one?
A woman, I dare say without vainglory,
Never yet branded with suspicion?
Have I with all my full affections
Still met the King? Loved him next Heaven?
  Obeyed him?   130
Been, out of fondness, superstitious to him?°
Almost forgot my prayers to content him?
And am I thus rewarded? 'Tis not well, lords.
Bring me a constant woman to her husband,
One that ne'er dreamed a joy beyond his pleasure,
And to that woman, when she has done most,   136
Yet will I add an honor, a great patience.
  wol. Madam, you wander from the good we aim
  at.
  q. kath. My lord, I dare not make myself so
  guilty
To give up willingly that noble title   140
Your master wed me to. Nothing but death
Shall e'er divorce my dignities.
  wol.   Pray hear me.
  q. kath. Would I had never trod this English
  earth,

Or felt the flatteries that grow upon it!
Ye have angels' faces, but Heaven knows your
  hearts.   145
What will become of me now, wretched lady!
I am the most unhappy woman living.
Alas, poor wenches, where are now your fortunes?
Shipwrecked upon a kingdom where no pity,
No friends, no hope, no kindred weep for me,   150
Almost no grave allowed me. Like the lily,
That once was mistress of the field and flourished,
I'll hang my head and perish.
  wol.   If your Grace
Could but be brought to know our ends are honest,
You'd feel more comfort. Why should we, good
  lady,   155
Upon what cause, wrong you? Alas, our places,
The way of our profession is against it.
We are to cure such sorrows, not to sow 'em.
For goodness' sake, consider what you do;
How you may hurt yourself, aye, utterly   160
Grow from the King's acquaintance,° by this car-
  riage.°
The hearts of princes kiss obedience,
So much they love it; but to stubborn spirits
They swell and grow as terrible as storms.
I know you have a gentle, noble temper,   165
A soul as even as a calm. Pray think us
Those we profess, peacemakers, friends, and serv-
  ants.
  cam. Madam, you'll find it so. You wrong your
  virtues
With these weak women's fears. A noble spirit,
As yours was put into you, ever casts   170
Such doubts, as false coin, from it. The King loves
  you;
Beware you lose it not. For us, if you please
To trust us in your business, we are ready
To use our utmost studies in your service.
  q. kath. Do what ye will, my lords; and pray
  forgive me   175
If I have used myself unmannerly.
You know I am a woman, lacking wit
To make a seemly answer to such persons.
Pray do my service° to His Majesty.
He has my heart yet, and shall have my prayers   180
While I shall have my life. Come, Reverend Fa-
  thers,
Bestow your counsels on me. She now begs
That little thought, when she set footing here,
She should have bought her dignities so dear.
                      [Exeunt.]

---

112. **mere distraction:** sheer madness.   113. **envy:** malice.
115. **professors:** professing Christians.   117. **churchmen's
habits:** only the clothes of churchmen; i.e., wolves in disguise.
123–24. **All . . . this:** take as much thought as you can, and
you will not be able to make my life more cursed than it
is now.   124. **worse:** i.e., things are not so bad as you fear.
131. **out . . . him:** in my foolish affection made a god of him.

161. **Grow . . . acquaintance:** lose the King's favor. **carriage:**
behavior.   179. **do my service:** express my loyalty.

SCENE II. *Antechamber to the* KING'S *apartment.*

[*Enter the* DUKE OF NORFOLK, *the* DUKE OF SUFFOLK, *the* EARL OF SURREY, *and the* LORD CHAMBERLAIN.]

NOR. If you will now unite in your complaints
And force them with a constancy,° the Cardinal
Cannot stand under them. If you omit
The offer of this time,° I cannot promise
But that you shall sustain moe new disgraces   5
With these you bear already.

SUR.   I am joyful
To meet the least occasion that may give me
Remembrance of my father-in-law, the Duke,°
To be revenged on him.

SUF.   Which of the peers
Have uncontemned° gone by him, or at least   10
Strangely neglected? When did he regard
The stamp of nobleness° in any person
Out of° himself?

CHAM.   My lords, you speak your pleasures.
What he deserves of you and me I know;
What we can do to him, though now the time   15
Gives way° to us, I much fear. If you cannot
Bar his access to the King, never attempt
Anything on him, for he hath a witchcraft
Over the King in 's tongue.

NOR.   Oh, fear him not.
His spell° in that is out. The King hath found   20
Matter against him that for ever mars
The honey of his language. No, he's settled,°
Not to come off,° in his displeasure.

SUR.   Sir,
I should be glad to hear such news as this
Once every hour.

NOR.   Believe it, this is true.   25
In the divorce his contrary proceedings
Are all unfolded, wherein he appears
As I would wish mine enemy.

SUR.   How came
His practices° to light?

SUF.   Most strangely.

SUR.   Oh, how, how?

SUF. The Cardinal's letters to the Pope miscarried   30
And came to the eye o' the King, wherein° was read
How that the Cardinal did entreat His Holiness
To stay° the judgment o' the divorce; for if
It did take place, "I do," quoth he, "perceive
My King is tangled in affection to   35

A creature of the Queen's, Lady Anne Bullen."

SUR. Has the King this?

SUF.   Believe it.

SUR.   Will this work?

CHAM. The King in this perceives him how he coasts
And hedges° his own way. But in this point
All his tricks founder, and he brings his physic   40
After his patient's death. The King already
Hath married the fair lady.

SUR.   Would he had!

SUF. May you be happy in your wish, my lord!
For, I profess, you have it.

SUR.   Now, all my joy
Trace the conjunction!°

SUF.   My amen to 't!

NOR.   All men's!   45

SUF. There's order given for her coronation.
Marry, this is yet but young,° and may be left
To some ears unrecounted. But, my lords,
She is a gallant creature and complete
In mind and feature. I persuade me, from her   50
Will fall some blessing to this land which shall
In it be memorized.°

SUR.   But will the King
Digest° this letter of the Cardinal's?
The Lord forbid!

NOR.   Marry, amen!

SUF.   No, no.
There be moe wasps that buzz about his nose   55
Will make this sting the sooner. Cardinal Campeius
Is stol'n away to Rome; hath ta'en no leave;
Has left the cause o' the King unhandled and
Is posted° as the agent of our Cardinal
To second° all his plot. I do assure you   60
The King cried "Ha!" at this.

CHAM.   Now God incense him,
And let him cry "Ha!" louder!

NOR.   But, my lord,
When returns Cranmer?

SUF. He is returned in his opinions, which
Have satisfied the King for his divorce,   65
Together with all famous colleges
Almost in Christendom. Shortly, I believe,
His second marriage shall be published, and
Her coronation. Katharine no more
Shall be called Queen, but Princess Dowager   70
And widow to Prince Arthur.

NOR.   This same Cranmer's
A worthy fellow and hath ta'en much pain
In the King's business.

Sc. ii. **2. constancy:** determination.   **4. offer . . . time:** this opportunity.   **8. Duke:** i.e., Buckingham. See II.i.43-44.   **10. uncontemned:** undespised.   **12. stamp of nobleness:** mark of nobility.   **13. Out of:** except.   **16. Gives way:** is favorable.   **20. spell:** power to bewitch.   **22. settled:** sure fixed.   **23. come off:** escape.   **29. practices:** underhand plots.   **31-36. wherein . . . Bullen.** See App. 28.   **33 stay:** stop.

38-39. coasts . . . hedges: i.e., like one who sneaks along under the cover of a hedge.   **44-45. all . . . conjunction:** I wish all joy to the marriage (*conjunction*).   **47. young:** just decided.   **50-52. from . . . memorized:** The only child to be born of the marriage was a daughter, afterward the famous Queen Elizabeth. See Genealogical Table C, p. 1652.   **53. Digest:** stomach, put up with.   **59. posted:** hastened.   **60. second:** support.

SUF.　　　　　　　He has, and we shall see him
For it an archbishop.
　NOR.　　　　So I hear.
　SUF.　　　　　　　　　'Tis so.
The Cardinal!
　　　　　[*Enter* WOLSEY *and* CROMWELL.]
　NOR.　　　　Observe, observe, he's moody.　　75
　WOL. The packet, Cromwell,
Gave 't you the King?
　CROM.　　　　To his own hand, in 's bedchamber.
　WOL. Looked he o' the inside of the paper?
　CROM.　　　　　　　　　Presently°
He did unseal them, and the first he viewed,
He did it with a serious mind. A heed　　80
Was in his countenance. You he bade
Attend him here this morning.
　WOL.　　　　　　　　Is he ready
To come abroad?
　CROM.　　　　I think by this he is.
　WOL. Leave me awhile.　　　[*Exit* CROMWELL.]
[*Aside*] It shall be to the Duchess of Alençon,　85
The French King's sister. He shall marry her.
Anne Bullen! No! I'll no Anne Bullens for him.
There's more in 't than fair visage. Bullen!
No, we'll no Bullens. Speedily I wish
To hear from Rome. The Marchioness of Pem-
　broke!　　　　　　　　　　　　　　　90
　NOR. He's discontented.
　SUF.　　　　　May be he hears the King
Does whet his anger to him.
　SUR.　　　　　　Sharp enough,
Lord, for thy justice!
　WOL. [*Aside*] The late Queen's gentlewoman, a
　knight's daughter,　　　　　　　　　94
To be her mistress' mistress! The Queen's Queen!
This candle burns not clear. 'Tis I must snuff it.°
Then out it goes. What though I know her virtu-
　ous
And well deserving? Yet I know her for
A spleeny° Lutheran, and not wholesome to
Our cause, that she should lie i' the bosom of　100
Our hard-ruled° King. Again, there is sprung up
A heretic, an arch one, Cranmer, one
Hath crawled in to the favor of the King
And is his oracle.
　NOR.　　　　He is vexed at something.
　SUR. I would 'twere something that would fret
　the string,　　　　　　　　　　　　105
The master cord° on 's heart!
　[*Enter* KING, *reading of a schedule, and* LOVELL.]
　SUF.　　　　　　The King, the King!
　KING. What piles of wealth hath he accumulated
To his own portion! And what expense by the
　hour

Seems to flow from him! How, i' the name of thrift,
Does he rake this together? Now, my lords,　110
Saw you the Cardinal?
　NOR.　　　　　My lord, we have
Stood here observing him. Some strange commo-
　tion
Is in his brain. He bites his lip and starts;
Stops on a sudden, looks upon the ground,
Then lays his finger on his temple; straight　115
Springs out into fast gait;° then stops again,
Strikes his breast hard, and anon he casts
His eye against the moon. In most strange postures
We have seen him set himself.
　KING.　　　　　　　It may well be;
There is a mutiny in 's mind. This morning　120
Papers of state he sent me to peruse
As I required; and wot° you what I found
There, on my conscience, put unwittingly?°
Forsooth, an inventory, thus importing
The several parcels° of his plate, his treasure,　125
Rich stuffs, and ornaments of household, which
I find at such proud rate that it outspeaks
Possession of a subject.
　NOR.　　　　　It's Heaven's will.
Some spirit put this paper in the packet
To bless your eye withal.
　KING.　　　　　　If we did think　130
His contemplation were above the earth,
And fixed on spiritual object, he should still
Dwell in his musings. But I am afraid
His thinkings are below the moon,° not worth
His serious considering.
　　　　[KING *takes his seat, whispers to* LOVELL,
　　　　　　　who goes to the CARDINAL.]
　WOL.　　　　　Heaven forgive me!　135
Ever God bless your Highness!
　KING.　　　　　　Good my lord,
You are full of heavenly stuff, and bear the inven-
　tory
Of your best graces in your mind, the which
You were now running o'er. You have scarce time
To steal from spiritual leisure a brief span　140
To keep your earthly audit. Sure, in that
I deem you an ill husband° and am glad
To have you therein my companion.
　WOL.　　　　　　　Sir,
For holy offices I have a time; a time
To think upon the part of business which　145
I bear i' the state; and nature does require
Her times of preservation, which perforce
I, her frail son, amongst my brethren mortal,
Must give my tendance° to.
　KING.　　　　　You have said well.

---

78. Presently: immediately.　**96. candle . . . it:** See *Haml,* IV.
vii.116,n.　**99. spleeny:** vindictive.　**101. hard-ruled:** difficult
to manage.　**105-06. fret . . . cord:** break his heartstring.

116. gait: walk.　**122. wot:** know.　**123. unwittingly:** unintentionally.　**125. parcels:** particulars.　**134. below. . . moon:** i.e.,
earthly.　**142. ill husband:** bad manager.　**149. tendance:** attention.

WOL. And ever may your Highness yoke to-
   gether,   150
As I will lend you cause, my doing well
With my well saying!
   KING.   'Tis well said again,
And 'tis a kind of good deed to say well.
And yet words are no deeds. My father loved you.
He said he did and with his deed did crown   155
His word° upon you. Since I had my office,
I have kept you next my heart; have not alone
Employed you where high profits might come
   home,
But pared my present havings° to bestow
My bounties upon you.
   WOL. [*Aside*]   What should this mean?   160
   SUR. [*Aside*] The Lord increase this business!
   KING.   Have I not made you
The prime man of the state? I pray you tell me
If what I now pronounce you have found true.
And, if you may confess it, say withal
If you are bound to us or no. What say you?   165
   WOL. My sovereign, I confess your royal graces,
Showered on me daily, have been more than could
My studied purposes requite,° which went
Beyond all man's endeavors. My endeavors
Have ever come too short of my desires,   170
Yet filed° with my abilities. Mine own ends
Have been mine so that evermore they pointed
To the good of your most sacred person and
The profit of the state. For your great graces
Heaped upon me, poor undeserver, I   175
Can nothing render but allegiant° thanks,
My prayers to Heaven for you, my loyalty,
Which ever has and ever shall be growing,
Till death, that winter, kill it.
   KING.   Fairly answered.
A loyal and obedient subject is   180
Therein illustrated. The honor of it
Does pay the act of it, as, i' the contrary,
The foulness is the punishment.° I presume
That, as my hand has opened bounty to you,
My heart dropped love, my power rained honor,
   more   185
On you than any, so your hand and heart,
Your brain, and every function of your power
Should, notwithstanding that your bond of duty,
As 'twere in love's particular, be more
To me,° your friend, than any.
   WOL.   I do profess   190
That for your Highness' good I ever labored

More than mine own, that am, have, and will be —
Though all the world should crack° their duty to
   you
And throw it from their soul, though perils did
Abound as thick as thought could make 'em, and
Appear in forms more horrid — yet my duty,   196
As doth a rock against the chiding flood,
Should the approach of this wild river break,
And stand unshaken yours.
   KING.   'Tis nobly spoken.
Take notice, lords, he has a loyal breast,   200
For you have seen him open 't. [*Giving him pa-
pers.*] Read o'er this;
And after, this. And then to breakfast with
What appetite you have.
   [*Exit* KING, *frowning upon the* CARDINAL. *The
nobles throng after him, smiling and whispering.*]
   WOL.   What should this mean?
What sudden anger's this? How have I reaped it?
He parted frowning from me, as if ruin   205
Leaped from his eyes. So looks the chafèd° lion
Upon the daring huntsman that has galled° him,
Then makes him nothing. I must read this paper;
I fear, the story of his anger. 'Tis so.
This paper has undone me. 'Tis the account   210
Of all that world of wealth I have drawn together
For mine own ends; indeed, to gain the popedom
And fee° my friends in Rome. Oh, negligence!
Fit for a fool to fall by. What cross° devil
Made me put this main secret in the packet   215
I sent the King? Is there no way to cure this?
No new device to beat this from his brains?
I know 'twill stir him strongly. Yet I know
A way, if it take right, in spite of fortune
Will bring me off again. What's this? " To the
   Pope! "   220
The letter, as I live, with all the business
I writ to 's Holiness. Nay then, farewell!
I have touched the highest point of all my greatness,
And from that full meridian° of my glory,
I haste now to my setting. I shall fall   225
Like a bright exhalation° in the evening,
And no man see me more.
   [*Re-enter to* WOLSEY *the* DUKES OF NORFOLK *and*
SUFFOLK, *the* EARL OF SURREY, *and the* LORD
CHAMBERLAIN.]
   NOR. Hear the King's pleasure, Cardinal, who
   commands you
To render up the Great Seal° presently
Into our hands, and to confine yourself   230
To Asher House, my Lord of Winchester's,
Till you hear further from His Highness.
   WOL.   Stay.

155–56. crown . . . word: showed the truth of his words by deeds.
159. pared . . . havings: reduced my own income. **168. My . . .
requite:** I could repay even if I studied how to think of ways.
171. filed: kept pace with. **176 allegiant:** loyal. **181–
83. The . . . punishment:** i.e., good deeds bring honor as their
reward; and, on the contrary, evil deeds bring disgrace. **188–
90. notwithstanding . . . me:** apart from the fact that as a loyal
subject (*bond of duty*) you should have particular love for me.

193. crack: strain to breaking. **206. chafed:** angered.
207. galled: wounded. **213. fee:** bribe. **214. cross:** perverse.
224. meridian: highest point of the sun's daily course. **226. exhalation:** falling star. **229. Great Seal:** See I.i.114,s.d.,n.

Where's your commission, lords? Words cannot
    carry
Authority so weighty.
    SUF.   Who dare cross 'em,   234
Bearing the King's will from his mouth expressly?
WOL. Till I find more than will or words to do
    it —
I mean your malice — know, officious lords,
I dare and must deny it. Now I feel
Of what coarse metal ye are molded — envy.
How eagerly ye follow my disgraces,   240
As if it fed ye! And how sleek and wanton
Ye appear in every thing may bring my ruin!
Follow your envious courses, men of malice.
You have Christian warrant for 'em and, no doubt,
In time will find their fit rewards. That Seal   245
You ask with such a violence, the King,
Mine and your master, with his own hand gave me,
Bade me enjoy it, with the place and honors,
During my life, and, to confirm his goodness,   249
Tied it by letters patents.° Now, who'll take it?
    SUR. The King, that gave it.
    WOL.   It must be himself, then.
    SUR. Thou art a proud traitor, priest.
    WOL.   Proud lord, thou liest.
Within these forty hours Surrey durst better
Have burnt that tongue than said so.
    SUR.   Thy ambition,
Thou scarlet sin,° robbed this bewailing land   255
Of noble Buckingham, my father-in-law.
The heads of all thy brother Cardinals,
With thee and all thy best parts bound together,
Weighed not° a hair of his. Plague of your policy!
You sent me Deputy for Ireland,°   260
Far from his succor, from the King, from all
That might have mercy on the fault thou gavest
    him,
Whilst your great goodness, out of holy pity,
Absolved him with an ax.
    WOL.   This, and all else
This talking lord can lay upon my credit,   265
I answer is most false. The Duke by law
Found his deserts. How innocent I was
From any private malice in his end,
His noble jury° and foul cause can witness.
If I loved many words, lord, I should tell you   270
You have as little honesty as honor
That in the way of loyalty and truth
Toward the King, my ever royal master,
Dare mate a sounder man than Surrey can be,
And all that love his follies.°

SUR.   By my soul,   275
Your long coat, priest, protects you. Thou shouldst
    feel
My sword i' the lifeblood of thee else. My lords,
Can ye endure to hear this arrogance?
And from this fellow? If we live thus tamely,
To be thus jaded by a piece of scarlet,   280
Farewell nobility. Let His Grace go forward
And dare us with his cap, like larks.°
    WOL.   All goodness
Is poison to thy stomach.
    SUR.   Yes, that goodness
Of gleaning all the land's wealth into one,
Into your own hands, Cardinal, by extortion;   285
The goodness of your intercepted packets
You writ to the Pope against the King. Your good-
    ness,
Since you provoke me, shall be most notorious.
My Lord of Norfolk,° as you are truly noble,
As you respect the common good, the state   290
Of our despised nobility, our issues,°
Who, if he live, will scarce be gentlemen,
Produce the grand sum of his sins, the articles
Collected from his life. I'll startle you
Worse than the sacring bell° when the brown
    wench   295
Lay kissing in your arms, Lord Cardinal.
WOL. How much, methinks, I could despise this
    man,
But that I am bound in charity against it!
    NOR. Those articles, my lord, are in the King's
    hand.
But, thus much, they are foul ones.
    WOL.   So much fairer   300
And spotless shall mine innocence arise
When the King knows my truth.
    SUR.   This cannot save you.
I thank my memory, I yet remember
Some of these articles, and out they shall.
Now, if you can blush and cry " guilty," Cardinal,
You'll show a little honesty.
    WOL.   Speak on, sir.   306
I dare your worst objections. If I blush,
It is to see a nobleman want manners.
    SUR. I had rather want those than my head. Have
    at you!°
First° that, without the King's assent or knowl-
    edge,   310

---

250. letters patents: formal confirmations. See Pl. 11b.
255. scarlet sin: The Cardinal wears the scarlet robes of his office; with an echo of Isaiah 1:18: "Though your sins be as scarlet, they shall be as white as snow." 259. Weighed not: were not equal to. 260. Deputy . . . Ireland: See II.i.43. 269. noble jury: the court composed of peers of the realm. 274–75. Dare . . . follies: i.e., if you pretend that you can rival me, a more loyal man than you, or those who love your follies, can ever be. 282. dare . . . larks: fascinate us with his scarlet hat as men catch larks. The lark nests and rests in the grass. To persuade it to stay cowering the lark catcher used to wave a piece of scarlet cloth until he had thrown a net over the bird. dare: dazzle, fascinate. 289. My . . . Norfolk: Actually Norfolk was Surrey's father. 291. issues: children. 295. sacring bell: a bell rung at the elevation of the Host, the most solemn moment in the Mass. 309. Have at you: See II.ii.85,n. 310–30. First . . . kingdom: These accusations made against the Cardinal were selected from the longer list in Holinshed.

You wrought to be a legate,° by which power
You maimed the jurisdiction of all bishops.
    NOR. Then that in all you writ to Rome, or else
To foreign princes, *Ego et Rex meus*°
Was still inscribed, in which you brought the King
To be your servant.
    SUF.   Then that, without the knowledge   316
Either of King or Council, when you went
Ambassador to the Emperor, you made bold
To carry into Flanders the Great Seal.°
    SUR. Item,° you sent a large commission°   320
To Gregory de Cassado to conclude,
Without the King's will or the state's allowance,
A league between His Highness and Ferrara.
    SUF. That out of mere ambition you have caused
Your holy hat to be stamped on the King's coin.
    SUR. Then, that you have sent innumerable sub-
        stance —   326
By what means got, I leave to your own con-
        science —
To furnish Rome, and to prepare the ways
You have for dignities, to the mere° undoing
Of all the kingdom. Many more there are,   330
Which, since they are of you and odious,
I will not taint my mouth with.
    CHAM.   O my lord!
Press not a falling man too far. 'Tis virtue.°
His faults lie open to the laws. Let them,
Not you, correct him. My heart weeps to see him
So little of his great self.
    SUR.   I forgive him.   336
    SUF. Lord Cardinal, the King's further pleasure
        is —
Because all those things you have done of late
By your power legatine° within this kingdom
Fall into the compass of a praemunire° —   340
That therefore such a writ be sued against you:
To forfeit all your goods, lands, tenements,
Chattels, and whatsoever, and to be
Out of the King's protection. This is my charge.
    NOR. And so we'll leave you to your meditations
How to live better. For your stubborn answer   346
About the giving back the Great Seal to us,

The King shall know it and, no doubt, shall thank
    you.
So fare you well, my little good Lord Cardinal.
                      [*Exeunt all but* WOLSEY.]
    WOL. So farewell to the little good you bear me.
Farewell! A long farewell, to all my greatness!   351
This is the state of man: Today he puts forth
The tender leaves of hopes; tomorrow blossoms
And bears his blushing honors thick upon him;
The third day comes a frost, a killing frost,   355
And, when he thinks, good easy° man, full surely
His greatness is aripening, nips his root,
And then he falls, as I do. I have ventured,
Like little wanton boys that swim on bladders,
This many summers in a sea of glory,   360
But far beyond my depth. My high-blown pride
At length broke under me, and now has left me,
Weary and old with service, to the mercy
Of a rude stream that must forever hide me.
Vain pomp and glory of this world, I hate ye.   365
I feel my heart new opened. Oh, how wretchèd
Is that poor man that hangs on princes' favors!
There is, betwixt that smile we would aspire to,
That sweet aspéct of princes, and their ruin,   369
More pangs and fears than wars or women have.
And when he falls, he falls like Lucifer,°
Never to hope again.
        [*Enter* CROMWELL, *and stands amazed.*]
                  Why, how now, Cromwell!
    CROM. I have no power to speak, sir.
    WOL.   What, amazed
At my misfortunes? Can thy spirit wonder   374
A great man should decline? Nay, an° you weep,
I am fall'n indeed.
    CROM.   How does your Grace?
    WOL.   Why, well.
Never so truly happy, my good Cromwell.
I know myself now, and I feel within me
A peace above all earthly dignities,
A still and quiet conscience. The King has cured
    me,   380
I humbly thank His Grace, and from these should-
    ers,
These ruined pillars, out of pity, taken
A load would sink a navy — too much honor.
Oh, 'tis a burden, Cromwell, 'tis a burden
Too heavy for a man that hopes for Heaven!   385
    CROM. I am glad your Grace has made that right
        use of it.
    WOL. I hope I have. I am able now, methinks,
Out of a fortitude of soul I feel,
To endure more miseries and greater far
Than my weak-hearted enemies dare offer.   390

---

311. legate: the Pope's representative in England, and so standing outside the ordinary law in ecclesiastical matters.   **314. Ego . . . meus:** I and my King. In Latin it is normal to put the first person first. Wolsey's actual offense was that he coupled his name with that of the King, not that he put himself first.   **319. Great Seal:** See I.i.114,n. The Great Seal is not allowed to be taken out of England; for that reason during his term of office the Lord Chancellor may not leave the country.   **320. Item:** also. See *T Gent*, III.i.274,n. **large commission:** commission with full powers to act.   **329. mere:** utter.   **333. virtue:** a good deed — not to strike a fallen man.   **339. power legatine:** power as Papal Legate.   **340. compass . . . praemunire:** within the penalties for breaking the Statute of Praemunire. This statute, passed in 1392, made it a penal offense to appeal to the Pope in an action against an English subject. The penalty was forfeiture of goods and imprisonment.

356. easy: easygoing, careless.   **371. Lucifer:** Satan, who with his angels was cast out of Heaven for aspiring to be equal with God. "How art thou fallen from Heaven, O Lucifer, son of the morning!" (Isaiah, 14:12.)   **375. an:** if.

What news abroad?

CROM.   The heaviest and the worst
Is your displeasure with the King.

WOL.   God bless him!

CROM. The next is that Sir Thomas More is chosen
Lord Chancellor in your place.

WOL.   That's somewhat sudden.
But he's a learned man. May he continue   395
Long in His Highness' favor and do justice
For truth's sake and his conscience, that his bones,
When he has run his course and sleeps in blessings,
May have a tomb of orphans' tears wept on 'em!
What more?

CROM.   That Cranmer is returned with welcome,
Installed Lord Archbishop of Canterbury.   401

WOL. That's news indeed.

CROM.   Last, that the Lady Anne,
Whom the King hath in secrecy long married,
This day was viewed in open as his Queen,
Going to chapel, and the voice° is now   405
Only about her coronation.

WOL. There was the weight that pulled me down.
Oh, Cromwell,
The King has gone beyond me. All my glories
In that one woman I have lost for ever.
No sun shall ever usher forth mine honors   410
Or gild again the noble troops that waited
Upon my smiles. Go, get thee from me, Cromwell.
I am a poor fall'n man, unworthy now
To be thy lord and master. Seek the King.   414
That sun, I pray, may never set! I have told him
What and how true thou art. He will advance thee.
Some little memory of me will stir him —
I know his noble nature — not to let
Thy hopeful service perish too. Good Cromwell,
Neglect him not. Make use° now, and provide   420
For thine own future safety.

CROM.   O my lord,
Must I then leave you? Must I needs forgo
So good, so noble and so true a master?
Bear witness, all that have not hearts of iron,
With what a sorrow Cromwell leaves his lord.   425
The King shall have my service, but my prayers
For ever and for ever shall be yours.

WOL. Cromwell, I did not think to shed a tear
In all my miseries, but thou hast forced me
Out of thy honest truth to play the woman.   430
Let's dry our eyes; and thus far hear me, Cromwell.
And, when I am forgotten, as I shall be,
And sleep in dull cold marble, where no mention
Of me more must be heard of, say I taught thee.
Say, Wolsey, that once trod the ways of glory   435
And sounded all the depths and shoals of honor,
Found thee a way, out of his wreck, to rise in —

A sure and safe one,° though thy master missed it.
Mark but my fall and that that ruined me.
Cromwell, I charge thee, fling away ambition.   440
By that sin fell the angels. How can man, then,
The image of his Maker, hope to win by it?
Love thyself last. Cherish those hearts that hate thee.
Corruption wins not more than honesty.
Still in thy right hand carry gentle peace   445
To silence envious tongues. Be just, and fear not.
Let all the ends thou aim'st at be thy country's,
Thy God's, and truth's. Then if thou fall'st, Cromwell,
Thou fall'st a blessed martyr! Serve the King.
And prithee lead me in.   450
There take an inventory of all I have
To the last penny. 'Tis the King's. My robe
And my integrity to Heaven is all
I dare now call mine own. Oh, Cromwell, Cromwell!
Had I but served my God with half the zeal   455
I served my King, he would not in mine age
Have left me naked to mine enemies.

CROM. Good sir, have patience.

WOL.   So I have. Farewell
The hopes of Court! My hopes in Heaven do dwell.

                           [*Exeunt.*]

Act IV

SCENE I. *A street in Westminster.*

[*Enter two* GENTLEMEN, *meeting one another.*]

1. GENT. You're well met once again.°

2. GENT.   So are you.

1. GENT. You come to take your stand here and behold
The Lady Anne pass from her coronation?

2. GENT. 'Tis all my business. At our last encounter
The Duke of Buckingham came from his trial.   5

1. GENT. 'Tis very true. But that time offered sorrow;
This, general joy.

2. GENT.   'Tis well. The citizens,
I am sure, have shown at full their royal° minds —
As, let 'em have their rights,° they are ever forward —

---

438. **sure . . . one:** This parting blessing and advice is bitter irony, for Cromwell ultimately succeeded Wolsey as the King's chief minister and was beheaded when he fell from favor.

    Act IV, Sc. i: 1. again: the previous meeting was in II.i. **8. royal:** loyal. **9. let . . . rights:** give them their due.

---

405. **voice:** talk.   420. **Make use:** take your advantage.

In celebration of this day with shows,   10
Pageants, and sights of honor.

1. GENT.   Never greater,
Nor, I'll assure you, better taken, sir.

2. GENT. May I be bold to ask what that contains,
That paper in your hand?

1. GENT.   Yes. 'Tis the list
Of those that claim their offices this day   15
By custom of the coronation.
The Duke of Suffolk is the first, and claims
To be High Steward; next, the Duke of Norfolk,
He to be Earl Marshal. You may read the rest.

2. GENT. I thank you, sir. Had I not known those
     customs,   20
I should have been beholding° to your paper.
But, I beseech you, what's become of Katharine,
The Princess Dowager? How goes her business?

1. GENT. That I can tell you too. The Archbishop
Of Canterbury, accompanied with other   25
Learned and reverend fathers of his order,°
Held a late court at Dunstable, six miles off
From Ampthill, where the princess lay, to which
She was often cited° by them, but appeared not.
And, to be short, for not appearance and   30
The King's late scruple, by the main assent
Of all these learned men she was divorced
And the late marriage° made of none effect.
Since which she was removed to Kimbolton,
Where she remains now sick.

2. GENT.   Alas, good lady! [*Trumpets.*]   35
The trumpets sound. Stand close, the Queen is
     coming.   [*Hautboys.°*]

[THE ORDER OF THE CORONATION

1. *A lively flourish°* of trumpets.

2. *Then two* JUDGES.

3. LORD CHANCELLOR, *with purse and mace before him.*

4. CHORISTERS, *singing.* MUSICIANS.

5. MAYOR OF LONDON, *bearing the mace. Then* GARTER,° *in his coat-of-arms, and on his head he wears a gilt copper crown.*

6. MARQUESS DORSET, *bearing a scepter of gold, on his head a demicoronal° of gold. With him, the* EARL OF SURREY, *bearing the rod of silver with the dove, crowned with an earl's coronet. Collars of SS.°*

7. DUKE OF SUFFOLK, *in his robe of estate, his coronet on his head, bearing a long white*

21. beholding: indebted.   26. his order: i.e., churchmen. 29. cited: summoned.   33. late marriage: i.e., the original marriage between Henry and Katharine.   36. s.d., Hautboys: oboes. The details of this procession are taken from Holinshed. For the lavishness of the original stage production, see Wotton's letter, p. 50b. flourish: trumpet notes denoting the approach of a procession. Garter: the chief herald, known as Garter King at Arms. See App. 9. demicoronal: coronet. Collars of SS: gold chains worn by high officials of the state, so called because the links resembled a series of SS–SS–SS. For similar collars, see Pls. 8d and 3b.

wand, as High Steward. With him, the DUKE OF NORFOLK, *with the rod of marshalship, a coronet on his head. Collars of SS.*

8. *A canopy borne by four of the* CINQUE PORTS;° *under it, the* QUEEN *in her robe; in her hair richly adorned with pearl, crowned. On each side her, the* BISHOPS OF LONDON *and* WINCHESTER.

9. *The old* DUCHESS OF NORFOLK, *in a coronal of gold wrought with flowers, bearing the* QUEEN's *train.*

10. *Certain* LADIES *or* COUNTESSES, *with plain circlets of gold without flowers.*
     They pass over the stage in order and state.]

2. GENT. A royal train, believe me. These I know.
Who's that that bears the scepter?

1. GENT.   Marquess Dorset;
And that the Earl of Surrey, with the rod.

2. GENT. A bold brave gentleman. That should
     be   40
The Duke of Suffolk?

1. GENT.   'Tis the same. High Steward.

2. GENT. And that my Lord of Norfolk?

1. GENT.   Yes.

2. GENT. [*Looking on the* QUEEN] Heaven bless
     thee!
Thou hast the sweetest face I ever looked on.
Sir, as I have a soul, she is an angel.
Our King has all the Indies° in his arms,   45
And more and richer, when he strains° that lady.
I cannot blame his conscience.

1. GENT.   They that bear
The cloth of honor over her are four Barons
Of the Cinque Ports.

2. GENT. Those men are happy, and so are all are
     near her.   50
I take it she that carries up the train
Is that old noble lady, Duchess of Norfolk.

1. GENT. It is, and all the rest are Countesses.

2. GENT. Their coronets say so. These are stars indeed,
And sometimes falling ones.

1. GENT.   No more of that.   55
[*Exit procession; and then a great flourish of
                         trumpets.*]
[*Enter a* THIRD GENTLEMAN.]
God save you, sir! Where have you been broiling?

3. GENT. Among the crowd i' the abbey, where a
     finger
Could not be wedged in more. I am stifled
With the mere rankness° of their joy.

2. GENT.   You saw
The ceremony?

36. s.d., four . . . Cinque Ports: Barons of the Five Channel Ports — the chief ports on the south coast of England. 45. Indies: i.e., all the riches of the Indies, i.e., South America. 46.. strains: hugs   59. rankness: strong smell.

3. GENT.   That I did.
1. GENT.   How was it?   60
3. GENT. Well worth the seeing.
2. GENT.   Good sir, speak it to us.
3. GENT. As well as I am able. The rich stream
Of lords and ladies, having brought the Queen
To a prepared place in the choir, fell off
A distance from her, while Her Grace sat down   65
To rest awhile, some half an hour or so,
In a rich chair of state, opposing° freely
The beauty of her person to the people.
Believe me, sir, she is the goodliest woman
That ever lay by man; which when the people   70
Had the full view of, such a noise arose
As the shrouds° make at sea in a stiff tempest,
As loud and to as many tunes. Hats, cloaks —
Doublets, I think — flew up, and had their faces
Been loose, this day they had been lost. Such joy
I never saw before. Great-bellied° women   76
That had not half a week to go, like rams°
In the old time of war, would shake the press°
And make 'em reel before 'em. No man living
Could say, "This is my wife" there, all were
       woven   80
So strangely in one piece.
   2. GENT.   But what followed?
   3. GENT. At length Her Grace rose and with mod-
       est paces
Came to the altar, where she kneeled and saintlike
Cast her fair eyes to Heaven and prayed devoutly;
Then rose again and bowed her to the people;   85
When by the Archbishop of Canterbury
She had all the royal makings° of a queen,
As holy oil, Edward Confessor's crown,°
The rod, and bird of peace,° and all such emblems
Laid nobly on her; which performed, the choir, 90
With all the choicest music° of the kingdom,
Together sung "*Te Deum.*" So she parted
And with the same full state paced° back again
To York Place, where the feast is held.
   1. GENT.   Sir,
You must no more call it York Place. That's past.
For, since the Cardinal fell, that title's lost.   96
'Tis now the King's and called Whitehall.
   3. GENT.   I know it,
But 'tis so lately altered that the old name
Is fresh about me.
   2. GENT.   What two reverend Bishops
Were those that went on each side of the Queen?

3. GENT. Stokesly and Gardiner; the one of Win-
       chester,   101
Newly preferred from° the King's secretary,
The other, London.
   2. GENT.   He of Winchester
Is held no great good lover of the Archbishop's,
The virtuous Cranmer.
   3. GENT.   All the land knows that.   105
However, yet there is no great breach. When it
       comes,
Cranmer will find a friend will° not shrink from
       him.
   2. GENT. Who may that be, I pray you?
   3. GENT.   Thomas Cromwell,
A man in much esteem with the King, and truly
A worthy friend. The King has made him master
O' the Jewel House,   111
And one, already, of the Privy Council.°
   2. GENT. He will deserve more.
   3. GENT.   Yes, without all doubt.
Come, gentlemen, ye shall go my way,
Which is to the Court, and there ye shall be my
       guests.   115
Something I can command.° As I walk thither,
I'll tell ye more.
   BOTH.   You may command us, sir. [*Exeunt.*]

SCENE II. *Kimbolton.*

[*Enter* KATHARINE, *Dowager, sick, led between*
GRIFFITH, *her* GENTLEMAN USHER,° *and* PATIENCE,
her woman.]

   GRIF. How does your Grace?
   KATH.   Oh, Griffith, sick to death!
My legs, like loaden branches, bow to the earth,
Willing to leave their burden. Reach a chair.
So; now, methinks, I feel a little ease.   4
Didst thou not tell me, Griffith, as thou led'st me,
That the great child of honor, Cardinal Wolsey,
Was dead?
   GRIF.   Yes, madam, but I think your Grace,
Out of the pain you suffered, gave no ear to 't.
   KATH. Prithee, good Griffith, tell me how he died.
If well, he stepped before me, happily°   10
For my example.
   GRIF.   Well, the voice goes, madam.
For after the stout Earl Northumberland
Arrested him at York and brought him forward
As a man sorely tainted to his answer,
He fell sick suddenly, and grew so ill   15
He could not sit his mule.
   KATH.   Alas, poor man!

67. opposing: exposing.   72. shrouds: rigging.   76. Great-
bellied: in the last stages of pregnancy.   77. rams: battering
rams.   78. shake . . . press: charge the crowd, head down.
87. royal makings: ceremonial befitting a coronation.   88. Edward . . . crown: the ancient crown of St. Edward (who died in
1066), used in crowning the kings of England.   89. rod . . .
peace: a scepter surmounted by a dove, one of the insignia of
royalty.   91. music: musicians.   93. paced: marched in procession.

102. preferred from: promoted from being. Gardiner was made
Bishop of Winchester.   107. will: i.e., who will.   112. Privy
Council: See Gen. Intro. pp. 24b–25a.   116. Something . . .
command: I have some influence there.
   Sc. ii: s.d., Usher: attendant.   10. happily: perhaps.

GRIF. At last, with easy roads,° he came to Leicester,
Lodged in the abbey, where the reverend abbot,
With all his covent,° honorably received him;
To whom he gave these words: " O Father Abbot,
An old man broken with the storms of state   21
Is come to lay his weary bones among ye.
Give him a little earth for charity! "
So went to bed, where eagerly his sickness
Pursued him still, and three nights after this,   25
About the hour of eight, which he himself
Foretold should be his last, full of repentance,
Continual meditations, tears, and sorrows,
He gave his honors to the world again,
His blessèd part to Heaven, and slept in peace.   30
   KATH. So may he rest. His faults lie gently on
him!
Yet thus far, Griffith, give me leave to speak him,
And yet with charity. He° was a man
Of an unbounded stomach,° ever ranking
Himself with princes, one that by suggestion°   35
Tied all the kingdom. Simony° was fair play.
His own opinion was his law. I' the presence°
He would say untruths and be ever double°
Both in his words and meaning. He was never,
But where he meant to ruin, pitiful.   40
His promises were, as he then was, mighty,
But his performance, as he is now, nothing.
Of his own body he was ill and gave
The clergy ill example.
   GRIF.   Noble madam,
Men's evil manners live in brass;° their virtues   45
We write in water. May it please your Highness
To hear me speak his good now?
   KATH.   Yes, good Griffith.
I were malicious else.
   GRIF.   This Cardinal,
Though from an humble stock, undoubtedly
Was fashioned to much honor from his cradle.   50
He was a scholar, and a ripe and good one,
Exceeding wise, fair-spoken, and persuading,
Lofty and sour to them that loved him not,
But to those men that sought him, sweet as summer.
And though he were unsatisfied in getting,   55
Which was a sin, yet in bestowing, madam,
He was most princely; ever witness for him
Those twins of learning that he raised in you,°
Ipswich and Oxford;° one of which fell with him,

Unwilling to outlive the good° that did it,   60
The other, though unfinished, yet so famous,
So excellent in art and still so rising,
That Christendom shall ever speak his virtue.
His overthrow heaped happiness upon him;
For then, and not till then, he felt himself,   65
And found the blessedness of being little.
And, to add greater honors to his age
Than man could give him, he died fearing God.
   KATH. After my death I wish no other herald,°
No other speaker of my living° actions,   70
To keep mine honor from corruption,
But such an honest chronicler as Griffith.
Whom I most hated living, thou hast made me,
With thy religious truth and modesty,
Now in his ashes honor. Peace be with him!   75
Patience, be near me still, and set me lower.
I have not long to trouble thee. Good Griffith,
Cause the musicians play me that sad note
I named my knell, whilst I sit meditating
On that celestial harmony I go to.   80
                    [*Sad and solemn music.*]
   GRIF. She is asleep. Good wench, let's sit down quiet,
For fear we wake her. Softly, gentle Patience.
[*The vision. Enter, solemnly tripping*° *one after
another, six personages, clad in white robes, wearing on their heads garlands of bays,*° *and golden
vizards*° *on their faces; branches of bays or palm in
their hands. They first congee*° *unto her, then
dance; and, at certain changes, the first two hold a
spare garland over her head, at which the other four
make reverent curtsies. Then the two that held the
garland deliver the same to the other next two, who
observe the same order in their changes, and holding the garland over her head; which done, they
deliver the same garland to the last two, who likewise observe the same order, at which, as it were
by inspiration, she makes in her sleep signs of rejoicing, and holdeth up her hands to heaven. And
so in their dancing vanish, carrying the garland
with them. The music continues.*]
   KATH. Spirits of peace, where are ye? Are ye all
gone
And leave me here in wretchedness behind ye?
   GRIF. Madam, we are here.
   KATH.   It is not you I call for.   85
Saw ye none enter since I slept?
   GRIF.   None, madam.
   KATH. No? Saw you not even now a blessèd
troop
Invite me to a banquet, whose bright faces
Cast thousand beams upon me, like the sun?

17. roads: journeys.   19. covent: convent.   33–44. He . . . example: For the original of this character sketch, see *Hen VIII*
Intro. p. 1504a.   34. stomach: pride.   35. suggestion: underhand dealing.   36. Simony: buying and selling sacred offices.
37. presence: i.e., presence chamber, before the King himself.
38. double: deceitful.   45. live in brass: i.e., are permanently
recorded.   58. in you: i.e., in your two cities.   59. Ipswich . . .
Oxford: Wolsey founded a college in Ipswich which was abandoned; his foundation at Oxford, first called Cardinal College,
was renamed Christ Church and remains the most magnificent
of all the college buildings.

60. good: good intention.   69. herald: one of whose duties was
to organize the funerals of the great. See App. 9.   70. living:
while still alive.   82. s.d., tripping: on the toes. garlands of bays:
crowns of bay leaves. vizards: masks. congee: bow.

They promised me eternal happiness   90
And brought me garlands, Griffith, which I feel
I am not worthy yet to wear. I shall, assuredly.
 GRIF. I am most joyful, madam, such good
      dreams
Possess your fancy.°
     KATH.   Bid the music leave.°
They are harsh and heavy to me.   [*Music ceases.*]
 PAT.   Do you note   95
How much Her Grace is altered on the sudden?
How long her face is drawn! How pale she looks,
And of an earthy cold! Mark her eyes!
 GRIF. She is going, wench. Pray, pray.
 PAT.   Heaven comfort her!
            [*Enter a* MESSENGER.]
 MESS. An 't like your Grace——
 KATH.   You are a saucy fellow.   100
Deserve we no more reverence?
 GRIF.   You are to blame,
Knowing she will not lose her wonted greatness,
To use so rude behavior. Go to, kneel.
 MESS. I humbly do entreat your Highness' par-
      don.
My haste made me unmannerly. There is staying
A gentleman, sent from the King, to see you.   106
 KATH. Admit him entrance, Griffith. But this fel-
      low
Let me ne'er see again.
        [*Exeunt* GRIFFITH *and* MESSENGER.]
      [*Re-enter* GRIFFITH, *with* CAPUCIUS.]
                  If my sight fail not,
You should be Lord Ambassador from the Emperor
My royal nephew, and your name Capucius.   110
 CAP. Madam, the same. Your servant.
 KATH.   Oh, my lord,
The times and titles now are altered strangely
With me since first you knew me. But, I pray you,
What is your pleasure with me?
 CAP.   Noble lady,
First, mine own service to your Grace; the next,
The King's request that I would visit you,   116
Who grieves much for your weakness, and by me
Sends you his princely commendations
And heartily entreats you take good comfort.
 KATH. Oh, my good lord, that comfort comes too
      late.   120
'Tis like a pardon after execution.
That gentle physic, given in time, had cured me,
But now I am past all comforts here but prayers.
How does His Highness?
 CAP.   Madam, in good health.
 KATH. So may he ever do, and ever flourish,   125
When I shall dwell with worms and my poor name
Banished the kingdom! Patience, is that letter,

I caused you write yet sent away?
 PAT.   No, madam. [*Giving it to* KATHARINE.]
 KATH. Sir, I most humbly pray you to deliver
This to my lord the King.
 CAP.   Most willing, madam.   130
 KATH. In which I have commended to his good-
      ness
The model of° our chaste loves, his young daugh-
      ter—
The dews of Heaven fall thick in blessings on
      her!—
Beseeching him to give her virtuous breeding°—
She is young and of a noble modest nature;   135
I hope she will deserve well—and a little
To love her for her mother's sake that loved him,
Heaven knows how dearly. My next poor petition
Is that his noble Grace would have some pity
Upon my wretched women, that so long   140
Have followed both° my fortunes faithfully;
Of which there is not one, I dare avow—
And now I should not lie—but will deserve,
For virtue and true beauty of the soul,
For honesty and decent carriage,   145
A right good husband—let him be a noble.
And, sure, those men are happy that shall have 'em.
The last is for my men—they are the poorest
(But poverty could never draw 'em from me)—
That they may have their wages duly paid 'em
And something over to remember me by.   151
If Heaven had pleased to have given me longer life
And able means, we had not parted thus.
These are the whole contents. And, good my lord,
By that you love the dearest in this world,   155
As you wish Christian peace to souls departed,
Stand these poor people's friend, and urge the King
To do me this last right.
 CAP.   By Heaven, I will,
Or let me lose the fashion of a man!   159
 KATH. I thank you, honest lord. Remember me
In all humility unto His Highness.
Say his long trouble now is passing
Out of this world. Tell him in death I blessed him,
For so I will. Mine eyes grow dim. Farewell,
My lord. Griffith, farewell. Nay, Patience,   165
You must not leave me yet. I must to bed.
Call in more women. When I am dead, good
      wench,
Let me be used with honor. Strew me over
With maiden flowers, that all the world may know
I was a chaste wife to my grave. Embalm me,   170
Then lay me forth. Although unqueened, yet like
A queen, and daughter to a king, inter me.
I can no more.   [*Exeunt, leading* KATHARINE.]

94. fancy: imagination. music leave: musicians cease.
132. model of: image created by.   134. breeding: education.
141. both: i.e., good and bad.

Act V

SCENE I. *London. A gallery in the palace.*

[*Enter* GARDINER, BISHOP OF WINCHESTER, *a* PAGE
with a torch before him, met by SIR THOMAS LOVELL.]

GARD. It's one o'clock, boy, is 't not?

BOY.   It hath struck.

GARD. These should be hours for necessities,
Not for delights; times to repair our nature
With comforting repose, and not for us
To waste these times. Good hour of night, Sir
    Thomas!   5
Whither so late?

LOV.   Came you from the King, my lord?

GARD. I did, Sir Thomas, and left him at primero°
With the Duke of Suffolk.

LOV.   I must to him, too,
Before he go to bed. I'll take my leave.

GARD. Not yet, Sir Thomas Lovell. What's the
    matter?   10
It seems you are in haste. An if there be
No great offense belongs to 't, give your friend
Some touch of your late business. Affairs that walk,
As they say spirits do, at midnight have
In them a wilder nature than the business   15
That seeks dispatch by day.

LOV.   My lord, I love you,
And durst commend a secret to your ear
Much weightier than this work. The Queen's in la-
    bor,
They say, in great extremity, and feared
She'll with the labor end.

GARD.   The fruit she goes with   20
I pray for heartily, that it may find
Good time° and live. But for the stock,° Sir
    Thomas,
I wish it grubbed up now.

LOV.   Methinks I could
Cry the amen; and yet my conscience says
She's a good creature and, sweet lady, does   25
Deserve our better wishes.

GARD.   But, sir, sir,
Hear me, Sir Thomas. You're a gentleman
Of mine own way.° I know you wise, religious;
And, let me tell you, it will ne'er be well —
'Twill not, Sir Thomas Lovell, take 't of me —   30
Till Cranmer, Cromwell, her two hands,° and she
Sleep in their graves.

LOV.   Now, sir, you speak of two
The most remarked i' the kingdom. As for Crom-
    well,
Beside that of the Jewel House, is made Master   34

Act V, Sc. i: **7. primero:** a card game. **22. Good time:**
good luck. **stock:** i.e., the new Queen, whom Gardiner dislikes because she favors the party of the Reformers (especially Cranmer
and Cromwell). **28. way:** i.e., faith. **31. hands:** supporters.

O' the Rolls,° and the King's secretary; further, sir,
Stands in the gap and trade° of moe preferments,
With which the time will load him. The Arch-
    bishop
Is the King's hand and tongue, and who dare speak
One syllable against him?

GARD.   Yes, yes, Sir Thomas,
There are that dare; and I myself have ventured 40
To speak my mind of him. And indeed this day,
Sir, I may tell it you, I think I have
Incensed° the Lords o' the Council that he is —
For so I know he is, they know he is —
A most archheretic,° a pestilence   45
That does infect the land; with which they moved
Have broken with° the King, who hath so far
Given ear to our complaint, of his great grace
And princely care foreseeing those fell° mischiefs
Our reasons laid before him, hath commanded   50
Tomórrow morning to the Council board
He be convented.° He's a rank weed, Sir Thomas,
And we must root him out. From your affairs
I hinder you too long. Good night, Sir Thomas.

LOV. Many good nights, my lord. I rest your serv-
    ant.   [*Exeunt* GARDINER *and* PAGE.]   55
                [*Enter* KING *and* SUFFOLK.]

KING. Charles, I will play no more tonight.
My mind's not on 't. You are too hard for me.

SUF. Sir, I did never win of you before.

KING. But little, Charles,
Nor shall not, when my fancy's on my play.   60
Now, Lovell, from the Queen what is the news?

LOV. I could not personally deliver to her
What you commanded me, but by her woman
I sent your message; who returned her thanks
In the great'st humbleness, and desired your High-
    ness   65
Most heartily to pray for her.

KING.   What say'st thou, ha?
To pray for her? What, is she crying out?

LOV. So said her woman, and that her suffer-
    ance°
Almost each pang a death.

KING.   Alas, good lady!

SUF. God safely quit° her of her burden, and   70
With gentle travail, to the gladding° of
Your Highness with an heir!

KING.   'Tis midnight, Charles.
Prithee, to bed, and in thy prayers remember
The estate° of my poor Queen. Leave me alone,
For I must think of that which company   75

34–35. Master . . . Rolls: Keeper of the Records. **36. gap . . .
trade:** open way. **43. Incensed:** made angry, with the accusation that. **45. archheretic:** Cranmer was one of the chief con-
trivers of the Reformation in the Church of England, especially
after the death of Henry VIII. **47. broken with:** given information to. **49. fell:** fearful. **52. convented:** summoned. **68. sufferance:** sufferings. **70. quit:** relieve. **71. gladding:** making
glad. **74. estate:** state, condition.

Would not be friendly to.

SUF.   I wish your Highness
A quiet night, and my good mistress will
Remember in my prayers.

    KING.   Charles, good night. [*Exit* SUFFOLK.]
       [*Enter* SIR ANTHONY DENNY.]
Well, sir, what follows?

    DEN. Sir, I have brought my lord the Archbishop,
As you commanded me.

    KING.   Ha! Canterbury?   81
    DEN. Aye, my good lord.
    KING.   'Tis true. Where is he, Denny?
    DEN. He attends your Highness' pleasure.
    KING.   Bring him to us. [*Exit* DENNY.]
    LOV. [*Aside*] This is about that which the Bish-
    op spake.

I am happily come hither.   85
    [*Re-enter* DENNY, *with* CRANMER.]
    KING. Avoid° the gallery. [LOVELL *seems to stay.*]
    Ha! I have said. Be gone.

What!   [*Exeunt* LOVELL *and* DENNY.]
    CRAN. [*Aside*] I am fearful.° Wherefore frowns
he thus?
'Tis his aspéct of terror.° All's not well.
    KING. How now, my lord! You do desire to know
Wherefore I sent for you.

    CRAN. [*Kneeling*]   It is my duty   90
To attend your Highness' pleasure.

    KING.   Pray you, arise,
My good and gracious Lord of Canterbury.
Come, you and I must walk a turn together.
I have news to tell you. Come, come, give me your
hand.
Ah, my good lord, I grieve at what I speak,   95
And am right sorry to repeat what follows.
I have, and most unwillingly, of late
Heard many grievous, I do say, my lord,
Grievous complaints of you; which, being consid-
ered,
Have moved us and our Council that you shall
This morning come before us; where, I know,   101
You cannot with such freedom purge yourself,
But that, till further trial in those charges
Which will require your answer, you must take
Your patience to you and be well contented   105
To make your house our Tower.° You a brother of
us,
It fits we thus proceed, or else no witness
Would come against you.°

    CRAN. [*Kneeling*]   I humbly thank your High-
ness,

And am right glad to catch this good occasion
Most throughly° to be winnowed° where my
chaff   110
And corn° shall fly asunder. For I know
There's none stands under more calumnious
tongues
Than I myself, poor man.

    KING.   Stand up, good Canterbury.
Thy truth and thy integrity is rooted
In us, thy friend. Give me thy hand, stand up. 115
Prithee, let's walk. Now, by my holidame,°
What manner of man are you? My lord, I looked
You would have given me your petition that
I should have ta'en some pains to bring together
Yourself and your accusers, and to have heard you
Without indurance° further.

    CRAN.   Most dread liege,   121
The good I stand on is my truth and honesty.
If they shall fail, I, with mine enemies,
Will triumph o'er my person, which I weigh not,
Being of those virtues vacant. I fear nothing   125
What can be said against me.

    KING.   Know you not
How your state stands i' the world, with the whole
world?
Your enemies are many, and not small. Their prac-
tices
Must bear the same proportion, and not ever°
The justice and the truth o' the question carries
The due o' the verdict with it. At what ease   131
Might corrupt minds procure knaves as corrupt
To swear against you? Such things have been done.
You are potently opposed, and with a malice
Of as great size. Ween you of° better luck —   135
I mean, in perjured witness — than your Master,°
Whose minister you are, whiles here He lived
Upon this naughty earth? Go to, go to.
You take a precipice for no leap of danger
And woo your own destruction.

    CRAN.   God and your Majesty   140
Protect mine innocence, or I fall into
The trap is laid for me!

    KING.   Be of good cheer.
They shall no more prevail than we give way to.
Keep comfort to you, and this morning see   144
You do appear before them. If they shall chance,
In charging you with matters, to commit° you,
The best persuasions to the contrary
Fail not to use, and with what vehemency
The occasion shall instruct you. If entreaties
Will render you no remedy, this ring°   150

---

86. Avoid: leave.   **87.** fearful: full of fear.   **88.** aspect of terror: frightening face.   **106.** To . . . Tower: to be housed in the Tower, where prisoners who had offended the sovereign were lodged. See Gen. Intro. p. 16a.   **106–08.** You . . . you: although as a Councilor you are one of my brethren, yet this proceeding is for the best, or else no testimony can be given against you. See below, V.iii.50,n.

110. throughly: thoroughly. winnowed: have my chaff sifted from my true grain. See *Cymb*, I.vi.177–78,n.   **111.** corn: grain.   **116.** holidame: holy relic; sometimes spelt halidom. See *R & J*, I.iii.43,n.   **121.** indurance: imprisonment.   **129.** ever: always.   **135.** Ween . . . of: do you imagine that you will have.   **136.** Master: i.e., Christ.   **146.** commit: send to prison.   **150.** ring: seal ring, engraved with the royal coat of arms.

Deliver them, and your appeal to us
There make before them. Look, the good man
    weeps!
He's honest, on mine honor. God's blest Mother!
I swear he is truehearted, and a soul
None better in my kingdom. Get you gone,   155
And do as I have bid you. [*Exit* CRANMER.] He has
    strangled°
His language in his tears.
       [*Enter* OLD LADY, LOVELL *following.*]
   GENT. [*Within*]   Come back. What mean you?
   OLD L. I'll not come back. The tidings that I
    bring
Will make my boldness manners. Now, good
    angels
Fly o'er thy royal head, and shade thy person   160
Under their blessed wings!
   KING.   Now, by thy looks
I guess thy message. Is the Queen delivered?
Say, aye, and of a boy.
   OLD L.   Aye, aye, my liege;
And of a lovely boy. The God of heaven
Both now and ever bless her! 'Tis a girl,   165
Promises boys hereafter. Sir, your Queen
Desires your visitation, and to be
Acquainted with this stranger. 'Tis as like you
As cherry is to cherry.
   KING.   Lovell!
   LOV.   Sir?
   KING. Give her an hundred marks.° I'll to the
   Queen.   [*Exit.*]   170
   OLD L. An hundred marks! By this light, I'll ha'
   more.
An ordinary groom is for such payment.
I will have more or scold it out of him.
Said I for this the girl was like to him?
I will have more or else unsay 't; and now,   175
While it is hot, I'll put it to the issue.   [*Exeunt.*]

SCENE II. *Before the Council Chamber.*

[PURSUIVANTS,° PAGES, *&c. attending.*
Enter CRANMER, *Archbishop of Canterbury.*]
   CRAN. I hope I am not too late; and yet the gen-
   tleman
That was sent to me from the Council prayed me
To make great haste. All fast?° What means this?
Ho!
Who waits there? Sure, you know me?
           [*Enter* KEEPER.]
   KEEP.   Yes, my lord;
But yet I cannot help you.   5

   CRAN. Why?
           [*Enter* DOCTOR BUTTS.]
   KEEP. Your Grace must wait till you be called
   for.
   CRAN.   So.
   BUTTS. [*Aside*] This is a piece of malice. I am
   glad
I came this way so happily. The King
Shall understand it presently.   [*Exit.*]
   CRAN. [*Aside*]   'Tis Butts,   10
The King's physician. As he passed along,
How earnestly he cast his eyes upon me!
Pray Heaven, he sound° not my disgrace! For cer-
   tain,
This is of purpose laid by some that hate me —
God turn their hearts! I never sought their malice —
To quench mine honor. They would shame° to
   make me   16
Wait else at door, a fellow councilor,
'Mong boys, grooms and lackeys. But their pleas-
   ures
Must be fulfilled, and I attend with patience.
[*Enter the* KING *and* BUTTS *at a window above.*]
   BUTTS. I'll show your Grace the strangest
   sight ——
   KING.   What's that, Butts?   20
   BUTTS. I think your Highness saw this many a
   day.
   KING. Body o' me, where is it?
   BUTTS.   There, my lord.
The high promotion of His Grace of Canterbury,
Who holds his state at door, 'mongst pursuivants,
Pages, and footboys.
   KING.   Ha! 'Tis he, indeed.   25
Is this the honor they do one another?
'Tis well there's one above 'em yet. I had thought
They had parted° so much honesty among 'em,
At least good manners, as not thus to suffer
A man of his place and so near our favor   30
To dance attendance on their lordships' pleasures,
And at the door, too, like a post with packets.°
By holy Mary, Butts, there's knavery.
Let 'em alone, and draw the curtain close.
We shall hear more anon.   [*Exeunt.*]   35

SCENE III. *The Council Chamber.*

[*Enter* LORD CHANCELLOR, *places himself at the upper end of the table on the left hand, a seat being
left void° above him, as for* CANTERBURY'S *seat.*
DUKE OF SUFFOLK, DUKE OF NORFOLK, SURREY, LORD
CHAMBERLAIN, GARDINER, *seat themselves in order on*

---

156. strangled: choked.   **170. marks:** A mark was worth two
thirds of a pound; the reward, £66. 13*s.* 4*d.*, was very handsome.
See App. 27.
   Sc. ii: s.d., Pursuivants: servants of the heralds.   **3. All fast:**
i.e., he tries the door and finds it locked.

13. sound: proclaim.   **16. shame:** be ashamed.   **28. parted:**
shared.   **32. post . . . packets:** postboy with letters waiting to
be admitted.
   Sc. iii: s.d., void: empty.

each side. CROMWELL *at lower end, as secretary.*
        KEEPER *at the door.*]
    CHAN. Speak to the business, Master Secretary.
Why are we met in Council?
    CROM.   Please your Honors,
The chief cause concerns His Grace of Canterbury.
    GARD. Has he had knowledge of it?
    CROM.   Yes.
    NOR.   Who waits there?
    KEEP. Without,° my noble lords?
    GARD.   Yes.
    KEEP.   My Lord Archbishop;   5
And has done half an hour, to know your pleas-
    ures.
    CHAN. Let him come in.
    KEEP.   Your Grace may enter now.
[CRANMER *enters and approaches the Council table.*]
    CHAN. My good Lord Archbishop, I'm very sorry
To sit here at this present and behold
That chair stand empty. But we all are men,   10
In our own natures frail and capable
Of° our flesh; few are angels; out of which frailty
And want of wisdom, you, that best should teach
    us,
Have misdemeaned yourself, and not a little:
Toward the King first, then his laws, in filling   15
The whole realm by your teaching and your chap-
    lains —
For so we are informed — with new opinions,
Divers and dangerous, which are heresies
And, not reformed, may prove pernicious.
    GARD. Which reformation must be sudden, too,
My noble lords; for those that tame wild horses   21
Pace 'em not in their hands° to make 'em gentle,
But stop their mouths with stubborn bits and spur
    'em
Till they obey the manage.° If we suffer,
Out of our easiness and childish pity   25
To one man's honor, this contagious sickness,
Farewell all physic. And what follows then?
Commotions, uproars, with a general taint
Of the whole state, as of late days our neighbors,
The upper Germany, can dearly witness,°   30
Yet freshly pitied in our memories.
    CRAN. My good lords, hitherto, in all the progress
Both of my life and office, I have labored,
And with no little study, that my teaching
And the strong course of my authority   35
Might go one way, and safely; and the end
Was ever to do well. Nor is there living —
I speak it with a single heart, my lords —
A man that more detests, more stirs against,

Both in his private conscience and his place,   40
Defacers of a public peace than I do.
Pray Heaven, the King may never find a heart
With less allegiance in it! Men that make
Envy and crooked malice nourishment°
Dare bite the best. I do beseech your lordships,   45
That, in this case of justice, my accusers,
Be what they will, may stand forth face to face
And freely urge° against me.
    SUF.   Nay, my lord,
That cannot be. You are a Councillor,
And by that virtue° no man dare accuse you.   50
    GARD. My lord, because we have business of more
    moment,
We will be short with you. 'Tis His Highness'
    pleasure,
And our consent, for better trial of you,
From hence you be committed to the Tower,
Where, being but a private man again,   55
You shall know many dare accuse you boldly,
More than, I fear, you are provided for.
    CRAN. Ah, my good Lord of Winchester, I thank
    you.
You are always my good friend. If your will pass,°
I shall both find your lordship judge and juror,   60
You are so merciful. I see your end.
'Tis my undoing. Love and meekness, lord,
Become a churchman better than ambition.
Win straying souls with modesty again,
Cast none away. That I shall clear myself,   65
Lay all the weight ye can upon my patience,
I make as little doubt as you do conscience
In doing daily wrongs. I could say more,
But reverence to your calling makes me modest.
    GARD. My lord, my lord, you are a sectary.°   70
That's the plain truth. Your painted gloss° discov-
    ers,°
To men that understand you, words and weakness.
    CROM. My Lord of Winchester, you are a little,
By your good favor, too sharp. Men so noble,
However faulty, yet should find respect   75
For what they have been. 'Tis a cruelty
To load° a falling man.
    GARD.   Good Master Secretary,
I cry your Honor mercy.° You may, worst
Of all this table, say so.
    CROM.   Why, my lord?
    GARD. Do not I know you for a favorer   80
Of this new sect? Ye are not sound.
    CROM.   Not sound?
    GARD. Not sound, I say.

---

5. **Without:** outside the door.   **11–12. capable Of:** liable to fail
through.   **22. Pace . . . hands:** do not train them by leading
them gently.   **24. manage:** horsemanship, the control by the
rider.   **29–30. neighbors . . . witness:** The Reformation movement in Germany led to risings in 1524 and 1535 which caused
much bloodshed.

43–44. make . . . nourishment: feed on.   **48. urge:** make their
accusations.   **50. virtue:** privilege. Privy Councilors had various privileges, including freedom from public accusation for
abuse of office.   **59. pass:** prevail.   **70. sectary:** follower of a
sect, i.e., Protestant.   **71. painted gloss:** showy exterior. **discovers:** reveals.   **77. load:** oppress.   **78. I . . . mercy:** I apologize — said sarcastically.

CROM.   Would you were half so honest!
Men's prayers then would seek you, not their fears.
  GARD. I shall remember this bold language.
  CROM.   Do.
Remember your bold life too.
  CHAN.   This is too much. 85
Forbear, for shame, my lords.
  GARD.   I have done.
  CROM.   And I.
  CHAN. Then thus for you, my lord. It stands
    agreed,
I take it, by all voices that forthwith
You be conveyed to the Tower a prisoner,
There to remain till the King's further pleasure 90
Be known unto us. Are you all agreed, lords?
  ALL. We are.
  CRAN.   Is there no other way of mercy,
But I must needs to the Tower, my lords?
  GARD.   What other
Would you expect? You are strangely troublesome.
Let some o' the guard be ready there.
              [*Enter* GUARD.]
  CRAN.   For me? 95
Must I go like a traitor thither?
  GARD.   Receive him,
And see him safe i' the Tower.
  CRAN.   Stay, good my lords,
I have a little yet to say. Look there, my lords.
By virtue of that ring, I take my cause
Out of the gripes° of cruel men and give it 100
To a most noble judge, the King, my master.
  CHAMB. This is the King's ring.
  SUR.   'Tis no counterfeit.
  SUF. 'Tis the right ring, by Heaven. I told ye all,
When we first put this dangerous stone arolling,
'Twould fall upon ourselves.
  NOR.   Do you think, my lords, 105
The King will suffer but° the little finger
Of this man to be vexed?
  CHAMB.   'Tis now too certain.
How much more is his life in value with him?°
Would I were fairly out on 't!
  CROM.   My mind gave° me,
In seeking tales and informations 110
Against this man, whose honesty the Devil
And his disciples only envy at,
Ye blew the fire that burns ye. Now have at ye!
  [*Enter* KING, *frowning on them; takes his seat.*]
  GARD. Dread sovereign, how much are we bound
    to Heaven
In daily thanks, that gave us such a prince, 115
Not only good and wise, but most religious;
One that, in all obedience, makes the Church
The chief aim of his honor; and, to strengthen
That holy duty, out of dear respect,
His royal self in judgment comes to hear 120
The cause betwixt her and this great offender.
  KING. You were ever good at sudden commenda-
    tions,
Bishop of Winchester. But know I come not
To hear such flattery now, and in my presence
They are too thin and bare to hide offenses. 125
To me you cannot reach you play the spaniel,
And think with wagging of your tongue to win me;
But, whatsoe'er thou takest me for, I'm sure
Thou hast a cruel nature and a bloody.
[*To* CRANMER] Good man, sit down. Now let me
    see the proudest 130
He that dares most, but wag his finger at thee.
By all that's holy, he had better starve
Than but once think this place becomes thee not.
  SUR. May it please your Grace ——
  KING.   No, sir, it does not please me.
I had thought I had had men of some understand-
    ing 135
And wisdom of my Council, but I find none.
Was it discretion, lords, to let this man,
This good man — few of you deserve that title —
This honest man, wait like a lousy footboy 139
At chamber door? And one as great as you are?
Why, what a shame was this! Did my commission
Bid ye so far forget yourselves? I gave ye
Power as he was a Councilor to try him,
Not as a groom. There's some of ye, I see,
More out of malice than integrity, 145
Would try him to the utmost, had ye mean,°
Which ye shall never have while I live.
  CHAN.   Thus far,
My most dread sovereign, may it like° your Grace
To let my tongue excuse all. What was purposed
Concerning his imprisonment was rather, 150
If there be faith in men, meant for his trial
And fair purgation° to the world than malice,
I'm sure, in me.
  KING.   Well, well, my lords, respect him.
Take him and use him well. He's worthy of it. 155
I will say thus much for him, if a prince
May be beholding° to a subject, I
Am, for his love and service, so to him.
Make me no more ado, but all embrace him.
Be friends, for shame, my lords! My Lord of Can-
    terbury, 160
I have a suit which you must not deny me;
That is, a fair young maid that yet wants baptism.
You must be godfather, and answer for her.
  CRAN. The greatest monarch now alive may glory
In such an honor. How may I deserve it 165
That am a poor and humble subject to you?

---

100. gripes: grip, handling.   **106. suffer but:** will not allow more than.   **108. How ... him:** i.e., the King values Cranmer's life far more than his little finger.   **109. gave:** misgave

146. mean: means.   **148. like:** please.   **152. purgation:** clearing of accusations.   **157. beholding:** indebted.

KING. Come, come, my lord, you'd spare your spoons.° You shall have two noble partners with you, the old Duchess of Norfolk, and Lady Marquess Dorset. Will these please you?   170
Once more, my Lord of Winchester, I charge you, Embrace and love this man.

GARD.   With a true heart
And brother love I do it.

CRAN.   And let Heaven
Witness how dear I hold this confirmation.

KING. Good man, those joyful tears show thy true
     heart.   175
The common voice, I see, is verified
Of thee, which says thus: " Do my Lord of Canterbury
A shrewd° turn, and he is your friend for ever."
Come, lords, we trifle time away. I long
To have this young one made a Christian.   180
As I have made ye one, lords, one remain;
So I grow stronger, you more honor gain.
                                        [*Exeunt.*]

SCENE IV. *The palace yard.*

[*Noise and tumult within. Enter* PORTER *and his*
            MAN.]

PORT. You'll leave your noise anon, ye rascals. Do you take the court for Paris Garden?° Ye rude slaves, leave your gaping.

[*Within*] Good Master Porter, I belong to the larder.°   5

PORT. Belong to the gallows and be hanged, ye rogue! Is this a place to roar in? Fetch me a dozen crab-tree staves,° and strong ones. These are but switches to 'em.° I'll scratch your heads. You must be seeing christenings? Do you look for ale and cakes° here, you rude rascals?   11

MAN. Pray, sir, be patient. 'Tis as much impossible —
Unless we sweep 'em from the door with cannons —
To scatter 'em as 'tis to make 'em sleep
On May Day morning,° which will never be.   15
We may as well push against Powle's° as stir 'em.

PORT. How got they in, and be hanged?

MAN. Alas, I know not. How gets the tide in?
As much as one sound cudgel of four foot —   19
You see the poor remainder — could distribute,
I made no spare, sir.

PORT.   You did nothing, sir.

MAN. I am not Samson,° nor Sir Guy,° nor Colbrand,°
To mow 'em down before me. But if I spared any
That had a head to hit, either young or old,
He or she, cuckold or cuckold maker,   25
Let me ne'er hope to see a chine° again;
And that I would not for a cow, God save her!°

[*Within*] Do you hear, Master Porter?

PORT. I shall be with you presently,° good Master Puppy. Keep the door close, sirrah.   30

MAN. What would you have me do?

PORT. What should you do, but knock 'em down by the dozens? Is this Moorfields° to muster in? Or have we some strange Indian with the great tool come to Court, the women so besiege us? Bless   35 me, what a fry of fornication° is at door! On my Christian conscience, this one christening will beget a thousand. Here will be father, godfather, and all together.   39

MAN. The spoons will be the bigger, sir. There is a fellow somewhat near the door, he should be a brazier° by his face, for, o' my conscience, twenty of the dog days° now reign in 's nose. All that stand about him are under the line,° they need no   45 other penance. That firedrake° did I hit three times on the head, and three times was his nose discharged against me. He stands there, like a mortar piece,° to blow us. There was a haberdasher's° wife of small wit near him that railed upon me till   50 her pinked porringer° fell off her head for kindling such a combustion in the state. I missed the meteor° once, and hit that woman, who cried out " Clubs! "° when I might see from far some forty truncheoners° draw to her succor which were the hope o'   55 the Strand,° where she was quartered. They fell on. I made good my place. At length they came to the broomstaff° to me. I defied 'em still; when suddenly a file° of boys behind 'em, loose shot, delivered such

---

167-68. spare . . . spoons: save yourself the cost of a christening gift. It is an English custom for godparents to present a godchild with a spoon at the christening.   178. shrewd: bitter.
Sc. iv: 2. Paris Garden: the name of the rowdy bearbaiting arena, situated near to the Globe Theater. See App. 5.   4-5. I . . . larder: i.e., I am one of the servants in the larder — and so entitled to come in.   8. crab-tree staves: cudgels made of crab-apple wood, hard and strong.   8-9. These . . . 'em: the sticks we now have are thin rods compared to a good crab-tree cudgel.   10-11. ale . . . cakes: free food.   15. May . . . morning: a general holiday, when people rose early to see the sunrise.   16. Powle's: St. Paul's Cathedral. See Gen. Intro. p. 17. Powle is the normal Elizabethan pronunciation of the word.

22. Samson . . . Sir Guy . . . Colbrand: famous heroes who performed deeds of ferocity.   26. chine: chine (back) of beef.   27. And . . . her: not satisfactorily explained.   29. presently: at once.   33. Moorfields: an open space near the City of London where the train bands held their annual parade.   36. fry of fornication: crowd of bastards.   42. brazier: worker in brass, whose occupation gives him a red face.   43. dog days: hot summer days in July and August.   45. under . . . line: living near the equator.   46. firedrake: man with a red nose, lit., fiery dragon.   48-49. mortar piece: a squat cannon used for firing bombshells.   49. haberdasher: dealer in women's goods.   51. pinked porringer: small hat with scalloped edge.   52. meteor: i.e., the man with the red nose.   53. Clubs: See *AYLI*, V.ii.45,n.   54-55. truncheoners: men with sticks.   55-56. hope . . . Strand: the pick of the London apprentices from the street called the Strand.   57-58. came . . . broomstaff: came within short range.   59. file: party.

a shower of pebbles that I was fain° to draw   60
mine honor in and let 'em win the work.° The
Devil was amongst 'em, I think, surely.

PORT. These are the youths that thunder at a
playhouse and fight for bitten apples;° that no audience, but the tribulation of Tower Hill,° or   65
the limbs° of Limehouse, their dear brothers, are
able to endure. I have some of 'em in Limbo Patrum,° and there they are like to dance these three
days, besides the running banquet of two beadles°
that is to come.   70

[*Enter* LORD CHAMBERLAIN.]

CHAM. Mercy o' me, what a multitude are here!
They grow still too. From all parts they are com-
        ing,
As if we kept a fair here. Where are these por-
        ters,
These lazy knaves? Ye have made a fine hand,
        fellows!
There's a trim° rabble let in. Are all these   75
Your faithful friends o' the suburbs?° We shall
        have
Great store of room, no doubt, left for the ladies
When they pass back from the christening.

PORT.   An 't please your Honor,
We are but men; and what so many may do,
Not being torn apieces, we have done.   80
An army cannot rule 'em.

CHAM.   As I live,
If the King blame me for 't, I'll lay ye all
By the heels, and suddenly; and on your heads
Clap round° fines for neglect. Ye're lazy knaves;
And here ye lie baiting of bombards° when   85
Ye should do service. Hark! The trumpets sound.
They're come already from the christening.
Go, break among the press, and find a way out
To let the troop pass fairly, or I'll find   89
A Marshalsea° shall hold ye play these two months.

PORT. Make way there for the Princess.

MAN.   You great fellow,
Stand close up, or I'll make your head ache.

PORT. You i' the camlet,° get up o' the rail;°
I'll peck you o'er the pales° else.   [*Exeunt.*]

---

60. **fain**: obliged.   61. **work**: fort.   64. **bitten apples**: i.e., the
half-eaten apples thrown down by better class playgoers. The
modern equivalent is cigarette ends.   65. **tribulation ... Hill**:
the rowdies of Tower Hill, a notoriously unruly district.
66. **limbs**: nuisances.   67–68. **Limbo Patrum**: slang for "lockup."   69. **running ... beadles**: a taste of the beadle's whip.
75. **trim**: fine.   76. **suburbs**: the disorderly parts of the City.
84. **round**: severe.   85. **baiting of bombards**: i.e., drinking. See
Pl. 17f.   90. **Marshalsea**: the prison of the Marshal where
those who offended in the neighborhood of the Court were imprisoned.   93. **camlet**: cloak made of rough material. **get ...
rail**: get down from the railings.   94. **peck ... pales**: pitch you
over the fence.

SCENE V. *The palace.*

[*Enter Trumpets, sounding; then two* ALDERMEN,
LORD MAYOR, GARTER,° CRANMER, DUKE OF NORFOLK
with his marshal's staff, DUKE OF SUFFOLK, *two*
NOBLEMEN *bearing great standing-bowls° for the
christening gifts; then four* NOBLEMEN *bearing a
canopy, under which the* DUCHESS OF NORFOLK, *godmother, bearing the child richly habited in a mantle, &c., train borne by a* LADY. *Then follows the*
MARCHIONESS DORSET, *the other godmother, and* LA-
DIES. *The troop pass once about the stage, and*
GARTER *speaks.*]

GART. Heaven, from Thy endless goodness, send
prosperous life, long, and ever happy, to the high
and mighty Princess of England, Elizabeth!

[*Flourish. Enter* KING *and* GUARD.]

CRAN. [*Kneeling*] And to your royal Grace, and
        the good Queen!   5
My noble partners and myself thus pray:
All comfort, joy, in this most gracious lady,
Heaven ever laid up to make parents happy,
May hourly fall upon ye!

KING.   Thank you, good Lord Archbishop.
What is her name?

CRAN.   Elizabeth.

KING. Stand up, lord. [*The* KING *kisses the child.*]
With this kiss take my blessing. God protect thee,
Into Whose hand I give thy life.

CRAN.   Amen.   12

KING. My noble gossips,° ye have been too prodi-
        gal.°
I thank ye heartily; so shall this lady
When she has so much English.

CRAN.   Let me speak, sir,   15
For Heaven now bids me; and the words I utter
Let none think flattery, for they'll find 'em truth.
This royal infant — Heaven still move about
        her! —
Though in her cradle, yet now promises
Upon this land a thousand thousand blessings,   20
Which time shall bring to ripeness. She shall be —
But few now living can behold that goodness —
A pattern to all princes living with her,
And all that shall succeed. Saba° was never
More covetous of wisdom and fair virtue   25
Than this pure soul shall be. All princely graces,
That mold° up such a mighty piece as this is,
With all the virtues that attend the good,
Shall still be doubled on her. Truth shall nurse her,
Holy and heavenly thoughts still counsel her.   30

Sc. v: s.d., **Garter**: See IV.i.36,s.d.,n. **standing-bowls**: See
Pl. 20h.   13. **gossips**: godparents. **prodigal**: generous in your
christening gifts.   24. **Saba**: the Queen of Sheba, who came to
visit King Solomon (I Kings 10:1–10).   27. **mold**: make, compose.

She shall be loved and feared. Her own shall bless
    her,
Her foes shake like a field of beaten corn,
And hang their heads with sorrow. Good grows
    with her.
In° her days every man shall eat in safety
Under his own vine what he plants, and sing   35
The merry songs of peace to all his neighbors.
God shall be truly known; and those about her
From her shall read the perfect ways of honor,
And by those claim their greatness, not by blood.
Nor shall this peace sleep with her; but, as when
The bird of wonder dies, the maiden phoenix,°   41
Her ashes new create another heir
As great in admiration° as herself,
So shall she leave her blessedness to one° —
When Heaven shall call her from this cloud of
    darkness —   45
Who from the sacred ashes of her honor
Shall starlike rise, as great in fame as she was,
And so stand fixed. Peace, plenty, love, truth, terror,
That were the servants to this chosen infant,
Shall then be his, and like a vine grow to him.   50
Wherever the bright sun of heaven shall shine,
His honor and the greatness of his name
Shall be, and make new nations. He shall flourish,
And, like a mountain cedar, reach his branches
To all the plains about him. Our children's children
Shall see this and bless Heaven.
      KING.   Thou speakest wonders.   56
      CRAN. She shall be, to the happiness of England,
An agèd Princess. Many days shall see her,
And yet no day without a deed to crown it.   59
Would I had known no more! But she must die.
She must. The saints must have her. Yet a virgin,

A most unspotted lily, shall she pass
To the ground, and all the world shall mourn her.
      KING. O Lord Archbishop,
Thou hast made me now a man! Never before   65
This happy child did I get° anything.
This oracle of comfort has so pleased me
That when I am in Heaven, I shall desire
To see what this child does, and praise my Maker.
I thank ye all. To you, my good Lord Mayor,   70
And your good brethren, I am much beholding.
I have received much honor by your presence,
And ye shall find me thankful. Lead the way, lords.
Ye must all see the Queen, and she must thank ye.
She will be sick else. This day no man think   75
Has° business at his house; for all shall stay.°
This little one shall make it holiday.   *[Exeunt.]*

THE EPILOGUE

'Tis ten to one this play can never please
All that are here. Some come to take their ease
And sleep an act or two; but those, we fear,
We have frighted with our trumpets, so, 'tis clear
They'll say 'tis naught; others, to hear the City   5
Abused extremely,° and to cry, " That's witty! "
Which we have not done neither; that I fear
All the expected good we're like to hear
For this play at this time is only in
The merciful construction° of good women;   10
For such a one we showed 'em. If they smile
And say 'twill do, I know within a while
All the best men are ours; for 'tis ill hap°
If they hold when their ladies bid 'em clap.

34–37. In . . . known: This prophecy of the golden age of Queen
Elizabeth owes something to Micah 4:3–7.   41. maiden
phoenix: See *Temp*, III.iii.23,n.   43. admiration: causing wonder.   44. one: i.e., King James I, then King, and patron of
Shakespeare's company.

66. get: beget.   76. Has: that he has. stay: stop work.
    Epilogue: 5–6. hear . . . extremely: Comedies at this time
were full of sarcastic abuse of London citizens.   10. construction: acceptance.   13. hap: luck.

VENUS AND ADONIS

Introduction

Venus and Adonis was entered in the Stationers' Register on April 18, 1593: " xviii° Aprilis. Richard Feild Assigned ouer to master Harrison senior 25 Junii 1594. Entred for his copie under thandes of the Archbisshop of Canterbury and master warden Stirrop, a booke intituled, Venus and Adonis, vjᵈ." The first edition followed soon afterward, with the title page: *VENUS AND ADONIS/Vilia miretur vulgus: mihi flauus Apollo/Pocula Castalia plena ministret aqua. London. Imprinted by Richard Field, and are to be sold at the signe of the white Greyhound in Paules Church-yard. 1593.* Richard Field, the printer, who had originally come from Stratford-on-Avon, was a man of good standing in the printing trade. The volume was finely printed in good, large type and was obviously intended for the better class of reader.

Venus and Adonis is one of several poems written in the 1590's in which the physical attractions of a young man are stressed. It was a very popular work, and though nowadays early copies are excessively rare, examples of editions printed in 1594, 1596, 1599 (2), 1602 (3), as well as undated fragments, survive. There are many references to the poem, which was much quoted; in *England's Parnassus* (1600), a collection of "the choicest flowers of our modern poets," there are twenty-six quotations. Sober-minded readers, however, regarded the poem as improper.

Venus and Adonis is written in a six-line stanza, each line having five stresses, the rhyme scheme being ababcc. This pattern was not common, but it had been used by Spenser in the First Eclogue in *The Shepherd's Calendar* (1579), and also by Thomas Lodge in *Scilla's Metamorphosis* (1589).

The story of Venus's passion for Adonis was well known and often retold. Shakespeare probably first met it in Ovid's *Metamorphoses,* and he could also have taken hints from Lodge's poem. The story was told also in Spenser's *Faerie Queene* (Book III, Canto i, 34–38; 1591), in

which there is given a luscious description of the Castle Joyous:

The walls were round about apparellèd
With costly cloths of Arras and of Tour,
In which with cunning hand was portrayèd
The love of Venus and her Paramour
The fair Adonis, turnèd to a flower,
A work of rare device, and wondrous wit.
First did it show the bitter baleful stour [conflict],
Which her assayed with many a fervent fit,
When first her tender heart was with his beauty
    smit.

.   .   .   .

And whilst he slept, she over him would spread
Her mantle, colored like the starry skies,
And her soft arm lay underneath his head,
And with ambrosial kisses bathe his eyes;
And whilst he bathed, with her two crafty spies,
She secretly would search each dainty limb,
And throw into the well sweet rosemaries,
And fragrant violets, and pansies trim,
And ever with sweet nectar she did sprinkle him.

So did she steal his heedless heart away,
And joyed his love in secret unespied.
But for she saw him bent to cruel play,
To hunt the savage beast in forest wide,
Dreadful of danger, that mote him betide,
She oft and oft advised him to refrain
From chase of greater beasts, whose brutish pride
Mote breed him scathe unwares: but all in vain;
For who can shun the chance, that dest'ny doth
    ordain?

Lo, where beyond he lieth languishing,
Deadly engorèd of a great wild Boar,
And by his side the Goddess groveling
Makes for him endless moan, and evermore
With her soft garment wipes away the gore,
Which stains his snowy skin with hateful hue:
But when she saw no help might him restore,
Him to a dainty flower she did transmew,
Which in that cloth was wrought, as if it lively
    grew.

A contemporary illustration of the story "with cunning hand portrayed" in needlework is shown in Pl. 7a.

Vilia miretur vulgus : mihi flavus Apollo
Pocula Castalia plena ministret aqua.°

TO THE

RIGHT HONORABLE HENRY WRIOTHESLEY,

EARL OF SOUTHAMPTON AND BARON OF TITCHFIELD.

RIGHT HONORABLE, I know not how I shall offend in dedicating my unpolished lines to your Lordship, nor how the world will censure me for choosing so strong a prop to support so weak a burden; only if your Honor seem but pleased, I account myself highly praised, and vow to take advantage of all idle hours till I have honored you with some graver labor. But if the first heir of my invention prove deformed, I shall be sorry it had so noble a godfather; and never after ear so barren a land, for fear it yield me still so bad a harvest. I leave it to your honorable survey, and your Honor to your heart's content, which I wish may always answer your own wish and the world's hopeful expectation.

Your Honor's in all duty,
WILLIAM SHAKESPEARE.

Even as the sun with purple-colored face
Had ta'en his last leave of the weeping° morn,
Rose-cheeked Adonis hied him to the chase.
Hunting he loved, but love he laughed to scorn.
   Sick-thoughted Venus makes amain° untò him,
   And like a bold-faced suitor 'gins to woo him. 6

" Thrice fairer than myself," thus she began,
" The field's chief flower, sweet above compare,
Stain to° all nymphs, more lovely than a man,
More white and red than doves or roses are;   10
   Nature that made thee, with herself at strife,
   Saith that the world hath ending with thy life.

" Vouchsafe, thou wonder, to alight thy steed
And rein his proud head to the saddlebow.°
If thou wilt deign this favor, for thy meed°   15
A thousand honey secrets shalt thou know.
   Here come and sit, where never serpent hisses,
   And being set, I'll smother thee with kisses,

" And yet not cloy thy lips with loathed satiety,
But rather famish them amid their plenty,   20
Making them red and pale with fresh variety;
Ten kisses short as one, one long as twenty.
   A summer's day will seem an hour but short,
   Being wasted in such time-beguiling sport."

With this she seizeth on his sweating palm,   25
The precedent of pith° and livelihood,°
And, trembling in her passion, calls it balm,
Earth's sovereign salve to do a goddess good.
   Being so enraged,° desire doth lend her force
   Courageously to pluck him from his horse.   30

Over one arm the lusty courser's° rein,
Under her other was the tender boy,
Who blushed and pouted in a dull disdain,
With leaden appetite, unapt to toy;
   She red and hot as coals of glowing fire,   35
   He red for shame, but frosty in desire.

The studded bridle on a raggèd° bough
Nimbly she fastens — oh, how quick is love! —
The steed is stallèd up, and even now
To tie the rider she begins to prove.°   40
   Backward she pushed him, as she would be thrust,
   And governed him in strength, though not in lust.

So soon was she along° as he was down,
Each leaning on their elbows and their hips.
Now doth she stroke his cheek, now doth he frown,
And 'gins to chide, but soon she stops his lips,   46
   And kissing speaks, with lustful language broken,
   " If thou wilt chide, thy lips shall never open."

He burns with bashful shame; she with her tears
Doth quench the maiden burning of his cheeks.   50
Then with her windy sighs and golden hairs

Motto: *Vilia . . . aqua.* Let the vulgar admire vile things; for me may golden-haired Apollo provide cups full of water from the Castalian spring; i.e., from the fountain whence the Muses drank inspiration. The lines are a quotation from Ovid's *Amores.* **2. weeping:** dewy. **5. makes amain:** hastens. **9. Stain to:** eclipsing. **14. saddlebow:** the arched pieces which make the front of a saddle. **15. meed:** reward.

26. precedent . . . livelihood: sign of lusty activity. **pith:** lit., marrow. **29. enraged:** full of passion. **31. courser:** horse. **37. ragged:** rough. **40. prove:** attempt. **43. along:** lying prostrate.

To fan and blow them dry again she seeks.
　He saith she is immodest, blames her miss.°
　What follows more she murders with a kiss.

Even as an empty eagle, sharp by fast,　　　55
Tires° with her beak on feathers, flesh, and bone,
Shaking her wings, devouring all in haste,
Till either gorge° be stuffed or prey be gone,
　Even so she kissed his brow, his cheek, his chin,
　And where she ends she doth anew begin.　60

Forced to content, but never to obey,
Panting he lies and breatheth in her face.
She feedeth on the steam as on a prey,
And calls it heavenly moisture, air of grace,　64
　Wishing her cheeks were gardens full of flowers,
　So they were dewed with such distilling showers.

Look, how a bird lies tangled in a net,
So fastened in her arms Adonis lies.
Pure shame and awed resistance° made him fret,
Which bred more beauty in his angry eyes.　70
　Rain added to a river that is rank°
　Perforce will force it overflow the bank.

Still she entreats, and prettily entreats,
For to a pretty ear she tunes her tale.
Still is he sullen, still he lours and frets,　75
'Twixt crimson shame, and anger ashy-pale.
　Being red, she loves him best, and, being white,
　Her best is bettered with a more delight.

Look how he can, she cannot choose but love,
And by her fair immortal hand she swears　80
From his soft bosom never to remove
Till he take truce with her contending tears,
　Which long have rained, making her cheeks all
　　wet;
　And one sweet kiss shall pay this countless debt.

Upon this promise did he raise his chin,　85
Like a dive-dapper° peering through a wave,
Who, being looked on, ducks as quickly in.
So offers he to give what she did crave;
　But when her lips were ready for his pay,
　He winks,° and turns his lips another way.　90

Never did passenger° in summer's heat
More thirst for drink than she for this good turn.
Her help she sees, but help she cannot get.
She bathes in water, yet her fire must burn.

" Oh, pity," gan she cry, " flint-hearted boy!　95
'Tis but a kiss I beg. Why art thou coy?

" I have been wooed, as I entreat thee now,
Even by the stern and direful God of War,
Whose sinewy neck in battle ne'er did bow,
Who conquers where he comes in every jar.°　100
　Yet hath he been my captive and my slave,
　And begged for that which thou unasked shalt
　　have.

" Over my altars hath he hung his lance,
His battered shield, his uncontrollèd crest,°
And for my sake hath learned to sport and dance,
To toy, to wanton, dally, smile and jest,　106
　Scorning his churlish drum and ensign red,
　Making my arms his field, his tent my bed.

" Thus he that overruled I overswayed,
Leading him prisoner in a red-rose chain.　110
Strong-tempered steel his stronger strength obeyed,
Yet was he servile to my coy disdain.
　Oh, be not proud, nor brag not of thy might,
　For mastering her that foiled° the god of fight!

" Touch but my lips with those fair lips of thine —
Though mine be not so fair, yet are they red —　116
The kiss shall be thine own as well as mine.
What seest thou in the ground? Hold up thy head.
　Look in mine eyeballs, there thy beauty lies.°
　Then why not lips on lips, since eyes in eyes?　120

" Art thou ashamed to kiss? Then wink again,
And I will wink; so shall the day seem night.
Love keeps his revels where there are but twain.
Be bold to play, our sport is not in sight.
　These blue-veined violets whereon we lean　125
　Never can blab, nor know not what we mean.

" The tender spring° upon thy tempting lip
Shews thee unripe. Yet mayst thou well be tasted.
Make use of time, let not advantage slip.
Beauty within itself should not be wasted.　130
　Fair flowers that are not gathered in their prime
　Rot and consume themselves in little time.

" Were I hard-favored,° foul, or wrinkled old,
Ill-nurtured, crooked, churlish, harsh in voice,
O'erworn, despisèd, rheúmatic and cold,　135
Thick-sighted, barren, lean, and lacking juice,
　Then mightst thou pause, for then I were not for
　　thee;
　But having no defects, why dost abhor me?

---

53. miss: light behavior.　56. Tires: tears.　58. gorge: stomach.　69. awed resistance: fear of resisting.　71. rank: overfull.　86. dive-dapper: a shy water bird, called a grebe, which lives in rushes.　90. winks: shuts his eyes.　91. passenger: traveler.

100. jar: fight.　104. uncontrolled crest: invincible helmet.　114. foiled: defeated.　119. there . . . lies: i.e., therein you will see your own reflection.　127. spring: i.e., down.　133. hard-favored: ugly.

" Thou canst not see one wrinkle in my brow.
Mine eyes are gray° and bright and quick in turn-
    ing.   140
My beauty as the spring doth yearly grow,
My flesh is soft and plump, my marrow burning.
    My smooth moist hand, were it with thy hand felt,
    Would in thy palm dissolve, or seem to melt.

" Bid me discourse, I will enchant thine ear,   145
Or, like a fairy, trip upon the green,
Or, like a nymph, with long disheveled hair,
Dance on the sands, and yet no footing° seen.
    Love is a spirit all compact of fire,
    Not gross to sink, but light, and will aspire.   150

" Witness this primrose bank whereon I lie.
These forceless° flowers like sturdy trees support
    me.
Two strengthless doves will draw me through the
    sky
From morn till night, even where I list to sport me.
    Is love so light, sweet boy, and may it be   155
    That thou shouldst think it heavy unto thee?

" Is thine own heart to thine own face affected?°
Can thy right hand seize love upon thy left?
Then woo thyself, be of thyself rejected,
Steal thine own freedom, and complain on theft.
    Narcissus° so himself himself forsook,   161
    And died to kiss his shadow in the brook.

" Torches are made to light, jewels to wear,
Dainties to taste, fresh beauty for the use,
Herbs for their smell, and sappy plants to bear.   165
Things growing to themselves are growth's abuse.
    Seeds spring from seeds and beauty breedeth
      beauty.
    Thou wast begot. To get° it is thy duty.

" Upon° the earth's increase why shouldst thou
    feed,
Unless the earth with thy increase be fed?   170
By law of nature thou art bound to breed,
That thine may live when thou thyself art dead;
    And so, in spite of death, thou dost survive,
    In that thy likeness still is left alive."

By this, the love-sick Queen began to sweat,   175
For, where they lay, the shadow had forsook them,
And Titan,° tirèd in the midday heat,
With burning eye did hotly overlook them,
    Wishing Adonis had his team° to guide,
    So he were like him and by Venus' side.   180

And now Adonis, with a lazy sprite,°
And with a heavy, dark, disliking eye,
His louring brows o'erwhelming his fair sight,
Like misty vapors when they blot the sky,
    Souring his cheeks, cries " Fie, no more of love!
    The sun doth burn my face. I must remove."   186

" Aye me," quoth Venus, " young, and so unkind!°
What bare excuses makest thou to be gone!
I'll sigh celestial breath, whose gentle wind
Shall cool the heat of this descending sun.   190
    I'll make a shadow for thee of my hairs.
    If they burn too, I'll quench them with my tears.

" The sun that shines from heaven shines but warm,
And, lo, I lie between that sun and thee.
The heat I have from thence doth little harm,   195
Thine eye darts forth the fire that burneth me;
    And were I not immortal, life were done
    Between this heavenly and earthly sun.

" Art thou obdurate, flinty, hard as steel?
Nay, more than flint, for stone at rain relenteth.°
Art thou a woman's son, and canst not feel   201
What 'tis to love? How want of love tormenteth?
    Oh, had thy mother borne so hard a mind,
    She had not brought forth thee, but died unkind.

" What am I, that thou shouldst contemn° me this?
Or what great danger dwells upon my suit?   206
What were thy lips the worse for one poor kiss?
Speak, fair, but speak fair words, or else be mute.
    Give me one kiss, I'll give it thee again,   209
    And one for interest, if thou wilt have twain.

" Fie, lifeless picture, cold and senseless stone,
Well-painted idol, image dull and dead,
Statue contenting but the eye alone,
Thing like a man, but of no woman bred!   214
    Thou art no man, though of a man's complexion,
    For men will kiss even by their own direction."°

This said, impatience chokes her pleading tongue,
And swelling passion doth provoke a pause.
Red cheeks and fiery eyes blaze forth her wrong.
Being judge in love, she cannot right her cause.   220
    And now she weeps, and now she fain would
      speak,
    And now her sobs do her intendments° break.

Sometimes she shakes her head, and then his hand,
Now gazeth she on him, now on the ground.
Sometimes her arms infold him like a band.   225

---

140. gray: blue.   148. footing: footprint.   152. forceless: without strength.   157. affected: in love with.   161. Narcissus:
See *Ant & Cleo*, II.v.96,n.   168. get: beget, be a father.
169–74. Upon . . . alive: See Sonnets 1–17, and especially 1.
177. Titan: the sun.   179. team: the horses that drew the
chariot of the sun.

181. sprite: spirit.   187. unkind: unnatural.   200. at . . . relenteth: is worn by.   205. contemn: despise.   216. by . . . direction: i.e., without being asked.   222. intendments: what she
intended to say.

She would, he will not in her arms be bound;
  And when from thence he struggles to be gone,
  She locks her lily fingers one in one.

"Fondling,"° she saith, "since I have hemmed
    thee here
Within the circuit of this ivory pale,°   230
I'll be a park, and thou shalt be my deer.
Feed where thou wilt, on mountain or in dale.
  Graze on my lips, and if those hills be dry,
  Stray lower, where the pleasant fountains lie.

"Within this limit is relief enough,   235
Sweet bottom-grass° and high delightful plain,
Round rising hillocks, brakes° obscure and rough,
To shelter thee from tempest and from rain.
  Then be my deer, since I am such a park.
  No dogs shall rouse° thee, though a thousand
    bark."   240

At this Adonis smiles as in disdain,
That in each cheek appears a pretty dimple.
Love made those hollows, if himself were slain,
He might be buried in a tomb so simple,
  Foreknowing well, if there he came to lie,   245
  Why, there Love lived, and there he could not
    die.

These lovely caves, these round enchanting pits,
Opened their mouths to swallow Venus' liking.
Being mad before, how doth she now for wits? 249
Struck dead at first, what needs a second striking?
  Poor Queen of Love, in thine own law forlorn,
  To love a cheek that smiles at thee in scorn!

Now which way shall she turn? What shall she say?
Her words are done, her woes the more increasing.
The time is spent, her object will away   255
And from her twining arms doth urge releasing.
  "Pity," she cries, "some favor, some remorse!"°
  Away he springs, and hasteth to his horse.

But, lo, from forth a copse that neighbors by,
A breeding° jennet,° lusty, young, and proud, 260
Adonis' trampling courser doth espy,
And forth she rushes, snorts, and neighs aloud.
  The strong-necked steed, being tied unto a tree,
  Breaketh his rein and to her straight goes he.

Imperiously he leaps, he neighs, he bounds, 265
And now his woven girths he breaks asunder.
The bearing earth with his hard hoof he wounds,
Whose hollow womb resounds like heaven's thun-
    der;

The iron bit he crusheth 'tween his teeth,
Controlling what he was controllèd with.   270

His ears up-pricked; his braided hanging mane
Upon his compassed° crest now stand on end.
His nostrils drink the air, and forth again,
As from a furnace, vapors doth he send.
  His eye, which scornfully glisters like fire,   275
  Shows his hot courage and his high desire.

Sometime he trots, as if he told° the steps,
With gentle majesty and modest pride.
Anon he rears upright, curvets,° and leaps,
As who should say "Lo, thus my strength is tried;
  And this I do to captivate the eye   281
  Of the fair breeder that is standing by."

What recketh he his rider's angry stir,
His flattering "Holla" or his "Stand, I say"?
What cares he now for curb or pricking spur? 285
For rich caparisons° or trappings gay?
  He sees his love, and nothing else he sees,
  For nothing else with his proud sight agrees.

Look, when a painter would surpass the life,
In limning° out a well-proportioned steed, 290
His art with nature's workmanship at strife,
As if the dead the living should exceed.
  So did this horse excel a common one
  In shape, in courage, color, pace, and bone.

Round-hoofed, short-jointed, fetlocks shag° and
    long,   295
Broad breast, full eye, small head, and nostril wide,
High crest, short ears, straight legs and passing°
    strong,
Thin mane, thick tail, broad buttocks, tender hide.
  Look, what a horse should have he did not lack,
  Save a proud rider on so proud a back.   300

Sometime he scuds far off, and there he stares.
Anon he starts at stirring of a feather.
To bid the wind a base° he now prepares,
And whether° he run or fly they know not whether.
  For through his mane and tail the high wind
    sings,   305
  Fanning the hairs, who wave like feathered
    wings.

He looks upon his love and neighs unto her.
She answers him, as if she knew his mind.   308
Being proud, as females are, to see him woo her,
She puts on outward strangeness, seems unkind,

---

229. **Fondling:** darling.   230. **pale:** fence.   236. **bottom-grass:**
grass growing in a damp valley. 237. **brakes:** bushes. 240. **rouse:**
disturb — a hunting term.   257. **remorse:** pity.   260. **breeding:** in heat. **jennet:** Spanish mare.

272. **compassed:** arched.   277. **told:** counted.   279. **curvets:**
jumps. 286. **caparisons:** harness. 290. **limning:** painting.
295. **shag:** shaggy. 297. **passing:** very. 303. **bid . . . base:**
challenge the wind to play "prisoners' base"; i.e., to chase him.
304. **whether:** pronounced where.

Spurns at his love and scorns the heat he feels,
Beating his kind embracements with her heels.

Then, like a melancholy malcontent,
He vails° his tail, that, like a falling plume,
Cool shadow to his melting buttock lent.   315
He stamps, and bites the poor flies in his fume.°
   His love, perceiving how he was enraged,
   Grew kinder, and his fury was assuaged.

His testy° master goeth about to take him,
When, lo, the unbacked breeder, full of fear,   320
Jealous of catching,° swiftly doth forsake him,
With her the horse, and left Adonis there.
   As° they were mad, unto the wood they hie them,
   Outstripping crows that strive to overfly them.

All swoln with chafing,° down Adonis sits,   325
Banning° his boisterous and unruly beast.
And now the happy season once more fits,
That lovesick Love by pleading may be blest;
   For lovers say, the heart hath treble wrong   329
   When it is barred the aidance° of the tongue.

An oven° that is stopped, or river stayed,
Burneth more hotly, swelleth with more rage.
So of concealèd sorrow may be said:
Free vent of words love's fire doth assuage,
   But when the heart's attorney once is mute,   335
   The client breaks,° as desperate in his suit.

He sees her coming, and begins to glow,
Even as a dying coal revives with wind,
And with his bonnet° hides his angry brow,
Looks on the dull earth with disturbèd mind,   340
   Taking no notice that she is so nigh,
   For all askance he holds her in his eye.

Oh, what a sight it was, wistly° to view
How she came stealing to the wayward boy!
To note the fighting conflict of her hue,   345
How white and red each other did destroy!
   But now her cheek was pale, and by and by
   It flashed forth fire, as lightning from the sky.

Now was she just before him as he sat,
And like a lowly lover down she kneels.   350
With one fair hand she heaveth up his hat,
Her other tender hand his fair cheek feels.
   His tenderer cheek receives her soft hand's print
   As apt as new-fallen snow takes any dint.°

Oh, what a war of looks was then between them!
Her eyes petitioners to his eyes suing;   356
His eyes saw her eyes as they had not seen them;
Her eyes wooed still, his eyes disdained the wooing.
   And all this dumb play had his acts made plain
   With tears, which choruslike her eyes did rain.°

Full gently now she takes him by the hand,   361
A lily prisoned in a jail of snow,
Or ivory in an alabaster band.
So white a friend engirts so white a foe.
   This beauteous combat, willful and unwilling,
   Showed like two silver doves that sit abilling.   366

Once more the engine° of her thoughts began:
" Oh fairest mover° on this mortal round,°
Would thou wert as I am, and I a man,
My heart all whole as thine, thy heart my wound.
   For one sweet look thy help° I would assure
     thee,   371
   Though nothing but my body's bane° would cure
     thee."

" Give me my hand," saith he. " Why dost thou
     feel it? "
" Give me my heart," saith she, " and thou shalt
     have it.
Oh, give it me, lest thy hard heart do steel it,   375
And being steeled, soft sighs can never grave° it.
   Then love's deep groans I never shall regard,
   Because Adonis' heart hath made mine hard."

" For shame! " he cries, " Let go, and let me go.
My day's delight is past, my horse is gone,   380
And 'tis your fault I am bereft° him so.
I pray you hence, and leave me here alone;
   For all my mind, my thought, my busy care,
   Is how to get my palfrey° from the mare."

Thus she replies: " Thy palfrey, as he should,   385
Welcomes the warm approach of sweet desire.
Affection is a coal that must be cooled,
Else, suffered,° it will set the heart on fire.   388
   The sea hath bounds, but deep desire hath none.
   Therefore no marvel though thy horse be gone.

" How like a jade° he stood, tied to the tree,
Servilely mastered with a leathern rein!
But when he saw his love, his youth's fair fee,°
He held such petty bondage in disdain;   394

---

314. vails: lowers.   316. fume: anger.   319. testy: angry.
321. Jealous of catching: afraid of being caught.   323. As: as if.
325. swoln . . . chafing: puffed with anger. 326. Banning:
cursing.   330. aidance: aid.   331. oven: i.e., the brick oven
which was filled with hot coals that were afterward raked out.
336. breaks: is bankrupt.   339. bonnet: cap.   343. wistly:
steadfastly.   354. dint: impression.

359–60. And . . . rain: and all these gestures were interpreted by
her tears, as a chorus interprets the dumb show of a play. For
the dumb show and the chorus in action, see *Haml.*, III.ii.145–64,
255,n.   367. engine: i.e., tongue.   368. mover: being. mortal
round: earth.   371. help: remedy.   372. bane: destruction.
376. grave: make an impression upon.   381. bereft: deprived
of.   384. palfrey: riding horse.   388. suffered: allowed to
remain hot.   391. jade: poor-spirited horse.   393. fee: reward.

Throwing the base thong from his bending crest,
Enfranchising° his mouth, his back, his breast.

"Who sees his true love in her naked bed,
Teaching the sheets a whiter hue than white,
But, when his glutton eye so full hath fed,
His other agents aim at like delight?   400
　Who is so faint, that dares not be so bold
　To touch the fire, the weather being cold?

"Let me excuse thy courser, gentle boy,
And learn of him, I heartily beseech thee,
To take advantage on presented joy.   405
Though I were dumb, yet his proceedings teach
　　thee.
　Oh, learn to love. The lesson is but plain,
　And once made perfect, never lost again."

"I know not love," quoth he, "nor will not know
　　it,
Unless it be a boar, and then I chase it.   410
'Tis much to borrow, and I will not owe it.
My love to love is love but to disgrace it;°
　For I have heard it is a life in death,
　That laughs, and weeps, and all but with a
　　breath.

"Who wears a garment shapeless and unfinished?
Who plucks the bud before one leaf put forth?   416
If springing° things be any jot diminished,
They wither in their prime, prove nothing worth.
　The colt that's backed and burdened being young
　Loseth his pride, and never waxeth strong.   420

"You hurt my hand with wringing. Let us part,
And leave this idle theme, this bootless° chat.
Remove your siege from my unyielding heart.
To love's alarms it will not ope the gate.
　Dismiss your vows, your feignèd tears, your flat-
　　tery;   425
　For where a heart is hard they make no battery."°

"What! Canst thou talk?" quoth she. "Hast thou
　　a tongue?
Oh, would thou hadst not, or I had no hearing!
Thy mermaid's° voice hath done me double wrong.
I had my load before, now pressed with bearing.°
　Melodious discord, heavenly tune harsh-sound-
　　ing,   431
　Ear's deep-sweet music, and heart's deep-sore
　　wounding.

"Had I no eyes but ears, my ears would love
That inward beauty and invisible;
Or were I deaf, thy outward parts would move   435
Each part in me that were but sensible.°
　Though neither eyes nor ears, to hear nor see,
　Yet should I be in love by touching thee.

"Say that the sense of feeling were bereft me
And that I could not see, nor hear, nor touch,   440
And nothing but the very smell were left me,
Yet would my love to thee be still as much;
　For from the stillitory° of thy face excelling
　Comes breath perfumed, that breedeth love by
　　smelling.

"But, oh, what banquet wert thou to the taste,
Being nurse and feeder of the other four!   446
Would they not wish the feast might ever last,
And bid Suspicion double-lock the door,
　Lest Jealousy, that sour unwelcome guest,
　Should by his stealing in disturb the feast?"   450

Once more the ruby-colored portal opened,
Which to his speech did honey passage yield,
Like a red morn, that ever yet betokened
Wreck to the seaman, tempest to the field,
　Sorrow to shepherds, woe unto the birds,   455
　Gusts and foul flaws° to herdmen and to herds.

This ill presage° advisedly she marketh.
Even as the wind is hushed before it raineth,
Or as the wolf doth grin before he barketh,
Or as the berry breaks before it staineth,   460
　Or like the deadly bullet of a gun,
　His meaning struck her ere his words begun.

And at his look she flatly falleth down,
For looks kill love, and love by looks reviveth.
A smile recures° the wounding of a frown,   465
But blessèd bankrupt, that by love so thriveth!
　The silly° boy, believing she is dead,
　Claps her pale cheek, till clapping makes it red,

And all amazed brake off his late intent,
For sharply he did think to reprehend her,   470
Which cunning love did wittily prevent.
Fair fall° the wit that can so well defend her!
　For on the grass she lies as she were slain,
　Till his breath breatheth life in her again.

He wrings her nose, he strikes her on the cheeks,
He bends her fingers, holds her pulses hard,   476
He chafes her lips. A thousand ways he seeks
To mend the hurt that his unkindness marred.

---

396. Enfranchising: freeing.   412. My . . . it: my only feeling
toward love is a desire to disgrace it.   417. springing: growing.
422. bootless: vain.   426. battery: bruise.   429. mermaid: The
mermaid, like the siren, was supposed to lure men to their destruction by sweet singing.   430. pressed . . . bearing: overcome
with its weight.

436. sensible: sensitive.   443. stillitory: distillery.   456. flaws:
squalls of wind.   457. presage: warning sign.   465. recures:
cures.   467. silly: simple.   472. Fair fall: good luck to.

He kisses her, and she, by her good will,
Will never rise, so° he will kiss her still.　　480

The night of sorrow now is turned to day.
Her two blue windows faintly she upheaveth,
Like the fair sun, when in his fresh array
He cheers the morn and all the earth relieveth.
　　And as the bright sun glorifies the sky,　　485
　　So is her face illumined with her eye,

Whose beams upon his hairless face are fixed,
As if from thence they borrowed all their shine.
Were never four such lamps together mixed,
Had not his clouded with his brow's repine;°　　490
　　But hers, which through the crystal tears gave
　　　　light,
　　Shone like the moon in water seen by night.

"Oh, where am I?" quoth she, "in earth or
　　heaven,
Or in the ocean drenched, or in the fire?
What hour is this? Or° morn or weary even?　　495
Do I delight to die, or life desire?
　　But now I lived, and life was death's annoy;°
　　But now I died, and death was lively joy.

"Oh, thou didst kill me. Kill me once again.　　499
Thy eyes' shrewd° tutor, that hard heart of thine,
Hath taught them scornful tricks, and such disdain
That they have murdered this poor heart of mine;
　　And these mine eyes, true leaders to their queen,
　　But for thy piteous lips no more had seen.

"Long may they kiss each other, for this cure!　　505
Oh, never let their crimson liveries wear!
And as they last, their verdure still endure
To drive infection° from the dangerous year!
　　That the stargazers,° having writ on death,　　509
　　May say the plague is banished by thy breath.

"Pure lips, sweet seals in my soft lips imprinted,
What bargains may I make, still to be sealing?
To sell myself I can be well contented,
So thou wilt buy, and pay, and use good dealing;
　　Which purchase if thou make, for fear of slips
　　Set thy seal manual° on my wax-red lips.　　516

"A thousand kisses buys my heart from me,
And pay them at thy leisure, one by one.
What is ten hundred touches unto thee?
Are they not quickly told and quickly gone?　　520

Say, for nonpayment that the debt should double,
Is twenty hundred kisses such a trouble?"

"Fair Queen," quoth he, "if any love you owe me,
Measure my strangeness with my unripe years.
Before I know myself, seek not to know me.　　525
No fisher but the ungrown fry forbears.°
　　The mellow plum doth fall, the green sticks fast,
　　Or being early plucked is sour to taste.

"Look, the world's comforter,° with weary gait,
His day's hot task hath ended in the west.　　530
The owl, night's herald, shrieks, 'tis very late.
The sheep are gone to fold, birds to their nest;
　　And coal-black clouds that shadow heaven's light
　　Do summon us to part, and bid good night.

"Now let me say 'Good night,' and so say you.
If you will say so, you shall have a kiss."
"Good night," quoth she, and, ere he says "Adieu,"
The honey fee of parting tendered° is.　　538
　　Her arms do lend his neck a sweet embrace.
　　Incorporate then they seem. Face grows to face.

Till breathless he disjoined, and backward drew
The heavenly moisture, that sweet coral mouth,
Whose precious taste her thirsty lips well knew,
Whereon they surfeit, yet complain on drouth.
　　He with her plenty pressed, she faint with dearth,
　　Their lips together glued, fall to the earth.　　546

Now quick desire hath caught the yielding prey,
And gluttonlike she feeds, yet never filleth.
Her lips are conquerors, his lips obey,
Paying what ransom the insulter willeth;　　550
　　Whose vulture thought doth pitch the price so
　　　　high
　　That she will draw his lips' rich treasure dry.

And having felt the sweetness of the spoil,
With blindfold fury she begins to forage.
Her face doth reek° and smoke, her blood doth
　　boil,　　555
And careless lust stirs up a desperate courage,
　　Planting oblivion, beating reason back,
　　Forgetting shame's pure blush and honor's
　　　　wrack.°

Hot, faint, and weary with her hard embracing,
Like a wild bird being tamed with too much han-
　　dling,　　560
Or as the fleet-foot roe that's tired with chasing,

---

480. so: so long as.　490. repine: dislike.　495. Or: either.
497. annoy: harm.　500. shrewd: ill-natured.　508. infection:
the plague. There was a very bad epidemic of plague in 1593,
the year of the writing of this poem.　509. stargazers: astrologers. See App. 2.　516. seal manual: impression of your seal.

526. No . . . forbears: i.e., every fisherman puts back the little
fishes.　529. world's comforter: i.e., the sun.　538. tendered:
offered.　555. reek: steam.　558. wrack: wreck.

Or like the froward° infant stilled° with dandling,
　He now obeys, and now no more resisteth,
　While she takes all she can, not all she listeth.

What wax so frozen but dissolves with tempering,°
And yields at last to every light impression?　566
Things out of hope are compassed oft with ventur-
　　ing,
Chiefly in love, whose leave exceeds commission.°
　Affection faints not like a pale-faced coward,
　But then woos best when most his choice is fro-
　　ward.　　　　　　　　　　　　　　　　570

When he did frown, oh, had she then gave over,
Such nectar from his lips she had not sucked.
Foul words and frowns must not repel a lover.
What though the rose have prickles, yet 'tis plucked.
　Were beauty under twenty locks kept fast,　575
　Yet love breaks through and picks them all at last.

For pity now she can no more detain him.
The poor fool prays her that he may depart.
She is resolved no longer to restrain him,
Bids him farewell, and look well to her heart,　580
　The which, by Cupid's bow she doth protest,
　He carries thence incagèd in his breast.

"Sweet boy," she says, "this night I'll waste in
　　sorrow,
For my sick heart commands mine eyes to watch.
Tell me, Love's master, shall we meet tomorrow?
Say, shall we? Shall we? Wilt thou make the
　　match?"　　　　　　　　　　　　　　　586
　He tells her, no; tomorrow he intends
　To hunt the boar with certain of his friends.

"The boar!" quoth she, whereat a sudden pale,
Like lawn° being spread upon the blushing rose,
Usurps her cheeks; she trembles at his tale,　591
And on his neck her yoking arms she throws;
　She sinketh down, still hanging by his neck,
　He on her belly falls, she on her back.

Now is she in the very lists° of love,　　　595
Her champion mounted for the hot encounter.
All is imaginary she doth prove,
He will not manage her, although he mount her;
　That worse than Tantalus'° is her annoy,
　To clip° Elysium,° and to lack her joy.　600

Even so poor birds, deceived with painted grapes,
Do surfeit by the eye and pine the maw,°
Even so she languisheth in her mishaps
As those poor birds that helpless° berries saw.
　The warm effects which she in him finds miss-
　　ing　　　　　　　　　　　　　　　　605
　She seeks to kindle with continual kissing.

But all in vain; good Queen, it will not be;
She hath assayed as much as may be proved.
Her pleading hath deserved a greater fee;
She's Love, she loves, and yet she is not loved.　610
　"Fie, fie," he says, "you crush me; let me go.
　You have no reason to withhold me so."

"Thou hadst been gone," quoth she, "sweet boy,
　　ere this,
But that thou toldst me thou wouldst hunt the boar.
Oh, be advised: thou knowst not what it is　615
With javelin's point a churlish swine to gore,
　Whose tushes° never sheathed he whetteth still,
　Like to a mortal° butcher, bent to kill.

"On his bow-back° he hath a battle° set
Of bristly pikes, that ever threat his foes.　620
His eyes, like glowworms, shine when he doth fret.
His snout digs sepulchers where'er he goes.
　Being moved, he strikes whate'er is in his way,
　And whom he strikes his crooked tushes slay.

"His brawny sides, with hairy bristles armed,　625
Are better proof° than thy spear's point can enter.
His short, thick neck cannot be easily harmed;
Being ireful, on the lion he will venture.
　The thorny brambles and embracing bushes,　629
　As fearful of him, part, through whom he rushes.

"Alas, he naught esteems that face of thine
To which Love's eyes pay tributary gazes;
Nor thy soft hands, sweet lips, and crystal eyne°
Whose full perfection all the world amazes.　634
　But having thee at vantage — wondrous dread!
　Would root these beauties as he roots the mead.°

"Oh, let him keep his loathsome cabin still.
Beauty hath naught to do with such foul fiends.
Come not within his danger° by thy will;　639
They that thrive well take counsel of their friends.
　When thou didst name the boar, not to dissemble,
　I feared thy fortune, and my joints did tremble.

"Didst thou not mark my face? Was it not white?
Saw'st thou not signs of fear lurk in mine eye?

---

562. **froward:** spoilt. **stilled:** quieted.　　565. **tempering:** softening with warmth.　　568. **whose . . . commission:** who takes
more than he is rightfully allowed.　　590. **lawn:** fine transparent
linen.　　595. **lists:** place of combat. See *Rich II*, I.iii.　599. **Tantalus:** Tantalus was punished in the underworld by a raging thirst
which he could never satisfy. He was set in the middle of a lake,
but whenever he stooped to drink, the water receded from him.
600. **clip:** embrace. **Elysium:** in classical mythology the place
of the blessed.

602. **pine . . . maw:** starve the stomach.　　604. **helpless:** useless.
617. **tushes:** boar's tusks.　　618. **mortal:** deadly.　　619. **bow-
back:** bent back. **battle:** army.　　626. **proof:** impenetrable armor.
633. **eyne:** eyes.　　636. **mead:** meadow.　　639. **danger:** power.

Grew I not faint? And fell I not downright?   645
Within my bosom, whereon thou dost lie,
    My boding heart pants, beats, and takes no rest,
    But, like an earthquake, shakes thee on my
       breast.

" For where Love reigns, disturbing Jealousy
Doth call himself Affection's sentinel;   650
Gives false alarms, suggesteth mutiny,
And in a peaceful hour doth cry " Kill, kill! "
    Distempering gentle Love in his desire,
    As air and water do abate the fire.

" This sour informer, this bate-breeding° spy,   655
This canker° that eats up Love's tender spring,
This carry-tale, dissentious Jealousy,
That sometime true news, sometime false doth
       bring,
    Knocks at my heart, and whispers in mine ear,
    That if I love thee, I thy death should fear.   660

" And more than so, presenteth to mine eye
The picture of an angry chafing boar,
Under whose sharp fangs on his back doth lie
An image like thyself, all stained with gore,
    Whose blood upon the fresh flowers being shed
    Doth make them droop with grief and hang the
       head.   666

" What should I do, seeing thee so indeed,
That tremble at the imagination?
The thought of it doth make my faint heart bleed,
And fear doth teach it divination.   670
    I prophesy thy death, my living sorrow,
    If thou encounter with the boar tomorrow.

" But if thou needs wilt hunt, be ruled by me.
Uncouple° at the timorous flying hare,
Or at the fox which lives by subtlety,
                                 675
Or at the roe which no encounter dare.
    Pursue these fearful creatures o'er the downs,
    And on thy well-breathed horse keep with thy
       hounds.

" And when thou hast on foot the purblind hare,
Mark the poor wretch, to overshoot his troubles,
How he outruns the wind, and with what care   681
He cranks° and crosses with a thousand doubles.
    The many musits° through the which he goes
    Are like a labyrinth to amaze his foes.

" Sometime he runs among a flock of sheep,   685
To make the cunning hounds mistake their smell,
And sometime where earth-delving conies° keep,

To stop the loud pursuers in their yell;
    And sometime sorteth° with a herd of deer.
    Danger deviseth shifts,° wit waits on fear.   690

" For there his smell with others being mingled,
The hot scent-snuffing hounds are driven to doubt,
Ceasing their clamorous cry till they have singled
With much ado the cold fault° cleanly out.
    Then do they spend their mouths: Echo replies,
    As if another chase were in the skies.   696

" By this, poor Wat,° far off upon a hill,
Stands on his hinder legs with listening ear,
To hearken if his foes pursue him still.
Anon their loud alarums he doth hear;   700
    And now his grief may be comparèd well
    To one sore sick that hears the passing bell.°

" Then shalt thou see the dew-bedabbled wretch
Turn, and return, indenting° with the ways.
Each envious brier his weary legs doth scratch, 705
Each shadow makes him stop, each murmur stay;
    For misery is trodden on by many,
    And being low never relieved by any.

" Lie quietly, and hear a little more.
Nay, do not struggle, for thou shalt not rise.   710
To make thee hate the hunting of the boar,
Unlike myself thou hear'st me moralize,
    Applying this to that, and so to so;
    For love can comment upon every woe.

" Where did I leave? "° " No matter where, "
       quoth he.   715
" Leave me, and then the story aptly ends:
The night is spent. " Why, what of that? " quoth
       she.
" I am, " quoth he, " expected of my friends,
    And now 'tis dark, and going I shall fall. "   719
    " In night, " quoth she, " desire sees best of all.

" But if thou fall, oh, then imagine this:
The earth, in love with thee, thy footing trips,
And all is but to rob thee of a kiss.
Rich preys make true men thieves; so do thy lips
    Make modest Dian° cloudy and forlorn,   725
    Lest she should steal a kiss, and die forsworn.°

" Now of this dark night I perceive the reason:
Cynthia° for shame obscures her silver shine,
Till forging Nature be condemned of treason,

689. sorteth: mingles.   690. shifts: tricks.   694. cold fault:
scent which has failed.   697. Wat: the hare.   702. passing
bell: See App. 19.   704. indenting: making a curved path.
715. leave: i.e., reach in my argument.   725. Dian: Diana,
goddess of chastity.   726. forsworn: having broken her oath
of chastity.   728. Cynthia: the moon. Diana was three-formed;
on earth she was Diana, in heaven Cynthia, in the underworld
Hecate.

655. bate-breeding: causing strife.   656. canker: worm.
674. Uncouple: loose your hounds.   682. cranks: makes sharp
turns.   683. musits: gaps in a hedge.   687. conies: rabbits.

For stealing molds from heaven that were divine.°
  Wherein she framed thee, in high heaven's
     despite,   731
  To shame the sun by day and her by night.

"And therefore hath she bribed the Destinies
To cross° the curious° workmanship of nature;
To mingle beauty with infirmities   735
And pure perfection with impure defeature,°
  Making it subject to the tyranny
  Of mad mischances and much misery,

"As burning fevers, agues pale and faint,
Life-poisoning pestilence and frenzies wood,° 740
The marrow-eating sickness, whose attaint
Disorder breeds° by heating of the blood.
  Surfeits, imposthumes,° grief and damned des-
    pair,
  Swear Nature's death for framing thee so fair.

"And not the least of all these maladies   745
But in one minute's fight brings beauty under.
Both favor,° savor, hue, and qualities,
Whereat the impartial gazer late did wonder,
  Are on the sudden wasted, thawed and done,
  As mountain snow melts with the midday sun.

"Therefore,° despite of fruitless chastity, 751
Love-lacking vestals and self-loving nuns,
That on the earth would breed a scarcity
And barren dearth of daughters and of sons,
  Be prodigal. The lamp that burns by night 755
  Dries up his oil to lend the world his light.

"What is thy body but a swallowing grave,
Seeming to bury that posterity
Which by the rights of time thou needs must have,
If thou destroy them not in dark obscurity? 760
  If so, the world will hold thee in disdain,
  Sith° in thy pride so fair a hope is slain.

"So in thyself thyself art made away;°
A mischief worse than civil homebred strife,
Or theirs whose desperate hands themselves do slay,
Or butcher sire that reaves° his son of life. 766
  Foul cankering rust the hidden treasure frets,°
  But gold that's put to use more gold begets."

"Nay, then," quoth Adon, "you will fall again
Into your idle overhandled theme.   770

The kiss I gave you is bestowed in vain,
And all in vain you strive against the stream,
  For, by this black-faced night, desire's foul nurse,
  Your treatise makes me like you worse and worse.

"If Love have lent you twenty thousand tongues,
And every tongue more moving than your own,
Bewitching like the wanton mermaid's songs, 777
Yet from mine ear the tempting tune is blown.
  For know, my heart stands armèd in mine ear,
  And will not let a false sound enter there 780

"Lest the deceiving harmony should run
Into the quiet closure° of my breast,
And then my little heart were quite undone,
In his bedchamber to be barred of rest.
  No, lady, no; my heart longs not to groan, 785
  But soundly sleeps, while now it sleeps alone.

"What have you urged that I cannot reprove?
The path is smooth that leadeth on to danger.
I hate not love, but your device in love
That lends embracements unto every stranger. 790
  You do it for increase; oh strange excuse,
  When reason is the bawd° to lust's abuse!

"Call it not love, for Love to heaven is fled
Since sweating Lust on earth usurped his name,
Under whose simple semblance he hath fed 795
Upon fresh beauty, blotting it with blame
  Which the hot tyrant stains and soon bereaves,
  As caterpillars do the tender leaves.

"Love comforteth like sunshine after rain,
But Lust's effect is tempest after sun.   800
Love's gentle spring doth always fresh remain,
Lust's winter comes ere summer half be done.
  Love surfeits not, Lust like a glutton dies.
  Love is all truth, Lust full of forgèd lies.

"More I could tell, but more I dare not say. 805
The text is old, the orator too green.
Therefore, in sadness, now I will away.
My face is full of shame, my heart of teen.°
  Mine ears, that to your wanton talk attended,
  Do burn themselves for having so offended." 810

With this, he breaketh from the sweet embrace
Of those fair arms which bound him to her breast,
And homeward through the dark lawnd° runs
    apace.
Leaves Love upon her back deeply distressed.
  Look, how a bright star shooteth from the sky,
  So glides he in the night from Venus' eye 816

Which after him she darts, as one on shore
Gazing upon a late-embarkèd friend,
Till the wild waves will have him seen no more,
Whose ridges with the meeting clouds contend.
    So did the merciless and pitchy° night   821
    Fold in the object that did feed her sight.

Whereat amazed, as one that unaware
Hath dropped a precious jewel in the flood,
Or 'stonished as night wanderers often are,   825
Their light blown out in some mistrustful° wood;
    Even so confounded in the dark she lay,
    Having lost the fair discovery of her way.

And now she beats her heart, whereat it groans,
That all the neighbor caves, as seeming troubled,
Make verbal repetition of her moans.   831
Passion on passion deeply is redoubled.
    " Aye me! " she cries, and twenty times, " Woe,
      woe! "
    And twenty echoes twenty times cry so.

She, marking them, begins a wailing note.   835
And sings extemporally a woeful ditty:
How love makes young men thrall,° and old men
    dote;
How love is wise in folly, foolish-witty.
    Her heavy anthem still concludes in woe,
    And still the choir of echoes answer so.   840

Her song was tedious, and outwore the night,
For lovers' hours are long, though seeming short.
If pleased themselves, others, they think, delight
In such-like circumstance, with such-like sport.
    Their copious stories, oftentimes begun,   845
    End without audience, and are never done.

For who hath she to spend the night withal,
But idle sounds resembling parasites,
Like shrill-tongued tapsters° answering every call,
Soothing the humor of fantastic° wits?   850
    She says " 'Tis so." They answer all " 'Tis so,"
    And would say after her, if she said " No."

Lo, here the gentle lark, weary of rest,
From his moist cabinet° mounts up on high,
And wakes the morning, from whose silver breast
The sun ariseth in his majesty.   856
    Who doth the world so gloriously behold,
    That cedar tops and hills seem burnished gold.

Venus salutes him with this fair good morrow:
" O thou clear god, and patron of all light,   860

From whom each lamp and shining star doth bor-
    row
The beauteous influence that makes him bright,
    There lives a son, that sucked an earthly mother,
    May lend thee light, as thou dost lend to other."

This said, she hasteth to a myrtle grove,   865
Musing the morning is so much o'erworn
And yet she hears no tidings of her love.
She hearkens for his hounds and for his horn.
    Anon she hears them chant it lustily,
    And all in haste she coasteth° to the cry.   870

And as she runs, the bushes in the way
Some catch her by the neck, some kiss her face,
Some twine about her thigh to make her stay.
She wildly breaketh from their strict embrace,
    Like a milch doe, whose swelling dugs do ache,
    Hasting to feed her fawn hid in some brake.   876

By this she hears the hounds are at a bay,°
Whereat she starts, like one that spies an adder
Wreathed up in fatal folds just in his way,
The fear whereof doth make him shake and shud-
    der.   880
    Even so the timorous yelping of the hounds
    Appals her senses and her spirit° confounds.

For now she knows it is no gentle chase,
But the blunt boar, rough bear, or lion proud,
Because the cry remaineth in one place,   885
Where fearfully the dogs exclaim aloud.
    Finding their enemy to be so curst,°
    They all strain courtesy° who shall cope° him
    first.

This dismal cry rings sadly in her ear,
Through which it enters to surprise her heart,   890
Who, overcome by doubt and bloodless fear,
With cold pale weakness numbs each feeling part
    Like soldiers, when their captain once doth yield,
    They basely fly, and dare not stay the field.

Thus stands she in a trembling ecstasy°   895
Till, cheering up her senses all dismayed,
She tells them 'tis a causeless fantasy,
And childish error, that they are afraid.   898
    Bids them leave quaking, bids them fear no more,
    And with that word she spied the hunted boar

Whose frothy mouth, bepainted all with red,
Like milk and blood being mingled both together,

---

821. **pitchy:** black.   826. **mistrustful:** causing doubt.   837. **thrall:** slave.   849. **tapsters:** bartenders.   850. **fantastic:** capricious.   854. **cabinet:** small room.

870. **coasteth:** makes toward.   877. **at a bay:** brought to a stand still round a quarry that has turned to face its pursuers 882. **spirit:** pronounced "sprite."   887: **curst:** bitter, vicious 888. **strain courtesy:** politely yield to each other. **cope:** encounter 895. **ecstasy:** excitement.

A second fear through all her sinews spread, 903
Which madly hurries her she knows not whither.
  This way she runs, and now she will no further,
  But back retires to rate° the boar for murther.°

A thousand spleens° bear her a thousand ways.
She treads the path that she untreads again.
Her more than haste is mated° with delays
Like the proceedings of a drunken brain: 910
  Full of respects, yet naught at all respecting;
  In hand with all things, naught at all effecting.°

Here kenneled in a brake she finds a hound,
And asks the weary caitiff° for his master.
And there another licking of his wound, 915
'Gainst venomed sores the only sovereign° plaster.
  And here she meets another sadly scowling,
  To whom she speaks, and he replies with howling.

When he hath ceased his ill-resounding noise,
Another flap-mouthed mourner, black and grim,
Against the welkin° volleys out his voice. 921
Another and another answer him,
  Clapping their proud tails to the ground below,
  Shaking their scratched ears, bleeding as they go.

Look, how the world's poor people are amazed 925
At apparitions, signs and prodigies
Whereon with fearful eyes they long have gazed,
Infusing them with dreadful prophecies.
  So she at these sad signs draws up her breath,
  And, sighing it again, exclaims on Death. 930

" Hard-favored tyrant, ugly, meager, lean,
Hateful divorce of love " — thus chides she
    Death —
" Grim-grinning ghost, earth's worm, what dost
    thou mean
To stifle beauty and to steal his breath,
  Who when he lived, his breath and beauty set
  Gloss on the rose, smell to the violet? 936

" If he be dead — oh, no, it cannot be,
Seeing his beauty, thou shouldst strike at it —
Oh, yes, it may. Thou hast no eyes to see,
But hatefully at random dost thou hit. 940
  Thy mark is feeble age; but thy false dart
  Mistakes that aim, and cleaves an infant's heart.

" Hadst thou but bid beware, then he had spoke,
And, hearing him, thy power had lost his power.
The Destinies will curse thee for this stroke. 945

They bid thee crop a weed, thou pluckst a flower.
  Love's golden arrow at him should have fled,
  And not Death's ebon° dart, to strike him dead.

" Dost thou drink tears, that thou provokest such
    weeping?
What may a heavy groan advantage thee? 950
Why hast thou cast into eternal sleeping
Those eyes that taught all other eyes to see?
  Now Nature cares not for thy mortal vigor,
  Since her best work is ruined with thy rigor."

Here overcome, as one full of despair, 955
She vailed her eyelids, who, like sluices, stopped
The crystal tide that from her two cheeks fair
In the sweet channel of her bosom dropped; 958
  But through the floodgates breaks the silver rain,
  And with his strong course opens them again.

Oh, how her eyes and tears did lend and borrow!
Her eye seen in the tears, tears in her eye.
Both crystals, where they viewed each other's sor-
    row,
Sorrow that friendly sighs sought still to dry.
  But like a stormy day, now wind, now rain, 965
  Sighs dry her cheeks, tears make them wet again.

Variable passions throng her constant woe,
As striving who should best become her grief;
All entertained, each passion labors so
That every present sorrow seemeth chief, 970
  But none is best: then join they all together,
  Like many clouds consulting for foul weather.

By this, far off she hears some huntsman holloa;
A nurse's song ne'er pleased her babe so well.
The dire imagination she did follow 975
This sound of hope doth labor to expel,
  For now reviving joy bids her rejoice,
  And flatters her it is Adonis' voice.

Whereat her tears began to turn their tide,
Being prisoned in her eye like pearls in glass. 980
Yet sometimes falls an orient° drop beside,
Which her cheek melts, as scorning it should pass
  To wash the foul face of the sluttish ground,
  Who is but drunken when she seemeth drowned.

Oh hard-believing love, how strange it seems 985
Not to believe, and yet too credulous!
Thy weal and woe are both of them extremes.
Despair and hope makes thee ridiculous:
  The one doth flatter thee in thoughts unlikely,
  In likely thoughts the other kills thee quickly.

---

906. rate: blame. **murther:** murder.   **907. spleens:** impulses.
909. mated: matched.   **911–12. Full . . . effecting:** full of ideas
but utterly careless; trying to do everything but accomplishing
nothing.   **914. caitiff:** wretch, lit., captive.   **916. sovereign:**
supreme, excellent.   **921. welkin:** sky.

948. ebon: black.   **981. orient:** pearly.

Now she unweaves the web that she hath wrought;
Adonis lives, and Death is not to blame;   992
It was not she that called him all to naught.°
Now she adds honors to his hateful name.
    She clepes° him king of graves, and grave for
        kings,   995
    Imperious supreme of all mortal things.

" No, no," quoth she, " sweet Death, I did but jest.
Yet pardon me, I felt a kind of fear
When as I met the boar, that bloody beast
Which knows no pity, but is still severe,   1000
    Then, gentle shadow — truth I must confess —
    I railed on thee, fearing my love's decease.

" 'Tis not my fault: the boar provoked my tongue.
Be wreaked° on him, invisible commander.
'Tis he, foul creature, that hath done thee wrong.
I did but act, he's author of thy slander.   1006
    Grief hath two tongues, and never woman yet
    Could rule them both without ten women's wit."

Thus hoping that Adonis is alive,
Her rash suspect° she doth extenuate,   1010
And that his beauty may the better thrive,
With Death she humbly doth insinuate;°
    Tells him of trophies, statues, tombs, and stories
    His victories, his triumphs, and his glories.

" O Jove," quoth she, " how much a fool was I
To be of such a weak and silly mind   1016
To wail his death who lives and must not die
Till mutual overthrow of mortal kind!°
    For he being dead, with him is beauty slain,
    And, beauty dead, black chaos comes again.

" Fie, fie, fond° love, thou art so full of fear   1021
As one with treasure laden, hemmed with thieves.
Trifles unwitnessèd with eye or ear
Thy coward heart with false bethinking grieves."
    Even at this word she hears a merry horn,   1025
    Whereat she leaps that was but late forlorn.

As falcons to the lure,° away she flies.
The grass stoops not, she treads on it so light,
And in her haste unfortunately spies
The foul boar's conquest on her fair delight;   1030
    Which seen, her eyes, as murdered with the view.
    Like stars ashamed of day, themselves withdrew;

Or, as the snail, whose tender horns being hit,
Shrinks backward in his shelly cave with pain,

And there all smothered up in shade doth sit,   1035
Long after fearing to creep forth again,
    So, at his bloody view, her eyes are fled
    Into the deep-dark cabins of her head,

Where they resign their office and their light
To the disposing of her troubled brain   1040
Who bids them still consort with ugly night,
And never wound the heart with looks again,
    Who, like a king perplexèd in his throne,
    By their suggestion gives a deadly groan,

Whereat each tributary subject quakes;   1045
As when the wind, imprisoned in the ground,
Struggling for passage, earth's foundation shakes,
Which with cold terror doth men's minds con-
        found.
    This mutiny each part doth so surprise,
    That from their dark beds once more leap her
        eyes,   1050

And being opened threw unwilling light
Upon the wide wound that the boar had trenched
In his soft flank whose wonted lily white
With purple tears, that his wound wept, was
        drenched.   1054
    No flower was nigh, no grass, herb, leaf, or weed,
    But stole his blood and seemed with him to bleed.

This solemn sympathy poor Venus noteth.
Over one shoulder doth she hang her head.
Dumbly she passions,° frantically she doteth.
She thinks he could not die, he is not dead.   1060
    Her voice is stopped, her joints forget to bow.
    Her eyes are mad that they have wept till now.

Upon his hurt she looks so steadfastly
That her sight dazzling makes the wound seem
        three,
And then she reprehends her mangling eye   1065
That makes more gashes where no breach should be.
    His face seems twain, each several° limb is dou-
        bled.
    For oft the eye mistakes, the brain being troubled.

" My tongue cannot express my grief for one,
And yet," quoth she, " behold two Adons dead!
My sighs are blown away, my salt tears gone,   1071
Mine eyes are turned to fire, my heart to lead.
    Heavy heart's lead, melt at mine eyes' red fire!
    So shall I die by drops of hot desire.

" Alas, poor world, what treasure hast thou lost!
What face remains alive that's worth the viewing?
Whose tongue is music now? What canst thou
        boast   1077

993. all to naught: worthless.   995. clepes: calls.   1004. Be
wreaked: take your revenge.   1010. suspect: suspicion.
1012. insinuate: flatter.   1018. Till . . . kind: until the general
(*mutual*) destruction of the human race.   1021. fond: foolish.
1027. falcons . . . lure: See App. 26.

1059. passions: grieves.   1067. several: separate, individual

Of things long since, or any thing ensuing?
  The flowers are sweet, their colors fresh and
    trim,
  But true sweet beauty lived and died with him.

"Bonnet nor veil henceforth no creature wear!
Nor sun nor wind will ever strive to kiss you. 1082
Having no fair° to lose, you need not fear.
The sun doth scorn you, and the wind doth hiss
   you,
  But when Adonis lived, sun and sharp air 1085
  Lurked like two thieves, to rob him of his fair.

"And therefore would he put his bonnet on,
Under whose brim the gaudy sun would peep.
The wind would blow it off, and, being gone,
Play with his locks; then would Adonis weep,
  And straight, in pity of his tender years, 1091
  They both would strive who first should dry his
   tears.

"To see his face the lion walked along
Behind some hedge, because he would not fear°
   him.
To recreate° himself when he hath sung, 1095
The tiger would be tame and gently hear him.
  If he had spoke, the wolf would leave his prey,
  And never fright the silly lamb that day.

"When he beheld his shadow in the brook
The fishes spread on it their golden gills. 1100
When he was by, the birds such pleasure took,
That some would sing, some other in their bills
  Would bring him mulberries and ripe-red cher-
   ries.
  He fed them with his sight, they him with ber-
   ries. 1104

"But this foul, grim, and urchin-snouted° boar,
Whose downward eye still looketh for a grave,
Ne'er saw the beauteous livery that he wore.
Witness the entertainment that he gave:
  If he did see his face, why then I know
  He thought to kiss him, and hath killed him so.

"'Tis true, 'tis true; thus was Adonis slain: 1111
He ran upon the boar with his sharp spear,
Who did not whet his teeth at him again,
But by a kiss thought to persuade him there,
  And nuzzling° in his flank, the loving swine 1115
  Sheathed unaware the tusk in his soft groin.

"Had I been toothed like him, I must confess,
With kissing him I should have killed him first.
But he is dead, and never did he bless
My youth with his; the more am I accurst." 1120
  With this, she falleth in the place she stood,
  And stains her face with his congealèd blood.

She looks upon his lips, and they are pale.
She takes him by the hand, and that is cold.
She whispers in his ears a heavy tale, 1125
As if they heard the woeful words she told.
  She lifts the coffer lids that close his eyes,
  Where, lo, two lamps, burnt out, in darkness lies.

Two glasses, where herself herself beheld
A thousand times, and now no more reflect; 1130
Their virtue lost, wherein they late excelled,
And every beauty robbed of his effect.°
  "Wonder of time," quoth she, "this is my spite,
  That, thou being dead, the day should yet be
   light.

"Since thou art dead, lo, here I prophesy, 1135
Sorrow on love hereafter shall attend.
It shall be waited on with jealousy,
Find sweet beginning but unsavory end;
  Ne'er settled equally, but high or low,
  That all love's pleasure shall not match his woe.

"It shall be fickle, false and full of fraud; 1141
Bud, and be blasted, in a breathing-while;
The bottom poison, and the top o'erstrawed°
With sweets that shall the truest sight beguile.
  The strongest body shall it make most weak,
  Strike the wise dumb, and teach the fool to speak.

"It shall be sparing and too full of riot, 1147
Teaching decrepit age to tread the measures.°
The staring ruffian shall it keep in quiet,
Pluck down the rich, enrich the poor with treas-
   ures. 1150
  It shall be raging-mad, and silly-mild,
  Make the young old, the old become a child.

"It shall suspect where is no cause of fear.
It shall not fear where it should most mistrust.
It shall be merciful and too severe, 1155
And most deceiving when it seems most just.
  Perverse it shall be where it shows most toward,°
  Put fear to valor, courage to the coward.

"It shall be cause of war and dire events,
And set dissension 'twixt the son and sire. 1160
Subject and servile to all discontents,

1083. **fair:** complexion. It was the high mark of beauty to have
a pink and white complexion, untouched by the sun. 1094. **fear:**
frighten. 1095. **recreate:** entertain. 1105. **urchin-snouted:**
with a snout like a hedgehog — which the wild boar somewhat
resembles.

1132. **robbed . . . effect:** deprived of its power to charm.
1143. **o'erstrawed:** strewn over. 1148. **tread . . . measures:**
dance. See App. 24. 1157. **toward:** docile.

As dry combustious matter is to fire,
  Sith in his prime death doth my love destroy,
  They that love best their loves shall not enjoy."

By this the boy that by her side lay killed   1165
Was melted like a vapor from her sight,
And in his blood, that on the ground lay spilled,
A purple flower sprung up, checkered with white,
  Resembling well his pale cheeks and the blood
  Which in round drops upon their whiteness
    stood.   1170

She bows her head, the new-sprung flower to smell,
Comparing it to her Adonis' breath,
And says, within her bosom it shall dwell,
Since he himself is reft from her by death.
  She crops the stalk, and in the breach appears
  Green-dropping sap, which she compares to
    tears.   1176

" Poor flower," quoth she, " this was thy father's
    guise —
Sweet issue of a more sweet-smelling sire —

For every little grief to wet his eyes,
To grow unto himself was his desire,   1180
  And so 'tis thine. But know, it is as good
  To wither in my breast as in his blood.

" Here was thy father's bed, here in my breast.
Thou art the next of blood, and 'tis thy right.
Lo, in this hollow cradle take thy rest.   1185
My throbbing heart shall rock thee day and night.
  There shall not be one minute in an hour
  Wherein I will not kiss my sweet love's flower."

Thus weary of the world, away she hies,
And yokes her silver doves,° by whose swift aid
Their mistress, mounted, through the empty skies
In her light chariot quickly is conveyed;   1192
  Holding their course to Paphos,° where their
    queen
  Means to immure herself and not be seen.

1190. doves: Venus was transported in a chariot drawn by doves
(or, according to another version, by swans). See Pl. 7a. 1193. Paphos: a town in the island of Cyprus, where there was a great
temple to Venus.

THE RAPE OF LUCRECE

Introduction

Lucrece was entered in the Stationers' Register on May 9, 1594: "9 Maij. Master Harrison Senior Entred for his copie vnder thand of Master Cawood Warden, a booke intituled the Ravyshement of Lucrece vj^d." The poem was soon after printed with the title page: *LUCRECE. London. Printed by Richard Field, for Iohn Harrison, and are to be sold at the signe of the white Greyhound in Paules Church-yard. 1594.*

Lucrece was a handsome piece of printing, in a similar style to *Venus and Adonis,* which was also the work of Richard Field. It was a popular success and went into several editions. Copies exist dated 1598, 1600 (2), and 1607; two other early editions, undated, are also known. The poem was much admired, especially by the graver kind of reader, and thirty-nine quotations from it are included in *England's Parnassus,* which was published in 1600.

The story of the fate of Lucrece was part of Roman legend and was told in Latin by Livy in his Roman history and by Ovid in his *Fasti.* Lucrece also appears among the heroines in Chaucer's *Legend of Good Women* where her tale is told at some length. No story was more popular in Elizabethan times, and references to it are very common.

The poem is written in the meter known as rhyme royal, which consists of stanzas of seven lines, rhymed ababbcc, each line bearing five stresses. This meter had been used by Chaucer and was common in the fifteenth and sixteenth centuries. It was also used by Samuel Daniel in *The Complaint of Rosamond,* one of several poems written in the 1590's which relate the sad fate of some distressed lady of legend.

TO THE RIGHT HONORABLE HENRY WRIOTHESLEY

Earl of Southampton and Baron of Tichfield.

The love I dedicate to your Lordship is without end; whereof this pamphlet, without beginning, is but a superfluous moiety. The warrant I have of your honorable disposition, not the worth of my untutored lines, makes it assured of acceptance. What I have done is yours; what I have to do is yours; being part in all I have, devoted yours. Were my worth greater, my duty would show greater; meantime, as it is, it is bound to your Lordship, to whom I wish long life, still lengthened with all happiness.

Your Lordship's in all duty,
WILLIAM SHAKESPEARE.

The Argument

Lucius Tarquinius, for his excessive pride surnamed Superbus, after he had caused his own father-in-law Servius Tullius to be cruelly murdered, and, contrary to the Roman laws and customs, not requiring or staying for the people's suffrages, had possessed himself of the kingdom, went, accompanied with his sons and other noblemen of Rome, to besiege Ardea. During which siege the principal men of the army meeting one evening at the tent of Sextus Tarquinius, the king's son, in their discourses after supper everyone commended the virtues of his own wife; among whom Collatinus extolled the incomparable chastity of his wife Lucretia. In that pleasant humor they all posted to Rome; and intending, by their secret and sudden arrival, to make trial of that which every one had before avouched, only Collatinus finds his wife, though it were late in the night, spinning amongst her maids: the other ladies were all found dancing and reveling, or in several disports. Whereupon the noblemen yielded Collatinus the victory, and his wife the fame. At that time Sextus Tarquinius being inflamed with Lucrece' beauty, yet smothering his passions for the present, departed with the rest back to the camp; from whence he shortly after privily withdrew himself, and was, according to his estate, royally entertained and lodged by Lucrece at Collatium. The same night he treacherously stealeth into her chamber, violently ravished her, and early in the morning speedeth away. Lucrece, in this lamentable plight, hastily dispatcheth messengers, one to Rome for her father, another to the camp for Collatine. They came, the one accompanied with Junius Brutus, the other with Publius Valerius; and finding Lucrece attired in mourning habit, demanded the cause of her sorrow. She, first taking an oath of them for her revenge, revealed the actor and whole manner of his dealing, and withal suddenly stabbed herself. Which done, with one consent they all vowed to root out the whole hated family of the Tarquins; and bearing the dead body to Rome, Brutus acquainted the people with the doer and manner of the vile deed, with a bitter invective against the tyranny of the King: wherewith the people were so moved, that with one consent and a general acclamation the Tarquins were all exiled, and the state government changed from kings to consuls.

From the besieged Ardea all in post,°
Borne by the trustless° wings of false desire,
Lust-breathèd° Tarquin leaves the Roman host,
And to Collatium bears the lightless° fire
Which, in pale embers hid, lurks to aspire,°   5
   And girdle with embracing flames the waist
   Of Collatine's fair love, Lucrece the chaste.

Haply that name of " chaste " unhappily set
This bateless° edge on his keen appetite,
When Collatine unwisely did not let°   10
To praise the clear unmatchèd red and white°
Which triumphed in that sky of his delight,
   Where mortal stars,° as bright as heaven's beauties,
   With pure aspects did him peculiar duties.°

For he the night before, in Tarquin's tent,   15
Unlocked the treasure of his happy state:
What priceless wealth the heavens had him lent
In the possession of his beauteous mate,
Reckoning his fortune at such high-proud rate
   That kings might be espousèd to more fame,   20
   But king nor peer to such a peerless dame.

Oh happiness enjoyed but of a few!
And, if possessed, as soon decayed and done
As is the morning's silver-melting dew
Against the golden splendor of the sun!   25
An expired date,° canceled ere well begun:
   Honor and beauty, in the owner's arms,
   Are weakly fortressed from a world of harms.

Beauty itself doth of itself persuade
The eyes of men without an orator.   30
What needeth then apologies be made,

To set forth that which is so singular?
Or why is Collatine the publisher
   Of that rich jewel he should keep unknown
   From thievish ears, because it is his own?   35

Perchance his boast of Lucrece' sovereignty
Suggested° this proud issue° of a king,
For by our ears our hearts oft tainted be.
Perchance that envy of so rich a thing,
Braving compare, disdainfully did sting   40
   His high-pitched° thoughts, that meaner men should vaunt
   That golden hap° which their superiors want.°

But some untimely thought did instigate
His all-too-timeless° speed, if none of those,
His honor, his affairs, his friends, his state   45
Neglected all, with swift intent he goes
To quench the coal which in his liver° glows.
   Oh rash-false heat, wrapped in repentant cold,
   Thy hasty spring still blasts, and ne'er grows old!

When at Collatium this false lord arrived,   50
Well was he welcomed by the Roman dame,
Within whose face beauty and virtue strived
Which of them both should underprop° her fame.
When virtue bragged, beauty would blush for shame;
   When beauty boasted blushes, in despite°   55
   Virtue would stain that o'er with silver white.

But° beauty, in that white intitulèd,°
From Venus' doves° doth challenge that fair field.
Then virtue claims from beauty beauty's red,

1. post: haste. See App. 17.   2. trustless: faithless.   3. Lust-breathed: urged on by lust.   4. lightless: showing no light.   5. aspire: break forth.   9. bateless: not to be blunted.   10. let: hesitate.   11. red . . . white: the colors of beauty and chastity.   13. stars: i.e., eyes.   14. did . . . duties: i.e., looked only on him.   26. expired date: state which disappears immediately.

37. Suggested: prompted to lust. issue: son.   41. high-pitched: soaring.   42. hap: good fortune. want: lack.   44. all-too-timeless: too rapid.   47. liver: regarded as the seat of the passions.   53. underprop: support.   55. in despite: in spite.   57-70. But . . . seat: The idea so elaborately worked out in these two stanzas is that Lucrece's beauty is set forth in her red and white; but the white of chastity is made red by modesty, and the red of beauty is made pale by virtue.   57. intituled: designated.   58. Venus' doves: love.

Which virtue gave the golden age to gild° 60
Their silver cheeks, and called it then their shield,
  Teaching them thus to use it in the fight,
  When shame assailed, the red should fence the
    white.

This heraldry° in Lucrece' face was seen,
Argued by beauty's red and virtue's white 65
Of either's color was the other queen,
Proving from world's minority° their right.
Yet their ambition makes them still to fight,
  The sovereignty of either being so great,
  That oft they interchange each other's seat. 70

This silent war of lilies and of roses,
Which Tarquin viewed in her fair face's field,
In their pure ranks his traitor eye encloses,
Where, lest between them both it should be killed,
The coward captive vanquishèd doth yield 75
  To those two armies, that would let him go
  Rather than triumph in so false a foe.

Now thinks he that her husband's shallow tongue,
The niggard prodigal that praised her so,
In that high task hath done her beauty wrong, 80
Which far exceeds his barren skill to show.
Therefore that praise which Collatine doth owe°
  Enchanted Tarquin answers with surmise,
  In silent wonder of still-gazing° eyes.

This earthly saint, adorèd by this devil, 85
Little suspecteth the false worshiper;
For unstained thoughts do seldom dream on evil,
Birds never limed° no secret bushes fear.
So guiltless she securely° gives good cheer
  And reverend welcome to her princely guest, 90
  Whose inward ill no outward harm expressed.

For that he colored° with his high estate,
Hiding base sin in plaits° of majesty
That nothing in him seemed inordinate
Save sometime too much wonder of his eye, 95
Which, having all, all could not satisfy,
  But, poorly rich, so wanteth in his store,
  That, cloyed with much, he pineth still for more.

But she, that never coped° with stranger eyes, 99
Could pick no meaning from their parling° looks,
Nor read the subtle-shining secrecies

Writ in the glassy margents° of such books.
She touch'd no unknown baits, nor feared no
    hooks,
  Nor could she moralize° his wanton sight 104
  More than° his eyes were opened to the light.

He stories° to her ears her husband's fame
Won in the fields of fruitful Italy,
And decks with praises Collatine's high name,
Made glorious by his manly chivalry
With bruisèd arms and wreaths of victory. 110
  Her joy with heaved-up hand she doth express,
  And wordless so greets heaven for his success.

Far from the purpose of his coming hither,
He makes excuses for his being there.
No cloudy show of stormy blustering weather 115
Doth yet in his fair welkin° once appear,
Till sable° Night, mother of dread and fear,
  Upon the world dim darkness doth display,
  And in her vaulty prison stows the day.

For then is Tarquin brought unto his bed, 120
Intending weariness with heavy sprite,°
For after supper long he questionèd°
With modest Lucrece, and wore out the night.
Now leaden slumber with life's strength doth fight,
  And every one to rest themselves betake, 125
  Save thieves and cares and troubled minds that
    wake.

As one of which doth Tarquin lie revolving
The sundry dangers of his will's obtaining,
Yet ever to obtain his will resolving,
Though weak-built hopes persuade him to abstain-
    ing. 130
Despair to gain doth traffic° oft for gaining,
  And when great treasure is the meed° proposed,
  Though death be adjunct,° there's no death sup-
    posed.

Those that much covet are with gain so fond°
That what they have not, that which they possess,
They scatter and unloose it from their bond,° 136
And so, by hoping more, they have but less,
Or, gaining more, the profit of excess
  Is but to surfeit, and such griefs sustain
  That they prove bankrupt in this poor-rich gain.

The aim of all is but to nurse the life 141
With honor, wealth, and ease, in waning age;

60. gild: Red and gold are often confused in Shakespeare's verse. See *Macb*, II.ii.55–57. 64. heraldry: painting. There is however a general idea of heraldic painting and symbolism running throughout these two stanzas. See App. 9. 67. world's minority: when the world was young. 82. owe: own; i.e., express. 84. still-gazing: ever staring. 88. limed: caught by birdlime. 89. securely: unsuspecting, without anxiety. 92. colored: concealed. 93. plaits: folds — as beneath a cloak. 99. coped: encountered. 100. parling: inviting to a parley.

102. margents: margins — where the commentary on the text was often printed. 104. moralize: draw a moral from, interpret. 105. than: than that. 106. stories: tells the story of. 116. welkin: sky. 117. sable: black. 121. sprite: spirit. 122. questioned: conversed. 131. traffic: makes great efforts. 132. meed: reward. 133. adjunct: added. 134. fond: foolish, infatuated. 136. bond: band, fastening.

And in this aim there is such thwarting strife
That one for all or all for one we gage:°
As life for honor in fell battle's rage;   145
   Honor for wealth; and oft that wealth doth cost
   The death of all, and all together lost.

So that in venturing ill we leave to be
The things we are for that which we expect.
And this ambitious foul infirmity,   150
In having much, torments us with defect
Of that we have. So then we do neglect
   The thing we have, and, all for want of wit,
   Make something nothing by augmenting it.

Such hazard now must doting Tarquin make,   155
Pawning his honor to obtain his lust,
And for himself himself he must forsake.
Then where is truth, if there be no self-trust?
When shall he think to find a stranger just,
   When he himself himself confounds, betrays
   To slanderous tongues and wretched, hateful
     days?   161

Now stole upon the time the dead of night,
When heavy sleep had closed up mortal eyes.
No comfortable star did lend his light,
No noise but owls' and wolves' death-boding cries.
Now serves the season that they may surprise   166
   The silly° lambs. Pure thoughts are dead and
     still,
   While lust and murder wakes to stain and kill.

And now this lustful lord leaped from his bed,
Throwing his mantle rudely o'er his arm.   170
Is madly tossed between desire and dread:
Th' one sweetly flatters, th' other feareth harm.
But honest fear, bewitched with lust's foul charm,
   Doth too too oft betake him to retire,
   Beaten away by brain-sick rude desire.   175

His falchion° on a flint he softly smiteth,
That from the cold stone sparks of fire do fly,
Whereat a waxen torch forthwith he lighteth,
Which must be lodestar° to his lustful eye,
And to the flame thus speaks advisedly: 180
   "As from this cold flint I enforced this fire,
   So Lucrece must I force to my desire."

Here pale with fear he doth premeditate
The dangers of his loathsome enterprise,
And in his inward mind he doth debate   185
What following sorrow may on this arise.
Then looking scornfully he doth despise

His naked armor of still-slaughtered lust,°
And justly thus controls his thoughts unjust.

"Fair torch, burn out thy light, and lend it not
To darken her whose light excelleth thine.   191
And die, unhallowed thoughts, before you blot
With your uncleanness that which is divine.
Offer pure incense to so pure a shrine.
   Let fair humanity abhor the deed   195
   That spots and stains love's modest snow-white
     weed.°

"Oh shame to knighthood and to shining arms!
Oh foul dishonor to my household's grave!°
Oh impious act, including all foul harms!
A martial man to be soft fancy's° slave!   200
True valor still a true respect should have.
   Then my digression is so vile, so base,
   That it will live engraven in my face.

"Yea, though I die, the scandal will survive,
And be an eyesore in my golden coat.   205
Some loathsome dash° the herald will contrive,
To cipher° me how fondly I did dote.
That my posterity, shamed with the note,
   Shall curse my bones, and hold it for no sin
   To wish that I their father had not been.   210

"What win I, if I gain the thing I seek?
A dream, a breath, a froth of fleeting joy.
Who buys a minute's mirth to wail a week?
Or sells eternity to get a toy?   214
For one sweet grape who will the vine destroy?
   Or what fond beggar, but to touch the crown,
   Would with the scepter straight be strucken
     down?

"If Collatinus dream of my intent,
Will he not wake, and in a desperate rage
Post hither, this vile purpose to prevent;   220
This siege that hath engirt his marriage,
This blur to youth, this sorrow to the sage,
   This dying virtue, this surviving shame,
   Whose crime will bear an ever-during blame?

"Oh, what excuse can my invention make,   225
When thou shalt charge me with so black a deed?
Will not my tongue be mute, my frail joints shake,
Mine eyes forgo their light, my false heart bleed?
The guilt being great, the fear doth still exceed,
   And extreme fear can neither fight nor fly,   230
   But coward-like with trembling terror die.

---

188. His . . . lust: his weak defense of lust that. . . . **196. weed:** garment. **198. household's grave:** family tomb. **200. fancy:** love. **206. loathsome dash:** ignominious mark. Books of heraldry include various symbols which were added to the coat of arms of a man who had committed offenses against honor. See App. 9. **207. cipher:** describe.

144. gage: pledge.   **167. silly:** simple.   **176. falchion:** curved sword.   **179. lodestar:** guiding star.

"Had Collatinus killed my son or sire,
Or lain in ambush to betray my life,
Or were he not my dear friend, this desire
Might have excuse to work upon his wife,   235
As in revenge or quittal of such strife.
   But as he is my kinsman, my dear friend,
   The shame and fault finds no excuse nor end.

"Shameful it is; aye, if the fact be known,
Hateful it is; there is no hate in loving.   240
I'll beg her love, but she is not her own.
The worst is but denial and reproving:
My will° is strong, past reason's weak removing.
   Who fears a sentence or an old man's saw°
   Shall by a painted cloth° be kept in awe."   245

Thus graceless holds he disputation
'Tween frozen conscience and hot-burning will,
And with good thoughts makes dispensation,°
Urging the worser sense for vantage° still,
Which in a moment doth confound and kill   250
   All pure effects, and doth so far proceed
   That what is vile shows like a virtuous deed.

Quoth he: " She took me kindly by the hand,
And gazed for tidings in my eager eyes,
Fearing some hard news from the warlike band,
Where her belovèd Collatinus lies.   256
Oh, how her fear did make her color rise!
   First red as roses that on lawn° we lay,
   Then white as lawn, the roses took away.

"And how her hand, in my hand being locked,
Forced it to tremble with her loyal fear!   261
Which struck her sad, and then it faster rocked,°
Until her husband's welfare she did hear;
Whereat she smilèd with so sweet a cheer
   That had Narcissus° seen her as she stood   265
   Self-love had never drowned him in the flood.

"Why hunt I then for color° or excuses?
All orators are dumb when beauty pleadeth.
Poor wretches have remorse° in poor abuses.
Love thrives not in the heart that shadows dreadeth.
Affection is my captain, and he leadeth,   271
   And when his gaudy banner is displayed,
   The coward fights, and will not be dismayed.

"Then, childish fear avaunt! Debating die!
Respect° and reason wait on wrinkled age!   275

My heart shall never countermand mine eye.
Sad pause and deep regard beseems the sage.
My part is Youth, and beats these from the stage.°
   Desire my pilot is, Beauty my prize;
   Then who fears sinking where such treasure
    lies? "   280

As corn o'ergrown by weeds, so heedful fear
Is almost choked by unresisted lust.
Away he steals with open listening ear,
Full of foul hope and full of fond mistrust,
Both which, as servitors to the unjust,   285
   So cross him with their opposite persuasion
   That now he vows a league, and now invasion.

Within his thought her heavenly image sits,
And in the self-same seat sits Collatine.
That eye which looks on her confounds his wits.
That eye which him beholds, as more divine,   291
Unto a view so false will not incline,
   But with a pure appeal seeks to the heart
   Which once corrupted takes the worser part.

And therein heartens up his servile powers,   295
Who, flattered by their leader's jocund show,
Stuff up his lust, as minutes fill up hours,
And as their captain, so their pride doth grow,
Paying more slavish tribute than they owe.°
   By reprobate desire thus madly led,   300
   The Roman lord marcheth to Lucrece' bed.

The locks between her chamber and his will,
Each one by him enforced, retires his ward.°
But, as they open, they all rate° his ill,   304
Which drives the creeping thief to some regard.
The threshold grates° the door to have him heard;
   Night-wandering weasels shriek to see him there;
   They fright him, yet he still pursues his fear.

As each unwilling portal yields him way,
Through little vents and crannies of the place   310
The wind wars with his torch to make him stay,
And blows the smoke of it into his face,
Extinguishing his conduct° in this case.
   But his hot heart, which fond desire doth scorch,
   Puffs forth another wind that fires the torch,   315

And being lighted, by the light he spies
Lucretia's glove, wherein her needle sticks
He takes it from the rushes° where it lies,
And griping it, the needle° his finger pricks

---

243. will: lust.   **244. saw:** proverb.   **245. painted cloth:** "Painted cloths" showing stories from Scripture or classical legend were used as wall coverings. The figures were often provided with labels issuing from their mouths which contained sage or moral sentences. See Pl. 6a.   **248. dispensation:** license to break a law.   **249. vantage:** his own profit.   **258. lawn:** fine white linen.   **262. rocked:** shook.   **265. Narcissus:** See *Ant & Cleo*, II.v.96,n.   **267. color:** pretext.   **269. remorse:** pity. **275. Respect:** prudence.

278. beats . . . stage: as in a morality play where Youth and Old Age appear as characters.   **299. owe:** own.   **303. retires . . . ward:** draws back its bar. A *ward* is lit. the ridge on the inside of a lock which corresponds with the incision in the key.   **304. rate:** blame — by their noise.   **306. grates:** scrapes on.   **313. conduct:** escort — the torch.   **318. rushes:** used as floor covering. **319. needle:** pronounced "neeld."

As who should say: " This glove to wanton tricks
  Is not inured. Return again in haste;   321
  Thou see'st our mistress' ornaments are chaste."

But all these poor forbiddings could not stay him.
He in the worst sense construes their denial.
The doors, the wind, the glove that did delay him,
He takes for accidental things of trial,   326
Or as those bars° which stop the hourly dial,°
  Who with a lingering stay his course doth let°
  Till every minute pays the hour his debt.

" So, so," quoth he, " these lets attend the time°
Like little frosts that sometime threat the spring
To add a more rejoicing to the prime   332
And give the sneapèd° birds more cause to sing.
Pain pays the income of each precious thing.
  Huge rocks, high winds, strong pirates, shelves
    and sands,   335
  The merchant fears, ere rich at home he lands."

Now is he come unto the chamber door
That shuts him from the heaven of his thought,
Which with a yielding latch, and with no more,
Hath barred him from the blessèd thing he sought.
So from himself impiety hath wrought,   341
  That for his prey to pray he doth begin,
  As if the heavens should countenance his sin.

But in the midst of his unfruitful prayer,
Having solicited the eternal power   345
That his foul thoughts might compass his fair fair,
And they would stand auspicious to the hour,
Even there he starts. Quoth he: " I must deflower.
  The powers to whom I pray abhor this fact;
  How can they then assist me in the act?   350

" Then Love and Fortune be my gods, my guide!
My will is backed with resolution:
Thoughts are but dreams till their effects be tried.
The blackest sin is cleared with absolution.
Against love's fire fear's frost hath dissolution.   355
  The eye of heaven is out, and misty night
  Covers the shame that follows sweet delight."

This said, his guilty hand plucked up the latch,
And with his knee the door he opens wide.
The dove sleeps fast that this night owl will catch.
Thus treason works ere traitors be espied.   361
  Who sees the lurking serpent steps aside,
    But she, sound sleeping, fearing no such thing,
    Lies at the mercy of his mortal sting.

Into the chamber wickedly he stalks   365
And gazeth on her yet unstainèd bed.
The curtains° being close, about he walks,
Rolling his greedy eyeballs in his head.
By their high treason is his heart misled,   369
  Which gives the watchword to his hand full soon
  To draw the cloud° that hides the silver moon.

Look, as the fair and fiery-pointed sun,
Rushing from forth a cloud, bereaves our sight.
Even so, the curtain drawn, his eyes begun
To wink,° being blinded with a greater light.   375
Whether it is that she reflects so bright,
  That dazzleth them, or else some shame sup-
    posed,
  But blind they are, and keep themselves enclosed.

Oh, had they in that darksome prison died!
Then had they seen the period° of their ill.   380
Then Collatine again, by Lucrece' side,
In his clear bed might have reposèd still.
But they must ope, this blessèd league to kill,
  And holy-thoughted Lucrece to their sight
  Must sell her joy, her life, her world's delight.

Her lily hand her rosy cheek lies under,   386
Cozening° the pillow of a lawful kiss,
Who, therefore angry, seems to part in sunder,
Swelling on either side to want° his bliss
Between whose hills her head entombèd is,   390
  Where, like a virtuous monument,° she lies,
  To be admired of lewd unhallowed eyes.

Without° the bed her other fair hand was,
On the green coverlet, whose perfect white
Showed like an April daisy on the grass,   395
With pearly sweat, resembling dew of night.
Her eyes, like marigolds, had sheathed their light,
  And canopied in darkness sweetly lay,
  Till they might open to adorn the day.

Her hair, like golden threads, played with her
  breath.   400
O modest wantons! Wanton modesty!
Showing life's triumph in the map of death,°
And death's dim look in life's mortality.
Each° in her sleep themselves so beautify
  As if between them twain there were no strife,
  But that life lived in death and death in life.   406

Her breasts, like ivory globes circled with blue,
A pair of maiden worlds unconquerèd,

---

327. bars: cogs. dial: clock.   328. let: hinder.   330. lets . . .
time: these difficulties are part of the affair.   333. sneaped:
nipped by cold.

367. curtains: i.e., of the bed. See Pl. 17b.   371. cloud: i.e., the
bed curtains.   375. wink: shut.   380. period: end.   387. Cozening: cheating.   389. want: be without.   391. virtuous monument: figure on a tomb. For an example see Pl. 2b.   393. Without: outside.   402. map of death: picture of death; i.e., sleep.
404. Each: i.e., life and death.

Save of their lord no bearing yoke they knew,
And him by oath they truly honorèd.   410
These worlds in Tarquin new ambition bred,
  Who, like a foul usurper, went about
  From this fair throne to heave the owner out.

What could he see but mightily he noted?
What did he note but strongly he desired?   415
What he beheld, on that he firmly doted,
And in his will his willful eye he tired.°
With more than admiration° he admired
  Her azure veins, her alabaster skin,
  Her coral lips, her snow-white dimpled chin.

As the grim lion fawneth o'er his prey,   421
Sharp hunger by the conquest satisfied,
So o'er this sleeping soul doth Tarquin stay,
His rage of lust by gazing qualified;°
Slacked, not suppressed, for standing by her side,
  His eye, which late this mutiny restrains,   426
  Unto a greater uproar tempts his veins;

And they, like straggling slaves for pillage fighting,
Obdurate vassals° fell exploits effecting,
In bloody death and ravishment delighting,   430
Nor children's tears nor mothers' groans respecting,
Swell in their pride, the onset still expecting.
  Anon his beating heart, alarum striking,
  Gives the hot charge, and bids them do their lik-
    ing.

His drumming heart cheers up his burning eye,
His eye commends the leading to his hand.   436
His hand, as proud of such a dignity,
Smoking with pride, marched on to make his stand
On her bare breast, the heart of all her land,
  Whose ranks of blue veins, as his hand did scale,
  Left their round turrets destitute and pale.   441

They, mustering to the quiet cabinet°
Where their dear governess and lady lies,
Do tell her she is dreadfully beset,
And fright her with confusion of their cries.   445
She, much amazed, breaks ope her locked-up eyes,
  Who, peeping forth this tumult to behold,
  Are by his flaming torch dimmed and controlled.

Imagine her as one in dead of night   449
From forth dull sleep by dreadful fancy waking,
That thinks she hath beheld some ghastly sprite,
Whose grim aspéct sets every joint ashaking.
What terror 'tis! But she, in worser taking,°
  From sleep disturbèd, heedfully doth view   454
  The sight which makes supposèd terror true.

Wrapped and confounded in a thousand fears,
Like to a new-killed bird she trembling lies;
She dares not look; yet, winking, there appears
Quick-shifting antics,° ugly in her eyes.
Such shadows are the weak brain's forgeries,   460
  Who, angry that the eyes fly from their lights,
  In darkness daunts them with more dreadful
    sights.

His hand, that yet remains upon her breast —
Rude ram,° to batter such an ivory wall! —
May feel her heart, poor citizen, distressed,   465
Wounding itself to death, rise up and fall,
Beating her bulk, that his hand shakes withal.
  This moves in him more rage and lesser pity,
  To make the breach and enter this sweet city.

First, like a trumpet, doth his tongue begin   470
To sound a parley to his heartless° foe;
Who o'er the white sheet peers her whiter chin,
The reason of this rash alarm to know,
Which he by dumb demeanor seeks to show.
  But she with vehement prayers urgeth still   475
  Under what color° he commits this ill.

Thus he replies: " The color in thy face,
That even for anger makes the lily pale
And the red rose blush at her own disgrace,
Shall plead for me and tell my loving tale.   480
Under that color am I come to scale
  Thy never-conquered fort. The fault is thine,
  For those thine eyes betray thee unto mine.

" Thus I forestall thee, if thou mean to chide.
Thy beauty hath ensnared thee to this night,   485
Where thou with patience must my will abide;°
My will that marks thee for my earth's° delight,
Which I to conquer sought with all my might.
  But as reproof and reason beat it dead,
  By thy bright beauty was it newly bred.   490

" I see what crosses° my attempt will bring.
I know what thorns the growing rose defends.
I think the honey guarded with a sting —
All this beforehand counsel comprehends.
But will is deaf and hears no heedful friends.   495
  Only he hath an eye to gaze on beauty,
  And dotes on what he looks, 'gainst law or duty.

" I have debated, even in my soul,
What wrong, what shame, what sorrow I shall
    breed,
But nothing can affection's course control,   500
Or stop the headlong fury of his speed.

417. tired: i.e., by gazing.   418. admiration: excessive wonder.
424. qualified: allayed.   429. vassals: slaves.   442. cabinet:
tent; i.e., the brain.   453. taking: distress.

459. antics: grotesque shapes.   464. ram: battering ram.
471. heartless: frightened.   476. color: pretext.   486. will
abide: endure my lust.   487. earth: body.   491. crosses:
troubles.

I know repentant tears ensue° the deed,
  Reproach, disdain and deadly enmity;
  Yet strive I to embrace mine infamy."

This said, he shakes aloft his Roman blade,   505
Which, like a falcon towering in the skies,
Coucheth° the fowl below with his wings' shade,
Whose crookèd beak threats if he mount he dies.
So under his insulting falchion lies
  Harmless Lucretia, marking what he tells   510
  With trembling fear, as fowl hear falcon's bells.°

"Lucrece," quoth he, "this night I must enjoy thee.
If thou deny, then force must work my way,
For in thy bed I purpose to destroy thee.
That done, some worthless slave of thine I'll slay,
To kill thine honor with thy life's decay,   516
  And in thy dead arms do I mean to place him,
  Swearing I slew him, seeing thee embrace him.

"So thy surviving husband shall remain
The scornful mark of every open eye.   520
Thy kinsmen hang their heads at this disdain,
Thy issue° blurred with nameless° bastardy.
And thou, the author of their obloquy,
  Shalt have thy trespass cited up in rhymes
  And sung by children in succeeding times.   525

"But if thou yield, I rest thy secret friend.
The fault unknown is as a thought unacted.
A little harm done to a great good end
For lawful policy remains enacted.°
The poisonous simple° sometime is compacted°
  In a pure compound. Being so applied,   531
  His venom in effect is purified.

"Then, for thy husband and thy children's sake,
Tender° my suit. Bequeath not to their lot
The shame that from them no device can take,
The blemish that will never be forgot,   536
Worse than a slavish wipe° or birth-hour's blot.
  For marks descried in men's nativity
  Are nature's faults, not their own infamy."

Here with a cockatrice'° dead-killing eye   540
He rouseth up himself, and makes a pause,
While she, the picture of pure piety,
Like a white hind under the gripe's° sharp claws,
Pleads, in a wilderness where are no laws,

To the rough beast that knows no gentle right,
  Nor aught obeys but his foul appetite.   546

But when a black-faced cloud the world doth threat,
In his dim mist the aspiring mountains hiding,
From earth's dark womb some gentle gust doth get,
Which blows these pitchy vapors from their biding,
Hindering their present fall by this dividing,   551
  So his unhallowed haste her words delays,
  And moody Pluto winks while Orpheus plays.°

Yet, foul night-waking cat, he doth but dally,
While in his hold-fast foot the weak mouse panteth.
Her sad behavior feeds his vulture folly,   556
A swallowing gulf° that even in plenty wanteth.
His ear her prayers admits, but his heart granteth
  No penetrable entrance to her plaining.
  Tears harden lust, though marble wear with rain-
  ing.   560

Her pity-pleading eyes are sadly fixed
In the remorseless wrinkles of his face.
Her modest eloquence with sighs is mixed,
Which to her oratory adds more grace.
She puts the period often from his place,°   565
  And midst the sentence so her accent breaks
  That twice she doth begin ere once she speaks.

She conjures him by high almighty Jove,
By knighthood, gentry,° and sweet friendship's
  oath,
By her untimely tears, her husband's love,   570
By holy human law and common troth,°
By heaven and earth, and all the power of both,
  That to his borrowed° bed he make retire,
  And stoop to honor, not to foul desire.

Quoth she: "Reward not hospitality   575
With such black payment as thou hast pretended.°
Mud not the fountain that gave drink to thee.
Mar not the thing that cannot be amended.
End thy ill aim before thy shoot be ended.
  He is no woodman that doth bend his bow   580
  To strike a poor unseasonable doe.

"My husband is thy friend; for his sake spare me.
Thyself art mighty; for thine own sake leave me.
Myself a weakling; do not then ensnare me.
Thou look'st not like deceit; do not deceive me.

---

502. ensue: come after.   507. Coucheth: causes to crouch.
511. falcon's bells: See App. 26.   522. issue: children. nameless: of unknown father.   529. For ... enacted: is regarded
as a rightful action.   530. simple: drug. compacted: mixed.
534. Tender: grant.   537. slavish wipe: the mark branded on
a slave.   540. cockatrice: a fabulous serpent, so deadly that it
could slay by its glance.   543. gripe: griffin, a fabulous beast
with the head and wings of an eagle and the body and limbs of a
lion.

553. And ... plays: Orpheus, the wonderful singer, seeking the
soul of his wife Eurydice charmed his way into the underworld.
Such was the power of his music that even Pluto, god of the
underworld, closed his eyes.   557. gulf: whirlpool.   565. puts
... place: i.e., she often stops in her sentences before each is
finished.   569. gentry: the code of a gentleman.   571. troth:
truth.   573. borrowed: guest.   576. pretended: offered.

My sighs, like whirlwinds, labor hence to heave
   thee.   586
  If ever man were moved with woman's moans,
  Be movèd with my tears, my sighs, my groans,

"All which together, like a troubled ocean,
Beat at thy rocky and wreck-threatening heart,
To soften it with their continual motion;   591
For stones dissolved to water do convert.
Oh, if no harder than a stone thou art,
  Melt at my tears, and be compassionate!
  Soft pity enters at an iron gate.   595

"In Tarquin's likeness I did entertain thee.
Hast thou put on his shape to do him shame?
To all the host of Heaven I complain me,
Thou wrong'st his honor, wound'st his princely
  name.   599
Thou art not what thou seem'st; and if the same,
  Thou seem'st not what thou art, a god, a King.
  For kings, like gods, should govern everything.

"How will thy shame be seeded° in thine age,
When thus thy vices bud before thy spring!
If in thy hope thou darest do such outrage,   605
What darest thou not when once thou art a King?
Oh, be remembered, no outrageous thing
  From vassal actors° can be wiped away.
  Then kings' misdeeds cannot be hid in clay.°

"This deed will make thee only loved for fear,   610
But happy monarchs still are feared for love.
With foul offenders thou perforce must bear,
When they in thee the like offenses prove.
If but for fear of this, thy will remove,   614
  For princes are the glass, the school, the book,
  Where subjects' eyes do learn, do read, do look.

"And wilt thou be the school where Lust shall
  learn?
Must he in thee read lectures of such shame?
Wilt thou be glass wherein it shall discern
Authority for sin, warrant for blame,   620
To privilege dishonor in thy name?
  Thou back'st reproach against long-living laud,
  And mak'st fair reputation but a bawd.°

"Hast thou command? By him that gave it thee,
From a pure heart command thy rebel will.   625
Draw not thy sword to guard iniquity,
For it was lent thee all that brood to kill.
Thy princely office how canst thou fulfill,
  When, patterned by thy fault, foul sin may say
  He learned to sin and thou didst teach the way?

"Think but how vile a spectacle it were   631
To view thy present trespass in another.
Men's faults do seldom to themselves appear.
Their own transgressions partially° they smother.
This guilt would seem death-worthy in thy brother.
  Oh, how are they wrapped in with infamies   636
  That from their own misdeeds askance° their
    eyes!

"To thee, to thee, my heaved-up hands appeal,
Not to seducing Lust, thy rash relier.°
I sue for exiled majesty's repeal;°   640
Let him return, and flattering thoughts retire.
His true respect will prison false desire,
  And wipe the dim mist from thy doting eyne,°
  That thou shalt see thy state and pity mine."

"Have done," quoth he. "My uncontrollèd tide
Turns not, but swells the higher by this let.°   646
Small lights are soon blown out, huge fires abide,
And with the wind in greater fury fret.
The petty streams that pay a daily debt
  To their salt sovereign, with their fresh falls' haste
  Add to his flow, but alter not his taste."   651

"Thou art," quoth she, "a sea, a sovereign King,
And, lo, there falls into thy boundless flood
Black lust, dishonor, shame, misgoverning,
Who seek to stain the ocean of thy blood.   655
If all these petty ills shall change thy good,
  Thy sea within a puddle's womb is hearsed,°
  And not the puddle in thy sea dispersed.

"So shall these slaves be king, and thou their slave.
Thou nobly base, they basely dignified.   660
Thou their fair life, and they thy fouler grave.
Thou loathèd in their shame, they in thy pride.
The lesser thing should not the greater hide.
  The cedar stoops not to the base shrub's foot,
  But low shrubs wither at the cedar's root.   665

"So let thy thoughts, low vassals to thy state" —
"No more," quoth he. "By Heaven, I will not hear
  thee.
Yield to my love; if not, enforcèd hate,
Instead of love's coy touch, shall rudely tear thee.
That done, despitefully I mean to bear thee   670
  Unto the base bed of some rascal groom,
  To be thy partner in this shameful doom."

This said, he sets his foot upon the light,
For light and lust are deadly enemies.

---

603. **seeded:** i.e., what sort of crop will it yield.   608. **vassal
actors:** inferior subjects of a king.   609. **hid in clay:** concealed
in the earth.   623. **bawd:** purveyor of lust.

634. **partially:** through partiality.   637. **askance:** turn aside
639. **thy . . . relier:** which rashly relies on your present mood.
640. **for . . . repeal:** for the recall from banishment (*repeal*)
of true kingship.   643. **eyne:** eyes.   646. **let:** hindrance.
657. **hearsed:** coffined.

Shame folded up in blind concealing night,   675
When most unseen, then most doth tyrannize.
The wolf hath seized his prey, the poor lamb cries,
   Till with her own white fleece her voice con-
     trolled
   Entombs her outcry in her lips' sweet fold.

For with the nightly linen that she wears   680
He pens her piteous clamors in her head,
Cooling his hot face in the chastest tears
That ever modest eyes with sorrow shed.
Oh, that prone lust should stain so pure a bed!
   The spots whereof could weeping purify,   685
   Her tears should drop on them perpetually.

But she hath lost a dearer thing than life,
And he hath won what he would lose again.
This forcèd league doth force a further strife;
This momentary joy breeds months of pain;   690
This hot desire converts to cold disdain.
   Pure Chastity is rifled of her store,
   And Lust, the thief, far poorer than before.

Look, as the full-fed hound or gorgèd hawk,
Unapt for tender smell or speedy flight,   695
Make slow pursuit, or altogether balk°
The prey wherein by nature they delight,
So surfeit-taking Tarquin fares this night.
   His taste delicious, in digestion souring,   699
   Devours his will, that lived by foul devouring.°

Oh, deeper sin than bottomless conceit°
Can comprehend in still imagination!
Drunken Desire must vomit his receipt,°
Ere he can see his own abomination.
While Lust is in his pride, no exclamation   705
   Can curb his heat or rein his rash desire,
   Till, like a jade,° Self-will himself doth tire.

And then with lank and lean discolored cheek,
With heavy eye, knit brow, and strengthless pace,
Feeble Desire, all recreant,° poor and meek,   710
Like to a bankrupt beggar wails his case.
The flesh being proud, Desire doth fight with
     Grace,°
   For there it revels, and when that decays,
   The guilty rebel for remission prays.

So fares it with this faultful lord of Rome,   715
Who this accomplishment so hotly chased;
For now against himself he sounds this doom,
That through the length of times he stands dis-
     graced.

696. balk: let slip.   699–700. His . . . devouring: See Sonnet 129.   701. conceit: imagination.   703. receipt: what it has taken in.   707. jade: poor-spirited horse. See *Caesar*, IV.ii.23–27. 710. recreant: cowardly.   712. Grace: i.e., divine help which encourages a man to subdue his evil passions.

Besides, his soul's fair temple is defaced,
   To whose weak ruins muster troops of cares,   720
   To ask the spotted princess° how she fares.

She says, her subjects with foul insurrection
Have battered down her consecrated wall,
And by their mortal fault brought in subjection
Her immortality, and made her thrall°   725
To living death and pain perpetual,
   Which in her prescience she controllèd still,
   But her foresight could not forestall their will.

Even in this thought through the dark night he
     stealeth,
A captive victor that hath lost in gain;   730
Bearing away the wound that nothing healeth,
The scar that will, despite of cure, remain,
Leaving his spoil perplexed in greater pain.
   She bears the load of lust he left behind,
   And he the burden of a guilty mind.   735

He like a thievish dog creeps sadly thence;
She like a wearied lamb lies panting there.
He scowls, and hates himself for his offense;
She, desperate, with her nails her flesh doth tear.
He faintly flies, sweating with guilty fear;   740
   She stays, exclaiming on the direful night.
   He runs, and chides his vanished, loathed delight.

He thence departs a heavy convertite;°
She there remains a hopeless castaway.
He in his speed looks for the morning light;   745
She prays she never may behold the day.
"For day," quoth she, "night's 'scapes° doth open
     lay,
   And my true eyes have never practiced how
   To cloak offenses with a cunning brow.

"They think not but that every eye can see   750
The same disgrace which they themselves behold,
And therefore would they still in darkness be,
To have their unseen sin remain untold.
For they their guilt with weeping will unfold,   754
   And grave,° like water that doth eat in steel,
   Upon my cheeks what helpless shame I feel."

Here she exclaims against repose and rest,
And bids her eyes hereafter still be blind.
She wakes her heart by beating on her breast,
And bids it leap from thence, where it may find
Some purer chest° to close° so pure a mind.   761
   Frantic with grief thus breathes she forth her
     spite
   Against the unseen secrecy of night:

721. princess: i.e., his soul.   725. thrall: slave.   743. convertite: convert, penitent.   747. 'scapes: escapades.   755. grave: engrave.   761. chest: coffer. close: enclose, contain.

"Oh comfort-killing Night, image of Hell!
Dim register and notary of shame!   765
Black stage° for tragedies and murders fell!
Vast sin-concealing chaos; nurse of blame!
Blind muffled bawd! Dark harbor for defame!
    Grim cave of death! Whispering conspirator
    With close-tongued Treason and the ravisher!

"O hateful, vaporous and foggy Night!   771
Since thou art guilty of my cureless crime,
Muster thy mists to meet the eastern light,
Make war against proportioned course° of time,
Or if thou wilt permit the sun to climb   775
    His wonted height, yet ere he go to bed,
    Knit poisonous clouds about his golden head.

"With rotten damps ravish the morning air.
Let their exhaled unwholesome breaths make sick
The life of purity, the supreme fair,°   780
Ere he arrive his weary noontide prick;°
And let thy misty vapors march so thick
    That in their smoky ranks his smothered light
    May set at noon and make perpetual night.

"Were Tarquin Night, as he is but Night's child,
The silver-shining Queen he would distain.°   786
Her twinkling handmaids° too, by him defiled,
Through Night's black bosom should not peep
        again.
So should I have co-partners in my pain —
    And fellowship in woe doth woe assuage,   790
    As palmers'° chat makes short their pilgrimage.

"Where now I have no one to blush with me,
To cross their arms and hang their heads with
        mine,
To mask their brows and hide their infamy,
But I alone alone must sit and pine,   795
Seasoning° the earth with showers of silver brine,
    Mingling my talk with tears, my grief with
        groans,
    Poor wasting monuments of lasting moans.

"O Night, thou furnace of foul-reeking smoke,
Let not the jealous Day behold that face   800
Which underneath thy black all-hiding cloak
Immodestly lies martyred with disgrace!
Keep still possession of thy gloomy place,
    That all the faults which in thy reign are made
    May likewise be sepulchred in thy shade!   805

"Make me not object to the telltale Day!
The light will show, charàctered° in my brow,
The story of sweet chastity's decay,
The impious breach of holy wedlock vow.
Yea, the illiterate, that know not how   810
    To cipher° what is writ in learnèd books,
    Will quote° my loathsome trespass in my looks.

"The nurse, to still her child, will tell my story,
And fright her crying babe with Tarquin's name;
The orator, to deck his oratory,   815
Will couple my reproach to Tarquin's shame;
Feast-finding minstrels, tuning° my defame,
    Will tie the hearers to attend each line,
    How Tarquin wrongèd me, I Collatine.

"Let my good name, that senseless reputation,   820
For Collatine's dear love be kept unspotted.
If that be made a theme for disputation,
The branches of another root are rotted,
And undeserved reproach to him allotted
    That is as clear from this attaint° of mine   825
    As I, ere this, was pure to Collatine.

"Oh, unseen shame! Invisible disgrace!
Oh, unfelt sore! Crest-wounding, private scar!
Reproach is stamped in Collatinus' face,
And Tarquin's eye may read the mot° afar,   830
How he in peace is wounded, not in war.
    Alas, how many bear such shameful blows,
    Which not themselves, but he that gives them
        knows!

"If, Collatine, thine honor lay in me,
From me by strong assault it is bereft.   835
My honey lost, and I, a dronelike bee,
Have no perfection of my summer left,
But robbed and ransacked by injurious theft.
    In thy weak hive a wandering wasp hath crept,
    And sucked the honey which thy chaste bee kept.

"Yet am I guilty of thy honor's wrack.°   841
Yet for thy honor did I entertain him.
Coming from thee, I could not put him back,
For it had been dishonor to disdain him.
Besides, of weariness he did complain him,   845
    And talked of virtue. Oh, unlooked-for evil,
    When virtue is profaned in such a devil!

"Why should the worm intrude the maiden bud?
Or hateful cuckoos° hatch in sparrows' nests?
Or toads infect fair founts with venom mud?   850
Or tyrant folly lurk in gentle breasts?

---

766. **Black stage:** The stage was hung with black curtains
when a tragedy was acted. See *I Hen VI*, I.i.1.   774. **proportioned course:** alternation of light and dark.   780. **supreme
fair:** the finest kind of beauty.   781. **prick:** the mark on the dial
of a clock denoting the hour.   786–87. **Queen . . . handmaids:**
the moon and the stars.   786. **distain:** stain.   791. **palmers:**
pilgrims.   796. **Seasoning:** making salt.

807. **charactered:** written.   811. **cipher:** decipher, read.
812. **quote:** note.   817. **tuning:** singing about.   825. **attaint:**
dishonor.   830. **mot:** inscription.   841. **wrack:** disaster.
849. **cuckoos:** See App. 11.

Or kings be breakers of their own behests?°
    But no perfection is so absolute
    That some impurity doth not pollute.

"The aged man that coffers up his gold   855
Is plagued with cramps and gouts and painful fits,
And scarce hath eyes his treasure to behold,
But like still-pining Tantalus° he sits
And useless barns the harvest of his wits,
    Having no other pleasure of his gain   860
    But torment that it cannot cure his pain.

"So then he hath it when he cannot use it,
And leaves it to be mastered by his young,
Who in their pride do presently abuse it.
Their father was too weak, and they too strong,   865
To hold their cursèd-blessèd fortune long.
    The sweets we wish for turn to loathèd sours
    Even in the moment that we call them ours.

"Unruly blasts wait on the tender spring.
Unwholesome weeds take root with precious flow-
    ers.   870
The adder hisses where the sweet birds sing;
What virtue breeds iniquity devours.
We have no good that we can say is ours
    But ill-annexèd Opportunity°
    Or° kills his life or else his quality.°   875

"O Opportunity, thy guilt is great!
'Tis thou that execut'st the traitor's treason.
Thou set'st the wolf where he the lamb may get.
Whoever plots the sin, thou 'point'st° the season.
'Tis thou that spurn'st at right, at law, at reason,
    And in thy shady cell, where none may spy him,
    Sits Sin, to seize the souls that wander by him.

"Thou mak'st the vestal° violate her oath;   883
Thou blow'st the fire when temperance is thawed;
Thou smother'st honesty, thou murder'st troth;
Thou foul abettor! Thou notorious bawd!   886
Thou plantest scandal and displacest laud!°
    Thou ravisher, thou traitor, thou false thief,
    Thy honey turns to gall, thy joy to grief!

"Thy secret pleasure turns to open shame,   890
Thy private feasting to a public fast,
Thy smoothing titles to a ragged name,
Thy sugared tongue to bitter wormwood taste.
Thy violent vanities can never last.
    How comes it then, vile Opportunity,   895
    Being so bad, such numbers seek for thee?

"When wilt thou be the humble suppliant's friend,
And bring him where his suit may be obtained?
When wilt thou sort° an hour great strifes to end,
Or free that soul which wretchedness hath chained?
Give physic to the sick, ease to the pained?   901
    The poor, lame, blind, halt, creep, cry out for
        thee,
    But they ne'er meet with Opportunity.

"The patient dies while the physician sleeps;
The orphan pines while the oppressor feeds;   905
Justice is feasting while the widow weeps;
Advice° is sporting while infection breeds.
Thou grant'st no time for charitable deeds.
    Wrath, envy, treason, rape, and murder's rages —
    Thy heinous hours wait on them as their pages.

"When Truth and Virtue have to do with thee,
A thousand crosses° keep them from thy aid.   912
They buy thy help, but Sin ne'er gives a fee;
He gratis comes, and thou art well appaid°
As well to hear as grant what he hath said.   915
    My Collatine would else have come to me
    When Tarquin did, but he was stayed by thee.

"Guilty thou art of murder and of theft,
Guilty of perjury and subornation,
Guilty of treason, forgery and shift,°   920
Guilty of incest, that abomination.
An accessáry by thine inclination
    To all sins past and all that are to come,
    From the creation to the general doom.

"Misshapen Time, copesmate° of ugly Night,   925
Swift subtle post,° carrier of grisly care,
Eater of youth, false slave to false delight,
Base watch of woes, sin's pack horse, virtue's snare,
Thou nursest all and murder'st all that are.
    O hear me then, injurious, shifting Time!   930
    Be guilty of my death, since of my crime.

"Why hath thy servant Opportunity
Betrayed the hours thou gavest me to repose,
Canceled my fortunes and enchainèd me
To endless date of never-ending woes?   935
Time's office is to fine° the hate of foes,
    To eat up errors by opinion bred,
    Not spend the dowry of a lawful bed.

"Time's glory is to calm contending kings,
To unmask falsehood and bring truth to light,
To stamp the seal of time in agèd things,   941
To wake the morn and sentinel the night,

---

852. **behests:** commands.   858. **Tantalus:** See *Venus*, l.599,n.
874. **Opportunity:** The word means both the occasion and the
desire to commit an action, usually evil.   875. **Or:** either.
quality: character, honor.   879. **'point'st:** appointest.   883. **vestal:** virgin priestess of Diana, the goddess of chastity.   887. **laud:**
praise.

899. **sort:** select.   907. **Advice:** careful judgment.   912. **crosses:**
impediments.   914. **appaid:** contented.   920. **shift:** swindle.
925. **copesmate:** companion.   926. **post:** messenger.   936. **fine:**
end.

To wrong the wronger till he render right,
　To ruinate proud buildings with thy hours
　And smear with dust their glittering golden
　　towers.　　　　　　　　　　　　945

"To fill with wormholes stately monuments,
To feed oblivion with decay of things,
To blot old books and alter their contents,
To pluck the quills from ancient ravens' wings.
To dry the old oak's sap and cherish springs, 950
　To spoil antiquities of hammered steel
　And turn the giddy round of Fortune's wheel.°

"To show the beldam° daughters of her daughter,
To make the child a man, the man a child,
To slay the tiger that doth live by slaughter, 955
To tame the unicorn and lion wild,
To mock the subtle in themselves beguiled,
　To cheer the plowman with increaseful crops,
　And waste huge stones with little water drops.

"Why work'st thou mischief in thy pilgrimage,
Unless thou couldst return to make amends? 961
One poor retiring° minute in an age
Would purchase thee a thousand thousand friends,
Lending him wit that to bad debtors lends.
　O this dread Night, wouldst thou one hour
　　come back,　　　　　　　　　　965
　I could prevent this storm and shun thy wrack!

"Thou ceaseless lackey to eternity,
With some mischance cross Tarquin in his flight.
Devise extremes beyond extremity,
To make him curse this cursèd crimeful night.
Let ghastly shadows his lewd eyes affright, 971
　And the dire thought of his committed evil
　Shape every bush a hideous shapeless devil.

"Disturb his hours of rest with restless trances.
Afflict him in his bed with bedrid groans. 975
Let there bechance him pitiful mischances,
To make him moan—but pity not his moans.
Stone him with hardened hearts, harder than
　　stones,
　And let mild women to him lose their mildness,
　Wilder to him than tigers in their wildness. 980

"Let him have time to tear his curlèd hair,
Let him have time against himself to rave,
Let him have time of Time's help to despair,
Let him have time to live a loathèd slave,
Let him have time a beggar's orts° to crave, 985
　And time to see one that by alms doth live
　Disdain to him disdainèd scraps to give.

"Let him have time to see his friends his foes,
And merry fools to mock at him resort.　989
Let him have time to mark how slow Time goes
In time of sorrow, and how swift and short
His time of folly and his time of sport,
　And ever let his unrecalling° crime
　Have time to wail the abusing of his time.

"Oh Time, thou tutor both to good and bad, 995
Teach me to curse him that thou taught'st this ill!
At his own shadow let the thief run mad,
Himself himself seek every hour to kill!
Such wretched hands such wretched blood should
　　spill.
　For who so base would such an office have 1000
　As slanderous deathsman° to so base a slave?

"The baser is he, coming from a King,
To shame his hope with deeds degenerate.
The mightier man, the mightier is the thing
That makes him honored or begets him hate, 1005
For greatest scandal waits on greatest state.
　The moon being clouded presently° is missed,
　But little stars may hide them when they list.

"The crow may bathe his coal-black wings in mire,
And unperceived fly with the filth away, 1010
But if the like the snow-white swan desire,
The stain upon his silver down will stay.
Poor grooms are sightless° night, kings glorious
　　day.
　Gnats are unnoted wheresoe'er they fly,
　But eagles gazed upon with every eye. 1015

"Out, idle words, servants to shallow fools!
Unprofitable sounds, weak arbitrators!
Busy yourselves in skill-contending schools.
Debate where leisure serves with dull debaters.
To trembling clients be you mediators. 1020
　For me, I force° not argument a straw,°
　Since that my case is past the help of law.

"In vain I rail at Opportunity,
At Time, at Tarquin, and uncheerful Night.
In vain I cavil with mine infamy, 1025
In vain I spurn at my confirmed despite.°
This helpless smoke of words doth me no right.
　The remedy indeed to do me good
　Is to let forth my foul defilèd blood.

"Poor hand, why quiver'st thou at this decree?
Honor thyself to rid me of this shame, 1031
For if I die, my honor lives in thee,

---

952. Fortune's wheel: See *Hen V*, III.vi.26–40.　953. beldam: old woman.　962. retiring: withdrawing; i.e., if only Time could go backward.　985. orts: scraps.

993. unrecalling: irrevocable.　1001. deathsman: executioner. 1007. presently: immediately.　1013. sightless: unseen. 1021. force . . . straw: have no use for arguments. force: value. 1026. despite: scorn.

But if I live, thou livest in my defame.
Since thou couldst not defend thy loyal dame
   And wast afeard to scratch her wicked foe,   1035
   Kill both thyself and her for yielding so."

This said, from her betumbled couch she starteth,
To find some desperate instrument of death,
But this no slaughterhouse no tool imparteth   1039
To make more vent° for passage of her breath
Which, thronging through her lips, so vanisheth
   As smoke from Aetna that in air consumes,
   Or that which from dischargèd cannon fumes.

"In vain," quoth she, "I live, and seek in vain
Some happy mean to end a hapless life.   1045
I feared by Tarquin's falchion to be slain,
Yet for the self-same purpose seek a knife.
But when I feared I was a loyal wife.
   So am I now. Oh, no, that cannot be!
   Of that true type° hath Tarquin rifled me.   1050

"Oh, that is gone for which I sought to live,
And therefore now I need not fear to die.
To clear this spot by death, at least I give
A badge° of fame to slander's livery,
A dying life to living infamy.   1055
   Poor helpless help, the treasure stolen away,
   To burn the guiltless casket where it lay!

"Well, well, dear Collatine, thou shalt not know
The stainèd taste of violated troth.
I will not wrong thy true affection so,   1060
To flatter thee with an infringèd oath.
This bastard graff° shall never come to growth.
   He shall not boast who did thy stock pollute
   That thou art doting father of his fruit.

"Nor shall he smile at thee in secret thought,   1065
Nor laugh with his companions at thy state.
But thou shalt know thy interest was not bought
Basely with gold, but stolen from forth thy gate.
For me, I am the mistress of my fate,
   And with my trespass never will dispense,   1070
   Till life to death acquit my forced offense.

"I will not poison thee with my attaint,
Nor fold my fault in cleanly coined excuses.
My sable° ground of sin I will not paint,
To hide the truth of this false night's abuses.   1075
My tongue shall utter all; mine eyes, like sluices,
   As from a mountain spring that feeds a dale,
   Shall gush pure streams to purge my impure
     tale."

By this, lamenting Philomel° had ended
The well-tuned warble of her nightly sorrow,   1080
And solemn night with slow sad gait descended
To ugly Hell, when lo, the blushing morrow
Lends light to all fair eyes that light will borrow.
   But cloudy Lucrece shames herself to see,
   And therefore still in night would cloistered be.

Revealing day through every cranny spies,   1086
And seems to point her out where she sits weeping,
To whom she sobbing speaks: "Oh eye of eyes,
Why pry'st thou through my window? Leave thy
    peeping.
Mock with thy tickling beams eyes that are sleep-
    ing.   1090
   Brand not my forehead with thy piercing light,
   For day hath naught to do what's done by night."

Thus cavils she with every thing she sees.
True grief is fond° and testy as a child,
Who wayward once, his mood with naught agrees.
Old woes, not infant sorrows, bear them mild;
Continuance tames the one, the other wild,   1097
   Like an unpracticed swimmer plunging still
   With too much labor drowns for want of skill.

So she, deep drenchèd in a sea of care,   1100
Holds disputation with each thing she views,
And to herself all sorrow doth compare.
No object but her passion's strength renews,
And as one shifts, another straight ensues.   1104
   Sometime her grief is dumb and hath no words.
   Sometime 'tis mad and too much talk affords.

The little birds that tune their morning's joy
Make her moans mad with their sweet melody,
For mirth doth search the bottom of annoy.
Sad souls are slain in merry company.   1110
Grief best is pleased with grief's society.
   True sorrow then is feelingly sufficed
   When with like semblance it is sympathized.

'Tis double death to drown in ken° of shore.
He ten times pines that pines beholding food.   1115
To see the salve doth make the wound ache more.
Great grief grieves most at that would do it good.
Deep woes roll forward like a gentle flood,
   Who, being stopped, the bounding banks o'er-
    flows.   1119
   Grief dallied with nor° law nor limit knows.

"You mocking birds," quoth she, "your tunes en-
    tomb
Within your hollow-swelling feathered breasts,
And in my hearing be you mute and dumb.

1040. **vent:** hole.   1050. **type:** pattern; i.e., loyalty as a wife.
1054. **badge:** device worn by a servant as part of his uniform
(*livery*) to denote that he belonged to his master.   1062. **graff:**
graft.   1074. **sable:** black.

1079. **Philomel:** See *T Andr* Intro. pp. 295b–96a.   1094. **fond:**
foolish.   1114. **ken:** sight.   1120. **nor:** neither.

My restless discord loves no stops nor rests.°
A woeful hostess brooks not merry guests.   1125
  Relish your nimble notes to pleasing ears.
  Distress likes dumps° when time is kept with
    tears.

"Come, Philomel,° that sing'st of ravishment,
Make thy sad grove in my disheveled hair.
As the dank earth weeps at thy languishment,
So I at each sad strain will strain a tear,   1131
And with deep groans the diapason° bear.
  For burden-wise° I'll hum on Tarquin still,
  While thou on Tereus descant'st better skill.

"And while against a thorn° thou bear'st thy part,
To keep thy sharp woes waking, wretched I,   1136
To imitate thee well, against my heart
Will fix a sharp knife, to affright mine eye,
Who, if it wink, shall thereon fall and die.   1139
  These means, as frets° upon an instrument,
  Shall tune our heartstrings to true languishment.

"And for,° poor bird, thou sing'st not in the day,
As shaming any eye should thee behold,
Some dark deep desert, seated from the way,°
That knows not parching heat nor freezing cold,
Will we find out, and there we will unfold   1146
  To creatures stern sad tunes, to change their
    kinds.°
  Since men prove beasts, let beasts bear gentle
    minds."

As the poor frighted deer, that stands at gaze,
Wildly determining which way to fly,   1150
Or one encompassed with a winding maze,
That cannot tread the way out readily,
So with herself is she in mutiny,
  To live or die, which of the twain were better,
  When life is shamed and death reproach's
    debtor.°
                       1155

"To kill myself," quoth she, "alack, what were it,
But with my body my poor soul's pollution?°
They that lose half with greater patience bear it
Than they whose whole is swallowed in confusion.
That mother tries a merciless conclusion   1160

Who, having two sweet babes, when death takes
  one,
Will slay the other and be nurse to none.

"My body or my soul, which was the dearer,
When the one pure, the other made divine?
Whose love of either to myself was nearer,   1165
When both were kept for Heaven and Collatine?
Aye me! The bark peeled from the lofty pine,
  His leaves will wither and his sap decay.
  So must my soul, her bark being peeled away.

"Her house is sacked, her quiet interrupted,   1170
Her mansion battered by the enemy.
Her sacred temple spotted, spoiled, corrupted,
Grossly engirt with daring infamy.
Then let it not be called impiety
  If in this blemished fort I make some hole   1175
  Through which I may convey this troubled soul.

"Yet die I will not till my Collatine
Have heard the cause of my untimely death,
That he may vow, in that sad hour of mine,
Revenge on him that made me stop my breath.
My stainèd blood to Tarquin I'll bequeath,   1181
  Which by him tainted shall for him be spent,
  And as his due writ in my testament.

"My honor I'll bequeath unto the knife
That wounds my body so dishonorèd.   1185
'Tis honor to deprive dishonored life.
The one will live, the other being dead.
So of shame's ashes shall my fame be bred,
  For in my death I murder shameful scorn.
  My shame so dead, mine honor is newborn.

"Dear lord of that dear jewel I have lost,   1191
What legacy shall I bequeath to thee?
My resolution,° love, shall be thy boast,
By whose example thou revenged mayst be.
How Tarquin must be used, read it in me.   1195
  Myself, thy friend, will kill myself, thy foe,
  And, for my sake, serve thou false Tarquin so.

"This brief abridgment of my will I make:
My soul and body to the skies and ground;
My resolution, Husband, do thou take;   1200
Mine honor be the knife's that makes my wound;
My shame be his that did my fame confound;
  And all my fame that lives disbursèd° be
  To those that live and think no shame of me.

"Thou, Collatine, shalt oversee° this will.   1205
How was I overseen° that thou shalt see it!

1124. **stops . . . rests:** pauses in a piece of music.   1127. **dumps:** melancholy tunes.   1128. **Philomel:** the nightingale. See l.1079,n.   1132. **diapason:** part in the music.   1133. **burden-wise:** like a refrain.   1135. **against a thorn:** The nightingale was supposed to sing with her breast touching a thorn. 1140. **frets:** the bars on a stringed instrument. See Pl. 18b. 1142. **for:** because.   1144. **seated . . . way:** situated in some obscure place.   1147. **kinds:** natures.   1155. **death . . . debtor:** reproach owes death a debt; i.e., shame demands suicide. 1157. **poor . . . pollution:** Suicide to a Christian is mortal sin; by the Romans it was regarded as an honorable end after defeat or disgrace.

1193. **resolution:** courage.   1203. **disbursed:** distributed. 1205. **oversee:** be executor of.   1206. **overseen:** bewitched.

My blood shall wash the slander of mine ill.
My life's foul deed, my life's fair end shall free it.
Faint not, faint heart, but stoutly say ' So be it.'
   Yield to my hand; my hand shall conquer thee.
   Thou dead, both die and both shall victors be."

This plot° of death when sadly she had laid,
And wiped the brinish pearl from her bright eyes,
With untuned tongue she hoarsely calls her maid,
Whose swift obedience to her mistress hies.   1215
For fleet-winged duty with thought's feathers flies.
   Poor Lucrece' cheeks unto her maid seem so
   As winter meads when sun doth melt their snow.

Her mistress she doth give demure good morrow,
With soft slow tongue, true mark of modesty,   1220
And sorts° a sad look to her lady's sorrow,
For why° her face wore sorrow's livery,
But durst not ask of her audaciously
   Why her two suns were cloud-eclipsèd so,
   Nor why her fair cheeks overwashed with woe.

But as the earth doth weep, the sun being set,   1226
Each flower moistened like a melting eye,
Even so the maid with swelling drops 'gan wet
Her circled eyne, enforced by sympathy
Of those fair suns set in her mistress' sky,   1230
   Who in a salt-waved ocean quench their light,
   Which makes the maid weep like the dewy night.

A pretty while these pretty creatures stand,
Like ivory conduits° coral cisterns filling.
One justly weeps; the other takes in hand   1235
No cause, but company, of her drops spilling.°
Their gentle sex to weep are often willing,
   Grieving themselves to guess at others' smarts,
   And then they drown their eyes or break their
      hearts.

For men have marble, women waxen, minds,   1240
And therefore are they formed as marble will.
The weak oppressed, the impression of strange
   kinds
Is formed in them by force, by fraud, or skill.
Then call them not the authors of their ill,
   No more than wax shall be accounted evil   1245
   Wherein is stamped the semblance of a devil.°

Their smoothness, like a goodly champaign° plain,
Lays open all the little worms° that creep.
In men, as in a rough-grown grove, remain
Cave-keeping evils that obscurely sleep.   1250

Through crystal walls each little mote° will peep.
   Though men can cover crimes with bold stern
      looks,
   Poor women's faces are their own faults' books.

No man inveigh against the withered flower,   1254
But chide rough winter that the flower hath killed.
Not that devoured, but that which doth devour,
Is worthy blame. Oh, let it not be hild°
Poor women's faults, that they are so fulfilled°
   With men's abuses. Those proud lords to blame
   Make weak-made women tenants to their shame.

The precedent° whereof in Lucrece view,   1261
Assailed by night with circumstances strong
Of present death, and shame that might ensue
By that her death, to do her husband wrong.
Such danger to resistance did belong,   1265
   That dying fear through all her body spread,
   And who cannot abuse° a body dead?

By this, mild patience bid fair Lucrece speak
To the poor counterfeit of her complaining.°
" My girl," quoth she, " on what occasion break
Those tears from thee, that down thy cheeks are
      raining?   1271
If thou dost weep for grief of my sustaining,
   Know, gentle wench, it small avails my mood.
   If tears could help, mine own would do me good.

" But tell me, girl, when went " — and there she
      stayed   1275
Till after a deep groan — " Tarquin from hence? "
" Madam, ere I was up," replied the maid,
" The more to blame my sluggard negligence.
Yet with the fault I thus far can dispense.
   Myself was stirring ere the break of day,   1280
   And ere I rose was Tarquin gone away.

" But, lady, if your maid may be so bold,
She would request to know your heaviness."
" Oh, peace! " quoth Lucrece, " if it should be told,
The repetition cannot make it less,   1285
For more it is than I can well express;
   And that deep torture may be called a hell
   When more is felt than one hath power to tell.

" Go, get me hither paper, ink, and pen.
Yet save that labor, for I have them here.   1290
What should I say? One of my husband's men
Bid thou be ready by and by to bear
A letter to my lord, my love, my dear.
   Bid him with speed prepare to carry it;   1294
   The cause craves haste and it will soon be writ."

1212. plot: plan.   1221. sorts: fits.   1222. For why: because.
1234. conduits: fountains.   1236. No . . . spilling: she (the maid) had no reason to weep except to keep her mistress company.   1245–46. evil . . . devil: pronounced "eale" and "deale."   1247. champaign: open meadow.   1248. worms: all creeping creatures.

1251. mote: speck of dust.   1257. hild: held.   1258. fulfilled: i.e., the woman should not be blamed for the lust of the man.   1261. precedent: example.   1267. abuse: outrage.   1269. counterfeit .. complaining: imitation of her sorrow; i.e., the weeping maid.

Her maid is gone, and she prepares to write,
First hovering o'er the paper with her quill.°
Conceit and grief an eager combat fight.
What wit sets down is blotted straight with will.°
This is too curious good,° this blunt and ill.   1300
  Much like a press of people at a door,
  Throng her inventions,° which shall go before.

At last she thus begins: "Thou worthy lord
Of that unworthy wife that greeteth thee,
Health to thy person! Next vouchsafe t' afford —
If ever, love, thy Lucrece thou wilt see —   1306
Some present speed to come and visit me.
  So, I commend me from our house in grief.
  My woes are tedious, though my words are brief."

Here folds she up the tenor° of her woe,   1310
Her certain sorrow writ uncertainly.
By this short schedule Collatine may know
Her grief, but not her grief's true quality.
She dares not thereof make discovery,
  Lest he should hold it her own gross abuse,   1315
  Ere she with blood had stained her stained ex-
  cuse.

Besides, the life and feeling of her passion
She hoards, to spend when he is by to hear her,
When sighs and groans and tears may grace the
  fashion
Of her disgrace, the better so to clear her   1320
From that suspicion which the world might bear
  her.
  To shun this blot, she would not blot the letter
  With words, till action might become them bet-
  ter.

To see sad sights moves more than hear them told,
For then the eye interprets to the ear   1325
The heavy motion that it doth behold,
When every part a part of woe doth bear.
'Tis but a part of sorrow that we hear.
  Deep sounds° make lesser noise than shallow
  fords,°
  And sorrow ebbs, being blown with wind of
  words.   1330

Her letter° now is sealed and on it writ
"At Ardea to my lord with more than haste."
The post attends,° and she delivers it,
Charging the sour-faced groom to hie as fast
As lagging fowls before the northern blast.   1335

Speed more than speed but dull and slow she
  deems.
  Extremity still urgeth such extremes.

The homely villain° curtsys to her low,
And blushing on her, with a steadfast eye
Receives the scroll without or yea or no,   1340
And forth with bashful innocence doth hie.
But they whose guilt within their bosoms lie
  Imagine every eye beholds their blame,
  For Lucrece thought he blushed to see her shame,

When, silly groom! God wot,° it was defect   1345
Of spirit, life, and bold audacity.
Such harmless creatures have a true respect
To talk in deeds, while others saucily
Promise more speed but do it leisurely.
  Even so this pattern of the worn-out age   1350
  Pawned honest looks, but laid no words to gage.°

His kindled° duty kindled her mistrust,
That two red fires in both their faces blazed.
She thought he blushed, as knowing Tarquin's lust,
And blushing with him, wistly° on him gazed.
Her earnest eye did make him more amazed.   1356
  The more she saw the blood his cheeks replenish,
  The more she thought he spied in her some blem-
  ish.

But long she thinks till he return again,
And yet the duteous vassal° scarce is gone.   1360
The weary time she cannot entertain,
For now 'tis stale to sigh, to weep and groan.
So woe hath wearied woe, moan tirèd moan,
  That she her plaints a little while doth stay,
  Pausing for means to mourn some newer way.

At last she calls to mind where hangs a piece 1366
Of skillful painting, made for Priam's Troy;°
Before the which is drawn the power of Greece,
For Helen's rape the city to destroy,
Threatening cloud-kissing Ilion° with annoy,   1370
  Which the conceited° painter drew so proud,
  As heaven, it seemed, to kiss the turrets bowed.

A thousand lamentable objects there,
In scorn of nature,° art gave lifeless life.

1297. quill: quill pen.   1299. will: desire — to avoid detailing
her shame.   1300. curious good: elaborately expressed.
1302. inventions: ideas, composition.   1310. tenor: summary —
a legal term meaning the substance of a document.   1329. sounds:
channels. fords: streams.   1331. letter: See App. 6: Letters.
1333. attends: waits.

1338. villain: servant.   1345. wot: knows.   1351. Pawned . . .
gage: promised to be faithful by his bashful look, but not by
words.   1352. kindled: blushing.   1355. wistly: steadfastly.
1360. vassal: servant.   1367. painting . . . Troy: Elaborate
pictures of battles were popular in Shakespeare's day, and the
theme of the great siege of Troy was common. For a long description of the sack, see *Haml*, II.ii.466–541. Shakespeare afterward dramatized parts of the saga in *Tr & Cr*, wherein Helen,
Ajax, Ulysses, Nestor, Achilles, Priam, Hecuba, and the rest
appear as characters.   1370. Ilion: the citadel of Troy.
1371. conceited: clever.   1374. In . . . nature: more realistically
than life.

Many a dry drop seemed a weeping tear, 1375
Shed for the slaughtered husband by the wife.
The red blood reeked,° to show the painter's strife,°
    And dying eyes gleamed forth their ashy lights
    Like dying coals burnt out in tedious nights.

There might you see the laboring pioner° 1380
Begrimed with sweat and smearèd all with dust,
And from the towers of Troy they would appear
The very eyes of men through loopholes thrust,
Gazing upon the Greeks with little lust.° 1384
    Such sweet observance in this work was had
    That one might see those far-off eyes look sad.

In great commanders grace and majesty
You might behold, triumphing in their faces,
In youth, quick bearing and dexterity.
And here and there the painter interlaces 1390
Pale cowards, marching on with trembling paces,
    Which heartless peasants did so well resemble
    That one would swear he saw them quake and
        tremble.

In Ajax and Ulysses, oh, what art
Of physiognomy might one behold!
The face of either ciphered° either's heart; 1395
Their face their manners most expressly told.
In Ajax' eyes blunt rage and rigor rolled,
    But the mild glance that sly Ulysses lent 1399
    Showed deep regard and smiling government.°

There pleading might you see grave Nestor stand,
As 'twere encouraging the Greeks to fight,
Making such sober action with his hand
That it beguiled attention, charmed the sight. 1404
In speech, it seemed, his beard all silver white
    Wagged up and down, and from his lips did fly
    Thin winding breath which purled° up to the
        sky.

About him were a press of gaping faces
Which seemed to swallow up his sound advice.
All jointly listening, but with several graces, 1410
As if some mermaid° did their ears entice,
Some high, some low, the painter was so nice.°
    The scalps of many, almost hid behind,
    To jump up higher seemed, to mock the mind.

Here one man's hand leaned on another's head,
His nose being shadowed by his neighbor's ear.
Here one being thronged° bears back, all bollen°
    and red; 1417

Another smothered seems to pelt° and swear,
And in their rage such signs of rage they bear
    As, but for loss of Nestor's golden words, 1420
    It seemed they would debate with angry swords.

For much imaginary work was there.
Conceit deceitful, so compact, so kind,°
That for Achilles' image stood his spear
Griped in an armèd hand; himself behind 1425
Was left unseen, save to the eye of mind.
    A hand, a foot, a face, a leg, a head,
    Stood for the whole to be imaginèd.

And from the walls of strong-besiegèd Troy
When their brave hope, bold Hector, marched to
        field, 1430
Stood many Trojan mothers sharing joy
To see their youthful sons bright weapons wield.
And to their hope they such odd° action yield
    That through their light joy seemèd to appear,
    Like bright things stained, a kind of heavy fear.

And from the strand of Dardan,° where they
        fought, 1436
To Simois'° reedy banks the red blood ran,
Whose waves to imitate the battle sought
With swelling ridges; and their ranks began
To break upon the gallèd shore, and than° 1440
    Retire again, till meeting greater ranks
    They join and shoot their foam at Simois' banks.

To this well-painted piece is Lucrece come,
To find a face where all distress is stelled.°
Many she sees where cares have carvèd some, 1445
But none where all distress and dolor dwelled,
Till she despairing Hecuba beheld,
    Staring on Priam's wounds with her old eyes,
    Which bleeding under Pyrrhus' proud foot lies.

In her the painter had anatomized° 1450
Time's ruin, beauty's wreck, and grim care's reign.
Her cheeks with chaps° and wrinkles were dis-
        guised.
Of what she was no semblance did remain.
Her blue blood changed to black in every vein,
    Wanting the spring that those shrunk pipes had
        fed, 1455
    Showed life imprisoned in a body dead.

On this sad shadow Lucrece spends her eyes,
And shapes her sorrow to the beldam's woes,
Who nothing wants to answer her but cries,
And bitter words to ban° her cruel foes. 1460

1377. reeked: steamed. strife: effort. 1380. pioner: pioneer,
miner. 1384. lust: eagerness. 1396. ciphered: displayed.
1400. government: self-control. 1407. purled: wreathed.
1411. mermaid: The mermaid was believed to entice mariners to destruction by her singing. 1412. nice: particular.
1417. thronged: crowded. bollen: swollen.

1418. pelt: assail with curses. 1423. kind: natural. 1433. odd:
extraordinary. 1436. strand of Dardan: the Trojan plain,
surrounding the city. 1437. Simois: a marshy river north of
Troy. 1440. than: then. 1444. stelled: fixed. 1450. anatomized: dissected, shown in minute detail. 1452. chaps: lower
part of the cheek. 1460. ban: curse.

The painter was no god to lend her those,
  And therefore Lucrece swears he did her wrong,
  To give her so much grief and not a tongue.

"Poor instrument," quoth she, "without a sound,
I'll tune thy woes with my lamenting tongue,   1465
And drop sweet balm in Priam's painted wound,
And rail on Pyrrhus that hath done him wrong,
And with my tears quench Troy that burns so long,
  And with my knife scratch out the angry eyes
  Of all the Greeks that are thine enemies.   1470

"Show me the strumpet° that began this stir,
That with my nails her beauty I may tear.
Thy heat of lust, fond Paris, did incur
This load of wrath that burning Troy doth bear.
Thy eye kindled the fire that burneth here,   1475
  And here in Troy, for trespass of thine eye,°
  The sire, the son, the dame and daughter die.

"Why should the private pleasure of some one
Become the public plague of many moe?°
Let sin, alone committed, light alone   1480
Upon his head that hath transgressèd so.
Let guiltless souls be freed from guilty woe.
  For one's offense why should so many fall,
  To plague a private sin in general?

"Lo, here weeps Hecuba, here Priam dies,   1485
Here manly Hector faints, here Troilus swounds,
Here friend by friend in bloody channel lies,
And friend to friend gives unadvisèd° wounds,
And one man's lust these many lives confounds.°
  Had doting Priam checked his son's desire,
  Troy had been bright with fame and not with
  fire."   1491

Here feelingly she weeps Troy's painted woes,
For sorrow, like a heavy-hanging bell
Once set on ringing, with his own weight goes.
Then little strength rings out the doleful knell:
So Lucrece, set a-work, sad tales doth tell   1496
  To penciled° pensiveness and colored sorrow.
  She lends them words, and she their looks doth
  borrow.

She throws her eyes about the painting round,
And who she finds forlorn she doth lament.   1500
At last she sees a wretched image bound,°
That piteous looks to Phrygian° shepherds lent.°
His face, though full of cares, yet showed content.
  Onward to Troy with the blunt swains he goes,
  So mild that Patience seemed to scorn his woes.

1471. **strumpet:** harlot; i.e., Helen.   1476. **for . . . eye:** because your eye sinned.   1479. **moe:** more.   1488. **unadvised:** unintentional.   1489. **confounds:** destroys.   1497. **penciled:** painted. 1501. **image bound:** figure fixed in the painting.   1502. **Phrygian:** of Asia Minor. **lent:** caused.

In him the painter labored with his skill   1506
To hide deceit and give the harmless show
An humble gait, calm looks, eyes wailing still,
A brow unbent that seemed to welcome woe,
Cheeks neither red nor pale, but mingled so   1510
  That blushing red no guilty instance° gave,
  Nor ashy pale the fear that false hearts have.

But, like a constant and confirmèd devil,
He entertained a show° so seeming just,
And therein so ensconced his secret evil,   1515
That jealousy° itself could not mistrust
False-creeping craft and perjury should thrust
  Into so bright a day such black-faced storms,
  Or blot with Hell-born sin such saintlike forms.

The well-skilled workman this mild image drew
For perjured Sinon,° whose enchanting° story
The credulous old Priam after slew.   1522
Whose words, like wildfire,° burnt the shining glory
Of rich-built Ilion, that the skies were sorry,
  And little stars shot from their fixèd places,
  When their glass fell wherein they viewed their
  faces.°   1526

This picture she advisedly° perused,
And chid the painter for his wondrous skill,
Saying some shape in Sinon's was abused —
So fair a form lodged not a mind so ill.   1530
And still on him she gazed, and gazing still
  Such signs of truth in his plain face she spied
  That she concludes the picture was belied.°

"It cannot be," quoth she, "that so much guile" —
She would have said "can lurk in such a look,"
But Tarquin's shape came in her mind the while,
And from her tongue "can lurk" from "cannot"
  took.   1537
"It cannot be" she in that sense forsook,
  And turned it thus: "It cannot be, I find,
  But such a face should bear a wicked mind.

"For even as subtle Sinon here is painted,   1541
So sober-sad, so weary and so mild,
As if with grief or travail° he had fainted,
To me came Tarquin armèd; so beguiled
With outward honesty, but yet defiled   1545
  With inward vice. As Priam him did cherish,
  So did I Tarquin; so my Troy did perish.

1511. **guilty instance:** appearance of guilt.   1514. **entertained a show:** assumed an appearance.   1516. **jealousy:** suspicion. 1521. **Sinon:** sent by the Greeks to persuade the Trojans to drag the Wooden Horse inside Troy. See III *Hen VI*, III.ii.190,n. **enchanting:** bewitching.   1523. **wildfire:** sometimes called "Greek fire," a primitive form of incendiary bomb.   1526. **When . . . faces:** a farfetched conceit, meaning that the towers of Ilion were so high and bright that they reflected the stars.   1527. **advisedly:** carefully.   1533. **belied:** false.   1543. **travail:** labor.

" Look, look, how listening Priam wets his eyes,
To see those borrowed° tears that Sinon sheds!
Priam, why art thou old and yet not wise?　　1550
For every tear he falls° a Trojan bleeds.
His eye drops fire, no water thence proceeds.
　　Those round clear pearls of his that move thy pity
　　Are balls of quenchless fire to burn thy city.

" Such devils steal effects° from lightless Hell,
For Sinon in his fire doth quake with cold,　　1556
And in that cold hot-burning fire doth dwell.
These contraries such unity do hold
Only to flatter fools and make them bold.
　　So Priam's trust false Sinon's tears doth flatter,
　　That he finds means to burn his Troy with
　　　water."°　　　　　　　　　　　　　　1561

Here, all enraged, such passion her assails,
That patience is quite beaten from her breast.
She tears the senseless Sinon with her nails,
Comparing him to that unhappy guest　　1565
Whose deed hath made herself herself detest.
　　At last she smilingly with this gives o'er.
　　" Fool, fool! " quoth she, " his wounds will not
　　　be sore."

Thus ebbs and flows the current of her sorrow,
And time doth weary time with her complaining.
She looks for night, and then she longs for morrow,
And both she thinks too long with her remaining.
Short time seems long in sorrow's sharp sustaining.
　　Though woe be heavy, yet it seldom sleeps,　　1574
　　And they that watch see time how slow it creeps.

Which all this time hath overslipped her thought,
That she with painted images hath spent,
Being from the feeling of her own grief brought
By deep surmise of others' detriment,
Losing her woes in shows of discontent.　　1580
　　It easeth some, though none it ever cured,
　　To think their dolor others have endured.

But now the mindful messenger come back
Brings home his lord and other company,
Who finds his Lucrece clad in mourning black.
And round about her tear-distainèd eye　　1586
Blue circles streamed, like rainbows in the sky.
　　These water-galls° in her dim element
　　Foretell new storms to those already spent.

Which when her sad-beholding husband saw,　　1590
Amazedly in her sad face he stares.

Her eyes, though sod° in tears, looked red and raw,
Her lively color killed with deadly cares.
He hath no power to ask her how she fares.
　　Both stood, like old acquaintance in a trance,
　　Met far from home, wondering each other's
　　　chance.°　　　　　　　　　　　　　1596

At last he takes her by the bloodless hand,
And thus begins: " What uncouth° ill event
Hath thee befallen, that thou dost trembling stand?
Sweet love, what spite° hath thy fair color spent?
Why art thou thus attired in discontent?　　1601
　　Unmask, dear dear, this moody heaviness,
　　And tell thy grief, that we may give redress.

Three times with sighs she gives her sorrow fire,
Ere once she can discharge one word of woe.　　1605
At length addressed° to answer his desire,
She modestly prepares to let them know
Her honor is ta'en prisoner by the foe;
　　While Collatine and his consorted lords
　　With sad attention long to hear her words.　　1610

And now this pale swan in her watery nest
Begins the sad dirge of her certain ending:°
" Few words," quoth she, " shall fit the trespass
　　best,　　　　　　　　　　　　　　1613
Where no excuse can give the fault amending.
In me moe woes than words are now depending,
　　And my laments would be drawn out too long,
　　To tell them all with one poor tirèd tongue.

" Then be this all the task it hath to say:
Dear Husband, in the interest of thy bed
A stranger came, and on that pillow lay　　1620
Where thou wast wont to rest thy weary head.
And what wrong else may be imaginèd
　　By foul enforcement might be done to me,
　　From that, alas, thy Lucrece is not free.

" For in the dreadful dead of dark midnight,　　1625
With shining falchion in my chamber came
A creeping creature, with a flaming light,
And softly cried ' Awake, thou Roman dame,
And entertain my love, else lasting shame
　　On thee and thine this night I will inflict,　　1630
　　If thou my love's desire do contradict.

" ' For some hard-favored° groom of thine,' quoth
　　he,
' Unless thou yoke thy liking to my will,
I'll murder straight, and then I'll slaughter thee,

1549. borrowed: false.　**1551. falls:** lets fall.　**1555. effects:** false outward signs.　**1561. That . . . water:** i.e., as a result of his feigned tears Troy is burned.　**1588. water-galls:** a secondary, reflected rainbow, regarded as a sure sign of rain.

1592. sod: sodden, boiled.　**1596. chance:** misfortune.　**1598. uncouth:** strange.　**1600. spite:** outrage.　**1606. addressed:** made ready.　**1611–12. swan . . . ending:** It was believed that the swan for the first and only time in its life burst into lovely song just before its death.　**1632. hard-favored:** ugly.

And swear I found you where you did fulfill 1635
The loathsome act of lust, and so did kill
   The lechers in their deed. This act will be
   My fame, and thy perpetual infamy.'

" With this, I did begin to start and cry,
And then against my heart he set his sword, 1640
Swearing, unless I took all patiently,
I should not live to speak another word.
So should my shame still rest upon record,
   And never be forgot in mighty Rome
   The adulterate death of Lucrece and her groom.

" Mine enemy was strong, my poor self weak, 1646
And far the weaker with so strong a fear.
My bloody judge forbade my tongue to speak,
No rightful plea might plead for justice there.
His scarlet lust came evidence to swear 1650
   That my poor beauty had purloined his eyes,
   And when the judge is robbed, the prisoner dies.

" Oh, teach me how to make mine own excuse,
Or, at the least, this refuge let me find: 1654
Though my gross blood be stained with this abuse
Immaculate and spotless is my mind.
That was not forced; that never was inclined
   To accessary° yieldings, but still pure
   Doth in her poisoned closet yet endure."

Lo, here, the hopeless merchant° of this loss, 1660
With head declined, and voice damned up with woe,
With sad-set eyes and wretched arms across,
From lips new-waxen pale begins to blow
The grief away that stops his answer so.
   But, wretched as he is, he strives in vain; 1665
   What he breathes out his breath drinks up again.

As° through an arch the violent roaring tide
Outruns the eye that doth behold his haste,
Yet in the eddy boundeth in his pride
Back to the strait° that forced him on so fast, 1670
In rage sent out, recalled in rage, being past.
   Even so his sighs, his sorrows, make a saw,°
   To push grief on and back the same grief draw.

Which speechless woe of his, poor she attendeth
And his untimely frenzy thus awaketh: 1675
" Dear lord, thy sorrow to my sorrow lendeth
Another power. No flood by raining slaketh.

My woe too sensible° thy passion maketh
   More feeling-painful. Let it then suffice 1679
   To drown one woe, one pair of weeping eyes.

" And for my sake, when I might charm thee so,
For she that was thy Lucrece, now attend me:
Be suddenly revengèd on my foe,
Thine, mine, his own. Suppose thou dost defend me
From what is past? The help that thou shalt lend
   me 1685
   Comes all too late, yet let the traitor die,
   For sparing justice feeds iniquity.

" But ere I name him, you fair lords," quoth she,
Speaking to those that came with Collatine,
" Shall plight your honorable faiths to me, 1690
With swift pursuit to venge this wrong of mine,
For 'tis a meritorious fair design
   To chase injustice with revengeful arms.
   Knights, by their oaths, should right poor ladies'
      harms."

At this request, with noble disposition 1695
Each present lord began to promise aid,
As bound in knighthood to her imposition,°
Longing to hear the hateful foe bewrayed.
But she, that yet her sad task hath not said, 1699
   The protestation stops. " Oh, speak," quoth she,
   " How may this forcèd stain be wiped from me?

" What is the quality of my offense,
Being constrained with dreadful circumstance?
May my pure mind with the foul act dispense,
My low-declinèd honor to advance?° 1705
May any terms acquit me from this chance?
   The poisoned fountain clears itself again,
   And why not I from this compellèd stain? "

With this, they all at once began to say,
Her body's stain her mind untainted clears, 1710
While with a joyless smile she turns away
The face, that map which deep impression bears
Of hard misfortune, carved in it with tears.
   " No, no," quoth she, " no dame hereafter living
   By my excuse shall claim excuse's giving." 1715

Here with a sigh, as if her heart would break,
She throws forth Tarquin's name: " He, he," she
   says,
But more than " he " her poor tongue could not
   speak
Till after many accents and delays,
Untimely breathing, sick and short assays, 1720
   She utters this: " He, he, fair lords, 'tis he,
   That guides this hand to give this wound to me."

1658. accessary: willing. 1660. merchant: owner. 1667–71. As
. . . past: When the water runs rapidly under a narrow bridge,
part of the stream at the edge of the main flow eddies round in a
circle until it is again caught up in the flow. Probably Shakespeare
took this image from the water which rushed under the narrow
piers of London Bridge, especially at high tide. 1670. strait:
narrow passage. 1672. make a saw: i.e., his sighs make a noise
like a saw, pushed to and fro through a plank.

1678. sensible: full of feeling. 1697. imposition: command.
1705. advance: raise up, promote.

Even here she sheathèd in her harmless breast
A harmful knife, that thence her soul unsheathed.
That blow did bail it from the deep unrest   1725
Of that polluted prison where it breathed.
Her contrite sighs unto the clouds bequeathed
    Her wingèd sprite, and through her wounds doth
        fly
    Life's lasting date from canceled destiny.°

Stone-still, astonished° with this deadly deed,   1730
Stood Collatine and all his lordly crew,
Till Lucrece' father, that beholds her bleed,
Himself on her self-slaughtered body threw,
And from the purple fountain Brutus° drew   1734
    The murderous knife, and, as it left the place,
    Her blood, in poor revenge, held it in chase.

And bubbling from her breast, it doth divide
In two slow rivers, that the crimson blood
Circles her body in on every side,
Who, like a late-sacked island, vastly stood   1740
Bare and unpeopled in this fearful flood.
    Some of her blood still pure and red remained,
    And some looked black, and that false Tarquin
        stained.

About the mourning and congealèd face
Of that black blood a watery rigol° goes,   1745
Which seems to weep upon the tainted place.
And ever since, as pitying Lucrece' woes,
Corrupted blood some watery token shows,
    And blood untainted still doth red abide,
    Blushing at that which is so putrified.   1750

"Daughter, dear daughter," old Lucretius cries,
"That life was mine which thou hast here deprived.
If in the child the father's image lies,
Where shall I live now Lucrece is unlived?°
Thou wast not to this end from me derived.   1755
    If children predecease progenitors,
    We are their offspring, and they none of ours.

"Poor broken glass, I often did behold
In thy sweet semblance my old age new born.
But now that fair fresh mirror, dim and old,   1760
Shows me a bare-boned death° by time outworn.
Oh, from thy cheeks my image thou hast torn,
    And shivered all the beauty of my glass,
    That I no more can see what once I was.°

1729. Life's . . . destiny: the end of life canceled by fate. The
image is that of a canceled lease.   **1730. astonished:** astounded.
1734. Brutus: Lucius Junius Brutus was the nephew of Tarquin
the Proud, tyrant of Rome and father of Tarquin who violated
Lucrece. Tarquin the Proud had murdered Brutus's elder brother,
but he spared Brutus, who had cunningly pretended to be an
idiot. After the suicide of Lucrece, Brutus dropped this pose
and became the leader of her avengers.   **1745. rigol:** circle.
1754. unlived: dead.   **1761. bare-boned death:** skeleton.
1763-64. And . . . was: See Sonnets 1 and 2.

"O Time, cease thou thy course and last no longer,
If they surcease to be that should survive.   1766
Shall rotten Death make conquest of the stronger
And leave the faltering feeble souls alive?
The old bees die, the young possess their hive.
    Then live, sweet Lucrece, live again, and see
    Thy father die, and not thy father thee!"   1771

By this, starts Collatine as from a dream,
And bids Lucretius give his sorrow place,
And then in key-cold Lucrece' bleeding stream
He falls, and bathes the pale fear in his face,
And counterfeits to die with her a space,   1776
    Till manly shame bids him possess his breath,
    And live to be revengèd on her death.

The deep vexation of his inward soul
Hath served a dumb arrest upon his tongue   1780
Who, mad that sorrow should his use control
Or keep him from heart-easing words so long,
Begins to talk; but through his lips do throng   1783
    Weak words, so thick come in his poor heart's aid
    That no man could distinguish what he said.

Yet sometime "Tarquin" was pronouncèd plain,
But through his teeth, as if the name he tore.
This windy tempest, till it blow up rain,
Held back his sorrow's tide, to make it more.
At last it rains, and busy winds give o'er.   1790
    Then son and father weep with equal strife,
    Who should weep most, for daughter or for wife.

The one doth call her his, the other his,
Yet neither may possess the claim they lay.
The father says "She's mine." "Oh, mine she is"
Replies her husband. "Do not take away   1796
My sorrow's interest; let no mourner say
    He weeps for her, for she was only mine,
    And only must be wailed by Collatine."

"Oh," quoth Lucretius, "I did give that life   1800
Which she too early and too late hath spilled."
"Woe, woe," quoth Collatine, "she was my wife.
I owed her, and 'tis mine that she hath killed."
"My daughter" and "my wife" with clamors
        filled
    The dispersed air, who, holding Lucrece' life,
    Answered their cries, "my daughter" and "my
        wife."   1806

Brutus, who plucked the knife from Lucrece' side,
Seeing such emulation in their woe,
Began to clothe his wit in state and pride,
Burying in Lucrece' wound his folly's show.   1810
He with the Romans was esteemèd so
    As silly-jeering idiots are with kings,
    For sportive words and uttering foolish things.

But now he throws that shallow habit by
Wherein deep policy did him disguise,   1815
And armed his long-hid wits advisedly
To cheek the tears in Collatinus' eyes.
"Thou wrongèd lord of Rome," quoth he, "arise.
    Let my unsounded self, supposed a fool,
    Now set thy long-experienced wit to school.°

"Why, Collatine, is woe the cure for woe?   1821
Do wounds help wounds, or grief help grievous
        deeds?
Is it revenge to give thyself a blow
For his foul act by whom thy fair wife bleeds?
Such childish humor from weak minds proceeds.
    Thy wretched wife mistook the matter so,   1826
    To slay herself, that should have slain her foe.

"Courageous Roman, do not steep thy heart
In such relenting dew of lamentations,
But kneel with me and help to bear thy part   1830
To rouse our Roman gods with invocations
That they will suffer these abominations,
    Since Rome herself in them doth stand disgraced,
    By our strong arms from forth her fair streets
        chased.

1820. set . . . school: i.e., become your teacher.

"Now, by the Capitol° that we adore,   1835
And by this chaste blood so unjustly stained,
By heaven's fair sun that breeds the fat earth's store,
By all our country rights in Rome maintained,
And by chaste Lucrece' soul that late complained
    Her wrongs to us, and by this bloody knife,   1840
    We will revenge the death of this true wife!"

This said, he struck his hand upon his breast,
And kissed the fatal knife, to end° his vow,
And to his protestation urged the rest,   1844
Who, wondering at him, did his words allow.°
Then jointly to the ground their knees they bow,
    And that deep vow, which Brutus made before,
    He doth again repeat, and that they swore.

When they had sworn to this advisèd° doom,
They did conclude to bear dead Lucrece thence,
To show her bleeding body thorough° Rome,   1851
And so to publish Tarquin's foul offense.
Which being done with speedy diligence,
    The Romans plausibly° did give consent
    To Tarquin's everlasting banishment.   1855

1835. Capitol: regarded as the center of government, law, and
order in Rome.   1843. end: confirm.   1845. allow: approve.
1849. advised: determined.   1851. thorough: through.
1854. plausibly: with applause.

THE PASSIONATE PILGRIM

Introduction

The Passionate Pilgrim is a prettily printed little volume, intended for the pocket of the poetry lover. Its pages measure only 4½ by 2¾ inches. It was first published in 1599, without entry in the Stationers' Register, carrying the title page: *THE PASSIONATE PILGRIME. By W. Shakespeare. At London. Printed for W. Iaggard and are to be sold by W. Leake, at the Greyhound in Paules Churchyard. 1599.* A second title page was inserted before XVI (" It was a lording's daughter ") reading *Sonnets To sundry notes of Music.*

The volume contains twenty-one poems (or twenty if XIV and XV are regarded as one poem). They were originally without numbers or titles but they have been numbered by editors for convenience. Actually only five poems in the collection were certainly written by Shakespeare: I — a version of Sonnet 138 with many differences of reading; II — a version of Sonnet 144 (these two sonnets had not hitherto appeared in print); III, V, and XVII — sonnets and love poems from *Love's Labor's Lost,* which had been printed in 1598.

Of the remaining poems, the following have been identified: VIII and XXI are from Richard Barnfield's *Poems in divers Humors,* printed in 1598; XI is from Bartholomew Griffin's *Fidessa* (1596); XVIII had appeared in Thomas Weekes' collection of *Madrigals* in 1597; XX is a version of Christopher Marlowe's famous poem " Come live with me and be my love," with one stanza of the answer said to have been written by Sir Walter Ralegh; a shortened version of XII was later included in Thomas Deloney's *Garland of Goodwill, 1631.* The origin of the rest is unknown.

A third edition of *The Passionate Pilgrim* was printed by Jaggard in 1612 with the title page: *The Passionate Pilgrime Or Certaine Amorous Sonnets, betweene Venus and Adonis, newly corrected and augmented. By W. Shakespeare. The third Edition. Whereunto is newly added two Loue-Epistles, the first from Paris to Hellen, and Hellens answere backe againe to Paris. Printed by W. Iaggard. 1612.* The additional " Love-Epistles " were actually written by Thomas Heywood. Heywood was annoyed at the unauthorized printing of his poems, and in his *Apology for Actors,* 1612, he protested:

" Here likewise, I must necessarily insert a manifest injury done me in that work, by taking the two Epistles of Paris to Helen, and Helen to Paris, and printing them in a less volume, under the name of another, which may put the world in opinion I might steal them from him; and he to do himself right, hath since published them in his own name: but as I must acknowledge my lines not worthy his patronage, under whom he hath published them, so the Author I know much offended with M. Jaggard that (altogether unknown to him) presumed to make so bold with his name."

The Passionate Pilgrim was thus a dishonest publication. Nor is it of any great interest, except as it shows that by 1599 Shakespeare's name on a title page was likely to attract a poetry lover.

1°

When my love swears that she is made of truth,
I do believe her, though I know she lies,
That she might think me some untutored youth,
Unskillful in the world's false forgeries.
Thus vainly thinking that she thinks me young, 5
Although I know my years be past the best,
I smiling credit her false-speaking tongue,
Outfacing faults in love with love's ill rest.°
But wherefore says my love that she is young?
And wherefore say not I that I am old? 10
Oh, love's best habit is a soothing tongue,
And age, in love, loves not to have years told.
    Therefore I'll lie with love, and love with me,
    Since that our faults in love thus smothered be.

I. another version of Sonnet 138.

8. **Outfacing ... rest:** an ambiguous sentence, perhaps meaning that her tongue putting a bold face on her faithlessness fills me with uneasiness.

II°

Two loves I have, of comfort and despair,
That like two spirits do suggest me still;
My better angel is a man right fair,
My worser spirit a woman colored ill.
To win me soon to hell, my female evil   5
Tempteth my better angel from my side,
And would corrupt my saint to be a devil,
Wooing his purity with her fair pride.
And whether that my angel be turned fiend,
Suspect I may, yet not directly tell.   10
For being both to me, both to each friend,
I guess one angel in another's hell.
 The truth I shall not know, but live in doubt,
 Till my bad angel fire my good one out.

III°

Did not the heavenly rhetoric of thine eye,
'Gainst whom the world could not hold argument,
Persuade my heart to this false perjury?
Vows for thee broke deserve not punishment.
A woman I forswore; but I will prove,   5
Thou being a goddess, I forswore not thee:
My vow was earthly, thou a heavenly love;
Thy grace being gained cures all disgrace in me.
My vow was breath, and breath a vapor is.
Then, thou fair sun, that on this earth doth shine,
Exhale this vapor vow; in thee it is.   11
If broken, then it is no fault of mine.
 If by me broke, what fool is not so wise
 To break an oath, to win a paradise?

IV

Sweet Cytherea,° sitting by a brook
With young Adonis, lovely, fresh, and green,
Did court the lad with many a lovely look,
Such looks as none could look but beauty's queen.
She told him stories to delight his ear,   5
She showed him favors to allure his eye.
To win his heart, she touched him here and there —
Touches so soft still conquer chastity.
But whether unripe years did want conceit,°
Or he refused to take her figured proffer,°   10
The tender nibbler would not touch the bait,
But smile and jest at every gentle offer.
 Then fell she on her back, fair queen, and
  toward.°
 He rose and ran away. Ah, fool too froward.°

v°

If love make me forsworn, how shall I swear to
 love?
Oh, never faith could hold, if not to beauty vowed.

II. another version of Sonnet 144.
III. a version of Longaville's sonnet in *LLL*, IV.iii.60–73.
IV. 1. Cytherea: Venus. 9. want conceit: lack understanding. 10. figured proffer: suggestive offer. 13. toward: willing. 14. froward: perverse.
V. Berowne's sonnet in *LLL*, IV.ii.109–22.

Though to myself forsworn, to thee I'll constant
 prove.
Those thoughts, to me like oaks, to thee like osiers
 bowed.°
Study his bias° leaves, and make his book thine
 eyes,   5
Where all those pleasures live that art can compre-
 hend.
If knowledge be the mark, to know thee shall suf-
 fice;
Well-learnèd is that tongue that well can thee com-
 mend.
All ignorant that soul that sees thee without won-
 der,
Which is to me some praise, that I thy parts admire.
Thine eye Jove's lightning seems, thy voice his
 dreadful thunder,   11
Which, not to anger bent, is music and sweet fire.
 Celestial as thou art, oh, do not love that wrong,
 To sing heaven's praise with such an earthly
  tongue.

VI

Scarce had the sun dried up the dewy morn,
And scarce the herd gone to the hedge for shade,
When Cytherea, all in love forlorn,
A longing tarriance° for Adonis made
Under an osier growing by a brook,   5
A brook where Adon used to cool his spleen.°
Hot was the day; she hotter that did look
For his approach, that often there had been.
Anon he comes, and throws his mantle by,
And stood stark naked on the brook's green brim.
The sun looked on the world with glorious eye,   11
Yet not so wistly° as this queen on him.
 He, spying her, bounced in, whereas° he stood:
 "O Jove," quoth she, "why was not I a flood!"

VII

Fair is my love, but not so fair as fickle,
Mild as a dove, but neither true nor trusty,
Brighter than glass and yet, as glass is, brittle,
Softer than wax and yet as iron rusty.
 A lily pale, with damask° dye to grace her,   5
 None fairer, nor none falser to deface° her.

Her lips to mine how often hath she joined,
Between each kiss her oaths of true love swearing!
How many tales to please me hath she coined,
Dreading my love, the loss thereof still fearing!   10
 Yet in the midst of all her pure protestings,
 Her faith, her oaths, her tears, and all were jest-
  ings.

4. osiers bowed: bent willow twigs. 5. bias: inclination, course
See App. 13.
VI. 4. tarriance: tarrying. 6. spleen: hot temper. 12. wistly:
eagerly. 13. whereas: just where.
VII. 5. damask: pink. 6. deface: cancel her beauty.

She burned with love, as straw with fire flameth;
She burned out love, as soon as straw outburneth;
She framed° the love, and yet she foiled° the fram-
    ing;   15
She bade love last, and yet she fell aturning.
    Was this a lover, or a lecher whether?°
    Bad in the best, though excellent in neither.

VIII

If music and sweet poetry agree,
As they must needs, the sister and the brother,
Then must the love be great 'twixt thee and me,
Because thou lov'st the one and I the other.
Dowland° to thee is dear, whose heavenly touch 5
Upon the lute doth ravish human sense.
Spenser to me, whose deep conceit is such
As passing° all conceit° needs no defense.
Thou lovest to hear the sweet melodious sound
That Phoebus'° lute,° the queen of music, makes;
And I in deep delight am chiefly drowned   11
When as himself to singing he betakes.
    One god is god of both, as poets feign;
    One knight loves both, and both in thee remain.

IX°

Fair was the morn when the fair queen of love,
Paler for sorrow than her milk-white dove,
For Adon's sake, a youngster proud and wild,
Her stand she takes upon a steep-up° hill.
Anon Adonis comes with horn and hounds.   5
She, silly queen, with more than love's good will,
Forbade the boy he should not pass those grounds.
" Once," quoth she, " did I see a fair sweet youth
Here in these brakes deep-wounded with a boar,
Deep in the thigh, a spectacle of ruth!°   10
See, in my thigh," quoth she, " here was the sore."
    She showèd hers. He saw more wounds than one,
    And blushing fled. and left her all alone.

X

Sweet rose, fair flower, untimely plucked, soon
    vaded,°
Plucked in the bud and vaded in the spring!
Bright orient pearl, alack, too timely shaded!
Fair creature, killed too soon by death's sharp sting!
    Like a green plum that hangs upon a tree,   5
    And falls through wind before the fall should be,

I weep for thee and yet no cause I have;
For why° thou left'st me nothing in thy will.

And yet thou left'st me more than I did crave,
For why I cravèd nothing of thee still.°   10
    Oh, yes, dear friend, I pardon crave of thee.
    Thy discontent thou didst bequeath to me.

XI

Venus, with young Adonis sitting by her
Under a myrtle shade, began to woo him.
She told the youngling how god Mars did try her,
And as he fell to her, so fell she to him.
" Even thus," quoth she, " the warlike god em-
    braced me,"   5
And then she clipped° Adonis in her arms.
" Even thus," quoth she, " the warlike god unlaced
    me,"
As if the boy should use like loving charms.
" Even thus," quoth she, " he seizèd on my lips,"
And with her lips on his did act the seizure.   10
And as she fetchèd breath, away he skips,
And would not take her meaning nor her pleasure.
    Ah, that I had my lady at this bay,°
    To kiss and clip me till I run away!

XII

Crabbèd age and youth cannot live together:
Youth is full of pleasance, age is full of care.
Youth like summer morn, age like winter weather;
Youth like summer brave,° age like winter bare.
Youth is full of sport, age's breath is short;   5
    Youth is nimble, age is lame;
Youth is hot and bold, age is weak and cold;
    Youth is wild, and age is tame.
Age, I do abhor thee; youth, I do adore thee.
    Oh, my love, my love is young!   10
Age, I do defy thee. Oh, sweet shepherd, hie° thee,
    For methinks thou stay'st too long.

XIII

Beauty is but a vain and doubtful good;
A shining gloss that vadeth suddenly;
A flower that dies when first it 'gins to bud;
A brittle glass that's broken presently.°
    A doubtful good, a gloss, a glass, a flower,   5
    Lost, vaded, broken, dead within an hour.

And as goods lost are seld° or never found,
As vaded gloss no rubbing will refresh,
As flowers dead lie withered on the ground,
As broken glass no cement can redress,   10
    So beauty blemished once 's for ever lost,
    In spite of physic, painting, pain and cost.

---

15. framed: caused. **foiled:** overthrew. **17. whether:** rather.
    VIII. 5. Dowland: John Dowland, the most popular com-
poser of songs and airs to be sung to the lute. **7–8. conceit . . .
conceit:** skill . . . imagination. **8. passing:** surpassing. **10. Phoebus:** Apollo, god of music and the arts. **lute:** See Pl. 18d.
    IX. In this poem the second line has been accidentally omitted.
4. steep-up: steep. **10. ruth:** pity.
    X. 1. vaded: faded. **8. For why:** because.

10. still: ever.
    XI. 6. clipped: held fast. **13. at . . . bay:** a metaphor from
stag hunting, when the stag turns to face his pursuers. Here the
man is the stag, and Venus the pursuer.
    XII. 4. brave: fine and gay. **11. hie:** hasten.
    XIII. 4. presently: at once. **7. seld:** seldom.

XIV

Good night, good rest. Ah, neither be my share.
She bade good night that kept my rest away;
And daffed° me to a cabin hanged with care,
To descant on the doubts of my decay.°
   "Farewell," quoth she, "and come again to-
     morrow."   5
   Fare well I could not, for I supped with sorrow.

Yet at my parting sweetly did she smile,
In scorn or friendship, nill° I construe whether.
'T may be, she joyed to jest at my exile,
'T may be, again to make me wander thither.   10
   "Wander," a word for shadows like myself,
   As take the pain, but cannot pluck the pelf.°

XV°

Lord, how mine eyes throw gazes to the east!
My heart doth charge the watch;° the morning rise
Doth cite° each moving sense from idle rest.
Not daring trust the office of mine eyes,   4
   While Philomela° sits and sings, I sit and mark,
   And wish her lays were tunèd like the lark.

For she doth welcome daylight with her ditty,
And drives away dark dreaming night.
The night so packed,° I post° unto my pretty.   9
Heart hath his hope and eyes their wishèd sight,
   Sorrow changed to solace and solace mixed with
     sorrow,
   For why, she sighed, and bade me come tomor-
     row.

Were I with her, the night would post too soon,
But now are minutes added to the hours.
To spite me now, each minute seems a moon,°   15
Yet not for me, shine sun to succor flowers!
   Pack night, peep day; good day, of night now
     borrow.
   Short, night, tonight, and length thyself tomor-
     row.

SONNETS

To Sundry notes of music.

XVI

It was a lording's° daughter, the fairest one of three,
That likèd of her master° as well as well might be,

XIV. 3. daffed: waved aside. 4. descant . . . decay: to
wonder whether I was ruined. descant: lit., to warble like a bird.
8. nill: will not. 12. pelf: profit.
   XV. Some editors regard these stanzas as part of XIV. In the
original, XIV ll. 1–12 are printed on one page, XVI ll. 1–12 on
the next, and ll. 13–18 on the third. 2. charge . . . watch: give
the watch their orders; i.e., stay awake all night. The town
watch went on duty at the beginning of the night. The process
is illustrated in M Ado, III.iii. 3. cite: summon. 5. Philomela: the nightingale. 9. packed: sent packing, dispatched.
post: hasten. 15. moon: month.
   XVI. 1. lording: a fancy word for lord. 2. master: schoolmaster, tutor.

Till looking on an Englishman, the fair'st that eye
   could see,
   Her fancy fell aturning.
Long was the combat doubtful that love with love
   did fight,   5
To leave the master loveless, or kill the gallant
   knight.
To put in practice either, alas, it was a spite
   Unto the silly damsel!
But one must be refused; more mickle° was the
   pain
That nothing could be used to turn them both to
   gain,   10
For of the two the trusty knight was wounded with
   disdain.
   Alas, she could not help it!
Thus art° with arms contending was victor of the
   day,
Which by a gift of learning did bear the maid away.
Then, lullaby, the learnèd man hath got the lady
   gay,   15
   For now my song is ended.

XVII°

On a day, alack the day!
Love, whose month was ever May,
Spied a blossom passing fair,
Playing in the wanton air.
Through the velvet leaves the wind   5
All unseen 'gan passage find.
That the lover, sick to death,
Wished himself the heaven's breath,
"Air," quoth he, "thy cheeks may blow.
Air, would I might triumph so!   10
But, alas! my hand hath sworn
Ne'er to pluck thee from thy thorn.
Vow, alack! for youth unmeet,°
Youth, so apt to pluck a sweet.
Thou for whom Jove would swear   15
Juno but an Ethiope were,
And deny himself for Jove,
Turning mortal for thy love."

XVIII

My flocks feed not,
My ewes breed not,
My rams speed not;
   All is amiss.
Love's denying,   5
Faith's defying,°
Heart's renying,°
   Causer of this.
All my merry jigs are quite forgot,

9. mickle: mighty. 13. art: learning.
   XVII. taken from Dumain's love poem, LLL, IV.iii.101–20.
13. unmeet: not fit.
   XVIII. 6. defying: rejecting. 7. renying: refusing.

All my lady's love is lost, God wot.   10
Where her faith was firmly fixed in love,
There a nay° is placed without remove.
One silly cross°
Wrought all my loss.
  O frowning Fortune, cursèd, ficklè dame!   15
For now I see
Inconstancy
  More in women than in men remain.

In black mourn I,
All fears scorn I,   20
Love hath forlorn me,
  Living in thrall.°
Heart is bleeding,
All help needing,
O cruel speeding,   25
  Fraughtèd° with gall.
My shepherd's pipe can sound no deal.°
My wether's bell° rings doleful knell.
My curtal° dog, that wont to have played,
Plays not at all, but seems afraid.   30
My sighs so deep
Procure° to weep,
  In howling wise, to see my doleful plight.
How sighs resound
Through heartless ground,   35
  Like a thousand vanquished men in bloody fight!

Clear wells spring not,
Sweet birds sing not,
Green plants bring not
  Forth their dye.   40
Herds stand weeping,
Flocks all sleeping,
Nymphs back peeping
  Fearfully.
All our pleasure known to us poor swains,   45
All our merry meetings on the plains,
All our evening sport from us is fled,
All our love is lost, for Love is dead.
Farewell, sweet lass,
Thy like ne'er was   50
  For a sweet content, the cause of all my moan.
Poor Corydon°
Must live alone.
  Other help for him I see that there is none.

XIX

When as thine eye hath chose the dame,
And stalled° the deer that thou shouldst strike,

Let reason rule things worthy blame,
As well as fancy,° partial wight.°
  Take counsel of some wiser head,   5
  Neither too young nor yet unwed.

And when thou comest thy tale to tell,
Smooth not thy tongue with filèd talk,°
Lest she some subtle practice° smell —
A cripple soon can find a halt° —   10
  But plainly say thou lovest her well,
  And set thy person forth to sell.

What though her frowning brows be bent,
Her cloudy looks will calm ere night:
And then too late she will repent   15
That thus dissembled her delight,
  And twice desire, ere it be day,
  That which with scorn she put away.

What though she strive to try her strength,
And ban° and brawl, and say thee nay,   20
Her feeble force will yield at length,
When craft hath taught her thus to say:
  "Had women been so strong as men,
  In faith, you had not had it then."

And to her will frame all thy ways.   25
Spare not to spend, and chiefly there
Where thy desert may merit praise,
By ringing in thy lady's ear.
  The strongest castle, tower and town,
  The golden bullet beats it down.   30

Serve always with assurèd° trust,
And in thy suit be humble true.
Unless thy lady prove unjust,°
Press never thou to choose anew.
  When time shall serve, be thou not slack   35
  To proffer, though she put thee back.

The wiles and guiles that women work,
Dissembled with an outward show,
The tricks and toys that in them lurk,
The cock that treads them shall not know.   40
  Have you not heard it said full oft,
  A woman's nay doth stand for naught?

Think° women still to strive with men,
To sin and never for to saint.

4. fancy: love. partial wight: biased lover. The original text reads "party-all might." 8. filed talk: smooth phrases. 9. practice: plot. 10. A . . . halt: a proverb meaning that a professional beggar will soon detect an impostor. 20. ban: curse. 31. assured: confident. 33. unjust: unfaithful. 43–46. Think . . . attaint: The stanza probably means "Women are as eager as men to commit sin and as reluctant to be saints: There is no joy when they are sullied (*attaint*) with age." by . . . then: if the reading is correct may mean "by that holy time." The whole stanza is difficult, and the text is probably corrupt.

12. nay: refusal.   13. cross: thwarting.   22. thrall: servitude.
26. Fraughted: laden.   27. no deal: not at all.   28. wether's
bell: the bell hung round the bellwether, or leader of a flock of
sheep.   29. curtal: with tail cut short.   32. Procure: cause.
52. Corydon: a name often given to a shepherd in pastoral poetry.
  XIX. 2. stalled: cornered.

There is no heaven, by holy then, 45
When time with age shall them attaint.
    Were kisses all the joys in bed,
    One woman would another wed.

But, soft! enough — too much, I fear —
Lest that my mistress hear my song. 50
She will not stick to round me on th' ear,°
To teach my tongue to be so long.
    Yet will she blush, here be it said,
    To hear her secrets so bewrayed.

xx°

Live with me, and be my love,
And we will all the pleasures prove
That hills and valleys, dales and fields,
And all the craggy mountains yields.

There will we sit upon the rocks, 5
And see the shepherds feed their flocks,
By shallow rivers, by whose falls
Melodious birds sing madrigals.°

There will I make thee a bed of roses,
With a thousand fragrant posies, 10
A cap of flowers, and a kirtle°
Embroidered all with leaves of myrtle.

A belt of straw and ivy buds,
With coral clasps and amber studs;
And if these pleasures may thee move, 15
Then live with me and be my love.

Love's Answer

If that the world and love were young,
And truth in every shepherd's tongue,
These pretty pleasures might me move
To live with thee and be thy love. 20

XXI

    As it fell upon a day
    In the merry month of May,
Sitting in a pleasant shade
Which a grove of myrtles made,
Beasts did leap and birds did sing, 5
Trees did grow and plants did spring.
Everything did banish moan,
Save the nightingale° alone.

She, poor bird, as all forlorn,
Leaned her breast up-till° a thorn, 10
And there sung the doleful'st ditty,
That to hear it was great pity.
"Fie, fie, fie," now would she cry;
"Tereu, Tereu!"° by and by.
That to hear her so complain, 15
Scarce I could from tears refrain.
For her griefs so lively shown
Made me think upon mine own.
Ah, thought I, thou mourn'st in vain!
None takes pity on thy pain: 20
Senseless trees they cannot hear thee;
Ruthess beasts they will not cheer thee.
King Pandion° he is dead.
All thy friends are lapped in lead.°
All thy fellow birds do sing, 25
Careless of thy sorrowing.
Even so, poor bird, like thee,
None alive will pity me.
Whilst as fickle Fortune smiled,
Thou and I were both beguiled. 30
    Everyone that flatters thee
Is no friend in misery.
Words are easy, like the wind;
Faithful friends are hard to find.
Every man will be thy friend 35
Whilst thou hast wherewith to spend,
But if store of crowns be scant,
No man will supply thy want.
If that one be prodigal,
Bountiful they will him call, 40
And with suchlike flattering,
"Pity but he were° a king."
If he be addict to vice,
Quickly him they will entice.
If to women he be bent, 45
They have at commandèment.
But if Fortune once do frown,
Then farewell his great renown.
They that fawned on him before
Use his company no more. 50
He that is thy friend indeed,
He will help thee in thy need.
If thou sorrow, he will weep;
If thou wake, he cannot sleep.
Thus of every grief in heart 55
He with thee doth bear a part.
These are certain signs to know
Faithful friend from flattering foe.

51. round . . . ear: usually means "to whisper," but here apparently "to strike."

XX. This is the famous and popular song attributed to Marlowe, with the reply by Sir Walter Ralegh. It appears in various versions. See *M Wives*, III.i.17–26. 8. madrigals: songs sung in parts. 11. kirtle: skirt.

XXI. 8. nightingale: For the sad tale of Philomela the nightingale, see *T Andr*, Intro. pp. 295b–96a.

10. up-till: against. 14. Tereu: the nightingale's cry of reproach against Tereus. 23. Pandion: the father of Procne and Philomela. 24. lapped in lead: in their leaden coffins. 42. but he were: that he is not.

THE PHOENIX AND THE TURTLE

Introduction

In 1601 a little collection of poems was published with the title *Love's Martyr: Or, Rosalins Complaint. Allegorically shadowing the truth of Loue, in the constant Fate of the Phoenix and Turtle. A Poeme interlaced with much varietie and raritie; now first translated out of the venerable Italian Torquato Caeliano, by Robert Chester. With the true legend of famous King Arthur, the last of the nine Worthies, being the first Essay of a new Brytish Poet: collected out of diuerse Authenticall Records. To these are added some new compositions, of seuerall moderne Writers whose names are subscribed to their seuerall workes, vpon the first subiect: viz. the Phoenix and Turtle. Mar: — Mutare dominum non potest liber notus. London Imprinted for E. B. 1601.* These " new compositions " are thus prefaced:

" Hereafter follow diverse Poeticall Essaies on the former Subiect; viz: the Turtle and Phoenix. Done by the best and chiefest of our moderne writers, with their names subscribed to their particular works: neuer before extant. And (now first) consecrated by them all generally, to the loue and merite of the true-noble Knight, Sir John Salisburie. Dignum laude virum Musa vetat mori. Anchora Spei. MDCI."

The writers' names are Shakespeare, John Marston, George Chapman, and Benjamin Jonson, as well as " Chorus Vatum " (the chorus of poets) and " Ignoto."

Shakespeare's little contribution to the collection is difficult and enigmatical, and no one has yet offered any satisfactory interpretation of its inner meaning. On the surface it celebrates, in obscure symbolism, the spiritual union of the Phoenix (true love) and the Turtledove (constancy). It is likely, however, that the poem has other and inner meanings that were well understood by the small circle of readers for whom it was originally intended. Until these persons and events are discovered, *The Phoenix and the Turtle* will remain an enigma.

Let the bird of loudest lay,°
On the sole Arabian tree,°
Herald sad and trumpet be,
To whose sound chaste wings obey.

But thou shrieking harbinger,°   5
Foul precurrer° of the fiend,
Augur° of the fever's end,
To this troop come thou not near!

From this session interdict°
Every fowl of tyrant wing,   10
Save the eagle, feathered king.
Keep the obsequy° so strict.

Let the priest in surplice white,
That defunctive° music can,°

Be the death-divining° swan,   15
Lest the requiem lack his° right.

And thou treble-dated° crow,
That thy sable gender makest
With the breath thou givest and takest,°
'Mongst our mourners shalt thou go.   20

Here the anthem doth commence:
Love and Constancy is dead,
Phoenix and the turtle fled
In a mutual flame from hence.

So they loved, as love in twain   25
Had the essence° but in one;
Two distincts, division none.
Number there in love was slain.°

1. **lay**: song.   2. **Arabian tree**: See *Temp*, III.iii.23,n.   5. **shrieking harbinger**: i.e., the screech owl. **harbinger**: prophet of disaster, lit., one who goes before to make preparations for a royal journey.   6. **precurrer**: forerunner.   7. **Augur**: prophet. See *MND*, V.i.383–85.   9. **interdict**: ban.   12. **obsequy**: funeral rite.   14. **defunctive**: belonging to the dead. **can**: is skillful in.

15. **death-divining**: foretelling death in its song. The swan was supposed to sing only once in its life — just before its death.   16. **his**: its.   17. **treble-dated**: The life of a crow was believed to be as long as three human lives.   18–19. **That . . . takest**: i.e., that shows your black nature (*sable gender*) in your dismal croakings.   26. **essence**: essential nature.   28. **Number . . . slain**: i.e., they are no longer two, but a single unity.

Hearts remote, yet not asunder;
Distance, and no space was seen   30
'Twixt the turtle and his Queen.
But° in them it were a wonder.

So between them love did shine,
That the turtle saw his right
Flaming in the phoenix' sight;   35
Either was the other's mine.°

Property was thus appalled,
That the self was not the same;
Single nature's double name
Neither two nor one was called.°   40

Reason, in itself confounded,
Saw division grow together,
To themselves yet either neither,
Simple were so well compounded°

That it cried, How true a twain   45
Seemeth this concordant one!

Love hath reason, reason none,
If what parts can so remain.

Whereupon it made this threne°
To the phoenix and the dove,   50
Co-supremes and stars of love,
As chorus to their tragic scene.

THRENOS

Beauty, Truth, and Rarity,
Grace in all simplicity,
Here enclosed in cinders lie.   55

Death is now the phoenix' nest,
And the turtle's loyal breast
To eternity doth rest,

Leaving no posterity.
'Twas not their infirmity,   60
It was married chastity.

Truth may seem, but cannot be;
Beauty brag, but 'tis not she;
Truth and Beauty buried be.

To this urn let those repair   65
That are either true or fair;
For these dead birds sigh a prayer.

32. But: except; i.e., in others this would be a marvel. **33–36. So . . mine:** The image of this stanza is of two lovers finding themselves in each other. **mine:** gold mine, treasure. **37–40. Property . . . called:** The idea is that two personalities have become so merged that neither can be distinguished. **Property:** lit., that which is proper (individual) to a person. **43–44. To . . . compounded:** The idea of the previous stanza is continued — both are now compounded into a new unity.

49. threne: in Greek literary terms "threnos," a dirge.

SONNETS AND A LOVER'S COMPLAINT

Introduction

Shakespeare's sonnets are the most discussed and disputed of all collections of poetry in the English language, and every conceivable view has been expressed about them. Most critics, however, tend to join one of two parties. Some agree with Wordsworth, who wrote:

> Scorn not the Sonnet; Critic, you have frowned,
> Mindless of its just honor; with this key
> Shakespeare unlocked his heart.

Others follow Matthew Arnold, who said:

> Others abide our question. Thou art free.
> We ask and ask — Thou smilest and art still,
> Out-topping knowledge.

These two observations sum up the main divisions between those who believe that Shakespeare was an inscrutable sphinx about whose personality we can know nothing and those who believe that Shakespeare has laid bare his heart in his plays and his sonnets.

There are indeed many lovers of poetry to whom all discussion of the personal and historical " problems " of the sonnets is distasteful, and who feel, not unreasonably, that such delicate works of art should not be dissected and anatomized. Such readers should leave these problems alone; indeed, theories about the sonnets are dreary unless the student studies the whole question for himself at first hand.

There are, however, certain indisputable facts. On May 20, 1609, Thomas Thorpe entered in the Stationers' Register " a Booke called Shakespeares sonnettes." On June 19, Edward Alleyn, in jotting down a list of purchases, noted " Shakspers Sonnets 5d." The title printed on Thorpe's quarto reads:

SHAKE-SPEARES
SONNETS

Neuer before Imprinted.

AT LONDON

By *G. Eld for T. T.* and are
to be solde by *John Wright,* dwelling
at Christ Church gate,
1609.

The volume is dedicated in a curious and enigmatic way:

TO . THE . ONLIE . BEGETTER . OF .
THESE . INSVING . SONNETS .
Mr W. H. ALL . HAPPINESSE .
AND . THAT . ETERNITIE .
PROMISED .
BY .
OVR . EVER-LIVING . POET .
WISHETH .
THE . WELL-WISHING .
ADVENTVRER . IN .
SETTING .
FORTH .

T. T.

By 1609 some of the sonnets were at least eleven years old. In 1598 Meres, in his *Palladis Tamia* (see pp. 11b–12a), in writing of Shakespeare as a poet said: " As the soul of Euphorbus was thought to live in Pythagoras: so the sweet witty soul of Ovid lives in mellifluous and honey-tongued Shakespeare, witness his *Venus and Adonis,* his *Lucrece,* his sugared Sonnets among his private friends, &c." In 1599, William Jaggard had issued a little book called *" The Passionate Pilgrime.* By W. Shakespeare." It contained twenty short poems, of which the first two were versions of Sonnets 138 and 144, and Nos. 3, 5, 17, poems taken from *Love's Labor's Lost.* The rest of the poems in the volume were by other authors.

The volume of Shakespeare's *Sonnets* printed by Thorpe contains in all one hundred and fifty-four sonnets. As arranged in his edition, they tell a story of sorts. The first seventeen sonnets form a series. They are addressed to a beautiful youth and call on him to marry so that his type may be preserved and continued in his children. From Sonnet 18 to Sonnet 126, the poet addresses the youth on various topics and occasions and in a variety of moods. A sense of intimacy increases; admiration becomes love; but there is little method in the arrangement and no continuous story. The poet at first is shy and tongue-tied in the presence of his friend, and can only express himself in writing (23). The poet is separated from him by travel, but thinks continuously of the youth (27). He is outcast, but comforted by the thought of his love (29). He warns his friend not to honor him publicly, lest he become tainted with scandal (36). The friend steals the poet's mistress, but is forgiven (40–42). The poet has the youth's picture, which he wears at his breast on a journey (47–49). The poet is elderly (73). He is jealous because others seek the youth's patronage, especially one poet whose verse bears " proud full sail " (78–86). The poet gently rebukes the youth for wantonness (96). After a spring and a summer of separation the poet comes back to his friend (97–98). The poet congratulates the youth on his escape from a " confined doom " (107). He is reconciled after absence (109). He is disgusted with his profession (110–11). He defends himself against the charge of ingratitude (117). He apologizes for giving away the " tables " which the youth had given him (122). The last of this series is Sonnet 126.

Then follow twenty-six sonnets addressed to a dark woman, whom the poet has loved passionately but reluctantly. She is skillful in playing on the virginals, faithless, wanton, physically unattractive, false to her husband, and yet irresistibly desirable. The collection ends with two conventional love sonnets on Cupid.

There are thus a number of problems. If only we could answer any one of a dozen questions for certain, the enigma of the sonnets might be solved and our knowledge of Shakespeare greatly increased. The mysteries begin with the dedication. Even this has been interpreted in more than one way. Most assume that T. T. regards Mr. W. H. as the only begetter of the sonnets; but some read the dedication as implying that Mr. W. H. is wishing happiness to the only begetter.

Before considering these problems it is well to look at the probable date when Shakespeare's sonnets were written and at their place in Elizabethan poetry.

The Elizabethan sonnet is the most famous of all verse forms, but its vogue was very short-lived. The sonnet form had first been introduced into English through Wyatt and Surrey's translations from Petrarch, in the 1530's, and a few other English poets had written sonnets before 1590; but the popularity of the form was directly due to the publication of Sir Philip Sidney's

Astrophel and Stella in the spring of 1591. Anything written by Sidney was eagerly read, and this series of sonnets was at times so personal and sincere that it revealed to English poets possibilities hitherto unrealized. The most important collections of sonnets — Daniel's *Delia*, Lodge's *Phyllis*, Constable's *Diana*, Drayton's *Idea*, Spenser's *Amoretti* — all appeared within the next five years, and thereafter for several years sonnets were seldom published. It is most likely, therefore, that most of Shakespeare's sonnets were written during this vogue; that is, not before 1592 and probably not much after 1598. In style, they are akin rather to *Venus and Adonis* and some of the earlier plays. The greatest number of parallels of phrase and idea are to be found in *Love's Labor's Lost, Two Gentlemen of Verona, Romeo and Juliet, Venus and Adonis, Lucrece, Richard the Second* and *Richard the Third,* all of which were written by 1595. Moreover, if the sonnets stand in approximately the order of their writing, it seems clear from Sonnet 104 that they cover a period of more than three years.

As for " Mr. W. H.," various candidates have been put forward. Sir Sidney Lee noted that an edition of the *Fourfold Meditations* of Father Robert Southwell, the Jesuit martyr, printed in 1606, was dedicated " To the Right Worshipful and Vertuous Gentleman, Matthew Saunders, Esquire. W. H. wisheth, with long life, a prosperous achievement of his good desires." Lee identified this W. H. with William Hall, a printer in a small way. Another guess is Sir William Harvey, who married the mother of the Earl of Southampton in 1598. If the Earl of Southampton was the beautiful youth, then this guess has much to recommend it; for Harvey was a likely person to have had access to the original manuscript. He has also a greater claim to be the " W. H." of Father Southwell's *Meditations,* for the Southampton family were strongly Catholic, whereas W. Hall, the printer, published anti-Catholic books.

A third candidate is William Herbert, Earl of Pembroke, but it seems unlikely that a nobleman of his standing would ever have been addressed as " Mr. W. H."

As for the fair youth, there are at present two main choices, Henry Wriothesley, Earl of Southampton, and William Herbert, Earl of Pembroke. Southampton was born on October 6,

1573 and succeeded to the title at the age of seven. He was therefore a ward (i.e., a minor needing a guardian) until he came of age. Lord Burleigh, Queen Elizabeth's great Minister, was his guardian. To Southampton Shakespeare dedicated *Venus and Adonis,* which was entered in the Stationers' Register on April 18, 1593 (see p. 10a). Just over a year later, Shakespeare dedicated *Lucrece* to Southampton in warmer terms (see p. 10a) which suggest that in the interval he had received considerable encouragement. As a young man Southampton was conspicuously handsome, but for some years he refused to marry, although Lord Burleigh himself proposed his own granddaughter as a suitable wife. In 1595, Southampton fell in love with Mistress Elizabeth Vernon, one of Queen Elizabeth's maids of honor, whom, to the Queen's great anger, he secretly married in 1598. Southampton was a personal friend and adoring follower of the Earl of Essex, and shared in his misfortune (see p. 24a–b).

The claims of William Herbert, Earl of Pembroke, are based principally on his initials and on the dedication to him and to his brother of the first folio in 1623, in which Heming and Condell declare " that their Lordships have been pleased to think these trifles somewhat heretofore, and have prosecuted both them and their Author living with so much favor." In 1595 there was a proposal to betroth Pembroke, then aged fifteen, to the daughter of Sir George Carey, son of the patron of the Lord Chamberlain's Company. Apart from this, there is no further known connection between him and Shakespeare.

With Pembroke, however, is linked the name of Mistress Mary Fitton, another of Queen Elizabeth's maids of honor. She was a lively lady who became the mother of three illegitimate children by different men, but afterward married richly and died very respectable. Pembroke was the father of her first child and there was much scandal in court about their behavior. Mistress Fitton is a candidate for the doubtful honor of being considered the " Dark Lady "; she was not, however, conspicuously dark. This theory is known as the " Herbert theory." Its great glory is that it was itself the " only begetter " of George Bernard Shaw's play *The Dark Lady of the Sonnets,* and its preface.

Various other candidates have been put forward. Some take Sonnet 20, line, 7, in its original spelling as a pointer:

A man in hew all *Hews* in his controwling.

There seems to be a pun in this line on the name Hughes. The theory is ancient, but Oscar Wilde championed it, claiming that the youth was a boy actor called William Hughes. The records of Elizabethan acting companies are fairly complete, and there is no trace of any actor of this name. There are many other theories, but until some further definite fact is indisputably established, they must remain theories, and the student of poetry can neglect them all.

The sonnet is one of the most difficult forms for sublime or permanent poetry. It is admirable for saying something short, pretty, effective, complimentary, but its very formality and rigidity are against it. There are very few perfect sonnets. The normal form is fixed at fourteen lines of iambic pentameters and a poet cannot always pack or expand his thoughts into so exact a mold. Moreover, Shakespeare chose the most difficult kind of sonnet pattern — three quatrains followed by a couplet. When successful, the couplet folds up the whole poem in a neat final conclusion, but too often the couplet is an awkward appendix to a twelve-line poem.

Shakespeare's sonnets, as poetry, are perhaps rather for private reading than public discussion, for they touch sensitive readers in secret ways. To such readers all discussion of the problems is impertinent and all criticism superfluous.

A Lover's Complaint, which tells the sad story of a girl seduced by a deceitful lover, was printed as an appendix to the Sonnets. It is one of several Elizabethan poems, such as Samuel Daniel's *Complaint of Rosamond* (1592) and Anthony Chute's *Beauty Dishonored* (1593), in which deserted ladies lament their bitter fate. Many critics doubt on grounds of style that the poem is Shakespeare's work.

Sonnets

1

From fairest creatures we desire increase,
That thereby beauty's rose° might never die,
But as the riper should by time decrease,
His tender heir might bear his memory.
But thou, contracted to thine own bright eyes,°   5
Feed'st thy light's flame with self-substantial° fuel,
Making a famine where abundance lies,
Thyself thy foe, to thy sweet self too cruel.
Thou that art now the world's fresh ornament
And only herald to the gaudy spring,   10
Within thine own bud buriest thy content°
And, tender churl,° makest waste in niggarding.°
   Pity the world, or else this glutton be,
   To eat the world's due, by the grave and thee.°

2

When forty winters shall besiege thy brow
And dig deep trenches in thy beauty's field,
Thy youth's proud livery, so gazed on now,
Will be a tattered weed,° of small worth held.
Then being asked where all thy beauty lies,   5
Where all the treasure of thy lusty days,
To say within thine own deep-sunken eyes
Were an all-eating° shame and thriftless° praise.
How much more praise deserved thy beauty's use
If thou couldst answer, " This fair child of mine   10
Shall sum my count° and make my old excuse,"°
Proving his beauty by succession° thine!
   This were to be new-made when thou art old,
   And see thy blood warm when thou feel'st it cold.

3

Look in thy glass, and tell the face thou viewest
Now is the time that face should form another,
Whose fresh repair° if now thou not renewest,
Thou dost beguile the world, unbless some mother.

For where is she so fair whose uneared° womb 5
Disdains the tillage of thy husbandry?
Or who is he so fond° will be the tomb
Of his self-love,° to stop posterity?
Thou art thy mother's glass,° and she in thee
Calls back the lovely April of her prime.   10
So thou through windows of thine age shalt see,
Despite of wrinkles, this thy golden time.
   But if thou live, remembered not to be,°
   Die single, and thine image dies with thee.

4

Unthrifty loveliness, why dost thou spend
Upon thyself thy beauty's legacy?°
Nature's bequest gives nothing, but doth lend,
And being frank,° she lends to those are free.°
Then, beauteous niggard, why dost thou abuse   5
The bounteous largess° given thee to give?
Profitless usurer, why dost thou use
So great a sum of sums, yet canst not live?°
For having traffic with thyself alone,
Thou of thyself thy sweet self dost deceive.   10
Then how, when nature calls thee to be gone,
What acceptable audit canst thou leave?
   Thy unused beauty must be tombed with thee,
   Which, used, lives th' executor° to be.

5

Those hours that with gentle work did frame
The lovely gaze° where every eye doth dwell
Will play the tyrants to the very same
And that unfair° which fairly doth excel.
For never-resting time leads summer on   5
To hideous winter and confounds° him there,
Sap checked with frost and lusty leaves quite gone,
Beauty o'ersnowed and bareness everywhere.
Then, were not summer's distillation° left,
A liquid prisoner pent in walls of glass,   10
Beauty's effect° with beauty were bereft,
Nor it, nor no remembrance what it was.

Sonnet 1: 2. beauty's rose: The rose is often used as a symbol of youthful perfection. Cf. *Haml*, III.i.160; *I Hen IV*, I.iii.175–76.   5. contracted . . . eyes: married to your own reflection. 6. self-substantial: of its own substance; i.e., consuming itself. 11. content: that which you contain; i.e., your child that might be. 12. churl: miser. niggarding: being niggardly. 14. To . . . thee: i.e., you and the grave will consume what is due to the world; viz., your posterity.

Sonnet 2: 4. tattered weed: ragged garment. 8. all-eating: devouring. thriftless: unprofitable. 11. sum my count: balance my account. old excuse: excuse for being old. 12. succession: right of succession as your child.

Sonnet 3: 3. repair: renewal.

5. uneared: unplowed. 7. fond: foolish. 8. Of . . . self-love: through sheer selfishness. 9. glass: reflection. 13. remembered . . . be: not to be remembered.

Sonnet 4: 2. beauty's legacy: the beauty bestowed on you by your parents. 4. frank: liberal. free: generous. 6. largess: bounty. 8. live: survive. 14. th' executor: i.e., the survivor who carries out the wishes of the dead.

Sonnet 5: 2. gaze: i.e., object. 4. unfair: make ugly. 6. confounds: destroys. 9. distillation: perfume distilled from summer's flowers. 11. effect: product; i.e., the perfume.

But flowers distilled, though they with winter
　　meet,
Leese° but their show. Their substance still lives
　　sweet.

6

Then let not winter's ragged hand deface
In thee thy summer, ere thou be distilled.
Make sweet some vial, treasure thou some place
With beauty's treasure, ere it be self-killed.
That use is not forbidden usury,°　　　　　　　5
Which happies° those that pay the willing loan.
That's for thyself to breed another thee,
Or ten times happier, be it ten for one.
Ten times thyself were happier than thou art
If ten of thine ten times refigured° thee.　　　10
Then what could death do if thou shouldst depart
Leaving thee living in posterity?
　　Be not self-willed, for thou art much too fair
　　To be death's conquest and make worms thine
　　　heir.

7

Lo, in the orient when the gracious light°
Lifts up his burning head, each undereye°
Doth homage to his new-appearing sight,
Serving with looks his sacred majesty.
And having climbed the steep-up heavenly hill,　5
Resembling strong youth in his middle age,
Yet mortal looks adore his beauty still,
Attending on his golden pilgrimage.
But when from highmost pitch,° with weary car,°
Like feeble age, he reeleth from the day,　　　10
The eyes, 'fore° duteous, now converted are
From his low tract,° and look another way.
　　So thou, thyself outgoing° in thy noon,
　　Unlooked on diest unless thou get° a son.

8

Music to hear,° why hear'st thou music sadly?
Sweets with sweets war not, joy delights in joy.

14. Leese: lose.
　　Sonnet 6: 5. forbidden usury: Usury — the lending of money at excessive rates of interest — was regarded as un-Christian but the law allowed an interest rate of 10%.　6. happies: makes happy.　10. refigured: reproduced.
　　Sonnet 7: 1. gracious light: i.e., the sun. The image of the sun in its course from dawn to sunset is sustained until l. 12. 2. undereye: eye in the earth beneath.　9. pitch: zenith; lit., the highest point in the flight of a hawk. See App. 26. car: chariot.　11. 'fore: before.　12. tract: track.　13. outgoing: going out, declining.　14. get: beget.
　　Sonnet 8: 1. Music to hear: you who are like music.

Why lovest thou that which thou receivest **not**
　　gladly,
Or else receivest with pleasure thine annoy?°
If the true concord of well-tunèd sounds,　　　5
By unions married, do offend thine ear,
They do but sweetly chide thee, who confounds
In singleness the parts that thou shouldst bear.
Mark how one string, sweet husband to another,
Strikes each in each by mutual ordering,　　　10
Resembling sire and child and happy mother,
Who, all in one, one pleasing note do sing.
　　Whose speechless song, being many, seeming one,
　　Sings this to thee: " Thou single wilt prove none."

9

Is it for fear to wet a widow's eye
That thou consumest thyself in single **life?**
Ah, if thou issueless shalt hap to die,
The world will wail thee, like a makeless° **wife.**
The world will be thy widow, and still° **weep**　5
That thou no form° of thee hast left behind,
When every private widow well may keep
By children's eyes her husband's shape in mind.
Look what an unthrift in the world doth spend
Shifts but his place, for still the world enjoys it,°
But beauty's waste hath in the world an **end,**　11
And kept unused, the user so destroys it.
　　No love toward others in that bosom **sits**
　　That on himself such murderous shame **commits.**

10

For shame! Deny that thou bear'st love **to any,**
Who for thyself art so unprovident.
Grant, if thou wilt, thou art beloved of many,
But that thou none lovest is most evident.
For thou art so possessed with murderous **hate**　5
That 'gainst thyself thou stick'st not to conspire,
Seeking that beauteous roof° to ruinate°
Which to repair should be thy chief desire.
Oh, change thy thought, that I may change my
　　mind!
Shall hate be fairer lodged than gentle love?　　10
Be, as thy presence is, gracious and kind,
Or to thyself at least kindhearted prove.
　　Make thee another self, for love of me,
　　That beauty still may live in thine or thee.

4. annoy: harm.
　　Sonnet 9: 4. makeless: without a mate.　5. still: always. 6. form: shape.　9–10. Look . . . it: i.e., the money which a waster (*unthrift*) spends remains in circulation.
　　Sonnet 10: 7. roof: house; i.e., family. ruinate: destroy.

11

As fast as thou shalt wane, so fast thou grow'st
In one of thine, from that which thou departest,°
And that fresh blood which youngly thou bestow'st
Thou mayst call thine when thou from youth con-
    vertest.°
Herein lives wisdom, beauty, and increase;   5
Without this, folly, age, and cold decay.
If all were minded so, the times° should cease
And threescore year would make the world away.
Let those whom Nature hath not made for store,°
Harsh, featureless, and rude, barrenly perish.   10
Look whom she best endowed she gave the more,
Which bounteous gift thou shouldst in bounty
    cherish.
    She carved thee for her seal,° and meant thereby
    Thou shouldst print more, not let that copy die.

12

When I do count the clock that tells the time
And see the brave day sunk in hideous night,
When I behold the violet past prime
And sable° curls all silvered o'er with white;
When lofty trees I see barren of leaves   5
Which erst from heat did canopy the herd,
And summer's green all girded up in sheaves,
Borne on the bier with white and bristly beard° —
Then of thy beauty do I question° make,
That thou among the wastes of time must go,   10
Since sweets and beauties do themselves forsake
And die as fast as they see others grow.
    And nothing 'gainst Time's scythe can make de-
    fense
    Save breed,° to brave° him when he takes thee
    hence.

13

Oh, that you were yourself! But, love, you are
No longer yours than you yourself here live.
Against this coming end you should prepare,
And your sweet semblance to some other give.
So should that beauty which you hold in lease°   5
Find no determination.° Then you were
Yourself again after yourself's decease,

When your sweet issue your sweet form should bear.
Who lets so fair a house fall to decay,
Which husbandry° in honor might uphold   10
Against the stormy gusts of winter's day
And barren rage of death's eternal cold?
    Oh, none but unthrifts. Dear my love, you know
    You had a father. Let your son say so.

14°

Not from the stars do I my judgment pluck,
And yet methinks I have astronomy,°
But not to tell of good or evil luck,
Of plagues, of dearths, or seasons' quality.
Nor can I fortune to brief minutes tell,   5
Pointing to each his thunder, rain, and wind,
Or say with princes if it shall go well
By oft predict° that I in heaven find.
But from thine eyes my knowledge I derive,
And, constant stars, in them I read such art°   10
As truth and beauty shall together thrive,
If from thyself to store thou wouldst convert.°
    Or else of thee this I prognosticate:
    Thy end is truth's and beauty's doom and date.°

15

When I consider everything that grows
Holds in perfection but a little moment,
That this huge stage presenteth naught but shows
Whereon the stars in secret influence° comment;
When I perceive that men as plants increase,   5
Cheerèd and checked even by the selfsame sky,
Vaunt° in their youthful sap, at height decrease,
And wear their brave state out of memory —
Then the conceit° of this inconstant stay
Sets you most rich in youth before my sight,   10
Where wasteful Time debateth with Decay,
To change your day of youth to sullied° night.
    And all in war with Time for love of you,
    As he takes from you, I engraft° you new.

16

But wherefore do not you a mightier way
Make war upon this bloody tyrant, Time?
And fortify yourself in your decay

Sonnet 11: 1–2. As . . . departest: i.e., as you fade, your child
waxes toward that prime from which you are departing.   4. con-
vertest: change.   7. times: i.e., this generation.   9. store:
breeding.   13. seal: i.e., that which makes impressions of itself.

Sonnet 12: 4. sable: black.   7–8. And . . . beard: i.e., the
barley, once green, now white and bearded, cut, stacked, and
carted.   9. question: matter for thought.   14. breed: offspring.
brave: taunt.

Sonnet 13: 5. hold in lease: i.e., as a temporary tenant.
6. determination: lit., the legal conclusion of a tenancy.

10. husbandry: good management.

Sonnet 14: The whole sonnet sustains the image of astrological
predictions. See App. 1 and 2.   2. astronomy: astrology.   8. oft
predict: frequent signs.   10. art: knowledge.   12. store . . .
convert: breed progeny.   14. doom . . . date: Doomsday.

Sonnet 15: 4. influence: See App. 1.   7. Vaunt: triumph.
9. conceit: thought.   12. sullied: dark.   14. engraft: i.e., graft
you into my verse.

With means more blessèd than my barren rhyme?
Now stand you on the top of happy hours,   5
And many maiden gardens, yet unset,
With virtuous wish would bear your living flowers
Much liker than your painted counterfeit.°
So should the lines of life° that life repair
Which this, Time's pencil, or my pupil pen,°   10
Neither in inward worth nor outward fair,°
Can make you live yourself in eyes of men.
   To give away yourself keeps yourself still,
   And you must live, drawn by your own sweet skill.

17°

Who will believe my verse in time to come
If it were filled with your most high deserts?
Though yet, Heaven knows, it is but as a tomb
Which hides your life and shows not half your
     parts.°
If I could write the beauty of your eyes   5
And in fresh numbers° number all your graces,
The age to come would say, "This poet lies,
Such heavenly touches ne'er touched earthly faces."
So should my papers, yellowed with their age,   9
Be scorned, like old men of less truth than tongue,
And your true rights be termed a poet's rage°
And stretchèd° meter of an antique song.
   But were some child of yours alive that time,
   You should live twice, in it and in my rhyme.

18

Shall I compare thee to a summer's day?
Thou art more lovely and more temperate.
Rough winds do shake the darling buds of May,
And summer's lease hath all too short a date.
Sometime too hot the eye of heaven° shines,   5
And often is his gold complexion dimmed.
And every fair from fair sometime declines,
By chance or nature's changing course untrimmed.°
But thy eternal summer shall not fade,
Nor lose possession of that fair thou owest,°   10
Nor shall Death brag thou wander'st in his shade

When in eternal lines to time thou grow'st.
   So long as men can breathe, or eyes can see,
   So long lives this, and this gives life to thee.°

19

Devouring Time, blunt thou the lion's paws,
And make the earth devour her own sweet brood.
Pluck the keen teeth from the fierce tiger's jaws,
And burn the long-lived phoenix° in her blood.
Make glad and sorry seasons as thou fleet'st,°   5
And do whate'er thou wilt, swift-footed Time,
To the wide world and all her fading sweets,
But I forbid thee one most heinous crime.
Oh, carve not with thy hours my love's fair brow,
Nor draw no lines there with thine antique pen.   10
Him in thy course untainted do allow
For beauty's pattern to succeeding men.
   Yet do thy worst, old Time. Despite thy wrong,
   My love shall in my verse ever live young.

20

A woman's face with Nature's own hand painted
Hast thou, the master-mistress of my passion,
A woman's gentle heart, but not acquainted
With shifting change, as is false women's fashion,
An eye more bright than theirs, less false in rolling,
Gilding the object whereupon it gazeth,°   6
A man in hue, all hues in his controlling,°
Which steals men's eyes and women's souls amazeth.
And for a woman wert thou first created,
Till Nature, as she wrought thee, fell a-doting,   10
And by addition me of thee defeated°
By adding one thing to my purpose nothing.
   But since she pricked thee out° for women's
     pleasure,
   Mine be thy love, and thy love's use their treasure.

21

So is it not with me as with that Muse°
Stirred° by a painted beauty to his verse,
Who Heaven itself for ornament doth use

Sonnet 16: 8. counterfeit: imitation, portrait.   9. lines of
life: living lines; i.e., children.   10. Which . . . pen: which a
portrait — Time's method of preserving a likeness — or my be-
ginner's verse. Some editors read "this time's pencil"; i.e., artists
of today.   11. fair: beauty.
   Sonnet 17: This sonnet concludes the first series in which
the young man is urged to marry.   4. parts: good qualities,
physical and mental.   6. numbers: verses.   11. rage: enthusiasm.   12. stretched: exaggerated.
   Sonnet 18: 5. eye of heaven: the sun.   8. untrimmed: shorn
of beauty.   10. fair . . . owest: beauty you possess.

13–14. So . . . thee: This sentiment — that the poet is giving
immortality to his subject — is a commonplace with sonneteers.
   Sonnet 19: 4. phoenix: a mythical Arabian bird which lived
for five hundred years. See Temp, III.iii.21–24,n.   5. fleet'st:
pass rapidly.
   Sonnet 20: 6. Gilding . . . gazeth: It was believed that the
eye, like a searchlight, shot out a beam which enabled the gazer
to see the object. Cf. Tr & Cr, III.iii.109–11.   7. A . . . controlling: See Sonnets Intro. p. 1594b.   11. defeated: cheated.
13. pricked . . . out: selected you.
   Sonnet 21: 1. Muse: poet.   2. Stirred: roused.

And every fair with his fair doth rehearse,°
Making a couplement° of proud compare　　　5
With sun and moon, with earth and sea's rich gems,
With April's first-born flowers, and all things rare
That heaven's air in this huge rondure° hems.
Oh, let me, true in love, but truly write,
And then believe me, my love is as fair　　　10
As any mother's child, though not so bright
As those gold candles° fixed in heaven's air.
　　Let them say more that like of hearsay well.
　　I will not praise that purpose not to sell.°

22

My glass shall not persuade me I am old
So long as youth and thou are of one date,
But when in thee time's furrows I behold,
Then look I death my days should expiate.°
For all that beauty that doth cover thee　　　5
Is but the seemly raiment of my heart,
Which in thy breast doth live, as thine in me.
How can I then be elder than thou art?
Oh, therefore, love, be of thyself so wary
As I, not for myself, but for thee will,　　　10
Bearing thy heart, which I will keep so chary
As tender nurse her babe from faring ill.
　　Presume not on thy heart when mine is slain.
　　Thou gavest me thine, not to give back again.

23

As an unperfect actor on the stage,
Who with his fear is put besides his part,
Or some fierce thing replete with too much rage,
Whose strength's abundance weakens his own heart,
So I, for fear of trust, forget to say　　　5
The perfect ceremony of love's rite,°
And in mine own love's strength seem to decay,
O'ercharged with burden of mine own love's might.
Oh, let my books be then the eloquence
And dumb presagers° of my speaking breast,　　　10
Who plead for love, and look for recompense,
More than that tongue that more hath more ex-
　　pressed.
　　Oh, learn to read what silent love hath writ.
　　To hear with eyes belongs to love's fine wit.

24

Mine eye hath played the painter and hath stelled°
Thy beauty's form in table° of my heart.
My body is the frame wherein 'tis held,
And pérspective it is best painter's art.
For through the painter must you see his skill,　　　5
To find where your true image pictured lies,
Which in my bosom's shop is hanging still,
That hath his windows glazèd with thine eyes.
Now see what good turns eyes for eyes have done.
Mine eyes have drawn thy shape, and thine for me
Are windows to my breast, wherethrough the sun
Delights to peep, to gaze therein on thee.　　　12
　　Yet eyes this cunning want° to grace their art,
　　They draw but what they see, know not the heart.

25

Let those who are in favor with their stars°
Of public honor and proud titles boast,
Whilst I, whom fortune of such triumph bars,
Unlooked for joy° in that I honor most.
Great princes' favorites their fair leaves spread　　　5
But as the marigold at the sun's eye,°
And in themselves their pride lies burièd,
For at a frown they in their glory die.
The painful° warrior famousèd for fight,
After a thousand victories once foiled,　　　10
Is from the book of honor razèd quite,
And all the rest forgot for which he toiled.
　　Then happy I, that love and am beloved
　　Where I may not remove nor be removed.

26°

Lord of my love, to whom in vassalage°
Thy merit hath my duty strongly knit,
To thee I send this written ambassage,
To witness duty, not to show my wit.
Duty so great, which wit so poor as mine　　　5
May make seem bare in wanting words to show it,
But that I hope some good conceit of thine
In thy soul's thought, all naked, will bestow it.
Till whatsoever star that guides my moving,
Points on me graciously with fair aspéct,°　　　10
And puts apparel on my tattered loving,

---

4. **And . . . rehearse:** compares his fair subject with every beautiful thing.　5. **couplement:** union.　8. **rondure:** orb; i.e., the earth.　12. **gold candles:** the stars.　14. **I . . . sell:** I do not praise you because I want to sell you.

Sonnet 22: 4. **expiate:** end.

Sonnet 23: 5–6. **So . . . rite:** so I, being too diffident, forget to show my love outwardly.　10. **dumb presagers:** like the dumb show that explains the action which is to follow. See *Haml,* III.ii.145,n.

Sonnet 24: 1. **stelled:** fixed.　2. **table:** the flat surface on which a portrait is painted.　13. **want:** lack.

Sonnet 25: 1. **in . . . stars:** lucky.　4. **Unlooked . . . joy:** rejoice inconspicuously.　6. **the . . . eye:** i.e., which closes when the sun ceases to shine on it.　9. **painful:** toiling.

Sonnet 26: Written to accompany some offering of poetry, possibly the *Rape of Lucrece.* See Gen. Intro. p. 10a.　1. **vassalage:** homage.　10. **aspect:** the "influence" of a star. See App. 1.

To show me worthy of thy sweet respect.
    Then may I dare to boast how I do love thee,
    Till then not show my head where thou mayst
        prove me.

27

Weary with toil, I haste me to my bed,
The dear repose for limbs with travel tired.
But then begins a journey in my head,
To work my mind, when body's work's expired.
For then my thoughts, from far where I abide,   5
Intend° a zealous pilgrimage to thee,
And keep my drooping eyelids open wide,
Looking on darkness which the blind do see.
Save that my soul's imaginary sight
Presents thy shadow° to my sightless view,   10
Which, like a jewel hung in ghastly night,
Makes black night beauteous and her old face new.
    Lo, thus by day my limbs, by night my mind,
    For thee and for myself no quiet find.

28

How can I then return in happy plight,
That am debarred the benefit of rest?
When day's oppression is not eased by night,
But day by night, and night by day, oppressed?
And each, though enemies to either's reign,   5
Do in consent shake hands to torture me,
The one by toil, the other to complain
How far I toil, still farther off from thee.
I tell the day, to please him° thou art bright,
And dost him grace when clouds do blot the heaven.
So flatter I the swart-complexioned night;   11
When sparkling stars twire° not thou gild'st the
    even.°
    But day doth daily draw my sorrows longer,
    And night doth nightly make grief's strength
        seem stronger.

29

When in disgrace with fortune and men's eyes
I all alone beweep my outcast state,
And trouble deaf Heaven with my bootless° cries,
And look upon myself and curse my fate,
Wishing me like to one more rich in hope,   5
Featured like him, like him with friends possessed,
Desiring this man's art and that man's scope,

With what I most enjoy contented least —
Yet in these thoughts myself almost despising,
Haply I think on thee, and then my state,   10
Like to the lark at break of day arising
From sullen earth, sings hymns at Heaven's gate.
    For thy sweet love remembered such wealth brings
    That then I scorn to change my state with kings.

30

When to the sessions° of sweet silent thought
I summon up remembrance of things past,
I sigh the lack of many a thing I sought,
And with old woes new wail my dear time's waste.
Then can I drown an eye, unused to flow,   5
For precious friends hid in death's dateless° night,
And weep afresh love's long since canceled woe,
And moan the expense° of many a vanished sight.
Then can I grieve at grievances foregone,°
And heavily from woe to woe tell o'er   10
The sad account of forebemoanèd moan,
Which I new-pay as if not paid before.
    But if the while I think on thee, dear friend,
    All losses are restored and sorrows end.

31°

Thy bosom is endearèd with all hearts,
Which I by lacking have supposèd dead.
And there reigns love, and all love's loving parts,
And all those friends which I thought burièd.
How many a holy and obsequious° tear   5
Hath dear religious love stol'n from mine eye,
As interest° of the dead, which now appear
But things removed that hidden in thee lie!
Thou art the grave where buried love doth live,
Hung with the trophies of my lovers° gone,   10
Who all their parts of me to thee did give,
That due of many now is thine alone.
    Their images I loved I view in thee,
    And thou, all they, hast all the all of me.

32

If thou survive my well-contented° day,
When that churl° Death my bones with dust shall
    cover,
And shalt by fortune once more resurvey

Sonnet 30: 1. **sessions**: lit., sittings of a law court. **6. dateless**: everlasting. **8. expense**: waste. **9. foregone**: past.
    Sonnet 31: The poet's friend being absent is as dead. This reminds him of his dead friends whose qualities are combined in his friend. **5. obsequious**: mourning. **7. interest**: i.e., tribute due to. **10. lovers**: dear friends.
    Sonnet 32: 1. **well-contented**: happy. **2. churl**: boor.

    Sonnet 27: 6. **Intend**: direct. **10. shadow**: reflection, image.
    Sonnet 28: 9. **to ... him**: to rejoice that. **12. twire**: twinkle, peep. **even**: evening.
    Sonnet 29: 3. **bootless**: vain.

These poor rude lines of thy deceasèd lover,
Compare them with the bettering of the time,°   5
And though they be outstripped by every pen,
Reserve them for my love, not for their rhyme,
Exceeded by the height of happier men.
Oh, then vouchsafe me but this loving thought:
"Had my friend's Muse grown with this growing
    age,   10
A dearer birth than this his love had brought,
To march in ranks of better equipage.
   But since he died, and poets better prove,
   Theirs for their style I'll read, his for his love."

33

Full many a glorious morning have I seen
Flatter the mountaintops with sovereign° eye,
Kissing with golden face the meadows green,
Gilding pale streams with heavenly alchemy,°
Anon permit the basest clouds to ride   5
With ugly rack° on his celestial face
And from the forlorn world his visage hide,
Stealing unseen to west with this disgrace.
Even so my sun one early morn did shine
With all-triumphant splendor on my brow.   10
But out, alack! he was but one hour mine,
The region° cloud hath masked him from me now.
   Yet him for this my love no whit disdaineth.
   Suns of the world may stain when heaven's sun
    staineth.

34

Why didst thou° promise such a beauteous day,
And make me travel forth without my cloak,
To let base clouds o'ertake me in my way,
Hiding thy bravery° in their rotten smoke?°
'Tis not enough that through the cloud thou break
To dry the rain on my storm-beaten face,   6
For no man well of such a salve° can speak
That heals the wound and cures not the disgrace.
Nor can thy shame give physic to my grief.
Though thou repent, yet I have still the loss.   10
The offender's sorrow lends but weak relief
To him that bears the strong offense's cross.°
   Ah, but those tears are pearl which thy love sheds,
   And they are rich and ransom all ill deeds.

35

No more be grieved at that which thou hast done.
Roses have thorns, and silver fountains mud,
Clouds and eclipses stain both moon and sun,
And loathsome canker° lives in sweetest bud.
All men make faults, and even I in this,   5
Authorizing thy trespass with compare,°
Myself corrupting, salving thy amiss,
Excusing thy sins more than thy sins are.
For to thy sensual fault I bring in sense° —
Thy adverse party is thy advocate —   10
And 'gainst myself a lawful plea commence.
Such civil war is in my love and hate,
   That I an accessory needs must be
   To that sweet thief which sourly robs from me.

36

Let me confess that we two must be twain,
Although our undivided loves are one.
So shall those blots that do with me remain,
Without thy help, by me be borne alone.
In our two loves there is but one respect,°   5
Though in our lives a separable° spite,
Which though it alter not love's sole effect,°
Yet doth it steal sweet hours from love's delight.
I may not evermore acknowledge thee,
Lest my bewailèd guilt should do thee shame,   10
Nor thou with public kindness honor me,
Unless thou take that honor from thy name.
   But do not so. I love thee in such sort,
   As thou being mine, mine is thy good report.

37

As a decrepit father takes delight
To see his active child do deeds of youth,
So I, made lame by fortune's dearest° spite,
Take all my comfort of thy worth and truth.
For whether beauty, birth, or wealth, or wit,   5
Or any of these all, or all, or more,
Entitled in° thy parts do crownèd sit,
I make my love engrafted° to this store.
So then I am not lame, poor, nor despised
Whilst that this shadow doth such substance give   10
That I in thy abundance am sufficed

---

5. bettering . . . time: finer verse which will then be written.
   Sonnet 33: 2. sovereign: supreme, glorious.   **4. alchemy:** transmutation of base metal to gold. See App. 21.   **6. rack:** mass of clouds.   **12. region:** of the air.
   Sonnet 34: 1. thou: i.e., the sun.   **4. bravery:** splendor. **smoke:** mist.   **7. salve:** healing ointment.   **12. cross:** burden.

   Sonnet 35: 4. canker: cankerworm.   **6. Authorizing . . . compare:** justifying your offense with my similes (e.g., of roses and thorns).   **9. sense:** reason (to allay my passion).
   Sonnet 36: 5. respect: consideration.   **6. separable:** separating.   **7. effect:** result.
   Sonnet 37: 3. dearest: bitterest.   **7. Entitled in:** having a right to.   **8. engrafted:** firmly joined.

And by a part of all thy glory live.
   Look, what is best, that best I wish in thee.
   This wish I have, then ten times happy me!

38

How can my Muse want subject to invent
While thou dost breathe, that pour'st into my verse
Thine own sweet argument,° too excellent
For every vulgar paper to rehearse?
Oh, give thyself the thanks if aught in me   5
Worthy perusal stand against thy sight,
For who's so dumb that cannot write to thee
When thou thyself dost give invention° light?
Be thou the tenth Muse,° ten times more in worth
Than those old nine which rhymers invocate,   10
And he that calls on thee, let him bring forth
Eternal numbers to outlive long date.
   If my slight Muse do please these curious days,
   The pain be mine, but thine shall be the praise.

39

Oh, how thy worth with manners° may I sing,
When thou art all the better part of me?
What can mine own praise to mine own self bring?
And what is 't but mine own when I praise thee?
Even for this let us divided live,   5
And our dear love lose name of single one,
That by this separation I may give
That due to thee which thou deservest alone.
O absence, what a torment wouldst thou prove,
Were it not thy sour leisure gave sweet leave   10
To entertain the time with thoughts of love,
Which time and thoughts so sweetly doth deceive,°
   And that thou teachest how to make one twain°
   By praising him here who doth hence remain!

40

Take all my loves, my love, yea, take them all.
What hast thou then more than thou hadst before?
No love, my love, that thou mayst truelove call,

All mine was thine before thou hadst this more.
Then, if for my love thou my love receivest,°   5
I cannot blame thee for my love thou usest,
But yet be blamed if thou thyself deceivest
By willful taste of what thyself refusest.°
I do forgive thy robbery, gentle thief,
Although thou steal thee all my poverty.   10
And yet, love knows, it is a greater grief
To bear love's wrong than hate's known injury.
   Lascivious grace, in whom all ill well shows,
   Kill me with spites,° yet we must not be foes.

41°

Those pretty wrongs that liberty commits,
When I am sometime absent from thy heart,
Thy beauty and thy years full well befits,
For still temptation follows where thou art.
Gentle° thou art, and therefore to be won,   5
Beauteous thou art, therefore to be assailed.
And when a woman woos, what woman's son
Will sourly leave her till she have prevailed?
Aye me! but yet thou mightst my seat° forbear,
And chide thy beauty and thy straying youth,   10
Who lead thee in their riot even there
Where thou art forced to break a twofold truth° —
   Hers, by thy beauty tempting her to thee,
   Thine, by thy beauty being false to me.

42°

That thou hast her it is not all my grief,
And yet it may be said I loved her dearly.
That she hath thee is of my wailing chief,
A loss in love that touches me more nearly.
Loving offenders, thus I will excuse ye —   5
Thou dost love her, because thou know'st I love her,
And for my sake even so doth she abuse me,
Suffering my friend for my sake to approve° her.
If I lose thee, my loss is my love's° gain,
And losing her, my friend hath found that loss.   10
Both find each other, and I lose both twain,
And both for my sake lay on me this cross.
   But here's the joy — my friend and I are one.
   Sweet flattery! Then she loves but me alone.

Sonnet 38: **3. argument:** topic for verse.   **8. invention:** the creative power.   **9. tenth Muse:** The Nine Muses were the patron goddesses of the different forms of art, particularly poetry, and were regarded by the ancients as directly inspiring the artist.

Sonnet 39: **1. with manners:** i.e., without immodesty.   **12. deceive:** beguile.   **13. make . . . twain:** make one person of two; i.e., though absent I am united with you in thought.

Sonnet 40: **5. Then . . . receivest:** if because you love me you take my mistress.   **8. By . . . refusest:** i.e., you take my love (mistress) but refuse my love (for you).   **14. spites:** vexations.

Sonnet 41: (Continuing 40). **5. Gentle:** of good birth. **9. seat:** place.   **12. truth:** loyalty.

Sonnet 42: (Continuing 41). **8. approve:** make trial of. **9. love's:** mistress's.

43

When most I wink,° then do mine eyes best see,
For all the day they view things unrespected,°
But when I sleep, in dreams they look on thee,
And, darkly bright, are bright in dark° directed.
Then thou, whose shadow° shadows doth make
    bright, 5
How would thy shadow's form form happy show
To the clear day with thy much clearer light
When to unseeing eyes thy shade shines so!
How would, I say, mine eyes be blessèd made
By looking on thee in the living day, 10
When in dead night thy fair imperfect° shade
Through heavy sleep on sightless eyes doth stay!
    All days are nights to see till I see thee,
    And nights bright days when dreams do show
      thee me.

44°

If the dull substance° of my flesh were thought,
Injurious distance should not stop my way.
For then, despite of space, I would be brought
From limits far remote where thou dost stay.
No matter then although my foot did stand 5
Upon the farthest earth removed from thee,
For nimble thought can jump both sea and land
As soon as think the place where he would be.
But, ah, thought kills me, that I am not thought,
To leap large lengths of miles when thou art gone,
But that, so much of earth and water wrought,° 11
I must attend time's leisure with my moan,
    Receiving naught by elements so slow
    But heavy tears, badges of either's woe.

45°

The other two, slight air and purging fire,
Are both with thee, wherever I abide.
The first my thought, the other my desire,
These present-absent with swift motion slide.
For when these quicker elements are gone 5
In tender embassy of love to thee,
My life, being made of four, with two alone
Sinks down to death, oppressed with melancholy,
Until life's composition° be recured°

By those swift messengers returned from thee, 10
Who even but now come back again, assured
Of thy fair health, recounting it to me.
    This told, I joy, but then no longer glad,
    I send them back again, and straight grow sad.

46

Mine eye and heart are at a mortal° war
How to divide the conquest of thy sight.°
Mine eye my heart thy picture's sight would bar,
My heart mine eye the freedom of that right.
My heart doth plead that thou in him dost lie, 5
A closet never pierced with crystal eyes.
But the defendant doth that plea deny,
And says in him thy fair appearance lies.
To 'cide° this title is impanelèd
A quest° of thoughts, all tenants to the heart, 10
And by their verdict is determinèd
The clear eye's moiety° and the dear heart's part.
    As thus: Mine eye s due is thine outward part,
    And my heart's right thine inward love of heart.

47°

Betwixt mine eye and heart a league is took,
And each doth good turns now unto the other.
When that mine eye is famished for a look,
Or heart in love with sighs himself doth smother,
With my love's picture then my eye doth feast 5
And to the painted banquet bids my heart.
Another time mine eye is my heart's guest
And in his thoughts of love doth share a part.
So, either by thy picture or my love,
Thyself away art present still with me, 10
For thou not farther than my thoughts canst move,
And I am still with them and they with thee.
    Or, if they sleep, thy picture in my sight
    Awakes my heart to heart's and eye's delight.

48

How careful was I when I took my way,
Each trifle under truest bars to thrust,
That to my use it might unusèd stay
From hands of falsehood, in sure wards° of trust!

Sonnet 43: 1. wink: close my eyes in sleep. 2. unrespected: unnoticed. 4. bright in dark: i.e., see clearly because of your brightness. 5. shadow: appearance, image (as seen in a dream). 11. imperfect: i.e., unreal.
    Sonnet 44: In this and the following sonnet the imagery is of the four elements. See App. 3. 1. dull substance: i.e., made of the two "dull" elements, earth and water. 11. so . . . wrought: I, being compounded (wrought) of these two elements.
    Sonnet 45: (Continuing 44). 9. life's composition: i.e., the combination of all four elements. recured: restored.

Sonnet 46: 1. mortal: deadly. 2. the . . . sight: the right to gaze on your picture. 9. 'cide: decide. 10. quest: jury. 12. moiety: share.
    Sonnet 47: (Continuing 46).
    Sonnet 48: 4. wards: bolts.

But thou, to whom my jewels trifles are,   5
Most worthy comfort, now my greatest grief,
Thou, best of dearest and mine only care,
Art left the prey of every vulgar thief.
Thee have I not locked up in any chest,
Save where thou art not, though I feel thou art,   10
Within the gentle closure° of my breast,
From whence at pleasure thou mayst come and part.
   And even thence thou wilt be stol'n, I fear,
   For truth proves thievish for a prize so dear.

49

Against that time, if ever that time come,
When I shall see thee frown on my defects,
When as thy love hath cast his utmost sum,°
Called to that audit by advised respects° —   4
Against that time when thou shalt strangely° pass,
And scarcely greet me with that sun, thine eye,
When love, converted from the thing it was,
Shall reasons find of settled gravity° —
Against that time do I ensconce° me here
Within the knowledge of mine own desert,   10
And this my hand against myself uprear,
To guard the lawful reasons on thy part.
   To leave poor me thou hast the strength of laws,
   Since why to love I can allege no cause.

50

How heavy do I journey on the way
When what I seek, my weary travel's end,
Doth teach that ease and that repose to say,
" Thus far the miles are measured from thy friend! "
The beast that bears me, tired with my woe,   5
Plods dully on, to bear that weight in me,
As if by some instínct the wretch did know
His rider loved not speed, being made° from thee.
The bloody spur cannot provoke him on
That sometimes anger thrusts into his hide,   10
Which heavily he answers with a groan
More sharp to me than spurring to his side.
   For that same groan doth put this in my mind:
   My grief lies onward, and my joy behind.

51°

Thus can my love excuse the slow offense°
Of my dull bearer when from thee I speed.
From where thou art why should I haste me thence?
Till I return, of posting° is no need.
Oh, what excuse will my poor beast then find,   5
When swift extremity° can seem but slow?
Then should I spur, though mounted on the wind,
In wingèd speed no motion shall I know.
Then can no horse with my desire keep pace,
Therefore desire, of perfect'st love being made,   10
Shall neigh — no dull flesh — in his fiery race,
But love, for love, thus shall excuse my jade:°
   Since from thee going he went willful-slow,
   Toward thee I'll run and give him leave to go.°

52

So am I as the rich, whose blessèd key
Can bring him to his sweet uplockèd treasure,
The which he will not every hour survey,
For blunting the fine point of seldom pleasure.
Therefore are feasts so solemn and so rare,   5
Since, seldom coming, in the long year set°
Like stones of worth they thinly placèd are,
Or captain° jewels in the carcanet.°
So is the time that keeps you as my chest,
Or as the wardrobe which the robe doth hide,   10
To make some special instant special blest
By new-unfolding his imprisoned pride.
   Blessèd are you, whose worthiness gives scope,
   Being had, to triumph — being lacked, to hope.

53°

What is your substance, whereof are you made,
That millions of strange° shadows on you tend?
Since every one hath, every one, one shade,
And you, but one, can every shadow lend.°
Describe Adonis,° and the counterfeit°   5
Is poorly imitated after you.
On Helen's cheek all art of beauty set,

And you in Grecian tires° are painted new.
Speak of the spring and foison° of the year,
The one doth shadow of your beauty show,   10
The other as your bounty doth appear,
And you in every blessèd shape we know.
  In all external grace you have some part,
  But you like none, none you, for constant heart.

54°

Oh, how much more doth beauty beauteous seem
By that sweet ornament which truth° doth give!
The rose looks fair, but fairer we it deem
For that sweet odor which doth in it live.
The canker blooms° have full as deep a dye   5
As the perfumèd tincture of the roses,
Hang on such thorns, and play as wantonly
When summer's breath their maskèd buds discloses.
But for° their virtue only is their show,
They live unwooed and unrespected fade,   10
Die to themselves. Sweet roses do not so.
Of their sweet deaths are sweetest odors made.
  And so of you, beauteous and lovely youth,
  When that shall vade,° by verse distills your truth.

55

Not marble, nor the gilded monuments
Of princes, shall outlive this powerful rhyme.
But you shall shine more bright in these contents
Than unswept stone,° besmeared with sluttish time.
When wasteful war shall statues overturn,   5
And broils root out the work of masonry,
Nor Mars his sword nor war's quick fire shall burn
The living record of your memory.
'Gainst death and all-oblivious enmity
Shall you pace forth. Your praise shall still find room
Even in the eyes of all posterity   11
That wear this world out to the ending doom.
  So, till the judgment° that° yourself arise,
  You live in this, and dwell in lovers' eyes.

56

Sweet love, renew thy force. Be it not said
Thy edge should blunter be than appetite,

---

8. **tires**: attire.   9. **foison**: plenty; i.e., autumn.
  Sonnet 54: (Continuing 53). 2. **truth**: constancy.   5. **canker blooms**: wild roses, which are odorless, contrasted with the sweet-scented garden rose.   9. **for**: since.   14. **vade**: fade.
  Sonnet 55: 4. **unswept stone**: the dusty inscribed slab over a grave on the floor in a church.   13. **judgment**: Day of Judgment. **that**: when.

Which but today by feeding is allayed,
Tomorrow sharpened in his former might.
So, love, be thou. Although today thou fill   5
Thy hungry eyes even till they wink with fullness,
Tomorrow see again, and do not kill
The spirit of love with a perpetual dullness.
Let this sad interim like the ocean be
Which parts the shore, where two contracted new°
Come daily to the banks, that when they see   11
Return of love, more blest may be the view.
  Or call it winter, which, being full of care,
  Makes summer's welcome thrice more wished,
    more rare.

57

Being your slave, what should I do but tend
Upon the hours and times of your desire?
I have no precious time at all to spend,
Nor services to do, till you require.
Nor dare I chide the world-without-end hour   5
Whilst I, my sovereign, watch the clock for you,
Nor think the bitterness of absence sour
When you have bid your servant once adieu.
Nor dare I question with my jealous thought
Where you may be, or your affairs suppose,°   10
But, like a sad slave, stay and think of naught
Save where you are how happy you make those.
  So true° a fool is love that in your will,
  Though you do anything, he thinks no ill.

58

That god forbid that made me first your slave,
I should in thought control your times of pleasure,
Or at your hand the account of hours to crave,
Being your vassal, bound to stay your leisure!
Oh, let me suffer, being at your beck,   5
The imprisoned absence of your liberty.°
And patience, tame to sufferance, bide each check°
Without accusing you of injury.
Be where you list, your charter is so strong
That you yourself may privilege your time   10
To what you will. To you it doth belong
Yourself to pardon of self-doing crime.
  I am to wait, though waiting so be Hell,
  Not blame your pleasure, be it ill or well.

  Sonnet 56: 10. **contracted new**: newly betrothed.
  Sonnet 57: 10. **suppose**: guess about.   13. **true**: faithful.
  Sonnet 58: 6. **The . . . liberty**: you are free to go as you please, and your absence makes me a prisoner.   7. **check**: rebuke.

59

If there be nothing new, but that which is
Hath been before, how are our brains beguiled,
Which, laboring for invention,° bear amiss
The second burden of a former child!°
Oh that recórd° could with a backward look,   5
Even of five hundred courses of the sun,
Show me your image in some antique book,
Since mind at first in character was done.°
That I might see what the old world could say
To this composèd wonder° of your frame —   10
Whether° we are mended, or whether better they,
Or whether revolution° be the same.
    Oh, sure I am the wits of former days
    To subjects worse have given admiring praise.

60

Like as the waves make toward the pebbled shore,
So do our minutes hasten to their end,
Each changing place with that which goes before,
In sequent toil all forward do contend.
Nativity,° once in the main of light,°   5
Crawls to maturity, wherewith being crowned,
Crookèd eclipses 'gainst his glory fight,
And Time that gave doth now his gift confound.
Time doth transfix the flourish set on youth
And delves the parallels in beauty's brow,   10
Feeds on the rarities of nature's truth,
And nothing stands but for his scythe to mow.
    And yet to times in hope my verse shall stand,
    Praising thy worth, despite his cruel hand.

61°

Is it thy will thy image should keep open
My heavy eyelids to the weary night?
Dost thou desire my slumbers should be broken
While shadows like to thee do mock my sight?
Is it thy spirit that thou send'st from thee   5
So far from home into my deeds to pry,
To find out shames and idle hours in me,
The scope and tenor° of thy jealousy?°
Oh, no! Thy love, though much, is not so great.
It is my love that keeps mine eye awake,   10

Mine own true love that doth my rest defeat,
To play the watchman ever for thy sake.
    For thee watch I whilst thou dost wake elsewhere,
    From me far off, with others all too near.

62

Sin of self-love possesseth all mine eye
And all my soul and all my every part,
And for this sin there is no remedy,
It is so grounded inward in my heart.
Methinks no face so gracious is as mine,   5
No shape so true, no truth of such account,
And for myself mine own worth do define,
As I all other in all worths surmount.
But when my glass shows me myself indeed,
Beated° and chopped° with tanned antiquity,   10
Mine own self-love quite contrary I read.
Self so self-loving were iniquity.
    'Tis thee, myself,° that for myself I praise,
    Painting my age with beauty of thy days.

63

Against° my love shall be, as I am now,
With Time's injurious hand crushed and o'erworn,
When hours have drained his blood and filled his
    brow
With lines and wrinkles, when his youthful morn
Hath traveled on to age's steepy night,   5
And all those beauties whereof now he's king
Are vanishing or vanished out of sight,
Stealing away the treasure of his spring.
For such a time do I now fortify
Against confounding age's cruel knife,   10
That he shall never cut from memory
My sweet love's beauty, though my lover's life.
    His beauty shall in these black lines be seen,
    And they shall live, and he in them still green.

64°

When I have seen by Time's fell hand defaced
The rich-proud cost of outworn buried age;°
When sometime lofty towers I see down-razed,
And brass eternal slave to mortal rage;
When I have seen the hungry ocean gain   5
Advantage on the kingdom of the shore,

Sonnet 59: 3. invention: new creation.   4. The ... child: a notion which has already been expressed by another.   5. record: research.   8. in ... done: recorded in writing.   10. composed wonder: marvel of construction.   11. Whether: pronounced "whe'er."   12. revolution: change.
    Sonnet 60: 5. Nativity: the moment of birth; i.e., the newborn infant. main of light: bright daylight.
    Sonnet 61: Cf. 43. 8. scope ... tenor: aim and intention. jealousy: suspicion.

Sonnet 62: 10. Beated: overpowered. chopped: chapped, roughened.   13. thee, myself: i.e., yourself, which is my other self.
    Sonnet 63: 1. Against: anticipating the time when.
    Sonnet 64: (Continuing 63). 2. rich-proud ... age: proud costly memorials of a bygone age.

And the firm soil win of the watery main,
Increasing store with loss and loss with store;
When I have seen such interchange of state,
Or state itself confounded to decay —   10
Ruin hath taught me thus to ruminate,
That Time will come and take my love away.
 This thought is as a death, which cannot choose
 But weep to have that which it fears to lose.

65°

Since brass, nor stone, nor earth, nor boundless sea
But° sad mortality o'ersways° their power,
How with this rage shall beauty hold a plea,
Whose action is no stronger than a flower?
Oh, how shall summer's honey breath hold out   5
Against the wreckful siege of battering days
When rocks impregnable are not so stout,
Nor gates of steel so strong, but Time decays?
O fearful meditation! Where, alack,   9
Shall Time's best jewel from Time's chest lie hid?
Or what strong hand can hold his swift foot back?
Or who his spoil of beauty can forbid?
 Oh, none, unless this miracle have might,
 That in black ink my love may still shine bright.

66

Tired with all these, for restful death I cry,
As, to behold desert a beggar born,
And needy nothing trimmed in jollity,°
And purest faith unhappily forsworn,
And gilded honor shamefully misplaced,   5
And maiden virtue rudely strumpeted,
And right perfection wrongfully disgraced,
And strength by limping sway disabled,
And art° made tongue-tied by authority,
And folly, doctorlike,° controlling skill,   10
And simple truth miscalled simplicity,°
And captive good attending captain ill.
 Tired with all these, from these would I be gone,
 Save that, to die I leave my love alone.

67

Ah, wherefore with infection° should he live
And with his presence grace impiety,
That sin by him advantage should achieve

And lace° itself with his society?
Why should false painting imitate his cheek,   5
And steal dead seeing° of his living hue?
Why should poor beauty indirectly seek
Roses of shadow,° since his rose is true?
Why should he live, now Nature bankrupt is,
Beggared of blood to blush through lively veins?
For she hath no exchequer now but his,°   11
And, proud of many, lives upon his gains.
 Oh, him she stores, to show what wealth she had
 In days long since, before these last so bad.

68

Thus is his cheek the map of days outworn,
When beauty lived and died as flowers do now.
Before these bastard signs of fair° were born
Or durst inhabit on a living brow;
Before the golden tresses of the dead,°   5
The right of sepulchers, were shorn away,
To live a second life on second head,
Ere beauty's dead fleece made another gay.
In him those holy antique hours are seen,
Without all ornament, itself° and true,   10
Making no summer of another's green,
Robbing no old to dress his beauty new.
 And him as for a map° doth Nature store,°
 To show false Art what beauty was of yore.

69

Those parts of thee that the world's eye doth view
Want nothing that the thought of hearts can mend.
All tongues, the voice of souls, give thee that due,
Uttering bare truth, even so as foes commend.°   4
Thy outward thus with outward praise is crowned,
But those same tongues that give thee so thine own
In other accents do this praise confound
By seeing farther than the eye hath shown.
They look into the beauty of thy mind,
And that, in guess, they measure by thy deeds.   10
Then, churls, their thoughts, although their eyes
  were kind,
To thy fair flower add the rank smell of weeds.
 But why° thy odor matcheth not thy show,
 The soil° is this, that thou dost common° grow.

4. lace: ornament. **6. dead seeing:** appearance of life which is in reality dead. **8. Roses of shadow:** i.e., imitation color. **11. exchequer . . . his:** i.e., he is the only beautiful specimen of nature now left.

 Sonnet 68: 3. bastard . . . fair: imitation beauty, cosmetics. **5. golden . . . dead:** See *M of Ven*, III.ii.92–96,n. **10. itself:** i.e., pure. **13. map:** pattern. **store:** hoard.

  Sonnet 69: 4. even . . . commend: i.e., which even an enemy would grant. **13. But why:** the reason why. **14. soil:** blemish. **common:** open to all comers.

  Sonnet 65: (Continuing 64). **1–2. Since . . . But:** since there is neither . . . but that. **2. o'ersways:** overpowers.

  Sonnet 66: 3. needy . . . jollity: i.e., the beggar born clad in gay clothes. **9. art:** skill. **10. doctorlike:** with the airs of a scholar. **11. simplicity:** silliness.

  Sonnet 67: 1. with infection: in these plaguey times.

70°

That thou art blamed shall not be thy defect.
For slander's mark was ever yet the fair.
The ornament of beauty is suspect,
A crow that flies in heaven's sweetest air.
So° thou be good, slander doth but approve°   5
Thy worth the greater, being wooed of time,
For canker vice the sweetest buds doth love,
And thou present'st a pure unstainèd prime.
Thou hast passed by the ambush of young days,
Either not assailed, or victor being charged.°   10
Yet this thy praise cannot be so thy praise,
To tie up envy evermore enlarged.°
    If some suspect° of ill masked° not thy show,
    Then thou alone kingdoms of hearts shouldst owe.

71

No longer mourn for me when I am dead
Than you shall hear the surly sullen bell°
Give warning to the world that I am fled
From this vile world, with vilest worms to dwell.
Nay, if you read this line, remember not   5
The hand that writ it, for I love you so
That I in your sweet thoughts would be forgot
If thinking on me then should make you woe.
Oh, if, I say, you look upon this verse
When I perhaps compounded am with clay,   10
Do not so much as my poor name rehearse,
But let your love even with my life decay,
    Lest the wise world should look into your moan,
    And mock you with me after I am gone.

72°

Oh, lest the world should task you to recite
What merit lived in me, that you should love
After my death, dear love, forget me quite.
For you in me can nothing worthy prove,
Unless you would devise some virtuous lie,   5
To do more for me than mine own desert,
And hang more praise upon deceasèd I
Than niggard truth would willingly impart.
Oh, lest your true love may seem false in this,
That you for love speak well of me untrue,   10
My name be buried where my body is,
And live no more to shame nor me nor you.
    For I am shamed by that which I bring forth,
    And so should you, to love things nothing worth.

73

That time of year thou mayst in me behold
When yellow leaves, or none, or few, do hang
Upon those boughs which shake against the cold,
Bare ruined choirs° where late the sweet birds sang.
In me thou see'st the twilight of such day   5
As after sunset fadeth in the west,
Which by and by black night doth take away,
Death's second self, that seals up° all in rest.
In me thou see'st the glowing of such fire,
That on the ashes of his youth doth lie   10
As the deathbed whereon it must expire,
Consumed with that which it was nourished by.
    This thou perceivest, which makes thy love more
      strong,
    To love that well which thou must leave ere long.

74°

But be contented. When that fell° arrest°
Without all bail shall carry me away,
My life hath in this line° some interest,
Which for memorial still with thee shall stay.
When thou reviewest this, thou dost review   5
The very part was consecrate to thee.
The earth can have but earth, which is his due,
My spirit is thine, the better part of me.
So then thou hast but lost the dregs of life,
The prey of worms, my body being dead,   10
The coward conquest of a wretch's knife,
Too base of thee to be rememberèd.
    The worth of that is that which it contains,
    And that is this, and this with thee remains.°

75

So are you to my thoughts as food to life,
Or as sweet-seasoned showers are to the ground.
And for the peace of you° I hold such strife
As 'twixt a miser and his wealth is found,
Now proud as an enjoyer, and anon   5
Doubting° the filching age will steal his treasure;
Now counting best to be with you alone,

Sonnet 70: (Continuing 69). 5. So: so long as. approve: prove.
10. charged: attacked. 12. enlarged: free to go to and fro.
13. suspect: suspicion. masked: concealed.
    Sonnet 71: 2. bell: See App. 19.
    Sonnet 72: (Continuing 71).

    Sonnet 73: 4. choirs: that part of a cathedral or large church
in which the services are conducted. The image was suggested
by the roofless choir of a ruined abbey, which resembles a leaf-
less avenue of tall trees. See Pl. 6c. 8. seals up: concludes.
    Sonnet 74: (Continuing 73). 1. fell: fearful. arrest: Cf. *Haml*,
V.ii.347–48. 3. this line: i.e., of verse. 13–14. The . . . remains: i.e, the worth of my body is the spirit which it contains,
and this verse is my spirit, which stays with you.
    Sonnet 75: 3. peace of you: the peace which comes through
your friendship. 6. Doubting: fearing.

Then bettered° that the world may see my pleasure.
Sometime all full with feasting on your sight,
And by and by clean starvèd for a look,   10
Possessing or pursuing no delight
Save what is had or must from you be took.
  Thus do I pine and surfeit day by day,
  Or gluttoning on all or all away.

76

Why is my verse so barren of new pride,°
So far from variation or quick change?
Why with the time° do I not glance aside
To new-found methods and to compounds strange?°
Why write I still all one, ever the same,   5
And keep invention in a noted weed,°
That every word doth almost tell my name,
Showing their birth and where they did proceed?
Oh, know, sweet love, I always write of you,
And you and love are still my argument.°   10
So all my best is dressing old words new,
Spending again what is already spent.
  For as the sun is daily new and old,
  So is my love still telling what is told.

77°

Thy glass will show thee how thy beauties wear,
Thy dial° how thy precious minutes waste.
The vacant° leaves thy mind's imprint will bear,
And of this book this learning mayst thou taste.
The wrinkles which thy glass will truly show   5
Of mouthèd° graves will give thee memory.
Thou by thy dial's shady stealth° mayst know
Time's thievish progress to eternity.
Look, what thy memory cannot contain   9
Commit to these waste blanks, and thou shalt find
Those children nursed, delivered from thy brain,
To take a new acquaintance of thy mind.
  These offices, so oft as thou wilt look,
  Shall profit thee and much enrich thy book.

78

So oft have I invoked thee for° my Muse
And found such fair assistance in my verse

8. **bettered:** made better.
  Sonnet 76: 1. new pride: novelty.   **3. time:** latest fashion.
4. compounds strange: fantastic compound words, such as some
poets were affecting.   **6. noted weed:** familiar garb.   **10. argument:** subject, theme.
  Sonnet 77: (Sent with the gift of a notebook). **2. dial:** sundial.
3. vacant: empty.   **6. mouthed:** gaping.   **7. shady stealth:**
stealthy shadow.
  Sonnet 78: 1. for: to be.

As° every alien pen hath got my use
And under thee° their poesy disperse.
Thine eyes, that taught the dumb on high to sing   5
And heavy ignorance aloft to fly,
Have added feathers to the learnèd's wing
And given grace a double majesty.
Yet be most proud of that which I compile,
Whose influence is thine and born of thee.   10
In others' works thou dost but mend the style,
And arts with thy sweet graces gracèd be,
  But thou art all my art, and dost advance
  As high as learning my rude ignorance.

79°

Whilst I alone did call upon thy aid,
My verse alone had all thy gentle grace,
But now my gracious numbers are decayed,
And my sick Muse doth give another place.
I grant, sweet love, thy lovely argument°   5
Deserves the travail of a worthier pen,
Yet what of thee thy poet doth invent
He robs thee of, and pays it thee again.
He lends thee virtue, and he stole that word
From thy behavior. Beauty doth he give,   10
And found it in thy cheek. He can afford
No praise to thee but what in thee doth live.
  Then thank him not for that which he doth say,
  Since what he owes thee thou thyself dost pay.

80

Oh, how I faint when I of you do write,
Knowing a better spirit° doth use your name,
And in the praise thereof spends all his might,
To make me tongue-tied, speaking of your fame!
But since your worth, wide as the ocean is,   5
The humble as the proudest sail doth bear,
My saucy bark,° inferior far to his,
On your broad main° doth willfully appear.
Your shallowest help will hold me up afloat,
Whilst he upon your soundless deep° doth ride,   10
Or, being wrecked, I am a worthless boat,°
He of tall° building and of goodly pride.
  Then if he thrive and I be cast away,
  The worst was this — my love was my decay.

3. As: that.   **4. under thee:** under your patronage.
  Sonnet 79: (Continuing 78). **5. thy . . . argument:** the theme
of thy loveliness.
  Sonnet 80: 2. better spirit: greater poet.   **7. bark:** small
ship.   **8. main:** ocean.   **10. soundless deep:** a sea too deep to
be sounded.   **11. boat:** i.e., little boat.   **12. tall:** fine.

81

Or° I shall live your epitaph to make,
Or you survive when I in earth am rotten,
From hence° your memory death cannot take,
Although in me each part will be forgotten.
Your name from hence immortal life shall have,   5
Though I, once gone, to all the world must die.
The earth can yield me but a common grave,
When you entombèd in men's eyes shall lie.
Your monument shall be my gentle verse,
Which eyes not yet created shall o'erread,   10
And tongues to be your being shall rehearse°
When all the breathers of this world are dead.
    You still shall live — such virtue hath my pen —
    Where breath most breathes, even in the mouths
    of men.

82

I grant thou wert not married° to my Muse,
And therefore mayst without attaint° o'erlook
The dedicated words° which writers use
Of their fair subject, blessing every book.
Thou art as fair in knowledge as in hue,   5
Finding thy worth a limit past my praise,
And therefore art enforced to seek anew
Some fresher stamp° of the time-bettering days.
And do so, love. Yet when they have devised
What strainèd touches rhetoric can lend,   10
Thou truly fair wert truly sympathized°
In true plain words by thy true-telling friend,
    And their gross painting° might be better used
    Where cheeks need blood — in thee it is abused.°

83°

I never saw that you did painting need,
And therefore to your fair° no painting set.
I found, or thought I found, you did exceed
The barren tender° of a poet's debt.
And therefore have I slept in your report,   5
That you yourself, being extant, well might show
How far a modern° quill° doth come too short

Speaking of worth, what worth in you doth grow.
This silence for my sin you did impute,
Which shall be most my glory, being dumb,   10
For I impair not beauty being mute,
When others would give life and bring a tomb.°
    There lives more life in one of your fair eyes
    Than both your poets can in praise devise.

84°

Who is it that says most? Which can say more
Than this rich praise, that you alone are you?
In whose confine immurèd is the store
Which should example where your equal grew.°
Lean penury within that pen doth dwell   5
That to his subject lends not some small glory.
But he that writes of you, if he can tell
That you are you, so dignifies his story.
Let him but copy what in you is writ,
Not making worse what Nature made so clear,   10
And such a counterpart shall fame° his wit,
Making his style admirèd everywhere.
    You to your beauteous blessings add a curse,
    Being fond on° praise, which makes your praises
    worse.

85

My tongue-tied Muse in manners holds her still,
While comments of your praise, richly compiled,
Reserve their character° with golden quill,
And precious phrase by all the Muses filed.°
I think good thoughts whilst other write good
    words,   5
And, like unlettered clerk,° still cry " Amen "
To every hymn that able spirit affords,
In polished form of well-refinèd pen.
Hearing you praised, I say, " 'Tis so, 'tis true,"
And to the most of praise add something more.   10
But that is in my thought, whose love to you,
Though words come hindmost, holds his rank be-
    fore.
    Then others for the breath of words respect,
    Me for my dumb thoughts, speaking in effect.°

    Sonnet 81: 1. Or: either.   **3. hence:** i.e., the epitaph.
11. rehearse: relate.
    Sonnet 82: 1. married: i.e., and therefore bound not to en-
courage others.   **2. attaint:** shame.   **3. dedicated words:** dedi-
cations (in books).   **8. stamp:** lit., that which makes an impression.   **11. sympathized:** expressed with feeling.   **13. painting:**
exaggeration.   **14. abused:** misused; i.e., your beauty needs no
exaggeration.
    Sonnet 83: (Continuing 82).   **2. fair:** beauty.   **4. tender:**
offering in repayment.   **7. modern:** slight. **quill:** pen.

    11–12. For . . . tomb: I do not harm your beauty when I say
nothing, but others in trying to make it live destroy it.
    Sonnet 84: (Continuing 83).   **3–4. In . . . grew:** within your-
self is contained (*immured;* lit., walled in) the whole stock of
beauty from which other examples might have been chosen.
11. fame: make famous.   **14. fond on:** foolishly eager for.
    Sonnet 85: 3. Reserve . . . character: preserve this style
(*character;* lit., writing).   **4. filed:** polished.   **6. clerk:** The
clerk said the responses to the prayers read by the parson.
14. in effect: in act.

86°

Was it the proud full sail of his great verse,
Bound for the prize of all too precious you,
That did my ripe thoughts in my brain inhearse,°
Making their tomb the womb wherein they grew?
Was it his spirit, by spirits taught to write   5
Above a mortal pitch, that struck me dead?
No, neither he, nor his compeers° by night
Giving him aid, my verse astonishèd.
He, nor that affable familiar ghost°
Which nightly gulls° him with intelligence,°   10
As victors, of my silence cannot boast.
I was not sick of any fear from thence.
　　But when your countenance filled up his line,
　　Then lacked I matter. That enfeebled mine.

87

Farewell! Thou art too dear for my possessing,
And like enough thou know'st thy estimate.°
The charter° of thy worth gives thee releasing,
My bonds in thee are all determinate.°
For how do I hold thee but by thy granting?   5
And for that riches where is my deserving?
The cause of this fair gift in me is wanting,
And so my patent° back again is swerving.
Thyself thou gavest, thy own worth then not know-
　　ing,
Or me, to whom thou gavest it, else mistaking.   10
So thy great gift, upon misprision° growing,
Comes home again, on better judgment making.
　　Thus have I had thee, as a dream doth flatter,
　　In sleep a king, but waking no such matter.

88

When thou shalt be disposed to set me light,°
And place my merit in the eye of scorn,
Upon thy side against myself I'll fight,
And prove thee virtuous, though thou art forsworn.
With mine own weakness being best acquainted,   5
Upon thy part I can set down a story
Of faults concealed, wherein I am attainted,°
That thou in losing me shalt win much glory.

And I by this will be a gainer too,
For bending all my loving thoughts on thee,   10
The injuries that to myself I do,
Doing thee vantage, double-vantage me.
　　Such is my love, to thee I so belong
　　That for thy right myself will bear all wrong.

89

Say that thou didst forsake me for some fault,
And I will comment upon that offense.
Speak of my lameness, and I straight will halt,
Against thy reasons making no defense.
Thou canst not, love, disgrace me half so ill,   5
To set a form° upon desirèd change,
As I'll myself disgrace. Knowing thy will,
I will acquaintance strangle° and look strange,
Be absent from thy walks, and in my tongue
Thy sweet belovèd name no more shall dwell,   10
Lest I, too much profane, should do it wrong,
And haply of our old acquaintance tell.
　　For thee, against myself I'll vow debate,
　　For I must ne'er love him whom thou dost hate.

90°

Then hate me when thou wilt. If ever, now,
Now while the world is bent my deeds to cross,
Join with the spite of fortune, make me bow,
And do not drop in for an afterloss.°
Ah, do not, when my heart hath 'scaped this sorrow,
Come in the rearward of a conquered woe.   6
Give not a windy night a rainy morrow,
To linger° out a purposed overthrow.
If thou wilt leave me, do not leave me last,
When other petty griefs have done their spite,   10
But in the onset come. So shall I taste
At first the very worst of fortune's might,
　　And other strains of woe, which now seem woe,
　　Compared with loss of thee will not seem so.

91

Some glory in their birth, some in their skill,
Some in their wealth, some in their body's force,
Some in their garments, though newfangled ill,°

Sonnet 86: (Continuing 85). The rival poet is by many believed to be George Chapman.   3. inhearse: entomb.   7. compeers: fellow students.   9. ghost: spirit.   10. gulls: cheats.
intelligence: news.
　　Sonnet 87: 2. estimate: value.   3. charter: lit., a right to
perform certain actions.   4. determinate: ended.   8. patent:
privilege.   11. misprision: misunderstanding.
　　Sonnet 88: 1. set me light: regard me lightly.   7. attainted:
dishonored.

Sonnet 89: 6. set a form: give a good appearance to.
8. strangle: destroy.
　　Sonnet 90: (Continuing 89).   4. afterloss: later misfortune.
8. linger: protract.
　　Sonnet 91: 3. newfangled ill: i.e., the latest ugly fashion.

Some in their hawks and hounds, some in their
    horse.
And every humor° hath his adjunct° pleasure,   5
Wherein it finds a joy above the rest.
But these particulars are not my measure,
All these I better in one general best.
Thy love is better than high birth to me,
Richer than wealth, prouder than garments' cost,
Of more delight than hawks or horses be.   11
And having thee, of all men's pride I boast,
    Wretched in this alone, that thou mayst take
    All this away and me most wretched make.

92°

But do thy worst to steal thyself away,
For term of life thou art assurèd mine.
And life no longer than thy love will stay,
For it depends upon that love of thine.
Then need I not to fear the worst of wrongs,   5
When in the least of them my life hath end.
I see a better state to me belongs
Than that which on thy humor doth depend.
Thou canst not vex me with inconstant mind,
Since that my life on thy revolt doth lie.°   10
Oh, what a happy title do I find,
Happy to have thy love, happy to die!
    But what's so blessèd-fair that fears no blot?
    Thou mayst be false, and yet I know it not.

93

So shall I live, supposing thou art true,
Like a deceivèd husband. So love's face
May still seem love to me, though altered new,
Thy looks with me, thy heart in other place.
For there can live no hatred in thine eye,   5
Therefore in that I cannot know thy change.
In many's looks the false heart's history
Is writ in moods and frowns and wrinkles strange,
But Heaven in thy creation did decree
That in thy face sweet love should ever dwell,   10
Whate'er thy thoughts or thy heart's workings be,
Thy looks should nothing thence but sweetness tell.
    How like Eve's apple° doth thy beauty grow
    If thy sweet virtue answer not° thy show!

94

They that have power to hurt and will do none,
That do not do the thing they most do show,°
Who, moving others, are themselves as stone,
Unmovèd, cold, and to temptation slow —
They rightly do inherit Heaven's graces   5
And husband nature's riches from expense.°
They are the lords and owners of their faces,
Others but stewards° of their excellence.
The summer's flower is to the summer sweet,
Though to itself it only live and die,   10
But if that flower with base infection meet,
The basest weed outbraves his dignity.°
    For sweetest things turn sourest by their deeds.
    Lilies that fester smell far worse than weeds.

95

How sweet and lovely dost thou make the shame
Which, like a canker in the fragrant rose,
Doth spot the beauty of thy budding name!
Oh, in what sweets dost thou thy sins enclose!
That tongue that tells the story of thy days,   5
Making lascivious comments on thy sport,
Cannot dispraise but in a kind of praise.
Naming thy name blesses an ill report.
Oh, what a mansion have those vices got
Which for their habitation chose out thee,   10
Where beauty's veil doth cover every blot
And all things turn to fair that eyes can see!
    Take heed, dear heart, of this large privilege.°
    The hardest knife ill-used doth lose his edge.

96°

Some say thy fault is youth, some wantonness,
Some say thy grace is youth and gentle sport.
Both grace and faults are loved of more and less,
Thou makest faults graces that to thee resort.
As on the finger of a thronèd queen   5
The basest jewel will be well esteemed,
So are those errors that in thee are seen
To truths translated° and for true things deemed.
How many lambs might the stern wolf betray
If like a lamb he could his looks translate!°   10
How many gazers mightst thou lead away
If thou wouldst use the strength of all thy state!
    But do not so. I love thee in such sort
    As thou being mine, mine is thy good report.

5. **humor:** whim. See App. 3. **adjunct:** annexed.
    Sonnet 92: (Continuing 91). **9–10. Thou . . . lie:** you cannot torment me by being inconstant for when you desert me (*revolt*), I die.
    Sonnet 93: 13. Eve's apple: i.e., lovely to look upon but disastrous in its effects. **14. answer not:** does not correspond with.

    Sonnet 94: 2. show: seem to do. **6. expense:** waste.
8. stewards: hired overseers. **12. dignity:** worth.
    Sonnet 95: 13. large privilege: freedom to go astray.
    Sonnet 96: (Continuing 95). **8. translated:** transformed.
10. like . . . translate: make himself like a lamb.

97

How like a winter hath my absence been
From thee, the pleasure of the fleeting year!
What freezings have I felt, what dark days seen!
What old December's bareness everywhere!
And yet this time removed° was summer's time, 5
The teeming autumn, big with rich increase,
Bearing the wanton burden of the prime,
Like widowed wombs after their lords' decease.
Yet this abundant issue seemed to me
But hope of orphans and unfathered fruit,° 10
For summer and his pleasures wait on thee,
And, thou away, the very birds are mute,
　Or if they sing, 'tis with so dull a cheer
　That leaves look pale, dreading the winter's near.

98

From you have I been absent in the spring,
When proud-pied° April, dressed in all his trim,
Hath put a spirit of youth in everything,
That heavy Saturn° laughed and leaped with him.
Yet nor the lays of birds, nor the sweet smell 5
Of different flowers in odor and in hue,
Could make me any summer's story tell,
Or from their proud lap pluck them where they
　　grew.
Nor did I wonder at the lily's white,
Nor praise the deep vermilion in the rose. 10
They were but sweet, but figures of delight,
Drawn after you, you pattern of all those.°
　Yet seemed it winter still and, you away,
　As with your shadow° I with these did play.

99°

The forward° violet thus did I chide:
Sweet thief, whence didst thou steal thy sweet that
　　smells
If not from my love's breath? The purple pride

Which on thy soft cheek for complexion dwells
In my love's veins thou hast too grossly dyed. 5
The lily I condemnèd for thy hand,°
And buds of marjoram had stol'n thy hair.
The roses fearfully on thorns did stand,°
One blushing shame, another white despair,
A third, nor red nor white, had stol'n of both 10
And to his robbery had annexed thy breath.
But for his theft, in pride of all his growth
A vengeful canker eat him up to death.
　More flowers I noted, yet I none could see
　But sweet or color it had stol'n from thee. 15

100

Where art thou, Muse, that thou forget'st so long
To speak of that which gives thee all thy might?
Spend'st thou thy fury° on some worthless song,
Darkening thy power to lend base subjects light?
Return, forgetful Muse, and straight redeem 5
In gentle numbers time so idly spent,
Sing to the ear that doth thy lays esteem
And gives thy pen both skill and argument.
Rise, resty° Muse, my love's sweet face survey,
If Time have any wrinkle graven there. 10
If any, be a satire to° decay,
And make Time's spoils despisèd everywhere.
　Give my love fame faster than Time wastes life.
　So thou prevent'st° his scythe and crooked knife.

101°

O truant Muse, what shall be thy amends
For thy neglect of truth in beauty dyed?
Both truth and beauty on my love depends,
So dost thou too, and therein dignified.°
Make answer, Muse. Wilt thou not haply say, 5
"Truth needs no color with his color fixed,
Beauty no pencil, beauty's truth to lay,°
But best is best if never intermixed"?
Because he needs no praise, wilt thou be dumb?
Excuse not silence so, for 't lies in thee 10
To make him much outlive a gilded tomb
And to be praised of ages yet to be.
　Then do thy office, Muse. I teach thee how
　To make him seem long hence as he shows now.

Sonnet 97: 5. **removed:** of absence.   **9–10. Yet . . . fruit:** yet this promise of plenty seemed to me (like the widow's posthumous child) to be a promise also of children who should be fatherless orphans.

Sonnet 98: 2. **proud-pied:** exulting in the variety of its colors. 4. **Saturn:** the planet. Those born under its influence were heavy and saturnine.   **11–12. They . . . those:** i.e., their sweetness was nothing in itself; it was a symbol of you, the pattern of all loveliness.   14. **shadow:** symbol. See Sonnet 53.

Sonnet 99: (Continuing 98). This sonnet contains 15 lines, a fifth line having been added to the first quatrain.   1. **forward:** precocious. The violet is one of the first flowers to appear in the spring.

6. **condemned . . . hand:** accused of stealing the whiteness of your hand.   8. **on . . . stand:** i.e., uneasily, like anxious thieves. Cf. the phrase "on tenterhooks."

Sonnet 100: 3. **fury:** enthusiasm.   9. **resty:** sluggish.   11. **be . . . to:** write satires on.   14. **prevent'st:** anticipate.

Sonnet 101: (Continuing 100). 4. **dignified:** are dignified.
7. **lay:** paint.

102

My love is strengthened, though more weak in seem-
    ing,
I love not less, though less the show appear.
That love is merchandised° whose rich esteeming°
The owner's tongue doth publish everywhere.
Our love was new, and then but in the spring,   5
When I was wont to greet it with my lays,
As Philomel° in summer's front° doth sing,
And stops her pipe in growth of riper days.
Not that the summer is less pleasant now
Than when her mournful hymns did hush the night,
But that wild music burdens every bough,   11
And sweets grown common lose their dear delight.
    Therefore, like her, I sometime hold my tongue,
    Because I would not dull you with my song.

103

Alack, what poverty my Muse brings forth,
That having such a scope to show her pride,
The argument, all bare, is of more worth
Than when it hath my added praise beside!
Oh, blame me not if I no more can write!   5
Look in your glass, and there appears a face
That overgoes° my blunt invention quite,
Dulling my lines and doing me disgrace.
Were it not sinful then, striving to mend,
To mar the subject that before was well?   10
For to no other pass° my verses tend
Than of your graces and your gifts to tell,
    And more, much more, than in my verse can sit,
    Your own glass shows you when you look in it.

104°

To me, fair friend, you never can be old,
For as you were when first your eye I eyed,
Such seems your beauty still. Three winters cold
Have from the forests shook three summers' pride,
Three beauteous springs to yellow autumn turned
In process of the seasons have I seen,   6
Three April perfumes in three hot Junes burned,
Since first I saw you fresh, which yet are green.
Ah, yet doth beauty, like a dial hand,°
Steal from his figure, and no pace perceived.   10

So your sweet hue, which methinks still doth **stand,**
Hath motion, and mine eye may be deceived.
    For fear of which, hear this, thou age unbred —
    Ere you were born was beauty's summer dead.

105

Let not my love be called idolatry,
Nor my belovèd as an idol show,°
Since all alike my songs and praises be
To one, of one, still such, and ever so.
Kind is my love today, tomorrow kind,   5
Still constant in a wondrous excellence,
Therefore my verse to constancy confined,
One thing expressing, leaves out difference.°
" Fair, kind, and true " is all my argument,
" Fair, kind, and true " varying to other words,   10
And in this change° is my invention spent,
Three themes in one, which wondrous scope affords.
    " Fair, kind, and true " have often lived alone,
    Which three till now never kept seat in one.

106

When in the chronicle of wasted° time
I see descriptions of the fairest wights,°
And beauty making beautiful old rhyme
In praise of ladies dead and lovely knights,
Then, in the blazon° of sweet beauty's best,   5
Of hand, of foot, of lip, of eye, of brow,
I see their antique pen would have expressed
Even such a beauty as you master now.
So all their praises are but prophecies
Of this our time, all you prefiguring,   10
And, for° they looked but with divining° eyes,
They had not skill enough your worth to sing.
    For we, which now behold these present days,
    Have eyes to wonder, but lack tongues to praise.

107

Not mine own fears, nor the prophetic soul
Of the wide world dreaming on things to come,
Can yet the lease of my true love control,

Sonnet 102: 3. merchandised: bought and sold. esteeming:
value.   7. Philomel: the nightingale, whose song is chiefly heard
in May. front: early days.
    Sonnet 103: 7. overgoes: surpasses.   11. pass: end.
    Sonnet 104: In this sonnet the poet shows that the friendship
has lasted for three years.   9. like . . . hand: like the stealthy
movement of the shadow on the sundial.

Sonnet 105: 2. show: appear.   8. difference: the quality
which distinguishes different specimens of the same kind.
11. change: variety; lit., the different orders in which a peal of
bells can be rung. See App. 19.
    Sonnet 106: 1. wasted: passed, dead and gone.   2. wights:
men, a poetic word.   5. blazon: praise; lit., heraldic description
of a coat of arms.   11. for: except that. divining: foreseeing.

Supposed as forfeit to a cónfined doom.°
The mortal moon hath her eclipse endured,°   5
And the sad augurs° mock their own presage.
Incertainties now crown themselves assured,
And peace proclaims olives° of endless age.
Now with the drops of this most balmy time
My love looks fresh, and Death to me subscribes,°
Since, spite of him, I'll live in this poor rhyme   11
While he insults° o'er dull and speechless° tribes.
　　And thou in this shalt find thy monument,
　　When tyrants' crests and tombs of brass are spent.

108

What's in the brain that ink may character°
Which hath not figured to thee my true spirit?
What's new to speak, what new to register,
That may express my love, or thy dear merit?
Nothing, sweet boy. But yet, like prayers divine,   5
I must each day say o'er the very same,
Counting no old thing old, thou mine, I thine,
Even as when first I hallowed° thy fair name.
So that eternal love in love's fresh case°
Weighs not the dust and injury of age,   10
Nor gives to necessary wrinkles place,
But makes antiquity° for aye his page,°
　　Finding the first conceit° of love there bred
　　Where time and outward form would show it
　　dead.

109

Oh, never say that I was false of heart,
Though absence seemed my flame to qualify.°
As easy might I from myself depart
As from my soul,° which in thy breast doth lie.
That is my home of love. If I have ranged,°   5
Like him that travels, I return again,

Just° to the time, not with the time exchanged,°
So that myself bring water for my stain.
Never believe, though in my nature reigned
All frailties that besiege all kinds of blood,   10
That it could so preposterously be stained,
To leave for nothing all thy sum of good.
　　For nothing this wide universe I call,
　　Save thou, my rose.° In it thou art my all.

110°

Alas, 'tis true I have gone here and there,
And made myself a motley° to the view,
Gored mine own thoughts, sold cheap what is most
　　dear,
Made old offenses of affections new.°
Most true it is that I have looked on truth   5
Askance and strangely. But, by all above,
These blenches° gave my heart another youth,
And worse essays proved thee my best of love.
Now all is done, have what shall have no end.
Mine appetite I never more will grind   10
On newer proof, to try° an older friend,
A god in love, to whom I am confined.
　　Then give me welcome, next my heaven the best,
　　Even to thy pure and most most loving breast.

111

Oh, for my sake do you with Fortune chide,
The guilty goddess of my harmful deeds,
That did not better for my life provide
Than public means which public manners breeds.°
Thence comes it that my name receives a brand,°   5
And almost thence my nature is subdued
To what it works in, like the dyer's hand.
Pity me, then, and wish I were renewed,°
Whilst, like a willing patient, I will drink
Potions of eisel 'gainst my strong infection.°   10
No bitterness that I will bitter think,
Nor double penance, to correct correction.
　　Pity me, then, dear friend, and I assure ye
　　Even that your pity is enough to cure me.

Sonnet 107: 4. Supposed . . . doom: if the *lease* is forfeit, the meaning of the quatrain is "those who declared that our love was ended have proved bad prophets." If *love* (i.e., my friend) is forfeit, the line means "believed to be condemned to imprisonment." **5. The . . . endured:** The mortal moon is Queen Elizabeth, but it is disputable whether the line means "has passed through an eclipse and emerged safely" or has been permanently eclipsed; i.e., has died. The Queen died on March 24, 1603. **6. sad augurs:** i.e., those who prophesied disaster. **8. olives:** The olive is the symbol of peace. **10. subscribes:** yields. **12. insults:** triumphs. **speechless:** who cannot express themselves.
　　Sonnet 108: 1. character: write. **8. hallowed:** made holy. **9. fresh case:** renewal. **12. antiquity:** old age. **page:** boy servant. **13. conceit:** thought.
　　Sonnet 109: 2. qualify: moderate. **4. my soul:** i.e., you my love. Cf. *T Night*, I.v.288. **5. ranged:** roamed.

7. Just: exactly. **exchanged:** changed. **14. rose:** See Sonnet 1.2.
　　Sonnet 110: (Continuing 109). **2. motley:** professional jester; lit., the fool's particolored dress. **4. Made . . . new:** offended old friends by making new ones. **7. blenches:** glances aside. **11. try:** test.
　　Sonnet 111: (Continuing 110). **4. public . . . breeds:** living on vulgar applause which produces vulgar manners. **5. brand:** mark of shame. **8. renewed:** revived. **10. eisel . . . infection:** vinegar, drunk as an antidote to the plague (*infection*).

112°

Your love and pity doth the impression fill°
Which vulgar scandal stamped upon my brow.
For what care I who calls me well or ill,
So you o'ergreen° my bad, my good allow?
You are my all the world, and I must strive   5
To know my shames and praises from your tongue,
None else to me, nor I to none alive,
That my steeled sense or changes right or wrong.°
In so profound abysm I throw all care
Of° others' voices, that my adder's sense°   10
To critic and to flatterer stoppèd are.
Mark how with my neglect I do dispense.°
   You are so strongly in my purpose bred
   That all the world besides methinks are dead.

113

Since I left you mine eye is in my mind,
And that which governs me to go about
Doth part his function° and is partly blind,
Seems seeing, but effectually° is out.
For it no form delivers to the heart   5
Of bird, of flower, or shape, which it doth latch.°
Of his quick objects hath the mind no part,
Nor his own vision holds what it doth catch.
For if it see the rudest or gentlest sight,
The most sweet favor° or deformed'st creature,   10
The mountain or the sea, the day or night,
The crow or dove, it shapes them to your feature.
   Incapable of more, replete with you,
   My most true mind thus maketh mine° untrue.

114°

Or whether° doth my mind, being crowned with
     you,
Drink up the monarch's plague, this flattery?°
Or whether shall I say mine eye saith true,
And that your love taught it this alchemy,°

To make of monsters and things indigest°   5
Such cherubins as your sweet self resemble,
Creating every bad a perfect best
As fast as objects to his beams° assemble?
Oh, 'tis the first, 'tis flattery in my seeing,
And my great mind most kingly drinks it up.   10
Mine eye well knows what with his gust° is 'gree-
     ing,
And to his palate doth prepare the cup.
   If it be poisoned, 'tis the lesser sin
   That mine eye loves it and doth first begin.

115

Those lines that I before have writ do lie,
Even those that said I could not love you dearer.
Yet then my judgment knew no reason why
My most full flame should afterward burn clearer.
But reckoning Time,° whose millioned accidents   5
Creep in 'twixt vows, and change decrees of kings,
Tan° sacred beauty, blunt the sharp'st intents,
Divert strong minds to the course of altering
     things —
Alas, why, fearing of Time's tyranny,
Might I not then say, "Now I love you best,"   10
When I was certain o'er incertainty,
Crowning the present, doubting of the rest?
   Love is a babe, then might I not say so,
   To give full growth to that which still doth grow?

116

Let me not to the marriage of true minds
Admit impediments. Love is not love
Which alters when it alteration finds,
Or bends with the remover to remove.°
Oh no! It is an ever-fixèd mark   5
That looks on tempests and is never shaken.
It is the star to every wandering bark,
Whose worth's unknown, although his height be
     taken.
Love's not Time's fool,° though rosy lips and cheeks
Within his bending sickle's compass come.   10
Love alters not with his brief hours and weeks,
But bears it out even to the edge of doom.°
   If this be error and upon me proved,
   I never writ, nor no man ever loved.

Sonnet 112: (Continuing 111). 1. impression fill: take away
the mark.   4. o'ergreen: cover over (as with new grass).
7–8. None . . . wrong: there is no one else for whom I care or
who cares for me that can change my firm feelings either to right
or wrong.   10. Of: for. adder's sense: an echo of Psalm 58:
The poison of the wicked "is like the poison of a serpent; they
are like the deaf adder that stoppeth her ear."   12. with . . .
dispense: I excuse my neglect.

     Sonnet 113: 3. part . . . function: divides its functions; i.e.,
the eye's function is to perceive objects and convey the impression to the mind, but the poet's eye is now only able to perceive
without conveying.   4. effectually: actually.   6. latch: lay hold
of.   10. favor: face.   14. mine: i.e., eye.

     Sonnet 114: (Continuing 113). 1. Or whether: is it that.
2. flattery: i.e., dressing up the truth to make it more palatable.
4. alchemy: power to transform. See App. 21.

5. indigest: shapeless.   8. beams: See Sonnet 20.6,n.   11. gust:
taste.

     Sonnet 115: 5. reckoning Time: i.e., remembering Time's
power.   7. Tan: make brown.

     Sonnet 116: 4. Or . . . remove: or wishes to change when the
loved one is inconstant.   9. Time's fool: i.e., mocked by Time.
Cf. *I Hen IV*, V.iv.81.   12. doom: Doomsday.

117

Accuse me thus: that I have scanted° all
Wherein I should your great deserts repay,
Forgot upon your dearest love to call,
Whereto all bonds do tie me day by day.
That I have frequent been with unknown minds, 5
And given to time your own dear-purchased right.
That I have hoisted sail to all the winds
Which should transport me farthest from your sight.
Book° both my willfulness and errors down,
And on just proof surmise accumulate.° 10
Bring me within the level° of your frown,
But shoot not at me in your wakened hate,
   Since my appeal says I did strive to prove
   The constancy and virtue of your love.

118°

Like as, to make our appetites more keen,
With eager° compounds we our palate urge —
As to prevent° our maladies unseen
We sicken° to shun sickness when we purge —
Even so, being full of your ne'er-cloying sweetness,
To bitter sauces did I frame my feeding, 6
And sick of welfare found a kind of meetness°
To be diseased, ere that there was true needing.
Thus policy in love, to anticipate
The ills that were not, grew to faults assured, 10
And brought to medicine° a healthful state,
Which, rank° of goodness, would by ill be cured.
   But thence I learn, and find the lesson true,
   Drugs poison him that so fell sick of you.

119

What potions have I drunk of Siren° tears,
Distilled from limbecks° foul as Hell within,
Applying fears to hopes and hopes to fears,
Still losing when I saw myself to win!
What wretched errors hath my heart committed 5
Whilst it hath thought itself so blessèd never!
How have mine eyes out of their spheres been fitted°
In the distraction of this madding fever!
O benefit of ill! Now I find true

That better is by evil still made better, 10
And ruined love, when it is built anew,
Grows fairer than at first, more strong, far greater.
   So I return rebuked to my content,
   And gain by ill thrice more than I have spent.

120

That you were once unkind befriends me now,
And for that sorrow which I then did feel
Needs must I under my transgression bow,
Unless my nerves° were brass or hammered steel.
For if you were by my unkindness shaken, 5
As I by yours, you've passed a hell of time,
And I, a tyrant, have no leisure taken
To weigh how once I suffered in your crime.
Oh, that our night of woe might have remembered°
My deepest sense, how hard true sorrow hits, 10
And soon to you, as you to me, then tendered
The humble salve° which wounded bosoms fits!
   But that your trespass now becomes a fee,
   Mine ransoms yours, and yours must ransom me.

121

'Tis better to be vile than vile esteemed,
When not to be receives reproach of being,
And the just pleasure lost, which is so° deemed
Not by our feeling, but by others' seeing.
For why should others' false adulterate eyes 5
Give salutation to° my sportive blood?
Or on my frailties why are frailer spies,
Which in their wills count bad what I think good?
No, I am that I am, and they that level
At my abuses reckon up their own. 10
I may be straight, though they themselves be bevel,°
By their rank thoughts my deeds must not be shown,
   Unless this general evil they maintain,
   All men are bad and in their badness reign.

122°

Thy gift, thy tables,° are within my brain
Full charactered° with lasting memory,
Which shall above that idle rank° remain
Beyond all date, even to eternity.

Sonnet 117: 1. **scanted:** neglected. 9. **Book:** record as a debit. 10. **on . . . accumulate:** add suspicion to proof. 11. **level:** aim.
   Sonnet 118: (Continuing 117 but in the medical imagery of purging). 2. **eager:** bitter. 3. **prevent:** forestall. 4. **sicken:** deliberately make ourselves ill by taking medicine. 7. **meetness:** fitness. 11. **brought to medicine:** caused to be sick. 12. **rank:** overfull.
   Sonnet 119: 1. **Siren:** temptress. The Sirens were creatures who by their beautiful songs lured mariners to their destruction. 2. **limbecks:** alembics, stills. 7. **fitted:** convulsed.

   Sonnet 120: 4. **nerves:** sinews. 9. **remembered:** reminded. 12. **salve:** healing ointment.
   Sonnet 121: 3. **so:** i.e., vile. 6. **Give . . . to:** salute as one of themselves. 11. **bevel:** slanting.
   Sonnet 122: The poet excuses himself for giving away his friend's gift of a notebook. 1. **tables:** notebook. 2. **charactered:** inscribed. 3. **idle rank:** empty series (of leaves).

Or, at the least, so long as brain and heart   5
Have faculty by nature to subsist,
Till each to razed oblivion yield his part
Of thee, thy record never can be missed.
That poor retention° could not so much hold,
Nor need I tallies° thy dear love to score.°   10
Therefore to give them from me° was I bold,
To trust those tables that receive thee more.
　　To keep an adjunct° to remember thee
　　Were to import° forgetfulness in me.

123

No, Time, thou shalt not boast that I do change.
Thy pyramids built up with newer might
To me are nothing novel, nothing strange,
They are but dressings of a former sight.°
Our dates are brief, and therefore we admire°   5
What thou dost foist upon us that is old,
And rather make them born to our desire
Than think that we before have heard them told.
Thy registers and thee I both defy,
Not wondering at the present nor the past,   10
For thy recórds and what we see doth lie,
Made more or less by thy continual haste.
　　This I do vow, and this shall ever be,
　　I will be true, despite thy scythe and thee.

124

If my dear love were but the child of state,°
It might for Fortune's bastard be unfathered,°
As subject to Time's love or to Time's hate,
Weeds among weeds, or flowers with flowers
　　gathered.
No, it was builded far from accident,   5
It suffers not in smiling pomp, nor falls
Under the blow of thrallèd discontent,°
Whereto the inviting time our fashion calls.°
It fears not policy, that heretic,
Which works on leases of short-numbered hours,
But all alone stands hugely politic,   11
That it nor grows with heat nor drowns with show-
　　ers.

To this I witness call the fools of time,
Which die for goodness, who have lived for
　　crime.°

125°

Were 't aught to me I bore the canopy,°
With my extern the outward honoring,
Or laid great bases for eternity,
Which prove more short than waste or ruining?
Have I not seen dwellers on form and favor°   5
Lose all, and more, by paying too much rent,
For compound sweet forgoing simple savor,
Pitiful thrivers, in their gazing spent?°
No, let me be obsequious in thy heart,
And take thou my oblation, poor but free,   10
Which is not mixed with seconds,° knows no art
But mutual render,° only me for thee.
　　Hence, thou suborned° informer! A true soul
　　When most impeached stands least in thy control.

126

O thou, my lovely boy, who in thy power
Dost hold Time's fickle glass, his sickle, hour,
Who hast by waning grown,° and therein show'st
Thy lovers withering as thy sweet self grow'st,
If Nature, sovereign mistress over wrack,°   5
As thou goest onwards, still will pluck thee back,
She keeps thee to this purpose, that her skill
May time disgrace and wretched minutes kill.
Yet fear her, O thou minion° of her pleasure!
She may detain, but not still keep, her treasure.   10
Her audit, though delayed, answered must be,
And her quietus° is to render° thee.

127°

In the old age black was not counted fair,
Or if it were, it bore not beauty's name,

13–14. fools . . . crime: those foolish heretics who when executed for crime declare that they are dying in a holy cause.
　　Sonnet 125: (Continuing 124). 1. bore . . . canopy: paid outward signs of respect. On state occasions, the sovereign walked or was carried under a canopy carried by courtiers. See Pl. 3b. 5. dwellers . . . favor: hopeful flatterers who pay much attention to ceremony and signs of favor. 8. Pitiful . . . spent: disappointed losers who lose all while they gape for promotion. 11. seconds: ulterior aims. 12. render: surrender, exchange. 13. suborned: perjured.
　　Sonnet 126: The last of the Sonnets to the fair youth, and probably an envoy (or conclusion) to the whole series, written in six rhymed couplets. 3. waning grown: i.e., growing more (and not less) beautiful as you grow older. 5. wrack: ruin. 9. minion: darling. 12. quietus: closing of the account. render: use you as payment.
　　Sonnet 127: The first of the series to the dark mistress.

9. retention: container; i.e., the book. 10. tallies: A tally was a stick on which notches were cut as a record of sums of money owed. score: record (a debt). 11. give . . . me: give away. 13. adjunct: object. 14. import: imply.
　　Sonnet 123: 4. dressings . . . sight: repetitions of what we have seen before. 5. admire: wonder at.
　　Sonnet 124: 1. child of state: born of circumstances; i.e., accidental. 2. Fortune's . . . unfathered: be neglected as a mere bastard. 7. thralled discontent: discontent held in subjugation. 8. the . . . calls: i.e., the discontent which is fashionable nowadays

But now is black beauty's successive° heir,
And beauty slandered with a bastard shame.
For since each hand hath put on Nature's power, 5
Fairing the foul° with art's false borrowed face,
Sweet beauty hath no name, no holy bower,
But is profaned, if not lives in disgrace.
Therefore my mistress' eyes are raven-black,
Her eyes so suited,° and they mourners seem   10
At such who, not born fair, no beauty lack,°
Slandering creation with a false esteem.
    Yet so they mourn, becoming of their woe,
    That every tongue says beauty should look so.

128

How oft, when thou, my music, music play'st
Upon that blessed wood° whose motion sounds
With thy sweet fingers, when thou gently sway'st
The wiry concord° that mine ear confounds,
Do I envy those jacks° that nimble leap   5
To kiss the tender inward of thy hand
Whilst my poor lips, which should that harvest reap,
At the wood's boldness by thee blushing stand!
To be so tickled, they would change their state
And situation with those dancing chips   10
O'er whom thy fingers walk with gentle gait,
Making dead wood more blest than living lips.
    Since saucy jacks so happy are in this,
    Give them thy fingers, me thy lips to kiss.

129

The expense of spirit in a waste of shame
Is lust in action, and till action, lust
Is perjured, murderous, bloody, full of blame,
Savage, extreme, rude, cruel, not to trust,
Enjoyed no sooner but despisèd straight,   5
Past reason hunted, and no sooner had,
Past reason hated, as a swallowed bait,
On purpose laid to make the taker mad.
Mad in pursuit, and in possession so,
Had, having, and in quest to have, extreme,   10
A bliss in proof, and proved,° a very woe.
Before, a joy proposed, behind, a dream.
    All this the world well knows, yet none knows
        well
    To shun the Heaven that leads men to this Hell.

130

My mistress' eyes are nothing like the sun,
Coral is far more red than her lips' red.
If snow be white, why then her breasts are dun,
If hairs be wires, black wires grow on her head.
I have seen roses damasked,° red and white,   5
But no such roses see I in her cheeks.
And in some perfumes is there more delight
Than in the breath that from my mistress reeks.
I love to hear her speak, yet well I know
That music hath a far more pleasing sound.   10
I grant I never saw a goddess go,°
My mistress, when she walks, treads on the ground.
    And yet, by Heaven, I think my love as rare
    As any she belied with false compare.

131

Thou art as tyrannous, so as thou art,°
As those whose beauties proudly make them cruel.
For well thou know'st to my dear doting heart
Thou art the fairest and most precious jewel.
Yet, in good faith, some say that thee behold,   5
Thy face hath not the power to make love groan.
To say they err I dare not be so bold,
Although I swear it to myself alone.
And to be sure that is not false I swear,
A thousand groans, but thinking on thy face,   10
One on another's neck,° do witness bear
Thy black is fairest in my judgment's place.
    In nothing art thou black save in thy deeds,
    And thence this slander, as I think, proceeds.

132

Thine eyes I love, and they, as pitying me,
Knowing thy heart torments me with disdain,
Have put on black and loving mourners be,
Looking with pretty ruth° upon my pain.
And truly not the morning sun of heaven   5
Better becomes the gray cheeks of the east,
Nor that full star that ushers in the even
Doth half that glory to the sober west,
As those two mourning eyes become thy face.
Oh, let it then as well beseem° thy heart   10
To mourn for me, since mourning doth thee grace,
And suit thy pity° like in every part.
    Then will I swear beauty herself is black,
    And all they foul that thy complexion lack.

3. successive: in order of succession.   6. Fairing . . . foul: making beautiful the ugly.   10. suited: matching.   11. no . . . lack: i.e., because they have beautified themselves.
    Sonnet 128: 2. wood: i.e., the keys of the virginal. See Pl. 19f.
4. wiry concord: harmony of wires.   5. jacks: keys.
    Sonnet 129: 11. proved: experienced.

    Sonnet 130: 5. damasked: variegated pink and white.
11. go: walk.
    Sonnet 131: 1. so . . . art: being what you are.   11. One . . . neck: one after the other.
    Sonnet 132: 4. ruth: pity.   10. beseem: be fitting for.
12. suit . . . pity: i.e., let your pity also wear black.

133°

Beshrew° that heart that makes my heart to groan
For that deep wound it gives my friend and me!
Is 't not enough to torture me alone,
But slave to slavery my sweet'st friend must be?
Me from myself thy cruel eye hath taken,   5
And my next self thou harder hast engrossed.°
Of him, myself, and thee I am forsaken,
A torment thrice threefold thus to be crossed.
Prison my heart in thy steel bosom's ward,°
But then my friend's heart let my poor heart bail.
Whoe'er keeps me, let my heart be his guard,   11
Thou canst not then use rigor in my jail.
    And yet thou wilt, for I, being pent in thee,
    Perforce am thine, and all that is in me.

134°

So, now I have confessed that he is thine
And I myself am mortgaged to thy will,
Myself I'll forfeit, so that other mine°
Thou wilt restore, to be my comfort still.
But thou wilt not, nor he will not be free,   5
For thou art covetous and he is kind.
He learned but surety-like to write° for me,
Under that bond that him as fast doth bind.
The statute of thy beauty thou wilt take,
Thou usurer, that put'st forth all to use,   10
And sue a friend came° debtor for my sake,
So him I lose through my unkind abuse.
    Him have I lost, thou hast both him and me.
    He pays the whole, and yet am I not free.

135

Whoever hath her wish, thou hast thy "Will,"°
And "Will" to boot,° and "Will" in overplus.
More than enough am I that vex thee still,
To thy sweet will making addition thus.
Wilt thou, whose will is large and spacious,   5
Not once vouchsafe to hide my will in thine?
Shall will in others seem right gracious
And in my will no fair acceptance shine?
The sea, all water, yet receives rain still,
And in abundance addeth to his store.   10
So thou, being rich in "Will," add to thy "Will"

One will of mine, to make thy large "Will" more
Let no unkind, no fair beseechers kill.
Think all but one, and me in that one "Will."

136°

If thy soul check° thee that I come so near,
Swear to thy blind soul that I was thy "Will,"
And will, thy soul knows, is admitted there.
Thus far for love, my love suit, sweet, fulfill.
"Will" will fulfill the treasure of thy love —   5
Aye, fill it full with wills, and my will one.
In things of great receipt° with ease we prove
Among a number one is reckoned none.
Then in the number let me pass untold,
Though in thy store's account I one must be,   10
For nothing hold me, so it please thee hold
That nothing me, a something sweet to thee.
    Make but my name° thy love, and love that still,
    And then thou lovest me, for my name is "Will."

137

Thou blind fool, Love, what dost thou to mine eyes,
That they behold, and see not what they see?
They know what beauty is, see where it lies,
Yet what the best is take the worst to be.°
If eyes, corrupt by overpartial looks,   5
Be anchored in the bay where all men ride,
Why of eyes' falsehood° hast thou forgèd hooks
Whereto the judgment of my heart is tied?
Why should my heart think that a several° plot
Which my heart knows the wide world's common
     place?   10
Or mine eyes seeing this, say this is not,
To put fair truth upon so foul a face?
    In things right true my heart and eyes have erred,
    And to this false plague are they now transferred.

138

When my love swears that she is made of truth,
I do believe her, though I know she lies,
That she might think me some untutored youth,
Unlearnèd in the world's false subtleties.
Thus vainly thinking that she thinks me young,   5
Although she knows my days are past the best,
Simply I credit her false-speaking tongue.
On both sides thus is simple truth suppressed.

Sonnet 133: Cf. Sonnets 40, 42. 1. Beshrew: ill luck take.
6. engrossed: bought up wholesale. 9. ward: cell.
    Sonnet 134: (Continuing 133). 3. other mine: my other self.
7. surety-like to write: to sign as surety. 11. came: who became.
    Sonnet 135: 1. Will: desire, and Will Shakespeare. 2. to
boot: in addition.

Sonnet 136: (Continuing 135). 1. check: rebuke. 7. receipt:
capacity. 13. my name: i.e., Will (desire).
    Sonnet 137: 4. what . . . be: take worst for the best. 7. false-
hood: deception. 9. several: private.

But wherefore says she not she is unjust?°
And wherefore say not I that I am old?   10
Oh, love's best habit° is in seeming trust,
And age in love loves not to have years told.°

    Therefore I lie with her and she with me,
    And in our faults by lies we flattered be.

139

Oh, call not me to justify the wrong
That thy unkindness lays upon my heart.
Wound me not with thine eye, but with thy tongue.
Use power with power,° and slay me not by art.°
Tell me thou lovest elsewhere, but in my sight,   5
Dear heart, forbear to glance thine eye aside.
What need'st thou wound with cunning when thy
    might
Is more than my o'erpressed defense can bide?
Let me excuse thee. Ah, my love well knows
Her pretty looks have been mine enemies,   10
And therefore from my face she turns my foes,
That they elsewhere might dart their injuries.

    Yet do not so, but since I am near slain,
    Kill me outright with looks, and rid my pain.

140

Be wise as thou art cruel. Do not press
My tongue-tied patience with too much disdain,
Lest sorrow lend me words, and words express
The manner of my pity-wanting° pain.
If I might teach thee wit, better it were,   5
Though not to love, yet, love, to tell me so,
As testy sick men, when their deaths be near,
No news but health from their physicians know.°
For if I should despair, I should grow mad,
And in my madness might speak ill of thee.   10
Now this ill-wresting° world is grown so bad,
Mad slanderers by mad ears believèd be.

    That I may not be so, nor thou belied,
    Bear thine eyes straight, though thy proud heart
    go wide.

141

In faith, I do not love thee with mine eyes,
For they in thee a thousand errors note,
But 'tis my heart that loves what they despise,

Who, in despite of view, is pleased to dote.
Nor are mine ears with thy tongue's tune delighted,
Nor tender feeling, to base touches prone,   6
Nor taste, nor smell, desire to be invited
To any sensual feast with thee alone.
But my five wits nor my five senses can
Dissuade one foolish heart from serving thee   10
Who leaves unswayed° the likeness of a man,
Thy proud heart's slave and vassal° wretch to be.

    Only my plague thus far I count my gain,
    That she that makes me sin awards me pain.

142

Love is my sin, and thy dear virtue hate,
Hate of my sin, grounded on sinful loving.
Oh, but with mine compare thou thine own state,
And thou shalt find it merits not reproving,
Or if it do, not from those lips of thine,   5
That have profaned their scarlet ornaments
And sealed false bonds of love as oft as mine,
Robbed others' beds' revénues of their rents.
Be it lawful I love thee, as thou lovest those
Whom thine eyes woo as mine importune thee.   10
Root pity in thy heart, that, when it grows,
Thy pity may deserve to pitied be.

    If thou dost seek to have what thou dost hide,°
    By self-example mayst thou be denied!

143

Lo, as a careful housewife runs to catch
One of her feathered creatures broke away,
Sets down her babe, and makes all swift dispatch
In pursuit of the thing she would have stay
Whilst her neglected child holds her in chase,   5
Cries to catch her whose busy care is bent
To follow that which flies before her face,
Not prizing her poor infant's discontent —
So runn'st thou after that which flies from thee
Whilst I thy babe chase thee afar behind.   10
But if thou catch thy hope, turn back to me,
And play the mother's part, kiss me, be kind.

    So will I pray that thou mayst have thy "Will,"
    If thou turn back and my loud crying still.

144

Two loves I have of comfort and despair,
Which like two spirits do suggest° me still.
The better angel is a man right fair,

Sonnet 138: 9. unjust: untrue. 11. habit: garment. 12. told: counted.
    Sonnet 139: 4. with power: powerfully. art: cunning; i.e., say outright that you do not love me.
    Sonnet 140: 4. pity-wanting: lacking pity. 8. know: learn.
11. ill-wresting: that puts an evil interpretation on everything.

Sonnet 141: 11. unswayed: without self-control. 12. vassal: slave.
    Sonnet 142: 13. what . . . hide: i.e., pity.
    Sonnet 144: 2. suggest: tempt.

The worser spirit a woman colored ill.
To win me soon to Hell, my female evil   5
Tempteth my better angel from my side,
And would corrupt my saint to be a devil,
Wooing his purity with her foul pride.
And whether that my angel be turned fiend
Suspect I may, yet not directly tell,   10
But being both from me, both to each friend,°
I guess one angel in another's Hell.
    Yet this shall I ne'er know, but live in doubt
    Till my bad angel fire my good one out.

145°

Those lips that Love's own hand did make
Breathed forth the sound that said " I hate,"
To me that languished for her sake.
But when she saw my woeful state,
Straight in her heart did mercy come,   5
Chiding that tongue that ever sweet
Was used in giving gentle doom,
And taught it thus anew to greet.
" I hate " she altered with an end
That followed it as gentle day   10
Doth follow night, who, like a fiend,
From Heaven to Hell is flown away.
    " I hate " from hate away she threw,
    And saved my life, saying " not you."

146

Poor soul, the center° of my sinful earth,
My sinful earth,° these rebel powers that thee array,
Why dost thou pine within and suffer dearth,
Painting thy outward walls so costly gay?
Why so large cost, having so short a lease,   5
Dost thou upon thy fading mansion spend?
Shall worms, inheritors of this excess,
Eat up thy charge?° Is this thy body's end?
Then, soul, live thou upon thy servant's° loss,
And let that pine to aggravate° thy store,   10
Buy terms divine° in selling hours of dross,
Within be fed, without be rich no more.
    So shalt thou feed on Death, that feeds on men,
    And Death once dead, there's no more dying then.

147

My love is as a fever, longing still°
For that which longer nurseth the disease,
Feeding on that which doth preserve the ill,
The uncertain sickly appetite to please.
My reason, the physician to my love,   5
Angry that his prescriptions are not kept,
Hath left me, and I desperate now approve°
Desire is death, which physic did except.°
Past cure I am, now reason is past care,
And frantic-mad with evermore unrest.   10
My thoughts and my discourse as madmen's are,
At random from the truth vainly expressed,
    For I have sworn thee fair, and thought thee
      bright,
    Who art as black as Hell, as dark as night.

148

Oh me, what eyes hath Love put in my head,
Which have no correspondence with true sight!
Or, if they have, where is my judgment fled,
That censures° falsely what they see aright?
If that be fair whereon my false eyes dote,   5
What means the world to say it is not so?
If it be not, then love doth well denote
Love's eye is not so true as all men's. No,
How can it? Oh, how can Love's eye be true,
That is so vexed with watching and with tears?   10
No marvel then, though I mistake my view.°
The sun itself sees not till heaven clears.
    O cunning Love! With tears thou keep'st me blind,
    Lest eyes well-seeing thy foul faults should find.

149

Canst thou, O cruel! say I love thee not,
When I against myself with thee partake?°
Do I not think on thee when I forgot
Am of myself, all tyrant,° for thy sake?
Who hateth thee that I do call my friend?   5
On whom frown'st thou that I do fawn upon?
Nay, if thou lour'st on me, do I not spend
Revenge upon myself with present moan?
What merit do I in myself respect,
That is so proud thy service to despise,   10
When all my best doth worship thy defect,°

11. **to . . . friend:** friends to each other.
    Sonnet 145: Written in an 8-syllable meter.
    Sonnet 146: 1. **center:** See App. 1.   2. **My . . . earth:** This is
the Q reading; the compositor has repeated "My sinful earth"
instead of the two syllables which should begin the line. There
have been many guesses. Some such word as "feeding" is required.   8. **charge:** what you have spent.   9. **servant:** i.e., the
body.   10. **aggravate:** increase.   11. **terms divine:** immortal life.

    Sonnet 147: 1. **still:** always.   7. **approve:** prove by experi-
ence.   8. **except:** forbid.
    Sonnet 148: 4. **censures:** judges.   11. **view:** what I see.
    Sonnet 149: 2. **partake:** take sides.   4. **all tyrant:** you com-
plete tyrant.   11. **defect:** lack of beauty.

Commanded by the motion of thine eyes?
But, love, hate on, for now I know thy mind.
Those that can see thou lovest, and I am blind.

150

Oh, from what power hast thou this powerful might
With insufficiency° my heart to sway?
To make me give the lie to my true sight,
And swear that brightness doth not grace the day?
Whence hast thou this becoming of things ill,° 5
That in the very refuse of thy deeds
There is such strength and warrantise° of skill
That, in my mind, thy worst all best exceeds?
Who taught thee how to make me love thee more,
The more I hear and see just cause of hate? 10
Oh, though I love what others do abhor,
With others thou shouldst not abhor my state.
  If thy unworthiness raised love in me,
  More worthy I to be beloved of thee.

151

Love is too young to know what conscience is,
Yet who knows not conscience is born of love?
Then, gentle cheater, urge° not my amiss,°
Lest guilty of my faults thy sweet self prove.
For, thou betraying me, I do betray 5
My nobler part to my gross body's treason.
My soul doth tell my body that he may
Triumph in love, flesh stays no farther reason,°
But rising at thy name doth point out thee
As his triumphant prize. Proud of this pride, 10
He is contented thy poor drudge to be,
To stand in thy affairs, fall by thy side.
  No want of conscience hold it that I call
  Her "love" for whose dear love I rise and fall.

152°

In loving thee thou know'st I am forsworn,
But thou art twice forsworn, to me love swearing,
In act thy bed vow° broke, and new faith torn,
In vowing new hate after new love bearing.
But why of two oaths' breach do I accuse thee 5

When I break twenty? I am perjured most,
For all my vows are oaths but to misuse° thee,
And all my honest faith in thee is lost.
For I have sworn deep oaths of thy deep kindness,
Oaths of thy love, thy truth, thy constancy, 10
And, to enlighten° thee, gave eyes to blindness,°
Or made them swear against the thing they see.
  For I have sworn thee fair, more perjured I,
  To swear against the truth so foul a lie!

153

Cupid laid by his brand° and fell asleep.
A maid of Dian's° this advantage found,
And his love-kindling fire did quickly steep
In a cold valley-fountain of that ground,
Which borrowed from this holy fire of Love 5
A dateless° lively heat, still to endure,
And grew a seething bath,° which yet men prove
Against strange maladies a sovereign cure.
But at my mistress' eye Love's brand new-fired,
The boy for trial needs would touch my breast. 10
I, sick withal, the help of bath desired,
And thither hied, a sad distempered guest,
  But found no cure. The bath for my help lies
  Where Cupid got new fire, my mistress' eyes.

154

The little Love god lying once asleep
Laid by his side his heart-inflaming brand
Whilst many nymphs that vowed chaste life to keep
Came tripping by. But in her maiden hand
The fairest votary° took up that fire 5
Which many legions of true hearts had warmed,
And so the general° of hot desire
Was sleeping by a virgin hand disarmed.
This brand she quenchèd in a cool well by,°
Which from Love's fire took heat perpetual, 10
Growing a bath and healthful remedy
For men diseased. But I, my mistress' thrall,
  Came there for cure, and this by that I prove,
  Love's fire heats water, water cools not love.

7. misuse: i.e., be false in saying that you are fair. 11. enlighten: make you appear light. gave . . . blindness: blinded my own eyes.
  Sonnet 153: 1. brand: torch. 2. Dian: Diana, goddess of virginity. 6. dateless: perpetual. 7. seething bath: hot bath; probably a reference to the natural hot springs of Bath, which were as famous in Shakespeare's day as in Roman times.
  Sonnet 154: 5. votary: one who has vowed to lead a chaste life. 7. general: commander; i.e., Love. 9. by: near by.

Sonnet 150: 2. With insufficiency: in spite of your defects.
5. becoming . . . ill: power to make evil attractive. 7. warrantise: guarantee.
  Sonnet 151: 3. urge: stress. amiss: trespass. 8. reason: argument.
  Sonnet 152: (The last of the series to the dark mistress).
3. bed vow: marriage vow.

A Lover's Complaint

From off a hill whose concave womb reworded°
A plaintful story from a sistering vale,
My spirits to attend° this double voice accorded,
And down I laid to list the sad-tuned tale;
Ere long espied a fickle maid full pale,   5
Tearing of papers,° breaking rings atwain,
Storming her world° with sorrow's wind and rain.

Upon her head a platted hive of straw,°
Which fortified° her visage from the sun,
Whereon the thought might think sometime it saw
The carcass of a beauty spent and done.   11
Time had not scythèd all that youth begun,
Nor youth all quit; but, spite of heaven's fell rage,
Some beauty peeped through lattice of seared age.°

Oft did she heave her napkin° to her eyne,°   15
Which on it had conceited characters,°
Laundering the silken figures in the brine
That seasoned° woe had pelleted° in tears,
And often reading what contents it bears;
As often shrieking undistinguished° woe,   20
In clamors of all size, both high and low.

Sometimes her leveled eyes their carriage ride,°
As they did battery to the spheres° intend.
Sometimes diverted their poor balls are tied
To the orbed earth; sometimes they do extend   25
Their view right on. Anon their gazes lend
To every place at once, and nowhere fixed
The mind and sight distractedly commixed.

Her hair, nor loose nor tied in formal plat,°
Proclaimed in her a careless hand of pride,°   30
For some, untucked, descended her sheaved° hat,
Hanging her pale and pinèd° cheek beside.
Some in her threaden fillet° still did bide,
And, true to bondage, would not break from thence,
Though slackly braided in loose negligence.   35

A thousand favors° from a maund° she drew
Of amber, crystal, and of beaded jet,
Which one by one she in a river threw,

Upon whose weeping margent° she was set;
Like usury,° applying wet to wet,   40
Or monarch's hands that lets not bounty fall
Where want cries some, but where excess begs all.

Of folded schedules° had she many a one
Which she perused, sighed, tore, and gave the flood.
Cracked many a ring of posied° gold and bone,   45
Bidding them find their sepulchres in mud.
Found yet moe° letters sadly penned in blood,
With sleided° silk feat and affectedly
Enswathed,° and sealed to curious° secrecy.

These often bathed she in her fluxive° eyes,   50
And often kissed, and often 'gan to tear.
Cried " O false blood, thou register of lies,
What unapprovèd° witness dost thou bear!
Ink would have seemed more black and damnèd
    here! "
This said, in top of° rage the lines she rents,   55
Big° discontent so breaking their contents.

A reverend man that grazed his cattle nigh —
Sometime a blusterer,° that the ruffle° knew
Of court, of city, and had let go by
The swiftest hours, observèd as they flew —   60
Toward this afflicted fancy° fastly° drew,
And, privileged by age, desires to know
In brief the grounds and motives of her woe.

So slides he down upon his grainèd bat,°
And comely distant sits he by her side,   65
When he again desires her, being sat,
Her grievance with his hearing to divide.
If that from him there may be aught applied
Which may her suffering ecstasy° assuage,
'Tis promised in the charity of age.   70

" Father," she says, " though in me you behold
The injury of many a blasting hour,
Let it not tell your judgment I am old.
Not age, but sorrow, over me hath power.
I might as yet have been a spreading flower,   75

---

1. **reworded:** echoed.   3. **spirits to attend:** scanned "sprites t'attend."   6. **papers:** love letters.   7. **Storming . . . world:** distressing her body.   8. **platted . . . straw:** straw hat. The ancient beehive was made of plaited straw in shape of an inverted U.   9. **fortified:** protected.   14. **lattice . . . age:** wrinkles like a lattice window.   15. **napkin:** handkerchief. **eyne:** eyes.   16. **conceited characters:** symbolical devices.   18. **seasoned:** salted. **pelleted:** hailed.   20. **undistinguished:** confused, inarticulate.   22. **carriage ride:** The image is that of a cannon aimed (*leveled*).   23. **spheres:** stars.   29. **plat:** knot.   30. **careless . . . pride:** one who had no pride in her appearance.   31. **sheaved:** made of straw.   32. **pined:** thin, worn.   33. **threaden fillet:** woven headband.   36. **favors:** gifts. **maund:** basket.

39. **margent:** margin, bank.   40. **Like usury:** i.e., which adds to the original sum.   43. **schedules:** papers.   45. **posied:** engraved with a motto. See *Haml,* III.ii.162,n.   47. **moe:** more.   48. **sleided:** unwrought or "floss." Personal letters, especially love letters, were often tied with a silk band over which the seal was applied. See App. 6: Letters.   48–49. **feat . . . Enswathed:** tied in a neat and fancy manner.   49. **curious:** elaborate.   50. **fluxive:** flowing.   53. **unapproved:** false, not proved by deeds.   55. **top of:** utmost.   56. **Big:** swelling.   58. **blusterer:** swaggerer. **ruffle:** showiness.   61. **fancy:** love. **fastly:** near.   64. **grained bat:** staff made of ash wood which shows the grain.   69. **ecstasy:** passion.

Fresh to myself, if I had self-applied
Love to myself, and to no love beside.

"But, woe is me! too early I attended
A youthful suit — it was to gain my grace —
Of one by nature's outwards so commended, 80
That maidens' eyes stuck over all his face.
Love lacked a dwelling and made him her place,
And when in his fair parts she did abide,
She was new lodged and newly deified.

"His browny locks did hang in crookèd curls, 85
And every light occasion of the wind
Upon his lips their silken parcels hurls.
What's sweet to do, to do will aptly find.
Each eye that saw him did enchant the mind,
For on his visage was in little drawn 90
What largeness thinks in Paradise was sawn.°

"Small show of man was yet upon his chin.
His phoenix down° began but to appear,
Like unshorn velvet, on that termless° skin,
Whose bare outbragged the web it seemed to
       wear.° 95
Yet showed his visage by that cost° more dear,
And nice affections° wavering stood in doubt
If best were as it was, or best without.

"His qualities were beauteous as his form,
For maiden-tongued he was, and thereof free, 100
Yet, if men moved him, was he such a storm
As oft 'twixt May and April is to see,
When winds breathe sweet, unruly though they be.
His rudeness so with his authórized youth
Did livery° falseness in a pride of truth.° 105

"Well could he ride, and often men would say,
'That horse his mettle from his rider takes.
Proud of subjection, noble by the sway,
What rounds, what bounds, what course, what stop
       he makes!'
And controversy hence a question takes, 110
Whether the horse by him became his deed,°
Or he his manage° by the well-doing steed.

"But quickly on this side the verdict went.
His real habitude° gave life and grace

To appertainings and to ornament, 115
Accomplished in himself, not in his case.°
All aids, themselves made fairer by their place,
Came for additions, yet their purposed trim
Pieced° not his grace, but were all graced by him.

"So on the tip of his subduing tongue 120
All kind of arguments and question deep,
All replication° prompt and reason strong,
For his advantage still did wake and sleep.
To make the weeper laugh, the laugher weep,
He had the dialect and different skill, 125
Catching all passions in his craft of will,°

"That he did in the general bosom reign
Of young, of old, and sexes both enchanted,
To dwell with him in thoughts, or to remain 129
In personal duty,° following where he haunted.
Consents bewitched, ere he desire, have granted,
And dialogued for him what he would say,
Asked their own wills and made their wills obey.

"Many there were that did his picture get,
To serve their eyes, and in it put their mind, 135
Like fools that in the imagination set
The goodly objects which abroad they find
Of lands and mansions, theirs in thought assigned,
And laboring in moe pleasures to bestow them
Than the true gouty landlord which doth owe°
       them. 140

"So many have, that never touched his hand,
Sweetly supposed them mistress of his heart.
My woeful self, that did in freedom stand,
And was my own fee simple,° not in part,°
What with his art in youth and youth in art, 145
Threw my affections in his charmèd power,
Reserved the stalk and gave him all my flower.

"Yet did I not, as some my equals did,
Demand of him, nor being desirèd yielded;
Finding myself in honor so forbid, 150
With safest distance I mine honor shielded.
Experience for me many bulwarks builded
Of proofs new-bleeding,° which remained the foil°
Of this false jewel, and his amorous spoil.

"But, ah, who ever shunned by precedent 155
The destined ill she must herself assay?°
Or forced examples,° 'gainst her own content,
To put the by-past perils in her way?

90–91. visage . . . sawn: in his face was drawn a miniature picture of the loveliness of Paradise. sawn: seen. 93. phoenix down: newborn fluff. The image — farfetched — is of the phoenix newly born from the ashes of the old phoenix. See *Temp, III*.iii.23,n. 94. termless: young. 95. Whose . . . wear: i.e., the skin was lovelier than its covering. 96. cost: lit., costly addition; i.e., golden down. 97. nice affections: inclination delicately balanced. 104–05. His . . . truth: his rough manner (when roused) as well as his true youth clothed his falseness with the fine appearance of truth. 105. livery: lit., the uniform of a great man's servant. 111. became . . . deed: showed his good qualities. 112. manage: horsemanship. 114 real habitude: true nature.

116. in . . . case: in what was belonging to him, his outward possessions. 119. Pieced: added to. 122. replication: reply. 126. craft of will: skill to do what he wished. 130. personal duty: i.e., as servants waiting on him. 140. owe: own. 144. fee simple: absolute possession. not in part: with no restrictions. 153. proofs new-bleeding: i.e., examples of others' ruin. foil: See *Rich III*, V.iii.250,n. 156. assay: attempt, experience. 157. forced examples: forcibly reminded herself of what had happened to others.

Counsel may stop awhile what will not stay;
For when we rage, advice is often seen   160
By blunting us to make our wits more keen.

"Nor gives it satisfaction to our blood,
That we must curb it upon others' proof;
To be forbod° the sweets that seem so good,
For fear of harms that preach in our behoof.   165
O appetite, from judgment stand aloof!
The one a palate hath that needs will taste,
Though Reason weep, and cry 'It is thy last.'

"For further I could say 'This man's untrue,'
And knew the patterns of his foul beguiling.°   170
Heard where his plants in others' orchards grew,
Saw how deceits were gilded in his smiling.
Knew vows were ever brokers to defiling.
Thought characters° and words merely but art
And bastards of his foul adulterate heart.   175

"And long upon these terms I held my city,
Till thus he 'gan besiege me: 'Gentle maid,
Have of my suffering youth some feeling pity,
And be not of my holy vows afraid.
That's to ye sworn to none was ever said,   180
For feasts of love I have been called unto,
Till now did ne'er invite, nor never woo.

"'All my offenses that abroad you see
Are errors of the blood,° none of the mind.
Love made them not. With acture they may be,   185
Where neither party is nor true nor kind.°
They sought their shame that so their shame did
     find,
And so much less of shame in me remains
By how much of me their reproach contains.

"'Among the many that mine eyes have seen,   190
Not one whose flame my heart so much as warmed,
Or my affection put to the smallest teen,°
Or any of my leisures ever charmed.
Harm have I done to them, but ne'er was harmed;
Kept hearts in liveries,° but mine own was free,
And reigned, commanding in his monarchy.   196

"'Look here, what tributes wounded fancies sent
     me,
Of palèd° pearls and rubies red as blood,
Figuring that they their passions likewise lent me
Of grief and blushes, aptly understood   200
In bloodless white and the encrimsoned mood;
Effects of terror and dear modesty,
Encamped in hearts, but fighting outwardly.

"'And, lo, behold these talents° of their hair,°
With twisted metal amorously impleached,°   205
I have received from many a several fair,°
Their kind acceptance weepingly beseeched,
With the annexions° of fair gems enriched,
And deep-brained sonnets that did amplify
Each stone's dear° nature, worth, and quality.   210

"'The diamond, why, 'twas beautiful and hard,
Whereto his invised° properties did tend;
The deep-green emerald, in whose fresh regard
Weak sights their sickly radiance do amend.°
The heaven-hued sapphire and the opal blend   215
With objects manifold; each several stone,
With wit well blazoned,° smiled or made some
     moan.

"'Lo, all these trophies of affections hot,
Of pensived and subdued desires the tender,°   219
Nature hath charged me that I hoard them not,
But yield them up where I myself must render,°
That is, to you, my origin and ender.
For these, of force, must your oblations be,
Since I their altar, you enpatron me.°

"'Oh, then, advance of yours that phraseless°
     hand,   225
Whose white weighs down the airy scale of praise.
Take all these similes° to your own command,
Hallowed with sighs that burning lungs did raise;
What me, your minister for you obeys,
Works under you,° and to your audit comes   230
Their distract parcels° in combinèd sums.

"'Lo, this device was sent me from a nun,
Or sister sanctified, of holiest note,
Which late her noble suit in court did shun,   234
Whose rarest havings° made the blossoms dote.
For she was sought by spirits° of richest coat,
But kept cold distance, and did thence remove,
To spend her living° in eternal love.

"'But, oh my sweet, what labor is 't to leave
The thing we have not, mastering what not strives,
Playing the place which did no form receive,   241

204. talents: riches. hair: i.e., rings or bracelets made of hair —
a common form of lover's gift.   205. impleached: intertwined.
206. several fair: different lady.   208. annexions: additions.
210. dear: valuable.   212. invised: invisible.   213–14. emerald
... amend: It was believed that the sight of an emerald was
good for tired eyes.   217. blazoned: described.   219. tender:
offer.   221. where ... render: i.e., to you to whom I must surrender myself.   223–24. For ... me: these must be offerings
made to you (your oblations), since you are the patron saint of
me, the altar on which they were offered.   225. phraseless:
indescribable.   227. similes: emblems — the jewels.   229–
30. What ... you: what obeys me, your servant (minister), works
for you: i.e., what was mine is yours.   231. distract parcels:
different items.   235. havings: possessions.   236. spirits: pronounced "sprites."   238. living: life.

164. forbod: forbidden.   170. patterns ... beguiling: those
whom he had seduced.   174. characters: letters.   184. blood:
lust.   185–86. With ... kind: i.e., where neither party is truly
in love, these are mere acts (acture) of passion.   192. teen: distress.   195. in liveries: as my servants.   198. paled: pale.

Playing patient sports in unconstrainèd gyves?°
She that her fame so to herself contrives,°
The scars of battle 'scapeth by the flight.
And makes her absence valiant, not her might. 245

" ' Oh, pardon me, in that my boast is true.
The accident which brought me to her eye
Upon the moment did her force subdue,
And now she would the cagèd cloister fly.
Religious love put out Religion's eye. 250
Not to be tempted, would she be immured,°
And now, to tempt all, liberty procured.

" ' How mighty then you are, oh, hear me tell!
The broken bosoms° that to me belong
Have emptied all their fountains in my well, 255
And mine I pour your ocean all among.
I strong o'er them, and you o'er me being strong,
Must for your victory us all congest,°
As compound love to physic° your cold breast.

" ' My parts° had power to charm a sacred nun,
Who disciplined, aye, dieted in grace, 261
Believed her eyes when they to assail begun,
All vows and consecrations giving place:
O most potential° love! vow, bond, nor space,
In thee hath neither sting, knot, nor confine, 265
For thou art all, and all things else are thine.

" ' When thou impressest, what are precepts worth
Of stale example? When thou wilt inflame,
How coldly those impediments stand forth
Of wealth, of filial fear, law, kindred, fame! 270
Love's arms are peace, 'gainst rule, 'gainst sense,
    'gainst shame,
And sweetens, in the suffering pangs it bears,
The aloes° of all forces, shocks, and fears.

" ' Now all these hearts that do on mine depend,
Feeling it break, with bleeding groans they pine,
And supplicant° their sighs to you extend, 276
To leave the battery that you make 'gainst mine,
Lending soft audience to my sweet design,
And credent soul to that strong-bonded oath
That shall prefer° and undertake my troth.'° 280

" This said, his watery eyes he did dismount,
Whose sights till then were leveled on my face,
Each cheek a river running from a fount
With brinish current downward flowed apace.

Oh, how the channel to the stream gave grace! 285
Who glazed with crystal gate° the glowing roses
That flame through water which their hue encloses.

" O father, what a hell of witchcraft lies
In the small orb of one particular tear!
But with the inundation of the eyes 290
What rocky heart to water will not wear?
What breast so cold that is not warmèd here?
Oh, cleft effect!° Cold modesty, hot wrath,
Both fire from hence and chill extincture hath.

" For, lo, his passion, but an art of craft, 295
Even there resolved my reason into tears.
There my white stole of chastity I daffed,°
Shook off my sober guards and civil° fears.
Appear to him, as he to me appears,
All melting, though our drops this difference bore,
His poisoned me, and mine did him restore. 301

" In him a plenitude of subtle matter,
Applied to cautels,° all strange forms receives,
Of burning blushes, or of weeping water,
Or swounding° paleness; and he takes and leaves,
In either's aptness, as it best deceives, 306
To blush at speeches rank,° to weep at woes,
Or to turn white and swound at tragic shows.

" That not a heart which in his level came
Could 'scape the hail of his all-hurting aim, 310
Showing fair nature is both kind and tame,
And, veiled in them, did win whom he would
    maim.
Against the thing he sought he would exclaim.
When he most burned in heart-wished luxury,°
He preached pure maid and praised cold chastity.

" Thus merely with the garment of a Grace 316
The naked and concealèd fiend he covered,
That the unexperient° gave the tempter place,
Which, like a cherubin, above them hovered.
Who, young and simple, would not be so lovered?
Aye me! I fell, and yet do question make 321
What I should do again for such a sake.

" Oh, that infected moisture of his eye,
Oh, that false fire which in his cheek so glowed,
Oh, that forced thunder from his heart did fly,
Oh, that sad breath his spongy lungs bestowed, 326
Oh, all that borrowed motion seeming owed,°
Would yet again betray the fore-betrayed,
And new pervert a reconcilèd° maid! "

241–42. **Playing . . . gyves:** The first "playing" seems to be a
misprint, the printer having taken up the word from l. 242. Perhaps the right reading is "Leaving." The general sense is that it
was no hardship to live a quiet life in fetters (*gyves*) that did not
constrain her. 243. **She . . . contrives:** one who is content to
be known only to herself. 251. **immured:** shut in. 254. **bos-**
oms: hearts. 258. **congest:** gather together. 259. **physic:**
cure. 260. **parts:** natural gifts, personal qualities. 264. **po-**
tential: powerful. 273. **aloes:** bitterness. 276. **supplicant:**
as supplicants. 280. **prefer:** promote. **troth:** faith, love.

286. **crystal gate:** glassy door. 293. **cleft effect:** cause of opposite results. 297. **daffed:** put off. 298. **civil:** orderly, moral.
303. **Applied to cautels:** used for crafty tricks. 305. **swounding:**
swooning. 307. **rank:** lustful. 314. **luxury:** lust. 318. **un-**
experient: inexperienced. 327. **seeming owed:** which seemed
to be his very own. 329. **reconciled:** a penitent received back
into the Church.

APPENDICES

1. THE ELIZABETHAN IDEA OF THE UNIVERSE, 1631

2. THE ALMANAC, 1631

3. THE HUMORS, 1632

4. THE MELANCHOLIC HUMOR, 1633

5. BEARBAITING AND BULLBAITING, 1634

6. LETTERS AND SEALS, 1635

7. HATS AND HEADS, 1635

8. BALLADS, 1636

9. HERALDS AND HERALDRY, 1637

10. TORTURES AND PUNISHMENTS, 1638

11. CUCKOLDS AND HORNS, 1639

12. SIGNS, 1639

13. BOWLS, 1639

14. THE GREAT HOUSEHOLD, 1640

15. MARRIAGE CUSTOMS, 1640

16. FUNERAL CUSTOMS, 1640

17. THE POST, 1641

18. NATURE AND ART, 1642

19. BELLS, 1642

20. EQUIVOCATION, 1642

21. ALCHEMY, 1643

22. TIME PROBLEMS, 1643

23. WITCHES AND WITCHCRAFT, 1644

24. DANCES, 1645

25. THE FENCING MATCH IN "HAMLET," 1647

26. HAWKS AND HAWKING, 1647

27. MONEY VALUES, 1648

28. THE HISTORY BEHIND THE HISTORY PLAYS, 1650

29. THE ORDER OF THE GARTER, 1657

30. THE SHAKESPEAREAN ADDITION TO "THE BOOKE OF SIR THOMAS MORE," 1658

Appendices

1. The Elizabethan Idea of the Universe

Although Copernicus's *De revolutionibus orbum Coelestium,* which first appeared in 1543, may be said to have revolutionized modern ideas about the physical structure of the universe, in Shakespeare's day the book was hardly known. Most Elizabethans still believed that the earth was the center of the universe and immovable, and that all matter on the earth was naturally drawn to its center, which was thus the absolute center of everything.

Around the earth moved the seven planets, each in its sphere, thus forming a series of concentric circles. Nearest was the moon; then came Mercury, Venus, Sol (the Sun), Mars, Jupiter, and Saturn. In an eighth circle were the fixed stars, which remained constant in their relationships to each other, and outside there was a ninth circle known as the *Primum Mobile,* or the First Mover. The *Primum Mobile* had the power to turn all the other circles around the earth from east to west once every twenty-four hours; yet each sphere had, at the same time, its own contrary motion as it moved from west to east in its own orbit.

The moon took twenty-eight days to complete its circle; Sol, Venus, and Mercury moved in a year; Mars in two years; Jupiter in twelve years; and Saturn in thirty. It was believed that the planets in their motion each made a musical note, the whole forming a perfect harmony of sound. Since the planets moved at different paces, their relationship to each other was constantly changing, and certain conjunctions of the planets were regarded as lucky, others as unlucky.

Planets were believed to give out a kind of ethereal fluid or "influence" (*influentia*), which greatly affected human beings. The moon, as the nearest and most easily observed, was known to affect the ebb and flow of tides and was believed to be peculiarly powerful. The other planets also were considered to have a direct bearing on the weather, and indeed on all earthly affairs. Accordingly, astrologers believed that as a result of their accumulation of observations they could by the pattern of the heavens decide what was likely to happen at any time. In the same way, by observing the various conjunctions of the heavenly bodies at the moment of a person's birth, a horoscope could be drawn up which would indicate the future course of his life. A man's fate was thus determined by the stars.

The movements of the heavenly bodies were usually discussed in terms of the zodiac. The zodiac is a belt of the heavens which lies eight degrees on either side of the sun's annual course. It forms a complete circle, which is divided into twelve houses or signs, each of thirty degrees. These signs are named Aries (the Ram), Taurus (the Bull), Gemini (the Twins), Cancer (the Crab), Leo (the Lion), Virgo (the Virgin), Libra (the Scales), Scorpio (the Scorpion), Sagittarius (the Archer), Capricornus (the Goat), Aquarius (the Water Carrier), and Pisces (the Fishes). During its annual course, the sun passes into and out of each house or sign. In astrological parlance, the season was described by the position of the sun in relation to the sign of the zodiac. Abnormal events in the heavens, and especially the appearance of a comet or an eclipse, were regarded as alarming portents of disaster.

2. The Almanac

Astrological language is common in Shakespeare and all Elizabethan writings, but much of the knowledge displayed came from no deeper source than the penny almanac, published annually. These little almanacs were of a pattern still preserved in the *Old Farmer's Almanac,* and gave miscellaneous information. Almanacs were printed in two colors, black for the text, with red for titles, special days, and other notable items. Thus Buckminster's *Almanac for the Year 1598* is described on the title page as:

An Almanacke and

Prognostication, for the
yeere of Christes incarnation
M. D. XCVIII.

Being the second after the leape yeere.

And the yeere of the worldes
creation. 5560

Seruing generally for all
England, but especially for the
Meridian of this honorable Citie
of London. Gathered and made by
Thomas Buckmynster.

Anno aetatis suae. 66.

imprinted at London by Richard
Watkins and James Roberts.

Cum priuilegio Regiæ Maiestatis

Next follows information of the movable feasts
of the Church (Easter, and so on). Then come
short notes for letting of blood, purging, bathing,
and so on; for example: " Let [that is, draw] the
melancholike blood when the Moone is in Libra
or Aquarius." Then comes a picture of a naked
man, showing the parts governed by the twelve
celestial signs.

The calendar proper follows, each month being given a page. The feasts of the Church are
noted, special feasts being printed in red, as is
also the day when the sun enters a new sign
of the zodiac. Thus in July it is noted that the sun
enters Leo on the thirteenth, and on the nineteenth " dog days " begin.

After the calendar follows the second part:

A Prognostication
for the yeere of
our Lord God.
M. D. XCVIII.

This contains certain notes on convenient times
for planting, for example: " You may sowe
seedes, especially in Gardens, betweene the
change and the full, when the Moone is in Virgo,
Sagittarius, or Pisces."

Then follow notes of the beginning and end
of the Law Terms; the dates when marriage may
not be solemnized without a license; the dates
of the two eclipses of the moon and one of the
sun which will occur during the year; a vague
prognostication of what is likely to happen in
each of the four quarters of the year; a table " to
know for ever how long the moon doth shine
every night "; and finally, a day-by-day weather
forecast for the whole year.

Astrologers and almanac-makers, needless to
say, were often mocked for their lack of success
as prophets. Their answer was that, though by
their science they could interpret the signs of the
heavens, they could not foresee the will of God,
which is unpredictable.

3. *The Humors*

It was believed that all matter in the universe
consisted of four elements or principles, each of
which was hostile to the other but could exist in
combination when in proper proportions. These
four elements were *earth, air, fire,* and *water*. It
followed that since the human body was also
matter, it must likewise be composed of the four
elements. Anatomy was much studied toward the
end of the sixteenth century, and the word became popular in literary jargon to denote what
is now called analysis or psychology. When
learned men examined the human body, they
were impressed by its all-pervading *humor* or
quality of dampness. But the " humors " of the
body were obviously of different kinds, and on
the assumption that the physical body must be
composed of four elements, " earth " was identified as black bile, " air " as blood, " fire " as bile,
and " water " as phlegm. Each element produced
a corresponding temperament, which was indicated outwardly by a man's complexion. Too
much earth produced the *melancholic* humor;
air, the *sanguine;* fire, the *choleric;* water, the
phlegmatic.

In a healthy body the four humors were accurately balanced, one against the other; but if one
humor became predominant or deficient, the individual became mentally and physically unbalanced.

In the 1590's the word " humor " rapidly became popular, as words sometimes will, and every
intelligent person began to talk of his humors.
Indeed, it became the mark of a would-be intellectual to have a humor, preferably melancholic,
which was the sign of a great mind. The type is
thus described by Samuel Rowlands in *The Letting of Humor's Blood in the Head-Vein:*

OF MASTER HUMORS
Ask Humors why a feather he doth wear?
" It is his humor, by the Lord," he'll swear.
Or what he doth with such a horsetail lock?
Or why upon a whore he spends his stock?
" He hath a humor doth determine so."

Why in that stop-throat fashion doth he go
With scarf about his neck? Hat without band?
" It is his humor, sweet sir, understand."
What cause his purse is so extreme distressed
That often times 'tis scarcely penny-blest?
" Only a humor." If you question why,
His tongue is ne'er unfurnished with a lie:
" It is his humor too," he doth protest.
Or why with sergeants he is so oppressed
That like to ghosts they haunt him every day?
A rascal humor doth not love to pay.
Object, why boots and spurs are still in season?
His humor answers; " humor is his reason."
If you perceive his wits in wetting shrunk,
It cometh of a humor to be drunk.
When you behold his looks pale, thin, and poor,
Th' occasion is his humor, and a whore.
And everything that he doth undertake,
It is a vein, for senseless humor's sake.

In Shakespeare's plays the word " humor " is very common and has a wide range of meanings. It may be used literally to mean moisture, or to imply one of the four humors, but its commonest meanings are whim, obsession, temperament, mood, temper, or inclination.

4. *The Melancholic Humor*

Of all kinds of humor the melancholic was the most often discussed. Melancholy characters appear fairly often in Elizabethan plays, and are usually treated seriously, though sometimes satirically. It is clear that in the late 1590's and early 1600's the melancholic intellectual was a common and recognized type. He was a man out of tune with his universe, who advertised himself by wearing a large black hat with the brim pulled down over his brow, a cloak, and a general air of moody aloofness.

Ben Jonson parodied the type in *Every Man in His Humor* (1598). Master Matheo, who tried to pose as an intellectual, was vastly impressed when he heard that Stephano, who was trying to learn fashionable behavior, was also melancholy, and he observed: " O Lord, sir, it's your only best humor, sir; your true melancholy breeds your perfect wit, sir. I am melancholy myself divers times, sir, and then do I no more but take your pen and paper presently, and write you your half score or your dozen of sonnets at a sitting." And he offers Stephano the use of his study. To which Stephano replies: " I thank you, sir; I shall be bold I warrant you. Have you a close stool there? " — for this piece of furniture was peculiarly devoted to melancholy contemplations.

Similarly John Davies in his epigram " On a Gull ":

See, yonder melancholy gentleman,
Which, hoodwinked with his hat, alone doth sit!
Think what he thinks, and tell me if you can
What great affairs troubles his little wit.
He thinks not of the war 'twixt France and Spain,
Whether it be for Europe's good or ill,
Nor whether the Empire can itself maintain
Against the Turkish power encroaching still;
Nor what great town in all the Netherlands,
The States determine to besiege this spring;
Nor how the Scottish policy now stands,
Nor what becomes of the Irish mutining.
But he doth seriously bethink him whether
Of the gulled people he be more esteemed
For his long cloak or for his great black feather,
By which each gull is now a gallant deemed.
Or of a journey he deliberates,
To Paris-garden, Cockpit or the Play;
Or how to steal a dog he meditates,
Or what he shall unto his mistress say.
    Yet with these thoughts he thinks himself most fit
    To be of counsel with a king for wit.

There were three main types of melancholic humor: lover's melancholy, politician's (or malcontent's) melancholy, and intellectual melancholy. The melancholy lover was thus described by Rosalind when she criticized Orlando for having none of the proper marks of a genuine specimen (*AYLI*, III.ii.391):

A lean cheek, which you have not, a blue eye and sunken, which you have not, an unquestionable spirit, which you have not, a beard neglected, which you have not; but I pardon you for that, for simply you having in beard, is a younger brother's revenue; then your hose should be ungartered, your bonnet unbanded, your sleeve unbuttoned, your shoe untied, and everything about you demonstrating a careless desolation.

The political or malcontent type was fairly common. Shakespeare's Thersites (in *Troilus and Cressida*) is a good example, but there were others in real life. For instance, Henry Cuffe, secretary and evil genius of the Earl of Essex, was described by Sir Henry Wotton, who at one time was his colleague, as " a man of secret ambitious ends of his own, and of proportionate counsels smothered under the habit of a scholar, and slubbered over with a certain rude and clownish fashion that had the semblance of integrity."

The third type was the intellectual melancholic; his was the true type of melancholic humor. Hamlet is Shakespeare's supreme example of this kind, and his famous soliloquy " To be or not to be " (III.i.56) sums up the intellectual's problems. He was a man who realized that the times were out of joint but could see no remedy or hope, either in this world or the next — if, indeed, there was a next. Most of the satirists suffered from this feeling of futility and frustration, and they revenged themselves on their fellows by snarling at their many follies.

Melancholy was recognized as a disease, and several treatises were written by physicians discussing its symptoms, causes, and cures. Special diets were prescribed or certain foods forbidden. The most elaborate study of the whole subject was *The Anatomy of Melancholy* that Robert Burton published in 1621.

One cause of melancholy was a foul smell. This led John Harington to connect melancholy with the Greek hero Ajax. Ajax (see *Troilus and Cressida*) was a great boaster, but he came to a sad end. After the death of Achilles, the armor which had been made for him by the god Vulcan was claimed both by Ulysses and by Ajax. When the armor was awarded to Ulysses, Ajax fell into such melancholy that he suffered hallucinations. He mistook a flock of sheep for his companions who had wronged him and he slaughtered them. In 1596 Harington wrote a Rabelaisian book called *The Metamorphosis of Ajax,* which was in fact a treatise on domestic sanitation and his invention of a primitive water closet. Harington used the name " Ajax " for the privy — a very foul-smelling convenience — and to describe his own invention of the first water closet. Thus, as he explained it, Ajax = A Jax = A Jakes (sometimes spelt Jaques); the word " jakes," it may be noted, was the coarse synonym for privy. Harington's book caused much scandalous amusement and was well known. Thereafter the name " Ajax " usually connoted at the same time both a privy and the melancholic humor. It is even possible that Shakespeare in giving the name " Jaques " to the melancholy philosopher in *As You Like It* was not unmindful of an anecdote in *The Metamorphosis:*

There was a very tall and serviceable gentleman, sometime Lieutenant of the Ordnance, called Master Jaques Wingfield, who coming one day, either of business or of kindness, to visit a great Lady of the Court, the Lady had her gentlewoman ask which of the Wingfields it was. He told her " Jaques Wingfield." The modest gentlewoman, that was not so well seen in the French to know that " Jaques " was but " James " in English, who so bashful, that to mend the matter (as she thought) she brought her Lady word not without blushing, that it was " Master Privy Wingfield," of which, I suppose the Lady then, I am sure the gentleman after, as long as he lived, was wont to make great sport.

Melancholy in its extreme form was also regarded as the cause of fearful visions and hallucinations. Thus Nashe in *Terrors of the Night* (1593) remarked:

Even as slime and dirt in a standing puddle engender toads and frogs and many other unsightly creatures, so this slimy melancholy humor still still thickening as it stands still engendreth many misshapen objects in our imaginations.

The term " melancholic humor " thus covered many forms of mental disturbance, from general depression to acute mania.

5. *Bearbaiting and Bullbaiting*

Among the Henslowe papers there is an advertisement which runs:

Tomorrowe beinge Thursdaie shalbe seen at the Beargardin on the banckside [See Pl. 2a] a greate mach plaid by the gamstirs of Essex who hath chalenged all comers what soeuer to plaie v dogges at the single beare for v pounds and also to wearie a bull dead at the stake and for your better content shall haue plasant sport with the horse and ape and whiping of the blind beare. Viuat Rex.

There are frequent references to the sport of bearbaiting, which took place twice a week, on Wednesday and Sunday, and Shakespeare used many poetic images drawn from it. Foreign visitors were particularly impressed by the sport.

In bearbaiting, the bear was tied by a long rope to a post. Four or five mastiffs were then let into the pit and attacked the bear, which retaliated fiercely. The surviving dogs, however, were pulled off before the bear had received fatal injuries. In bullbaiting, the bull was usually free, but the sport continued until the animal was worried to death.

Other forms of sport were mentioned in the advertisement. A pony was led into the ring with an ape fastened on its back. The amusement consisted in watching the pony, terrified by the screams of the ape, lashing out at the dogs which tried to pull it down.

For the whipping of the blind bear, half a dozen men armed with whips surrounded the bear, and beat it until they drew blood. The bear defended itself vigorously, striking the whips out of the hands of its tormentors and breaking them, and even clawing the men themselves.

For further details, see E. K. Chambers, *The Elizabethan Stage,* Vol. II, pp. 448–71.

6. *Letters and Seals*

LEGAL AGREEMENTS

There are many poetic images in Shakespeare's plays drawn from the preparation and the completion of legal documents. When a legal agreement was drawn up between two or more parties the different copies were written out on a single sheet of parchment, thus:

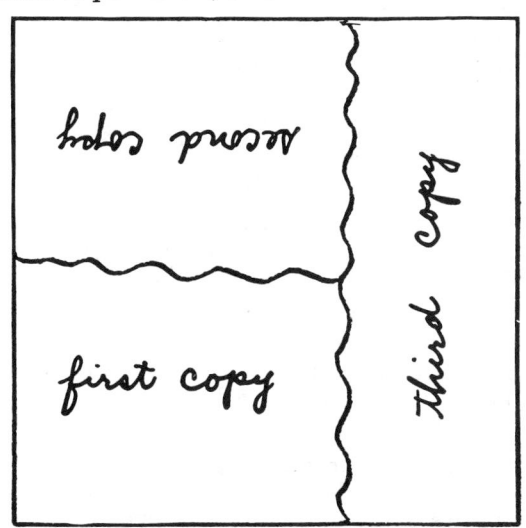

The copies were then cut apart with a wavy or indented cut; hence agreements were (and in legal language still are) known as *indentures* (see Pl. 11a). The purpose of the indentation was to prevent forgery. If the genuineness of any copy was called in question, it could be compared with and fitted against the other copy. When the copies had been separated, about an inch of the parchment at the bottom of each was folded over, and through the folds slits were made. Ribbons, or "labels" of parchment, were then inserted, one for each of the parties to the agreement. These labels hung down some three or four inches. The parties signed their names on the folded portion across the upper end of the label. The bottom of the label was then enclosed in a small ball of softened wax, into which the party pressed his seal. The impressing of the seal was the final act in making the formal agreement. Normally indentures were made between two parties, but indentures "tripartite" were quite common.

LETTERS

The letters presented by messengers in modern stage performances of Shakespeare's plays usually resemble a college diploma — a rolled scroll tied with a ribbon. Actually, however, Elizabethan letters were not in this form. A letter of any importance was written with generous margins on a double sheet of paper. This was then folded over, with the writing inside, in such a way that at the back the top edge overlapped the lower. Thus two thicknesses of paper intervened between the writing and the outside. The address or superscription was written on the front. The back was then secured by sealing wax impressed with the sender's seal. An unbroken seal showed the recipient that the letter had not been opened in transit. Hence the reading of a letter is sometimes referred to as "breaking open." Envelopes had not yet been invented.

7. *Hats and Heads*

In Shakespeare's time, the outward signs of courtesy toward those of higher rank were strictly demanded and observed. In the presence of a superior, the inferior stood bareheaded, hat in hand, with his head slightly bent forward in an attitude of humility. The inferior, especially if a servant, also "made a leg," or curtsied. This was done by bending both knees, the right behind the left, as low as possible.

Great men wore their hats, indoors and out, on all ceremonial occasions as a sign of their importance; and the etiquette of rank was exact even in moments of crisis. Thus on the memorable occasion of Essex's rebellion (see Gen. Intro. p. 24a), a deputation consisting of the Lord Keeper of the Great Seal and other members of the Privy Council appeared at Essex House. They were admitted to the courtyard. The Lord Keeper removed his hat as a mark of respect to Essex, who was his senior in rank. Essex and his friends removed their hats in respect to the Lord Keeper as representing the Queen. When, however, the Lord Keeper began to speak in the Queen's name as her representative, he put on his hat and commanded Essex and his company on their allegiance to lay down their weapons. In reply to this command, Essex's party put on their hats as a deliberate sign of contempt. It is small wonder that so precise a courtier as Osric was embarrassed when Hamlet bade him " put his bonnet to its right use " (*Haml*, v.ii.94).

8. *Ballads*

Students of literature are accustomed to think of the ballad as a folk poem of early origin with certain metrical characteristics. In Shakespeare's time, the commonest form was the news ballad. Hundreds of these ballads were written on every manner of topic: battles and victories, royal progresses, grievances, marvelous events, crimes and executions (particularly in the form of a lament by the criminal for his wicked life and deserved end), and scandals of all kinds. The news ballad was a crude and popular form of publication that appealed to the kind of person who nowadays is interested only in comic strips or tabloids.

Wherever there was a crowd ballads were hawked by a ballad-singer, who first sang the ballad and then sold copies at a penny apiece. They were vilely printed on a single sheet of paper, headed with any woodcut, more or less appropriate, which happened to be available in the printer's workshop. A typical specimen by Thomas Deloney, one of the most famous ballad-writers, runs as follows:

The Lamentation of Mr. Page's Wife [1]

of Plymouth, who, being forced to wed him, consented to his
Murder, for the love of G. Strangwidge: for
which they suffered at Barnstable
in Devonshire.

[1] The case caused a great sensation. The parents of Ulalia forced her to marry a rich old man called Page, although her true love, George Strangwidge, was an entirely suitable husband. At

The Tune is Fortune my Foe, etc.

Unhappy she whom Fortune hath forlorn,
Despised of grace that proffered grace did scorn,
My lawless love hath luckless wrought my woe,
My discontent content did overthrow.

My loathèd life too late I do lament,
My woeful deeds in heart I do repent;
A wife I was that willful went awry,
And for that fault am here prepared to die.

In blooming years my father's greedy mind,
Against my will, a match for me did find.
Great wealth there was, yea, gold and silver store,
But yet my heart had chosen one before.

Mine eyes disliked my father's liking quite,
My heart did loathe my parent's fond delight;
My childish mind and fancy told to me,
That with his age my youth could not agree.

On knees I prayed they would not me constrain;
With tears I cried their purpose to refrain;
With sighs and sobs I did them often move,
I might not wed whereas I could not love.

But all in vain my speeches still I spent.
My mother's will my wishes did prevent.
Though wealthy Page possessed the outward part,
George Strangwidge still was lodgèd in my heart.

I wedded was and wrappèd all in woe;
Great discontent within my heart did grow;
I loathed to live, yet lived in deadly strife,
Because perforce I was made Page's wife.

My closen eyes could not his sight abide;
My tender youth did loathe his agèd side:
Scant could I taste the meat whereon he fed;
My legs did loathe to lodge within his bed.

Cause knew I none I should despise him so,
That such disdain within my heart should grow,
Save only this, that fancy did me move,
And told me still, George Strangwidge was my love.

Lo! here began my downfall and decay,
In mind I mused to make him straight away.
I that became his discontented wife,
Contented was he should be rid of life.

Methinks the heavens cry vengeance for my fact,
Methinks the world condemns my monstrous act,
Methinks within my conscience tells me true,
That for that deed hell-fire is my due.

My pensive soul doth sorrow for my sin,
For which offense my soul doth bleed within;

Ulalia's request, Strangwidge and two accomplices strangled Page in bed. All four were subsequently hanged. There was very general sympathy with the girl as the victim of her parents' stupid greed.

But mercy, Lord! for mercy still I cry:
Save thou my soul, and let my body die.

Well could I wish that Page enjoyed his life,
So that he had some other to his wife:
But never could I wish, of low or high,
A longer life than see sweet Strangwidge die.

Oh woe is me! that had no greater grace
To stay till he had run out Nature's race.
My deeds I rue, but I do repent
That to the same my Strangwidge gave consent.

You parents fond, that greedy-minded be,
And seek to graft upon the golden tree,
Consider well and rightful judges be,
And give you doom twixt parents' love and me.

I was their child, and bound for to obey,
Yet not to love where I no love could lay.
I married was to muck and endless strife;
But faith before had made me Strangwidge' wife.

O wretched world, who cankered rust doth blind!
And cursèd men who bear a greedy mind!
And hapless I, whom parents did force so,
To end my days in sorrow, shame, and woe.

You Denshire dames, and courteous Cornwall
    knights,
That here are come to visit woeful wights,
Regard my grief, and mark my woeful end,
But to your children be a better friend.

And thou, my dear, that for my fault must die,
Be not afraid the sting of death to try.
Like as we lived and loved together true,
So both at once we'll bid the world adieu.

Ulalia, thy friend, doth take her last farewell,
Whose soul with thee in Heaven shall ever dwell.
Sweet Saviour Christ, do thou my soul receive!
The world I do with all my heart forgive.

And parents now, whose greedy minds do show
Your heart's desire, and inward beauty woe,
Mourn you no more, for now my heart doth tell,
Ere day be done my soul shall be full well.

And Plymouth proud, I bid thee now farewell.
Take heed, you wives, let not your hands rebel.
And farewell, life, wherein such sorrow shows,
And welcome, death, that doth my corpse enclose.

And now, sweet Lord, forgive me my misdeeds!
Repentance cries for soul that inward bleeds.
My soul and body I commend to thee,
That with thy blood from death redeemèd me.

Lord! Bless our Queen with long and happy life,
And send true peace betwixt each man and wife;

And give all parents wisdom to foresee
The match is marred where minds do not agree.

                          T. D.

London. Printed by Thomas Scarlet 1591.

9. *Heralds and Heraldry*

Heralds, wearing their sleeveless coats embroidered with the royal arms, still have their place in state pageantry in England, but nowadays they are little more than a picturesque survival from the Middle Ages. Their greatest age was in the fourteenth century. Nevertheless in Shakespeare's time the heralds had an important place in the social and noble life, and a knowledge of the elaborate science of heraldry was part of the education of a gentleman. Heralds were under the control of the Earl Marshal, a court official of considerable importance. They were (and still are) organized in a College, in which each herald bore a romantic name. The three seniors were known as "Kings"—Garter King at Arms, Clarenceux King at Arms, and Norroy King at Arms. Under them were the heralds known as York, Richmond, Somerset, Lancaster, Chester, and Windsor, and four pursuivants, or junior heralds, called Rouge Dragon, Blue Mantle, Portcullis, and Rouge Croix.

The heralds were concerned with matters that affected the dignities and the honor of kings, noblemen, and gentlemen. They organized all important state ceremonies, especially those at the accession of kings, royal weddings, coronations, funerals, and the solemnities of the special orders of knighthood, such as the Garter or the Bath. In the Middle Ages they were also the official and inviolable messengers of kings in war and peace and as such read royal proclamations (see, for example, *Hen V*, III.vi.120; IV.iii.79–127). They directed proceedings at combats of honor (see, for example, *Rich II*, I.iii.), though trial by combat was no longer officially allowed in Shakespeare's time. Apart from their duties at Court they undertook to direct lesser ceremonies, particularly the funerals of noble or wealthy persons.

The most important function, however, of the College of Heralds was to preserve the records of noble families and to grant coats of arms to persons worthy to be considered gentlemen. From time to time, during visitations in the counties, they examined the claims of those who declared themselves to be of gentle birth, and recorded their findings. They thus acted as a kind of *Social Register* and *Who's Who* of the time.

The granting of a coat of arms was the official recognition that the recipient was a "gentleman." As might be expected, the privilege encouraged much petty snobbery. New-made gentlemen irritated alike those who lacked the privilege and those who had enjoyed it for many generations. Indeed in Shakespeare's time it was openly said, and with much truth, that any man with money could buy a coat of arms from the heralds quite regardless of a claim to merit. The truth is that in England the qualities that distinguish gentlemen from common men have always been very vague.

Heraldry was originally a means of distinguishing one warrior enclosed in armor from another. Each assumed a recognizable badge, which he painted on his shield. By the thirteenth century a regular system of recording and painting these badges had developed, and coats of arms were passed down from father to son. Coats of arms were not only useful in war; they are also a pleasing and picturesque form of decoration. In time, heraldry developed into an elaborate science with a considerable vocabulary to describe the colors, ornaments, and arrangement of innumerable devices in such a way that anyone could recognize or reproduce the design from the description.

Seven colors were used in painting (or *blazoning*) a shield, usually designated by French names, viz., *or* (yellow or gold), *argent* (white or silver), *gules* (red), *azure* (blue), *sable* (black), *vert* (green), *purpure* (purple). The shield was divided in many different ways, each of which had its technical name. Many shields contained only a geometrical pattern, but more commonly devices or *charges* were used, which were often appropriate to the name or the deeds of the first wearer. Coats of arms descended from father to children, but members of the same family often made a distinction in their coats by adding a border or changing the color of the background or making a slight variation in the device; this was known as a *difference*. Daughters bore the coats of arms of their fathers; and when a gentleman married the daughter of a distinguished house, especially if she was also an heiress, the coats of arms of the two families were combined, either by *impaling* (that is, by dividing the shield vertically and blazoning the two coats of arms side by side) or by *halving* (where

each coat was cut in two horizontally) or by quartering (when the shield was divided into four and the two coats repeated at the opposite corners).

A gentleman who was descended from several illustrious families often had a most elaborate shield subdivided into a dozen or more coats of arms. The expert in heraldry by reading the shield would be able to identify the wearer from the details of his descent thus set out. Coats of arms were not confined to noblemen or gentlemen; cities, corporations, bishops, universities, colleges, dioceses, guilds, were all entitled to appropriate arms.

In addition to the shield, the heralds granted a *crest*. This was originally a device worn on top of the helmet by a knight in full armor and was therefore something simple, such as an eagle, a lion, a swan's head.

The coat of arms and the crest granted to Shakespeare's father in 1596 will illustrate heraldic language. The coat was *Gold, on a bend sable, a spear of the first, steeled argent*. Gold (or yellow), the first color mentioned, is that of the background of the shield. The *bend* is a band running diagonally from the top right corner (i.e., the wearer's right); it is sable (or black). On the bend is a spear "of the first," that is, the first-mentioned color — gold, with its point silver. The spear is chosen as a pun on the name Shakespeare. The crest (or cognizance) was a *falcon, his wings displayed, argent, standing on a wreath of his colors;* that is, a silver falcon with wings outstretched standing on a silver wreath. Coat of arms and crest are illustrated on the title page of this book.

10. *Tortures and Punishments*

Torture was seldom practiced in England. Only in cases of high treason was the rack used to encourage a reluctant witness to talk. The *rack* was a large frame set out on the ground. At each end there were rollers around which a pair of ropes were wound. The hands and feet of the victim were fastened to these ropes and tension was applied by means of levers. The victim was thus stretched until he was persuaded to give the necessary information. In other countries other means of torture were used. The " strappado," several times mentioned by Shakespeare, was an

Italian torment. The victim was drawn up to a height by means of a rope passed through his elbows, and then let down with a jerk.

Various methods of punishment were used on convicted offenders. The court of the Star Chamber often sentenced an offender to stand in the *pillory*. This was a heavy framework of wood with holes through which the victim's hands and head were thrust. Thus fixed, he was subjected to the gaze and the abuse of the crowd. Over his head was fixed a paper setting out the details of his offense. Sometimes he was nailed to the pillory by one of his ears. The punishment of standing in the pillory often included the cutting off of one or both ears or slitting the nose. Petty malefactors and vagabonds were made to sit in the *stocks*. Here the legs were secured through holes in a heavy board. Rogues and vagabonds were whipped on the back until bloody. Convicted prostitutes were led through the streets tied to the back of a cart and whipped while metal basins were sounded to draw the attention of passers-by.

Debtors were imprisoned until the debt was discharged. The jailer was made responsible for producing his prisoner on demand, and if the prisoner escaped, the jailer himself had to pay the debt. Prisoners were obliged to pay for their keep and were not released until they had discharged their fees to the jailer. Poor prisoners were allowed to beg for the charity of passers-by; they would otherwise have starved, as no free rations were provided. It was not, however, usual to sentence an offender to long terms of imprisonment.

11. *Cuckolds and Horns*

Elizabethan plays abound in jokes about cuckolds and horns. A cuckold is a husband deceived by a faithless wife, and therefore regarded as an object of derision. The name derives from cuckoo, a bird of unusual and disorderly habits. It is a migrant which appears in northern Europe toward the end of April and disappears in July. It is remarkable for its distinctive and monotonous cry of " cuck-oo cuck-oo." It was and is regarded as a foolish bird, probably because of its cry, which is at first welcomed as a sign of spring but afterward disliked because of its irritating monotony. Unlike most birds, it makes no nest; instead it lays an egg in the nest of some smaller bird, who innocently hatches and feeds the foster child even after the latter has shouldered the legitimate offspring out of the nest. The origin of the name " cuckold " may thus be one who has been cheated by a cuckoo — an adulterer who has foisted his own offspring on an innocent victim. To " cry cuckoo " after a husband was to warn him that his wife's lover was near.

A cuckold was also supposed to wear a pair of invisible horns as a sign of his unhappy fate. The origin of this curious myth is unknown, though there have been many guesses, none very convincing. The simplest explanation is that horns are appropriate to a cuckold because he has shown himself to be a dull, stupid, oxlike creature. Once, however, a connection between horns and infidelity had been established, writers and wits showed endless ingenuity in making play on the word " horn " in all its possible meanings and uses.

12. *Signs*

In Elizabethan England the practice of numbering houses or shops in large towns had not yet been introduced. Instead each house or shop in a street displayed a sign jutting out at right angles, in the form of a painted board suspended from a bracket (see Pls. 3a, 6b). The sign was some simple and easily recognizable device, such as a bell, an angel, a white hart, a fox, or a green dragon. The sign of Cupid blindfolded denoted a brothel. The sign-painters' trade was therefore much in evidence. In England signs are still displayed over or beside inns.

As well as the pictorial signs, certain trades also had their own recognized symbols. The barber's shop was (and sometimes still is) designated by a pole painted spirally in red and white. A bush was the token of a wine shop, a garland of an ale house, while the lattice windows of a tavern were painted red.

13. *Bowls*

Shakespeare frequently used poetic imagery taken from the game of bowls. In that game a small bowl (or ball), called the *jack* or the *mistress,* was set as a mark at one end of the green; from the other end the players rolled their bowls toward the jack, the player whose bowl finally rested nearest the jack scoring highest. A bowl which touched the jack was said to " kiss."

The bowl was not a perfect sphere, but so made that one side somewhat protruded. This protrusion was called the *bias;* it caused the bowl to take a curving and indirect course. The game was played in bowling alleys and on greens; but the bowling green lacked the perfect and smooth surface of a modern green. Lumps and impediments in the turf which diverted the bowl were called *rubs.*

14. *The Great Household*

Some understanding of the organization of a great house is required to appreciate many of Shakespeare's plays. It was the fashion to employ as many servants as possible. A nobleman or a man of wealth lived in a small palace, and each department of the household had its own staff under the control of a gentleman, who was assisted by a yeoman. The "gentleman serving-man" was usually the younger son of a man of good family, and employment in a great house was regarded as a normal occupation which carried with it no sense of social inferiority. Promising and ambitious young scholars, fresh from the universities, often took service as tutors or secretaries and in time rose to high positions. Similarly, the lady of the house was served by young gentlewomen of good family, who in this way learned polite behavior and domestic economy until such time as a marriage was arranged for them. Thus in *Twelfth Night,* Malvolio, Olivia's steward, was a man of good family, and Maria was a lady of birth and the social equal of Sir Toby.

15. *Marriage Customs*

In a marriage where all forms were observed the first step was the formal betrothal of the two parties. This was a private affair. Then came the publication of the banns: according to law, on three successive Sundays the minister must publicly announce in church the intention of the parties to be married and call on any person who knew any cause why the marriage should not lawfully be performed to come forward and declare it. If for any reason it was necessary to hasten the marriage, a special license was procured from the bishop of the diocese.

Elizabethan life was essentially a small-town or village affair. As a result, in most marriages the parties lived within walking distance of each other. A wedding celebrated with full ceremony was an uproarious all-day event. It began very early in the morning in the bride's house, when the bridesmaids awakened and dressed the bride. Soon the bridegroom, accompanied by his groomsmen, friends, and musicians, arrived to claim the bride. Then the whole party of friends and relations set out in procession to the church, the bride, dressed in white, with her hair loose, being the center of attraction.

After the ceremony had been performed, the party moved off to the bridegroom's house, where a great feast was prepared, and the guests settled down to enjoy themselves for the rest of the day with eating, drinking, dancing, and games. If there was a poet among the party, he would present an epithalamium, or wedding poem; or a masque or other form of entertainment might be given.

The merriment increased as night came on. At length the bridesmaids led the bride away to the wedding chamber, where she was undressed and put into bed. Then they took her garters and threw them among the bachelor guests, who scrambled for them. The bridegroom's friends then led him away, undressed him, and brought him to the wedding chamber, where he was put into bed with his bride, after which, with much noise, laughter, and coarse jesting, the two were sewed together into the sheets. Bridegroom and bride were then left alone to begin their married life while the guests went back to continue their revelry.

Early in the morning, the newly married couple were greeted with a song at their bedroom window. Thereafter, bride and bridegroom took their places among the married folk. There was no honeymoon.

A more idealized account of an Elizabethan wedding will be found in Spenser's *Epithalamium.*

16. *Funeral Customs*

Funeral customs in Shakespeare's time were elaborate. Great men were buried with much ceremonial, pomp, and ostentation. The body, enclosed in a coffin and covered with a pall, was borne to the grave by bearers wearing black, and followed by a long procession of mourners, friends, and servants, who wore hooded black cloaks which completely covered them. The coats of arms of the great man in the form of scutcheons painted on buckram and resembling stiff flags were carried in the procession, and the whole ceremony was elaborately ordered and arranged by one of the heralds, who drew a fee for his services. After the funeral the mourners were feasted, and sometimes money was given to the poor. To omit any of the proper ceremony was a sign of disrespect for the dead and cast a slur on his name and family, as Laertes complained when he heard that his father had been buried "hugger-mugger" (*Haml,* IV.v.213–17).

Of all state funerals during Shakespeare's life in London, that of Queen Elizabeth, on April 28, 1603, was the most elaborate and splendid. First came the Knight Marshal's men to clear the way; then two hundred and forty poor women, walking four and four; then servants of gentlemen, esquires, and knights, followed by the servants from the many departments of the Royal Household. In the next section of the procession walked the grooms of the household and the servants of earls and countesses. Then came two equerries, leading the Queen's horse, trapped with velvet; next the clerks and sergeants, the musicians, the apothecaries and surgeons, the Master of the Hall, the groom porter, the chief clerks. Next in ascending order were the clerks of the great Departments of State — the Privy Council, the Privy Seal, the Signet, the Parliament — doctors of physic, the Queen's chaplains. In the next section went the aldermen of London, the Solicitor General, the Attorney General, knights bachelors, the Lord Chief Baron, the Lord Chief Justice, knights ambassadors, and esquires of the body. After them came the Master of Requests, the agents for Venice and the States of the Low Countries, the Lord Mayor of London, Sir Robert Cecil (Principal Secretary), barons, bishops, viscounts, earls, marquises, the Lord Keeper of the Great Seal, the French Ambassador, and the Archbishop of Canterbury. They were followed by the heralds and gentlemen ushers, and then the chariot itself containing the body of the Queen, embalmed and enclosed in a lead coffin, surmounted by her recumbent effigy, crowned and in her Parliament robes. Over the chariot was a canopy borne by four noblemen, and immediately following the Earl of Worcester, Master of the Horse, leading the palfrey of honor. Next came the Lady Mar-

chioness of Northampton, who, as senior peeress, was the chief mourner, supported by the Lord Treasurer and the Lord Admiral. She was followed by the gentlewomen of the Queen's chamber, countesses, viscountesses, earls' daughters, baronesses, and maids of honor; and, last of all, Sir Walter Ralegh, Captain of the Guard, with all the guard following, five by five, with their halberds downward.

As the procession passed along, "the City of Westminster was surcharged with multitudes of all sorts of people in their streets, houses, windows, leads, and gutters, that came to see the obsequy; and when they beheld her statue or picture lying upon the coffin set forth in royal robes, having a crown upon the head thereof, and a ball and scepter in either hand, there was such a general sighing, groaning, and weeping as the like hath not been seen or known in the memory of man, neither doth any history mention any people, time, or state, to make like lamentation for the death of their Sovereign."

Sovereigns, noblemen, and men of wealth were buried inside the church beneath an elaborate monument, which they had usually taken care to erect for themselves while still living. Lesser men were buried more simply. The common man, indeed, was carried on a bier, uncoffined, and wrapped in a shroud which was simply a sheet knotted at head and foot, sometimes leaving the face exposed. He was buried in a shallow grave in the open churchyard. The practice of erecting headstones over graves had not yet come into fashion, and the dead were regarded only as temporary tenants of consecrated ground. After a time the grave would be used for some newcomer and the bones then thrown up were cast in the charnel house until they decayed or were thrown out.

Suicides were not permitted burial in holy ground. They were buried without ceremony in some open place, such as a crossroads (see *Haml,* V.i.).

17. The Post

There was in Elizabethan days no postal service for the general public. For official use, however, there was a regular system of post horses kept constantly ready by the local "postmaster" at various stages along the main highways. These saddle horses were available also for wealthy travelers who wished to make a fast journey, but they were intended mainly for official messengers, who carried their letters at top speed. In times of emergency the postmaster was empowered to impress riding horses as required. The post boy carried a horn which he blew to give warning of his approach. In Shakespeare's plays there are many images, usually denoting speed, derived from the post.

Some idea of the speed of the post boy can be gathered from the endorsements on letters. Thus a very urgent letter written by Essex on October 26, 1597, was dispatched from Plymouth about 10 A.M. It reached Ashburton (25 miles) at 4:30 P.M., Exeter (19 miles) after 8 P.M., Honiton (15 miles) at 10:30 P.M., Crewkerne (20 miles) at 1:30 A.M., Sherborne (12 miles) at 4:30 A.M., Shafton (14 miles) at 7 A.M., Salisbury (17 miles) at 9 A.M., Andover (16 miles) at noon, and Basingstoke (16 miles) at 3:30 P.M. This means that in less than 30 hours the letter was carried a distance of approximately 165 miles over unlit country roads, with nine pauses for change of horses.

18. Nature and Art

Nature and art are constantly contrasted by writers in the sixteenth and seventeenth centuries. In Elizabethan English, "nature" meant that which was born in a man — that is, natural ability; art was that which came with study and training. Ben Jonson in his conversations with the Scottish poet William Drummond of Hawthornden grumbled that Shakespeare "wanted art"; in his ode on Shakespeare, prefaced to the first folio (see Gen. Intro. p. 73a), he was more generous. By lack of art, Jonson meant that though Shakespeare had natural genius, he did not always take sufficient pains to design or polish his work or to observe the critical rules. Jonson himself was far more indebted to art than to nature, for his work was most conscientiously and deliberately wrought.

Art thus meant technical skill. Today the word "artist" implies also a touch of genius, and is confined chiefly to experts in painting, sculpture, music, literature, and acting. In Shakespeare's time an artist was a skilled craftsman. When Bacon contrasted "arts" and "sciences," he meant by "art" almost what is now called applied science and by "science," pure knowledge.

Art implied also study and conscious effort. Cassius admiring Brutus's stoic acceptance of the news of Portia's death says (*Caesar*, IV.iii.194):

> I have as much of this in art as you,
> But yet my nature could not bear it so.

Art and matter are likewise contrasted, "art" meaning style and "matter" content. When Polonius begins his lecture on Hamlet's madness, he is so pleased with his own style and artistic phrasing that the Queen interrupts him with (*Haml*, II.ii.95):

> More matter with less art.

Nature and Fortune also provide natural contrasts, as in the lighthearted argument between Celia and Rosalind (*AYLI*, I.ii.34–58): Nature bestows or withholds natural gifts such as ability, beauty, or goodness, which are born in a man; Fortune brings those accidental good or evil gifts which come to a man from without, such as wealth, friendship, promotion, poverty, or ill luck. Moreover, since Fortune is very capricious in her gifts, she is painted as a blind woman, as Ancient Pistol very learnedly explains (*Hen V*, III.vi.31–40).

19. Bells

Shakespeare constantly refers to church bells. They were rung on many occasions, to summon worshipers to church on Sunday and holy days, to announce good tidings, to give the alarm for fire or invasion, to celebrate the sovereign's accession, or for weddings and funerals. The bell was also tolled to announce the passing of a sick man, if possible at the moment of death, so that his soul might be accompanied by the prayers of his friends. It was tolled again at his funeral. In times of plague the sound of the passing bell was never still, and added to the general gloom. In many country churches there was a peal (or set) of bells, and bell-ringing was an art much practiced. For all joyous occasions peals of bells were rung, but one solitary bell was used for deaths and burials.

20. Equivocation

The theory of equivocation was much discussed between the years 1598 and 1606. In 1598 a great controversy arose among English Roman Catholics. Those who wished to practice their religion in peace realized that most of the bitter feeling against Catholics was caused by the actions of the English Jesuits on the Continent, who were regarded as being the instigators of the many plots against the life of Queen Elizabeth. The controversy led to a pamphlet war between the Jesuits and the Catholic secular priests in England, in which the Anglican Bishop of London took a hand, for he encouraged the seculars and even arranged for their pamphlets to be printed. One doctrine, hotly disputed and very generally abhorred by Protestant Englishmen, was the principle of equivocation by which a man might conceal the truth when giving evidence on oath. Equivocation was defended by Father Robert Parsons, the chief propagandist for the Jesuits, in a book called *A Brief Apology or Defense of the Catholic Ecclesiastical Hierarchy,* which appeared in 1602, wherein he claimed that in certain special circumstances "amphibology," or hiding the truth by dissimulation, was lawful. On March 28, 1606, Father Henry Garnet was tried and condemned to death for being accessory to the Gunpowder Plot. Equivocation was one of the major issues in the trial, for it was shown that some of the conspirators had deliberately concealed the truth when under oath. Garnet in his defense justified equivocation in particular cases. At his execution on May 6, he was urged not to equivocate with his last breath but to speak the truth. It is likely that the Porter's remarks in *Macbeth* (II.iii.9–12) are a direct reference to this event.

21. *Alchemy*

Chemistry as now studied was unknown in Shakespeare's time, but there was a considerable practical knowledge of chemical processes, especially among those who worked in the various metals. "Alchemists," basing their notions on the theories of the four humors (see App. 3), believed that all metals were composed of earth, water, and air in varying proportions; pure gold was the perfect metal in which all qualities were perfectly combined. On this assumption alchemists were concerned mainly with trying to find the "philosopher's stone" which would transmute baser metals into gold and would also produce the "elixir of life" or *aurum potabile* (tincture of

gold) which would reconcile the discords of the bodily humors and so be a cure for all diseases, including old age. The lure of boundless wealth attracted the credulous and the greedy, and there were many rascals ready to fleece them. Much magic and mystic symbolism were mingled with the study of alchemy, genuine and bogus. Ben Jonson's play *The Alchemist* gives an amusing picture of one group and contains much of the jargon actually used by alchemists. Nevertheless, many alchemists were genuine students; and even if they never succeeded in finding the philosopher's stone, they were at least conducting original experiments and not relying solely on tradition.

22. *Time Problems*

Critics, especially those who are not overfamiliar with the customs of the Elizabethan stage, are often disturbed by time problems in Shakespeare's plays. The most famous occurs in *Othello.* When the play is read carefully, there is a noticeable inconsistency. The action begins in Venice on the night of the runaway marriage of Othello and Desdemona. Almost at once Othello is summoned to the Council and dispatched forthwith to take command in Cyprus, leaving Desdemona to follow him. Cassio, Desdemona, and Othello reach Cyprus in different ships. Othello and Desdemona are reunited. That same night, Cassio is made drunk on guard by Iago and is immediately dismissed from his post by Othello. Early next morning, by Iago's advice Cassio comes to Desdemona to ask her to intercede for him with Othello, and directly afterwards — as Cassio is going out — Iago begins his plot to persuade Othello that Desdemona has deceived him and has long been Cassio's mistress. As the story is unfolded, there has been no possible chance or opportunity for Desdemona and Cassio even to have been alone together. This inconsistency in the story undoubtedly exists when the play is read and dissected; but *Othello,* and all Shakespeare's plays, were written for acting, and in the rush and excitement of events on the stage the difficulty passes unnoticed.

Shakespeare was indeed very free with time in a play. He was concerned with creating a succession of impressions in the minds of his audience, and not with presenting a series of mathematical problems of time. Months and even years pass unnoticed and unmentioned during the action of many Elizabethan plays. There are in fact other instances of compression of time, even in *Othello,* which disturb no one. Thus in II.i, the arrival of Cassio's ship in the harbor is announced at line 26; he enters at line 42. At line 51 another ship is sighted at sea; 14 lines later the arrival of Iago is announced, and he appears with Desdemona at line 81. The third ship is sighted at line 93, and Othello enters at line 183. Thus in a matter of less than a quarter of an hour of unbroken acting time three separate ships — and sailing ships at that — are sighted, enter the harbor, and are tied up. In real life the whole process between sighting and docking would have taken at least six hours.

Another instance which causes no comment is to be found in *Richard II.* In I.iv, Richard and Aumerle (who has just parted from Bolingbroke) discuss Bolingbroke's behavior as he went away to banishment. At line 52 Bushy announces that John of Gaunt is dying. Richard at once goes out to visit him, and arrives at II.i.68. Shortly afterward Gaunt is carried out, and his death is announced at line 147. Richard, having declared that he will seize Gaunt's wealth, makes his exit at line 223. At line 276 Northumberland announces that Bolingbroke has *already* gathered an expedition in Britanny to invade England.

These and many other apparent inconsistencies are quite unimportant on the stage. Indeed, the actual passing of time in drama is seldom noticed unless for some particular reason it obtrudes and causes a feeling of doubt or of questioning in the spectator.

23. Witches and Witchcraft

It is popularly supposed that in Shakespeare's England every Englishman believed in witches and that witchcraft was commonly practiced. Actually there were far more skeptics than believers, and the reports of the cases tried in the courts, of which there are many, make disappointingly unromantic reading.

The most famous and elaborate work on witchcraft to be published in Shakespeare's lifetime was Reginald Scot's *Discovery of Witchcraft* (1584). Scot had been greatly disturbed at the flimsy evidence offered at the trial of certain witches in his own part of the country, and he studied the subject carefully in many authorities, classical, foreign, and English. He set out to prove " that the compacts and contracts of witches with all Devils and all Infernal Spirits or Familiars are but erroneous novelties and imaginary conceptions." Scot's sturdy Protestant skepticism was not, however, acceptable to all his readers, because he made light of the evidence of the Bible.

In 1587 George Gifford, a minister of religion and a learned theologian, answered Scot in *A Discourse of the Subtle Practises of Devils by Witches and Sorcerers,* and six years later in a more popular *Dialogue Concerning Witches.* Gifford compromised between Scot's skepticism and vulgar credulity. In 1597 King James VI of Scotland, later King James I of England and patron of Shakespeare's company, published his *Daemonology,* to refute the " damnable opinions " of Scot. The book is well written in the form of a dialogue, and is a valuable summary of contemporary beliefs in the occult. King James had good reasons for his beliefs. In 1591 a number of Scottish witches of both sexes were brought to trial for endeavoring to murder him by witchcraft. King James was himself present at some of the examinations, and the evidence was sensational. When one of the witches named Agnes Sampson had made such strange confessions that the King exclaimed that they were all liars, she took him aside and " declared unto him the very words which passed between the King's Majesty and his Queen at Upslo in Norway the first night of their marriage; whereat the King wondered greatly and swore by the living God that he believed that all the devils in Hell could not have discovered the same." As a popular account of the trials was published in England in 1592, Shakespeare may have read it; the witches in *Macbeth* behave in much the same way as the witches in this case.

There is considerable evidence that in the Middle Ages and in Shakespeare's own time secret societies of witches flourished both in France and in Scotland. The members of these groups practiced an anti-Christian cult with various obscene rites, and they had a considerable knowledge of simple poisons. But there is little trace of any widespread witch cult in England. Individual witches, of both sexes, were accused of doing harm, sometimes resulting in death. If condemned, the witch was executed not for witchcraft, but for murder by witchcraft. For the most part the accused were lonely and malicious old women. Scot thus describes the type:

One sort of such as are said to be witches are women which be commonly old, lame, blear-eyed, pale, foul, and full of wrinkles; poor, sullen, superstitious, and papists; or such as know no religion: in whose drowsy minds the Devil hath gotten a fine seat; so as, what mischief, mischance, calamity, or slaughter is brought to pass, they are easily persuaded the same is done by themselves, imprinting in their minds an earnest and constant imagination thereof. They are lean and deformed, showing melancholy in their faces, to the horror of all that see them. They are doting, scolds, mad, devilish; and not much differing from them that are thought to be possessed with spirits; so firm and steadfast in their opinions, as whosoever shall only have respect to the constancy of their words uttered would easily believe they were true indeed.

These miserable wretches are so odious unto all their neighbors, and so feared, as few dare offend them, or deny them anything they ask. Whereby they take upon them — yea, and sometimes think that they can do — such things as are beyond the ability of human nature. These go from house to house, and from door to door, for a pot full of milk, yeast, drink, pottage, or some such relief; without the which they could hardly live; neither obtaining for their service and pains, nor by their art, nor yet at the Devil's hands (with whom they are said to make a perfect and visible bargain) either beauty, money, promotion, wealth, worship, pleasure, honor, knowledge, learning, or any other benefit whatsoever.

It falleth out many times that neither their necessities nor their expectation is answered or served, in those places where they beg or borrow; but rather their lewdness is by their neighbors reproved. And further, in tract of time the witch waxeth odious and tedious to her neighbors; and they again are despised and despited of her: so as sometimes she curseth one and sometimes another; and from that the master of the house, his wife, children, cattle, etc. to the little pig that lieth in the sty. Thus in process of time they have all displeased her, and she hath wished evil luck unto them all; perhaps with curses and imprecations made in form. Doubtless (at length) some of her neighbors die, or fall sick; or some of their children are visited with diseases that vex them strangely: as apoplexies, epilepsies, convulsions, hot fevers, worms, etc. Which by ignorant parents are supposed to be the vengeance of witches. Yea, and their opinions and conceits are confirmed and maintained by unskillful physicians: according to the common saying: *Inscitiæ pallium maleficium et incantatio,* Witchcraft and enchantment is the cloak of ignorance: whereas indeed evil humors, and not strange words, witches, or spirits are the causes of such diseases. Also some of their cattle perish, either by disease or mischance. Then they upon whom such adversities fall, weighing the fame that goeth upon this woman (her words, displeasure, and curses meeting so justly with their misfortune), do not only conceive, but also are resolved, that all their mishaps are brought to pass by her only means.

The witch, on the other side, expecting her neighbors' mischances, and seeing things sometimes come to pass according to her wishes, curses, and incantations (for *Bodin* himself confesseth that not one above two in a hundred of their witchings or wishings take effect) being called before a Justice, by due examination of the circumstances is driven to see her imprecations and desires and her neighbors' harms and losses to concur, and as it were to take effect: and so confesseth that she (as a goddess) hath brought such things to pass. Wherein not only she, but the accuser, and also the Justice, are fouly deceived and abused; as being through her confession and other circumstances persuaded (to the injury of God's glory) that she hath done, or can do, that which is proper only to God himself.

In general most Englishmen scoffed at witchcraft, but with the sneaking suspicion that " there might be something in it." An Elizabethan play about witches thus produced much the same reaction in an audience as a modern horror film.

24. *Dances*

Dancing [1] in the sixteenth century was as popular with all classes as today, and as severely condemned by extreme puritans. Of the dances practiced by gentlemen and their ladies, those most frequently mentioned by Shakespeare are:

THE MEASURE

The measure was a slow, solemn dance full of stately movement and suitable for the elderly and for formal occasions. It is thus described by Sir John Davies in *Orchestra, or The Poem of Dancing:*

But after these, as men more civil grew,
He [Love] did more grave and solemn measures frame,
With such fair order and proportion true,

[1] For a full note, see *Shakespeare's England*, Vol. II, pp. 437-50.

And correspondence every way the same,
That no faultfinding eye did ever blame;
   For every eye was movèd at the sight
   With sober wond'ring, and with sweet delight.

Not those old students of the heavenly book,
Atlas the great, Prometheus the wise,
Which on the stars did all their lifetime look,
Could ever find such measures in the skies,
So full of change and rare varieties;
   Yet all the feet whereon these measures go,
   Are only spondees, solemn, grave, and slow.

The measure was danced by Capulet's guests (*R & J*, I.v.) and in *Much Ado*, II.i.

THE PAVAN

The pavan " was a stately, dignified, processional dance suitable to the gala mantles of princes and the robes of magistrats. ' Every pavane has its galliard ' says the Spanish proverb, as if to say every solemnity must have its moment of levity. The measured steps were two simple and a double one forward, and the same number backward, to the music of hautboys and trumpets." [2]

THE GALLIARD

The galliard, known also as a cinquepace or five-step, was a much quicker, livelier dance, of which Davies wrote:

But for more divers and more pleasing show,
A swift and wandering dance she did invent.
With passages uncertain to and fro,
Yet with a certain answer and consent
To the quick music of the instrument.
   Five was the number of the music's feet,
   Which still the dance did with five paces meet.

A gallant dance, that lively doth bewray
A spirit and a virtue masculine;
Impatient that her house on earth should stay
Since she herself is fiery and divine;
Oft doth she make her body upward fline [3]
   With lofty turns and capriols in the air,
   Which with the lusty tunes accordeth fair.

THE CAPRIOL

The capriol or caper was a movement that is still common in ballet dancing, where the dancer leaps upward beating the feet together while still in the air.

CORANTO AND LAVOLTA

The coranto and the lavolta were varieties of the galliard. In the coranto the movement was swift and gliding; in the lavolta the dancers leaped into the air. Davies describes them thus:

Coranto
What shall I name those current travases [4]
That on a triple dactile foot do run
Close by the ground with sliding passages,
Wherein that dancer greatest praise hath won
Which with best order can all orders shun;
   For everywhere he wantonly must range,
   And turn, and wind, with unexpected change.

Lavolta
Yet is there one, the most delightful kind,
A lofty jumping, or a leaping round,
Where arm in arm two dancers are entwined
And whirl themselves with strict embracements
   bound,
And still their feet an anapest do sound.
   An anapest is all their music's song,
   Whose first two feet are short, and third is long.

Much Ado ends with a coranto.

THE BRAWL

The brawl was originally a French dance in which a pair of dancers led the movement and the rest followed.

COUNTRY DANCES

Country dances were common, especially at holiday time. On Mayday the painted maypole was set up and boys and girls danced a round dance about it. Whitsun (Pentecost, which follows seven weeks after Easter, in May or June) was the time for morris dancing. The morris (originally Moorish) dance was a primitive kind of ballet in which the various dancers were in character, usually Robin Hood, Friar Tuck, Maid Marian, and Little John. There was also a member of the party who wore the hobbyhorse — a frame fastened to his waist resembling a horse, with trappings reaching down to the ground and concealing the human legs. Thus equipped, the dancer pranced and cavorted around. Morris dancers wore bells around their knees. See Pl. 13d.

---

[2] *Shakespeare's England*, Vol. II, 444.   [3] That is, fly.   [4] That is, traverses.

THE JIG

There were two kinds of jig, the one a lively round dance with movements like a Scottish reel, and the other danced after the performance of a play (see *Caesar* Intro. p. 529a). The stage jig was a pantomime dance performed by two or more dancers in character, often with dialogue and frequently very bawdy. Will Kempe, the clown of Shakespeare's company, was especially famous for dancing jigs.

25. The Fencing Match in " Hamlet "

THE BET

(V.ii.171–77)

Laertes fancies himself an expert fencer and is therefore prepared to give Hamlet a handicap. He has bet the King that he will hit Hamlet twelve times before Hamlet hits him nine times. Hamlet's handicap is, then, plus three in twelve hits.

THE MATCH

(V.ii.290–316)

Hamlet scores the first two hits and is thus two up. Laertes then presses his attack and scores a hit with his pointed foil. Both men are now roused. Hamlet, realizing from his wound that Laertes is fighting with a pointed foil, carries out a textbook movement to exchange rapiers. This is illustrated in Sainct-Didier's *Traicté contenant les secrets du premier livre sur l'espée seule* (see Pl. 13b), where the opponents are called the Lieutenant (=Laertes) and the Provost (=Hamlet). In the maneuver, the Lieutenant makes a short thrust. The Provost parries, drawing back his left foot; then with his foil he pushes the Lieutenant's blade to one side. Whereupon, bringing up his left foot, he swings round and with his left hand grasps the hilt of his opponent's foil and twists it backward. If the Lieutenant holds onto his own foil, it will be twisted out of his hand, and his fingers broken as well. His only answer to this movement is to drop his own foil and retaliate by similarly grasping the Provost's hilt with his left hand and twisting it out of his grasp. Each opponent now has the other's foil in his left hand. Each steps back, transfers the exchanged foil to the right hand, and resumes the contest.

Hamlet, having thus exchanged rapiers, now presses home the attack and scores his third hit with Laertes' pointed (and poisoned) rapier. At this moment the Queen swoons and the contest is broken off.

It may be noted that the stage direction in Q1 is "*They catch one another's Rapiers, and both are wounded.*" F1 reads "*In scuffling they change Rapiers.*" There is no stage direction in Q2.

26. Hawks and Hawking

Hawking, which was a very popular sport with gentlemen, had an elaborate vocabulary. Various types of hawk were used for the different kinds of game, the best being imported from the Continent. In training the hawk and keeping it in good condition, considerable skill and experience were necessary, and the professional falconer was an expert.

Hawks were not bred in captivity. They were captured wild and tamed. If taken from the nest (eyrie) they were called *eyasses,* and were brought up by hand. *Eyasses* were naturally more easily trained, but less skillful in taking the game. Mature wild hawks were called *haggards;* they were more difficult to tame, but having hunted naturally before capture, they needed less training.

The first stage in taming a wild hawk was to *seel* its eyes. This was done by passing a needle and thread through the lower eyelid of each eye; the thread was then tied over the head and the eyes could be closed at the will of the falconer. A blinded hawk does not resist handling. When the hawk was taken out, a hood was placed over its head, and little straps called *jesses,* by which the bird was held and controlled, were fastened to each leg. If the haggard remained wild it could usually be tamed by keeping it awake until it was exhausted. The process of taming a hawk was known as *manning.*

When the hawk was ready for field training, it was first induced to return to an artificial prey or bait known as a *lure.* When fully trained, the hawk was taken out and sent up to attack its *quarry.* Bells were attached to its legs, which enabled the falconer to locate his hawk if it brought down the quarry in thick country.

Of the various other technical words used in hawking the commonest were:

fly — to loose the hawk after the game

pitch — the highest point in the upward flight of the hawk as it hovers waiting for the game to be put up

stoop — the hawk's downward swoop on the quarry

bate — to flap the wings

imp — to insert a feather in a hawk's wing in place of one that was broken

For a fuller note see *Shakespeare's England,* Vol. II, pp. 351–66.

27. *Money Values*

One of the problems which confronts the student is to try to translate sums of Elizabethan English money into the equivalent in modern American dollars. This is exceedingly difficult, especially at the present time, when the value of the pound in dollars is unstable and the purchasing power of the dollar is constantly shifting. At the beginning of this century, when exchange was stable, £1 was worth about $4.80 — that is, one halfpenny was equivalent to one cent; by 1967 it was worth $2.80; in November 1967 it was devalued to about $2.40. To add to the difficulty, the actual value of coins in the sixteenth and seventeenth centuries varied from time to time as the relative value of gold and silver fluctuated. Gold and silver coins contained their actual value of metal, though in earlier times the coinage had been debased. Paper money and bank checks were unknown.

The English pound in Shakespeare's time (as today) contained 20 shillings; each shilling contained 12 pennies, and each penny 4 farthings. The pound was a gold coin, as were also the angel (10s.), the noble (6s. 8d., or one-third of a pound), and the crown (5s.). The commonest silver coins were shilling, sixpence, groat (fourpence), half-groat (twopence), and one penny (see Pl. 10a–e). The mark (13s. 4d., or two-thirds of a pound) was used as a sum in accounts, but there was no equivalent coin.

Historians from time to time make rough-and-ready calculations to express an approximate equivalent of the purchasing power of the pound at various dates. Thus £1 in 1600 was worth roughly £6 in 1914 and £10 in 1947. But this kind of calculation can never be at all accurate, because the values of commodities, wages, and needs have not changed uniformly. Moreover, modern men need far more. In Shakespeare's time television, newspapers, cars, telephones, and social services (such as free education, public health, and sanitation) did not exist, so were not part of the individual's normal expenses. The standard of living, especially for those in the low-income brackets, was very low. It may, however, give a general idea of comparative standards of prices if the Elizabethan pound is taken as roughly equivalent in modern times to $60, the shilling as worth $3, and a penny as 25 cents.

Some actual figures from various sources will illustrate the changes in values:

SKILLED WORKERS' WAGES IN THE CITY OF LONDON

	In Elizabethan Money	Approximate Modern Equivalent
By the year, with maintenance:	£3 6s. 8d. to £6 13s. 4d.	$ 200 to $ 400
By the day with food and drink:	6d. to 9d.	$1.50 to $2.25
By the day without food and drink:	10d. to 14d.	$2.50 to $3.50

SOLDIERS' PAY

In 1596 the pay of the various ranks in the army serving in France was laid down as follows:

IN A COMPANY OF 200 MEN	In Elizabethan Money		Approximate Modern Equivalent	
	DAILY PAY	WEEKLY ALLOWANCE FOR MAINTENANCE	DAILY PAY	WEEKLY ALLOWANCE FOR MAINTENANCE
Captain	8s.	56s.	$24	$168
Lieutenant	4s.	28s.	$12	$ 84
Ensign	2s.	14s.	$ 6	$ 42
Sergeant Drummer Surgeon	12d.	7s.	$ 3	$ 21
Soldier	8d.	7s.	$ 2	$ 21

CEILING PRICES OF FOOD IN 1599

During the mobilization in August 1599 a scale of maximum prices was laid down which included the following:

	In Elizabethan Money	Approximate Modern Equivalent
Beer, best quality	1*d.* per quart	$0.25
Beer, weak	½*d.* per quart	$0.13
Butter	4*d.* per lb.	$1
Cheese	1½*d.* to 2*d.* per lb.	$0.38 to 0.50
Eggs, best quality	2*d.* for 7	$0.85 per doz.
Beef, best quality	14*d.* for 8 lbs.	$0.45 per lb.
A fat pig, best quality	16*d.*	$4
Fat chickens (capons)	20*d.* a pair	$2.50 each
Tallow candles	4*d.* per lb.	$1

MISCELLANEOUS PRICES

Items (chiefly clothing) from Henslowe's *Diary* (see Gen. Intro. p. 38b):

	In Elizabethan Money	Approximate Modern Equivalent
A boy's wages	3*s.* a week	$ 9
An ordinary dinner	6*d.* to 9*d.* per person	$1.50 to 2.25
Soldier's sword and dagger	8*s.*	$ 24
Soldier's helmet	8*s.*	$ 24
A sackbut (musical instrument)	40*s.*	$120
Tailor's charges for making		
(a) a suit	18*s.*	$ 54
(b) woman's bodice and a pair of sleeves	6*s.* 7*d.*	$ 19.75
A short velvet cloak embroidered with bugles		
(beads) and a hood cape	£4	$240
Satin doublets (see Pl. 8b)	40*s.* to 45*s.* each	$120 to 135
A woman's gown	£10	$600
A woman's gray gown (a working dress)	20*s.*	$ 60
Two pile (second-grade) velvet of carnadine (red)	20*s.* a yard	$ 60
Satin	12*s.* a yard	$ 36
Taffeta	12*s.* 6*d.* a yard	$ 37.50
A plume of feathers	10*s.*	$ 30

PAYMENTS FOR PLAYS

	In Elizabethan Money	Approximate Modern Equivalent
To Jonson & Dekker for *Page of Plymouth,* 1599 (see Gen. Intro. p. 43b.)	£8	$480
To Drayton, Hathway, Munday, and Wilson for the two parts of *Sir John Oldcastle,* 1599 (see Gen. Intro. p. 43b.)	£14	$840
with a special present of 10*s.* at the first performance		$ 30
To Heywood for *A Woman Killed with Kindness,* 1603 (see Gen. Intro. p. 46b.)	£6	$360
Fee for licensing a play, paid to the Master of Revels	7*s.*	$ 21

As these figures show, food was rather less than it is now; clothing was far more expensive; wages, especially those of working-men, were much less. Since plays were usually short-lived, payments to dramatists were generous.

28. *The History Behind the History Plays*

KING JOHN

John, in English school history books, has the reputation of being " England's worst king." He was the youngest and spoiled child of King Henry II and Queen Elinor. As a man he was lustful, mean, vindictive, and treacherous, and his reign was " troublesome."

Richard, known as Coeur-de-lion for his physical courage, succeeded Henry II in 1189. Soon after his accession, he went on crusade to recover Jerusalem from the Saracens. While on crusade, he quarreled with a fellow warrior, Leopold, Duke of Austria. At the end of 1192 a truce was made with the Saracens, and Richard set out for England. On his way across Europe he was captured by Austria, and held prisoner.

It was during the period of his captivity that the famous (but legendary) episode of the lion is said to have occurred. Richard was suddenly confronted with a fierce lion which was set loose upon him. The heroic King plunged his arm down the lion's throat and pulled out the heart through its mouth. Richard thereafter wore the lion's skin as a memorial of this feat.

Richard was released in 1194 on payment of an enormous ransom. He died in France in 1199 as the result of an arrow-shot wound received while attacking a castle belonging to the Count of Limoges. In the play, Austria (who had actually died in 1194) and Limoges are merged into one person who wears the famous lion skin as a trophy of victory over Richard.

Richard Coeur-de-lion left no son, and on his death John was chosen King of England by the barons; but the Angevin lords refused to recognize him, and declared that the true heir was Arthur, posthumous son of Geoffrey, John's elder brother, who had died in 1187. A long and indecisive war followed between John and Philip of France, who was supporting Arthur, but in 1200 a truce was made by which Philip recognized John as King of England and Duke of Normandy, and Arthur as Duke of Brittany. The next year Arthur's mother died, and he was betrothed to the French King's daughter, a girl of six. The war broke out again in 1202, and in April 1203 John captured Arthur, who was then aged sixteen. Arthur was never seen again.

In 1205 John quarreled with the Pope. The see of Canterbury was vacant and the Pope appointed Stephen Langton to be Archbishop. John refused to admit Langton and was placed under a papal interdict; this did not greatly disturb John who lived for some years on the plunder of religious houses. However, he was formally excommunicated; in 1212 the Pope ordered him to be deposed from his throne and called on Philip to carry out the deposition. John prepared to fight, but his barons showed such hatred of his arbitrary actions that John sent to Pandulph, the Papal Legate, offering to submit and become the Pope's subject, which he did on May 15, 1212. In 1214 John again invaded France, but he was defeated by Louis the Dauphin and returned to England. By this time his barons were so incensed that they forcibly demanded a solemn promise of reforms. They met the King at Runnymede near Windsor and on June 15, 1215, John set his seal to the famous declaration known as the Great Charter (Magna Carta). This document in later ages was regarded as the foundation of civil liberty in England, and endowed with the same kind of reverence as the Declaration of Independence in the United States. In Shakespeare's time, writers seldom mentioned it, and it is entirely ignored in both versions of the play.

John soon tried to get even with his barons, but they appealed to Louis for help. The Pope, however, was now on John's side and the Papal Legate ineffectively ordered Louis to desist. Louis landed in England and many came over to him. John fought a losing fight against the rebels, and in crossing the Wash — the treacherous sandy coast between the counties of Lincoln and Norfolk — part of his army and all his baggage were overwhelmed by the incoming tide. John, raging with grief and indignation, went on to the Abbey of Swinstead where he became fatally ill. Reports vary as to the cause of death; some said too much strong beer, others too many ripe peaches, and others that he had been poisoned by a monk — the last being the version accepted by the author of *The Troublesome Reign*.

On John's death his eldest son, Henry, a boy of nine years, became King. The barons, having no quarrel with the new King, closed round the Regent, William Marshal, Earl of Pembroke. Peace was made and the French withdrew to their own country.

THE LANCASTER AND YORK PLAYS

Richard II, I and II Henry IV,
and Henry V

Except for *King John* and *Henry VIII,* Shakespeare's ten history plays are concerned with one central theme — the rise and fall of the House of Lancaster. They cover a period of nearly a century of complex events.

Edward III reigned fifty years (1327–77). He had seven sons, of whom the eldest was Edward, the Black Prince. Both Edwards were passionately devoted to war and were constantly campaigning in France or Spain. In his later days, Edward III became senile, but he outlived his eldest son; the Black Prince died in 1376, Edward III a few months later, in 1377. Thereupon the King's eleven-year-old grandson, Richard II, son of the Black Prince, became King, under the regency of John of Gaunt, Duke of Lancaster, the eldest surviving son of Edward III. In 1381 occurred the Peasants' Revolt. The boy King behaved with great bravery and pacified the rebels by promises of redress of their grievances, promises which were afterward broken by his advisers. In 1382, at the age of sixteen, Richard married Anne of Bohemia. By this time, Gaunt had left the country and was warring in Spain; the control of the kingdom had passed to Thomas of Woodstock, Duke of Gloucester, sixth son of Edward III.

Richard was now growing up; to Gloucester's alarm, he formed a Court party of his own friends. Gloucester and his supporters (called the Lords Appellant), who included Henry Bolingbroke, Duke of Hereford (son of John of Gaunt), and Thomas Mowbray (Earl of Nottingham and afterward Duke of Norfolk), seized Richard's friends by force and executed them. In 1389, Richard suddenly declared that he was now of age, and Gloucester was obliged to resign his regency. Thereafter for some years Richard ruled competently and moderately; he even seemed to be reconciled with the Lords Appellant; but when Gloucester again began his intrigues he was arrested, sent to Calais (then an English possession), and there murdered.

Richard meanwhile had lost his first wife and had married again. His character changed. He became reckless and extravagant, and his Court was filled with favorites and parasites. As a result he was constantly in need of money, which he raised by forced loans, benevolences ("voluntary" gifts from wealthy men), and by farming out the taxes; that is, in return for cash down he granted some financier the right to collect the taxes — a system of raising money which led to great abuses.

In 1398, Bolingbroke and Norfolk quarreled. At this point, Shakespeare's *Richard II* begins. Richard banished both noblemen — Norfolk for life and Bolingbroke for six years — but with the promise that the great estates which should come to Bolingbroke on the death of his father (John of Gaunt, Duke of Lancaster), should not be violated. Nevertheless, when Gaunt died a few months later, Richard broke his promise and seized the Lancaster estates to pay for his expedition to subdue a rebellion in Ireland. While Richard was away, Bolingbroke landed in Yorkshire, declaring that he had come to recover his rights as Duke of Lancaster. The Percies of Northumberland — the greatest and most powerful family in the Northern parts — joined him, together with all Richard's enemies. When Richard returned to England, he found himself deserted. Bolingbroke now claimed the throne, and Richard was obliged to abdicate in favor of Bolingbroke, who became king as Henry IV. Plotting against the new King began almost at once. In 1400 Richard II was murdered. Here the play of *Richard II* ends.

The First Part of Henry IV covers the period of the next two and a half years, that is 1400–03.

Richard II left no children. The line of the Black Prince being thus extinct, the next heir to the throne by right of birth was therefore the senior surviving descendant of Lionel, Duke of Clarence (second son of Edward III). Lionel's daughter Phillipa had married Edmund Mortimer, third Earl of March. She had three children, Roger (who became fourth Earl of March), Elizabeth (who married Henry Percy, called "Hotspur," son of the Earl of Northumberland, and who is Lady Percy in the play), and Edmund. Roger had died in Ireland in 1398 and *his* son Edmund, fifth Earl of March, was thus the legal heir to the throne.

The reign of Henry IV was full of troubles. The first serious rebellion occurred in 1403 when Owen Glendower, a Welsh chieftain, led a national rising against the English. **King Henry**

Genealogical Tables

These tables show the complicated family relationship of the Houses of Lancaster, York, and Tudor. They have been much simplified and include only the major persons.

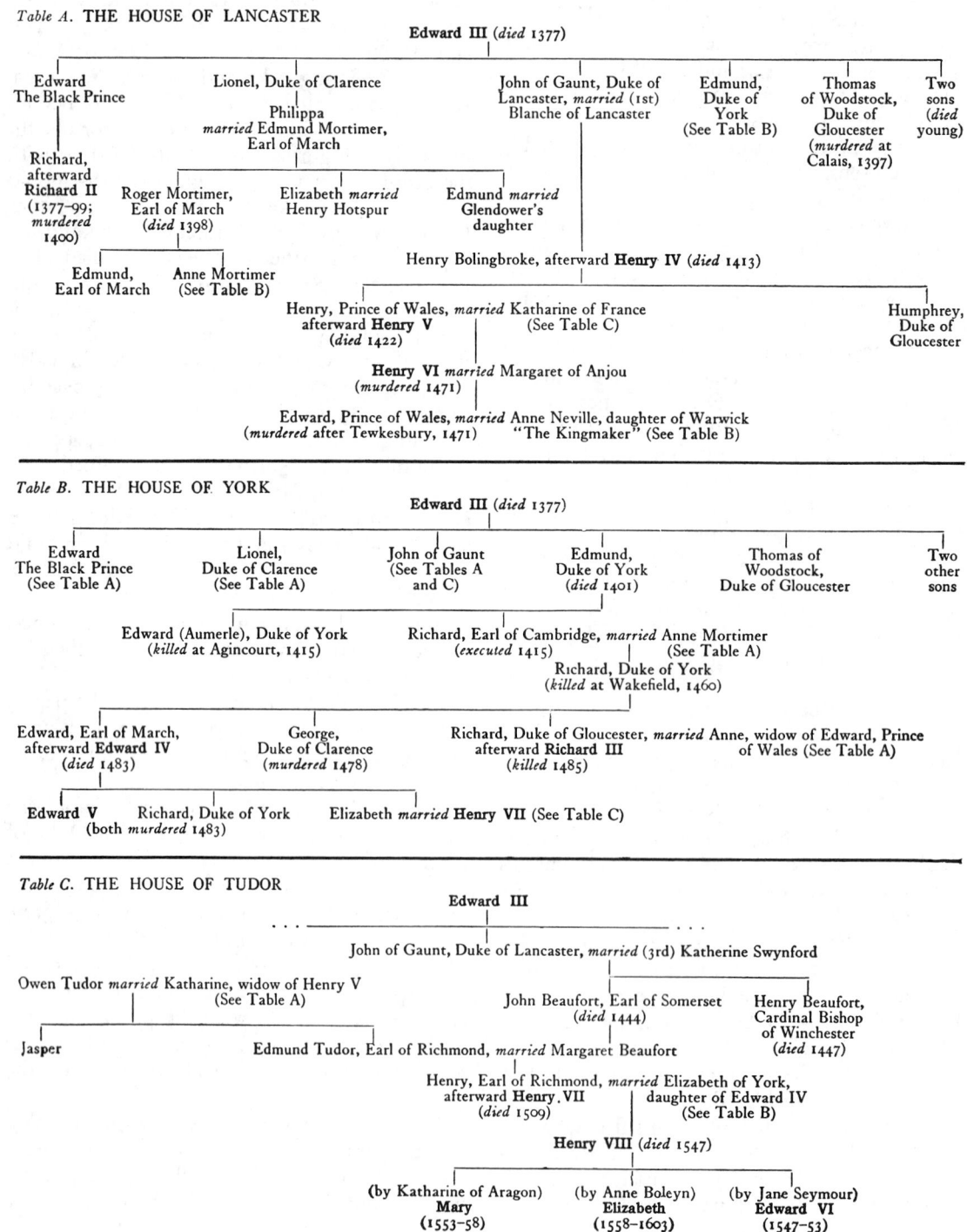

Table A. **THE HOUSE OF LANCASTER**

Edward III (*died* 1377)

Edward The Black Prince — Lionel, Duke of Clarence — John of Gaunt, Duke of Lancaster, *married* (1st) Blanche of Lancaster (See Table B) — Edmund, Duke of York (See Table B) — Thomas of Woodstock, Duke of Gloucester (*murdered* at Calais, 1397) — Two sons (*died* young)

Richard, afterward **Richard II** (1377–99; *murdered* 1400)

Philippa *married* Edmund Mortimer, Earl of March

Roger Mortimer, Earl of March (*died* 1398) — Elizabeth *married* Henry Hotspur — Edmund *married* Glendower's daughter

Henry Bolingbroke, afterward **Henry IV** (*died* 1413)

Edmund, Earl of March — Anne Mortimer (See Table B)

Henry, Prince of Wales, *married* Katharine of France afterward **Henry V** (See Table C) (*died* 1422) — Humphrey, Duke of Gloucester

Henry VI *married* Margaret of Anjou (*murdered* 1471)

Edward, Prince of Wales, *married* Anne Neville, daughter of Warwick (*murdered* after Tewkesbury, 1471) "The Kingmaker" (See Table B)

Table B. **THE HOUSE OF YORK**

Edward III (*died* 1377)

Edward The Black Prince (See Table A) — Lionel, Duke of Clarence (See Table A) — John of Gaunt (See Tables A and C) — Edmund, Duke of York (*died* 1401) — Thomas of Woodstock, Duke of Gloucester — Two other sons

Edward (Aumerle), Duke of York (*killed* at Agincourt, 1415) — Richard, Earl of Cambridge, *married* Anne Mortimer (*executed* 1415) (See Table A)

Richard, Duke of York (*killed* at Wakefield, 1460)

Edward, Earl of March, afterward **Edward IV** (*died* 1483) — George, Duke of Clarence (*murdered* 1478) — Richard, Duke of Gloucester, *married* Anne, widow of Edward, **Prince** afterward **Richard III** of Wales (See Table A) (*killed* 1485)

Edward V — Richard, Duke of York (both *murdered* 1483) — Elizabeth *married* **Henry VII** (See Table C)

Table C. **THE HOUSE OF TUDOR**

Edward III

· · · John of Gaunt, Duke of Lancaster, *married* (3rd) Katherine Swynford · · ·

Owen Tudor *married* Katharine, widow of Henry V (See Table A)

John Beaufort, Earl of Somerset (*died* 1444) — Henry Beaufort, Cardinal Bishop of Winchester (*died* 1447)

Jasper — Edmund Tudor, Earl of Richmond, *married* Margaret Beaufort

Henry, Earl of Richmond, *married* Elizabeth of York, afterward **Henry VII** daughter of Edward IV (*died* 1509) (See Table B)

Henry VIII (*died* 1547)

(by Katharine of Aragon) **Mary** (1553–58) — (by Anne Boleyn) **Elizabeth** (1558–1603) — (by Jane Seymour) **Edward VI** (1547–53)

went against him, but without success. He therefore left the command to Hotspur and Edmund Mortimer (uncle of Edmund, Earl of March) [1] and returned to London. Mortimer was captured by Glendower, but the two men became friends, and Mortimer married Glendower's daughter. Hotspur went back to the North, where at Holmedon Hill he defeated a large army of invading Scots under Douglas.

Soon afterward the Percies quarreled with the King. The chief members of the family were Henry, Earl of Northumberland, Henry "Hotspur" (his son), and Thomas Percy, Earl of Worcester (his brother). When the King demanded that the Percies should hand over the valuable ransoms exacted from the prisoners taken at Holmedon, the Percies refused and rebelled. They planned to gather a combined force to meet the King, their allies being Mortimer, Glendower, and Douglas with his Scots. Hotspur and Douglas marched south to join with Glendower. The issue was decided at the Battle of Shrewsbury (1403). Hotspur was killed, Worcester captured and beheaded, and Douglas captured and ransomed; Northumberland, who was not present at the battle, submitted.

It is difficult nowadays to realize the vast power of these great nobles, most of whom were related by marriage to the royal family. Moreover, by their various intermarriages and alliances they amassed great wealth and owned much land, which meant also the services of those who lived and worked on the land. Their castles were fortified palaces, and it was easy for a nobleman to raise and maintain a private army of retainers from his estates, especially in days when a soldier needed little further equipment than a sword, a helmet, a bow, and a bundle of arrows.

The First Part of Henry IV comes to an end with the Battle of Shrewsbury.

The Second Part of Henry IV covers a period of about nine years. In 1403, Scroop, Archbishop of York, with Northumberland and Mowbray (son of the Duke of Norfolk of *Richard II*), rebelled in the North, and they were defeated. Scroop and Mowbray were executed; Northumberland escaped, but again attempted rebellion

in 1408 and was killed. Henry IV, after a long period of sickness, died in 1413. *The Second Part of Henry IV* ends with the accession of his son Prince Hal, who then became Henry V.

Henry V, like his great-grandfather Edward III, was ambitious for military glory. At this time France was in great confusion, with civil war raging between the Orleanists and the Burgundians. Henry therefore claimed the throne of France, as the great-grandson of Edward III, for reasons detailed by Shakespeare (*II Hen IV*, IV. v.213–16, and *Hen V*, I.ii.), and prepared an expeditionary force. He was about to embark at Southampton when a plot against his life was discovered. The chief plotters were Richard, Earl of Cambridge (son of Edmund, Duke of York), Scroop (a kinsman of the late Archbishop of York), and Lord Thomas Grey; all three were executed. Henry landed opposite Le Havre, at the mouth of the Seine, at Harfleur, which he captured after a five weeks' siege. He then went on with an army greatly reduced by sickness, intending to embark at Calais; but he was intercepted by the French Army. On October 25, 1415, Henry defeated the French against great odds at the Battle of Agincourt; but his army was too weak for further action, and he returned to England by way of Calais.

These events are dramatized in Acts I, II, and III of *Henry V*. In 1417 Henry again invaded France and captured Caen. In January 1419 he captured Rouen, thereby establishing control of Normandy. In May 1420 he made peace with the Burgundians in France. By the treaty it was agreed that Henry should become Regent of France so long as the imbecile French King lived, and thereafter should succeed as King of France, excluding the Dauphin (the French King's eldest son) from the throne. As part of the bargain, Henry married Katharine, the French King's daughter. Henry returned to England with his Queen in 1421, leaving his eldest brother, Thomas, Duke of Clarence, in command in France. Clarence was killed in action by the Dauphin. Henry was therefore forced to invade France for the third time, but on August 31, 1422, he died of dysentery. Shakespeare's *Henry V* covers the period from Henry's demand for the French crown to his marriage with Katharine; that is, from 1413 to 1420.

---

[1] Shakespeare, it may be noted, confused the two Edmunds. The Edmund who married the Welsh lady was *not* heir to the throne. See Table A.

I, II and III Henry VI

English history from the death of Henry V (1422) to the accession of Henry VII (1485) was the theme of four of Shakespeare's earliest plays — the three parts of *Henry VI*, and *Richard III*. It was a period of constant strife, treachery, murder, and civil war between the various great noblemen who were descended from or closely related to the family of Edward III. When Henry V died in 1422, he left the throne to his son Henry VI, then an infant of nine months. Once more England was ruled by Regents and Protectors, each in turn striving to oust the other. Between them they lost all France except Calais, and then fell to squabbling and civil war at home.

Just before Henry V had set out for France, he discovered a conspiracy against himself (see above). It was led, among others, by Richard, Earl of Cambridge, who was the son of Edmund, Duke of York (fourth son of Edward III). Cambridge had married Anne, daughter of Roger Mortimer, the grandson of Lionel, Duke of Clarence (second son of Edward III; see Table B). The children of Richard, Earl of Cambridge, were thus in a more direct line of descent than was Henry V.

The First Part of Henry VI opens with the funeral of Henry V. At this time a large part of France was in English hands and the remainder was in a state of civil war and chaos, with the Burgundians supporting the English against Charles the Dauphin. In 1428 the English were besieging Orleans and likely to extend their conquests; but in January 1429 Joan of Arc appeared at the court of Charles, and thereafter the French began to take the offensive. Orleans was relieved in May 1429. In June, Sir John Talbot, the most successful and valiant of the English commanders, was captured; he remained a prisoner in French hands for four years. On July 14, the French, inspired by Joan's enthusiasm, retook Rheims and two days later Charles was crowned King of France. This was the zenith of the Maid's success. Ten months later (May 1430) she was captured by the Burgundians and handed over to the English.

In the following December the boy King was brought over to Paris and there crowned King of France. Joan endured a year in prison; at length, after many examinations and a trial which resulted in her condemnation for heresy,

she was burned in Rouen on May 30, 1431.

Henry was now taking a precocious interest in state affairs. In 1432 — at the age of ten — he opened the English Parliament in person, and in the stormy session which followed he showed that he favored the party of the Beauforts. Three years later the Duke of Bedford died, and the Burgundians deserted the English side. By this time Charles had discarded his frivolous favorites, and, ably supported by competent commanders, in 1436 he recaptured Paris. The war was now very much in favor of the French and the English garrisons were steadily pushed out of France.

In 1442 the young King became of legal age, and the next year he was betrothed to Margaret, daughter of the Duke of Lorraine, but the marriage was not celebrated until 1445 when the Princess arrived in England escorted by the Earl of Suffolk. Meanwhile a truce had been made at Tours. The war broke out again in 1451, and Sir John Talbot (who had been created Earl of Shrewsbury) was sent over to take command of the English forces in Aquitaine; he was now aged nearly seventy. He was killed in a battle at Castillon on July 17, 1453. Soon afterward the Hundred Years' War between England and France came to an end, leaving only Calais in English possession.

The First Part of Henry VI is concerned mainly with the wars in France, which are dramatized with complete disregard for chronology. The Second and Third Parts tell of the civil Wars of the Roses which lasted intermittently from 1455 to 1485. During his minority, the boy King had been ruled by his uncles, especially by Humphrey, Duke of Gloucester, son of Henry IV, and by the Beauforts — John, Earl of Somerset, and Henry, Cardinal Beaufort, Bishop of Winchester, sons of John of Gaunt by his third wife (see Table B). As a King, Henry showed himself quite incompetent; throughout his life he remained a saintly innocent, the puppet of the party in power. Margaret his wife, however, was a woman of strong and ferocious character. In 1447, Gloucester was accused of high treason by his enemies of the Queen's party and was murdered in prison.

At first the marriage between Henry and Margaret was childless, and failing an heir the next in succession was Richard, Duke of York (son of Richard, Earl of Cambridge). The Beauforts grew jealous of him, and an open quarrel broke out between them. York took as his symbol a white rose; Somerset chose a red rose. The King associated himself with the party of the Red Rose.

In 1453 Queen Margaret gave birth to a son, Prince Edward, who thus was the heir to the throne; but in the next year Henry VI for a while became insane, and York was made Regent. When the King recovered, the Somerset party returned to power. York in self-protection raised an army and rebelled. At the Battle of St. Albans (1455) York defeated and killed Somerset and captured Henry VI. York thus again became Regent. Forced by York, the King agreed to an arrangement whereby he was to hold the crown during life, but at his death York was to be his successor.

Nevertheless, though the Lancastrians — that is, the Somerset party, called Lancastrians because of their descent from John of Gaunt, Duke of Lancaster — were defeated, Margaret did not give up, even when her new forces were defeated in the first engagements. York then made formal claim to the throne for himself; but a few weeks later in an unlucky battle at Wakefield in Yorkshire (1460) he was defeated and killed by Margaret's forces. Margaret sent his head, crowned with a paper crown, to be set up in York.

York's son was Edward, fifth Earl of March. He carried on the fight, and in 1461 at the Battle of Towton he wiped out the Lancastrian army; but he failed to capture Margaret, who fled to France. Edward, Earl of March, now became King of England with the title of Edward IV. His chief supporter hitherto had been Richard Neville, Earl of Warwick, known as " Warwick the Kingmaker." Edward did not wish to be dependent on the Nevilles; and while Warwick was negotiating a French marriage for him, he secretly married a lady of no rank, Elizabeth Woodville, the widow of a Lancastrian knight. To strengthen his party, Edward IV promoted his wife's relatives to the greatest offices in the state. Warwick retaliated for this snub by arranging the marriage of his own daughter to George, Duke of Clarence (Edward IV's brother), who thus showed open hostility to the King.

In 1469 the Lancastrians were again gathering. Warwick deserted the Yorkists, and by persua-sion of the French King, Louis XI, he was reconciled with Margaret, who was still an exile in France. Edward IV fled from England. Warwick then declared for Henry VI, and the new alliance between Warwick and Margaret was cemented by the marriage of Anne, Warwick's daughter, to Edward, the son of Margaret and Henry VI. Warwick's forces captured London; Henry VI was brought out of the Tower, where he had long been a prisoner, and was once more set on the throne.

Henry VI's second period as puppet King did not last long. Edward, aided by his brother Richard, Duke of Gloucester, landed at Ravenspur in Yorkshire with a small force. The little army marched southward. Clarence deserted Warwick and became reconciled to his brother Edward IV. The decisive battle was fought at Barnet, a few miles north of London, in 1471; Edward was victorious and Warwick was killed. The final rout of the Lancastrians came a few weeks later at Tewkesbury in Gloucestershire, where Margaret's last army was utterly defeated. Among those captured was Edward, Margaret's son; he was murdered after the battle by Richard, Duke of Gloucester, and the surviving Lancastrian noblemen were executed. The only relic of the Lancastrian line now left was Henry Tudor, Earl of Richmond (see Table C).

So Edward IV once more returned to London as King; on the same day Henry VI was murdered in the Tower of London by Gloucester. At this point the Third Part of Shakespeare's *Henry VI* ends.

Richard III

The play of *Richard III* begins shortly before the death of Edward IV in 1483 and covers a period of about two years. Edward was pleasure-loving and voluptuous, his love affair with Jane Shore, the wife of a London citizen, being particularly notorious. The King's brother Richard, Duke of Gloucester, who had married the widow of Prince Edward (whom he had murdered), was regarded as the strong man behind the throne; he had already amply shown his ruthless nature. Gloucester persuaded Edward that Clarence was again becoming dangerous. So Clarence was sent to the Tower and there murdered. But Gloucester had many enemies; the Queen's family and relations — the Woodvilles and the Greys — hated him; the King was ailing, and Gloucester knew that if they should retain their power after the King's death, his own chances of survival were small.

As soon as Edward IV was dead, Gloucester acted quickly. With the aid of the Duke of Buckingham, he captured the young King, Edward V, from his uncles, the Earl Rivers and Sir Richard Grey, whom he imprisoned and later caused to be beheaded. Then he was made Protector of the boy King. Gloucester was now aiming directly at the crown for himself, and when he found that the Lord Chamberlain, Lord Hastings, was not with him, he quarreled with Hastings at a meeting of the Council and ordered him to be beheaded out of hand.

Meanwhile the younger son of Edward IV, Richard, Duke of York, had been taken into sanctuary at Westminster by his mother. Gloucester persuaded her to release him to be a companion to his brother in the Tower. Gloucester was now ready for the next open step. Backed by Buckingham and his own retainers, he " accepted " the throne of England as Richard III when it was offered him by a deputation of London citizens; and to make his position more secure, he sent to have the two young Princes murdered in the Tower. However, Richard's ruthlessness caused general disgust, and his many enemies began plotting to bring in Henry of Richmond as King. Even Buckingham turned against him, but by bad luck he was captured and executed.

Richard's next plan was to get rid of his wife and marry his niece, Elizabeth of York, daughter of Edward IV; but before this scheme could be carried out Henry of Richmond landed in Wales. The last battle of the Wars of the Roses was fought at Bosworth near Leicester in 1485. Henry's chances seemed poor, for Richard's army was far larger; but in the battle many of Richard's supporters deserted to the other side, and Richard himself was killed fighting desperately. So Henry of Richmond became King as Henry VII, and by marrying Elizabeth of York united the White Rose and the Red.

The son of Henry VII was Henry VIII; Queen Elizabeth was his granddaughter. The last battles of the Wars of the Roses were almost as close to Shakespeare and his audiences as the American Civil War to modern times. Much of the fighting had occurred in places familiar to Shakespeare; Tewkesbury, where the most ghastly slaughter was made, is less than thirty miles from Stratford-on-Avon. Moreover, to Englishmen in those times it seemed only too likely that chaos would come again at the death of Elizabeth. There was thus an immediate and keen interest in any play which told of the events and personalities of those brutal and not far distant days.

HENRY VIII

Henry VIII, second son of Henry VII, was born in 1491. He became heir to the throne in 1502 on the death of his elder brother Arthur, Prince of Wales, a youth of fifteen. Shortly before his death Arthur had been married to Katharine of Aragon, daughter of Ferdinand and Isabella of Spain. A dispensation was now sought from the Pope to allow Henry to be betrothed — at the age of nine — to his brother's widow. By canon law a marriage between a man and his brother's widow is not allowed; but the dispensation was claimed and granted on the grounds that the original marriage between Arthur and Katharine had never been consummated and was thus invalid. Henry became King on April 22, 1509, and married Katharine seven weeks later.

The young King took as his adviser and chief minister Thomas Wolsey, a man of humble birth but of great ability and overweening pride and cupidity; and the two worked closely together. Wolsey, as were so many administrators in the ages before the Reformation, was a churchman and derived a vast income from Church benefices, of which he held many. He amassed enormous wealth and lived in ostentatious magnificence. He was made a Cardinal in 1515. In 1520 Wolsey arranged a ceremonious meeting between Henry and the French King, Francis I, known as the Field of the Cloth of Gold because of the extravagant display shown by all who took part. In the following year the Duke of Buckingham was executed on slight charges, an act which showed that Henry was an autocrat whom it was dangerous to attempt to thwart.

The King's marriage with Katharine was not a success, for the Queen failed to produce a male heir, and Henry tired of her. By 1522 he was beginning to grant great favors to the family of Sir Thomas Boleyn, whose two daughters had attracted him. Mary Boleyn was for some time the King's mistress; Anne resisted his advances, which greatly increased the King's infatuation, but the first rumors of a divorce were not heard until 1527. The King now sought to have his first marriage set aside, and he asked the Pope to declare that it was invalid and that he was living in sin with Katharine. Cardinal Campeggio was sent over from Rome to examine the evidence and a court was opened on May 31, 1529, but the Cardinal adjourned the case till the autumn and then referred the question to Rome.

The King was incensed at the delays; and Wolsey's many enemies, especially Anne Boleyn, took their chance of laying the blame on the much-hated minister. Wolsey was ordered to give up the Great Seal, and he retired to private life. In the following months he yielded up most of his vast wealth to the King. About a year after his fall he was summoned to London to face a charge of high treason, but he died on the journey on November 29, 1530.

Meanwhile the proceedings for the annulment of the King's marriage dragged on without any decision from Rome. The opinions of theologians in the European universities were sought, and on May 31, 1531, a deputation of noblemen went to Queen Katharine, asking her to submit the case to arbitration. She refused.

By this time the Reformation movement, which had begun in Germany in 1517, had gained great strength, and there were many in England who favored the new doctrines. The King, however, always maintained that he was a true Catholic, but when the Pope was unwilling to grant what he wanted, Henry declared himself to be the Supreme Head of the Church in England (1531) and as such proceeded to appoint his own bishops and to regulate the doctrine and discipline of the Anglican Church. In ecclesiastical matters Henry was now being advised by Thomas Cranmer, a man of very different character from Wolsey, and one who supported the Protestant doctrines. In 1532, on the death of Archbishop Warham, the King appointed Cranmer to be Archbishop of Canterbury. In January 1533, the King secretly went through a form of marriage with Anne, and in the following May Cranmer pronounced the marriage between Henry and Katharine invalid and the new marriage with Anne valid. Anne was, therefore, publicly crowned as Queen, and on September 7 she gave birth to a daughter, afterward the famous Queen Elizabeth. Kath-

arine lived on in dignified retirement until her death in 1536.

The marriage with Anne was in every way disastrous and lasted less than three years. She too failed to produce the wanted male heir and the King soon turned his affections elsewhere. In 1536 she was accused of adultery and beheaded, Cranmer having first declared the marriage invalid.

29. *The Order of the Garter*

The Order of the Garter, sometimes known as the Order of St. George, was founded by Edward III about 1344. It is the most ancient and honorable order of chivalry still surviving in Europe.

The origin of the Order is said to have been an incident at the Court of Edward III. One day when there was dancing in Court, a garter belonging to Joan, Countess of Salisbury, fell to the ground; the Countess was a lady of great beauty with whom the King was on terms of familiarity. When the King picked up the garter, his courtiers began to laugh; but he rebuked them for their evil thoughts and declared that he would make that garter an object of great honor. Thereupon he founded the Order.

The Order is very exclusive; it consists of the English Sovereign and only twenty-five members at one time, all being persons chosen for their distinguished service to the state. In addition, living kings and princes of other countries are sometimes admitted. In Shakespeare's day, the Order met once a year for a solemn Feast on the eve of St. George's Day (April 23). Next day they went in procession to worship in St. George's Chapel, in the precincts of Windsor Castle. Here each knight has his stall, above which is hung his banner. Knights of the Garter wear as their emblem on solemn occasions a garter buckled on the left leg below the knee. The garter is of blue velvet, embroidered in gold thread with the motto *Honi Soit Qui Mal Y Pense* (Shame be to him who thinks evil), with a gold buckle. In addition, a Knight wears an enameled collar round the neck, from which hangs the figure of St. George slaying the dragon, and a mantle of purple velvet.

In Pl. 8d the Earl of Leicester and in Pl. 3b four other noblemen are shown wearing both garter and collar.

30. *The Shakespearean Addition to* The Booke of Sir Thomas More [1]

Among the manuscripts in the British Museum, London, is the draft of a play inscribed *The Booke of Sir Thomas More*. This play was never acted or printed until modern times. The manuscript contains twenty folio pages, of which half are in the known handwriting of Anthony Munday, a professional writer of considerable versatility. Scenes and smaller insertions have been contributed in the handwriting of Henry Chettle (see p. 9b) and of Thomas Dekker (see pp. 45b–46a). Sir Edward Tyllney, Master of the Revels at the Court of Queen Elizabeth and, by virtue of his office, licenser and censor of plays, added some notes showing his disapproval of certain passages and demanding emendation. Other passages are in handwritings designated Hand C and Hand D. Hand D is the author of a whole scene of 147 lines wherein Sir Thomas More, as Sheriff of London, quiets a riotous mob which has been roused to attack the aliens in the city of London as the cause of the rising cost of living. It has been claimed that Hand D is Shakespeare's.

The case for Shakespeare has been argued hotly for many years, and though not proved, yet most scholars who have examined the evidence agree on a verdict of " most probable."

Sir Thomas More was first printed in 1844, edited by Alexander Dyce in a modernized edition. In 1908, C. F. Tucker Brooke included the play in *The Shakespeare Apocrypha,* a collection of plays which have some connection with Shakespeare but were not included in the First Folio. In 1910, a photographic facsimile was published by J. S. Farmer; and in 1911 a type-facsimile, reproducing so far as type permits the peculiarities of the manuscript, was edited by W. W. Greg for the Malone Society.

The first attempt to present a case for Shakespeare's hand was made by Richard Simpson in 1871, but it was not taken very seriously until Sir Edward Maunde Thompson, an expert palaeographer, was led to re-examine the manuscript while preparing his chapter on handwriting for *Shakespeare's England,* 1916. Soon afterwards he published a study, *Shakespeare's Handwriting,* and claimed that the Three Pages had been written by Shakespeare.

By this time so much interest had been aroused that in 1923 five scholars combined to state the case for Shakespeare in *Shakespeare's Hand in the Play of " Sir Thomas More."* Their claim rested mainly on three arguments. (1) The evidence from handwriting. The only indisputable specimens of Shakespeare's handwriting are a signature on his deposition in the suit of *Bellot* vs. *Mountjoy* (see p. 14b); two signatures on deeds connected with the purchase of property in the Blackfriars (see p. 15a); and three signatures and the words " by me " on his last will, dated March 25, 1616 (see p. 15a–b). The evidence from the handwriting is thus too slight to be conclusive, but Maunde Thompson did at least establish two points — that the handwriting in the Three Pages is similar to Shakespeare's, and that it does not resemble the known handwriting of any other Elizabethan dramatist.

(2) J. Dover Wilson argued from the peculiar spellings in the Three Pages. He noted that in the printed quartos (see pp. 61–66) certain words were sometimes abnormally spelt and that some of these spellings were to be found in the Three Pages. He noted also that the forms of the letters were such that certain kinds of misprint were likely to arise, and that in fact such misprints are to be found in the quartos.

(3) R. W. Chambers argued that the ideas and literary quality of More's speech on Loyalty and Order were essentially Shakespearean. This argument, which to ordinary readers is the most convincing, is the least provable, for it depends mainly on literary tact.

In some ways, however, the case presented in *Shakespeare's Hand in the Play of " Sir Thomas More"* was weak. They argued, for instance, that Shakespeare made his contribution to the play in 1593–95. But if Shakespeare did write the scene, then he must have done it later by several years, for stylistically the speech belongs not to the period of *Romeo and Juliet* and *Richard II* (1593–95) but rather to the period of *Julius Caesar* and *Troilus and Cressida* (1599–1601). However, a good case has been made by D. C. Collins (*Review of English Studies,* 1934, Vol. X, pp. 401–11) for 1600 or 1601 as the date of the play, when the excitement caused by the Earl of Essex's rebellion was enough to cause the cautious Tyllney to object to any episode or speech which could possibly be regarded as topical or remotely seditious.

---

[1] See also pp. 85–86.

Shakespeare's hand in *Sir Thomas More* is thus one of the major controversies in Shakespearean scholarship. For those interested, the evidence is skillfully summarized by R. C. Bald in *Shakespeare Survey,* 1949, Vol. II. There is enough agreement among scholars to demand that the "Shakespearean contribution" to the play should be included in *Shakespeare: The Complete Works.*

On pp. 85–86 of the General Introduction lines 58–116 are transcribed in the original spelling.

From SIR THOMAS MORE

London. A street.

[*Enter* LINCOLN, DOLL, CLOWN, GEORGE BETTS, WILLIAMSON, *and others.*]

LINC. Peace, hear me! He that will not see a red herring° at a Harry groat,° butter at eleven pence a pound,° meal at nine shillings a bushel, and beef at four nobles a stone,° list to me!

BETTS. It will come to that pass if strangers be suffered. Mark him!   6

LINC. Our country is a great eating country; argo,° they eat more in our country than they do in their own.

CLOWN. By a half-penny loaf a day, troy° weight.   11

LINC. They bring in strange roots,° which is merely to the undoing of poor prentices; for what's a sorry parsnip to a good heart?

WILL. Trash, trash! They breed sore eyes, and 'tis enough to infect the city with the palsy.   16

LINC. Nay, it has infected it with the palsy: for these bastards of dung° — as you know they grow in dung — have infected us, and it is our infection will make the city shake, which partly comes through the eating of parsnips.   21

CLOWN. True, and pumpions° together!

[*Enter a* SERGEANT AT ARMS.]

SERG. What say ye to the mercy of the King? Do you refuse it?   24

LINC. You would have us upon th' hip,° would you? No, marry, do we not; we accept of the King's mercy, but we will show no mercy upon the strangers.

SERG. You are the simplest things that ev'° stood in such a question.   30

LINC. How say you now? Prentices, prentices simple!° Down with him!

ALL. Prentices simple! Prentices simple!

[*Enter* LORD MAYOR, SHERIFF MORE, EARLS OF SURREY *and* SHREWSBURY, SIR THOMAS PALMER, *and* SIR ROGER CHOLMLEY.]

MAYOR. Hold, in the King's name! Hold!

SUR. Friends! Masters! Countrymen!   35

MAYOR. Peace, how! Peace! I charge you keep the peace.

SHREW. My masters! Countrymen —

WILL. The noble Earl of Shrewsbury! Let's hear him.   40

BETTS. We'll hear the Earl of Surrey!

LINC. The Earl of Shrewsbury!

BETTS. We'll hear both.

ALL. Both! Both! Both! Both!

LINC. Peace, I say! Peace! Are you men of wisdom, or what are you?   46

SUR. What you will have them, but not men of wisdom.

ALL. We'll not hear my Lord of Surrey! No, no, no, no, no! Shrewsbury! Shrewsbury!   50

MORE. Whiles they are o'er the bank of their obedience,°

Thus will they bear down° all things.

LINC. Sheriff More speaks. Shall we hear Sheriff More speak?   54

DOLL. Let's hear him! He keeps a plentiful shrievalty,° and he made my brother, Arthur Watchins, Sergeant Safe's yeoman.° Let's hear Shrieve More!

ALL. Shrieve More! More! More! Shrieve More!

MORE. Even by the rule you have among yourselves,

Command still audience.   60

SOME. Surrey! Surrey!

OTHERS. More! More!

LINC. & BETTS. Peace! Peace! Silence! Peace!

MORE. You that have voice and credit with the number,°

Command them to a stillness.   65

LINC. A plague on them, they will not hold their peace.

The devil cannot rule them.

MORE. Then what a rough and riotous charge° have you,

1–2. **red herring:** a herring dried, salted, and smoked — a poor man's dish. **Harry groat:** a groat (worth 4*d.*) of the reign of Henry VIII. 2–3. **butter . . . pound:** The usual price of butter was 4*d.* a pound; see App. 28. 3–4. **beef . . . stone:** A noble was worth 6*s.* 8*d.* The stone was a measure of weight which varied from 8 lbs. to 14 lbs., according to the commodity. A stone of beef was 8 lbs., and the usual cost about 14*d.* 8. **argo:** for *ergo* — therefore. 10. **troy:** a standard of weight used for bread, in which the pound contains 12 ounces. 12. **strange roots:** One of the commoner, but more irrational, causes of interracial misunderstanding is that foreigners have different eating habits from natives. 18. **bastards of dung:** things bred out of manure. 22. **pumpions:** pumpkins. 25. **upon th' hip:** at a disadvantage — a wrestling term.

29. **ev':** ever. 31–32. **prentices simple:** Are you daring to say that apprentices are simpletons? 51. **o'er . . . obedience:** have overflowed the restraints of law. 52. **bear down:** overwhelm, like a flood. 55–56. **keep . . . shrievalty:** is generous in his office as sheriff (shrieve). The Sheriff of London was an important civic official; he was responsible for keeping public order. 57. **yeoman:** servant, assistant. 64. **number:** multitude. 68. **charge:** responsibility.

To lead those that the devil cannot rule!
Good masters, hear me speak! 70
   DOLL. Aye, by th' mass will we, More! Th' art a
good housekeeper,° and I thank thy good worship
for my brother Arthur Watchins.
   ALL. Peace! Peace! 74
   MORE. Look, what you do offend° you cry upon!°
That is the peace. Not [one] of you here pres-
  ent,
Had there such fellows lived when you were babes
That could have topped° the peace as now you
   would,
The peace wherein you have till now grown up
Had been ta'en from you, and the bloody times 80
Could not have brought you to the state of men.
Alas, poor things, what is it you have got,
Although we grant you get the thing you seek?
   BETTS. Marry,° the removing of the strangers
which cannot choose but much advantage the poor
handicrafts° of the city. 86
   MORE. Grant them removed, and grant that this
   your noise
Hath chid down° all the majesty of England.
Imagine that you see the wretched strangers, 89
Their babies at their backs, and their poor luggage,
Plodding to th' ports and coasts for transportation,
And that you sit as kings in your desires,
Authority quite silenced by your brawl,
And you in ruff of your opinions clothed° — 94
What had you got? I'll tell you. You had taught
How insolence and strong hand should prevail,
How order should be quelled, and by this pattern
Not one of you should live an aged man,
For other ruffians as their fancies wrought 99
With self same hand, self reasons, and self right
Would shark° on you; and men, like ravenous
   fishes,
Would feed on one another.
   DOLL. Before God, that's as true as the gospel.
   LINC. Nay, this's a sound fellow, I tell you. Let's
mark him. 105
   MORE. Let me set up before your thoughts, good
   friends,
One supposition, which if you will mark,
You shall perceive how horrible a shape
Your innovation° bears. First, 'tis a sin
Which oft th' apostle did forewarn us of, 110
Urging obedience to authority;°
And 'twere no error if I told you all

You were in arms 'gainst G[od].
   ALL. Marry, God forbid that!
   MORE. Nay, certainly you are: 115
For to the King God hath his office lent
Of dread, of justice, power, and command,
Hath bid him rule, and willed you to obey:
And, to add ampler majesty to this,
He hath not only lent the King his figure, 120
His throne, sword, but given him his own name,
Calls him a god on earth. What do you then,
Rising 'gainst him that God himself installs,
But rise 'gainst God? What do you to your
   souls
In doing this? O desperate as you are. 125
Wash your foul minds with tears, and those same
   hands,
That you like rebels lift against the peace,
Lift up for peace, and your unreverent knees,
Make them your feet to kneel to be forgiven!°
Tell me but this: what rebel captain, 130
As mutinies are incident,° by his name
Can still the rout?° Who will obey a traitor?
Or how can well that proclamation sound,
When there is no addition° but a rebel 134
To qualify° a rebel?° You'll put down strangers,
Kill them, cut their throats, possess their houses,
And lead the majesty of law in liom°
To slip him like a hound. Say now the King,
As he is clement if th' offender mourn,
Should so much come too short of your great tres-
   pass 140
As but to banish you, whither would you go?
What country, by the nature of your error,
Should give you harbor? Go you to France or
   Flanders,
To any German province, Spain or Portugal,
Nay, anywhere that not adheres to England — 145
Why you must needs be strangers. Would you be
   pleased
To find a nation of such barbarous temper,
That, breaking out in hideous violence,
Would not afford you an abode on earth, 149
Whet their detested knives against your throats,
Spurn you like dogs, and like as if that God
Owed° not nor made not you, nor that the elements
Were not all appropriate° to your comforts,
But chartered° unto them? What would you think
To be thus used? This is the strangers' case, 155

---

72. good housekeeper: i.e., hospitable and generous. 75. offend: hurt. cry upon: cry after, seek — i.e., peace. 78. topped: overthrown. 84. Marry: by the Virgin Mary. 86. handicrafts: craftsmen, workers. 88. chid down: silenced by your chiding. 94. ruff . . . clothed: giving yourselves airs of authority. The ruff (see note j.i. on p. 94) was worn only by gentlemen. 101. shark: prey, feed. 109. innovation: riot, violence; see *I Hen IV*, V.i.78, "hurly-burly innovation." 109–11. sin . . . authority: The reference is to Romans 13:1–7, where St. Paul urges his converts to obey lawful authority.

129. feet . . . forgiven: i.e., go to the King on your knees to ask for pardon. 131. as . . . incident: i.e., when there is a state of mutiny. 132. still the rout: quiet the unruly mob. 133–35. how . . . rebel: i.e., what sort of authority can a rebellious leader claim, except that he is a rebel? 134. addition: lit., a title added to a man's name. 135. qualify: describe. 137. liom: leash, strap used to restrain a greyhound until he is released (slipped) to pursue a hare. 152. Owed: owned. 153. appropriate: common to. 154. chartered: reserved solely for.

And this your momtanish° inhumanity.

ALL. Faith! He says true; let's us do as we may be done by.

LINC. We'll be ruled by you, Master More, if you'll stand by our friend to procure our pardon.   160

MORE. Submit you to these noble gentlemen,

156. momtanish: This is the reading of the manuscript. The word is not otherwise known and has been much disputed. From the context it must have some such meaning as "monstrous," "barbarous," or "enormous."

Entreat their mediation to the King,
Give up yourself to form,° obey the magistrate,
And there's no doubt but mercy may be found
If you so seek it.   165

163. form: orderly behavior.

A photograph of manuscript lines 114–34 will be found on Plate 14a; the following is a literal transcript of these lines:

all	marry god forbid that

moo   nay certainly you ar
for to the king god hath his offyc lent
of dread of Juſtyce, power and Comaund
hath bid him rule, and willd you to obay
and to add ampler maͭie to this
he ~~god~~ hath not ~~le~~ only lent the king his figure
                     &
his throne ~~his~~ ſword, but gyven him his owne name
calls him a god on earth, what do you then
ryſing gainſt him that god himſealf enſtalls
but ryſe gainſt god, what do you to yor fowles
in doing this o deſperat ~~ar~~ as you are.
waſh your foule mynds wt teares and thoſe ſame handes
that you lyke rebells lyft againſt the peace
lift vp for peace, and your vnreuerent knees
~~that~~ make them your feet to kneele to be forgyven
~~is ſafer warrs, then euer you can make~~
                        ~~in in to yor obedienc.~~
~~whoſe diſcipline is ryot; why euen yor warrs hurly~~
     tell me but this
~~cannot peeed but by obedienc~~ what rebell captaine
       n
as mutyes ar incident, by his name
can ſtill the rout who will obay ~~th~~ a traytor
or howe can well that pclamation founde
when ther is no adicion but a rebell

Reading List

This Reading List is in three parts. Part I contains a selection of books that are likely to be of use and interest to the general student. Part II directs the reader to some important classics of Shakespearean criticism. Part III is an extensive list of works that are of particular interest to modern critics.[1]

Part I: General Works

A. Bibliography

The Cambridge Bibliography of English Literature, ed. by F. W. Bateson, 4 vols., Cambridge University Press, 1947 (orig. publ. 1940).

For general purposes this is the most useful of all bibliographies for the student. Shakespeare and his contemporaries are included in Volume I. The *Bibliography* includes works published to the end of 1938. A Supplementary Volume (V) carries the *Bibliography* down to the beginning of 1955.

New work is listed annually in the *Shakespeare Quarterly,* Shakespeare Association of New York, and is briefly reviewed in *Shakespeare Survey,* Cambridge University Press. A useful bibliography will be found in *The Reader's Encyclopedia of Shakespeare,* T. Y. Crowell, 1966.

B. Facsimile Texts

Facsimiles of Original Quartos
  a. *The Merchant of Venice, The Merry Wives of Windsor, Hamlet* (Q1), *King Lear, Pericles, Love's Labor's Lost, Henry V, Troilus and Cressida, Hamlet* (Q1), and *Romeo and Juliet* have been reproduced in collotype, ed. by W. W. Greg, Oxford University Press, 1939–57.
  b. *Hamlet* (Q1), Harvard University Press, 1931; *Titus Andronicus* (Q1), Scribners, 1936; *Hamlet* (Q2), Huntington Library, 1938; and *Shakespeare's Poems,* The Elizabethan Club, Yale University Press, 1964, are collotype reproductions.

Photographic Facsimiles of the First
  Folio of 1623
  a. In collotype, ed. by Sidney Lee, Oxford University Press, 1902.
  b. By line process, ed. by H. Kökeritz and C. T. Prouty, Yale University Press, 1954. The size of the type has been reduced but the text is adequate

[1] Paperback editions are noted by asterisks.

for normal use. The process used in the reproduction does not give absolute accuracy, for the plates must sometimes be doctored to eliminate imperfections in the original, especially " show-through " due to too absorbent paper. Though not suitable for the minutest bibliographical research, the volume is a most desirable possession for any serious student.

Xerox facsimiles of any text can be obtained at a reasonable price from University Microfilms, Ann Arbor, Michigan.

C. Shakespeare's Times

Stow, John, *A Survey of London,* London, 1598, ed. by C. L. Kingsford, 2 vols., Oxford University Press, 1908; Dutton (Everyman), 1956. An elaborate contemporary and historical description of London.

Stow, John, *Annales; or, a General Chronicle of England, Begun by John Stow; Continued by Edmund Howes . . . unto . . . 1631,* London, 1631. A contemporary chronicle, year by year, of the most sensational events in English life.

Nichols, John, *The Progresses and Public Processions of Queen Elizabeth,* 3 vols., London, 1823; *The Progresses, Processions, and Magnificent Festivities, of King James the First,* 4 vols., London, 1828.

Both are full and valuable collections of records and contemporary pamphlets dealing with ceremonials, pageants, masques, and entertainments of the Court.

Gardiner, S. R., *History of England from the Accession of James I to the Outbreak of the Civil War, 1603–1642,* new ed., 10 vols., Longmans, Green, 1894–96. With Cheyney (see below), the most comprehensive and generally useful of the longer histories of the period.

Madden, D. H., *The Diary of Master William Silence: A Study of Shakespeare & of Elizabethan Sport,* Longmans, Green, 1897.

Cheyney, Edward P., *A History of England from the Defeat of the Armada to the Death of Elizabeth,* 2 vols., Longmans, Green, 1914–26.

Shakespeare's England, ed. by Walter Raleigh, Sidney Lee, and C. T. Onions, 2 vols., Oxford University Press, 1917. An account of the life and manners of his age. An essential book for any student of Shakespeare. It contains chapters by experts on almost every aspect of life in Shakespeare's England, with particular reference to the plays. There are many illustrations.

Byrne, Muriel St. C., *Elizabethan Life in Town and Country*, British Book, 1954 (orig. publ. 1925). An interesting book for the student.

Harrison, G. B., *The Elizabethan Journals, 1591–1603*, University of Michigan Press, 1955 (orig. publ. 1929, 1931, 1933); *A Jacobean Journal . . . 1603–1606*, Macmillan, 1941; *A Second Jacobean Journal . . . 1607–1610*, University of Michigan Press, 1958. A detailed day-by-day account of those matters great and small which chiefly interested Shakespeare and his contemporaries.

Judges, A. V., *The Elizabethan Underworld*, Kegan Paul, Trench, Trubner, 1930. A useful collection of the more important contemporary pamphlets about Elizabethan rogues and vagabonds.

Wright, Louis B., *Middle-Class Culture in Elizabethan England*, University of North Carolina Press (Huntington Library Publications), 1935. An account of the mentality and culture of the average middle-class citizens who formed the greater part of Shakespeare's audiences.

Black, J. B., *The Reign of Elizabeth, 1558–1603*, Oxford University Press, 1936. A useful general account of the reign in most of its aspects, with a general historical bibliography.

Craig, Hardin, *The Enchanted Glass*, Essential Books, 1952 (orig. publ. 1936). A scholarly account of the intellectual background of the age.

The Letters of John Chamberlain, ed. by N. E. McClure, 2 vols., American Philosophical Society, 1939. John Chamberlain was the best of the Elizabethan letter writers. He had a keen zest for gossip and his letters provide a racy running commentary on the period from 1597 to 1626.

Spencer, Theodore, *Shakespeare and the Nature of Man*, Macmillan, 1942. A discussion of the turmoil of contemporary ideas on man's place in the universe and their reflections in Shakespeare's plays.

Tillyard, E. M. W., *The Elizabethan World Picture*, Macmillan, 1943; Random House (Vintage*), n.d. An attempt to set out the theory of the universe as understood by Shakespeare's contemporaries.

Akrigg, G. P. V., *Jacobean Pageant: The Court of King James I*, Harvard University Press, 1962. A lively account of the King and Court for which Shakespeare wrote his greatest plays.

Shakespeare in His Own Age, ed. by Allardyce Nicoll, Shakespeare Survey, 17, Cambridge University Press, 1964. Seventeen essays on the daily life, philosophy and fancy, art and entertainment; with many good illustrations.

Halliday, F. E., *Shakespeare: A Pictorial Biography*, Crowell, 1957; Nicoll, Allardyce, *The Elizabethans*, Cambridge University Press, 1957. Two picture books of considerable value to any student

who is not familiar with the outward appearance of Shakespeare's age.

D. Elizabethan Theatrical Conditions

Henslowe's Diary (2 vols.) and *Henslowe's Papers* (1 vol.), ed. by W. W. Greg, Bullen, London, 1904–08. See Gen. Intro. pp. 38b, 65a, 84b. The accounts and various papers concerning their theatrical ventures left by Philip Henslowe and Edward Alleyn. The most fascinating of all original documents concerning the Elizabethan theater. A more modern and accessible edition is *Henslowe's Diary*, edited with supplementary material, introduction, and notes by R. A. Foakes and R. T. Rickert, Cambridge University Press, 1961. The text is preferable to Greg's, but this edition lacks Greg's full and valuable commentary.

Adams, Joseph Quincy, *Shakespearean Playhouses*, Houghton Mifflin, 1917. A lively and interesting account of the various London playhouses.

Chambers, E. K., *The Elizabethan Stage*, 4 vols., Oxford University Press, 1923. An essential work for the advanced student and the scholar. It exhaustively summarizes the facts about Elizabethan plays, dramatists, theaters, and companies, with many extracts from original sources.

Noble, Richmond, *Shakespeare's Use of Song*, Oxford University Press, 1923. Discusses the purpose of the songs in the plays.

Baldwin, T. W., *Organization and Personnel of the Shakespearean Company*, Princeton University Press, 1927. An elaborate and detailed account of the Elizabethan acting company.

Nungezer, Edwin, *A Dictionary of Actors . . . before 1642*, Cornell University Press, 1929. A valuable book of reference.

Greg, W. W., *Dramatic Documents from the Elizabethan Playhouses*, 2 vols., Oxford University Press, 1931. Facsimiles of the most important documents of stage history. Most valuable and interesting for the serious student.

Naylor, Edward W., *Shakespeare and Music*, rev. ed., Dutton, 1931 (orig. ed., 1896). A useful account of Elizabethan music and musical instruments.

Linthicum, Marie C., *Costume in Elizabethan Drama*, Oxford University Press, 1936. An essential book of reference for all matters of fabrics, colors, and costumes.

Sisson, C. J., *Lost Plays of Shakespeare's Age*, Cambridge University Press, 1936. A record of researches, chiefly in the Public Record Office in London, which throws much light on the murkier corners of Elizabethan social life and the drama. It is, moreover, fascinating and amusing reading.

Harrison, G. B., *Elizabethan Plays and Players*,

University of Michigan Press (Ann Arbor *), 1956 (orig. publ. 1940). An account of the chief personalities in Elizabethan dramatic history from 1570 to 1603.

Harbage, Alfred, *Shakespeare's Audience,* Columbia University Press, 1941. An important and stimulating study of the size, social composition, behavior, and intelligence of Shakespeare's audiences.

Adams, John Cranford, *The Globe Playhouse: Its Design and Equipment,* Harvard University Press, 1942. Although many of Adams' conjectures have been rejected by modern experts on the Elizabethan stage, this is still an important book for the serious student.

Hodges, C. Walter, *The Globe Restored,* Coward-McCann, 1954. More conservative than Adams. Particularly valuable for its illustrations, especially of the development of the Elizabethan stage from the inn yard to the elaborate Second Globe of 1614.

Smith, Irwin, *Shakespeare's Globe Playhouse,* Scribner's, 1957. A modern reconstruction, with text and plans, based upon Adams' *The Globe Playhouse.*

Shakespeare Survey, 12, ed. by Allardyce Nicoll, Cambridge University Press, 1959. This volume contains several articles on the Elizabethan theater which should be read alongside Adams' *The Globe Playhouse.*

E. The Text and Its Problems

Greg, W. W., *Shakespeare's Merry Wives of Windsor,* Oxford University Press, 1910. The first serious study of a "bad quarto" by a modern scholar.

Pollard, A. W., *Shakespeare's Fight with the Pirates and the Problems of the Transmission of His Text,* 2nd ed., Cambridge University Press, 1937 (orig. publ. 1917). This book, more than any other single volume, was responsible for the modern interest in the exact study of the early texts of Shakespeare. See Gen. Intro. p. 85a.

Pollard, A. W., Greg, W. W., Thompson, E. M., Wilson, J. Dover, and Chambers, R. W., *Shakespeare's Hand in the Play of "Sir Thomas More,"* Cambridge University Press, 1923. See Gen. Intro. pp. 85b–86a and App. 30.

McKerrow, R. B., *An Introduction to Bibliography for Literary Students,* Oxford University Press, 1927. An indispensable introduction to the scholarly study of the problems of the text.

Willoughby, Edwin E., *The Printing of the First Folio of Shakespeare,* Oxford University Press, 1932. A study of the making of the most important volume in English literature.

McKerrow, R. B., *Prolegomena to the Oxford Shakespeare: A Study in Editorial Method,* Oxford

University Press, 1939. Shortly before his death in 1940 McKerrow planned to produce a new text of Shakespeare based on sound bibliographical principles. In this book he laid down the plan he proposed to follow.

Greg, W. W., *The Editorial Problem in Shakespeare,* Oxford University Press, 1954 (orig. publ. 1942). A discussion of the problems and principles of editing the plays. It should be read in conjunction with the preceding.

Duthie, G. I., *The "Bad" Quarto of Hamlet,* Cambridge University Press, 1941. A full discussion of the origins of the most famous of the "bad quartos."

Hoppe, Harry R., *The Bad Quarto of Romeo and Juliet,* Cornell University Press, 1948. A good example of modern scholarly textual study.

Greg, W. W., *The Shakespeare First Folio: Its Bibliographical and Textual History,* Oxford University Press, 1955. The most generally important and comprehensive of all works on the Shakespeare text.

F. Sources

Holinshed, Raphael, *Chronicles of England, Scotland and Ireland,* 2 vols., London, 1577; 2nd ed., 1587. The source book for the History Plays and for *Macbeth.* Copious extracts of the passages Shakespeare used in writing the History Plays are given in *Shakespeare's Holinshed,* ed. by W. G. Boswell-Stone, London, 1896, and *Holinshed's Chronicles as Used in Shakespeare's Plays,* ed. by A. and J. Nicoll, Dutton (Everyman), 1927.

Plutarch, *The Lives of the Noble Grecians and Romans,* trans. from the French by Sir Thomas North, London, 1579, and later editions. See *Caesar* Intro. p. 809b. *Shakespeare's Plutarch,* ed. by T. J. B. Spencer, Penguin,* 1964, contains the Lives of Julius Caesar, Brutus, Marcus Antonius, and Coriolanus in the North translation.

Narrative and Dramatic Sources of Shakespeare, ed. by Geoffrey Bullough, 6 vols. (vol. 7 in preparation), Columbia University Press, 1957——. A full and elaborate collection of all major sources and analogues of Shakespeare's plays, with discussions on the ways he used them. An essential collection for the serious student.

G. Shakespeare the Man

Bagehot, Walter, "Shakespeare, the Man," in *Literary Studies,* Longmans, Green, 1879; Dutton (Everyman), 1911. A sensible short essay by the sanest of Victorian critics, nowadays unjustly neglected.

Adams, Joseph Quincy, *A Life of William Shake-*

speare, Houghton Mifflin, 1923. The best of the earlier scholarly biographies.

Fripp, E. I., *Master Richard Quyny, Bailiff of Stratford-upon-Avon and Friend of William Shakespeare*, Oxford University Press, 1924, and *Shakespeare's Stratford*, Oxford University Press, 1928. Good accounts of the social and intellectual background of the Shakespeare family in Stratford-on-Avon.

Hotson, Leslie, *Shakespeare versus Shallow*, Little, Brown, 1931. Dr. Hotson's own account of his discovery of a new fact about Shakespeare. See Gen. Intro. pp. 10b–11a.

Harrison, G. B., *Shakespeare under Elizabeth*, Holt, 1933; also published as *Shakespeare at Work, 1592–1603*, University of Michigan Press (Ann Arbor*), 1956. An attempt to show how Shakespeare's plays reflected current interest and events.

Hotson, Leslie, *I, William Shakespeare*, Cape, 1937. An account of the man whom Shakespeare appointed as executor of his will and of the circle in which Shakespeare was well known. Valuable for any student interested in Shakespeare's biography and personal background.

Baldwin, T. W., *William Shakspere's Small Latine and Lesse Greeke*, 2 vols., University of Illinois Press, 1944. A vast and illuminating study of education at English schools in Shakespeare's time.

Chute, Marchette, *Shakespeare of London*, Dutton,* 1949; and Halliday, F. E., *The Life of Shakespeare*, Penguin,* 1964. Two readable and popular biographies.

H. General and Reference

Bartlett, John, *Complete Concordance . . . to . . . Shakespeare*, St. Martin's, 1953 (orig. publ. 1889). An essential reference book.

Onions, C. T., *A Shakespeare Glossary*, 2nd rev. ed., Oxford University Press, 1919 (orig. publ. 1911). A most useful reference book for the general student.

Chambers, E. K., *William Shakespeare: A Study of Facts and Problems*, 2 vols., Oxford University Press, 1930. An essential work of reference for any serious student, as it contains all the material for advanced study of the facts and problems of Shakespeare the man and his work. The common reader will find it almost incomprehensibly technical, and even the scholar, while he can rely on the facts, should beware of taking on trust Chambers' curt summaries of theories and opinions with which he disagrees. Nevertheless, it is one of the first books that should be bought for the student's private Shakespearean library.

Munro, J. J., ed., *The Shakspere Allusion Book:*

A Collection of Allusions to Shakspere from 1591 to 1700, 2 vols., Oxford University Press, 1931. Apart from its interest, the collection reveals, so far as is now possible, the contemporary popularity of Shakespeare's plays and characters.

Shakespeare Survey, Cambridge University Press, 1949——. An annual survey of Shakespearean study and production.

Shakespeare Quarterly, Shakespeare Association of New York, 1950——. A quarterly dealing with every kind of Shakespearean interest, particularly on the American continent.

Tilley, Morris Palmer, *A Dictionary of the Proverbs in England in the Sixteenth and Seventeenth Centuries*, University of Michigan Press, 1950. This work, which is especially concerned with Shakespeare's use of proverbs, is one of great value to all students of Shakespeare's language and imagery.

Kökeritz, Helge, *Shakespeare's Pronunciation*, Yale University Press, 1953. An extensive study, based on rhymes, puns, and spellings, of Shakespeare's pronunciation. A book for the specialist, but an important reminder that the sounds of Shakespeare's own English differed in many ways from modern " standard English." Also, by the same author, *Shakespeare's Names: A Pronouncing Dictionary*, Yale University Press, 1959. A warning to the American reader to be wary of how he pronounces English names, ancient or modern.

Halliday, F. E., *A Shakespeare Companion 1564–1964*, Penguin,* 1964. Similar to *The Reader's Encyclopedia of Shakespeare*, but more modest in scope (and price).

Campbell, Oscar James, and Quinn, Edward G., *The Readers Encyclopedia of Shakespeare*, T. Y. Crowell, 1966. A vast and most useful compendium of all kinds of information concerning Shakespeare, his works and times, his critics, and other relevant matters. An essential reference book.

Part II: Classic Critical Works

Ralli, Augustus, *A History of Shakespearian Criticism*, 2 vols., Oxford University Press, 1932. An elaborate collection of summaries of the critical work on Shakespeare from the beginnings to 1925.

Smith, D. Nichol, ed., *Eighteenth Century Essays on Shakespeare*, MacLehose, Glasgow, 1903.

Smith, D. Nichol, ed., *Shakespeare Criticism* (from the beginnings to Carlyle), Oxford University Press, 1916. A very useful short selection of the most important critical pronouncements, including Dryden, Rowe, Pope, Johnson, Morgann, Lamb, Coleridge, Hazlitt, De Quincey, and Carlyle. See Gen. Intro. pp. 73a–82a.

Bradby, Anne, ed., *Shakespeare Criticism, 1919–*

1935, Oxford University Press, 1936. A collection of modern critical essays from the first third of the twentieth century.

Lamb, Charles, *On the Tragedies of Shakespeare Considered with Reference to Their Fitness for Stage Representation*, London, 1811. See Gen. Intro. p. 78a.

Coleridge, S. T., *Shakespearean Criticism* (1811–1834), ed. by T. M. Raysor, 2 vols., Harvard University Press, 1930. The standard edition. See also *Lectures on Shakespeare*, Dutton (Everyman), 1907. See Gen. Intro. pp. 79a–80a. Coleridge was the most important of the critics of the " Romantic Revival," and was largely responsible for the excessive veneration of Shakespeare's genius in the Victorian era.

Hazlitt, William, *Characters of Shakespeare's Plays*, 1817. Included in Vol. IV of the *Complete Works*, ed. by P. P. Howe, 21 vols., Dent, 1932–34; Dutton (Everyman), 1906. See Gen. Intro. pp. 80a–81a. Sane appreciations of the chief characters, written with much sense and gusto.

Dowden, Edward, *Shakespere: A Critical Study of His Mind and Art*, Kegan Paul, Trench, Trubner, 1875; 3rd ed., Barnes & Noble, 1962. See Gen. Intro. pp. 82b–83a. The first critical work based on an accurate knowledge of the general development of Shakespeare's plays.

Moulton, R. G., *Shakespeare as a Dramatic Artist*, Oxford University Press, 1885. A study of the technique of drama and of Shakespeare's methods as a dramatist; a useful book.

Shaw, George Bernard, *Shaw on Shakespeare,* ed. by Edwin Wilson, Dutton,* 1961. Throughout his long life, Shaw wrote many penetrating criticisms and comments on Shakespeare, which are always worth reading alongside the more exuberant pronouncements of modern critics. The most important were made in the 1890's, when Shaw was drama critic for *The Saturday Review* of London.

Bradley, A. C., *Shakespearean Tragedy*, Macmillan, 1904; Fawcett (Premier*), 1965. See Gen. Intro. pp. 83a–84b. The book considers the principles of Shakespearean tragedy, and in detail, *Hamlet, Othello, Lear,* and *Macbeth.*

Raleigh, Walter, *Shakespeare*, Macmillan, 1907; St. Martin's,* 1957. A lively and human general introduction to the enjoyment of Shakespeare's plays.

MacCallum, M. W., *Shakespeare's Roman Plays and Their Background*, Macmillan, 1910. Full and elaborate studies of the three Roman tragedies— *Julius Caesar, Antony and Cleopatra,* and *Coriolanus* — with a discussion of Roman stories on the French and English stage.

Quiller-Couch, A. T., *Shakespeare's Workmanship*, Cambridge University Press, 1931 (orig. publ. 1918). Lively, common-sense lectures on the plays as specimens of theatrical art.

Eliot, T. S., " Hamlet and His Problems," 1919 (reprinted in *Selected Essays of T. S. Eliot*, rev. ed., Harcourt, Brace, 1950). In this famous short essay (originally a review), Eliot declared that in *Hamlet* " Shakespeare tackled a problem which proved too much for him." He also propagated for the first time the notion of the " objective correlative."

Schücking, Levin L., *Character Problems in Shakespeare's Plays*, Harrap, 1922. Critical studies from the scholar's point of view.

Granville-Barker, Harley, *Prefaces to Shakespeare*, 2 vols., Princeton University Press, 1946, 1947. See Gen. Intro. p. 87a. The first of the prefaces was originally published in 1923; others followed at intervals until 1947, the year after Granville-Barker's death. Volume 1, *Hamlet, Lear, Merchant of Venice, Antony and Cleopatra, Cymbeline.* Volume 2, *Othello, Coriolanus, Romeo and Juliet, Julius Caesar, Love's Labor's Lost.* A four-volume paperback edition was published by Princeton University Press in 1965.

Stoll, Elmer E., *Shakespeare Studies*, Macmillan, 1927. Essays on various topics — including " Literature and Life," " Characterization," " The Ghosts," " Shylock," " The Criminals," " Falstaff " — written in this author's usual pungent style.

Campbell, Lily B., *Shakespeare's Tragic Heroes; Slaves of Passion*, Barnes & Noble,* 1952 (orig. publ. 1930). A discussion of the tragic heroes in the light of Elizabethan ideas on moral philosophy and psychology.

Knight, G. Wilson, *The Wheel of Fire*, Oxford University Press, 1930; Meridian,* 1957. A subjective and imaginative interpretation of the ideas suggested by Shakespeare's poetic imagery. It was followed by *The Imperial Theme*, Oxford University Press, 1931, and *The Crown of Life*, Oxford University Press, 1947. See Gen. Intro. p. 89a.

Lawrence, W. W., *Shakespeare's Problem Comedies*, Macmillan, 1931. Valuable studies of *All's Well, Measure for Measure, Troilus and Cressida,* and *Cymbeline*, particularly considered in the light of medieval and Elizabethan ideas.

Knights, L. C., *How Many Children Had Lady Macbeth?*, W. Heffer, 1933; reprinted in *Explorations*, New York University Press,* 1964. The first important attack on A. C. Bradley's critical methods in *Shakespearean Tragedy.*

Stoll, Elmer E., *Art and Artifice in Shakespeare*, Barnes & Noble, 1933. Considers especially *Othello, Macbeth, Hamlet,* and *Lear.* See Gen. Intro. p. 87b.

Granville-Barker, Harley, and Harrison, G. B., eds., *A Companion to Shakespeare Studies*, Cambridge University Press, 1934; Doubleday (Anchor*), 1960. A collection of chapters by different authors on the principal topics that interest students of Shakespeare.

Spurgeon, Caroline F. E., *Shakespeare's Imagery and What It Tells Us,* Cambridge University Press, 1952 (orig. publ. 1935); Beacon,* 1958. See Gen. Intro. p. 88b.

Murry, J. Middleton, *Shakespeare,* Harcourt, Brace, 1936. A general study by a modern critic of the first rank.

Van Doren, Mark, *Shakespeare,* Holt, 1939; Doubleday (Anchor*), 1953. Short, stimulating essays on each of the plays and the poems.

Campbell, Oscar James, *Shakespeare's Satire,* Oxford University Press, 1943. A stimulating picture of the varieties of satire in the plays.

Campbell, Lily B., *Shakespeare's " Histories,"* Huntington Library, 1947. A study of the history plays in the light of contemporary ideas on history.

Heilman, R. B., *This Great Stage,* Louisiana State University Press, 1948. An elaborate study of the imagery of *King Lear* and a good example of the latest kind of study of Shakespeare's poetic processes. It was followed by *Magic in the Web* (a study of action and language in *Othello*), University of Kentucky Press, 1956.

Jones, Ernest, *Hamlet and Oedipus,* Norton, 1949; Doubleday (Anchor*), 1954. A psychoanalysis of Hamlet by the biographer of Sigmund Freud. Jones wrote several versions of this, the first of which appeared as an article in *American Journal of Psychology,* XXI, 1910.

Stauffer, Donald, *Shakespeare's World of Images: The Development of His Moral Ideas,* Norton, 1949. A mid-twentieth century version of what Dowden attempted in *Shakespere . . . His Mind and Art* in 1875.

Clemen, Wolfgang H., *The Development of Shakespeare's Imagery,* Harvard University Press, 1951 (orig. publ. in German, 1936). One of the sanest surveys of Shakespeare's use of imagery, and particularly valuable because it makes no extravagant claims.

Fluchère, Henri, *Shakespeare,* trans. by Guy Hamilton, Longmans, Green, 1953; *Shakespeare and the Elizabethans,* Hill & Wang (Dramabooks*), 1957. An excellent introduction to the understanding of Shakespeare's plays as a whole, and especially useful as an introduction to modern criticism.

Harbage, Alfred, *Shakespeare and the Rival Tradition,* Macmillan, 1953. Part dramatic history, part criticism. It shows that in Shakespeare's age, as today, there were two kinds of theater: the public theater, for which Shakespeare wrote, and the private playhouse, which catered to a coterie of intellectuals.

Hubler, Edward, *The Sense of Shakespeare's Sonnets,* Princeton University Press, 1954. A discussion of the Sonnets and what they say, leading to the contents of Shakespeare's mind.

Part III: Modern Critical Works

No attempt is made here to cover the vast expanse of Shakespearean criticism but only to provide crucial items that will give the reader a grasp of the chief issues and the directions taken by criticism in this century. Where works have been simultaneously published in England and the United States, the American publisher is given, not the English. In the case of articles and excerpts reprinted in paperback collections, a short title of the volume containing the reprint is provided.

Citations of many books are followed by a brief description of the contents or argument. In the case of articles, where the title usually reveals the contents, a description follows only if the article is of unusual importance or if some fact about it requires comment. For convenience of reference, the bibliography is in two sections, each with a number of subsections. Section A contains general books and articles dealing with major aspects of Shakespeare's style and subject matter. Section B contains criticism of each of Shakespeare's plays and poems.

A. Craftsmanship and Subject Matter

Critical Discussion of All Shakespeare's Plays

Goddard, Harold, *The Meaning of Shakespeare,* University of Chicago Press,* 1951. Excellent readings of individual plays that see Shakespeare as the continuing champion of liberal and democratic attitudes.

Traversi, Derek, *An Approach to Shakespeare,* 2nd rev. ed., Doubleday (Anchor*), 1956. The best single-volume treatment of the entire sweep of the plays.

Van Doren, Mark, *Shakespeare,* Holt, 1939; Doubleday (Anchor*), 1953. Very short but very perceptive sketches of the plays. Concentration on the poetry.

Use of the Stage

Brown, J. R., *Shakespeare's Plays in Performance,* St. Martin's, 1967. The concept of the " subtext " developed, the life of movement, gesture, expression, and intonation that lies below the printed text and is only realized in stage performance. Several histories of stage interpretation followed and analyzed.

Granville-Barker, Harley, *Prefaces to Shake-*

speare, 2 vols., Princeton University Press, 1946–47; 4 vols.,* 1965. Interpretations of ten plays turning on the meanings revealed as they are produced on stage. The plays treated in the four-volume paperback edition are: Vol. 1, *King Lear, Cymbeline, Julius Caesar;* Vol. 2, *Love's Labour's Lost, Romeo and Juliet, The Merchant of Venice, Othello;* Vol. 3, *Antony and Cleopatra, Coriolanus;* Vol. 4, *Hamlet.*

Knight, G. Wilson, *Shakespearean Production,* Northwestern University Press, 1964. Reverses to some extent the arguments of Brown and Granville-Barker and maintains that the symbolism and effects in the text provide the stage producer with clues about what to stress.

Dramatic Construction

Beckerman, Bernard, *Shakespeare at the Globe, 1599–1609,* Macmillan,* 1962. Reconstructs the theatrical conditions at the Globe and the types of plays Shakespeare and others were writing for that stage and company.

Ellis-Fermor, Una, *Shakespeare the Dramatist,* ed. by Kenneth Muir, Barnes & Noble, 1961. Posthumous collection of essays that in general argue that Shakespeare's greatness comes from his understanding of the fundamental nature of drama and particularly of character and plot.

Price, H. T., *Construction in Shakespeare,* University of Michigan Press, 1951. Examines the ways in which plays are built and assembled.

Treatment of Character

Sewall, Arthur, *Character and Society in Shakespeare,* Oxford University Press, 1951. Characters are best understood not as imitations of actual people or types of humanity but as parts of a central vision broken up as by a prism.

Stewart, J. I. M., *Character and Motive in Shakespeare: Some Recent Appraisals Examined,* Longmans, Green, 1949. A defense of the "truth" of Shakespeare's characters against charges of earlier critics like Schücking and Stoll that they are psychologically improbable.

Stoll, E. E., "Source and Motive in *Macbeth* and *Othello,*" *Review of English Studies,* 19 (1943), 25. See also Stoll's *Shakespeare and Other Masters,* Harvard University Press, 1940. Stoll's continuing argument is that Shakespeare did not create consistent and probable characters but manipulated them to create the maximum theatrical effect, shock, or thrills.

Psychoanalysis and the Plays

Holland, Norman, *Psychoanalysis and Shakespeare,* McGraw-Hill, 1966. A complete review of psychoanalytic criticism of the poet and the plays,

offered with a theory that attempts to reconcile psychoanalytic insights with more conventional criticism. Contains a summary of major psychoanalytic theories advanced on each play.

Jones, Ernest, *Hamlet and Oedipus,* Norton, 1949; Doubleday (Anchor*), 1954. The classic psychoanalytic treatment of Shakespeare, which explains Hamlet's delay by an unresolved Oedipal complex.

Style, General

Cruttwell, Patrick, *The Shakespearean Moment and Its Place in the Poetry of the Seventeenth Century,* Chatto & Windus, 1954; Random House (Vintage*), 1960. A careful description of an aspect of the style, considered as both language and arrangement of scenes, that focuses on a tension between opposing beliefs and values.

Evans, B. I., *The Language of Shakespeare's Plays,* Methuen, 1952; 3rd ed., Barnes & Noble (University Paperbacks*), 1964. Discusses the major stylistic devices in a number of plays and draws conclusions about the nature of the style.

Rylands, George, "Shakespeare the Poet," in *A Companion to Shakespeare Studies,* rev. ed., ed. by H. Granville-Barker and G. B. Harrison, Doubleday (Anchor*), 1960. Excellent short summary of the characteristics of three main periods of the style.

Imagery

Clemen, Wolfgang, *The Development of Shakespeare's Imagery,* Harvard University Press, 1951; Hill & Wang,* 1962. Patient and careful description of chief patterns of imagery in the major works, with discussions of various ways imagery functions in the drama.

Spurgeon, Caroline, *Shakespeare's Imagery and What It Tells Us,* Cambridge University Press, 1935; Beacon,* 1958. Pioneering study that attempts to catalogue the imagery and draw conclusions, chiefly about Shakespeare the man, from frequencies and "cluster" patterns. Good starting place.

Rhetoric

Joseph, Sister Miriam, *Shakespeare's Use of the Arts of Language,* Columbia University Press, 1947; as *Rhetoric in Shakespeare's Time,* Harcourt, Brace & World (Harbinger*), 1962. Excellent example of the influential school of critics who have sought the key to Shakespeare's style in his use of the formal practices of rhetoric taught in the schools.

Puns

Mahood, M. M., *Shakespeare's Wordplay,* Barnes & Noble, 1957. Examines the functions of the frequent puns, concentrating on five plays (*Romeo and Juliet, Richard II, Hamlet, Macbeth,* and *The Winter's Tale*), and argues that the puns lead to the vision of reality at the center of the play.

Elizabethan English

Willcock, Gladys D., "Shakespeare and Elizabethan English," *Shakespeare Survey, 7,* Cambridge University Press, 1954, 12–24.

Specialized Studies in Particular Themes and Subjects

Bush, Geoffrey, *Shakespeare and the Natural Condition,* Harvard University Press, 1956. Brief but effective treatment of Shakespeare's understanding of nature.

Frye, Roland Mushat, *Shakespeare and Christian Doctrine,* Princeton University Press, 1963; Princeton,* 1965. Tries the plays against several theologies of the time and concludes that Shakespeare was a secular poet with humane rather than specifically religious interests.

Halliday, F. E., *Shakespeare and His Critics,* Duckworth, 1949; Schocken,* 1963. Good collection of major criticism from Ben Jonson to T. S. Eliot.

Harbage, Alfred, *As They Liked It,* Macmillan, 1947; Harper (Torchbooks*), 1961. Excellent reconstruction of Shakespeare's audience and its expectations in the theater.

Rabkin, Norman, *Shakespeare and the Common Understanding,* Free Press,* 1967. Discussion of many Shakespearean plays in the framework of "complementarity," a way of seeing the world that permits absolutely opposite views of reality to exist together. Excellent synthesis and explanation of opposing critical readings of the plays.

Righter, Anne, *Shakespeare and the Idea of the Play,* Barnes & Noble, 1963; Penguin,* 1967. The special use Shakespeare made of the "all the world's a stage" metaphor and its relation to the status of the play in reality.

Spencer, Theodore, *Shakespeare and the Nature of Man,* Macmillan, 1942; 2nd ed., Collier,* 1961. Relates plays to the Elizabethan understanding of the physical and moral order of the universe.

Sternfeld, F. W., *Music in Shakespearean Tragedy,* Dover, 1963. To be followed by a work on music in the comedies, this is the most complete and competent work on the subject from both dramatic and musical points of view.

Watson, C. B., *Shakespeare and the Renaissance Concept of Honor,* Princeton University Press, 1961. Traces the theme of honor through the plays and compares the views expressed in the plays with nondramatic writings on the subject.

Whitaker, Virgil K., *Shakespeare's Use of Learning,* Huntington Library, 1953. Works out Shakespeare's probable reading and discusses the ways in which it contributed to his plays.

B. The Plays and Poems

The Early Comedies, General

Barber, C. L., *Shakespeare's Festive Comedy,* Princeton University Press, 1959; Meridian,* 1963. Fascinating study of the major comedies as dramatic versions of a pattern of release and clarification also found in such social festivities as Maying and the Feast of Misrule.

Bradbrook, M. C., *Growth and Structure of Elizabethan Comedy,* Chatto & Windus, 1955. Places Shakespeare's comedies in the tradition of other comic writers and in the conventions of comedy.

Brown, John Russell, *Shakespeare and His Comedies,* 2nd ed., Barnes & Noble, 1962. Careful reading of each of the comedies and tracing of Shakespeare's development as a comic dramatist.

Crane, Milton, "Shakespeare's Comedies and the Critics," in *Shakespeare 400,* ed. by J. G. McManaway, Holt, Rinehart, and Winston, 1964. Good summary of various theories of Shakespeare's comedies that have developed in recent years.

Frye, Northrop, *A Natural Perspective: The Development of Shakespearean Comedy and Romance,* Columbia University Press, 1965. Looks at the comedies from "the middle distance" in an attempt to see them as a group and to distinguish the recurring images and structural devices.

Shakespeare, the Comedies, ed. by Kenneth Muir, Prentice-Hall,* 1965. Good collection of essays on the individual comedies. Interesting introduction that surveys the field and argues that the comedies are best approached as distinct plays, not as instances of "comedy."

Welsford, Enid, *The Fool, His Social and Literary History,* Faber & Faber, 1935. Fascinating account of the history of the Fool and the meaning of this strange figure in life and literature. Contains a valuable treatment of the Fool in *King Lear* also.

The Comedy of Errors

Brooks, Harold F., "Themes and Structure in *The Comedy of Errors,*" *Stratford-Upon-Avon Studies 3: Early Shakespeare,* St. Martin's,* 1961.

Levin, Harry, Introduction in *The Comedy of Errors,* New American Library,* 1965.

Williams, Gwyn, "*The Comedy of Errors* Rescued from Tragedy," *Review of English Literature,* 5 (1964), 63–71.

The Taming of the Shrew

Bradbrook, M. C., "Dramatic Role as a Social Image: A Study of *The Taming of the Shrew,*" *Shakespeare Jahrbuch,* 94 (1958), 132–50.

Hosley, Richard, "Sources and Analogues of *The Taming of the Shrew*," *Huntington Library Quarterly*, 27 (1963–64), 289–308. Collection of critical views of the play and discussion of problems relating to it, including its relationship to an earlier play, *The Taming of a Shrew*.

Mack, Maynard, "Engagement and Detachment in Shakespeare's Plays," *Essays on Shakespeare and Elizabethan Drama in Honor of Hardin Craig*, ed. by Richard Hosley, University of Missouri Press, 1962. See especially pp. 279–80 for discussion of *The Taming of the Shrew*, but article traces a pattern of special importance in comedies.

The Two Gentlemen of Verona

Brooks, Harold F., "Two Clowns in a Comedy (to Say Nothing of the Dog): Speed, Launce (and Crab) in *The Two Gentlemen of Verona*," *Essays and Studies 1963*, ed. by S. Gorley Putt, 1963, pp. 91–100.

Danby, John F., "Shakespeare Criticism and *Two Gentlemen of Verona*," *Critical Quarterly*, 2 (1960), 309–21.

Evans, Bertrand, Introduction in *The Two Gentlemen of Verona*, New American Library,* 1964.

Love's Labor's Lost

Frye, Northrop, "The Argument of Comedy," *English Institute Essays, 1948*, ed. by D. A. Robertson, Columbia University Press, 1949. (Reprinted in numerous paperback collections of and on comedy.) Basis of chapter on comedy in Frye's *Anatomy of Criticism*, Atheneum,* 1966, which sketches the most useful general theory of comedy.

Roesen, Bobbyann, "*Love's Labour's Lost*," *Shakespeare Quarterly*, 4 (1953), 411–26.

Yates, F. A., *A Study of "Love's Labour's Lost*," Cambridge University Press, 1936.

A Midsummer Night's Dream

Nemerov, Howard, "The Marriage of Theseus and Hippolyta," *Kenyon Review*, 18 (1956), 633–41.

Schanzer, Ernest, "The Moon and the Fairies in *A Midsummer Night's Dream*," *University of Toronto Quarterly*, 24 (1955), 234–46.

Young, David P., *Something of Great Constancy; The Art of "A Midsummer Night's Dream*," Yale University Press, 1966. Approaches the play from several directions to show the play's center in a view of reality and art that transcends the usual split between reason and imagination, reality and playing.

The Merchant of Venice

Barber, C. L., *Shakespeare's Festive Comedy*, Princeton University Press,* 1959.

Brown, John Russell, "Creating a Role: Shy-lock," *Shakespeare's Plays in Performance*, St. Martin's 1967. Excellent history of the ways various actors have realized the "subtext" below the words of the printed play.

Much Ado About Nothing

Craik, T. W., "*Much Ado About Nothing*," *Scrutiny*, 19 (1953), 297–316.

Jorgensen, Paul A., "*Much Ado About Nothing*," *Shakespeare Quarterly*, 5 (1954), 287–95.

Rossiter, A. P., "*Angel with Horns*" and Other *Shakespeare Lectures*, ed. by Graham Storey, Longmans, Green, 1961. Includes an excellent essay on *Much Ado About Nothing*.

Smith, J., "*Much Ado About Nothing*," *Scrutiny*, 13 (1946), 242–57.

As You Like It

Gardner, Helen, "*As You Like It*," *More Talking of Shakespeare*, ed. by John W. P. Garrett, Longmans, Green, 1959. An excellent essay, distinguished chiefly by its concise but far-reaching theories of the ultimate nature of comedy and tragedy.

Halio, Jay L., "'No Clock in the Forest': Time in *As You Like It*," *Studies in English Literature: 1500–1900*, 2 (1962), 197–207.

Jenkins, H., "*As You Like It*," *Shakespeare Survey*, 8, Cambridge University Press, 1955, 40–51.

Shaw, John, "Fortune and Nature in *As You Like It*," *Shakespeare Quarterly*, 6 (1955), 45–50.

Twelfth Night

Frye, Northrop, "Characterization in Shakespearian Comedy," *Shakespeare Quarterly*, 4 (1953), 271–77.

Hollander, John, "*Twelfth Night* and the Morality of Indulgence," *Sewanee Review*, 67 (1959), 220–38.

Salingar, L. D., "The Design of *Twelfth Night*," *Shakespeare Quarterly*, 9 (1959), 117–39.

The Merry Wives of Windsor

Charlton, H. B., *Shakespearean Comedy*, Barnes & Noble, 1938.

Green, William, *Shakespeare's "Merry Wives of Windsor*," Princeton University Press, 1962.

Later Comedies and Romances, General

Bethell, S. L., *Shakespeare and the Popular Dramatic Tradition*, Duke University Press, 1945.

Knight, G. Wilson, *The Shakespearean Tempest*, Oxford, 1932; 3rd ed., Barnes & Noble,* 1960. Works out several continuing symbols in Shakespeare, particularly the tempest and the sounds of music, and details their appearance and effect in the last plays.

Lawrence, W. W., *Shakespeare's Problem Comedies*, Macmillan, 1931. An excellent introduction to the questions and problems of the middle and late plays that baffled and confused older realistic critical approaches. Should be read in conjunction with a book like Bethell's or Knight's employing a different view of dramatic poetry.

Shakespeare Survey, 11, Cambridge University Press, 1958. An issue given to the last plays with excellent articles on the history, staging, and structure of these works.

Tillyard, E. M. W., *Shakespeare's Last Plays*, Chatto & Windus, 1938; 6th ed., Barnes & Noble, 1964. One of the first and best descriptions of the common elements in the last plays, arguing that Shakespeare was trying a new form in *Pericles* and *Cymbeline* that was perfected in *The Winter's Tale* and *The Tempest*.

Traversi, Derek, *Shakespeare: The Last Phase*, Harcourt, Brace, 1955. Careful reading of these plays, concentrating on developing imagery and themes rather than character.

Wells, Stanley, "Shakespeare and Romance," *Stratford-upon-Avon Studies 8: Later Shakespeare*, St. Martin's,* 1967. Summation of present knowledge of the romance tradition and the ways in which Shakespeare adapted it.

All's Well That Ends Well

Halio, Jay L., "*All's Well That Ends Well*," *Shakespeare Quarterly*, 15 (1964), 33–43.

Hunter, G. K., Introduction in *Arden Edition of the Works of William Shakespeare: "All's Well That Ends Well*," 3rd rev. ed., Harvard University Press, 1959; also in *Shakespeare, the Comedies*, ed. by Kenneth Muir, Prentice-Hall,* 1965.

Knight, G. Wilson, "The Third Eye," in *The Sovereign Flower: On Shakespeare as the Poet of Royalism*, Macmillan, 1958.

Measure for Measure

Chambers, R. W., "*Measure for Measure*," *Man's Unconquerable Mind*, Jonathan Cape, 1952; also in *Measure for Measure*, New American Library,* 1964.

Knight, G. Wilson, "*Measure for Measure* and the Gospels," *The Wheel of Fire*, Oxford University Press, 1930; 4th rev. ed., British Book Centre, 1949, Meridian,* 1957.

Lascelles, Mary, *Shakespeare's "Measure for Measure*," De Graff, 1954.

Stevenson, David L., "Design and Structure in *Measure for Measure*: A New Appraisal," *ELH*, 23 (1956), 256–78.

Pericles

Arthos, John, "*Pericles, Prince of Tyre*: A Study in the Dramatic Use of Romantic Narrative," *Shakespeare Quarterly*, 4 (1953), 257–70.

Danby, John F., "Sidney and the Late-Shakespearian Romance," in *Poets on Fortune's Hill*, Faber & Faber,* 1952. See especially pp. 186–92.

Knight, G. Wilson, "*Pericles*," *The Crown of Life*, Oxford University Press, 1947; Barnes & Noble,* 1961.

Cymbeline

Harris, Bernard, "'What's Past Is Prologue': *Cymbeline* and *Henry VIII*," *Stratford-upon-Avon Studies 8: Later Shakespeare*, St. Martin's, 1967.

Stephenson, A. A., "The Significance of *Cymbeline*," *Scrutiny*, 10 (1942), 329–38.

Tinkler, F. C., "*Cymbeline*," *Scrutiny*, 7 (1938), 5–20.

The Winter's Tale

Bethell, S. L., "*The Winter's Tale*": A Study, Staples Press, 1947.

Frye, Northrop, "Recognition in *The Winter's Tale*," *Essays on Shakespeare and Elizabethan Drama*, ed. by Richard Hosley, University of Missouri Press, 1962.

Hoeniger, F. D., "The Meaning of *The Winter's Tale*," *University of Toronto Quarterly*, 20 (1950), 11–26.

Leavis, F. R., "A Criticism of Shakespeare's Last Plays," *Scrutiny*, 10 (1942), 339–45. Reprinted in *The Common Pursuit*, Chatto & Windus, 1952; Penguin,* 1962.

Mahood, M. M., "*The Winter's Tale*," *Shakespeare's Wordplay*, Barnes & Noble, 1957.

The Tempest

Auden, W. H., "The Sea and the Mirror: A Commentary on Shakespeare's *The Tempest*," *The Collected Poetry*, Random House, 1945.

Brower, R. A., "The Mirror of Analogy: *The Tempest*," *The Fields of Light*, Oxford University Press, 1951; Galaxy Books,* 1951.

Knox, Bernard, "*The Tempest* and the Ancient Comic Tradition," *English Stage Comedy*, ed. by W. K. Wimsatt, Jr., English Institute Essays 1954, Columbia University Press, 1955; also in *The Tempest*, New American Library,* 1964.

Spencer, Theodore, "Appearance and Reality in Shakespeare's Last Plays," *Modern Philology*, 39 (1942), 265–74.

The History Plays, General

Shakespeare, the Histories, ed. by E. M. Waith, Prentice-Hall,* 1965. A collection of essays on the history plays, with an excellent introduction describing the change in critical attitudes toward these plays.

Tillyard, E. M. W., *Shakespeare's History Plays*, Macmillan, 1946; Collier,* 1962. Traces the relationship between the events and actions of the history plays and received Elizabethan views of political and social order.

Traversi, Derek, *Shakespeare from "Richard II" to "Henry V,"* Stanford University Press, 1957. Close, careful analysis of the plays of the second tetralogy that widens considerably the view of history advanced by Tillyard.

Henry VI, Part One

Brockbank, J. P., "The Frame of Disorder — *Henry VI,*" *Stratford-upon-Avon Studies 3: Early Shakespeare,* ed. by John Russell Brown and Bernard Harris, St. Martin's, 1961.

Clemen, Wolfgang H., "Anticipation and Foreboding in Shakespeare's Early Histories," *Shakespeare Survey,* 6, ed. by Allardyce Nicoll, Cambridge University Press, 1953.

Kirschbaum, Leo, "The Authorship of *1 Henry VI,*" *PMLA,* 67 (1952), 809–22.

Henry VI, Part Two

Berman, Ronald S., "Fathers and Sons in the *Henry VI* Plays," *Shakespeare Quarterly,* 13 (1962), 487–97.

Leech, Clifford, "The Two-Part Play: Marlowe and the Early Shakespeare," *Shakespeare Jahrbuch,* 92 (1958), 90–106.

Turner, Robert Y., "Shakespeare and the Public Confrontation Scene in Early History Plays," *Modern Philology,* 72 (1964), 1–12.

Henry VI, Part Three

Kernan, Alvin, "A Comparison of the Imagery in *3 Henry VI* and *The True Tragedie of Richard Duke of York,*" *Studies in Philology,* 51 (1954), 431–42.

Ribner, Irving, *The English History Play in the Age of Shakespeare,* Princeton University Press, 1957.

Richard III

Kott, Jan, "The Kings," *Shakespeare Our Contemporary,* trans. by B. Taborski, Doubleday (Anchor*), 1966, pp. 3–55.

Krieger, Murray, "The Dark Generations of *Richard III,*" *Criticism,* 1 (1959), 32–48.

Rossiter, A. P., "The Unity of *Richard III,*" *Angel With Horns,* Longmans, Green, 1961, pp. 1–22.

Richard II

Altick, Richard D., "Symphonic Imagery in *Richard II,*" *PMLA,* 62 (1947), 339–65; also in *Richard II,* New American Library,* 1963.

Bogard, Travis, "Shakespeare's Second Richard," *PMLA,* 70 (1955), 192–209.

Dean, Leonard F., "*Richard II:* The State and the Image of the Theater," *PMLA,* 67 (1952), 211–18; also in *Shakespeare Criticism,* ed. by Leonard Dean, Oxford University Press,* 1966.

King John

Bonjour, Adrien, "The Road to Swinstead Abbey: A Study of the Sense and Structure of *King John,*" *ELH,* 18 (1951), 253–74.

Calderwood, James L., "Commodity and Honour in *King John,*" *University of Toronto Quarterly,* 29 (1960), 341–56.

Elliott, John R., "Shakespeare and the Double Image of King John," *Shakespeare Studies,* 1 (1965), 64–84.

Henry IV, Part One

Barber, C. L., "From Ritual to Comedy: An Examination of *Henry IV,*" *English Stage Comedy,* ed. by W. K. Wimsatt, Jr., English Institute Essays 1954, Columbia University Press, 1954, pp. 22–51; also in Barber's *Shakespeare's Festive Comedy,* Meridian,* 1963.

Spivack, Bernard, "Falstaff and the Psychomachia," *Shakespeare Quarterly,* 8 (1957), 449–59.

Wilson, J. Dover, *The Fortunes of Falstaff,* Cambridge University Press, 1943; Cambridge,* 1964.

Henry IV, Part Two

Bradley, Andrew Cecil, "The Rejection of Falstaff," *Oxford Lectures on Poetry,* Macmillan, 1909; Indiana University Press,* 1961.

Jenkins, Harold, *The Structural Problem in Shakespeare's "Henry the Fourth,"* Methuen, 1956; also in *Henry IV, Part Two,* New American Library,* 1965.

Leech, Clifford, "The Unity of *2 Henry IV,*" *Shakespeare Survey,* 6, ed. by Allardyce Nicoll, Cambridge University Press, 1953, 16–24.

Henry V

Dorius, R. J., "A Little More Than a Little," *Shakespeare Quarterly,* 11 (1960), 13–26; also in *Shakespeare, the Histories,* ed. by E. M. Waith, Prentice-Hall,* 1965.

Reese, Max Meredith, *The Cease of Majesty: A Study of Shakespeare's History Plays,* St. Martin's, 1962.

Walter, J. H., Introduction in *The Arden Edition of the Works of William Shakespeare: King Henry V,* Harvard University Press, 1954.

Henry VIII

Harris, Bernard, "'What's Past Is Prologue': *Cymbeline* and *Henry VIII,*" *Stratford-upon-Avon Studies 8: Later Shakespeare,* ed. by J. R. Brown and Bernard Harris, St. Martin's, 1967.

Kermode, Frank, "What Is Shakespeare's *Henry VIII* About?" *Durham University Journal,* n.s. 9 (1948), 48–55; also in *Shakespeare, the Histories,* ed. by E. M. Waith, Prentice-Hall,* 1965.

Hamlet

Holland, Norman, *Psychoanalysis and Shakespeare*, McGraw-Hill, 1966. Contains an excellent summary (pp. 163–206) of the varying views of the psychoanalytic critics from Sigmund Freud and Ernest Jones to the present.

Knight, G. Wilson, " The Embassy of Death: An Essay on *Hamlet*," and " *Hamlet* Reconsidered (1947)," *The Wheel of Fire*, 4th rev. ed., British Book Centre, 1949, Meridian,* 1957. The famous attack on Hamlet as a death-bringer.

Levin, Harry, *The Question of Hamlet*, Oxford University Press, 1959; Viking (Compass*), 1961. Approaches the play primarily through its rhetoric to trace the path of Hamlet from a condition of " question," through " doubt," to a final acceptance of unreconciled opposites in " irony."

Mack, Maynard, " The World of *Hamlet*," *Yale Review*, 41 (1952), 502–23. A basic piece of *Hamlet* criticism, reprinted in numerous collections of criticism.

Mahood, M. M., " *Hamlet*," *Shakespeare's Wordplay*, Barnes & Noble, 1957.

Prosser, Eleanor, *Hamlet and Revenge*, Stanford University Press, 1967. The most recent and comprehensive investigation of the ethics of revenge in the play and in Elizabethan England.

Wilson, J. Dover, *What Happens in " Hamlet*," 3rd ed., Cambridge University Press, 1951; Cambridge,* 1959. Good place to start. Examines in detail the most fundamental realistic questions about ghosts and revenge.

Troilus and Cressida

Foakes, R. A., " *Troilus and Cressida* Reconsidered," *University of Toronto Quarterly*, 32 (1963), 142–54.

Gérard, Albert, " Meaning and Structure in *Troilus and Cressida*," *English Studies*, 40 (1959), 148–57.

Nowottny, Winifred M. T., " 'Opinion' and 'Value' in *Troilus and Cressida*," *Essays in Criticism*, 4 (1954), 282–96.

Othello

Heilman, Robert B., *Magic in the Web: Action and Language in " Othello*," University of Kentucky Press, 1956. Line-by-line analysis of the most distinguished kind that develops a conflict between wit and witchcraft.

Kernan, Alvin, Introduction in *Othello*, New American Library,* 1963; also in *Shakespeare, the Tragedies*, ed. by A. Harbage, Prentice-Hall,* 1964.

Knight, G. Wilson, " The *Othello* Music," *The Wheel of Fire*, Oxford University Press, 1930; Meridian,* 1957.

Nowottny, Winifred M. T., " Justice and Love in *Othello*," *University of Toronto Quarterly*, 21 (1951–52), 330–44.

Seltzer, Daniel, " Elizabethan Acting in *Othello*," *Shakespeare Quarterly*, 10 (1959), 201–10.

King Lear

Danby, John F., *Shakespeare's Doctrine of Nature: A Study of " King Lear*," Faber & Faber, 1949.

Fraser, Russell A., *Shakespeare's Poetics in Relation to " King Lear*," Routledge & Kegan Paul, 1962.

Heilman, Robert B., *This Great Stage: Image and Structure in " King Lear*," Louisiana State University Press, 1948; University of Washington Press,* 1963.

Kernan, Alvin, " Formalism and Realism in Elizabethan Drama: The Miracles in *King Lear*," *Renaissance Drama*, 9, ed. by S. Schoenbaum, Northwestern University Press, 1966.

Knight, G. Wilson, " *King Lear* and the Comedy of the Grotesque " and " The *Lear* Universe," *The Wheel of Fire*, Oxford University Press, 1930; 4th rev. ed., British Book Centre, 1949, Meridian,* 1957.

Levin, Harry, " The Heights and the Depths: A Scene from *King Lear*," *More Talking of Shakespeare*, ed. by John Garrett, Theater Arts Books, 1959; also in *King Lear*, New American Library,* 1963. On the " miracle " Edgar contrives for his father.

Mack, Maynard, *" King Lear" in Our Time*, University of California Press, 1965. Complete study of *King Lear* in terms of its archetypes and its stage history.

Macbeth

Elliott, G. R., *Dramatic Providence in " Macbeth*," Princeton University Press, 1958.

Knights, L. C., *Some Shakespearean Themes*, Stanford University Press,* 1960.

Paul, Henry N., *The Royal Play of " Macbeth*," Macmillan, 1951. Recreates the situation in the court of James I, where play may have been first presented, and stresses the King's interest in witchcraft and history.

A famous and most interesting controversy over methods of criticism is contained in two articles on *Macbeth*: Brooks, Cleanth, " The Naked Babe and the Cloak of Manliness," *The Well Wrought Urn*, Harcourt, Brace, 1947, Harcourt (Harvest*), 1956; and Campbell, O. J., " Shakespeare and the 'New Critics'," *Joseph Quincy Adams: Memorial Studies*,

Knight, G. Wilson, "*Henry VIII* and the Poetry of Conversion," *The Crown of Life*, Oxford University Press, 1947; Barnes & Noble,* 1961.

The Tragedies, General

Bradley, A. C., *Shakespearean Tragedy*, Macmillan, 1904; Fawcett (Premier*), 1965. The great standard work on the tragedies that remains the classic. The book considers the principles of Shakespearean tragedy, focusing on *Hamlet, Othello, King Lear,* and *Macbeth.* Bradley approaches the plays through close observation and analysis of characters, and his method can profitably be compared to the very different methods of Knight and Holloway.

Frye, Northrop, *Fools of Time: Studies in Shakespearean Tragedy,* University of Toronto Press, 1967. Frye's application to Shakespeare's tragedies of the general theory of tragedy he developed in *Anatomy of Criticism.* Finds the basis of tragedy in the sense of being in time, in the one-directional flow of life, and follows this through three broad categories: the tragedy of the loss of order, the tragedy of failed passion, and the tragedy of isolation.

Holloway, John, *The Story of the Night,* Routledge and Kegan Paul, 1961; University of Nebraska Press,* 1963. Develops a mythic pattern in the tragedies in which the hero is gradually isolated from the world and society and is at last killed as a scapegoat. Good example of " mythic " criticism.

James, D. G., *The Dream of Learning,* Oxford University Press, 1951. Approaches tragedy, particularly *Hamlet* and *King Lear,* as a contrasting mode of knowledge and view of life to that of Bacon in *The Advancement of Learning,* where poetry is called "a dream of learning."

Knight, G. Wilson, *The Wheel of Fire,* Oxford University Press, 1930; 4th rev. ed., British Book Centre, 1949, Meridian,* 1957. One of the first great works of modern literary criticism, in which Knight explains his method of " interpretation " with its concentration on the whole design of the plays and applies his method to the major tragedies. The paperback edition contains several new essays.

Mack, Maynard, " The Jacobean Shakespeare: Some Observations on the Construction of the Tragedies," *Stratford-upon-Avon Studies 1: Jacobean Theater,* St. Martin's, 1960; also in *Othello,* New American Library,* 1963. A brief and most useful statement of the situations and plot patterns common to the great tragedies.

Siegel, Paul N., *Shakespearean Tragedy and the Elizabethan Compromise,* New York University Press, 1957. Relates the tragedies to the Elizabethan social and political situation and presents Shakespeare as spokesman for conservative world view and social order.

Wilson, Harold S., *On the Design of Shakespearean Tragedy,* University of Toronto Press, 1957. Treats ten plays as different kinds of tragedies and seeks their unity not in a common formula but in an interrelationship of different tragic points of view. The plays considered are *Romeo and Juliet, Hamlet, Othello, Macbeth, Julius Caesar, Coriolanus, Troilus and Cressida, Timon of Athens, Antony and Cleopatra,* and *King Lear.*

Titus Andronicus

Hamilton, A. C., " *Titus Andronicus:* The Form of Shakespearian Tragedy," *Shakespeare Quarterly,* 14 (1963), 201–13.

Price, H. T., "Construction in *Titus Andronicus,*" *Journal of English and Germanic Philology,* 47 (1943), 55–81; also in *Shakespeare, the Tragedies,* ed. by A. Harbage, Prentice-Hall,* 1964. Crucial part of Price's argument on basis of structure that *Titus Andronicus* is the work of Shakespeare.

Sommers, Alan, " ' Wilderness of Tigers ': Structure and Symbolism in *Titus Andronicus,*" *Essays in Criticism,* 10 (1960), 275–89.

Waith, Eugene M., " The Metamorphosis of Violence in *Titus Andronicus,*" *Shakespeare Survey,* 10, ed. by Allardyce Nicoll, Cambridge University Press, 1957, 39–49.

Romeo and Juliet

Kernan, Alvin, "*Romeo and Juliet,*" *Writing and Literature in the Secondary School,* ed. by E. J. Gordon, Holt, Rinehart and Winston,* 1965.

Levin, Harry, " Form and Formality in *Romeo and Juliet,*" *Shakespeare Quarterly,* 11 (1960), 3–11.

Mahood, M. M., "*Romeo and Juliet,*" *Shakespeare's Wordplay,* Barnes & Noble, 1957.

Julius Caesar

Bonjour, Adrien, *The Structure of " Julius Caesar,"* University Press of Liverpool, 1958.

Charney, Maurice, *Shakespeare's Roman Plays,* Harvard University Press, 1961.

Dean, Leonard, " *Julius Caesar* and Modern Criticism," *The English Journal* (October 1961), 451–56; also in *Julius Caesar,* New American Library,* 1963. Excellent summary of changing critical views.

Foakes, R. A., " An Approach to *Julius Caesar,*" *Shakespeare Quarterly,* 5 (1954), 259–70.

Mack, Maynard, " Teaching Drama: *Julius Caesar,*" *Essays on the Teaching of English,* ed. by E. J. Gordon and E. S. Noyes, Appleton-Century-Crofts,* 1960.

to the questions and problems of the middle and late plays that baffled and confused older realistic critical approaches. Should be read in conjunction with a book like Bethell's or Knight's employing a different view of dramatic poetry.

Shakespeare Survey, 11, Cambridge University Press, 1958. An issue given to the last plays with excellent articles on the history, staging, and structure of these works.

Tillyard, E. M. W., *Shakespeare's Last Plays*, Chatto & Windus, 1938; 6th ed., Barnes & Noble, 1964. One of the first and best descriptions of the common elements in the last plays, arguing that Shakespeare was trying a new form in *Pericles* and *Cymbeline* that was perfected in *The Winter's Tale* and *The Tempest*.

Traversi, Derek, *Shakespeare: The Last Phase*, Harcourt, Brace, 1955. Careful reading of these plays, concentrating on developing imagery and themes rather than character.

Wells, Stanley, "Shakespeare and Romance," *Stratford-upon-Avon Studies 8: Later Shakespeare*, St. Martin's,* 1967. Summation of present knowledge of the romance tradition and the ways in which Shakespeare adapted it.

All's Well That Ends Well

Halio, Jay L., "*All's Well That Ends Well*," *Shakespeare Quarterly*, 15 (1964), 33–43.

Hunter, G. K., Introduction in *Arden Edition of the Works of William Shakespeare: "All's Well That Ends Well*," 3rd rev. ed., Harvard University Press, 1959; also in *Shakespeare, the Comedies*, ed. by Kenneth Muir, Prentice-Hall,* 1965.

Knight, G. Wilson, "The Third Eye," in *The Sovereign Flower: On Shakespeare as the Poet of Royalism*, Macmillan, 1958.

Measure for Measure

Chambers, R. W., "*Measure for Measure*," *Man's Unconquerable Mind*, Jonathan Cape, 1952; also in *Measure for Measure*, New American Library,* 1964.

Knight, G. Wilson, "*Measure for Measure* and the Gospels," *The Wheel of Fire*, Oxford University Press, 1930; 4th rev. ed., British Book Centre, 1949, Meridian,* 1957.

Lascelles, Mary, *Shakespeare's "Measure for Measure*," De Graff, 1954.

Stevenson, David L., "Design and Structure in *Measure for Measure*: A New Appraisal," *ELH*, 23 (1956), 256–78.

Pericles

Arthos, John, "*Pericles, Prince of Tyre*: A Study in the Dramatic Use of Romantic Narrative," *Shakespeare Quarterly*, 4 (1953), 257–70.

Danby, John F., "Sidney and the Late-Shake-spearian Romance," in *Poets on Fortune's Hill*, Faber & Faber,* 1952. See especially pp. 186–92.

Knight, G. Wilson, "*Pericles*," *The Crown of Life*, Oxford University Press, 1947; Barnes & Noble,* 1961.

Cymbeline

Harris, Bernard, "'What's Past Is Prologue': *Cymbeline* and *Henry VIII*," *Stratford-upon-Avon Studies 8: Later Shakespeare*, St. Martin's, 1967.

Stephenson, A. A., "The Significance of *Cymbeline*," *Scrutiny*, 10 (1942), 329–38.

Tinkler, F. C., "*Cymbeline*," *Scrutiny*, 7 (1938), 5–20.

The Winter's Tale

Bethell, S. L., "*The Winter's Tale*": A Study, Staples Press, 1947.

Frye, Northrop, "Recognition in *The Winter's Tale*," *Essays on Shakespeare and Elizabethan Drama*, ed. by Richard Hosley, University of Missouri Press, 1962.

Hoeniger, F. D., "The Meaning of *The Winter's Tale*," *University of Toronto Quarterly*, 20 (1950), 11–26.

Leavis, F. R., "A Criticism of Shakespeare's Last Plays," *Scrutiny*, 10 (1942), 339–45. Reprinted in *The Common Pursuit*, Chatto & Windus, 1952; Penguin,* 1962.

Mahood, M. M., "*The Winter's Tale*," *Shakespeare's Wordplay*, Barnes & Noble, 1957.

The Tempest

Auden, W. H., "The Sea and the Mirror: A Commentary on Shakespeare's *The Tempest*," *The Collected Poetry*, Random House, 1945.

Brower, R. A., "The Mirror of Analogy: *The Tempest*," *The Fields of Light*, Oxford University Press, 1951; Galaxy Books,* 1951.

Knox, Bernard, "*The Tempest* and the Ancient Comic Tradition," *English Stage Comedy*, ed. by W. K. Wimsatt, Jr., English Institute Essays 1954, Columbia University Press, 1955; also in *The Tempest*, New American Library,* 1964.

Spencer, Theodore, "Appearance and Reality in Shakespeare's Last Plays," *Modern Philology*, 39 (1942), 265–74.

The History Plays, General

Shakespeare, the Histories, ed. by E. M. Waith, Prentice-Hall,* 1965. A collection of essays on the history plays, with an excellent introduction describing the change in critical attitudes toward these plays.

Tillyard, E. M. W., *Shakespeare's History Plays*, Macmillan, 1946; Collier,* 1962. Traces the relationship between the events and actions of the history plays and received Elizabethan views of political and social order.

Traversi, Derek, *Shakespeare from "Richard II" to "Henry V,"* Stanford University Press, 1957. Close, careful analysis of the plays of the second tetralogy that widens considerably the view of history advanced by Tillyard.

Henry VI, Part One

Brockbank, J. P., "The Frame of Disorder — *Henry VI,*" *Stratford-upon-Avon Studies 3: Early Shakespeare,* ed. by John Russell Brown and Bernard Harris, St. Martin's, 1961.

Clemen, Wolfgang H., "Anticipation and Foreboding in Shakespeare's Early Histories," *Shakespeare Survey,* 6, ed. by Allardyce Nicoll, Cambridge University Press, 1953.

Kirschbaum, Leo, "The Authorship of *1 Henry VI,*" *PMLA,* 67 (1952), 809–22.

Henry VI, Part Two

Berman, Ronald S., "Fathers and Sons in the *Henry VI* Plays," *Shakespeare Quarterly,* 13 (1962), 487–97.

Leech, Clifford, "The Two-Part Play: Marlowe and the Early Shakespeare," *Shakespeare Jahrbuch,* 92 (1958), 90–106.

Turner, Robert Y., "Shakespeare and the Public Confrontation Scene in Early History Plays," *Modern Philology,* 72 (1964), 1–12.

Henry VI, Part Three

Kernan, Alvin, "A Comparison of the Imagery in *3 Henry VI* and *The True Tragedie of Richard Duke of York,*" *Studies in Philology,* 51 (1954), 431–42.

Ribner, Irving, *The English History Play in the Age of Shakespeare,* Princeton University Press, 1957.

Richard III

Kott, Jan, "The Kings," *Shakespeare Our Contemporary,* trans. by B. Taborski, Doubleday (Anchor*), 1966, pp. 3–55.

Krieger, Murray, "The Dark Generations of *Richard III,*" *Criticism,* 1 (1959), 32–48.

Rossiter, A. P., "The Unity of *Richard III,*" *Angel With Horns,* Longmans, Green, 1961, pp. 1–22.

Richard II

Altick, Richard D., "Symphonic Imagery in *Richard II,*" *PMLA,* 62 (1947), 339–65; also in *Richard II,* New American Library,* 1963.

Bogard, Travis, "Shakespeare's Second Richard," *PMLA,* 70 (1955), 192–209.

Dean, Leonard F., "*Richard II:* The State and the Image of the Theater," *PMLA,* 67 (1952), 211–18; also in *Shakespeare Criticism,* ed. by Leonard Dean, Oxford University Press,* 1966.

King John

Bonjour, Adrien, "The Road to Swinstead Abbey: A Study of the Sense and Structure of *King John,*" *ELH,* 18 (1951), 253–74.

Calderwood, James L., "Commodity and Honour in *King John,*" *University of Toronto Quarterly,* 29 (1960), 341–56.

Elliott, John R., "Shakespeare and the Double Image of King John," *Shakespeare Studies,* 1 (1965), 64–84.

Henry IV, Part One

Barber, C. L., "From Ritual to Comedy: An Examination of *Henry IV,*" *English Stage Comedy,* ed. by W. K. Wimsatt, Jr., English Institute Essays 1954, Columbia University Press, 1954, pp. 22–51; also in Barber's *Shakespeare's Festive Comedy,* Meridian,* 1963.

Spivack, Bernard, "Falstaff and the Psychomachia," *Shakespeare Quarterly,* 8 (1957), 449–59.

Wilson, J. Dover, *The Fortunes of Falstaff,* Cambridge University Press, 1943; Cambridge,* 1964.

Henry IV, Part Two

Bradley, Andrew Cecil, "The Rejection of Falstaff," *Oxford Lectures on Poetry,* Macmillan, 1909; Indiana University Press,* 1961.

Jenkins, Harold, *The Structural Problem in Shakespeare's "Henry the Fourth,"* Methuen, 1956; also in *Henry IV, Part Two,* New American Library,* 1965.

Leech, Clifford, "The Unity of *2 Henry IV,*" *Shakespeare Survey,* 6, ed. by Allardyce Nicoll, Cambridge University Press, 1953, 16–24.

Henry V

Dorius, R. J., "A Little More Than a Little," *Shakespeare Quarterly,* 11 (1960), 13–26; also in *Shakespeare, the Histories,* ed. by E. M. Waith, Prentice-Hall,* 1965.

Reese, Max Meredith, *The Cease of Majesty: A Study of Shakespeare's History Plays,* St. Martin's, 1962.

Walter, J. H., Introduction in *The Arden Edition of the Works of William Shakespeare: King Henry V,* Harvard University Press, 1954.

Henry VIII

Harris, Bernard, "'What's Past Is Prologue': *Cymbeline* and *Henry VIII,*" *Stratford-upon-Avon Studies 8: Later Shakespeare,* ed. by J. R. Brown and Bernard Harris, St. Martin's, 1967.

Kermode, Frank, "What Is Shakespeare's *Henry VIII* About?" *Durham University Journal,* n.s. 9 (1948), 48–55; also in *Shakespeare, the Histories,* ed. by E. M. Waith, Prentice-Hall,* 1965.

ed. by J. G. McManaway *et al.,* Folger Library, 1948.

Antony and Cleopatra

Barnet, Sylvan, "Recognition and Reversal in *Antony and Cleopatra,*" *Shakespeare Quarterly,* 8 (1957), 331–34.

Holloway, John, "Antony and Cleopatra," *The Story of the Night,* Routledge & Kegan Paul, 1961; University of Nebraska Press,* 1963.

Knight, G. Wilson, *The Imperial Theme,* British Book Centre, 1951; 3rd ed., Barnes & Noble,* 1966.

Ornstein, Robert, "The Ethic of the Imagination: Love and Art in *Antony and Cleopatra,*" *Stratford-upon-Avon Studies 8: Later Shakespeare,* ed. by J. R. Brown and B. Harris, St. Martin's, 1967.

Coriolanus

Discussions of Shakespeare's Roman Plays, ed. by Maurice Charney, D. C. Heath,* 1964.

Ellis-Fermor, Una, Chapter 4 in *Shakespeare the Dramatist,* ed. by Kenneth Muir, Barnes & Noble, 1961.

Levin, Harry, Introduction in *Coriolanus,* Penguin,* 1956.

Waith, Eugene, *The Herculean Hero,* Columbia University Press, 1962. Places Coriolanus in the tradition of the Herculean type of tragic hero.

Timon of Athens

Cook, David, "*Timon of Athens,*" *Shakespeare Survey,* 16, Cambridge University Press, 1963, 83–94; also in *Timon of Athens,* New American Library,* 1965.

Ellis-Fermor, Una, "*Timon of Athens:* An Unfinished Play," *Review of English Studies,* 18 (1942), 270–83. Reprinted in *Shakespeare the Dramatist,* ed. by Kenneth Muir, Barnes & Noble, 1961.

Kernan, Alvin, *The Cankered Muse: Satire of the English Renaissance,* Yale University Press, 1959. Places *Timon of Athens* in context of Elizabethan satire.

Spencer, Terence, "Shakespeare Learns the Value of Money: The Dramatist at Work on *Timon of Athens,*" *Shakespeare Survey,* 6, ed. by Allardyce Nicoll, Cambridge University Press, 1953, 75–78.

The Poetry, General

Shakespeare Survey, 15, Cambridge University Press, 1962, is devoted to articles on the poems, with several summaries of twentieth-century criticism on this subject. This volume contains bibliog-

raphy for several of the minor poems, not referred to here, the authorship of which is disputed.

Venus and Adonis

Bonjour, Adrien, "From Shakespeare's Venus to Cleopatra's Cupids," *Shakespeare Survey,* 15, Cambridge University Press, 1962, 73–80.

Bradbrook, M. C., *Shakespeare and Elizabethan Poetry,* Chatto & Windus, 1951. Interpretation stresses the freshness and open paganism of the poem rather than taking the moral point of view.

Lewis, C. S., *English Literature in the Sixteenth Century,* Oxford University Press, 1954. Discusses this and other Shakespeare poems in the context of the poetry of the age.

The Rape of Lucrece

Bradbrook, M. C., *Shakespeare and Elizabethan Poetry,* Chatto & Windus, 1951. Lewis, C. S., *English Literature in the Sixteenth Century,* Oxford University Press, 1954. Both books discuss this and other Shakespearean poems in context of Elizabethan poetry. A history of modern attitudes toward the poem is provided by J. W. Lever in *Shakespeare Survey,* 15, Cambridge University Press, 1962, 22–25.

The Phoenix and the Turtle

Ellrodt, Robert, "An Anatomy of *The Phoenix and the Turtle,*" *Shakespeare Survey,* 15, Cambridge University Press, 1962, 99–110.

Knight, G. Wilson, *The Mutual Flame,* Macmillan, 1955. Contains an elaborate analysis of the poem.

Prince, F. T., Introduction in *The New Arden Shakespeare: The Poems,* Harvard University Press, 1960. The best general discussion of the textual histories, sources, and interpretations of this and other Shakespeare poems.

The Sonnets

Cruttwell, Patrick, *The Shakespearean Moment and Its Place in the Poetry of the Seventeenth Century,* Chatto & Windus, 1953; Random House (Vintage*), 1960. Cruttwell's first two chapters make heavy use of the sonnets to construct a theory of Shakespeare's style.

Hubler, Edward, *The Sense of Shakespeare's Sonnets,* Princeton University Press, 1954.

Hubler, Edward, *et al., The Riddle of Shakespeare's Sonnets,* Basic Books, 1962.

Knight, G. Wilson, *The Mutual Flame,* Macmillan, 1955.

Lever, J. W., *The Elizabethan Love Sonnet,* British Book Service, 1956. A good history of the literary background of the sonnet sequence.